Contemporary Authors®
Cumulative Index

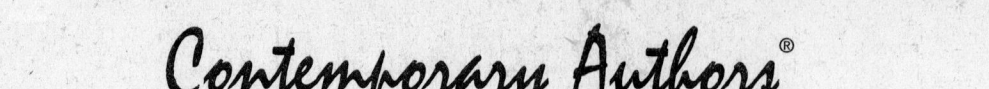

Cumulative Index

Contemporary Authors Volumes 1-239

Contemporary Authors New Revision Series Volumes 1-144

Citations to entries in Contemporary Authors are identified as follows:

R after number	•	*Contemporary Authors* First Revision Volumes 1-44
Volume number only	•	*Contemporary Authors* Original Volumes 45-239
CANR	•	*Contemporary Authors New Revision Series,* Volumes 1-144
CAP	•	*Contemporary Authors Permanent Series,* Volumes 1-2
CAAS	•	*Contemporary Authors Autobiography Series,* Volumes 1-30
CABS	•	*Contemporary Authors Bibliographical Series,* Volumes 1-3

Citations to entries in other reference works are identified as follows:

- **AAL** • *Asian American Literature*
- **AAYA** • *Authors and Artists for Young Adults,* Volumes 1-67
- **AFAW** • *African American Writers,* Volumes 1-2 (Charles Scribner's Sons, an imprint of Gale)
- **AFW** • *African Writers* (Charles Scribner's Sons, an imprint of Gale)
- **AITN** • *Authors in the News,* Volumes 1-2
- **AMW** • *American Writers* (Charles Scribner's Sons, an imprint of Gale)
- **AMWC** • *American Writers—The Classics,* Volumes 1-2 (Charles Scribner's Sons, an imprint of Gale)
- **AMWR** • *American Writers Retrospective Supplement,* Volumes 1-2 (Charles Scribner's Sons, an imprint of Gale)
- **AMWS** • *American Writers Supplement,* Volumes 1-15 (Charles Scribner's Sons, an imprint of Gale)
- **ANW** • *American Nature Writers* (Charles Scribner's Sons, an imprint of Gale)
- **AW** • *Ancient Writers,* Volumes 1-2 (Charles Scribner's Sons, an imprint of Gale)
- **BEST** • *Bestsellers* (quarterly; citations appear as Year: Issue number)
- **BG** • *Beat Generation,* Volumes 2-3
- **BLC** • *Black Literature Criticism,* Volumes 1-3; **BLCS:** *Black Literature Criticism Supplement*
- **BPFB** • *Beacham's Encyclopedia of Popular Fiction: Biography and Resources,* Volumes 1-3
- **BRW** • *British Writers,* Volumes 1-7 (Charles Scribner's Sons, an imprint of Gale)
- **BRWC** • *British Writers—The Classics,* Volumes 1-2 (Charles Scribner's Sons, an imprint of Gale)
- **BRWR** • *British Writers Retrospective Supplement,* Volumes 1-2 (Charles Scribner's Sons, an imprint of Gale)
- **BRWS** • *British Writers Supplement,* Volumes 1-11 (Charles Scribner's Sons, an imprint of Gale)
- **BW** • *Black Writers,* Editions 1-3
- **BYA** • *Beacham's Guide to Literature for Young Adults,* Volumes 1-16
- **CAD** • *Contemporary American Dramatists* (St. James Press, an imprint of Gale)
- **CBD** • *Contemporary British Dramatists* (St. James Press, an imprint of Gale)
- **CCA** • *Contemporary Canadian Authors,* Volume 1
- **CD** • *Contemporary Dramatists,* 5th edition (St. James Press, an imprint of Gale)
- **CDALB** • *Concise Dictionary of American Literary Biography,* 1640-1865, 1865-1917, 1917-1929, 1929-1941, 1941-1968, 1968-1988; **CDALBS:** *Concise Dictionary of American Literary Biography Supplement*
- **CDBLB** • *Concise Dictionary of British Literary Biography,* Before 1660, 1660-1789, 1789-1832, 1832-1890, 1890-1914, 1914-1945, 1945-1960, 1960 to Present
- **CDWLB** • *Concise Dictionary of World Literary Biography,* Volumes 1-4
- **CLC** • *Contemporary Literary Criticism,* Volumes 1-212
- **CLR** • *Children's Literature Review,* Volumes 1-104
- **CMW** • *St. James Guide to Crime & Mystery Writers,* 4th edition (St. James Press, an imprint of Gale)
- **CN** • *Contemporary Novelists,* 7th edition (St. James Press, an imprint of Gale)
- **CP** • *Contemporary Poets,* 7th edition (St. James Press, an imprint of Gale)
- **CPW** • *Contemporary Popular Writers* (St. James Press, an imprint of Gale)
- **CSW** • *Contemporary Southern Writers* (St. James Press, an imprint of Gale)
- **CWD** • *Contemporary Women Dramatists* (St. James Press, an imprint of Gale)
- **CWP** • *Contemporary Women Poets* (St. James Press, an imprint of Gale)
- **CWRI** • *St. James Guide to Children's Writers,* 5th edition (St. James Press, an imprint of Gale)
- **CWW** • *Contemporary World Writers,* (St. James Press, an imprint of Gale)
- **DA** • *DISCovering Authors*
- **DA3** • *DISCovering Authors 3.0*
- **DAB** • *DISCovering Authors: British Edition*
- **DAC** • *DISCovering Authors: Canadian Edition*
- **DAM** • *DISCovering Authors: Modules*
  - **DRAM:** *Dramatists Module;* **MST:** *Most-Studied Authors Module;*
  - **MULT:** *Multicultural Authors Module;* **NOV:** *Novelists Module;*
  - **POET:** *Poets Module;* **POP:** *Popular Fiction and Genre Authors Module*
- **DC** • *Drama Criticism,* Volumes 1-26
- **DFS** • *Drama for Students,* Volumes 1-22
- **DLB** • *Dictionary of Literary Biography,* Volumes 1-322
- **DLBD** • *Dictionary of Literary Biography Documentary Series,* Volumes 1-18
- **DLBY** • *Dictionary of Literary Biography Yearbook,* 1980-2002

MONTGOMERY COLLEGE
ROCKVILLE CAMPUS LIBRARY
ROCKVILLE, MARYLAND

- **DNFS** • *Literature of Developing Nations for Students,* Volumes 1-2
- **EFS** • *Epics for Students,* Volumes 1-2
- **EW** • *European Writers,* Volumes 1-13 (Charles Scribner's Sons, an imprint of Gale)
- **EWL** • *Encyclopedia of World Literature in the 20th Century,* 2nd and 3rd editions (St. James Press, an imprint of Gale)
- **EXPN** • *Exploring Novels*
- **EXPP** • *Exploring Poetry*
- **EXPS** • *Exploring Short Stories*
- **FANT** • *St. James Guide to Fantasy Writers* (St. James Press, an imprint of Gale)
- **FL** • *Feminism in Literature,* Volumes 1-6
- **FW** • *Feminist Writers* (St. James Press, an imprint of Gale)
- **GFL** • *Guide to French Literature,* Beginnings to 1789, 1789 to the Present (St. James Press, an imprint of Gale)
- **GLL** • *Gay and Lesbian Literature,* Volumes 1-2 (St. James Press, an imprint of Gale)
- **HGG** • *St. James Guide to Horror, Ghost & Gothic Writers* (St. James Press, an imprint of Gale)
- **HLC** • *Hispanic Literature Criticism,* Volumes 1-2; **HLCS:** *Hispanic Literature Criticism Supplement,* Volumes 1-2
- **HR** • *Harlem Renaissance,* Volumes 2-3
- **HW** • *Hispanic Writers,* Editions 1-2
- **IDFW** • *International Dictionary of Films and Filmmakers: Writers and Production Artists,* Editions 3-4 (St. James Press, an imprint of Gale)
- **IDTP** • *International Dictionary of Theatre: Playwrights* (St. James Press, an imprint of Gale)
- **JRDA** • *Junior DISCovering Authors*
- **LAIT** • *Literature and Its Times,* Volumes 1-5; **LATS:** *Literature and Its Times Supplement*
- **LAW** • *Latin American Writers* (Charles Scribner's Sons, an imprint of Gale); **LAWS:** *Latin American Writers Supplement* (Charles Scribner's Sons, an imprint of Gale)
- **LLW** • *Latino and Latina Writers* (Charles Scribner's Sons, an imprint of Gale)
- **LMFS** • *Literary Movements for Students,* Volumes 1-2
- **MAICYA** • *Major Authors and Illustrators for Children and Young Adults,* Editions 1-2; **MAICYAS:** *Major Authors and Illustrators for Children and Young Adults Supplement*
- **MAL** • *Modern American Literature,* Edition 5 (St. James Press, an imprint of Gale)
- **MAWW** • *Modern American Women Writers* (Charles Scribner's Sons, an imprint of Gale)
- **MJW** • *Modern Japanese Writers* (Charles Scribner's Sons, an imprint of Gale)
- **MSW** • *Mystery and Suspense Writers* (Charles Scribner's Sons, an imprint of Gale)
- **MTCW** • *Major 20th-Century Writers,* Editions 1-2
- **MTFW** • *Major 21st-Century Writers (eBook),* 2005 edition
- **NCFS** • *Nonfiction Classics for Students,* Volumes 1-5
- **NFS** • *Novels for Students,* Volumes 1-22
- **NNAL** • *Native North American Literature*
- **PAB** • *Poets: American and British* (Charles Scribner's Sons, an imprint of Gale)
- **PC** • *Poetry Criticism,* Volumes 1-68
- **PFS** • *Poetry for Students,* Volumes 1-23
- **RGAL** • *Reference Guide to American Literature,* 4th edition (St. James Press, an imprint of Gale)
- **RGEL** • *Reference Guide to English Literature,* 2nd edition (St. James Press, an imprint of Gale)
- **RGSF** • *Reference Guide to Short Fiction,* 2nd edition (St. James Press, an imprint of Gale)
- **RGWL** • *Reference Guide to World Literature,* 2nd and 3rd editions (St. James Press, an imprint of Gale)
- **RHW** • *Twentieth-Century Romance and Historical Writers* (St. James Press, an imprint of Gale)
- **SAAS** • *Something about the Author Autobiography Series,* Volumes 1-26
- **SATA** • *Something about the Author,* Volumes 1-163
- **SCFW** • *Science Fiction Writers,* 2nd edition (Charles Scribner's Sons, an imprint of Gale)
- **SFW** • *St. James Guide to Science Fiction Writers,* 4th edition (St. James Press, an imprint of Gale)
- **SSC** • *Short Story Criticism,* Volumes 1-85
- **SSFS** • *Short Stories for Students,* Volumes 1-21
- **SUFW** • *Supernatural Fiction Writers* 1st and 2nd editions (Charles Scribner's Sons, an imprint of Gale)
- **TCLC** • *Twentieth-Century Literary Criticism,* Volumes 1-169
- **TCLE** • *Twayne Companion to Contemporary Literature in English* (Twayne Publishers, an imprint of Gale)
- **TCWW** • *Twentieth-Century Western Writers,* 1st and 2nd editions (St. James Press, an imprint of Gale)
- **TEA** • *Twayne's English Authors Series* (Twayne Publishers, an imprint of Gale)
- **TUS** • *Twayne's United States Authors Series* (Twayne Publishers, an imprint of Gale)
- **TWA** • *Twayne's World Authors Series* (Twayne Publishers, an imprint of Gale)
- **WCH** • *Writers for Children* (Charles Scribner's Sons, an imprint of Gale)
- **WLC** • *World Literature Criticism;* **WLCS:** *World Literature Criticism Supplement*
- **WLIT** • *World Literature and Its Times,* Volumes 1-7
- **WP** • *World Poets* (Charles Scribner's Sons, an imprint of Gale)
- **WWE** • *World Writers in English* (Charles Scribner's Sons, an imprint of Gale)
- **WYA** • *Writers for Young Adults* (Charles Scribner's Sons, an imprint of Gale); **WYAS:** *Writers for Young Adults Supplement* (Charles Scribner's Sons, an imprint of Gale)
- **YABC** • *Yesterday's Authors of Books for Children,* Volumes 1-2
- **YAW** • *St. James Guide to Young Adult Writers* (St. James Press, an imprint of Gale)

Note: This cumulative index supersedes all lower-numbered CA indexes and is not bound in any CA volume.

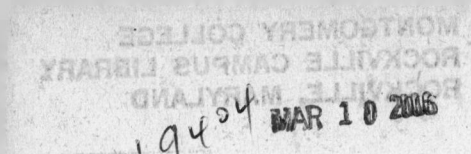

Staff

Index Coordinator
Michelle Kazensky

This publication is a creative work fully protected by all applicable copyright laws, as well as by misappropriation, trade secret, unfair competition, and other applicable laws. The authors and editors of this work have added value to the underlying factual material herein through one or more of the following: unique and original selection, coordination, expression, arrangement, and classification of the information.

All rights to this publication will be vigorously defended.

Copyright © 2006 Thomson Gale, a part of the Thomson Corporation.
27500 Drake Rd.
Farmington Hills, MI 48331-3535
ISBN 0-7876-9057-0

Gale Group and Design is a trademark used herein under license.

Printed in the United States of America

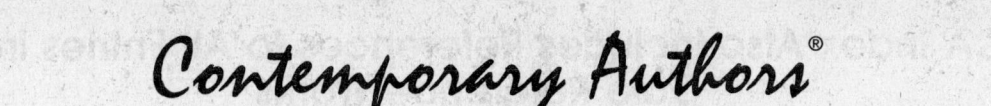

Cumulative Index

Contemporary Authors Volumes 1-239

Contemporary Authors New Revision Series Volumes 1-144

This Index Includes References to All Entries in the *Contemporary Authors* Series

Contemporary Authors—Volume 239 brings the total coverage to approximately 152,000 writers, both living and deceased, a large portion of whom cannot be found in other reference works. Writers in fiction, general nonfiction, poetry, journalism, drama, motion pictures, television, and other fields are included in CA. Each new volume contains sketches on authors not previously listed in the series. Cumulative index published separately and distributed with even-numbered original volumes. All volumes in the series are in print.

Contemporary Authors New Revision Series—Provides completely updated information on authors listed in previous volumes of CA. Sketches from a number of volumes are assessed, and only entries requiring significant change are revised and published in the CA New Revision Series. Volumes 1-144 are in print. (All volumes published under the former revision system, 1-4 through 41-44 First Revision, will remain in print.)

Contemporary Authors Permanent Series—Consists of updated listings for deceased and inactive authors removed from original volumes 9-36 when these volumes were revised. Two volumes only; both are in print.

Contemporary Authors Autobiography Series—Presents specially commissioned autobiographies by leading writers. Volumes 1-30 are in print.

Contemporary Authors Bibliographical Series—Contains primary and secondary bibliographies as well as analytical bibliographical essays. Volumes 1-2 are in print.

A Sample Index Entry:

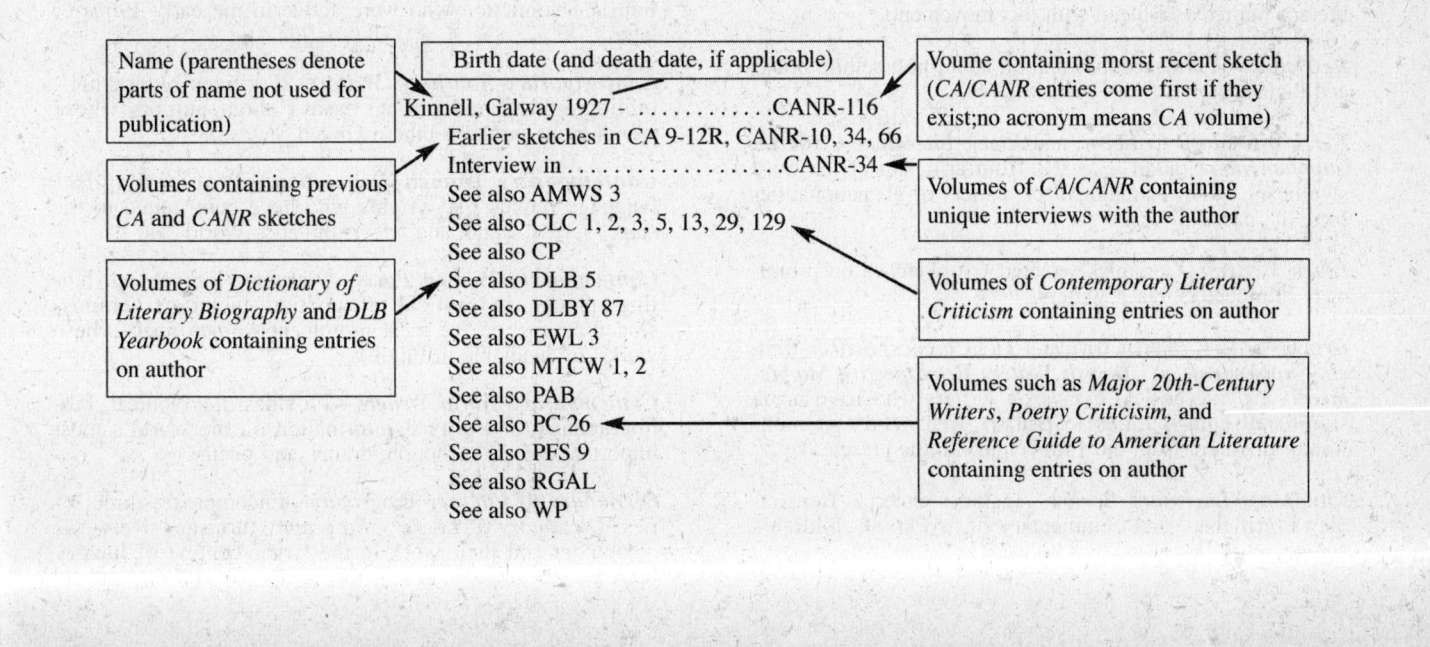

The CA Index Also Includes References to All Entries in These Gale Reference Works

African American Writers—Offers biographical and critical essays on prominent African American novelists, poets, dramatists, and essayists.

African Writers—Provides essays on African writers from seventeen countries writing in English, French, Portuguese, Arabic, and indigenous languages.

American Nature Writers—Furnishes biographical and critical essays on writers from this literary genre, as well as general subject essays.

American Writers, *American Writers—The Classics*, *American Writers Supplement*, and *American Writers Retrospective Supplement*—Provide critical and biographical articles covering notable authors from the 17th century to the present day.

Ancient Writers—Provides a survey of western literature in the classical period.

Asian American Literature—Contains biographical sketches and excerpts from literature criticism on frequently studied Asian American writers.

Authors and Artists for Young Adults—Provides sketches on prominent young adult authors and creative artists of all eras and nationalities.

Authors in the News—Reprints articles from American periodicals covering authors and members of the communications media. Two volumes, 1976-77.

Beacham's Encyclopedia of Popular Fiction: Biography and Resources—Contains bibliographical and biographical information on prominent novelists and short story writers of all nationalities.

Beacham's Guide to Literature for Young Adults—Presents bibliographical and biographical information on authors of fiction and nonfiction for young adults, as well as critical analysis of their work.

Beat Generation—A Gale Critical Companion series providing comprehensive collections of criticism about major literary figures associated with this movement.

Bestsellers—Furnishes information about best-selling books and their authors for the years 1989-90.

Black Literature Criticism and *Black Literature Criticism Supplement*—Contain excerpts from criticism of the most significant works of major black writers of all nationalities from the past 200 years.

Black Writers—Compiles selected CA sketches on prominent 20th-century black writers.

British Writers, *British Writers—The Classics*, *British Writers Supplement*, and *British Writers Retrospective Supplement*—Provide critical essays on writers who have made significant contributions to British, Irish, and Commonwealth literature from the 14th century to the present day.

Children's Literature Review—Includes excerpts from reviews, criticism, and commentary on works of children's authors and illustrators.

Concise Dictionary of American Literary Biography and *Concise Dictionary of American Literary Biography Supplement*—Contain selected entries on major American authors from the Dictionary of Literary Biography.

Concise Dictionary of British Literary Biography—Provides selected entries on major British authors from the Dictionary of Literary Biography.

Concise Dictionary of World Literary Biography—Furnishes selected entries on major international authors from the Dictionary of Literary Biography.

Contemporary American Dramatists—Offers critical, biographical, and bibliographical information on the most important American dramatists since the end of World War II.

Contemporary British Dramatists—Furnishes critical, biographical, and bibliographical information on the most influential British dramatists of the mid to late 20th century.

Contemporary Canadian Authors—Provides biographical information on Canadian novelists, playwrights, journalists, and scriptwriters.

Contemporary Literary Criticism—Presents excerpts from current criticism of the works of today's novelists, poets, playwrights, short story writers, scriptwriters, and other creative writers.

Contemporary Dramatists—Provides biographical, bibliographical, and critical information, including commissioned essays, on important and influential contemporary playwrights.

Contemporary Novelists—Contains biographies, bibliographies, and critical essays on the world's most important novelists.

Contemporary Poets—Provides biographical, bibliographical, and critical information, including commissioned essays, about the world's most important English-language poets.

Contemporary Popular Writers—Contains biographies, bibliographies, and critical essays on prominent authors of fiction and nonfiction who were active in the early 1960s or later.

Contemporary Southern Writers—Provides biographies, bibliographies, and critical essays about authors whose works focus on the southern United States.

Contemporary Women Dramatists—Profiles English-language female playwrights who have contributed to the stage, screen, radio, and television since World War II.

Contemporary Women Poets—Presents biographical, bibliographical, and critical information, including commissioned essays, on the most prominent women poets whose works are available in English.

Contemporary World Writers—Provides biographical, bibliographical, and critical information on the world's most important writers of fiction, drama, and poetry.

Dictionary of Literary Biography—Encompasses three series. *Dictionary of Literary Biography* furnishes overviews of authors and their work in the larger context of literary history. *Dictionary of Literary Biography Documentary Series* illuminates the careers of major figures through a selection of literary documents. *Dictionary of Literary Biography Yearbook* summarizes the year's literary activity.

DISCovering Authors—1997 CD-ROM of 300 biographical sketches and critical excerpts for the most-studied authors of all eras and nationalities. *DISCovering Authors: British Edition* 1997 CD-ROM includes 46 additional authors who figure prominently in British literature and curriculum. *DISCovering Authors: Canadian Edition* 1997 CD-ROM includes over 50 additional authors who figure prominently in Canadian literature and curriculum.

DISCovering Authors Modules—1997 CD-ROM divided into six modules, with each module offering biographical and critical information on authors within a specific genre: *DISCovering Most-Studied Authors, DISCovering Novelists, DISCovering Multicultural Authors, DISCovering Poets, DISCovering Dramatists,* and *DISCovering Popular Fiction and Genre Authors.*

DISCovering Authors 3.0—presents biographical and critical information on more than 600 of the most-studied authors at the high-school level, including novelists, poets, dramatists, popular, and multicultural writers of all eras and nationalities.

Drama Criticism—Furnishes excerpts from criticism of the works of most-studied dramatists of all eras and nationalities.

Drama for Students—Contains discussions of the literary and historical background of most-studied plays from various cultures and eras.

Encyclopedia of World Literature in the 20th Century—Presents in-depth information on the major aspects of literature in the 20th century, including more than 2,000 entries on individual authors.

Epics for Students—Presents analysis, context, and criticism on epic literature that is most studied in classrooms.

European Writers—Contains biographical and critical information on prominent European authors of all eras, as well as general subject essays.

Exploring Novels—1997 CD-ROM offering critical analysis of the novels most studied in high school and college undergraduate courses.

Exploring Poetry—1997 CD-ROM providing full text and in-depth explications of 275 poems most frequently studied in high schools.

Exploring Short Stories—1997 CD-ROM furnishing coverage of 100 classic, contemporary, and multicultural short stories studied in high school and college undergraduate courses.

Feminism in Literature—A Gale Critical Companion series providing criticism and interpretation of Feminism throughout history. The 6-volume set offers an inclusive range of critical and scholarly responses to authors and topics widely studied in high school and undergraduate classes.

Feminist Writers—Presents biographical, bibliographical, and critical information, including commissioned essays, about authors whose works reflect trends in feminist thought.

Gay and Lesbian Literature—Furnishes biographical, bibliographical, and critical information on authors who have figured prominently in gay and lesbian literature and culture since 1900.

Guide to French Literature—Surveys the lives and works of famous French writers from the roots of French literature to the present.

Harlem Renaissance—A Gale Critical Companion series offering biographical, bibliographical, and critical information on major literary figures and their works from this period.

Hispanic Literature Criticism and *Hispanic Literature Criticism Supplement*—Compile excerpts from criticism of the works of Hispanic writers of the late 19th and 20th centuries.

Hispanic Writers—Contains selected CA sketches on prominent 20th-century Hispanic writers.

International Dictionary of Film and Filmmakers: Writers and Production Artists—Provides coverage of legendary film writers and other production artists through detailed essays, filmographies, and bibliographies.

International Dictionary of Theatre: Playwrights—Contains biographical, bibliographical, and critical entries on major writers for the stage.

Junior DISCovering Authors—1997 CD-ROM product containing biographical sketches and critical excerpts for over 300 authors, from all eras, nationalities and genres, most studied by middle-school students.

Latin American Writers and *Latin American Writers Supplement*—Furnishes biographical and critical essays on Latin American novelists, poets, journalists, and playwrights from the 16th century to the present.

Latino and Latina Writers—Presents biographical and critical essays on writers of Hispanic ethnic origins.

Literary Movements for Students—Provides historical background information on literary movements, modern critical interpretation of each movement's characteristic styles and themes, and thumbnail sketches of representative authors and works.

Literature and Its Times and *Literature and Its Times Supplement*—Offer historical background on 300 of the most-studied literary works—novels, plays, poems, speeches, and short stories, both foreign and American.

Literature of Developing Nations for Students—Profiles authors and works from developing regions, including Africa, Latin America, Asia/Pacific Rim, India, and the Caribbean.

Major Authors and Illustrators for Children and Young Adults—Contains both newly written and completely updated *Something about the Author* sketches on authors and illustrators for young people. *Major Authors and Illustrators for Children and Young Adults Supplement* includes entries on more than 150 authors and illustrators.

Major 20th-Century Writers—Presents in two multi-volume editions selected CA sketches on the most influential novelists, poets, playwrights, and other creative writers in the twentieth century.

Major 21st-Century Writers—eBook first released in 2005, encompassing detailed biographical and bibliographical information on over 1,000 of the most-studied authors at the turn of the 21st century. Available through Gale Virtual Reference Library.

Modern American Literature—Provides a broad and instructive overview of the most significant authors of the modern period in American literature.

Modern American Women Writers—Furnishes critical and biographical essays on women writers since 1870.

Modern Japanese Writers—Presents biographical and bibliographical information on the most widely translated Japanese authors.

Mystery and Suspense Writers—Provides articles on the most influential and popular writers of mystery, detective, and espionage fiction.

Native North American Literature—Features sketches on prominent Native North American writers.

Nonfiction Classics for Students—Presents literary and historical background on the most commonly studied nonfiction essays, books, biographies and memoirs, as well as author profiles.

Novels for Students—Contains discussions of the literary and historical background of most-studied works by novelists of all nationalities and time periods.

Poetry Criticism—Furnishes excerpts from criticism of the works of the most-studied poets of all eras and nationalities.

Poetry for Students—Provides analysis of the most frequently studied poems from a variety of cultures and time periods.

Poets: American and British—Furnishes biographical and critical information on the lives and works of classic poets.

Reference Guide to American Literature—Presents bibliographical information and critical essays on American novelists, dramatists, poets, and essayists, and offers more than 100 essays on notable works of American literature.

Reference Guide to English Literature—Provides bibliographical and critical information on notable writers from Britain, Ireland, Australia, Canada, New Zealand and English-speaking Africa, Asia and the Caribbean.

Reference Guide to Short Fiction—Offers bibliographical information and a critical essay on often-studied authors, as well as essays discussing important works of short fiction.

Reference Guide to World Literature—Presents biographical and bibliographical entries on poets, dramatists, novelists and such nonfiction writers from the ancient Greeks to the 20th century.

St. James Guide to Children's Writers—Provides biographical, bibliographical, and critical information, including commissioned essays, about prominent authors of fiction, poetry, drama, and nonfiction for children.

St. James Guide to Crime & Mystery Writers—Presents biographical and bibliographical information, as well as critical essays, about authors of crime, mystery, and thriller fiction.

St. James Guide to Fantasy Writers—Provides biographical, bibliographical, and critical information, including commissioned essays, about authors of fantasy fiction.

St. James Guide to Horror, Ghost & Gothic Writers—Presents biographical and bibliographical information, as well as critical essays, about authors of horror and gothic fiction.

St. James Guide to Science Fiction Writers—Provides biographical, bibliographical, and critical information, including commissioned essays, about authors of science fiction and other forms of speculative fiction.

St. James Guide to Young Adult Writers—Presents biographical and bibliographical information, as well as critical essays, about prominent authors of fiction, poetry, drama, and nonfiction for young adults.

Science Fiction Writers—Offers biographical information and critical commentary about major authors of science fiction.

Short Stories for Students—Provides analysis of most-studied short stories from various cultures and time periods.

Short Story Criticism—Provides excerpts from criticism of the works of the most-studied short story writers of all eras and nationalities.

Something about the Author—Contains heavily illustrated sketches on juvenile and young adult authors and illustrators of all eras and nationalities.

Something about the Author Autobiography Series—Presents specially commissioned autobiographical essays by prominent juvenile and young adult authors and illustrators from all eras and nationalities.

Supernatural Fiction Writers—Offers critical essays about the most widely-read authors in fantasy and horror genres.

Twayne Companion to Contemporary Literature in English—Compiles critical appraisals of 101 authors, originally published 1975-2000 in the esteemed journal The Hollins Critic. Updated primary bibliographies and personal profiles accompany all articles. In 2 volumes.

Twayne's English Authors Series—Presents concise critical introductions to influential writers from the United Kingdom and their works.

Twayne's United States Authors Series—Features critical, interpretive studies of the works of important American authors.

Twayne's World Authors Series—Offers critical interpretation and discussion of the works of widely-read international writers.

Twentieth-Century Literary Criticism—Furnishes excerpts from criticism of the works of the most-studied novelists, poets, playwrights, short story writers, nonfiction writers, scriptwriters, and various other creative writers who died between 1900 and 1999.

Twentieth-Century Romance and Historical Writers—Provides biographical and bibliographical information, as well as critical essays, about authors of romance and historical fiction.

Twentieth-Century Western Writers—Features biographical and bibliographical information, as well as critical essays, about authors of western fiction.

World Literature and Its Times—Offers historical background on major works of fiction, poetry, and nonfiction from Africa, Europe, Latin America, and the Middle East.

World Literature Criticism—Contains in six volumes excerpts from criticism of the works of over 200 major writers from 1500 to the present. *World Literature Criticism Supplement*—Contains 50 additional writers of all eras.

World Poets—Offers biographical portraits of the world's most influential poets, as well as general topic essays.

World Writers in English—Contains biographical and critical essays on the lives and works of key writers from every part of the English speaking world.

Writers for Children—Provides biographical and bibliographical information about major children's authors.

Writers for Young Adults and *Writers for Young Adults Supplement*—Offer biographical and bibliographical information, as well as critical essays, about prominent authors for adolescents.

Yesterday's Authors of Books for Children—Consists of heavily illustrated sketches on children's authors who died before 1961. Two volumes only.

Contemporary Authors

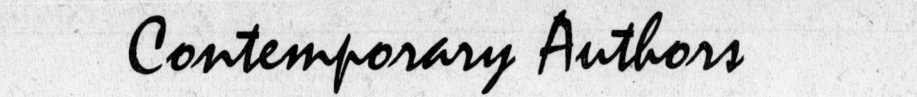

Cumulative Index

20/1631
See Upward, Allen
A/C Cross
See Lawrence, T(homas) E(dward)
A. M.
See Megged, Aharon
Aach, Herb(ert) 1923-1985
Obituary 118
Aaker, David A(llen) 1938- CANR-130
Earlier sketches in CA 49-52, CANR-31
Aaker, Everett 1954- 169
Aakjaer, Jeppe 1866-1930 .... DLB 214
Aakjer, Jeppe
See Aakjaer, Jeppe
Aalben, Patrick
See Jones, Noel
Aallyn, Alysse
See Clark, Melissa
Aalto, (Hugo) Alvar (Henrik) 1898-1976 181
Obituary 65-68
Aaltonen, Sirkku 1952- 202
Aamodt, Donald 166
See also FANT
Aardema, Verna 1911-2000 .... CANR-39
Obituary 189
Earlier sketches in CA 5-8R, CANR-3, 18
See also Vugteveen, Verna Aardema
See also CWRI 5
Aarestrup, Emil 1800-1856 .... DLB 300
Aaron, Benjamin 1915- 21-24R
Aaron, Betsy 1938- 139
Aaron, Chester 1923- CANR-102
Earlier sketches in CA 21-24R, CANR-8, 38
See also CWRI 5
See also MAICYA 1, 2
See also SAAS 12
See also SATA 9, 74
Aaron, Daniel 1912- CANR-7
Earlier sketch in CA 13-16R
Aaron, David (Laurence) 1938- CANR-107
Earlier sketch in CA 126
Aaron, Hank 1934- 147
Brief entry 104
Aaron, Henry (Jacob) 1936- 129
Aaron, Henry Louis
See Aaron, Hank
Aaron, James Ethridge 1927- 21-24R
Aaron, R. I.
See Aaron, Richard Ithamar
Aaron, Richard Ithamar 1901-1987 177
Obituary 122
Aaron, Shale
See Boswell, Robert
Aaron, Shirley L. 1941- 123
Aaron, Sidney
See Chayefsky, Sidney
Aaron, Stephen 1936- 124
Aaronovitch, Sam 1919- 13-16R
Aarons, Edward S(idney)
1916-1975 .... CANR-58
Obituary 57-60
Earlier sketch in CA 93-96
See also CMW 4
Aarons, Leroy (F.) 1933-2004 150
Obituary 233
Aarons, Slim 1916- 180
Brief entry 106
Aaronson, Bernard S(eymour)
1924-1990 .... 29-32R
Aarsleff, Hans 1925- 21-24R
Aaseng, Nate
See Aaseng, Nathan
Aaseng, Nathan 1953- CANR-103
Earlier sketches in CA 106, CANR-36
See also AAYA 27
See also CLR 54
See also JRDA
See also MAICYA 1, 2
See also SAAS 12
See also SATA 51, 88
See also SATA-Brief 38
Aaseng, Rolf E(dward) 1923- CANR-27
Earlier sketch in CA 49-52
Aasheim, Ashley 1942- 115
Abadi, Jennifer Felicia 1967(?)- 238
Abadinsky, Howard 1941- 110
Abagnale, Frank W., Jr. 1948- CANR-95
Earlier sketch in CA 112
Abajian, James De Tar 1914-1986 65-68
Abarbanel, Karin 1950- 65-68
Abarbanel, Sam X. 1914-
Brief entry 106
Abas, Syed Jan 1936- 154
Abasiyanik, Sait Faik 1906-1954 231
Brief entry 123
See also Sait Faik
Abata, Russell M(ary) 1930- 113
Abate, Frank R(obert) 1951- 118
Abayakoon, Cyrus D. F. 1912-
Brief entry 115
Abbagnano, Nicola 1901-1990 .... 33-36R
Abbas 1934- 149
Abbas, Abdul
See Hamza, Khidhir (Abdul Abbas)
Abbas, Jailan 1952- 155
See also SATA 91
Abbas, Khwaja Ahmad 1914-1987 ... CANR-69
Earlier sketch in CA 57-60
See also CN 1, 2, 3, 4, 5, 6
See also IDFW 3, 4
Abbate, Janet 197
Abbazia, Patrick 1937- 57-60
Abbe, Elfriede (Martha) 1919- 13-16R
Abbe, George (Bancroft) 1911-1989 . CANR-10
Earlier sketch in CA 25-28R
Abbe, Kathryn McLaughlin 1919- 142
Abbensetts, Michael 1938- CANR-67
Earlier sketches in CA 104, CANR-37
See also CBD
See also CD 5, 6
Abberley, Aldwyn
See Cowie, Donald
Abbey, Edward 1927-1989 .... CANR-131
Obituary 128
Earlier sketches in CA 45-48, CANR-2, 41
See also AMWS 13
See also ANW
See also CLC 36, 59
See also DA3
See also DLB 256, 275
See also LATS 1:2
See also MTCW 2
See also MTFW 2005
See also TCLC 160
See also TCWW 1, 2
Abbey, Edwin Austin 1852-1911 198
See also DLB 188
Abbey, Kieran
See Reilly, Helen
Abbey, Lloyd (Robert) 1943- 125
Brief entry 104
Abbey, Lynn
See Abbey, Marilyn Lorraine
Abbey, Maj. J. R. 1894-1969 .... DLB 201
Abbey, Margaret
See York, Margaret Elizabeth
Abbey, Marilyn Lorraine 1948- CANR-140
Earlier sketches in CA 119, CANR-62
See also FANT
See also SATA 156
Abbey, Merrill R(ay) 1905-1996 .... CANR-3
Obituary 171
Earlier sketch in CA 1-4R
Abbington, John
See Gibson, Walter B(rown)
Abbot, Anthony
See Oursler, (Charles) Fulton
Abbot, Charles G(reeley) 1872-1973 77-80
Obituary 45-48
Abbot, Francis Ellingwood 1836-1903 204
Abbot, Rick
See Sharkey, John Michael
Abbot, W(illiam) W(right) 1922-
Brief entry 110
Abbot, Willis J(ohn) 1863-1934 194
Brief entry 119
See also DLB 29
Abbott, Alice
See Borland, Kathryn Kilby and Speicher, Helen Ross S(mith)
Abbott, Anthony S. 1935- 17-20R
Abbott, Berenice 1898-1991 .... CANR-76
Obituary 136
Earlier sketch in CA 106
See also AAYA 40
Abbott, Carl (John) 1944- CANR-11
Earlier sketch in CA 65-68
Abbott, Claude Colleer 1889-1971 .. CANR-75
Obituary 89-92
Earlier sketch in CA 5-8R
Abbott, Craig S. 1941- 194
Abbott, E(ric) S(ymes) 1906-1983
Obituary 110
Abbott, Edith 1876-1957 226
See also FW
Abbott, Edwin A. 1838-1926 .... DLB 178
See also TCLC 139
Abbott, Freeland K(night) 1919-1971 .... CAP-2
Earlier sketch in CA 25-28
Abbott, George (Francis)
1887-1995 .... CANR-72
Obituary 147
Earlier sketch in CA 93-96
Abbott, Gerry 194
Abbott, H(orace) Porter 1940- 45-48
Abbott, Hailey 239
Abbott, Jack Henry
See Abbott, Rufus Henry
Abbott, Jacob 1803-1879 .... DLB 1, 42, 243
See also SATA 22
Abbott, James H(amilton) 1924- 77-80
Abbott, Jerry (Lynn) 1938- 45-48
Abbott, John J(amison) 1930- 17-20R
Abbott, Keith 1944- CANR-104
Earlier sketches in CA 121, CANR-47
Abbott, L(enwood) B(allard) 1908-1985 177
Obituary 117
Abbott, Lee K(ittredge) 1947- CANR-101
Earlier sketches in CA 124, CANR-51
See also CLC 48
See also DLB 130
Abbott, Lyman 1835-1922 179
See also DLB 79
Abbott, Manager Henry
See Stratemeyer, Edward L.
Abbott, Margaret Evans 1896-1976 177
Obituary 110
Abbott, Martin 1922-1977 .... 33-36R
Abbott, May L(aura) 1916- 9-12R
Abbott, Pamela 1947- 135
Abbott, Philip (R.) 1944-1998 126
Brief entry 106
Abbott, R(obert) Tucker 1919-1995 .. CANR-37
Obituary 150
Earlier sketches in CA 9-12R, CANR-4
See also SATA 61
See also SATA-Obit 87
Abbott, Raymond H(erbert) 1942- 57-60
Abbott, Richard H(enry) 1936- 33-36R
Abbott, Robert S. 1868-1940 .... DLB 29, 91
Abbott, Rowland A(ubrey) S(amuel)
1909- 53-56
Abbott, Rufus Henry 1944-2002 107
Obituary 205
Abbott, Sarah
See Zolotow, Charlotte (Gertrude) S(hapiro)
Abbott, Scott 1949- 138
Abbott, Shirley 1934- 113
Abbott, Sidney 1937- 41-44R
Abbott, Tony 1952- 235
See also SATA 159
Abbott, Walter M(atthew) 1923- 9-12R
Abbott-Hoduski, Bernadine E. 1938- 238
Abbotts, John 1947- 73-76
Abboushi, W(asif) F(ahmi) 1931- 29-32R
Abbs, Peter 1942- 93-96
ABC
See Caddick, Arthur
Abcarian, Richard 1929- 33-36R
'Abd al-Hamid al-Katib c. 689-750 .... DLB 311
'Abd Al-Khaliq, Jabir
See Herbert, Nick
Abdallah, Omar
See Humbaraci, D(emir) Arslan
Abd al-Sabur, Salah 1931-1981 .... WLIT 6
Abdel-Magid, Isam Mohammed
1952- CANR-112
Earlier sketch in CA 152
Abdel-Malek, Anouar 1924- CANR-44
Earlier sketch in CA 29-32R
Abdel-Quddous, Ihsan (Mohammad)
1920(?)-1990 177
Obituary 130
Abdelsamad, Moustafa H(assan) 1941- ... 53-56
Abdelsayed, Cindy 1962- .... SATA 123
Abdoh, Salar 221
Abdul, Raoul 1929- 29-32R
See also SATA 12
Abdul-baki, Mahmud 1526-1600
See Baki
Abdul-Jabbar, Kareem 1947- 139
See also BW 2
Abdullah, Achmed 1881-1945
Brief entry 115
See also FANT
Abdullahi, Guda 1946- 93-96
Abdul-Masih, Marguerite Thabit 1956- 220
Abdul-Rauf, Muhammad 1917- 101
Abe, Kobo 1924-1993 .... CANR-60
Obituary 140
Earlier sketches in CA 65-68, CANR-24
See also CLC 8, 22, 53, 81
See also DAM NOV
See also DFS 14
See also DLB 182
See also EWL 3
See also MJW
See also MTCW 1, 2
See also MTFW 2005
See also NFS 22
See also RGWL 3
See also SFW 4
See also SSC 61
See also TCLC 131
Abeel, Erica (Hennefeld) 1937- 113
Brief entry 109
Abegglen, James C. 1926- 217
Abe Kobo
See Abe, Kobo
Abel, Alan (Irwin) 1928- CANR-12
Earlier sketch in CA 17-20R
Abel, Bob
See Abel, Robert
Abel, Christopher (Graham) 1946- 127
Abel, Elie 1920-2004 .... CANR-36
Obituary 230
Earlier sketches in CA 61-64, CANR-8
Abel, Emily K. 1942- CANR-118
Earlier sketch in CA 153
Abel, Ernest L(awrence) 1943- CANR-123
Earlier sketches in CA 41-44R, CANR-14
Abel, I(orwith) W(ilbur) 1908-1987 186
Obituary 123
Brief entry 105
Abel, Jeanne 1937- 17-20R
Abel, Jessica 1969- 197
Abel, Lionel 1910-2001 61-64
Obituary 195
Abel, Raymond 1911- .... SATA 12
Abel, Reuben 1911-1997 .... 37-40R
Obituary 160
Abel, Richard (Owen) 1941- 129
Abel, Richard L. 1941- 131
Abel, Robert 1913(?)-1987 181
Obituary 122
Abel, Robert 1931-1981 .... CANR-11
Obituary 105
Earlier sketch in CA 65-68
Abel, Robert H(alsall) 1941- CANR-37
Earlier sketch in CA 102
Abel, Sam 1957- 156
Abel, Theodora M(ead) 1899-1998 57-60
Obituary 172
Abel, Theodore (Fred) 1896-1988 .... 21-24R
Obituary 180
Abel, Wilhelm 1904-
Brief entry 119
Abelaira, Augusto 1926- .... DLB 287
Abelard, Peter c. 1079-c. 1142 ... DLB 115, 208
Abeles, Elvin (V. I.) 1907-1997 104
Obituary 174
Abell, Arunah S. 1806-1888 .... DLB 43
Abell, George O(gden) 1927-1983 ... CANR-75
Obituary 111
Earlier sketches in CA 9-12R, CANR-3
Abell, Kathleen 1938- 49-52
See also SATA 9
Abell, Kjeld 1901-1961 191
Obituary 111
See also CLC 15
See also DLB 214
See also EWL 3
Abell, Ron(ald F.) 1932- 119
Abella, Alex 1950- CANR-106
Earlier sketch in CA 93-96
Abella, Irving (Martin) 1940- CANR-28
Earlier sketch in CA 49-52
Abellan, Jose Luis 1933- 206
Abelove, Joan CANR-122
Earlier sketch in CA 172
See also AAYA 36
See also SATA 110
Abels, Harriette S(heffer) 1926- 121
See also SATA 50
Abels, Jules 1913-1977 61-64
Abels, Richard Philip 1951- 196
Abel-Smith, Brian 1926- CANR-9
Earlier sketch in CA 21-24R
Abelson, Alan 1925- 136
Abelson, Philip H(auge) 1913-2004 155
Obituary 229
Brief entry 107
Abelson, Raziel A(lter) 1921- CANR-6
Earlier sketch in CA 9-12R
Abelson, Robert P(aul) 1928- 41-44R
Abend, Norman A(nchel) 1931- 33-36R
Aber, William M(cKee) 1929- 57-60
Aberbach, David 1953- 135
Aberbach, Joel D(avid) 1940- CANR-20
Earlier sketch in CA 45-48
Abercrombie, Barbara (Mattes)
1939- CANR-127
Earlier sketch in CA 81-84
See also SATA 16
Abercrombie, Lascelles 1881-1938
Brief entry 112
See also DLB 19
See also RGEL 2
See also TCLC 141
Abercrombie, M(innie) L(ouie) J(ohnson)
1909(?)-1984 177
Obituary 115
Abercrombie, M. L. Johnson
See Abercrombie, M(innie) L(ouie) J(ohnson)
Abercrombie, Michael 1912-1979
Obituary 115
Abercrombie, Nicholas 1944- CANR-125
Earlier sketches in CA 128, CANR-59

Abercrombie 2 CONTEMPORARY AUTHORS

Abercrombie, Nigel J(ames)
1908-1986 .... CANR-75
Obituary 118
Earlier sketch in CA 101
Abercrombie, Stanley 1935- 117
Aberg, Sherrill E. 1924- 21-24R
Aberle, David F(riend) 1918- 21-24R
Aberle, John Wayne 1919- 1-4R
Aberle, Kathleen Gough 1925- CANR-5
Earlier sketch in CA 13-16R
Abernathy, David M(yles) 1933- CANR-37
Earlier sketch in CA 53-56
Abernathy, Donzaleigh (Avis) 222
Abernathy, (M.) Elton 1913-1992 .... 17-20R
Abernathy, M(abra) Glenn
1921-1990 .... CANR-76
Obituary 131
Earlier sketch in CA 13-16R
Abernathy, Ralph David 1926-1990 133
Obituary 131
Abernathy, William J(ackson)
1933-1983 .... CANR-37
Obituary 111
Earlier sketch in CA 93-96
Abernethy, Francis Edward 1925- CANR-8
Earlier sketch in CA 21-24R, 175
Abernethy, George Lawrence 1910-1996 .. 1-4R
Abernethy, Peter L(ink) 1935- 69-72
Abernethy, Robert G(ordon) 1927- 21-24R
See also SATA 5
Abernethy, Thomas Perkins
1890-1975 .... CANR-75
Obituary 111
Earlier sketches in CAP-1, CA 19-20
Abernethy, Virginia 1934- 93-96
Abert, Donald B. 1907-1985
Obituary 116
Aberth, John 1963- 230
Abhavananda
See Crowley, Edward Alexander
See also GLL 1
Abhedananda, Svami 1866-1939 218
Abhedananda, Swami
See Abhedananda, Svami
ab Hugh, Dafydd 1960- 154
See also BYA 10
See also FANT
Abildskov, Marilyn 1961- 235
Abisch, Roslyn Kroop 1927- CANR-10
Earlier sketch in CA 21-24R
See also SATA 9
Abisch, Roz
See Abisch, Roslyn Kroop
Abish, Walter 1931- CANR-114
Earlier sketches in CA 101, CANR-37
See also CLC 22
See also CN 3, 4, 5, 6
See also DLB 130, 227
See also MAL 5
See also SSC 44
Able, James A(ugustus), Jr. 1928- 93-96
Able, Kenneth P(aul) 228
Able, Mark
See Krooth, Richard
Ableman, Michael 1954- 170
Ableman, Paul 1927- CANR-67
Earlier sketches in CA 61-64, CANR-12
See also CBD
See also CN 1, 2, 3
Abler, Ronald F. 1939- CANR-4
Earlier sketch in CA 53-56
Abler, Thomas S(truthers) 1941- 101
Ablesimov, Aleksandr Onisimovich
1742-1783 .... DLB 150
Abley, Mark 1955- CANR-104
Earlier sketches in CA 120, CANR-50
Ablow, Keith Russell 1961- CANR-121
Earlier sketch in CA 141
Abma, G(erben) Willem 1942-2002 209
Abodaher, David J. (Naiph) 1919- CANR-10
Earlier sketch in CA 17-20R
See also SATA 17
Abolafia, Yossi 1944- 142
See also SATA 60
See also SATA-Brief 46
Abou El Fadl, Khaled 1963- 220
Abourezk, James G(eorge) 1931- 135
Abou-Saif, Laila 1941- 147
Abouzeid, Leila 1950- 200
Abrahall, Clare Hoskyns
See Hoskyns-Abrahall, Clare (Constance Drury)
Abraham, A(ntoine) J. 1942- 175
Abraham, Claude K(urt) 1931- CANR-36
Earlier sketch in CA 21-24R
Abraham, David 1946- 129
Abraham, Doc
See Abraham, George
Abraham, George 1915-2005 110
Obituary 235
Abraham, Gerald Ernest Heal
1904-1988 .... CANR-75
Obituary 125
Earlier sketch in CA 89-92
Abraham, Henry Julian 1921- CANR-18
Earlier sketches in CA 5-8R, CANR-2
Abraham, Katherine 1922-2005 110
Obituary 239
Abraham, Katy
See Abraham, Katherine
Abraham, Louis Arnold 1893-1983 177
Obituary 108
Abraham, M(annamplakkal) Francis 1939- . 110
Abraham, Margaret 1961- 197
Abraham, Pearl 152
Abraham, Willard 1916-1999 .... CANR-5
Earlier sketch in CA 13-16R
Abraham, William E. 1934- 13-16R
Abraham, William I(srael) 1919- 25-28R
Abraham a Sancta Clara 1644-1709 ... DLB 168
Abrahami, Izzy 1930-
Brief entry 110
Abrahamian, Ervand 1940- 110
Abrahams, Doris Caroline 1901(?)-1982(?) . 129
Obituary 108
Abrahams, Edward 1949- 122
Abrahams, Gerald 1907-1980 102
Obituary 97-100
Abrahams, Hilary (Ruth) 1938- .... SATA 29
Abrahams, Howard Phineas 1904-1997 .. 57-60
Abrahams, Jim 1944- 138
Abrahams, Lionel (Isaac)
1928-2004 .... CANR-92
Obituary 227
Earlier sketch in CA 145
Abrahams, Peter (Henry) 1919- CANR-125
Earlier sketches in CA 57-60, CANR-26
See also AFW
See also BW 1
See also CDWLB 3
See also CLC 4
See also CN 1, 2, 3, 4, 5, 6
See also DLB 117, 225
See also EWL 3
See also MTCW 1, 2
See also RGEL 2
See also WLIT 2
Abrahams, Peter 1947- CANR-91
Earlier sketch in CA 152
Abrahams, R(aphael) G(arvin) 1934- 25-28R
Abrahams, Robert David 1905-1998 .... CAP-2
Earlier sketch in CA 33-36
See also SATA 4
Abrahams, Roger D(avid) 1933- CANR-49
Earlier sketches in CA 9-12R, CANR-5, 24
Abrahams, William (Miller)
1919-1998 .... CANR-43
Obituary 169
Earlier sketch in CA 61-64
Abrahamsen, Christine Elizabeth 1916- 101
Abrahamsen, David 1903-2002 65-68
Obituary 206
Abrahamson, Irving 1925- CANR-65
Earlier sketch in CA 129
Abrahamson, Mark J. 1939- 101
Abrahamsson, Bengt 1937- 97-100
Abrahms, Sally (Ellen) 1953- 113
Abram, H(arry) S(hore) 1931-1977 .... 29-32R
Abram, Morris Berthold 1918-2000 108
Obituary 190
Abramo, J(oe) L. 217
Abramo, J(oseph) L.
See Abramo, J(oe) L.
Abramov, Emil
See Draitser, Emil
Abramov, Fedor Aleksandrovich
See Abramov, Fyodor Aleksandrovich
See also DLB 302
Abramov, Fyodor Aleksandrovich
1920-1983 133
Obituary 109
See also Abramov, Fedor Aleksandrovich
See also EWL 3
Abramov, S(hene'ur) Zalman 1908-1997 134
Brief entry 108
Abramovitz, Anita (Zeltner Brooks)
1914- 97-100
See also Brooks, Anita
Abramowitz, Jack 1918- CANR-6
Earlier sketch in CA 5-8R
Abramowitz, Shalom Jacob 1835(?)-1917 ... 177
Brief entry 118
Abrams, Alan E(dwin) 1941- 89-92
Abrams, Ann Uhry 1934- 198
Abrams, Charles 1901-1970 .... CAP-2
Earlier sketch in CA 23-24
Abrams, Douglas Carl 1950- 143
Abrams, Elliott 1948- 140
Abrams, George J(oseph)
1918-1978 .... CANR-12
Earlier sketch in CA 61-64
Abrams, Harry N(athan) 1904-1979
Obituary 93-96
Abrams, J. J.
See Abrams, Jeffrey
Abrams, Jeffrey 1966- 226
See also AAYA 61
Abrams, Joy 1941- 77-80
See also SATA 16
Abrams, Judith Z. 235
Abrams, Lawrence F. 124
See also SATA 58
See also SATA-Brief 47
Abrams, Linsey 1951- CANR-18
Earlier sketch in CA 102
Abrams, M(eyer) H(oward) 1912- CANR-33
Earlier sketches in CA 57-60, CANR-13
See also CLC 24
See also DLB 67
Abrams, Mark 1906-1994 124
Abrams, Nancy 1963- 192
Abrams, Nita 1953- 208
Abrams, Ovid (S. McL.) 1939- 173
Abrams, Peter D(avid) 1936- 33-36R
Abrams, Philip 1933(?)-1981 129
Obituary 105
Abrams, Richard M. 1932- 13-16R
Abrams, Roger I. 1945- 177
Abrams, Sam(uel) 1935- 21-24R
Abramsky, Chimen 1916-
Brief entry 109
Abramson, Albert 1922- 155
Abramson, Doris E. 1925- 25-28R
Abramson, Edward A. 1944- 143
Abramson, Glenda 1938- 220
Abramson, Harold A(lexander) 1889-1980 . 200
Abramson, Harold Alexander 1889-1980
Obituary 102
Abramson, Harold J(ulian) 1934- 45-48
Abramson, Jesse P. 1904-1979 .... CANR-123
Obituary 89-92
Earlier sketch in CA 177
See also DLB 241
Abramson, Jill 1954- 156
Abramson, Joan 1932- CANR-37
Earlier sketch in CA 25-28R
Abramson, Leslie W. 166
Abramson, Martin 1921- 49-52
Abramson, Michael 1944- 69-72
Abramson, Paul R(obert) 1937- CANR-94
Earlier sketches in CA 61-64, CANR-8, 37
Abramson, Rudy 1937- 152
Abrash, Merritt 1930- 21-24R
Abrashkin, Raymond 1911-1960 115
See also SATA 50
Abravanel, Elizabeth 1944- 112
Abravanel, Elliot D(on) 1942- 112
Abrecht, Mary Ellen (Benson) 1945- 69-72
Abresch, Peter E. 1931- CANR-123
Earlier sketch in CA 169
Abreu, Maria Isabel 1919-2000 45-48
Obituary 190
Abromowitz, Joe
See Adams, Joey
Abruzzo, Ben(jamine Lawrence)
1930-1985 177
Obituary 115
Absalom, Roger Neil Lewis 1929- CANR-57
Earlier sketches in CA 111, CANR-31
Abschatz, Hans Assmann von
See Abschatz, Hans Aßmann von
Abschatz, Hans Aßmann von
1646-1699 .... DLB 168
Abse, Dannie 1923- CANR-124
Earlier sketches in CA 53-56, CANR-4, 46, 74
See also CAAS 1
See also CBD
See also CLC 7, 29
See also CN 1, 2, 3
See also CP 1, 2, 3, 4, 5, 6, 7
See also DAB
See also DAM POET
See also DLB 27, 245
See also MTCW 2
See also PC 41
Abse, David Wilfred 1915- 49-52
Abse, Joan 1926- CANR-123
Earlier sketch in CA 108
Abse, Leo 1917- 137
Abshire, David M. 1926- CANR-37
Earlier sketches in CA 21-24R, CANR-8
Abt, Clark C(laus) 1929- CANR-21
Earlier sketch in CA 69-72
Abt, Jeffrey 1940- 208
Abt, Lawrence Edwin 1915-1994 .... CANR-13
Obituary 176
Earlier sketch in CA 33-36R
Abt, Vicki 1942- 120
Abu al-'Atahiyah 748-825(?) .... DLB 311
Abu al-Harith Ghaylan ibn 'Uqbah
See Dhu al-Rummah
Abuba, Ernest Hawkins 1947- 133
Abu-Jaber, Diana 1959- 142
Abu Jaber, Kamel S(aleh) 1932- CANR-14
Earlier sketch in CA 21-24R
Abu-Jamal, Mumia 1954- CANR-113
Earlier sketch in CA 154
Abu-Lughod, Ibrahim Ali
1929-2001 .... CANR-10
Obituary 197
Earlier sketch in CA 5-8R
Abu-Lughod, Janet L(ouise) 1928- CANR-10
Earlier sketch in CA 65-68
Abu-Lughod, Lila 1952- CANR-94
Earlier sketch in CA 150
Abu Madi, Iliyya 1889-1957 .... EWL 3
Abun-Nasr, Jamil Miri 1932- 69-72
Abu Nuwas 760(?)-815(?) .... DLB 311
See also WLIT 6
Aburdene, Patricia 1947(?)- 140
Aburish, Said K. 1935- CANR-85
Earlier sketch in CA 140
Abutsu 1222(?)-1283
See Abutsu-ni
Abutsu-ni
See Abutsu
See also DLB 203
Abu Zayd, Layla
See Abouzeid, Leila
Aby, Stephen H. 1949- 123
Abzug, Bella S(avitsky) 1920-1998 137
Obituary 165
Brief entry 104
Abzug, Martin 1916-1986 210
Obituary 119
Abzug, Robert H(enry) 1945- CANR-21
Earlier sketch in CA 104
Academicus Mentor
See Montagu, Ashley
Academic Investor
See Reddaway, W(illiam) Brian
Accad, Evelyne 1943- 162
See also EWL 3
See also RGWL 3
Accattoli, Luigi 231
Accawi, Anwar F. 1943- 217
Accinelli, Robert 1939- 160
Accius c. 170B.C.-c. 80B.C. .... DLB 211
Accola, Louis W(ayne) 1937- CANR-12
Earlier sketch in CA 29-32R
Accomando, Claire Hsu 1937- 142
Acconci, Vito 1940- .... CP 1
Accordino, John J. 236
Accrocca, Elio Filippo 1923-1996 238
See also DLB 128
Ace, Goodman 1899-1982 .... CANR-77
Obituary 106
Earlier sketch in CA 61-64
Aceto, Vincent J(ohn) 1932- 106
Acevedo Diaz, Eduardo 1851-1921 .... LAW
Achard, George
See Torres-Levin, Tereska (Szwarc)
Achard, Marcel -1974
See Ferreol, Marcel Auguste
See also IDFW 3
Achdiat, Karta Mihardja 1911- .... EWL 3
Achebe, (Albert) Chinua(lumogu)
1930- CANR-124
Earlier sketches in CA 1-4R, CANR-6, 26, 47
See also AAYA 15
See also AFW
See also BLC 1
See also BPFB 1
See also BRWC 2
See also BW 2, 3
See also CDWLB 3
See also CLC 1, 3, 5, 7, 11, 26, 51, 75, 127, 152
See also CLR 20
See also CN 1, 2, 3, 4, 5, 6, 7
See also CP 2, 3, 4, 5, 6, 7
See also CWRI 5
See also DA
See also DA3
See also DAB
See also DAC
See also DAM MST, MULT, NOV
See also DLB 117
See also DNFS 1
See also EWL 3
See also EXPN
See also EXPS
See also LAIT 2
See also LATS 1:2
See also MAICYA 1, 2
See also MTCW 1, 2
See also MTFW 2005
See also NFS 2
See also RGEL 2
See also RGSF 2
See also SATA 38, 40
See also SATA-Brief 38
See also SSFS 3, 13
See also TWA
See also WLC
See also WLIT 2
See also WWE 1
Achenbach, Joel 231
Achenbaum, W(ilbert) Andrew
1947- CANR-88
Earlier sketches in CA 89-92, CANR-15, 34
Acheson, David C(ampion) 1921- 132
Acheson, Dean (Gooderham)
1893-1971 .... CAP-2
Obituary 33-36R
Earlier sketch in CA 25-28
Acheson, Patricia Castles 1924- 1-4R
Achilles
See Lamb, Charles Bentall
Achinstein, Peter Jacob 1935- 111
Achinstein, Sharon 1963- 234
Acholonu, Catherine Obianuju 1951- 180
Achord, James L(ee) 1931- 230
Achtemeier, Elizabeth (Rice)
1926-2002 .... CANR-8
Obituary 210
Earlier sketch in CA 17-20R
Achtemeier, Paul J(ohn) 1927- CANR-8
Earlier sketch in CA 17-20R
Achterberg, Gerrit 1905-1962 .... EWL 3
Achternbusch, Herbert 1938- 182
See also DLB 124
Achyut
See Birla, Lakshminiwas N.
Aciman, Andre A. 1808(?)-1866 188
Acito, Marc 1966- 232
Ackart, Robert 1921- 109
Ackelsberg, Martha A. 1946- 139
Acker, Alison 1928- 125
Acker, Bertie (Wilcox Naylor) 1922- 147
Acker, Duane Calvin 1931- 33-36R
Acker, Helen 73-76
Acker, Kathy 1948-1997 .... CANR-55
Obituary 162
Brief entry 117
Earlier sketch in CA 122
See also AMWS 12
See also CLC 45, 111
See also CN 5, 6
See also MAL 5
Acker, Robert Flint 1920- 89-92
Acker, William R(eynolds) B(eal)
1910(?)-1974 176
Obituary 49-52
Ackerley, Chris(topher John) 1947- 129
Ackerley, J(oe) R(andolph) 1896-1967 102
Obituary 89-92
Ackerman, Bruce A. 1943- CANR-95
Earlier sketch in CA 53-56
Ackerman, Carl W(illiam) 1890-1970 73-76
Obituary 29-32R

Cumulative Index 3 Adams

Ackerman, Diane 1948- ... CANR-112
Earlier sketches in CA 57-60, CANR-31, 54
See also CAAS 20
See also ANW
See also CP 4, 5, 6, 7
See also CWP
See also DLB 120
See also PFS 19
See also SATA 102
Ackerman, Edward A. 1911-1973
Obituary ... 41-44R
Ackerman, Edward A(ugustus) 1911-1973 .. 200
Ackerman, Eugene (Francis)
1888-1974 ... SATA 10
Ackerman, Forrest J(ames) 1916- ... CANR-78
Earlier sketch in CA 102
Interview in ... CA-102
Ackerman, Gerald M(artin) 1928- ... CANR-1
Earlier sketch in CA 45-48
Ackerman, J. Mark 1939- ... 53-56
Ackerman, James D. 1950- ... 153
Ackerman, James S(loss) 1919- ... 9-12R
Ackerman, Jennifer G. 1959- ... 203
Ackerman, Karen 1951- ... SATA 126
Ackerman, Kenneth David ... 223
Ackerman, Lowell J. 1956- ... 224
Ackerman, Nathan W(ard) 1908-1971 .. CAP-2
Earlier sketch in CA 29-32
Ackerman, Robert E(dwin) 1928- ... CANR-43
Earlier sketches in CA 45-48, CANR-20
Ackerman, Robert K. 1933- ... 123
Ackerman, Robert W(illiam) 1910-1980 ... 103
Ackerman, Susan ... 221
Ackerman, Susan Rose
See Rose-Ackerman, Susan
Ackerman, Susan Yoder 1945- ... 156
See also SATA 92
Ackermann, Joan ... DFS 22
Ackermann, Paul Kurt 1919- ... 180
Brief entry ... 104
Ackermann, Robert John 1933-
Brief entry ... 108
Ackerson, Duane (Wright), Jr. 1942- ... 33-36R
Ackison, Wendy Wassink 1956- ... SATA 103
Ackland, Len 1944- ... 199
Ackland, Rodney 1908-1991 ... 57-60
See also CBD
Ackles, David 1937-1999 ... 183
Ackley, Charles Walton 1913-1975 ... 41-44R
Ackley, Hugh Gardner 1915-1998 ... 61-64
Obituary ... 164
Ackley, Peggy Jo 1955- ... SATA 58
Ackley, Randall William 1931- ... CANR-6
Earlier sketch in CA 53-56
Ackley Bean, Heather Ann 1966- ... 188
Ackmann, Martha (A.) 1951- ... 225
Ackoff, Russell L(incoln) 1919- ... CANR-32
Earlier sketches in CA 41-44R, CANR-15
Ackroyd, Joyce Irene ... 103
Ackroyd, Peter 1949- ... CANR-132
Brief entry ... 123
Earlier sketches in CA 127, CANR-51, 74, 99
Interview in ... CA-127
See also BRWS 6
See also CLC 34, 52, 140
See also CN 4, 5, 6, 7
See also DLB 155, 231
See also HGG
See also MTCW 2
See also MTFW 2005
See also RHW
See also SATA 153
See also SUFW 2
Ackroyd, Peter R(unham)
1917-2005 ... CANR-31
Obituary ... 235
Earlier sketch in CA 25-28R
Ackworth, Robert Charles 1923- ... 5-8R
Acland, Alice
See Wignall, Anne
Acland, James H. 1917-1976 ... 41-44R
Acocella, Joan Ross 1945- ... 188
Acocella, Marisa 1960(?)- ... 156
Acomb (Walker), Evelyn Martha 1910- ... 85-88
Acomb, Frances (Dorothy) 1907-1984 ... 215
Brief entry ... 109
Acomb-Walker, Evelyn Martha
See Acomb (Walker), Evelyn Martha
Acorn, John (Harrison) 1958- ... SATA 79
Acorn, Milton 1923-1986 ... 103
Interview in ... CA-103
See also CCA 1
See also CLC 15
See also CP 1, 2, 3, 4
See also DAC
See also DLB 53
Acosta, Jose de 1540-1600 ... DLB 318
Acosta, Juvenal 1961- ... 172
Autobiographical Essay in ... 172
See also CAAS 27
Acosta, Oscar Zeta 1935(?)- ... 131
See also DLB 82
See also HW 1
Acosta, Teresa Palomo 1949- ... EXPP
See also PFS 12
Acosta Torres, Jose
See Torres, Jose Acosta
Acquaviva, Sabino Samele 1927- ... 101
Acquaye, Alfred Allotey 1939- ... 25-28R
Acre, Stephen
See Gruber, Frank
Acred, Arthur 1926- ... 25-28R
Acredolo, Linda (Potter) 1947- ... 195
See also SATA 159
Acs, Laszlo (Bela) 1931- ... SATA 42
See also SATA-Brief 32
Acsadi, Gwendolyn
See Johnson-Acsadi, Gwendolyn
Actaea
See Agassiz, Elizabeth Cary
Acton, Edward J. 1949- ... CANR-2
Earlier sketch in CA 45-48
Acton, Harold Mario Mitchell
1904-1994 ... CANR-75
Obituary ... 144
Earlier sketches in CA 1-4R, CANR-3
Acton, Jay
See Acton, Edward J.
Acton, Thomas (Alan) 1948- ... 57-60
Acuff, Frederick Gene 1931-
Brief entry ... 110
Acuff, Jerry 1949- ... 233
Acuff, Selma Boyd 1924- ... 111
See also SATA 45
Acula, Dr.
See Ackerman, Forrest J(ames)
Acuna, Rodolfo
See Acuna, Rodolfo F(rancis)
Acuna, Rodolfo F(rancis) 1932- ... CANR-72
Brief entry ... 108
Earlier sketch in CA 131
See also HW 1, 2
Acuna, Rudy
See Acuna, Rodolfo F(rancis)
Aczel, Amir D. 1950- ... CANR-99
Earlier sketch in CA 164
Aczel, Tamas 1921-1994 ... CANR-29
Earlier sketch in CA 49-52
Ada, Alma Flor 1938- ... CANR-122
Earlier sketches in CA 123, CANR-87
See also CLR 62
See also MAICYA 2
See also SATA 43, 84, 143
Adachi, Barbara (Curtis) 1924- ... CANR-27
Earlier sketch in CA 49-52
Adachi, Jiro 1965- ... 231
Adachi, Ken 1929(?)-1989 ... 176
Obituary ... 128
Adair, Aaron J. 1980- ... 227
Adair, Cecil
See Everett-Green, Evelyn
Adair, Cherry 1951- ... 232
Adair, Christy 1949- ... 147
Adair, Dennis 1945- ... 107
Adair, Gilbert 1944- ... CANR-125
Earlier sketch in CA 157
See also DLB 194
See also FANT
See also SATA 98
Adair, Ian 1942- ... CANR-11
Earlier sketch in CA 69-72
See also SATA 53
Adair, Jack
See Pavey, Don
Adair, James 1709(?)-1783(?) ... DLB 30
Adair, James R. 1923- ... 17-20R
Adair, John G(lenn) 1933- ... 49-52
Adair, Margaret Weeks (?)-1971 ... CAP-1
Earlier sketch in CA 13-14
See also SATA 10
Adair, Robert Kemp 1924- ... 136
Adair, Virginia Hamilton
1913-2004 ... CANR-94
Obituary ... 231
Earlier sketch in CA 156
Adair, Vivyan C. 1953- ... 234
Adam, Ben
See Drachman, Julian M(oses)
Adam, Christina ... 203
Adam, Cornel
See Lengyel, Cornel Adam
Adam, David 1936- ... 208
Adam, Graeme Mercer 1839-1912 ... 179
See also DLB 99
Adam, Hans Christian 1948- ... 131
Adam, Helen (Douglas) 1909-1993 .. CANR-75
Obituary ... 143
Earlier sketches in CA 17-20R, CANR-7
See also CP 1, 3, 4
Adam, Heribert 1936- ... 105
Adam, Jan 1920- ... CANR-38
Earlier sketch in CA 115
Adam, Ken 1921- ... IDFW 3, 4
Adam, Mark
See Alexander, Marc
Adam, Michael 1919- ... CANR-37
Earlier sketch in CA 53-56
Adam, Paul 1951- ... CANR-123
Earlier sketch in CA 145
Adam, Peter 1929- ... CANR-123
Earlier sketches in CA 127, CANR-51
Adam, Robert 1948- ... 158
See also SATA 93
Adam, Robert Borthwick II 1863-1940 ... 184
See also DLB 187
Adam, Ruth (Augusta) 1907-1977 ... 21-24R
Adam, Thomas R(itchie) 1900-1990 ... CAP-1
Earlier sketch in CA 19-20
Adamashvili, Mikhail 1880-1937
See Djavakhishvili, Mikheil
Adamczewski, Zygmunt 1921-1990 ... 13-16R
Adame, Leonard 1947- ... 131
See also DLB 82
See also HW 1
Adamec, Christine 1949- ... CANR-123
Earlier sketch in CA 141
Adamec, Ludwig W(arren) 1924- ... CANR-104
Earlier sketches in CA 21-24R, CANR-9, 24, 49
Adamesteanu, Gabriela 1942- ... DLB 232
Adamic, Alojzij 1899(?)-1951
Brief entry ... 109
See also Adamic, Louis
Adamic, Louis (?)- ... 177
See also Adamic, Alojzij
See also DLB 9
Adamov, Arthur 1908-1970 ... CAP-2
Obituary ... 25-28R
Earlier sketch in CA 17-18
See also CLC 4, 25
See also DAM DRAM
See also DLB 321
See also EWL 3
See also GFL 1789 to the Present
See also MTCW 1
See also RGWL 2, 3
Adamovich, Georgii 1894-1972 ... DLB 317
Adams, A. Don
See Cleveland, Philip Jerome
Adams, A. John 1931- ... 33-36R
Adams, Abby 1939- ... 154
Adams, Abigail 1744-1818 ... DLB 183, 200
Adams, Adrienne 1906- ... CANR-104
Earlier sketches in CA 49-52, CANR-1, 35
See also CLR 73
See also MAICYA 2
See also MAICYAS 1
See also SATA 8, 90
Adams, Alexander B. 1917(?)-1984 ... 202
Obituary ... 112
Adams, Alice (Boyd) 1926-1999 ... CANR-136
Obituary ... 179
Earlier sketches in CA 81-84, CANR-26, 53, 75, 88
Interview in ... CANR-26
See also CLC 6, 13, 46
See also CN 4, 5, 6
See also CSW
See also DLB 234
See also DLBY 1986
See also MTCW 1, 2
See also MTFW 2005
See also SSC 24
See also SSFS 14, 21
Adams, Andy
See Gibson, Walter B(rown)
Adams, Andy 1859-1935 ... TCLC 56
See also TCWW 1, 2
See also YABC 1
Adams, Anne H(utchinson)
1935-1980 ... CANR-27
Earlier sketch in CA 41-44R
Adams, Annette
See Rowland, D(onald) S(ydney)
Adams, Ansel (Easton) 1902-1984 ... CANR-10
Obituary ... 112
Earlier sketch in CA 21-24R
Interview in ... CANR-10
See also AAYA 14
See also AITN 1
Adams, Art(hur) 1963- ... 224
Adams, Arthur E(ugene) 1917- ... CANR-4
Earlier sketch in CA 5-8R
Adams, Arthur Gray, (Jr.) 1935- ... CANR-46
Earlier sketches in CA 107, CANR-23
Adams, Arthur Merrihew 1908-1979 ... 53-56
Adams, Arthur Stanton 1896-1980 ... 177
Obituary ... 102
Adams, B. B.
See Adams, Barbara
Adams, Barbara
See Gardner, Virginia (Marberry)
Adams, Barbara 1932- ... 187
Adams, Barbara Johnston 1943- ... SATA 60
Adams, Bart
See Bingley, David Ernest
Adams, Benjamin 1966- ... 215
Adams, Bernard (Paul Fornaro)
1915-2002 ... 128
Obituary ... 210
Adams, Bertha Leith 1837(?)-1912 ... 215
See also DLB 240
Adams, Bertha Leith c. 1837-1912 ... 215
Adams, Betsy
See Pitcher, Gladys
Adams, Bronte (Jane) 1963- ... 140
Adams, (Henry) Brooks 1848-1927 ... 193
Brief entry ... 123
See also DLB 47
See also TCLC 80
Adams, Bruin
See Ellis, Edward S(ylvester)
Adams, Captain Bruin
See Ellis, Edward S(ylvester)
Adams, Captain J. F. C.
See Ellis, Edward S(ylvester)
Adams, Caren 1946- ... 135
Adams, Carol J. 1951- ... 134
Adams, Cedric M. 1902-1961 ... 176
Obituary ... 89-92
Adams, Charles
See Stephens, Charles Asbury
Adams, Charles 1930- ... 150
Adams, Charles Francis, Jr. 1835-1915 ... 203
Brief entry ... 113
See also DLB 47
Adams, Charles J. III 1947- ... CANR-100
Earlier sketch in CA 150
Adams, Charles J(oseph) 1924- ... CANR-24
Earlier sketches in CA 17-20R, CANR-8
Adams, Charles Lynford 1929- ... 113
Adams, Charlotte 1899-1996
Brief entry ... 107
Adams(-Butch), Christine A(nn) 1935- ... 237
Adams, Chuck
See Tubb, E(dwin) C(harles)
Adams, Cindy (Heller) 1930- ... CANR-136
Earlier sketches in CA 21-24R, CANR-17
Adams, Cleve F(ranklin) 1895-1949 ... 184
Brief entry ... 112
See also CMW 4
Adams, Clifton 1919-1971 ... CANR-63
Earlier sketches in CA 13-16R, CANR-21
See also TCWW 1, 2
Adams, Clinton 1918-2002 ... 33-36R
Obituary ... 206
Adams, Colin C. 1956- ... 152
Adams, Dale
See Quinn, Elisabeth
Adams, Daniel
See Nicole, Christopher (Robin)
Adams, Deborah 1956- ... CANR-141
Earlier sketch in CA 170
Adams, Debra
See Speregen, Devra Newberger
Adams, Don(ald Kendrick) 1925- ... 33-36R
Adams, Donald K(napp) 1924-1987 ... 176
Obituary ... 123
Brief entry ... 111
Adams, Donald R., Jr. 1940-
Brief entry ... 113
Adams, Douglas (Noel)
1952-2001 ... CANR-124
Obituary ... 197
Earlier sketches in CA 106, CANR-34, 64
See also AAYA 4, 33
See also BEST 89:3
See also BYA 14
See also CLC 27, 60
See also CPW
See also DA3
See also DAM POP
See also DLB 261
See also DLBY 1983
See also JRDA
See also MTCW 2
See also MTFW 2005
See also NFS 7
See also SATA 116
See also SATA-Obit 128
See also SFW 4
Adams, E(lie) M(aynard) 1919-2003 . CANR-97
Obituary ... 221
Earlier sketch in CA 1-4R
Adams, Edie 1929- ... 173
Adams, Edith
See Shine, Deborah
Adams, Edward E. 1921- ... 155
Adams, Elsie B(onita) 1932- ... 69-72
Adams, Eugenia
See Owens, Virginia Stem
Adams, Evangeline (Smith) 1872(?)-1932 ... 177
Brief entry ... 121
Adams, F(rank) Ramsay 1883-1963 .. CANR-61
Earlier sketch in CA 5-8R
See also TCWW 2
Adams, Faith 1960- ... 121
Adams, Florence 1932- ... 49-52
See also SATA 61
Adams, Francis A(lexandre) 1874-1975 ... 177
Obituary ... 61-64
Adams, Frank C(lyde) 1916- ... 69-72
Adams, Franklin P(ierce) 1881-1960 ... 178
Obituary ... 93-96
See also DLB 29
Adams, Fred C(hester) 1961- ... 198
Adams, Frederick C(harles) 1941-
Brief entry ... 105
Adams, Gail Galloway 1943- ... 128
Adams, George Matthew 1878-1962 ... 201
Obituary ... 93-96
Adams, George Worthington
1905-1981 ... 41-44R
Adams, Georgia Sachs 1913-1984 ... 37-40R
Adams, Gerald R. 1946- ... 144
Adams, Glenda 1939- ... CANR-62
Earlier sketch in CA 104
See also CN 6, 7
Adams, Graham, Jr. 1928- ... 17-20R
Adams, Hannah 1755-1832 ... DLB 200
Adams, Harlen M(artin) 1904-1997 ... CAP-1
Obituary ... 164
Earlier sketch in CA 13-14
Adams, Harold 1923- ... CANR-83
Earlier sketches in CA 126, CANR-58
See also CMW 4
Adams, Harriet S(tratemeyer)
1892(?)-1982 ... CANR-27
Obituary ... 106
Earlier sketch in CA 17-20R
See also AITN 2
See also MAICYA 1, 2
See also SATA 1
See also SATA-Obit 29
Adams, Harrison ... CANR-26
Earlier sketches in CAP-2, CA 19-20
See also Rathborne, St. George (Henry) and Stratemeyer, Edward L.
Adams, Harry Baker 1924- ... 180
Brief entry ... 106
Adams, Hazard 1926- ... 9-12R
See also SATA 6

Adams 4 CONTEMPORARY AUTHORS

Adams, Henry (Brooks) 1838-1918 .. CANR-77
Brief entry ... 104
Earlier sketch in CA 133
See also AMW
See also DA
See also DAB
See also DAC
See also DAM MST
See also DLB 12, 47, 189, 284
See also EWL 3
See also MAL 5
See also MTCW 2
See also NCFS 1
See also RGAL 4
See also TCLC 4, 52
See also TUS
Adams, Henry 1949- ... 132
Adams, Henry H(itch) 1917- ... CANR-13
Earlier sketch in CA 21-24R
Adams, Henry Mason 1907-1992 ... CAP-1
Earlier sketch in CA 17-18
Adams, Henry T.
See Ransom, Jay Ellis
Adams, Herbert Baxter 1850-1901
Obituary ... 162
See also DLB 47
Adams, Herbert Mayow 1893-1985 ... CAP-2
Obituary ... 115
Earlier sketch in CA 25-28
Adams, Howard (Joseph) 1928- ... 89-92
Adams, Hunter
See Adams, Patch
Adams, J(ames) Donald 1891-1968 .... CANR-1
Earlier sketch in CA 1-4R
Adams, J(ames) Mack 1933- ... 85-88
Adams, Jad 1954- ... CANR-99
Earlier sketch in CA 142
Adams, James (Macgregor David) 1951- 138
Adams, James E(dward) 1941- ... 73-76
Adams, James F(rederick) 1927- ... 17-20R
Adams, James Luther 1901-1994 ... 41-44R
Adams, James R(owe) 1934- ... 41-44R
Adams, James Truslow 1878-1949 ... 173
Brief entry ... 115
See also DLB 17
See also DLBD 17
Adams, Jane (Ellen) 1940- ... CANR-87
Earlier sketch in CA 116
Adams, Jay Edward 1929- ... 126
Brief entry ... 108
Adams, Jeanie ... CWRI 5
Adams, Jeanne Clare 1921- ... 169
Adams, Jerome R(obertson) 1938- ... 139
Adams, Joanna Z.
See Koch, Joanne
Adams, Jody 1957- ... 208
Adams, Joey 1911-1999 ... CANR-1
Obituary ... 187
Earlier sketch in CA 49-52
Adams, John 1735-1826 ... DLB 31, 183
Adams, John 1938- ... 111
Adams, John Anthony 1944- ... 134
See also SATA 67
Adams, John Clarke 1910-2000 ... 1-4R
Adams, John Coldwell 1927- ... 121
Adams, John Cranford 1903-1986 ... 217
Obituary ... 121
Adams, John D(avid) 1942- ... 115
Adams, John F(estus) 1930- ... 33-36R
Adams, John M(ilton) 1905-1981 ... 107
Adams, John P. 1922(?)-1983 ... 122
Obituary ... 111
Adams, John Paul
See Kinnaird, Clark
Adams, John Quincy 1767-1848 ... DLB 37
Adams, John R. 1900-1994 ... 25-28R
Adams, Jonathan S(eth) 1961- ... 141
Adams, Julian 1919- ... CANR-11
Earlier sketch in CA 25-28R
Adams, Julius J. 1901(?)-1989 ... 177
Obituary ... 130
Adams, Justin
See Cameron, Lou
Adams, Kathleen M(arie) 1957- ... 204
Adams, Kenneth Menzies 1922- ... 103
Adams, Kramer A. 1920- ... 9-12R
Adams, L(ouis) Jerold 1939- ... 49-52
Adams, Laura 1943- ... 53-56
Adams, Laurie 1941- ... 53-56
See also SATA 33
Adams, Lee (Richard) 1924- ... 186
Brief entry ... 111
Adams, Leon D(avid) 1905-1995 ... 45-48
Obituary ... 149
Adams, Leonie (Fuller) 1899-1988 ... CAP-1
Obituary ... 125
Earlier sketch in CA 9-10
See also CP 1, 2, 3, 4
See also DLB 48
See also MAL 5
Adams, Les 1934- ... 97-100
Adams, Levi 1802(?)-1832 ... DLB 99
Adams, Lorraine ... 233
Adams, Lowell
See Joseph, James (Herz)
Adams, Marilyn Jager 1948- ... 136
Adams, Marion 1932- ... 41-44R
Adams, Mary (Grace Agnes) 1898-1984 181
Obituary ... 113
Adams, Maurice 1915(?)-1985 ... 176
Obituary ... 116
Adams, Michael (Evelyn) 1920-2005 .... 33-36R
Obituary ... 236
Adams, Michael C(harles) C(orringham)
1945- ... 89-92
Adams, Mike S. 1964- ... 234
Adams, Mildred
See Kenyon, Mildred Adams
Adams, Mrs. Leith
See Adams, Bertha Leith
Adams, Nancy 1943(?)-1987 ... 176
Obituary ... 123
Adams, Nathan Miller 1934- ... 45-48
Adams, Neil 1941- ... AAYA 64
Adams, Nicholas
See Pine, Nicholas
Adams, Nicholas
See Smith, Sherwood
Adams, Nicholas
See Doyle, Debra and Macdonald, James D.
Adams, Nicholas 1947- ... 127
Adams, Norman (Edward Albert)
1927-2005 ... 114
Obituary ... 237
Adams, Orvill 1950- ... 144
Adams, Pam 1919- ... 184
See also SATA 112
Adams, Patch 1945(?)- ... 199
Adams, Paul L(ieber) 1924- ... 61-64
Adams, Percy G(uy) 1914- ... CANR-4
Earlier sketch in CA 1-4R
Adams, Perseus 1933- ... 107
See also CP 1, 3, 4, 7
Adams, Philip R. 1908-1993 ... 85-88
Adams, Phoebe-Lou 1918- ... 125
Brief entry ... 121
Adams, R(alph) J(ames) Q(uincy) 1943- 128
Adams, Rachel (Elizabeth) 1968- ... 206
Adams, Rachel Leona White 1905(?)-1979 . 176
Obituary ... 93-96
Adams, Ramon F(rederick) 1889-1976 ... 179
Obituary ... 65-68
Adams, Ramona Shepherd 1921- ... 106
Adams, Richard (George) 1920- CANR-128
Earlier sketches in CA 49-52, CANR-3, 35
See also AAYA 16
See also AITN 1, 2
See also BPFB 1
See also BYA 5
See also CLC 4, 5, 18
See also CLR 20
See also CN 4, 5, 6, 7
See also DAM NOV
See also DLB 261
See also FANT
See also JRDA
See also LAIT 5
See also MAICYA 1, 2
See also MTCW 1, 2
See also NFS 11
See also SATA 7, 69
See also YAW
Adams, Richard E(dward) W(ood) 1931- 106
Adams, Richard N(ewbold) 1924- CANR-12
Earlier sketch in CA 29-32R
Adams, Richard P(errill) 1917-1977 ... CAP-2
Obituary ... 69-72
Earlier sketch in CA 33-36
Adams, (Franklin) Robert
1932-1990 ... CANR-66
Earlier sketch in CA 69-72
Adams, Robert H(ickman) 1937- CANR-22
Earlier sketch in CA 105
Adams, Robert Martin 1915-1996 ...... CANR-4
Obituary ... 155
Earlier sketch in CA 5-8R
Adams, Robert McCormick 1926- CANR-39
Earlier sketches in CA 61-64, CANR-12
Adams, Robert Merrihew 1937- ... CANR-96
Earlier sketch in CA 135
Adams, Robert Pardee 1910-1994 ... 13-16R
Adams, Rolland Leroy 1905(?)-1979 ... 177
Obituary ... 89-92
Adams, Roy J(oseph) 1940- ... 154
Adams, Russell B(aird), Jr. 1937- ... 69-72
Adams, Russell L. 1930- ... 53-56
Adams, Ruth Joyce ... SATA 14
Adams, Sally Pepper (?)-197(?) ... 41-44R
Adams, Sam 1934- ... 57-60
Adams, Samuel 1722-1803 ... DLB 31, 43
Adams, Samuel A. 1933(?)-1988 ... 177
Obituary ... 126
Adams, Samuel Hopkins 1871-1958 ... 220
Adams, Sarah Fuller Flower
1805-1848 ... DLB 199
Adams, Scott
See Adams, Charles
Adams, Scott 1957- ... 168
See also AAYA 27
Adams, Sexton 1936- ... CANR-37
Earlier sketch in CA 25-28R
Adams, Sheila Kay 1953- ... 150
Adams, Shelby Lee 1950- ... 223
Adams, (Llewellyn) Sherman 1899-1986 199
Obituary ... 120
Adams, Stanley 1927- ... 135
Adams, Stephen J(on) 1945- ... 111
Adams, Susan S.
See Kissel, Susan S.
Adams, T(homas) W(illiam) 1933- ... 25-28R
Adams, Terrence Dean 1935- ... 33-36R
Adams, Theodore Floyd 1898-1980 ...... CAP-1
Obituary ... 97-100
Earlier sketch in CA 11-12
Adams, Thomas 1582(?)-c. 1652 ... DLB 151
Adams, Thomas Boylston 1910-1997 ... 114
Obituary ... 158
Adams, Thomas F. 1927- ... 13-16R
Adams, Thomas Randolph 1921- ... 107
Adams, Timothy Dow 1943- ... 133
Adams, Tony (Alexander) 1966- ... 190
Adams, Tricia
See Kite, Pat
Adams, Tricia
See Kite, (L.) Patricia
Adams, Val 1917(?)-1983 ... 177
Obituary ... 109
Adams, Walter 1922-1998 ... CANR-37
Obituary ... 170
Earlier sketches in CA 1-4R, CANR-3
Adams, Willi Paul 1940- ... 105
Adams, William Howard ... 129
Brief entry ... 105
Adams, William James 1947- ... 148
Adams, William Taylor 1822-1897 ... DLB 42
See also SATA 28
Adams, William Yewdale 1927-
Brief entry ... 104
Adamski, George 1891-1965 ... 179
Obituary ... 112
Adam Smith, Janet (Buchanan)
1905-1999 ... CANR-35
Earlier sketch in CA 113
See also SATA 63
Adam-Smith, Patricia Jean 1926- ... 105
Adam-Smith, Patsy
See Adam-Smith, Patricia Jean
Adamson, Alan (Herbert) 1919- ... 81-84
Adamson, David Grant 1927- ... 13-16R
Adamson, Donald 1939- ... CANR-39
Earlier sketch in CA 53-56
Adamson, Ed(ward Joseph) 1915(?)-1972 ... 176
Obituary ... 37-40R
Adamson, Frank
See Adams, (Franklin) Robert
Adamson, Gareth 1925-1982(?) ... CANR-11
Obituary ... 106
Earlier sketch in CA 13-16R
See also SATA 46
See also SATA-Obit 30
Adamson, George 1906-1989 ... 129
See also SATA-Obit 63
Adamson, George (Worsley) 1913-2005 107
Obituary ... 237
See also SATA 30
Adamson, Graham
See Groom, Arthur William
Adamson, Hans Christian 1890-1968 ... 5-8R
Adamson, Harold 1906-1980 ... DLB 265
Adamson, Joe
See Adamson, Joseph III
Adamson, Sir John (Ernest) 1867-1950 ... 162
See also DLB 98
Adamson, Joseph III 1945- ... CANR-21
Earlier sketches in CA 45-48, CANR-1
Adamson, Joy(-Friederike Victoria)
1910-1980 ... CANR-22
Obituary ... 93-96
Earlier sketch in CA 69-72
See also CLC 17
See also MTCW 1
See also SATA 11
See also SATA-Obit 22
Adamson, Lesley
See Grant-Adamson, Lesley
Adamson, Lynda G. 1945- ... 187
Adamson, M. J.
See Adamson, Mary Jo
Adamson, Margot Robert 1898- ... CP 1
Adamson, Mary Jo 1935- ... CANR-123
Earlier sketch in CA 134
Adamson, Robert 1943- ... CANR-94
Earlier sketch in CA 153
See also CP 3, 4, 5, 6, 7
See also DLB 289
Adamson, Walter L(uiz) 1946- ... 107
Adamson, Wendy Writson 1942- ... 53-56
See also SATA 22
Adamson, William Robert 1927- ... 21-24R
Adamz-Bogus, SDiane 1946- ... 141
See also BW 2
Adas, Michael 1943- ... 53-56
Adastra
See Mirepoix, Camille
Adatto, Kiku 1947- ... 153
Adburgham, Alison Haig 1912-1997 ..... CAP-1
Earlier sketch in CA 9-10
Adcock, Almey St. John 1894- ... 65-68
Adcock, Arthur St. John 1864-1930 .... DLB 135
Adcock, Betty
See Adcock, Elizabeth S(harp)
See also DLB 105
Adcock, C(yril) John 1904-1987 ... CAP-1
Earlier sketch in CA 19-20
Adcock, Elizabeth S(harp) 1938- ... 57-60
See also Adcock, Betty
See also CSW
Adcock, Fleur 1934- ... 182
Earlier sketches in CA 25-28R, CANR-11, 34, 69, 101
Autobiographical Essay in ... 182
See also CAAS 23
See also CLC 41
See also CP 1, 2, 3, 4, 5, 6, 7
See also CWP
See also DLB 40
See also FW
See also WWE 1
Adcock, Franz Ezra 1886-1968 ... 183
Obituary ... 106
Adcock, Thomas 1947- ... CANR-59
Earlier sketch in CA 138
Addae, Akili
See Obika, Akili Addae
Addams, Charles (Samuel)
1912-1988 ... CANR-79
Obituary ... 126
Earlier sketches in CA 61-64, CANR-12
See also CLC 30
Addams, (Laura) Jane 1860-1935 ... 194
See also AMWS 1
See also DLB 303
See also FW
See also TCLC 76
Addanki, Sam 1932- ... 109
Adde, Leo 1927(?)-1975 ... 177
Obituary ... 57-60
Addeo, Jovita A. 1939- ... 103
Adderson, Caroline 1963- ... CANR-96
Earlier sketch in CA 146
Addica, Milo 1963- ... 212
Addie, Bob 1911(?)-1982 ... 177
Obituary ... 105
Addie, Pauline Betz 1919(?)-
Brief entry ... 105
Addinall, Peter 1932- ... 141
Addington, Arthur Charles 1939- ... 105
Addington, Larry H(olbrook) 1932- 33-36R
Addinsell, Richard 1904-1977 ... IDFW 4
Addis, Caren ... 194
Addison, Gwen
See Harris, Alf(red)
Addison, Herbert 1889-1982
Obituary ... 108
Addison, Jan
See Foster, Jeannette Howard
See also GLL 1
Addison, Joseph 1672-1719 ... BRW 3
See also CDBLB 1660-1789
See also DLB 101
See also RGEL 2
See also WLIT 3
Addison, Linda D. 1952- ... 217
Addison, Lloyd 1937- ... 45-48
Addison, Paul S. 1966- ... 170
Addison, William Wilkinson
1905-1992 ... CANR-5
Earlier sketch in CA 13-16R
Addiss, Stephen 1935- ... 120
Addleshaw, George William Outram
1907(?)-1982 ... 176
Obituary ... 107
Addleton, Jonathan S. 1957- ... 164
Addona, Angelo F. 1925- ... 25-28R
See also SATA 14
Addonizio, Kim (Theresa) 1954- ... 173
Earlier sketches in CA 169, CANR-123
Autobiographical Essay in ... 173
See also CAAS 28
Addy, George M(ilton) 1927- ... 21-24R
Addy, John 1915- ... 69-72
Addy, Sharon Hart 1943- ... 178
See also SATA 108
Addy, Ted
See Winterbotham, R(ussell) R(obert)
Ade, George 1866-1944 ... 238
Brief entry ... 110
See also DLB 11, 25
See also RGAL 4
Ade, Walter Frank Charles 1910-1995 53-56
Adelberg, Doris
See Orgel, Doris
Adelberg, Roy P. 1928-1993 ... 17-20R
Adeler, Max
See Clark, Charles Heber
Adelkhah, Fariba 1959- ... 215
Adell, Sandra 1946- ... CANR-87
Earlier sketch in CA 150
See also BW 3
Adelman, Bob 1930- ... CANR-143
Earlier sketch in CA 69-72
Adelman, Clifford 1942- ... 41-44R
Adelman, Deborah 1958- ... 141
Adelman, Gary 1935- ... 33-36R
Adelman, Howard 1938- ... 25-28R
Adelman, Irma Glicman ... CANR-3
Earlier sketch in CA 5-8R
Adelman, Irving 1926- ... 21-24R
Adelman, Janet (Ann) 1941- ... 61-64
Adelman, M(orris) A(lbert) 1917- ... 126
Brief entry ... 104
Adelman, Saul J(oseph) 1944- ... 104
Adelmann, Frederick J(oseph)
1915-1996 ... CANR-27
Earlier sketch in CA 49-52
Adelsberger, Lucie 1895-1971 ... 177
Obituary ... 33-36R
Adelson, Alan (Merrill) 1943- ... CANR-93
Earlier sketch in CA 145
Adelson, Bruce ... 192
Adelson, Daniel 1918-1989 ... 69-72
Adelson, Joseph (Bernard) 1925- ... 17-20R
Adelson, Leone 1908- ... 61-64
See also SATA 11
Adelson, Roger 1942- ... 150
Adelson, Sandra 1934- ... 105
Adelstein, Michael E. 1922- ... CANR-15
Earlier sketch in CA 33-36R
Aden, John M(ichael) 1918-1993 ... 97-100
Adenauer, Konrad 1876-1967 ... 179
Obituary ... 112
Adeney, David Howard 1911-1994 ... 53-56
Adeney, Martin 1942- ... 128
Adepoju, Aderanti 1945- ... CANR-87
Earlier sketch in CA 154
Ader, Paul (Fassett) 1919- ... 65-68
Aderman, Ralph M(erl) 1919- ... 5-8R
Ades, Dawn 1943- ... CANR-104
Earlier sketch in CA 103
Adey, Lionel 1925- ... 132
Adichie, Amanda N.
See Adichie, Chimamanda Ngozi
Adichie, Chimamanda Ngozi 1977- ... 231
Adickes, Roland 1930- ... 206
Adickes, Sandra 1933- ... 139
Adiele, Faith (E.) ... 235

Cumulative Index 5 Agresto

Adisa, Opal Palmer 1954- ... 178
See also BW 3
Adiseshiah, Malcolm S(athianathan) 1910-1994 ... 81-84
Obituary ... 147
Adivar, Halide Edib 1884-1964 ... EWL 3
Adizes, Ichak 1937- ... 33-36R
Adjibolosoo, Senyo B.-S.K. 1953- ... 175
Adjudge, Daphne
See Odjig, Daphne
Adkin, Mark 1936- ... 139
Adkins, Arthur W(illiam) H(ope) 1929- ... 111
Brief entry ... 104
Adkins, Cecil (Dale) 1932- ... 115
Adkins, Dorothy C.
See Wood, Dorothy Adkins
Adkins, Jan 1944- ... CANR-126
Earlier sketches in CA 33-36R, CANR-103
See also CLR 7, 77
See also MAICYA 1, 2
See also SAAS 19
See also SATA 8, 69, 144
Adkins, Lesley 1955- ... 221
Adkins, Nelson F(rederick) 1897-1976 ... 73-76
Obituary ... 65-68
Adkins, Patrick H. 1948- ... 126
See also FANT
Adkins, Roy 1951- ... 219
Adlard, John 1929- ... CANR-21
Earlier sketches in CA 57-60, CANR-6
Adlard, (Peter) Mark 1932- ... CANR-57
Earlier sketch in CA 65-68
See also DLB 261
See also SFW 4
Adleman, Robert H. 1919-1995 ... CANR-55
Obituary ... 150
Earlier sketch in CA 25-28R
Adler, Alfred (F.) 1870-1937 ... 159
Brief entry ... 119
See also TCLC 61
Adler, B.
See Adler, William
Adler, Betty 1918-1973 ... CAP-1
Earlier sketch in CA 13-14
Adler, Bill
See Adler, William
Adler, C(arole) S(chwerdtfeger) 1932- ... CANR-101
Earlier sketches in CA 89-92, CANR-19, 40
See also AAYA 4, 41
See also CLC 35
See also CLR 78
See also JRDA
See also MAICYA 1, 2
See also SAAS 15
See also SATA 26, 63, 102, 126
See also YAW
Adler, Carol 1938- ... 61-64
Adler, Christopher Edward 1954(?)-1984 ... 177
Obituary ... 114
Adler, Cyrus 1863-1940 ... 180
Brief entry ... 122
Adler, David A. 1947- ... CANR-88
Earlier sketches in CA 57-60, CANR-7, 23
See also MAICYA 1, 2
See also SATA 14, 70, 106, 151
Adler, Denise Rinker 1908-2000 ... 102
Adler, Elizabeth ... CANR-89
Earlier sketch in CA 144
Adler, Elmer 1884-1962 ... 210
Obituary ... 89-92
Adler, Felix 1851-1933 ... 204
Adler, France-Michele 1942- ... 105
Adler, Freda 1934- ... CANR-56
Earlier sketches in CA 69-72, CANR-11, 27
Adler, Gerhard 1904-1989(?)
Obituary ... 128
Adler, H(ans) G(unther) 1910- ... CANR-91
Earlier sketches in CA 25-28R, CANR-10
Adler, Hans A(rnold) 1921-2005 ... 49-52
Obituary ... 235
Adler, Helmut E(rnest) 1920- ... 33-36R
Adler, Irene
See Penzler, Otto and Storr, Catherine (Cole)
Adler, Irving 1913- ... CANR-114
Earlier sketches in CA 5-8R, CANR-2, 47
See also CLR 27
See also MAICYA 1, 2
See also SAAS 15
See also SATA 1, 29
Adler, Isidore 1925(?)-1990 ... 177
Obituary ... 131
Adler, Jack ... 73-76
Adler, Jacob (P.) 1873(?)-1974 ... 202
Obituary ... 53-56
Adler, Jacob 1913-1999 ... 17-20R
Adler, Jacob H(enry) 1919- ... 13-16R
Adler, Jeffrey S(cott) 1957- ... 141
Adler, John Hans 1912-1980 ... 185
Obituary ... 97-100
Adler, Joyce
See Adler, Joyce Sparer
Adler, Joyce Sparer 1915-1999 ... 128
Adler, Kathleen
See Jones, Kathleen Eve
Adler, Larissa 1932- ... 150
Adler, Larry 1939- ... 105
See also SATA 36
Adler, Lucile 1922- ... 105
Adler, Lulla
See Rosenfeld, Lulla
Adler, Manfred 1936- ... 49-52
Adler, Margot 1946- ... 107
Adler, Max K(urt) 1905- ... CANR-3
Earlier sketch in CA 9-12R
Adler, Mortimer J(erome) 1902-2001 ... CANR-73
Obituary ... 198
Earlier sketches in CA 65-68, CANR-7, 33
Interview in ... CANR-7
See also MTCW 1, 2
Adler, Norman Tenner 1941- ... CANR-20
Earlier sketch in CA 69-72
Adler, Peggy ... SATA 22
Adler, Renata 1938- ... CANR-95
Earlier sketch in CA 49-52
See also CLC 8, 31
See also CN 4, 5, 6
See also MTCW 1
Adler, Richard 1921- ... DLB 265
Adler, Ruth 1915-1968 ... CANR-4
Obituary ... 25-28R
Earlier sketch in CA 5-8R
See also SATA 1
Adler, Selig 1909-1984 ... 5-8R
Obituary ... 114
Adler, Sol 1925-1993 ... CANR-22
Earlier sketches in CA 17-20R, CANR-7
Adler, Stephen J. 1956(?)- ... 235
Adler, Warren 1927- ... CANR-113
Earlier sketches in CA 69-72, CANR-11
Adler, William 1929- ... CANR-49
Earlier sketches in CA 9-12R, CANR-7
Adler, William 1951- ... 124
Adlerblum, Nina H. 1882-1974 ... 177
Obituary ... 49-52
Adlerman, Daniel (Ezra) 1963- ... CANR-142
Earlier sketch in CA 161
See also SATA 96, 163
Adlerman, Kim
See Adlerman, Kimberly M(arie)
Adlerman, Kimberly M(arie) 1964- ... CANR-135
Earlier sketch in CA 161
See also SATA 96, 163
Adloff, Virginia Thompson 1903-1990 ... 201
Obituary ... 130
Adnan, Etel 1925- ... 154
See also CWP
See also FW
Adoff, Arnold 1935- ... CANR-126
Earlier sketches in CA 41-44R, CANR-20, 37, 67
See also AAYA 3, 50
See also AITN 1
See also CLR 7
See also CWRI 5
See also DLBY 2001
See also JRDA
See also MAICYA 1, 2
See also SAAS 15
See also SATA 5, 57, 96
Adoff, Jaime (Levi) ... 239
See also SATA 163
Adolph, E. F.
See Adolph, Edward F(rederick)
Adolph, Edward F(rederick) 1895-1986 ... 176
Obituary ... 121
Adomeit, Ruth E(lizabeth) 1910-1996 ... 111
Adon, Aaron Bar
See Bar-Adon, Aaron
Adonias Filho
See Filho, Adonias
Adonis
See Sa'id, Ali Ahmad
See also RGWL 3
Adony, Raoul
See Launay, Andre (Joseph)
Adorjan, Carol (Madden) 1934- ... CANR-109
Earlier sketches in CA 41-44R, CANR-14, 31, 56
See also SATA 10, 71
Adorno, Theodor W(iesengrund) 1903-1969 ... CANR-89
Obituary ... 25-28R
Earlier sketch in CA 89-92
See also DLB 242
See also EWL 3
See also TCLC 111
Adoum, Jorge Enrique 1926- ... 152
See also DLB 283
See also HW 1, 2
Adrian, (Gilbert) 1903-1959 ... IDFW 3, 4
Adrian, Arthur A(llen) 1906-1996 ... CAP-2
Earlier sketch in CA 19-20
Adrian, Charles R. 1922- ... CANR-3
Earlier sketch in CA 1-4R
Adrian, Chris 1970- ... 196
Adrian, Edgar Douglas 1889-1977 ... 159
Obituary ... 73-76
Adrian, Frances
See Polland, Madeleine A(ngela Cahill)
Adrian, L. A.
See Griffiths, Rhys Adrian
Adrian, Mary
See Jorgensen, Mary Venn
Adrian, Rhys
Brief entry ... 106
See also Griffiths, Rhys Adrian
Adrouny, A. Richard 1952- ... 237
Adshead, Gladys L(ucy) 1896-1985 ... 29-32R
Obituary ... 180
See also SATA 3
Adshead, S(amuel) A(drian) M(iles) ... 167
Adunis
See Sa'id, Ali Ahmad
See also CWW 2
See also EWL 3
See also WLIT 6
Advani, Rukun 1955- ... 119
Ady, Endre 1877-1919
Brief entry ... 107
See also CDWLB 4
See also DLB 215
See also EW 9
See also EWL 3
See also TCLC 11
Ady, Ronald W(illiam) 1934- ... 117
Adytum
See Curl, James Stevens
Adzigian, Denise Allard 1952- ... 97-100
A.E.
See Russell, George William
See also DLB 19
See also TCLC 3, 10
Aebi, Ormond 1916- ... 89-92
Aeby, Jacquelyn ... CANR-24
Earlier sketch in CA 29-32R
Aelfric c. 955-c. 1010 ... DLB 146
Aero, Rita ... 112
Aers, David 1946- ... CANR-8
Earlier sketch in CA 61-64
Aeschines c. 390B.C.-c. 320B.C. ... DLB 176
Aeschliman, Michael D(avid) 1948- ... 113
Aeschylus 525(?)B.C.-456(?)B.C. ... AW 1
See also CDWLB 1
See also DA
See also DAB
See also DAC
See also DAM DRAM, MST
See also DC 8
See also DFS 5, 10
See also DLB 176
See also LMFS 1
See also RGWL 2, 3
See also TWA
See also WLCS
Aesop
See Blake, Lillie Devereux
Aesop 620(?)B.C.-560(?)B.C. ... CLR 14
See also MAICYA 1, 2
See also SATA 64
Aesop, Abraham
See Newbery, John
Affabee, Eric
See Stine, R(obert) L(awrence)
Affable Hawk
See MacCarthy, Sir (Charles Otto) Desmond
Affinito, Alfonso G. 1930- ... 225
Affleck, Ben(jamin G.) 1972- ... 168
Affron, Charles 1935- ... CANR-102
Earlier sketch in CA 21-24R
Afkhami, Mahnaz 1941- ... CANR-98
Earlier sketch in CA 146
Afnan, Ruhi Muhsen 1899-1971 ... CAP-2
Earlier sketch in CA 29-32
Africa, Ben
See Bosman, Herman Charles
Africa, Thomas Wilson 1927- ... 17-20R
Africano, Lillian 1935- ... CANR-29
Earlier sketches in CA 69-72, CANR-11
Afrika, Tatamkhulu 1920-2002 ... 217
Aftel, Mandy 1948- ... 108
Afterman, Allen 1941-1992 ... 103
Afton, Effie
See Harper, Frances Ellen Watkins
Afzal, Omar 1939- ... 159
Agan, Patrick 1943- ... CANR-10
Earlier sketch in CA 65-68
Agan, Raymond J(ohn) 1919- ... 33-36R
Agan, (Anna) Tessie 1897-1988 ... CAP-1
Obituary ... 171
Earlier sketch in CA 17-18
Ağaoğlu, Adalet 1929- ... EWL 3
Agapida, Fray Antonio
See Irving, Washington
Agar, Brian
See Ballard, (Willis) Todhunter
Agar, Emile
See Kacew, Romain
Agar, Herbert (Sebastian) 1897-1980 ... 65-68
Obituary ... 102
Agar, Michael H(enry) 1945- ... CANR-2
Earlier sketch in CA 45-48
Agar, William (Macdonough) 1894-1972 ... 176
Obituary ... 37-40R
Agard, H. E.
See Evans, Hilary
Agard, John ... 208
See also CWRI 5
See also SATA 138
Agard, Nadema 1948- ... SATA 18
Agarossi, Elena 1940- ... CANR-20
Earlier sketch in CA 97-100
Agarwal, Deepa 1947- ... 212
See also SATA 141
Agarwala, Amar N. 1917- ... CANR-13
Earlier sketch in CA 21-24R
Agassi, Joseph 1927- ... CANR-41
Earlier sketches in CA 41-44R, CANR-15
Agassiz, Elizabeth Cary 1822-1907 ... 182
See also DLB 189
Agassiz, Jean Louis Rodolphe 1807-1873 ... DLB 1, 235
Agathocleous, Tanya 1970- ... 228
Agatstein, Mieczyslaw
See Jastrun, Mieczyslaw
Agatston, Arthur ... 223
Agawa, Hiroyuki 1920- ... 134
Agay, Denes 1911- ... 69-72
Agbodeka, Francis 1931- ... CANR-4
Earlier sketch in CA 53-56
Age 1919-
See Age and Scarpelli
Agee, Chris 1956- ... 170
Agee, James (Rufus) 1909-1955 ... CANR-131
Brief entry ... 108
Earlier sketch in CA 148
See also AAYA 44
See also AITN 1
See also AMW
See also CDALB 1941-1968
See also DAM NOV
See also DLB 2, 26, 152
See also DLBY 1989
See also EWL 3
See also LAIT 3
See also LATS 1:2
See also MAL 5
See also MTCW 2
See also MTFW 2005
See also NFS 22
See also RGAL 4
See also TCLC 1, 19
See also TUS
Agee, Joel 1940-
Brief entry ... 105
Agee, Jon 1960- ... CANR-142
Earlier sketch in CA 180
See also SATA 116, 157
Agee, Jonis 1943- ... CANR-88
Earlier sketch in CA 139
Agee, Philip 1935- ... 135
Brief entry ... 104
Agee, Warren Kendall 1916- ... 17-20R
Agell, Charlotte 1959- ... CANR-117
Earlier sketch in CA 167
See also SATA 99, 150
A Gentlewoman
See Moore, Doris Langley
Agent Orange
See Moseley, James W(illett)
Ager, Cecelia 1902-1981 ... 177
Obituary ... 103
Ager, Derek Victor 1923-1993 ... 107
Obituary ... 140
Ageton, Arthur Ainsley 1900-1971 ... CANR-1
Obituary ... 29-32R
Earlier sketch in CA 1-4R
Aggeler, Geoffrey D(onovan) 1939- ... 97-100
Aggertt, Otis J. 1916-1973 ... 33-36R
Agha-Jaffar, Tamara 1952- ... 234
Aghill, Gordon
See Garrett, (Gordon) Randall (Phillip) and Silverberg, Robert
Agich, George J. 1947- ... 146
Agins, Teri 1953- ... 234
Aginsky, Bernard W(illard) 1905-2000 ... 85-88
Aginsky, Burt W.
See Aginsky, Bernard W(illard)
Aginsky, Ethel G(oldberg) 1910-1990 ... 41-44R
Agle, Nan Hayden 1905- ... CANR-3
Earlier sketch in CA 1-4R
See also SAAS 10
See also SATA 3
Agnelli, Marella 1927(?)- ... 230
Agnelli, Susanna 1922- ... CANR-28
Earlier sketch in CA 109
Agnew, Edith J(osephine) 1897-1988 ... CAP-1
Obituary ... 180
Earlier sketch in CA 17-18
See also SATA 11
Agnew, Eleanor 1948- ... 168
Agnew, James Barron 1930- ... 89-92
Agnew, Patience McCormick-Goodhart 1913(?)-1976
Obituary ... 69-72
Agnew, Peter L(awrence) 1901-1969 ... CAP-2
Earlier sketch in CA 21-22
Agnew, Spiro T(heodore) 1918-1996 ... 135
Obituary ... 153
Brief entry ... 110
Agniel, Lucien D. 1919-1988 ... 29-32R
Agnon, S(hmuel) Y(osef Halevi) 1888-1970 ... CANR-102
Obituary ... 25-28R
Earlier sketches in CAP-2, CA 17-18, CANR-60
See also CLC 4, 8, 14
See also EWL 3
See also MTCW 1, 2
See also RGSF 2
See also RGWL 2, 3
See also SSC 30
See also TCLC 151
See also WLIT 6
Agolli, Dritero 1931- ... EWL 3
Agonito, Rosemary (Giambattista) 1937- ... 122
Brief entry ... 112
Agoos, Julie 1956- ... CANR-55
Earlier sketch in CA 127
Agor, Weston H(arris) 1939- ... CANR-29
Earlier sketch in CA 49-52
Agosin, Marjorie (Stella) 1955- ... CANR-92
Earlier sketches in CA 131, CANR-53
See also CWP
See also HW 1
See also LLW
Agosta, William C(arleton) 1933- ... 197
Agostinelli, Maria Enrica 1929- ... 33-36R
Agovi, Kofi Ermeleh 1944- ... 168
Agran, Edward G. 1949- ... 202
Agranoff, Robert 1936- ... CANR-14
Earlier sketch in CA 37-40R
Agrawal, Govind P. 1951- ... 233
Agree, Rose H. 1913- ... 21-24R
Agress, Hyman 1931- ... 89-92
Agress, Lynne 1941- ... 112
Agresto, John 1946- ... 115

Agronsky, Martin (Zama) 1915-1999 ... CA-109
Obituary ... 185
Interview in ... 109
See also AITN 2
Aguero, Kathleen 1949- ... 73-76
Agueros, Jack 1934- ... LLW
See also SSFS 13
Aguila, Pancho 1945- ... 105
See also HW 1
Aguilar, Luis E. 1926- ... 21-24R
Aguilar, Ricardo
See Aguilar Melantzon, Ricardo
Aguilar, Rodolfo J(esus) 1936- ... 53-56
Aguilar, Rosario (Fiallos de) 1938- .. CANR-128
Earlier sketch in CA 160
Aguilar Melantzon, Ricardo 1947-2004 ... 152
Obituary ... 231
See also HW 1
Aguilera, Carolina Garcia
See Garcia-Aguilera, Carolina
Aguilera, Donna Conant ... 37-40R
Aguilera, Jaime Roldos
See Roldos Aguilera, Jaime
Aguilera Malta, Demetrio
1909-1981 ... CANR-87
Brief entry ... 111
Earlier sketch in CA 124
See also DAM MULT, NOV
See also DLB 145
See also EWL 3
See also HLCS 1
See also HW 1
See also RGWL 3
Aguinis, Marcos 1935- ... 206
Aguirre, Isidora 1919- ... DLB 305
Aguolu, Christian Chukwunedu
1940- ... CANR-42
Earlier sketches in CA 101, CANR-19
Agus, Irving A(braham) 1910-1984 ... CAP-2
Obituary ... 113
Earlier sketch in CA 33-36
Agus, Jacob Bernard 1911-1986 ... CANR-2
Obituary ... 120
Earlier sketch in CA 5-8R
Agustin, Jose 1944- ... 179
See also EWL 3
Agustini, Delmira 1886-1914 ... 166
See also DLB 290
See also HLCS 1
See also HW 1, 2
See also LAW
Agutter, Jennifer Ann 1952- ... 133
Agutter, Jenny
See Agutter, Jennifer Ann
Aguzzi-Barbagli, Danilo 1924- ... 49-52
Agwani, Mohammed Shafi 1928- ... CANR-7
Earlier sketch in CA 17-20R
Agyeman, Opoku 1942- ... 145
Agyeya
See Vatsyayan, Sachchidanand Hiranand
Aharoni, Reuben 1943- ... 151
Aharoni, Re'uven 1943-
See Aharoni, Reuben
Aharoni, Yohanan 1919-1976 ... CANR-15
Earlier sketch in CA 25-28R
Ahearn, (Edward) Allen 1937- ... CANR-137
Earlier sketch in CA 151
Ahearn, Barry 1950- ... 110
Ahearn, Catherine 1949- ... 114
Ahearn, Patricia 1937- ... 151
Ahern, Barnabas M(ary) 1915-1995 ... CANR-3
Obituary ... 180
Earlier sketch in CA 5-8R
Ahern, Cecelia 1981- ... 228
Ahern, Emily M(artin)
See Martin, Emily
Ahern, James
See Ahern, Barnabas M(ary)
Ahern, James F(rancis) 1932-1986 ... 41-44R
Obituary ... 118
Ahern, John F(rancis) 1936- ... 61-64
Ahern, Margaret McCrohan 1921- ... 13-16R
See also SATA 10
Ahern, Thomas Francis 1947- ... CANR-21
Earlier sketches in CA 45-48, CANR-1
Ahern, Tim(othy James) 1952- ... 115
Ahern, Tom
See Ahern, Thomas Francis
Aherne, Brian (de Lacy) 1902-1986 ... 135
Obituary ... 118
Brief entry ... 117
Aherne, Owen
See Cassill, R(onald) V(erlin)
Ahituv, Niv 1943- ... 117
Ahl, Anna Maria 1926- ... SATA 32
Ahl, Frederick Michael 1941- ... CANR-30
Earlier sketch in CA 111
Ahlberg, Allan 1938- ... CANR-98
Brief entry ... 111
Earlier sketches in CA 114, CANR-38, 70
See also CLR 18
See also CWRI 5
See also MAICYA 1, 2
See also SATA 68, 120
See also SATA-Brief 35
Ahlberg, Janet 1944-1994 ... CANR-104
Obituary ... 147
Brief entry ... 111
Earlier sketches in CA 114, CANR-79
See also CLR 18
See also CWRI 5
See also MAICYA 1, 2
See also MAICYAS 1
See also SATA 68, 120
See also SATA-Brief 32
See also SATA-Obit 83
Ahlberg, William A. 1922(?)-1985
Obituary ... 116
Ahlborn, Richard Eighme 1933- ... 108
Ahlers, John C(larke) 1927-1983
Obituary ... 110
Ahlert, Richard 1921-1985
Obituary ... 117
Ahles, Carol Laflin 1948- ... 209
Ahlfors, Lars V(alerian) 1907-1996 ... 155
Ahlgren, Gillian T. W. 1910- ... 157
Ahlin, Janne 1942- ... 136
Ahlin, Lars 1915-1997 ... 194
See also DLB 257
See also EWL 3
Ahlstroem, G(oesta) W(erner)
1918-1992 ... CANR-21
Obituary ... 136
Earlier sketch in CA 45-48
Ahlstrom, G(osta) W(erner)
See Ahlstroem, G(oesta) W(erner)
Ahlstrom, Sydney E(ckman)
1919-1984 ... 21-24R
Obituary ... 113
Ahlswede, Ann 1928- ... TCWW 1, 2
Ahmad, Eqbal 1931-1999 ... 188
Ahmad, Ishtiaq 1937- ... 53-56
Ahmad, Jalal Al-i
See Al-E Ahmad, Jalal
See also WLIT 6
Ahmad, Mirza Ghulam Hazrat 1835-1908 . 212
Ahmad, Nafis 1913- ... 17-20R
Ahmad, Suleiman M(uhammad) 1943- ... 110
Ahmad, Zakaria Haji
See Zakaria, Haji Ahmad
Ahmann, Mathew H(all) 1931-2001 ... 9-12R
Obituary ... 200
Ahmed, Akbar S(alahudin) 1943- ... 141
Ahmed, Faiz
See Faiz, Faiz Ahmad
Ahmed, Leila 1940- ... 140
Ahn, Byong Man 1941- ... 229
Ahnebrink, Lars 1915- ... 5-8R
Ahnstrom, D(oris) N. 1915-1991 ... 5-8R
Aho, James (Alfred) 1942- ... 107
Ahokas, Jaakko (Alfred) 1923- ... 65-68
Ahrari, Mohammed E. 1945- ... 120
Ahrendt, Delilah (Anna) 1975(?)- ... 230
Ahrons, Constance (Ruth) 1937- ... 233
Ahrweiler, Helene
See Ahrweiler, Helene
Ahrweiler, Helene 1926- ... 197
Ahsen, Akhter 1931- ... CANR-25
Earlier sketches in CA 61-64, CANR-10
Ahuja, Savitri 1924- ... 112
Ai 1947- ... CANR-70
Earlier sketch in CA 85-88
See also CAAS 13
See also CLC 4, 14, 69
See also DLB 120
See also PFS 16
Ai, Ch'ing
See Chiang Hai-ch'eng
Ai, Wu 1904- ... 168
Aichele, George, Jr. 1944- ... 206
Ai Ch'ing
See Chiang Hai-ch'eng
See also EWL 3
Aichinger, Helga 1937- ... CANR-19
Earlier sketch in CA 25-28R
See also SATA 4
Aichinger, Ilse 1921- ... 85-88
See also CWW 2
See also DLB 85, 299
See also EWL 3
See also RGSF 2
Aichinger, Peter 1933- ... CANR-11
Earlier sketch in CA 61-64
Aickman, Robert (Fordyce)
1914-1981 ... CANR-100
Earlier sketches in CA 5-8R, CANR-3, 72
See also CLC 57
See also DLB 261
See also HGG
See also SUFW 1, 2
Aidala, Thomas R(ichard) 1933-
Brief entry ... 112
Aidells, Bruce 1944- ... 138
Aidenoff, Abraham 1913-1976 ... 37-40R
Obituary ... 61-64
Aidinoff, Elsie V. 1931(?)- ... 234
Aidoo, (Christina) Ama Ata 1942- .. CANR-144
Earlier sketches in CA 101, CANR-62
See also AFW
See also BLCS
See also BW 1
See also CD 5, 6
See also CDWLB 3
See also CLC 177
See also CN 6, 7
See also CWD
See also CWP
See also DLB 117
See also DNFS 1, 2
See also EWL 3
See also FW
See also WLIT 2
Aig-Imoukhuede, Frank Abiodun 1935- ... CP 1
Aiguillette
See Hargreaves, Reginald (Charles)
Aiken, Clarissa (M.) Lorenz 1899-1992 . CAP-2
Obituary ... 171
Earlier sketch in CA 21-22
See also SATA 12
See also SATA-Obit 109
Aiken, Conrad (Potter) 1889-1973 ... CANR-60
Obituary ... 45-48
Earlier sketches in CA 5-8R, CANR-4
See also AMW
See also CDALB 1929-1941
See also CLC 1, 3, 5, 10, 52
See also CN 1
See also CP 1
See also DAM NOV, POET
See also DLB 9, 45, 102
See also EWL 3
See also EXPS
See also HGG
See also MAL 5
See also MTCW 1, 2
See also MTFW 2005
See also PC 26
See also RGAL 4
See also RGSF 2
See also SATA 3, 30
See also SSC 9
See also SSFS 8
See also TUS
Aiken, George D(avid) 1892-1984 ... 183
Obituary ... 114
Brief entry ... 111
Aiken, Henry David 1912-1982 ... CANR-79
Obituary ... 106
Earlier sketches in CA 1-4R, CANR-1
Aiken, Irene (Nixon) ... 93-96
Aiken, Joan (Delano) 1924-2004 ... 182
Obituary ... 223
Earlier sketches in CA 9-12R, CANR-4, 23, 34, 64, 121
Autobiographical Essay in ... 182
See also AAYA 1, 25
See also CLC 35
See also CLR 1, 19, 90
See also DLB 161
See also FANT
See also HGG
See also JRDA
See also MAICYA 1, 2
See also MTCW 1
See also RHW
See also SAAS 1
See also SATA 2, 30, 73
See also SATA-Essay 109
See also SATA-Obit 152
See also SUFW 2
See also WYA
See also YAW
Aiken, John (Kempton) 1913-1990 ... 101
Aiken, John R(obert) 1927- ... 33-36R
Aiken, Lewis R(oscoe), Jr. 1931- ... CANR-10
Earlier sketch in CA 25-28R
Aiken, Maurice C. 1909(?)-1983
Obituary ... 109
Aiken, Michael Thomas 1932- ... CANR-9
Earlier sketch in CA 21-24R
Aikens, Tom Pitt
See Pitt-Aikens, Tom
Aikin, Charles 1901-1974 ... 5-8R
Aikin, Lucy 1781-1864 ... DLB 144, 163
Aikman, Ann
See McQuade, Ann Aikman
Aikman, David (B. T.) 1944- ... 65-68
Aikman, Lonnelle (Davison) 1901(?)-1986
Obituary ... 121
Aimes, Angelica 1943- ... CANR-14
Earlier sketch in CA 81-84
Aini, Sadriddin 1878-1954 ... EWL 3
Ainsbury, Ray
See Paine, Lauran (Bosworth)
Ainsbury, Roy
See Paine, Lauran (Bosworth)
Ainsley, Alix
See Steiner, Barbara A(nnette)
Ainslie, Peter III 1867-1934 ... 209
Ainslie, Rosalynde 1932- ... 25-28R
Ainslie, Tom
See Carter, Richard
Ainsworth, Catherine Harris 1910- ... SATA 56
Ainsworth, Charles H(arold) 1935- ... 49-52
Ainsworth, Dorothy Sears 1894-1976
Obituary ... 69-72
Ainsworth, Ed(ward Maddin)
1902-1968 ... CANR-4
Earlier sketch in CA 5-8R
Ainsworth, G(eoffrey) C(lough)
1905-1998 ... 73-76
Obituary ... 171
Ainsworth, Harriet
See Cadell, (Violet) Elizabeth
Ainsworth, Katherine 1908-1989 ... 29-32R
Ainsworth, Mary D(insmore) Salter
1913-1999 ... CANR-8
Obituary ... 177
Earlier sketch in CA 21-24R
Ainsworth, Maryan W(ynn) 1949- ... 188
Ainsworth, Norma ... CANR-5
Earlier sketch in CA 13-16R
See also SATA 9
Ainsworth, Patricia
See Bigg, Patricia Nina
Ainsworth, Ray
See Paine, Lauran (Bosworth)
Ainsworth, Roy
See Paine, Lauran (Bosworth)
Ainsworth, Ruth (Gallard) 1908- ... CANR-106
Earlier sketch in CANR-37, 79
See also CWRI 5
See also MAICYA 1, 2
See also SATA 7, 73
Ainsworth, Thomas Hargraves, Jr.
1920-1999 ... 123
Ainsworth, William Harrison
1805-1882 ... DLB 21
See also HGG
See also RGEL 2
See also SATA 24
See also SUFW 1
Ainsworthy, Roy
See Paine, Lauran (Bosworth)
Ainsztein, Reuben 1917-1981 ... 110
Obituary ... 108
Aira, Cesar 1949- ... 234
Air Chief Marshal Lord Dowding
See Dowding, Hugh Caswell Tremenheere
Aird, Catherine
See McIntosh, Kinn Hamilton
Aird, Eileen M(argaret) 1945- ... 49-52
Airlie, Catherine
See MacLeod, Jean Sutherland
Airola, Paavo (Olavi) 1915-1983 ... 81-84
Airth, Rennie 1935- ... 190
Aisenberg, Nadya 1928-1999 ... 135
Aislin
See Mosher, (Christopher) Terry
Aisse, Charlotte-Elisabeth
1694(?)-1733 ... DLB 313
Aistis, Jonas 1904-1973
Obituary ... 41-44R
See also CDWLB 4
See also DLB 220
See also EWL 3
Aistrop, Jack 1916- ... CANR-3
Earlier sketch in CA 1-4R
See also SATA 14
Aitchison, James 1938- ... 137
See also CP 7
Aitchison, Janet 1962- ... 57-60
Aitken, A(dam) J(ack) 1921- ... CANR-7
Earlier sketch in CA 13-16R
Aitken, Amy 1952- ... 108
See also SATA 54
See also SATA-Brief 40
Aitken, Dorothy 1916- ... CANR-2
Earlier sketch in CA 49-52
See also SATA 10
Aitken, Douglas 1933- ... 115
Aitken, George A(therton) 1860-1917 . DLB 149
Aitken, Hugh G(eorge) J(effrey)
1922-1994 ... CANR-3
Earlier sketch in CA 1-4R
Aitken, Jonathan (William Patrick)
1942- ... 21-24R
Aitken, (John William) Max(well) 1910-1985
Obituary ... 116
Aitken, Robert (Baker) 1917- ... 130
Aitken, Rosemary 1942- ... 226
Aitken, Thomas, Jr. 1910-1992 ... 1-4R
Aitken, W(illiam) R(ussell) 1913-1998 ... 41-44R
Aitken, William Maxwell
See Beaverbrook, William Maxwell Aitken
Aitkin, Don(ald Alexander) 1937- ... CANR-15
Earlier sketch in CA 93-96
Aitmatov, Chingiz (Torekulovich)
1928- ... CANR-38
Earlier sketch in CA 103
See also Aytmatov, Chingiz
See also CLC 71
See also CWW 2
See also DLB 302
See also MTCW 1
See also RGSF 2
See also SATA 56
Aiyejina, Funso 1949- ... 194
Aizley, Harlyn ... 225
Ajami, Alfred M(ichel) 1948-
Brief entry ... 110
Ajami, Fouad 1946- ... 167
Ajar, Emile
See Kacew, Romain
Ajay, Betty 1918- ... 69-72
Ajayi, J(acob) F(estus) Ade(niyi)
1929- ... CANR-40
Earlier sketches in CA 61-64, CANR-18
Ajegbo, Keith 1946- ... 122
Ajilvsgi, Geyata 1933- ... 124
Ajmera, Maya ... 238
Ajpu', Kaji
See Carey, David, Jr.
Akaba, Suekichi 1910- ... SATA 46
Akaha, Tsuneo 1949- ... 120
Akalaitis, JoAnne 1937- ... 138
See also CAD
See also CD 5, 6
See also CWD
Akamatsu, Ken 1968- ... 232
Akanji, Sangodare
See Beier, Ulli
Akar, John J(oseph) 1927-1975 ... 153
See also BW 2
Akare, Thomas 1950- ... 109
Akarli, Engin Deniz 1945- ... 146
Akashi, Yoji 1928- ... 33-36R
Akasofu, Syun-Ichi 1930- ... 212
Akass, John Ewart 1933-1990
Obituary ... 131
Akass, Jon
See Akass, John Ewart
Ake, Claude 1939-1996 ... CANR-87
Obituary ... 154
Earlier sketches in CA 21-24R, CANR-10
Ake, David (Andrew) 1961- ... 209
Akehurst, M(ichael) B(arton) 1940- ... 25-28R
Aken, Piet van
See van Aken, Piet
Akens, David S. 1921- ... CANR-12
Earlier sketch in CA 25-28R
Akenside, Mark 1721-1770 ... DLB 109
See also RGEL 2

Cumulative Index 7 Alcorn

Akenson, Donald Harman 1941- CANR-88
Earlier sketches in CA 57-60, CANR-7, 22, 45
Aker, George F(rederick)
1927-1987 ..... CANR-15
Earlier sketch in CA 41-44R
Akeret, Robert U(lrich) 1928- 45-48
Akerman, Chantal (Anne) 1950- 127
Akerman, Susanna (Kristina) 1959- 139
Akers, Alan Burt
See Bulmer, (Henry) Kenneth
Akers, Charles W(esley) 1920- 13-16R
Akers, Floyd
See Baum, L(yman) Frank
Akers, Keith 1949- CANR-101
Earlier sketch in CA 112
Akers, Monte (E.) 1950- 228
Akers, Norman 1958- 211
Akers, Ronald L(ouis) 1939- CANR-1
Earlier sketch in CA 45-48
Akers, Susan Grey 1889-1984
Obituary 112
Akesson, Sonja 1926-1977 ..... EWL 3
Akhmadulina, Bella Akhatovna 1937- 65-68
See also CLC 53
See also CWP
See also CWW 2
See also DAM POET
See also EWL 3
See also PC 43
Akhmatova, Anna 1888-1966 ..... CANR-35
Obituary 25-28R
Earlier sketches in CAP-1, CA 19-20
See also CLC 11, 25, 64, 126
See also DA3
See also DAM POET
See also DLB 295
See also EW 10
See also EWL 3
See also FL 1:5
See also MTCW 1, 2
See also PC 2, 55
See also PFS 18
See also RGWL 2, 3
Akhnaton, Askia
See Eckels, Jon
Akhtar, Shabbir 1960- 139
Akhurst, Bertram A. 1928- 45-48
Akiba Sullivan Harper, Donna
See Sullivan Harper, Donna Akiba
Akin, Wallace E(lmus) 1923- 25-28R
Akin, William E(rnest) 1936- CANR-39
Earlier sketch in CA 116
Akinjogbin, I(saac) A(deagbo) 1930- . CANR-29
Earlier sketches in CA 21-24R, CANR-12
Akins, Ellen 135
Akins, Zoe 1886-1958 181
Brief entry 115
See also DLB 26
See also RGAL 4
Akinsha, Konstantin 1960- 155
Akita, George 1926- 17-20R
Akitsu, Saburo
See Miyazaki, Hayao
Akmakjian, Alan P(aul) 1948- 200
Akmakjian, Hiag 1926- 57-60
Akpabot, Samuel Ekpe 1932- 101
Akrigg, G(eorge) P(hillip) V(ernon)
1913- 25-28R
Aks, Patricia 1926-1994 136
See also SATA 68
Aksakov, Ivan Sergeevich 1823-1886 . DLB 277
Aksakov, Sergei Timofeyvich
1791-1859 ..... DLB 198
Aksenov, Vasilii (Pavlovich)
See Aksyonov, Vassily (Pavlovich)
See also CWW 2
Aksenov, Vassily
See Aksyonov, Vassily (Pavlovich)
Akst, Daniel 1956- CANR-110
Earlier sketch in CA 161
See also CLC 109
Aksyonov, Vassily (Pavlovich)
1932- CANR-77
Earlier sketches in CA 53-56, CANR-12, 48
See also Aksenov, Vasilii (Pavlovich)
See also CLC 22, 37, 101
See also DLB 302
See also EWL 3
Akunin, Boris
See Chkhartishvili, Grigorii Shalvovich and Chkhartishvili, Grigory (Shalvovich)
See also DLB 285
Akurgal, Ekrem 1911- 130
Akutagawa Ryunosuke 1892-1927 154
Brief entry 117
See also DLB 180
See also EWL 3
See also MJW
See also RGSF 2
See also RGWL 2, 3
See also SSC 44
See also TCLC 16
Akyeampong, Emmanuel K(waku) 1962- 166
Alabaster, William 1568-1640 ..... DLB 132
See also RGEL 2
Aladjem, Henrietta H. 1917- 105
Alagoa, Ebiegberi Joe 1933- CANR-138
Earlier sketch in CA 167
See also BW 3
See also SATA 108
Alai 1959- 216
Alailima, Fay C. 1921- 33-36R
Alain
See Brustlein, Daniel
Alain 1868-1951 163
See also EWL 3
See also GFL 1789 to the Present
See also TCLC 41
Alain de Lille c. 1116-c. 1203 ..... DLB 208
Alain-Fournier
See Fournier, Henri-Alban
See also DLB 65
See also EWL 3
See also GFL 1789 to the Present
See also RGWL 2, 3
See also TCLC 6
Alajalov, Constantin 1900-1987
Obituary 123
See also SATA-Obit 53
Alali, A. Odasuo 1957- 140
Alama, Pauline J. 1964- 211
Alameddine, Rabih 173
Al-Amin, Jamil Abdullah 1943- CANR-82
Brief entry 112
Earlier sketch in CA 125
See also BLC 1
See also BW 1, 3
See also DAM MULT
Alan, David
See Horsfield, Alan
Alan, Jack
See Green, Alan (Baer)
Alan, Robert
See Silverstein, Robert Alan
Alan, Sandy
See Ullman, Allan
Alan, Theresa 1972- 234
Aland, Kurt 1915- CANR-12
Earlier sketch in CA 25-28R
Alanus de Insluis
See Alain de Lille
al-A'Raj, Wasini 1954- ..... EWL 3
Alarcon, Francisco X(avier) 1954- ... CANR-113
Alarcon, Francisco X(avier) 1954- 147
See also DLB 122
See also SATA 104
Alarcon, Justo S. 1930- ..... DLB 209
Alarcon, Pedro Antonio de 1833-1891 .. SSC 64
Alare, Anthony W(ard) 1942- 177
Alas (y Urena), Leopoldo (Enrique Garcia)
1852-1901 131
Brief entry 113
See also HW 1
See also RGSF 2
See also TCLC 29
Alavi, Buzurg 1907-1997 ..... EWL 3
Alaya, Flavia (M.) 1935- CANR-91
Earlier sketch in CA 33-36R
al-Azm, Sadik J. 1934- CANR-9
Earlier sketch in CA 21-24R
Alazraki, Jaime 1934- CANR-21
Earlier sketch in CA 33-36R
Alba, Bernardo Dominguez 1904(?)-1994 .. 176
See also Sinan, Rogelio
See also HW 2
Alba, Nanina 1915-1968 141
See also BW 2
See also DLB 41
Alba, Richard D(enis) 1942- 109
Alba, Victor 1916- CANR-25
Earlier sketches in CA 21-24R, CANR-10
Alba de Gamez, Cielo Cayetana 1920- ... 93-96
Albahari, David 1948- 172
Albala, Ken(neth) 1964- 220
Albanese, Antonio 1964- 215
Albanese, Catherine L(ouise) 1940- .. CANR-24
Earlier sketches in CA 65-68, CANR-9
Albanese, Laurie Lico 1959- 234
Albanov, Valerian Ivanovich 1881-1919 211
Albany, A(my) J(o) 1962- 223
Albany, James
See Rae, Hugh C(rauford)
Albarella, Joan K. 1944- 199
Albaret, Celeste (Gineste) 1891-1984 73-76
Obituary 112
Albarn, Keith 1939- 135
Albarran, Alan B. 1954- 222
Albaugh, Edwin (Doll, Jr.) 1935- 89-92
Albaugh, Ralph M(attern) 1909-1976 .... CAP-1
Obituary 171
Earlier sketch in CA 13-14
Albaum, Gerald (Sherwin) 1933- CANR-38
Earlier sketches in CA 37-40R, CANR-14
Albaum, Melvin 1936- 53-56
al-Bayyati, Abd al-Wahhab 1926-
See Bayati, al- 'Abdal-Wahhab
See also EWL 3
Albee, Edward (Franklin) (III)
1928- CANR-124
Earlier sketches in CA 5-8R, CANR-8, 54, 74
Interview in CANR-8
See also CABS 3
See also AAYA 51
See also AITN 1
See also AMW
See also CAD
See also CD 5, 6
See also CDALB 1941-1968
See also CLC 1, 2, 3, 5, 9, 11, 13, 25, 53, 86, 113
See also DA
See also DA3
See also DAB
See also DAC
See also DAM DRAM, MST
See also DC 11
See also DFS 2, 3, 8, 10, 13, 14
See also DLB 7, 266
See also EWL 3
See also LAIT 4
See also LMFS 2
See also MAL 5
See also MTCW 1, 2
See also MTFW 2005
See also RGAL 4
See also TUS
See also WLC
Albee, George Sumner 1905-1964 ..... 1-4R
Alber, Mike 1938- 25-28R
Alberdi, Juan Bautista 1810-1884 ..... LAW
Alberigo, Giuseppe 1926- 220
Alberoni, Francesco (Saverio) 1929- 130
Albers, Anni 1899-1994 ..... CANR-78
Obituary 145
Earlier sketches in CA 1-4R, CANR-2
Albers, Henry H. 1919- CANR-6
Earlier sketch in CA 1-4R
Albers, Jan 1952- 187
Albers, Josef 1888-1976 ..... CANR-3
Obituary 65-68
Earlier sketch in CA 1-4R
Albers, Patricia 1949- 206
Albert, A(braham) Adrian 1905-1972
Obituary 37-40R
Albert, Alexa 1968- 200
Albert, Allan (Praigrod) 1945-
Brief entry 116
Albert, Bill 1942- 164
Albert, Burton 1936- CANR-46
Earlier sketches in CA 61-64, CANR-8, 23
See also SATA 22
Albert, Carl (Bert) 1908-2000 132
Obituary 188
Albert, David Z. 230
Albert, Ethel M(ary) 1918-1989 ..... 21-24R
Albert, Fred 1957- 140
Albert, Gail 1942- 108
Albert, Hans 1921- 141
Albert, Harold A. 1909-1997 ..... 29-32R
Obituary 162
See also Cathcart, Helen
Albert, Linda 1939- CANR-27
Earlier sketch in CA 110
Albert, Louise 1928- CANR-141
Earlier sketch in CA 69-72
See also SATA 157
Albert, Marv 1943- 101
Albert, Marvin H(ubert) 1924-1996 .. CANR-58
Obituary 151
Earlier sketches in CA 73-76, CANR-30
See also CMW 4
See also TCWW 1, 2
Albert, Michael 1947- 224
Albert, Mimi (Abriel) 1940- 175
Earlier sketch in CA 73-76
Autobiographical Essay in 175
See also CAAS 30
Albert, Neil 1950- 160
Albert, Octavia 1853-c. 1889 ..... DLB 221
Albert, Peter J(oseph) 1946- 114
Albert, Richard E. 1909-1999 149
See also SATA 82
Albert, Richard N(orman) 1930- 176
Albert, Stephen P.
See Albert, Steve
Albert, Steve 1950- 147
Albert, Susan Wittig 1940- CANR-101
Earlier sketch in CA 167
See also SATA 107
Albert, Walter E. 1930- 21-24R
Albertazzie, Ralph 1923- 101
Alberti, Johanna 1940- 136
Alberti (Merello), Rafael
See Alberti, Rafael
See also CWW 2
Alberti, Rafael 1902-1999 ..... CANR-81
Obituary 185
Earlier sketch in CA 85-88
See also Alberti (Merello), Rafael
See also CLC 7
See also DLB 108
See also EWL 3
See also HW 2
See also RGWL 2, 3
Alberti, Robert E(dward) 1938- CANR-7
Earlier sketch in CA 61-64
Albertinus, Aegidius c. 1560-1620 ..... DLB 164
Alberts, David Stephen 1942- 29-32R
Alberts, Frances Jacobs 1907-1989 ..... 5-8R
See also SATA 14
Alberts, Laurie 1953- 234
Alberts, Robert C(arman) 1907-1996 ..... 33-36R
Obituary 154
Alberts, William W. 1925- 21-24R
Albertson, Chris 1931- 57-60
Albertson, Dean 1920-1989 ..... CANR-78
Obituary 128
Earlier sketches in CA 1-4R, CANR-3
Albertson, Susan
See Wojciechowski, Susan
Albert the Great 1193(?)-1280 ..... DLB 115
Albertyn, Dorothy
See Black, Dorothy
Albery, Nicholas 1948-2001 209
Albery, Nobuko 1940- CANR-135
Earlier sketch in CA 81-84
Albiach, Anne-Marie 1937- ..... CWP
Albin, Peter S(teigman) 1934- 85-88
Albini, Joseph L(ouis) 1930- 61-64
Albinski, Henry Stephen 1931- CANR-23
Earlier sketches in CA 21-24R, CANR-8
Albinson, Jack
See Albinson, James P.
Albinson, James P. 1932- 57-60
Albion, Ken
See King, Albert
Albion, Lee Smith ..... SATA 29
Albion, Mark S. 1951- 213
Albion, Robert Greenhalgh
1896-1983 ..... CANR-78
Obituary 110
Earlier sketches in CA 1-4R, CANR-3
Al-Bisatie, Mohamed 1937- 181
See also El-Bisatie, Mohamed
Albo, Mike 1969- 207
Albom, Mitch (David) 1958- CANR-128
Earlier sketches in CA 140, CANR-91
See also AAYA 38
See also MTFW 2005
Albornoz, Claudio Sanchez
See Sanchez Albornoz (y Mediuna), Claudio
Alborough, Jez 1959- CANR-133
Earlier sketch in CA 131
See also SATA 86, 149
Albran, Kehlog
See Shacket, Sheldon R(ubin)
Albrand, Martha (a pseudonym)
1914-1981 ..... CANR-79
Obituary 108
Earlier sketches in CA 13-16R, CANR-11
Albrecht, Ernest (Jacob) 1937- 152
Albrecht, Gary L(ouis) 1937- CANR-105
Earlier sketch in CA 147
Albrecht, H.
See Munchhausen, Borries von
Albrecht, Karl (G.) 1941- 221
Albrecht, Lillie (Vanderveer H.)
1894-1985 ..... 5-8R
Obituary 180
See also SATA 12
Albrecht, Milton C(harles)
1904-1990 ..... CANR-13
Earlier sketch in CA 33-36R
Albrecht, Robert C(harles) 1933- 21-24R
Albrecht, Ruth E(sther Martha)
1905-1994 ..... 17-20R
Albrecht, Steve 1963- 146
Albrecht, William P(rice) 1907-1986 73-76
Albrecht-Carrie, Rene 1904-1978 ..... CANR-1
Earlier sketch in CA 1-4R
Albright, Bets Parker
See Albright, Elizabeth A.
Albright, Bliss (James F.) 1903-1984 ..... 33-36R
Albright, Carol Rausch 1936- 205
Albright, Daniel 1945- 125
Albright, Elizabeth A. 1920- 108
Albright, Horace M(arden) 1890-1987 124
Obituary 122
Albright, John Brannon 1930- 65-68
Albright, Joseph (Medill Patterson)
1937- 97-100
Albright, Madeleine Korbel 1937- 158
Albright, Peter 1926- 108
Albright, Raymond W(olf) 1901-1965 ... CAP-1
Earlier sketch in CA 9-10
Albright, Roger (Lynch) 1922- 106
Albright, Thomas 1935-1984
Obituary 112
Albright, William F(oxwell) 1891-1971
Obituary 33-36R
Albritton, Robert 1941- 235
Albrow, Martin 1937- 33-36R
Albus, James Sacra 1935- 124
Albyn, Carole Lisa 1955- 150
See also SATA 83
Alcaeus c. 620B.C.- ..... DLB 176
Alcala, Kathleen
See Alcala, Kathleen
Alcala, Kathleen 1954- CANR-101
Earlier sketch in CA 158
Alcala-Galiano, Juan Valera y
See Valera y Alcala-Galiano, Juan
Alcalde, E. L.
See Chaij, Fernando
Alcalde, Miguel
See Burgess, Michael (Roy)
Alcaly, Roger E. 1941- 229
Alcantara, Ruben R(eyes) 1940- 105
Alcayaga, Lucila Godoy
See Godoy Alcayaga, Lucila
Alcena, Valiere 1934- 198
Alchemy, Jack
See Gershator, David
Alchian, Armen A(lbert) 1914- 127
Brief entry 110
Alcibiade
See Praz, Mario
Alcindor, (Ferdinand) Lew(is)
See Abdul-Jabbar, Kareem
Alcock, Gudrun 1908- ..... SATA 56
See also SATA-Brief 33
Alcock, John 1942- CANR-113
Earlier sketches in CA 125, CANR-52
Alcock, Susan E. 212
Alcock, Vivien (Dolores)
1924-2003 ..... CANR-105
Obituary 222
Earlier sketches in CA 110, CANR-41
See also AAYA 8, 57
See also BYA 5, 6
See also CLR 26
See also JRDA
See also MAICYA 1, 2
See also SATA 45, 76
See also SATA-Brief 38
See also SATA-Obit 148
See also YAW
Alcoriza, Luis 1920-1992 ..... IDFW 3, 4
Alcorn, Alfred 1941- CANR-85
Earlier sketch in CA 122
Alcorn, John 1935- ..... SATA 31
See also SATA-Brief 30
Alcorn, Marvin D(ouglas) 1902-1972 .... 13-16R
Obituary 180
Alcorn, Pat B(arker) 1948- 107

Alcorn, Randy (C.) 1954- ... 189
Alcorn, Robert Hayden 1909-1980 ... 5-8R
Alcorn, Stephen 1958- ... SATA 110
Alcosser, Sandra (B.) 1944- ... 142
  Brief entry ... 124
Alcott, Amos Bronson 1799-1888 .. DLB 1, 223
Alcott, John 1931-1986 ... IDFW 3, 4
Alcott, Julia
  See Cudlipp, Edythe
Alcott, Louisa May 1832-1888 ... AAYA 20
  See also AMWS 1
  See also BPFB 1
  See also BYA 2
  See also CDALB 1865-1917
  See also CLR 1, 38
  See also DA
  See also DA3
  See also DAB
  See also DAC
  See also DAM MST, NOV
  See also DLB 1, 42, 79, 223, 239, 242
  See also DLBD 14
  See also FL 1:2
  See also FW
  See also JRDA
  See also LAIT 2
  See also MAICYA 1, 2
  See also NFS 12
  See also RGAL 4
  See also SATA 100
  See also SSC 27
  See also TUS
  See also WCH
  See also WLC
  See also WYA
  See also YABC 1
  See also YAW
Alcott, William Andrus 1789-1859 . DLB 1, 243
Alcuin c. 730-804 ... DLB 148
Alcyone
  See Krishnamurti, Jiddu
Ald, Roy A(llison) ... CANR-24
  Earlier sketch in CA 73-76
Alda, Alan 1936- ... 103
Alda, Arlene 1933- ... CANR-142
  Earlier sketch in CA 114
  See also CLR 93
  See also SATA 44, 106, 158
  See also SATA-Brief 36
Aldan, Daisy 1923- ... CANR-25
  Earlier sketches in CA 13-16R, CANR-8
Aldana, Francisco de 1537-1578 ... DLB 318
Aldanov, M. A.
  See Aldanov, Mark (Alexandrovich)
Aldanov, Mark (Alexandrovich)
  1886-1957 ... 181
  Brief entry ... 118
  See also DLB 317
  See also TCLC 23
Aldcroft, Derek H(oward) 1936- ... CANR-116
  Earlier sketches in CA 25-28R, CANR-12, 29, 55
Aldecoa, Ignacio 1925-1969 ... 206
Alden, Carella
  See Remington, Ella-Carrie
Alden, Dauril 1926- ... CANR-110
  Earlier sketch in CA 105
Alden, Douglas William 1912-1998 . CANR-93
  Obituary ... 172
  Earlier sketch in CA 69-72
Alden, Henry Mills 1836-1919 ... 179
  See also DLB 79
Alden, Isabella (Macdonald) 1841-1930 ... 179
  Brief entry ... 120
  See also DLB 42
  See also SATA 115
  See also YABC 2
Alden, Jack
  See Barrows, (Ruth) Marjorie
Alden, Joan 1944- ... 144
Alden, John D. 1921- ... 17-20R
Alden, John R(ichard) 1908-1991 ... CANR-78
  Obituary ... 135
  Earlier sketches in CA 61-64, CANR-11
Alden, Michele
  See Avallone, Michael (Angelo, Jr.)
Alden, Patricia ... 193
Alden, Robert L(eslie) 1937- ... 65-68
Alden, Sue
  See Francis, Dorothy Brenner
Alder, Francis A(nthony) 1937- ... 61-64
Alder, Henry (Ludwig) 1922- ... 49-52
Alder, Ken(neth L.) ... CANR-127
  Earlier sketch in CA 172
Alderfer, Clayton P. 1940- ... 37-40R
Alderfer, E. G.
  See Alderfer, E(verett) Gordon
Alderfer, E(verett) Gordon 1915-1996 ... 121
  Obituary ... 176
Alderfer, Harold F(reed) 1903-1983 ... 9-12R
  Obituary ... 174
Alderman, Clifford Lindsey
  1902-1988 ... CANR-3
  Earlier sketch in CA 1-4R
  See also SATA 3
Alderman, Ellen 1957(?)- ... 162
Alderman, Geoffrey 1944- ... CANR-55
  Earlier sketches in CA 93-96, CANR-29
Alderman, (Barbara) Joy 1931- ... 61-64
Aldersey-Williams, Hugh 1959- ... 138
Alderson, Jo(anne) Bartels 1930- ... 65-68
Alderson, Maggie ... 205
Alderson, Michael (Rowland) 1931-1988
  Obituary ... 126
Alderson, (Arthur) Stanley 1927- ... 5-8R
Alderson, Sue Ann 1940- ... CWRI 5
  See also SATA 59
  See also SATA-Brief 48
Alderson, William T(homas), Jr. 1926- ... 9-12R
Alding, Peter
  See Jeffries, Roderic (Graeme)
Aldington, Richard 1892-1962 ... CANR-45
  Earlier sketch in CA 85-88
  See also CLC 49
  See also DLB 20, 36, 100, 149
  See also LMFS 2
  See also RGEL 2
Aldis, Dorothy (Keeley) 1896-1966 .. CANR-34
  Earlier sketch in CA 1-4R
  See also DLB 22
  See also SATA 2
Aldis, H. G. 1863-1919 ... DLB 184
Aldiss, Brian W(ilson) 1925- ... 190
  Earlier sketches in CA 5-8R, CANR-5, 28, 64, 121
  Autobiographical Essay in ... 190
  See also CAAS 2
  See also AAYA 42
  See also CLC 5, 14, 40
  See also CN 1, 2, 3, 4, 5, 6, 7
  See also DAM NOV
  See also DLB 14, 261, 271
  See also MTCW 1, 2
  See also MTFW 2005
  See also SATA 34
  See also SCFW 1, 2
  See also SFW 4
  See also SSC 36
Aldo, G. R. 1902-1953 ... IDFW 3, 4
Aldon, Adair
  See Meigs, Cornelia Lynde
Aldon, Howard
  See Wilson, (Alan) Doric
  See also GLL 1
Aldouby, Zwy H(erbert) 1931- ... 33-36R
Aldous, Allan (Charles) 1911- ... SATA 27
Aldous, Anthony Michael 1935- ... CANR-25
  Earlier sketch in CA 69-72
Aldous, Tony
  See Aldous, Anthony Michael
Aldred, Cyril 1914-1991 ... CANR-78
  Obituary ... 134
  Earlier sketches in CA 57-60, CANR-6
Aldrich, Ann
  See Meaker, Marijane (Agnes)
  See also GLL 2
Aldrich, Bess Streeter 1881-1954 ... CLR 70
  See also TCLC 125
  See also TCWW 2
Aldrich, C(larence) Knight 1914- ... 25-28R
Aldrich, Frederic DeLong 1899-1998 .... CAP-1
  Earlier sketch in CA 11-12
Aldrich, Jonathan 1936- ... 180
  Brief entry ... 112
Aldrich, Joseph C(offin) 1940- ... CANR-37
  Earlier sketch in CA 114
Aldrich, Marcia ... 180
Aldrich, Nelson W(ilmarth), Jr. 1935- ... 141
  Brief entry ... 110
Aldrich, Richard (Stoddard) 1902-1986
  Obituary ... 119
Aldrich, Richard James 1961- ... 197
Aldrich, Robert (Joseph) 1954- ... 187
Aldrich, Ruth I(sabelle) ... 105
Aldrich, Sandra Picklesimer 1945- ... 111
Aldrich, Thomas (Bailey) 1836-1907 ... 179
  Brief entry ... 111
  See also DLB 42, 71, 74, 79
  See also SATA 17, 114
Aldridge, A(lfred) Owen 1915- ... 17-20R
Aldridge, Adele 1934- ... CANR-28
  Earlier sketch in CA 49-52
Aldridge, Alan 1943- ... 125
  See also SATA-Brief 33
Aldridge, Delores P(atricia) ... 142
  See also BW 2
Aldridge, (Harold Edward) James
  1918- ... CANR-51
  Earlier sketches in CA 61-64, CANR-13
  See also CN 1, 2, 3, 4, 5, 6, 7
  See also SATA 87
  See also YAW
Aldridge, Jeffrey 1938- ... 25-28R
Aldridge, John W(atson) 1922- ... CANR-3
  Earlier sketch in CA 1-4R
Aldridge, Josephine Haskell ... 73-76
  See also SATA 14
Aldridge, Richard (Boughton)
  1930- ... CANR-107
  Earlier sketches in CA 9-12R, CANR-3
Aldridge, Sarah
  See Marchant, Anyda
Aldrin, Edwin E(ugene), Jr. 1930- ... 89-92
Aldwinckle, Russell (Foster) 1911-1996 ... 69-72
Aldyne, Nathan
  See McDowell, Michael (McEachern)
Al-E Ahmad, Jalal 1923-1969 ... 152
  See also Ahmad, Jalal Al-i
  See also EWL 3
  See also RGWL 3
Aleandri, Emelise (Francesca) ... 219
Alef, Daniel 1944- ... 192
Alegria, Ciro 1909-1967 ... CANR-72
  Earlier sketch in CA 131
  See also DLB 113
  See also EWL 3
  See also LAW
Alegria, Claribel
  See Alegria, Claribel (Joy)
  See also CWW 2
  See also DLB 145, 283
Alegria, Claribel (Joy) 1924- ... CANR-134
  Earlier sketches in CA 131, CANR-66, 94
  See also Alegria, Claribel
  See also CAAS 15
  See also CLC 75
  See also DAM MULT
  See also EWL 3
  See also HLCS 1
  See also HW 1
  See also MTCW 2
  See also MTFW 2005
  See also PC 26
  See also PFS 21
Alegria, Fernando 1918- ... CANR-72
  Earlier sketches in CA 9-12R, CANR-5, 32
  See also CLC 57
  See also EWL 3
  See also HW 1, 2
Alegria, Ricardo E(nrique) 1921- ... CANR-72
  Earlier sketches in CA 25-28R, CANR-15, 32
  See also HW 1, 2
  See also SATA 6
Aleichem, Sholom
  See Rabinovitch, Sholem
  See also SSC 33
  See also TCLC 1, 35
  See also TWA
Aleinikoff, T. Alexander
  See Aleinikoff, Thomas Alexander
Aleinikoff, Thomas Alexander 1952- ... 237
Aleixandre, Vicente 1898-1984 ... CANR-81
  See also DLB 108
  See also EWL 3
  See also HLCS 1
  See also HW 2
  See also MTCW 1, 2
  See also RGWL 2, 3
  See also TCLC 113
Alejandro, Carlos F(ederico) Diaz
  See Diaz-Alejandro, Carlos F(ederico)
Alekan, Henri 1909- ... IDFW 3, 4
Aleksandravicius, Jonas
  See Aistis, Jonas
Aleksandrov, Aleksandr Andreevich
  See Durova, Nadezhda Andreevna
Aleksandrov, Pavel S(ergeevich)
  1896-1982 ... 159
Alekseeva, Marina Anatol'evna
  See Marinina, Aleksandra
Aleksin, Anatolii Georgievich 1924- . CANR-29
  Earlier sketch in CA 109
  See also SATA 36
Aleman, Miguel 1903(?)-1983
  Obituary ... 110
Alemany-Galway, Mary 1944- ... 229
Alembert, Jean(-Baptiste) le Rond d'
  1717-1783 ... DLB 313
  See also GFL Beginnings to 1789
Alencar, Jose de 1829-1877 ... DLB 307
  See also LAW
  See also WLIT 1
Alencon, Marguerite d'
  See de Navarre, Marguerite
Alenov, Lydia 1948- ... SATA 61
Alent, Rose Marie Bachem
  See Bachem Alent, Rose M(arie Baake)
Alepoudelis, Odysseus
  See Elytis, Odysseus
  See also CWW 2
Aleramo, Sibilla 1876-1960 ... DLB 114, 264
  See also WLIT 7
Alers, Rochelle 1943- ... 178
  See also BW 3
Aleshire, Peter 1952- ... 199
Aleshkovsky, Joseph 1929- ... 128
  Brief entry ... 121
  See also Aleshkovsky, Yuz
Aleshkovsky, Petr Markovich 1957- .... DLB 285
Aleshkovsky, Yuz
  See Aleshkovsky, Joseph
  See also CLC 44
  See also DLB 317
Alessandra, Anthony J(oseph)
  1947- ... CANR-141
  Earlier sketch in CA 103
Alessandra, Tony ... 160
Alessandrini, Federico 1906(?)-1983
  Obituary ... 109
Alex, Ben (a pseudonym) 1946- ... 114
  See also SATA 45
Alex, Marlee (a pseudonym) 1948- ... 114
  See also SATA 45
Alexander, Adele Logan 1938- ... CANR-91
  Earlier sketch in CA 142
Alexander, Agnes B(aldwin) 1875-1971 ... 213
Alexander, Albert 1914- ... 25-28R
Alexander, Alfred 1908-1983
  Obituary ... 110
Alexander, Alma
  See Hromic, Alma A.
Alexander, Anna B(arbara Cooke) 1913- . 57-60
  See also SATA 1
Alexander, Anne
  See Alexander, Anna B(arbara Cooke)
Alexander, Anthony Francis 1920- ... 1-4R
Alexander, Arthur (Wilson) 1927- ... 5-8R
Alexander, Bevin (Ray) 1928- ... CANR-120
  Earlier sketches in CA 122, CANR-48
Alexander, Bill 1910-2000 ... 130
  Obituary ... 188
Alexander, Boyd 1913-1980 ... 53-56
  Obituary ... 97-100
Alexander, Bruce 1932- ... 166
  See also Cook, Bruce
Alexander, Caroline 1956- ... CANR-115
  Earlier sketch in CA 132
Alexander, Cecil Frances 1818-1895 .. DLB 199
Alexander, Charles
  See Hadfield, (Ellis) Charles (Raymond)
Alexander, Charles 1868-1923 ... 205
  See also DLB 91
Alexander, Charles C(omer) 1935- CANR-91
  Earlier sketch in CA 13-16R
Alexander, Charles Stevenson 1916- .. CANR-2
  Earlier sketch in CA 5-8R
Alexander, Christine 1893-1975
  Obituary ... 61-64
Alexander, Christine (Anne) 1949- ... 117
Alexander, Colin James 1920- ... 13-16R
Alexander, Conel Hugh O'Donel
  1909-1974 ... 73-76
Alexander, David 1907-1973 ... 1-4R
  Obituary ... 41-44R
  See also CMW 4
Alexander, David M(ichael) 1945- ... 81-84
Alexander, Denis 1945- ... 45-48
Alexander, Donna
  See Vitek, Donna Kimel
Alexander, Donnell ... 223
Alexander, Doris (Muriel) 1922- ... 143
Alexander, Edward 1936- ... CANR-97
  Earlier sketch in CA 13-16R
Alexander, Edward P(orter) 1907-2003 .. 33-36R
  Obituary ... 218
Alexander, Edwin P. 1905-1981 ... 29-32R
Alexander, Elizabeth 1962- ... CANR-112
  Earlier sketch in CA 135
  See also PFS 22
Alexander, Ellen 1938- ... SATA 91
Alexander, Eric 1910(?)-1982
  Obituary ... 106
Alexander, Ernest R(obert) 1933- ... 103
Alexander, Estella Conwill 1949- ... 143
  See also BW 2
Alexander, Faith
  See Bentley, Margaret
Alexander, Floyce 1938- ... CANR-13
  Earlier sketch in CA 33-36R
Alexander, Frances (Laura)
  1888-1979 ... CANR-35
  Earlier sketch in CA 25-28R
  See also SATA 4
Alexander, Frank 1943- ... 65-68
Alexander, Franklin Osborne
  1897-1993 ... CAP-2
  Earlier sketch in CA 25-28
Alexander, Franz (Gabriel) 1891-1964 ... 5-8R
Alexander, Gary 1941- ... CANR-81
  Earlier sketch in CA 135
Alexander, George Jonathan 1931- ... 73-76
Alexander, George M(oyer) 1914-1983 ... 5-8R
Alexander, Gil
  See Ralston, Gilbert A(lexander)
Alexander, H. G. ... 129
  See also Alexander, Horace G(undry)
Alexander, Harold Lee 1934- ... 69-72
Alexander, Harriet Semmes 1949- ... 156
Alexander, Henry
  See McAllister, Alister
Alexander, Herbert (Mortimer) 1910-1988
  Obituary ... 127
Alexander, Herbert E(phraim) 1927- ... 41-44R
Alexander, Holmes (Moss)
  1906-1985 ... CANR-36
  Obituary ... 118
  Earlier sketch in CA 61-64
Alexander, Horace G(undry) 1889-1989
  Obituary ... 129
  See also Alexander, H. G.
Alexander, Hubert G(riggs) 1909-1998 .. 21-24R
Alexander, I. J. 1905(?)-1974
  Obituary ... 53-56
Alexander, Ian W(elsh) 1911-1979 ... 13-16R
Alexander, J(onathan) J(ames) G(raham)
  1935- ... CANR-13
  Earlier sketch in CA 21-24R
Alexander, James 1691-1756 ... DLB 24
Alexander, James E(ckert) 1913- ... 73-76
Alexander, Jan
  See Banis, Victor J(erome)
Alexander, Jane 1939- ... CANR-124
  Earlier sketch in CA 172
Alexander, Janet 1907-1994 ... CANR-79
  Earlier sketches in CA 9-12R, CANR-4
  See also McNeill, Janet
  See also CWRI 5
Alexander, Jean 1926- ... CANR-27
  Earlier sketch in CA 49-52
Alexander, Jeb 1899-1965 ... 146
Alexander, Jeffrey C(harles) 1947- ... 211
Alexander, Joan
  See Wetherell-Pepper, Joan Alexander
Alexander, Jocelyn Anne Arundel
  1930- ... CANR-4
  Earlier sketch in CA 1-4R
  See also SATA 22
Alexander, John A(leck) 1912-1982 ... 9-12R
Alexander, John Kurt 1941- ... 102
Alexander, John N. 1941- ... 69-72
Alexander, John T(horndike) 1940- ... 33-36R
Alexander, John W(esley) 1918- ... CANR-3
  Earlier sketch in CA 5-8R
Alexander, Jon 1940- ... 33-36R
Alexander, Joseph H(ammond) 1938- ... 150
Alexander, Josephine 1909- ... 104
Alexander, (Charles) K(halil) 1923-1980
  Obituary ... 103
Alexander, Karl 1944- ... 134
Alexander, Kate
  See Armstrong, Tilly
Alexander, Kathryn
  See Caldwell, Kathryn (Smoot)
Alexander, Kelly D., Jr. 1938- ... 223

Cumulative Index 9 Allbery

Alexander, Ken
See Alexander, Kenneth John Wilson
Alexander, Kenneth John Wilson
1922-2001 ... 61-64
Obituary ... 194
Alexander, L(ouis) G(eorge)
1932-2002 ... CANR-42
Obituary ... 206
Earlier sketches in CA 102, CANR-19
Alexander, Lawrence 1939-
Brief entry ... 122
Alexander, Leo 1905-1985
Obituary ... 116
Alexander, Lewis M(cElwain) 1921- ... 21-24R
Alexander, Linda 1935- ... 21-24R
See also SATA 2
Alexander, Liza
See Campbell, Louisa D.
Alexander, Lloyd (Chudley) 1924- .. CANR-113
Earlier sketches in CA 1-4R, CANR-1, 24, 38, 55
See also AAYA 1, 27
See also BPFB 1
See also BYA 5, 6, 7, 9, 10, 11
See also CLC 35
See also CLR 1, 5, 48
See also CWRI 5
See also DLB 52
See also FANT
See also JRDA
See also MAICYA 1, 2
See also MAICYAS 1
See also MTCW 1
See also SAAS 19
See also SATA 3, 49, 81, 129, 135
See also SUFW
See also TUS
See also WYA
See also YAW
Alexander, Louis 1917- ... 121
Alexander, Marc 1929- ... CANR-82
Earlier sketches in CA 5-8R, CANR-14, 34
See also FANT
See also SATA 117
Alexander, Marge
See Edwards, Roselyn
Alexander, Martha 1920- ... CANR-106
Earlier sketches in CA 85-88, CANR-44
See also MAICYA 1, 2
See also SATA 11, 70, 136
Alexander, Marthann 1907- ... 53-56
Alexander, Martin 1930- ... CANR-27
Earlier sketch in CA 49-52
Alexander, Mary Jean McCutcheon ... 9-12R
Alexander, Meena 1951- ... CANR-70
Earlier sketches in CA 115, CANR-38
See also CLC 121
See also CP 7
See also CWP
See also FW
Alexander, Michael (Joseph) 1941- ... CANR-45
Earlier sketches in CA 45-48, CANR-22
Alexander, Michael 1970- ... 218
Alexander, Michael Van Cleave 1937- ... 102
Alexander, Milton 1917-1998 ... 17-20R
Alexander, Pamela 1948- ... 122
Alexander, Pat(ricia June) 1937- ... 113
Alexander, Paul 1955- ... CANR-142
Earlier sketch in CA 149
Alexander, Peter F. 1949- ... 138
Alexander, R(obert) McNeill 1934- . CANR-109
Earlier sketches in CA 124, CANR-51
Alexander, R(obert) P(ercival) 1905(?)-1985
Obituary ... 117
Alexander, Rae Pace
See Alexander, Raymond Pace
Alexander, Ralph (Holland) 1936- ... 115
Alexander, Raymond Pace 1898-1974 .. 97-100
See also SATA 22
Alexander, Ric
See Long, Richard A(lexander)
Alexander, Richard Dale 1929- ... 110
Alexander, Robert
See Legat, Michael (Ronald)
Alexander, Robert
See Gross, Michael (Robert)
Alexander, Robert J. 1918- ... CANR-39
Earlier sketches in CA 1-4R, CANR-3, 18
Alexander, Robert Lester 1920- ... 108
Alexander, Robert William 1906(?)-1980
Obituary ... 97-100
Alexander, Rod
See Pellowski, Michael (Joseph)
Alexander, Ron 1930-1998 ... 189
Alexander, (Eben) Roy 1899(?)-1978 ... 85-88
Obituary ... 81-84
Alexander, Roy 1928- ... CANR-42
Earlier sketch in CA 118
Alexander, Ruth M. 1954- ... 154
Alexander, Sally Hobart 1943- ... CANR-114
Earlier sketch in CA 150
See also SATA 84
Alexander, Samuel 1859-1938 ... TCLC 77
Alexander, Shana 1925- ... CANR-97
Earlier sketches in CA 61-64, CANR-26, 58
Interview in ... CANR-26
Alexander, Sidney 1912-1999 ... CANR-6
Obituary ... 187
Earlier sketch in CA 9-12R
Alexander, Stanley Walter 1895-1980
Obituary ... 97-100
Alexander, Stella Tucker 1912- ... 105
Alexander, Sue 1933- ... CANR-113
Earlier sketches in CA 53-56, CANR-4, 19, 57
See also SAAS 15
See also SATA 12, 89, 136
Alexander, Taylor Richard 1915- ... 107
Alexander, Theron 1913- ... CANR-3
Earlier sketch in CA 5-8R
Alexander, Thomas G(len) 1935- ... 65-68
Alexander, Thomas W(illiamson), Jr.
1930- ... 9-12R
Alexander, Victoria ... 228
Alexander, Victoria N. 1965- ... 152
Alexander, Vincent Arthur 1925-1980
Obituary ... 101
See also SATA-Obit 23
Alexander, W(illiam) M(ortimer) 1928- ... 69-72
Alexander, Will 1948- ... 209
Alexander, Sir William 1557(?)-1640 .. DLB 121
Alexander, William M(arvin)
1912-1996 ... 33-36R
Alexander, Yonah 1931- ... 61-64
Alexander, Zane
See Alexander, Harold Lee
Alexanderson, Gerald L(ee) 1933- ... CANR-42
Earlier sketch in CA 118
Alexandersson, Gunnar V(ilhelm)
1922- ... 17-20R
Alexandre, Philippe 1932- ... 41-44R
Alexandrowicz, Charles Henry
1902-1975 ... CANR-1
Earlier sketch in CA 1-4R
Alexeev, Wassilij 1906- ... 89-92
Alexeieff, Alexandre A. 1901-1979 .. IDFW 3, 4
See also SATA 14
Alexeyev, Constantin (Sergeivich)
See Stanislavsky, Konstantin (Sergeivich)
Alexeyeva, Ludmilla 1927- ... 144
Alexie, Sherman (Joseph, Jr.)
1966- ... CANR-133
Earlier sketches in CA 138, CANR-65, 95
See also AAYA 28
See also BYA 15
See also CLC 96, 154
See also CN 7
See also DA3
See also DAM MULT
See also DLB 175, 206, 278
See also LATS 1:2
See also MTCW 2
See also MTFW 2005
See also NFS 17
See also NNAL
See also PC 53
See also SSFS 18
Alexiou, Margaret 1939- ... 69-72
Alexis, Andre 1957- ... 173
See also CN 7
Alexis, Katina
See Strauch, Katina (Parthemos)
Alexis, Willibald 1798-1871 ... DLB 133
Aley, Albert 1919-1986
Obituary ... 118
Alfandary-Alexander, Mark 1923- ... 5-8R
al-Farabi 870(?)-950 ... DLB 115
al-Farid, Ibn 'Umar
See Ibn al-Farid, 'Umar
al-Faruqi, Isma'il Raji 1921- ... CANR-13
Earlier sketch in CA 69-72
Alfau, Felipe 1902-1999 ... 137
See also CLC 66
Alfeyeva, Valeria ... 171
Alfieri, Vittorio 1749-1803 ... EW 4
See also RGWL 2, 3
See also WLIT 7
Alfino, Mark (R) 1959- ... 176
Alf laylah wa laylah 9th cent. - ... DLB 311
Alford, Bernard William Ernest 1937- ... 101
Alford, C(harles) Fred(erick) 1947- ... 131
Alford, Edna 1947- ... 152
Alford, Henry 1962- ... 230
Alford, Jeffrey ... 175
Alford, Kenneth D. 1939- ... 150
Alford, Norman (William) 1929- ... 37-40R
Alford, Robert R(oss) 1928- ... 41-44R
Alford, Terry (L.) 1945- ... 181
Brief entry ... 110
Alfred, King 849-901 ... DLB 146
Alfred, Jean Gaston
See Ponge, Francis
Alfred, Richard
See Haverstock, Nathan Alfred
Alfred, William 1922-1999 ... CANR-67
Obituary ... 179
Earlier sketch in CA 13-16R
See also CAD
See also MAL 5
Alfven, Hannes O(lof) G(oesta)
1908-1995 ... 29-32R
Obituary ... 148
Algarin, Miguel 1941- ... CANR-20
Earlier sketch in CA 69-72
See also LLW
Algeo, John (Thomas) 1930- ... CANR-123
Earlier sketches in CA 17-20R, CANR-7
Alger, Horatio, Jr.
See Stratemeyer, Edward L.
Alger, Horatio, Jr. 1832-1899 ... CLR 87
See also DLB 42
See also LAIT 2
See also RGAL 4
See also SATA 16
See also TUS
Alger, Leclaire (Gowans)
1898-1969 ... CANR-79
Earlier sketch in CA 73-76
See also CWRI 5
See also MAICYA 1, 2
See also SATA 15
Alger, Philip Langdon 1894-1979
Obituary ... 109
Algery, Andre
See Coulet du Gard, Rene
Al-Ghazali, Muhammad ibn Muhammad
1058-1111 ... DLB 115
al-Ghitani, Jamal
See Ghitani, Jamal al-
Algren, Nelson 1909-1981 ... CANR-61
Obituary ... 103
Earlier sketches in CA 13-16R, CANR-20
See also AMWS 9
See also BPFB 1
See also CDALB 1941-1968
See also CLC 4, 10, 33
See also CN 1, 2
See also DLB 9
See also DLBY 1981, 1982, 2000
See also EWL 3
See also MAL 5
See also MTCW 1, 2
See also MTFW 2005
See also RGAL 4
See also RGSF 2
See also SSC 33
Alhadeff, Gini q 1951- ... 164
Alhaique, Claudio 1913- ... 29-32R
al-Hajj, Unsi Luwis
See Hajj, Unsi Luwis al-
al-Hariri, al-Qasim ibn 'Ali Abu Muhammad
al-Basri 1054-1122 ... RGWL 3
Al Hussein, Noor 1951- ... 211
Ali, Agha Shahid 1949-2001 ... 153
Obituary ... 203
See also CP 7
See also PFS 18
See also WWE 1
Ali, Ahmed 1908-1998 ... CANR-34
Earlier sketches in CA 25-28R, CANR-15
See also CLC 69
See also CN 1, 2, 3, 4, 5
See also EWL 3
Ali, Chaudhri Mohamad 1905-1980
Obituary ... 105
Ali, Monica 1967- ... 219
See also AAYA 67
Ali, Muhammad 1942- ... 179
Brief entry ... 116
Ali, Salim (A.) 1896-1987 ... 132
Obituary ... 123
Ali, Samina 1969- ... 231
Ali, Schavi M.
See Ali, Schavi Mali Oghomaria Meritra
Ali, Schavi Mali Oghomaria Meritra
1948- ... CANR-95
Earlier sketch in CA 61-64
Ali, Shahrazad 1947- ... CANR-87
Earlier sketch in CA 152
See also BW 2
Ali, Sheikh R(ustum) 1932-1994 ... 141
Obituary ... 161
Ali, Tariq 1943- ... CANR-99
Earlier sketches in CA 25-28R, CANR-10
See also CLC 173
Ali, Thalassa ... 218
Alia, Valerie 1942- ... 196
Aliano, Richard Anthony 1946- ... CANR-10
Earlier sketch in CA 65-68
Aliav, Ruth
See Kluger, Ruth
Alibek, Ken ... 190
Aliber, Robert Z. 1930- ... CANR-25
Earlier sketches in CA 21-24R, CANR-8
Alibrandi, Tom 1941- ... CANR-12
Earlier sketch in CA 65-68
Alicea, Gil C. 1979- ... 152
Aliesan, Jody 1943- ... CANR-109
Earlier sketches in CA 57-60, CANR-7
Alighieri, Dante
See Dante
See also WLIT 7
Alihan, Milla ... CAP-2
Earlier sketch in CA 29-32
'Ali ibn Abi Talib c. 600-661 ... DLB 311
Ali Khan, Shirley 1951- ... 118
Aliki
See Brandenberg, Aliki (Liacouras)
See also CLR 9, 71
Alilunas, Leo John 1912- ... 17-20R
Alimayo, Chikuyo
See Franklin, Harold L(eroy)
Alinder, Martha Wheelock
See Wheelock, Martha E.
Alinder, Mary Street 1946- ... 141
Aline
See Quintanilla, (Maria) Aline (Griffith y Dexter)
Alinsky, Saul (David) 1909-1972 ... 133
Obituary ... 37-40R
Alioto, Robert F(ranklyn) 1933- ... 45-48
Alisky, Marvin (Howard)
1923-1995 ... CANR-42
Earlier sketches in CA 13-16R, CANR-5, 20
Alison, Jane 1961- ... 220
Alisov, Boris P. 1892-1972
Obituary ... 37-40R
Al-Issa, Ihsan 1931- ... 109
Alitto, Guy S(alvatore) 1942- ... 93-96
Alix, Ernest Kahlar 1939-
Brief entry ... 112
Alkalay-Gut, Karen 1945- ... 129
Alkali, Zaynab 1950- ... 172
Alkazi, Roshen 1923- ... CP 1
Alkema, Chester Jay 1932- ... 53-56
See also SATA 12
Alker, Hayward R(ose), Jr. 1937- ... 17-20R
al-Khal, Yusuf
See Khal, Yusuf al-
al-Khalil, Samir a pseudonym ... 140
Al-Khalili, Jim 1962- ... SATA 124
Al-Khansa' 575(?)-646 ... DLB 311
See also RGWL 3
al-Kharrat, Edwar 1926- ... 136
See also Kharrat, Edwar al-
Alkire, Leland George, (Jr.) 1937- ... 101
Alkire, William Henry 1935- ... 107
Alkiviades, Alkis 1953- ... CANR-138
Earlier sketch in CA 173
See also SATA 105
Alkon, Paul K. ... 150
al-Kuni, Ibrahim
See Kuni, Ibrahim al-
Allaback, Steven Lee 1939- ... 97-100
Allaby, (John) Michael 1933- ... CANR-134
Earlier sketches in CA 45-48, CANR-1, 20, 42
Allahar, Anton L. 1949- ... 153
Allain, Marie-Francoise 1945- ... 142
Allaire, Bernard 1960- ... 218
Allaire, Joseph L(eo) 1929- ... 41-44R
Allamand, Pascale 1942- ... CANR-12
Earlier sketch in CA 69-72
See also SATA 12
Allan, Adrian R. ... 168
Allan, Alfred K. 1930- ... 17-20R
Allan, Andrew (Edward Fairbairn)
1907-1974 ... 145
See also DLB 88
Allan, D(avid) G(uy) C(harles)
1925- ... CANR-15
Earlier sketch in CA 25-28R
Allan, Dan ... 229
Allan, David 1964- ... 148
Allan, Elkan 1922- ... 101
Allan, Harry T. 1928- ... 25-28R
Allan, J(ohn) David 1945- ... 41-44R
Allan, John B.
See Westlake, Donald E(dwin)
Allan, Keith 1943- ... 141
Allan, Lewis
See Meeropol, Abel
Allan, Luke
See Amy, William Lacey
See also TCWW 1, 2
Allan, Mabel Esther 1915-1998 ... CANR-104
Obituary ... 167
Earlier sketches in CA 5-8R, CANR-2, 18, 47
See also CLR 43
See also CWRI 5
See also MAICYA 1, 2
See also SAAS 11
See also SATA 5, 32, 75
Allan, Margaret
See Quick, W(illiam) T(homas)
Allan, Maud 1873-1956 ... 205
Allan, Mea 1909-1982 ... CANR-2
Obituary ... 107
Earlier sketch in CA 5-8R
Allan, Nicholas 1956- ... 194
See also SATA 79, 123
Allan, Robert Alexander 1914-1979
Obituary ... 106
Allan, Robin 1934- ... 107
Allan, Sidney
See Hartmann, Sadakichi
Allan, Sydney
See Hartmann, Sadakichi
Allan, Ted 1918(?)-1995 ... CANR-67
Obituary ... 149
Earlier sketch in CA 77-80
See also CD 5, 6
See also DLB 68
Allana, Ghulam Ali 1906-1985
Obituary ... 115
See also CP 1
Allana, Ghulamali
See Allana, Ghulam Ali
Allanbrook, Douglas 1921- ... 151
Allanbrook, Wye J(amison) 1943- ... 110
Alland, Alexander, Jr. 1931- ... CANR-128
Earlier sketch in CA 21-24R
Alland, Guy 1944- ... 69-72
Allan-Meyer, Kathleen 1918- ... CANR-105
Earlier sketches in CA 123, CANR-50
See also SATA 51
See also SATA-Brief 46
Allard, Bessie Butler Newsom (?)-1987
Obituary ... 122
Allard, Dean C(onrad) 1933- ... CANR-1
Earlier sketch in CA 45-48
Allard, Harry
See Allard, Harry G(rover), Jr.
Allard, Harry G(rover), Jr. 1928- ... CANR-38
Earlier sketch in CA 113
Interview in ... CA-113
See also CLR 85
See also MAICYA 1, 2
See also SATA 42, 102
Allard, Janet ... CLC 59
Allard, Michel (Adrien) 1924-1976
Obituary ... 65-68
Allard, Sven 1896-1975 ... CAP-2
Earlier sketch in CA 29-32
Allard, William Albert 1937- ... 115
Allardt, Erik 1925- ... CANR-116
Earlier sketches in CA 73-76, CANR-13, 30, 56
Allardt, Linda 1926- ... 126
Brief entry ... 104
Allardyce, Gilbert Daniel 1932- ... 33-36R
Allardyce, Paula
See Torday, Ursula
Allason, Rupert (W. S.) 1951- ... 171
Earlier sketch in CA 132
Allaun, Frank (Julian) 1913-2002 ... 103
Obituary ... 210
Allbeck, Willard Dow 1898-1994 ... 21-24R
Allbery, Debra 1957- ... 141

Allbeury, Ted
See Allbeury, Theodore Edward le Bouthillier
See also DLB 87
Allbeury, Theodore Edward le Bouthillier 1917- ... CANR-72
Earlier sketches in CA 53-56, CANR-5, 34
See also Allbeury, Ted
See also CMW 4
Allchin, A(rthur) M(acdonald) 1930- . CANR-38
Earlier sketches in CA 25-28R, CANR-17
Allcorn, Seth 1946- ... 138
Alldridge, James Charles 1910- ... 29-32R
Alldritt, Keith 1935- ... CANR-42
Earlier sketch in CA 25-28R
See also DLB 14
Allee, John Gage, (Jr.) 1918-1987
Obituary ... 121
Allee, Marjorie Hill 1890-1945 ... SATA 17
Alleger, Daniel E(ugene) 1903-2001 ... 33-36R
Allegretto, Michael 1944- ... 167
See also CMW 4
Allegro, John Marco 1923-1988 ... CANR-79
Obituary ... 124
Earlier sketches in CA 9-12R, CANR-4, 20
Allen, A(sa) A(lonzo) 1911-1970 ... 218
Allen, A(rthur) B(ruce) 1903-1975 ... CAP-2
Earlier sketch in CA 23-24
Allen, A(rvon) Dale, Jr. 1935- ... 21-24R
Allen, Adam
See Epstein, Beryl (M. Williams) and Epstein, Samuel
Allen, Agnes Rogers 1893-1986
Obituary ... 121
Allen, Alex B.
See Heide, Florence Parry
Allen, Allyn
See Eberle, Irmengarde
Allen, Anita
See Schenck, Anita A(llen)
Allen, Arthur A(ugustus) 1885-1964 . CANR-19
Earlier sketch in CA 1-4R
Allen, Barbara
See Stuart, (Violet) Vivian (Finlay)
Allen, Barry 1957- ... CANR-94
Earlier sketch in CA 145
Allen, Betsy
See Harrison, Elizabeth (Allen) Cavanna
Allen, Betty (Jeanne) 1929- ... 113
Allen, Bob 1948- ... 118
Allen, Bob 1961- ... 143
See also SATA 76
Allen, Brian 1952- ... 126
Allen, Captain Quincy ... CANR-26
Earlier sketches in CAP-2, CA 19-20
Allen, Carl 1961- ... 69-72
Allen, Catherine B(ryant) 1942- ... 129
Allen, Cecil J(ohn) 1886-1973 ... CAP-2
Earlier sketch in CA 25-28
Allen, Charles 1940- ... 222
Allen, Charles L(ivingstone) 1913- ... CANR-56
Earlier sketches in CA 111, CANR-28
Allen, Charlotte Hale 1928- ... 130
Allen, Charlotte Vale 1941- ... CANR-54
Earlier sketches in CA 69-72, CANR-12, 30
See also RHW
Allen, Chester
See Ingham, Henry Lloyd
See also TCWW 2
Allen, Chris 1929- ... 29-32R
Allen, Clabon Walter 1904-1987
Obituary ... 124
Allen, Clay
See Paine, Lauran (Bosworth)
Allen, Clifford Edward 1902- ... CAP-1
Earlier sketch in CA 9-10
Allen, Clifton Judson 1901-1986 ... 108
Allen, Conrad
See Miles, Keith
Allen, Craig M(itchell) 1954- ... CANR-92
Earlier sketch in CA 145
Allen, Daniel 1947- ... 125
Allen, David 1925- ... 33-36R
Allen, David 1939- ... 115
Allen, David Elliston 1932- ... 25-28R
Allen, David F(ranklyn) 1943- ... 103
Allen, David Grayson 1943- ... 115
Allen, David Rayvern 1938- ... 129
Allen, David W. 1922-
Brief entry ... 113
Allen, Dean 1950- ... 173
Allen, Debbie 1953- ... 210
Allen, Dede 1925- ... IDFW 3, 4
Allen, Derek Fortrose 1910-1975
Obituary ... 114
Allen, Dick 1939- ... 33-36R
See also CAAS 11
See also DLB 282
Allen, Diogenes 1932- ... CANR-25
Earlier sketches in CA 25-28R, CANR-10
Allen, Dizzy
See Allen, H(ubert) R(aymond)
Allen, Don Cameron 1903-1972 ... CANR-4
Earlier sketch in CA 5-8R
Allen, Donald Emerson 1917- ... 45-48
Allen, Donald M(erriam) 1912-2004 ... CANR-10
Obituary ... 229
Earlier sketch in CA 17-20R
Allen, Donald R. 1930- ... 45-48
Allen, Douglas (Malcolm) 1941- ... 113
Allen, Durward L(eon) 1910-1997 ... 41-44R
Allen, Dwight 1951- ... 198
Allen, Dwight W(illiam) 1931- ... 13-16R
Allen, E. C.
See Ward, Elizabeth Campbell
Allen, E. John B. 1933- ... 146
Allen, Edith Beavers 1920- ... 9-12R
Allen, Edith Marion ... CAP-1
Earlier sketch in CA 13-16
Allen, Edward 1948- ... CLC 59
Allen, Edward (Hathaway) 1948- ... 161
Allen, Edward D(avid) 1923- ... CANR-31
Earlier sketch in CA 49-52
Allen, Edward Heron
See Heron-Allen, Edward
Allen, Edward J(oseph) 1907-1990 ... CAP-1
Earlier sketch in CA 17-18
Allen, Edward Lawrence 1913-1989
Obituary ... 130
Allen, Edward Switzer 1887-1985
Obituary ... 116
Allen, Elisabeth Offutt 1895-1980 ... 57-60
Allen, Elizabeth
See Thompson, Elizabeth Allen
Allen, (Evelyn) Elizabeth 1918- ... 121
Allen, Elizabeth 1955- ... 122
Allen, Elizabeth Cooper
See Allen, Betty (Jeanne)
Allen, Eric 1916- ... 133
Brief entry ... 111
Allen, Esther 1962- ... CANR-116
Earlier sketch in CA 158
Allen, Ethan 1738-1789 ... DLB 31
Allen, Everett S(locum) 1916-1990 ... 147
Brief entry ... 110
Allen, Felicity 1924- ... 198
Allen, Fergus 1921- ... 162
Allen, Francis A(lfred) 1919- ... 13-16R
Allen, Francis R(obbins) 1908-1992 ... 77-80
Allen, Frank 1939- ... CANR-26
Earlier sketch in CA 109
Allen, Franklin 1956- ... 236
Allen, Fred 1894-1956 ... TCLC 87
Allen, Frederick G(arfield) 1936-1986 ... CANR-26
Obituary ... 121
Earlier sketch in CA 57-60
Allen, Frederick Lewis 1890-1954 ... 186
See also DLB 137
Allen, Frederick S(tetson) 1930-
Brief entry ... 112
Allen, G(eorge) C(yril) 1900-1982 ... CANR-32
Obituary ... 107
Earlier sketches in CA 1-4R, CANR-3
Allen, G(eorge) Francis 1907- ... CAP-1
Earlier sketch in CA 9-10
Allen, Garland E(dward) 1936- ... 53-56
Allen, Gary
See Allen, Frederick G(arfield)
Allen, Gay Wilson 1903-1995 ... CANR-3
Obituary ... 149
Earlier sketch in CA 5-8R
See also DLB 103
See also DLBY 1995
Allen, Geoffrey Francis 1902-1982 ... CAP-1
Earlier sketch in CA 13-14
Allen, George 1808-1876 ... DLB 59
Allen, George (Herbert) 1922-1990 ... 111
Allen, Gerald 1942- ... CANR-16
Earlier sketch in CA 93-96
Allen, Gertrude E(lizabeth) 1888-1984 ... 61-64
See also SATA 9
Allen, Gilbert (Bruce) 1951- ... CANR-109
Earlier sketch in CA 111
Allen, Gina 1918- ... CANR-43
Earlier sketch in CA 1-4R
Allen, Grace
See Hogarth, Grace (Weston Allen)
Allen, Grant 1848-1899 ... DLB 70, 92, 178
Allen, (Charles) Grant (Blairfindie) 1848-1899 ... HGG
Allen, Gwenfread Elaine 1904-1987 ... 61-64
Allen, H. Fredericka
See Allen, H(elena) G(ronlund)
Allen, H(elena) G(ronlund) ... 29-32R
Allen, H(ubert) R(aymond) 1919-1987
Obituary ... 122
Allen, Harold B(yron) 1902-1988 ... CANR-10
Earlier sketch in CA 17-20R
Allen, Harold J(oseph) 1925- ... 45-48
Allen, Harriette Bias
See Insignares, Harriette Bias
Allen, Harry Cranbrook 1917-1998 ... 5-8R
Allen, Hazel
See Hershberger, Hazel Kuhns
Allen, Heather 1953- ... 172
Allen, Henry
See Adams, Henry H(itch)
Allen, Henry Wilson 1912-1991 ... CANR-64
Obituary ... 135
Earlier sketch in CA 89-92
See also DLBY 1985
See also TCWW 1, 2
Allen, Herman R. 1913(?)-1979
Obituary ... 89-92
Allen, (William) Hervey, (Jr.) 1889-1949 ... 169
Brief entry ... 108
See also DLB 9, 45, 316
See also RHW
Allen, Howard W. 1931- ... 33-36R
Allen, Hugh
See Rathborne, St. George (Henry)
Allen, Ida (Cogswell) Bailey 1885-1973
Obituary ... 110
Allen, Ira R. 1948- ... 65-68
Allen, Irene 1903- ... CAP-1
Earlier sketch in CA 13-16
Allen, Irving L(ewis), Jr. 1931- ... 110
Allen, Ivan (Earnest), Jr. 1911-2003 ... 109
Obituary ... 218
Allen, J(ames) Timothy 1959- ... 235
Allen, Jack 1899- ... SATA-Brief 29
Allen, Jack 1914- ... CANR-4
Earlier sketch in CA 9-12R
Allen, James
See Ader, Paul (Fassett)
Allen, James 1739-1808 ... DLB 31
Allen, James B(rown) 1927- ... 105
Allen, James B(eekman) 1931- ... 105
Allen, James Egert 1896-1980
Obituary ... 97-100
Allen, James L(ovic), Jr. 1929- ... CANR-17
Earlier sketch in CA 33-36R
Allen, James Lane 1849-1925 ... 205
See also DLB 71
See also RGAL 4
Allen, James S. 1906(?)-1986
Obituary ... 120
Allen, James Smith 1949- ... 111
Allen, Jane 1941- ... 235
Allen, Jay Presson 1922- ... CANR-45
Earlier sketch in CA 73-76
See also DLB 26
See also IDFW 3, 4
Allen, Jeffery Renard 1962- ... 230
Allen, Jeffner 1947- ... 155
See also GLL 2
Allen, Jeffrey (Yale) 1948- ... 112
See also SATA 42
Allen, Jeffrey G(rant) 1943- ... 116
Allen, Jerry 1911-1994 ... CANR-94
Obituary ... 147
Earlier sketch in CA 9-12R
Allen, Jim
See Allen, James L(ovic), Jr.
Allen, Jim 1926-1999 ... 189
Allen, Jo Harvey 1943- ... 206
Allen, Johannes 1916-1973 ... CANR-14
Earlier sketch in CA 29-32R
Allen, John
See Perry, Ritchie (John Allen)
Allen, John Alexander 1922- ... 25-28R
Allen, John D(aniel) 1898-1972 ... CAP-2
Earlier sketch in CA 33-36
Allen, John Jay 1932- ... CANR-18
Earlier sketch in CA 33-36R
Allen, John Logan 1941- ... 85-88
Allen, John Stuart 1907-1982
Obituary ... 109
Allen, Jon L(ewis) 1931- ... 57-60
Allen, Jonathan B(urgess) 1957-
See Allen, Jonathan Dean
See also SATA 131
Allen, Jonathan Dean
See Allen, Jonathan B(urgess)
See also CWRI 5
Allen, Jordan
See Dumke, Glenn S.
Allen, Judson B(oyce) 1932- ... CANR-17
Earlier sketch in CA 81-84
Allen, Judy (Christina) 1941- ... SATA 80, 124
Allen, K. Eileen 1918- ... 113
Allen, Katharine Martin 1906(?)-1984
Obituary ... 115
Allen, Kenneth (William) 1941- ... 69-72
Allen, Kenneth S. 1913-1981 ... CANR-32
Earlier sketch in CA 77-80
See also SATA 56
Allen, Kieran 1954- ... 234
Allen, L(ouis) David 1940- ... 130
Brief entry ... 117
Allen, Lafe Franklin 1914-2000
Brief entry ... 111
Allen, Laura Jean ... 133
Brief entry ... 110
See also SATA-Brief 53
Allen, Lawrence A. 1926- ... 45-48
Allen, Layman E(dward) 1927- ... 5-8R
Allen, Lee 1915-1969 ... CANR-1
Earlier sketch in CA 1-4R
Allen, Leonard 1915(?)-1981
Obituary ... 102
Allen, Leroy 1912- ... 65-68
See also SATA 11
Allen, Leslie Christopher 1935- ... CANR-13
Earlier sketch in CA 73-76
Allen, Leslie H. 1887(?)-1973
Obituary ... 49-52
Allen, Lillian 1951- ... 196
Allen, Linda 1925- ... 102
See also SATA 33
Allen, Loring
See Allen, Robert Loring
Allen, Louis 1922-1991 ... 41-44R
Obituary ... 136
Allen, Louis A. 1917- ... 5-8R
Allen, M(arion) C(arroll) 1914-1995 ... 9-12R
Obituary ... 171
Allen, M(alcolm) D(ennis) 1951- ... 138
Allen, Marcus
See Donicht, Mark Allen
Allen, Marjorie 1931- ... 69-72
See also SATA 22
Allen, Marjory (Gill) 1897-1976 ... CAP-1
Earlier sketch in CA 9-10
Allen, Mark
See Donicht, Mark Allen
Allen, Martha Mitten 1937- ... 125
Allen, Mary
See Cleveland, Mary
Allen, Mary (Charlotte Chocqueel) 1909- ... 109
Allen, Maury 1932- ... CANR-95
Earlier sketch in CA 17-20R
See also SATA 26
Allen, Merrill J(ames) 1918- ... 69-72
Allen, Merritt Parmelee 1892-1954 ... SATA 22
Allen, Michael (Derek) 1939- ... CANR-39
Earlier sketch in CA 77-80
Allen, Michael J(ohn) B(ridgman) 1941- ... 102
Allen, Michael Patrick 1945- ... 137
Allen, Minerva C(rantz) 1935- ... CANR-6
Earlier sketch in CA 57-60
Allen, Miriam Marx 1927- ... 138
Allen, Moira (Anderson) 1959- ... 222
Allen, Myron B. 1954- ... 171
Allen, Myron Sheppard 1901-1995 ... CAP-1
Earlier sketch in CA 9-10
Allen, Nancy 1938- ... 165
Allen, Nancy Kelly 1949- ... SATA 127
Allen, Nina (Stroemgren) 1935- ... SATA 22
Allen, Oliver E. 1922- ... CANR-53
Earlier sketch in CA 126
Allen, Pamela (Kay) 1934- ... CANR-118
Earlier sketches in CA 126, CANR-53
See also CLR 44
See also CWRI 5
See also MAICYA 2
See also SATA 50, 81, 123
Allen, Pat 1938- ... 118
Allen, Paul (E.) 1945- ... 196
Allen, Paul 1948- ... 81-84
Allen, Paula Gunn 1939- ... CANR-130
Brief entry ... 112
Earlier sketches in CA 143, CANR-63
See also AMWS 4
See also CLC 84, 202
See also CWP
See also DA3
See also DAM MULT
See also DLB 175
See also FW
See also MTCW 2
See also MTFW 2005
See also NNAL
See also RGAL 4
See also TCWW 2
Allen, Paula Smith 1951- ... 188
Allen, Peter Christopher 1905-1993 ... 108
Allen, Philip M(ark) 1932- ... 150
Allen, Phyllis (Greig) ... 65-68
Allen, Phyllis S(loan) 1908- ... 65-68
Allen, Polly Reynolds 1940- ... 110
Allen, R. Earl 1922- ... CANR-6
Earlier sketch in CA 9-12R
Allen, Reginald E. 1931- ... CANR-13
Earlier sketch in CA 33-36R
Allen, Richard 1760-1831 ... AFAW 2
Allen, Richard (Hugh Sedley) 1903-1996 ... 25-28R
Obituary ... 151
Allen, (Alexander) Richard 1929- ... CANR-11
Earlier sketch in CA 65-68
Allen, Richard C.
See Taylor, John M(axwell)
Allen, Richard C. 1926- ... CANR-17
Earlier sketch in CA 25-28R
Allen, Richard Sanders 1917- ... CANR-94
Earlier sketch in CA 21-24R
Allen, Richard V(incent) 1936- ... 21-24R
Allen, Roach Van 1917-1998 ... 9-12R
Allen, Robert
See Garfinkel, Bernard Max
Allen, Robert 1946- ... 97-100
Allen, Robert C(lyde) 1950- ... CANR-41
Earlier sketch in CA 117
Allen, Robert Day 1927-1986 ... 107
Obituary ... 125
Allen, Robert F(rancis) 1928-1987 ... CANR-36
Obituary ... 123
Earlier sketch in CA 33-36R
Allen, Robert G. 1948- ... 218
Allen, Robert J. 1930- ... 13-16R
Allen, Robert L(ee) 1942- ... CANR-138
Earlier sketch in CA 101
See also BW 1
Allen, Robert Livingston 1916- ... 17-20R
Allen, Robert Loring 1921- ... CANR-6
Earlier sketch in CA 1-4R
Allen, Robert M. 1909-1979 ... CANR-2
Earlier sketch in CA 1-4R
Allen, Robert Porter 1905-1963 ... CANR-94
Earlier sketch in CA 5-8R
Allen, Robert S(haron) 1900-1981 ... CANR-6
Obituary ... 103
Earlier sketch in CA 57-60
Allen, Robert Thomas 1911-1990
Brief entry ... 110
Allen, Roberta L. 1945- ... CANR-104
Earlier sketch in CA 144
Allen, Rodney F. 1938-1999 ... 61-64
See also SATA 27
Allen, Roger M(ichael) A(shley) 1942- ... CANR-51
Earlier sketches in CA 111, CANR-28
Allen, Roger MacBride 1957- ... CANR-139
Earlier sketch in CA 162
See also SATA 105
See also SFW 4
Allen, Roland
See Ayckbourn, Alan
Allen, Ronald B(arclay) 1941- ... 114
Allen, Ronald J(ay) 1948- ... CANR-123
Earlier sketch in CA 170
Allen, Ronald Royce 1930- ... CANR-32
Earlier sketch in CA 17-20R, 113
Allen, Ross R(oundy) 1928- ... 33-36R
Allen, Roy (George Douglas) 1906-1983
Obituary ... 110
Allen, Roy E. 1957- ... 188
Allen, Rupert C(lyde) 1927- ... 65-68
Allen, Ruth
See Peterson, Esther (Allen)
Allen, Ruth Finney 1898-1979 ... 93-96
Obituary ... 85-88
Allen, Sam
See Allen, M(arion) C(arroll)

Cumulative Index 11 AlRoy

Allen, Samuel W(ashington) 1917- ... CANR-26
Earlier sketch in CA 49-52
See also BW 1
See also DLB 41
See also EXPP
See also SATA 9
Allen, Sarah A.
See Hopkins, Pauline Elizabeth
Allen, Sarah (Pearson) Sawyer 1920- 89-92
Allen, Sheila Rosalynd 1942- 135
Allen, Shirley Seifried 1921- 57-60
Allen, Shirley Walter 1883-1968 .... CAP-2
Earlier sketch in CA 25-28
Allen, Sidney H.
See Hartmann, Sadakichi
Allen, Stephen (Valentine Patrick William)
1921-2000 .... CANR-109
Obituary 191
Earlier sketches in CA 25-28R, CANR-18, 46
Allen, Steve
See Allen, Stephen (Valentine Patrick William)
Allen, Stuart
See Tubb, E(dwin) C(harles)
Allen, Sue P. 1913-1987 .... 25-28R
Allen, Susan Heuck 1952- 197
Allen, Sydney (Earl), Jr. 1929- 29-32R
Allen, T. D.
See Allen, Terril Diener
See also TCWW 1, 2
Allen, Terril Diener 1908- CANR-61
Earlier sketches in CA 5-8R, CANR-2
See also Allen, T. D.
See also SATA 35
Allen, Terry D.
See Allen, Terril Diener
Allen, Thomas B(enton) 1929- CANR-119
Earlier sketches in CA 13-16R, CANR-5, 20, 45, 79
See also SATA 45, 140
Allen, Tim 1953- 158
See also AAYA 24
Allen, Tom
See Allen, Thomas B(enton)
Allen, Tony 1945- 77-80
Allen, Vernon L(esley) 1933- 29-32R
Allen, W(illiam) Sidney 1918-2004 49-52
Obituary 227
Allen, Wallace (Wilbur) 1919- 118
Allen, Walter Ernest 1911-1994 .... CANR-25
Obituary 147
Earlier sketch in CA 61-64
See also CAAS 6
See also CN 1, 2, 3, 4, 5
Allen, William 1940- 65-68
Allen, William A(ustin) 1916- CANR-13
Earlier sketch in CA 33-36R
Allen, William R(ichard) 1924- 17-20R
Allen, William Sheridan 1932- 13-16R
Allen, William Stannard 1913- 101
Allen, Woody 1935- CANR-128
Earlier sketches in CA 33-36R, CANR-27, 38, 63
See also AAYA 10, 51
See also AMWS 15
See also CLC 16, 52, 195
See also DAM POP
See also DLB 44
See also MTCW 1
See also SSFS 21
Allenbaugh, Kay 208
Allende, Isabel 1942- CANR-129
Brief entry 125
Earlier sketches in CA 130, CANR-51, 74
Interview in CA-130
See also AAYA 18
See also CDWLB 3
See also CLC 39, 57, 97, 170
See also CLR 99
See also CWW 2
See also DA3
See also DAM MULT, NOV
See also DLB 145
See also DNFS 1
See also EWL 3
See also FL 1:5
See also FW
See also HLC 1
See also HW 1, 2
See also LAIT 5
See also LAWS 1
See also LMFS 2
See also MTCW 1, 2
See also MTFW 2005
See also NCFS 1
See also NFS 6, 18
See also RGSF 2
See also RGWL 3
See also SATA 163
See also SSC 65
See also SSFS 11, 16
See also WLCS
See also WLIT 1
Allendoerfer, Carl B(arnett)
1911-1974 .... CANR-11
Earlier sketches in CAP-2, CA 17-18
Allen of Hurtwood, Lady
See Allen, Marjory (Gill)
Allentuch, Harriet Ray 1933- 13-16R
Allentuck, Andrew 1943- 111
Allentuck, Marcia Epstein 1928- 33-36R
Allerton, Mary
See Govan, (Mary) Christine Noble
Alletzhauser, Albert J. 1960- 136
Alley, Brian 1933- 111
Alley, Henry Melton 1943- CANR-109
Earlier sketches in CA 112, CANR-35
Alley, Louis Edward 1914-1991 .... 17-20R
Alley, Norman William 1895-1981
Obituary 115
Alley, Rewi 1897-1987 .... CANR-36
Obituary 124
Earlier sketches in CA 73-76, CANR-13
See also CP 1, 2, 3
Alley, Robert S. 1932- 33-36R
Alley, Stephen L(ewis) 1915-1997
Brief entry 110
Alleyn, Ellen
See Rossetti, Christina (Georgina)
Alleyne, Carla D. .... CLC 65
Alleyne, Mervyn (C.) 1933- 130
Allfrey, Anthony 1930- 137
Allgire, Mildred J. 1910-1988 .... CAP-2
Earlier sketch in CA 25-28
Allgood, Myralyn F(rizzelle) 1939- 137
Allgor, Catherine 1958- 207
Allibone, T(homas) E(dward)
1903-2003 .... CANR-96
Obituary 220
Earlier sketch in CA 131
Allie, Scott 232
Alliluyeva, Svetlana (Iosifovna Stalina)
1926- 57-60
Allin, Clinton Harrop
See Harrop-Allin, Clinton
Allin, Craig Willard 1946- CANR-51
Earlier sketches in CA 108, CANR-25
Allin, Lou 1945- 227
Allin, Michael 1944- 178
Alline, Henry 1748-1784 .... DLB 99
Allingham, Margery (Louise)
1904-1966 .... CANR-58
Obituary 25-28R
Earlier sketches in CA 5-8R, CANR-4
See also CLC 19
See also CMW 4
See also DLB 77
See also MSW
See also MTCW 1, 2
Allingham, Michael 1943- 97-100
Allingham, William 1824-1889 .... DLB 35
See also RGEL 2
Allington, Maynard 1931- 148
Allington, Richard L(loyd) 1947- CANR-57
Earlier sketches in CA 112, CANR-30
See also SATA 39
See also SATA-Brief 35
Allinsmith, Wesley 1923- 85-88
Allinson, Beverley (Lynn Rouse)
1936- CANR-4
Earlier sketch in CA 49-52
Allinson, Gary D(ean) 1942- CANR-91
Earlier sketch in CA 77-80
Allis, Frederick Scouller, Jr. 1913-1993 115
Allis, Oswald T(hompson) 1880-1973
Obituary 37-40R
Allison, A(ntony) F(rancis) 1916- 106
Allison, Alexander Ward 1919-1973 .... 5-8R
Allison, Amy 1956- 208
See also SATA 138
Allison, Anne Marie 1931- 114
Allison, Anthony C(lifford) 1928- CANR-25
Earlier sketch in CA 29-32R
Allison, Bob .... SATA 14
Allison, C(hristopher) FitzSimons
1927- CANR-4
Earlier sketch in CA 1-4R
Allison, Clay
See Keevill, Henry J(ohn)
See also TCWW 1, 2
Allison, Diane Worfolk .... SATA 78
Allison, Dorothy E. 1949- CANR-107
Earlier sketches in CA 140, CANR-66
See also AAYA 53
See also CLC 78, 153
See also CN 7
See also CSW
See also DA3
See also FW
See also MTCW 2
See also MTFW 2005
See also NFS 11
See also RGAL 4
Allison, E. M. A.
See Allison, Eric W(illiam) and Allison, Mary Ann
Allison, Eric W(illiam) 1947- 122
Allison, Graham T(illett), Jr. 1940- CANR-35
Earlier sketches in CA 49-52, CANR-2
Allison, Harrison C(larke) 1917- CANR-35
Earlier sketch in CA 49-52
Allison, Henry E(dward) 1937- 133
Brief entry 110
Allison, John Murray 1889-1977 73-76
Allison, Joseph D(avid) 1950- 111
Allison, Linda 1948- CANR-144
Earlier sketch in CA 113
See also SATA 43
Allison, Marian
See Reid, Frances (Marion) P(ugh)
Allison, Mary Ann 1949- 122
Allison, Michael Frederick Lister 1936- ... 57-60
Allison, Mike
See Allison, Michael Frederick Lister
Allison, Oliver Claude 1908-1989 129
Allison, Penny
See Katz, Carol
Allison, R(ichard) Bruce 1949- CANR-19
Earlier sketches in CA 49-52, CANR-3
Allison, Ralph B(rewster) 1931- 101
Allison, Rand
See McCormick, Wilfred
Allison, Rosemary 1953- 93-96
Allison, Roy (Anthony) 1957- 119
Allison, Sam
See Loomis, Noel M(iller)
Allitt, Patrick N. 1956- 188
Allman, Barbara 1950- 207
See also SATA 137
Allman, Eileen Jorge 1940- 128
Allman, James 1943- 112
Allman, John 1935- CANR-25
Earlier sketch in CA 85-88
See also CAAS 15
Allman, T. D. 1944- CANR-17
Earlier sketch in CA 93-96
Allman Brothers .... CWRI 5
Allmand, C. T. 154
Allmand, Christopher
See Allmand, C. T.
Allmendinger, David F(rederick), Jr.
1938- CANR-97
Earlier sketch in CA 61-64
See also SATA 35
Allnutt, Gillian (Marguerite) 1949- 128
Allon, Yigal 1918-1980 .... CANR-36
Obituary 97-100
Earlier sketch in CA 73-76
Allott, Kenneth 1912-1973 129
Obituary 89-92
See also CP 1
See also DLB 20
Allott, Miriam 1920- 112
Allouache, Merzak 1944- 180
Alloula, Malek .... CLC 65
Alloway, David N(elson) 1927- CANR-10
Earlier sketch in CA 21-24R
Alloway, Lawrence 1926-1990 .... 41-44R
Allport, Gordon (Willard) 1897-1967 . CANR-3
Obituary 25-28R
Earlier sketch in CA 1-4R
Allport, Susan 1950- CANR-122
Earlier sketches in CA 124, CANR-54, 72
Allred, Alexandra Powe 1965- 217
See also SATA 144
Allred, Dorald M(ervin) 1923- 65-68
Allred, G. Hugh 1932- CANR-8
Earlier sketch in CA 61-64
Allred, Gordon T(hatcher) 1930- CANR-10
Earlier sketch in CA 17-20R
See also SATA 10
Allred, Ruel A(cord) 1929- 106
Allred, Rulon C(lark) 1906-1977 218
Allsen, Philip E(dmond) 1932- CANR-4
Earlier sketch in CA 53-56
Allsobrook, David Ian 1940- 151
Allsop, Kenneth 1920-1973 .... CANR-6
Earlier sketch in CA 1-4R
See also SATA 17
Allsopp, (Harold) Bruce 1912-2000 . CANR-98
Obituary 188
Earlier sketches in CA 5-8R, CANR-2, 18
Allsopp, (Stanley Reginald) Richard 1923- . 166
See also BW 3
Allston, Aaron 1960- 171
Allston, Washington 1779-1843 ..... DLB 1, 235
Allswang, John M(yers) 1937- 41-44R
Allum, Nancy (Patricia Eaton) 1920- CAP-1
Earlier sketch in CA 9-10
Allvine, Fred C. 1936- 61-64
Allvine, Glendon 1893(?)-1977
Obituary 73-76
Allward, Maurice (Frank) 1923- CANR-19
Earlier sketches in CA 5-8R, CANR-3
Allwood, Martin (Samuel) 1916- CANR-29
Earlier sketch in CA 110
Allworth, Edward (Alfred) 1920- CANR-43
Earlier sketch in CA 101
Allyn, David S(mith) 1969- 196
Allyn, Doug 1942- CANR-81
Earlier sketch in CA 148
See also CMW 4
Allyn, Jennifer
See Jones, Jeannette
Allyn, Paul
See Schosberg, Paul A.
Allyson, Kym
See Kimbro, John M.
Alma, Peter
See Nemeshegyi, Peter
al-Maghut, Muhammad
See Maghut, al- Muhammad
Alman, David 1919- CANR-95
Earlier sketch in CA 9-12R
Al-Marayati, Abid A(min) 1931- 33-36R
Almaraz, Felix D(iaz), Jr. 1933- 33-36R
Almasi, Janice F. 1963- 165
Almaz, Michael 1921- 81-84
Almedingen, E. M.
See Almedingen, Martha Edith von
See also CLC 12
See also SATA 3
Almedingen, Martha Edith von
1898-1971 .... CANR-1
Earlier sketch in CA 1-4R
See also Almedingen, E. M.
Almeida, Manuel Antonio de
1831-1861 .... DLB 307
Almeida Garrett, Joao Baptista da Silva Leitao de
See Garrett, Almeida
Almendros, Nestor 1930-1992 142
See also IDFW 3, 4
Almodovar, Norma Jean 1951- 142
Almodovar, Pedro 1949(?)- CANR-72
Earlier sketch in CA 133
See also CLC 114
See also HLCS 1
See also HW 2
Almog, Ruth 1936- 193
Almog, Shmuel 1926- 187
Almon, Bert 1943- 110
Almon, Clopper, Jr. 1934- 21-24R
Almon, Russell
See Clevenger, William R(ussell) and Downing, David A(lmon)
Almon, Sophie M.
See Hensley, Sophie Almon
Almond, Brenda 1937- CANR-112
Earlier sketch in CA 151
Almond, David 1951- CANR-142
Earlier sketch in CA 186
See also AAYA 38
See also BYA 16
See also CLR 85
See also MAICYA 2
See also SATA 114, 158
Almond, Gabriel A(braham)
1911-2002 .... CANR-18
Obituary 210
Earlier sketch in CA 101
Almond, Linda Stevens 1881(?)-1987
Obituary 121
See also SATA-Obit 50
Almond, Paul 1931- 73-76
Almond, Richard 1938- 53-56
Almond, Steven 1967(?)- 221
Almonte, Rosa
See Paine, Lauran (Bosworth)
Almquist, Don 1929- .... SATA 11
Almquist, Gregg (Andrew) 1948- 126
Almquist, L. Arden 1921- 29-32R
al-Mutanabbi, Ahmad ibn al-Husayn Abu al-Tayyib al-Jufi al-Kindi 915-965
See Mutanabbi, Al-
See also RGWL 3
Almy, Millie C. 1915-2001 85-88
Obituary 199
Alnaes, Finn
See Alnaes, Finn
Alnasrawi, Abbas 140
Aloff, Mindy 1947- 135
Alofsin, Anthony 1949- CANR-140
Earlier sketch in CA 146
Aloian, David 1928-1986 .... 25-28R
Aloma, Rene R(amon) 1947- 113
Alomes, Stephen 1949- 190
Aloni, Nissim 1926-1998 .... EWL 3
Alonie de Lestres, Lionel Montal
See Groulx, Lionel (Adolphe)
Alonso, Damaso 1898-1990 .... CANR-72
Obituary 130
Brief entry 110
Earlier sketch in CA 131
See also CLC 14
See also DLB 108
See also EWL 3
See also HW 1, 2
Alonso, J(uan) M(anuel) 1936- 102
Alonso, Maria Teresa Manjon
See Manjon De Read, Maria Teresa
Alonso, William 1933- CANR-6
Earlier sketch in CA 9-12R
Alonzo, John A. 1934-2001 .... IDFW 3, 4
Alotta, Robert I(gnatius) 1937- CANR-14
Earlier sketch in CA 65-68
Alov
See Gogol, Nikolai (Vasilyevich)
Aloysius, Sister Mary
See Schaldenbrand, Mary
Alpar, Murat 1943- .... EWL 3
Alpaugh, Craig 1945- 117
Alper, Benedict S(olomon)
1905-1994 .... CANR-27
Earlier sketch in CA 49-52
Alper, M(ax) Victor 1944- 69-72
Alpern, Andrew 1938- CANR-52
Earlier sketches in CA 69-72, CANR-11, 27
Alpern, David M(ark) 1942- 73-76
Alpern, Gerald D(avid) 1932- 53-56
Alpern, Sara 1942- 128
Alperovitz, Gar 1936- CANR-29
Earlier sketch in CA 49-52
Alpers, Antony (Francis George)
1919-1997 .... CANR-82
Earlier sketches in CA 1-4R, CANR-3, 35
Alpers, Bernard J. 1900-1981
Obituary 105
Alpers, Edward Alter 1941- 109
Alpers, Paul (Joel) 1932- 85-88
Alpers, Svetlana (Leontief) 1936- 115
Alpert, Cathryn 1952- 151
Alpert, Hollis 1916- CANR-46
Earlier sketches in CA 1-4R, CANR-6, 23
Alpert, Jane (Lauren) 1947- 107
Alpert, Mark I(ra) 1942- 61-64
Alpert, Paul 1907-1996 .... 41-44R
Alpert, Richard 1931- 89-92
Alpha and Omega
See Gogarty, Oliver St. John
Alphin, Elaine Marie 1955- 199
See also MAICYA 2
See also SATA 80, 130, 139
See also SATA-Essay 139
Alphonso-Karkala, John B. 1923- CANR-14
Earlier sketch in CA 37-40R
Alplaus, N. Y.
See Rubin, Cynthia Elyce
al-Qays, Imru 526(?)-565(?)
See Imru al-Qays
See also RGWL 3
Al-Qazzaz, Ayad (Sayyid Ali) 1941- 112
al-Radi, Nuha
See Radi, Nuha
Alred, Gerald J(ames) 1943- 105
AlRoy, Gil Carl 1924-1985 .... CANR-17
Obituary 116
Earlier sketch in CA 41-44R

Als 12 CONTEMPORARY AUTHORS

Als, Hilton 162
al'Sadaawi, Nawal
See El Saadawi, Nawal
See also FW
al-Samman, Ghadah 1942- 233
Alschuler, Albert W. 1940- 197
Alschuler, Rose Haas 1887-1979 .... CAP-2
Obituary 89-92
Earlier sketch in CA 25-28
Alschuler, William R. 234
Alsen, Eberhard 1939- 110
Al Sharouni, Youssef 1924- 131
Alshawi, Hiyan 1957- 143
al-Shaykh, Hanan 1945- CANR-111
Earlier sketch in CA 135
See also Shaykh, al- Hanan
See also WLIT 6
Al Siddik
See Rolfe, Frederick (William Serafino Austin Lewis Mary)
See also GLL 1
See also RGEL 2
Alsobrook, Rosalyn R. 228
Alson, Peter (H.) 1955- 156
Alsop, George 1636-(?) .... DLB 24
Alsop, Gulielma Fell 1881-1978
Obituary 77-80
Alsop, Joseph (Wright) 1910-1989 129
Obituary 122
Alsop, Mary O'Hara 1885-1980 .... CANR-65
Obituary 102
Earlier sketches in CA 9-12R, CANR-4
See also O'Hara, Mary
See also CWRI 5
See also MAICYA 1, 2
See also SATA 2, 34
See also SATA-Obit 24
Alsop, Richard 1761-1815 .... DLB 37
Alsop, Stewart (Johonnot Oliver)
1914-1974 89-92
Obituary 49-52
Alstad, Diana 147
Alsterlund, Betty
See Pilkington, Betty
Alstern, Fred
See Stern, Alfred
Alston, J(ames) M(axwell) 1901(?)-1990
Obituary 131
Alston, Mary Niven 1918- 33-36R
Alston, Patrick L(ionel) 1926- 25-28R
Alston, Philip 1950- 140
Alston, Robin (Carfrae) 1933- 131
Alston, Walter Emmons 1911-1984
Obituary 113
Alston, William P(ayne) 1921- CANR-37
Earlier sketches in CA 5-8R, CANR-7
Alswang, Betty 1920(?)-1978
Obituary 77-80
Alt, Betty Sowers 1931- CANR-85
Earlier sketch in CA 133
Alt, David D. 1933- CANR-27
Earlier sketch in CA 49-52
Alt, Herschel 1897(?)-1981
Obituary 105
Alt, (Arthur) Tilo 1931- 41-44R
Alta 1942- 57-60
See also CLC 19
Altaba (Rebeles), Dolors 1934- 236
Altaba-Artal, Dolors
See Altaba (Rebeles), Dolors
Altabe, Joan B. 1935- 53-56
Altbach, Edith Hoshino 1941- 57-60
Altbach, Philip G(eoffrey) 1941- CANR-10
Earlier sketch in CA 25-28R
Altemeyer, Bob 1940- 163
Alten, Steve 1959- CANR-104
Earlier sketch in CA 165
Altenberg, Peter 1859-1919 178
See also DLB 81
Altenbernd, (August) Lynn 1918- CANR-1
Earlier sketch in CA 45-48
Altenburg, Matthias 1958- 233
Alter, Anna 1974- .... SATA 135
Alter, J(ohn) Cecil 1879-1964 .... 5-8R
Alter, Jean V(ictor) 1925- 45-48
Alter, Jonathan Hammerman 1957- 129
Alter, Joseph Dinsmore 1923- 111
Alter, Judith (MacBain) 1938- CANR-31
Earlier sketches in CA 81-84, CANR-14
See also SATA 52, 101
Alter, Judy
See Alter, Judith (MacBain)
Alter, Nora M. 167
Alter, Robert B(ernard) 1935- CANR-100
Earlier sketches in CA 49-52, CANR-1, 47
See also CLC 34
Alter, Robert Edmond 1925-1965 .... CANR-1
Earlier sketch in CA 1-4R
See also SATA 9
Alter, Stephen 1956- 109
Alteras, Isaac 1938- 144
Alterman, Eric (Ross) 1960- CANR-89
Earlier sketch in CA 151
Alterman, Glenn 1946- 225
Alterman, Natan 1910-1970 .... EWL 3
Alterman, Nathan 1910-1970
Obituary 25-28R
Altfest, Karen Caplan 105
Alth, Max O(ctavious) 1927- CANR-17
Earlier sketch in CA 41-44R
Althauser, Robert P(ierce) 1939- 57-60
Althea
See Braithwaite, Althea
Alther, Lisa 1944- CANR-51
Earlier sketches in CA 65-68, CANR-12, 30
See also CAAS 30
See also BPFB 1
See also CLC 7, 41
See also CN 4, 5, 6, 7
See also CSW
See also GLL 2
See also MTCW 1
Althoff, Phillip 1941- 33-36R
Altholz, Josef L(ewis) 1933- CANR-86
Earlier sketches in CA 9-12R, CANR-35
Althouse, Larry
See Althouse, Lawrence Wilson
Althouse, LaVonne 1932- 17-20R
Althouse, Lawrence Wilson 1930- 101
Althusser, L.
See Althusser, Louis
Althusser, Louis 1918-1990 .... CANR-102
Obituary 132
Earlier sketch in CA 131
See also CLC 106
See also DLB 242
Altick, Richard Daniel 1915- CANR-40
Earlier sketches in CA 1-4R, CANR-4, 19
Altieri, Charles F(rancis) 1942- 106
Altizer, Thomas J(onathan) J(ackson)
1927- CANR-3
Earlier sketch in CA 1-4R
Altman, Dennis 1943- CANR-90
Earlier sketches in CA 33-36R, CANR-15, 34
See also GLL 1
Altman, Edward I(ra) 1941- CANR-22
Earlier sketches in CA 57-60, CANR-7
Altman, Frances 1937- 65-68
Altman, Ira 1944- 192
Altman, Irwin 1928- 81-84
Altman, Irwin 1930- CANR-21
Earlier sketch in CA 69-72
Altman, Jack 1938- 21-24R
Altman, Janet Gurkin 1945- 128
Altman, Larry
See Altman, Irwin
Altman, Lawrence Kimball 1937- 172
Altman, Linda Jacobs 1943- CANR-123
Earlier sketches in CA 29-32R, CANR-30
See also SATA 21
Altman, Nathaniel 1948- CANR-116
Earlier sketches in CA 57-60, CANR-6, 21, 44
Altman, Richard Charles 1932- 41-44R
Altman, Rick 1945- 128
Altman, Robert 1925- CANR-43
Earlier sketch in CA 73-76
See also CLC 16, 116
Altman, Robert A. 1943- 29-32R
Altman, Suzanne
See Orgel, Doris and Schecter, Ellen
Altman, Thomas
See Black, Campbell
Altman, Wilfred 1927- CAP-1
Earlier sketch in CA 9-10
Altmann, Alexander 1906-1987 .... CANR-35
Obituary 122
Earlier sketches in CA 61-64, CANR-8
Altmann, Berthold 1902(?)-1977
Obituary 69-72
Altmann, Simon L(eonardo) 1924- 143
Altobello, Brian J. 1948- 206
Altoff, Gerard T(homas) 1949- 170
Altolaguirre, Manuel 1905(?)-1959 174
See also DLB 108
See also HW 2
Altoma, Salih J(awad) 1929- 49-52
Alton, John 1901-1996 .... IDFW 4
Alton, Thomas
See Bryant, T(homas) Alton
Altrocchi, Julia Cooley 1893-1972 .... CAP-1
Earlier sketch in CA 13-14
Altschul, Aaron Mayer 1914-1994 105
Obituary 146
Altschul, b j 1948- 114
Altschul, Selig 1914-1992 108
Altschuler, Franz 1923- .... SATA 45
Altschuler, Glenn C. 1950- 225
Altsheler, Joseph A(lexander) 1862-1919 167
See also YABC 1
Altshuler, Alan Anthony 1936- 108
Altshuler, Edward A. 1919- 17-20R
Altshuler, Harry 1913(?)-1990
Obituary 131
Aluko, T(imothy) M(ofolorunso)
1918(?)- CANR-62
Earlier sketches in CA 65-68, CANR-10
See also BW 1
See also CN 1, 2, 3, 4, 5, 6
See also DLB 117
Alumit, Noel 1968- 209
Alurista 45-48R
See also Urista (Heredia), Alberto (Baltazar)
See also DLB 82
See also HLCS 1
See also LLW
See also PC 34
Al-Van-Gar
See Radwanski, Pierre A(rthur)
Alvarado (green), Manuel (Bernardo)
1948- 147
Alvararez Quintero, Serafin 1871-1938 .. EWL 3
Alvarez, A(lfred) 1929- CANR-134
Earlier sketches in CA 1-4R, CANR-3, 33, 63, 101
See also CLC 5, 13
See also CN 3, 4, 5, 6
See also CP 1, 2, 3, 4, 5, 6, 7
See also DLB 14, 40
See also MTFW 2005
Alvarez, Alejandro Rodriguez 1903-1965 ... 131
Obituary 93-96
See also Casona, Alejandro
See also HW 1
Alvarez, Alex 1963- 209
Alvarez, David J. 220
Alvarez, Eugene 1932- CANR-128
Earlier sketch in CA 57-60
Alvarez, John
See del Rey, Lester
Alvarez, Jose E. 1955- 192
Alvarez, Josefina 1936- 185
Alvarez, Joseph A. 1930- CANR-17
Earlier sketch in CA 33-36R
See also SATA 18
Alvarez, Julia 1950- CANR-133
Earlier sketches in CA 147, CANR-69, 101
See also AAYA 25
See also AMWS 7
See also CLC 93
See also DA3
See also DLB 282
See also HLCS 1
See also LATS 1:2
See also LLW
See also MTCW 2
See also MTFW 2005
See also NFS 5, 9
See also SATA 129
See also WLIT 1
Alvarez, Luis W(alter) 1911-1988
Obituary 126
Alvarez, Lynne 131
See also HW 1
Alvarez, Max Joseph 1960- 112
Alvarez, Walter C(lement)
1884-1978 .... CANR-10
Earlier sketch in CA 61-64
Alvarez-Altman, Grace (DeJesus)
1926- 33-36R
Alvarez-Bravo, Manuel 1902-2002 ..... AAYA 59
Alvarez del Vayo, Julio 1891-1975
Obituary 61-64
Alvarez Gardeazabal, Gustavo 1945- ..... EWL 3
Alvarez Murena, Hector Alberto 1923- ... HW 1
Alvarez Quintero, Joaquin 1873-1944 ... EWL 3
Alvaro, Corrado 1896-1956 163
See also DLB 264
See also EWL 3
See also TCLC 60
Alver, Betti 1906-1989 .... CDWLB 4
See also DLB 220
See also EWL 3
Alverson, Charles (E.) 1935- CANR-13
Earlier sketch in CA 25-28R
Alverson, Donna 1933- 65-68
Alverson, Marianne 1942- 126
Alves, Colin 1930- CANR-2
Earlier sketch in CA 5-8R
Alves, Marcio Moreira 1936- CANR-2
Earlier sketch in CA 45-48
Alves, Michael (Joseph) 1956- 118
Alvey, Edward, Jr. 1902-1999 53-56
Alvey, R(ichard) Gerald 1935- 121
Alvi, Moniza 1954- 153
See also CP 7
See also CWP
Alvin, Juliette (Louise) (?)-1982 77-80
Obituary 108
Alvord, Burt
See Keevill, Henry J(ohn)
See also TCWW 2
al-Windawi, Thura
See Windawi, Thura al-
Alworth, E. P(aul) 1918- 25-28R
Alwyn, William 1905-1985
Obituary 117
See also IDFW 3, 4
Aly, Bower 1903-1977 .... CANR-5
Earlier sketch in CA 5-8R
Aly, Lucile Folse 1913-1990 .... 21-24R
Alyer, Philip A.
See Stratemeyer, Edward L.
Alyeshmerni, Mansoor 1943- 29-32R
Alyn, Marc (a pseudonym) 1937- 101
Alzado, Lyle (Martin) 1949-1992
Brief entry 110
Alzaga, Florinda 1930- 73-76
al-Zayyat, Latifa 1923-1996 201
Amabile, George 1936- 33-36R
See also CP 1
Amacher, Richard Earl 1917- CANR-3
Earlier sketch in CA 1-4R
Amacher, Ryan C(uster) 1945- 105
Amadi, Elechi (Emmanuel) 1934- CANR-63
Earlier sketches in CA 29-32R, CANR-16, 38
See also BW 1
See also CN 3, 4, 5, 6, 7
See also DLB 117
See also EWL 3
See also WLIT 2
Amado, Jorge 1912-2001 .... CANR-135
Obituary 201
Earlier sketches in CA 77-80, CANR-35, 74
See also CLC 13, 40, 106
See also CWW 2
See also DAM MULT, NOV
See also DLB 113, 307
See also EWL 3
See also HLC 1
See also HW 2
See also LAW
See also LAWS 1
See also MTCW 1, 2
See also MTFW 2005
See also RGWL 2, 3
See also TWA
See also WLIT 1
Amadon, Dean 1912-2003 61-64
Obituary 213
Amalrik, Andrei Alekseyevich 1938-1980 .. 155
Obituary 102
See also DLB 302
Amamoo, Joseph Godson 1931- 13-16R
Aman, Mohammed M(ohammed)
1940- CANR-16
Earlier sketches in CA 49-52, CANR-1
Amanda
See Wynne-Tyson, Esme
Amann, Janet 1951- 147
See also SATA 79
Amann, Peter H. 1927- 61-64
Amann, Richard 1945- 106
Amann, Ronald 1943- 112
Amann, Victor F(rancis) 1927- 41-44R
Amanuddin, Syed 1934- CANR-17
Earlier sketches in CA 49-52, CANR-1
Amar, Akhil Reed 1958- 167
Amaral, Anthony 1930-1982 .... CANR-11
Earlier sketch in CA 21-24R
Amaral, Jose Vazquez
See Vazquez Amaral, Jose
Amare, Rothayne
See Byrne, Stuart J(ames)
Amaron, Douglas 1914-1985
Obituary 117
Amary, Issam B(ahjat) 1942- CANR-8
Earlier sketch in CA 61-64
Amato, Antony
See Klein, Daniel M(artin)
Amato, Carol A. 1942- CANR-135
Earlier sketch in CA 156
See also SATA 92
Amato, Joseph Anthony 1938- CANR-89
Earlier sketches in CA 57-60, CANR-6
Amato, Mary 1961- 211
See also SATA 140
Amatora, Sister Mary 9-12R
Amaya, Manuel E(liseo) 1928-1986
Obituary 120
Amaya, Mario (Anthony)
1933-1986 .... CANR-36
Obituary 119
Earlier sketches in CA 61-64, CANR-9
Amazing Randi, The
See Randi, James
Ambasz, Emilio 1943- 73-76
Amberg, George H. 1901-1971
Obituary 110
Amberg, (Martin) Hans 1913-1993 77-80
Amberg, Richard H(iller), Jr. 1942- 77-80
Amberg, Richard Hiller 1912-1967
Obituary 114
Amberhill, Bevan
See Burnett, Virgil
Ambert, Anne-Marie 1940- CANR-93
Earlier sketch in CA 145
Ambhanwong, Suthilak 1924- CANR-18
Earlier sketch in CA 73-76
Ambirajan, Srinivasa 1936- CANR-7
Earlier sketch in CA 17-20R
Ambler, C(hristopher) Gifford
1886- .... SATA-Brief 29
Ambler, Effie 1936- 77-80
Ambler, Eric 1909-1998 .... CANR-74
Obituary 171
Earlier sketches in CA 9-12R, CANR-7, 38
See also BRWS 4
See also CLC 4, 6, 9
See also CMW 4
See also CN 1, 2, 3, 4, 5, 6
See also DLB 77
See also MSW
See also MTCW 1, 2
See also TEA
Ambler, John S(teward) 1932- CANR-27
Earlier sketch in CA 49-52
Ambler, Marjane 1948- 135
Ambler, Scott W. 1966- 169
Ambrose, Alice
See Lazerowitz, Alice Ambrose
Ambrose, Bonnie Holt 1943- 171
Ambrose, David (Edwin) 1943- 144
Brief entry 116
Ambrose, Eric (Samuel) 1908- CAP-1
Earlier sketch in CA 11-12
Ambrose, John W(illiam), Jr. 1931- 57-60
Ambrose, Stephen E(dward)
1936-2002 .... CANR-105
Obituary 209
Earlier sketches in CA 1-4R, CANR-3, 43, 57, 83
See also AAYA 44
See also CLC 145
See also MTFW 2005
See also NCFS 2
See also SATA 40, 138
Ambrose, W. Haydn 1922- 25-28R

Cumulative Index 13 **Anders**

Ambrosi, Hans Georg 1925- ... 103
Ambrosini, Maria Luisa ... 33-36R
Ambrosini, Richard 1955- ... 143
Ambroz, Oton 1905-1994 ... 41-44R
Ambrus, Gyozo Laszlo 1935- ... CANR-104
  Earlier sketches in CA 25-28R, CANR-11, 28, 53
  See also Ambrus, Victor G.
  See also MAICYA 1, 2
  See also SATA 41
Ambrus, Victor G.
  See Ambrus, Gyozo Laszlo
  See also SAAS 4
  See also SATA 1
Ambrus, Zoltan 1861-1932 ... EWL 3
Amburn, Ellis 1933- ... CANR-119
  Earlier sketch in CA 138
Amdur, Neil 1939- ... 106
Amdur, Nikki 1950- ... 111
Amelio, Gianni 1945- ... 156
Amelio, Ralph J. 1939- ... 37-40R
Amen, Carol 1934(?)-1987
  Obituary ... 123
Amen, Daniel G. ... 233
Amend, Bill 1962- ... 221
  See also AAYA 52
  See also SATA 147
Amend, Victor E(arl) 1916- ... 33-36R
Ament, Deloris Tarzan 1934- ... 220
Ament, Pat 1946- ... 85-88
Amerika, Mark ... CANR-110
  Earlier sketch in CA 152
Amerine, Maynard A(ndrew) 1911-1998 ... 41-44R
  Obituary ... 166
Ameringer, Charles D. 1926- ... 57-60
Amerman, Lockhart 1911-1969 ... CAP-2
  Earlier sketch in CA 29-32
  See also SATA 3
Amert, Susan ... 237
Amery, Francis
  See Stableford, Brian (Michael)
Amery, Jean
  See Mayer, Hans
Amery, (Harold) Julian 1919- ... 61-64
Ames, Charles Edgar 1895-1972 ... CAP-2
  Earlier sketch in CA 25-28
Ames, Christopher 1956- ... 164
Ames, Delano L. 1906-1987 ... 107
Ames, Edward Scribner 1870-1958 ... 218
Ames, Elinor
  See Ranzini, Addis Durning
Ames, Evelyn 1908-1990 ... 57-60
  Obituary ... 130
  See also SATA 13
  See also SATA-Obit 64
Ames, Felicia
  See Burden, Jean
Ames, Fisher 1758-1808 ... DLB 37
Ames, Francis H. 1900-1986 ... 17-20R
Ames, Gerald 1906-1993 ... 73-76
  Obituary ... 140
  See also SATA 11
  See also SATA-Obit 74
Ames, Jennifer
  See Greig, Maysie
Ames, Jocelyn Green ... 5-8R
Ames, John 1944- ... 111
Ames, John Dawes 1904-1987
  Obituary ... 122
Ames, Jonathan 1964- ... 216
Ames, Joye
  See Lavene, Jim and Lavene, Joyce
Ames, Kenneth L. 1942- ... 143
Ames, Lee J(udah) 1921- ... CANR-18
  Earlier sketches in CA 1-4R, CANR-3
  See also SATA 3, 151
Ames, Leslie
  See Rigoni, Orlando (Joseph) and Ross, W(illiam) E(dward) D(aniel)
Ames, Lois (Winslow Sisson) 1931- ... 101
Ames, Louise Bates 1908-1996 ... CANR-39
  Obituary ... 154
  Earlier sketches in CA 1-4R, CANR-3, 18
Ames, Mary Clemmer 1831-1884 ... DLB 23
Ames, Mildred 1919-1994 ... CANR-11
  Obituary ... 146
  Earlier sketch in CA 69-72
  See also SATA 22, 81, 85
Ames, Noel
  See Barrows, (Ruth) Marjorie
Ames, Norma 1920- ... CANR-12
  Earlier sketch in CA 29-32R
Ames, Preston ... IDFW 3, 4
Ames, Rachel 1922-1999 ... 97-100
Ames, Ruth M(argaret) 1918- ... 29-32R
Ames, (Polly) Scribner 1908-1993 ... 69-72
Ames, Van Meter 1898-1985 ... CAP-1
  Obituary ... 117
  Earlier sketch in CA 13-16
Ames, Walter Lansing 1946- ... 106
Ames, William 1576-1633 ... DLB 281
Ames, Winslow 1907-1990 ... CAP-2
  Earlier sketch in CA 25-28
Ames-Lewis, Francis 1943- ... CANR-104
  Earlier sketch in CA 108
Amey, Lloyd Ronald 1922- ... CANR-20
  Earlier sketch in CA 45-48
Amfiteatrov, Aleksandr 1862-1938 ... DLB 317
Amfitheatrof, Erik 1931- ... 89-92
Amft, M(arian) J(anet) 1920-1985
  Obituary ... 117
Amherst, Wes
  See Shaver, Richard S(harpe)
Ami, Ben
  See Eliav, Arie L(ova)
Ami, Shlomo Ben
  See Ben-Ami, Shlomo
Amichai, Yehuda 1924-2000 ... CANR-132
  Obituary ... 189
  Earlier sketches in CA 85-88, CANR-46, 60, 99
  See also CLC 9, 22, 57, 116
  See also CWW 2
  See also EWL 3
  See also MTCW 1, 2
  See also MTFW 2005
  See also PC 38
  See also WLIT 6
Amichai, Yehudah
  See Amichai, Yehuda
Amick, Robert Gene 1933- ... 33-36R
Amidei, Sergio 1904-1981 ... IDFW 3, 4
Amidon, Bill (Vincent) 1935-1979 ... 45-48
  Obituary ... 103
Amidon, Stephen 1959- ... CANR-92
  Earlier sketch in CA 132
Amiel, Barbara 1940- ... 101
Amiel, Henri Frederic 1821-1881 ... DLB 217
Amiel, Joseph 1937- ... 101
Amies, (Edwin) Hardy 1909-2003 ... 129
  Obituary ... 214
Amin, Ali 1913(?)-1976
  Obituary ... 65-68
Amin, Mohamed 1943-1996 ... 158
Amin, Samir 1931- ... CANR-35
  Earlier sketches in CA 89-92, CANR-15
Amini, Fari(borz) -2004 ... 192
  Obituary ... 228
Amini, Johari M.
  See Kunjufu, Johari M. Amini
  See also DLB 41
Amiotte, Arthur (Douglas) 1942- ... 211
Amir, Javed 1945- ... 174
Amir, Menachem 1930- ... 45-48
Amis, Breton
  See Best, Rayleigh Breton Amis
Amis, Kingsley (William) 1922-1995 ... CANR-54
  Obituary ... 150
  Earlier sketches in CA 9-12R, CANR-8, 28
  Interview in ... CANR-8
  See also AITN 2
  See also BPFB 1
  See also BRWS 2
  See also CDBLB 1945-1960
  See also CLC 1, 2, 3, 5, 8, 13, 40, 44, 129
  See also CN 1, 2, 3, 4, 5, 6
  See also CP 1, 2, 3, 4
  See also DA
  See also DA3
  See also DAB
  See also DAC
  See also DAM MST, NOV
  See also DLB 15, 27, 100, 139
  See also DLBY 1996
  See also EWL 3
  See also HGG
  See also MTCW 1, 2
  See also MTFW 2005
  See also RGEL 2
  See also RGSF 2
  See also SFW 4
Amis, Martin (Louis) 1949- ... CANR-132
  Earlier sketches in CA 65-68, CANR-8, 27, 54, 73, 95
  Interview in ... CANR-27
  See also BEST 90:3
  See also BRWS 4
  See also CLC 4, 9, 38, 62, 101, 213
  See also CN 5, 6, 7
  See also DA3
  See also DLB 14, 194
  See also EWL 3
  See also MTCW 2
  See also MTFW 2005
Amishai-Maisels, Ziva
  See Maisels, Maxine S.
Amling, Frederick 1926- ... 133
  Brief entry ... 112
Amlund, Curtis Arthur 1927- ... 21-24R
Ammaniti, Niccolo 1966- ... 238
Ammar, Abbas 1907(?)-1974
  Obituary ... 53-56
Amme, Carl H., Jr. 1913-1990 ... 25-28R
Ammer, Christine (Parker) 1931- ... 106
Ammer, Dean S. 1926-1999 ... CANR-7
  Earlier sketch in CA 17-20R
Ammerman, David L(eon) 1938- ... 57-60
Ammerman, Gale Richard 1923- ... 107
Ammerman, Leila T(remaine) 1912-1998 ... 33-36R
Ammerman, Nancy T(atom) 1950- ... 167
Ammerman, Robert R(ay) 1927- ... 13-16R
Ammianus Marcellinus c. 330-c. 395 ... AW 2
  See also DLB 211
Ammon, Harry 1917- ... 73-76
Ammon, Richard 1942- ... SATA 124
Ammons, A(rchie) R(andolph) 1926-2001 ... CANR-107
  Obituary ... 193
  Earlier sketches in CA 9-12R, CANR-6, 36, 51, 73
  See also AITN 1
  See also AMWS 7
  See also CLC 2, 3, 5, 8, 9, 25, 57, 108
  See also CP 1, 2, 3, 4, 5, 6, 7
  See also CSW
  See also DAM POET
  See also DLB 5, 165
  See also EWL 3
  See also MAL 5
  See also MTCW 1, 2
  See also PC 16
  See also PFS 19
  See also RGAL 4
  See also TCLE 1:1
Amo, Tauraatua i
  See Adams, Henry (Brooks)
Amoaku, J. K. 1936- ... 45-48
Amoia, Alba della Fazia 1928- ... 144
Amon, Aline 1928- ... CANR-8
  Earlier sketch in CA 61-64
  See also SATA 9
Amor, Amos
  See Harrell, (Mildred) Irene B(urk)
Amor, Anne Clark 1933- ... CANR-59
  Earlier sketches in CA 112, CANR-31
Amore, Roy Clayton 1942- ... 105
Amorim, Enrique (Manuel) 1900-1960 ... EWL 3
  See also HW 1
Amoroso Lima, Alceu 1893-1983 ... 206
  See also LAW
Amory, Anne Reinberg 1931- ... 17-20R
Amory, Cleveland 1917-1998 ... CANR-29
  Obituary ... 171
  Earlier sketch in CA 69-72
  Interview in ... CANR-29
  See also AITN 1
  See also CPW
  See also DAM POP
Amory, Mark 1941- ... CANR-88
  Earlier sketches in CA 114, CANR-36
Amory, Robert, Jr. 1915-1989
  Obituary ... 128
Amory, Thomas 1691(?)-1788 ... DLB 39
Amos, James H., Jr. 1946- ... 132
Amos, Wallace, Jr. ... 197
Amos, Wally 1936-
  See Amos, Wallace, Jr.
Amos, William (David) 1933- ... 146
Amos, William E. 1926- ... 17-20R
Amos, Winsom 1921- ... CANR-27
  Earlier sketch in CA 49-52
Amosoff, N(ikolai) M(ikhailovich)
  See Amosov, N(ikolai) M(ikhailovich)
Amosov, N.
  See Amosov, N(ikolai) M(ikhailovich)
Amosov, N(ikolai) M(ikhailovich) 1913-2002
  Obituary ... 212
  Brief entry ... 112
Amoss, Benjamin McRae, Jr. 1960- ... 139
Amoss, Berthe 1925- ... CANR-14
  Earlier sketch in CA 21-24R
  See also SATA 5, 112
Amplegirth, Antony
  See Dent, Anthony Austen
Amprimoz, Alexandre 1948- ... CANR-15
  Earlier sketch in CA 37-40R
Amram, David (Werner) (III) 1930- ... CANR-119
  Earlier sketches in CA 29-32R, CANR-28
Amram, Philip Werner 1900-1990
  Obituary ... 131
Amrine, Michael 1919(?)-1974 ... 73-76
  Obituary ... 49-52
Amritanandamayi, Mataji 1953- ... 208
Amsden, David 1980- ... 225
Amsel, Abram 1922- ... CANR-82
  Earlier sketches in CA 114, CANR-35
Amstead, B(illy) H(oward) 1921- ... 21-24R
Amster, Linda 1938- ... CANR-22
  Earlier sketch in CA 45-48
Amsterdam, Morey 1908(?)-1996 ... 148
  Obituary ... 154
  Brief entry ... 111
Amstutz, Arnold E. 1936- ... 21-24R
Amstutz, Mark R(obert) 1944- ... CANR-93
  Earlier sketch in CA 105
Amter, Joseph A. (?)-1982
  Obituary ... 109
Amundsen, Kirsten 1932- ... 37-40R
Amundsen, Roald Engelbregt Gravning 1872-1928 ... 170
  Brief entry ... 117
Amusart, Joseph
  See Sulte, Benjamin
Amusin, Joseph 1910-1984
  Obituary ... 113
Amuzegar, Jahangir 1920- ... CANR-15
  Earlier sketch in CA 41-44R
A M V
  See Cruickshank, Helen B(urness)
Amy, William Lacey -1962
  See Allan, Luke
A N A
  See Cruickshank, Helen B(urness)
Anacreon c. 582B.C.-c. 475B.C. ... RGWL 2, 3
Analyticus
  See Wise, James Waterman
Anand, Mulk Raj 1905-2004 ... CANR-64
  Obituary ... 231
  Earlier sketches in CA 65-68, CANR-32
  See also CLC 23, 93
  See also CN 1, 2, 3, 4, 5, 6, 7
  See also DAM NOV
  See also EWL 3
  See also MTCW 1, 2
  See also MTFW 2005
  See also RGSF 2
Anand, Valerie 1937- ... CANR-104
  Earlier sketches in CA 73-76, CANR-13, 61
  See also RHW
Anandamurti, Shrii Shrii 1923-1990 ... 219
Anania, Michael 1939- ... 25-28R
  See also CP 2, 3, 4, 5, 6, 7
  See also DLB 193
Anasi, Robert 1966- ... 205
Anastaplo, George 1925- ... CANR-92
  Earlier sketch in CA 37-40R
Anastas, Benjamin 1971- ... CANR-119
  Earlier sketch in CA 169
  See also DLBY 1998
Anastas, Lila L. 1940- ... 122
Anastas, Peter 1937- ... CANR-1
  Earlier sketch in CA 45-48
Anastasi, Anne 1908-2001 ... CANR-17
  Obituary ... 197
  Earlier sketches in CA 5-8R, CANR-2
Anastasio, Dina 1941- ... CANR-68
  Earlier sketch in CA 107
  See also SATA 37, 94
  See also SATA-Brief 30
Anastasiou, Clifford (John) 1929- ... CANR-18
  Earlier sketches in CA 49-52, CANR-3
Anastos, Andrea La Sonde (Melrose) 1951- ... 117
Anatol
  See Schnitzler, Arthur
Anatol, A.
  See Kuznetsov, Anatoli(i)
Anaya, Rudolfo A(lfonso) 1937- ... CANR-124
  Earlier sketches in CA 45-48, CANR-1, 32, 51
  See also CAAS 4
  See also AAYA 20
  See also BYA 13
  See also CLC 23, 148
  See also CN 4, 5, 6, 7
  See also DAM MULT, NOV
  See also DLB 82, 206, 278
  See also HLC 1
  See also HW 1
  See also LAIT 4
  See also LLW
  See also MAL 5
  See also MTCW 1, 2
  See also MTFW 2005
  See also NFS 12
  See also RGAL 4
  See also RGSF 2
  See also TCWW 2
  See also WLIT 1
Anber, Paul
  See Baker, Pauline H(alpern)
Anbinder, Tyler (Gregory) 1962- ... CANR-118
  Earlier sketch in CA 141
Ancel, Marc 1902-1990 ... CANR-12
  Earlier sketch in CA 69-72
Ancelet, Barry Jean 1951- ... 131
Anchell, Melvin 1919- ... 25-28R
Anchor, Robert 1937- ... 69-72
Anckarsvard, Karin Inez Maria 1915-1969 ... 9-12R
  Obituary ... 103
  See also SATA 6
Ancona, George 1929- ... CANR-126
  Earlier sketches in CA 53-56, CANR-4, 19, 102
  See also CWRI 5
  See also MAICYA 2
  See also MAICYAS 1
  See also SAAS 18
  See also SATA 12, 85, 145
Anctil, Pierre 1952- ... 209
Andahazi, Federico 1963- ... 188
Anday, Melih Cevdet 1915- ... EWL 3
Andel, Jiri
  See Andel, Jiri
Andel, Jiri 1939- ... 206
Andelin, Helen B. 1920- ... 89-92
Andelman, Eddie 1936- ... 57-60
Andelman, Samuel L(ouis) 1916-
  Brief entry ... 114
Andelson, Robert V(ernon) 1931- ... 33-36R
Andenaes, Johannes 1912- ... CANR-68
  Earlier sketch in CA 129
Anderegg, Karen Klok 1940- ... 137
Andereich, Justus
  See Steiner, Gerolf
Anderman, Janusz 1949- ... 142
Anders, Allison 1954- ... 165
Anders, C. J.
  See Bennett, Cherie
Anders, Donna Carolyn 1938- ... 125
Anders, Edith (Mary) England 1899-1979 ... CAP-1
  Earlier sketch in CA 13-16
Anders, Evelyn 1916- ... 29-32R
Anders, Georg
  See Soyfer, Jura
Anders, Isabel 1946- ... CANR-137
  Earlier sketch in CA 161
  See also SATA 101
Anders, Jeanne
  See Anderson, Joan Wester
Anders, Leslie 1922- ... 13-16R

Anders, Rex
See Barrett, Geoffrey John
Anders, Sarah Frances 1927- ... 105
Andersch, Alfred 1914-1980 ... CANR-37
Obituary ... 93-96
Earlier sketch in CA 33-36R
See also DLB 69
See also EWL 3
See also MTCW 1
Andersch, Elizabeth Genevieve 1913-1974 ... 5-8R
Andersdatter, Karla M(argaret) 1938- ... CANR-44
Earlier sketches in CA 104, CANR-21
See also SATA 34
Andersen, Arlow W. 1906-1996 ... CAP-1
Earlier sketch in CA 11-12
Andersen, Benny (Allan) 1929- ... 101
See also DLB 214
See also EWL 3
Andersen, Christopher P(eter) 1949- ... CANR-127
Earlier sketches in CA 69-72, CANR-14, 31
Andersen, D(ennis) R(ichard) 1947- ... 108
Andersen, Dennis Alan ... 226
Andersen, Doris 1909- ... CANR-11
Earlier sketch in CA 21-24R
Andersen, Francis Ian 1925- ... CANR-27
Earlier sketch in CA 108
Andersen, Georg 1941- ... 112
Andersen, Hans Christian 1805-1875 . AAYA 57
See also CLR 6
See also DA
See also DA3
See also DAB
See also DAC
See also DAM MST, POP
See also EW 6
See also MAICYA 1, 2
See also RGSF 2
See also RGWL 2, 3
See also SATA 100
See also SSC 6, 56
See also TWA
See also WCH
See also WLC
See also YABC 1
Andersen, Jefferson 1955(?)-1979
Obituary ... 85-88
Andersen, Juel 1923- ... CANR-22
Earlier sketch in CA 105
Andersen, Kenneth E(ldon) 1933- ... 37-40R
Andersen, Kurt Byars 1954- ... CANR-101
Earlier sketches in CA 106, CANR-23
Andersen, Marianne S(inger) 1934- ... 65-68
Andersen, Marion Lineaweaver 1912(?)-1971
Obituary ... 29-32R
Andersen, Martin Edwin 1954(?)- ... 231
Andersen, R(udolph) Clifton 1933- ... 33-36R
Andersen, Richard 1931- ... CANR-24
Earlier sketches in CA 57-60, CANR-8
Andersen, Richard 1946- ... 102
Andersen, Susan ... 197
Andersen, Ted
See Boyd, Waldo T.
Andersen, Uell Stanley 1917-1986 ... 1-4R
Andersen, Wayne V. 1928- ... 9-12R
Andersen, Wilhelm 1911-1980 ... 29-32R
Andersen, Yvonne 1932- ... 29-32R
See also SATA 27
Anderson, A(rthur) J(ames) 1933- ... 106
Anderson, Alan B(rauer) 1934- ... 133
Anderson, Alan H., Jr. 1943- ... 69-72
Anderson, Alan Ross 1925-1973 ... CAP-2
Obituary ... 45-48
Earlier sketch in CA 17-18
Anderson, Alexander 1775-1870 ... DLB 188
Anderson, Alison 1950- ... 174
Autobiographical Essay in ... 174
See also CAAS 30
Anderson, Allan 1915-1994 ... 97-100
Anderson, Alpha E. 1914-1970 ... CAP-2
Earlier sketch in CA 23-24
Anderson, Ann Kiemel 1945- ... 121
Anderson, Arthur J(ames) O(utram) 1907-1996 ... CANR-15
Earlier sketch in CA 85-88
Anderson, Atholl ... 218
Anderson, B(asil) W(illiam) 1901-1984
Obituary ... 112
Anderson, Barbara (Lilias) 1926- ... 188
See also CN 5, 6
Anderson, Barbara 1948- ... 93-96
Anderson, Barbara Gallatin 1926- ... 190
Brief entry ... 111
See also CN 7
Anderson, Barry (Franklin) 1935- ... 17-20R
Anderson, Bern 1900-1963 ... 1-4R
Anderson, Bernard Eric 1936- ... CANR-5
Earlier sketch in CA 53-56
Anderson, Bernhard Word 1916- ... CANR-8
Earlier sketch in CA 57-60
Anderson, Bernice G(oudy) 1894-1997 ... 101
See also SATA 33
Anderson, Bertha Moore 1892-1973 ... 5-8R
Anderson, Beverly
See Nemiro, Beverly Anderson
Anderson, Beverly M.
See Nemiro, Beverly Anderson
Anderson, Bob 1944- ... SATA 136, 139
Anderson, Bob 1947- ... 69-72
Anderson, Bonnie S. 1943- ... 192
Anderson, Brad(ley Jay) 1924- ... 106
See also SATA 33
See also SATA-Brief 31
Anderson, Burton 1938- ... 149
Anderson, C. C.
See Anderson, Catherine Corley
Anderson, C. Farley
See Mencken, H(enry) L(ouis) and Nathan, George Jean
Anderson, C(arl) L(eonard) 1901-1987 .. 25-28R
Anderson, C(harles) P(almerston) 1864-1930 ... 224
Anderson, C(larence) W(illiam) 1891-1971 ... CANR-79
Obituary ... 29-32R
Earlier sketch in CA 73-76
See also CWRI 5
See also SATA 11
Anderson, Camilla M(ay) 1904-2001 ... 33-36R
Anderson, Carl Dicmann 1912-1998 ... 33-36R
Anderson, Carl L(ennart) 1919- ... 41-44R
Anderson, Carlotta R. 1929- ... 203
Anderson, Carol 1951- ... 205
Anderson, Carolyn 1941- ... 73-76
Anderson, Catherine 1948- ... 220
Anderson, Catherine C.
See Anderson, Catherine Corley
Anderson, Catherine Corley 1909-2001 ... 1-4R
See also SATA 72
Anderson, Charles 1933- ... CANR-27
Earlier sketch in CA 49-52
Anderson, Charles Burroughs 1905-1985 ... 65-68
Obituary ... 115
Anderson, Charles C. 1931- ... 29-32R
Anderson, Charles Roberts 1902-1999 ... CANR-3
Earlier sketch in CA 1-4R
Anderson, Charles W(illiam) 1934- ... 9-12R
Anderson, Charlotte Maria 1923- ... 81-84
Anderson, Chester 1932-1991 ... 131
Brief entry ... 117
Anderson, Chester G(rant) 1923- ... 25-28R
Anderson, Chuck
See Anderson, Charles
Anderson, Clifford
See Gardner, Richard (M.)
Anderson, Colena M(ichael) 1891-1988 ... CANR-11
Earlier sketch in CA 21-24R
Anderson, Cortland 1935-1985
Obituary ... 118
Anderson, Courtney 1906- ... CAP-1
Earlier sketch in CA 19-20
Anderson, Daphne 1919- ... 130
Anderson, Daryl Shon 1963- ... SATA 93
Anderson, Dave
See Anderson, David (Poole)
Anderson, David
See Anderson, David (Poole)
See also DLB 241
Anderson, David (Poole) 1929- ... CANR-122
Earlier sketch in CA 89-92
See also SATA 60
Anderson, David 1952- ... 130
Anderson, David D(aniel) 1924- ... CANR-5
Earlier sketch in CA 13-16R
Anderson, David L(eonard) 1919- ... 5-8R
Anderson, Dillon 1906-1974 ... 1-4R
Obituary ... 45-48
Anderson, Don 1939- ... 128
Anderson, Donald F(rancis) 1938- ... 53-56
Anderson, Donald K(ennedy), Jr. 1922- . 37-40R
Anderson, Donna K. 1935- ... 142
Anderson, Doris (Hilda) 1925- ... 89-92
Anderson, Douglas A(llen) 1959- ... 147
Anderson, Duane 1943- ... 193
Anderson, Dwight G(ale) 1938- ... 107
Anderson, E. Ruth 1907-1989 ... 93-96
Anderson, E. W. 1901-1981
Obituary ... 104
Anderson, Earl Robert 1943- ... 111
Anderson, Edgar 1920- ... CANR-30
Earlier sketches in CA 33-36R, CANR-13
Anderson, Edward F. 1932- ... CANR-93
Earlier sketch in CA 146
Anderson, Einar 1909-1995 ... 13-16R
Anderson, Elbridge Gerry 1907-1984 ... 69-72
Anderson, Elijah 1943- ... CANR-89
Earlier sketch in CA 140
Anderson, Elizabeth (S.) 1959- ... 147
Anderson, Elliott 1944- ... 93-96
Anderson, Eloise Adell 1927- ... 53-56
See also SATA 9
Anderson, Elwood G. 1929- ... 220
Anderson, Emily 1891-1962 ... 124
Anderson, Eric (Douglas) 1949- ... 106
Anderson, Erica 1914-1976 ... 57-60
Anderson, Erland G. 1946- ... 224
Anderson, Eugene N(ewton) 1900-1984 ... 29-32R
Anderson, (William) Ferguson 1914-2001 .. 107
Anderson, Frank J(ohn) 1919- ... CANR-4
Earlier sketch in CA 9-12R
Anderson, Fred 1949- ... CANR-92
Earlier sketch in CA 117
Anderson, Frederick Irving 1877-1947
Brief entry ... 112
See also CMW 4
See also DLB 202
Anderson, Freeman B(urket) 1922- ... 41-44R
Anderson, Gary Clayton 1948- ... 117
Anderson, Gary L. 1948- ... 167
Anderson, Gary Lee 1939-
Brief entry ... 115
Anderson, George
See Groom, Arthur William
Anderson, George
See Weissman, Jack
Anderson, George B. 1908(?)-1985
Obituary ... 114
Anderson, George Christian 1907-1976 ... CAP-2
Obituary ... 69-72
Earlier sketch in CA 29-32
Anderson, George K(umler) 1901-1980 . CAP-2
Earlier sketch in CA 23-24
Anderson, George L(aVerne) 1905-1971 ... CANR-9
Earlier sketch in CA 13-16R
Anderson, George Lee 1934-
Brief entry ... 111
Anderson, Gerald Dwight 1944- ... CANR-37
Earlier sketch in CA 115
Anderson, Gerald H(arry) 1930- ... CANR-7
Earlier sketch in CA 17-20R
Anderson, Gloria T. 1955- ... 220
Anderson, Godfrey Tryggve 1909-1986 . 41-44R
Anderson, Grace Fox 1932- ... 121
See also SATA 43
Anderson, Gregory 1946- ... 135
Anderson, H(ugh) Allen, (Jr.) 1950- ... 120
Anderson, H(obson) Dewey 1897-1975 .. 65-68
Obituary ... 61-64
Anderson, H(ugh) George 1932- ... 204
Anderson, Harold H(omer) 1897-1990 .. CAP-2
Earlier sketch in CA 21-22
Anderson, Harry 1952- ... 152
Anderson, Harry V(ernon) 1903-1983
Obituary ... 110
Anderson, Henry L(ee Norman) 1934- ... 142
See also BW 2
Anderson, Henry P. 1927- ... 33-36R
Anderson, Ho Che 1970(?)- ... AAYA 55
Anderson, Howard Jeremy 1915(?)-1983
Obituary ... 111
Anderson, Howard Peter 1932- ... 61-64
Anderson, Hugh 1920- ... 9-12R
Anderson, Ian Gibson 1933- ... 85-88
Anderson, Irvine H(enry) 1928- ... CANR-11
Earlier sketch in CA 69-72
Anderson, J(ohn) E(dward) 1903- ... 37-40R
Anderson, J(ohn) K(inloch) 1924- ... CANR-28
Earlier sketches in CA 17-20R, CANR-10
Anderson, J(ohn) Kerby 1951- ... 97-100
Anderson, J. N.
See Anderson, (James) Norman (Dalrymple)
Anderson, J(ohn) R(ichard) L(ane) 1911-1981 ... CANR-18
Obituary ... 104
Earlier sketch in CA 25-28R
See also SATA 15
See also SATA-Obit 27
Anderson, Jack(son Northman) 1922- ... CANR-44
Earlier sketches in CA 57-60, CANR-6
See also AITN 1
Anderson, Jack 1935- ... CANR-24
Earlier sketch in CA 33-36R
Anderson, James 1936- ... 232
See also CMW 4
Anderson, James C(letus) 1943- ... 111
Anderson, James D(esmond) 1933- .. CANR-27
Earlier sketch in CA 49-52
Anderson, James E(lliott) 1933- ... CANR-21
Earlier sketches in CA 9-12R, CANR-6
Anderson, James F(rancis) 1910-1981 ... 41-44R
Anderson, James G(eorge) 1936- ... 25-28R
Anderson, James LaVerne 1940-
Brief entry ... 111
Anderson, James M(axwell) 1933- ... 33-36R
Anderson, Janet A. 1934-2002 ... 140
Anderson, (Helen) Jean 1931- ... CANR-57
Earlier sketches in CA 41-44R, CANR-14, 31
Anderson, Jeanne 1934(?)-1979
Obituary ... 85-88
Anderson, Jennifer 1942- ... 57-60
Anderson, Jerry M(aynard) 1933- ... 41-44R
Anderson, Jervis 1936(?)-2000 ... 141
Obituary ... 187
See also BW 2
Anderson, Jessica 1916- ... 205
Anderson, Jessica (Margaret) Queale 1916- ... CANR-62
Earlier sketches in CA 9-12R, CANR-4
See also CLC 37
See also CN 4, 5, 6, 7
Anderson, Jim 1937- ... 134
Anderson, Joan 1943- ... 212
Anderson, Joan Wester 1938- ... CANR-24
Earlier sketches in CA 65-68, CANR-9
Anderson, Joanne M. 1949- ... 169
Anderson, John Bayard 1922- ... 33-36R
Anderson, John F(reeman) 1945- ... 53-56
Anderson, John K.
See Anderson, J(ohn) K(inloch)
Anderson, John L(onzo) 1905- ... CANR-35
Earlier sketch in CA 25-28R
See also Anderson, Lonzo
Anderson, John M(ueller) 1914-1999 ... 17-20R
Anderson, John Q. 1916-1975 ... CANR-3
Earlier sketch in CA 1-4R
Anderson, Jon (Stephen) 1936- ... 133
Anderson, Jon (Victor) 1940- ... CANR-20
Earlier sketch in CA 25-28R
See also CLC 9
See also CP 1, 3, 4
See also DAM POET
Anderson, Jon Lee 1957- ... 175
Anderson, Joy 1928- ... 25-28R
See also SATA 1
Anderson, Judith H(elena) 1940- ... CANR-50
Earlier sketch in CA 123
Anderson, Judith I(cke) 1939- ... 112
Anderson, Judy 1943- ... 149
Anderson, Kare 1950- ... 142
Anderson, Karen (Kruse) 1932- ... 136
See also BYA 8
Anderson, Karl E.
See Evanzz, Karl
Anderson, Kay 1958- ... 152
Anderson, Ken 1917- ... 25-28R
Anderson, Kenneth Norman 1921- ... CANR-18
Earlier sketch in CA 102
Anderson, Kent 1945- ... 171
Anderson, Kevin J(ames) 1962- ... CANR-102
Earlier sketches in CA 161, CANR-94
See also AAYA 34
See also SATA 74, 117
See also SFW 4
Anderson, Kirk 1965- ... 140
Anderson, Kirsty 1978- ... 178
See also SATA 108
Anderson, Kristin
See Du Breuil, (Elizabeth) L(or)inda
Anderson, Lars ... 235
Anderson, Lauri (Arvid) 1942- ... 193
Anderson, Laurie 1947- ... 156
Anderson, Laurie Halse 1961- ... CANR-135
Earlier sketches in CA 160, CANR-103
See also AAYA 39
See also BYA 16
See also MTFW 2005
See also SATA 95, 132
Anderson, LaVere Francis Shoenfelt 1907-1998 ... 101
See also SATA 27
Anderson, Lee 1896-1972 ... 1-4R
Obituary ... 37-40R
Anderson, Lee Stratton 1925- ... 101
Anderson, Leone Castell 1923- ... 126
See also SATA 53
See also SATA-Brief 49
Anderson, Lester William 1918-1973 ... 5-8R
Obituary ... 103
Anderson, Lindsay (Gordon) 1923-1994 ... CANR-77
Obituary ... 146
Brief entry ... 125
Earlier sketch in CA 128
See also CLC 20
Anderson, Lisa G. 1963- ... 178
See also SATA 108
Anderson, Loni 1945(?)- ... 171
Anderson, Lonzo
See Anderson, John L(onzo)
See also SATA 2
Anderson, Louie 1953(?)- ... CANR-137
Earlier sketch in CA 139
Anderson, Lucia (Lewis) 1922- ... 41-44R
See also SATA 10
Anderson, Luther A(dolph) ... 65-68
Anderson, M(ary) D(esiree) 1902-1973 ... 9-12R
Anderson, M(atthew) T(obin) 1968- ... CANR-125
Earlier sketch in CA 163
See also AAYA 60
See also SATA 97, 146
Anderson, Madeleine Paltenghi 1899- .. CAP-1
Earlier sketch in CA 19-20
Anderson, Madelyn Klein ... CANR-28
Earlier sketches in CA 69-72, CANR-11
See also SATA 28
Anderson, Maggie
See Anderson, Margaret
Anderson, Malcolm 1934- ... 33-36R
Anderson, Margaret (Vance) 1917- ... 21-24R
Anderson, Margaret 1948- ... 101
Anderson, Margaret Bartlett 1922- ... 9-12R
Anderson, Margaret C(aroline) 1886-1973 ... CANR-74
Obituary ... 45-48
Earlier sketch in CA 108
See also DLB 4, 91
Anderson, Margaret J(ohnson) 1909-1993 ... CANR-3
Earlier sketch in CA 1-4R
Anderson, Margaret J(ean) 1931- ... CANR-26
Earlier sketches in CA 69-72, CANR-11
See also SAAS 8
See also SATA 27
See also YAW
Anderson, Marilyn D. 1943- ... 217
See also SATA 144
Anderson, Mark M. 1955- ... 139
Anderson, Martha G. 1948- ... 221
Anderson, Martin 1936- ... CANR-102
Earlier sketches in CA 13-16R, CANR-9
Anderson, Marvin Walter 1933- ... 41-44R
Anderson, Mary 1939- ... CANR-16
Earlier sketches in CA 49-52, CANR-1
See also SAAS 23
See also SATA 7, 82
Anderson, Mary M. 1919- ... 136
Anderson, Matthew Smith 1922- ... 13-16R
Anderson, Maxie (Leroy) 1934-1983
Obituary ... 115
Anderson, Maxwell 1888-1959 ... 152
Brief entry ... 105
See also DAM DRAM
See also DFS 16, 20
See also DLB 7, 228
See also MAL 5
See also MTCW 2
See also MTFW 2005
See also RGAL 4
See also TCLC 2, 144
Anderson, Michael Falconer 1947- ... 136
Anderson, Molly D(elCarmen) 1955- ... 147
Anderson, Mona 1910-2004 ... CANR-6
Earlier sketch in CA 57-60
See also SATA 40
Anderson, Mrs. Melvin
See Anderson, Catherine Corley
Anderson, Nancy Fix 1941- ... 126

Cumulative Index 15 **Andrews**

Anderson, Nancy Scott 1939- ... 137
Anderson, (James) Norman (Dalrymple)
1908-1994 ... CANR-4
Earlier sketch in CA 9-12R
Anderson, Norman Dean 1928- ... CANR-42
Earlier sketches in CA 33-36R, CANR-15
See also SATA 22
Anderson, Norman G(ulden) 1913-1991 ... 133
Brief entry ... 114
Anderson, O(rvil) Roger 1937- ... 33-36R
Anderson, Odin W(aldemar)
1914-2003 ... 25-28R
Anderson, Olive M(ary) 1915- ... CANR-42
Earlier sketches in CA 81-84, CANR-14
Anderson, Olive Ruth 1926- ... 107
Anderson, P(aul) Howard 1947- ... 61-64
Anderson, Patricia J(eanne) 1950- ... CANR-110
Earlier sketch in CA 152
Anderson, Patrick (John MacAllister)
1915-1979 ... 93-96
Obituary ... 85-88
See also CP 1, 2
See also DLB 68
Anderson, Patrick 1936- ... 33-36R
Anderson, Paul E. 1925- ... 33-36R
Anderson, Paul Seward 1913-1975 ... CANR-6
Earlier sketch in CA 1-4R
Anderson, Paul Thomas 1970- ... 223
Anderson, Paul Y(ewell) 1893-1938 ... 174
See also DLB 29
Anderson, Peggy 1938- ... 93-96
Anderson, Peggy Perry 1953- ... SATA 84
Anderson, Perry 1938- ... CANR-139
Earlier sketch in CA 151
Anderson, Philip 1956- ... 158
Anderson, Philip Warren 1923- ... 159
Anderson, Poul (William) 1926-2001 ... 181
Obituary ... 199
Earlier sketches in CA 1-4R, CANR-2, 15, 34, 64, 110
Interview in ... CANR-15
Autobiographical Essay in ... 181
See also CAAS 2
See also AAYA 5, 34
See also BPFB 1
See also BYA 6, 8, 9
See also CLC 15
See also CLR 58
See also DLB 8
See also FANT
See also MTCW 1, 2
See also MTFW 2005
See also SATA 90
See also SATA-Brief 39
See also SATA-Essay 106
See also SCFW 1, 2
See also SFW 4
See also SUFW 1, 2
Anderson, Quentin 1912-2003 ... CANR-3
Obituary ... 213
Earlier sketch in CA 1-4R
Anderson, R. C. 1883(?)-1976
Obituary ... 69-72
Anderson, R(oy) C(laude) 1931- ... 124
Anderson, Rachel 1943- ... CANR-107
Earlier sketches in CA 21-24R, CANR-9, 24, 50
See also SAAS 18
See also SATA 34, 86
Anderson, Randall C. 1934- ... 41-44R
Anderson, Ray Sherman 1925- ... CANR-10
Earlier sketch in CA 65-68
Anderson, Raymond L(loyd) 1927- ... 106
Anderson, Richard
See Anderson, J(ohn) R(ichard) L(ane)
Anderson, Richard Chase 1934- ... 185
Brief entry ... 112
Anderson, Richard Lloyd 1926- ... 37-40R
Anderson, Robert 1750-1830 ... CAD
See also CD 5
See also DLB 142
See also RGAL 4
Anderson, Robert (Woodruff) 1917- ... CANR-32
Earlier sketch in CA 21-24R
See also AITN 1
See also CD 6
See also CLC 23
See also DAM DRAM
See also DLB 7
See also LAIT 5
Anderson, Robert (David) 1927- ... 150
Anderson, Robert 1964- ... 238
Anderson, Robert A(ndrew) 1944- ... 109
Anderson, Robert C(harles) 1930-1990 ... 85-88
Obituary ... 130
Anderson, Robert David 1942- ... 73-76
Anderson, Robert H(enry) 1918- ... CANR-27
Earlier sketch in CA 49-52
Anderson, Robert Mapes 1929- ... 108
Anderson, Robert N(orris) 1944- ... 126
Anderson, Robert Newton 1929- ... 49-52
Anderson, Robert T(homas) 1926- ... 9-12R
Anderson, Robert W(illiam) 1926- ... 17-20R
Anderson, Roberta 1942- ... CANR-42
Brief entry ... 111
Earlier sketch in CA 115
Anderson, Roberta Joan
See Mitchell, Joni
Anderson, Rodney Dean 1938- ... 108
Anderson, Ronald Kinloch 1911-1984
Obituary ... 111
Anderson, Roy
See Anderson, R(oy) C(laude)
Anderson, Roy 1926- 13-16R
Anderson, Roy Allan 1895-1985 ... CANR-9
Earlier sketch in CA 13-16R
Anderson, Ruth I(rene) 1919- ... CANR-18
Earlier sketch in CA 1-4R
Anderson, Ruth Nathan 1934- ... 69-72
Anderson, S. Catherine ... 229
Anderson, Sarah 1947- ... CANR-122
Earlier sketch in CA 168
Anderson, Scarvia (Bateman) 1926- ... CANR-14
Earlier sketch in CA 41-44R
Anderson, (Tom) Scoular ... 209
See also SATA 138
Anderson, Sherwood 1876-1941 ... CANR-61
Brief entry ... 104
Earlier sketch in CA 121
See also AAYA 30
See also AMW
See also AMWC 2
See also BPFB 1
See also CDALB 1917-1929
See also DA
See also DA3
See also DAB
See also DAC
See also DAM MST, NOV
See also DLB 4, 9, 86
See also DLBD 1
See also EWL 3
See also EXPS
See also GLL 2
See also MAL 5
See also MTCW 1, 2
See also MTFW 2005
See also NFS 4
See also RGAL 4
See also RGSF 2
See also SSC 1, 46
See also SSFS 4, 10, 11
See also TCLC 1, 10, 24, 123
See also TUS
See also WLC
Anderson, Sheryl J. 1958- ... 234
Anderson, Sparky
See Anderson, George Lee
Anderson, Stanford 1934- ... 25-28R
Anderson, Stanley Edwin 1900-1977 ... CANR-3
Earlier sketch in CA 1-4R
Anderson, Stanley V(ictor) 1928- ... 21-24R
Anderson, Susan 1946- ... 182
Anderson, Susan 1952- ... SATA 90
Anderson, Sydney 1927- ... 106
Anderson, T(heodore) W(ilbur)
1918- ... CANR-29
Earlier sketch in CA 49-52
Anderson, Teresa 1944- ... 85-88
Anderson, Terry (A.) 1949- ... 147
Anderson, Terry H(oward) 1946- ... 128
Anderson, Theodore R(obert) 1927- ... 41-44R
Anderson, Thomas 1929- ... 1-4R
Anderson, Thomas D. 1929- ... 111
Anderson, Tom 1910- ... 69-72
Anderson, Tommy (Nolan) 1918- ... 45-48
Anderson, Totton J(ames) 1909-1992 ... 1-4R
Obituary ... 136
Anderson, Trevor A(ndrew) 1959- ... 154
Anderson, Verily (Bruce) 1915- ... CANR-3
Earlier sketch in CA 5-8R
Anderson, Vernon E(llsworth)
1908-1994 ... CANR-5
Earlier sketch in CA 1-4R
Anderson, Victor H. 1917-2001 ... 235
Anderson, Violet Louise 1906- ... CP 1
Anderson, Virgil Antris 1899-1994 ... CANR-16
Earlier sketch in CA 1-4R
Anderson, Virginia (R. Cronin) 1920- ... 21-24R
Anderson, Virginia DeJohn 1954- ... 150
Anderson, Vivienne 1916- ... 17-20R
Anderson, W. B.
See Schultz, James Willard
Anderson, Wallace Ludwig 1917- ... 17-20R
Anderson, Walt
See Anderson, Walter Truett
Anderson, Walter 1944- ... 101
Anderson, Walter Truett 1933- ... CANR-128
Earlier sketch in CA 105
Anderson, Warren DeWitt 1920- ... 17-20R
Anderson, Wayne 1946- ... 107
See also SATA 56, 147
Anderson, Wayne Jeremy 1908-1993 ... 49-52
Anderson, Wendell B(ernhard) 1920- ... 105
Anderson, Wes 1969- ... 214
Anderson, Wilda (Christine) 1951- ... 139
Anderson, William A(verette) 1937-
Brief entry ... 114
Anderson, William Charles
1920-2003 ... CANR-2
Obituary ... 216
Earlier sketch in CA 5-8R
Anderson, William Davis 1938- ... 33-36R
Anderson, William Eugene 1926-
Brief entry ... 111
Anderson, William G(ary) 1945- ... 115
Anderson, William H(arry) 1905-1972 ... 49-52
Anderson, William L(ouis) 1941- ... 135
Anderson, William Robert 1921- ... 5-8R
Anderson, William Scovil 1927- ... 61-64
Anderson, Wilton T(homas) 1916- ... 17-20R
Anderson-Dargatz, Gail 1963- ... CANR-89
Earlier sketch in CA 158
Anderson Imbert, Enrique (Eduardo)
1910-2000 ... CANR-26
Earlier sketches in CA 17-20R, CANR-10
See also HW 1
See also LAW
Andersons, Edgars
See Anderson, Edgar
Anders-Richards, Donald 1928- ... 25-28R
Andersson, Claes 1937- ... 195
Andersson, Ingvar 1899(?)-1974
Obituary ... 53-56
Andersson, Lars Gunnar 1954- ... 192
Andersson, Theodore 1903-1994 ... CANR-29
Earlier sketch in CA 49-52
Andersson, Theodore M(urdock) 1934- ... 25-28R
Anderton, David A(lbin) 1919-1989 ... CANR-9
Earlier sketch in CA 65-68
Anderton, Joanne (Marie) Gast 1930- ... 61-64
Anderton, Johana Gast
See Anderton, Joanne (Marie) Gast
Anderton, Stephen 1955- ... 178
Andervont, Howard Bancroft 1898-1981
Obituary ... 103
Andes, Karen 1956- ... 154
Andier, Pierre
See Desnos, Robert
Andonian, Jeanne (Beghian) 1891(?)-1976
Obituary ... 65-68
Andonov-Poljanski, Hristo 1927- ... CANR-9
Earlier sketch in CA 21-24R
Andouard
See Giraudoux, Jean(-Hippolyte)
Andrade, Carlos Drummond de
See Drummond de Andrade, Carlos
See also CLC 18
See also EWL 3
See also RGWL 2, 3
Andrade, E(dward) N(eville) da C(osta)
1887-1971 ... CAP-1
Earlier sketch in CA 11-12
Andrade, Eugenio de
See Fontinhas, Jose
See also EWL 3
Andrade, Jorge 1922-1984 ... DLB 307
Andrade, Jorge Carrera
See Carrera Andrade, Jorge
Andrade, Jose Oswald de Sousa
See de Andrade, Oswald
Andrade, Mario de
See de Andrade, Mario
See also DLB 307
See also EWL 3
See also LAW
See also RGWL 2, 3
See also TCLC 43
See also WLIT 1
Andrade, Oswald de
See de Andrade, Oswald
See also DLB 307
See also EWL 3
See also LAWS 1
Andrade, Victor (Manuel) 1905- ... 69-72
Andrade Franco, Aluisio Jorge
See Andrade, Jorge
Andrain, Charles F(ranklin) 1937- ... 69-72
Andre, Alix
See Kimberly, Gail
Andre, Evelyn M(arie) 1924- ... CANR-11
Earlier sketch in CA 69-72
See also SATA 27
Andre, Judith 1941- ... 140
Andre, (Kenneth) Michael 1946- ... CANR-108
Earlier sketch in CA 114
See also CAAS 13
Andre, Rae 1946- ... 116
Andreach, Robert J. 1930- ... 33-36R
Andreae, Christine 1942- ... 222
Andreae, Johann V(alentin)
1586-1654 ... DLB 164
Andreano, Ralph L(ouis) 1929- ... CANR-6
Earlier sketch in CA 5-8R
Andreas, Burton G(ould) 1921-1989 ... 81-84
Andreas, Thomas
See Williams, Thomas (Andrew)
Andreas Capellanus fl. c. 1185- ... DLB 208
Andreasen, Alan R(obert) 1934- ... 65-68
Andreasen, Nancy C(oover) 1938- ... 108
Andreas-Salome, Lou 1861-1937 ... 178
See also DLB 66
See also TCLC 56
Andreassen, Karl
See Boyd, Waldo T.
Andree, Louise
See Coury, Louise Andree
Andree, R(ichard) V(ernon)
1919-1987 ... CANR-8
Earlier sketch in CA 57-60
Andree, Robert G(erald) 1912-1987 ... 29-32R
Obituary ... 124
Andreev, Leonid
See Andreyev, Leonid (Nikolaevich)
See also DLB 295
See also EWL 3
Andreev, Nikolay
See Trofimenko, Henry (Alexandrovich)
Andreissen, David
See Poyer, David
Andrejew, Andre 1887-1966 ... IDFW 3, 4
Andreopoulos, George J. 1953- ... 168
Andreopoulos, Spyros (George) 1929- ... 77-80
Andres, Glenn M(erle) 1941- ... 73-76
Andres, Stefan Paul 1906-1970 ... 179
Obituary ... 29-32R
See also DLB 69
See also EWL 3
Andresen, Jack
See Andresen, John H(enry), Jr.
Andresen, John H(enry), Jr. 1917- ... 57-60
Andresen, Julie Tetel
See Tetel, Julie
Andresen, Sophia de Mello Breyner
1919- ... DLB 287
See also EWL 3
Andreski, Iris
See Gillespie, I(ris) S(ylvia)
Andreski, Stanislav Leonard 1919- ... 61-64
Andress, Lesley
See Sanders, Lawrence
Andreu, Blanca 1959- ... DLB 134
Andrew, Christopher (Maurice) 1941- ... 136
Andrew, David S. 1943- ... 123
Andrew, Donna T. 1944(?)- ... 212
Andrew, Edward G. 1941- ... 175
Andrew, Geoff 1954- ... 192
Andrew, Ian (Peter) 1962- ... SATA 116
Andrew, J(ames) Dudley 1945- ... CANR-9
Earlier sketch in CA 65-68
Andrew, John A(lfred III)
1943-2000 ... CANR-143
Earlier sketch in CA 165
Andrew, Joseph J(erald) 1960- ... 143
Andrew, Joseph Maree
See Occomy, Marita (Odette) Bonner
Andrew, Malcolm (Ross) 1945- ... 105
Andrew, Paige G. 1957- ... 197
Andrew, Prudence (Hastings) 1924- ... CANR-52
Earlier sketches in CA 1-4R, CANR-1
See also CWRI 5
See also SATA 87
Andrew, Sheila M. 1938- ... 165
Andrew, Warren 1910-1982 ... 21-24R
Andrewes, Christopher Howard
1896-1988 ... 17-20R
Andrewes, Lancelot 1555-1626 ... DLB 151, 172
Andrewes, Patience
See Bradford, Patience Andrewes
Andrews, A. A.
See Paine, Lauran (Bosworth)
Andrews, Allen 1913- ... CANR-1
Earlier sketch in CA 49-52
Andrews, Andy 1959- ... 225
Andrews, Arthur (Douglas, Jr.) 1923- ... 69-72
Andrews, Barry G(eoffrey)
1943-1987 ... CANR-2
Earlier sketch in CA 49-52
Andrews, Bart 1945- ... CANR-24
Earlier sketches in CA 65-68, CANR-9
Andrews, Benny 1930- ... 106
See also SATA 31
Andrews, Bruce 1948- ... CANR-10
Earlier sketch in CA 49-52
Andrews, Burton (Allen) 1906-1992 ... CAP-2
Earlier sketch in CA 33-36
Andrews, Charles M(cLean) 1863-1943 ... 183
Brief entry ... 119
See also DLB 17
Andrews, Cicily Fairfield
See West, Rebecca
Andrews, Claire 1940- ... 33-36R
Andrews, Clarence A(delbert)
1912-2002 ... CANR-20
Earlier sketch in CA 33-36R
Andrews, Claudia Emerson
See Emerson, Claudia
See also CSW
Andrews, Colin 1946- ... 133
Andrews, Donald H(atch)
1898-1973(?) ... CAP-2
Earlier sketch in CA 23-24
Andrews, Dorothea Harris 1916-1976
Obituary ... 69-72
Andrews, E(ric) M(ontgomery) 1933- ... 93-96
Andrews, Eamonn 1922-1987 ... 120
Obituary ... 124
Andrews, Edgar Harold 1932- ... 105
Andrews, Eleanor Lattimore
See Lattimore, Eleanor Frances
Andrews, Elmer 1948- ... 132
Andrews, Elton V.
See Pohl, Frederik
Andrews, Ernest E(ugene) 1932- ... 57-60
Andrews, F(rank) Emerson
1902-1978 ... CANR-1
Obituary ... 81-84
Earlier sketch in CA 1-4R
See also SATA 22
Andrews, Felicia
See Grant, Charles L(ewis)
Andrews, (Earl) Frank 1937- ... 61-64
Andrews, Frank M(eredith) 1935- ... CANR-14
Earlier sketch in CA 41-44R
Andrews, George (Clinton) 1926- ... 21-24R
Andrews, George F(redrick) 1918- ... 65-68
Andrews, George Reid 1951- ... 141
Andrews, Henry N(athaniel), Jr. 1910- ... 93-96
Andrews, J. Cutler 1908-1972
Obituary ... 37-40R
Andrews, J(ames) S(ydney) 1934- ... 29-32R
See also CWRI 5
See also SATA 4
Andrews, James David 1924- ... 53-56
Andrews, James Frederick 1936-1980
Obituary ... 107
Andrews, James J. C. 1943(?)-1985
Obituary ... 116
Andrews, James R(obertson) 1936- ... 129
Brief entry ... 117
Andrews, Jan 1942- ... 122
See also MAICYA 2
See also SATA 58, 98
See also SATA-Brief 49
Andrews, Jay
See Wynorski, Jim
Andrews, John (Malcolm) 1936- ... CANR-127
Earlier sketches in CA 117, CANR-41, 67
See also CMW 4
Andrews, John F(rank) 1942- ... CANR-48
Earlier sketch in CA 119
Andrews, John Henry 1939- ... 107
Andrews, John Williams 1898-1973
Obituary ... 57-60
Andrews, Julia F(rances) 1951- ... 197

Andrews, Julie 1935- ... CANR-139
Earlier sketch in CA 37-40R
See also CLR 85
See also SATA 7, 153
Andrews, Keith 1930- ... 33-36R
Andrews, Keith William
See Keith, William H(enry), Jr., Jr.
Andrews, Kenneth R(ichmond)
1916- ... CANR-37
Earlier sketches in CA 1-4R, CANR-16
Andrews, Kevin 1924- ... 124
Andrews, Laura
See Coury, Louise Andree
Andrews, Lewis M. 1946- ... 65-68
Andrews, Linda Wasmer 1957- ... 238
Andrews, (William) Linton 1886-1972 ... 9-12R
Obituary ... 120
Andrews, Lori B. 1952- ... 192
Andrews, Lucilla (Mathew) ... CANR-61
Brief entry ... 116
Earlier sketch in CA 128
See also RHW
Andrews, Lyman 1938- ... 49-52
Andrews, Lynn V. ... CANR-114
Brief entry ... 125
Earlier sketch in CA 129
Andrews, Margaret E(lizabeth) ... 33-36R
Andrews, Mark Edwin 1903-1992 ... CAP-1
Earlier sketch in CA 19-20
Andrews, (Daniel) Marshall 1899(?)-1973
Obituary ... 45-48
Andrews, Mary Evans ... 5-8R
Andrews, Michael
See Andrews, Michael Alford
Andrews, Michael Alford 1939- ... 116
Andrews, Michael F(rank)
1916-1988 ... CANR-27
Earlier sketch in CA 49-52
Andrews, Mike
See Andrews, Michael Alford
Andrews, Miles Peter (?)-1814 ... DLB 89
Andrews, Nicocla
See Papazoglou, Orania
Andrews, Nin 1958- ... 176
Andrews, Patrick E. 1936- ... TCWW 2
Andrews, Paul 1949- ... 189
Andrews, Paul Revere 1906-1983
Obituary ... 110
Andrews, Peter 1931- ... CANR-11
Earlier sketch in CA 17-20R
Andrews, Ralph W(arren) 1897-1988 ... 9-12R
Andrews, Raymond 1934-1991 ... CANR-42
Obituary ... 136
Earlier sketches in CA 81-84, CANR-15
See also BW 2
Andrews, Richard N(igel) L(yon) 1944- ... 189
Andrews, Robert D.
See Andrews, (Charles) Robert Douglas (Hardy)
Andrews, (Charles) Robert Douglas (Hardy)
1908-1999 ... CAP-1
Earlier sketch in CA 9-10
Andrews, Roy Chapman 1884-1960 ... SATA 19
Andrews, Russell
See Gethers, Peter and Handler, David
Andrews, Sam S. 1942- ... 169
Andrews, Sarah 1949(?)- ... CANR-127
Earlier sketch in CA 175
Andrews, Stanley 1894-1994 ... CANR-22
Earlier sketch in CA 45-48
Andrews, Stephen Pearl 1812-1886 ... DLB 250
Andrews, Tamra 1959- ... 198
See also SATA 129
Andrews, Tom 1961- ... 147
Andrews, V. C.
See Neiderman, Andrew
Andrews, V(irginia) C(leo)
1924(?)-1986 ... CANR-21
Obituary ... 121
Earlier sketch in CA 97-100
See also AAYA 4, 41
See also CPW
See also DA3
See also DAM POP
See also HGG
See also MTCW 1
See also SATA-Obit 50
See also YAW
Andrews, Wayne 1913-1987 ... CANR-70
Obituary ... 123
Earlier sketches in CA 9-12R, CANR-3
Andrews, Wendy
See Sharmat, Marjorie Weinman
Andrews, William G(eorge) 1930- ... CANR-48
Earlier sketches in CA 5-8R, CANR-7
See also SATA 74
Andrews, William L(eake) 1946- ... 136
Andrews, William R(obert) 1937- ... 53-56
Andreyev, Leonid (Nikolaevich)
1871-1919 ... 185
Brief entry ... 104
See also Andreev, Leonid
See also TCLC 3
Andreyev, Nikolay Efremych 1908-1982
Obituary ... 106
Andrezel, Pierre
See Blixen, Karen (Christentze Dinesen)
Andrian, Gustave W(illiam) 1918- ... 181
Brief entry ... 114
Andrian, Leopold von 1875-1951 ... 174
See also DLB 81
Andriani, Renee
See Williams-Andriani, Renee
Andric, Ivo 1892-1975 ... CANR-60
Obituary ... 57-60
Earlier sketches in CA 81-84, CANR-43
See also CDWLB 4
See also CLC 8
See also DLB 147
See also EW 11
See also EWL 3
See also MTCW 1
See also RGSF 2
See also RGWL 2, 3
See also SSC 36
See also TCLC 135
Andric, Stanko
See Andric, Stanko
Andric, Stanko 1967- ... 209
Andriekus, (Kazimieras) Leonardas
1914-2003 ... 25-28R
Andrien, Kenneth James 1951- ... 120
Andriessen, Hendrik (Franciscus) 1892-1981
Obituary ... 108
Andriola, Alfred J. 1912-1983
Obituary ... 109
See also SATA-Obit 34
Andriot, Laurie A. 1955- ... 202
Andriote, John-Manuel 1959- ... 220
Andrist, Ralph K. 1914-2004 ... CANR-20
Obituary ... 231
Earlier sketches in CA 9-12R, CANR-5
See also SATA 45
Andropov, Yuri (Vladimirovich)
1914-1984 ... 193
Obituary ... 111
Andros, Dee G(us) 1924-2003 ... 69-72
Obituary ... 220
Andros, Phil
See Steward, Samuel M(orris)
See also GLL 1
Androvar
See Prado (Calvo), Pedro
Andrus, (Vincent) Dyckman 1942- ... 102
Andrus, Hyrum L(eslie) 1924- ... 37-40R
Andrus, Jeff 1947- ... 155
Andrus, Paul 1931- ... 65-68
Andrus, Vera 1895-1979 ... CAP-2
Earlier sketch in CA 21-22
Andryszewski, Tricia 1956- ... CANR-121
Earlier sketch in CA 152
See also SATA 88, 148
Andrzejewski, Jerzy 1909-1983 ... CANR-79
Obituary ... 109
Earlier sketches in CA 25-28R, CANR-29
See also DLB 215
See also EWL 3
See also RGWL 2, 3
Andrzejewski, Julie 1945- ... 129
Andrzeyevski, George
See Andrzejewski, Jerzy
Anduze-Dufy, Raphael
See Coulet du Gard, Rene
Anees, Munawar Ahmad 1948- ... 123
An Elderly Spinster
See Wilson, Margaret (Wilhelmina)
An English Mother
See Butler, Josephine (Elizabeth)
Anfinsen, Christian Boehmer 1916-1995 ... 159
Anfousse, Ginette 1944- ... SATA-Brief 48
Ang, Ien 1954- ... CANR-144
Earlier sketch in CA 133
Angebert, Jean
See Bertrand, Michel
Angebert, Jean-Michel
See Bertrand, Michel
Angebert, Michel
See Bertrand, Michel
Angel, Daniel D. 1939- ... 33-36R
Angel, Heather 1941- ... CANR-25
Earlier sketch in CA 69-72
Angel, J(ohn) Lawrence 1915-1986 ... 101
Obituary ... 120
Angel, Marc D(wight) 1945- ... 101
Angel, Marie 1923- ... CANR-15
Earlier sketch in CA 29-32R
See also SATA 47
Angela, Alberto 1962- ... 144
Angelella, Michael 1953- ... 97-100
Angeles, Carlos A. 1921- ... CP 1, 3
Angeles, Jose 1930- ... 33-36R
Angeles, Peter A. 1931- ... 33-36R
See also SATA 40
Angeles, Philip 1909- ... 5-8R
Angeletti, Roberta 1964- ... SATA 124
Angeli, Marguerite (Lofft) de
See de Angeli, Marguerite (Lofft)
Angelilli, Frank Joseph
See Angell, Frank Joseph
Angelin, Patricia ... 119
Angelino, Marie
See Garbutt, Janice (D.) Lovoos
Angelique, Pierre
See Bataille, Georges
Angelis, Barbara (Ann) De
See De Angelis, Barbara (Ann)
Angelis, Milo de
See De Angelis, Milo
Angell, David (F.) ... 170
Angell, David F.
See Angell, David (F.)
Angell, Ernest 1889-1973
Obituary ... 37-40R
Angell, Frank Joseph 1919- ... 17-20R
Angell, George 1945- ... 101
Angell, James Burrill 1829-1916 ... DLB 64
Angell, James W(aterhouse) 1898-1986
Obituary ... 119
Angell, Judie
See Gaberman, Judie Angell
See also WYA
Angell, Madeline 1919- ... CANR-10
Earlier sketch in CA 65-68
See also SATA 18
Angell, Marcia 1939- ... 236
Angell, (Ralph) Norman 1874(?)-1967 ... CAP-1
Earlier sketch in CA 13-14
Angell, Richard B(radshaw) 1918- ... 13-16R
Angell, Robert Cooley 1899-1984 ... 101
Angell, Roger 1920- ... CANR-144
Earlier sketches in CA 57-60, CANR-13, 44, 70
See also CLC 26
See also DLB 171, 185
Angell, Tony 1940- ... CANR-4
Earlier sketch in CA 53-56
Angelo, Bonnie ... CANR-104
Brief entry ... 113
Angelo, Frank 1914-2000 ... CANR-4
Earlier sketch in CA 53-56
Angelo, Ivan 1937- ... WLIT 1
Angelo, Valenti 1897- ... CANR-68
Earlier sketch in CA 73-76
See also BYA 1
See also SATA 14
Angelocci, Angelo 1926- ... 21-24R
Angelou, Maya 1928- ... CANR-133
Earlier sketches in CA 65-68, CANR-19, 42, 65, 111
See also AAYA 7, 20
See also AMWS 4
See also BLC 1
See also BPFB 1
See also BW 2, 3
See also BYA 2
See also CDALBS
See also CLC 12, 35, 64, 77, 155
See also CLR 53
See also CP 4, 5, 6, 7
See also CPW
See also CSW
See also CWP
See also DA
See also DA3
See also DAB
See also DAC
See also DAM MST, MULT, POET, POP
See also DLB 38
See also EWL 3
See also EXPN
See also EXPP
See also FL 1:5
See also LAIT 4
See also MAICYA 2
See also MAICYAS 1
See also MAL 5
See also MAWW
See also MTCW 1, 2
See also MTFW 2005
See also NCFS 2
See also NFS 2
See also PC 32
See also PFS 2, 3
See also RGAL 4
See also SATA 49, 136
See also TCLE 1:1
See also WLCS
See also WYA
See also YAW
Anger, Jane ... DLB 136
Anger, Kenneth 1930- ... 106
Interview in ... CA-106
Angermann, Gerhard O(tto) 1904-1981 ... 65-68
Angers, Felicite
See Conan, Laure
Anggraeni, Dewi 1945- ... 197
Anghelaki-Rooke, Katerina 1939- ... CWW 2
Angier, Bradford -1997 ... CANR-7
Earlier sketch in CA 5-8R
See also SATA 12
Angier, Carole 1943- ... CANR-123
Earlier sketch in CA 120
Angier, Natalie Marie 1958- ... 188
Angier, Roswell P. 1940- ... 101
Angiolillo, Paul F(rancis) 1917- ... 105
Anglade, Jean 1915- ... CANR-43
Earlier sketches in CA 103, CANR-20
Angle, Barbara 1947- ... 150
Angle, Jim 1946- ... 133
Angle, Kurt (Steven) 1968- ... 235
Angle, Paul M(cClelland) 1900-1975 ... CAP-2
Obituary ... 57-60
Earlier sketch in CA 21-22
See also SATA-Obit 20
Anglesey, Zoe (Rita) 1941- ... 147
Angley, Ernest (W.) 1921- ... 206
Anglim, Christopher Thomas 1957- ... 201
Anglin, Douglas G(eorge) 1923- ... CANR-14
Earlier sketch in CA 37-40R
Anglin, Patty ... 232
Anglo, Sydney 1934- ... 89-92
Anglund, Joan Walsh 1926- ... CANR-15
Earlier sketch in CA 5-8R
See also CLR 1, 94
See also MAICYA 2
See also SATA 2
Ango 1906-1955 ... MJW
Ango, Fan D.
See Longyear, Barry B(rookes)
Angoff, Allan 1910-1998 ... CANR-20
Earlier sketch in CA 45-48
Angoff, Charles 1902-1979 ... CANR-68
Obituary ... 85-88
Earlier sketches in CA 5-8R, CANR-4
Angold, Michael ... 209
Angouleme, Marguerite d'
See de Navarre, Marguerite
Angremy, Jean-Pierre 1937- ... 106
Angress, R(uth) K(lueger) 1931- ... 37-40R
Angress, Werner T(homas) 1920- ... 13-16R
Angrist, Shirley S(arah) 1933- ... 25-28R
Angrist, Stanley W(olff) 1933- ... 25-28R
See also SATA 4
Anguelov, Zlatko 1946- ... 209
Anguizola, G. A.
See Anguizola, Gustave (A.)
Anguizola, Gustave (A.) 1927-
Brief entry ... 116
Angus, Christopher (K.) 1950- ... 235
Angus, Colin 1971- ... 212
Angus, David L. 1933-1999 ... 194
Angus, Douglas Ross 1909- ... CANR-3
Earlier sketch in CA 1-4R
Angus, Fay 1929- ... CANR-33
Earlier sketches in CA 89-92, CANR-15
Angus, Ian
See Mackay, James (Alexander)
Angus, J(ohn) Colin 1907- ... 107
Angus, Margaret 1908- ... 21-24R
Angus, Sylvia 1921-1982 ... CANR-10
Earlier sketch in CA 61-64
Angus, Tom
See Powell, Geoffrey (Stewart)
Angus-Butterworth, Lionel Milner
1900- ... CANR-4
Earlier sketch in CA 53-56
Anhalt, Edward 1914-2000 ... CANR-29
Obituary ... 189
Earlier sketch in CA 85-88
See also DLB 26
Anholt, Catherine 1958- ... MAICYA 2
See also SATA 74, 131
Anholt, Laurence 1959- ... 212
See also MAICYA 2
See also SATA 74, 141
Anicar, Tom
See Raucina, Thomas Frank
Aniebo, I(feanyichukwu) N(dubuisi) C(hikezie)
1939- ... CANR-62
Earlier sketch in CA 134
See also CN 4, 5, 6, 7
Anikouchine, William A(lexander) 1929-
Brief entry ... 117
Anissimov, Myriam 1943- ... DLB 299
Anita
See Daniel, Anita
Ankenbrand, Frank, Jr. 1905-1972 ... CAP-2
Earlier sketch in CA 19-20
Anker, Charlotte 1934- ... 93-96
Anker, Nini Magdalene Roll
1873-1942 ... DLB 297
Anker, Roy M. 1945- ... 196
Ankerberg, John (F.) 1945- ... 207
Ankerson, Dudley (Charles) 1948- ... CANR-53
Earlier sketch in CA 126
Anmar, Frank
See Nolan, William F(rancis)
Anna, Timothy E. 1944- ... 101
Annan, Noel Gilroy 1916-2000 ... CANR-123
Obituary ... 188
Earlier sketches in CA 61-64, CANR-63
Annand, J(ames) K(ing) 1908-1993 ... CANR-18
Earlier sketch in CA 101
Annandale, Barbara
See Bowden, Jean
Annaqtussi Tulurialik, Ruth 1934- ... 211
Annas, George J. 1945- ... 77-80
Annas, Julia ... 190
Annaud, Jean-Jacques 1943- ... 213
Anne (Elizabeth Alice Louise Windsor), Princess
1950- ... 140
Anne-Mariel
See Goud, Anne
Annenkov, Georges 1889-1974 ... IDFW 3, 4
Annenkov, Pavel Vasil'evich
1813(?)-1887 ... DLB 277
Annensky, Innokentii Fedorovich
See Annensky, Innokenty (Fyodorovich)
See also DLB 295
Annensky, Innokenty (Fyodorovich)
1856-1909 ... 155
Brief entry ... 110
See also EWL 3
See also TCLC 14
Annerino, John ... 144
Annesley, James 1968- ... 188
Anness, Milford E(dwin) 1918-1992 ... 17-20R
Annett, Cora
See Scott, Cora Annett (Pipitone)
Annett, John 1930- ... 29-32R
Annie, Apple
See Maddux, (Juanita) Rachel
Annie-Jo
See Blanchard, Patricia and Suhr, Joanne
Annigoni, Pietro 1910-1988
Obituary ... 127
Annikova, Galina
See Dutkina, Galina (Borisovna)
Annis, Linda Ferrill 1943- ... 85-88
Annixter, Jane
See Sturtzel, Jane Levington
Annixter, Paul
See Sturtzel, Howard A(llison)
Anno, Mitsumasa 1926- ... CANR-141
Earlier sketches in CA 49-52, CANR-4, 44
See also CLR 2, 14
See also MAICYA 1, 2
See also SATA 5, 38, 77, 157
Annunzio, Gabriele d'
See D'Annunzio, Gabriele
Anobile, Richard J(oseph) 1947- ... CANR-5
Earlier sketch in CA 53-56

Cumulative Index 17 **Appelbaum**

Anobile, Ulla (Kakonen) 1945- 111
Anodos
See Coleridge, Mary E(lizabeth)
Anoff, I(sador) S(amuel) 1892-1995 45-48
Anon, Charles Robert
See Pessoa, Fernando (Antonio Nogueira)
Another
See Hensley, Sophie Almon
Anouilh, Jean (Marie Lucien Pierre)
1910-1987 .... CANR-32
Obituary 123
Earlier sketch in CA 17-20R
See also AAYA 67
See also CLC 1, 3, 8, 13, 40, 50
See also DAM DRAM
See also DC 8, 21
See also DFS 9, 10, 19
See also DLB 321
See also EW 13
See also EWL 3
See also GFL 1789 to the Present
See also MTCW 1, 2
See also MTFW 2005
See also RGWL 2, 3
See also TWA
Anozie, Sunday O(gbonna) 1942- 143
See also BW 2
Anquillare, John 1942- 105
Anreus, Alejandro 1960- 209
Anrooy, Francine Van
See Van Anrooy, Francine
Ansa, Tina McElroy 1949- CANR-143
Earlier sketch in CA 142
See also BW 2
See also CSW
Ansara, Michael
See Crowther, Bruce (Ian)
Ansary, Mir Tamim 1948- 211
See also SATA 140
Ansay, A. Manette 1964- CANR-89
Earlier sketch in CA 148
Ansbacher, Heinz L(udwig) 1904- CAP-1
Earlier sketch in CA 9-10
Ansbacher, Max G. 1935- 89-92
Ansberry, Clare 1957- 199
Ansberry, William F. 1926- 33-36R
Anschel, Eugene 1907-1990 53-56
Anschel, Kurt R. 1936- 41-44R
Anscombe, Elizabeth
See Anscombe, G(ertrude) E(lizabeth) M(argaret)
Anscombe, Francis John 1918-2001 219
Anscombe, G(ertrude) E(lizabeth) M(argaret)
1919-2001 129
Obituary 192
Brief entry 122
See also DLB 262
Anscombe, Isabelle (Mary) 1954- 108
Anscombe, Roderick 1947- 147
Ansel, Talvikki 1962- 164
Ansel, Walter (Charles) 1897-1977 45-48
Obituary 73-76
Ansell, Amy E(lizabeth) 1964- 182
Ansell, Helen 1940- 25-28R
Ansell, Jack 1925-1976 .... 17-20R
Obituary 69-72
Anselm, Felix
See Pollak, Felix
Anselm of Canterbury 1033(?)-1109 .... DLB 115
Ansen, Alan 1922- CANR-4
Earlier sketch in CA 1-4R
See also CP 1
Anshaw, Carol 1946- CANR-139
Earlier sketch in CA 164
Anshen, Melvin (Leon) 1912-1997 124
Ansky, S.
See Rappoport, Shloyme Zanul
Ansky, Solomon 1863-1920
Ansley, Gladys Piatt 1906-1995 .... 5-8R
Anslinger, Harry Jacob 1892-1975 ... CANR-70
Obituary 61-64
Earlier sketches in CAP-1, CA 11-12
Ansolabehere, Stephen 174
Anson, Bill 1907-1983
Obituary 110
Anson, Cyril J(oseph) 1923- 49-52
Anson, Jay 1921-1980 .... CANR-29
Obituary 97-100
Earlier sketch in CA 81-84
Anson, John
See Firth, (Frederick) Anson
Anson, Peter Frederick 1889-1975 .... 9-12R
Anson, Robert Sam 1945- CANR-52
Brief entry 115
Earlier sketch in CA 125
Interview in CA-125
Anspach, Donald F. 1942- 69-72
Anstee, Margaret Joan 1926- 230
Anstey, Caroline 1958- .... SATA 81
Anstey, Edgar
See Slusser, George Edgar
Anstey, Edgar 1917- CANR-3
Earlier sketch in CA 5-8R
Anstey, F.
See Guthrie, Thomas Anstey
See also DLB 141, 178
See also SUFW
Anstey, Roger T(homas) 1927-1979 .... 13-16R
Anstey, Vera (Powell) 1889-1976 .... CAP-1
Earlier sketch in CA 17-18
Anstruther, Godfrey 1903-1988
Obituary 126
Anstruther, Ian 1922- CANR-129
Earlier sketches in CA 128, CANR-59
Anstruther, James
See Maxtone Graham, James Anstruther
An Tai-sung 1931- 188
Brief entry 113
Antal, Dan 1954- 152
Antal, Sandy 1950- 188
Antar, Johanna 1953- 140
'Antarah (?)-7th cent. (?) .... DLB 311
'Antar ibn Shaddad al-'Absi
See 'Antarah
Antell, Gerson 1926- 53-56
Antell, Will D. 1935- 104
See also SATA 31
Antelme, Robert 1917-1990
Anthes, Richard A(llen) 1944- 107
Anthony
See Taber, Anthony Scott
Anthony, Barbara 1932- CANR-21
Earlier sketch in CA 103
See also SATA 29, 163
Anthony, C. L.
See Smith, Dorothy Gladys
Anthony, Carolyn (Taylor) 1928- 147
Anthony, Catherine
See Adachi, Barbara (Curtis)
Anthony, Crystal McCrary 232
Anthony, David
See Smith, William Dale
Anthony, Diana 1951- 114
Anthony, Edward 1895-1971 .... CANR-68
Obituary 33-36R
Earlier sketch in CA 73-76
See also SATA 21
Anthony, Evelyn
See Ward-Thomas, Evelyn Bridget Patricia Stephens
Anthony, Felix
See Millus, Donald (J.)
Anthony, Florence
See Ai
Anthony, Geraldine (Cecilia) 1919- .. CANR-52
Earlier sketches in CA 69-72, CANR-11, 28
Anthony, Gordon
See Stannus, (James) Gordon (Dawson)
Anthony, Inid E. 1925- 104
Anthony, J(oseph) Garner 1899-1982 61-64
Anthony, James R(aymond) 1922- CANR-27
Earlier sketch in CA 49-52
Anthony, John
See Beckett, Ronald Brymer and Ciardi, John (Anthony) and Sabini, John Anthony
Anthony, Joseph Patrick 1964- CANR-135
Earlier sketch in CA 170
See also SATA 103
Anthony, Julie 1948- 106
Anthony, Katharine (Susan) 1877-1965
Obituary 25-28R
Anthony, Mark (Russell Lee) 1966- 192
Anthony, Michael 1932- CANR-43
Earlier sketches in CA 17-20R, CANR-10, 27
See also CAAS 18
See also BW 2
See also CN 1, 2, 3, 4, 5, 6, 7
See also DLB 125
See also EWL 3
Anthony, Patricia 1947- 166
See also SATA 109
Anthony, Peter
See Shaffer, Anthony (Joshua) and Shaffer, Peter (Levin)
Anthony, Piers 1934- 200
Earlier sketch in CANR-28, 56, 73, 102, 133
Autobiographical Essay in 200
See also AAYA 11, 48
See also BYA 7
See also CLC 35
See also CPW
See also DAM POP
See also DLB 8
See also FANT
See also MAICYA 2
See also MAICYAS 1
See also MTCW 1, 2
See also MTFW 2005
See also SAAS 22
See also SATA 84, 129
See also SATA-Essay 129
See also SFW 4
See also SUFW 1, 2
See also YAW
Anthony, Rebecca (Jespersen) 1950- 118
Anthony, Robert N(ewton) 1916- CANR-5
Earlier sketch in CA 13-16R
Anthony, Sterling 1949- 230
Anthony, Susan B(rownell) 1820-1906 211
See also FW
See also TCLC 84
Anthony, Susan B(rownell) 1916-1991 89-92
Obituary 134
Anthony, Susan C(arol) 1953- .... SATA 87
Anthony, Susanna 1726-1791 .... DLB 200
Anthony, Tony
See Alessandra, Tony
Anthony, William G. 1934- 17-20R
Anthony, William P(hilip) 1943- CANR-29
Earlier sketches in CA 77-80, CANR-13
Anthrop, Donald F. 1935-
Brief entry 111
Anticaglia, Elizabeth 1939- CANR-1
Earlier sketch in CA 45-48
See also SATA 12
Antico, John 1924- 29-32R
Antieau, Kim 224
Antill, James Macquarie 1912-1994 . CANR-13
Earlier sketch in CA 33-36R
Antin, David 1932- 73-76
See also CP 1, 3, 4, 5, 6, 7
See also DLB 169
Antin, Mary 1881-1949 181
Brief entry 118
See also DLB 221
See also DLBY 1984
Antin, Steve
See Antin, Steven (Howard)
Antin, Steven (Howard) 1961- 226
Antle, Nancy 1955- .... SATA 102
Antler 1946- .... TCLE 1:1
Antoine, Marc
See Proust, (Valentin-Louis-George-Eugene) Marcel
Antoine-Dariaux, Genevieve 1914- 57-60
Antokoletz, Elliott (Maxim) 1942- 129
Antol, Marie Nadine 1930- 152
Antol, Nikki
See Antol, Marie Nadine
Antolini, Margaret Fishback 1904-1985
Obituary 117
See also SATA-Obit 45
Anton, Frank Robert 1920- 41-44R
Anton, Hector R(oque) 1919- 73-76
Anton, John P(eter) 1920- CANR-9
Earlier sketch in CA 21-24R
Anton, Michael J(ames) 1940- 57-60
See also SATA 12
Anton, Rita (Kenter) 1920- 9-12R
Anton, Ted 1957- 153
Antonacci, Robert J(oseph) 1916- CANR-9
Earlier sketch in CA 5-8R
See also SATA 45
See also SATA-Brief 37
Antoncich, Betty (Kennedy)
1913-1982 .... 13-16R
Antone, Evan Haywood 1922- 126
Antonetta, Susanne 1956- 203
Antoni
See Iranek-Osmecki, Kazimierz
Antoni, Brian 1959- 147
Antoni, Robert (William) 1958- 139
Antoniak, Helen Elizabeth 1947- 105
Antonick, Robert J. 1939- 37-40R
Antoninus, Brother
See Everson, William (Oliver)
See also CP 1
Antonio, Emile de
See de Antonio, Emile
Antonio, Robert J(ohn) 1945- 120
Antonioni, Michelangelo 1912- CANR-77
Earlier sketches in CA 73-76, CANR-45
See also CLC 20, 144
Antoniutti, Ildebrando 1898-1974
Obituary 53-56
Antonovsky, Aaron 1923-1994 .... CANR-12
Earlier sketch in CA 29-32R
Antonucci, Francesco 1956- 149
Antony, Jonquil 1916(?)-1980 .... 13-16R
Obituary 120
Antoun, Richard T(aft) 1932- 65-68
Antreasian, Garo Z(areh) 1922- 81-84
Antrim, Donald 1959(?)- CANR-111
Earlier sketch in CA 167
Antrim, Harry Thomas 1936- 33-36R
Antrim, William H. 1928- 69-72
Antrobus, John 1933- CANR-67
Earlier sketches in CA 57-60, CANR-11
See also CBD
See also CD 5, 6
Antschel, Paul 1920-1970 .... CANR-61
Earlier sketches in CA 85-88, CANR-33
See also Celan, Paul
See also MTCW 1
See also PFS 21
Anttila, Raimo (Aulis) 1935- 33-36R
Antunes, Antonio Lobo 1942- .... DLB 287
Anunobi, Fredoline O. 1956- 146
Anvic, Frank
See Sherman, Jory (Tecumseh)
Anvil, Christopher
See Crosby, Harry C., Jr.
Anwar, Chairil 1922-1949 219
Brief entry 121
See also Chairil Anwar
See also RGWL 3
See also TCLC 22
Anweiler, Oskar 1925- CANR-9
Earlier sketch in CA 65-68
Anyidoho, Kofi 1947- 178
See also BW 3
See also CP 7
See also DLB 157
See also EWL 3
Anyon, G(eorge) Jay 1909-1974 .... 5-8R
Anzaldua, Gloria (Evanjelina) 1942-2004 ... 175
Obituary 227
See also CLC 200
See also CSW
See also CWP
See also DLB 122
See also FW
See also HLCS 1
See also LLW
See also RGAL 4
See also SATA-Obit 154
Anzengruber, Ludwig 1839-1889 .... DLB 129
Anzetti, Toni
See Zeddies, Ann Tonsor
Anzovin, Steven 1954- 124
Aoki, Haruo 1930- CANR-52
Earlier sketches in CA 49-52, CANR-27
Aoki, Hisako 1942- 115
See also SATA 45
Aoki, Michiko Y(amaguchi) 107
Aos, Foel
See ter Balkt, H(erman) H(endrik)
Aparain, Mario Delgado
See Delgado Aparain, Mario
Apatow, Judd 1968- 206
See also AAYA 49
Apel, Dora 1952- 234
Apel, Karl-Otto 1922- CANR-46
Earlier sketches in CA 105, CANR-22
Apel, Willi 1893-1988 .... CANR-2
Earlier sketch in CA 1-4R
Apelian, Albert Solomon 1893-1986
Obituary 121
Apess, William 1798-1839(?) .... DAM MULT
See also DLB 175, 243
See also NNAL
Apfel, Necia H(alpern) 1930- CANR-46
Earlier sketches in CA 107, CANR-23
See also SATA 51
See also SATA-Brief 41
Apffel, Edmund R., Jr. 1948- 107
Apgar, Virginia 1909-1974 73-76
Obituary 53-56
Aphrodite, J.
See Livingston, Carole
Aphrontis, Hippoclides
See Humez, Nicholas (David)
Apikuni
See Schultz, James Willard
Apilentz
See Apelian, Albert Solomon
Apitz, Bruno 1900-1979
Obituary 85-88
Aplon, Roger 1937- 119
Apodaca, Jennifer 214
Apodaca, Rudy S(amuel) 1939- 131
See also DLB 82
See also HW 1
Apolinar, Danny 1934- 61-64
Apolito, Paolo 1947- 188
Apollinaire, Guillaume 1880-1918 152
See also Kostrowitzki, Wilhelm Apollinaris de
See also DAM POET
See also DLB 258, 321
See also EW 9
See also EWL 3
See also GFL 1789 to the Present
See also MTCW 2
See also PC 7
See also RGWL 2, 3
See also TCLC 3, 8, 51
See also TWA
See also WP
Apollonius of Rhodes
See Apollonius Rhodius
See also AW 1
See also RGWL 2, 3
Apollonius Rhodius c. 300B.C.-c. 220B.C.
See Apollonius of Rhodes
See also DLB 176
Aponte, Barbara (Ann) Bockus 1936-
Brief entry 111
Aponte, Harry J. 1935- 149
Apostle, Chris(tos) N(icholas) 1935- 21-24R
Apostolides, Marianne 196
Apostolon, Billy (Michael) 1930- 97-100
Apostolos-Cappadona, Diane 1948- . CANR-30
Earlier sketch in CA 112
Apostolou, Christine Hale 1955- . SATA 82, 128
Apostolou, John L. 1930- 127
Apostolous, Anna
See Doherty, P(aul) C.
App, Austin Joseph 1902-1984 101
Obituary 112
Appachana, Anjana 1956- CANR-99
Earlier sketch in CA 148
Appadorai, A(ngadipuram) 1902- 102
Appel, Alfred, Jr. 1934- CANR-127
Brief entry 113
Earlier sketch in CA 133
Appel, Allan 1946- CANR-110
Earlier sketch in CA 77-80
Appel, Allen (R.) 1945- 138
See also AAYA 33
See also SATA 115
Appel, Benjamin 1907-1977 .... CANR-69
Obituary 69-72
Earlier sketches in CA 13-16R, CANR-6
See also SATA 39
See also SATA-Obit 21
Appel, Frederic C. 1935(?)-1984
Obituary 112
Appel, John J. 1921- 33-36R
Appel, Kenneth Ellmaker 1896-1979
Obituary 89-92
Appel, Libby E(ve Sundel) 1937- 117
Appel, Martin E(liot) 1948- CANR-15
Earlier sketch in CA 85-88
See also SATA 45
Appel, Marty
See Appel, Martin E(liot)
Appel, Willa 1946- 117
Appel, William 1939- 114
Appelbaum, Diana Muir Karter
1953- CANR-100
Earlier sketch in CA 122
See also SATA 132
Appelbaum, Judith (Pilpel) 1939- CANR-14
Earlier sketch in CA 77-80
Interview in CANR-14
Appelbaum, Paul S(tuart) 1951- 108
Appelbaum, Stephen A(rthur) 1926- 101

Appelfeld, Aharon 1932- CANR-86
Brief entry 112
Earlier sketch in CA 133
See also CLC 23, 47
See also CWW 2
See also DLB 299
See also EWL 3
See also RGSF 2
See also SSC 42
See also WLIT 6
Appell, Don 1917(?)-1990
Obituary 131
Appell, Scott D. 1954- 201
Appelman, Hyman (Jedidiah) 1902-1983 .. 5-8R
Appelt, Kathi 1954- CANR-108
Earlier sketch in CA 150
See also SATA 83, 129
Appere, Guy 1923- CANR-41
Earlier sketch in CA 117
Apperley, Dawn 1969- SATA 135
Appiah, (Kwame) Anthony 1954- ... CANR-123
Earlier sketch in CA 140
See also BW 2
Appiah, Peggy 1921- CANR-116
Earlier sketches in CA 41-44R, CANR-53
See also CWRI 5
See also SAAS 19
See also SATA 15, 84
Appignanesi, Lisa 1946- CANR-106
Earlier sketches in CA 49-52, CANR-27, 50
See also RHW
Applbaum, Ronald L. 1943- CANR-7
Earlier sketch in CA 57-60
Apple, Hope 1942- 152
Apple, Jacki 1941- 127
Apple, Margot SATA 64, 152
See also SATA-Brief 42
Apple, Max (Isaac) 1941- CANR-54
Earlier sketches in CA 81-84, CANR-19
See also CLC 9, 33
See also DLB 130
See also SSC 50
Apple, Michael W(hitman) 1942- 109
Apple, R(aymond) W(alter), Jr. 1934- 89-92
Apple, Rima D. 1944- 147
Applebaum, Anne 1964- 149
Applebaum, Edmond L(ewis) 1924- 117
Applebaum, Samuel 1904-1986 65-68
Applebaum, Stan 1922- 85-88
See also SATA 45
Applebaum, William 1906-1979(?) CANR-6
Earlier sketch in CA 9-12R
Applebee, Arthur N(oble) 1946- CANR-57
Earlier sketches in CA 81-84, CANR-14, 31
Applebome, Peter CANR-127
Earlier sketch in CA 169
Appleby, Andrew Bell 1929-1980 108
Appleby, David P. 1925- 110
Appleby, John T. 1907-1974
Obituary 53-56
Appleby, Jon 1948- 33-36R
Appleby, Joyce Oldham 1929- CANR-97
Earlier sketches in CA 69-72, CANR-11
Appleby, Louis 1955- 146
Applegarth, Margaret Tyson 1886-1976
Obituary 69-72
Applegate, Edd
See Applegate, Edward
Applegate, Edward 1947- 174
Applegate, James (Earl) 1923- 33-36R
Applegate, K. A.
See Applegate, Katherine (Alice)
See also AAYA 37
See also BYA 14, 16
See also CLR 90
See also WYAS 1
Applegate, Katherine (Alice) 1956- . CANR-138
Earlier sketch in CA 171
See also Applegate, K. A.
See also SATA 109, 162
Applegate, Richard 1913(?)-1979
Obituary 85-88
Applegath, John 1935- 115
Appleman, John Alan 1912-1982 CANR-2
Obituary 108
Earlier sketch in CA 5-8R
Appleman, M(arjorie) H. 1928- CANR-43
Earlier sketch in CA 118
Appleman, Margie
See Appleman, M(arjorie) H.
Appleman, Mark J(erome) 1917-1989 ... 29-32R
Appleman, Philip (Dean) 1926- CANR-56
Earlier sketches in CA 13-16R, CANR-6, 29
See also CAAS 18
See also CLC 51
Appleman, Roy Edgar 1904-1993 CAP-1
Earlier sketch in CA 9-10
Appleton, Arthur 1913-1997 93-96
Appleton, George 1902-1993 126
Appleton, James Henry 1919- CANR-2
Earlier sketch in CA 5-8R
Appleton, Jane (Frances) 1934- 102
Appleton, Jay
See Appleton, James Henry
Appleton, Lawrence
See Lovecraft, H(oward) P(hillips)
Appleton, Marion Brymner 1906- 105
Appleton, Sarah 1930- 37-40R
See also CP 3
Appleton, Sheldon Lee 1933- 1-4R
Appleton, Victor CANR-27
Earlier sketches in CAP-2, CA 19-20
See also Barrett, Neal, Jr. and
Doyle, Debra and Macdonald, James D. and
Rotsler, (Charles) William and
Stratemeyer, Edward L. and Vardeman, Robert
E(dward)
See also SATA 1, 67
Appleton, Victor II CANR-27
Earlier sketch in CA 17-20R
See also Goulart, Ron(ald Joseph)
See also SATA 1, 67
Appleton, William S. 1934- 101
Appleton, William W(orthen) 1915-
Brief entry 113
Applewhite, Cynthia 89-92
Applewhite, E(dgar) J(arratt, Jr.)
1919-2005 89-92
Obituary 236
Applewhite, Harriet Branson 1940- 106
Applewhite, James W(illiam) 1935- .. CANR-50
Earlier sketches in CA 85-88, CANR-25
See also CSW
See also DLB 105
Applewhite, Philip B(oatman) 1938- 112
Appley, Lawrence A. 1904-1997 121
Appley, M(ortimer) H(erbert) 1921- 13-16R
Appleyard, Bryan (Edward) 1951- 141
Appleyard, Donald 1928-1982 CANR-4
Earlier sketch in CA 5-8R
Appleyard, Reginald Thomas 1927- 17-20R
Applezweig, M. H.
See Appley, M(ortimer) H(erbert)
Apps, Jerold W(illard) 1934- CANR-37
Earlier sketches in CA 49-52, CANR-1, 16
Apps, Jerry
See Apps, Jerold W(illard)
Appy, Christian G. 225
April, Jean-Pierre 1948- DLB 251
apRoberts, Ruth 111
Apsler, Alfred 1907-1982 CANR-3
Earlier sketch in CA 5-8R
See also SATA 10
Apstein, Theodore 1918-1998 131
Obituary 169
Apt, Bryan 1965- 183
Apt, (Jerome) Leon 1929- 53-56
Apte, Helen Jacobus 1886-1946 185
Apte, Mahadev L(akshuman) 1931- 117
Apted, M(ichael) R. 1919- 25-28R
Aptekar, Jane 1935- 81-84
Apter, David Ernest 1924- CANR-93
Earlier sketches in CA 1-4R, CANR-3
Apter, Emily (S.) 1954- 137
Apter, Michael J(ohn) 1939- 29-32R
Apter, Ronnie 1943- 194
Apter, Samson "Sam" 1905-1986 104
Apter, Shimshon
See Apter, Samson "Sam"
Apter, T(erri) E. 1949- 134
Apteryx
See Eliot, T(homas) S(tearns)
Aptheker, Bettina 1944- CANR-6
Earlier sketch in CA 29-32R
Aptheker, Herbert 1915-2003 CANR-6
Obituary 214
Earlier sketch in CA 5-8R
Interview in CANR-6
Apukhtin, Aleksei Nikolaevich
1840-1893 DLB 277
Apuleius, (Lucius Madaurensis)
125(?)-175(?) AW 2
See also CDWLB 1
See also DLB 211
See also RGWL 2, 3
See also SUFW
Aql, Sa'id 1912- EWL 3
Aquarius, Qass
See Buskirk, Richard H(obart)
Aquilano, Nicholas Joseph 1930- 112
Aquin, Hubert 1929-1977 105
See also CLC 15
See also DLB 53
See also EWL 3
Aquina, Sister Mary
See Weinrich, A(nna) K(atharina) H(ildegard)
Aquinas, Thomas 1224(?)-1274 DLB 115
See also EW 1
See also TWA
Aquino, Benigno S(imeon, Jr.) 1932-1983 .. 192
Obituary 110
Aquino, Luis Hernandez
See Hernandez Aquino, Luis
Aquino, Michael A. 1946- 209
Aquino, Ninoy
See Aquino, Benigno S(imeon, Jr.)
Arac, Jonathan 1945- 198
Arad, Yitshak 1926- 134
Arafat, Ibtihaj Said 1934- 85-88
Aragbabalu, Omidiji
See Beier, Ulli
Aragon, Louis 1897-1982 CANR-71
Obituary 108
Earlier sketches in CA 69-72, CANR-28
See also CLC 3, 22
See also DAM NOV, POET
See also DLB 72, 258
See also EW 11
See also EWL 3
See also GFL 1789 to the Present
See also GLL 2
See also LMFS 2
See also MTCW 1, 2
See also RGWL 2, 3
See also TCLC 123
Aragon, Luis Cardoza y
See Cardoza y Aragon, Luis
Aragon, Ray John de
See de Aragon, Ray John
Aragones, Sergio 1937- CANR-125
Earlier sketch in CA 122
See also AAYA 56
See also SATA 48
See also SATA-Brief 39
Arai, Masami 1953- 140
Arakawa, Yoichi 1962- CANR-122
Earlier sketch in CA 163
Araki, James T(omomasa) 1925-1991 .... 13-16R
Aralica, Ivan 1930- DLB 181
See also EWL 3
Arana, Marie 1949- 205
Arango, Jorge Sanin 1916- 61-64
Aranha, Jose (Pereira) da Graca
1868-1931 179
See also EWL 3
Aranha, Ray 1939- 180
Brief entry 112
Aranow, Edward Ross 1909-1993 41-44R
Obituary 143
Aranyos, Kakay 1847-1910
See Mikszath, Kalman
Araoz, Daniel Leon 1930- 108
Arapoff, Nancy 1930- 29-32R
Arasteh, A(bdol) Reza 1927-1992 CANR-46
Obituary 139
Earlier sketch in CA 105
Arata, Esther S(pring) 1918- 89-92
Arata, Luis O(scar) 1950- 115
Aratus of Soli c. 315B.C.-c. 240B.C. .. DLB 176
Araugo, Tess de
See De Araugo, Tess (S.)
Araujo, Frank P. 1937- CANR-87
Earlier sketch in CA 151
See also SATA 86
Arax, Mark 1956- 154
Arbasino, Alberto 1930- DLB 196
Arbatov, G. A.
See Arbatov, Georgi (Arkadevich)
Arbatov, Georgi (Arkadevich) 1923- 116
Arbatov, Yuri Arkadevich
See Arbatov, Georgi (Arkadevich)
Arbeiter, Jean S(onkin) 1937- CANR-143
Earlier sketch in CA 106
Arberry, A(rthur) J(ohn) 1905-1969 CANR-4
Earlier sketch in CA 1-4R
See also CP 1
Arbib, Robert
See Arbib, Robert S(imeon), Jr.
Arbib, Robert S(imeon), Jr.
1915-1987 CANR-80
Obituary 123
Earlier sketch in CA 33-36R
Arbingast, Stanley A(lan) 1910- CANR-10
Earlier sketch in CA 17-20R
Arbo, Cris 1950- SATA 103
Arbogast, William F. 1908-1979
Obituary 89-92
Arbuckle, Dorothy Fry 1910-1982
Obituary 108
See also SATA-Obit 33
Arbuckle, Dugald S(inclair) 1912- 13-16R
Arbuckle, Robert D(ean) 1940- 61-64
Arbuckle, W(endell) S(herwood) 1911-1987
Obituary 122
Arbuckle, Wanda Rector 1910-2000 41-44R
Arbus, Amy 1954- 127
Arbus, Diane 1923-1971 166
Arbuthnot, John 1667-1735 DLB 101
Arbuthnot, May Hill 1884-1969 9-12R
See also SATA 2
Arbuthnott, Hugh (James) 1936- 125
Arbuzov, Alexei Nikolaevich 1908-1986 . 69-72
Obituary 119
Arca, Julie Anne 1953- 111
Arcana, Judith 1943- 103
Arcand, Bernard 164
Arcand, Denys 1941- 133
Arce, Hector 1935-1980 97-100
Arce, Julio G.
See Ulica, Jorge
Arceneaux, Jean
See Ancelet, Barry Jean
Arceneaux, Thelma Hoffmann Tyler AITN 1
Arch, E. L.
See Payes, Rachel (Ruth) C(osgrove)
ar C'halan, Reun
See Galand, Rene
Archambault, John CANR-103
Earlier sketch in CA 135
See also MAICYA 1, 2
See also SATA 67, 112, 163
Archambault, Paul 1937- 81-84
Archbold, Rick 1950- CANR-144
Earlier sketch in CA 154
See also SATA 97
Archdeacon, Thomas J(ohn) 1942- 65-68
Archer, A. A.
See Joscelyn, Archie L(ynn)
Archer, Chalmers, Jr. 1938- 138
See also BW 2
Archer, Christon I(rving) 1940- 218
Archer, Dennis
See Paine, Lauran (Bosworth)
Archer, Frank
See O'Connor, Richard
Archer, Fred 1915- CANR-7
Earlier sketch in CA 57-60
Archer, Fred C. 1916(?)-1974
Obituary 53-56
Archer, Gleason Leonard, Jr. 1916- 65-68
Archer, H(orace) Richard 1911-1978 .. CANR-6
Obituary 89-92
Earlier sketch in CA 13-16R
Archer, Herbert Winslow
See Mencken, H(enry) L(ouis)
Archer, Ian W. 1960- 135
Archer, Jane (a pseudonym) 113
Archer, Jeffrey (Howard) 1940- CANR-136
Earlier sketches in CA 77-80, CANR-22, 52, 95
Interview in CANR-22
See also AAYA 16
See also BEST 89:3
See also BPFB 1
See also CLC 28
See also CPW
See also DA3
See also DAM POP
See also MTFW 2005
Archer, John H(all) 1914- 101
Archer, Jules 1915- CANR-69
Earlier sketches in CA 9-12R, CANR-6
See also CLC 12
See also SAAS 5
See also SATA 4, 85
Archer, Keith (Allan) 1955- 135
Archer, Lee
See Ellison, Harlan (Jay)
Archer, Leonie (Jane) 1955- 132
Archer, Marion Fuller 1917- 5-8R
See also SATA 11
Archer, Mildred (Agnes) 1911-2005 104
Obituary 236
Archer, Myrtle (Lilly) 1926- 102
Archer, Nathan 1958- 154
Archer, Nuala 1955- CANR-59
Earlier sketch in CA 121
Archer, Peter Kingsley 1926- CANR-2
Earlier sketch in CA 5-8R
Archer, Richard 1941- 209
Archer, Ron
See White, Theodore Edwin
Archer, S. E.
See Soderberg, Percy Measday
Archer, Sellers G. 1908-1980 17-20R
Obituary 134
Archer, Stanley (Louis) 1935- 145
Archer, Stephen H(unt) 1928- 17-20R
Archer, Stephen M(urphy) 1934- 105
Archer, W(illiam) G(eorge) 1907-1979 57-60
Obituary 125
Archer, William 1856-1924 179
Brief entry 108
See also DLB 10
Archerd, Armand 115
Brief entry 110
Archerd, Army
See Archerd, Armand
Archer Houblon, Doreen (Lindsay)
1899-1977 106
Archery, Helen
See Argers, Helen
Archibald, (Rupert) Douglas 1919- 101
Archibald, Douglas N(elson) 1933- 128
Brief entry 113
Archibald, James Montgomery 1920-1983
Obituary 110
Archibald, Joe
See Archibald, Joseph S(topford)
Archibald, John J. 1925- 5-8R
Archibald, Joseph S(topford)
1898-1986 CANR-5
Obituary 118
Earlier sketch in CA 9-12R
See also SATA 3
See also SATA-Obit 47
Archibald, Sandra O(rr) 1945- 113
Archibald, William 1924-1970
Obituary 29-32R
Archilochus c. 7th cent. B.C.- DLB 176
Archpoet, The c. 1130-(?) DLB 148
Arciniegas, German 1900-1999 CANR-29
Obituary 186
Earlier sketches in CA 61-64, CANR-10
See also HW 1
See also LAW
Arcone, Sonya 1925-1978 21-24R
Obituary 77-80
Ard, Ben N(eal), Jr. 1922- CANR-12
Earlier sketch in CA 33-36R
Ard, Patricia M. 1955- 191
Ard, William (Thomas) 1922-1960 ... CANR-72
Earlier sketch in CA 5-8R
See also Ward, Jonas
See also CMW 4
Ardagh, John 1928- CANR-50
Earlier sketch in CA 25-28R
Ardagh, Philip 1961- 229
See also SATA 154
Ardai, Charles 1969- 136
See also SATA 85
Ardalan, Nader 1939- 69-72
Arden, Barbi
See Stoutenburg, Adrien (Pearl)
Arden, Gothard Everett 1905-1978 CAP-1
Earlier sketch in CA 11-12
Arden, Harvey 190
Arden, J. E. M.
See Conquest, (George) Robert (Acworth)
Arden, Jane 61-64
See also CBD
See also CWD

Arden, John 1930- ... CANR-124
Earlier sketches in CA 13-16R, CANR-31, 65, 67
See also CAAS 4
See also BRWS 2
See also CBD
See also CD 5, 6
See also CLC 6, 13, 15
See also DAM DRAM
See also DFS 9
See also DLB 13, 245
See also EWL 3
See also MTCW 1
Arden, Judith
See Saxton, Judith
Arden, Leon 1932- ... 107
Arden, Noele
See Dambrauskas, Joan Arden
Arden, William
See Lynds, Dennis
Ardener, Edwin (William) 1927-1987 ... 5-8R
Obituary ... 123
Ardies, Tom 1931- ... CANR-59
Earlier sketch in CA 33-36R
See also CMW 4
Arditti, Rita 1934- ... 188
Ardizzone, Edward (Jeffrey Irving) 1900-1979 ... CANR-78
Obituary ... 89-92
Earlier sketches in CA 5-8R, CANR-8
See also CLR 3
See also CWRI 5
See also DLB 160
See also MAICYA 1, 2
See also SATA 1, 28
See also SATA-Obit 21
See also WCH
Ardizzone, Heidi ... 220
Ardizzone, Tony 1949- ... 85-88
Ardley, Gavin 1915- ... 129
Ardley, Neil (Richard) 1937- ... CANR-99
Earlier sketches in CA 115, CANR-39
See also SATA 43, 121
Ardmore, Jane Kesner 1915-2000 ... 5-8R
Obituary ... 189
Ardoin, John (Louis) 1935-2001 ... CANR-91
Obituary ... 195
Earlier sketch in CA 57-60
Ardrey, Robert 1908-1980 ... 33-36R
Obituary ... 93-96
See also CAD
Arecco, Vera Lustig
See Lustig-Arecco, Vera
Areeda, Phillip E. 1930-1995 ... 21-24R
Obituary ... 150
Arehart-Treichel, Joan 1942- ... CANR-6
Earlier sketch in CA 57-60
See also SATA 22
Arellanes, Audrey Spencer 1920- ... 33-36R
Arellano, Diana Ramirez de
See Ramirez de Arellano, Diana (T. Clotilde)
Arellano, Juan Estevan 1947- ... 175
See also DLB 122
See also HW 2
Arellano, Rafael W(illiam) Ramirez de
See Ramirez de Arellano, Rafael W(illiam)
Arem, Joel E(dward) 1943- ... 89-92
Arena, Felice 1968- ... 226
See also SATA 151
Arena, Jay M(orris) 1909-1996 ... 107
Arena, John I. 1929- ... CANR-20
Earlier sketch in CA 45-48
Arenas, Reinaldo 1943-1990 ... CANR-106
Obituary ... 133
Brief entry ... 124
Earlier sketches in CA 128, CANR-73
See also CLC 41
See also DAM MULT
See also DLB 145
See also EWL 3
See also GLL 2
See also HLC 1
See also HW 1
See also LAW
See also LAWS 1
See also MTCW 2
See also MTFW 2005
See also RGSF 2
See also RGWL 3
See also WLIT 1
Arends, Carolyn ... 199
Arendt, Hannah 1906-1975 ... CANR-60
Obituary ... 61-64
Earlier sketches in CA 17-20R, CANR-26
See also CLC 66, 98
See also DLB 242
See also MTCW 1, 2
Arenella, Roy 1939- ... SATA 14
Arens, Katherine (Marie) 1953- ... 164
Arens, Richard 1921-1984 ... 73-76
Obituary ... 112
Arens, William 1940- ... 89-92
Arensberg, Ann 1937- ... CANR-85
Earlier sketch in CA 114
Interview in ... CA-114
See also DLBY 1982
Arensberg, Conrad Maynadier 1910-1997 ... 61-64
Obituary ... 156
Arenson, Gloria 1935- ... 118
Arent, Arthur 1904-1972 ... CAP-2
Obituary ... 33-36R
Earlier sketch in CA 23-24
Areskoug, Kaj 1933- ... 29-32R
Arestis, Philip 1941- ... CANR-105
Earlier sketch in CA 148
Aresty, Esther B(radford) 1908(?)-2000 ... 9-12R
Obituary ... 190
Areta, Mavis
See Winder, Mavis Areta
Aretino, Pietro 1492-1556 ... RGWL 2, 3
Aretxaga, Begona
See Aretxaga, Begona
Aretxaga, Begona ... 193
Arevalo Martinez, Rafael 1884-1975 ... HW 1
Arey, James A(rthur) 1936-1988 ... 41-44R
Obituary ... 125
Arey, Leslie Brainerd 1891-1988
Obituary ... 125
Argan, Giulio Carlo 1909-1992 ... CANR-46
Obituary ... 139
Earlier sketch in CA 65-68
Argent, Kerry 1960- ... SATA 138
Argenti, John 1926- ... 115
Argenti, Philip 1891-1974
Obituary ... 49-52
Argenzio, Victor 1902-1983 ... 53-56
Argers, Helen ... 148
Argersinger, Peter H(ayes) 1944-
Brief entry ... 112
Arghezi, Tudor ... 167
See also Theodorescu, Ion N.
See also CDWLB 4
See also CLC 80
See also DLB 220
See also EWL 3
Argiri, Laura 1958- ... 163
Argiro, Larry 1909-1988 ... 5-8R
Argo, Ellen
See Johnson, Ellen Argo
Argow, Waldemar 1916-1996 ... 21-24R
Arguedas, Alcides 1879-1946 ... 178
See also EWL 3
See also HW 2
Arguedas, Jose Maria 1911-1969 ... CANR-73
Earlier sketch in CA 89-92
See also CLC 10, 18
See also DLB 113
See also EWL 3
See also HLCS 1
See also HW 1
See also LAW
See also RGWL 2, 3
See also TCLC 147
See also WLIT 1
Arguelles, Hugo 1932-2003 ... DLB 305
Arguelles, Ivan (Wallace) 1939- ... CANR-91
Earlier sketch in CA 158
See also CAAS 24
Arguelles, Jose A(nthony) 1939- ... CANR-20
Earlier sketch in CA 45-48
Arguelles, Miriam Tarcov 1943- ... 45-48
Argueta, Manlio 1936- ... CANR-73
Earlier sketch in CA 131
See also CLC 31
See also CWW 2
See also DLB 145
See also EWL 3
See also HW 1
See also RGWL 3
Arguiles, Cheryl ... 180
Argus
See Osusky, Stefan and Phillips-Birt, Douglas Hextall Chedzey
Argyle, Aubrey William 1910- ... CAP-1
Earlier sketch in CA 17-18
Argyle, Gisela 1939- ... 230
Argyle, (John) Michael 1925-2002 ... CANR-50
Obituary ... 210
Earlier sketches in CA 21-24R, CANR-9, 25
Argyris, Chris 1923- ... CANR-20
Earlier sketches in CA 1-4R, CANR-5
Arian, Alan (Asher) 1938- ... CANR-1
Earlier sketch in CA 49-52
Arian, Edward 1921- ... 33-36R
Arias, Ron(ald Francis) 1941- ... CANR-136
Earlier sketches in CA 131, CANR-81
See also DAM MULT
See also DLB 82
See also HLC 1
See also HW 1, 2
See also MTCW 2
See also MTFW 2005
Arias-Misson, Alain 1936- ... 77-80
Arias Sanchez, Oscar 1941- ... HW 1
'Arib al-Ma'muniyah 797-890 ... DLB 311
Aricha, Amos 1933- ... 162
Arico, Santo L. 1938- ... 162
Aridas, Chris 1947- ... CANR-42
Earlier sketch in CA 112
Aridjis, Homero 1940- ... CANR-123
Earlier sketch in CA 131
See also CWW 2
See also HW 1
Ariel
See Moraes, Frank Robert
Ariel, David S. 1949- ... 180
Aries, Philippe 1914-1984 ... 89-92
Obituary ... 112
Arieti, James Alexander 1948- ... 108
Arieti, Silvano 1914-1981 ... CANR-10
Obituary ... 104
Earlier sketch in CA 21-24R
Ariff, Mohamed 1942- ... 199
Arimond, Carroll 1909-1979
Obituary ... 89-92
Aring, Charles D(air) 1904-1998 ... 49-52
Arinze, Cardinal Francis
See Arinze, Francis A.
Arinze, Francis A. 1932- ... CANR-119
Earlier sketch in CA 138
Ariosto, Lodovico
See Ariosto, Ludovico
See also WLIT 7
Ariosto, Ludovico 1474-1533
See Ariosto, Lodovico
See also EW 2
See also PC 42
See also RGWL 2, 3
Aris, Michael V(aillancourt) 1946-1999 ... 182
Aris, Rutherford 1929- ... 117
Arishima Takeo 1878-1923 ... DLB 180
Arismendi, Rodney 1913-1989
Obituary ... 130
Aristide, Jean-Bertrand 1953- ... CANR-101
Earlier sketch in CA 147
Aristides
See Epstein, Joseph
Aristophanes 450B.C.-385B.C. ... AW 1
See also CDWLB 1
See also DA
See also DA3
See also DAB
See also DAC
See also DAM DRAM, MST
See also DC 2
See also DFS 10
See also DLB 176
See also LMFS 1
See also RGWL 2, 3
See also TWA
See also WLCS
Aristotle 384B.C.-322B.C. ... AW 1
See also CDWLB 1
See also DA
See also DA3
See also DAB
See also DAC
See also DAM MST
See also DLB 176
See also RGWL 2, 3
See also TWA
See also WLCS
Ariyoshi, Sawako 1931-1984 ... 105
Obituary ... 113
See also Ariyoshi Sawako and Ariyoshi Sawako
Ariyoshi, Shoichiro 1939(?)-1979
Obituary ... 89-92
Ariyoshi Sawako
See Ariyoshi, Sawako
See also EWL 3
Ariyoshi Sawako
See Ariyoshi, Sawako
See also DLB 182
Arjouni, Jakob 1964- ... 189
Arkadius
See Frosterus, Theodor Oskar
Arkadyev, N.
See Shevchenko, Arkady N(ikolaevich)
Arkell, Anthony John 1898-1980 ... 102
Obituary ... 97-100
Arkell, David 1913-1997 ... 142
Arkhurst, Frederick S(iegfried) 1920- ... CANR-25
Earlier sketch in CA 29-32R
Arkhurst, Joyce Cooper 1921- ... 17-20R
Arkin, Alan (Wolf) 1934- ... 112
Brief entry ... 110
See also SATA 59
See also SATA-Brief 32
Arkin, David 1906-1980 ... 21-24R
Arkin, Frieda 1917- ... CANR-11
Earlier sketch in CA 65-68
Arkin, Herbert 1906- ... 5-8R
Arkin, Joseph 1922- ... 5-8R
Arkin, Marcus 1926- ... 53-56
Arkley, Arthur J(ames) 1919- ... 112
Arkoun, Mohammed 1928- ... CANR-110
Earlier sketch in CA 156
Arkow, Phil 1947- ... 128
Arksey, Laura L(ee) 1936- ... 119
Arksey, Neil ... 234
See also SATA 158
Arkush, Arthur Spencer 1925-1979
Obituary ... 85-88
Arkush, Michael 1958- ... 148
Arland, Marcel 1899-1986 ... 183
See also DLB 72
Arlandson, Leone 1917- ... 29-32R
Arledge, Roone (Pinckney, Jr.) 1931-2002 ... 226
Arlen, Alice ... 169
Arlen, Leslie
See Nicole, Christopher (Robin)
Arlen, Michael 1895-1956 ... 202
Brief entry ... 120
See also DLB 36, 77, 162
See also HGG
See also RHW
Arlen, Michael J. 1930- ... CANR-13
Earlier sketch in CA 61-64
Arleo, Joseph 1933- ... 29-32R
Arley, Catherine 1935- ... CANR-2
Earlier sketch in CA 45-48
Arley, Robert
See Jackson, Mike
Arlington, Taryn
See Palmer, Randy
Arliss, Leslie 1901-1987
Obituary ... 124
Arlott, (Leslie Thomas) John 1914-1991 ... 9-12R
Obituary ... 136
Arlotto, Anthony (Thomas) 1939- ... 33-36R
Arlow, Jacob A. 1912-2004 ... 53-56
Obituary ... 227
Arlt, Roberto (Godofredo Christophersen) 1900-1942 ... CANR-67
Brief entry ... 123
Earlier sketch in CA 131
See also DAM MULT
See also DLB 305
See also EWL 3
See also HLC 1
See also HW 1, 2
See also IDTP
See also LAW
See also TCLC 29
Arluke, Arnold 1947- ... 162
Armacost, Michael Hayden 1937- ... 101
Armah, Ayi Kwei 1939- ... CANR-64
Earlier sketches in CA 61-64, CANR-21
See also AFW
See also BLC 1
See also BRWS 10
See also BW 1
See also CDWLB 3
See also CLC 5, 33, 136
See also CN 1, 2, 3, 4, 5, 6, 7
See also DAM MULT, POET
See also DLB 117
See also EWL 3
See also MTCW 1
See also WLIT 2
Armand, Louis 1905-1971 ... CAP-2
Obituary ... 33-36R
Earlier sketch in CA 29-32
Armand, Octavio Rafael 1946- ... 131
See also HW 1, 2
Armantrout, (Mary) Rae 1947- ... 179
Earlier sketches in CA 153, CANR-69
Autobiographical Essay in ... 179
See also CAAS 25
See also CP 7
See also CWP
See also DLB 193
Armas, Frederick A(lfred) de
See De Armas, Frederick A(lfred)
Armas, Jose R(afael) de
See de Armas, Jose R(afael)
Armas Marcelo, J(uan) J(esu) 1946- ... 206
Armatas, James P. 1931- ... 41-44R
Armatrading, Joan 1950- ... 186
Brief entry ... 114
See also CLC 17
Armbrister, Trevor 1933- ... 89-92
Armbruster, Ann ... 233
Armbruster, Carl J. 1929- ... 33-36R
Armbruster, F(ranz) O(wen) 1929- ... 49-52
Armbruster, Francis E(dward) 1923- ... 29-32R
Armbruster, Frank
See Armbruster, Francis E(dward)
Armbruster, Maxim Ethan 1902-1982 ... 1-4R
arme Hartmann, Der (?)-c. 1150(?) ... DLB 148
Armens, Sven 1921- ... 21-24R
Armentrout, Donald S. 1939- ... 191
Armentrout, Fred S(herman) 1946- ... 119
Armentrout, William W(infield) 1918- ... 33-36R
Armer, Alberta (Roller) 1904-1986 ... 5-8R
See also SATA 9
Armer, J(ohn) Michael 1937- ... 106
Armer, Laura Adams 1874-1963 ... 65-68
See also BYA 3
See also MAICYA 1, 2
See also SATA 13
Armerding, Carl Edwin 1936- ... 104
Armerding, George D. 1899-1986 ... 85-88
Armerding, Hudson Taylor 1918- ... CANR-11
Earlier sketch in CA 21-24R
Armes, Roy (Philip) 1937- ... CANR-13
Earlier sketch in CA 73-76
Armin, Robert 1952- ... 220
Armington, John Calvin 1923-1995 ... 53-56
Armington, R(aymond) Q(uintin) 1907-1993 ... 131
Armistead, John 1941- ... CANR-110
Earlier sketches in CA 150, CANR-81
See also SATA 130
Armistead, Samuel (Gordon) 1927- ... 53-56
Armitage, A(rthur) L(lewellyn) 1916-1984
Obituary ... 112
Armitage, Angus 1902-1976 ... CAP-1
Earlier sketch in CA 13-14
Armitage, David 1943- ... CANR-114
Earlier sketch in CA 167
See also SATA 99, 155
See also SATA-Brief 38
Armitage, E(dward) Liddall 1887- ... CAP-1
Earlier sketch in CA 9-10
Armitage, Frank
See Carpenter, John (Howard)
Armitage, G(ary) E(dric) 1956- ... CANR-113
Earlier sketch in CA 121
See also DLB 267
Armitage, Merle 1893-1975
Obituary ... 61-64
Armitage, Michael 1930- ... CANR-41
Earlier sketch in CA 117
Armitage, Ronda (Jacqueline) 1943- ... CANR-114
Earlier sketches in CA 121, CANR-47
See also CWRI 5
See also SATA 47, 99, 155
See also SATA-Brief 38
Armitage, Shelley S(ue) 1947- ... CANR-99
Earlier sketches in CA 121, CANR-47
Armitage, Simon 1963- ... CANR-91
Earlier sketch in CA 134
See also BRWS 8
See also CP 7
Armour, John
See Paine, Lauran (Bosworth)
Armour, Leslie 1931- ... 110

Armour 20 CONTEMPORARY AUTHORS

Armour, Lloyd R. 1922- 29-32R
Armour, Peter (James) 1940-2002 ..... CANR-59
Obituary 207
Earlier sketch in CA 128
Armour, Richard (Willard)
1906-1989 .... CANR-32
Obituary 128
Earlier sketches in CA 1-4R, CANR-4
See also SATA 14
See also SATA-Obit 61
Armour, Rollin Stely 1929- 33-36R
Arms, George (Warren) 1912-1992 .... 5-8R
Arms, Johnson
See Halliwell, David (William)
Arms, Suzanne 1944- 57-60
Armstrong, (Walter) Alan 1936- 73-76
Armstrong, Alexandra 1939- 142
Armstrong, Ann Seidel 1917- 9-12R
Armstrong, Anne(tte) 1924- 13-16R
Armstrong, Anthony
See Willis, (George) Anthony Armstrong
Armstrong, Anthony C.
See Armstrong, Christopher J(ohn) R(ichard)
Armstrong, (Grace) April (Oursler)
1926- 89-92
Armstrong, Arthur Hilary 1909-1997 69-72
Obituary 162
Armstrong, Benjamin Leighton 1923- 93-96
Armstrong, Brian G(ary) 1936- 69-72
Armstrong, Charles B. 1923-1985
Obituary 115
Armstrong, Charlotte 1905-1969 ...... CANR-71
Obituary 25-28R
Earlier sketches in CA 1-4R, CANR-3
See also CMW 4
Armstrong, Christopher J(ohn) R(ichard)
1935- 69-72
Armstrong, Claude Blakely 1889-1982
Obituary 108
Armstrong, D(avid) M(alet) 1926- CANR-31
Earlier sketches in CA 25-28R, CANR-11
Armstrong, (James) David 1945- 107
Armstrong, David 1946- 226
Armstrong, David M(ichael) 1944- 57-60
Armstrong, Diana 1943- 107
Armstrong, Diane (Julie) 1939- 203
Armstrong, Douglas Albert 1920- 9-12R
Armstrong, Edward Allworthy
1900-1978 .... CANR-4
Earlier sketch in CA 5-8R
Armstrong, (Annette) Elizabeth
1917-2001 .... 25-28R
Obituary 202
Armstrong, F. W.
See Wright, T(errance) M(ichael)
Armstrong, Frank III 1944(?)- 237
Armstrong, Frederick H(enry) 1926- 33-36R
Armstrong, Garner Ted 1930-2003 169
Obituary 220
Brief entry 113
Armstrong, Geoffrey
See Fearn, John Russell
Armstrong, George D. 1927- .... SATA 10
Armstrong, Gerry (Breen) 1929- 13-16R
See also SATA 10
Armstrong, Gillian (May) 1950- 173
Armstrong, Gregory T(imon) 1933- 9-12R
Armstrong, Hamilton Fish 1893-1973 93-96
Obituary 41-44R
Armstrong, Henry
See Jackson, Henry
Armstrong, Henry H.
See Arvay, Harry
Armstrong, Herbert W. 1892-1986 142
Obituary 118
Brief entry 116
Armstrong, J(on) Scott 1937- CANR-1
Earlier sketch in CA 45-48
Armstrong, (A.) James 1924- 29-32R
Armstrong, Jeannette (C.) 1948- 149
See also CCA 1
See also CN 6, 7
See also DAC
See also NNAL
See also SATA 102
Armstrong, Jennifer 1961- CANR-134
Earlier sketches in CA 145, CANR-67
See also AAYA 28
See also CLR 66
See also SAAS 24
See also SATA 77, 111
See also SATA-Essay 120
See also YAW
Armstrong, Joe C. W.
See Armstrong, Joseph Charles Woodland
Armstrong, John 1966- 224
Armstrong, John A(lexander, Jr.)
1922- CANR-3
Earlier sketch in CA 1-4R
Armstrong, John Borden 1926- 33-36R
Armstrong, John Byron 1917-1976 .... 5-8R
Obituary 65-68
Armstrong, Joseph Charles Woodland
1934- CANR-57
Earlier sketch in CA 127
Armstrong, Joseph Gravitt 1943- 101
Armstrong, Joshua 1957- 198
Armstrong, Judith Mary 1935- 102
Armstrong, Karen 1945(?)- CANR-95
Earlier sketch in CA 147
Armstrong, Keith F(rancis) W(hitfield)
1950- 29-32R
Armstrong, Kelley L. 1968- 204
Armstrong, Lance 1971- 211
Armstrong, Leslie 1940- 124
Armstrong, Lindsay 239
See also RHW
Armstrong, (Daniel) Louis 1901-1971
Obituary 29-32R
Armstrong, Louise 117
Brief entry 111
See also SATA 43
See also SATA-Brief 33
Armstrong, Luanne (A.) 1949- 233
Armstrong, Marjorie Moore 1912- 89-92
Armstrong, Martin Donisthorpe
1882-1974 179
Obituary 49-52
See also DLB 197
See also SATA 115
Armstrong, Mary (Elizabeth) Willems
1957- 134
Armstrong, Nancy 1938- 192
Armstrong, Neil (Alden) 1930- 155
Armstrong, Norman
See Toy, Barbara
Armstrong, O(rland) K(ay) 1893-1987 93-96
Obituary 122
Armstrong, (Raymond) Paul
1912-1988 .... 37-40R
Armstrong, Paul B(radford) 1949- 112
Armstrong, Richard 1903-1986 .... CANR-70
Earlier sketch in CA 77-80
See also CWRI 5
See also DLB 160
See also SATA 11
Armstrong, Richard B(yron) 1956- 134
Armstrong, Richard G. 1932- 73-76
Armstrong, Robert H(oward) 1936- 108
Armstrong, Robert L(aurence) 1926- 29-32R
Armstrong, Robert Plant 1919-1984 ...... 41-44R
Obituary 113
Armstrong, Roger D. 1939- 17-20R
Armstrong, Ruth Gallup 1891-1972 ...... CAP-1
Earlier sketch in CA 9-10
Armstrong, Sally (Wishart) 1943- 221
Armstrong, (Russell) Scott 1945- 108
Interview in CA-108
Armstrong, Terence Ian Fytton
1912-1970 .... CAP-2
Obituary 29-32R
Earlier sketch in CA 17-18
See also Gawsworth, John
Armstrong, Thomas 1899-1978 .... 5-8R
Obituary 103
Armstrong, Tilly 1927- CANR-47
Earlier sketches in CA 107, CANR-23
See also RHW
Armstrong, Wallace Edwin 1896-1980
Obituary 97-100
Armstrong, Warren B(ruce) 1933-2004 185
Obituary 232
Armstrong, William A(lexander)
1912-1997 .... 13-16R
Armstrong, William A(rthur) 1915- 17-20R
Armstrong, William H(oward)
1914-1999 .... CANR-104
Obituary 177
Earlier sketches in CA 17-20R, CANR-9, 69
See also AAYA 18
See also AITN 1
See also BYA 3
See also CLR 1
See also JRDA
See also MAICYA 1, 2
See also SAAS 7
See also SATA 4
See also SATA-Obit 111
See also YAW
Armstrong, William M(artin) 1919- 49-52
Armstrong-Ellis, Carey (Fraser) 1956- . SATA 145
Armstrong-Jones, Antony (Charles Robert)
1930- CANR-43
Earlier sketch in CA 118
Armstrong Jones, Tony
See Armstrong-Jones, Antony (Charles Robert)
Armytage, R.
See Watson, Rosamund Marriott
Armytage, Walter Harry Green
1915-1998 .... 9-12R
Obituary 181
Arnade, Charles W(olfgang) 1927- 33-36R
Arnandez, Richard 1912- CANR-6
Earlier sketch in CA 13-16R
Arnason, David 1940- 114
Arnason, Eleanor (Atwood) 1942- 156
See also FANT
See also SFW 4
Arnason, H(jorvardur) H(arvard)
1909-1986 .... CANR-13
Obituary 119
Earlier sketch in CA 61-64
Arnau, Frank
See Schmitt, Heinrich
Arnaud, Claude 1955- 143
Arnaud, Georges
See Girard, Henri Georges Charles Achille
Arnauld, Antoine 1612-1694 .... DLB 268
Arnaz, Desi
See Arnaz y de Acha, Desiderio Alberto III
Arnaz y de Acha, Desiderio Alberto III
1917(?)-1986
Obituary 121
Brief entry 114
Arncliffe, Andrew
See Walker, Peter N.
Arndottir, Nina Bjork 1941-2000 .... DLB 293
Arndt, Elise 1943- 116
Arndt, Ernst H(einrich) D(aniel) 1899- ... CAP-2
Earlier sketch in CA 23-24
Arndt, Ernst Moritz 1769-1860 .... DLB 90
Arndt, H(einz) W(olfgang) 1915- CANR-29
Earlier sketches in CA 21-24R, CANR-10
Arndt, Karl John Richard
1903-1991 .... CANR-23
Earlier sketches in CA 17-20R, CANR-7
Arndt, Ursula (Martha H.) .... SATA 56
See also SATA-Brief 39
Arndt, Walter W(erner) 1916- CANR-5
Earlier sketch in CA 13-16R
Arnebeck, Bob 1947- 108
Arner, Sivar
See Arner, (Ernst Nils) Sivar (Erik)
Arner, (Ernst Nils) Sivar (Erik)
1909(?)-1997 .... EWL 3
Arneson, D(on) J(on) 1935- 106
See also SATA 37
Arnett, Caroline
See Cole, Lois Dwight
Arnett, Carroll 1927-1997 .... CANR-93
Earlier sketches in CA 21-24R, CANR-11
Arnett, Harold E(dward) 1931- CANR-8
Earlier sketch in CA 21-24R
Arnett, Jack
See Goulart, Ron(ald Joseph)
Arnett, Peter (Gregg) 1934- 152
Arnett, Ronald C. 1952- 144
Arnett, Ross H(arold), Jr. 1919-1999 . CANR-17
Earlier sketches in CA 49-52, CANR-2
Arnette, Robert
See Silverberg, Robert
Arney, James
See Russell, Martin
Arney, William Ray 1950- CANR-43
Earlier sketch in CA 110
Arnez, Nancy Levi 1928- 29-32R
Arnheim, Daniel D(avid) 1930- CANR-5
Earlier sketch in CA 9-12R
Arnheim, Rudolf 1904- CANR-69
Earlier sketches in CA 1-4R, CANR-3
Arniches (y Barrera), Carlos (Jorge German)
1866-1943 .... EWL 3
Arnim, Achim von (Ludwig Joachim von Arnim)
1781-1831 .... DLB 90
See also SSC 29
Arnim, Bettina von 1785-1859 .... DLB 90
See also RGWL 2, 3
Arno, Enrico 1913-1981 .... SATA 43
See also SATA-Obit 28
Arno, Peter 1904-1968 73-76
Obituary 25-28R
Arno, Stephen F. 1943- 230
Arnold, A(lbert) James, (Jr.) 1939- 132
Arnold, Adlai F(ranklin) 1914-1992 .... 33-36R
Arnold, Alan 1922- 5-8R
Arnold, Alvin L(incoln) 1929- 93-96
Arnold, Anthony 1928- 111
Arnold, Armin H. 1931- CANR-18
Earlier sketches in CA 9-12R, CANR-3
Arnold, Arnold (Ferdinand) 1921- CANR-44
Earlier sketches in CA 17-20R, CANR-10, 27
Arnold, Benjamin 1943- 144
Arnold, Bob 1952- 185
Earlier sketches in CA 105, CANR-21
Autobiographical Essay in 185
See also CAAS 25
Arnold, Bruce 1936- 93-96
See also TCLE 1:1
Arnold, Bruce (Edward) 1955- 177
Arnold, Carl
See Raknes, Ola
Arnold, Caroline 1944- CANR-137
Earlier sketches in CA 107, CANR-24
See also CLR 61
See also SAAS 23
See also SATA 36, 85, 131
See also SATA-Brief 34
Arnold, Carroll C(lyde) 1912-1997 184
Brief entry 116
Arnold, Catharine 1959- 125
Arnold, Charles Harvey 1920- 65-68
Arnold, Charlotte E(lizabeth) Cramer
-2001 57-60
Obituary 198
Arnold, Corliss Richard 1926- 49-52
Arnold, Denis Midgley 1926-1986 ...... CANR-2
Obituary 119
Earlier sketch in CA 5-8R
Arnold, Duane W(ade-) H(ampton) 1953- .. 127
Arnold, Eberhard 1883-1935 204
Arnold, Ed N. 1952- 228
Arnold, Edmund C(larence) 1913- CANR-3
Earlier sketch in CA 1-4R
Arnold, Edwin 1832-1904 209
See also DLB 35
Arnold, Edwin L(ester Linden)
1857(?)-1935 154
Brief entry 109
See also DLB 178
See also FANT
See also SFW 4
Arnold, Edwin T. 1947- 134
Arnold, Eleanor 1929- 143
Arnold, Elliott 1912-1980 .... CANR-65
Obituary 97-100
Earlier sketches in CA 17-20R, CANR-24
See also SATA 5
See also SATA-Obit 22
See also TCWW 1, 2
Arnold, Elsie 1925- 236
Arnold, Emily 1939- CANR-103
Earlier sketch in CA 109, 180
See also McCully, Emily Arnold
See also CWRI 5
See also MAICYA 1, 2
See also MAICYAS 1
See also SATA 50, 76
Arnold, Emmy (von Hollander)
1884-1980 .... CANR-9
Earlier sketch in CA 21-24R
Arnold, Eve 1913- CANR-125
Earlier sketches in CA 112, CANR-31, 52
Arnold, Francena H(arriet Long)
1888-1972 .... CAP-1
Earlier sketch in CA 17-18
Arnold, G. L.
See Lichtheim, George
Arnold, Gary Howard 1942-
Brief entry 117
Arnold, Gladys (M.) 1905- 128
Arnold, Guy 1932- CANR-53
Earlier sketches in CA 25-28R, CANR-11, 28
Arnold, H(arry) J(ohn) P(hilip) 1932- .. CANR-2
Earlier sketch in CA 5-8R
Arnold, Heini
See Arnold, Johann Heinrich
Arnold, Herbert 1935- 37-40R
Arnold, Janet 1932-1998 .... CANR-93
Obituary 172
Earlier sketch in CA 93-96
Arnold, Janis 160
Arnold, Johann Christoph 1940- 189
Arnold, Johann Heinrich 1913-1982 122
Obituary 111
Arnold, John D(avid) 1933- 111
Arnold, Joseph H.
See Hayes, Joseph
Arnold, June (Davis) 1926-1982 .... CANR-58
Obituary 133
Earlier sketch in CA 21-24R
See also FW
Arnold, Katya 1947- 186
See also SATA 82, 115
Arnold, Kenneth L. 1957- 148
Arnold, L. J.
See Cameron, Lou
Arnold, Leslie
See Lazarus, A(rnold) L(eslie)
Arnold, Lloyd R. 1906-1970 .... CAP-2
Earlier sketch in CA 25-28
Arnold, Lois B(arber) 107
Arnold, Madelyn M. a pseudonym 1948- ... 129
Arnold, Magda B(londiau) 1903- 5-8R
Arnold, Malcolm 1921- .... IDFW 3, 4
Arnold, Margot
See Cook, Petronelle Marguerite Mary
Arnold, Marilyn 1935- CANR-144
Earlier sketch in CA 122
Arnold, Marsha Diane 1948- CANR-121
Earlier sketch in CA 158
See also SATA 93, 147
Arnold, Mary Ann 1918- 65-68
Arnold, Matthew 1822-1888 .... BRW 5
See also CDBLB 1832-1890
See also DA
See also DAB
See also DAC
See also DAM MST, POET
See also DLB 32, 57
See also EXPP
See also PAB
See also PC 5
See also PFS 2
See also TEA
See also WLC
See also WP
Arnold, Milo Lawrence 1903-1987 57-60
Arnold, Nick 1961- 185
See also SATA 113
Arnold, Olga Moore 1900-1981
Obituary 102
Arnold, Oren 1900-1980 .... CANR-2
Earlier sketch in CA 5-8R
See also SATA 4
Arnold, Pauline 1894-1974 .... CANR-2
Earlier sketch in CA 1-4R
Arnold, Peter 1931- 123
Arnold, Peter 1943- CANR-1
Earlier sketch in CA 49-52
Arnold, R. Douglas 1950- 101
Arnold, Ray Henry 1895-1973 .... 5-8R
Arnold, Richard 1912- CANR-3
Earlier sketch in CA 9-12R
Arnold, Richard E(ugene) 1908- CAP-2
Earlier sketch in CA 33-36
Arnold, Richard K(lein) 1923- 69-72
Arnold, Robert E(vans) 1932- 49-52
Arnold, Rollo (Davis) 1926-1998 .... 21-24R
Arnold, Ron 1937- CANR-25
Earlier sketch in CA 108
Arnold, Roseanne 1952- 139
See also BEST 90:1
Arnold, Stephen H. 1942- 117
Arnold, Susan (Riser) 1951- .... SATA 58
Arnold, Tedd 1949- 137
See also SATA 69, 116, 160
Arnold, Terrell E. 1925- 130
Arnold, Thomas 1795-1842 .... DLB 55
Arnold, Thurman Wesley 1891-1969 .... CAP-1
Earlier sketch in CA 13-16
Arnold, Tom 1959- 218
Arnold, William Robert 1933- 29-32R
Arnold, William Van 1941- 110
Arnold-Baker, Charles 1918- 5-8R
Arnold-Forster, Mark 1920-1981 65-68
Obituary 105
Arnoldi, Katie 1959- 200
Arnoldy, Julie
See Bischoff, Julia Bristol
Arnosky, James Edward 1946- CANR-126
Earlier sketches in CA 69-72, CANR-12, 32
See also Arnosky, Jim
See also CLR 15, 93
See also SATA 22, 160

Cumulative Index 21 **Ascher**

Arnosky, Jim
  See Arnosky, James Edward
  See also CLR 93
  See also MAICYA 1, 2
  See also SATA 70, 118
Arnot, Bob
  See Arnot, Robert (Burns)
Arnot, Robert (Burns) 1947(?)- 238
Arnote, Ralph 1926-1998 170
Arnothy, Christine 1930- CANR-10
  Earlier sketch in CA 65-68
Arnott, (Margaret) Anne 1916- CANR-13
  Earlier sketch in CA 73-76
Arnott, J(ames) F(ullarton) 1914-1982
  Obituary 108
Arnott, Kathleen 1914- 57-60
  See also SATA 20
Arnott, Peter 1962- 217
  See also DLB 233
Arnott, Peter D(ouglas) 1931- CANR-3
  Earlier sketch in CA 1-4R
Arnoux, Alexandre (Paul) 1884-1973
  Obituary 37-40R
Arnov, Boris, Jr. 1926- CANR-3
  Earlier sketch in CA 1-4R
  See also SATA 12
Arnove, Robert Fred 1937- 111
Arnow, Harriette (Louisa) Simpson
  1908-1986 .... CANR-14
  Obituary 118
  Earlier sketch in CA 9-12R
  See also BPFB 1
  See also CLC 2, 7, 18
  See also CN 2, 3, 4
  See also DLB 6
  See also FW
  See also MTCW 1, 2
  See also RHW
  See also SATA 42
  See also SATA-Obit 47
Arnow, L(eslie) Earle 1909- 69-72
Arnsteen, Katy Keck 1934- 136
  See also SATA 68
Arnstein, Flora Jacobi 1885-1990 .... 5-8R
Arnstein, Helene S(olomon) 1915- 57-60
  See also SATA 12
Arnstein, Walter L(eonard) 1930- CANR-46
  Earlier sketches in CA 13-16R, CANR-5, 23
Arntson, Herbert E(dward) 1911-1982 ... 17-20R
  See also SATA 12
Arny, Mary (Travis) 1909-1997 61-64
Arny, Thomas Travis 1940- 85-88
Arnzen, Michael A. 1967- 175
Arocena, Felipe 1963- 238
Arom, Simha 1930- 139
Aron, Cindy S(ondik) 1945- 223
Aron, Jean-Paul 1925(?)-1988
  Obituary 126
Aron, Leon (Rabinovich) 1954- 197
Aron, Michael 1946- 146
Aron, Raymond (Claude Ferdinand)
  1905-1983 .... CANR-82
  Obituary 111
  Earlier sketches in CA 49-52, CANR-2
Aron, Robert 1898-1975 93-96
  Obituary 57-60
Arond, Miriam 1955- 127
Aroner, Miriam 149
  See also SATA 82
Aronfreed, Justin 1930- 25-28R
Aronie, Nancy S(lonim) 1941- 176
Aronin, Ben 1904-1980
  Obituary 102
  See also SATA-Obit 25
Aronoff, Craig E(llis) 1951- 145
Aronoff, Myron J(oel) 1940- CANR-24
  Earlier sketch in CA 107
Aronowitz, Stanley 1933- CANR-100
  Earlier sketch in CA 131
Arons, Arnold B. 1916- 162
Aronson, Alex 1912- 45-48
Aronson, Alvin 1928- 25-28R
Aronson, David 1894-1988
  Obituary 126
Aronson, Elliot 1932- CANR-12
  Earlier sketch in CA 33-36R
Aronson, Harvey 1929- 85-88
Aronson, I(rwin) Michael 1942- 137
Aronson, J(ay) Richard 1937- CANR-86
  Earlier sketches in CA 81-84, CANR-34
Aronson, James (Allan) 1915-1988 ... CANR-80
  Obituary 126
  Earlier sketch in CA 29-32R
Aronson, Joseph 1898-1976 .... CAP-1
  Earlier sketch in CA 19-20
Aronson, Marc 1948- CANR-137
  Earlier sketch in CA 196
  See also AAYA 67
  See also MAICYA 2
  See also MTFW 2005
  See also SATA 126
Aronson, Marvin L. 1925- 41-44R
Aronson, Ronald 1938- 133
Aronson, Shlomo 1936- 73-76
Aronson, Steven M. L. 153
Aronson, Theo(dore Ian Wilson)
  1930-2003 .... CANR-25
  Obituary 216
  Earlier sketches in CA 9-12R, CANR-4
Aronson, Virginia 1954- CANR-100
  Earlier sketches in CA 108, CANR-25
  See also SATA 122
Arora, Shirley (Lease) 1930- 1-4R
  See also SATA 2
Aros, Andrew A(lexandre) 1944- 97-100
Arouet, Francois-Marie
  See Voltaire
Arout, Gabriel 1909-1982
  Obituary 106
Aroutunova, Bayara 1926- 152
Arozarena, Marcelino 1912- .... HW 1
Arp, Bill
  See Smith, Charles Henry
Arp, Hans
  See Arp, Jean
Arp, Jean 1887-1966 .... CANR-77
  Obituary 25-28R
  Earlier sketches in CA 81-84, CANR-42
  See also CLC 5
  See also EW 10
  See also TCLC 115
Arpad, Joseph J(ohn) 1937- 49-52
Arpel, Adrien
  See Newman, Adrien Ann
Arpino, Giovanni 1927-1987 199
  See also DLB 177
Arps, Louisa Ward 1901-1986
  Obituary 118
Arquette, Cliff(ord) 1905-1974
  Obituary 53-56
Arquilla, John 209
Arrabal
  See Arrabal, Fernando
Arrabal (Teran), Fernando
  See Arrabal, Fernando
  See also CWW 2
Arrabal, Fernando 1932- CANR-15
  Earlier sketch in CA 9-12R
  See also Arrabal (Teran), Fernando
  See also CLC 2, 9, 18, 58
  See also DLB 321
  See also EWL 3
  See also LMFS 2
Arre, Helen
  See Ross, Zola Helen
Arre, John
  See Holt, John (Robert)
Arrebo, Anders 1587-1637 .... DLB 300
Arreola, Juan Jose 1918-2001 .... CANR-81
  Obituary 200
  Brief entry 113
  Earlier sketch in CA 131
  See also CLC 147
  See also CWW 2
  See also DAM MULT
  See also DLB 113
  See also DNFS 2
  See also EWL 3
  See also HLC 1
  See also HW 1, 2
  See also LAW
  See also RGSF 2
  See also SSC 38
Arrian c. 89(?)-c. 155(?) .... DLB 176
Arrick, Fran
  See Gaberman, Judie Angell
  See also BYA 6
  See also CLC 30
Arrigan, Mary 1943- 213
  See also SATA 142
Arrighi, Mel 1933-1986 .... CANR-18
  Obituary 120
  Earlier sketches in CA 49-52, CANR-1
Arrillaga, Maria
  See Arrillaga, Maria
Arrillaga, Maria 1940- 190
Arrington, Leonard J(ames)
  1917-1999 .... CANR-30
  Obituary 177
  Earlier sketches in CA 17-20R, CANR-9
Arrington, Stephen L(ee) 1948- 163
  See also SATA 97
Arriola, Gus 1917- 129
Arrizon, Alicia 210
Arrley, Richmond
  See Delany, Samuel R(ay), Jr.
Arrow, Kenneth J(oseph) 1921- CANR-13
  Earlier sketch in CA 13-16R
Arrow, William
  See Rotsler, (Charles) William
Arroway, Francis M.
  See Rosmond, Babette
Arrowood, (McKendrick Lee) Clinton
  1939- .... SATA 19
Arrowsmith, Marvin Lawrence 1913-1995
  Obituary 150
  Brief entry 116
Arrowsmith, Pat 1930- 101
  See also Barton, Pat
Arrowsmith, William Ayres
  1924-1992 .... CANR-79
  Obituary 136
  Earlier sketches in CA 9-12R, CANR-4
Arroyo, Antonio M. Stevens
  See Stevens-Arroyo, Antonio M.
Arroyo, Stephen J(oseph) 1946- 61-64
Arrufat, Anton B. 1935- .... DLB 305
  See also HW 1
Arscott, David 174
  See also FANT 1
Arseniev, Vladimir K(lavdievich)
  1872-1930 218
Arsiennieva, Natalla 1903- .... EWL 3
Art, Robert (Jeffrey) 1942- 65-68
Artaud, Antonin (Marie Joseph)
  1896-1948 149
  Brief entry 104
  See also DA3
  See also DAM DRAM
  See also DC 14
  See also DFS 22
  See also DLB 258, 321
  See also EW 11
  See also EWL 3
  See also GFL 1789 to the Present
  See also MTCW 2
  See also MTFW 2005
  See also RGWL 2, 3
  See also TCLC 3, 36
Arteaga, Alfred 1950- 163
  See also HW 2
Arteaga, Lucio 1924- 49-52
Arteaga, William De
  See De Arteaga, William
Artel, Jorge 1909-1994 .... DLB 283
  See also HW 1
Artell, Mike 1948- CANR-113
  Earlier sketch in CA 155
  See also SATA 89, 134
Arter, David 201
Arterburn, Stephen (Forrest) 1953- 147
Artes, Dorothy Beecher 1919- 57-60
Arther, Richard O. 1928- 17-20R
Arthos, John 1908-2000 .... 9-12R
Arthur, Alan
  See Edmonds, Arthur Denis
Arthur, Anthony 1937- 119
Arthur, Art(hur) 1911-1985
  Obituary 116
Arthur, Burt
  See Shappiro, Herbert (Arthur)
  See also TCWW 1, 2
Arthur, C. J.
  See Arthur, Chris
Arthur, Chris 1955- 211
Arthur, Don(ald) R(amsay) 1917-1984 ... 29-32R
  Obituary 114
Arthur, Elizabeth 1953- CANR-90
  Earlier sketches in CA 105, CANR-21
Arthur, Eric (Ross) 1898-1982
  Obituary 112
Arthur, Frank
  See Ebert, Arthur Frank
Arthur, George
  See Phillips, Bluebell Stewart
Arthur, Gladys
  See Osborne, Dorothy (Gladys) Yeo
Arthur, Herbert
  See Shappiro, Herbert (Arthur)
Arthur, Hugh
  See Christie-Murray, David (Hugh Arthur)
Arthur, Karl 1952- 181
Arthur, Kay L(ee) 1933- CANR-42
  Earlier sketch in CA 118
Arthur, Lee 122
Arthur, Lowell J. 1951- 191
Arthur, Martin (Forest) 1951- 116
Arthur, Max 1939- 121
Arthur, Percy E. 1910-1988 .... CAP-1
  Earlier sketch in CA 9-10
Arthur, Robert, (Jr.) 1909-1969 188
  See also Arthur, Robert (Andrew)
  See also SATA 118
Arthur, Robert (Andrew) 1909-1969
  See Arthur, Robert, (Jr.)
  See also HGG
Arthur, Ruth M(abel) 1905-1979 .... CANR-4
  Obituary 85-88
  Earlier sketch in CA 9-12R
  See also CLC 12
  See also CWRI 5
  See also SATA 7, 26
Arthur, T. S.
  See Arthur, Timothy Shay
  See also DLB 42, 250
  See also DLBD 13
Arthur, Thomas H. 1937- 122
Arthur, Tiffany
  See Pelton, Robert W(ayne)
Arthur, Timothy Shay 1809-1885
  See Arthur, T. S.
  See also DLB 3, 79
  See also RGAL 4
Arthur, Tom
  See Arthur, Thomas H.
Arthur, William
  See Neubauer, William Arthur
Arthurs, Peter 1933- 106
Arthus-Bertrand, Yann 1946- 212
Artin, Thomas 1938- 180
  Brief entry 116
Artin, Tom
  See Artin, Thomas
Artis, Vicki Kimmel 1945- 53-56
  See also SATA 12
Artmann, H(ans) C(arl) 1921-2000 101
  See also DLB 85
  See also EWL 3
Artobolevsky, Ivan I. 1905-1977
  Obituary 73-76
Artom, Guido 1906-1982 .... CANR-12
  Earlier sketch in CA 29-32R
Arts, Herwig (W. J.) 1935- CANR-32
  Earlier sketch in CA 113
Artsybashev, Mikhail (Petrovich)
  1878-1927 170
  See also DLB 295
  See also TCLC 31
Artus, Nancy
  See Dargel, Nancy
Artz, Frederick B(inkerd)
  1894-1983 .... CANR-18
  Earlier sketch in CA 1-4R
Artzybasheff, Boris (Miklailovich)
  1899-1965 .... SATA 14
Aruego, Ariane
  See Dewey, Ariane
Aruego, Jose (Espiritu) 1932- CANR-105
  Earlier sketches in CA 37-40R, CANR-42
  See also CLR 5
  See also MAICYA 1, 2
  See also SATA 6, 68, 125
Arundale, G. S.
  See Arundale, George S(ydney)
Arundale, George S(ydney) 1878-1945
  Brief entry 119
Arundel, Honor (Morfydd) 1919-1973 .. CAP-2
  Obituary 41-44R
  Earlier sketch in CA 21-22
  See also CLC 17
  See also CLR 35
  See also CWRI 5
  See also SATA 4
  See also SATA-Obit 24
Arundel, Jocelyn
  See Alexander, Jocelyn Anne Arundel
Arundel, Russell M. 1903-1978
  Obituary 77-80
Arundell, Dennis Drew 1898-1988
  Obituary 127
Aruri, Naseer H. 1934- CANR-135
  Earlier sketch in CA 161
Arvay, Harry 1925- CANR-8
  Earlier sketch in CA 57-60
Arvay, Stephen 1937- 114
Arvensis, Alauda
  See Furdyna, Anna M.
Arvey, Michael 1948- 147
  See also SATA 79
Arvey, Verna 1910-1987 157
Arvigo, Rosita 1941- 232
Arvill, Robert
  See Boote, Robert Edward
Arvin, Kay K(rehbiel) 1922- 65-68
Arvin, (Frederic) Newton, (Jr.) 1900-1963 ... 177
  Obituary 116
  See also DLB 103
Arvin, Nick 236
Arvin, Reed 233
Arvio, Raymond Paavo 1930-1986 77-80
  Obituary 120
Arvio, Sarah 1954- 213
  See also PFS 21
Ary, Donald E(ugene) 1930- 41-44R
Ary, Sheila M(ary Littleboy) 1929- 13-16R
Arya, Usharbudh 1934- 105
Arzhak, Nikolai
  See Daniel, Yuli (Markovich)
Arzner, Dorothy 1900-1979 .... CLC 98
Arzoomanian, Raffi
  See Arzoomanian, Ralph Sarkis
Arzoomanian, Ralph Sarkis 1937- 118
Arzt, Max 1897-1975
  Obituary 61-64
Asalache, Khadambi .... CP 1
Asals, Frederick (John) 1935- 124
Asamani, Joseph Owusu 1934- 49-52
Asante, Molefi Kete 1942- CANR-126
  Earlier sketches in CA 33-36R, CANR-21
  See also BW 2
Asare, Bediako
  See Konadu, S(amuel) A(sare)
Asare, Meshack (Yaw) 1945- CANR-118
  Earlier sketches in CA 61-64, CANR-11, 52
  See also CWRI 5
  See also SATA 86, 139
Asaro, Catherine (Ann) 1955- CANR-116
  Earlier sketch in CA 161
  See also AAYA 47
  See also SATA 101
Asay, Donna Day 1945- .... SATA 127
Asayesh, Gelareh 1962- 189
Asbell, Bernard 1923-2001 .... CANR-50
  Obituary 193
  Earlier sketches in CA 45-48, CANR-1, 25
Asbjornsen, Peter Christen
  1812-1885 .... MAICYA 1, 2
  See also SATA 15
  See also WCH
Asbury, Herbert 1891-1963
  Obituary 116
Ascani, Sparky (Wilson) 1922- 111
Ascanio, Pam 1950- 142
Ascasubi, Hilario 1807-1875 .... LAW
Asch, Frank 1946- CANR-128
  Earlier sketch in CA 41-44R
  See also CWRI 5
  See also SATA 5, 66, 102, 154
Asch, Nathan 1902-1964 109
  See also DLB 4, 28
Asch, Peter 1937-1990 133
  Brief entry 114
Asch, Sholem 1880-1957
  Brief entry 105
  See also EWL 3
  See also GLL 2
  See also TCLC 3
Ascham, Roger 1516(?)-1568 .... DLB 236
Aschan, Ulf 1937- 138
Ascheim, Skip 1943- 53-56
Aschenbrenner, Joyce 1931- 219
Ascher, Abraham 1928- CANR-123
  Earlier sketch in CA 81-84
Ascher, Barbara Lazear 1946(?)- 138
  Brief entry 130
  Interview in CA-138

Ascher, Carol 1941- ... CANR-29
Earlier sketch in CA 105
Ascher, Kate (J.) 1958- ... 128
Ascher, Marcia 1935- ... 231
Ascher, Maria Louise ... 140
Ascher, Sheila ... CANR-23
Earlier sketch in CA 105
Ascher/Straus
See Ascher, Sheila and Straus, Dennis
Ascher, William (Louis) 1947- ... 114
Ascherson, (Charles) Neal 1932- ... CANR-140
Earlier sketches in CA 13-16R, CANR-57
Aschmann, Alberta 1921- ... CANR-7
Earlier sketch in CA 13-16R
Aschmann, Helen Tann ... 13-16R
Ascoli, Max 1898-1978
Obituary ... 77-80
Aseev, Nikolai Nikolaevich
1889-1963 ... DLB 295
Asen, Robert 1968- ... 210
Ash, Anthony Lee 1931- ... CANR-3
Earlier sketch in CA 49-52
Ash, Bernard 1910- ... CAP-1
Earlier sketch in CA 19-20
Ash, Brian 1936-
Brief entry ... 114
Ash, Christopher (Edward) 1914- ... 1-4R
Ash, Constance (Lee) 1950- ... 154
See also FANT
Ash, David W(ilfred) 1923- ... 9-12R
Ash, Douglas 1914- ... CANR-2
Earlier sketch in CA 5-8R
Ash, Fenton
See Atkins, Francis Henry
Ash, J(ohn) S(idney) 1925- ... 179
Ash, Jennifer 1964- ... 149
Ash, John 1948- ... CANR-77
Brief entry ... 123
Earlier sketch in CA 127
Interview in ... CA-127
See also CP 4, 5, 6, 7
See also DLB 40
Ash, Jutta 1942- ... SATA 38
Ash, Lee (Michael) 1917- ... 110
Ash, Mary Kay (Wagner) 1971(?)-2001 ... 112
Obituary ... 204
Ash, Maurice Anthony 1917-2003 ... 101
Obituary ... 212
Ash, Rene Lee 1939- ... 57-60
Ash, Roberta
See Garner, Roberta
Ash, Sarah Leeds 1904-1994 ... CAP-1
Earlier sketch in CA 9-10
Ash, Shalom
See Asch, Sholem
Ash, Stephen V. 1948- ... CANR-141
Earlier sketch in CA 153
Ash, Timothy Garton
See Garton Ash, Timothy
Ash, William Franklin 1917- ... CANR-18
Earlier sketches in CA 5-8R, CANR-2
Ashabranner, Brent (Kenneth)
1921- ... CANR-110
Earlier sketches in CA 5-8R, CANR-10, 27, 57
See also AAYA 6, 46
See also BYA 1
See also CLR 28
See also JRDA
See also MAICYA 1, 2
See also SAAS 14
See also SATA 1, 67, 130
See also YAW
Ashabranner, Melissa 1950- ... 134
Ashall, Frank 1957- ... 146
Ashbaugh, Nancy 1929- ... 73-76
Ashbee, C(harles) R(obert) 1863-1942 ... 209
Ashbee, Paul 1918- ... 93-96
Ashbery, John (Lawrence) 1927- ... CANR-132
Earlier sketches in CA 5-8R, CANR-9, 37, 66, 102
Interview in ... CANR-9
See also Berry, Jonas
See also AMWS 3
See also CLC 2, 3, 4, 6, 9, 13, 15, 25, 41, 77, 125
See also CP 1, 2, 3, 4, 5, 6, 7
See also DA3
See also DAM POET
See also DLB 5, 165
See also DLBY 1981
See also EWL 3
See also MAL 5
See also MTCW 1, 2
See also MTFW 2005
See also PAB
See also PC 26
See also PFS 11
See also RGAL 4
See also TCLE 1:1
See also WP
Ashbless, William
See Powers, Tim(othy Thomas)
Ashbolt, Allan Campbell 1921- ... 104
Ashbridge, Elizabeth 1713-1755 ... DLB 200
Ashbrook, James B(arbour)
1925-1999 ... CANR-118
Earlier sketches in CA 37-40R, CANR-14, 31, 57
Ashbrook, Joseph 1918-1980 ... 122
Obituary ... 117
Ashbrook, William (Sinclair) 1922- ... 29-32R
Ashburne, Jim G. 1912-1996 ... 1-4R
Ashburnham, Bertram Lord
1797-1878 ... DLB 184
Ashby, Carter
See Paine, Lauran (Bosworth)
Ashby, Cliff 1919- ... 25-28R
See also CAAS 6
Ashby, Eric 1904-1992 ... 61-64
Obituary ... 139
Ashby, Franklin C. 1954- ... 227
Ashby, Gil 1958- ... SATA 146
Ashby, Godfrey W. 1930- ... 170
Ashby, Gwynneth 1922- ... 25-28R
See also SATA 44
Ashby, LaVerne 1922- ... 21-24R
Ashby, (Darrel) LeRoy 1938- ... 33-36R
Ashby, Lloyd W. 1905-1992 ... 89-92
Ashby, Lynn 1938- ... 127
Ashby, Neal 1924-1986 ... 89-92
Ashby, Nora
See Africano, Lillian
Ashby, Philip Harrison 1916- ... 17-20R
Ashby, Yvonne 1955- ... SATA 121
Ashcom, Robert L. 1940- ... 188
Ashcraft, Allan Coleman 1928-1990 ... 9-12R
Ashcraft, Laura 1945- ... 107
Ashcraft, Laurie
See Ashcraft, Laura
Ashcraft, Morris 1922- ... 45-48
Ashcraft, W. Michael 1955- ... 237
Ashcroft, John (David) 1942- ... 112
Ashdown, Clifford
See Freeman, R(ichard) Austin
Ashdown, Dulcie M(argaret) 1946- ... 122
Brief entry ... 112
Ashdown, Paul G(eorge) 1944- ... 119
Ashe, Arthur (Robert, Jr.)
1943-1993 ... CANR-42
Earlier sketches in CA 65-68, CANR-18, 35
See also BW 2
See also SATA 65
See also SATA-Obit 87
Ashe, Douglas
See Bardin, John Franklin
Ashe, Geoffrey (Thomas) 1923- ... 192
Earlier sketches in CA 5-8R, CANR-12, 31, 57
Autobiographical Essay in ... 192
See also SATA 17
See also SATA-Essay 125
Ashe, Gerald C. 1924(?)-1984
Obituary ... 112
Ashe, Gordon
See Creasey, John
Ashe, Mary Ann
See Lewis, Mary (Christianna)
Ashe, Penelope
See Greene, Robert W. and
Karman, Mal and
Young, Billie
Ashe, Rebecca
See Meluch, R(ebecca) M.
Asheim, Lester E(ugene) 1914-1997 ... 17-20R
Obituary ... 159
Ashenfelter, David L. 1948- ... 108
Ashenfelter, Orley C(lark) 1942- ... CANR-8
Earlier sketch in CA 61-64
Asher, Don 1926- ... 73-76
Asher, Harry
See Freemantle, Brian (Harry)
Asher, Harry (Maurice Felix) 1909- ... CANR-2
Earlier sketch in CA 5-8R
Asher, Jane 1946- ... CANR-82
Earlier sketch in CA 133
Asher, Jim ... 219
Asher, John A(lexander) 1921-1996 ... 21-24R
Asher, Kenneth George ... 177
Asher, Maxine 1930- ... 105
Asher, Michael 1953- ... 151
Asher, Miriam
See Mundis, Hester
Asher, R. E. 1926- ... CANR-106
Earlier sketch in CA 149
Asher, Ramona M. 1945- ... 143
Asher, Robert 1944- ... 111
Asher, Robert Eller 1910- ... 61-64
Asher, Sandra Fenichel 1942- ... CANR-97
Earlier sketches in CA 105, CANR-22, 53, 77
See also Asher, Sandy
See also JRDA
See also MAICYA 1, 2
See also SATA 118, 158
See also SATA-Essay 158
See also YAW
Asher, Sandy
See Asher, Sandra Fenichel
See also AAYA 17
See also BYA 6, 8
See also DLBY 1983
See also SAAS 13
See also SATA 36, 71
See also SATA-Brief 34
See also WYA
Asheron, Sara
See Moore, Lilian
Ashey, Bella
See Breinburg, Petronella
Ashfield, Christian Marion 1946-2002 ... 239
See also Fraser, Christine Marion
Ashfield, Helen
See Bennetts, Pamela
Ashford, Daisy
See Ashford, Margaret Mary
Ashford, Douglas E(lliott) 1928- ... CANR-37
Earlier sketches in CA 73-76, CANR-16
Ashford, Gerald 1907-1981 ... 41-44R
Ashford, Janet Isaacs 1949- ... 113
Ashford, Jeffrey
See Jeffries, Roderic (Graeme)
Ashford, Margaret Mary 1881-1972
Obituary ... 33-36R
See also SATA 10
Ashford, Nicholas 1943(?)-1990
Obituary ... 130
Ashford, Nigel (John Gladwell) 1952- ... 137
Ashford, (H.) Ray 1926- ... 65-68
Ashford, Theodore Askounes 1908-1987
Obituary ... 122
Ashihara, Yoshinobu 1918- ... CANR-65
Earlier sketch in CA 129
Ashkenazy, Vladimir D(avidovich) 1937- ... 137
Ashley, A.
See Aasheim, Ashley
Ashley, Amanda
See Baker, Madeline
Ashley, Benedict M. 1915- ... 232
Ashley, Bernard (John) 1935- ... CANR-140
Earlier sketches in CA 93-96, CANR-25, 44
See also CLR 4
See also MAICYA 1, 2
See also SATA 47, 79, 155
See also SATA-Brief 39
See also YAW
Ashley, Douglas ... 155
Ashley, Elizabeth
See Salmon, Annie Elizabeth
Ashley, Ellen
See Gasparotti, Elizabeth Seifert
Ashley, (Arthur) Ernest 1906- ... CAP-1
Earlier sketch in CA 13-16
Ashley, Franklin 1942- ... CANR-1
Earlier sketch in CA 45-48
Ashley, Fred
See Atkins, Francis Henry
Ashley, Graham
See Organ, John
Ashley, Jack 1922- ... 106
Ashley, Leonard R(aymond) N(elligan)
1928- ... CANR-24
Earlier sketches in CA 13-16R, CANR-9
Ashley, Maurice (Percy) 1907-1994 ... 41-44R
Ashley, Michael (Raymond Donald)
1948- ... CANR-110
Earlier sketches in CA 69-72, CANR-13, 30, 56
Ashley, Nova Trimble 1911-1980 ... 65-68
Ashley, Paul P(ritchard) 1896-1979 ... CANR-10
Obituary ... 85-88
Earlier sketch in CA 21-24R
Ashley, Perry J(onathan) 1928- ... 120
Ashley, Ray
See Abrashkin, Raymond
Ashley, Renee 1949- ... CANR-108
Earlier sketch in CA 148
Ashley, Robert P(aul), Jr. 1915- ... 17-20R
Ashley, Rosalind Minor 1923- ... 69-72
Ashley, Sally 1935- ... 109
Ashley, Steven
See McCaig, Donald
Ashley, Trisha ... 226
Ashley-Montagu, Montague Francis
See Montagu, Ashley
Ashlin, John
See Cutforth, John Ashlin
Ashlock, Patrick (Robert) 1937- ... 61-64
Ashlock, Robert B. 1930- ... CANR-28
Earlier sketches in CA 29-32R, CANR-12
Ashman, Howard (Elliott)
1950-1991 ... CANR-75
Obituary ... 133
Brief entry ... 122
Earlier sketch in CA 131
Ashman, Linda 1960- ... SATA 150
Ashmead, John, Jr. 1917-1992 ... CANR-28
Obituary ... 136
Earlier sketch in CA 1-4R
Ashmole, Bernard 1894-1988 ... CANR-75
Obituary ... 124
Earlier sketch in CA 106
Ashmore, Harry S(cott) 1916-1998 ... 13-16R
Obituary ... 163
Ashmore, Jerome 1901-1985 ... CAP-2
Earlier sketch in CA 33-36
Ashmore, Lewis
See Raborg, Frederick A(shton), Jr.
Ashmore, Owen 1920- ... 106
Ashner, Sonie Shapiro 1938- ... 57-60
Ashrawi, Hanan (Mikhail) 1946- ... 162
Ashrawi-Mikhail, Hanan
See Ashrawi, Hanan (Mikhail)
Ashton, Ann
See Kimbro, John M.
Ashton, Dianne 1949- ... CANR-124
Earlier sketch in CA 170
Ashton, Dore 1928- ... CANR-57
Earlier sketches in CA 5-8R, CANR-2, 30
Ashton, (Arthur) Leigh (Bolland) 1897-1983
Obituary ... 114
Ashton, Lorayne
See Gottfried, Theodore Mark
Ashton, Robert 1924- ... CANR-3
Earlier sketch in CA 1-4R
Ashton, Rosemary 1947- ... CANR-75
Earlier sketch in CA 138
Ashton, Sharon
See Van Slyke, Helen (Lenore)
Ashton, (Margery) Violet 1908-1996 ... 73-76
Ashton, Warren T.
See Adams, William Taylor
Ashton, Winifred 1888-1965
Obituary ... 93-96
See also Dane, Clemence
See also RHW
Ashton-Warner, Sylvia (Constance)
1908-1984 ... CANR-29
Obituary ... 112
Earlier sketch in CA 69-72
See also CLC 19
See also CN 1, 2, 3
See also MTCW 1, 2
Ashworth, Adele ... 219
Ashworth, Andrea 1969- ... 170
Ashworth, Kenneth H(ayden) 1932- ... 41-44R
Ashworth, Mary Wells Knight 1903-1992 ... 5-8R
Ashworth, Phyll ... 196
Ashworth, Robert A(rchibald) 1871-1959 ... 226
Ashworth, Wilfred 1912- ... 13-16R
Ashworth, William 1920-1991 ... CANR-76
Obituary ... 134
Earlier sketch in CA 5-8R
Ashworth, (Lewis) William 1942- ... 133
Asimov, Isaac 1920-1992 ... CANR-125
Obituary ... 137
Earlier sketches in CA 1-4R, CANR-2, 19, 36, 60
Interview in ... CANR-19
See also AAYA 13
See also BEST 90:2
See also BPFB 1
See also BYA 4, 6, 7, 9
See also CLC 1, 3, 9, 19, 26, 76, 92
See also CLR 12, 79
See also CMW 4
See also CN 1, 2, 3, 4, 5
See also CPW
See also DA3
See also DAM POP
See also DLB 8
See also DLBY 1992
See also JRDA
See also LAIT 5
See also LMFS 2
See also MAICYA 1, 2
See also MAL 5
See also MTCW 1, 2
See also MTFW 2005
See also RGAL 4
See also SATA 1, 26, 74
See also SCFW 1, 2
See also SFW 4
See also SSFS 17
See also TUS
See also YAW
Asimov, Janet (Jeppson) 1926- ... CANR-84
Earlier sketch in CANR-36
See also BYA 7
Asimow, Michael 1939- ... 154
Asin, Alfredo Quispez
See Moro, Cesar
Asin, Cesar Quispez
See Moro, Cesar
Asinof, Eliot 1919- ... CANR-7
Earlier sketch in CA 9-12R
See also MTFW 2005
See also SATA 6
Ask, Upendranath 1910- ... CWW 2
Aska, Warabe
See Masuda, Takeshi
See also SATA 56
Askari, Hussaini Muhammad
See Pereira, Harold Bertram
Askenasy, Hans George 1930- ... 77-80
Askew, Amanda Jane 1955- ... 218
Askew, Anne 1521(?)-1546 ... DLB 136
Askew, Jack
See Hivnor, Robert
Askew, Rilla 1951- ... 209
Askew, Thomas A(delbert, Jr.) 1931- ... 130
Askew, William C(larence) 1910-1999 ... 49-52
Askham, Francis
See Greenwood, Julia Eileen Courtney
Askin, A. Bradley 1943- ... 73-76
Askin, Alma 1911- ... 57-60
Askin, I(da) Jayne 1940- ... 109
Askins, Renee 1959(?)- ... 213
Askonas, Peter 1919- ... 177
Askwith, Betty Ellen 1909-1995 ... CANR-13
Obituary ... 148
Earlier sketch in CA 61-64
Askwith, Herbert 1889-1985
Obituary ... 117
Brief entry ... 113
Aslanapa, Oktay 1914- ... 37-40R
Aslet, Clive (William) 1955- ... CANR-139
Earlier sketches in CA 113, CANR-32
Aslin, Elizabeth (Mary) 1923-1989
Obituary ... 128
Asman, David 1954- ... 127
Aspaturian, Vernon V. 1922- ... 105
Aspazija 1865-1943 ... CDWLB 4
See also DLB 220
Aspel, Michael (Terence) 1933- ... 180
Brief entry ... 117
Aspell, Patrick J(oseph) 1930- ... 25-28R
Aspenstroem, Werner
See Aspenstrom, (Karl) Werner
Aspenstrom, (Karl) Werner 1918-1997 ... 192
See also CWW 2
See also EWL 3
Asper, Kathrin 1941- ... 146
Aspin, Les(lie, Jr.) 1938-1995 ... 108
Obituary ... 148
Aspinall, (Honor) Ruth (Alastair)
1922- ... CANR-2
Earlier sketch in CA 5-8R
Aspinwall, Dorothy B(rown) 1910- ... 49-52
Aspiz, Harold 1921- ... 105
Aspler, Tony 1939- ... CANR-25
Earlier sketch in CA 105

Cumulative Index 23 Atwood

Asprey, Robert B(rown) 1923- CANR-105
Earlier sketches in CA 5-8R, CANR-6
Asprin, Robert L(ynn) 1946- CANR-137
Earlier sketches in CA 85-88, CANR-57
See also AAYA 33
See also FANT
See also SATA 92
See also SFW 4
Aspy, David N(athanial) 1930- CANR-20
Earlier sketch in CA 45-48
Asquith, Cynthia Mary Evelyn (Charteris)
1887-1960 166
Obituary 110
See also HGG
See also SATA 107
Asquith, Glenn Hackney 1904- CANR-16
Earlier sketches in CA 1-4R, CANR-1
Asquith, Nan
See Pattinson, Nancy Evelyn
See also RHW
Asquith, Ros 228
See also SATA 153
Asquith, Stewart 1948- 116
Assael, Henry 1935- 41-44R
Assagioli, Roberto 1888-1974
Obituary 53-56
Asselbroke, Archibald Algernon 1923- 77-80
Asselin, E(dward) Donald 1903-1970 .... CAP-1
Earlier sketch in CA 11-12
Asselin, (Jean-Francois) Olivar 1874-1937 .. 174
See also DLB 92
Asselineau, Roger (Maurice) 1915- ... CANR-26
Earlier sketch in CA 97-100
Assensoh, A(kwasi) B(retuo) 1946(?)- 120
Assiac
See Fraenkel, Heinrich
Assiniwi, Bernard 1935-2000 205
Assis, Joaquim Maria Machado de
See Machado de Assis, Joaquim Maria
Assmann, Jan 1938- CANR-120
Earlier sketch in CA 168
Assouline, Pierre 1953- 162
Assuncao, Leilah 1943- 225
Astafyev, Victor 1924-2001 218
Astaire, Fred 1899-1987
Obituary 122
Astarita, Tommaso 1961- 143
Astell, Ann W. 225
Astell, Mary 1666-1731 .... DLB 252
See also FW
Aster, Sidney 1942- CANR-10
Earlier sketch in CA 65-68
Astier, Pierre A(rthur) G(eorges)
1927-1994 .... CANR-20
Earlier sketch in CA 45-48
Astill, Kenneth N. 1923- 53-56
Astin, Alexander W(illiam) 1932- CANR-53
Earlier sketches in CA 17-20R, CANR-7, 28
Astin, Helen S(tavridou) 1932- CANR-28
Earlier sketch in CA 29-32R
Astin, Patty Duke
See Duke, Anna Marie
Astin, Sean (Patrick) 1971- 237
Astiz, Carlos A. 1933- 25-28R
Astley, Joan Bright 1910- 33-36R
Astley, Juliet
See Lofts, Norah (Robinson)
Astley, Neil 1953- CANR-82
Earlier sketch in CA 132
Astley, Thea (Beatrice May)
1925-2004 .... CANR-78
Obituary 229
Earlier sketches in CA 65-68, CANR-11, 43
See also CLC 41
See also CN 1, 2, 3, 4, 5, 6, 7
See also DLB 289
See also EWL 3
Astley, William 1855-1911
See Warung, Price
Aston, Athina (Leka) 1934- 117
Aston, James
See White, T(erence) H(anbury)
Aston, Margaret 1932- 73-76
Aston, Michael (Anthony) 1946- 61-64
Aston, Trevor Henry 1925-1985
Obituary 118
Astor, Brooke 1902- 148
Astor, (Francis) David (Langhorne) 1912-2001
Obituary 201
Brief entry 113
Astor, Gavin 1918-1984
Obituary 113
Astor, Gerald (Morton) 1926- CANR-24
Earlier sketch in CA 107
Astor, Mary 1906-1987 .... CANR-75
Obituary 123
Earlier sketches in CA 5-8R, CANR-3
Astor, Michael Langhorne
1916-1980 .... CANR-75
Obituary 97-100
Earlier sketch in CA 61-64
Astor, Susan 1946- 105
Astrachan, Samuel 1934- 69-72
Astro, Richard 1941- CANR-27
Earlier sketch in CA 29-32R
Asturias, Miguel Angel 1899-1974 ... CANR-32
Obituary 49-52
Earlier sketches in CAP-2, CA 25-28
See also CDWLB 3
See also CLC 3, 8, 13
See also DA3
See also DAM MULT, NOV
See also DLB 113, 290
See also EWL 3
See also HLC 1
See also HW 1
See also LAW
See also LMFS 2
See also MTCW 1, 2
See also RGWL 2, 3
See also WLIT 1
Aswad, Betsy (Becker) 1939- CANR-25
Earlier sketch in CA 104
Aswell, Mary Louise 1902-1984
Obituary 114
Aswin
See Nandakumar, Prema
Ata, Te 1895-1995 190
See also SATA 119
Atamian, David 1892(?)-1978
Obituary 81-84
Atangan, Patrick 236
Atares, Carlos Saura
See Saura (Atares), Carlos
Atava, S.
See Terpigorev, Sergei Nikolaevich
Atcheson, Richard 1934- 29-32R
Atchity, Kenneth John 1944- CANR-16
Earlier sketches in CA 49-52, CANR-1
Atchley, Bob
See Atchley, Robert C.
Atchley, Dana W(inslow) 1941-2000 61-64
Obituary 190
Atchley, Robert C. 1939- CANR-1
Earlier sketch in CA 45-48
Atencia, Maria Victoria 1931- .... EWL 3
Atene, Ann
See Atene, (Rita) Anna
Atene, (Rita) Anna 1922- .... SATA 12
Athanas, (William) Verne
1917-1962 .... TCWW 1, 2
Athanasiadis, Harris 237
Athanassiadis, Nikos 1904-1990 ...... CANR-17
Earlier sketch in CA 33-36R
Athans, George (Stanley), Jr. 1952- 104
Athar
See Afzal, Omar
Athas, Daphne 1923- CANR-3
Earlier sketch in CA 1-4R
Athay, R(obert) E. 1925- 33-36R
Athearn, Robert G(reenleaf)
1914-1983 .... CANR-70
Earlier sketches in CA 1-4R, CANR-3
Atheling, William
See Pound, Ezra (Weston Loomis)
Atheling, William, Jr.
See Blish, James (Benjamin)
Atherden, Margaret Ann 1947- CANR-119
Earlier sketch in CA 147
Atherton, Alexine 1930- 37-40R
Atherton, Gertrude (Franklin Horn)
1857-1948 155
Brief entry 104
See also DLB 9, 78, 186
See also HGG
See also RGAL 4
See also SUFW 1
See also TCLC 2
See also TCWW 1, 2
Atherton, James C(hristian) 1915-1998 49-52
Atherton, James S(tephen) 1910- CAP-1
Earlier sketch in CA 13-16
Atherton, Lewis E. 1905-1989 .... 1-4R
Atherton, Lucius
See Masters, Edgar Lee
Atherton, Maxine 5-8R
Atherton, Michael (Andrew) 1968- 221
Atherton, Mike
See Atherton, Michael (Andrew)
Atherton, Nancy 191
Atherton, Pauline
See Cochrane, Pauline A(therton)
Atherton, Sarah
See Bridgman, Sarah Atherton
Atherton, Wallace N(ewman)
1927-1982 49-52
Athey, Irene J(owett) 1919-1998 61-64
Athill, Diana 1917- CANR-102
Earlier sketches in CA 1-4R, CANR-2
Atholl, Desmond 1956- 134
Athos
See Walkerley, Rodney Lewis (de Burgh)
Athos, Anthony G(eorge) 1934- CANR-19
Earlier sketch in CA 25-28R
Athos, Jonathan
See Mallett, Daryl F(urumi)
Atil, Esin 1938- CANR-67
Earlier sketches in CA 113, CANR-32
Atiya, Aziz S. 1898-1988 .... 5-8R
Atiya, Nayra 1943- 128
Atiyah, Michael Francis 1929- 169
Atiyah, P(atrick) S(elim) 1931- 37-40R
Atiyeh, George N(icholas) 1923- 57-60
Atkeson, Roy A. 1907-1990 .... CANR-11
Obituary 131
Earlier sketch in CA 69-72
Atkey, Philip 1908-1985 148
Obituary 118
Brief entry 112
See also CMW 4
Atkin, Douglas 236
Atkin, Flora B(lumenthal) 1919- CANR-37
Earlier sketches in CA 93-96, CANR-16
Atkin, Grace Murray 1894-1964 .... RHW
Atkin, J. Myron 1927- 45-48
Atkin, Mary Gage 1929- 81-84
Atkin, William Wilson 1912(?)-1976
Obituary 65-68
Atkins, Ace 206
Atkins, Burton M(ark) 1944-
Brief entry 115
Atkins, Catherine 236
See also BYA 14
See also SATA 160
Atkins, Charles 233
Atkins, Chester Burton 1924-2001
Obituary 198
Brief entry 113
Atkins, Chester G(reenough) 1948- 45-48
Atkins, Chet
See Atkins, Chester Burton
Atkins, E. Taylor 1967- 233
Atkins, E(dward) Wulstan (Ivor)
1904-2003 128
Obituary 216
Atkins, Eileen 1934- 206
Atkins, Francis Henry 1840-1927 167
See also SFW 4
Atkins, Frank
See Atkins, Francis Henry
Atkins, G(eorge) Douglas 1943- 114
Atkins, G(eorge) Pope 1934- CANR-17
Earlier sketch in CA 33-36R
Atkins, Gary 1949- 126
Atkins, (Arthur) Harold (Foweraker)
1910- CANR-127
Earlier sketch in CA 105
Atkins, Harry 1933- 25-28R
Atkins, Hedley (John Barnard) 1905-1983
Obituary 111
Atkins, Jack
See Harris, Mark
Atkins, James G. 1932- 17-20R
Atkins, Jeannine 1953- 185
See also SATA 113
Atkins, Jim
See Atkins, James G.
Atkins, John (Alfred) 1916- CANR-19
Earlier sketches in CA 9-12R, CANR-3
Atkins, Josiah 1755(?)-1781 .... DLB 31
Atkins, Kenneth R(obert) 1920- 73-76
Atkins, Linda 1939- 172
Atkins, Mary
See Sternau, Cynthia
Atkins, Meg Elizabeth 102
Atkins, Oliver F. 1916-1977 73-76
Atkins, Ollie
See Atkins, Oliver F.
Atkins, P(eter) W(illiam) 1940- CANR-41
Earlier sketch in CA 117
Atkins, Paul Moody 1892-1977
Obituary 69-72
Atkins, Peter 1955- .... HGG
Atkins, Robert C(oleman)
1930-2003 .... CANR-105
Obituary 215
Earlier sketch in CA 128
Atkins, Russell 1926- CANR-82
Earlier sketches in CA 45-48, CANR-1, 25, 53
See also CAAS 16
See also BW 1, 3
See also DLB 41
Atkins, Stephen E. 1941- 144
Atkins, Stuart (Pratt) 1914-2000 .... 25-28R
Atkins, Thomas R(adcliffe) 1939- CANR-8
Earlier sketch in CA 61-64
Atkinson, Allen G. 1953(?)-1987 .... SATA 60
See also SATA-Brief 46
See also SATA-Obit 55
Atkinson, Anthony Barnes 1944- CANR-96
Earlier sketches in CA 69-72, CANR-11
Atkinson, Basil F(erris) C(ampbell) 1895- .. 5-8R
Atkinson, (Justin) Brooks
1894-1984 .... CANR-14
Obituary 111
Earlier sketch in CA 61-64
Atkinson, Carroll (Holloway)
1896-1988 .... CAP-1
Earlier sketch in CA 13-16
Atkinson, Dan 1961- 174
Atkinson, David J(ohn) 1943- 107
Atkinson, David N. 196
Atkinson, Frank 1922- 108
Atkinson, Geoffrey 1955- 118
Atkinson, Harley (T.) 1951- 219
Atkinson, Henry A(very) 1877-1960 227
Atkinson, Hugh C(raig) 1933-1986 ... CANR-28
Obituary 120
Earlier sketch in CA 49-52
Atkinson, James 1914- 25-28R
Atkinson, James B(lakely) 1934- 119
Atkinson, Jay 1957- 209
Atkinson, Jennifer (Elizabeth) McCabe
1937- 232
Brief entry 116
Atkinson, John W(illiam) 1923- CANR-11
Earlier sketch in CA 21-24R
Atkinson, Kate 1951- CANR-101
Earlier sketch in CA 166
See also CLC 99
See also DLB 267
Atkinson, Linda 1941- 135
Atkinson, Louisa 1834-1872 .... DLB 230
Atkinson, M. E.
See Frankau, Mary Evelyn Atkinson
Atkinson, Margaret Fleming 73-76
See also SATA 14
Atkinson, Mary
See Hardwick, Mary Atkinson
Atkinson, Michael (J.) 167
Atkinson, Michael 1942- 177
Atkinson, Phillip S. 1921- 25-28R
Atkinson, R(ichard) C(hatham) 1929- 17-20R
Atkinson, Rick 1952- CANR-124
Earlier sketch in CA 133
See also BEST 90:2
Atkinson, Ron 1932- 57-60
Atkinson, Ronald Field 1928- 17-20R
Atkinson, W. W.
See Atkinson, William Walker
Atkinson, Walter S(ydney) 1891-1978
Obituary 73-76
Atkinson, William Christopher 1902-1992 . 109
Obituary 139
Atkinson, William Walker 1862-1932
Brief entry 120
Atkisson, Arthur A(lbert, Jr.) 1930- 61-64
Atkyns, Glenn C(hadwick) 1921- 49-52
Atlas, Helen Vincent 1931- 101
Atlas, James (Robert) 1949- CANR-100
Earlier sketch in CA 138
Atlas, Martin 1914-1997 .... 5-8R
Atlas, Samuel 1899-1977
Obituary 73-76
Atmore, Anthony 1932- 25-28R
Attanasio, A(lfred) A(ngelo) 1951- CANR-69
Earlier sketch in CA 137
See also AAYA 45
See also SFW 4
Attanasio, Paul 1959- 160
Attar, Farid al-Din Abu Hamid Mohammad c.
1116-c. 1220 .... RGWL 2, 3
See also WLIT 6
Attaway, Robert J(oseph) 1942- 49-52
Attaway, William (Alexander)
1911-1986 .... CANR-82
Earlier sketch in CA 143
See also BLC 1
See also BW 2, 3
See also CLC 92
See also DAM MULT
See also DLB 76
See also MAL 5
Attea, Mary
See Spahn, Mary Attea
Atteberry, William L(ouis) 1939- 53-56
Attema, Martha 1949- CANR-116
Earlier sketch in CA 159
See also SATA 94, 156
Attenborough, Bernard George CANR-2
Earlier sketch in CA 49-52
Attenborough, David (Frederick)
1926- CANR-125
Earlier sketches in CA 1-4R, CANR-6, 30
Attenborough, John 1908-1994 101
Obituary 146
Attenborough, Richard (Samuel)
1923- CANR-78
Brief entry 127
Earlier sketch in CA 139
Atterton, Julian (Harold) 1956- 122
Attfield, Robin 137
Atthill, Robin 1912-1997 69-72
Atticus
See Davies, Hunter and
Fleming, Ian (Lancaster) and
Pawle, Gerald Strachan and
Wilson, (Thomas) Woodrow
Attiyeh, Richard E. 1937-
Brief entry 113
Attlee, C. R.
See Attlee, Clement R(ichard)
Attlee, Clement R(ichard) 1883-1967
Obituary 112
Attneave, Carolyn L(ewis)
1920-1992 .... CANR-1
Earlier sketch in CA 45-48
Attner, Paul (Thomas) 1947- 180
Attridge, Derek 1945- CANR-105
Earlier sketch in CA 105
Attwell, Arthur A(lbert) 1917-1990 49-52
Attwood, William (Hollingsworth)
1919-1989 .... 21-24R
Obituary 128
Atwater, C(onstance) Elizabeth (Sullivan)
1923- 13-16R
Atwater, Eastwood 1925- 110
Atwater, Florence (Hasseltine Carroll)
1896-1979 135
See also CLR 19
See also MAICYA 1, 2
See also SATA 16, 66
Atwater, James David 1928-1996 101
Obituary 151
Atwater, Lynn 1935- 111
Atwater, Montgomery Meigs
1904-1976 .... CANR-70
Earlier sketch in CA 73-76
See also SATA 15
Atwater, P. M. H. CANR-116
Earlier sketch in CA 133
Atwater, Richard (Tupper) 1892-1948 135
Brief entry 111
See also CLR 19
See also CWRI 5
See also MAICYA 1, 2
See also SATA 54, 66
See also SATA-Brief 27
Atwater-Rhodes, Amelia 1984- 198
See also AAYA 40
See also SATA 124
Atwell, Debby 1953- .... SATA 87, 150
Atwood, Ann (Margaret) 1913-1992 ...... 41-44R
See also SATA 7

Atwood 24 CONTEMPORARY AUTHORS

Atwood, Drucy
See Morrison, Eula Atwood
Atwood, I(saac) M(organ) 1838-1917 228
Atwood, Margaret (Eleanor) 1939- .. CANR-133
Earlier sketches in CA 49-52, CANR-3, 24, 33, 59, 95
Interview in CANR-24
See also AAYA 12, 47
See also AMWS 13
See also BEST 89:2
See also BPFB 1
See also CLC 2, 3, 4, 8, 13, 15, 25, 44, 84, 135
See also CN 2, 3, 4, 5, 6, 7
See also CP 1, 2, 3, 4, 5, 6, 7
See also CPW
See also CWP
See also DA
See also DA3
See also DAB
See also DAC
See also DAM MST, NOV, POET
See also DLB 53, 251
See also EWL 3
See also EXPN
See also FL 1:5
See also FW
See also GL 2
See also LAIT 5
See also MTCW 1, 2
See also MTFW 2005
See also NFS 4, 12, 13, 14, 19
See also PC 8
See also PFS 7
See also RGSF 2
See also SATA 50
See also SSC 2, 46
See also SSFS 3, 13
See also TCLE 1:1
See also TWA
See also WLC
See also WWE 1
See also YAW
Atwood, Nina 168
Atwood, Robert B. 1907-1997 .... AITN 2
Atwood, William G(oodson) 1932- .. CANR-92
Earlier sketch in CA 142
Atxaga, Bernardo
See Garmendia, Joseba Irazu
Atyeo, Don 1950- 93-96
Atzeni, Sergio 1952-1995 168
Aub, Max 1903-1972 .... DLB 322
See also EWL 3
Auberjonois, Fernand 1910-2004 77-80
Obituary 231
Aubert, Alvin (Bernard) 1930- CANR-82
Earlier sketches in CA 81-84, CANR-26
See also CAAS 20
See also BW 1, 3
See also CP 2, 3, 4, 5, 6, 7
See also CSW
See also DLB 41
Aubert, Brigitte 1956- 217
Aubert, Jacques 1932- 147
Aubert, Rosemary 1946- CANR-89
Earlier sketch in CA 113
Aubert de Gaspe, Philippe-Ignace-Francois 1814-1841 .... DLB 99
Aubert de Gaspe, Philippe-Joseph 1786-1871 .... DLB 99
Aubery, Pierre 1920- 37-40R
Aubey, Robert T(haddeus) 1930- 21-24R
Aubigne, Theodore Agrippa d' 1552-1630 .... GFL Beginnings to 1789
Aubigny, Pierre d'
See Mencken, H(enry) L(ouis)
Aubin, Henry (Trocme) 1942- CANR-122
Earlier sketch in CA 77-80
Aubin, Napoleon 1812-1890 .... DLB 99
Aubin, Penelope 1685-1731(?) .... DLB 39
Aubrac, Lucie 1912- 151
Aubrey, Crispin 1946- 129
Aubrey, Frank
See Atkins, Francis Henry
Aubrey, Meg Kelleher 1963- .... SATA 83
Aubrey-Fletcher, Henry Lancelot 1887-1969
Obituary 111
See also Wade, Henry
See also CMW 4
Aubry, Claude B. 1914-1984 106
See also SATA 29
See also SATA-Obit 40
Auburn, David 1969- 196
See also DFS 21
Auburn, Mark Stuart 1945- 89-92
Auch, Mary Jane 208
See also SATA 138
Auchincloss, Louis (Stanton) 1917- CANR-130
Earlier sketches in CA 1-4R, CANR-6, 29, 55, 87
Interview in CANR-29
See also AMWS 4
See also CLC 4, 6, 9, 18, 45
See also CN 1, 2, 3, 4, 5, 6, 7
See also DAM NOV
See also DLB 2, 244
See also DLBY 1980
See also EWL 3
See also MAL 5
See also MTCW 1
See also RGAL 4
See also SSC 22
Auchmuty, James Johnston 1909-1981 101
Obituary 109
Auchterlonie, Dorothy
See Green, Dorothy (Auchterlonie)
See also CP 1
Auclair, Joan 1960- .... SATA 68
Aucoin, Kevyn 1962-2002 169
Obituary 205
Audax
See Oakesey, John
Audeh, Azmi S. 1932- 170
Audemars, Pierre 1909-1989 .... CANR-58
Earlier sketches in CA 17-20R, CANR-7
See also CMW 4
Auden, Renee
See West, Uta
Auden, W(ystan) H(ugh) 1907-1973 .... CANR-105
Obituary 45-48
Earlier sketches in CA 9-12R, CANR-5, 61
See also AAYA 18
See also AMWS 2
See also BRW 7
See also BRWR 1
See also CDBLB 1914-1945
See also CLC 1, 2, 3, 4, 6, 9, 11, 14, 43, 123
See also CP 1, 2
See also DA
See also DA3
See also DAB
See also DAC
See also DAM DRAM, MST, POET
See also DLB 10, 20
See also EWL 3
See also EXPP
See also MAL 5
See also MTCW 1, 2
See also MTFW 2005
See also PAB
See also PC 1
See also PFS 1, 3, 4, 10
See also TUS
See also WLC
See also WP
Audi, Robert (N.) 1941- 123
Audiard, Michel 1920-1985
Obituary 116
Audiberti, Jacques 1899-1965
Obituary 25-28R
See also CLC 38
See also DAM DRAM
See also DLB 321
See also EWL 3
Audouard, Antoine 1956- 235
Audubon, John James 1785-1851 .... ANW
See also DLB 248
Audubon, John Woodhouse 1812-1862 .... DLB 183
Auel, Jean M(arie) 1936- CANR-115
Earlier sketches in CA 103, CANR-21, 64
Interview in CANR-21
See also AAYA 7, 51
See also BEST 90:4
See also BPFB 1
See also CLC 31, 107
See also CPW
See also DA3
See also DAM POP
See also NFS 11
See also RHW
See also SATA 91
Auer, J(ohn) Jeffery 1913-1999 .... CANR-6
Earlier sketch in CA 9-12R
Auer, James M(atthew) 1928- CANR-85
Earlier sketch in CA 133
Auer, Martin 1951- 145
See also SATA 77
Auerbach, Aline B.
See Auerbach, Aline Sophie (Buchman)
Auerbach, Aline Sophie (Buchman) 1899(?)-1985
Obituary 116
Auerbach, Arnold (Jacob) 1917- 131
Auerbach, Arnold M. 1912-1998 .... 17-20R
Obituary 171
Auerbach, Berthold 1812-1882 .... DLB 133
Auerbach, Erich 1892-1957 155
Brief entry 118
See also EWL 3
See also TCLC 43
Auerbach, Erna (?)-1975
Obituary 61-64
Auerbach, George 1905-1973
Obituary 45-48
Auerbach, Jeffrey A. 213
Auerbach, Jerold S(tephen) 1936- ... CANR-112
Earlier sketches in CA 21-24R, CANR-69
Auerbach, Jessica (Lynn) 1947- 114
Auerbach, John 1922-2002 225
Auerbach, Loyd 1956- 166
Auerbach, Marjorie (Hoffberg) 9-12R
Auerbach, Michael 1949- 170
Auerbach, Nina 1943- CANR-96
Earlier sketches in CA 85-88, CANR-15, 34
Auerbach, Red
See Auerbach, Arnold (Jacob)
Auerbach, Stevanne 1938- CANR-24
Earlier sketches in CA 57-60, CANR-8
Auerbach, Stuart C(harles) 1935-2003 89-92
Obituary 222
Auerbach, Sylvia CANR-4
Earlier sketch in CA 53-56
Auernheimer, Raoul (Othmar) 1876-1948 .. 179
See also DLB 81
Auezov, Mukhtar Omarkhan-uli .... EWL 3
Auf der Maur, Nick 1942- 129
Aufricht, Hans 1902-1973 45-48
Augarde, Steve(n Andre) 1950- CANR-21
Earlier sketch in CA 104
See also SATA 25, 159
Augarde, Tony 1936- 118
Augarten, Stan 1952- 115
Auge, Bud
See Auge, Henry J., Jr.
Auge, Henry J., Jr. 1930(?)-1983
Obituary 109
Augelli, John P(at) 1921- 17-20R
See also SATA 46
Augenbraum, Harold 1953- 142
Auger, C(harles) P(eter) 1931- CANR-98
Earlier sketch in CA 147
Aughey, Arthur 212
Aughtry, Charles Edward 1925-1978 .... 5-8R
Augier, Emile 1820-1889 .... DLB 192
See also GFL 1789 to the Present
Augsburger, A(aron) Don(ald) 1925- 21-24R
Augsburger, David W. 1938- CANR-13
Earlier sketch in CA 33-36R
Augsburger, Myron S. 1929- CANR-6
Earlier sketch in CA 13-16R
Augspurger, Everett F. 1904(?)-1986
Obituary 118
Augstein, Rudolf (Karl) 1923-2002 110
Obituary 210
Auguet, Roland (Jacques) 1935- 105
August, Andrew 1962- 194
August, Bille 1948- 144
August, Eugene R(obert) 1935- CANR-27
Earlier sketch in CA 49-52
August, John
See De Voto, Bernard (Augustine)
August, Joseph H. 1890-1947 .... IDFW 3, 4
Augustin, Ann Sutherland 1934- 57-60
Augustin, Pius 1934- 17-20R
Augustine, St. 354-430 .... DA
See also DA3
See also DAB
See also DAC
See also DAM MST
See also DLB 115
See also EW 1
See also RGWL 2, 3
See also WLCS
Augustine, Erich
See Stoil, Michael Jon
Augustine, Mildred
See Benson, Mildred (Augustine Wirt)
Augustine, Norman R(alph) 1935- 121
Augustinos, Gerasimos 1939- 145
Augustson, Ernest
See Ryden, Ernest Edwin
Augustus, Albert, Jr.
See Nuetzel, Charles (Alexander)
Auiler, Dan Rose 202
Aukerman, Dale 1930-1999 112
Aukerman, Robert C. 1910- 33-36R
Aukofer, Frank A(lexander) 1935- 65-68
Aukrust, Olav 1883-1929 194
Auld, Rhoda L(andsman) 105
Auleta, Michael S. 1909-1998 .... CAP-2
Earlier sketch in CA 25-28
Auletta, Ken 1942- CANR-72
Earlier sketches in CA 69-72, CANR-12
See also DLBY 1997
Auletta, Richard P(aul) 1942- 53-56
Auletta, Robert 1940- CANR-99
Brief entry 115
Earlier sketches in CA 119, CANR-48
Interview in CA-119
Aulich, James 1952- 132
Aulicino, Armand 1920(?)-1983
Obituary 109
Aulick, June L. 1906- 25-28R
Ault, Donald D(uane) 1942- 81-84
Ault, James M(ase), Jr. 1946- 236
Ault, Phil
See Ault, Phillip H(alliday)
Ault, Phillip H(alliday) 1914- CANR-18
Earlier sketch in CA 101
See also SATA 23
Ault, Rosalie Sain 1942- 107
See also SATA 38
Ault, Roz
See Ault, Rosalie Sain
Aultman, Donald S. 1930- 17-20R
Aultman, Richard E(ugene) 1933- CANR-9
Earlier sketch in CA 65-68
Aulus Gellius c. 125-c. 180 .... DLB 211
Aumann, Francis R(obert) 1901-1995 ... 41-44R
Aumbry, Alan
See Bayley, Barrington J(ohn)
Aumont, Jean-Pierre 1913-2001 .... 29-32R
Obituary 192
Aune, Bruce (Arthur) 1933- 73-76
Aune, James Arnt 1953- 201
Aung, (Maung) Htin 1909- CANR-3
Earlier sketch in CA 5-8R
See also SATA 21
Aunger, Edmund A(lexander) 1949- 112
Aunt Belinda
See Braddon, Mary Elizabeth
Auntie Deb
See Coury, Louise Andree
Auntie Louise
See Coury, Louise Andree
Aunt Weedy
See Alcott, Louisa May
Aurand, Harold Wilson 1940- 41-44R
Aurand, L(eonard) W(illiam) 1920- 53-56
Aurandt, Paul (Harvey II) 1948- 129
Aurandt, Paul Harvey 1918- 102
Aurelio, John R. 1937- CANR-28
Earlier sketch in CA 111
Aurelius
See Bourne, Randolph S(illiman)
Aurelius, Marcus 121-180
See Marcus Aurelius
See also RGWL 2, 3
Aurell, Tage 1895-1976
Obituary 113
See also EWL 3
Aurenche, Jean 1904-1992 .... IDFW 3, 4
Auric, Georges 1899-1983 .... IDFW 3, 4
Aurner, Robert R(ay) 1898-1990 .... 5-8R
Aurobindo, Sri
See Ghose, Aurabinda
Aurobindo Ghose
See Ghose, Aurabinda
Aurthur, Robert Alan 1922-1978 ...... CANR-34
Earlier sketch in CA 81-84
Aury, Dominique 1907-1998 237
Ausland, John C(ampbell) 1920-1996 93-96
Obituary 152
Auslander, Audrey (May) Wurdemann 1911-1960
Obituary 116
Auslander, Joseph 1897-1965
Obituary 116
Ausmus, Harry Jack 1937- 115
Ausonius, Decimus Magnus c. 310-c. 395 .... RGWL 2, 3
Austen, Carrie
See Bennett, Cherie
Austen, Jane 1775-1817 .... AAYA 19
See also BRW 4
See also BRWC 1
See also BRWR 2
See also BYA 3
See also CDBLB 1789-1832
See also DA
See also DA3
See also DAB
See also DAC
See also DAM MST, NOV
See also DLB 116
See also EXPN
See also FL 1:2
See also GL 2
See also LAIT 2
See also LATS 1:1
See also LMFS 1
See also NFS 1, 14, 18, 20, 21
See also TEA
See also WLC
See also WLIT 3
See also WYAS 1
Austen, Michael (Edward) 1951- 109
Austen, Ralph A. 1937- 25-28R
Auster, Nancy (Eileen) R(oss) 1926- 65-68
Auster, Paul 1947- CANR-129
Earlier sketches in CA 69-72, CANR-23, 52, 75
See also AMWS 12
See also CLC 47, 131
See also CMW 4
See also CN 5, 6, 7
See also DA3
See also DLB 227
See also MAL 5
See also MTCW 2
See also MTFW 2005
See also SUFW 2
See also TCLE 1:1
Austerlitz, Paul 1957- 165
Austerlitz, Robert Paul 1923-1994 111
Obituary 146
Austerman, Wayne R. 1948- 122
Austgen, Robert Joseph 1932- 21-24R
Austin, Alfred 1835-1913 179
See also DLB 35
Austin, Allan Edward 1929- 73-76
Austin, Allen 1922- 33-36R
Austin, Anthony 1919- 33-36R
Austin, (Mildred) Aurelia 53-56
Austin, Barbara Leslie
See Linton, Barbara Leslie
Austin, Brett
See Floren, Lee
Austin, Bunny
See Austin, Henry Wilfred
Austin, Carrie
See Seuling, Barbara
Austin, Charles M(arshall) 1941- 69-72
Austin, David E(dwards) 1926- 29-32R
Austin, Denise 1957- 223
Austin, E. V.
See Wilcox, Patricia (Anne Florence)
Austin, Elizabeth S. 1907-1977 .... CAP-2
Earlier sketch in CA 25-28
See also SATA 5
Austin, Frank
See Faust, Frederick (Schiller)
Austin, Guy 1966- 163
Austin, Harry
See McInerny, Ralph (Matthew)
Austin, Henry Wilfred 1906-2000 101
Obituary 189
Austin, James C(layton) 1923- 13-16R
Austin, James Henry 1925- 188
Austin, Jane Goodwin 1831-1894 ...... DLB 202
Austin, Jeannette Holland 1936- 239
Austin, Joe Alan 1957- 213
Austin, John 1790-1859 .... DLB 262
Austin, John 1922- 61-64
Austin, John Langshaw 1911-1960
Obituary 112
See also DLB 261
Austin, K(enneth) A(shurst) 1911- 102
Austin, Lettie J(ane) 1925- 65-68
Austin, Lewis 1936- 73-76

Cumulative Index 25 Aylesworth

Austin, Lloyd James 1915-1994 ... CAP-1
Obituary ... 147
Earlier sketch in CA 13-14
Austin, Lynn (N.) 1949- ... 222
Austin, M(ichel) M(ervyn) 1943- ... CANR-19
Earlier sketch in CA 85-88
Austin, Margot 1909(?)-1990 ... CAP-1
Obituary ... 132
Earlier sketch in CA 9-10
See also SATA 11
See also SATA-Obit 66
Austin, Mary (Hunter) 1868-1934 ... 178
Brief entry ... 109
See also ANW
See also DLB 9, 78, 206, 221, 275
See also FW
See also TCLC 25
See also TCWW 1, 2
Austin, Mary C(arrington) 1915- ... 5-8R
Austin, Michael ... 165
Austin, Neal F(uller) 1926- ... 25-28R
Austin, (John) Norman 1937- ... 89-92
Austin, Oliver L(uther), Jr. 1903-1988 ... 49-52
Obituary ... 127
See also SATA 7
See also SATA-Obit 59
Austin, Patricia 1950- ... SATA 137
Austin, R. G.
See Gelman, Rita Golden and Lamb, Nancy
Austin, (Stewart) Reid 1931- ... 89-92
Austin, Richard B(uckner), Jr. 1930- ... 73-76
Austin, Stephen
See Stevens, Austin N(eil)
Austin, Timothy R(obert) 1952- ... 117
Austin, Virginia 1951- ... SATA 80, 152
Austin, William 1778-1841 ... DLB 74
See also SUFW
Austin, William W(eaver) 1920- ... 21-24R
Australie
See Manning, Emily
Austwick, John
See Lee, Austin
Ausubel, Herman 1920-1977 ... 1-4R
Obituary ... 69-72
Ausubel, Marynn H. 1913(?)-1980
Obituary ... 97-100
Auten, James H(udson) 1938- ... 41-44R
Auteur, Hillary
See Gottfried, Theodore Mark
Auth, Tony
See Auth, William Anthony, Jr.
Auth, William Anthony, Jr. 1942- ... CANR-72
Brief entry ... 108
Earlier sketch in CA 111
Interview in ... CA-111
See also SATA 51
Author of Elizabeth and Her German Garden
See Russell, Mary Annette Beauchamp
Autrey, C. E. 1904-1993 ... CANR-2
Earlier sketch in CA 1-4R
Autry, Ewart (Arthur) 1900-1981 ... 13-16R
Autry, (Orvon) Gene 1907(?)-1998 ... 169
Obituary ... 171
Brief entry ... 112
Autry, Gloria Diener
See Allen, Terril Diener
Autry, James A(rthur) 1933- ... 135
Brief entry ... 115
Autton, Norman William James 1920- ... 101
Auty, Phyllis 1910-1998 ... CANR-2
Earlier sketch in CA 5-8R
Auty, Robert 1914-1978
Obituary ... 111
Auvert, Elizabeth ... CANR-14
Earlier sketch in CA 37-40R
Auvil, Kenneth W(illiam) 1925-1999 ... 17-20R
Auvil, Peggy A(ppleby) 1954- ... 194
See also SATA 122
Avabhasa, Da
See Jones, Franklin Albert
Avadian, Brenda 1959- ... 187
Avakian, Arlene Voski 1939- ... 139
Avakian, Arra S(teve) 1912- ... 85-88
Avakumovic, Ivan 1926- ... 41-44R
Avalle-Arce, Juan Bautista de 1927- ... CANR-87
Earlier sketches in CA 33-36R, CANR-13, 32
See also HW 1
Avallone, Michael (Angelo, Jr.)
1924-1999 ... CANR-77
Obituary ... 177
Earlier sketches in CA 5-8R, CANR-4, 39
Interview in ... CANR-4
See also CMW 4
See also DLB 306
See also DLBY 1999
Avalon, Arthur
See Woodroffe, John George
Avalos, Luis 1946- ... 206
Avancini, Nicolaus 1611-1686 ... DLB 164
Avanzini, John F. 1936- ... CANR-49
Earlier sketch in CA 122
Avarius
See Stolk, Anthonie
Avedis, Hikmet ... 132
Avedis, Howard
See Avedis, Hikmet
Aveline, Claude 1901-1992 ... CANR-6
Earlier sketch in CA 5-8R
Aveling, Hugh
See Aveling, J(ohn) C(edric) H(ugh)
Aveling, J(ohn) C(edric) H(ugh) 1917-1993 . 131
Obituary ... 140
Avella, Steven M. 1951- ... 145
Avellano, Albert
See Marlowe, Dan J(ames)
Avena, Thomas ... 236
Avendano, Fausto 1941- ... CANR-87
Earlier sketch in CA 131
See also DLB 82
See also HW 1
Aveni, Anthony F(rancis) 1938- ... CANR-143
Earlier sketch in CA 81-84
Averbach, Albert 1902-1975 ... CAP-2
Earlier sketch in CA 21-22
Averill, E(dgar) W(aite) 1906-1980 ... 53-56
Averill, Esther (Holden) 1902-1992 ... CANR-12
Obituary ... 139
Earlier sketch in CA 29-32R
See also CWRI 5
See also SATA 1, 28
See also SATA-Obit 72
Averill, Gage 1954- ... 166
Averill, H. C.
See Snow, Charles H(orace)
Averill, James H(alsey) 1947- ... 129
Averill, John Hillier 1923-1984
Obituary ... 111
Averill, Lloyd J(ames) 1923- ... CANR-10
Earlier sketch in CA 21-24R
Averill, Thomas Fox 1949- ... 205
Averitt, Robert T(abor) 1931- ... 21-24R
Averroes 1126-1198 ... DLB 115
Avers, Charlotte J(o) 1926-1990
Obituary ... 131
Aversa, Elizabeth Smith 1946- ... 127
Avery, A. A.
See Montgomery, Rutherford George
Avery, Al
See Montgomery, Rutherford George
Avery, Anne
See Holmberg, Anne
Avery, Burniece 1908-1993 ... 73-76
Avery, Catherine B(arber) 1909-1987 ... 57-60
Avery, Don H(oward) 1938- ... 229
Avery, Edwina Austin 1896-1983
Obituary ... 110
Avery, Evelyn 1940- ... 211
Avery, Fiona Kai ... 226
Avery, George C(ostas) 1926- ... 25-28R
Avery, Gillian (Elise) 1926- ... CANR-69
Earlier sketches in CA 9-12R, CANR-4
See also CWRI 5
See also DLB 161
See also MAICYA 1, 2
See also SAAS 6
See also SATA 7, 75, 137
See also SATA-Essay 137
Avery, Ira 1914-1984 ... 81-84
Avery, James S. 1923- ... 126
Avery, Jeanne 1931- ... 111
Avery, June
See Rees, Joan
Avery, Kay 1908- ... 1-4R
See also SATA 5
Avery, Kevin J. 1950- ... CANR-100
Earlier sketch in CA 149
Avery, Laurence G(reen) 1934- ... 33-36R
Avery, Lorraine
See Older, Effin and Older, Jules
Avery, Lynn
See Cole, Lois Dwight
Avery, Martin 1955- ... 113
Avery, Mary Ellen 1927- ... 118
Avery, Morgan
See Kennett, Shirley
Avery, Peter 1923- ... 13-16R
Avery, Richard
See Cooper, Edmund
Avery, Robert J., Jr. 1911(?)-1983
Obituary ... 110
Avery, Robert Sterling 1917- ... 13-16R
Avery, Tex 1907-1980 ... IDFW 3, 4
Avery, Valeen Tippetts 1936- ... 129
Avery, Valerie 1940- ... 111
Avery, Anne C. 1946- ... 127
Avey, Albert E(dwin) 1886-1963 ... CAP-1
Earlier sketch in CA 17-18
Avey, Ruby 1927- ... CANR-39
Earlier sketches in CA 89-92, CANR-16
Avi
See Wortis, Avi
See also AAYA 10, 37
See also BYA 1, 10
See also CLR 24, 68
See also SATA 71, 108
See also WYA
Aviad, Janet 1942- ... 115
Avice, Claude (Pierre Marie)
1925-1995 ... CANR-49
Earlier sketches in CA 61-64, CANR-8, 24
Avicenna 980-1037 ... DLB 115
Avidan, David 1934-1995 ... 238
Avigad, Nachman 1905-1992 ... CANR-80
Obituary ... 136
Earlier sketch in CA 129
Avila, Alexander 1961- ... 212
Avila, Charles 1945- ... 129
Avila, Lilian Estelle ... 45-48
Avila (Penagos), Rafael 1941- ... CANR-93
Earlier sketch in CA 132
Avila Jimenez, Antonio 1898-1965 ... DLB 283
Aviles Fabila, Rene 1940- ... 192
Avineri, Shlomo 1933- ... 25-28R
Avins, Styra ... 174
Avirgan, Anthony Lance 1944- ... CANR-31
Earlier sketch in CA 112
Avirgan, Tony
See Avirgan, Anthony Lance
Avis, Paul (David Loup) 1947- ... CANR-45
Earlier sketch in CA 120
Avise, John C. ... 170
Avishai, Susan 1949- ... SATA 82
Avison, Margaret (Kirkland) 1918- ... CANR-134
Earlier sketch in CA 17-20R
See also CLC 2, 4, 97
See also CP 1, 2, 3, 4, 5, 6, 7
See also DAC
See also DAM POET
See also DLB 53
See also MTCW 1
Avison, N(eville) Howard 1934- ... 29-32R
Avi-Yonah, M(ichael) 1904-1974 ... CANR-6
Earlier sketch in CA 5-8R
Avlon, John P. ... 230
Avnery, Uri 1923- ... CANR-25
Earlier sketch in CA 105
Avnet, Jon(athan Michael) 1949- ... 177
Avni, Abraham Albert 1921-1995 ... 33-36R
Avni, Haim 1930- ... 133
Avomieli, Antero
See Kianto, Ilmari
Avramides, Anita 1952- ... CANR-86
Earlier sketch in CA 133
Avramovic, Dragoslav 1919-2001 ... CANR-17
Obituary ... 194
Earlier sketch in CA 41-44R
Avrelin, M.
See Steinberg, Aaron Zacharovich
Avrett, Robert 1901-1975 ... 1-4R
Avrett, Rosalind Case 1933- ... 110
Avrett, Roz
See Avrett, Rosalind Case
Avrich, Paul (Henry) 1931- ... CANR-5
Earlier sketch in CA 49-52
Avriel, Ehud 1917-1980 ... 69-72
Obituary ... 133
Avril, Pierre 1930- ... 29-32R
Avruch, Kevin Andrew 1950- ... CANR-50
Earlier sketch in CA 123
Avrutis, Raymond 1948- ... 69-72
Avvakum (Petrovich), Archpriest
1620(?)-1682 ... DLB 150
Avyzius, Jonas 1922-1999 ... DLB 220
AvZ
See Von Zelewsky, Alexander
Aw, Tash ... 239
Awa, Eme Onuoha 1921- ... 13-16R
Awad, Elias M. 1934- ... CANR-11
Earlier sketch in CA 17-20R
Awdry, Christopher Vere 1940- ... 136
See also SATA 67
Awdry, Wilbert Vere 1911-1997 ... 103
Obituary ... 157
See also CLR 23
See also CWRI 5
See also DLB 160
See also MAICYA 2
See also MAICYAS 1
See also SATA 94
Awe, Chulho 1927- ... 33-36R
Awe, Susan C. 1948- ... 166
Awiakta, Marilou 1936- ... 148
See also CSW
See also FW
Awkward, Michael ... 209
Awolowo, Obafemi Awo
1909-1987 ... CANR-14
Obituary ... 122
Earlier sketch in CA 65-68
See also BW 2
Awoonor, Kofi (Nyidevu) 1935- ... CANR-82
Earlier sketches in CA 29-32R, CANR-15, 42
See also CAAS 13
See also AFW
See also BW 2, 3
See also CP 1, 2, 3, 4, 5, 6, 7
See also DLB 117
See also EWL 3
Awoonor-Williams, George
See Awoonor, Kofi (Nyidevu)
Awret, Irene 1921- ... 131
Awwad, Tawfiq Yusuf 1911-1988 ... 154
See also EWL 3
Axell, Herbert (Ernest) 1915-2001 ... CANR-14
Obituary ... 200
Earlier sketch in CA 81-84
Axelrad, Jacob 1899-1977 ... 61-64
Axelrad, Sidney 1913-1976 ... 122
Obituary ... 110
Axelrad, Sylvia Brody 1914- ... 104
Axelrod, Alan 1952- ... CANR-99
Earlier sketch in CA 110
Axelrod, Amy ... 200
See also SATA 131
Axelrod, D(avid) B(ruce) 1943- ... CANR-94
Earlier sketches in CA 45-48, CANR-1
Axelrod, George 1922-2003 ... 65-68
Obituary ... 218
See also CAD
See also CD 5, 6
Axelrod, Herbert Richard 1927- ... 85-88
Axelrod, Joseph 1918- ... 33-36R
Axelrod, Marian Thurm ... CANR-110
See also Thurm, Marian
Axelrod, Mark (R.) 1946- ... CANR-108
Earlier sketch in CA 145
Axelrod, Paul (Douglas) 1949- ... 110
Axelrod, Robert 1943- ... 33-36R
Axelrod, Steven Gould 1944- ... 81-84
Axelson, Eric (Victor) 1913-1998 ... CANR-89
Earlier sketches in CA 21-24R, CANR-9, 25
Axford, Elizabeth C. 1958- ... 187
Axford, H. William 1925-1980 ... 37-40R
Axford, Joseph Mack 1879-1970 ... CAP-2
Earlier sketch in CA 25-28
Axford, LaVonne B(rady) 1928- ... 33-36R
Axford, Roger W(illiam) 1920- ... 33-36R
Axinn, Donald E(verett) 1929- ... CANR-53
Brief entry ... 115
Earlier sketch in CA 125
Axinn, June 1923- ... 89-92
Axler, James
See James, Laurence
Axler, Leo
See Lazuta, Gene
Axline, W. Andrew 1940- ... 25-28R
Axtell, James Lewis 1941- ... CANR-111
Earlier sketches in CA 108, CANR-25, 54
Axthelm, Peter M(acrae) 1943-1991 ... 107
Interview in ... CA-107
Axton, David
See Koontz, Dean R(ay)
Axton, Hoyt (Wayne) 1938-1999 ... 173
Obituary ... 185
Axton, W(illiam) F(itch) 1926-2000 ... 21-24R
Ayal, Igal 1942- ... 37-40R
Ayala, Cesar J.
See Ayala (Casas), Cesar J.
Ayala (Casas), Cesar J. 1960- ... 190
Ayala, Emilie Smith
See Smith-Ayala, Emilie
Ayala, Francisco (de Paula y Garcia Duarte)
1906- ... 208
See also CWW 2
See also DLB 322
See also EWL 3
See also RGSF 2
Ayala, Francisco 1934- ... 85-88
Ayala, Mitzi 1941- ... 110
Ayandele, E(mmanuel) A(yankanmi)
1936- ... CANR-13
Earlier sketch in CA 21-24R
Ayars, Albert L(ee) 1917- ... 29-32R
Ayars, James S(terling) 1898-1986 ... CANR-2
Earlier sketch in CA 5-8R
See also SATA 4
Ayatey, Siegfried B. Y. 1934- ... 25-28R
Aybek
See Tashmuhammad-oghli, Musa
See also EWL 3
Ayckbourn, Alan 1939- ... CANR-118
Earlier sketches in CA 21-24R, CANR-31, 59
See also BRWS 5
See also CBD
See also CD 5, 6
See also CLC 5, 8, 18, 33, 74
See also DAB
See also DAM DRAM
See also DC 13
See also DFS 7
See also DLB 13, 245
See also EWL 3
See also MTCW 1, 2
See also MTFW 2005
Aycliffe, Jonathan
See MacEoin, Denis
Aycoberry, Pierre ... 221
Aycock, Don M(ilton) 1951- ... 106
Aydelotte, William Osgood 1910-1996 ... 57-60
Obituary ... 151
Aydy, Catherine
See Tennant, Emma (Christina)
Aye, A. K.
See Edwards, Hazel (Eileen)
Ayearst, Morley 1899-1983 ... CAP-2
Obituary ... 109
Earlier sketch in CA 29-32
Ayer, A(lfred) J(ules) 1910-1989 ... CANR-34
Obituary ... 129
Earlier sketches in CA 5-8R, 129, CANR-5
See also DLB 262
See also MTCW 2
Ayer, Eleanor H. 1947-1998 ... CANR-99
Earlier sketch in CA 146
See also SATA 78, 121
Ayer, Frederick, Jr. 1917(?)-1974 ... CANR-70
Obituary ... 45-48
Earlier sketch in CA 73-76
Ayer, H(arry) D(ouglas Sandy) 1952- ... 220
Ayer, Jacqueline 1930- ... CANR-70
Earlier sketch in CA 69-72
See also SATA 13
Ayer, Margaret (?)-1981 ... CANR-13
Earlier sketch in CA 65-68
See also SATA 15
Ayers, Bill
See Ayers, William
Ayers, Bradley Earl 1935- ... 69-72
Ayers, Donald Murray 1923- ... 17-20R
Ayers, Edward L(ynn) 1953- ... CANR-127
Earlier sketch in CA 115
Ayers, M(ichael) R(ichard) 1935- ... 25-28R
Ayers, Robert H(yman) 1918- ... 45-48
Ayers, Ronald 1948- ... 61-64
Ayers, Rose
See Greenwood, Lillian Bethel
Ayers, William 1944- ... 204
Ayerst, David (George Ogilvy) 1904-
Brief entry ... 113
Ayim, Maryann E. Neely 1943- ... 179
Ayim, May 1960-1986 ... 139
See also BW 2
Ayittey, George B. N. 1945- ... 167
See also BW 3
Aykroyd, Dan(iel Edward) 1952- ... 123
Aykroyd, Wallace Ruddell 1899-1979
Obituary ... 110
Aylen, Leo (William) 1935- ... CANR-19
Earlier sketch in CA 102
Aylesworth, Jim 1943- ... CANR-45
Earlier sketches in CA 106, CANR-22
See also CLR 89
See also CWRI 5
See also SATA 38, 89, 139

Aylesworth, Thomas G(ibbons) 1927-1995 ... CANR-26
Obituary ... 149
Earlier sketches in CA 25-28R, CANR-10
See also CLR 6
See also SAAS 17
See also SATA 4, 88
Aylett, Steve 1967- ... 195
Ayling, (Harold) Keith (Oliver) 1898-1976 ... 73-76
Obituary ... 69-72
Ayling, Stanley (Edward) 1909- ... CANR-44
Earlier sketches in CA 45-48, CANR-21
Aylmer, Felix
See Jones, Felix Edward Aylmer
Aylmer, G(erald) E(dward) 1926-2000 ... CANR-5
Obituary ... 190
Earlier sketch in CA 13-16R
Aylward, Gladys 1902(?)-1970
Obituary ... 111
Aylward, Marcus
See Alexander, Marc
Aymar, Brandt 1911- ... CANR-37
Earlier sketches in CA 1-4R, CANR-16
See also SATA 22
Aymar, Gordon C(hristian) 1893-1989 ... 5-8R
Ayme, Marcel (Andre) 1902-1967 ... CANR-137
Earlier sketches in CA 89-92, CANR-67
See also CLC 11
See also CLR 25
See also DLB 72
See also EW 12
See also EWL 3
See also GFL 1789 to the Present
See also RGSF 2
See also RGWL 2, 3
See also SATA 91
See also SSC 41
Aymes, Sister Maria de la Cruz ... 21-24R
Aynes, Edith A(nnette) 1909-1980 ... 45-48
Aynes, Pat Edith
See Aynes, Edith A(nnette)
Aynesworth, Hugh (G.) 1931- ... 120
Brief entry ... 115
Interview in ... CA-120
Ayrault, Evelyn West 1922- ... 9-12R
Ayre, Jessica
See Appignanesi, Lisa
Ayre, Robert (Hugh) 1900-1980 ... 1-4R
Ayre, Thornton
See Fearn, John Russell
Ayres, Alison
See Carter, Robert A(yres)
Ayres, Becky
See Hickox, Rebecca (Ayres)
Ayres, Carole Briggs
See Briggs, Carole S(uzanne)
Ayres, E. C. 1946- ... CANR-72
Ayres, Gene
See Ayres, E. C.
Ayres, Ian 1959- ... 144
Ayres, James (Eyvind) 1939- ... CANR-89
Earlier sketch in CA 103
Ayres, Mary Jo 1953- ... 162
Ayres, Pam 1947- ... 155
See also SATA 90
Ayres, Patricia Miller 1923-1985
Obituary ... 117
See also SATA-Obit 46
Ayres, Paul
See Aarons, Edward S(idney)
Ayres, Philip 1944- ... CANR-90
Earlier sketch in CA 134
Ayres, Robert U(nderwood) 1932- ... CANR-16
Earlier sketch in CA 93-96
Ayres, Ruby M(ildred) 1883-1955
Brief entry ... 117
See also RHW
Ayres, Thomas (R.) 1936- ... 203
Ayrton, Elisabeth Walshe 1910(?)-1991 ... CANR-21
Obituary ... 136
Earlier sketches in CA 5-8R, CANR-3
Ayrton, Michael 1921-1975 ... CANR-21
Obituary ... 61-64
Earlier sketches in CA 5-8R, CANR-9
See also CLC 7
Aytmatov, Chingiz
See Aitmatov, Chingiz (Torekulovich)
See also EWL 3
Ayto, Russell 1960- ... SATA 111
Aytoun, Sir Robert 1570-1638 ... DLB 121
Aytoun, William Edmonstoune 1813-1865 ... DLB 32, 159
Ayub Khan, Mohammad 1907-1974 ... CAP-2
Earlier sketch in CA 23-24
Ayvazian, L. Fred 1919- ... 69-72
Azaid
See Zaidenberg, Arthur
Azana, Manuel 1880-1940 ... 216
Azania, Malcolm 1970(?)- ... 236
Azar, Edward E(lias) 1938-1991 ... CANR-28
Obituary ... 134
Earlier sketch in CA 49-52
Azar, Penny 1952- ... SATA 121
Azarian, Mary 1940- ... 118
See also MAICYA 2
See also SATA 112
Azarya, Victor 1946- ... 129
Azbel, Mark Ya. 1932- ... 105
Azcarate y Florez, Pablo de 1890-1971
Obituary ... 113
Azevedo, Aluisio 1857-1913 ... DLB 307
See also LAW
See also WLIT 1
Azevedo, Carlos de 1918- ... 136
Azevedo, Manuel Antonio Alvares de 1831-1852 ... DLB 307
Azevedo, Ross E(ames) ... 105
Azicri, Max 1934- ... 207
Azikiwe, Uche 1947- ... 177
Aziz, Sartaj 1929- ... 111
Aznavour, Charles ... 173
See also Aznavourian, Varenagh
Aznavourian, Varenagh
Brief entry ... 112
See also Aznavour, Charles
Aznavurjian, Shahnour Varenagh
See Aznavour, Charles
Azneer, J. Leonard 1921- ... 33-36R
Azorin
See Martinez Ruiz, Jose
See also CLC 11
See also DLB 322
See also EW 9
See also EWL 3
Azoulay, Dan 1960- ... CANR-124
Earlier sketch in CA 170
Azoy, A(nastasio) C. M. 1891-1965 ... CAP-1
Earlier sketch in CA 13-14
Azoy, G. Whitney 1940- ... 128
Azrael, Judith Anne 1938- ... CANR-10
Earlier sketch in CA 65-68
Azrin, Nathan H(arold) 1930- ... CANR-16
Earlier sketches in CA 45-48, CANR-1
Azua, Felix de 1944- ... 208
Azuela, Arturo 1938- ... 178
Earlier sketch in CA 131
See also EWL 3
See also HW 1, 2
Azuela, Mariano 1873-1952 ... CANR-81
Brief entry ... 104
Earlier sketch in CA 131
See also DAM MULT
See also EWL 3
See also HLC 1
See also HW 1, 2
See also LAW
See also MTCW 1, 2
See also MTFW 2005
See also TCLC 3, 145
Azumi, Atsushi 1907- ... 102
Azumi, Koya 1930- ... 29-32R
Azzi, Stephen (Corrado) 1965- ... 187

B

Ba, (Mallam) Amadou Hampate 1920(?)-1991 ... 186
Ba, Mariama 1929-1981 ... CANR-87
Earlier sketch in CA 141
See also AFW
See also BLCS
See also BW 2
See also DNFS 2
See also WLIT 2
Baack, Lawrence James 1943- ... 109
Baade, (Wilhelm Heinrich) W(alter) 1893-1960
Obituary ... 112
Baaklini, Abdo I(skandar) 1938-2003 ... 198
Obituary ... 221
Baali, Fuad (G.) 1930- ... 184
Brief entry ... 117
Baal-Teshuva, Jacob 1929- ... 5-8R
Baantjer, Albert Cornelis 1923- ... 141
Baar, James A. 1929- ... 102
Baars, Bernard J(oseph) 1946- ... 171
Baars, Conrad W(alterus) 1919-1981 ... CANR-8
Earlier sketch in CA 57-60
Baars, Donald Lee 1928- ... 121
Baarslag, Karl Herman William 1900-1984
Obituary ... 111
Baastad, Babbis Friis
See Friis-Baastad, Babbis Ellinor
Baatz, Charles A(lbert) 1916-1982 ... 104
Obituary ... 162
Baatz, Olga K. 1921- ... 104
Bab
See Gilbert, W(illiam) S(chwenck)
Baba, Ali
See Hubbard, Elbert
Baba, Meher 1894-1969 ... 109
Obituary ... 106
Babb, Howard S(elden) 1924-1978 ... 13-16R
Obituary ... 120
Babb, Hugh Webster 1887-1971(?) ... CAP-1
Earlier sketch in CA 13-14
Babb, Janice Barbara
See Bentley, Janice Babb
Babb, Lawrence 1902-1979 ... CAP-2
Obituary ... 162
Earlier sketch in CA 33-36
Babb, Lawrence Alan 1941-
Brief entry ... 105
Babb, Sanora 1907- ... 13-16R
Babb, Sarah L. 1966- ... 220
Babb, Valerie (Melissa) 1955- ... 142
See also BW 2
Babbage, Stuart Barton 1916- ... CANR-8
Earlier sketch in CA 5-8R
Babbidge, Homer D(aniels), Jr. 1925-1984 ... CANR-13
Obituary ... 112
Earlier sketch in CA 61-64
Babbie, Earl (Robert) 1938- ... CANR-48
Earlier sketches in CA 61-64, CANR-8, 23
Babbis, Eleanor
See Friis-Baastad, Babbis Ellinor
Babbitt, Bruce E(dward) 1938- ... 97-100
Babbitt, Irving 1865-1933 ... 178
See also DLB 63
See also MAL 5
Babbitt, Kathleen 1948- ... 184
Babbitt, Lucy Cullyford 1960- ... 151
See also SATA 85
Babbitt, Natalie (Zane Moore) 1932- ... CANR-126
Earlier sketches in CA 49-52, CANR-2, 19, 38
See also AAYA 51
See also BYA 5
See also CLR 2, 53
See also CWRI 5
See also DLB 52
See also JRDA
See also MAICYA 1, 2
See also SAAS 5
See also SATA 6, 68, 106
Babbitt, Robert
See Bangs, Robert B(abbitt)
Babbitt, Susan E. 1953- ... 159
Babbs, Ken 1936- ... 158
Babcock, C(larence) Merton 1908- ... CANR-5
Earlier sketch in CA 5-8R
Babcock, Chris 1963- ... 150
See also SATA 83
Babcock, Dennis Arthur 1948- ... 61-64
See also SATA 22
Babcock, Dorothy E(llen) 1931- ... 65-68
Babcock, Frederic 1896-1979 ... 5-8R
Babcock, Frederick Morrison 1897(?)-1983
Obituary ... 110
Babcock, Havilah 1898-1964 ... 122
Obituary ... 110
Babcock, Leland S. 1922- ... 180
Brief entry ... 106
Babcock, Nicolas
See Lewis, Tom
Babcock, Richard (Felt, Jr.) 1947- ... 222
Babcock, Robert J(oseph) 1928- ... 13-16R
Babe, Thomas 1941-2000 ... CANR-67
Obituary ... 190
Earlier sketch in CA 101
Interview in ... CA-101
See also CAD
See also CD 5, 6
Babel, Isaac
See Babel, Isaak (Emmanuilovich)
See also EW 11
See also SSFS 10
Babel, Isaak (Emmanuilovich) 1894-1941(?) ... CANR-113
Brief entry ... 104
Earlier sketch in CA 155
See also Babel, Isaac
See also DLB 272
See also EWL 3
See also MTCW 2
See also MTFW 2005
See also RGSF 2
See also RGWL 2, 3
See also SSC 16, 78
See also TCLC 2, 13
See also TWA
Babenco, Hector (Eduardo) 1946- ... 230
Baber, Asa 1936-2003 ... 140
Obituary ... 218
Baber, Carolyn Stonnell 1936- ... 161
See also SATA 96
Baber, Walter F(rank) 1953- ... 120
Babich, Babette E. 1956- ... CANR-108
Earlier sketch in CA 149
Babiiha, Thaddeo K(itasimbwa) 1945- ... 110
Babin, David E. 1925- ... 21-24R
Babin, Maria-Teresa 1910-1989 ... 173
Brief entry ... 107
See also HW 1, 2
Babington, Anthony (Patrick) 1920-2004 . 61-64
Obituary ... 227
Babington Smith, Constance 1912-2000 ... 131
Obituary ... 189
Babits, Lawrence E. 1943- ... 172
Babits, Mihaly 1883-1941
Brief entry ... 114
See also CDWLB 4
See also DLB 215
See also EWL 3
See also TCLC 14
Babitz, Eve 1943- ... CANR-91
Earlier sketches in CA 81-84, CANR-28
Babitz, Sol 1911-1982 ... CANR-28
Earlier sketch in CA 41-44R
Babladelis, Georgia 1931- ... CANR-8
Earlier sketch in CA 21-24R
Babris, Peter J. 1917-1995 ... CANR-10
Earlier sketch in CA 21-24R
Babrius c. 150-c. 200 ... DLB 176
Babson, Marian 1929- ... CANR-104
Earlier sketches in CA 102, CANR-66
See also DLB 276
Babson, Roger W(ard) 1875-1967
Obituary ... 89-92
Babula, William 1943- ... CANR-45
Earlier sketches in CA 105, CANR-21
Babushka
See Malamud-Goti, Jaime
Babylas 1898-1962
See Ghelderode, Michel de
Baca, Jimmy Santiago 1952- ... CANR-90
Earlier sketches in CA 131, CANR-81
See also CP 7
See also DAM MULT
See also DLB 122
See also HLC 1
See also HW 1, 2
See also LLW
See also MAL 5
See also PC 41
Baca, Jose Santiago
See Baca, Jimmy Santiago
Baca, Manuel Cabeza de
See Cabeza de Baca, Manuel
See also DLB 122
Baca, Maria 1951- ... SATA 104
Baca, Murtha ... 154
Bacall, Lauren 1924- ... 93-96
Bacchelli, Riccardo 1891-1985 ... 29-32R
Obituary ... 117
See also CLC 19
See also DLB 264
See also EWL 3
Bacciocco, Edward J(oseph), Jr. 1935- ... 45-48
Bacevich, Andrew J. 1947- ... 218
Bach, Alice (Hendricks) 1942- ... CANR-60
Earlier sketch in CA 101
See also SATA 30, 93
See also SATA-Brief 27
See also YAW
Bach, Bellamy
See Windling, Terri
Bach, Bert C(oates) 1936- ... 21-24R
Bach, George Leland 1915-1994 ... CANR-3
Earlier sketch in CA 1-4R
Bach, George Robert 1914-1986 ... 104
Bach, Ira J(ohn) 1906-1985 ... 115
Bach, Jean
See Greif, Martin
Bach, Kent 1943- ... 85-88
Bach, Lauren
See Holzapfel, Kathleen G.
Bach, Marcus (Louis) 1906-1995
Brief entry ... 115
Bach, Mary 1960- ... SATA 125
Bach, Orville E(uing), Jr. 1946- ... 115
Bach, P. D. Q.
See Schickele, Peter
Bach, Richard (David) 1936- ... CANR-93
Earlier sketches in CA 9-12R, CANR-18
See also AITN 1
See also BEST 89:2
See also BPFB 1
See also BYA 5
See also CLC 14
See also CPW
See also DAM NOV, POP
See also FANT
See also MTCW 1
See also SATA 13
Bach, Steven 1940- ... CANR-115
Earlier sketch in CA 141
Bach, Wilfrid 1936- ... CANR-10
Earlier sketch in CA 61-64
Bacharach, Alfred L(ouis) 1891-1966 ... CAP-1
Earlier sketch in CA 11-12
Bacharach, Bert(ram Mark) 1898-1983
Obituary ... 110
Bacharach, Burt 1928- ... IDFW 3, 4
Bachchan, Harivansh Rai 1907-2003 ... 235
Bache, Benjamin Franklin 1769-1798 .. DLB 43
Bache, Ellyn 1942- ... CANR-129
Earlier sketches in CA 129, CANR-65
See also SATA 124
Bache, William B. 1922- ... 25-28R
Bachel, Beverly K. 1957- ... 213
See also SATA 142
Bachelard, Gaston 1884-1962 ... 97-100
Obituary ... 89-92
See also DLB 296
See also GFL 1789 to the Present
See also TCLC 128
Bachelder, Chris 1971- ... 205
Bachelder, Thomas 1958- ... 139
Bacheller, Irving 1859-1950 ... DLB 202
See also RHW
Bacheller, Irving (Addison) 1859-1950 ... 202
Bachem Alent, Rose M(arie Baake) ... 49-52
Bacher, John 1954- ... 225
Bacher, June Masters 1918-1993 ... 108
Bachkatov, Nina 1946- ... 134
Bachman, David C(hristian) 1934- ... 124
Bachman, Fred 1949- ... 53-56
See also SATA 12
Bachman, Jerald G(raybill) 1936- ... 41-44R
Bachman, John (Walter) 1916-2003 ... 5-8R
Obituary ... 219
Bachman, Richard
See King, Stephen (Edwin)
Bachman, W(illiam) Bryant, Jr. 1941- ... 145
Bachmann, Gideon 1927- ... 104
Bachmann, Ingeborg 1926-1973 ... CANR-69
Obituary ... 45-48
Earlier sketch in CA 93-96
See also CLC 69
See also DLB 85
See also EWL 3
See also RGWL 2, 3
Bachmura, Frank T(homas) 1922-1975 ... 45-48
Bacho, Peter 1950- ... 167
See also BYA 10
Bachrach, Bernard S. 1939- ... CANR-104
Earlier sketch in CA 113
Bachrach, Deborah ... 147
See also SATA 80
Bachrach, Judy 1948- ... 114
Bachrach, Susan D. 1948- ... 223

Cumulative Index 27 Bailey

Bacigalupo, Massimo 196
Bacik, James Joseph 1936- 105
Bacinskaite-Buciene, Salomeja
See Neris, Salomeja
Back, Joe (W.) 1899-1986 .... CANR-75
Obituary 120
Earlier sketches in CAP-2, CA 17-18
Back, Kurt W(olfgang) 1919-1999 .... 13-16R
Backer, Dorothy 1925- 85-88
Backer, John H. 1902-1985 .... 33-36R
Obituary 116
Backer, Morton 1918-2000 .... 17-20R
Backer, Sara 1957- 204
Backes, Clarus 1935-1988
Obituary 127
Backes, David James 1957- 166
Backgammon, Daisy
See Murray, John F(rancis)
Backhouse, Janet 1938-2004 .... CANR-109
Obituary 233
Earlier sketches in CA 109, CANR-26, 54
Backhouse, Sally 1927- 21-24R
Backlund, Ralph T. 1918-1994 73-76
Backman, Carl W(ard) 1923- 17-20R
Backman, Jules 1910-1982 .... CANR-3
Earlier sketch in CA 1-4R
Backman, Melvin (Abraham) 1919- 21-24R
Backman, Milton V., Jr. 1927- CANR-13
Earlier sketch in CA 33-36R
Backscheider, Paula R(ice) 1943- CANR-98
Earlier sketch in CA 138
Backstrom, Charles H(erbert) 1926- 13-16R
Backus, James Gilmore 1913-1989
Obituary 129
See also SATA-Obit 63
Backus, Jean L(ouise) 1914-1986 .... 33-36R
Obituary 119
Backus, Jim
See Backus, James Gilmore
Backus, Oswald P(rentiss) III
1921-1972 .... CAP-2
Obituary 37-40R
Earlier sketch in CA 33-36
Backus, (D.) William 1926- 135
Bacle, Claude
See Grignon, Claude-Henri
See also CCA 1
Bacmeister, Rhoda W(arner)
1893-1991 .... CAP-1
Obituary 133
Earlier sketch in CA 13-16
See also SATA 11
Bacon, Betty
See Bacon, Elizabeth
Bacon, Charlotte 1965- 231
Bacon, Daisy Sarah 1899(?)-1986
Obituary 118
Bacon, Delia 1811-1859 .... DLB 1, 243
Bacon, Donald C(onrad) 1935- 133
Bacon, Edmund N(orwood) 1910- 41-44R
Bacon, Edward 1906-1981 .... 29-32R
Obituary 102
Bacon, Elizabeth 1914-2001 .... 29-32R
Obituary 201
See also SATA 3
See also SATA-Obit 131
Bacon, Elizabeth E(maline) 1904-1972 .. CAP-1
Earlier sketch in CA 19-20
Bacon, Ernst 1898-1990
Obituary 131
Bacon, Frances Atchinson 1903-1982 .... 1-4R
Bacon, Francis 1561-1626 .... BRW 1
See also CDBLB Before 1660
See also DLB 151, 236, 252
See also RGEL 2
See also TEA
Bacon, Joan Chase
See Bowden, Joan Chase
Bacon, John 1940- 53-56
Bacon, Josephine Dodge (Daskam)
1876-1961 97-100
See also SATA 48
Bacon, Lenice Ingram 1895-1978 45-48
Bacon, Leonard 1887-1954 201
Bacon, Mardges 1944- 223
Bacon, Margaret 106
Bacon, Margaret Frances
See Bacon, Peggy
See also SATA-Obit 50
Bacon, Margaret Hope 1921- CANR-123
Earlier sketch in CA 25-28R
See also SATA 6
Bacon, Marion 1901(?)-1975
Obituary 57-60
Bacon, Mark S. 1948- CANR-137
Earlier sketch in CA 151
Bacon, Martha Sherman 1917-1981 85-88
Obituary 104
See also CLR 3
See also CWRI 5
See also SATA 18
See also SATA-Obit 27
Bacon, Melvin (L.) 1950- 159
See also SATA 93
Bacon, Nancy 1940- 93-96
Bacon, Sir Nicholas c. 1510-1579 .... DLB 132
Bacon, Peggy 1895-1987 .... CAP-2
Obituary 121
Earlier sketch in CA 23-24
See also Bacon, Margaret Frances
See also SATA 2
Bacon, Phillip 1922- 41-44R
Bacon, R(onald) L(eonard) 1924- CANR-51
Earlier sketch in CA 104
See also CWRI 5
See also SATA 26, 84
Bacon, Roger 1214(?)-1294 .... DLB 115
Bacon, Thomas 1700(?)-1768 .... DLB 31
Bacon, Wallace A(lger) 1914-2001 .... 17-20R
Obituary 193
Bacote, Clarence A(lbert) 1906-1981 .... CAP-2
Earlier sketch in CA 33-36
Bacovia, G.
See Vasiliu, Gheorghe
Bacovia, George 1881-1957
See Vasiliu, Gheorghe
See also CDWLB 4
See also DLB 220
See also EWL 3
See also TCLC 24
Bacque, James 1929- CANR-81
Earlier sketch in CA 101
Bada, Constantina 1950- 145
Badalamenti, Angelo 1937- .... IDFW 4
Badami, Anita Rau 1962- 203
Badanes, Jerome 1937-1995 234
See also CLC 59
Badash, Lawrence 1934- CANR-14
Earlier sketch in CA 37-40R
Badawi, M(ohamed) M(ustafa) 1925- . CANR-1
Earlier sketch in CA 49-52
Badawi, Muhammed Mustafa
See Badawi, M(ohamed) M(ustafa)
Badcock, Christopher Robert 1946- 101
Badcock, Gary D. 1961- 164
Baddeley, Alan D(avid) 1934- 69-72
Baddeley, Hermione 1906(?)-1986 133
Obituary 120
Baddeley, V. C. Clinton
See Clinton-Baddeley, V(ictor) (Vaughan Reynolds Geraint) C(linton)
Baddock, James 1950- 137
Bade, Jane (Ruth) 1932- 89-92
Bade, Patrick 1951- 89-92
Baden, John A. 1939- 172
Baden, Robert 1936- 138
See also SATA 70
Badenoch, Andrea 1951-2004 227
Baden-Powell, Dorothy 1920- 103
Baden-Powell, Robert (Stephenson Smyth)
1857-1941
Brief entry 114
See also SATA 16
Bader, Carol H. 1949- 192
Bader, Douglas (Robert Steuart)
1910-1982 101
Obituary 107
Bader, Julia 1944- 69-72
Bader, Michael 205
Bader, Robert S(mith) 1925- 120
Badger, John d'Arcy 1917- 45-48
Badger, Ralph E(astman) 1890-1978 .... CAP-2
Obituary 73-76
Earlier sketch in CA 21-22
Badger, Reid 1942- 97-100
Badgley, John 1930- 37-40R
Badgley, Robin F(rancis) 1931- 101
Badham, Leslie (Stephen Ronald) 1908-1975
Obituary 114
Badham, Roger A. 167
Badia, Leonard F(rancis) 1934- 113
Badian, Ernst 1925- 37-40R
Badillo, Herman 1929- 85-88
Badinter, Elisabeth 1944- 118
Badius, J. van Zomeren
See Greshoff, Jan
Badough, Rose Marie 1938- 117
Badovinac, Zdenka 1958- 206
Badt, Karin L(uisa) 1963- 155
See also SATA 91
Badura-Skoda, Eva 1929- CANR-14
Earlier sketch in CA 37-40R
Bae, Youngsoo 222
Baechler, Jean 1937- CANR-116
Earlier sketches in CA 73-76, CANR-13, 30, 56
Baeck, Leo 1873-1956
Brief entry 115
Baeder, John 1938- 111
Baehr, Consuelo 1938- 103
Baehr, Harry William 1907-1987
Obituary 123
Baehr, Kingsley M. 1937- 155
See also SATA 89
Baehr, Patricia (Goehner) 1952- CANR-35
Earlier sketch in CA 103
See also SATA 65
Baen, James P. 1943-
Brief entry 112
Baena, Julio 1955- 179
Baensch, Willy E(dward) 1893-1972
Obituary 37-40R
Baenziger, Hans 1917- 49-52
Baepler, Paul 1961- 192
Baer, Adela S(wenson) 1931- 101
Baer, Curtis O. 1898-1976 49-52
Baer, Daniel J(oseph) 1929- 33-36R
Baer, Donald Merle 1931- 81-84
Baer, Earl E. 1928- 57-60
Baer, Edith R(uth) 1920- CANR-21
Earlier sketch in CA 104
Baer, Eleanora A(gnes) 1907-1998 .... 9-12R
Baer, Gabriel 1919- CANR-2
Earlier sketch in CA 5-8R
Baer, George Webster 1935- 21-24R
Baer, Greg 226
Baer, Hans A. 1944- CANR-139
Earlier sketches in CA 119, CANR-44
Baer, Jean L. CANR-9
Earlier sketch in CA 13-16R
Interview in CANR-9
Baer, Jill
See Gilbert, (Agnes) Joan (Sewell)
Baer, John 1886-1970
Obituary 29-32R
Baer, Judith A(bbott) 1945- 81-84
Baer, Judy 1951- .... SATA 71
Baer, Julie 1960- .... SATA 161
Baer, Marc (Bradley) 1945- 138
Baer, Marianne 1932- 81-84
Baer, Martha 1961- 158
Baer, Max Frank 1912-1994 .... 9-12R
Baer, Morley 1916-1995 218
Baer, Robert 223
Baer, Rosemary 1913- 41-44R
Baer, Walter S. III 1937- 65-68
Baer, Werner 1931- 9-12R
Baer, William E. 1948- 180
Baerg, Harry J(ohn) 1909-1996 .... CANR-4
Earlier sketch in CA 9-12R
See also SATA 12
Baerwald, Hans H(erman) 1927- 33-36R
Baerwald, Sara 1948- 61-64
Baeten, Lieve 1954- .... SATA 83
Baetjer, Anna M(edora) 1899-1984
Obituary 112
Baetzhold, Howard G(eorge) 1923- 29-32R
Baeuml, Franz H(einrich) 1926- 49-52
Baez, Joan (Chandos) 1941- CANR-87
Earlier sketches in CA 21-24R, CANR-26, 55
See also HW 1
Bagarag, Shibli
See Lawlor, Patrick Anthony
Bagby, George
See Stein, Aaron Marc
Bagby, Meredith E. 1974(?)- 180
Bagby, Wesley M(arvin) 1922- CANR-37
Earlier sketches in CA 1-4R, CANR-16
Bagdasarian, Adam .... AAYA 58
Bagdikian, Ben Haig 1920- CANR-6
Earlier sketch in CA 9-12R
Bage, Robert 1728-1801 .... DLB 39
See also RGEL 2
Bagehot, Walter 1826-1877 .... DLB 55
Bagert, Brod 1947- 147
See also SATA 80
Bagg, Graham (William) 1917- 57-60
Bagg, Robert Ely 1935- CANR-42
Earlier sketches in CA 65-68, CANR-15
Baggaley, Andrew R(obert) 1923- 13-16R
Bagge, Peter (Christian Paul) 1957- 224
Baggesen, Jens 1764-1826 .... DLB 300
Baggett, Nancy 1943- CANR-111
Earlier sketch in CA 117
Baggette, Susan K. 1942- .... SATA 126
Baggley, John (Samuel) 1940- 124
Baggott, Julianna 1970(?)- 211
Baggott, Rob 1960- 205
Bagin, Don(ald Richard) 1938- 77-80
Baginski, Frank 1938- 93-96
Bagley, Christopher 1937- 119
Bagley, Desmond 1923-1983 .... CANR-29
Obituary 109
Earlier sketch in CA 17-20R
See also DLB 87
Bagley, Edward R(osecrans) 1926- CANR-5
Earlier sketch in CA 53-56
Bagley, J(ohn) J(oseph) 1908-1989 .... CANR-2
Obituary 127
Earlier sketch in CA 5-8R
Bagley, Mary (C.) 1958- 208
Bagley, Michael 1947- 129
Bagley, Sarah G. 1806-1848(?) .... DLB 239
Bagnall, Nigel Thomas 1927-2002 136
Obituary 205
Bagnel, Joan 1933- 49-52
Bagni, Gwen
See Dubov, Gwen Bagni
Bagnold, Enid 1889-1981 .... CANR-40
Obituary 103
Earlier sketches in CA 5-8R, CANR-5
See also BYA 2
See also CBD
See also CLC 25
See also CN 2
See also CWD
See also CWRI 5
See also DAM DRAM
See also DLB 13, 160, 191, 245
See also FW
See also MAICYA 1, 2
See also RGEL 2
See also SATA 1, 25
Bagnold, Ralph Alger 1896-1990
Obituary 131
Bagramian, Ivan K(ristoforovich) 1897-1982
Obituary 107
Bagritsky, Eduard
See Dzyubin, Eduard Georgievich
See also TCLC 60
Bagritsky, Edvard
See Dzyubin, Eduard Georgievich
See also EWL 3
Bagrjana, Elisaveta
See Belcheva, Elisaveta Lyubomirova
Bagryana, Elisaveta 178
See also Belcheva, Elisaveta Lyubomirova
See also CDWLB 4
See also CLC 10
See also DLB 147
See also EWL 3
Bagster, Hubert
See Trumper, Hubert Bagster
Bagwell, Philip S(idney) 1914- CANR-70
Earlier sketches in CA 33-36R, CANR-13, 29
Bagwell, Stella 1953- 228
Bagwell, William Francis, Jr. 1923- .. CANR-31
Earlier sketch in CA 33-36R
Bahadur, K(rishna) P(rakash) 1924- ... CANR-28
Earlier sketch in CA 57-60
Bahal, Aniruddha 1967- 226
Bahat, Dan 1938- 77-80
Bahdanovich, Maksim 1891-1917 .... EWL 3
Bahl, Roy W., (Jr.) 1939- 21-24R
Bahlke, George W(ilbon) 1934- 29-32R
Bahlke, Valerie Worth 1933-1994 .... CANR-44
Obituary 146
Earlier sketches in CA 41-44R, CANR-15
See also Worth, Valerie
See also CWRI 5
See also SATA 81
Bahlman, Dudley Ward Rhodes 1923- 85-88
Bahlmann, Shirley 1958- 239
Bahm, Archie J(ohn) 1907-1996 .... CANR-3
Earlier sketch in CA 9-12R
Bahmueller, Charles F(erdinand) 1942- 112
Bahn, Eugene 1906-1991 .... 21-24R
Bahn, Margaret (Elizabeth) Linton
1907-1969 .... CAP-2
Earlier sketch in CA 25-28
Bahn, Paul (Gerard) 1953- CANR-100
Earlier sketch in CA 146
Bahous, Sally 1939- .... SATA 86
Bahr, Alice Harrison 1946- 208
Bahr, Edith-Jane 1926-1991 65-68
Bahr, Erhard 1932- 33-36R
Bahr, Hermann 1863-1934 189
Brief entry 121
See also DLB 81, 118
See also EWL 3
Bahr, Howard (Leslie) 1946- 190
Bahr, Howard M. 1938- CANR-12
Earlier sketch in CA 29-32R
Bahr, Jerome 1909-1993 .... 33-36R
Bahr, Mary (Madelyn) 1946- CANR-124
Earlier sketches in CA 136, CANR-65
See also SATA 95
Bahr, Robert 1940- CANR-9
Earlier sketch in CA 65-68
See also SATA 38
Bahro, Rudolf 1935-1997 189
Bahti, Tom 1926-1972 .... SATA 57
See also SATA-Brief 31
Baicker-McKee, Carol 1958- 226
Baida, Peter 1950-1999 202
Baier, Kurt Erich 1917- 65-68
Baif, Jean-Antoine de
1532-1589 .... GFL Beginnings to 1789
Baigell, Matthew 1933- CANR-138
Earlier sketch in CA 107
Bai Jieming
See Barme, Geremie
Bai Juyi 772-846 .... RGWL 2, 3
Bail, Murray 1941- CANR-62
Earlier sketch in CA 127
See also CN 4, 5, 6, 7
Bailes, Kendall E(ugene) 1940-1988
Brief entry 112
Bailey, Abigail Abbot 1746-1815 .... DLB 200
Bailey, Alfred Goldsworthy 1905-1997 . 25-28R
See also CP 1
See also DLB 68
Bailey, Alfred M(arshall) 1894-1978 .... 41-44R
Bailey, Alice A(nne La Trobe-Bateman)
1880(?)-1949
Brief entry 116
Bailey, Alice Cooper 1890-1978 .... CANR-70
Earlier sketches in CAP-1, CA 13-16
See also SATA 12
Bailey, Anne 1958- .... SATA 71
Bailey, Anne C(aroline) 1964- 239
Bailey, Anthony 1933- CANR-105
Earlier sketches in CA 1-4R, CANR-3, 44
Bailey, Barry 1926- 107
Bailey, Bernadine (Freeman)
1901-1995 .... CANR-7
Earlier sketch in CA 5-8R
See also SATA 14
Bailey, Beryl Loftman 1920(?)-1977
Obituary 69-72
Bailey, Beth L. 1957- CANR-118
Earlier sketch in CA 142
Bailey, Carolyn Sherwin 1875-1961 73-76
See also BYA 5
See also CWRI 5
See also MAICYA 1, 2
See also SATA 14
Bailey, Charles W(aldo) II 1929- CANR-1
Earlier sketch in CA 1-4R
Bailey, Chris H(arvey) 1946- 65-68
Bailey, Conrad Charles Maitland 1922- 105
Bailey, Cornelia Walker 1945- 195
Bailey, D. F. 1950- 125
Bailey, D. R. Shackleton
See Shackleton Bailey, D(avid) R(oy)
Bailey, Dale 1968- 228
Bailey, David (Royston) 1938- 120
Bailey, David C(harles) 1930- 45-48
Bailey, Debbie 1954- .... SATA 123
Bailey, Derrick Sherwin 1910-1984 .... CANR-2
Obituary 112
Earlier sketch in CA 5-8R
Bailey, Don 1942- 93-96
Bailey, Donna (Veronica Anne) 1938- 136
See also SATA 68
Bailey, Dudley 1918- 17-20R
Bailey, Eric 1933-1997 .... 33-36R
Bailey, F(rancis) Lee 1933- 89-92
Bailey, Florence Merriam 1863-1948 .... ANW
Bailey, Fred Arthur 1947- CANR-72
Earlier sketch in CA 129
Bailey, (John) Frederick (II) 1946- 133
Bailey, Frederick George 1924- CANR-9
Earlier sketch in CA 13-16R
Bailey, Frederick Marshman
1882-1967 .... CAP-1
Earlier sketch in CA 13-14

Bailey, George 1919- ... CANR-38
Earlier sketches in CA 25-28R, CANR-17
Bailey, Gerald Earl 1929- ... CANR-10
Earlier sketch in CA 25-28R
Bailey, Gordon Keith 1936- ... 112
Bailey, H(enry) C(hristopher) 1878-1961
Obituary ... 108
See also DLB 77
See also RHW
Bailey, Harold (Walter) 1899-1996 ... 109
Obituary ... 151
Bailey, Harry A(ugustine), Jr. 1932- ... 21-24R
Bailey, Helen Miller 1909- ... 13-16R
Bailey, Herbert S(mith), Jr. 1921-
Brief entry ... 112
Bailey, Hilary 1936- ... 158
Bailey, Hillary G(oodsell) 1894-1988 ... 57-60
Bailey, Hugh C(oleman) 1929- ... 9-12R
Bailey, J(ames) Martin 1929- ... 49-52
Bailey, J(ames) O(sler) 1903-1979 ... 17-20R
Obituary ... 126
Bailey, Jackson Holbrook
1925-1996 ... CANR-21
Obituary ... 153
Earlier sketch in CA 45-48
Bailey, Jacob 1731-1808 ... DLB 99
Bailey, James 1946- ... 238
Bailey, James H(enry) 1919- ... 106
Bailey, James R(ichard) A(be) 1919- ... 53-56
Bailey, (Corinne) Jane 1943- ... 77-80
Bailey, Jane H(orton) 1916- ... CANR-4
Earlier sketch in CA 53-56
See also SATA 12
Bailey, Joan H(auser) 1922- ... 21-24R
Bailey, Joe A(llen) 1929- ... 37-40R
Bailey, John (Robert) 1940- ... 121
See also SATA 52
Bailey, John A(medee) 1929- ... 37-40R
Bailey, K. C.
See Bailey, Kathleen C.
Bailey, Kathleen C. 1949- ... 149
Bailey, Kathryn ... 175
Bailey, Kenneth K(yle) 1923- ... 21-24R
Bailey, Kenneth P. 1912-2000 ... CANR-4
Earlier sketch in CA 53-56
Bailey, Lee 1926-2003 ... CANR-141
Obituary ... 221
Earlier sketch in CA 144
Bailey, Linda 1948- ... CANR-123
Earlier sketch in CA 166
See also SATA 107
Bailey, Lloyd Richard 1936- ... CANR-15
Earlier sketch in CA 85-88
Bailey, M(innie Elizabeth) Thomas ... 57-60
Bailey, Maralyn Collins (Harrison) 1941- . 53-56
See also SATA 12
Bailey, Maria T. ... 224
Bailey, Martha (J.) 1929- ... CANR-108
Earlier sketch in CA 151
Bailey, Martin 1947- ... 134
Bailey, Matilda
See Radford, Ruby L(orraine)
Bailey, Maurice Charles 1932- ... 53-56
See also SATA 12
Bailey, Norman A(lishan) 1931- ... CANR-13
Earlier sketch in CA 21-24R
Bailey, Patrick 1925-1998 ... 57-60
Bailey, Paul 1937- ... CANR-124
Earlier sketches in CA 21-24R, CANR-16, 62
See also CLC 45
See also CN 1, 2, 3, 4, 5, 6, 7
See also DLB 14, 271
See also GLL 2
Bailey, Paul Dayton 1906-1987 ... CANR-75
Obituary ... 124
Earlier sketches in CA 5-8R, CANR-6
Bailey, Pearl (Mae) 1918-1990 ... CANR-87
Obituary ... 132
Earlier sketches in CA 61-64, CANR-14, 42
See also BW 2
See also SATA 81
Bailey, Peter J. 1946- ... 201
Bailey, Philip James 1816-1902 ... 179
See also DLB 32
See also RGEL 2
Bailey, Ralph Edgar 1893-1982 ... CANR-70
Earlier sketches in CAP-1, CA 17-18
See also SATA 11
Bailey, Raymond H(amby) 1938- ... CANR-8
Earlier sketch in CA 61-64
Bailey, Richard W(eld) 1939- ... CANR-10
Earlier sketch in CA 25-28R
Bailey, Robert, Jr. 1945- ... 49-52
Bailey, Robert W(ilson) 1943- ... CANR-21
Earlier sketch in CA 69-72
Bailey, Robin W(ayne) 1952- ... 154
See also FANT
Bailey, Rosemary 1953- ... 227
Bailey, Sheila (Lucas) 1960- ... SATA 155
Bailey, Stephen Kemp 1916-1982 ... CANR-76
Obituary ... 106
Earlier sketches in CA 1-4R, CANR-4
Bailey, Sydney D(awson)
1916-1995 ... CANR-31
Obituary ... 150
Earlier sketches in CA 69-72, CANR-12
Bailey, Thomas A(ndrew)
1902-1983 ... CANR-18
Obituary ... 110
Earlier sketch in CA 17-20R
Bailey, Victor 1948- ... 125
Bailie, Victoria Worley 1894-1991 ... CAP-1
Earlier sketch in CA 13-16
Bailin, George 1928- ... 208
Bailkey, Nels M(artin) 1911- ... 33-36R
Baillargeon, Pierre 1916-1967 ... 152
See also Brulard, Henri
See also CCA 1
See also DLB 88
Baillen, Claude
See Delay(-Tubiana), Claude
Baillie, Allan (Stuart) 1943- ... CANR-135
Earlier sketches in CA 118, CANR-42
See also AAYA 25
See also CLR 49
See also SAAS 21
See also SATA 87, 151
See also YAW
Baillie, Hugh 1890-1966 ... 183
Obituary ... 89-92
See also DLB 29
Baillie, Isobel 1895-1983
Obituary ... 110
Baillie, Joanna 1762-1851 ... DLB 93
See also GL 2
See also RGEL 2
Baillie, Kate 1957- ... 124
Baillie-Hamilton, George 1894-1986
Obituary ... 121
Baily, Charles M(ichael) 1944- ... 117
Baily, Leslie 1906-1976 ... CAP-2
Earlier sketch in CA 25-28
Baily, Nathan A(riel) 1920-2003 ... CANR-6
Obituary ... 214
Earlier sketch in CA 9-12R
Baily, Samuel L(ongstreth) 1936- ... 29-32R
Bailyn, Bernard 1922- ... CANR-140
Earlier sketches in CA 61-64, CANR-8, 46
See also DLB 17
Bailyn, Lotte 1930- ... 146
Bain, A(ndrew) D(avid) 1936- ... 180
Brief entry ... 111
Bain, Carl E. 1930- ... 85-88
Bain, Chester A(rthur) 1912-1991 ... 29-32R
Bain, Chester Ward 1919- ... 85-88
Bain, David Haward 1949- ... CANR-91
Earlier sketch in CA 141
Bain, Donald 1935- ... 180
Bain, George Sayers 1939- ... 132
Bain, Joe S. 1912-1991 ... 33-36R
Bain, Kenneth (Ross) 1923- ... 130
Bain, Kenneth Bruce Findlater
1921-1985 ... CANR-75
Obituary ... 115
Earlier sketch in CA 93-96
Bain, Kenneth Ray 1942- ... 104
Bain, Robert 1932- ... 77-80
Bain, Ted
See Tubb, E(dwin) C(harles)
Bain, Trevor 1931- ... 145
Bain, Willard S., Jr. 1938- ... 25-28R
Bainbridge, Beryl (Margaret) 1934- . CANR-128
Earlier sketches in CA 21-24R, CANR-24, 55, 75, 88
See also BRWS 6
See also CLC 4, 5, 8, 10, 14, 18, 22, 62, 130
See also CN 2, 3, 4, 5, 6, 7
See also DAM NOV
See also DLB 14, 231
See also EWL 3
See also MTCW 1, 2
See also MTFW 2005
Bainbridge, Cyril 1928- ... 129
Bainbridge, David ... 229
Bainbridge, Geoffrey 1923- ... 5-8R
Bainbridge, John (Lakin) 1913-1992 . CANR-46
Obituary ... 139
Earlier sketch in CA 13-16R
Bainbridge, William Sims 1940- ... 120
Baine, Rodney M(ontgomery)
1913-2000 ... 69-72
Baines, Anthony C(uthbert) 1912-1997 ... 5-8R
Baines, Frank 1915-1987
Obituary ... 124
Baines, Jocelyn 1925-1973 ... 106
Obituary ... 104
Baines, John (David) 1943- ... SATA 71
Baines, John M. 1935- ... 41-44R
Baines, John Robert 1946- ... 123
Bains, Larry
See Sabin, Louis
Bains, William (Arthur) 1955- ... 145
Bainton, Roland H(erbert)
1894-1984 ... CANR-5
Obituary ... 113
Earlier sketch in CA 1-4R
Bair, Deirdre 1935- ... 81-84
See also BEST 90:4
Bair, Frank E. 1927- ... 102
Baird, A(lbert) Craig 1883-1979 ... CAP-1
Earlier sketch in CA 13-14
Baird, Alexander (John) 1925- ... 9-12R
See also CP 1
Baird, Alison 1963- ... 208
See also SATA 138
Baird, Bil 1904-1987 ... 106
Obituary ... 122
See also SATA 30
See also SATA-Obit 52
Baird, Duncan H. 1917- ... 65-68
Baird, Forrest J. 1905-2001 ... CAP-1
Earlier sketch in CA 19-20
Baird, Irene (Todd) 1901-1981 ... 145
See also DLB 68
Baird, J(oseph) Arthur 1922- ... CANR-3
Earlier sketch in CA 5-8R
Baird, J(oseph) L. 1933- ... 85-88
Baird, Jack
See Baird, John Charlton
Baird, Jay Warren 1936- ... 41-44R
Baird, Jesse Hays 1889-1976 ... 13-16R
Baird, John Charlton 1938- ... 126
Baird, John D. 1941- ... 109
Baird, John Edward 1922- ... 17-20R
Baird, Jonathan 1972- ... 203
Baird, Joseph Armstrong, (Jr.)
1922-1992 ... CANR-57
Obituary ... 142
Earlier sketches in CA 33-36R, CANR-12
Baird, Lorrayne Y. 1927- ... 112
Baird, Marie-Terese 1918- ... 57-60
Baird, Martha (Joanna) 1921-1981 ... CANR-9
Earlier sketch in CA 61-64
Baird, Nancy Disher 1935- ... CANR-32
Earlier sketches in CA 89-92, CANR-15
Baird, Nicola ... 237
Baird, Patrick D(ouglas) 1912-1984
Obituary ... 112
Baird, Robert D(ahlen) 1933- ... 53-56
Baird, Robert M. 1937- ... 139
Baird, Ronald J(ames) 1929- ... 53-56
Baird, Russell N. 1922-1993 ... 17-20R
Baird, Thomas (P.) 1923-1990 ... CANR-21
Obituary ... 131
Earlier sketches in CA 53-56, CANR-4
See also SATA 45
See also SATA-Brief 39
See also SATA-Obit 64
See also YAW
Baird, W(illiam) David 1939- ... 41-44R
Baird, Wilhelmina 1935- ... 163
See also SFW 4
Baird, William (Robb) 1924- ... CANR-104
Earlier sketch in CA 13-16R
Baird, William Britton
See Baird, Bil
Baird-Smith, Robin 1946- ... 123
Bairstow, Jeffrey N(oel) 1939- ... CANR-8
Earlier sketch in CA 61-64
Baisden, Michael 1963- ... 218
Baistow, (Enoch) Thomas 1914-1999 ... 183
Baistow, Tom
See Baistow, (Enoch) Thomas
Baity, Elizabeth Chesley 1907-1989 ... 29-32R
See also SATA 1
Baitz, Jon Robin 1961- ... CANR-72
Earlier sketch in CA 134
See also CAD
See also CD 5, 6
Baiul, Oksana 1977- ... 170
See also SATA 108
Bai Xianyong
See Pai Hsien-yung
Bajema, Carl Jay 1937- ... CANR-12
Earlier sketch in CA 33-36R
Ba Jin
See Li Fei-kan
See also CWW 2
Bajwa, Rupa 1976- ... 231
Bakal, Carl 1918-2004 ... 21-24R
Obituary ... 225
Bakalar, James B. 1943- ... 97-100
Bakalar, Nicholas ... 228
Bakalar, Nick
See Bakalar, Nicholas
Bakalian, Anny 1951- ... 145
Bakalis, Michael J. 1938- ... 85-88
Bakan, David 1921- ... 25-28R
Bakan, Paul 1928- ... 21-24R
Bakaric, Vladimir 1912-1983
Obituary ... 114
Bake, William A(lbert) 1938- ... 110
Bakeless, John (Edwin) 1894-1978 ... CANR-5
Obituary ... 118
Earlier sketch in CA 5-8R
See also SATA 9
Bakeless, Katherine Little 1895-1992 ... 5-8R
See also SATA 9
Bakely, Don(ald Carlisle) 1928- ... 65-68
Baker, A(lbert) A(llen) 1910-1996 ... 104
Baker, A(rthur) D(avidson) III 1941- ... 161
Baker, Adelaide N(ichols)
1894-1974 ... CANR-80
Obituary ... 134
Earlier sketch in CA 45-48
Baker, Adolph 1917- ... 53-56
Baker, Al ... AITN 1
Baker, Alan 1951- ... CANR-129
Earlier sketches in CA 97-100, CANR-16, 38, 68
See also SATA 22, 93, 146
Baker, Alfred Thornton 1915(?)-1983
Obituary ... 110
Baker, Alison 1953- ... 144
Baker, Allison
See Crumbaker, Alice
Baker, Alton Wesley 1912-1992 ... 33-36R
Baker, Asa
See Dresser, Davis
Baker, Augusta 1911-1998 ... CANR-17
Obituary ... 164
Earlier sketch in CA 1-4R
See also BW 1
See also SATA 3
Baker, Augustine 1575-1641 ... DLB 151
Baker, Barbara 1952- ... 235
Baker, Benjamin 1915- ... 1-4R
Baker, Betty D(oreen Flook) 1916- ... CANR-6
Earlier sketch in CA 9-12R
See also RHW
Baker, Betty Lou 1928-1987 ... CANR-38
Earlier sketches in CA 1-4R, CANR-2
See also CWRI 5
See also JRDA
See also MAICYA 1, 2
See also SATA 5, 73
See also SATA-Obit 54
Baker, Bill
See Baker, C(harles) William
Baker, Bill 1936- ... 77-80
Baker, Bill Russell 1933- ... 57-60
Baker, Bobby
See Baker, Alfred Thornton and Baker, Robert G.
Baker, C. Edwin 1947- ... 172
Baker, C. J.
See Baker, Christopher John
Baker, C(harles) William 1919- ... 57-60
Baker, Calvin 1972- ... 163
See also BW 3
Baker, Carin Greenberg 1959- ... SATA 79
Baker, Carlos (Heard) 1909-1987 ... CANR-63
Obituary ... 122
Earlier sketches in CA 5-8R, CANR-3
See also DLB 103
See also TCLC 119
Baker, Carroll 1931- ... 142
Baker, Charlotte 1910- ... 17-20R
See also SATA 2
Baker, Christina Looper 1939- ... 161
Baker, Christopher John 1948- ... 135
Brief entry ... 117
Baker, Christopher W. 1952- ... 217
See also SATA 144
Baker, D(onald) Philip 1937- ... 102
Baker, David (Anthony) 1954- ... CANR-119
Earlier sketch in CA 118
See also DLB 120
Baker, Deborah 1959- ... 158
See also HGG
Baker, Dennis 1942- ... 107
Baker, Denys Val 1917-1984 ... CANR-72
Obituary ... 113
Earlier sketches in CA 9-12R, CANR-6
See also HGG
Baker, Donald G(ene) 1932- ... 33-36R
Baker, Donald N(oel) 1936- ... 21-24R
Baker, Donald W(hitelaw) 1923- ... CANR-12
Earlier sketch in CA 73-76
Baker, Dorothy 1907-1968 ... CANR-1
Obituary ... 25-28R
Earlier sketch in CA 1-4R
Baker, Eleanor Z(uckerman) 1932- ... CANR-8
Earlier sketch in CA 57-60
Baker, (Mary) Elizabeth (Gillette)
1923- ... CANR-70
Earlier sketches in CA 1-4R, CANR-3
See also SATA 7
Baker, Elizabeth Faulkner 1886(?)-1973 . CAP-1
Obituary ... 41-44R
Earlier sketch in CA 13-16
Baker, Elliott 1922- ... CANR-63
Earlier sketches in CA 45-48, CANR-2
See also CLC 8
See also CN 1, 2, 3, 4, 5, 6, 7
Baker, Elsie 1929- ... 65-68
Baker, Elsworth F. 1903-1985 ... CAP-2
Earlier sketch in CA 25-28
Baker, Emerson W(oods II) ... 174
Baker, Eric Wilfred 1899-1973
Obituary ... 45-48
Baker, Ernest W., Jr. 1926- ... 208
Baker, Eugene H. ... SATA-Brief 50
Baker, F(rederick) Sherman 1902-1976
Obituary ... 65-68
Baker, Falcon (O., Jr.) 1916-1994 ... 135
Baker, Frank (Edgar) 1908-1982 ... FANT
See also SUFW
Baker, Frank 1910-1999 ... 9-12R
Baker, Frank 1936-1982 ... CANR-18
Earlier sketches in CA 49-52, CANR-2
Baker, Frank S. 1899(?)-1983
Obituary ... 109
Baker, Frank S(heaffer) 1910-2005 ... 17-20R
Obituary ... 239
Baker, G. P.
See Baker, Gordon (Park)
Baker, G(eorge) W(alter) 1915-2003 ... 21-24R
Obituary ... 217
Baker, G(eorge) W(alter) 1915-2003
Obituary ... 217
Baker, Gary G. 1939- ... 21-24R
Baker, Gayle Cunningham 1950- ... 105
See also SATA 39
Baker, George 1915-1975 ... 93-96
Obituary ... 57-60
Baker, George Pierce 1866-1935 ... DLB 266
Baker, Gilbert
See Baker, John Gilbert Hindley
Baker, Gladys L(ucille) 1910-1991 ... 41-44R
Baker, Glenn A. 1952- ... 197
Baker, Gordon (Park) 1938-2002 ... CANR-86
Obituary ... 206
Earlier sketch in CA 130
Baker, Gordon Pratt 1910-1994 ... 1-4R
Baker, Herbert G(eorge) 1920- ... 41-44R
Baker, Herschel Clay 1914-1990 ... 61-64
See also DLB 111
Baker, Houston A., Jr. 1943- ... CANR-87
Earlier sketches in CA 41-44R, CANR-14, 42
See also BW 2
See also DLB 67
Baker, Howard (James) 1946- ... 218
Baker, Howard H(enry), Jr. 1925- ... 124
Brief entry ... 113
Baker, Howard Wilson 1905-1990 ... CAP-2
Obituary ... 132
Earlier sketch in CA 19-20
See also CP 1, 2, 3, 4
Baker, Hugh D. R. 1937- ... CANR-12
Earlier sketch in CA 25-28R
Baker, Ivon 1928- ... 73-76
Baker, J(ohn) A(lec) 1926- ... 25-28R
Baker, James C(alvin) 1935- ... CANR-55
Brief entry ... 117
Earlier sketch in CA 125

Cumulative Index 29 **Baldwin**

Baker, James Chamberlain 1879-1969 213
Baker, James Lawrence 1941- 53-56
Baker, James R(upert) 1925- 29-32R
Baker, James T. 1940- 85-88
Baker, James Volant 1903-1977 57-60
Baker, James W. 1924- 77-80
  See also SATA 22, 65
Baker, James W. 1926- CANR-86
  Earlier sketch in CA 133
  See also SATA 122
Baker, Jameson
  See Spencer, David
Baker, Jane Howard 1950- 110
Baker, Janice E(dla) 1941- 57-60
  See also SATA 22
Baker, Jean H.
  See Russell, George William
  See also TCLC 3, 10
Baker, Jean H(ogarth Harvey)
  1933- CANR-127
  Earlier sketches in CA 41-44R, CANR-59
Baker, Jean M. 1927- 171
Baker, Jean-Claude 1943- CANR-104
  Earlier sketch in CA 150
Baker, Jeannie 1950- CANR-102
  Earlier sketches in CA 97-100, CANR-69
  See also CLR 28
  See also CWRI 5
  See also MAICYA 2
  See also MAICYAS 1
  See also SATA 23, 88, 156
Baker, Jeffrey J(ohn) W(heeler) 1931- .. CANR-1
  Earlier sketch in CA 49-52
  See also SATA 5
Baker, Jerry 105
  See also AITN 2
Baker, Jill 1951- 127
Baker, Jim
  See Baker, James W.
Baker, John 1901(?)-1971
  Obituary 104
Baker, John 1942- 229
Baker, John C(hester) 1909-1999 106
  Obituary 185
Baker, John F(leetwood) 1901-1985
  Obituary 117
Baker, John F. 1931- 85-88
Baker, John Gilbert Hindley 1910-1986
  Obituary 119
Baker, John H(enry) 1936- 33-36R
Baker, John R(andal) 1900-1984 .... CANR-27
  Obituary 113
  Earlier sketch in CA 49-52
Baker, John W(esley) 1920- 61-64
Baker, Joseph E(llis) 1905-1985 .... 33-36R
Baker, Josephine 1906-1975
  Obituary 105
Baker, Kage 1952- 221
  Earlier sketches in CA 164, CANR-104
  Autobiographical Essay in 221
Baker, Keith Michael 1938- 57-60
Baker, Ken 1962- .... SATA 133
Baker, Kenneth F(rank) 1908-1996 ... CANR-27
  Earlier sketch in CA 49-52
Baker, Kevin (Breen) 1958- CANR-140
  Earlier sketch in CA 143
Baker, Kyle 1965- 226
Baker, Larry 173
Baker, Laura Nelson 1911- CANR-70
  Earlier sketches in CA 5-8R, CANR-5
  See also SATA 3
Baker, Lawrence M(anning) 1907- CAP-1
  Earlier sketch in CA 13-14
Baker, Leonard S(tanley) 1931-1984 ...... 21-24R
  Obituary 114
Baker, Letha Elizabeth (Mitts) 1913- 33-36R
Baker, Lewis
  See Baker, Lewis T(urner) III
Baker, Lewis T(urner) III 1953- 129
Baker, Liliane L.
  See Baker, Lillian (L.)
Baker, Lillian (L.) 1921-1996 139
Baker, Lise S. 235
Baker, Liva 1930- 29-32R
Baker, Lori 1962- 156
Baker, Lucinda 1916- 65-68
Baker, Lynn S. 1948- 109
Baker, M(ary) E(llen) Penny 45-48
Baker, Madeline CANR-90
  Earlier sketch in CA 177
Baker, Margaret 1890-1965 .... CANR-6
  Earlier sketch in CA 13-16R
  See also SATA 4
Baker, Margaret J(oyce) 1918- CANR-22
  Earlier sketches in CA 13-16R, CANR-7
  See also SAAS 8
  See also SATA 12
Baker, Marilyn 1929-
  Brief entry 111
Baker, Mark 1950- 143
Baker, Mark (Raphael) 1959-
Baker, Mary Gladys Steel 1892-1974 .... CAP-1
  Earlier sketch in CA 13-16
  See also SATA 12
Baker, Maureen 1948- CANR-130
  Earlier sketch in CA 162
Baker, (Robert) Michael (Graham)
  1938- 25-28R
  See also SATA 4
Baker, Michael H(enry) C(hadwick)
  1937- CANR-23
  Earlier sketches in CA 57-60, CANR-8
Baker, Miriam Hawthorn
  See Nye, Miriam (Maurine Hawthorn) Baker
Baker, Nancy C(arolyn Moll) 1944- 81-84
Baker, Nancy V. 1952- 144
Baker, Nelson B(laisdell) 1905-1994 ..... 17-20R
Baker, Nicholson 1957- CANR-138
  Earlier sketches in CA 135, CANR-63, 120
  See also AMWS 13
  See also CLC 61, 165
  See also CN 6
  See also CPW
  See also DA3
  See also DAM POP
  See also DLB 227
  See also MTFW 2005
Baker, Nikki 1962- 137
  See also BW 2
Baker, Nina (Brown) 1888-1957 .... SATA 15
Baker, Norma Jean 1926-1962 129
  Obituary 113
Baker, Olaf 1870(?)-1964 129
Baker, Oleda 1934- 69-72
Baker, Pamela J. 1947- 127
  See also SATA 66
Baker, Paul R(aymond) 1927- CANR-41
  Earlier sketches in CA 9-12R, CANR-4, 19
Baker, Paul T(hornell) 1927- 33-36R
Baker, Pauline H(alpern) 1941- 105
Baker, Pearl Biddlecome 1907-1992 ..... 17-20R
Baker, Peter (Gorton) 1926- CANR-10
  Earlier sketch in CA 21-24R
Baker, Philip John Noel
  See Noel-Baker, Philip John
Baker, R(onald) J(ames) 1924- 33-36R
Baker, R. R.
  See Baker, R(eginald) Robin
Baker, R(eginald) Robin 1944- 110
Baker, Rachel 1904-1978 .... 5-8R
  Obituary 103
  See also SATA 2
  See also SATA-Obit 26
Baker, Ray Stannard 1870-1946
  Brief entry 118
  See also TCLC 47
Baker, Richard A(llan) 1940- 140
Baker, Richard E. 1950- 148
Baker, Richard M(ason), Jr. 1924-1978 .. 13-16R
  Obituary 135
Baker, Richard St. Barbe 1889-1982 ...... CAP-1
  Obituary 110
  Earlier sketch in CA 11-12
Baker, Richard Terrill 1913-1981 .... 1-4R
  Obituary 104
Baker, Rick 1950- .... IDFW 3, 4
Baker, Robert Allen, Jr. 1921- 108
Baker, Robert Andrew 1910-1992 109
Baker, Robert B(ernard) 1937- CANR-6
  Earlier sketch in CA 53-56
Baker, Robert D(onald) 1927- 121
Baker, Robert G. 1928- 85-88
Baker, Robert J(unior) 1920- 116
Baker, Robert K(erry) 1948- 108
Baker, Robin
  See Baker, R(eginald) Robin
Baker, Robin Campbell 1941- 17-20R
Baker, (John) Roger 1934-1993 .... 25-28R
  Obituary 143
Baker, Rollin H(arold) 1916- 118
Baker, Ronald L(ee) 1937- 105
Baker, Ross K(enneth) 1938- 29-32R
Baker, Russell (Wayne) 1925- CANR-137
  Earlier sketches in CA 57-60, CANR-11, 41, 59
  See also BEST 89:4
  See also CLC 31
  See also MTCW 1, 2
  See also MTFW 2005
Baker, S. H.
  See Baker, Sarah H.
Baker, Samm Sinclair 1909-1997 ..... CANR-21
  Obituary 157
  Earlier sketches in CA 5-8R, CANR-3
  See also SATA 12
  See also SATA-Obit 96
Baker, Samuel White 1821-1893 .... DLB 166
Baker, Sarah H. 229
Baker, Scott (MacMartin) 1947- CANR-72
  Earlier sketch in CA 93-96
  See also HGG
Baker, Sharlene 1954- 136
Baker, Sharon 1938-1991 117
  See also SFW 4
Baker, Sheridan (Warner, Jr.)
  1918-2000 .... CANR-18
  Earlier sketches in CA 5-8R, CANR-2
Baker, Stephen 1921-2004 .... CANR-19
  Obituary 231
  Earlier sketches in CA 1-4R, CANR-3
Baker, Susan (Catherine) 1942-1991 105
  See also SATA 29
Baker, T(homas) F(rancis) Timothy
  1935- 25-28R
Baker, T(homas) Lindsay 1947- CANR-98
  Earlier sketches in CA 121, CANR-47
Baker, Thomas 1656-1740 .... DLB 213
Baker, Thomas George Adames
  1920-2000 108
Baker, Thomas Harrison 1933- 33-36R
Baker, Trudy
  See Bain, Donald
Baker, Van R. 1925- 236
Baker, Victor Richard 1945- 109
Baker, W. B.
  See Baker, William B(uck)
Baker, W. Buck
  See Baker, William B(uck)
Baker, Wesley C. 21-24R
Baker, Will(iam Edwin) 1935- CANR-102
  Earlier sketch in CA 21-24R
Baker, William 1944- CANR-131
  Earlier sketch in CA 163
Baker, William Avery 1911-1981 .... CANR-2
  Earlier sketch in CA 5-8R
Baker, William B(uck) 1954- 235
Baker, William D. 1924- 105
Baker, William F. 1942- 172
Baker, William Howard
  See McNeilly, Wilfred (Glassford)
Baker, William Joseph 1938- CANR-24
  Earlier sketch in CA 97-100
Baker, William W(allace) 1921- 73-76
Baker-Carr, Janet 1934- 93-96
Baker Roshi, Richard 1936- 209
Baker White, John 1902-1988 101
Bakewell, K(enneth) G(raham) B(artlett)
  1931- CANR-42
  Earlier sketches in CA 102, CANR-19
Bakewell, Paul, Jr. 1889-1972 .... CAP-1
  Earlier sketch in CA 11-12
Bakewell, Peter J(ohn) 1943- 119
Bakhtiar, Laleh Mehree 1938- 69-72
Bakhtiari, Soraya Esfandiari 1932-2001 234
Bakhtin, M.
  See Bakhtin, Mikhail Mikhailovich
Bakhtin, M. M.
  See Bakhtin, Mikhail Mikhailovich
Bakhtin, Mikhail
  See Bakhtin, Mikhail Mikhailovich
Bakhtin, Mikhail Mikhailovich 1895-1975 . 128
  Obituary 113
  See also CLC 83
  See also DLB 242
  See also EWL 3
  See also TCLC 160
Baki
  See Abdul-baki, Mahmud
  See also WLIT 6
Bakis, Kirsten 1968(?)- CANR-113
  Earlier sketch in CA 159
Bakish, David (Joseph) 1937- 45-48
Bakjian, Andy 1915-1986 53-56
Bakke, E(dward) Wight 1903-1971
  Obituary 110
Bakke, Mary S(terling) 1904-1987 .... 37-40R
  Obituary 121
Bakken, Dick 1941- CANR-25
  Earlier sketch in CA 106
Bakken, Henry Harrison 1896-1987 . CANR-11
  Earlier sketch in CA 65-68
Bakker, Cornelius B(ernardus) 1929- 57-60
Bakker, Elna S(undquist) 1921-1995 69-72
  Obituary 149
Bakker, James Orson 1940- 128
Bakker, Jim
  See Bakker, James Orson
Bakker, Robert T. 1946(?)- 152
Bakker, Tamara Faye 128
Bakker, Tammy Faye
  See Bakker, Tamara Faye
Bakker-Rabdau, Marianne K(atherine)
  1935- 73-76
Baklanoff, Eric N. 1925- CANR-13
  Earlier sketch in CA 33-36R
Bakr, Abd Al-Wahhab 1933- 139
Bakr, Salwa 1949- .... CWW 2
Bakr el Toure, Askia Muhammad Abu
  See Toure, Askia Muhammad Abu Bakr el
Bakshi, Ralph 1938(?)- 138
  Brief entry 112
  See also CLC 26
  See also IDFW 3
Bakshian, Aram 1944- 102
Bakst, Harold 1953- 142
Bakula, William J(ohn), Jr. 1936- 49-52
Bakunin, Mikhail (Alexandrovich)
  1814-1876 .... DLB 277
Bakwin, Harry 1894-1973 .... CAP-2
  Obituary 45-48
  Earlier sketch in CA 19-20
Bakwin, Ruth Morris 1898-1985 .... 17-20R
Bal, Mieke (Maria Gertrudis) 1946- .. CANR-99
  Earlier sketch in CA 156
Balaam
  See Lamb, G(eoffrey) F(rederick)
Balaam, David N(orman) 1950- 112
Balaban, Barney 1887-1971 .... IDFW 3, 4
Balaban, Bob
  See Balaban, Robert Elmer
Balaban, John B. 1943- CANR-70
  Earlier sketches in CA 65-68, CANR-12, 29
  See also DLB 120
Balaban, Nancy 1928- 126
Balaban, Robert Elmer 1945- 206
Balabkins, Nicholas (W.) 1926- 9-12R
Balachandran, M(adhavarao)
  1938-2000 .... CANR-40
  Obituary 193
  Earlier sketch in CA 102
Balachandran, Sarojini 1934- CANR-40
  Earlier sketches in CA 102, CANR-18
Balagura, Saul 1943- 81-84
Balaguru, P(erumalsamy) N(aidu) 1947- ... 144
Balakian, Anna (Elizabeth) 1916-1997 129
  Obituary 160
Balakian, Nona 1919-1991 85-88
  Obituary 134
Balakian, Peter 1951- CANR-69
  Earlier sketch in CA 102
Balakrishnan, N. 1956- CANR-114
  Earlier sketch in CA 157
Balan, Bruce 1959- 174
  See also SATA 113
Balanchine, George 1904-1983 111
  Obituary 109
Balancy, Pierre Guy Girald 1924-1979
  Obituary 89-92
Balandier, Georges (Leon) 1920- CANR-8
  Earlier sketch in CA 61-64
Balas, David L(aszlo) 1929- 33-36R
Balaskas, Arthur 1940- 103
Balaskas, Janet (Marion) 1946- 117
Balassa, Bela 1928-1991 .... CANR-3
  Obituary 134
  Earlier sketch in CA 1-4R
Balawyder, Aloysius 1924- CANR-15
  Earlier sketch in CA 41-44R
Balay, Robert 1930- 220
Balbontin, Jose Antonio 1893- CAP-1
  Earlier sketch in CA 11-12
Balbuena, Bernardo de 1561(?)-1627 .... LAW
Balbus
  See Huxley, Julian (Sorell)
Balcar, Gerald P. 1932- 194
Balcarce, Alberto G. 1946- 128
Balcavage, Dynise 1965- 207
  See also SATA 137
Balch, Glenn 1902-1989 .... CANR-3
  Earlier sketch in CA 1-4R
  See also SAAS 11
  See also SATA 3
  See also SATA-Obit 83
Balch, James F. 1933- 202
Balchen, Bernt 1899-1973
  Obituary 45-48
Balchin, John Frederick 1937- 122
Balchin, Nigel (Marlin) 1908-1970 ... CANR-21
  Obituary 29-32R
  Earlier sketch in CA 97-100
Balchin, W(illiam) G(eorge) V(ictor)
  1916- CANR-18
  Earlier sketch in CA 101
Balcomb, Mary N. 1928- 149
Balcomb, Raymond E. 1923- 21-24R
Balcon, Michael 1896-1977 77-80
  Obituary 73-76
  See also IDFW 3, 4
Bald, F(rederick) Clever 1897-1970 .... CAP-1
  Earlier sketch in CA 13-14
Bald, Margaret (Marion) 1948- 187
Bald, R(obert) C(ecil) 1901-1965 .... CANR-6
  Earlier sketch in CA 5-8R
Bald, Wambly 1902-1990 170
  See also DLB 4
Baldacci, David 1960- 187
  See also AAYA 60
Baldanza, Frank 1924- 1-4R
Baldassarri, Mario 1946- 146
Baldasty, Gerald J. 193
Balde, Jacob 1604-1668 .... DLB 164
Baldelli, Giovanni 1914-1986 45-48
Baldeosingh, Kevin 1963- 156
Balderose, Nancy Ward 1952- 158
  See also SATA 93
Balderson, Margaret 1935- CANR-79
  Earlier sketch in CA 25-28R
  See also SATA 151
Balderston, Daniel 1952- 144
Balderston, Frederick E(mery) 1923- 133
  Brief entry 112
Balderston, John L.
  See Balderston, John Lloyd
Balderston, John Lloyd 1889-1954
  Brief entry 121
  See also DLB 26
Balderston, Katharine Canby 1895-1979
  Obituary 93-96
Baldi, Pierre 220
Baldick, Chris(topher Giles) 1954- 128
Baldick, Robert 1927-1972
  Obituary 89-92
Baldinger, Stanley 1932- 29-32R
Baldinger, Wallace S(pencer) 1905-1993 .. 1-4R
Baldini, Antonio 1889-1962 208
Baldree, J(asper) Martin, Jr. 1927- 53-56
Baldrey, Keith (Donald) 1958- 133
Baldridge, Cates 1958- 197
Baldridge, Cyrus LeRoy 1889- .... SATA-Brief 29
Baldridge, Mary Humphrey 1937- 114
Baldrige, Letitia (Katherine)
  1927(?)- CANR-124
  Earlier sketches in CA 25-28R, CANR-17
Baldry, Cherith 1947- .... SATA 72
Baldry, Harold (Caparne) 1907-1991 .... 17-20R
Balducci, Carolyn (Feleppa) 1946- 33-36R
  See also SATA 5
Balducci, Ernesto 1922-1992 .... CANR-28
  Earlier sketches in CA 29-32R, CANR-12
Baldwin, Alex
  See Butterworth, W(illiam) E(dmund III)
Baldwin, Anna P. 1947- 128
Baldwin, Anne fl. 1680-1713 .... DLB 170
Baldwin, Anne Norris 1938- 29-32R
  See also SATA 5
Baldwin, Arthur W. 1904(?)-1976
  Obituary 69-72
Baldwin, Bates
  See Jennings, John (Edward, Jr.)
Baldwin, Billy
  See Baldwin, William, Jr.
Baldwin, Christina 1946- CANR-31
  Earlier sketches in CA 77-80, CANR-13
Baldwin, Cinda K. 1954- 147
Baldwin, Clara 61-64
  See also SATA 11
Baldwin, David A. 1936- 17-20R
Baldwin, Dick
  See Raborg, Frederick A(shton), Jr.
Baldwin, Ed(ward A.) 1935-1998 118
Baldwin, Edward R(obinson) 1935- .. CANR-21
  Earlier sketch in CA 45-48
Baldwin, Faith 1893-1978 .... CANR-59
  Obituary 77-80
  Earlier sketches in CA 5-8R, CANR-4
  See also AITN 1
  See also RHW

Baldwin, Frank 1963- CANR-113
Earlier sketch in CA 171
Baldwin, Gordo
See Baldwin, Gordon C(ortis)
Baldwin, Gordon C(ortis)
1908-1983 .... CANR-62
Earlier sketches in CA 1-4R, CANR-3
See also SATA 12
See also TCWW 1, 2
Baldwin, Hanson W(eightman)
1903-1991 .... CANR-70
Obituary 136
Earlier sketch in CA 61-64
Baldwin, James 1841-1925
Brief entry 111
See also BYA 4
See also SATA 24
Baldwin, James (Arthur) 1924-1987 . CANR-24
Obituary 124
Earlier sketches in CA 1-4R, CANR-3
See also CABS 1
See also AAYA 4, 34
See also AFAW 1, 2
See also AMWR 2
See also AMWS 1
See also BLC 1
See also BPFB 1
See also BW 1
See also CAD
See also CDALB 1941-1968
See also CLC 1, 2, 3, 4, 5, 8, 13, 15, 17, 42, 50, 67, 90, 127
See also CN 1, 2, 3, 4
See also CPW
See also DA
See also DA3
See also DAB
See also DAC
See also DAM MST, MULT, NOV, POP
See also DC 1
See also DFS 11, 15
See also DLB 2, 7, 33, 249, 278
See also DLBY 1987
See also EWL 3
See also EXPS
See also LAIT 5
See also MAL 5
See also MTCW 1, 2
See also MTFW 2005
See also NCFS 4
See also NFS 4
See also RGAL 4
See also RGSF 2
See also SATA 9
See also SATA-Obit 54
See also SSC 10, 33
See also SSFS 2, 18
See also TUS
See also WLC
Baldwin, John D. 1930- 101
Baldwin, John W(esley) 1929- 105
Baldwin, Joseph B(urkette) 1918-1994 111
Obituary 147
Baldwin, Joseph Glover 1815-1864 . DLB 3, 11, 248
See also RGAL 4
Baldwin, Joyce G(ertrude) 1921- CANR-8
Earlier sketch in CA 61-64
Baldwin, Leland D(ewitt) 1897-1981 .... 41-44R
Obituary 103
Baldwin, Lewis V. 1949- 135
Baldwin, Louis 1919- 180
See also SATA 110
Baldwin, Louisa 1845-1925 .... DLB 240
Baldwin, Margaret
See Weis, Margaret (Edith)
Baldwin, Marshall W(hithed)
1903-1975 61-64
Obituary 57-60
Baldwin, Michael 1930- CANR-3
Earlier sketch in CA 9-12R
Baldwin, Monica 1896(?)-1975
Obituary 104
Baldwin, Mrs. Alfred
See Baldwin, Louisa
Baldwin, Ned
See Baldwin, Edward R(obinson)
Baldwin, Neil 1947- CANR-112
Earlier sketch in CA 130
Baldwin, Peter 1956- 218
Baldwin, Raymond Earl 1893-1986
Obituary 121
Baldwin, Rebecca
See Chappell, Helen
Baldwin, Richard c. 1653-1698 .... DLB 170
Baldwin, Richard S(heridan) 1910- 105
Baldwin, Robert E(dward) 1924- 41-44R
Baldwin, Roger (Nash) 1884-1981
Obituary 105
Baldwin, Roger E(dwin) 1929- 49-52
Baldwin, Shauna Singh 1962- 205
Baldwin, Stan(ley C.) 1929- CANR-38
Earlier sketches in CA 49-52, CANR-2, 17
See also SATA 62
See also SATA-Brief 28
Baldwin, William, Jr. 1903-1983 129
Obituary 111
Baldwin, William c. 1515-1563 .... DLB 132
Baldwin, William 1944- 152
See also CSW
Baldwin, William J. 1937- 211
Baldwin, William Lee 1928- CANR-3
Earlier sketch in CA 1-4R
Bale, G. F.
See Cox, Patricia Bale
Bale, John 1495-1563 .... DLB 132
See also RGEL 2
See also TEA
Bale, Robert Osborne 1912- 1-4R
Balen, Malcolm 1956- 227
Bales, Carol Ann 1940- 45-48
See also SATA 57
See also SATA-Brief 29
Bales, Jack
See Bales, James E(dward)
Bales, James D(avid) 1915- 5-8R
Bales, James E(dward) 1951- CANR-30
Earlier sketch in CA 107
Bales, Kevin 1952- 140
Bales, Richard F. 1951- 232
Bales, Robert F(reed) 1916- 93-96
Bales, William Alan 1917-1996 .... 5-8R
Obituary 152
Balester, Valerie M. 1952- 147
Balestrini, Nanni 1935- .... DLB 128, 196
Balet, Jan (Bernard) 1913- 85-88
See also SATA 11
Baley, James A. 1918- CANR-5
Earlier sketch in CA 13-16R
Balf, Todd 1961- 197
Balfort, Neil
See Fanthorpe, R(obert) Lionel
Balfour, A. J.
See Balfour, Arthur James
Balfour, Sir Andrew 1630-1694 .... DLB 213
Balfour, Arthur J.
See Balfour, Arthur James
Balfour, Arthur James 1848-1930 191
Brief entry 120
See also DLB 190
Balfour, Conrad George 1928- 53-56
Balfour, Henry H(allowell), Jr. 1940- 117
Balfour, James 1925-1992 .... 25-28R
Balfour, Sir James 1600-1657 .... DLB 213
Balfour, John
See Moore, James
Balfour, Michael (Leonard) Graham
1908- CANR-6
Obituary 150
Earlier sketch in CA 9-12R
Balfour, (John) Patrick Douglas
1904-1976 .... CANR-6
Earlier sketch in CA 9-12R
Balfour, Sandy 1962- 239
Balfour, Victoria 1954- 129
Balfour-Kinnear, George Purvis Russell
1888- 5-8R
Balgassi, Haemi 1971- 200
See also SATA 131
Balian, Lorna 1929- CANR-40
Earlier sketches in CA 53-56, CANR-4, 19
See also SATA 9, 91
Baligh, Helmy H. 1931- 21-24R
Balikci, Asen 1929- 29-32R
Balinky, Alexander 1919-1998 .... 21-24R
Balint, Christine 1975- 207
Balint, Michael 1896-1970 .... CAP-1
Earlier sketch in CA 9-10
Balis, Andrea F. 1948- 108
Balit, Christina 1961- CANR-124
Earlier sketch in CA 169
See also SATA 102, 159
Balizet, Carol 1933- 114
Baljeu, Joost 1925- 97-100
Balk, Alfred (W.) 1930- 25-28R
Balk, H(oward) Wesley 1932-
Brief entry 111
Balka, Marie
See Balkany, Marie (Romoka Zelinger) de
Balkany, Marie (Romoka Zelinger) de
1930- 104
Balke, Willem 1933- 107
Balken, Debra Bricker 1954- CANR-128
Earlier sketch in CA 168
Balkey, Rita 1922- CANR-30
Earlier sketch in CA 111
Balkin, Richard 1938- 77-80
Balkoff, Zuri
See Stavans, Ilan
Balkt, H. H. ter
See ter Balkt, H(erman) H(endrik)
Ball, Angela 1952- 135
Ball, Ann (E. Bolton) 1944- CANR-98
Earlier sketch in CA 148
Ball, B. N.
See Ball, Brian N(eville)
Ball, Brian N(eville) 1932- 33-36R
Ball, (Frederick) Clive 1941-
Brief entry 114
Ball, David 1937- 65-68
Ball, David (W.) 1950(?)- 236
Ball, Desmond (John) 1947- CANR-89
Earlier sketches in CA 106, CANR-24
Ball, Donald W(inston) 1934-1976 122
Obituary 110
Ball, Donna 1951- 175
Earlier sketch in CA 108
Ball, Doris Bell (Collier) 1897-1987 . CANR-58
Obituary 122
Earlier sketches in CA 1-4R, CANR-2, 18
Ball, Duncan 1941- .... SATA 73
Ball, Edith L. 1905-1996 85-88
Ball, Edward 1959- CANR-111
Earlier sketch in CA 167
Ball, (Katherine) Eve(lyn) 1890-1984 122
Obituary 114
Ball, F(rederick) Carlton 1911-1992 ...... 17-20R
Ball, George W(ildman) 1909-1994 73-76
Obituary 145
Ball, Gordon 1944- 201
Ball, Howard 1937- CANR-17
Earlier sketch in CA 33-36R
Ball, Hugo 1886-1927 .... TCLC 104
Ball, Jane Eklund 1921- 33-36R
Ball, Jennifer (M. V.) 1958- 136
Ball, John (Dudley, Jr.) 1911-1988 .... CANR-58
Obituary 126
Earlier sketches in CA 5-8R, CANR-3, 18
Ball, John C. 1924- CANR-103
Earlier sketches in CA 5-8R, CANR-8
Ball, John M(iller) 1923- 33-36R
Ball, Joseph H(urst) 1905-1993 .... CAP-2
Obituary 143
Earlier sketch in CA 23-24
Ball, Karen (M.) 1957- 239
Ball, Larry Durwood Sr. 1940- 123
Ball, Lucille (Desiree) 1911-1989 164
Ball, M(ary) Margaret 1909-1999 .... 25-28R
Ball, Marion J(okl) 1940- CANR-15
Earlier sketch in CA 89-92
Ball, Nelson 1942- 134
See also CP 1
Ball, Nicole (Janice) 1948- CANR-31
Earlier sketch in CA 112
Ball, Philip (Charles) 1962- 180
Ball, Robert Edward 1911-1990 108
Ball, Robert Hamilton 1902-1988 .... CANR-80
Obituary 127
Earlier sketch in CA 9-12R
Ball, Robert J(erome) 1941- 128
Ball, Robert M(yers) 1914- 97-100
Ball, Stuart 1956- CANR-105
Earlier sketch in CA 130
Ball, Sylvia Patricia 1936- 57-60
Ball, Terence 1944- 138
Ball, Zachary
See Janas, Frankie-Lee and Masters, Kelly R(ay)
Ballagas (y Cubenas), Emilio 1908-1954 179
See also EWL 3
See also LAW
Ballantine, Bill 1911-1999 106
Obituary 179
See also Ballantine, William (Oliver)
Ballantine, David 1926- CANR-106
Earlier sketch in CA 115
Ballantine, John
See da Cruz, Daniel, Jr.
Ballantine, John (Winthrop) 1920- 53-56
Ballantine, Joseph W. 1888-1973
Obituary 41-44R
Ballantine, Lesley Frost
See Frost, Lesley
Ballantine, Poe 1955- 214
Ballantine, Richard 1940- CANR-1
Earlier sketch in CA 45-48
Ballantine, William (Oliver) 106
Obituary 179
See also Ballantine, Bill
Ballantyne, Andrew 233
Ballantyne, David (Watt)
1924-1986 .... CANR-10
Earlier sketch in CA 65-68
See also CN 1, 2, 3, 4
Ballantyne, Dorothy Joan (Smith) 1922- 5-8R
Ballantyne, R(obert) M(ichael)
1825-1894 .... DLB 163
See also JRDA
See also RGEL 2
See also SATA 24
Ballantyne, Sheila 1936- CANR-25
Earlier sketch in CA 101
Ballard, Allen B(utler, Jr.) 1930- CANR-100
Earlier sketch in CA 61-64
Ballard, Charles E. 1914(?)-1987
Obituary 123
Ballard, Dean
See Wilkes-Hunter, R(ichard)
Ballard, Edward Goodwin
1910-1989 .... CANR-30
Earlier sketches in CA 33-36R, CANR-13
Ballard, Eric Allen 1908-1968 .... CWRI 5
Ballard, Guy W(arren) 1878-1939 211
Ballard, Holley
See Rubinsky, Holley
Ballard, I. Edward 1909(?)-1985
Obituary 117
Ballard, J(ames) G(raham) 1930- CANR-133
Earlier sketches in CA 5-8R, CANR-15, 39, 65, 107
See also AAYA 3, 52
See also BRWS 5
See also CLC 3, 6, 14, 36, 137
See also CN 1, 2, 3, 4, 5, 6, 7
See also DA3
See also DAM NOV, POP
See also DLB 14, 207, 261, 319
See also EWL 3
See also HGG
See also MTCW 1, 2
See also MTFW 2005
See also NFS 8
See also RGEL 2
See also RGSF 2
See also SATA 93
See also SCFW 1, 2
See also SFW 4
See also SSC 1, 53
Ballard, Jane
See Gorman, Carol
Ballard, Joan Kadey 1928- 5-8R
Ballard, John 1945- 180
See also SATA 110
Ballard, K. G.
See Roth, Holly
Ballard, Lowell C(lyne) 1904-1986 .... CAP-1
Obituary 120
Earlier sketch in CA 11-12
See also SATA 12
See also SATA-Obit 49
Ballard, Lucien 1908-1988 .... IDFW 3, 4
Ballard, Martha Moore 1735-1812 ..... DLB 200
Ballard, (Charles) Martin 1929- 25-28R
See also SATA 1
Ballard, Michael B. 1946- CANR-137
Earlier sketch in CA 156
Ballard, Mignon F(ranklin) 1934- CANR-90
Earlier sketch in CA 121
See also SATA 64
See also SATA-Brief 49
Ballard, P. D.
See Ballard, (Willis) Todhunter
Ballard, Robert D(uane) 1942- CANR-96
Earlier sketch in CA 112
See also CLR 60
See also SATA 85
Ballard, Robin 1965- .... SATA 126
Ballard, Terry 1946- 163
Ballard, (Willis) Todhunter
1903-1980 .... CANR-59
Earlier sketches in CA 13-16R, CANR-29
See also TCWW 1, 2
Ballard, W. T.
See Ballard, (Willis) Todhunter
Ballard, Willis T.
See Ballard, (Willis) Todhunter
Ballem, John 1925- 81-84
Ballen, Roger 1950- 103
Ballendorf, Dirk Anthony 1939- 165
Ballentine, Lee (Kenney) 1954- 162
Ballentine, Rudolph 1941- 114
Baller, Warren Robert 1900-1988 69-72
Ballerini, Luigi 1940- 197
See also DLB 128
Ballet, Arthur H(arold) 1924-
Brief entry 111
Ballew, Charles
See Snow, Charles H(orace)
Ballhaus, Michael 1935- .... IDFW 3, 4
Balliett, Blue 1955- 231
See also SATA 156
Balliett, Whitney 1926- CANR-143
Earlier sketches in CA 17-20R, CANR-13, 30, 57
Ballin, Caroline 17-20R
Balling, Robert C., Jr. 1952- 138
Ballingall, James (Gordon Mackie) 1958- ... 117
Ballinger, Bill S.
See Ballinger, William Sanborn
Ballinger, Bryan 1968- .... SATA 161
Ballinger, Harry (Russell) 1892-1993 ..... CAP-2
Earlier sketch in CA 23-24
Ballinger, James Lawrence 1919- 17-20R
Ballinger, Louise Bowen 1909-1998 ...... 13-16R
Ballinger, (Violet) Margaret (Livingstone)
1894-1980 .... CANR-13
Obituary 105
Earlier sketch in CA 61-64
Ballinger, Raymond A. 1907-1985 .... 5-8R
Ballinger, W. A.
See McNeilly, Wilfred (Glassford)
Ballinger, William Sanborn
1912-1980 .... CANR-58
Obituary 97-100
Earlier sketches in CA 1-4R, CANR-1
Ballon, Robert J(ean) 1919- CANR-44
Earlier sketches in CA 45-48, CANR-21
Ballonoff, Paul A(lan) 1943- 57-60
Ballou, Arthur W. 1915-1981 .... 25-28R
Obituary 134
Ballou, Ellen B(artlett) 1905-1995 .... CAP-2
Earlier sketch in CA 29-32
Ballou, Maturin Murray 1820-1895 ..... DLB 79, 189
Ballouhey, Pierre 1944- .... SATA 90
Ballowe, James 1933- CANR-12
Earlier sketch in CA 29-32R
Ballstadt, Carl A. 1931- CANR-54
Earlier sketch in CA 124
Balma, Michael J(ames) 1930- 17-20R
Balmain, Lydia
See Saxton, Judith
Balmain, Pierre (Alexandre) 1914-1982
Obituary 107
Balme, Maurice (George) 1925- 61-64
Balmer, Edwin 1883-1959
Brief entry 114
Balmer, Randall (Herbert) 1954- 199
Balmes, Kathy
See Kiefer, Kathleen Balmes
Balmont, Konstantin (Dmitriyevich)
1867-1943 155
Brief entry 109
See also DLB 295
See also EWL 3
See also TCLC 11
Balmuth, Daniel 1929- 208
Balmuth, Miriam S(charf) 1925(?)-2004 124
Obituary 228
Balodis, Janis (Maris) 1950- CANR-67
Earlier sketch in CA 134
See also CD 5, 6
Balogh, Mary 1944- CANR-112
Earlier sketch in CA 161
See also RHW
Balogh, Penelope 1916-1975 .... CAP-2
Earlier sketch in CA 25-28
See also SATA 1
See also SATA-Obit 34
Balogh, Thomas 1905-1985 57-60
Obituary 115
Balota, D(avid) A. 1954- 135

Cumulative Index 31 Banning

Balow, Tom 1931- 45-48
See also SATA 12
Baloyra, Enrique Antonio 1942- 111
Balsdon, (John Percy Vyvian) Dacre 1901-1977 .... CANR-13
Obituary 73-76
Earlier sketch in CA 5-8R
Balsdon, J. P. V. D.
See Balsdon, (John Percy Vyvian) Dacre
Balseiro, Jose Agustin 1900-1992 .... CANR-72
Earlier sketch in CA 81-84
See also AITN 1
See also HW 1, 2
Balsiger, Dave
See Balsiger, David (Wayne)
Balsiger, David (Wayne) 1945- CANR-28
Earlier sketches in CA 61-64, CANR-11
Balsley, Howard L(loyd) 1913-1996 ... CANR-4
Earlier sketch in CA 1-4R
Balsley, Irol Whitmore 1912-1989 .... 13-16R
Balswick, Jack Orville 136
Balswick, Judith K. 1939- 136
Baltake, Joe 1945- 118
Baltausis, Vincas 1847-1910
See Mikszath, Kalman
Baltazar, Eulalio R. 1925- 17-20R
Baltazzi, Evan S(erge) 1921- CANR-57
Earlier sketch in CA 65-68
See also SATA 90
Baltensperger, Peter 1938- 115
Balterman, Marcia Ridlon 1942- 25-28R
See also Ridlon, Marci
Baltes, Paul B. 1939- 89-92
Balthasar, Hans Urs von
See von Balthasar, Hans Urs
Balthazar, Earl E(dward) 1918-1993 53-56
Baltimore, J.
See Catherall, Arthur
Baltz, Howard B(url) 1930- 29-32R
Baltzell, E(dward) Digby 1915-1996 .... CANR-48
Obituary 153
Earlier sketch in CA 33-36R
Baltzer, Hans (Adolf) 1900- .... SATA 40
Balukas, Jean 1959- 193
Brief entry 111
Balutansky, Kathleen M(arie) 1954- 145
Balwers, Renato
See La Barre, Weston
Baly, (Alfred) Denis 1913-1987 .... 17-20R
Baly, Monica Eileen 1914-1998 .... CANR-93
Obituary 172
Earlier sketch in CA 102
Balzac, Guez de (?)-
See Balzac, Jean-Louis Guez de
See also DLB 268
Balzac, Honore de 1799-1850 .... DA
See also DA3
See also DAB
See also DAC
See also DAM MST, NOV
See also DLB 119
See also EW 5
See also GFL 1789 to the Present
See also LMFS 1
See also RGSF 2
See also RGWL 2, 3
See also SSC 5, 59
See also SSFS 10
See also SUFW
See also TWA
See also WLC
Balzac, Jean-Louis Guez de 1597-1654
See Balzac, Guez de
See also GFL Beginnings to 1789
Balzano, Jeanne (Koppel) 1912- 5-8R
See also Iannone, Jeanne
Balzer, Richard J(ay) 1944- 45-48
Balzer, Robert Lawrence 1912- 103
Bambach, Carmen C. 1959- 169
Bambara, Toni Cade 1939-1995 .... CANR-81
Obituary 150
Earlier sketches in CA 29-32R, CANR-24, 49
See also AAYA 5, 49
See also AFAW 2
See also AMWS 11
See also BLC 1
See also BW 2, 3
See also BYA 12, 14
See also CDALBS
See also CLC 19, 88
See also DA
See also DA3
See also DAC
See also DAM MST, MULT
See also DLB 38, 218
See also EXPS
See also MAL 5
See also MTCW 1, 2
See also MTFW 2005
See also RGAL 4
See also RGSF 2
See also SATA 112
See also SSC 35
See also SSFS 4, 7, 12, 21
See also TCLC 116
See also WLCS
Bamber, Linda 1945- 109
Bamberger, Bernard J(acob) 1904-1980 .... CANR-6
Obituary 101
Earlier sketch in CA 13-16R
Bamberger, Carl 1902-1987 .... CAP-2
Earlier sketch in CA 21-22
Bamberger, Fritz 1902-1984
Obituary 113
Bamberger, Michael (F.) 1960- 134
Bambola, Sylvia 1945- 202
Bambrough, (John) Renford 1926-1999 ... 61-64
Obituary 173
Bamdad, A.
See Shamlu, Ahmad
Bamdad, Alef
See Shamlu, Ahmad
Bamford, James 1946- CANR-119
Earlier sketch in CA 123
Bamford, Paul W(alden) 1921- 41-44R
Bamford, Samuel 1788-1872 .... DLB 190
Bamfylde, Walter
See Bevan, Tom
Bamm, Peter
See Emmrich, Curt
Bamman, Gerry 1941- 174
Bamman, Henry A. 1918- CANR-7
Earlier sketch in CA 5-8R
See also SATA 12
Ban, (Maria) Eva 1934- 73-76
Ban, Joseph D(aniel) 1926- CANR-23
Earlier sketches in CA 21-24R, CANR-8
Ban, Thomas A. 1929- CANR-10
Earlier sketch in CA 21-24R
Bana, Eric 1968- 213
Banani, Amin 1926- 33-36R
Banash, Stan
See Banash, Stanley D.
Banash, Stanley D. 1940- 171
Banash, "Tex"
See Banash, Stanley D.
Banat, D. R.
See Bradbury, Ray (Douglas)
Banazek, Jeanne M. (Carpenter) 1943- 156
Banbury, Jen(nifer Marie) 1966- CANR-139
Earlier sketch in CA 167
Banbury, Philip 1914- 102
Bance, Alan F. 1939- 111
Banchs, Enrique J. 1888-1968 .... HW 1
Bancquart, Marie-Claire 1930- 214
Bancroft, Anne 1923- 57-60
Bancroft, Caroline 1900-1985 .... CAP-2
Earlier sketch in CA 21-22
Bancroft, George 1800-1891 .... DLB 1, 30, 59, 243
Bancroft, Griffing 1907-1999 .... 29-32R
See also AITN 1
See also SATA 6
Bancroft, Hubert Howe 1832-1918 179
See also DLB 47, 140
Bancroft, Iris (May Nelson) 1922- CANR-19
Earlier sketch in CA 102
Interview in CANR-19
Bancroft, Laura
See Baum, L(yman) Frank
Bancroft, Mary 1903-1997 118
Obituary 156
Bancroft, Peter 1916- 41-44R
Bancroft, Robert
See Kirsch, Robert R.
Bancroft, Stephanie
See Bond, Stephanie
Bandarage, Asoka 1950- 167
Bandeira (Filho), Manuel (Carneiro de Sousa) 1886-1968
Obituary 115
See also DLB 307
See also EWL 3
See also LAW
Bandel, Betty 1912- 106
See also SATA 47
Bandele, Biyi 1967- 167
See also Bandele-Thomas, Biyi
See also BW 3
See also CD 5
Bandele-Thomas, Biyi
See Bandele, Biyi
See also CD 6
Bandelier, Adolph F(rancis) 1840-1914 230
See also DLB 186
Bander, Edward J. 1923- CANR-5
Earlier sketch in CA 13-16R
Bandera, V(ladimir) N(icholas) 1932- 33-36R
Bandi, Hans-Georg 1920- 85-88
Bandinelli, Ranuccio Bianchi 1900-1975
Obituary 53-56
Bandman, Bertram 1930- 21-24R
Bandoff, Hope
See Guthrie, Thomas Anstey
Bandow, Doug(las) 1957- 127
Bandrauk, Andre D. 1941- 149
Bandura, Albert 1925- 13-16R
Bandy, (Eugene) Franklin 1914-1987 .... CANR-24
Obituary 122
Earlier sketch in CA 33-36R
Bandy, Leland A. 1935- 77-80
Bandy, Melanie 1932- 114
Bandy, W(illiam) T(homas) 1903-1989 .. 37-40R
Obituary 129
Bandy, Way 1941(?)-1986 123
Obituary 120
Bandyopadhyay, Bidisha 1978- 232
Bane, Diana
See Day, Dianne
Bane, Mary Jo 1942- 126
Brief entry 112
Bane, Michael 1950- 108
Banel, Joseph 1943- 45-48
Baner, Skulda Vanadis 1897-1964 .... CAP-1
Earlier sketch in CA 13-14
See also SATA 10
Banerjee, Asit 1940- 146
Banerjee, Dillon 1968- 205
Banerjee, H(emendra) N(ath) 1929-
Brief entry 111
Banerjee, Mukulika 239
Banerji, Bibhuti-Bhusan 1894-1950 .... EWL 3
Banerji, Ranan B(ihari) 1928- CANR-11
Earlier sketch in CA 29-32R
Banerji, S(riranjan) 1938- 147
Banerji, Sara 1932- 126
Banet, Doris Beatrice Robinson 1925- 5-8R
Banfield, A(lexander) W(illiam) F(rancis) 1918- 61-64
Banfield, Edward C(hristie) 1916-1999 57-60
Obituary 185
See also AITN 1
Banfield, Stephen 1951- CANR-144
Earlier sketch in CA 149
Banfill, A. Scott 1956- .... SATA 98
Bang, Betsy 1912- 102
See also SATA 48
See also SATA-Brief 37
Bang, Garrett
See Bang, Molly Garrett
Bang, Herman 1857-1912 .... DLB 300
Bang, Mary Jo 1946- 194
See also PFS 23
Bang, Molly Garrett 1943- CANR-126
Earlier sketch in CA 102
See also CLR 8
See also CWRI 5
See also MAICYA 1, 2
See also SATA 24, 69, 111, 158
Bang-Campbell, Monika 211
See also SATA 140
Bangert, Ethel E(lizabeth) 1912- CANR-1
Earlier sketch in CA 45-48
Bangert, Sharon 1951- 146
Bangert, William V(alentine) 1911-1985 . 45-48
Bangerter, Lowell A(llen) 1941- CANR-26
Earlier sketches in CA 69-72, CANR-11
Bangham, Mary Dickerson 1896-1973 .. CAP-2
Earlier sketch in CA 23-24
Banghart, Charles K(enneth) 1910(?)-1980
Obituary 97-100
Banghart, Kenneth
See Banghart, Charles K(enneth)
Bangley, Bernard K. 1935- CANR-51
Earlier sketches in CA 110, CANR-28
Bangs, Carl (Oliver) 1922- CANR-7
Earlier sketch in CA 17-20R
Bangs, Carol Jane 1949- 114
Bangs, John Kendrick 1862-1922
Brief entry 110
See also DLB 11, 79
See also FANT
See also SUFW
Bangs, Lester 1948-1982
Obituary 106
Bangs, Nina 226
Bangs, Richard 1950- CANR-125
Earlier sketch in CA 122
Bangs, Robert B(abbitt) 1914-1986 .... 37-40R
Bangura, Abdul Karim 1953- 196
Banham, (Peter) Reyner 1922-1988 .. CANR-35
Obituary 125
Earlier sketch in CA 29-32R
Banim, John 1798-1842 .... DLB 116, 158, 159
See also RGEL 2
Banim, Michael 1796-1874 .... DLB 158, 159
Banis, Victor J(erome) 1937- 81-84
Bani-Sadr, Abolhassan 1933- 143
Banish, Roslyn 1942- 232
Banister, Gary L. 1948- 57-60
Banister, Judith 1943- CANR-57
Earlier sketch in CA 127
Banister, Manly (Miles) 1914-1986 .... 41-44R
Obituary 171
Banister, Margaret 1894(?)-1977
Obituary 73-76
Banjo, The
See Paterson, A(ndrew) B(arton)
Bank, Dena Citron 1912-1993 123
Bank, Melissa 1961- 190
See also DLBY 1998
Bank, Mirra 1945- 102
Bank, Stephen Paul 1941- 110
Bank, Ted
See Bank, Theodore P(aul) II
Bank, Theodore P(aul) II 1923- 41-44R
Banke, Cecile de
See de Banke, Cecile
Banker, James R. 1938- 132
Banker, Mark T(ollie) 1951- 143
Bankier, David 1947- 145
Bank-Jensen, Thea
See Ottesen, Thea Tauber
Bankoff, George Alexis
See Milkomane, George Alexis Milkomanovich
Bankowsky, Richard James 1928- 1-4R
Banks, A. L.
See Banks, Arthur Leslie
Banks, A. Leslie
See Banks, Arthur Leslie
Banks, Ann 1943- 105
Banks, Arthur Leslie 1904-1989
Obituary 129
Banks, Arthur S. 1926- CANR-27
Earlier sketch in CA 33-36R
Banks, Brian R. 1956- 138
Banks, Carolyn 1941- CANR-23
Earlier sketch in CA 105
Banks, Dennis J. 1932- 238
Banks, Geraldine 1942- 147
Banks, Hal N(orman) 1921- 102
Banks, Harlan Parker 1913-1998 89-92
Banks, Iain
See Banks, Iain M(enzies)
See also BRWS 11
Banks, Iain M(enzies) 1954- CANR-106
Brief entry 123
Earlier sketches in CA 128, CANR-61
Interview in CA-128
See also Banks, Iain
See also CLC 34
See also DLB 194, 261
See also EWL 3
See also HGG
See also MTFW 2005
See also SFW 4
Banks, J(ohn) Houston 1911-1996 .... 33-36R
Banks, James A(lbert) 1941- CANR-68
Earlier sketches in CA 33-36R, CANR-13, 32
Banks, James Houston 1925- 89-92
Banks, Jane 1913- 65-68
Banks, Jeri
See Banks, Geraldine
Banks, Jimmy
See Banks, James Houston
Banks, John 1653(?)-1706 .... DLB 80
See also RGEL 2
Banks, Kate 1960- .... SATA 134
Banks, L. A.
See Banks, Leslie Esdaile
Banks, Laura Stockton Voorhees 1908(?)-1980
Obituary 101
See also SATA-Obit 23
Banks, Leslie
See Banks, Leslie Esdaile
Banks, Leslie 1920- 145
Banks, Leslie E.
See Banks, Leslie Esdaile
Banks, Lynne Reid
See Reid Banks, Lynne
See also AAYA 6
See also BYA 7
See also CLC 23
See also CLR 86
See also CN 4, 5, 6
Banks, Margaret A(melia) 1928- 209
Banks, Michael A. 1951- 161
See also SATA 101
Banks, Oliver 1941- 107
Banks, Richard L. 1920- 9-12R
Banks, Roger 1929- 107
Banks, Ronald F(illmore) 1934- 29-32R
Banks, Russell (Earl) 1940- CANR-118
Earlier sketches in CA 65-68, CANR-19, 52, 73
See also CAAS 15
See also AAYA 45
See also AMWS 5
See also CLC 37, 72, 187
See also CN 4, 5, 6, 7
See also DLB 130, 278
See also EWL 3
See also MAL 5
See also MTCW 2
See also MTFW 2005
See also NFS 13
See also SSC 42
Banks, Sara (Jeanne Gordon Harrell)
See Harrell, Sara (Jeanne) Gordon
See also SATA 26
Banks, Taylor
See Banks, Jane
Banks, William L(ove) 1928- 112
Banks, William M(aron III) 1943- 195
Bankson, Douglas (Henneck) 1920- . CANR-31
Earlier sketch in CA 45-48
Bankwitz, Philip Charles Farwell 1924- 33-36R
Bann, Stephen 1942- 137
Bannatyne-Cugnet, (Elizabeth) Jo(-Anne) 1951- 160
See also SATA 101
Banner, Angela
See Maddison, Angela Mary
See also CLR 24
Banner, Charla Ann Leibenguth 1942- CANR-24
Earlier sketch in CA 106
Banner, Hubert Stewart 1891-1964 .... CAP-1
Earlier sketch in CA 11-12
Banner, James M(orrill), Jr. 1935- CANR-95
Earlier sketch in CA 49-52
Banner, Keith 1965- 184
Banner, Lois W(endland) 1939- CANR-88
Earlier sketches in CA 49-52, CANR-1
Banner, Melvin Edward 1914-1997 53-56
Banner, Stuart 1963- 221
Banner, William Augustus 1915- 45-48
Banner-Haley, Charles T. 1948- 148
Bannerman, Helen (Brodie Cowan Watson) 1862(?)-1946 111
Earlier sketch in CA 136
See also CLR 21
See also CWRI 5
See also DLB 141
See also MAICYA 1, 2
See also SATA 19
Bannerman, Mark
See Lewing, Anthony Charles
Bannerman, Roland
See Hartston, W(illiam) R(oland)
Bannerman, W. Mary 1894-1984
Obituary 114
Bannet, Eve Tavor CANR-55
Earlier sketch in CA 127
Bannick, Nancy (Meredith) 1926- 41-44R
Banning, Evelyn I. 1903-1993 73-76
See also SATA 36
Banning, Lance (Gilbert) 1942- CANR-52
Earlier sketch in CA 89-92

Banning, Margaret Culkin 1891-1982 .... CANR-70
Obituary 105
Earlier sketches in CA 5-8R, CANR-4
Bannister, Don
See Bannister, Donald
Bannister, Donald 1928- CANR-9
Earlier sketch in CA 61-64
Bannister, Jo 1951- CANR-96
Earlier sketches in CA 119, CANR-48
Bannister, Nathaniel (H.) 1813-1847 .... RGAL 4
Bannister, Pat
See Davis, Lou Ellen
Bannister, Patricia Valeria 1923- CANR-134
Brief entry 115
Earlier sketch in CA 150
See also RHW
Bannister, Robert C(orwin), Jr. 1935- 21-24R
Bannister, Roger (Gilbert) 1929- 237
Bannister, Sally
See Pratt, James Norwood
Bannock, Graham 1932- 33-36R
Bannon, Ann 1932- 213
See also GLL 1
Bannon, Barbara Anne 1928- 101
Bannon, David Race 1963(?)- 227
Bannon, John Francis 1905-1986 .... CANR-4
Obituary 119
Earlier sketch in CA 1-4R
Bannon, Laura (?)-1963 .... 1-4R
See also SATA 6
Bannon, Peter
See Durst, Paul
Bannor, Brett 1959- 215
See also SATA 143
Bansal, Vipul K. 1959- 142
Bansemer, Roger 1948- 137
Banta, Martha 1928- CANR-29
Earlier sketch in CA 81-84
Banta, R(ichard) E(lwell) 1904-1977 ...... CAP-2
Earlier sketch in CA 33-36
Banta, Trudy W. CANR-98
Earlier sketch in CA 148
Bantel, Linda 1943- 113
Banti, Anna
See Lopresti, Lucia (Longhi)
See also DLB 177
See also WLIT 7
Banting, Keith G. 1947- CANR-93
Earlier sketch in CA 129
Banting, Peter M(yles) 1936- 112
Bantleman, Lawrence 1942- .... CP 1
Bantock, G(eoffrey) H(erman) 1914-1997 .... CANR-11
Earlier sketch in CA 25-28R
Bantock, Gavin (Marcus August) 1939- . 33-36R
See also CP 1, 2, 3, 4, 5, 6, 7
Bantock, Nick 1950(?)- CANR-100
Earlier sketches in CA 142, CANR-65
See also DAM POP
See also SATA 95
Banton, Coy
See Norwood, Victor G(eorge) C(harles)
Banton, Michael (Parker) 1926- CANR-2
Earlier sketch in CA 5-8R
Banton, Travis 1894-1958 .... IDFW 3, 4
Banville, John 1945- CANR-104
Brief entry 117
Earlier sketch in CA 128
Interview in CA-128
See also CLC 46, 118
See also CN 4, 5, 6, 7
See also DLB 14, 271
Banville, Theodore (Faullain) de 1832-1891 .... DLB 217
See also GFL 1789 to the Present
Banville, Thomas G(eorge) 1924- 81-84
Bany, Mary A. 1913-1993 .... 9-12R
Banz, George 1928- 29-32R
Banziger, Hans
See Baenziger, Hans
Baofu, Peter 1962- 234
Baptist, Edward E. 1970- 233
Bapu
See Khare, Narayan Bhaskar
Barabas, Gabor 1948- 134
Barabas, Steven 1904-1983 .... 5-8R
Obituary 109
Barabas, SuzAnne 1949- 134
Barabasi, Albert-Laszlo 1967- 234
Barabtarlo, Gene
See Barabtarlo, Gennady
Barabtarlo, Gennady 1949- CANR-120
Earlier sketch in CA 147
Barach, Alvan L(eroy) 1895-1977
Obituary 73-76
Barach, Arnold B(auer) 1913-1987 97-100
Obituary 122
Barack, Nathan A. 1913-1999 .... 13-16R
Barackman, Floyd Hays, Jr. 1923- 115
Barackman, Paul F(reeman) 1894-1989 .... 1-4R
Baracks, Barbara 1951- 106
Barada, Bill
See Barada, William Richard
Barada, William Richard 1913-1998 45-48
Bar-Adon, Aaron 1923-
Brief entry 114
Baraheni, Reza 1935- CANR-126
Earlier sketch in CA 69-72
Barak, Gregg 1948- CANR-35
Earlier sketch in CA 114
Barak, Michael
See Bar-Zohar, Michael
Baraka, Amiri 1934- CANR-133
Earlier sketches in CA 21-24R, CANR-27, 38, 61
See also Jones, LeRoi
See also CABS 3
See also AAYA 63
See also AFAW 1, 2
See also AMWS 2
See also BLC 1
See also BW 2, 3
See also CAD
See also CD 3, 5, 6
See also CDALB 1941-1968
See also CLC 1, 2, 3, 5, 10, 14, 33, 115, 213
See also CP 4, 5, 6, 7
See also CPW
See also DA
See also DA3
See also DAC
See also DAM MST, MULT, POET, POP
See also DC 6
See also DFS 3, 11, 16
See also DLB 5, 7, 16, 38
See also DLBD 8
See also EWL 3
See also MAL 5
See also MTCW 1, 2
See also MTFW 2005
See also PC 4
See also PFS 9
See also RGAL 4
See also TCLE 1:1
See also TUS
See also WLCS
See also WP
Barakat, Hoda 1954(?)- .... EWL 3
Baral, Robert 1905-1980 .... CAP-1
Earlier sketch in CA 9-10
Baram, Amatzia 1938- 146
Baram, Phillip J(ason) 1938- 85-88
Baram, Robert 1919-2005 234
Obituary 238
Brief entry 112
Baran, Annette 1927- 185
Brief entry 114
Baran, Susan 206
Baranczak, Stanislaw 1946- CANR-77
Earlier sketch in CA 149
See also CWW 2
See also DLB 232
See also EWL 3
Baranet, Nancy Neiman 1933- 41-44R
Baranov, Alexander A. 1931(?)-1983
Obituary 109
Baranskaia, Natal'ia Vladimirovna 1908- .... DLB 302
Baranson, Jack 1924- 119
Barany, George 1922- 25-28R
Barasch, Frances K. 1928- 37-40R
Barasch, Lynne 1939- .... SATA 74, 126
Barasch, Marc Ian 1949- CANR-103
Earlier sketch in CA 113
Barasch, Moshe 1920- 97-100
Barash, David P(hilip) 1946- CANR-141
Earlier sketch in CA 144
Barash, Meyer 1916- 1-4R
Barash, Samuel T(heodore) 1921- 107
Barat, Kahar 1950- 227
Baratay, Eric 236
Baratta, Don 1932- 209
Baratta, Joseph Preston 1943- 154
Barattini, Kathryn DeFatta 1968- 192
Baratynsky, Evgenii Abramovich 1800-1844 .... DLB 205
Barayon, Ramon Sender
See Sender Barayon, Ramon
Barazangi, Nimat Hafez 1943- CANR-116
Earlier sketch in CA 160
Barba, Harry 1922- CANR-1
Earlier sketch in CA 1-4R
Barbach, Lonnie (Villoldo) 1946- CANR-25
Earlier sketches in CA 61-64, CANR-9
Barba-Jacob, Porfirio 1883-1942 .... DLB 283
Barbalet, Margaret 1949- CANR-92
Earlier sketch in CA 145
See also SATA 77
Barbanell, Maurice 1902-1981
Obituary 113
Barbara, Dominick A. 1914-2002 .... 37-40R
Barbare, Rholf
See Volkoff, Vladimir
Barbarese, J. T. 1948- 135
Barbary, James
See Beeching, Jack
Barbash, Jack 1910-1994 .... CANR-80
Obituary 145
Earlier sketches in CA 1-4R, CANR-16
Barbash, Shepard 1957- 150
See also SATA 84
Barbash, Tom 216
Barbato, Joseph 1944- 150
Barbauld, Anna Laetitia 1743-1825 ... DLB 107, 109, 142, 158
See also RGEL 2
Barbe, Walter Burke 1926- 13-16R
See also SATA 45
Barbeau, Arthur E(dward) 1936- 49-52
Barbeau, Clayton C(harles) 1930- 73-76
Barbeau, Edward J(oseph) 1938- 159
Barbeau, Jean 1945-
Barbeau, (Frederic Charles Joseph) Marius 1883-1969 148
Obituary 25-28R
See also DLB 92
Barbee, David E(dwin) 1936- 57-60
Barbee, Phillips
See Sheckley, Robert
Barbellion, W. N. P.
See Cummings, Bruce F(rederick)
See also TCLC 24
Barber, Antonia
See Anthony, Barbara
Barber, Benjamin R. 1939- CANR-119
Earlier sketches in CA 29-32R, CANR-12, 32, 64
See also CLC 141
Barber, Bernard 1918- CANR-14
Earlier sketch in CA 65-68
Barber, Charles (Laurence) 1915-2000 .... CANR-22
Earlier sketches in CA 17-20R, CANR-7
Barber, Cyril J(ohn) 1934- CANR-9
Earlier sketch in CA 65-68
Barber, D(ulan) F(riar Whilberton) 1940-1988 .... CANR-71
Earlier sketches in CA 61-64, CANR-21
See also CMW 4
See also HGG
Barber, E(lizabeth) J. W(ayland) 1940- CANR-89
Earlier sketch in CA 146
Barber, James David 1930-2004 .... CANR-6
Obituary 231
Earlier sketch in CA 13-16R
Barber, James G(eoffrey) 1952- 110
Barber, Jesse (Belmont) 1893-1979
Obituary 85-88
Barber, John 1944- 128
Barber, John Warner 1798-1885 .... DLB 30
Barber, Joseph 1909-1982
Obituary 107
Barber, Karin 138
Barber, Lucie W(elles) 1922- 108
Barber, Lucy G(race) 1964- 224
Barber, Lucy L(ombardi) 1882(?)-1974
Obituary 49-52
Barber, Lynda
See Graham-Barber, Lynda
Barber, Lynda Graham
See Graham-Barber, Lynda
Barber, Lynn 1944- 97-100
Barber, Nigel (William Thomas) 1955- 236
Barber, Noel (John Lysberg) 1909-1988
Obituary 126
Brief entry 115
See also RHW
Barber, Patricia 1946- CANR-48
Barber, Paul (Thomas) 1941- 134
Barber, Philip W(ilson) 1903-1981
Obituary 103
Barber, Phyllis (Nelson) 1943- 139
Barber, Red
See Barber, Walter Lanier
Barber, Richard (William) 1941- CANR-72
Earlier sketches in CA 33-36R, CANR-13, 32
See also SATA 35
Barber, Richard J. 1932- 29-32R
Barber, Samuel 1910-1981
Obituary 103
Barber, Stephen Guy 1921-1980 69-72
Obituary 97-100
Barber, T(heodore) X(enophon) 1927- ... 41-44R
Barber, Walter Lanier 1908-1992 141
Brief entry 113
Barber, Willard F(oster) 1909-2002 .... CAP-2
Obituary 210
Earlier sketch in CA 21-22
Barber, William Henry 1918-2004 .... 5-8R
Obituary 225
Barber, William Joseph 1925- CANR-8
Earlier sketch in CA 61-64
Barbera, Henry 1929- 105
Barbera, Jack (Vincent) 1945- CANR-45
Earlier sketch in CA 110
See also CLC 44
Barbera, Joe
See Barbera, Joseph Roland
Barbera, Joseph Roland 1911- 150
See also IDFW 3, 4
See also SATA 51
Barberis
See Barberis, Franco
Barberis, Franco 1905-1992 .... 25-28R
Barberis, Juan C(arlos) 1920- .... SATA 61
Barberi Squarotti, Giorgio 1929- 209
See also DLB 128
Barbero, Yves Regis Francois 1943- 57-60
Barbet, Pierre
See Avice, Claude (Pierre Marie)
Barbette, Jay
See Spicer, Bart
Barbey d'Aurevilly, Jules-Amedee 1808-1889 .... DLB 119
See also GFL 1789 to the Present
See also SSC 17
Barbier, Auguste 1805-1882 .... DLB 217
Barbier, Patrick 1956- 157
Barbieri, Elaine 1936- 138
Barbilian, Dan
See Barbu, Ion
Barbotin, Edmond 1920- 57-60
Barbour, Alan G. 1933-2002
Brief entry 117
Barbour, Arthur Joseph 1926- 57-60
Barbour, Brian M(ichael) 1943- 49-52
Barbour, Douglas (Fleming) 1940- CANR-54
Earlier sketches in CA 69-72, CANR-11, 27
See also CP 2, 3, 4, 5, 6, 7
Barbour, Frances Martha 1895-1979 ..... 17-20R
Barbour, George B(rown) 1890-1977
Obituary 73-76
Barbour, Hugh (Stewart) 1921- 21-24R
Barbour, Ian G(raeme) 1923- CANR-96
Earlier sketches in CA 21-24R, CANR-8
Barbour, J(ames) Murray 1897-1970 ...... CAP-1
Earlier sketch in CA 11-12
Barbour, John c. 1316-1395 .... DLB 146
Barbour, John D. 1951- 150
Barbour, Julian B. 1937- CANR-92
Earlier sketch in CA 133
Barbour, Karen 1956- CANR-99
Earlier sketch in CA 127
See also SATA 63, 121
Barbour, (Kenneth) Michael 1921-2004 .... CANR-7
Obituary 232
Earlier sketch in CA 5-8R
Barbour, Michael G(eorge) 1942- CANR-2
Earlier sketch in CA 49-52
Barbour, Nevill 1895-1972 .... CANR-80
Obituary 103
Earlier sketch in CA 5-8R
Barbour, Philip L(emont) 1898-1980 .... 9-12R
Barbour, Ralph Henry 1870-1944 .... DLB 22
See also SATA 16
Barbour, Roger W(illiam) 1919- 61-64
Barbour, Russell B. 1906-1993 .... CAP-2
Earlier sketch in CA 23-24
Barbour, Ruth P(eeling) 1924- 89-92
Barbour, Thomas L.
See Lesure, Thomas B(arbour)
Barbrook, Alec
See Barbrook, Alexander Thomas
Barbrook, Alexander Thomas 1927-2001 45-48
Obituary 203
Barbu, Ion 1895-1961 .... CDWLB 4
See also DLB 220
See also EWL 3
Barbusse, Henri 1873-1935 154
Brief entry 105
See also DLB 65
See also EWL 3
See also RGWL 2, 3
See also TCLC 5
Barchek, James Robert 1935- 41-44R
Barchiesi, Robert 1955- 137
Barchilon, Jacques 1923- CANR-5
Earlier sketch in CA 13-16R
Barchus, Agnes J(osephine) 1893-1983 . 97-100
Barcia, Jose Rubia
See Rubia Barcia, Jose
Barck, Oscar Theodore, Jr. 1902-1993 .. 21-24R
Barclay, Alexander c. 1475-1552 .... DLB 132
Barclay, Andrew M(ichael) 1941- 113
Barclay, Ann
See Greig, Maysie
Barclay, Barbara 1938- 29-32R
Barclay, Bill
See Moorcock, Michael (John)
Barclay, Cyril Nelson 1896-1979 .... 5-8R
Barclay, Donald A. 1958- 217
Barclay, Florence L(ouisa Charlesworth) 1862-1921 157
See also RHW
Barclay, Glen St. J(ohn) 1930- 77-80
Barclay, Harold B. 1924- 9-12R
Barclay, Hartley Wade 1903-1978 85-88
Obituary 81-84
Barclay, Isabel
See Dobell, I(sabel) M(arian) B(arclay)
Barclay, Max
See Sherwood, Ben
Barclay, Oliver R(ainsford) 1919- CANR-8
Earlier sketch in CA 57-60
Barclay, Paris 1957- .... AAYA 55
Barclay, Robert 1946- 143
Barclay, Tessa
See Bowden, Jean
Barclay, Virginia
See McDonnell, Virginia B(leecker)
Barclay, William 1907-1978 .... CANR-29
Obituary 73-76
Earlier sketch in CA 77-80
Barclay, William Ewert
See Moorcock, Michael (John)
Barcus, James E(dgar) 1938- 21-24R
Barcus, Nancy B(idwell) 1937- CANR-40
Earlier sketch in CA 117
Barcynski, Leon Roger 1949- CANR-10
Earlier sketch in CA 93-96
Barcynski, Vivian G(odfrey) 1917- CANR-10
Earlier sketch in CA 61-64
Bard, Bernard 1927- 25-28R
Bard, Harry 1906-1976 .... 33-36R
Bard, James (Alan) 1925- 102
Bard, Mitchell G. 1959- CANR-104
Earlier sketch in CA 148
Bard, Morton 1924- 97-100
Obituary 163
Bard, Patti 1935- 21-24R
Bard, Rachel 1921- 117
Bardach, John E(ugene) 1915- 41-44R
Bardarson, Hjalmar R(oegnvaldur) 1918- 57-60
Bardemeyer, Geert
See Brunclair, Victor
Barden, Dan 171
Barden, Leonard (William) 1929- CANR-2
Earlier sketch in CA 1-4R
Barden, Thomas E(arl) 1946- CANR-96
Earlier sketch in CA 136
Bardens, Amey E. 1894(?)-1974
Obituary 53-56
Bardens, Dennis (Conrad) 1911-2004 .... 5-8R
Obituary 223
Bardhan, Pranab 1939- 139
Bardi, Pietro Maria 1900-1999 .... CANR-42
Earlier sketches in CA 85-88, CANR-19

Cumulative Index 33 Barnard

Bardin, John Franklin 1916-1981 ... CANR-66
Obituary ... 104
Earlier sketch in CA 81-84
Bardis, Panos D(emetrios) 1924-1996 ... CANR-46
Earlier sketches in CA 25-28R, CANR-10
Bard of Avondale
See Jacobs, Howard
Bardolph, Richard 1915- ... 61-64
Bardon, Edward J(ohn) 1933- ... 81-84
Bardon, Jack Irving 1925-1993 ... 101
Bardos, Marie (Dupuis) 1935- ... 13-16R
Bardot, Louis 1896-1975
Obituary ... 61-64
Bardsley, Cuthbert K(illick) N(orman) 1907-1991 ... CANR-78
Obituary ... 133
Earlier sketches in CAP-2, CA 25-28
Bardwell, Denver
See Sayers, James Denson
See also TCWW 1, 2
Bardwell, George E(ldred) 1924- ... 1-4R
Bardwell, Leland 1928- ... 225
See also CN 7
Bardwick, Judith M(arcia) 1933- ... CANR-19
Earlier sketch in CA 103
Bare, Arnold Edwin 1920- ... SATA 16
Bare, Colleen Stanley ... 102
See also SATA 32
Barea, Arturo 1897-1957 ... 201
Brief entry ... 111
See also TCLC 14
Bareham, Lindsey 1948- ... 140
Bareham, Terence 1937- ... 109
Barell, John 1938- ... 111
Barendrecht, Cor W(illiam) 1934- ... 114
Barenholtz, Bernard 1914-1989 .. SATA-Obit 64
Barer, Burl (Roger) 1947- ... CANR-136
Earlier sketch in CA 162
Baretski, Charles Allan 1918- ... 77-80
Barfield, (Arthur) Owen 1898-1997 .... CANR-2
Obituary ... 163
Earlier sketch in CA 5-8R
Barfield, Ray 1939- ... 187
Barfield, Rhonda 1953(?)- ... 239
Barfield, Woodrow 1950- ... 168
Barfoot, Audrey Ilma 1918-1964 ... 5-8R
Barfoot, Joan 1946- ... CANR-141
Earlier sketch in CA 105
See also CLC 18
Barford, Carol 1931- ... 89-92
Barford, Philip (Trevelyan) 1925- ... 93-96
Barga, Corpus
See Barga y Gomez de la Serna, Andres Garcia de la
Bargad, Warren 1940- ... CANR-49
Earlier sketch in CA 122
Bargar, B(radley) D(uffee) 1924- ... 17-20R
Bargar, Gary W. 1947-1985 ... SATA 63
Bargate, Verity 1941(?)-1981
Obituary ... 103
Bargebuhr, Frederick P(erez) 1904-1978 ... CAP-2
Earlier sketch in CA 33-36
Bargellini, Piero 1897-1980(?)
Obituary ... 97-100
Barger, Harold 1907-1989 ... CAP-2
Earlier sketch in CA 19-20
Barger, James (David) 1947- ... 57-60
Barger, Jan 1948- ... SATA 147
Barger, Ralph 1939- ... 212
Barger, Ralph Sonny
See Barger, Ralph
Barghouti, Mourid 1944- ... 215
Bargum, Johan 1943- ... 209
See also EWL 3
Barham, Patte B. ... 143
Barham, Richard Harris 1788-1845 .... DLB 159
Bar-Hillel, Yehoshua 1915-1975
Obituary ... 115
Bari, Nina Karlovna 1901-1961 ... 161
Bari, Ruth Aaronson 1917- ... 161
Baricco, Alessandro 1958- ... 171
Barich, Bill 1943- ... CANR-68
Earlier sketch in CA 149
See also DLB 185
Barille, Elisabeth 1960- ... 137
Baring, Arnulf Martin 1932- ... 41-44R
Baring, Maurice 1874-1945 ... 168
Brief entry ... 105
See also DLB 34
See also HGG
See also TCLC 8
Baringer, William E(ldon) 1909-2000 ... 1-4R
Baring-Gould, Sabine 1834-1924 ... DLB 156, 190
See also TCLC 88
Baring-Gould, William Stuart 1913-1967
Obituary ... 25-28R
Barish, Evelyn 1935- ... 132
Barish, Jonas A. 1922-1998 ... 21-24R
Obituary ... 165
Barish, Matthew 1907-2000 ... 57-60
See also SATA 12
Baritz, Loren 1928- ... 13-16R
Barjavel, Rene (Gustave Henri) 1911-1985 . 162
Brief entry ... 107
See also SFW 4
Bar-Joseph, Uri 1949- ... 155
Bark, Dennis L(aistner) 1942- ... CANR-41
Earlier sketch in CA 117
Bark, William (Carroll) 1908-1996 ... CAP-1
Obituary ... 154
Earlier sketch in CA 13-14
Barkalow, Frederick Schenck, Jr. 1914-1982 ... 61-64
Barkan, Elliott Robert 1940- ... 21-24R
Barkan, Joanne ... CANR-91
Earlier sketch in CA 145
See also SATA 77, 127
Barkan, Leonard 1944- ... CANR-101
Brief entry ... 116
Earlier sketch in CA 122
Barkas, J. L.
See Yager, Jan
Barkas, Janet
See Yager, Jan
Barkdoll, Robert S. 1913(?)-1984
Obituary ... 112
Barkee, Asouff
See Strung, Norman
Barker, A(rthur) J(ames) 1918-1981 ... CANR-70
Obituary ... 104
Earlier sketches in CA 13-16R, CANR-7
Barker, A(udrey) L(ilian) 1918-2002 .. CANR-88
Obituary ... 205
Earlier sketches in CA 9-12R, CANR-3, 27, 53
See also CN 1, 2, 3, 4, 5, 6, 7
See also DLB 14, 139
Barker, A(nthony) W(ilhelm) 1930- ... CANR-32
Earlier sketch in CA 113
Barker, Albert W. 1900- ... CANR-14
Earlier sketch in CA 73-76
See also SATA 8
Barker, Andrew (Dennison) 1943- ... 130
Barker, Bill
See Barker, William J(ohn)
Barker, Carol (Minturn) 1938- ... 107
See also SATA 31
Barker, Carol M. 1942- ... 45-48
Barker, Charles Albro 1904-1993 ... CANR-78
Obituary ... 142
Earlier sketch in CA 93-96
Barker, Charles M., Jr. 1926- ... 13-16R
Barker, Cicely Mary 1895-1973 ... 121
Obituary ... 117
See also CLR 88
See also CWRI 5
See also SATA 49
See also SATA-Brief 39
Barker, Clive 1952- ... CANR-133
Brief entry ... 121
Earlier sketches in CA 129, CANR-71, 111
Interview in ... CA-129
See also AAYA 10, 54
See also BEST 90:3
See also BPFB 1
See also CLC 52, 205
See also CPW
See also DA3
See also DAM POP
See also DLB 261
See also HGG
See also MTCW 1, 2
See also MTFW 2005
See also SSC 53
See also SUFW 2
Barker, D(erek) R(oland) 1930- ... 5-8R
Barker, Dennis (Malcolm) 1929- ... CANR-32
Earlier sketches in CA 25-28R, CANR-14
Barker, Dudley 1910-1980(?) ... CANR-58
Obituary ... 102
Earlier sketches in CA 1-4R, CANR-1
See also Black, Lionel
Barker, E. M.
See Barker, Elsa (McCormick)
Barker, Elisabeth 1910-1986 ... 136
Obituary ... 118
Barker, Elliott S(peer) 1886-1988 ... CANR-78
Obituary ... 125
Earlier sketch in CA 89-92
Barker, Elsa (McCormick) 1906-1996 .... CAP-2
Earlier sketch in CA 17-18
Barker, Elspeth 1940- ... 138
Barker, Elver A. 1920- ... 25-28R
Barker, Eric 1905-1973 ... CANR-27
Obituary ... 41-44R
Earlier sketch in CA 1-4R
See also CP 1
Barker, Ernest 1874-1960 ... 103
Obituary ... 93-96
Barker, Esther T(emperley) 1910-2002 ... CANR-2
Earlier sketch in CA 49-52
Barker, (Richard) Felix (Raine) 1917-1997 ... CANR-95
Earlier sketch in CA 130
Barker, Frank Granville 1923- ... CAP-1
Earlier sketch in CA 11-12
Barker, Garry 1943- ... 140
Barker, George Granville 1913-1991 ... CANR-38
Obituary ... 135
Earlier sketches in CA 9-12R, CANR-7
See also CLC 8, 48
See also CP 1, 2, 3, 4
See also DAM POET
See also DLB 20
See also EWL 3
See also MTCW 1
Barker, Gerard A(rthur) 1930- ... 69-72
Barker, Graham H(arold) 1949- ... 106
Barker, Harley Granville
See Granville-Barker, Harley
See also DLB 10
Barker, Howard 1946- ... 102
See also CBD
See also CD 5, 6
See also CLC 37
See also DLB 13, 233
Barker, Jack M. 1925-1985
Obituary ... 117
Barker, James Nelson 1784-1858 ... DLB 37
See also RGAL 4
Barker, Jane 1652-1732 ... DLB 39, 131
Barker, Jane Valentine 1930- ... CANR-11
Earlier sketch in CA 65-68
Barker, John W(alton, Jr.) 1933- ... 17-20R
Barker, Jonathan 1949- ... 139
Barker, Joseph 1929- ... 103
Barker, Keith 1947-1998 ... 135
Barker, Kenneth S(tacey) 1932- ... 110
Barker, Larry L(ee) 1941- ... CANR-17
Earlier sketch in CA 81-84
Barker, M(uhammad) A(bd-Al-)R(ahman) 1929- ... 116
Barker, Margaret 1944- ... CANR-105
Earlier sketch in CA 138
Barker, Lady Mary Anne 1831-1911
See Stewart, Mary Anne
See also DLB 166
Barker, Melvern 1907-1989 ... CAP-1
Earlier sketch in CA 9-10
See also SATA 11
Barker, Myrtie Lillian 1910-1983 ... 5-8R
Barker, Nancy Nichols 1925-
Brief entry ... 114
Barker, Nicola (Jane) 1966- ... CANR-101
Earlier sketch in CA 141
Barker, Nicolas (John) 1932- ... CANR-43
Earlier sketch in CA 102
Barker, Pat(ricia) 1943- ... CANR-101
Brief entry ... 117
Earlier sketches in CA 122, CANR-50
Interview in ... CA-122
See also BRWS 4
See also CLC 32, 94, 146
See also CN 6, 7
See also DLB 271
Barker, Paul 1935- ... CANR-123
Earlier sketch in CA 171
Barker, Philip 1929- ... 114
Barker, Raffaella 1964- ... CANR-94
Earlier sketch in CA 146
Barker, Ralph 1917- ... CANR-38
Earlier sketches in CA 1-4R, CANR-1, 16
Barker, Robert L(ee) 1937- ... 25-28R
Barker, Rocky
See Barker, Roland
Barker, Rodney (Steven) 1942- ... 45-48
Barker, Rodney 1946- ... 160
Barker, Roger Garlock 1903-1990 .... CANR-11
Earlier sketches in CAP-1, CA 11-12
Barker, Roland 1953- ... 146
Barker, Ronald E(rnest) 1921(?)-1976
Obituary ... 65-68
Barker, S(quire) Omar 1894-1985 ... CANR-64
Earlier sketches in CAP-2, CA 17-18
See also SATA 10
See also TCWW 1, 2
Barker, Sally
See McMurry, Sarah L.
Barker, Sebastian 1945- ... CANR-54
Earlier sketch in CA 124
Barker, Shirley Frances 1911-1965 ... CANR-70
Earlier sketch in CA 5-8R
Barker, T(heodore Cardwell) 1923-2001 ... CANR-5
Obituary ... 203
Earlier sketch in CA 13-16R
Barker, T(erence) S(narr) 1941- ... CANR-21
Earlier sketch in CA 45-48
Barker, Thomas M. 1929- ... 21-24R
Barker, W(illiam) Alan 1923-1988(?) .. CANR-1
Obituary ... 125
Earlier sketch in CA 1-4R
Barker, Wendy B. 1942- ... CANR-52
Earlier sketch in CA 125
Barker, Will 1913-1983 ... 9-12R
Obituary ... 110
See also SATA 8
Barker, William c. 1520-1576(?) ... DLB 132
Barker, William George 1867-1951 . IDFW 3, 4
Barker, William J(ohn) ... 65-68
Barker, William P(ierson) 1927- ... 9-12R
Barker-Benfield, G(raham) J(ohn) 1941-
Brief entry ... 113
Barkey, Karen 1958- ... 168
Barkhouse, Joyce 1913- ... 93-96
See also SATA-Brief 48
Barkin, Carol 1944- ... 135
Brief entry ... 118
See also SATA 42, 52
Barkin, David Peter 1942- ... 37-40R
Barkin, Kenneth D(avid) 1939- ... 41-44R
Barkin, Solomon 1907-2000 ... 9-12R
Obituary ... 190
Barkins, Evelyn (Warner) 1919- ... 29-32R
Barklem, Jill 1951- ... CANR-137
Earlier sketch in CA 161
See also CLR 31
See also SATA 96
Barkley, Charles (Wade) 1963- ... 214
Barkley, Deanne 1931-
Brief entry ... 114
Barkley, James Edward 1941- ... SATA 6
Barkley, T(heodore) M(itchell) 1934- ... 120
Barkley, Vada Lee 1919- ... 57-60
Barkman, Alma 1939- ... CANR-82
Earlier sketches in CA 114, CANR-35
Barkman, Paul Friesen 1921- ... 17-20R
Barkov, Ivan Semenovich 1732-1768 . DLB 150
Barkow, Al 1932- ... CANR-114
Earlier sketches in CA 53-56, CANR-4
Barks, Carl 1901-2000 ... 115
Obituary ... 189
See also AAYA 55
See also SATA 37
Barks, Coleman (Bryan) 1937- ... CANR-118
Earlier sketches in CA 25-28R, CANR-12
See also CP 4
See also DLB 5
Barksdale, E(thelbert) C(ourtland) 1944- .. 57-60
Barksdale, Hiram C(ollier) 1921- ... 9-12R
Barksdale, Richard (Kenneth) 1915-1993 ... 49-52
Barkton, S. Rush
See Brav, Stanley R(osenbaum)
Barkun, Michael 1938- ... 135
Brief entry ... 114
Barkworth, Peter (Wynn) 1929- ... 107
Barlach, Ernst (Heinrich) 1870-1938 ... 178
See also DLB 56, 118
See also EWL 3
See also TCLC 84
Barlay, Bennett
See Crossen, Kendell Foster
Barlay, Stephen 1930- ... CANR-12
Earlier sketch in CA 25-28R
Barlett, Donald L(eon) 1936- ... CANR-101
Earlier sketches in CA 115, CANR-68
Interview in ... CA-115
Barlett, Peggy F. 1947- ... 144
Barletta, Martha 1954- ... 228
Barley, Janet Crane 1934- ... 160
See also SATA 95
Barley, M. W.
See Barley, Maurice Willmore
Barley, Maurice Willmore 1909-1991 ... CANR-78
Obituary ... 134
Earlier sketch in CA 122
Barlin, Anne L(ief) 1916- ... 97-100
Barling, Charles
See Barling, Muriel Vere Mant
Barling, Muriel Vere Mant 1904- ... 5-8R
Barlough, Jeffrey Ernest 1953- ... CANR-100
Earlier sketch in CA 49-52
Barlow, Claude W(illis) 1907-1976 ... CAP-2
Earlier sketch in CA 33-36
Barlow, Connie 1952- ... CANR-113
Earlier sketch in CA 154
Barlow, Frank 1911- ... CANR-30
Earlier sketches in CA 9-12R, CANR-3
Barlow, Genevieve 1895-1992 ... 21-24R
Barlow, Grant
See Meares, Leonard Frank
Barlow, J(ames) Stanley, (Jr.) 1924- ... 41-44R
Barlow, James 1921-1973 ... CANR-69
Obituary ... 41-44R
Earlier sketches in CAP-1, CA 13-14
Barlow, Jane 1857(?)-1917 ... 190
Brief entry ... 115
Barlow, Joel 1754-1812 ... AMWS 2
See also DLB 37
See also RGAL 4
Barlow, John A(lfred) 1924-1991 ... 21-24R
Barlow, John D(enison) 1934- ... 120
Barlow, Judith E(llen) 1946- ... 107
Barlow, Maude (Victoria) 1947- ... CANR-127
Earlier sketch in CA 135
Barlow, (Emma) Nora 1885- ... CAP-2
Earlier sketch in CA 25-28
Barlow, Robert O.
See Meyer, Heinrich
Barlow, Roger
See Leckie, Robert (Hugh)
Barlow, Ronald S. 1936- ... 142
Barlow, Samuel L(atham) M(itchell) 1892-1982
Obituary ... 107
Barlow, Sanna Morrison
See Rossi, Sanna Morrison Barlow
Barlow, T(homas) Edward 1931- ... CANR-3
Earlier sketch in CA 45-48
Barlow, Tani E. 1950- ... 130
Barlow, Wilfred 1915-1991 ... 101
Barlow, William 1943- ... 139
Barlowe, Raleigh 1914- ... 17-20R
Barlowe, Wayne Douglas 1958- ... 134
Barltrop, Robert 1922- ... CANR-19
Earlier sketch in CA 73-76
Barman, Alicerose 1919- ... 65-68
Barman, Charles R(oy) 1945- ... 106
Barmann, Lawrence Francis 1932- ... 9-12R
Barmash, Isadore 1921- ... CANR-17
Earlier sketches in CA 45-48, CANR-1
Barme, Geremie 1954- ... CANR-90
Earlier sketch in CA 131
Barmine, Alexander (G.) 1899-1987
Obituary ... 125
Barna, George 1954- ... 114
Barna, Joel Warren 1951- ... 138
Barna, Yon 1927- ... 53-56
Barnabas
See Blandford, Brian E(rnest) and West, Charles Converse
Barnaby, (Charles) Frank 1927- ... CANR-56
Earlier sketches in CA 33-36R, CANR-13, 29
Barnaby, Ralph S(tanton) 1893-1986 ... 61-64
See also SATA 9
Barnacle, Hugo 1958- ... 172
Barnao, Jack
See Wood, Edward John
Barnard, A. M.
See Alcott, Louisa May
Barnard, (James) Alan 1928- ... 9-12R
Barnard, Bryn 1956- ... SATA 115
Barnard, Charles N(elson III) 1924- CANR-1
Earlier sketch in CA 49-52
Barnard, Christiaan (Neethling) 1922-2001 ... CANR-110
Obituary ... 198
Earlier sketches in CA 61-64, CANR-14
Barnard, Ellsworth 1907- ... CANR-26
Earlier sketches in CA 21-24R, CANR-11

Barnard 34 CONTEMPORARY AUTHORS

Barnard, F(rederick) M(echner) 1921- ... 25-28R
Barnard, Harry 1906-1982 .... CANR-78
Obituary 107
Earlier sketches in CA 5-8R, CANR-3
Barnard, Howard Clive 1884-1985 85-88
Obituary 117
Barnard, J(ohn) Darrell 1906- 5-8R
Barnard, J(ohn) Lawrence 1912-1977 77-80
Obituary 73-76
Barnard, John 1681-1770 .... DLB 24
Barnard, (Virgil) John 1932- CANR-45
Earlier sketch in CA 33-36R
Barnard, Judith 1934- 139
See also CPW
See also DAM POP
Barnard, Larry
See Barnard, Lawrence T.
Barnard, Lawrence T. 1970- 221
Barnard, Marjorie Faith 1897-1987 156
See also DLB 260
See also SFW 4
Barnard, Mary (Ethel) 1909- CAP-2
Earlier sketch in CA 21-22
See also CLC 48
See also CP 1
Barnard, Nicholas 1958- 139
Barnard, Robert 1936- CANR-54
Earlier sketches in CA 77-80, CANR-20
Interview in CANR-20
See also DLB 276
See also MSW
Barnard, Tom
See Geldenhuys, Deon
Barnard, William Dean 1942- 69-72
Bar-Natan, Moshe
See Louvish, Misha
Barne, Kitty
See Barne, Marion Catherine
See also DLB 160
Barne, Marion Catherine 1883-1957 154
Brief entry 112
See also Barne, Kitty
See also CWRI 5
See also SATA 97
Barner, Bob 1947- 93-96
See also SATA 29, 136
Bar Ner, R.
See Brenner, Reeve R(obert)
Barnes, Adrienne Martine
See Martine-Barnes, Adrienne
Barnes, Annie S. 1932- 146
Barnes, Barnabe 1571-1609 .... DLB 132
Barnes, Barry 1943- 97-100
Barnes, Burton V(erne) 1930- 130
Barnes, Chesley Virginia
See Young, Chesley Virginia
Barnes, Christopher J(on) 1942- CANR-90
Earlier sketch in CA 132
Barnes, Clara Ernst 1895-1986 .... 5-8R
Barnes, Clive (Alexander) 1927- CANR-26
Earlier sketch in CA 77-80
See also AITN 2
Barnes, Djuna 1892-1982 .... CANR-55
Obituary 107
Earlier sketches in CA 9-12R, CANR-16
See also Steptoe, Lydia
See also AMWS 3
See also CAD
See also CLC 3, 4, 8, 11, 29, 127
See also CN 1, 2, 3
See also CWD
See also DLB 4, 9, 45
See also EWL 3
See also GLL 1
See also MAL 5
See also MTCW 1, 2
See also MTFW 2005
See also RGAL 4
See also SSC 3
See also TCLE 1:1
See also TUS
Barnes, Douglas 1927- CANR-41
Earlier sketches in CA 103, CANR-19
Barnes, Duncan 1935- 127
Barnes, Edward F.
See Marquis, Max
Barnes, Elmer Tracey CANR-26
Earlier sketches in CAP-2, CA 19-20
Barnes, (Frank) Eric Wollencott
1907-1962 .... SATA 22
Barnes, George S. 1893-1953 .... IDFW 3, 4
Barnes, Gregory Allen 1934- CANR-25
Earlier sketches in CA 25-28R, CANR-10
Barnes, H. Lee 1944- 199
Barnes, Harry Elmer 1889-1968 89-92
Obituary 25-28R
Barnes, Hazel E(stella) 1915- CANR-3
Earlier sketch in CA 5-8R
Barnes, Henry A. 1906-1968 .... CAP-1
Earlier sketch in CA 13-16
Barnes, Irston Roberts 1904-1988
Obituary 124
Barnes, J. 1944- 85-88
Barnes, J(ohn) A(rundel) 1918- 101
Barnes, Jack 1920- 89-92
Barnes, Jack 1940- CANR-9
Earlier sketch in CA 61-64
Barnes, James A(nderson) 1898-1980 ...... 9-12R
Barnes, James J(ohn) 1931- CANR-4
Earlier sketch in CA 9-12R
Barnes, James N(eil) 1944- 117
Barnes, Jane
See Casey, Jane Barnes
Barnes, Jay 1958- 154
Barnes, Jim 1933- 175
Earlier sketch in CA 108
Autobiographical Essay in 175
See also CAAS 28
See also DLB 175
See also NNAL
Barnes, Joanna 1934- 57-60
Barnes, John 1908-1997 .... CANR-2
Earlier sketch in CA 45-48
Barnes, (Ernest) John (Ward) 1917-1992 108
Barnes, John (Allen) 1957- CANR-115
Earlier sketch in CA 137
See also SFW 4
Barnes, John B(ertram) 1924- 33-36R
Barnes, Joseph Fels 1907-1970
Obituary 104
Barnes, Joyce Annette 1958- CANR-135
Earlier sketch in CA 151
See also SATA 85
Barnes, Julian (Patrick) 1946- CANR-137
Earlier sketches in CA 102, CANR-19, 54, 115
See also BRWS 4
See also CLC 42, 141
See also CN 4, 5, 6, 7
See also DAB
See also DLB 194
See also DLBY 1993
See also EWL 3
See also MTCW 2
See also MTFW 2005
Barnes, Kenneth Charles 1903-1998 106
Barnes, Kim CANR-98
Earlier sketch in CA 163
Barnes, Laura T. 1958- 190
See also SATA 119
Barnes, Leonard (John) 1895-1977 .... CAP-2
Earlier sketch in CA 29-32
Barnes, Lilly I. 1935- 126
Barnes, Linda
See Barnes, Linda J(oyce)
Barnes, Linda J(oyce) 1949- CANR-62
Earlier sketch in CA 132
Barnes, Loutricia
See Barnes-Svarney, Patricia L(ou)
Barnes, Lynard 1948- 173
Barnes, Malcolm 1909(?)-1984
Obituary 114
See also SATA-Obit 41
Barnes, Margaret Ayer 1886-1967 178
Obituary 25-28R
See also DLB 9
Barnes, Mary 1923-2001 85-88
Obituary 198
Barnes, Melvyn (Peter Keith) 1942- 122
Barnes, Michael 1934- .... SATA 55
Barnes, Michael (Anthony) 1947- 137
Barnes, Mike 1955- 224
Barnes, Patience P(lummer) 1932- 108
Barnes, Peter 1931-2004 .... CANR-113
Obituary 230
Earlier sketches in CA 65-68, CANR-33, 34, 64
See also CAAS 12
See also CBD
See also CD 5, 6
See also CLC 5, 56
See also DFS 6
See also DLB 13, 233
See also MTCW 1
Barnes, Phoebe 1908- CAP-2
Earlier sketch in CA 23-24
Barnes, R(ichard) G(ordon) 1932-2000 . 33-36R
Barnes, Ralph M(osser) 1900-1984 .... CAP-2
Obituary 114
Earlier sketch in CA 17-18
Barnes, Robert J(ay) 1925- 21-24R
Barnes, Robert M(orson) 1940- CANR-25
Earlier sketch in CA 45-48
Barnes, Sam(uel) G(ill) 1913-1976 .... 13-16R
Barnes, Samuel H(enry) 1931- 21-24R
Barnes, Simon 1951- 130
Barnes, Stephen Emory 1952- CANR-122
Earlier sketches in CA 105, CANR-55
See also SFW 4
Barnes, Steven
See Barnes, Stephen Emory
Barnes, Suzanne Falter
See Falter-Barns, Suzanne
Barnes, Thomas Garden 1930- CANR-1
Earlier sketch in CA 1-4R
Barnes, Timothy David 1942- 114
Barnes, Trevor 1955- 143
Barnes, Valerie 115
Barnes, Viola Florence 1885-1979 .... 1-4R
Barnes, Walter 1880-1969
Obituary 116
Barnes, William 1801-1886 .... DLB 32
Barnes-Murphy, Frances 1951- .... SATA 88
Barnes-Murphy, Rowan 1952- .... SATA 88
Barness, Richard 1917- 65-68
Barnes-Svarney, Patricia L(ou)
1953- CANR-143
Earlier sketch in CA 135
See also SATA 67
Barnet, Miguel 1940- 175
See also DLB 145
See also HW 2
See also WLIT 1
Barnet, Nancy 1954- .... SATA 84
Barnet, Richard J(ackson)
1929-2004 .... CANR-49
Obituary 234
Earlier sketch in CA 13-16R
Barnet, Sylvan 1926- CANR-4
Earlier sketch in CA 1-4R
Barnetson, William Denholm 1917-1981
Obituary 103
Barnett, A(rthur) Doak 1921-1999 .... CANR-15
Obituary 177
Earlier sketch in CA 5-8R
Barnett, Adam
See Fast, Julius
Barnett, Anthony 175
Barnett, Correlli (Douglas) 1927- CANR-46
Earlier sketches in CA 13-16R, CANR-15
Barnett, Franklin 1903-1982 69-72
Barnett, George L(eonard) 1915- 29-32R
Barnett, (Nicolas) Guy 1928- 17-20R
Barnett, H(omer) G(arner) 1906- 45-48
Barnett, Isobel (Morag) 1918-1980
Obituary 105
Barnett, Ivan 1947- .... SATA 70
Barnett, James Monroe 1925- 114
Barnett, Joe R(ichard) 1933- 106
Barnett, Joel 1923- 129
Barnett, L. David
See Laschever, Barnett D.
Barnett, LaShonda K. 1974- 191
Barnett, Le Roy G. 1941- 206
Barnett, Leo 1925- 29-32R
Barnett, Leonard (Palin) 1919- CANR-12
Earlier sketches in CAP-1, CA 13-14
Barnett, Lincoln (Kinnear) 1909-1979 102
Obituary 89-92
See also SATA 36
Barnett, Lisa A. 212
Barnett, Louise K. 192
Barnett, Malcolm Joel 1941- 45-48
Barnett, Marva T(uttle) 1913- 57-60
Barnett, Matthew 1974- 203
Barnett, Maurice 1917-1980
Obituary 97-100
Barnett, Michael 1930- 57-60
Barnett, Michael N. 1960- 235
Barnett, Moneta 1922-1976 .... SATA 33
Barnett, Naomi 1927- CANR-7
Earlier sketch in CA 5-8R
See also SATA 40
Barnett, Paul 1935- 172
Barnett, Peter Herbert 1945- 124
Barnett, Richard B(aity) 1941- 105
Barnett, Richard C(hambers) 1932- 33-36R
Barnett, Robert W(arren) 1911-1997 126
Obituary 159
Barnett, Rosalind C(hait) 1937- 129
Barnett, S(amuel) A(nthony) 1915- CANR-6
Earlier sketch in CA 13-16R
Barnett, Sanford 1909(?)-1988
Obituary 125
Barnett, Stephen 1954- 236
Barnett, Suzanne Wilson 1940- 120
Barnett, Thomas P. M. 236
Barnett, Ursula A(nnemarie) 1924- 123
Barnett, Victoria (Joan) 1950- 147
Barnett, Vivian E(ndicott) 1944- 115
Barnette, Henlee H(ulix) 1911-2004 . CANR-31
Obituary 232
Earlier sketch in CA 49-52
Barnette, Martha 1957- 136
Barnette, W(arren) Leslie, Jr.
1910-1980 .... CAP-1
Earlier sketch in CA 11-12
Barnewall, Gordon G(ouverneur) 1924- 121
Barney, Harry
See Lottman, Eileen
Barney, Kenneth D. 1921- 69-72
Barney, Laura D(reyfus) 1880(?)-1974
Obituary 53-56
Barney, LeRoy 1930- 33-36R
Barney, Maginel Wright 1881(?)-1966
Obituary 111
See also SATA 39
See also SATA-Brief 32
Barney, Natalie (Clifford) 1878(?)-1972 177
Obituary 33-36R
See also DLB 4
Barney, Stephen A(llen) 1942- 102
Barney, William L(esko) 1943- 41-44R
Barnfield, Richard 1574-1627 .... DLB 172
Barnhardt, Deanna
See Kawatski, Deanna
Barnhardt, Wilton 1960- 148
See also CN 7
Barnhart, Clarence L(ewis) 1900-1993 .. 13-16R
Obituary 143
See also SATA 48
See also SATA-Obit 78
Barnhart, Joe Edward 1931- 41-44R
Barnhart, Michael A(ndrew) 1951- 127
Barnhart, Robert K. 1933- 127
Barnhill, David Landis 1949- 227
Barnhill, Myrtle Fait 1896-1986 .... CAP-1
Obituary 119
Earlier sketch in CA 13-16
Barnhouse, Donald 103
Barnhouse, Donald Grey 1895-1960 123
Obituary 113
Barnhouse, Ruth Tiffany 1923- CANR-15
Earlier sketch in CA 85-88
Barnhurst, Kevin G. 1951- 223
Barnie, John 1941- 57-60
Barnitt, Nedda Lemmon 9-12R
Barnitz, Harry W. 1920-1973 .... CAP-2
Earlier sketch in CA 25-28
Barnoon, Shlomo 1940- 41-44R
Barnouw, Adriaan Jacob 1877-1968
Obituary 104
See also SATA-Obit 27
Barnouw, Dagmar 1936- 139
Barnouw, Erik 1908-2001 .... CANR-72
Obituary 199
Earlier sketches in CA 13-16R, CANR-12
Barnouw, Victor 1915-1989 85-88
See also SATA 43
See also SATA-Brief 28
Barn Owl
See Howells, Roscoe
Barnright, Julia
See Bancroft, Iris (May Nelson)
Barns, John W(intour) B(aldwin) 1912-1974
Obituary 49-52
Barns, Suzanne Falter
See Falter-Barns, Suzanne
Barnsley, Alan Gabriel 1916-1986 .... 13-16R
Obituary 121
See also Fielding, Gabriel
Barnstone, Aliki 1956- 105
Barnstone, Howard 1923-1987
Obituary 122
Barnstone, Willis 1927- CANR-68
Earlier sketches in CA 17-20R, CANR-45
See also CAAS 15
See also SATA 20
Barnum, Barbara (J.) Stevens 1937- 162
Barnum, Jay Hyde 1888(?)-1962 .... SATA 20
Barnum, P. T., Jr.
See Stratemeyer, Edward L.
Barnum, Richard CANR-26
Earlier sketches in CAP-2, CA 19-20
See also SATA 1, 67
Barnum, Theodore
See Stratemeyer, Edward L.
Barnum, Vance CANR-26
Earlier sketches in CAP-2, CA 19-20
Barnum, W(illiam) Paul 1933- 29-32R
Barnwell, D. Robinson 1915- 17-20R
Barnwell, J. O.
See Caruso, Joseph
See also TCWW 2
Barnwell, John (Gibbes, Jr.) 1947- 113
Barnwell, William Curtis 1943- 103
Baro, Gene 1924-1982
Obituary 112
See also CP 1, 2, 3
Baroff, David 1961- 186
Baroff, George Stanley 1924- 101
Baroja (y Nessi), Pio 1872-1956
Brief entry 104
See also EW 9
See also HLC 1
See also TCLC 8
Baroja (y Nessi), Pio 1872-1956 .... DLB 322
See also EWL 3
Barolini, Antonio 1910-1971 .... CANR-1
Earlier sketch in CA 1-4R
Barolini, Helen 1925- CANR-108
Earlier sketches in CA 73-76, CANR-16, 39, 45
Barolini, Teodolinda 1951- 124
Barolsky, Paul 1941- 81-84
Baron, Alexander 1917-1999 .... CANR-14
Obituary 187
Earlier sketch in CA 5-8R
Baron, Beth 1958- 138
Bar-On, Dan 1938- 139
Baron, David
See Pinter, Harold
Baron, Dennis E(mery) 1944- CANR-54
Earlier sketches in CA 110, CANR-27
Baron, Elizabeth Frank
See Frank-Baron, Elizabeth
Baron, Frank 1936- 119
Baron, Hans 1900-1988 .... 17-20R
Baron, Herman 1941- 61-64
Baron, J. W.
See Krauzer, Steven M(ark)
Baron, Jill S. 1954- 237
Baron, Joseph Alexander
See Baron, Alexander
Baron, Kathy 1954- .... SATA 90
Baron, Mary (Kelley) 1944- CANR-2
Earlier sketch in CA 49-52
Baron, Mikan
See Barba, Harry
Baron, Mike 1949- 227
Baron, Naomi S(usan) 1946- CANR-98
Earlier sketch in CA 140
Baron, Oscar 1908(?)-1976
Obituary 65-68
Baron, Othello
See Fanthorpe, R(obert) Lionel
Baron, Robert Alex 1920- 41-44R
Baron, Robert C. 1934- 239
Baron, Salo W(ittmayer) 1895-1989 . CANR-82
Obituary 130
Earlier sketch in CA 69-72
Baron, Samuel H(askell) 1921- CANR-119
Earlier sketches in CA 9-12R, CANR-3
Baron, Virginia Olsen 1931- 25-28R
See also SATA 46
See also SATA-Brief 28
Baron, (Ora) Wendy 1937- 41-44R
Baron Amulree
See Mackenzie, Basil William Sholto
Baron-Cohen, Simon 1958- 151
Baron Corvo
See Rolfe, Frederick (William Serafino Austin Lewis Mary)
Baron Denning
See Denning, Alfred Thompson
Barondes, Samuel H(erbert) 1933- 181
Barondess, Sue K(aufman)
1926-1977 .... CANR-1
Obituary 69-72
Earlier sketch in CA 1-4R
See also Kaufman, Sue
See also CLC 8
Baron de Teive
See Pessoa, Fernando (Antonio Nogueira)

Cumulative Index 35 **Barrow**

Barone, Dennis 1955- 192
Barone, Michael 1944- 93-96
Barone, Mike
See Albert, Marvin H(ubert)
Baroness Hart of South Lanark
See Hart, Judith (Constance Mary)
Baroness Strange
See Evans, (Jean) Cherry (Drummond)
Baroness Von S.
See Zangwill, Israel
Baron Lloyd of Hampstead
See Lloyd, Dennis
Baron of Remenham
See Thomas, (William) Miles (Webster)
Baron of West Kirby
See Sheppard, David Stuart
Baron Raglan
See Raglan, FitzRoy (Richard Somerset)
Baron Supervielle, Silvia 1934- 190
Baron Tebbit of Chingford
See Tebbit, Norman
Baroody, Jamil Murad 1905-1979
Obituary 85-88
Barooshian, (Dickran) Vahan 1932- 85-88
Barovsky, Sharon Daley 1939- 128
Barquist, David L. 218
Barr, Alfred H(amilton), Jr.
1902-1981 .... CANR-29
Obituary 105
Earlier sketch in CA 49-52
Barr, (Chester) Alwyn, (Jr.) 1938- CANR-101
Earlier sketch in CA 33-36R
Barr, Amelia Edith (Huddleston)
1831-1919 181
See also DLB 202, 221
Barr, Andrew 1961- 130
Barr, Anthony 1921-2002 109
Obituary 210
Barr, Betty 1932- 97-100
Barr, Beverly 61-64
Barr, Densil Neve
See Buttrey, Douglas N(orton)
Barr, Donald 1921-2004 .... 9-12R
Obituary 223
See also SATA 20
See also SATA-Obit 152
Barr, Donald Roy 1938- 69-72
Barr, Doris W(ilson) 1923- 33-36R
Barr, Emily 218
Barr, George 1907-1992 .... CANR-1
Earlier sketch in CA 1-4R
See also SATA 2
Barr, Gladys Hutchison 1904-1976 .... CANR-6
Earlier sketch in CA 1-4R
Barr, James 1924-1995 .... CANR-20
Earlier sketches in CA 1-4R, CANR-4
See also GLL 2
Barr, Jeff 1941- 69-72
Barr, Jene 1922-1985
See Cohen, Jene Barr
See also SATA 16
See also SATA-Obit 42
Barr, Jennifer 1945- 102
Barr, John J(ay) 1942- 61-64
Barr, Lyn
See Sherwood, Lyn
Barr, Lynne
See Sherwood, Lyn
Barr, Margaret Scolari 1901-1987
Obituary 124
Barr, Marleen Sandra 1953- 120
Barr, Murray L(lewellyn) 1908-1995 130
Barr, Nevada 1952- CANR-95
Earlier sketch in CA 161
See also AAYA 33
See also SATA 115, 126
Barr, Nicholas 1943- 143
Barr, O(rlando) Sydney 1919- 13-16R
Barr, Pat(ricia Miriam) 1934- CANR-60
Earlier sketches in CA 21-24R, CANR-12, 30, 56
See also RHW
Barr, Robert 1850-1912 179
See also DLB 70, 92
Barr, Robert R(ussell) 1931- 110
Barr, Sheldon 1938- 176
Barr, Stephen 1904-1989 .... CAP-1
Earlier sketch in CA 13-16
Barr, Stephen M. 1953- 232
Barr, Stringfellow 1897-1982 .... CANR-75
Obituary 106
Earlier sketches in CA 1-4R, CANR-1
Barr, Tony
See Barr, Anthony
Barr, William G. 1920(?)-1987
Obituary 121
Barra, Allen 233
Barraclough, Geoffrey 1908-1984 101
Obituary 114
Barraclough, June (Mary) 1930- 132
Barraclough, Solon L(ovett) 1922-2002 . 41-44R
Obituary 213
Barraga, Natalie Carter 1915- 41-44R
Barral, Carlos 1928(?)-1989 177
Obituary 130
See also DLB 134
See also HW 2
Barral, Mary-Rose 1925- 33-36R
Barranger, M(illy) S(later) 1937- CANR-53
Earlier sketches in CA 29-32R, CANR-12, 28
Barratt, Barnaby B. 147
Barratt, G. R.
See Barratt, Glynn (Richard V.)
Barratt, G. R. V.
See Barratt, Glynn (Richard V.)
Barratt, Glynn (Richard V.) 1944- 127
Brief entry 110
Barratt, Iris K. 1954- 172
Barratt-Brown, Michael 1918- CANR-38
Earlier sketches in CA 97-100, CANR-17
Barrault, Jean-Louis 1910-1994 .... CANR-79
Obituary 143
Earlier sketch in CA 105
Barrax, Gerald William 1933- CANR-10
Earlier sketch in CA 65-68
See also BW 2
See also DLB 41, 120
Barre, Michael Lee 1943- 118
Barre, Richard 1943- CANR-139
Earlier sketches in CA 150, CANR-72
Barreca, Regina 1957- CANR-96
Earlier sketch in CA 145
Barreiro, Alvaro 1936- 131
Barrell, Geoffrey Richard 1917-1983
Obituary 111
Barrell, Rex A(rthur) 1921- CANR-65
Earlier sketch in CA 129
Barrell, Sarah Webb 1946(?)-1979
Obituary 89-92
Barren, Charles (MacKinnon) 1913- CANR-4
Earlier sketch in CA 9-12R
Barreno, Maria Isabel
See Martins, Maria Isabel Barreno de Faria
See also AITN 1
Barrer, Gertrude
See Barrer-Russell, Gertrude
Barrera, Mario 1939- 97-100
Barrer-Russell, Gertrude 1921- .... SATA 27
Barres, (Auguste-)Maurice 1862-1923 164
See also DLB 123
See also GFL 1789 to the Present
See also TCLC 47
Barres, Oliver 1921- 13-16R
Barresi, Dorothy 1957- 196
Barreto, A. de Mascarenhas
See Barreto, Augusto Cassiano Neves da Sylveira Mascarenhas
Barreto, Afonso Henrique de Lima
See Lima Barreto, Afonso Henrique de
Barreto, Amilcar Antonio 1965- 217
Barreto, Augusto Cassiano Neves da Sylveira Mascarenhas 1923- 172
Barreto, Mascarenhas
See Barreto, Augusto Cassiano Neves da Sylveira Mascarenhas
Barrett, Andrea 1954- CANR-92
Earlier sketch in CA 156
See also CLC 150
See also CN 7
Barrett, Angela (Jane) 1955- .... SATA 75, 145
Barrett, Anne Mainwaring (Gillett)
1911-1987 .... CAP-2
Earlier sketch in CA 29-32
Barrett, Anthony A(rthur) 1941- 134
Barrett, Bob 1925- 73-76
Barrett, Buckley Barry 1948- CANR-104
Earlier sketch in CA 149
Barrett, C(harles) Kingsley 1917- CANR-50
Earlier sketches in CA 21-24R, CANR-10, 25
Barrett, C(lifton) Waller 1901-1991 .... 41-44R
Barrett, Clifford L(eslie) 1894-1971
Obituary 33-36R
Barrett, (Denis) Cyril 1925-2003 233
Barrett, David M(arshall) 1951- 154
Barrett, Dean 1942- CANR-93
Earlier sketch in CA 69-72
Barrett, Deirdre 1954- 177
Barrett, Donald N(eil) 1920- 13-16R
Barrett, Eaton Stannard 1786-1820 .... DLB 116
Barrett, Edward L(ouis), Jr. 1917- 25-28R
Barrett, Edward W(are) 1910-1989
Obituary 130
Barrett, Ethel 134
See also SATA 87
See also SATA-Brief 44
Barrett, Eugene F(rancis) 1921- 57-60
Barrett, Geoffrey John 1928- .... TCWW 2
Barrett, George W(est) 1908-2000 .... 17-20R
Obituary 190
Barrett, George W. 1913(?)-1984
Obituary 114
Barrett, Gerald Van 1936- 37-40R
Barrett, Harold 1925- 81-84
Barrett, Harrison D(elivan) 1863-1911 206
Barrett, Harry B(emister) 1922- 85-88
Barrett, Henry Charles 1923- 53-56
Barrett, Ivan J. 1910-1999 49-52
Barrett, J(ohn) Edward 1932- 37-40R
Barrett, James H(enry) 1906- 33-36R
Barrett, James Lee 1929-1989 .... CANR-126
Earlier sketch in CA 81-84
Barrett, James R. 1950- 234
Barrett, Jennifer
See Plecas, Jennifer
Barrett, John Gilchrist 1921- CANR-2
Earlier sketch in CA 5-8R
Barrett, John Henry 1913- 101
Barrett, Joyce Durham 1943- CANR-117
Earlier sketch in CA 138
See also SATA 138
Barrett, Judi
See Barrett, Judith
Barrett, Judith 1941- 103
See also CLR 98
See also MAICYA 2
See also SATA 26
Barrett, Julia
See Kessler, Julia Braun
Barrett, Kate Harwood Waller 1857-1925 .. 204
Barrett, Kim E(laine) 1958- 208
Barrett, Laurence I(rwin) 1935- 69-72
Barrett, Leonard E(manuel) 1920- 65-68
Barrett, (Eseoghene) Lindsay 1941- 143
See also BW 2
Barrett, Linton Lomas 1904-1972 .... CANR-79
Obituary 134
Earlier sketch in CA 5-8R
Barrett, Lois (Yvonne) 1947- CANR-53
Earlier sketch in CA 125
Barrett, Lynne 192
Barrett, Marvin 1920- CANR-119
Earlier sketches in CA 69-72, CANR-11
Barrett, Mary Ellin 1927- 17-20R
Barrett, Max 81-84
Barrett, Maye
See Barrett, Max
Barrett, Michael Dennis 1947- 85-88
Barrett, Michele .... CLC 65
Barrett, N. S.
See Barrett, Norman (S.)
Barrett, Nancy Smith 1942- 37-40R
Barrett, Nathan N(oble) 1933- 17-20R
Barrett, Neal, Jr. 237
See also Appleton, Victor and Dixon, Franklin W.
See also SFW 4
Barrett, Norman (S.) 1935- CANR-24
Earlier sketch in CA 107
Barrett, Patricia 1914-1987 .... 5-8R
Obituary 121
Barrett, Paul F(rancis) 1943-2004 117
Obituary 232
Barrett, Raina
See Kelly, Pauline Agnes
Barrett, Robert T(heodore) 1949- .... SATA 92
Barrett, Ron 1937- .... SATA 14
Barrett, Rona 1936- 103
Interview in CA-103
See also AITN 1
Barrett, Russel H(unter) 1919- 17-20R
Barrett, Stanley R. 1938- 128
Barrett, Susan (Mary) 1938- 138
Brief entry 109
See also SATA 113
Barrett, (Roger) Syd 1946- .... CLC 35
Barrett, Sylvia 1914- 25-28R
Barrett, Tracy 1955- CANR-98
Earlier sketch in CA 150
See also SATA 84, 115, 156
Barrett, Ward J. 1927- 29-32R
Barrett, William (Christopher)
1913-1992 .... CANR-67
Obituary 139
Earlier sketches in CA 13-16R, CANR-11
Interview in CANR-11
See also CLC 27
Barrett, William E(dmund)
1900-1986 .... CANR-22
Obituary 120
Earlier sketch in CA 5-8R
See also SATA-Obit 49
Barrett, William R. 1922(?)-1977
Obituary 73-76
Barrett Browning, Elizabeth
1806-1861 .... AAYA 63
See also BRW 4
See also CDBLB 1832-1890
See also DA
See also DA3
See also DAB
See also DAC
See also DAM MST, POET
See also DLB 32, 199
See also EXPP
See also FL 1:2
See also PAB
See also PC 6, 62
See also PFS 2, 16, 23
See also TEA
See also WLC
See also WLIT 4
See also WP
Barretto, Larry
See Barretto, Laurence Brevoort
Barretto, Laurence Brevoort 1890-1971
Obituary 33-36R
Barretton, Grandall
See Garrett, (Gordon) Randall (Phillip)
Barriault, Arthur 1915(?)-1976
Obituary 65-68
Barricelli, Jean-Pierre 1924-1997 .... CANR-45
Earlier sketches in CA 105, CANR-21
Barrick, Mac E(ugene) 1933- 33-36R
Barrie, Alexander 1923- CANR-5
Earlier sketch in CA 1-4R
Barrie, Donald C(onway) 1905-1985 .... 17-20R
Barrie, J(ames) M(atthew)
1860-1937 .... CANR-77
Brief entry 104
Earlier sketch in CA 136
See also BRWS 3
See also BYA 4, 5
See also CDBLB 1890-1914
See also CLR 16
See also CWRI 5
See also DA3
See also DAB
See also DAM DRAM
See also DFS 7
See also DLB 10, 141, 156
See also EWL 3
See also FANT
See also MAICYA 1, 2
See also MTCW 2
See also MTFW 2005
See also SATA 100
See also SUFW
See also TCLC 2, 164
See also WCH
See also WLIT 4
See also YABC 1
Barrie, Jane
See Savage, Mildred (Spitz)
Barrie, Patricia
See Barber, Patricia
Barrie, Thomas (Matthew) 1955- 161
Barrier, (John) Michael 1940- CANR-87
Earlier sketch in CA 109
Barrier, Norman G(erald) 1940- CANR-4
Earlier sketch in CA 53-56
Barriger, John Walker 1899-1976
Obituary 69-72
Barrile, Jackie 1943- 117
Barringer, Tim(othy) J. 238
Barringer, T.J.
See Barringer, Tim(othy) J.
Barringer, William 1940-1996 .... SATA 153
Barringer Gordon, Sarah 1955- 209
Barrington, H. W.
See Brannon, William T.
Barrington, Judith 1944- 187
Barrington, Maurice
See Brogan, D(enis) W(illiam)
Barrington, Michael
See Moorcock, Michael (John)
Barrington, P. V.
See Barling, Muriel Vere Mant
Barrington, Pamela
See Barling, Muriel Vere Mant
Barrington, Thomas Joseph 1916- 104
Barrio, Raymond 1921-1996 .... CANR-32
Earlier sketches in CA 25-28R, CANR-11
See also CAAS 15
See also DLB 82
See also HW 1
Barrio-Garay, Jose Luis 1932- 81-84
Barrios, Eduardo 1884-1963 .... EWL 3
See also HW 1
See also LAW
Barrios, Greg 1945- 175
See also DLB 122
See also HW 2
Barrios, Pilar E. 1889-1979 .... HW 1
Barris, Alex 1922- 61-64
Barris, Chuck 1929- CANR-142
Brief entry 109
Earlier sketch in CA 169
Barris, George 1925- 169
See also SATA 47
Barritt, Denis P(hillips) 1914- 21-24R
Barro, Robert Joseph 1944- 97-100
Barrol, Grady
See Bograd, Larry
Barroll, John Leeds III 1928- CANR-106
Earlier sketch in CA 101
Barroll, Leeds
See Barroll, John Leeds III
Barron, Ann Forman -1998 69-72
Barron, Bruce 1960- 123
Barron, Charlie Nelms 1922-1977
Obituary 69-72
Barron, Ed
See Bernhardt, Clyde Edric Barron
Barron, Francis (Xavier) 1922-2002 .... CANR-8
Obituary 209
Earlier sketch in CA 5-8R
Barron, Frank
See Barron, Francis (Xavier)
Barron, Fred CANR-41
Earlier sketch in CA 117
Barron, Gayle 1945- 109
Barron, Gloria Joan 1934- 81-84
Barron, Greg 1952- 110
Barron, Jerome A(ure) 1933- CANR-49
Earlier sketches in CA 45-48, CANR-24
Barron, Jonathan N. 1962- 195
Barron, Judy 1939- 137
Barron, Milton L. 1918-1994 .... CANR-18
Earlier sketch in CA 1-4R
Barron, (Richard) Neil 1934- CANR-37
Earlier sketch in CA 102
Barron, Rex 1951- .... SATA 84
Barron, Stephanie 1950- CANR-105
Earlier sketch in CA 169
Barron, T(homas) A(rchibald)
1952- CANR-122
Earlier sketches in CA 150, CANR-105
See also AAYA 30
See also BYA 12, 13, 14
See also CLR 86
See also SATA 83, 126
See also YAW
Barron, Tom
See Barron, T(homas) A(rchibald)
Barron-Tieger, Barbara 203
Barrosse, Thomas 1926-1994 .... 9-12R
Barrow, Adam 180
Barrow, Andrew 1945- CANR-137
Earlier sketches in CA 97-100, CANR-73
Barrow, Clyde W. 1956- 197
Barrow, Geoffrey W(allis) S(teuart)
1924- CANR-30
Earlier sketches in CA 17-20R, CANR-7
Barrow, Harold M(arion) 1909- 106
Barrow, Henry 1906(?)-1985
Obituary 117
Barrow, Jedediah
See Benson, Gerard
Barrow, John D(avid) 1952- CANR-105
Earlier sketch in CA 115
Barrow, Joseph Louis 1914-1981
Obituary 103
Barrow, Keith E. 1954-1983
Obituary 111
Barrow, Kenneth 1945-1993 119
Obituary 142
Barrow, Leo (Lebron) 1925-
Brief entry 110

Barrow, Lloyd H. 1942- ... SATA 73
Barrow, Marilyn ... GLL 1
Barrow, Mark V., Jr. 1960- ... 230
Barrow, Pamela
See Howarth, Pamela
Barrow, R. H. 1894(?)-1984
Obituary ... 114
Barrow, Raymond 1920- ... CP 1
Barrow, Rhoda
See Lederer, Rhoda Catharine (Kitto)
Barrow, Robin 1944- ... CANR-10
Earlier sketch in CA 65-68
Barrow, Terence 1923- ... 41-44R
Barrow, Thomas C(hurchill) 1929- ... 21-24R
Barrow, William
See Fuller, Hoyt (William)
Barrowcliffe, Mark 1964- ... 207
Barrows, Anita 1947- ... CANR-31
Earlier sketch in CA 49-52
Barrows, Chester L. 1892(?)-1975
Obituary ... 104
Barrows, (Ruth) Marjorie
1892(?)-1983 ... CANR-76
Obituary ... 109
Earlier sketches in CAP-2, CA 21-22
Barrows, R. M.
See Barrows, (Ruth) Marjorie
Barrows, Ruth
See Barrows, (Ruth) Marjorie
Barrows, Susanna Isabel 1944- ... 108
Barrows, Sydney (Biddle) 1952- ... 126
Barry, Ann 1942-1996 ... 152
Barry, Anne 1940- ... 85-88
Barry, Barbara R. 1949- ... 198
Barry, Clive 1922- ... CN 1, 2, 3
Barry, Colman J(ames) 1921-1994 ... CANR-75
Obituary ... 143
Earlier sketch in CA 13-16R
Barry, Dana (Marie Malloy) 1949- ... 210
See also SATA 139
Barry, Dave 1947- ... CANR-131
Brief entry ... 129
Earlier sketches in CA 134, CANR-77
Interview in ... CA-134
See also AAYA 14
See also BEST 90:4
See also CPW
See also CSW
Barry, Herbert III 1930- ... CANR-43
Earlier sketches in CA 37-40R, CANR-14
Barry, Iris 1895-1969
Obituary ... 104
Barry, Jack 1939- ... 69-72
Barry, Jackson G(ranville) 1926- ... 29-32R
Barry, James Donald 1926- ... 33-36R
Barry, James P(otvin) 1918- ... CANR-24
Earlier sketch in CA 37-40R
See also SATA 14
Barry, Jane (Powell) 1925- ... CANR-62
Earlier sketch in CA 5-8R
See also TCWW 1, 2
Barry, Jerome B(enedict) 1894-1975 . CANR-68
Obituary ... 61-64
Earlier sketch in CA 1-4R
Barry, Jocelyn
See Bowden, Jean
Barry, John 1933- ... IDFW 3, 4
Barry, John A(bbott) 1948- ... 139
Barry, John M. 1947- ... CANR-119
Earlier sketch in CA 165
Barry, John Vincent William
1903-1969 ... CANR-76
Obituary ... 103
Earlier sketch in CA 1-4R
Barry, Joseph (Amber) 1917-1994 ... CANR-76
Obituary ... 144
Earlier sketches in CA 57-60, CANR-14
Barry, Katharina Watjen 1936- ... 9-12R
See also SATA 4
Barry, Kathleen (L.) 1941- ... 129
Barry, Kevin
See Laffan, Kevin (Barry)
Barry, Kristen Lawton 1947- ... 212
Barry, Laurel D. 1922- ... 144
Barry, Lucy (Brown) 1934- ... 17-20R
Barry, Lynda (Jean) 1956- ... CANR-134
Earlier sketches in CA 138, CANR-102
See also AAYA 9, 54
See also DAM POP
See also MTFW 2005
Barry, Margaret Stuart 1927- ... CANR-25
Earlier sketch in CA 106
See also CWRI 5
Barry, Mary J(ane) 1928- ... 49-52
Barry, Maxx
See Barry, Max
Barry, Mike
See Malzberg, Barry N(athaniel)
Barry, Noeline 1915- ... CP 1
Barry, Norman P. 1944- ... 134
Barry, P(atricia) S(teepee) 1926- ... 140
Barry, Philip 1896-1949 ... 199
Brief entry ... 109
See also DFS 9
See also DLB 7, 228
See also MAL 5
See also RGAL 4
See also TCLC 11
Barry, Raymond Walker 1894-1983 ... CAP-1
Earlier sketch in CA 17-18
Barry, Robert (Everett) 1931- ... CANR-2
Earlier sketch in CA 5-8R
See also SATA 6
Barry, Roger Graham 1935- ... 102
Barry, Roxana
See Robinson, Roxana (Barry)
Barry, Scott 1952- ... 89-92
See also SATA 32
Barry, Sebastian 1955- ... CANR-122
Earlier sketch in CA 117
See also CD 5, 6
See also DLB 245
Barry, Sheila Anne -2003 ... CANR-116
Earlier sketches in CA 135, CANR-57
See also SATA 91
Barry, Spranger
See Kauffmann, Stanley
Barry, Stephen P. 1948(?)-1986 ... 123
Obituary ... 120
Barry, Tom 1950- ... 139
Barry, William A(nthony) 1930- ... CANR-38
Earlier sketch in CA 115
Barry, William David 1946- ... 114
Barrymore, Drew 1975- ... 139
Barrymore, Jaid 1946- ... 213
Barsacq, Andre 1909-1973
Obituary ... 41-44R
Barsacq, Leon 1906-1969
Obituary ... 113
See also IDFW 3, 4
Barsamian, David ... 233
Barsby, John A. 1935- ... CANR-90
Earlier sketch in CA 121
Barsh, Russel Lawrence 1950- ... 105
Barsis, Max 1894(?)-1973
Obituary ... 41-44R
Barsky, Arthur 1900(?)-1982(?)
Obituary ... 106
Barsky, Robert F. 1961- ... CANR-137
Earlier sketch in CA 161
Barsness, John 1952- ... 139
Barson, John 1936- ... 85-88
Barson, Michael 1951- ... CANR-100
Earlier sketch in CA 129
Barsotti, C(harles) 1933- ... 65-68
Barstow, Anne Llewellyn 1929- ... 111
Barstow, Phyllida 1937- ... CANR-27
Earlier sketch in CA 121
Barstow, Stan(ley) 1928- ... CANR-114
Earlier sketches in CA 1-4R, CANR-1, 44, 62
See also CN 1, 2, 3, 4, 5, 6, 7
See also DLB 14, 139, 207
Bart, Andre Schwarz
See Schwarz-Bart, Andre
Bart, Benjamin F(ranklin) 1917-1994 ... 25-28R
Bart, Lionel 1930-1999 ... 65-68
Obituary ... 177
Bart, Pauline B(ernice) 1930- ... 53-56
Bart, Peter 1932- ... CANR-142
Earlier sketches in CA 93-96, CANR-19
Bartek, E(dward) J(ohn) 1921- ... 37-40R
Bartel, Pauline C(hristine) 1952- ... 81-84
Bartel, Roland 1919- ... 17-20R
Bartell, Ernest 1932- ... 33-36R
Bartell, Linda Lang 1948- ... 125
Bartels, Robert 1913- ... 13-16R
Bartels, Robert A. 1923-1989 ... CANR-16
Earlier sketch in CA 1-4R
Bartels, Susan Ludvigson
See Ludvigson, Susan
Barten, Harvey H(arold) 1933- ... 33-36R
Bartenbach, Jean 1918- ... 115
See also SATA 40
Bartenieff, Irmgard 1900(?)-1981
Obituary ... 105
Barter, A(lice) K(nar) 1918- ... 57-60
Barter, Judith A(nn) 1951- ... 186
Barth, Alan 1906-1979 ... CANR-5
Obituary ... 104
Earlier sketch in CA 1-4R
Barth, Charles P. 1895-1976 ... CAP-2
Earlier sketch in CA 25-28
Barth, Christoph F. 1917- ... 29-32R
Barth, Edna 1914-1980 ... CANR-27
Obituary ... 102
Earlier sketch in CA 41-44R
See also SATA 7
See also SATA-Obit 24
Barth, Fredrik 1928- ... CANR-11
Earlier sketch in CA 65-68
Barth, Gunther 1925-2004 ... 103
Obituary ... 225
Barth, Ilene Joan 1944- ... 134
Barth, J(ohn) Robert 1931- ... 29-32R
Barth, John (Simmons) 1930- ... CANR-113
Earlier sketches in CA 1-4R, CANR-5, 23, 49, 64
See also CABS 1
See also AITN 1, 2
See also AMW
See also BPFB 1
See also CLC 1, 2, 3, 5, 7, 9, 10, 14, 27, 51, 89
See also CN 1, 2, 3, 4, 5, 6, 7
See also DAM NOV
See also DLB 2, 227
See also EWL 3
See also FANT
See also MAL 5
See also MTCW 1
See also RGAL 4
See also RGSF 2
See also RHW
See also SSC 10
See also SSFS 6
See also TUS
Barth, Karl 1886-1968 ... CANR-77
Obituary ... 25-28R
Earlier sketch in CA 134
Barth, Kelly L. 1964- ... 227
See also SATA 152
Barth, Lois
See Freihofer, Lois Diane
Barth, Markus Karl 1915-1994 ... CANR-2
Earlier sketch in CA 5-8R
Barth, Peter S. 1937- ... CANR-25
Earlier sketch in CA 106
Barth, R(obert) L(awrence) 1947- ... 203
Barth, Richard 1943- ... CANR-100
Earlier sketch in CA 81-84
Barth, Roland S(awyer) 1937- ... CANR-1
Earlier sketch in CA 45-48
Barthel, Diane L(ee) 1949- ... 115
Barthel, Joan 1932- ... 114
Brief entry ... 111
Interview in ... CA-114
Barthelme, Donald 1931-1989 ... CANR-58
Obituary ... 129
Earlier sketches in CA 21-24R, CANR-20
See also AMWS 4
See also BPFB 1
See also CLC 1, 2, 3, 5, 6, 8, 13, 23, 46, 59, 115
See also CN 1, 2, 3, 4
See also DA3
See also DAM NOV
See also DLB 2, 234
See also DLBY 1980, 1989
See also EWL 3
See also FANT
See also LMFS 2
See also MAL 5
See also MTCW 1, 2
See also MTFW 2005
See also RGAL 4
See also RGSF 2
See also SATA 7
See also SATA-Obit 62
See also SSC 2, 55
See also SSFS 17
Barthelme, Frederick 1943- ... CANR-77
Brief entry ... 114
Earlier sketch in CA 122
Interview in ... CA-122
See also AMWS 11
See also CLC 36, 117
See also CN 4, 5, 6, 7
See also CSW
See also DLB 244
See also DLBY 1985
See also EWL 3
Barthelme, Peter R. 1939- ... 127
Barthelme, Steve(n) 1947- ... CANR-98
Earlier sketch in CA 136
See also CSW
Barthelmes, (Albert) Wes(ley, Jr.)
1922-1976 ... 69-72
Obituary ... 65-68
Barthes, Roland (Gerard)
1915-1980 ... CANR-66
Obituary ... 97-100
Earlier sketch in CA 130
See also CLC 24, 83
See also DLB 296
See also EW 13
See also EWL 3
See also GFL 1789 to the Present
See also MTCW 1, 2
See also TCLC 135
See also TWA
Bartholet, Elizabeth 1940- ... 141
Bartholomay, Julia A. 1923- ... 45-48
Bartholomeusz, Dennis 1930- ... 130
Bartholomew, Barbara 1941- ... 135
Brief entry ... 118
See also SATA 86
See also SATA-Brief 42
Bartholomew, Bart
See Bartholomew, Frank H(armon)
Bartholomew, Cecilia 1907-1992 ... CAP-1
Earlier sketch in CA 13-14
Bartholomew, Ed(ward Ellsworth)
1914- ... 25-28R
Bartholomew, Frank H(armon) 1898-1985 . 174
Obituary ... 115
See also DLB 127
Bartholomew, James 1950- ... 132
Bartholomew, Jean
See Beatty, Patricia (Robbins)
Bartholomew, John Eric
See Morecambe, Eric
Bartholomew, Nancy ... 221
Bartholomew, Paul C(harles)
1907-1975 ... CANR-10
Earlier sketch in CA 17-20R
Bartier, Pierre 1945- ... 21-24R
Bartiromo, Maria Sara 1967- ... 207
Bartky, Sandra Lee 1935- ... CANR-109
Earlier sketch in CA 154
See also FW
Bartlett, Alison ... SATA 153
Bartlett, Amy 1949- ... 124
Bartlett, Basil Hardington 1905-1985
Obituary ... 115
Bartlett, Bruce R(eeves) 1951- ... CANR-19
Earlier sketch in CA 89-92
Bartlett, C(hristopher) J(ohn) 1931- ... 17-20R
Bartlett, Charles (Leffingwell) 1921- ... 29-32R
Bartlett, David
See Mason, Madeline
Bartlett, Donald L.
Brief entry ... 110
Bartlett, Elizabeth (Winters) 1924- ... CANR-9
Earlier sketch in CA 17-20R
See also CP 7
Bartlett, Elsa Jaffe 1935- ... CANR-15
Earlier sketch in CA 33-36R
Bartlett, Eric George 1920- ... CANR-41
Earlier sketches in CA 5-8R, CANR-2, 19
Bartlett, F. C.
See Bartlett, Frederic Charles
Bartlett, Frederic Charles 1886-1969
Obituary ... 115
Bartlett, Gene E(bert) 1910-1989
Obituary ... 130
Bartlett, Gerald (Robert) 1935-2003 ... 21-24R
Obituary ... 214
Bartlett, Harriett M(oulton) 1897-1987
Obituary ... 121
Bartlett, Hubert Moyse
See Moyse-Bartlett, Hubert
Bartlett, Irving H(enry) 1923- ... CANR-9
Earlier sketch in CA 21-24R
Bartlett, Jean Anne 1927- ... 97-100
Bartlett, Jennifer Losch 1941- ... 136
Bartlett, John 1820-1905 ... 185
See also DLB 1, 235
Bartlett, Jonathan 1931- ... 93-96
Bartlett, Kathleen
See Paine, Lauran (Bosworth)
Bartlett, Kim 1941- ... 89-92
Bartlett, Lee Anthony 1950- ... 114
Bartlett, Margaret Farrington
1896-1982 ... CANR-5
Earlier sketch in CA 5-8R
Bartlett, Marie (Swan) 1918- ... 21-24R
Bartlett, Merrill L(ewis) 1939- ... 117
Bartlett, Nancy
See Strong, Charles S(tanley)
Bartlett, Nancy W(hite) 1913-1972 ... CAP-2
Obituary ... 41-44R
Earlier sketch in CA 23-24
Bartlett, Neil 1958- ... 188
See also CBD
See also CD 5, 6
See also GLL 1
Bartlett, Paul (Alexander) 1909-1990 ... CAP-2
Earlier sketch in CA 17-18
Bartlett, Philip A. ... CANR-26
Earlier sketches in CAP-2, CA 19-20
See also SATA 1
Bartlett, Phyllis 1908(?)-1973
Obituary ... 41-44R
Bartlett, Richard A(dams) 1920- ... CANR-2
Earlier sketch in CA 5-8R
Bartlett, Robert (John) 1950- ... 125
Bartlett, Robert Merrill 1899-1995 ... CANR-68
Earlier sketches in CA 5-8R, CANR-2
See also SATA 12
Bartlett, Robert V(irgil) 1953- ... CANR-22
Earlier sketch in CA 104
Bartlett, Ruhl J. 1897- ... CAP-1
Earlier sketch in CA 11-12
Bartlett, Ruth ... 17-20R
Bartlett, Sarah 1955- ... 140
Bartlett, Thomas ... 239
Bartlett, (Charles) Vernon (Oldfield)
1894-1983 ... CANR-75
Obituary ... 108
Earlier sketches in CA 61-64, CANR-68
Bartley, Diana E(sther) Pelaez-Rivera
1940- ... 69-72
Bartley, Leigh
See Riker, Leigh
Bartley, Numan V(ache) 1934- ... CANR-12
Earlier sketch in CA 69-72
Bartley, Robert L(eRoy) 1937-2003 ... 97-100
Obituary ... 226
Interview in ... CA-97-100
Bartley, William Warren III 1934- ... CANR-15
Earlier sketch in CA 37-40R
Bartman, Elizabeth ... 238
Bartocci, Gianni 1925- ... 21-24R
Bartol, Cyrus Augustus 1813-1900 ... 178
See also DLB 1, 235
Bartole, Genevieve 1927- ... 101
Bartoletti, Susan Campbell 1958- ... CANR-113
Earlier sketch in CA 152
See also AAYA 44
See also BYA 10, 16
See also MAICYA 2
See also SATA 88, 129, 135
Bartoli, Jill Sunday 1945- ... 238
Bartolome de Roxas, Juan
See Rubia Barcia, Jose
Bartolomeo, Christina 1962(?)- ... CANR-142
Earlier sketch in CA 174
Bartolomeo, Joseph F(rancis)
1958- ... CANR-137
Earlier sketch in CA 151
Barton, Allen H(oisington) 1924- ... CANR-10
Earlier sketch in CA 25-28R
Barton, Anne 1933- ... 144
Barton, Bernard 1784-1849 ... DLB 96
Barton, Beverly ... 207
Barton, Bruce (Fairchild) 1886-1967 ... 211
Barton, Bruce Walter 1935- ... 89-92
Barton, Byron 1930- ... CANR-105
Earlier sketches in CA 57-60, CANR-13, 57
See also SATA 9, 90, 126
Barton, Carlin A. ... 231
Barton, Charles (Albert) 1920- ... 139
Barton, Dan ... 235
Barton, Del 1925-1971
Obituary ... 103
Barton, Emily 1969- ... 222
Barton, Erle
See Fanthorpe, R(obert) Lionel
Barton, Eustace Robert 1854-1943
Brief entry ... 114
Barton, Fredrick (Preston) 1948- ... CANR-43
Earlier sketch in CA 119
Barton, H. Arnold 1929- ... 77-80
Barton, Harriett ... SATA-Brief 43

Cumulative Index 37 **Bate**

Barton, Humphrey (Douglas Elliott)
1900-1963(?) CAP-2
Earlier sketch in CA 19-20
Barton, Jack
See Chadwick, Joseph (L.)
Barton, Jill(ian) 1940- .... SATA 75
Barton, Jim Tom 123
Barton, John 1610-1675 .... DLB 236
Barton, John 1948- CANR-119
Earlier sketch in CA 137
Barton, John (Stuart) 1957- 114
Barton, John Bernard Adie 1928- 81-84
Barton, John H(ays) 1936- 111
Barton, John Mackintosh Tilney
1898-1977 .... CAP-1
Earlier sketch in CA 17-18
Barton, Jon
See Harvey, John (Barton)
Barton, Lee
See Fanthorpe, R(obert) Lionel
Barton, Lew(is Randolph) 1918- 73-76
Barton, M. Xaveria 1910-
Brief entry 105
Barton, Margaret D(over) 1902-1986 ..... CAP-1
Earlier sketch in CA 13-16
Barton, Marlin 1961- 210
Barton, Mary Neill 1899- CAP-2
Earlier sketch in CA 19-20
Barton, May Hollis CANR-26
Earlier sketches in CAP-2, CA 19-20
See also SATA 1, 67
Barton, Michael (Lee) 1943- 110
Barton, Pat
See Arrowsmith, Pat
See also SATA 59
Barton, Richard F(leming) 1924- 61-64
Barton, Roger A(very) 1903-1976
Obituary 65-68
Barton, S. W.
See Whaley, Barton Stewart
Barton, Tamsyn (S.) 1962- 151
Barton, Thomas Frank 1905-1985 ...... CANR-1
Earlier sketch in CA 45-48
Barton, Thomas Pennant 1803-1869 .. DLB 140
Barton, V(ernon) Wayne 1-4R
Barton, Walter Elbert 1886-1983
Obituary 111
Barton, (Samuel) Wayne 1944- CANR-140
Earlier sketches in CA 124, CANR-64
See also TCWW 2
Barton, Weldon V. 1938- 21-24R
Barton, William (Renald III) 1950- CANR-1
Earlier sketch in CA 45-48
Bartos, Otomar J(an) 1927- 105
Bartos-Hoeppner, Barbara 1923- CANR-10
Earlier sketch in CA 25-28R
See also SATA 5
Bartoszewski, Wladyslaw T(eofil) 1955- 146
Bartov, Hanoch 1926- CANR-124
Brief entry 117
Earlier sketches in CA 129, CANR-65
Bartov, Omer 1954- CANR-100
Earlier sketch in CA 135
Bartram, George
See Cameron, Kenneth M.
Bartram, Graham 1946- 116
Bartram, John 1699-1777 .... DLB 31
Bartram, Simon .... SATA 156
Bartram, William 1739-1823 .... ANW
See also DLB 37
Bartran, Margaret 1913-1976 .... CAP-2
Earlier sketch in CA 29-32
Bartrum, Douglas A(lbert) 1907- CANR-6
Earlier sketch in CA 9-12R
Bartrum, Giulia 226
Bartsch, Jochen 1906- .... SATA 39
Bartsch, William H. 1933- 138
Bartscht, Waltraud 1924-1996 .... 41-44R
Bartusiak, Marcia 1950- CANR-104
Earlier sketch in CA 129
Bartusis, Mary Ann 1930- 101
Bart-Williams, Gaston 1938- .... BW 2
See also CP 1
Bartz, Albert E(dward) 1933- 21-24R
Bartz, Patricia McBride 1921- 102
Bartz, Wayne R(onald) 1938- 111
Baruah, Sanjib (Kumar) 1951- 195
Baruch, Dorothy W(alter) 1899-1962 .. SATA 21
Baruch, Elaine Hoffman 171
Baruch, Grace K. 1936(?)-1988
Obituary 126
Baruch, Ruth-Marion 1922- 29-32R
Baruchello, Gianfranco 1924- 153
Baruk, Henri Marc 1897-1999 85-88
Barunga, Albert 1912(?)-1977 .... SATA 120
Barwick, Steven 1921- 13-16R
Barwin, Gary 1964- 213
Barwood, Hal 129
Brief entry 125
Bary, Brett de
See Nee, Brett de Bary
Barykova, Anna Pavlovna 1839-1893 . DLB 277
Barylski, Robert V. 185
Baryshnikov, Mikhail (Nikolayevich)
1948- CANR-72
Brief entry 113
Earlier sketch in CA 133
Barzanti, Sergio 1925- 17-20R
Barzilay, Isaac Eisenstein 1915- 113
Barzini, Luigi (Giorgio, Jr.)
1908-1984 .... CANR-23
Obituary 112
Earlier sketch in CA 13-16R
Barzman, Ben 1912-1989 132
Barzman, Norma 1920- 224
Bar-Zohar, Michael 1938- CANR-80
Earlier sketches in CA 21-24R, CANR-12, 35
Barzun, Jacques (Martin) 1907- CANR-95
Earlier sketches in CA 61-64, CANR-22
See also CLC 51, 145
Bas, Joe 1932- 53-56
Bas, Rutger
See Rutgers van der Loeff-Basenau, An(na) Maria Margaretha
Basa, Eniko Molnar 1939- 77-80
Basart, Ann Phillips 1931- CANR-1
Earlier sketch in CA 1-4R
Basbanes, Nicholas A. 1943- 209
Basch, Michael Franz 130
Basch, Rachel 1959- 168
Basche, James 1926-1988 .... 29-32R
Bascio, Patrick 1927- CANR-44
Earlier sketch in CA 119
Bascom, David 1912-1985 93-96
Bascom, Harold A(dolphus) 1951- 135
Bascom, Willard Newell 1916-2000 .. CANR-6
Obituary 189
Earlier sketch in CA 1-4R
Bascom, William R(ussel)
1912-1981 .... CANR-75
Obituary 125
Earlier sketch in CA 17-20R
Bascomb, Neal 1971(?)- 235
Basdekis, Demetrios 1930- 25-28R
Base, Giulio 1964- 235
Base, Graeme (Rowland) 1958- CANR-128
Earlier sketches in CA 134, CANR-69
See also CLR 22
See also CWRI 5
See also MAICYA 1, 2
See also SATA 67, 101, 162
Baseley, Godfrey 1904-1997 102
Obituary 156
Basevi, James 1890- .... IDFW 3, 4
Basgoz, M(ehmet) Ilhan 1921- 113
Bash, Barbara 1948- .... SATA 132
Bash, Deborah M. Blumenthal 1940- 109
Bash, Frank N(ess) 1937- 107
Bash, Harry H(arvey) 1926- 89-92
Basham, Don W(ilson) 1926- 65-68
Basham, Richard Dalton 1945- 111
Basham, William Randolph 1933(?)-1986
Obituary 118
Bashe, Patricia Ann Romanowski 1956- 127
Bashe, Philip (Scott) 1954- CANR-100
Earlier sketch in CA 134
Bashevis, Isaac
See Singer, Isaac Bashevis
Bashevkin, Sylvia B. 1954- 121
Bashford, H(enry) H(owarth) 1880-1961 220
Bashira, Damali 1951- 57-60
Basho, Matsuo
See Matsuo Basho
See also RGWL 2, 3
See also WP
Bashshar ibn Burd c. 714-c. 784 .... DLB 311
Bashshur, Rashid L. 1933- 89-92
Basichis, Gordon (Allen) 1947- 85-88
Basie, Count
See Basie, William James
Basie, William James 1904(?)-1984 134
Basil, Douglas C. 1923- 41-44R
Basil, Otto 1901-1983 .... CANR-75
Obituary 113
Earlier sketch in CA 49-52
Basile, Gloria Vitanza 1929- CANR-12
Earlier sketch in CA 69-72
Basile, Joseph 1912- CANR-11
Earlier sketch in CA 25-28R
Basile, Leon 1955- 113
Basile, Robert M(anlius) 1916- 53-56
Basil-Hart, James
See Hough, Harold
Basilius, Harold A. 1905-1977 .... CANR-2
Earlier sketch in CA 1-4R
Basille, Theodore 1512(?)-1567
See Becon, Thomas
Basinger, Jeanine (Deyling) 1936- CANR-90
Earlier sketches in CA 97-100, CANR-18
Basinski, Michael 1950- 173
Earlier sketch in CANR-142
Autobiographical Essay in 173
See also CAAS 29
Basiuk, Victor 1932- 93-96
Basker, James G(lynn) 1952- 218
Baskerville, Barnet 1916- 1-4R
Baskerville, Patricia 1951- 108
Basket, Raney
See Edgerton, Clyde (Carlyle)
Baskett, John 1930- 97-100
Baskette, Floyd K(enneth)
1910-1979 .... CANR-29
Earlier sketch in CA 33-36R
Baskin, Barbara H(olland) 1929- CANR-22
Earlier sketch in CA 103
Baskin, Esther Tane 1926(?)-1973
Obituary 37-40R
Baskin, Judith R. 1950- 137
Baskin, Leonard 1922-2000 106
Obituary 188
See also CWRI 5
See also SATA 30, 120
See also SATA-Brief 27
Baskin, Nora Raleigh 1961- 198
See also SATA 129
Baskin, Robert E(dward) 1917-1983
Obituary 110
Baskin, Samuel 1921- 17-20R
Baskin, Wade 1924-1974 .... CAP-2
Earlier sketch in CA 23-24
Basler, Roy P(rentice) 1906-1989 ..... CANR-77
Obituary 130
Earlier sketches in CA 5-8R, CANR-4
Basler, Thomas G(ordon) 1940- 103
Bason, Fred
See Bason, Frederick (Thomas)
Bason, Frederick (Thomas)
1907-1973 .... CANR-75
Obituary 89-92
Earlier sketch in CA 5-8R
Bason, Lillian 1913- 69-72
See also SATA 20
Basra, Amarjit S(ingh) 1958- CANR-138
Earlier sketch in CA 151
Bass, Altha Leah (Bierbower)
1892-1988 .... CAP-2
Obituary 126
Earlier sketch in CA 23-24
Bass, Althea
See Bass, Altha Leah (Bierbower)
Bass, Amy 218
Bass, Bernard M(orris) 1925- CANR-19
Earlier sketches in CA 1-4R, CANR-4
Bass, Bill
See Bass, William M(arvin III)
Bass, Clarence B(eaty) 1922- 5-8R
Bass, Cynthia 1949- 160
Bass, Dorothy C. 1949- 188
Bass, Eben E(dward) 1924-1994 107
Bass, Ellen 1947- CANR-2
Earlier sketch in CA 49-52
See also PFS 19
Bass, Frank
See Peeples, Samuel Anthony
Bass, George F(letcher) 1932- CANR-48
Earlier sketch in CA 122
Bass, Harold F. 1948- 202
Bass, Henry B(enjamin) 1897-1975
Obituary 57-60
Bass, Herbert Jacob 1929- CANR-1
Earlier sketch in CA 1-4R
Bass, Howard 1923- CANR-2
Earlier sketch in CA 5-8R
Bass, Howard L(arry) 1942- 69-72
Bass, Jack 1934- CANR-19
Earlier sketch in CA 29-32R
Bass, Jack A(lexander) 1946- 97-100
Bass, Kingsley B., Jr.
See Bullins, Ed
Bass, Lawrence W(ade) 1898-1982 49-52
Bass, Madeline Tiger
See Tiger, Madeline
Bass, Milton R. 1923- 25-28R
Bass, Nelson Estupinan
See Estupinan Bass, Nelson
Bass, Rick 1958- CANR-93
Earlier sketches in CA 126, CANR-53
See also ANW
See also CLC 79, 143
See also CSW
See also DLB 212, 275
See also SSC 60
Bass, Robert D(uncan) 1904-1983 61-64
Bass, Ron
See Bass, Ronald
Bass, Ronald 165
See also IDFW 4
Bass, Saul 1920-1996 .... IDFW 3, 4
Bass, T. J.
See Bassler, Thomas J(oseph)
See also DLBY 1981
Bass, Thomas A. 1951- CANR-90
Earlier sketch in CA 124
Bass, Virginia W(auchope) 1905-1998 61-64
Bass, William M(arvin III) 1928- CANR-31
Earlier sketch in CA 41-44R
Bassan, Maurice 1929- 25-28R
Bassani, Giorgio 1916-2000 .... CANR-33
Obituary 190
Earlier sketch in CA 65-68
See also CLC 9
See also CWW 2
See also DLB 128, 177, 299
See also EWL 3
See also MTCW 1
See also RGWL 2, 3
Basse, Eli 1904-1979
Obituary 93-96
Basse, William 1583(?)-1653 .... DLB 121
Basseches, Michael 1950- 114
Bassermann, Lujo
See Schreiber, Hermann (Otto Ludwig)
Basset, Bernard 1909-1988 .... CANR-6
Obituary 125
Earlier sketch in CA 9-12R
Bassett, Edward Eryl 1940- 33-36R
Bassett, Elizabeth 1950- 171
Bassett, Flora Marjorie 1890(?)-1980
Obituary 97-100
Bassett, George William 1910-1999 102
Bassett, Glenn Arthur 1930- 17-20R
Bassett, (Mary) Grace 1927- 73-76
Bassett, Jack
See Rowland, D(onald) S(ydney)
Bassett, James E(lias) 1912-1978 61-64
Obituary 81-84
Bassett, Jan(ice Mary) 1953-1999 145
Bassett, Jeni 1959- .... SATA 64
See also SATA-Brief 43
Bassett, John Earl, Jr. 1942- 123
Bassett, John Keith
See Keating, Lawrence A.
Bassett, John Spencer 1867-1928
Brief entry 122
See also DLB 17
Bassett, Lisa 1958- CANR-53
Earlier sketch in CA 126
See also SATA 61
Bassett, Marnie
See Bassett, Flora Marjorie
Bassett, Richard 1900-1995 .... CAP-2
Earlier sketch in CA 25-28
Bassett, Ronald 1924- 81-84
Bassett, T(homas) D(ay) Seymour
1913-2001 .... CANR-8
Earlier sketch in CA 21-24R
Bassett, William B. K. 1908-1991 .... CAP-1
Earlier sketch in CA 9-10
Bassett, William Travis 1923- 9-12R
Bassett, William W. 1932- CANR-34
Earlier sketch in CA 25-28R
Bassford, Christopher 1953- 152
Bassil, Andrea 1948- CANR-128
Earlier sketch in CA 161
See also SATA 96
Bassin, Donna 1950- 148
Bassiouni, M. Cherif 1937- CANR-34
Earlier sketch in CA 29-32R
Bassis, Vladimir (M.) 1959- 174
Bassler, Gerhard P. 1937- 200
Bassler, Thomas J(oseph) 1932- 115
See also Bass, T. J.
See also SFW 4
Bassnett, Susan (Edna) 1947- 128
Bassnett-McGuire, Susan
See Bassnett, Susan (Edna)
Basso, Aldo P(eter) 1922- 65-68
Basso, (Joseph) Hamilton
1904-1964 .... CANR-67
Earlier sketch in CA 89-92
Basso, Keith H(amilton) 1940- CANR-86
Earlier sketch in CA 131
Bassoff, Bruce 1941- 69-72
Bassoff, Evelyn S(ilten) 1944- 166
Basson, Helene Carol Weldt
See Weldt-Basson, Helene Carol
Basta, Lofty L. 1933- 156
Basta, Samir Sanad 1943- 199
Bastable, Bernard
See Barnard, Robert
Basten, Fred E(rnest) CANR-137
Earlier sketches in CA 57-60, CANR-7, 22
Bastian, Ann .... CLC 70
Bastian, F(rank) 1913- 128
Bastianich, Lidia Matticchio 1947- . CANR-126
Earlier sketch in CA 170
Bastias, Constantine 1901(?)-1972
Obituary 37-40R
Bastico, Ettore 1876-1972
Obituary 37-40R
Bastien, Joseph William 1935- 193
Bastin, J(ohn) S(turgus) 1927- CANR-11
Earlier sketch in CA 21-24R
Bastlund, Knud 1925- 21-24R
Baston, Lewis 216
Bastos, Augusto (Antonio) Roa
See Roa Bastos, Augusto (Jose Antonio)
Bastyra, Judy 178
See also SATA 108
Basu, Alaka Malwade 1949- 235
Basu, Arindam 1948- 61-64
Basu, Asoke (Kumar) 1940- 106
Basu, Dipak R. 1951- 112
Basu, Kaushik 1952- CANR-38
Earlier sketch in CA 115
Basu, Romen 1923- CANR-116
Earlier sketches in CA 77-80, CANR-13, 30, 56
Baswell, Christopher 1952- 149
Bataille, Christophe 1971- CANR-129
Earlier sketch in CA 170
Bataille, Georges 1897-1962 101
Obituary 89-92
See also CLC 29
See also EWL 3
See also TCLC 155
Bataille, Gretchen M. 1944- 102
Bataille, Henri 1872-1922 ...... GFL 1789 to the Present
Batali, Mario 1960- 211
Bat-Ami, Miriam 1950- CANR-100
Earlier sketch in CA 150
See also AAYA 38
See also BYA 9, 14
See also MAICYA 2
See also SATA 82, 122, 150
See also SATA-Essay 150
Batatu, Hanna 1926-2000 199
Batbedat, Jean 1926- 37-40R
Batchelder, Alan Bruce 1931- 21-24R
Batchelder, Howard T(imothy)
1909-1984 .... CAP-2
Earlier sketch in CA 19-20
Batcheller, John M. 1918- 45-48
Batchelor, C(larence) D(aniel) 1888-1977
Obituary 73-76
Batchelor, David 1943- CANR-18
Earlier sketch in CA 101
Batchelor, Edward, Jr. 1930- 110
Batchelor, John 1942- CANR-97
Earlier sketch in CA 93-96
Batchelor, John (Dennis) 1947- 109
Batchelor, John Calvin 1948- CANR-45
Earlier sketch in CA 105
See also SFW 4
Batchelor, Joy 1914- .... IDFW 3
See also SATA-Brief 29
Batchelor, Julie F(rances) E(lizabeth) 1947- . 109
Batchelor, R. E. 1934- 146
Batchelor, Reg
See Paine, Lauran (Bosworth)
Batchelor, Stephen 1953- 233
Batchen, Geoffrey 231
Batcher, Elaine Kotler 1944- 109
Bate, Jonathan 1958- CANR-101
Earlier sketch in CA 134

Bate 38 CONTEMPORARY AUTHORS

Bate, Lucy 1939- ... 69-72
See also SATA 18
Bate, Norman (Arthur) 1916- ... 1-4R
See also SATA 5
Bate, Sam 1907- ... 102
Bate, W(alter) Jackson 1918-1999 ... 5-8R
Obituary ... 185
See also DLB 67, 103
Bateham, Josephine (Abiah) Penfield (Cushman) 1829-1901 ... 203
Bateman, Barbara Dee 1933- ... 41-44R
Bateman, Christopher fl. 1684-1731 ... DLB 170
Bateman, Colin 1962- ... 153
Bateman, Geoffrey (Wayne) 1974- ... 239
Bateman, Robert (Moyes Carruthers) 1922-1973 ... CANR-7
Earlier sketch in CA 5-8R
Bateman, Robert L. 1967- ... 233
Bateman, Stephen 1510(?)-1584 ... DLB 136
Bateman, Teresa 1957- ... 184
See also SATA 112
Bateman, Walter L(ewis) 1916- ... 29-32R
Bates, Alan Lawrence 1923- ... 17-20R
Bates, Arthenia J.
See Millican, Arthenia Jackson Bates
Bates, Barbara S(nedeker) 1919- ... 17-20R
See also SATA 12
Bates, Betty
See Bates, Elizabeth
See also SATA 19
Bates, Carol Neuls
See Neuls-Bates, Carol
Bates, Caroline (Philbrick) 1932- ... 103
Bates, Catherine 1964- ... 139
Bates, Charles C(arpenter) 1918- ... 121
Bates, Craig D. 1952- ... 140
Bates, Daisy (Lee) 1914-1999 ... 127
Obituary ... 186
Bates, (Julian) Darrell 1913-1989 ... CAP-1
Obituary ... 129
Earlier sketch in CA 9-10
Bates, David Vincent 1922- ... 110
Bates, Dianne 1948- ... 221
See also SATA 147
Bates, Elizabeth 1921- ... CANR-32
Earlier sketches in CA 77-80, CANR-14
See also Bates, Betty
Bates, H(erbert) E(rnest) 1905-1974 ... CANR-34
Obituary ... 45-48
Earlier sketch in CA 93-96
See also CLC 46
See also CN 1
See also DA3
See also DAB
See also DAM POP
See also DLB 162, 191
See also EWL 3
See also EXPS
See also MTCW 1, 2
See also RGSF 2
See also SSC 10
See also SSFS 7
Bates, Harry 1900-1981 ... 162
See also SFW 4
Bates, Helen L. Z.
See Yakobson, Helen B(ates)
Bates, J. Douglas 1946- ... 142
Bates, J(ames) Leonard 1919- ... 13-16R
Bates, Jefferson D(avis) 1920-2002 ... CANR-86
Obituary ... 205
Earlier sketches in CA 81-84, CANR-15, 34
Bates, Jerome E. 1917- ... 17-20R
Bates, Judy Fong 1949- ... 239
Bates, Karen Grigsby 1951(?)- ... 211
Bates, Katharine Lee 1859-1929 ... 177
See also Lincoln, James
See also DLB 71
See also SATA 113
Bates, Kenneth Francis 1904-1994 ... CAP-1
Earlier sketch in CA 13-14
Bates, Lucius Christopher 1901(?)-1980
Obituary ... 101
Bates, Margaret J(ane) 1918- ... 17-20R
Bates, Marston 1906-1974 ... CANR-7
Obituary ... 49-52
Earlier sketch in CA 5-8R
Bates, Martine
See Leavitt, Martine
Bates, Milton J(ames) 1945- ... 128
Bates, Paul A(llen) 1920- ... 37-40R
Bates, Peter Watson 1920- ... 102
Bates, Ralph Samuel 1906- ... 1-4R
Bates, Robert H(inrichs) 1942- ... CANR-103
Earlier sketches in CA 69-72, CANR-11, 28
Bates, Robert L(atimer) 1912-1994 ... CANR-46
Obituary ... 145
Brief entry ... 116
Earlier sketch in CA 121
Bates, Ronald (Gordon Nudell) 1924- ... 25-28R
See also CP 1
Bates, Scott 1923- ... 49-52
Bates, Stephen 1958- ... 122
Bates, Steven Latimer 1940- ... 114
Bates, Su
See Bates, Susannah (Vacella)
Bates, Susannah (Vacella) 1941- ... 112
Bates, Timothy M(ason) 1946- ... 53-56
Bates, Tom 1944-1999 ... 143
Obituary ... 187
Bateson, Catherine 1960- ... 233
See also SATA 157
Bateson, Charles (Henry) 1903-1975 ... 69-72
Bateson, F(rederick) W(ilse) 1901-1978 ... CANR-6
Earlier sketch in CA 5-8R
Bateson, Gregory 1904-1980 ... CANR-80
Obituary ... 101
Earlier sketch in CA 41-44R
Bateson, Mary Catherine 1939- ... CANR-97
Earlier sketch in CA 137
Batey, Mavis 1921- ... CANR-51
Earlier sketch in CA 125
Batey, Richard (Alexander) 1933- ... 33-36R
Batey, Tom 1946- ... 107
See also SATA 52
See also SATA-Brief 41
Bath, Philip Ernest 1898- ... CAP-1
Earlier sketch in CA 9-10
Batherman, Muriel
See Sheldon, Muriel
Bathke, Edwin A(lbert) 1936- ... 57-60
Bathke, Nancy E(dna) 1938- ... 57-60
Batho, Edith C(lara) 1895-1986 ... CAP-1
Earlier sketch in CA 11-12
Bathurst, Bella 1969- ... 237
Bathurst, Sheila
See Sullivan, Sheila
Batista, Fulgencio
See Batista y Zaldivar, Fulgencio
Batista y Zaldivar, Fulgencio 1901-1973
Obituary ... 111
Batiuk, Thomas M(artin) 1947- ... 69-72
See also SATA-Brief 40
Batiushkov, Konstantin Nikolaevich 1787-1855 ... DLB 205
Batki, John 1942- ... 45-48
Batman, Richard (Dale) 1932- ... 124
Batonyi, Gabor 1961- ... 188
Bator, Robert 1939- ... 115
Batra, Raveendra N(ath) 1943- ... CANR-87
Earlier sketches in CA 89-92, CANR-31
Interview in ... CANR-31
Batra, Ravi
See Batra, Raveendra N(ath)
Batson, C(harles) Daniel 1943- ... 129
Batson, George (Donald) 1918-1977 ... 33-36R
Obituary ... 73-76
Batson, Larry 1930- ... 57-60
See also SATA 35
Batson, Wade Thomas 1912- ... 125
Batt, Tanya Robyn 1970- ... 200
See also SATA 131
Battaglia, Anthony 1939- ... 108
Battaglia, Aurelius 1910- ... SATA 50
See also SATA-Brief 33
Battaglia, Elio Lee 1928- ... CANR-1
Earlier sketch in CA 1-4R
Battaglia, Pasqual ... 210
Battaglia, Pat
See Battaglia, Pasqual
Battalia, O. William 1928- ... 45-48
Battan, Louis J(oseph) 1923- ... 13-16R
Battcock, Gregory 1938-1980 ... CANR-11
Obituary ... 105
Earlier sketch in CA 21-24R
Battelle, Phyllis (Marie) 1922- ... 77-80
Batten, Charles Linwood, Jr. 1942- ... 85-88
Batten, Frank 1927- ... 214
Batten, H(arry) Mortimer 1888-1958 ... 203
Brief entry ... 112
See also SATA 25
Batten, Jack (Hubert, Jr.) 1932- ... CANR-44
Earlier sketch in CA 49-52
Batten, James Knox 1936-1995 ... 102
Obituary ... 148
Batten, James William 1919- ... 33-36R
Batten, Jean (Gardner) 1909-1982 ... 106
Obituary ... 123
Batten, Joyce Mortimer
See Mankowska, Joyce Kells Batten
Batten, Mary 1937- ... 41-44R
See also SATA 5, 102, 162
Batten, (Richard) Peter 1916- ... 97-100
Batten, Thomas Reginald 1904- ... 13-16R
Battenhouse, Roy W(esley) 1912-1995 ... 13-16R
Obituary ... 148
Batterberry, Ariane Ruskin 1935- ... CANR-13
Earlier sketch in CA 69-72
See also SATA 13
Batterberry, Michael Carver 1932- ... 77-80
See also SATA 32
Battersby, Christine 1946- ... 132
Battersby, James L(yons) 1936- ... 41-44R
Battersby, Martin 1914(?)-1982
Obituary ... 106
Battersby, William J(ohn) 1904-1976 ... CANR-4
Earlier sketch in CA 5-8R
Battestin, Martin C(arey) 1930- ... 13-16R
Batteux, Charles 1713-1780 ... DLB 313
Battie, David 1942- ... 135
Battin, B(rinton) W(arner) 1941- ... CANR-57
Earlier sketches in CA 112, CANR-30
Battin, R(osabell) Ray 1925- ... CANR-6
Earlier sketch in CA 9-12R
Battin, Wendy 1953- ... 121
Battis, Emery John 1915- ... 1-4R
Battiscombe, E(sther) Georgina (Harwood) 1905- ... CANR-53
Earlier sketches in CAP-1, CA 9-10, CANR-14
See also DLB 155
Battison, Brian 1939- ... 147
Battista, Miriam 1912(?)-1980
Obituary ... 103
Battista, O(rlando) A(loysius) 1917- ... CANR-7
Earlier sketch in CA 13-16R
Battisti, Eugenio 1924- ... 37-40R
Battle, Allen Overton 1927- ... 41-44R
Battle, Gerald N(ichols) 1914- ... 57-60
Battle, Jean Allen 1914- ... 25-28R
Battle, Lois 1942- ... CANR-104
Earlier sketches in CA 106, CANR-27
Battle, Richard John Vulliamy 1907-1982
Obituary ... 106
Battle, Richard V. 1951- ... 226
Battle, Sol(omon Oden) 1934- ... 25-28R
Battle-Lavert, Gwendolyn 1951- ... CANR-140
Earlier sketch in CA 151
See also Lavert, Gwendolyn Battle
See also SATA 85, 155
Battles, (Roxy) Edith 1921- ... 41-44R
See also SATA 7
Battles, Ford Lewis 1915-1979 ... 13-16R
Battles, Matthew ... 225
Battle-Walters, Kim(berly) (A.) ... 210
Batto, Bernard Frank 1941- ... 57-60
Batts, Michael S. 1929- ... 41-44R
Batty, C(harles) D(avid) 1932- ... 17-20R
Batty, Joyce D(orothea) 1919- ... 17-20R
Batty, Linda Schmidt 1940- ... 61-64
Battye, Gladys Starkey 1915-1975
Brief entry ... 111
Battye, Louis Neville 1923- ... 5-8R
Baty, Gordon B(ruce) 1938- ... 57-60
Baty, Roger M(endenhall) 1937- ... 77-80
Baty, Wayne 1925- ... CANR-5
Earlier sketch in CA 13-16R
Bau, Joseph -2002 ... 175
Obituary ... 206
Bauby, Cathrina 1927- ... 49-52
Bauby, Jean-Dominique 1952(?)-1997 ... 163
Bauchart
See Camus, Albert
Bauchau, Henry 1913- ... 166
Baucom, Donald R. 1940- ... 145
Baudelaire, Charles 1821-1867 ... DA
See also DA3
See also DAB
See also DAC
See also DAM MST, POET
See also DLB 217
See also EW 7
See also GFL 1789 to the Present
See also LMFS 2
See also PC 1
See also PFS 21
See also RGWL 2, 3
See also SSC 18
See also TWA
See also WLC
Baudet, Henri 1919- ... 134
Baudhuin, John S. 1948- ... 112
Baudino, Gael 1955(?)- ... 154
See also FANT
Baudot, Georges 1935- ... 162
Baudouin, Marcel
See Peguy, Charles (Pierre)
Baudouin, Pierre
See Peguy, Charles (Pierre)
Baudouy, Michel-Aime 1909- ... CAP-2
Earlier sketch in CA 33-36
See also SATA 7
Baudrillard, Jean 1929- ... CLC 60
See also DLB 296
Baudry, Bernard
See Guindey, Guillaume Louis
Bauduc, R.
See Segre, Dan V(ittorio)
Baudy, Nicolas 1904(?)-1971
Obituary ... 33-36R
Bauer, Bruno 1809-1882 ... DLB 133
Bauer, Caroline Feller 1935- ... CANR-67
Earlier sketch in CA 77-80
See also SAAS 24
See also SATA 52, 98
See also SATA-Brief 46
Bauer, Cat ... 209
Bauer, Craig (A.) 1947- ... 197
Bauer, Dale M. 1956- ... 174
Bauer, Douglas 1945- ... 166
Bauer, E. Charles 1916- ... 9-12R
Bauer, Erwin A(dam) 1919-2004 ... CANR-122
Obituary ... 225
Earlier sketches in CA 9-12R, CANR-6
Bauer, Florence Marvyne ... CAP-2
Earlier sketch in CA 17-18
Bauer, Fred 1934- ... CANR-13
Earlier sketch in CA 29-32R
See also SATA 36
Bauer, George C. 1942- ... 73-76
Bauer, George Howard 1933-1996 ... CANR-15
Obituary ... 152
Earlier sketch in CA 29-32R
Bauer, (Jo) Hanna R(uth Goldsmith) 1918- ... 57-60
Bauer, Harry C(harles) 1902-1979 ... CAP-1
Obituary ... 85-88
Earlier sketch in CA 13-14
Bauer, Helen 1900-1988 ... 5-8R
See also SATA 2
Bauer, Henry H. 1931- ... 149
Bauer, Joan 1951- ... 190
See also AAYA 34
See also BYA 11, 15
See also MAICYA 2
See also SATA 117, 160
See also WYA
Bauer, Josef Martin 1901-2001 ... CANR-5
Earlier sketch in CA 5-8R
Bauer, Jutta 1955- ... 225
See also SATA 150
Bauer, K(arl) Jack 1926-1987 ... CANR-10
Obituary ... 123
Earlier sketch in CA 25-28R
Bauer, Malcolm Clair 1914-1996 ... 102
Bauer, Maria 1919- ... 117
Bauer, Marion Dane 1938- ... CANR-103
Earlier sketches in CA 69-72, CANR-11, 26, 50
See also AAYA 19
See also BYA 12
See also JRDA
See also MAICYA 1, 2
See also SAAS 9
See also SATA 20, 69, 113, 144
See also SATA-Essay 144
See also WYA
See also YAW
Bauer, Nancy 1934- ... 113
Bauer, Peggy 1932-2004 ... 172
Obituary ... 226
Bauer, Peter (Thomas) 1915-2002 ... 103
Obituary ... 206
Bauer, Raymond A(ugustine) 1916-1977 ... CANR-11
Obituary ... 73-76
Earlier sketch in CA 61-64
Bauer, Robert A(lbert) 1910-2003 ... 69-72
Obituary ... 220
Bauer, Roy A. 1945- ... 137
Bauer, Royal D(aniel) M(ichael) 1889-1983 ... 33-36R
Bauer, Steven 1948- ... CANR-90
Earlier sketch in CA 128
See also SATA 125
Bauer, Susan Wise 1968- ... 224
Bauer, Tricia ... CANR-99
Earlier sketch in CA 153
Bauer, Walter 1904-1976 ... 101
See also EWL 3
Bauer, William R. 1957- ... 212
Bauer, William Waldo 1892-1967 ... CANR-7
Earlier sketch in CA 5-8R
Bauer, Wolfgang 1941- ... 151
See also DLB 124
See also EWL 3
Bauer, Wolfgang L(eander) 1930- ... 13-16R
Bauer, Yehuda 1926- ... CANR-104
Earlier sketches in CA 29-32R, CANR-12
Bauerle, Ruth (Ellen) H(awkins) 1924- ... 112
Bauerlein, Mark (Weightman) 1959- ... 141
Bauernfeind, Harry B. 1904-1989 ... CAP-2
Earlier sketch in CA 19-20
Bauerschmidt, Marjorie 1926- ... SATA 15
Baugh, Albert C(roll) 1891-1981 ... 107
Obituary ... 103
Baugh, Daniel A(lbert) 1931- ... 69-72
Baughan, Peter E(dward) 1934- ... 107
Baughman, Dorothy 1940- ... 65-68
See also SATA 61
Baughman, Ernest W(arren) 1916- ... 33-36R
Baughman, James L(ewis) 1952- ... CANR-41
Earlier sketch in CA 118
Baughman, James P(orter) 1936- ... 25-28R
Baughman, John Lee 1913-1989 ... 97-100
Baughman, M(illard) Dale 1919- ... 41-44R
Baughman, Michael 1937- ... 150
Baughman, Ray Edward 1925- ... CANR-22
Earlier sketches in CA 9-12R, CANR-4
Baughman, Ronald 1940- ... 122
Baughman, T. H. 1947- ... 145
Baughman, Urbanus E., Jr. 1905(?)-1978
Obituary ... 81-84
Baughn, William Hubert 1918- ... CANR-17
Earlier sketch in CA 1-4R
Baukhage, Hilmar Robert 1889-1976
Obituary ... 65-68
See also AITN 2
Baul, Lee Khepa
See Lozowick, Lee
Bauland, Peter 1932- ... 25-28R
Baulch, Jerry T. 1913-1985 ... 77-80
Baulch, Lawrence 1926- ... 25-28R
Baum, Allyn Z(elton) 1924-1997 ... 17-20R
Obituary ... 158
See also SATA 20, 98
Baum, Bernard H(elmut) 1926- ... 37-40R
Baum, Dale 1943- ... 118
Baum, Dan 1956- ... 197
Baum, Daniel (Jay) 1934- ... CANR-6
Earlier sketch in CA 13-16R
Baum, David William 1940- ... 53-56
Baum, Gregory 1923- ... CANR-15
Earlier sketch in CA 25-28R
Baum, Joan 1937- ... 134
Baum, L. Frank
See Thompson, Ruth Plumly
Baum, L(yman) Frank 1856-1919 ... 133
Brief entry ... 108
See also AAYA 46
See also BYA 16
See also CLR 15
See also CWRI 5
See also DLB 22
See also FANT
See also JRDA
See also MAICYA 1, 2
See also MTCW 1, 2
See also NFS 13
See also RGAL 4
See also SATA 18, 100
See also TCLC 7, 132
See also WCH
Baum, Louis 1948- ... 124
See also SATA 64
See also SATA-Brief 52
Baum, Louis F.
See Baum, L(yman) Frank
Baum, Markus 1963- ... 185
Baum, Paull F(ranklin) 1886-1964 ... 5-8R
Obituary ... 103
Baum, Rainer C(arl) 1934- ... 107
Baum, Richard (Dennis) 1940- ... 57-60

Cumulative Index 39 Beagle

Baum, Richard Fitzgerald 1913-1985 .... 5-8R
Baum, Robert J(ames) 1941- CANR-17
Earlier sketch in CA 85-88
Baum, Thomas 1940- 65-68
Baum, Vicki 1888-1960 93-96
Interview in CA-93-96
See also DLB 85
Baum, Willi 1931- 29-32R
See also SATA 4
Bauman, Christian 1970- 216
Bauman, Clarence 1928- CANR-32
Earlier sketch in CA 45-48
Bauman, Edward Walter 1927- 106
Bauman, H(erman) Carl 1913-2001 .... 9-12R
Bauman, Janina (G.) 1926- 134
Bauman, Karl R. 1902(?)-1989
Obituary 130
Bauman, Louis S(ylvester) 1875-1950 214
Bauman, M. Garrett 1948- 191
Bauman, Paul 1955- 186
Bauman, Richard W. 1951- 163
Bauman, Zygmunt 1925- 127
Baumann, Amy (Brown) Beeching
1922- 21-24R
See also SATA 10
Baumann, Carol Edler 1932- 33-36R
Baumann, Charles Henry 1926- 73-76
Baumann, Charly 1928-2001 89-92
Obituary 195
Baumann, Edward (Weston) 1925- 109
Baumann, Elwood D. -1988 185
Brief entry 111
See also SATA-Brief 33
Baumann, Gerd 1953- 125
Baumann, Hans 1914- CANR-3
Earlier sketch in CA 5-8R
See also CLR 35
See also SATA 2
Baumann, Hans Felix S(iegismund) 1893-1985
Obituary 115
Baumann, Kurt 1935- CANR-13
Earlier sketch in CA 77-80
See also SATA 21
Baumann, Walter 1935- 29-32R
Baumbach, Jonathan 1933- CANR-140
Earlier sketches in CA 13-16R, CANR-12, 66
Interview in CANR-12
See also CAAS 5
See also CLC 6, 23
See also CN 3, 4, 5, 6, 7
See also DLBY 1980
See also MTCW 1
Baumback, Clifford M(ason) 1915- CANR-6
Earlier sketch in CA 57-60
Baumber, Michael (Leslie) 1935- 133
Baume, Michael 1930- 25-28R
Baumeister, Roy Frederick 1953- 187
Baumel, Judith 1956- CANR-124
Earlier sketch in CA 125
Baumer, Franklin L(e Van) 1913-1990 186
Brief entry 110
Baumer, William H(enry) 1909-1989 . CANR-1
Obituary 127
Earlier sketch in CA 1-4R
Baumgaertel, (Max) Walter 1902- 69-72
Baumgard, Herbert Mark 1920- CANR-135
Earlier sketch in CA 13-16R
Baumgardner, Jennifer 1970- 201
Baumgardt, David 1890-1963 .... CANR-15
Obituary 103
Earlier sketch in CA 1-4R
Baumgartel, Walter
See Baumgaertel, (Max) Walter
Baumgarten, Sylvia 1933- 112
Baumgartner, A. Marguerite 1909- 145
Baumgartner, Barbara 1939- .... SATA 86
Baumgartner, Frederic J(oseph)
1945- CANR-88
Earlier sketches in CA 110, CANR-27, 52
Baumgartner, Frederick Milton 1910-1996 . 154
Baumgartner, John Stanley 1924- 9-12R
Bauml, Franz H.
See Baeuml, Franz H(einrich)
Baumol, William J(ack) 1922- CANR-100
Earlier sketches in CA 13-16R, CANR-7, 24, 49
Baumrin, Bernard H(erbert) 1934- 9-12R
Baumrin, Stefan
See Baumrin, Bernard H(erbert)
Baums, Roosevelt 171
Baumslag, Naomi 1936- 167
Baur, Francis G. 1930- 111
Baur, John E(dward) 1922-1993 .... 9-12R
Baur, John I(reland) H(owe) 1909-1987
Obituary 122
Baur, Susan (Whiting) 1940- CANR-139
Earlier sketch in CANR-40, 62
See also Schlee, Susan
Baurys, Flo(rence) 1938- 194
See also SATA 122
Baus, Herbert M(ichael) 1914-1999 .. CANR-11
Obituary 178
Earlier sketch in CA 25-28R
Bausani, Alessandro 1921- CANR-43
Earlier sketch in CA 45-48
Bausch, Richard (Carl) 1945- CANR-87
Earlier sketches in CA 101, CANR-43, 61
See also CAAS 14
See also AMWS 7
See also CLC 51
See also CN 7
See also CSW
See also DLB 130
See also MAL 5
Bausch, Robert (Charles) 1945- 219
Earlier sketches in CA 109, CANR-97
Autobiographical Essay in 219
See also CAAS 14
See also DLB 218
Bausch, William J. 1929- CANR-11
Earlier sketch in CA 29-32R
Bausher, Mildred Jordan 1901-1982
Obituary 133
Bavarel, Michel (Joseph) 1940- CANR-82
Earlier sketches in CA 114, CANR-35
Bavier, Robert Newton, (Jr.) 1918- 115
Bavin, Bill 1919- 73-76
Bavinck, J(ohan) H(erman) 1895-1965
Obituary 113
Bavly, Dan (Abraham) 1929- 130
Bawcutt, Priscilla (June) 1931- CANR-120
Earlier sketch in CA 141
Bawden, Nina (Mary Mabey) 1925- . CANR-54
Earlier sketches in CA 17-20R, CANR-8, 29
See also Kark, Nina Mary
See also CLR 2, 51
See also CN 1, 2, 3, 4, 5, 6, 7
See also DAB
See also DLB 14, 161, 207
See also JRDA
See also MAICYA 1, 2
See also SAAS 16
See also SATA 4, 72
See also YAW
Bawer, (Theodore) Bruce 1956- CANR-144
Earlier sketch in CA 144
Bawly, Dan
See Bavly, Dan (Abraham)
Bawn, Mary
See Wright, Mary Pamela Godwin
Bax
See Baxter, Gordon F(rancis), Jr.
Bax, Clifford 1886-1962
Obituary 113
See also DLB 10, 100
Bax, Martin C(harles) O(wen) 1933- 65-68
Bax, Roger
See Winterton, Paul
Baxandall, Rosalyn (Fraad) 1939- CANR-92
Earlier sketch in CA 81-84
Baxt, George (Leonard) 1923-2003 .... 21-24R
Obituary 218
Baxter, Angus 1912- CANR-28
Earlier sketch in CA 111
Baxter, Anne 1923-1985 114
Obituary 118
Brief entry 111
Baxter, Annette Kar 1926- CANR-4
Earlier sketch in CA 1-4R
Baxter, Batsell Barrett 1916-1982 .... 33-36R
Baxter, Charles (Morley) 1947- CANR-133
Earlier sketches in CA 57-60, CANR-40, 64, 104
See also CLC 45, 78
See also CPW
See also DAM POP
See also DLB 130
See also MAL 5
See also MTCW 2
See also MTFW 2005
See also TCLE 1:1
Baxter, Craig 1929- CANR-52
Earlier sketches in CA 25-28R, CANR-11, 26
Baxter, Douglas Clark 1942- 85-88
Baxter, Edna May 1890-1985 .... CAP-1
Earlier sketch in CA 17-18
Baxter, Eric George 1918- 17-20R
Baxter, Eric P(eter) 1913- 9-12R
Baxter, (William John) Ern(est) 1914-1993 .. 214
Baxter, George Owen
See Faust, Frederick (Schiller)
Baxter, Glen 1944- CANR-56
Earlier sketches in CA 109, CANR-28
Baxter, Gordon F(rancis), Jr. 1923- CANR-1
Earlier sketch in CA 45-48
Baxter, Hazel
See Rowland, D(onald) S(ydney)
Baxter, Ian F. G. CANR-11
Earlier sketch in CA 21-24R
Baxter, James K(eir) 1926-1972 77-80
See also CLC 14
See also CP 1
See also EWL 3
Baxter, James P(hinney) III 1893-1975 65-68
Obituary 57-60
Baxter, James Sidlow 1903-1999 73-76
Baxter, John
See Hunt, E(verette) Howard, (Jr.)
Baxter, John 1939- CANR-25
Earlier sketch in CA 29-32R
See also SFW 4
Baxter(-Wright), Keith (Stanley) 1935- 135
Baxter, Mary Lynn 1943- CANR-108
Earlier sketch in CA 152
Baxter, Maurice Glen 1920- CANR-105
Earlier sketch in CA 13-16R
Baxter, Michael John 1944- 103
Interview in CA-103
Baxter, Mike
See Baxter, Michael John
Baxter, Patricia E. W. 107
Baxter, Paula A. 1954- 203
Baxter, Phyllis
See Wallmann, Jeffrey M(iner)
Baxter, Shane V.
See Norwood, Victor G(eorge) C(harles)
Baxter, Stephen 1957- 204
Earlier sketch in CA 161
Autobiographical Essay in 204
See also AAYA 67
See also SFW 4
Baxter, Stephen B(artow) 1929- 17-20R
Baxter, Valerie
See Meynell, Laurence Walter
Baxter, Virginia
See Hilton, Margaret Lynette
Baxter, William F(rancis)
1929-1998 .... CANR-93
Obituary 172
Earlier sketch in CA 89-92
Baxter, William T(hreipland) 1906- 107
Bay, Austin 1951- 131
Bay, Christian 1921-1990 .... 33-36R
Obituary 131
Bay, Howard 1912-1986 81-84
Obituary 121
Bay, Jeanette Graham 1928- 152
See also SATA 88
Bayan, Matthew J. 1951- 218
Bayard, Jean 1923- 114
Bayati, al- 'Abdal-Wahhab
See al-Bayyati, Abd al-Wahhab
See also CWW 2
Baybars, Taner 1936- CANR-4
Earlier sketch in CA 53-56
See also CP 1, 2, 3, 4, 5, 6, 7
Bayer, Eleanor
See Perry, Eleanor (Rosenfeld Bayer)
Bayer, Harold
See Gregg, Andrew K.
Bayer, Herbert 1900-1985
Obituary 117
Bayer, Jane E. (?)-1985
Obituary 116
See also SATA-Obit 44
Bayer, Konrad 1932-1964 214
See also DLB 85
Bayer, Linda 1948- CANR-26
Earlier sketch in CA 107
Bayer, Oliver Weld
See Perry, Eleanor (Rosenfeld Bayer)
Bayer, Patricia 1952- 141
Bayer, Richard C. 221
Bayer, Ronald 1943- 106
Bayer, Sandra Lee 1945- 127
Bayer, Sandy
See Bayer, Sandra Lee
Bayer, Sylvia
See Glassco, John
Bayer, Valerie Townsend 1924- 141
Bayer, William 1939- CANR-130
Earlier sketches in CA 33-36R, CANR-48
Bayer-Berenbaum, Linda
See Bayer, Linda
Bayerle, Gustav 1931- 53-56
Bayes, Marjorie 1934- 115
Bayes, Ronald H(omer) 1932- CANR-10
Earlier sketch in CA 25-28R
Bayh, Birch E(vans), Jr. 1928- 41-44R
Bayh, Marvella (Hern) 1933-1979 93-96
Obituary 85-88
Bay Laurel, Alicia
See Laurel, Alicia Bay
Bayle, Pierre 1647-1706 .... DLB 268, 313
See also GFL Beginnings to 1789
Baylen, Joseph O(scar) 1920- CANR-10
Earlier sketch in CA 25-28R
Bayles, Ernest E(dward) 1897-1977 73-76
Bayles, Martha 1948- 134
Bayles, Michael D(ale) 1941- CANR-18
Earlier sketches in CA 49-52, CANR-1
Bayless, John 1913(?)-1983
Obituary 109
Bayless, Kenneth 1913(?)-1972
Obituary 104
Bayless, Raymond G(ordon) 1920-2004 .. 85-88
Obituary 227
Bayley, Barrington J(ohn) 1937- CANR-43
Earlier sketches in CA 37-40R, CANR-14
See also DLB 261
See also SFW 4
Bayley, Charles C(alvert) 1907-1982 ..... 33-36R
Bayley, David H(ume) 1933- 13-16R
Bayley, Edwin (Richard) 1918-2002 108
Obituary 209
Bayley, John (Oliver) 1925- CANR-85
Earlier sketch in CA 85-88
Bayley, Monica Worsley 1919- 111
Bayley, Nicola 1949- 118
See also MAICYA 1, 2
See also SATA 41, 69, 129
Bayley, Peter Charles 1921- 101
Bayley, Stephen 1951- 106
Bayley, Viola (Clare Powles) 1911- CANR-5
Earlier sketch in CA 5-8R
Baylis, Janice H(inshaw) 1928- 161
Baylis, John 1946- CANR-39
Earlier sketches in CA 101, CANR-18
Bayliss, John Clifford 1919- 13-16R
See also Clifford, John
See also CP 1
Bayliss, Timothy
See Baybars, Taner
Bayliss, William Maddock 1860-1924 159
Baylor, Byrd 1924- CANR-115
Earlier sketch in CA 81-84
See also CLR 3
See also MAICYA 1, 2
See also SATA 16, 69, 136
Baylor, Robert 1925- 13-16R
Bayly, Joseph T(ate) 1920- 17-20R
Baym, Max I. 1895-1979 .... 41-44R
Baym, Nina 1936- CANR-127
Earlier sketches in CA 112, CANR-32, 64
Bayme, Steven 1950- CANR-109
Earlier sketch in CA 151
Bayne, David C(owan) 1918- 41-44R
Bayne, Nicholas (Peter) 1937- 130
Bayne, Robin L. 1962- 228
Bayne, Stephen F(ielding), Jr. 1908-1974
Obituary 45-48
Bayne-Jardine, C(olin) C(harles) 1932- .. 25-28R
Baynes, Cary F. 1873(?)-1977
Obituary 104
Baynes, Dorothy Colston
See Colston-Baynes, Dorothy
Baynes, John (Christopher Malcolm)
1928- 21-24R
Baynes, Ken 1934- 193
Brief entry 110
Baynes, Kenneth R(ichard) 1954- 141
Baynes, Pauline (Diana) 1922- CANR-111
Earlier sketches in CA 120, CANR-37
See also DLB 160
See also MAICYA 1, 2
See also SATA 19, 59, 133
Baynham, Henry (W. F.) 1933- 29-32R
Baynton, Barbara 1857-1929 .... DLB 230
See also RGSF 2
See also TCLC 57
Bayor, Ronald H(oward) 1944- CANR-60
Earlier sketch in CA 128
Bayrd, Edwin 1944- 97-100
Bays, Gwendolyn McKee 13-16R
Bayyati, al- Abd al-Wahhab
See al-Bayyati, Abd al-Wahhab
Bazell, Robert (Joseph) 1945- 181
Bazelon, David T(homas) 1923-2005 .... 17-20R
Obituary 239
Bazelon, Irwin 1922-1995 102
Bazerman, Charles 1945- 191
Bazin, Andre 1918-1958 185
Brief entry 113
Bazin, Germain (Rene Michel)
1901-1990 .... CANR-79
Obituary 131
Earlier sketches in CA 5-8R, CANR-12
Bazin, Herve
See Herve-Bazin, Jean Pierre Marie
See also DLB 83
Bazin, Nancy Topping 1934- 41-44R
Bazley, Margaret C. 1938- 106
Bazzana, Kevin 1963- 233
Bazzoni, Jana O'Keefe 1941- 154
BB
See Watkins-Pitchford, Denys James
Beach, Bert Beverly 1928- 57-60
Beach, Charles
See Reid, (Thomas) Mayne
Beach, Charles Amory CANR-26
Earlier sketches in CAP-2, CA 19-20
See also SATA 1
Beach, Christopher (John) 1959- 186
Beach, Dale S. 1923- 13-16R
Beach, David (Williams) 1938- 115
Beach, David N. 1943-1999 202
Beach, Earl F(rancis) 1912- 13-16R
Beach, Edward L(atimer) 1918-2002 .. CANR-6
Obituary 211
Earlier sketch in CA 5-8R
See also SATA 12
See also SATA-Obit 140
Beach, Eric 1947- 160
Beach, Frank Ambrose 1911-1988 110
Obituary 125
Beach, Hugh 1949- CANR-101
Earlier sketch in CA 143
Beach, Lisa 1957- 182
See also SATA 111
Beach, Lynn
See Lance, Kathryn
Beach, Mark B. 1937- 69-72
Beach, Milo Cleveland 1939- 194
Beach, Rex 1877-1949 .... TCWW 1, 2
Beach, Robert C. 1935-1998 139
Beach, Stewart T(aft) 1899-1979 93-96
Obituary 85-88
See also SATA 23
Beach, Sylvia (Woodbridge) 1887-1962 108
See also DLB 4
See also DLBD 15
Beach, Vincent W(oodrow) 1917- 33-36R
Beach, (William) Waldo 1916- 61-64
Beacham, Richard C. 1946- CANR-98
Earlier sketch in CA 141
Beachcomber
See Morton, John (Cameron Andrieu) Bingham (Michael)
Beachcroft, Nina 1931- CANR-19
Earlier sketch in CA 97-100
See also CWRI 5
See also SATA 18
Beachcroft, T(homas) O(wen)
1902-1988 .... CAP-1
Earlier sketch in CA 9-10
Beachey, Duane 1948- 112
Beachum, Larry M(ahon) 1948 113
Beachy, Lucille 1935- 77-80
Beadell, Len 1923-1995 102
Beadle, G. W.
See Beadle, George Wells
Beadle, George
See Beadle, George Wells
Beadle, George Wells 1903-1989 159
Obituary 128
Beadle, Leigh P(atric) 1941- 65-68
Beadle, Muriel (McClure Barnett)
1915-1994 .... 21-24R
Obituary 144
Beadles, William T(homas) 1902-1991 . 17-20R
Beaglo, J. Robert
See Regalbuto, Robert J.

Beagle, Peter S(oyer) 1939- CANR-110
Earlier sketches in CA 9-12R, CANR-4, 51, 73
Interview in CANR-4
See also AAYA 47
See also BPFB 1
See also BYA 9, 10, 16
See also CLC 7, 104
See also DA3
See also DLBY 1980
See also FANT
See also MTCW 2
See also MTFW 2005
See also SATA 60, 130
See also SUFW 1, 2
See also YAW
Beaglehole, Helen 1946- 189
See also SATA 117
Beaglehole, J(ohn) C(awte) 1901-1971 .. CAP-2
Obituary 33-36R
Earlier sketch in CA 21-22
Beagley, Brenda E. 1962- 211
Beakley, George Carroll, Jr. 1922- CANR-16
Earlier sketches in CA 45-48, CANR-1
Beal, Anthony (Ridley) 1925-2003 9-12R
Obituary 220
Beal, Bob 1949- 130
Beal, George M(elvin) 1917- CANR-13
Earlier sketch in CA 21-24R
Beal, Graham W(illiam) J(ohn) 1947- 118
Beal, Gwyneth 1943- 69-72
Beal, John Robinson 1906(?)-1985
Obituary 116
Beal, M. F. 1937- 73-76
See also DLBY 1981
Beal, Merrill D. 1898-1990 CANR-5
Earlier sketch in CA 1-4R
Beal, Peter 1944- 203
Beal, Richard S(mith) 1945-1984 122
Obituary 114
Beal, Virginia
See Dabney, Virginia Bell
Beale, Betty 73-76
Beale, Calvin L(unsford) 1923- 1-4R
Beale, Christopher Griffin
See Griffin-Beale, Christopher
Beale, Dorothea 1831-1906 232
See also FW
Beale, Fleur SATA 107
Beale, Howard 1898-1983 109
Beale, Howard K(ennedy) 1899-1959 209
See also DLB 17
Beale, Paul (Christian) 1933-1999 130
Obituary 186
Beale, Walter H(enry) 1945-
Brief entry 118
Bealer, Alex W(inkler III) 1921-1980 .. CANR-2
Obituary 97-100
Earlier sketch in CA 45-48
See also SATA 8
See also SATA-Obit 22
Bealer, George Persson 1944- CANR-32
Earlier sketch in CA 113
Beales, Derek (Edward Dawson)
1931- CANR-16
Earlier sketch in CA 73-76
Beales, H(ugh) L(ancelot) 1889-1988
Obituary 125
Beales, Peter 1936- CANR-119
Earlier sketches in CA 122, CANR-48
Beales, Valerie 1915- SATA 74
Bealey, (Frank) William 1922- CANR-2
Earlier sketch in CA 5-8R
Beall, Anne E. 1966- 147
Beall, James Lee 1924- CANR-11
Earlier sketch in CA 65-68
Beall, Karen F(riedmann) 1938- 106
Beall, Otho T(hompson), Jr. 1908-1977
Obituary 113
Beals, Alan R(obin) 1928- 37-40R
Beals, Carleton 1893-1979 CANR-66
Earlier sketches in CA 1-4R, CANR-3
See also SATA 12
Beals, Frank Lee 1881-1972 5-8R
Obituary 103
See also SATA-Obit 26
Beals, Melba Patillo
See Beals, Melba Pattillo
Beals, Melba Pattillo 1941- 159
Beals, Ralph L(eon) 1901-1985 21-24R
Beam, Alex 1954- CANR-116
Earlier sketches in CA 135, CANR-115
Beam, Alvin Wesley 1912-1982
Obituary 107
Beam, C. Richard 45-48
Beam, George D(ahl) 1934- 69-72
Beam, Philip C(onway) 1910- 97-100
Beaman, Joyce Proctor 1931- 29-32R
Beame, Rona 1934- 45-48
See also SATA 12
Beamer, (George) Charles (Jr.) 1942- 121
See also SATA 43
Beamer, Lisa 1969- 211
Beamer, Yvonne
See Dennis, Yvonne Wakim
Beamish, Annie O'Meara de Vic 1883- . 13-16R
Beamish, Anthony Hamilton (?)-1983
Obituary 109
Beamish, Caroline 1941- 194
Beamish, Huldine V. 1904- CAP-1
Earlier sketch in CA 13-14
Beamish, Noel de Vic
See Beamish, Annie O'Meara de Vic
Beamish, Paul W(illiam) 1953- 191
Beamish, Tufton Victor Hamilton
See Chelwood, Tufton Victor Hamilton
Bean, (Myrtle) Amelia TCWW 1, 2
Bean, Constance A(ustin) 41-44R
Bean, George E(wart) 1903-1977 25-28R
Obituary 133
Bean, Gregory (K.) 1952- CANR-72
Earlier sketch in CA 152
Bean, Henry (Schorr) 1945- CANR-123
Earlier sketch in CA 109
Bean, Jonathan J. 1962- CANR-97
Earlier sketch in CA 164
Bean, Judith M(attson) 1945- 214
Bean, Keith F(enwick) 1911-1980 CAP-1
Earlier sketch in CA 11-12
Bean, Lowell John 1931- 41-44R
Bean, Mabel Greene 1898(?)-1977
Obituary 73-76
Bean, Normal
See Burroughs, Edgar Rice
Bean, Orson 1928- 77-80
Bean, Walton (Elbert) 1914-1978 25-28R
Bean, William B(ennett) 1909-1989 . CANR-79
Obituary 128
Earlier sketch in CA 111
Beane, Douglas Carter DFS 21
Beaney, Jan
See Udall, Jan Beaney
Beaney, Jane
See Udall, Jan Beaney
Bear, Bullen
See Donnelly, Austin Stanislaus
Bear, David 1949- 106
Bear, Greg(ory Dale) 1951- CANR-81
Earlier sketches in CA 113, CANR-35
See also AAYA 24
See also BPFB 1
See also BYA 9, 10
See also CN 7
See also SATA 65, 105
See also SCFW 2
See also SFW 4
Bear, James A(dam), Jr. 1919- 21-24R
Bear, Joan 1918- 57-60
Bear, John (Boris) 1938- CANR-29
Earlier sketches in CA 73-76, CANR-13
Bear, O. L.
See Putnam, William L(owell)
Bear, Roberta Meyer 1942- 21-24R
Bearanger, Marie
See Messier, Claire
Bearce, George D(onham) 1922- 9-12R
Bearchell, Charles 1925- 93-96
Beard, Belle Boone 1898-1984
Obituary 114
Beard, Bernice 1927- 180
Beard, Charles A(ustin) 1874-1948 189
Brief entry 115
See also DLB 17
See also SATA 18
See also TCLC 15
Beard, Dan(iel Carter) 1850-1941 SATA 22
Beard, Darleen Bailey 1961- CANR-142
Earlier sketch in CA 161
See also SATA 96
Beard, Estle S. 1908-1983 111
Beard, Geoffrey 1929- CANR-86
Earlier sketch in CA 130
Beard, Helen 1931- CANR-32
Earlier sketch in CA 113
Beard, James (Andrews) 1903-1985 . CANR-15
Obituary 114
Earlier sketch in CA 81-84
Beard, James F(ranklin) 1919-1989 1-4R
Obituary 130
Beard, Jo Ann 1955- 169
Beard, Julie 218
Beard, Marna L(ouise) 1942- 112
Beard, Mary 1955- 189
Beard, Mary Ritter 1876-1958 232
See also FW
Beard, Patricia 1947(?)- 224
Beard, Peter H. 1938- 13-16R
Beard, Richard 1967- 169
Beard, Robert Eric 1911-1983
Obituary 111
Beard, William R. 1946- 226
Bearden, James Hudson 1933- 21-24R
Bearden, Milton 1940- 171
Bearden, Romare (Howard)
1914(?)-1988 CANR-80
Obituary 125
Earlier sketch in CA 102
See also AAYA 67
See also SATA 22
See also SATA-Obit 56
Beardmore, Cedric
See Beardmore, George
Beardmore, George 1908-1979 69-72
Obituary 126
See also SATA 20
Beardon, Milton 1940- 171
Beardsell, Peter R. 1940- 143
Beardslee, John W(alter) III 1914-2001 . 37-40R
Beardslee, Karen E. 1965- 211
Beardsley, Charles Noel 1914-1994 ... CANR-2
Earlier sketch in CA 1-4R
Beardsley, (John) Douglas 1941- 113
Beardsley, Elizabeth Lane 29-32R
Beardsley, John 1952- CANR-28
Earlier sketch in CA 109
Beardsley, (Betty) Lou 1925- 118
Beardsley, Martyn R. 1957- SATA 150
Beardsley, Monroe C(urtis) 1915-1985 .. 17-20R
Obituary 117
Beardsley, Richard K(ing)
1918-1978 CANR-11
Obituary 77-80
Earlier sketch in CA 17-20R
Beardsley, Theodore S(terling), Jr.
1930- 33-36R
Beardsworth, Millicent Monica 1915- 103
Beardwood, Roger 1932- 89-92
Beardwood, Valerie Fairfield 5-8R
Beare, Francis W(right)
1902-1982(?) CANR-16
Earlier sketch in CA 1-4R
Beare, (M. A.) Nikki 1928- 37-40R
Bearman, Jane (Ruth) 1917- 105
See also SATA 29
Bearne, C(olin) G(erald) 1939- 97-100
Bearss, Edwin C(ole) 1923- CANR-10
Earlier sketch in CA 25-28R
Beary, Michael J. 1956- 224
Beasecker, Robert F(rancis) 1946- 177
Beaser, Herbert W. 1913(?)-1979
Obituary 85-88
Beasley, Bruce 1958- CANR-105
Earlier sketch in CA 159
Beasley, David 1931- 206
Beasley, Faith E. 1958- 139
Beasley, Jerry C(arr) 1940- CANR-14
Earlier sketch in CA 37-40R
Beasley, M. Robert 1918- 9-12R
Beasley, Maurine 1936- CANR-42
Earlier sketches in CA 104, CANR-20
Beasley, Rex 1925- 9-12R
Beasley, Ruth 1942- 135
Beasley, W(illiam) Conger, Jr. 1940- ... CANR-4
Earlier sketch in CA 53-56
Beasley, W(illiam) G(erald) 1919- 53-56
Beasley-Murray, George Raymond
1916-2000 65-68
Beasley-Topliffe, Keith 1951- 205
Beason, Doug 1953- 164
Beason, Robert G(ayle) 1927- 114
Beath, Paul Robert 1905-1982 5-8R
Beath, Warren Newton 1951- 136
Beaton, Alan A. 1947- 123
Beaton, Anne
See Washington, (Catherine) Marguerite Beauchamp
Beaton, Arthur
See Kennedy, Leo
Beaton, Cecil (Walter Hardy)
1904-1980 CANR-68
Obituary 93-96
Earlier sketch in CA 81-84
See also IDFW 3, 4
Beaton, Clare 1947- SATA 125
Beaton, George
See Brenan, (Edward Fitz)Gerald
Beaton, (Donald) Leonard
1929-1971 CANR-4
Obituary 29-32R
Earlier sketch in CA 5-8R
Beaton, M. C.
See Chesney, Marion
Beaton-Jones, Cynon 1921- 5-8R
Beattie, Ann 1947- CANR-128
Earlier sketches in CA 81-84, CANR-53, 73
See also AMWS 5
See also BEST 90:2
See also BPFB 1
See also CLC 8, 13, 18, 40, 63, 146
See also CN 4, 5, 6, 7
See also CPW
See also DA3
See also DAM NOV, POP
See also DLB 218, 278
See also DLBY 1982
See also EWL 3
See also MAL 5
See also MTCW 1, 2
See also MTFW 2005
See also RGAL 4
See also RGSF 2
See also SSC 11
See also SSFS 9
See also TUS
Beattie, Carol 1918- 29-32R
Beattie, Edward J(ames), Jr. 1918- 106
Beattie, Geoffrey 228
Beattie, James 1735-1803 DLB 109
Beattie, Jessie Louise 1896-1985 ...... CANR-17
Earlier sketches in CA 5-8R, CANR-2
Beattie, John (Hugh Marshall)
1915-1990 37-40R
Obituary 131
Beattie, L(inda) Elisabeth 1953- 193
Beattie, Melody (Lynn) 1948- 141
See also BEST 90:4
Beattie, Sally 1941- 122
Beattie, Susan 1938- 123
Beatts, Anne Patricia 1947- 102
Beatty, Barbara (R.) 1946- 152
Beatty, Bernard 1938- 127
Beatty, Chester 1875-1968 DLB 201
Beatty, (Alfred) Chester 1875-1968 216
Beatty, Elizabeth
See Holloway, Teresa (Bragunier)
Beatty, Hetty Burlingame 1907-1971 1-4R
Obituary 103
See also SATA 5
Beatty, Jack 1945- 169
Beatty, Jerome, Jr. 1918- CANR-3
Earlier sketch in CA 9-12R
See also SATA 5
Beatty, John CWRI 5
Beatty, John (Louis) 1922-1975 CANR-4
Obituary 57-60
Earlier sketch in CA 5-8R
See also BYA 2
See also SATA 6
See also SATA-Obit 25
Beatty, Morgan 1902-1975
Obituary 61-64
Beatty, Patricia (Robbins)
1922-1991 CANR-55
Obituary 134
Earlier sketches in CA 1-4R, CANR-3
See also AAYA 16
See also BYA 2, 6, 8
See also CWRI 5
See also JRDA
See also MAICYA 1, 2
See also SAAS 4
See also SATA 1, 30, 73
See also SATA-Obit 68
See also YAW
Beatty, Paul 1963(?)- CANR-94
Earlier sketch in CA 154
Beatty, Rita Gray 1930- 45-48
Beatty, Robert Owen 1924-1976
Obituary 69-72
Beatty, Scott 1969- 237
Beatty, Warren
See Beaty, Warren
Beatty, William Alfred 1912-1979(?) CAP-1
Earlier sketch in CA 13-14
Beatty, William K(ave) 1926-2002 41-44R
Obituary 210
Beaty, Betty CANR-18
Earlier sketch in CA 73-76
Beaty, (Arthur) David 1919-1999 CANR-18
Obituary 187
Earlier sketches in CA 1-4R, CANR-2
See also CN 1, 2, 3, 4
Beaty, Janice J(anowski) 1930- 13-16R
Beaty, Jerome 1924- 85-88
Beaty, Mary (T.) 1947- 220
See also SATA 146
Beaty, Shirley MacLean
See MacLaine, Shirley
Beaty, Warren 1937(?)- 126
Brief entry 109
Beaubien, Anne K(athleen) 1947- 123
Beauchamp, Cari 167
Beauchamp, Edward R(obert) 1933- 61-64
Beauchamp, Gorman 1938- 121
Beauchamp, Kathleen Mansfield
1888-1923 134
Brief entry 104
See also Mansfield, Katherine and Petrovsky, Boris
See also DA
See also DA3
See also DAC
See also DAM MST
See also MTCW 2
See also TEA
Beauchamp, Kenneth L(loyd) 1939- 29-32R
Beauchamp, Pat
See Washington, (Catherine) Marguerite Beauchamp
Beauchamp, Tom L. 1939- CANR-13
Earlier sketch in CA 73-76
Beauchemin, Neree 1850-1931 DLB 92
Beauchemin, Yves 1941- 129
See also CCA 1
See also DLB 60
Beauclerk, Helen De Vere 1892-1969
Obituary 114
See also FANT
Beauclerk, Jane
See Engh, M(ary) J(ane)
Beaud, Michel 1935- 146
Beaudoin, Kenneth Lawrence
1913-1995 29-32R
Beaudoin, Tom 173
Beaudouin, John T(yrell) 1920-
Brief entry 114
Beaufitz, William
See Critchley, Julian (Michael Gordon)
Beaufort, John (David) 1912-1992 104
Beaufort, Simon 181
Beaufoy, Simon 1967- 172
Beaufre, Andre 1902-1975 65-68
Obituary 57-60
Beaugrand, Honore 1848-1906 DLB 99
Beaulac, Willard L(eon) 1899-1990 9-12R
Obituary 132
Beaulieu, Victor-Levy 1945- 146
See also DLB 53
Beauman, E(ric) Bentley 1891-1989 9-12R
Obituary 129
Beauman, Katharine (Burgoyne) Bentley
1902- 102
Beauman, Nicola 1944- 152
Beauman, Sally 1944(?)- CANR-112
Earlier sketch in CA 134
Beaumarchais, Pierre-Augustin Caron de
1732-1799 DAM DRAM
See also DC 4
See also DFS 14, 16
See also DLB 313
See also EW 4
See also GFL Beginnings to 1789
See also RGWL 2, 3
Beaumer, Mme. de (?)-1766 DLB 313
Beaumont, Beverly
See von Block, Sylvia
Beaumont, Charles 1929-1967 CANR-73
Obituary 103
Earlier sketch in CA 5-8R
See also HGG
See also SFW 4
Beaumont, Charles Allen 1926- 1-4R
Beaumont, Cyril William
1891-1976 CANR-68
Obituary 65-68
Earlier sketch in CA 13-16R

Cumulative Index 41 Beckwith

Beaumont, Francis 1584(?)-1616 .... BRW 2
See also CDBLB Before 1660
See also DC 6
See also DLB 58
See also TEA
Beaumont, George Ernest 1888-1974
Obituary 49-52
Beaumont, Sir John 1583(?)-1627 .... DLB 121
Beaumont, Joseph 1616-1699 .... DLB 126
Beaumont, Keith (Stanley) 1944- 118
Beaumont, Robert 1954- 220
Beaumont, Roger A(lban) 1935- 65-68
Beauregard, Erving E. 1920- CANR-43
Earlier sketch in CA 111
Beauregard, Georges de
See de Beauregard, Georges
Beaurline, L(ester) A(lbert) 1927-1999 ... 21-24R
Beausang, Michael F(rancis), Jr. 1936- 57-60
Beausay, Florence E(dith) 1911-1991 .... 21-24R
BeauSeigneur, James 1953- 226
Beausobre, Iulia de
See Namier, Julia
Beausoleil, Beau 1941- CANR-14
Earlier sketch in CA 81-84
Beauvais, Robert 1911- 104
Beauvoir, Simone (Lucie Ernestine Marie Bertrand) de 1908-1986 .... CANR-61
Obituary 118
Earlier sketches in CA 9-12R, CANR-28
See also BPFB 1
See also CLC 1, 2, 4, 8, 14, 31, 44, 50, 71, 124
See also DA
See also DA3
See also DAB
See also DAC
See also DAM MST, NOV
See also DLB 72
See also DLBY 1986
See also EW 12
See also EWL 3
See also FL 1:5
See also FW
See also GFL 1789 to the Present
See also LMFS 2
See also MTCW 1, 2
See also MTFW 2005
See also RGSF 2
See also RGWL 2, 3
See also SSC 35
See also TWA
See also WLC
Beavan, Colin 203
Beaven, Derek 172
Beaver, Bruce (Victor) 1928- 97-100
See also CP 1, 2, 3, 4, 5, 6, 7
See also DLB 289
Beaver, Frank E(ugene) 1938- 114
Beaver, Harold (Lothar) 1929-2002 .... 21-24R
Obituary 208
Beaver, (Jack) Patrick 1923- 33-36R
Beaver, Paul (Eli) 1953- CANR-40
Earlier sketch in CA 115
Beaver, R(obert) Pierce 1906- CANR-7
Earlier sketch in CA 5-8R
Beaver, Stanley H(enry) 1907-1984
Obituary 114
Beaverbrook, William Maxwell Aitken 1879-1964 103
Obituary 89-92
Beazley, John Davidson 1885-1970
Obituary 115
Bebb, Russ(ell H.), Jr. 1930- 49-52
Bebbington, D(avid) W(illiam) 1949- 133
Bebel, (Ferdinand) August 1840-1913 .... FW
Bebell, Mildred Hoyt 1909- CAP-1
Earlier sketch in CA 13-16
Bebey, Francis 1929-2001 .... CANR-25
Obituary 197
Earlier sketch in CA 69-72
See also BW 1
Bebler, A(lex) Anton 1937- CANR-2
Earlier sketch in CA 49-52
Becerra, Rosina M. 1939- CANR-48
Earlier sketch in CA 122
Bechard, Margaret 1953- CANR-139
Earlier sketch in CA 151
See also SATA 85
Bechdel, Alison 1960- CANR-97
Earlier sketch in CA 138
See also GLL 2
Bechdolt, Frederick R(itchie) 1874-1950 .... TCWW 1, 2
Becher, Anne 1963- 181
Becher, Johannes R. 1891-1958 194
Becher, Ronald E. 1943- 195
Becher, Ulrich 1910- 101
See also DLB 69
Bechert, Heinz 1932- 136
Bechervaise, John Mayston 1910-1998 .... CANR-5
Earlier sketch in CA 13-16R
Bechhoefer, Bernhard G. 1904-1998 .... 1-4R
Obituary 171
Bechko, P(eggy) A(nne) 1950- CANR-63
Earlier sketches in CA 49-52, CANR-2
See also TCWW 1, 2
Bechler, Curt 1958- 145
Bechmann, Roland 1919- 136
Becht, J. Edwin 1918- 29-32R
Bechtel, Louise Seaman 1894-1985 ...... CAP-2
Obituary 116
Earlier sketch in CA 29-32
See also SATA 4
See also SATA-Obit 43
Bechtel, Paul M(oyer) 1909-1998 116
Bechtel, Stefan D. 1951- CANR-128
Earlier sketch in CA 163
Bechtol, William M(ilton) 1931-1998 .... CANR-34
Earlier sketch in CA 49-52
Beck, Aaron T(emkin) 1921- CANR-91
Earlier sketches in CA 21-24R, CANR-11
Beck, Alan M(arshall) 1942- CANR-21
Earlier sketch in CA 45-48
Beck, Barbara L. 1927- 17-20R
See also SATA 12
Beck, Calvin Thomas 1937-1989 97-100
Beck, Carl 1930- CANR-1
Earlier sketch in CA 1-4R
Beck, Clive 1939- CANR-27
Earlier sketch in CA 49-52
Beck, Doc
See Beck, Earl Clifton
Beck, Earl Clifton 1891-1977
Obituary 110
Beck, Earl R(ay) 1916- 33-36R
Beck, Emily M(orison) 1915-2004 114
Obituary 225
Beck, Evelyn Torton 1933- CANR-13
Earlier sketch in CA 33-36R
Beck, Harry
See Paine, Lauran (Bosworth)
Beck, Helen L(ouise) 1908-1992 73-76
Beck, Henry G(abriel) J(ustin) 1914- 9-12R
Beck, Horace P(almer) 1920- 77-80
Beck, Hubert (F.) 1931- CANR-12
Earlier sketch in CA 29-32R
Beck, Ian (Archibald) 1947- .... SATA 138
Beck, James (Henry) 1930- CANR-89
Earlier sketch in CA 85-88
Beck, James Murray 1914- 101
Beck, Joan (Wagner) 1923-1998
Obituary 172
Brief entry 118
Beck, John C. 216
Beck, John Jacob, Jr. 1941- 53-56
Beck, Julian 1925-1985 .... CANR-78
Obituary 117
Earlier sketch in CA 102
Beck, K(athrine) K(ristine) 1950- CANR-144
Earlier sketch in CA 142
Beck, Leslie 1907(?)-1978
Obituary 104
Beck, Lewis White 1913-1997 .... CANR-2
Earlier sketch in CA 5-8R
Beck, Lois (Conchita Grant) 1944- 236
Beck, M. Susan 1941- 113
Beck, Marilyn (Mohr) 1928- 65-68
Beck, Martha (Nibley) 1962- 185
Beck, Mary L. (Giraudo) 1924- 131
Beck, Mike 1947- .... CWRI 5
Beck, Pamela 1954- 120
Beck, Paul 1933(?)-1985
Obituary 116
Beck, Phineas
See Chamberlain, Samuel
Beck, Robert Edward 1941- 104
Beck, Robert H(olmes) 1918-1991 .... 29-32R
Beck, Robert J. 1961- 149
Beck, Robert Nelson 1924-1980 .... CANR-4
Earlier sketch in CA 1-4R
Beck, Thomas D(avis) 1943- 57-60
Beck, Timothy James
See Cochrane, Becky
Beck, Toni 1925- 57-60
Beck, Victor Emanuel 1894-1963 .... 5-8R
Beck, Warren 1896-1986 .... CANR-68
Obituary 119
Earlier sketches in CA 1-4R, CANR-3
See also CN 1, 2
Beck, Warren Albert 1918-1991 .... CANR-78
Obituary 135
Earlier sketches in CA 5-8R, CANR-6
Beckel, Annamarie (L.) 186
Beckel, Graham 1913-2002 .... 1-4R
Beckelhymer, (Paul) Hunter 1919- CANR-3
Earlier sketch in CA 1-4R
Becker, A(dolph) C(arl), Jr. 1920- 65-68
Becker, Abraham S(amuel) 1927-2003 .. 33-36R
Obituary 218
Becker, Albert B. 1903-1972 .... CAP-2
Earlier sketch in CA 29-32
Becker, Arthur P(eter) 1918- 29-32R
Becker, B. Jay 1904-1987 65-68
Obituary 123
Becker, Beril 1901-1999 .... CAP-1
Earlier sketch in CA 9-10
See also SATA 11
Becker, Bill
See Becker, William
Becker, Bruce 57-60
Becker, Carl (Lotus) 1873-1945 157
See also DLB 17
See also TCLC 63
Becker, Carol 1947- 124
Becker, Charles M(axwell) 1954- 146
Becker, Deborah Zimmett 1955- 209
See also SATA 138
Becker, Elizabeth 1947- 141
Becker, Ernest 1925-1974 97-100
Becker, Ethan 1945- CANR-128
Earlier sketch in CA 169
Becker, Florence
See Lennon, Florence Becker (Tanenbaum)
Becker, Gary S(tanley) 1930- CANR-122
Earlier sketches in CA 61-64, CANR-11
Becker, George J(oseph) 1908-1989 . CANR-78
Obituary 130
Earlier sketches in CA 5-8R, CANR-7
Becker, Harold K(auffman) 1922- CANR-10
Earlier sketch in CA 29-32R
Becker, Helaine 1961- 213
See also SATA 142
Becker, Howard S(aul) 1928- 134
Brief entry 115
Becker, Hyam Yona 1953- 180
Becker, Irving 1945- 122
Becker, Jasper 1956- CANR-103
Earlier sketches in CA 139, CANR-62
Becker, Jillian (Ruth) 1932- CANR-141
Earlier sketches in CA 77-80, CANR-25
Becker, John (Leonard) 1901- CAP-1
Earlier sketch in CA 11-12
See also SATA 12
Becker, John E(dward) 1930- 49-52
Becker, John E(mil) 1942- 222
See also SATA 148
Becker, Joseph M(aria) 1908-2001 ...... CANR-7
Obituary 201
Earlier sketch in CA 17-20R
Becker, Josh 1958- 226
Becker, Joyce 1936- .... SATA 39
Becker, Juergen 1932- 154
See also DLB 75
Becker, Jurek 1937-1997 .... CANR-117
Obituary 157
Earlier sketches in CA 85-88, CANR-60
See also CLC 7, 19
See also CWW 2
See also DLB 75, 299
See also EWL 3
Becker, Jurgen
See Becker, Juergen
Becker, Klaus
See Koch, Kurt E(mil)
Becker, Lawrence C(arlyle) 1939- ... CANR-105
Earlier sketch in CA 85-88
Becker, Leslee 1945- 189
Becker, Lucille F(rackman) 1929- CANR-12
Earlier sketch in CA 29-32R
Becker, Manning H. 1922- 13-16R
Becker, Marion Rombauer 1903-1976 .. 37-40R
Obituary 69-72
Becker, Marvin Burton 1922- 107
Becker, May Lamberton 1873-1958 201
Brief entry 112
See also SATA 33
Becker, Murray 1909(?)-1986
Obituary 118
Becker, Neesa 1951- .... SATA 123
Becker, Olga
See Frank, Rudolf
Becker, Palmer (Joseph) 1936- 143
Becker, Paula Lee 1941- 17-20R
Becker, Peter 1921- 53-56
Becker, Robert O(tto) 1923- 123
Becker, Robin (G.) 1951- CANR-109
Earlier sketches in CA 110, CANR-70
See also CWP
Becker, Ruby Wirt 1915- 33-36R
Becker, Russell J(ames) 1923- 37-40R
Becker, Samuel L(eo) 1923- CANR-7
Earlier sketch in CA 13-16R
Becker, Seymour 1934- 25-28R
Becker, Stephen (David) 1927-1999 . CANR-62
Earlier sketches in CA 5-8R, CANR-3
See also CAAS 1
See also CN 1, 2, 3, 4, 5, 6, 7
Becker, Suzy 231
Becker, Ted
See Becker, Theodore L(ewis)
Becker, Theodore L(ewis) 1932-
Brief entry 116
Becker, Thomas W(illiam) 1933- 5-8R
Becker, Walter 1950- .... CLC 26
Becker, Wesley C(lemence) 1928- 33-36R
Becker, William 1903(?)-1983
Obituary 110
Becker, William H(enry) 1943- 125
Beckerman, Bernard 1921-1985 .... CANR-19
Obituary 117
Earlier sketch in CA 1-4R
Beckerman, Ilene 1935- CANR-99
Earlier sketch in CA 151
Beckerman, Paul 1948- 141
Beckerman, Wilfred 1925- CANR-7
Earlier sketch in CA 17-20R
Beckert, Sven 1965- 200
Becket, Henry S. A.
See Goulden, Joseph C. (Jr.)
Beckett, Ian F(rederick) W(illiam) 1950- CANR-91
Earlier sketches in CA 120, CANR-45
Beckett, J(ames) C(amlin) 1912-1996
Obituary 151
Brief entry 114
Beckett, John A(ngus) 1916- 33-36R
Beckett, Kenneth A(lbert) 1929- CANR-51
Earlier sketches in CA 65-68, CANR-10, 28
Beckett, Lucy 1942- 49-52
Beckett, Mary 1926- 127
See also CN 7
See also DLB 319
Beckett, Ralph L(awrence) (Sr.) 1923-2005 .... 5-8R
Obituary 237
Beckett, Ronald Brymer 1891-1970 .... 5-8R
Beckett, Samuel (Barclay) 1906-1989 .... CANR-61
Obituary 130
Earlier sketches in CA 5-8R, CANR-33
See also BRWC 2
See also BRWR 1
See also BRWS 1
See also CBD
See also CDBLB 1945-1960
See also CLC 1, 2, 3, 4, 6, 9, 10, 11, 14, 18, 29, 57, 59, 83
See also CN 1, 2, 3, 4
See also CP 1, 2, 3, 4
See also DA
See also DA3
See also DAB
See also DAC
See also DAM DRAM, MST, NOV
See also DC 22
See also DFS 2, 7, 18
See also DLB 13, 15, 233, 319, 321
See also DLBY 1990
See also EWL 3
See also GFL 1789 to the Present
See also LATS 1:2
See also LMFS 2
See also MTCW 1, 2
See also MTFW 2005
See also RGSF 2
See also RGWL 2, 3
See also SSC 16, 74
See also SSFS 15
See also TCLC 145
See also TEA
See also WLC
See also WLIT 4
Beckett, Sandra L. 1953- 177
Beckett, Sheilah 1913- .... SATA 33
Beckett, Wendy 1930- 207
Beckey, Fred W(olfgang) 1923- 109
Beckford, George L(eslie Fitz-Gerald) 1934- 97-100
Beckford, Ruth 1925- 195
Beckford, William 1760-1844 .... BRW 3
See also DLB 39, 213
See also GL 2
See also HGG
See also LMFS 1
See also SUFW
Beckham, Barry (Earl) 1944- CANR-62
Earlier sketches in CA 29-32R, CANR-26
See also BLC 1
See also BW 1
See also CN 1, 2, 3, 4, 5, 6
See also DAM MULT
See also DLB 33
Beckham, Stephen Dow 1941- CANR-51
Earlier sketches in CA 61-64, CANR-12, 28
Beckhart, Benjamin Haggott 1897-1975
Obituary 57-60
Beckingham, Charles Fraser 1914-1998 .. 61-64
Obituary 170
Beckinsale, Monica 1914- 69-72
Beckinsale, Robert Percy 1908-1998 .. CANR-2
Obituary 169
Earlier sketch in CA 5-8R
Becklake, Sue 1943- 120
Beckler, Marion Floyd 1889-1978 .... CAP-1
Earlier sketch in CA 11-12
Beckles, Hilary McD(onald) 1955- 218
Beckles Willson, Robina (Elizabeth) 1930- CANR-43
Earlier sketches in CA 13-16R, CANR-5, 20
See also Willson, Robina Beckles
Beckley, Harlan R. 1943- 145
Beckman, Aldo Bruce 1934- 73-76
Beckman, Delores 1914-1994 121
See also SATA 51
Beckman, Gail McKnight 1938- 53-56
Beckman, Gunnel 1910- CANR-114
Earlier sketches in CA 33-36R, CANR-15
See also CLC 26
See also CLR 25
See also MAICYA 1, 2
See also SAAS 9
See also SATA 6
Beckman, Joshua (Saul) 180
Beckman, Kaj
See Beckman, Karin
Beckman, Karin 1913- .... SATA 45
Beckman, Linda Hunt 209
Beckman, Patti
See Boeckman, Patti
Beckman, Per (Frithiof) 1913- .... SATA 45
Beckman, Robert C(harles) 1934- 120
Beckmann, David M(ilton) 1948- CANR-8
Earlier sketch in CA 61-64
Beckmann, George Michael 1926- 5-8R
Beckmann, Martin J(osef) 1924- 37-40R
Beckmann, Petr 1924- 69-72
Beckner, Weldon (Earnest) 1933- 33-36R
Beckovic, Matiia 1939- 33-36R
See also Beckovic, Matija
See also DLB 181
Beckovic, Matija
See Beckovic, Matiia
See also EWL 3
Beckson, Karl 1926- CANR-92
Earlier sketches in CA 5-8R, CANR-2
Beckwith, B(rainerd) K(ellogg) 1902-1981 73-76
Beckwith, Burnham Putnam 1904-1989 .... 33-36R
Beckwith, Carol 1945- 195
Beckwith, Charles E(milio) 1917- 37-40R
Beckwith, Charlie A(lvin) 1929-1994 216
Beckwith, Harry 1949- 168

Beckwith 42 CONTEMPORARY AUTHORS

Beckwith, John Gordon 1918-1991 .... 9-12R
Beckwith, Jon
  See Beckwith, Jonathan R(oger)
Beckwith, Jonathan R(oger) 1935- 224
Beckwith, Lillian
  See Comber, Lillian
Beckwith, Paul 1905-1975
  Obituary 113
Beckwith, Yvonne 106
Becon, Thomas 1512(?)-1567
  See Basille, Theodore
  See also DLB 136
Becque, Henri 1837-1899 .... DC 21
  See also DLB 192
  See also GFL 1789 to the Present
Becquer, Gustavo Adolfo
  1836-1870 .... DAM MULT
  See also HLCS 1
Bedard, Anthony 233
Bedard, Michael 233
Bedard, Michael 1949- CANR-118
  Earlier sketch in CA 159
  See also AAYA 22
  See also CLR 35
  See also CWRI 5
  See also MAICYA 2
  See also MAICYAS 1
  See also SATA 93, 154
Bedard, Michelle
  See Finnigan, Joan (MacKenzie)
Bedard, Patrick Joseph 1941- 112
Bedard, Tony
  See Bedard, Anthony
Bedau, Hugo Adam 1926- CANR-41
  Earlier sketches in CA 9-12R, CANR-4, 19
Beddall, Barbara G(ould) 1919-1999 .... 33-36R
Beddall-Smith, Charles John 1916- 13-16R
Beddoe, Ellaruth
  See Elkins, Ella Ruth
Beddoes, Richard H(erbert) 1926- 37-40R
Beddoes, Thomas 1760-1808 .... DLB 158
Beddoes, Thomas Lovell 1803-1849 .. BRWS 11
  See also DC 15
  See also DLB 96
Beddows, Eric
  See Nutt, Ken
Bede c. 673-735 .... DLB 146
  See also TEA
Bede, Andrew
  See Beha, Ernest
Bede, Jean-Albert 1903-1977
  Obituary 69-72
Bedeian, Arthur G(eorge) 1946- 110
Bedell, George C(hester) 1928- 41-44R
Bedell, Geraldine 174
Bedell, L. Frank 1888-1984 .... CAP-1
  Earlier sketch in CA 13-16
Bedell, Madelon (Jane Berns)
  1922(?)-1986 136
  Obituary 119
Bedells, Phyllis 1893-1985
  Obituary 116
Bederman, Gail 1952- 151
Bedford, A. N.
  See Watson, Jane Werner
Bedford, Ann
  See Rees, Joan
Bedford, Annie North
  See Watson, Jane Werner
Bedford, Charles Harold 1929- 57-60
Bedford, David .... SATA 159
Bedford, Deborah 1958- 200
Bedford, Denton R. 1907-(?) .... NNAL
Bedford, Donald F.
  See Fearing, Kenneth (Flexner)
Bedford, Emmett G(runer) 1922- 45-48
Bedford, Henry F(rederick) 1931- 9-12R
Bedford, John
  See Hastings, Phyllis (Dora Hodge)
Bedford, Kenneth
  See Paine, Lauran (Bosworth)
Bedford, Martyn 1959- CANR-105
  Earlier sketch in CA 154
Bedford, Norton M(oore) 1916- 5-8R
Bedford, Steven McLeod 1953- 198
Bedford, Sybille 1911- CANR-106
  Earlier sketches in CA 9-12R, CANR-47
  See also CN 1, 2, 3, 4, 5, 6, 7
Bedford, Victoria Hilkevitch 177
Bedford-Jones, H(enry James O'Brien)
  1887-1949 157
  See also DLB 251
  See also FANT
Bedi, Ashok (R.) 1948- 189
Bediako, Kwabena Asare
  See Konadu, S(amuel) A(sare)
Bedikian, Antriganik A. 1886(?)-1980
  Obituary 93-96
Bedinger, Margery 1891-1983 57-60
Bedinger, Singleton B(erry) 1907-1985 49-52
Bedini, Silvio A. 1917- CANR-55
  Earlier sketches in CA 33-36R, CANR-13, 29
Bednar, Alfonz 1914-1989 .... EWL 3
Bednarek, Janet R. Daly 1959- 220
Bednarik, Charles (Philip) 1925- 77-80
Bednarik, Chuck
  See Bednarik, Charles (Philip)
Bedoukian, Kerop 1907-1981 93-96
  See also SATA 53
Bedoyere, Michael De La
  See De La Bedoyere, Michael
Bedregal, Yolanda 1913-1999 .... DLB 283
Bedrij, Orest (John) 1933- CANR-16
  Earlier sketch in CA 85-88
Bedsole, Adolph 1914- 13-16R
Bedts, Ralph F(ortes) de
  See de Bedts, Ralph F(ortes)
Bee, Clair (Francis) 1900-1983 .... CANR-78
  Obituary 109
  Earlier sketch in CA 1-4R
Bee, (John) David (Ashford) 1931- 17-20R
Bee, Helen L. 1939- CANR-16
  Earlier sketch in CA 89-92
Bee, Jay
  See Brainerd, John W(hiting)
Bee, Robert L(awrence) 1938- 113
Bee, Ronald J. 1955- 140
Beebe, (Ida) Ann 1919- 41-44R
Beebe, B(urdetta) F(aye)
  See Johnson, B(urdetta) F(aye)
  See also SATA 1
Beebe, Frank L(yman) 1914- 89-92
Beebe, Frederick S(essions) 1914-1973
  Obituary 41-44R
Beebe, H. Keith 1921- 29-32R
Beebe, Lucius 1902-1966
  Obituary 25-28R
Beebe, Maurice (Laverne) 1926- CANR-1
  Earlier sketch in CA 1-4R
Beebe, Ralph K(enneth) 1932- 33-36R
Beebe, (Charles) William 1877-1962 73-76
  See also DLB 275
  See also SATA 19
Beebee, Thomas O(liver) 1955- 222
Beeby, Betty 1923- .... SATA 25
Beeby, C(larence) E(dward) 1902-1998 109
Beeby, Dean 1954- CANR-117
  Earlier sketch in CA 151
Beech, George T(homas) 1931- 9-12R
Beech, Harold Reginald 1925- 25-28R
Beech, Keyes 1913-1990 .... CANR-78
  Obituary 130
  Earlier sketch in CA 33-36R
Beech, Robert (Paul) 1940- 33-36R
Beech, Webb
  See Butterworth, W(illiam) E(dmund III)
Beecham, Alice
  See Tubb, E(dwin) C(harles)
Beecham, Jahnna 237
  See also SATA 161
Beecham, Justin
  See Wintle, Justin (Beecham)
Beecham, Thomas 1879-1961
  Obituary 112
Beechcroft, William
  See Hallstead, William F(inn III)
Beecher, Catharine Esther 1800-1878 .... DLB 1, 243
Beecher, Donald A(llen) 1942- 135
Beecher, Henry Ward 1813-1887 .... DLB 3, 43, 250
Beecher, John 1904-1980 .... CANR-8
  Obituary 105
  Earlier sketch in CA 5-8R
  See also AITN 1
  See also CLC 6
  See also CP 1, 2, 3
Beecher, Jonathan French 1937- CANR-120
  Earlier sketch in CA 128
Beecher, Maureen Ursenbach 1935- 137
Beecher, William (M.) 1933- 65-68
Beechert, Edward D. 1920- 124
Beechhold, Henry F(rank) 1928- 33-36R
Beechick, Ruth 1925- CANR-25
  Earlier sketch in CA 108
Beeching, Jack 1922- CANR-13
  Earlier sketch in CA 21-24R
  See also SATA 14
Beechy, Winifred
  See Beechy, Winifred Nelson
Beechy, Winifred Nelson 1915- 116
Beeck, Franz Jozef van
  See van Beeck, Frans Jozef
Beecroft, John William Richard
  1902-1966 .... 5-8R
Beedell, Suzanne (Mollie) 1921- CANR-20
  Earlier sketch in CA 69-72
Beeding, Francis
  See Palmer, John (Leslie) and Saunders, Hilary Aidan St. George
Beegle, Charles William 1928- 106
Beegle, Dewey Maurice 1919-1995 .... 5-8R
Beegle, J(oseph) Allan 1918- 119
Beehler, Bruce M(cPherson) 1951- ... CANR-55
  Earlier sketch in CA 127
Beek, Martin(us) A(drianus) 1909- 13-16R
Beeke, Tiphanie .... SATA 163
Beekman, Allan 1913-2001 .... 33-36R
Beekman, E(ric) M(ontague) 1939- ... CANR-14
  Earlier sketch in CA 33-36R
Beekman, John 1918-1980 61-64
  Obituary 135
Beekman, Ross
  See Dey, Frederic (Merrill) Van Rensselaer
Beeks, Graydon 1919- 65-68
Beeler, Cecil Freeman 1915- 139
Beeler, Janet
  See Shaw, Janet
Beeler, Nelson F(rederick) 1910-1978 69-72
  See also SATA 13
Beeler, Selby B. 180
Beeler, Stephen P. 1943- 220
Beeman, Randal S(cott) 1963- 206
Beeman, Richard R(oy) 1942- 77-80
Beeman, Robin 1940- CANR-141
  Earlier sketch in CA 151
Beer, Barrett L(ynn) 1936- 49-52
Beer, Edith Hahn 1914- 235
Beer, Edith Lynn 1930- CANR-28
  Earlier sketches in CA 61-64, CANR-11
Beer, Eloise C. S. 1903-1979 .... 13-16R
Beer, Ethel S(ophia) 1897-1975 .... CAP-2
  Obituary 57-60
  Earlier sketch in CA 25-28
Beer, Francis Anthony 1939- CANR-10
  Earlier sketch in CA 25-28R
Beer, Gavin R(ylands) de
  See de Beer, Gavin R(ylands)
Beer, George L(ouis) 1872-1920 211
  See also DLB 47
Beer, Gillian (Patricia Kempster)
  1935- CANR-128
  Earlier sketch in CA 142
Beer, Jeanette (Mary Ayres) CANR-112
  Earlier sketches in CA 124, CANR-51
Beer, Johann 1655-1700 .... DLB 168
Beer, John B(ernard) 1926- CANR-49
  Earlier sketches in CA 5-8R, CANR-7, 23
Beer, Kathleen Costello 1926-2001 .... 25-28R
  Obituary 200
Beer, Lawrence W(ard) 1932- 37-40R
Beer, Lisl
  See Beer, Eloise C. S.
Beer, P. de
  See Bosman, Herman Charles
Beer, Patricia 1924- CANR-46
  Obituary 183
  Earlier sketches in CA 61-64, CANR-13
  See also CLC 58
  See also CP 1, 2, 3, 4
  See also CWP
  See also DLB 40
  See also FW
Beer, Ralph (Robert) 1947- CANR-64
  Earlier sketch in CA 120
  See also TCWW 2
Beer, Samuel Hutchison 1911- CANR-31
  Earlier sketch in CA 61-64
Beer, Vic
  See Bird, Vivian
Beer, William Reed 1943- CANR-31
  Earlier sketch in CA 112
Beerbohm, Max
  See Beerbohm, (Henry) Max(imilian)
Beerbohm, (Henry) Max(imilian)
  1872-1956 .... CANR-79
  Brief entry 104
  Earlier sketch in CA 154
  See also BRWS 2
  See also DLB 34, 100
  See also FANT
  See also MTCW 2
  See also TCLC 1, 24
Beere, Peter 1951- 151
  See also SATA 97
Beer-Hofmann, Richard 1866-1945 160
  See also DLB 81
  See also TCLC 60
Beers, Burton F(loyd) 1927- CANR-41
  Earlier sketches in CA 1-4R, CANR-19
Beers, Dorothy Sands 1917- 49-52
  See also SATA 9
Beers, Henry A(ugustin) 1847-1926 209
  See also DLB 71
Beers, Henry Putney 1907-1996 .... 13-16R
Beers, Lorna 1897-1989 49-52
  See also SATA 14
Beers, Mark H. 1954- CANR-138
  Earlier sketch in CA 140
Beers, Paul Benjamin 1931- 102
Beers, V(ictor) Gilbert 1928- CANR-90
  Earlier sketches in CA 49-52, CANR-1, 16, 36
  See also SATA 9, 130
Beers, William 1948- 137
Beery, Mary 1907-1999 .... 5-8R
Beesley, Amanda 1967- 221
Beesly, Patrick 1913-1986 .... CANR-15
  Obituary 120
  Earlier sketch in CA 85-88
Beeson, Trevor Randall 1926- 93-96
Beeth, Howard 1942- 144
Beeton, Max
  See Redding, Robert Hull
Beeton, (Douglas) Ridley 1929- 93-96
Beevers, John (Leonard) 1911-1975 61-64
Beevor, Antony 1946- CANR-124
  Earlier sketches in CA 129, CANR-67
Beevor, Kinta 1911-1995 189
Beezley, P(aul) C. 1895-1975 .... 5-8R
Beezley, William H(oward Taft)
  1942- CANR-27
  Earlier sketch in CA 49-52
Befu, Harumi 1930- 53-56
Beg, Shemus
  See Stephens, James
Beg, Toran
  See McKillop, Norman
Begam, Robert G(eorge) 1928- 127
Begay, Shonto 1954- .... CWRI 5
  See also SATA 137
Begaye, Lisa Shook
  See Beach, Lisa
Begelman, Mitchell (Craig) 1953- 154
Begg, A(lexander) Charles 1912-1991 102
Begg, Howard Bolton 1896-1967 .... 5-8R
Begg, Neil Colquhoun 1915-1995 102
Beggs, David W(hiteford) III
  1931-1966 .... CAP-1
  Earlier sketch in CA 13-16
Beggs, Donald L(ee) 1941- 33-36R
Beggs, Edward Larry 1933- CANR-56
  Earlier sketch in CA 89-92
Begiebing, Robert J(ohn) 1946- CANR-88
  Earlier sketches in CA 122, CANR-40
  See also CLC 70
Begin, Maryjane 1963- .... SATA 82
Begin, Menachem 1913-1992 186
  Brief entry 109
Begin, Menahem
  See Begin, Menachem
Begin-Callanan, Maryjane
  See Begin, Maryjane
Begleiter, Henri 1935- 119
Begley, James 1929- 25-28R
Begley, Kathleen A(nne) 1948- 77-80
  See also SATA 21
Begley, Louis 1933- CANR-98
  Earlier sketch in CA 140
  See also CLC 197
  See also DLB 299
  See also TCLE 1:1
Begley, Sharon (Lynn) 1956- 218
Begnal, Michael H(enry) 1939- 73-76
Begner, Edith 1918-1989 .... CANR-3
  Obituary 129
  Earlier sketch in CA 1-4R
Bego, Mark 1952- CANR-111
  Earlier sketch in CA 145
Begon, Elisabeth 1696-1755 .... DLB 99
Begoun, Paula 1953- 172
Begovic, Milan 1876-1948 .... EWL 3
Beha, Ernest 1908- CAP-1
  Earlier sketch in CA 13-14
Beha, Sister Helen Marie 1926- 21-24R
Behan, Brendan (Francis)
  1923-1964 .... CANR-121
  Earlier sketches in CA 73-76, CANR-33
  See also BRWS 2
  See also CBD
  See also CDBLB 1945-1960
  See also CLC 1, 8, 11, 15, 79
  See also DAM DRAM
  See also DFS 7
  See also DLB 13, 233
  See also EWL 3
  See also MTCW 1, 2
Behan, Brian 1926-2002 227
Behan, Dominic 1928(?)-1989
  Obituary 129
Behan, Leslie
  See Gottfried, Theodore Mark
Behar, Joy 1943- 223
Behar, Ruth 1956- 159
  See also HW 2
Behara, Devendra Nath 1940- 41-44R
Behbudiy, Mahmud Khoja 1874-1919 ... EWL 3
Behdad, Ali 1961- 206
Behee, John 1933- 112
Beher, Joy
  See Behar, Joy
Behle, William H(arroun) 1909- 5-8R
Behler, Deborah A. 1947- 218
  See also SATA 145
Behler, Ernst 1928- 41-44R
Behler, John L. 1943- 218
  See also SATA 145
Behling, Laura L. 1967- 214
Behlmer, George K(inkel) 1948- 123
Behlmer, Rudy 1926- CANR-8
  Earlier sketch in CA 57-60
Behm, Marc 1925- 101
Behm, William H(erman), Jr. 1922- 13-16R
Behme, Robert Lee 1924- 57-60
Behn, Aphra 1640(?)-1689 .... BRWS 3
  See also DA
  See also DA3
  See also DAB
  See also DAC
  See also DAM DRAM, MST, NOV, POET
  See also DC 4
  See also DFS 16
  See also DLB 39, 80, 131
  See also FW
  See also PC 13
  See also TEA
  See also WLC
  See also WLIT 3
Behn, Harry 1898-1973 .... CANR-5
  Obituary 53-56
  Earlier sketch in CA 5-8R
  See also CWRI 5
  See also DLB 61
  See also SATA 2
  See also SATA-Obit 34
  See also YAW
Behn, Noel 1928-1998 129
  Obituary 169
  Brief entry 116
Behn, Robert Dietrich 1941- 137
Behn, Robin .... PFS 21
Behney, John Bruce 1905-1987 101
Behnke, Charles A(lbert) 1891-1967 ...... CAP-2
  Earlier sketch in CA 19-20
Behnke, Frances L. 33-36R
  See also SATA 8
Behnke, John 1945- 69-72
Behnke, Leo 1933- 111
Behnke, Patricia (C.) 1954- 197
Behnke, Robert H. 1929- 215
Behr, Edward (Samuel) 1926- CANR-42
  Earlier sketches in CA 1-4R, CANR-3
Behr, Ira Steven 1953- 239
Behr, Joyce 1929- .... SATA 15
Behr, Marion 1939- 105
Behr, Mark 152
Behrend, Jeanne 1911-1988 .... 17-20R
Behrens, Earl (Charles) 1892-1985
  Obituary 116
Behrens, Ellen 1957- 153
Behrens, Helen Kindler 1922-1995 61-64
  Obituary 148
Behrens, Herman D(aniel) 1901-1988 .. 33-36R
Behrens, John C. 1933- CANR-14
  Earlier sketch in CA 37-40R
Behrens, June York 1925- CANR-24
  Earlier sketches in CA 17-20R, CANR-8
  See also SATA 19

Cumulative Index 43 Bell

Behrens, Roy R(ichard) 1946- 110
Behrman, Carol H(elen) 1925- CANR-124
Earlier sketches in CA 61-64, CANR-7, 22, 46
See also SATA 14, 144
Behrman, Cynthia F(ansler) 1931- 123
Behrman, Daniel 1923-1990 65-68
Obituary 131
Behrman, Jack N(ewton) 1922- CANR-30
Earlier sketch in CA 29-32R
Behrman, Lucy Creevey
See Creevey, Lucy E.
Behrman, S(amuel) N(athaniel)
1893-1973 .... CAP-1
Obituary 45-48
Earlier sketch in CA 13-16
See also CAD
See also CLC 40
See also DLB 7, 44
See also IDFW 3
See also MAL 5
See also RGAL 4
Behrstock, Barry 1948- 106
Bei, Dao 139
See also Shi Mo and
Zhenkai, Zhao
See also RGWL 3
Beichman, Arnold 1913- CANR-31
Earlier sketch in CA 49-52
Beichner, Paul E(dward) 1912- 33-36R
Bei Dao
See Zhenkai, Zhao
See also CWW 2
See also EWL 3
Beidelman, T(homas) O(wen) 1931- 129
Beiderwell, Bruce 1952- 137
Beidler, Peter G. 1940- 193
Beier, Ernst G(unter) 1916- 21-24R
Beier, Ulli 1922- CANR-4
Earlier sketch in CA 9-12R
Beierle, Andrew W. M. 238
Beifuss, John, (Jr.) 1959- 156
See also SATA 92
Beigbeder, Frederic 1965- 207
Beigel, Allan 1940-1996 101
Obituary 152
Beigel, Herbert 1944- 97-100
Beigel, Hugo George 1897-1978 .... 37-40R
Beik, Paul H(arold) 1915- 13-16R
Beik, William (Humphrey) 1941- 123
Beil, Karen Magnuson 1950- 180
See also SATA 124
Beilenson, Edna 1909-1981 .... CANR-29
Obituary 103
Earlier sketch in CA 85-88
Beilenson, Laurence W. 1899-1988 ...... 29-32R
Obituary 125
Beiler, Edna 1923- CANR-1
Earlier sketch in CA 1-4R
See also SATA 61
Beilhart, Jacob 1867-1908 211
Beilharz, Edwin Alanson
1907-1986 .... CANR-27
Obituary 120
Earlier sketch in CA 33-36R
Beilharz, Peter (Michael) 1953- CANR-112
Earlier sketches in CA 127, CANR-55
Beim, Norman 1923- 85-88
See also DFS 18
Beine, George Holmes 1893-1987 93-96
Beineix, Jean-Jacques 1946- 124
Beiner, Ronald 1953- CANR-42
Earlier sketch in CA 117
Beinhart, Larry 1947- 138
Beinicke, Steve 1956- .... SATA 69
Beining, Guy 1938- .... CAAS 30
Beirne, Barbara 1933- .... SATA 71
Beirne, Brother Kilian 1896-1976 .... 21-24R
Obituary 134
Beirne, Gerald E(dward) 1936- 118
Beirne, Joseph Anthony 1911-1974 45-48
Obituary 53-56
Beiser, Arthur 1931- 93-96
See also SATA 22
Beiser, Frederick C. 1949- 128
Beiser, Germaine 1931- .... SATA 11
Beisner, Robert L(ee) 1936- CANR-129
Earlier sketch in CA 25-28R
Beissel, Henry Eric 1929- CANR-10
Earlier sketch in CA 65-68
See also CP 1, 2, 3, 4
Beisser, Arnold R(ay) 1925-1991 .... 25-28R
Beissinger, Steven R. 1953- 146
Beistle, Shirley
See Climo, Shirley
Beit-Hallahmi, Benjamin 1943- 105
Beitler, Ethel Jane (Heinkel)
1906-1983 .... CANR-2
Earlier sketch in CA 5-8R
Beitler, Stanley (Samuel) 1924- 5-8R
Beitz, Charles R(ichard) 1949- CANR-1
Earlier sketch in CA 49-52
Beitzell, Edwin Warfield 1905(?)-1984
Obituary 114
Beitzell, Robert (E.) 1930-
Brief entry 115
Beitzinger, A(lfons) J(oseph) 1918- 45-48
Beizer, Boris 1934- 105
Beja, Morris 1935- 29-32R
Bejerot, Nils 1921- 29-32R
Bekederemo, J. P. Clark
See Clark Bekederemo, J(ohnson) P(epper)
See also CD 6
Bekessy, Janos
See Habe, Hans
Bekker, Hugo 1925- 41-44R
Bekker-Nielsen, Hans 1933- CANR-18
Earlier sketch in CA 25-28R
Beklemishev, Iurii Solomonovich
See Krymov, Iurii Solomonovich
Bekoff, Marc 1945- 218
Belair, Felix, Jr. 1907-1978
Obituary 77-80
Belair, Richard L. 1934- 13-16R
See also SATA 45
Belamri, Rabah 1946-1995 .... EWL 3
Beland, Pierre 1947- 153
Belaney, Archibald Stansfeld 1888-1938
Brief entry 114
See also Grey Owl
See also DLBD 17
See also SATA 24
Belanger, Andre J. 1935- 189
Belanger, Jerome D(avid) 1938- 69-72
Belasco, David 1853-1931 168
Brief entry 104
See also DLB 7
See also MAL 5
See also RGAL 4
See also TCLC 3
Belbel, Sergi 1963- 208
Belbin, David 1958- 175
See also SATA 106
Belbin, Joseph 1958- 175
Belcastro, Joseph 1910-1989 .... CAP-2
Earlier sketch in CA 19-20
Belch, Caroline Jean 1916- 45-48
Belchem, David
See Belchem, R(onald) F(rederick) K(ing)
Belchem, John (Charles) 1948- 238
Belchem, R(onald) F(rederick) K(ing)
1911-1981 122
Obituary 108
Belcher, Jerry 1930-1987
Obituary 124
Belcher, Wendy (Laura) 1962- CANR-86
Earlier sketch in CA 130
Belcheva, Elisaveta Lyubomirova 1893-1991
See Bagryana, Elisaveta
See also CLC 10
Belden, Gail
See Belden, Louise Conway
Belden, Jack 1910-1989
Obituary 128
Belden, Louise Conway 1910- 104
Belden, Wilanne Schneider 1925- CANR-23
Earlier sketch in CA 106
See also SATA 56
Belding, Robert E(dward) 1911-1989 ..... 33-36R
Beldone, Phil "Cheech"
See Ellison, Harlan (Jay)
Belehradek, Jan 1896-1980
Obituary 97-100
Belen
See Kaplan, Nelly
Beleno
See Azuela, Mariano
Beletsky, Les
See Beletsky, Les D.
Beletsky, Les D. 1956- 192
Belew, M. Wendell 1922- 33-36R
Belfer, Nancy 1930- 85-88
Belfield, Eversley (Michael Gallimore)
1918- CANR-11
Earlier sketch in CA 25-28R
Belfiglio, Valentine J(ohn) 1934- CANR-51
Earlier sketches in CA 49-52, CANR-11, 28
Belford, Barbara 1935- CANR-104
Earlier sketches in CA 136, CANR-59
Belford, Lee A(rcher) 1913-1988 .... 17-20R
Belfrage, Cedric H. 1904-1990 .... CANR-3
Obituary 132
Earlier sketch in CA 9-12R
Belfrage, Sally 1936-1994 .... CANR-45
Obituary 144
Earlier sketch in CA 105
See also SATA 65
See also SATA-Obit 79
Bel Geddes, Joan
See Geddes, Joan Bel
Belgion, (Harold) Montgomery
1892-1973 .... CAP-1
Earlier sketch in CA 13-14
Belgrad, Daniel 1964- 209
Belgum, David 1922- CANR-6
Earlier sketch in CA 13-16R
Belieu, Erin 1965- CANR-100
Earlier sketch in CA 160
Belin, David W. 1928-1999 85-88
Obituary 173
Belin, Esther G. 1968- 202
Beling, Willard A(dolf) 1919- 53-56
Belinkov, Arkady Viktorovich 1922(?)-1970
Obituary 29-32R
Belinski, Vissarion Grigoryevich
1811-1848 .... DLB 198
Belisle, Louis-Alexandre 1902-1985
Obituary 117
Belitsky, A(braham) Harvey 1929- 33-36R
Belitt, Ben 1911- CANR-77
Earlier sketches in CA 13-16R, CANR-7
See also CAAS 4
See also CLC 22
See also CP 1, 2, 3, 4
See also DLB 5
Belk, Fred Richard 1937- 115
Belkaoui, Ahmed R.
See Riahi-Belkaoui, Ahmed
Belkin, Aaron 1966- 235
Belkin, Gary S(tuart) 1945- 114
Belkin, Kristin Lohse 180
Belkin, Lisa 1960- CANR-139
Earlier sketch in CA 141
Belkin, Samuel 1911-1976 .... CANR-6
Obituary 65-68
Earlier sketch in CA 1-4R
Belkind, Allen 1927- 29-32R
Belknap, B. H.
See Ellis, Edward S(ylvester)
Belknap, Boynton
See Ellis, Edward S(ylvester)
Belknap, Boynton M.D.
See Ellis, Edward S(ylvester)
Belknap, Ivan (Carl) 1916- 5-8R
Belknap, Jeremy 1744-1798 .... DLB 30, 37
Belknap, Robert H(arlan) 1917- 45-48
Belknap, Robert L(amont) 1929- 33-36R
Belknap, S(ally) Yancey 1895-1987 .... CAP-1
Earlier sketch in CA 11-12
Bell, A(rthur) Donald 1920- 25-28R
Bell, Adrian (Hanbury) 1901-1980 ... CANR-69
Obituary 102
Earlier sketch in CA 97-100
See also DLB 191
Bell, Alan P(aul) 1932-2002 .... CANR-13
Obituary 208
Earlier sketch in CA 33-36R
Bell, Albert A., Jr. 1945- 142
Bell, Anne Olivier 1916- 112
Bell, Anthea 1936- CANR-140
Earlier sketch in CA 152
See also SATA 88, 148
Bell, Arthur 1939-1984 .... CANR-72
Obituary 112
Earlier sketch in CA 85-88
Bell, Barbara Currier 1941- 115
Bell, Barbara Mosallai 1937- 150
Bell, Bernard Iddings 1886-1958 204
Bell, Bernard W(illiam) 1936-
Brief entry 117
Bell, Betty
See Bell, Lorna Beatrice
Bell, Betty Louise 1949- 145
Bell, Carol
See Flavell, Carol Willsey Bell
Bell, Carolyn L.
See Rigoni, Orlando (Joseph)
Bell, Carolyn Shaw 1920- 29-32R
Bell, Charles G. 1929- 37-40R
See also CP 3
Bell, Charles Greenleaf 1916- CANR-2
Earlier sketch in CA 1-4R
See also CAAS 12
See also CP 1, 2
Bell, Chip R(ay) 1944- CANR-101
Earlier sketch in CA 121
Bell, Clare (Louise) 1952- CANR-122
Earlier sketch in CA 157
See also BYA 6
See also FANT
See also SATA 99
Bell, (Arthur) Clive (Howard)
1881-1964 .... CANR-72
Obituary 89-92
Earlier sketch in CA 97-100
See also DLBD 10
See also MTCW 1
Bell, Colin (John) 1938- CANR-32
Earlier sketch in CA 29-32R
Bell, Corydon Whitten 1894-1980 .... 5-8R
See also SATA 3
Bell, Daniel 1919- CANR-117
Earlier sketches in CA 1-4R, CANR-4
See also DLB 246
Bell, David A(rnold) 1945- 156
Bell, David Owen 1949- 167
See also SATA 99
Bell, David R(obert) 1932- 93-96
Bell, David S(heffield) 1945- CANR-141
Earlier sketch in CA 61-64
Bell, David Victor John 1944- CANR-38
Earlier sketches in CA 45-48, CANR-1, 17
Bell, Derrick
See Bell, Derrick A(lbert), Jr.
Bell, Derrick A(lbert), Jr. 1930- CANR-124
Earlier sketch in CA 104
See also BW 2
Bell, Diane 1943- 197
Bell, Earl Hoyt 1903-1963 .... 1-4R
Bell, Edward L. 1963- 213
Bell, Eileen 1907-2005 .... 33-36R
Obituary 235
Bell, Elizabeth Rose 1912- 106
Bell, Elizabeth S. 1946- 128
Bell, Elliot V(allance) 1902-1983
Obituary 108
Bell, Emerson
See Stratemeyer, Edward L.
Bell, Emily Mary
See Cason, Mabel Earp
Bell, Eric Temple 1883-1960 200
See also Taine, John
See also SFW 4
Bell, Eudorus N. 1866-1923 215
Bell, Frank
See Benson, Mildred (Augustine Wirt)
Bell, Gail Winther 1936- 41-44R
Bell, Gavin 229
Bell, Gawain (Westray) 1909-1995 131
Bell, Geoffrey (Lakin) 1939-
Brief entry 114
Bell, Geoffrey Foxall 1896-1984
Obituary 111
Bell, Georgianna
See Rundle, Anne
Bell, Gerald D(ean) 1937- 49-52
Bell, Gertrude (Margaret Lowthian)
1868-1926 .... CANR-110
Earlier sketch in CA 167
See also DLB 174
See also TCLC 67
Bell, Gertrude (Wood) 1911-1987 .... 13-16R
See also SATA 12
Bell, Gina
See Balzano, Jeanne (Koppel)
Bell, Gordon Bennett 1934- 104
Bell, H(arold) Idris 1879-1967 .... CAP-1
Earlier sketch in CA 13-14
Bell, Harry McAra 1899- CAP-1
Earlier sketch in CA 13-14
Bell, Hazel K(athleen) 1935- 227
Bell, Herbert C(lifford Francis) 1881-1966
Obituary 113
Bell, Herbert W. 1922- 123
Bell, Hilari 1958- 231
See also SATA 151
Bell, Hilary 1966- 235
See also CD 5, 6
Bell, Ian A.
See Bell, Ian F. A.
Bell, Ian F. A. 1932- 152
Bell, Ilona 194
Bell, Irene Wood 1944- 89-92
Bell, J(ohn) Bowyer 1931-2003 .... 17-20R
Obituary 219
Bell, J. Freeman
See Zangwill, Israel
Bell, Jack L. 1904-1975 .... CANR-6
Obituary 61-64
Earlier sketch in CA 1-4R
Bell, Jadrien
See Golden, Christie
Bell, James (Adrian) 1917-1992 73-76
Bell, James B. 1932- 101
Bell, James Edward 1941- 33-36R
Bell, James K(enton) 1937- 25-28R
Bell, James Madison 1826-1902 124
Brief entry 122
See also BLC 1
See also BW 1
See also DAM MULT
See also DLB 50
See also TCLC 43
Bell, James Scott 1954- 207
Bell, Janet
See Clymer, Eleanor
Bell, Janet Cheatham 1937- 197
See also SATA 127
Bell, John
See Johnson, Victor Hugo
Bell, John (Donnelly) 1944- 97-100
Bell, John C. 1902(?)-1981
Obituary 103
Bell, John Elderkin 1913-1995 81-84
Bell, John Patrick 1935- 101
Bell, Joseph N. 1921- 5-8R
Bell, Josephine
See Ball, Doris Bell (Collier)
Bell, Joyce 1920- CANR-8
Earlier sketch in CA 57-60
Bell, Joyce Denebrink 1936- 17-20R
Bell, Julian (Heward) 1908-1937 158
Bell, Julian 1952- 185
Bell, Krista (Anne Blakeney) 1950- 196
See also SATA 126
Bell, L. Nelson 1894-1973 .... CAP-1
Obituary 45-48
Earlier sketch in CA 19-20
Bell, Leland V(irgil) 1934- 49-52
Bell, Linda R. 1949- 117
Bell, Lorna Beatrice 1902-1996 117
Bell, Louise Price CAP-1
Earlier sketch in CA 9-10
Bell, Madison Smartt 1957- 183
Earlier sketches in CA 111, CANR-28, 54, 73, 134
Autobiographical Essay in 183
See also AMWS 10
See also BPFB 1
See also CLC 41, 102
See also CN 5, 6, 7
See also CSW
See also DLB 218, 278
See also MTCW 2
See also MTFW 2005
Bell, Malcolm (H.) 1931- 122
Bell, Margaret E(lizabeth) 1898-1990 . CANR-1
Earlier sketch in CA 1-4R
See also SATA 2
Bell, Mark R(obert) 1975- 236
Bell, Martin 1918- .... CP 1, 2
Bell, Marvin (Hartley) 1937- CANR-102
Earlier sketches in CA 21-24R, CANR-59
See also CAAS 14
See also CLC 8, 31
See also CP 1, 2, 3, 4, 5, 6, 7
See also DAM POET
See also DLB 5
See also MAL 5
See also MTCW 1
Bell, Mary Hayley
See Hayley Bell, Mary
Bell, Mary Reeves 1946- 152
See also SATA 88
Bell, Michael Davitt 1941- CANR-15
Earlier sketch in CA 81-84
Bell, Millicent (L.) CANR-36
Earlier sketch in CA 114
See also DLB 111
Bell, Nancy 1932- CANR-144
Earlier sketch in CA 171
Bell, Neil 1887-1964 .... HGG

Bell 44 CONTEMPORARY AUTHORS

Bell, Neill 1946- 118
See also SATA-Brief 50
Bell, Norman (Edward) 1899- 61-64
See also SATA 11
Bell, Norman W. 1928- CANR-1
Earlier sketch in CA 1-4R
Bell, Oliver (Sydney) 1913-1980 53-56
Bell, Philip W(ilkes) 1924- CANR-26
Earlier sketch in CA 29-32R
Bell, Quentin (Claudian Stephen) 1910-1996 .... CANR-51
Obituary 155
Earlier sketch in CA 57-60
See also DLB 155
Bell, R(obert) C(harles) 1917- CANR-24
Earlier sketches in CA 17-20R, CANR-7
Bell, Raymond Martin 1907-1999 .... 29-32R
See also SATA 13
Bell, Richard H. 1938- 145
Bell, Robert (Ivan) 1942- 101
Bell, Robert E(ugene) 1914- 37-40R
Bell, Robert E(ugene) 1926- 138
Bell, Robert Roy 1924- CANR-1
Earlier sketch in CA 1-4R
Bell, Robert S(tanley) W(arren) 1871-1921
Brief entry 115
See also SATA-Brief 27
Bell, Robert Vaughn 1924-1997 .... CANR-64
Earlier sketch in CA 110
See also TCWW 2
Bell, Robin
See Jones, John F(inbar)
Bell, Roger 1947- CANR-48
Earlier sketch in CA 122
Bell, (Caroline) Rose (Buchanan) 1939- 29-32R
Bell, Roseann P. 1945- 120
See also BW 2
Bell, Rudolph M(ark) 1942- CANR-85
Earlier sketches in CA 45-48, CANR-48
Bell, Sallie Lee -1970 .... CANR-1
Earlier sketch in CA 1-4R
Bell, Sarah Fore 1920- 53-56
Bell, Sidney 1929- 41-44R
Bell, Stephen (Scott) 1935- 65-68
Bell, Ted 1947- 223
Bell, Terrel H(oward) 1921-1996 144
Obituary 152
Bell, Thelma Harrington 1896-1985 . CANR-69
Earlier sketch in CA 1-4R
See also SATA 3
Bell, Thornton
See Fanthorpe, R(obert) Lionel
Bell, Vanessa 1879-1961 145
See also DLBD 10
Bell, Vicars W(alker) 1904-1988 .... CAP-1
Earlier sketch in CA 13-16
Bell, W. L. D.
See Mencken, H(enry) L(ouis)
Bell, Wendell 1924- CANR-4
Earlier sketch in CA 1-4R
Bell, Whitfield Jenks, Jr. 1914- 105
Bell, William 1945- CANR-123
Earlier sketch in CA 155
See also CLR 91
See also MAICYA 2
See also SATA 90
See also YAW
Bell, William J. .... AITN 1
Bell, William Stewart 1921-1980 .... 1-4R
Bell, Winifred 1914- CANR-9
Earlier sketch in CA 17-20R
Bellacera, Carole 207
Bellah, James Warner 1899-1976 .... CANR-61
Obituary 69-72
Earlier sketch in CA 5-8R
See also TCWW 1, 2
Bellah, Robert N(eelly) 1927- 21-24R
Bellairs, George
See Blundell, Harold
Bellairs, John (Anthony) 1938-1991 . CANR-24
Obituary 133
Earlier sketches in CA 21-24R, CANR-8
See also BYA 4, 5
See also CLR 37
See also FANT
See also JRDA
See also MAICYA 1, 2
See also SATA 2, 68, 160
See also SATA-Obit 66
Bellak, Leopold 1916-2000 .... CANR-40
Obituary 190
Earlier sketches in CA 85-88, CANR-16
Bellamann, Henry 1882-1945 .... RHW
Bellamy, Atwood C.
See Mencken, H(enry) L(ouis)
Bellamy, Christopher (David) 1955- 157
Bellamy, David (James) 1933- 180
Brief entry 114
Bellamy, Edward 1850-1898 .... DLB 12
See also NFS 15
See also RGAL 4
See also SFW 4
Bellamy, Francis Rufus 1886-1972
Obituary 33-36R
Bellamy, Guy 1935- CANR-34
Earlier sketches in CA 65-68, CANR-9
Bellamy, Harmon
See Bloom, Herman Irving
Bellamy, J(ohn) G. 1930- 174
Bellamy, James A(ndrew) 1925- 49-52
Bellamy, Joe David 1941- CANR-34
Earlier sketches in CA 41-44R, CANR-15
Bellamy, John fl. 1620-1651 .... DLB 170
Bellamy, Joseph 1719-1790 .... DLB 31
Bellamy, Joyce (M.) 1921-2002 216
Bellamy, Peter 1914-1989
Brief entry 117
Bellamy, Ralph (Rexford) 1904-1991 101
Obituary 136
Bellamy, Richard (Paul) 1957- 141
Bellan, Ruben C. 1918- 13-16R
Belle, Jennifer 1968- 194
Belle, Kathryn
See Lynn (Ruiz), Kathryn
Belle, Pamela 1952- CANR-61
Earlier sketches in CA 115, CANR-38
See also RHW
Belleau, Remy 1528-1577 ... GFL Beginnings to 1789
Bellechild, Karen
See Stein, Karen
Beller, Anne Scott 77-80
Beller, Elmer Adolph 1894-1980
Obituary 97-100
Beller, Jacob 1896- CAP-2
Earlier sketch in CA 25-28
Beller, Joel 1926- 113
Beller, Miles 1951- CANR-101
Earlier sketch in CA 134
Beller, Steven (Peter) 1958- 133
Beller, Susan Provost 1949- CANR-109
Earlier sketch in CA 151
See also SATA 84, 128
Beller, Thomas
See Beller, Tom
Beller, Tom 1965- 150
Beller, William Stern 1919- 5-8R
Bellerby, (Mary Eireen) Frances Parker 1899-1975 101
See also CP 1, 2
Bellesiles, Michael A. 217
Belleville, Bill 1945- 220
Bellezza, Dario 1944-1995 209
See also DLB 128
Bellhouse, Alan Robert 1914-1980
Obituary 108
Belli, Angela 1935- 37-40R
Belli, Carlos German
See Belli, Carlos German
See also DLB 290
Belli, Carlos German 1927- 131
See also Belli, Carlos German
See also DLB 290
See also EWL 3
See also HW 1
Belli, Gioconda 1948- CANR-143
Earlier sketch in CA 152
See also CWW 2
See also DLB 290
See also EWL 3
See also HLCS 1
See also RGWL 3
Belli, Melvin M(ouron) 1907-1996 ... CANR-34
Obituary 152
Earlier sketch in CA 104
Bellin, Andy 1968(?)- 210
Bellin, Edward J.
See Kuttner, Henry
Bellingham, Brenda 1931- CANR-54
Earlier sketch in CA 123
See also SATA 99
See also SATA-Brief 51
Bellingham, Helen Mary Dorothea
See Beauclerk, Helen De Vere
Bellini delle Stelle, Pier Luigi 1920(?)-1984
Obituary 111
Belliotti, Raymond A(ngelo) 1948- 143
Bellis, David James 1944- 108
Bellisario, Donald P. 1935- 151
Belliveau, G(regory) K(enneth) 1965- 188
Bellm, Dan 1952- 170
Bellman, Richard (Ernest) 1920-1984 .... CANR-80
Obituary 112
Earlier sketches in CA 69-72, CANR-12
Bellman, Samuel Irving 1926- CANR-7
Earlier sketch in CA 17-20R
Bellman, Willard F. 1920- 113
Bell-Metereau, Rebecca 1949- 122
Bellmon, Patricia 1948- 140
Bello, Andres 1781-1865 .... LAW
Bello, Francis (Cesare) 1917-1987
Obituary 121
Bello, Rosario de
See De Bello, Rosario
Belloc, (Joseph) Hilaire (Pierre Sebastien Rene Swanton) 1870-1953 152
Brief entry 106
See also CLR 102
See also CWRI 5
See also DAM POET
See also DLB 19, 100, 141, 174
See also EWL 3
See also MTCW 2
See also MTFW 2005
See also PC 24
See also SATA 112
See also TCLC 7, 18
See also WCH
See also YABC 1
Belloc, Joseph Peter Rene Hilaire
See Belloc, (Joseph) Hilaire (Pierre Sebastien Rene Swanton)
Belloc, Joseph Pierre Hilaire
See Belloc, (Joseph) Hilaire (Pierre Sebastien Rene Swanton)
Belloc, M. A.
See Lowndes, Marie Adelaide (Belloc)
Belloc, Madame
See Parkes, Bessie Rayner
Bellochio, Marco 1939- 110
Belloc-Lowndes, Mrs.
See Lowndes, Marie Adelaide (Belloc)
Bellocq, Louise
See Boudat, Marie-Louise
Belloli, Andrea P. A. 1947- CANR-144
Earlier sketch in CA 151
See also SATA 86
Bellonci, Maria 1902-1986 218
Obituary 120
See also DLB 196
Bellone, Enrico 1938- 106
Bellony, Alice 1925- 118
Bellony-Rewald, Alice
See Bellony, Alice
Bellos, David 1945- CANR-92
Earlier sketch in CA 153
Bellosi, Luciano 1936- 218
Bellot, Leland J(oseph) 1936-
Brief entry 115
Bellotti, Laura Golden 1947- 137
Bellow, Adam 1957- 225
Bellow, Saul 1915-2005 .... CANR-132
Obituary 238
Earlier sketches in CA 5-8R, CANR-29, 53, 95
See also CABS 1
See also AITN 2
See also AMW
See also AMWC 2
See also AMWR 2
See also BEST 89:3
See also BPFB 1
See also CDALB 1941-1968
See also CLC 1, 2, 3, 6, 8, 10, 13, 15, 25, 33, 34, 63, 79, 190, 200
See also CN 1, 2, 3, 4, 5, 6, 7
See also DA
See also DA3
See also DAB
See also DAC
See also DAM MST, NOV, POP
See also DLB 2, 28, 299
See also DLBD 3
See also DLBY 1982
See also EWL 3
See also MAL 5
See also MTCW 1, 2
See also MTFW 2005
See also NFS 4, 14
See also RGAL 4
See also RGSF 2
See also SSC 14
See also SSFS 12
See also TUS
See also WLC
Bellows, Barbara L(awrence) 1950- 145
Bellows, James G(ilbert) 1922- CANR-123
Earlier sketch in CA 102
Interview in CA-102
Bellows, Nathaniel 1972- 226
Bellows, Roger Marion 1905- 1-4R
Bellows, Thomas J(ohn) 1935-1997 .. CANR-31
Earlier sketch in CA 45-48
Bellush, Bernard 1917- 132
Brief entry 120
Bellush, Jewel (Lubin) 1959- 152
Bell-Villada, Gene Harold 1941- 105
Bellville, Cheryl Walsh 1944- CANR-71
Earlier sketch in CA 109
See also SATA 54
See also SATA-Brief 49
Bellville, Rod 1944- 117
Bell-Zano, Gina
See Balzano, Jeanne (Koppel)
Belmondo, Jean-Paul 1933- 174
Belmont, Bob
See Reynolds, Dallas McCord
Belmont, Eleanor Robson 1879-1979
Obituary 97-100
Belmont(-Pelorson), Georges (Jean-Claude) 1909- CANR-139
Earlier sketch in CA 29-32R
Belmont, Herman S. 1920- 41-44R
Belmonte, Kevin Charles 224
Belmonte, Thomas 1946-1995 93-96
Obituary 148
Belnap, Nuel 1930- 144
Belo, Fernando 1933- 131
Beloff, John 1920- 147
Beloff, Max 1913-1999 .... CANR-18
Obituary 177
Earlier sketch in CA 5-8R
Beloff, Michael 1942- 21-24R
Beloff, Nora 1919-1997 106
Obituary 156
Belok, Michael V(ictor) 1923- 33-36R
Beloof, Robert 1923- 21-24R
See also CP 1
Belote, James H(ine) 1922-1988 .... 33-36R
Belote, Julianne 1929- 61-64
Belote, William Milton 1922- 49-52
Belotserkovsky, Vladimir Naumovich Bill
See Bill-Belotserkovsky, Vladimir Naumovich
Belous, Russell E. 1925- 25-28R
Belov, Vasilii Vladimirovna 1932- .... DLB 302
Belozersky, Andrei (Nicolaevich) 1905-1972
Obituary 37-40R
Belpre, Pura 1899-1982 73-76
Obituary 109
See also SATA 16
See also SATA-Obit 30
Bels, Alberts 1938- .... DLB 232
See also EWL 3
Belser, Lee 1925(?)-1988 73-76
Obituary 127
Belser, Reimond Karel Maria de 1929- 152
See also Ruyslinck, Ward
Belsevica, Vizma 1931- .... CDWLB 4
See also DLB 232
Belsey, Catherine 1940- 142
Belshaw, Cyril S(hirley) 1921- 9-12R
Belshaw, John Douglas 1957- 238
Belshaw, Michael (Horace) 1928- 21-24R
Belshaw, Patrick (Edward Blakiston) 1936- . 148
Belsky, Dick 1945- CANR-48
Earlier sketch in CA 122
Belsky, R(ichard) G. 174
Belsley, David A(lan) 1939- 29-32R
Belth, Joseph M(orton) 1929- 112
Belth, Nathan C. 1909(?)-1989
Obituary 128
Belting, Hans 1951- CANR-140
Earlier sketch in CA 155
Belting, Natalia Maree 1915-1997 ... CANR-70
Earlier sketches in CA 1-4R, CANR-3
See also SATA 6
Beltman, Brian W. 1945- 156
Belton, John Raynor 1931- 69-72
See also SATA 22
Belton, Sandra (Yvonne) 1939- CANR-115
Earlier sketch in CA 151
See also SATA 85, 134
Beltrametti, Franco 1937- .... CAAS 13
Beltran, Alberto 1923- .... SATA 43
Beltran, Miriam 1914- 33-36R
Beltran, Pedro (Gerardo) 1897-1979 93-96
Obituary 85-88
Beltran-Hernandez, Irene 1945- .... SATA 74
Belue, Ted Franklin 1954- CANR-124
Earlier sketch in CA 171
Belushi, John 1949-1982
Obituary 106
Belveal, L(orenzo) Dee 1918- 21-24R
Belvedere, Lee
See Grayland, Valerie (Merle Spanner)
Bely, Andrey
See Bugayev, Boris Nikolayevich
See also DLB 295
See also EW 9
See also EWL 3
See also PC 11
See also TCLC 7
Bely, Jeanette L(obach) 1916-1995 .... 33-36R
Belyaev, Aleksandr 1884-1942(?) 166
See also SFW 4
Belyi, Andrei
See Bugayev, Boris Nikolayevich
See also RGWL 2, 3
Belz, Carl 1937- CANR-26
Earlier sketches in CA 29-32R, CANR-11
Belz, Herman (Julius) 1937- 65-68
Belzer, Richard 1944- 206
Bem, Sandra Lipsitz 183
Bemba, Sylvain 1934-1995 .... EWL 3
Bemberg, Maria Luisa 1922-1995 233
Bembo, Pietro 1470-1547 .... RGWL 2, 3
Bemelmans, Ludwig 1898-1962 .... CANR-81
Earlier sketch in CA 73-76
See also CLR 6, 93
See also CWRI 5
See also DLB 22
See also MAICYA 1, 2
See also RGAL 4
See also SATA 15, 100
See also WCH
Bemis, Samuel Flagg 1891-1973 .... 9-12R
Obituary 45-48
See also DLB 17
Bemis, Stephen Edward 1937-1985
Obituary 115
Bemister, Henry
See Barrett, Harry B(emister)
Bemporad, Jules (Richard) 1937- 122
Bemrose, John 1947- 234
Ben, Ilke
See Harper, Carol Ely
Benabib, Kim 174
Benacerraf, Baruj 1920- 171
Benagh, Jim 1937- CANR-9
Earlier sketch in CA 57-60
Benaissa, Slimane 1943- 239
Ben-Ami, Shlomo 1943- 116
Ben-Ami, Yitshaq 1913-1984 130
Ben Ammi 1939- 207
Ben-Amos, Dan 1934- CANR-123
Earlier sketches in CA 69-72, CANR-11
Ben-Amotz, Dahn
See Ben-Amotz, Dan
Ben-Amotz, Dan 1923(?)-1989
Obituary 130
See also Ben-Amotz, Dahn
Benamou, Michel J(ean) 1929-1978 ... CANR-3
Earlier sketch in CA 5-8R
Benander, Carl D. 1941- 141
See also SATA 74
Benante, Joseph P(hilip) 1936- 33-36R
Benard, Cheryl 1953- 209
Benarde, Melvin A(lbert) 1923- 25-28R
Benardete, Jane Johnson 1930- 45-48
Benario, Herbert W. 1929- 25-28R
Benarria, Allan
See Goldenthal, Allan Benarria
Benary, Margot
See Benary-Isbert, Margot
Benary-Isbert, Margot 1889-1979 .... CANR-72
Obituary 89-92
Earlier sketches in CA 5-8R, CANR-4
See also CLC 12
See also CLR 12
See also MAICYA 1, 2
See also SATA 2
See also SATA-Obit 21
Benasutti, Marion 1908-1992 .... 21-24R
See also SATA 6

Cumulative Index 45 Benner

Benatar, Stephen (Royce) 1937- 110
Benaud, Richard 1930- 131
Benaud, Richie
  See Benaud, Richard
Benavente (y Martinez), Jacinto
  1866-1954 .... CANR-81
  Brief entry 106
  Earlier sketch in CA 131
  See also DAM DRAM, MULT
  See also DC 26
  See also EWL 3
  See also GLL 2
  See also HLCS 1
  See also HW 1, 2
  See also MTCW 1, 2
  See also TCLC 3
Benavie, Arthur 238
Benavie, Barbara
  See Harshav, Barbara
Ben-Avraham, Chofetz Chaim
  See Pickering, Stephen
Benbow, Charles (Clarence) 1929- 122
Benbow, Dave 238
Bencastro, Mario 1949- 183
Bence, Evelyn 110
Bence-Jones, Mark 1930- CANR-48
  Earlier sketches in CA 13-16R, CANR-5
Bench, Johnny (Lee) 1947- 133
  Brief entry 113
Benchley, Nathaniel (Goddard)
  1915-1981 .... CANR-12
  Obituary 105
  Earlier sketches in CA 1-4R, CANR-2
  See also SATA 3, 25
  See also SATA-Obit 28
  See also YAW
Benchley, Peter (Bradford) 1940- CANR-115
  Earlier sketches in CA 17-20R, CANR-12, 35, 66
  See also AAYA 14
  See also AITN 2
  See also BPFB 1
  See also CLC 4, 8
  See also CPW
  See also DAM NOV, POP
  See also HGG
  See also MTCW 1, 2
  See also MTFW 2005
  See also SATA 3, 89
Benchley, Robert (Charles) 1889-1945 153
  Brief entry 105
  See also DLB 11
  See also MAL 5
  See also RGAL 4
  See also TCLC 1, 55
Bencke, Matthew
  See Von Bencke, Matthew Justin
Bencur, Matej
  See Kukucin, Martin
Benda, Harry J(indrich) 1919-1971 .... 9-12R
  Obituary 134
Benda, Julien 1867-1956 154
  Brief entry 120
  See also GFL 1789 to the Present
  See also TCLC 60
Bendall, Molly 1961- 170
Bendat, Julius S. 1923- 198
Bendavid, Avrom 1942- 41-44R
Ben-David, Joseph 1920-1986 157
  Obituary 118
Bendell, Frederick H.
  See McCarty, Hanoch
Bender, Aimee 194
Bender, Arnold Eric 1918-1999 183
Bender, Coleman C. 1921- 33-36R
Bender, Daniel Henry 1866-1945 215
Bender, David L(eo) 1936- 123
Bender, David R(ay) 1942- 102
Bender, Edna 1941- .... SATA 92
Bender, Esther 1942- 152
  See also SATA 88
Bender, Frederic L(awrence) 1943- 69-72
Bender, Harold S(tauffer) 1897-1962 211
Bender, Henry E(dwin), Jr. 1937- 33-36R
Bender, James F(rederick) 1905-1997 .... 17-20R
  Obituary 162
Bender, Jay
  See Deindorfer, Robert Greene
Bender, John B(ryant) 1940- 65-68
Bender, Louis W. 1927- CANR-32
  Earlier sketches in CA 33-36R, CANR-14
Bender, Lucy Ellen 1942- 25-28R
  See also SATA 22
Bender, Marylin 1925- CANR-12
  Earlier sketch in CA 21-24R
Bender, Norman J(ohn) 1927- 118
Bender, Richard 1930- 45-48
Bender, Robert 1962- .... SATA 79, 160
Bender, Robert M. 1936- 33-36R
Bender, Ross Thomas 1929- 61-64
Bender, Sheila 1948- 203
Bender, Stephen (Joseph) 1942- 61-64
Bender, Thomas 1944- CANR-86
  Earlier sketches in CA 73-76, CANR-12, 35
Bender, Todd K. 1936- CANR-24
  Earlier sketches in CA 21-24R, CANR-9
Bender, Tom 1941- 184
Benderly, Beryl Lieff 1943- CANR-120
  Earlier sketches in CA 108, CANR-30
Bendersky, Margaret (Irene) 1949- 151
Bendick, Jeanne 1919- CANR-113
  Earlier sketches in CA 5-8R, CANR-2, 48
  See also CLR 5
  See also MAICYA 1, 2
  See also SAAS 4
  See also SATA 2, 68, 135
Bendick, Marc, Jr. 1946- 118
Bendick, Robert L(ouis) 1917- 61-64
  See also SATA 11
Bendiner, Elmer 1916- CANR-7
  Earlier sketch in CA 57-60
Bendiner, Kenneth Paul 1947- 119
Bendiner, Robert 1909- 9-12R
Bendis, Brian Michael 232
Bendit, Gladys Williams 1885-1975 ...... CAP-1
  Earlier sketch in CA 13-14
Bendit, Laurence John 1898-1974 .... CAP-2
  Earlier sketch in CA 25-28
Bendix, Deanna Marohn 1938- 152
Bendix, Reinhard 1916-1991 .... CANR-4
  Obituary 133
  Earlier sketch in CA 1-4R
Bendixen, Alfred 1952- 128
Bendixson, Terence 1934- 93-96
Ben-Dov, Meir
  See Bernet, Michael M.
Bendroth, Margaret Lamberts
  1954- CANR-142
  Earlier sketch in CA 151
Benecke, Gerhard (?)-1985
  Obituary 117
Benedek, Barbara 165
Benedek, Emily 221
Benedek, Therese 1892-1977 .... 41-44R
Benedetti, Jean (Norman) 1930- 160
Benedetti, Mario 1920- 152
  See also DAM MULT
  See also DLB 113
  See also EWL 3
  See also HW 1, 2
  See also LAW
Benedetti, Robert L(awrence) 1939- 29-32R
Benedetto, Antonio di
  See di Benedetto, Antonio
Benedetto, Arnold J(oseph) 1916-1966 ...... 5-8R
Benedict, Andrew
  See Arthur, Robert, (Jr.)
Benedict, Barbara M. 1955- 151
Benedict, Bertram 1892(?)-1978
  Obituary 77-80
Benedict, Burton 1923- 109
Benedict, Dianne 1941- 110
Benedict, Dorothy Potter
  1889-1979 .... CANR-75
  Obituary 93-96
  Earlier sketches in CAP-1, CA 13-14
  See also SATA 11
  See also SATA-Obit 23
Benedict, Elinor Divine 1931- 207
Benedict, Elizabeth 1954- CANR-90
  Brief entry 126
  Earlier sketches in CA 131, CANR-69
  Interview in CA-131
Benedict, Helen 1952- CANR-99
  Earlier sketch in CA 140
Benedict, Howard (S.) 1928-2005 147
  Obituary 239
Benedict, Lois Trimble 1902-1967 .... CAP-2
  Earlier sketch in CA 19-20
  See also SATA 12
Benedict, Marion 1923- 109
Benedict, Michael Les 1945- 45-48
Benedict, Morgan
  See Morgan, Fidelis
Benedict, Philip (Joseph) 1949- CANR-86
  Earlier sketch in CA 130
Benedict, Pinckney 1964- CANR-138
  Earlier sketch in CA 170
  See also DLB 244
Benedict, Rex 1920-1995 .... 17-20R
  See also CWRI 5
  See also SATA 8
Benedict, Robert P(hilip)
  1924-1986 .... CANR-75
  Obituary 119
  Earlier sketch in CA 41-44R
Benedict, Ruth (Fulton) 1887-1948 158
  See also DLB 246
  See also TCLC 60
Benedict, Stewart H(urd) 1924- 13-16R
  See also SATA 26
Benedictus, David (Henry) 1938- CANR-66
  Earlier sketches in CA 73-76, CANR-24
  See also CN 1, 2, 3, 4, 5, 6
  See also DLB 14
Benediksdottir Bjarklind, Unnur
  See Bjarklind, Unnur Benekiktsdottir
Benedikt, Michael 1935- CANR-7
  Earlier sketch in CA 13-16R
  See also CLC 4, 14
  See also CP 1, 2, 3, 4, 5, 6, 7
  See also DLB 5
Benediktov, Vladimir Grigor'evich
  1807-1873 .... DLB 205
Benediktsson, Einar 1864-1940 .... DLB 293
Beneduce, Ann Keay 198
  See also SATA 128
Benefield, June 1921- 45-48
Beneke, Walter 1923- .... HW 1
Benell, Florence B(elle) 1912-1988 .... 33-36R
Benell, Julie 1906(?)-1982
  Obituary 105
Benello, C. George 1926- 33-36R
Ben-Ephraim, Gavriel 1946- 116
Beneria, Lourdes 1939- CANR-139
  Earlier sketch in CA 161
Benes, Jan 1936- 29-32R
Benesch, Klaus (T.) 1958- 220
Benet, Edouard
  See Edwards, William B(ennett)
Benet, James 1914- CANR-8
  Earlier sketch in CA 61-64
Benet, Juan 1927-1993 143
  See also CLC 28
  See also EWL 3
Benet, Laura 1884-1979 .... CANR-70
  Obituary 85-88
  Earlier sketches in CA 9-12R, CANR-6
  See also SATA 3
  See also SATA-Obit 23
Benet, Mary Kathleen 1943- 57-60
Benet, Stephen Vincent 1898-1943 152
  Brief entry 104
  See also AMWS 11
  See also DA3
  See also DAM POET
  See also DLB 4, 48, 102, 249, 284
  See also DLBY 1997
  See also EWL 3
  See also HGG
  See also MAL 5
  See also MTCW 2
  See also MTFW 2005
  See also PC 64
  See also RGAL 4
  See also RGSF 2
  See also SSC 10
  See also SUFW
  See also TCLC 7
  See also WP
  See also YABC 1
Benet, Sula 1906-1982 .... CANR-75
  Obituary 108
  Earlier sketch in CA 89-92
  See also SATA 21
  See also SATA-Obit 33
Benet, William Rose 1886-1950 152
  Brief entry 118
  See also DAM POET
  See also DLB 45
  See also RGAL 4
  See also TCLC 28
Benetar, Judith 1941- 53-56
Benevolo, Leonardo 1923- 89-92
Ben-Ezer, Ehud 1936- CANR-142
  Earlier sketches in CA 61-64, CANR-8, 24
  See also SATA 122
Benezra, Barbara (Beardsley) 1921- .. CANR-72
  Earlier sketch in CA 13-16R
  See also SATA 10
Benezra, Neal 1953- 141
Benfey, Christopher 1954- 191
Benfield, Derek 1926- CANR-56
  Earlier sketches in CA 21-24R, CANR-10, 30
Benfield, G(raham) J(ohn) Barker
  See Barker-Benfield, G(raham) J(ohn)
Benfield, Richard E. 1940- 77-80
Benford, Gregory (Albert) 1941- 175
  Earlier sketches in CA 69-72, CANR-12, 24, 49, 95, 134
  Autobiographical Essay in 175
  See also CAAS 27
  See also BPFB 1
  See also CLC 52
  See also CN 7
  See also CSW
  See also DLBY 1982
  See also MTFW 2005
  See also SCFW 2
  See also SFW 4
Benford, Harry (Bell) 1917- 89-92
Benford, Timothy B(artholomew)
  1941- CANR-11
  Earlier sketch in CA 69-72
Benge, Eugene J(ackson) 1896-1990 .. CANR-9
  Earlier sketch in CA 57-60
Bengelsdorf, Irving S. 1922- 57-60
Bengis, Ingrid 1944- 223
Bengtson, Vern L. 1941- CANR-4
  Earlier sketch in CA 49-52
Bengtsson, Arvid 1916- 33-36R
Bengtsson, Frans (Gunnar) 1894-1954 170
  See also EWL 3
  See also TCLC 48
Ben-Gurion, David 1886-1973 101
  Obituary 45-48
Benham, Leslie 1922- 9-12R
  See also SATA 48
Benham, Lois (Dakin) 1924- 9-12R
  See also SATA 48
Benham, Mary Lile 1914-1991 102
  See also SATA 55
Ben-Horav, Naphthali
  See Kravitz, Nathaniel
Ben-Horin, Meir 1918- CANR-14
  Earlier sketch in CA 29-32R
Benichou, Paul 1908-2001 57-60
Benig, Irving 1944- 152
Beniger, James R. 1946- 111
Benigni, Roberto 1952- 230
Benington, John (Elson) 1921-1969 .. CANR-76
  Obituary 134
  Earlier sketch in CA 5-8R
Benison, C. C.
  See Whiteway, Doug(las) Alfred
Ben-Israel, Ben Ammi
  See Ben Ammi and
  Ben-Israel, Ben Ami
Ben-Israel-Kidron, Hedva 33-36R
Benitez, Fernando 1911(?)-2000 152
  Obituary 188
  See also HW 1
Benitez, Sandra
  See Benitez, Sandra (Ables)
  See also DLB 292
Benitez, Sandra (Ables) 1941- CANR-120
  Earlier sketches in CA 144, CANR-86
  See also MTFW 2005
Benitez-Rojo, Antonio 1931-2005 .. CANR-103
  Obituary 235
  Earlier sketch in CA 137
  See also Rojo, Antonio Benitez
Benjamin, Alice
  See Brooke, Avery (Rogers)
Benjamin, Anna Shaw 1925- 41-44R
Benjamin, Annette Francis 1928- 17-20R
Benjamin, Bry 1924- 17-20R
Benjamin, Burton Richard
  1917-1988 .... CANR-75
  Obituary 126
  Earlier sketch in CA 101
Benjamin, Carol Lea 217
Benjamin, Claude (Max Edward Pohlman)
  1911- 9-12R
Benjamin, Curtis G. 1901-1983 122
  Obituary 111
Benjamin, David
  See Slavitt, David R(ytman)
Benjamin, Denis R(ichard) 1945- 154
Benjamin, E. M. J.
  See Bache, Ellyn
Benjamin, Edward Bernard 1897-1980 ... 69-72
  Obituary 133
Benjamin, Gerald 1945- CANR-93
  Earlier sketches in CA 49-52, CANR-46
Benjamin, Harold H. 1924-2004 154
  Obituary 234
Benjamin, Harry 1885-1986 .... CAP-1
  Obituary 120
  Earlier sketch in CA 11-12
Benjamin, Herbert S(tanley) 1922- 5-8R
Benjamin, Joan 1956- 167
Benjamin, Joseph 1921- 57-60
Benjamin, Judy-Lynn
  See del Rey, Judy-Lynn
Benjamin, Kathleen Kelly
  See Kelly-Benjamin, Kathleen
Benjamin, Laszlo 1915- .... EWL 3
Benjamin, Lois
  See Gould, Lois
Benjamin, Nora
  See Kubie, Nora Gottheil Benjamin
Benjamin, Park 1809-1864 .... DLB 3, 59, 73, 250
Benjamin, Peter
  See Cunningham, Peter
Benjamin, Philip (Robert) 1922-1966 .... 5-8R
  Obituary 25-28R
Benjamin, Robert (Irving) 1949- 109
Benjamin, Roger W. 1942- 37-40R
Benjamin, Ruth 1934- 125
Benjamin, S(amuel) G(reen) W(heeler)
  1837-1914 183
  See also DLB 189
Benjamin, Saragail Katzman 1953- 151
  See also SATA 86
Benjamin, Walter 1892-1940 164
  See also DLB 242
  See also EW 11
  See also EWL 3
  See also TCLC 39
Benjamin, William E(arl) 1942- 25-28R
Benjamine, Elbert 1882-1951 213
Benjaminson, Peter 1945- CANR-12
  Earlier sketch in CA 73-76
Ben Jelloun, Tahar 1944- 135
  See also Jelloun, Tahar ben
  See also CWW 2
  See also EWL 3
  See also RGWL 3
  See also WLIT 2
Benji, Thomas
  See Robinson, Frank M(alcolm)
ben-Jochannan, Yosef 1918- CANR-12
  Earlier sketch in CA 69-72
  See also BW 2
Benko, Stephen 1924- 9-12R
Benkovitz, Miriam J(eanette)
  1911-1986 .... CANR-4
  Obituary 119
  Earlier sketch in CA 9-12R
Benlowes, Edward 1602-1676 .... DLB 126
Benn, Anthony Neil Wedgwood 1925- 131
Benn, Gottfried 1886-1956 153
  Brief entry 106
  See also DLB 56
  See also EWL 3
  See also PC 35
  See also RGWL 2, 3
  See also TCLC 3
Benn, John Andrews 1904-1984
  Obituary 115
Benn, June
  See Barraclough, June (Mary)
Benn, June Wedgwood
  See Barraclough, June (Mary)
Benn, Matthew
  See Siegel, Benjamin
Benn, Melissa 180
Benn, Piers 197
Benn, S. I.
  See Benn, Stanley I(saac)
Benn, Stanley I(saac) 1920-1986 129
Benn, Tony
  See Benn, Anthony Neil Wedgwood
Bennahum, David S. 1968- 193
Bennahum, Judith Chazin 1937- 146
Bennani, B(en) M(ohammed) 1946- . CANR-13
  Earlier sketch in CA 61-64
Bennassar, Bartolome 1929- CANR-116
  Earlier sketch in CA 158
Benne, Kenneth D(ean) 1908-1992 .. CANR-46
  Obituary 139
  Earlier sketch in CA 33-36R
Benner, Cheryl 1962- .... SATA 80

Benner 46 CONTEMPORARY AUTHORS

Benner, Judith Ann 1942- CANR-62
Earlier sketch in CA 122
See also SATA 94
Benner, Ralph Eugene (Jr.) 1932- 33-36R
Bennet, Glin 1927- 123
Bennet, Richard Bruce 1957- 150
Bennet, Rick
See Bennet, Richard Bruce
Bennet, Ruth
See Straubing, Harold (Elk)
Bennett, A(bram) E(lting Hasbrouck)
1898-1985 65-68
Bennett, Addison C(urtis) 1918- CANR-7
Earlier sketch in CA 5-8R
Bennett, Adrian A(rthur) 1941- 53-56
Bennett, Alan 1934- CANR-106
Earlier sketches in CA 103, CANR-35, 55
See also BRWS 8
See also CBD
See also CD 5, 6
See also CLC 45, 77
See also DAB
See also DAM MST
See also DLB 310
See also MTCW 1, 2
See also MTFW 2005
Bennett, Alice
See Ziner, Florence
Bennett, Anna Elizabeth 1914- 17-20R
Bennett, Archibald F. 1896-1965 .... CAP-1
Earlier sketch in CA 13-16
Bennett, (Enoch) Arnold 1867-1931 155
Brief entry 106
See also BRW 6
See also CDBLB 1890-1914
See also DLB 10, 34, 98, 135
See also EWL 3
See also MTCW 2
See also TCLC 5, 20
Bennett, Barbara 1959- 190
Bennett, Betty T. 115
Bennett, Boyce McLean, Jr. 1928-1996 115
Bennett, Brian (Scott) 1953- 170
Bennett, Bruce (Harry) 1941- 229
Bennett, Bruce (William) 1952- 110
Bennett, Bruce L(anyon) 1917- 25-28R
Bennett, Carl D(ouglas) 1917- 140
Bennett, Charles 1899-1995 146
Obituary 149
See also DLB 44
Bennett, Charles 1901-1968 .... CAP-1
Earlier sketch in CA 13-16
Bennett, Charles 1932- 25-28R
Bennett, Charles A. 1947- 199
Bennett, Charles E(dward) 1910-2003 ..... 9-12R
Obituary 220
Bennett, Cherie 1960- CANR-130
Earlier sketch in CA 163
See also AAYA 29
See also SATA 97, 158
Bennett, Christine
See Neubauer, William Arthur
Bennett, Clinton 1955- 157
Bennett, Colin J. 1955- 138
Bennett, Daniel
See Gilmore, Joseph L(ee)
Bennett, Daphne Nicholson 41-44R
Bennett, David H. 1935- 25-28R
Bennett, Dean B. 1935- 228
Bennett, Deborah J. 1950- 180
Bennett, Dennis J. 1917-1991 .... CANR-20
Earlier sketch in CA 49-52
Bennett, Dorothea
See Young, Dorothea Bennett
Bennett, Dwight
See Newton, D(wight) B(ennett)
Bennett, E(thel) M. Granger 1891- CAP-1
Earlier sketch in CA 13-14
Bennett, E. N.
See Bennett, Ernest N(athaniel)
Bennett, Edward (Martin) 1924- 5-8R
Bennett, Edward M(oore) 1927- 33-36R
Bennett, Elizabeth
See Mitchell, Margaret (Munnerlyn)
Bennett, Elizabeth
See Harrod-Eagles, Cynthia
Bennett, Elizabeth Deare
See Merwin, (W.) Sam(uel Kimball), Jr.
Bennett, Emerson 1822-1905 197
See also DLB 202
Bennett, Ernest N(athaniel) 1868-1947
Brief entry 119
Bennett, Frances Grant 1899-1995 .... CAP-2
Earlier sketch in CA 25-28
Bennett, Frederick 1928- 218
Bennett, Fredna W(illis) 1906-1987 .... CAP-1
Earlier sketch in CA 9-10
Bennett, G. V.
See Bennett, Gareth Vaughan
Bennett, Gareth Vaughan 1929-1987
Obituary 124
Bennett, Gary L. 1940- 138
Bennett, Geoffrey (Martin) 1909-1983 .. 13-16R
Obituary 110
Bennett, George 1920-1969 .... 5-8R
Obituary 134
Bennett, George Harold 1930- CANR-87
Earlier sketch in CA 97-100
See also Bennett, Hal
See also BW 1
Bennett, Georgette 1946- 143
Bennett, Gertrude Ryder 53-56
Bennett, Gordon A(nderson) 1940- 29-32R
Bennett, Gordon C. 1935- CANR-31
Earlier sketches in CA 33-36R, CANR-14
Bennett, Gwendolyn B. 1902-1981 125
See also BW 1
See also DLB 51
See also HR 1:2
See also WP
Bennett, Hal
See Bennett, George Harold
See also CLC 5
See also DLB 33
Bennett, Hal 1930- .... CAAS 13
Bennett, Hal Zina 1936- CANR-40
Earlier sketch in CA 41-44R
Bennett, Hall
See Hall, Bennie Caroline (Humble)
Bennett, Harve
See Fischman, Harve
Bennett, Howard Franklin 1911-1974 .... 1-4R
Bennett, Ian (Hamilton William) 1924- 214
Bennett, Isadora 1900-1980
Obituary 93-96
Bennett, J(ohn) G(odolphin) 1897-1974
Obituary 111
Bennett, Jack Arthur Walter
1911-1981 .... CANR-6
Obituary 103
Earlier sketch in CA 9-12R
Bennett, James (W.) 1942- CANR-131
Earlier sketch in CA 158
See also AAYA 26
See also SATA 93, 148, 153
See also SATA-Essay 153
Bennett, James D(avid) 1926- 61-64
Bennett, James Gordon, Jr. 1841-1918 . DLB 23
Bennett, James Gordon 1795-1872 ...... DLB 43
Bennett, James R(ichard) 1932- 33-36R
Bennett, James Thomas 1942- CANR-23
Earlier sketch in CA 106
Bennett, Jay 1912- CANR-79
Earlier sketches in CA 69-72, CANR-11, 42
See also AAYA 10
See also CLC 35
See also JRDA
See also SAAS 4
See also SATA 41, 87
See also SATA-Brief 27
See also WYA
See also YAW
Bennett, Jean Francis
See Dorcy, Sister Mary Jean
Bennett, Jeremy
See Bennett, John Jerome Nelson
Bennett, Jill (Crawford) 1934- .... SATA 41
Bennett, Jill 1947- 106
Bennett, Joan S. 1941- 132
Bennett, John 1865-1956 204
See also DLB 42
See also YABC 1
Bennett, John (Frederic) 1920-1991 ...... 29-32R
Bennett, John Jerome Nelson 1939- 21-24R
Bennett, John M(ichael) 1942- CANR-41
Earlier sketches in CA 49-52, CANR-2, 18
See also CAAS 25
Bennett, John W. 1918- 69-72
Bennett, John William 1915- CANR-4
Earlier sketch in CA 1-4R
Bennett, Jon 1955- 127
Bennett, Jonathan (Francis) 1930- CANR-1
Earlier sketch in CA 45-48
Bennett, Joseph D. 1922-1972 .... 1-4R
Obituary 33-36R
Bennett, Josephine Waters 1899-1975 ...... 1-4R
Obituary 103
Bennett, Judith (?)-1979
Obituary 85-88
Bennett, Kathleen 1946- 138
Bennett, Kay Curley 1922-1997 .... 17-20R
Obituary 162
Bennett, Kenneth A(lan) 1935- 131
Bennett, Lerone, Jr. 1928- CANR-25
Earlier sketches in CA 45-48, CANR-2
See also BW 2
See also CSW
Bennett, Linda L(eveque) 1946- 115
Bennett, Louise (Simone) 1919- 151
See also BLC 1
See also BW 2, 3
See also CDWLB 3
See also CLC 28
See also CP 1, 2, 3, 4, 5, 6, 7
See also DAM MULT
See also DLB 117
See also EWL 3
Bennett, M. J.
See Bennett, Marcia J(oanne)
Bennett, Marcia J(oanne) 1945- CANR-35
Earlier sketch in CA 114
Bennett, Margaret E(laine) 1893-1980 .... 5-8R
Bennett, Margot 1912-1980
Obituary 105
Bennett, Marion T(insley) 1914-2000 ...... 9-12R
Obituary 192
Bennett, Melba Berry 1901-1968 .... CAP-2
Earlier sketch in CA 19-20
Bennett, Meridan 1927- 25-28R
Bennett, Merit 1947- 160
Bennett, Michael 1943-1987 .... CANR-79
Obituary 122
Earlier sketch in CA 101
Bennett, Mildred R. 1909-1989 .... CAP-2
Obituary 130
Earlier sketch in CA 25-28
Bennett, Neil G. 228
Bennett, Neville 1937- CANR-41
Earlier sketches in CA 102, CANR-19
Bennett, Noel 1939- 45-48
Bennett, Norman Robert 1932- CANR-39
Earlier sketches in CA 9-12R, CANR-3, 18
Bennett, O. H. 1957- 219
Bennett, Patrick (H.) 1931- 122
Bennett, Paul Lewis 1921-2002 .... CANR-4
Obituary 208
Earlier sketch in CA 1-4R
Bennett, Penelope (Agnes) 1938- CANR-65
Earlier sketch in CA 13-16R
See also SATA 94
Bennett, Rachel
See Hill, Margaret (Ohler)
Bennett, Rainey 1907-1998
Obituary 172
See also SATA 15
See also SATA-Obit 111
Bennett, Reginald George Stephen 1928-
See Long, Elliot
Bennett, Richard 1899- .... SATA 21
Bennett, Richard Rodney 1936- .... IDFW 4
Bennett, Rita (Marie) 1934- CANR-20
Earlier sketch in CA 69-72
Bennett, Robert A(ndrew) 1927- CANR-5
Earlier sketch in CA 13-16R
Bennett, Robert D(onald) 1947- 118
Bennett, Robert L. 1931- 41-44R
Bennett, Robert Russell 1894-1981
Obituary 105
Bennett, Ronan 1956- CANR-90
Earlier sketch in CA 142
Bennett, Russell H(oradley) 1896- .... SATA 25
Bennett, Saxon 1961- 163
Bennett, Scott (Boyce) 1939- 33-36R
Bennett, Shelley M. 1947- 131
Bennett, Thomas L(eroy) 1942- 85-88
Bennett, Tony 1926- 180
Bennett, Victor 1919- CANR-7
Earlier sketch in CA 5-8R
Bennett, W(illiam) R(obert) 1921- 13-16R
Bennett, Wilhelmine 1933- 167
Bennett, William (Ira) 1941- 107
Bennett, William (John) 1943- CANR-111
Earlier sketch in CA 153
See also SATA 102
Bennett, William L. 1924- 17-20R
Bennett-England, Rodney Charles 1936- . 61-64
Bennett-Goleman, Tara 217
Bennetts, Pamela 1922-1986 .... CANR-60
Earlier sketch in CA 37-40R
See also RHW
Benni, Stefano 1947- .... DLB 196
Bennie, William A(ndrew) 1921- 69-72
Bennigsen, Alexandre (A.) 1913-1988(?)
Obituary 125
Benning, Elizabeth
See Rice, Bebe Faas
Benning, (Barbara) Lee Edwards 1934- 53-56
Bennion, Barbara Elisabeth 1930- 110
Bennion, Sherilyn Cox 1935- 137
Bennis, Warren G. 1925- CANR-5
Earlier sketch in CA 53-56
Ben no Naishi 1228(?)-1271(?) .... DLB 203
Benoff, Mac 1915(?)-1972
Obituary 37-40R
Benoist, Francoise-Albine Puzin de La
Martiniere 1731-c. 1809 .... DLB 313
Benoist-Mechin, Jacques 1901-1983 105
Obituary 109
Benoit, Brent 1974- 213
Benoit, Charles 235
Benoit, Emile 1910-1978 .... CANR-3
Obituary 77-80
Earlier sketch in CA 5-8R
Benoit, Jacques 1941- 209
See also DLB 60
Benoit, Leroy James 1913- 33-36R
Benoit, Pierre 1886-1962
Obituary 93-96
Benoit, Pierre Maurice 1906-1987 ... CANR-75
Obituary 122
Earlier sketch in CA 41-44R
Benoit, Richard 1899(?)-1969
Obituary 104
Benoit, William L. 1953- CANR-130
Earlier sketch in CA 163
Benoliel, Jeanne Quint 1919- CANR-27
Earlier sketch in CA 49-52
Ben-Rafael, Eliezer 1938- 141
Bense, Walter F(rederick) 1932- CANR-1
Earlier sketch in CA 45-48
Bensel, Richard Franklin 1949- 141
Bensen, Alice Rhodus 1911- 69-72
Bensen, Donald R. 1927-1997 .... CANR-20
Earlier sketches in CA 9-12R, CANR-5
Bensko, John 1949- 105
Bensley, Connie 1929- 135
Bensman, David 1949- 144
Bensman, Joseph 1922-1986 .... CANR-10
Earlier sketch in CA 21-24R
Bensman, Marvin R. 1937- 214
Bensol, Oscar
See Gilbert, Willie
Benson, A. C. 1862-1925 .... DLB 98
See also TCLC 123
Benson, A(rthur) C(hristopher) 1862-1925 .. 203
Benson, A. George 1924- 69-72
Benson, Amy 1972(?)- 236
Benson, Angela 178
See also BW 3
Benson, Ann 170
Benson, B. A.
See Beyea, Basil
Benson, Ben(jamin) 1915-1959
Brief entry 112
Benson, C(arl) David 1942- 123
Benson, C. Randolph 1923- 29-32R
Benson, Carmen 1921- 57-60
Benson, Charles S(cott) 1922-1994 .. CANR-79
Obituary 146
Earlier sketches in CA 17-20R, CANR-8
Benson, Constantine Walter 1909-1982
Obituary 108
Benson, D(avid) Frank 1928- 151
Benson, Daniel
See Cooper, Colin Symons
Benson, Dennis C(arroll) 1936- 37-40R
Benson, E(dward) F(rederic) 1867-1940 157
Brief entry 114
See also DLB 135, 153
See also HGG
See also SUFW 1
See also TCLC 27
Benson, Elizabeth P(olk) 1924- CANR-86
Earlier sketches in CA 93-96, CANR-35
See also SATA 65
Benson, Eugene 1928- 89-92
Benson, Evelyn Rose 1924- 167
Benson, Frederick R. 1934- 33-36R
Benson, Frederick William 1948- CANR-43
Earlier sketches in CA 101, CANR-19
Benson, George C(harles) S(umner)
1908-1999 182
Benson, Gerard 1931- 144
Benson, Gigi (Dian Daniels) 1941- 108
Benson, Ginny
See Benson, Virginia
Benson, Harry 1929- CANR-116
Earlier sketch in CA 108
Benson, Herbert 1935- 85-88
Benson, J(ack) L(eonard) 1920- 105
Benson, Jackson J. 1930- 25-28R
See also CLC 34
See also DLB 111
Benson, Jeffrey 1937- 120
Benson, John 1945- 131
Benson, Judi 1947- 147
Benson, Kathleen 1947- CANR-117
Earlier sketch in CA 85-88
See also SATA 62, 111
Benson, Larry D(ean) 1929- 37-40R
Benson, Linda M(aria) 1959- .... SATA 84
Benson, Lyman (David) 1909-1993 .. CANR-32
Earlier sketch in CA 49-52
Benson, Margaret H. Benson 1899-1982 .. 5-8R
Benson, Mary 1919-2000 .... CANR-17
Obituary 188
Earlier sketches in CA 49-52, CANR-1
Benson, Maxine (Frances) 1939- 65-68
Benson, Mildred (Augustine Wirt)
1905-2002 134
Obituary 209
See also Keene, Carolyn
See also MAICYA 1, 2
See also SATA 65, 100
See also SATA-Obit 135
Benson, Mildred Wirt
See Benson, Mildred (Augustine Wirt)
Benson, Millie
See Benson, Mildred (Augustine Wirt)
Benson, Patrick 1956- .... SATA 147
Benson, Peter 1956- 137
Benson, R(obert) H(ugh) 1871-1914 167
See also DLB 153
See also HGG
Benson, Rachel
See Jowitt, Deborah
Benson, Raymond 1955- CANR-121
Earlier sketch in CA 118
Benson, Richard
See Cooper, Saul
Benson, Robby 1956- 171
Benson, Robert G(reen) 1930- 29-32R
Benson, Robert S(later) 1942- 33-36R
Benson, Rolf Eric 1951- 102
Benson, Ruth Crego 1937- 41-44R
Benson, Sally 1900-1972 .... CAP-1
Obituary 37-40R
Earlier sketch in CA 19-20
See also CLC 17
See also SATA 1, 35
See also SATA-Obit 27
Benson, Stella 1892-1933 155
Brief entry 117
Earlier sketch in CA 154
See also DLB 36, 162
See also FANT
See also TCLC 17
See also TEA
Benson, Stephana Vere 1909- 13-16R
Benson, Ted
See Benson, Frederick William
Benson, Thomas Godfrey 1899- CAP-1
Earlier sketch in CA 11-12
Benson, Thomas W(alter) 1937- CANR-19
Earlier sketch in CA 29-32R
Benson, Virginia 1923- 57-60
Benson, Warren S(ten) 1929- 114
Benson, William Howard 1902-1984 .... 1-4R
Bensserade, Isaac de
1613-1691 .... GFL Beginnings to 1789
Benstead, Steven 1951- 113
Bensted-Smith, Richard (Brian) 1929- ... 13-16R
Benstock, Bernard 1930-1994 .... CANR-29
Earlier sketches in CA 17-20R, CANR-7
Benstock, Shari 1944- CANR-116
Earlier sketches in CA 97-100, CANR-29, 115
Bent, Alan Edward 1939- CANR-4
Earlier sketch in CA 49-52
Bent, Charles N. 1935- 21-24R
Bent, James Theodore 1852-1897 .... DLB 174
Bent, Mabel Virginia Anna (?)-(?) .... DLB 174
Bent, Robert D. 1928- 228
Bent, Rudyard K(ipling) 1901-1987 .. CANR-18
Earlier sketch in CA 1-4R

Cumulative Index 47 Berger

Bent, Timothy (David) 1955- 157
Benteen, John
See Haas, Ben(jamin) L(eopold) and Linaker, Mike
Bentel, Pearl B(ucklen) 1901-1986 .... CAP-2
Earlier sketch in CA 21-22
Benthall, Jonathan 1941- 41-44R
Bentham, Fred (Percy)
See Bentham, Frederick (Percy)
Bentham, Frederick (Percy) 1911-2001 105
Bentham, Jay
See Bensman, Joseph
Bentham, Jeremy 1748-1832 ..... DLB 107, 158, 252
Benthic, Arch E.
See Stewart, Harris B(ates), Jr.
Benthul, Herman F(orrest) 1911-1998 ... 33-36R
Bentivoglio, Fabrizio 1957- 206
Bentley, Beth (Rita) 1928- 101
Bentley, Bill
See Bentley, William (George)
Bentley, Colin 1936- 118
Bentley, E(dmund) C(lerihew) 1875-1956 ... 232
Brief entry 108
See also DLB 70
See also MSW
See also TCLC 12
Bentley, Eric (Russell) 1916- CANR-67
Earlier sketches in CA 5-8R, CANR-6
Interview in CANR-6
See also CAD
See also CBD
See also CD 5, 6
See also CLC 24
Bentley, G(erald) E(ades), Jr. 1930- . CANR-113
Earlier sketches in CA 1-4R, CANR-4
Bentley, Gene
See Fearn, John Russell
Bentley, Gerald Eades 1901-1994 .... 41-44R
Obituary 146
Bentley, Howard Beebe 1925- 9-12R
Bentley, James 1937-2000 208
Bentley, Janice Babb 1933- 13-16R
Bentley, Jayne
See Krentz, Jayne Ann
Bentley, Jeffery W(estwood) 1955- 143
Bentley, Jerry H(arrell) 1949- CANR-55
Earlier sketch in CA 127
Bentley, Joanne 1928- 130
Bentley, Joyce 1928- 144
Bentley, Judith (McBride) 1945- CANR-48
Earlier sketches in CA 107, CANR-23
See also SATA 40, 89
Bentley, Margaret 1926- CANR-25
Earlier sketch in CA 108
Bentley, Michael (John) 1948- CANR-121
Earlier sketch in CA 145
Bentley, Nancy (L.) 1946- 146
See also SATA 78
Bentley, Nicolas Clerihew 1907-1978 .... CANR-11
Obituary 81-84
Earlier sketch in CA 65-68
See also SATA-Obit 24
Bentley, Phyllis Eleanor 1894-1977 .. CANR-59
Earlier sketches in CA 1-4R, CANR-3
See also DLB 191
See also RHW
See also SATA 6
See also SATA-Obit 25
Bentley, Richard
See Browning, Alice C(rolley)
Bentley, Richard 1662-1742 .... DLB 252
Bentley, Roy 1947- 127
See also SATA 46
Bentley, Sarah 1946- 29-32R
Bentley, Toni 1958- CANR-116
Earlier sketches in CA 123, CANR-56
Bentley, Ursula 1945-2004 125
Obituary 227
Bentley, Virginia W(illiams) 1908- 57-60
Bentley, William (George) 1916- 150
See also SATA 84
Bentley-Taylor, David 1915-2005 ..... CANR-14
Obituary 236
Earlier sketch in CA 77-80
Benton, D(ebra) A. 1953- 141
Benton, Dorothy Gilchrist 1919- 57-60
Benton, F(red) Warren 1948- 119
Benton, Helen Hemingway 1902(?)-1974
Obituary 104
Benton, John Frederic 1931-1988 69-72
Obituary 124
Benton, John W. 1933- CANR-12
Earlier sketch in CA 29-32R
Benton, Josephine Moffett 1905-1978 .... 5-8R
Benton, Karla
See Rowland, D(onald) S(ydney)
Benton, Kenneth (Carter) 1909-1999 .. CANR-1
Earlier sketch in CA 49-52
Benton, Lewis R(obert) 1920- 17-20R
Benton, Megan L. 1954- 201
Benton, (Joseph) Nelson (Jr.) 1924-1988 112
Obituary 124
Brief entry 110
Interview in CA-112
Benton, Patricia 1907-1983 .... 5-8R
Benton, Peggie 1906- CANR-31
Earlier sketch in CA 49-52
Benton, Richard G(lasscock) 1938- 81-84
Benton, Robert
See Buse, Renee
Benton, Robert (Douglass) 1932- CANR-2
Earlier sketch in CA 1-4R
See also DLB 44
Benton, Stuart
See Viereck, George S(ylvester)
Benton, Thomas Hart 1889-1975 93-96
Obituary 53-56
Benton, Wilbourn Eugene 1917-1996 .... 1-4R
Benton, Will
See Paine, Lauran (Bosworth)
Benton, William 1900-1973 .... CAP-1
Obituary 41-44R
Earlier sketch in CA 13-16
Bentov, Itzhak 1923(?)-1979
Obituary 85-88
Bentsen, Cheryl 1950- 138
Bentwich, Norman (De Mattos) 1883-1971
Obituary 111
Bentz, Thomas 1943- 112
Bentz, William F(rederick) 1940- 53-56
ben Uzair, Salem
See Horne, Richard Henry Hengist
Benveniste, Asa 1925-1990 .... CANR-33
Obituary 131
Earlier sketch in CA 69-72
See also CP 2, 3, 4
Benveniste, Emile 1902-1976
Obituary 115
Benveniste, Guy 1927- CANR-8
Earlier sketch in CA 61-64
Ben-Veniste, Richard 1943-
Brief entry 114
Benvenisti, Meron (Shmuel) 1934- ... CANR-35
Earlier sketches in CA 65-68, CANR-12
Benvenuto, Christine 232
Benward, Bruce (Charles) 1921- CANR-9
Earlier sketch in CA 9-12R
Beny, Roloff
See Beny, Wilfred Roy
Beny, Wilfred Roy 1924-1984 .... CANR-32
Obituary 112
Earlier sketch in CA 21-24R
Ben-Yehuda, Nachman 1948- CANR-117
Earlier sketch in CA 159
Ben-Yishai, Yonatan
See Wachsmann, Shelley
Ben-Yitzhak, Avraham 1883-1950 206
Benyo, Richard (Stephen) 1946- CANR-29
Earlier sketches in CA 77-80, CANR-13
Ben-Yosef, Avraham C(haim)
See Matsuba, Moshe
Benz, Ernst (Wilhelm) 1907-1978 ..... CANR-13
Earlier sketch in CA 13-16R
Benz, Frank L(eonard) 1930- 41-44R
Benz, Maude 1951- 174
Benzie, William 1930- 37-40R
Benziger, Barbara Field 1918-1984 180
Brief entry 115
Benziger, James 1914-1985 .... 13-16R
Ben-Zion
See Weinman, Benzion
Benzoni, Juliette (Andree Marguerite) 1920- CANR-18
Earlier sketch in CA 101
Beorse, Bryn 1896-1980 45-48
Bequaert, Lucia H(umes) 65-68
Beran, Michael Knox 1966- 232
Beranbaum, Rose Levy 1944(?)- 185
Beranek, Leo L(eroy) 1914- 5-8R
Beranek, William 1922- 5-8R
Berard, J(ules) Aram 1933- 17-20R
Berardo, Felix M(ario) 1934- CANR-24
Earlier sketches in CA 57-60, CANR-8
Berberian, Viken 216
Berberick, Nancy Varian 1951- CANR-143
Earlier sketch in CA 154
See also FANT
Berberova, Nina (Nikolaevna) 1901-1993 .... CANR-90
Obituary 142
Earlier sketches in CA 33-36R, CANR-14, 56
See also DLB 317
Berbrich, Joan D. 1925-1995 .... CANR-12
Earlier sketch in CA 29-32R
Berbusse, Edward J(oseph) 1912-2000 .. 21-24R
Bercaw, Edna Coe 1961- .... SATA 124
Berch, Bettina 1950- CANR-94
Earlier sketch in CA 129
Berch, William O.
See Coyne, Joseph E.
Berchen, Ursula 1919- 65-68
Berchen, William 1920- 65-68
Berck, Judith 1960- 142
See also SATA 75
Berck, Martin G(ans) 1928- 65-68
Berckman, Evelyn Domenica 1900-1978 .... CANR-71
Obituary 174
Earlier sketches in CA 1-4R, CANR-1
Bercovici, Rion 1903(?)-1976
Obituary 69-72
Bercovitch, Jacob 169
Bercovitch, Reuben 1923- 104
Bercovitch, Sacvan 1933- 41-44R
Berczeller, Richard 1902-1994 .... 9-12R
Obituary 143
Berdahl, Daphne 1966- 190
Berdanier, Carolyn D. 1936- 150
Berdes, George R. 1931- 29-32R
Berdie, Douglas R(alph) 1946- 53-56
Berdie, Ralph F(reimuth) 1916-1974 . CANR-11
Earlier sketch in CA 17-20R
Berding, Andrew H(enry) 1902-1989 .... 5-8R
Berdyaev, Nicolas
See Berdyaev, Nikolai (Aleksandrovich)
Berdyaev, Nikolai (Aleksandrovich) 1874-1948 157
Brief entry 120
See also TCLC 67
Berdyayev, Nikolai (Aleksandrovich)
See Berdyaev, Nikolai (Aleksandrovich)
Bere, Rennie Montague 1907-1991 65-68
Berebitsky, Julie 203
Bereday, George Z(ygmunt) F(ijalkowski) 1920-1983 .... CANR-4
Obituary 111
Earlier sketch in CA 1-4R
Bereiter, Carl 1930-
Brief entry 113
Berelson, Bernard R(euben) 1912-1979 .... CANR-3
Obituary 89-92
Earlier sketch in CA 5-8R
Berelson, David 1943- 25-28R
Berelson, Howard 1940- .... SATA 5
Berenbaum, Linda Bayer
See Bayer, Linda
Berenbaum, Michael 1945- CANR-100
Earlier sketch in CA 146
Berends, Polly Berrien 1939- 108
See also SATA 50
See also SATA-Brief 38
Berendsohn, Walter A(rthur) 1884-1984(?) CANR-34
Earlier sketch in CA 33-36R
Berendt, Joachim Ernst 1922-2000 ... CANR-30
Obituary 188
Earlier sketches in CA 69-72, CANR-12
Berendt, John (Lawrence) 1939- CANR-93
Earlier sketches in CA 146, CANR-75
See also CLC 86
See also DA3
See also MTCW 2
See also MTFW 2005
Berendzen, Richard (Earl) 1938- 85-88
Berenson, Conrad 1930- 9-12R
Berenson, F(rances) M(aria) 1929- CANR-64
Earlier sketch in CA 129
Berenson, Laurien 192
Berenstain, Jan(ice) 1923- CANR-108
Earlier sketches in CA 25-28R, CANR-14, 36, 77
See also CLR 19
See also CWRI 5
See also MAICYA 1, 2
See also SAAS 20
See also SATA 12, 64, 129, 135
Berenstain, Michael 1951- CANR-36
Earlier sketches in CA 97-100, CANR-14
See also SATA 45
Berenstain, Stan(ley) 1923- CANR-108
Earlier sketches in CA 25-28R, CANR-14, 36
See also CLR 19
See also CWRI 5
See also MAICYA 1, 2
See also SAAS 20
See also SATA 12, 64, 129, 135
Berent, Waclaw 1873-1940 .... DLB 215
Bereny, Gail Rubin 1942- 85-88
Berenzy, Alix 1957- 133
See also SATA 65
Beresford, Anne 1929- CANR-133
Earlier sketches in CA 97-100, CANR-70
See also CP 1, 2, 3, 4, 5, 6, 7
See also CWP
See also DLB 40
Beresford, Bruce 1940- 213
Beresford, Elisabeth 1928- CANR-112
Earlier sketches in CA 102, CANR-53
See also SAAS 20
See also SATA 25, 86, 141
Beresford, J(ohn) D(avys) 1873-1947 155
Brief entry 112
See also DLB 162, 178, 197
See also SFW 4
See also SUFW 1
See also TCLC 81
Beresford, Maurice Warwick 1920- .. CANR-72
Earlier sketch in CA 13-16R
Beresford, Peter
See Horsley, (Beresford) Peter (Torrington)
Beresford-Howe, Constance 1922- . CANR-134
Earlier sketch in CA 53-56
See also AITN 2
See also DLB 88
Beresiner, Yasha 1940- CANR-12
Earlier sketch in CA 69-72
Beretta, Lia 1934- 17-20R
Berg, A(ndrew) Scott 1949(?)- CANR-85
Earlier sketch in CA 81-84
See also BEST 89:3
See also NCFS 1
Berg, Adriane G(ilda) 1948- CANR-136
Earlier sketch in CA 119
See also SATA 152
Berg, Alan (David) 1932- CANR-22
Earlier sketch in CA 45-48
Berg, Barbara J. 124
Berg, Bjoern 1923- .... SATA-Brief 47
Berg, Darrel E. 1920- 17-20R
Berg, Dave
See Berg, David
Berg, David 1920-2002 .... CANR-10
Obituary 207
Earlier sketch in CA 21-24R
See also SATA 27
See also SATA-Obit 137
Berg, Elizabeth 1948- CANR-98
Earlier sketch in CA 147
See also DLB 292
See also SATA 104
Berg, Fred Anderson 1948- 37-40R
Berg, Frederick S(ven) 1928- 53-56
Berg, Friedrich Kantor
See Kantor-Berg, Friedrich
Berg, Goesta 1903-1993 69-72
Berg, Irwin August 1913-2001 .... 13-16R
Berg, Ivar E(lis), Jr. 1929- CANR-13
Earlier sketch in CA 21-24R
Berg, James J. 1964- 215
Berg, Jean Horton 1913-1995 .... CANR-4
Earlier sketch in CA 53-56
See also SATA 6
Berg, Joan
See Victor, Joan Berg
Berg, John C. 1943- 150
Berg, Larry L(ee) 1939- 41-44R
Berg, Lasse 1943- CANR-12
Earlier sketch in CA 73-76
Berg, Leila Rita 1917- 101
See also CWRI 5
Berg, Louis 1901-1972
Obituary 37-40R
Berg, M. C.
See Berg, Michael C(hristian)
Berg, Mary
See Wattenberg, Miriam
Berg, Michael C(hristian) 1955- 215
Berg, Orley M. 1918- 17-20R
Berg, Paul Conrad 1921- 33-36R
Berg, Richard F(rederick) 1936- 115
Berg, Rick 1951- 93-96
Berg, Ron 1952- .... SATA 48
Berg, Stephen (Walter) 1934- CANR-106
Earlier sketches in CA 13-16R, CANR-8
See also CP 1, 2, 3, 4, 5, 6, 7
See also DLB 5
Berg, Thomas L(eRoy) 1930- 69-72
Berg, Viola Jacobson 1918- CANR-5
Earlier sketch in CA 53-56
Berg, William 1938- 97-100
Berg, William J. 1942- 215
Bergamini, David H(owland) 1928-1983 .... CANR-15
Obituary 110
Earlier sketch in CA 1-4R
Bergamini, John D. 1925(?)-1982
Obituary 108
Bergan, Ronald 194
Bergaust, Erik 1925-1978 .... CANR-32
Obituary 77-80
Earlier sketch in CA 73-76
See also SATA 20
Berge, Carol 1928- CANR-7
Earlier sketch in CA 13-16R
See also CAAS 10
See also CP 1, 2, 3, 4, 5, 6, 7
Berge, H(ans) C(ornelius) ten
See ten Berge, Hans Cornelis
See also CWW 2
See also EWL 3
Begel, Colin J. 1963- 207
See also SATA 137
Bergel, Egon Ernst 1894-1969 .... CAP-2
Earlier sketch in CA 21-22
Bergelson, David (Rafailovich) 1884-1952 . 220
See also Bergelson, Dovid
See also TCLC 81
Bergelson, Dovid
See Bergelson, David (Rafailovich)
See also EWL 3
Bergen, Candice 1946- 142
Bergen, David 1957- CANR-125
Earlier sketch in CA 161
Bergen, Joyce 1949- .... SATA 95
Bergen, Peter L(ampert) 1962- 198
Bergen, Polly 1930- 57-60
Bergendoff, Conrad J(ohn) I(mmanuel) 1895-1997 .... CANR-13
Earlier sketch in CA 33-36R
Bergengruen, Werner 1892-1964
Obituary 114
See also DLB 56
Berger, Alan L. 1939- 198
Berger, Andrew J(ohn) 1915-2000 .... CANR-14
Earlier sketch in CA 41-44R
Berger, Anna Maria Busse 146
Berger, Arthur Asa 1933- CANR-51
Earlier sketches in CA 25-28R, CANR-10, 26
Berger, Arthur S. 1920- 176
Berger, Barbara (Helen) 1945- CANR-141
Earlier sketch in CA 145
See also SATA 77
Berger, Bennett Maurice 1926- CANR-4
Earlier sketch in CA 1-4R
Berger, Brigitte (M. L.) 1928- 131
Berger, Bruce 1938- CANR-117
Earlier sketches in CA 112, CANR-30, 56
Berger, Carl 1925- 9-12R
Berger, Charles R. 167
Berger, Colonel
See Malraux, (Georges-)Andre
Berger, David 1943- CANR-105
Earlier sketch in CA 115
Berger, David G. 1941- 129
Berger, Elmer 1908-1996 61-64
Obituary 154
Berger, Evelyn Miller 1896-1990 ...... CANR-14
Earlier sketch in CA 37-40R
Berger, Fredericka 1932- 131
Berger, Gilda 1935- 134
Brief entry 118
See also SATA 88
See also SATA-Brief 42
Berger, H. Jean 1924- 13-16R
Berger, Harry, Jr. 1924- 110
Berger, Hilbert J. 1920- 57-60
Berger, Ivan (Bennett) 1939- CANR-17
Earlier sketch in CA 97-100
Berger, John (Peter) 1926- CANR-117
Earlier sketches in CA 81-84, CANR-51, 78
See also BRWS 4
See also CLC 2, 19
See also CN 1, 2, 3, 4, 5, 6, 7
See also DLB 14, 207, 319
Berger, John J(oseph) 1945- 69-72

Berger, Josef 1903-1971 ... 5-8R
Obituary ... 33-36R
See also SATA 36
Berger, Joseph 1924- ... 41-44R
Berger, Joseph 1945- ... 201
Berger, Joyce 1924- ... 176
Berger, Karen 1944- ... 122
Berger, Keith 1952- ... 171
Berger, Klaus 1901-2000 ... CAP-1
Earlier sketch in CA 13-14
Berger, Marilyn 1935- ... 101
Berger, Marjorie Sue 1916- ... 13-16R
Berger, Mark L(ewis) 1942-
Brief entry ... 109
Berger, Maurice 1956- ... 192
Berger, Melvin H. 1927- ... CANR-142
Earlier sketches in CA 5-8R, CANR-4
See also CLC 12
See also CLR 32
See also SAAS 2
See also SATA 5, 88, 158
See also SATA-Essay 124
Berger, Meyer 1898-1959(?) ... 154
Brief entry ... 120
See also DLB 29
Berger, Michael L(ouis) 1943- ... CANR-32
Earlier sketches in CA 77-80, CANR-14
Berger, Morroe 1917-1981 ... CANR-4
Obituary ... 103
Earlier sketch in CA 1-4R
Berger, Nan 1914-1998 ... 113
Berger, Peter Ludwig 1929- ... CANR-1
Earlier sketch in CA 1-4R
Berger, Phil 1942-2001 ... CANR-100
Obituary ... 194
Earlier sketches in CA 61-64, CANR-12, 55
See also SATA 62
Berger, Rainer 1930- ... 37-40R
Berger, Raoul 1901-2000 ... CANR-44
Obituary ... 189
Earlier sketch in CA 93-96
Berger, Raymond M(ark) 1950- ... 109
Berger, Robert W(illiam) 1936- ... 49-52
Berger, Ronald J. 1951- ... 222
Berger, Samantha (Allison) 1969- ... 211
See also SATA 140
Berger, Sidney 1936- ... 176
Berger, Stefan 1964- ... CANR-112
Earlier sketch in CA 154
Berger, Stuart 1953-1994 ... 112
Obituary ... 144
Berger, Suzanne E(lizabeth) 1944- ... 105
Berger, Terry 1933- ... 37-40R
See also SATA 8
Berger, Thomas (Louis) 1924- ... CANR-128
Earlier sketches in CA 1-4R, CANR-5, 28, 51
Interview in ... CANR-28
See also BPFB 1
See also CLC 3, 5, 8, 11, 18, 38
See also CN 1, 2, 3, 4, 5, 6, 7
See also DAM NOV
See also DLB 2
See also DLBY 1980
See also EWL 3
See also FANT
See also MAL 5
See also MTCW 1, 2
See also MTFW 2005
See also RHW
See also TCLE 1:1
See also TCWW 1, 2
Berger, Thomas R(odney) 1933- ... CANR-139
Earlier sketch in CA 143
Berger, Todd R. 1968- ... 218
Berger, Yves 1934-2004 ... 85-88
Obituary ... 233
Bergeret, Ida Treat 1889(?)-1978
Obituary ... 77-80
Berger-Kiss, Andres 1927- ... 175
Bergeron, Arthur W(illiam), Jr. 1946- ... 141
Bergeron, David M(oore) 1938- ... CANR-2
Earlier sketch in CA 45-48
Bergeron, Paul H. 1938- ... 101
Bergeron, Victor (Jules, Jr.) 1902-1984 ... 89-92
Obituary ... 114
Bergerud, Eric M. 1948- ... CANR-143
Earlier sketch in CA 141
Berges, Emily Trafford 1937- ... 132
Berges, Marshall (William) 1921(?)-1988
Obituary ... 126
Bergesen, Albert J. 1942- ... 209
Bergeson, John B(rian) 1935- ... 69-72
Bergevin, Paul (Emile) 1906-1993 ... CANR-2
Earlier sketch in CA 5-8R
Bergey, Alyce (Mae) 1934- ... CANR-7
Earlier sketch in CA 5-8R
See also SATA 45
Berggren, W(illiam) A(lfred) 1931- ... 123
Berghahn, Volker R(olf) 1938- ... CANR-115
Earlier sketches in CA 103, CANR-20
Bergier, Jacques 1912-1978 ... CANR-37
Obituary ... 81-84
Earlier sketch in CA 85-88
Bergin, Allen E. 1934- ... 45-48
Bergin, John 1966- ... 148
Bergin, Kenneth Glenny 1911-1981
Obituary ... 103
Bergin, Mark 1961- ... 186
See also SATA 114, 160
Bergin, Thomas Goddard
1904-1987 ... CANR-79
Obituary ... 124
Earlier sketches in CA 9-12R, CANR-3
Bergin, Thomas J. (Tim) 1940- ... 160
Bergland, Martha 1945- ... CANR-86
Earlier sketches in CA 130, CANR-68
Berglas, Steven 1949- ... CANR-113
Earlier sketch in CA 142
Bergman, Andrew 1945- ... CANR-106
Earlier sketch in CA 149
Bergman, Arlene Eisen 1942- ... 61-64
Bergman, Bernard A(aron) 1894-1980 ... 102
Obituary ... 97-100
Bergman, Bo Hjalmar 1869-1967
Obituary ... 25-28R
Bergman, David (L.) 1950- ... CANR-94
Earlier sketches in CA 106, CANR-22, 51
Bergman, Donna 1934- ... SATA 73
Bergman, Eugene 1930- ... 135
Bergman, Floyd L(awrence) 1927- ... CANR-17
Earlier sketches in CA 49-52, CANR-2
Bergman, Hannah E(stermann)
1925-1981 ... 69-72
Obituary ... 135
Bergman, Hjalmar (Frederik Elgerus)
1883-1931 ... 185
Brief entry ... 119
See also DLB 259
See also EWL 3
Bergman, (Shmuel) Hugo 1883-1975
Obituary ... 57-60
Bergman, (Ernst) Ingmar 1918- ... CANR-70
Earlier sketches in CA 81-84, CANR-33
See also AAYA 61
See also CLC 16, 72, 210
See also CWW 2
See also DLB 257
See also MTCW 2
See also MTFW 2005
Bergman, Ingrid 1915-1982 ... 132
Obituary ... 107
Bergman, Jay Asa 1948- ... 110
Bergman, Jules (Verne) 1929-1987 ... CANR-79
Obituary ... 121
Earlier sketch in CA 108
Interview in ... CA-108
Bergman, Lewis 1918-1988
Obituary ... 127
Bergman, Stephen J. 1944- ... CANR-80
Bergman, Susan ... 172
Bergman, Tamar 1939- ... CANR-68
Earlier sketch in CA 138
See also SATA 95
Bergmann, Ernst W. 1896(?)-1977
Obituary ... 69-72
Bergmann, Fred L(ouis) 1916- ... 61-64
Bergmann, Frithjof H. 1930- ... 101
Bergmann, Peter G(abriel) 1915-2002 ... 21-24R
Obituary ... 209
Bergner, Daniel ... 234
Bergo, Bettina (G.) 1957- ... 189
Bergon, Frank 1943- ... 152
Bergonzi, Bernard 1929- ... CANR-8
Earlier sketch in CA 17-20R
Bergonzo, Jean Louis 1939-(?) ... CAP-2
Earlier sketch in CA 25-28
Bergquist, Charles 1942- ... 234
Bergquist, Laura (Cecella) 1918-1982
Obituary ... 108
Bergquist, William Hastings 1940- ... 144
Bergreen, Laurence R. 1950- ... CANR-72
Earlier sketches in CA 104, CANR-42
See also BEST 90:4
Bergsma, Jody Lynn ... SATA 163
Bergson, Abram 1914-2003 ... 13-16R
Obituary ... 215
Bergson, Henri(-Louis) 1859-1941 ... 164
See also EW 8
See also EWL 3
See also GFL 1789 to the Present
See also TCLC 32
Bergson, Leo
See Stebel, S(idney) L(eo)
Bergsson, Gudbergur 1932- ... DLB 293
See also EWL 3
Bergstein, Eleanor 1938- ... CANR-5
Earlier sketch in CA 53-56
See also CLC 4
Bergsten, C. Fred 1941- ... 111
Bergsten, Staffan 1932- ... CANR-6
Earlier sketch in CA 57-60
Bergstrom, Elaine 1946- ... 149
Bergstrom, Joan M(argosian) 1940- ... 144
Bergstrom, Louise 1914- ... 29-32R
Bergum, Constance R. 1952- ... SATA 121
Bergvall, Caroline 1963- ... CWP
Beria, Sergo 1924-2000 ... 213
Beringause, Arthur F. 1919- ... 33-36R
Beringer, Richard E. 1933- ... 81-84
Berio, Luciano 1925-2003 ... 146
Obituary ... 216
Berk, Fred 1911(?)-1980
Obituary ... 97-100
Berke, Joel S(ommers) 1936-1981 ... 110
Obituary ... 105
Berke, Joseph H(erman) 1939- ... 57-60
Berke, Roberta 1943- ... CANR-43
Earlier sketch in CA 106
Berkebile, Don(ald) H(erbert) 1926- ... CANR-8
Earlier sketch in CA 61-64
Berkebile, Fred D(onovan) 1900-1978 ... 5-8R
Obituary ... 103
See also SATA-Obit 26
Berkeley, Anthony
See Cox, A(nthony) B(erkeley)
See also DLB 77
Berkeley, David S(helley) 1917- ... 41-44R
Berkeley, Edmund 1912-1993 ... 133
Brief entry ... 112
Berkeley, Ellen Perry 1931- ... 110
Berkeley, George 1685-1753 ... DLB 31, 101, 252
Berkeley, Sara 1967- ... CANR-100
Earlier sketch in CA 152
See also CWP
Berkemeyer, William C. 1908-2000 ... CAP-2
Earlier sketch in CA 25-28
Berkenstadt, Jim 1956- ... 176
Berkey, Barry Robert 1935- ... 69-72
See also SATA 24
Berkey, Helen 1898-1977 ... CAP-2
Earlier sketch in CA 23-24
Berkey, Jonathan P. 1959- ... 140
Berkhof, Louis 1873-1957 ... 221
Berkhofer, Robert Frederick, Jr. 1931- ... 13-16R
Berkin, Carol (Ruth) 1942- ... CANR-134
Earlier sketches in CA 69-72, CANR-11
Berkley, George E(ugene) 1928- ... 127
Brief entry ... 113
Berkman, Alexander 1870-1936 ... DLB 303
Berkman, Edward O(scar) 1914- ... CANR-9
Earlier sketch in CA 61-64
Berkman, Harold W(illiam) 1926- ... CANR-44
Earlier sketches in CA 53-56, CANR-5, 21
Berkman, Pamela Rafael ... 232
Berkman, Richard Lyle 1946- ... CANR-1
Earlier sketch in CA 45-48
Berkman, Sue 1936- ... 45-48
Berkman, Ted
See Berkman, Edward O(scar)
Berkoff, Steven 1937- ... CANR-72
Earlier sketch in CA 104
See also CBD
See also CD 5, 6
See also CLC 56
Berkove, Lawrence Ivan 1930- ... CANR-82
Earlier sketches in CA 106, CANR-36
Berkovich, Felix 1932- ... 197
Berkovitch, Nitza 1955- ... 211
Berkovits, Eliezer 1908-1992 ... CANR-37
Earlier sketches in CA 1-4R, CANR-2
Berkovitz, Irving H(erbert) 1924- ... 57-60
Berkovitz, Jay R. 1951- ... 134
Berkow, Ira 1940- ... CANR-99
Earlier sketch in CA 97-100
Berkowitz, Bernard 1909- ... AITN 1
Berkowitz, Dan ... 224
Berkowitz, David Sandler 1913-1983 ... 33-36R
Berkowitz, Freda Pastor 1908-1994 ... CAP-1
Earlier sketch in CA 9-10
See also SATA 12
Berkowitz, Gerald M(artin) 1942- ... 110
Berkowitz, Henry 1857-1924 ... 220
Berkowitz, Leonard 1926- ... 125
Berkowitz, Luci 1938- ... 33-36R
Berkowitz, Marvin 1938- ... CANR-30
Earlier sketch in CA 29-32R
Berkowitz, Monroe 1919- ... CANR-86
Earlier sketch in CA 130
Berkowitz, Morris Ira 1931- ... 53-56
Berkowitz, Pearl H(enriette) 1921- ... 21-24R
Berkowitz, Peter 1959- ... 151
Berkowitz, Sol 1922- ... CANR-1
Earlier sketch in CA 45-48
Berkowitz, William R(obby) 1939- ... CANR-43
Earlier sketch in CA 112
Berkson, Bill 1939- ... 180
Earlier sketches in CA 21-24R, CANR-9, 24, 49
Autobiographical Essay in ... 180
See also CP 1, 2, 3, 4, 5, 6, 7
Berkson, William Koller 1944- ... 102
Berkus, Clara Widess 1909- ... 146
See also SATA 78
Berlak, Harold 1932- ... 33-36R
Berlan, Kathryn Hook 1946- ... 146
See also SATA 78
Berland, Alwyn 1920- ... 125
Berland, Theodore 1929- ... CANR-18
Earlier sketches in CA 5-8R, CANR-2
Berlanstein, Lenard R(ussell) 1947- ... 69-72
Berlant, Anthony 1941- ... 184
Brief entry ... 112
Berlant, Tony
See Berlant, Anthony
Berle, Adolf A(ugustus), Jr. 1895-1971 ... CAP-2
Obituary ... 29-32R
Earlier sketch in CA 23-24
Berle, Beatrice Bishop 1902-1993 ... CANR-80
Obituary ... 141
Earlier sketch in CA 114
Berle, Gustav 1920-1996 ... 140
Obituary ... 153
Berle, Milton 1908-2002 ... 77-80
Obituary ... 209
See also AITN 1
Berleant, Arnold 1932- ... 29-32R
Berler, Beatrice (Adele) 1915- ... 139
Berlfein, Judy Reiss 1958- ... 147
See also SATA 79
Berlin, Adam 1966- ... 235
Berlin, Ellin (Mackay) 1902(?)-1988 ... 65-68
Obituary ... 126
Berlin, Ira 1941- ... CANR-98
Earlier sketches in CA 101, CANR-56
Berlin, Irving 1888-1989 ... CANR-79
Obituary ... 129
Earlier sketch in CA 108
See also DLB 265
See also IDFW 3, 4
Berlin, Irving N. 1917- ... CANR-13
Earlier sketch in CA 21-24R
Berlin, Isaiah 1909-1997 ... 85-88
Obituary ... 162
See also TCLC 105
Berlin, Jean V. 1962- ... 150
Berlin, Lucia 1936- ... 198
See also DLB 130
Berlin, Michael J(oseph) 1938- ... 69-72
Berlin, Normand 1931- ... 57-60
Berlin, Richard Emmett 1894(?)-1986
Obituary ... 118
Berlin, Sven (Paul) 1911-1999 ... CANR-15
Earlier sketch in CA 85-88
Berlind, Bruce 1926- ... 33-36R
Berliner, Don 1930- ... CANR-45
Earlier sketches in CA 105, CANR-21
See also SATA 33
Berliner, Franz 1930- ... CANR-29
Earlier sketches in CA 29-32R, CANR-12
See also SATA 13
Berliner, Herman A(lbert) 1944- ... 77-80
Berliner, Janet 1939- ... CANR-114
Earlier sketch in CA 163
Berliner, Joseph S(cholom) 1921-2001 ... 69-72
Obituary ... 201
Berliner, Michael S. 1938- ... 153
Berlinger, Joe 1961- ... 216
Berlinski, David 1942- ... 196
Berlioz, Hector 1803-1869 ... EW 6
Berlitz, Charles (L. Frambach)
1914-2003 ... CANR-9
Obituary ... 224
Earlier sketch in CA 5-8R
Interview in ... CANR-9
See also SATA 32
See also SATA-Obit 151
Berl-Lee, Maria
See Lee, Maria Berl
Berlo, Janet Catherine ... 200
Berloni, William 1956- ... 77-80
Berlow, Alan 1950- ... 159
Berlye, Milton K. 1915-1986 ... CANR-31
Earlier sketch in CA 49-52
Berlyn, Phillippa 1923- ... CP 1
Berlyne, D(aniel) E(llis) 1924- ... 13-16R
Berman, Alex 1914-2000 ... 215
Berman, Arthur I(rwin) 1925- ... 97-100
Berman, Bennett H(erbert) 1927- ... 105
Berman, Bob ... 238
Berman, Bruce D(avid) 1944- ... 41-44R
Berman, Claire 1936- ... CANR-10
Earlier sketch in CA 25-28R
Berman, Connie 1949- ... 93-96
Berman, Daniel M(arvin) 1928-1967 ... CANR-1
Earlier sketch in CA 1-4R
Berman, David 1942- ... CANR-108
Earlier sketch in CA 135, 147
Berman, Ed 1941- ... 106
Berman, Edgar F(rank) 1915(?)-1987 ... 97-100
Obituary ... 124
Berman, Eleanor 1934- ... 85-88
Berman, Emile Zola 1902-1981
Obituary ... 104
Berman, Harold Joseph 1918- ... CANR-15
Earlier sketch in CA 89-92
Berman, Jeffrey 1945- ... CANR-90
Earlier sketch in CA 134
Berman, Larry 1951- ... CANR-113
Earlier sketches in CA 93-96, CANR-48
Berman, Linda 1948- ... 113
See also SATA 38
Berman, Louise M(arguerite) 1928- ... 21-24R
Berman, Marshall 1940- ... CANR-144
Earlier sketch in CA 29-32R
See also DLB 246
Berman, Milton 1924- ... 1-4R
Berman, Mitch 1956- ... 136
Berman, Morris 1944- ... 139
Berman, Morton 1924- ... CANR-2
Earlier sketch in CA 5-8R
Berman, Morton M(ayer) 1899-1986
Obituary ... 118
Berman, Pandro S. 1905-1996 ... IDFW 3, 4
Berman, Paul (Lawrence) 1949- ... CANR-135
Earlier sketch in CA 110
See also SATA 66
Berman, Ronald 1930- ... 13-16R
Berman, Ruth 1958- ... CANR-139
Earlier sketch in CA 156
Berman, Sabina 1955- ... DLB 305
Berman, Sanford 1933- ... 37-40R
Berman, Simeon M(oses) 1935- ... 49-52
Berman, Susan 1945-2000 ... CANR-17
Obituary ... 190
Earlier sketch in CA 65-68
Berman, William C(arl) 1932- ... 41-44R
Bermange, Barry 1933- ... CANR-67
Earlier sketch in CA 57-60
See also CBD
See also CD 5, 6
Bermann, Sandra L. 1947- ... 156
Bermant, Chaim (Icyk) 1929-1998 ... CANR-105
Earlier sketches in CA 57-60, CANR-6, 31, 57
See also CLC 40
See also CN 2, 3, 4, 5, 6
Bermant, Gordon 1936- ... 120
Bermel, Albert (Cyril) 1927- ... CANR-11
Earlier sketch in CA 69-72
Bermeo, Nancy 1951- ... 131
Bermingham, Ann 1948- ... CANR-96
Earlier sketch in CA 128
Bermont, Hubert Ingram 1924- ... CANR-5
Earlier sketch in CA 9-12R
Bermosk, Loretta Sue 1918-1982 ... CANR-3
Earlier sketch in CA 9-12R
Bern, Maria Rasputin Soloviev 1900(?)-1977
Obituary ... 73-76
Bern, Victoria
See Fisher, M(ary) F(rances) K(ennedy)
Berna, Paul 1910-1994 ... CANR-78
Obituary ... 143
Earlier sketch in CA 73-76
See also CLR 19
See also SATA 15
See also SATA-Obit 78

Cumulative Index 49 Berry

Bernabei, Alfio 1941- CANR-14
Earlier sketch in CA 77-80
Bernadette
See Watts, (Anna) Bernadette
Bernadotte, Folke 1895-1948 213
Bernal (y Garcia y Pimentel), Ignacio
1910-1992 .... CANR-78
Obituary 136
Earlier sketches in CA 9-12R, CANR-5
Bernal, J(ohn) D(esmond) 1901-1971 97-100
Obituary 33-36R
Bernal, Judith F. 1939- 57-60
Bernal, Martin (Gardiner) 1937- CANR-110
Earlier sketch in CA 104
Bernal, Vicente J. 1888-1915 .... DLB 82
See also HW 1
Bernanos, (Paul Louis) Georges
1888-1948 .... CANR-94
Brief entry 104
Earlier sketch in CA 130
See also DLB 72
See also EWL 3
See also GFL 1789 to the Present
See also RGWL 2, 3
See also TCLC 3
Bernanos, Michel 1924-1964 167
Bernard, Andre 1956- 132
Bernard, April 1956- CANR-144
Earlier sketch in CA 131
See also CLC 59
Bernard, Bruce 1928-2000 152
Obituary 190
See also SATA 78
See also SATA-Obit 124
Bernard, Catherine 1633(?)-1712 .... DLB 268
Bernard, Christopher 1950- 180
Autobiographical Essay in 180
Bernard, Emily 1967- 201
Bernard, George 1939- 73-76
Bernard, George I. 1949- .... SATA 39
Bernard, Guy
See Barber, Stephen Guy
Bernard, H(arvey) Russell 1940- 41-44R
Bernard, Harold W. 1908-1998 .... CANR-4
Earlier sketch in CA 1-4R
Bernard, Harry 1898-1979 145
See also CCA 1
See also DLB 92
Bernard, Hugh Y(ancey), Jr. 1919- 21-24R
Bernard, Jack F. 1930- 21-24R
Bernard, Jacqueline (de Sieyes)
1921-1983 .... CANR-78
Obituary 117
Earlier sketch in CA 21-24R
See also BYA 2
See also SATA 8
See also SATA-Obit 45
Bernard, James 1925-2001 .... IDFW 3, 4
Bernard, Jami 1956- CANR-126
Earlier sketch in CA 152
Bernard, Jay
See Sawkins, Raymond H(arold)
Bernard, Jean-Jacques 1888-1972
Obituary 37-40R
Bernard, Jessie (Shirley) 1903-1996 151
See also FW
Bernard, John 1756-1828 .... DLB 37
Bernard, Kenneth 1930- CANR-137
Earlier sketches in CA 41-44R, CANR-67
See also CAD
See also CD 5, 6
Bernard, Kenneth A(nderson) 1906- 29-32R
Bernard, Laureat J(oseph) 1922- 25-28R
Bernard, Marley
See Graves, Susan B(ernard)
Bernard, Nelson T(ed), Jr. 1925- 123
Bernard, Oliver 1925- 13-16R
See also CP 1
Bernard, Patricia 1942- 175
See also SATA 106
Bernard, Paul Peter 1929- 89-92
Bernard, Richard 1568-c. 1641 .... DLB 281
Bernard, Richard Marion 1948- 105
Bernard, Robert
See Martin, Robert Bernard
Bernard, Sidney 1918- 29-32R
Bernard, Stefan
See Baumrin, Bernard H(erbert)
Bernard, Thelma Rene 1940- 57-60
Bernard, Thomas J(oseph) 1945- 138
Bernard, Will 1915- 93-96
Bernard, William Spencer 1907-1986
Obituary 118
Bernardi, Adria 1957- 234
Bernardi, Daniel (Leonard) 1964- 175
Bernardin, James (B.) 1966- .... SATA 112
Bernardin, Joseph (Louis Cardinal)
1928-1996 .... CANR-113
Earlier sketch in CA 160
Bernardin de Saint-Pierre, Jacques-Henri
1737-1814 .... DLB 313
See also GFL Beginnings to 1789
Bernardini, Joe 1937- 136
Bernardo, Aldo S(isto) 1920- CANR-4
Earlier sketch in CA 1-4R
Bernardo, Anilu .... BYA 9
Bernardo, James V. 1913-1996 .... 17-20R
Bernardo, Jose Raul .... DNFS 2
Bernardo, Stephanie
See Johns, Stephanie Bernardo
Bernard of Chartres 1060(?)-1124(?) .... DLB 115
Bernard of Clairvaux 1090-1153 .... DLB 208
Bernards, Neal 1963- .... SATA 71
Bernard Silvestris fl. c. 1130-fl. c.
1160 .... DLB 208
Bernari, Carlo 1909-1992 .... DLB 177
See also EWL 3
Bernarn, Terrave
See Burnett, David (Benjamin Foley)
Bernau, George 1945- 127
Bernauer, George F. 1941- 29-32R
Bernauer, Thomas 1963- 194
Bernays, Anne
See Kaplan, Anne Bernays
Bernays, Edward L. 1891-1995 .... CANR-78
Obituary 147
Earlier sketch in CA 17-20R
Bernazza, Ann Marie
See Haase, Ann Marie Bernazza
Bernbach, William 1911-1982
Obituary 108
Bernd, Joseph Laurence 1923- 17-20R
Berndt, Ronald Murray 1916-1990 ... CANR-19
Earlier sketches in CA 5-8R, CANR-3
Berndt, Walter 1899-1979
Obituary 89-92
Berndtson, Arthur 1913-1997 108
Berne, Eric (Lennard) 1910-1970 .... CANR-4
Obituary 25-28R
Earlier sketch in CA 5-8R
See also Gandalac, Lennard and
Horsely, Ramsbottom and
Pinto, Peter
See also MTCW 1
Berne, Leo
See Davies, L(eslie) P(urnell)
Berne, Patricia H(iggins) 1934- 110
Berne, Stanley 1923- CANR-72
Earlier sketches in CA 45-48, CANR-1
Berne, Suzanne 1961- 228
Berne, Victoria
See Fisher, M(ary) F(rances) K(ennedy)
Berner, Carl Walter 1902-1997 .... CANR-37
Earlier sketch in CA 49-52
Berner, Jeff 1940- CANR-108
Earlier sketch in CA 89-92
Berner, Robert A(rbuckle) 1935- 155
Berner, Robert B(arry) 1940- 41-44R
Berners-Lee, Tim 1955- 187
Bernert, Eleanor H.
See Sheldon, Eleanor Bernert
Bernet, Michael M. 1930- 25-28R
Bernhard, Durga T. 1961- .... SATA 80
Bernhard, Emery 1950- .... SATA 80
Bernhard, Sandra 1955(?)- 137
Bernhard, Thomas 1931-1989 .... CANR-57
Obituary 127
Earlier sketches in CA 85-88, CANR-32
See also CDWLB 2
See also CLC 3, 32, 61
See also DC 14
See also DLB 85, 124
See also EWL 3
See also MTCW 1
See also RGWL 2, 3
See also TCLC 165
Bernhard, Virginia Purington
1937- CANR-107
Earlier sketch in CA 112
Bernhardsen, Bris
See Bernhardsen, (Einar) Christian (Rosenvinge)
Bernhardsen, (Einar) Christian (Rosenvinge)
1923- 29-32R
Bernhardt, Clyde Edric Barron 1905-1986
Obituary 119
Bernhardt, Frances Simonsen 1932- 103
Bernhardt, Karl S. 1901-1967 .... CAP-1
Earlier sketch in CA 13-14
Bernhardt, Sarah (Henriette Rosine)
1844-1923 157
See also TCLC 75
Bernhardt, William 1960- CANR-108
Earlier sketch in CA 151
Bernheim, Emmanuelle 1955- 148
Bernheim, Evelyne 1935- 21-24R
Bernheim, Kayla F. 1946- 108
Bernheim, Marc 1924- 21-24R
Bernheimer, Charles 1942- 134
Bernheimer, Martin 1936- 69-72
Bernier, Alexis 1956- 130
Bernier, Olivier 1941- CANR-93
Earlier sketches in CA 105, CANR-30
Bernieres, Louis de
See de Bernieres, Louis
See also DLB 271
Bernikow, Louise 1940- CANR-105
Earlier sketch in CA 132
Berninghausen, David K(nipe) 1916- 111
Bernlef, J.
See Marsman, Hendrik Jan
Berns, Julie 1899(?)-1983
Obituary 111
Berns, Walter (Fred) 1919- CANR-107
Earlier sketches in CA 101, CANR-24
Bernstam, Mikhail S. 1943- 130
Bernstein, Alvin H(owell) 1939- 89-92
Bernstein, Anne C(arolyn) 1944- 105
Bernstein, Arnold 1920- 29-32R
Bernstein, Barton J(annen) 1936- 37-40R
Bernstein, Basil (Bernard) 1924-2000
Obituary 189
Brief entry 119
Bernstein, Blanche 1912-1993 .... CANR-78
Obituary 140
Earlier sketch in CA 110
Bernstein, Burton 1932- CANR-21
Earlier sketches in CA 1-4R, CANR-4
Bernstein, Carl 1944- 81-84
See also AITN 1
Bernstein, Charles 1950- CANR-90
Earlier sketch in CA 129
See also CAAS 24
See also CLC 142,
See also CP 4, 5, 6, 7
See also DLB 169
Bernstein, Daryl (Evan) 1976- 149
See also SATA 81
Bernstein, David 1915-1974
Obituary 53-56
Bernstein, David E(liot) 1967- 224
Bernstein, Dorothy Lewis 1914-1988 161
Bernstein, Douglas A. 1942- 45-48
Bernstein, Eduard 1850-1932 211
Bernstein, Ellen 1953- 171
Bernstein, Elmer 1922-2004 .... IDFW 3, 4
Bernstein, Gail Lee 1939- 115
Bernstein, Gerry 1927- 105
Bernstein, Harry 1909-1993 .... CANR-1
Earlier sketch in CA 1-4R
Bernstein, Hilda 1915- 130
Bernstein, Hillel 1892(?)-1977
Obituary 69-72
Bernstein, Ingrid
See Kirsch, Sarah
Bernstein, Irving 1916-2001
Obituary 199
Brief entry 114
Bernstein, J(erome) S(traus) 1936- 25-28R
Bernstein, Jacob 1946- 104
Bernstein, Jane 1949- CANR-93
Earlier sketch in CA 104
Bernstein, Jared 1955- 145
Bernstein, Jeremy 1929- CANR-27
Earlier sketch in CA 13-16R
Bernstein, Jerry Marx 1908-1969 .... CAP-2
Earlier sketch in CA 25-28
Bernstein, Joanne E(ckstein) 1943- ... CANR-29
Earlier sketches in CA 77-80, CANR-13
See also SATA 15
Bernstein, John Andrew 1944- 124
Bernstein, Joseph M(ilton) 1908-1975
Obituary 57-60
Bernstein, Laurie 201
Bernstein, Leonard 1918-1990 .... CANR-79
Obituary 132
Earlier sketches in CA 1-4R, CANR-2, 21
See also LAIT 4
See also MTFW 2005
Bernstein, Lewis 1915- 33-36R
Bernstein, Margery 1933- 186
Earlier sketch in CA 57-60
See also SATA 114
Bernstein, Marilyn 1929- 21-24R
Bernstein, Mark 1950- 224
Bernstein, Marver H(illel) 1919-1990 . CANR-2
Earlier sketch in CA 1-4R
Bernstein, Marvin David 1923- 45-48
Bernstein, Merton C(lay) 1923- 17-20R
Bernstein, Michael Andre 1947- CANR-122
Earlier sketches in CA 124, CANR-51
Bernstein, Mordechai 1893-1983
Obituary 109
Bernstein, Morey 1919-1999 .... 21-24R
Obituary 177
Bernstein, Nina 223
Bernstein, Norman R. 1927- CANR-13
Earlier sketch in CA 33-36R
Bernstein, Paula 1944- 125
Bernstein, Peter L. 1919- 209
Bernstein, Philip S(idney)
1901-1985 .... CANR-28
Earlier sketch in CA 49-52
Bernstein, Richard 1944- 203
Bernstein, Richard J(acob) 1932-
Brief entry 113
Bernstein, Richard K. 1934- 105
Bernstein, Seymour CANR-26
Earlier sketch in CA 109
Bernstein, Theodore M(enline)
1904-1979 .... CANR-3
Earlier sketch in CA 1-4R
See also SATA 12
See also SATA-Obit 27
Bernstein, Thomas P(aul) 1937- 113
Bernstein, Walter 1919- CANR-90
Earlier sketch in CA 106
Interview in CA-106
See also IDFW 4
Bernstein, William J. 236
Bernzweig, Eli P. 1927- CANR-26
Earlier sketch in CA 29-32R
Berofsky, Bernard 1935- 89-92
Berque, Jacques Augustin 1910-1995 85-88
Obituary 149
Berquist, Goodwin F(auntleroy) 1930- .. 21-24R
Berrada, Mohamed
See Berrada, Mohammed
See also EWL 3
Berrada, Mohammed 1938-
See Berrada, Mohamed
Berrellez, Robert 1920(?)-1985
Obituary 116
Berres, Thomas Edward 1953- 239
Berrett, Delwyn G(reen) 1935- 128
Berrett, LaMar C(ecil) 1926- 53-56
Berri, Claude 1934- 152
Berrian, Albert H. 1925- 37-40R
Berriault, Gina 1926-1999 .... CANR-66
Obituary 185
Brief entry 116
Earlier sketch in CA 129
See also CLC 54, 109
See also DLB 130
See also SSC 30
See also SSFS 7,11
Berridge, Celia 1943- CANR-28
Earlier sketch in CA 110
Berridge, Elizabeth 1921- CANR-6
Earlier sketch in CA 57-60
Berridge, G(eoffrey) R(aymond)
1947- CANR-95
Earlier sketch in CA 146
Berridge, P(ercy) S(tuart) A(ttwood)
1901- 29-32R
Berrien, Edith Heal
See Heal, Edith
Berrien, F. Kenneth 1909-1971 .... CANR-1
Obituary 29-32R
Earlier sketch in CA 1-4R
Berrigan, Daniel 1921- 187
Earlier sketches in CA 33-36R, CANR-11, 43, 78
Autobiographical Essay in 187
See also CAAS 1
See also CLC 4
See also CP 1, 2, 3, 4, 5, 6, 7
See also DLB 5
Berrigan, Edmund Joseph Michael, Jr.
1934-1983 .... CANR-102
Obituary 110
Earlier sketches in CA 61-64, CANR-14
See also Berrigan, Ted
Berrigan, Philip (Francis)
1923-2002 .... CANR-11
Obituary 210
Earlier sketch in CA 13-16R
Interview in CANR-11
Berrigan, Ted
See Berrigan, Edmund Joseph Michael, Jr.
See also CLC 37
See also CP 1, 2, 3
See also DLB 5, 169
See also WP
Berrill, Jacquelyn (Batsel) 1905- 17-20R
See also SATA 12
Berrill, N(orman) J(ohn) 1903-1996 .... 17-20R
Berrington, Hugh B(ayard) 1928- 49-52
Berrington, John
See Brownjohn, Alan
Berrisford, Judith Mary
See Lewis, Judith Mary
Berry, Adrian M(ichael) 1937- CANR-25
Earlier sketches in CA 57-60, CANR-9
Berry, Andrew 226
Berry, B. J.
See Berry, Barbara J.
Berry, Barbara J. 1937- 33-36R
See also SATA 7
Berry, Bertice 1960- 190
Berry, Boyd M(cCulloch) 1939- 69-72
Berry, Brewton 1901-1993 .... CANR-3
Earlier sketch in CA 1-4R
Berry, Brian J(oe) L(obley) 1934- CANR-5
Earlier sketch in CA 13-16R
Berry, Bryan 1930-1955 177
Brief entry 112
Berry, Burton Yost 1901-1985 85-88
Berry, Carmen Renee 1953(?)- 227
Berry, Carole 167
Berry, Chad 1963- 216
Berry, Charles Edward Anderson 1931- 115
See also Berry, Chuck
Berry, Charles H. 1930- 69-72
Berry, Chuck
See Berry, Charles Edward Anderson
See also CLC 17
Berry, Cicely 1926- 93-96
Berry, D. C.
See Berry, David (Chapman)
Berry, David (Chapman) 1942- CANR-27
Earlier sketch in CA 45-48
Berry, David (Ronald) 1942- 29-32R
Berry, David (Adams) 1943- 108
Berry, Don (George) 1932- CANR-67
Earlier sketch in CA 106
See also TCWW 1, 2
Berry, Donald K(ent) 1953- 190
Berry, Edmund G(rindlay) 1915- 1-4R
Berry, Edward I. 1940- 57-60
Berry, Eliot 1949- 139
Berry, (Julia) Elizabeth 1920- 21-24R
Berry, Erick
See Best, (Evangel) Allena Champlin
Berry, Faith 1939- 133
Berry, Francis 1915- CANR-5
Earlier sketch in CA 5-8R
See also CP 1, 2, 3, 4, 5, 6, 7
Berry, Frederic Aroyce, Jr. 1906-1978
Obituary 77-80
Berry, Geoffrey 1912-1988
Obituary 124
Berry, Helen
See Rowland, D(onald) S(ydney)
Berry, Henry 1926- 85-88
Berry, Herbert 1922- CANR-29
Earlier sketch in CA 111
Berry, I. William 1934- CANR-25
Earlier sketch in CA 105
Berry, J. Bill 1945- 137
Berry, J. W. 1939- 149
Berry, Jack 1918-1984 .... 37-40R
Berry, Jake 1959- .... CAAS 24
Berry, James 1925- CANR-102
Earlier sketch in CA 135
See also AAYA 30
See also BYA 9
See also CLR 22
See also CWRI 5
See also JRDA
See also MAICYA 2
See also MAICYAS 1
See also SATA 67, 110

Berry, James 1932- 21-24R
Berry, James Gomer 1883-1968
Obituary 89-92
Berry, Jane Cobb 1915(?)-1979
Obituary 85-88
See also SATA-Obit 22
Berry, Jason 1949- 45-48
Berry, Jeffrey M. 1948- 199
Berry, Jim
See Berry, James
Berry, Jim 1946- 107
Berry, Jo(ycelyn) 1933- CANR-18
Earlier sketch in CA 102
Berry, John Nichols (III) 1933-
Brief entry 113
Berry, John Stevens 1938- 132
Berry, Jonas
See Ashbery, John (Lawrence)
See also GLL 1
Berry, Joy
See Berry, Joy Wilt
Berry, Joy Wilt 1944- 134
See also SATA 58
See also SATA-Brief 46
Berry, Katherine F(iske) 1877-1972(?) CAP-2
Earlier sketch in CA 17-18
Berry, Leonidas Harris 1902-1995 159
Berry, Linda 1940- 202
Berry, Lloyd E(ason) 1935-1977 .... 13-16R
Obituary 133
Berry, Lynn 1948- 61-64
Berry, Mary Frances 1938- CANR-92
Earlier sketches in CA 33-36R, CANR-14
See also BW 1
Berry, Michelle 1968- 213
Berry, Neil 1952- 228
Berry, Nicholas O(rlando) 1936- 93-96
Berry, Paul 1919-1999 102
Obituary 179
Berry, Philippa 1955- 201
Berry, R(obert) J(ames) 1934- 121
Berry, R(alph) M(arion) 1947- CANR-105
Earlier sketch in CA 128
Berry, Roland (Brian) 1951- 93-96
Berry, Ron(ald Anthony) 1920-1997 ...... 25-28R
Obituary 159
Berry, Rynn 1945- 164
Berry, Scyld 1954- 136
Berry, Sheila Martin 1947- 206
Berry, Sister Mary Virginia 1908(?)-1987
Obituary 122
Berry, Stephen Ames 1947- 118
Berry, Steve 1955- 234
Berry, Thomas (Mary) 1914- CANR-100
Earlier sketch in CA 21-24R
Berry, Thomas Edwin 1930- 102
Berry, Thomas Elliott 1917- 33-36R
Berry, Venise T(orriana) 1956- 221
Berry, Wallace Taft 1928-1983 .... CANR-8
Earlier sketch in CA 17-20R
Berry, Wendell (Erdman) 1934- CANR-132
Earlier sketches in CA 73-76, CANR-50, 73, 101
See also AITN 1
See also AMWS 10
See also ANW
See also CLC 4, 6, 8, 27, 46
See also CP 1, 2, 3, 4, 5, 6, 7
See also CSW
See also DAM POET
See also DLB 5, 6, 234, 275
See also MTCW 2
See also MTFW 2005
See also PC 28
See also TCLE 1:1
Berry, William D(avid) 1926- 73-76
See also SATA 14
Berry, William Turner 1888- CAP-2
Earlier sketch in CA 23-24
Berryman, Charles (Beecher) 1939- 112
Berryman, Jack W. 1947- 143
Berryman, James Thomas 1902-1971
Obituary 93-96
Berryman, Jim
See Berryman, James Thomas
Berryman, John 1914-1972 .... CANR-35
Obituary 33-36R
Earlier sketches in CAP-1, CA 13-16
See also CABS 2
See also AMW
See also CDALB 1941-1968
See also CLC 1, 2, 3, 4, 6, 8, 10, 13, 25, 62
See also CP 1
See also DAM POET
See also DLB 48
See also EWL 3
See also MAL 5
See also MTCW 1, 2
See also MTFW 2005
See also PAB
See also RGAL 4
See also WP
Berryman, Phillip E. 1938- 158
Bers, Lipman 1914-1993 159
Bersani, Leo 1931- CANR-5
Earlier sketch in CA 53-56
Berscheid, Ellen 1936- 25-28R
Bershadsky, Luba 1916-1986 131
Obituary 162
Bershtel, Sara 1947- 139
Bersia, John C(esar) 1956- 220
Bersianik, Louky 1930- 231
See also DLB 60
Berson, Harold 1926- 33-36R
See also SATA 4
Berson, Lenora E. 1926- 93-96
Berssenbrugge, Mei-mei 1947- 104
See also DLB 312
Berst, Charles A(shton) 1932- 41-44R
Berst, Jesse 116
Bert, Norman A(llen) 1942- 149
Bertagna, Julie 1962- 226
See also SATA 151
Bertcher, Harvey (Joseph) 1929- 85-88
Bertelli, Sergio 209
Bertelson, David (Earl) 1934- 21-24R
Bertematti, Richard 1971- 160
Berthelet, Thomas fl. 1524(?)-1555 ..... DLB 170
Berthelot, Helen Washburn 1904-1996 159
Berthelot, Joseph A. 1927- 21-24R
Berthoff, Ann (Rhys) E(vans) 1924- ... CANR-65
Earlier sketch in CA 129
Berthoff, Rowland (Tappan) 1921- 33-36R
Berthoff, Warner (Bement) 1925- CANR-2
Earlier sketch in CA 5-8R
Berthold, Dennis (Alfred) 1942- 117
Berthold, Margot 1922- CANR-48
Earlier sketch in CA 73-76
Berthold, Mary Paddock 1909-1997 53-56
Berthold, Richard M(artin) 1946- 131
Bertholf, Diana 1946- 115
Bertholf, Robert J. 238
Berthoud, Jacques (Alexandre)
1935- CANR-10
Earlier sketch in CA 17-20R
Berthoud, Roger 1934- 128
Berthrong, Donald J(ohn) 1922- 81-84
Berthrong, Evelyn Nagai
See Nagai Berthrong, Evelyn
Bertin, Charles 1919- 192
Bertin, Charles-Francois
See Berlitz, Charles (L. Frambach)
Bertin, Jack
See Bertin, John and
Germano, Peter B.
Bertin, John 1904-1963
Obituary 116
Bertin, Leonard M. 1918- 13-16R
Bertling, Tom 1956- CANR-122
Earlier sketch in CA 167
Bertman, Stephen (Samuel) 1937- 45-48
Berto, Giuseppe 1912-1978 202
See also DLB 177
See also EWL 3
Bertocci, Peter A(nthony) 1910-1989 .... 17-20R
See also DLB 279
Bertolet, Paul
See McLaughlin, Frank
Bertolino, James 1942- CANR-17
Earlier sketches in CA 45-48, CANR-1
See also CP 1, 2, 3, 4, 5, 6, 7
Bertolucci, Attilio 1911-2000 181
Obituary 188
See also DLB 128
Bertolucci, Bernardo 1940- CANR-125
Earlier sketch in CA 106
See also CLC 16, 157
Berton, Dick
See Roquebrune, Robert (Laroque) de
Berton, Peter (Alexander Menquez)
1922- 77-80
Berton, Pierre (Francis de Marigny)
1920-2004 .... CANR-144
Obituary 233
Earlier sketches in CA 1-4R, CANR-2, 56
See also CLC 104
See also CPW
See also DLB 68
See also SATA 99
See also SATA-Obit 158
Berton, Ralph 1910-1993 49-52
Obituary 143
Bertonasco, Marc F(rancis) 1934- 89-92
Bertram, Anthony 1897-1978
Obituary 104
Bertram, (George) Colin (Lawder)
1911-2001 .... 13-16R
Bertram, James Munro 1910-1993 65-68
Bertram, Jean De Sales CANR-12
Earlier sketch in CA 45-48
Bertram, Noel
See Fanthorpe, R(obert) Lionel
Bertram-Cox, Jean De Sales
See Bertram, Jean De Sales
Bertrand, Aloysius 1807-1841
See Bertrand, Louis "Aloysius"
Bertrand, Alvin L(ee) 1918- CANR-30
Earlier sketch in CA 45-48
Bertrand, Cecile 1953- 143
See also SATA 76
Bertrand, Charles
See Carter, David C(harles)
Bertrand, Diane Gonzales 1956- 175
See also SATA 106
Bertrand, Lewis 1897(?)-1974
Obituary 53-56
Bertrand, Louis "Aloysius"
See Bertrand, Aloysius
See also DLB 217
Bertrand, Lynne 1963- 149
See also SATA 81
Bertrand, Marsha 1950- 162
Bertrand, Michel 1944- CANR-13
Earlier sketch in CA 73-76
Bertrand, Sandra 1943- CANR-86
Earlier sketch in CA 130
Berube, Allan
See Berube, Allan
See also GLL 1
Berube, Allan 229
See also Berube, Allan
Berube, Maurice R. 1933- 139
Berwanger, Eugene H. 21-24R
Berwick, Jean Shepherd 1929- 9-12R
Berwick, Keith (Bennet) 1928- 33-36R
Berzensky, Steven Michael 1940- 200
Berzin, Alexander 1944- 184
Besag, Frank P. 1935- 119
Besanceney, Paul H. 1924- 45-48
Besancon, Alain J. 1932- 130
Besant, Annie (Wood) 1847-1933 185
Brief entry 105
See also TCLC 9
Besant, Sir Walter 1836-1901 ..... DLB 135, 190
Besas, Peter 1933- 77-80
Beschloss, Michael R(ichard)
1955- CANR-142
Earlier sketches in CA 101, CANR-42, 73
Besdine, Matthew 1905(?)-1986
Obituary 120
Besemeres, Mary 1972- 232
Beshers, James M(onahan) 1931- 1-4R
Beshoar, Barron B(enedict) 1907-1987 69-72
Beskow, Bo 1906- CANR-11
Earlier sketch in CA 61-64
Beskow, Elsa (Maartman) 1874-1953 135
See also CLR 17
See also MAICYA 1, 2
See also SATA 20
Besmann, Wendy Lowe 1954- 237
Besner, Hilda F. 1950- 157
Besner, Neil K. 1949- 137
Besoyan, Rick 1924(?)-1970
Obituary 25-28R
Bess, Clayton
See Locke, Robert
See also CLR 39
Bess, Savitri L. 1940- 178
Bessa-Luis, Agustina 1922- .... DLB 287
Bessborough, Tenth Earl of
See Ponsonby, Frederick Edward Neuflize
Bessel, Richard 1948- 145
Bessell, Peter (Joseph) 1921-1985
Obituary 117
Besser, Gretchen R(ous) 1928- CANR-14
Earlier sketch in CA 41-44R
Besser, Joe 1907-1988
Obituary 124
Besser, Milton 1911-1976 69-72
Obituary 65-68
Besserman, Perle 1948- 174
Bessette, Gerard 1920- CANR-14
Earlier sketch in CA 37-40R
See also CCA 1
See also DLB 53
See also EWL 3
Bessette, Roland L. 193
bes-Shahar, Eluki 1956- 168
Bessie, Alvah 1904-1985 .... CANR-80
Obituary 116
Earlier sketches in CA 5-8R, CANR-2
See also CLC 23
See also DLB 26
Bessie, Constance Ernst 1918(?)-1985
Obituary 115
Bessinger, Jess B(alsor), Jr. 1921-1994 ... 13-16R
Obituary 146
Bessire, Mark H. C. 1964- 218
Bessler, John D. 1967- 232
Bessom, Malcolm E(ugene) 1940-1988 ... 57-60
Obituary 126
Besson, Luc 1959- 152
Bessy, Maurice 1910-1993 .... CANR-26
Obituary 143
Earlier sketches in CA 65-68, CANR-10
Best, Adam
See Carmichael, William Edward
Best, Alan C. G. 1939- 111
Best, (Evangel) Allena Champlin
1892-1974 .... CANR-71
Earlier sketches in CAP-2, CA 25-28
See also SATA 2
See also SATA-Obit 25
Best, Cari 1951- .... SATA 107, 149
Best, Charles H(erbert) 1899-1978 ... CANR-29
Obituary 103
Earlier sketch in CA 45-48
Best, D. Minor
See Best, Don(ald M.)
Best, Don(ald M.) 1949- 147
Best, Ernest 1917-2004 .... CANR-35
Obituary 232
Earlier sketch in CA 114
Best, Ernest E. 1919- 112
Best, G. F. A.
See Best, Geoffrey (Francis Andrew)
Best, Gary A(llen) 1939- 33-36R
Best, Gary Dean 1936- CANR-40
Earlier sketch in CA 117
Best, Geoffrey (Francis Andrew) 1928- 142
Brief entry 114
Best, (Oswald) Herbert 1894-1980 ... CANR-71
Obituary 176
Earlier sketches in CAP-2, CA 25-28
See also SATA 2
Best, Hugh 1920- 115
Best, James J(oseph) 1938- 37-40R
Best, Joel 1946- 139
Best, John Wesley 1909- 17-20R
Best, Judith A. 1938- 69-72
Best, Marc
See Lemieux, Marc
Best, Marshall A. 1901(?)-1982
Obituary 106
Best, Michael R. 37-40R
Best, Nicholas 1948- 138
Best, Otto F(erdinand) 1929- CANR-25
Earlier sketch in CA 69-72
Best, Rayleigh Breton Amis 1905- CAP-1
Earlier sketch in CA 13-16
Best, Robin Hewitson (?)-1984
Obituary 113
Best, Thomas W(aring) 1939- 29-32R
Bestall, A(lfred) E(dmeades) 1892-1986 155
Obituary 119
See also SATA 97
See also SATA-Obit 48
Beste, R(aymond) Vernon 1908- CANR-4
Earlier sketch in CA 1-4R
Bester, Alfred 1913-1987 .... CANR-36
Obituary 123
Earlier sketches in CA 13-16R, CANR-12
See also BPFB 1
See also DLB 8
See also MTCW 1
See also SCFW 1, 2
See also SFW 4
Besterman, Theodore (Deocatus Nathaniel)
1904-1976
Obituary 105
See also DLB 201
Bestic, Alan Kent 1922- 13-16R
Beston, Henry 1888-1968
Obituary 25-28R
See also ANW
See also DLB 275
Bestor, Arthur (Eugene, Jr.)
1908-1994 .... CANR-6
Earlier sketch in CA 1-4R
Bestor, Dorothy K(och) 118
Bestul, Thomas H(oward) 1942- 53-56
Bestuzhev, Aleksandr Aleksandrovich
1797-1837 .... DLB 198
Bestuzhev, Nikolai Aleksandrovich
1791-1855 .... DLB 198
Betancourt, Cressy de
See Dobkin De Rios, Marlene
Betancourt, Ingrid 1961- 199
Betancourt, Jeanne 1941- CANR-131
Earlier sketches in CA 49-52, CANR-31, 67
See also SATA 55, 96, 148
See also SATA-Brief 43
Betancourt, John (Gregory) 1963- ... CANR-143
Earlier sketch in CA 149
Betancourt, Romulo 1908-1981 104
Beteille, Andre 1934- 130
Betenson, Lula Parker 1884-1980 61-64
Obituary 133
Beth
See Winship, Elizabeth
Beth, Loren Peter 1920- CANR-3
Earlier sketch in CA 1-4R
Beth, Mary
See Miller, Mary Beth
Betham-Edwards, Matilda Barbara
1836-1919 .... DLB 174
Bethancourt, T. Ernesto
See Paisley, Tom
See also AAYA 20
See also CLR 3
See also SATA 11
See also WYA
Bethe, H. A.
See Bethe, Hans (Albrecht)
Bethe, Hans (Albrecht) 1906-2005
Obituary 237
Brief entry 115
Bethe, Hans A.
See Bethe, Hans (Albrecht)
Bethea, David M. 1948- 209
Bethea, J. D.
See Bethea, James D.
Bethea, James D. 1933(?)-1990
Obituary 130
Bethel, Dell 1929- CANR-26
Earlier sketch in CA 29-32R
See also SATA 52
Bethel, Elizabeth Rauh 1942- 106
Bethel, Leonard L(eslie) 1939- 213
Bethel, Paul D(uane) 1919- 25-28R
Bethelard, Faith 1953(?)- 224
Bethell, Jean (Frankenberry) 1922- CANR-3
Earlier sketch in CA 9-12R
See also SATA 8
Bethell, Nicholas William 1938- CANR-1
Earlier sketch in CA 45-48
Bethell, Tom 1940- 77-80
Bethers, Ray 1902-1973 .... CAP-1
Earlier sketch in CA 11-12
See also SATA 6
Bethge, Eberhard 1909-2000 85-88
Obituary 190
Bethke, Bruce Raymond 1955- 177
See also SATA 114
Bethlen, T. D.
See Silverberg, Robert
Bethmann, Erich Waldemar
1904-1993 .... CAP-2
Obituary 141
Earlier sketch in CA 23-24
Bethune, J. G.
See Ellis, Edward S(ylvester)
Bethune, J. H.
See Ellis, Edward S(ylvester)
Bethurum, F(rances) Dorothy
1897-1999 .... CAP-2
Earlier sketch in CA 17-18
Beti, Mongo CANR-79
See also Biyidi, Alexandre
See also AFW
See also BLC 1
See also CLC 27
See also DAM MULT
See also EWL 3
See also WLIT 2

Cumulative Index 51 **Bidermann**

Betjeman, John 1906-1984 .... CANR-56
  Obituary 112
  Earlier sketches in CA 9-12R, CANR-33
  See also BRW 7
  See also CDBLB 1945-1960
  See also CLC 2, 6, 10, 34, 43
  See also CP 1, 2, 3
  See also DA3
  See also DAB
  See also DAM MST, POET
  See also DLB 20
  See also DLBY 1984
  See also EWL 3
  See also MTCW 1, 2
Betjeman, Penelope Chetwode
  See Chetwode, Penelope
Betocchi, Carlo 1899-1986 .... CANR-4
  Earlier sketch in CA 9-12R
  See also DLB 128
  See also EWL 3
Betsko, Kathleen
  See Yale, Kathleen Betsko
Betsky, Aaron 1958- 185
Bett, Walter R(eginald) 1903-1968 .... CAP-1
  Earlier sketch in CA 13-14
Bettarini, Mariella 1942- CANR-139
  Earlier sketch in CA 156
  See also DLB 128
Bettelheim, Bruno 1903-1990 .... CANR-61
  Obituary 131
  Earlier sketches in CA 81-84, CANR-23
  See also CLC 79
  See also DA3
  See also MTCW 1, 2
  See also TCLC 143
Bettelheim, Charles 1913- CANR-13
  Earlier sketch in CA 73-76
Bettelheim, Frederick A(braham)
  1923-2004 49-52
  Obituary 223
Betten, Neil B. 1939- 105
Bettenbender, John (I.) 1921-1988
  Obituary 125
Bettenson, Henry (Scowcroft) 1908- 13-16R
Better, Cathy Drinkwater 1952- 213
Betteridge, Anne 169
  See also Potter, Margaret (Newman)
Betteridge, Don
  See Newman, Bernard (Charles)
Betteridge, H(arold) T(homas) 1910-1993 . 5-8R
Bettersworth, John K(nox) 1909-1991 . CANR-2
  Earlier sketch in CA 5-8R
Bettey, J(oseph) H(arold) 1932- CANR-87
  Earlier sketch in CA 130
Betti, Laura 1934-2004 215
  Obituary 229
Betti, Liliana 1939- 101
Betti, Ugo 1892-1953 155
  Brief entry 104
  See also EWL 3
  See also RGWL 2, 3
  See also TCLC 5
Bettina
  See Ehrlich, Bettina Bauer
Bettini, Maurizio 1947- CANR-101
  Earlier sketch in CA 139
Bettis, Joseph Dabney 1936- 33-36R
Bettmann, Otto Ludwig 1903-1998 .... 17-20R
  Obituary 167
  See also SATA 46
Betts, Charles L(ancaster), Jr. 1908-1997 101
Betts, Clive 1943- 153
Betts, Donni 1948- CANR-5
  Earlier sketch in CA 53-56
Betts, Doris (Waugh) 1932- CANR-77
  Earlier sketches in CA 13-16R, CANR-9, 66
  Interview in CANR-9
  See also CLC 3, 6, 28
  See also CN 6, 7
  See also CSW
  See also DLB 218
  See also DLBY 1982
  See also RGAL 4
  See also SSC 45
Betts, Emmett Albert 1903-1987 .... 33-36R
Betts, George 1944- CANR-2
  Earlier sketch in CA 45-48
Betts, Glynne Robinson 1934- 105
Betts, James
  See Haynes, Betsy
Betts, John (Edward) 1939- 106
Betts, Raymond F. 1925- CANR-3
  Earlier sketch in CA 1-4R
Betts, Richard K(evin) 1947- CANR-40
  Earlier sketches in CA 85-88, CANR-16
Betts, William W(ilson), Jr. 1926- 33-36R
Betty, L(ewis) Stafford 1942- CANR-42
  Earlier sketch in CA 118
Betz, Betty 1920- 1-4R
Betz, Eva Kelly 1897-1968 .... CAP-1
  Earlier sketch in CA 11-12
  See also SATA 10
Betz, Hans Dieter 1931- CANR-41
  Earlier sketches in CA 53-56, CANR-4, 19
Beuf, Ann H(ill) 1939- 85-88
Beum, Robert (Lawrence) 1929- 9-12R
Beumers, Birgit 1963- 200
Beurdeley, (Jean-)Michel 1911- CANR-30
  Earlier sketch in CA 49-52
Beus, Jacobus Gysbertus de
  See de Beus, Jacobus Gysbertus
Beutel, William Charles 1930- 101
Beuttler, Edward Ivan Oakley
  1909-1998 73-76
Beuve-Mery, Hubert 1902-1989
  Obituary 129
Bevan, Alistair
  See Roberts, Keith (John Kingston)
Bevan, Aneurin 1897-1960
  Obituary 106
Bevan, Bryan 1913-1999 .... 13-16R
Bevan, E. Dean 1938- 33-36R
Bevan, Gloria (Isabel) CANR-59
  Brief entry 117
  Earlier sketch in CA 134
  See also RHW
Bevan, Jack 1920- 13-16R
Bevan, James (Stuart) 1930- 106
Bevan, Tom 1868-1930(?) .... YABC 2
Bevans, Stephen B(ennett) 1944- 233
Bevenot, Maurice 1897-1980
  Obituary 105
Beveridge, Albert J(eremiah) 1862-1927 213
  See also DLB 17
Beveridge, Andrew A(lan) 1945- 93-96
Beveridge, George David, Jr. 1922-1987 102
  Obituary 121
Beveridge, Judith 1956- 238
Beveridge, Oscar Maltman 1913- 9-12R
Beveridge, William (Henry) 1879-1963
  Obituary 112
Beveridge, William (Ian Beardmore) 1908- . 106
Beverley, Jo 1947- CANR-123
  Earlier sketch in CA 166
Beverley, Mary Frances 1925- 120
Beverley, Robert 1673(?)-1722 .... DLB 24, 30
Beverly, Fred
  See Ober, Frederick Albion
BeVier, Michael J(udson) 97-100
Bevilacqua, Alberto 1934- CANR-26
  Earlier sketch in CA 29-32R
  See also DLB 196
Bevington, David M(artin) 1931- CANR-141
  Earlier sketches in CA 1-4R, CANR-3
Bevington, Helen (Smith)
  1906-2001 .... CANR-69
  Obituary 195
  Earlier sketch in CA 13-16R
Bevington, Louisa Sarah 1845-1895 ... DLB 199
Bevis, Charles W. 1954- 237
Bevis, Charlie
  See Bevis, Charles W.
Bevis, Em Olivia 1932- CANR-1
  Earlier sketch in CA 49-52
Bevis, H(erbert) U(rlin) 1902- CAP-2
  Earlier sketch in CA 29-32
Bevis, James
  See Cumberland, Marten
Bevis, Richard W(ade) 1937- 213
Bevis, William W. 1941- 153
Bevlin, Marjorie Elliott 1917- 9-12R
Bew, Paul Anthony 1950- 169
Bewes, Richard 1934- CANR-20
  Earlier sketch in CA 102
Bewick, Thomas 1753-1828 .... SATA 16
Bewkes, Eugene Garrett 1895-1992 .... 5-8R
Bewley, Charles Henry 1888-1969 .... 5-8R
Bewley, Christina (Mary Erskine) 1924- 129
Bewley, Marius 1918-1973 .... CANR-3
  Obituary 41-44R
  Earlier sketch in CA 5-8R
Bexar, Phil
  See Borg, Jack
Bey, Isabelle
  See Bosticco, (Isabel Lucy) Mary
Bey, Pilaff
  See Douglas, (George) Norman
Beyala, Calixthe 1961- .... EWL 3
Beye, Charles Rowan 1930- 93-96
Beyea, Basil 1910-1986 61-64
Beyer, (Richard) Andrew 1943- CANR-11
  Earlier sketch in CA 69-72
Beyer, Audrey White 1916- CANR-72
  Earlier sketch in CA 13-16R
  See also SATA 9
Beyer, Edvard (Freydar) 1920- 121
  Brief entry 116
Beyer, Evelyn M. 1907- CAP-2
  Earlier sketch in CA 25-28
Beyer, Glenn H. 1913-1969 .... CANR-2
  Earlier sketch in CA 1-4R
Beyer, Paul J. III 1950- .... SATA 74
Beyer, Robert 1913(?)-1978
  Obituary 77-80
Beyer, Steven L(arsen) 1943- 123
Beyer, Werner William 1911- 9-12R
Beyerchen, Alan 1945- 81-84
Beyerhaus, Peter (Paul Johannes)
  1929- CANR-38
  Earlier sketches in CA 93-96, CANR-16
Beyerlin, Walter W(ilhelm) 1929- 124
Beyers, Charlotte K(empner) 1931-2005 .. 85-88
  Obituary 237
Beyfus, Drusilla 1927- 107
Beyle, Hank
  See Buchanan, James David
Beyle, Thad L. 1934- 37-40R
Beynon, Huw 1942- 107
Beynon, John
  See Harris, John (Wyndham Parkes Lucas) Beynon
Beytagh, Francis (X.) 1935- 215
Beytagh, Gonville (Aubie) ffrench
  See ffrench-Beytagh, Gonville (Aubie)
Bezencon, Jacqueline (Buxcel) 1924- .. SATA 48
Bezilla, Michael 1950- 111
Bezio, May Rowland (?)-1977
  Obituary 69-72
Bezmozgis, David 1973- 236
Bezruc, Petr
  See Vasek, Vladimir
  See also EWL 3
Bezruchka, Stephen (Anthony) 1943- 107
Bezwoda, Eva Susanne 1942- .... CP 1
Bhabra, H(argurchet) S(ingh) 1955-2000 145
Bhagat, G(oberdhan) 1928- 29-32R
Bhagavatula, Murty S. 1921- 29-32R
Bhagwati, Jagdish N. 1934- CANR-89
  Earlier sketch in CA 17-20R
Bhajan, Yogi
  See Yogiji, Harbhajan Singh Khalsa
Bhaktivedanta Swami, A. C.
  See Prabhupada, A. C. Bhaktivedanta
Bhala, Raj K. 1962- 151
Bhalla, A. S. 1939- 236
Bhana, Surendra 1939- CANR-105
  Earlier sketch in CA 57-60
Bhanjdeo, Asha 185
Bharath, Ramachandran 1935- 148
Bharati, Agehananda 1923-1991 .... CANR-4
  Obituary 134
  Earlier sketch in CA 1-4R
Bharati, Subramania
  See Iyer, C. Subramania
  See also EWL 3
Bhardwaj, Surinder Mohan 1934- 45-48
Bharti, Dharmvir 1926- .... CWW 2
Bharti, Ma Satya 1942- 102
Bhasin, Kamla 1946- 185
Bhaskaran, M.P. 1921- .... CP 1
Bhatia, Hans Raj 1904-1979 53-56
  Obituary 133
Bhatia, Jamunadevi 1919- CANR-45
  Earlier sketch in CA 101
  See also Edwards, June and Forrester, Helen
  See also RHW
Bhatia, June
  See Bhatia, Jamunadevi
Bhatia, Krishan 1926(?)-1974
  Obituary 53-56
Bhatnagar, Joti 1935- 41-44R
Bhatt, Jagdish J(eyshanker) 1939- CANR-31
  Earlier sketches in CA 77-80, CANR-14
Bhatt, Sujata 1956- CANR-120
  Earlier sketch in CA 153
  See also CP 7
  See also CWP
Bhattacharji, Sukumari 1921- 33-36R
Bhattacharya, Bhabani 1906- CANR-9
  Earlier sketch in CA 5-8R
  See also CN 1, 2, 3, 4
Bhattacharya, Nalinaksha 1949- 163
Bhave, Vinoba 1895-1982
  Obituary 108
Bhide, Amar 1955- 130
Bhote, Keki R. 1925- 142
Bhutto, Benazir 1953- 131
Bhutto, Zulfikar Ali 1928-1979 .... CANR-11
  Earlier sketch in CA 53-56
Biaggini, Adriana Ivancich 1930(?)-1983
  Obituary 109
Biagi, Shirley 1944- CANR-32
  Earlier sketches in CA 85-88, CANR-15
Bial, Morrison David 1917- 61-64
  See also SATA 62
Bial, Raymond 1948- CANR-95
  Earlier sketch in CA 143
  See also SATA 76, 116
Biala
  See Brustlein, Janice Tworkov
Biale, Rachel 1952- 167
  See also SATA 99
Bialik, Chaim Nachman 1873-1934 170
  See also Bialik, Hayyim Nahman
  See also EWL 3
  See also TCLC 25
Bialik, Hayyim Nahman
  See Bialik, Chaim Nachman
  See also WLIT 6
Bialk, Elisa
  See Krautter, Elisa (Bialk)
Bialosky, Jill 1957- 212
  See also PFS 19
Bialostocki, Jan 1921- CANR-48
  Earlier sketch in CA 104
Bialostosky, Don H(oward) 1947- 120
Bialoszewski, Miron 1922-1983 .... DLB 232
  See also EWL 3
Bialy, Harvey 1945- .... CP 1
Bianchi, Eugene C(arl) 1930- CANR-134
  Earlier sketch in CA 25-28R
Bianchi, Hombert 1912(?)-1980
  Obituary 97-100
Bianchi, John 1947- .... SATA 91
Bianchi, Robert S(teven) 1943- CANR-54
  Earlier sketch in CA 109
  See also SATA 92
Bianciardi, Luciano 1922-1971 206
Bianco, Anthony 1953- CANR-81
  Earlier sketch in CA 134
Bianco, Lucien Andre 1930- CANR-15
  Earlier sketch in CA 85-88
Bianco, Margery
  See Bianco, Margery Williams
Bianco, Margery Williams 1881-1944 155
  Brief entry 109
  See also CLR 19
  See also CWRI 5
  See also DLB 160
  See also MAICYA 1, 2
  See also SATA 15
  See also WCH
Bianco, Pamela 1906- 85-88
  See also SATA 28
Biancolli, Louis Leopold 1907-1992 65-68
  Obituary 139
Bianconi, Lorenzo (Gennaro) 1946- 121
Bianculli, Anthony J. 1925- 236
Biasin, Gian-Paolo 1933- 25-28R
Bibaud, Adele 1854-1941 .... DLB 92
Bibaud, Michel 1782-1857 .... DLB 99
Bibb, (David) Porter III 1937- 65-68
Bibby, Cyril 1914-1987 .... CANR-7
  Earlier sketch in CA 13-16R
Bibby, John F(ranklin) 1934- CANR-35
  Earlier sketch in CA 45-48
Bibby, T(homas) Geoffrey 1917-2001 . CANR-4
  Obituary 195
  Earlier sketch in CA 1-4R
Bibby, Violet 1908- 102
  See also SATA 24
Bibee, John 1954- 112
Biber, Jacob 1915- 211
Biber, Ya'akov
  See Biber, Jacob
Biberman, Edward 1904-1986 49-52
  Obituary 118
Biberman, Herbert 1900-1971 .... CAP-1
  Obituary 33-36R
  Earlier sketch in CA 13-16
Bibesco, Marthe Lucie 1887-1973 ... CANR-68
  Obituary 49-52
  Earlier sketch in CA 93-96
Bible, Charles 1937- 69-72
  See also SATA 13
Bibo, Bobette
  See Gugliotta, Bobette
Bicanic, Rudolf 1905-1968 85-88
Bicat, Tony 1945- 130
Bicchieri, Cristina 1950- 149
Bice, Clare 1909-1976 .... SATA 22
Bicerano, Jozef 1952- 145
Bichakjian, Bernard H. 1937- 136
Bichler, Joyce 1954- 107
Bichsel, Peter 1935- CANR-71
  Earlier sketch in CA 81-84
  See also DLB 75
  See also EWL 3
Bick, Edgar Milton 1902-1978
  Obituary 77-80
Bickel, Alexander M(ordecai)
  1924-1974 .... CANR-1
  Obituary 53-56
  Earlier sketch in CA 1-4R
Bickelhaupt, David L(ynn) 1929- 69-72
Bickerman, Elias J(oseph)
  1897-1981 .... CANR-20
  Obituary 104
  Earlier sketch in CA 25-28R
Bickers, Richard (Leslie) Townshend
  1917- CANR-42
  Earlier sketches in CA 45-48, CANR-1
Bickerstaff, Isaac
  See Swift, Jonathan
Bickerstaff, Isaac John 1733-1808 .... DLB 89
Bickersteth, Geoffrey Langdale 1884-1974
  Obituary 49-52
Bickerton, David M. 1944- 201
Bickerton, Derek 1926- CANR-66
  Earlier sketch in CA 61-64
Bicket, Zenas J(ohan) 1932- 37-40R
Bickford, David 1953- 133
Bickford, Elwood Dale 1927- 61-64
Bickford, Lawrence 1921- 147
Bickford-Smith, Vivian 1955- 150
Bickham, Jack M(iles) 1930-1997 ..... CANR-23
  Obituary 159
  Earlier sketches in CA 5-8R, CANR-8
  See also TCWW 1, 2
Bickle, Judith Brundrett (?)-(?) CANR-66
  Earlier sketches in CAP-1, CA 13-14
Bickley, R(obert) Bruce, Jr. 1942- CANR-9
  Earlier sketch in CA 65-68
Bickman, Martin 1945- 104
Bida, Constantine 1916- CANR-13
  Earlier sketch in CA 61-64
Bidart, Frank 1939- CANR-106
  Earlier sketch in CA 140
  See also AMWS 15
  See also CLC 33
  See also CP 7
Bidault, Georges 1899-1983
  Obituary 109
Biddiscombe, Perry 1959- 231
Biddiss, Michael Denis 1942- CANR-4
  Earlier sketch in CA 53-56
Biddle, Adrian .... IDFW 4
Biddle, Arthur W(illiam) 1936- CANR-105
  Earlier sketch in CA 45-48
Biddle, Bruce J(esse) 1928- CANR-7
  Earlier sketch in CA 17-20R
Biddle, Cordelia Frances 1947- 234
Biddle, Flora Miller 1928- 191
Biddle, Francis (Beverley) 1886-1968 .... 5-8R
  Obituary 103
Biddle, George 1885-1973
  Obituary 45-48
Biddle, Katherine Garrison Chapin
  1890-1977 .... CANR-5
  Obituary 73-76
  Earlier sketch in CA 5-8R
Biddle, Marcia McKenna 1931- 112
Biddle, Martin 1937- 193
Biddle, Perry H(arvey), Jr. 1932- 57-60
Biddle, Phillips R. 1933- 37-40R
Biddle, Wayne 1948- 106
Biddle, William W(ishart) 1900-(?) CAP-2
  Earlier sketch in CA 17-18
Biddulph, Steve CANR-138
  Earlier sketch in CA 175
Biderman, Abraham (Hersz) 1924-
Biderman, Albert D. 1923-2003 .... CANR-47
  Obituary 217
  Earlier sketches in CA 5-8R, CANR-8, 23
Biderman, Sol 1936- 25-28R
Bidermann, Jacob 1577-1639 .... DLB 164

Bidini, Dave 1963(?)- 211
Bidisha
See Bandyopadhyay, Bidisha
Bidney, David 1908-1987 9-12R
Bidney, Martin 1943- 165
Bidwell, Dafne (Mary) 1929- 97-100
Bidwell, Marjory Elizabeth Sarah (?)-1985 CANR-79
Earlier sketch in CA 77-80
Bidwell, Percy W(ells) 1888-1970(?) CAP-1
Earlier sketch in CA 9-10
Bidwell, Walter Hilliard 1798-1881 DLB 79
Biebel, David B. 1949- 125
Bieber, Konrad (F.) 1916- 141
Bieber, Margarete 1879-1978 CANR-11
Obituary 77-80
Earlier sketch in CA 17-20R
Biebuyck, Daniel P. 1925- CANR-30
Earlier sketches in CA 25-28R, CANR-11
Bieder, Robert E. 1938- 152
Biederman, Marcia (Squire) 1949- 127
Biederman, Pat
See Biederman, Patricia Ward
Biederman, Patricia Ward 180
Biederwolf, William Edward 1867-1939 214
Biegel, John E(dward) 1925- 49-52
Biegel, Paul 1925- CANR-73
Earlier sketches in CA 77-80, CANR-14, 32
See also CLR 27
See also SAAS 18
See also SATA 16, 79
Biehl, Charlotta Dorothea 1731-1788 DLB 300
Biehl, Michael (Melvin) 1951- 213
Biehler, Robert F(rederick) 1927- 37-40R
Biek, David E. 1952- 199
Biel, Steven 1960- CANR-114
Earlier sketch in CA 159
Bielakiewicz, Gerilyn J. 1968- 238
Bielby, Cliff 1919-1984
Obituary 111
Bielby, Denise D. 155
Biele, Joelle PFS 21
Bielenberg, Christabel (Mary Burton) 1909-2003 29-32R
Obituary 221
Bieler, Ludwig 1906-1981 5-8R
Obituary 103
Bieler, Manfred 1934- 192
Bielfield, Sidney 1904(?)-1984
Obituary 112
Bielski, Alison Joy 1925- CP 1
Bielski, Feliks
See Giergielewicz, Mieczyslaw F.
Bielyi, Sergei
See Hollo, Anselm
Bieman, Elizabeth 1923- 137
Biemiller, Carl L(udwig), Jr.) 1912-1979 121
Obituary 106
See also SATA 40
See also SATA-Obit 21
Biemiller, Ruth Cobbett 1914- 37-40R
Bien, David Duckworth 1930- 5-8R
Bien, Joseph Julius 1936- CANR-31
Earlier sketches in CA 53-56, CANR-5
Bien, Peter (Adolph) 1930- 9-12R
Bien, Thomas (H.) 1953- 225
Bienek, Horst 1930- 73-76
See also CLC 7, 11
See also DLB 75
Bienen, Henry Samuel 1939- 81-84
Bienenfeld, Florence L(ucille) 1929- CANR-23
Earlier sketch in CA 106
See also SATA 39
Bienes, Nicholas Peter 1952- CANR-141
Earlier sketch in CA 136
Bienstock, Mike
See Bienstock, Myron Joseph
Bienstock, Myron Joseph 1922- 9-12R
Bienvenu, Bernard J(efferson) 1925- 53-56
See also SSFS 2
Bienvenu, Marcelle 1945- 154
Bienvenu, Richard (Thomas) 1936- 61-64
Bier, Jesse 1925- CANR-3
Earlier sketch in CA 5-8R
Bier, William C(hristian) 1911-1980 33-36R
Obituary 97-100
Bierbaum, Margaret 1916- 33-36R
Bierbaum, Otto Julius 1865-1910 DLB 66
Bierbrier, M(orris) L(eonard) 1947- CANR-60
Earlier sketch in CA 128
Bierce, Ambrose (Gwinett) 1842-1914(?) CANR-78
Brief entry 104
Earlier sketch in CA 139
See also AAYA 55
See also AMW
See also BYA 11
See also CDALB 1865-1917
See also DA
See also DA3
See also DAC
See also DAM MST
See also DLB 11, 12, 23, 71, 74, 186
See also EWL 3
See also EXPS
See also HGG
See also LAIT 2
See also MAL 5
See also RGAL 4
See also RGSF 2
See also SSC 9, 72
See also SSFS 9
See also SUFW 1
See also TCLC 1, 7, 44
See also WLC
Bierce, Jane 1940- 144
Bierds, Linda 1945- CANR-101
Earlier sketch in CA 147
Bierhorst, John (William) 1936- CANR-51
Earlier sketches in CA 33-36R, CANR-13, 28
See also MAICYA 2
See also MAICYAS 1
See also SAAS 10
See also SATA 6, 91, 149
See also SATA-Essay 149
Bieri, Arthur Peter 1931- 61-64
Bieringer, R(eimund) 1957- 226
Bierley, Paul E(dmund) 1926- CANR-13
Earlier sketch in CA 77-80
Bierman, Arthur K(almer) 1923- 85-88
Bierman, Harold, Jr. 1924- CANR-9
Earlier sketch in CA 17-20R
Bierman, John 232
Bierman, Judah 1917- 114
Bierman, Mildred Thornton 1912- 5-8R
Bierman, Stanley M(elvin) 1935- 106
Biermann, Lillian
See Wehmeyer, Lillian (Mabel) Biermann
Biermann, Pieke 1950- 153
Biermann, Wolf 1936- 81-84
See also CWW 2
See also EWL 3
Biernat, Len 1946- 219
Biernatzki, William E(ugene) 1931- CANR-6
Earlier sketch in CA 57-60
Biers, William Richard 1938- CANR-23
Earlier sketch in CA 106
Bierstedt, Robert 1913-1998 CANR-2
Obituary 170
Earlier sketch in CA 1-4R
Biery, William (Richard) 1933- 57-60
Biesanz, Mavis Hiltunen 1919- 33-36R
Biesanz, Richard 1944- 112
Biesel, David B. 1931- 140
Biesterveld, Betty Parsons 1923- CANR-1
Earlier sketch in CA 1-4R
Bietenholz, Peter G(erard) 1933- 101
Biezanek, Anne C(ampbell) 1927- 17-20R
Bigard, (Albany) Barney (Leon) 1906-1980 134
Bigart, Robert James 1947- 33-36R
Bigelow, Brian J(ohn) 1947- 164
Bigelow, Donald N(evius) 1918- 41-44R
Bigelow, Gordon Ellsworth 1919- 110
Bigelow, Karl Worth 1898-1980
Obituary 97-100
Bigelow, Kathryn 1951- 139
Bigelow, Marybelle S(chmidt) 1923- 25-28R
Bigelow, Robert P(ratt) 1927-
Brief entry 118
Bigelow, Robert Sydney 1918- 102
Bigelow, William F. 1879-1966 DLB 91
Biger, Gideon 1945- 144
Bigg, Patricia Nina 1932- 102
See also RHW
Biggar, Joan R(awlins) 1936- 191
See also SATA 120
Bigge, Morris L. 1908-2000 9-12R
Biggers, Earl Derr 1884-1933 153
Brief entry 108
See also DLB 306
See also TCLC 65
Biggers, John Thomas 1924-2001 CANR-2
Obituary 193
Earlier sketch in CA 1-4R
Biggle, Lloyd, Jr. 1923-2002 CANR-35
Earlier sketches in CA 13-16R, CANR-5, 20
See also DLB 8
See also SATA 65
See also SFW 4
Biggs, Anselm G. 1914-2001 33-36R
Biggs, Bradley 1920- 124
Biggs, Cheryl 1947- 152
Biggs, Cheryln
See Biggs, Cheryl
Biggs, Chester M(axwell), Jr. 1921- 151
Biggs, John, Jr. 1895-1979
Obituary 85-88
Biggs, John B(urville) 1934- CANR-6
Earlier sketch in CA 57-60
Biggs, Margaret Key 1933- 114
Biggs, Mary 1944- 137
Biggs, Matthew 238
Biggs, (Marvin) Mouzon, Jr. 1941- 111
Biggs, Peter
See Rimel, Duane (Weldon)
Biggs-Davison, John (Alec) 1918- 13-16R
Bigham, Darrel E. 1942- CANR-122
Earlier sketch in CA 169
Bigiaretti, Libero 1906- CANR-12
Earlier sketch in CA 29-32R
See also DLB 177
Bigland, Eileen 1898-1970 DLB 195
Bigler, Vernon 1922-1998 21-24R
Bignell, Alan 1928- 103
Bignell, Jonathan (Charles) 1963- 224
Bigo, Pierre (Auguste) 1906- 136
Bigongiari, Piero 1914-1997 DLB 128
See also EWL 3
Bigsby, C(hristopher) W(illiam) E(dgar) 1941- CANR-128
Earlier sketches in CA 25-28R, CANR-11, 28, 55
Bihalji-Merin, Oto 1904-1993 CANR-34
Earlier sketches in CA 81-84, CANR-15
Bihler, Penny
See Harter, Penny
Bijou, Sidney W(illiam) 1908- CANR-14
Earlier sketch in CA 37-40R
Bikel, Theodore 1924- CANR-1
Earlier sketch in CA 1-4R
Bikkie, James A(ndrew) 1929- 53-56
Biklen, Douglas Paul 1945- CANR-15
Earlier sketch in CA 85-88
Bilac, Olavo (Braz Martinos dos Guimaraes) 1865-1918 178
See also DLB 307
See also HW 2
Bilal, Abdel W(ahab) 1970- SATA 92
Bilal, Enki 1951- 227
Bilas, Richard A(llen) 1935- 53-56
Bilbo, Queenie (?)-1972
Obituary 37-40R
Bilbow, Antony 1932- 25-28R
Bilbrough, Norman 1941- 182
See also SATA 111
Bilby, Joanne Stroud 1927- 149
Bilderback, Dean Loy 1932- 97-100
Bilderback, Diane E(lizabeth) 1951- 110
Bilderdijk, Willem 1756-1831 RGWL 2, 3
Bileck, Marvin 1920- SATA 40
Bilek, Arthur J(ohn) 1929- 115
Bilenchi, Romano 1909-1989 DLB 264
Bilgrami, Akeel 1950- 140
Bilibin, Ivan (Iakolevich) 1876-1942 SATA 61
Bilich, Marion Yellin 1949- 114
Bilinsky, Yaroslav 1932- 13-16R
Bilkey, Warren J(oseph) 1920- 29-32R
Bill, Alfred Hoyt 1879-1964 CANR-68
Earlier sketch in CA 107
See also SATA 44
Bill, J(ohn) Brent 1951- CANR-98
Earlier sketch in CA 117
Bill, James A(lban) 1939- CANR-120
Brief entry 114
Bill, Stephen 1948- 230
See also CBD
See also CD 5, 6
Bill, Valentine T. 13-16R
Billam, Rosemary 1952- 123
See also SATA 61
Billard, Pierre 1921(?)- 230
Bill-Belotserkovsky, Vladimir Naumovich 1884-1970
Obituary 104
Billcliffe, Roger (George) 1946- 132
Biller, Henry B(urt) 1940- CANR-35
Earlier sketch in CA 114
Billetdoux, Francois (Paul) 1927-1991 21-24R
Billetdoux, Raphaele 1951- 159
Billett, Roy O(ren) 1891-1973 13-16R
Billheimer, John (W.) 218
Billias, George Athan 1919- CANR-6
Earlier sketch in CA 9-12R
Billig, Otto 1910-1989 129
Billiken, Bud
See Motley, Willard (Francis)
Billing, Graham (John) 1936- 147
See also CN 4, 5, 6
Billinger, Richard 1890-1965 DLB 124
Billingham, Mark 229
Billings, Charlene W(interer) 1941- CANR-49
Earlier sketches in CA 107, CANR-24
See also SATA 41
Billings, Charles E(dward) 1938- 121
Billings, Evelyn L(ivingston) 1918- 112
Billings, Ezra
See Halla, (Robert) Chris(tian)
Billings, Hammatt 1818-1874 DLB 188
Billings, Harold (Wayne) 1931- 25-28R
Billings, John Shaw 1898-1975
Obituary 104
See also DLB 137
Billings, Josh
See Shaw, Henry Wheeler
Billings, Peggy 1928- 25-28R
Billings, Richard N. 1930- 103
Billings, Robert 1949- 113
Billings, Warren M(artin) 1940- 61-64
Billings, William Dwight 1910-1997 113
Billingsley, Andrew 1926- 57-60
See also BW 2
Billingsley, Edward Baxter 1910-1997 CAP-2
Earlier sketch in CA 25-28
Billingsley, Franny 1954- 195
See also AAYA 41
See also MAICYA 2
See also SATA 132
Billingsley, (Kenneth) Lloyd 1949- 173
Billington, David P(erkins) 1927- 134
Billington, Dora May 1890-1968 CAP-1
Earlier sketch in CA 13-14
Billington, Elizabeth T(hain) 101
See also SATA 50
See also SATA-Brief 43
Billington, James H(adley) 1929- CANR-141
Brief entry 117
Earlier sketch in CA 132
Interview in CA-132
Billington, John
See Beaver, (Jack) Patrick
Billington, Joy 1931- 77-80
Billington, Michael 1939- CANR-134
Earlier sketch in CA 102
Billington, Monroe Lee 1928- 21-24R
Billington, (Lady) Rachel (Mary) 1942- CANR-44
Earlier sketch in CA 33-36R
See also AITN 2
See also CLC 43
See also CN 4, 5, 6, 7
Billington, Ray Allen 1903-1981 CANR-5
Obituary 103
Earlier sketch in CA 1-4R
Billington, Raymond John 1930- 110
Billmeyer, Fred Wallace, Jr. 1919- 85-88
Billout, Guy (Rene) 1941- CANR-124
Earlier sketches in CA 85-88, CANR-26
See also CLR 33
See also SATA 10, 144
Bills, Robert E(dgar) 1916- 107
Bills, Scott L(aurence) 1948- CANR-38
Earlier sketch in CA 112
Billson, Anne 1954- CANR-72
Earlier sketch in CA 143
See also HGG
Billson, Janet Mancini 1941- CANR-124
Earlier sketch in CA 152
Billy, Andre 1882-1971
Obituary 29-32R
Bilow, Pat 1941- 106
Bilsker, Richard L. 1968- 220
Bilsland, Bilko
See Bilsland, E(rnest) C(harles)
Bilsland, E(rnest) C(harles) 1931- 69-72
Bilson, Geoffrey 1938-1987 160
See also SATA 99
Bimler, Richard William 1940- CANR-14
Earlier sketch in CA 41-44R
Bina, Cyrus 1946- 140
Binch, Caroline (Lesley) 1947- MAICYA 2
See also MAICYAS 1
See also SATA 81, 140
Binchy, Maeve 1940- CANR-134
Brief entry 127
Earlier sketches in CA 134, CANR-50, 96
Interview in CA-134
See also BEST 90:1
See also BPFB 1
See also CLC 153
See also CN 5, 6, 7
See also CPW
See also DA3
See also DAM POP
See also DLB 319
See also MTCW 2
See also MTFW 2005
See also RHW
Bindas, Kenneth J. 1959- 212
Binder, Aaron 1927- 57-60
Binder, David 1931- 65-68
Binder, Eando
See Binder, Otto O(scar)
Binder, Frederick M(elvin) 1931- 29-32R
Binder, Frederick Moore 1920-2004 41-44R
Obituary 222
Binder, Leonard 1927- 61-64
Binder, Otto O(scar) 1911-1974 CANR-3
Obituary 53-56
Earlier sketch in CA 1-4R
See also SFW 4
Binder, Pearl
See Elwyn-Jones, Pearl Binder
Binder, Rudolf F. 1924- 178
Binding, Paul 1943- 173
Binding, Rudolf G. 1867-1938 DLB 66
Binding, Tim 1947- CANR-144
Earlier sketch in CA 169
Bindloss, Harold 1866-1945 TCWW 1, 2
Bindman, Arthur J(oseph) 1925- 45-48
Bindman, David L. 1963- 229
Bindoff, Stanley Thomas 1908-1980 73-76
Obituary 102
Bindra, Dalbir 1922-1980 122
Obituary 117
Binford, Chapman H(unter) 1900-1990
Obituary 130
Binford, Lewis R(oberts) 1930- 131
Bing, Christopher (H.) SATA 126
Bing, Elisabeth D. 1914- CANR-11
Earlier sketch in CA 69-72
Bing, Jonathan 238
Bing, Leon 1950- 140
Bing, Rudolf 1902-1997 89-92
Obituary 161
Bing, Stanley
See Schwartz, Gil (Stanley Bing)
Bingaman, Ron 1936- 61-64
Bingay, Malcolm 1884-1953 DLB 241
Bingay, Malcolm Wallace 1884-1953 203
Bingel, Horst 1933- 195
Binger, Carl A(lfred) L(anning) 1889-1976 73-76
Obituary 65-68
Binger, Norman H(enry) 1914-1988 33-36R
Binger, Walter 1888(?)-1979
Obituary 85-88
Bingham, (George) Barry, Jr. 1933- 106
Interview in CA-106
Bingham, (George) Barry 1906-1988
Obituary 126
See also DLB 127
Bingham, Caleb 1757-1817 DLB 42
Bingham, Caroline 1938-1998 CANR-90
Earlier sketches in CA 57-60, CANR-10
Bingham, Caroline 1962- SATA 158
Bingham, Carson
See Cassiday, Bruce (Bingham)
Bingham, Charlotte (Mary Therese) 1942- CANR-129
Earlier sketches in CA 105, CANR-11
Bingham, David A(ndrew) 1926- 53-56
Bingham, Edwin R(alph) 1920- CANR-2
Earlier sketch in CA 5-8R
Bingham, Emily 229
Bingham, Evangeline M(arguerite) L(adys) (Elliot) 1899- 65-68
Bingham, Howard L. 1939- 239
Bingham, Jane M(arie) 1941- 104
See also SATA 163
Bingham, John (Michael Ward) 1908-1988 CANR-58
Obituary 126
Earlier sketches in CA 21-24R, CANR-11
Bingham, Jonathan Brewster 1914-1986 33-36R
Obituary 119
Bingham, June Rossbach 1919- 1-4R

Cumulative Index 53 Bishop

Bingham, M(orley) P(aul) 1918- 49-52
Bingham, Madeleine (Mary Ebel)
1912-1988 .... CANR-11
Obituary 124
Earlier sketch in CA 13-16R
Bingham, Melinda 1950- 119
Bingham, Mindy
See Bingham, Melinda
Bingham, Richard D. 1937- 112
Bingham, Robert 1966(?)-1999 186
Bingham, Robert C(harles) 1927- 21-24R
Bingham, Robert E. 1925- 29-32R
Bingham, Robert Kamerer 1925(?)-1982
Obituary 107
Bingham, Sallie
See Bingham, Sarah (Montague)
Bingham, Sam(uel A.) 1944- 161
See also SATA 96
Bingham, Sarah (Montague) 1937- 217
Earlier sketches in CA 1-4R, CANR-18, 55
Autobiographical Essay in 217
See also CSW
See also DLB 234
Bingham, Woodbridge 1901-1986
Obituary 119
Bingley, Clive (Hamilton) 1936- 17-20R
Bingley, D. E.
See Bingley, David Ernest
Bingley, David Ernest 1920-1985 ..... CANR-42
Earlier sketches in CA 45-48, CANR-2, 18
See also Wigan, Christopher
See also TCWW 2
Bingley, Margaret (Jane Kirby) 1947- 180
See also HGG
See also SATA 72
Binham, Philip Frank 1924- 107
Binion, Rudolph 1927- CANR-4
Earlier sketch in CA 1-4R
bin Ishak, Yusof
See Ishak, Yusof bin
Binkley, Anne
See Rand, Ann (Binkley)
Binkley, Luther John 1925- 5-8R
Binkley, Olin T(rivette) 1908-1999 45-48
Obituary 185
Binkley, Thomas (Eden) 1931- 135
Binkley, William Campbell 1889-1970 107
Obituary 104
Binnema, Theodore 1963- 211
Binnie, G(eoffrey) M(orse) 1908-1989
Obituary 128
Binns, Archie (Fred) 1899-1971 .... CANR-71
Obituary 133
Earlier sketch in CA 73-76
Binns, Brigit (Legere) 161
Binns, J(ames) W(allace) 1940- 53-56
Binns, Jack R. 1933- 202
Binski, Paul 1956- 150
Binstock, R. C. 1958- CANR-63
Earlier sketch in CA 138
Binswanger, Ludwig 1881-1966
Obituary 107
Binswanger, Mathias 1962- 212
Binyon, Claude 1905-1978
Obituary 77-80
Binyon, Helen 1904-1982(?)
Obituary 114
Binyon, (Robert) Laurence 1869-1943 181
Brief entry 115
See also DLB 19
See also RGEL 2
Binyon, Michael (Roger) 1944- 142
Binyon, T(imothy) J(ohn)
1936-2004 .... CANR-140
Obituary 232
Earlier sketches in CA 111, CANR-28
See also CLC 34
Binzen, Bill
See Binzen, William
See also SATA 24
Binzen, Peter (Husted) 1922- 136
Binzen, William 89-92
See also Binzen, Bill
Biossat, Bruce 1910(?)-1974
Obituary 104
Biot, Francois 1923- 13-16R
Biow, Milton H. 1882(?)-1976
Obituary 65-68
Bioy Casares, Adolfo 1914-1999 ...... CANR-66
Obituary 177
Earlier sketches in CA 29-32R, CANR-19, 43
See also Casares, Adolfo Bioy and
Miranda, Javier and
Sacastru, Martin
See also CLC 4, 8, 13, 88
See also CWW 2
See also DAM MULT
See also DLB 113
See also EWL 3
See also HLC 1
See also HW 1, 2
See also LAW
See also MTCW 1, 2
See also MTFW 2005
See also SSC 17
Biram, Brenda 1930(?)-1984
Obituary 112
Biran, Michal 1965- 209
Birch, Alison Wyrley 1922- 85-88
Birch, Allison .... CLC 65
Birch, Anthony H(arold) 1924- CANR-5
Earlier sketch in CA 13-16R
Birch, Beryl Bender 1942- CANR-101
Earlier sketch in CA 147
Birch, Bruce C(harles) 1941- CANR-51
Earlier sketches in CA 65-68, CANR-10, 25
Birch, Carol 1951- 127
Birch, Charles
See Birch, L(ouis) C(harles)
Birch, Cyril 1925- 85-88
Birch, Daniel R(ichard) 1937- 101
Birch, David (W.) 1913-1996 155
See also SATA 89
Birch, David L. 1937- CANR-16
Earlier sketch in CA 25-28R
Birch, Geraldine 1943- 205
Birch, Herbert G. 1918-1973
Obituary 41-44R
Birch, L(ouis) C(harles) 1918- CANR-44
Earlier sketch in CA 120
Birch, Leo Bedrich 1902-1982 .... 33-36R
Birch, Lionel (?)-1982(?)
Obituary 106
Birch, (Evelyn) Nigel (Chetwode) 1906-1981
Obituary 108
Birch, Reginald B(athurst) 1856-1943 .. SATA 19
Birch, William G(arry) 1909-1996 53-56
Birchall, Diana 1945- 234
Birchall, Ian H(arry) 1939- 97-100
Bircham, Deric Neale 1934- 89-92
Bircher, Urs 1947- 232
Birchman, David 1949- .... SATA 72
Birchmore, Daniel A. 1951- 156
See also SATA 92
Birchmore, Fred (Agnew) 1911- 153
Bird, Al
See Mandel, Leon III
Bird, Anthony (Cole) 1917-1974 .... 13-16R
Obituary 135
Bird, Brandon
See Evans, George Bird and
Evans, Kay Harris
Bird, Carmel 1940- 128
See also SATA 124
Bird, Caroline 1915- CANR-139
Earlier sketches in CA 17-20R, CANR-11
Bird, Christiane 235
Bird, Cordwainer
See Ellison, Harlan (Jay)
Bird, David 1926(?)-1987
Obituary 121
Bird, Dennis L(eslie) 1930- 116
Bird, Dorothy Maywood 1899-1989 ..... CAP-1
Earlier sketch in CA 17-18
Bird, E(lzy) J(ay) 1911- .... SATA 58
Bird, Florence (Bayard) 1908-1998 97-100
Bird, George L(loyd) 1900-1996 .... CANR-2
Earlier sketch in CA 5-8R
Bird, Harrison K. 1910- 85-88
Bird, Isabella Lucy
See Bishop, Isabella Lucy (Bird)
See also BRWS 10
See also DLB 166
Bird, James Harold 1923- 102
Bird, John 1941- 130
Bird, Junius Bouton 1907-1982
Obituary 106
Bird, Kai 180
Bird, (Cyril) Kenneth 1887-1965 .... CAP-1
Earlier sketch in CA 13-14
Bird, Larry (Joe) 1956- 139
Bird, Lewis P(enhall) 1933- CANR-17
Earlier sketch in CA 97-100
Bird, Patricia Amy 1941- CANR-46
Earlier sketches in CA 61-64, CANR-7, 22
Bird, Richard (Miller) 1938- CANR-19
Earlier sketches in CA 9-12R, CANR-4
Bird, Robert Montgomery 1806-1854 . DLB 202
See also RGAL 4
Bird, Sarah McCabe 1949- CANR-44
Earlier sketch in CA 111
Bird, Veronica 1932- 112
Bird, Vivian 1910-2000 102
Bird, W(illiam) Ernest 1890-1975 .... CAP-1
Earlier sketch in CA 19-20
Bird, Wendell R(aleigh) CANR-40
Earlier sketch in CA 116
Bird, Will R. 1891-1984 .... 13-16R
Bird, William 1889-1963
Obituary 112
See also DLB 4
See also DLBD 15
Birdsall, Steve 1944- CANR-7
Earlier sketch in CA 53-56
Birdsell, Joseph B(enjamin) 1908-1994 119
Birdsell, Sandra 1942- CANR-123
Earlier sketch in CA 130
Birdseye, Clarence (Frank) 1886-1956 172
Brief entry 122
Birdseye, Tom 1951- CANR-131
Earlier sketch in CA 133
See also SATA 66, 98, 148
Birdwell, Russell (Juarez) 1903-1977
Obituary 107
Birdwhistell, Ray L. 1918-1994 45-48
Birdzell, L(uther) E(arle), Jr. 1916- 154
Bireley, Robert 1933- 137
Birenbaum, Arnold 1939- 108
Birenbaum, Barbara 1941- 136
See also SATA 65
Birenbaum, Halina 1929- 45-48
Birenbaum, Harvey 1936- 109
Birenbaum, William M. 1923- 29-32R
Birimisa, George 1924- CANR-122
Earlier sketches in CA 89-92, CANR-67
Interview in CA-89-92
See also CAD
See also CD 5, 6
Birkenhead, Lord
See Smith, Frederick Winston Furneaux
Birkenmayer, Sigmund Stanley 1923- 21-24R
Birkerts, Sven 1951- 176
Brief entry 128
Earlier sketch in CA 133
Interview in CA-133
Autobiographical Essay in 176
See also CAAS 29
See also CLC 116
Birket-Smith, Kaj 1893-1977 .... CAP-1
Earlier sketch in CA 13-14
Birkett, Dea 1958- 172
Birkhoff, George David 1884-1944 155
Birkin, Andrew (Timothy) 1945- CANR-41
Earlier sketch in CA 97-100
Birkin, Charles (Lloyd) 1907-1986 .... CANR-72
Earlier sketch in CA 69-72
See also HGG
Birkinshaw, Margaret 1907-2003 237
Birkland, Thomas A. 1961- 170
Birkley, Marilyn 1916-1999 .... 41-44R
Birkner, Michael John 1950- 125
Birkos, Alexander S(ergei) 1936- 25-28R
Birks, Tony 1937- CANR-50
Earlier sketches in CA 69-72, CANR-12
Birksted-Breen, Dana 1946- 102
Birla, Ghanshyamdas 1894-1983
Obituary 110
Birla, Lakshminiwas N. 1909-1994 ...... CAP-1
Earlier sketch in CA 13-14
Birley, Anthony (Richard) 1937- 129
Birley, Anthony R.
See Birley, Anthony (Richard)
Birley, Julia (Davies) 1928- 13-16R
Birley, Robert 1903-1982
Obituary 110
Birmelin, Blair T. 1939- 117
Birmingham, David (Bevis) 1938- 17-20R
Birmingham, F(rederic) A(lexander)
1911-1982 .... CANR-11
Obituary 107
Earlier sketch in CA 17-20R
Birmingham, Frances A(therton) 1920- .. 17-20R
Birmingham, John 1951- 45-48
Birmingham, John 1964- 239
Birmingham, Lloyd P(aul) 1924- .... SATA 12, 83
Birmingham, Maisie 1914- 101
Birmingham, Ruth
See Sorrells, Walter
Birmingham, Stephen 1932- CANR-20
Earlier sketches in CA 49-52, CANR-2
Interview in CANR-20
See also AITN 1
Birmingham, Walter (Barr) 1913-2004 .. 17-20R
Obituary 229
Birn, Donald S. 1937- 132
Birn, Randi (Marie) 1935- 73-76
Birn, Raymond Francis 1935- 102
Birnbach, Lisa 1957- 164
Birnbach, Martin 1929- 1-4R
Birnbaum, Eleazar 1929- 37-40R
Birnbaum, Jeffrey H. 204
Birnbaum, Louis 1909-1983 125
Birnbaum, Milton 1919- 33-36R
Birnbaum, Norman 1926- CANR-103
Earlier sketches in CA 53-56, CANR-5
Birnbaum, Philip 1904-1988 .... CANR-1
Obituary 125
Earlier sketch in CA 49-52
Birnbaum, Phyllis 1945- CANR-89
Earlier sketch in CA 102
Birnbaum, Pierre 1940- 191
Birnbaum, Solomon Asher 1891-1989
Obituary 130
Birnbaum, Stephen (Norman)
1937-1991 .... CANR-80
Obituary 136
Brief entry 125
Earlier sketch in CA 129
Birnbaum, Steve
See Birnbaum, Stephen (Norman)
Birnberg, Thomas B.
See Brooks, Thomas
Birne, Henry 1921- 17-20R
Birney, Alice L(otvin) 1938- 33-36R
Birney, Betty G. 1947- 165
See also SATA 98
Birney, (Alfred) Earle 1904-1995 ...... CANR-20
Earlier sketches in CA 1-4R, CANR-5
See also CLC 1, 4, 6, 11
See also CN 1, 2, 3, 4
See also CP 1, 2, 3, 4
See also DAC
See also DAM MST, POET
See also DLB 88
See also MTCW 1
See also PC 52
See also PFS 8
See also RGEL 2
Birney, (Herman) Hoffman
1891-1958 .... TCWW 1, 2
Birnie, Whittlesey 1945- 97-100
Birnkrant, Arthur 1906(?)-1983
Obituary 108
Biro, B.
See Biro, B(alint) S(tephen)
Biro, B(alint) S(tephen) 1921- CANR-77
Earlier sketches in CA 25-28R, CANR-11, 39
See also Biro, Val
See also CWRI 5
See also MAICYA 1, 2
See also SATA 67
Biro, Brian D. 1954- 206
Biro, Charlotte Slovak 1904-1995 57-60
Biro, David (Eric) 1964- 191
Biro, Lajos 1880-1948 .... IDFW 3, 4
Biro, Val
See Biro, B(alint) S(tephen)
See also CLR 28
See also SAAS 13
See also SATA 1
Biro, Yvette 111
Biroc, Joseph 1903-1996 .... IDFW 3, 4
Birrell, Anne (Margaret) 130
Birrell, Augustine 1850-1933 181
See also DLB 98
Birren, Faber 1900-1988 .... CANR-7
Obituary 180
Earlier sketch in CA 13-16R
Birren, James E(mmett) 1918- 17-20R
Birringer, Johannes (H.) 1953- 158
Birse, A(rthur) H(erbert) 1889-1981 .... CAP-2
Earlier sketch in CA 23-24
Birstein, Ann 1927- CANR-28
Earlier sketch in CA 17-20R
Birstein, Vadim J. 1944- 221
Birt, David 1936- CANR-35
Earlier sketches in CA 73-76, CANR-13
Birtha, Becky 1948- 142
See also BW 2
See also GLL 1
Biryukov, Nikolai (Ivanovich) 1949- 149
Bischof, Guenter
See Bischof, Gunter
Bischof, Gunter
See Bischof, Gunter
Bischof, Gunter 1953- 206
Bischof, Ledford Julius 1914- 9-12R
Bischoff, David F(redrick) 1951- 81-84
See also SFW 4
Bischoff, F(rederick) A(lexander) 1928- 89-92
Bischoff, Julia Bristol 1909-1970 .... CAP-2
Earlier sketch in CA 21-22
See also SATA 12
Bish, Robert L(ee) 1942- 53-56
Bishai, Wilson B. 1923- 33-36R
Bi Shang-guan
See Shen, Congwen
Bisher, Furman 1918- 182
See also DLB 171
Bisher, James F(urman) 1918- CANR-2
Earlier sketch in CA 5-8R
Bishin, William R(obert) 1939- 61-64
Bishir, John (William) 1933- 41-44R
Bishop, Anne 238
Bishop, Bonnie 1943- 103
See also SATA 37
Bishop, Claire Huchet
1899(?)-1993 .... CANR-36
Obituary 140
Earlier sketch in CA 73-76
See also CLR 80
See also CWRI 5
See also MAICYA 1, 2
See also SATA 14
See also SATA-Obit 74
Bishop, Claudia
See Stanton, Mary
Bishop, Courtney
See Ruemmler, John D(avid)
Bishop, Crawford M. 1885-1972 .... CAP-2
Earlier sketch in CA 17-18
Bishop, Curtis (Kent) 1912-1967 ...... CANR-88
Earlier sketches in CAP-1, CA 11-12
See also SATA 6
Bishop, Donald
See Steward, Samuel M(orris)
See also GLL 1
Bishop, Donald G. 1907-1987 .... CANR-3
Earlier sketch in CA 1-4R
Bishop, Donald H(arold) 1920- 105
Bishop, E. Morchard
See Stonor, Oliver
Bishop, Elizabeth 1911-1979 .... CANR-108
Obituary 89-92
Earlier sketches in CA 5-8R, CANR-26, 61
See also CABS 2
See also AMWR 2
See also AMWS 1
See also CDALB 1968-1988
See also CLC 1, 4, 9, 13, 15, 32
See also CP 1, 2, 3
See also DA
See also DA3
See also DAC
See also DAM MST, POET
See also DLB 5, 169
See also EWL 3
See also GLL 2
See also MAL 5
See also MAWW
See also MTCW 1, 2
See also PAB
See also PC 3, 34
See also PFS 6, 12
See also RGAL 4
See also SATA-Obit 24
See also TCLC 121
See also TUS
See also WP
Bishop, Eugene C. 1909-1983
Obituary 109
Bishop, Ferman 1922-1997 .... 21-24R
Bishop, Gavin 1946- CANR-126
Earlier sketches in CA 121, CANR-48
See also SATA 97, 144
Bishop, George (Victor) 1924- CANR-2
Earlier sketch in CA 49-52
Bishop, George Archibald
See Crowley, Edward Alexander
Bishop, George W(esley), Jr.
1910-1974 .... 13-16R
Bishop, Gordon (Bruce) 1938- 118

Bishop, Ian Benjamin 1927- ... 106
Bishop, Isabella Bird
See Bishop, Isabella Lucy (Bird)
Bishop, Isabella L.
See Bishop, Isabella Lucy (Bird)
Bishop, Isabella Lucy (Bird) 1831-1904 ... 185
Brief entry ... 123
See also Bird, Isabella Lucy
Bishop, James, Jr. 1936- ... 154
Bishop, James 1929-1999 ... 97-100
Bishop, James Alonzo 1907-1987 ... CANR-71
Obituary ... 123
Earlier sketch in CA 17-20R
See also Bishop, Jim
Bishop, Jerry E. 1931- ... 142
Bishop, Jim
See Bishop, James Alonzo
See also AITN 1, 2
Bishop, John
See Willis, Edward Henry
Bishop, John 1908-1994 ... 65-68
Bishop, John 1935- ... 105
See also CLC 10
Bishop, John L(yman) 1913-1974 ... CAP-2
Earlier sketch in CA 33-36
Bishop, John Melville 1946- ... CANR-13
Earlier sketch in CA 77-80
Bishop, John Peale 1892-1944 ... 155
Brief entry ... 107
See also DLB 4, 9, 45
See also MAL 5
See also RGAL 4
See also TCLC 103
Bishop, John Wesley 1927- ... 128
Bishop, Jonathan P(eale) 1927- ... 129
Bishop, Joseph W(arren), Jr.
1915-1985 ... 33-36R
Obituary ... 116
Bishop, Kathleen Wong 1954- ... SATA 120
Bishop, Kathy
See Bishop, Kathleen Wong
Bishop, Leonard 1922- ... CANR-70
Earlier sketch in CA 13-16R
Bishop, Lloyd (Ormond) 1933- ... 114
Bishop, Louis Faugeres 1901(?)-1986 ... 122
Obituary ... 119
Bishop, Martin
See Paine, Lauran (Bosworth)
See also TCWW 2
Bishop, Maurice 1944-1983 ... 123
Obituary ... 111
See also BW 1
Bishop, Maxine H. 1919- ... 25-28R
Bishop, Michael 1945- ... 178
Earlier sketches in CA 61-64, CANR-9, 49
Autobiographical Essay in ... 178
See also CAAS 26
See also AITN 2
See also SCFW 2
See also SFW 4
See also SUFW 2
Bishop, Morchard
See Stonor, Oliver
Bishop, Morris 1893-1973 ... CANR-88
Obituary ... 45-48
Earlier sketches in CA 1-4R, CANR-6
Bishop, Mrs. J. F.
See Bishop, Isabella Lucy (Bird)
Bishop, Nic 1955- ... 200
See also MAICYA 2
See also SATA 107, 161
Bishop, Patrick 1952- ... 132
Bishop, Pike
See Obstfeld, Raymond
Bishop, Robert 1938-1991 ... CANR-35
Obituary ... 135
Earlier sketches in CA 81-84, CANR-15
Bishop, Robert Lee 1931- ... 13-16R
Bishop, Ron 1922(?)-1988
Obituary ... 124
Bishop, Ryan 1959- ... 236
Bishop, Samuel P.
See Hutson, Shaun
See also TCWW 2
Bishop, Sheila (Grencarn) 1918- ... RHW
Bishop, Shelton Hale 1889-1962 ... 213
Bishop, Susan M. 1921(?)-1970
Obituary ... 104
Bishop, Tania Kroitor 1906-1996 ... CAP-2
Earlier sketch in CA 29-32
Bishop, Thomas W(alter) 1929- ... CANR-18
Earlier sketches in CA 1-4R, CANR-1
Bishop, Tom
See Bishop, Thomas W(alter)
Bishop, W(illiam) Arthur 1923- ... 21-24R
Bishop, Wendy 1953- ... 137
Bishop, William W(arner), Jr. 1906- ... 17-20R
Bishop of Marsland
See Duncan, Ronald
Bishop of Truro
See Leonard, Graham Douglas
Bisignani, J(oseph) D(aniel) 1947- ... CANR-35
Earlier sketch in CA 112
Biskin, Miriam 1920- ... 21-24R
Biskind, Peter ... 172
Bismarck, Otto von 1815-1898 ... DLB 129
Bisnow, Mark (C.) 1952- ... 130
Bisque, Anatole
See Bosquet, Alain
Biss, Eula 1977- ... 210
Bissell, Claude T(homas) 1916-2000 ... 101
Bissell, Elaine ... 81-84
Bissell, LeClair 1928- ... 133
Bissell, Richard (Pike) 1913-1977 ... CANR-88
Obituary ... 69-72
Earlier sketches in CA 1-4R, CANR-6
Bissell, Sallie ... 203
Bissell, Tom 1974- ... 238
Bissessar, Ann Marie 1958- ... 236
Bisset, Donald 1910-1995 ... CANR-51
Earlier sketches in CA 33-36R, CANR-13
See also CWRI 5
See also SATA 7, 86
Bisset, Robert c. 1759-1805 ... DLB 142
Bisset, Ronald 1950- ... 103
Bissett, Bill 1939- ... CANR-15
Earlier sketch in CA 69-72
See also CAAS 19
See also CCA 1
See also CLC 18
See also CP 1, 2, 3, 4, 5, 6, 7
See also DLB 53
See also MTCW 1
See also PC 14
Bissett, Donald J(ohn) 1930- ... 97-100
Bissette, Stephen R. 1955- ... 231
Bissinger, H(arry) G(erard III) 1954- ... 140
Bisson, Terry (Ballantine) 1942- ... CANR-100
Earlier sketches in CA 127, CANR-59
See also AAYA 43:
See also FANT
See also SATA 99
See also SFW 4
See also SSFS 18
Bisson, Thomas N(oel) 1931- ... 119
Bissoondath, Neil (Devindra)
1955- ... CANR-123
Earlier sketch in CA 136
See also CLC 120
See also CN 6, 7
See also DAC
Bissoondoyal, Basdeo 1906- ... CANR-11
Earlier sketch in CA 25-28R
Biswas, Anil 1914- ... IDFW 3, 4
Bisztray, George 1938- ... 106
Bita, Lili
See Zaller, Angeliki Bita
Bite, Ben
See Schneck, Stephen
Bitker, Marjorie M(arks) 1901-1990 ... 77-80
Obituary ... 132
Bitov, Andrei (Georgievich) 1937- ... 142
See also CLC 57
See also DLB 302
Bitsios, Dimitri S. 1915-1984
Obituary ... 111
Bittel, Lester Robert 1918- ... CANR-45
Earlier sketches in CA 13-16R, CANR-6, 21
Bitter, Francis 1902-1967
Obituary ... 113
Bitter, Gary G(len) 1940- ... CANR-31
Earlier sketches in CA 69-72, CANR-14
See also SATA 22
Bittermann, Henry J(ohn) 1904- ... 33-36R
Bittinger, Desmond W(right)
1905-1991 ... 37-40R
Bittinger, Emmert F(oster) 1925- ... 37-40R
Bittker, Boris I(rving) 1916-
Brief entry ... 109
Bittle, William E(lmer) 1926- ... 53-56
Bittlinger, Arnold (Georg) 1928- ... CANR-31
Earlier sketch in CA 49-52
Bittman, Mark ... 177
Bittner, Donald F(rancis) 1941- ... 122
Bittner, Rosanne 1945- ... CANR-123
Earlier sketch in CA 143
Bittner, Vernon (John) 1932- ... 69-72
Bittner, William (Robert) 1921- ... 5-8R
Bitton, Davis 1930- ... CANR-31
Earlier sketches in CA 33-36R, CANR-14
Bitton, Livia Elvira
See Bitton Jackson, Livia E(lvira)
Bitton-Jackson, Livia
See Bitton Jackson, Livia E(lvira)
Bitton Jackson, Livia E(lvira) 1931- ... 130
See also MAICYA 2
Bitzer, Billy 1872-1944 ... IDFW 3, 4
Biven, W(illiam) Carl 1925- ... 21-24R
Bivins, John 1940- ... 85-88
Bix, Herbert P(hilip) 1938- ... 195
Bixby, Jay Lewis
See Bixby, Jerome Lewis
Bixby, Jerome Lewis 1923-1998 ... 17-20R
Bixby, Ray Z.
See Tralins, S(andor) Robert
Bixby, William (Courtney)
1920-1986 ... CANR-71
Obituary ... 118
Earlier sketches in CA 1-4R, CANR-6
See also SATA 6
See also SATA-Obit 47
Bixler, Julius Seelye 1894-1985
Obituary ... 115
Bixler, Norma 1905-1998 ... 49-52
Bixler, Paul (Howard) 1899-1991 ... 69-72
Bixler, R(oy) Russell, Jr. 1927- ... 61-64
Biyidi, Alexandre 1932- ... CANR-81
Brief entry ... 114
Earlier sketch in CA 124
See also Beti, Mongo
See also BW 1, 3
See also DA3
See also MTCW 1, 2
Bizardel, Yvon 1891- ... 61-64
Biziou, Peter ... IDFW 4
Bizzarro, Salvatore 1939- ... 53-56
Bizzarro, Tina Waldeier 1950- ... 144
Bizzell, Patricia (Lynn) 1948- ... 139
Bjarklind, Unnur Benekiktsdottir 1881-1946
See Hulda
Bjarkman, Peter C(hristian) 1941- ... CANR-100
Earlier sketches in CA 130, CANR-86
Bjarme, Brynjolf
See Ibsen, Henrik (Johan)
Bjelic, Dusan I.
See Bjelic, Dusan I.
Bjelic, Dusan I. ... 229
Bjell, Ernst Barany
See Wiechert, Ernst (Emil)
Bjerke, (Jarl) Andre 1918-1985 ... 197
See also EWL 3
Bjerke, Robert Alan 1939- ... 41-44R
Bjerke, Ward (Ollie) 1920-
Brief entry ... 108
Bjerre, Jens 1921- ... 9-12R
Bjoerk, Christina 1938- ... 135
See also CLR 22
See also SATA 67, 99
Bjoerneboe, Jens 1920-1976 ... CANR-28
Obituary ... 65-68
Earlier sketch in CA 69-72
See also Bjorneboe, Jens
Bjoernson, Bjoernstjerne (Martinius) 1832-1910
Brief entry ... 104
See also TCLC 7, 37
Bjorge, Gary J(ohn) 1940- ... CANR-90
Earlier sketch in CA 130
Bjork, Christina
See Bjoerk, Christina
Bjork, Daniel W. 1940- ... 143
Bjorkelo, Anders 1947- ... 138
Bjorklund, Lorence F. 1913-1978 ... SATA 35
See also SATA-Brief 32
Bjorkman, Steve ... SATA 163
Bjorling, Gunnar 1887-1960 ... EWL 3
Bjorn, Thyra Ferre 1905-1975 ... CANR-69
Obituary ... 57-60
Earlier sketches in CA 5-8R, CANR-3
Bjornard, Reidar B(ernhard) 1917- ... 33-36R
Bjorneboe, Jens
See Bjoerneboe, Jens
See also DLB 297
See also EWL 3
Bjornson, Bjornstjerne (Martinius)
1832-1910 ... RGWL 2, 3
Bjornson, Richard 1938- ... 77-80
Bjornson, (Kristjan) Val(dimar) 1906-1987
Obituary ... 121
Bjornstad, James 1940- ... 29-32R
Bjornvig, Thorkild (Strange) 1918- ... 194
See also DLB 214
See also EWL 3
Bjornvig, Thorkild Strange
See Bjornvig, Thorkild (Strange)
Bjorset, Bryniolf
See Beorse, Bryn
Blaazer, David (Paul) 1957- ... 141
Blachford, George 1913- ... 9-12R
Blachly, Frederick (Frank) 1881(?)-1975
Obituary ... 57-60
Blachly, Lou 1889-1965 ... CAP-1
Earlier sketch in CA 13-14
Black, Albert George 1928- ... 45-48
Black, Algernon David 1900-1993 ... CANR-2
Obituary ... 141
Earlier sketch in CA 1-4R
See also SATA 12
See also SATA-Obit 76
Black, Angus 1943- ... 29-32R
Black, Antony 1936- ... 121
Black, Arthur (Raymond) 1943- ... 138
Black, Baxter 1945- ... CANR-119
Earlier sketch in CA 147
Black, Betty
See Schwartz, Betty
Black, Bonnie Lee 1945- ... 107
Black, Brady Forrest 1908-1994 ... 102
Black, Campbell 1944- ... CANR-72
Earlier sketch in CA 89-92
See also HGG
Black, Cara 1951- ... 190
Black, Charles
See Black, Charles L(und), Jr.
Black, Charles 1928- ... 132
Black, Charles L(und), Jr. 1915-2001 ... CANR-3
Obituary ... 197
Earlier sketch in CA 1-4R
Black, Cheryl 1954- ... 223
Black, Clinton V(ane De Brosse)
1918- ... CANR-30
Earlier sketch in CA 102
Black, Conrad (Moffat) 1944- ... 231
Black, Creed C(arter) 1925- ... 73-76
Black, Cyril Edwin 1915-1989 ... CANR-3
Obituary ... 129
Earlier sketch in CA 1-4R
Black, D. M.
See Black, David (Macleod)
Black, David
See Way, Robert E(dward)
Black, David (Macleod) 1941- ... 25-28R
See also CP 1, 2, 3, 4, 5, 6, 7
See also DLB 40
Black, David 1945- ... CANR-91
Earlier sketch in CA 136
Black, Dianne (a pseudonym) 1940- ... 97-100
Black, Donald 1941- ... 146
Black, Dorothy 1899-1985
Obituary ... 115
Black, Dorothy 1914- ... CANR-30
Earlier sketch in CA 111
Black, Douglas M. 1895-1977
Obituary ... 104
Black, Duncan 1908-1991 ... CAP-2
Earlier sketch in CA 19-20
Black, E(dward) L(oring) 1915- ... 9-12R
Black, Earl 1942- ... CANR-121
Earlier sketch in CA 101
Black, Edwin ... 230
Black, Elizabeth 1908(?)-1987
Obituary ... 122
Black, Ethan ... 239
Black, Eugene C(harlton) 1927- ... 9-12R
Black, Eugene R(obert) 1898-1992 ... CAP-2
Earlier sketch in CA 25-28
Black, Floyd H. 1888-1983
Obituary ... 111
Black, Gavin
See Wynd, Oswald Morris
See also DLB 276
Black, Hallie 1943- ... 108
Black, Harry George 1933- ... 61-64
Black, Holly 1971- ... 213
See also SATA 147
Black, Hugh C(leon) 1920- ... 37-40R
Black, Hugo Lafayette 1886-1971
Obituary ... 33-36R
Black, Ian Stuart 1915-1997 ... CANR-6
Obituary ... 171
Earlier sketch in CA 9-12R
Black, Ingrid
See McConnel, Ian and
O'Hanlon, Ellis
Black, Irma Simonton 1906-1972 ... CANR-68
Obituary ... 37-40R
Earlier sketches in CA 1-4R, CANR-6
See also SATA 2
See also SATA-Obit 25
Black, Ishi
See Gibson, Walter B(rown)
Black, Ivan 1904(?)-1979
Obituary ... 85-88
Black, Ivory
See Janvier, Thomas A(llibone)
Black, J. L. 1937- ... 206
Black, Jack 1969- ... 213
Black, James A(llen) 1937- ... 121
Black, James Menzies 1913-1982 ... CANR-5
Earlier sketch in CA 5-8R
Black, Jeremy (Martin) 1955- ... CANR-110
Earlier sketch in CA 136
Black, John N(icholson) 1922- ... CANR-13
Earlier sketch in CA 33-36R
Black, John Wilson 1906- ... CAP-1
Earlier sketch in CA 17-18
Black, Jonathan
See von Block, Bela W(illiam)
Black, Joseph E. 1921- ... 9-12R
Black, Kenneth, Jr. 1925- ... CANR-7
Earlier sketch in CA 13-16R
Black, Kitty
See Black, Dorothy
Black, Laura 1929-2000 ... RHW
Black, Lionel
See Barker, Dudley
See also DLB 276
Black, Maggie
See Black, Margaret K(atherine)
Black, Malacai
See D'Amato, Barbara
Black, Malcolm Charles Lamont 1928- ... 85-88
Black, Mansell
See Trevor, Elleston
Black, Margaret K(atherine)
1921-1999 ... CANR-32
Earlier sketches in CA 29-32R, CANR-14
Black, Martha E(llen) 1901-1980 ... 33-36R
Black, Mary (Childs) 1922-1992 ... CANR-13
Obituary ... 137
Earlier sketch in CA 21-24R
Black, MaryAnn
See Easley, MaryAnn
Black, Matthew W(ilson) 1895-1978 ... CAP-2
Earlier sketch in CA 25-28
Black, Max 1909-1988 ... 61-64
Black, Michael (Hugo) 1928- ... CANR-90
Earlier sketch in CA 131
Black, Michael A. 1949- ... 235
Black, Michael L(awrence) 1940- ... 121
Black, Millard H. 1912-2000 ... 25-28R
Black, Misha 1912-1977 ... CAP-1
Obituary ... 133
Earlier sketch in CA 11-12
Black, Nancy B(reMiller) 1941-
Brief entry ... 107
Black, Noel (Anthony) 1937- ... 171
Black, Percy 1922- ... 33-36R
Black, R(obert) D(enis) Collison
1922- ... CANR-86
Earlier sketch in CA 131
Black, Robert
See Holdstock, Robert P.
Black, Robert 1946- ... 121
Black, Robert B(ruce) 1920- ... 109
Black, Robert C(lifford) III 1914-2001 ... 41-44R
Black, Roe C(oddington) 1926-1985 ... 89-92
Black, Roger David 1948- ... 175
Black, Shane 1962(?)- ... 152
Black, Shirley Temple 1928- ... BEST 89:2
Black, Stanley Warren III 1939- ... CANR-31
Earlier sketch in CA 45-48
Black, Stephen A(mes) 1935- ... 228
Black, Susan Adams 1953- ... 105
See also SATA 40
Black, Theodore Michael 1919-1994 ... 109
Obituary ... 144
Black, Veronica
See Peters, Maureen
Black, William Joseph 1934(?)-1977
Obituary ... 73-76
Black, Winifred 1863-1936 ... 178
See also DLB 25
Blackaby, Henry T. 1935- ... 197
Blackall, Bernie 1956- ... 196
See also SATA 126
Blackall, Eric Albert 1914-1989 ... 65-68
Obituary ... 130
Blackamore, Arthur 1679-(?) ... DLB 24, 39

Cumulative Index 55 Blaisdell

Blackbeard, Bill 1926- ... CANR-66
Earlier sketch in CA 97-100
Interview in ... CA-97-100
Blackbourn, David 1949- ... 132
Blackbridge, Persimmon 1951- ... 185
Blackburn, Alexander (Lambert) 1929- ... CANR-113
Earlier sketch in CA 97-100
See also DLBY 1985
Blackburn, Barbara
See Leader, (Evelyn) Barbara (Blackburn)
Blackburn, Claire
See Altman, Linda Jacobs
Blackburn, Fred M(onroe) 1950- ... 166
Blackburn, George M. III 1950- ... 123
Blackburn, Graham (John) 1940- ... CANR-22
Earlier sketch in CA 69-72
Blackburn, John (Fenwick) 1923-1993 ... CANR-58
Earlier sketches in CA 1-4R, CANR-2, 22
See also DLB 261
See also HGG
Blackburn, John(ny) Brewton 1952- ... SATA 15
Blackburn, John O. 1929- ... 127
Blackburn, Joyce Knight 1920- ... 17-20R
See also SATA 29
Blackburn, Julia 1948- ... CANR-143
Earlier sketch in CA 172
Blackburn, Laurence Henry 1897-1990 .. 57-60
Blackburn, Michael 1954- ... CANR-43
Earlier sketch in CA 118
Blackburn, Norma Davis 1914- ... 69-72
Blackburn, Norman 1904(?)-1990
Obituary ... 131
Blackburn, Paul 1926-1971 ... CANR-34
Obituary ... 33-36R
Earlier sketch in CA 81-84
See also BG 1:2
See also CLC 9, 43
See also CP 1
See also DLB 16
See also DLBY 1981
Blackburn, R(obert) M(artin) 1934- ... 119
Blackburn, Robert T. 1923- ... 121
Blackburn, Robin 1940- ... CANR-139
Earlier sketches in CA 128, CANR-63
Blackburn, Simon 1944- ... CANR-89
Earlier sketches in CA 49-52, CANR-40
Blackburn, Thomas (Eliel Fenwick) 1916-1977 ... CANR-69
Obituary ... 113
Earlier sketch in CA 73-76
See also CP 1, 2
See also DLB 27
Blackburn, Thomas C(arl) 1936- ... CANR-22
Earlier sketch in CA 69-72
Blackburne, Kenneth (William) 1907-1980
Obituary ... 105
Blackburne, Neville Alfred Edmund 1913-1999 ... 53-56
Black Elk 1863-1950 ... 144
See also DAM MULT
See also MTCW 2
See also MTFW 2005
See also NNAL
See also TCLC 33
See also WP
Blacker, C(arlos) P(aton) 1895-1975
Obituary ... 57-60
Blacker, Carmen Elizabeth 1924- ... 9-12R
Blacker, Irwin R(obert) 1919-1985 ... CANR-3
Obituary ... 115
Earlier sketch in CA 1-4R
Blacker, Terence 1948- ... 206
See also DLB 271
Blackett, Patrick (Maynard Stuart) 1897-1974
Obituary ... 49-52
Blackett, Veronica Heath 1927- ... 53-56
See also SATA 12
Blackey, Robert 1941- ... CANR-4
Earlier sketch in CA 53-56
Blackford, Charles Minor III 1898-1985 .. 69-72
Blackford, Mansel G(riffiths) 1944- ... 142
Blackford, Staige D(avis) 1931-2003 ... 103
Obituary ... 217
Blackhall, David Scott 1910- ... 5-8R
Blackham, Garth J. 1926- ... 33-36R
Blackham, H(arold) J(ohn) 1903- ... 21-24R
Black Hawk 1767-1838 ... NNAL
Black Hobart
See Sanders, (James) Ed(ward)
Blackie, Bruce L(othian) 1936- ... 57-60
Blackie, Jean Cutler 1943- ... SATA 79
Blackie, John (Ernest Haldane) 1904-1985 ... 73-76
Obituary ... 116
Blackie, Pamela 1917- ... 103
Blacking, John (Anthony Randoll) 1928- ... CANR-3
Earlier sketch in CA 9-12R
Blackledge, Ethel H(ale) ... CANR-11
Earlier sketch in CA 21-24R
Blacklin, Malcolm
See Chambers, Aidan
Blacklock, Dyan 1951- ... 184
See also SATA 112
Blackman, Ann ... 185
Blackman, Audrey (Babette) 1907-1990(?) .. 109
Obituary ... 132
Blackman, Malorie 1962- ... CANR-107
Earlier sketch in CA 150
See also CWRI 5
See also SATA 83, 128
Blackman, Raymond V(ictor) B(ernard) 1910-1989
Obituary ... 128
Blackman, Sheldon 1935- ... 33-36R
Blackman, Sue Anne Batey 1948- ... CANR-89
Earlier sketch in CA 132
Blackman, Victor 1922- ... 103
Blackmer, Donald L. M. 1929- ... 33-36R
Black-Michaud, Jacob 1938- ... 61-64
Blackmon, C(harles) Robert 1925- ... 33-36R
Blackmon, Rosemary Barnsdall 1921(?)-1983
Obituary ... 111
Blackmore, Charles (David) 1957- ... 124
Blackmore, Dorothy S. 1914-1998 ... 41-44R
Blackmore, John T(homas) 1931- ... CANR-15
Earlier sketch in CA 41-44R
Blackmore, Peter 1909-1984 ... 9-12R
Obituary ... 114
Blackmore, R(ichard) D(oddridge) 1825-1900
Brief entry ... 120
See also DLB 18
See also RGEL 2
See also TCLC 27
Blackmore, Richard 1654-1729 ... DLB 131
See also RGEL 2
Blackmore, Robert Long 1919- ... 113
Blackmore, Susan (Jane) 1951- ... CANR-93
Earlier sketch in CA 146
Blackmur, R(ichard) P(almer) 1904-1965 ... CANR-71
Obituary ... 25-28R
Earlier sketches in CAP-1, CA 11-12
See also AMWS 2
See also CLC 2, 24
See also DLB 63
See also EWL 3
See also MAL 5
Blackoff, Edward M. 1934- ... 9-12R
Blackshear, Helen F(riedman) 1911- . CANR-10
Earlier sketch in CA 25-28R
Blacksnake, George
See Richardson, Gladwell
Blackstock, Charity
See Torday, Ursula
Blackstock, David T. 1930- ... 197
Blackstock, Lee
See Torday, Ursula
Blackstock, Nelson 1944- ... 97-100
Blackstock, Paul W(illiam) 1913-1978 ... CANR-69
Earlier sketch in CA 13-16R
Blackstock, Terri 1957- ... CANR-119
Earlier sketch in CA 153
Blackstock, Walter 1917-1976 ... CANR-9
Earlier sketch in CA 5-8R
Blackston, Ray ... 237
Blackstone, Bernard 1911-1983 ... 69-72
Obituary ... 111
Blackstone, Geoffrey Vaughan 1910-1989 ... CAP-1
Earlier sketch in CA 9-10
Blackstone, Harry
See Blackstone, Harry (Bouton), Jr.
Blackstone, Harry (Bouton), Jr. 1934-1997 .. 114
Obituary ... 158
See also MTFW 2005
Blackstone, James
See Brosnan, John and Brosnan, John
Blackstone, Tessa Ann Vosper 1942- ... CANR-42
Earlier sketches in CA 102, CANR-19
Blackstone, William T(homas) 1931- ... CANR-11
Earlier sketch in CA 17-20R
Black Tarantula
See Acker, Kathy
Blackton, Peter
See Wilson, Lionel
Blackwelder, Bernice Fowler 1902-1986 ... 1-4R
Blackwelder, Boyce W(atson) 1913-1976 ... 17-20R
Obituary ... 135
Blackwelder, Jerry 1950- ... 122
Blackwell, Alice Stone 1857-1950 ... DLB 303
Blackwell, Antoinette (Louisa) Brown 1825-1921 ... 215
Blackwell, Basil (Henry) 1889-1984
Obituary ... 112
Blackwell, Betsy Talbot 1905(?)-1985
Obituary ... 115
Blackwell, David (Harold) 1919- ... 169
See also BW 3
Blackwell, (Samuel) Earl, (Jr.) 1913-1995 . 81-84
Obituary ... 148
Blackwell, James
See Blackwell, James A., Jr.
Blackwell, James A., Jr. ... 140
Blackwell, James E(dward) 1926- ... 133
Brief entry ... 114
Blackwell, Leslie 1885- ... 9-12R
Blackwell, Lois S. 1943- ... 85-88
Blackwell, (Annie) Louise 1919-1977 ... 37-40R
Blackwell, Marilyn Johns 1948- ... 116
Blackwell, Michael C. 1942- ... 219
Blackwell, Muriel F(ontenot) 1929- ... 108
Blackwell, Richard Joseph 1929- ... 33-36R
Blackwell, Roger D(ale) 1940- ... 93-96
Blackwell, William L. 1929- ... 21-24R
Blackwill, Robert D. 1939- ... 173
Blackwood, Alan 1932- ... CANR-53
Earlier sketches in CA 110, CANR-28
See also SATA 70
Blackwood, Algernon (Henry) 1869-1951 .. 150
Brief entry ... 105
See also DLB 153, 156, 178
See also HGG
See also SUFW 1
See also TCLC 5
Blackwood, Andrew W(atterson), Jr. 1915-1987 ... CANR-5
Earlier sketch in CA 1-4R
Blackwood, Andrew W(atterson) 1882-1966 ... CANR-69
Obituary ... 103
Earlier sketch in CA 5-8R
Blackwood, Caroline (Maureen) 1931-1996 ... CANR-65
Obituary ... 151
Earlier sketches in CA 85-88, CANR-32, 61
See also BRWS 9
See also CLC 6, 9, 100
See also CN 3, 4, 5, 6
See also DLB 14, 207
See also HGG
See also MTCW 1
Blackwood, Cheryl Prewitt 1957- ... 108
Blackwood, Easley 1903-1992 ... 115
Blackwood, Gary L. 1945- ... CANR-96
Earlier sketch in CA 185
See also AAYA 40
See also BYA 8, 10
See also SATA 72, 118
Blackwood, George D(ouglas) 1919- ... 13-16R
Blackwood, James R. 1918- ... 21-24R
Blackwood, Margaret 1959- ... 144
Blackwood, Paul Everett 1913-1997 ... 102
Blade, Alexander
See Garrett, (Gordon) Randall (Phillip) and Hamilton, Edmond and Silverberg, Robert
Bladel, Roderick L(eRoy) ... 97-100
Bladen, Ashby 1929- ... 106
Bladen, V(incent) W(heeler) 1900-1981 .. 61-64
Blades, Ann (Sager) 1947- ... CANR-48
Earlier sketches in CA 77-80, CANR-13
See also CLR 15
See also CWRI 5
See also JRDA
See also MAICYA 1, 2
See also SATA 16, 69
Blades, Brian Brewer 1906-1977
Obituary ... 73-76
Blades, James 1901-1999 ... 65-68
Obituary ... 179
Blades, Joe
See Blades, Joseph Wendell
Blades, John (D.) 1936- ... 140
Blades, Joseph Wendell 1961-
See Blades, Joe
Blades, Ruben 1948- ... CANR-81
Earlier sketch in CA 131
See also HW 1, 2
Blades, William 1824-1890 ... DLB 184
Bladow, Suzanne Wilson 1937- ... 61-64
See also SATA 14
Blaeser, Kimberly M. 1955- ... 210
Blaffer, Sarah C.
See Hrdy, Sarah Blaffer
Blaga, Lucian 1895-1961 ... 157
See also CLC 75
See also DLB 220
See also EWL 3
Blagden, Cyprian 1906-1962 ... 1-4R
Blagden, David 1944- ... 53-56
Blagden, Isabella 1817(?)-1873 ... DLB 199
Blagojevic, Ljiljana 1960- ... 224
Blagowidow, George 1923- ... 77-80
Blaher, Damian J(oseph) 1913- ... 21-24R
Blaich, Theodore Paul 1902-1977 ... CAP-1
Earlier sketch in CA 13-14
Blaike, Avona
See MacIntosh, Joan
Blaikie, Robert J. 1923- ... 33-36R
Blaiklock, Edward Musgrave 1903- ... CANR-7
Earlier sketch in CA 17-20R
Blain, W. Edward 1951- ... 139
Blaine, Celia
See Murphey, Cecil B(laine)
Blaine, David 1973- ... 222
Blaine, James
See Avallone, Michael (Angelo, Jr.)
Blaine, Jeff
See Barrett, Geoffrey John
Blaine, John
See Goodwin, Harold L(eland)
Blaine, Marge
See Blaine, Margery Kay
Blaine, Margery Kay 1937- ... 61-64
See also SATA 11
Blaine, Michael ... 239
Blaine, Thomas R(obert) 1895-1984 ... 106
Blaine, Tom R.
See Blaine, Thomas R(obert)
Blaine, William L(ee) 1931- ... 65-68
Blainey, Ann (Warriner) 1935- ... CANR-104
Earlier sketch in CA 25-28R
Blainey, Geoffrey (Norman) 1930- .. CANR-120
Earlier sketches in CA 25-28R, CANR-69
Blair
See Blair-Fish, Wallace Wilfrid
Blair, Alison
See Lerangis, Peter
Blair, Anne Denton 1914-1993 ... 110
See also SATA 46
Blair, Betsy 1923- ... 228
Blair, Calvin Patton 1924- ... 13-16R
Blair, Carvel Hall 1924-1995 ... 49-52
Blair, Charles E. 1920- ... 25-28R
Blair, Claude 1922- ... CANR-11
Earlier sketch in CA 5-8R
Blair, Clay Drewry, Jr., Jr. 1925-1998 ... CANR-68
Obituary ... 172
Earlier sketch in CA 77-80
See also AITN 2
Blair, Cynthia 1953- ... 118
Blair, David Nelson 1954- ... 147
See also SATA 80
Blair, (Robert) Dike 1919- ... 9-12R
Blair, Don 1933- ... 65-68
Blair, Dorothy L. 1890-1989 ... 114
Blair, Dorothy S(ara Greene) 1913-1998
Brief entry ... 113
Blair, E(lizabeth) Anne 1946- ... CANR-112
Earlier sketch in CA 153
Blair, Edward H. 1938- ... CANR-7
Earlier sketch in CA 17-20R
Blair, Edward P(ayson) 1910- ... CANR-26
Earlier sketches in CAP-1, CA 13-14, CANR-11
Blair, Emma 1942- ... RHW
Blair, Eric (Arthur) 1903-1950 ... 132
Brief entry ... 104
See also Orwell, George
See also DA
See also DA3
See also DAB
See also DAC
See also DAM MST, NOV
See also MTCW 1, 2
See also MTFW 2005
See also SATA 29
See also TCLC 123
Blair, Everetta Love 1907-1978 ... CAP-2
Earlier sketch in CA 25-28
Blair, Francis Preston 1791-1876 ... DLB 43
Blair, Frank 1915-1995 ... 93-96
Obituary ... 148
Blair, George S(imms) 1924- ... 17-20R
Blair, Glenn Myers 1908-1994 ... 5-8R
Blair, Gwenda (Linda) 1943- ... CANR-100
Earlier sketch in CA 125
Blair, Harry Wallace 1938- ... 109
Blair, Helen 1910- ... SATA-Brief 29
Blair, J(oseph) Allen 1913- ... 89-92
Blair, James 1655(?)-1743 ... DLB 24
Blair, Jane N(emec) 1911- ... 57-60
Blair, Jay 1953- ... SATA 45
Blair, Jessica
See Spence, William John Duncan
Blair, John Durburrow 1759-1823 ... DLB 37
Blair, John G(eorge) 1934- ... 13-16R
Blair, John M(alcolm) 1914-1976 ... 73-76
Obituary ... 69-72
Blair, Kathryn ... RHW
Blair, Kay Reynolds 1942- ... 33-36R
Blair, Leon Borden 1917- ... 29-32R
Blair, Leona ... 165
Blair, Lorraine Louise 1899(?)-1984
Obituary ... 114
Blair, Lucile
See Yeakley, Marjory Hall
Blair, Margaret Whitman 1951- ... SATA 124
Blair, Pauline Hunter
See Clarke, Pauline
Blair, Paxton 1892-1974
Obituary ... 53-56
Blair, Peter Hunter
See Hunter Blair, Peter
Blair, Philip M(ark) 1928-1979 ... 41-44R
Obituary ... 133
Blair, Ruth Van Ness 1912-1999 ... 21-24R
See also SATA 12
Blair, Sam 1932- ... 53-56
Blair, Shannon
See Kaye, Marilyn
Blair, Sheila ... 166
Blair, Thomas (Lucien Vincent) 1926- ... 106
Blair, Toni
See Blake, Toni
Blair, Walter 1900-1992 ... CANR-18
Obituary ... 139
Earlier sketches in CA 5-8R, CANR-3
See also SATA 12
See also SATA-Obit 72
Blair, Wilfrid
See Blair-Fish, Wallace Wilfrid
Blair, William (Alan) ... 185
Blair-Fish, Wallace Wilfrid 1889-1968 .. CAP-2
Earlier sketch in CA 29-32
Blais, Andre 1947- ... CANR-123
Earlier sketch in CA 167
Blais, Madeleine 1947- ... CANR-126
Earlier sketch in CA 104
See also MTFW 2005
Blais, Marie-Claire 1939- ... CANR-93
Earlier sketches in CA 21-24R, CANR-38, 75
See also CAAS 4
See also CLC 2, 4, 6, 13, 22
See also CWW 2
See also DAC
See also DAM MST
See also DLB 53
See also EWL 3
See also FW
See also MTCW 1, 2
See also MTFW 2005
See also TWA
Blaisdell, Bob
See Blaisdell, Robert
Blaisdell, Donald C(hristy) 1899-1988 .. 37-40R
Obituary ... 126
Blaisdell, Foster W(arren) 1927- ... 69-72
Blaisdell, Harold F. 1914-1985 ... 65-68
Blaisdell, Paul H(enry) 1908-1983 ... 61-64
Blaisdell, Robert 1959- ... 173
See also SATA 105
Blaisdell, Thomas C(harles), Jr. 1895-1988
Obituary ... 127

Blaise, Clark 1940- 231
Earlier sketches in CA 53-56, CANR-5, 66, 106
Autobiographical Essay in 231
See also CAAS 3
See also AITN 2
See also CLC 29
See also CN 4, 5, 6, 7
See also DLB 53
See also RGSF 2
Blake, Alfred
See Janifer, Laurence M(ark)
Blake, Andrea
See Weale, Anne
Blake, Andrew
See Janifer, Laurence M(ark)
Blake, Ann 1941- 195
Blake, Anthony
See Tubb, E(dwin) C(harles)
Blake, Brian 1918-1991 109
Blake, Bronwyn 1940- 223
See also SATA 149
Blake, Bud
See Blake, Julian Watson
Blake, Christina
See Chandler, Bryn
Blake, David H(aven) 1940- 41-44R
Blake, Eubie
See Blake, James Hubert
Blake, Eugene Carson 1906-1985
Obituary 116
Blake, Fairley
See De Voto, Bernard (Augustine)
Blake, Fay M(ontaug) 1920- 53-56
Blake, Forrester .... TCWW 1, 2
Blake, Gary 1944- CANR-15
Earlier sketch in CA 85-88
Blake, George 1893-1961 183
See also DLB 191
Blake, Gerald H(enry) 1936- CANR-51
Earlier sketch in CA 124
Blake, Harlan Morse 1923- 25-28R
Blake, I(srael) George 1902-1982 .... 21-24R
Blake, J. W.
See Blake, John William
Blake, James 1922-1979 93-96
Obituary 85-88
Blake, James Carlos 1948- CANR-97
Earlier sketch in CA 158
Blake, James Hubert 1883-1983
Obituary 109
Blake, Jennifer
See Maxwell, Patricia
Blake, John W.
See Blake, John William
Blake, John William 1911-1987
Obituary 122
Blake, Jon 1954- 135
See also SATA 78
Blake, Judith (Kincade) 1926-1993 ... CANR-47
Obituary 141
Earlier sketch in CA 1-4R
Blake, Julian Watson 1918- 65-68
Blake, Justin
See Bowen, John (Griffith)
Blake, Katherine
See Walter, Dorothy Blake
Blake, Kathleen 1944- 57-60
Blake, Kay
See Walter, Dorothy Blake
Blake, Ken
See Bulmer, (Henry) Kenneth
Blake, L(eslie) J(ames) 1913- CANR-11
Earlier sketch in CA 25-28R
Blake, Laurel
See Palencia, Elaine Fowler
Blake, Lillie Devereux 1833-1913 186
See also DLB 202, 221
Blake, Margaret
See Trimble, Barbara Margaret
Blake, Michael 1945- 140
Blake, Michelle
See Simons, Michelle Blake
Blake, Mike 1950- 148
Blake, Minden V(aughan) 1913-1981 69-72
Blake, Mindy
See Blake, Minden V(aughan)
Blake, Monica
See Muir, Marie
Blake, Nelson Manfred 1908-1996 .. CANR-71
Earlier sketches in CA 1-4R, CANR-3
Blake, Nicholas
See Day Lewis, C(ecil)
See also DLB 77
See also MSW
Blake, Nick
See Hutson, Shaun
Blake, Norman (Francis) 1934- 93-96
Blake, Olive
See Supraner, Robyn
Blake, Patricia 1933- CANR-46
Earlier sketch in CA 49-52
Blake, Patrick
See Egleton, Clive (Frederick)
Blake, Paul C. 1916- 25-28R
Blake, Peter (Jost) 1920- CANR-14
Earlier sketch in CA 65-68
Blake, Quentin (Saxby) 1932- CANR-105
Earlier sketches in CA 25-28R, CANR-11, 37, 67
See also CLR 31
See also CWRI 5
See also MAICYA 1, 2
See also SATA 9, 52, 96, 125
Blake, Raymond B(enjamin) 1958- ... CANR-99
Earlier sketch in CA 148
Blake, Reed H(arris) 1933- 57-60
Blake, Richard A(loysius) 1939- 93-96
Blake, Robert
See Davies, L(eslie) P(urnell)
Blake, Robert (Norman William) 1916-2003 .... CANR-45
Obituary 220
Earlier sketches in CA 9-12R, CANR-22
Blake, Robert 1949- .... SATA 42
Blake, Robert J. .... SATA 160
Blake, Robert R(ogers) 1918- CANR-13
Earlier sketch in CA 21-24R
Blake, Robert W(illiam) 1930- CANR-31
Earlier sketch in CA 33-36R
Blake, Robin (James) 1948- CANR-88
Earlier sketch in CA 127
Blake, Sally
See Saunders, Jean
Blake, Sally Mirliss 1925-1986 .... 17-20R
Obituary 118
Blake, Stephanie
See Pearl, Jacques Bain
Blake, Stephen P. 1942- 139
Blake, Sterling
See Benford, Gregory (Albert)
Blake, Toni 1965- 210
Blake, Vanessa
See Brown, May
Blake, Walker E.
See Butterworth, W(illiam) E(dmund III)
Blake, Wendon
See Holden, Donald
Blake, William 1757-1827 .... AAYA 47
See also BRW 3
See also BRWR 1
See also CDBLB 1789-1832
See also CLR 52
See also DA
See also DA3
See also DAB
See also DAC
See also DAM MST, POET
See also DLB 93, 163
See also EXPP
See also LATS 1:1
See also LMFS 1
See also MAICYA 1, 2
See also PAB
See also PC 12, 63
See also PFS 2, 12
See also SATA 30
See also TEA
See also WCH
See also WLC
See also WLIT 3
See also WP
Blake, William J(ames) 1894-1969 .... 5-8R
Obituary 25-28R
Blakeborough, Jack Fairfax
See Fairfax-Blakeborough, John Freeman
Blakeborough, John Freeman Fairfax
See Fairfax-Blakeborough, John Freeman
Blakeley, Phyllis (Ruth) 1922- 61-64
Blakeley, Thomas J(ohn) 1931- CANR-3
Earlier sketch in CA 9-12R
Blakely, Alexander J. 1969- 212
Blakely, Allison 1940- CANR-51
Earlier sketch in CA 125
Blakely, Diann
See Shoaf, Diann Blakely
See also CSW
Blakely, Gloria 1950- 210
See also SATA 139
Blakely, Mary Kay 1948- 131
Blakely, Mike 1958- 207
Blakely, R(obert) J(ohn) 1915-1994 .... 37-40R
Obituary 147
Blakely, Roger K. 1922- 149
See also SATA 82
Blakemore, Colin (Brian) 1944- CANR-140
Earlier sketch in CA 85-88
Blakemore, Harold 1930-1991 146
Blakemore, Michael (Howell) 1928- 216
Blakeney, Jay D.
See Chester, Deborah
Blaker, Alfred A(rthur) 1928- 65-68
Blaker, Kimberly Kae 1965- 220
Blakeslee, Alton (Lauren) 1913-1997 105
Obituary 158
Blakeslee, Mermer 180
Blakeslee, Sandra 1943- CANR-98
Earlier sketch in CA 131
Blakeslee, Thomas R(obert) 1937- 101
Blakesley, Christopher L. 1945- 146
Blakeston, Oswell 1907(?)-1985(?)
Obituary 116
Blakey, George T., Jr. 1939- 120
Blakey, Nancy 1955- 159
See also SATA 94
Blakey, Scott 1936- 85-88
Blakey, Walker Jameson 1940- 69-72
Blakiston, Georgiana 1903-1995 69-72
Obituary 150
Blakiston, Noel 1905-1984
Obituary 115
Blakney, Raymond D. 1897(?)-1970
Obituary 104
Blalock, Hubert M(orse), Jr. 1926-1991 .... CANR-5
Obituary 133
Earlier sketch in CA 13-16R
Blalock, Jane B. 1945-
Brief entry 112
Blaman, Anna
See Vrugt, Johanna Petronella
See also EWL 3
See also GLL 2
Blamires, Alcuin (Godfrey) 1946- 141
Blamires, David (Malcolm) 1936- CANR-14
Earlier sketch in CA 65-68
Blamires, Harry 1916- CANR-42
Earlier sketches in CA 9-12R, CANR-5, 20
Blanc, Esther S. 1913-1997 131
See also SATA 66
Blanc, Mel 1908-1989 .... IDFW 3, 4
See also SATA-Obit 64
Blanc, Michel H(enri) A(mbroise) 1929- 133
Blanc, Nero
See Biddle, Cordelia Frances and Zettler, Steve
Blanc, Suzanne 1915-1999 181
Blance, Ellen 1931- CANR-7
Earlier sketch in CA 57-60
Blanch, Lesley 1907- CANR-70
Earlier sketch in CA 102
Blanch, Robert J. 1938- 21-24R
Blanch, Stuart Yarworth 1918-1994 106
Obituary 145
Blanchard, Alice 1959- CANR-121
Earlier sketch in CA 163
Blanchard, Allan E(dward) 1929- 69-72
Blanchard, B(irdsall) Everard 1909- 41-44R
Blanchard, Carroll Henry, Jr. 1928- 13-16R
Blanchard, Charles Albert 1848-1925 215
Blanchard, Fessenden Seaver 1888-1963 .. 5-8R
Blanchard, Howard L(awrence) 1909- 5-8R
Blanchard, J. Richard 1912-1996 89-92
Blanchard, Kendall A(llan) 1942- CANR-11
Earlier sketch in CA 69-72
Blanchard, Kenneth H(artley) 1939- CANR-123
Earlier sketch in CA 111
Blanchard, Mary Warner 1934- 180
Blanchard, Nina 101
Blanchard, Olivier Jean 1948- 141
Blanchard, Patricia .... SATA 125
Blanchard, Paula (Barber) 1936- 81-84
Blanchard, Peter 1946- 117
Blanchard, Ralph Harrub 1890-1973 .... CAP-1
Earlier sketch in CA 13-14
Blanchard, Scott 238
Blanchard, Stephen (Thomas) 1950- 161
See also DLB 267
Blanchard, William H(enry) 1922- CANR-8
Earlier sketch in CA 21-24R
Blanche, Pierre 1927- 25-28R
Blanchet, Eileen 1924- 57-60
Blanchet, M(uriel) Wylie 1891-1961 168
See also SATA 106
Blanchette, Oliva 1929- CANR-92
Earlier sketch in CA 53-56
Blanchot, Maurice 1907-2003 .... CANR-138
Obituary 213
Brief entry 117
Earlier sketch in CA 144
See also CLC 135
See also DLB 72, 296
See also EWL 3
Blanck, Gertrude 1914-2001 85-88
Blanck, Jacob Nathaniel 1906-1974 . CANR-69
Obituary 53-56
Earlier sketches in CAP-1, CA 11-12
Blanck, Rubin 1914-1995 .... 25-28R
Blanckenburg, Chrisitian Friedrich von 1744-1796 .... DLB 94
Blanco, Luis Anado 1903(?)-1975
Obituary 104
Blanco, Richard 1968- 200
Blanco, Richard L(idio) 1926- 57-60
See also SATA 63
Blanco Fombona, Rufino 1874-1944 ...... HW 1
See also LAW
Blanco White, Amber 1887-1981
Obituary 105
Bland, Alexander
See Gosling, Nigel
Bland, E.
See Nesbit, E(dith)
Bland, Edith Nesbit
See Nesbit, E(dith)
Bland, Eleanor Taylor CANR-116
Earlier sketch in CA 166
Bland, Fabian
See Nesbit, E(dith)
Bland, Hester Beth 1906-1998 57-60
Bland, Jeffrey 1946- 106
Bland, Jennifer
See Bowden, Jean
Bland, Larry I(rvin) 1940- 109
Bland, Lucy 158
Bland, Peter 1934- 153
See also CP 1, 7
Bland, Randall Walton 1942- CANR-5
Earlier sketch in CA 53-56
Blanda, George (Frederick) 1927-
Brief entry 114
Blandford, Brian E(rnest) 1937- 118
Blandford, Percy William 1912- 9-12R
Blandiana, Ana 1942- 152
See also CDWLB 4
See also CWW 2
See also DLB 232
See also EWL 3
Blanding, Forrest H(arvey) 1917- 111
Blandino, Giovanni 1923- 21-24R
Blandy, Doug(las E.) 1951- 138
Blane, Gertrude
See Blumenthal, Gertrude
Blane, Howard T(homas) 1926- CANR-51
Earlier sketches in CA 25-28R, CANR-10, 28
Blanford, James T. 1917- 33-36R
Blank, Blanche D(avis) 1923(?)-2003 .... 41-44R
Obituary 222
Blank, Clarissa Mabel 1915-1965 .... SATA 62
Blank, G(regory) Kim 1952- CANR-108
Earlier sketch in CA 151
Blank, George (W. III) 1945- 110
Blank, Harrod 1963(?)- 211
Blank, Joost de
See de Blank, Joost
Blank, Joseph P. 1919- 93-96
Blank, Leonard 1927- CANR-12
Earlier sketch in CA 33-36R
Blank, Les 1935- 131
Blank, Robert H(enry) 1943- 148
Blank, Sheldon H(aas) 1896-1989 .... 1-4R
Blanke, Henry 1901-1981 .... IDFW 3, 4
Blankenhorn, David (George) III 1955- CANR-119
Earlier sketch in CA 151
Blankenship, A(lbert) B. 1914-1998 .... CANR-7
Earlier sketch in CA 13-16R
Blankenship, Edward Gary 1943- 45-48
Blankenship, Lela (McDowell) 1886-1966 .... 5-8R
Blankenship, William D(ouglas) 1934- .. 33-36R
Blankfort, (Seymour) Michael 1907-1982 .... CANR-70
Obituary 107
Earlier sketches in CA 1-4R, CANR-2
Blanksten, George I(rving) 1917- CANR-1
Earlier sketch in CA 1-4R
Blanpied, Pamela Wharton 1937- 102
Blanshard, Brand 1892-1987 .... CANR-16
Obituary 124
Earlier sketch in CA 1-4R
See also DLB 279
Blanshard, Paul (Beecher) 1892-1980 135
Obituary 93-96
Blanton, (Martha) Catherine 1907- ... CANR-70
Earlier sketch in CA 1-4R
Blanton, DeAnne 1964- 223
Blanton, Thomas S. 1955- 184
Blantz, Thomas E(dward) 1934- CANR-96
Earlier sketch in CA 111
Blanzaco, Andre C. 1934- 29-32R
Blasband, Philippe 1964- 195
Blasco Ibanez, Vicente 1867-1928 ... CANR-81
Brief entry 110
Earlier sketch in CA 131
See also Ibanez, Vicente Blasco
See also BPFB 1
See also DA3
See also DAM NOV
See also EW 8
See also EWL 3
See also HW 1, 2
See also MTCW 1
See also TCLC 12
Blase, Melvin G(eorge) 1933- 33-36R
Blaser, Robin (Francis) 1925- CANR-8
Earlier sketch in CA 57-60
See also CP 1, 2, 3, 4, 5, 6, 7
See also DLB 165
Blaser, Werner 1924- CANR-141
Earlier sketch in CA 136
Blashford-Snell, John (Nicholas) 1936- CANR-135
Earlier sketches in CA 102, CANR-19, 42
Blasi, Anthony J(oseph) 1946- 140
Blasier, (Stewart) Cole 1925- 21-24R
Blasing, Mutlu Konuk 1944- CANR-82
Earlier sketches in CA 89-92, CANR-35
Blasing, Randy 1943- CANR-50
Earlier sketches in CA 114, CANR-35
Blasis, Celeste De
See De Blasis, Celeste (Ninette)
Blass, Bill 1922-2002 221
Blass, Birgit A(nnelise) 1940- 29-32R
Blass, Ron(ald J.) 1922-1984
Obituary 114
Blass, Thomas 233
Blassingame, John W(esley) 1940-2000 .... CANR-25
Obituary 188
Earlier sketch in CA 49-52
See also BW 1
Blassingame, Wyatt Rainey 1909-1985 .... CANR-68
Obituary 114
Earlier sketches in CA 1-4R, CANR-3
See also SATA 1, 34
See also SATA-Obit 41
Blatch, Harriot Eaton Stanton 1856-1940 ... 222
See also FW
Blatchford, Christie 1951- 73-76
Blatchford, Claire H. 1944- CANR-123
Earlier sketch in CA 159
See also SATA 94
Blathwayt, Jean 1918- 106
Blatner, David 1966- CANR-135
Earlier sketch in CA 168
Blatt, Burton 1927-1985 .... CANR-14
Earlier sketch in CA 41-44R
Blatt, Martin H(enry) 1951- 191
Blatt, Sidney J(ules) 1928- 37-40R
Blatt, Thomas 1927-
Blatter, Dorothy (Gertrude) 1901-1977 .. CAP-1
Earlier sketch in CA 11-12
Blatter, Silvio 1946- .... EWL 3
Blatty, William Peter 1928- CANR-124
Earlier sketches in CA 5-8R, CANR-9
See also CLC 2
See also DAM POP
See also HGG
Blau, Abram 1907-1979
Obituary 85-88
Blau, Eric 1921- 85-88
Blau, Francine D(ee) 1946- CANR-51
Earlier sketches in CA 106, CANR-25

Cumulative Index 57 Blocksma

Blau, Herbert 1926- CANR-102
Earlier sketches in CA 111, CANR-36
Blau, Joel 1945- CANR-90
Earlier sketch in CA 137
Blau, Joseph L(eon) 1909-1986 .... 9-12R
Obituary 121
Blau, Joshua 1919- CANR-7
Earlier sketch in CA 13-16R
Blau, Judith R. 1942- CANR-48
Earlier sketch in CA 122
Blau, Milton
See Blau, Eric
Blau, Peter M(ichael) 1918- CANR-1
Earlier sketch in CA 1-4R
Blau, Sheldon Paul 1935- 57-60
Blau, Tom 1913(?)-1984
Obituary 113
Blau, Yehoshua
See Blau, Joshua
Blau, Zena Smith 1922- CANR-1
Earlier sketch in CA 45-48
Blauer, Ettagale 1940- CANR-24
Earlier sketch in CA 103
See also SATA 49
Blaufarb, Douglas S(amuel) 1918-2000 ... 85-88
Obituary 190
Blaug, Mark 1927- CANR-16
Earlier sketches in CA 1-4R, CANR-1
Blaukopf, Herta 1924- 131
Blaukopf, Kurt 1914-1999 186
Brief entry 114
Blaumanis, Rudolfs 1863-1908 .... DLB 220
Blauner, Bob 1929-
See Blauner, Robert
Blauner, Laurie (Ann) 1953- 222
Blauner, Peter 1959- CANR-141
Earlier sketches in CA 136, CANR-73
Blauner, Robert 1929- 210
Blauner, Susan Rose 1965- 213
Blaustein, Albert Paul 1921-1994 ..... CANR-19
Obituary 171
Earlier sketches in CA 1-4R, CANR-1
Blaustein, Arthur I. 1933- CANR-10
Earlier sketch in CA 25-28R
Blaustein, Elliott H(arold) 1915- 41-44R
Blaustein, Esther 1935- 45-48
Blauw, Johannes 1912- 9-12R
Blauw, Pieter Wilhelmus 1942- 137
Blauw, Wim
See Blauw, Pieter Wilhelmus
Blaxland, John 1917- 5-8R
Blaxland, W(illiam) Gregory 1918- CANR-3
Earlier sketch in CA 9-12R
Blaylock, James P(aul) 1950- CANR-107
Earlier sketches in CA 110, CANR-27, 53
See also AAYA 64
See also FANT
See also SFW 4
See also SUFW 2
Blayn, Hugo
See Fearn, John Russell
Blayne, Diana
See Kyle, Susan (Spaeth)
Blayne, Sara
See Howl, Marcia (Yvonne Hurt)
Blayney, Margaret S(tatler) 1926- 53-56
Blayre, Christopher
See Heron-Allen, Edward
Blaze, Wayne 1951- 61-64
Blazek, Douglas 1941- 25-28R
Blazek, Ron(ald David) 1936- 111
Blazer, Dan G(erman) II 1944- 110
Blazer, J. S.
See Scott, Justin
Blazier, Kenneth D(ean) 1933- CANR-11
Earlier sketch in CA 69-72
Bleakley, David (Wylie) 1925- 102
Bleamer, Burton 1906(?)-1986
Obituary 118
Bleasdale, Alan 1946- 215
See also CBD
See also CD 5, 6
See also DLB 245
Blecher, M(arcel) 1909-1938 .... EWL 3
Blechman, Barry M. 1943- 97-100
Blechman, Burt 1927- CANR-72
Earlier sketches in CA 21-24R, CANR-65
See also CN 1, 2, 3, 4, 5, 6
Blechman, Elaine A(nn) 1943- 170
Blechta, Rick 1951- 220
Blecker, Robert A. 1956- CANR-91
Earlier sketch in CA 145
Bledlow, John
See Vale, (Henry) Edmund (Theodoric)
Bledsoe, Albert Taylor 1809- .... DLB 3, 79, 248
Bledsoe, Glen L(eonard) 1951- 170
See also SATA 108
Bledsoe, Jerry 1941- CANR-90
Earlier sketches in CA 85-88, CANR-49
See also CSW
Bledsoe, Joseph C(ullie) 1918- 33-36R
Bledsoe, Karen E(lizabeth) 1962- 170
See also SATA 108
Bledsoe, Lucy Jane 1957- CANR-131
Earlier sketch in CA 152
See also SATA 97, 162
Bledsoe, Thomas (Alexander)
1914-1968 .... CANR-9
Earlier sketch in CA 13-16R
Bledsoe, Timothy 1953- 146
Bledsoe, William Ambrose 1906-1981
Obituary 104
Blee, Kathleen M. 211
Bleeck, Oliver
See Thomas, Ross (Elmore)
Bleeker, Ann Eliza 1752-1783 .... DLB 200
Bleeker, Mordecia
See Morgan, Fred Troy
Bleeker, Sonia
See Zim, Sonia Bleeker
See also SATA 2
See also SATA-Obit 26
Blees, Robert A(rthur) 1922-1985(?) 17-20R
Blegen, Carl (William) 1887-1971
Obituary 33-36R
Blegen, Daniel M. 1950- 156
See also SATA 92
Blegen, Theodore C(hristian)
1891-1969 .... CANR-69
Earlier sketches in CA 5-8R, CANR-3
Blegvad, Erik 1923- 97-100
See also CWRI 5
See also MAICYA 1, 2
See also SATA 14, 66, 132
Blegvad, Lenore 1926- CANR-31
Earlier sketches in CA 69-72, CANR-14
See also SATA 14, 66
Blehl, Vincent Ferrer 1921-2001 .... 9-12R
Obituary 204
Blei, Norbert 1935- 143
Bleiberg, Robert Marvin 1924-1997 103
Obituary 162
Bleich, Alan R. 1913-1995 .... 13-16R
Bleich, Harold 1930(?)-1980
Obituary 93-96
Bleich, J(udah) David 1936- CANR-90
Earlier sketch in CA 116
Bleicher, Michael N(athaniel) 1935- 37-40R
Bleier, Robert Patrick 1946- 85-88
Bleier, Rocky
See Bleier, Robert Patrick
Bleiler, Everett F(ranklin) 1920- 164
Bleiler, Richard 229
Blench, J(ohn) W(heatley) 1926- 13-16R
Blend, Charles D(aniels) 1918-1971 ..... 21-24R
Obituary 134
Blenk, K. T.
See Blenk, Katie
Blenk, Katie 1954- 152
Blenkinsopp, Joseph 1927- 37-40R
Blennerhassett, Margaret Agnew
1773-1842 .... DLB 99
Bleser, Carol K. 1935- 107
Blesh, Rudi
See Blesh, Rudolph Pickett
Blesh, Rudolph Pickett 1899-1985 ... CANR-72
Obituary 117
Earlier sketch in CA 17-20R
Blessing, Lee (Knowlton) 1949- 236
See also CAD
See also CD 5, 6
See also CLC 54
Blessing, Richard Allen 1939- 53-56
See also YAW
Blessington, Francis C(harles) 1942- . CANR-86
Earlier sketch in CA 130
Blessington, Marguerite 1789-1849 .... DLB 166
Blest Gana, Alberto 1830-1920 .... LAW
Blet, Pierre 1918- 193
Blethen, H(arold) Tyler 1945- 166
Bletter, Robert 1933(?)-1976
Obituary 61-64
Bletter, Rosemarie Haag 1939- 57-60
Blevins, James Lowell 1936- 106
Blevins, Leon W(ilford) 1937- 57-60
Blevins, William L. 1937- 33-36R
Blevins, Win
See Blevins, Winfred (Ernest, Jr.)
Blevins, Winfred (Ernest, Jr.) 1938- ... CANR-88
Earlier sketches in CA 45-48, CANR-1
Blew, Mary Clearman 1939- 213
See also DLB 256
Blewett, Daniel K(eith) 1957- 152
Blewett, Mary (H.) 1938- 205
Bleything, Dennis H(ugh) 1946- 61-64
Bleznick, Donald W(illiam) 1924- 21-24R
Blezzard, Judith 1944- 134
Blicher, Steen Steensen 1782-1848 ..... DLB 300
Blicker, Seymour 1940- 77-80
Blickle, Peter 1938- CANR-143
Earlier sketch in CA 144
Blicq, Anthony 1926- 33-36R
Blier, Bertrand 1939- 143
Bligh, Norman
See Neubauer, William Arthur
Blight, David W. 1949- CANR-106
Earlier sketch in CA 147
Blight, James G. 217
Blight, John 1913-1995 .... CANR-22
Earlier sketch in CA 69-72
See also CP 1, 2, 3, 4
Blight, Rose
See Greer, Germaine
Blij, Harm J(an) de
See de Blij, Harm J(an)
Blincoe, Nicholas 180
Blind, Mathilde 1841-1896 .... DLB 199
Blinder, Alan S(tuart) 1945- CANR-32
Earlier sketch in CA 113
Blinder, Elliot 1949- 106
Blinder, Martin 190
Blinderman, Abraham 1916-1997 61-64
Blinderman, Charles 1930- 135
Blinn, Johna
See Dorsey, Helen
Blinn, Keith Wayne 1917-1990
Obituary 131
Blinn, Walter Craig 1930- 61-64
Blischke, Wallace R. 1934- 206
Blish, James (Benjamin) 1921-1975 .... CANR-3
Obituary 57-60
Earlier sketch in CA 1-4R
See also BPFB 1
See also CLC 14
See also CN 2
See also DLB 8
See also MTCW 1
See also SATA 66
See also SCFW 1, 2
See also SFW 4
Blishen, Bernard Russell 1919- CANR-3
Earlier sketch in CA 1-4R
Blishen, Edward (William)
1920-1996 .... CANR-27
Obituary 155
Earlier sketches in CA 17-20R, CANR-11
See also SATA 8, 66
See also SATA-Obit 93
Bliss, A. J.
See Bliss, Alan (Joseph)
Bliss, Alan (Joseph) 1921-1985 134
Obituary 118
Bliss, Carey S(tillman) 1914-1994 .... 41-44R
Obituary 145
Bliss, Carolyn (Jane) 1947- 128
Bliss, Corinne Demas 1947- CANR-28
Earlier sketch in CA 104
See also Demas, Corinne
See also SATA 37
Bliss, Dorothy E(lizabeth) 1916-1987 118
Obituary 124
Bliss, Edward, Jr. 1912-2002 .... 41-44R
Obituary 210
Bliss, Edwin C(rosby) 1923- 131
Bliss, Frederick
See Card, Orson Scott
Bliss, George William 1918-1978 85-88
Obituary 81-84
Bliss, Harry 1964- 231
See also SATA 156
Bliss, Lee 1943- CANR-49
Earlier sketch in CA 122
Bliss, (John) Michael 1941- CANR-95
Earlier sketches in CA 103, CANR-31, 60
Bliss, Michael (J.) 1947- 150
Bliss, Patricia Lounsbury 1929- CANR-109
Earlier sketches in CA 127, CANR-55
Bliss, Reginald
See Wells, H(erbert) G(eorge)
Bliss, Ronald G(ene) 1942- 53-56
See also SATA 12
Bliss, William D(wight) P(orter)
1856-1926 212
Blissett, Luther
See Home, Stewart
Blissett, Marlan 1938- 41-44R
Blistein, Elmer M(ilton) 1920-1993 .... 9-12R
Obituary 142
Blitch, Fleming Lee
See Lee, Fleming
Blitchington, Evelyn G(rant) 1947- 114
Blits, Jan H. 1943- 110
Blitzer, Wolf 1948- 136
Blitzstein, Marc 1905-1964
Obituary 110
Bliven, Bruce, Jr. 1916-2002 .... CANR-7
Obituary 208
Earlier sketch in CA 17-20R
See also SATA 2
Bliven, Bruce 1889-1977 .... CANR-70
Obituary 69-72
Earlier sketch in CA 37-40R
See also DLB 137
Bliven, Naomi 1925-2002 .... 33-36R
Obituary 208
Blix, Hans (Martin) 1928- 230
Blix, Jacqueline 1949- 163
Blixen, Karen (Christentze Dinesen)
1885-1962 .... CANR-50
Earlier sketches in CAP-2, CA 25-28, CANR-22
See also Dinesen, Isak
See also DA3
See also DLB 214
See also LMFS 1
See also MTCW 1, 2
See also SATA 44
See also SSFS 20
Blizzard, Gladys S. (?)-1992 .... SATA 79
Blizzard, S(amuel) W(ilson, Jr.) 1914(?)-1976
Obituary 65-68
Blobaum, Cindy 1966- 194
See also SATA 123
Bloch, Alice 1947- .... GLL 2
Bloch, Ariel A(lfred Karl) 1933- 41-44R
Bloch, Arthur McBride 1938- 128
Bloch, Barbara 1925- CANR-49
Earlier sketches in CA 106, CANR-24
Bloch, Bertram 1892-1987
Obituary 122
Bloch, Blanche 1890-1980
Obituary 97-100
Bloch, Chana 1940- CANR-107
Earlier sketches in CA 105, CANR-70
See also CWP
Bloch, Dan 1943- 140
Bloch, Dorothy 1912- 93-96
Bloch, Douglas 1949- 138
Bloch, E. Maurice 25-28R
Bloch, Ernst 1885-1977 .... CANR-34
Obituary 73-76
Earlier sketch in CA 29-32R
See also DLB 296
Bloch, Herbert A(aron David) 1904-1965 . 1-4R
Obituary 134
Bloch, Herman D(avid) 1914-1976 .... 29-32R
Bloch, Jeff(rey W.) 1959- 130
Bloch, Konrad E. 1912-2000 150
Obituary 191
Bloch, Lucienne 1909-1999 .... SATA 10
Bloch, Lucienne S(chupf) 1937- 93-96
Bloch, Marc (Leopold Benjamin)
1886-1944 201
Brief entry 118
Bloch, Marie Halun 1910-1998 .... CANR-19
Earlier sketches in CA 1-4R, CANR-4
See also SAAS 9
See also SATA 6
Bloch, Robert (Albert) 1917-1994 179
Obituary 146
Earlier sketches in CA 5-8R, CANR-5, 78
Interview in CANR-5
Autobiographical Essay in 179
See also CAAS 20
See also AAYA 29
See also CLC 33
See also DA3
See also DLB 44
See also HGG
See also MTCW 2
See also SATA 12
See also SATA-Obit 82
See also SFW 4
See also SUFW 1, 2
Blocher, Henri (Arthur) 1937- CANR-10
Earlier sketch in CA 65-68
Blochman, Lawrence G(oldtree)
1900-1975 .... CANR-58
Obituary 53-56
Earlier sketches in CAP-2, CA 19-20
See also SATA 22
Block, Adrienne (Fried) 1921- 185
Block, Allan (Forrest) 1923- CANR-31
Earlier sketch in CA 49-52
Block, Andrew 1892-1985
Obituary 118
Block, Arthur John 1916(?)-1981
Obituary 105
Block, Brett Ellen 235
Block, Cathy Collins 1948- 233
Block, Daniel I. 1943- 173
Block, Eugene B. 1890-1988 .... CANR-72
Earlier sketches in CA 5-8R, CANR-2
Block, Francesca Lia 1962- CANR-135
Earlier sketches in CA 131, CANR-56, 77, 94
See also AAYA 13, 34
See also BYA 8, 10
See also CLR 33
See also MAICYA 2
See also MAICYAS 1
See also MTFW 2005
See also SAAS 21
See also SATA 80, 116, 158
See also WYA
See also YAW
Block, Geoffrey 1948- CANR-141
Earlier sketch in CA 162
Block, Hal 1914(?)-1981
Obituary 104
Block, Herbert (Lawrence) 1909-2001 111
Obituary 200
Block, Irvin 1917- 17-20R
See also SATA 12
Block, Irving (Leonard) 1930- 118
Block, Jack 1921- 33-36R
Block, Jack 1931- 53-56
Block, James E. 1946- 239
Block, Jean Libman 5-8R
Block, Joel D(avid) 1943- CANR-15
Earlier sketch in CA 89-92
Block, Joyce 1951- 145
Block, Julian 1934- 106
Block, Laurie S. 1951- 127
Block, Lawrence 1938- 214
Earlier sketches in CA 1-4R, CANR-6, 45, 63, 105
Autobiographical Essay in 214
See also CAAS 11
See also BPFB 1
See also CPW
See also DAM POP
See also DLB 226
See also MSW
See also MTCW 2
Block, Libbie 1910(?)-1972
Obituary 33-36R
Block, Marvin Avram 1903-1989 ..... CANR-80
Obituary 128
Earlier sketch in CA 106
Block, Michael 1942- 101
Block, Ned Joel 1942- 117
Block, Paul, Jr. 1911-1987
Obituary 122
Block, Ralph 1889-1974
Obituary 45-48
Block, Ron (ald D.) 1955- 174
Block, Rudolph
See Lessing, Bruno
Block, Seymour Stanton 1918- 89-92
Block, Stanley Byron 1939- 85-88
Block, Thomas H(arris) 1945- CANR-18
Earlier sketch in CA 101
Block, Walter (Edward) 1941- CANR-22
Earlier sketches in CA 57-60, CANR-6
Block, Zenas 1916- 107
Blocker, Clyde (Edward) 1918-1980 ...... 33-36R
Blocker, H(arry) Gene 1937- 116
Blockinger, Betty
See Blocklinger, Peggy O'More
Blockley, John 1921-2002 217
Blocklinger, Peggy O'More 1895-1970 ..... 5-8R
Blocksma, Mary 1942- 130
See also SATA-Brief 44

Blockson, Charles L(eRoy) 1933- 141
See also BW 2
Blodgett, Beverley 1926- 57-60
Blodgett, E(dward) D(ickinson) 1935- 112
Blodgett, Geoffrey Thomas 1931- 17-20R
Blodgett, Harold William 1900-1994 .... 13-16R
Blodgett, Harriet Eleanor 1919- 33-36R
Blodgett, (Anita) Jan 1954- 175
Blodgett, Peter J. 1954- 203
Blodgett, Richard 1940- CANR-1
Earlier sketch in CA 49-52
Bloem, Diane Brummel 1935- CANR-16
Earlier sketch in CA 85-88
Bloesch, Donald G. 1928- 13-16R
Bloesser, Robert 1930- 37-40R
Blofeld, John (Eaton Calthorpe)
1913-1987 .... CANR-19
Obituary 123
Earlier sketches in CA 53-56, CANR-4
Blois, Marsden S(cott, Jr.) 1919-1988 132
Blok, Alexander (Alexandrovich)
1880-1921 183
Brief entry 104
See also DLB 295
See also EW 9
See also EWL 3
See also LMFS 2
See also PC 21
See also RGWL 2, 3
See also TCLC 5
Blok, Anton 1935- 97-100
Blom, Gaston E(ugene) 1920- 25-28R
Blom, Jan
See Breytenbach, Breyten
Blom, Karl Arne 1946- CANR-51
Earlier sketches in CA 69-72, CANR-11, 28
Blom, Lynne Anne 1942- 120
Blom, Philipp
See Sievert, Philipp
Blomain, Karen 1944- 210
Blomberg, Thomas G. 1944- 222
Blom-Cooper, Louis Jacques 1926- 5-8R
Blomgren, Jennifer (Alice) 1954- .... SATA 136
Blond, Anthony 1928- CANR-100
Earlier sketch in CA 106
Blondal, Patricia (Jenkins) 1926-1959 177
See also DLB 88
Blondel, Jean Fernand Pierre 1929- 101
Blondel, Nathalie 1960- CANR-115
Earlier sketch in CA 138
Blondell, (Rose) Joan 1912(?)-1979 115
Obituary 93-96
Blonder, Ellen Leong 1950- 214
Blood, Bob
See Blood, Robert O(scar), Jr.
Blood, Charles Lewis 1929- 73-76
See also SATA 28
Blood, Jerome W. 1926- 9-12R
Blood, Marje 41-44R
Blood, Matthew
See Dresser, Davis
Blood, Robert O(scar), Jr. 1921- CANR-3
Earlier sketch in CA 1-4R
Bloodmelt, Evian
See Headmess, Violet
Bloodstein, Oliver 1920- 146
Bloodstone, John
See Byrne, Stuart J(ames)
Bloodstone, Mark
See McNaughton, Brian
Bloodworth, Linda (Joyce)
See Bloodworth-Thomason, Linda (Joyce)
Bloodworth-Thomason, Linda (Joyce)
1947- 239
Bloom, Alan (Herbert Vawser)
1906-2005 .... CANR-3
Obituary 237
Earlier sketch in CA 9-12R
Bloom, Alexander 1947- 114
Bloom, Allan (David) 1930-1992 ..... CANR-80
Obituary 139
Brief entry 125
Earlier sketch in CA 131
Interview in CA-131
Bloom, Amy 1953- CANR-136
Earlier sketches in CA 144, CANR-61, 99
See also MTFW 2005
See also SSFS 11
Bloom, Barbara Lee 1943- 220
See also SATA 146
Bloom, Claire 1931- CANR-59
Earlier sketch in CA 114
Bloom, Clive 1953- 131
Bloom, Daniel Halevi 1949- 120
Bloom, Edward A(lan) 1914-1994 .... CANR-2
Earlier sketch in CA 1-4R
Bloom, Erick Franklin 1944- 57-60
Bloom, Floyd E(lliott) 1936- 120
Bloom, Freddy 1914-2000 101
Obituary 189
See also SATA 37
See also SATA-Obit 121
Bloom, Gordon F. 1918- 13-16R
Bloom, Harold 1930- CANR-133
Earlier sketches in CA 13-16R, CANR-39, 75, 92
See also CLC 24, 103
See also DLB 67
See also EWL 3
See also MTCW 2
See also MTFW 2005
See also RGAL 4
Bloom, Harry 1913(?)-1981
Obituary 104
Bloom, Herman Irving 1908-1992 102
Bloom, James D. 1951- 163
Bloom, John 1921- 5-8R
Bloom, John Porter 1924- 49-52
Bloom, Jonathan M(ax) 1950- 150
Bloom, Ken(neth) 1949- CANR-38
Earlier sketch in CA 115
Bloom, Lillian D. 1920- CANR-11
Earlier sketch in CA 17-20R
Bloom, Lisa E. 1958- 144
Bloom, Lloyd 1947- .... SATA 108
See also SATA-Brief 43
Bloom, Lynn (Marie) Z(immerman)
1934- CANR-100
Earlier sketches in CA 13-16R, CANR-6, 21, 49
Bloom, Melvyn H(arold) 1938- 45-48
Bloom, Miriam 1934- 151
Bloom, Murray Teigh 1916- CANR-69
Earlier sketch in CA 17-20R
Bloom, Patrice 1936- 128
Bloom, Paul 1963- 231
Bloom, Pauline 41-44R
Bloom, Peter H(erbert) 1949- 194
Bloom, Rebecca (S.) 1975- 224
Bloom, Reginald
See Stine, Scott A(aron)
Bloom, Robert 1930- 17-20R
Bloom, Samuel William 1921- CANR-3
Earlier sketch in CA 9-12R
Bloom, Steven 1942- 159
Bloom, Ursula (Harvey) 1893-1984 . CANR-77
Obituary 114
Earlier sketches in CA 25-28R, CANR-48
See also RHW
Blooman, Percy A. 1906- CAP-1
Earlier sketch in CA 11-12
Bloomberg, Beverly 198
Bloomberg, Edward (Michael) 1937- 41-44R
Bloomberg, Marty
See Bloomberg, Max Arthur
Bloomberg, Max Arthur 1938- 101
Bloomberg, Michael (Rubens) 1942- 160
Bloomberg, Morton 1936- 53-56
Bloome, Enid P. 1925- 85-88
Bloomer, Amelia 1818-1894 .... DLB 79
Bloomer, Kent C(ress) 1935- 125
Bloomfield, Anthony (John Westgate)
1922- CANR-49
Earlier sketch in CA 1-4R
Bloomfield, Arthur (John) 1931- 65-68
Bloomfield, Arthur Irving 1914-1998 .... 41-44R
Bloomfield, Aurelius
See Bourne, Randolph S(illiman)
Bloomfield, B(arry) C(ambray)
1931-2002 .... CANR-5
Obituary 209
Earlier sketch in CA 9-12R
Bloomfield, Harold H. 1944- CANR-123
Earlier sketches in CA 57-60, CANR-9
Bloomfield, Lincoln Palmer 1920- CANR-5
Earlier sketch in CA 1-4R
Bloomfield, Louis A(ub) 1956- 163
Bloomfield, Masse 1923- CANR-8
Earlier sketch in CA 61-64
Bloomfield, Maxwell H(erron III)
1931- CANR-99
Brief entry 118
Earlier sketch in CA 122
Bloomfield, Michaela 1966- .... SATA 70
Bloomfield, Morton W(ilfred)
1913-1987 .... CANR-2
Obituary 122
Earlier sketch in CA 5-8R
Bloomfield, Robert 1766-1823 .... DLB 93
Bloomingdale, Teresa 1930- CANR-21
Earlier sketch in CA 105
Bloomquist, Edward R. 1924- 29-32R
Bloomstein, Morris J. 1928- 25-28R
Bloor, Edward (William) 1950- CANR-140
Earlier sketch in CA 166
See also AAYA 43
See also MAICYA 2
See also SATA 98, 155
Bloor, Ella Reeve 1862-1951 .... DLB 303
Blos, Joan W(insor) 1928- CANR-128
Earlier sketches in CA 101, CANR-21
See also BYA 1
See also CLR 18
See also CWRI 5
See also JRDA
See also MAICYA 1, 2
See also SAAS 11
See also SATA 33, 69, 109, 153
See also SATA-Brief 27
See also SATA-Essay 153
See also YAW
Blos, Peter 1904-1997 89-92
Obituary 158
Bloss, F(red) Donald 1920- 53-56
Bloss, Meredith 1908-1982
Obituary 107
Blossfeld, Hans-Peter 1954- CANR-123
Earlier sketch in CA 170
Blossom, Frederick A. 1878(?)-1974
Obituary 49-52
Blossom, Laurel 1943- 209
Blossom, Thomas 1912-1992 .... 21-24R
Blotner, Joseph (Leo) 1923- CANR-35
Earlier sketches in CA 17-20R, CANR-13
See also CAAS 25
See also AITN 1
See also DLB 111
Blotnick, Elihu 1939- 106
Blotnick, Srully (D.) 1941- 136
Brief entry 123
Blouet, Brian Walter 1936- CANR-15
Earlier sketches in CA 93-96, CANR-32
Blouet, Olwyn M(ary) 1948- 130
Blough, Glenn O(rlando)
1907-1995 .... CANR-68
Earlier sketches in CAP-1, CA 11-12
See also SATA 1
Blough, Roger M(iles) 1904-1985
Obituary 117
Blouin, Lenora P. 1941- 199
Blount, Charles (Harold Clavell) 1913- . 17-20R
Blount, Margaret 1924- 69-72
Blount, Roy (Alton), Jr. 1941- CANR-125
Earlier sketches in CA 53-56, CANR-10, 28, 61
Interview in CANR-28
See also CLC 38
See also CSW
See also MTCW 1, 2
See also MTFW 2005
Blount, Thomas 1618(?)-1679 .... DLB 236
Bloustein, Edward J. 1925-1989 .... 41-44R
Blovits, Larry (John) 1936- 236
Blow, Michael 1930- 130
Blow, Simon 236
Blow, Suzanne (Katherine) 1932- 45-48
Blowsnake, Sam 1875-(?) .... NNAL
Bloy, Leon 1846-1917 183
Brief entry 121
See also DLB 123
See also GFL 1789 to the Present
See also TCLC 22
Blu, Karen I(sobell) 1941- 121
Blue, Betty (Anne) 1922- CANR-1
Earlier sketch in CA 45-48
Blue, Frederick Judd 1937- 53-56
Blue, Martha Ward 1942- 104
Blue, Rose 1931- CANR-60
Earlier sketches in CA 41-44R, CANR-14
See also SAAS 24
See also SATA 5, 91, 93
See also SATA-Essay 117
Blue, Vida (Rochelle) 1949- 185
Brief entry 112
Blue, Wallace
See Kraenzel, Margaret (Powell)
Blue, Zachary
See Stine, R(obert) L(awrence)
Bluebond-Langner, Myra 1948- 81-84
Blue Cloud, Peter (Aroniawenrate)
1933- CANR-40
Earlier sketch in CA 117
See also DAM MULT
See also NNAL
Blue Eagle, Acee 1909(?)-1959 216
Bluefarb, Samuel 1919- 37-40R
Bluemel, Kristin 1964- 166
Bluemle, Andrew (Waltz) 1929- 1-4R
Blues, Elwood
See Aykroyd, Dan(iel Edward)
Bluestein, Barry (M.) 1950-2000 154
Obituary 188
Bluestein, Daniel Thomas 1943- 65-68
Bluestein, Gene 1928- 81-84
Bluestone, Barry A(lan) 1944- CANR-123
Earlier sketch in CA 115
Bluestone, George 1928- CANR-1
Earlier sketch in CA 1-4R
Bluestone, Irving 1917- 136
Bluestone, Max 1926- 13-16R
Bluestone, Naomi 1936-1999 199
Bluger, Marianne Sasha 1945- 177
Bluggage, Oranthy
See Alcott, Louisa May
Bluh, Bonnie (Charles) 1926- CANR-93
Earlier sketch in CA 97-100
Bluhm, Heinz 1907-1993 .... CAP-1
Earlier sketch in CA 17-18
Bluhm, William T(heodore) 1923- 13-16R
Blum, Albert A(lexander) 1924- CANR-11
Earlier sketch in CA 5-8R
Blum, Bruce I(van) 1931- 144
Blum, Carol (Kathlyn) O'Brien
1934- CANR-17
Earlier sketch in CA 101
Blum, D. Steven 1951- 118
Blum, David 1935-1998 .... CANR-94
Obituary 166
Earlier sketch in CA 107
Blum, Deborah (Leigh) 1954- CANR-142
Earlier sketches in CA 151, CANR-81
Blum, Eleanor 1914- 1-4R
Blum, Fred 1932- 13-16R
Blum, Harold P. 1929- 103
Blum, Henrik L(eo) 1915- CANR-6
Earlier sketch in CA 9-12R
Blum, Howard 1948- CANR-110
Earlier sketch in CA 146
Blum, Jenna 1970- 229
Blum, Jerome 1913-1993 .... CANR-19
Obituary 141
Earlier sketch in CA 1-4R
Blum, John Morton 1921- CANR-72
Earlier sketches in CA 5-8R, CANR-2
Blum, Kristen Raub 1967- 175
Blum, Lawrence A. 1943- CANR-144
Earlier sketches in CA 124, CANR-54
Blum, Lenore (Carol) 1943- 170
Blum, Leon 1872-1950 180
Brief entry 119
Blum, Linda M. 1956- 236
Blum, Louise A(gnes) 1960- 210
Blum, Lucille Hollander 1904- 101
Blum, Mark E. 1937- 121
Blum, Ralph .... AITN 1
Blum, Richard H(osmer Adams)
1927- CANR-69
Earlier sketch in CA 13-16R
Blum, Rudolf 1909-1998 144
Blum, Shirley Neilsen 1932- 33-36R
Blum, Stella 1916-1985 97-100
Obituary 116
Blum, Virgil C(larence) 1913-1990 .... 13-16R
Blum, William (Henry) 1933- CANR-99
Earlier sketches in CA 125, CANR-51
Blumberg, Arnold 1925- 33-36R
Blumberg, Dorothy Rose 1904-1988 ..... CAP-2
Earlier sketch in CA 25-28
Blumberg, Gary 1938- CANR-2
Earlier sketch in CA 45-48
Blumberg, Harry 1903-1983 73-76
Blumberg, Leda 1956- .... SATA 59
Blumberg, Leonard U. 1920- 101
Blumberg, Mark S. 1961- 229
Blumberg, Morris B. 1917- 123
Blumberg, Myrna 1932- 21-24R
Blumberg, Nathan(iel) Bernard 1922- 41-44R
Blumberg, Paul (Marvin) 1935-
Brief entry 113
Blumberg, Phillip I(rvin) 1919- CANR-82
Earlier sketches in CA 101, CANR-35
Blumberg, Rena J(oy) 1934- 109
Blumberg, Rhoda 1917- CANR-101
Earlier sketches in CA 65-68, CANR-9, 26
See also CLR 21
See also MAICYA 1, 2
See also SATA 35, 70, 123
Blumberg, Rhoda L(ois Goldstein)
1926- CANR-30
Earlier sketches in CA 57-60, CANR-6
Blumberg, Richard E(lliot) 1944- 113
Blumberg, Robert S(tephen) 1945- 57-60
Blumberg, Stanley A. 1912-1996 136
Blume, Friedrich 1893-1975 73-76
Blume, Harvey 1946- 141
Blume, Helmut 1920- 138
Blume, Judy (Sussman) 1938- CANR-124
Earlier sketches in CA 29-32R, CANR-13, 37, 66
See also AAYA 3, 26
See also BYA 1, 8, 12
See also CLC 12, 30
See also CLR 2, 15, 69
See also CPW
See also DA3
See also DAM NOV, POP
See also DLB 52
See also JRDA
See also MAICYA 1, 2
See also MAICYAS 1
See also MTCW 1, 2
See also MTFW 2005
See also SATA 2, 31, 79, 142
See also WYA
See also YAW
Blumenfeld, Erwin 1897-1969 201
Blumenfeld, Gerry 1906- 21-24R
Blumenfeld, Hans 1892-1988 .... CAP-2
Earlier sketch in CA 21-22
Blumenfeld, Harold 1905(?)-1991 97-100
Obituary 133
Blumenfeld, Laura 1964(?)- 211
Blumenfeld, Meyer 1905-1980
Obituary 97-100
Blumenfeld, Robert 1943- 239
Blumenfeld, Samuel L(eon) 1926- 41-44R
Blumenfeld, Yorick 1932- CANR-108
Earlier sketch in CA 25-28R
Blumenkrantz, Jeff 1965- 216
Blumenson, Martin 1918-2005 .... CANR-21
Obituary 238
Earlier sketches in CA 1-4R, CANR-4
Blumenstock, David Irving 1913-1963
Obituary 116
Blumenthal, Arthur L. 1936- 29-32R
Blumenthal, David Reuben 1938- 112
Blumenthal, Deborah .... SATA 161
Blumenthal, Eileen (Flinder) 1948- ... CANR-99
Earlier sketch in CA 120
Blumenthal, Fred(erick G.) 1919(?)-1986
Obituary 118
Blumenthal, Gerda Renee 1923-2004 .... 1-4R
Obituary 227
Blumenthal, Gertrude 1907-1971
Obituary 104
See also SATA-Obit 27
Blumenthal, Henry 1911-1987 .... 29-32R
Obituary 121
Blumenthal, Howard J. 1952- 136
Blumenthal, John 1949- CANR-98
Earlier sketch in CA 129
Blumenthal, L. Roy 1908-1975
Obituary 61-64
Blumenthal, Lassor Agoos 1926- 25-28R
Blumenthal, Michael C. 1949- CANR-142
Earlier sketch in CA 110
See also PFS 7
Blumenthal, Monica David 1930-1981 ... 73-76
Obituary 103
Blumenthal, Norm 97-100
Blumenthal, Ralph 198
Blumenthal, Shirley 1943- 108
See also SATA 46
Blumenthal, Sid
See Blumenthal, Sidney
Blumenthal, Sidney 1909- 106
Blumenthal, Sidney 1948- CANR-144
Earlier sketch in CA 142
Blumenthal, Susan
See Tribich, Susan
Blumenthal, Walter Hart 1883-1969 ..... CAP-1
Earlier sketch in CA 11-12
Blumer, Herbert 1900-1987 216
Blumhofer, Edith L. 1950- 239
Blumhofer, Edith Waldvogel
See Blumhofer, Edith L.

Cumulative Index 59 **Bodker**

Blumin, Stuart M(ack) 1940- .... CANR 97
Earlier sketch in CA 65-68
Bluming, Mildred G. 1919- 106
Blumlein, Michael 1948- 156
See also SFW 4
Blumrich, Josef F(ranz) 1913-2002 93-96
Blumrosen, Alfred W(illiam) 1928- 53-56
Blunck, Hans Friedrich 1888-1961 .... DLB 66
Blundel, Anne
See Conley, Enid Mary
Blundell, (Walter) Derek (George) 1929- 135
Blundell, Derek (John) 1933- 144
Blundell, Harold 1902-1982 101
Blundell, Sue 1947- CANR-109
Earlier sketch in CA 151
Blunden, Caroline 1948- 132
Blunden, Edmund (Charles)
1896-1974 .... CANR-54
Obituary 45-48
Earlier sketches in CAP-2, CA 17-18
See also BRW 6
See also BRWS 11
See also CLC 2, 56
See also CP 1, 2
See also DLB 20, 100, 155
See also MTCW 1
See also PAB
See also PC 66
Blunden, Margaret (Anne) 1939- 21-24R
Blundeville, Thomas 1522-1606 .... DLB 236
Blunk, Frank M. 1897(?)-1976
Obituary 69-72
Blunsden, John (Beresford) 1930- 57-60
Blunsdon, Norman (Victor Charles)
1915-1968 .... CAP-1
Earlier sketch in CA 13-14
Blunt, Alison 237
Blunt, Lady Anne Isabella Noel
1837-1917 182
See also DLB 174
Blunt, Anthony (Frederick) 1907-1983 113
Obituary 109
Blunt, Don
See Booth, Edwin
Blunt, Giles 1952- 203
Blunt, Judy 1954- 205
Blunt, Wilfrid (Jasper Walter)
1901-1987 .... CANR-68
Obituary 121
Earlier sketches in CA 13-16R, CANR-5, 21
Blunt, Wilfrid Scawen 1840-1922 211
See also DLB 19, 174
Bluphocks, Lucien
See Seldes, Gilbert (Vivian)
Blush, Steven 1962- 229
Blustein, Paul 231
Bluth, B(etty) J(ean) 1934- CANR-49
Earlier sketches in CA 106, CANR-24
Bluth, Don 1938- 156
Blutig, Eduard
See Gorey, Edward (St. John)
Bly, Amy Sprecher 1955- 126
Bly, Carol(yn) 1930- CANR-93
Earlier sketches in CA 108, CANR-26, 51
Bly, Janet (Chester) 1945- CANR-40
Earlier sketch in CA 116
See also SATA 43
Bly, Mark J. 1949- 165
Bly, Nellie
See Cochrane, Elizabeth
Bly, Peter A(nthony) 1944- CANR-38
Earlier sketch in CA 116
Bly, Robert (Elwood) 1926- CANR-125
Earlier sketches in CA 5-8R, CANR-41, 73
See also AMWS 4
See also CLC 1, 2, 5, 10, 15, 38, 128
See also CP 1, 2, 3, 4, 5, 6, 7
See also DA3
See also DAM POET
See also DLB 5
See also EWL 3
See also MAL 5
See also MTCW 1, 2
See also MTFW 2005
See also PC 39
See also PFS 6, 17
See also RGAL 4
Bly, Robert W(ayne) 1957- CANR-40
Earlier sketch in CA 117
See also SATA-Brief 48
Bly, Stephen A(rthur) 1944- CANR-95
Earlier sketches in CA 121, CANR-40
See also SATA 43, 116
Bly, Thomas J. 1918(?)-1979
Obituary 85-88
Blyler, Allison Lee 1966- .... SATA 74
Blyn, George 1919- CANR-14
Earlier sketch in CA 37-40R
Blyth, Alan 1929- CANR-1
Earlier sketch in CA 49-52
Blyth, Chay 1940- 185
Brief entry 110
Blyth, Estelle 1882(?)-1983
Obituary 109
Blyth, Henry 1910-1983 .... CANR-69
Obituary 110
Earlier sketch in CA 21-24R
Blyth, Jeffrey 1926- 65-68
Blyth, John
See Hibbs, John
Blyth, Myrna 1939- CANR-10
Earlier sketch in CA 65-68
Blythe, (William) LeGette
1900-1993 .... CANR-68
Earlier sketches in CA 1-4R, CANR-1
Blythe, Martin 1954- 149
Blythe, Ronald (George) 1922- CANR-89
Earlier sketches in CA 5-8R, CANR-48
Blythe, Will(iam Legette II) 1957- 179
Blyton, Carey 1932-2002 49-52
Obituary 207
See also SATA 9
See also SATA-Obit 138
Blyton, Enid (Mary) 1897-1968 .... CANR-33
Obituary 25-28R
Earlier sketch in CA 77-80
See also CLR 31
See also CWRI 5
See also DLB 160
See also MAICYA 1, 2
See also SATA 25
Boa, Kenneth 1945- CANR-27
Earlier sketches in CA 61-64, CANR-8
Boadella, David 1931- 53-56
Boaden, James 1762-1839 .... DLB 89
Boadt, Lawrence 1942- 114
Boag, Peter G. 1961- 147
Boak, Arthur Edward Romilly 1888-1962 .. 5-8R
Boak, (Charles) Denis 1932- 13-16R
Boal, Augusto 1931- CANR-113
Earlier sketch in CA 158
See also DLB 307
See also EWL 3
Boalch, Donald (Howard) 1914-1999 ..... 9-12R
Boalt, (Hans) Gunnar 1910- CANR-7
Earlier sketch in CA 57-60
Board, C(hester) Stephen 1942- 57-60
Board, Joseph B(reckinridge), Jr. 1931- .. 29-32R
Boardman, Arthur 1927- 61-64
Boardman, Barrington 1933- 130
Boardman, Brigid M. 1931- CANR-134
Earlier sketches in CA 129, CANR-65
Boardman, Charles C. 1932- 29-32R
Boardman, Eunice
See Meske, Eunice Boardman
Boardman, Fon Wyman, Jr.
1911-2000 .... CANR-72
Earlier sketches in CA 1-4R, CANR-3
See also SATA 6
Boardman, Francis 1915-1976
Obituary 69-72
Boardman, Gwenn R.
See Petersen, Gwenn Boardman
See also SATA 12
Boardman, John 1927- CANR-123
Earlier sketches in CA 101, CANR-72
Boardman, Michael Moore 1945- 118
Boardman, Neil S(ervis) 1907-1974 ...... CAP-1
Earlier sketch in CA 13-14
Boardman, Peter (David) 1950-1982 97-100
Obituary 108
Boardman, Robert (B.) 1943- 138
Boardman, Thomas Leslie 1919-1990 176
Obituary 131
Brief entry 111
Boardwell, Robert Lee 1926- 103
Boaretto, Claire 1947- 134
Boarino, Gerald L(ouis) 1931- 21-24R
Boarman, Patrick M(adigan) 1922- ... CANR-28
Earlier sketches in CA 13-16R, CANR-9
Boas, Claudio Villas
See Villas Boas, Claudio
Boas, Franz 1858-1942 181
Brief entry 115
See also TCLC 56
Boas, Frederick S(amuel) 1862-1957 .. DLB 149
Boas, Guy (Herman Sidney)
1896-1966 .... CAP-1
Earlier sketch in CA 11-12
Boas, Jacob 1943- 120
Boas, Louise Schutz 1885-1973 .... CANR-70
Earlier sketch in CA 5-8R
Boas, Marie
See Hall, Marie Boas
Boas, Maurits Ignatius 1892-1986 ...... CANR-5
Earlier sketch in CA 1-4R
Boas, Orlando Villas
See Villas Boas, Orlando
Boase, Alan Martin 1902-1982 .... CANR-10
Obituary 108
Earlier sketch in CA 5-8R
Boase, Paul H(enshaw) 1915- 37-40R
Boase, Thomas Sherrer Ross
1898-1974 .... CANR-70
Earlier sketches in CAP-2, CA 23-24
Boase, Wendy 1944-1999 106
Obituary 177
See also SATA 28
See also SATA-Obit 110
Boast, Philip 1952- 135
Boateng, E(rnest) A(mano)
1920-1997 .... CANR-28
Earlier sketches in CA 21-24R, CANR-11
Boateng, Yaw Maurice
See Brunner, Maurice Yaw
Boatman, Don Earl 1913- 1-4R
Boatner, Mark Mayo III 1921- 21-24R
See also SATA 29
Boatright, John Raymond 1941- 191
Boatright, Mody Coggin 1896-1970 . CANR-72
Obituary 89-92
Earlier sketches in CA 5-8R, CANR-3
Boatwright, Howard (Leake, Jr.)
1918-1999 53-56
Obituary 177
Boatwright, James III 1933-1988 119
Obituary 126
Boatwright, Mary T(aliaferro) 231
Boaz, David 1953- CANR-143
Earlier sketch in CA 144
Boaz, Martha (Terosse) CANR-19
Earlier sketches in CA 9-12R, CANR-3
Boaz, Noel T(homas) 1952- CANR-142
Earlier sketches in CA 146, CANR-72
Boba, Imre 1919- 69-72
Bobb, Bernard E(arl) 1917- 5-8R
Bobbe, Dorothie de Bear 1905-1975 .... CAP-2
Obituary 57-60
Earlier sketch in CA 25-28
See also SATA 1
See also SATA-Obit 25
Bobbio, Norberto 1909-2004 230
Bobbitt, Philip (Chase) 1948- CANR-142
Earlier sketch in CA 108
Bober, Harry 1915-1988
Obituary 125
Bober, Natalie S. 1930- CANR-111
Earlier sketch in CA 151
See also AAYA 46
See also SAAS 23
See also SATA 87, 134
Bober, P(hyllis) P(ray) 1920-2002 ... CANR-112
Obituary 207
Earlier sketches in CA 127, CANR-55
Bober, Stanley 1932- CANR-11
Earlier sketch in CA 21-24R
Bobette
See Simenon, Georges (Jacques Christian)
Bobette, Bibo
See Gugliotta, Bobette
Bobinski, George S(ylvan) 1929- 29-32R
Bobker, Lee R(obert) 1925-1999 .... CANR-9
Obituary 187
Earlier sketch in CA 53-56
Bobo, Lawrence (Douglas) 1958- ... CANR-107
Earlier sketch in CA 124
Boborykin, Petr Dmitrievich 1836-1921 206
See also DLB 238
Bobri, Vladimir V. 1898-1986 105
See also Bobritsky, Vladimir
Bobrick, Benson 1947- CANR-130
Earlier sketch in CA 169
Bobritsky, Vladimir
See Bobri, Vladimir V.
See also SATA 47
See also SATA-Brief 32
Bobroff, Edith
See Marks, Edith Bobroff
Bobrov, Semen Sergeevich
1763(?)-1810 .... DLB 150
Bobrow, Davis Bernard 1936- CANR-7
Earlier sketch in CA 57-60
Bobrow, Edwin E. 1928- CANR-24
Earlier sketches in CA 21-24R, CANR-8
Bobrowski, Johannes 1917-1965 ...... CANR-33
Earlier sketch in CA 77-80
See also DLB 75
See also EWL 3
See also RGWL 2, 3
Bobst, Elmer H(olmes) 1884-1978 122
Obituary 113
Bocage, Manuel Maria Barbosa du
1765-1805 .... DLB 287
Bocardo, Claire 1939- 141
Bocca, Al
See Winter, Bevis (Peter)
Bocca, Geoffrey 1923-1983
Obituary 110
Boccaccio, Giovanni 1313-1375 .... EW 2
See also RGSF 2
See also RGWL 2, 3
See also SSC 10
See also TWA
See also WLIT 7
Bochak, Grayce 1956- .... SATA 76
Bochco, Steven 1943- 138
Brief entry 124
See also AAYA 11
See also CLC 35
Bochenski, Innocentius M.
See Bochenski, Joseph M.
Bochenski, Joseph M. 1902-1995 .... CANR-7
Earlier sketch in CA 5-8R
Bochin, Hal W(illiam) 1942- 137
Bochner, Salomon 1899-1982 .... 41-44R
Bochroch, Albert R(obert)
1909-1989 .... CANR-39
Earlier sketch in CA 111
Bock, Alan W(illiam) 1943- 41-44R
Bock, Carl H(einz) 1930-(?) CAP-2
Earlier sketch in CA 19-20
Bock, Darrell L(ane) 1953- 232
Bock, Dennis 1964- 186
Bock, Fred 1939-1998 .... CANR-10
Obituary 169
Earlier sketch in CA 25-28R
Bock, Frederick 1916- 9-12R
Bock, Gisela 1942- 138
Bock, Hal
See Bock, Harold I.
Bock, Harold I. 1939- 29-32R
See also SATA 10
Bock, Joanne 1940- 57-60
Bock, Paul J(ohn) 1922- 53-56
Bock, Philip K. 1934- CANR-11
Earlier sketch in CA 25-28R
Bock, William Sauts Netamux'we
1939- .... SATA 14
Bockelman, Wilfred 1920- 37-40R
Bockl, George 1909- 61-64
Bockle, Franz
See Boeckle, Franz
Bockmon, Guy Alan 1926- 5-8R
Bockmuehl, Markus N. A. 214
Bockstoce, John R(oberts) 1944- 121
Bockus, H(erman) William 1915- 53-56
Bocock, Maclin 1920- 184
Bocock, Robert (James) 1940- CANR-28
Earlier sketches in CA 69-72, CANR-12
Boczek, Boleslaw Adam 1922- CANR-4
Earlier sketch in CA 1-4R
Bod, Peter
See Vesenyi, Paul E.
Bodanis, David 209
See also MTFW 2005
Bodansky, Oscar 1901-1977
Obituary 73-76
Bodansky, Yossef 233
Bodard, Lucien (Albert) 1914-1998 149
Obituary 165
Brief entry 116
Bodart, Joni
See Bodart-Talbot, Joni
Bodart-Talbot, Joni 1947- CANR-23
Earlier sketch in CA 106
Boddewyn, J(ean) J. 1929- CANR-39
Earlier sketches in CA 25-28R, CANR-17
Boddie, Charles Emerson 1911-1997 65-68
Boddington, Craig Thornton 1952- ... CANR-28
Earlier sketch in CA 111
Boddy, David 1940- 119
Boddy, Frederick A(rthur) 1914- 61-64
Boddy, Janice 1951- 134
Boddy, William Charles 1913- 101
Bode, Carl 1911-1993 .... CANR-20
Obituary 140
Earlier sketches in CA 1-4R, CANR-3
Bode, Elroy 1931- CANR-10
Earlier sketch in CA 25-28R
Bode, Janet 1943-1999 .... CANR-67
Obituary 187
Earlier sketches in CA 69-72, CANR-12
See also AAYA 21
See also MAICYA 2
See also MAICYAS 1
See also SATA 60, 96
See also SATA-Obit 118
See also YAW
Bode, Roy E. 1948- 77-80
Bode, Sigmund
See O'Doherty, Brian
Bodecker, N(iels) M(ogens)
1922-1988 .... CANR-114
Obituary 124
Earlier sketches in CA 49-52, CANR-4, 40
See also CWRI 5
See also MAICYA 1, 2
See also SATA 8, 73
See also SATA-Obit 54
Bodeen, DeWitt 1908-1988 .... CANR-10
Obituary 125
Earlier sketch in CA 25-28R
Bodek, Richard 1961- 233
Bodell, Mary
See Pecsok, Mary Bodell
Bodelsen, Anders 1937- 128
See also CWW 2
See also EWL 3
Boden, Hilda
See Bodenham, Hilda Morris
Boden, Margaret A. 1936- 93-96
Bodenham, Hilda Morris 1901- CANR-6
Earlier sketch in CA 9-12R
See also SATA 13
Bodenhamer, David J(ackson) 1947- 142
Bodenheim, Maxwell 1892-1954 187
Brief entry 110
See also DLB 9, 45
See also MAL 5
See also RGAL 4
See also TCLC 44
Bodenheimer, Edgar 1908-1991 .... CANR-20
Earlier sketch in CA 33-36R
Bodenheimer, Maxwell
See Bodenheim, Maxwell
Bodenstedt, Friedrich von
1819-1892 .... DLB 129
Bodenwieser, Gertrud 1890-1959 205
Bodet, Jaime Torres
See Torres Bodet, Jaime
Bodett, Thomas Edward 1955- CANR-64
Earlier sketches in CA 123, CANR-44
See also Bodett, Tom
Bodett, Tom
See Bodett, Thomas Edward
See also SATA 70
Bodey, Donald 1946- 128
Bodey, Hugh (Arthur) 1939- CANR-12
Earlier sketch in CA 61-64
Bodger, Joan
See Mercer, Joan Bodger
Bodian, Nat G. 1921- CANR-44
Earlier sketches in CA 103, CANR-20
Bodie, Idella F(allaw) 1925- CANR-55
Earlier sketch in CA 41-44R
See also SATA 12, 89
Bodin, Jean 1529(?)-1596 ..... GFL Beginnings to 1789
Bodin, Paul 1909- 65-68
Bodine, Eunice
See Lapp, Eunice Willis Bodine
Bodine, J. D.
See Cunningham, Chet
Bodington, Nancy H(ermione)
1912- CANR-67
Earlier sketch in CA 53-56
See also CMW 4
Bodington, Stephen 1909- 123
Bodini, Vittorio 1914-1970 .... DLB 128
Bodker, Cecil 1927-
See Bodker, Cecil

Bodker, Cecil 1927- ... CANR-111
Earlier sketches in CA 73-76, CANR-13, 44
See also CLC 21
See also CLR 23
See also MAICYA 1, 2
See also SATA 14, 133
Bodkin, Cora 1944- ... 69-72
Bodkin, M(atthias) M'Donnell 1850-1933
Brief entry ... 114
See also DLB 70
Bodkin, Maud 1875-1967 ... CAP-1
Earlier sketch in CA 11-12
Bodkin, Ronald G(eorge) 1936- ... 33-36R
Bodle, Yvonne Gallegos 1939- ... 33-36R
Bodley, Hal
See Bodley, Harley Ryan, Jr.
Bodley, Harley Ryan, Jr. 1936- ... 126
Bodley, Sir Thomas 1545-1613 ... DLB 213
Bodmer, Johann Jakob 1698-1783 ... DLB 97
Bodmer, Walter Fred 1936- ... 102
Bodmershof, Imma von 1895-1982 ... 177
See also DLB 85
Bodnar, John (Edward) 1944- ... CANR-144
Earlier sketch in CA 110
Bodo, Murray 1937- ... CANR-46
Earlier sketches in CA 57-60, CANR-7, 23
Bodo, Peter T. 1949- ... 85-88
Bodoh, John J(ames) 1931- ... 45-48
Bodsworth, (Charles) Fred(erick)
1918- ... CANR-66
Earlier sketches in CA 1-4R, CANR-3
See also CN 1, 2, 3, 4, 5, 6, 7
See also DLB 68
See also SATA 27
Bodvarsson, Gudmundur
See Bodvarsson, Gudmundur
Bodvarsson, Gudmundur 1904-1974 .. DLB 293
Bodwell, Richard
See Spring, Gerald M(ax)
Boeckle, Franz 1921- ... 101
Boeckman, Charles 1920- ... 13-16R
See also SATA 12
Boeckman, Patti ... CANR-28
Earlier sketch in CA 109
Boege, Ulrich Gustav 1940- ... 97-100
Boegehold, Alan L(indley) 1927- ... CANR-93
Earlier sketch in CA 146
Boegehold, Betty (Doyle)
1913-1985 ... CANR-12
Obituary ... 115
Earlier sketch in CA 69-72
See also SATA-Obit 42
Boegner, Marc 1881-1970
Obituary ... 29-32R
Boehling, Rebecca L. 1955- ... 164
Boehlke, Frederick J(ohn), Jr. 1926- ... 21-24R
Boehlke, Robert R(ichard) 1925- ... 5-8R
Boehlow, Robert H(enry) 1925- ... 53-56
Boehm, Christopher 1937- ... 121
Boehm, Eric H. 1918- ... 13-16R
Boehm, Herb
See Varley, John (Herbert)
Boehm, Karl 1894-1981
Obituary ... 105
Boehm, Sydney 1908-1990 ... 147
See also DLB 44
Boehm, William D(ryden) 1946- ... 61-64
Boehme, Gernot 1937- ... 145
Boehme, Lillian R.
See Rodberg, Lillian
Boehmer, Elleke 1961- ... CANR-108
Earlier sketch in CA 164
Boehmer, Ulrike 1959- ... 226
Boehning, W. R.
See Bohning, W(olf) R(uediger)
Boehrer, Bruce Thomas ... 174
Boehringer, Robert 1885(?)-1974
Obituary ... 53-56
Boelcke, Willi A(lfred) 1929-
Brief entry ... 107
Boelen, Bernard J(acques) 1916- ... 41-44R
Boell, Heinrich (Theodor)
1917-1985 ... CANR-24
Obituary ... 116
Earlier sketch in CA 21-24R
See also Boll, Heinrich (Theodor)
See also CLC 2, 3, 6, 9, 11, 15, 27, 32, 72
See also DA
See also DA3
See also DAB
See also DAC
See also DAM MST, NOV
See also DLB 69
See also DLBY 1985
See also MTCW 1, 2
See also MTFW 2005
See also SSC 23
See also SSFS 20
See also TWA
See also WLC
Boelts, Maribeth 1964- ... 146
See also SATA 78, 163
Boeman, John (Sigler) 1923- ... 108
Boennelycke, Emil
See Bonnelycke, Emil (Christian Theodor)
Boer, Charles 1939- ... 69-72
See also CP 1, 2, 3, 4
See also DLB 5
Boer, Harry R(einier) 1913-1999 ... CANR-4
Earlier sketch in CA 1-4R
Boerne, Alfred
See Doeblin, Alfred
Boers, Arthur Paul 1957- ... CANR-144
Earlier sketch in CA 138
Boerst, William J. 1939- ... 192
See also SATA 121

Boesch, Hans Heinrich 1911-1978
Obituary ... 116
Boesch, Mark J(oseph) 1917- ... 21-24R
See also SATA 12
Boeschenstein, Warren 1940- ... 190
Boese, Alex 1968- ... 220
Boesel, David 1938- ... 41-44R
Boesen, Victor 1908- ... CANR-107
Earlier sketch in CA 37-40R
See also SATA 16
Boesiger, Willi 1904-1990 ... 102
Boessenecker, John 1953- ... 138
Boeth, Richard 1933-1982
Obituary ... 107
Boethius c. 480-c. 524 ... DLB 115
See also RGWL 2, 3
Boethius of Dacia 1240(?)-(?) ... DLB 115
Boetie, Dugmore 1920(?)-1966
Obituary ... 109
Boetius, Henning 1939- ... 209
Boettcher, Henry J. 1893-1979 ... CAP-1
Earlier sketch in CA 19-20
Boettcher, Robert B. 1941(?)-1984
Obituary ... 112
Boettcher, Thomas D. 1944- ... 129
Boetticher, Budd 1916-2001 ... 157
See also Boetticher, Oscar, Jr.
Boetticher, Oscar, Jr. 1916-2001
Obituary ... 204
See also Boetticher, Budd
Boettinger, Henry M(aurice) 1924- ... 73-76
Boeve, Edgar G. 1929- ... 21-24R
Boewe, Charles (Ernst) 1924- ... 9-12R
Boff, Leonardo (Genezio Darci) 1938- ... 150
See also CLC 70
See also DAM MULT
See also HLC 1
See also HW 2
Boff, Vic 1915- ... 103
Boffa, Giuseppe 1923- ... 140
Boffey, David Barnes 1945- ... 110
Bogacki, Tomek 1950- ... CANR-117
Earlier sketch in CA 170
See also SATA 138
Bogaduck
See Lindsay, Harold Arthur
Bogaerts, Gert 1965- ... SATA 80
Bogan, Christopher E(ric) 1954- ... 144
Bogan, James 1945- ... 103
Bogan, Louise 1897-1970 ... CANR-82
Obituary ... 25-28R
Earlier sketches in CA 73-76, CANR-33
See also AMWS 3
See also CLC 4, 39, 46, 93
See also CP 1
See also DAM POET
See also DLB 45, 169
See also EWL 3
See also MAL 5
See also MAWW
See also MTCW 1, 2
See also PC 12
See also PFS 21
See also RGAL 4
Bogan, Paulette 1960- ... SATA 129
Bogard, Travis (Miller) 1918-1997 ... 69-72
Obituary ... 157
Bogarde, Dirk
See Van Den Bogarde, Derek Jules Gaspard Ulric Niven
See also DLB 14
Bogardus, Emory Stephen 1882-1973
Obituary ... 116
Bogart, Carlotta 1929- ... 61-64
Bogart, E. A.
See Bogart, Eleanor A(nne)
Bogart, Eleanor A(nne) 1928- ... 137
Bogart, Frank L. 1914-1993 ... 161
Bogart, Jo Ellen 1945- ... CANR-110
Earlier sketch in CA 156
See also CLR 59
See also SATA 92
Bogart, Leo 1921- ... CANR-14
Earlier sketch in CA 41-44R
Bogart, Mary Hattan 1916- ... CANR-123
Earlier sketch in CA 161
Bogart, Stephen Humphrey 1949- ... CANR-72
Earlier sketch in CA 150
Bogart, W. A. 1950- ... 212
Bogat, Shatan
See Kacew, Romain
Bogatyryov, Konstantin 1924(?)-1976
Obituary ... 65-68
Bogdan, Radu J. ... 173
Bogdan, Robert 1941- ... 128
Bogdanor, Vernon 1943- ... CANR-89
Earlier sketches in CA 81-84, CANR-14, 35, 82
Bogdanov, Aleksandr Aleksandrovich
See Malinovsky, Aleksandr Aleksandrovich (Bogdanov)
See also DLB 295
Bogdanov, Michael 1938- ... 129
Bogdanovich, Ippolit Fedorovich c.
1743-1803 ... DLB 150
Bogdanovich, Peter 1939- ... CANR-71
Earlier sketches in CA 5-8R, CANR-21
Bogen, Hyman 1924- ... 140
Bogen, James Benjamin 1935- ... 89-92
Bogen, Laurel Ann 1950- ... CANR-123
Earlier sketches in CA 112, CANR-35
Bogen, Nancy R(uth) 1932- ... 97-100
Boger, Louise Ade 1909-
Brief entry ... 115
Bogert, L(otta) Jean 1888-1970 ... CAP-1
Earlier sketch in CA 11-12
Boggan, E(lton) Carrington 1943- ... 101

Boggess, Louise Bradford
1912-2002 ... CANR-53
Earlier sketches in CA 13-16R, CANR-7, 28
Boggs, Bill
See Boggs, William III
Boggs, James 1919-1993 ... 77-80
Boggs, Jean Sutherland 1922- ... 108
Boggs, Johnny D. 1962- ... 214
Boggs, Marcus 1947- ... 108
Boggs, Ralph Steele 1901-1994 ... CAP-1
Earlier sketch in CA 11-12
See also SATA 7
Boggs, W(ilmot) Arthur 1916- ... 17-20R
Boggs, Wade Hamilton, Jr. 1916- ... 13-16R
Boggs, William III 1942- ... 102
Bogin, George 1920- ... 104
Bogin, Magda 1950- ... 148
Bogin, Meg
See Bogin, Magda
Bogin, Ruth 1920- ... 122
Bogle, Donald ... 211
See also AITN 1
Bogle, Warren
See Bergman, Andrew
Bogner, Norman 1935- ... CANR-99
Earlier sketches in CA 5-8R, CANR-15
See also AITN 2
Bogomolny, Robert L(ee) 1938- ... 121
Bogosian, Eric 1953- ... CANR-102
Earlier sketch in CA 138
See also CAD
See also CD 5, 6
See also CLC 45, 141
Bogoslovsky, Christina Stael 1888(?)-1974
Obituary ... 49-52
Bograd, Larry 1953- ... CANR-57
Earlier sketch in CA 93-96
See also CLC 35
See also SAAS 21
See also SATA 33, 89
See also WYA
Bogue, Allan G(eorge Britton) 1921- ... 107
Bogue, Jesse C. 1912(?)-1983
Obituary ... 111
Bogue, Lucile 1911-2005 ... CANR-13
Obituary ... 236
Earlier sketch in CA 37-40R
Bogue, Margaret Beattie 1924- ... 212
Bogue, Merwyn (Alton) 1908-1994 ... 131
Obituary ... 145
Bogumil, Mary L. 1955- ... 236
Boguraev, Branimir Konstantinov 1950- ... 163
Bogus, Carl T. 1948- ... 228
Boguslaw, Robert 1919-1993 ... 132
Boguslawski, Dorothy Beers 1911(?)-1978
Obituary ... 77-80
Bohan, Peter ... 33-36R
Bohana, Aileen Stein 1951- ... 103
Bohannan, Paul (James) 1920- ... 9-12R
Bohdal, Susi 1951- ... 97-100
See also SATA 22, 101
Bohem, Endre 1901(?)-1990
Obituary ... 131
Bohen, Halcyone H(arger) 1937- ... 108
Bohen, Sister Marian 1930- ... 5-8R
Bohi, Charles W(esley) 1940- ... 89-92
Bohi, M. Janette 1927- ... 25-28R
Bohjalian, Chris(topher A.) 1960- ... CANR-130
Earlier sketches in CA 139, CANR-85
See also DLB 292
Bohlander, Jill 1936- ... 37-40R
Bohle, Bruce 1918- ... CANR-9
Earlier sketch in CA 21-24R
Bohle, Edgar (Henry) 1909- ... 1-4R
Bohlen, Charles Eustis 1904-1973
Obituary ... 111
Bohlen, Joe M(erl) 1919- ... 5-8R
Bohlen, Nina 1931- ... SATA 58
Bohlke, L(andall) Brent 1942-1987 ... 124
Bohlman, (Mary) Edna McCaull
1897-1989 ... CAP-1
Earlier sketch in CA 9-10
Bohlman, Herbert W(illiam)
1896-1968 ... CAP-1
Earlier sketch in CA 19-20
Bohlmeijer, Arno 1956- ... 156
See also SATA 94
Bohman, James F. ... 171
Bohm-Duchen, Monica 1957- ... 189
Bohme, Gernot
See Boehme, Gernot
Bohme, Jakob 1575-1624 ... DLB 164
Bohn, Frank 1878-1975
Obituary ... 57-60
Bohn, Joyce Illig 1940(?)-1976
Obituary ... 69-72
Bohn, Martin J(ohn), Jr. 1938- ... 116
Bohn, Ralph C. 1930- ... CANR-11
Earlier sketch in CA 17-20R
Bohner, Charles (Henry) 1927- ... 118
See also BYA 6
See also SATA 62
Bohnet, Michael 1937- ... 102
Bohnhoff, Maya Kaathryn 1954- ... 152
See also SATA 88
Bohning, W(olf) R(uediger) 1942- ... 111
Bohn-Spector, Claudia ... 239
Bohnstedt, John W(olfgang) 1927- ... 33-36R
Bohntinsky, Dori 1951- ... 211
Bohr, Niels (Henrik David) 1885-1962 ... 155
Obituary ... 112
Bohr, R(ussell) L(eRoi) 1916- ... 25-28R
Bohr, Theophilus
See Thistle, Mel(ville William)
Bohren, Craig F. 1940- ... CANR-60
Earlier sketch in CA 128

Bohrnstedt, George W(illiam) 1938- . CANR-44
Earlier sketches in CA 33-36R, CANR-20
Bohrod, Aaron 1907-1992 ... 21-24R
Bohse, August 1661-1742 ... DLB 168
Boice, James Montgomery
1938-2000 ... CANR-51
Earlier sketches in CA 29-32R, CANR-12, 28
Boie, Heinrich Christian 1744-1806 ... DLB 94
Boiko, Claire Taylor 1925- ... 93-96
Boileau, Pierre 1906-1989 ... 209
Boileau-Despreaux, Nicolas
1636-1711 ... DLB 268
See also EW 3
See also GFL Beginnings to 1789
See also RGWL 2, 3
Boiles, Charles Lafayette (Jr.) 1932- ... 65-68
Boime, Albert 1933- ... 125
Bois, J(oseph) Samuel 1892-1978 ... 33-36R
Bois, Wilhelmina J. E. de
See de Bois, Wilhelmina J. E.
Boisen, Anton T(heophilus) 1876-1965 ... 225
Boisgilbert, Edmund M.D.
See Donnelly, Ignatius
Boissard, Janine 1932- ... SATA 59
See also YAW
Boissard, Maurice
See Leautaud, Paul
Boisseau, Michelle 1955- ... 216
Boisset, Caroline 1955- ... 134
Boissevain, Jeremy 1928- ... CANR-21
Earlier sketches in CA 57-60, CANR-6
Boissiere, Robert 1914-2002 ... 119
Boissoneau, Robert 1937- ... 105
Boissonneau, Alice ... 101
Boisvert, Raymond D. 1947- ... 172
Boitani, Piero 1947- ... 137
Bojanowski, Marc 1977(?)- ... 235
Bojaxhiu, Agnes Gonxha
See Mother Teresa
Bojer, Johan 1872-1959 ... 189
See also EWL 3
See also TCLC 64
Bojunga, Lygia
See Nunes, Lygia Bojunga
See also DLB 307
Bojunga-Nunes, Lygia
See Nunes, Lygia Bojunga
Bok, Bart J(an) 1906-1983 ... CANR-30
Obituary ... 110
Earlier sketch in CA 49-52
Bok, Cary W(illiam) 1905-1970
Obituary ... 29-32R
Bok, Christian 1966- ... 235
Bok, Derek (Curtis) 1930- ... CANR-108
Earlier sketches in CA 106, CANR-64
Bok, Edward W(illiam) 1863-1930 ... 217
See also DLB 91
See also DLBD 16
See also TCLC 101
Bok, Hannes (Vajn) 1914-1964 ... 154
See also FANT
Bok, Priscilla F(airfield) 1896-1975 ... 49-52
Bok, Sissela Ann 1934- ... CANR-32
Earlier sketch in CA 112
Bokenkotter, Thomas 1924- ... CANR-17
Earlier sketch in CA 85-88
Boker, George Henry 1823-1890 ... RGAL 4
Bokina, John 1948- ... CANR-120
Earlier sketch in CA 148
Bokser, Ben Zion 1907-1984 ... CANR-69
Obituary ... 111
Earlier sketches in CA 65-68, CANR-11
Bokum, Fanny Butcher 1888-1987 ... 37-40R
Obituary ... 122
Bokun, Branko 1920- ... 45-48
Bolam, Robyn
See Lomax, Marion
Boland, Bridget 1913-1988 ... CANR-125
Obituary ... 124
Earlier sketch in CA 101
See also CBD
See also CWD
Boland, Charles Michael 1917- ... 9-12R
Boland, Daniel 1891- ... CAP-1
Earlier sketch in CA 13-14
Boland, Eavan (Aisling) 1944- ... 207
Earlier sketches in CA 143, CANR-61
Autobiographical Essay in ... 207
See also BRWS 5
See also CLC 40, 67, 113
See also CP 1, 7
See also CWP
See also DAM POET
See also DLB 40
See also FW
See also MTCW 2
See also MTFW 2005
See also PC 58
See also PFS 12, 22
Boland, Janice ... CANR-129
Earlier sketch in CA 165
See also SATA 98
Boland, (Bertram) John 1913-1976 ... CANR-10
Earlier sketch in CA 9-12R
Boland, Lillian C(anon) 1919- ... 29-32R
Bolano, Roberto 1953-2003 ... 229
Bolch, Ben W(ilsman) 1938- ... 57-60
Bolcom, William E(lden) 1938- ... CANR-123
Earlier sketch in CA 93-96
Bold, Alan Norman 1943- ... CANR-30
Earlier sketch in CA 25-28R
See also CP 1, 2, 3, 4
Bolden, Tonya (Wilyce) 1959- ... CANR-107
Earlier sketch in CA 147
See also SATA 79, 138
Bolding, Amy 1910-1994 ... 73-76

Cumulative Index 61 Bonham

Boldizsar, Ivan 1912-1988
Obituary ... 127
Boldrewood, Rolf
See Browne, Thomas Alexander
Boldrewoood, Rolf
See Browne, Thomas Alexander
Boldt, Laurence G. ... 235
Boldt, Menno 1930- ... CANR-46
Earlier sketch in CA 120
Bolen, Jean Shinoda 1936- ... 110
Boles, Donald Edward 1926- ... CANR-18
Earlier sketch in CA 1-4R
Boles, Harold W(ilson) 1915- ... 17-20R
Boles, John B. 1943- ... CANR-48
Earlier sketches in CA 37-40R, CANR-14
Boles, Paul Darcy 1916-1984 ... CANR-4
Obituary ... 112
Earlier sketch in CA 9-12R
See also SATA 9
See also SATA-Obit 38
Boles, Philana Marie ... 225
Boles, Robert (E.) 1943- ... BW 2, 3
Bolgan, Anne C(atherine) 1923-1992(?) . 41-44R
Obituary ... 136
Bolgar, (Caius Coriolanus) R(obert) R(alph) 1913-1985
Obituary ... 117
Bolger, Daniel P(atrick) 1957- ... 150
Bolger, Dermot 1959- ... CANR-91
Earlier sketch in CA 145
See also CN 7
Bolger, Philip C(unningham) 1927- CANR-6
Earlier sketch in CA 57-60
Bolgiano, Chris(tina) 1948- ... CANR-109
Earlier sketch in CA 151
Bolian, Polly 1925- ... 33-36R
See also SATA 4
Bolin, Inge ... 197
Bolin, Luis (A.) 1894-1969 ... CAP-2
Earlier sketch in CA 23-24
Boling, Fredrick W. 1926- ... 226
Boling, Katharine (Singleton) 1933- ... 57-60
Bolingbroke, Viscount
See St. John, Henry
Bolinger, Dwight (L.) 1907-1992 ... CANR-7
Obituary ... 137
Earlier sketch in CA 13-16R
Bolino, August C(onstantino) 1922- .. CANR-18
Earlier sketch in CA 1-4R
Bolitho, Archie A(rdella) 1886-1975 ... CAP-1
Earlier sketch in CA 9-10
Bolitho, Harold 1939- ... 103
Bolitho, (Henry) Hector 1897-1974 .. CANR-68
Obituary ... 53-56
Earlier sketches in CAP-1, CA 9-10
Bolitho, Ray D.
See Blair, Dorothy S(ara Greene)
Bolkhovitinov, Nikolai Nikolaevich 1930- ... 97-100
Bolkosky, Sidney M(arvin) 1944- ... 65-68
Boll, Carl R. 1894-1981 ... CAP-1
Earlier sketch in CA 17-18
Boll, David 1931- ... 21-24R
Boll, Ernest
See Boll, Theophilus E(rnest) M(artin)
Boll, Heinrich (Theodor)
See Boell, Heinrich (Theodor)
See also BPFB 1
See also CDWLB 2
See also EW 13
See also EWL 3
See also RGSF 2
See also RGWL 2, 3
Boll, Theo
See Boll, Theophilus E(rnest) M(artin)
Boll, Theophilus E(rnest) M(artin) 1902-1994 ... 37-40R
Bolland, Brian 1951- ... 228
Bolland, O(rlando) Nigel 1943- ... 110
Bolle, Kees W. 1927- ... CANR-17
Earlier sketch in CA 25-28R
Bollen, Roger 1941(?)- ... AITN 1
See also MAICYA 2
See also SATA 83
See also SATA-Brief 29
Bollens, John C(onstantinus) 1920-1983 ... CANR-3
Obituary ... 111
Earlier sketch in CA 1-4R
Boller, Paul Franklin, Jr. 1916- ... CANR-104
Earlier sketches in CA 1-4R, CANR-3, 19, 41
Bolles, (Edmund) Blair 1911-1990 ... 9-12R
Obituary ... 130
Bolles, Donald F. 1928-1976 ... 73-76
Obituary ... 65-68
Bolles, Edmund Blair 1942- ... 188
Bolles, Richard Nelson 1927- ... CANR-1
Earlier sketch in CA 45-48
Bolles, Robert C(harles) 1928- ... 21-24R
Bollettieri, Nick J(ames) 1931- ... 110
Bolliger, Max 1929- ... 25-28R
See also SATA 7
Bolling, Hal
See Schwalberg, Carol(yn Ernestine Stein)
Bolling, Richard (Walker) 1916-1991 .... 17-20R
Obituary ... 134
Bolling, Robert 1738-1775 ... DLB 31
Bollinger, Lee C. 1946- ... 138
Bolloten, Burnett 1909-1987 ... 93-96
Obituary ... 123
Bolls, Imogene (Lamb) 1938- ... CANR-105
Earlier sketch in CA 149
Bolman, Frederick deWolfe, Jr. 1912-1985
Obituary ... 117
Bolman, Lee G. 1941- ... 149
Bolner, James (Jerome) 1936- ... 61-64
Bologna, Joseph ... 77-80
Bolognese, Don(ald Alan) 1934- CANR-108
Earlier sketches in CA 97-100, CANR-45
See also MAICYA 1, 2
See also SATA 24, 71, 129
Bolognese, Elaine (Raphael Chionchio) 1933- ... 97-100
See also Raphael, Elaine
Bolotin, Norman (Phillip) 1951- ... 159
See also SATA 93
Bolotov, Andrei Timofeevich 1738-1833 ... DLB 150
Bolotowsky, Ilya 1907-1981
Obituary ... 108
Bolshakoff, Serge 1901-1991 ... 93-96
Bolster, John 1910-1984 ... 89-92
Obituary ... 111
Bolster, Richard (H.) ... 203
Bolster, W(illiam) Jeffrey 1954- ... CANR-135
Earlier sketch in CA 161
Bolsterli, Margaret Jones 1931- ... 111
Bolt, Bruce A(lan) 1930-2005 ... CANR-10
Earlier sketch in CA 65-68
Bolt, Carol 1941- ... CANR-70
Earlier sketch in CA 101
See also CD 5, 6
See also CWD
See also DLB 60
Bolt, Clarence 1951- ... 220
Bolt, David (Michael) Langstone 1927- ... CANR-6
Earlier sketch in CA 1-4R
Bolt, Ernest C(ollier), Jr. 1936- ... 77-80
Bolt, Jonathan 1935- ... 145
Bolt, Lee
See Faust, Frederick (Schiller)
Bolt, Martin 1944- ... 118
Bolt, Robert (Oxton) 1924-1995 ... CANR-67
Obituary ... 147
Earlier sketches in CA 17-20R, CANR-35
See also CBD
See also CLC 14
See also DAM DRAM
See also DFS 2
See also DLB 13, 233
See also EWL 3
See also LAIT 1
See also MTCW 1
Bolten, Steven E. 1941- ... 37-40R
Boltho, Andrea 1939- ... CANR-42
Earlier sketch in CA 69-72
Bolton, Carole 1926- ... CANR-1
Earlier sketch in CA 49-52
See also SATA 6
Bolton, Elizabeth
See St. John, Nicole
Bolton, Evelyn
See Bunting, (Anne) Eve(lyn)
Bolton, Guy (Reginald) 1884-1979 ... CANR-80
Obituary ... 89-92
Earlier sketch in CA 5-8R
Bolton, H(arold) Philip 1944- ... 127
Bolton, Herbert E(ugene) 1870-1953 ... 179
See also DLB 17
Bolton, Isabel
See Miller, Mary Britton
Bolton, James 1917(?)-1981
Obituary ... 103
Bolton, John Robert 1948- ... 115
Bolton, Kenneth (Ewart) 1914- ... 9-12R
Bolton, Maisie Sharman 1915- ... 9-12R
Bolton, Michele Kremen 1952- ... 236
Bolton, Muriel Roy 1909(?)-1983
Obituary ... 109
Bolton, Ruthie 1961- ... 147
Bolton, Theodore 1889(?)-1973
Obituary ... 45-48
Bolton, W(hitney) F(rench) 1930- ... 17-20R
Bolton, Whitney 1900-1969
Obituary ... 25-28R
Bolus, James Michael 1943- ... 111
Bolus, Jim
See Bolus, James Michael
Bolz, Frank A., Jr. 1930- ... 127
Boman, Thorleif Gustav 1894- ... 21-24R
Bomans, Godfried J(an) A(rnold) 1913-1971 ... CAP-2
Earlier sketch in CA 29-32
Bomar, Cora Paul 1913- ... 41-44R
Bombal, Maria Luisa 1910-1980 ... CANR-72
Earlier sketch in CA 127
See also EWL 3
See also HLCS 1
See also HW 1
See also LAW
See also RGSF 2
See also SSC 37
Bombardieri, Merle 1949- ... 107
Bombeck, Erma (Louise) 1927-1996 . CANR-39
Obituary ... 151
Earlier sketches in CA 21-24R, CANR-12
Interview in ... CANR-12
See also AITN 1
See also BEST 89:4
See also CPW
See also DAM POP
See also MTCW 1
Bombelles, Joseph T. 1930- ... 25-28R
Bombet, Louis-Alexandre-Cesar
See Stendhal
Bomeli, Edwin C(larence) 1920- ... 21-24R
Bomkauf
See Kaufman, Bob (Garnell)
Bommarito, James W. 1922- ... 121
Bompas, William C(arpenter) 1834-1906 ... 215
Bona, Mercy
See Ziegler, Alan
Bonachea, E(nrique) Rolando 1943- ... 41-44R
Bonacich, Edna 1940- ... 45-48
Bonadio, Felice A. ... 173
Bonadio, William 1955- ... 201
Bonald, Jose Manuel Caballero 1926- ... 175
See also Caballero Bonald, Jose Manuel
See also HW 2
Bonanno, Bill
See Bonanno, Salvatore
Bonanno, Joseph 1905-2002 ... 170
Obituary ... 209
Bonanno, Margaret Wander 1950- ... CANR-40
Earlier sketch in CA 85-88
Bonanno, Salvatore 1932- ... 238
Bonansea, Bernardino M(aria) 1908- ... CANR-14
Earlier sketch in CA 41-44R
Bonansinga, Jay R. ... 166
Bonaparte, Felicia 1937- ... CANR-11
Earlier sketch in CA 61-64
Bonar, Veronica
See Bailey, Donna (Veronica Anne)
Bonatti, Walter 1930- ... CANR-110
Earlier sketches in CA 106, CANR-23, 48
Bonaventura ... DLB 90
Bonaventure 1217(?)-1274 ... DLB 115
See also LMFS 1
Bonavia, David Michael 1940-1988 ... 106
Obituary ... 126
Bonavia-Hunt, Noel Aubrey 1882-1965 ... CAP-1
Earlier sketch in CA 9-10
Bonaviri, Giuseppe 1924- ... DLB 177
Bonbright, James C(ummings) 1891-1985 . 1-4R
Obituary ... 117
Bond, Alma H(albert) 1923- ... 130
Bond, B. J.
See Heneghan, James
Bond, Brian 1936- ... CANR-6
Earlier sketch in CA 57-60
Bond, Bruce 1939- ... SATA 61
Bond, Bruce 1954- ... 190
Bond, Charles R(ankin), Jr. 1915- ... 124
Bond, Christopher Godfrey 1945- ... 101
See also CBD
See also CD 5, 6
Bond, Donald F(rederic) 1898-1987 ... 13-16R
Obituary ... 121
Bond, Douglas Danford 1911-1976
Obituary ... 69-72
Bond, E(dward) J(arvis) 1930- ... 114
Bond, Edward 1934- ... CANR-106
Earlier sketches in CA 25-28R, CANR-38, 67
See also AAYA 50
See also BRWS 1
See also CBD
See also CD 5, 6
See also CLC 4, 6, 13, 23
See also DAM DRAM
See also DFS 3, 8
See also DLB 13, 310
See also EWL 3
See also MTCW 1
Bond, Elaine 1924-1984
Obituary ... 112
Bond, Evelyn
See Hershman, Morris
Bond, Felicia 1954- ... CANR-105
Earlier sketch in CA 127
See also SATA 49, 126
Bond, Geoffrey 1924-1978 ... 29-32R
Obituary ... 134
Bond, George C(lement) 1936- ... CANR-120
Earlier sketch in CA 147
Bond, Gladys Baker 1912- ... CANR-2
Earlier sketch in CA 5-8R
See also SATA 14
Bond, Harold 1939-2000 ... CANR-11
Earlier sketch in CA 65-68
Bond, Higgins 1951- ... SATA 83
Bond, Horace Mann 1904-1972 ... CANR-1
Obituary ... 37-40R
Earlier sketch in CA 1-4R
Bond, J. Harvey
See Winterbotham, R(ussell) R(obert)
Bond, James 1900-1989
Obituary ... 127
Bond, Jean Carey ... 106
Bond, Julian 1940- ... 49-52
See also BW 1
Bond, Larry 1951- ... 171
Bond, Lewis H.
See Paine, Lauran (Bosworth)
Bond, Marshall, Jr. 1908-1983 ... CAP-2
Earlier sketch in CA 25-28
Bond, Mary Fanning Wickham 1898-1997 ... 21-24R
Bond, Maurice Francis 1916-1983
Obituary ... 111
Bond, (Thomas) Michael 1926- ... CANR-101
Earlier sketches in CA 5-8R, CANR-4, 24, 49
Interview in ... CANR-24
See also CLR 1, 95
See also CWRI 5
See also DLB 161
See also MAICYA 1, 2
See also SAAS 3
See also SATA 6, 58, 157
Bond, Mrs. James
See Bond, Mary Fanning Wickham
Bond, Nancy (Barbara) 1945- ... CANR-36
Earlier sketches in CA 65-68, CANR-9
See also CLR 11
See also JRDA
See also MAICYA 1, 2
See also SAAS 13
See also SATA 22, 82, 159
See also SATA-Essay 159
See also YAW
Bond, Nelson S(lade) 1908- ... CANR-58
Earlier sketches in CAP-1, CA 19-20
See also SFW 4
Bond, Otto F(erdinand) 1885-1980 ... 1-4R
Bond, Ray
See Smith, Richard Rein
Bond, Raymond T. 1893(?)-1981
Obituary ... 104
Bond, Rebecca 1972- ... SATA 130
Bond, Richmond Pugh 1899-1979 ... CAP-2
Earlier sketch in CA 33-36
Bond, Ruskin 1934- ... CANR-52
Earlier sketches in CA 29-32R, CANR-14, 31
See also CWRI 5
See also RGSF 2
See also SATA 14, 87
Bond, Simon 1947- ... 104
Bond, Stephanie ... 213
Bond, Ted
See Bond, E(dward) J(arvis)
Bond, William Henry 1915- ... CANR-54
Earlier sketch in CA 124
Bond, William J(oseph) 1941- ... CANR-51
Earlier sketches in CA 108, CANR-26
Bondanella, Peter Eugene 1943- ... CANR-29
Earlier sketches in CA 65-68, CANR-10
Bondarev, Iurii Vasil'evich 1924- ... DLB 302
Bonder, Nilton 1957- ... CANR-116
Earlier sketch in CA 164
Bonderoff, Jason (Dennis) 1946- ... 97-100
Bondeson, Jan 1962- ... 195
Bondeson, Ulla V(iveka) 1937- ... 237
Bondi, Joseph C. 1936- ... CANR-28
Earlier sketches in CA 29-32R, CANR-11
Bondoc, Anna 1969- ... 197
Bondurant, Joan V(alerie) 1918- ... 41-44R
Bondy, Sebastian Salazar
See Salazar Bondy, Sebastian
Bone, Edith 1889(?)-1975
Obituary ... 57-60
Bone, Hugh A(lvin) 1909-1994 ... CANR-3
Earlier sketch in CA 1-4R
Bone, Ian 1956- ... CANR-142
Earlier sketch in CA 189
See also SATA 117, 158
Bone, J. F.
See Bone, Jesse F(ranklin)
Bone, Jesse F(ranklin) 1916- ... CANR-55
Earlier sketch in CA 57-60
See also SFW 4
Bone, Quentin 1918- ... 85-88
Bone, Robert (Adamson) 1924- ... 69-72
Bone, Robert C(larke) 1917- ... 37-40R
Bonehill, Captain Ralph
See Stratemeyer, Edward L.
Bonelli, Robert Allen 1950- ... 112
Bonellie, Helen-Janet 1937- ... 41-44R
Bonello, Frank J. 1939- ... 154
Bones, James C., Jr. 1943- ... 125
Bones, Jim, Jr.
See Bones, James C., Jr.
Boness, A. James 1928- ... 37-40R
Bonesteel, Michael ... 238
Bonestell, Chesley 1888-1986
Obituary ... 119
See also SATA-Obit 48
Bonett, Emery
See Coulson, Felicity Carter
Bonett, John
See Coulson, John H(ubert) A(rthur)
Bonetti, Edward 1928- ... 93-96
Bonewits, Isaac
See Bonewits, P(hilip) E(mmons) I(saac)
Bonewits, P(hilip) E(mmons) I(saac) 1949- ... 93-96
Boney, Elaine E(mesette) 1921-
Brief entry ... 110
Boney, F(rancis) N(ash) 1929- ... CANR-46
Earlier sketches in CA 41-44R, CANR-15
Boney, Mary Lily
See Sheats, Mary Boney
Boney, William Jerry 1930- ... 21-24R
Bonfante, Giuliano 1904- ... 158
Bonfante, Larissa ... CANR-11
Earlier sketch in CA 69-72
Bongar, Emmet W(ald) 1919- ... 33-36R
Bongard, David L(awrence) 1959- ... 140
Bongartz, Heinz
See Thorwald, Juergen
Bongartz, Roy 1924-1989 ... 13-16R
Obituary ... 128
Bongie, Chris 1960- ... 188
Bongie, Laurence L(ouis) 1929- ... CANR-85
Earlier sketch in CA 61-64
Bonham, Barbara Thomas 1926- ... CANR-7
Earlier sketch in CA 17-20R
See also SATA 7

Bonham 62 CONTEMPORARY AUTHORS

Bonham, Frank 1914-1989 .... CANR-36
Earlier sketches in CA 9-12R, CANR-4
See also AAYA 1
See also BYA 1, 3
See also CLC 12
See also JRDA
See also MAICYA 1, 2
See also SAAS 3
See also SATA 1, 49
See also SATA-Obit 62
See also TCWW 1, 2
See also YAW
Bonham-Carter, Victor 1913- 9-12R
Bonham Carter, (Helen) Violet (Asquith)
1887-1969 .... CAP-2
Earlier sketch in CA 17-18
Bonheim, Helmut 1930- CANR-4
Earlier sketch in CA 1-4R
Bonhoeffer, Dietrich 1906-1945 148
Brief entry 122
Bonhomme, Denise 1926- 104
Boni, Albert 1892-1981 65-68
Obituary 104
Boni, Franz 1952- .... EWL 3
Boni, Margaret Bradford 1893(?)-1974
Obituary 53-56
Boni, Tanella S(usane) 1954- .... EWL 3
Boniface, William 1963- 169
See also SATA 102
Bonifacio, Amelia Lapena
See Lapena-Bonifacio, Amelia
Bonilla-Silva, Eduardo 1962- 213
Bonime, Florence 1907-1990 49-52
Bonime, Walter 1909- CAP-2
Earlier sketch in CA 17-18
Bonine, Gladys Nichols 1907- CAP-1
Earlier sketch in CA 13-16
Bonington, Chris(tian John Storey)
1934- CANR-91
Earlier sketches in CA 45-48, CANR-1, 34
Bonini, Charles P(ius) 1933- 13-16R
Bonino, Louise
See Williams, Louise Bonino
Bonjean, Charles M. 1935- 41-44R
Bonjour, Laurence Alan 1943- 176
Bonk, Ecke 181
Bonk, James 1932- 123
Bonk, Wallace J. 1923- 9-12R
Bonn, Pat
See Bonn, Patricia Carolyn
Bonn, Patricia Carolyn 1948- .... SATA 43
Bonn, Robert Lewis 1937- 125
Bonn, Thomas L. 1939- 109
Bonnamy, Francis
See Walz, Audrey Boyers
Bonnar, Alphonsus 1895-1968 .... CAP-1
Earlier sketch in CA 9-10
Bonnay, Charles (Louis) 1930-1986
Obituary 119
Bonnefoy, Yves 1923- CANR-136
Earlier sketches in CA 85-88, CANR-33, 75, 97
See also CLC 9, 15, 58
See also CWW 2
See also DAM MST, POET
See also DLB 258
See also EWL 3
See also GFL 1789 to the Present
See also MTCW 1, 2
See also MTFW 2005
See also PC 58
Bonnell, Dorothy Haworth
1914-1999 .... CANR-3
Earlier sketch in CA 1-4R
Bonnell, F(raser) C(larence) 1908-1983 118
Bonnell, F(lorence Rhodes) W(inn) 1915- ... 118
Bonnell, John Sutherland 1893-1992 .... 5-8R
Obituary 136
Bonner, Arthur 1922- CANR-101
Earlier sketch in CA 135
Bonner, Brian 1917- CANR-21
Earlier sketch in CA 104
Bonner, Cindy 1953- 139
See also CSW
Bonner, Gerald 1926- CANR-5
Earlier sketch in CA 9-12R
Bonner, Jack
See Paine, Lauran (Bosworth)
Bonner, James Calvin 1904-1989 .... CANR-9
Earlier sketch in CA 9-12R
Bonner, Joey 1948- 122
Bonner, John Tyler 1920- CANR-98
Earlier sketches in CA 49-52, CANR-48
Bonner, Kieran (Martin) 1951- 175
Bonner, Marita
See Occomy, Marita (Odette) Bonner
See also HR 1:2
Bonner, Mary Graham 1890-1974 .... CANR-68
Obituary 49-52
Earlier sketch in CA 73-76
See also SATA 19
Bonner, Michael
See Glasscock, Anne Bonner
See also TCWW 1, 2
Bonner, Mike 1951- 192
See also SATA 121
Bonner, Parker
See Ballard, (Willis) Todhunter
Bonner, Paul Hyde 1893-1968 .... CANR-72
Obituary 103
Earlier sketch in CA 1-4R
See also DLBD 17
Bonner, Raymond T(homas) 1942- 117
Bonner, Sherwood
See McDowell, Katharine Sherwood Bonner
See also DLB 202
Bonner, Terry Nelsen
See Krauzer, Steven M(ark) and Raeschild, Sheila and Yarbro, Chelsea Quinn
Bonner, Thomas, Jr. 1942- 110
Bonner, Thomas N(eville)
1923-2003 .... CANR-117
Obituary 220
Earlier sketch in CA 9-12R
Bonner, William H(omer) 1924- 53-56
Bonner, William Hallam 1899-1980
Obituary 115
Bonners, Susan 1947- 219
See also MAICYA 2
See also SATA 85
See also SATA-Brief 48
Bonnette, Jeanne 1907-1983 .... 41-44R
Bonnette, Victor
See Roy, Ewell Paul
Bonneville, Douglas A(lan) 1931- 21-24R
Bonney, Bill
See Keevill, Henry J(ohn)
Bonney, H(anning) Orrin 1903-1979 .... 9-12R
Obituary 103
Bonney, Lorraine G(agnon) 1922- CANR-1
Earlier sketch in CA 45-48
Bonney, Merl E(dwin) 1902- CAP-2
Earlier sketch in CA 33-36
Bonney, Richard (John) 1947- 191
Bonney, (Mabel) Therese 1897-1978
Obituary 73-76
Bonnice, Joseph G(regory) 1930- 49-52
Bonnie, Fred 1945-2000 127
Bonnie, Richard J(effrey) 1945- CANR-4
Earlier sketch in CA 53-56
Bonnifield, Paul 1937- 104
Bonnin, Gertrude 1876-1938 150
See also Zitkala-Sa
See also DAM MULT
See also NNAL
Bonnor, William (Bowen) 1920- 9-12R
Bonny, Helen L(indquist) 1921- CANR-19
Earlier sketches in CA 49-52, CANR-2
Bono, Chastity 1969- CANR-144
Earlier sketch in CA 177
Bono, Philip 1921- 101
Bono, Sonny 1935-1998 201
Bonoma, T(homas) V(incent) 1946- .. CANR-33
Earlier sketches in CA 85-88, CANR-15
Bonomelli, Charles J(ames) 1948- 169
Bonomi, Patricia U(pdegraff) 1928- 85-88
Bononno, Robert 1949- CANR-117
Earlier sketch in CA 159
Bonosky, Phillip 1916- 128
Bonsal, Philip Wilson 1903-1995 85-88
Bonsal, Stephen 1865-1950 217
Bonsall, Crosby Barbara (Newell)
1921-1995 .... CANR-72
Obituary 147
Earlier sketch in CA 73-76
See also CWRI 5
See also SATA 23
See also SATA-Obit 84
Bonsall, Joseph S. 1948- 190
See also SATA 119
Bonsanti, Alessandro 1904-1984 .... DLB 177
Bonsignore, Joan 1959- 211
See also SATA 140
Bonta, Marcia Myers 1940- CANR-119
Earlier sketch in CA 148
Bonta, Vanna 152
Bontatibus, Donna R. 1968- 187
Bonte, Pierre 1942- 143
Bontebal, Henk
See Heertje, Arnold
Bontecou, Eleanor 1890(?)-1976
Obituary 65-68
Bontempelli, Massimo 1878-1960 ...... DLB 264
See also EWL 3
Bontempo, Charles J(oseph) 1931- 61-64
Bontemps, Arna(ud Wendell)
1902-1973 .... CANR-35
Obituary 41-44R
Earlier sketches in CA 1-4R, CANR-4
See also BLC 1
See also BW 1
See also CLC 1, 18
See also CLR 6
See also CP 1
See also CWRI 5
See also DA3
See also DAM MULT, NOV, POET
See also DLB 48, 51
See also HR 1:2
See also JRDA
See also MAICYA 1, 2
See also MAL 5
See also MTCW 1, 2
See also SATA 2, 44
See also SATA-Obit 24
See also WCH
See also WP
Bontly, Thomas (John) 1939- 57-60
Bontrager, G(erald) Edwin 1939- 114
Bontrager, John K(enneth) 1923- 65-68
Bonvie, Thomas L. 1940- 114
Bony, Jean (Victor) 1908-1995 101
Bonzon, Paul-Jacques 1908-1978 93-96
See also SATA 22
Boock, Paula 1964- 203
See also SATA 134
Boodman, David M(orris) 1923- 21-24R
Boody, Shirley Bright 1919- 89-92
Boog Watson, Elspeth Janet 1900- CAP-1
Earlier sketch in CA 11-12
Booher, Dianna Daniels 1948- 103
See also SATA 33
Book, Rick 1949- 190
See also BYA 15
See also SATA 119
Book, Rita
See Holub, Joan
Bookbinder, David J(oel) 1951- 101
Bookbinder, Robert 1950- 110
Bookchin, Debbie 234
Bookchin, Murray 1921- CANR-48
Earlier sketches in CA 1-4R, CANR-1
Booker, Anton S.
See Randolph, Vance
Booker, Cedella Marley 1926- 225
Booker, Christopher (John Penrice) 1937- ... 136
Booker, M. Keith 1953- 185
Booker, Malcolm (Richard) 1915- 108
Booker, Simeon Saunders 1918- 9-12R
Booker, Sue
See Thandeka
Bookman, Charlotte
See Zolotow, Charlotte (Gertrude) S(hapiro)
Bookman, Terry Allen 1950- 202
Book-Senninger, Claude 1928- 45-48
Bookspan, Martin 1926- 41-44R
Bookstein, Abraham 1940- 53-56
Boole, Ella Alexander 1858-1952 204
Boom, Alfred B. 1928- CANR-14
Earlier sketch in CA 25-28R
Boom, Corrie ten
See ten Boom, Corrie
Boomgaard, Peter 1946- 212
Boomhauer, Charlie
See Cook, Will(iam Everett)
Boon, Debbie 1960- 170
See also SATA 103
Boon, Emilie (Laetitia) 1958- 131
See also SATA 86
Boon, Francis
See Bacon, Edward
Boon, Kevin A(lexander) 1956- 195
Boon, Louis-Paul 1912-1979 .... CANR-13
Earlier sketch in CA 73-76
See also EWL 3
Boon, Marcus 1963- 219
Boone, Bruce 1940- 112
Boone, Buford 1909(?)-1983
Obituary 109
Boone, Catherine 1958- 144
Boone, Charles Eugene
See Boone, Pat
Boone, Daniel R. 1927- CANR-12
Earlier sketch in CA 33-36R
Boone, Debby
See Boone, Deborah Ann
Boone, Deborah Ann 1956- 110
Boone, Eugene 1962- CANR-86
See also Boone, Gene
Boone, Gene CANR-33
Earlier sketch in CA 113
See also Boone, Eugene
Boone, Gray Davis 1938- 93-96
Boone, Ike
See Athanas, (William) Verne
Boone, Jack W. 1922- 207
Boone, Louis E(ugene) 1941-2005 .... CANR-15
Obituary 235
Earlier sketch in CA 41-44R
Boone, Muriel 1893-1990 69-72
Boone, Pat 1934- CANR-2
Earlier sketch in CA 1-4R
See also SATA 7
Boontje
See Boon, Louis-Paul
Boorde, Andrew 1490(?)-1549 .... DLB 136
Boore, W(alter) H(ugh) 1904- CANR-5
Earlier sketch in CA 5-8R
Boorer, Wendy 1931- CANR-6
Earlier sketch in CA 57-60
Boorman, Howard L(yon) 1920- 41-44R
Boorman, John 1933- 121
Brief entry 112
See also AAYA 3
Boorman, Linda (Kay) 1940- 121
See also SATA 46
Boorman, Scott A(rcher) 1949- 29-32R
Boorman, Stanley (Harold) 1939- 127
Boorstein, Edward 1915- 73-76
Boorstein, Sylvia 216
Boorstin, Daniel J(oseph)
1914-2004 .... CANR-71
Obituary 224
Earlier sketches in CA 1-4R, CANR-1, 28
Interview in CANR-28
See also AITN 2
See also DLB 17
See also SATA 52
Boorstin, Jon 1946- CANR-136
Earlier sketch in CA 134
See also MTFW 2005
Boorstin, Paul (Terry) 1944- 103
Boorstin, Ruth F.
See Boorstin, Ruth (Carolyn) Frankel
Boorstin, Ruth (Carolyn) Frankel 1917- 134
Boos, Frank Holgate 1893-1968 .... CAP-2
Earlier sketch in CA 33-36
Boostrom, Robert E(dward) 1949- 147
Boot, John C. G. 1936- 17-20R
Boot, Max 1968- 180
Boot, William
See Stoppard, Tom
Boote, Robert Edward 1920- 65-68
Booth, Alan R(undlett) 1934- 185
Brief entry 107
Booth, Ballington 1857-1940 224
Booth, Bradford A(llen) 1909-1968
Obituary 116
Booth, Brian 1936- 143
Booth, Catherine Bramwell
See Bramwell-Booth, Catherine
Booth, Charles Orrell 1918- 13-16R
Booth, Edward
See Booth, Geoffrey Thornton
Booth, Edwin CANR-63
Earlier sketches in CA 17-20R, CANR-7
See also TCWW 1, 2
Booth, Ernest Sheldon 1915-1984 53-56
See also SATA 43
Booth, Evangeline Cory 1865-1950 232
Booth, Franklin 1874-1948 185
See also DLB 188
Booth, Geoffrey
See Tann, Jennifer
Booth, Geoffrey Thornton 1928- CANR-89
Earlier sketch in CA 132
Booth, George C(live) 1901-1973 .... CAP-1
Earlier sketch in CA 11-12
Booth, Graham (Charles) 1935- .... SATA 37
Booth, Helen Sutton 1890(?)-1985
Obituary 117
Booth, Irwin
See Hoch, Edward D(entinger)
Booth, James 1945- CANR-144
Earlier sketch in CA 119
Booth, John A(llan) 1946- CANR-28
Earlier sketch in CA 111
Booth, John E(rlanger) 1919- 9-12R
Booth, Ken 1943- 102
Booth, L(aVaughn) Venchael 1919-2002 209
Booth, Margaret 1898-2002 .... IDFW 3, 4
Booth, Mark Warren 1943- 107
Booth, Martin 1944-2004 188
Obituary 223
Earlier sketches in CA 93-96, CANR-92
Autobiographical Essay in 188
See also CAAS 2
See also CLC 13
See also CP 1, 2, 3, 4
Booth, Mary L. 1831-1889 .... DLB 79
Booth, Maud Ballington 1865-1948 203
Booth, Nyla 121
Booth, Pat(rick John) 1929- CAP-1
Earlier sketch in CA 9-10
Booth, Pat 1942- 130
See also BEST 90:1
See also DA3
See also DAM POP
Booth, Paul Henry Gore
See Gore-Booth, Paul Henry
Booth, Philip 1907-1981 106
Booth, Philip 1925- CANR-88
Earlier sketches in CA 5-8R, CANR-5
See also CLC 23
See also CP 1, 2, 3, 4, 5, 6, 7
See also DLBY 1982
Booth, Rosemary Frances 1928- 53-56
See also RHW
Booth, Stanley 1942- 136
Booth, Stephen 1933- CANR-114
Earlier sketch in CA 69-72
Booth, Stephen 1952- 198
Booth, Taylor L(ockwood) 1933- 53-56
Booth, Warren Scripps 1894-1987
Obituary 121
Booth, Wayne C(layson)
1921-2005 .... CANR-117
Earlier sketches in CA 1-4R, CANR-3, 43
See also CAAS 5
See also CLC 24
See also DLB 67
Booth, William 1829-1912 188
See also DLB 190
Booth, Windsor Peyton 1912-1989
Obituary 130
Boothby, Guy (Newell) 1867-1905 .... HGG
Boothby, Robert
See Boothby, Robert John Graham
Boothby, Robert John Graham 1900-1986 .. 117
Obituary 120
Boothroyd, (John) Basil 1910-1988 .. CANR-13
Obituary 124
Earlier sketch in CA 33-36R
Bootle, Stan Kelly
See Kelly-Bootle, Stan
Bootman, Colin .... SATA 159
Booton, (Catherine) Kage 1919-1994 61-64
Booty, John Everitt 1925- CANR-43
Earlier sketches in CA 85-88, CANR-17
Bopp, Karl Richard 1906-1979
Obituary 107
Bopp, Mary S.
See Strow, Mary R.
Bor, Jonathan (Steven) 1953- 133
Bor, Josef 1906-1979
Obituary 115
See also DLB 299
Bor, Norman 1893(?)-1973
Obituary 104
Boraas, Roger S(tuart) 1926- 33-36R
Borah, Timm
See Zech, Paul
Borah, Woodrow (Wilson)
1912-1999 .... CANR-3
Obituary 187
Earlier sketch in CA 5-8R
Boraine, Alex(ander) 202
Borch, Ted
See Lund, A. Morten
Borchard, Ruth (Berendsohn) 1910- 13-16R
Borchard, Therese Johnson 234
Borchardt, Alice 198
Borchardt, D(ietrich) H(ans) 1916- ... CANR-49
Earlier sketches in CA 21-24R, CANR-9, 24
Borchardt, Frank L(ouis) 1938- 33-36R

Cumulative Index 63 **Bosmajian**

Borchardt, Rudolf 1877-1945 183
See also DLB 66
Borchers, Gladys L. 1891-1988 .... CAP-1
Earlier sketch in CA 17-18
Borchert, Gerald L(eo) 1932- CANR-36
Earlier sketches in CA 37-40R, CANR-14
Borchert, James 1941- CANR-94
Earlier sketch in CA 104
Borchert, Till-Holger 1967- 227
Borchert, Wolfgang 1921-1947 188
Brief entry 104
See also DLB 69, 124
See also EWL 3
See also TCLC 5
Borch-Jacobsen, Mikkel 163
Borcz, Geri 224
Borden, Bob
See Rees, Clair (Francis)
Borden, Charles A. 1912-1968 .... 5-8R
Borden, Henry 1901-1989 .... 41-44R
Borden, Iain 1962- 195
Borden, Lee
See Deal, Borden
Borden, Leigh
See Deal, Borden
Borden, Linda 1951(?)- 125
Borden, Lizzie
See Borden, Linda
Borden, Louise (Walker) 1949- CANR-119
Earlier sketch in CA 136
See also SATA 68, 104, 141
See also SATA-Essay 141
Borden, M.
See Saxon, Gladys Relyea
Borden, Mary 1886-1968 .... CANR-59
Obituary 25-28R
Earlier sketches in CAP-1, CA 13-16
See also RHW
Borden, Morton 1925- 9-12R
Borden, Neil Hopper 1895-1980 .... CANR-6
Earlier sketch in CA 1-4R
Borden, Norman E(aston), Jr.
1907-1978 .... 17-20R
Borden, Richard Carman 1900-1986 ..... CAP-1
Earlier sketch in CA 11-12
Borden, William (Vickers) 1938- CANR-144
Earlier sketches in CA 25-28R, CANR-10, 25
Borden-Turner, Mary
See Borden, Mary
Borderieux, Carita 1874-1953 176
Brief entry 113
Borders, William Alexander 1939- 134
Bordes, Francois 1919-1981
Obituary 103
Bordewijk, Ferdinand 1884-1965 202
See also EWL 3
Bordier, Georgette 1924- .... SATA 16
Bordill, Judith
See Eccles, Marjorie
Bordin, Edward S. 1913-1992 57-60
Bordin, Ruth B(irgitta) Anderson
1917-1994 .... CANR-56
Earlier sketches in CA 21-24R, CANR-11, 27
Bording, Anders 1619-1677 .... DLB 300
Bordley, James III 1900-1979 69-72
Obituary 133
Bordman, Gerald 1931- 107
Bordo, Susan (Rebecca) 1947- 159
Bordo, Susan R.
See Bordo, Susan (Rebecca)
Bordow, Joan (Wiener) 1944- 85-88
Bordowitz, Hank 1955- 176
Borea, Phyllis Gilbert 1924- 29-32R
Boreham, Gordon F. 1928- 41-44R
Borek, Ernest 1911-1986 106
Obituary 118
Borel, Jacques 1925- CANR-101
Earlier sketches in CA 33-36R, CANR-13, 49
Borel, Petrus 1809-1859 .... DLB 119
See also GFL 1789 to the Present
Borel, Raymond C. 1927- 73-76
Borell, Helene
See Hegeler, Sten
Boreman, Jean 1909- CAP-2
Earlier sketch in CA 21-22
Boren, Henry C(harles) 1921- 17-20R
Boren, James H(arlan) 1925- 41-44R
Boren, Lynda S. 1941- 194
Borenstein, Audrey F(arrell) 1930- CANR-28
Earlier sketches in CA 77-80, CANR-13
Borenstein, Emily 1923- 104
Borer, Mary (Irene) Cathcart
1906-1994 .... CANR-4
Earlier sketch in CA 9-12R
Boretz, Allen 1900-1986
Obituary 119
Boretz, Alvin 1919- CANR-48
Brief entry 118
Earlier sketch in CA 124
Interview in CA-124
Boretz, Benjamin (Aaron) 1934- CANR-43
Earlier sketch in CA 69-72
Borg, Bjoern (Rune) 1956- 134
Brief entry 114
Borg, Bjorn
See Borg, Bjoern (Rune)
Borg, Dorothy 1902-1993 .... 21-24R
Obituary 143
Borg, Jack .... TCWW 1, 2
Borg, Marcus J(oel) 1942- 200
Borg, Susan 1947- 131
Borg, Walter R(aymond) 1921- CANR-13
Earlier sketch in CA 33-36R
Borge, Bernhard
See Bjerke, (Jarl) Andre
Borgen, Johan 1902-1979 185
See also DLB 297
See also EWL 3
Borgen, Robert 1945- 124
Borgenicht, David 1968- 202
Borges, Jorge Luis 1899-1986 .... CANR-133
Earlier sketches in CA 21-24R, CANR-19, 33, 75, 105
See also AAYA 26
See also BPFB 1
See also CDWLB 3
See also CLC 1, 2, 3, 4, 6, 8, 9, 10, 13, 19, 44, 48, 83
See also DA
See also DA3
See also DAB
See also DAC
See also DAM MST, MULT
See also DLB 113, 283
See also DLBY 1986
See also DNFS 1, 2
See also EWL 3
See also HLC 1
See also HW 1, 2
See also LAW
See also LMFS 2
See also MSW
See also MTCW 1, 2
See also MTFW 2005
See also PC 22, 32
See also RGSF 2
See also RGWL 2, 3
See also SFW 4
See also SSC 4, 41
See also SSFS 17
See also TCLC 109
See also TWA
See also WLC
See also WLIT 1
Borgese, Elisabeth Mann
1918-2002 .... CANR-24
Obituary 209
Earlier sketch in CA 73-76
Borgese, Giuseppe Antonio 1882-1952 206
See also DLB 264
Borghese, Junio Valerio 1906(?)-1974
Obituary 53-56
Borglum, (James) Lincoln (De La Mothe)
1912-1986 122
Obituary 118
Borgman, James (Mark) 1954- CANR-100
Earlier sketch in CA 133
See also SATA 122
Borgman, Jim
See Borgman, James (Mark)
Borgmann, Albert 1937- 117
Borgmann, Dmitri A(lfred) 1927-1985 ... 17-20R
Obituary 118
Borgo, Ludovico 1930- 65-68
Borgos, Seth 1952- 119
Borgstrom, Georg A(rne) 1912-1990 ..... 17-20R
Obituary 130
Borgzinner, Jon A. 1938-1980 108
Obituary 97-100
Borhek, Mary V(irginia) 1922- 113
Borich, Barrie Jean 1959- 191
Borich, Michael 1949- 105
Boring, Edwin G(arrigues)
1886-1968 .... CANR-6
Earlier sketch in CA 1-4R
Boring, M(aynard) Eugene 1935- 107
Boring, Mel 1939- 106
See also SATA 35
Boring, Phyllis Zatlin
See Zatlin, Phyllis
Boris, Edna Z(wick) 1943- 113
Boris, Martin 1930- 89-92
Borish, Elaine 132
Boritt, Gabor S(zappanos) 1940- CANR-116
Earlier sketches in CA 147, CANR-115
Borja, Corinne 1929- 97-100
See also SATA 22
Borja, Robert 1923- 97-100
See also SATA 22
Borjas, George J(esus) 1950- 193
Bork, Alfred M. 1926- 17-20R
Bork, Robert H(eron) 1927- CANR-78
Brief entry 111
Earlier sketch in CA 130
See also BEST 90:2
Borkin, Joseph 1911-1979 97-100
Obituary 89-92
Borklund, C(arl) W(ilbur) 1930- 21-24R
Borko, Harold 1922- 13-16R
Borkovec, Thomas D. 1944- 45-48
Borland, Barbara Dodge 1904(?)-1991 .. CAP-1
Obituary 133
Earlier sketch in CA 9-10
Borland, Hal
See Borland, Harold Glen
See also BYA 10
See also NFS 18
See also SATA 5
See also SATA-Obit 24
See also TCWW 1, 2
Borland, Harold Glen 1900-1978 .... CANR-63
Obituary 77-80
Earlier sketches in CA 1-4R, CANR-6
See also Borland, Hal
Borland, Kathryn Kilby 1916- CANR-4
Earlier sketch in CA 53-56
See also SATA 16
Borlenghi, Patricia 1951- .... SATA 79
Borley, Lester 1931- 181
Borman, Kathryn M. 1941- 117
Borman, William Alan 1940- .... [illegible]
Bormann, Ernest G(ordon) 1925- 17-20R
Born, Adolf 1930- .... SATA 49
Born, Ernest Alexander 1898-1992 102
Born, Heidi von
See von Born, Heidi
Born, Max 1882-1970 .... 5-8R
Obituary 25-28R
Borne, Dorothy
See Rice, Dorothy Mary
Borne, Lawrence Roger 1939- 121
Borne, Ludwig 1786-1837 .... DLB 90
Borneman, Ernest 1915- CANR-41
Earlier sketches in CA 9-12R, CANR-3, 19
Borneman, H.
See Gottshall, Franklin Henry
Borneman, John 1952- 140
Bornemann, Alfred H(enry) 1908-1991 . 13-16R
Obituary 134
Bornet, Vaughn Davis 1917- CANR-42
Earlier sketches in CA 1-4R, CANR-5, 20
Bornheimer, Deane G(ordon) 1935- 89-92
Bornholdt, Jennifer Mary 1960- 153
See also CP 7
See also CWP
Bornholdt, Jenny
See Bornholdt, Jennifer Mary
Borning, Bernard C(arl) 1913- CANR-3
Earlier sketch in CA 1-4R
Bornkamm, Guenther 1905-
Brief entry 116
Bornstein, Diane (Dorothy)
1942-1984 .... CANR-8
Obituary 112
Earlier sketch in CA 57-60
Bornstein, George (Jay) 1941- CANR-117
Earlier sketch in CA 29-32R
Bornstein, Miriam
See Bornstein-Somoza, Miriam
See also DLB 209
Bornstein, Morris 1927- CANR-2
Earlier sketch in CA 5-8R
Bornstein, Ruth Lercher
See Bornstein-Lercher, Ruth
See also SATA-Essay 107
Bornstein, Sam 1913-
Brief entry 112
Bornstein-Lercher, Ruth 1927- CANR-8
Earlier sketch in CA 61-64
See also Bornstein, Ruth Lercher
See also SATA 14, 88
Bornstein-Somoza, Miriam 1950-
See Bornstein, Miriam
See also HW 1
Borntrager, Karl A. 1892-1990 89-92
Borntrager, Mary Christner 1921- ... CANR-143
Earlier sketch in CA 144
Borodacz, William (?)-1986
Obituary 118
Borodin, George
See Milkomane, George Alexis Milkomanovich
Boroff, David 1917-1965 .... CAP-1
Obituary 29-32R
Earlier sketch in CA 11-12
Borofka, David 1954- 181
Boroson, Warren 1935- 21-24R
Borovik, Artyom 1960-2000 141
Borovik, Genrikh (Aviezerovich) 1929- 151
Borovitz, Mark 1951- 238
Borovski, Conrad 1930- 37-40R
Borovsky, Natasha 1924- 121
Borowiec, Andrew 1928- 127
Borowitz, Albert (Ira) 1930- CANR-32
Earlier sketches in CA 85-88, CANR-15
Borowitz, Andy (Seth) 1958- 225
Borowitz, Eugene B(ernard) 1924- CANR-1
Earlier sketch in CA 49-52
Borowski, Oded 1939- 219
Borowski, Tadeusz 1922-1951 154
Brief entry 106
See also CDWLB 4
See also DLB 215
See also EWL 3
See also RGSF 2
See also RGWL 3
See also SSC 48
See also SSFS 13
See also TCLC 9
Borras, Frank Marshall (?)-1980
Obituary 102
Borregaard, Ebbe 1933- .... CP 1
Borrell, D(orothy) E(lizabeth) 1928- .... CP 1
Borrelli, Karen (Troxel) 1958- 217
Borrello, Alfred 1931- 29-32R
Borrie, John 1915- 103
Borrie, Wilfred David 1913-2000 109
Borroff, Edith 1925- 65-68
Borroff, Marie 1923- CANR-2
Earlier sketch in CA 5-8R
Borror, Donald J(oyce) 1907-1988 .... CANR-29
Earlier sketch in CA 1-4R
Borror, Gordon L(amar) 1936- 117
Borrow, George (Henry) 1803-1881 .... DLB 21, 55, 166
Borrus, Michael (Glen) 1956- 141
Borsch, Frederick Houk 1935- CANR-25
Earlier sketches in CA 25-28R, CANR-10
Borski, Lucia Merecka 73-76
See also SATA 18
Borsodi, Ralph 1888-1977
Obituary 73-76
Borson, Roo
See Borson, Ruth Elizabeth
Borson, Ruth Elizabeth 1952- CANR-95
Earlier sketches in CA 112, CANR-46
See also CP 7
See also CWP
Borsook, Eve 1929- 180
Borst, Raymond R(ichard) 1909-2001 107
Obituary 197
Borstelmann, Thomas 1958- 142
Borsten, Orin 1912- 85-88
Borsten, Rick 1955- 140
Borten, Helen Jacobson 1930- CANR-3
Earlier sketch in CA 5-8R
See also SATA 5
Borth, Christian C. 1895(?)-1976
Obituary 65-68
Borthwick, J. S.
See Creighton, Joan Scott
Bortin, George 114
Bortin, V. G.
See Bortin, George and Bortin, Virginia
Bortin, Virginia 1936- 114
Bortner, Doyle M(cClean) 1915- 33-36R
Bortner, Morton 1925- 33-36R
Bortnik, Aida (Beatriz) 1938- 163
See also HW 2
Bortoli, Georges 1923- 65-68
Bortolotti, Dan 1969- 233
See also SATA 157
Borton, D. B.
See Carpenter, Lynette
Borton, Douglas 1960- .... HGG
Borton, Elizabeth
See Trevino, Elizabeth B(orton) de
Borton, John C., Jr. 1938- CANR-27
Earlier sketch in CA 29-32R
Borton, Lady 1942- 147
See also SATA 98
Borton, Terry
See Borton, John C., Jr.
Borton de Trevino, Elizabeth
See Trevino, Elizabeth B(orton) de
Bortstein, Larry 1942- 33-36R
See also SATA 16
Bortz, Alfred B(enjamin) 1944- CANR-118
Earlier sketch in CA 141
See also SATA 74, 139
Bortz, Daniel 1943- 177
Bortz, Edward L(eRoy) 1896-1970 .... CAP-1
Earlier sketch in CA 11-12
Bortz, Fred
See Bortz, Alfred B(enjamin)
Boruch, Robert F(rancis) 1942- 69-72
Borum, Poul 1934-1996 202
Borus, Michael E(liot) 1938-1987 .... 37-40R
Obituary 122
Bory, Jean-Louis 1919-1979 187
Borysenko, Joan 1945- 201
Borza, Eugene N(icholas) 1935- 25-28R
Borzutzky, Silvia 1946- 234
Bosanquet, Bernard 1848-1923 .... DLB 262
Bosanquet, N(icholas) F(rancis) G(ustavus)
1942- 131
Bosanquet, Nick
See Bosanquet, N(icholas) F(rancis) G(ustavus)
Bosanquet, Reggie
See Bosanquet, Reginald
Bosanquet, Reginald 1932-1984
Obituary 113
Boscan, Juan c. 1490-1542 .... DLB 318
Bosch, David J(acobus) 1929- 118
Bosch, Henry G(erard) 1914-1995 135
Bosch, Hieronymus c. 1450-1516 ...... AAYA 65
Bosch (Gavino), Juan 1909-2001 151
Obituary 204
See also DAM MST, MULT
See also DLB 145
See also HLCS 1
See also HW 1, 2
Bosch, William Joseph 1928- 29-32R
Boschken, Herman L. 1944- 233
Bosco, Antoinette (Oppedisano) 1928- .. 13-16R
Bosco, Dominick 1948- 145
Bosco, (Fernand Joseph Marius) Henri
1888-1976 69-72
Obituary 65-68
See also DLB 72
Bosco, Jack
See Holliday, Joseph
Bosco, Joseph (Augustus) 1948- 147
Bosco, Monique 1927- 160
See also DLB 53
Bose, Buddhadeva 1908-
Brief entry 119
Bose, Irene Mott 1899(?)-1974
Obituary 53-56
Bose, N(irmal) K(umar) 1901-1972 .... CAP-2
Earlier sketch in CA 23-24
Bose, Sumantra 228
Bose, Tarun Chandra 1931- CANR-48
Earlier sketch in CA 45-48
Boserup, Ester (Talke) 1910-1999 57-60
Boshell, Buris R(aye) 1923- 105
Boshell, Gordon 1908- 77-80
See also SATA 15
Bosher, J(ohn) F(rancis) 1929- 186
Boshinski, Blanche 1922- 21-24R
See also SATA 10
Boskin, Joseph 1929- 25-28R
Boskoff, Alvin 1924- 13-16R
Bosland, Chelcie Clayton 1901-1997 .... 5-8R
Bosler, Raymond Thomas 1915- 112
Bosley, Harold A(ugustus) 1907-1975 49-52
Obituary 53-56
Bosley, Keith 1937- CANR-6
Earlier sketch in CA 57-60
See also CP 2, 3, 4
Boslooper, Thomas 1923- 81-84
Bosmajian, Haig Aram 1928- CANR-7
Earlier sketch in CA 17-20R
Bosmajian, Hamida 1936- 107

Bosman, Herman Charles 1905-1951 160
See also Malan, Herman
See also DLB 225
See also RGSF 2
See also TCLC 49
Bosman, Paul 1929- .... SATA 107
Bosna, Valerie 237
Bosoni, Anthony J. 1952- 151
Bosquet, Alain 1919-1998 .... 13-16R
Obituary 166
Boss, Jeremy M. 237
Boss, Judy 1935- 57-60
Boss, Pauline 1934- 211
Boss, Richard W(oodruff) 1937- 103
Bosschere, Jean de 1878(?)-1953 186
Brief entry 115
See also TCLC 19
Bosse, Malcolm (Joseph, Jr.)
1926-2002 .... CANR-49
Obituary 209
Earlier sketch in CA 106
See also AAYA 16
See also MAICYAS 1, 2
See also SATA 35, 136
See also YAW
Bosselaar, Laure-Anne 1943- CANR-132
Earlier sketch in CA 170
Bosserman, (Charles) Phillip 1931- 102
See also SATA 84
Bossert, Steven T(homas) 1948- 104
Bossom, Naomi 1933- 102
See also SATA 35
Bossone, Richard M. 1924- 33-36R
Bossuet, Jacques-Benigne 1627-1704 . DLB 268
See also EW 3
See also GFL Beginnings to 1789
Bost, Pierre 1901-1976 .... IDFW 3, 4
Bostdorff, Denise M. 1959- CANR-98
Earlier sketch in CA 147
Bostic, Joe 1908-1988 216
See also DLB 241
Bosticco, (Isabel Lucy) Mary 102
Bostick, William A(llison) 1913- 89-92
Bostock, Mike 1962- .... SATA 114
Boston, Anne 1945- 130
Boston, Bruce 1943- 177
Earlier sketch in CA 146
Autobiographical Essay in 177
See also CAAS 30
Boston, Charles K.
See Gruber, Frank
Boston, Jonathan 1957- 140
Boston, L(ucy) M(aria Wood)
1892-1990 .... CANR-58
Obituary 131
Earlier sketch in CA 73-76
See also CLR 3
See also CWRI 5
See also DLB 161
See also FANT
See also JRDA
See also MAICYA 1, 2
See also SATA 19
See also SATA-Obit 64
See also YAW
Boston, Noel 1910-1966 .... CAP-1
Earlier sketch in CA 13-16
Boston, Ray(mond J.) 1927- 128
Boston, Robert 1940- CANR-60
Earlier sketch in CA 65-68
Bostridge, Mark 194
Bostrom, Kathleen (Susan) Long 1954- 210
See also SATA 139
Bostrom, Kathy
See Bostrom, Kathleen (Susan) Long
Bostwick, Burdette Edwards 1908-1995 106
Bosustow, Stephen 1911-1981 .... IDFW 3, 4
Boswell
See Gordon, Giles (Alexander Esme)
Boswell, Barbara (S.) 1946- 122
Boswell, Charles (Meigs, Jr.) 1909- 5-8R
Boswell, Jackson Campbell 1934- 61-64
Boswell, James 1740-1795 .... BRW 3
See also CDBLB 1660-1789
See also DA
See also DAB
See also DAC
See also DAM MST
See also DLB 104, 142
See also TEA
See also WLC
See also WLIT 3
Boswell, Jeanetta 1922- CANR-22
Earlier sketch in CA 106
Boswell, John (Eastburn)
1947-1994 .... CANR-138
Obituary 147
Earlier sketches in CA 121, CANR-79
See also MTFW 2005
Boswell, Marshall 1965- 223
Boswell, Robert 1953- CANR-124
Earlier sketch in CA 136
See also DLB 234
Boswell, Thomas 1947- 118
Bosworth, Allan R(ucker)
1901-1986 .... CANR-64
Obituary 120
Earlier sketch in CA 1-4R
See also TCWW 1, 2
Bosworth, Clifford Edmund 1928- CANR-7
Earlier sketch in CA 13-16R
Bosworth, David 1947- 113
Bosworth, Frank
See Paine, Lauran (Bosworth)
Bosworth, J. Allan 1925- .... SATA 19
Bosworth, Patricia 1933- CANR-113
Earlier sketches in CA 77-80, CANR-65
Bosworth, R(ichard) J(ames) B(oon)
1943- CANR-46
Earlier sketches in CA 106, CANR-23
Bosworth, Sheila 1950- 233
See also CSW
Bote, Hermann c. 1460-c. 1520 .... DLB 179
Boteach, Shmuel 216
Botein, Bernard 1900-1974
Obituary 45-48
Botel, Morton 1925- 105
Botello, Judy Goldstein 1943- 180
Botev, Khristo 1847-1876 .... DLB 147
Botha, Ted 235
Botham, Noel 1940- CANR-139
Earlier sketch in CA 104
Bothmer, Dietrich Felix von
See von Bothmer, Dietrich Felix
Bothwell, Jean (?)-1977 .... CANR-68
Earlier sketches in CA 1-4R, CANR-3
See also SATA 2
Bothwell, Robert (Selkirk) 1944- 143
Botjer, George (Francis) 1937- 97-100
Botkin, B(enjamin) A(lbert) 1901-1975 .. CAP-1
Obituary 57-60
Earlier sketch in CA 13-16
See also SATA 40
Botkin, Daniel B. 1937- CANR-113
Earlier sketch in CA 136
Botkin, James W. 1943- 112
Botkin, Vasilii Petrovich 1811-1869 .... DLB 277
Botman, Selma 1950- 135
Boto, Eza
See Biyidi, Alexandre
Botsch, Robert Emil 1947- 104
Botsford, Gardner 1917- 232
Botsford, Keith 1928- 9-12R
Botsford, Ward 1927-2004 110
Obituary 227
See also SATA 66
Bott, Anita F. 1970- 151
Bott, George 1920- 104
Bott, Raoul 1923- 164
Botta, Anne Charlotte (Lynch)
1815-1891 .... DLB 3, 250
Bottel, Helen 1914-1999 .... 25-28R
Botterill, Cal(vin Bruce) 1947- 57-60
Botterill, Joyce 1939- 138
Bottigheimer, Ruth B. 1939- 125
Bottiglia, William F(ilbert) 1912- 21-24R
Botting, Douglas (Scott) 1934- CANR-113
Earlier sketches in CA 45-48, CANR-1, 16, 37
See also SATA 43
Bottner, Barbara 1943- CANR-60
Earlier sketches in CA 61-64, CANR-8, 23
See also SAAS 26
See also SATA 14, 93
See also SATA-Essay 121
Botto, Jan
See Krasko, Ivan
Bottom, Raymond 1927- 33-36R
Bottome, Edgar M. 1937- 33-36R
Bottome, Margaret McDonald 1827-1906 .. 204
Bottome, Phyllis 179
See also Forbes-Dennis, Phyllis
See also DLB 197
Bottomley, Gordon 1874-1948 192
Brief entry 120
See also DLB 10
See also TCLC 107
Bottomly, Heath 1919- 105
Bottomore, T(homas) B(urton)
1920-1992 .... CANR-79
Obituary 140
Earlier sketches in CA 9-12R, CANR-4, 20
Bottoms, A(nthony) E(dward) 1939- 73-76
Bottoms, David 1949- CANR-22
Earlier sketch in CA 105
See also CLC 53
See also CSW
See also DLB 120
See also DLBY 1983
Bottoms, Lawrence W(endell)
1908-1994 89-92
Bottone, Frank G., Jr. 1969- 212
See also SATA 141
Bottrall, Margaret Florence Saumarez
1909- 104
Bottrall, (Francis James) Ronald
1906-1989 53-56
Obituary 129
See also CP 1, 2, 3, 4
See also DLB 20
Botvinnik, Mikhail Moiseyevich
1911-1995 112
Obituary 148
Botwin, Carol 1929-1997 159
Botwinick, Jack 1923- 41-44R
Bouazza, Hafid 1970- 195
Bouce, Paul-Gabriel 1936- 73-76
Bouchard, Constance B(rittain)
1948- CANR-115
Earlier sketches in CA 128, CANR-60
Bouchard, David 1952- 189
See also SATA 117
Bouchard, Lois Kalb 1938- 25-28R
Bouchard, Michel Marc 1958- 197
Bouchard, Robert H. 1923- 17-20R
Bouchardy, Joseph 1810-1870 .... DLB 192
Bouchelle, Joan Hoiness 1928- 146
Boucher, Alan (Estcourt) 1918-1996 . CANR-54
Earlier sketches in CA 5-8R, CANR-9, 24
Boucher, Anthony
See White, William A(nthony) P(arker)
See also DLB 8
Boucher, Bruce (Ambler) 1948- CANR-93
Earlier sketch in CA 146
Boucher, (Clarence) Carter 1954- ...... SATA 129
Boucher, David 1951- 135
Boucher, Frank 1901-1977 122
Obituary 110
Boucher, John G(regory) 1930- 37-40R
Boucher, Jonathan 1738-1804 .... DLB 31
Boucher, Paul Edward 1893-1981 .... CAP-1
Earlier sketch in CA 13-14
Boucher, Philip P. 1944- CANR-93
Earlier sketch in CA 146
Boucher, Sandy 1936- CANR-100
Earlier sketch in CA 110
Boucher, Wayne I(rving) 1934- 53-56
Boucherville, Georges Boucher de
1814-1894 .... DLB 99
Bouchez, Colette 1960- 219
Boucolon, Maryse
See Conde, Maryse
Boudat, Marie-Louise 1909- CAP-1
Earlier sketch in CA 11-12
Boudelang, Bob
See Pell, Ed(ward)
Boudjedra, Rachid 1941- .... EWL 3
Boudon, Raymond 1934- CANR-118
Earlier sketches in CA 49-52, CANR-30, 56
Boudreau, Eugene H(oward) 1934- 45-48
Boudreau, R(obert) L(ouis) 1951- 217
Boudreaux, Patricia Duncan 1941- 33-36R
Bough, Lee
See Huser, (La)Verne (Carl)
Boughey, Arthur S(tanley) 1913-2000
Brief entry 113
Boughner, Daniel C(liness) 1909-1974 .. CAP-2
Obituary 49-52
Earlier sketch in CA 23-24
Boughton, Doug(las Gordon) 1944- 163
Boughton, James M(urray) 1940- 41-44R
Boughton, Richard 1954- 142
See also SATA 75
Boughton, Willis A(rnold) 1885-1977
Obituary 73-76
Bouhours, Dominique 1628-1702 ...... DLB 268
Bouissac, Paul (Antoine Rene) 1934- 65-68
Boukreev, Anatoli 1958(?)-1997 ...... CANR-114
Earlier sketch in CA 166
Boulanger, Nadia (Juliette) 1887-1979 127
Boularan, Jacques 1890-1972
Obituary 37-40R
Boulby, Mark 1929- 37-40R
Boulding, Elise (Biorn-Hansen)
1920- CANR-51
Earlier sketches in CA 21-24R, CANR-8, 26
Boulding, Kenneth E(wart)
1910-1993 .... CANR-77
Obituary 140
Earlier sketches in CA 5-8R, CANR-7, 26
Boulet, Susan Seddon 1941- .... SATA 50
Boulez, Pierre 1925- CANR-101
Earlier sketch in CA 148
Boulger, James Denis 1931-1979 109
Boullata, Issa J. 1929- CANR-124
Earlier sketch in CA 169
Boulle, Pierre (Francois Marie-Louis)
1912-1994 .... CANR-24
Obituary 143
Earlier sketch in CA 9-12R
See also SATA 22
See also SATA-Obit 78
See also SFW 4
See also TWA
Boullosa, Carmen 1954- 190
Boulogne, Jean 1942- 93-96
Boult, Adrian (Cedric) 1889-1983 114
Obituary 109
Boult, S. Kye
See Cochrane, William E.
Boulter, Eric Thomas 1917-1989
Obituary 129
Boulting, John (Edward) 1913-1985
Obituary 116
Boulton, David 1935- CANR-15
Earlier sketch in CA 25-28R
Boulton, James T(hompson) 1924- .. CANR-113
Earlier sketch in CA 29-32R
Boulton, Jane 1921- CANR-57
Earlier sketch in CA 65-68
See also SATA 91
Boulton, Laura Theresa Craytor 1899(?)-1980
Obituary 110
Boulton, Marjorie 1924- CANR-9
Earlier sketch in CA 65-68
Boulton, Wayne G(ranberry) 1941- 115
Boultwood, Alban (Henry) 1911- 118
Boulware, Marcus H(anna)
1907-1981 .... CANR-1
Earlier sketch in CA 45-48
Bouma, Donald H(erbert) 1918- 41-44R
Bouma, J(ohanas) L. -c. 1979 .... TCWW 1, 2
Bouma, Mary La Grand 93-96
Bouma, Paddy 1947- .... SATA 128
Bouman, Pieter M(arinus) 1938- CANR-12
Earlier sketch in CA 29-32R
Bouman, Walter Richard 1929- 29-32R
Boumelha, Penelope Ann 1950- 110
Boumelha, Penny
See Boumelha, Penelope Ann
Boumphrey, Robert Stavely 1916(?)-1987
Obituary 123
Bouquet, Alan Coates 1884-1976 217
Bouquet, Mary (Rose) 1955- 146
Bour, Daniele 1939- .... SATA 62
Bouraoui, H(edi) A(ndre) 1932- CANR-25
Earlier sketches in CA 65-68, CANR-9
Bourassa, Napoleon 1827-1916 .... DLB 99
Bourbaki, Nicolas
See Cartan, Henri (Paul) and
Weil, Andre
Bourbon, Ken
See Bauer, Erwin A(dam)
Bourdain, Anthony 1957(?)- CANR-98
Earlier sketch in CA 154
Bourdeaux, Michael 1934- CANR-14
Earlier sketch in CA 33-36R
Bourdier, James A(aron) 1929-1987
Obituary 124
Bourdieu, Pierre 1930-2002 130
Obituary 204
See also CLC 198
Bourdon, David 1934-1998 .... CANR-46
Earlier sketches in CA 37-40R, CANR-13
See also SATA 46
Bourdon, Sylvia Diane Eve 1949- 85-88
Bourdouxhe, Madeleine 1906-1996 171
Boureau, Alain 209
Bouregy, Thomas 1909(?)-1978
Obituary 104
Bouret, Jean 1914- 85-88
Bourgeois, Paulette 1951- CANR-137
Earlier sketch in CA 137
See also SATA 153
Bourget, Paul (Charles Joseph) 1852-1935 .. 196
Brief entry 107
See also DLB 123
See also GFL 1789 to the Present
See also TCLC 12
Bourgholtzer, Frank 1919- 25-28R
Bourguignon, Erika (Eichhorn) 1924- 85-88
Bourinot, Arthur Stanley 1893-1969 159
Bourinot, John George 1837-1902 .... DLB 99
Bourjaily, Monte Ferris 1894-1979 97-100
Obituary 85-88
Bourjaily, Vance (Nye) 1922- CANR-72
Earlier sketches in CA 1-4R, CANR-2
See also CAAS 1
See also CLC 8, 62
See also CN 1, 2, 3, 4, 5, 6, 7
See also DLB 2, 143
See also MAL 5
Bourke, Angela 1952- 199
Bourke, Joanna 195
Bourke, Vernon J(oseph) 1907-1998 ... CANR-3
Earlier sketch in CA 9-12R
Bourke-White, Margaret 1904-1971 ...... CAP-1
Obituary 29-32R
Earlier sketch in CA 13-16
See also AAYA 51
Bourliaguet, Leonce 1895-1965 102
Bourliere, Francois (Marie Gabriel)
1913-1993 159
Brief entry 113
Bourne, Aleck William 1885(?)-1974
Obituary 53-56
Bourne, Charles P. 1931- 9-12R
Bourne, Dorothy D(ulles) 1893-1969(?) . CAP-2
Earlier sketch in CA 23-24
Bourne, Edward Gaylord 1860-1908 186
See also DLB 47
Bourne, Eulalia 97-100
Bourne, Frank Card 1914-1983 .... 17-20R
Bourne, Geoffrey Howard
1909-1988 .... CANR-79
Obituary 126
Earlier sketch in CA 33-36R
Bourne, J(ohn) M. 1949- 124
Bourne, James R. 1897-1973(?) CAP-2
Earlier sketch in CA 21-22
Bourne, Joanna Watkins 1949- 112
Bourne, John
See John, Owen
Bourne, Joyce 1933- 175
Bourne, Kenneth 1930-1992 .... CANR-11
Obituary 140
Earlier sketch in CA 25-28R
Bourne, L(arry) S(tuart) 1939- CANR-56
Earlier sketches in CA 33-36R, CANR-12, 27
Bourne, Lesley
See Marshall, Evelyn
Bourne, Lyle E(ugene), Jr. 1932- 53-56
Bourne, Miriam Anne 1931-1989 ..... CANR-10
Earlier sketch in CA 21-24R, 129
See also SATA 16
See also SATA-Obit 63
Bourne, Peter
See Jeffries, Graham Montague
Bourne, Peter Geoffrey 1939- CANR-64
Earlier sketches in CA 57-60, CANR-7
Bourne, Randolph S(illiman) 1886-1918 155
Brief entry 117
See also AMW
See also DLB 63
See also MAL 5
See also TCLC 16
Bourne, Russell 1928- CANR-141
Earlier sketch in CA 133
Bourne, Ruth (May) 1897-1986 .... 33-36R
Obituary 120
Bourneuf, Alice E. 1912-1980
Obituary 102
Bourniquel, Camille (Rene) 1918- 194
Bournoutian, George A. 1943- 191
Bourque, Antoine
See Brasseaux, Carl A(nthony)
Bourricaud, Francois 1922- CANR-26
Earlier sketch in CA 29-32R
Bourtchouladze, Rusiko 230
Bouscaren, Anthony Trawick 1920- .. CANR-69
Earlier sketches in CA 1-4R, CANR-5
Bouscaren, T(imothy) Lincoln
1884-1971 .... CAP-1
Earlier sketch in CA 11-12
Bousfield, (Gerald) Arthur (Harvey) 1943- .. 213
Bouson, J. Brooks CANR-123
Earlier sketch in CA 151

Cumulative Index 65 Bowman

Bousono, Carlos 1923- 178
See also DLB 108
See also HW 2
Bousquet, Joe 1897-1950 177
See also DLB 72
Bousquet, Marie-Louis Valentin 1887(?)-1975
Obituary 104
Boussard, Jacques Marie 1910- 29-32R
Boustani, Rafic 1942- 141
Boustead, John Edmund Hugh 1895-1980
Obituary 97-100
Boutell, Clarence Burley 1908-1981
Obituary 104
Boutell, Clip
See Boutell, Clarence Burley
Boutelle, Ann Edwards 1943- 131
Boutelle, Sara Holmes
1909(?)-1999 .... CANR-86
Obituary 179
Earlier sketch in CA 130
Boutens, P(ieter) C(ornelis) 1870-1943 193
See also EWL 3
Boutet de Monvel, (Louis) M(aurice)
1850(?)-1913 177
See also CLR 32
See also MAICYA 2
See also MAICYAS 1
See also SATA 30
Boutilier, Mary A(nn) 1943- 105
Boutilier, Robert 1950- 145
Bouton, Gary David 1953- 169
Bouton, James Alan 1939- 89-92
Bouton, Jim
See Bouton, James Alan
Boutros-Ghali, Boutros 1922- 166
See also BW 3
Bouts, Dirk
See Greshoff, Jan
Bouvard, Marguerite Guzman 1937- 149
Bouvier, Emile 1906- 37-40R
Bouvier, Leon F(rancis) 1922- CANR-100
Earlier sketch in CA 105
Bouvier, Nicolas 1929- 153
Bouwsma, William J. 1923-2004 196
Obituary 225
Bova, Ben(jamin William) 1932- CANR-111
Earlier sketches in CA 5-8R, CANR-11, 56, 94
Interview in CANR-11
See also CAAS 18
See also AAYA 16
See also CLC 45
See also CLR 3, 96
See also DLBY 1981
See also MAICYA 1, 2
See also MTCW 1
See also SATA 6, 68, 133
See also SFW 4
Bovaird, Anne E(lizabeth) 1960- 155
See also SATA 90
Bovard, Oliver K. 1872-1945 177
See also DLB 25
Bovasso, Julie 1930-1991 .... 25-28R
See also CAD
See also CWD
Bove, Emmanuel 1898-1945 177
See also DLB 72
Bove, Paul A(nthony) 1949- 125
Bovee, Courtland L(owell) 1944- CANR-27
Earlier sketch in CA 49-52
Bovee, Ruth
See Paine, Lauran (Bosworth)
Bovell, Andrew (John) 1962- 231
See also CD 5, 6
Boven, William 1887(?)-1970
Obituary 104
Bovet, Eric D(avid) 1900-2000 118
Obituary 188
Bovey, John (Alden, Jr.) 1913-2001 107
Bovie, Palmer
See Bovie, Smith Palmer
Bovie, Smith Palmer 1917-1999 238
Bovis, H(enry) Eugene 1928- 29-32R
Bovon, Francois 1938- 199
Bow, Russell 1925- 21-24R
Bowden, Betsy 1948- 107
Bowden, Charles 1945(?)- CANR-120
Earlier sketch in CA 156
Bowden, Edwin T(urner), Jr. 1924- CANR-8
Earlier sketch in CA 13-16R
Bowden, Elbert Victor 1924- CANR-48
Earlier sketches in CA 41-44R, CANR-15
Bowden, Gregory Houston 1948- 41-44R
Bowden, Henry Warner 1939- CANR-27
Earlier sketch in CA 49-52
Bowden, J(ocelyn) J(ean) 1927- 29-32R
Bowden, Jean 1925(?)- CANR-136
Earlier sketches in CA 53-56, CANR-7
See also RHW
Bowden, Jim
See Spence, William John Duncan
See also TCWW 1, 2
Bowden, Joan Chase 1925- 89-92
See also SATA 51
See also SATA-Brief 38
Bowden, Leonard (Walter) 1933-1979 .. 17-20R
Obituary 134
Bowden, Mark 1951- CANR-90
Earlier sketch in CA 148
Bowden, Mary Weatherspoon 1941- 110
Bowden, Roland Heywood 1916- CANR-24
Earlier sketch in CA 106
Bowden, Susan White
See White-Bowden, Susan
Bowder, Diana (Ruth) 1942- 109
Bowditch, James L(owell) 1939- 89-92
Bowdle, Donald N(elson) 1935- 49-52
Bowdler, Roger 1934- 97-100
Bowdring, Paul (Edward) 1946- 135
Bowe, Frank 1947- 104
Bowe, Gabriel P(aul) 1923- 21-24R
Bowe, Kate
See Taylor, Mary Ann
Bowe, (Paul Thomas) Patrick 1945- 106
Bowen, Alexandria Russell 163
See also SATA 97
Bowen, Andy Russell
See Bowen, Alexandria Russell
Bowen, Barbara C(herry) 1937- 37-40R
Bowen, Betty Morgan
See West, Betty
Bowen, Catherine (Shober) Drinker
1897-1973 .... CANR-68
Obituary 45-48
Earlier sketches in CA 5-8R, CANR-15
See also SATA 7
Bowen, Croswell 1905-1971
Obituary 33-36R
Bowen, David
See Bowen, Joshua David
Bowen, Desmond 1921- 33-36R
Bowen, Earl Kenneth 1918- 5-8R
Bowen, Edmund (John) 1898-1980
Obituary 105
Bowen, Elbert Russell 1918- 13-16R
Bowen, Elizabeth (Dorothea Cole)
1899-1973 .... CANR-105
Obituary 41-44R
Earlier sketches in CAP-2, CA 17-18,
CANR-35
See also BRWS 2
See also CDBLB 1945-1960
See also CLC 1, 3, 6, 11, 15, 22, 118
See also CN 1
See also DA3
See also DAM NOV
See also DLB 15, 162
See also EWL 3
See also EXPS
See also FW
See also HGG
See also MTCW 1, 2
See also MTFW 2005
See also NFS 13
See also RGSF 2
See also SSC 3, 28, 66
See also SSFS 5
See also SUFW 1
See also TCLC 148
See also TEA
See also WLIT 4
Bowen, Emrys George 1900-1983
Obituary 111
Bowen, Ezra 1927- 85-88
Bowen, Francis 1811-1890 .... DLB 1, 59, 235
Bowen, Fred 1953- 205
See also SATA 136
Bowen, Gail 1942- CANR-135
Earlier sketch in CA 138
Bowen, Haskell L. 1929- 41-44R
Bowen, Howard R(othmann)
1908-1989 .... CANR-8
Obituary 130
Earlier sketch in CA 21-24R
Bowen, (Ivor) Ian 1908-1984 105
Obituary 115
Bowen, J(ean) Donald 1922- CANR-8
Earlier sketch in CA 17-20R
Bowen, James Keith 1932- 37-40R
Bowen, Jeremy 1960- 239
Bowen, John 1916- 103
See also CBD
Bowen, John (Griffith) 1924- CANR-67
Earlier sketches in CA 1-4R, CANR-2
See also CD 5, 6
See also CN 1, 2, 3, 4, 5, 6, 7
See also DLB 13
Bowen, Joshua David 1930- 105
See also SATA 22
Bowen, Marjorie
See Campbell, (Gabrielle) Margaret (Vere)
See also DLB 153
Bowen, Mary
See Hall, Mary Bowen
Bowen, Michael 1951- 134
Bowen, Peter 1939- 57-60
Bowen, Peter 1945- 229
Bowen, Ralph H(enry) 1919- 69-72
Bowen, Rhys 179
See also Quin-Harkin, Janet
Bowen, Richard M. 1928- 21-24R
Bowen, Robert O. 1920- 9-12R
See also CN 1, 2
Bowen, Robert Sydney 1900-1977 .... CANR-28
Obituary 69-72
Earlier sketch in CA 73-76
See also SATA 52
See also SATA-Obit 21
Bowen, Roger W. 1947- 146
Bowen, Wayne H. 1968- 198
Bowen, Zack (Rhollie) 1934- CANR-120
Earlier sketch in CA 29-32R
Bowen-Judd, Sara (Hutton)
1922-1985 .... CANR-58
Obituary 117
Earlier sketches in CA 9-12R, CANR-5
See also CMW 4
Bower, B(ertha) M(uzzy) 1871-1940 . TCWW 1,
2
Bower, Barbara
See Todd, Barbara Euphan
Bower, David A(llan) 1945- 37-40R
Bower, Donald E(dward) 1920- 77-80
Bower, Eli M(ichael) 1917- 89-92
Bower, Fay Louise 1929- 53-56
Bower, Gordon H(oward) 1932- 17-20R
Bower, John Morton 1942- 143
Bower, Joseph L(yon) 1938- 112
Bower, Julia Wells 1903-1999 .... 41-44R
Bower, Keith
See Beckett, Kenneth A(lbert)
Bower, Louise 1900-1977 .... CAP-2
Earlier sketch in CA 21-22
Bower, Muriel 1921- 49-52
Bower, Robert T(urrell) 1919-1990 .... CANR-27
Obituary 132
Earlier sketch in CA 49-52
Bower, Sharon Anthony 1932- 65-68
Bower, Tom 1946- CANR-72
Earlier sketch in CA 144
Bower, Ursula Violet Graham 1914-1988
Obituary 127
Bower, William Clayton 1878-1982 .... 5-8R
Bowering, George 1935- CANR-10
Earlier sketch in CA 21-24R
See also CAAS 16
See also CLC 15, 47
See also CN 7
See also CP 1, 2, 3, 4, 5, 6, 7
See also DLB 53
Bowering, Marilyn R(uthe) 1949- CANR-49
Earlier sketch in CA 101
See also CLC 32
See also CP 4, 5, 6, 7
See also CWP
Bowermaster, Jon 1954- CANR-113
Earlier sketch in CA 127
See also SATA 77, 135
Bowers, Bathsheba 1671-1718 .... DLB 200
Bowers, C. A. 1935- 29-32R
Bowers, Claude G(ernade) 1878-1958 179
See also DLB 17
Bowers, Edgar 1924-2000 .... CANR-24
Obituary 188
Earlier sketch in CA 5-8R
See also CLC 9
See also CP 1, 2, 3, 4, 5, 6, 7
See also CSW
See also DLB 5
Bowers, Faubion 1917-1999 .... 5-8R
Obituary 186
Bowers, Fredson (Thayer)
1905-1991 .... CANR-48
Obituary 134
Earlier sketches in CA 5-8R, CANR-2
See also DLB 140
See also DLBY 1991
Bowers, George K. 1916- CANR-2
Earlier sketch in CA 1-4R
Bowers, Mrs. J. Milton 1842-1914
See Bierce, Ambrose (Gwinett)
Bowers, Jane Palatini 1945- 145
Bowers, Janice Emily 1950- CANR-93
Earlier sketch in CA 162
Bowers, John 1928- 33-36R
Bowers, John M. 1949- 126
Bowers, John Waite 1935- 41-44R
Bowers, Kenneth S. 1937- 97-100
Bowers, Margaretta K(eller) 1908-1999 .... 5-8R
Bowers, Mary Beacom 1932- 105
Bowers, Neal 1948- CANR-102
Earlier sketches in CA 110, CANR-28, 55
Bowers, Q(uentin) David 1938- CANR-37
Earlier sketches in CA 41-44R, CANR-16
Bowers, Ronald (Lee) 1941- 41-44R
Bowers, Terrell L. 1945- CANR-130
Earlier sketch in CA 168
See also SATA 101
See also TCWW 2
Bowers, Terry
See Bowers, Terrell L.
Bowers, Warner Fremont 1906- 61-64
Bowers, William 1916-1987 102
Obituary 122
Interview in CA-102
Bowers, William J(oseph) 1935- 97-100
Bowers, William L(avalle) 1930-
Brief entry 114
Bowersock, G(len) W(arren) 1936- 81-84
Bowes, Anne LaBastille
See LaBastille, Anne
Bowes, Richard (D.) 238
Bowett, Derek William 1927- CANR-6
Earlier sketch in CA 9-12R
Bowick, Dorothy Mueller
See Mueller, Dorothy
Bowie, Andrew (S.) 1952- 134
Bowie, C. W.
See Old, Wendie C(orbin) and
Wirths, Claudine (Turner) G(ibson)
Bowie, David
See Jones, David Robert
See also CLC 17
Bowie, Janetta (Hamilton) 1907-1996 102
Bowie, Jim
See Norwood, Victor G(eorge) C(harles) and
Stratemeyer, Edward L.
Bowie, Malcolm (McNaughtan)
1943- CANR-105
Earlier sketch in CA 128
Bowie, Norman E. 1942- CANR-29
Earlier sketches in CA 33-36R, CANR-13
Bowie, Robert R(ichardson) 1909- CAP-1
Earlier sketch in CA 11-12
Bowie, Sam
See Ballard, (Willis) Todhunter
Bowie, Walter Russell 1882-1969 .... CANR-3
Earlier sketch in CA 5-8R
Bowker, Francis E. 1917- 41-44R
Bowker, Gordon 1934- CANR-116
Earlier sketches in CA 155, CANR-115
Bowker, John (Westerdale) 1935- CANR-122
Earlier sketches in CA 25-28R, CANR-12
Bowker, Lee Harrington 1940- CANR-25
Earlier sketch in CA 108
Bowker, Margaret 1936- 25-28R
Bowker, R(obin) M(arsland) 1920- 65-68
Bowker, Richard (J.) 1950- 127
Bowkett, Stephen 1953- 134
See also HGG
See also SATA 67
Bowlby, Alex 1924- 237
Bowlby, (Edward) John (Mostyn)
1907-1990 .... CANR-34
Obituary 132
Earlier sketch in CA 49-52
Bowlby, Rachel 1957- CANR-86
Earlier sketch in CA 130
Bowle, John (Edward) 1905-1985 .... CANR-1
Obituary 117
Earlier sketch in CA 1-4R
Bowler, Jan Brett
See Brett, Jan (Churchill)
Bowler, Peter J(ohn) 1944- CANR-122
Earlier sketches in CA 129, CANR-65
Bowler, R(eginald) Arthur 1930- 57-60
Bowler, Tim 1953- CANR-133
Earlier sketch in CA 200
See also MAICYA 2
See also SATA 149
Bowles, Chester (Bliss) 1901-1986 69-72
Obituary 119
Bowles, D(elbert) Richard 1910-1990 ... 33-36R
Bowles, Edmund A(ddison) 1925- CANR-32
Earlier sketch in CA 33-36R
Bowles, Ella Shannon 1886-1975
Obituary 57-60
Bowles, Frank H(amilton) 1907-1975 ... 13-16R
Obituary 57-60
Bowles, George A., Jr. 1924(?)-1986
Obituary 118
Bowles, Gordon Townsend 1904-1991 . CAP-1
Earlier sketch in CA 11-12
Bowles, Jane (Sydney) 1917-1973 .... CAP-2
Obituary 41-44R
Earlier sketch in CA 19-20
See also Bowles, Jane Auer
See also CLC 3, 68
See also CN 1
See also MAL 5
Bowles, Jane Auer
See Bowles, Jane (Sydney)
See also EWL 3
Bowles, John 1938- 106
Bowles, Kerwin
See Abeles, Elvin (V. I.)
Bowles, Norma L(ouise) 77-80
Bowles, Paul (Frederick) 1910-1999 . CANR-75
Obituary 186
Earlier sketches in CA 1-4R, CANR-1, 19, 50
See also CAAS 1
See also AMWS 4
See also CLC 1, 2, 19, 53
See also CN 1, 2, 3, 4, 5, 6
See also DA3
See also DLB 5, 6, 218
See also EWL 3
See also MAL 5
See also MTCW 1, 2
See also MTFW 2005
See also RGAL 4
See also SSC 3
See also SSFS 17
Bowles, Samuel III 1826-1878 .... DLB 43
Bowles, Samuel 1939- 211
Bowles, William Lisle 1762-1850 .... DLB 93
Bowley, Rex Lyon 1925- 103
Bowling, Ann (Patricia) 1951- 113
Bowling, Harry .... RHW
Bowling, Jackson M(ichael) 1934- 5-8R
Bowling, Lewis 1959- 226
Bowling, Tim 1964- 196
Bowlt, John E(llis) 1943- CANR-86
Earlier sketch in CA 130
Bowman, Albert Hall 1921- 41-44R
Bowman, Alfred C(onner) 1904-1982 117
Bowman, Bob
See Bowman, Robert T(urnbull)
Bowman, Bruce 1938- 65-68
Bowman, Buck
See Bowman, J. Wilson
Bowman, Clell Edgar 1904-1984 105
Bowman, Crystal 1951- 165
See also SATA 105
Bowman, David 1957- 140
Bowman, David J. 1919-1993 .... 9-12R
Obituary 142
Bowman, Derek 1931- 102
Bowman, Frank Paul 1927- 33-36R
Bowman, Henry A(delbert) 1903-1977 .. CAP-1
Earlier sketch in CA 13-14
Bowman, Herbert E(ugene) 1917- 65-68
Bowman, J. Wilson CANR-87
Earlier sketch in CA 151
Bowman, James Cloyd 1880-1961 97-100
See also SATA 23
Bowman, Jeanne
See Blocklinger, Peggy O'More
Bowman, John S(tewart) 1931- CANR-41
Earlier sketches in CA 9-12R, CANR-5, 19
See also SATA 16
Bowman, John Wick 1894-1986 .... CANR-6
Earlier sketch in CA 1-4R
Bowman, Karl M. 1888-1973
Obituary 41-44R
Bowman, Kathleen (Gill) 1942- 69-72
See also SATA 52
See also SATA-Brief 40

Bowman, Larry G(ene) 1935-
Brief entry ... 115
Bowman, LeRoy 1887-1971
Obituary ... 33-36R
Bowman, Locke E., Jr. 1927- ... CANR-2
Earlier sketch in CA 5-8R
Bowman, Louise Morey 1882-1944 ... 177
See also DLB 68
Bowman, Marcelle 1914-1989 ... 25-28R
Bowman, Mary D. 1924- ... 25-28R
Bowman, Mary Jean 1908- ... 33-36R
Bowman, Ned A(lan) 1932- ... 41-44R
Bowman, Paul Hoover 1914- ... 33-36R
Bowman, Peter 1917(?)-1985
Obituary ... 114
Bowman, Raymond Albert 1903-1979
Obituary ... 89-92
Bowman, Robert 1928- ... 25-28R
Bowman, Robert T(urnbull) 1910-1984 ... 73-76
Bowman, Shayne 1969- ... 238
Bowman, Sylvia E(dmonia) 1914-1989 ... 1-4R
Bowman, Ward S(imon), Jr. 1911-1992 ... 49-52
Bowmer, Angus L(ivingston) 1904-1979
Obituary ... 85-88
Bown, Deni 1944- ... 154
Bown, Stephen R. ... 236
Bowne, (William) Alan 1945(?)-1989
Obituary ... 130
Bowne, Borden Parker 1847-1919 ... DLB 270
Bowne, Ford
See Brown, Forrest
Bowness, Alan 1928- ... 130
Bowood, Richard
See Daniell, Albert Scott
Bowra, (Cecil) Maurice 1898-1971 .. CANR-69
Obituary ... 29-32R
Earlier sketches in CA 1-4R, CANR-2
Bowring, Richard (John) 1947- ... 114
Bowron, Edgar Peters 1943- ... 130
Bowser, Benjamin P(aul) 1946- ... CANR-116
Earlier sketch in CA 146
Bowser, Eileen 1928- ... CANR-51
Earlier sketches in CA 69-72, CANR-11, 26
Bowser, Frederick P(ark) 1937-1996 ... 49-52
Bowser, Hallowell 1922(?)-1990
Obituary ... 130
Bowser, Joan
See Bowser, Pearl
Bowser, Pearl 1931- ... CANR-113
Earlier sketches in CA 33-36R, CANR-13
Bowskill, Derek 1928- ... CANR-47
Earlier sketches in CA 77-80, CANR-13
Bowyer, (Raymond) Chaz 1926- ... CANR-72
Earlier sketches in CA 93-96, CANR-15, 33
Bowyer, John W(alter) 1921- ... 37-40R
Bowyer, Mathew J(ustice) 1926- ... CANR-13
Earlier sketch in CA 37-40R
Box, Betty 1920-1999 ... IDFW 3
Box, C. J. ... 214
Box, Edgar
See Vidal, (Eugene Luther) Gore
See also GLL 1
Box, John 1920-2005 ... IDFW 3
Box, Muriel 1905-1991 ... 235
Box, Sydney 1907-1983
Obituary ... 109
Boxer, Charles Ralph 1904-2000 ... CANR-72
Obituary ... 190
Earlier sketch in CA 102
Boxer, (Charles) Mark (Edward) 1931-1988
Obituary ... 126
Boxerman, David Samuel 1945- ... 61-64
Boxill, Roger 1928- ... 126
Boxleitner, Bruce 1950- ... 198
Boxman
See Chambliss, William J(oseph)
Boy, Angelo V(ictor) 1929- ... 69-72
Boyajian, Cecile
See Starr, Cecile
Boyars, Arthur 1925- ... CP 1
Boyarsky, Bill 1936- ... 25-28R
Boyatzis, Richard E(leftherios) 1946- ... 209
Boyce, (Joseph) Chris(topher)
1943-1999 ... 73-76
Boyce, David George 1942- ... CANR-93
Earlier sketch in CA 103
Boyce, George A(rthur) 1898- ... 53-56
See also SATA 19
Boyce, Gray Cowan 1899-1981 ... 5-8R
Boyce, Joseph Nelson 1937- ... 102
Boyce, Richard Fyfe 1896-1985 ... 69-72
Obituary ... 116
Boyce, Ronald R(eed) 1931- ... CANR-18
Earlier sketches in CA 9-12R, CANR-3
Boyce Davies, Carole Elizabeth 1947- ... 187
Boycott, Desmond (Lionel) Morse
See Morse-Boycott, Desmond (Lionel)
Boycott, Geoff(rey) 1940- ... CANR-101
Earlier sketch in CA 131
Boycott, Rosie 1951- ... 132
Boyd, Alamo
See Bosworth, Allan R(ucker)
Boyd, Andrew (Kirk Henry)
1920-2003 ... CANR-48
Obituary ... 212
Earlier sketch in CA 1-4R
Boyd, Ann S.
See Schoonmaker, Ann
Boyd, Anne Morris 1884-1974
Obituary ... 113
Boyd, Beverly M(ary) 1925- ... 69-72
Boyd, Blanche M.
See Boyd, Blanche McCrary
Boyd, Blanche McCrary 1945- ... 162
Boyd, Bob
See Boyd, Robert T(hompson)
Boyd, Brian (David) 1952- ... CANR-99
Earlier sketch in CA 139
Boyd, Candy Dawson 1946- ... CANR-81
Earlier sketch in CA 138
See also BW 2, 3
See also CLR 50
See also JRDA
See also MAICYA 2
See also SATA 72
Boyd, Carl 1936- ... 141
Boyd, Carolyn Patricia 1944- ... 112
Boyd, Carse
See Stacton, David (Derek)
Boyd, Claude E. 1939- ... 151
Boyd, Dean (Wallace) ... 5-8R
Boyd, Donna
See Ball, Donna
Boyd, E(lizabeth) 1904(?)-1974
Obituary ... 53-56
Boyd, Edward M. 1927- ... 120
Boyd, Frank
See Kane, Frank
Boyd, Greg 1957- ... 218
Boyd, Gregory A. 1957- ... 219
Boyd, Harper W(hite), Jr. 1917- ... 13-16R
Boyd, Herb 1938- ... CANR-130
Earlier sketch in CA 110
Boyd, J(ohn) Francis 1910-1995 ... 5-8R
Boyd, Jack 1932- ... CANR-86
Earlier sketches in CA 49-52, CANR-34
Boyd, James 1888-1944 ... 186
See also DLB 9
See also DLBD 16
See also RGAL 4
See also RHW
See also TCLC 115
Boyd, James M(oore) 1919- ... 33-36R
Boyd, James S(terling) 1917- ... 49-52
Boyd, Jerry 1930-2002 ... 234
Boyd, John
See Upchurch, Boyd (Bradfield)
See also DLB 8
Boyd, John 1912-2002 ... DLB 310
Boyd, John D. 1916- ... 25-28R
Boyd, Julian P(arks) 1903-1980 ... 65-68
Obituary ... 97-100
Boyd, Malcolm 1923- ... CANR-139
Earlier sketches in CA 5-8R, CANR-4, 26, 51
Interview in ... CANR-26
See also CAAS 11
See also GLL 1
Boyd, (Charles) Malcolm 1932- ... 126
Boyd, Marion M.
See Havighurst, Marion (M.)
Boyd, Martin a Beckett 1893-1972 ... CAP-1
Earlier sketch in CA 13-14
See also CN 1
See also DLB 260
Boyd, Maurice 1921- ... 9-12R
Boyd, Melba Joyce 1950- ... 195
Boyd, Mildred Worthy 1921- ... 17-20R
Boyd, Myron F(enton) 1909-1978 ... 41-44R
Boyd, Nan Alamilla ... 225
Boyd, Nancy
See Millay, Edna St. Vincent
See also GLL 1
Boyd, Neil
See DeRosa, Peter (Clement)
Boyd, Neil 1951- ... 129
Boyd, Pauline
See Schock, Pauline
Boyd, R(obert) L(ewis) F(ullarton)
1922-2004 ... 57-60
Obituary ... 224
Boyd, Robert H. 1912-1997 ... 53-56
Boyd, Robert S. 1928- ... 13-16R
Boyd, Robert T(hompson) 1914-2001 ... 108
Boyd, Robin (Gerard Penleigh)
1919-1971 ... 17-20R
Obituary ... 133
Boyd, Russell 1944- ... IDFW 4
Boyd, Selma
See Acuff, Selma Boyd
Boyd, Shylah 1945- ... 61-64
Boyd, Steven R(ay) 1946- ... 146
Boyd, Sue Abbott 1921- ... CANR-14
Earlier sketch in CA 65-68
Boyd, Thomas (Alexander) 1898-1935 ... 183
Brief entry ... 111
See also DLB 9
See also DLBD 16, 316
See also TCLC 111
Boyd, Waldo T. 1918- ... CANR-12
Earlier sketch in CA 29-32R
See also SATA 18
Boyd, William 1885-1979 ... 41-44R
Obituary ... 135
Boyd, William (Andrew Murray)
1952- ... CANR-131
Brief entry ... 114
Earlier sketches in CA 120, CANR-51, 71
See also CLC 28, 53, 70
See also CN 4, 5, 6, 7
See also DLB 231
Boyd, William C(louser) 1903-1983
Obituary ... 109
Boyd, William Harland 1912- ... CANR-11
Earlier sketch in CA 69-72
Boyd-Carpenter, John (Archibald)
1908-1998 ... 131
Obituary ... 169
Boyden, David D(odge) 1910-1986
Obituary ... 120
Boyden, Donald P. 1957- ... 128
Boyden, Linda 1948- ... 215
See also SATA 143
Boyden, Matthew 1956- ... 194
Boyden, Sarah B. (?)-1989
Obituary ... 128
Boydston, Jo Ann 1924- ... 29-32R
Boye, Alan 1950- ... 189
Boye, Karin
See Boye, Karin Maria
See also DLB 259
See also EWL 3
Boye, Karin Maria 1900-1941 ... 165
See also Boye, Karin
See also GLL 2
See also SFW 4
Boyens, Philippa ... 237
Boyer, Allen B. 1963- ... 228
See also SATA 153
Boyer, Brian D. 1939- ... 45-48
Boyer, Bruce Hatton 1946- ... 101
Boyer, Carl B(enjamin) 1906-1976
Obituary ... 65-68
Boyer, Dwight 1912-1977 ... 65-68
Boyer, Elizabeth (Mary) 1913-2002 ... 81-84
Boyer, Elizabeth H. ... FANT
Boyer, Ernest LeRoy 1928-1995 ... 110
Obituary ... 150
Boyer, G. G.
See Boyer, Glenn G.
Boyer, Glenn G. 1924- ... 130
Boyer, Harold W. 1908-1993 ... 1-4R
Boyer, Jay 1947- ... 147
Boyer, John (William) 1946- ... 103
Boyer, Mildred (Vinson) 1926- ... 112
Boyer, Pascal (Robert) ... 210
Boyer, Paul Samuel 1935- ... CANR-96
Earlier sketches in CA 49-52, CANR-1, 18, 41
Boyer, Richard Edwin 1932- ... 21-24R
Boyer, Richard Lewis 1943- ... CANR-62
Earlier sketches in CA 69-72, CANR-11, 27
Boyer, Richard O. 1903-1973
Obituary ... 45-48
Boyer, Rick
See Boyer, Richard Lewis
Boyer, Robert
See Lake, Kenneth R(obert)
Boyer, Robert E(rnst) 1929- ... 41-44R
See also SATA 22
Boyer, Ruth Gasink 1913-1998 ... 114
Boyer, Sophia Ames 1907(?)-1972
Obituary ... 37-40R
Boyer, William H(arrison) 1924- ... CANR-22
Earlier sketch in CA 106
Boyer, William W., (Jr.) 1923- ... 13-16R
Boyers, Margaret Anne ... CANR-144
Earlier sketch in CA 118
Boyers, Peg
See Boyers, Margaret Anne
Boyers, Peggy
See Boyers, Margaret Anne
Boyers, Robert 1942- ... CANR-4
Earlier sketch in CA 53-56
Boyes, Vivien (Elizabeth) 1952- ... 175
See also SATA 106
Boyesen, Hjalmar Hjorth 1848-1895 ... DLB 12, 71
See also DLBD 13
See also RGAL 4
Boyett, Jimmie T. 1948- ... 149
Boyett, Joseph H. 1945- ... 149
Boyett, Steven R. 1960- ... 154
See also FANT
Boyington, (Gregory) Pappy 1912-1988
Obituary ... 124
Boykin, J. Robert III 1944- ... 225
Boykin, James H(andy) 1914- ... CANR-2
Earlier sketch in CA 5-8R
Boykin, Keith 1965- ... CANR-139
Earlier sketch in CA 156
Boylan, Anne M. 1947- ... 187
Boylan, Bernard R(obert) 1927- ... 127
Boylan, Boyd
See Whiton, James Nelson
Boylan, Brian Richard 1936- ... 81-84
Boylan, Clare (Catherine) 1948- ... 136
See also CN 4, 5, 6, 7
See also DLB 267
Boylan, Eleanor 1916- ... CANR-141
Earlier sketch in CA 132
Boylan, James (Richard) 1927- ... CANR-16
Earlier sketches in CA 1-4R, CANR-1
Boylan, James Finney
See Boylan, Jennifer Finney
Boylan, Jennifer Finney 1958- ... 235
Boylan, Leona Davis 1910- ... 61-64
Boylan, Lucile 1906- ... CAP-1
Earlier sketch in CA 11-12
Boylan, Mary 1913(?)-1984
Obituary ... 112
Boylan, Roger 1951- ... CANR-135
Earlier sketch in CA 183
Boyle, Alistair 1952- ... CANR-142
Earlier sketch in CA 157
Boyle, Andrew (Philip More) 1919-1991 ... 102
Obituary ... 134
Boyle, Ann (Peters) 1916- ... CANR-26
Earlier sketch in CA 29-32R
See also SATA 10
Boyle, Charles 1951- ... CANR-144
Earlier sketch in CA 113
Boyle, David (Courtney) 1958- ... CANR-82
Earlier sketch in CA 133
Boyle, Deirdre 1949- ... CANR-28
Earlier sketch in CA 110
Boyle, Edward Charles Gurney 1923-1981
Obituary ... 108
Boyle, Eleanor Vere (Gordon)
1825-1916 ... SATA 28
Boyle, Freddie M. 1915(?)-1984
Obituary ... 113
Boyle, Gerry 1956- ... CANR-72
Earlier sketch in CA 144
Boyle, Hal
See Boyle, Harold V(incent)
Boyle, Harold V(incent) 1911-1974 ... 101
Obituary ... 89-92
Boyle, Harry Joseph 1915- ... CANR-7
Earlier sketch in CA 13-16R
Boyle, J(ohn) A(ndrew) 1916-1979 ... CANR-9
Obituary ... 85-88
Earlier sketch in CA 61-64
Boyle, Jimmy 1944- ... CANR-89
Earlier sketch in CA 130
Boyle, John Hunter 1930- ... 41-44R
Boyle, John P(hillips) 1931-
Brief entry ... 114
Boyle, Josephine 1935- ... 148
Boyle, (Emily) Joyce 1901- ... CAP-1
Earlier sketch in CA 13-14
Boyle, Kay 1902-1992 ... CANR-110
Obituary ... 140
Earlier sketches in CA 13-16R, CANR-29, 61
See also CAAS 1
See also CLC 1, 5, 19, 58, 121
See also CN 1, 2, 3, 4, 5
See also CP 1, 2, 3, 4
See also DLB 4, 9, 48, 86
See also DLBY 1993
See also EWL 3
See also MAL 5
See also MTCW 1, 2
See also MTFW 2005
See also RGAL 4
See also RGSF 2
See also SSC 5
See also SSFS 10, 13, 14
Boyle, (C.) Kevin 1943- ... CANR-50
Earlier sketch in CA 123
Boyle, Kevin 1960- ... 239
Boyle, Leonard E(ugene) 1923-1999 ... 127
Boyle, Mark
See Kienzle, William X(avier)
Boyle, Mary 1882(?)-1975
Obituary ... 53-56
Boyle, Nicholas 1946- ... CANR-101
Earlier sketch in CA 140
Boyle, Patrick 1905-1982 ... 127
See also CLC 19
Boyle, Richard J(ohn) 1932- ... 129
Boyle, Robert 1910- ... IDFW 3, 4
Boyle, Robert (Richard) 1915- ... 13-16R
Boyle, Robert H. 1928- ... CANR-12
Earlier sketch in CA 17-20R
See also SATA 65
Boyle, Roger 1621-1679 ... DLB 80
See also RGEL 2
Boyle, Samuel J. III 1920-1985
Obituary ... 118
Boyle, Sarah Patton 1906-1994 ... CAP-1
Obituary ... 144
Earlier sketch in CA 13-16
Boyle, Stanley E(ugene) 1927- ... 41-44R
Boyle, T. C.
See Boyle, T(homas) Coraghessan
See also AMWS 8
Boyle, T(homas) Coraghessan
1948- ... CANR-132
Earlier sketches in CA 120, CANR-44, 76, 89
See also Boyle, T. C.
See also AAYA 47
See also BEST 90:4
See also BPFB 1
See also CLC 36, 55, 90
See also CN 6, 7
See also CPW
See also DA3
See also DAM POP
See also DLB 218, 278
See also DLBY 1986
See also EWL 3
See also MAL 5
See also MTCW 2
See also MTFW 2005
See also SSC 16
See also SSFS 13, 19
Boyle, Ted Eugene 1933- ... 21-24R
Boyle, Thomas 1939- ... CANR-44
Earlier sketch in CA 118
Boyle, Thomas A. 1922- ... 161
Boyle, Timm
See Boyle, Timothy R(obert)
Boyle, Timothy R(obert) 1953- ... 118
Boylen, Margaret Currier 1921-1967 ... 1-4R
Obituary ... 103
Boyles, C(larence) S(cott), Jr.
1905-1995 ... CANR-64
Earlier sketch in CA 1-4R
See also Brown, Will C.
Boyles, Denis 1946- ... 140
Boyll, (James) Randall 1962- ... 232
See also HGG
Boylston, Helen Dore 1895-1984 ... CANR-21
Obituary ... 113
Earlier sketch in CA 73-76
See also CWRI 5
See also MAICYA 1, 2
See also SATA 23
See also SATA-Obit 39
Boym, Svetlana 1959- ... 139
Boyne, Daniel J. 1959- ... 202
Boyne, Walter J(ames) 1929- ... CANR-136
Earlier sketch in CA 107
Boynton, Lewis Delano 1909- ... CANR-6
Earlier sketch in CA 5-8R
Boynton, Peter S. 1920(?)-1971
Obituary ... 104

Cumulative Index 67 Bradley

Boynton, Robert W(hitney) 1921-
Brief entry 117
Boynton, Sandra (Keith) 1953- CANR-136
Earlier sketches in CA 126, CANR-53
See also MAICYA 2
See also SATA 57, 107, 152
See also SATA-Brief 38
Boynton, Searles Roland 1926- 77-80
Boyriven, Mariette Hartley
See Hartley, Mariette
Boysson-Bardies, Benedicte
See de Boysson-Bardies, Benedicte
Boyum, Joy Gould 1934- 33-36R
Boyum, Keith O(rel) 1945- 102
Boz
See Dickens, Charles (John Huffam)
Boz, George R.
See Rosenbaum, Ron
Boza, Maria del Carmen 1952- 185
Bozarth-Campbell, Alla (Linda Renee)
1947- 105
Boze, Arthur Phillip 1945- 57-60
Bozell, L. Brent III 1925- 237
Bozeman, Adda B(ruemmer)
1908-1994 .... CANR-3
Earlier sketch in CA 5-8R
Bozeman, Theodore Dwight 1942- 85-88
Bozic, Mirko 1919- .... DLB 181
Bozzetto, Bruno 1938- .... IDFW 3, 4
Braasch, William Frederick 1878-1975 . CAP-2
Earlier sketch in CA 29-32
Braaten, Carl E. 1929- 219
Brabazon, James
See Seth-Smith, Leslie James
Brabb, George J(acob) 1925- 41-44R
Brabec, Barbara 1937- CANR-65
Earlier sketches in CA 93-96, CANR-15, 32
Brabson, George Dana 1900-1999 .... CAP-1
Earlier sketch in CA 19-20
Brace, Edward Roy 1936- CANR-19
Earlier sketch in CA 102
Brace, Geoffrey (Arthur) 1930- CANR-11
Earlier sketch in CA 69-72
Brace, Gerald Warner 1901-1978 .... CANR-71
Obituary 81-84
Earlier sketch in CA 13-16R
Brace, Paul (R.) 1954- 145
Brace, Richard Munthe 1915-1977 .. CANR-15
Obituary 69-72
Earlier sketch in CA 1-4R
Brace, Timothy
See Pratt, Theodore
Braceairdle, Cyril 1920- 45-48
Bracegirdle, Brian 1933- 101
Braceland, Francis J(ames) 1900-1985
Obituary 115
Bracewell, Michael 1958- CANR-129
Earlier sketch in CA 135
Bracewell, Ronald N(ewbold) 1921- 57-60
Bracewell-Milnes, (John) Barry
1931- CANR-37
Earlier sketches in CA 33-36R, CANR-13
Bracey, Howard E(dwin) 1905- 13-16R
Bracey, John H(enry, Jr.) 1941- 29-32R
Brach, Gerard 1927- 138
Brach, Tara 226
Bracher, Frederick (George) 1905- 111
Bracher, Karl Dietrich 1922- CANR-40
Earlier sketches in CA 45-48, CANR-1, 17
Bracher, Marjory (Louise) 1906- CAP-1
Earlier sketch in CA 13-16
Brack, Harold Arthur 1923- 17-20R
Brack, O M, Jr. 1938- 41-44R
Brack, Vektris
See Humphrys, Leslie George
Brack, William Dennis 1939- 136
Brackbill, Yvonne 1928- 21-24R
Brackeen, Steve
See Farris, John
Bracken, Charles
See Pellowski, Michael (Joseph)
Bracken, Dorothy K(endall) 21-24R
Bracken, James K. 1952- 142
Bracken, Joseph Andrew 1930- 37-40R
Bracken, Len 1961- CANR-125
Earlier sketch in CA 166
Bracken, Paul 1948- 115
Bracken, Peg 1920- CANR-6
Earlier sketch in CA 1-4R
Brackenbury, Alison 1953- 136
See also CP 7
See also CWP
See also DLB 40
Brackenridge, Hugh Henry
1748-1816 .... DLB 11, 37
See also RGAL 4
Brackenridge, R(obert) Douglas 1932- 101
Bracker, Jon 1936- 17-20R
Brackers de Hugo, Pierre 1960- 186
See also SATA 115
Brackett, Charles 1892-1969
Obituary 113
See also DLB 26
See also IDFW 3, 4
Brackett, Dolli Tingle 1911-1993 .... CANR-10
Earlier sketch in CA 25-28R
See also SATA 137
Brackett, Leigh (Douglass)
1915-1978 .... CANR-1
Obituary 77-80
Earlier sketch in CA 1-4R
See also DLB 8, 26
See also IDFW 3, 4
See also SFW 4
See also SUFW 1
Brackett, Peter
See Collins, Max Allan, (Jr.)
Brackett, Virginia (Roberts Meredith)
1950- 192
See also SATA 121
Brackman, Arnold C(harles)
1923-1983 .... CANR-2
Obituary 111
Earlier sketch in CA 5-8R
See also AITN 1
Brackman, Barbara 1945- CANR-141
Earlier sketch in CA 146
Brackney, William (Henry) 1948- CANR-50
Earlier sketch in CA 123
Bracy, Ihsan 1957(?)- 239
Bracy, William 1915- 61-64
Bradbrook, M(uriel) C(lara)
1909-1993 .... CANR-80
Obituary 141
Earlier sketches in CA 13-16R, CANR-7, 23
Bradburn, Norman M. 1933- CANR-13
Earlier sketch in CA 37-40R
Bradburne, E(lizabeth) S. 1915- 25-28R
Bradbury, Bianca (Ryley)
1908-1982 .... CANR-37
Earlier sketches in CA 13-16R, CANR-5
See also MAICYA 1, 2
See also SATA 3, 56
Bradbury, Dorothy E(dith) 1902-1984
Obituary 113
Bradbury, Edward P.
See Moorcock, Michael (John)
See also MTCW 2
Bradbury, Jim 1937- 140
Bradbury, John M(ason) 1908-1969 .... CAP-1
Earlier sketch in CA 13-16
Bradbury, Katharine L(orraine) 1946- 111
Bradbury, Malcolm (Stanley)
1932-2000 .... CANR-137
Earlier sketches in CA 1-4R, CANR-1, 33, 91, 98
See also CLC 32, 61
See also CN 1, 2, 3, 4, 5, 6, 7
See also CP 1
See also DA3
See also DAM NOV
See also DLB 14, 207
See also EWL 3
See also MTCW 1, 2
See also MTFW 2005
Bradbury, Parnell 1904- 13-16R
Bradbury, Peggy 1930- 65-68
Bradbury, Ray (Douglas) 1920- CANR-125
Earlier sketches in CA 1-4R, CANR-2, 30, 75
See also AAYA 15
See also AITN 1, 2
See also AMWS 4
See also BPFB 1
See also BYA 4, 5, 11
See also CDALB 1968-1988
See also CLC 1, 3, 10, 15, 42, 98
See also CN 1, 2, 3, 4, 5, 6, 7
See also CPW
See also DA
See also DA3
See also DAB
See also DAC
See also DAM MST, NOV, POP
See also DLB 2, 8
See also EXPN
See also EXPS
See also HGG
See also LAIT 3, 5
See also LATS 1:2
See also LMFS 2
See also MAL 5
See also MTCW 1, 2
See also MTFW 2005
See also NFS 1, 22
See also RGAL 4
See also RGSF 2
See also SATA 11, 64, 123
See also SCFW 1, 2
See also SFW 4
See also SSC 29, 53
See also SSFS 1, 20
See also SUFW 1, 2
See also TUS
See also WLC
See also YAW
Bradby, Marie 237
See also SATA 161
Bradby, Tom 1967- 228
Braddock, Joseph (Edward) 1902-
Brief entry 117
Braddock, Richard R(eed) 1920-1974 .... 1-4R
Obituary 103
Braddon, George
See Milkomane, George Alexis Milkomanovich
Braddon, Mary Elizabeth 1837-1915 179
Brief entry 108
See also BRWS 8
See also CMW 4
See also DLB 18, 70, 156
See also HGG
See also TCLC 111
Braddon, Russell (Reading)
1921-1995 .... CANR-71
Obituary 148
Earlier sketches in CA 1-4R, CANR-2
Braddy, Haldeen 1908-1980 .... 17-20R
Obituary 101
Brade-Birks, S(tanley) Graham
1887-1982 .... CAP-1
Earlier sketch in CA 13-16
Braden, Charles Samuel 1887-?2000 .... 5-8R
Braden, Donna R. 1953- CANR-90
Earlier sketch in CA 130
Braden, Gordon 1947- 198
Braden, Irene A.
See Hoadley, Irene Braden
Braden, Spruille 1894-1978
Obituary 115
Braden, Thomas (Wardell) 1918-
Brief entry 113
Braden, Tom
See Braden, Thomas (Wardell)
Braden, Waldo W(arder) 1911-1991 ... CANR-5
Earlier sketch in CA 5-8R
Braden, William 1930- 21-24R
Bradfield, Carl 1942- .... SATA 91
Bradfield, James McComb 1917- 5-8R
Bradfield, Jolly Roger
See Bradfield, Roger
Bradfield, Nancy 1913- 29-32R
Bradfield, Richard 1896-1981 .... CAP-2
Earlier sketch in CA 23-24
Bradfield, Roger 1924- 17-20R
Bradfield, Scott (Michael) 1955- CANR-90
Earlier sketch in CA 147
See also HGG
See also SSC 65
See also SUFW 2
Bradford, Adam M.D.
See Wassersug, Joseph D.
Bradford, Alex 1927-1978
Obituary 112
Bradford, Andrew 1686-1742 .... DLB 43, 73
Bradford, Ann (Liddell) 1917-
Brief entry 116
See also SATA 56
See also SATA-Brief 38
Bradford, Arthur 1969- 209
Bradford, Barbara Taylor 1933- CANR-98
Earlier sketches in CA 89-92, CANR-32, 56
See also BEST 89:1
See also CPW
See also DA3
See also DAM POP
See also MTCW 1
See also RHW
See also SATA 66
Bradford, Benjamin 1925- CANR-47
Earlier sketch in CA 85-88
Bradford, David F(rantz) 1939-2005 124
Obituary 236
Bradford, Dennis E(arle) 1946- 118
Bradford, Ernle (Dusgate Selby)
1922-1986 .... CANR-68
Obituary 119
Earlier sketch in CA 101
Bradford, Gamaliel 1863-1932 160
See also DLB 17
See also TCLC 36
Bradford, James C(hapin) 1945- CANR-29
Earlier sketch in CA 111
Bradford, John 1749-1830 .... DLB 43
Bradford, Karleen 1936- CANR-127
Earlier sketches in CA 112, CANR-67
See also SATA 48, 96
See also YAW
Bradford, Leland P(owers)
1905-1981 .... CANR-9
Earlier sketch in CA 13-16R
Bradford, Leroy 1922- 105
Bradford, Lois J(ean) 1936- 104
See also SATA 36
Bradford, M(elvin) E(ustace)
1934-1993 .... CANR-46
Obituary 140
Earlier sketches in CA 77-80, CANR-13
Bradford, Patience Andrewes 1918- 33-36R
Bradford, Peter Amory 1942- 61-64
Bradford, Reed H(oward) 1912-1994 49-52
Bradford, Richard (Roark)
1932-2002 .... CANR-64
Obituary 209
Earlier sketches in CA 49-52, CANR-2
See also LAIT 4
See also SATA 59
See also SATA-Obit 135
See also TCWW 1, 2
Bradford, Richard H(eadlee) 1938- 89-92
Bradford, Roark (Whitney Wickliffe)
1896-1948 162
See also DLB 86
See also RGAL 4
Bradford, Robert W(hitmore) 1918- 77-80
Bradford, Roy Hamilton 1920-1998 109
Obituary 170
Bradford, S. W.
See Battin, B(rinton) W(arner)
Bradford, Sarah (Mary Malet)
1938- CANR-109
Earlier sketches in CA 128, CANR-60, 65
Bradford, Sax(ton) 1907-1966 .... 1-4R
Bradford, Will
See Paine, Lauran (Bosworth)
Bradford, William III 1722-1791 .... DLB 43, 73
Bradford, William 1590-1657 .... DLB 24, 30
See also RGAL 4
Bradford, William C(astle) 1910- 9-12R
Brading, D. A. 1936- CANR-122
Earlier sketch in CA 136
Bradlaugh, Charles 1833-1891 .... DLB 57
Bradlee, Benjamin C(rowninshield)
1921- 61-64
See also AITN 2
Bradlee, Frederic 1920-2003 .... 21-24R
Obituary 218
Bradlee, Frederic 1920-2003
Obituary 218
Bradley, Alfred 1925-1991 105
Obituary 134
Bradley, Bert E(dward) 1926- 41-44R
Bradley, Bill
See Bradley, William Warren
Bradley, Brigitte L(ooke) 1924- 37-40R
Bradley, C. Paul 1918- 106
Bradley, Celeste 237
Bradley, Concho
See Paine, Lauran (Bosworth)
Bradley, David (Henry), Jr. 1950- CANR-81
Earlier sketches in CA 104, CANR-26
See also BLC 1
See also BW 1, 3
See also CLC 23, 118
See also CN 4, 5, 6, 7
See also DAM MULT
See also DLB 33
Bradley, David G. 1916- 13-16R
Bradley, Duane
See Sanborn, Duane
Bradley, Ed 1911(?)-1983
Obituary 110
Bradley, Ed(ward R.) 1941- 113
Brief entry 108
Interview in CA-113
See also BW 1
Bradley, Edwin M(cKinley) 1958- 158
Bradley, Erwin S(tanley) 1906- CAP-2
Earlier sketch in CA 33-36
Bradley, F. H. 1846-1924 .... DLB 262
Bradley, George 1953- CANR-113
Earlier sketch in CA 134
Bradley, Harold Whitman 1903-1990 ... 33-36R
Bradley, Hassell 1930- 65-68
Bradley, Helen G(enevieve) 1932- 112
Bradley, Ian (Campbell) 1950- CANR-123
Earlier sketch in CA 103
Bradley, James 1967- 190
Bradley, James E. 1944- 136
Bradley, James V(andiver) 1924- 37-40R
Bradley, Jerry (Wayne) 1948- 137
Bradley, John (Francis Nejez) 1930- . CANR-10
Earlier sketch in CA 25-28R
Bradley, John Ed(mund, Jr.) 1958- CANR-99
Earlier sketch in CA 139
See also CLC 55
See also CN 6, 7
See also CSW
Bradley, John Lewis 1917- 29-32R
Bradley, Joseph (C., Jr.) 1945- 207
Bradley, Joseph F(rancis) 1917- 21-24R
Bradley, Katherine Harris 1846-1914
See Field, Michael
Bradley, Kenneth (Granville)
1904-1977 .... CAP-1
Earlier sketch in CA 13-14
Bradley, Kimberly Brubaker 1967- .... AAYA 59
Bradley, Marion Zimmer
1930-1999 .... CANR-107
Obituary 185
Earlier sketches in CA 57-60, CANR-7, 31, 51, 75
See also Chapman, Lee and
Dexter, John and
Gardner, Miriam and
Ives, Morgan and
Rivers, Elfrida
See also CAAS 10
See also AAYA 40
See also BPFB 1
See also CLC 30
See also CPW
See also DA3
See also DAM POP
See also DLB 8
See also FANT
See also FW
See also MTCW 1, 2
See also MTFW 2005
See also SATA 90, 139
See also SATA-Obit 116
See also SFW 4
See also SUFW 2
See also YAW
Bradley, Marjorie D. 1931- 25-28R
Bradley, Matt 1947- 105
Bradley, Melanie (Rose) Choukas
See Choukas-Bradley, Melanie (Rose)
Bradley, Michael
See Blumberg, Gary
Bradley, Michael 1944- 129
Bradley, Omar Nelson 1893-1981
Obituary 103
Bradley, Patricia 1941- 193
Bradley, Preston 1888-1983
Obituary 110
Bradley, R. C. 1929-1995 .... CANR-14
Earlier sketch in CA 33-36R
Bradley, Richard 1961- 237
Bradley, Ritamary 1916- 49-52
Bradley, Robert A(ustin) 1917- 21-24R
Bradley, Sam(uel McKee) 1917-1998 .... 21-24R
See also CP 1
Bradley, (Edward) Sculley 1897-1987 89-92
Bradley, Shelley 1968- 217
Bradley, Thomas Iver 1954- 218
Bradley, Tom
See Bradley, Thomas Iver
Bradley, Van Allen 1913-1984 .... 37-40R
Obituary 114
Bradley, Virginia 1912- CANR-8
Earlier sketch in CA 61-64
See also SATA 23
Bradley, Will
See Strickland, (William) Brad(ley)
Bradley, William 1934- 45-48
Bradley, William Aspenwall 1878-1939 193
Brief entry 107
See also DLB 4

Bradley 68 CONTEMPORARY AUTHORS

Bradley, William L(ee) 1918- 21-24R
Bradley, William Warren 1943- CANR-55
Earlier sketch in CA 101
Bradlow, Edna Rom CAP-1
Earlier sketch in CA 9-10
Bradlow, Frank R(osslyn)
1913-2000 .... CANR-13
Earlier sketches in CAP-1, CA 9-10
Bradman, Tony 1954- CANR-136
Earlier sketches in CA 149, CANR-78
See also CWRI 5
See also SATA 81, 152
Bradner, Enos 1892-1984 57-60
Obituary 111
Bradshaw, Anne C. 1942- 239
Bradshaw, Brendan 1937- 73-76
Bradshaw, Buck
See Paine, Lauran (Bosworth)
Bradshaw, George 1909(?)-1973
Obituary 45-48
Bradshaw, Gillian (Joan) 1949- .... SATA 118
Bradshaw, Gillian (Marucha) 1956- .. CANR-93
Earlier sketches in CA 103, CANR-58
See also BPFB 1
See also FANT
See also SATA 127
Bradshaw, Henry 1831-1886 .... DLB 184
Bradshaw, John 1933- CANR-61
Earlier sketch in CA 138
See also CLC 70
Bradshaw, Jon (Wayne) 1937-1986 145
Obituary 121
Bradshaw, Michael 1935- 143
Bradshaw, Terry (Paxton) 1948- CANR-110
Earlier sketch in CA 111
Bradshaw, Thornton F(rederick)
1917-1988 108
Bradshaw, Timothy 1950- 170
Bradsher, Henry S(t. Amant) 1931- 133
Bradsher, Keith (Vinson) 1964- 228
Bradstock, Andrew (William) 1955- 127
Bradstreet, Anne 1612(?)-1672 .... AMWS 1
See also CDALB 1640-1865
See also DA
See also DA3
See also DAC
See also DAM MST, POET
See also DLB 24
See also EXPP
See also FW
See also PC 10
See also PFS 6
See also RGAL 4
See also TUS
See also WP
Bradstreet, T. J.
See Thesman, Jean
Bradstreet, Vallerie
See Roby, Mary Linn
Bradt, A(cken) Gordon 1896-1983 57-60
Obituary 110
Bradunas, Kazys 1917- .... DLB 220
Bradwardine, Thomas 1295(?)-1349 ... DLB 115
Bradway, Becky 1957- 238
Bradway, John S(aeger) 1890-1985 .... CAP-2
Earlier sketch in CA 33-36
Bradwell, James
See Kent, Arthur William Charles
Brady, Alexander 1896-1985
Obituary 117
Brady, Ann 1947- 138
Brady, Catherine 1955- 232
Brady, Charles Andrew 1912-1995 .... 5-8R
Brady, Darlene A(nn) 1951- 102
Brady, Dave 1913(?)-1988
Obituary 125
Brady, David W(illiam) 1940-
Brief entry 114
Brady, Esther Wood 1905-1987 93-96
Obituary 123
See also SATA 31
See also SATA-Obit 53
Brady, Frank 1924-1986 .... 13-16R
Obituary 120
See also DLB 111
Brady, Frank 1934- CANR-9
Earlier sketch in CA 61-64
Brady, Gene P(aul) 1927- 107
Brady, George Stuart 1887-1977
Obituary 73-76
Brady, Gerald Peter 1929- 5-8R
Brady, Ian 1938- 223
Brady, Ignatius Charles 1911-1990 113
Brady, Irene 1943- CANR-20
Earlier sketch in CA 33-36R
See also SATA 4
Brady, James (Winston) 1928- CANR-93
Earlier sketches in CA 101, CANR-21
Brady, James B. 1939- 143
Brady, Jane 1934- 181
Brief entry 113
Brady, Joan 1939- 141
See also CLC 86
Brady, John (Joseph) 1942- CANR-113
Earlier sketches in CA 65-68, CANR-10
Brady, John (Mary) 1955- CANR-53
Earlier sketch in CA 130
Brady, John Paul 1928- CANR-5
Earlier sketch in CA 13-16R
Brady, Kathleen 1947- 129
Brady, Kimberley S(mith) 1953- 168
See also SATA 101
Brady, Kristin 1949- 109
Brady, Leo 1917-1984 69-72
Obituary 114
Brady, Lillian 1902- 105
See also SATA 28
Brady, Mary Lou 1937- 106
Brady, Maureen 1943- 112
Brady, Maxine L. 1941- 69-72
Brady, Michael 1928- 93-96
Brady, Nicholas
See Levinson, Leonard
Brady, Patricia 1943- 136
Brady, Patrick 1933- 191
Brady, Peter
See Daniels, Norman
Brady, Rose 1956- 235
Brady, Sally Ryder 1939- 103
Brady, Taylor
See Ball, Donna
Brady, Terence 1939- 106
Brady, William S.
See Harvey, John (Barton)
Brady, William S.
See Wells, Angus
Braeker, Ulrich 1735-1798 .... DLB 94
Braenne, Berit 1918- 21-24R
Braestrup, Carl Bjorn 1897-1982
Obituary 107
Braestrup, Peter 1929-1997 97-100
Obituary 160
Braff, Allan James 1930- 108
Braff, Joshua 1967- 237
Braffet, Kelly 1976- 239
Braga, Newton C. 1946- 217
Braga, Rubem 1913-1990 .... DLB 307
Braganti, Nancy (Sue) 1941- CANR-40
Earlier sketch in CA 117
Bragdon, Clifford R(ichardson) 1940- 57-60
Bragdon, Elspeth MacDuffie
1897-1980 .... CANR-5
Earlier sketch in CA 5-8R
See also SATA 6
Bragdon, Henry Wilkinson
1906-1980 .... CANR-3
Obituary 97-100
Earlier sketch in CA 5-8R
Bragdon, Kathleen J. 163
Bragdon, Lillian Jacot 73-76
See also SATA 24
Brager, Bruce L. 1949- 220
See also SATA 146
Bragg, Arthur N(orris) 1897-1968 .... CAP-1
Earlier sketch in CA 17-18
Bragg, Bill
See Bragg, William Fredrick, Jr.
Bragg, Dobby
See Sykes, Roosevelt
Bragg, George Freeman, Jr. 1863-1940 205
Bragg, Mabel Caroline 1870-1945 ...... SATA 24
Bragg, Melvyn 1939- CANR-89
Earlier sketches in CA 57-60, CANR-10, 48
See also BEST 89:3
See also CLC 10
See also CN 1, 2, 3, 4, 5, 6, 7
See also DLB 14, 271
See also RHW
Bragg, Michael 1948- 128
See also SATA 46
Bragg, Richard Geoffrey 1909-1998 121
Bragg, Rick 1959- CANR-137
Earlier sketches in CA 165, CANR-112
See also MTFW 2005
Bragg, Ruth Gembicki 1943- .... SATA 77
Bragg, Sir William Henry
See Bragg, William Henry
Bragg, Steven M. 1960- 162
Bragg, W(illiam) F(rederick)
1892-1967 .... TCWW 1, 2
Bragg, Sir W. H.
See Bragg, William Henry
Bragg, Sir William
See Bragg, William Henry
Bragg, William Fredrick, Jr. 1922- 109
Bragg, William Henry 1862-1942 155
Brief entry 123
Bragg, William Lawrence 1890-1971 155
Obituary 115
Braggin, Mary Vetterling
See Vetterling-Braggin, Mary (Katherine)
Braginsky, Vladimir B. 1931- 145
Braham, Allan (John Witney) 1937- 105
Braham, (E.) Jeanne 1940- CANR-143
Earlier sketch in CA 150
Braham, Randolph L(ewis) 1922- ... CANR-105
Earlier sketches in CA 1-4R, CANR-5, 19, 41
Brahe, Tycho 1546-1601 .... DLB 300
Brahm, Sumishta 1954- .... SATA 58
Brahms, Caryl
See Abrahams, Doris Caroline
Brahs, Stuart J(ohn) 1940- 57-60
Brahtz, John F(rederick) Peel 1918-1996 . 73-76
Braider, Donald 1923-1976 .... CAP-2
Obituary 65-68
Earlier sketch in CA 33-36
Braidwood, Robert John 1907-2003 108
Obituary 212
Braiker, Harriet B. 1948-2004 141
Obituary 226
Brailsford, Dennis 1925- 218
Brailsford, Frances
See Wosmek, Frances
Braimah, Joseph Adam 1916- 61-64
Braiman, Susan 1943- 97-100
Brain, George B(ernard) 1920- 41-44R
Brain, J(oy) B(lundell) 1926- CANR-41
Earlier sketch in CA 118
Brain, James Lewton
See Lewton-Brain, James
Brain, Joseph J. 1920- 13-16R
Brain, Robert 1933- 73-76
Brainard, Cecilia Manguerra 1947- 146
Brainard, Harry Gray 1907-1996 .... 1-4R
Brainard, Joe 1942-1994 .... CANR-12
Obituary 145
Earlier sketch in CA 65-68
Braine, David 1940- 155
Braine, John (Gerard) 1922-1986 ..... CANR-33
Obituary 120
Earlier sketches in CA 1-4R, CANR-1
See also CDBLB 1945-1960
See also CLC 1, 3, 41
See also CN 1, 2, 3, 4
See also DLB 15
See also DLBY 1986
See also EWL 3
See also MTCW 1
Brainerd, Barron 1928- 33-36R
Brainerd, Charles Jon 1944- 103
Brainerd, John W(hiting) 1918- 57-60
See also SATA 65
Braithwaite, Althea 1940- CANR-18
Earlier sketch in CA 97-100
See also SAAS 24
See also SATA 23
See also SATA-Essay 119
Braithwaite, (Eustace) E(dward) R(icardo)
1920- CANR-25
Earlier sketch in CA 106
See also BW 1
See also CN 1
Braithwaite, Kenneth James
See Barrow, Kenneth
Braithwaite, Max 1911-1995 93-96
Braithwaite, Richard Bevan 1900-1990
Obituary 131
Braithwaite, William Stanley (Beaumont)
1878-1962 125
See also BLC 1
See also BW 1
See also DAM MULT
See also DLB 50, 54
See also HR 1:2
See also MAL 5
See also PC 52
Brake, Laurel 1941- 138
Brake, Mike 1936- 93-96
Brakel, Samuel J(ohannes) 1943- 33-36R
Brakhage, (James) Stanley
1933-2003 .... CANR-96
Obituary 214
Earlier sketches in CA 41-44R, CANR-15
Brakman, Willem 1922- 194
Bralver, Eleanor 1913- 97-100
Braly, Malcolm 1925-1980 .... CANR-12
Obituary 97-100
Earlier sketch in CA 17-20R
Bram, Chris
See Bram, Christopher
Bram, Christopher 1952- CANR-86
Earlier sketch in CA 126
See also GLL 1
Bram, Elizabeth 1948- CANR-9
Earlier sketch in CA 65-68
See also SATA 30
Bram, Joseph 1904-1974
Obituary 110
Bramah, Ernest 1868-1942 156
See also CMW 4
See also DLB 70
See also FANT
See also TCLC 72
Bramall, Eric 1927- 9-12R
Braman, Sandra 1951- 114
Bramann, Jorn K(arl) 1938- CANR-43
Earlier sketch in CA 119
Brambell, Wilfrid 1912-1985 113
Brambeus, Baron
See Senkovsky, Osip Ivanovich
Bramble, Forbes 1939- 89-92
Brame, Charles L. 1926- 169
Brameld, Theodore (Burghard Hurt)
1904-1987 .... 17-20R
Obituary 123
Bramer, Jennie (Perkins) 1900-1983 ...... CAP-1
Earlier sketch in CA 13-14
Bramer, John C(onrad) Jr. 1924- 1-4R
Bramesco, Norton J. 1924- 106
Bramlett, John
See Pierce, John Leonard, Jr.
Bramly, Serge 1949- 142
Brammell, P(aris) Roy 1900-1996 65-68
Brammer, Billy Lee
See Brammer, William
Brammer, Lawrence M(artin) 1922- 13-16R
Brammer, William 1929-1978 235
Obituary 77-80
See also CLC 31
Brampton, Sally (Jane) 1955- 171
Brams, Stanley Howard 1910-1999 .... 9-12R
Brams, Steven J(ohn) 1940- CANR-52
Earlier sketches in CA 61-64, CANR-10, 26
Bramsch, Joan 1936- 122
Bramson, Leon 1930- CANR-4
Earlier sketch in CA 1-4R
Bramson, Robert M(ark) 1925- CANR-54
Earlier sketches in CA 108, CANR-25
Bramson, Susan (Jane) 1940- 128
Bramwell, Charlotte
See Kimbro, John M.
Bramwell, Dana G. 1948- 57-60
Bramwell, James Guy 1911- 9-12R
Bramwell-Booth, Catherine 1883-1987
Obituary 123
Branagan, Thomas 1774-1843 .... DLB 37
Branagh, Kenneth 1960- 156
See also AAYA 20, 59
Brana-Shute, Gary 1945- 111
Branca, Albert A. 1916- 13-16R
Branca, Vittore (Felice Giovanni)
1913- CANR-114
Earlier sketch in CA 154
Brancaccio, David 198
Brancaforte, Benito 1934- 37-40R
Brancati, Vitaliano 1907-1954
Brief entry 109
See also DLB 264
See also EWL 3
See also TCLC 12
Brancato, Gilda 1949- 107
Brancato, Robin F(idler) 1936- CANR-45
Earlier sketches in CA 69-72, CANR-11
See also AAYA 9
See also BYA 6
See also CLC 35
See also CLR 32
See also JRDA
See also MAICYA 2
See also MAICYAS 1
See also SAAS 9
See also SATA 97
See also WYA
See also YAW
Branch, Alan E(dward) 1933- CANR-101
Earlier sketches in CA 105, CANR-25, 50
Branch, Daniel Paulk 1931- 17-20R
Branch, Edgar Marquess 1913- CANR-91
Earlier sketch in CA 13-16R
Branch, Harold F(rancis) 1894-1966 .... 5-8R
Branch, Kip 1947- 108
Branch, Mary 1910-1997 .... CANR-10
Earlier sketch in CA 25-28R
Branch, Melville C(ampbell) 1913- .. CANR-14
Earlier sketch in CA 41-44R
Branch, Michael P. 203
Branch, Muriel Miller 1943- CANR-115
Earlier sketch in CA 159
See also SATA 94, 152
Branch, Taylor 1947- CANR-78
Earlier sketch in CA 131
Interview in CA-131
See also BEST 89:2
Branch, William (Blackwell) 1927- ... CANR-40
Earlier sketches in CA 81-84, CANR-16
See also BW 2
See also DLB 76
Branciforte, Suzanne 1961- 213
Branco, Paulo 1950- .... IDFW 3, 4
Brancusi, Constantin 1876-1957 .... AAYA 62
Brand, Adolf 1874-1945 .... GLL 2
Brand, Alice Glarden 1938- CANR-98
Earlier sketch in CA 148
Brand, C(larence) E(ugene) 1895-1969 .. CAP-2
Earlier sketch in CA 23-24
Brand, Carl F(remont) 1892-1981 .... 13-16R
Obituary 133
Brand, Charles M(acy) 1932- 21-24R
Brand, Charles Peter 1923- 13-16R
Brand, Christianna
See Lewis, Mary (Christianna)
See also DLB 276
Brand, Clay
See Norwood, Victor G(eorge) C(harles)
Brand, Dionne 1953- CANR-143
Earlier sketch in CA 143
See also BW 2
See also CLC 192
See also CWP
Brand, Eugene L(ouis) 1931- CANR-8
Earlier sketch in CA 61-64
Brand, Garrison
See Brandner, Gary (Phil)
Brand, Gerd 1921-
Brief entry 113
Brand, Irene B. 1929- CANR-123
Earlier sketch in CA 124
Brand, Jeanne L(aurel) 1919- 13-16R
Brand, Max
See Faust, Frederick (Schiller)
See also BPFB 1
See also TCWW 1, 2
Brand, Millen 1906-1980 .... CANR-72
Obituary 97-100
Earlier sketch in CA 21-24R
See also CLC 7
Brand, Myles 1942- 37-40R
Brand, Oscar 1920- CANR-4
Earlier sketch in CA 1-4R
Brand, Peter
See Larsen, Erling
Brand, Rebecca
See Charnas, Suzy McKee
Brand, Sandra 1918- 85-88
Brand, Stewart 1938- CANR-44
Earlier sketch in CA 81-84
See also AITN 1
Brand, Susan
See Roper, Susan Bonthron
Brandabur, Edward 1930- 41-44R
Brandane, John
See MacIntyre, John
Brandao, Fiama Hasse Pais 1938- .... EWL 3
Brandao, Raul
See Brandao, Raul
See also DLB 287
Brandao, Raul 1867-1930
See Brandao, Raul
See also EWL 3
Brandauer, Klaus Maria 1944- 216
Brande, Ralph T. 1921- 25-28R
Brandeis, Gayle 1968- 230
Brandeis, Irma 1906(?)-1990
Obituary 130
Brandeis, Louis Dembitz 1856-1941 166
Brief entry 118

Cumulative Index 69 **Braunbeck**

Brandel, Arthur Meyer 1913(?)-1980
Obituary ... 102
Brandel, Marc 1919- ... CANR-25
Earlier sketch in CA 108
See also SATA 71
Brandell, (Erik) Gunnar 1916- ... CANR-42
Earlier sketches in CA 103, CANR-20
Branden, Barbara ... 148
See also CLC 44
Branden, Nathaniel 1930- ... CANR-27
Earlier sketch in CA 33-36R
Interview in ... CANR-27
Branden, Victoria (Fremlin) ... 101
Brandenberg, Alexa (Demetria) 1966- ... 163
See also SATA 97
Brandenberg, Aliki (Liacouras)
1929- ... CANR-102
Earlier sketches in CA 1-4R, CANR-4, 12, 30
See also Aliki
See also CWRI 5
See also MAICYA 1, 2
See also SATA 2, 35, 75, 113, 157
Brandenberg, Franz 1932- ... CANR-30
Earlier sketches in CA 29-32R, CANR-12
See also MAICYA 1, 2
See also SATA 8, 35, 75
Brandenburg, David J(ohn) 1920-1987
Obituary ... 123
Brandenburg, Frank R(alph) 1926- ... 13-16R
Brandenburg, Jim 1945- ... 151
See also SATA 87
Brander, Michael (William) 1924- ... CANR-7
Earlier sketch in CA 53-56
Brandes, Georg (Morris Cohen)
1842-1927 ... 189
Brief entry ... 105
See also DLB 300
See also TCLC 10
Brandes, Joseph 1928- ... CANR-96
Earlier sketch in CA 5-8R
Brandes, Norman Scott 1923- ... 57-60
Brandes, Paul D(ickerson) 1920- ... CANR-2
Earlier sketch in CA 45-48
Brandes, Stuart D. 1940- ... 160
Brandewyne, (Mary) Rebecca (Wadsworth)
1955- ... CANR-60
Earlier sketches in CA 107, CANR-23
See also RHW
Brandhorst, Carl T(heodore)
1898-1988 ... CAP-2
Earlier sketch in CA 25-28
See also SATA 23
Brandi, John 1943- ... CANR-47
Earlier sketches in CA 73-76, CANR-12
See also CP 2, 3, 4, 5, 6, 7
Brandis, Marianne 1938- ... CANR-132
Earlier sketches in CA 117, CANR-67
See also SATA 59, 96, 149
Brandner, Gary (Phil) 1933- ... CANR-72
Earlier sketches in CA 45-48, CANR-1, 17, 38
See also HGG
Brando, Marlon, (Jr.) 1924-2004 ... 148
Obituary ... 230
Brandom, Robert B(oyce) 1950- ... 192
Brandon, Beatrice
See Krepps, Robert W(ilson)
Brandon, Brumsic, Jr. 1927- ... 61-64
See also SATA 9
Brandon, Carl
See Carr, Terry (Gene)
Brandon, Craig 1950- ... 187
Brandon, Curt
See Bishop, Curtis (Kent)
Brandon, Dick H. 1934-1981 ... CANR-10
Earlier sketch in CA 17-20R
Brandon, Donald (Wayne) 1926- ... 69-72
Brandon, Dorothy 1899(?)-1977
Obituary ... 69-72
Brandon, Frances Sweeney 1916- ... 9-12R
Brandon, Frank
See Bulmer, (Henry) Kenneth
Brandon, (Oscar) Henry 1916-1993 . CANR-48
Obituary ... 141
Earlier sketch in CA 49-52
Brandon, James Rodger 1927- ... CANR-11
Earlier sketch in CA 69-72
Brandon, Jay (Robert) 1953- ... CANR-93
Earlier sketch in CA 119
Brandon, Joe
See Davis, Robert P.
Brandon, John G(ordon) 1879(?)-1941
Brief entry ... 112
Brandon, Johnny 1920(?)- ... CANR-96
Earlier sketches in CA 105, CANR-45
Brandon, Joyce A(lmeta) 1938- ... CANR-42
Earlier sketch in CA 118
Brandon, Robert Joseph 1918- ... 105
Brandon, Robin
See Brandon, Robert Joseph
Brandon, S(amuel) G(eorge) F(rederick)
1907-1971 ... CANR-69
Earlier sketch in CA 102
Brandon, Sheila
See Rayner, Claire (Berenice)
Brandon, William 1914-2002 ... 77-80
Brandon-Cox, Hugh 1917-2003 ... 93-96
Obituary ... 225
Brandreth, Gyles 1948- ... 65-68
See also SATA 28
Brandreth, Gyles (Daubeney)
1948- ... CANR-114
Brandreth, Henry R(enaud) T(urner) 1914-1984
Obituary ... 114
Brands, H. W. 1953- ... CANR-100
Earlier sketches in CA 147, CANR-69
Brands, Joh. G.
See Greshoff, Jan
Brandstatter, A(rthur) F. 1914- ... 107
Brandstetter, Alois 1938- ... 193
Brandt, Allan M(orris) 1953- ... 144
Brandt, Alvin G. 1922- ... 13-16R
Brandt, Anthony 1936- ... CANR-115
Earlier sketch in CA 69-72
Brandt, Beverly ... 219
Brandt, Bill 1904(?)-1983
Obituary ... 111
Brandt, Carol 1904-1984
Obituary ... 114
Brandt, Catharine 1905-1997 ... 106
See also SATA 40
Brandt, Charles 1942- ... 128
Brandt, Clare 1934- ... 145
Brandt, Deborah 1951- ... 138
Brandt, Di(onne)
See Brandt, Di(ana)
See also CWP
Brandt, Di(ana) 1952- ... 231
See also Brandt, Di(onne)
Brandt, Dionne
See Brandt, Di(ana)
Brandt, Edward R(eimer) 1931- ... 234
Brandt, Floyd S(tanley) 1930- ... 21-24R
Brandt, George W(illiam) 1920- ... 131
Brandt, Harvey
See Edwards, William B(ennett)
Brandt, Jane Lewis 1915- ... 97-100
Brandt, Jorgen Gustava 1929- ... 194
See also EWL 3
Brandt, Keith
See Sabin, Louis
Brandt, Leslie F. 1919- ... CANR-46
Earlier sketches in CA 21-24R, CANR-8, 23
Brandt, Lucile (Long Strayer) 1900- .. CANR-13
Earlier sketch in CA 61-64
Brandt, Lyle
See Newton, Michael
Brandt, Nat
See Brandt, Nathan Henry, Jr.
Brandt, Nathan Henry, Jr. 1929- ... CANR-18
Earlier sketch in CA 102
Brandt, Rex(ford Elson) 1914-2000 ... CANR-5
Earlier sketch in CA 13-16R
Brandt, Richard B(ooker) 1910-
Brief entry ... 114
Brandt, Richard M(artin) 1922-1997 ... 33-36R
Brandt, Robert 1941- ... 187
Brandt, Roger
See Crawford, William (Elbert)
Brandt, Sue R(eading) 1916- ... 25-28R
See also SATA 59
Brandt, Tom
See Dewey, Thomas B(lanchard)
Brandt, Vincent S. R. 1924- ... 37-40R
Brandt, William E(dward) 1920- ... 5-8R
Brandt, Willy 1913-1992 ... 85-88
Brandt, Yanna Kroyt 1933- ... 104
Brandts, Robert (Percival) 1930- ... 69-72
Brandwein, Chaim N(aftali) 1920- ... 21-24R
Brandys, Kazimierz 1916-2000 ... 239
See also CLC 62
See also EWL 3
Brandys, Marian 1912- ... 57-60
Branegan, James Augustus III 1950- ... 124
Branfield, John (Charles) 1931- ... CANR-72
Earlier sketches in CA 41-44R, CANR-14, 33
See also CWRI 5
See also SATA 11
Branfoot, Gwynneth
See Holder, Gwynneth
Branford, Henrietta 1946-1999 ... 175
See also MAICYA 2
See also SATA 106
Branham, Mary 1929- ... 199
Branham, Mary Edith 1909-1999 ... 192
Branham, Robert J(ames) 1953-1998 ... 227
Branham, William M(arrion) 1909-1965 ... 206
Branick, Vincent P(atrick) 1941- ... 113
Branigan, Keith 1940- ... CANR-110
Earlier sketches in CA 124, CANR-51
Branin, M(anlif) Lelyn 1901-1995 ... 85-88
Branley, Franklyn M(ansfield)
1915-2002 ... CANR-39
Obituary ... 207
Earlier sketches in CA 33-36R, CANR-14
See also CLC 21
See also CLR 13
See also MAICYA 1, 2
See also SAAS 16
See also SATA 4, 68, 136
Brann, Eva T(oni) H(elene) 1929- ... 93-96
Brann, Ross 1949- ... 238
Brannan, Robert Louis 1927- ... 21-24R
Brannen, J. P. 1927- ... 156
Brannen, Julia (M.) 1944- ... 130
Brannen, Noah S(amuel) 1924- ... CANR-11
Earlier sketch in CA 25-28R
Brannen, Ted R. 1924- ... 17-20R
Branner, H. C.
See Branner, Hans Christian
See also DLB 214
Branner, Hans Christian 1903-1966 ... 97-100
Obituary ... 89-92
See also Branner, H. C.
See also EWL 3
Branner, R(obert) 1927-1973 ... CANR-3
Obituary ... 45-48
Earlier sketch in CA 5-8R
Brannigan, Bill
See Brannigan, William
Brannigan, Gary G(eorge) 1947- ... 139
Brannigan, Russ ... TCWW 2
Brannigan, William 1936- ... 65-68
Brannon, William T. 1906- ... CAP-1
Earlier sketch in CA 13-16
Branon, Bill 1937- ... 149
Branover, Herman 1931- ... CANR-90
Earlier sketch in CA 130
Branscomb, (Bennett) Harvie 1894-1998 ... 106
Obituary ... 169
Branscum, Robbie (Tilley)
1937-1997 ... CANR-8
Obituary ... 158
Earlier sketch in CA 61-64
See also AAYA 19
See also JRDA
See also MAICYA 1, 2
See also MAICYAS 1
See also SAAS 17
See also SATA 23, 72
See also SATA-Obit 96
See also WYA
See also YAW
Bransford, Kent Jackson 1953- ... 97-100
Bransford, Stephen 1949- ... 134
Bransom, (John) Paul 1885-1979 ... SATA 43
Branson, David 1909- ... CANR-21
Earlier sketch in CA 41-44R
Branson, Douglas M. 1945- ... 194
Branson, H(enry) C(lay) 1905-1981 ... 237
See also CMW 4
Branson, Louise ... 219
Branson, Margaret Stimmann 1922- ... CANR-1
Earlier sketch in CA 49-52
Branston, (Ronald Victor) Brian 1914- ... 53-56
Brant, Beth (E.) 1941- ... 144
See also FW
See also NNAL
Brant, Charles S(tanford) 1919- ... 25-28R
Brant, Irving (Newton) 1885-1976 ... CANR-68
Obituary ... 69-72
Earlier sketch in CA 9-12R
Brant, Lewis
See Rowland, D(onald) S(ydney)
Brant, Marley 1950- ... CANR-137
Earlier sketch in CA 140
Brant, Sebastian 1457-1521 ... DLB 179
See also RGWL 2, 3
Brantenberg, Gerd 1941- ... 162
See also CWW 2
See also GLL 2
Brantley, Cynthia Louise 1943- ... 109
Brantlinger, Patrick (Morgan) 1941- .. CANR-91
Earlier sketch in CA 145
Brantome, Pierre de Bourdeille
1540-1614 ... GFL Beginnings to 1789
Branyan, Brenda
See Branyan-Broadbent, Brenda
Branyan, Robert L(ester) 1930- ... 104
Branyan-Broadbent, Brenda 1932- ... 128
Branzburg, Paul M(arshal) 1941- ... 73-76
Braoude, Patrick ... 207
Braque, Georges 1882-1963
Obituary ... 112
Brasch, Charles (Orwell) 1909-1973 ... 114
Obituary ... 104
See also CP 1
Brasch, Ila Wales 1945- ... 57-60
Brasch, James D(aniel) 1929- ... 116
Brasch, Rudolph 1912- ... CANR-51
Earlier sketches in CA 21-24R, CANR-8, 27
Brasch, Walter Milton 1945- ... CANR-100
Earlier sketches in CA 57-60, CANR-6, 23, 49
Braschi, Giannina 1953- ... 146
See also LLW
Braselton, Jeanne 1962-2003 ... 220
Brasfield, James 1952- ... 189
Brashares, Ann 1967- ... 218
See also AAYA 52
See also SATA 145
Brashear, Charles (Ross) 1930- ... CANR-8
Earlier sketch in CA 5-8R
Brashear, Jean 1949- ... 226
Brasher, Brenda E. 1952- ... 200
Brasher, Chris(topher William)
1928-2003 ... 5-8R
Obituary ... 213
Brasher, N(orman) H(enry) 1922-2003 .. 25-28R
Brasher, Nell 1912-1992 ... CANR-7
Earlier sketch in CA 61-64
Brasher, Thomas L(owber) 1912-1979 ... 69-72
Brashers, H(oward) C(harles)
See Brashear, Charles (Ross)
Brashers, Howard C.
See Brashear, Charles (Ross)
Brashler, William 1947- ... CANR-2
Earlier sketch in CA 45-48
Brasier, Virginia (Rossmore) 1910-1994 ... 61-64
Brasier-Creagh, Patrick
See Creagh, Patrick
Brasil, Emanuel 1940- ... 130
Brasillach, Robert 1909-1945 . GFL 1789 to the Present
See also RGWL 2, 3
Brasnett, Bertrand R(ippington) 1893-1988
Obituary ... 124
Brason, Gill 1942- ... 112
Brass, Paul Richard 1936- ... 17-20R
Brassai
See Halasz, Gyula
Brasseaux, Carl A(nthony) 1951- ... CANR-101
Earlier sketch in CA 143
Brasselle, Keefe 1923(?)-1981
Obituary ... 104
Brassens, Georges 1921-1981
Obituary ... 105
Brasseur, Pierre
See Espinasse, Albert
Brassey, Lady Annie (Allnutt)
1839-1887 ... DLB 166
Brassloff, Audrey 1934- ... 200
Braswell, George Wilbur, Jr. 1936- ... 112
Brata, Sasthi 1939- ... 143
See also CN 3, 4, 5, 6, 7
Brater, Enoch 1944- ... CANR-48
Earlier sketch in CA 122
Brathwait, Richard c. 1588-1673 ... DLB 151
Brathwaite, Edward Kamau 1930- .. CANR-107
Earlier sketches in CA 25-28R, CANR-11, 26, 47
See also BLCS
See also BW 2, 3
See also CDWLB 3
See also CLC 11
See also CP 1, 2, 3, 4, 5, 6, 7
See also DAM POET
See also DLB 125
See also EWL 3
See also PC 56
Brathwaite, Errol (Freeman) 1924- ... CANR-66
Earlier sketches in CA 57-60, CANR-7, 11
See also CN 1, 2, 3, 4, 5, 6
Brathwaite, Kamau
See Brathwaite, Edward Kamau
Brathwaite, Sheila R. 1914- ... 25-28R
Bratt, Elmer Clark 1901-1970 ... 1-4R
Obituary ... 103
Bratt, James D. 1949- ... 170
Bratt, John H(arold) 1909- ... CANR-9
Earlier sketch in CA 17-20R
Bratter, Herbert Max 1900-1976
Obituary ... 65-68
Bratter, Thomas Edward 1939- ... 120
Brattgarg, Helge (Axel Kristian) 1920- ... 5-8R
Bratton, Daniel L(ance) 1950- ... 206
Bratton, Fred Gladstone
1896-1970(?) ... CANR-69
Earlier sketches in CAP-1, CA 11-12
Bratton, Helen 1899-1986 ... CAP-2
Earlier sketch in CA 23-24
See also SATA 4
Bratton, Susan Power 1948- ... 145
Brattstrom, Bayard H(olmes) 1929- ... 57-60
Bratun, Katy 1950- ... SATA 83, 160
Brauchli, Bernard 1944- ... 188
Braude, Ann (Deborah) 1955- ... CANR-89
Earlier sketch in CA 132
Braude, Benjamin 1945- ... 111
Braude, Jacob M(orton) 1896-1970 ... CANR-5
Earlier sketch in CA 5-8R
Braude, Michael 1909-1986
Obituary ... 121
Braude, Michael 1936- ... 17-20R
See also SATA 23
Braude, William Gordon 1907-1988 ... 33-36R
Braudel, Fernand (Paul) 1902-1985 .. CANR-42
Obituary ... 117
Earlier sketches in CA 93-96, CANR-14
Braudy, Leo 1941- ... CANR-138
Earlier sketch in CA 37-40R
Braudy, Susan (Orr) 1941- ... CANR-10
Earlier sketch in CA 65-68
Brauer, Carl M(alcolm) 1946- ... 85-88
Brauer, George C(harles), Jr. 1925-
Brief entry ... 113
Brauer, Jerald C(arl) 1921-1999 ... CANR-13
Obituary ... 185
Earlier sketch in CA 33-36R
Brauer, Kinley J(ules) 1935- ... 21-24R
Brault, Gerard Joseph 1929- ... CANR-3
Earlier sketch in CA 5-8R
Brault, Jacques 1933- ... 161
See also DLB 53
Braun, Armin C(harles John) 1911-1986
Obituary ... 120
Braun, Arthur E. 1876-1976
Obituary ... 69-72
Braun, Barbara 1939- ... CANR-113
Earlier sketch in CA 162
Braun, Bev(erly) Kirschner 1952- ... 213
Braun, Edward 1936- ... 134
Brief entry ... 115
Braun, Eric 1921- ... 102
Braun, Henry 1930- ... 25-28R
See also CP 1
Braun, Hugh 1902-1968(?) ... CANR-70
Earlier sketch in CA 25-28R
Braun, J(oachim) Werner 1914-1972
Obituary ... 37-40R
Braun, John R(ichard) 1928- ... 33-36R
Braun, Kazimierz (P.) 1936- ... 174
Braun, Lev 1913- ... 41-44R
Braun, Lilian Jackson 1916(?)- ... CANR-92
Earlier sketches in CA 140, CANR-59
See also AAYA 29
See also BPFB 1
See also CMW 4
See also DA3
See also DAM POP
See also SATA 109
Braun, Marta (A.) 1946- ... 141
Braun, Matt 1932- ... 209
See also DLB 212
See also TCWW 1, 2
Braun, Richard Emil 1934- ... 9-12R
See also CP 3, 4
Braun, Sidney D(avid) 1912-1992 ... CANR-10
Earlier sketch in CA 65-68
Braun, Stephen R. 1957- ... CANR-131
Earlier sketch in CA 162
Braun, Theodore E. D. 1933- ... CANR-7
Earlier sketch in CA 13-16R
Braun, Thomas (Felix Rudry Gerhart)
1935- ... 115
Braun, Volker 1939- ... 194
See also CWW 2
See also DLB 75, 124
See also EWL 3
Braunbeck, Gary A. 1960(?)- ... 236

Braunbehrens 70 CONTEMPORARY AUTHORS

Braunbehrens, Volkmar 1941- 134
Braunberger, Pierre 1905-1990 .... IDFW 3, 4
Braunburg, Rudolf 1924- CANR-29
Earlier sketch in CA 109
Braund, Hal
See Braund, Harold
Braund, Harold 1913-1988 61-64
Obituary 124
Braund, Kathryn E. Holland 1955- 145
Braunmuller, A(lbert) R(ichard)
1945- CANR-89
Earlier sketch in CA 132
Braunrot, Bruno 1936- 114
Braunstein, Daniel N(orman) 1938- 111
Braunstein, Mark M(athew) 1951- .. CANR-105
Earlier sketches in CA 113, CANR-50
Braunthal, Alfred 1898(?)-1980
Obituary 93-96
Braunthal, Gerard 1923- 13-16R
Braunthal, Julius 1891-1972 .... CAP-2
Earlier sketch in CA 23-24
Brautigan, Richard (Gary)
1935-1984 .... CANR-34
Obituary 113
Earlier sketch in CA 53-56
See also BPFB 1
See also CLC 1, 3, 5, 9, 12, 34, 42
See also CN 1, 2, 3
See also CP 1, 2, 3, 4
See also DA3
See also DAM NOV
See also DLB 2, 5, 206
See also DLBY 1980, 1984
See also FANT
See also MAL 5
See also MTCW 1
See also RGAL 4
See also SATA 56
See also TCLC 133
Brav, Stanley R(osenbaum) 1908-1992 .. 25-28R
Brave Bird, Mary
See Crow Dog, Mary (Ellen)
See also NNAL
Braveboy-Wagner, Jacqueline Anne 1948- . 168
Braver, Adam 1963- 229
Braver, Gary
See Goshgarian, Gary
Braverman, Harry 1920-1976 53-56
Obituary 69-72
Braverman, Kate 1950- CANR-141
Earlier sketch in CA 89-92
See also CLC 67
Braverman, Melanie 1960- CANR-139
Earlier sketch in CA 156
Braverman, Terry 1953- 156
Bravmann, Rene A. 1939- 85-88
Brawer, Florence B(lum) 1922- 37-40R
Brawley, Benjamin (Griffith) 1882-1939 125
See also BW 1
Brawley, Ernest 1937- 53-56
Brawley, Paul Holm
See Brawley, Paul L(eroy)
Brawley, Paul L(eroy) 1942-1988 73-76
Obituary 126
Brawley, Robert L. 1939- 156
Brawn, Dympna 1931- 25-28R
Brawne, Michael 1925-2003 73-76
Obituary 218
Braxton, Joanne M(argaret) 1950- 140
See also BW 2
See also DLB 41
Braxton, Jodi
See Braxton, Joanne M(argaret)
Bray, Alan 1948-2001 209
Bray, Alison
See Rowland, D(onald) S(ydney)
Bray, Allen Farris III 1926- 9-12R
Bray, Anna Eliza 1790-1883 .... DLB 116
Bray, Douglas W. 1918- 13-16R
Bray, Howard 1929- 105
Bray, J(ohn) J(efferson) 1912-1995 102
Bray, J. R. 1879-1978 .... IDFW 3, 4
Bray, Libba 235
See also SATA 159
Bray, Nicholas 1948- 135
Bray, Rosemary L. 1955- 177
See also BW 3
Bray, Thomas 1656-1730 .... DLB 24
Bray, Virginia Elizabeth Nuckolls 1895(?)-1979
Obituary 93-96
Bray, Warwick 1936- CANR-15
Earlier sketch in CA 25-28R
Braybon, (Charmian) Gail 1952- CANR-90
Earlier sketch in CA 131
Braybrooke, David 1924- CANR-98
Earlier sketches in CA 9-12R, CANR-3, 18
Braybrooke, Neville (Patrick Bellairs)
1923-2001 .... 5-8R
Obituary 201
Brayce, William
See Rowland, D(onald) S(ydney)
Brayfield, Celia 1945- 128
Brayman, Harold 1900-1988 73-76
Obituary 124
Braymer, Marguerite
See Dodd, Marguerite (Annetta)
Braymer, Marjorie Elizabeth 1911-1988 .... 1-4R
See also BYA 3
See also SATA 6
Braynard, Frank O(sborn) 1916- CANR-45
Earlier sketches in CA 17-20R, CANR-8
Braza, Jacque
See McKeag, Ernest L(ionel)
Brazaitis, Mark 1966- 172
Brazdzionis, Bernardas 1907-2002 239
See also DLB 220
Brazeau, Jay 1945- 213
Brazeau, Peter (Alden) 1942-1986 111
Obituary 119
Brazell, Karen 1938- CANR-31
Earlier sketch in CA 45-48
Brazelton, T(homas) Berry 1918- 97-100
Brazelton, W. Robert 1933- 223
Brazer, Harvey E(lliott) 1922-1991 111
Obituary 134
Brazil, Angela 1869(?)-1947
Brief entry 112
See also CWRI 5
Brazile, Donna L. 1959- 236
Brazill, William J., Jr. 1935- 53-56
Brazos, Waco
See Jennings, Michael Glenn
Brdecka, Jiri 1917-1982 .... IDFW 3, 4
Breach, Robert Walter 1927- 13-16R
Breakwell, Glynis M(arie) 1952- 122
Brealey, Richard A. 1936- 53-56
Brean, Herbert (J.) 1907-1973 .... CANR-58
Obituary 41-44R
Earlier sketch in CA 93-96
See also CMW 4
Brearley, Denis 1940- 37-40R
Brears, Peter C(harles) D(avid) 1944- 102
Breashears, David 1956- 186
Breasted, Charles 1898(?)-1980
Obituary 93-96
Breasted, James Henry, Jr. 1908-1983
Obituary 109
Breasted, James Henry 1865-1935 179
See also DLB 47
Breathed, (Guy) Berke(ley) 1957- CANR-27
Earlier sketch in CA 110
See also AAYA 5, 61
See also SATA 86, 161
Breathett, George 1925- 13-16R
Breatnac, Seamus
See Walsh, James P(atrick)
Breault, William 1926- CANR-6
Earlier sketch in CA 57-60
Brebner, Philip 1955- 139
Brecher, Charles Martin 1945- CANR-4
Earlier sketch in CA 53-56
Brecher, Edward M(oritz) 1911-1989 .. CANR-7
Obituary 128
Earlier sketch in CA 13-16R
Brecher, Frank W. 1931- 235
Brecher, Jeremy 1946- CANR-12
Earlier sketch in CA 69-72
Brecher, Michael 1925- CANR-72
Earlier sketches in CA 1-4R, CANR-4
Brecher, Ruth E(rnestine) 1911-1966 ..... CAP-1
Earlier sketch in CA 13-14
Brechner, Irv 1951- 110
Brecht, Arnold 1884-1977 .... CANR-72
Obituary 73-76
Earlier sketch in CA 77-80
Brecht, (Eugen) Bertolt (Friedrich)
1898-1956 .... CANR-62
Brief entry 104
Earlier sketch in CA 133
See also CDWLB 2
See also DA
See also DA3
See also DAB
See also DAC
See also DAM DRAM, MST
See also DC 3
See also DFS 4, 5, 9
See also DLB 56, 124
See also EW 11
See also EWL 3
See also IDTP
See also MTCW 1, 2
See also MTFW 2005
See also RGWL 2, 3
See also TCLC 1, 6, 13, 35, 169
See also TWA
See also WLC
Brecht, Edith 1895-1975 .... CAP-2
Earlier sketch in CA 25-28
See also SATA 6
See also SATA-Obit 25
Brecht, Eugen Berthold Friedrich
See Brecht, (Eugen) Bertolt (Friedrich)
Brecht, George 1924- 106
Breck, Allen duPont 1914- CANR-9
Earlier sketch in CA 13-16R
Breck, Vivian
See Breckenfeld, Vivian Gurney
Breckenfeld, Vivian Gurney
1895-1992 .... CANR-69
Earlier sketch in CA 5-8R
See also SATA 1
Breckenridge, Adam Carlyle 1916- 29-32R
Breckinridge, Mary 1881-1965
Obituary 114
Breckler, Rosemary 1920- 101
Breda, Tjalmar
See DeJong, David C(ornel)
Bredel, Willi 1901-1964 183
See also DLB 56
Bredemeier, Harry Charles 1920- CANR-8
Earlier sketch in CA 5-8R
Bredemeier, Mary E(lizabeth) 1924- 81-84
Bredero, Adriaan H(endrick) 1921- 159
Bredero, Gerbrand Adriaensz
1585-1618 .... RGWL 2, 3
Bredes, Don(ald) 1947- CANR-110
Earlier sketch in CA 110
Bredeson, Carmen 1944- 166
See also SATA 98, 163
Bredow, Miriam
See Wolf, Miriam Bredow
Bredsdorff, Bodil 235
Bredsdorff, Elias Lunn 1912-2002 .... CAP-1
Obituary 209
Earlier sketch in CA 9-10
Bredsdorff, Jan 1942- CANR-13
Earlier sketch in CA 21-24R
Bredvold, Louis I(gnatius) 1888-1977 .... 1-4R
Obituary 103
Bree, Germaine 1907-2001 .... CANR-4
Obituary 199
Earlier sketch in CA 1-4R
See also CAAS 15
Breech, (Earl) James 1944- 114
Breecher, Maury M. 1944- CANR-125
Earlier sketch in CA 156
Breed, Paul F. 1916- 33-36R
Breeden, David 1958- 189
Breeden, Joann Elizabeth 1934- 145
Breeden, Stanley 1938- 106
Breedlove, Lynn 1959(?)- 211
Breem, Wallace (Wilfred Swinburne)
1926-1990 229
Brief entry 113
Breen, Dana
See Birksted-Breen, Dana
Breen, (Joseph) John 1942-1999 149
Obituary 185
Breen, Jon L(inn) 1943- CANR-63
Earlier sketch in CA 119
See also CMW 4
Breen, Quirinus 1896-1975 .... CAP-2
Earlier sketch in CA 33-36
Breen, Richard 1935- 110
Breen, Richard L. 1919-1967
Obituary 111
Breen, T(imothy) H(all) 1942- 101
Breen, William J(ames) 1937- 118
Breer, Robert 1926- .... IDFW 3, 4
Breese, Dave
See Breese, David W(illiam)
Breese, David W(illiam) 1926-2002 118
Breese, Gerald (William) 1912-1995 ..... 41-44R
Breeskin, Adelyn Dohme 1896-1986 .... 33-36R
Obituary 119
Breetveld, Jim Patrick 1925- CANR-69
Earlier sketches in CA 1-4R, CANR-2
Breeze, Billy
See Brocksmith, Roy
Breeze, Jean Binta 1956- 194
Breeze, Katie 1929- 111
Breffort, Alexandre 1901-1971
Obituary 29-32R
Bregendahl, Marie 1867-1940 .... DLB 214
Breger, Louis 1935- CANR-102
Earlier sketch in CA 69-72
Breggin, Peter R(oger) 1936- CANR-92
Earlier sketches in CA 81-84, CANR-15, 34
Bregman, Ahron 238
Bregman, Jacob I(srael Jack) 1923- 41-44R
Bregman, Jay 1940- 109
Brehm, Sharon S(tephens) 1945- CANR-30
Earlier sketch in CA 112
Brehm, Shirley A(lice) 1926- 69-72
Brehony, Kathleen A. 199
Breig, Joseph A(nthony) 1905-1982 .... 5-8R
Breihan, Carl W(illiam) 1916- CANR-1
Earlier sketch in CA 1-4R
Breillat, Catherine 1950- 33-36R
Breimyer, Harold F(rederick) 1914- 17-20R
Breinburg, Petronella 1927- CANR-4
Earlier sketch in CA 53-56
See also CLR 31
See also SATA 11
Breiner, Laurence A. 233
Breines, Paul 1941- 61-64
Breines, Simon 1906-2003
Obituary 220
Brief entry 114
Breines, Winifred 1942- 113
Breisach, Ernst Adolf 1923- CANR-18
Earlier sketch in CA 1-4R
Breisky, William J(ohn) 1928- 53-56
See also SATA 22
Breit, Harvey 1909-1968 .... CANR-6
Obituary 25-28R
Earlier sketch in CA 5-8R
Breit, Marquita E(laine) 1942- 57-60
Breit, William (Leo) 1933- CANR-13
Earlier sketch in CA 33-36R
Breitbart, Vicki 1942- 93-96
Breitenkamp, Edward C(arlton)
1913-1995 .... CANR-25
Earlier sketches in CA 25-28R, CANR-10
Breitinger, Johann Jakob 1701-1776 ..... DLB 97
Breitman, George 1916-1986 .... CANR-7
Obituary 119
Earlier sketch in CA 61-64
Breitman, Richard D(avid) 1947- CANR-21
Earlier sketch in CA 105
Breitner, I. Emery 1929- 57-60
Breivik, Patricia Senn 1939- 170
Brekke, Paal (Emanuel) 1923-1993 192
See also DLB 297
Brekus, Catherine A. 1963- 197
Breland, Osmond P(hilip)
1910-1984 .... CANR-69
Earlier sketch in CA 9-12R
Brelis, Dean 1924- CANR-72
Earlier sketch in CA 9-12R
Brelis, Matthew 1957- 132
Brief entry 126
Interview in CA-132
Brelis, Nancy (Burns) 1929- 21-24R
Brelsford, W(illiam) V(ernon) 1907- CAP-1
Earlier sketch in CA 13-14
Breman, Paul 1931- 21-24R
Brembeck, Winston Lamont 1912-
Brief entry 115
Bremer, Arthur H(erman) 1950-
Brief entry 113
Bremer, Francis J(ohn) 1947- CANR-144
Earlier sketch in CA 93-96
Bremer, Fredrika 1801-1865 .... DLB 254
Bremer, Lisa
See Janas, Frankie-Lee
Bremermann, Hans-Joachim 1926-1996 170
Bremmer, Ian A. 1969- 143
Bremner, Geoffrey 1930- CANR-38
Earlier sketch in CA 115
Bremner, John B(urton) 1920-1987
Obituary 123
Bremner, Robert H(amlett)
1917-2002 .... CANR-9
Obituary 210
Earlier sketch in CA 21-24R
Brems, Hans 1915-2000 .... CANR-10
Obituary 192
Earlier sketch in CA 25-28R
Bremser, Bonnie 1939- 153
See also DLB 16
Bremser, Ray 1934- 17-20R
See also CP 1, 2, 3, 4
See also DLB 16
Bremyer, Jayne Dickey 1924- 61-64
Brenan, (Edward Fitz)Gerald
1894-1987 .... CANR-72
Obituary 121
Earlier sketches in CA 1-4R, CANR-3
Brenchley, Chaz 1959- 238
See also HGG
Brend, Ruth M(argaret) 1927- 105
Brende, Eric 237
Brendel, Alfred 1931- 225
Brendel, Otto Johannes 1901-1973 97-100
Brendon, Piers (George Rundle)
1940- CANR-99
Earlier sketches in CA 101, CANR-31, 57
Brendtro, Larry K. 1940- 29-32R
Brener, Milton E. 1930- 29-32R
Brengelman, Fred(erick Henry) 1928- 134
Brief entry 115
Brengelmann, Johannes Clemens 1920- 5-8R
Brenlove, Milovan S. 1948- 126
Brenna, Duff CANR-143
Earlier sketch in CA 170
Brenna, Dwayne 1955- 220
Brennan, Anne 1936- 109
Brennan, Bernard P(atrick) 1918- 5-8R
Brennan, Carol
See Slate, Caroline
Brennan, Christine 235
Brennan, Christopher
See Kininmonth, Christopher
Brennan, Christopher John 1870-1932 188
Brief entry 117
See also DLB 230
See also EWL 3
See also TCLC 17
Brennan, Donald (George) 1926-1980
Obituary 97-100
Brennan, Gale (Patrick) 1927- 125
See also SATA 64
See also SATA-Brief 53
Brennan, (Harold) Geoffrey 1944- 128
Brennan, Herbie
See Brennan, J(ames) H(erbert)
Brennan, J(ames) H(erbert) 1940- 211
See also SATA 140
Brennan, Jan
See Brennan, J(ames) H(erbert)
Brennan, John N(eedham) H(uggard)
1914- CANR-64
Earlier sketches in CA 1-4R, CANR-4, 20
See also CMW 4
Brennan, Joseph Gerard 1910- CANR-69
Earlier sketches in CA 1-4R, CANR-3
Brennan, Joseph K(illorin) 1952- 121
Brennan, Joseph Lomas 1903-2000 .... CANR-2
Earlier sketch in CA 5-8R
See also SATA 6
Brennan, Joseph Payne 1918-1990 .. CANR-72
Obituary 180
Earlier sketches in CA 1-4R, CANR-4, 19
See also HGG
Brennan, Lawrence D(avid) 1915- 5-8R
Brennan, Linda Crotta 1952- .... SATA 130
Brennan, Louis A(rthur) 1911-1983 .. CANR-71
Obituary 109
Earlier sketch in CA 17-20R
Brennan, Maeve 1917-1993 .... CANR-100
Earlier sketches in CA 81-84, CANR-72
See also CLC 5
See also TCLC 124
Brennan, Martin 1942- 194
Brennan, Mary C. 1959- 152
Brennan, Matthew
See Bateman, Robert L.
Brennan, Matthew C(annon) 1955- . CANR-117
Earlier sketch in CA 165
Brennan, Matthew J. 1917- 106
Brennan, Maynard J. 1921- 13-16R
Brennan, Michael Joseph, Jr. 1928- 13-16R
Brennan, Neil F(rancis) 1923- 37-40R
Brennan, Niall 1918- 13-16R
Brennan, Nicholas (Stephen) 1948- 106
Brennan, Ray 1908(?)-1972
Obituary 37-40R
Brennan, Richard O(liver) 1916- 89-92
Brennan, Thomas 1965- 238
Brennan, Tim
See Conroy, John Wesley
Brennan, Timothy (Andres) 1953- 181
Brennan, Tom
See Brennan, Thomas

Cumulative Index 71 Bridenbaugh

Brennan, Walt
See King, Albert
Brennan, Ward
See Meares, Leonard Frank
Brennan, Will
See Paine, Lauran (Bosworth)
Brennan, William J(oseph), Jr. 1906-1997 ... 163
Brennand, Frank
See Lambert, Eric
Brennecke, John H(enry) 1934- ... 37-40R
Brenneman, Helen Good
1925-1994 ... CANR-46
Obituary ... 146
Earlier sketch in CA 21-24R
Brennen, Bonnie (Sue) 1952- ... 213
Brenner, Anita 1905-1974 ... CANR-71
Obituary ... 53-56
Earlier sketch in CA 49-52
See also SATA 56
Brenner, Barbara (Johnes) 1925- ... CANR-57
Earlier sketches in CA 9-12R, CANR-12, 31
See also JRDA
See also MAICYA 1, 2
See also SAAS 14
See also SATA 4, 42, 76, 124
Brenner, David 1945- ... 133
Brenner, Elizabeth 1954- ... 123
Brenner, Erma 1911-2001 ... 69-72
Brenner, Fred 1920- ... MAICYA 1, 2
See also SATA 36
See also SATA-Brief 34
Brenner, Gerry 1937- ... 110
Brenner, Isabel
See Schuchman, Joan
Brenner, Joel Glenn 1966- ... 193
Brenner, Johanna ... 200
Brenner, Jooel
See Brenner, Joel Glenn
Brenner, Lenni 1937- ... 117
Brenner, Marie 1949- ... CANR-71
Earlier sketch in CA 73-76
Brenner, Mayer Alan 1956- ... 154
See also FANT
Brenner, Michael 1964- ... 208
Brenner, Philip (Joseph) 1946- ... 224
Brenner, Rebecca Summer 1945- ... CANR-10
Earlier sketch in CA 61-64
Brenner, Reeve R(obert) 1936-
Brief entry ... 116
Brenner, Reuven 1947- ... 142
Brenner, Robert 1945- ... 162
Brenner, Summer
See Brenner, Rebecca Summer
Brenner, Wendy 1966- ... CANR-114
Earlier sketch in CA 166
Brenner, Yehojachin Simon 1926- ... CANR-11
Earlier sketch in CA 21-24R
Brenner, Yosef H(ayyim)
See Brenner, Joseph Hayyim
Brennert, Alan (Michael) 1954- ... CANR-72
Earlier sketch in CA 118
See also HGG
Brenni, Vito J(oseph) 1923- ... CANR-31
Earlier sketch in CA 49-52
Brenson, Michael 1942- ... 196
Brent, Beryl
See Ince, Martin (Jeffrey)
Brent, Harold Patrick 1943- ... 33-36R
Brent, Harry
See Brent, Harold Patrick
Brent, Hope 1935(?)-1984 ... SATA-Obit 39
Brent, Iris
See Bancroft, Iris (May Nelson)
Brent, Jonathan 1949- ... CANR-144
Earlier sketch in CA 113
Brent, Linda
See Jacobs, Harriet A(nn)
Brent, Madeleine
See O'Donnell, Peter
See also RHW
Brent, Peter (Ludwig) 1931-1984 ... CANR-13
Obituary ... 114
Earlier sketch in CA 65-68
Brent, Stuart ... 73-76
See also SATA 14
Brentano, Bernard von 1901-1964 ... 185
See also DLB 56
Brentano, Clemens (Maria) 1778-1842 . DLB 90
See also RGWL 2, 3
Brentano, Franz Clement 1838-1917 .. DLB 296
Brentano, Robert 1926-2002 ... 21-24R
Obituary ... 210
Brent-Dyer, Elinor Mary 1895-1969 ... 101
See also CWRI 5
Brentlinger, John 1934- ... 152
Brent of Bin Bin
See Franklin, (Stella Maria Sarah) Miles (Lampe)
Brenton, Howard 1942- ... CANR-67
Earlier sketches in CA 69-72, CANR-33
See also CBD
See also CD 5, 6
See also CLC 31
See also DLB 13
See also MTCW 1
Brenton and
Soupault
Soupault ... CWRI 5
Breo, Dennis L. 1942- ... 124
Brereton, Geoffrey 1906-1979 ... CANR-20
Earlier sketch in CA 25-28R
Bresee, Clyde W. 1916- ... CANR-48
Earlier sketch in CA 122
Breskin, David ... 233
[illegible]
Breslau, Alan Jeffry 1926- ... 69-72
Breslauer, George W. 1946- ... CANR-142
Earlier sketches in CA 29-32R, CANR-12
Breslauer, Samuel Daniel 1942- ... 102
Bresler, Fenton S(hea) 1929-2003 ... 191
Obituary ... 222
Breslin, Catherine 1936- ... 93-96
Breslin, Herbert H. 1924- ... 53-56
Breslin, James 1930- ... CANR-139
Earlier sketches in CA 73-76, CANR-31, 75
See also Breslin, Jimmy
See also DAM NOV
See also MTCW 1, 2
See also MTFW 2005
Breslin, James E. B. 1935-1996 ... 33-36R
Obituary ... 151
Breslin, Jimmy
See Breslin, James
See also AITN 1
See also CLC 4, 43
See also DLB 185
See also MTCW 2
Breslin, John B. 1943- ... 132
Breslin, Mark 1952- ... 121
Breslin, Paul 1946- ... 111
Breslin, Rosemary 1957-2004 ... 162
Obituary ... 228
Breslin, Theresa ... 138
See also AAYA 54
See also SATA 70, 128
See also SATA-Essay 128
Breslove, David 1891- ... 9-12R
Breslow, Lester 1915- ... 115
Breslow, Lou 1900(?)-1987
Obituary ... 124
Breslow, Maurice (A.) 1935- ... CANR-82
Earlier sketch in CA 133
See also SATA 72
Breslow, Susan 1951- ... 137
See also SATA 69
Bressett, Kenneth E(dward) 1928- ... 93-96
Bressler, Leo A(lbert) 1911-1995 ... 57-60
Bressler, Marion Ann 1921- ... 57-60
Bresson, Robert 1901(?)-1999 ... CANR-49
Obituary ... 187
Earlier sketch in CA 110
See also CLC 16
Bressoud, David M(arius) 1950- ... 141
Brestin, Dee 1944- ... 114
Brestol, Betsey Ann
See Ritchie, (Harry) Ward
Bret, David 1952- ... 134
Bretall, Robert Walter 1913-1980
Obituary ... 110
Bretecher, Claire 1940-
Brief entry ... 113
Bretnor, (Alfred) Reginald
1911-1992 ... CANR-25
Obituary ... 176
Earlier sketches in CA 65-68, CANR-10
See also SFW 4
Breton, Albert 1929- ... 61-64
Breton, Andre 1896-1966 ... CANR-60
Obituary ... 25-28R
Earlier sketches in CAP-2, CA 19-20, CANR-40
See also CLC 2, 9, 15, 54
See also DLB 65, 258
See also EW 11
See also EWL 3
See also GFL 1789 to the Present
See also LMFS 2
See also MTCW 1, 2
See also MTFW 2005
See also PC 15
See also RGWL 2, 3
See also TWA
See also WP
Breton, Marcela
See Jenkins, Marcella
Breton, Mary Joy 1924- ... 191
Breton, Nicholas 1555(?)-1626(?) ... DLB 136
Bretscher, Paul G(erhardt) 1921- ... CANR-8
Earlier sketch in CA 17-20R
Brett, Bernard 1925- ... CANR-17
Earlier sketch in CA 97-100
See also SATA 22
Brett, Bill 1922- ... 122
Brett, Brian 1950- ... 139
Brett, Catherine
See Humphreys, Helen (Caroline)
Brett, David
See Campbell, Will D(avis)
Brett, Donna W(hitson) 1947- ... 134
Brett, Dorothy 1883-1977
Obituary ... 73-76
Brett, Edward T(racy) 1944- ... 134
Brett, George P(latt), Jr. 1893-1984
Obituary ... 112
Brett, Grace N(eff) 1900-1975 ... 9-12R
Obituary ... 120
See also SATA 23
Brett, Hawksley
See Bell, Robert S(tanley) W(arren)
Brett, Jan (Churchill) 1949- ... CANR-110
Earlier sketches in CA 116, CANR-41
See also CLR 27
See also CWRI 5
See also MAICYA 1, 2
See also SATA 42, 71, 130
Brett, John Michael
See Tripp, Miles (Barton)
Brett, Leo
See Fanthorpe, R(obert) Lionel
Brett, Lily 1946- ... 195
Brett, Lionel (Gordon Baliol) 1913-2004 ... 131
Obituary ... [illegible]
Brett, Mary Elizabeth ... 9-12R
Brett, Michael
See Tripp, Miles (Barton)
Brett, Molly
See Brett, Mary Elizabeth
Brett, Peter David 1943- ... 77-80
Brett, Philip 1937-2002 ... 129
Obituary ... 208
Brett, Raymond Laurence 1917-1996 . CANR-3
Earlier sketch in CA 1-4R
Brett, Simon (Anthony Lee) 1945- ... CANR-113
Earlier sketches in CA 69-72, CANR-29, 63
See also CMW 4
See also DLB 276
Brettell, Caroline B. 1950- ... CANR-111
Earlier sketches in CA 127, CANR-55
Brettell, Noel Harry 1908- ... CP 1
Brettell, Richard (Robson) 1949- ... 124
Brett-James, (Eliot) Antony
1920-1984 ... CANR-7
Obituary ... 112
Earlier sketch in CA 5-8R
Bretton, Barbara 1950- ... CANR-113
Earlier sketch in CA 162
Bretton, Henry L. 1916- ... CANR-2
Earlier sketch in CA 5-8R
Brettschneider, Bertram D(onald)
1924-1986 ... 33-36R
Obituary ... 121
Brett-Smith, Richard 1923- ... 21-24R
Brett-Young, Jessica (Hankinson)
1883-1970 ... CAP-1
Earlier sketch in CA 9-10
Bretuo, Akwasi
See Assensoh, A(kwasi) B(retuo)
Breuer, Bessie 1893-1975 ... CANR-70
Obituary ... 61-64
Earlier sketches in CAP-2, CA 17-18
Breuer, Ernest Henry 1902-1972 ... CAP-2
Earlier sketch in CA 19-20
Breuer, Georg 1919- ... 105
Breuer, Gustav J. 1915-1985
Obituary ... 114
Breuer, Gustl
See Breuer, Gustav J.
Breuer, Lee 1937- ... CANR-143
Earlier sketches in CA 110, CANR-68
See also CAD
See also CD 5, 6
Breuer, Marcel 1902-1981 ... CANR-5
Obituary ... 104
Earlier sketch in CA 5-8R
Breuer, Miles J(ohn) 1888-1947 ... 235
Brief entry ... 112
Breuer, Reinhard 1946- ... CANR-38
Earlier sketch in CA 115
Breuer, William B(entley) 1926- ... CANR-100
Earlier sketch in CA 118
Breugelmans, Rene 1925- ... 103
Breunig, Jerome Edward 1917- ... CANR-45
Earlier sketch in CA 13-16R
Breunig, LeRoy C(linton) 1915-1996 ... 61-64
Obituary ... 151
Brevard, Aleshia 1937- ... 215
Brew, Douglas James 1949(?)-1985
Obituary ... 117
Brew, J(ohn) O(tis) 1906- ... 61-64
Brew, (Osborne Henry) Kwesi 1928- ... 142
See also BW 2
See also CP 1, 2, 3, 4, 5, 6, 7
Breward, Christopher 1965- ... 151
Brewer, Annie M. 1925- ... 107
Brewer, D(erek) S(tanley) 1923- ... CANR-4
Earlier sketch in CA 1-4R
Brewer, Edward S(amuel) 1933- ... CANR-13
Earlier sketch in CA 33-36R
Brewer, (Lucie) Elisabeth 1923- ... 115
Brewer, Frances Joan 1913-1965 ... CAP-1
Earlier sketch in CA 11-12
Brewer, Fredric (Aldwyn) 1921- ... 17-20R
Brewer, Garry Dwight 1941- ... CANR-14
Earlier sketch in CA 33-36R
Brewer, Gay 1965- ... 146
Brewer, Gene 1937- ... 222
Brewer, Gil 1922-1983 ... 237
See also CMW 4
See also DLB 306
Brewer, J(ohn) Mason 1896-1975 ... CAP-2
Earlier sketch in CA 25-28
Brewer, Jack A. 1933- ... 21-24R
Brewer, James D. 1951- ... 178
See also SATA 108
Brewer, James H. Fitzgerald 1916- ... 9-12R
Brewer, Jeannie A. 1960- ... 158
Brewer, Jeutonne P. 1939- ... CANR-14
Earlier sketch in CA 77-80
Brewer, John 1947- ... 232
Brewer, John D(avid) 1951- ... CANR-88
Earlier sketch in CA 131
Brewer, Kenneth W(ayne) 1941- ... CANR-92
Earlier sketch in CA 110
Brewer, Luther Albertus 1858-1933 ... 184
See also DLB 187
Brewer, Margaret L. 1929- ... 29-32R
Brewer, Priscilla J. 1956- ... 122
Brewer, Sally King 1947- ... SATA 33
Brewer, Sam Pope 1909(?)-1976
Obituary ... 65-68
Brewer, Steve 1957- ... 198
Brewer, Thomas B. 1932- ... 21-24R
Brewer, William C. 1897(?)-1974
Obituary ... 53-56
Brewer, William D(ean) 1955- ... 151
Brewer, Wilmon 1895-1998 ... 5-8R
Brewerton, Derick (Arthur) 1924- ... 115
Brewi, Janice 1933- ... 110
Brewington, Marion Vernon
1902-1974 ... CANR-3
Obituary ... 53-56
Earlier sketch in CA 5-8R
Brewster, Benjamin
See Folsom, Franklin (Brewster)
Brewster, David (C.) 1939- ... 139
Brewster, Dorothy 1883-1979 ... CANR-70
Obituary ... 85-88
Earlier sketches in CA 1-4R, CANR-3
Brewster, Elizabeth (Winifred) 1922- ... 230
Earlier sketches in CA 25-28R, CANR-10, 25, 68
Autobiographical Essay in ... 230
See also CAAS 15
See also CP 1, 2, 3, 4, 5, 6, 7
See also CWP
See also DLB 60
Brewster, Eva 1922- ... 132
Brewster, Hugh 1950- ... CANR-144
Earlier sketch in CA 160
See also SATA 95
Brewster, Patience 1952- ... CANR-46
Earlier sketch in CA 121
See also SATA 97
Brewster, Townsend 1924- ... CANR-29
Earlier sketch in CA 105
Brewton, John E(dmund) 1898-1982 .. CANR-3
Earlier sketch in CA 5-8R
See also SATA 5
Brewton, Sara Westbrook (?)-1976 ... 122
Breyer, Chloe ... 199
Breyer, N(orman) L(ane) 1942- ... CANR-31
Earlier sketch in CA 49-52
Breyer, Stephen G(erald) 1938- ... CANR-64
Earlier sketch in CA 107
Breyman, Steve 1960- ... 170
Breytenbach, Breyten 1939(?)- ... CANR-122
Brief entry ... 113
Earlier sketches in CA 129, CANR-61
See also CLC 23, 37, 126
See also CWW 2
See also DAM POET
See also DLB 225
See also EWL 3
Breza, Tadeusz 1905(?)-1970
Obituary ... 29-32R
Brezhnev, L. I.
See Brezhnev, Leonid I(lyich)
Brezhnev, Leonid
See Brezhnev, Leonid I(lyich)
Brezhnev, Leonid I(lyich) 1906-1982 ... 132
Obituary ... 108
Brezianu, Andrei 1934- ... 200
Brezina, Otokar
See Jebavy, Vaclav Ignac
See also EWL 3
Breznitz, Shlomo 1936- ... 140
Brian
See Powell, Brian S(harples)
Brian, Alan B.
See Parulski, George R(ichard), Jr.
Brian, Cynthia 1951- ... 217
Brian, Denis 1923- ... CANR-121
Earlier sketch in CA 25-28R
Brian, Janeen (Paulette) 1948- ... 212
See also SATA 141
Briand, Paul L., Jr. 1920- ... CANR-4
Earlier sketch in CA 1-4R
Briand, Rena 1935- ... 29-32R
Brians, Paul 1942- ... CANR-112
Earlier sketches in CA 127, CANR-55
Briarton, Grendel
See Bretnor, (Alfred) Reginald
Brice, Douglas 1916- ... 21-24R
Brice, Marshall Moore 1898-1978 ... 17-20R
Brice, Valerie Kack
See Kack-Brice, Valerie
Brichant, Colette Dubois 1926- ... 13-16R
Brichoux, Karen ... 234
Brichto, Herbert Chanan
1925-1996 ... CANR-107
Earlier sketch in CA 147
Brick, Howard 1953- ... 126
Brick, John 1922-1973 ... CANR-70
Obituary ... 45-48
Earlier sketches in CAP-1, CA 13-14
See also SATA 10
Brick, Michael 1922-1974 ... CANR-9
Earlier sketch in CA 13-16R
Bricker, Victoria Reifler 1940- ... 53-56
Brickhill, Paul Chester Jerome
1916-1991 ... CANR-69
Obituary ... 134
Earlier sketch in CA 9-12R
Bricklin, Mark Harris 1939- ... 111
Brickman, Marshall 1941- ... 81-84
Brickman, Robin D. 1954- ... SATA 155
Brickman, William Wolfgang
1913-1986 ... CANR-17
Obituary ... 119
Earlier sketches in CA 1-4R, CANR-1
Brickner, Balfour 1926- ... 216
Brickner, Richard P(ilpel) 1933- ... CANR-2
Earlier sketch in CA 5-8R
Bricktop
See Smith, Ada Beatrice Queen Victoria Louisa Virginia
Bricmont, Jean ... 197
Bricuth, John
See Irwin, John T(homas)
Bridal, Tessa ... NFS 17
Bride, Nadja
See Nobisso, Josephine
Bridenbaugh, Carl 1903-1992 ... CANR-69
Obituary ... 130
Earlier sketches in CA 9-12R, CANR-4

Bridge, Ann
See O'Malley, Lady Mary Dolling (Sanders)
Bridge, Don(ald) U(lysses) 1894-1984
Obituary 112
Bridge, Horatio 1806-1893 ..... DLB 183
Bridge, Raymond 1943- CANR-32
Earlier sketch in CA 69-72
Bridgecross, Peter
See Cardinal, Roger (Thomas)
Bridgeman, Harriet 1942- 85-88
Bridgeman, Richard
See Davies, L(eslie) P(urnell)
Bridgeman, William Barton 1916- 9-12R
Bridger, Adam
See Bingley, David Ernest
Bridger, Gordon (Frederick) 1932- 65-68
Bridgers, Sue Ellen 1942- CANR-36
Earlier sketches in CA 65-68, CANR-11
See also AAYA 8, 49
See also BYA 7, 8
See also CLC 26
See also CLR 18
See also DLB 52
See also JRDA
See also MAICYA 1, 2
See also SAAS 1
See also SATA 22, 90
See also SATA-Essay 109
See also WYA
See also YAW
Bridges, Ben
See Whitehead, David
Bridges, Emily
See Bruggen, Carol (Holmes)
Bridges, Hal 1918- 1-4R
Bridges, Herb 1929- 110
Bridges, James 1936-1993 ..... CANR-80
Obituary 141
Brief entry 116
Earlier sketch in CA 127
Bridges, Kate 209
Bridges, Laurie 147
See also Bruck, Lorraine
Bridges, Peter (S.) 1932- 239
Bridges, Robert (Seymour) 1844-1930 152
Brief entry 104
See also BRW 6
See also CDBLB 1890-1914
See also DAM POET
See also DLB 19, 98
See also PC 28
See also TCLC 1
Bridges, Ruby (Nell) 1954- 199
See also SATA 131
Bridges, William (Andrew)
1901-1984 ..... CANR-69
Earlier sketch in CA 33-36R
See also SATA 5
Bridges, William (Emery) 1933- CANR-13
Earlier sketch in CA 33-36R
Bridges-Adams, William 1889-1965 ..... CAP-1
Earlier sketch in CA 13-14
Bridgland, Fred 1941- 176
Bridgman, Elizabeth 1921- 73-76
Bridgman, Richard M. 1927-2005 129
Obituary 236
Bridgman, Sarah Atherton 1889(?)-1975
Obituary 57-60
Bridgwater, (William) Patrick 1931- 5-8R
Bridie, James
See Mavor, Osborne Henry
See also DLB 10
See also EWL 3
See also TCLC 3
Bridson, Gavin (Douglas Ruthven) 1936- ... 105
Bridwell, Norman (Ray) 1928- CANR-117
Earlier sketches in CA 13-16R, CANR-5, 20, 46
See also CLR 96
See also CWRI 5
See also MAICYA 1, 2
See also SATA 4, 68, 138
Briefs, Goetz Antony 1889-1974 ..... CAP-2
Obituary 49-52
Earlier sketch in CA 21-22
Briegel, Ann C(arrick) 1915- 33-36R
Brien, Alan 1925- 147
Brien, Mimi 1929- 111
Brien, Nell
See Palmer, Shirley
Brien, Raley
See McCulley, Johnston
Brier, Bob 1943- 102
Brier, Howard M(axwell)
1903-1969 ..... CANR-69
Earlier sketches in CAP-1, CA 13-14
See also SATA 8
Brier, Peter A. 1935- 105
Brier, Royce 1894-1975
Obituary 93-96
Brier, Warren Judson 1931- 25-28R
Brierley, (Louise) 1958- ..... SATA 59
Brierley, Barry 1937- 153
Brierley, David 1936- 107
Brierley, Susan S.
See Isaacs, Susan (Sutherland Fairhurst)
Briers, Richard (David) 1934- 190
Brietzke, Zander 1960- 213
Brieux, Eugene 1858-1932 182
See also DLB 192
Briffault, Herma 1898-1981
Obituary 104
Brigadere, Anna 1861-1933 ..... CDWLB 4
See also DLB 220
See also EWL 3
Briggs, Asa 1921- CANR-125
Earlier sketches in CA 5-8R, CANR-7
Briggs, Austin (Eugene), Jr. 1931- 29-32R
Briggs, B(arry B.) Bruce
See Bruce-Briggs, B(arry B.)
Briggs, Berta N. 1884(?)-1976
Obituary 69-72
Briggs, Carl 1925- 114
Briggs, Carole S(uzanne) 1950- 110
See also SATA-Brief 47
Briggs, Charles Augustus 1841-1913 220
Briggs, Charles Frederick 1804-1877 ..... DLB 3, 250
Briggs, Charlie 1927- CANR-1
Earlier sketch in CA 49-52
Briggs, Clarence E. III 1960- 136
Briggs, Desmond Lawther 1931- CANR-25
Earlier sketch in CA 108
Briggs, Dorothy Corkille 1924- 29-32R
Briggs, Ellis O(rmsbee) 1899-1976 73-76
Obituary 65-68
Briggs, F(red) Allen 1916- 33-36R
Briggs, Fred 1932-1995 73-76
Obituary 147
Briggs, G. A. 1891(?)-1978
Obituary 104
Briggs, George M(cSpadden) 1919- 33-36R
Briggs, Jean 1925- 93-96
Briggs, Jean L(ouise) 1929- 177
Briggs, Joe Bob 1959- CANR-130
Earlier sketch in CA 131
Briggs, John 1945- CANR-94
Earlier sketch in CA 132
Briggs, Julia 1943- 147
Briggs, Katharine Mary 1898-1980 ... CANR-58
Obituary 102
Earlier sketches in CA 9-12R, CANR-12
See also CWRI 5
See also FANT
See also SATA 101
See also SATA-Obit 25
Briggs, Kenneth Arthur 1941- 101
Briggs, Kenneth R. 1934- 33-36R
Briggs, L(loyd) Cabot 1909-1975 ..... CANR-3
Obituary 57-60
Earlier sketch in CA 5-8R
Briggs, Matt(hew D.) 1970- 188
Briggs, Michael (David) 1951- 135
Briggs, Peter 1921-1975 ..... CANR-70
Obituary 57-60
Earlier sketches in CAP-2, CA 25-28
See also SATA 39
See also SATA-Obit 31
Briggs, R(obert) C(ook) 1915- 37-40R
Briggs, Raymond (Redvers) 1934- CANR-70
Earlier sketch in CA 73-76
See also CLR 10
See also CWRI 5
See also MAICYA 1, 2
See also SATA 23, 66, 131
Briggs, Shirley Ann 1918-2004 106
Obituary 233
Briggs, Vernon M(ason), Jr. 1937- 73-76
Briggs, Walter Ladd 1919- 69-72
Briggs, Ward W(right, Jr.) 1945- 135
Brigham, Besmilr 1923- CANR-12
Earlier sketch in CA 29-32R
Brigham, John C(arl) 1942- 41-44R
Brighouse, Harold 1882-1958 169
Brief entry 110
See also DLB 10
Bright, Bill
See Bright, William Rohl
Bright, Chris(topher) 182
Bright, Deborah (Sue Tomberg) 1949- ... 97-100
Bright, Freda 1929- 136
Bright, Greg 1951- 93-96
Bright, John M. 1908-1989 ..... CANR-70
Obituary 129
Earlier sketch in CA 5-8R
Bright, Myron H. 1919- 134
Bright, Pamela Mia 1914- 109
Bright, Richard (Eugene) 1931- 69-72
Bright, Robert (Douglas Sr.)
1902-1988 ..... CANR-70
Obituary 127
Earlier sketch in CA 73-76
See also CWRI 5
See also SATA 24, 63
See also SATA-Obit 60
Bright, Sarah
See Shine, Deborah
Bright, Susannah 1958- CANR-138
Earlier sketch in CA 172
See also Bright, Susie
Bright, Susie
See Bright, Susannah
See also GLL 2
Bright, William 1928- 33-36R
Bright, William Rohl 1921-2003 220
Brightbill, Charles K(estner) 1910-1966 ..... 1-4R
Obituary 103
Brightfield, Richard 1927- CANR-35
Earlier sketch in CA 118
See also SATA 65
See also SATA-Brief 53
Brightfield, Rick
See Brightfield, Richard
Brightman, Carol 1939- 158
Brightman, Edgar S(heffield) 1884-1953 220
See also DLB 270
Brightman, Robert 1920- 105
Brighton, Catherine 1943- 130
See also SATA 65, 107
Brighton, Howard 1925- 57-60
Brighton, Wesley, Jr.
See Lovin, Roger Robert
Brightwell, Emily
See Arguiles, Cheryl
Brightwell, L(eonard) R(obert)
1889- ..... SATA-Brief 29
Brignano, Russell C(arl) 1935- 57-60
Brignetti, Raffaello 1922(?)-1978
Obituary 104
Brigola, Alfredo L(uigi) 1923- 41-44R
Brijbhushan, Jamila 1918-1990 130
Briles, Judith 1946- 106
Briley, John (Richard) 1925- CANR-44
Earlier sketch in CA 101
Brilhart, John K. 1929- 21-24R
Brill, Alida 1949- 142
Brill, Earl H(ubert) 1925- 17-20R
Brill, Leon 1915- 110
Brill, Marlene Targ 1945- CANR-97
Earlier sketch in CA 145
See also SATA 77, 124
Brill, Steve 1949- 223
Brill, Steven 1950- CANR-142
Earlier sketch in CA 85-88
Brill, Wildman Steve
See Brill, Steve
Brilliant, Alan 1936- ..... CP 1, 2
Brilliant, Ashleigh (Ellwood) 1933- ... CANR-45
Earlier sketches in CA 65-68, CANR-11
Brilliant, Eleanor L(uria) 1930- 112
Brilliant, Richard 1929- 33-36R
Brillstein, Bernie (J.) 1931- 188
Briloff, Abraham J(acob) 1917- 61-64
Brim, Orville G(ilbert), Jr. 1923- CANR-2
Earlier sketch in CA 5-8R
Brimberg, Stanlee 1947- 49-52
See also SATA 9
Brimblecombe, Peter 1949- 128
Brimelow, Peter 1947- CANR-71
Earlier sketch in CA 133
Brimner, Larry Dane 1949- 221
See also SATA 79
See also SATA-Essay 112
Brin, David 1950- CANR-127
Earlier sketches in CA 102, CANR-24, 70, 125
Interview in CANR-24
See also AAYA 21
See also CLC 34
See also SATA 65
See also SCFW 2
See also SFW 4
Brin, Herb(ert Henry) 1915-2003 ..... CANR-27
Obituary 213
Earlier sketch in CA 49-52
Brin, Ruth Firestone 1921- CANR-8
Earlier sketch in CA 17-20R
See also SATA 22
Brinckerhoff, Sidney B(urr) 1933- 185
Brief entry 117
Brinckloe, Julie (Lorraine) 1950- 65-68
See also SATA 13
Brindel, June (Rachuy) 1919- CANR-31
Earlier sketch in CA 49-52
See also SATA 7
Brindle, Jane
See Cox, Josephine
Brindle, Max
See Fleischman, (Albert) Sid(ney)
Brindle, Reginald Smith -2003
Obituary 220
See also Smith Brindle, Reginald
Brindze, Ruth 1903-1984 ..... CANR-70
Earlier sketch in CA 73-76
See also SATA 23
Brine, Adrian 1936- 197
Brinegar, David F(ranklin) 1910-1998 77-80
Briner, Bob 1935-1999 162
Obituary 181
Brines, Francisco 1932- ..... DLB 134
Brines, Russell (Dean) 1911-1982 69-72
Briney, Robert E(dward) 1933- CANR-19
Earlier sketches in CA 53-56, CANR-4
Bring, Mitchell 1951- 106
Bringhurst, Robert 1946- CANR-91
Earlier sketches in CA 57-60, CANR-6, 21, 44
See also CP 4, 5, 6, 7
Bringuier, Jean-Claude 1925- 133
Brinig, Myron 1900-1991 ..... TCWW 2
Brinitzer, Carl 1907-1974 ..... CANR-3
Obituary 53-56
Earlier sketch in CA 5-8R
Brink, Andre (Philippus) 1935- CANR-133
Earlier sketches in CA 104, CANR-39, 62, 109
Interview in CA-103
See also AFW
See also BRWS 6
See also CLC 18, 36, 106
See also CN 4, 5, 6, 7
See also DLB 225
See also EWL 3
See also LATS 1:2
See also MTCW 1, 2
See also MTFW 2005
See also WLIT 2
Brink, Carol Ryrie 1895-1981 ..... CANR-65
Obituary 104
Earlier sketches in CA 1-4R, CANR-3
See also BYA 1
See also CLR 30
See also CWRI 5
See also JRDA
See also MAICYA 1, 2
See also SATA 1, 31, 100
See also SATA-Obit 27
See also TCWW 2
See also WCH
Brink, Jean R. 1942- 137
Brink, T(erry) L(ee) 1949- CANR-86
Earlier sketches in CA 89-92, CANR-15, 34
Brink, Wellington 1895-1979
Obituary 85-88
Brinker, Nancy (Goodman) 1946- 134
Brinker, Paul A. 1919- 25-28R
Brinker, Robert Durie 1901-1983
Obituary 111
Brinkerhoff, Dericksen Morgan 1921- 85-88
Brinkley, Alan 1949- CANR-96
Earlier sketches in CA 107, CANR-45
Brinkley, Christie 1953- 122
Brinkley, David (McClure) 1920-2003 ... 97-100
Obituary 217
Brinkley, Douglas 1961(?)- 170
Brinkley, George A. (Jr.) 1931- 17-20R
Brinkley, Joel (Graham) 1952- CANR-103
Earlier sketches in CA 102, CANR-61
Brinkley, Roberta Florence 1892(?)-1967
Obituary 112
Brinkley, William (Clark)
1917-1993 ..... CANR-11
Obituary 143
Earlier sketch in CA 21-24R
Brinkman, George L(oris) 1942- 53-56
Brinkman, Grover 1903-1999 73-76
Brinkmann, Rolf Dieter 1940-1975 192
See also EWL 3
Brinks, Herbert J(ohn) 1935- CANR-44
Earlier sketches in CA 29-32R, CANR-12
Brinley, Bertrand R(ussell) 1917-1994 ... 29-32R
Obituary 147
Brinley, George, Jr. 1817-1875 ..... DLB 140
Brinley, Maryann B(ucknum)
1949- CANR-142
Earlier sketch in CA 130
Brinner, William M(ichael) 1924- CANR-55
Earlier sketches in CA 111, CANR-29
Brinnin, John Malcolm 1916-1998 ... CANR-70
Earlier sketches in CA 1-4R, CANR-1
See also CP 1, 2, 3, 4
See also DLB 48
Brinsmead, H. F(ay)
See Aalben, Patrick and Brinsmead, H(esba) F(ay)
Brinsmead, H. F.
See Brinsmead, H(esba) F(ay)
Brinsmead, H(esba) F(ay) 1922- CANR-10
Earlier sketch in CA 21-24R
See also CLC 21
See also CLR 47
See also CWRI 5
See also MAICYA 1, 2
See also SAAS 5
See also SATA 18, 78
Brint, Armand Ian 1952- 105
Brint, Michael (E.) 1955- 140
Brinton, Alexander
See Battin, B(rinton) W(arner)
Brinton, (Clarence) Crane
1898-1968 ..... CANR-69
Obituary 25-28R
Earlier sketch in CA 5-8R
Brinton, Henry 1901-1977 ..... CANR-70
Earlier sketches in CA 1-4R, CANR-4
Brinton, Howard Haines 1884-1973 .. CANR-3
Earlier sketch in CA 5-8R
Brinzeu, Pia 1948- 214
Briody, Dan 236
Briody, Thomas Gately 1960- 188
Brion, Guy
See Madsen, Axel
Brion, Irene 1919- 167
Brion, John M. 1922- 21-24R
Brion, Marcel 1895-1984 124
Obituary 114
Briquebec, John
See Rowland-Entwistle, (Arthur) Theodore (Henry)
Brisbane, Albert 1809-1890 ..... DLB 3, 250
Brisbane, Arthur 1864-1936 182
See also DLB 25
Brisbane, Henry R.
See Ellis, Edward S(ylvester)
Brisbane, Holly E. 1927- 33-36R
Brisbane, Katharine 1932- CANR-23
Earlier sketch in CA 107
Brisbane, Robert Hughes 1913-1998 77-80
Obituary 163
Brisco, P. A.
See Matthews, Patricia (Anne)
Brisco, Patty
See Matthews, Clayton (Hartley) and Matthews, Patricia (Anne)
Brisco, Thomas V. 1947- 214
Briscoe, Connie 1952- CANR-122
Earlier sketch in CA 162
Briscoe, D(avid) Stuart 1930- CANR-50
Earlier sketches in CA 17-20R, CANR-9, 25
Briscoe, Jill (Pauline) 1935- CANR-8
Earlier sketch in CA 61-64
See also SATA 56
See also SATA-Brief 47
Briscoe, Joanna 169
Briscoe, John 1938- 118
Briscoe, Marsha 217
Briscoe, Mary Louise 1937- 109
Brisk, Melvin J. 1924-1981
Obituary 104
Briskin, Alan 1954- 218
Briskin, Jacqueline 1927- CANR-60
Earlier sketches in CA 29-32R, CANR-13
See also BEST 89:4
See also CPW
See also DAM POP
See also RHW
Briskin, Mae 1924- CANR-139
Earlier sketch in CA 134

Brisley, Joyce Lankester 1896-1978 ... 97-100
Obituary ... 147
See also CWRI 5
See also SATA 22
See also SATA-Obit 84
Brisman, Leslie 1944- ... 61-64
Brison, Susan J. ... 207
Brissenden, Alan (Theo) 1932- ... 132
Brissenden, Connie
See Brissenden, Constance
Brissenden, Constance 1947- ... CANR-134
Earlier sketch in CA 215
See also SATA 150
Brissenden, Paul F(rederick)
1885-1974 ... CAP-2
Obituary ... 53-56
Earlier sketch in CA 17-18
Brissenden, R(obert) F(rancis) 1928- . CANR-10
Earlier sketch in CA 21-24R
Brisset, Jean-Pierre 1837-1919 ... 232
Brisson, Pat 1951- ... CANR-107
Earlier sketch in CA 134
See also MAICYA 2
See also SATA 67, 128, 133
See also SATA-Essay 133
Brister, C(ommodore) W(ebster), Jr.
1926- ... CANR-7
Earlier sketch in CA 13-16R
Brister, Richard 1915- ... 13-16R
Bristol, Goldie M(ae) 1918- ... 121
Bristol, Julius
See Abel, Alan (Irwin)
Bristol, Lee Hastings, Jr. 1923-1979 ... CANR-4
Obituary ... 89-92
Earlier sketch in CA 5-8R
Bristol, Leigh
See Ball, Donna
Bristol, Michael D. 1940- ... 209
Bristow, Allen P. 1929- ... CANR-57
Earlier sketches in CA 21-24R, CANR-8
Bristow, Gwen 1903-1980 ... CANR-59
Obituary ... 102
Earlier sketches in CA 17-20R, CANR-12
See also RHW
See also TCWW 2
Bristow, Robert O'Neil 1926- ... 25-28R
Bristowe, Anthony (Lynn) 1921-(?) ... CAP-1
Earlier sketch in CA 11-12
Britain, Dan
See Pendleton, Don(ald Eugene)
Britain, Ian (Michael) 1948- ... CANR-86
Earlier sketch in CA 130
Britchky, Seymour 1930-2004 ... 102
Obituary ... 228
Brite, Poppy Z. 1967- ... CANR-108
Earlier sketch in CA 141
See also AAYA 44
See also HGG
See also SUFW 2
Britindian
See Solomon, Samuel
Britnell, R(ichard) H. 1944- ... 142
Brito, Aristeo 1942- ... 204
See also DLB 122
See also HW 1
Britsch, Ralph A(dam) 1912-1994 ... 101
Britsch, Todd A(dam) 1937- ... 101
Britt, Albert 1874-1969 ... CANR-70
Obituary ... 103
Earlier sketch in CA 5-8R
See also SATA-Obit 28
Britt, Brian (Michael) 1964- ... 170
Britt, Dell 1934- ... 25-28R
See also SATA 1
Britt, George (William Hughes) 1895-1988
Obituary ... 124
Britt, Steuart Henderson 1907-1979 ... CANR-2
Obituary ... 85-88
Earlier sketch in CA 1-4R
Brittain, Bill
See Brittain, William (E.)
See also JRDA
See also SAAS 7
Brittain, C. Dale 1948- ... 149
See also SATA 82
Brittain, Frederick (?)-1969 ... CANR-3
Earlier sketch in CA 5-8R
Brittain, Joan Tucker 1928- ... 37-40R
Brittain, John A(shleigh) 1923- ... 73-76
Brittain, Vera (Mary) 1893(?)-1970 ... CANR-58
Obituary ... 25-28R
Earlier sketches in CAP-1, CA 13-16
See also BRWS 10
See also CLC 23
See also DLB 191
See also FW
See also MTCW 1, 2
Brittain, Victoria ... 198
Brittain, William (E.) 1930- ... CANR-57
Earlier sketches in CA 77-80, CANR-13, 30
See also Brittain, Bill
See also CWRI 5
See also MAICYA 1, 2
See also SATA 36, 76
Brittan, Gordon G(oodhue), Jr. 1939- ... 89-92
Brittan, Leon 1939- ... 177
Brittan, Samuel 1933- ... 29-32R
Britten, Milton R(eese) 1924-1985 ... 125
Obituary ... 115
Britten, Rhonda ... 236
Britten Austin, Paul 1922- ... CANR-13
Earlier sketch in CA 21-24R
Britter, Eric V(alentine) B(lakeney) 1906-1977
Obituary ... 73-76
Brittin, Norman A(ylsworth) 1906- ... 17-20R
Brittin, Phil (Henry) 1953- ... 108
Brittingham, Geoffrey (Hugh) 1959- ... SATA 76
Britton, Bill
See Britton, Charles William
Britton, Bruce K. 1944- ... 145
Britton, Bryce 1943- ... 110
Britton, Celia (Margaret) 1946- ... 216
Britton, Charles William 1918-1985 ... 220
Britton, Christopher (Q.) 1943-
Brief entry ... 118
Britton, David 1945- ... HGG
Britton, Dorothea S(prague) 1926- ... CANR-16
Earlier sketches in CA 45-48, CANR-1
Britton, Dorothy (Guyver) 1922- ... 107
Britton, John A(ndrew) 1943- ... CANR-55
Earlier sketch in CA 126
Britton, Karl (William) 1909-1983 ... CANR-47
Obituary ... 110
Earlier sketch in CA 29-32R
Britton, Kate
See Stegeman, Janet Allais
See also SATA 49
Britton, Louisa
See McGuire, Leslie (Sarah)
Britton, Mattie Lula Cooper 1914-2002 ... 5-8R
Britton, Pamela ... 228
Britton, Peter Ewart 1936- ... CANR-40
Earlier sketches in CA 97-100, CANR-18
Britton, Rick 1952- ... SATA 82
Briusov, Valerii Iakovlevich
1873-1924 ... DLB 295
Brivic, Sheldon Roy 1943- ... 122
Brizeux, Auguste 1803-1858 ... DLB 217
Brkic, Courtney Angela 1972- ... 227
Brkic, Jovan 1927- ... 41-44R
Bro, Bernard (Gerard Marie) 1925- ... CANR-39
Earlier sketches in CA 97-100, CANR-17
Bro, Harmon Hartzell 1919-1997 ... 25-28R
Obituary ... 161
Bro, Marguerite (Harmon)
1894-1977 ... CANR-71
Earlier sketch in CA 77-80
See also SATA 19
See also SATA-Obit 27
Broad, C(harlie) D(unbar)
1887-1971 ... CANR-70
Obituary ... 89-92
Earlier sketch in CA 101
Broad, Charles Lewis 1900- ... CANR-81
Earlier sketch in CA 5-8R
Broad, Jay 1930- ... CANR-19
Earlier sketch in CA 97-100
Broad, Kendal L. 1966- ... 170
Broad, Robin 1954- ... 143
Broad, William J. ... 210
Broadbent, Donald E(ric) 1926-1993 ... 105
Broadbent, Edward 1936- ... 45-48
Broadbent, (John) Michael 1927- ... 231
Broadbent, W. W. 1919- ... 69-72
Broaddus, Dorothy C. ... 185
Broaddus, J(ohn) Morgan, Jr. 1929- ... 21-24R
Broadfoot, Barry 1926-2003 ... 89-92
Obituary ... 222
Broadhead, Helen Cross 1913- ... 103
See also SATA 25
Broadhurst, Allan R. 1932- ... 5-8R
Broadhurst, Kent 1940- ... 137
Broadhurst, Ronald Joseph Callender
1906- ... CAP-1
Earlier sketch in CA 11-12
Broadley, Margaret E(ricson)
1904-1985 ... 97-100
Obituary ... 117
Broadribb, Violet ... 41-44R
Broadus, Calvin
See Snoop Doggy Dogg
Broadus, Catherine 1929- ... 37-40R
Broadus, Loren, Jr. 1928- ... 37-40R
Broadus, Robert N(ewton) 1922- ... 73-76
Broadwater, Jeff 1955- ... 144
Broadwell, Martin M. 1927- ... CANR-28
Earlier sketches in CA 73-76, CANR-13
Broadwin, John A. 1944- ... CANR-124
Earlier sketch in CA 164
Broat, I(sidore) G(erald) 1927- ... 97-100
Brobeck, Florence 1895-1979
Obituary ... 85-88
Brobeck, Stephen 1944- ... 169
Broby-Johansen, R(udolf)
1900-1987 ... CANR-12
Earlier sketch in CA 25-28R
Broccoli, Albert R. 1909-1996 ... IDFW 3, 4
Broce, Thomas Edward 1935- ... 69-72
Broch, Harald Beyer 1944- ... 135
Broch, Hermann 1886-1951 ... 211
Brief entry ... 117
See also CDWLB 2
See also DLB 85, 124
See also EW 10
See also EWL 3
See also RGWL 2, 3
See also TCLC 20
Brochmann, Elizabeth 1938- ... 112
See also SATA 41
Brochu, Andre 1942- ... CANR-140
Earlier sketch in CA 162
See also DLB 53
Brock, Alice May 1941- ... 41-44R
Brock, Arthur Guy Clutton
See Clutton-Brock, Arthur Guy
Brock, Ben
See Howells, Roscoe
Brock, Betty (Carter) 1923-2003 ... 29-32R
Obituary ... 224
See also SATA 4
See also SATA-Obit 150
Brock, C(harles) E(dmund) 1870-1938 . SATA 42
See also SATA-Brief 32
Brock, D(ewey) Heyward 1941- ... 53-56
Brock, Darryl ... 239
Brock, David 1962- ... 212
Brock, Delia
See Ephron, Delia
Brock, Dewey Clifton, Jr. 1930- ... 5-8R
Brock, Edwin 1927- ... 130
Brief entry ... 119
See also CP 1, 2, 3, 4
See also DLB 40
Brock, Eleanor (Hope) 1921- ... 130
Brock, Emma L(illian) 1886-1974 ... 5-8R
Obituary ... 103
See also SATA 8
Brock, Gavin
See Lindsay, (John) Maurice
Brock, Gerald Wayne 1948- ... 57-60
Brock, H(enry) M(atthew) 1875-1960 .. SATA 42
Brock, Horace 1908(?)-1981
Obituary ... 105
Brock, Horace Rhea 1927- ... CANR-33
Earlier sketch in CA 113
Brock, James 1958- ... 160
Brock, Lou(is Clark) 1939- ... 184
Brief entry ... 113
Brock, Lynn
See McAllister, Alister
Brock, Mary Duncan Howe 1909(?)-1984
Obituary ... 112
Brock, Michael George 1920- ... 93-96
Brock, P. W.
See Brock, Patrick Willet
Brock, Patrick Willet 1902-1988 ... 112
Brock, Peter (de Beauvoir) 1920- ... CANR-5
Earlier sketch in CA 9-12R
Brock, Pope 1950(?)- ... 235
Brock, Rita Nakashima 1950- ... 209
Brock, Rose
See Hansen, Joseph
See also GLL 1
Brock, Russell Claude 1903-1980
Obituary ... 105
Brock, Stanley E(dmunde) 1936- ... 57-60
Brock, Stuart
See Trimble, Louis P(reston)
Brock, Van(dall) K(line) 1932- ... CANR-11
Earlier sketch in CA 61-64
Brock, W(illiam) H(odson) 1936- ... CANR-106
Earlier sketch in CA 21-24R
Brock, William R(anulf) 1916- ... CANR-20
Earlier sketches in CA 1-4R, CANR-4
Brockbank, (John) Philip 1922-1989
Obituary ... 129
Brockbank, Reed 1923- ... 21-24R
Brock-Broido, Lucie 1956- ... CANR-111
Earlier sketch in CA 153
See also CP 7
See also CWP
Brockelman, Paul T(aylor) 1935- ... 110
Brockes, Barthold Heinrich
1680-1747 ... DLB 168
Brockett, Eleanor Hall 1913-1967 ... CAP-1
Earlier sketch in CA 9-10
See also SATA 10
Brockett, Oscar Gross 1923- ... CANR-22
Earlier sketches in CA 13-16R, CANR-7
Brockington, J(ohn) L(eonard) 1940- . CANR-91
Earlier sketch in CA 146
Brockley, Fenton
See Rowland, D(onald) S(ydney)
Brockman, C(hristian) Frank 1902-1985 ... 5-8R
See also SATA 26
Brockman, David Drake
See Drake-Brockman, David
Brockman, Harold 1902-1980
Obituary ... 101
Brockman, James R(aymond) 1926- .. CANR-53
Earlier sketches in CA 110, CANR-28
Brockman, John 1941- ... 192
Brockman, Norbert 1934- ... 177
Earlier sketch in CA 73-76
Brockmann, R. John 1951- ... 209
Brockmann, Suzanne ... 196
Brockmeier, Kevin 1972- ... 230
Brockriede, Wayne Elmer 1922- ... CANR-4
Earlier sketch in CA 1-4R
Brocksmith, Roy 1945-2001 ... 173
Obituary ... 200
Brockway, Allan R(eitz) 1932- ... 21-24R
Brockway, Connie 1954- ... CANR-121
Earlier sketch in CA 162
Brockway, Edith E. 1914-1998 ... 17-20R
Brockway, (Archibald) Fenner
1888-1988 ... CANR-83
Obituary ... 125
Earlier sketches in CAP-1, CA 11-12
Brockway, George P(ond)
1915-2001 ... CANR-49
Obituary ... 202
Earlier sketch in CA 123
Brockway, George Pond
See Brockway, George P(ond)
Brockway, Thomas P(armelee)
1898-1999 ... CAP-2
Earlier sketch in CA 17-18
Brockway, Wallace 1905-1972
Obituary ... 37-40R
Brod, Harry 1951- ... 143
Brod, Max 1884-1968 ... CANR-7
Obituary ... 25-28R
Earlier sketch in CA 5-8R
See also DLB 81
See also EWL 3
See also TCLC 115
Brod, Ruth Hagy 1911-1980 ... 166
Obituary ... 97-100
Brodatz, Philip 1915- ... 57-60
Brodbeck, L. Emma 1893(?)-1989
Obituary ... 130
Brodber, Erna (May) 1940- ... 143
See also BW 2
See also CN 6, 7
See also DLB 157
Brode, Douglas (Isaac) 1943- ... CANR-116
Earlier sketch in CA 57-60
Brode, Patrick 1950- ... CANR-89
Earlier sketch in CA 132
Brode, Wallace R. 1900(?)-1974
Obituary ... 53-56
Broder, David S(alzer) 1929- ... CANR-102
Earlier sketches in CA 97-100, CANR-58, 65
Broder, Patricia Janis 1935- ... CANR-6
Earlier sketch in CA 57-60
Broderick, Carlfred B(artholomew)
1932-1999 ... CANR-10
Earlier sketch in CA 25-28R
Broderick, Damien (Francis) 1944- ... CANR-90
Earlier sketches in CA 111, CANR-28, 58
See also SFW 4
Broderick, Dorothy M. 1929- ... 13-16R
See also SATA 5
Broderick, Francis L(yons)
1922-1992 ... CANR-46
Obituary ... 139
Earlier sketch in CA 101
Broderick, John 1927-1989 ... 143
See also CN 4
Broderick, John C(aruthers) 1926- ... 1-4R
Broderick, John F. 1909- ... CAP-2
Earlier sketch in CA 33-36
Broderick, Richard L(awrence) 1927- . CANR-1
Earlier sketch in CA 45-48
Broderick, Robert C(arlton)
1913-1991 ... CANR-8
Earlier sketch in CA 21-24R
Brodeur, Nicole ... 220
Brodeur, Paul (Adrian, Jr.) 1931- ... CANR-65
Earlier sketches in CA 5-8R, CANR-25
See also CN 1, 2
Brodeur, Ruth Wallace
See Wallace-Brodeur, Ruth
Brodey, James Miles 1942- ... CP 1
Brodhead, John R. 1814-1873 ... DLB 30
Brodhead, Michael John 1935- ... 105
Brodie, Bernard 1910-1978 ... CANR-81
Obituary ... 81-84
Earlier sketches in CA 17-20R, CANR-10
Brodie, Fawn M(cKay) 1915-1981 ... CANR-71
Obituary ... 102
Earlier sketches in CA 17-20R, CANR-10
Brodie, H(arlowe) Keith H(ammond)
1939- ... 103
Brodie, Janet Farrell ... 229
Brodie, John (Riley) 1935-
Brief entry ... 115
Brodie, Sally
See Cavin, Ruth (Brodie)
Brodie-Innes, J(ohn) W(illiam) 1848-1923 .. 169
See also HGG
Brodin, Pierre Eugene 1909-1997 ... 85-88
Obituary ... 156
Brodine, Karen 1947- ... 123
Brodine, Virginia Warner 1915- ... 41-44R
Brodkey, Harold (Roy) 1930-1996 ... CANR-71
Obituary ... 151
Earlier sketch in CA 111
See also CLC 56
See also CN 4, 5, 6
See also DLB 130
See also TCLC 123
Brodman, James W(illiam) 1945- ... 210
Brodoff, Ami Sands 1955- ... 186
Brodribb, (Arthur) Gerald (Norcott)
1915-1999 ... CANR-72
Earlier sketches in CA 113, CANR-33
Brodrick, William 1960- ... 223
Brodskii, Iosif (Alexandrovich)
See Brodsky, Iosif Alexandrovich
See also CWW 2
Brodsky, Alyn 1928- ... 225
Brodsky, Archie 1945- ... CANR-7
Earlier sketch in CA 61-64
Brodsky, Beverly
See McDermott, Beverly Brodsky
Brodsky, Iosif Alexandrovich
1940-1996 ... CANR-106
Obituary ... 151
Earlier sketches in CA 41-44R, CANR-37
See also Brodskii, Iosif (Alexandrovich) and
Brodsky, Joseph
See also AITN 1
See also DA3
See also DAM POET
See also MTCW 1, 2
See also MTFW 2005
See also RGWL 2, 3
Brodsky, Joseph
See Brodsky, Iosif Alexandrovich
See also AMWS 8
See also CLC 4, 6, 13, 36, 100
See also CWW 2
See also DLB 285
See also EWL 3
See also MTCW 1
See also PC 9
Brodsky, Louis Daniel 1941- ... 111
Brodsky, Michael (Mark) 1948- ... CANR-58
Earlier sketches in CA 102, CANR-18, 41
See also CLC 19
See also DLB 244
Brodsky, Stanley L. 1939- ... CANR-29
Earlier sketch in CA 29-32R
Brodsky, Vera
See Lawrence, Vera Brodsky

Brodwin 74 CONTEMPORARY AUTHORS

Brodwin, Leonora Leet 1929- ... 53-56
Brody, Baruch A(lter) 1943- ... CANR-14
Earlier sketch in CA 33-36R
Brody, David 1930- ... 33-36R
Brody, Elaine 1923-1987 ... 37-40R
Obituary ... 123
Brody, J(acob) J(erome) 1929- ... CANR-32
Earlier sketch in CA 113
Brody, Jane E(llen) 1941- ... CANR-23
Earlier sketch in CA 102
Interview in ... CANR-23
Brody, Jean ... 148
Brody, Jennifer DeVere ... 198
Brody, Jules 1928- ... CANR-9
Earlier sketch in CA 13-16R
Brody, Marc
See Wilkes-Hunter, R(ichard)
Brody, Miriam 1940- ... CANR-120
Earlier sketch in CA 147
Brody, Nathan 1935- ... 111
Brody, Polly 1919- ... 57-60
Brody, Sandor 1863-1924 ... EWL 3
Brody, Saul Nathaniel 1938- ... 53-56
Brody, Stuart 1959- ... 171
Brody, Sylvia
See Axelrad, Sylvia Brody
Brody, Wendy
See Staub, Wendy Corsi
Brodzki, Bella ed. ... CLC 65
Broe, Mary Lynn 1946- ... 110
Broe, Ruth Hammond 1912(?)-1983
Obituary ... 110
Broeg, Bob
See Broeg, Robert M.
See also DLB 171
Broeg, Robert M. 1918- ... CANR-62
Earlier sketches in CA 13-16R, CANR-5
See also Broeg, Bob
Broeger, Achim 1944- ... CANR-48
Earlier sketch in CA 107
See also SATA 31
Broegger, Fredrik Chr(istian) 1945- ... 138
Broehl, Wayne G(ottlieb), Jr. 1922- ... 9-12R
Broek, J(an) O(tto) M(arius) 1904-1974 . CAP-2
Earlier sketch in CA 19-20
Broekel, Rainer Lothar 1923- ... CANR-45
Earlier sketches in CA 9-12R, CANR-3, 19
See also SATA 38
Broekel, Ray
See Broekel, Rainer Lothar
Broeker, Galen 1920-1978 ... 41-44R
Obituary ... 133
Broekman, Marcel 1922- ... 57-60
Broekstra, Lorette 1964- ... SATA 124
Broer, Lawrence R(ichard) 1938- ... 69-72
Broer, Marion Ruth 1910- ... 13-16R
Broerman, Bruce M(artin) 1945- ... 126
Broesamle, John J(oseph) 1941- ... 57-60
Broeze, Frank 1945- ... 148
Brof, Janet 1929- ... 37-40R
Brog, Molly (Jane) 1950- ... 113
Brogan, D(enis) W(illiam)
1900-1974 ... CANR-71
Obituary ... 45-48
Earlier sketch in CA 97-100
Brogan, Elise
See Urch, Elizabeth
Brogan, Frankie Fonde 1922- ... 109
Brogan, Gerald E(dward) 1924-1981 ... 29-32R
Obituary ... 104
Brogan, (Denis) Hugh (Vercingetorix)
1936- ... CANR-143
Earlier sketch in CA 144
Brogan, Jacque Vaught
See Brogan, Jacqueline Vaught
Brogan, Jacqueline Vaught 1952- ... CANR-57
Earlier sketch in CA 125
Brogan, James
See Hodder-Williams, (John) Christopher (Glazebrook)
Brogan, James E(dmund) 1941- ... 41-44R
Brogan, Phil(ip) F(rancis) 1896-1983 ... 9-12R
Brogan, T(erry) V. F. 1951- ... 119
Broger, Achim
See Broeger, Achim
Brogger, Fredrik Chr.
See Broegger, Fredrik Chr(istian)
Brogger, Suzanne 1944- ... CWW 2
See also DLB 214
Broglie, Louis (Victor Pierre Raymond) de
See de Broglie, Louis (Victor Pierre Raymond)
Broglie, Marguerite de 1897-1973
Obituary ... 37-40R
Broh, C(harles) Anthony 1945- ... 61-64
Broh-Kahn, Eleanor 1924- ... 45-48
Broida, Marian ... 229
See also SATA 154
Broido, Ethel 1917- ... 143
Broido, Vera
See Cohn, Vera
Brokamp, Marilyn 1920- ... CANR-46
Earlier sketch in CA 49-52
See also SATA 10
Brokaw, Thomas John 1940- ... CANR-83
Earlier sketch in CA 108
Brokaw, Tom
See Brokaw, Thomas John
Brokensha, David W(arwick) 1923- ... 25-28R
Broker, Ignatia 1919-1987 ... 227
Brokhin, Yuri 1934- ... 57-60
Brokhoff, John R(udolph) 1913- ... CANR-23
Earlier sketches in CA 61-64, CANR-8
Brolin, Brent C(ruse) 1940- ... 65-68
Bromage, Mary Cogan 1906- ... CAP-1
Earlier sketch in CA 13-16
Broman, Fred
See Moseley, James W(illett)
Broman, Sarah Harman 1927(?)-1999 ... 186
Bromberg, Nicolette A. ... 216
Bromberg, Walter 1900-2000 ... 65-68
Bromberger, Merry (Marie Louis) 1906-1979
Obituary ... 110
Bromberger, Serge Paul 1912- ... 29-32R
Brombert, Victor (Henri) 1923- ... CANR-84
Earlier sketches in CA 13-16R, CANR-7, 45
Brome, Richard 1590(?)-1652 ... BRWS 10
See also DLB 58
Brome, (Herbert) Vincent
1910-2004 ... CANR-52
Obituary ... 232
Earlier sketches in CA 77-80, CANR-14
See also DLB 155
Bromell, Henry 1947- ... CANR-116
Earlier sketches in CA 53-56, CANR-9, 115
See also CLC 5
Bromfield, Louis (Brucker) 1896-1956 ... 155
Brief entry ... 107
See also DLB 4, 9, 86
See also RGAL 4
See also RHW
See also TCLC 11
Bromhall, Winifred ... SATA 26
Bromhead, Peter (Alexander) 1919- ... 61-64
Bromige, David (Mansfield) 1933- ... CANR-16
Earlier sketch in CA 25-28R
See also CAAS 26
See also CP 1, 2, 3, 4, 5, 6, 7
See also DLB 193
Bromige, Iris (Amy Edna) 1910- ... RHW
Bromiley, Geoffrey W(illiam) 1915- .. CANR-19
Earlier sketches in CA 5-8R, CANR-4
Bromke, Adam 1928- ... 13-16R
Bromley, David G(rover) 1941- ... 41-44R
Bromley, Dorothy Dunbar 1896-1986
Obituary ... 118
Bromley, Dudley 1948- ... 77-80
See also SATA-Brief 51
Bromley, Gordon 1910- ... 112
Bromley, John Carter 1937- ... 33-36R
Bromley, John Selwyn 1913-1985
Obituary ... 116
Bromley, Simon 1961- ... 147
Bromley, Yulian Vladimirovich 1921-1990
Obituary ... 131
Brommer, Gerald F(rederick) 1927- .. CANR-21
Earlier sketch in CA 105
See also SATA 28
Bromwich, David (Lee) 1951- ... CANR-87
Brief entry ... 121
Earlier sketch in CA 127
Interview in ... CA-127
Bron, Eleanor 1938- ... 156
Bronaugh, Robert Brett 1947- ... 106
Brondfield, Jerome 1913-1998 ... 73-76
See also SATA 22
Brondfield, Jerry
See Brondfield, Jerome
Broneer, Oscar (Theodore) 1894-1992 ... 168
Broner, E(sther) M(asserman) 1930- .. CANR-72
Earlier sketches in CA 17-20R, CANR-8, 25
See also CLC 19
See also CN 4, 5, 6
See also DLB 28
Bronfeld, Stewart 1929- ... 109
Bronfen, Elisabeth (Eve) 1958- ... 192
Bronfenbrenner, Martin 1914-1997 ... 13-16R
Bronfenbrenner, Urie 1917-2005 ... CANR-16
Earlier sketch in CA 97-100
Bronfman, Edgar M(iles) 1929- ... 179
Broniewski, Wladyslaw 1897-1962 ... EWL 3
Bronin, Andrew 1947- ... 45-48
Bronk, William (M.) 1918-1999 ... CANR-23
Obituary ... 177
Earlier sketch in CA 89-92
See also CLC 10
See also CP 3, 4, 5, 6, 7
See also DLB 165
Bronnen, Arnolt 1895-1959 ... DLB 124
Bronner, Edwin B(laine) 1920- ... CANR-22
Earlier sketches in CA 5-8R, CANR-7
Bronner, Ethan (Samuel) 1954- ... 140
Bronner, Leila Leah 1930- ... 155
Bronner, Simon J. 1954- ... CANR-96
Earlier sketches in CA 121, CANR-46
Bronner, Stephen Eric 1949- ... CANR-72
Earlier sketches in CA 113, CANR-32
See also SATA 101
Bronowski, Jacob 1908-1974 ... CANR-71
Obituary ... 53-56
Earlier sketches in CA 1-4R, CANR-3
See also SATA 55
Bronsen, David 1926- ... 37-40R
Bronski, Michael 1945- ... 228
Bronson, Bertrand Harris
1902-1986 ... CANR-71
Obituary ... 118
Earlier sketch in CA 61-64
Bronson, Jill (Dorothy) Ireland 1936-1990
Obituary ... 131
Bronson, L. T.
See Tubb, E(dwin) C(harles)
Bronson, Lee
See King, Albert
Bronson, Lita
See Bell, Louise Price
Bronson, Lynn
See Lampman, Evelyn Sibley
Bronson, Oliver
See Rowland, D(onald) S(ydney)
Bronson, Po 1964- ... CANR-143
Earlier sketch in CA 153
Bronson, Wilfrid Swancourt 1894-1985 .. 73-76
Obituary ... 116
See also SATA-Obit 43
Bronson, William (Knox) 1926-1976 ... 41-44R
Obituary ... 65-68
Bronson, Wolfe
See Raborg, Frederick A(shton), Jr.
Bronstein, Arthur J. 1914- ... 9-12R
Bronstein, Jamie L. 1968- ... 195
Bronstein, Leo 1903(?)-1976
Obituary ... 65-68
Bronstein, Lev Davidovich
See Trotsky, Leon
Bronstein, Lynne 1950- ... 77-80
Bronstein, Yetta
See Abel, Jeanne
Bronte, Anne 1820-1849 ... BRW 5
See also BRWR 1
See also DA3
See also DLB 21, 199
See also TEA
Bronte, Charlotte 1816-1855 ... AAYA 17
See also BRW 5
See also BRWC 2
See also BRWR 1
See also BYA 2
See also CDBLB 1832-1890
See also DA
See also DA3
See also DAB
See also DAC
See also DAM MST, NOV
See also DLB 21, 159, 199
See also EXPN
See also FL 1:2
See also GL 2
See also LAIT 2
See also NFS 4
See also TEA
See also WLC
See also WLIT 4
Bronte, D(iana) Lydia 1938- ... 125
Bronte, Emily (Jane) 1818-1848 ... AAYA 17
See also BPFB 1
See also BRW 5
See also BRWC 1
See also BRWR 1
See also BYA 3
See also CDBLB 1832-1890
See also DA
See also DA3
See also DAB
See also DAC
See also DAM MST, NOV, POET
See also DLB 21, 32, 199
See also EXPN
See also FL 1:2
See also GL 2
See also LAIT 1
See also PC 8
See also TEA
See also WLC
See also WLIT 3
Bronte, Louisa
See Roberts, Janet Louise
Brontes
See Bronte, Anne and
Bronte, Charlotte and
Bronte, Emily (Jane)
Bronwell, Arthur B. 1909-1985 ... 33-36R
Bronzino, Joseph D. 1937- ... 136
Brook, Andrew ... 214
Brook, Barry S(helley) 1918-1997 ... CANR-16
Obituary ... 163
Earlier sketch in CA 25-28R
Brook, David 1932- ... 13-16R
Brook, Elaine (Isabel) 1949- ... 143
Brook, G. L.
See Brook, George Leslie
Brook, George Leslie 1910-1987 ... CANR-80
Obituary ... 123
Earlier sketches in CA 9-12R, CANR-5
Brook, Judith (Penelope) 1926- ... 122
See also SATA 59
See also SATA-Brief 51
Brook, Judy
See Brook, Judith (Penelope)
Brook, Peter (Stephen Paul) 1925- ... CANR-38
Earlier sketch in CA 105
See also MTCW 1
Brook, Rhidian ... 230
Brook, Stephen 1947- ... CANR-106
Earlier sketch in CA 147
See also DLB 204
Brook, Timothy (James) 1951- ... 140
Brook, Victor John Knight 1887-1974 ... 1-4R
Obituary ... 103
Brook, Vincent 1946- ... 239
Brooke, A. B.
See Jennings, Leslie Nelson
Brooke, Avery (Rogers) 1923- ... CANR-21
Earlier sketches in CA 57-60, CANR-6
Brooke, Brian 1911- ... 85-88
Brooke, Bryan (Nicholas) 1915-1998 . CANR-1
Obituary ... 170
Earlier sketch in CA 45-48
Brooke, Carol
See Ramskill, Valerie Patricia Roskams
Brooke, Christopher N(ugent) L(awrence)
1927- ... CANR-109
Earlier sketches in CA 5-8R, CANR-2, 18, 40, 42
Brooke, Dinah 1936- ... CANR-4
Earlier sketch in CA 49-52
Brooke, Eleanor (Golden) 1905(?)-1987
Obituary ... 122
Brooke, Frances 1724-1789 ... DLB 39, 99
Brooke, George Mercer, Jr. 1914- ... 122
Brooke, Harold 1910-
Brief entry ... 113
Brooke, Henry 1703(?)-1783 ... DLB 39
Brooke, James B. 1955- ... 135
Brooke, Jill 1959- ... 203
Brooke, (Bernard) Jocelyn 1908-1966 ... 5-8R
Brooke, John 1920-1985
Obituary ... 118
Brooke, John L. 1953- ... 140
Brooke, Joshua
See Miller, Victor (Brooke)
Brooke, L(eonard) Leslie 1862-1940 ... CLR 20
See also CWRI 5
See also DLB 141
See also MAICYA 1, 2
See also SATA 17
Brooke, Margaret (Alice Lilly de Windt)
1849-1936 ... 183
See also DLB 174
Brooke, Maxey 1913-1994 ... 9-12R
Brooke, Nicholas Stanton 1924- ... 25-28R
Brooke, Rosalind B(eckford) 1925- ... 148
Brooke, Rupert (Chawner)
1887-1915 ... CANR-61
Brief entry ... 104
Earlier sketch in CA 132
See also BRWS 3
See also CDBLB 1914-1945
See also DA
See also DAB
See also DAC
See also DAM MST, POET
See also DLB 19, 216
See also EXPP
See also GLL 2
See also MTCW 1, 2
See also MTFW 2005
See also PC 24
See also PFS 7
See also TCLC 2, 7
See also TEA
See also WLC
Brooke, Simon 1963- ... 238
Brooke, (Robert) Tal(iaferro) 1945- ... 93-96
Brooke, William J. 1946- ... 134
See also CWRI 5
See also SATA 139
Brooke-Haven, P.
See Wodehouse, P(elham) G(renville)
Brooke-Little, John 1927- ... CANR-10
Earlier sketch in CA 21-24R
Brooker, Barbara 1936- ... 127
Brooker, Bertram (Richard) 1888-1955 . DLB 88
Brooker, Clark
See Fowler, Kenneth A(brams)
Brooker, Jewel Spears 1940- ... CANR-134
Earlier sketches in CA 135, CANR-69
Brooke-Rose, Christine 1926(?)- ... CANR-118
Earlier sketches in CA 13-16R, CANR-58
See also BRWS 4
See also CLC 40, 184
See also CN 1, 2, 3, 4, 5, 6, 7
See also DLB 14, 231
See also EWL 3
See also SFW 4
Brookes, Edgar Harry 1897-1979 ... CANR-70
Earlier sketches in CA 1-4R, CANR-3
Brookes, John A. 1933- ... 137
Brookes, Kenneth John 1909-1984
Obituary ... 111
Brookes, Owen
See Barber, D(ulan) F(riar Whilberton)
Brookes, Pamela 1922- ... 25-28R
Brookes, Reuben Solomon 1914- ... CAP-1
Earlier sketch in CA 9-10
Brookes, Tim 1953- ... CANR-99
Earlier sketch in CA 147
Brookhiser, Richard 1955- ... CANR-87
Earlier sketch in CA 139
Brookhouse, (John) Christopher
1938- ... CANR-107
Earlier sketches in CA 29-32R, CANR-52
Brookhouser, Frank 1912(?)-1975 ... 1-4R
Obituary ... 61-64
Brookins, Dana 1931- ... 69-72
See also SATA 28
Brookman, Denise Cass 1921- ... 1-4R
Brookman, Rosina Francesca 1932- ... 61-64
Brookmyre, Christopher 1968- ... 184
Brookner, Anita 1928- ... CANR-130
Brief entry ... 114
Earlier sketches in CA 120, CANR-37, 56, 87
See also BRWS 4
See also CLC 32, 34, 51, 136
See also CN 4, 5, 6, 7
See also CPW
See also DA3
See also DAB
See also DAM POP
See also DLB 194
See also DLBY 1987
See also EWL 3
See also MTCW 1, 2
See also MTFW 2005
See also TEA
Brookover, Wilbur B(one) 1911- ... 33-36R
Brooks, A(lfred) Russell 1906- ... CAP-2
Earlier sketch in CA 33-36
Brooks, Albert 1947- ... CANR-37
Brief entry ... 109
Earlier sketch in CA 113
Brooks, Andree (Nicole) Aelion
1937- ... CANR-125
Earlier sketch in CA 133
Brooks, Anita
See Abramovitz, Anita (Zeltner Brooks)
See also SATA 5
Brooks, Anne Tedlock 1905-1980 ... CANR-1
Earlier sketch in CA 1-4R

Cumulative Index 75 **Browder**

Brooks, B. David 1938- 113
Brooks, Barbara 1947- 195
Brooks, Betty 1936- 162
Brooks, Bill 1939- .... SATA 59
Brooks, Bill 1943- 235
Brooks, Bruce 1950- CANR-140
Earlier sketch in CA 137
See also AAYA 8, 36
See also BYA 7, 9
See also CLR 25
See also JRDA
See also MAICYA 1, 2
See also SATA 72, 112
See also SATA-Brief 53
See also WYA
See also YAW
Brooks, C(larence) Carlyle 1888-1983 ... CAP-1
Earlier sketch in CA 13-14
Brooks, Caroline
See Chappell, Helen
Brooks, Caryl 1924- 150
See also SATA 84
Brooks, Charles (Gordon) 1920- 115
Brooks, Charles B(enton) 1921- 1-4R
Brooks, Charles E(dward) 1921- 53-56
Brooks, Charles Timothy 1813-1883 ..... DLB 1, 243
Brooks, Charles V. W. 1912-1991 77-80
Brooks, Charlotte K(endrick)
1918-1998 .... CANR-45
Obituary 172
Earlier sketch in CA 89-92
See also SATA 24
See also SATA-Obit 112
Brooks, Cleanth 1906-1994 .... CANR-35
Obituary 145
Earlier sketches in CA 17-20R, CANR-33
Interview in CANR-35
See also AMWS 14
See also CLC 24, 86, 110
See also CSW
See also DLB 63
See also DLBY 1994
See also EWL 3
See also MAL 5
See also MTCW 1, 2
See also MTFW 2005
Brooks, Colette 230
Brooks, D(avid) P. 1915- CANR-11
Earlier sketch in CA 25-28R
Brooks, David (Gordon) 1953- 140
Brooks, David 1961- 235
Brooks, David H(opkinson) 1929- 61-64
Brooks, Deems M(arkham) 1934- 69-72
Brooks, Douglas
See Brooks-Davies, Douglas
Brooks, Douglas L(ee) 1916- CANR-86
Earlier sketches in CA 114, CANR-35
Brooks, Elston (Harwood) 1930- 125
Brooks, Emerson M. 1905(?)-1982
Obituary 108
Brooks, Erik 1972- 227
See also SATA 152
Brooks, Fairleigh 1953- 224
Brooks, Fern Field 1934- 229
Brooks, Gary D(onald) 1942- 41-44R
Brooks, George
See Baum, L(yman) Frank
Brooks, George E(dward), Jr. 1933- 33-36R
Brooks, Geraldine 170
Brooks, Gladys Rice 1886(?)-1984
Obituary 111
Brooks, Glenn E(llis), Jr. 1931- 1-4R
Brooks, Gregory 1961- 102
Brooks, Gwendolyn (Elizabeth)
1917-2000 .... CANR-132
Obituary 190
Earlier sketches in CA 1-4R, CANR-1, 27, 52, 75
See also AAYA 20
See also AFAW 1, 2
See also AITN 1
See also AMWS 3
See also BLC 1
See also BW 2, 3
See also CDALB 1941-1968
See also CLC 1, 2, 4, 5, 15, 49, 125
See also CLR 27
See also CP 1, 2, 3, 4, 5, 6, 7
See also CWP
See also DA
See also DA3
See also DAC
See also DAM MST, MULT, POET
See also DLB 5, 76, 165
See also EWL 3
See also EXPP
See also FL 1:5
See also MAL 5
See also MAWW
See also MTCW 1, 2
See also MTFW 2005
See also PC 7
See also PFS 1, 2, 4, 6
See also RGAL 4
See also SATA 6
See also SATA-Obit 123
See also TUS
See also WLC
See also WP
Brooks, H(arold) Allen 1925- CANR-31
Earlier sketches in CA 81-84, CANR-14
Brooks, Harold F(letcher) 1907-1990 128
Brooks, Harvey 1915-2004 .... 25-28R
Obituary 227
Brooks, Hindi 185
Brief entry 115
Brooks, Hugh C. 1922- 29-32R
Brooks, Hunter O(tis) 1929- 77-80
Brooks, James L. 1940- CANR-124
Earlier sketches in CA 73-76, CANR-32, 54
See also AAYA 17
Brooks, Janice Young 1943- CANR-104
Earlier sketches in CA 65-68, CANR-9, 39, 69
Brooks, Jeanne
See Brooks-Gunn, Jeanne
Brooks, Jeremy 1926-1994 .... CANR-7
Obituary 146
Earlier sketch in CA 5-8R
See also CN 1, 2
See also DLB 14
Brooks, Jerome 1931- CANR-2
Earlier sketch in CA 49-52
See also SATA 23
Brooks, Jerome E(dmund) 1895(?)-1983
Obituary 109
Brooks, John
See Sugar, Bert Randolph
Brooks, John (Nixon) 1920-1993 ...... CANR-55
Obituary 142
Earlier sketches in CA 13-16R, CANR-6
Brooks, Juanita 1898-
Brief entry 114
Brooks, Karen 1949- 57-60
Brooks, Keith 1923- 17-20R
Brooks, Kevin M. 1959- 225
See also SATA 150
Brooks, (Frank) Leonard 1911- 13-16R
Brooks, LeRoy D(avis) II 1943-
Brief entry 113
Brooks, Lester 1924- CANR-42
Earlier sketches in CA 33-36R, CANR-13
See also SATA 7
Brooks, (Mary) Louise 1906-1985 .. CANR-120
Obituary 117
Earlier sketch in CA 134
Brooks, Lyman Beecher 1910-1984 122
Obituary 112
Brooks, Maggie
See Brooks, Margaret Ann
Brooks, Margaret Ann 1951- 132
Brooks, Maria (Zagorska) 1933- 41-44R
Brooks, Martha 1944- CANR-110
Earlier sketch in CA 136
See also AAYA 37
See also BYA 12, 16
See also MAICYA 2
See also SATA 68, 121, 134
See also SATA-Essay 134
See also YAW
Brooks, Maurice (Graham) 1900- .... SATA 45
Brooks, Mel
See Kaminsky, Melvin
See also AAYA 13, 48
See also CLC 12
See also DLB 26
Brooks, Nelson Herbert 1902-1978
Obituary 77-80
Brooks, Noah 1830-1903 216
See also DLB 42
See also DLBD 13
Brooks, Pat 1931- CANR-7
Earlier sketch in CA 57-60
Brooks, Patricia 1926- CANR-11
Earlier sketch in CA 25-28R
Brooks, Paul 1909-1998 .... CANR-70
Earlier sketches in CA 13-16R, CANR-7
Brooks, Peter (Preston) 1938- CANR-107
Earlier sketches in CA 45-48, CANR-1
See also CLC 34
Brooks, Peter Newman 1931- CANR-86
Earlier sketch in CA 131
Brooks, Peter W(right) 1920-1996 .... 9-12R
Brooks, Philip 1899(?)-1975
Obituary 104
Brooks, Polly Schoyer 1912- CANR-17
Earlier sketch in CA 1-4R
See also SATA 12
Brooks, Richard 1912-1992 73-76
Obituary 137
See also DLB 44
Brooks, Richard A. 1931- 153
Brooks, Richard Oliver 1934- 112
Brooks, Robert A(ngus) 1920-1976
Obituary 65-68
Brooks, Robert Emanuel 1941- 57-60
Brooks, Rodney (A.) 1954- 216
Brooks, Romaine 1874-1970 163
See also GLL 1
Brooks, Ron(ald George) 1948- 159
Brief entry 111
See also SATA 94
See also SATA-Brief 33
Brooks, Roy L(avon) 1950- 166
Brooks, Seth Rogers 1901-1987
Obituary 123
Brooks, Stewart M. 1923- CANR-9
Earlier sketch in CA 17-20R
Brooks, Terry 1944- CANR-135
Earlier sketches in CA 77-80, CANR-14, 51, 100
See also AAYA 18
See also CPW
See also DAM POP
See also FANT
See also MTFW 2005
See also SATA 60
See also SUFW 2
See also YAW
Brooks, Thomas 1941- 120
Brooks, Thomas R(eed) 1925- CANR-34
Earlier sketch in CA 73-76
Brooks, Tim(othy Haley) 1942- CANR-19
Earlier sketch in CA 102
Brooks, Van Wyck 1886-1963 .... CANR-6
Earlier sketch in CA 1-4R
See also AMW
See also CLC 29
See also DLB 45, 63, 103
See also MAL 5
See also TUS
Brooks, W. Hal 1933- 57-60
Brooks, Walter R(ollin) 1886-1958
Brief entry 111
See also CWRI 5
See also SATA 17
Brooks, William D(ean) 1929- 33-36R
Brooks-Davies, Douglas 1942- CANR-12
Earlier sketch in CA 73-76
Brooks-Gunn, Jeanne 1946- 135
Brook-Shepherd, (Frederick) Gordon
1918-2004 .... CANR-70
Obituary 226
Earlier sketches in CA 9-12R, CANR-3
Brookshier, Frank 93-96
Brooks-Hill, Helen (Mason)
1908-1994 .... SATA 59
Brookter, Marie 1934(?)- .... AITN 1
Broom, Leonard 1911- CANR-5
Earlier sketch in CA 13-16R
Broom, Neil D. 203
Broomall, Robert W(alter) 1946- CANR-44
Earlier sketch in CA 119
See also TCWW 2
Broome, Charles L(arue) 1925- 41-44R
Broome, Errol 1937- CANR-139
Earlier sketch in CA 173
See also SATA 105, 158
Broome, Harvey 1902-1968 122
Obituary 110
Broomell, Myron H(enry) 1906-1970 .... CAP-1
Earlier sketch in CA 9-10
Broomfield, Gerald W(ebb) 1895-1976 ..... 5-8R
Obituary 103
Broomfield, J(ohn) H(indle) 1935- 25-28R
Brophy, Ann 1931- 106
Brophy, Brigid (Antonia) 1929-1995 . CANR-53
Obituary 149
Earlier sketches in CA 5-8R, CANR-25
See also CAAS 4
See also CBD
See also CLC 6, 11, 29, 105
See also CN 1, 2, 3, 4, 5, 6
See also CWD
See also DA3
See also DLB 14, 271
See also EWL 3
See also MTCW 1, 2
Brophy, Donald F(rancis) 1934- CANR-10
Earlier sketch in CA 21-24R
Brophy, Elizabeth Bergen 1929- 61-64
Brophy, James David, Jr. 1926- CANR-3
Earlier sketch in CA 1-4R
Brophy, James J(oseph) 1912-1986 65-68
Brophy, Jere E(dward) 1940- CANR-2
Earlier sketch in CA 45-48
Brophy, Jim
See Brophy, James J(oseph)
Brophy, John 1899-1965 .... CANR-71
Earlier sketches in CAP-1, CA 11-12
See also DLB 191
Brophy, Liam 1910- 9-12R
Brophy, Nannette 1963- .... SATA 73
Brophy, Robert J(oseph) 1928- CANR-5
Earlier sketch in CA 53-56
Brorson, Hans Adolph 1694-1764 ...... DLB 300
Brose, Olive J(ohnson) 1919- 41-44R
Brosio, Richard A(nthony) 1938- 198
Brosman, Catharine Savage 1934- CANR-46
Earlier sketches in CA 61-64, CANR-21
See also CLC 9
Brosnahan, Leger (Nicholas) 1929- 208
Brosnahan, Leonard Francis 1922- 102
Brosnahan, Tom 1945- 119
Brosnan, James Patrick 1929- CANR-3
Earlier sketch in CA 1-4R
See also SATA 14
Brosnan, Jim
See Brosnan, James Patrick
Brosnan, John 1947-2005 160
See also Blackstone, James and Knight, Harry Adam
See also SFW 4
Bross, Donald G. 1932- 154
Bross, Irwin D(udley) J(ackson)
1921-2004 .... 37-40R
Obituary 229
Brossa, Joan 1919-1998 211
Brossard, Chandler 1922-1993 .... CANR-56
Obituary 142
Earlier sketches in CA 61-64, CANR-8
See also CAAS 2
See also BG 1:2
See also CN 1, 2, 3
See also DLB 16
Brossard, Nicole 1943- CANR-140
Earlier sketch in CA 122
See also CAAS 16
See also CCA 1
See also CLC 115, 169
See also CWP
See also CWW 2
See also DLB 53
See also EWL 3
See also FW
See also GLL 2
See also RGWL 3
Brossier, Margaret 1918(?)-1984
Obituary 113
Broster, Dorothy Kathleen 1877-1950 202
See also DLB 160
See also HGG
See also RHW
Brostoff, Anita 1931- 201
See also SATA 132
Brostowin, Patrick Ronald 1931- 13-16R
Broszat, Martin 1926-1989
Obituary 130
Brotchie, Alastair 1952- 189
Brother Anonymous
See Desbiens, Jean-Paul
Brother Antoninus
See Everson, William (Oliver)
Brother Bob
See Buell, Robert Kingery
Brother Choleric
See van Zeller, Claud
Brothers, (M.) Jay 1931-1979 103
Brothers, Joyce (Diane Bauer)
1929- CANR-13
Earlier sketch in CA 21-24R
See also AITN 1
Brothers Hildebrandt, The
See Hildebrandt, Greg and Hildebrandt, Tim(othy)
The Brothers Quay
See Quay, Stephen and Quay, Timothy
Brotherston, James Gordon 1939- CANR-11
Earlier sketch in CA 25-28R
Brotherton, Lord 1856-1930 .... DLB 184
Brotherton, Edward Allen 1856-1930 186
Brotherton, Manfred 1900(?)-1981
Obituary 102
Brottman, Mikita 1966- 175
Broude, Norma (Freedman) 1941- 113
Broudy, Harry S(amuel) 1905-1998 .... CANR-3
Earlier sketch in CA 1-4R
Broue, Pierre 1926- CANR-12
Earlier sketch in CA 69-72
Brough, James 1918- 111
Brough, John 1917-1984
Obituary 111
Brough, R(obert) Clayton 1950- CANR-7
Earlier sketch in CA 57-60
Brougham, Henry Peter 1778-1868 ... DLB 110, 158
Brougham, John 1810-1880 .... DLB 11
See also RGAL 4
Broughton, Bradford B. 1926-1997 .... 21-24R
Broughton, Diane 1943- 81-84
Broughton, Geoffrey 1927- 102
Broughton, Jack(sel Markham) 1925- 73-76
Broughton, James (Richard)
1913-1999 .... CANR-57
Obituary 179
Earlier sketches in CA 49-52, CANR-2, 30
See also CAAS 12
See also CP 1, 2
See also DLB 5
Broughton, John Marcus 1947- .... CD 5, 6
Broughton, R(obert) Peter 1940- 148
Broughton, Rhoda 1840-1920 183
See also DLB 18
See also HGG
Broughton, T(homas) Alan 1936- CANR-111
Earlier sketches in CA 45-48, CANR-2, 23, 48
See also CLC 19
Broughton, Trev Lynn 1959- 209
Brouillette, Jeanne S. -1995 .... 1-4R
Broumas, Olga 1949- CANR-110
Earlier sketches in CA 85-88, CANR-20, 69
See also CLC 10, 73
See also CP 7
See also CWP
See also GLL 2
Broun, Emily
See Sterne, Emma Gelders
Broun, Heywood 1888-1939 .... DLB 29, 171
See also TCLC 104
Broun, Heywood Hale 1918-2001 ... CANR-12
Obituary 202
Earlier sketch in CA 17-20R
Broun, Heywood Oren 1950(?)-1987 144
Obituary 124
Broun, Hob
See Broun, Heywood Oren
Broussard, Louis 1922- 25-28R
Broussard, Meredith (K.) 1974- 234
Broussard, Vivian L.
See Martinetz, V(ivian) L.
Brouwer, J(elle) H(indriks) 1900-1981 209
Brouwer, Joel 1968- .... PFS 14
Brouwer, Luitzen Egbertus Jan 1881-1966
Obituary 116
Brouwer, S. W.
See Brouwer, Sigmund (W.)
Brouwer, Sigmund (W.) 1959- CANR-113
Earlier sketch in CA 164
See also SATA 109
Brouwer, Sigmund (W.) 1959- CANR-113
Brouwers, Jeroen 1940- .... EWL 3
Brovka, Petr (Pyatrus Ustinovich) 1905-1980
Obituary 105
Brovkin, Vladimir N. 1951- 137
Brow, Robert 1924- CANR-10
Earlier sketch in CA 21-24R
Brow, Thea 1934- .... SATA 60
Broward, Donn
See Halleran, E(ugene) E(dward)
Broward, Robert C. 1926- 122
Browder, Earl Russell 1891-1973
Obituary 45-48
See also DLB 303
Browder, Lesley H(ughes), Jr. 1935- 45-48
Browder, Olin L(orraine), Jr. 1913- 41-44R

Browder, Robert P(aul) 1921- 122
Browder, Sue 1946- 77-80
Browder, Walter Everett 1939- 53-56
Brower, Brock (Hendrickson) 1931- 25-28R
Brower, Charles Hendrickson 1901-1984 ... 102
Obituary 113
Brower, Charlie
See Brower, Charles Hendrickson
Brower, Daniel R(oberts) 1936- 41-44R
Brower, David (Ross) 1912-2000 .... CANR-9
Obituary 191
Earlier sketch in CA 61-64
Brower, Kenneth (David) 1944- CANR-10
Earlier sketch in CA 25-28R
Brower, Linda A. 1945- 33-36R
Brower, Millicent CANR-15
Earlier sketch in CA 41-44R
See also SATA 8
Brower, Pauline 1929- 77-80
See also SATA 22
Brower, Reuben Arthur 1908-1975 ... CANR-69
Obituary 57-60
Earlier sketches in CA 1-4R, CANR-6
Browin, Frances Williams
1898-1986 .... CANR-69
Earlier sketches in CAP-1, CA 19-20
See also SATA 5
Brown, A(lfred) R(eginald) Radcliffe
See Radcliffe-Brown, A(lfred) R(eginald)
Brown, Alan 163
Brown, Alan 1950- 156
See also CLC 99
Brown, Alan A. 1929- CANR-16
Earlier sketch in CA 25-28R
Brown, Alan R. 1938- 105
Brown, Alberta L(ouise) 1894-1987 .... CAP-1
Earlier sketch in CA 11-12
Brown, Alexander (Crosby)
1905-1993 .... CANR-3
Earlier sketch in CA 1-4R
Brown, Alexis
See Baumann, Amy (Brown) Beeching
Brown, Alice 1856-1948 178
See also DLB 78
Brown, Alice Very
See Very, Alice (N.)
Brown, Allen 1926- 13-16R
Brown, Amanda 223
Brown, Andreas Le 1933- 108
Brown, Andrew 197
Brown, Anne Ensign 1937- 101
See also SATA 61
Brown, Anne M. Wyatt
See Wyatt-Brown, Anne M(arbury)
Brown, Anne S(eddon) K(insolving)
1906-1985 .... 17-20R
Obituary 117
Brown, Annice Harris 1897-1982 45-48
Brown, Annora 1899-1987(?)
Obituary 121
Brown, Anthony Cave 1930- 139
Brown, Anthony Eugene 1937- 89-92
Brown, Archibald Haworth 1938- CANR-44
Earlier sketches in CA 103, CANR-20
Brown, Arnold 1927- 117
Brown, Arthur A(llen) 1900-1988 73-76
Brown, Arthur Wayne 1917- CANR-8
Earlier sketch in CA 5-8R
Brown, Ashley 1923- CANR-20
Earlier sketches in CA 1-4R, CANR-3
Brown, B(artley) Frank 1917- CANR-4
Earlier sketch in CA 9-12R
Brown, B(essie) Katherine (Taylor)
1917- 13-16R
Brown, Barbara B(anker) 1917- 69-72
Brown, Barbara W(ood) 1928- 105
Brown, Beatrice C.
See Curtis Brown, Beatrice
Brown, Benjamin F. 1930-1999 .... CANR-1
Earlier sketch in CA 45-48
Brown, Bernard E(dward) 1925- CANR-21
Earlier sketches in CA 1-4R, CANR-4
Brown, Bert R(obert) 1936- 41-44R
Brown, Beth CANR-69
Earlier sketches in CAP-2, CA 21-22
Brown, Betty
See Jones, Elizabeth B(rown)
Brown, Beverly Swerdlow .... SATA 97
Brown, Bill
See Brown, William L(ouis)
Brown, Billye Walker
See Cutchen, Billye Walker
Brown, Blanche R. (Levine) 1915- 13-16R
Brown, Bob
See Brown, Robert Carlton
See also DLB 4, 45
Brown, Bob
See Brown, Robert Joseph
Brown, Bob Burton 1925- 21-24R
Brown, Brian A. 1942- 161
Brown, Brooks 1981(?)- 226
Brown, Bryan T(urner) 1952- 139
Brown, Buck 1936- .... SATA 45
Brown, Byron 1952- 181
Brown, Calvin S(mith) 1909- 49-52
Brown, Camille 1917- 9-12R
Brown, Carl F(raser) 1910- 41-44R
Brown, Carol Williams 1941- 111
Brown, Carolyn S. 1950- 127
Brown, Carrie
See Brown, Carolyn S.
Brown, Carter
See Yates, A(lan) G(eoffrey)
See also CMW 4
Brown, Cassie 1919-1986 .... CANR-23
Earlier sketch in CA 45-48
See also SATA 55
Brown, Cecil 1907-1987
Obituary 123
Brown, Cecil H(ooper) 1944- 109
Brown, Cecil M(orris) 1943- CANR-27
Earlier sketch in CA 73-76
See also BW 1
See also DLB 33
Brown, Charles
See Cadet, John
Brown, Charles Brockden
1771-1810 .... AMWS 1
See also CDALB 1640-1865
See also DLB 37, 59, 73
See also FW
See also GL 2
See also HGG
See also LMFS 1
See also RGAL 4
See also TUS
Brown, Charles Henry 1910-1993 .... 21-24R
Brown, Charles N(ikki) 1937- 93-96
Brown, Charles T(homas) 1912- 41-44R
Brown, Chester 1960- 184
Brown, Christopher P(aterson)
1939- CANR-10
Earlier sketch in CA 65-68
Brown, Christy 1932-1981 .... CANR-72
Obituary 104
Earlier sketch in CA 105
See also BYA 13
See also CLC 63
See also DLB 14
Brown, Clair 1946- 171
Brown, Clarence (Fleetwood, Jr.) 1929-
Brief entry 112
Brown, Clark 1935- 25-28R
Brown, Claude 1937-2002 .... CANR-81
Obituary 205
Earlier sketch in CA 73-76
See also AAYA 7
See also BLC 1
See also BW 1, 3
See also CLC 30
See also DAM MULT
Brown, Clifford Waters, Jr. 1942- 77-80
Brown, (John) Clive (Anthony) 1947- 121
Brown, Conrad 1922- .... SATA 31
Brown, Constantine 1889-1966 .... CAP-1
Earlier sketch in CA 11-12
Brown, Corinne Joy 1948- 222
Brown, Courtney C(onrades) 1904-1990 . 77-80
Obituary 131
Brown, Craig McFarland 1947- .... SATA 73
Brown, Croswell 1905(?)-1971
Obituary 104
Brown, Curtis F(ranklin) 1925- 61-64
Brown, Cynthia 1952- 121
Brown, Dale 1956(?)- CANR-117
Brief entry 129
Earlier sketches in CA 138, CANR-60
See also BEST 89:4
Brown, Dale W. 1926- 37-40R
Brown, Dan 1964- 217
See also AAYA 55
See also CLC 209
See also MTFW 2005
Brown, Daniel G(ilbert) 1924- 45-48
Brown, Daniel Russell
See Curzon, Daniel
Brown, Daphne Faunce
See Faunce-Brown, Daphne (Bridget)
Brown, David
See Brown, David A(lan) and
Myller, Rolf
Brown, David 1916- 13-16R
Brown, David (Clifford) 1929- CANR-141
Earlier sketch in CA 57-60
Brown, David A.
See Brown, David A(lan)
Brown, David A(lan) 1922-1982 129
Obituary 110
Brown, David E(arl) 1938- CANR-64
Earlier sketches in CA 113, CANR-32
Brown, David Grant 1936- 13-16R
Brown, David S(pringer) 1915- 29-32R
Brown, Deaver David 1943- 102
Brown, Dee (Alexander) 1908-2002 . CANR-60
Obituary 212
Earlier sketches in CA 13-16R, CANR-11, 45
See also CAAS 6
See also AAYA 30
See also CLC 18, 47
See also CPW
See also CSW
See also DA3
See also DAM POP
See also DLBY 1980
See also LAIT 2
See also MTCW 1, 2
See also MTFW 2005
See also NCFS 5
See also SATA 5, 110
See also SATA-Obit 141
See also TCWW 1, 2
Brown, Delwin (Wray) 1935- 135
Brief entry 117
Brown, Deming 1919-1999 147
Brown, Denise Scott 1931- 41-44R
Brown, Dennis A(lbert) 1926-1978 ... CANR-13
Earlier sketch in CA 61-64
Brown, Derek Ernest Denny
See Denny-Brown, Derek Ernest
Brown, Diana 1928- CANR-40
Earlier sketches in CA 101, CANR-18
Brown, Dona 1956- CANR-111
Earlier sketch in CA 151
Brown, Donald Eugene 1909-1996 .... CAP-1
Obituary 155
Earlier sketch in CA 13-16
Brown, Donald Fowler 1909-1989 .... 41-44R
Brown, Donald Robert 1925- 41-44R
Brown, Doris E. 1910(?)-1975
Obituary 61-64
Brown, Dorothy
See Oxley, Dorothy (Anne)
Brown, Dorothy M. 1932- 125
Brown, Douglas
See Gibson, Walter B(rown)
Brown, Douglas (Frank Lambert)
1907- 25-28R
Brown, Drew T. III 1955- 150
See also SATA 83
Brown, Drollene P. 1939- CANR-48
Earlier sketch in CA 122
See also SATA 53
Brown, Duane 1937- 33-36R
Brown, E(dward) K(illoran) 1905-1951
Brief entry 107
Brown, E(ugene) Richard 1942- CANR-40
Earlier sketches in CA 97-100, CANR-18
Brown, Edgar S., Jr. 1922- 9-12R
Brown, Edmund G. (Pat)
See Brown, Edmund G(erald)
Brown, Edmund G(erald) 1905-1996 132
Obituary 151
Brown, Edward J(ames) 1909-1991 .. CANR-69
Earlier sketch in CA 25-28R
Brown, Elaine 1943- CANR-140
Earlier sketch in CA 142
See also BW 2
Brown, Eleanor Frances 1908-1987 ...... 29-32R
See also SATA 3
Brown, Eleanor Gertrude 1887-1968
Obituary 104
Brown, Elisabeth Potts 1939- 133
Brown, Elizabeth Ferguson 1937- 228
See also SATA 153
Brown, Elizabeth Louise 1924- 53-56
Brown, Elizabeth M(yers) 1915- 107
See also SATA 43
Brown, Emily Clara 1911-2001 53-56
Brown, Eric 1960- 197
See also SFW 4
Brown, Erik 1932- 114
Brown, Ernest Henry Phelps 1906-1994 108
Brown, Evelyn M(arjorie) 1911- 21-24R
Brown, F(rancis) Andrew 1915- 41-44R
Brown, F. Keith 1913(?)-1976
Obituary 69-72
Brown, F(rancis Charles Claypon) Yeats
See Yeats-Brown, F(rancis Charles Claypon)
Brown, Felicia M. Jefferson 1971- 162
Brown, Fern G. 1918- CANR-40
Earlier sketches in CA 97-100, CANR-17
See also SATA 34
Brown, (Robert) Fletch 1923- 116
See also SATA 42
Brown, Fornan 1901-1996 .... SATA 71
See also SATA-Obit 88
Brown, Forrest 49-52
Brown, (Ernest) Francis 1903-1995 ... CANR-69
Obituary 150
Earlier sketch in CA 73-76
Brown, Francis R(obert) 1914-2001 ...... 41-44R
Brown, Frank A(rthur), Jr. 1908-1983 69-72
Brown, Frank E(dward) 1908-1988 101
Brown, Frank London 1927-1962 141
See also BW 2
See also DLB 76
Brown, Fred 1923- 179
Brown, Frederick 1934- CANR-66
Earlier sketch in CA 25-28R
Brown, Frederick G(ramm) 1932- CANR-12
Earlier sketch in CA 29-32R
Brown, Fredric (William)
1906-1972 .... CANR-117
Obituary 33-36R
Earlier sketches in CA 121, CANR-59
See also CMW 4
See also DLB 8
See also SFW 4
Brown, G(eorge) Neville 1932- 17-20R
Brown, Geoff 1932- 61-64
Brown, George
See Wertmueller, Lina
Brown, George Alfred George
See George-Brown, George Alfred
Brown, George Douglas 1869-1902 162
See also Douglas, George
See also TCLC 28
Brown, George Earl 1883-1964 .... 5-8R
See also SATA 11
Brown, George Isaac 1923- 73-76
Brown, George Mackay 1921-1996 . CANR-67
Obituary 151
Earlier sketches in CA 21-24R, CANR-12, 37
See also CAAS 6
See also BRWS 6
See also CLC 5, 48, 100
See also CN 1, 2, 3, 4, 5, 6
See also CP 1, 2
See also DLB 14, 27, 139, 271
See also MTCW 1
See also RGSF 2
See also SATA 35
Brown, George Thompson 1921- 111
Brown, Gerald Saxon 1911-1999 .... 9-12R
Brown, Gerald W(illiam) 1916- 33-36R
Brown, Giles T(yler) 1916- 17-20R
Brown, Ginny
See Brown, Virginia Sharpe
Brown, Gordon S. 1936- 238
Brown, Gwilym Slater 1928-1974 .... 9-12R
Obituary 53-56
Brown, H. Jackson, Jr. 1940- 140
Brown, H. Rap
See Al-Amin, Jamil Abdullah
Brown, Hamish M. 1934- 129
Brown, Harcourt 1900-1990 .... CANR-20
Obituary 141
Earlier sketch in CA 101
Brown, Harold O(gden) J(oseph)
1933- CANR-10
Earlier sketch in CA 25-28R
Brown, Harriet N(ancy) 1958- 173
Brown, Harriett M. 1897-1987 .... 5-8R
Brown, Harrison Scott 1917-1986 69-72
Obituary 121
Brown, Harry (Peter McNab, Jr.)
1917-1986 .... CANR-72
Obituary 120
Earlier sketch in CA 69-72
See also DLB 26
Brown, Harry Clifford 1953- 168
Brown, Harry G(unnison) 1880-1975
Obituary 57-60
Brown, Harry M(atthew) 1921- CANR-10
Earlier sketch in CA 25-28R
Brown, Hazel E(lizabeth) 1893-1986 57-60
Brown, Helen Gurley 1922- CANR-91
Earlier sketches in CA 5-8R, CANR-5
Interview in CANR-5
Brown, Herbert Ross 1902-1988 .... CAP-1
Earlier sketch in CA 13-16
Brown, Howard Mayer 1930-1993 .. CANR-49
Obituary 140
Earlier sketches in CA 1-4R, CANR-3
Brown, Hugh Auchincloss 1879-1975
Obituary 61-64
Brown, Huntington 1899-1985 .... CAP-1
Earlier sketch in CA 19-20
Brown, Ian 1945- .... DLB 310
Brown, Ian 1954(?)- 156
Brown, Ida Mae 1908- CAP-2
Earlier sketch in CA 29-32
Brown, Ina Corinne 5-8R
Brown, Ina Ladd 1905-1985 .... CAP-1
Earlier sketch in CA 13-14
Brown, Ira Vernon 1922- 5-8R
Brown, Irene Bennett 1932- CANR-12
Earlier sketch in CA 29-32R
See also SATA 3
Brown, Irene Quenzler 1938- 224
Brown, Irving
See Adams, William Taylor
Brown, Irwin
See Murray, David Stark
Brown, Ivor (John Carnegie)
1891-1974 .... CANR-69
Obituary 49-52
Earlier sketches in CA 9-12R, CANR-12
See also SATA 5
See also SATA-Obit 26
Brown, J(ames) Douglas 1898-1986 169
Obituary 118
Brown, J(oseph) P(aul) S(ummers)
1930- CANR-63
Earlier sketch in CA 61-64
See also TCWW 1, 2
Brown, James (Wiley) 1909-1983 77-80
Obituary 135
Brown, James (Montgomery) 1921-2005 ... 1-4R
Obituary 238
Brown, James (Joe, Jr.) 1928(?)- 146
Brown, James 1934- CANR-27
Earlier sketches in CA 65-68, 139, CANR-10
Brown, James 1957- 139
Brown, James Alan Calvert 1922-1984
Obituary 114
Brown, James Bush
See Bush-Brown, James
Brown, James Cooke 1921-1987 .... 29-32R
Brown, James I(saac) 1908- CANR-7
Earlier sketch in CA 17-20R
Brown, James Patrick 1948- 29-32R
Brown, James S(eay), Jr. 1944- 120
Brown, James Wilson 1913-1987 .... 41-44R
Brown, Jamie 1945- CANR-20
Earlier sketch in CA 101
Brown, Jane 1938- 207
Brown, Jane Clark 1930- .... SATA 81
Brown, Janet 1947- 69-72
Brown, Janet Mitsui 151
See also SATA 87
Brown, Jared Allen 1936- 142
Brown, Jared M(cDaniel) 1964- 182
Brown, Jason 1969- .... SSFS 14
Brown, Jay A(llen) 1935- 110
Brown, Jeff
See Brown, Sevellon III
Brown, Jeff 1926-2003 232
Brown, Jennifer S. H. 1940- 130
Brown, Jerry Earl 1940- 105
Brown, Jerry Wayne 1936- 25-28R
Brown, Jim 1936- 207
Brown, Jim (M.) 1940- 69-72
Brown, Jim 1956- 205
Brown, Jo Ann
See Ferguson, Jo Ann
Brown, Jo Giese 1947- 108
Brown, Joan Sayers 1925(?)-1983
Obituary 110
Brown, Joanne 1933- 221
See also SATA 147
Brown, Joe David 1915-1976 .... CANR-70
Obituary 65-68
Earlier sketch in CA 13-16R
See also SATA 44
Brown, John 1800-1859 .... LAIT 2

Cumulative Index 77 **Brown**

Brown, John 1887-1975 .... CAP-1
Earlier sketch in CA 13-14
Brown, John 1920- 5-8R
Brown, John (E.) 1934- CANR-45
Earlier sketch in CA 25-28R
Brown, John A. 1898-1996 112
Brown, John Arthur 1914- CANR-11
Earlier sketch in CA 17-20R
Brown, John Buchanan
See Buchanan-Brown, John
Brown, John Gracen 1936- CANR-44
Earlier sketch in CA 104
Brown, John Gregory CANR-113
Earlier sketch in CA 160
Brown, John J. 1916- 13-16R
Brown, John L(ackey) 1914-2002 ..... CANR-46
Obituary 210
Earlier sketch in CA 49-52
Brown, John Mason 1900-1969 .... CANR-70
Obituary 25-28R
Earlier sketch in CA 9-12R
Brown, John Pairman 1923- 33-36R
Brown, John Russell 1923- CANR-70
Earlier sketches in CA 21-24R, CANR-11
Brown, Jonathan (Mayer) 1939- 188
Brief entry 112
Brown, Jones
See Munby, Arthur Joseph
Brown, Joseph E(dward) 1929- CANR-6
Earlier sketch in CA 53-56
See also SATA 59
See also SATA-Brief 51
Brown, Judith C(ora) 136
Brown, Judith Gwyn 1933- CANR-21
Earlier sketch in CA 93-96
See also SATA 20
Brown, Judith K. CANR-51
Earlier sketch in CA 124
Brown, Judith M(argaret) 1944- CANR-72
Earlier sketches in CA 41-44R, CANR-15, 32
Brown, Julia (Prewitt) 1948- 93-96
Brown, Karl 1895(?)-1970
Obituary 104
Brown, Karl 1897-1990
Obituary 131
See also IDFW 3, 4
Brown, Kathi Ann 1958- 187
Brown, Kathryn 1955- 166
See also SATA 98
Brown, Ken (James) .... SATA 129
Brown, Kenneth H. 1936- CANR-69
Earlier sketch in CA 13-16R
See also CAD
See also CD 5, 6
Brown, Kevin 1960- CANR-116
Earlier sketches in CA 148, CANR-115
See also SATA 101
Brown, Kevin V. 1922- 89-92
Brown, Kitt
See Vandergriff, (Lola) Aola
Brown, L(aurence) B(inet) 1927- 65-68
Brown, L. Carl
See Brown, Leon Carl
Brown, L. J.
See Du Breuil, (Elizabeth) L(or)inda
Brown, Larry
See Brown, Lawrence, Jr.
See also DLB 234, 292
Brown, (William) Larry 1951-2004 . CANR-117
Obituary 233
Brief entry 130
Earlier sketch in CA 134
Interview in CA-134
See also CLC 73
See also CSW
See also DLB 234
Brown, Laurene Krasny 1945- CANR-54
Earlier sketch in CA 117
See also SATA 54, 99
Brown, Laurie Krasny
See Brown, Laurene Krasny
Brown, Lawrence, Jr. 1947-
Brief entry 114
See also Brown, Larry
Brown, Lawrence R. 1904(?)-1986
Obituary 119
Brown, Lee Ann 1964- 226
Brown, Lee Dolph 1890-1971
Obituary 29-32R
Brown, Leigh 65-68
Brown, Leland 1914-1994 .... 1-4R
Brown, Lennox (John) 1934- 93-96
Brown, Leon Carl 1928-
Brief entry 117
Brown, LeRoy Chester 1908-1991 .... CANR-13
Earlier sketches in CAP-1, CA 11-12
Brown, Les(ter Louis) 1928- CANR-13
Earlier sketch in CA 33-36R
Brown, Leslie H(ilton) 1917-1980 ...... CANR-7
Earlier sketch in CA 9-12R
Brown, Leslie Wilfrid 1912-1999 .... 17-20R
Obituary 187
Brown, Lester
See Brown, Lester R(ussell)
Brown, Lester R(ussell) 1934- CANR-117
Earlier sketch in CA 132
Brown, Letitia Woods 1915-1976 73-76
Obituary 69-72
Brown, Lew 1893-1958 .... DLB 265
Brown, Linda Beatrice 1939- 148
See also CSW
Brown, Lloyd Arnold 1907-1966 .... CAP-1
Earlier sketch in CA 11-12
See also SATA 36
Brown, Lloyd L(ouis) 1913-2003 143
Obituary 215
See also BW 2
Brown, Loranne 1955- 223
Brown, Louis M(orris) 1909-1996 ..... CANR-47
Obituary 154
Earlier sketch in CA 49-52
Brown, Lyle C(larence) 1926- CANR-15
Earlier sketch in CA 41-44R
Brown, Lyn Mikel 140
Brown, Lynne P. 1952- 138
Brown, M(ary) L(oretta) T(herese) 13-16R
Brown, Mac Alister 1924- 89-92
Brown, Mahlon A.
See Ellis, Edward S(ylvester)
Brown, Mandy
See Brown, May
Brown, Marc (Tolon) 1946- CANR-130
Earlier sketches in CA 69-72, CANR-36, 79
See also CLR 29
See also CWRI 5
See also MAICYA 1, 2
See also SATA 10, 53, 80, 145
Brown, Marcia (Joan) 1918- CANR-46
Earlier sketch in CA 41-44R
See also CLR 12
See also CWRI 5
See also DLB 61
See also MAICYA 1, 2
See also MAICYAS 1
See also SATA 7, 47
Brown, Marel 1899-1991 102
Brown, Margaret (Isobel) Gillies 1929- 190
Brown, Margaret J. 1948- 216
Brown, Margaret Lynn 1958- 216
Brown, Margaret Wise 1910-1952 ... CANR-78
Brief entry 108
Earlier sketch in CA 136
See also CLR 10
See also CWRI 5
See also DLB 22
See also MAICYA 1, 2
See also SATA 100
See also YABC 2
Brown, Margery (Wheeler) CANR-26
Earlier sketch in CA 25-28R
See also BW 2
See also SATA 5, 78
Brown, Marian A. 1911-1994 73-76
Brown, Marilyn McMeen Miller
1938- CANR-6
Earlier sketch in CA 57-60
Brown, Marion Marsh 1908-2001 .... CANR-70
Earlier sketches in CA 1-4R, CANR-3
See also SATA 6
Brown, Mark 165
Brown, Mark H(erbert) 1900-1988 ... CANR-70
Earlier sketches in CAP-2, CA 21-22
Brown, Marshall 1945- CANR-113
Earlier sketches in CA 111, CANR-48
Brown, Marshall L. 1924- 21-24R
Brown, Marvin L(uther), Jr. 1920- CANR-70
Earlier sketch in CA 53-56
Brown, Mary 1929- .... FANT
Brown, Mary Ellen 1939- CANR-144
Earlier sketches in CA 117, CANR-41
Brown, Mary Ward 1917- CANR-128
Earlier sketch in CA 133
Brown, Maurice F(red) 1928-1985 .... 41-44R
Obituary 116
Brown, May 1913- 118
Brown, Melissa Mather 1917- 121
Brown, Merle Elliott 1925-1978 108
Brown, Michael 1931- CANR-55
Earlier sketch in CA 33-36R
Brown, Michael 1938- 127
Brown, Michael Barratt
See Barratt-Brown, Michael
Brown, Michael F(obes) 1950- 142
Brown, Michael H(arold) 1952- 121
Brown, Michael John 1932- 29-32R
Brown, Michael P. 1966- 168
Brown, Michelle P(atricia) 1959- 139
Brown, Mick 1950- 239
Brown, Milton Perry, Jr. 1928- 9-12R
Brown, Milton W(olf) 1911-1998
Obituary 164
Brief entry 113
Brown, Molly 222
Brown, Molly Young 1942- 190
Brown, Montague 1952- 162
Brown, Morna Doris 1907-1995 ...... CANR-59
Obituary 148
Earlier sketches in CA 5-8R, CANR-5
See also Ferrars, Elizabeth
See also CMW 4
Brown, Morris Cecil 1943- 37-40R
Brown, Moses
See Barrett, William (Christopher)
Brown, Muriel 1938- 107
Brown, Muriel W(hitbeck) 1892-1989 ... CAP-2
Earlier sketch in CA 23-24
Brown, Murray 1929- 37-40R
Brown, Myra Berry 1918- CANR-3
Earlier sketch in CA 1-4R
See also SATA 6
Brown, Nacio Herb 1896-1964 .... IDFW 3, 4
Brown, Nathaniel Hapgood 1929- 101
Brown, Ned 1882(?)-1976
Obituary 65-68
Brown, Neville (George) 1932- 9-12R
Brown, Newell 1917-2000 97-100
Obituary 190
Brown, Norman D(onald) 1935- 53-56
Brown, Norman O(liver)
1913-2002 .... CANR-70
Obituary 209
Earlier sketch in CA 21-24R
Brown, Oliver Madox 1855-1874 .... DLB 21
Brown, Palmer 1919- CANR-69
Earlier sketch in CA 107
See also SATA 36
Brown, Pamela (Beatrice)
1924-1989 .... CANR-70
Obituary 127
Earlier sketch in CA 13-16R
See also CWRI 5
See also SATA 5
See also SATA-Obit 61
Brown, Parker B(oyd) 1928- 53-56
Brown, Pat
See Brown, Edmund G(erald)
Brown, Patricia Fortini 1936- CANR-138
Earlier sketches in CA 131, CANR-72
Brown, Paul B. 1954- 138
Brown, Paula 1925- CANR-47
Earlier sketch in CA 110
Brown, Peter 1926(?)-1984(?)
Obituary 112
Brown, Peter (Robert Lamont)
1935- CANR-13
Earlier sketch in CA 21-24R
Brown, Peter A. 1949- 138
Brown, Peter Carter
See Yates, A(lan) G(eoffrey)
Brown, Peter Douglas 1925- CANR-16
Earlier sketch in CA 25-28R
Brown, Peter G. 1940- 151
Brown, Peter Harry 1939- CANR-143
Earlier sketch in CA 143
Brown, Peter Lancaster
See Lancaster-Brown, Peter
Brown, R(eginald) Allen 1924-1989 . CANR-11
Obituary 128
Earlier sketch in CA 5-8R
Brown, R(onald) G(ordon) S(clater)
1929-1978 .... CANR-48
Earlier sketch in CA 29-32R
Brown, Rae
See Brown, Forrest
Brown, Rajeswary Ampalavanar 227
Brown, Ralph Adams 1908-1986 .... 33-36R
Brown, Raymond Bryan 1923-1977 ...... 17-20R
Obituary 133
Brown, Raymond E(dward)
1928-1998 .... CANR-17
Obituary 169
Earlier sketch in CA 97-100
Brown, Raymond George 1924- 109
Brown, Raymond Kay 1936- 102
Brown, Raymond Lamont
See Lamont-Brown, Raymond
Brown, Re Mona 1917- 41-44R
Brown, Rebecca
See Ore, Rebecca
Brown, Rebecca 1956- CANR-81
Earlier sketch in CA 124
Brown, Reeve Lindbergh
See Lindbergh, Reeve
Brown, Rex V(andesteene) 1933- 53-56
Brown, Ricardo J. 1927-1999 229
Brown, Richard 1935- 114
Brown, Richard C(arl) 1917- CANR-17
Earlier sketches in CA 5-8R, CANR-2
Brown, Richard D(avid) 1939- CANR-136
Earlier sketch in CA 53-56
Brown, Richard E(ugene) 1937- 73-76
Brown, Richard E. 1946- 130
See also SATA 61
Brown, Richard E(arl) 1948- 149
Brown, Richard H(olbrook) 1927- 9-12R
Brown, Richard H(arvey)
1940-2003 .... CANR-38
Obituary 220
Earlier sketch in CA 109
Brown, Richard Howard 1929- 57-60
Brown, Richard Maxwell 1927- CANR-11
Earlier sketch in CA 17-20R
Brown, Rita Mae 1944- CANR-138
Earlier sketches in CA 45-48, CANR-2, 11, 35, 62, 95
Interview in CANR-11
See also BPFB 1
See also CLC 18, 43, 79
See also CN 5, 6, 7
See also CPW
See also CSW
See also DA3
See also DAM NOV, POP
See also FW
See also MAL 5
See also MTCW 1, 2
See also MTFW 2005
See also NFS 9
See also RGAL 4
See also TUS
Brown, Robert C.
See Brown, Robert Carlton
Brown, Robert Carlton 1886-1959 202
Brief entry 107
See also Brown, Bob
Brown, Robert Craig 1935- 101
Brown, Robert D. 1924- CANR-20
Earlier sketch in CA 104
Brown, Robert E(ldon) 1907- 5-8R
Brown, Robert Edward 1945- CANR-15
Earlier sketch in CA 65-68
Brown, Robert Fath 1941- CANR-91
Earlier sketch in CA 111
Brown, Robert Goodell 1923- 33-36R
Brown, Robert Hanbury 1916-2002 112
Obituary 204
Brown, Robert Joseph 1907-1989 .... CANR-13
Earlier sketches in CAP-1, CA 9-10
See also SATA 14
Brown, Robert L. 1921- 21-24R
Brown, Robert McAfee 1920-2001 ... CANR-69
Obituary 202
Earlier sketches in CA 13-16R, CANR-7
Brown, Robert T(homas) 1943- 113
Brown, Roberta Simpson 1939- 150
Brown, Robin 1937- 97-100
Brown, Roderick (Langmere) Haig-
See Haig-Brown, Roderick (Langmere)
Brown, Roger Glenn 1941- 77-80
Brown, Roger H(amilton) 1931- 9-12R
Brown, Roger William 1925-1997 .... 13-16R
Obituary 163
Brown, Ronald 1900- 81-84
Brown, Rosalie
See Moore, Rosalie (Gertrude)
See also SATA 9
Brown, Rosel George 1926-1967
Obituary 102
See also SFW 4
Brown, Rosellen 1939- CANR-98
Earlier sketches in CA 77-80, CANR-14, 44
See also CAAS 10
See also CLC 32, 170
See also CN 6, 7
Brown, Rosemary Eleanor 1916-2001
Obituary 209
Brief entry 115
Brown, Roswell
See Webb, Jean Francis (III)
Brown, Roy (Frederick) 1921-1982 65-68
Obituary 117
See also CWRI 5
See also SATA 51
See also SATA-Obit 39
Brown, Rustie 1930(?)-1988
Obituary 125
Brown, Ruth 1941- 173
See also MAICYA 2
See also SATA 105
Brown, Ruth Murray 1927-2002 220
Brown, Sanborn C(onner)
1913-1981 .... CANR-11
Obituary 106
Earlier sketch in CA 17-20R
Brown, Sandra 1948- CANR-108
Earlier sketches in CA 139, CANR-63
See also CPW
See also CSW
See also DA3
See also RHW
Brown, Sanford J(ay) 1946- 118
Brown, Scott 1971- 203
See also SATA 134
Brown, Sevellon III 1913-1983
Obituary 110
Brown, Seyom 1933- CANR-17
Earlier sketch in CA 65-68
Brown, Sheldon S. 1933- 122
Brown, Sheldon S. 1937- CANR-7
Earlier sketch in CA 53-56
Brown, Sidney DeVere 1925- 33-36R
Brown, Spencer 1909-1989 130
Brown, Stanley (Branson) 1914- 49-52
Brown, Stanley C(oleman) 1928- 77-80
Brown, Stanley H(arold) 1927- 45-48
Brown, Stephen W. 1940- CANR-13
Earlier sketch in CA 33-36R
Brown, Sterling Allen 1901-1989 ..... CANR-26
Obituary 127
Earlier sketch in CA 85-88
See also AFAW 1, 2
See also BLC 1
See also BW 1, 3
See also CLC 1, 23, 59
See also DA3
See also DAM MULT, POET
See also DLB 48, 51, 63
See also HR 1:2
See also MAL 5
See also MTCW 1, 2
See also MTFW 2005
See also PC 55
See also RGAL 4
See also WP
Brown, Steve 1944- 201
Brown, Steven P(reston) 1964- 239
Brown, Steven R(andall) 1939- 49-52
Brown, Stewart 1951- 135
Brown, Stuart C(ampbell) 1938- CANR-50
Earlier sketches in CA 29-32R, CANR-25
Brown, Stuart Gerry 1912-1991 .... CANR-70
Obituary 135
Earlier sketch in CA 21-24R
Brown, Sue Ellen 1954- .... SATA 81
Brown, Susan Jenkins 1896-1982 85-88
Brown, T. E. 1830-1897 .... DLB 35
Brown, T(illman) Merritt 1913-1973 ..... 41-44R
Brown, Terence 1944- CANR-90
Earlier sketches in CA 102, CANR-19, 41
Brown, Theo W(atts) 1934- CANR-8
Earlier sketch in CA 61-64
Brown, Theodore L(awrence) 1928- 33-36R
Brown, Theodore M(orey) 1925- 33-36R
Brown, Thomas H., Jr. 1950- CANR-56
Earlier sketch in CA 127
Brown, Thomas H. 1930- 57-60
Brown, Thomas J. 1960- 201
Brown, Thomas McPherson 1906-1989
Obituary 128
Brown, Tim W. 1961- 164
Brown, Timothy C(harles) 1938- 218
Brown, Tina 1953- 118
Brief entry 116
Brown, Tom, Jr.
See Brown, Thomas H., Jr.
Brown, Tricia 1954- 186
See also SATA 114

Brown, Truesdell S(parhawk) 1906- ... 13-16R
Brown, Turner, Jr.
See Hample, Stuart
Brown, V(ictor) I(vy) 1949- ... 216
Brown, Velma Darbo 1921- ... 97-100
Brown, Vinson 1912-1991 ... CANR-1
Earlier sketch in CA 1-4R
See also SATA 19
Brown, Virginia (Suggs) 1924- ... 69-72
Brown, Virginia Pounds 1916- ... 114
Brown, Virginia Sharpe 1916- ... 13-16R
Brown, W(illiam) Norman 1892-1975 ... 61-64
Obituary ... 57-60
Brown, Wallace 1933- ... 17-20R
Brown, Walter Lee 1924- ... 33-36R
Brown, Walter R(eed) 1929- ... CANR-2
Earlier sketch in CA 45-48
See also SATA 19
Brown, Warner
See Boroson, Warren
Brown, Warren (William)
1894-1978 ... CANR-144
Obituary ... 81-84
Earlier sketch in CA 85-88
See also DLB 241
Brown, Warren A. 1917(?)-1985
Obituary ... 117
Brown, Wayne 1944- ... 101
See also CP 2, 3, 4, 5, 6, 7
Brown, Weldon A(mzy) 1911-1996 ... 65-68
Brown, Wenzell 1912-1981 ... CANR-70
Obituary ... 162
Earlier sketches in CA 1-4R, CANR-5
Brown, Wesley 1945- ... CANR-98
Earlier sketch in CA 125
See also BW 2
See also CN 7
Brown, Wilfred (Banks Duncan)
1908-1985 ... 9-12R
Obituary ... 116
Brown, Wilfred A(rthur) Gavin
See Gavin-Brown, Wilfred A(rthur)
Brown, Will
See Ainsworth, William Harrison
Brown, Will C.
See Boyles, C(larence) S(cott), Jr.
See also TCWW 2
Brown, William Anthony 1933- ... 125
Brief entry ... 110
See also BW 1
Brown, William Campbell 1928- ... 57-60
Brown, William E(nglish) 1907-1975 ... CAP-2
Earlier sketch in CA 29-32
Brown, William Edward 1904-1989 ... 126
Brown, William F. 1900(?)-1989
Obituary ... 131
Brown, William F(rank) 1920- ... 33-36R
Brown, William F(erdinand) 1928- ... 33-36R
Brown, William Hill 1765-1793 ... DLB 37
Brown, William J. ... 97-100
Brown, William James 1889-1970 ... 5-8R
Brown, William L(ouis) 1910-1964 .. CANR-70
Earlier sketch in CA 1-4R
See also SATA 5
Brown, William Montgomery 1855-1937 ... 220
Brown, William Wells 1815-1884 ... BLC 1
See also DAM MULT
See also DC 1
See also DLB 3, 50, 183, 248
See also RGAL 4
Brown, Zenith Jones 1898-1983 ... 9-12R
Obituary ... 110
See also CMW 4
Brown-Azarowicz, Marjory F. 1922- ... 33-36R
Brownback, Paul 1940- ... 113
Browne, Anthony (Edward Tudor)
1946- ... CANR-82
Earlier sketches in CA 97-100, CANR-36, 78
See also CLR 19
See also CWRI 5
See also MAICYA 1, 2
See also MAICYAS 1
See also SATA 45, 61, 105, 163
See also SATA-Brief 44
Browne, Barum
See Saunders, Hilary Aidan St. George
Browne, Charles Farrar 1834-1867
See Ward, Artemus
See also DLB 11
Browne, Colette (Victoria) 1950- ... 121
Browne, Courtney 1915- ... 21-24R
Browne, Dik
See Browne, Richard Arthur Allen
See also AITN 1
Browne, E(lliott) Martin 1900-1980 ... CAP-2
Obituary ... 97-100
Earlier sketch in CA 25-28
Browne, Frances 1816-1879 ... DLB 199
Browne, Francis Fisher 1843-1913 ... 179
See also DLB 79
Browne, G(erald) P(eter) 1930- ... 21-24R
Browne, Gary Lawson 1939- ... 101
Browne, George Stephenson
1890-1970 ... CAP-2
Earlier sketch in CA 29-32
Browne, Gerald A(ustin) 1928- ... 166
Browne, Hablot Knight 1815-1882 ... SATA 21
Browne, Harry
See Browne, Henry
Browne, Harry 1933- ... CANR-3
Earlier sketch in CA 49-52
Browne, Henry 1918- ... 102
Browne, Howard 1908-1999 ... 73-76
See also CMW 4
See also DLB 226
Browne, J. Ross 1821-1875 ... DLB 202
Browne, (Clyde) Jackson 1948(?)- ... 120
See also CLC 21
Browne, Janet 1950- ... 214
Browne, Joseph William 1914-1991 ... 105
Browne, Joy 1944- ... CANR-123
Earlier sketch in CA 97-100
Browne, Kingsley R. ... 230
Browne, Malcolm W(ilde) 1931- ... 17-20R
Browne, Marshall 1935- ... 188
Browne, Mary T. 1955- ... 148
Browne, Matthew
See Rands, William Brighty
Browne, Michael Dennis 1940- ... CANR-15
Earlier sketch in CA 29-32R
See also CAAS 20
See also CP 1, 2, 3, 4, 5, 6, 7
See also DLB 40
Browne, N(icky) M(atthews) ... 231
Browne, Ray B(roadus) 1922- ... CANR-49
Earlier sketches in CA 17-20R, CANR-11
Browne, Raymond 1897-1988 ... 73-76
Browne, Richard Arthur Allen 1917-1989
Obituary ... 128
See also Browne, Dik
See also SATA 67
See also SATA-Brief 38
Browne, Robert
See Karlins, Marvin
Browne, Robert S(pan) 1924-2004 ... CANR-14
Obituary ... 229
Earlier sketch in CA 37-40R
Browne, Roland A(ndrew) 1910-1995 ... 65-68
Browne, Sam
See Smith, Ronald Gregor
Browne, Theodore R. 1911(?)-1979
Obituary ... 81-84
Browne, Sir Thomas 1605-1682 ... BRW 2
See also DLB 151
Browne, Thomas Alexander 1826-1915 ... 205
See also DLB 230
Browne, Vee F(rances) 1956- ... SATA 90
Browne, Walter A(nderson) 1895-1987 . 37-40R
Browne, William P(aul) 1945- ... CANR-112
Earlier sketches in CA 109, CANR-25, 54
Browne, Wynyard (Barry) 1911-1964 ... 178
Obituary ... 113
See also DLB 13, 233
Brownell, Blaine Allison 1942- ... 65-68
Brownell, Charles E(dward III) 1943- ... 139
Brownell, John Arnold 1924- ... 21-24R
Brownell, Kelly D. 1951- ... CANR-144
Earlier sketch in CA 172
Brownell, Susan 1960- ... CANR-115
Earlier sketch in CA 155
Brownell, W(illiam) C(rary) 1851-1928 ... 179
See also DLB 71
Browne Miller, Angela 1952- ... 135
Browne of Tavistock, William
1590-1645 ... DLB 121
Browning, Alice C(rolley) 1907-1985
Obituary ... 117
Browning, Christopher R(obert)
1944- ... CANR-113
Earlier sketch in CA 112
Browning, Columban
See Browning, William
Browning, David (George) 1938- ... 37-40R
Browning, Dixie (Burrus) 1930- ... CANR-121
Earlier sketches in CA 110, CANR-64, 66
See also RHW
Browning, Don S(pencer) 1934- ... CANR-123
Earlier sketches in CA 49-52, CANR-2
Browning, (Grayson) Douglas 1929- ... 13-16R
Browning, Elizabeth 1924- ... 57-60
Browning, Frank 1946- ... 107
Browning, Gordon 1938- ... 37-40R
Browning, Iben 1918-
Brief entry ... 113
Browning, J(ohn) D. 1942- ... 125
Browning, John S.
See Williams, Robert Moore
Browning, L. J.
See Du Breuil, (Elizabeth) L(or)inda
Browning, Mary 1887-1989 ... CAP-1
Earlier sketch in CA 11-12
Browning, Norma Lee 1914-2001 ... CANR-8
Obituary ... 198
Earlier sketch in CA 61-64
Browning, Peter 1928- ... 104
Browning, Preston M(ercer), Jr. 1929- ... 57-60
Browning, Reed 1938- ... CANR-94
Earlier sketch in CA 57-60
Browning, Robert 1812-1889 ... BRW 4
See also BRWC 2
See also BRWR 2
See also CDBLB 1832-1890
See also CLR 97
See also DA
See also DA3
See also DAB
See also DAC
See also DAM MST, POET
See also DLB 32, 163
See also EXPP
See also LATS 1:1
See also PAB
See also PC 2, 61
See also PFS 1, 15
See also RGEL 2
See also TEA
See also WLCS
See also WLIT 4
See also WP
See also YABC 1
Browning, Robert 1914-1997 ... CANR-13
Obituary ... 157
Earlier sketch in CA 33-36R
Browning, Robert L(ynn) 1924- ... CANR-16
Earlier sketch in CA 85-88
Browning, Rufus P(utnam) 1934- ... 124
Browning, (Zerilda) Sinclair 1946- ... CANR-49
Earlier sketch in CA 112
Browning, Sterry
See Gribble, Leonard (Reginald)
Browning, Susan 1941- ... 239
Browning, Tod 1882-1962 ... 141
Obituary ... 117
See also CLC 16
Browning, Wilfrid (Robert Francis) 1918- .. 5-8R
Browning, William 1921- ... 113
Brownjohn, Alan 1931- ... CANR-73
Earlier sketches in CA 25-28R, CANR-72
See also CP 1, 2, 3, 4, 5, 6, 7
See also DLB 40
See also SATA 6
Brownjohn, J(ohn Nevil) Maxwell
1929- ... CANR-90
Earlier sketch in CA 129
Brownlee, David B(ruce) 1951- ... 132
Brownlee, Donald E(ugene) 1943- ... 233
Brownlee, O(swald) H(arvey) 1917- ... 65-68
Brownlee, W(ilson) Elliot, Jr. 1941- ... 69-72
Brownlee, W(illiam) H(ugh) 1917- ... 9-12R
Brownlee, Walter 1930- ... 57-60
See also SATA 62
Brownlie, Betty 1946- ... SATA 159
Brownlie, Ian 1932- ... CANR-2
Earlier sketch in CA 5-8R
Brownlow, Cecil Alexander III 1926-1988
Obituary ... 124
Brownlow, Kevin 1938- ... CANR-12
Earlier sketch in CA 25-28R
See also SATA 65
Brownlow, (David) Timothy 1941- ... CP 1
Brownmiller, Susan 1935- ... CANR-137
Earlier sketches in CA 103, CANR-35, 75
See also CLC 159
See also DAM NOV
See also FW
See also MTCW 1, 2
See also MTFW 2005
Brownridge, William R(oy) 1932- ... 159
See also SATA 94
Brownrigg, Sylvia ... 192
Brownrigg, Walter Grant 1940- ... 110
Brownson, Orestes Augustus
1803-1876 ... DLB 1, 59, 73, 243
Brownson, William C(larence), Jr. 1928- . 69-72
Brownstein, Elizabeth Smith 1930- ... 192
Brownstein, Gabriel 1966- ... 211
Brownstein, Karen (Osney) 1944-1989 ... 124
Obituary ... 130
Brownstein, Michael 1943- ... CANR-130
Earlier sketch in CA 33-36R
See also CP 1, 2
Brownstein, Oscar Lee 1928- ... 113
Brownstein, Rachel M. 1937- ... 122
Brownstein, Ronald J. 1958- ... 106
Brownstein, Samuel C. 1909-1996 ... 5-8R
Obituary ... 155
Brownstone, David M. 1928- ... CANR-65
Earlier sketches in CA 104, CANR-21
Brox, Jane (Martha) 1956- ... 153
Broxholme, John Franklin
1930-2000 ... CANR-31
Earlier sketches in CA 65-68, CANR-12
See also CMW 4
Broxon, Mildred Downey 1944- ... CANR-58
Earlier sketch in CA 107
See also FANT
Broy, Anthony 1916- ... 102
Broyard, Anatole 1920-1990 ... CANR-44
Obituary ... 132
Earlier sketch in CA 105
Broyard, Bliss ... 194
See also BYA 14
Broyles, J(ohn) Allen 1934- ... 9-12R
Broyles, Michael 1939- ... 146
Broyles, William Dodson, Jr. 1944- ... 73-76
Broz, J. Lawrence 1956- ... 167
Brozek, Josef (Maria) 1913- ... CANR-48
Earlier sketch in CA 45-48
Brozen, Yale 1917-1998 ... 109
Obituary ... 166
Bru, Hedin
See Jacobsen, Hans Jacob
Brubach, Holly 1953- ... 110
Brubacher, John Seiler 1898-1988 ... CANR-1
Obituary ... 162
Earlier sketch in CA 1-4R
Brubaker, Carol
See Stolk, Anthonie
Brubaker, Dale L(ee) 1937- ... CANR-4
Earlier sketch in CA 53-56
Brubaker, Earl R(oy) 1932- ... 107
Brubaker, Sterling 1924- ... 21-24R
Bruccoli, Matthew J(oseph) 1931- ... CANR-87
Earlier sketches in CA 9-12R, CANR-7
See also CLC 34
See also DLB 103
Bruce, Arthur Loring
See Crowninshield, Francis (Welch)
Bruce, Ben F., Jr. 1920- ... 13-16R
Bruce, Charles (Tory) 1906-1971 ... 152
See also CP 1
See also DLB 68
Bruce, Colin John 1960- ... 150
Bruce, Curt 1946- ... 97-100
Bruce, David (Kirkpatrick Este) 1898-1977
Obituary ... 105
Bruce, Debra 1951- ... CANR-94
Earlier sketch in CA 118
Bruce, Dickson D., Jr. 1946- ... CANR-139
Earlier sketch in CA 53-56
Bruce, Donald (James) 1930- ... 17-20R
Bruce, Dorita Fairlie 1885-1970
Obituary ... 107
See also CWRI 5
See also SATA-Obit 27
Bruce, Duncan A. 1932- ... 237
Bruce, Evangeline ... 153
Bruce, F(rederick) F(yvie)
1910-1990 ... CANR-41
Earlier sketches in CA 1-4R, CANR-3, 19
Bruce, George 1909-2002 ... CANR-69
Obituary ... 207
Earlier sketch in CA 65-68
See also CP 1, 2, 3, 4, 5, 6, 7
Bruce, Harold (R., Jr.) 1934(?)-1987
Obituary ... 122
Bruce, (William) Harry 1934- ... 145
See also SATA 77
Bruce, Harry J. 1931- ... 21-24R
Bruce, Janet
See Campbell, Janet Bruce
Bruce, Jeannette M. 1922- ... 5-8R
Bruce, Lennart 1919- ... CANR-13
Earlier sketch in CA 33-36R
See also CAAS 27
Bruce, Lenny
See Schneider, Leonard Alfred
See also CLC 21
Bruce, Leo
See Croft-Cooke, Rupert
See also DLB 77
Bruce, Mary 1927- ... 25-28R
See also SATA 1
Bruce, Mary Grant 1878-1958 ... CWRI 5
See also DLB 230
Bruce, Maurice 1913(?)-1988
Obituary ... 125
Bruce, Mildred Mary 1896(?)-1990
Obituary ... 131
Bruce, Monica
See Melaro, Constance L(oraine)
Bruce, Philip Alexander 1856-1933 ... 181
See also DLB 47
Bruce, R(aymon) R(ene) 1934- ... 89-92
Bruce, Richard
See Nugent, Richard Bruce
Bruce, Robert 1927- ... CAP-1
Earlier sketch in CA 9-10
Bruce, Robert S. 1955- ... 224
Bruce, Robert V(ance) 1923- ... CANR-116
Earlier sketch in CA 53-56
Bruce, Shelley
See Merklinghaus, Michele
Bruce, Sylvia (Valerie) 1936- ... 33-36R
Bruce, Victoria ... 203
Bruce, Violet R(ose) ... 29-32R
Bruce, William Cabell 1860-1946 ... 218
Bruce-Briggs, B(arry B.) ... 112
Bruce-Gardyne, Jock
See Bruce-Gardyne, John
Bruce-Gardyne, John 1930-1990
Obituary ... 131
Bruce Lockhart, Robin 1920- ... 25-28R
Bruce-Novoa
See Bruce-Novoa, Juan D.
Bruce-Novoa, John David
See Bruce-Novoa, Juan D.
Bruce-Novoa, Juan D. 1944- ... CANR-32
Brief entry ... 117
See also CAAS 18
See also DLB 82
See also HW 1
Bruch, Hilde ... 53-56
See also AITN 1
Bruchac, Joseph III 1942- ... CANR-137
Earlier sketches in CA 33-36R, CANR-13, 47, 75, 94
See also AAYA 19
See also CLR 46
See also CWRI 5
See also DAM MULT
See also JRDA
See also MAICYA 2
See also MAICYAS 1
See also MTCW 2
See also MTFW 2005
See also NNAL
See also SATA 42, 89, 131
Bruchey, Stuart (Weems) 1917- ... 33-36R
Bruck, Connie 1946- ... CANR-144
Earlier sketch in CA 140
Bruck, Edith
See Steinschreiber, Edith
Bruck, Julie 1957- ... 198
Bruck, Lilly 1918- ... 109
Bruck, Lorraine 1921- ... 147
See also Bridges, Laurie
See also SATA 55
See also SATA-Brief 46
Brucker, Clara (Hantel) 1892(?)-1980
Obituary ... 97-100
Brucker, Gene (Adam) 1924-
Brief entry ... 114
Brucker, Herbert 1898-1977 ... CANR-4
Obituary ... 69-72
Earlier sketch in CA 5-8R
Brucker, Roger W(arren) 1929- ... CANR-11
Earlier sketch in CA 65-68
Bruckheimer, Linda 1946(?)- ... 234
Bruckman, Clyde (Adolph) 1894-1955 ... 178
See also DLB 26
See also IDFW 3, 4
Bruckner, D. J. R. 1933- ... 132
Bruckner, Ferdinand
See Tagger, Theodor
See also DLB 118
See also EWL 3

Cumulative Index 79 **Bryde**

Bruckner, Pascal 1948- 150
Bruder, Judith 97-100
Bruder, Mary Newton 1939- 127
Brudny, Yitzhak M. 198
Bruegel, Johann Wolfgang 1905-1986 77-80
Obituary 121
Bruegel, John Wolfgang
See Bruegel, Johann Wolfgang
Brueggemann, Walter (A.) 1933- 237
Brief entry 117
Bruegmann, Robert 1948- 101
Bruehl, Anton 1900-1982
Obituary 110
Bruemmer, Fred 1929- CANR-69
Earlier sketch in CA 102
See also SATA 47
Bruen, Ken 1951- 221
Bruening, William H(arry) 1943- 57-60
Bruer, John T. 1949- 193
Bruess, Clint E. 1941- 33-36R
Bruff, Nancy
See Gardner, Nancy Bruff
Bruffee, Kenneth A. 1934- 37-40R
Bruford, Walter Horace 1894-1988
Obituary 126
Bruggen, Carol (Holmes) 1932- 117
Brugger, Bill
See Brugger, William (Christian)
Brugger, Robert J(ohn) 1943- CANR-38
Earlier sketches in CA 85-88, CANR-16
Brugger, William (Christian) 1941- ... CANR-44
Earlier sketches in CA 73-76, CANR-12
Bruggink, Donald J. 1929- CANR-7
Earlier sketch in CA 13-16R
Brugioni, Dino A. 1921- CANR-88
Earlier sketch in CA 137
Brugman, Alyssa (F.) 1974- 227
See also SATA 152
Bruhn, Eric (Belton Evers) 1928-1986
Obituary 118
Bruhn, John Glyndon 1934- 89-92
Bruhn, Siglind 1951- 185
Bruhns, Karen Olsen 1941- 154
Bruin, John
See Brutus, Dennis
Bruins, Elton J(ohn) 1927- 53-56
Bruland, Esther (Byle) 1956- 116
Brulard, Henri
See Baillargeon, Pierre
See also CCA 1
Brulard, Henri
See Stendhal
Brulez, Raymond 1895-1972 .... EWL 3
Brull, Mariano 1891-1956 .... LAWS 1
Brulle, Robert J. 207
Bruller, Jean (Marcel) 1902-1991 ...... CANR-47
Obituary 134
Earlier sketches in CA 65-68, CANR-12
See also Vercors
See also SFW 4
Brulls, Christian
See Simenon, Georges (Jacques Christian)
Brulotte, Gaetan 1945- CANR-100
See also Brulotte, Gaetan A.
Brulotte, Gaetan A. 150
See also Brulotte, Gaetan
Brumback, Carl V. 1917(?)-1987
Obituary 123
Brumbaugh, Robert Sherrick
1918-1992 .... CANR-70
Earlier sketches in CA 5-8R, CANR-3
Brumbaugh, Thomas B(rendle) 1921- ... 49-52
Brumbeau, Jeff 1955- .... SATA 157
Brumble, H(erbert) David III 1943- 107
Brumfield, William C.
See Brumfield, William Craft
Brumfield, William Craft 1944- CANR-144
Earlier sketch in CA 144
Brumgardt, John R(aymond) 1946- 97-100
Brumm, Ursula 1919- 29-32R
Brummel, Mark Joseph 1933- 103
Brummet, R. Lee 1921- 21-24R
Brummitt, Wyatt B. 1897-1984 .... 9-12R
Brun, Ellen 1933- 103
Brun, Henri 1939- 53-56
Bruna, Dick 1927- CANR-36
Earlier sketch in CA 112
See also CLR 7
See also MAICYA 1, 2
See also SATA 43, 76
See also SATA-Brief 30
Brundage, Burr Cartwright
1912-1993 .... CANR-70
Earlier sketch in CA 41-44R
Brundage, Dorothy J(une) 1930- 104
Brundage, Elizabeth 237
Brundage, James A(rthur) 1929- CANR-7
Earlier sketch in CA 5-8R
Brundage, John Herbert 1926-2001 101
Obituary 198
See also Herbert, John
See also CD 5
Brundage, Percival F(lack) 1892-1979 101
Obituary 89-92
Brundage, W(illiam) Fitzhugh 1959- 142
Brundige, Donald G. 1940- 170
Brundige, Sharron L(ea) 1943- 170
Brune, Lester H(ugo) 1926- CANR-101
Earlier sketches in CA 33-36R, CANR-13, 48
Bruneau, Carol 1956- 219
Bruneau, Jean
See Sylvestre, (Joseph Jean) Guy
Bruneau, Thomas C. 1939- 53-56
Brunelli, Jean 1934- 138
Bruner, Edward M. 1924 121
Bruner, Herbert B. 1894(?)-1974
Obituary 53-56
Bruner, Jerome S(eymour) 1915- CANR-123
Earlier sketches in CA 45-48, CANR-1
Bruner, Margaret E. (Baggerly)
1886-1970(?) CAP-1
Earlier sketch in CA 17-18
Bruner, Phillip L. 1944- 127
Bruner, Richard W(allace) 1926- 49-52
Bruner, Wally 1931-1997 49-52
Obituary 162
Brunet, Michel 1917-1985 .... CANR-18
Obituary 117
Earlier sketch in CA 102
Brunette, Peter (Clark), Jr. 1943- CANR-53
Earlier sketch in CA 126
Brunetti, Cledo 1910-1971 .... CAP-2
Earlier sketch in CA 29-32
Brunetti, Mendor Thomas 1894-1979
Obituary 89-92
Brunhoff, Jean de 1899-1937 137
Brief entry 118
See also CLR 4
See also MAICYA 1, 2
See also SATA 24
See also TWA
See also WCH
Brunhoff, Laurent de 1925- CANR-129
Earlier sketches in CA 73-76, CANR-45
See also CLR 4
See also MAICYA 1, 2
See also SATA 24, 71, 150
Brunhouse, Robert Levere
1908-1996 .... CANR-2
Obituary 162
Earlier sketch in CA 49-52
Bruning, Nancy P(auline) 1948- CANR-46
Earlier sketches in CA 106, CANR-23
Brunk, Samuel 1958- 189
Brunkhorst, Alex 239
Brunn, Harry O(tis), Jr. 1919- 1-4R
Brunner, Edmund de S(chweinitz)
1889-1973 .... CAP-1
Obituary 45-48
Earlier sketch in CA 13-16
Brunner, Edward J. 1946- 127
Brunner, Elizabeth 1920-1983
Obituary 111
Brunner, Ernst 1950- 190
Brunner, James A(lbertus) 1923- 37-40R
Brunner, John (Kilian Houston)
1934-1995 .... CANR-37
Obituary 149
Earlier sketches in CA 1-4R, CANR-2
See also CAAS 8
See also CLC 8, 10
See also CPW
See also DAM POP
See also DLB 261
See also MTCW 1, 2
See also SCFW 1, 2
See also SFW 4
Brunner, Jose
See Brunner, Jose
Brunner, Jose 1954- 232
Brunner, Karl 1916-1989
Obituary 128
Brunner, Maurice Yaw 1950- 103
Brunner, Theodore F(riederich) 1934- ... 33-36R
Brunner, Warren E. 1928- 180
Brunnings, Florence E(mery) 1916- 112
Bruno, Carole A. 1942- 144
Bruno, Frank
See St. Bruno, Albert Francis
Bruno, Frank J(oe) 1930- 107
Bruno, Giordano 1548-1600 .... RGWL 2, 3
Bruno, Harold R., Jr. 1928- 77-80
Bruno, James Edward 1940- 41-44R
Bruno, Michael 1921- 33-36R
Bruno, Richard L(ouis) 1954- 216
Bruno, Vincent J. 1926- 65-68
Bruns, Don 1947- 216
Bruns, Frederick R., Jr. 1913(?)-1979
Obituary 85-88
Bruns, George 1914(?)-1983
Obituary 109
Bruns, J(ames) Edgar 1923- CANR-2
Earlier sketch in CA 5-8R
Bruns, Joe
See Altshuler, Harry
Bruns, Roger A. 1941- CANR-97
Earlier sketch in CA 144
Bruns, William A(lan) 1942- 113
Bruns, William J(ohn), Jr. 1935- 37-40R
Brunschwig, Henri 1904-1989 169
Brunschwig, Jacques 1929- 198
Brunskill, Elizabeth Ann Flatt 1966- .... SATA 88
Brunskill, Ronald (William) 1929- 85-88
Brunstein, Karl (Avrum) 1933- 97-100
Brunswick, Heinrich Julius of
1564-1613 .... DLB 164
Brunt, P(eter) A(stbury) 1917- 101
Brunt, Stephen 232
Bruntjen, Scott 1943- 111
Brunton, David W(alter) 1929- 41-44R
Brunton, Mary 1778-1818 .... RGEL 2
Brunton, Paul 1898-1981
Obituary 115
Bruntz, George G. 1901-1991 .... 5-8R
Brunvand, Jan Harold 1933- CANR-99
Earlier sketches in CA 108, CANR-26, 51
Brus, Wlodzimierz 1921- 73-76
Brusati, Franco 1927-1993 148
Brush, Craig B(alcombe) 1930- 21-24R
Brush, Douglas P(eirce) 1930- CANR-7
Earlier sketch in CA 57-60
Brush, John E(dwin) 1919- 33-36R
Brush, Judith M(arie) 1938- CANR-7
Earlier sketch in CA 57-60
Brush, Karen A(lexandra) 1960- 127
See also SATA 85
Brush, Kathleen (E.) 1956- 202
Brush, Stephanie 1954- 138
Brush, Stephen G(eorge) 73-76
Brushwood, John S(tubbs) 1920- CANR-9
Earlier sketch in CA 21-24R
Brusiloff, Phyllis 1935- 57-60
Bruss, Elizabeth W(issman) 1944-1981 108
Brussat, Frederic 172
Brussat, Mary Ann 171
Brussel, Jacob 1900(?)-1979
Obituary 104
Brussel, James Arnold 1905-1982 ..... CANR-70
Earlier sketches in CA 1-4R, CANR-3
Brussel-Smith, Bernard 1914- .... SATA 58
Brust, Harold
See Cheyney, (Reginald Evelyn) Peter (Southouse)
Brust, Steven K. (Zoltan) 1955- CANR-99
Earlier sketches in CA 115, CANR-37
See also AAYA 36
See also FANT
See also SATA 86, 121
See also SUFW 2
Brustein, Robert S(anford) 1927- CANR-71
Earlier sketches in CA 9-12R, CANR-7
Brustein, William I. 1947- 162
Bruster, Bill(y) G(lenn) 1940- 111
Brustlein, Daniel 1904- .... SATA 40
Brustlein, Janice Tworkov -2000 .... 9-12R
Obituary 191
See also SATA 40
See also SATA-Obit 126
Bruteau, Beatrice 1930- 57-60
Bruton, Eric (Moore) 1915-2000 ...... CANR-23
Earlier sketches in CA 13-16R, CANR-5
Bruton, Henry J(ackson) 1921- 21-24R
Bruton, J(ack) G(ordon) 1914-1970 .... 9-12R
Brutschy, Jennifer 1960- .... SATA 84
Brutten, Gene J. 1928- 37-40R
Brutten, Milton 1922-2000 45-48
Obituary 190
Brutus
See Spooner, John D.
Brutus, Dennis 1924- CANR-81
Earlier sketches in CA 49-52, CANR-2, 27, 42
See also CAAS 14
See also AFW
See also BLC 1
See also BW 2, 3
See also CDWLB 3
See also CLC 43
See also CP 1, 2, 3, 4, 5, 6, 7
See also DAM MULT, POET
See also DLB 117, 225
See also EWL 3
See also PC 24
Bruun, Bertel 1937- 45-48
Bruun, (Arthur) Geoffrey
1898-1988 .... CANR-70
Obituary 126
Earlier sketch in CA 1-4R
Bruun, Ruth Dowling 1937- 108
Bruyn, Kathleen 1903-1983 .... CAP-2
Earlier sketch in CA 33-36
Bruzelius, Caroline 1949- 121
Bry, Adelaide 1920- 33-36R
Bry, Gerhard 1911-1996 .... 41-44R
Bryan, Ashley F. 1923- CANR-43
Earlier sketches in CA 107, CANR-26
See also BW 2
See also CLR 18, 66
See also CWRI 5
See also MAICYA 1, 2
See also MAICYAS 1
See also SATA 31, 72, 132
Bryan, C(ourtlandt) D(ixon) B(arnes)
1936- CANR-68
Earlier sketches in CA 73-76, CANR-13
Interview in CANR-13
See also CLC 29
See also DLB 185
Bryan, Carter R(oyston) 1911-1986 .... 33-36R
Obituary 162
Bryan, Christopher 1935- CANR-43
Earlier sketches in CA 104, CANR-20
Bryan, Dorothy M. 1896(?)-1984
Obituary 114
See also SATA-Obit 39
Bryan, Ferald J. 1958- 212
Bryan, Ford R. 1912- 134
Bryan, G(eorge) McLeod 1920- 1-4R
Bryan, George B(arton) 1939- 117
Bryan, J(oseph) III 1904-1993 .... CANR-47
Obituary 141
Earlier sketches in CA 61-64, CANR-11
Bryan, J(ack) Y(eaman) 1907-1988 73-76
Bryan, John 1911-1969 .... IDFW 4
Bryan, John E. 1931- CANR-4
Earlier sketch in CA 53-56
Bryan, Julien (Hequembourg) 1899-1974
Obituary 53-56
Bryan, Lynne 1961- CANR-105
Earlier sketch in CA 149
Bryan, M(erwyn) Leonard 1937- 103
Bryan, Marian K(nighton) 1900(?)-1974
Obituary 53-56
Bryan, Mark A. 1953(?)- 176
Bryan, Martin 1908-1982 .... 1-4R
Bryan, Mavis
See O'Brien, Marian P(lowman)
Bryan, Michael
See Moore, Brian
See also CCA 1
Bryan, Mike 236
Bryan, Mina R(uese) 1908-1985
Obituary 115
Bryan, Sharon 1943- CANR-37
Earlier sketch in CA 115
Bryan, William Jennings 1860-1925 ... DLB 303
See also TCLC 99
Bryan, (William) Wright 1905-1991 77-80
Obituary 133
Bryans, Robert Harbinson 1928- CANR-11
Earlier sketch in CA 5-8R
Bryans, Robin
See Bryans, Robert Harbinson
Bryant, Al
See Bryant, T(homas) Alton
Bryant, Anita
See Green, Anita Jane
Bryant, Arthur (Wynne Morgan)
1899-1985 .... CANR-72
Obituary 114
Earlier sketch in CA 105
See also DLB 149
Bryant, Bear
See Bryant, Paul W(illiam)
Bryant, Bernice (Morgan) 1908-1976 .... CAP-1
Earlier sketch in CA 9-10
See also SATA 11
Bryant, Beth Elaine 1936- 13-16R
Bryant, Betty 1922-1999 203
Bryant, Chris(topher) 1962- 239
Bryant, Christopher G. A. 1944- CANR-126
Earlier sketch in CA 164
Bryant, Cyril E(ric, Jr.) 1917- 61-64
Bryant, Donald C(ross) 1905-1987 .... 13-16R
Bryant, Dorothy 1930- 179
Earlier sketches in CA 53-56, CANR-4, 19, 41
Autobiographical Essay in 179
See also CAAS 26
See also FW
Bryant, Edward (Albert) 1928- CANR-11
Earlier sketch in CA 9-12R
Bryant, Edward (Winslow, Jr.) 1945- . CANR-72
Earlier sketches in CA 45-48, CANR-1
See also HGG
See also SFW 4
Bryant, Edward (Arnot) 1948- 141
Bryant, Gay 1945- CANR-13
Earlier sketch in CA 73-76
Bryant, Geoff 229
Bryant, Henry A(llen), Jr. 1943- CANR-4
Earlier sketch in CA 53-56
Bryant, Howard 1968- 216
Bryant, J(oseph) A(llen), Jr. 1919-1999 ...... 5-8R
Bryant, J. M.
See Bryant, Jonathan M.
Bryant, James C(ecil), Jr. 1931- CANR-99
Earlier sketches in CA 49-52, CANR-48
Bryant, Jennifer F(isher) 1960- CANR-115
Earlier sketch in CA 159
See also SATA 94
Bryant, Jerry H(olt) 1928- 33-36R
Bryant, Jon
See Bryant, Jonathan M.
Bryant, Jonathan M. 1957- 161
Bryant, Katherine Cliffton 1912-1992 ... 13-16R
Bryant, Keith L(ynn), Jr. 1937- CANR-141
Earlier sketch in CA 49-52
Bryant, Lynwood S(ilvester) 1908-2005 139
Obituary 237
Bryant, Margaret M. 1900-1993 .... CANR-83
Obituary 141
Earlier sketches in CA 1-4R, CANR-4
Bryant, Mark 1953- 231
Bryant, Michael
See Brennert, Alan (Michael)
Bryant, Paul W(illiam) 1913-1983 111
Obituary 108
Bryant, Ralph C(lement) 1938- 117
Bryant, Robert H(arry) 1925- 21-24R
Bryant, Shasta M(onroe) 1924- 41-44R
Bryant, T(homas) Alton 1926- CANR-29
Earlier sketches in CA 25-28R, CANR-10
Bryant, Traphes L(emon) 1914-1986 77-80
Bryant, Verda Evelyn 1910- CAP-2
Earlier sketch in CA 21-22
Bryant, William Cullen 1794-1878 ..... AMWS 1
See also CDALB 1640-1865
See also DA
See also DAB
See also DAC
See also DAM MST, POET
See also DLB 3, 43, 59, 189, 250
See also EXPP
See also PAB
See also PC 20
See also RGAL 4
See also TUS
Bryant, Willis Rooks 1892-1965 .... 5-8R
Obituary 103
Bryce, Gladysann 1934- 116
Bryce, Herrington J. 212
Bryce, James
See Mobley, James Bryce
Bryce, James 1838-1922 .... DLB 166, 190
Bryce, Murray D(avidson) 1917- 13-16R
Bryce, Robert 235
Bryce, Trevor R. 1940- 229
Bryce Echenique, Alfredo 1939- 175
See also CDWLB 3
See also DLB 145
See also EWL 3
See also HW 2
See also LAWS 1
Brychta, Alex 1956- CANR-20
Earlier sketch in CA 103
See also SATA 21
Bryde, John F(rancis) 1920- 33-36R

Bryden, Bill
See Bryden, William Campbell Rough
See also DLB 233
Bryden, John (Herbert) 1943- 134
Bryden, John Marshall 1941- CANR-1
Earlier sketch in CA 49-52
Bryden, John R(ennie) 1913-2001 .... 33-36R
Bryden, William Campbell Rough 1942- 105
See also Bryden, Bill
Brydges, Samuel Egerton 1762-1837 . DLB 107, 142
Bryer, Jackson R(obert) 1937- CANR-97
Earlier sketches in CA 9-12R, CANR-3, 18, 40
Bryer, (Alastair) Robin (Mornington) 1944- .. 111
Bryers, Paul 1945- CANR-89
Earlier sketch in CA 73-76
Bryfonski, Dedria (Anne) 1947- 101
Bryher 1894-1983 .... CANR-60
Obituary 108
Earlier sketch in CA 104
See also Ellerman, Annie Winifred
See also CN 1, 2, 3
Bryks, Rachmil 1912-1974 97-100
Brymer, Jack 1915- 110
Bryner, Gary C. 1951- 145
Brynie, Faith H(ickman) 1946- 185
See also SATA 113
Brynildsen, Ken(neth) 1944- 110
Bryning, Frank (Francis) B(ertram) 1907-1999 .... SFW 4
Brynner, Yul
See Khan, Taidje
Brysac, Shareen Blair 1939- 186
Brysk, Alison 1960- 202
Bryskett, Lodowick 1546(?)-1612 .... DLB 167
Bryson, Bernarda 1903-2004 .... CANR-70
Obituary 234
Earlier sketch in CA 49-52
See also Shahn, Bernarda Bryson
See also BYA 4
See also SATA 9
Bryson, Bill
See Bryson, William
Bryson, Conrey 1905-1994 93-96
Bryson, John 1923- 133
Bryson, John (Noel) 1935- 142
Bryson, Norman 1949- 147
Bryson, Phillip J(ames) 1939- 69-72
Bryson, Reid Allen 1920- 101
Bryson, W(illiam) Hamilton 1941- ... CANR-82
Earlier sketches in CA 114, CANR-36
Bryson, William 1951(?)- CANR-131
Earlier sketches in CA 142, CANR-72
See also MTFW 2005
Bryusov, Valery Yakovlevich 1873-1924 155
Brief entry 107
See also EWL 3
See also SFW 4
See also TCLC 10
Brzezinski, Zbigniew K(azimierz) 1928- CANR-81
Earlier sketches in CA 1-4R, CANR-5, 41
See also BEST 89:3
Buarque, Chico
See Buarque de Hollanda, Francisco
See also EWL 3
Buarque De Holanda (Ferreira), Aurelio 1911(?)-1989
Obituary 128
Buarque de Hollanda, Francisco 1944-
See Buarque, Chico
Buba, Joy Flinsch 1904- .... SATA 44
Bubar, Margaret Weber 1920(?)-1978
Obituary 77-80
Bubb, Mel
See Whitcomb, Ian
Bube, Richard H. 1927- CANR-8
Earlier sketch in CA 21-24R
Bubeck, Mark I(rving) 1928- 61-64
Buber, Martin 1878-1965 125
Obituary 25-28R
See also EWL 3
See also MTCW 1, 2
See also MTFW 2005
See also TWA
Bubner, Rudiger
See Bubner, Ruediger
Bubner, Ruediger 1941- 121
Bucaille, Laetitia 236
Bucaille, Maurice 1920- 137
Buccellati, Giorgio 1937- 41-44R
Bucchieri, Theresa F. 1908- 73-76
Buccini, Stefania 1959- 166
Bucco, Martin 1929- CANR-105
Earlier sketches in CA 29-32R, CANR-14
Buch, Esteban 1963- 224
Buchan, Alastair (Francis) 1918-1976 73-76
Obituary 65-68
Buchan, Bryan 1945- 107
See also SATA 36
Buchan, David
See Womack, David A(lfred)
Buchan, Elizabeth (Mary) 1948- 228
See also RHW
Buchan, James 1916- 130
Brief entry 119
Buchan, James (Ernest) 1954- 194
Buchan, John 1875-1940 145
Brief entry 108
See also CMW 4
See also DAB
See also DAM POP
See also DLB 34, 70, 156
See also HGG
See also MSW
See also MTCW 2
See also RGEL 2
See also RHW
See also TCLC 41
See also YABC 2
Buchan, Kate
See Erskine, Barbara
Buchan, Norman Findlay 1922-1990 109
Obituary 132
Buchan, Perdita 1940- 21-24R
Buchan, Stuart 1942-1987 57-60
Obituary 123
See also SATA-Obit 54
Buchan, Thomas Buchanan 1931- ... CANR-16
Earlier sketch in CA 25-28R
See also Buchan, Tom
Buchan, Tom
See Buchan, Thomas Buchanan
See also CP 1, 2, 3, 4, 5, 6, 7
Buchan, Ursula 1953- CANR-141
Earlier sketch in CA 128
Buchan, William (James de l'Aigle) 1916- .. 161
Buchanan, A(lbert) Russell 1906- 13-16R
Buchanan, Andrea 223
Buchanan, Anne L. 1960- 176
Buchanan, Annette 1933- 118
Buchanan, Betty (Joan) 1923- 101
Buchanan, Chuck
See Rowland, D(onald) S(ydney)
Buchanan, Colin 1907-2001 216
Buchanan, Colin O(gilvie) 1934- 25-28R
Buchanan, Cynthia 1942- CANR-1
Earlier sketch in CA 45-48
Buchanan, Cynthia D(ee) 1937- 5-8R
Buchanan, Daniel C(rump) 1892-1982 . 17-20R
Buchanan, (Eric) David 1933- 57-60
Buchanan, David A(lan) 1949- 118
Buchanan(-Berrigan), Dawna Lisa 1954- 137
Buchanan, Debby 1952- 149
See also SATA 82
Buchanan, Deborah Leevonne
See Buchanan, Debby
Buchanan, Donald W(illiam) 1908-1966(?) CAP-1
Earlier sketch in CA 11-12
Buchanan, Edna (Rydzik) 1939(?)- ... CANR-111
Brief entry 125
Earlier sketches in CA 132, CANR-52
Interview in CA-132
See also CMW 4
Buchanan, George 1506-1582 .... DLB 132
Buchanan, George (Henry Perrott) 1904-1989 .... CANR-3
Obituary 129
Earlier sketch in CA 9-12R
See also CN 1, 2, 3
See also CP 1, 2
Buchanan, George Wesley 1921- CANR-14
Earlier sketch in CA 37-40R
Buchanan, Jack
See Newton, Michael
Buchanan, James David 1929- 130
Buchanan, James J(unkin) 1925- 33-36R
Buchanan, James McGill 1919- CANR-22
Earlier sketches in CA 5-8R, CANR-3
Buchanan, Jane 1956- 236
See also SATA 160
Buchanan, Keith 1919- CANR-10
Earlier sketch in CA 21-24R
Buchanan, Ken 1952- 149
Buchanan, Laura
See King, Florence
Buchanan, Leonard 221
Buchanan, Lyn
See Buchanan, Leonard
Buchanan, Marie 1922- CANR-72
Earlier sketches in CA 65-68, CANR-10, 25
See also CMW 4
Buchanan, Patrick
See Corley, Edwin (Raymond)
Buchanan, Patrick J(oseph) 1938- 186
Buchanan, Paul 1959- 188
See also SATA 116
Buchanan, Paul G. 1954- 154
Buchanan, Pegasus 1920- 9-12R
Buchanan, R(obert) A(ngus) 1930- CANR-7
Earlier sketch in CA 17-20R
Buchanan, Robert 1841-1901 179
See also DLB 18, 35
See also TCLC 107
Buchanan, Sue 1939- 210
See also SATA 139
Buchanan, Thomas G(ittings) 1919-1988 .. 1-4R
Obituary 174
Buchanan, Wiley T(homas), Jr. 1914-1986
Obituary 118
Buchanan, William
See Buck, William Ray
Buchanan, William J(esse) 1926- CANR-39
Earlier sketch in CA 73-76
Buchanan-Brown, John 1929- 102
Buchard, Robert 1931- 33-36R
Buchdahl, Gerd 1914-2001 57-60
Bucheister, Patt 1942- CANR-98
Earlier sketches in CA 122, CANR-48
Buchele, William Martin 1895-1977 57-60
Buchen, Irving H. 1930- 25-28R
Bucher, Bradley 1932- 37-40R
Bucher, Charles A(ugustus) 1912-1988 .... CANR-3
Earlier sketch in CA 9-12R
Bucher, Francois 1927- CANR-3
Earlier sketch in CA 5-8R
Bucher, Glenn R(ichard) 1940- 57-60
Bucher, Magnus 1927- 41-44R
Buchheim, Lothar-Guenther 1918- 85-88
See also CLC 6
Buchheimer, Naomi Barnett
See Barnett, Naomi
Buchheit, Lee C(harles) 1950- 81-84
Buchholz, Todd G. 1961- 150
Buchignani, Walter 1965- 150
See also SATA 84
Buchler, Justus 1914-1991 .... 5-8R
Obituary 134
See also DLB 279
Buchman, Dian Dincin CANR-8
Earlier sketch in CA 61-64
Buchman, Frank N(athan) D(aniel) 1878-1961
Obituary 112
Buchman, Herman 1920- 41-44R
Buchman, Marion 121
Buchman, Randall L(oren) 1929- CANR-1
Earlier sketch in CA 45-48
Buchman, Sidney 1902-1975 93-96
Obituary 61-64
See also DLB 26
See also IDFW 3, 4
Buchmann, Stephen L. 162
Buchner, Augustus 1591-1661 .... DLB 164
Buchner, (Karl) Georg 1813-1837 ..... CDWLB 2
See also DLB 133
See also EW 6
See also RGSF 2
See also RGWL 2, 3
See also TWA
Bucholtz, Andreas Heinrich 1607-1671 .... DLB 168
Bucholz, Arden 1936- CANR-91
Earlier sketch in CA 167
Buchsbaum, Tony 1961- 128
Buchwald, Ann 1920-1994 128
Obituary 146
Buchwald, Art(hur) 1925- CANR-107
Earlier sketches in CA 5-8R, CANR-21, 67
See also AITN 1
See also CLC 33
See also MTCW 1, 2
See also SATA 10
Buchwald, Emilie 1935- CANR-2
Earlier sketch in CA 49-52
See also SATA 7
Buchwalter, Andrew 1949- 145
Buck, Ashley (?)-1980
Obituary 97-100
Buck, Bob
See Buck, Robert N.
Buck, Charles (Henry, Jr.) 1915- 33-36R
Buck, Craig 1952- 141
Buck, D. W.
See Buck, Detlev
Buck, David 1934(?)-1989
Obituary 128
Buck, Detlev 1962- 201
Buck, Doris P(itkin) 1898(?)-1980
Obituary 102
Buck, Edith V(irginia) 1919- 117
Buck, Frederick Silas 5-8R
Buck, George C(rawford) 1918- 69-72
Buck, Gisela 1941- 168
See also SATA 101
Buck, Harry M(erwyn, Jr.) 1921- CANR-13
Earlier sketch in CA 33-36R
Buck, Heather 1926- .... CWP
Buck, James H. 1924- 104
Buck, Joan Juliet 1948- CANR-25
Earlier sketch in CA 108
Buck, John Lossing 1890-1975 .... CANR-2
Obituary 61-64
Earlier sketch in CA 45-48
Buck, John N(elson) 1906- CAP-2
Earlier sketch in CA 29-32
Buck, Lewis 1925- 73-76
See also SATA 18
Buck, Margaret Waring 1905-1997 .. CANR-70
Earlier sketch in CA 5-8R
See also SATA 3
Buck, Marion A(shby) 1909- CAP-1
Earlier sketch in CA 13-14
Buck, Paul H(erman) 1899-1978 219
Obituary 81-84
Buck, Pearl S(ydenstricker) 1892-1973 .... CANR-34
Obituary 41-44R
Earlier sketches in CA 1-4R, CANR-1
See also AAYA 42
See also AITN 1
See also AMWS 2
See also BPFB 1
See also CDALBS
See also CLC 7, 11, 18, 127
See also CN 1
See also DA
See also DA3
See also DAB
See also DAC
See also DAM MST, NOV
See also DLB 9, 102
See also EWL 3
See also LAIT 3
See also MAL 5
See also MTCW 1, 2
See also MTFW 2005
See also RGAL 4
See also RHW
See also SATA 1, 25
See also TUS
Buck, Peggy S(ullivan) 1930- 65-68
Buck, Philip W(allenstein) 1900-1985 65-68
Buck, Rinker 1951(?)- CANR-143
Earlier sketch in CA 166
Buck, Robert N. 1914- 103
Buck, Ross (Workman) 1941- 128
Buck, Siegfried 1941- 168
See also SATA 101
Buck, Stratton 1906- CAP-2
Earlier sketch in CA 17-18
Buck, Susan J. 1947- 141
Buck, Vernon E(llis) 1934- 37-40R
Buck, William Ray 1930- 1-4R
Buckaway, C. M.
See Buckaway, Catherine M(argaret)
Buckaway, Catherine M(argaret) 1919-1996 130
Bucke, Charles 1781-1846 .... DLB 110
Bucke, Richard Maurice 1837-1902 178
See also DLB 99
Buckelew, Albert R., Jr. 1942- 150
Buckeridge, Anthony (Malcolm) 1912-2004 .... CANR-52
Obituary 228
Earlier sketches in CA 49-52, CANR-2
See also SATA 6, 85
Buckey, Sarah Masters 1955- 239
Buckeye, Donald A(ndrew) 1930- CANR-98
Earlier sketches in CA 49-52, CANR-47
Buckhanon, Kalisha 1977- 239
Buckholdt, David R. 1942- 101
Buckholtz, Eileen (Garber) 1949- 117
See also SATA 54
See also SATA-Brief 47
Buckhout, Robert 1935-1990 45-48
Obituary 133
Buckingham, Burdette H. 1907(?)-1977
Obituary 73-76
Buckingham, Clyde E(dwin) 1907-1981 .... CAP-1
Earlier sketch in CA 13-16
Buckingham, Edwin 1810-1833 .... DLB 73
Buckingham, George Villiers 1628-1687 .... RGEL 2
Buckingham, James (William) 1932-1992 .... CANR-47
Obituary 136
Earlier sketch in CA 29-32R
Buckingham, Jamie
See Buckingham, James (William)
Buckingham, Joseph Tinker 1779-1861 .... DLB 73
Buckingham, Nancy 1924-1990 .... RHW
Buckingham, Robert W(illiam) III 113
Buckingham, Walter S(amuel), Jr. 1924-1967 .... 1-4R
Obituary 103
Buckingham, Willis J(ohn) 1938- 29-32R
Buckland, Gail Susan 1948- 180
Buckland, Michael K(eeble) 1941- 97-100
Buckland, Raymond 1934- 73-76
Buckland, Wilfred 1866-1946 .... IDFW 3, 4
Buckle, (Christopher) Richard (Sandford) 1916-2001 .... CANR-70
Obituary 200
Earlier sketch in CA 97-100
Buckler, Beatrice 1933- 127
Buckler, Ernest 1908-1984 .... CAP-1
Obituary 114
Earlier sketch in CA 11-12
See also CCA 1
See also CLC 13
See also CN 1, 2, 3
See also DAC
See also DAM MST
See also DLB 68
See also SATA 47
Buckler, John 1945- 121
Buckler, William Earl 1924- CANR-20
Earlier sketches in CA 1-4R, CANR-5
Buckless, Andrea K. 1968- 189
See also SATA 117
Buckley, Anthony D. 1945- CANR-98
Earlier sketches in CA 120, CANR-47
Buckley, Christopher (Taylor) 1952- CANR-119
Earlier sketch in CA 139
See also CLC 165
Buckley, Cornelius M(ichael) 1925- 138
Buckley, Fergus Reid 1930- 21-24R
Buckley, Fiona
See Anand, Valerie
Buckley, Francis J(oseph) 1928- CANR-13
Earlier sketch in CA 33-36R
Buckley, Gail Lumet 1937- 142
See also BW 2
Buckley, Heather
See Buckley Neville, Doris Heather
Buckley, Helen 1923- 144
Buckley, Helen E(lizabeth) 1918- CANR-3
Earlier sketch in CA 5-8R
See also SATA 2, 90
Buckley, J(ames) Taylor, Jr. 1939- 127
Buckley, James, Jr. 1963- 186
See also SATA 114
Buckley, James Lane 1923- 61-64
Buckley, James Monroe 1836-1920 206
Buckley, Jerome Hamilton 1917- CANR-70
Earlier sketches in CA 1-4R, CANR-3
Buckley, John (F.) 1961- 148
Buckley, Jonathan 1956- 183
Buckley, Julian Gerard 1905-1997 .... 41-44R
Buckley, Kevin 1941(?)- 140
Buckley, Mary (Elizabeth Anne) 1951- 227
Buckley, Mary L(orraine) 53-56
Buckley, Michael F. 1880(?)-1977
Obituary 69-72
Buckley, Michael J(oseph) 1931- 73-76
Buckley, Paul 1938- 162
Buckley, Peter 1938-1991 112
Obituary 134
Buckley, Priscilla 1921-1992 81-84
Buckley, Roger N(orman) 1937- CANR-90
Earlier sketch in CA 97-100
Buckley, Shawn 1943- 93-96

Cumulative Index 81 Bull

Buckley, Suzanne Shelton 1946- 108
Buckley, Thomas H(ugh) 1932- 29-32R
Buckley, Vincent (Thomas) 1925-1988 101
See also CLC 57
See also CP 1, 2
See also DLB 289
Buckley, Walter (Frederick) 1921- 121
Buckley, William F(rank), Jr. 1925- . CANR-133
Earlier sketches in CA 1-4R, CANR-1, 24, 53, 93
Interview in CANR-24
See also AITN 1
See also BPFB 1
See also CLC 7, 18, 37
See also CMW 4
See also CPW
See also DA3
See also DAM POP
See also DLB 137
See also DLBY 1980
See also MTCW 1, 2
See also MTFW 2005
See also TUS
Buckley Neville, Doris Heather
1910-2000 103
Bucklin, Louis P(ierre) 1928- 97-100
Buckman, Peter 1941- CANR-11
Earlier sketch in CA 65-68
Buckman, Rob
See Buckman, Robert (Alexander Amiel)
Buckman, Robert (Alexander Amiel)
1948- 128
Buckmaster, Henrietta
See Stephens, Henrietta Henkle
See also SATA 6
Buckminster, Joseph Stevens
1784-1812 .... DLB 37
Bucknall, Barbara J(ane) 1933- CANR-14
Earlier sketch in CA 33-36R
Bucknell, Howard III 1924-1986 125
Buckner, M. M. 236
Buckner, Rheuben
See McCoy, Max
Buckner, Robert (Henry) 1906-1989 .... 1-4R
Obituary 171
See also DLB 26
Buckner, Sally Beaver 1931- 61-64
Bucko, Raymond A. 185
Bucks, Brad
See Holub, Joan
Buckser, Andrew (S.) 1964- 164
Buckstaff, Kathryn 1947- CANR-139
Earlier sketch in CA 147
Buckstead, Richard C(hris) 1929- 49-52
Buckstone, John Baldwin 1802-1879 .... RGEL 2
Buckvar, Felice (Spitz) 1938- 107
Bucuvalas, Tina 1951- 149
Buczkowski, Leopold 1905- 41-44R
Budapest, Zsuzsanna E(mese) 1940- 154
Buday, George
See Buday, Gyorgy
Buday, Gyorgy 1907-1990(?) 107
Obituary 132
Budberg, Moura 1892(?)-1974
Obituary 53-56
Budbill, David 1940- 73-76
Budd, Carol (Pellegrini) 1951- 128
Budd, E. S.
See Sirimarco, Elizabeth
Budd, Edward C(arhart) 1920- 21-24R
Budd, Elaine 1925- 101
Budd, Holly
See Petty, Alan Edwin
Budd, John (M.) 1953- 238
Budd, Kenneth George 1904-1972 .... CAP-1
Earlier sketch in CA 13-14
Budd, Lillian (Peterson) 1897-1989 .. CANR-72
Earlier sketches in CA 1-4R, CANR-4
See also SATA 7
Budd, Louis J(ohn) 1921- CANR-3
Earlier sketch in CA 1-4R
Budd, Mavis CANR-19
Earlier sketch in CA 102
Budd, Richard W. 1934- 21-24R
Budd, Thomas (?)-1698 .... DLB 24
Budd, William C(laude) 1923- 49-52
Budde, Michael L(eo) 1958- CANR-120
Earlier sketch in CA 168
Buddee, Paul Edgar 1913- 103
Budden, Julian (Medforth) 1924- 130
Budden, Laura M(adeline) 1894- 5-8R
Budden, Sandra C.
See Campbell, Sandra
Buddensieg, Tilmann 1928- 138
Bude, Guillaume 1468-1540 .... GFL Beginnings to 1789
Bude, John
See Elmore, Ernest Carpenter
Budenz, Louis F(rancis) 1891-1972
Obituary 89-92
Buderi, Robert 1954- CANR-142
Earlier sketch in CA 162
Budge, Ian 1936- CANR-12
Earlier sketch in CA 29-32R
Budgen, Frank Spencer Curtis 1882-1971
Obituary 29-32R
Budhos, Marina Tamar 192
Budiansky, Stephen (Philip) 1957- 150
Budick, Sanford 1942- CANR-71
Earlier sketch in CA 33-36R
Budimir, (Simo) Velimir 1926- 65-68
Budinger, Peyton Bailey 1939- 114
Budnitz, Judy 1973- 169
Budny, Mildred 235
Budoff, Penny Wise 1939- 110
Budra, Paul (Vincent) 1957- 185
Budrys, Algirdas Jonas 1931- CANR-20
Earlier sketches in CA 1-4R, CANR-4
See also Budrys, Algis
See also DLB 8
See also SFW 4
Budrys, Algis
See Budrys, Algirdas Jonas
See also CAAS 14
See also SCFW 1, 2
Budurowycz, Bohdan B(asil) 1921- CANR-3
Earlier sketch in CA 5-8R
Budy, Andrea (Hollander) 1947- 189
Budz, Mark 1960- 234
Budzik, Janet K. Sims 1942- 37-40R
Budziszewski, J(ay Dalton) 1952- 125
Buechner, (Carl) Frederick 1926- CANR-138
Earlier sketches in CA 13-16R, CANR-11, 39, 64, 114
Interview in CANR-11
See also AMWS 12
See also BPFB 1
See also CLC 2, 4, 6, 9
See also CN 1, 2, 3, 4, 5, 6, 7
See also DAM NOV
See also DLBY 1980
See also MAL 5
See also MTCW 1, 2
See also MTFW 2005
See also TCLE 1:1
Buechner, John C(harles) 1934- 21-24R
Buechner, Thomas S(charman)
1926- CANR-101
Earlier sketches in CA 49-52, CANR-47
Buehler, Curt F(erdinand) 1905-1985 .... 1-4R
Obituary 117
Buehler, Evelyn Judy 1953- 167
See also BW 3
Buehler, Stephanie Jona 1956- 150
See also SATA 83
Buehlmann, Walbert 1916- CANR-38
Earlier sketch in CA 115
Buehnau, Ludwig
See Schreiber, Hermann (Otto Ludwig)
Buehner, Andrew J(ohn) 1905-1984 .... 17-20R
Buehner, Caralyn (M.) 1963- CANR-142
Earlier sketch in CA 171
See also SATA 104, 159
Buehner, Mark 1959- .... SATA 104, 159
Buehr, Walter Franklin 1897-1971 .... CANR-3
Obituary 33-36R
Earlier sketch in CA 5-8R
See also SATA 3
Buehrig, Edward H(enry) 1910-1986 .... 37-40R
Buehrig, Gordon M. 1904-1990 101
Buel, Richard (Van Wyck), Jr. 1933- . CANR-13
Earlier sketch in CA 73-76
Bueler, Lois E(aton) 1940- 57-60
Bueler, William Merwin 1934- 37-40R
Buell, Ellen Lewis
See Cash, Ellen Lewis Buell
Buell, Emmett H., Jr. 1941- 138
Buell, Frederick H(enderson) 1942- 33-36R
Buell, Janet 1945- 127
Buell, Janet 1952- .... SATA 106
Buell, John (Edward) 1927- CANR-71
Earlier sketch in CA 1-4R
See also CLC 10
See also DLB 53
Buell, John W. 1945- 197
Buell, Jon A. 1939- 102
Buell, Lawrence (Ingalls) 1939- CANR-112
Earlier sketches in CA 49-52, CANR-47
Buell, Robert Kingery 1908-1971 .... CANR-71
Earlier sketches in CAP-2, CA 25-28
Buell, Victor P(aul) 1914- CANR-8
Earlier sketch in CA 21-24R
Buelow, George J. 1929- 21-24R
Buenaventura, Enrique 1925-2003 151
See also DAM MULT
See also DLB 305
See also EWL 3
See also HW 1, 2
Buendia, Manuel
See Giron, Manuel Buendia Tellez
Buenker, John D(avid) 1937- CANR-16
Earlier sketches in CA 45-48, CANR-1
Bueno, Jose de la Torre 1905(?)-1980
Obituary 93-96
Bueno de Mesquita, Bruce James 1946- 108
Buergel, Paul-Hermann H. 1949- .... SATA 83
Buergenthal, Thomas 1934- 37-40R
Buerger, Peter 1936- 144
Buerkle, Jack Vincent 1923-2000 .... 41-44R
Buero Vallejo, Antonio 1916-2000 ... CANR-75
Obituary 189
Earlier sketches in CA 106, CANR-24, 49
See also CLC 15, 46, 139
See also CWW 2
See also DC 18
See also DFS 11
See also EWL 3
See also HW 1
See also MTCW 1, 2
Bueschel, Richard M. 1926- CANR-26
Earlier sketches in CA 25-28R, CANR-11
Buetow, Harold A(ndrew) 1919- 53-56
Buettner, Dan 1960- 160
See also SATA 95
Buettner-Janusch, John 1924-1992 49-52
Obituary 138
Bufalari, Giuseppe 1927- CANR-16
Earlier sketch in CA 25-28R
Bufalino, Gesualdo 1920-1996 209
See also CLC 74
See also CWW 2
See also DLB 196
Buferd, Norma Bradley 1937- 69-72
Buff, Conrad 1886-1975 135
See also MAICYA 1, 2
See also SATA 19
Buff, Joe 1955(?)- 221
Buff, Mary (E. Marsh) 1890-1970 135
Obituary 116
See also MAICYA 1, 2
See also SATA 19
Buffa, D. W.
See Buffa, Dudley W.
Buffa, Dudley
See Buffa, Dudley W.
Buffa, Dudley W. 1940- CANR-143
Earlier sketch in CA 121
Buffalo Bird Woman 1839-1929 220
Buffalo Chuck
See Barth, Charles P.
Buffaloe, Neal D(ollison) 1924- 53-56
Buffett, Jimmy 1946- 141
See also BEST 90:2
See also BPFB 1
See also CPW
See also CSW
See also SATA 76, 110
Buffi, Roberta 1968- 238
Buffie, Margaret 1945- 160
See also AAYA 23
See also CLR 39
See also CWRI 5
See also JRDA
See also MAICYA 2
See also MAICYAS 1
See also SATA 71, 107, 161
Buffington, Albert F(ranklin)
1905-1980 .... 33-36R
Obituary 162
Buffington, Robert (Ray) 1933- 21-24R
Buffon, Georges-Louis Leclerc
1707-1788 .... DLB 313
See also GFL Beginnings to 1789
Bufkin, Ernest Claude, Jr. 1929- 101
Buford, Bill 1954- 143
Buford, Kate 192
Buford, Thomas O(liver) 1932- 29-32R
Buford, William Holmes
See Buford, Bill
Bugajski, Janusz 1954- CANR-143
Earlier sketch in CA 144
Bugayev, Boris Nikolayevich 1880-1934 165
Brief entry 104
See also Bely, Andrey and Belyi, Andrei
See also MTCW 2
See also MTFW 2005
See also PC 11
See also TCLC 7
Bugbee, Emma 1888(?)-1981
Obituary 105
See also SATA-Obit 29
Bugbee, Ruth Carson 1903-1989 .... CANR-1
Earlier sketch in CA 1-4R
Bugeja, Michael J. 1952- CANR-114
Earlier sketch in CA 138
See also CAAS 29
Bugental, James F(rederick) T(homas)
1915- CANR-50
Earlier sketches in CA 21-24R, CANR-10, 25
Bugg, James L(uckin), Jr. 1920- 5-8R
Bugg, Ralph 1922- 73-76
Buggie, Frederick D(enman) 1929- 97-100
Buglass, Leslie J. 1917- 13-16R
Bugliarello, George 1927- 41-44R
Bugliosi, Vincent (T.) 1934- CANR-110
Earlier sketches in CA 73-76, CANR-13, 46
Bugnet, Georges (-Charles-Jules)
1879-1981 148
See also Doutremont, Henri
See also DLB 92
Bugni, Alice 1951- 194
See also SATA 122
Bugos, Glenn E. 1961- 164
Bugul, Ken
See Mbaye, Marietou (Bileoma)
See also EWL 3
Buhagiar, Marion 1932- 141
Buhite, Russell D(evere) 1938- 101
Buhle, Mari Jo 1943- 108
Buhle, Paul 1944- CANR-110
Earlier sketches in CA 127, CANR-63
Buhler, Charlotte B(ertha)
1893-1974(?) CANR-72
Earlier sketches in CAP-2, CA 17-18
Buhler, Charlotte Malachowski
See Buhler, Charlotte B(ertha)
Buhler, Curt F(erdinand)
See Buehler, Curt F(erdinand)
Buhler, Stephen M. 1954- 223
Buhlmann, Walbert
See Buehlmann, Walbert
Buhner, Stephen Harrod 1952- 171
Buhturi, al- 821-897 .... DLB 311
Buida, Lurii
See Buida, Yuri
Buida, Yuri 1954- 232
Buies, Arthur 1840-1901 178
See also DLB 99
Buigues, Pierre (A.) 1949- 214
Buisseret, David 1934- 124
Buist, Charlotte
See Patterson, Charlotte (Buist)
Buist, Vincent 1919(?)-1979
Obituary 89-92
Buitenhuis, Peter (Martinus) 1925- 25-28R
Buitrago, Ann Mari 1929- 105
Bujold, Lois McMaster 1949- CANR-115
Earlier sketches in CA 139, CANR-87
See also AAYA 19, 54
See also CN 7
See also SATA 136
See also SFW 4
Bujor, Flavia 1989- 239
Bukalski, Peter J(ulian) 1941- CANR-15
Earlier sketch in CA 41-44R
Bukatman, Scott 1957- 151
Buker, George E(dward) 1923- 53-56
Bukey, Evan Burr 1940- CANR-93
Earlier sketch in CA 131
Bukharin, Nikolai (Ivanovich) 1858-1938
Brief entry 120
Bukiet, Melvin Jules CANR-93
Earlier sketch in CA 154
See also DLB 299
Bukowczyk, John J(oseph) 1950- 125
Bukowski, Charles 1920-1994 .... CANR-105
Obituary 144
Earlier sketches in CA 17-20R, CANR-40, 62
See also CLC 2, 5, 9, 41, 82, 108
See also CN 4, 5
See also CP 1, 2
See also CPW
See also DA3
See also DAM NOV, POET
See also DLB 5, 130, 169
See also EWL 3
See also MAL 5
See also MTCW 1, 2
See also MTFW 2005
See also PC 18
See also SSC 45
Buktenica, Norman A(ugust) 1930- 33-36R
Bulanda, Susan 1946- 181
Bulatkin, Eleanor Webster 1913-1998 ... 33-36R
Bulatovic, Miodrag 1930-1991 .... CANR-72
Obituary 133
Earlier sketches in CA 5-8R, CANR-21
See also CDWLB 4
See also DLB 181
See also EWL 3
Bulbeck, Chilla 1951- 145
Buley, R(oscoe) Carlyle 1893-1968 .... CAP-2
Obituary 25-28R
Earlier sketch in CA 21-22
Bulfinch, Thomas 1796-1867 .... SATA 35
Bulgakov, Mikhail (Afanas'evich)
1891-1940 152
Brief entry 105
See also BPFB 1
See also DAM DRAM, NOV
See also DLB 272
See also EWL 3
See also MTCW 2
See also MTFW 2005
See also NFS 8
See also RGSF 2
See also RGWL 2, 3
See also SFW 4
See also SSC 18
See also TCLC 2, 16, 159
See also TWA
Bulgarin, Faddei Venediktovich
1789-1859 .... DLB 198
Bulger, Bozeman 1877-1932 192
See also DLB 171
Bulger, Margaret Anne
See Bulger, Peggy A.
Bulger, Peggy A. 1949- 149
Bulger, William M. 1934- 153
Bulger, William T(homas) 1927- 69-72
Bulgya, Alexander Alexandrovich
1901-1956 181
Brief entry 117
See also Fadeev, Aleksandr Aleksandrovich and Fadeev, Alexandr Alexandrovich and Fadeyev, Alexander
See also TCLC 53
Bulion, Leslie 1958- 237
See also SATA 161
Bulka, Reuven P(inchas) 1944- CANR-128
Earlier sketches in CA 113, CANR-49
Bulkeley, Christy C. .... AITN 2
Bulkeley, Kelly 1962- 175
Bulkeley, William M. 1950- 135
Bulkley, Dwight H(atfield) 1919- 105
Bulkowski, Thomas N. 1957- 227
Bull, Angela (Mary) 1936- CANR-24
Earlier sketches in CA 21-24R, CANR-9
See also CWRI 5
See also SATA 45
Bull, Barry L. 1947- CANR-93
Earlier sketch in CA 146
Bull, Bartle 1939- 193
Bull, Christopher Neil 1940- 145
Bull, Emma 1954- 127
See also AAYA 31
See also FANT
See also SATA 99
See also SATA-Essay 103
See also SFW 4
Bull, Geoffrey Taylor 1921- CANR-3
Earlier sketch in CA 9-12R
Bull, George (Anthony) 1929-2001 .. CANR-39
Obituary 194
Earlier sketch in CA 115
Bull, Guyon B(oys) G(arrett) 1912- CANR-5
Earlier sketch in CA 5-8R
Bull, Hedley Norman 1932-1985 .... 5-8R
Obituary 116
Bull, John 1914- 69-72
Bull, Norman John 1916- CANR-16
Earlier sketch in CA 93-96
See also SATA 41

Bull, Odd 1907- ... 81-84
Bull, Olaf (Jacob Martin Luther)
1883-1933 ... 191
See also DLB 297
See also EWL 3
Bull, Peter (Cecil) 1912-1984 ... CANR-11
Obituary ... 112
Earlier sketch in CA 25-28R
See also SATA-Obit 39
Bull, Robert J(ehu) 1920- ... 97-100
Bull, Schuyler M. 1974- ... 208
See also SATA 138
Bull, Storm 1913- ... 9-12R
Bull, William E(merson) 1909-1972 ... CAP-1
Earlier sketch in CA 13-16
Bulla, Clyde Robert 1914- ... CANR-118
Earlier sketches in CA 5-8R, CANR-3, 18, 40
See also CWRI 5
See also MAICYA 1, 2
See also SAAS 6
See also SATA 2, 41, 91, 139
Bullard, Beth 1939- ... CANR-100
Earlier sketch in CA 149
Bullard, E(dgar) John III 1942- ... 33-36R
Bullard, Fred Mason 1901-1994 ... 25-28R
Bullard, Helen 1902-1996 ... CANR-7
Earlier sketch in CA 17-20R
Bullard, Lisa 1961- ... 213
See also SATA 142
Bullard, Oral 1922- ... CANR-23
Earlier sketches in CA 61-64, CANR-8
Bullard, Pamela 1948- ... 106
Bullard, Roger A(ubrey) 1937- ... 33-36R
Bulle, Florence (Elizabeth) 1925- ... CANR-15
Earlier sketch in CA 93-96
Bulleid, H(enry) A(nthony) V(aughan)
1912- ... CANR-13
Earlier sketches in CAP-1, CA 9-10
Bullein, William c. 1520-1576 ... DLB 167
Bullen, Dana R(ipley) 1931- ... 73-76
Bullen, Fiona ... 184
Bullen, Keith Edward 1906-1976
Obituary ... 106
Bullen, Leonard
See Kennedy, Leo
Bullen, Robert 1926(?)-1976
Obituary ... 69-72
Buller, Herman 1923- ... 61-64
Bullett, Gerald (William) 1893-1958 ... 155
See also FANT
Bulliet, Richard W(illiams) 1940- ... CANR-7
Earlier sketch in CA 57-60
Bullingham, Rodney
See Sladen, Norman St. Barbe
Bullins, Ed 1935- ... CANR-134
Earlier sketches in CA 49-52, CANR-24, 46, 73
See also CAAS 16
See also BLC 1
See also BW 2, 3
See also CAD
See also CD 5, 6
See also CLC 1, 5, 7
See also DAM DRAM, MULT
See also DC 6
See also DLB 7, 38, 249
See also EWL 3
See also MAL 5
See also MTCW 1, 2
See also MTFW 2005
See also RGAL 4
Bullis, Harry Amos 1890-1963 ... CAP-2
Earlier sketch in CA 17-18
Bullis, Jerald 1944- ... CANR-1
Earlier sketch in CA 49-52
Bullitt, Dorothy 1955- ... 171
Bullitt, John M(arshall) 1921-1985
Obituary ... 117
Bullitt, Orville H(orwitz) 1894-1979 ... 33-36R
Obituary ... 89-92
Bullitt, Stimson 1919- ... 112
Bullitt, William C(hristian) 1891-1967
Obituary ... 89-92
Bullitt-Jonas, Margaret 1951- ... 184
Bulloch, John 1928- ... 134
Bullock, Lord Alan (Louis Charles)
1914-2004 ... CANR-141
Obituary ... 224
Earlier sketches in CA 1-4R, CANR-41
Bullock, Alice 1904-1986 ... 89-92
Bullock, Barbara
See Bullock-Wilson, Barbara
Bullock, C(larence) Hassell 1939- ... 89-92
Bullock, Charles S(pencer) III 1942- . CANR-13
Earlier sketch in CA 33-36R
Bullock, Frederick W(illiam) B(agshawe)
1903-(?) ... CANR-4
Earlier sketch in CA 5-8R
Bullock, Henry 1907(?)-1973
Obituary ... 41-44R
Bullock, Kathleen (Mary) 1946- ... SATA 77
Bullock, Michael 1918- ... CANR-78
Earlier sketches in CA 17-20R, CANR-7, 38
See also CP 1, 2, 3, 4, 5, 6, 7
Bullock, Paul 1924-1986 ... CANR-11
Obituary ... 118
Earlier sketch in CA 29-32R
Bullock, Robert (D.) 1947- ... SATA 92
Bullock-Wilson, Barbara 1945- ... 65-68
Bullough, Bonnie 1927-1996 ... CANR-49
Earlier sketches in CA 69-72, CANR-11
Bullough, D(onald) A(uberon) 1928- ... 107
Bullough, Geoffrey 1901-1982 ... CANR-5
Obituary ... 106
Earlier sketch in CA 1-4R
Bullough, Robert V., Jr. 1949- ... 135
Bullough, Vern (LeRoy) 1928- ... CANR-52
Earlier sketches in CA 9-12R, CANR-4, 11, 26
Bullough, William A(lfred) 1933- ... 101
Bullrich (Palenque), Silvina 1915-1990 ... HW 1
Bulman, Joan (Carroll Boone) 1904- ... 103
Bulman, Oliver (Meredith Boone) 1902-1974
Obituary ... 49-52
Bulmer, (Henry) Kenneth 1921- ... CANR-9
Earlier sketch in CA 13-16R
See also SFW 4
Bulmer, Martin 1943- ... 113
Bulmer, Ralph N(eville) H(ermon) 1928-1988
Obituary ... 126
Bulmer-Thomas, Ivor 1905-1993 ... CAP-1
Obituary ... 143
Earlier sketch in CA 11-12
Buloff, Joseph 1899-1985 ... 141
Obituary ... 115
Bulosan, Carlos 1911-1956 ... 216
See also AAL
See also DLB 312
See also RGAL 4
Bulpin, T(homas) V(ictor) 1918- ... CANR-4
Earlier sketch in CA 9-12R
Bulpin, (Barbara) Vicki ... 156
See also SATA 92
Bultmann, Rudolf Karl 1884-1976 ... CANR-29
Obituary ... 65-68
Earlier sketch in CA 5-8R
See also MTCW 1
Bulwer, John 1606(?)-1656 ... DLB 236
Bulwer-Lytton, Edward (George Earle Lytton)
1803-1873 ... DLB 21
See also RGEL 2
See also SFW 4
See also SUFW 1
See also TEA
Bumagin, Victoria E. 1923- ... 89-92
Bumiller, Elisabeth 1956- ... 153
Bump, Jerome 1943- ... 109
Bumpers, Dale L(eon) 1925- ... 219
Bumppo, Nathaniel John Balthazar
1940- ... 97-100
Bumppo, Natty
See Bumppo, Nathaniel John Balthazar
Bumpus, Jerry 1937- ... CANR-44
Earlier sketches in CA 65-68, CANR-10
See also DLBY 1981
Bumstead, Henry 1915- ... IDFW 3, 4
Bumstead, Kathleen Mary 1918-1987 ... 121
See also SATA 53
Bumsted, J(ohn) M(ichael) 1938- ... 41-44R
Bunao, G(odofredo) Burce 1926- ... CP 1
Bunce, Alan 1939- ... 77-80
Bunce, Frank David 1907-1980 ... CAP-1
Earlier sketch in CA 11-12
Bunce, Linda Susan (Staines) 1956- ... 107
Bunch, Charlotte (Anne) 1944- ... CANR-72
Earlier sketch in CA 126
See also FW
Bunch, Chris(topher R.) 1943-2005 ... 163
See also FANT 1
Bunch, Clarence ... 53-56
Bunch, David R(oosevelt) 1925-2000 ... 29-32R
Bunch, Richard Alan 1945- ... 194
Bunche, Ralph J(ohnson) 1904-1971 ... 125
Obituary ... 33-36R
See also BW 2
See also DAM MULT
Bunch-Weeks, Charlotte
See Bunch, Charlotte (Anne)
Bunck, Julie Marie 1960- ... 148
Bundles, A'Lelia Perry 1952- ... CANR-103
Earlier sketch in CA 144
See also SATA 76
Bundtzen, Lynda K(athryn) 1947- ... 127
Bundy, Clarence E(verett) 1906- ... 85-88
Bundy, McGeorge 1919-1996 ... 160
Bundy, William P(utnam) 1917-2000 ... 104
Obituary ... 191
Bungay, Stephen 1954- ... 127
Bunge, Mario A(ugusto) 1919- ... CANR-113
Earlier sketch in CA 163
See also HW 2
Bunge, Nancy L(iddell) 1942- ... 124
Bunge, Robert Pierce 1930- ... 124
Bunge, Walter R(ichard) 1911-1999 ... 25-28R
Bungert, D. Edward 1957- ... 140
Bung Karno
See Sukarno, (Ahmed)
Buni, Andrew 1931- ... 21-24R
Bunim, Amos 1929- ... 132
Bunim, Irving M. 1901(?)-1980
Obituary ... 103
Bunin, Catherine 1967- ... 93-96
See also SATA 30
Bunin, Ivan Alexeyevich 1870-1953
Brief entry ... 104
See also DLB 317
See also EWL 3
See also RGSF 2
See also RGWL 2, 3
See also SSC 5
See also TCLC 6
See also TWA
Bunin, Sherry 1925- ... 93-96
See also SATA 30
Buning, Sietze
See Wiersma, Stanley M(arvin)
Bunke, H(arvey) Charles 1922- ... 9-12R
Bunker, Edward 1933-2005 ... CANR-103
Earlier sketches in CA 41-44R, CANR-65
Bunker, Gerald Edward 1938- ... 37-40R
Bunker, Linda K. 1947- ... CANR-29
Earlier sketch in CA 111
Bunkers, Suzanne L. 1950- ... CANR-115
Earlier sketch in CA 160
See also SATA 136
Bunkley, Anita Richmond ... 178
See also BW 3
Bunn, John T(homas) 1924- ... 37-40R
Bunn, John W(illiam) 1898-1979 ... CAP-2
Earlier sketch in CA 23-24
Bunn, Ronald F(reeze) 1929- ... 21-24R
Bunn, Scott (Middelton) 1943- ... 111
Bunn, T. Davis 1952- ... 221
Bunn, Thomas 1944- ... 69-72
Bunnell, Peter C(urtis) 1937- ... CANR-30
Earlier sketches in CA 33-36R, CANR-12
Bunnell, William S(tanley) 1925- ... CAP-1
Earlier sketch in CA 11-12
Bunner, H. C. 1855-1896 ... DLB 78, 79
Bunt, Gary R. ... 203
Bunt, Lucas N(icolaas) H(endrik)
1905-1984 ... 69-72
Bunting, A. E.
See Bunting, (Anne) Eve(lyn)
Bunting, Bainbridge 1913-1981 ... CANR-8
Earlier sketch in CA 61-64
Bunting, Basil 1900-1985 ... CANR-7
Obituary ... 115
Earlier sketch in CA 53-56
See also BRWS 7
See also CLC 10, 39, 47
See also CP 1, 2
See also DAM POET
See also DLB 20
See also EWL 3
See also RGEL 2
Bunting, Eve
See Bunting, (Anne) Eve(lyn)
See also JRDA
See also WYA
Bunting, (Anne) Eve(lyn) 1928- ... CANR-142
Earlier sketches in CA 53-56, CANR-5, 19, 59
See also Bunting, Eve
See also AAYA 5, 61
See also BYA 8
See also CLR 28, 56, 82
See also JRDA
See also MAICYA 1, 2
See also MAICYAS 1
See also SATA 18, 64, 110, 158
See also WYA
See also YAW
Bunting, Glenn (Davison) 1957- ... SATA 22
Bunting, Josiah III 1939- ... CANR-71
Earlier sketch in CA 45-48
Buntline, Ned
See Judson, Edward Zane Carroll
Bunuan, Josefina S(antiago) 1935- ... 33-36R
Bunuel, Luis 1900-1983 ... CANR-77
Obituary ... 110
Earlier sketches in CA 101, CANR-32
See also CLC 16, 80
See also DAM MULT
See also HLC 1
See also HW 1
Bunyan, John 1628-1688 ... BRW 2
See also BYA 5
See also CDBLB 1660-1789
See also DA
See also DAB
See also DAC
See also DAM MST
See also DLB 39
See also RGEL 2
See also TEA
See also WCH
See also WLC
See also WLIT 3
Bunzel, John H(arvey) 1924- ... 17-20R
Bunzel, Ruth L(eah) 1898-1990
Obituary ... 130
Buol, S(tanley) W(alter) 1934- ... 49-52
Bupp, Walter
See Garrett, (Gordon) Randall (Phillip)
Burack, Abraham Saul 1908-1978 ... CANR-4
Obituary ... 77-80
Earlier sketch in CA 9-12R
Burack, Elmer H(oward) 1927- ... CANR-37
Earlier sketches in CA 37-40R, CANR-16
Burack, Sylvia K. 1916-2003 ... CANR-9
Obituary ... 216
Earlier sketch in CA 21-24R
See also SATA 35
See also SATA-Obit 143
Burak, Carl S. 1942- ... 147
Burak, Linda (Gallina) ... 116
Burana, Lily 1968(?)- ... 203
Buranelli, Vincent 1919- ... CANR-43
Earlier sketches in CA 9-12R, CANR-5, 20
Buravsky, Alexandr ... CLC 59
Burayidi, Michael A. 1958- ... 175
Burbank, Addison (Buswell)
1895-1961 ... SATA 37
Burbank, Garin 1940- ... 69-72
Burbank, Natt B(ryant) 1903-1995 ... CAP-2
Earlier sketch in CA 25-28
Burbank, Nelson L(incoln) 1898-1977 .. CAP-1
Earlier sketch in CA 11-12
Burbank, Rex James 1925- ... CANR-18
Earlier sketch in CA 1-4R
Burbidge, Peter George 1919-1985
Obituary ... 116
Burbridge, Branse 1921- ... 97-100
Burby, Raymond J(oseph) III 1942- ... CANR-11
Earlier sketch in CA 69-72
Burby, William E(dward) 1893-1982 ... CAP-1
Earlier sketch in CA 11-12
Burce, Suzanne Lorraine 1929- ... 208
Burch, Claire R. 1925- ... 101
Burch, Francis F(loyd) 1932- ... 29-32R
Burch, Geoff 1951- ... CANR-111
Earlier sketch in CA 156
Burch, George Bosworth 1902-1973 ... 122
Obituary ... 109
Burch, Jennings Michael 1941- ... 118
Burch, Joann J(ohansen) ... 142
See also SATA 75
Burch, Mark H(etzel) 1953- ... 122
Burch, Mary Lou 1914- ... 104
Burch, Monte G. 1943- ... 103
Burch, Pat 1944- ... 57-60
Burch, Philip H. 1930- ... 106
Burch, Preston M. 1884-1978
Obituary ... 77-80
Burch, Robert J(oseph) 1925- ... CANR-71
Earlier sketches in CA 5-8R, CANR-2, 17
See also BYA 3
See also CLR 63
See also DLB 52
See also JRDA
See also MAICYA 1, 2
See also SATA 1, 74
See also YAW
Burcham, Nancy A(nn) 1942- ... 89-92
Burchard, John Ely 1898-1975 ... CANR-6
Obituary ... 61-64
Earlier sketch in CA 1-4R
Burchard, Max N(orman) 1925- ... 21-24R
Burchard, Peter Duncan 1921- ... CANR-121
Earlier sketches in CA 5-8R, CANR-3, 18, 39
See also MAICYA 1, 2
See also SAAS 13
See also SATA 5, 74, 143
Burchard, Rachael C(aroline) 1921- ... 33-36R
Burchard, S. H.
See Burchard, Sue
Burchard, Sue 1937- ... CANR-19
Earlier sketches in CA 53-56, CANR-4
See also SATA 22
Burchardt, Bill
See Burchardt, William Robert
See also TCWW 1, 2
Burchardt, Nellie 1921- ... 21-24R
See also SATA 7
Burchardt, William Robert
1917-1990 ... CANR-16
Earlier sketch in CA 89-92
See also Burchardt, Bill
Burchell, Mary
See Cook, Ida
See also RHW
Burchell, R(obert) A(rthur) 1941- ... 106
Burchett, Randall E. (?)-1971 ... 1-4R
Obituary ... 103
Burchett, Wilfred (Graham)
1911-1983 ... CANR-72
Obituary ... 110
Earlier sketches in CA 49-52, CANR-2
Burchfield, Joe D(onald) 1937- ... 85-88
Burchfield, Robert William
1923-2004 ... CANR-99
Obituary ... 230
Earlier sketches in CA 41-44R, CANR-14, 35
Burchill, Julie 1959- ... CANR-116
Earlier sketches in CA 135, CANR-115
Burchwood, Katharine T(yler) ... 57-60
Burciaga, Jose Antonio 1940-1996 . CANR-110
Obituary ... 154
Earlier sketch in CA 131
See also DLB 82
See also HW 1
Burck, Jacob 1904-1982
Obituary ... 106
Burckel, Nicholas C(lare) 1943- ... CANR-19
Earlier sketch in CA 103
Burckhardt, C(arl) J(akob) 1891-1974 ... 93-96
Obituary ... 49-52
Burckhardt, Jacob (Christoph)
1818-1897 ... EW 6
Burckhardt, Titus 1908-1984 ... 235
Burd, Laurence Hull 1915-1983
Obituary ... 109
Burd, Van Akin 1914- ... 41-44R
Burda, R(obert) W(arren) 1932- ... 73-76
Burdekin, Katharine (Penelope)
1896-1963 ... 162
See also DLB 255
See also FW
See also SFW 4
Burdekin, Kay
See Burdekin, Katharine (Penelope)
Burden, Jean 1914- ... CANR-3
Earlier sketch in CA 9-12R
See also CP 1
Burden, Michael 1960- ... 206
Burden, Shirley C. 1909(?)-1989
Obituary ... 128
Burden, William Douglas 1898-1978
Obituary ... 81-84
Burder, John 1940- ... 110
Burdett, John 1951- ... CANR-141
Earlier sketch in CA 151
Burdett, Lois ... 189
See also SATA 117
Burdett, Winston 1913-1993 ... 29-32R
Burdette, Franklin L. 1911-1975 ... 65-68
Obituary ... 61-64
Burdge, Rabel J(ames) 1937- ... 69-72
Burdick, Carol (Ruth) 1928- ... CANR-93
Earlier sketch in CA 132
Burdick, Donald W(alter) 1917- ... 53-56
Burdick, Eric 1934- ... 29-32R

Cumulative Index 83 **Burling**

Burdick, Eugene (Leonard)
1918-1965 .... CANR-71
Obituary 25-28R
Earlier sketch in CA 5-8R
See also SATA 22
Burdick, Loraine 1929- 57-60
Burdon, Eric 1941- 210
Burdon, R. H.
See Burdon, Roy H(unter)
Burdon, R(andal) M(athews) 1896- CAP-1
Earlier sketch in CA 13-14
Burdon, Roy H(unter) 1938- 238
Bureau, William H(obbs) 1913-1991 102
Burel, Leonce-Henry 1892-1977 ...... IDFW 3, 4
Buren, Martha Margareta Elisabet
1910- CAP-1
Earlier sketch in CA 13-14
Burenstam Linder, Staffan
See Linder, Staffan Burenstam
Burfield, Eva
See Ebbett, (Frances) Eva
Burford, Anne M(cGill) 1942-2004 127
Obituary 230
Burford, E(phraim) J(ohn) 1905- CANR-52
Earlier sketch in CA 124
Burford, Eleanor
See Hibbert, Eleanor Alice Burford
Burford, Lolah 1931- CANR-58
Earlier sketch in CA 41-44R
See also RHW
Burford, Roger L(ewis) 1930- 41-44R
Burford, William (Skelly) 1927- CANR-71
Earlier sketches in CA 5-8R, CANR-7
See also CP 1, 2
Burg, B(arry) R(ichard) 1938- 129
Burg, Dale R(onda) 1942- CANR-100
Earlier sketches in CA 106, CANR-23, 47
Burg, David
See Dolberg, Alexander
Burg, David F(rederick) 1936- 116
Burg, Steven L. 1950- 193
Burgan, Michael 1960- 190
See also SATA 118
Burgauer, Steven 1952- 176
Burge, Doris 1909- 120
Burge, Ethel 1916- 65-68
Burge, Wendy 221
Burgeon, G. A. L.
See Barfield, (Arthur) Owen
Burger, Albert E. 1941- 37-40R
Burger, Alfred 1905-2000 122
Burger, Angela Sutherland (Brown)
1936- 81-84
Burger, Carl 1888-1967 .... CAP-2
Earlier sketch in CA 19-20
See also SATA 9
Burger, Chester 1921- 9-12R
Burger, Edward J(ames), Jr. 1933- 110
Burger, George V(anderkarr) 1927-1998 .. 57-60
Obituary 169
Burger, Gottfried August 1747-1794 ..... DLB 94
Burger, Henry G. 1923- CANR-15
Earlier sketch in CA 41-44R
Burger, Hermann 1942-1989
Obituary 128
Burger, Jack
See Burger, John R(obert)
Burger, Joanna 1941- CANR-114
Earlier sketch in CA 136
Burger, John
See Marquard, Leo(pold)
Burger, John R(obert) 1942- 81-84
Burger, Nash K(err) 1908-1996 .... CAP-2
Earlier sketch in CA 23-24
Burger, Peter
See Buerger, Peter
Burger, Robert E(ugene) 1931- 85-88
Burger, Robert S. 1913-1998 .... 29-32R
Obituary 169
Burger, Ronna Cheryl 1947- 117
Burger, Ruth (Pazen) 1917- 17-20R
Burger, Sarah Greene 1935- 69-72
Burges, Dennis 225
Burgess, Ann Marie
See Gerson, Noel Bertram
Burgess, Anthony
See Wilson, John (Anthony) Burgess
See also AAYA 25
See also AITN 1
See also BRWS 1
See also CDBLB 1960 to Present
See also CLC 1, 2, 4, 5, 8, 10, 13, 15, 22, 40, 62, 81, 94
See also CN 1, 2, 3, 4, 5
See also DAB
See also DLB 14, 194, 261
See also DLBY 1998
See also EWL 3
See also RGEL 2
See also RHW
See also SFW 4
See also YAW
Burgess, Barbara Hood 1926- 138
See also SATA 69
Burgess, C(hester) F(rancis) 1922- 21-24R
Burgess, Charles (Orville) 1932- 33-36R
Burgess, Christopher Victor 1921- 9-12R
Burgess, David (Stewart) 1917- 222
Burgess, Em
See Burgess, Mary Wyche
Burgess, Eric (Alexander) 1912- 101
Burgess, Eric 1920- CANR-42
Earlier sketches in CA 5-8R, CANR-3, 18
Burgess, (Frank) Gelett 1866-1951
Brief entry 113
See also DLB 11
See also SATA 32
See also SATA-Brief 30
Burgess, Granville Wyche 1947- 137
Burgess, Helen S(teers) 1906-1987
Obituary 123
Burgess, Jackson (Visscher) 1927-1981 .... 9-12R
Burgess, Jane K. 1928- CANR-42
Earlier sketches in CA 73-76, CANR-13
Burgess, John H(enry) 1923- 33-36R
Burgess, John Lawie 1912-1987
Obituary 121
Burgess, John W(illiam) 1844-1931 178
See also DLB 47
Burgess, Jonathan S. 1960- 229
Burgess, Linda Cannon 1911-2000 73-76
Obituary 189
Burgess, Lorraine Marshall 1913-1996 106
Burgess, M(argaret) Elaine 13-16R
Burgess, M. R.
See Burgess, Michael (Roy)
Burgess, Mark .... SATA 157
Burgess, Mary A(lice Wickizer) 1938- 211
Burgess, Mary Wyche 1916- 61-64
See also SATA 18
Burgess, Melvin 1954- CANR-118
Earlier sketch in CA 161
See also AAYA 28
See also BYA 12
See also MAICYA 2
See also SATA 96, 146
Burgess, Michael
See Gerson, Noel Bertram
Burgess, Michael (Roy) 1948- CANR-112
Earlier sketches in CA 57-60, CANR-6, 42
Burgess, Mike
See Burgess, Michael (Roy)
Burgess, Moira 1936- 188
Burgess, Norman 1923- 25-28R
Burgess, Patricia 1947- 151
Burgess, Philip M(ark) 1939- CANR-16
Earlier sketch in CA 25-28R
Burgess, Robert F(orrest) 1927- CANR-11
Earlier sketch in CA 25-28R
See also SATA 4
Burgess, Robert H(errmann) 1913- CANR-5
Earlier sketch in CA 9-12R
Burgess, Robert J(ohn) 1961- 143
Burgess, Robert L. 1938- 29-32R
Burgess, Scott (A.) 1964- 189
Burgess, Stephen F(ranklin) 1952- 216
Burgess, Thornton Waldo
1874-1965 .... CANR-79
Earlier sketches in CA 73-76, CANR-41
See also CWRI 5
See also DLB 22
See also MAICYA 1, 2
See also SATA 17
Burgess, Trevor
See Trevor, Elleston
Burgess, W(arren) Randolph
1889-1978 .... CAP-2
Obituary 81-84
Earlier sketch in CA 29-32
Burgess-Kohn, Jane
See Burgess, Jane K.
Burgett, Donald R(obert) 1925- 21-24R
Burgett, Gordon (Lee) 1938- 182
Burggraaff, Winfield J. 1940-
Brief entry 114
Burgh, Anita 1937- .... RHW
Burghard, August 1901-1987 .... CANR-7
Earlier sketch in CA 17-20R
See also AITN 2
Burghardt, Andrew Frank 1924- 5-8R
Burghardt, Linda 234
Burghardt, Walter J(ohn) 1914- CANR-41
Earlier sketches in CA 1-4R, CANR-4, 19
Burgin, C(harles) David 1939- 73-76
Burgin, G(eorge) B(rown) 1856-1944 .... RHW
Burgin, (Weston) Richard 1947- CANR-88
Earlier sketch in CA 25-28R
Burgos, Joseph A(gner), Jr. 1945- 106
Burgos, Julia de
See de Burgos, Julia
See also DLB 290
Burgoyne, Bruce E. 1924- 135
Burgoyne, Elizabeth
See Pickles, M(abel) Elizabeth
Burgoyne, John 1722-1792 .... RGEL 2
Burgwyn, Diana 1937- 108
Burgwyn, Mebane Holoman
1914-1992 .... CANR-71
Earlier sketch in CA 49-52
See also SATA 7
Burhoe, Ralph Wendell 1911-1997 .... 17-20R
Buri, Fritz 1907-1995 .... CANR-8
Earlier sketch in CA 17-20R
Burian, Jarka M(arsano) 1927- 33-36R
Burian, Richard M(artin) 1941- CANR-47
Earlier sketch in CA 121
Burich, Nancy J(ane) 1943- 29-32R
Burick, Si(mon) 1909-1986 .... CANR-62
Obituary 121
Earlier sketch in CA 85-88
See also DLB 171
Burk, Bill E(ugene) 1932- 65-68
Burk, Bruce 1917- 61-64
Burk, Frank 1942- 170
Burk, John Daly 1772(?)-1808 .... DLB 37
Burk, Kathleen 1946- CANR-116
Earlier sketch in CA 130
Burk, Robert F(redrick) 1955- CANR-106
Earlier sketch in CA 134
Burk, Ronnie 1955- .... DLB 209
Burkard, Michael 1947- CANR-107
Earlier sketch in CA 132
Burke, Alan Dennis 1949- 106
Burke, Anna Mae Walsh 1938- 111
Burke, Anne 197
Burke, Avid J. 1906- 21-24R
Burke, C(letus) J(oseph) 1917-1973 45-48
Burke, Carl F(rancis) 1917- 25-28R
Burke, Carol 1950- CANR-14
Earlier sketch in CA 65-68
Burke, Carolyn 175
Burke, Christopher 1967- 197
Burke, Colin Bradley 1936- CANR-50
Earlier sketch in CA 113
Burke, David 1927- CANR-111
Earlier sketches in CA 105, CANR-23, 47
See also SATA 46
Burke, Delta (Ramona Leah) 1956- 171
Burke, Desmond William Lardner
See Lardner-Burke, Desmond William
Burke, Diana G.
See Gallagher, Diana G.
Burke, Diana Gallagher
See Gallagher, Diana G.
Burke, Dianne O'Quinn 1940- .... SATA 89
Burke, Edmund 1729(?)-1797 .... BRW 3
See also DA
See also DA3
See also DAB
See also DAC
See also DAM MST
See also DLB 104, 252
See also RGEL 2
See also TEA
See also WLC
Burke, Edmund M. 1928- 9-12R
Burke, Fielding
See Dargan, Olive (Tilford)
Burke, Fred G(eorge) 1926-2005 .... 13-16R
Obituary 237
Burke, Gerald 1914- CANR-1
Earlier sketch in CA 45-48
Burke, J(ohn) Bruce 1933- 37-40R
Burke, J(ackson) F(rederick Augustine)
1915- CANR-12
Earlier sketch in CA 65-68
Burke, James 1936- CANR-136
Earlier sketches in CA 102, CANR-28
Burke, James Lee 1936- CANR-106
Earlier sketches in CA 13-16R, CANR-7, 22, 41, 64
See also CAAS 19
See also AMWS 14
See also CMW 4
See also CN 6, 7
See also CSW
See also DLB 226
Burke, James Wakefield 1916- CANR-1
Earlier sketch in CA 45-48
Burke, Jan 1953- CANR-87
Earlier sketch in CA 142
Burke, Janine 1952- 210
See also SATA 139
Burke, John
See O'Connor, Richard
Burke, John (Frederick) 1922- CANR-50
Earlier sketches in CA 5-8R, CANR-9, 25
See also HGG
Burke, John Emmett 1908-1991 .... 37-40R
Burke, John Garrett 1917- 77-80
Burke, John J(oseph), Jr. 1942- 114
Burke, John J(oseph) 1875-1936 220
Burke, Johnny 1908-1964 .... DLB 265
Burke, Jonathan
See Burke, John (Frederick)
Burke, Joseph (Terence Anthony)
1913-1992 103
Burke, Kenneth (Duva) 1897-1993 . CANR-136
Obituary 143
Earlier sketches in CA 5-8R, CANR-39, 74
See also AMW
See also CLC 2, 24
See also CN 1, 2
See also CP 1, 2
See also DLB 45, 63
See also EWL 3
See also MAL 5
See also MTCW 1, 2
See also MTFW 2005
See also RGAL 4
Burke, Leda
See Garnett, David
Burke, Maggie
See Snyder, Marilyn
Burke, Martyn 1947(?)- 144
Burke, Matthew Aloysius
See Baroff, David
Burke, (Omar) Michael 1927- 73-76
Burke, Owen
See Burke, John (Frederick)
Burke, Patrick 1958- 186
See also SATA 114
Burke, (Ulick) Peter 1937- CANR-63
Earlier sketches in CA 25-28R, CANR-16
Burke, Phyllis 1951- 164
Burke, Ralph
See Garrett, (Gordon) Randall (Phillip) and Silverberg, Robert
Burke, Richard C(ullen) 1932- 53-56
Burke, Richard E. 1953- 143
Burke, Robert E(ugene) 1921- 21-24R
Burke, Russell 1946- 33-36R
Burke, S(amuel) M(artin) 1906- 49-52
Burke, Sean 1961- 151
Burke, Shannon 1966(?)- 239
Burke, Shifty
See Benton, Peggie
Burke, Stanley 1923- 101
Burke, T(homas) Patrick 1934- 121
Burke, Ted 1934(?)-1978
Obituary 77-80
Burke, Thomas 1886-1945 155
Brief entry 113
See also CMW 4
See also DLB 197
See also TCLC 63
Burke, Tom 73-76
Burke, Vee
See Burke, Velma Whitgrove
Burke, Velma Whitgrove 1921- CANR-4
Earlier sketch in CA 53-56
Burke, Vincent John 1919-1973 122
Obituary 111
Burke, Virginia M. 1916- 45-48
Burke, W. Warner 1935- CANR-14
Earlier sketch in CA 37-40R
Burke, Warren
See Braun, Matt
Burke, William F., Jr. 221
Burkert, Nancy Ekholm 1933- ...... MAICYA 1, 2
See also SAAS 14
See also SATA 24
Burkert, Walter 1931- CANR-90
Earlier sketches in CA 103, CANR-34
Burket, Harriet 1908- 37-40R
Burkett, David (Young III) 1934- CANR-9
Earlier sketch in CA 65-68
Burkett, Elinor 177
Burkett, Eva M(ae) 1903-1994 .... 33-36R
Burkett, Jack 1914- 101
Burkett, Larry 1939- CANR-107
Earlier sketch in CA 140
Burkett, Molly 1932- CANR-9
Earlier sketch in CA 53-56
Burke-Weiner, Kimberly 1962- 160
See also SATA 95
Burkey, Richard M(ichael) 1930- 93-96
Burkey, Stan 1938- 144
Burkhalter, Barton R. 1938- CANR-11
Earlier sketch in CA 25-28R
Burkhardt, Richard Wellington 1918- 1-4R
Burkhart, Charles 1924- 13-16R
Burkhart, James A(ustin) 1914-1979 .... 9-12R
Burkhart, John E(rnest) 1927- 116
Burkhart, Kathryn Watterson 1942- .. CANR-34
Earlier sketch in CA 45-48
Burkhart, Kitsi
See Burkhart, Kathryn Watterson
Burkhart, Robert E(dward) 1937- 29-32R
Burkhead, Jesse 1916- CANR-3
Earlier sketch in CA 1-4R
Burkholder, J(ames) Peter 1954- 119
Burkholder, John Richard 1928- CANR-37
Earlier sketch in CA 115
Burkholder, Vicky (E.) 1952- 217
Burkholz, Herbert 1932- CANR-41
Earlier sketches in CA 25-28R, CANR-11
Burkill, T(om) A(lec) 1912- 33-36R
Burkitt, Denis (Parsons) 1911-1993 112
Obituary 141
Burkitt, Ian 1956- 144
Burkle, Howard R(ussell) 1925-
Brief entry 107
Burkman, Katherine H. 1934- 29-32R
Burkowsky, Mitchell R(oy) 1931- 29-32R
Burks, Ardath Walter 1915- 107
Burks, Arthur J. 1898-1974 231
See also HGG
Burks, Arthur W(alter) 1915- CANR-48
Earlier sketch in CA 49-52
Burks, Brian 1955- 160
See also SATA 95
Burks, Cris 220
Burks, David D. 1924- 33-36R
Burks, Edward C. 1921(?)-1983
Obituary 111
Burks, Gordon E(ngledow) 1904-1992 ...... 1-4R
Burks, Jean M. 1949- 151
Burks, Ned
See Burks, Edward C.
Burks, Robert 1910-1968 .... IDFW 3, 4
Burl, (Harry) Aubrey (Woodruff)
1926- CANR-135
Earlier sketch in CA 97-100
Burland, Brian (Berkeley) 1931- CANR-23
Earlier sketches in CA 13-16R, CANR-7
See also SATA 34
Burland, C. A.
See Burland, Cottie (Arthur)
Burland, Cottie (Arthur) 1905-1983 .. CANR-72
Earlier sketches in CA 5-8R, CANR-5
See also SATA 5
Burleigh, Anne Husted 1941- 29-32R
Burleigh, David Robert 1907-1984 .... 1-4R
Burleigh, John H. S. 1894-1985
Obituary 116
Burleigh, Michael 1955- CANR-102
Earlier sketch in CA 135
Burleigh, Nina 195
Burleigh, Robert 1936- CANR-127
Earlier sketch in CA 166
See also SATA 55, 98, 146
Burlew, A(nn) Kathleen 145
Burley, Dan(iel Gardner) 1907-1962 201
See also DLB 241
Burley, George (Joseph) 1939-
Brief entry 107
Burley, W(illiam) J(ohn)
1914-2002 .... CANR-115
Earlier sketches in CA 33-36R, CANR-13, 29, 55
See also CMW 4
See also DLB 276
Burling, Robbins 1926- 17-20R

Burling, William J. 1949- ... CANR-91
Earlier sketch in CA 145
Burlingame, Edward Livermore
1848-1922 ... 178
See also DLB 79
Burlingame, Michael 1941- ... 169
Burlingame, (William) Roger
1889-1967 ... CANR-72
Earlier sketch in CA 5-8R
See also SATA 2
Burlingame, Virginia (Struble)
1900-1993 ... CAP-2
Earlier sketch in CA 23-24
Burlingham, Dorothy (Tiffany) 1891-1979 .. 109
Obituary ... 93-96
Burliuk, David 1882-1967 ... DLB 317
Burma, John H(armon) 1913- ... CANR-5
Earlier sketch in CA 1-4R
Burman, Alice Caddy
1896(?)-1977 ... SATA-Obit 24
Burman, Ben Lucien 1896-1984 ... CANR-32
Obituary ... 114
Earlier sketches in CA 5-8R, CANR-8
See also CWRI 5
See also SATA 6
See also SATA-Obit 40
Burman, Carina 1960- ... DLB 257
Burman, Edward 1947- ... 134
Burman, Jose Lionel 1917- ... CANR-53
Earlier sketches in CA 109, CANR-28
Burman, S. D. 1906-1977 ... IDFW 3, 4
Burmeister, Edwin 1939- ... CANR-26
Earlier sketch in CA 29-32R
Burmeister, Eva (Elizabeth) 1899-1969 .. CAP-1
Earlier sketch in CA 13-14
Burmeister, Jon 1933- ... 29-32R
Burmeister, Lou E(lla) 1928- ... CANR-26
Earlier sketch in CA 45-48
Burn, A(ndrew) R(obert) 1902-1991 . CANR-72
Earlier sketches in CA 1-4R, CANR-1, 17
Burn, Barbara 1940- ... CANR-17
Earlier sketch in CA 85-88
Burn, Doris 1923- ... 29-32R
See also SATA 1
Burn, Duncan (Lyall) 1902-1988
Obituary ... 124
Burn, Gordon 1948- ... CANR-118
Earlier sketch in CA 123
Burn, J(oshua) Harold 1892-1982 ... CAP-1
Obituary ... 108
Earlier sketch in CA 11-12
Burn, Mary (Wynn) 1910- ... 122
Burn, Ted
See Burn, Thomas E.
Burn, Thomas E. 1940- ... SATA 150
Burnaby, John 1891-1978 ... CAP-1
Obituary ... 104
Earlier sketch in CA 13-14
Burnaby, Mrs. Fred
See Le Blond, (Elizabeth) Aubrey
Burnam, Tom 1913-1991 ... 61-64
Burnard, Bonnie 1945- ... 196
See also CN 7
Burnard, Damon 1963- ... 186
See also SATA 115
Burne, Glen
See Green, Alan (Baer)
Burne, Glenn S. 1921- ... 21-24R
Burne, Kevin G. 1925- ... 13-16R
Burnell, George E(dwin) 1863-1948 ... 220
Burnell, Mark 1964- ... HGG
Burner, David (B.) 1937- ... CANR-48
Earlier sketches in CA 25-28R, CANR-10
Burnes, Caroline
See Haines, Carolyn
Burness, Pete 1910- ... IDFW 3
Burness, Tad
See Burness, Wallace B(inny)
Burness, Wallace B(inny) 1933- ... CANR-21
Earlier sketch in CA 69-72
Burnet, George Bain 1894- ... CAP-2
Earlier sketch in CA 23-24
Burnet, Gilbert 1643-1715 ... DLB 101
Burnet, Jean R. 1920- ... 130
Burnet, (Frank) Macfarlane
1899-1985 ... CANR-70
Obituary ... 117
Earlier sketch in CA 73-76
Burnet, Mary E(dith) 1911-1996 ... 53-56
Burnett, Alan 1932- ... 146
Burnett, Alfred David 1937- ... CANR-41
Earlier sketches in CA 102, CANR-19
Burnett, Allison (James) ... 236
Burnett, Anne Pippin 1925- ... 113
Burnett, Archie ... 198
Burnett, Avis 1937- ... 41-44R
Burnett, Ben G(eorge) 1924-1975 ... CANR-3
Earlier sketch in CA 1-4R
Burnett, Calvin 1921- ... 33-36R
Burnett, Carol 1933- ... 127
Burnett, Charles 1944- ... 171
Burnett, Collins W. 1914-1993 ... CANR-3
Earlier sketch in CA 9-12R
Burnett, Constance Buel 1893-1975 . CANR-72
Earlier sketch in CA 5-8R
See also SATA 36
Burnett, David (Benjamin Foley)
1931-1971 ... 9-12R
Obituary ... 33-36R
Burnett, David (Alan) 1946- ... 121
Burnett, Dorothy Kirk 1924- ... 5-8R
Burnett, Frances (Eliza) Hodgson
1849-1924 ... 136
Brief entry ... 108
See also BYA 3
See also CLR 24
See also CWRI 5
See also DLB 42, 141
See also DLBD 13, 14
See also JRDA
See also MAICYA 1, 2
See also MTFW 2005
See also RGAL 4
See also RGEL 2
See also SATA 100
See also TEA
See also WCH
See also YABC 2
Burnett, Gail Lemley 1953- ... 151
Burnett, Hallie Southgate (Zeisel)
1909(?)-1991 ... CANR-37
Obituary ... 135
Earlier sketches in CA 13-16R, CANR-6
Burnett, Janet 1915-1988 ... 49-52
Burnett, Joe Ray 1928- ... 17-20R
Burnett, John 1925- ... 57-60
Burnett, June 1936- ... 113
Burnett, Laurence 1907-1982 ... 49-52
Burnett, Leo 1891-1971
Obituary ... 116
Burnett, Leon R. 1925(?)-1983
Obituary ... 109
Burnett, Ron 1947- ... 157
Burnett, Virgil 1928- ... CANR-128
Earlier sketch in CA 161
Burnett, W(illiam) R(iley)
1899-1982 ... CANR-59
Obituary ... 106
Earlier sketches in CA 5-8R, CANR-22
See also CMW 4
See also DLB 9, 226
See also TCWW 1, 2
Burnett, Whit(ney Ewing) 1899-1973 ... CAP-2
Obituary ... 41-44R
Earlier sketch in CA 13-14
See also DLB 137
Burnette, O(llen) Lawrence, Jr. 1927- ... 33-36R
Burney, Anton
See Hopkins, (Hector) Kenneth
Burney, Elizabeth (Mary) 1934- ... 21-24R
Burney, Eugenia 1913- ... 29-32R
Burney, Fanny 1752-1840 ... BRWS 3
See also DLB 39
See also FL 1:2
See also NFS 16
See also RGEL 2
See also TEA
Burney, Frances
See Burney, Fanny
Burnford, S. D.
See Burnford, Sheila (Philip Cochrane Every)
Burnford, Sheila (Philip Cochrane Every)
1918-1984 ... CANR-49
Obituary ... 112
Earlier sketches in CA 1-4R, CANR-1
See also CLR 2
See also CWRI 5
See also JRDA
See also MAICYA 1, 2
See also SATA 3
See also SATA-Obit 38
Burnham, Alan 1913-1984 ... 13-16R
Obituary ... 112
Burnham, Charles
See Paine, Lauran (Bosworth)
Burnham, Daniel H(udson) 1846-1912 ... 184
Burnham, David (Bright) 1933- ... CANR-48
Earlier sketch in CA 122
Burnham, Dorothy E(dith) 1921- ... 65-68
Burnham, (Linden) Forbes (Sampson)
1923-1985
Obituary ... 117
Burnham, J. W.
See Burnham, Jack (Wesley)
Burnham, Jack (Wesley) 1931- ... 115
Burnham, James 1905-1987
Obituary ... 123
Burnham, John
See Beckwith, Burnham Putnam
Burnham, John C(hynoweth) 1929- ... 33-36R
Burnham, Linda Frye 1940- ... 125
Burnham, Nicole 1970- ... 230
See also SATA 161
Burnham, Niki
See Burnham, Nicole
Burnham, Philip D(rover) 1951- ... 212
Burnham, Richard 1940- ... 118
Burnham, Robert Ward, Jr. 1913-1977 .. 17-20R
Burnham, Sophy 1936- ... CANR-123
Earlier sketches in CA 41-44R, CANR-38
See also AITN 1
See also SATA 65
Burnham, Terence (Charles) ... 201
Burnham, Terry
See Burnham, Terence (Charles)
Burnham, Walter Dean 1930- ... 101
Burnie, David ... 207
Burnim, Kalman A(aron) 1928- ... 1-4R
Burningham, John (Mackintosh)
1936- ... CANR-78
Earlier sketches in CA 73-76, CANR-36
See also CLR 9
See also CWRI 5
See also MAICYA 1, 2
See also SATA 16, 59, 111, 160
Burnley, (John) David 1941-2001 ... CANR-40
Obituary ... 199
Earlier sketch in CA 117
Burnley, Judith ... CANR-16
Earlier sketch in CA 97-100
Interview in ... CANR-16
Burns, Aidan 1943- ... 121
Burns, Ailsa (Milligan) 1930- ... 148
Burns, Alan 1929- ... CANR-34
Earlier sketches in CA 9-12R, CANR-5
See also CN 1, 2, 3, 4, 5, 6, 7
See also DLB 14, 194
Burns, Alan Cuthbert 1887-1980
Obituary ... 102
Burns, Allan P. 1935- ... 125
Burns, Alma 1919- ... 81-84
Burns, Anna 1962- ... 201
Burns, Arthur F(rank) 1904-1987 ... CANR-46
Obituary ... 122
Earlier sketch in CA 13-16R
Burns, Betty 1909- ... CAP-2
Earlier sketch in CA 19-20
Burns, Bobby
See Burns, Vincent Godfrey
Burns, Carol 1934- ... 29-32R
Burns, Chester R(ay) 1937- ... 103
Burns, David D. 1942- ... 114
Burns, Deborah E(dwards) 1951- ... 147
Burns, Diane L. 1950- ... CANR-55
Earlier sketch in CA 135
See also SAAS 24
See also SATA 81
Burns, E(dward) Bradford 1932- ... CANR-72
Earlier sketch in CA 17-20R
Burns, Edward 1946- ... 170
See also MTFW 2005
Burns, Edward 1955- ... 173
Burns, Edward McNall 1897-1972 ... 1-4R
Obituary ... 103
Burns, Eedson Louis Millard
1897-1985 ... CANR-5
Obituary ... 117
Earlier sketch in CA 5-8R
Burns, Elizabeth 1959- ... 222
Burns, Eloise Wilkin
See Wilkin, Eloise
Burns, Eveline M(abel Richardson) 1900-1985
Obituary ... 117
Burns, Florence M. 1905-1988 ... SATA 61
Burns, Geoff 1954- ... 115
Burns, George 1896-1996 ... CANR-63
Obituary ... 151
Earlier sketch in CA 112
See also BEST 89:2
Burns, Gerald P(hillip) 1918- ... 17-20R
Burns, Grant (Francis) 1947- ... 146
Burns, Helen M(arie) 1922- ... 110
Burns, Hobert Warren 1925- ... CANR-47
Earlier sketch in CA 1-4R
Burns, James MacGregor 1918- ... CANR-91
Earlier sketches in CA 5-8R, CANR-19, 43, 78
Burns, James W(illiam) 1937- ... 33-36R
Burns, Jean (Ellen) 1934- ... 103
Burns, Jim 1936- ... 101
See also CP 1, 2, 3, 4, 5, 6, 7
Burns, Jimmy 1953- ... 134
Burns, Joan Simpson 1927- ... 65-68
Burns, Joanne 1945- ... DLB 289
Burns, John Horne 1916-1953 ... 198
Brief entry ... 115
See also DLBY 1985
See also MAL 5
Burns, John McLauren 1932-
Brief entry ... 109
Burns, John V. 1907-1982 ... CAP-2
Earlier sketch in CA 33-36
Burns, Kathryn (Jane) 1959- ... 235
Burns, Ken(neth Lauren) 1953- ... CANR-136
Earlier sketches in CA 141, CANR-79
See also AAYA 42
See also MTFW 2005
Burns, Khephra 1950- ... CANR-136
Earlier sketch in CA 156
See also SATA 92
Burns, Marilyn 1941- ... CANR-139
Earlier sketch in CA 161
See also SATA 96
See also SATA-Brief 33
Burns, Michael 1947- ... 121
Burns, Michael D. 1953- ... 191
Burns, Norman T(homas) 1930- ... 69-72
Burns, Olive Ann 1924-1990 ... CANR-41
Obituary ... 132
Earlier sketch in CA 120
See also AAYA 32
See also BPFB 1
See also LAIT 3
See also SATA 65
See also WYA
See also YAW
Burns, Paul C. ... CANR-4
Earlier sketch in CA 1-4R
See also SATA 5
Burns, Ralph 1949- ... 162
Burns, Ralph J. 1901- ... CAP-2
Earlier sketch in CA 25-28
Burns, Ray
See Burns, Raymond (Howard)
Burns, Raymond (Howard) 1924- ... SATA 9
Burns, Rex (Sehler) 1935- ... CANR-13
Earlier sketch in CA 77-80
See also CMW 4
Burns, Ric 1955- ... CANR-91
Earlier sketch in CA 141
Burns, Richard (William)
1958-1992 ... CANR-60
Obituary ... 139
Earlier sketch in CA 128
See also FANT
Burns, Richard Dean 1929- ... CANR-8
Earlier sketch in CA 17-20R
Burns, Richard Gordon 1925- ... 142
Burns, Richard W(ebster) 1920- ... 69-72
Burns, Rio
See Burns, Deborah E(dwards)
Burns, Robert 1759-1796 ... AAYA 51
See also BRW 3
See also CDBLB 1789-1832
See also DA
See also DA3
See also DAB
See also DAC
See also DAM MST, POET
See also DLB 109
See also EXPP
See also PAB
See also PC 6
See also RGEL 2
See also TEA
See also WLC
See also WP
Burns, Robert E(lliott) 1891(?)-1955 ... 138
Burns, Robert Edward 1919-2000 ... 111
Burns, Robert Grant 1938- ... CANR-16
Earlier sketch in CA 25-28R
Burns, Robert I(gnatius) 1921- ... CANR-52
Earlier sketches in CA 17-20R, CANR-7, 26
Burns, Robert M(ilton) C(lark), Jr. 1940- ... 102
Burns, Ruby V(ermillion) 1901-1993 ... 106
Burns, Scott
See Burns, Robert M(ilton) C(lark), Jr.
Burns, Sheila
See Bloom, Ursula (Harvey)
Burns, Stanley B(enjamin) 1938- ... 147
Burns, Stuart L(eroy) 1932- ... 127
Burns, Tex
See L'Amour, Louis (Dearborn)
Burns, Theresa 1961- ... SATA 84
Burns, Thomas (Jr.) 1928- ... CANR-14
Earlier sketch in CA 41-44R
Burns, Thomas J. 1942- ... 127
Burns, Thomas Stephen 1927- ... CANR-45
Earlier sketch in CA 49-52
Burns, Tom 1913-2001 ... CANR-22
Earlier sketches in CA 5-8R, CANR-5
Burns, Vincent Godfrey 1893-1979 ... 41-44R
Obituary ... 85-88
See also AITN 2
Burns, Walter Noble 1872-1932 ... TCWW 1, 2
Burns, Wayne 1918- ... CANR-1
Earlier sketch in CA 1-4R
Burns, William A. 1909-1999 ... CANR-11
Earlier sketches in CAP-1, CA 13-14
See also SATA 5
Burns, Zed H(ouston) 1903-1987 ... 33-36R
Burns-Bisogno, Louisa 1936- ... 134
Burnshaw, Stanley 1906- ... 9-12R
See also CLC 3, 13, 44
See also CP 1, 2, 3, 4, 5, 6, 7
See also DLB 48
See also DLBY 1997
Burnside, John 1955- ... 153
See also CP 7
Burnside, Wesley M(ason) 1918- ... 65-68
Buros, Oscar Krisen 1905-1978
Obituary ... 77-80
Burow, Daniel R(obert) 1931- ... CANR-11
Earlier sketch in CA 29-32R
Burr, Alfred Gray 1919- ... 25-28R
Burr, Anne 1937- ... 25-28R
See also CLC 6
Burr, C. Chauncey 1815(?)-1883 ... DLB 79
Burr, Chandler 1963- ... 230
Burr, Charles 1922(?)-1976
Obituary ... 69-72
Burr, Dan 1951- ... SATA 65
Burr, David (Dwight) 1934- ... 216
Burr, Esther Edwards 1732-1758 ... DLB 200
Burr, Gray 1919- ... 69-72
Burr, John R(oy) 1933- ... CANR-94
Earlier sketches in CA 45-48, CANR-45
Burr, Keith 1946- ... 115
Burr, Lonnie 1943- ... 103
See also SATA 47
Burr, Samuel Engle, Jr. 1897-1987
Obituary ... 124
Burr, Wesley R(ay) 1936- ... 37-40R
Burrage, A(lfred) M(cLelland) 1889-1956 . HGG
Burrell, Berkeley G(raham) 1919-1979 . 33-36R
Obituary ... 89-92
Burrell, David B(akewell) 1933- ... 33-36R
Burrell, Evelyn Patterson 1920- ... CANR-7
Earlier sketch in CA 53-56
Burrell, Roy E(ric) C(harles) 1923- ... 33-36R
See also SATA 72
Burreson, Jay ... 227
Burridge, Kenelm (Oswald Lancelot)
1922- ... CANR-122
Earlier sketches in CA 93-96, CANR-70
Burridge, Trevor David 1932- ... 137
Burrin, Frank K. 1920- ... 25-28R
Burrington, David E. 1931- ... 73-76
Burris, B. C(ullen) 1924- ... 21-24R
Burris, John L. 1945- ... 185
Burris-Meyer, Harold 1902-1984 ... 41-44R
Burros, Marian (Fox) ... CANR-30
Earlier sketch in CA 89-92
Burrough, Bryan 1961- ... CANR-90
Earlier sketch in CA 140
See also BEST 90:3
Burroughs, Augusten 1965- ... 214
Burroughs, Ben(jamin F.) 1918-1980 ... 65-68
Obituary ... 122

Cumulative Index 85 Bush

Burroughs, Edgar Rice 1875-1950 .. CANR-131
Brief entry 104
Earlier sketch in CA 132
See also AAYA 11
See also BPFB 1
See also BYA 4, 9
See also DA3
See also DAM NOV
See also DLB 8
See also FANT
See also MTCW 1, 2
See also MTFW 2005
See also RGAL 4
See also SATA 41
See also SCFW 1, 2
See also SFW 4
See also TCLC 2, 32
See also TCWW 1, 2
See also TUS
See also YAW
Burroughs, Franklin (Gorham, Jr.) 1942- 235
See also CSW
Burroughs, Jean Mitchell 1908- 65-68
See also SATA 28
Burroughs, John 1837-1921 167
Brief entry 109
See also ANW
See also DLB 64, 275
Burroughs, Margaret G.
See Burroughs, Margaret Taylor (Goss)
Burroughs, Margaret Taylor (Goss)
1917- CANR-25
Earlier sketch in CA 21-24R
See also BW 1
See also DLB 41
Burroughs, Polly 1925- CANR-113
Earlier sketch in CA 25-28R
See also SATA 2
Burroughs, Raleigh (Simpson) 1901-1998 ... 106
Burroughs, William (Seward), Jr.
1947-1981 73-76
Obituary 112
See also DLB 16
Burroughs, William James 1942- 144
Burroughs, William S(eward)
1914-1997 .... CANR-104
Obituary 160
Earlier sketches in CA 9-12R, CANR-20, 52
See also Lee, William and
Lee, Willy
See also AAYA 60
See also AITN 2
See also AMWS 3
See also BG 1:2
See also BPFB 1
See also CLC 1, 2, 5, 15, 22, 42, 75, 109
See also CN 1, 2, 3, 4, 5, 6
See also CPW
See also DA
See also DA3
See also DAB
See also DAC
See also DAM MST, NOV, POP
See also DLB 2, 8, 16, 152, 237
See also DLBY 1981, 1997
See also EWL 3
See also HGG
See also LMFS 2
See also MAL 5
See also MTCW 1, 2
See also MTFW 2005
See also RGAL 4
See also SFW 4
See also TCLC 121
See also WLC
Burrow, James Gordon 1922- CANR-2
Earlier sketch in CA 5-8R
Burrow, John A(nthony) 1932- 97-100
Burrow, John W(yon) 1935- CANR-30
Earlier sketches in CA 21-24R, CANR-12
Burroway, Janet (Gay) 1936- 208
Earlier sketches in CA 21-24R, CANR-12, 44, 97
Autobiographical Essay in 208
See also CAAS 6
See also CN 1, 2, 3, 4, 5, 6, 7
See also DLB 6
See also SATA 23
Burrowes, Michael Anthony Bernard
1937- 103
Burrowes, Mike
See Burrowes, Michael Anthony Bernard
Burrows, Abe
See Burrows, Abram Solman
Burrows, Abram Solman
1910-1985 .... CANR-82
Obituary 116
Earlier sketch in CA 110
Burrows, David J(ames) 1936- 41-44R
Burrows, Donald (James) 1945- 222
Burrows, E(dwin) G(ladding) 1917- .. CANR-14
Earlier sketch in CA 77-80
Burrows, Edwin G(wynne) 1943- 200
Burrows, Fredrika Alexander 1908- CANR-6
Earlier sketch in CA 57-60
Burrows, James C. 1944- 29-32R
Burrows, John 1945- CANR-69
Earlier sketch in CA 101
See also CBD
See also CD 5, 6
Burrows, Miles 1936- 21-24R
See also CP 1
Burrows, Millar 1889-1980 .... CANR-72
Obituary 97-100
Earlier sketch in CA 81-84
Burrows, William E. 1937- CANR-122
Earlier sketch in CA 65-68
Burrows, William R(ichard) 1942- 117
Burrup, Percy E(dward) 1910-1982 .... 1-4R
Bursk, Christopher 1943- CANR-24
Earlier sketch in CA 85-88
Bursk, Edward C(ollins) 1907-1990 .... CANR-5
Obituary 130
Earlier sketch in CA 1-4R
Burstall, Aubrey F(rederic) 1902-1984
Obituary 113
Burstein, Alvin G(eorge) 1931- 85-88
Burstein, Andrew 193
Burstein, Chaya M(alamud) 1923- .. CANR-111
Earlier sketches in CA 126, CANR-53
See also SATA 64
Burstein, Fred 1950- 151
See also SATA 83
Burstein, John 1949- CANR-21
Earlier sketch in CA 69-72
See also SATA 54
See also SATA-Brief 40
Burstein, Michael A. 1970- 233
Burstein, Patricia (Ann) 1945- 108
Burstein, Paul 1946- 123
Burstiner, Irving 1919- 104
Burston, Daniel 1954- CANR-144
Earlier sketch in CA 158
Burston, Paul 1965- 236
Burston, W. H. 1915-1981
Obituary 103
Burstow, Bonnie 1945- 145
Burstyn, Harold L(ewis) 1930- CANR-5
Earlier sketch in CA 9-12R
Bursztynski, Sue 1953- 186
See also SATA 114
Burt, Al(vin Victor, Jr.) 1927- 25-28R
Burt, Alfred LeRoy 1888-1971 .... CAP-1
Earlier sketch in CA 9-10
Burt, Christopher C(linton) 1954- 239
Burt, Cyril (Lodowic) 1883-1971 .... CAP-1
Obituary 33-36R
Earlier sketch in CA 13-14
Burt, Donald X(avier) 1929- CANR-39
Earlier sketch in CA 116
Burt, Frances R(iemer) 1917- 69-72
Burt, Guy 1972- 209
Burt, Jesse Clifton 1921-1976 .... CANR-4
Earlier sketch in CA 9-12R
See also SATA 46
See also SATA-Obit 20
Burt, John 1955- 179
Burt, John J. 1934- CANR-11
Earlier sketch in CA 29-32R
Burt, Katharine 1882-1977 .... TCWW 1, 2
Burt, Larry W(ayne) 1950- 122
Burt, Leonard James 1892-1983
Obituary 114
Burt, Mala S(chuster) 1943- 112
Burt, Maxwell Struthers 1882-1954 179
See also DLB 86
See also DLBD 16
Burt, Nathaniel 1913- CANR-72
Earlier sketch in CA 17-20R
Burt, Olive Woolley 1894-1981 .... CANR-71
Earlier sketches in CA 5-8R, CANR-5
See also SATA 4
Burt, Richard 1954- 197
Burt, Robert Amsterdam 1939- 102
Burt, Roger B(ivens) 1939- 113
Burt, Samuel M(athew) 1915- 21-24R
Burt, Simon 1947- 123
Burt, Stephen (Louis) 1971- 221
Burt, Struthers
See Burt, Maxwell Struthers
Burt, Wendy 1970- 214
Burt, William Henry 1903-1987 106
Burtch, Brian 1949- 148
Burtchaell, James Tunstead 1934- CANR-52
Earlier sketches in CA 25-28R, CANR-11, 27
Burtis, C(harles) Edward 1907-1994 ...... 41-44R
Burtle, James (L.) 1919-
Brief entry 113
Burtless, Gary 1950- 144
Burtness, Paul Sidney 1923- 17-20R
Burton, Anne
See Bowen-Judd, Sara (Hutton)
Burton, Anthony 1933- 61-64
Burton, Anthony 1934- 97-100
Burton, Arthur 1914-1982 .... CANR-10
Earlier sketch in CA 21-24R
Burton, Carl D. 1913- 1-4R
Burton, David H(enry) 1925- CANR-3
Earlier sketch in CA 49-52
Burton, Dolores Marie 1932- 25-28R
Burton, Dwight L(owell) 1922- 61-64
Burton, Edward J. 1917- 21-24R
Burton, (Alice) Elizabeth 1908- CANR-72
Earlier sketches in CA 65-68, CANR-15
See also FANT
Burton, Gabrielle 1939- 45-48
Burton, Genevieve 1912- 33-36R
Burton, Gennett 1945- 160
See also SATA 95
Burton, Georganne B. 233
Burton, H(arry) M(cGuire Philip) 1898(?)-1979
Obituary 93-96
Burton, Hal
See Burton, Harold Bernard
Burton, Harold Bernard 1908-1992 .. CANR-70
Earlier sketch in CA 97-100
Burton, Hester (Wood-Hill)
1913-2000 .... CANR-10
Earlier sketch in CA 9-12R
See also CLR 1
See also DLB 161
See also MAICYA 1, 2
See also SAAS 8
See also SATA 7, 74
See also YAW
Burton, Humphrey (McGuire) 1931- 200
Burton, Ian 1935- 17-20R
Burton, Isabel Arundell 1831-1896 ..... DLB 166
Burton, Ivor Flower 1923- 109
Burton, Jane 1933- CANR-123
Earlier sketches in CA 105, CANR-29
Burton, Jimalee 1906-2000 220
Burton, Joe Wright 1907-1976 107
Burton, John A(ndrew) 1944- CANR-14
Earlier sketch in CA 65-68
Burton, John Wear 1915- 103
Burton, Katherine (Kurz) 1890-1969 . CANR-71
Earlier sketch in CA 77-80
Burton, L(awrence) DeVere 1943- 156
Burton, Leslie
See McGuire, Leslie (Sarah)
Burton, Levar 1957- 166
See also BW 3
Burton, Lindy 1937- 25-28R
Burton, Lloyd E. 1922- 53-56
Burton, M. Garlinda 1958- 156
Burton, Marilee Robin 1950- CANR-46
Earlier sketch in CA 121
See also SATA 46, 82
Burton, Martin A. 1911-1984
Obituary 114
Burton, Mary E(lizabeth) 1900-1997 106
Burton, Maurice 1898-1992 .... CANR-29
Obituary 139
Earlier sketches in CA 65-68, CANR-9
See also SATA 23
Burton, Miles
See Street, Cecil J(ohn) C(harles)
Burton, Nelson, Jr. 1942- 57-60
Burton, Orville Vernon 1947- CANR-141
Earlier sketch in CA 126
Burton, Philip 1904-1995 .... 25-28R
Obituary 147
Burton, Raymond L.
See Tubb, E(dwin) C(harles)
Burton, Rebecca B(rown) 1940- 216
Burton, Richard 1925-1984
Obituary 113
Burton, Sir Richard F(rancis)
1821-1890 .... DLB 55, 166, 184
See also SSFS 21
Burton, Robert 1577-1640 .... DLB 151
See also RGEL 2
Burton, Robert (Wellesley) 1941- CANR-118
Earlier sketches in CA 45-48, CANR-1, 17, 29
See also SATA 22
Burton, Robert E(dward) 1927- CANR-13
Earlier sketch in CA 61-64
Burton, Robert H(enderson) 1934- 37-40R
Burton, Roger V(ernon) 1928- 45-48
Burton, S(amuel) H(olroyd) 1919- 102
Burton, Sandra 1941(?)-2004 132
Obituary 226
Burton, Thomas
See Longstreet, Stephen
Burton, Thomas G(len) 1935- 145
Burton, Tim 1958- CANR-108
Earlier sketch in CA 148
See also AAYA 14, 65
Burton, Virginia Lee 1909-1968 .... CANR-86
Obituary 25-28R
Earlier sketches in CAP-1, CA 13-14
See also CLR 11
See also CWRI 5
See also DLB 22
See also MAICYA 1, 2
See also SATA 2, 100
See also WCH
Burton, William Evans 1804-1860 .... DLB 73
Burton, William H(enry) 1890-1964 ... CANR-1
Earlier sketch in CA 1-4R
See also SATA 11
Burton, William L(ester) 1928- 21-24R
Burton-Bradley, Burton Gyrth
1914-1994 77-80
Burtschi, Mary (Pauline) 1911- CANR-19
Earlier sketches in CA 9-12R, CANR-5
Burtt, Ben 1948- .... IDFW 3, 4
Burtt, Edwin Arthur 1892-1989 .... 5-8R
Obituary 129
Burtt, Everett Johnson, Jr. 1914-1989 .... 9-12R
Burtt, George 1914-1984 .... CANR-11
Earlier sketch in CA 61-64
Burtt, Harold E(rnest) 1890-1991 .... CAP-2
Earlier sketch in CA 17-18
Burtt, Shelley 1959- 139
Buruma, Ian 1951- CANR-141
Earlier sketches in CA 128, CANR-65
See also CLC 163
Burwash, Peter 1945- 119
Burwell, Adam Hood 1790-1849 .... DLB 99
Burwell, Carter 1955- .... IDFW 4
Burwell, Jennifer 1962- 166
Bury, Frank
See Harris, Herbert
Bury, J(ohn) P(atrick) T(uer) 1908- 17-20R
Bury, Lady Charlotte 1775-1861 .... DLB 116
Buryn, Ed(ward Casimir) 1934- 85-88
Busbee, Shirlee (Elaine) 1941- CANR-114
Earlier sketches in CA 77-80, CANR-60
See also RHW
Busby, Cylin 1970- 190
See also SATA 118
Busby, Edith (A. Lake) (?)-1964
Obituary 109
See also SATA-Obit 29
Busby, F. M. 1921-2005 .... CANR-49
Earlier sketches in CA 65-68, CANR-9, 24
See also SFW 4
Busby, John 1928- CANR-39
Earlier sketch in CA 116
Busby, Mabel Janice
See Stanford, Sally
Busby, Mark 1945- 151
Busby, Roger (Charles) 1941- CANR-60
Earlier sketch in CA 105
See also CMW 4
Buscaglia, (Felice) Leo(nardo)
1924-1998 .... CANR-30
Obituary 169
Brief entry 110
Earlier sketch in CA 112
Interview in CANR-30
See also Buscaglia, Leo F.
See also CPW
See also DAM POP
See also SATA 65
Buscaglia, Leo F.
See Buscaglia, (Felice) Leo(nardo)
See also BEST 89:4
Buscall, Jon 1970- 217
Busch, Briton Cooper 1936- CANR-82
Earlier sketches in CA 21-24R, CANR-8, 36
Busch, Charles (Louis) 1954- CANR-94
Earlier sketch in CA 145
See also CAD
See also CD 5, 6
See also GLL 2
Busch, Francis X(avier) 1879-1975 .... CAP-1
Obituary 61-64
Earlier sketch in CA 13-14
Busch, Frederick 1941- CANR-92
Earlier sketches in CA 33-36R, CANR-45, 73
See also CAAS 1
See also CLC 7, 10, 18, 47, 166
See also CN 1, 2, 3, 4, 5, 6, 7
See also DLB 6, 218
Busch, Hans (Peter) 1914-1996 109
Obituary 153
Busch, Julia 1940- CANR-39
Earlier sketch in CA 57-60
Busch, Lawrence (Michael) 1945- .. CANR-126
Earlier sketch in CA 161
Busch, Niven 1903-1991 .... CANR-74
Obituary 135
Earlier sketches in CA 13-16R, CANR-7
See also DLB 44
See also TCWW 1, 2
Busch, Noel F(airchild) 1906-1985 49-52
Obituary 117
Busch, Phyllis S. 1909- CANR-71
Earlier sketch in CA 107
See also SATA 30
Busch, Ronald 1928-1987
Obituary 123
Buschkuehl, Matthias 1953- CANR-47
Earlier sketch in CA 121
Buschkuhl, Matthias
See Buschkuehl, Matthias
Buse, D(ieter) K(urt) 1941- 137
Buse, R. F.
See Buse, Renee
Buse, Renee 1914(?)-1979
Obituary 85-88
Buse, Rueben C. 1932- 109
Buser, Pierre 1921- 146
Busey, James L. 1916- 5-8R
Bush, Alan (Dudley) 1900-1995 110
Obituary 150
Bush, Anne Kelleher 1959- 151
See also SATA 97
Bush, Barbara (Pierce) 1925- 141
Bush, Barbara Holstein 1935- CANR-12
Earlier sketch in CA 69-72
Bush, Barney (Furman) 1946- 145
See also NNAL
Bush, Barry (Michael) 1938- 110
Bush, Catherine 1961- CANR-114
Earlier sketches in CA 151, CANR-101
See also SATA 128
Bush, Charlie Christmas 1885-1973 . CANR-58
Obituary 104
Earlier sketch in CA 107
See also CMW 4
Bush, Christopher
See Bush, Charlie Christmas
Bush, Clifford L(ewis) 1915- 33-36R
Bush, Donald J(ohn) 114
Bush, (John Nash) Douglas
1896-1983 .... CANR-41
Obituary 109
Earlier sketch in CA 37-40R
Bush, Duncan 1946- 153
See also CP 7
Bush, Eric Wheler 1899-1985 65-68
Obituary 117
Bush, Frederic W(illiam) 1929- 125
Bush, George Edward, Jr. 1938- 109
Bush, George P(ollock) 1892-1977 .... 17-20R
Bush, George S(idney) 1925- 110
Bush, George W(alker) 1946- 197
Bush, Grace A(bhau) 1936- 104
Bush, Ian (Elcock) 1928-1986 157
Bush, Jim 1926- 57-60
Bush, John W(illiam) 1917-1976 .... CAP-2
Earlier sketch in CA 33-36
Bush, L(uther) Russ(ell III) 1944- CANR-47
Earlier sketch in CA 121
Bush, Larry
See Bush, Lawrence Dana

Bush, Lawrence Dana 1951- ... 109
Bush, Lewis William 1907- ... 81-84
Bush, M(ichael) L(accohee) 1938- ... 132
Bush, Mark 1943- ... 178
Bush, Martin H(arry) 1930- ... CANR-71
  Earlier sketches in CA 29-32R, CANR-12
Bush, Patricia (Jahns) 1932- ... CANR-24
  Earlier sketch in CA 105
Bush, Perry 1959- ... 188
Bush, Richard C(larence, Jr.) 1923- ... 185
  Brief entry ... 114
Bush, Robert (Burton) 1917- ... 116
Bush, Robert (Ray) 1920-1972
  Obituary ... 33-36R
Bush, Ronald 1946- ... 136
  See also CLC 34
Bush, Sargent, Jr. 1937- ... CANR-115
  Earlier sketches in CA 65-68, CANR-29, 56
Bush, Susan 1933- ... 127
Bush, Ted J. 1922- ... 17-20R
Bush, Vannevar 1890-1974 ... 97-100
  Obituary ... 53-56
Bush, William (Shirley, Jr.) 1929- ... CANR-32
  Earlier sketches in CA 37-40R, CANR-14
Busha, Charles Henry 1931- ... CANR-5
  Earlier sketch in CA 53-56
Bush-Brown, Albert 1926- ... 128
Bush-Brown, James 1892-1985 ... 5-8R
  Obituary ... 118
Bush-Brown, Louise 1896(?)-1973
  Obituary ... 49-52
Bushell, Agnes (Barr) 1949- ... CANR-142
  Earlier sketch in CA 135
Bushell, Don(ald Gair), Jr. 1934-
  Brief entry ... 113
Bushell, Raymond 1910-1998 ... CANR-20
  Obituary ... 164
  Earlier sketches in CA 13-16R, CANR-5
Bushey, Jeanne 1944- ... 149
Bushey, Jerry 1941- ... CANR-25
  Earlier sketch in CA 108
Bushinsky, Jay (Joseph Mason) 1932- ... 77-80
Bushman, Claudia L(auper) 1934- ... CANR-22
  Earlier sketch in CA 106
Bushman, Richard L(yman) 1931- ... CANR-116
  Earlier sketches in CA 21-24R, CANR-22
Bushmiller, Ernest Paul 1905-1982 ... 29-32R
  Obituary ... 107
  See also Bushmiller, Ernie
  See also AITN 1
Bushmiller, Ernie
  See Bushmiller, Ernest Paul
  See also SATA-Obit 31
Bushnell, Candace 1959(?)- ... CANR-104
  Earlier sketch in CA 163
Bushnell, David S(herman) 1927- ... 41-44R
Bushnell, Horace 1802-1876 ... DLBD 13
Bushnell, Jack 1952- ... 151
  See also SATA 86
Bushnell, Rebecca W. 1952- ... 232
Bushong, Carolyn N(ordin) 1947- ... 164
Bushrui, S(uheil) B(adi) 1929- ... CANR-87
  Earlier sketch in CA 17-20R
Bushyager, Linda E(yster) 1947- ... 154
  Earlier sketch in CA 93-96
  See also FANT
Busi, Aldo 1948- ... 206
  See also GLL 1
Busia, Akosua ... 161
Busia, Kofi Abrefa 1913-1978 ... CANR-46
  Obituary ... 126
  Earlier sketch in CA 69-72
  See also BW 2
Busiek, Kurt 1960- ... 234
  See also AAYA 53
  See also MTFW 2005
Buske, Morris (Roger) 1912-2005 ... 13-16R
  Obituary ... 235
Buskin, Martin 1930-1976
  Obituary ... 65-68
Buskin, Richard 1959- ... 164
Buskirk, Richard H(obart) 1927-1994 ... CANR-1
  Obituary ... 145
  Earlier sketch in CA 1-4R
Buslik, Gary 1946- ... 173
Busoni, Rafaello 1900-1962
  Obituary ... 117
  See also SATA 16
Buss, Arnold H. 1924- ... CANR-4
  Earlier sketch in CA 1-4R
Buss, Claude Albert 1903-1998 ... 109
Buss, David M. 1953- ... CANR-103
  Earlier sketch in CA 151
Buss, Gerald (Vere Austen) 1936- ... 127
Buss, Helen M.
  See Clarke, Margaret
Buss, Leo W. 1953- ... 121
Buss, Martin J(ohn) 1930- ... 33-36R
Buss, Robin (Caron) 1939- ... 141
Bussard, Paul 1904-1983
  Obituary ... 109
Bussche, Henri O(mer) A(ntoine) Van den
  1920-1965 ... CANR-5
  Earlier sketch in CA 5-8R
Busse, Heribert Hermann 1926- ... 185
Busse, Thomas V(alentine) 1941-1986 ... 77-80
  Obituary ... 119
Bussell, Harold L. 1941- ... 125
Busselle, Rebecca 1941- ... 135
  See also SATA 80
Bussey, Ellen M(arion) 1926- ... CANR-2
  Earlier sketch in CA 49-52
Bussieres, Arthur de 1877-1913 ... DLB 92
Bussieres, Simone 1918- ... 53-56
Bussing-Burks, Marie 1958- ... 200
Bussmann, Klaus 1941- ... 185
Bussy, Roger de Rabutin
  1618-1693 ... GFL Beginnings to 1789
Bustad, Leo Kenneth 1920-1998 ... 106
Bustamante, A(gustin) Jorge 1938- ... 33-36R
Bustanoby, Andre S(teven) 1930- ... 101
Bustard, Bruce I. 1954- ... 214
Bustard, Robert 1938- ... 65-68
Busteed, Marilyn 1937- ... 61-64
Bustos, F(rancisco)
  See Borges, Jorge Luis
Bustos Domecq, H(onorio)
  See Bioy Casares, Adolfo and
  Borges, Jorge Luis
Buswell, J(ames) Oliver, Jr. 1895-1977 ... 5-8R
Butala, Sharon (Annette) 1940- ... CANR-136
  Earlier sketch in CA 170
Butalia, Urvashi ... 198
Butazzoni, Fernando 1953- ... EWL 3
Butcher, Fanny
  See Bokum, Fanny Butcher
Butcher, Geoffrey (Arthur John) 1936- ... 111
Butcher, Grace 1934- ... 25-28R
Butcher, H(arold) J(ohn) 1920- ... 21-24R
Butcher, Harry Cecil 1901-1985
  Obituary ... 115
Butcher, James Neal 1933- ... CANR-14
  Earlier sketch in CA 33-36R
Butcher, Jim 1971- ... 238
Butcher, (Anne) Judith 1927- ... 57-60
Butcher, Kristin 1951- ... 211
  See also SATA 140
Butcher, (Charles) Philip 1918- ... CANR-4
  Earlier sketch in CA 1-4R
Butcher, Russell Devereux 1938- ... CANR-8
  Earlier sketch in CA 61-64
Butcher, Thomas Kennedy 1914- ... CAP-1
  Earlier sketch in CA 11-12
Butcher, (Charles) William 1951- ... CANR-90
  Earlier sketch in CA 131
Butchvarov, Panayot K. 1933- ... 33-36R
Butck, Zulie
  See Jones, Thomas W(arren)
Bute, Mary Ellen 1908-1983 ... IDFW 3
Butel, Jane
  See de Calles, Jane F. Butel
Butenko, Bohdan 1931- ... SATA 90
Butera, Mary C. 1925- ... 21-24R
Buteux, Paul E. 1939- ... 121
Buth, Lenore 1932- ... 89-92
Buthelezi, Gatsha 1928- ... 102
Butland, Gilbert J(ames) 1910- ... 21-24R
Butler, Albert 1923- ... CANR-5
  Earlier sketch in CA 13-16R
Butler, Annie L(ouise) 1920-1979 ... CANR-28
  Earlier sketch in CA 33-36R
  See also BW 2
Butler, Arthur D. 1923- ... 1-4R
Butler, B. C.
  See Butler, Basil Christopher
Butler, Basil Christopher 1902-1986 ... CANR-2
  Obituary ... 120
  Earlier sketch in CA 1-4R
Butler, Beverly Kathleen 1932- ... CANR-72
  Earlier sketches in CA 1-4R, CANR-4
  See also SATA 7
Butler, Bill
  See Butler, Ernest Alton and
  Butler, William Huxford and
  Butler, William (Arthur) Vivian
Butler, Bishop B. C.
  See Butler, Basil Christopher
Butler, Charles 1560(?)-1647 ... DLB 236
Butler, Charles (Cadman) 1963- ... 192
  See also SATA 121
Butler, Charles Henry 1894-1970(?) ... CAP-2
  Earlier sketch in CA 23-24
Butler, Christina Violet 1884-1982
  Obituary ... 106
Butler, Christopher
  See Butler, Basil Christopher
Butler, Colin Gasking 1913- ... 109
Butler, Daniel Allen 1957- ... 170
Butler, David Edgeworth 1924- ... CANR-13
  Earlier sketch in CA 5-8R
Butler, David Francis 1928- ... 41-44R
Butler, David Jonathon 1946- ... 69-72
Butler, Dorothy 1925- ... 133
  See also SATA 73
Butler, E(dward) H(arry) 1913-1993 ... 13-16R
Butler, Edgar W(ilbur) 1929- ... 77-80
Butler, Erica Bracher 1905- ... CAP-2
  Earlier sketch in CA 17-18
Butler, Ernest Alton 1926- ... 33-36R
Butler, Francelia McWilliams
  1913-1998 ... CANR-3
  Obituary ... 170
  Earlier sketch in CA 9-12R
Butler, G(eorge) Paul 1900-1977 ... CAP-2
  Earlier sketch in CA 17-18
Butler, Geoff 1945- ... 159
  See also SATA 94
Butler, George D. 1893-1985 ... 17-20R
Butler, George Tyssen 1943- ... 103
Butler, Grace Kipp Pratt
  See Pratt-Butler, Grace Kipp
Butler, Gregory S. 1961- ... 145
Butler, (Frederick) Guy 1918-2001 ... CANR-41
  Obituary ... 195
  Earlier sketches in CA 101, CANR-18
  See also CP 1, 2, 3, 4, 5, 6, 7
  See also DLB 225
  See also RGEL 2
Butler, Gwendoline Williams
  1922- ... CANR-108
  Earlier sketches in CA 9-12R, CANR-6, 63
  See also CMW 4
Butler, Hal 1913-2002 ... 57-60
Butler, Iris (Mary) 1905-2002 ... 21-24R
  Obituary ... 210
Butler, Ivan
  See Beuttler, Edward Ivan Oakley
Butler, J. Donald 1908-1994 ... 1-4R
Butler, Jack 1944- ... CANR-53
  Earlier sketch in CA 114
  See also BPFB 1
  See also CSW
Butler, James 1904- ... CAP-1
  Earlier sketch in CA 11-12
Butler, James H(armon) 1908-1985 ... 41-44R
Butler, James R(amsay) M(ontagu)
  1889-1975 ... CAP-1
  Earlier sketch in CA 13-14
Butler, Jean Campbell (MacLaurin)
  1918- ... 9-12R
Butler, Jean Rouverol 1916- ... CANR-118
  Earlier sketch in CA 97-100
Butler, Jeffrey (Ernest) 1922- ... 65-68
Butler, Jerry P. 1944- ... 65-68
Butler, Joan
  See Alexander, Robert William
Butler, John Alfred Valentine
  1899-1977 ... CANR-5
  Obituary ... 106
  Earlier sketch in CA 5-8R
Butler, Jon 1940- ... CANR-94
  Earlier sketch in CA 134
Butler, Joseph 1692-1752 ... DLB 252
Butler, Joseph Thomas 1932- ... 13-16R
Butler, Josephine (Elizabeth) 1828-1906 ... 182
  See also DLB 190
Butler, Joyce 1933- ... CANR-25
  Earlier sketches in CA 65-68, CANR-9
Butler, Juan (Antonio) 1942-1981 ... 146
  See also DLB 53
Butler, Judith P. ... CANR-106
  Earlier sketch in CA 154
  See also DLB 246
  See also FW
Butler, Lance St. John 1947- ... 144
Butler, Linda ... 233
Butler, Lindley S(mith) 1939- ... 191
Butler, Lionel Harry 1923-1981 ... 110
  Obituary ... 105
Butler, Lucius (Albert, Jr.) 1928- ... 69-72
Butler, M. Christina 1934- ... SATA 72
Butler, Margaret Gwendoline ... 104
Butler, Marilyn (Speers) 1937- ... 102
Butler, Mildred Allen 1897-1987 ... CAP-2
  Earlier sketch in CA 29-32
Butler, Mollie 1907- ... 128
Butler, Natalie Sturges 1908- ... 53-56
Butler, Nathan
  See Sohl, Jerry
Butler, Octavia E(stelle) 1947- ... CANR-73
  Earlier sketches in CA 73-76, CANR-12, 24, 38
  See also AAYA 18, 48
  See also AFAW 2
  See also AMWS 13
  See also BLCS
  See also BPFB 1
  See also BW 2, 3
  See also CLC 38, 121
  See also CLR 65
  See also CN 7
  See also CPW
  See also DA3
  See also DAM MULT, POP
  See also DLB 33
  See also LATS 1:2
  See also MTCW 1, 2
  See also MTFW 2005
  See also NFS 8, 21
  See also SATA 84
  See also SCFW 2
  See also SFW 4
  See also SSFS 6
  See also TCLE 1:1
  See also YAW
Butler, Pat(rick) (Trevor) 1929- ... 5-8R
Butler, Pierce 1884-1953 ... 204
  See also DLB 187
Butler, Pierce A. 1952- ... 146
Butler, Rab
  See Butler, Richard Austen
Butler, Rebecca R. 1945- ... 214
Butler, Richard
  See Allbeury, Theodore Edward le Bouthillier
Butler, Richard 1925- ... CANR-8
  Earlier sketch in CA 57-60
Butler, Richard Austen 1902-1982
  Obituary ... 106
Butler, Rick 1946- ... 97-100
Butler, Robert Albert 1934- ... CANR-11
  Earlier sketch in CA 61-64
Butler, Robert Lee 1918- ... 57-60
Butler, Robert M. 1928(?)-1989
  Obituary ... 129
Butler, Robert N(eil) 1927- ... 41-44R
Butler, Robert Olen, (Jr.) 1945- ... CANR-138
  Earlier sketches in CA 112, CANR-66
  Interview in ... CA-112
  See also AMWS 12
  See also BPFB 1
  See also CLC 81, 162
  See also CN 7
  See also CSW
  See also DAM POP
  See also DLB 173
  See also MAL 5
  See also MTCW 2
  See also MTFW 2005
  See also SSFS 11
Butler, Rohan D'Olier 1917-1996 ... 109
  Obituary ... 154
Butler, Ron(ald William) 1934- ... 69-72
Butler, Ronnie 1931- ... 130
Butler, Ruth (Ann) 1931- ... CANR-108
  Earlier sketch in CA 151
Butler, Samuel 1612-1680 ... DLB 101, 126
  See also RGEL 2
Butler, Samuel 1835-1902 ... 143
  See also BRWS 2
  See also CDBLB 1890-1914
  See also DA
  See also DA3
  See also DAB
  See also DAC
  See also DAM MST, NOV
  See also DLB 18, 57, 174
  See also RGEL 2
  See also SFW 4
  See also TCLC 1, 33
  See also TEA
  See also WLC
Butler, Sandra (Ada) 1938- ... 105
Butler, Stanley 1914- ... 57-60
Butler, Stefan Congrat
  See Congrat-Butler, Stefan
Butler, Stuart Thomas 1926- ... 107
Butler, Suzanne
  See Perreard, Suzanne Louise Butler
Butler, Tajuana ... 229
Butler, Ted
  See Schweitzer, Darrell (Charles)
Butler, Vivian
  See Butler, William (Arthur) Vivian
Butler, Walter C.
  See Faust, Frederick (Schiller)
Butler, Walter E(rnest) 1898- ... CANR-5
  Earlier sketch in CA 5-8R
Butler, William
  See Butler, William (Arthur) Vivian
Butler, William 1929- ... CANR-70
  Earlier sketch in CA 107
Butler, William E(lliot II) 1939- ... CANR-38
  Earlier sketches in CA 25-28R, CANR-11
Butler, William F(rank) 1917-1972
  Obituary ... 113
Butler, William Francis 1838-1910 ... 183
  See also DLB 166
Butler, William Huxford 1934-1977 ... 57-60
  Obituary ... 133
Butler, William (Arthur) Vivian 1927-1987 ... 135
  See also Marric, J. J.
  See also SATA 79
Butlin, Martin (Richard Fletcher)
  1929- ... CANR-19
  Earlier sketches in CA 5-8R, CANR-2
Butlin, Ron 1949- ... CANR-143
  Earlier sketch in CA 136
  See also CP 7
Butman, John (Campbell) 1951- ... CANR-135
  Earlier sketch in CA 142
Butor, Michel (Marie Francois)
  1926- ... CANR-66
  Earlier sketches in CA 9-12R, CANR-33
  See also CLC 1, 3, 8, 11, 15, 161
  See also CWW 2
  See also DLB 83
  See also EW 13
  See also EWL 3
  See also GFL 1789 to the Present
  See also MTCW 1, 2
  See also MTFW 2005
Butow, Robert J. C. 1924- ... 13-16R
Butrym, Zofia Teresa 1927- ... 103
Butsch, Richard (J.) 1943- ... 135
Butscher, Edward 1943- ... 97-100
Butson, Thomas G(ordon) 1932(?)-2000 ... 186
Butt, (Howard) Edward, Jr. 1927- ... 57-60
Butt, (Dorcas) Susan 1938- ... 89-92
Buttaci, Sal(vatore) St. John 1941- ... CANR-9
  Earlier sketch in CA 65-68
Buttel, Robert (William) 1923- ... 102
Buttenwieser, Ann L. 1935- ... 128
Buttenwieser, Paul (Arthur) 1938- ... CANR-35
  Earlier sketch in CA 104
Butter, Nathaniel fl. 1604-1663 ... DLB 170
Butter, Peter (Herbert) 1921-1999 ... 5-8R
  Obituary ... 178
Butterfield, Fox 1939- ... CANR-55
  Earlier sketch in CA 119
  Interview in ... CA-119
Butterfield, Herbert 1900-1979 ... CANR-46
  Earlier sketch in CA 1-4R
Butterfield, Lyman H(enry) 1909-1982
  Obituary ... 106
Butterfield, Roger (Place) 1907-1981 ... CAP-1
  Obituary ... 103
  Earlier sketch in CA 9-10
Butterfield, Stephen T(homas) 1942- ... 57-60
Butterick, George F. 1942-1988 ... CANR-27
  Obituary ... 126
  Earlier sketches in CA 69-72, CANR-11
Butters, Dorothy Gilman
  See Gilman, Dorothy
  See also SATA 5
Butterworth, Brian 1944- ... 187
Butterworth, Douglas Stanley 1930- ... 108
Butterworth, Emma Macalik 1928- ... 105
  See also SATA 43
Butterworth, (Wilfred) Eric 1916-2003 ... 204
  Obituary ... 216
Butterworth, F(rank) Edward, (Jr.)
  1917- ... 29-32R
Butterworth, Hezekiah 1839-1905 ... 217
  See also DLB 42
Butterworth, Jeremy c. 1969- ... 234
  See also Butterworth, Jez

Cumulative Index 87 Cabot

Butterworth, Jez
See Butterworth, Jeremy
See also CD 5, 6
Butterworth, Lionel Milner Angus
See Angus-Butterworth, Lionel Milner
Butterworth, Michael 1924-1986 ..... CANR-96
Obituary 121
Earlier sketches in CA 25-28R, CANR-10
See also RHW
Butterworth, Neil 1934- CANR-56
Earlier sketch in CA 125
Butterworth, Nick 1946- CANR-134
Earlier sketch in CA 175
See also MAICYA 2
See also SATA 106, 149
Butterworth, Oliver 1915-1990 ..... CANR-37
Obituary 132
Earlier sketch in CA 1-4R
See also BYA 4
See also CWRI 5
See also MAICYA 1, 2
See also SATA 1
See also SATA-Obit 66
Butterworth, W(illiam) E(dmund III)
1929- CANR-64
Earlier sketches in CA 1-4R, CANR-2, 18, 40
See also Griffin, W. E. B.
See also CPW
See also SATA 5
Butti, Ken(neth Michael) 1950- 104
Buttigeig, Anton 1912-1983
Obituary 109
Buttimer, Anne 1938- 37-40R
Buttinger, Joseph 1906-1992 ..... CANR-46
Obituary 138
Earlier sketch in CA 21-24R
Buttinger, Muriel Gardiner
1901-1985 ..... CANR-39
Obituary 115
Earlier sketch in CA 77-80
Buttitta, Anthony 1907- 81-84
Buttitta, Ignazio 1899-1997 ..... DLB 114
Buttitta, Tony
See Buttitta, Anthony
Buttlar, Lois J(acqueline) 1934- 112
Buttle, Myra
See Purcell, Victor
Button, Daniel E(van) 1917- 89-92
Button, Dick 1929- 9-12R
Button, James W(ickham) 1942- 81-84
Button, Kenneth John 1948- CANR-20
Earlier sketch in CA 103
Button, (Henry) Warren 1922- 97-100
Buttress, Frederick Arthur 1908- 33-36R
Buttrey, Douglas N(orton) CANR-40
Earlier sketches in CA 101, CANR-18
Buttrick, George Arthur 1892-1980 61-64
Obituary 93-96
Butts, Anthony 1969- CANR-123
Earlier sketch in CA 168
Butts, David P. 1932- 9-12R
Butts, Dennis 1932- 145
Butts, Edward 1951- 128
Butts, Ellen R(ubinstein) 1942- 158
See also SATA 93
Butts, Jane Roberts 1929-1984 ..... CANR-15
Earlier sketch in CA 41-44R
Butts, Mary 1890(?)-1937 148
See also DLB 240
See also TCLC 77
Butts, Porter (Freeman) 1903-1991 ..... 41-44R
Butts, R(obert) Freeman 1910- 13-16R
Butwell, Richard 1929- CANR-1
Earlier sketch in CA 45-48
Butzer, Karl W(ilhelm) 1934- CANR-8
Earlier sketch in CA 21-24R
Buultjens, (Edward) Ralph 1936- CANR-4
Earlier sketch in CA 53-56
Buxbaum, Edith 1902-1982 ..... CAP-2
Earlier sketch in CA 25-28
Buxbaum, Martin (David) 1912-1991 ... 17-20R
Obituary 134
Buxbaum, Melvin H. 1934- 53-56
Buxbaum, Robert C(ourtney) 1930- 97-100
Buxton, Anne (Arundel)
Brief entry 115
Buxton, Anthony 1892(?)-1970
Obituary 104
Buxton, (Evelyn June) Bonnie 1940- 69-72
Buxton, Charles R(oberts) 1913-1997 65-68
Buxton, Cindy 1950- 132
Buxton, Claude E(lmo) 1912-1991
Brief entry 114
Buxton, David Roden 1910-2003 104
Obituary 221
Buxton, Edward F(ulton) 1917-1990 ..... 41-44R
Obituary 132
Buxton, Harold J(ocelyn) 1880-1976
Obituary 104
Buxton, (Edward) John (Mawby)
1912-1989 ..... CANR-31
Earlier sketches in CA 9-12R, CANR-5
Buxton, Ralph
See Silverstein, Alvin and
Silverstein, Virginia B(arbara Opshelor)
Buxton, Thomas H(amilton) 1940- 57-60
Buys, Donna 1944- 102
Buys, Paul
See Greshoff, Jan
Buysse, Cyriel 1859-1932 209
Buzan, Barry 1946- CANR-44
Earlier sketch in CA 119
Buzard, James 1959- 141
Buzo, Adrian 197
Buzo, Alex
See Buzo, Alexander (John)
See also DLB 289
Buzo, Alexander (John) 1944- CANR-69
Earlier sketches in CA 97-100, CANR-17, 39
See also CD 5, 6
See also CLC 61
Buzzard, John Huxley 1912-1984
Obituary 112
Buzzati, Dino 1906-1972 160
Obituary 33-36R
See also CLC 36
See also DLB 177
See also RGWL 2, 3
See also SFW 4
Buzzell, Robert (Dow) 1933-2004 104
Obituary 233
Buzzeo, Toni 1951- 204
See also SATA 135
Buzzi, Aldo 1910- 181
Buzzle, Buck
See Rubin, Charles J.
Buzzotta, V. R(alph) 1931- 37-40R
Byalick, Marcia 1947- CANR-120
Earlier sketch in CA 154
See also SATA 97, 141
Byard, Carole (Marie) 1941- ..... SATA 57
Byars, Betsy (Cromer) 1928- 183
Earlier sketches in CA 33-36R, CANR-18, 36, 57, 102
Interview in CANR-18
Autobiographical Essay in 183
See also AAYA 19
See also BYA 3
See also CLC 35
See also CLR 1, 16, 72
See also DLB 52
See also JRDA
See also MAICYA 1, 2
See also MAICYAS 1
See also MTCW 1
See also SAAS 1
See also SATA 4, 46, 80, 163
See also SATA-Essay 108
See also WYA
See also YAW
Byatt, A(ntonia) S(usan Drabble)
1936- CANR-133
Earlier sketches in CA 13-16R, CANR-13, 33, 50, 75, 96
See also BPFB 1
See also BRWC 2
See also BRWS 4
See also CLC 19, 65, 136
See also CN 1, 2, 3, 4, 5, 6
See also DA3
See also DAM NOV, POP
See also DLB 14, 194
See also EWL 3
See also MTCW 1, 2
See also MTFW 2005
See also RGSF 2
See also RHW
See also TEA
Bychowski, Gustav 1895-1972
Obituary 33-36R
Byck, Robert 1933-1999 109
Obituary 183
Bye, Beryl (Joyce Rayment) 1926- CANR-11
Earlier sketch in CA 61-64
Bye, Ranulph (deBayeux) 1916- 53-56
Bye, Raymond T(aylor) 1892-1976 ..... 5-8R
Byer, Kathryn Stripling 1944- CANR-138
Earlier sketch in CA 142
Byerly, Greg (W.) 1949- 130
Byerly, Henry Clement 1935- 53-56
Byerly, Kenneth R(hodes) 1908-1998 ..... 1-4R
Byerly, Victoria 1949- 127
Byers, David (Milner) 1941- 53-56
Byers, Edward A(dams) 1939-1989 119
Obituary 129
Byers, Edward E. 1921- CANR-3
Earlier sketch in CA 1-4R
Byers, (Amy) Irene 1906- CANR-3
Earlier sketch in CA 9-12R
Byers, John A. 1948- 169
Byers, Michael 1969- 192
Byers, R(ichard) McCulloch 1913- 69-72
Byfield, Barbara Ninde 1930- CANR-4
Earlier sketch in CA 1-4R
See also SATA 8
Byham, William C(larence) 1936- CANR-17
Earlier sketch in CA 25-28R
Bykau, Vasilii Uladzimiravich
See Bykov, Vasily Vladimirovich
Bykaw, Vasil
See Bykov, Vasily Vladimirovich
See also EWL 3
See also RGWL 2, 3
Bykov, Vasily Vladimirovich 1924-2003 102
Obituary 217
See also Bykaw, Vasil
Byles, Mather 1707-1788 ..... DLB 24
Bylinsky, Gene Michae 1930- 77-80
Byman, Jeremy 1944- 198
See also SATA 129
Bynagle, Hans E(dward) 1946- 120
Byng, Douglas 1893-1987
Obituary 123
Bynneman, Henry fl. 1566-1583 ..... DLB 170
Bynner, Witter 1881-1968 ..... CANR-4
Obituary 25-28R
Earlier sketch in CA 1-4R
See also AMWS 15
See also DLB 54
Bynum, David E(liab) 1936- CANR-20
Earlier sketch in CA 37-40R
Bynum, Jamie ..... SATA 133
Bynum, Sarah Shun-lien 233
Bynum, Terrell Ward 1941- CANR-18
Earlier sketch in CA 101
Bynum, Victoria E. 1947- CANR-93
Earlier sketch in CA 146
Byock, Jesse L(ewis) 1945- 110
Byrd, Adrianne 239
Byrd, Bobby
See Byrd, Robert James
Byrd, C. L.
See Rosenkrantz, Linda
Byrd, Cecil Kash 1913-1997 ..... 17-20R
Byrd, Don 1944- 230
Byrd, Eldon A(rthur) 1939- 45-48
Byrd, Elizabeth 1912-1989 ..... CANR-5
Earlier sketch in CA 5-8R
See also SATA 34
Byrd, Emmett
See Hinden, Michael C(harles)
Byrd, John Crowe
See Hinden, Michael C(harles)
Byrd, Martha 1930- 29-32R
Byrd, Max (W.) 1942- CANR-72
Earlier sketch in CA 142
See also CMW 4
Byrd, Nicole
See Zach, Cheryl (Byrd)
Byrd, Richard E(dward) 1931- CANR-7
Earlier sketch in CA 57-60
Byrd, Robert (John) 1942- CANR-142
Earlier sketch in CA 184
See also SATA 33, 112, 158
Byrd, Robert C(arlyle) 1917- 238
Byrd, Robert James 1942- 65-68
Byrd, William II 1674-1744 ..... DLB 24, 140
See also RGAL 4
Byrd, William c. 1543-1623 ..... DLB 172
Byrne, Charles Raymond 1916-1983
Obituary 111
Byrne, David 1952- 127
See also CLC 26
Byrne, Donald E(dward), Jr. 1942- 73-76
Byrne, Donn 1889-1928 ..... RHW
Byrne, Donn (Erwin) 1931- CANR-78
Earlier sketches in CA 9-12R, CANR-5, 20
Byrne, Edmund F(rancis) 1933- 29-32R
Byrne, Edward M. 1935- 29-32R
Byrne, Elena Karina 1959- ..... PFS 20
Byrne, Frank L(oyola) 1928- 21-24R
Byrne, Gary C. 1942- 49-52
Byrne, Herbert Winston 1917- 1-4R
Byrne, James E. 1945- 81-84
Byrne, Janet 174
Byrne, John 1940- CANR-69
Earlier sketch in CA 104
See also AAYA 66
See also CBD
See also CD 5, 6
Byrne, John Keyes 1926- CANR-140
Earlier sketches in CA 102, CANR-78
Interview in CA-102
See also Leonard, Hugh
Byrne, Malcolm 1955- 127
Byrne, Mary Gregg 1951- ..... SATA 162
Byrne, Muriel St. Clare 1895-1983 ..... CAP-1
Obituary 111
Earlier sketch in CA 17-18
Byrne, Peter 1925- 65-68
Byrne, Ralph
See Burns, Ralph J.
Byrne, Richard Hill 1915- 21-24R
Byrne, Robert (Eugene) 1928- 185
Brief entry 110
Byrne, Robert 1930- CANR-82
Earlier sketches in CA 73-76, CANR-13, 35
Byrne, Stuart J(ames) 1913- 102
Byrnes, Edward T(homas) 1929- 53-56
Byrnes, Eugene F. 1890(?)-1974
Obituary 49-52
Byrnes, Garrett D(avis) 1904(?)-1985
Obituary 118
Byrnes, James Francis 1879-1972
Obituary 112
Byrnes, James T. 1960- 220
Byrnes, John D. 1945- 236
Byrnes, Joseph Francis 1939- 114
Byrnes, Robert F(rancis) 1917-1997 ..... CANR-10
Obituary 158
Earlier sketch in CA 25-28R
Byrnes, Thomas Edmund 1911-1986 ..... 13-16R
Byrom, James
See Bramwell, James Guy
Byrom, John 1692-1763 ..... RGEL 2
Byrom, (Robert) Michael 1925- 5-8R
Byron, A(nne) M. 1932- 171
Byron, Carl R(oscoe) 1948- 97-100
Byron, Christopher M. 1944- CANR-113
Earlier sketch in CA 77-80
Byron, George Gordon (Noel)
1788-1824 ..... AAYA 64
See also BRW 4
See also BRWC 2
See also CDBLB 1789-1832
See also DA
See also DA3
See also DAB
See also DAC
See also DAM MST, POET
See also DC 24
See also DLB 96, 110
See also EXPP
See also LMFS 1
See also PAB
See also PC 16
See also PFS 1, 14
See also RGEL 2
See also TEA
See also WLC
See also WLIT 3
See also WP
Byron, Gilbert (Valliant) 1903-1991 ..... 17-20R
Obituary 134
Byron, H(enry) J(ames) 1835-1884 ..... RGEL 2
Byron, John
See Armstrong, John Byron
Byron, Robert 1905-1941 160
See also DLB 195
See also TCLC 67
Byron, William J(ames) 1927- 81-84
Bystander
See Smith, Goldwin
Bytwerk, Randall Lee 1950- 109
Bywater, William G(len), Jr. 1940- 61-64

C

C. 3. 3.
See Wilde, Oscar (Fingal O'Flahertie Wills)
C. E. M.
See Mastrangelo, Charles E(lmer)
C. F. H.
See Heartman, Charles F(rederick)
Caballero, Ann Mallory 1928- 17-20R
Caballero, Fernan 1796-1877
Caballero, Manuel 1931- 132
See also HW 1
Caballero, Nicolas Moreno 1935- 205
Caballero Bonald, Jose Manuel 1926-
See Bonald, Jose Manuel Caballero
See also DLB 108
Caballero Calderon, E.
See Caballero Calderon, Eduardo
Caballero Calderon, Eduardo
1910-1993 ..... EWL 3
See also HW 1
Cabanero, Eladio 1930-2000 209
See also DLB 134
Cabanis, Jose 1922- 185
Brief entry 111
Cabaniss, J(ames) Allen 1911-1997 ..... 1-4R
See also SATA 5
Cabarga, Leslie 1954- CANR-114
Earlier sketches in CA 77-80, CANR-13
Cabassa, Victoria 1912- 49-52
Cabat, Erni 1914- ..... SATA 74
Cabbell, Edward J. 1946- 121
Cabbell, Paul 1942- 53-56
Cabeen, David Clark 1886-1965(?) CAP-1
Earlier sketch in CA 13-14
Cabell, Branch
See Cabell, James Branch
Cabell, James Branch 1879-1958 152
Brief entry 105
See also DLB 9, 78
See also FANT
See also MAL 5
See also MTCW 2
See also RGAL 4
See also SUFW 1
See also TCLC 6
Cabeza de Baca, Manuel 1853-1915 174
See also Baca, Manuel Cabeza de
See also HW 2
Cabeza de Baca Gilbert, Fabiola
See Gilbert, Fabiola Cabeza de Baca
See also DLB 122
Cabezas (Lacayo), Omar 1951(?)- CANR-81
Earlier sketch in CA 131
See also HW 1, 2
Cabibi, John F(rank) J(oseph) 1912-1994 . 53-56
Cable, George Washington 1844-1925 155
Brief entry 104
See also DLB 12, 74
See also DLBD 13
See also RGAL 4
See also SSC 4
See also TCLC 4
See also TUS
Cable, James (Eric) 1920-2001 ..... CANR-106
Obituary 201
Earlier sketches in CA 85-88, CANR-15, 33
Cable, John L(aurence) 1934- CANR-21
Earlier sketch in CA 69-72
Cable, Mary 1920- CANR-28
Earlier sketches in CA 25-28R, CANR-11
See also SATA 9
Cable, Mildred 1878-1952 ..... DLB 195
Cable, Thomas Monroe 1942- 180
Brief entry 106
Cabot, Blake 1905(?)-1974
Obituary 53-56
Cabot, John Moors 1901-1981
Obituary 103

Cabot, Laurie 1933- 206
Cabot, Meg(gin) 1967- 197
See also AAYA 50
See also BYA 16
See also CLR 85
See also SATA 127
Cabot, Patricia
See Cabot, Meg(gin)
Cabot, Robert (Moors) 1924- CANR-97
Earlier sketch in CA 29-32R
Cabot, Thomas Dudley 1897-1995 93-96
Cabot, Tracy 1941- 81-84
Cabral, Alberto
See White, Richard Alan
Cabral, Amilcar 1924-1973
Obituary 111
See also EWL 3
Cabral, Joao de Pina
See Pina-Cabral, Joao de
Cabral, Manuel del 1907-1999 .... DLB 283
Cabral, O. M.
See Cabral, Olga
Cabral, Olga 1909- CANR-10
Earlier sketch in CA 25-28R
See also SATA 46
Cabral de Melo Neto, Joao 1920-1999 151
See also Melo Neto, Joao Cabral de
See also CLC 76
See also DAM MULT
See also DLB 307
See also LAW
See also LAWS 1
Cabrera, James C. 1935-1997 109
Obituary 161
Cabrera, Jane 1968- 170
See also SATA 103, 152
Cabrera, Lydia 1900-1991 178
See also DLB 145
See also EWL 3
See also HW 1
See also LAWS 1
Cabrera, Marcela 1966- .... SATA 90
Cabrera Infante, G(uillermo)
1929-2005 .... CANR-110
Obituary 236
Earlier sketches in CA 85-88, CANR-29, 65
See also CDWLB 3
See also CLC 5, 25, 45, 120
See also CWW 2
See also DA3
See also DAM MULT
See also DLB 113
See also EWL 3
See also HLC 1
See also HW 1, 2
See also LAW
See also LAWS 1
See also MTCW 1, 2
See also MTFW 2005
See also RGSF 2
See also SSC 39
See also WLIT 1
Cabrujas, Jose Ignacio 1937-1995 ...... DLB 305
Cacaci, Joe 233
Caccia-Dominioni, Paolo 1896-1992 .... 21-24R
Cacciatore, Vera (Signorelli) 1911- CANR-5
Earlier sketch in CA 5-8R
Cach, Lisa 210
Cachia, Pierre J. E. 1921- CANR-11
Earlier sketch in CA 25-28R
Cacoyannis, Michael 1922- 101
Cacucci, Pino 1955- 238
Cadbury, Deborah 235
Cadbury, Henry J(oel) 1883-1974 .... CAP-1
Obituary 53-56
Earlier sketch in CA 13-16
Cadbury, Paul Strangman 1895-1984
Obituary 114
Caddel, Richard (Ivo) 1949-2003 137
Obituary 215
Cadden, Joseph E. 1911(?)-1980
Obituary 101
Cadden, Thomas Scott 1923- 131
Cadden, Tom Scott
See Cadden, Thomas Scott
Caddick, Arthur 1911-1987
Obituary 122
Caddy, Alice
See Burman, Alice Caddy
Caddy, Caroline 1944- 153
See also CP 7
See also CWP
Caddy, (Michael) Douglas 1938- 136
Cade, Alexander
See Methold, Kenneth (Walter)
Cade, Jared
See Cade, John
Cade, John 1942- 193
Cade, Robin
See Nicole, Christopher (Robin)
Cade, Toni
See Bambara, Toni Cade
Cadell, (Violet) Elizabeth
1903-1989 .... CANR-72
Earlier sketches in CA 57-60, CANR-11
See also RHW
Cadenhead, Ivie E(dward), Jr. 1923- 41-44R
Cader, Michael 1961- CANR-143
Earlier sketch in CA 147
Cadet, John 1935- 77-80
Cadieux, Charles L. 1919- 57-60
Cadieux, (Joseph Arthur) Lorenzo
1903-1976 49-52
Obituary 103
Cadieux, (Joseph David Romeo) Marcel
1915-1981
Obituary 108
Cadigan, Pat(ricia Kearney) 1953- ... CANR-111
Earlier sketch in CA 165
See also AAYA 53
See also SFW 4
See also SUFW 2
Cadle, Dean 1920- 25-28R
Cadle, Farris W(illiam) 1952- 135
Cadman, S(amuel) Parkes 1864-1936 212
Cadmus and
Harmonia
Harmonia
See Buchan, John
Cadnum, Michael 1949- CANR-90
Earlier sketch in CA 151
See also AAYA 23
See also BYA 9, 11, 13
See also CLR 78
See also HGG
See also SATA 87, 121
See also WYAS 1
See also YAW
Cadogan, Alexander (George Montagu)
1884-1968
Obituary 106
Cadogan, Mary (Rose) 1928- 106
Caduto, Michael J. 1955- CANR-109
Earlier sketch in CA 153
See also SATA 103
Cadwallader, Clyde T(homas) 5-8R
Cadwallader, Sharon 1936- CANR-17
Earlier sketches in CA 49-52, CANR-1
See also SATA 7
Cady, Arthur 1920-1983
Obituary 109
Cady, Edwin Harrison 1917- CANR-70
Earlier sketches in CA 1-4R, CANR-4
See also DLB 103
Cady, Ernest (Albert) 1899-1985
Obituary 117
Cady, H(arriet) Emilie 1848-1941 221
Cady, (Walter) Harrison 1877(?)-1970
Obituary 116
See also SATA 19
Cady, Howard Stevenson 1914-1990
Obituary 132
Cady, Jack A(ndrew) 1932-2004 .... CANR-72
Obituary 223
Earlier sketches in CA 65-68, CANR-9
See also HGG
Cady, John Frank 1901-1996 .... CANR-72
Earlier sketches in CA 1-4R, CANR-4
Cady, Steve (Noel) 1927-1995 45-48
Obituary 149
Caedmon fl. 658-680 .... DLB 146
Caedmon, Father
See Wahl, Thomas (Peter)
Caefer, Raymond J(ohn) 1926- 17-20R
Caeiro, Alberto
See Pessoa, Fernando (Antonio Nogueira)
Caemmerer, Richard R(udolph)
1904-1984 .... CANR-5
Earlier sketch in CA 1-4R
Caen, Herb (Eugene) 1916-1997 .... CANR-1
Obituary 156
Earlier sketch in CA 1-4R
See also AITN 1
Caesar, Adrian (David) 1955- 195
Caesar, Ann (Hallamore) 228
Caesar, (Eu)Gene (Lee) 1927- CANR-72
Earlier sketches in CA 1-4R, CANR-1
Caesar, Irving 1895-1996 .... DLB 265
Caesar, Judith 1946- 167
Caesar, Julius
See Julius Caesar
See also AW 1
See also RGWL 2, 3
Caesar, (Isaac) Sid(ney) 1922- 143
Cafferky, Michael E. 197
Cafferty, Bernard 1934- 41-44R
Cafferty, Pastora San Juan 1940- 114
Caffey, David L(uther) 1947- 45-48
Caffey, Donna (J.) 1954- 180
See also SATA 110
Caffrey, John G(ordon) 1922- 17-20R
Caffrey, Kate CANR-1
Earlier sketch in CA 49-52
Caffrey, Margaret M. 1947- 135
Cagan, Phillip D(avid) 1927- 17-20R
Cagan, Stephen M(ichael) 1943- 139
Cage, John (Milton), (Jr.) 1912-1992 . CANR-78
Obituary 169
Earlier sketches in CA 13-16R, CANR-9
Interview in CANR-9
See also CLC 41
See also DLB 193
See also PC 58
See also TCLE 1:1
Cagen, Sasha 236
Caggiano, Philip 1949- 114
Cagle, Malcolm W(infield) 1918- 108
See also SATA 32
Cagle, William R(ea) 1933- 65-68
Cagney, James (Francis, Jr.) 1899(?)-1986 ... 144
Obituary 118
Brief entry 115
Cagney, Peter
See Winter, Bevis (Peter)
Cahalan, (John) Don(ald) 1912-1992 102
Cahalan, James M(ichael) 1953- CANR-144
Earlier sketch in CA 145
Cahalane, Victor H(arrison) 1901-1993 . CAP-2
Earlier sketch in CA 23-24
Cahan, Abraham 1860-1951 154
Brief entry 108
See also DLB 9, 25, 28
See also MAL 5
See also RGAL 4
See also TCLC 71
Cahan, David 198
Cahan, William G(eorge) 1914-2001 139
Obituary 201
Cahen, Alfred B. 1932- 17-20R
Cahill, Audrey Fawcett 1929- 21-24R
Cahill, Barry 1953- 197
Cahill, Daniel J(oseph) 1929- 69-72
Cahill, Fred V(irgil), Jr. 1916-1984
Obituary 112
Cahill, Gilbert A. 1912-1985
Brief entry 107
Cahill, Jack
See Cahill, John Denis
Cahill, James F(rancis) 1926- CANR-6
Earlier sketch in CA 1-4R
Cahill, Jane (Miller) 1901-1986 .... CAP-2
Earlier sketch in CA 23-24
Cahill, John Denis 1926- 131
Cahill, Kevin Michael 1936- CANR-63
Earlier sketches in CA 102, CANR-18, 40
Cahill, Laura 211
Cahill, Nicholas D. 227
Cahill, Rick 1950- 126
Cahill, Robert S. 1933- 13-16R
Cahill, Susan Neunzig 1940- 37-40R
Cahill, Thomas (Quinn) 1940- CANR-92
Earlier sketches in CA 49-52, CANR-53, 90
Cahill, Tim 1944- CANR-101
Earlier sketch in CA 164
See also AAYA 25
Cahill, Tom
See Cahill, Thomas (Quinn)
Cahn, Edgar S. 1935- 29-32R
Cahn, Rhoda 1922- 81-84
See also SATA 37
Cahn, Robert 1917-1997 108
Obituary 162
Cahn, Sammy 1913-1993 85-88
Obituary 140
See also DLB 265
See also IDFW 3, 4
Cahn, Steven M. 1942- CANR-53
Earlier sketches in CA 21-24R, CANR-13, 29
Cahn, Walter 1933- 129
Cahn, William 1912-1976 .... CANR-71
Obituary 69-72
Earlier sketch in CA 21-24R
See also SATA 37
Cahn, Zvi 1896- CAP-2
Earlier sketch in CA 23-24
Cahnman, Werner J(acob) 1902-1980 49-52
Caiden, Gerald E(lliot) 1936- CANR-14
Earlier sketch in CA 29-32R
Caidin, Martin 1927-1997 .... CANR-58
Obituary 157
Earlier sketches in CA 1-4R, CANR-2
See also AITN 2
See also SFW 4
Caiger-Smith, Alan 1930- 13-16R
Cail, Carol 1937- CANR-136
Earlier sketches in CA 140, CANR-71
Caillois, Roger 1913-1978 .... CANR-13
Obituary 85-88
Earlier sketch in CA 25-28R
Caillou, Alan
See Lyle-Smythe, Alan
Caimita Hostert, Anna 1949- 178
Cain, Arthur H(omer) 1913-1981 .... CANR-4
Earlier sketch in CA 1-4R
See also SATA 3
Cain, Bob
See Cain, Robert Owen
Cain, Bruce E. 1948- 122
Cain, G.
See Cabrera Infante, G(uillermo)
Cain, George (M.) 1943- 142
See also BW 2
See also DLB 33
Cain, Glen G. 1933- 21-24R
Cain, Guillermo
See Cabrera Infante, G(uillermo)
Cain, Jackson
See Gleason, Robert
Cain, James M(allahan) 1892-1977 .. CANR-61
Obituary 73-76
Earlier sketches in CA 17-20R, CANR-8, 34
See also AITN 1
See also BPFB 1
See also CLC 3, 11, 28
See also CMW 4
See also CN 1, 2
See also DLB 226
See also EWL 3
See also MAL 5
See also MSW
See also MTCW 1
See also RGAL 4
Cain, Kenneth 236
Cain, Mary (Dawson) 1904-1984
Obituary 112
Cain, Maureen 1938- 73-76
Cain, Michael Peter 1941- 93-96
Cain, Paul
See Sims, George (Carrol)
See also CMW 4
See also DLB 306
Cain, Robert
See Keith, William H(enry), Jr., Jr.
Cain, Robert Owen 1934- 65-68
Cain, T. G. S. 1944- 124
Cain, Thomas H(enry) 1931- 93-96
Caine, Barbara 1948- 143
Caine, Geoffrey
See Walker, Robert W(ayne)
Caine, (Thomas Henry) Hall 1853(?)-1931
Brief entry 122
Caine, Hall 1853-1931 .... RHW
See also TCLC 97
Caine, Jeffrey (Andrew) 1944- 85-88
Caine, Lynn 1924(?)-1987
Obituary 124
Caine, Mark
See Raphael, Frederic (Michael)
Caine, Michael 1933- 146
Caine, Mitchell
See Sparkia, Roy (Bernard)
Caine, Peter
See Hornig, Doug
Caine, Stanley P(aul) 1940- 41-44R
Caine, Sydney 1902-1991 .... CAP-2
Earlier sketch in CA 25-28
Caines, Jeannette (Franklin) 1938- 152
See also BW 2
See also CLR 24
See also SATA 78
See also SATA-Brief 43
Caird, Edward 1835-1908 .... DLB 262
Caird, George Bradford 1917-1984 61-64
Obituary 112
Caird, Janet 1913- CANR-2
Earlier sketch in CA 49-52
Caird, John (Newport) 1948- 156
Caird, Mona 1854-1932 .... DLB 197
Cairncross, Alec
See Cairncross, Alexander Kirkland
Cairncross, Alexander Kirkland
1911-1998 .... CANR-57
Obituary 171
Earlier sketches in CA 61-64, CANR-8
Cairncross, Frances (Anne) 1944- ... CANR-120
Earlier sketch in CA 57-60
Cairney, John 1930- 105
Cairns, (Hugh) Alan C(raig) 1930- 220
Cairns, David 1904-1992 .... CANR-11
Obituary 140
Earlier sketch in CA 61-64
Cairns, (Thomas) Dorian 1901-1972
Obituary 37-40R
Cairns, Earle E(dwin) 1910- CANR-18
Earlier sketch in CA 1-4R
Cairns, (Samuel) Ed(mund) 1945- CANR-66
Earlier sketch in CA 128
Cairns, Grace Edith 1907-2000 .... CANR-18
Earlier sketch in CA 1-4R
Cairns, Huntington 1904-1985 .... CANR-79
Obituary 114
Earlier sketches in CA 53-56, CANR-5
Cairns, J(ames) F(ord) 1914-2003 105
Obituary 220
Cairns, John C(ampbell) 1924- CANR-5
Earlier sketch in CA 13-16R
Cairns, Scott 1954- CANR-91
Earlier sketch in CA 146
Cairns, Thomas W(illiam) 1931- 21-24R
Cairns, Trevor 1922- 33-36R
See also SATA 14
Cairns-Smith, A(lexander) G(raham) 1931- . 123
Cairo, Jon
See Romano, Deane Louis
Caitlin, Elise 1953- 111
Cake, Patrick
See Welch, Timothy L.
Caks, Aleksandrs 1901-1950 .... CDWLB 4
See also DLB 220
See also EWL 3
Calabrese, Alphonse F. X. 1923- 69-72
Calabrese, Anthony 1938- 89-92
Calabrese, Richard J. 1942- 171
Calabresi, Guido 1932- CANR-20
Earlier sketch in CA 41-44R
Calabro, Marian 1954- CANR-105
Earlier sketch in CA 147
See also SATA 79
Calaferte, Louis 1928- CANR-17
Earlier sketches in CA 45-48, CANR-1
Calais, Jean
See Rodefer, Stephen
Calamandrei, Mauro 1925- 69-72
Calamari, John D(aniel) 1921- 37-40R
Calame, Claude 1943- 191
Calamnius-Kianto, Ilmari
See Kianto, Ilmari
Calas, Nicholas 1907-1988
Obituary 127
Calasibetta, Charlotte M(ankey) 1917- 103
Calasso, Roberto 1941- CANR-89
Earlier sketch in CA 143
See also CLC 81
Calbert, Cathleen 1955- 170
Calbom, Cherie 1947- CANR-144
Earlier sketch in CA 138
Calcagno, Anne 1957- 191
Caldarelli, Nazareno 1887-1959 178
See also Cardarelli, Vincenzo
Calde, Mark A(ugustine) 1945- 69-72
Caldecott, Moyra 1927- CANR-30
Earlier sketches in CA 77-80, CANR-13
See also FANT
See also SATA 22
Caldecott, Randolph (J.) 1846-1886 .... AAYA 64
See also CLR 14
See also DLB 163
See also MAICYA 1, 2
See also SATA 17, 100
Calder, Alexander 1898-1976 167
Obituary 111
See also AAYA 25

Cumulative Index 89 Calvin

Calder, Angus 1942- CANR-38
Earlier sketch in CA 29-32R
Calder, Bruce J. 1940- 132
Calder, C(larence) R(oy), Jr. 1928- 81-84
Calder, Charlotte 1952- 196
See also SATA 125
Calder, Daniel Gillmore 1939-1994 103
Calder, David 1932-1997 173
See also SATA 105
Calder, Iain 1939- 237
Calder, Jason
See Dunmore, John
Calder, Jenni 1941- CANR-38
Earlier sketches in CA 45-48, CANR-1
Calder, John (Mackenzie) 1927- CANR-91
Earlier sketch in CA 133
Calder, Kent E(yring) 1948- 107
Calder, Lendol (Glen) 1958- 192
Calder, Lyn
See Calmenson, Stephanie
Calder, Marie D(onais) 1948- 161
See also SATA 96
Calder, Nigel (David Ritchie) 1931- . CANR-38
Earlier sketches in CA 21-24R, CANR-11
See also MTCW 1
Calder, Ritchie
See Ritchie-Calder, Peter Ritchie
Calder, Robert
See Mundis, Jerrold
Calder, Robert Lorin 1941- 65-68
Calder-Marshall, Arthur 1908-1992 .. CANR-72
Obituary 137
Earlier sketch in CA 61-64
See also CN 1, 2, 3
See also HGG
Calderon, Eduardo Caballero
See Caballero Calderon, Eduardo
Calderon, Hector (Valle) 1945- 179
Calderon, Jose Vasconcelos
See Vasconcelos (Calderon), Jose
Calderon de la Barca, Pedro 1600-1681 .. DC 3
See also EW 2
See also HLCS 1
See also RGWL 2, 3
See also TWA
Calderone, Mary S(teichen) 1904-1998 104
Obituary 171
See also AITN 1
Calderone-Stewart, Lisa
See Calderone-Stewart, Lisa-Marie
Calderone-Stewart, Lisa-Marie 1958- 194
See also SATA 123
Calders, Pere 1912-1994 206
See also EWL 3
Calderwood, Ivan E. 1899-1998 57-60
Calderwood, James D(ixon) 1917- CANR-3
Earlier sketch in CA 5-8R
Calderwood, James L(ee) 1930- 21-24R
Caldicott, Helen (Mary) 1938- CANR-124
Brief entry 114
Earlier sketches in CA 124, CANR-66
Interview in CA-124
See also MTCW 1, 2
Caldwell, Ben(jamin) 1937- 124
Brief entry 117
See also BW 1
See also DLB 38
Caldwell, Bettye (McDonald) 1924- 104
Caldwell, C(harles) Edson 1906-1974 ... CAP-2
Earlier sketch in CA 29-32
Caldwell, Dan (Edward) 1948- 112
Caldwell, David H(epburn) 1951- CANR-93
Earlier sketch in CA 132
Caldwell, Doreen (Mary) 1942- .... SATA 71
Caldwell, Edward S(abiston) 1928- 65-68
Caldwell, Erskine (Preston)
1903-1987 .... CANR-33
Obituary 121
Earlier sketches in CA 1-4R, CANR-2
See also CAAS 1
See also AITN 1
See also AMW
See also BPFB 1
See also CLC 1, 8, 14, 50, 60
See also CN 1, 2, 3, 4
See also DA3
See also DAM NOV
See also DLB 9, 86
See also EWL 3
See also MAL 5
See also MTCW 1, 2
See also MTFW 2005
See also RGAL 4
See also RGSF 2
See also SSC 19
See also TCLC 117
See also TUS
Caldwell, Gaylon L(oray) 1920- 33-36R
Caldwell, Grant 1947- 159
Caldwell, Harry B(oynton) 1935- 37-40R
Caldwell, Helen F. 1904-1987 77-80
Caldwell, Inga Gilson 1897-1985 61-64
Caldwell, Irene Catherine (Smith)
1908-1979 .... 9-12R
Obituary 103
Caldwell, James
See Lowry, Robert (James Collas)
Caldwell, John 1928- CANR-12
Earlier sketch in CA 73-76
Caldwell, John C(ope) 1913-1984 ..... CANR-13
Earlier sketch in CA 21-24R
See also SATA 7
Caldwell, Joseph 1938- 209
Caldwell, Joseph H(erman) 1934- 21-24R
Caldwell, Kathryn (Smoot) 1942- 69-72
Caldwell, Louis O(liver) 1935- 69-72
Caldwell, Lynton (Keith) 1913- CANR-12
Earlier sketch in CA 29-32R
Caldwell, (James Alexander) Malcolm
1931-1978 .... CANR-17
Earlier sketch in CA 25-28R
Caldwell, Marge 1914- 97-100
Caldwell, Mark 238
Caldwell, Nat(han Green) 1912-1985
Obituary 115
Caldwell, Norm(an) 1943- 200
Caldwell, Oliver Johnson 1904-1990 .... 37-40R
Caldwell, Robert G(ranville) 1882-1976
Obituary 65-68
Caldwell, Robert Graham 1904-1978 ... 17-20R
Caldwell, Stratton F(ranklin) 1926- 136
Caldwell, (Janet Miriam) Taylor (Holland)
1900-1985 .... CANR-5
Obituary 116
Earlier sketch in CA 5-8R
See also BPFB 1
See also CLC 2, 28, 39
See also DA3
See also DAM NOV, POP
See also DLBD 17
See also MTCW 2
See also RHW
Caldwell, William A(nthony) 1906-1986
Obituary 119
Cale, John 1940(?)- 196
Calef, George (Waller) 1944- 132
Calef, Wesley (Carr) 1914- 13-16R
Caletti, Deb 1963- 234
Caley, Rod
See Rowland, D(onald) S(ydney)
Calhoon, Richard P(ercival) 1909- 57-60
Calhoon, Robert M(cCluer) 1935- CANR-4
Earlier sketch in CA 53-56
Calhoun, B. B. 1961- 165
See also SATA 98
Calhoun, Calfrey C. 1928- 37-40R
Calhoun, Chad
See Barrett, Neal, Jr. and
Cunningham, Chet and Goulart, Ron(ald Joseph)
Calhoun, Charles W(illiam) 1948- 125
Calhoun, Conyus 1946- 111
Calhoun, Craig (Jackson) 1952- 130
Calhoun, Daniel F(airchild) 1929- 65-68
Calhoun, Dia 1959- 198
See also AAYA 44
See also BYA 15, 16
See also SATA 129
Calhoun, Don Gilmore 1914- 85-88
Calhoun, Donald W(allace) 1917- 104
Calhoun, Eric
See Turner, Robert (Harry)
Calhoun, Jackie 1936- 138
Calhoun, James Frank 1941- 109
Calhoun, John Caldwell 1782-1850 ...... DLB 3, 248
Calhoun, Mary
See Wilkins, Mary Huiskamp
See also CLR 42
See also SATA 2
Calhoun, Richard James 1926- 33-36R
Calhoun, Robert L(owery) 1896-1983
Obituary 110
Calhoun, T. B.
See Bisson, Terry (Ballantine)
Calhoun, Thomas 1940- 89-92
Calhoun, Wes
See Sadler, Jeff
Calia, Charles Laird 179
Calia, Vincent F(rank) 1926- 53-56
Calian, Carnegie Samuel 1933- 25-28R
Caliban
See Reid, J(ohn) C(owie)
Calif, Ruth 1922- 134
See also SATA 67
Califano, Joseph A(nthony), Jr. 1931- .. CANR-2
Earlier sketch in CA 45-48
Califia, Pat 1954- 133
See also GLL 1
Calimani, Riccardo 1946- 137
Calin, William (Compaine) 1936- CANR-27
Earlier sketches in CA 21-24R, CANR-11
Calinescu, George 1899-1965 .... DLB 220
See also EWL 3
Calinescu, Matei (Alexe) 1934- 131
Calinger, Ronald (Steve) 1942- 194
Calisch, Edith Lindeman 1898-1984
Obituary 114
Calisher, Hortense 1911- CANR-117
Earlier sketches in CA 1-4R, CANR-1, 22
Interview in CANR-22
See also CLC 2, 4, 8, 38, 134
See also CN 1, 2, 3, 4, 5, 6, 7
See also DA3
See also DAM NOV
See also DLB 2, 218
See also MAL 5
See also MTCW 1, 2
See also MTFW 2005
See also RGAL 4
See also RGSF 2
See also SSC 15
Calistro, Paddy
See Calistro McAuley, Patricia Ann
Calistro McAuley, Patricia Ann
1948- CANR-41
Earlier sketch in CA 118
Calitri, Charles J(oseph) 1916-1984 .. CANR-70
Earlier sketch in CA 5-8R
Calitri, Princine 33-36R
Calkin, Homer Leonard 1912-1995 ...... 41-44R
Calkin, Ruth Harms 1910- 102
Calkins, Fay
See Alailima, Fay C.
Calkins, Franklin
See Stratemeyer, Edward L.
Calkins, Lucy McCormick CANR-72
Earlier sketch in CA 125
Calkins, Mary Whiton 1863-1930 ...... DLB 270
Calkins, Robert G. 1932- 130
Calkins, Rodello 1920- 185
Brief entry 105
Call, Alice E(lizabeth) LaPlant
1914-1986 .... 13-16R
Call, Hughie Florence 1890-1969 .... CANR-70
Earlier sketch in CA 5-8R
See also SATA 1
Calladine, Andrew G(arfield) 1941- 102
Calladine, Carole E(lizabeth) 1942- 102
Callado, Antonio 1917-1997 208
See also EWL 3
Callaghan, Barry 1937- 101
Interview in CA-101
See also CP 7
Callaghan, Catherine A. 1931- 33-36R
Callaghan, Mary Rose 1944- CANR-43
Earlier sketch in CA 118
See also BYA 7
See also DLB 207
Callaghan, Morley Edward
1903-1990 .... CANR-73
Obituary 132
Earlier sketches in CA 9-12R, CANR-33
See also CLC 3, 14, 41, 65
See also CN 1, 2, 3, 4
See also DAC
See also DAM MST
See also DLB 68
See also EWL 3
See also MTCW 1, 2
See also MTFW 2005
See also RGEL 2
See also RGSF 2
See also SSFS 19
See also TCLC 145
Callaghan, Thomas 1924- 114
Callahan, Bob 1942- 138
Callahan, Charles C(lifford) 1910-1973 . CAP-2
Earlier sketch in CA 17-18
Callahan, Claire Wallis 1890-1974 .. CANR-92
Earlier sketch in CA 5-8R
Callahan, Daniel 1930- CANR-127
Earlier sketch in CA 21-24R
Callahan, David 1965(?)- 140
Callahan, Dorothy M(onahan) 1934- 114
See also SATA 39
See also SATA-Brief 35
Callahan, Gerald N. 190
Callahan, John
See Gallun, Raymond Z(inke)
Callahan, John
See Chadwick, Joseph (L.)
Callahan, John F(rancis) 1912- 33-36R
Callahan, Mary
See Randazzo, Mary Callahan
Callahan, Nelson J. 1927- 33-36R
Callahan, North 1908- CANR-72
Earlier sketches in CA 1-4R, CANR-2
Callahan, Philip Serna 1923- 102
See also SATA 25
Callahan, Raymond (Aloysius) 1938- 69-72
Callahan, S. Alice 1868-1894 ..... DLB 175, 221
See also RGAL 4
Callahan, Sidney Cornelia 1933- 17-20R
Callahan, Sterling G. 1916- 21-24R
Callahan, Steven (Patrick) 1952- 120
Callan, Edward T. 1917- 17-20R
Callan, Jamie 1954- 109
See also SATA 59
Callan, John P(atrick) 1939- 111
Callan, Richard J(erome) 1932- 53-56
Callanan, Frank 1956- 144
Callanan, Liam 229
Callander, Don 1930- 146
Callard, D(avid) A(rthur) 1950- 144
Callard, Maurice (Frederick Thomas)
1912-1993 .... CANR-3
Earlier sketch in CA 1-4R
Callard, Thomas Henry 1912- 9-12R
Callas, Theo
See McCarthy, Shaun (Lloyd)
Callaway, Ben (Anderson) 1927- 131
Callaway, Bernice (Anne) 1923- 121
See also SATA 48
Callaway, C. Wayne 1941- 138
Callaway, Joseph A(tlee) 1920- 65-68
Callaway, Kathy 1943- 107
See also SATA 36
Callaway, Trey 232
Callcott, George H(ardy) 1929- 29-32R
Callcott, Margaret Law 1929- 61-64
Callcott, Wilfrid H(ardy) 1895-1969
Obituary 112
Calle, Francisco Rosillo
See Rosillo-Calle, Francisco
Callen, Larry
See Callen, Lawrence Willard, Jr.
Callen, Lawrence Willard, Jr. 1927- . CANR-12
Earlier sketch in CA 73-76
See also SATA 19
Callen, Michael (Lane) 1955-1993 ... CANR-74
Obituary 143
Earlier sketch in CA 139
Callen, William B. 1930- 21-24R
Callenbach, Ernest 1929- CANR-21
Earlier sketches in CA 57-60, CANR-6
See also SFW 4
Callendar, Newgate
See Schonberg, Harold C(harles)
Callender, Charles 1928- 41-44R
Callender, George 1916-1992 136
Callender, Julian
See Lee, Austin
Callender, Red
See Callender, George
Callender, Wesley P(ayne), Jr. 1923- 17-20R
Calleo, David P(atrick) 1934- CANR-129
Earlier sketches in CA 17-20R, CANR-10, 31, 57
Calles, Jane F. Butel de
See de Calles, Jane F. Butel
Calley, Karin 1965- .... SATA 92
Callicott, J(ohn) Baird 1941- CANR-90
Earlier sketch in CA 135
Callihan, E(lmer) L(ee) 1903-1987 .... CAP-2
Earlier sketch in CA 25-28
Callimachus c. 305B.C.-c. 240B.C. .... AW 1
See also DLB 176
See also RGWL 2, 3
Callinan, Bernard James 1913-1995 110
Callis, Helmut G(unther) 1906- CANR-5
Earlier sketch in CA 53-56
Callis, Robert 1920- 37-40R
Callison, Brian (Richard) 1934- CANR-60
Earlier sketches in CA 29-32R, CANR-31
Callister, Frank 1916- 13-16R
Callmann, Rudolf 1892-1976 69-72
Obituary 65-68
Callow, Alexander B., Jr. 1925- 21-24R
Callow, James T(homas) 1928- 41-44R
Callow, Philip (Kenneth) 1924- CANR-73
Earlier sketches in CA 13-16R, CANR-6, 21
See also CN 2, 3, 4, 5, 6, 7
Callow, Simon 1949- CANR-87
Earlier sketch in CA 138
Calloway, Cab(ell III) 1907-1994 182
Brief entry 113
Calloway, Colin G(ordon) 1953- 135
Calloway, Doris Howes 1923-2001 ...... 21-24R
Obituary 200
Callum, Myles 1934- 9-12R
Callwood, June 1924- CANR-101
Earlier sketches in CA 101, CANR-24, 49
Calman, Alvin R(ose) 1895-1983
Obituary 110
Calman, Mel 1931-1994 126
Obituary 144
Calmann, John 1935-1980 .... 21-24R
Obituary 97-100
Calmann-Levy, Robert 1899-1982
Obituary 108
Calmenson, Stephanie 1952- CANR-118
Earlier sketches in CA 107, CANR-24
See also SATA 51, 84, 139
See also SATA-Brief 37
Calmer, Edgar 1907-1986 .... CANR-20
Obituary 118
Earlier sketch in CA 69-72
See also DLB 4
Calmer, Ned
See Calmer, Edgar
Calmus, Lawrence 1943- 111
Calnan, T(homas) D(aniel) 1915- 29-32R
Calne, Donald B. 1936- 203
Calne, Roy Yorke 1930- 61-64
Calonne, David Stephen 1953- 114
Calprenede
See La Calprenede, Gautier de Costes
Calta, Louis 1913(?)-1990
Obituary 132
Caltagirone, Carmen L(illian) 1950- 114
Calter, Paul (Arthur) 1934- CANR-57
Earlier sketches in CA 41-44R, CANR-14, 31
Calverley, Charles Stuart 1831-1884 ..... DLB 35
See also RGEL 2
Calvert, Elinor H.
See Lasell, Elinor H.
Calvert, Gene 1943- 144
Calvert, George Henry 1803-1889 .. DLB 1, 64, 248
Calvert, John
See Leaf, (Wilbur) Munro
Calvert, Laura D. 1922- 37-40R
Calvert, Monte A(lan) 1938- 21-24R
Calvert, Patricia 1931- CANR-114
Earlier sketches in CA 105, CANR-21
See also AAYA 18
See also BYA 7
See also JRDA
See also MAICYA 1, 2
See also MAICYAS 1
See also SAAS 17
See also SATA 45, 69, 132
See also YAW
Calvert, Peter (Anthony Richard)
1936- CANR-71
Earlier sketches in CA 25-28R, CANR-11
Calvert, Robert, Jr. 1922- 25-28R
Calvert, Theodora 1898-1988
Obituary 128
Calverton, V. F.
See Goetz, George
See also DLB 303
Calvez, Jean-Yves 1927- 57-60
Calvin, Henry
See Hanley, Clifford (Leonard Clark)
Calvin, Jean
See Calvin, John
See also GFL Beginnings to 1789
Calvin, John 1509-1564
See Calvin, Jean
Calvin, Melvin 1911-1997 155
Calvin, Ross 1890(?)-1970
Obituary 101
Calvin, William H(oward) 1939- CANR-98
Earlier sketch in CA 123

Calvino 90 CONTEMPORARY AUTHORS

Calvino, Italo 1923-1985 ... CANR-132
Obituary ... 116
Earlier sketches in CA 85-88, CANR-23, 61
See also AAYA 58
See also CLC 5, 8, 11, 22, 33, 39, 73
See also DAM NOV
See also DLB 196
See also EW 13
See also EWL 3
See also MTCW 1, 2
See also MTFW 2005
See also RGSF 2
See also RGWL 2, 3
See also SFW 4
See also SSC 3, 48
See also SSFS 12
See also WLIT 7
Calvo, Lino Novas
See Novas Calvo, Lino
Calvocoressi, Peter (John Ambrose)
1912- ... CANR-81
Earlier sketch in CA 65-68
Cam, Helen Maud 1885-1968 ... CAP-1
Earlier sketch in CA 13-14
Camaiti Hostert, Anna 1949- ... 178
Camaj, Martin 1925-1992 ... EWL 3
Camara, Helder Pessoa 1909-1999 ... 61-64
Obituary ... 183
Camara Laye
See Laye, Camara
See also EWL 3
Camarillo, Albert (M.) 1948- ... 132
Camarillo, Alberto
See Camarillo, Albert (M.)
Camazine, S(cott) 1952- ... 129
Cambaceres, Eugenio 1843-1889 ... LAW
Camber, Andrew
See Bingley, David Ernest
Cambie, R(ichard) C(onrad) 1931- ... 143
Cambon, Glauco (Gianlorenzo)
1921-1988 ... CANR-7
Obituary ... 125
Earlier sketch in CA 17-20R
Cambridge, A Gentleman of the University of
See Crowley, Edward Alexander
Cambridge, Ada ... DLB 230
Camburn, Carol A.
See Camburn-Bracalente, Carol A.
Camburn-Bracalente, Carol A. 1962- . SATA 118
Camden, Archie 1888-1979 ... 114
Camden, William 1551-1623 ... DLB 172
Cameja, Pedro
See Camejo, Peter (Miguel)
Camejo, Pedro
See Camejo, Peter (Miguel)
Camejo, Pedro M.
See Camejo, Peter (Miguel)
Camejo, Peter (Miguel) 1939- ... 125
Brief entry ... 105
Camerini, Mario 1895-1981
Obituary ... 103
Cameron, A(rchibald) J(ames) 1920- ... 73-76
Cameron, Alan (Douglas Edward)
1938- ... CANR-8
Earlier sketch in CA 61-64
Cameron, Alexander
See Gibson, Alexander Cameron
Cameron, Allan Gillies 1930- ... 102
Cameron, Allan W(illiams) 1938- ... 33-36R
Cameron, Angus de Mille 1913-1996 ... 102
Cameron, Angus Fraser 1941-1983 ... 122
Obituary ... 109
Cameron, Ann 1943- ... CANR-108
Earlier sketches in CA 101, CANR-57
See also AAYA 59
See also MAICYA 2
See also MAICYAS 1
See also SAAS 20
See also SATA 27, 89, 129
Cameron, (Barbara) Anne 1938- ... 136
Cameron, Berl
See Glasby, John S.
Cameron, Betsy 1949- ... 101
Cameron, (Jack) Bruce 1913-1979 ... 1-4R
Obituary ... 133
Cameron, Carey 1952- ... 135
See also CLC 59
Cameron, Caryn
See Harper, Karen
Cameron, Catherine M(ary) ... 175
Cameron, Charla
See Skinner, Gloria Dale
Cameron, Christian 1962- ... 234
Cameron, Constance Carpenter 1937- ... 49-52
Cameron, D. A.
See Cameron, Donald (Allan)
Cameron, D. Y.
See Cook, Dorothy Mary
Cameron, David R(obertson) 1941- ... 73-76
Cameron, Deborah 1958- ... CANR-53
Earlier sketch in CA 126
Cameron, Donald
See Bryans, Robert Harbinson
Cameron, Donald (Allan) 1937- ... CANR-8
Earlier sketch in CA 21-24R
Cameron, Edna M. 1905-1999 ... CAP-1
Earlier sketch in CA 9-10
See also SATA 3
Cameron, Eleanor (Frances)
1912-1996 ... CANR-22
Obituary ... 154
Earlier sketches in CA 1-4R, CANR-2
See also BYA 3, 5
See also CLR 1, 72
See also DLB 52
See also JRDA
See also MAICYA 1, 2
See also MAICYAS 1
See also MTCW 1
See also SAAS 10
See also SATA 1, 25
See also SATA-Obit 93
See also YAW
Cameron, Eleanor Cranston ... 118
Cameron, Eleanor Elford 1910-1981 ... 77-80
Cameron, Elizabeth
See Nowell, Elizabeth Cameron
Cameron, Elizabeth Jane 1910-1976 .. CANR-1
Obituary ... 69-72
Earlier sketch in CA 1-4R
See also CWRI 5
See also SATA 32
See also SATA-Obit 30
Cameron, Elspeth 1943- ... 113
Cameron, Frank T. 1909-1984 ... CAP-1
Earlier sketch in CA 19-20
Cameron, George Frederick
1854-1885 ... DLB 99
Cameron, George Glenn 1905-1979
Obituary ... 89-92
Cameron, Harold W. 1905-1986 ... 81-84
Cameron, Hope
See Morritt, Hope
Cameron, Ian
See Payne, Donald Gordon
Cameron, J(ames) M(unro)
1910-1995 ... CANR-2
Earlier sketch in CA 5-8R
Cameron, (Mark) James (Walter)
1911-1985 ... CANR-73
Obituary ... 114
Earlier sketch in CA 21-24R
Cameron, James 1954- ... CANR-71
Earlier sketch in CA 137
See also AAYA 9, 27
See also CCA 1
Cameron, James R(eese) 1929- ... 33-36R
Cameron, James Sorel
See Sorel-Cameron, James (Robert)
Cameron, John 1914-2003 ... 29-32R
Obituary ... 222
Cameron, Joy 1912- ... 132
Cameron, Julia ... 217
Cameron, Julie
See Cameron, Lou
Cameron, Kate
See Du Breuil, (Elizabeth) L(or)inda and McGlamry, Beverly
Cameron, Kenneth 1922-2001 ... 103
Obituary ... 194
Cameron, Kenneth M. 1931- ... 129
Cameron, Kenneth Neill
1908-1994 ... CANR-81
Obituary ... 144
Earlier sketches in CA 9-12R, CANR-3
Cameron, Kenneth Walter 1908- ... CANR-49
Earlier sketches in CA 21-24R, CANR-8, 24
Cameron, Kim S(terling) 1946- ... 109
Cameron, Lorna
See Fraser, Anthea
Cameron, Lou 1924- ... CANR-101
Earlier sketches in CA 1-4R, CANR-4, 21
See also TCWW 1, 2
Cameron, Louis
See Cameron, Lou
Cameron, Lucy Lyttelton 1781-1858 .. DLB 163
Cameron, M(alcolm) G(ordon) Graham
See Graham-Cameron, M(alcolm) G(ordon)
Cameron, M. Graham
See Graham-Cameron, M(alcolm) G(ordon)
Cameron, M(alcolm) L(aurence) 1918- ... 146
Cameron, Mary Owen 1915- ... 13-16R
Cameron, Maxwell A. 1961- ... 151
Cameron, Meribeth E(lliott) 1905-1997 ... 1-4R
Obituary ... 159
Cameron, Mike Graham
See Graham-Cameron, M(alcolm) G(ordon)
Cameron, Neil 1920-1985
Obituary ... 115
Cameron, (John) Norman 1905-1953 .. BRWS 9
See also RGEL 2
Cameron, Peter 1959- ... CANR-117
Earlier sketches in CA 125, CANR-50
See also AMWS 12
See also CLC 44
See also DLB 234
See also GLL 2
Cameron, Polly 1928- ... 17-20R
See also SATA 2
Cameron, Roderick (William)
1913-1985 ... CANR-72
Obituary ... 117
Brief entry ... 113
Cameron, Rondo (Emmett) 1925- ... CANR-5
Earlier sketch in CA 1-4R
Cameron, Scott 1962- ... SATA 84
Cameron, Sharon 1947- ... 123
Cameron, Silver Donald
See Cameron, Donald (Allan)
Cameron, Stella ... 193
Cameron, Sue 1944- ... 171
Cameron, Theresa 1954- ... 209
Cameron, William Bleasdell 1862-1951 ... 177
See also DLB 99
Cameron, William Bruce 1920- ... 37-40R
Cameron, William J(ames) 1926-
Brief entry ... 116
Cameron Watt, Donald 1928- ... CANR-14
Earlier sketch in CA 77-80
Camille, Michael 1958-2002 ... 137
Obituary ... 209
Camilleri, Andrea 1925- ... 217
See also WLIT 7
Camilleri, Joseph A. 1944- ... CANR-41
Earlier sketch in CA 117
Caminada, Jerome (Charles) 1911-1985
Obituary ... 117
Caminals-Heath, Roser 1956- ... 137
Camm, John 1718-1778 ... DLB 31
Cammack, Floyd M(cKee) 1933- ... CANR-6
Earlier sketch in CA 9-12R
Cammann, Schuyler (van Rensselaer)
1912-1991 ... 9-12R
Cammarata, Jerry F(rank) 1947- ... 81-84
Cammer, Leonard 1913-1979 ... 65-68
Cammermeyer, Margarethe 1942- ... 152
Camner, James 1950- ... 108
Camnitzer, Luis 1937- ... 152
Camoens, Luis Vaz de 1524(?)-1580
See Camoes, Luis de
See also EW 2
Camoes, Luis de 1524(?)-1580
See Camoens, Luis Vaz de
See also DLB 287
See also HLCS 1
See also PC 31
See also RGWL 2, 3
Camoin, Francois Andre 1939- ... 61-64
Camon, Ferdinando 1935- ... DLB 196
Camp, Candace (Pauline) 1949- ... CANR-116
Earlier sketches in CA 102, CANR-42
Camp, Charles L. 1893-1975
Obituary ... 61-64
See also SATA-Obit 31
Camp, Dalton Kingsley 1920- ... 61-64
Camp, Fred V(alterma) 1911-1986 ... 49-52
Camp, Helen C(ollier) 1939- ... 152
Camp, James 1923- ... 33-36R
Camp, Joe
See Camp, Joseph Shelton, Jr.
Camp, John (Michael Francis) 1915- ... 93-96
Camp, John (Roswell) 1944- ... CANR-134
Earlier sketches in CA 138, CANR-98
See also MTFW 2005
Camp, Joseph Shelton, Jr. 1939- ... 129
Camp, Lindsay 1957- ... SATA 133
Camp, Robert C. 1935- ... 150
Camp, Roderic (Ai) 1945- ... CANR-41
Earlier sketches in CA 102, CANR-18
Camp, T(homas) Edward 1929- ... 13-16R
Camp, Walter (Chauncey) 1859-1925 ... 200
See also DLB 241
See also YABC 1
Camp, Wesley D(ouglass) 1915- ... 17-20R
Camp, William (Newton Alexander)
1926-2002 ... 61-64
Obituary ... 205
Campa, Arthur L(eon) 1905-1978 ... CANR-40
Obituary ... 171
Earlier sketch in CA 73-76
See also HW 1
Campa, Arturo Leon
See Campa, Arthur L(eon)
Campagna, Palmiro 1954- ... 225
Campaigne, Jameson Gilbert 1914-1985 .. 1-4R
Obituary ... 114
Campana, Dino 1885-1932
Brief entry ... 117
See also DLB 114
See also EWL 3
See also TCLC 20
Campana, Richard J(ohn) 1918- ... 199
Campanella, Francis B. 1936- ... 53-56
Campanella, Tommaso 1568-1639 . RGWL 2, 3
Campanile, Archille 1900(?)-1977
Obituary ... 69-72
Campanile, Pasquale Festa
See Festa Campanile, Pasquale
Campbell, A. C.
See Campbell, Andrew C.
Campbell, Alan K(eith) 1923-1998 ... CANR-3
Obituary ... 164
Earlier sketch in CA 5-8R
Campbell, Alasdair Iain
See Hamilton, Iain (Bertram)
Campbell, Albert A.
See Campbell, (Albert) Angus
Campbell, Alexander 1912-1977 ... 61-64
Obituary ... 69-72
Campbell, Alexandra 1954- ... 203
Campbell, Alistair 1907-1974 ... CAP-1
Earlier sketch in CA 17-18
Campbell, Alistair (Te Ariki) 1925- ... CP 1, 2, 3, 4, 5, 6, 7
See also RGEL 2
Campbell, Alla (Linda Renee) Bozarth
See Bozarth-Campbell, Alla (Linda Renee)
Campbell, (Elizabeth) Andrea 1963- ... SATA 50
Campbell, Andrea S. 1949- ... 221
Campbell, Andrew C. 1923-
Brief entry ... 114
Campbell, Angus
See Chetwynd-Hayes, R(onald Henry Glynn)
Campbell, (Albert) Angus 1910-1980 ... 129
Obituary ... 105
Campbell, Ann R. 1925- ... 21-24R
See also SATA 11
Campbell, Archibald Bruce 1881-1966 . CAP-1
Earlier sketch in CA 13-16
Campbell, Arnold Everitt 1906-1980
Obituary ... 108
Campbell, Arthur A(ndrews) 1924- ... CANR-43
Earlier sketch in CA 1-4R
Campbell, Ballard Crooker, Jr.
1940- ... CANR-135
Earlier sketch in CA 104
Campbell, Beatrice Murphy
See Murphy, Beatrice M.
Campbell, Beatrix 1947- ... 138
Campbell, Bebe Moore 1950- ... CANR-134
Earlier sketches in CA 139, CANR-81
See also AAYA 26
See also BW 2, 3
See also DLB 227
See also MTCW 2
See also MTFW 2005
Campbell, Bernard G(rant) 1930- ... 21-24R
Campbell, Bill 1960- ... SATA 89
Campbell, Blanche 1902-1977 ... 5-8R
Campbell, Bonnie Jo 1962- ... 187
Campbell, Bruce
See Epstein, Samuel
Campbell, Bruce 1958- ... 214
Campbell, Camilla 1905-1992 ... CANR-72
Earlier sketches in CAP-2, CA 25-28
See also SATA 26
Campbell, Carlos Cardozo 1937- ... 102
Campbell, Carole R. 1939- ... 196
See also SATA 125
Campbell, Charles Arthur 1897-1974
Obituary ... 49-52
Campbell, Charles S(outter) 1911- ... 69-72
Campbell, Christopher 1951- ... 231
Campbell, Christy
See Campbell, Christopher
Campbell, Clarice (Marjorie) T(hompson)
1907-2000 ... 166
Campbell, Claude 1929- ... 228
Campbell, Cliff
See Heckelmann, Charles N(ewman)
Campbell, Clive
See MacRae, Donald G.
Campbell, Clyde Crane
See Gold, H(orace) L(eonard)
Campbell, Colin Dearborn 1917- ... 33-36R
Campbell, Cy(ril Calvin) 1925- ... 97-100
Campbell, D(onald)
See Gilford, C(harles) B(ernard)
Campbell, D(onald) Ross 1939- ... 117
Campbell, Dan H(ampton) 1907-1974
Obituary ... 112
Campbell, David (Watt Ian)
1915-1979 ... 97-100
See also CP 1, 2
See also DLB 260
Campbell, David 1961- ... 146
Campbell, David A(itken) 1927- ... CANR-11
Earlier sketch in CA 25-28R
Campbell, David (John) Graham
See Graham-Campbell, David (John)
Campbell, David P. 1934- ... 21-24R
Campbell, Dennis M(arion) 1945- ... 73-76
Campbell, Don(ald Guy) 1922-1991 ... 17-20R
Obituary ... 135
Campbell, Donald 1940- ... CANR-56
Earlier sketches in CA 69-72, CANR-30
See also CP 2
Campbell, Donald E. 1943- ... 138
Campbell, Drusilla ... 227
Campbell, Duane E(ugene) 1941- ... 116
Campbell, E(lwood) G(ordon) 1923- ... 107
Campbell, E. Simms 1906-1971
Obituary ... 93-96
Campbell, Eddie 1955- ... 224
Campbell, Edward D(unscomb) C(hristian), Jr.
1946- ... CANR-26
Earlier sketch in CA 106
Campbell, Edward F(ay), Jr. 1932- ... 13-16R
Campbell, Elizabeth McClure
1891-1989 ... 37-40R
Campbell, Enid (Mona) 1932- ... 109
Campbell, Eric 1941- ... 239
Campbell, Ernest Q(ueener) 1926- ... 37-40R
Campbell, Eugene Edward 1915- ... 21-24R
Campbell, Ewing 1940- ... CANR-53
Earlier sketches in CA 73-76, CANR-13, 29
Campbell, F(enton) Gregory, Jr. 1939- ... 69-72
Campbell, Francis Stuart
See Kuehnelt-Leddihn, Erik (Maria) Ritter von
Campbell, G(aylon) S(anford) 1940- ... 107
Campbell, George ... CP 1
Campbell, George F(rederick)
1915- ... CANR-14
Earlier sketch in CA 65-68
Campbell, Georgia Arianna Ziadie 1949- ... 140
Campbell, Graeme 1931- ... 77-80
Campbell, Hannah ... 9-12R
Campbell, Herbert James 1925- ... 97-100
Campbell, Hope 1925- ... CANR-10
Earlier sketch in CA 61-64
See also SATA 20
Campbell, Howard E(rnest) 1925- ... CANR-7
Earlier sketch in CA 57-60
Campbell, Hugh 1930- ... SATA 90
Campbell, Ian 1899-1978 ... 53-56
Obituary ... 103
Campbell, Ian 1942- ... CANR-25
Earlier sketches in CA 65-68, CANR-9
Campbell, J(ames) Arthur 1916- ... 53-56
Campbell, Jack K(enagy) 1927- ... 21-24R
Campbell, James (M.) ... 239
Campbell, James 1920- ... 57-60
Campbell, James B. 1944- ... 165
Campbell, James Dykes 1838-1895 ... DLB 144
Campbell, James E(dward) 1945- ... 107
Campbell, James Edwin 1867-1896 ... DLB 50
Campbell, James Howard 1928-1998 ... 113

Cumulative Index 91 Cann

Campbell, James Marshall 1895-1977 73-76
Obituary 69-72
Campbell, Jane
See Edwards, Jane Campbell
Campbell, Jane 1934- 41-44R
Campbell, Janet Bruce 1955- 121
Campbell, (Mary) Jean 1943- 115
Campbell, Jeff(erson) H(olland) 1931- ... 41-44R
Campbell, Jeffrey
See Black, Campbell
Campbell, Jeremy 1931- CANR-113
Earlier sketches in CA 109, CANR-29
Interview in CANR-29
Campbell, Jim
See Campbell, James Howard
Campbell, Jo Ann (L.) 1958- 157
Campbell, Joan 1929- 109
Campbell, Joanna
See Bly, Carol(yn)
Campbell, John 1653-1728 ..... DLB 43
Campbell, John 1947- CANR-82
Earlier sketches in CA 114, CANR-35
Campbell, John 1956- 149
Campbell, John Coert 1911-2000 ..... CANR-3
Obituary 188
Earlier sketch in CA 1-4R
Campbell, John Creighton 1941- 111
Campbell, John Franklin 1940(?)-1971
Obituary 33-36R
Campbell, John Lorne 1906- 29-32R
Campbell, John R(oy) 1933- 53-56
Campbell, John W(ood, Jr.)
1910-1971 ..... CANR-34
Obituary 29-32R
Earlier sketches in CAP-2, CA 21-22
See also CLC 32
See also DLB 8
See also MTCW 1
See also SCFW 1, 2
See also SFW 4
Campbell, Joseph 1904-1987 ..... CANR-107
Obituary 124
Earlier sketches in CA 1-4R, CANR-3, 28, 61
See also AAYA 3, 66
See also BEST 89:2
See also CLC 69
See also DA3
See also MTCW 1, 2
See also TCLC 140
Campbell, Judith
See Pares, Marion (Stapylton)
Campbell, Julie
See Tatham, Julie Campbell
Campbell, Karen
See Beaty, Betty
Campbell, Karlyn Kohrs 1937- CANR-39
Earlier sketches in CA 53-56, CANR-4, 18
Campbell, Katie 1957- 136
Campbell, Keith 1938- CANR-102
Earlier sketch in CA 106
Campbell, Keith Oliver 1920- 110
Campbell, Ken 1941- 77-80
Campbell, Ken M. 1940- 198
Campbell, Kenneth 1901(?)-1979
Obituary 85-88
Campbell, Lady Colin
See Campbell, Georgia Arianna Ziadie
Campbell, Laurence R(andolph)
1903-1987 126
Campbell, Lawrence James 1931- 106
Campbell, Litta Belle 1886-1980 ..... CANR-5
Earlier sketch in CA 5-8R
Campbell, Louisa D. 1958- 121
Campbell, Louisa Dresser 1907-1989
Obituary 129
Campbell, Luke
See Madison, Thomas A(lvin)
Campbell, Malcolm J(ames) 1930- ... CANR-21
Earlier sketches in CA 57-60, CANR-6
Campbell, Margaret 69-72
Campbell, (Gabrielle) Margaret (Vere)
1886-1952
Brief entry 116
See also Bowen, Marjorie and
Shearing, Joseph
See also HGG
See also RHW
Campbell, Margaret 1916- 106
Campbell, Maria 1940- CANR-54
Earlier sketch in CA 102
See also CCA 1
See also CLC 85
See also DAC
See also NNAL
Campbell, Marion 1919- 162
Campbell, Marion (May) 1948- ..... CN 5, 6, 7
Campbell, Marjorie Wilkins 97-100
Campbell, Mary B(aine) 1954- 136
Campbell, Matthew (J. B.) 1962- 191
Campbell, Mavis C. CANR-119
Earlier sketch in CA 148
Campbell, Michael Mussen 1924-1984 102
Obituary 113
Campbell, Oscar James, Jr. 1879-1970
Obituary 29-32R
Campbell, Patricia J(ean) 1930- CANR-86
Earlier sketches in CA 103, CANR-35
See also SATA 45
Campbell, Patricia Piatt 1901-1976 ..... 25-28R
Campbell, Patrick Gordon 1913-1980
Obituary 102
Campbell, Patty
See Campbell, Patricia J(ean)
Campbell, Paul N. 1923- 21-24R
Campbell, Penelope 1935- 33-36R
Campbell, Peter (Walter) 1926- CANR-11
Earlier sketches in CAP-1, CA 13-14
Campbell, Peter A. 1948- CANR-137
Earlier sketch in CA 167
See also SATA 99
Campbell, Peter Anthony 1935- 21-24R
Campbell, R. T.
See Todd, Ruthven
Campbell, R. W.
See Campbell, Rosemae Wells
Campbell, R(obert) Wayne 1941- 167
Campbell, R(obert) Wright
1927-2000 ..... CANR-60
Obituary 189
Earlier sketches in CA 57-60, CANR-6, 21, 24
See also CMW 4
See also DLB 306
Campbell, (John) Ramsey 1946- 228
Earlier sketches in CA 57-60, CANR-7, 102
Interview in CANR-7
Autobiographical Essay in 228
See also AAYA 51
See also CLC 42
See also DLB 261
See also HGG
See also SSC 19
See also SUFW 1, 2
Campbell, Randolph B(luford)
1940- CANR-143
Earlier sketch in CA 41-44R
Campbell, Rebecca 1967- 238
Campbell, Rex R. 1931- 41-44R
Campbell, Rhonda 1962- 167
See also BW 3
Campbell, Rita Ricardo
See Ricardo-Campbell, Rita
Campbell, Robert
See Campbell, R(obert) Wright
Campbell, Robert 1922-1977 ..... CANR-8
Obituary 73-76
Earlier sketch in CA 53-56
Campbell, Robert B(lair) 1923- 69-72
Campbell, Robert C(harles) 1924- 49-52
Campbell, Robert Dale 1914-1993 ..... 9-12R
Campbell, Robert Wellington 1926- ... CANR-3
Earlier sketch in CA 1-4R
Campbell, Robin
See Strachan, Ian
Campbell, Rod 1945- 155
See also SATA 51, 98
See also SATA-Brief 44
Campbell, Rosemae Wells 1909- 13-16R
See also SATA 1
Campbell, (Ignatius) Roy (Dunnachie)
1901-1957 155
Brief entry 104
See also AFW
See also DLB 20, 225
See also EWL 3
See also MTCW 2
See also RGEL 2
See also TCLC 5
Campbell, Sandra 1946- 230
Campbell, Sheldon 1919- 41-44R
Campbell, Sid 1944- CANR-48
Earlier sketch in CA 118
Campbell, Siobhan 1962- 171
Campbell, Stanley W(allace) 1926- 49-52
Campbell, Stephen K(ent) 1935- 49-52
Campbell, Thomas 1777-1844 ..... DLB 93, 144
See also RGEL 2
Campbell, Thomas E.
See Campbell, Tom
Campbell, Thomas F. 1924- 21-24R
Campbell, Thomas M(oody)
1936-1993 ..... CANR-53
Obituary 142
Earlier sketch in CA 49-52
Campbell, Tom 1938- 150
Campbell, Tom D. 1938- CANR-112
Earlier sketches in CA 126, CANR-54
Campbell, Tracy (A.) 1962- 146
Campbell, Wallace Justin 1910-1998 135
Obituary 163
Campbell, Wilfred
See Campbell, William
See also TCLC 9
Campbell, Will D(avis) 1924- CANR-130
Earlier sketches in CA 5-8R, CANR-7, 22, 45
See also CSW
Campbell, William 1858(?)-1918
Brief entry 106
See also Campbell, Wilfred
See also DLB 92
Campbell, William Edward March 1893-1954
Brief entry 108
See also March, William
Campbell-Culver, Maggie 211
Campbell-Johnson, Alan 1913-1998 65-68
Campbell-Kelly, Martin 1945- 217
Campbell-Purdie, Wendy 1925- 21-24R
Campen, Richard N(ewman) 1912-1997 . 69-72
Camper, Carol 1954- 149
Camper, Shirley
See Soman, Shirley Camper
Campert, Remco Wouter 1929- 192
Camping, Harold 1921- 205
Campion, Anna 1952- 190
Campion, Dan(iel Ray) 1949- 157
Campion, Donald Richard 1921-1988
Obituary 128
Campion, Edmund 1539-1581 ..... DLB 167
Campion, Jane 1954- CANR-87
Earlier sketch in CA 138
See also AAYA 33
See also CLC 95
Campion, Joan 1940- 124
Campion, Nardi Reeder 1917- CANR-6
Earlier sketch in CA 1-4R
See also SATA 22
Campion, Nicholas 1953- 162
Campion, Rosamond
See Rosmond, Babette
Campion, Sidney R(onald) 1891-1978 .. CAP-1
Earlier sketch in CA 9-10
Campion, Thomas 1567-1620 ... CDBLB Before 1660
See also DAM POET
See also DLB 58, 172
See also RGEL 2
Camplin, Jamie (Robert) 1947- 97-100
Campling, Christopher R(ussell) 1925- 113
Campling, Elizabeth 1948- 123
See also SATA 53
Campo, Rafael 1964- 193
See also DLB 282
See also GLL 2
See also LLW
Campobello, Nellie (Francisca Ernestina)
1912-1986 131
See also HW 1
Campolo, Anthony, Jr. 1935- CANR-107
Earlier sketches in CA 69-72, CANR-11, 26
Campolo, Tony
See Campolo, Anthony, Jr.
Campos, Augusto de 1931- 218
Campos, Paul F. 1959- 172
Campoy, F. Isabel (Coronado) 1946- 215
See also SATA 143
Camps, Arnulf (P. H. J. M.) 1925- CANR-86
Earlier sketch in CA 131
Camps, Francis Edward 1905-1972 ..... 37-40R
Camps, Luis 1928- ..... SATA 66
Campton, David 1924- CANR-47
Earlier sketches in CA 5-8R, CANR-5, 20
See also CBD
See also CD 5, 6
See also DLB 245
Camus, Albert 1913-1960 ..... CANR-131
Earlier sketch in CA 89-92
See also AAYA 36
See also AFW
See also BPFB 1
See also CLC 1, 2, 4, 9, 11, 14, 32, 63, 69, 124
See also DA
See also DA3
See also DAB
See also DAC
See also DAM DRAM, MST, NOV
See also DC 2
See also DLB 72, 321
See also EW 13
See also EWL 3
See also EXPN
See also EXPS
See also GFL 1789 to the Present
See also LATS 1:2
See also LMFS 2
See also MTCW 1, 2
See also MTFW 2005
See also NFS 6, 16
See also RGSF 2
See also RGWL 2, 3
See also SSC 9, 76
See also SSFS 4
See also TWA
See also WLC
Camus, Jean-Pierre 1584-1652 ..... DLB 268
Camus, Raoul Francois 1930- 65-68
Camus, (Jean) Renaud (Gabriel) 1946- 108
Camuti, Louis J(oseph) 1893-1981 101
Obituary 103
Canada, Geoffrey 1954- 165
Canada, Lena 1942- 93-96
Canaday, John E(dwin) 1907-1985 ... CANR-79
Obituary 116
Earlier sketches in CA 13-16R, CANR-7
See also CMW 4
Canales, Nemesio R. 1878-1923 194
Canales, Viola 1957- 212
See also SATA 141
Canan, James William 1929- 61-64
Canan, Janine 1942- 181
Autobiographical Essay in 181
Canary
See Conn, Canary Denise
Canary, Robert H(ughes) 1939- CANR-11
Earlier sketch in CA 29-32R
Canavaggio, Jean (Francois) 1936- .. CANR-113
Earlier sketch in CA 167
Canavan, Francis 1917- 118
Canaway, W(illiam) H(amilton) 1925- 93-96
See also CN 1, 2, 3
Canby, C. C.
See Jackson, Sid J.
Canby, Courtlandt 1914- 118
Canby, Henry Seidel 1878-1961 179
Obituary 89-92
See also DLB 91
Canby, Vincent 1924-2000 81-84
Obituary 191
See also CLC 13
Cancale
See Desnos, Robert
Cancellare, Frank 1910-1985
Obituary 116
Cancian, Francesca M(icaela) 1937- 57-60
Cancian, Francis Alexander 1934- CANR-7
Earlier sketch in CA 53-56
Cancian, Frank
See Cancian, Francis Alexander
Candelaria, Cordelia (Chavez) 1943- 131
See also DLB 82
See also HW 1
Candelaria, Frederick (Henry) 1929- 17-20R
Candelaria, Nash 1928- CANR-72
Earlier sketches in CA 69-72, CANR-11, 32
See also DLB 82
See also HW 1, 2
Candell, Victor 1903-1977 ..... SATA-Obit 24
can der Alm, Aart
See Donkersloot, Nicolaas-Anthonie
Candida
See Hoffman, Lisa
Candilis, Wray O. 1927- CANR-10
Earlier sketch in CA 25-28R
Candis, Judy 239
Candisky, Catherine A. 1961- 144
Candland, Douglas Keith 1934- CANR-2
Earlier sketch in CA 5-8R
Candler, Julie 1919- 65-68
Candler, Warren A(kin) 1857-1941 215
Candlin, Enid Saunders 1909- CANR-1
Earlier sketch in CA 45-48
Candy, Edward
See Neville, B(arbara) Alison (Boodson)
Candy, John (Franklin) 1950-1994 155
Candy, Philip C(arne) 1950- 140
Cane, Melville (Henry) 1879-1980 ... CANR-72
Obituary 97-100
Earlier sketches in CA 1-4R, CANR-6, 8
Canellopoulos, Panayiotis 1902-1986
Obituary 120
Canemaker, John 1943- CANR-122
Earlier sketch in CA 81-84
Caner, Mary Paul 1893-1985 ..... CAP-2
Earlier sketch in CA 21-22
Canetti, Elias 1905-1994 ..... CANR-79
Obituary 146
Earlier sketches in CA 21-24R, CANR-23, 61
See also CDWLB 2
See also CLC 3, 14, 25, 75, 86
See also CWW 2
See also DA3
See also DLB 85, 124
See also EW 12
See also EWL 3
See also MTCW 1, 2
See also MTFW 2005
See also RGWL 2, 3
See also TCLC 157
See also TWA
Caney, Steven 1941- 104
Canfield, Cass 1897-1986 ..... CANR-75
Obituary 118
Earlier sketch in CA 41-44R
Canfield, (Fayette) Curtis 1903-1986
Obituary 120
Canfield, D(elos) Lincoln 1903-1991 .... 25-28R
Canfield, Dorothea F.
See Fisher, Dorothy (Frances) Canfield
Canfield, Dorothea Frances
See Fisher, Dorothy (Frances) Canfield
Canfield, Dorothy
See Fisher, Dorothy (Frances) Canfield
Canfield, Gae Whitney 1931- 113
Canfield, J. Douglas 1941- 191
Canfield, Jack 1944- CANR-108
Earlier sketch in CA 159
Canfield, James D(avid) 1937- 117
Canfield, James K(eith) 1925- 25-28R
Canfield, James Lewis 1942- 121
Canfield, Jane White 1897-1984 ..... CANR-76
Obituary 112
Earlier sketch in CA 109
See also SATA 32
See also SATA-Obit 38
Canfield, John A(lan) 1941- 37-40R
Canfield, Kenneth French 1909- CAP-1
Earlier sketch in CA 13-16
Canfield, Leon Hardy 1886-1980 ..... 1-4R
Canfield, Muriel 1935- 115
See also SATA 94
Canfield, Sandra (Kay Patterson) 1944- 146
Canfora, Luciano 1942- 177
Cang, Joel 1899-1974 ..... CAP-2
Earlier sketch in CA 29-32
Cangemi, Sister Marie Lucita 1920- 21-24R
Canham, Erwin D(ain) 1904-1982 .... CANR-76
Obituary 105
Earlier sketches in CAP-1, CA 13-14
See also DLB 127
Canham, Kingsley 1945- 57-60
Canham, Marsha 201
Caniff, Milton (Arthur) 1907-1988 .. CANR-141
Obituary 125
Earlier sketches in CA 85-88, CANR-47
See also AAYA 55
See also AITN 1
See also SATA-Obit 58
Canin, Ethan 1960- 135
Brief entry 131
See also CLC 55
See also MAL 5
See also SSC 70
Canine, Craig 234
Canino, Frank 1939(?)- 207
Canitz, Friedrich Rudolph Ludwig von
1654-1699 ..... DLB 168
Cankar, Ivan 1876-1918 ..... CDWLB 4
See also DLB 147
See also EWL 3
See also TCLC 105
Cann, Helen 1969- ..... SATA 124
Cann, Jack
See Cann, John P.
Cann, John P. 1941- 174

Cann, Kate 1954- CANR-136
Earlier sketch in CA 170
See also SATA 103, 152
Cann, Marjorie Mitchell 1924- 89-92
Cannadine, David 1950- CANR-110
Earlier sketch in CA 151
Cannam, Peggie 1925- 13-16R
Cannan, Denis 1919- CANR-68
Earlier sketches in CA 57-60, CANR-7
See also CBD
Cannan, Gilbert E. 1884-1955
Brief entry 111
See also DLB 10, 197
Cannan, Joanna
See Pullein-Thompson, Joanna Maxwell
See also DLB 191
See also SATA 82
Cannell, Charles (Henry) 1882-1947 155
See also Vivian, E. Charles
See also FANT
Cannell, Dorothy (Reddish) 1943- .. CANR-135
Earlier sketch in CA 165
See also CMW 4
Cannell, Kathleen Biggar (Eaton)
1891-1974 106
See also DLB 4
Cannell, (Humberston) Skipwith, Jr.
1887-1957 200
Cannell, Skipwith 1887-1957 .... DLB 45
Cannell, Stephen J(oseph) 1941- CANR-105
Earlier sketch in CA 138
Canney, Donald L. 1947- 147
Canning, George 1770-1827 .... DLB 158
Canning, Jeff(rey Michael) 1947- 73-76
Canning, John 1920- 89-92
Canning, Paul 1947- 126
Canning, Peter 1937- 159
Canning, Ray R(ussell) 1920- 41-44R
Canning, Victor 1911-1986 .... CANR-63
Obituary 118
Earlier sketches in CA 13-16R, CANR-6
See also CMW 4
Cannistraro, Philip V(incent) 1942- 141
Cannold, Leslie 1965- 197
Cannon, A(nn) E(dwards) 239
See also SATA 93, 163
Cannon, Alexander 1896-1963(?)
Obituary 111
Cannon, Beth 1951- 69-72
Cannon, Bettie (Waddell) 1922- 126
See also SATA 59
Cannon, Bill
See Cannon, William S.
Cannon, C. W. 1966- 220
Cannon, Cornelia (James) 1876-1969
Obituary 109
See also SATA-Brief 28
Cannon, Curt
See Hunter, Evan
Cannon, David Wadsworth, Jr. 1911-1938 . 155
See also BW 2
Cannon, Devereaux D(unlap), Jr. 1954- 175
Cannon, Dolores Eilene 1931- 166
Cannon, Dyan 1937- 167
Cannon, Eileen E(mily) 1948- CANR-141
Earlier sketch in CA 165
See also SATA 119
Cannon, Frank
See Mayhar, Ardath
Cannon, Garland (Hampton) 1924- .. CANR-57
Earlier sketches in CA 33-36R, CANR-13, 30
Cannon, George Q.
See Cannon, Frank(lin) J(enne)
Cannon, George Q(uayle) 1827-1901 218
Cannon, Grant Groesbeck 1911-1969
Obituary 117
Cannon, Harold C(harles) 1930- 45-48
Cannon, Helen 1921- 101
Cannon, James Monroe III 1918- 1-4R
Cannon, James P. 1890(?)-1974
Obituary 53-56
Cannon, Janell 1957- .... MAICYA 2
See also SATA 78, 128
Cannon, Jimmy 1910-1973 199
Cannon, Jimmy 1910-1973 199
Obituary 104
See also DLB 171
Cannon, John
See Newton, Michael
Cannon, John (Darcy) 1918- 154
Cannon, John Ashton 1926- 202
Cannon, Le Grand, Jr. 1899-1979
Obituary 93-96
Cannon, Lou(is S.) 1933- CANR-123
Earlier sketches in CA 29-32R, CANR-43
Cannon, Marian G. 1923- 151
See also SATA 85
Cannon, Mark W(ilcox) 1928- 13-16R
Cannon, Michael 1929- 150
Cannon, Moya 1956- 190
Cannon, P. H.
See Cannon, Peter (Hughes)
Cannon, Peter (Hughes) 1951- 187
Cannon, Peter H.
See Cannon, Peter (Hughes)
Cannon, Poppy
See White, Poppy Cannon
Cannon, Sarah Ophelia Colley 1912-1996 . 129
Obituary 151
Cannon, Taffy
See Cannon, Eileen E(mily)
Cannon, William Ragsdale
1916-1997 .... CANR-18
Obituary 158
Earlier sketches in CA 1-4R, CANR-4
Cannon, William S. 1918- 29-32R
Canny, Nicholas P(atrick) 1944- CANR-113
Earlier sketch in CA 69-72
Cano, Daniel 1947- CANR-87
Earlier sketch in CA 155
See also DLB 209
Cano-Ballesta, Juan 1932- CANR-1
Earlier sketch in CA 49-52
Canon, David (T.) 1959- 189
Canon, Lance Kirkpatrick 1939- 45-48
Canovan, Margaret 1939- 81-84
Cansdale, George (Soper)
1909-1993 .... CANR-75
Obituary 142
Earlier sketch in CA 9-12R
Cansever, Edip 1928-1986 .... EWL 3
Cant, Gilbert 1909-1982
Obituary 107
Cant, Reginald (Edward) 1914-1987
Obituary 122
Cantacuzene, Julia 1876-1975
Obituary 61-64
Cantacuzino, Sherban 1928- 118
Cantalupo, Barbara 1947- 209
Cantalupo, Charles 1951- 126
Cantelon, John E(dward) 1924- 9-12R
Cantelon, Philip L(ouis) 1940- 124
Canter, Mark 1952- 152
Canterbery, E(stes) Ray 1935- 41-44R
Cantin, Eileen 1931- 53-56
Cantin, Eugene Thorpe 1944- 45-48
Cantinat, Jean 1902- 29-32R
Cantlupe, Joe 1951- 140
Canton, Katia 1962- CANR-87
Earlier sketch in CA 152
Cantone, Vic 1933- 138
Cantor, Arthur 1920-2001 .... 29-32R
Obituary 195
Cantor, Eli 1913- CANR-14
Earlier sketch in CA 77-80
Cantor, Geoffrey 1943- 135
Cantor, George (Nathan) 1941- CANR-92
Earlier sketch in CA 138
Cantor, Gilbert M. 1929(?)-1987
Obituary 122
Cantor, Harold 1926- 136
Cantor, (Alfred) Jay 1948- 224
Cantor, Leonard M(artin) 1927- 69-72
Cantor, Louis 1934- 29-32R
Cantor, Milton 1925- 226
Brief entry 112
Cantor, Muriel G. 1923- CANR-12
Earlier sketch in CA 33-36R
Cantor, Norman F(rank)
1929-2004 .... CANR-111
Obituary 231
Earlier sketch in CA 102
Cantor, Paul A(rthur) 1945- CANR-117
Earlier sketch in CA 89-92
Cantor, Paul David 1916-1979
Obituary 89-92
Cantori, Louis J. 1934- 29-32R
Cantrell, Gregg 1958- 188
Cantrell, J(ohn) A(nthony) 1952- 123
Cantrell, Lisa W. 1945- 166
See also HGG
Cantril, Albert H(adley) 1940- 111
Cantsin, Monty
See Home, Stewart
Cantu, Norma Elia 1947- CANR-81
Earlier sketch in CA 152
See also DLB 209
See also HW 2
Cantu, Robert Clark 1938- 108
Cantwell, Aston
See Platt, Charles
Cantwell, Dennis P(atrick) 1940-1997 57-60
Obituary 157
Cantwell, Lois 1951- 121
Cantwell, Mary 1930(?)-2000 140
Obituary 188
Cantwell, Robert Emmett
1908-1978 .... CANR-81
Obituary 81-84
Earlier sketches in CA 5-8R, CANR-4
See also CN 1, 2, 3
See also DLB 9
Canty, Kevin 1954(?)- CANR-108
Earlier sketch in CA 151
Cantzlaar, George La Fond 1906-1967 .. CAP-1
Earlier sketch in CA 13-16
Canuck, Abe
See Bingley, David Ernest
Canuck, Janey
See Murphy, Emily (Gowan Ferguson)
Canusi, Jose
See Barker, S(quire) Omar
Canutt, Enos Edward 1895(?)-1986 155
Obituary 119
Brief entry 114
See also Canutt, Yakima
Canutt, Yakima -1986
See Canutt, Enos Edward
See also IDFW 3, 4
Can Xue
See Deng, Xiao Hua
Canyon, Christopher 1966- .... SATA 104, 150
Canzoneri, Robert (Wilburn) 1925- 17-20R
Cao, Guanlong 163
Cao, Lan 1961- 165
See also CLC 109
Cao Yu
See Wan Chia-pao
See also CWW 2
Capa, Robert 1913-1954 .... AAYA 66
Capacchione, Lucia 232
Capaldi, Nicholas 1939- 21-24R
Cape, Judith
See Page, P(atricia) K(athleen)
See also CCA 1
Cape, Peter (Irwin) 1929- 108
Cape, William H(enry) 1920- 9-12R
Capeci, Anne 239
Capeci, Dominic Joseph, Jr. 1940- 77-80
Capecia, Mayotte
See Combette, Josephe
See also EWL 3
Capek, Joseph 1887-1945 .... DFS 11
Capek, Karel 1890-1938 140
Brief entry 104
See also CDWLB 4
See also DA
See also DA3
See also DAB
See also DAC
See also DAM DRAM, MST, NOV
See also DC 1
See also DFS 7, 11
See also DLB 215
See also EW 10
See also EWL 3
See also MTCW 2
See also MTFW 2005
See also RGSF 2
See also RGWL 2, 3
See also SCFW 1, 2
See also SFW 4
See also SSC 36
See also TCLC 6, 37
See also WLC
Capek, Michael 1947- CANR-121
Earlier sketches in CA 150, CANR-100
See also SATA 96, 142
Capek, Milic 1909- CANR-4
Earlier sketch in CA 1-4R
Capel, Roger
See Sheppard, Lancelot C(apel)
Capella, Anthony 1963(?)- 238
Capelle, Russell B(eckett) 1917- 5-8R
Capelotti, P(eter) J(oseph) 1960- 218
Capen, Joseph 1658-1725 .... DLB 24
Capers, Gerald Mortimer, Jr. 1909- ... CANR-70
Earlier sketch in CA 5-8R
Capes, Bernard (Edward Joseph)
1854-1918 183
See also DLB 156
See also HGG
See also SATA 116
Capie, Forrest H(unter) 1940- 146
Capitan, William H(arry) 1933- 29-32R
Capitanchik, Maurice 1929(?)-1985
Obituary 118
Capitman, Barbara Baer 1920-1990
Obituary 131
Capitman, William G(ardiner) 1921-1975 .. 122
Obituary 111
Capizzi, Michael 1941- 41-44R
Caplan, Arthur L(eonard) 1950- CANR-22
Earlier sketch in CA 106
Caplan, David 1947- 105
Caplan, Edwin H(arvey) 41-44R
Caplan, Frank 1911(?)-1988 .... CANR-75
Obituary 126
Earlier sketch in CA 110
Caplan, Gerald 1917- CANR-40
Earlier sketches in CA 25-28R, CANR-18
Caplan, Harry 1896-1980 .... CAP-2
Earlier sketch in CA 23-24
Caplan, Lincoln 1950- 138
Caplan, Lionel 33-36R
Caplan, Mariana 1969- CANR-123
Earlier sketch in CA 167
Caplan, Paula J(oan) 1947- 129
Caplan, Ralph 1925- 13-16R
Caplan, Ronald Mervyn 1937- 107
Caplan, Suzanne H. 1943- 202
Caplan, Theresa 110
Caplan, Thomas (Mark) 1946- 107
Caples, John 1900-1990 .... CANR-76
Obituary 131
Earlier sketch in CA 21-24R
Caplin, Alfred Gerald 1909-1979 ..... CANR-75
Obituary 89-92
Earlier sketch in CA 57-60
See also Capp, Al
See also SATA-Obit 21
Caplovitz, David 1928-1992 .... CANR-75
Obituary 139
Earlier sketch in CA 41-44R
Caplow, Theodore 1920- CANR-20
Earlier sketches in CA 1-4R, CANR-4
Capmany (Farnes), Maria Aurelia
1918-1991 208
Capobianco, Michael Victor 1950- 172
Capon, Edmund (George) 1940- 107
Capon, (Harry) Paul 1912-1969 .... CANR-55
Obituary 103
Earlier sketch in CA 5-8R
See also SFW 4
Capon, Peter
See Oakley, Eric Gilbert
Capon, Robert Farrar 1925- CANR-103
Brief entry 106
Earlier sketch in CA 136
Caponigri, A(loysius) Robert
1915-1983 .... CANR-43
Earlier sketch in CA 37-40R
Caponigro, Jeffrey R. 1957- 170
Caponigro, John Paul 1965- .... SATA 84
Caporale, Rocco 1927- 37-40R
Capote, Truman 1924-1984 .... CANR-62
Obituary 113
Earlier sketches in CA 5-8R, CANR-18
See also AAYA 61
See also AMWS 3
See also BPFB 1
See also CDALB 1941-1968
See also CLC 1, 3, 8, 13, 19, 34, 38, 58
See also CN 1, 2, 3
See also CPW
See also DA
See also DA3
See also DAB
See also DAC
See also DAM MST, NOV, POP
See also DLB 2, 185, 227
See also DLBY 1980, 1984
See also EWL 3
See also EXPS
See also GLL 1
See also LAIT 3
See also MAL 5
See also MTCW 1, 2
See also MTFW 2005
See also NCFS 2
See also RGAL 4
See also RGSF 2
See also SATA 91
See also SSC 2, 47
See also SSFS 2
See also TCLC 164
See also TUS
See also WLC
Capouya, Emile CANR-139
Brief entry 118
Earlier sketch in CA 122
Capp, Al
See Caplin, Alfred Gerald
See also SATA 61
Capp, B. S.
See Capp, Bernard (Stuart)
Capp, Bernard (Stuart) 1943- 130
Capp, Fiona 1963- 190
Capp, Glenn Richard 1910-1998 .... CANR-3
Earlier sketch in CA 1-4R
Capp, Richard 1935- 81-84
Cappadona, Diane Apostolos
See Apostolos-Cappadona, Diane
Cappas, Alberto O. 206
Cappel, Carmen Bambach
See Bambach, Carmen C.
Cappel, Constance 1936- CANR-10
Earlier sketch in CA 21-24R
See also SATA 22
Cappelin, Maria
See Fearn, John Russell
Cappelli, Peter 1956- 171
Cappelluti, Frank Joseph 1935-1972 ..... 37-40R
Capper, Douglas Parode 1898(?)-1979 .... 9-12R
Obituary 103
Cappetta, Cynthia 1949- .... SATA 125
Cappo, Joseph 1936- 77-80
Cappo, Nan Willard 1955- 215
See also SATA 143
Cappon, Daniel 1921- 17-20R
Cappon, Lester J(esse) 1900-1981 106
Obituary 104
Capps, Benjamin (Franklin) 1922- .. CANR-143
Earlier sketches in CA 5-8R, CANR-7, 61
See also DLB 256
See also SATA 9
See also TCWW 1, 2
Capps, Carroll M. 1917(?)-1971
Obituary 112
See also SFW 4
Capps, Clifford Lucille Sheats
1902-1976 .... 37-40R
Capps, Donald (Eric) 1939- CANR-93
Earlier sketches in CA 29-32R, CANR-12
Capps, Jack Lee 1926- 21-24R
Capps, Walter H(olden) 1934-1997 .. CANR-12
Obituary 162
Earlier sketch in CA 29-32R
Cappy Dick
See Cleveland, George
Capra, Frank 1897-1991 61-64
Obituary 135
See also AAYA 52
See also CLC 16
Capra, Fritjof 1939- CANR-135
Earlier sketch in CA 107
Capretta, Patrick J(ohn) 1929-1982 .... 21-24R
Obituary 135
Caprio, Betsy
See Caprio, Elizabeth (Blair) Whitworth
Caprio, Elizabeth (Blair) Whitworth
1933- CANR-44
Earlier sketches in CA 110, CANR-30
Caprio, Frank S(amuel) 1906- 101
Capriolo, Paola 1962- 233
Capron, Alexander Morgan 1944- 115
Capron, Jean F. 1924- 21-24R
Capron, Louis (Bishop) 1891-1971 ... CANR-71
Earlier sketches in CAP-1, CA 9-10
Capron, Walter Clark 1904-1979 .... CAP-1
Obituary 89-92
Earlier sketch in CA 17-18
Capron, William M(osher) 1920-2002 ... 29-32R
Obituary 209
Caproni, Giorgio 1912-1990 .... DLB 128
Capshew, James H. 1954- 232
Capstick, Peter Hathaway 1940-1996 102
Captain Kangaroo
See Keeshan, Robert J.
Captain Wheeler
See Ellis, Edward S(ylvester)

Cumulative Index 93 **Carlisle**

Captain X
  See Power-Waters, Brian
Captain Young of Yale
  See Stratemeyer, Edward L.
Capucilli, Alyssa Satin 1957- 186
  See also SATA 115, 163
Capucine
  See Mazille, Capucine
Caputi, Anthony (Francis) 1924- CANR-3
  Earlier sketch in CA 1-4R
Caputi, Jane 1953- CANR-86
  Earlier sketch in CA 129
Caputo, David A(rmand) 1943- 65-68
Caputo, John D. 1940- 205
Caputo, Philip 1941- CANR-135
  Earlier sketches in CA 73-76, CANR-40
  See also AAYA 60
  See also CLC 32
  See also YAW
Caputo, Richard K. 1948- 139
Caputo, Robert 1949- 101
Capuzzo, Michael 1957- 223
Carabelli, Giancarlo 1939- 154
Caradon, Lord
  See Foot, Hugh Mackintosh
Caragiale, Ion Luca 1852-1912 157
  See also TCLC 76
Caragiale, Mateiu Ioan 1885-1936 ..... DLB 220
  See also EWL 3
Caraher, Kim(berley Elizabeth) 1961- 173
  See also SATA 105
Caraion, Ion 1923-1986 .... EWL 3
Caraker, Mary 1929- .... SATA 74
Caraley, Demetrios 1932- 103
Caram, Eve (La Salle) 1934- 206
Caraman, Philip (George)
    1911-1998 .... CANR-70
  Obituary 167
  Earlier sketches in CA 9-12R, CANR-6, 21
Caramello, Charles 1948- 112
Caranfa, Angelo 1942- 199
Carano, Paul 1919- 17-20R
Caras, Roger A(ndrew) 1928-2001 ... CANR-47
  Obituary 195
  Earlier sketches in CA 1-4R, CANR-5
  See also SATA 12
  See also SATA-Obit 127
Caras, Tracy 1953- 113
Caravantes, Peggy 1935- 211
  See also SATA 140
Carawan, Candie
  See Carawan, Carolanne M.
Carawan, Carolanne M. 1939- 17-20R
Carawan, Guy H., Jr. 1927- 17-20R
Caraway, Caren 1939- .... SATA 57
Caraway, Charless 1888-1977 125
Carbajal, Xavier Joseph 1958- 163
  See also HW 2
Carballido (Fentanes), Emilio
  See Carballido, Emilio
  See also CWW 2
Carballido, Emilio 1925- CANR-87
  Earlier sketches in CA 33-36R, CANR-54
  See also Carballido (Fentanes), Emilio
  See also DFS 4
  See also DLB 305
  See also EWL 3
  See also HW 1
  See also LAW
Carbaugh, Robert J(ohn) 1946- 65-68
Carberry, Ann
  See Child, Maureen
Carberry, H.D. 1921- .... CP 1
Carbery, Mary 1867-1949 218
Carbery, Thomas F. 29-32R
Carbine, Patricia (Theresa) 1931- 107
Carbo, Nick 1964- CANR-118
  Earlier sketch in CA 176
Carbone, Elisa
  See Carbone, Elisa Lynn
Carbone, Elisa Lynn 1954- CANR-116
  Earlier sketch in CA 149
  See also AAYA 67
  See also SATA 81, 137
Carbonell, Reyes 1917- 9-12R
Carbonnier, Jeanne 1894-1974 .... CANR-71
  Earlier sketches in CAP-2, CA 33-36
  See also SATA 3
  See also SATA-Obit 34
Carbury, A. B.
  See Carr, Albert H. Z(olotkoff)
Carby, Hazel V. 1948- CANR-86
  Earlier sketch in CA 154
Carcaterra, Lorenzo 1954- CANR-107
  Earlier sketch in CA 140
Carcopino, Jerome 1881(?)-1970
  Obituary 104
Card, Orson Scott 1951- CANR-133
  Earlier sketches in CA 102, CANR-27, 47, 73, 102, 106
  Interview in CANR-27
  See also AAYA 11, 42
  See also BPFB 1
  See also BYA 5, 8
  See also CLC 44, 47, 50
  See also CPW
  See also DA3
  See also DAM POP
  See also FANT
  See also MTCW 1, 2
  See also MTFW 2005
  See also NFS 5
  See also SATA 83, 127
  See also SCFW 2
  See also SFW 4
  See also SUFW 2
  See also WWW
Card, Tim(othy) S. B. 1931-2001 .... CANR-125
  Earlier sketch in CA 147
Cardan, Paul
  See Castoriadis, Cornelius
Cardarelli, Joseph 1944- 77-80
Cardarelli, Vincenzo
  See Caldarelli, Nazareno
  See also DLB 114
  See also EWL 3
Cardella, Lara 1969- 206
Carden, Karen W(ilson) 1946- CANR-1
  Earlier sketch in CA 49-52
Carden, Maren Lockwood 53-56
Carden, Patricia J. 1935- 41-44R
Cardenal, Ernesto 1925- CANR-138
  Earlier sketches in CA 49-52, CANR-2, 32, 66
  See also CLC 31, 161
  See also CWW 2
  See also DAM MULT, POET
  See also DLB 290
  See also EWL 3
  See also HLC 1
  See also HW 1, 2
  See also LAWS 1
  See also MTCW 1, 2
  See also MTFW 2005
  See also PC 22
  See also RGWL 2, 3
Cardenas, Daniel N(egrete) 1917- CANR-26
  Earlier sketch in CA 45-48
Cardenas, Enrique 1954- 212
Cardenas, Gilbert 1947- 97-100
Cardenas, Nancy 1934-1994 .... GLL 2
Cardenas, Reyes
  See Cardenas, Reyes
  See also DLB 122
Cardenas, Reyes 1948- 152
  See also Cardenas, Reyes
  See also HW 1
Carder, Leigh
  See Cunningham, Eugene
Cardew, Cornelius 1936-1981 130
  Obituary 108
Cardew, Michael (Ambrose)
    1901-1983 .... CANR-30
  Obituary 109
  Earlier sketch in CA 49-52
Cardiff, Gray Emerson 1949- 89-92
Cardiff, Jack 1914- 237
  See also IDFW 3, 4
Cardiff, John
  See Cardiff, Jack
Cardinal, Douglas Joseph 1934- 210
Cardinal, Marie 1929-2001 177
  See also CLC 189
  See also CWW 2
  See also DLB 83
  See also FW
Cardinal, Ora 1913-1994 111
Cardinal, Roger (Thomas) 1940- CANR-40
  Earlier sketches in CA 45-48, CANR-1, 18
Cardinal, Sister Mary Ora
  See Cardinal, Ora
Cardinale, Claudia 1938- 201
Cardona, George 1936- 119
Cardona, Manuel 1934- 156
Cardona-Hine, Alvaro 1926- CANR-5
  Earlier sketch in CA 9-12R
Cardone, Samuel S(teve) 1938- 17-20R
Cardoso, Lucio 1913-1968 178
  See also HW 2
Cardoso, Onelio Jorge 1914-1986 .... HW 1
Cardoso, Rafael
  See Denis, Rafael Cardoso
Cardoso Pires, Jose (Augusto Neves)
  See Pires, Jose Cardoso
  See also CWW 2
Cardoza y Aragon, Luis
  See Cardoza y Aragon, Luis
  See also DLB 290
Cardoza y Aragon, Luis 1904-1992
  See Cardoza y Aragon, Luis
  See also HW 1
Cardozo, Arlene Rossen 1938- CANR-19
  Earlier sketch in CA 102
Cardozo, Benjamin N(athan) 1870-1938 164
  Brief entry 117
  See also TCLC 65
Cardozo, Michael H(art IV) 1910-1996 . 33-36R
  Obituary 154
Cardozo, Nancy 103
Cardozo, Peter 1916- 61-64
Cardozo-Freeman, Inez 1928- 131
  See also HW 1
Carducci, Giosue (Alessandro Giuseppe)
    1835-1907 163
  See also EW 7
  See also PC 46
  See also RGWL 2, 3
  See also TCLC 32
Cardui, Van
  See Wayman, Tony Russell
Cardui, Vanessa
  See Wayman, Tony Russell
Cardullo, Bert
  See Cardullo, Robert James
Cardullo, Robert James 1948- 222
Cardus, Neville 1889-1975 .... CANR-70
  Obituary 57-60
  Earlier sketches in CA 61-64, CANR-11
Cardwell, D(onald) S(tephen) L(owell)
    1919- 101
Cardwell, Guy A(dams) 1905- 13-16R
Cardwell, Harold D(ouglas) Sr. 1926- 232
Care, Felicity
  See Coury, Louise Andree
Care, Norman S. 1937- 25-28R
Careless, J(ames) M(aurice) S(tockford)
    1919- 102
Carens, James Francis 1927- CANR-12
  Earlier sketch in CA 61-64
Carerra, Kathleen
  See Carr, Jess(e Crowe, Jr.)
Cares, Paul B(enjamin) 1911-1998 .... 9-12R
Caress, James M. 1947- 122
Caress, Jay
  See Caress, James M.
Carette, Louis 1913- 85-88
Carew, Dorothy 1910(?)-1973
  Obituary 41-44R
Carew, Dudley Charles 1903-1981
  Obituary 103
Carew, Jan (Rynveld) 1925- 77-80
  See also BW 2
  See also CN 1, 2
  See also DLB 157
  See also EWL 3
  See also SATA 51
  See also SATA-Brief 40
Carew, Jocelyn
  See Aeby, Jacquelyn
Carew, John Mohun 1921-1980 .... CANR-7
  Earlier sketch in CA 13-16R
Carew, Rivers Vervain 1935- .... CP 1
Carew, Rod(ney Cline) 1945- 104
Carew, Thomas 1595(?)-1640 .... BRW 2
  See also DLB 126
  See also PAB
  See also PC 29
  See also RGEL 2
Carew, Tim
  See Carew, John Mohun
Carewe, S. C.
  See Du Breuil, (Elizabeth) L(or)inda
Carey, Anne
  See Nevill, Barry St-John
Carey, Bonnie
  See Marshall, Bonnie C.
Carey, David, Jr. 1967- 220
Carey, Diane 1954- 122
Carey, Drew 1958- 166
Carey, Eileen
  See O'Casey, Eileen (Kathleen Reynolds)
Carey, Ernestine Gilbreth 1908- CANR-71
  Earlier sketch in CA 5-8R
  See also CLC 17
  See also SATA 2
Carey, Gary 1938- CANR-34
  Earlier sketches in CA 57-60, CANR-15
Carey, George (Leonard) 1935- 171
Carey, George Wescott 1933- CANR-138
  Earlier sketch in CA 173
Carey, Harry, Jr., Jr. 1921- 172
Carey, Henry 1687(?)-1743 .... DLB 84
  See also RGEL 2
Carey, Jacqueline 1954- CANR-116
  Earlier sketch in CA 162
Carey, Jacqueline 1964- 208
Carey, James Charles 1915- 13-16R
Carey, Jane Perry (Clark) 1898-1981 73-76
  Obituary 105
Carey, John 1934- CANR-82
  Earlier sketches in CA 57-60, CANR-6, 35
Carey, John A(ndrew) 1949- 109
Carey, Joseph Kuhn 1957- 135
Carey, Julian
  See Tubb, E(dwin) C(harles)
Carey, Kenneth Moir 1908-1979
  Obituary 108
Carey, Lisa 169
  See also SATA 110
Carey, M. V.
  See Carey, Mary V(irginia)
Carey, Mary V(irginia) 1925-1994 .... CANR-38
  Earlier sketches in CA 81-84, CANR-17
  See also SATA 44
  See also SATA-Brief 39
Carey, Mathew 1760-1839 .... DLB 37, 73
Carey, Michael
  See Burton, Edward J.
Carey, Michael (Sausmarez) 1913-1985
  Obituary 118
Carey, Michael L(awrence) 1948- 65-68
Carey, Mike 1959- 227
Carey, Mother Marme Aimee 1931- 13-16R
Carey, Omer L. 1929- CANR-23
  Earlier sketches in CA 21-24R, CANR-8
Carey, Patrick W. 1940- 145
Carey, Peter 1943- CANR-117
  Brief entry 123
  Earlier sketches in CA 127, CANR-53, 76
  Interview in CA-127
  See also CLC 40, 55, 96, 183
  See also CN 4, 5, 6, 7
  See also DLB 289
  See also EWL 3
  See also MTCW 1, 2
  See also MTFW 2005
  See also RGSF 2
  See also SATA 94
Carey, Richard John 1925- 53-56
Carey, Roane 235
Carey, Robert George 1926-
  Brief entry 108
Carey, Steven Harry 1946(?)-1989
  Obituary 129
Carey, Valerie Scho 1949- 128
  See also SATA 60
Carey Evans, Olwen (Elizabeth)
    1892-1990 126
Carey-Jones, N(orman) S(tewart)
    1911-1997 .... 21-24R
Carfagne, Cyril
  See Jennings, Leslie Nelson
Carfagno, Vincent R. 1935- 41-44R
Carfax, Catherine
  See Fairburn, Eleanor
Cargas, Harry J(ames) 1932- CANR-21
  Earlier sketches in CA 13-16R, CANR-6
Cargill, Jennifer S(ue) 1944- 109
Cargill, Oscar 1898-1972 .... CANR-15
  Obituary 33-36R
  Earlier sketch in CA 1-4R
Cargill, Robert L. 1929- 25-28R
Cargo, David N(iels) 1932- 57-60
Cargo, Robert T. 1933- 85-88
Cargoe, Richard
  See Payne, (Pierre Stephen) Robert
Carhart, Arthur Hawthorne
    1892-1978 .... CANR-71
  Earlier sketches in CAP-1, CA 9-10
Cariaga, Catalina 1958- 218
Caridi, Ronald J. 1941- 25-28R
Carigiet, Alois 1902-1985 73-76
  Obituary 119
  See also CLR 38
  See also SATA 24
  See also SATA-Obit 47
Carim, Enver 1938- 136
Carin, Arthur A. 1928- 29-32R
Carin, Michael 1951- 132
Carini, Edward 1923- 61-64
  See also SATA 9
Carisella, P(asquale) J. 1922- 134
Caristi, Dom(inic) 1956- 143
Carkeet, David 1946- CANR-38
  Earlier sketch in CA 102
  See also SATA 75
Carl, Beverly May 1932- CANR-4
  Earlier sketch in CA 53-56
Carl, Leo Darwin 1918(?)-2001 218
Carl, Lillian Stewart 1949- CANR-128
  Earlier sketches in CA 118, CANR-42
Carle, Eric 1929- CANR-98
  Earlier sketches in CA 25-28R, CANR-10, 25
  See also CLR 10, 72
  See also CWRI 5
  See also MAICYA 1, 2
  See also SAAS 6
  See also SATA 4, 65, 120, 163
Carlebach, Michael L(loyd) 1945- 143
Carlell, Lodowick 1602-1675 .... DLB 58
Carlen, Claudia 1906- 106
Carles, Emilie 1900-1979 141
Carless, Jennifer 1960- 146
Carleton, Barbara 1925- 169
Carleton, Barbee Oliver 1917- CANR-71
  Earlier sketch in CA 21-24R
Carleton, Captain L. C.
  See Ellis, Edward S(ylvester)
Carleton, Captain Latham C.
  See Ellis, Edward S(ylvester)
Carleton, Latham C.
  See Ellis, Edward S(ylvester)
Carleton, Mark T. 1935-1995 .... CANR-12
  Earlier sketch in CA 33-36R
Carleton, R(eginald) Milton
    1899-1986 .... CANR-77
  Obituary 120
  Earlier sketch in CA 69-72
Carleton, Will(iam McKendree)
    1845-1912 204
  Brief entry 115
Carleton, William 1794-1869 .... DLB 159
  See also RGEL 2
  See also RGSF 2
Carleton, William G(raves) 1903-1982 .. CAP-2
  Earlier sketch in CA 25-28
Carley, Larry W. 1950- 139
Carley, Lionel (Kenneth) 1936- 132
Carley, Michael Jabara 1945- 205
Carley, V(an Ness) Royal 1906-1976 ..... CAP-2
  Earlier sketch in CA 29-32
  See also SATA-Obit 20
Carli, Angelo 1937- 49-52
Carli, Enzo 1910-1999 197
Carlile, Clancy 1930-1998 128
  Obituary 169
Carlile, Clark S(tites) 1912- 41-44R
Carlile, Henry 1934- 33-36R
Carlile, Richard 1790-1843 .... DLB 110, 158
Carlin, Gabriel S. 1921- 1-4R
Carlin, George (Denis) 1937- CANR-112
  Earlier sketch in CA 158
Carlin, Martha 159
Carlin, Thomas W(illard) 1918-1980 ..... 25-28R
Carlin, Vivian F. 1919- 131
Carline, Richard (Cotton) 1896-1980
  Obituary 105
Carling, Alan H(ugh) 1949- 143
Carling, Amelia Lau 1949- .... SATA 119
Carling, Finn 1925-2004 194
  See also EWL 3
Carling, Francis 1945- 25-28R
Carling, Paul J. 1945- 151
Carling, Will(iam David Charles) 1965- 193
Carlino, Lewis John 1932- CANR-67
  Earlier sketch in CA 77-80
  See also CAD
  See also CD 5, 6
Carlinsky, Dan 1944- CANR-47
  Earlier sketches in CA 21-24R, CANR-8, 23
Carlip, Hillary 1956- 150
Carlise, Carris
  See Pemberton, Margaret
Carlisle, Carol Jones 1919- 29-32R
Carlisle, Clark
  See Holding, James (Clark Carlisle, Jr.)
Carlisle, D. M.
  See Cook, Dorothy Mary

Carlisle, Donna
See Ball, Donna
Carlisle, Douglas H(ilton) 1921- 45-48
Carlisle, E(rvin) Fred 1935- 53-56
Carlisle, Elizabeth Pendergast 231
Carlisle, Fred 1915- 73-76
Carlisle, Henry (Coffin) 1926- CANR-85
Earlier sketches in CA 13-16R, CANR-15
See also CLC 33
Carlisle, Howard M(yron) 1928- 69-72
Carlisle, Lilian (Matarose) Baker 1912- 53-56
Carlisle, Olga Andreyev 1930- CANR-85
Earlier sketches in CA 13-16R, CANR-7
See also SATA 35
Carlisle, Rodney P. 1936- CANR-49
Earlier sketch in CA 45-48
Carlisle, Thomas (Fiske) 1944- 53-56
Carlisle, Thomas John 1913-1992 CANR-40
Earlier sketches in CA 101, CANR-18
Carlock, John R(obert) 1921- 33-36R
Carlock, Lynn
See Cunningham, Marilyn
Carlon, Patricia Bernardette 1927- CANR-86
Earlier sketches in CA 13-16R, CANR-56
Carlquist, Sherwin 1930- 13-16R
Carls, (John) Norman 1907-1985 CAP-2
Earlier sketch in CA 17-18
Carls, Stephen D(ouglas) 1944- CANR-119
Earlier sketch in CA 148
Carlsen, Chris
See Holdstock, Robert P.
Carlsen, G(eorge) Robert 1917- CANR-24
Earlier sketches in CA 17-20R, CANR-8
See also SATA 30
Carlsen, James C(aldwell) 1927- 25-28R
Carlsen, Ruth C(hristoffer) 1918- CANR-24
Earlier sketches in CA 17-20R, CANR-8
See also SATA 2
Carlson, Allan C(onstantine) 1949- 198
Carlson, Andrew R(aymond) 1934- CANR-71
Earlier sketch in CA 29-32R
Carlson, Arthur E(ugene) 1923- 37-40R
Carlson, Avis D(ungan) 1896-1987 CANR-75
Obituary 121
Earlier sketch in CA 73-76
Carlson, Bernice Wells 1910- CANR-2
Earlier sketch in CA 5-8R
See also SATA 8
Carlson, Betty 1919- CANR-2
Earlier sketch in CA 1-4R
Carlson, C. C.
See Carlson, Carole C.
Carlson, Carl Walter 1907-1989 49-52
Carlson, Carole C. 1925- 113
Carlson, Dale (Bick) 1935- CANR-100
Earlier sketches in CA 9-12R, CANR-3, 49
See also SATA 1
Carlson, Daniel (Bick) 1960- 105
See also SATA 27
Carlson, Edgar M(agnus) 1908-1992 105
Carlson, Ellsworth C. 1917-
Brief entry 105
Carlson, Elof Axel 1931- CANR-44
Earlier sketch in CA 45-48
Carlson, Eric W(alter) 1910- CANR-113
Earlier sketch in CA 25-28R
Carlson, Esther Elisabeth 1920- 5-8R
Carlson, Harry Gilbert 1930- CANR-29
Earlier sketch in CA 109
Carlson, John A(llyn) 1933- 29-32R
Carlson, Judith Lee 1952- 104
Carlson, Keith Thor 1966- 211
Carlson, Laurie (Winn) 1952- CANR-95
Earlier sketch in CA 140
See also SATA 101
Carlson, Leland H(enry) 1908-1995 17-20R
Carlson, Lewis H(erbert) 1934- CANR-122
Earlier sketch in CA 41-44R
Carlson, Loraine 1923- CANR-14
Earlier sketch in CA 37-40R
Carlson, Lori Marie 1957- 204
Carlson, Marvin 1935- CANR-71
Earlier sketches in CA 21-24R, CANR-8
Carlson, Maureen 1947- 163
Carlson, Melody 1956- 185
See also SATA 113
Carlson, Nancy L.
See Carlson, Nancy L(ee)
Carlson, Nancy L(ee) 1953- CANR-124
Earlier sketches in CA 110, CANR-57
See also SATA 56, 90, 144
See also SATA-Brief 45
Carlson, Natalie Savage 1906-1997 CANR-57
Earlier sketches in CA 1-4R, CANR-3
See also CWRI 5
See also JRDA
See also MAICYA 1, 2
See also SAAS 4
See also SATA 2, 68
Carlson, P. M.
See Carlson, Patricia M(cElroy)
Carlson, Patricia M(cElroy) 1940- CANR-128
Earlier sketches in CA 114, CANR-36
See also CMW 4
Carlson, Paul Robins 1928- 101
Carlson, Raymond 1906-1983
Obituary 109
Carlson, Reynold Edgar 1901-1997 CANR-4
Earlier sketch in CA 1-4R
Carlson, Richard 1912(?)-1977
Obituary 73-76
Carlson, Richard A. 1956- 169
Carlson, Richard C. 1942- 149
Carlson, Richard Stocks 1942- 57-60
Carlson, Rick J. 1940- CANR-134
Earlier sketch in CA 65-68
Carlson, Robert E(ugene) 1922- 41-44R
Carlson, Ron(ald F.) 1947- 189
Earlier sketches in CA 105, CANR-27
Autobiographical Essay in 189
See also CLC 54
See also DLB 244
Carlson, Ronald L. 1934- CANR-75
Earlier sketches in CA 33-36R, CANR-13, 35
Carlson, Roy L(incoln) 1930- 41-44R
Carlson, Ruth (Elizabeth) Kearney
1911-1979 29-32R
Carlson, Susan Johnston 1953- SATA 88
Carlson, Theodore L(eonard) 1905-1981 45-48
Carlson, Vada F. 1897- CANR-28
Earlier sketches in CA 21-24R, CANR-10
See also SATA 16
Carlson, William H(ugh) 1898-1990 CAP-2
Earlier sketch in CA 23-24
Carlson, William S(amuel)
1905-1994 CANR-75
Obituary 145
Earlier sketch in CA 1-4R
Carlston, Kenneth S. 1904-1969 5-8R
Carlstrom, Nancy White 1948- CANR-114
Earlier sketches in CA 121, CANR-57
See also MAICYA 2
See also MAICYAS 1
See also SATA 53, 92, 156
See also SATA-Brief 48
Carlton, Alva
See Delk, Robert Carlton
Carlton, Charles 1941- 53-56
Carlton, Charles Merritt 1928- CANR-43
Earlier sketch in CA 45-48
Carlton, David 1938- 103
Carlton, Henry F(isk) 1893(?)-1973
Obituary 41-44R
Carlton, Jay
See Obrecht, Jas
Carlton, Jim 1955- 167
Carlton, Keith
See Robertson, Keith (Carlton)
Carlton, Lessie 1903-1978 49-52
Carlton, Robert G(oodrich) 1927- 17-20R
Carlton, Roger
See Rowland, D(onald) S(ydney)
Carlton, Wendy 1949- 101
Carlut, Charles E. 1911- 153
Brief entry 107
Carlyle, Jane Welsh 1801-1866 DLB 55
Carlyle, Liz
See Woodhouse, S. T.
Carlyle, Thomas 1795-1881 BRW 4
See also CDBLB 1789-1832
See also DA
See also DAB
See also DAC
See also DAM MST
See also DLB 55, 144, 254
See also RGEL 2
See also TEA
Carlyon, Les 1942- 214
Carlyon, Richard SATA 55
Carm, Mac
See Armstrong, Keith F(rancis) W(hitfield)
Carmack, John 1970- AAYA 59
Carmack, Robert M. 1934- 45-48
Carmack, Sharon DeBartolo 1956- CANR-141
Earlier sketch in CA 174
Carman, Barry (Francis) 1922- 118
Carman, (William) Bliss 1861-1929 152
Brief entry 104
See also DAC
See also DLB 92
See also PC 34
See also RGEL 2
See also TCLC 7
Carman, Dominic 211
Carman, Dulce
See Drummond, Edith Marie Dulce Carman
Carman, J(ustice) Neale 1897-1972 CAP-1
Earlier sketch in CA 9-10
Carman, Judith E. 1940- 215
Carman, Patrick SATA 161
Carman, Robert A(rchibald) 1931- CANR-7
Earlier sketch in CA 57-60
Carman, Tim J. 1947- 238
Carman, William Y(oung) 1909- 13-16R
Carmean, Kelli 1960- 237
Carmel, Catherine 1939- CANR-46
Earlier sketch in CA 69-72
Carmel, Hesi 1937- 103
Carmell, Aryeh 1917- 118
Carmen, Arlene 1936- 69-72
Carmen, Ira H. 1934- 128
Carmen, Leon 1950- 164
Carmen, Sister (M.) Joann 1941- 21-24R
Carmen Sylva
See Elisabeth (Ottilie Luise), Queen (Pauline)
Carmer, Carl (Lamson) 1893-1976 CANR-70
Obituary 69-72
Earlier sketches in CA 5-8R, CANR-4
See also SATA 37
See also SATA-Obit 30
Carmer, Elizabeth Black 1904- SATA 24
Carmi, Giora 1944- SATA 79, 149
Carmi, T.
See Charny, Carmi
See also CWW 2
Carmichael, Ann
See MacAlpine, Margaret H(esketh Murray)
Carmichael, Ann G(ayton) 1947- 125
Carmichael, Calum M. 1938- 53-56
Carmichael, Carrie
See Carmichael, Harriet
See also SATA 40
Carmichael, Claire
See McNab, Claire
Carmichael, D(ouglas) R(oy) 1941- 33-36R
Carmichael, Fred 1924- CANR-51
Earlier sketches in CA 17-20R, CANR-10, 25
Carmichael, Harriet 115
See also Carmichael, Carrie
Carmichael, Harry
See Ognall, Leopold Horace
Carmichael, Hoagland Howard 1899-1981
Obituary 108
See also Carmichael, Hoagy
Carmichael, Hoagy -1981
See Carmichael, Hoagland Howard
See also IDFW 3, 4
Carmichael, Ian (Gillett) 1920- 129
Carmichael, Joel 1915- CANR-71
Earlier sketches in CA 1-4R, CANR-2
Carmichael, John P(eerless) 1902-1986
Obituary 119
Carmichael, Leonard 1898-1973 41-44R
Obituary 45-48
Carmichael, Marie
See Stonov, Natasha
Carmichael, Oliver C(romwell)
1891-1966 CAP-1
Earlier sketch in CA 9-10
Carmichael, Peter A(rchibald)
1897-1981 CAP-2
Earlier sketch in CA 17-18
Carmichael, Peter S. 1966- 152
Carmichael, Stokely 1941-1998 CANR-92
Obituary 172
Earlier sketches in CA 57-60, CANR-25
See also BW 1
Carmichael, Thomas N(ichols)
1919-1972 CAP-2
Earlier sketch in CA 29-32
Carmichael, William Edward 1922- 37-40R
Carmilly, Moshe 1908- 41-44R
Carmines, Al(vin Allison, Jr.) 1936- 103
Carmody, Denise Lardner 1935- 93-96
Carmody, Isobelle (Jane) 1958- 192
See also SATA 161
Carmody, Jay 1900(?)-1973
Obituary 41-44R
Carmody, John (Tully) 1939-1995 186
Carmoy, Guy de 1907-1997 89-92
Carnac, Carol
See Rivett, Edith Caroline
Carnac, Levin
See Griffith(-Jones), George (Chetwynd)
Carnahan, Walter H(ervey) 1891-1983 CAP-1
Earlier sketch in CA 9-10
Carnall, Geoffrey 1927- 13-16R
Carnap, Rudolf P. 1891-1970 CAP-1
Obituary 29-32R
Earlier sketch in CA 9-10
See also DLB 270
Carnarvon, The Earl of
See Herbert, Henry George Alfred Marius Victor Francis
Carne, Judy
See Botterill, Joyce
Carnegie, Charles V. 1952- 236
Carnegie, Dale 1888-1955 218
See also TCLC 53
Carnegie, Dorothy Vanderpool AITN 1
Carnegie, Raymond Alexander
1920-1999 CANR-11
Earlier sketch in CA 21-24R
Carnegie, Sacha
See Carnegie, Raymond Alexander
Carnegy, Patrick 1940- 81-84
Carneiro, Maurina Pereira
See Pereira Carneiro, Maurina
Carnell, Corbin Scott 1929- CANR-10
Earlier sketch in CA 65-68
Carnell, E. J.
See Carnell, (Edward) John
Carnell, Edward John 1919-1967 CAP-1
Earlier sketch in CA 13-14
Carnell, (Edward) John 1912-1972 CANR-76
Obituary 104
Earlier sketch in CA 25-28R
Carner, Gary 1955- 140
Carner, Mosco 1904-1985 CANR-38
Obituary 116
Earlier sketches in CAP-1, CA 11-12, CANR-12
Carnero, Guillermo 1947- 179
See also DLB 108
Carnes, Conrad D(ew) 1936- 85-88
Carnes, Mark C(hristopher) 1950- CANR-103
Earlier sketches in CA 112, CANR-30, 56
Carnes, Paul N(athaniel) 1921-1979
Obituary 85-88
Carnes, Ralph L(ee) 1931- 33-36R
Carnes, Valerie Folts-Bohanan 1945- 33-36R
Carnesale, Albert 1936- 142
Carnevale, Anthony P(atrick) 1946- 135
Carnevali, Doris L(orrain) CANR-44
Earlier sketches in CA 69-72, CANR-21
Carney, Daniel 1944- 119
Carney, Dora Sanders 1903-1986
Obituary 120
Carney, Edward John 1913-1989
Obituary 128
Carney, James (Patrick) 1914-1989 21-24R
Carney, John J(oseph), Jr. 1932- 69-72
Carney, John Otis 1922- CANR-3
Earlier sketch in CA 1-4R
Carney, Judith A(nn) 201
Carney, Matthew 1922- CANR-25
Earlier sketch in CA 108
Carney, Pat 1935- 203
Carney, Raymond 1950- CANR-115
Earlier sketch in CA 137
Carney, Richard Edward 1929- 37-40R
Carney, T(homas) F(rancis) 1931- CANR-39
Earlier sketches in CA 49-52, CANR-1, 17
Carney, W(illiam) Alderman 1922- 25-28R
Carney, William Wray 1950- 220
Carnicelli, D(omenick) D. 1931- 61-64
Carnochan, W(alter) B(liss) 1930- 33-36R
Carnot, Joseph B(arry) 1941- 45-48
Carnoy, Martin 1938- CANR-137
Earlier sketches in CA 65-68, CANR-10
Caro, Francis G(eorge) 1936- CANR-54
Earlier sketches in CA 69-72, CANR-11, 28
Caro, Miguel Antonio 1843-1909 LAW
Caro, Robert A(llan) 1935- CANR-115
Earlier sketches in CA 101, CANR-40
See also BEST 90:2
Caroe, Olaf Kirkpatrick 1892-1981 113
Carol, Bill J.
See Knott, William C(ecil, Jr.)
Carol, Jacqueline
See Cooper, Jacqueline
Carol, Phyllis
See Humphrey, Phyllis
Caroli, Betty Boyd 1938- CANR-43
Earlier sketch in CA 118
Caroll, Nonie 1926- 103
Caron, Ann F. 177
Caron, Leslie (Claire Margaret) 1931- 152
Caron, Roger 1938- 89-92
Caron, Romi
See Caron-Kyselkova', Romana
Carona, Philip B(en) 1925- CANR-4
Earlier sketch in CA 1-4R
Caronia, Guiseppe 1884(?)-1977
Obituary 69-72
Caron-Kyselkova', Romana 1967- SATA 94
Caroselli, Remus F(rancis) 1916- 97-100
See also SATA 36
Carossa, Hans 1878-1956 170
See also DLB 66
See also EWL 3
See also TCLC 48
Carosso, Vincent P(hillip)
1922-1993 CANR-48
Obituary 141
Earlier sketches in CA 9-12R, CANR-3
Carothers, J. Edward 1907-2000 41-44R
Obituary 189
Carothers, Robert Lee 1942- CANR-45
Earlier sketch in CA 45-48
Carothers, Thomas 1956- 199
Carousso, Georges 1909- 89-92
Carozzi, Albert V(ictor) 1925- 53-56
Carp, E. Wayne 1946- 185
Carp, Frances Merchant 1918- 21-24R
Carpelan, Bo (Gustaf Bertelsson)
1926- CANR-52
Earlier sketches in CA 49-52, CANR-2, 27
See also CWW 2
See also EWL 3
See also SATA 8
Carpenter
See Arnold, June (Davis)
Carpenter, (John) Allan 1917- CANR-42
Earlier sketches in CA 9-12R, CANR-3
See also SATA 3, 81
Carpenter, Andrew 1943- 93-96
Carpenter, Angelica Shirley 1945- 228
See also SATA 71, 153
Carpenter, Bogdana 1941- 135
Carpenter, Cal
See Carpenter, Clarence A(lfred)
Carpenter, Candice 1952- 236
Carpenter, Charles A. (Jr.) 1929- 33-36R
Carpenter, Charles H(ope), Jr. 1916- 111
Carpenter, Clarence A(lfred) 1921- 116
Carpenter, Clarence Ray 1905-1975
Obituary 57-60
Carpenter, D(avid) A(rscott) 1946- 134
Carpenter, David A(llen) 1949- 111
Carpenter, David C. 1941- 121
Carpenter, (J.) Delores Bird 1942- CANR-91
Earlier sketches in CA 126, CANR-53
Carpenter, Don(ald Richard)
1931-1995 CANR-71
Obituary 149
Earlier sketches in CA 45-48, CANR-1
See also CLC 41
Carpenter, Duffy
See Hurley, John J(erome)
Carpenter, Edward 1844-1929 163
See also GLL 1
See also TCLC 88
Carpenter, Elizabeth Sutherland 1920- 41-44R
Carpenter, Frances 1890-1972 CANR-71
Obituary 37-40R
Earlier sketches in CA 5-8R, CANR-4
See also SATA 3
See also SATA-Obit 27
Carpenter, Francis Ross 1925- 101
Carpenter, Fred
See Hand, (Andrus) Jackson
Carpenter, Frederic I.
See Carpenter, Frederic Ives (Jr.)
Carpenter, Frederic Ives (Jr.)
1903-1991 CANR-38
Obituary 134
Earlier sketch in CA 5-8R
Carpenter, Humphrey (William Bouverie)
1946-2005 CANR-53
Obituary 235
Earlier sketches in CA 89-92, CANR-13
Interview in CANR-13
See also DLB 155
Carpenter, J(ohn) D(avid) 1948- 115
Carpenter, James A. 1928- 37-40R
Carpenter, John (Randell) 1936- CANR-38
Earlier sketches in CA 65-68, CANR-9

Cumulative Index 95 **Carroll**

Carpenter, John (Howard) 1948- 134
See also AAYA 2
See also CLC 161
See also SATA 58
Carpenter, John A(lcott) 1921-1978 .... 9-12R
Obituary 77-80
Carpenter, John Jo
See Reese, John (Henry)
Carpenter, Johnny
See Wood, Edward D(avis), Jr.
Carpenter, Johnny
See Carpenter, John (Howard)
Carpenter, Joyce Frances 33-36R
Carpenter, Kenneth E(dward) 1936- 137
Carpenter, Kenneth J(ohn) 1923- CANR-50
Earlier sketch in CA 124
Carpenter, Liz
See Carpenter, Elizabeth Sutherland
Carpenter, Lucas 1947- CANR-109
Earlier sketches in CA 126, CANR-53
Carpenter, Lynette 1951- 138
Carpenter, Margaret Haley (?)-1985 .. CANR-75
Obituary 116
Earlier sketch in CA 5-8R
Carpenter, Marjorie 1896-1979 45-48
Carpenter, Michael (Anthony) 1940- 119
Carpenter, Mimi Gregoire 1947- CANR-30
Earlier sketch in CA 111
Carpenter, Morley
See Tubb, E(dwin) C(harles)
Carpenter, Nan Cooke 1912-1999 .... 25-28R
Carpenter, Patricia (Healy Evans)
1920- 29-32R
See also SATA 11
Carpenter, Peter 1922- 13-16R
Carpenter, Rhys 1889-1980 .... CANR-71
Obituary 93-96
Earlier sketch in CA 57-60
Carpenter, Richard C(oles) 1916- 13-16R
Carpenter, Stephen Cullen (?)-1820(?) ... DLB 73
Carpenter, Sue 1966- 234
Carpenter, Teresa (Suzanne) 1948- . CANR-130
Earlier sketch in CA 162
Carpenter, William 1940- CANR-108
Earlier sketch in CA 106
Carpenter, Willow
See Browning, (Zerilda) Sinclair
Carpentier (y Valmont), Alejo
1904-1980 .... CANR-70
Obituary 97-100
Earlier sketches in CA 65-68, CANR-11
See also CDWLB 3
See also CLC 8, 11, 38, 110
See also DAM MULT
See also DLB 113
See also EWL 3
See also HLC 1
See also HW 1, 2
See also LAW
See also LMFS 2
See also RGSF 2
See also RGWL 2, 3
See also SSC 35
See also WLIT 1
Carper, Jean Elinor 1932- CANR-7
Earlier sketch in CA 17-20R
Carper, L. Dean 1931- 49-52
Carpi, Daniel (V.) 1926- CANR-105
Earlier sketch in CA 149
Carpozi, George, Jr. 1920- CANR-71
Earlier sketches in CA 13-16R, CANR-11
Carr, A. H. Z.
See Carr, Albert H. Z(olotkoff)
Carr, Albert H. Z(olotkoff)
1902-1971 .... CANR-71
Obituary 33-36R
Earlier sketches in CA 1-4R, CANR-1
Carr, Alice
See Myers, Amy
Carr, Annemarie Weyl 1941- 144
Carr, Annie Roe CANR-26
Earlier sketches in CAP-2, CA 19-20
Carr, Archie (Fairly, Jr.) 1909-1987 ... CANR-71
Obituary 122
Earlier sketch in CA 13-16R
Carr, Arthur C(harles) 1918- 37-40R
Carr, Arthur Japheth 1914-1991 57-60
Carr, Blair 166
Carr, Bruce (A.) 1938- 114
Carr, C(harles) T(elford) 1905-1976
Obituary 65-68
Carr, Caleb 1955- CANR-134
Earlier sketches in CA 147, CANR-73
See also CLC 86
See also DA3
Carr, Catharine
See Wade, Rosalind Herschel
Carr, Christopher
See Benson, A(rthur) C(hristopher)
Carr, David William 1911- 37-40R
Carr, Donald Eaton 1903-1986 .... CANR-71
Earlier sketch in CA 13-16R
Carr, Dorothy Stevenson Laird
1912-2000 .... 9-12R
Obituary 190
Carr, Duane 1934- 166
Carr, Edward Hallet 1892-1982 .... CANR-14
Obituary 108
Earlier sketch in CA 61-64
Carr, Edwin George 1937- 61-64
Carr, Emily 1871-1945 159
See also DLB 68
See also FW
See also GLL 2
See also TCLC 32
Carr, Gerald F(rancis) 1930- CANR-114
Earlier sketch in CA 118
Carr, Glyn
See Styles, (Frank) Showell
Carr, Gwen B. 1924- 41-44R
Carr, H. D.
See Crowley, Edward Alexander
Carr, Harriett H(elen) 1899-1977 ...... CANR-71
Earlier sketches in CAP-1, CA 9-10
See also SATA 3
Carr, Herbert R(eginald) C(ulling) 1896-1986
Obituary 119
Carr, Ian (Henry Randell) 1933- CANR-46
Earlier sketch in CA 110
Carr, J(ames Joseph) L(loyd)
1912-1994 .... CANR-107
Obituary 144
Earlier sketches in CA 102, CANR-37
See also CN 4, 5
Carr, J(ames) Revell 1939- 234
Carr, Jan 1953- 155
See also SATA 89, 132
Carr, Janet Baker
See Baker-Carr, Janet
Carr, Jay Phillip 1936- 89-92
Carr, Jayge 1940- 158
See also Krueger, Marj
See also SFW 4
Carr, Jess(e Crowe, Jr.) 1930-1990 .... CANR-29
Obituary 130
Earlier sketches in CA 29-32R, CANR-12
Carr, (Bettye) Jo (Crisler) 1926- 21-24R
Carr, John C(harles) 1929-1999 53-56
Obituary 187
Carr, John Dickson 1906-1977 .... CANR-60
Obituary 69-72
Earlier sketches in CA 49-52, CANR-3, 33
See also Fairbairn, Roger
See also CLC 3
See also CMW 4
See also DLB 306
See also MSW
See also MTCW 1, 2
Carr, John Laurence 1916- 49-52
Carr, Jonathan 170
Carr, Josephine 1952- 111
Carr, Karen L. 1960- 142
Carr, Lois Green 1922- 61-64
Carr, M. J.
See Carr, Jan
Carr, Margaret 1935- 105
Carr, Marina 1964- 185
See also DLB 245
Carr, Marvin (N.) 1927- 148
Carr, Mary Jane 1899-1988 .... CAP-1
Obituary 124
Earlier sketch in CA 9-10
See also SATA 2
See also SATA-Obit 55
Carr, Michael Harold 1935- 109
Carr, Pat 1932- CANR-57
Earlier sketches in CA 65-68, CANR-14, 31
Carr, Philippa
See Hibbert, Eleanor Alice Burford
Carr, Raymond 1919- CANR-100
Earlier sketches in CA 17-20R, CANR-8
Carr, Robert K(enneth) 1908-1979 93-96
Obituary 85-88
Carr, Roberta
See Roberts, Irene
Carr, Robyn 1951- CANR-38
Earlier sketch in CA 115
See also RHW
Carr, Roger Vaughan 1937- 160
See also SATA 95
Carr, Roland T. 1908(?)-1983 122
Obituary 111
Carr, Rosamond Halsey 1914(?)- 194
Carr, Stephen L(amoni) 57-60
Carr, Steven Alan 1964- 187
Carr, Terry (Gene) 1937-1987 81-84
Obituary 180
See also SFW 4
Carr, Virginia Mason
See Vaughan, Virginia M(ason)
Carr, Virginia Spencer 1929- 61-64
See also CLC 34
See also DLB 111
Carr, Warren Tyree 1917- 5-8R
Carr, William 1921- 73-76
Carr, William G(eorge) 1901-1996 53-56
Obituary 151
Carr, William H(enry) A(lexander)
1924- CANR-7
Earlier sketch in CA 13-16R
Carraco, Carol Crowe
See Crowe-Carraco, Carol
Carradice, Ian A. 1953- CANR-123
Earlier sketch in CA 163
Carradine, Beverly 1848-1919 211
Carradine, David 1936- 206
Carradine, John Arthur
See Carradine, David
Carraher, Charles E. (Jr.) 1941- 135
Carranco, Lynwood 1921- CANR-21
Earlier sketches in CA 57-60, CANR-6
Carranza, Eduardo 1913-1985 .... EWL 3
Carras, Mary C(alliope) 85-88
Carrasco, David 1944- CANR-124
Earlier sketch in CA 112
Carrasquilla, Tomas 1858-1940 .... EWL 3
See also LAW
Carre, Ben 1883-1978 .... IDFW 3, 4
Carrel, Alexis (Marie Joseph Auguste Billiard)
1873-1944 157
Brief entry 120
Carrel, Annette Felder 1929- 155
See also SATA 90
Carrel, Mark
See Paine, Lauran (Bosworth)
Carrell, Norman (Gerald) 1905- CAP-2
Earlier sketch in CA 25-28
Carrera Andrade, Jorge 1903-1978 155
Obituary 85-88
See also DLB 283
See also EWL 3
See also HW 1
See also LAWS 1
Carreras, James 1909-1990 .... IDFW 3, 4
Carreras, Jose 1946- 141
Carrere, Emmanuel 1957- 200
See also CLC 89
Carrere d'Encausse, Helene 1929- 216
Carretta, Vincent (Albert) 1945- 131
Carrey, James Eugene 1962- 207
Carrey, Jim
See Carrey, James Eugene
Carr-Hill, Roy A. 1943- 141
Carrick, A. B.
See Lindsay, Harold Arthur
Carrick, Burt
See Cassiday, Bruce (Bingham)
Carrick, Carol (Hatfield) 1935- CANR-96
Earlier sketches in CA 45-48, CANR-1, 17, 37, 70
See also MAICYA 1, 2
See also SAAS 18
See also SATA 7, 63, 118
Carrick, Donald (F.) 1929-1989 .... CANR-37
Earlier sketches in CA 53-56, CANR-5, 20
See also MAICYA 1, 2
See also SATA 7, 63
Carrick, Edward
See Craig, Edward Anthony
Carrick, John
See Crosbie, (Hugh) Provan
Carrick, Malcolm 1945- CANR-14
Earlier sketch in CA 77-80
See also SATA 28
Carrier, Constance 1908-1991 .... 33-36R
See also CP 1
Carrier, Esther Jane 1925- 17-20R
Carrier, James G(olden) 1947- 149
Carrier, Jean-Guy 1945- 101
Carrier, Lark 1947- .... SATA 71
See also SATA-Brief 50
Carrier, Roch 1937- CANR-61
Earlier sketch in CA 130
See also CCA 1
See also CLC 13, 78
See also DAC
See also DAM MST
See also DLB 53
See also SATA 105
Carrier, Scott 1957- 200
Carrier, Thomas J. 1956- 224
Carrier, Warren (Pendleton) 1918- CANR-71
Earlier sketches in CA 9-12R, CANR-3, 18
See also CP 1
Carriere, Jean-Claude 1931- 140
See also IDFW 3, 4
Carrigan, Andrew G(ardner) 1935- CANR-1
Earlier sketch in CA 45-48
Carrigan, D(avid) Owen 1933- 25-28R
Carrigan, Richard A(lfred), Jr. 1932- . CANR-30
Earlier sketch in CA 112
Carrighar, Sally 1898-1985 .... CANR-70
Earlier sketch in CA 93-96
See also ANW
See also SATA 24
Carriker, Robert C(harles) 1940- 69-72
Carriker, S. David 1951- 172
Carrillo, Adolfo 1855-1926 174
See also DLB 122
See also HW 2
Carrillo, Lawrence W(ilbert)
1920-1995 .... 13-16R
Carringer, Robert L. 1941- CANR-17
Earlier sketch in CA 97-100
Carrington, Charles Edmund
1897-1990 .... CANR-71
Obituary 132
Earlier sketch in CA 5-8R
Carrington, (Frederica) Dorothy (Violet)
1910-2002 217
Carrington, Frank G(amble, Jr.) 1936- 57-60
Carrington, G. A.
See Cunningham, Chet
Carrington, George C(abell), Jr.
1928-1990 122
Obituary 132
Brief entry 118
Carrington, Grant 1938- 104
Carrington, Leonora 1917- 124
Brief entry 114
Carrington, Marsha Gray 1954- .... SATA 111
Carrington, Molly
See Matthews, C(onstance) M(ary)
Carrington, Paul D(eWitt) 1931- 29-32R
Carrington, Richard (Temple Murray)
1921- CANR-79
Earlier sketch in CA 9-12R
Carrington, Roslyn 235
Carrington, William Langley
1900-1970 .... CAP-1
Earlier sketch in CA 13-14
Carrio de la Vandera, Alonso c.
1715-1783 .... LAW
Carrion, Arturo Morales
See Morales Carrion, Arturo
Carris, Joan Davenport 1938- CANR-27
Earlier sketch in CA 106
See also SATA 44
See also SATA-Brief 42
Carrison, Daniel J. 1917- 37-40R
Carrison, Muriel Paskin 1928- 127
Carrithers, David W. 1943- 110
Carrithers, Gale H(emphill), Jr. 1932- 41-44R
Carrithers, Wallace M(axwell)
1911-1993 .... 25-28R
Carrol, Kathleen
See Creighton, Kathleen
Carrol, Shana
See Newcomb, Kerry and Schaefer, Frank
Carroll, Anne Kristin
See Gales, Barbara J.
Carroll, Archie B(enjamin III) 1943- 109
Carroll, B(illy) D(an) 1940- 53-56
Carroll, Benajah Harvey 1843-1914 215
Carroll, Berenice A(nita) 1932- 41-44R
Carroll, Bob 1936- CANR-65
Earlier sketch in CA 129
Carroll, Brendan G. 1952- 164
Carroll, C(armal) Edward 1923- 29-32R
Carroll, Carroll 1902-1991 101
Obituary 133
Carroll, Cathryn 226
Carroll, Charles Francis 1936- 53-56
Carroll, Christina
See Henderson, M(arilyn) R(uth)
Carroll, Colleen 1974- 216
Carroll, Curt
See Bishop, Curtis (Kent)
Carroll, Daniel B(ernard) 1928-1977 ..... 41-44R
Carroll, David
See Carroll, David L.
Carroll, David L. 1942- 129
Carroll, David M. 230
Carroll, Dennis 1940- 114
Carroll, Diahann 1935- 201
Carroll, Donald K(ingery) 1909- CAP-2
Earlier sketch in CA 17-18
Carroll, Elizabeth
See Barkin, Carol and James, Elizabeth
Carroll, Faye 1937- 21-24R
Carroll, Francis M(artin) 1938- 225
Carroll, Gerry 1947-1993 151
Carroll, Ginny 1948-2001 130
Obituary 197
Carroll, Gladys Hasty 1904-1999 .... CANR-5
Obituary 177
Earlier sketch in CA 1-4R
See also DLB 9
Carroll, Herbert A(llen) 1897-1983 .... CAP-1
Obituary 176
Earlier sketch in CA 11-12
Carroll, J. Larry 1946- 129
Carroll, Jackson W(alker) 1932- CANR-16
Earlier sketch in CA 85-88
Carroll, James Dennis
See Carroll, Jim
Carroll, James P. 1943(?)- CANR-139
Earlier sketches in CA 81-84, CANR-73
See also CLC 38
See also MTCW 2
See also MTFW 2005
Carroll, Jeffrey 1950- 85-88
Carroll, Jenny
See Cabot, Meg(gin)
Carroll, Jim 1951- CANR-115
Earlier sketches in CA 45-48, CANR-42
See also AAYA 17
See also CLC 35, 143
See also NCFS 5
Carroll, John 1735-1815 .... DLB 37
Carroll, John 1809-1884 .... DLB 99
Carroll, John 1944- CANR-7
Earlier sketch in CA 57-60
Carroll, John B(issell) 1916- CANR-3
Earlier sketch in CA 1-4R
Carroll, John D.
See Daly, Carroll John
Carroll, John J(oseph) 1924- 13-16R
Carroll, John M(elvin) 1928- 37-40R
Carroll, John Millar 1925- CANR-23
Earlier sketches in CA 5-8R, CANR-8
Carroll, Jonathan 1949- CANR-74
Earlier sketches in CA 105, CANR-21
See also FANT
See also HGG
See also MTFW 2005
See also SUFW 2
Carroll, Joseph 1912(?)-1989
Obituary 128
Carroll, Joseph T(homas) 1935- 102
Carroll, Joy 1924- 102
Carroll, Kenneth Lane 1924- 37-40R
Carroll, L(awrence) Patrick 1936- 111
Carroll, (Archer) Latrobe 1894-1996 ... CANR-3
Obituary 180
Earlier sketch in CA 1-4R
See also SATA 7
Carroll, Laura
See Parr, Lucy

Carroll, Lewis
See Dodgson, Charles L(utwidge)
See also AAYA 39
See also BRW 5
See also BYA 5, 13
See also CDBLB 1832-1890
See also CLR 2, 18
See also DLB 18, 163, 178
See also DLBY 1998
See also EXPN
See also EXPP
See also FANT
See also JRDA
See also LAIT 1
See also NFS 7
See also PC 18
See also PFS 11
See also RGEL 2
See also SUFW 1
See also TEA
See also WCH
See also WLC
Carroll, Loren 1904-1978 85-88
Obituary 81-84
Carroll, Martin
See Carr, Margaret
Carroll, Mary
See Sanford, Annette
Carroll, Matthew S. 1955- 152
Carroll, Noel
See Munson, Carol (Barr) Swayze and Munson, Noel J.
Carroll, Paul 1927- 25-28R
See also CP 1, 2
See also DLB 16
Carroll, Paul Vincent 1900-1968 .... 9-12R
Obituary 25-28R
See also CLC 10
See also DLB 10
See also EWL 3
See also RGEL 2
Carroll, Peter N(eil) 1943- 102
Carroll, Phil 1895-1971 .... CAP-1
Earlier sketch in CA 13-14
Carroll, Raymond 1924- 126
See also SATA 86
See also SATA-Brief 47
Carroll, Rebecca 1969- 147
Carroll, Richard J. 1957- 175
Carroll, Robert
See Alpert, Hollis
Carroll, Robert P(eter) 1941-2000 .... CANR-43
Obituary 189
Earlier sketch in CA 105
Carroll, Rodney (James) 1957- 232
Carroll, Rosalynn
See Katz, Carol
Carroll, Ruth (Robinson) 1899-1999 . CANR-79
Earlier sketches in CA 1-4R, CANR-1
Carroll, St. Thomas Marion
See Carroll, Tom M.
Carroll, Sheila Baker 1918(?)-1984
Obituary 113
Carroll, Sister Mary Gerald 1913- 21-24R
Carroll, Stephen J(ohn), Jr. 1930- 41-44R
Carroll, Susan 235
Carroll, Ted
See Carroll, Thomas Theodore, Jr.
Carroll, Theodus (Catherine) 1928- .. CANR-49
Earlier sketch in CA 69-72
Carroll, Thomas J. 1909-1971 .... 1-4R
Obituary 103
Carroll, Thomas Theodore, Jr. 1925- 9-12R
Carroll, Tom M. 1950- 53-56
Carroll, Vern 1933- 57-60
Carroll, Vinnette (Justine) -2002 .... CANR-78
Obituary 210
Brief entry 114
Earlier sketch in CA 123
Interview in CA-123
See also BW 1
Carron, Malcolm 1917-2005
Obituary 238
Brief entry 105
Carrott, Richard G. 1924-1990 85-88
Carrouges, Michel
See Couturier, Louis (Joseph)
Carrow, Milton M(ichael) 1912- CANR-16
Earlier sketch in CA 25-28R
Carr-Saunders, Alexander (Morris)
1886-1966 .... CANR-20
Obituary 103
Earlier sketch in CA 1-4R
Carruth, Estelle 1910- 9-12R
Carruth, Gorton Veeder 1925- CANR-6
Earlier sketch in CA 57-60
Carruth, Hayden 1921- CANR-110
Earlier sketches in CA 9-12R, CANR-4, 38, 59
Interview in CANR-4
See also CLC 4, 7, 10, 18, 84
See also CP 1, 2, 3, 4, 5, 6, 7
See also DLB 5, 165
See also MTCW 1, 2
See also MTFW 2005
See also PC 10
See also SATA 47
Carruthers, Ben F(rederick) 1911-1985 114
Carruthers, Malcolm Euan 1938- 102
Carruthers, Peter 1952- 126
Carry, (Benjamin) Peter 1942- 105
Carryaway, Nick
See Murray, John F(rancis)
Carryl, Charles E(dward) 1841-1920 178
See also DLB 42
See also SATA 114
Carsac, Francis
See Bordes, Francois
Carsberg, Bryan Victor 1939- CANR-29
Earlier sketches in CA 29-32R, CANR-12
Carse, James P(earce) 1932- 21-24R
Carse, Robert 1902-1971 .... CANR-82
Obituary 29-32R
Earlier sketches in CA 1-4R, CANR-1
See also SATA 5
Carskadon, Thomas R. 1901(?)-1983(?)
Obituary 108
Carson, Ada Lou 1932- 110
Carson, Alan 1951- 115
Carson, Anne (Regina) 1950- CANR-53
Earlier sketch in CA 132
Carson, Anne 1950- 203
See also AMWS 12
See also CLC 185
See also DLB 193
See also PC 64
See also PFS 18
See also TCLE 1:1
Carson, Anne Conover
See Conover, Anne
Carson, Barbara Harrell 1943- 143
Carson, Ben
See Carson, Benjamin S(olomon) Sr.
Carson, Benjamin S(olomon) Sr.
1951- CANR-80
Earlier sketch in CA 157
See also BW 3
Carson, Captain James CANR-26
Earlier sketches in CAP-2, CA 19-20
Carson, Ciaran 1948- CANR-113
Brief entry 112
Earlier sketch in CA 153
See also CLC 201
See also CP 7
Carson, Clarence B. 1925- 130
Carson, Clayborne 1944- CANR-116
Earlier sketches in CA 105, CANR-62, 115
Carson, D(onald) A(rthur) 1946- 142
Carson, Donald W. 1933- 201
Carson, F(ranklin) John 1920- 9-12R
Carson, Gerald (Hewes) 1899-1989 . CANR-82
Obituary 130
Earlier sketches in CA 1-4R, CANR-1, 16
Carson, Hampton L(awrence) 1914- 5-8R
Carson, Hank
See Fearn, John Russell
Carson, Herbert L(ee) 1929- 29-32R
Carson, J(ohn) Franklin 1920-1981 .... 13-16R
Obituary 171
See also SATA 1
See also SATA-Obit 107
Carson, Jane Dennison (?)-1984
Obituary 114
Carson, John William 1925-2005 205
Obituary 235
Carson, Johnny
See Carson, John William
Carson, Josephine 1919- .... CAAS 28
Carson, Kit
See Carson, Xanthus
Carson, Mary 1934- 41-44R
Carson, Mary Kay 1964- 225
See also SATA 150
Carson, Michael (Charles) 1946- 130
Carson, Rachel
See Carson, Rachel Louise
See also AAYA 49
See also DLB 275
Carson, Rachel Louise 1907-1964 .... CANR-35
Earlier sketch in CA 77-80
See also Carson, Rachel
See also AMWS 9
See also ANW
See also CLC 71
See also DA3
See also DAM POP
See also FW
See also LAIT 4
See also MAL 5
See also MTCW 1, 2
See also MTFW 2005
See also NCFS 1
See also SATA 23
Carson, Ray F(ritziof) 1939- 61-64
Carson, Robert 1909-1983 .... CANR-81
Obituary 108
Earlier sketch in CA 21-24R
Carson, Robert B. 1934- CANR-6
Earlier sketch in CA 57-60
Carson, Robert C(harles) 1930- 29-32R
Carson, Ronald A(lan) 1940- 119
Carson, Rosalind
See Chittenden, Margaret
Carson, Ruth
See Bugbee, Ruth Carson
Carson, S. M.
See Gorsline, (Sally) Marie
Carson, Tom 1956- 220
Carson, William C. 1928- .... SATA 154
Carson, William Glasgow Bruce
1891-1976 .... 5-8R
Carson, Xanthus 1910-1977 57-60
Carstairs, George Morrison 1916-1991 69-72
Carstairs, Kathleen
See Pendower, Jacques
Carsten, Francis Ludwig 1911-1998 . CANR-79
Earlier sketch in CA 13-16R
Carstens, Catherine Mansell
See Mayo, C(atherine) M(ansell)
Carstens, Grace Pearce -1989 .... 1-4R
Carstensen, Roger Norwood
1920-1996 .... CANR-2
Earlier sketch in CA 5-8R
Carswell, Catherine (McFarlane Jackson)
1879-1946 178
See also DLB 36
Carswell, Evelyn M(edicus) 1919- 57-60
Carswell, John (Patrick) 1918-1997 .. CANR-21
Obituary 162
Earlier sketch in CA 9-12R
Carswell, Leslie
See Stephens, Rosemary
Cart, Michael 1941- 217
See also GLL 2
Cartagena, Alfonso de c. 1384-1456 .. DLB 286
Cartagena, Teresa de 1425(?)- .... DLB 286
Cartan, Henri (Paul) 1904- 164
Cartano, Tony 1944- 129
Cartarescu, Mircea 1956- .... DLB 232
Carte, Gene E(dward) 1938- 61-64
Cartelli, Thomas 192
Carter, Alan 1936- 33-36R
Carter, Albert Howard 1913-1970 .... CAP-2
Earlier sketch in CA 25-28
Carter, Alden R(ichardson) 1947- CANR-114
Earlier sketches in CA 135, CANR-58
See also AAYA 17, 54
See also CLR 22
See also SAAS 18
See also SATA 67, 137
See also WYA
See also YAW
Carter, Alfred Edward 1914-1979 .... 33-36R
Carter, Allene G. 221
Carter, Amon Giles, Jr. 1919-1982
Obituary 111
Carter, Andy 1948- 203
See also SATA 134
Carter, Angela (Olive) 1940-1992 ... CANR-106
Obituary 136
Earlier sketches in CA 53-56, CANR-12, 36, 61
See also BRWS 3
See also CLC 5, 41, 76
See also CN 3, 4, 5
See also DA3
See also DLB 14, 207, 261, 319
See also EXPS
See also FANT
See also FW
See also GL 2
See also MTCW 1, 2
See also MTFW 2005
See also RGSF 2
See also SATA 66
See also SATA-Obit 70
See also SFW 4
See also SSC 13, 85
See also SSFS 4, 12
See also SUFW 2
See also TCLC 139
See also WLIT 4
Carter, Ann
See Brooks, Anne Tedlock
Carter, Anne
See Brooks, Anne Tedlock
Carter, Anne 184
Carter, Anne Laurel 1953- CANR-113
See also SATA 135
Carter, Anne Pitts 1925-
Brief entry 106
Carter, Arthur B. 214
Carter, Arthur M. 1911-1988
Obituary 125
Carter, Asa Earl
See Carter, Forrest
Carter, Ashley
See Whittington, Harry (Benjamin)
See also RHW
Carter, Ashton B. 1954- 137
Carter, Avis Murton
See Allen, Kenneth S.
Carter, Barbara (Ellen) 1925-1988 .... CANR-10
Obituary 126
Earlier sketch in CA 53-56
Carter, Ben
See Ben Ammi
Carter, Betty 1944- 170
Carter, Betty Smartt 1965- CANR-142
Earlier sketch in CA 169
Carter, Bill
See Carter, William E.
Carter, Boyd (George) 1908-1980 .... CANR-7
Earlier sketch in CA 13-16R
Carter, Bruce
See Hough, Richard (Alexander)
Carter, Burnham 1901(?)-1979
Obituary 89-92
Carter, Byron L. 1924- 21-24R
Carter, C(edric) O(swald) 1917-1984
Obituary 112
Carter, Carmen 1954- 128
Carter, Carol S(hadis) 1948- .... SATA 124
Carter, Carolle J(ean) 1934- 81-84
Carter, Charles Frederick
1919-2002 .... CANR-20
Obituary 208
Earlier sketches in CA 1-4R, CANR-4
Carter, Charles H(oward) 1927- 9-12R
Carter, Charles W(ebb) 1905-1996 .... 21-24R
Carter, Charlotte 172
Carter, Chris 1956- 160
See also AAYA 23
Carter, Dan T. 1940- CANR-52
Earlier sketch in CA 65-68
Carter, David A. 1957- 186
See also SATA 114
Carter, David C(harles) 1946- 45-48
Carter, Dixie 1939- 207
Carter, Don 1958- .... SATA 124
Carter, Don E(arl) 1917- 73-76
Carter, Dorothy Sharp 1921- 49-52
See also SATA 8
Carter, E. Lawrence 1910-1997 .... 25-28R
Obituary 158
Carter, Edward Julian 1902-1982 .... 5-8R
Obituary 107
Carter, Elizabeth 1717-1806 .... DLB 109
Carter, Elizabeth Eliot
See Holland, Cecelia (Anastasia)
Carter, Elliott Cook 1908- 89-92
Carter, Emily 1960- 199
Carter, Ernestine (Marie) (?)-1983 130
Obituary 110
Carter, Everett 1919- 13-16R
Carter, Forrest 1927(?)-1979 .... CANR-114
Earlier sketch in CA 107
See also BYA 16
See also DAM POP
See also SATA 32
See also TCWW 1, 2
Carter, Frances Monet 1923- 37-40R
Carter, Frances Tunnell 37-40R
Carter, Gari 1940- 214
Carter, George F(rancis) 1912- CANR-4
Earlier sketch in CA 5-8R
Carter, Gwendolen M(argaret)
1906-1991 .... CANR-82
Obituary 133
Earlier sketches in CA 1-4R, CANR-4, 19
Carter, Harold 1925- 33-36R
Carter, Harry Graham 1901-1982
Obituary 106
Carter, Harvey L(ewis) 1904-1994 .... 21-24R
Carter, Helene 1887-1960 .... SATA 15
Carter, Henry
See Leslie, Frank
Carter, Henry Hare 1905- 41-44R
Carter, (William) Hodding, Jr.
1907-1972 .... CAP-1
Obituary 33-36R
Earlier sketch in CA 13-14
See also DLB 127
See also SATA 2
See also SATA-Obit 27
Carter, Hugh 1895-1988 .... 37-40R
Carter, Hurricane
See Carter, Rubin
Carter, J(ohn) Anthony 1943- 61-64
Carter, James E(dward) 1935- CANR-22
Earlier sketches in CA 57-60, CANR-7
Carter, James Earl, Jr. 1924- CANR-109
Earlier sketches in CA 69-72, CANR-32
See also MTCW 1
See also SATA 79
Carter, James Puckette 1933- 33-36R
Carter, James Richard 1940- 33-36R
Carter, Jane Robbins
See Robbins, Jane (Borsch)
Carter, Janet 1938- 104
Carter, Jared 1939- 145
See also DLB 282
Carter, Jeanne Wilmot
See Wilmot, Jeanne
Carter, Jennifer 193
Carter, Jimmy
See Carter, James Earl, Jr.
Carter, John (Waynflete) 1905-1975 . CANR-82
Obituary 57-60
Earlier sketch in CA 5-8R
See also DLB 201
Carter, John (J.) 1955- 191
Carter, John E. 1950- 141
Carter, John Franklin 1897-1967
Obituary 25-28R
Carter, John Mack 1928- 103
Carter, John Marshall 1949- 143
Carter, John Stewart 1912-1965 .... CAP-1
Earlier sketch in CA 11-12
Carter, John T(homas) 1921- 33-36R
Carter, Joseph 1912-1984 49-52
Obituary 112
Carter, Joseph H(enry Sr.) 1932- 139
Carter, K(ay) Codell 1939- 110
Carter, Katharine J(ones) 1905-1984 .... 5-8R
See also SATA 2
Carter, Landon 1710-1778 .... DLB 31
Carter, Lief Hastings 1940- CANR-6
Earlier sketch in CA 57-60
Carter, (Bessie) Lillian (Gordy) 1898-1983 .. 118
Obituary 111
Brief entry 105
Carter, Lin(wood Vrooman)
1930-1988 .... CANR-30
Earlier sketch in CA 41-44R
See also DLBY 1981
See also FANT
See also SATA 91
See also SFW 4
Carter, Lonnie 1942- CANR-67
Earlier sketches in CA 65-68, CANR-9
See also CAD
See also CD 5, 6
Carter, Luther J(ordan) 1927- 57-60
Carter, M(argaret) L(ouise) 1948- 33-36R
Carter, Margaret (Mary) 1923- 107
Carter, Marilyn
See Ross, W(illiam) E(dward) D(aniel)
Carter, Martin (Wylde) 1927- CANR-42
Earlier sketch in CA 102
See also BW 2
See also CDWLB 3
See also CP 1, 2
See also DLB 117
See also EWL 3
Carter, Martin R(oger) 1946- CANR-107
Earlier sketch in CA 147

Cumulative Index 97 Casey

Carter, Mary CANR-5
Earlier sketch in CA 9-12R
Carter, Mary Ellen 1923-1997 .... 25-28R
Carter, Mary Kennedy 65-68
Carter, Merri Sue 1964- 215
Carter, Mike 1936- 208
See also SATA 138
Carter, Miranda 1965- 234
Carter, Neil 1913- 17-20R
Carter, Nevada
See Paine, Lauran (Bosworth)
Carter, Nicholas
See Dey, Frederic (Merrill) Van Rensselaer
Carter, Nick
See Avallone, Michael (Angelo, Jr.) and
Ballard, (Willis) Todhunter and
Cassiday, Bruce (Bingham) and
Chastain, Thomas and
Crider, (Allen) Bill(y) and
Dey, Frederic (Merrill) Van Rensselaer and
Garside, (Clifford) Jack and
Hayes, Ralph E(ugene) and
Henderson, M(arilyn) R(uth) and
Lynds, Dennis and
Lynds, Gayle (Hallenbeck) and
Randisi, Robert J(oseph) and
Rasof, Henry and
Smith, Martin Cruz and
Stratemeyer, Edward L. and
Swain, Dwight V(reeland) and
Vardeman, Robert E(dward) and
Wallmann, Jeffrey M(iner) and
White, Lionel
Carter, Paul (Hugh) 1951- 129
Carter, Paul A(llen) 1926- CANR-13
Earlier sketch in CA 33-36R
Carter, Paul J(efferson), Jr. 1912-1975 .... CAP-2
Earlier sketch in CA 21-22
Carter, Peter 1929- CANR-44
Earlier sketch in CA 69-72
See also CWRI 5
See also SATA 57
Carter, Phyllis Ann
See Eberle, Irmengarde
Carter, Ralph
See Neubauer, William Arthur
Carter, Randolph 1914-1998 101
Obituary 171
Carter, Raphael 164
Carter, Richard 1918- CANR-8
Earlier sketch in CA 61-64
Carter, Richard D(uane) 1929- 111
Carter, Robert 1945- 128
Carter, Robert A(yres) 1923- CANR-104
Earlier sketch in CA 33-36R
Carter, Robert M(ack) 1925- 33-36R
Carter, Roger 1939- CANR-43
Earlier sketch in CA 119
Carter, (Eleanor) Rosalynn (Smith) 1927- 113
Carter, Rubin 1937- 191
Brief entry 113
Carter, Samuel (Thomson) III
1904-1988 .... CANR-82
Obituary 127
Earlier sketch in CA 57-60
See also SATA 37
See also SATA-Obit 60
Carter, Sebastian 1941- 126
Carter, Stephen L(isle) 1954- CANR-106
Earlier sketch in CA 147
Carter, Steven 1956- 137
Carter, Steven R(ay) 1942- 141
Carter, (Elizabeth) Susanne 1950- 141
Carter, Thomas Earl 1947- CANR-100
Earlier sketch in CA 133
Carter, Tom
See Carter, Thomas Earl
Carter, Victor A(lbert) 1902- CAP-1
Earlier sketch in CA 9-10
Carter, W(illiam) Hodding 1963(?)- 232
Carter, Walter 1950- 149
Carter, Warren 1955- 225
Carter, William 1934- 33-36R
Carter, William Ambrose 1899-1984 ..... CAP-1
Earlier sketch in CA 17-18
Carter, William Beverly, Jr. 1921-1982
Obituary 110
Carter, William E. 1926-1983 .... 17-20R
Obituary 110
See also SATA 1
See also SATA-Obit 35
Carter, William E. 1939- 216
Carter, William Lee 1925- 1-4R
Carter, Worrall Reed 1885(?)-1975
Obituary 57-60
Carter-Brown, Peter
See Yates, A(lan) G(eoffrey)
Carterette, Edward C(alvin) 1921- 41-44R
Carter-Harrison, Paul
See Harrison, Paul Carter
Carter-Ruck, Peter F(rederick)
1914-2003 97-100
Obituary 222
Carter-Scott, Cherie (Untermeyer) 1949- 185
Cartey, Wilfred (George Onslow)
1931-1992 .... CANR-25
Obituary 137
Earlier sketch in CA 73-76
See also BW 2
Carthy, Mother Mary Peter 1911-1992 .. 13-16R
Cartier, Xam Wilson 1949(?)- 125
See also BW 2
Cartier-Bresson, Henri 1908-2004 ...... AAYA 63
Cartland, Barbara (Hamilton)
1901-2000 .... CANR-74
Obituary 189
Earlier sketches in CA 9-12R, CANR-6, 34
Interview in CANR-6
See also CAAS 8
See also CPW
See also DA3
See also DAM POP
See also MTCW 1, 2
See also RHW
Cartledge, Paul 1947- CANR-93
Earlier sketches in CA 124, CANR-51
Cartledge, Samuel Antoine 1903-1991 ...... 1-4R
Cartledgehayes, Mary 1949- 219
Cartlidge, Barbara 1922- 121
Cartlidge, Michelle 1950- CANR-129
Earlier sketches in CA 93-96, CANR-68
See also SATA 49, 96
See also SATA-Brief 37
Cartmill, Cleve 1908-1964 161
See also SFW 4
Cartmill, Matt 1943- 146
Cartnal, Alan 1950- 105
Cartner, William Carruthers 1910- 73-76
See also SATA 11
Carto, Willis A(llison) 1926- 114
Carton, Bernice 1922- 169
Cartter, Allan Murray 1922-1976 .... CANR-8
Earlier sketch in CA 5-8R
Cartwright, Ann 1940- .... SATA 78
Cartwright, Anthony 1973- 239
Cartwright, Desmond S(pencer) 1924- 89-92
Cartwright, Frederick (Fox) 1909-2001 228
Cartwright, Gary 1934- 89-92
Cartwright, Gene 238
Cartwright, James McGregor
See Jennings, Leslie Nelson
Cartwright, Jim 1958- 230
See also CBD
See also CD 5, 6
See also DLB 245
Cartwright, John 1740-1824 .... DLB 158
Cartwright, Joseph H. 1939- 73-76
Cartwright, Justin 1933- CANR-108
Earlier sketches in CA 144, CANR-87
Cartwright, N.
See Scofield, Norma Margaret Cartwright
Cartwright, Reg(inald Ainsley) 1938- ... SATA 64
Cartwright, Rosalind Dymond 1922- 81-84
Cartwright, Sally 1923- CANR-2
Earlier sketch in CA 49-52
See also SATA 9
Cartwright, Vanessa
See Preston, Harry
Cartwright, William 1611(?)-1643 .... DLB 126
See also RGEL 2
Cartwright, William H(olman)
1915-2004 .... 9-12R
Obituary 232
Carty, David 1955- 139
Carty, James William, Jr. 1925- 53-56
Caruba, Alan 1937- 65-68
Carus, Paul 1852-1919 213
Caruso, Enrico 1873-1921
Brief entry 115
Caruso, John Anthony 1907-1997 .... CANR-79
Earlier sketch in CA 33-36R
Caruso, Joseph
See Barnwell, J. O.
Carusone, Al 1949- 155
See also SATA 89
Carus-Wilson, Eleanora M(ary)
1897-1977 .... 5-8R
Caruth, Donald L(ewis) 1935- 29-32R
Caruthers, Osgood 1915-1985
Obituary 117
Caruthers, William Alexander
1802-1846 .... DLB 3, 248
Carvajal, Ricardo
See Meneses, Enrique
Carvalho-Neto, Paulo de 1923- CANR-4
Earlier sketch in CA 53-56
Carvell, Fred J. 1934- 29-32R
Carver, Caroline 215
Carver, Dave
See Bingley, David Ernest
Carver, Frank G(ould) 1928- CANR-94
Earlier sketches in CA 49-52, CANR-45
Carver, Fred D(onald) 1936- 29-32R
Carver, Henry
See Bingley, David Ernest
Carver, Jeffrey A(llan) 1949- CANR-108
Earlier sketches in CA 101, CANR-18
See also SFW 4
Carver, John
See Gardner, Richard (M.)
Carver, Jonathan 1710-1780 .... DLB 31
Carver, M. O. H.
See Carver, Martin
Carver, Martin 1941- CANR-94
Earlier sketches in CA 145, CANR-87
Carver, (Richard) Michael (Power)
1915-2001 .... CANR-14
Obituary 203
Earlier sketch in CA 69-72
Carver, Norman F., Jr. 1928- 41-44R
Carver, Raymond 1938-1988 .... CANR-103
Obituary 126
Earlier sketches in CA 33-36R, CANR-17, 34, 61
See also AAYA 44
See also AMWS 3
See also BPFB 1
See also CLC 22, 36, 53, 55, 126
See also CN 4
See also CPW
See also DA3
See also DAM NOV
See also DLB 130
See also DLBY 1984, 1988
See also EWL 3
See also MAL 5
See also MTCW 1, 2
See also MTFW 2005
See also PC 54
See also PFS 17
See also RGAL 4
See also RGSF 2
See also SSC 8, 51
See also SSFS 3, 6, 12, 13
See also TCLE 1:1
See also TCWW 2
See also TUS
Carver, Robert 194
Carver, Saxon Rowe 1905-1999 .... CAP-1
Earlier sketch in CA 13-14
Carver, Terrell 1946- CANR-86
Earlier sketch in CA 133
Carvey, Dana 1955- 174
Carvic, Heron 1917(?)-1980 .... CANR-72
Obituary 103
Earlier sketch in CA 53-56
See also DLB 276
Carville, (Chester) James, (Jr.)
1944- CANR-142
Earlier sketch in CA 147
Carwardine, Richard J(ohn) 1947- 146
Carwell, L'Ann
See McKissack, Patricia (L'Ann) C(arwell)
Cary
See Cary, Louis F(avreau)
Cary, Alice 1820-1871 .... DLB 202
Cary, Arthur
See Cary, (Arthur) Joyce (Lunel)
Cary, Barbara Knapp 1912(?)-1975
Obituary 61-64
See also SATA-Obit 31
Cary, Bob 1921- 105
Cary, Diana Serra
See Cary, Peggy-Jean Montgomery
Cary, Falkland L. 1897-1989
Obituary 128
Cary, Harold Whiting 1903-1994 .... CAP-1
Earlier sketch in CA 9-10
Cary, James Donald 1919- 5-8R
Cary, John H. 1926- 9-12R
Cary, (Arthur) Joyce (Lunel) 1888-1957 164
Brief entry 104
See also BRW 7
See also CDBLB 1914-1945
See also DLB 15, 100
See also EWL 3
See also MTCW 2
See also RGEL 2
See also TCLC 1, 29
See also TEA
Cary, Jud
See Tubb, E(dwin) C(harles)
Cary, Julian
See Tubb, E(dwin) C(harles)
Cary, Lee J(ames) 1925- 29-32R
Cary, Lorene 1956- 135
See also BW 2
Cary, Louis F(avreau) 1915- .... SATA 9
Cary, Lucian 1886-1971 .... 33-36R
Cary, Margaret 199
Cary, Otis 1921- 61-64
Cary, Patrick 1623(?)-1657 .... DLB 131
Cary, Peggy-Jean Montgomery 1918- 57-60
Cary, Richard 1909-1990 .... 21-24R
Cary, William L(ucius) 1910-1983
Obituary 109
Cary, Zenja Saft 1932(?)-1983
Obituary 110
Caryl, Jean
See Kaplan, Jean Caryl Korn
Caryl, Warren 1920- 21-24R
Casaccia, Gabriel
See Casaccia Bibolini, G(abriel)
Casaccia Bibolini, G(abriel) 1907- .... HW 1
Casada, James A(llen) 1942- CANR-43
Earlier sketch in CA 109
Casado, Pablo Gil 1931- CANR-47
Earlier sketch in CA 49-52
Casady, Cort (Boon) 1947- CANR-22
Earlier sketch in CA 105
Casady, Donald Rex 1926- 13-16R
Casal, Julian del 1863-1893 .... DLB 283
See also LAW
Casal, Mary 1864-c. 1930 .... GLL 2
Casalandra, Estelle
See Estelle, Sister Mary
Casale, Anne L. 1930- 146
Casale, Joan T(herese) 1935- 61-64
Casale, Ottavio M(ark) 1934- 104
Casals, Pablo
See Casals, Pau Carlos Salvador Defillo de
Casals, Pau Carlos Salvador Defillo de
1876-1973 93-96
Obituary 45-48
Casanova, Giacomo
See Casanova de Seingalt, Giovanni Jacopo
See also WLIT 7
Casanova, Mary 1957- CANR-136
Earlier sketch in CA 159
See also SATA 94, 136
Casanova de Seingalt, Giovanni Jacopo
1725-1798
See Casanova, Giacomo
Casares, Adolfo Bioy
See Bioy Casares, Adolfo
See also RGSF 2
Casart, Jonathan
See St. Martin, Hardie
Casart, Julian
See St. Martin, Hardie
Casas, Bartolome de las 1474-1566
See Las Casas, Bartolome de
See also WLIT 1
Casas, Penelope 1943- 114
Casati, Roberto 1961- CANR-144
Earlier sketch in CA 148
Casavini, Pierallesandro
See Wainhouse, Austryn
Casberg, Melvin Augustus 1909- 104
Cascardi, Anthony J(oseph) 1953- 132
Cascio, Chuck 1946- 93-96
Cascone, A.G.
See Cascone, Annette and
Cascone, Gina
Cascone, Annette 1960- 170
See also SATA 103
Cascone, Gina 1955- CANR-144
Earlier sketch in CA 170
See also SATA 103
Casdorph, Herman Richard 1928- 101
Casdorph, Paul D(ouglas) 1932- 106
Case, Bill
See Case, Theodore Willard
Case, Brian (David) 1937- 25-28R
Case, (Brian) David (Francis) 1937- .. CANR-72
Earlier sketch in CA 107
See also HGG
Case, Elinor Rutt 1914-2003 .... 1-4R
Case, Fred E. 1918-2000 .... CANR-31
Earlier sketches in CA 5-8R, CANR-4
Case, Geoffrey 77-80
Case, George (Andrew Thomas) 1967- 164
Case, Jack Gaylord 1918(?)-1970
Obituary 104
Case, John
See Hougan, James Richard
Case, John c. 1540-1600 .... DLB 281
Case, John 1944- 114
Case, Josephine Young 1907-1990 .... CAP-2
Obituary 130
Earlier sketch in CA 25-28
Case, Justin
See Gleadow, Rupert Seeley
Case, L. L.
See Lewin, Leonard C(ase)
Case, Leland D(avidson) 1900-1986 ..... 17-20R
Case, Lynn M(arshall) 1903-1996 .... 13-16R
Case, Marshal T(aylor) 1941- 57-60
See also SATA 9
Case, Maurice 1910-1968 .... CAP-2
Earlier sketch in CA 19-20
Case, Michael
See Howard, Robert West
Case, Patricia J(une) 1952- CANR-53
Earlier sketches in CA 110, CANR-27
Case, Robert Ormond 1895-1964 . TCWW 1, 2
Case, Shirley Jackson 1872-1947 225
Case, Theodore Willard 1920- 133
Case, Victoria 1897-1973 .... 5-8R
Case, Walter 1909(?)-1983
Obituary 110
Casebier, Allan (Frank) 1934- 65-68
Casebier, Marjorie
See McCoy, Marjorie Casebier
Casebier, Virginia (Eleanor) 1918- 41-44R
Caseley, Judith 1951- CANR-143
Earlier sketches in CA 121, CANR-48
See also SATA 87, 159
See also SATA-Brief 53
Caseleyr, Cam(ille Auguste Marie)
1909- CAP-1
Earlier sketch in CA 9-10
Casely-Hayford, Gladys May
1904-1950 .... CANR-87
Earlier sketch in CA 152
See also BW 2
Casely-Hayford, J(oseph) E(phraim)
1866-1903 152
Brief entry 123
See also BLC 1
See also BW 2
See also DAM MULT
See also TCLC 24
Casement, Richard 1942-1982
Obituary 108
Casemore, Robert 1915- CANR-35
Earlier sketch in CA 73-76
Casewit, Curtis W(erner)
1922-2002 .... CANR-21
Earlier sketches in CA 13-16R, CANR-6
See also SATA 4
Casey, Barbara (Louise) 1944- 225
See also SATA 79, 147
Casey, Beatrice Vivian 1898(?)-1986
Obituary 120
Casey, Bernard Terry 1939- 152
See also BW 2, 3
Casey, Bernie
See Casey, Bernard Terry
Casey, Bill Harris 1930- 1-4R
Casey, Brigid 1950- CANR-28
Earlier sketch in CA 49-52
See also SATA 9

Casey 98 CONTEMPORARY AUTHORS

Casey, Daniel J(oseph) 1937- CANR-22
Earlier sketches in CA 57-60, CANR-6
Casey, Don 233
Casey, Douglas R(obert) 1946-
Brief entry 118
Casey, Edward Scott 1939- 102
Casey, Gavin (Stoddart) 1907-1964 .... DLB 260
Casey, Genevieve M(ary) 1916- CANR-39
Earlier sketch in CA 116
Casey, Gladys
See Grier, Barbara G(ene Damon)
See also GLL 1
Casey, Jack
See Casey, John
Casey, Jane Barnes 1942- 104
Casey, John (Dudley) 1939- CANR-100
Earlier sketches in CA 69-72, CANR-23
See also BEST 90:2
See also CLC 59
Casey, John 1950- 120
Casey, Juanita 1925- CANR-45
Earlier sketch in CA 49-52
See also DLB 14
Casey, Kevin 1940- 25-28R
Casey, Lawrence B. 1905-1977 73-76
Obituary 69-72
Casey, Linda M. 136
Casey, Mart
See Casey, Michael T.
Casey, Maud 200
Casey, Michael 1947- CANR-109
Earlier sketch in CA 65-68
See also CLC 2
See also CP 2
See also DLB 5
Casey, Michael T. 1922- 21-24R
Casey, Patrick
See Thurman, Wallace (Henry)
Casey, Philip 1950- 185
Casey, Richard Gardiner 1890-1976 61-64
Obituary 65-68
Casey, Robert J(oseph) 1890-1962
Obituary 89-92
Casey, Rosemary 1904-1976
Obituary 65-68
Casey, Rosemary Alice (Christmann)
1922- 5-8R
Casey, Thomas Francis 1923- 13-16R
Casey, Tina 1959- 212
See also SATA 141
Casey, W. Wilson 1954- 107
Casey, Warren (Peter) 1935-1988 101
Obituary 127
Interview in CA-101
See also CLC 12
Casey, William J(oseph) 1913-1987
Obituary 122
Casey, William Van Etten 1914-1990 57-60
Obituary 131
Casgrain, Therese F. 1896(?)-1981 110
Obituary 108
Cash, Anthony 1933- 102
Cash, Arthur H(ill) 1922-
Brief entry 110
Cash, Catherine 1939- 141
Cash, Ellen Lewis Buell 1905-1989
Obituary 130
See also SATA-Obit 64
Cash, Grace (Savannah) 1915- 21-24R
Cash, Grady
See Cash, Grace (Savannah)
Cash, J(ames) Allan 1901- CANR-4
Earlier sketch in CA 5-8R
Cash, Jean W(ampler) 1938- 216
Cash, John R.
See Cash, Johnny
Cash, Johnny 1932-2003 142
Obituary 220
Brief entry 110
See also AAYA 63
Cash, Joseph H(arper) 1927- 41-44R
Cash, Kevin (Richard) 1926-1985 77-80
Obituary 115
Cash, Megan Montague .... SATA 160
Cash, Philip 1931- 106
Cash, Sebastian
See Smithells, Roger (William)
Cash, Steve 1946- 239
Cashdan, Linda 1942- 132
Cashen, Richard A(nthony) 1938- 112
Cashin, Edward J(oseph, Jr.) 1927- CANR-9
Earlier sketch in CA 21-24R
Cashin, Edward L(awrence)
See Cashin, Edward J(oseph, Jr.)
Cashin, James A. 1911-1982 .... CANR-10
Earlier sketch in CA 17-20R
Cashin, Sheryll 237
Cashman, John
See Davis, Timothy Francis Tothill
Cashman, Paul Harrison 1924- 13-16R
Cashman, Sean Dennis 1943- 107
Cashmore, E. Ellis 1949- 116
Cashmore, Ernest
See Cashmore, E. Ellis
Casil, Amy Sterling 1962- 225
Casilla, Robert 1959- .... SATA 75, 146
Casimir, H(endrik) B(rugt) G(erhard)
1909-2000 129
Obituary 192
Casimir, Hendrik
See Casimir, H(endrik) B(rugt) G(erhard)
Casing, James
See Burridge, Kenelm (Oswald Lancelot)
Caskey, John L. 1908-1981 .... 13-16R
Casler, Lawrence (Ray) 1932- 49-52
Casmier, Adam A(nthony) 1934- 33-36R
Casmir, Fred L. 1928- 37-40R
Casner, A(ndrew) James 1907-1990 .... CANR-4
Obituary 132
Earlier sketch in CA 5-8R
Caso, Adolph 1934- CANR-7
Earlier sketch in CA 57-60
Casolaro, Daniel 1949- 114
Cason, Ann 1942- 207
Cason, Mabel Earp 1892-1965 .... CAP-1
Earlier sketch in CA 13-14
See also SATA 10
Casona, Alejandro
See Alvarez, Alejandro Rodriguez
See also CLC 49
See also EWL 3
Casotti, Fred 1923- 93-96
Caspari, Ernest W(olfgang) 1909- 41-44R
Caspary, Vera 1904-1987 .... CANR-59
Obituary 122
Earlier sketches in CA 13-16R, CANR-9
See also CMW 4
Casper, Barry M(ichael) 1939- 69-72
Casper, Bill, Jr.
See Casper, William Earl, Jr.
Casper, Billy
See Casper, William Earl, Jr.
Casper, Claudia 1957(?)- 171
Casper, Henry W. 1909- 37-40R
Casper, Jonathan D(avid) 1942- 53-56
Casper, Joseph Andrew 1941- 65-68
Casper, Lawrence E. 1948- 214
Casper, Leonard Ralph 1923- CANR-106
Earlier sketch in CA 1-4R
Casper, Linda Ty
See Ty-Casper, Linda
Casper, Monica J. 1966- 169
Casper, Scott E. 1964- 193
Casper, William Earl, Jr. 1931- 121
Casque, Sammy
See Davis, Sydney Charles Houghton
Casriel, H(arold) Daniel 1924-1983 ...... 13-16R
Obituary 110
Cass, Carl Bartholomew 1901-1980 ...... CAP-1
Earlier sketch in CA 9-10
Cass, James (Michael) 1915-1992 101
Obituary 140
Cass, Joan E(velyn) CANR-20
Earlier sketches in CA 1-4R, CANR-5
See also SATA 1
Cass, Ronald A(ndrew) 1949- 106
Cass, Zoe
See Low, Lois Dorothea
Cassady, Carolyn (Elizabeth Robinson)
1923- CANR-107
Earlier sketch in CA 133
See also DLB 16
Cassady, Claude
See Paine, Lauran (Bosworth)
Cassady, Marsh 1936- 167
Cassady, Neal 1926-1968 141
See also BG 1:2
See also DLB 16, 237
See also LMFS 2
Cassady, Ralph, Jr. 1900-1978 .... CANR-4
Obituary 77-80
Earlier sketch in CA 1-4R
Cassandra
See Connor, William (Neil)
Cassara, Ernest 1925- 41-44R
Cassata, Mary B. 1930- 121
Cassatt, Mary 1845-1926 .... AAYA 22
Cassavant, Sharron Greer 1939- 125
Cassavetes, John 1929-1989 .... CANR-82
Obituary 127
Earlier sketch in CA 85-88
See also CLC 20
Cassavetes, Nick 1959- 206
Cass-Beggs, Barbara 1904- .... SATA 62
Cassedy, James H(iggins) 1919- CANR-46
Earlier sketch in CA 1-4R
Cassedy, Patrice (Rinaldo) 1953- 223
See also SATA 149
Cassedy, Sylvia 1930-1989 .... CANR-22
Earlier sketch in CA 105
See also CLR 26
See also CWRI 5
See also JRDA
See also MAICYA 2
See also MAICYAS 1
See also SATA 27, 77
See also SATA-Obit 61
See also YAW
Cassel, Don 1942- CANR-28
Earlier sketch in CA 110
Cassel, Lili
See Wronker, Lili Cassel
Cassel, Mana-Zucca 1891-1981
Obituary 103
Cassel, Russell N(apoleon) 1911-2004 .. 37-40R
Obituary 227
Cassel, Susie Lan 1966- 239
Cassel, Virginia Cunningham 105
Cassell, Anthony K. 1941- CANR-48
Earlier sketch in CA 120
Cassell, Eric J. 1928- 137
Cassell, Frank A(llan) 1941- 33-36R
Cassell, Frank H(yde) 1916-1999 .... 37-40R
Obituary 186
Cassell, Joan 1929- 135
Cassell, Richard A(llan) 1921- 21-24R
Cassell, Sylvia 1924- 5-8R
Cassells, Cyrus (Curtis III) 1957- CANR-49
Earlier sketch in CA 112
Cassells, John
See Duncan, W(illiam) Murdoch
Casselman, Karen Leigh 1942- 107
Cassels, Alan 1929- CANR-13
Earlier sketch in CA 33-36R
Cassels, J(ohn) W(illiam) S(cott) 1922- 142
Cassels, Louis 1922-1974 .... CANR-4
Obituary 45-48
Earlier sketch in CA 9-12R
Casserley, H(enry) C(yril) 1903- CANR-9
Earlier sketch in CA 65-68
Casserley, Julian Victor Langmead
1909-1978 .... 9-12R
Obituary 133
Casserly, Jack
See Casserly, John J(oseph)
Casserly, John J(oseph) 1927- CANR-44
Earlier sketch in CA 120
Cassian, Nina 1924- .... CWP
See also CWW 2
See also PC 17
Cassiday, Bruce (Bingham)
1920-2005 .... CANR-47
Obituary 235
Earlier sketches in CA 1-4R, CANR-4, 19
Cassidy, Daniel J(ames) 1956- 119
Cassidy, David (Bruce) 1950- 153
Cassidy, David C(harles) 1945- 140
Cassidy, Frederic Gomes 1907-2000 .... 1-4R
Obituary 188
Cassidy, George
See Vance, William E.
Cassidy, Harold G(omes) 1906- 25-28R
Cassidy, John 1928- CANR-35
Earlier sketch in CA 114
Cassidy, John 1963- 237
Cassidy, John A(lbert) 1908-1977 .... 33-36R
Cassidy, John R(ufus) 1922- 89-92
Cassidy, Jude (Anne) 1955- 121
Cassidy, Michael 1936- 97-100
Cassidy, Richard J(oseph) 1942- 114
Cassidy, Vincent H. 1923- 21-24R
Cassidy, William L(awrence Robert) 103
Cassilis, Robert
See Edwardes, Michael (F. H.)
Cassill, Kay 89-92
Cassill, R(onald) V(erlin) 1919-2002 . CANR-45
Obituary 208
Earlier sketches in CA 9-12R, CANR-7
See also CAAS 1
See also CLC 4, 23
See also CN 1, 2, 3, 4, 5, 6, 7
See also DLB 6, 218
See also DLBY 2002
Cassils, Peter
See Keele, Kenneth D(avid)
Cassin, Rene Samuel 1887-1976
Obituary 65-68
Cassinelli, C(harles) W(illiam, Jr.) 1925- 1-4R
Cassini, Igor (Loiewski) 1915-2002 129
Obituary 205
Cassirer, Ernst 1874-1945 157
See also TCLC 61
Cassity, (Allen) Turner 1929- 223
Earlier sketches in CA 17-20R, CANR-11
Autobiographical Essay in 223
See also CAAS 8
See also CLC 6, 42
See also CSW
See also DLB 105
Cassius Dio c. 155-c. 229 .... DLB 176
Casso, Evans J(oseph) 1914-1996 57-60
Cassola, Albert M(aria) 1915- CAP-1
Earlier sketch in CA 9-10
Cassola, Carlo 1917-1987 .... CANR-71
Obituary 121
Earlier sketch in CA 101
See also DLB 177
See also EWL 3
See also RGWL 2, 3
Casson, Hugh Maxwell 1910-1999 .. CANR-36
Obituary 183
Earlier sketches in CA 103, CANR-20
See also SATA 65
See also SATA-Obit 115
Casson, Lionel 1914- CANR-79
Earlier sketches in CA 9-12R, CANR-3
Casson, Mark (Christopher) 1945- 143
Casstevens, Thomas W(illiam) 1937- 17-20R
Cassuto, David N(athan) 1963- 145
Cassuto, Leonard 1960- 190
Cassutt, Michael (Joseph) 1954- 146
See also SATA 78
Cast, David (Jesse Dale) 1942- 109
Castagna, Edwin 1909-1983 .... CAP-2
Obituary 111
Earlier sketch in CA 17-18
Castagnola, Lawrence A. 1933- CANR-12
Earlier sketch in CA 29-32R
Castaldo, Nancy Fusco 1962- CANR-135
Obituary 152
See also SATA 93, 151
Castaneda, Carlos (Cesar Aranha)
1931(?)-1998 .... CANR-105
Earlier sketches in CA 25-28R, CANR-32, 66
See also CLC 12, 119
See also DNFS 1
See also HW 1
See also MTCW 1
Castaneda, Christopher James
1959- CANR-93
Earlier sketch in CA 145
Castaneda, Eliza C. 1958- 238
Castaneda, Hector-Neri 1924- CANR-19
Earlier sketches in CA 5-8R, CANR-3
Castaneda, James A(gustin) 1933- 41-44R
Castaneda, Jorge G. 1953- CANR-105
Earlier sketch in CA 144
Castaneda, Omar S. 1954- 135
See also DNFS
See also SATA 71
Castedo, Elena 1937- 132
See also CLC 65
Castedo-Ellerman, Elena
See Castedo, Elena
Castel, Albert 1928- CANR-119
Earlier sketches in CA 1-4R, CANR-5
Castel, J(ean) G(abriel) 1928- CANR-106
Earlier sketches in CA 21-24R, CANR-9, 25, 50
Castel, Robert 1933- CANR-126
Earlier sketches in CA 129, CANR-68
Castelao, Alfonso (Daniel) R(odriguez)
1886-1950 208
Casteleyn, Mary (Teresa) 1941- 131
Castell, Megan
See Williams, Jeanne
Castellan, N(orman) John, Jr. 1939- 37-40R
Castellaneta, Carlo 1930- CANR-11
Earlier sketch in CA 13-16R
Castellani, Catherine 1965- 224
Castellani, Christopher 1972- 219
Castellano, Giuseppe 1893-1977
Obituary 73-76
Castellano, Olivia Guerrero 1944- 175
See also DLB 122
See also HW 2
Castellanos, Jane Mollie Robinson
1913-2001 .... 9-12R
See also SATA 9
Castellanos, Rosario 1925-1974 .... CANR-58
Obituary 53-56
Earlier sketch in CA 131
See also CDWLB 3
See also CLC 66
See also DAM MULT
See also DLB 113, 290
See also EWL 3
See also FW
See also HLC 1
See also HW 1
See also LAW
See also MTCW 2
See also MTFW 2005
See also RGSF 2
See also RGWL 2, 3
See also SSC 39, 68
Castellon, Federico 1914-1971 .... SATA 48
Castells, Manuel 1942- CANR-37
Earlier sketch in CA 115
Castells, Matilde O(livella) 1929- 69-72
Castelnuovo-Tedesco, P(ietro) 1925- 21-24R
Castelo Branco, Camilo 1825-1890 ..... DLB 287
Caster, Andrew I. 1954- 165
Castetter, William Benjamin 1914- CANR-4
Earlier sketch in CA 1-4R
Casti, J.
See Casti, John L(ouis)
Casti, J. L.
See Casti, John L(ouis)
Casti, John
See Casti, John L(ouis)
Casti, John L(ouis) 1943- 141
Castiglione, Baldassare 1478-1529
See Castiglione, Baldesar
See also LMFS 1
See also RGWL 2, 3
Castiglione, Baldesar
See Castiglione, Baldassare
See also EW 2
See also WLIT 7
Castile, Rand 1938- 138
Castillejo, Cristobal de 1490(?)-1550 .. DLB 318
Castillo, Amelia del 1920- 193
Castillo, Ana (Hernandez Del)
1953- CANR-128
Earlier sketches in CA 131, CANR-51, 86
See also AAYA 42
See also CLC 151
See also CWP
See also DLB 122, 227
See also DNFS 2
See also FW
See also HW 1
See also LLW
See also PFS 21
Castillo, Debra A(nn Garsow) 1953- 136
Castillo, Edmund L. 1924- 29-32R
See also SATA 1
Castillo, Rafael C. 1950- .... DLB 209
Castillo, Richard Griswold del
See Griswold del Castillo, Richard
Castillo, Susan 1948- 214
Castillo Puche, Jose Luis 1919-
Brief entry 110
Castle, Alfred L. 1948- 139
Castle, Anthony (Percy) 1938- CANR-73
Earlier sketches in CA 113, CANR-32
Castle, Barbara (Anne) 1910-2002 ... CANR-86
Obituary 205
Earlier sketch in CA 130
Castle, Charles 1939- 33-36R
Castle, Coralie 1924- 57-60
Castle, Damon
See Smith, Richard Rein
Castle, Edgar Bradshaw 1897-1973
Obituary 104
Castle, Emery N(eal) 1923- 1-4R
Castle, Frances
See Leader, (Evelyn) Barbara (Blackburn)
Castle, Frederick Ted 1938- 137
Castle, Jayne
See Krentz, Jayne Ann
Castle, Kate 123
Castle, Kathryn 164
Castle, Keith 1927(?)-1985
Obituary 118

Cumulative Index 99 Cavazos-Gaither

Castle, Lee
See Ogan, George F. and Ogan, Margaret E. (Nettles)
Castle, Leonard L. 1912(?)-1989 ... 129
Castle, Linda
See Crockett, Linda Lea
Castle, Marian (Johnson) ... CAP-2
Earlier sketch in CA 17-18
Castle, Mort 1946- ... CANR-14
Earlier sketch in CA 81-84
Castle, Nick 1947- ... 156
Castle, Paul
See Howard, Vernon (Linwood)
Castle, Robert
See Hamilton, Edmond
Castle, Robert W., Jr. 1929- ... 25-28R
Castle, Sue G(aronzik) 1942- ... 105
Castle, Terry (Jacqueline) 1953- ... 112
Castle, Tony
See Castle, Anthony (Percy)
Castle, William 1914-1977 ... 77-80
Obituary ... 69-72
Castleden, Rodney 1945- ... 138
Castle-Kanerova, Mita 1948- ... 142
Castleman, Harry 1953- ... 109
Castleman, Michael 1950- ... 108
Castleman, (Esther) Riva 1930- ... CANR-40
Brief entry ... 117
Earlier sketch in CA 128
Castlemon, Harry
See Fosdick, Charles Austin
Castles, Francis G(eoffrey) 1943- ... CANR-17
Earlier sketch in CA 25-28R
Castles, Lance 1937- ... 25-28R
Castleton, Virginia 1925- ... 49-52
Castor, Grahame (Douglas) 1932- ... CANR-7
Earlier sketch in CA 13-16R
Castor, Henry 1909-1999 ... CANR-82
Earlier sketch in CA 17-20R
Castoriadis, Cornelius 1922-1997 ... 138
Castoro, Laura (Ann) 1948- ... CANR-143
Earlier sketch in CA 124
Castro (y Quesada), Americo 1885-1972 ... 37-40R
See also HW 1
Castro, Antonio 1946- ... 53-56
Castro, Brian (Albert) 1950- ... CANR-130
Earlier sketch in CA 167
See also CN 6, 7
Castro, Consuelo de 1946- ... DLB 307
Castro (Ruz), Fidel 1926(?)- ... CANR-81
Brief entry ... 110
Earlier sketch in CA 129
See also DAM MULT
See also HLC 1
See also HW 2
Castro, Jan Garden 1945- ... 120
Castro, Jose Maria Ferreira de
See Ferreira de Castro, Jose Maria
See also EWL 3
Castro, Michael 1945- ... 132
Castro, Rosalia de 1837-1885 ... DAM MULT
See also PC 41
Castro, Tony
See Castro, Antonio
Castro Alves, Antonio de 1847-1871 .. DLB 307
See also LAW
Castro-Klaren, Sara 1942- ... 61-64
Castronovo, David 1945- ... CANR-82
Earlier sketches in CA 114, CANR-35, 55
Casty, Alan Howard 1929- ... CANR-4
Earlier sketch in CA 1-4R
Casule, Kole 1921- ... 182
See also DLB 181
Caswall, Edward 1814-1878 ... DLB 32
Caswell, Brian 1954- ... 163
See also SATA 97
Caswell, Helen (Rayburn) 1923- ... 33-36R
See also SATA 12
Caswell, Margaret (Betsy) R(oss) 1903(?)-1982
Obituary ... 107
Catacalos, Rosemary 1944- ... 177
See also DLB 122
See also HW 2
Catala, Rafael 1942- ... CANR-80
Earlier sketches in CA 73-76, CANR-13, 32
See also HW 1
Catala, Victor
See Albert i Paradis, Caterina
Catalano, Dominic 1956- ... SATA 76, 163
Catalano, Donald B(ernard) 1920- ... 57-60
Catalano, Grace (A.) 1961- ... 141
See also SATA 99
Catalano, Joseph S(tellario) 1928- ... 102
Catalano, Nick 1940(?)- ... 204
Catalano, Stephen 1952- ... 135
Catalanotto, Peter 1959- ... CANR-68
Earlier sketch in CA 138
See also CLR 68
See also MAICYA 2
See also MAICYAS 1
See also SAAS 25
See also SATA 70, 114, 159
See also SATA-Essay 113
Cataldi, Lee Ann 1942- ... CWP
Cataldo, Michael F. 1947- ... 122
Catanese, Anthony James (Jr.) 1942- . CANR-32
Earlier sketches in CA 29-32R, CANR-14
Catania, A(nthony) Charles 1936- ... 37-40R
Catanzariti, John 1942- ... CANR-51
Earlier sketch in CA 124
Catanzaro, Thomas E. 1944- ... 198
Cate, Benjamin W(ilson) 1931- ... 73-76
Cate, Curtis 1924- ... CANR-144
Earlier sketches in CA 53-56, CANR-9
Cate, Curtis Wolsey 1884-1976
Obituary ... 61-64
Cate, Dick
See Cate, Richard Edward Nelson
Cate, Richard Edward Nelson 1932- ... 73-76
See also SATA 28
Cate, Robert L(ouis) 1932- ... CANR-28
Earlier sketch in CA 111
Cate, William Burke 1924- ... 13-16R
Cateora, Philip Rene 1932- ... 5-8R
Cater, (Silas) Douglass, (Jr.) 1923-1995 ... CANR-1
Obituary ... 149
Earlier sketch in CA 1-4R
Cates, Jo A. 1958- ... 134
Cates, Ray A., Jr. 1940- ... 29-32R
Cates, Tory
See Bird, Sarah McCabe
Cateura, Linda Brandi 1924- ... 135
Cath, Stanley H. 1921- ... 224
Cathcart, Helen ... CANR-2
Earlier sketch in CA 5-8R
See also Albert, Harold A.
Cathcart, Jim 1946- ... 176
Cathcart, Noble Aydelotte 1898-1988
Obituary ... 126
Cathcart, Robert S(tephen) 1923- ... 101
Cather, Willa (Sibert) 1873-1947 ... 128
Brief entry ... 104
See also AAYA 24
See also AMW
See also AMWC 1
See also AMWR 1
See also BPFB 1
See also CDALB 1865-1917
See also CLR 98
See also DA
See also DA3
See also DAB
See also DAC
See also DAM MST, NOV
See also DLB 9, 54, 78, 256
See also DLBD 1
See also EWL 3
See also EXPN
See also EXPS
See also FL 1:5
See also LAIT 3
See also LATS 1:1
See also MAL 5
See also MAWW
See also MTCW 1, 2
See also MTFW 2005
See also NFS 2, 19
See also RGAL 4
See also RGSF 2
See also RHW
See also SATA 30
See also SSC 2, 50
See also SSFS 2, 7, 16
See also TCLC 1, 11, 31, 99, 132, 152
See also TCWW 1, 2
See also TUS
See also WLC
Catherall, Arthur 1906-1980 ... CANR-38
Earlier sketch in CA 5-8R
See also Ruthin, Margaret
See also CWRI 5
See also MAICYA 1, 2
See also SATA 3, 74
Catherine II
See Catherine the Great
See also DLB 150
Catherine the Great 1729-1796
See Catherine II
Cathers, David M. 1941- ... 111
Cathers, Ken 1951- ... 112
Catherwood, (Henry) Frederick (Ross) 1925- ... 106
Catherwood, Mary Hartwell 1847-1902 ... 178
See also DLB 78
Cathey, Cornelius Oliver 1908-1986 ... 1-4R
Cathon, Laura E(lizabeth) 1908-1991 ... 5-8R
See also SATA 27
Cathy, S. Truett 1921- ... 215
Catledge, Turner 1901-1983 ... 57-60
Obituary ... 109
See also AITN 1
See also DLB 127
Catlett, Elizabeth 1919(?)- ... SATA 82
Catlin, George 1796-1872 ... DLB 186, 189
Catlin, George E(dward) G(ordon) 1896-1979 ... 13-16R
Obituary ... 85-88
Catlin, Warren Benjamin 1881-1968 ... 1-4R
Obituary ... 103
Catlin, Wynelle 1930- ... 65-68
See also SATA 13
Catling, Darrel (Charles) 1909- ... 5-8R
Catling, Patrick Skene 1925- ... 209
Brief entry ... 115
Catlow, Joanna
See Lowry, Joan (Catlow)
Cato
See Howard, Peter D(unsmore)
Cato, Ann
See Stewart, Sally
Cato, Heather ... 173
See also SATA 105
Cato, Marcus Porcius 234B.C.-149B.C.
See Cato the Elder
Cato, Marcus Porcius, the Elder
See Cato, Marcus Porcius
Cato, Nancy (Fotheringham) 1917-2000 ... CAP-1
Earlier sketch in CA 49-52
See also CP 1
See also RHW
Cato, Sheila ... 186
See also SATA 114
Catoir, John T. 1931- ... CANR-11
Earlier sketch in CA 25-28R
Caton, Charles E(dwin) 1928- ... 9-12R
Caton, Donald 1937- ... 194
Caton, Hiram P. 1936- ... CANR-4
Earlier sketch in CA 53-56
Caton, Steven (Charles) 1950- ... 219
Caton-Thompson, Gertrude 1888-1985 ... 122
Obituary ... 116
Cato the Elder
See Cato, Marcus Porcius
See also DLB 211
Catran, Jack 1933-2001 ... 128
Catron, Louis E. 1932- ... 45-48
Catrow, David
See Catrow, David J. III
Catrow, David J. III ... 227
See also SATA 152
Catt, Carrie Chapman 1859-1947 ... FW
Cattafi, Bartolo 1922-1979 ... DLB 128
Cattan, Henry 1906-1992 ... 29-32R
Cattaui, Georges 1896-1974 ... CAP-2
Earlier sketch in CA 25-28
Cattell, Everett L(ewis) 1905-1981 ... 1-4R
Cattell, James 1954- ... 194
See also SATA 123
Cattell, Psyche 1893-1989 ... 41-44R
Cattell, Raymond Bernard 1905- ... CANR-86
Earlier sketches in CA 5-8R, CANR-2
Catterall, Lee 1944- ... 141
Catterall, Peter 1961- ... 134
Catto, Henry E(dward), Jr. 1930- ... 187
Catto, Max(well Jeffrey) 1909-1992 .. CANR-82
Obituary ... 137
Earlier sketch in CA 105
Catton, (Charles) Bruce 1899-1978 .. CANR-74
Obituary ... 81-84
Earlier sketches in CA 5-8R, CANR-7
See also AITN 1
See also CLC 35
See also DLB 17
See also MTCW 2
See also MTFW 2005
See also SATA 2
See also SATA-Obit 24
Catton, William Bruce 1926- ... CANR-1
Earlier sketch in CA 1-4R
Catton, William R(obert), Jr. 1926- ... 109
Catty, Charles ... GLL 1
Catudal, Honore M(arc, Jr.) 1944- ... CANR-12
Earlier sketch in CA 69-72
Catullus c. 84B.C.-54B.C. ... AW 2
See also CDWLB 1
See also DLB 211
See also RGWL 2, 3
Catz, Max
See Glaser, Milton
Caubraith, Robert
See Galbraith, Robert
Caudell, Marian 1930- ... 121
See also SATA 52
Caudill, (Charles) Edward 1953- ... 170
Caudill, Harry M(onroe) 1922-1990 . CANR-71
Obituary ... 133
Earlier sketches in CA 33-36R, CANR-14
Caudill, Rebecca 1899-1985 ... CANR-44
Obituary ... 117
Earlier sketches in CA 5-8R, CANR-2
See also MAICYA 1, 2
See also SATA 1
See also SATA-Obit 44
See also YAW
Caudill, William W(ayne) 1914-1983
Obituary ... 110
Caudle, Neil 1952- ... 132
Caudwell, Christopher
See Sprigg, C(hristopher) St. John
See also BRWS 9
Caudwell, Sarah
See Cockburn, Sarah
See also CMW 4
Cauffiel, Lowell 1951- ... 132
Caufield, Catherine ... 161
Caughey, John L(yon) 1941- ... 115
Caughey, John Walton 1902-1995
Obituary ... 150
Brief entry ... 106
Caughman, Ginger Morris
See Caughman, Virginia Morris
Caughman, Virginia Morris 1939- ... 212
Caulder, Colline 1945- ... 113
Cauldwell, Frank
See King, Francis (Henry)
Cauley, John R(owan) 1908-1976
Obituary ... 65-68
Cauley, Lorinda Bryan 1951- ... 101
See also SATA 46
See also SATA-Brief 43
Cauley, Terry
See Cauley, Troy Jesse
Cauley, Troy Jesse 1902-1990 ... CANR-1
Earlier sketch in CA 1-4R
Caulfield, Carlota 1953- ... 176
See also CAAS 25
Caulfield, Malachy Francis 1915- ... CANR-14
Earlier sketch in CA 77-80
Caulfield, Max
See Caulfield, Malachy Francis
Caulfield, Peggy F. 1926-1987 ... 5-8R
Obituary ... 123
See also SATA-Obit 53
Caulfield, Sean 1925- ... 108
Caulflower, Sebastian
See Seldes, Gilbert (Vivian)
Cauman, Samuel 1910-1971 ... CAP-2
Earlier sketch in CA 23-24
See also SATA 48
Caumont, Jacques 1932- ... 239
Caunitz, William J. 1933-1996 ... CANR-73
Obituary ... 152
Brief entry ... 125
Earlier sketch in CA 130
Interview in ... CA-130
See also BEST 89:3
See also CLC 34
Causley, Charles (Stanley) 1917-2003 ... CANR-94
Obituary ... 223
Earlier sketches in CA 9-12R, CANR-5, 35
See also CLC 7
See also CLR 30
See also CP 1, 2
See also CWRI 5
See also DLB 27
See also MTCW 1
See also SATA 3, 66
See also SATA-Obit 149
Causse, Michele ... GLL 2
Caute, (John) David 1936- ... CANR-120
Earlier sketches in CA 1-4R, CANR-1, 33, 64
See also CAAS 4
See also CBD
See also CD 5, 6
See also CLC 29
See also CN 1, 2, 3, 4, 5, 6, 7
See also DAM NOV
See also DLB 14, 231
Cautela, Joseph R(ichard) 1927- ... 106
Cauthen, Baker James 1909-1985
Obituary ... 115
Cauthen, Irby Bruce, Jr. 1919-1994 ... 111
Obituary ... 180
Cauthen, W(ilfred) Kenneth 1930- ... CANR-7
Earlier sketch in CA 5-8R
Cauveren, Sydney (Raymond) 1947- ... 196
Cauvin, Jean-Pierre (Bernard) 1936- ... 116
Cauwelaert, Didier van 1960- ... 231
Cauwels, Janice M(arie) 1949- ... 110
Cava, Esther Laden 1916- ... 37-40R
Cavafy, C(onstantine) P(eter) ... 148
See also Kavafis, Konstantinos Petrou
See also DA3
See also DAM POET
See also EW 8
See also EWL 3
See also MTCW 2
See also PC 36
See also PFS 19
See also RGWL 2, 3
See also TCLC 2, 7
See also WP
Cavafy, Constantin
See Kavafis, Konstantinos Petrou
Cavaiani, Mabel 1919- ... CANR-45
Earlier sketches in CA 57-60, CANR-6, 21
Cavaioli, Frank J. 1930- ... 221
Cavalcanti, Alberto (de Almeida) 1897-1982
Obituary ... 107
Cavalcanti, Guido c. 1250-c. 1300 . RGWL 2, 3
See also WLIT 7
Cavalier, Julian 1931- ... CANR-2
Earlier sketch in CA 49-52
Cavaliero, Glen 1927- ... CANR-53
Earlier sketches in CA 73-76, CANR-13, 29
Cavallari, Alberto 1927-1998 ... CANR-10
Obituary ... 169
Earlier sketch in CA 21-24R
Cavallaro, Ann (Abelson) 1918- ... 5-8R
See also SATA 62
Cavalletti, Sofia 1917- ... CANR-87
Earlier sketch in CA 130
Cavalli, Thom F(rank) 1947- ... 214
Cavallo, Diana 1931- ... CANR-2
Earlier sketch in CA 1-4R
See also SATA 7
Cavallo, Evelyn
See Spark, Muriel (Sarah)
Cavallo, Robert M. 1932- ... CANR-10
Earlier sketch in CA 65-68
Cavan, Romilly 1914(?)-1975
Obituary ... 61-64
Cavan, Sherri 1938- ... 17-20R
Cavanagh, Gerald F(rancis) 1931- ... 41-44R
Cavanagh, Helen (Carol) 1939- ... 104
See also SATA 48, 98
See also SATA-Brief 37
Cavanagh, John B. 1908-1983
Obituary ... 110
Cavanagh, John Richard 1904-1981 ... CAP-2
Earlier sketch in CA 19-20
Cavanagh, Richard E(dward) 1946- ... 121
Cavanah, Frances 1899-1982 ... CANR-89
Obituary ... 133
Earlier sketch in CA 13-16R
See also SATA 1, 31
Cavanaugh, Arthur 1926- ... 17-20R
Cavanaugh, Matt ... 219
Cavani, Liliana 1936- ... 110
Cavanna, Betty
See Harrison, Elizabeth (Allen) Cavanna
See also CLC 12
See also JRDA
See also MAICYA 1
See also SAAS 4
See also SATA 1, 30
Cavanna, Elizabeth
See Harrison, Elizabeth (Allen) Cavanna
Cavanna, Elizabeth Allen
See Harrison, Elizabeth (Allen) Cavanna
Cavazos-Gaither, Alma E(lisa) 1955- ... 165

Cave, Alfred A. 1935- CANR-94
Earlier sketch in CA 37-40R
Cave, (John) David 1957- 138
Cave, Eric M. 1965- 170
Cave, Hugh B(arnett) 1910-2004 ...... CANR-72
Obituary 228
Earlier sketches in CA 5-8R, CANR-2
See also HGG
Cave, Kathryn 1948- 194
Earlier sketch in CA 143
See also SATA 76, 123
Cave, Roderick (George James Munro)
1935- CANR-2
Earlier sketch in CA 5-8R
Cave, Stephanie F(eehan) 1944- 223
Cave, Terence (Christopher) 1938- ... CANR-88
Earlier sketch in CA 142, 185
Cave, Thomas
See Steward, Samuel M(orris)
See also GLL 1
Cave Brown, Anthony
See Brown, Anthony Cave
Cavell, Benjamin 224
Cavell, Marcia 1931- 147
Cavell, Stanley (Louis) 1926- CANR-11
Earlier sketch in CA 61-64
Cavelti, Peter C(hristian) 1948- 116
Cavendish, J(ean) M(avis) 1932- 118
Cavendish, Margaret Lucas
1623-1673 .... DLB 131, 252, 281
See also RGEL 2
Cavendish, Peter
See Horler, Sydney
Cavendish, Richard 1930- CANR-20
Earlier sketches in CA 9-12R, CANR-5
Cavendish, (Michael) William (Patrick)
1964- 143
Caveney, Graham 173
Caveney, Philip (Richard) 1951- CANR-19
Earlier sketch in CA 102
Caverhill, Nicholas
See Kirk-Greene, Anthony (Hamilton Millard)
Caverhill, William Melville 1910-1983
Obituary 111
Cavers, David F(arquhar) 1902-1988 .... 17-20R
Obituary 125
Cavert, Samuel McCrea 1888-1976 ...... 37-40R
Cavert, Walter Dudley 1891-1986 .... 1-4R
Caves, Richard E(arl) 1931- CANR-41
Earlier sketches in CA 1-4R, CANR-4, 19
Cavett, Dick
See Cavett, Richard A.
Cavett, Richard A. 1936- 108
Caviedes, Juan del Valle y
1645(?)-1697(?) .... LAW
Cavin, Ruth (Brodie) 1918- CANR-8
Earlier sketch in CA 61-64
See also SATA 38
Cavitch, David 1933- 29-32R
Cavnes, Max P(arvin) 1922- 9-12R
Cavoukian, Raffi 1948- 136
See also SATA 68
Cavrell, Jean 1927- 107
Cawein, Madison 1865-1914 178
See also DLB 54
Cawein, Wanda 1937- 174
Cawelti, John G(eorge) 1929- CANR-90
Earlier sketch in CA 21-24R
Cawley, Linda 1949- 113
Cawley, Robert Ralston 1893-1973 .... CAP-2
Obituary 41-44R
Earlier sketch in CA 21-22
Cawley, Winifred 1915- 69-72
See also SATA 13
Cawood, John W. 1931- 33-36R
Caws, Ian 1945- 118
Caws, Mary Ann 1933- CANR-55
Earlier sketches in CA 25-28R, CANR-10, 31
Caws, Peter (James) 1931- CANR-8
Earlier sketch in CA 17-20R
Cawse, James N. 1945- 237
Cawthorne, Graham 1906(?)-1980
Obituary 97-100
Cawthorne, Nigel 1951- 136
Caxton, Pisistratus
See Lytton, Edward G(eorge) E(arle) L(ytton)
Bulwer-Lytton Baron
Caxton, William 1421(?)-1491(?) .... DLB 170
Cayce, Edgar 1877-1945 191
Cayce, Edgar E(vans) 1918- 21-24R
Cayce, Hugh Lynn 1907-1982 .... CANR-34
Obituary 107
Earlier sketch in CA 25-28R
Cayer, D. M.
See Duffy, Maureen (Patricia)
Cayleff, Susan E. 1954- CANR-120
Earlier sketch in CA 147
Cayley, Michael (Forde) 1950- 53-56
Caylor, O. P. 1849-1897 .... DLB 241
Caylus, Marthe-Marguerite de
1671-1729 .... DLB 313
Cayrol, Jean 1911-2005 89-92
Obituary 236
See also CLC 11
See also DLB 83
See also EWL 3
Cayson, Joyce A. 1952- 222
Cayton, Andrew R(obert) L(ee) 1954- 126
Cayton, Horace R(oscoe) 1903-1970 .... CAP-1
Obituary 29-32R
Earlier sketch in CA 13-14
Cayton, Mary Kupiec 1954- 137
Cazalet-Keir, Thelma 1900(?)-1989 .... 25-28R
Obituary 127
Cazamian, Louis Francois 1877-1965
Obituary 93-96
Cazden, Courtney B(orden) 1925- 146
Cazden, Elizabeth 1950- 65-68
Cazden, Norman 1914-1980 .... 37-40R
Cazden, Robert E. 1930- 33-36R
Cazeau, Charles J(ay) 1931- 104
See also SATA 65
Cazeaux, Isabelle 1926- 53-56
Cazel, Fred A(ugustus), Jr. 1921- 9-12R
Cazelles, Brigitte Jacqueline 1944- 102
Cazemajou, Jean 1924- 73-76
Cazenave, Noel A(nthony) 1948- 214
Cazet, Denys 1938- 108
See also SATA 52, 99, 163
See also SATA-Brief 41
Ca'Zorci, Giacomo 1898-1960 209
See also Noventa, Giacomo
Cazotte, Jacques 1719-1792 .... SUFW
Cazzola, Gus 1934- CANR-46
Earlier sketch in CA 108
See also SATA 73
Ceadel, Martin (Eric) 1948- CANR-127
Earlier sketch in CA 128
Cebrian, Juan Luis (Echarri) 1944- 205
Cebula, Richard J(ohn) 1944- 111
Cebulash, Mel 1937- CANR-57
Earlier sketches in CA 29-32R, CANR-12, 30
See also SATA 10, 91
Cecchetti, Giovanni 1922-1998 180
Brief entry 107
Cecchi D'amico, Susanna 1914- 239
Cecchi D'amico, Suso
See Cecchi D'amico, Susanna
Cecchi D'Amico, Suso 1914- .... IDFW 3, 4
Cecelski, Elizabeth 1953- 119
Cech, John O(tto) 1944- CANR-46
Earlier sketch in CA 120
Cecil, (Edward Christian) David (Gascoyne)
1902-1986 .... CANR-34
Obituary 118
Earlier sketches in CA 61-64, CANR-13
See also DLB 155
Cecil, Henry
See Keller, David H(enry) and
Leon, Henry Cecil
Cecil, Hugh Mortimer
See Roberts, William
Cecil, Lamar (John Ryan, Jr.) 1932- 21-24R
Cecil, Lord David
See Cecil, (Edward Christian) David (Gascoyne)
Cecil, R. H.
See Hewitt, Cecil Rolph
Cecil, Robert 1913-1994 .... CANR-72
Obituary 144
Earlier sketch in CA 53-56
Cecil-Fronsman, Bill 1953- 143
Ceder, Georgiana Dorcas -1985 .... 1-4R
See also SATA 10
Cedering, Siv 1939- CANR-129
Earlier sketch in CA 41-44R
Ceely, Jonatha 229
Cefkin, J. Leo 1916- 25-28R
Cegielka, Francis A(nthony) 1908- 37-40R
Ceitho, Dewi
See Jones, Evan David
Cejka, Jaroslav 1943- 132
Cela (y Trulock), Camilo Jose
See Cela, Camilo Jose
See also CWW 2
Cela, Camilo Jose 1916-2002 .... CANR-139
Obituary 206
Earlier sketches in CA 21-24R, CANR-21, 32, 76
See also Cela (y Trulock), Camilo Jose
See also CAAS 10
See also BEST 90:2
See also CLC 4, 13, 59, 122
See also DAM MULT
See also DLB 322
See also DLBY 1989
See also EW 13
See also EWL 3
See also HLC 1
See also HW 1
See also MTCW 1, 2
See also MTFW 2005
See also RGSF 2
See also RGWL 2, 3
See also SSC 71
Celaeno
See Harper, George W(illiam)
Celan, Paul
See Antschel, Paul
See also CDWLB 2
See also CLC 10, 19, 53, 82
See also DLB 69
See also EWL 3
See also PC 10
See also RGWL 2, 3
Celati, Gianni 1937- .... CWW 2
See also DLB 196
Celaya, Gabriel 1911-1991 174
See also DLB 108
See also EWL 3
See also HW 2
Celenza, Anna Harwell 202
See also SATA 133
Celeste, Sister Marie CANR-30
Earlier sketch in CA 49-52
Celestino, Martha Laing 1951- 107
See also SATA 39
Celine, Louis-Ferdinand
See Destouches, Louis-Ferdinand
See also CLC 1, 3, 4, 7, 9, 15, 47, 124
See also DLB 72
See also EW 11
See also EWL 3
See also GFL 1789 to the Present
See also RGWL 2, 3
Celizic, Mike 1948- 135
Cell, Edward (Charles) 1928- 21-24R
Cell, John W(hitson) 1935- 41-44R
Cellario, Alberto R. 1910(?)-1984
Obituary 112
Celler, Emanuel 1888-1981
Obituary 108
Cellini, Benvenuto 1500-1571 .... WLIT 7
Celnik, Max 1933- 17-20R
Celoria, Francis (S. C.) 1926- 102
Celtis, Conrad 1459-1508 .... DLB 179
Cemach, Harry P(aul) 1917- 57-60
Cenci, Louis 1918- 17-20R
Cendrars, Blaise
See Sauser-Hall, Frederic
See also CLC 18, 106
See also DLB 258
See also EWL 3
See also GFL 1789 to the Present
See also RGWL 2, 3
See also WP
Censer, Jane T(urner) 1951- 123
Cente, H. F.
See Rocklin, Ross Louis
Center, Allen Harry 1912- CANR-4
Earlier sketch in CA 5-8R
Centlivre, Susanna 1669(?)-1723 .... DC 25
See also DLB 84
See also RGEL 2
Cento
See Cobbing, Bob
Centolella, Thomas Carmen 1952- 140
Centore, F. F. 1938- 25-28R
Cepeda, Joe .... SATA 159
Ceram, C. W.
See Marek, Kurt W(illi)
Cerami, Charles A. 225
Ceravolo, Joseph 1934-1988 102
Obituary 126
See also CP 1, 2
Cercas, Javier 1962- 231
Cercignani, Carlo 1939- 202
Ceren, Sandra L. 223
Cerf, Bennett (Alfred) 1898-1971 .... CAP-2
Obituary 29-32R
Earlier sketch in CA 19-20
See also SATA 7
Cerf, Christopher (Bennett) 1941- CANR-48
Earlier sketch in CA 25-28R
See also SATA 2
Cerf, Jay H(enry) 1923-1974 .... CAP-2
Obituary 53-56
Earlier sketch in CA 19-20
Cerling, Charles (Edward), Jr. 1943- 111
Cermak, Laird S(cott) 1942- CANR-4
Earlier sketch in CA 53-56
Cermak, Martin
See Duchacek, Ivo D(uka)
Cerminara, Gina -1983 .... 17-20R
Cernada, George P. CANR-128
Earlier sketch in CA 166
Cerney, James Vincent 1914-1987 .... 21-24R
Cernuda (y Bidon), Luis 1902-1963 131
Obituary 89-92
See also CLC 54
See also DAM POET
See also DLB 134
See also EWL 3
See also GLL 1
See also HW 1
See also PC 62
See also RGWL 2, 3
Cerny, Frank J. 1946- 217
Cerra, Frances 1946- 97-100
Cerri, Lawrence J. 1923- CANR-17
Earlier sketch in CA 89-92
Cerruti, James Smith 1918-1997 103
Obituary 158
Cerruto, Oscar 1912-1981 .... DLB 283
Certner, Simon 1909(?)-1979
Obituary 89-92
Cerullo, Mary M. 1949- CANR-125
Earlier sketch in CA 151
See also SATA 86, 145
Cerullo, Morris 1931- 232
Cerutti, Maria Antonietta 1932- 25-28R
Cerutti, Toni
See Cerutti, Maria Antonietta
Cerutty, Percy Wells 1895-1975 .... CAP-2
Obituary 61-64
Earlier sketch in CA 25-28
Ceruzzi, Paul Edward 1949- 193
Cervantes, Alfonso J(uan) 1920-1983
Obituary 110
Cervantes, Lorna Dee 1954- CANR-80
Earlier sketch in CA 131
See also CWP
See also DLB 82
See also EXPP
See also HLCS 1
See also HW 1
See also LLW
See also PC 35
Cervantes, Lucius F. 1914- 13-16R
Cervantes (Saavedra), Miguel de
1547-1616 .... AAYA 56
See also BYA 1, 14
See also DA
See also DAB
See also DAC
See also DAM MST, NOV
See also EW 2
See also HLCS
See also LAIT 1
See also LATS 1:1
See also LMFS 1
See also NFS 8
See also RGSF 2
See also RGWL 2, 3
See also SSC 12
See also TWA
See also WLC
Cervenka, Jarda
See Cervenka, Jaroslav
Cervenka, Jaroslav 1933- CANR-94
Earlier sketch in CA 152
Cervera, Alejo de
See de Cervera, Alejo
Cerveri, Doris 1914- 101
Cervon, Jacqueline
See Moussard, Jacqueline
Cerwinske, Laura 1948- 111
Cerych, Ladislav 1925- CANR-7
Earlier sketch in CA 13-16R
Cesaire, Aime (Fernand) 1913- CANR-81
Earlier sketches in CA 65-68, CANR-24, 43
See also BLC 1
See also BW 2, 3
See also CLC 19, 32, 112
See also CWW 2
See also DA3
See also DAM MULT, POET
See also DC 22
See also DLB 321
See also EWL 3
See also GFL 1789 to the Present
See also MTCW 1, 2
See also MTFW 2005
See also PC 25
See also WP
Cesara, Manda
See Poewe, Karla
Cesarani, David 229
Cespedes, Frank V. 1950- 154
Cessac, Catherine 1952- 153
Cetin, Frank Stanley 1921- 1-4R
See also SATA 2
Cetina, Gutierre de 1514(?)-1556 .... DLB 318
Cetinski, Tugomir
See Begovic, Milan
Cetron, Marvin Jerome 1930- 107
Cetta, Lewis T(homas) 1933- 53-56
Cevasco, George A(nthony) 1924- CANR-2
Earlier sketch in CA 5-8R
Cezair-Thompson, Margaret 1956- 223
Cezanne, Paul 1839-1906 .... AAYA 54
Ch., T.
See Marchenko, Anastasiia Iakovlevna
Cha, Theresa Hak Kyung 1951-1982 217
See also DLB 312
Chaadaev, Petr Iakovlevich
1794-1856 .... DLB 198
Chabal, Patrick (Enri) 1951- 207
Chabe, Alexander M(ichael) 1923- 53-56
Chaber, M. E.
See Crossen, Kendell Foster
Chabod, Federico 1901-1960
Obituary 116
Chabon, Michael 1963- CANR-138
Earlier sketches in CA 139, CANR-57, 96, 127
See also AAYA 45
See also AMWS 11
See also CLC 55, 149
See also DLB 278
See also MAL 5
See also MTFW 2005
See also SATA 145
See also SSC 59
Chabrol, Claude 1930- 110
See also CLC 16
Chace, Isobel
See de Guise, Elizabeth (Mary Teresa)
Chace, James (Clarke) 1931-2004 .... CANR-30
Obituary 232
Earlier sketches in CA 1-4R, CANR-1
Chace, Rebecca 1960- CANR-87
Earlier sketch in CA 144
Chace, William M(urdough) 1938- 69-72
Chacel (Arimon), Rosa
See Chacel, Rosa
See also CWW 2
Chacel, Rosa 1898-1994
See Chacel (Arimon), Rosa
See also DLB 134, 322
See also EWL 3
Chacholiades, Miltiades 1937- CANR-1
Earlier sketch in CA 45-48
Chacko, David 1942- CANR-31
Earlier sketch in CA 49-52
Chacko, George K(uttickal) 1930- CANR-13
Earlier sketch in CA 73-76
Chacon, Eusebio 1869-1948 .... CANR-89
Earlier sketch in CA 131
See also DLB 82
See also HW 1
Chacon, Felipe Maximiliano 1873-(?) ... DLB 82
Chaconas, D(oris) J. 1938- CANR-126
Earlier sketch in CA 21-24R
See also SATA 145
Chaconas, Dori
See Chaconas, D(oris) J.

Cumulative Index **101** **Chan**

Chadbourn, Mark ... HGG
Chadbourne, Richard M(cClain) 1922- ... 21-24R
Chadeayne, Lee 1933- ... 53-56
Chadourne, Marc 1896(?)-1975
Obituary ... 53-56
Chadwick, Alex
See Zoss, Joel
Chadwick, Bruce (V.) ... 209
Chadwick, Bruce A(lbert) 1940- ... 97-100
Chadwick, Cydney 1959- ... CANR-123
Earlier sketch in CA 164
Chadwick, Elizabeth
See Herndon, Nancy
Chadwick, Geoffrey 1950- ... 207
Chadwick, Henry 1824-1908 ... 201
See also DLB 241
Chadwick, Henry 1920- ... CANR-50
Earlier sketches in CA 21-24R, CANR-9, 25
Chadwick, Irene Kooi 1936- ... 229
Chadwick, James 1891-1974 ... 157
Obituary ... 49-52
Chadwick, Janet (Bachand) 1933- ... 97-100
Chadwick, (Gerald William St.) John
1920-1998 ... 25-28R
Chadwick, John 1920-1998 ... 1-4R
Obituary ... 172
Chadwick, John White 1840-1904 ... 214
Chadwick, Joselyn
See Chadwick, Joseph (L.)
Chadwick, Joseph (L.) ... TCWW 2
Chadwick, Lee 1909- ... 69-72
Chadwick, Lester ... CANR-27
Earlier sketches in CAP-2, CA 19-20
See also SATA 1, 67
Chadwick, Margaret Lee (Gill) 1893-1984
Obituary ... 112
Chadwick, Nora Kershaw
1891-1972 ... CANR-81
Earlier sketches in CAP-1, CA 13-16
Chadwick, (William) Owen 1916- ... CANR-41
Earlier sketches in CA 1-4R, CANR-1, 19
Chadwick, Paul 1957- ... AAYA 35
Chadwick, Ronald P(aul) 1935- ... 116
Chadwick, Whitney 1943- ... 132
Chadwin, Dean 1966(?)- ... 237
Chadwin, Mark Lincoln 1939- ... CANR-17
Earlier sketch in CA 25-28R
Chae, Man-Sik 1902-1950 ... 166
Chaet, Bernard 1924- ... 69-72
Chafe, Wallace L. 1927- ... 29-32R
Chafe, William H(enry) 1942- ... CANR-12
Earlier sketch in CA 49-52
Chafel, Judith A. 1945- ... 149
Chafer, Lewis Sperry 1871-1952 ... 218
Chafets, Ze'ev 1947(?)- ... 137
Chafets, Zev
See Chafets, Ze'ev
Chafetz, Gary S. 1947- ... 145
Chafetz, Henry 1916-1978 ... CANR-79
Obituary ... 73-76
Earlier sketches in CA 1-4R, CANR-3
Chafetz, Janet Saltzman 1942- ... 69-72
Chafetz, Morris E(dward) 1924- ... CANR-5
Earlier sketch in CA 13-16R
Chaffee, Allen ... CAP-1
Earlier sketch in CA 9-10
See also SATA 3
Chaffee, John 1946- ... CANR-128
Earlier sketch in CA 85-88
Chaffee, Steven Henry 1935-2001 ... 106
Obituary ... 197
Chaffee, Wilber Albert ... CANR-140
Earlier sketch in CA 174
Chaffin, J. Thomas 1952- ... 215
Chaffin, James B.
See Lutz, Giles A(lfred)
Chaffin, Lillie D(orton) 1925- ... CANR-13
Earlier sketch in CA 33-36R
See also SATA 4
Chaffin, Tom
See Chaffin, J. Thomas
Chaffin, Yule M. 1914-2003 ... 21-24R
Chafin, Andrew 1937- ... 53-56
Chagall, David 1930- ... CANR-3
Earlier sketch in CA 9-12R
Chagall, Marc 1887-1985 ... 122
Obituary ... 114
See also AAYA 24
Chagla, M(ohamedali) C(urrim) 1900-1981
Obituary ... 108
Chagnon, Napoleon A. 1938- ... 130
Chah, Ajahn 1919-1992 ... 231
Chai, Arlene J. 1955- ... 155
Chai, Chen kang 1916- ... 21-24R
Chai, Ch'u 1906- ... 9-12R
Chai, Hon-chan 1931- ... 21-24R
Chai, May-Lee ... 202
Chai, Winberg 1932- ... CANR-113
Earlier sketches in CA 5-8R, CANR-9
Chaij, Fernando 1909- ... CANR-8
Earlier sketch in CA 21-24R
Chaikin, Miriam 1924- ... CANR-136
Earlier sketches in CA 81-84, CANR-14
See also SATA 24, 102, 152
Chairil Anwar
See Anwar, Chairil
See also EWL 3
Chais, Pamela (Herbert) 1930- ... 73-76
Chaisson, Eric (Joseph) 1946- ... CANR-25
Earlier sketch in CA 108
Chaiton, Sam 1950- ... 221
Chajkowsky, William E(ugene) 1938- ... 116
Chakerian, Charles (Garabed)
1904-1994 ... 45-48
Chakour, Charles M. 1929- ... 33-36R
Chakovsky, Sergei 1949- ... 144
Chakravarty, Amiya (Chandra)
1901-1986 ... CANR-1
Earlier sketch in CA 1-4R
Chakravarty, Birendra Narayan
1904-1980(?) ... 102
Chakravarty, Sumita S(inha) 1951- ... 148
Cha'lay
See Tillman, Deborah Lindsay
Chaleff, Ira 1945- ... 150
Chalfant, Edward Allan 1921- ... CANR-111
Earlier sketch in CA 111
Chalfant, William Y. 1928- ... 149
Chalfont, Alun
See Jones, (Alun) Arthur Gwynne
Chalfoun, Michelle 1967(?)- ... 174
Chalhoub, Michael 1932- ... 89-92
Chalidze, Valery Nikolaevich 1938- ... 103
Chalk, John Allen 1937- ... 57-60
Chalk, Ocania 1927- ... CANR-1
Earlier sketch in CA 45-48
Chalker, Dennis ... 233
Chalker, Jack L(aurence) 1944-2005 ... CANR-97
Obituary ... 236
Earlier sketches in CA 73-76, CANR-47
See also SFW 4
Chalker, Sylvia ... 146
Chall, Jeanne S(ternlicht)
1921-1999 ... CANR-10
Obituary ... 186
Earlier sketch in CA 25-28R
Chall, Marsha Wilson ... CANR-134
Earlier sketch in CA 177
See also SATA 150
Challand, Helen J(ean) 1921- ... 121
Brief entry ... 118
See also SATA 64
Challans, Mary 1905-1983 ... CANR-74
Obituary ... 111
Earlier sketch in CA 81-84
See also Renault, Mary
See also DA3
See also MTCW 2
See also MTFW 2005
See also SATA 23
See also SATA-Obit 36
See also TEA
Challe, Robert 1659-c. 1720 ... GFL Beginnings to 1789
Challens, Mary ... GLL 1
Challice, Kenneth
See Hutchin, Kenneth Charles
Challinor, John 1894-1990 ... 73-76
Challis, Chris ... 131
Challis, Christopher 1919- ... IDFW 4
Challis, George
See Faust, Frederick (Schiller)
Challis, (Cecil) Gordon 1932- ... CP 1
Challis, Mary
See Bowen-Judd, Sara (Hutton)
Challis, Sarah ... 227
Challis, Simon
See Phillips, D(ennis) J(ohn Andrew)
Challoner, H. K.
See Mills, J(anet) M(elanie) A(ilsa)
Challoner, Robert
See Butterworth, Michael
Chalmers, Alan D(ouglas) 1957- ... 152
Chalmers, David Mark 1927- ... 25-28R
Chalmers, Eric Brownlie 1929- ... 102
Chalmers, Floyd S(herman) 1898-1993 ... CAP-2
Earlier sketch in CA 25-28
Chalmers, George 1742-1825 ... DLB 30
Chalmers, Harvey II 1890-1971
Obituary ... 33-36R
Chalmers, John West 1910- ... 93-96
Chalmers, Malcolm 1956- ... 120
Chalmers, Mary (Eileen) 1927- ... CANR-79
Earlier sketch in CA 5-8R
See also CWRI 5
See also SAAS 14
See also SATA 6
Chalmers, Penny
See Kemp, Penn
Chalon, Jean 1935- ... CANR-40
Earlier sketches in CA 97-100, CANR-16
Chalon, Jon
See Chaloner, John Seymour
Chaloner, John Seymour 1924- ... 93-96
Chaloner, Sir Thomas 1520-1565 ... DLB 167
Chaloner, W. H.
See Chaloner, William Henry
Chaloner, William Henry 1914-1987
Obituary ... 122
Chamberlain, Anne 1917- ... 77-80
Chamberlain, Betty 1908-1983 ... 33-36R
Obituary ... 109
Chamberlain, Brenda Irene 1912- ... CP 1
Chamberlain, Diane 1950- ... 182
Chamberlain, Elinor 1901-1990 ... CAP-1
Earlier sketch in CA 13-16
Chamberlain, Elwyn M. 1928- ... 131
Chamberlain, Ena
See Cooper, Penny
Chamberlain, Houston Stewart 1855-1927(?)
Brief entry ... 120
Chamberlain, John (Rensselaer)
1903-1995 ... 57-60
Obituary ... 148
Chamberlain, Jonathan Mack 1928- ... 101
Chamberlain, Joseph Miles 1923- ... 107
Chamberlain, Kathleen P. 1947- ... 191
Chamberlain, Kent Clair 1943- ... 234
Chamberlain, Lesley 1951- ... CANR-104
Earlier sketch in CA 137
Chamberlain, Lorna M(arie) 1915- ... 140
Chamberlain, Margaret 1954- ... SATA 46
Chamberlain, Mary (Christina)
1947- ... CANR-44
Earlier sketch in CA 115
Chamberlain, Muriel Evelyn 1932- ... CANR-16
Earlier sketch in CA 93-96
Chamberlain, Narcisse 1924- ... 13-16R
Chamberlain, Neil Wolverton 1915- ... CANR-6
Earlier sketch in CA 13-16R
Chamberlain, (Arthur) Neville 1869-1940
Brief entry ... 113
Chamberlain, Robert Lyall 1923- ... 13-16R
Chamberlain, Safford 1926- ... 206
Chamberlain, Samuel 1895-1975 ... CAP-2
Obituary ... 53-56
Earlier sketch in CA 23-24
Chamberlain, Samuel S(elwyn) 1851-1916 ... 177
See also DLB 25
Chamberlain, Wilson
See Crandall, Norma
Chamberlain, Wilt(on Norman)
1936-1999 ... 103
Chamberland, Paul 1939- ... 177
See also DLB 60
Chamberlin, Ann 1954- ... 159
Chamberlin, E(ric) R(ussell) 1926- ... CANR-75
Earlier sketches in CA 97-100, CANR-19
Chamberlin, Enid C. S. 1900(?)-1982(?)
Obituary ... 106
Chamberlin, J. E(dward) 1943- ... 85-88
Chamberlin, J(ohn) Gordon 1914- ... CANR-4
Earlier sketch in CA 1-4R
Chamberlin, Judi 1944- ... 81-84
Chamberlin, Kate 1945- ... 173
See also SATA 105
Chamberlin, Lee
See La Pallo, A. Elise
Chamberlin, Leslie J(oseph) 1926- ... 53-56
Chamberlin, M. Hope 1920-1974 ... 45-48
Obituary ... 49-52
Chamberlin, Mary 1914- ... 45-48
Chamberlin, Thomas Chrowder
1843-1928 ... 158
Chamberlin, Waldo 1905-1986 ... 65-68
Chamberlin, William Henry 1897-1969 ... 5-8R
See also DLB 29
Chambers, Aidan 1934- ... CANR-116
Earlier sketches in CA 25-28R, CANR-12, 31, 58
See also AAYA 27
See also CLC 35
See also JRDA
See also MAICYA 1, 2
See also SAAS 12
See also SATA 1, 69, 108
See also WYA
See also YAW
Chambers, Anne 1949- ... CANR-53
Earlier sketch in CA 126
Chambers, Anthony H(ood) 1943- ... 108
Chambers, Bradford 1922-1984
Obituary ... 113
See also SATA-Obit 39
Chambers, Catherine E.
See St. John, Nicole
Chambers, Charles Sr. 1927- ... 169
See also BW 3
Chambers, Charles Haddon 1860-1921
Brief entry ... 110
See also DLB 10
Chambers, Chris ... 231
Chambers, Christopher 1963- ... 234
Chambers, Clarke A(lexander)
1921- ... CANR-75
Earlier sketch in CA 41-44R
Chambers, Colin 1950- ... 134
Chambers, Dewey W. 1929- ... CANR-12
Earlier sketch in CA 29-32R
Chambers, Edmund (Kerchever)
1866-1954 ... 199
Chambers, Edward J(ames) 1925- ... 17-20R
Chambers, Frances 1940- ... CANR-29
Earlier sketch in CA 111
Chambers, Frank P(entland) 1900- ... CAP-1
Earlier sketch in CA 9-10
Chambers, Howard V.
See Lowenkopf, Shelly A(lan)
Chambers, Iain 1949- ... 126
Chambers, James 1948-
Brief entry ... 124
See also Cliff, Jimmy
Chambers, Jandy 1965- ... 171
Chambers, Jane 1937-1983 ... 85-88
Obituary ... 109
Chambers, Jessie
See Lawrence, D(avid) H(erbert Richards)
See also GLL 1
Chambers, John W. 1933- ... 124
See also SATA 57
See also SATA-Brief 46
Chambers, John Whiteclay II 1936- ... 137
Chambers, Jonathan David
1898-1970 ... CANR-3
Earlier sketch in CA 1-4R
Chambers, Kate
See St. John, Nicole
Chambers, Leland H. 1928- ... 140
Chambers, Lenoir 1891-1970 ... CANR-75
Obituary ... 104
Earlier sketch in CA 111
Chambers, Lucille Arcola 1909(?)-1988
Obituary ... 125
Chambers, M(erritt) M(adison)
1899-1985 ... CANR-5
Earlier sketch in CA 9-12R
Chambers, Margaret Ada Eastwood
1911- ... 9-12R
See also SATA 2
Chambers, Maria Cristina
See Mena, Maria Cristina
Chambers, Mortimer Hardin, Jr.
1927- ... CANR-6
Earlier sketch in CA 9-12R
Chambers, Peggy
See Chambers, Margaret Ada Eastwood
Chambers, Peter
See Phillips, D(ennis) J(ohn Andrew)
Chambers, R(aymond) J(ohn) 1917- ... 17-20R
Chambers, Robert W(illiam) 1865-1933 ... 165
See also DLB 202
See also HGG
See also SATA 107
See also SUFW 1
See also TCLC 41
Chambers, Robin Bernard 1942- ... 103
Chambers, Ross ... 221
Chambers, Stephen M. 1980- ... 215
Chambers, Veronica 1970(?)- ... CANR-142
Earlier sketch in CA 167
See also AAYA 54
Chambers, W(illiam) Walker 1913- ... 29-32R
Chambers, (David) Whittaker 1901-1961
Obituary ... 89-92
See also DLB 303
See also TCLC 129
Chambers, William E. 1943- ... 73-76
Chambers, William Nisbet 1916- ... CANR-8
Earlier sketch in CA 5-8R
Chambers, William Trout 1896-1986 ... CAP-1
Earlier sketch in CA 13-14
Chambers-Schiller, Lee Virginia 1948- ... 120
Chambertin, Ilya
See von Block, Bela W(illiam) and von Block, Sylvia
Chambliss, Bill
See Chambliss, William J(oseph)
Chambliss, William C. 1908(?)-1975
Obituary ... 57-60
Chambliss, William J(ones) 1923- ... 13-16R
Chambliss, William J(oseph) 1933- ... CANR-14
Earlier sketch in CA 77-80
Chamelin, Neil Charles 1942- ... 69-72
Chametzky, Jules 1928- ... 33-36R
Chamfort, Sebastien-Roch Nicolas de
1740-1794 ... DLB 313
See also GFL Beginnings to 1789
Chamico
See Nale Roxlo, Conrado
Chamisso, Adelbert von 1781-1838 ... DLB 90
See also RGWL 2, 3
See also SUFW 1
Chamlee, Ruth Miller 1893(?)-1983
Obituary ... 110
Chamoiseau, Patrick 1953- ... CANR-88
Earlier sketch in CA 162
See also EWL 3
See also RGWL 3
Champagne, Duane (Willard) 1951- ... 193
Champagne, Marian 1915- ... 5-8R
Champe, Flavia Waters 1902-1992 ... 115
Champernowne, David (Gawen)
1912-2000 ... 104
Obituary ... 189
Champfleury 1821-1889 ... DLB 119
See also GFL 1789 to the Present
Champigny, Robert J(ean) 1922- ... 33-36R
Champion, Dick
See Champion, Richard Gordon
Champion, J(ustin) A. I. 1960- ... 141
Champion, John C(arr) 1923- ... CANR-8
Earlier sketch in CA 17-20R
Champion, John E(lmer) 1922- ... 13-16R
Champion, Larry S(tephen) 1932- ... CANR-73
Earlier sketches in CA 21-24R, CANR-9
Champion, R(ichard) A(nnells) 1925- ... 29-32R
Champion, Richard Gordon 1931- ... 77-80
Champion, Sarah 1970- ... 236
Champkin, Peter 1918-1989 ... 5-8R
Champlin, Charles (Davenport)
1926- ... CANR-142
Earlier sketch in CA 69-72
Champlin, James R(aymond) 1928- ... 21-24R
Champlin, John Michael 1937- ... CANR-52
Earlier sketches in CA 110, CANR-27
See also Champlin, Tim
Champlin, Joseph M(asson) 1930- ... CANR-20
Earlier sketches in CA 49-52, CANR-1
Champlin, Margaret Derby 1925- ... 148
Champlin, Peggy
See Champlin, Margaret Derby
Champlin, Tim
See Champlin, John Michael
See also TCWW 2
Champney, Freeman 1911-1998 ... 25-28R
Champourcin, Ernestina de 1905- ... 208
See also EWL 3
Champy, James 1942- ... 192
Chamson, Andre J(ules) L(ouis)
1900-1983 ... CANR-77
Obituary ... 111
Earlier sketches in CA 5-8R, CANR-2
See also GFL 1789 to the Present
Ch'An, Chu
See Blofeld, John (Eaton Calthorpe)
Ch'an, Chu
See Blofeld, John (Eaton Calthorpe)
Chan, David Marshall 1970- ... 237
Chan, Gerald ... 199
Chan, Gillian 1954- ... CANR-120
Earlier sketch in CA 160
See also SATA 102, 147
Chan, Jackie 1954- ... 174
Chan, Jacky
See Chan, Jackie
Chan, James W(ah Kong) 1949- ... 196

Chan, Jeffery Paul 1942- .... DLB 312
Chan, Kong-Sang
See Chan, Jackie
Chan, Kwong Sang
See Chan, Jackie
Chan, Loren Briggs 1943- CANR-8
Earlier sketch in CA 57-60
Chan, Mary 1940- 191
Chanaidh, Fear
See Campbell, John Lorne
Chanakya
See Panikkar, K(avalam) Madhava
Chanan, Ben
See Yaffe, Richard
Chanan, Gabriel 1942- CANR-7
Earlier sketch in CA 57-60
Chanan, Michael 1946- 106
Chance, Britton 1913- 157
Chance, James T.
See Carpenter, John (Howard)
Chance, Jane 1945- CANR-108
Earlier sketches in CA 57-60, CANR-8
See also Nitzsche, Jane Chance
Chance, John Newton 1911-1983 .... CANR-59
Obituary 110
Earlier sketch in CA 102
See also CMW 4
See also SFW 4
Chance, John T.
See Carpenter, John (Howard)
Chance, Jonathan
See Chance, John Newton
Chance, Megan 1959- CANR-126
Earlier sketch in CA 167
Chance, Michael R(obin) A(lexander)
1915- 85-88
Chance, Roger (James Ferguson) 1893-1987
Obituary 122
Chance, Stephen
See Turner, Philip (William)
Chancellor, Edward 1962- 194
Chancellor, John 1900-1971 .... CAP-2
Earlier sketch in CA 23-24
Chancellor, John (William) 1927-1996 109
Obituary 152
Interview in CA-109
See also AITN 1
See also BEST 90:4
Chancellor, Paul 1900-1975
Obituary 57-60
Chancer, Lynn S. 1955- 144
Chancy, Myriam J(oseph) A(imee) 1970- 176
Chand, Meira (Angela) 1942- 106
Chand, Munshi Prem
See Srivastava, Dhanpat Rai
Chand, Prem
See Srivastava, Dhanpat Rai
Chanda, Asok Kumar 1902- 17-20R
Chandler, A(rthur) Bertram
1912-1984 .... CANR-13
Earlier sketch in CA 21-24R
See also SFW 4
Chandler, Alfred D(upont), Jr.
1918- CANR-116
Earlier sketches in CA 9-12R, CANR-4
Chandler, Alice 1931- 53-56
Chandler, Allison 1906- CAP-1
Earlier sketch in CA 9-10
Chandler, B. J. 1921- 1-4R
Chandler, Billy Jaynes 1932- 122
Chandler, Bryn 1945- 118
Chandler, Caroline A(ugusta)
1906-1979 .... CANR-73
Obituary 93-96
Earlier sketch in CA 17-20R
See also SATA 22
See also SATA-Obit 24
Chandler, Daniel Ross 1937- 175
Chandler, David (Geoffrey)
1934-2004 .... CANR-52
Obituary 232
Earlier sketches in CA 25-28R, CANR-11, 28
Chandler, David Leon 1937(?)-1994 . CANR-38
Obituary 143
Earlier sketches in CA 49-52, CANR-1, 16
Chandler, David P(orter) 1933- CANR-97
Earlier sketches in CA 45-48, CANR-29, 54
See also SATA 28
Chandler, E(dwin) Russell, Jr. 1932- 77-80
Chandler, Edna Walker 1908-1982 ..... CANR-4
Obituary 108
Earlier sketch in CA 1-4R
See also SATA 11
See also SATA-Obit 31
Chandler, Elizabeth
See Helldorfer, M(ary) C(laire)
Chandler, Elizabeth 177
Chandler, Frank
See Harknett, Terry (Williams)
Chandler, George 1915-1992 .... CANR-5
Earlier sketch in CA 9-12R
Chandler, Harry 1864-1944 .... DLB 29
Chandler, Howard 1915(?)-1981
Obituary 104
Chandler, James 1948- 168
Chandler, James K. 203
Chandler, Jennifer
See Westwood, Jennifer
Chandler, Jon A. 1951- 220
Chandler, Karen 1959- .... SATA 122
Chandler, Laurel
See Holder, Nancy L.
Chandler, Lester Vernon 1905-1988
Obituary 126
Chandler, Linda S(mith) 1929- CANR-23
Earlier sketch in CA 106
See also SATA 39
Chandler, Margaret Kueffner 1922- 17-20R
Chandler, Marilyn R(uth) 1949- 140
Chandler, Norman 1899-1973 .... CANR-80
Obituary 89-92
See also DLB 127
Chandler, Otis 1927- CANR-80
Earlier sketch in CA 111
See also DLB 127
Chandler, Raymond (Thornton)
1888-1959 .... CANR-107
Brief entry 104
Earlier sketches in CA 129, CANR-60
See also AAYA 25
See also AMWC 2
See also AMWS 4
See also BPFB 1
See also CDALB 1929-1941
See also CMW 4
See also DA3
See also DLB 226, 253
See also DLBD 6
See also EWL 3
See also MAL 5
See also MSW
See also MTCW 1, 2
See also MTFW 2005
See also NFS 17
See also RGAL 4
See also SSC 23
See also TCLC 1, 7.
See also TUS
Chandler, Richard Eugene 1916- 5-8R
Chandler, Robert 1953- 112
See also SATA 40
Chandler, Robert Wilbur 1921- 102
Chandler, Ruth Forbes 1894-1978 .... CANR-73
Obituary 103
Earlier sketch in CA 1-4R
See also SATA 2
See also SATA-Obit 26
Chandler, S(tanley) Bernard 1921- 21-24R
Chandler, T(ony) J(ohn) 1928- 107
Chandler, Tertius 1915- CANR-19
Earlier sketch in CA 102
Chandola, Anoop C. 1937- CANR-107
Earlier sketches in CA 37-40R, CANR-14
Chandonnet, Ann F. 1943- CANR-47
Earlier sketches in CA 61-64, CANR-8, 23
See also SATA 92
Chandor, (Peter John) Anthony
1932- CANR-26
Earlier sketch in CA 29-32R
Chandos, Fay
See Swatridge, Irene Maude (Mossop)
Chandos, John
See McConnell, John Lithgow Chandos
Chandra, G. S. Sharat
See Sharat Chandra, G(ubbi) S(hankara Chetty)
Chandra, Pramod 1930- 77-80
Chandra, Sarat
See Chatterje, Sarat Chandra
Chandra, Smita 1960- 138
Chandra, Vikram 1961- CANR-97
Earlier sketch in CA 149
See also SSFS 16
Chandragupta, Bansi 1924-1981 ...... IDFW 3, 4
Chandrasekhar, Sripati 1918-2001 89-92
Obituary 198
Chandrasekhar, Subrahmanyan
1910-1995 157
Chaneles, Sol 1926- 41-44R
Chaney, Edward (Paul de Gruyter) 1951- ... 131
Chaney, Jill 1932- CANR-52
Earlier sketches in CA 25-28R, CANR-11
See also CWRI 5
See also SATA 87
Chaney, Norman 1935- 110
Chaney, Otto Preston, Jr. 1931- 33-36R
Chaney, William A(lbert) 1922- CANR-74
Earlier sketch in CA 33-36R
Chang, Chen-chi 1920- 153
Brief entry 115
Chang, Ch'eng-chi
See Chang, Chen-chi
Chang, Chih-Wei 1966- .... SATA 111
Chang, Chung-yuan 1900-1984 117
Chang, Cindy 1968- .... SATA 90
Chang, Constance D(an) 1917- 61-64
Chang, Dae H(ong) 1928- CANR-6
Earlier sketch in CA 57-60
Chang, David Wen-wei 1929- 130
Chang, Diana 1934- 228
See also AAL
See also CWP
See also DLB 312
See also EXPP
Chang, Eileen 1921-1995 166
See also Chang Ai-Ling and
Zhang Ailing
See also AAL
See also SSC 28
Chang, Garma C. C.
See Chang, Chen-chi
Chang, Hsin-hai 1898(?)-1972 .... CANR-73
Earlier sketch in CA 5-8R
Chang, Iris 1968-2004 .... CANR-129
Obituary 233
Earlier sketch in CA 169
See also MTFW 2005
Chang, Isabelle C(hin) 1924- 21-24R
Chang, Jen-chi 1903-1997 .... CAP-1
Earlier sketch in CA 11-12
Chang, Joan Chiung-huei 1962- 216
Chang, Jung 1952- 142
See also CLC 71
Chang, Kang-i Sun 1944- 200
Chang, Kevin O'Brien 1958- 168
Chang, Kia-Ngau 1889-1979 .... 5-8R
Chang, Kwang-chih 1931-2001 .... CANR-15
Obituary 193
Earlier sketch in CA 41-44R
Chang, Lan Samantha 1965- 238
Chang, Lee
See Levinson, Leonard
Chang, Leonard 1968- CANR-109
Earlier sketch in CA 168
Chang, Leslie 239
Chang, Margaret (Scrogin) 1941- .... SATA 71
Chang, Maria Hsia 1950- 170
Chang, Pang-Mei Natasha 1965- 156
Chang, Parris (Hsu-Cheng) 1936- CANR-6
Earlier sketch in CA 57-60
Chang, Raymond 1939- CANR-121
Earlier sketches in CA 121, CANR-47, 99
See also SATA 71, 142 PEN, 142
Chang, Richard T(aiwon) 1933- 61-64
Chang Ai-Ling
See Chang, Eileen
See also EWL 3
Chang Chieh
See Zhang, Jie
Chang Chien
See Zhang, Jie
Changeux, Jean-Pierre 1936- CANR-104
Earlier sketch in CA 134
Chang-Rodriguez, Eugenio 1926- CANR-21
Earlier sketches in CA 9-12R, CANR-6
Chanin, Abraham (Solomon) 1921- 89-92
Chanin, Michael 1952- .... SATA 84
Chankin, Donald O(liver) 1934- 57-60
Channel, A. R.
See Catherall, Arthur
Channels, Vera G(race) 1915- 69-72
Channer, Colin 1963- 214
Channing, Carol 1923- 214
Channing, Edward (Perkins) 1856-1931
Brief entry 122
See also DLB 17
Channing, Edward Tyrrell 1790-1856 .... DLB 1,
59, 235
Channing, Steven A. 1940- CANR-29
Earlier sketches in CA 33-36R, CANR-13
Channing, William Ellery II 1817-1901 215
See also DLB 1, 223
Channing, William Ellery 1780-1842 .... DLB 1,
59, 235
See also RGAL 4
Channing, William Henry 1810-1884 ... DLB 1,
59, 243
Channon, Henry 1897-1958
Brief entry 121
Chanoff, David 1943- CANR-123
Earlier sketch in CA 138
Chanover, E(dmond) Pierre 1932- 29-32R
Chanover, Hyman 1920- CANR-2
Earlier sketch in CA 49-52
Chansky, Norman M(orton) 1929- 21-24R
Chant, Barry (Mostyn) 1938- CANR-29
Earlier sketches in CA 65-68, CANR-11
Chant, Donald (Alfred) 1928- CANR-18
Earlier sketch in CA 101
Chant, Joy
See Rutter, Eileen Joyce
Chant, (Eileen) Joy
See Rutter, Eileen Joyce
See also FANT
Chant, Ken(neth David) 1933- 89-92
Chant, Sylvia (H.) 1958- 226
Chantiles, Vilma Liacouras 1925- CANR-6
Earlier sketch in CA 57-60
Chantler, David T(homas) 1925- 93-96
Chao, Buwei Yang 1889-1981 61-64
Obituary 120
Chao, Evelina 1949- 120
Chao, Kang 1929- 33-36R
Chao, Lien 1950- 236
Chao, Patricia 1955- 163
See also CLC 119
Chao, Paul 1919- 114
Chao, Yuen Ren 1892-1982 .... CAP-2
Obituary 106
Earlier sketch in CA 21-22
Chaon, Dan 1964- 207
Chao Shu-li 1906-1970 .... EWL 3
Chapel, Paul 1926- 25-28R
Chapelain, Jean 1595-1674 .... DLB 268
See also GFL Beginnings to 1789
Chapell, Bryan 1954- 223
Chapelle, Howard I(rving) 1901-1975 ... CAP-2
Obituary 57-60
Earlier sketch in CA 25-28
Chapian, Marie 1938- CANR-22
Earlier sketch in CA 106
See also SATA 29
Chapin, Alene Olsen Dalton 1915(?)-1986
Obituary 119
See also SATA-Obit 47
Chapin, Dwight Allan 1938- 41-44R
Chapin, F(rancis) Stuart, Jr. 1916- CANR-2
Earlier sketch in CA 5-8R
Chapin, Harry (Forster) 1942-1981 105
Obituary 104
Chapin, Henry 1893-1983 93-96
Obituary 110
Chapin, June Roediger 1931- CANR-13
Earlier sketch in CA 37-40R
Chapin, Katherine Garrison
See Biddle, Katherine Garrison Chapin
Chapin, Kim 1942- CANR-9
Earlier sketch in CA 53-56
Chapin, Louis Le Bourgeois, Jr. 1918-1981 . 103
Chapin, Miles 1954- 147
Chapin, Ned 1927- 13-16R
Chapin, Sarah 1931- CANR-120
Earlier sketch in CA 148
Chapin, Schuyler G(arrison) 1923- 77-80
Chapin, Tom 1945- .... SATA 83
Chapin, Victor 1919(?)-1983
Obituary 109
Chapin, William 1918- 37-40R
Chaplin, Bill
See Chaplin, W. W.
Chaplin, Charles Spencer 1889-1977 81-84
Obituary 73-76
See also Chaplin, Charlie
See also CLC 16
Chaplin, Charlie
See Chaplin, Charles Spencer
See also AAYA 61
See also DLB 44
Chaplin, Dora P. 1906(?)-1990
Obituary 132
Chaplin, Elizabeth
See McGown, Jill
Chaplin, George 1914-2003 69-72
Obituary 214
See also AITN 2
Chaplin, Gordon 194
Chaplin, James P(atrick) 1919- CANR-1
Earlier sketch in CA 1-4R
Chaplin, L(inda) Tarin 1941- CANR-40
Earlier sketch in CA 116
Chaplin, Sid(ney) 1916-1986 .... CANR-39
Obituary 118
Earlier sketches in CAP-1, CA 9-10, CANR-16
See also CN 1, 2, 3
Chaplin, W. W. 1895(?)-1978
Obituary 81-84
Chapman, A(rthur) H(arry) 1924- CANR-19
Earlier sketch in CA 25-28R
Chapman, Abraham 1915- 45-48
Chapman, Allen CANR-27
Earlier sketches in CAP-2, CA 19-20
See also SATA 1, 67
Chapman, Alvah H., Jr. .... AITN 2
Chapman, Audrey R. 184
Chapman, Brian 1923- 9-12R
Chapman, C. Stuart 1970(?)- 219
Chapman, Carl H(aley) 1915-1987 133
Chapman, Carleton B(urke) 1915- 69-72
Chapman, Charles F(rederic) 1881-1976
Obituary 65-68
Chapman, Cheryl O(rth) 1948- .... SATA 80
Chapman, Christine 1933- CANR-12
Earlier sketch in CA 73-76
Chapman, Clark Russell 1945- CANR-28
Earlier sketch in CA 110
Chapman, Clay McLeod 222
Chapman, Colin 1937- CANR-26
Earlier sketch in CA 29-32R
Chapman, David L. 1948- 148
Chapman, (William) Donald 1923- 109
Chapman, Dorothy Hilton 1934-1995 57-60
Chapman, Edmund H(aupt) 1906- CAP-1
Earlier sketch in CA 13-16
Chapman, (Constance) Elizabeth (Mann)
1919- CAP-1
Earlier sketch in CA 9-10
See also SATA 10
Chapman, Elwood N. 1916- 37-40R
Chapman, Fern Schumer 1954- 187
Chapman, Frances
See Chapman, Frank M(onroe)
Chapman, Frank
See Chapman, Frank M(onroe)
Chapman, Frank M(onroe) 1930- 113
Chapman, G(eorge) W(arren) Vernon
1925- CANR-26
Earlier sketch in CA 29-32R
Chapman, Gaynor 1935- .... SATA 32
Chapman, George 1559(?)-1634 .... BRW 1
See also DAM DRAM
See also DC 19
See also DLB 62, 121
See also LMFS 1
See also RGEL 2
Chapman, Gillian 1955- 191
See also SATA 120
Chapman, Graham 1941-1989 .... CANR-95
Obituary 129
Earlier sketches in CA 116, CANR-35
See also Monty Python
See also CLC 21
Chapman, Guy (Patterson) 1889-1972 101
Obituary 89-92
Chapman, Herb 1951- 200
Chapman, Hester W(olferstan)
1899-1976 .... CANR-9
Obituary 65-68
Earlier sketch in CA 9-12R
See also RHW
Chapman, J. Dudley 1928- CANR-8
Earlier sketch in CA 21-24R
Chapman, J(ohn) Wilbur 1859-1918 214
Chapman, James (Keith) 1919- CANR-33
Earlier sketches in CA 41-44R, CANR-15
Chapman, James B(laine) 1884-1947 215
Chapman, Jane 1970- .... SATA 122
Chapman, Jean 97-100
See also CLR 65
See also SATA 34, 104
Chapman, Jennifer 1950- CANR-42
Earlier sketch in CA 118
Chapman, John 1900-1972
Obituary 33-36R
Chapman, John Jay 1862-1933 191
Brief entry 104
See also AMWS 14
See also TCLC 7
Chapman, John L(eslie) 1920- 1-4R

Cumulative Index 103 Chase

Chapman, John Roy 1927-2001 .... CANR-15
Obituary 199
Earlier sketch in CA 77-80
Chapman, John Stanton Higham 1891-1972
Obituary 107
See also SATA-Obit 27
Chapman, Joseph Irvine 1912-2001 61-64
Chapman, June R(amey) 1918- 5-8R
Chapman, Karen C. 1942- 65-68
Chapman, Kenneth F(rancis) 1910- CAP-1
Earlier sketch in CA 13-16
Chapman, Kenneth G. 1927- 13-16R
Chapman, Laura 1935- 105
Chapman, Lee
See Bradley, Marion Zimmer
See also GLL 1
Chapman, Loren J(ames) 1927- 53-56
Chapman, Lynne F(erguson) 1963- . CANR-134
Earlier sketch in CA 159
See also SATA 94, 150
Chapman, M(ary) Winslow 1903-1995 ... 93-96
Chapman, Marie M(anire) 1917- CANR-11
Earlier sketch in CA 61-64
Chapman, Maristan
See Chapman, John Stanton Higham
Chapman, Matthew 1950- 207
Chapman, Nancy W(hisnant) Collins
See Collins-Chapman, Nancy W(hisnant)
Chapman, Olive Murray 1892-1977 .. DLB 195
Chapman, Paul K. 1931- 139
Chapman, Phil 1944- 121
Chapman, R. W. 1881-1960 .... DLB 201
Chapman, Raymond 1924- CANR-42
Earlier sketches in CA 5-8R, CANR-2
Chapman, Richard A(rnold) 1937- CANR-86
Brief entry 105
Earlier sketch in CA 133
Chapman, Rick M. 1943- 49-52
Chapman, Robert (DeWitt) 1937- 107
Chapman, Robert L(undquist) 1920-2002 ... 122
Obituary 208
Chapman, Roger E(ddington) 1916- 21-24R
Chapman, Ronald (George) 1917-1994 ..... 5-8R
Obituary 147
Chapman, Ruth 1912(?)-1979
Obituary 104
Chapman, Samuel Greeley 1929- CANR-9
Earlier sketch in CA 17-20R
Chapman, Stanley D(avid) 1935- CANR-9
Earlier sketch in CA 21-24R
Chapman, Stepan CANR-97
Earlier sketch in CA 41-44R
Chapman, Steven
See Chapman, Stepan
Chapman, Sydney 1888-1970 106
Chapman, Vera (Ivy May)
1898-1996 .... CANR-58
Obituary 180
Earlier sketch in CA 81-84
See also FANT
See also SATA 33
Chapman, Victoria L(ynn) 1944- 57-60
Chapman, Walker
See Silverberg, Robert
Chapman, William 1850-1917 .... DLB 99
Chapman, (George) William (Alfred)
1850-1917 177
Chapman-Mortimer, William Charles
1907-1988 .... 13-16R
Chapnick, Howard 1922-1996 65-68
Obituary 152
Chappel, Bernice M(arie) 1910- CANR-37
Earlier sketches in CA 89-92, CANR-16
Chappell, Audrey 1954- 140
See also SATA 72
Chappell, Booie
See Chappell, Ruth Paterson
Chappell, Clovis G(illham) 1882-1972 65-68
Chappell, Fred (Davis) 1936- 198
Earlier sketches in CA 5-8R, CANR-8, 33, 67, 110
Autobiographical Essay in 198
See also CAAS 4
See also CLC 40, 78, 162
See also CN 6
See also CP 7
See also CSW
See also DLB 6, 105
See also HGG
Chappell, Gordon (Stelling) 1939- 57-60
Chappell, Helen 1947- CANR-142
Earlier sketch in CA 104
Chappell, Jeannette
See Kalt, Jeannette Chappell
Chappell, Mollie 102
See also RHW
Chappell, Ruth Paterson 169
Chappell, Vere Claiborne 1930- 5-8R
Chappell, Warren 1904-1991 .... CANR-47
Obituary 134
Earlier sketches in CA 17-20R, CANR-8
See also MAICYA 1, 2
See also SAAS 10
See also SATA 6, 68
See also SATA-Obit 67
Chappell, William (Evelyn) 1908-1994 106
Obituary 143
See also DLB 236
Chapple, Christopher Key 1954- CANR-109
Earlier sketches in CA 126, CANR-52
Chapple, Eliot D(ismore) 1909- 41-44R
Chapple, (Clement) Gerald 1937- 111
Chapple, J(ohn) A(lfred) V(ictor) 1928- .. 21-24R
Chapple, Richard L(ynn) 1944- 112
Chapple, Steve 1949- 77-80
Chaput, Donald (Charles) 1933- 122
Brief entry 117
Chaqueri, Cosroe
See Shakeri, Khosrow
Char, K. T. Narasimha
See Narasimha Char, K. T.
Char, Rene(-Emile) 1907-1988 .... CANR-32
Obituary 124
Earlier sketch in CA 13-16R
See also CLC 9, 11, 14, 55
See also DAM POET
See also DLB 258
See also EWL 3
See also GFL 1789 to the Present
See also MTCW 1, 2
See also PC 56
See also RGWL 2, 3
Char, Tin-Yuke 1905-1990 57-60
Char, Wai Jane Chun 1912-1991 118
Char, Yum
See Barrett, Dean
Charanis, Peter 1908-1985 .... 37-40R
Obituary 115
Charap, John M. 1935- 221
Charbonneau, Eileen 1951- CANR-96
Earlier sketch in CA 150
See also AAYA 35
See also SATA 84, 118
Charbonneau, Jean 1875-1960 177
See also DLB 92
Charbonneau, Louis (Henry) 1924- .. CANR-55
Earlier sketch in CA 85-88
See also Young, Carter Travis
See also SFW 4
Charbonneau, Robert 1911-1967 177
See also CCA 1
See also DLB 68
Charbonnet, Gabrielle 1961- 149
See also SATA 81
Charby, Jay
See Ellison, Harlan (Jay)
Charchat, Isaac 1904(?)-1985
Obituary 116
Chard, (Maire) Brigid 1934- 105
Chard, Judy 1916- CANR-86
Earlier sketches in CA 77-80, CANR-14, 31
See also RHW
Chard, Leslie F. II 1934- 33-36R
Chardiet, Bernice (Kroll) 1927(?)- 103
See also SATA 27
Chardin, Pierre Teilhard de
See Teilhard de Chardin, (Marie Joseph) Pierre
Charen, Mona 1957- 229
Charents, Eghishe
See Soghomonian, Eghishe
See also EWL 3
Charfield, Cheryl A. 175
Chargaff, Erwin 1905-2002 .... CANR-39
Obituary 207
Earlier sketches in CA 101, CANR-18
Charhadi, Driss ben Hamed 13-16R
Chari, V. Krishna 1924- 17-20R
Charland, William (Alfred), Jr. 1937- 97-100
Charle, Christophe 1951- 212
Charlebois, Lucile C. 1950- 170
Charles, Amy M(arie) 1922- 116
Charles, C(arol) M(organ) 1931- CANR-1
Earlier sketch in CA 49-52
Charles, David
See Mondey, David (Charles) and Taylor, Charles D(oonan)
Charles, Don C(laude) 1918- 9-12R
Charles, Donald
See Meighan, Donald Charles
Charles, Franklin
See Adams, Cleve F(ranklin)
Charles, Gerda 1914-1996 .... CANR-68
Earlier sketches in CA 1-4R, CANR-1
See also CN 1, 2, 3, 4, 5, 6
See also DLB 14
Charles, Gordon H(ull) 1920- 104
Charles, Henry
See Harris, Marion Rose (Young)
Charles, John 1965- 201
Charles, Kate 1950- CANR-72
Earlier sketch in CA 141
Charles, Louis
See Stratemeyer, Edward L.
Charles, Maggi
See Koehler, Margaret (Hudson)
Charles, Mark
See Bickers, Richard (Leslie) Townshend
Charles, Nathanael
See Franklin, Benjamin V
Charles, Nicholas J.
See Kuskin, Karla (Seidman)
Charles, Norma 228
See also SATA 153
Charles, Ray
See Robinson, Ray Charles
Charles, Robert
See Smith, Robert Charles
Charles, Rupaul Andre 1960- 177
See also HW 2
Charles, Sara C(onnor) 1934- CANR-89
Earlier sketch in CA 132
Charles, Sascha 1896(?)-1972
Obituary 37-40R
Charles, Searle F(ranklin) 1923- 9-12R
Charles, Steven
See Grant, Charles L(ewis)
Charles, Theresa
See Swatridge, Charles (John)
Charles, Will
See Willeford, Charles (Ray III)
Charles d'Orleans 1394-1465 .... DLB 208
Charles-Roux, Edmonde 1920- 85-88
Charles the Clown
See Kraus, Charles E.
Charleston, Robert E.
See Robinson, Charles M. III
Charleston, Robert Jesse 1916-1994 102
Charlesworth, Arthur Riggs 1911-1975 53-56
Charlesworth, Edward A(llison) 1949- 125
Charlesworth, James Clyde 1900-1974 ... 9-12R
Obituary 45-48
Charlesworth, James H(amilton) 1940- 130
Charlesworth, John Kaye 1889-1972 ..... CAP-1
Earlier sketch in CA 9-10
Charlesworth, Maxwell John 1925- .. CANR-40
Earlier sketches in CA 1-4R, CANR-2, 18
Charlesworth, Monique 1951- 239
Charlier, Patricia (Mary) Simonet
1923- 37-40R
Charlier, Roger H(enri) 1921- CANR-60
Earlier sketches in CA 37-40R, CANR-13, 31
Charlip, Remy 1929- CANR-97
Earlier sketches in CA 33-36R, CANR-44
See also CLR 8
See also MAICYA 1, 2
See also SATA 4, 68, 119
Charlot, Anita M. 1965- 202
Charlot, Jean 1898-1979 .... CANR-4
Earlier sketch in CA 5-8R
See also SATA 8
See also SATA-Obit 31
Charlot, John (Pierre) 1941- 120
Charlot, Martin (Day) 1944- CANR-35
Earlier sketch in CA 114
See also SATA 64
Charlotte, Susan 1954- 109
Charlson, David
See Holmes, David Charles
Charlton, David 1946- 127
Charlton, Donald Geoffrey 1925- CANR-17
Earlier sketches in CA 1-4R, CANR-1
Charlton, Evan 1912-1983
Obituary 110
Charlton, Hilda 1910(?)-1988 215
Charlton, Jack
See Charlton, John
Charlton, James (Mervyn) 1939- 81-84
Charlton, John
See Woodhouse, Martin (Charlton)
Charlton, John 1935- 109
Charlton, Linda
See Murray, Linda Charlton
Charlton, Michael (Alan) 1923- .... SATA 34
Charlwood, D(onald) E(rnest) 1915- ... CANR-9
Earlier sketch in CA 21-24R
Charlwood, Don
See Charlwood, D(onald) E(rnest)
Charmatz, Bill 1925- 29-32R
See also SATA 7
Charme, Stuart Zane 1951- 137
Charmley, John 1955- 143
Charnance, L. P.
See Hannaway, Patricia H(inman)
Charnas, Suzy McKee 1939- CANR-73
Earlier sketches in CA 93-96, CANR-18, 39
See also AAYA 43
See also BPFB 1
See also BYA 6
See also HGG
See also SATA 61, 110
See also SFW 4
Charney, Ann CANR-111
Earlier sketch in CA 102
Charney, David H. 1923- CANR-15
Earlier sketch in CA 81-84
Charney, George 1905(?)-1975
Obituary 61-64
Charney, Hanna (Kurz) 1931- CANR-29
Earlier sketch in CA 49-52
Charney, Mark J. 1956- 141
Charney, Maurice (Myron) 1929- CANR-40
Earlier sketches in CA 9-12R, CANR-3, 18
Charnin, Martin (Jay) 1934- 103
Charnley, John 1911-1982
Obituary 107
Charnley, Mitchell V(aughn) 1898-1991 .. 69-72
Charnock, Joan 1903- CAP-2
Earlier sketch in CA 33-36
Charnon-Deutsch, Lou 1946- CANR-123
Earlier sketch in CA 162
Charny, Carmi 1925- CANR-45
Earlier sketches in CA 13-16R, CANR-7
See also Carmi, T.
Charny, Israel W(olf) 1931- 57-60
Charosh, Mannis 1906- 29-32R
See also SATA 5
Charpak, Georges 1924- CANR-128
Earlier sketch in CA 157
Charpentier, Henri 1880-1961 224
Charques, Dorothy (Taylor) 1899-1976 ... 73-76
Obituary 65-68
Charren, Peggy 1928- 129
Charrette, Robert N. 1953- CANR-144
Earlier sketch in CA 160
See also FANT
Charriere, Henri 1906-1973 101
Charriere, Isabelle de 1740-1805 .... DLB 313
Charron, Pierre 1541-1603 .. GFL Beginnings to 1789
Charron, Shirley 1935- 69-72
Charry, Elias 1906- 69-72
Charskaia, Lidiia
See Voronova, Lidiia Alekseevna
See also DLB 295
Charter, S(teve) P. R. 1915(?)-1984
Obituary 114
Charteris, Hugo (Francis Guy) 1922-1970 .. 105
Obituary 89-92
Charteris, James Donald 1948- 117
Charteris, Leslie 1907-1993 .... CANR-58
Obituary 141
Earlier sketches in CA 5-8R, CANR-10
See also CMW 4
See also DLB 77
See also MSW
Charters, Alexander N(athaniel) 1916- 120
Charters, Ann (Danberg) 1936- CANR-93
Earlier sketches in CA 17-20R, CANR-9, 34
Charters, Lowell
See Maxwell, Ann (Elizabeth)
Charters, Samuel (Barclay) 1929- CANR-34
Earlier sketches in CA 9-12R, CANR-9
Chartham, Robert
See Seth, Ronald (Sydney)
Chartier, Alain c. 1392-1430 .... DLB 208
Chartier, Emile-Auguste
See Alain
Chartier, Emilio
See Estenssoro, Hugo
Chartier, JoAnn 223
Chartier, Normand L. 1945- .... SATA 66
Chartier, Roger 1945- CANR-100
Earlier sketch in CA 137
Chartkoff, Joseph L(ouis) 1942- 119
Chartkoff, Kerry K(ona) 1943- 119
Chart Korbjitti 1954- .... EWL 3
Charvat, Frank John 1918- 1-4R
Charvet, John 1938- CANR-15
Earlier sketch in CA 85-88
Chary, Frederick B(arry) 1939- 49-52
Charyn, Jerome 1937- CANR-101
Earlier sketches in CA 5-8R, CANR-7, 61
See also CAAS 1
See also CLC 5, 8, 18
See also CMW 4
See also CN 1, 2, 3, 4, 5, 6, 7
See also DLBY 1983
See also MTCW 1
Chasan, Daniel Jack 1943- 29-32R
Chasca, Edmund V(illela) de
See de Chasca, Edmund V(illela)
Chasdi, Richard J. 1958- 219
Chase, A(lice) Elizabeth 1906- CAP-1
Earlier sketch in CA 11-12
Chase, Adam
See Fairman, Paul W. and Marlowe, Stephen and Thomson, James C(utting)
Chase, Alan (Louis) 1929- 1-4R
Chase, Alice
See McHargue, Georgess
Chase, Alston Hurd 1906-1994 .... 5-8R
Chase, Alyssa 1965- 156
See also SATA 92
Chase, Andra 1942- .... SATA 91
Chase, Borden
See Fowler, Frank
See also DLB 26
See also IDFW 3, 4
See also TCWW 1, 2
Chase, Caroline
See DuBay, Sandra
Chase, Carolyn
See Simmons, Trana Mae
Chase, Carter
See Hanle, Dorothea Zack
Chase, Chevy 1943- 164
Chase, Chris .... AITN 1
Chase, Cleveland B(ruce) 1904(?)-1975
Obituary 53-56
Chase, Clinton I(rvin) 1927- 106
Chase, Cora G(ingrich) 1898-1983 ..... CANR-7
Earlier sketch in CA 61-64
Chase, Donald 1943- 53-56
Chase, Edna Woolman 1877-1957 178
See also DLB 91
Chase, Elaine R(aco) 1949- CANR-82
Earlier sketches in CA 114, CANR-36
See also RHW
Chase, Emily
See Aks, Patricia and Garwood, Julie and Sachs, Judith and White, Carol
Chase, Gilbert 1906-1992 .... 17-20R
Obituary 137
Chase, Glen
See Fox, G(ardner) F(rancis) and Levinson, Leonard
Chase, Harold W(illiam) 1922- CANR-4
Earlier sketch in CA 9-12R
Chase, Ilka 1905-1978 .... CANR-9
Obituary 77-80
Earlier sketch in CA 61-64
Chase, James Hadley
See Raymond, Rene (Brabazon)
See also DLB 276
Chase, James S(taton) 1932- 85-88
Chase, Joan 134
Brief entry 129
Interview in CA-134
Chase, John Leighton 1953- 204
Chase, Judith Wragg 1907-1995 .... 41-44R
Chase, Karen 1943- 202
Chase, Karen Susan 1952- 201
Chase, Larry
See Chase, Lawrence
Chase, Lawrence 1943- 97-100
Chase, Loretta Lynda 1949- 203
Chase, Loriene Eck 102
Chase, Loring D. 1916- 25-28R
Chase, Lyndon
See Chard, Judy
Chase, Marilyn 1949- 222

Chase, Mary (Coyle) 1907-1981 77-80
Obituary 105
See also CAD
See also CWD
See also DC 1
See also DFS 11
See also DLB 228
See also SATA 17
See also SATA-Obit 29
Chase, Mary Ellen 1887-1973 .... CAP-1
Obituary 41-44R
Earlier sketch in CA 13-16
See also CLC 2
See also SATA 10
See also TCLC 124
Chase, Mildred Portney 1921- 106
Chase, Naomi Feigelson 1932- 104
Chase, Nicholas
See Hyde, Anthony
See also CCA 1
Chase, Otta Louise 1909-1987 .... CANR-32
Earlier sketch in CA 49-52
Chase, Philander D(ean) 1943- CANR-94
Earlier sketches in CA 124, CANR-51
Chase, Richard 1904-1988 61-64
Obituary 125
See also SATA 64
See also SATA-Obit 56
Chase, Robert David
See Gorman, Edward
Chase, Robin
See Robinson, Charles
Chase, Samantha
See Glick, Ruth (Burtnick)
Chase, Samuel B(rown), Jr. 1932- 5-8R
Chase, Stuart 1888-1985 65-68
Obituary 117
Chase, Sylvia (Belle) 1938- 115
Brief entry 110
Interview in CA-115
Chase, Thornton 1847-1912 212
Chase, Truddi 1937(?)- 142
Chase, Virginia Lowell
See Perkins, Virginia Chase
Chase, W. Linwood 1897(?)-1983
Obituary 110
Chasen, Nancy H. 1945- 130
Chase-Riboud, Barbara (Dewayne Tosi)
1939- CANR-76
Earlier sketch in CA 113
See also BW 2
See also DAM MULT
See also DLB 33
See also MTCW 2
Chasin, Barbara 1940- 69-72
Chasin, Helen .... CP 1
Chasins, Abram 1903-1987 .... CANR-14
Obituary 122
Earlier sketch in CA 37-40R
Chasles, Robert de
See Challe, Robert
Chasman, Herbert 1938- 121
Chast, Roz 1954- 149
See also SATA 97
Chastain, Madye Lee 1908-1989 .... 5-8R
See also SATA 4
Chastain, Sandra 177
Chastain, Thomas 1921-1994 235
See also CMW 4
Chasteen, Edgar R(ay) 1935- 33-36R
Chasteen, John Charles 1955- 196
Chastel, Andre (Adrien) 1912-1990
Obituary 132
Chastenet de Castaing, Jacques 1893-1978
Obituary 77-80
Chaston, Gloria Duncan 1929- 69-72
Chatalbash, Ron 1959- 111
Chataway, Carol 1955- 211
See also SATA 140
Chateaubriand, Francois Rene de
1768-1848 .... DLB 119
See also EW 5
See also GFL 1789 to the Present
See also RGWL 2, 3
See also TWA
Chateauclair, Wilfrid
See Lighthall, William Douw
Chatelain, Nicolas 1913-1976
Obituary 65-68
Chatelet, Albert 1928- CANR-6
Earlier sketch in CA 13-16R
Chatelet, Gabrielle-Emilie Du
See du Chatelet, Emilie
See also DLB 313
Chatellerault, Victor de
See Beaudoin, Kenneth Lawrence
Chatellier, Louis 1935- CANR-143
Earlier sketch in CA 161
Chater, Elizabeth (Eileen Moore)
1910-2004 111
Chatfield, (Earl) Charles (Jr.) 1934- 37-40R
Chatfield, Cheryl A. 175
Chatfield, Hale 1936- CANR-13
Earlier sketch in CA 33-36R
Chatfield, Michael 1934- CANR-10
Earlier sketch in CA 25-28R
Chatham, Doug(las) M. 1938- CANR-8
Earlier sketch in CA 61-64
Chatham, James R(ay) 1931- 33-36R
Chatham, Josiah G(eorge) 1914-1988 49-52
Chatham, Larry
See Bingley, David Ernest
Chatham, Russell 1939- 69-72
Chatman, Seymour B(enjamin) 1928- ... 37-40R
Chatov, Robert 1927- 105
Chatt, Orville K(eith) 1924- 53-56
Chatterje, Sarat Chandra 1876-1936(?)
Brief entry 109
See also Chatterji, Saratchandra
Chatterjee, Debjani 1952- 150
See also SATA 83
Chatterjee, Margaret (Gantzer)
1925- CANR-20
Earlier sketches in CA 5-8R, CANR-3
Chatterjee, Sankar 1943- 198
Chatterjee, Saratchandra
See Chatterje, Sarat Chandra
Chatterjee, Upamanyu 1959- 160
See also CN 6, 7
Chatterji, Joya 1964- 149
Chatterji, Saratchandra 186
See also Chatterje, Sarat Chandra
See also EWL 3
See also TCLC 13
Chatterji, Suniti Kumar 1890-1977 ... CANR-46
Earlier sketch in CA 81-84
Chatterton, Thomas 1752-1770 ...... DAM POET
See also DLB 109
See also RGEL 2
Chatterton, Wayne 1921- 37-40R
Chatto, Beth 1923- 227
Chatto, James 1955- 176
Chattopadhyay, Saratchandra
See Chatterje, Sarat Chandra
Chatwin, (Charles) Bruce 1940-1989 85-88
Obituary 127
See also AAYA 4
See also BEST 90:1
See also BRWS 4
See also CLC 28, 57, 59
See also CPW
See also DAM POP
See also DLB 194, 204
See also EWL 3
See also MTFW 2005
Chatzky, Jean 1964- 239
Chatzky, Jean Sherman
See Chatzky, Jean
Chaucer, Daniel
See Ford, Ford Madox
See also RHW
Chaucer, Geoffrey 1340(?)-1400 .... BRW 1
See also BRWC 1
See also BRWR 2
See also CDBLB Before 1660
See also DA
See also DA3
See also DAB
See also DAC
See also DAM MST, POET
See also DLB 146
See also LAIT 1
See also PAB
See also PC 19, 58
See also PFS 14
See also RGEL 2
See also TEA
See also WLCS
See also WLIT 3
See also WP
Chaudhuri, Amit (Prakash) 1962- CANR-99
Earlier sketch in CA 146
See also DLB 267
Chaudhuri, Haridas 1913-1975 .... CANR-4
Earlier sketch in CA 5-8R
Chaudhuri, Nirad C(handra) 1897-1999 128
Obituary 183
Chaudhuri, Pranay 1957- 143
Chaudhuri, Sukanta 1950- 57-60
See also CP 1
Chauffard, Rene-Jacques 1920(?)-1972
Obituary 37-40R
Chaulieu, Pierre
See Castoriadis, Cornelius
Chauncey, George 152
Chauncy, Charles 1705-1787 .... DLB 24
Chauncy, Nan(cen Beryl Masterman)
1900-1970 .... CANR-4
Earlier sketch in CA 1-4R
See also CLR 6
See also CWRI 5
See also MAICYA 1, 2
See also SATA 6
Chaundler, Christine 1887-1972 .... CAP-2
Earlier sketch in CA 29-32
See also CWRI 5
See also SATA 1
See also SATA-Obit 25
Chaurette, Normand 1954- 165
Chauveau, Pierre-Joseph-Olivier
1820-1890 .... DLB 99
Chauvin, Remy 1913- 108
Chavarria, Daniel 1933- 212
Chavasse, Michael Louis Maude 1923-1983
Obituary 110
Chavchavadze, Paul 1899-1971 .... CAP-2
Obituary 29-32R
Earlier sketch in CA 25-28
Chave, Anna C. 155
Chavel, Charles Ber 1906- CANR-4
Earlier sketch in CA 49-52
Chaves, Jonathan 1943- CANR-9
Earlier sketch in CA 65-68
Chaves, Mark (Alan) 1960- 232
Chavez, Angelico
See Chavez, Manuel
Chavez, Denise (Elia) 1948- CANR-137
Earlier sketches in CA 131, CANR-56, 81
See also DAM MULT
See also DLB 122
See also FW
See also HLC 1
See also HW 1, 2
See also LLW
See also MAL 5
See also MTCW 2
See also MTFW 2005
Chavez, Fray Angelico
See Chavez, Manuel
Chavez, Fray Angelico 1910-1996
See Chavez, Manuel
See also DLB 82
See also RGAL 4
Chavez, Jeffrey A. 1971- 164
Chavez, John R(ichard) 1949- CANR-87
Earlier sketch in CA 118
See also HW 1
Chavez, Lisa D. 1961- 196
Chavez, Lydia 1951- 182
Chavez, Manuel 1910-1996 .... CANR-32
Obituary 151
Earlier sketch in CA 93-96
See also Chavez, Fray Angelico
See also HW 1
Chavez, Patricia 1934- 103
Chaviaras, Strates 1935- 105
See also Haviaras, Stratis
Chavis Othow, Helen 1932- 213
Chayefsky, Paddy
See Chayefsky, Sidney
See also CAD
See also CLC 23
See also DLB 7, 44
See also DLBY 1981
See also RGAL 4
Chayefsky, Sidney 1923-1981 .... CANR-18
Obituary 104
Earlier sketch in CA 9-12R
See also Chayefsky, Paddy
See also DAM DRAM
Chayes, Abram 1922-2000 .... CANR-14
Obituary 190
Earlier sketch in CA 65-68
Chaytor, Lee
See Chater, Elizabeth (Eileen Moore)
Chazanof, William 1915- 33-36R
Chaze, (Lewis) Elliott 1915-1990 113
Chazin, Suzanne 1961- 207
Cheal, David 1945- 190
Cheape, Charles Windsor 1945- CANR-28
Earlier sketch in CA 105
Cheatham, Karyn Follis 1943- CANR-98
Earlier sketch in CA 81-84
Cheavens, (Sam) Frank 1905-1999 .... 33-36R
Cheavens, Martha Louise (Schuck) 1898-1975
Obituary 57-60
Cheboukiarian, Daniel 1884-1915
See Varoujan, Daniel
Checchi, Mary Jane 219
Check, Otto Premier
See Berman, Ed
Check, William A. 1943- 118
Checkel, Jeffrey T(aylor) 1959- 234
Checkland, (Edith) Olive 1920-2004 152
Obituary 231
Checkland, S(ydney) G(eorge)
1916-1986 .... 17-20R
Obituary 118
Checkoway, Julie 1963- 160
Chedid, Andree 1920- CANR-95
Earlier sketch in CA 145
See also CLC 47
See also EWL 3
Chee, Alexander 1967- 210
Chee, Cheng-Khee 1934- .... SATA 79
Cheech
See Marin, Richard Anthony
Cheek, Frances Edith 1923- 41-44R
Cheek, H(oward) Lee, Jr. 1960- 223
Cheek, Mavis 1948- 128
Cheeks, James E. 1930- 124
Cheers, D(uane) Michael 231
Cheese, Chloe 1952- .... SATA 118
Cheesman, (Lucy) Evelyn 1881-1969 . DLB 195
Cheesman, Paul R. 1921- CANR-1
Earlier sketch in CA 49-52
Cheetham, Erika (McMahon-Turner)
1939-1998 .... CANR-30
Obituary 167
Earlier sketch in CA 109
Cheetham, Hal
See Cheetham, J(ames) H(arold)
Cheetham, J(ames) H(arold) 1921- 108
Cheetham, Nicholas (John Alexander)
1910-2002 .... CANR-15
Obituary 209
Earlier sketch in CA 81-84
Cheever, Benjamin 1948- 187
Cheever, Ezekiel 1615-1708 .... DLB 24
Cheever, George Barrell 1807-1890 ..... DLB 59
Cheever, John 1912-1982 .... CANR-76
Obituary 106
Earlier sketches in CA 5-8R, CANR-5, 27
Interview in CANR-5
See also CABS 1
See also AAYA 65
See also AMWS 1
See also BPFB 1
See also CDALB 1941-1968
See also CLC 3, 7, 8, 11, 15, 25, 64
See also CN 1, 2, 3
See also CPW
See also DA
See also DA3
See also DAB
See also DAC
See also DAM MST, NOV, POP
See also DLB 2, 102, 227
See also DLBY 1980, 1982
See also EWL 3
See also EXPS
See also MAL 5
See also MTCW 1, 2
See also MTFW 2005
See also RGAL 4
See also RGSF 2
See also SSC 1, 38, 57
See also SSFS 2, 14
See also TUS
See also WLC
Cheever, Susan 1943- CANR-92
Earlier sketches in CA 103, CANR-27, 51
Interview in CANR-27
See also CLC 18, 48
See also DLBY 1982
Cheffins, Ronald I. 1930- 45-48
Chehak, Susan Taylor 1951- CANR-52
Earlier sketch in CA 130
Cheifetz, Dan 1926- 69-72
Cheifetz, Philip M(orris) 1944- 53-56
Cheim, John 1953- 138
Chein, Isidor 1912-1981 185
Brief entry 105
Chejne, Anwar G(eorge) 1923-1983 . CANR-18
Earlier sketch in CA 25-28R
Cheke, Sir John 1514-1557 .... DLB 132
Chekenian, Aram Haigaz 1900-1986
Obituary 119
Chekenian, Jane
See Gerard, Jane
Chekhonte, Antosha
See Chekhov, Anton (Pavlovich)
Chekhov, Anton (Pavlovich) 1860-1904 124
Brief entry 104
See also BYA 14
See also DA
See also DA3
See also DAB
See also DAC
See also DAM DRAM, MST
See also DC 9
See also DFS 1, 5, 10, 12
See also DLB 277
See also EW 7
See also EWL 3
See also EXPS
See also LAIT 3
See also LATS 1:1
See also RGSF 2
See also RGWL 2, 3
See also SATA 90
See also SSC 2, 28, 41, 51, 85
See also SSFS 5, 13, 14
See also TCLC 3, 10, 31, 55, 96, 163
See also TWA
See also WLC
Chekhova, Olga 1897-1980
Obituary 97-100
Chekki, Dan(esh) A(yyappa) 1935- ... CANR-47
Earlier sketches in CA 61-64, CANR-7, 23
Cheldelin, Larry V(ernon) 1945- 116
Cheles, Luciano 1948- CANR-138
Earlier sketches in CA 127, CANR-55
Chelf, Carl P. 1937- 37-40R
Chelius, James R(obert) 1943- 115
Chellis, Marcia 1940- 121
Chelminski, Rudolph 1934- 93-96
Chelsea, David 1959- 148
Chelsom, Peter (Anthony) 1956- 214
Chelton, John
See Durst, Paul
Chelwood, Tufton Victor Hamilton
1917-1989 65-68
Obituary 128
Chen, Anthony 1929- CANR-14
Earlier sketch in CA 37-40R
See also SATA 6
Chen, Chih-Yuan 1975- .... SATA 155
Chen, Ching-chih 1937- CANR-45
Earlier sketches in CA 106, CANR-22
Ch'En, Chi-yun 1933- 108
Chen, Chung-Hwan 1906- 45-48
Chen, Da 1962- 212
Chen, Edwin 1948- 159
Brief entry 116
Chen, Jack 1908-1995 .... CANR-15
Earlier sketch in CA 41-44R
Chen, Janey 1922- 73-76
Ch'en, Jerome 1921- CANR-9
Earlier sketch in CA 13-16R
Chen, Joan 1961- 223
Chen, Joseph Tao 1925- 37-40R
Chen, Ju-Hong 1941- .... SATA 78
Chen, Kan 1928- CANR-45
Earlier sketch in CA 49-52
Chen, Kenneth K(uan-) S(heng)
1907-1993 .... 17-20R

Cumulative Index 105 **Cheuse**

Chen, King C(hing) 1926- CANR-4
  Earlier sketch in CA 53-56
Chen, Kuan I. 1926- 41-44R
Chen, Lincoln C(hih-ho) 1942- CANR-47
  Earlier sketch in CA 49-52
Chen, Nai-Ruenn 1927- CANR-9
  Earlier sketch in CA 21-24R
Chen, Patrizia 1948- 224
Chen, Philip S(tanley) 1903-1978 .... CANR-5
  Earlier sketch in CA 9-12R
Chen, Ping 233
Chen, Samuel Shih-Tsai 1915- 41-44R
Chen, Sara
  See Odgers, Sally Farrell
Chen, Theodore Hsi-En 1902-1991 .. CANR-17
  Earlier sketches in CA 1-4R, CANR-1
Chen, Tony
  See Chen, Anthony
Chen, Vincent 1917- 37-40R
Chen, Ying 1961- 232
Chen, Yuan-tsung 1932- 106
  See also SATA 65
Chenault, Lawrence R(oyce)
  1897-1990 .... CAP-2
  Earlier sketch in CA 17-18
Chenault, Nell
  See Smith, Linell Nash
Chenedolle, Charles de 1769-1833 .... DLB 217
Chenery, Hollis Burnley 1918-1994 111
Chenery, Janet (Dai) 1923- 103
  See also SATA 25
Chenery, William Ludlow 1884-1974 ... 97-100
  Obituary 53-56
Chenetier, Marc 1946- 143
Cheney, Anne 1944- 61-64
Cheney, Brainard (Bartwell) 1900-1990 . CAP-2
  Obituary 130
  Earlier sketch in CA 25-28
Cheney, C. R.
  See Cheney, Christopher Robert
Cheney, Charles Edward 1836-1916 212
Cheney, Christopher Robert 1906-1987
  Obituary 123
Cheney, Cora 1916-1999 .... CANR-4
  Obituary 177
  Earlier sketch in CA 1-4R
  See also SATA 3
  See also SATA-Obit 110
Cheney, Ednah Dow (Littlehale)
  1824-1904 209
  See also DLB 1, 223
Cheney, Frances Neel 1906- 33-36R
Cheney, Glenn (Alan) 1951- CANR-119
  Earlier sketches in CA 109, CANR-70
  See also SATA 99
Cheney, Harriet Vaughan 1796-1889 ... DLB 99
Cheney, Jean E. 1921- 118
Cheney, Lois A. 1931- 29-32R
Cheney, Lynne V. 1941- CANR-117
  Earlier sketches in CA 89-92, CANR-58
  See also CLC 70
  See also SATA 152
Cheney, Margaret 1921- CANR-102
  Earlier sketch in CA 101
Cheney, Martha 1953- 171
Cheney, Richard B(ruce) 1941- 113
Cheney, Robert S(impson) 1922- 118
Cheney, Roberta Carkeek 1912- 73-76
Cheney, Ruth G(ordon) 1908-1998 113
Cheney, Sheldon Warren 1886-1980
  Obituary 102
Cheney, Ted
  See Cheney, Theodore Albert
Cheney, Theodore A. Rees
  See Cheney, Theodore Albert
Cheney, Theodore Albert 1928- CANR-23
  Earlier sketches in CA 61-64, CANR-8
  See also SATA 11
Cheney, Thomas E. 1901-1993 .... 41-44R
Cheney-Coker, Syl 1945- 153
  Earlier sketch in CA 101
  See also Cheyney-Coker, Syl
  See also EWL 3
Cheng, Andrea 1957- .... SATA 128
Cheng, Christopher 1959- 175
  See also SATA 106
Cheng, Chu-yuan 1927- CANR-42
  Earlier sketches in CA 13-16R, CANR-5, 20
Cheng, F.T.
  See Cheng, Tien-hsi
Cheng, Hang-Sheng 1927- 69-72
Cheng, Hou-Tien 1944- 69-72
Cheng, J(ames) Chester 1926- 9-12R
Cheng, James K(uo) C(hiang) 1936- 25-28R
Cheng, Judith 1955- .... SATA 36
Cheng, Lung
  See Chan, Jackie
Cheng, Naishan 167
Cheng, Ronald Ye-lin 1933- 41-44R
Cheng, Shan
  See Jiang, Cheng An
Cheng, Tien-hsi 1884-1970
  Obituary 104
Cheng, Yi
  See Cheng, James K(uo) C(hiang)
Cheng, Ying-wan 41-44R
Chen Gang, Shen
  See Chan, Jackie
Chenier, Andre-Marie de 1762-1794 .... EW 4
  See also GFL Beginnings to 1789
  See also TWA
Chenier, Marie-Joseph 1764-1811 ...... DLB 192
Chen Jia
  See Shen, Congwen
Chen Jo hsi
  See Tuann, Lucy H(siu-mei) C(hen)
Chennault, Anna (Chan) 1925- 61-64
Chennells, David W. 1967- 228
Chennells, Roy D. 1912(?)-1981
  Obituary 105
Chenneviere, Daniel
  See Rudhyar, Dane
Chenoweth, Vida S. 1928- CANR-11
  Earlier sketch in CA 25-28R
Chen Ruoxi
  See Tuann, Lucy H(siu-mei) C(hen)
  See also CWW 2
Chen Yuan, Long
  See Chan, Jackie
Chen Yuen, Lung
  See Chan, Jackie
Chepaitis, Barbara 205
Cher 1946- 174
Cher, Ming 1947- 149
Cheraskin, Emanuel 1916- 53-56
Cherchi-Usai, Paolo 1957- 216
Cheremisinoff, Paul N(icholas) 1929-1995 . 228
Cherim, Stanley M(arshall) 1929- 53-56
Cherington, Paul Whiton 1918-1974 . CANR-6
  Obituary 53-56
  Earlier sketch in CA 1-4R
Cheripko, Jan 1951- CANR-139
  Earlier sketch in CA 150
  See also SATA 83, 155
Cherkovski, Neeli 1945- 158
  See also CAAS 24
Chermayeff, Ivan 1932- 97-100
  See also SATA 47
Chermayeff, Serge (Ivan) 1900-1996 ..... 21-24R
  Obituary 152
Chernaik, Judith 1934- CANR-39
  Earlier sketches in CA 61-64, CANR-11
Chernaik, Warren L(ewis) 1931- 151
Chernenko, K. U.
  See Chernenko, Konstantin U(stinovich)
Chernenko, Konstantin U(stinovich)
  1911-1985 132
  Obituary 115
Cherner, Anne 1954- 109
Chernev, Irving 1900-1981
  Obituary 105
Cherniavsky, Michael 1923(?)-1973
  Obituary 41-44R
Chernick, Michael R(oss) 1947- 206
Chernik, Barbara E(ileen) 1938- 117
Chernin, Kim 1940- CANR-63
  Earlier sketch in CA 107
Cherniss, Harold
  See Cherniss, Harold Fredrik
Cherniss, Harold Fredrik 1904-1987 93-96
  Obituary 123
Cherniss, Michael D(avid) 1940- 37-40R
Cherniss, Norman A(rnold) 1926-1984 122
  Obituary 114
Chernoff, Dorothy A.
  See Ernst, (Lyman) John
Chernoff, Goldie Taub 1909- 33-36R
  See also SATA 10
Chernoff, John Miller 1947- 105
Chernoff, Maxine 1952- CANR-88
  Earlier sketch in CA 136
  See also CP 7
  See also CWP
Chernofsky, Barbara J. 1949- 152
Chernofsky, Jacob L. 1928- 73-76
Chernow, Barbara A. 1948- 144
Chernow, Burt 1933-1997 .... CANR-140
  Obituary 158
  Earlier sketch in CA 110
Chernow, Carol 1934- 57-60
Chernow, Fred B. 1932- 57-60
Chernow, Ron 1949- CANR-73
  Earlier sketch in CA 142
Chernowitz, Maurice E. 1909-1977
  Obituary 73-76
Cherns, Albert
  See Cherns, Albert B(ernard)
Cherns, Albert B(ernard) 1921-1987
  Obituary 122
Cherny, Andrei 1975- 201
Cherny, Robert W(allace) 1943- 131
Cherny, Sasha
  See Glikberg, Aleksandr Mikhailovich
  See also DLB 317
Chernykh, E(vgenij) N(ikolaevich) 1935- 147
Chernyshevsky, Nikolai Gavrilovich
  See Chernyshevsky, Nikolay Gavrilovich
  See also DLB 238
Chernyshevsky, Nikolay Gavrilovich 1828-1889
  See Chernyshevsky, Nikolai Gavrilovich
Cherrington, Ernest H(urst), Jr. 1909- 33-36R
Cherrington, John 1909-1988 116
Cherrington, Leon G. 1926- 33-36R
Cherry, Bridget (Katherine) 1941- 193
Cherry, C. Conrad 1937- CANR-11
  Earlier sketch in CA 21-24R
Cherry, Caroline L(ockett) 1942- 57-60
Cherry, Carolyn Janice 1942- CANR-10
  Earlier sketch in CA 65-68
  See also Cherryh, C. J.
Cherry, Charles L(ester) 1942- 57-60
Cherry, (Edward) Colin 1914-1979 .... CANR-12
  Obituary 93-96
  Earlier sketch in CA 69-72
Cherry, George Loy 1905-1978 .... 5-8R
Cherry, Gordon E(manuel) 1931- CANR-57
  Earlier sketch in CA 125
Cherry, Kelly 1940- 209
  Earlier sketches in CA 49-52, CANR-3, 47, 68
  Autobiographical Essay in 209
  See also MTCW 1
  See also DLBY 1983
Cherry, Kittredge 1957- 235
Cherry, Lynne 1952- 167
  See also SATA 34, 99
Cherry, Neeli
  See Cherkovski, Neeli
Cherry, Sheldon H(arold) 1934- CANR-27
  Earlier sketch in CA 49-52
Cherry-Garrard, Apsley (George Benet)
  1886-1959 238
Cherryh, C. J.
  See Cherry, Carolyn Janice
  See also AAYA 24
  See also BPFB 1
  See also CLC 35
  See also DLBY 1980
  See also FANT
  See also SATA 93
  See also SCFW 2
  See also SFW 4
  See also YAW
Cherryholmes, Anne
  See Price, Olive
Chertok, Haim
  See Chertok, Harvey
Chertok, Harvey 1938- CANR-55
  Earlier sketch in CA 127
Chertow, Marian R. 1955- 170
Chervin, Ronda 1937- CANR-21
  Earlier sketches in CA 57-60, CANR-6
Chervokas, John V(incent) 1936- 129
Cherwinski, Joseph 1915- CANR-5
  Earlier sketch in CA 13-16R
Chesbro, George C(lark) 1940- CANR-116
  Earlier sketches in CA 77-80, CANR-58
  See also CMW 4
Cheseborough, Steve 1956- 198
Chesebro', Caroline 1825-1873 .... DLB 202
Chesebro, James William 1944- CANR-106
  Earlier sketch in CA 108
Chesebrough, David B. 1932-2004 164
Chesen, Eli S. 1944- 37-40R
Chesham, Henry
  See Bingley, David Ernest
Chesham, Sallie CANR-26
  Earlier sketch in CA 29-32R
Chesher, Kim 1955- CANR-19
  Earlier sketch in CA 102
Chesher, Richard (Harvey) 1940- 106
Cheshin, Amir (S.) 1944- 189
Cheshire, David 1944- 97-100
Cheshire, Geoffrey Leonard
  1917-1992 .... CAP-1
  Earlier sketch in CA 13-14
Cheshire, Giff(ord Paul) 1905-(?) .... TCWW 2
Cheshire, Herbert 1925(?)-1985
  Obituary 118
Cheshire, Maxine 1930- 108
Cheska, Anna
  See Henley, Jan (S.)
Cheskin, Lawrence J. 1958- 213
Cheskin, Louis 1909-1981 .... CANR-5
  Obituary 105
  Earlier sketch in CA 5-8R
Chesler, Bernice 1932-2002 .... CANR-16
  Obituary 210
  Earlier sketch in CA 25-28R
  See also SATA 59
Chesler, Ellen 1947- 140
Chesler, Phyllis 1940- CANR-140
  Earlier sketches in CA 49-52, CANR-4, 59
  See also FW
Chesley, Robert c. 1943-1990 220
  See also GLL 1
Cheslock, Louis 1898-1981 .... CAP-1
  Earlier sketch in CA 11-12
Chesman, Andrea 1952- 135
Chesney, Ann
  See Dummett, (Agnes Margaret) Ann
Chesney, Elizabeth Anne
  See Zegura, Elizabeth Chesney
Chesney, Sir George Tomkyns
  1830-1895 .... DLB 190
Chesney, Inga L. 1928- 45-48
Chesney, Kellow (Robert) 1914- 29-32R
Chesney, Marion 1936- CANR-90
  Brief entry 111
  Earlier sketches in CA 115, CANR-53
  Interview in CA-115
  See also RHW
Chesney, Weatherby
  See Hyne, C(harles) J(ohn) Cutcliffe (Wright)
Chesney-Lind, Meda 1947- 220
Chesnoff, Richard Z(eltner) 1937- CANR-91
  Earlier sketches in CA 25-28R, CANR-10
Chesnut, J(ames) Stanley 1926- 21-24R
Chesnut, Mary Boykin 1823-1886 ...... DLB 239
Chesnutt, Charles W(addell)
  1858-1932 .... CANR-76
  Brief entry 106
  Earlier sketch in CA 125
  See also AFAW 1, 2
  See also AMWS 14
  See also BLC 1
  See also BW 1, 3
  See also DAM MULT
  See also DLB 12, 50, 78
  See also EWL 3
  See also MAL 5
  See also MTCW 1, 2
  See also MTFW 2005
  See also RGAL 4
  See also RGSF 2
  See also SSC 7, 54
  See also SSFS 11
  See also TCLC 5, 39
Chesnutt, David R(ogers) 1940- 122
Chess, Richard 1953- 150
Chess, Stella 1914- 85-88
Chess, Victoria (Dickerson) 1939- .. CANR-104
  Earlier sketch in CA 107
  See also MAICYA 2
  See also MAICYAS 1
  See also SATA 33, 92
Chessare, Michele .... SATA-Brief 42
Chesser, Eustace 1902-1973 .... CANR-4
  Obituary 45-48
  Earlier sketch in CA 9-12R
Chessex, Jacques 1934- 65-68
  See also CWW 2
Chesshyre, Robert (Coxhead) 1941- 128
Chessick, Richard D. 1931- 238
Chessman, Caryl (Whittier) 1921-1960 ... 73-76
Chessman, G(eorge) Wallace 1919- 13-16R
Chessman, Harriet Scott 205
Chessman, Ruth (Green) 1910-2000 ..... CAP-2
  Earlier sketch in CA 17-18
Chesson, Mrs. Nora
  See Hopper, Nora
Chester, Alfred 1929(?)-1971 196
  Obituary 33-36R
  See also CLC 49
  See also DLB 130
  See also MAL 5
Chester, Allan Griffith 1900-1976
  Obituary 111
Chester, Deborah 1957- CANR-72
  Earlier sketches in CA 102, CANR-18, 41
  See also SATA 85
Chester, Edward W(illiam) 1935- CANR-13
  Earlier sketch in CA 21-24R
Chester, Eric Thomas 1943- 152
Chester, George Randolph 1869-1924 179
  See also DLB 78
Chester, Kate
  See Guccione, Leslie Davis
Chester, Laura 1949- CANR-108
  Earlier sketches in CA 65-68, CANR-9, 50
Chester, Mark (S.) 1945- 144
Chester, Michael (Arthur) 1928- CANR-1
  Earlier sketch in CA 1-4R
Chester, (Daniel) Norman 1907-1986 109
  Obituary 120
Chester, Peter
  See Phillips, D(ennis) J(ohn Andrew)
Chester, (Charles) Ronald 1944- 194
Chester, Tessa Rose 1950- 130
Chesterman, Charles W(esley) 1913-1991 .. 107
Chesterman, Clement (Clapton) 1894-1983
  Obituary 110
Chesterson, Denise
  See Robins, Denise (Naomi)
Chesterton, A(rthur) K(enneth)
  1899-1973 .... CAP-1
  Earlier sketch in CA 11-12
Chesterton, G(ilbert) K(eith)
  1874-1936 .... CANR-131
  Brief entry 104
  Earlier sketches in CA 132, CANR-73
  See also AAYA 57
  See also BRW 6
  See also CDBLB 1914-1945
  See also CMW 4
  See also DAM NOV, POET
  See also DLB 10, 19, 34, 70, 98, 149, 178
  See also EWL 3
  See also FANT
  See also MSW
  See also MTCW 1, 2
  See also MTFW 2005
  See also PC 28
  See also RGEL 2
  See also RGSF 2
  See also SATA 27
  See also SSC 1, 46
  See also SUFW 1
  See also TCLC 1, 6, 64
Chestnut, Harold 1917- 157
Chestor, Rui
  See Courtier, S(idney) H(obson)
Chesworth, Michael .... SATA 160
Chetham, Deirdre 1954- 236
Chetham-Strode, Warren 1896-1974 ..... CAP-1
  Earlier sketch in CA 13-14
Chethimattam, John B(ritto) 1922- 25-28R
Chetin, Helen 1922- CANR-12
  Earlier sketch in CA 29-32R
  See also SATA 6
Chetkovich, Carol A. 1948- 164
Chettle, Henry 1560-1607(?) .... DLB 136
  See also RGEL 2
Chetwin, Grace CANR-52
  Earlier sketch in CA 123
  See also FANT
  See also SATA 86
  See also SATA-Brief 50
  See also YAW
Chetwode, Penelope 1910-1986 102
  Obituary 119
Chetwynd, Berry
  See Rayner, Claire (Berenice)
Chetwynd, Lionel 1940- 137
Chetwynd, Tom 1938- 45-48
Chetwynd-Hayes, R(onald Henry Glynn)
  1919-2001 .... CANR-58
  Earlier sketches in CA 61-64, CANR-12, 30
  See also HGG
Chetwynd-Talbot, Edward Hugh Frederick
  1909- 116
Cheung, Steven N(g-) S(heong) 1935- ... 25-28R
Cheung, Theresa (Francis) 1965- 214
Cheuse, Alan 1940- CANR-116
  Earlier sketches in CA 49-52, CANR-27, 52
  See also CN 6, 7
  See also DLB 244

Chevalier, Christa 1937- CANR-24
Earlier sketch in CA 107
See also SATA 35
Chevalier, Elizabeth (Pickett) 1896-1984
Obituary 111
Chevalier, Haakon (Maurice) 1901-1985 . 61-64
Obituary 116
Chevalier, Louis 1911-2001 .... CANR-35
Earlier sketch in CA 85-88
Chevalier, Maurice 1888-1972
Obituary 33-36R
Chevalier, Paul
See Moure, Nancy D(ustin) W(all)
Chevalier, Paul Eugene George 1925- 106
Chevalier, Tracy 1962- CANR-137
Earlier sketch in CA 193
See also AAYA 46
See also MTFW 2005
See also SATA 128
Chevallier, Gabriel 1895-1969
Obituary 113
Chevallier, Raymond 1929- 103
Chevigny, Bell Gale 1936- 57-60
Chevigny, Paul G. 1935- 97-100
Cheville, Roy A(rthur) 1897-1986 97-100
Chevremont, Evaristo Ribera
See Ribera Chevremont, Evaristo
Chew, Ada Nield 1870-1945 .... DLB 135
Chew, Allen F. 1924- 33-36R
Chew, Geoffrey Foucar 1924- 157
Chew, Peter 1924- 57-60
Chew, Ruth 1920- CANR-14
Earlier sketches in CA 41-44R, CANR-31
See also SATA 7
Cheyette, Bryan (Henry) 1959- CANR-112
Earlier sketch in CA 146
Cheyette, Irving 1904-1999 .... CANR-22
Earlier sketch in CA 69-72
Cheyney, Arnold B. 1926- CANR-23
Earlier sketches in CA 21-24R, CANR-8
Cheyney, Edward P(otts) 1861-1947 183
See also DLB 47
Cheyney, (Reginald Evelyn) Peter (Southouse)
1896-1951 213
Brief entry 113
See also CMW 4
Cheyney-Coker, Syl
See Cheney-Coker, Syl
See also CP 2, 3, 4, 5, 6, 7
Chi, Hsin Ying 1951- 190
Chi, Madeleine 1930- CANR-11
Earlier sketch in CA 69-72
Chi, Richard Hu See-Yee 1918- 37-40R
Chi, Wen-shun 1910-1984 .... 13-16R
Chia, Mantak 1944- 232
Chiang, Kai-shek 1886(?)-1975
Obituary 112
Chiang, Pin-chin 1904-1986
Obituary 118
See also Ding Ling and
Ting Ling
Chiang, Ted 1967- 212
See also AAYA 66
Chiang Hai-ch'eng 1910-
See Ai Ch'ing
Chiang Ping-chih
See Chiang, Pin-chin
Chiang Yee 1903-1977 .... CANR-15
Obituary 73-76
Earlier sketch in CA 65-68
See also DLB 312
Ch'iao, Sung
See Chou, Eric
Chiappelli, Fredi 1921-1990
Obituary 131
Chiara, Piero 1913-1986 .... CANR-8
Obituary 121
Earlier sketch in CA 53-56
See also DLB 177
Chiarella, Tom 1961- 161
Chiarelli, Luigi 1880-1947
Chiarello, Michael 1962- 149
Chiarenza, Carl 1935- CANR-29
Earlier sketch in CA 109
Chiari, Joseph 1911-1989 .... CANR-29
Earlier sketches in CA 5-8R, CANR-4
Chiaromonte, Nicola (?)-1972
Obituary 104
Chiaverini, Jennifer 220
Chiba, Atsuko 1941(?)-1987
Obituary 123
Chibbaro, Julie 1955- 237
Chibnall, Marjorie (McCallum)
1915- CANR-108
Earlier sketch in CA 29-32R
Chicago, Judy 1939- CANR-64
Earlier sketches in CA 85-88, CANR-21
See also AAYA 46
Chichester, Francis (Charles)
1901-1972 .... CAP-1
Obituary 37-40R
Earlier sketch in CA 13-14
Chichester, Jane
See Longrigg, Jane Chichester
Chichester Clark, Emma 1955- CANR-140
Earlier sketch in CA 132
See also Clark, Emma Chichester
See also CWRI 5
See also MAICYA 2
See also SATA 117, 156
Chichetto, James W. 1941- 191
Chick, Edson M(arland) 1924- 21-24R
Chick, Jean M.
See Snook, Jean M(cGregor)
Chickering, Arthur W. 1927- 29-32R
Chickering, Roger (Philip) 1942- CANR-97
Earlier sketch in CA 73-76
Chickos, James Speros 1941- 49-52
Chicorel, Marietta 85-88
Chideya, Farai 1969- CANR-86
Earlier sketch in CA 156
Chidgey, Catherine 1970- 212
Chidsey, Donald Barr 1902-1981 .... CANR-2
Obituary 103
Earlier sketch in CA 5-8R
See also SATA 3
See also SATA-Obit 27
Chidzero, Bernard Thomas Gibson 1927- . 1-4R
Chiefari, Janet D. 1942- .... SATA 58
Chief Eagle, Dallas 1925-1978 144
Chief Joseph 1840-1904 152
See also DA3
See also DAM MULT
See also NNAL
Chief Seattle 1786(?)-1866 .... DA3
See also DAM MULT
See also NNAL
Chief Standing Bear
See Standing Bear, Luther
Chieger, Bob 1945- 114
Chielens, Edward E(rnest) 1943- 53-56
Ch'ien, Chung-shu 1910-1998 .... CANR-73
Earlier sketch in CA 130
See also Qian Zhongshu
See also CLC 22
See also MTCW 1, 2
Ch'ien, Hsiao
See Qian, Xiao
Ch'ien, Ts'un-hsun
See Tsien, Tsuen-hsuin
Chien-min, Lin
See Rumford, James
Chiesa, Francesco 1871(?)-1973
Obituary 104
Chiffolo, Anthony F. 1959- 216
Chignon, Niles
See Lingeman, Richard R(oberts)
Chigounis, Evans 1931- 45-48
Chihuly, Dale 1941- .... AAYA 46
Chikamatsu Monzaemon 1653-1724 . RGWL 2, 3
Chilcote, Ronald H. 1935- CANR-100
Earlier sketches in CA 21-24R, CANR-8, 24, 49
Chilcott, John H(enry) 1924-1998 .... 41-44R
Child, Alan
See Langner, Lawrence
Child, Charles Manning 1869-1954 157
Child, Francis James 1825-1896 ...... DLB 1, 64, 235
Child, Greg CANR-130
Earlier sketch in CA 177
Child, Heather 1912-1997 .... 9-12R
Child, Irvin L(ong) 1915- 41-44R
Child, John 1922- 93-96
Child, Julia 1912-2004 .... CANR-113
Obituary 229
Earlier sketches in CA 41-44R, CANR-19
Child, Kenneth 1916-1983
Obituary 111
Child, L. Maria
See Child, Lydia Maria
Child, Lauren 1965- 190
See also SATA 119, 160
Child, Lee 1954- 194
Child, Lincoln B. 1957- 176
See also AAYA 32
See also SATA 113
Child, Lydia Maria 1802-1880 . DLB 1, 74, 243
See also RGAL 4
See also SATA 67
Child, Maureen 1951- 232
Child, Mrs.
See Child, Lydia Maria
Child, Philip 1898-1978 .... CAP-1
Earlier sketch in CA 13-14
See also CLC 19, 68
See also CP 1
See also DLB 68
See also RHW
See also SATA 47
Child, Roderick 1949- 25-28R
Childer, Simon Ian
See Brosnan, John
Childers, (Robert) Erskine 1870-1922 153
Brief entry 113
See also DLB 70
See also TCLC 65
Childers, Thomas 1946- 221
Childers, Thomas A(llen) 1940- CANR-143
Earlier sketch in CA 37-40R
Children's Shepherd, The
See Westphal, Arnold Carl
Childress, Alice 1920-1994 .... CANR-74
Obituary 146
Earlier sketches in CA 45-48, CANR-3, 27, 50
See also AAYA 8
See also BLC 1
See also BW 2, 3
See also BYA 2
See also CAD
See also CLC 12, 15, 86, 96
See also CLR 14
See also CWD
See also DA3
See also DAM DRAM, MULT, NOV
See also DC 4
See also DFS 2, 8, 14
See also DLB 7, 38, 249
See also JRDA
See also LAIT 5
See also MAICYA 1, 2
See also MAICYAS 1
See also MAL 5
See also MTCW 1, 2
See also MTFW 2005
See also RGAL 4
See also SATA 7, 48, 81
See also TCLC 116
See also TUS
See also WYA
See also YAW
Childress, James Franklin 1940- CANR-11
Earlier sketch in CA 65-68
Childress, Mark 1957- 134
See also CN 7
See also CSW
See also DLB 292
Childress, William 1933- CANR-34
Earlier sketch in CA 41-44R
Childs, Barney 1926-2000 .... 21-24R
Obituary 188
Childs, Brevard S(prings) 1923- 128
Brief entry 117
Childs, C. Sand
See Childs, Maryanna (Claire)
Childs, Christopher 1949- 171
Childs, Craig 1967- CANR-119
Earlier sketch in CA 163
Childs, David (Haslam) 1933- CANR-58
Earlier sketches in CA 37-40R, CANR-14, 31
Childs, Elizabeth C(atharine) 1954- 138
Childs, George W. 1829-1894 .... DLB 23
Childs, H(alla) Fay (Cochrane)
1890-1971 .... CAP-1
Earlier sketch in CA 13-16
See also SATA 1
See also SATA-Obit 25
Childs, Harwood Lawrence 1898-1972 . CAP-2
Obituary 37-40R
Earlier sketch in CA 25-28
Childs, J(ames) Rives 1893-1987
Obituary 123
Childs, James Bennett 1896-1977
Obituary 73-76
Childs, John Steven 1947- 128
Childs, Marilyn Grace Carlson 1923- 9-12R
Childs, Marquis W(illiam)
1903-1990 .... CANR-12
Obituary 132
Earlier sketch in CA 61-64
Childs, Maryanna (Claire) 1910- 9-12R
Childs, Michael J. 1956- 146
Childs, Timothy 1941- 97-100
Childs, W(illiam) H(arold) J(oseph)
1905(?)-1983
Obituary 109
Chiles, Nick 1965- 191
Chiles, Robert E(ugene) 1923- 17-20R
Chiles, Webb 1941- 108
Chill, Dan S(amuel) 1945- 69-72
Chilman, Catherine (Earles) S(treet) 1914- .. 121
Chilson, Peter 1961- 225
Chilson, Richard William 1943- CANR-6
Earlier sketch in CA 57-60
Chilson, Rob(ert Dean) 1945- CANR-58
Earlier sketch in CA 69-72
See also SFW 4
Chilson, Robert
See Chilson, Rob(ert Dean)
Chilton, Bruce 1949- CANR-104
Earlier sketch in CA 158
Chilton, Charles (Frederick William)
1917- 163
See also SATA 102
See also SFW 4
Chilton, Irma 1930- CANR-19
Earlier sketch in CA 103
Chilton, John (James) 1932- CANR-91
Earlier sketches in CA 61-64, CANR-8
Chilton, Lance 1944- 123
Chilton, Shirley R(ay) 1923- 77-80
Chilver, Guy (Edward Farquhar)
1910-1982 109
Obituary 107
Chilver, Peter 1933- CANR-38
Earlier sketches in CA 25-28R, CANR-17
Chimaera
See Farjeon, Eleanor
Chin, Chuan
See Chi, Richard Hu See-Yee
Chin, Elizabeth (J.) 1963- 223
Chin, Frank (Chew, Jr.) 1940- CANR-71
Earlier sketch in CA 33-36R
See also AAL
See also CAD
See also CD 5, 6
See also CLC 135
See also DAM MULT
See also DC 7
See also DLB 206, 312
See also LAIT 5
See also RGAL 4
Chin, Justin 1969- 216
See also DLB 312
Chin, M. Lucie .... FANT
Chin, Marilyn (Mei Ling) 1955- CANR-113
Earlier sketches in CA 129, CANR-70
See also CWP
See also DLB 312
See also PC 40
Chin, Richard (M.) 1946- 121
See also SATA 52
Chin, Robert 1918- 61-64
Chin, Yin-lien C. 1930- 141
Chinard, Gilbert 1882(?)-1972
Obituary 104
Chinas, Beverly N(ewbold) 1924- 89-92
Chinen, Nate 227
Chinery, Michael 1938- CANR-20
Earlier sketch in CA 103
See also SATA 26
Ching, Frank 1940- 129
Ching, James C(hristopher) 1926- 37-40R
Ching, Julia (Chia-yi) 1934- CANR-95
Earlier sketches in CA 101, CANR-37
Chinitz, Benjamin 1924- 9-12R
Chin-Lee, Cynthia D. 1958- 169
See also SATA 102
Chinmayananda, Swami 1916-1993 215
Chinmoy, Sri 1931- CANR-107
Earlier sketches in CA 49-52, CANR-2
Chinn, Carl 1956- 150
Chinn, Laurene Chambers 1902-1978 ...... 1-4R
Obituary 103
Chinn, Robert (Edward) 1928- 69-72
Chinn, William G. 1919- 33-36R
Chinnov, Igor' 1909-1996 .... DLB 317
Chinodya, Shimmer 1957- 139
See also CN 6, 7
See also EWL 3
Chinoy, Ely 1921-1975 .... CANR-1
Obituary 57-60
Earlier sketch in CA 1-4R
Chinoy, Helen Krich 1922- 17-20R
Chinweizu 1943- CANR-81
Earlier sketch in CA 103
See also BW 3
See also DLB 157
Chiocca, Olindo Romeo 1959- 193
Chioino, Joan D. Koss
See Koss-Chioino, Joan D.
Chipasula, Frank (Mkalawile) 1949- 121
Chipman, Bruce L(ewis) 1946- 37-40R
Chipman, Donald E(ugene) 1928- 29-32R
Chipman, John S(omerset) 1926- 104
Chipp, D(onald) L(eslie) 1925- 108
Chipp, Herschel B(rowning)
1913-1992 .... 25-28R
Chippendale, Lisa A. 234
See also SATA 158
Chipperfield, Joseph Eugene
1912-1980(?) CANR-6
Earlier sketch in CA 9-12R
See also CWRI 5
See also SATA 2, 87
Chipperfield, Richard 1904-1988
Obituary 125
Chira, Susan 170
Chiras, Daniel D. 1950- 143
Chiraska, B. S.
See Chinodya, Shimmer
Chirenje, J. Mutero 1935- 65-68
Chirico, Giorgio de
See de Chirico, Giorgio
Chironis, Nicholas P. 1921-1993 140
Chirot, Daniel 1942- 132
Chirovsky, Nicholas L. 1919- CANR-4
Earlier sketch in CA 53-56
Chisholm, A(rthur) M(urray)
1872-1960 .... CANR-64
Obituary 114
See also TCWW 1, 2
Chisholm, A(lan) R(owland) 1888-1981 .... 5-8R
Chisholm, Anne 109
Chisholm, Clive Scott 1936- 224
Chisholm, Dianne 1953- 137
Chisholm, Hugh J., Jr. 1913-1972
Obituary 37-40R
Chisholm, K. Lomneth 1919- 61-64
Chisholm, Mary K(athleen) 1924- 37-40R
Chisholm, Matt
See Watts, Peter Christopher
See also TCWW 1, 2
Chisholm, Michael (Donald Inglis)
1931- 37-40R
Chisholm, P. F.
See Finney, Patricia
Chisholm, R(obert) F(erguson) 1904- CAP-2
Earlier sketch in CA 29-32
Chisholm, Roderick Milton 1916-1999 102
Obituary 173
Chisholm, Roger K. 1937- 33-36R
Chisholm, Sam(uel) Whitten 1919- 5-8R
Chisholm, Shirley (Anita St. Hill)
1924-2005 .... CANR-27
Obituary 235
Earlier sketch in CA 29-32R
See also BW 1

Cumulative Index **107** **Christian**

Chisholm, William S(herman), Jr.
1931- CANR-27
Earlier sketch in CA 49-52
Chishti, Hakim M.
See Thomson, Robert
Chislett, (Margaret) Anne 1943- 151
See also CLC 34
Chislett, Gail (Elaine) 1948- .... SATA 58
Chisolm, Lawrence W(ashington) 1929- . 9-12R
Chissell, Joan Olive 61-64
Chitakasem, Manas 194
Chitham, Edward (Harry Gordon)
1932- CANR-41
Earlier sketches in CA 103, CANR-19
See also DLB 155
Chitnis, Anand C. 1942- 123
Chitrabhanu, Gurudev Shree 1922- 89-92
Chittenden, Elizabeth F. 1903-1999 61-64
See also SATA 9
Chittenden, Hiram Martin 1858(?)-1917 178
See also DLB 47
Chittenden, Margaret 1935- CANR-141
Earlier sketches in CA 53-56, CANR-4, 19, 59
See also SATA 28
Chittick, Donald Ernest 1932- 115
Chittick, William O(liver) 1937- 41-44R
Chittister, Joan (Daugherty) 1936- 236
Chittum, Ida 1918- CANR-14
Earlier sketch in CA 37-40R
See also SATA 7
Chitty, Arthur Benjamin 1914-2003 .. CANR-20
Earlier sketches in CA 53-56, CANR-4
Chitty, Letitia 1897-1982
Obituary 108
Chitty, Susan Elspeth 1929- CAP-1
Earlier sketch in CA 9-10
Chitty, Thomas Willes 1926- 5-8R
See also Hinde, Thomas
See also CLC 11
See also CN 7
Chitwood, B(illy) J(ames) 1931- 97-100
Chitwood, Marie Downs 1918- 9-12R
Chitwood, Michael 1958- 170
Chitwood, Oliver Perry 1874-1971 .... CAP-1
Earlier sketch in CA 13-14
Chitwood, Suzanne Tanner 1958- ..... SATA 160
Chiu, Christina 200
Chiu, Hong-Yee 1932- 53-56
Chiu, Hungdah 1936- CANR-60
Earlier sketches in CA 37-40R, CANR-14, 31
Chiu, Tony CANR-143
Earlier sketch in CA 143
Chivers, Thomas Holley 1809-1858 ...... DLB 3, 248
See also RGAL 4
Chivian, Eric 1942- 147
Chi-wei
See Shu, Austin Chi-wei
Chizmar, Richard T(homas) 1965- 227
Chkhartishvili, Grigorii Shalvovich
See Chkhartishvili, Grigory (Shalvovich)
Chkhartishvili, Grigory (Shalvovich) 1956- . 229
See also Akunin, Boris
Chkheidze, Otar 1920- .... EWL 3
Chlamyda, Jehudil
See Peshkov, Alexei Maximovich
Chlomoudis, Constantinos I. 1957- 238
Chloros, A(lexander) G(eorge) 1926-1982
Obituary 108
Chloros, Aleck George
See Chloros, A(lexander) G(eorge)
Chmaj, Betty E. 1930- 97-100
Chmielarz, Sharon Lee 1940- CANR-110
Earlier sketch in CA 121
See also SATA 72
Chmielewski, Edward 1928- 13-16R
Chmielewski, Wendy E. 1955- 139
Ch'o, Chou
See Shu-Jen, Chou
Cho, Yong Hyo 1934-
Brief entry 105
Cho, Yong Sam 1925- 5-8R
Choate, Ernest A(lfred) 1900-1980 49-52
Choate, Gwen Peterson 1922- 1-4R
Choate, J(ulian) E(rnest, Jr.) 1916- 33-36R
Choate, Jean (Marie) 1935- 216
Choate, Judith (Newkirk) 1940- 105
See also SATA 30
Choate, Pat 1941(?)- 146
Choate, R. G.
See Choate, Gwen Peterson
Chobanian, Aram V(an) 1929- 108
Chocano, Jose Santos 1875-1934 131
See also DLB 290
See also EWL 3
See also HW 1
See also LAW
Chochlik
See Radwanski, Pierre A(rthur)
Chociolko, Christina 1958- 149
Chocolate, Debbi 1954- 161
See also SATA 96
Chocolate, Deborah M. Newton
See Chocolate, Debbi
Chodes, John 1939- CANR-25
Earlier sketches in CA 61-64, CANR-9
Chodorov, Edward 1904-1988 102
Obituary 126
Chodorov, Jerome 1911-2004 .... CANR-15
Obituary 231
Earlier sketch in CA 65-68
Chodorov, Stephan 1934- 17-20R
Chodorow, Nancy (Julia) 1944- CANR-139
Earlier sketches in CA 105, CANR-59
See also FW
Chodos, Robert 1947- 142
Chodos-Irvine, Margaret .... SATA 152
Chodron, (Ane) Pema 1936- CANR-111
Earlier sketch in CA 162
Chodron, Thubten 1950- 184
Chogyam Trungpa 1939-1987 .... CANR-42
Obituary 122
Earlier sketches in CA 25-28R, CANR-12
Choi, Frederick D. S. 1942- 167
Choi, Hyaeweol 1962- 147
Choi, Sook Nyul 1937- 197
Autobiographical Essay in 197
See also AAYA 38
See also CLR 53
See also MAICYA 2
See also MAICYAS 1
See also SATA 73
See also SATA-Essay 126
Choi, Sunu 1916-1984
Obituary 115
Choi, Susan 1969- 223
See also CLC 119
Choiseul, Tristan
See Dugas, Marcel
Choku, Shaku
See Origuchi, Shinobu
Cholakian, Patricia Francis 1933- 228
Choldenko, Gennifer 1957- 204
See also SATA 135
Choldin, Marianna Tax 1942- CANR-26
Earlier sketch in CA 109
Choleric, Brother
See van Zeller, Claud
Cholmondeley, Alice
See Russell, Mary Annette Beauchamp
Cholmondeley, Mary 1859-1925 .... DLB 197
Chomette, Rene Lucien 1898-1981
Obituary 103
See also Clair, Rene
Chommie, John C(ampbell) 1914-1974 . CAP-2
Earlier sketch in CA 29-32
Chomsky, Aviva 1957- 167
Chomsky, (Avram) Noam 1928- CANR-132
Earlier sketches in CA 17-20R, CANR-28, 62, 110
See also CLC 132
See also DA3
See also DLB 246
See also MTCW 1, 2
See also MTFW 2005
Chomsky, William 1896-1977 77-80
Obituary 73-76
Chona, Maria 1845(?)-1936 144
See also NNAL
Chong
See Chong, Tommy
Chong, Denise CANR-101
Earlier sketch in CA 159
Chong, Kevin 205
Chong, Kyona-Jo
See Chung, Kyung Cho
Chong, Peng-Khuan 25-28R
Chong, Tommy 1938- 164
Brief entry 112
Choper, Jesse H(erbert) 1935- CANR-5
Earlier sketch in CA 13-16R
Chopey, Nicholas P. 147
Chopin, Kate
See Chopin, Katherine
See also AAYA 33
See also AMWR 2
See also AMWS 1
See also BYA 11, 15
See also CDALB 1865-1917
See also DA
See also DAB
See also DLB 12, 78
See also EXPN
See also EXPS
See also FL 1:3
See also FW
See also LAIT 3
See also MAL 5
See also MAWW
See also NFS 3
See also RGAL 4
See also RGSF 2
See also SSC 8, 68
See also SSFS 2, 13, 17
See also TCLC 127
See also TUS
See also WLCS
Chopin, Katherine 1851-1904 122
Brief entry 104
See also Chopin, Kate
See also DA3
See also DAC
See also DAM MST, NOV
Chopin, Rene 1885-1953 177
See also DLB 92
Chopra, Deepak (K.) 1946- CANR-128
Earlier sketches in CA 153, CANR-91
See also CPW
Choquette, Adrienne 1915-1973 177
See also CCA 1
See also DLB 68
Choquette, Robert 1905-1991 177
See also DLB 68
Choquette, Sonia (Loraine) 1957- 238
Chorafas, Dimitris N. 1926- CANR-48
Earlier sketches in CA 5-8R, CANR-4, 20
Chorao, Ian 219
Chorao, (Ann Mc)Kay (Sproat)
1936- CANR-104
Earlier sketches in CA 49-52, CANR-1, 19
See also MAICYA 1, 2
See also SATA 8, 69, 162
Chorbajian, Levon 1942- 154
Chorell, Walentin 1912-1984 189
Obituary 111
See also EWL 3
Chorley, Katharine Campbell (Hopkinson)
1897-1986
Obituary 120
Chorley, R. J.
See Chorley, Richard J(ohn)
Chorley, Richard J(ohn) 1927-2002 121
Obituary 209
Brief entry 116
Chorlton, David 1948- 144
Chorny, Merron 1922- 41-44R
Choron, Jacques 1904-1972 .... CAP-1
Obituary 33-36R
Earlier sketch in CA 9-10
Choron, Sandra (Zena Samelson) 1950- 220
See also SATA 146
Chorpenning, Charlotte (Lee Barrows)
1872-1955
Brief entry 114
See also CWRI 5
See also SATA-Brief 37
Chothia, Jean 1944- 105
Chotjewitz, David 239
Chotjewitz, Peter O(tto) 1934- 129
Chotzinoff, Robin 1958- 193
Chotzinoff, Samuel 1889-1964
Obituary 93-96
Chou, En-lai 1898-1976
Obituary 112
Chou, Eric 1915- 132
Chou, Mark 1910-1988
Obituary 128
Chou, Tsu-Wei 1940- 144
Chou, Ya-luu 1924- 41-44R
Chou, Yu-jui
See Chou, Eric
Choucri, Nazli 1943- CANR-14
Earlier sketch in CA 81-84
Choudhury, Ashok 1957- 145
Choudhury, G(olam) W(ahed)
1926- CANR-17
Earlier sketch in CA 25-28R
Choudhury, Malay Roy
See Roy Choudhury, Malay
Choudhury, Masudul Alam 1948- CANR-94
Earlier sketch in CA 146
Choueiri, Youssef M. 1948- CANR-120
Earlier sketch in CA 136
Choukas, Michael (Eugene) 1901-1989 . CAP-2
Obituary 129
Earlier sketch in CA 17-18
Choukas-Bradley, Melanie (Rose) 1952- 124
Choukri, Mohamed 1935-2003 136
Obituary 221
Chou Li-po 1908-1979 .... EWL 3
Chouraqui, Andre (Nathanael)
1917- CANR-10
Earlier sketch in CA 65-68
Chow, Claire S. 1952- 166
Chow, Gregory C. 1929- 13-16R
Chow, Yung-Teh 1916- 37-40R
Chowder, Ken 1950- CANR-48
Earlier sketch in CA 102
Chowdhary, Savitri Devi (Dumra)
1907-1996 .... CAP-1
Earlier sketch in CA 11-12
Chowdhury, Bernie 1959- 193
Chowdhury, Subir 1967- 200
Chown, Marcus 1959- 198
See also SATA 137
Chowning, Larry S(hepherd) 1949- 111
Choy, Bong-youn 1914- 69-72
Choyce, Lesley 1951- 211
Earlier sketches in CA 130, CANR-68
Autobiographical Essay in 211
See also DLB 251
See also SATA 94
See also YAW
Chraibi, Driss 1926- 151
See also CWW 2
See also EWL 3
Chretien, Jean-Pierre 227
Chretien de Troyes c. 12th cent. - ...... DLB 208
See also EW 1
See also RGWL 2, 3
See also TWA
Chrimes, Stanley Bertram 1907-1984 .... 5-8R
Obituary 113
Chrislock, Carl H(endrick) 1917- 45-48
Chrisman, Arthur Bowie 1889-1953 188
See also BYA 4
See also SATA 124
See also YABC 1
Chrisman, Harry E. 1906-1993 .... CANR-45
Earlier sketch in CA 1-4R
Chrisman, Katherine (G.) 1940(?)-1987
Obituary 122
Chrisman, Miriam Usher 1920- CANR-88
Earlier sketch in CA 131
Chriss, Nicholas C. 1928(?)-1990
Obituary 131
Christ, Carl F(inley) 1923- 21-24R
Christ, Carol P(atrice) 1945- 154
Christ, Carol T(ecla) 1944- 93-96
Christ, Henry I(rvine) 1915- CANR-2
Earlier sketch in CA 5-8R
Christ, John M(ichael) 1934- 106
Christ, Karl 1923- CANR-91
Earlier sketches in CA 120, CANR-45
Christ, Ronald 1936- CANR-10
Earlier sketch in CA 25-28R
Christain, David
See Gaulden, Albert Clayton
Christaller, Walter 1893-1969
Obituary 115
Christe, Ian 224
Christelow, Eileen 1943- CANR-57
Earlier sketch in CA 111
See also SATA 38, 90
See also SATA-Brief 35
See also SATA-Essay 120
Christen, Robert J. 1928-1981
Obituary 108
Brief entry 107
Christen, William L. 1942- 149
Christenbury, Leila 1950- 206
Christensen, Allan Conrad 1940- 170
Christensen, Ann 1946- 108
Christensen, Anna
See Mayer, Deborah Anne
Christensen, Bonnie 1951- CANR-141
Earlier sketch in CA 180
See also SATA 110, 157
Christensen, C(lement) B(yrne) 1911- .... CP 1
Christensen, Clyde M. 1905-1993 53-56
Christensen, Damascene 173
Christensen, David E(mun) 1921- 13-16R
Christensen, Edward L. 1913- 25-28R
Christensen, Eleanor Ingalls 1913-2001 .. 53-56
Christensen, Erwin O(ttomar)
1890-1976 .... CAP-1
Earlier sketch in CA 13-14
Christensen, Father Damascene
See Christensen, Damascene
Christensen, Francis 1902-1970(?) CAP-2
Earlier sketch in CA 23-24
Christensen, Gardell Dano 1907-1991 .... 9-12R
See also SATA 1
Christensen, Harold T(aylor) 1909- 45-48
Christensen, Inger 1935- .... DLB 214
See also EWL 3
Christensen, J(ack) A(rden) 1927- 53-56
Christensen, James L(ee) 1922- 97-100
Christensen, Jerome 1948- 110
Christensen, Jo Ippolito
See Christensen, Yolanda Maria Ippolito
Christensen, Kate 1962- 217
Christensen, Kathleen E(lizabeth) 1951- 233
Christensen, Kit Richard 1953- 175
Christensen, Lars Saabye
See Saabye Christensen, Lars
Christensen, Laurie
See Steding, Laurie
Christensen, Mark 235
Christensen, Otto H(enry) 1898-1979 ... 33-36R
Christensen, Paul 1943- CANR-108
Earlier sketches in CA 77-80, CANR-15
Christensen, Sandra 1944- 110
Christensen, Terry 1944- 127
Christensen, Yolanda Maria Ippolito
1943- CANR-7
Earlier sketch in CA 57-60
Christenson, Cornelia V(os) 1903-1993 . CAP-2
Earlier sketch in CA 33-36
Christenson, Evelyn (Carol) 1922- 117
Christenson, James A. 1944- 143
Christenson, Larry 1928- CANR-8
Earlier sketch in CA 57-60
Christenson, Nordis 1929- 108
Christenson, Reo M. 1918- 37-40R
Christesen, Barbara 1940- 107
See also SATA 40
Christesen, Clement Byrne 1912- 102
Christgau, Alice Erickson 1902-1977 ..... CAP-2
Earlier sketch in CA 17-18
See also SATA 13
Christgau, John (Frederick) 1934- 103
Christgau, Robert (Thomas) 1942- 65-68
Christian, A. B.
See Yabes, Leopoldo Y(abes)
Christian, Barbara T. 1943-2000 .... CANR-57
Earlier sketch in CA 188
See also BW 1
See also FW
Christian, C(urtis) W(allace) 1927- 21-24R
Christian, Carol (Cathay) 1923- 53-56
Christian, Deborah 221
Christian, Frederick
See Gehman, Richard (Boyd)
Christian, Frederick H.
See Nolan, Frederick William
See also TCWW 1, 2
Christian, Garna L. 1935- 151
Christian, Garth Hood 1921-1967 .... CAP-1
Earlier sketch in CA 9-10
Christian, George (Eastland) 1927-2002 .. 65-68
Obituary 212
Christian, Glynn 1942- 115
Christian, Henry A(rthur) 1931- CANR-14
Earlier sketch in CA 33-36R
Christian, James L(ee) 1927- 57-60
Christian, Jeffrey E. 1956- 225
Christian, Jill
See Dilcock, Noreen
Christian, John
See Dixon, Roger
Christian, Louise
See Grill, Nannette L.
Christian, Marcus Bruce 1900-1976 73-76
Christian, Mary Blount 1933- CANR-17
Earlier sketches in CA 45-48, CANR-1
See also SATA 9
Christian, Nick
See Pollitz, Edward A(lan), Jr.
Christian, Peter
See Steinbrunner, (Peter) Chris(tian)
Christian, Portia 1908-1996 103
Christian, Rebecca 1952- 107
Christian, Reginald Frank 1924- CANR-2
Earlier sketch in CA 5-8R
Christian, Roy Cloberry 1914- 93-96

Christian, Shirley (Ann) 1938- CANR-78
Brief entry 119
Earlier sketch in CA 125
Interview in CA-125
Christian, William 1945- 150
Christian, William A(rmistead), Jr. 1944- 107
Christiani, Dounia Bunis 1913-1983 ..... 13-16R
Christians, Clifford Glenn 1939- 104
Christiansen, Arthur 1904-1963 .... 1-4R
Christiansen, Eugene Martin 1944- 121
Christiansen, Harley Duane 1930- CANR-4
Earlier sketch in CA 53-56
Christiansen, Keith 1947- CANR-124
Earlier sketch in CA 112
Christiansen, Michael Robin 1927-1984
Obituary 113
Christiansen, Richard (Dean) 1931- 121
Christiansen, Rupert (Elliott Niels)
1954- CANR-142
Earlier sketch in CA 135
Christianson, Elin B(allantyne) 1936- 111
Christianson, Gale E. 1942- CANR-87
Earlier sketch in CA 81-84
Christianson, John Robert 1934- CANR-92
Earlier sketch in CA 21-24R
Christianson, Paul 1937- 169
Christianson, Sven-Ake 1954- 161
Christie
See Ichikawa, Kon
Christie, Agatha (Mary Clarissa)
1890-1976 .... CANR-108
Obituary 61-64
Earlier sketches in CA 17-20R, CANR-10, 37
See also AAYA 9
See also AITN 1, 2
See also BPFB 1
See also BRWS 2
See also CBD
See also CDBLB 1914-1945
See also CLC 1, 6, 8, 12, 39, 48, 110
See also CMW 4
See also CN 1, 2
See also CPW
See also CWD
See also DA3
See also DAB
See also DAC
See also DAM NOV
See also DFS 2
See also DLB 13, 77, 245
See also MSW
See also MTCW 1, 2
See also MTFW 2005
See also NFS 8
See also RGEL 2
See also RHW
See also SATA 36
See also TEA
See also YAW
Christie, George C(ustis) 1934- 37-40R
Christie, Gregory
See Christie, R. Gregory
Christie, Hugh
See Christie-Murray, David (Hugh Arthur)
Christie, Ian 1956- 145
Christie, Ian R(alph) 1919-1998 .... CANR-51
Obituary 172
Earlier sketches in CA 5-8R, CANR-2, 20, 42
Christie, James R(ichard) 1952- 129
Christie, Jean 1912- 101
Christie, John Aldrich 1920- 65-68
Christie, Keith
See Haynes, Alfred H(enry)
Christie, Lindsay H. 1906(?)-1976
Obituary 61-64
Christie, Milton 1921- 17-20R
Christie, Philippa CANR-109
See also Pearce, Philippa
See also BYA 5
See also CLC 21
See also CLR 9
See also DLB 161
See also MAICYA 1
See also SATA 1, 67, 129
Christie, R. Gregory 1971- .... SATA 127
Christie, Trevor L. 1905-1969 .... CAP-2
Earlier sketch in CA 21-22
Christie, William 1960- 140
Christie-Murray, David (Hugh Arthur)
1913- CANR-4
Earlier sketch in CA 53-56
Christina, Teresa
See Taylor, Delores
Christine, Charles T(hornton) 1936- 33-36R
Christine, Dorothy Weaver 1934- 33-36R
Christine de Pizan 1365(?)-1431(?) ..... DLB 208
See also PC 68
See also RGWL 2, 3
Christ-Janer, Albert W. 1910-1973 ...... CANR-4
Obituary 45-48
Earlier sketch in CA 1-4R
Christman, Al(bert B.) 1923- 168
Christman, Don(ald) R. 1919- 17-20R
Christman, Elizabeth 1914- 89-92
Christman, Henry 1906-1980
Obituary 103
Christman, Henry Max 1932- 65-68
Christman, Luther (Parmalee) 1915- 124
Christman, Paul J. 1952- 132
Christman, R(aymond) J(ohn) 1919- 89-92
Christmas, Joyce 1939- CANR-105
Earlier sketches in CA 123, CANR-50, 72
Christmas, Linda (Irene) 1943- 149
Christo 1935- .... AAYA 53
Christodoulou, Anastasios 1932-2002 120
Obituary 208
Christodoulou, Demetrios 1919- 136
Christoff, Peter K. 1911-1998 121
Christofferson, April 235
Christol, Carl Quimby 1914- CANR-4
Earlier sketch in CA 5-8R
Christoph, Florence A(nna) 1937- 137
Christoph, James B(ernard) 1928- CANR-4
Earlier sketch in CA 5-8R
Christoph, Peter R(ichard) 1938- 137
Christopher, Beth
See Steinke, Ann E(lizabeth)
Christopher, Georgia B. 1932- 111
Christopher, Joe R(andell) 1935- CANR-4
Earlier sketch in CA 53-56
Christopher, John
See Youd, (Christopher) Samuel
See also AAYA 22
See also BYA 4, 8
See also CLR 2
See also DLB 255
See also SFW 4
See also YAW
Christopher, John B. 1914-1988 .... 13-16R
Christopher, Kenneth
See Brophy, Donald F(rancis)
Christopher, Louise
See Hale, Arlene
Christopher, Matt(hew Frederick)
1917-1997 .... CANR-104
Obituary 161
Earlier sketches in CA 1-4R, CANR-5, 36
See also BYA 8
See also CLR 33
See also JRDA
See also MAICYA 1, 2
See also SAAS 9
See also SATA 2, 47, 80
See also SATA-Obit 99
Christopher, Maurine (Brooks) 65-68
Christopher, Milbourne 1914(?)-1984 105
Obituary 113
See also SATA 46
Christopher, Nicholas 1951- CANR-91
Earlier sketches in CA 108, CANR-43
Christopher, Paula
See Michaels, Lynn
Christopher, Renny (Teresa) 1957- .. CANR-123
Earlier sketch in CA 159
Christopher, Robert Collins
1924-1992 .... CANR-46
Obituary 138
Earlier sketch in CA 102
Christopher, Warren 1925- 171
Christophersen, Paul (Hans) 1911-1999 188
Christov, Solveig
See Grieg, Solveig Christov
See also EWL 3
Christowe, Stoyan 1898- 65-68
Christy, Betty 1924- 57-60
Christy, George 9-12R
Christy, Howard Chandler 1873-1952 178
See also DLB 188
See also SATA 21
Christy, Jim 1945- 138
Christy, Joe
See Christy, Joseph M.
Christy, Joseph M. 1919- CANR-14
Earlier sketch in CA 29-32R
Christy, Marian 1932- 65-68
Christy, Teresa E(lizabeth) 1927- 73-76
Chroman, Eleanor 1937- 45-48
Chroman, Nathan 1929- 77-80
Chronic, Halka (Pattison) 1923- 118
Chroust, Anton-Hermann 1907- CAP-1
Earlier sketch in CA 9-10
Chruden, Herbert J(efferson) 1918- 5-8R
Chryssavgis, John 1958- 227
Chryssides, Helen 167
Chryssochoou, Dimitris N. 1970- 212
Chrystie, Frances N(icholson)
1904-1986 .... SATA 60
Chrystos 1946- 205
Chu, Arthur (T. S.) 1916-1979 81-84
Obituary 133
Chu, Daniel 1933- 13-16R
See also SATA 11
Chu, Godwin C(hien) 1927- 114
Chu, Grace (Goodyear) 1916- 81-84
Chu, Grace Zia 1899-1999 .... CANR-4
Obituary 177
Earlier sketch in CA 5-8R
Chu, Kong 1926- 49-52
Chu, Louis H. 1915-1970 .... 13-16R
See also DLB 312
See also LAIT 4
Chu, Petra ten-Doesschate 1942- ... CANR-137
Earlier sketch in CA 138
Chu, Samuel C. 1929- 69-72
Ch'u, Tung-tsu 1910- CANR-2
Earlier sketch in CA 1-4R
Chu, Valentin (Yuan-ling) 1919- 9-12R
Chu, W. R.
See Chu, Arthur (T. S.)
Chua, Amy (Lynn) 1962- 222
Chua, Lawrence 1966- 174
Chuan-Hsiang
See Shih, Chih-yu
Chubak, Sadeq 1916- .... EWL 3
Chubb, Elmer
See Masters, Edgar Lee
Chubb, Judith (Ann) 1947- 113
Chubb, Mary 1903-2003 224
Chubb, Thomas Caldecot 1899-1972 . CANR-6
Obituary 33-36R
Earlier sketch in CA 1-4R
Chubin, Barry 1943- 124
Chuck D
See Ridenhour, Carlton
Chuck-Yiu, Clara Law
See Law, Clara
Chudacoff, Howard P(eter) 1943- 45-48
Chudley, Ron(ald Alexander) 1937- 110
Chughtai, Ismat 1915-1991 166
Chuikov, Vasili Ivanovich 1900-1982
Obituary 106
Chukovskaia, Lidiia
See Chukovskaya, Lydia (Korneeva)
See also DLB 302
Chukovskaya, Lydia (Korneeva)
1907-1996 128
Obituary 151
Brief entry 117
Chukovsky, Kornei (Ivanovich)
1882-1969 .... CANR-42
Obituary 25-28R
Earlier sketches in CA 5-8R, CANR-4
See also MAICYA 1, 2
See also SATA 5, 34
Chulak, Armando (?)-1975
Obituary 109
Chulkov, Mikhail Dmitrievich
1743-1792 .... DLB 150
Chumacero, Ali 1918- .... HW 1
Chumachenko, Tatyana A. 1958- 238
Chuman, Frank Fujio 1917- 69-72
Chun, Gloria Heyung 1961- 214
Chun, Jinsie K(yung) S(hien) 1902-1995 .. 49-52
Chun, Richard 1935- 65-68
Chung, Connie
See Chung, Constance Yu-Hwa
Chung, Constance Yu-Hwa 1946- 132
Brief entry 119
Chung, Edward K(oo-Young) 1931- 107
Chung, Hyung C(han) 1931- 57-60
Chung, Joseph Sang-hoon 1929- 49-52
Chung, Kyung Cho 1921- 33-36R
Chung, Lily CANR-122
Earlier sketch in CA 170
Chung, Sung Wook 1966- 236
Chung-yu, Chu
See Hsu, Benedict (Pei-Hsiung)
Chunn, Jay Carrington II 1938- 116
Chupack, Cindy 1973(?)- 226
Chupack, Henry 1915- 49-52
Church, Albert M(arion) 1940- 111
Church, Alonzo 1903-1995 157
Church, Benjamin 1734-1778 .... DLB 31
Church, F(rank) Forrester (IV) 1948- 133
Church, Francis Pharcellus 1839-1906 218
See also DLB 79
Church, Jeffrey
See Kirk, Richard (Edmund)
Church, Joseph 1918-2003 .... 1-4R
Obituary 224
Church, Kristine
See Jensen, Kristine Mary
Church, Margaret 1920- 13-16R
Church, Peggy Pond 1903-1986 .... DLB 212
Church, Peter
See Nuttall, Jeff
Church, Ralph (Bruce) 1927- 37-40R
Church, Richard 1893-1972 .... CANR-3
Obituary 33-36R
Earlier sketch in CA 1-4R
See also CN 1
See also CP 1
See also CWRI 5
See also DLB 191
See also SATA 3
Church, Robert L(eValley) 1938- 61-64
Church, Ronald James Harrison
See Harrison-Church, Ronald James
Church, Roy A. 1935- 124
Church, Ruth Ellen (Lovrien)
1910(?)-1991 .... CANR-75
Obituary 135
Earlier sketches in CA 5-8R, CANR-7
Church, Suzanne
See Bates, Susannah (Vacella)
Church, William Conant 1836-1917 179
See also DLB 79
Church, William Farr 1912-1977
Brief entry 105
Churchett, Stephen 1947- 163
Churchill, Allen 1911-1988 .... CANR-75
Obituary 124
Earlier sketch in CA 97-100
Churchill, Bill
See Churchill, Gail Winston
Churchill, Caryl 1938- CANR-108
Earlier sketches in CA 102, CANR-22, 46
See also Churchill, Chick
See also BRWS 4
See also CBD
See also CD 6
See also CLC 31, 55, 157
See also CWD
See also DC 5
See also DFS 12, 16
See also DLB 13, 310
See also EWL 3
See also FW
See also MTCW 1
See also RGEL 2
Churchill, Charles 1731-1764 .... DLB 109
See also RGEL 2
Churchill, Chick
See Churchill, Caryl
See also CD 5
Churchill, Creighton 1912-1984 .... CANR-76
Obituary 114
Earlier sketch in CA 69-72
Churchill, David 1935- 106
Churchill, E(lmer) Richard 1937- CANR-56
Earlier sketches in CA 17-20R, CANR-11, 30
See also SATA 11
Churchill, Edward Delos 1895-1972
Obituary 37-40R
Churchill, Elizabeth
See Hough, Richard (Alexander)
Churchill, Gail Winston 1903(?)-1984
Obituary 112
Churchill, Guy E. 1926- 29-32R
Churchill, J(ohn) H(oward) 1920-1990
Obituary 131
Churchill, Jill
See Brooks, Janice Young
Churchill, Joyce
See Harrison, M(ichael) John
Churchill, Linda R. 1938- CANR-11
Earlier sketch in CA 21-24R
Churchill, R(eginald) C(harles) 1916- 9-12R
Churchill, Randolph (Frederick Edward Spencer)
1911-1968
Obituary 89-92
Churchill, Reba 1932(?)-1985
Obituary 116
Churchill, Rhona Adelaide 1913- 5-8R
Churchill, Rogers Platt 1902-1989
Obituary 129
Churchill, Samuel 1911-1991 .... 17-20R
Churchill, Sarah (Millicent Hermione)
1914-1982 129
Obituary 107
Churchill, Thomas Bell Lindsay 1907-1990
Obituary 131
Churchill, Ward 1947- 135
Churchill, Winston 1871-1947 211
See also DLB 202
See also RGAL 4
See also RHW
Churchill, Sir Winston (Leonard Spencer)
1874-1965 97-100
See also BRW 6
See also CDBLB 1890-1914
See also DA3
See also DLB 100
See also DLBD 16
See also LAIT 4
See also MTCW 1, 2
See also TCLC 113
Churchill, Winston S(pencer) 1940- 131
Churchland, Patricia Smith 1943- CANR-50
Earlier sketch in CA 123
Churchland, Paul M. 1942- 152
Churchman, C(harles) West 1913- CANR-9
Earlier sketch in CA 21-24R
Churchman, Michael 1929- 37-40R
Churchyard, Thomas 1520(?)-1604 ..... DLB 132
See also RGEL 2
Churella, Albert J(ohn) 1964- 178
Churton, Henry
See Tourgee, Albion W.
Chusid, Irwin 1951- 222
Chute, B(eatrice) J(oy) 1913-1987 .... CANR-76
Obituary 123
Earlier sketch in CA 1-4R
See also SATA 2
See also SATA-Obit 53
Chute, Carolyn 1947- CANR-135
Earlier sketch in CA 123
See also CLC 39
See also CN 7
Chute, Janet E. 1952- 178
Chute, Marchette (Gaylord)
1909-1994 .... CANR-75
Obituary 145
Earlier sketches in CA 1-4R, CANR-5
See also DLB 103
See also SATA 1
See also YAW
Chute, Robert M. 1926- 109
Chute, Rupert
See Cleveland, Philip Jerome
Chute, William J(oseph) 1914-1994 .... 9-12R
Chutkow, Paul 1947- 172
Chvidkovski, Dmitri
See Shvidkovsky, Dimitri
Chwalek, Henryka C. 1918- 17-20R
Chwast, Jacqueline 1932- CANR-5
Earlier sketch in CA 49-52
See also SATA 6
Chwast, Seymour 1931- CANR-142
Earlier sketch in CA 161
See also SATA 18, 96, 146
Chyet, Stanley F. 1931-2002 .... 33-36R
Obituary 209
Cialente, Fausta
See Terni-Cialente, Fausta
Cianciolo, Patricia Jean 1929- CANR-13
Earlier sketch in CA 37-40R
Ciaramitaro, Andrew James 1955- 110
Ciaramitaro, Barbara 1946- 107
Ciaravino, Helene 1972- 202
Ciarcia, Steve 1947- 110

Cumulative Index 109 Clark

Ciardi, John (Anthony) 1916-1986 ... CANR-33
Obituary ... 118
Earlier sketches in CA 5-8R, CANR-5
Interview in ... CANR-5
See also CAAS 2
See also CLC 10, 40, 44, 129
See also CLR 19
See also CP 1, 2
See also CWRI 5
See also DAM POET
See also DLB 5
See also DLBY 1986
See also MAICYA 1, 2
See also MAL 5
See also MTCW 1, 2
See also MTFW 2005
See also RGAL 4
See also SAAS 26
See also SATA 1, 65
See also SATA-Obit 46
Ciavolella, Massimo 1942- ... 135
Cibber, Colley 1671-1757 ... DLB 84
See also RGEL 2
Ciccone, Madonna Louise Veronica
See Madonna
Ciccorella, Aubra Dair ... 65-68
Cicellis, Kay 1926- ... CANR-3
Earlier sketch in CA 1-4R
See also CN 1, 2
Cicero, Marcus Tullius 106B.C.-43B.C. ... AW 1
See also CDWLB 1
See also DLB 211
See also RGWL 2, 3
Cicognani, Amleto Giovanni Cardinal
1883-1973
Obituary ... 45-48
Cicora, Mary A. 1957- ... 176
Cicourel, Aaron V. 1928- ... 53-56
Cid Perez, Jose (Diego) 1906-1994 ... CANR-4
Earlier sketch in CA 53-56
Ciechanowski, Jan 1888(?)-1973
Obituary ... 41-44R
Ciee, Grace 1961- ... 140
See also BW 2
Cienciala, Anna M(aria) 1929- ... CANR-105
Earlier sketch in CA 89-92
Cieplak, Tadeusz N(owak) 1918- ... CANR-11
Earlier sketch in CA 69-72
Cigan, Janko
See Krasko, Ivan
Cigar, Norman ... 228
Cigler, Allan J(ames) 1943- ... CANR-29
Earlier sketch in CA 111
Cikovsky, Nicolai, Jr. 1933- ... 113
Ciletti, Barbara 1950- ... 194
Cilffriw, Gwynfor
See Griffith, Thomas Gwynfor
Cilliers, Charl Jean Francois 1941- ... CP 1
Cima, Annalisa 1941- ... 237
See also DLB 128
Cimbala, Stephen J. 1943- ... 142
Cimbollek, Robert (Carl) 1937- ... 57-60
Ciment, James D. 1958- ... 211
See also SATA 140
Ciment, Jill 1953- ... 154
Ciment, Michel 1938- ... CANR-44
Earlier sketch in CA 97-100
Cimera, Robert E(vert) 1968- ... 238
Cimino, Michael 1943- ... 105
See also CLC 16
Cimino, Richard P. ... 200
Cimprich, John (V.) 1949- ... 191
Cinberg, Bernard L. 1905-1979
Obituary ... 85-88
Cincinnatus
See Currey, Cecil B(arr)
Cinderella 1878-1958
See Bruce, Mary Grant
Cinel, Dino 1941- ... 111
Cingo, Zivko 1935-1987 ... DLB 181
Cinquin, Emmanuelle 1908- ... CANR-82
Earlier sketch in CA 131
Cinquin, Sister Emmanuelle
See Cinquin, Emmanuelle
Ciochon, Russell L. 1948- ... 145
Cioffari, Vincenzo 1905-1997 ... 17-20R
Cioffi, Frank Louis 1951- ... 195
Cioffi, Lou(is James) 1926-1998 ... 120
Obituary ... 167
Brief entry ... 109
Interview in ... CA-120
Cioran, E(mil) M. 1911-1995 ... CANR-91
Obituary ... 149
Earlier sketch in CA 25-28R
See also CLC 64
See also DLB 220
See also EWL 3
Cipes, Robert M. 1930- ... 21-24R
Cipkus, Alfonsas
See Nyka-Niliunas, Alfonsas
Ciplijauskaite, Birute 1929- ... CANR-14
Earlier sketches in CA 37-40R, CANR-31
Cipolla, Carlo M(anlio) 1922-2000 ... CANR-39
Obituary ... 189
Earlier sketches in CA 5-8R, CANR-2, 18
Cipolla, Joan Bagnel
See Bagnel, Joan
Cipriano, Anthony (John) 1941- ... 102
Circus, Anthony
See Hoch, Edward D(entinger)
Circus, Jim
See Roseyear, John
Cire
See Hayden, Eric W(illiam)
Cirese, Eugenio 1884-1955 ... 178
See also DLB 114
Ciresi, Rita 1960- ... CANR-98
Earlier sketch in CA 149
Ciria, Alberto 1934- ... 73-76
Cirino, Linda D(avis) 1941- ... CANR-92
Earlier sketch in CA 65-68
Cirino, Robert 1937- ... 61-64
Cirulis, Janis
See Bels, Alberts
Cismaru, Alfred 1933- ... 61-64
Cisneros, Antonio 1942- ... CANR-72
Earlier sketch in CA 131
See also CWW 2
See also DLB 290
See also HW 1, 2
Cisneros, Domingo 1942- ... 229
Cisneros, Pedro (Ruben) Treto 1939- ... 237
Cisneros, Sandra 1954- ... CANR-118
Earlier sketches in CA 131, CANR-64
See also AAYA 9, 53
See also AMWS 7
See also CLC 69, 118, 193
See also CN 7
See also CWP
See also DA3
See also DAM MULT
See also DLB 122, 152
See also EWL 3
See also EXPN
See also FL 1:5
See also FW
See also HLC 1
See also HW 1, 2
See also LAIT 5
See also LATS 1:2
See also LLW
See also MAICYA 2
See also MAL 5
See also MTCW 2
See also MTFW 2005
See also NFS 2
See also PC 52
See also PFS 19
See also RGAL 4
See also RGSF 2
See also SSC 32, 72
See also SSFS 3, 13
See also WLIT 1
See also YAW
Cissna, Kenneth N. 1948- ... 192
Ciszek, Walter 1904-1984 ... CAP-1
Earlier sketch in CA 13-14
Citati, Pietro 1930- ... CANR-43
Earlier sketches in CA 53-56, CANR-4
Citino, David 1947- ... CANR-108
Earlier sketch in CA 104
Citino, Robert (M.) 1958- ... 196
Citra, Becky 1954- ... 207
See also SATA 137
Citrine, Walter McLennan 1887-1983
Obituary ... 109
Citro, Joseph A. ... 176
See also HGG
Citron, Stephen ... 239
Cittafino, Ricardo
See Bickers, Richard (Leslie) Townshend
Ciuba, Edward J(oseph) 1935- ... 61-64
Civil-Brown, Sue
See Lee, Rachel
Civille, John R(aphael) 1940- ... CANR-11
Earlier sketch in CA 69-72
Cixous, Helene 1937- ... CANR-123
Earlier sketches in CA 126, CANR-55
See also CLC 92
See also CWW 2
See also DLB 83, 242
See also EWL 3
See also FL 1:5
See also FW
See also GLL 2
See also MTCW 1, 2
See also MTFW 2005
See also TWA
Cizek, Gregory J. 1958- ... 205
Cizmar, Paula 1949- ... 122
Claassen, Harold 1905-1986 ... CAP-2
Earlier sketch in CA 19-20
Claassen, William 1948- ... 197
Clabaugh, Gary K(enneth) 1940- ... 69-72
Clabby, John 1911-1990 ... 104
Clack, Robert Wood 1886-1964 ... 122
Obituary ... 110
Cladis, Mark S. 1958- ... 195
Claerbaut, David 1946- ... CANR-1
Earlier sketch in CA 45-48
Claes, Ernest 1885-1968 ... EWL 3
Claesson, Stig 1928- ... 194
Claeys, Gregory (Richard) 1953- ... 205
Claeyssens, Astere E(varist) 1924-1990
Obituary ... 132
Claffey, William J. 1925- ... 21-24R
Claflin, Edward 1949- ... 97-100
Clagett, John (Henry) 1916- ... CANR-6
Earlier sketch in CA 5-8R
Clagett, Marshall 1916-2005 ... CANR-5
Earlier sketch in CA 1-4R
Claghorn, Charles E.
See Claghorn, Charles Eugene
Claghorn, Charles Eugene 1911- ... CANR-44
Earlier sketch in CA 57-60
Claghorn, Gene
See Claghorn, Charles Eugene
Clague, Christopher K. 1938- ... 141
Clague, Ewan 1896-1987 ... 29-32R
Obituary ... 122
Clague, Maryhelen 1930- ... 81-84
Claiborne, Craig 1920-2000 ... CANR-94
Earlier sketches in CA 1-4R, CANR-5
Claiborne, Robert (Watson, Jr.)
1919-1990 ... CANR-31
Obituary ... 130
Earlier sketches in CA 29-32R, CANR-12
Claiborne, Sybil 1923-1992 ... 128
Obituary ... 140
Clain-Stefanelli, Vladimir 1914-1982 ... 111
Obituary ... 108
Clair, Andree ... 29-32R
See also SATA 19
Clair, Bernard (Eddy) 1951- ... 102
Clair, Louis
See Coser, Lewis A(lfred)
Clair, Maxine ... 179
Clair, Rene
See Chomette, Rene Lucien
See also CLC 20
Claire, Cherie
See Coen, Chere (Dastugue)
Claire, Edie ... 236
Claire, Keith
See Andrews, Claire and
Andrews, Keith
Claire, Rodger W(illiam) ... 235
Claire, William Francis 1935- ... CANR-7
Earlier sketch in CA 57-60
Clairmont, Elva 1937- ... 117
Clamer, Adrien
See Laberge, Albert
Clamer, Adrien ... CCA 1
Clammer, David 1943- ... 69-72
Clampett, Bob 1914(?)-1985
Obituary ... 112
See also Clampett, Robert
See also AITN 1
See also IDFW 3, 4
See also SATA-Obit 38
Clampett, Robert
See Clampett, Bob
See also SATA 44
Clampitt, Amy 1920-1994 ... CANR-79
Obituary ... 146
Earlier sketches in CA 110, CANR-29
See also AMWS 9
See also CLC 32
See also DLB 105
See also MAL 5
See also PC 19
Clance, Pauline Rose 1938- ... 126
Clanchy, Kate 1965- ... CWP
Clanchy, M(ichael) T. ... 182
Clancy, Clarence Lawson 1930-1998
See Carlile, Clancy
Clancy, Flora Simmons ... 226
Clancy, Francis Michael 1903-1986
Obituary ... 121
Clancy, John Gregory 1922- ... 13-16R
Clancy, Joseph P(atrick) 1928- ... CANR-18
Earlier sketch in CA 101
See also BYA 2
Clancy, King
See Clancy, Francis Michael
Clancy, Laurence James 1942- ... 108
Clancy, Laurie
See Clancy, Laurence James
Clancy, Thomas H(anley) 1923- ... CANR-7
Earlier sketch in CA 13-16R
Clancy, Thomas L., Jr. 1947- ... CANR-105
Brief entry ... 125
Earlier sketches in CA 131, CANR-62
Interview in ... CA-131
See also Clancy, Tom
See also DA3
See also MTCW 1, 2
See also MTFW 2005
Clancy, Tom ... CANR-132
See also Clancy, Thomas L., Jr.
See also AAYA 9, 51
See also BEST 89:1, 90:1
See also BPFB 1
See also BYA 10, 11
See also CLC 45, 112
See also CMW 4
See also CPW
See also DAM NOV, POP
See also DLB 227
Clancy, William 1922-1982
Obituary ... 106
Clanton, (Orval) Gene 1934- ... 41-44R
Clanton, Gordon 1942- ... 57-60
Clapham, Arthur Roy 1904-1990 ... 109
Obituary ... 133
Clapham, Christopher (S.) 1941- ... CANR-60
Earlier sketch in CA 128
Clapham, John 1908-1992 ... CANR-10
Earlier sketch in CA 25-28R
Clapp, James Gordon 1909-1970 ... CAP-1
Earlier sketch in CA 9-10
Clapp, John 1968- ... SATA 109
Clapp, Margaret (Antoinette) 1910-1974
Obituary ... 49-52
Clapp, Nicholas 1936- ... CANR-129
Earlier sketch in CA 170
Clapp, Patricia 1912- ... CANR-114
Earlier sketches in CA 25-28R, CANR-10, 37
See also BYA 10
See also JRDA
See also MAICYA 1, 2
See also SAAS 4
See also SATA 4, 74
See also YAW
Clapp, Rodney ... 176
Clapp, Verner W(arren) 1901-1972
Obituary ... 37-40R
Clapper, Gregory S(cott) 1951- ... 166
Clapper, Raymond 1892-1944 ... 175
See also DLB 29
Clapperton, Richard 1934- ... 25-28R
Clar, C(harles) Raymond 1903-1996 ... 37-40R
Clardy, Andrea Fleck 1943- ... CANR-17
Earlier sketch in CA 97-100
Clardy, Brian K(eith) 1967- ... 219
Clardy, J(esse) V. 1929- ... 33-36R
Clare, Anthony W(ard) 1942- ... 177
Clare, Baxter
See Trautman, Victoria B.
Clare, Elizabeth
See Cook, Dorothy Mary
Clare, Ellen
See Sinclair, Olga
Clare, Francis D.
See Aschmann, Alberta
Clare, George P. 1920- ... 111
Clare, Helen ... CANR-45
See also Clarke, Pauline
Clare, John 1793-1864 ... BRWS 11
See also DAB
See also DAM POET
See also DLB 55, 96
See also PC 23
See also RGEL 2
Clare, Josephine 1933- ... 73-76
Clare, Margaret
See Maison, Margaret M(ary Bowles)
Clare, Samantha
See Dawson, Janis
Claremont, Chris(topher Simon) 1950- ... 151
See also SATA 87
Clarens, Carlos (Figueredo y)
1936(?)-1987 ... 21-24R
Obituary ... 121
Clareson, Thomas D(ean)
1926-1993 ... CANR-83
Obituary ... 141
Earlier sketches in CA 1-4R, CANR-2, 18, 39
Clarfield, Gerard Howard 1936- ... 103
Claridge, Gordon S. 1932- ... 21-24R
Claridge, Laura P. ... 221
Clarie, Thomas C(ashin) 1943- ... 93-96
Clarin
See Alas (y Urena), Leopoldo (Enrique Garcia)
Clarizio, Harvey F(rank) 1934- ... 33-36R
Clark, A(ndrea) Kim 1964- ... 173
Clark, A(ilsa) M. 1926- ... 144
Clark, Admont Gulick 1919- ... 53-56
Clark, Al C.
See Goines, Donald
Clark, Alan 1928-1999 ... 13-16R
Obituary ... 185
Clark, Alfred Alexander Gordon
1900-1958 ... 221
Brief entry ... 112
See also Hare, Cyril
See also CMW 4
Clark, Alice S(andell) 1922- ... 41-44R
Clark, Andrew 1966- ... 234
Clark, Andrew F. ... 193
Clark, Andrew Hill 1911-1975 ... CAP-2
Earlier sketch in CA 25-28
Clark, Andy 1957- ... CANR-144
Earlier sketch in CA 163
Clark, Ann L(ivezey) 1913- ... CANR-7
Earlier sketch in CA 17-20R
Clark, Ann Nolan 1896-1995 ... CANR-48
Obituary ... 150
Earlier sketches in CA 5-8R, CANR-2
See also BYA 4
See also CLR 16
See also CWRI 5
See also DLB 52
See also MAICYA 1, 2
See also MAICYAS 1
See also SAAS 16
See also SATA 4, 82
See also SATA-Obit 87
Clark, Anna (K.) ... 234
Clark, Anne
See Amor, Anne Clark
Clark, Anne 1909-1989 ... 29-32R
Clark (of Herriotshall), Arthur Melville
1895-1990 ... 9-12R
Clark, Badger
See Paine, Lauran (Bosworth)
Clark, Ben T. 1928- ... 53-56
Clark, Benjamin
See Clark, Bob
Clark, Bill
See Clark, William A(rthur)
Clark, Billy C(urtis) 1928- ... CANR-22
Earlier sketch in CA 1-4R
Clark, Blue
See Clark, C(arter) Blue
Clark, Bob ... 201
Clark, Brian (Robert)
See Clark, (Robert) Brian
See also CD 6
Clark, (Robert) Brian 1932- ... CANR-67
Earlier sketch in CA 41-44R
See also Clark, Brian (Robert)
See also CBD
See also CD 5
See also CLC 29
Clark, Bruce B(udge) 1918- ... 69-72
Clark, Burton R(obert) 1921- ... CANR-52
Earlier sketches in CA 110, CANR-28
Clark, C(arter) Blue 1946- ... 150
Clark, C. E. Frazer, Jr. 1925-2001 ... 33-36R
See also Clark, Charles Elliot Frazer, Jr.
See also DLB 187
Clark, C. H. Douglas 1890- ... CAP-2
Earlier sketch in CA 23-24

Clark, C(harles) M(anning) H(ope)
1915-1991 ... 97-100
Obituary ... 134
Earlier sketch in CA 9-12R
Clark, Carol (Lois) 1948- ... 57-60
Clark, Carol Higgins 1956(?)- ... CANR-136
Earlier sketches in CA 152, CANR-102
See also MTFW 2005
Clark, Catherine Anthony (Smith)
1892-1977 ... CAP-1
Earlier sketch in CA 11-12
See also CWRI 5
See also DLB 68
See also JRDA
Clark, Champ 1923-2002 ... 108
Obituary ... 214
See also SATA 47
Clark, Charles E(dwin) 1929- ... 29-32R
Clark, Charles Elliot Frazer, Jr.
See Clark, C. E. Frazer, Jr.
See also DLBY 01
Clark, Charles Heber 1841-1915
Brief entry ... 111
See also DLB 11
See also SFW 4
Clark, Charles Michael Andres 1960- ... 144
Clark, Charles Tallifero 1917- ... 13-16R
Clark, China (Debra) 1950- ... 45-48
Clark, Christopher (Anthony) Stuart
See Stuart-Clark, Christopher (Anthony)
Clark, Clara Gillow 1951- ... CANR-139
Earlier sketch in CA 150
See also SATA 84, 154
Clark, Clifford E(dward), Jr. 1941- ... 81-84
Clark, Colin (Grant) 1905-1989 ... CANR-8
Obituary ... 129
Earlier sketch in CA 61-64
Clark, Colin (MacArthur) 1932-2002 ... 224
Clark, Curt
See Westlake, Donald E(dwin)
Clark, D. M. J.
See Clark, Douglas (Malcolm Jackson)
Clark, Daniel Matthew 1966-1998 ... 205
Clark, David
See Hardcastle, Michael
Clark, David (George) 1939- ... CANR-86
Earlier sketch in CA 130
Clark, David Aaron 1963(?)- ... 222
Clark, David Allen
See Ernst, (Lyman) John
Clark, David Gillis 1933- ... 53-56
Clark, David Lindsey 1926- ... 175
Clark, David Ridgley 1920- ... CANR-9
Earlier sketch in CA 17-20R
Clark, Davis Wasgatt 1812-1871 ... DLB 79
Clark, Dennis E. 1916- ... 29-32R
Clark, Dennis J. 1927-1993 ... CANR-53
Obituary ... 142
Earlier sketches in CA 1-4R, CANR-1
Clark, Diana Cooper
See Cooper-Clark, Diana
Clark, Dick
See Clark, Richard Wagstaff
Clark, Don(ald Rowlee) 1925- ... 57-60
Clark, Don(ald Henry) 1930- ... 29-32R
Clark, Donald E. 1933- ... CANR-8
Earlier sketch in CA 21-24R
Clark, Dora Mae 1893-1987 ... 41-44R
Clark, Dorothy Park 1899-1983 ... 5-8R
Clark, Douglas (Malcolm Jackson)
1919-1993 ... CANR-71
Earlier sketch in CA 114
See also CMW 4
See also DLB 276
Clark, Douglas W. ... 171
Clark, E. Ritchie 1912- ... 122
Clark, Edward W(illiam) 1943- ... 123
Clark, Eleanor 1913-1996 ... CANR-41
Obituary ... 151
Earlier sketch in CA 9-12R
See also CLC 5, 19
See also CN 1, 2, 3, 4, 5, 6
See also DLB 6
Clark, Electa 1910- ... 69-72
Clark, Eliot (Candee) 1883-1980
Obituary ... 97-100
Clark, Ella E(lizabeth) 1896-1984 ... 105
Clark, Ellery Harding, Jr. 1909-1997 . CANR-10
Obituary ... 160
Earlier sketch in CA 65-68
Clark, Elmer Talmage 1886-1966 ... 5-8R
Clark, Emma Chichester
See Chichester Clark, Emma
See also SATA 69
Clark, Eric 1911- ... CANR-9
Earlier sketch in CA 13-16R
Clark, Eric 1937- ... 102
Clark, Eugenie 1922- ... 49-52
Clark, Evans 1888-1970
Obituary ... 104
Clark, Evert 1926(?)-1988
Obituary ... 126
Clark, F(rederick) Stephen
1908-1977 ... CANR-14
Earlier sketch in CA 21-24R
Clark, Francis 1919- ... 17-20R
Clark, Francis E(dward) 1851-1927 ... 203
Clark, Frank J(ames) 1922- ... CANR-17
Earlier sketch in CA 13-16R
See also SATA 18
Clark, Fred George 1890-1972
Obituary ... 37-40R
Clark, Gail 1944- ... CANR-16
Earlier sketch in CA 97-100
Clark, Garel
See Garelick, May
Clark, Garth (Reginald) 1947- ... 115
Clark, Geoffrey (D.) 1940- ... CANR-115
Earlier sketch in CA 144
Clark, George 1932- ... 136
Clark, George Norman 1890-1979 ... 65-68
Obituary ... 85-88
Clark, George Sidney Roberts Kitson
See Kitson Clark, George Sydney Roberts
Clark, Gerald 1918- ... 13-16R
Clark, Glenn 1882-1956 ... 219
Clark, Gordon H(addon)
1902-1985 ... CANR-17
Earlier sketches in CA 1-4R, CANR-1
Clark, Gordon L. 1950- ... 148
Clark, (John) Grahame (Douglas)
1907-1995 ... CANR-10
Obituary ... 149
Earlier sketch in CA 65-68
Clark, Gregory 1892-1977
Obituary ... 89-92
Clark, Halsey
See Deming, Richard
Clark, Harry 1917- ... 61-64
Clark, Harry Hayden 1901-1971 ... CAP-2
Earlier sketch in CA 29-32
Clark, Henry B(alsley) II 1930- ... CANR-8
Earlier sketch in CA 5-8R
Clark, Howard
See Haskin, Dorothy C(lark)
Clark, Hunter R. 1955- ... 141
Clark, Ira G(ranville, Jr.) 1909- ... 127
Clark, J(onathan) C(harles) D(ouglas)
1951- ... CANR-47
Earlier sketch in CA 121
Clark, J(ohn) H(oward) 1929- ... 106
Clark, J(ustus) Kent 1917- ... 128
Clark, J. P.
See Clark Bekederemo, J(ohnson) P(epper)
See also CDWLB 3
See also DLB 117
Clark, J. R.
See Clark, John R(ussell)
Clark, J(eff) R(ay) 1947- ... CANR-22
Earlier sketch in CA 106
Clark, James Anthony 1907- ... 65-68
Clark, James C. 1947- ... CANR-92
Earlier sketches in CA 122, CANR-48
Clark, James M(ilford) 1930- ... 21-24R
Clark, James V(aughan) 1927- ... 13-16R
Clark, Janie 1956- ... 138
Clark, Jean C(ashman) 1920- ... 93-96
Clark, Jere Walton 1922- ... 21-24R
Clark, Jerome 1946- ... 143
Clark, Jerome L. 1928- ... 37-40R
Clark, Jerry E(ugene) 1942- ... 73-76
Clark, Jim 1944- ... 183
Clark, Joan
See Benson, Mildred (Augustine Wirt)
Clark, Joan 1934- ... CANR-119
Earlier sketches in CA 93-96, CANR-67
See also MAICYA 2
See also SATA 59, 96
Clark, John Desmond 1916-2002 ... 61-64
Obituary ... 205
Clark, John Drury 1907- ... 37-40R
Clark, John G(arretson) 1932- ... 17-20R
Clark, John Maurice 1884-1963 ... 5-8R
Clark, John Pepper
See Clark Bekederemo, J(ohnson) P(epper)
See also AFW
See also CD 5
See also CP 1, 2, 3, 4, 5, 6, 7
See also RGEL 2
Clark, John R(ussell) 1927- ... 120
Clark, John R(ichard) 1930- ... 37-40R
Clark, John R(alph) K(ukeakalani) 1946- ... 101
Clark, John T. 1968- ... 171
Clark, John W(illiams) 1907- ... 13-16R
Clark, Joseph 1958- ... 194
Clark, Joseph D(eadrick) 1893-1985 ... CAP-2
Earlier sketch in CA 33-36
Clark, Joseph James 1893-1971 ... CAP-2
Obituary ... 29-32R
Earlier sketch in CA 19-20
Clark, Joseph L(ynn) 1881-1969 ... CAP-2
Earlier sketch in CA 17-18
Clark, Joseph S(ill, Jr.) 1901-1990
Obituary ... 130
Clark, Joshua Reuben, Jr. 1871-1961 ... 165
Clark, Katerina 1941- ... CANR-58
Earlier sketch in CA 110
Clark, Katharine
See Flora, Kate Clark
Clark, Katharine (Jarman) 1911(?)-1986
Obituary ... 118
Clark, Katherine ... 205
Clark, Keith 1939- ... 124
Clark, Kelly James 1956- ... CANR-100
Earlier sketch in CA 173
Clark, Kenneth (Mackenzie)
1903-1983 ... CANR-36
Obituary ... 109
Earlier sketch in CA 93-96
See also MTCW 1, 2
See also MTFW 2005
See also TCLC 147
Clark, Kenneth B(ancroft) 1914-2005 ... 33-36R
Obituary ... 239
See also BW 1
Clark, L. D. 1922- ... CANR-1
Earlier sketch in CA 1-4R
Clark, Larry ... 170
Clark, Laurence (Walter) 1914- ... 13-16R
Clark, LaVerne Harrell 1929- ... CANR-46
Earlier sketches in CA 13-16R, CANR-11
Clark, Leonard 1905-1981 ... CANR-82
Obituary ... 105
Earlier sketches in CA 13-16R, CANR-7
See also CWRI 5
See also SATA 30
See also SATA-Obit 29
Clark, Leonard H(ill) 1915- ... CANR-4
Earlier sketch in CA 53-56
Clark, Leroy D. ... CANR-11
Earlier sketch in CA 61-64
Clark, Lewis Gaylord 1808-1873 ... DLB 3, 64, 73, 250
Clark, Lindley H(oag), Jr. 1920- ... 65-68
Clark, Lydia Benson
See Meaker, Eloise
Clark, Lynn Schofield ... 223
Clark, M. R.
See Clark, Mavis Thorpe
Clark, Mabel Margaret (Cowie)
1903-1975 ... 101
Clark, Malcolm (Hamilton), Jr. 1917- ... 106
Clark, Marcia (Rachel) 1953- ... 161
Clark, Marden J. 1916- ... 61-64
Clark, Margaret (D.) 1943- ... 196
See also SATA 126
Clark, Margaret Goff 1913- ... CANR-43
Earlier sketches in CA 1-4R, CANR-5, 20
See also SATA 8, 82
Clark, Marguerite Sheridan 1892(?)-1982
Obituary ... 107
Clark, Maria Louisa Guidish 1926- ... 5-8R
Clark, Marion L. 1943-1977 ... 77-80
Obituary ... 73-76
Clark, Marjorie A(gnes) 1911- ... 33-36R
Clark, Mark (Wayne) 1896-1984
Obituary ... 112
Clark, (Bennett) Marsh 1928-1985 ... 122
Obituary ... 117
Clark, Martin Fillmore, Jr. 1959- ... 202
Clark, Mary T. ... 37-40R
Clark, Mary Higgins 1929- ... CANR-133
Earlier sketches in CA 81-84, CANR-16, 36, 51, 76, 102
See also AAYA 10, 55
See also BEST 89:4
See also BPFB 1
See also CMW 4
See also CPW
See also DA3
See also DAM POP
See also DLB 306
See also HGG
See also JRDA
See also MTCW 1, 2
See also MTFW 2005
See also SATA 46
See also YAW
Clark, Mary Jane 1915- ... 57-60
Clark, Mary Jane Behrends ... 225
Clark, Mary Lou
See Clark, Maria Louisa Guidish
Clark, Mary Margaret 1929- ... 113
Clark, Mary T(wibill) ... 102
Clark, Mavis Thorpe 1909-1999 ... CANR-107
Earlier sketches in CA 57-60, CANR-8, 37
See also CLC 12
See also CLR 30
See also CWRI 5
See also MAICYA 1, 2
See also SAAS 5
See also SATA 8, 74
Clark, Melissa 1949- ... CANR-22
Earlier sketch in CA 104
Clark, Merle
See Gessner, Lynne
Clark, Michael D(orsey) 1937- ... 111
Clark, Miles (Morton) 1920- ... 21-24R
Clark, Nancy 1952- ... 220
Clark, Naomi 1932- ... 77-80
Clark, Neal 1950- ... 113
Clark, Neil M(cCullough) 1890-1980 ... 5-8R
Clark, Nicholas (Alexander) 1959-1984 ... 132
Clark, Norman H(arold) 1925-2004 ... 69-72
Clark, Parlin
See Trigg, Harry Davis
Clark, Patricia Denise 1921- ... CANR-79
See also Lorrimer, Claire
See also SATA 117
Clark, Patricia Finrow 1929- ... 17-20R
See also SATA 11
Clark, Paul F. 1954- ... 138
Clark, R. Milton
See Clark, Reginald M.
Clark, (William) Ramsey 1927- ... 29-32R
Clark, Randall 1957- ... 120
Clark, Reginald M. 1949- ... 128
Clark, Richard Charles 1935- ... 133
Brief entry ... 114
Clark, Richard Wagstaff 1929- ... 130
Brief entry ... 113
Clark, Robert 1952- ... 238
Clark, Robert Alfred 1908-2001 ... 101
Clark, Robert E(ugene) 1912- ... 41-44R
Clark, Robert E(dward) D(avid)
1906-1984 ... CANR-21
Earlier sketch in CA 5-8R
Clark, Robert L(loyd), Jr. 1945- ... 103
Clark, Robert P(hillips) 1921- ... 126
Clark, Rolf 1937- ... 114
Clark, Romane Lewis 1925- ... 17-20R
Clark, Ron(ald) 1972(?)- ... 223
Clark, Ronald Harry 1904-1999 ... 110
Clark, Ronald William 1916-1987 ... CANR-47
Obituary ... 122
Earlier sketch in CA 25-28R
See also SATA 2
See also SATA-Obit 52
Clark, Ruth C(ampbell) 1920- ... 69-72
Clark, Sally 1953- ... 171
See also CD 6
Clark, Samuel 1945- ... 89-92
Clark, Samuel Delbert 1910- ... CANR-11
Earlier sketches in CAP-1, CA 13-14
Clark, Septima Poinsette 1898-1987 ... 5-8R
Obituary ... 124
Clark, Sherryl 1956- ... 223
See also SATA 149
Clark, Simon 1958- ... HGG
Clark, Stephen R(ichard) L(yster)
1945- ... CANR-72
Earlier sketches in CA 77-80, CANR-13, 32
Clark, Sue C(assidy) 1935- ... 41-44R
Clark, Suzanne ... 199
Clark, Sydney A(ylmer) 1890-1975 ... CANR-4
Obituary ... 57-60
Earlier sketch in CA 5-8R
Clark, T(imothy) J(ames) ... 203
Clark, Terry N(ichols) 1940- ... 25-28R
Clark, Thomas A. 1944- ... CP 1
Clark, Thomas D(ionysious)
1903-2005 ... CANR-4
Earlier sketch in CA 5-8R
Clark, Thomas Willard 1941- ... CANR-80
Earlier sketches in CA 81-84, CANR-43
See also Clark, Tom
See also CAAS 22
Clark, Tom
See Clark, Thomas Willard
See also CP 1, 2, 3, 4, 5, 6, 7
Clark, Truman R(oss) 1935- ... 61-64
Clark, Van D(eusen) 1909-1974 ... CAP-1
Earlier sketch in CA 13-14
See also SATA 2
Clark, Virginia
See Gray, Patricia (Clark)
Clark, Walter Houston 1902-1994 ... 37-40R
Clark, Walter Van Tilburg
1909-1971 ... CANR-113
Obituary ... 33-36R
Earlier sketches in CA 9-12R, CANR-63
See also CLC 28
See also CN 1
See also DLB 9, 206
See also LAIT 2
See also MAL 5
See also RGAL 4
See also SATA 8
See also TCWW 1, 2
Clark, Wesley James 1950- ... CANR-31
Earlier sketch in CA 112
Clark, Wesley K. 1944- ... 203
Clark, Will 1939- ... 166
Clark, William 1770-1838 ... DLB 183, 186
Clark, William (Donaldson)
1916-1985 ... 29-32R
Obituary ... 116
Clark, William A(rthur) 1931- ... 33-36R
Clark, William Andrews, Jr. 1877-1934 ... 197
See also DLB 187
Clark, William Bedford 1947- ... CANR-51
Earlier sketches in CA 109, CANR-27
Clark, William R. 1938- ... CANR-88
Earlier sketch in CA 152
Clark, William Smith II 1900-1969 ... CAP-2
Earlier sketch in CA 25-28
Clark Bekederemo, J(ohnson) P(epper)
1935- ... CANR-72
Earlier sketches in CA 65-68, CANR-16
See also Bekederemo, J. P. Clark and Clark, J. P. and Clark, John Pepper
See also BLC 1
See also BW 1
See also CLC 38
See also DAM DRAM, MULT
See also DC 5
See also DFS 13
See also EWL 3
See also MTCW 2
See also MTFW 2005
Clarke, A. F. N. 1948- ... 128
Clarke, Adele E. ... 185
Clarke, Alison (Jane) ... 225
Clarke, Anna 1919-2004 ... CANR-39
Obituary ... 233
Earlier sketches in CA 102, CANR-18
See also CMW 4
Clarke, Arthur C(harles) 1917- ... CANR-130
Earlier sketches in CA 1-4R, CANR-2, 28, 55, 74
See also AAYA 4, 33
See also BPFB 1
See also BYA 13
See also CLC 1, 4, 13, 18, 35, 136
See also CN 1, 2, 3, 4, 5, 6, 7
See also CPW
See also DA3
See also DAM POP
See also DLB 261
See also JRDA
See also LAIT 5
See also MAICYA 1, 2
See also MTCW 1, 2
See also MTFW 2005
See also SATA 13, 70, 115
See also SCFW 1, 2
See also SFW 4
See also SSC 3
See also SSFS 4, 18
See also TCLE 1:1
See also YAW
Clarke, Arthur G(ladstone) 1887- ... CAP-2
Earlier sketch in CA 17-18

Cumulative Index 111 Clayton

Clarke, Austin 1896-1974 ... CAP-2
Obituary ... 49-52
Earlier sketch in CA 29-32
See also CLC 6, 9
See also CP 1, 2
See also DAM POET
See also DLB 10, 20
See also EWL 3
See also RGEL 2
Clarke, Austin C(hesterfield) 1934- ... CANR-140
Earlier sketches in CA 25-28R, CANR-14, 32, 68
See also CAAS 16
See also BLC 1
See also BW 1
See also CLC 8, 53
See also CN 1, 2, 3, 4, 5, 6, 7
See also DAC
See also DAM MULT
See also DLB 53, 125
See also DNFS 2
See also MTCW 2
See also MTFW 2005
See also RGSF 2
See also SSC 45
Clarke, Basil F(ulford) L(owther) 1908-1978 ... CANR-4
Obituary ... 89-92
Earlier sketch in CA 5-8R
Clarke, Boden
See Burgess, Michael (Roy)
Clarke, Breena 1951- ... 182
Clarke, Brenda (Margaret Lilian) 1926- ... CANR-102
Earlier sketches in CA 65-68, CANR-9, 24, 49
See also RHW
Clarke, Brian ... 237
Clarke, Captain Jafar
See Nesmith, Robert I.
Clarke, Charles (Richard Astley) 1944- ... 118
Clarke, Charles Galloway 1899-1983
Obituary ... 110
See also IDFW 3, 4
Clarke, Cheryl 1947- ... 143
See also BW 2
See also GLL 2
Clarke, Clorinda 1917- ... 25-28R
See also SATA 7
Clarke, D(erek) A(shdown) 1921- ... 125
Clarke, D(avid) Waldo 1907- ... 9-12R
See also Waldo, Dale and Waldo, Dave
Clarke, David E(gerton) 1920- ... 17-20R
Clarke, David Leonard 1937-1976
Obituary ... 111
Clarke, Derrick Harry 1919- ... 103
Clarke, Dorothy Clotelle
See Shadi, Dorothy Clotelle Clarke
Clarke, Dudley (Wrangel) 1899-1974 ... CAP-1
Earlier sketch in CA 13-16
Clarke, Duncan L(ynn) 1941- ... CANR-16
Earlier sketch in CA 97-100
Clarke, Dwight Lancelot 1885-1971 ... 1-4R
Obituary ... 103
Clarke, Edith 1883-1959 ... 157
Clarke, Elizabeth ... 173
Clarke, Ernest George 1927- ... 102
Clarke, Garry E(vans) 1943- ... 77-80
Clarke, George Elliott 1960- ... 192
Clarke, George Timothy ... CANR-1
Earlier sketch in CA 1-4R
Clarke, George Wallace
See Wallace-Clarke, George
Clarke, Gerald ... 206
Clarke, Gillian 1937- ... 106
See also CLC 61
See also CP 7
See also CWP
See also DLB 40
Clarke, Gus 1948- ... SATA 134
Clarke, H. Harrison 1902-1995 ... CANR-5
Earlier sketch in CA 1-4R
Clarke, Hans Thacher 1887-1972
Obituary ... 37-40R
Clarke, Harry Eugene, Jr. 1921- ... 5-8R
Clarke, Henry Charles 1899-1992 ... 102
Clarke, Hockley
See Clarke, Henry Charles
Clarke, Howard William 1929- ... 37-40R
Clarke, Hugh Vincent 1919-1996 ... CANR-41
Earlier sketches in CA 102, CANR-19
Clarke, I. F.
See Clarke, Ignatius (Ian) Frederick
Clarke, Ian
See Clarke, Ignatius (Ian) Frederick
Clarke, Ignatius (Ian) Frederick 1918- ... CANR-130
Earlier sketch in CA 116
Clarke, J.
See Clarke, Judith
Clarke, J(ohn) F(rederick) Gates 1905-1990 ... CAP-1
Obituary ... 132
Earlier sketch in CA 13-14
Clarke, Jack Alden 1924- ... 29-32R
Clarke, Jaime 1971- ... 207
Clarke, James 1934- ... 127
Clarke, James F(ranklin) 1906-1982 ... 69-72
Clarke, James Freeman 1810-1888 .. DLB 1, 59, 235
Clarke, James Hall
See Rowland-Entwistle, (Arthur) Theodore (Henry)
Clarke, James W(eston) 1937- ... CANR-42
Earlier sketch in CA 110
Clarke, Joan (Lorraine) 1920- ... 104
Clarke, Joan B. 1921- ... SATA 42
See also SATA-Brief 27
Clarke, Joan Dorn 1924- ... 9-12R
Clarke, John
See Laklan, Carli and Sontup, Dan(iel)
Clarke, John c. 1596-1658 ... DLB 281
Clarke, John (Campbell) 1913-(?) ... CAP-1
Earlier sketch in CA 13-16
Clarke, John Henrik 1915-1998 ... CANR-43
Obituary ... 169
Earlier sketches in CA 53-56, CANR-24
See also AITN 1
See also BW 2
Clarke, John Joseph 1879-1960 ... CANR-5
Earlier sketch in CA 5-8R
Clarke, John R. 1945- ... 141
Clarke, Judith 1943- ... CANR-123
Earlier sketch in CA 142
See also AAYA 34
See also CLR 61
See also SATA 75, 110
Clarke, Julia 1950-
Autobiographical Essay in ... 209 ... SATA 138
Clarke, Katherine ... 228
Clarke, Kenneth 1957- ... CANR-122
Earlier sketch in CA 169
See also SATA 107
Clarke, Kenneth W(endell) 1917- ... 17-20R
Clarke, Lea
See Rowland-Entwistle, (Arthur) Theodore (Henry)
Clarke, Lige 1942- ... 41-44R
Clarke, (Victor) Lindsay 1939- ... CANR-119
Earlier sketch in CA 127
See also DLB 231
Clarke, Marcus (Andrew Hislop) 1846-1881 ... DLB 230
See also RGEL 2
See also RGSF 2
Clarke, Margaret 1941- ... 130
See also CLR 99
Clarke, Martin Lowther 1909- ... CANR-2
Earlier sketch in CA 5-8R
Clarke, Mary 1923- ... 104
Clarke, Mary Stetson 1911-1994 ... CANR-8
Earlier sketch in CA 21-24R
See also SATA 5
Clarke, Mary Washington 1913-1999 ... CANR-11
Earlier sketch in CA 25-28R
Clarke, Mary Whatley 1899-1990 ... CANR-2
Earlier sketch in CA 5-8R
Clarke, Michael
See Newlon, (Frank) Clarke
Clarke, Nicholas Goodrick
See Goodrick-Clarke, Nicholas
Clarke, Nick ... 186
Clarke, Norman F. 1928- ... 196
Clarke, P(eter) F(rederick) 1942- ... 73-76
Clarke, Patricia 1926- ... 143
Clarke, Patsy 1929- ... 201
Clarke, Pauline 1921- ... CANR-45
See also Clare, Helen and Hunter Blair, Pauline
See also CLR 28
See also CWRI 5
See also DLB 161
See also MAICYA 1, 2
See also SATA 131
Clarke, Peter ... CP 1
Clarke, Peter 1936- ... CANR-121
Earlier sketch in CA 104
Clarke, Rebecca Sophia 1833-1906
Brief entry ... 119
See also DLB 42
Clarke, Richard
See Paine, Lauran (Bosworth)
Clarke, Richard (William Barnes) 1910-1975
Obituary ... 115
Clarke, Richard A. 1951- ... 223
Clarke, Robert
See Paine, Lauran (Bosworth) and Platt, Charles
Clarke, Robert B. 1942- ... 214
Clarke, Robin Harwood 1937- ... CANR-9
Earlier sketch in CA 13-16R
Clarke, Ron 1937- ... 107
Clarke, Ronald Francis 1933- ... 21-24R
Clarke, Sam 1948- ... CWRI 5
Clarke, Samuel 1676-1729 ... DLB 252
Clarke, Sarah 1919-2002 ... 219
Clarke, Shirley 1925-1997 ... 189
See also CLC 16
Clarke, Simon 1946- ... 122
Clarke, Stephan P(aul) 1945- ... 69-72
Clarke, Susanna 1959- ... 228
Clarke, Terence 1943- ... 172
Autobiographical Essay in ... 172
See also CAAS 28
Clarke, Thomas E(mmet) 1918- ... 53-56
Clarke, Thomas Ernest Bennett 1907-1989 ... CANR-19
Obituary ... 127
Earlier sketch in CA 103
See also IDFW 3, 4
Clarke, Thurston 1946- ... CANR-63
Earlier sketches in CA 77-80, CANR-13
Clarke, Tom E(ugene) 1915- ... 5-8R
Clarke, Victoria Mary ... 222
Clarke, William Dixon 1927- ... 5-8R
Clarke, William Kendall 1911(?)-1981
Obituary ... 104
Clarke, William M(alpas) 1922- ... CANR-34
Earlier sketches in CA 41-44R, CANR-15
Clarke, William Newton 1841-1912 ... 219
Clarke, William Thomas 1932- ... 57-60
Clarke-Rich, Elizabeth L. 1934- ... 170
See also SATA 103
Clarke-Stewart, K(athleen) Alison 1943- ... CANR-32
Earlier sketch in CA 113
Clark-Kennedy, A. E.
See Clark-Kennedy, Archibald Edmund
Clark-Kennedy, Archibald Edmund 1893-1985 ... 134
Obituary ... 117
Clark-Pendarvis, China 1950- ... 129
Clarkson, Adrienne 1939- ... 49-52
Clarkson, E(dith) Margaret 1915- ... CANR-20
Earlier sketches in CA 1-4R, CANR-5
See also SATA 37
Clarkson, Ewan 1929- ... CANR-17
Earlier sketch in CA 25-28R
See also SATA 9
Clarkson, Geoffrey P. E. 1934- ... CANR-2
Earlier sketch in CA 5-8R
Clarkson, Helen
See McCloy, Helen (Worrell Clarkson)
Clarkson, J. F.
See Tubb, E(dwin) C(harles)
Clarkson, Jan Nagel 1943- ... 93-96
Clarkson, Jesse Dunsmore 1897-1973 ... 5-8R
Obituary ... 45-48
Clarkson, John 1947- ... 177
Clarkson, L(eslie) A(lbert) 1933- ... 73-76
Clarkson, Ormand
See Richardson, Gladwell
Clarkson, Paul S(tephen) 1905-1998 ... 29-32R
Clarkson, Stephen 1937- ... 41-44R
Clarkson, Thomas 1760-1846 ... DLB 158
Clarkson, Tom 1913- ... 103
Clarkson, Wensley 1956- ... CANR-144
Earlier sketch in CA 156
Clarvoe, Jennifer ... 201
Clary, Jack 1932- ... 57-60
Clary, Killarney 1953- ... 148
Clary, Margie Willis 1931- ... 164
Clasen, Claus-Peter 1931- ... 41-44R
Clash, The
See Headon, (Nicky) Topper and Jones, Mick and Simonon, Paul and Strummer, Joe
Clason, Clyde B(urt) 1903-1987 ... 233
See also CMW 4
Clasper, Paul D(udley) 1923- ... 1-4R
Claspy, Everett M. 1907(?)-1973
Obituary ... 41-44R
Claster, Daniel S(tuart) 1932- ... 21-24R
Clatworthy, Nancy M(oore) K. 1924- ... 124
Claude, Richard (P.) 1934- ... 29-32R
Claudel, Alice Moser ... CANR-2
Earlier sketch in CA 49-52
Claudel, Paul (Louis Charles Marie) 1868-1955 ... 165
Brief entry ... 104
See also DLB 192, 258, 321
See also EW 8
See also EWL 3
See also GFL 1789 to the Present
See also RGWL 2, 3
See also TCLC 2, 10
See also TWA
Claude-Pierre, Peggy ... 176
Claudia, Sister Mary 1906- ... CAP-1
Earlier sketch in CA 9-10
Claudia, Susan
See Goulart, Ron(ald Joseph) and Johnston, William
Claudian 370(?)-404(?) ... RGWL 2, 3
Claudius, Matthias 1740-1815 ... DLB 97
Claus, Hugo (Maurice Julien) 1929- ... 168
Brief entry ... 116
See also CWW 2
See also EWL 3
See also RGWL 3
Claus, Marshall R. 1936-1970 ... CAP-2
Earlier sketch in CA 29-32
Clausen, Aage R. 1932- ... 49-52
Clausen, Andy 1943- ... 227
Brief entry ... 117
See also DLB 16
Clausen, Christopher (John) 1942- ... CANR-86
Earlier sketch in CA 130
Clausen, Connie 1923-1997 ... 1-4R
Obituary ... 161
Clausen, Dennis M(onroe) 1943- ... 106
Clausen, Jan 1950- ... 186
Clausen, Lowen ... 226
Clausen, Meredith L(eslie) 1942- ... 151
Clausen, W. V.
See Clausen, Wendell (Vernon)
Clausen, Wendell (Vernon) 1923- ... 121
Clauser, Suzanne (P.) 1929- ... 37-40R
Claussen, Sophus 1865-1931 ... DLB 300
Clavel, Bernard (Charles Henri) 1923- ... CANR-2
Earlier sketch in CA 45-48
Clavel, Maurice 1920-1979
Obituary ... 85-88
Clavel, Pierre ... 143
Clavell, James (duMaresq) 1925-1994 ... CANR-48
Obituary ... 146
Earlier sketches in CA 25-28R, CANR-26
See also BPFB 1
See also CLC 6, 25, 87
See also CN 5
See also CPW
See also DA3
See also DAM NOV, POP
See also MTCW 1, 2
See also MTFW 2005
See also NFS 10
See also RHW
Claverie, Jean 1946- ... SATA 38
Clavir, Miriam (Lisa) 1948- ... 207
Clawson, Calvin C. 1941- ... 148
Clawson, Dan 1948- ... 182
Clawson, James G. 1947- ... CANR-91
Earlier sketch in CA 145
Clawson, John L. 1865-1933 ... DLB 187
Clawson, Marion 1905-1998 ... CANR-10
Obituary ... 165
Earlier sketch in CA 65-68
Clawson, Robert W(ayne) 1939- ... CANR-25
Earlier sketch in CA 108
Claxton, Guy Lennox 1947- ... 186
Clay, Alison
See Keevill, Henry J(ohn)
Clay, Bertha M.
See Dey, Frederic (Merrill) Van Rensselaer
Clay, Cassius
See Ali, Muhammad
Clay, Cassius Marcellus 1810-1903
Brief entry ... 120
See also DLB 43
Clay, Charles Travis 1885-1978
Obituary ... 77-80
Clay, Christopher (G. A.) 1940- ... 128
Clay, Comer 1910- ... 45-48
Clay, Diskin 1938- ... 115
Clay, Edith 1910- ... 125
Clay, Floyd M(artin) 1927- ... 45-48
Clay, G. A.
See Trotter, Michael H(amilton)
Clay, Grady E. 1916- ... 93-96
Clay, James 1924- ... 17-20R
Clay, Jenny Strauss ... 125
Clay, Jim
See Clay, James
Clay, Lucius D(uBignon) 1897-1978 ... 81-84
Obituary ... 77-80
Clay, Marie M(ildred) 1926- ... CANR-22
Earlier sketches in CA 61-64, CANR-8
Clay, Patrice 1947- ... 106
See also SATA 47
Clay, Rita
See Estrada, Rita Clay
Clay, Roberta 1900-1974 ... CAP-2
Earlier sketch in CA 29-32
Clay, Rosamund
See Oakley, Ann (Rosamund)
Claybaugh, Amos L(incoln) 1917- ... 69-72
Claybourne, Casey ... 167
Claydon, Leslie Francis 1923- ... 53-56
Clayes, Stanley A(rnold) 1922- ... 29-32R
Clayman, Gregory ... CLC 65
Claypool, Jane
See Miner, Jane Claypool
See also SATA 103
Clayre, Alasdair 1935-1984 ... 102
Obituary ... 111
See also CP 1
Clayson, Alan 1951- ... 145
Clayson, (Susan) Hollis 1946- ... CANR-135
Earlier sketch in CA 140
Clayton, Aileen Bowen 1918-1981 ... 113
Clayton, Barbara
See Pluff, Barbara Littlefield
Clayton, Bruce 1939- ... 69-72
Clayton, C. Guy 1936- ... 122
See also RHW
Clayton, Charles C(urtis) 1902-1988 ... 73-76
Clayton, Donald D(elbert) 1935- ... 65-68
Clayton, Elaine 1961- ... 159
See also SATA 94, 159
Clayton, (Francis) Howard 1918- ... CANR-12
Earlier sketch in CA 29-32R
Clayton, Howard 1929- ... 65-68
Clayton, James E(dwin) 1929- ... 9-12R
Clayton, James L. 1931- ... CANR-12
Earlier sketch in CA 29-32R
Clayton, Jo 1939-1998 ... 81-84
Obituary ... 164
Clayton, John
See Beevers, John (Leonard)
Clayton, John 1892-1979 ... 33-36R
Obituary ... 89-92
Clayton, John J(acob) 1935- ... CANR-11
Earlier sketch in CA 25-28R
Clayton, Keith (M.) 1928- ... CANR-11
Earlier sketch in CA 21-24R
Clayton, Lawrence (Ray) 1938- ... CANR-92
Earlier sketch in CA 137
Clayton, Lawrence (Otto, Jr.) 1945- ... 142
See also SATA 75
Clayton, Martin 1967- ... 152
Clayton, Mary 1954- ... 136
Clayton, Michael 1934- ... 144
Clayton, Paul 1948- ... 224
Clayton, Paul C(lark) 1932- ... 61-64
Clayton, Peter A(rthur) 1937- ... 130

Clayton, Richard Henry Michael 1907-1993 ... CANR-79
Obituary ... 143
Earlier sketches in CA 5-8R, CANR-4, 29, 62
See also Haggard, William
See also CMW 4
Clayton, Sandra 1951- ... 180
See also SATA 110
Clayton, Susan
See Bailey, Alfred Goldsworthy
Clayton, Sylvia ... 103
Clayton, Thomas (Swoverland) 1932- ... CANR-100
Earlier sketch in CA 41-44R
Clayton, Thompson B(owker) 1904-1983 ... 57-60
Claytor, Gertrude Boatwright 1890(?)-1973
Obituary ... 45-48
Cleage, Albert B., Jr. 1911-2000 ... 65-68
Cleage, Pearl (Michelle) 1948- ... CANR-27
Earlier sketch in CA 41-44R
See also BW 2
See also DFS 14, 16
See also DLB 228
See also NFS 17
Cleall, Charles 1927- ... 5-8R
Clear, Todd R. 1949- ... 117
Cleare, John 1936- ... 65-68
Clearman, Brian (Patrick Joseph) 1941- ... CANR-38
Earlier sketch in CA 115
Cleary, Beverly (Atlee Bunn) 1916- ... CANR-129
Earlier sketches in CA 1-4R, CANR-2, 19, 36, 66, 85
Interview in ... CANR-19
See also AAYA 6, 62
See also BYA 1
See also CLR 2, 8, 72
See also CWRI 5
See also DA3
See also DLB 52
See also JRDA
See also MAICYA 1, 2
See also MTCW 1, 2
See also MTFW 2005
See also SAAS 20
See also SATA 2, 43, 79, 121
See also TUS
Cleary, Brian P. 1959- ... 159
See also SATA 93, 132
Cleary, David Powers 1915- ... 106
Cleary, Edward L. 1929- ... 140
Cleary, Florence Damon 1896-1982 ... 81-84
Obituary ... 133
Cleary, James W(illiam) 1927- ... 17-20R
Cleary, Johanna L. 1961- ... 122
Cleary, Jon (Stephen) 1917- ... CANR-52
Earlier sketches in CA 1-4R, CANR-3, 26
See also CMW 4
See also CN 1, 2, 3, 4, 5, 6
See also CPW
Cleary, Kate McPhelim 1863-1905 ... DLB 221
Cleary, Melissa ... CANR-141
Earlier sketch in CA 171
Cleary, Richard L(ouis) ... 185
Cleary, Robert E(dward) 1932- ... 41-44R
Cleator, P(hilip) E(llaby) 1908-1994 ... 102
Cleaver, Anastasia N. ... CANR-18
Earlier sketch in CA 97-100
Cleaver, Bill
See Cleaver, William J(oseph)
See also BYA 3
See also CLR 6
See also DLB 52
See also SATA 22
See also SATA-Obit 27
See also WYA
Cleaver, Carole 1934- ... 49-52
See also SATA 6
Cleaver, Dale G. 1928- ... 17-20R
Cleaver, (Leroy) Eldridge 1935-1998 ... CANR-75
Obituary ... 167
Earlier sketches in CA 21-24R, CANR-16
See also BLC 1
See also BW 1, 3
See also CLC 30, 119
See also DA3
See also DAM MULT
See also MTCW 2
See also YAW
Cleaver, Elizabeth (Ann Mrazik) 1939-1985 ... 97-100
Obituary ... 117
See also CLR 13
See also MAICYA 2
See also MAICYAS 1
See also SATA 23
See also SATA-Obit 43
Cleaver, Hylton Reginald 1891-1961 ... 73-76
See also SATA 49
Cleaver, Nancy
See Mathews, Evelyn Craw
Cleaver, Vera (Allen) 1919-1993 ... CANR-38
Obituary ... 161
Earlier sketch in CA 73-76
See also AAYA 12
See also BYA 3
See also CLR 6
See also DLB 52
See also JRDA
See also MAICYA 1, 2
See also SATA 22, 76
See also WYA
See also YAW 1
Cleaver, William J(oseph) 1920-1981 ... CANR-38
Obituary ... 104
Earlier sketch in CA 175
See also Cleaver, Bill
See also JRDA
See also MAICYA 1, 2
See also YAW
Cleaves, Emery N(udd) 1902-1989 ... 33-36R
Cleaves, Freeman 1904-1988 ... 1-4R
Cleaves, Peter S(hurtleff) 1943- ... 69-72
Clebsch, William Anthony 1923-1984 .. 13-16R
Obituary ... 113
Clecak, Peter (E.) 1938- ... 41-44R
Cleckley, Hervey Milton 1903-1984 ... 122
Obituary ... 111
Cleek, Richard K. 1945- ... 151
Cleese, John (Marwood) 1939- ... CANR-35
Brief entry ... 112
Earlier sketch in CA 116
See also Monty Python
See also CLC 21
See also MTCW 1
Cleeve, Brian (Talbot) 1921- ... CANR-16
Earlier sketches in CA 49-52, CANR-1
See also CMW 4
See also DLB 276
See also RHW
Cleeves, Ann 1954- ... 219
See also CMW 4
Clegg, Alec
See Clegg, Alexander Bradshaw
Clegg, Alexander Bradshaw 1909-1986 .. 85-88
Clegg, Brian ... 229
Clegg, Charles (Myron, Jr.) 1916- ... CANR-17
Earlier sketch in CA 25-28R
Clegg, Douglas 1958- ... 239
See also HGG
Clegg, Eileen M. 1952- ... 237
Clegg, Holly Berkowitz 1955- ... 154
Clegg, Jerry S(tephen) 1933- ... 77-80
Clegg, John 1909-1998 ... 118
Clegg, Reed K. 1907- ... CAP-1
Earlier sketch in CA 13-14
Clegg, Stewart (Roger) 1947- ... CANR-27
Earlier sketches in CA 69-72, CANR-11
Cleghorn, Reese 1930- ... 25-28R
Cleishbotham, Jebediah
See Scott, Sir Walter
Cleland, Charles C(arr) 1924- ... CANR-14
Earlier sketch in CA 41-44R
Cleland, Charles E(dward) 1936- ... 111
Cleland, David I. 1926- ... CANR-10
Earlier sketch in CA 25-28R
Cleland, Hugh
See Clarke, John (Campbell)
Cleland, John 1710-1789 ... DLB 39
See also RGEL 2
Cleland, Mabel
See Widdemer, Mabel Cleland
Cleland, (Joseph) Max(well) 1942- ... 129
Brief entry ... 113
Cleland, Morton
See Rennie, James Alan
Cleland, W(illiam) Wendell 1888-1972
Obituary ... 37-40R
Clelland, Catherine
See Townsend, Doris McFerran
Clelland, Richard C(ook) 1921- ... 17-20R
Clem, Alan L(eland) 1929- ... CANR-3
Earlier sketch in CA 9-12R
Clem, Margaret H(ollingsworth) 1923- ... 155
See also SATA 90
Clemeau, Carol
See Esler, Carol Clemeau
Clemen, Jane 1951(?)- ... 237
Clemen, Wolfgang Hermann 1909-1990 ... CANR-2
Earlier sketch in CA 1-4R
Clemence, Richard V(ernon) 1910-1982 ... 1-4R
Clemenceau, Georges (Eugene Benjamin) 1841-1929
Brief entry ... 114
Clemenko, Harold B. 1905-1984
Obituary ... 113
Clemens, Alphonse H. 1905-1977
Obituary ... 73-76
Clemens, Brian (Horace) 1931- ... 167
Clemens, Bryan T. 1934- ... 97-100
Clemens, Cyril 1902-1999 ... AITN 2
Clemens, Diane S(haver) 1936- ... 29-32R
Clemens, Rodgers
See Lovin, Roger Robert
Clemens, Samuel Langhorne 1835-1910 ... 135
Brief entry ... 104
See also Twain, Mark
See also CDALB 1865-1917
See also DA
See also DA3
See also DAB
See also DAC
See also DAM MST, NOV
See also DLB 12, 23, 64, 74, 186, 189
See also JRDA
See also LMFS 1
See also MAICYA 1, 2
See also NCFS 4
See also NFS 20
See also SATA 100
See also YABC 2
Clemens, Virginia Phelps 1941- ... CANR-15
Earlier sketch in CA 85-88
See also SATA 35
Clemens, Walter C., Jr. 1933- ... CANR-7
Earlier sketch in CA 17-20R
Clemens, Will 1970- ... 209
Clement, A(lfred) J(ohn) 1915- ... 25-28R
Clement, Aeron 1936(?)-1989
Obituary ... 127
Clement, Alison ... 207
Clement, Catherine 1939- ... 205
Clement, Charles B(axter) 1940-2002 ... 105
Obituary ... 210
Clement, Evelyn Geer 1926- ... 53-56
Clement, George H. 1909- ... 29-32R
Clement, Hal
See Stubbs, Harry C(lement)
See also CAAS 16
See also DLB 8
See also SCFW 1, 2
Clement, Herbert F(lint) 1927- ... 81-84
Clement, Jane Tyson 1917- ... 25-28R
Clement, Mary H. 1943- ... 193
Clement, Rod ... 163
See also SATA 97
Clement, Roland C(harles) 1912- ... 49-52
Clement, Russell T. 1952- ... 195
Clement, Wallace 1949- ... CANR-28
Earlier sketch in CA 111
Clement-Davies, David 1964- ... 194
Clemente, Maribeth 1962- ... 220
Clemente, Vince(nt L.) 1932- ... CANR-55
Earlier sketch in CA 127
Clements, A(rthur) L(eo) 1932- ... 29-32R
Clements, Alan 1948- ... CANR-138
Earlier sketch in CA 172
Clements, Alan 1951(?)- ... 172
Clements, Andrew 1949- ... CANR-126
Earlier sketch in CA 171
See also MAICYA 2
See also SATA 104, 158
Clements, Barbara Evans 1945- ... 89-92
Clements, Bruce 1931- ... CANR-68
Earlier sketches in CA 53-56, CANR-5
See also SATA 27, 94
See also YAW
Clements, Colleen D(ianne) 1936- ... 110
Clements, E(llen) Catherine (Scott) 1920- ... 13-16R
Clements, E(ileen) H(elen) 1905- ... CAP-1
Earlier sketch in CA 9-10
Clements, Frank A. 1942- ... 93-96
Clements, Harold M. Sr. 1907- ... 69-72
Clements, John 1916- ... CANR-11
Earlier sketch in CA 69-72
Clements, Jonathan 1963- ... 164
Clements, Julia 1906- ... CAP-1
Earlier sketch in CA 13-14
Clements, Kendrick Alling 1939- ... 110
Clements, Marcelle 1948- ... CANR-138
Earlier sketch in CA 121
Clements, Marie ... 180
Clements, Mark A. 1955- ... 136
Clements, Robert John 1912-1993 ... CANR-47
Obituary ... 142
Earlier sketches in CA 1-4R, CANR-5
Clements, Robert W(illiam) 1939- ... 110
Clements, Ronald Ernest 1929- ... 13-16R
Clements, Tad S. 1922- ... 25-28R
Clements, Traverse 1900(?)-1977
Obituary ... 69-72
Clements, William 1933(?)-1983
Obituary ... 110
Clements, William M(orris) 1943- ... 106
Clemhout, Simone 1934- ... 73-76
Cleminshaw, Clarence Higbee 1902-1985 . 134
Obituary ... 116
Brief entry ... 106
Clemmer, Richard O. 1945- ... 158
Clemmons, Francois 1945- ... 41-44R
Clemmons, Larry 1906(?)-1988
Obituary ... 127
Clemmons, Robert S(tarr) 1910-1995 ... CAP-2
Earlier sketch in CA 21-22
Clemmons, William (Preston) 1932- ... 57-60
Clemo, Jack
See Clemo, Reginald John
See also CP 1, 2
See also DLB 27
Clemo, Reginald John 1916-1994 ... CANR-6
Obituary ... 146
Earlier sketch in CA 13-16R
See also Clemo, Jack
Clemo, Richard F(rederick) 1920-1976
Obituary ... 65-68
Clemoes, Peter Alan Martin 1920-1996 ... 102
Obituary ... 151
Clemons, Elizabeth
See Nowell, Elizabeth Cameron
Clemons, Harry 1879-1968(?) ... CAP-1
Earlier sketch in CA 13-14
Clemons, Lulamae 1917- ... 73-76
Clemons, Walter, Jr. 1929-1994 ... CANR-6
Obituary ... 146
Earlier sketch in CA 1-4R
Clendenen, Clarence Clemens 1899-1977 ... 1-4R
Clendenin, Daniel B. ... 171
Clendenin, John C(ameron) 1903-1993 . 17-20R
Clendenin, William R(itchie) 1917-1979 ... 13-16R
Obituary ... 120
Clendenning, John 1934- ... 123
Clendenning, Sheila T. 1939- ... 25-28R
Clendinen, Dudley ... 233
Clendinnen, Inga 1934- ... CANR-120
Earlier sketch in CA 138
Cleobury, Frank Harold 1892- ... CAP-1
Earlier sketch in CA 13-14
Cleophil
See Congreve, William
Clephane, Elizabeth Cecilia 1830-1869 ... 166
See also DLB 199
Clephane, Irene (Amy) ... 13-16R
Clepper, Henry (Edward) 1901-1987 .. CANR-1
Obituary ... 122
Earlier sketch in CA 45-48
Clepper, Irene E(lizabeth) ... 53-56
Clerc, Charles 1926- ... CANR-14
Earlier sketch in CA 37-40R
Clergue, Lucien (Georges) 1934- ... CANR-129
Earlier sketch in CA 163
Clerici, Gianni 1930- ... 65-68
Clerihew, E.
See Bentley, E(dmund) C(lerihew)
Clerk, N. W.
See Lewis, C(live) S(taples)
Clery, (Reginald) Val(entine) 1924- ... CANR-3
Earlier sketch in CA 49-52
Cleugh, Mary F(rances) 1913- ... CANR-4
Earlier sketch in CA 1-4R
Cleugh, Sophia ... RHW
Cleve, Janita
See Rowland, D(onald) S(ydney)
Cleve, John
See Edmondson, G(arry) C(otton) and Green, Roland (James) and Haldeman, Jack C(arroll) II and Offutt, Andrew J(efferson V) and Proctor, Geo(rge W.) and Swain, Dwight V(reeland)
Cleveland, Bob
See Cleveland, George
Cleveland, Carles 1952- ... 85-88
Cleveland, Ceil 1940- ... CANR-140
Earlier sketch in CA 173
Cleveland, Clifford S.
See Goldsmith, David H(irsh)
Cleveland, George 1903(?)-1985
Obituary ... 116
See also SATA-Obit 43
Cleveland, (James) Harlan 1918- ... CANR-4
Earlier sketch in CA 1-4R
Cleveland, Harold van B(uren) 1916-1993 ... CANR-13
Obituary ... 140
Earlier sketch in CA 21-24R
Cleveland, Jim
See King, Albert
Cleveland, John
See McElfresh, (Elizabeth) Adeline
Cleveland, John 1613-1658 ... DLB 126
See also RGEL 2
Cleveland, Leslie 1921- ... 102
Cleveland, Mary 1917- ... 104
Cleveland, Philip Jerome 1903-1995 ... 9-12R
Cleveland, Ray L(eRoy) 1929- ... 21-24R
Cleveland, Sidney E(arl) 1919- ... 9-12R
Cleveland-Peck, Patricia ... CANR-105
Earlier sketch in CA 147
See also SATA 80
Cleven, Cathrine
See Cleven, Kathryn Seward
Cleven, Kathryn Seward ... 1-4R
See also SATA 2
Clevenger, Ernest Allen, Jr. 1929- ... CANR-8
Earlier sketch in CA 57-60
Clevenger, Theodore, Jr. 1929- ... 41-44R
Clevenger, William R(ussell) 1954- ... 150
See also SATA 84
Clever, (Warren) Glenn 1918- ... 57-60
Cleverdon, (Thomas) Douglas (James) 1903-1987 ... 29-32R
Obituary ... 123
Cleverley Ford, D(ouglas) W(illiam) 1914-1996 ... CANR-52
Earlier sketches in CA 25-28R, CANR-11, 28
Cleverly, Barbara ... 238
Cleves, Bernard
See Moore, Bernard
Clevin, Joergen 1920- ... 29-32R
See also SATA 7
Clevin, Jorgen
See Clevin, Joergen
Clew, Jeffrey Robert 1928- ... CANR-44
Earlier sketches in CA 57-60, CANR-6, 21
Clew, William J(oseph) 1904-1981 ... 77-80
Clewell, David 1955- ... 147
Clewes, Dorothy (Mary) 1907-2003 . CANR-52
Obituary ... 208
Earlier sketches in CA 5-8R, CANR-3
See also CWRI 5
See also SATA 1, 86
See also SATA-Obit 138
Clewes, Howard (Charles Vivian) 1912(?)-1988
Obituary ... 125
Clews, Roy 1937- ... 65-68
Click, J(ohn) W(illiam) 1936- ... 57-60
Cliff, Jimmy ... 193
See also Chambers, James
See also CLC 21
Cliff, Michelle 1946- ... CANR-72
Earlier sketches in CA 116, CANR-39
See also BLCS
See also BW 2
See also CDWLB 3
See also CLC 120
See also DLB 157
See also FW
See also GLL 2
Clifford, Alexandra
See Smith-Brown, Fern
Clifford, Lady Anne 1590-1676 ... DLB 151
Clifford, Barry 1945- ... 215
Clifford, Christine 1954- ... CANR-130
Earlier sketch in CA 164
Clifford, Clark (McAdams) 1906-1998 ... 140
Obituary ... 171
Clifford, Craig Edward 1951- ... 125
Clifford, David
See Rosenberg, Eth(el) Clifford

Cumulative Index 113 Coan

Clifford, Deborah Pickman 1933- 138
Clifford, Derek Plint 1915-2003 .... CANR-4
Obituary 221
Earlier sketch in CA 5-8R
Clifford, Eth
See Rosenberg, Eth(el) Clifford
See also MAICYAS 1
See also SAAS 22
See also SATA 92
Clifford, Francis
See Thompson, A(rthur) L(eonard) B(ell)
See also CN 2
Clifford, George 1934(?)-1985
Obituary 118
Clifford, Geraldine Joncich 1931- 25-28R
Clifford, H(enry) Dalton 1911- 9-12R
Clifford, Harold B(urton) 1893-1988 ..... CAP-1
Earlier sketch in CA 11-12
See also SATA 10
Clifford, J(ohn) Garry 1942- CANR-40
Earlier sketch in CA 53-56
Clifford, James L(owry) 1901-1978 ..... CANR-6
Obituary 77-80
Earlier sketch in CA 1-4R
See also DLB 103
Clifford, John
See Bayliss, John Clifford
See also CBD
Clifford, John E(dward) 1935- 37-40R
Clifford, John McLean 1904-1979 85-88
Clifford, John W(illiam) 1918- 17-20R
Clifford, Laurie B(erry) 1948- 112
Clifford, Lucy Lane 1853-1929 .. DLB 135, 141, 197
Clifford, Margaret Cort 1929- CANR-23
Earlier sketch in CA 25-28R
See also SATA 1
Clifford, Mark L. 1957- 222
Clifford, Martin
See Hamilton, Charles (Harold St. John)
Clifford, Martin 1910-2001 .... CANR-11
Earlier sketch in CA 25-28R
Clifford, Mary Louise Beneway
1926- CANR-3
Earlier sketch in CA 5-8R
See also SATA 23
Clifford, Nicholas R(owland) 1930- 21-24R
Clifford, Peggy
See Clifford, Margaret Cort
Clifford, Rachel Mark
See Lewis, Brenda Ralph
Clifford, Richard J(ohn) 1934- 112
Clifford, Sarah 1916-1976 .... CANR-11
Earlier sketch in CA 25-28R
Clifford, Theodore
See von Block, Sylvia
Clifford, Tony
See Slide, Anthony (Clifford)
Cliffton, Katherine Potter
See Bryant, Katherine Cliffton
Clift, Charmian 1923-1969 .... DLB 260
Clift, Elayne 1943- 179
Clift, Virgil Alfred 1912-1997 .... 9-12R
Clift, Wallace Bruce 1926- 110
Clifton, Bernice Marie 1901(?)-1985 .... 5-8R
Obituary 116
Clifton, Bud
See Stacton, David (Derek)
Clifton, Chas S. 1951- 144
Clifton, Frank M.
See Marion, Frances
Clifton, Fred J. 1935(?)-1984
Obituary 114
Clifton, Harry 1952- 195
See also CP 7
Clifton, Jack (Whitney) 1912-1990 106
Clifton, James A(lfonso) 1927- CANR-25
Earlier sketches in CA 25-28R, CANR-10
Clifton, James M(alcolm) 1930- 112
Clifton, Lewis
See Linedecker, Clifford L.
Clifton, (Thelma) Lucille 1936- CANR-138
Earlier sketches in CA 49-52, CANR-2, 24, 42, 76, 97
See also AFAW 2
See also BLC 1
See also BW 2, 3
See also CLC 19, 66, 162
See also CLR 5
See also CP 2, 3, 4, 5, 6, 7
See also CSW
See also CWP
See also CWRI 5
See also DA3
See also DAM MULT, POET
See also DLB 5, 41
See also EXPP
See also MAICYA 1, 2
See also MTCW 1, 2
See also MTFW 2005
See also PC 17
See also PFS 1, 14
See also SATA 20, 69, 128
See also WP
Clifton, Marguerite Ann 1925- 13-16R
Clifton, Mark (Irvin) 1906-1963 136
Obituary 117
See also SFW 4
Clifton, Oliver Lee
See Rathborne, St. George (Henry)
Clifton-Taylor, Alec 1907-1985 125
Clignot, Remi Pierre 1931- 104
Climo, Shirley 1928- CANR-91
Earlier sketches in CA 107, CANR-24, 49
See also CLR 69
See also CWRI 5
See also SATA 39, 77
See also SATA-Brief 35
See also SATA-Essay 110
Clinard, Dorothy Long 1909-1994 .... 5-8R
Clinard, Helen Hall 1931- 124
Clinard, Marshall B(arron) 1911- CANR-4
Earlier sketch in CA 5-8R
Clinard, Turner N(orman) 1917-1981 .... 37-40R
Obituary 135
Clinch, Nicholas (Bayard) 1930- 111
Clinchy, Everett R(oss) 1896-1986
Obituary 118
Cline, Bev
See Fink Cline, Beverly
Cline, Beverly
See Fink Cline, Beverly
Cline, Beverly Fink
See Fink Cline, Beverly
Cline, C(harles) Terry, Jr. 1935- CANR-50
Earlier sketches in CA 61-64, CANR-8, 25
Cline, Catherine Ann 1927- 17-20R
Cline, Charles (William) 1937- CANR-7
Earlier sketch in CA 61-64
Cline, Denzel C(ecil) 1903-1985 .... CAP-2
Earlier sketch in CA 21-22
Cline, Edward 1946- CANR-93
Earlier sketches in CA 101, CANR-40
Cline, Foster W. 1940- 145
Cline, Gloria Griffen 1929-1973 .... 5-8R
Obituary 125
Cline, Joan
See Hamilton, Joan Lesley
Cline, Leonard (Lanson) 1893-1929 .... HGG
Cline, Linda 1941- 65-68
Cline, Lynn Hunter 1961- 167
Cline, Rachel 229
Cline, Ray S(teiner) 1918-1996 133
Brief entry 106
Cline, Rodney 1903-1987 61-64
Cline, S(arah) L(ouise) 1948- 129
Cline, Victor (Bailey) 1925- 65-68
Cline, Wayne 1945- 172
Cline, William R. 1941- 145
Clinebell, Howard J., Jr. 1922-2005 . CANR-13
Obituary 238
Earlier sketch in CA 33-36R
Clines, Francis X. 1938- 183
See also DLB 185
Clinton, Bill
See Clinton, William Jefferson
Clinton, Catherine 1952- CANR-98
Earlier sketch in CA 130
Clinton, Cathryn
See Hoellwarth, Cathryn Clinton
Clinton, (Lloyd) D(eWitt) 1946- CANR-38
Earlier sketch in CA 116
Clinton, Dirk
See Silverberg, Robert
Clinton, F. G.
See Campbell, R(obert) Wright
Clinton, Hillary Rodham 1947- 153
Clinton, Iris A. (Corbin) 1901- CAP-1
Earlier sketch in CA 11-12
Clinton, James H(armon) 1946- 166
Clinton, James W(illiam) 1929- 163
Clinton, Jeff
See Bickham, Jack M(iles)
Clinton, Jerome W(right) 1937-2003 238
Clinton, Jon
See Prince, J(ack) H(arvey)
Clinton, Kate 1951- 172
Clinton, Richard Lee 1938- CANR-23
Earlier sketches in CA 61-64, CANR-8
Clinton, Rupert
See Bulmer, (Henry) Kenneth
Clinton, William Jefferson 1946- 165
Clinton-Baddeley, V(ictor) (Vaughan Reynolds Geraint) C(linton) 1911(?)-1970
Obituary 104
See also CMW 4
Clipman, William 1954- CANR-46
Earlier sketch in CA 106
Clipper, Lawrence Jon 1930- 49-52
Clish, (Lee) Marian 1946- .... SATA 43
Clissmann, Anne
See Clune, Anne
Clissold, (John) Stephen (Hallet)
1913-1982 110
Obituary 107
Clistier, Adeline
See Denny, Alma
Clithero, Myrtle E(ly) 1906-1983 .... CAP-2
Earlier sketch in CA 25-28
Clithero, Sally
See Clithero, Myrtle E(ly)
Clive, Caroline (V) 1801-1873 .... DLB 199
Clive, Clifford
See Hamilton, Charles (Harold St. John)
Clive, Dennis
See Fearn, John Russell
Clive, Geoffrey 1927-1976 .... 33-36R
Clive, John
See Clive, John Leonard
Clive, John 1933- 103
Clive, John Leonard 1924-1990 .... CANR-43
Obituary 130
Earlier sketch in CA 85-88
Clive, Mary 1907- 21-24R
Clive, William
See Bassett, Ronald
Cloake, John (Cecil) 1924- 133
Clodfelter, (William) Frank(lin) 1911-1984 .. 103
Clodfelter, Micheal D. 1946- CANR-31
Earlier sketch in CA 69-72
Cloeren, Hermann J(osef) 1934- 41-44R
Cloete, Stuart 1897-1976 .... CANR-3
Obituary 65-68
Earlier sketch in CA 1-4R
See also CN 1, 2
Clogan, Paul M(aurice) 1934- 33-36R
Clogg, Clifford C(ollier) 1949-1995 112
Obituary 148
Clogg, Richard 1939- 207
Cloke, Richard 1916- CANR-11
Earlier sketch in CA 69-72
Clokey, Art 1921- .... SATA 59
Clokey, Richard M(ontgomery) 1936- 127
Brief entry 107
Clones, N(icholas) J. 97-100
Clopper, Lawrence M., Jr. 1941- 230
Clopton, Beverly Virginia B(eck) 106
Cloquet, Ghislain 1924-1981 .... IDFW 3, 4
Clor, Harry M(ortimer) 1929- 53-56
Clore, Gerald L(ewis, Jr.) 1939- 37-40R
Close, A. Kathryn 1908(?)-1973
Obituary 41-44R
Close, Ajay 233
Close, Chuck 1940- .... AAYA 28
Close, Frank (E.) 1945- CANR-100
Earlier sketch in CA 126
Close, Henry T(hompson) 1928- 1-4R
Close, Reginald Arthur 1909-1996 .... 17-20R
Obituary 154
Close, Upton
See Hall, Josef Washington
Closen, Michael L. 1949- 121
Closs, August 1898-1990 .... CANR-2
Obituary 132
Earlier sketch in CA 5-8R
Closs, Elizabeth
See Traugott, Elizabeth Closs
Clot, Andre 1909- 156
Clotfelter, Beryl E(dward) 1926- 53-56
Clotfelter, Cecil F. 1929- 53-56
Clotfelter, Charles T. 1947- CANR-90
Earlier sketch in CA 131
Clotfelter, Mary (Eunice) L(ong) 103
Clothier, Peter (Dean) 1936- 65-68
Clothier, William H. 1903-1996 ...... IDFW 3, 4
Cloud, Dan
See Cloud, Daniel Tuttle, Jr.
Cloud, Daniel Tuttle, Jr. 1925- 199
Cloud, Darrah 1955- 231
See also CAD
See also CD 5, 6
See also CWD
Cloud, (Joseph) Fred (Jr.) 1925- 13-16R
Cloud, Patricia
See Strother, Pat Wallace
Cloud, Preston (Ercelle) 1912-1991 93-96
Obituary 133
Cloud, Yvonne
See Kapp, Yvonne (Mayer)
Cloudsley-Thompson, J(ohn) L(eonard)
1921- CANR-23
Earlier sketches in CA 17-20R, CANR-8
See also SATA 19
Clough, Arthur Hugh 1819-1861 .... BRW 5
See also DLB 32
See also RGEL 2
Clough, B(renda) W(ang) 1955- CANR-65
Earlier sketch in CA 116
Clough, Brenda
See Clough, B(renda) W(ang)
Clough, Francis F(rederick) 1912- CAP-1
Earlier sketch in CA 9-10
Clough, Neil 1950- 112
Clough, Ralph Nelson 1916-
Brief entry 105
Clough, Rosa Trillo 1906-2001 .... 13-16R
Clough, Shepard B(ancroft)
1901-1990 .... CANR-4
Obituary 131
Earlier sketch in CA 1-4R
Clough, William 1911(?)-1976
Obituary 69-72
Clough, William A. 1899-1974 .... CAP-2
Earlier sketch in CA 21-22
Clough, Wilson O(ber) 1894-1990 .... 17-20R
Obituary 161
Clouse, Nancy L. 1938- .... SATA 78
Clouse, Robert Gordon 1931- CANR-12
Earlier sketch in CA 29-32R
Clouser, John William 1932- 61-64
Clouser, Roy A. 1937- 146
Clout, Hugh Donald 1944- CANR-90
Earlier sketches in CA 41-44R, CANR-15, 34
Cloutier, Cecile
See Cloutier-Wojciechowska, Cecile
See also DLB 60
Cloutier, David 1951- CANR-49
Earlier sketches in CA 57-60, CANR-7
Cloutier-Wojciechowska, Cecile
1930- CANR-12
Earlier sketch in CA 65-68
See also Cloutier, Cecile
Clouts, Sydney 1926-1982 207
See also CP 1, 2
See also DLB 225
Clover, Frank Metlar III 1940- 101
Clover, Peter 1952- 227
See also SATA 152
Clovis, Allen M. 1953- 143
Clow, Barbara Hand 1943- CANR-82
Earlier sketch in CA 133
Clow, Martha de Mev 1932- 29-32R
Cloward, Richard Andrew 1926-2001 ... 41-44R
Obituary 201
Clower, Robert W(ayne) 1926- 89-92
Clowes, Daniel 1961- 191
See also AAYA 42
See also MTFW 2005
Clowes, E. M.
See Wiehe, Evelyn May Clowes
Clowney, Edmund P(rosper) 1917- CANR-8
Earlier sketch in CA 5-8R
Clowse, Barbara Barksdale 1937- 195
Clowse, Converse Dilworth 1929- 127
Brief entry 108
Clubb, Louise George 1930- 69-72
Clubb, O(liver) Edmund 1901-1989 ...... 37-40R
Obituary 128
Clubb, Oliver E., Jr. 1929- 5-8R
Clubbe, John 1938- CANR-119
Earlier sketches in CA 25-28R, CANR-11
Clube, (Stace) Victor (Murray) 1934- 130
Cluchey, (Douglas) Rick(land) 1933- 231
See also CAD
See also CD 5
Cluff, Charles E. 1937- 65-68
Cluff, Russell M. 1946- 154
Clugston, Richard 1938- 41-44R
Clulee, Nicholas H(arkins) 1945- 187
Clum, John M(acKenzie) 1941- CANR-121
Earlier sketch in CA 69-72
Clun, Arthur
See Polsby, Nelson W(oolf)
Clune, Anne 1945- 103
Clune, Francis Patrick 1893-1971 .... CAP-2
Obituary 29-32R
Earlier sketch in CA 23-24
Clune, Frank
See Clune, Francis Patrick
Clune, Henry W. 1890-1995 .... CANR-5
Obituary 161
Earlier sketch in CA 1-4R
Clunies Ross, Anthony (Ian) 1932- 53-56
Clunis, D. Merilee 166
Clurman, Harold 1901-1980 .... CANR-2
Obituary 101
Earlier sketch in CA 1-4R
Cluster, Dick 1947- 97-100
Clute, John 1940- 205
Clute, Morrel J. 1912-1995 .... 13-16R
Clute, Robert E(ugene) 1924- 41-44R
Clutha, Janet Paterson Frame
1924-2004 .... CANR-135
Obituary 224
Earlier sketches in CA 1-4R, CANR-2, 36, 76
See also Frame, Janet
See also MTCW 1, 2
See also SATA 119
Clutterbuck, David Ashley 1947- 113
Clutterbuck, Richard 1917-1998 ...... CANR-50
Obituary 163
Earlier sketches in CA 21-24R, CANR-9, 25
Clutton-Brock, Arthur 1868-1924 .... DLB 98
Clutton-Brock, Arthur Guy 1906-1995 110
Obituary 147
Cluver, Eustace Henry 1894-1982 .... CAP-1
Earlier sketch in CA 9-10
Cluysenaar, Anne (Alice Andree Jackson)
1936- 102
See also CP 1, 2, 3, 4, 5, 6, 7
See also CWP
Clybourn, Craig
See Hensley, Dennis
Clyde, Laurel Anne 1946- 207
Clyde, Leslie
See Kipps, Harriet C(lyde)
Clyde, Mary 1953- 190
Clyde, Norman Asa 1885-1972 .... 41-44R
Clyde Cool
See Frazier, Walt(er)
Clymer, Adam 1937- 188
Clymer, Eleanor 1906-2001 .... CANR-51
Obituary 194
Earlier sketches in CA 61-64, CANR-9
See also CWRI 5
See also SAAS 17
See also SATA 9, 85
See also SATA-Obit 126
Clymer, (Joseph) Floyd 1895-1970
Obituary 104
Clymer, Kenton James 1943- 127
Brief entry 109
Clymer, Reuben Swinburne 1878-1966 . CAP-1
Earlier sketch in CA 11-12
Clynder, Monica
See Muir, Marie
Clyne, James F. 1898(?)-1977
Obituary 69-72
Clyne, Patricia (Edwards) 101
See also SATA 31
Clyne, Terence
See Blatty, William Peter
Clynes, Michael
See Doherty, P(aul) C.
Clytus, John 1929- 29-32R
Cnudde, Charles F(rancis) 1938- CANR-26
Earlier sketch in CA 29-32R
Coad, F(rederick) Roy 1925- 103
Coad, Oral Sumner 1887-1976 45-48
Coade, Jessie 1911- 120
Coady, Lynn 1970- 189
Coakley, Lakme 1912-2002 69-72
Coakley, Mary Lewis CAP-1
Earlier sketch in CA 13-16
Coakley, Michael 1947(?)-1988
Obituary 126
Coale, Samuel Chase 1943- CANR-52
Earlier sketches in CA 65-68, CANR-11, 27
Coalson, Glo 1946- CANR-68
Earlier sketch in CA 103
See also SATA 26, 94
Coan, Eugene V(ictor) 1943- 110

Coan, Otis W(elton) 1895-1984 ... CAP-2
Earlier sketch in CA 33-36
Coan, Richard Welton 1928- ... CANR-12
Earlier sketch in CA 69-72
Coarelli, Filippo 1936- ... 233
Coates, Anna 1958- ... SATA 73
Coates, Austin 1922- ... 102
Coates, Belle 1896-1986 ... 5-8R
Obituary ... 161
See also SATA 2
Coates, Carrol F(ranklin) 1930- ... 199
Coates, Charles (K.) 1929- ... 146
Coates, Charles R(obert) 1915- ... 106
Coates, David 1946- ... CANR-93
Earlier sketches in CA 125, CANR-57
Coates, Deborah 1954- ... 204
Coates, Donald R(obert) 1922- ... CANR-2
Earlier sketch in CA 49-52
Coates, Doreen (Frances) 1912- ... 107
Coates, Gary J(oseph) 1947- ... 110
Coates, Geoffrey Edward 1917- ... 37-40R
Coates, J(ohn) F(rancis) 1922- ... CANR-108
Earlier sketches in CA 123, CANR-49
Coates, K. S.
See Coates, Kenneth (Stephen)
Coates, Ken
See Coates, Kenneth (Stephen)
Coates, Ken 1930- ... CANR-50
Earlier sketch in CA 123
Coates, Ken S.
See Coates, Kenneth (Stephen)
Coates, Kenneth (Stephen) 1956- ... 130
Coates, Lawrence 1956- ... 206
Coates, Robert C(rawford) 1937- ... 134
Coates, Robert M(yron) 1897-1973 ... 5-8R
Obituary ... 41-44R
See also CN 1
See also DLB 4, 9, 102
Coates, Ruth Allison 1915- ... 57-60
See also SATA 11
Coates, Sheila
See Holland, Sheila
Coates, Steven L. 1955- ... 232
Coates, W. Paul 1945- ... 136
Coates, William Ames 1916-1973 ... 37-40R
Coates, Willson H(avelock) 1899-1976 ... CANR-33
Obituary ... 69-72
Earlier sketch in CA 37-40R
Coats, Alice M(argaret) 1905-1976 ... 53-56
See also SATA 11
Coats, Daniel R(ay) 1943- ... 193
Coats, George W. 1936- ... 21-24R
Coats, Peter 1910-1990 ... CANR-78
Obituary ... 132
Earlier sketches in CA 49-52, CANR-1
Coats, Wendell John, Jr. 1947- ... 202
Coatsworth, Elizabeth (Jane) 1893-1986 ... CANR-78
Obituary ... 120
Earlier sketches in CA 5-8R, CANR-4
See also BYA 5
See also CLR 2
See also CWRI 5
See also DLB 22
See also MAICYA 1, 2
See also SATA 2, 56, 100
See also SATA-Obit 49
See also YAW
Coatsworth, John H(enry) 1940- ... 148
Cobain, Kurt (Donald) 1967-1994 ... 226
Cobalt, Martin
See Mayne, William (James Carter)
Cobb, Alice 1909-1995 ... 5-8R
Cobb, Carl W(esley) 1926- ... 21-24R
Cobb, Charles E(arl), Jr. 1943- ... CANR-138
Earlier sketch in CA 142
See also BW 2
See also DLB 41
Cobb, Clifford (William) 1951- ... 162
Cobb, David 1934- ... 112
Cobb, Faye Davis 1932- ... 9-12R
Cobb, Frank I(rving) 1869-1923 ... 175
See also DLB 25
Cobb, Geoffrey Belton 1892(?)-1971
Obituary ... 104
Cobb, Irvin S(hrewsbury) 1876-1944 ... 175
See also DLB 11, 25, 86
See also TCLC 77
Cobb, James Charles 1947- ... CANR-31
Earlier sketch in CA 112
Cobb, James H(arvey) 1953- ... CANR-88
Earlier sketch in CA 154
Cobb, Jane
See Berry, Jane Cobb
Cobb, John B(oswell), Jr. 1925- ... CANR-2
Earlier sketch in CA 1-4R
Cobb, Jonathan 1946- ... 93-96
Cobb, Mary 1931- ... SATA 88
Cobb, Nancy (Howard) 1949- ... 137
Cobb, Nathan 1943- ... 105
Cobb, R. C.
See Cobb, Richard (Charles)
Cobb, Richard (Charles) 1917-1996 ... 128
Obituary ... 151
Brief entry ... 116
Cobb, Robert A. 1941- ... 69-72
Cobb, Roger W(illiam) 1941- ... 104
Cobb, Thomas 1947- ... 136
Cobb, Vicki 1938- ... CANR-14
Earlier sketch in CA 33-36R
See also CLR 2
See also JRDA
See also MAICYA 1, 2
See also SAAS 6
See also SATA 8, 69, 131, 136
See also SATA-Essay 136
Cobb, William (Sledge) 1937- ... 196
See also CN 6, 7
See also CSW
Cobban, Alfred 1901-1968
Obituary ... 111
Cobbe, Frances Power 1822-1904 ... 182
See also DLB 190
See also FW
Cobbett
See Ludovici, Anthony M(ario)
Cobbett, Richard
See Pluckrose, Henry (Arthur)
Cobbett, William 1763-1835 ... DLB 43, 107, 158
See also RGEL 2
Cobbing, Bob 1920-2002 ... 101
Obituary ... 210
See also CP 1, 2, 3, 4, 5, 6, 7
Cobble, Dorothy Sue 1949- ... 237
Cobbledick, Gordon 1898-1969 ... 202
See also DLB 171
Cobbledick, James R. 1935- ... 97-100
Cobbold, Marika ... 236
Cobbs, Elizabeth Anne 1956- ... 144
Cobbs, John L(ewis) 1917- ... 176
Brief entry ... 115
Cobbs, Lisa
See Cobbs, Elizabeth Anne
Cobbs, Price M(ashaw) 1928- ... CANR-130
Earlier sketch in CA 21-24R
Coben, Harlan 1962- ... 164
Coben, Lawrence A(llan) 1926- ... 111
Coben, Stanley 1929- ... 122
Cober, Alan E(dwin) 1935-1998 ... SATA 7
See also SATA-Obit 101
Coberly, Lenore McComas 1925- ... 229
Cobham, Sir Alan
See Hamilton, Charles (Harold St. John)
Coble, John (Lawrence) 1924- ... 9-12R
Cobleigh, Ira U(nderwood) 1903-1995 ... 81-84
Coblentz, Stanton A(rthur) 1896-1982 ... CANR-21
Obituary ... 161
Earlier sketch in CA 5-8R
See also SFW 4
Cobley, John 1914-1989 ... 13-16R
Cobos, Ruben 1911- ... 135
Cobrin, Harry Aaron 1902-1989 ... CAP-2
Earlier sketch in CA 29-32
Coburn, Andrew 1932- ... CANR-108
Earlier sketches in CA 53-56, CANR-4, 36
See also CMW 4
Coburn, Ann ... CANR-121
Earlier sketch in CA 172
Coburn, Broughton 1951- ... 111
Coburn, D(onald) L(ee) 1938- ... 89-92
See also CLC 10
Coburn, Jake 1978- ... 229
See also SATA 155
Coburn, John Bowen 1914- ... CANR-2
Earlier sketch in CA 1-4R
Coburn, Karen Levin 1941- ... 65-68
Coburn, Kathleen 1905-1991 ... CANR-78
Obituary ... 135
Earlier sketch in CA 93-96
Coburn, L. J.
See Harvey, John (Barton) and James, Laurence
Coburn, Louis 1915-2003 ... 104
Obituary ... 215
Coburn, Thomas B(owen) 1944- ... 110
Coburn, Walt(er John) 1889-1971 ... CANR-61
Obituary ... 161
Earlier sketches in CAP-1, CA 9-10
See also TCWW 1, 2
Coca, Jordi 1947- ... 206
Cocagnac, Augustin Maurice(-Jean) 1924- ... CANR-17
Earlier sketch in CA 25-28R
See also SATA 7
Cocca-Leffler, Maryann 1958- ... SATA 80, 136
Coccioli, Carlo 1920- ... CANR-9
Earlier sketches in CA 13-16R, CANR-31
Cochard, Thomas S(ylvester) 1893-1975 . 57-60
Cochet, Gabriel 1888-1973
Obituary ... 45-48
Cochran, Bert 1917-1984 ... CANR-78
Obituary ... 113
Earlier sketch in CA 45-48
Cochran, Bobbye A. 1949- ... SATA 11
Cochran, Charles L(eo) 1940- ... 57-60
Cochran, Clarke E(dward) 1945- ... 107
Cochran, Elizabeth
See Cochrane, Elizabeth
Cochran, Hamilton 1898-1977 ... CANR-6
Obituary ... 73-76
Earlier sketch in CA 1-4R
Cochran, Jacqueline 1910(?)-1980
Obituary ... 101
Cochran, Jeff
See Durst, Paul
Cochran, John A(rthur) 1921- ... 122
Cochran, John R(obert) 1937- ... 41-44R
Cochran, Johnnie L., Jr. 1937-2005 ... 217
Obituary ... 237
Cochran, Leslie H(ershel) 1939- ... CANR-2
Earlier sketch in CA 49-52
Cochran, Mary E. 1916- ... 214
Cochran, Molly ... 156
See also FANT
Cochran, Rice E.
See Monroe, Keith
Cochran, Robert (Brady) 1943- ... CANR-144
Earlier sketch in CA 141
Cochran, Thomas C(hilds) 1902-1999 ... CANR-8
Obituary ... 179
Earlier sketch in CA 61-64
See also DLB 17
Cochrane, A(rchibald) L(eman) 1909(?)-1988
Obituary ... 125
Cochrane, Arthur C(aspersz) 1909- ... CANR-4
Earlier sketch in CA 5-8R
Cochrane, Becky ... 229
Cochrane, Elizabeth 1864-1922
Brief entry ... 118
See also Seaman, Elizabeth Cochrane
See also DLB 25, 189
Cochrane, Eric W. 1928-1985 ... CANR-28
Obituary ... 118
Earlier sketch in CA 49-52
Cochrane, Feargal 1965- ... 177
Cochrane, Glynn 1940- ... 53-56
Cochrane, Hugh (Ferrier) 1923- ... 103
Cochrane, James D(avid) 1938- ... 29-32R
Cochrane, James L. 1941- ... CANR-13
Earlier sketch in CA 33-36R
Cochrane, Jennifer (Ann Frances) 1936- ... 102
Cochrane, Louise Morley 1918- ... 9-12R
Cochrane, Pauline A(therton) 1929- ... 110
Cochrane, Willard W(esley) 1914- ... CANR-11
Earlier sketch in CA 21-24R
Cochrane, William E. 1926- ... 97-100
Cochrane de Alencar, Gertrude E. L. 1906- ... 5-8R
Cochran-Smith, Marilyn 1951- ... 115
Coch-y-Bonddhu
See Arnold, Richard
Cockburn, Alexander 1941- ... CANR-104
Brief entry ... 123
Earlier sketch in CA 144
Cockburn, Andrew 1947- ... 188
Cockburn, (Francis) Claud 1904-1981 ... CANR-78
Obituary ... 105
Earlier sketch in CA 102
Cockburn, Patricia (Evangeline Anne) 1914-1989 ... 144
Cockburn, Patrick 1950- ... 203
Cockburn, Sarah 1939-2000 ... 199
See also Caudwell, Sarah
Cockburn, Thomas Aiden 1912-1981 ... 9-12R
Cockcroft, George Powers 1932- ... 116
Cockcroft, James D(onald) 1935- ... CANR-65
Earlier sketches in CA 25-28R, CANR-10, 25
Cockcroft, John (Douglas) 1897-1967 ... CAP-2
Earlier sketch in CA 21-22
Cocker, Mark 1959- ... CANR-141
Earlier sketch in CA 176
Cockerell, H(ugh) A(nthony) L(ewis) 1909-1996 ... CAP-1
Earlier sketch in CA 13-14
Cockerell, Sir Sydney 1867-1962 ... DLB 201
Cockerell, Sydney M(orris) 1906-1987
Obituary ... 124
Cockerill, A(rthur) W(illiam) 1929- ... 131
Cockerill, John A. 1845-1896 ... DLB 23
Cockett, Mary ... CANR-19
Earlier sketches in CA 9-12R, CANR-4
See also CWRI 5
See also SATA 3
Cockfield, Jamie (Hartwell) 1945- ... 115
Cocking, Clive 1938- ... 105
Cocking, J(ohn) M(artin) 1914-1986 ... 53-56
Cockrell, Amanda 1948- ... 101
Cockrell, Marian (Brown) 1909-1999 ... CAP-2
Earlier sketch in CA 17-18
See also RHW
Cockrell, Thomas D(errell) 1949- ... 154
Cocks, Geoffrey (Campbell) 1948- ... CANR-98
Earlier sketches in CA 121, CANR-47
Cocks, Nancy L. ... 226
Cockshut, A(nthony) O(liver) J(ohn) 1927- ... CANR-10
Earlier sketch in CA 17-20R
Cocles, Angelo ... GLL 2
Coco, James (Emil) 1930(?)-1987
Obituary ... 121
Cocozzella, Peter 1937- ... 37-40R
Cocozzoli, Gary R(ichard) 1951- ... 119
Cocquyt, Kathryn Marie 1960- ... 147
Cocteau, Jean (Maurice Eugene Clement) 1889-1963 ... CANR-40
Earlier sketches in CAP-2, CA 25-28
See also CLC 1, 8, 15, 16, 43
See also DA
See also DA3
See also DAB
See also DAC
See also DAM DRAM, MST, NOV
See also DC 17
See also DLB 65, 258, 321
See also EW 10
See also EWL 3
See also GFL 1789 to the Present
See also MTCW 1, 2
See also RGWL 2, 3
See also TCLC 119
See also TWA
See also WLC
Codd, Carson
See Sommers, Robert (Thomas)
Coddell, Esme Raji
See Codell, Esme Raji
Codding, George A(rthur), Jr. 1923- ... CANR-13
Earlier sketch in CA 33-36R
Code, Grant Hyde 1896-1974 ... 49-52
Codel, Martin 1903(?)-1973
Obituary ... 41-44R
Codel, Michael R(ichard) 1939- ... 73-76
Codell, Esme Raji 1968- ... 191
See also SATA 160
Coder, S(amuel) Maxwell 1902-1997 ... CANR-14
Obituary ... 159
Earlier sketch in CA 37-40R
Codere, Helen (Frances) 1917- ... 69-72
Coderre, Emile 1893-1970 ... 148
See also Narrache, Jean
See also CCA 1
Codevilla, (Maria) Angelo 1943- ... 61-64
Codrescu, Andrei 1946- ... CANR-125
Earlier sketches in CA 33-36R, CANR-13, 34, 53, 76
See also CAAS 19
See also CLC 46, 121
See also CN 7
See also DA3
See also DAM POET
See also MAL 5
See also MTCW 2
See also MTFW 2005
Codrington, Kenneth de Burgh 1899-1986
Obituary ... 118
Cody, Al
See Joscelyn, Archie L(ynn)
Cody, C. S.
See Waller, Leslie
Cody, D(ouglas) Thane R(omney) 1932- .. 57-60
Cody, Fred 1916- ... 107
Cody, James P.
See Rohrbach, Peter Thomas
Cody, Jeffrey W. 1950- ... 216
Cody, Jess
See Cunningham, Chet
Cody, John
See Repp, Ed(ward) Earl
Cody, John 1925- ... 101
Cody, John J. 1930- ... 29-32R
Cody, Liza 1944- ... CANR-71
Brief entry ... 125
Earlier sketch in CA 129
See also CMW 4
See also DLB 276
Cody, Martin L(eonard) 1941- ... 53-56
Cody, Morrill 1901-1987 ... 125
Obituary ... 161
Cody, Paul 1953- ... 153
Cody, Robin 1943- ... 153
Cody, Stetson
See Gribble, Leonard (Reginald)
See also TCWW 1
Cody, Walt
See Norwood, Victor G(eorge) C(harles)
Coe, Anne (E.) 1949- ... SATA 95
Coe, Charles Norton 1915- ... 1-4R
Coe, Christine Sadler
See Sadler, Christine
Coe, David B. 1963- ... 214
Coe, Douglas
See Epstein, Beryl (M. Williams) and Epstein, Samuel
Coe, Fred(erick) 1914-1979
Obituary ... 85-88
Coe, George Albert 1862-1951 ... 219
Coe, Jonathan (Roger) 1961- ... CANR-82
Earlier sketch in CA 133
See also CN 6, 7
See also DLB 231
Coe, Lewis 1911- ... 154
Coe, Lloyd 1899(?)-1976
Obituary ... 69-72
See also SATA-Obit 30
Coe, Malcolm (James) 1930- ... 123
Coe, Marian 1931- ... 219
Coe, Max
See Bourne, Randolph S(illiman)
Coe, Michael Douglas 1929- ... CANR-121
Earlier sketches in CA 1-4R, CANR-4, 19, 41
Coe, Michelle E(ileen) 1917- ... 106
Coe, Peter 1929-1987
Obituary ... 122
Coe, Ralph T(racy) 1929- ... CANR-1
Earlier sketch in CA 1-4R
Coe, Richard L(ivingston) 1916- ... 65-68
Coe, Richard N(elson) 1923- ... CANR-12
Earlier sketch in CA 25-28R
Coe, Rodney Michael 1933- ... 41-44R
Coe, Sue 1951- ... CANR-116
Earlier sketches in CA 151, CANR-115
Coe, Tucker
See Westlake, Donald E(dwin)
Coe, William C(harles) 1930- ... 37-40R
Coel, Margaret 1937- ... 222
Earlier sketches in CA 106, CANR-39, 72
Autobiographical Essay in ... 222
Coelho, George Victor 1918- ... CANR-1
Earlier sketch in CA 45-48
Coelho, Ivo 1958- ... 239
Coelho, Paulo 1947- ... CANR-93
Earlier sketches in CA 152, CANR-80
Coelho, Susie ... 218
Coelho Neto, Henrique 1864-1934 ... 178
See also HW 2
Coello, Dennis (L.) ... 129
Coen, Chere (Dastugue) 1960- ... 216
Coen, Ethan 1958- ... CANR-85
Earlier sketch in CA 126
See also AAYA 54
See also CLC 108
Coen, Joel 1955- ... CANR-119
Earlier sketch in CA 126
See also AAYA 54
See also CLC 108
Coen, Rena Neumann 1925- ... 13-16R
See also SATA 20

Cumulative Index 115 Cohen

The Coen Brothers
See Coen, Ethan and
Coen, Joel
Coens, Sister Mary Xavier 1918- 21-24R
Coerr, Eleanor (Beatrice) 1922- CANR-11
Earlier sketch in CA 25-28R
See also CWRI 5
See also MAICYA 1, 2
See also SATA 1, 67
Coers, Donald V. 1941- 139
Coetzee, J(ohn) M(axwell) 1940- CANR-133
Earlier sketches in CA 77-80, CANR-41, 54, 74, 114
See also AAYA 37
See also AFW
See also BRWS 6
See also CLC 23, 33, 66, 117, 161, 162
See also CN 4, 5, 6, 7
See also DA3
See also DAM NOV
See also DLB 225
See also EWL 3
See also LMFS 2
See also MTCW 1, 2
See also MTFW 2005
See also NFS 21
See also WLIT 2
See also WWE 1
Cofacci, Gino P. 1914(?)-1989
Obituary 128
Cofer, Charles N(orval) 1916-1998 .... 37-40R
Cofer, Judith Ortiz 1952- CANR-130
Earlier sketches in CA 115, CANR-32, 72
See also Ortiz Cofer, Judith
See also AAYA 30
See also BYA 12
See also CSW
See also HW 1, 2
See also RGAL 4
See also SATA 110
See also YAW
Coffe, M.
See Gourmont, Remy(-Marie-Charles) de
Coffee, Lenore J. 1897(?)-1984 175
Obituary 113
See also DLB 44
Coffey, Alan R. 1931- 33-36R
Coffey, Brian
See Koontz, Dean R(ay)
Coffey, (Helen) Dairine 1933- 21-24R
Coffey, Daniel 1950- 131
Coffey, Frank 136
Coffey, J(oseph) I(rving) 1916- 41-44R
Coffey, Jan
See McGoldrick, James A. and
McGoldrick, Nikoo
Coffey, John W(ill), Jr. 1925- 45-48
Coffey, Marilyn 1937- CANR-2
Earlier sketch in CA 45-48
Coffey, Michael 1926- 139
Coffey, Michael 1954- 228
Coffey, Rebecca 166
Coffey, Robert E(dward) 1931- 65-68
Coffey, Thomas Patrick 1928- 120
Coffey, Tom 1958- 188
Coffey, Wayne 218
Coffin, Arthur B. 1929- 29-32R
Coffin, Berton 1910-1987 .... CANR-5
Earlier sketch in CA 9-12R
Coffin, David R(obbins) 1918-2003 .... 5-8R
Obituary 221
Coffin, Dean (Fiske) 1911-1992 .... 33-36R
Obituary 139
Coffin, Frank M(orey) 1919- 9-12R
Coffin, Geoffrey
See Mason, F(rancis) van Wyck
Coffin, George S(turgis) 1903-1994 .... 5-8R
Coffin, Harold 1905(?)-1981
Obituary 104
Coffin, Harold Glen 1926- 115
Coffin, Henry Sloane 1877-1954 219
Coffin, Howard 1942- 215
Coffin, Joseph (John) 1899- 57-60
Coffin, Lewis A(ugustus) III 1932- 61-64
Coffin, Lyn 1943- 110
Coffin, M. T.
See Stanley, George Edward
Coffin, Patricia 1912-1974 .... CAP-2
Obituary 49-52
Earlier sketch in CA 33-36
Coffin, Robert P(eter) Tristram 1892-1955 .. 169
Brief entry 123
See also DLB 45
See also TCLC 95
Coffin, Tristram 1912-1997 .... 21-24R
Obituary 158
Coffin, Tristram Potter 1922- CANR-2
Earlier sketch in CA 5-8R
Coffin, William Sloane, Jr. 1924- 103
Coffinet, Julien 1907- 61-64
Coffman, Barbara Frances 1907-1993 ... CAP-1
Earlier sketch in CA 13-16
Coffman, Charles DeWitt 1909-1982 102
Coffman, Edward M. 1929- 33-36R
Coffman, Paul B(rown) 1900-1990 .... CAP-2
Earlier sketch in CA 21-22
Coffman, Ramon Peyton 1896-1989 ..... CAP-2
Obituary 161
Earlier sketch in CA 17-18
See also SATA 4
Coffman, Virginia (Edith) 1914- CANR-2
Earlier sketch in CA 49-52
Cofyn, Cornelius
See Saunders, Hilary Aidan St. George
Cogan, Karen 1951- .... SATA 125
Cogan, Marc 231
Cogan, Mike
See Lottman, Eileen
Cogane, Gerald
See Fonarow, Jerry
Coger, Leslie Irene 1912-1999 .... 21-24R
Cogeval, Guy (Louis Antonio) 1955- 223
Coggan, (Frederick) Donald
1909-2000 .... 17-20R
Obituary 189
Coggin, Philip A(nnett) 1917- 117
Coggins, Jack (Banham) 1914- CANR-2
Earlier sketch in CA 5-8R
See also SATA 2
Coggins, Mark 1957- 222
Coggins, Paul E. 1951- 126
Coggins, Ross 1927- 13-16R
Coghill, Mrs. Harry
See Walker, Anna Louisa
Coghill, Nevill (Henry Kendall Aylmer)
1899-1980 .... CANR-11
Obituary 102
Earlier sketch in CA 13-16R
Coghill, Rhoda 1903- .... CP 1
Coghlan, Brian (Laurence Dillon)
1926- 17-20R
Coghlan, Margaret M. 1920- CANR-134
Earlier sketch in CA 106
See also Coghlan, Peggie and
Stirling, Jessica
Coghlan, Peggie .... RHW
Cogley, John 1916-1976 .... CANR-2
Obituary 65-68
Earlier sketch in CA 45-48
Cogley, Richard W. 1950- 218
Cogswell, Coralie (Norris) 1930- 13-16R
Cogswell, Fred(erick William)
1917- CANR-43
Earlier sketches in CA 5-8R, CANR-3, 18
See also CP 1, 2, 3, 4, 5, 6, 7
See also DLB 60
Cogswell, James A(rthur) 1922- 33-36R
Cogswell, Mason Fitch 1761-1830 .... DLB 37
Cogswell, Theodore R(ose)
1918-1987 .... CANR-4
Obituary 161
Earlier sketch in CA 1-4R
See also SFW 4
Cohan, Avery B(erlow) 1914-1977 61-64
Obituary 69-72
Cohan, George M(ichael) 1878-1942 157
See also DLB 249
See also RGAL 4
See also TCLC 60
Cohan, Tony 1939- CANR-90
Earlier sketch in CA 108
Cohane, John Philip 1911-1981 101
Cohane, Tim(othy Sylvester) 1912-1989 .. 9-12R
Obituary 161
Cohart, Mary 1911- 57-60
Cohassey, John (Frederick) 1961- 213
Cohen, Aaron (Samuel) 1935- 110
Cohen, Aharon 1910-1980 69-72
Cohen, Albert 1895(?)-1981
Obituary 105
Cohen, Albert J. 1903(?)-1984
Obituary 114
Cohen, Albert Kircidel 1918- 13-16R
Cohen, Allan R(ay) 1938- CANR-119
Earlier sketch in CA 148
Cohen, Allan Y. 1939- 33-36R
Cohen, Allen 1940-2004 139
Obituary 226
Cohen, Alvin 1931- 145
Cohen, Amnon 1936- 85-88
Cohen, Andrew (Z.) 1955- 135
Cohen, Anne Billings 1937- 57-60
Cohen, Anthea 1913- CANR-40
Earlier sketches in CA 97-100, CANR-18
See also CMW 4
Cohen, Arthur A(llen) 1928-1986 ..... CANR-42
Obituary 120
Earlier sketches in CA 1-4R, CANR-1, 17
See also CLC 7, 31
See also DLB 28
Cohen, Arthur M. 1927- 33-36R
Cohen, Avner 1951- 203
Cohen, B(enjamin) Bernard 1922- 9-12R
Cohen, Barbara 1932-1992 .... CANR-81
Obituary 140
Earlier sketches in CA 53-56, CANR-4, 19
See also AAYA 24
See also CWRI 5
See also JRDA
See also MAICYA 2
See also MAICYAS 1
See also SAAS 7
See also SATA 10, 77
See also SATA-Obit 74
Cohen, Bella
See Spewack, Bella
Cohen, Benjamin J(erry) 1937- CANR-18
Earlier sketch in CA 101
Cohen, Benjamin Victor 1894-1983 ...... CAP-1
Obituary 110
Earlier sketch in CA 11-12
Cohen, Bernard 1937- 103
Cohen, Bernard 1956- 166
Cohen, Bernard 1963- 167
Cohen, Bernard Lande 1902-1997 .... 29-32R
Cohen, Bernard P. 1930- 45-48
Cohen, Brenda
See Almond, Brenda
Cohen, Bruce J. 1938- 89-92
Cohen, Carl 1931- CANR-111
Earlier sketches in CA 1-4R, CANR-5
Cohen, Cary 1955- 224
Cohen, Charles 1943- 111
Cohen, Daniel (E.) 1936- CANR-44
Earlier sketches in CA 45-48, CANR-1, 20
See also AAYA 7
See also CLR 3, 43
See also JRDA
See also MAICYA 1, 2
See also SAAS 4
See also SATA 8, 70
Cohen, Daniel A. 1957- 144
Cohen, David 1946- 129
Cohen, David 1952- 108
Cohen, David Elliot 1955- 186
Cohen, David Steven 1943- 53-56
Cohen, Debra Nussbaum 1964- 203
Cohen, Donald J(ay) 1940-2001 145
Obituary 202
Cohen, Donna 1947- 122
Cohen, Dorothy H. 1915- 186
Brief entry 105
Cohen, Edgar H. 1913- 29-32R
Cohen, Edmund D(avid) 1943- 57-60
Cohen, Edward H. 1941-
Brief entry 115
Cohen, Edward M(artin) 1936- 21-24R
Cohen, Elaine (Marsha Perlman) 1938- 110
Cohen, Elie Aron 1909-1993 53-56
Cohen, Eliot A(sher) 1956- CANR-121
Earlier sketch in CA 113
Cohen (Van Pelt), Elizabeth 223
Cohen, Elliot D. 1951- CANR-144
Earlier sketch in CA 138
Cohen, Florence Chanock 1927-2003 ...... 5-8R
Obituary 212
Cohen, G(erald) A(llan) 1941- 207
Cohen, Gabriel 1961- 213
Cohen, Gary B(ennett) 1948- 107
Cohen, Gary G. 1934- CANR-7
Earlier sketch in CA 57-60
Cohen, George Michael 1931- 81-84
Cohen, Haim
See Cohn, Haim H(erman)
Cohen, Harry 1936- 106
Cohen, (Henry) Hennig 1919-1996 .... CANR-5
Earlier sketch in CA 1-4R
Cohen, Henry 1933- 33-36R
Cohen, Hiyaguha (Rachelle) 1951- 152
Cohen, Howard Martin 1926-
Brief entry 107
Cohen, hubert I. 1930- 155
Cohen, I. Bernard 1914-2003 .... CANR-106
Obituary 217
Earlier sketches in CA 69-72, CANR-56
Cohen, Ira Sheldon 1924- CANR-10
Earlier sketch in CA 5-8R
Cohen, J. M.
See Cohen, John Michael
Cohen, Jack S(idney) 1938- 130
Cohen, Jacob
See Dangerfield, Rodney
Cohen, Jacob 1918- 123
Cohen, James (E.) 1956- 137
Cohen, Jan Barger
See Barger, Jan
Cohen, Jane R(abb) 1938- 130
Cohen, Janet 1940- CANR-89
Earlier sketches in CA 126, CANR-55
See also CMW 4
Cohen, Janet Langhart 1941- 236
Cohen, Jason 1967- 152
Cohen, Jay S. 1945- 230
Cohen, Jayne 218
Cohen, Jean Louise 1946- 111
Cohen, Jeffrey A. 1952- 141
Cohen, Jene Barr CANR-42
Obituary 115
See also Barr, Jene
Cohen, Jeremy 1953- 130
Cohen, Jerome Alan 1930- CANR-30
Earlier sketches in CA 49-52, CANR-13
Cohen, Jerome B(ernard) 1915-1986 .... 9-12R
Obituary 121
Cohen, Joan Lebold 1932- CANR-30
Earlier sketches in CA 25-28R, CANR-13
See also SATA 4
Cohen, John 1911- CANR-6
Earlier sketch in CA 13-16R
Cohen, John Michael 1903-1989 .... CANR-4
Obituary 129
Earlier sketch in CA 5-8R
Cohen, Jon 196
Cohen, Jon S. 197
Cohen, Joseph 1926- CANR-10
Earlier sketch in CA 65-68
Cohen, Josh 1970- 210
Cohen, Jozef (B.) 1921-1995 .... 29-32R
Obituary 161
Cohen, Judith Beth 1943- 118
Cohen, Judith Love 1933- 146
See also SATA 78
Cohen, Kalman J(oseph) 1931- 13-16R
Cohen, Karl F. 1940- 167
Cohen, Kathleen Rogers 1933- 53-56
Cohen, Keith 1945- 101
Cohen, Larry 1945- 142
Cohen, Lawrence Jonathan 1923- 65-68
Cohen, Lawrence M. 186
Cohen, Leah Hager 1967- CANR-144
Earlier sketch in CA 170
Cohen, Lenard J. 200
Cohen, Leonard (Norman) 1934- CANR-69
Earlier sketches in CA 21-24R, CANR-14
See also CLC 3, 38
See also CN 1, 2, 3, 4, 5, 6
See also CP 1, 2, 3, 4, 5, 6, 7
See also DAC
See also DAM MST
See also DLB 53
See also EWL 3
See also MTCW 1
Cohen, Lizabeth (Ann) 1952- 224
Cohen, Lynne 1944- 224
Cohen, Marcel 1937- CANR-143
Earlier sketch in CA 153
Cohen, Margie K(anter) 1912-2000 109
Cohen, Mark 1958- 231
Cohen, Mark Nathan 1943- 135
Cohen, (Stephen) Marshall 1929- CANR-23
Earlier sketches in CA 45-48, CANR-2
Cohen, Martin A(aron) 1928- 193
Brief entry 113
Cohen, Marty 1947- 216
Cohen, Marvin 1931- CANR-17
Earlier sketch in CA 25-28R
Cohen, Matt(hew) 1942-1999 .... CANR-40
Obituary 187
Earlier sketch in CA 61-64
See also CAAS 18
See also CLC 19
See also CN 1, 2, 3, 4, 5, 6
See also DAC
See also DLB 53
Cohen, Michael J. 1940- CANR-65
Earlier sketch in CA 129
Cohen, Michael P. 1944- CANR-47
Earlier sketch in CA 121
Cohen, Mike
See Cohen, Morris
Cohen, Miriam 1926-1955 .... CANR-139
Earlier sketch in CA 106
See also SAAS 11
See also SATA 29, 106, 155
Cohen, Misha Ruth 1951(?)- 218
Cohen, Morris 1912- 17-20R
Cohen, Morris L(eo) 1927- CANR-53
Earlier sketches in CA 49-52, CANR-29
Cohen, Morris Raphael 1880-1947 .... DLB 270
Cohen, Mortimer J. 1894-1972
Obituary 104
Cohen, Morton N(orton) 1921- CANR-56
Earlier sketches in CA 1-4R, CANR-5, 28
Cohen, Myron 1903(?)-1986
Obituary 118
Cohen, Nancy J. 1948- 198
Cohen, Nancy Wainer 1947- 111
Cohen, Naomi W(iener) 1927- 195
Brief entry 114
Cohen, Nick 194
Cohen, Nora .... SATA 75
Cohen, Norm(an) 1936- 109
Cohen, Norman J. 1943- 193
Cohen, Octavus Roy 1891-1959
Brief entry 112
See also CMW 4
Cohen, Patricia Cline 1946- 185
Cohen, Paul (M.) 1955- 199
Cohen, Paul Andrew 1934- 115
Cohen, Paul S. 1945- 123
See also SATA 58
Cohen, Peter Zachary 1931- CANR-135
Earlier sketches in CA 33-36R, CANR-12
See also SATA 4, 150
Cohen, Philip G(ary) 1954- 136
Cohen, Rachel 235
Cohen, Ralph 1917- 138
Cohen, Randy 1948- 210
Cohen, Rich 1968- 173
Cohen, Richard 1952- 140
Cohen, Richard E. 222
Cohen, Richard M(artin) 1941- 146
Cohen, Richard Murry 1938- CANR-19
Earlier sketch in CA 103
Cohen, Robert 1938- CANR-90
Earlier sketches in CA 29-32R, CANR-12, 34
Cohen, Robert 1957- 131
Cohen, Robert Carl 1930- 57-60
See also SATA 8
Cohen, Roberta G. 1937- 49-52
Cohen, Robin 1944- 134
Cohen, Roger 1955- 180
Cohen, Ronald 1930- CANR-29
Earlier sketches in CA 33-36R, CANR-13
Cohen, Ronald Dennis 1940- 105
Cohen, Ronald Jay 1949- 97-100
Cohen, Rosalyn
See Higgins, Rosalyn (Cohen)
Cohen, S. Alan 1933- 29-32R
Cohen, S. Ralph 1917-1983
Obituary 110
Cohen, Sandy 1946- 198
Cohen, Sanford 1920- 1-4R
Cohen, Sara Kay Sherman 1943- 102
Cohen, Sarah Blacher 1936- 81-84
Cohen, Saul Bernard 1925- 130
Cohen, Scott 1946- 116
Cohen, Selma Jeanne 1920- 25-28R
Cohen, Seymour Jay 1922-2001 .... 25-28R
Obituary 195
Cohen, Sharleen Cooper CANR-41
Earlier sketches in CA 97-100, CANR-19
Cohen, Sheldon S. 1931- 25-28R
Cohen, Sherry Suib 1934- 102
Cohen, Sholom 1951- 159
See also SATA 94
Cohen, Sidney 1910-1987 .... 13-16R
Obituary 122

Cohen, Stanley 1928- CANR-34
Earlier sketches in CA 29-32R, CANR-15
Cohen, Stephen 1941- 118
Cohen, Stephen D(avid) 1942- 111
Cohen, Stephen F(rand) 1938- CANR-112
Earlier sketches in CA 49-52, CANR-35, 75
Cohen, Stephen S. 1941- 33-36R
Cohen, Stephen Z(olman) 1931- 121
Cohen, Steve (Michael) 1951- 114
Cohen, Steven (A.) 1953- 142
Cohen, Stewart 1940- 65-68
Cohen, Stuart 1958- 172
Cohen, Susan (Lois) 1938- CANR-44
Earlier sketches in CA 53-56, CANR-5, 20
Cohen, Warren I. 1934- CANR-127
Earlier sketches in CA 21-24R, CANR-9
Cohen, Wilbur J(oseph) 1913-1987 .. CANR-17
Obituary 122
Earlier sketch in CA 25-28R
Cohen, William A(lan) 1937- CANR-42
Earlier sketches in CA 103, CANR-19
Cohen, William B(enjamin) 1941-2002 . 37-40R
Obituary 210
Cohen, William Howard 1927- 17-20R
Cohen, William S(ebastian) 1940- CANR-27
Earlier sketch in CA 108
Cohen, Yehudi A(ryeh) 1928- 113
Cohen, Youssef 1947- 151
Cohen-Shalev, Amir 1951- 231
Cohen-Solal, Annie 1948- 239
See also CLC 50
Cohen-Stratyner, Barbara Naomi 1951- 113
Cohl, Emile 1857-1938 IDFW 3, 4
Cohler, Anne M(eyers) 1940(?)-1989
Obituary 130
Cohler, Bertram J(oseph) 1938- 109
Cohler, David Keith 1940- 104
Cohn, Adrian A. 1922- 25-28R
Cohn, Alan M(artin) 1926-1989 110
Obituary 129
Cohn, Angelo 1914-1997 CANR-4
Earlier sketch in CA 5-8R
See also SATA 19
Cohn, Arthur 1910-1998 110
Obituary 164
Cohn, David 1954- 216
Cohn, Dorrit 1924- CANR-108
Earlier sketch in CA 93-96
Cohn, Elchanan 1941- 73-76
Cohn, Haim H(erman) 1911-2002 45-48
Obituary 208
Cohn, Harry 1891-1958 IDFW 3, 4
Cohn, Helen Desfosses
See Desfosses, Helen
Cohn, Henry S. 1945- 141
Cohn, Jan K(adetsky) 1933-2004 102
Obituary 230
Cohn, Jules 1930- 33-36R
Cohn, Keith E(van) 1935- 107
Cohn, Laura 1930- 196
Cohn, Leopold 1862-1937 218
Cohn, Lester
See Cole, Lester
Cohn, Marguerite A. 1898(?)-1984
Obituary 113
Cohn, Marthe 1920- 227
Cohn, Marvin L(ester) 1924-1990 105
Obituary 131
Cohn, Nik 1946- CANR-88
Earlier sketch in CA 102
Cohn, Norman 1915- 57-60
Cohn, Rachel 1968- 235
See also AAYA 65
See also SATA 161
Cohn, Robert Greer 1921- 9-12R
Cohn, Roy M(arcus) 1927-1986 CANR-29
Obituary 119
Earlier sketch in CA 108
Cohn, Rubin (Goodman) 1911-1986 57-60
Obituary 119
Cohn, Ruby 1922- CANR-32
Earlier sketch in CA 93-96
Cohn, Samuel K(line), Jr. 1949- CANR-137
Earlier sketches in CA 125, CANR-52
Cohn, Stanley H(arold) 1922- 29-32R
Cohn, Theodore 1923- 89-92
Cohn, Vera 1907- 97-100
Cohn, Victor (Edward) 1919-2000 188
Cohn-Sherbok, Dan 1945- 174
Earlier sketch in CA 137
Cohoe, Grey 1944-1991 216
Cohon, Barry
See Cohon, Baruch J(oseph)
Cohon, Baruch J(oseph) 1926- 29-32R
Cohon, Beryl David 1898-1976 CANR-6
Earlier sketch in CA 1-4R
Cohon, Samuel S(olomon) 1888-1959 216
Coigney, Virginia 1917-1997 103
Coiner, Constance 1948-1996 201
Coit, Davida
See Scudder, Vida Dutton
Coit, John Hamilton 1947(?)-1986
Obituary 118
Coit, Lew Garrison 1897(?)-1985
Obituary 116
Coit, Margaret Louise 1922-2003 CANR-5
Obituary 214
Earlier sketch in CA 1-4R
See also SATA 2
See also SATA-Obit 142
Cojeen, Robert H. 1920- 37-40R
Cokal, Susann 1965- 203
Cokayne, Aston 1608-1684 RGEL 2
Coke, Allison Adelle Hedge 194
Coke, Tom S(tephen) 1943- 115
Coke, (Frank) Van Deren
1921-2004 CANR-22
Obituary 230
Earlier sketches in CA 13-16R, CANR-7
Coker, C(harles) F(rederick) W(illiams)
1932-1983
Obituary 110
Coker, Carolyn CANR-142
Earlier sketch in CA 125
Coker, Christopher CANR-89
Earlier sketch in CA 158
Coker, Elizabeth Boatwright 1909-1993 .. 45-48
Obituary 142
Coker, Gylbert 1944- 93-96
Coker, Jerry 1932- CANR-6
Earlier sketch in CA 9-12R
Coker, Syl Cheney
See Cheney-Coker, Syl
Cokinos, Christopher A. 1963- 187
Colacci, Mario 1910-1968 5-8R
Obituary 135
Colacello, Bob 1947- CANR-141
Earlier sketch in CA 138
Coladarci, Arthur Paul 1917-1991 5-8R
Obituary 161
Colaiaco, James A(lfred) 1945- 115
Colaianni, Louis 1959- 219
Colalillo-Kates, Isabella 1948- 216
Colalillo-Katz, Isabella
See Colalillo-Kates, Isabella
Colander, Pat(ricia) 1952- 110
Colander, Valerie Nieman
See Nieman, Valerie Gail
Colaneri, John Nunzio 1930- 103
Colapinto, John 195
Colas, Emily 1966(?)- 177
Colasanti, Marina 1937- DLB 307
Colaw, Emerson S. 1921- 13-16R
Colbach, Edward M(ichael) 1939- 69-72
Colbeck, Maurice 1925- CANR-34
Earlier sketches in CA 13-16R, CANR-5
Colbeck, Norman 1903-1987 DLB 201
Colberg, Marshall R(udolph)
1913-2000 CANR-1
Earlier sketch in CA 1-4R
Colbert, Anthony 1934- 89-92
See also SATA 15
Colbert, David CANR-144
Earlier sketch in CA 177
Colbert, Douglas A(lbert) 1933- 57-60
Colbert, Edwin Harris 1905-2001 CANR-8
Obituary 206
Earlier sketch in CA 61-64
Colbert, Evelyn S(peyer) 1918- 102
Colbert, Jaimee Wriston 1951- 187
Colbert, James 1951- CANR-54
Earlier sketch in CA 122
Colbert, Nancy A. 1936- 210
See also SATA 139
Colbert, Roman 1921- 53-56
Colbert, Stephen 1964- 223
Colborn, Nigel 1944- 128
Colbourn, H(arold) Trevor 1927- 33-36R
Colburn, C(lyde) William 1939- 37-40R
Colburn, David Richard 1942- 110
Colburn, George A(bbott) 1938- 41-44R
Colby, Averil 1900-1983(?)
Obituary 108
Colby, Benjamin N(ick) 1931- 61-64
Colby, C(arroll) B(urleigh) 1904-1977 . CANR-6
Earlier sketch in CA 1-4R
See also SATA 3, 35
Colby, Douglas (Steven) 1954- 116
Colby, Elbridge 1891-1982 CAP-1
Obituary 108
Earlier sketch in CA 13-16
Colby, Jean Poindexter 1909-1993 CANR-5
Earlier sketch in CA 1-4R
See also SATA 23
Colby, Joan 1939- CANR-13
Earlier sketch in CA 77-80
Colby, Robert A(lan) 1920-2004 53-56
Obituary 235
Colby, Roy (Edward) 1910-1994 25-28R
Colby, Vineta (Blumoff) 1922- 9-12R
Colby, William Egan 1920-1996 81-84
Obituary 151
Colby, William H. 1955- 218
Colchie, Elizabeth Schneider
See Schneider, Elizabeth (Susan)
Colden, Cadwallader 1688-1776 .. DLB 24, 30, 270
Colden, Jane 1724-1766 DLB 200
Coldham, James D(esmond Bowden)
1924-1987 113
Obituary 121
Coldiron, A. E. B. 1959- 215
Coldrey, Jennifer (M.) 1940- 121
Coldsmith, Don(ald Charles)
1926- CANR-100
Earlier sketches in CA 105, CANR-21, 50
See also TCWW 1, 2
Coldwell, David F(rederick) C(larke)
1923-1973 17-20R
Obituary 134
Coldwell, Joan 1936- 106
Coldwell, M(ichael) J. 1888-1974
Obituary 53-56
Cole, Adrian 1949- CANR-59
Earlier sketch in CA 121
Cole, Allan 1943- 150
See also FANT 1
Cole, Allison
See Coker, Carolyn
Cole, Ann 1937- 65-68
Cole, Ann Kilborn
See Callahan, Claire Wallis
Cole, Annette
See Steiner, Barbara A(nnette)
Cole, Arthur C(harles) 1886-1976
Obituary 65-68
Cole, Babette 1949- CANR-114
Earlier sketch in CA 161
See also CWRI 5
See also MAICYA 2
See also MAICYAS 1
See also SATA 61, 96, 155
Cole, Barry 1936- CANR-68
Earlier sketches in CA 25-28R, CANR-16
See also CN 1, 2, 3, 4, 5, 6, 7
See also CP 1, 2
See also DLB 14
Cole, Basil (Burr) 1937- 187
Cole, Bernard D. 1943- 215
Cole, Betsy 1940- 150
See also SATA 83
Cole, Bill
See Cole, William Shadrack
Cole, Brock 1938- CANR-115
Earlier sketch in CA 136
See also AAYA 15, 45
See also BYA 10
See also CLR 18
See also JRDA
See also MAICYA 1, 2
See also SATA 72, 136
See also WYA
See also YAW
Cole, Bruce 1938- CANR-15
Earlier sketch in CA 65-68
Cole, Burt 1930- 73-76
Cole, C. Donald 1923- 125
Cole, C(harles) Robert 1939- 65-68
Cole, Cannon
See Cook, Arlene Ethel
Cole, Charles C(hester), Jr. 1922- 118
Cole, Charles L(eland) 1927- 69-72
Cole, Charles Woolsey 1906-1978 ... CANR-22
Obituary 77-80
Earlier sketch in CA 69-72
Cole, Clifford A. 1915- 13-16R
Cole, Cornelius 1822-1924 218
Cole, Cozy
See Cole, William R.
Cole, Dandridge MacFarlan 1921- 13-16R
Cole, David C(hamberlin) 1928- 127
Brief entry 106
Cole, Davis
See Elting, Mary
Cole, Davis
See Elting, Mary
Cole, Diane 1952- 138
Cole, Donald Barnard 1922- 5-8R
Cole, Doris 1938- 89-92
Cole, Douglas 1934- CANR-2
Earlier sketch in CA 5-8R
Cole, E(ugene) R(oger) 1930- CANR-31
Earlier sketches in CA 53-56, CANR-4, 19
Cole, Eddie-Lou 1909-1995 65-68
Cole, Edward B(ender) 1923- 107
Cole, Edward C(yrus) 1904-1984 13-16R
Cole, Frank R(aymond) 1892-1988 69-72
Cole, G(eorge) D(ouglas) H(oward)
1889-1959 209
Brief entry 108
See also CMW 4
Cole, George F(raser) 1935- 65-68
Cole, George Watson 1850-1939 201
See also DLB 140
Cole, Gordon
See Cole, Gordon H(enry)
Cole, Gordon H(enry) 1912-1988
Obituary 125
Cole, H. S. D.
See Cole, (Hugh) Sam(uel David)
Cole, Hank
See Fearn, John Russell
Cole, Hannah 1954- SATA 74
Cole, (Roger) Henri 1956- 121
Cole, Howard C(handler) 1934- 49-52
Cole, Hubert (Archibald Noel) 1908- . CANR-5
Earlier sketch in CA 5-8R
Cole, J(ohn) A(lfred) 1905- CAP-1
Earlier sketch in CA 13-16
Cole, J. P.
See Cole, John P(eter)
Cole, J. Timothy 1959- 238
Cole, Jack -1974
See Stewart, John (William)
See also IDFW 3, 4
Cole, Jack 1914-1958 AAYA 65
Cole, Jackson
See Curry, Thomas Albert and
Germano, Peter B. and
Heckelmann, Charles N(ewman) and
Newton, D(wight) B(ennett) and
Schisgall, Oscar
Cole, Janet
See Hunter, Kim
Cole, Jean Hascall 1922- 139
Cole, Jean Murray 1927- 215
Cole, Jennifer
See Zach, Cheryl (Byrd)
Cole, Joan 1957- 113
Cole, Joanna 1944- CANR-98
Earlier sketches in CA 115, CANR-36, 55, 70
See also CLR 5, 40
See also MAICYA 1, 2
See also SATA 49, 81, 120
See also SATA-Brief 37
Cole, John N(elson) 1923-2003 93-96
Obituary 212
Cole, John P(eter) 1928- CANR-41
Earlier sketches in CA 5-8R, CANR-3, 19
Cole, John Y(oung), Jr. 1940- CANR-41
Earlier sketches in CA 103, CANR-19
Cole, Johnnetta B(etsch) 1936- CANR-87
Earlier sketch in CA 157
Cole, Jonathan 1951- 174
Cole, Jonathan R(ichard) 1942- 53-56
Cole, Juan R(icardo) I(rfan) 1952- CANR-93
Earlier sketch in CA 121
Cole, Justine
See Phillips, Susan Elizabeth
Cole, K. C. 1946- CANR-102
Earlier sketch in CA 105
Cole, Kay
See Colominas, Kathleen Adele
Cole, (Edmund) Keith 1919- CANR-19
Earlier sketch in CA 102
Cole, Laramee
See Gribble, Leonard (Reginald)
Cole, Larry 1936- 45-48
Cole, Leonard A(aron) 1933- 81-84
Cole, Leonard Leslie 1909-1980 103
Cole, Lester 1904(?)-1985
Obituary 117
Cole, Lewis 1946- 109
Cole, Lois Dwight 1903-1979 CANR-4
Obituary 104
Earlier sketch in CA 1-4R
See also RHW
See also SATA 10
See also SATA-Obit 26
Cole, Luella (Winifred) 1893-1970(?) CAP-1
Earlier sketch in CA 19-20
Cole, Margaret CMW 4
Cole, Margaret Alice CANR-6
Earlier sketch in CA 9-12R
Cole, Margaret Isabel 1893-1980 CANR-4
Obituary 97-100
Earlier sketch in CA 5-8R
Cole, Martha 1916(?)-1986
Obituary 118
Cole, Mary
See Hanna, Mary T.
Cole, Michael 1938- 97-100
Cole, Michael 1947- SATA 59
Cole, Michelle 1940- 29-32R
Cole, Monica M(ary) 1922-1994 1-4R
Obituary 144
Cole, Nora (Marie) 1953- 171
See also BW 3
Cole, Norma 1945- CWP
Cole, Phyllis (Blum) 1944- 172
Cole, Richard
See Barrett, Geoffrey John
Cole, Richard Cargill 1926- CANR-109
Earlier sketches in CA 124, CANR-51
Cole, Rick 1953- CMW 4
Cole, Robert
See Snow, Charles H(orace)
Cole, Robert 1939- CANR-91
Earlier sketch in CA 146
Cole, Robert E(van) 1937- 69-72
Cole, Robert H. 1918- 33-36R
Cole, Robert J(ason) 1925- 133
Cole, Roger L. 1933- 25-28R
Cole, (Hugh) Sam(uel David) 1943- 130
Cole, Sandi Gelles
See Gelles-Cole, Sandi
Cole, Sheila R(otenberg) 1939- CANR-68
Earlier sketches in CA 53-56, CANR-4
See also SATA 24, 95
Cole, Simon A. 227
Cole, Sonia (Mary) 1918-1982 93-96
Obituary 106
Cole, Stephanie 1941- 235
Cole, Stephen
See Webbe, Gale D(udley)
Cole, Stephen 1941- 29-32R
Cole, Stephen 1971- 237
See also SATA 161
Cole, Stephen A. 1955- 211
Cole, Susan Letzler 1940- CANR-122
Earlier sketch in CA 168
Cole, Sylvan, Jr. 1918- 69-72
Cole, Terrence (Michael) 1953- 135
Cole, (Andrew) Thomas (Jr.) 1933- 102
Cole, Thomas R(ichard) 1949- 141
Cole, Tim (J.) 1970- 236
Cole, Toby 1916- 153
Cole, Tom
See Cole, Thomas R(ichard)
Cole, W(illiam) Owen 1931- CANR-43
Earlier sketch in CA 118
Cole, Wayne S. 1922- 21-24R
Cole, Wendell 1914- 21-24R
Cole, William (Rossa) 1919-2000 CANR-47
Obituary 189
Earlier sketches in CA 9-12R, CANR-7
See also MAICYA 1, 2
See also SAAS 9
See also SATA 9, 71
Cole, William Earle 1904-1979 17-20R
Obituary 126
Cole, William Graham 1917- 17-20R
Cole, William R. 1909-1981
Obituary 108
Cole, William Shadrack 1937- 101
Colean, Miles Lanier 1898-1980 CAP-2
Obituary 161
Earlier sketch in CA 21-22
Colebatch, Hal G(ibson) P(ateshall) 1948- .. 191
Coleburt, J(ames) Russell 1920-1995 13-16R
Colecchia, Francesca Maria 89-92

Cumulative Index 117 **Collins**

Colegate, Isabel 1931- CANR-74
Earlier sketches in CA 17-20R, CANR-8, 22
Interview in CANR-22
See also CLC 36
See also CN 4, 5, 6, 7
See also DLB 14, 231
See also MTCW 1
Colegrove, Kenneth 1886-1975 .... CANR-4
Obituary 53-56
Earlier sketch in CA 5-8R
Coleman, A(llan) D(ouglass) 1943- ... CANR-15
Earlier sketch in CA 73-76
Coleman, A. Eugene 1942- 198
Coleman, Almand R(ouse) 1905-1996 ... CAP-2
Obituary 161
Earlier sketch in CA 29-32
Coleman, Andrew
See Pine, Nicholas
Coleman, Arthur 1924- 81-84
Coleman, Bernard D(avid) 1919- 25-28R
Coleman, Bill
See Coleman, William V(incent)
Coleman, Bob
See Coleman, Robert David
Coleman, Bruce P(umphrey) 1931- 37-40R
Coleman, Buck
See Richardson, Gladwell
Coleman, C. Norman 1945- 175
Coleman, Clare
See Bell, Clare (Louise) and
Easton, M(alcolm) Coleman
Coleman, Clayton W(ebster)
1901-1979 .... 29-32R
Coleman, D(onald) C(uthbert)
1920-1995 .... 13-16R
Coleman, Dabney 1932- 172
Coleman, Daniel 1961- 187
Coleman, David (Firth) 1945- 153
Coleman, Dorothy Gabe
1935-1992 .... CANR-46
Obituary 139
Earlier sketch in CA 93-96
Coleman, Elliott 1906-1980 .... 17-20R
Obituary 97-100
See also CP 1, 2
Coleman, Emily Holmes 1899-1974 105
See also DLB 4
Coleman, Emily R. 1947- 135
Coleman, Emmett
See Reed, Ishmael (Scott)
Coleman, Evelyn 1948- 222
Coleman, Evelyn Scherabon
See Firchow, Evelyn Scherabon
Coleman, Felicia Slatkin 1916(?)-1981
Obituary 102
Coleman, Francis Xavier Jerome 1939- 108
Coleman, Gene
See Coleman, A. Eugene
Coleman, J(ohn) Winston, Jr.
1898-1983 .... CANR-27
Earlier sketch in CA 49-52
Coleman, Jack 1958- 213
Coleman, James A(ndrew) 1921- 5-8R
Coleman, James C(ovington)
1914-1997 .... CANR-1
Earlier sketch in CA 1-4R
Coleman, James S(amuel) 1926-1995 ... 13-16R
Coleman, James Smoot 1919- 1-4R
Coleman, Jane Candia 1939- CANR-127
Earlier sketch in CA 136
Coleman, John R(oyston) 1921- CANR-1
Earlier sketch in CA 1-4R
See also AITN 1
Coleman, Jonathan (Mark) 1951- CANR-70
Brief entry 129
Earlier sketch in CA 138
Interview in CA-138
Coleman, Kenneth 1916-1999 .... CANR-33
Earlier sketches in CA 21-24R, CANR-8
Coleman, Lee
See Lapidus, Elaine
Coleman, Lonnie
See Coleman, William Laurence
Coleman, Loren (Elwood, Jr.) 1947- 133
Coleman, Lucile 73-76
Coleman, Marion (Reeves) Moore
1900-1993 .... CANR-11
Earlier sketch in CA 17-20R
Coleman, Mary Ann 1928- 150
See also SATA 83
Coleman, Mary DeLorse 1954- 143
Coleman, Michael (Lee) 1946- .... MAICYA 2
See also SATA 108, 133
See also SATA-Essay 133
Coleman, Michael C(hristopher)
1946- CANR-43
Earlier sketch in CA 119
Coleman, Patricia R(egister) 1936- ... CANR-51
Earlier sketches in CA 109, CANR-25
Coleman, Patty R.
See Coleman, Patricia R(egister)
Coleman, Peter J(arrett) 1926- 5-8R
Coleman, Ray 1937-1996 137
Obituary 153
Coleman, Raymond James 1923- CANR-36
Earlier sketch in CA 49-52
Coleman, Reed Farrel 1956- 231
Coleman, Richard J(ames) 1941- 41-44R
Coleman, Richard M(ark) 1951- 121
Coleman, Richard Patrick 1927- 33-36R
Coleman, Robert David 1951- 121
Coleman, Robert E(merson) 1928- CANR-82
Earlier sketches in CA 13-16R, CANR-7, 35
Coleman, Robert William Alfred 1916- ... 9-12R
Coleman, Roy V. 1885-1971
Obituary 104
Coleman, Terry 1931- CANR-108
Earlier sketches in CA 13-16R, CANR-10, 27, 58
Coleman, Thomas R. 1942- 57-60
Coleman, Verna (Scott) 134
Coleman, Vernon 1946- 81-84
Coleman, Victor (Art) 1944- 153
See also CP 7
Coleman, Wanda 1946- CANR-86
Earlier sketches in CA 119, CANR-43
See also CAAS 29
See also AMWS 11
See also BW 2, 3
See also DLB 130
Coleman, William L(eRoy) 1938- CANR-21
Earlier sketch in CA 69-72
See also SATA 49
See also SATA-Brief 34
Coleman, William Laurence
1920-1982 .... CANR-39
Coleman, William Oliver 154
Coleman, William V(incent) 1932- ... CANR-51
Earlier sketches in CA 57-60, CANR-9, 25
Coleman-Norton, P(aul) R(obinson) 1898-1971
Obituary 29-32R
Colen, B. D. 1946- CANR-23
Earlier sketch in CA 65-68
Colenbrander, Joanna 1908- 121
Coleridge, Hartley 1796-1849 .... DLB 96
Coleridge, John
See Binder, Otto O(scar)
Coleridge, M. E.
See Coleridge, Mary E(lizabeth)
Coleridge, Mary E(lizabeth) 1861-1907 166
Brief entry 116
See also DLB 19, 98
See also TCLC 73
Coleridge, Nicholas (David) 1957- 144
Coleridge, Samuel Taylor 1772-1834 . AAYA 66
See also BRW 4
See also BRWR 2
See also BYA 4
See also CDBLB 1789-1832
See also DA
See also DA3
See also DAB
See also DAC
See also DAM MST, POET
See also DLB 93, 107
See also EXPP
See also LATS 1:1
See also LMFS 1
See also PAB
See also PC 11, 39, 67
See also PFS 4, 5
See also RGEL 2
See also TEA
See also WLC
See also WLIT 3
See also WP
Coleridge, Sara 1802-1852 .... DLB 199
Coles, Alan 1927- 124
Coles, Cyril Henry 1899-1965 .... CANR-62
Earlier sketches in CAP-1, CA 9-10
See also Coles, Manning
See also CMW 4
Coles, Don 1928- CANR-38
Earlier sketch in CA 115
See also CLC 46
See also CP 7
Coles, Flournoy (Arthur), Jr. 1915- 57-60
Coles, Harry L(ewis) 1920- 9-12R
Coles, Janis
See Dawson, Janis
Coles, Joan M(yers) 1947- 133
Coles, John M(orton) 1930- CANR-90
Earlier sketches in CA 29-32R, CANR-12, 34
Coles, Kaines Adlard 1901-1985 .... CAP-1
Obituary 117
Earlier sketch in CA 13-14
Coles, Manning
See Coles, Cyril Henry
See also CMW 4
Coles, Robert (Martin) 1929- CANR-135
Earlier sketches in CA 45-48, CANR-3, 32, 66, 70
Interview in CANR-32
See also CLC 108
See also SATA 23
Coles, Robert R(eed) 1908(?)-1985
Obituary 116
Coles, S(ydney) F(rederick) Arthur 1896- ... 5-8R
Coles, Susan Vaughan Ebershoff
See Ebershoff-Coles, Susan Vaughan
Coles, William Allan 1930- 33-36R
Coles, William E., Jr. 1932- CANR-10
Earlier sketch in CA 61-64
Colet, John 1446-1519 .... DLB 132
Coletta, Paolo Enrico 1916- CANR-56
Earlier sketches in CA 41-44R, CANR-14, 31
Colette, (Sidonie-Gabrielle) 1873-1954 131
Brief entry 104
See also Willy, Colette
See also DA3
See also DAM NOV
See also DLB 65
See also EW 9
See also EWL 3
See also GFL 1789 to the Present
See also MTCW 1, 2
See also MTFW 2005
See also RGWL 2, 3
See also SSC 10
See also TCLC 1, 5, 16
See also TWA
Colette, Jacques 1929- 89-92
Cole-Whittaker, Terry 1939- 207
Colfax, David (John) 1936- 140
Colfax, J. David
See Colfax, David (John)
Colfer, Eoin 1965- CANR-131
Earlier sketch in CA 205
See also AAYA 48
See also BYA 16
See also SATA 148
Colford, Paul D(ennis) 1953- 110
Colford, William E(dward) 1908-1971 ...... 5-8R
Obituary 33-36R
Colgan, Jenny 1971- 235
Colgin, Russell W(eymount) 1925- 121
Colgrass, Michael 1932- 211
Colgrave, Bertram 1888-1968 .... CAP-2
Earlier sketch in CA 25-28
Colicchio, Joseph 1952- 235
Colie, Rosalie L(ittell) 1924-1972
Obituary 106
Colimore, Vincent J(erome) 1914-1998 . 37-40R
Colin, Ann
See Ure, Jean
Colin, Chris 1975(?)- 234
Colin, Jean
See Bell, Joyce
Colina, Tessa Patterson 1915- CANR-7
Earlier sketch in CA 17-20R
Colinas, Antonio 1946- .... DLB 134
Colinet, Paul 1898-1957 212
Colinvaux, Paul (Alfred) 1930- CANR-14
Earlier sketch in CA 41-44R
Colish, Marcia L. 1937- CANR-10
Earlier sketch in CA 25-28R
Coll, Alberto R(aoul) 1955- 145
Coll, Joseph Clement 1881-1921 .... DLB 188
Coll, Regina A(udrey) 1929- 112
Coll, Steve 1958- 137
Coll, Susan 239
Collard, Cyril 1957-1993 152
See also GLL 2
Collard, Edgar Andrew 1911-2000 102
Collard, Sneed B. III 1959- CANR-101
Earlier sketch in CA 150
See also SATA 84, 139
Collas, J. P. 1911-1984
Obituary 114
Collector, Stephen 1951- 139
Colledge, Anne 1939- 213
See also SATA 142
Colledge, Malcolm A(ndrew) R(ichard)
1939- CANR-10
Earlier sketch in CA 25-28R
Collee, John (Gerald) 1955- 145
Collen, Neil
See Lee, Lincoln
Coller, Richard Walter 1925- 119
Collery, Arnold (Peter) 1927-1989
Obituary 128
Collett, Barry 1934- CANR-64
Earlier sketch in CA 128
Collett, Rosemary K(ing) 1931- 69-72
Colletta, Lisa 239
Colletta, Nat J(oseph) 1944- 104
Collette, Christine 1947- 132
Colley, Ann C(heetham) 1940- CANR-30
Earlier sketch in CA 112
Colley, Barbara 1947- 211
Colley, Iain 1940- 97-100
Colley, Linda 1949- CANR-144
Earlier sketch in CA 130
Collias, Joe G. 1928- CANR-14
Earlier sketch in CA 41-44R
Collias, Nicholas E(lias) 1914- 131
Collicott, Sharleen 1937- CANR-122
Earlier sketch in CA 165
See also SATA 98, 143
Collie, Michael (John) 1929- CANR-39
Earlier sketches in CA 49-52, CANR-3, 18
See also CP 1
Collier, Andrea King 1956- 228
Collier, (John) Basil 1908- CANR-2
Earlier sketch in CA 5-8R
Collier, Boyd D(ean) 1938- 57-60
Collier, Bryan .... MAICYA 2
See also SATA 126
Collier, Calhoun C(rofford) 1916- 25-28R
Collier, Christopher 1930- CANR-102
Earlier sketches in CA 33-36R, CANR-13, 33
See also AAYA 13
See also BYA 2
See also CLC 30
See also JRDA
See also MAICYA 1, 2
See also SATA 16, 70
See also WYA
See also YAW 1
Collier, David 1942- 69-72
Collier, David S(wanson) 1923-1983 ..... 21-24R
Obituary 111
Collier, Douglas
See Fellowes-Gordon, Ian (Douglas)
Collier, Ethel 1903-1999 65-68
See also SATA 22
Collier, Eugenia W(illiams) 1928- 49-52
See also BW 2
Collier, Gary 1947- 138
Collier, Gaydell M(aier) 1935- CANR-135
Earlier sketches in CA 93-96, CANR-70
Collier, Gaylan Jane 1924- 37-40R
Collier, (Alan) Graham 1923- 17-20R
Collier, (James) Graham 1937- 105
Collier, Herbert L(eon) 1933- 103
Collier, James Lincoln 1928- CANR-102
Earlier sketches in CA 9-12R, CANR-4, 33, 60
See also AAYA 13
See also BYA 2
See also CLC 30
See also CLR 3
See also DAM POP
See also JRDA
See also MAICYA 1, 2
See also SAAS 21
See also SATA 8, 70
See also WYA
See also YAW 1
Collier, Jane
See Collier, Zena
Collier, John 1901-1980 .... CANR-10
Obituary 97-100
Earlier sketch in CA 65-68
See also CN 1, 2
See also DLB 77, 255
See also FANT
See also SSC 19
See also SUFW 1
See also TCLC 127
Collier, John Payne 1789-1883 .... DLB 184
Collier, Johnnie Lucille
See Collier, Lucille Ann
Collier, Joy
See Millar, (Minna Henrietta) Joy
Collier, Kenneth Gerald 1910-1998 .. CANR-18
Earlier sketch in CA 85-88
Collier, Leo(nard) D(awson) 1908- 5-8R
Collier, Louise Wilbourn 1925- 109
Collier, Lucille Ann 1919(?)-2004
Obituary 222
Brief entry 109
Collier, Lucy Ann
See Collier, Lucille Ann
Collier, Margaret
See Taylor, Margaret Stewart
Collier, Mary 1690-1762 .... DLB 95
Collier, Michael 1953- CANR-96
Earlier sketch in CA 137
Collier, Peter 1939- CANR-44
Earlier sketch in CA 65-68
Collier, Phyllis K(ay) 1939- 110
Collier, Richard 1924- CANR-25
Earlier sketches in CA 1-4R, CANR-5
Collier, Robert J. 1876-1918 175
See also DLB 91
Collier, Simon 1938- CANR-96
Earlier sketch in CA 21-24R
Collier, Steven 1942- .... SATA 61
Collier, Zena 1926- CANR-43
See also Collier, Jane
See also SATA 23
Colligan, Francis J(ames) 1908-1974(?) .. CAP-2
Earlier sketch in CA 19-20
Collignon, Jean Henri 1918- 1-4R
Collignon, Jeff 1953- 137
Collignon, Joseph 1930- 89-92
Collignon, Rick 1948- CANR-140
Earlier sketch in CA 167
See also HW 2
Collin, Marion (Cripps) 1928- CANR-5
Earlier sketch in CA 9-12R
See also RHW
Collin, Matthew 171
Collin, Richard H(arvey) 1932- 122
Collin, Richard Oliver 1940- 105
Collinge, William B. 1949- 162
Collings, Ellsworth 1887-1970 73-76
Collings, Gillian 1939- 169
See also SATA 102
Collings, I. J(illie) CANR-38
Earlier sketch in CA 115
Collings, Matthew 1955- 225
Collings, Michael R(obert) 1947- CANR-56
Earlier sketches in CA 111, CANR-30
Collington, Peter 1948- 127
See also SATA 59, 99
Collingwood, Charles (Cummings)
1917-1985 .... 29-32R
Obituary 117
Collingwood, Donna K. 145
Collingwood, R(obin) G(eorge)
1889(?)-1943 155
Brief entry 117
See also DLB 262
See also TCLC 67
Collingwood, W(illiam) G(ershom)
1854-1932 .... DLB 149
Collins, Ace 1953- 149
See also SATA 82
Collins, Alan 1928- 132
Collins, Alice H(esslein) 1907- 65-68
Collins, An fl. c. 1653- .... DLB 131
Collins, Andrew J.
See Collins, Ace
Collins, Anthony 1676-1729 .... DLB 252
Collins, Arnold Quint 1935- 73-76
Collins, Arthur Worth, Jr. 1929- 131
Collins, Barbara J(ane) 1929- CANR-6
Earlier sketch in CA 57-60
Collins, Barry 1941- 102
See also CBD
See also CD 5, 6
Collins, Barry E(merson) 1937- CANR-7
Earlier sketch in CA 13-16R
Collins, Beulah Stowe 1923-1983 122
Obituary 110
Collins, Billy 1941- CANR-92
Earlier sketch in CA 151
See also AAYA 64
See also MTFW 2005
See also PC 68
See also PFS 18

Collins 118 CONTEMPORARY AUTHORS

Collins, Brandilyn 1956- 220
Collins, Bud
See Collins, Arthur Worth, Jr.
Collins, Carvel 1912-1990 .... CANR-8
Obituary 131
Earlier sketch in CA 17-20R
Collins, Catherine Fisher CANR-127
Earlier sketch in CA 165
Collins, Cecil (James Henry) 1908-1989
Obituary 128
Collins, Charles C. 1919- 25-28R
Collins, Charles William 1880-1964
Obituary 89-92
Collins, Christopher 1936- 49-52
Collins, Cindy
See Smith, Richard Rein
Collins, Clark
See Reynolds, Dallas McCord
Collins, Colette
See Knaack, Twila
Collins, D.
See Bulleid, H(enry) A(nthony) V(aughan)
Collins, Dan 1959- 223
Collins, David (Joseph) 1962- 208
Collins, David A(lmon) 1931- 21-24R
Collins, David R(aymond)
1940-2001 .... CANR-99
Earlier sketches in CA 29-32R, CANR-11, 26, 51
See also SATA 7, 121
Collins, Desmond 1940- CANR-14
Earlier sketch in CA 73-76
Collins, Donald E(dward) 1934- 122
Collins, Douglas 1912-1972
Obituary 33-36R
Collins, Eamon 1954-1999 233
Collins, Eliza G. C. 1938- 129
Collins, F(rederick) Herbert 1890-1967 . CAP-1
Earlier sketch in CA 11-12
Collins, Fletcher, Jr. 1906-2005 53-56
Obituary 239
Collins, Freda
See Collins, Frederica Joan Hale
Collins, Frederica Joan Hale 1904- CAP-1
Earlier sketch in CA 13-14
Collins, Gary (Ross) 1934- CANR-45
Earlier sketches in CA 57-60, CANR-7, 22
Collins, George R(oseborough)
1917-1993 .... CANR-1
Obituary 140
Earlier sketch in CA 1-4R
Collins, Harold R(eeves) 1915- 25-28R
Collins, Harry M. 1943- 220
Collins, Heather 1946- .... SATA 81
Collins, Helen (Francis) 141
Collins, Henry 1917- 17-20R
Collins, Henry B(ascom), Jr. 1899-1987
Obituary 123
Collins, Herbert Ridgeway 1932- 118
Collins, Hugh 1953- 158
Collins, Hunt
See Hunter, Evan
Collins, Irene 1925- 151
Collins, Jackie 1941- CANR-98
Earlier sketches in CA 102, CANR-22, 64
See also BEST 90:4
See also BPFB 1
See also CPW
See also DAM POP
Collins, James Daniel 1917- CANR-5
Earlier sketch in CA 1-4R
Collins, Jean E(lizabeth) 1948- 110
Collins, Joan 1933- 116
Collins, Jodie 1941- 121
Collins, John H. 1893-1981 .... 1-4R
Collins, John J(oseph) 1946- 112
Collins, John Lawrence, Jr.
1929-2005 .... CANR-77
Earlier sketches in CA 65-68, CANR-19
Interview in CANR-19
Collins, John M(artin) 1921- CANR-117
Earlier sketches in CA 49-52, CANR-31, 56
Collins, Joseph B. 1898(?)-1975
Obituary 53-56
Collins, Joseph T. 1939- CANR-96
Earlier sketches in CA 120, CANR-45
Collins, Josie
See Bentley, Joyce
Collins, Judith Graham 1942- 115
Collins, Judy (Marjorie) 1939- CANR-95
Earlier sketches in CA 103, CANR-79
Collins, Julie (Hubbard) 1959- 131
Collins, June Irene 1935- 37-40R
Collins, Kathleen 1931- 119
Collins, L(ewis) John 1905-1982 .... CAP-1
Obituary 108
Earlier sketch in CA 13-14
Collins, Larry
See Collins, John Lawrence, Jr.
Collins, Lawrence D. 1907- 149
Collins, Linda 1931- 125
See also CLC 44
Collins, Lorraine (Hill) 1931- 57-60
Collins, Mabel
See Cook, Mabel Collins
Collins, Margaret (Brandon James)
1909- 89-92
Collins, Marie (Margaret) 1935- 53-56
Collins, Marjorie A(nn) 1930- CANR-11
Earlier sketch in CA 65-68
Collins, Marva (Deloise Nettles) 1936- 111
Collins, Mary Clementine 1846-1920 225
Collins, Max
See Collins, Max Allan, (Jr.)
Collins, Max Allan, (Jr.) 1948- CANR-138
Earlier sketches in CA 103, CANR-27, 58, 88
See also AAYA 51
See also MTFW 2005
Collins, Meghan 1926- 101
Collins, Merle 1950- 175
See also BW 3
See also DLB 157
Collins, Michael
See Lynds, Dennis
Collins, Michael 1930- CANR-5
Earlier sketch in CA 53-56
See also SATA 58
Collins, Michael 1964- 211
See also DLB 267
Collins, Miki (Dickey) 1959- 131
Collins, Mortimer 1827-1876 .... DLB 21, 35
Collins, Myron D(ean) 1901-1991 .... CAP-1
Earlier sketch in CA 13-16
Collins, Myrtle T(elleen) 1915- 101
Collins, Nancy A(verill) 1959- CANR-134
Earlier sketches in CA 148, CANR-73
See also HGG
See also SUFW 2
Collins, Nancy W.
See Collins-Chapman, Nancy W(hisnant)
Collins, Norman Richard 1907-1982 105
Obituary 107
Collins, Orvis F(loyd) 1918- 69-72
Collins, P. Elizabeth
See Collins, P(atricia) Elizabeth
Collins, P(atricia) Elizabeth 1950- 184
Collins, Pat(ricia) Lowery 1932- CANR-105
Earlier sketches in CA 107, CANR-24, 49
See also SATA 31, 151
Collins, Patricia Hill 1948- 154
See also FW
Collins, Paul 1936- CANR-87
Earlier sketch in CA 153, 196
See also SATA 126
Collins, Paul 1969- 235
Collins, Peter (Sheridan) 1942- 77-80
Collins, Philip (Arthur William)
1923- CANR-125
Earlier sketches in CA 5-8R, CANR-8, 22
Collins, R(obert) G(eorge) 1926- 112
Collins, Randall 1941- 189
Collins, Raymond F(rancis) 1935- 112
Collins, Richard (Wayne) 1952- 235
Collins, Robert 1924- CANR-15
Earlier sketch in CA 89-92
Collins, Robert E(mmet) 1927- 69-72
Collins, Robert M. 1943- 110
Collins, Robert O(akley) 1933- CANR-48
Earlier sketches in CA 1-4R, CANR-4, 22
Collins, Ronald K. L. 1949- CANR-130
Earlier sketch in CA 154
Collins, Rowland Lee 1934-1985 .... 9-12R
Obituary 116
Collins, Ruth Philpott 1890-1975 .... CANR-4
Obituary 53-56
Earlier sketch in CA 1-4R
See also SATA-Obit 30
Collins, Stephen 1947- 201
Collins, Stephen L. 1949- 140
Collins, Tess 170
Collins, Thomas Hightower 1910-1978 102
Collins, Tom
See Furphy, Joseph
See also RGEL 2
Collins, Trish 1927- 106
Collins, (William) Wilkie 1824-1889 ... BRWS 6
See also CDBLB 1832-1890
See also CMW 4
See also DLB 18, 70, 159
See also GL 2
See also MSW
See also RGEL 2
See also RGSF 2
See also SUFW 1
See also WLIT 4
Collins, Will
See Corley, Edwin (Raymond)
Collins, William 1721-1759 .... BRW 3
See also DAM POET
See also DLB 109
See also RGEL 2
Collins, William Alexander Roy 1900-1976
Obituary 69-72
Collins, William Bernard 1913- 5-8R
Collins-Chapman, Nancy W(hisnant)
1933- 112
Collinson, A. S.
See Collinson, Alan S.
Collinson, Alan S. 1934- 147
See also SATA 80
Collinson, Laurence (Henry) 1925-1986 103
See also CP 1, 2
Collinson, Roger (Alfred) 1936- CANR-111
Earlier sketch in CA 110
See also SATA 133
Collinson, Sarah 1965- 147
Collins-Queen, Niki 1950- 182
Collis, John Stewart 1900-1984 61-64
Obituary 112
Collis, Kevin F(rancis) 1930- 107
Collis, Louise 1925- 21-24R
Collis, Maurice 1889-1973 .... CANR-4
Obituary 89-92
Earlier sketch in CA 5-8R
See also DLB 195
Collis, Rose 1959- 224
Collis, William Robert Fitzgerald
1900-1975 .... CAP-1
Earlier sketch in CA 9-10
Collischan, Judy 1940- 192
Collison, David (John) 1937- 105
Collison, Gary 1947- 158
Collison, Kerry B(oyd) 1944- 193
Collison, Koder M(acklin) 1910-1979 53-56
Collison, Robert Lewis Wright
1914-1989 .... CANR-2
Earlier sketch in CA 5-8R
Colliss, Gertrude Florence Mary (Jones)
1908- 5-8R
Collodi, Carlo
See Lorenzini, Carlo
See also CLR 5
See also WCH
See also WLIT 7
Collom, Jack 1931- 77-80
Colloms, Brenda 1919- CANR-7
Earlier sketch in CA 61-64
See also SATA 40
Collon, Dominique 1940- 186
Collum, Danny Duncan 1954- 193
Collura, Mary-Ellen Lang 1949- 165
Collver, Michael 1953- 165
Collyer, Mary 1716(?)-1763(?) .... DLB 39
Collymore, Frank Appleton 1893- .... CP 1, 2
Collyns, Robin 1940- 69-72
Colm, Gerhard 1897-1968 .... 5-8R
Obituary 103
Colman, Arthur D. 1937- 33-36R
Colman, Benjamin 1673-1747 .... DLB 24
Colman, Carol 224
Colman, E(rnest) A(drian) M(ackenzie)
1930- 57-60
Colman, George
See Glassco, John
Colman, George, the Elder 1732-1794 . RGEL 2
Colman, George, the Younger
1762-1836 .... DLB 89
See also RGEL 2
Colman, Hila CANR-103
Earlier sketches in CA 13-16R, CANR-7
See also AAYA 1
See also JRDA
See also MAICYA 1, 2
See also SAAS 14
See also SATA 1, 53
See also WYA
Colman, John E. 1923- 21-24R
Colman, Juliet Benita 1944- 61-64
Colman, Libby Lee 1940- 33-36R
Colman, Morris 1899(?)-1981 ..... SATA-Obit 25
Colman, Penny (Morgan) 1944- 145
See also AAYA 42
See also SATA 77, 114, 160
See also SATA-Essay 160
Colman, Warren (David) 1944- 136
See also SATA 67
Colmer, John (Anthony) 1921-1994 .. CANR-34
Earlier sketches in CA 85-88, CANR-15
Colmer, Michael (J.) 1942- CANR-21
Earlier sketch in CA 69-72
Colodny, Len 1938- 162
Colodny, Robert G. 1915- CANR-14
Earlier sketch in CA 37-40R
Cologne-Brookes, Gavin (John) 1961- 152
Colombo, Dale
See Monroe, Keith
Colombo, Furio 1931- CANR-30
Earlier sketch in CA 111
Colombo, John Robert 1936- CANR-48
Earlier sketches in CA 25-28R, CANR-11
See also CAAS 22
See also CP 1, 2, 3, 4, 5, 6, 7
See also DLB 53
See also SATA 50
Colominas, Kathleen Adele 1948- 134
Colon, Jesus 1901-1974 .... CANR-72
Earlier sketch in CA 131
See also HW 1
Colon, Raul .... SATA 156
Colonel Sanders
See Sanders, Harland
Colonius, Lillian 1911-1992 .... 21-24R
See also SATA 3
Colonna, Vittoria 1492-1547 .... RGWL 2, 3
Colony, Horatio 1900-1977 .... 37-40R
Colorado, Antonio J.
See Colorado (Capella), Antonio J(ulio)
Colorado (Capella), Antonio J(ulio)
1903-1994 .... CANR-32
Obituary 144
Earlier sketch in CA 17-20R
See also HW 1
See also SATA 23
See also SATA-Obit 79
Colp, Ralph, Jr. 1924- 126
Colpi, Henri 1921- .... IDFW 3, 4
Colquhoun, Archibald 1912-1964 129
Obituary 89-92
Colquhoun, Frank 1909-1997 106
Obituary 157
Colquhoun, Ithell 1906-1988 .... 13-16R
Obituary 125
Colquhoun, Keith 1927- 102
Colquhoun, Patrick 1745-1820 .... DLB 158
Colquitt, Betsy Feagan 1926- 53-56
Colson, Bill
See Athanas, (William) Verne
Colson, Charles W(endell) 1931- CANR-111
Earlier sketches in CA 102, CANR-29, 54
Colson, Elizabeth 1917- 53-56
Colson, Frederick
See Geis, Richard E(rwin)
Colson, Greta (Scotchmur) 1913- CAP-1
Earlier sketch in CA 9-10
Colson, Howard P(aul) 1910-1993 .... 29-32R
Colson, Laramie
See Richardson, Gladwell
Colston, Fifi E. 1960- 225
See also SATA 150
Colston, Lowell G(wen) 1919-1985 53-56
Obituary 118
Colston-Baynes, Dorothy 1881(?)-1973
Obituary 104
Colt, Clem
See Nye, Nelson C(oral)
Colt, George Howe 227
Colt, John W. 1900(?)-1983
Obituary 111
Colt, Martin
See Epstein, Beryl (M. Williams) and Epstein, Samuel
Colt, Winchester Remington
See Hubbard, L(afayette) Ron(ald)
Colt, Zandra
See Stevenson, Florence
Coltart, James M(ilne) 1903-1986
Obituary 120
Coltart, Nina 1927-1997 144
Obituary 159
Colter, Cyrus J. 1910-2002 .... CANR-66
Obituary 205
Earlier sketches in CA 65-68, CANR-10
See also BW 1
See also CLC 58
See also CN 2, 3, 4, 5, 6
See also DLB 33
Colter, Dale
See Broomall, Robert W(alter)
Colter, Shayne
See Norwood, Victor G(eorge) C(harles)
Coltharp, Lurline H(ughes) 1913-1998 .. 17-20R
Coltman, Ernest Vivian
See Dudley, Ernest
Coltman, Paul Curtis 1917- .... CP 1
Coltman, Will
See Bingley, David Ernest
Colton, C(larence) E(ugene) 1914- CANR-2
Earlier sketch in CA 5-8R
Colton, Harold S(ellers) 1881-1970 .... CANR-3
Earlier sketch in CA 1-4R
Colton, Helen 1918- 57-60
Colton, James
See Hansen, Joseph
See also GLL 1
Colton, James B(yers) II 1908-1983 .... 37-40R
Colton, Joel 1918- CANR-2
Earlier sketch in CA 1-4R
Colton, Timothy J. 1947- CANR-63
Earlier sketch in CA 124
Coltrane, James
See Wohl, James P(aul)
Colum, Padraic 1881-1972 .... CANR-35
Obituary 33-36R
Earlier sketch in CA 73-76
See also BYA 4
See also CLC 28
See also CLR 36
See also CP 1
See also CWRI 5
See also DLB 19
See also MAICYA 1, 2
See also MTCW 1
See also RGEL 2
See also SATA 15
See also WCH
Columbu, Franco 1941- 125
Columbus, Chris(topher) 1959- 154
See also SATA 97
Columbus, Christopher 1451-1506 ..... DLB 318
Columella
See Moore, Clement Clarke
Columella fl. 1st cent. - .... DLB 211
Colver, A(nthony) Wayne 1923- 93-96
Colver, Alice Mary (Ross) 1892-1988 69-72
Obituary 161
Colver, Anne 1908- CANR-2
Earlier sketch in CA 45-48
See also SATA 7
Colvert, James B(rumley) 1921- 116
Colvett, Latayne
See Scott, Latayne Colvett
Colvile, Georgiana M. M. 171
Colville, Derek Kent 1923-
Brief entry 105
Colville, John Rupert 1915-1987 ...... CANR-10
Obituary 124
Earlier sketch in CA 61-64
Colville, W(illiam Wilberforce) J(uvenal)
1859(?)-1917 214
Colvin, Brenda 1897-1981
Obituary 108
Colvin, Clare 1943- 123
Colvin, Elaine Wright 1942- 106
Colvin, Howard Montagu 1919- 61-64
Colvin, Ian G(oodhope) 1912-1975 ...... CAP-2
Obituary 57-60
Earlier sketch in CA 19-20
Colvin, James
See Moorcock, Michael (John)
Colvin, John (Horace Ragnar) 1922-2003 ... 189
Obituary 221
Colvin, Ralph W(hitmore) 1920-1981 107
Obituary 104
Colvin, Sidney 1845-1927 182
See also DLB 149
Colwell, C(harles) Carter 1932- 41-44R
Colwell, Eileen (Hilda) 1904-2002 ... CANR-12
Obituary 211
Earlier sketch in CA 29-32R
See also SATA 2
Colwell, Ernest Cadman 1901-1974 ... CANR-4
Obituary 53-56
Earlier sketch in CA 5-8R
Colwell, Richard J(ames) 1930- 69-72

Cumulative Index 119 Conklin

Colwell, Rita R. 1934- 157
Colwell, Robert 1931- 33-36R
Colwin, Laurie (E.) 1944-1992 CANR-46
Obituary 139
Earlier sketches in CA 89-92, CANR-20
See also CLC 5, 13, 23, 84
See also DLB 218
See also DLBY 1980
See also MTCW 1
Colwyn, Stewart
See Pepper, Frank S.
Colyer, Penrose 1940- CANR-20
Earlier sketches in CA 65-68, CANR-14
Colyer, Richard Moore
See Moore-Colyer, Richard
Coma, Javier 1939- 180
Coman, Carolyn 195
See also AAYA 41
See also BYA 11
See also MAICYA 2
See also SATA 127
Coman, Dale Rex 1906-1993 81-84
Coman, Edwin Truman, Jr. 1903-1995 9-12R
Obituary 161
Coman, Otilia-Valeria
See Blandiana, Ana
Comaroff, Jean 1946- 139
Comaroff, John L(ionel) 1945- CANR-57
Earlier sketch in CA 125
Comaromi, John P(hillip) 1937- 111
Comarow, Avery 1945- 127
Comay, Joan 103
Combe, William 1742-1823 RGEL 2
Comber, Lillian 1916- CANR-3
Earlier sketch in CA 9-12R
Combes, Simon (Glenton) 1940-2004 176
Obituary 234
Combette, Josephe 1916-1955
See Capecia, Mayotte
Comblin, Jose 1923-1988 214
Combs, A(rthur) W(right)
1912-1999 CANR-141
Earlier sketches in CA 17-20R, CANR-10
Combs, Ann 1935- 117
Combs, David 1934- 108
Combs, Eugene 1934- 118
Combs, Harry (Benjamin) 1913-2003 129
Obituary 222
Combs, James E(verett) 1941- CANR-19
Earlier sketch in CA 101
Combs, Jerald A(rthur) 1937- 110
Combs, Lisa M.
See McCourt, Lisa
Combs, Maxine 1937- 195
Combs, Maxine Solow
See Combs, Maxine
Combs, Patrick 230
Combs, Richard Earl 1934- 33-36R
Combs, Robert
See Murray, John
Combs, (Elisha) Tram(mell, Jr.) 1924- 13-16R
Combuchen, Sigrid
See Combuechen, Sigrid
Combuechen, Sigrid 1942- 136
Comden, Betty 1917- CANR-140
Earlier sketches in CA 49-52, CANR-2, 40
See also DLB 44, 265
See also IDFW 3, 4
Comeau, Arthur M. 1938- 61-64
Comencini, Luigi 1916- 149
Comer, James P(ierpont) 1934- CANR-43
Earlier sketch in CA 61-64
See also BW 2
Comer, Krista 1958- 209
Comey, Dennis J. 1896-1987
Obituary 123
Comey, James Hugh 1947- 65-68
Comfort, Alex(ander) 1920-2000 CANR-45
Obituary 190
Earlier sketches in CA 1-4R, CANR-1
See also CLC 7
See also CN 1, 2, 3, 4
See also CP 1, 2, 3, 4, 5, 6, 7
See also DAM POP
See also MTCW 2
Comfort, B(arbara) 1916- CANR-72
Earlier sketch in CA 150
Comfort, Claudette Hegel
See Hegel, Claudette
Comfort, Howard 1904-1993 37-40R
Obituary 161
Comfort, Iris Tracy CANR-6
Earlier sketch in CA 13-16R
Comfort, Jane Levington
See Sturtzel, Jane Levington
Comfort, Mildred Houghton 1886-1976 9-12R
See also SATA 3
Comfort, Montgomery
See Campbell, (John) Ramsey
Comfort, Philip W(esley) 1950- 211
Comfort, Ray 1949- 150
Comfort, Richard A(llen) 1933- 21-24R
Comfort, Will Levington 1878-1932 TCWW 1, 2
Comi, Girolamo 1890-1968 175
See also DLB 114
Comidas, Chinas
See Genser, Cynthia
Comini, Alessandra 1934- 93-96
Comins, Ethel M(ae) CANR-8
Earlier sketch in CA 61-64
See also SATA 11
Comins, Jeremy 1933- CANR-14
Earlier sketch in CA 65-68
See also SATA 28
Comisso, Giovanni 1895-1969 DLB 264
Comitas, Lambros 1927- 185
Brief entry 113
Comito, Terry (Allen) 1935- CANR-29
Earlier sketch in CA 109
Commager, Henry Steele
1902-1998 CANR-68
Obituary 165
Earlier sketches in CA 21-24R, CANR-26
See also DLB 17
See also MTCW 1, 2
See also MTFW 2005
See also SATA 23
See also SATA-Obit 102
Commager, (Henry) Steele, (Jr.) 1932-1984
Obituary 112
Commins, William Dollard Sr. 1899-1983
Obituary 109
Commire, Anne CANR-44
Earlier sketches in CA 69-72, CANR-21
Committe, Thomas C. 1922- 65-68
Commoner, Barry 1917- CANR-93
Earlier sketches in CA 65-68, CANR-33, 76
See also MTCW 1, 2
Commons, Dorman L(eland) 1918- 129
Commons, Giselle GLL 1
Commynes, Phillippe de c.
1447-1511 DLB 208
Como, (Michael) William 1925-1989 69-72
Obituary 127
Comparetti, Alice (Pattee) 1907-1996 37-40R
Obituary 161
Compere, Mickie
See Davidson, Margaret
Compestine, Ying Chang 1963- 211
See also SATA 140
Compitello, Malcolm Alan 1946- 136
Complo, Sister Jannita Marie 1935- 57-60
Compo, Susan 1955- 134
Comprone, Joseph J(ohn) 1943- CANR-35
Earlier sketches in CA 53-56, CANR-5
Compton, Ann
See Prebble, Marjorie Mary Curtis
Compton, Arthur Holly 1892-1962 158
Obituary 116
Compton, D(avid) G(uy) 1930- CANR-17
Earlier sketch in CA 25-28R
See also DLB 261
See also SFW 4
Compton, Guy
See Compton, D(avid) G(uy)
Compton, Henry (Pasfield) 1909- 9-12R
Compton, James V(incent) 1928- 29-32R
Compton, Patricia A. 1936- 142
See also SATA 75
Compton, Piers 1903- 122
Compton, Susan P. 236
Compton-Burnett, I(vy) 1892(?)-1969 CANR-4
Obituary 25-28R
Earlier sketch in CA 1-4R
See also BRW 7
See also CLC 1, 3, 10, 15, 34
See also DAM NOV
See also DLB 36
See also EWL 3
See also MTCW 1, 2
See also RGEL 2
Compton-Hall, (Patrick) Richard
1929- CANR-49
Earlier sketches in CA 107, CANR-24
Comrey, Andrew Laurence 1923- 189
Brief entry 106
Comroe, Julius H(iram), Jr. 1911-1984 122
Obituary 113
Comstock, Anna Botsford 1854-1930 ANW
Comstock, Anthony 1844-1915 169
Brief entry 110
See also TCLC 13
Comstock, Christine 1942- CANR-20
Earlier sketch in CA 104
Comstock, Gary 1954- 127
Comstock, Gary D(avid) 1945- CANR-125
Earlier sketch in CA 162
Comstock, George Adolphe 1932- 124
Comstock, Helen 1893-1970 CANR-4
Obituary 89-92
Earlier sketch in CA 5-8R
Comstock, Henry B. 1908- CAP-2
Earlier sketch in CA 33-36
Comstock, Mary Bryce 1934- 105
Comstock, W(illiam) Richard 1928- 73-76
Comte, P. D. Q.
See Hilbert, Richard A.
Comte, The Great
See Hawkesworth, Eric
Comus
See Ballantyne, R(obert) M(ichael)
Comyns, Barbara
See Comyns-Carr, Barbara Irene Veronica
See also BRWS 8
Comyns, Nance
See Comyns-Toohey, Nantz
Comyns-Carr, Barbara Irene Veronica
1912-1992 5-8R
See also Comyns, Barbara
Comyns-Toohey, Nantz 1956- SATA 86
Conacher, D(esmond) J(ohn) 1918- 25-28R
Conacher, J(ames) B(lennerhasset)
1916- 25-28R
Conan, Laure 1845-1924 175
See also DLB 99
Conan Doyle, Adrian Malcolm
1910-1970 5-8R
Obituary 29-32R
Conan Doyle, Arthur
See Doyle, Sir Arthur Conan
See also BPFB 1
See also BYA 4, 5, 11
Conant, Eaton H. 1930- 53-56
Conant, Howard (Somers) 1921- CANR-8
Earlier sketch in CA 17-20R
Conant, James Bryant 1893-1978 13-16R
Obituary 77-80
Conant, Kenneth John 1894-1984 1-4R
Obituary 161
Conant, Michael 1924- 138
Conant, Ralph W(endell) 1926- CANR-31
Earlier sketches in CA 29-32R, CANR-14
Conant, Roger 1909-
Brief entry 107
Conant, Susan CANR-142
Earlier sketches in CA 139, CANR-72
Conard, Alfred Fletcher 1911- 13-16R
Conard, Joseph W(ickersham)
1911-1965 13-16R
Conard, Rebecca 1946- 162
Conard, Robert C. 1933- CANR-111
Earlier sketches in CA 126, CANR-53
Conarroe, Joel (Osborne) 1934- 29-32R
Conarroe, Richard R(iley) 1928- 69-72
Conason, Joe 1954(?)- 218
Conati, Marcello 1928- 154
Conaway, James (Alley) 1941- CANR-142
Earlier sketch in CA 33-36R
Concannon, Winifred
See Ament, Deloris Tarzan
Conchon, Georges 1925-1990
Obituary 132
Conconi, Charles N. 1938- 77-80
Conde, Alfredo 1945- EWL 3
Conde (Abellan), Carmen 1901-1996 177
See also CWW 2
See also DLB 108
See also EWL 3
See also HLCS 1
See also HW 2
Conde, Jesse C(lay) 1912-1994 57-60
Conde, Maryse 1937- 190
Earlier sketches in CA 110, CANR-30, 53, 76
Autobiographical Essay in 190
See also BLCS
See also BW 2, 3
See also CLC 52, 92
See also CWW 2
See also DAM MULT
See also EWL 3
See also MTCW 2
See also MTFW 2005
Condee, Ralph Waterbury 1916- 17-20R
Condee, William Faricy 1954- 239
Condell, Bruce 1941- 215
Condillac, Etienne Bonnot de
1714-1780 DLB 313
Condit, Carl Wilbur 1914-1997 CANR-4
Earlier sketch in CA 1-4R
Condit, Martha Olson 1913- 73-76
See also SATA 28
Condliffe, John B(ell) 1891-1981 CAP-1
Obituary 106
Earlier sketch in CA 13-16
Condon, Bill 1949- 213
See also SATA 142
Condon, David Rensing 1924-1994 114
Obituary 147
Condon, E(dward) U(hler) 1902-1974
Obituary 112
Condon, Eddie 1905-1973
Obituary 45-48
Condon, George Edward 1916- CANR-1
Earlier sketch in CA 45-48
Condon, Jack
See Condon, John C(arl), Jr.
Condon, Jane 1951- 128
Condon, John C(arl), Jr. 1938- CANR-10
Earlier sketch in CA 21-24R
Condon, Judith 150
See also SATA 83
Condon, Richard (Thomas)
1915-1996 CANR-23
Obituary 151
Earlier sketches in CA 1-4R, CANR-2
Interview in CANR-23
See also CAAS 1
See also BEST 90:3
See also BPFB 1
See also CLC 4, 6, 8, 10, 45, 100
See also CMW 4
See also CN 1, 2, 3, 4, 5, 6
See also DAM NOV
See also MAL 5
See also MTCW 1, 2
Condon, Robert 1921(?)-1972
Obituary 37-40R
Condor, Gladyn
See Davison, Gladys Patton
Condorcet
See Condorcet, marquis de Marie-Jean-Antoine-Nicolas Caritat
See also GFL Beginnings to 1789
Condorcet, marquis de
Marie-Jean-Antoine-Nicolas Caritat
1743-1794
See Condorcet
See also DLB 313
Condray, Bruno
See Humphrys, Leslie George
Condry, William Moreton 1918-1998 103
Condy, Roy 1942- SATA 96
Cone, Carl B(ruce) 1916-1995 9-12R
Obituary 161
Cone, Edward T(oner) 1917-2004 110
Obituary 232
Cone, Fairfax Mastick 1903-1977 73-76
Obituary 69-72
Cone, Ferne Geller 1921- 107
See also SATA 39
Cone, James H. 1938- CANR-90
Earlier sketch in CA 33-36R
Cone, John F(rederick) 1926- 17-20R
Cone, Molly (Lamken) 1918- CANR-37
Earlier sketches in CA 1-4R, CANR-1, 16
See also SAAS 11
See also SATA 1, 28, 115, 151
See also SATA-Essay 151
Cone, Patrick 1954- SATA 89
Cone, William F. 1919- 57-60
Conejo, Carlos A. 1956- 212
Conerly, Perian Collier 1926- 5-8R
Cones, John W. 1945- 172
Coney, Michael G(reatrex) 1932- CANR-56
Earlier sketch in CA 97-100
See also SATA 61
See also SFW 4
Coney, Michael Greatrex
See Coney, Michael G(reatrex)
Coney, Mike
See Coney, Michael G(reatrex)
Coney, Sandra 1944- 150
Confer, Dennis W. 1941- 157
Confer, Vincent 1913-1998 21-24R
Confiant, Raphael 1951- 199
Conford, Ellen 1942- CANR-111
Earlier sketches in CA 33-36R, CANR-13, 29, 54
See also AAYA 10
See also CLR 10, 71
See also JRDA
See also MAICYA 1, 2
See also SATA 6, 68, 110, 162
See also YAW
Confucius
See Lund, Philip R(eginald)
Confucius 551B.C.-479B.C. DA
See also DA3
See also DAB
See also DAC
See also DAM MST
See also WLCS
Congar, Marie Joseph
See Congar, (Georges) Yves Marie-Joseph
Congar, Y. M.
See Congar, (Georges) Yves Marie-Joseph
Congar, Yves
See Congar, (Georges) Yves Marie-Joseph
Congar, Yves M.-J.
See Congar, (Georges) Yves Marie-Joseph
Congar, Yves M. J.
See Congar, (Georges) Yves Marie-Joseph
Congar, (Georges) Yves Marie-Joseph
1904-1995 130
Obituary 149
Congdon, Constance S. 1944- CANR-67
Earlier sketch in CA 123
See also CAD
See also CD 5, 6
See also CWD
Congdon, Herbert Wheaton 1876-1965 5-8R
Congdon, Kirby 1924- CANR-7
Earlier sketch in CA 13-16R
Congdon, Kristin G. 1948- 138
Congdon, Lee (Walter) 1939- 130
Congdon, William Grosvenor
1912-1998 CANR-24
Earlier sketches in CA 17-20R, CANR-7
Conger, (Seymour) Beach III 1912-1969
Obituary 115
Conger, Jay A. 1952- 132
Conger, John (Janeway) 1921- CANR-6
Earlier sketch in CA 13-16R
Conger, Lesley
See Suttles, Shirley (Smith)
Conger, Marion (C.) 1915-1990
Obituary 130
Conger, Syndy McMillen 1942- 152
Congrat-Butler, Stefan 1914(?)-1979 103
Obituary 89-92
Congress, Richard 1943- 216
Congreve, Willard J(ohn) 1921-1979 57-60
Obituary 134
Congreve, William 1670-1729 BRW 2
See also CDBLB 1660-1789
See also DA
See also DAB
See also DAC
See also DAM DRAM, MST, POET
See also DC 2
See also DFS 15
See also DLB 39, 84
See also RGEL 2
See also WLC
See also WLIT 3
Conigliaro, Vincenzo 1928- 165
Conil, Jean 1917-2003 CANR-53
Obituary 215
Earlier sketches in CA 13-16R, CANR-13, 29
Conine, (Odie) Ernest 1925- 69-72
Coniston, Ed
See Bingley, David Ernest
Conkin, Paul K(eith) 1929- CANR-95
Earlier sketch in CA 33-36R
Conkle, E(llsworth) P(routy)
1899-1994 CANR-83
Obituary 144
Earlier sketch in CA 65-68
Conklin, Barbara P. 1927- 109
Conklin, Gladys Plemon 1903- CANR-4
Earlier sketch in CA 1-4R
See also SATA 2
Conklin, Groff 1904-1968 CANR-3
Earlier sketch in CA 1-4R
Conklin, Harold C(olyer) 1926- 118

Conklin 120 CONTEMPORARY AUTHORS

Conklin, John E(van) 1943- ... CANR-14
Earlier sketch in CA 37-40R
Conklin, Mike 1944- ... 120
Conklin, Paul S. 1929(?)-2003 ... 115
Obituary ... 221
Brief entry ... 111
See also SATA 43
See also SATA-Brief 33
See also SATA-Obit 147
Conkling, Hilda 1910-1986 ... SATA 23
Conlan, Kathleen Elizabeth 1950- ... 218
See also SATA 145
Conlan, Kathy
See Conlan, Kathleen Elizabeth
Conlay, Iris 1910- ... CAP-1
Earlier sketch in CA 11-12
Conley, Brenda (Joyce) Edgerton 1948- ... 239
Conley, Carolyn A. ... CANR-92
Earlier sketch in CA 145
Conley, Dalton ... 200
Conley, Ellen Alexander 1938- ... CANR-20
Earlier sketch in CA 103
Conley, Enid Mary 1917- ... CANR-10
Earlier sketch in CA 65-68
Conley, John (Allan) 1912-1999 ... 61-64
Conley, Katharine 1956- ... 236
Conley, Phillip Mallory 1887-1979 ... 69-72
Conley, Robert J(ackson) 1940- ... CANR-96
Earlier sketches in CA 41-44R, CANR-15, 34, 45
See also DAM MULT
See also NNAL
See also TCWW 2
Conley, Tom (Clark) 1943- ... 155
Conley, Verena Andermatt 1943- ... 117
Conley-Weaver, Robyn 1963- ... 196
See also SATA 125
Conlin, David A. 1897-1987 ... 17-20R
Conlin, Diane Atnally ... 173
Conlin, Joseph Robert 1940- ... CANR-40
Earlier sketch in CA 49-52
Conlon, Denis J. 1932- ... 37-40R
Conlon, Evelyn 1952- ... 176
See also DLB 319
Conlon, John J. 1945- ... 188
Conlon, Kathleen (Annie) 1943- ... CANR-86
Brief entry ... 114
Earlier sketch in CA 130
Conlon-McIvor, Maura ... 236
Conlon-McKenna, Marita 1956- ... 210
See also CWRI 5
See also SATA 71
Conly, Jane Leslie 1948- ... AAYA 32
See also SATA 80, 112
See also YAW
Conly, Robert Leslie 1918(?)-1973 ... 73-76
Obituary ... 41-44R
See also O'Brien, Robert C.
See also MAICYA 1, 2
See also SATA 23
See also YAW
Conn, Canary Denise 1949- ... 57-60
Conn, Charles Paul 1945- ... CANR-6
Earlier sketch in CA 57-60
Conn, Charles William 1920- ... CANR-10
Earlier sketch in CA 21-24R
Conn, Didi 1951- ... 226
Conn, Frances G. 1925- ... 33-36R
Conn, Jan E(velyn) 1952- ... CANR-31
Earlier sketch in CA 110
Conn, Martha Orr 1935- ... 93-96
Conn, Nicole 1959- ... CANR-137
Earlier sketch in CA 144
Conn, Peter J. 1942- ... 33-36R
Conn, Stetson 1908- ... CAP-1
Earlier sketch in CA 9-10
Conn, Stewart 1936- ... CANR-123
Brief entry ... 117
Earlier sketch in CA 153
See also CBD
See also CD 5, 6
See also CP 1, 2, 3, 4, 5, 6, 7
See also DLB 233
Conn, Walter E(ugene) 1940- ... CANR-92
Earlier sketch in CA 110
Connable, Alfred 1931- ... 81-84
Connally, Eugenia (Maye) Horstman 1931- ... 103
Connally, John (Bowden, Jr.) 1917-1993 ... 145
Connaughton, Shane ... CN 7
Connell, Brian (Reginald) 1916-1999 ... CANR-4
Obituary ... 183
Earlier sketch in CA 1-4R
Connell, Evan S(helby), Jr. 1924- ... CANR-140
Earlier sketches in CA 1-4R, CANR-2, 39, 76, 97
See also CAAS 2
See also AAYA 7
See also AMWS 14
See also CLC 4, 6, 45
See also CN 1, 2, 3, 4, 5, 6
See also DAM NOV
See also DLB 2
See also DLBY 1981
See also MAL 5
See also MTCW 1, 2
See also MTFW 2005
Connell, Francis J. 1888-1967 ... CAP-1
Earlier sketch in CA 13-14
Connell, George B(oyce II) 1957- ... 141
Connell, Jan
See Connell, Janice T(imchak)
Connell, Janice T(imchak) 1939- ... 140
Connell, John 1946- ... 203
Connell, Jon 1952- ... 97-100
Connell, K(enneth) H(ugh) 1917-1973 ... CAP-2
Earlier sketch in CA 25-28
Connell, Kirk
See Chapman, John Stanton Higham
Connell, Maureen 1931- ... 104
Connell, Richard Edward 1893-1949 ... BYA 14
See also EXPS
See also LAIT 3
See also SSFS 1
Connell, William Fraser 1916- ... 104
Connellan, Leo 1928-2001 ... 81-84
Obituary ... 193
Connelly, Bridget 1941- ... 127
Connelly, Douglas 1949- ... 121
Connelly, Frances S(usan) ... 151
Connelly, Joe 1963- ... 169
Connelly, Karen 1969- ... 149
Connelly, Marc(us Cook) 1890-1980 ... CANR-30
Obituary ... 102
Earlier sketch in CA 85-88
See also CAD
See also CLC 7
See also DFS 12
See also DLB 7
See also DLBY 1980
See also MAL 5
See also RGAL 4
See also SATA-Obit 25
Connelly, Merval Hannah
See Hoare, Merval Hannah
See also CP 1
Connelly, Michael 1956- ... CANR-91
Earlier sketch in CA 158
See also CMW 4
Connelly, Neil (O'Boyle) ... 237
Connelly, Neil O., Jr.
See Connelly, Neil (O'Boyle)
Connelly, Owen (Sergeson, Jr.) 1924- ... 17-20R
Connelly, Philip M(arshal) 1904(?)-1981
Obituary ... 104
Connelly, Thomas L(awrence) 1938- ... CANR-11
Earlier sketch in CA 17-20R
Connely, Willard 1888-1967 ... CAP-2
Earlier sketch in CA 17-18
Conner, Berenice Gillete 1908-1989 ... 65-68
Conner, Daryl R(iles) 1946- ... 142
Conner, Floyd D(avis) 1951- ... 119
Conner, K. Patrick 1952- ... CANR-54
Earlier sketch in CA 127
Conner, Lester I. 1919- ... 177
Conner, Patrick (Roy Mountifort) 1947- ... 106
Conner, Patrick Reardon 1907- ... 5-8R
Conner, Paul Willard 1937-1984 ... 17-20R
Obituary ... 114
Conner, Rearden
See Conner, Patrick Reardon
Conner, Valerie Jean 1945- ... 114
Conner, Walter T(homas) 1877-1952 ... 219
Connerly, Ward(ell) (Anthony) 1939- ... 229
Conners, Bernard F. 1926- ... CANR-140
Earlier sketch in CA 41-44R
Conners, Kenneth Wray 1909- ... 29-32R
Connery, Donald S(tuart) 1926-
Brief entry ... 114
Connery, George Edward 1907(?)-1985
Obituary ... 116
Connery, John (R.) 1913-1987
Obituary ... 124
Connery, Robert H(owe) 1907-1998 ... 41-44R
Obituary ... 169
Connery, Thomas Bernard ... 196
Connett, Eugene Virginius III 1891-1969 ... CAP-1
Earlier sketch in CA 13-14
Connette, Earle 1910-1984 ... CAP-1
Earlier sketch in CA 13-16
Connick, C(harles) Milo 1917- ... 1-4R
Conniff, Frank 1914-1971
Obituary ... 93-96
Conniff, James C(lifford) G(regory) ... 21-24R
Conniff, Michael L(ee) 1942- ... 118
Conniff, Richard 1951- ... CANR-137
Earlier sketch in CA 124
Connington, J. J.
See Stewart, A(lfred) W(alter)
See also CMW 4
Connolly, Cressida 1960- ... 194
Connolly, Cyril (Vernon) 1903-1974 ... CANR-61
Obituary ... 53-56
Earlier sketches in CAP-2, CA 21-22
See also BRWS 3
See also CN 1
See also DLB 98
See also MTCW 1, 2
See also RGEL 2
Connolly, Francis X(avier) 1909-1965 ... CAP-1
Earlier sketch in CA 13-14
Connolly, Geraldine 1947- ... 213
Connolly, James Brendan 1868-1957 ... 178
See also DLB 78
Connolly, Jerome P(atrick) 1931- ... SATA 8
Connolly, John 1968- ... 217
Connolly, Joseph 1950- ... 130
Connolly, Pat 1943- ... SATA 74
Connolly, Paul
See Wicker, Thomas Grey
Connolly, Peter 1935- ... 103
See also SATA 47, 105
Connolly, Ray 1940- ... 101
Connolly, Robert D(uggan, Jr.) 1917- ... 69-72
Connolly, S(ean) J. 1951- ... 138
Connolly, Thomas Edmund 1918- ... CANR-4
Earlier sketch in CA 1-4R
Connolly, Vivian 1925- ... CANR-1
Earlier sketch in CA 49-52
Connolly, William E(ugene) 1938- ... 201
Connon, Bryan (James Milne) 1927- ... 137
Connor, Anthony J(oseph) 1946- ... 144
Connor, Bernadette Y. 1952- ... 180
Connor, Catherine
See Rock, Gail
Connor, Daniel F. 1953- ... 234
Connor, J. Robert 1927- ... 123
Connor, James A. 1951- ... 229
Connor, Jim 1935- ... 107
Connor, Joan 1954- ... CANR-102
Earlier sketch in CA 168
Connor, John Anthony 1930- ... 13-16R
See also Connor, Tony
Connor, Joyce Mary 1929- ... CANR-10
Earlier sketch in CA 65-68
Connor, Kevin
See O'Rourke, Frank
Connor, Lawrence S(tanton) 1925- ... 89-92
Connor, Patricia 1943- ... 25-28R
Connor, Ralph
See Gordon, Charles William
See also DLB 92
See also TCLC 31
See also TCWW 1, 2
Connor, Seymour V(aughan) 1923- ... 53-56
Connor, Steven 1955- ... CANR-117
Earlier sketch in CA 141
Connor, Susanna Pflaum
See Pflaum, Susanna Whitney
Connor, Tony
See Connor, John Anthony
See also CP 1, 2
See also DLB 40
Connor, W(alter) Robert 1934- ... 41-44R
Connor, Walter Downing 1942- ... 106
Connor, William (Neil) 1909(?)-1967
Obituary ... 25-28R
Connor, William S. P. 1958- ... 169
Connors, Bruton
See Rohen, Edward
See also CP 1
Connors, Dorsey ... 45-48
Connors, John Stanley 1925-1984
Obituary ... 112
Connors, Joseph 1945- ... 106
Connors, Libby 1960- ... 194
Conoley, Gillian F. 1955- ... 197
Conolly, L(eonard) W(illiam) 1941- ... 106
Conolly, Violet 1901(?)-1988(?)
Obituary ... 124
Conolly-Smith, Peter 1964- ... 209
Conolly-Smith, Peter 1964- ... 208
Conor, Glen
See Cooney, Michael
Conot, Robert E. 1929- ... CANR-2
Earlier sketch in CA 45-48
Conover, Anne 1937- ... 230
Conover, C(harles) Eugene 1903-1983 ... 5-8R
Conover, Carole 1941- ... 89-92
Conover, Chris 1950- ... 128
See also SATA 31
Conover, David (Beals) 1919-1983 ... 115
Conover, Hobart H. 1914- ... 13-16R
Conover, Jessica Arline Wilcox
See Jones, Candy
Conover, Roger L(loyd) 1950- ... 130
Conover, Ted 1958- ... CANR-94
Earlier sketch in CA 129
Conquest, Edwin Parker, Jr. 1931- ... 29-32R
Conquest, John 1943- ... 144
Conquest, Ned
See Conquest, Edwin Parker, Jr.
Conquest, Owen
See Hamilton, Charles (Harold St. John)
Conquest, (George) Robert (Acworth) 1917- ... CANR-89
Earlier sketches in CA 13-16R, CANR-9, 25, 50
See also CN 1
See also CP 1, 2, 3, 4, 5, 6, 7
See also DLB 27
Conrad, Alfred Borys 1899(?)-1979
Obituary ... 104
Conrad, Andree 1945- ... 29-32R
Conrad, Barnaby (Jr.) 1922- ... CANR-6
Earlier sketch in CA 9-12R
Conrad, Brenda
See Brown, Zenith Jones
Conrad, David Eugene 1928- ... 17-20R
Conrad, Earl 1912-1986 ... CANR-78
Obituary ... 118
Earlier sketches in CA 1-4R, CANR-10
Conrad, Edna (G.) 1893-1991 ... CAP-2
Earlier sketch in CA 33-36
Conrad, Hal
See Conrad, Harold
Conrad, Harold 1911-1991 ... CANR-78
Obituary ... 134
Earlier sketch in CA 112
Conrad, Jack (Randolph) 1923- ... 9-12R
Conrad, Jean
See Martinez, Nancy C.
Conrad, John W(ilfred) 1935- ... CANR-4
Earlier sketch in CA 53-56
Conrad, Jon(athan) J(ames) 1920- ... 114
Conrad, Joseph 1857-1924 ... CANR-60
Brief entry ... 104
Earlier sketch in CA 131
See also AAYA 26
See also BPFB 1
See also BRW 6
See also BRWC 1
See also BRWR 2
See also BYA 2
See also CDBLB 1890-1914
See also DA
See also DA3
See also DAB
See also DAC
See also DAM MST, NOV
See also DLB 10, 34, 98, 156
See also EWL 3
See also EXPN
See also EXPS
See also LAIT 2
See also LATS 1:1
See also LMFS 1
See also MTCW 1, 2
See also MTFW 2005
See also NFS 2, 16
See also RGEL 2
See also RGSF 2
See also SATA 27
See also SSC 9, 67, 69, 71
See also SSFS 1, 12
See also TCLC 1, 6, 13, 25, 43, 57
See also TEA
See also WLC
See also WLIT 4
Conrad, Kenneth
See Lottich, Kenneth V(erne)
Conrad, L. K.
See Conrad, Andree
Conrad, Margaret R. 1946- ... 211
Conrad, Mark J. 1957- ... 164
Conrad, Pam 1947-1996 ... CANR-111
Obituary ... 151
Earlier sketches in CA 121, CANR-36, 78
See also AAYA 18
See also BYA 7, 8
See also CLR 18
See also JRDA
See also MAICYA 1, 2
See also MAICYAS 1
See also SAAS 19
See also SATA 52, 80, 133
See also SATA-Brief 49
See also SATA-Obit 90
See also YAW
Conrad, Paul (Francis) 1924- ... CANR-38
Earlier sketch in CA 113
Interview in ... CA-113
Conrad, Peter 1945- ... CANR-88
Earlier sketch in CA 139
Conrad, Robert 1928- ... 41-44R
Conrad, Robert Arnold
See Hart, Moss
Conrad, Susan P(hinney) 1941-
Brief entry ... 113
Conrad, Sybil 1921- ... 21-24R
Conrad, Tex
See Yates, A(lan) G(eoffrey)
Conrad, Tod
See Wilkes-Hunter, R(ichard)
Conrad, Will C. 1882-1970 ... CAP-1
Earlier sketch in CA 13-14
Conradi, Peter J(ohn) 1945- ... CANR-86
Earlier sketch in CA 133
Conradis, Heinz 1907- ... CAP-1
Earlier sketch in CA 13-14
Conrads, Ulrich 1923- ... 9-12R
Conran, Anthony 1931- ... CANR-14
Earlier sketch in CA 65-68
See also CP 1, 2
Conran, Shirley (Ida) 1932- ... CANR-22
Earlier sketch in CA 103
See also MTCW 1
Conran, Terence Orby 1931- ... CANR-120
Earlier sketch in CA 85-88
Conron, (Alfred) Brandon 1919- ... 17-20R
Conrow, Robert 1942- ... 57-60
Conroy, Al
See Albert, Marvin H(ubert)
Conroy, Albert
See Albert, Marvin H(ubert)
Conroy, Barbara 1934- ... 111
Conroy, Charles W. 1922- ... 13-16R
Conroy, Frank 1936-2005 ... CANR-88
Obituary ... 238
Earlier sketch in CA 77-80
See also NFS 11
Conroy, (Francis) Hilary 1919- ... CANR-39
Earlier sketch in CA 115
Conroy, Jack
See Conroy, John Wesley
See also CN 1, 2, 3
See also DLBY 1981
See also SATA 19
Conroy, Jim
See Chadwick, Joseph (L.)
Conroy, John 1951- ... CANR-120
Earlier sketch in CA 136
Conroy, John Wesley 1899-1990 ... CANR-78
Obituary ... 131
Earlier sketches in CA 5-8R, CANR-3
See also Conroy, Jack
See also SATA-Obit 65
Conroy, Mary 1941- ... 110
Conroy, Michael R(alph) 1945- ... CANR-9
Earlier sketch in CA 53-56

Cumulative Index 121 Cooke

Conroy, (Donald) Pat(rick) 1945- ... CANR-129
Earlier sketches in CA 85-88, CANR-24, 53
See also AAYA 8, 52
See also AITN 1
See also BPFB 1
See also CLC 30, 74
See also CN 7
See also CPW
See also CSW
See also DA3
See also DAM NOV, POP
See also DLB 6
See also LAIT 5
See also MAL 5
See also MTCW 1, 2
See also MTFW 2005
Conroy, Patricia 1941- ... 93-96
Conroy, Peter V(incent), Jr. 1944- ... 53-56
Conroy, Robert
See Goldston, Robert (Conroy)
Conroy, Thomas F(rancis) 1935- ... 143
Considine, Bob
See Considine, Robert (Bernard)
See also AITN 2
See also DLB 241
Considine, Douglas M(axwell)
1915- ... CANR-11
Earlier sketch in CA 69-72
Considine, Jennifer I(rene) 1962- ... 230
Considine, John 1938- ... 201
Considine, John J(oseph) 1897-1982 ... 1-4R
Considine, Robert (Bernard) 1906-1975 .. 93-96
Obituary ... 61-64
See also Considine, Bob
See also DLB 241
Considine, Shaun 1940- ... 137
Consilvio, Thomas 1947- ... 57-60
Consolmagno, Guy J. 1952- ... 218
Consolo, Dominick P(eter) 1923- ... 33-36R
Consolo, Vincenzo 1933- ... 232
See also DLB 196
Constable, George 1941(?)- ... 160
Constable, Giles 1929- ... 159
Constable, Henry 1562-1613 ... DLB 136
See also RGEL 2
Constable, John W. 1922- ... 81-84
Constable, Trevor James 1925- ... 89-92
Constable, W(illiam) G(eorge) 1887-1976 . 5-8R
Obituary ... 65-68
Constant, Alberta Wilson
1908-1981 ... CANR-78
Obituary ... 109
Earlier sketches in CA 1-4R, CANR-4
See also SATA 22
See also SATA-Obit 28
Constant (de Rebecque), (Henri) Benjamin
1767-1830 ... DLB 119
See also EW 4
See also GFL 1789 to the Present
Constant, Jan
See Dawson, Janis
Constante, Lena 1909- ... 156
Constantelos, Demetrios J. 1927- ... CANR-100
Earlier sketches in CA 21-24R, CANR-8, 24, 49
Constantin, James A. 1922- ... 13-16R
Constantin, Maurice
See Constantin-Weyer, Maurice
See also CCA 1
Constantin, Robert W(ilfrid) 1937- ... 25-28R
Constantine, David (John) 1944- ... CANR-120
Earlier sketch in CA 142
See also CP 7
See also DLB 40
Constantine, Greg(ory John) 1938- ... 117
Constantine, J. Robert 1924- ... 154
Constantine, K. C. 1934- ... CANR-71
Brief entry ... 114
Earlier sketch in CA 138
See also BPFB 1
See also CMW 4
See also MSW
Constantine, Larry L(eRoy) 1943- ... CANR-14
Earlier sketch in CA 81-84
Constantine, Mildred 1914- ... 112
Brief entry ... 105
Constantine, Murray
See Burdekin, Katharine (Penelope)
Constantine, Peter 1963- ... 188
Constantine, Stephen 1947- ... CANR-45
Earlier sketch in CA 120
Constantine, Storm 1956- ... CANR-92
Earlier sketch in CA 156
See also SFW 4
See also SUFW 2
Constantinescu, Gheorghe M(ircea) 1932- .. 237
Constantine-Simms, Delroy 1964- ... 227
Constantino, Renato 1919- ... CANR-42
Earlier sketch in CA 118
Constantin-Weyer, Maurice 1881-1964 ... 148
See also Constantin, Maurice
See also DLB 92
Constiner, Merle 1902-1979 ... TCWW 1, 2
Conte, Gian Biagio 1941- ... 136
Conteh-Morgan, Earl 1950- ... 175
Contento, William G(uy) 1947- ... 194
Conti, Bill 1942- ... IDFW 4
Conti, Gregory ... 199
Conti, Haroldo 1925-1976(?) ... 179
See also HW 2
Contini, Gianfranco 1912-1990
Obituary ... 130
Conton, William (Farquhar) 1925- ... 1-4R
Contoski, Victor 1936- ... CANR-17
Earlier sketch in CA 25-28R
Contosta, David R(ichard) 1945- ... CANR-92
Earlier sketch in CA 104
Contreras, Heles 1933- ... CANR-14
Earlier sketch in CA 37-40R
Converse, John Marquis 1909-1980
Obituary ... 102
Converse, Paul D(ulaney) 1889-1968 ... CAP-2
Earlier sketch in CA 17-18
Converse, Philip E. 1928- ... CANR-6
Earlier sketch in CA 13-16R
Conway, Alan (Arthur) 1920- ... CANR-2
Earlier sketch in CA 1-4R
Conway, Anne 1631-1679 ... DLB 252
Conway, Arlington B.
See Burns, Eedson Louis Millard
Conway, D. J. 1939- ... 154
Conway, David 1939- ... CANR-88
Earlier sketch in CA 106
Conway, Denise
See Prebble, Marjorie Mary Curtis
Conway, Diana C(ohen) 1943- ... 155
See also SATA 91
Conway, Freda 1911- ... 25-28R
Conway, Gordon
See Hamilton, Charles (Harold St. John)
Conway, Harry 1927- ... 154
Conway, J(ohn) D(onald) 1905-1967 .. CANR-2
Earlier sketch in CA 1-4R
Conway, J(ack) North 1949- ... 145
Conway, Jill K(er) 1934- ... CANR-94
Earlier sketch in CA 130
See also CLC 152
Conway, Jim 1932- ... CANR-39
Earlier sketch in CA 116
Conway, Joan Ditzel 1933- ... 97-100
Conway, John
See Chadwick, Joseph (L.)
Conway, John Seymour 1929- ... 25-28R
Conway, Lynn Ann 1938- ... 157
Conway, (Mary) Margaret 1935- ... 37-40R
Conway, Martha ... 226
Conway, Moncure Daniel 1832-1907 ... 179
See also DLB 1, 223
Conway, Olive
See Brighouse, Harold
Conway, Peter
See Milkomane, George Alexis Milkomanovich
Conway, Sally 1934- ... CANR-39
Earlier sketch in CA 116
Conway, Sara 1962- ... 219
Conway, Theresa (Ann) 1951- ... CANR-19
Earlier sketch in CA 103
Conway, Thomas D(aniel) 1934- ... 21-24R
Conway, Thomas Daniel 1933- ... 112
Conway, Tim
See Conway, Thomas Daniel
Conway, Tom
See Yates, A(lan) G(eoffrey)
Conway, Troy
See Avallone, Michael (Angelo, Jr.)
Conway, Ward
See Westmoreland, Reg(inald Conway)
Conway, William J. 1904-1983
Obituary ... 110
Conwell, Russell H(erman) 1843(?)-1925 ... 214
Conybeare, Charles Augustus
See Eliot, T(homas) S(tearns)
Conyers, James E(rnest) 1932- ... 41-44R
Conyers, James L., Jr. 1961- ... 208
Conyngham, William Joseph 1924- ... 53-56
Conyus
See Calhoun, Conyus
Conzalez, Maria Concepcion Zardoya
1914-1995
See Zardoya, Concha
Conze, Edward J. D. 1904-1979 ... 13-16R
Conzelman, James Gleason 1898-1970
Obituary ... 104
Conzelman, Jimmy
See Conzelman, James Gleason
Coogan, Daniel (Francis, Jr.)
1915-1980 ... CANR-75
Obituary ... 134
Earlier sketch in CA 21-24R
Coogan, John W(illiam) 1947- ... 107
Coogan, Joseph Patrick 1925- ... CANR-4
Earlier sketch in CA 1-4R
Coogan, Keith 1970- ... 172
Coogan, Michael David 1942- ... 204
Brief entry ... 112
Coogan, Tim(othy) Pat(rick) 1935- .. CANR-112
Earlier sketches in CA 145, CANR-62
Cook, Adrian 1940- ... 49-52
Cook, Alan (Hugh) 1922-2004 ... 106
Obituary ... 230
Cook, Albert S(paulding) 1925-1998 ... 176
Earlier sketches in CA 1-4R, CANR-1, 16, 37
Autobiographical Essay in ... 176
See also CAAS 27
Cook, Alice H(anson) 1903-1998 ... CANR-94
Obituary ... 164
Earlier sketch in CA 115
Cook, Alice Rice 1899-1973
Obituary ... 41-44R
Cook, Ann Jennalie 1934- ... 105
Cook, Ann Mariah 1955- ... 191
Cook, Arlene Ethel 1936- ... 65-68
Cook, Bernadine 1924- ... SATA 11
Cook, Beverly Blair 1926- ... 37-40R
Cook, Blanche Wiesen 1941- ... CANR-123
Earlier sketches in CA 53-56, CANR-4
See also MTFW 2005
See also NCFS 3
Cook, Bob 1961- ... 134
Cook, Bruce 1932-2003 ... 176
Obituary ... 221
Earlier sketches in CA 33-36R, CANR-101
Autobiographical Essay in ... 176
See also Alexander, Bruce
See also CAAS 28
Cook, Chris(topher) 1945- ... CANR-104
Earlier sketches in CA 57-60, CANR-6, 23
Cook, Claire 1955- ... 235
Cook, Daniel 1914-1986 ... 33-36R
Cook, Daniel J(oseph) 1938- ... 53-56
Cook, David (John) 1929- ... 107
Cook, David 1940- ... CANR-48
Earlier sketches in CA 103, CANR-22
See also CN 4, 5, 6, 7
Cook, David A. 1945- ... CANR-105
Earlier sketch in CA 107
Cook, David C(harles) III 1912-1990 ... 57-60
Cook, David T. 1946- ... 65-68
Cook, Deanna F. ... 156
Cook, Don(ald Paul) 1920-1995 ... CANR-14
Obituary ... 148
Earlier sketch in CA 13-16R
Cook, Don Lewis 1928- ... 69-72
Cook, Dorothy Mary 1907- ... CANR-20
Earlier sketch in CA 103
Cook, Ebenezer 1667(?)-1732(?) ... DLB 24
Cook, Edward M(arks), Jr. 1944- ... 123
Brief entry ... 118
Cook, Edward Tyas 1857-1919 ... 183
See also DLB 149
Cook, Eliza 1818-1889 ... DLB 199
Cook, Elsa E(stelle) 1932- ... 125
Cook, Eugene 1917(?)-1986
Obituary ... 120
Cook, F(rederick) P. 1937- ... 93-96
Cook, Ferris 1950- ... 145
Cook, Fred J(ames) 1911-2003 ... CANR-78
Obituary ... 217
Earlier sketches in CA 9-12R, CANR-3, 23
Interview in ... CANR-23
See also SATA 2
See also SATA-Obit 145
Cook, Geoffrey 1946- ... 77-80
Cook, George Allan 1916- ... 21-24R
Cook, George Cram 1873-1924 ... DLB 266
Cook, George S. 1920- ... 49-52
Cook, Gervis Frere
See Frere-Cook, Gervis
Cook, Gladys Emerson 1899-1976 ... 5-8R
Cook, Gladys Moon 1907- ... 33-36R
Cook, Glen (Charles) 1944- ... CANR-99
Earlier sketches in CA 122, CANR-58
See also FANT
See also SATA 108
See also SFW 4
See also SUFW 2
Cook, Glenn J. 1913-1991 ... 25-28R
Cook, Gregory M(orton) 1942- ... 117
Cook, Harold John 1952- ... CANR-124
Earlier sketch in CA 120
Cook, Harold Reed 1902-1975 ... 13-16R
Cook, Hugh 1942- ... 232
Cook, Hugh (Walter Gilbert) 1956- ... 132
See also FANT
See also SATA 85
Cook, Hugh C(hristopher) B(ult) 1910- ... 57-60
Cook, Ida (?)-1987(?) ... 153
Obituary ... 121
See also Burchell, Mary
Cook, J(ames) Gordon 1916- ... 9-12R
Cook, J(ohn) M(anuel) 1910-1994 ... 130
Cook, Jack
See Cook, John Augustine
Cook, (Harold) James 1926- ... 73-76
Cook, James Graham 1925-1966 ... CANR-78
Obituary ... 103
Earlier sketch in CA 1-4R
Cook, James L(ister) 1932- ... 142
Cook, James W(yatt) 1932- ... 69-72
Cook, Jean Thor 1930- ... 159
See also SATA 94
Cook, Jeffrey (Ross) 1934-2003 ... 97-100
Obituary ... 214
Cook, Joan Marble 1920- ... 57-60
Cook, Joel 1934- ... SATA 79
Cook, John Augustine 1940- ... 45-48
Cook, John Lennox 1923- ... 106
Cook, Joseph Jay 1924- ... CANR-2
Earlier sketch in CA 1-4R
See also SATA 8
Cook, Judith (Anne) 1933-2004 ... 132
Obituary ... 227
Cook, K(enneth) L. ... 238
Cook, Kenneth (Bernard) 1929-1987 ... 130
Cook, Lennox
See Cook, John Lennox
Cook, Lila
See Africano, Lillian
Cook, Lisa Broadie ... SATA 157
Cook, Louise (Celia) 1942-1984
Obituary ... 112
Cook, Luther T(ownsend) 1901-1982 ... 89-92
Cook, Lyn
See Waddell, Evelyn Margaret
Cook, Mabel Collins 1851-1927(?)
Brief entry ... 121
Cook, Margaret G(erry) 1903-1983 ... 5-8R
Cook, Marjorie 1920- ... 81-84
Cook, Mark 1942- ... CANR-14
Earlier sketch in CA 37-40R
Cook, Mary Jane 1929- ... 93-96
Cook, Melva Janice 1919- ... CANR-9
Earlier sketch in CA 21-24R
Cook, Melvin A(lonzo) 1911-2000 ... CANR-2
Obituary ... 191
Earlier sketch in CA 49-52
Cook, (Will) Mercer 1903-1987 ... CANR-25
Obituary ... 124
Earlier sketch in CA 77-80
See also BW 1
Cook, Michael 1931- ... CANR-50
Earlier sketch in CA 123
Cook, Michael 1933-1994 ... CANR-68
Earlier sketch in CA 93-96
See also CLC 58
See also DLB 53
Cook, Michael (L.) 1936- ... 196
Cook, Michael Lewis 1929- ... 112
Cook, Monte ... AAYA 63
Cook, Myra B. 1933- ... 21-24R
Cook, Nicholas (John) 1950- ... 128
Cook, Nick 1959- ... 228
Cook, Nilla Cram 1908-1982
Obituary ... 108
Cook, Olive 1912-2002 ... CANR-19
Obituary ... 206
Earlier sketches in CA 5-8R, CANR-3
Cook, Olive Rambo 1892-1981 ... 13-16R
Cook, P(auline) Lesley 1922- ... 13-16R
Cook, Paul 1950- ... CANR-125
Earlier sketch in CA 163
Cook, Peter D(onald) 1939- ... 112
Cook, Petronelle Marguerite Mary
1925- ... CANR-15
Earlier sketch in CA 81-84
Cook, Philip J. 1946- ... CANR-86
Earlier sketch in CA 133
Cook, Ramona Graham ... 5-8R
Cook, Ramsay 1931- ... CANR-50
Earlier sketches in CA 102, CANR-25
Cook, Raymond Allen 1919- ... 45-48
Cook, Rebecca J. 1946- ... 168
Cook, Reginald L. 1903-1997 ... 65-68
Cook, Richard I(rving) 1927- ... 21-24R
Cook, Robert 1958- ... 149
Cook, Robert Andrew 1912-1991 ... 117
Obituary ... 133
Cook, Robert I. 1920- ... 33-36R
Cook, Robert William Arthur
1931-1994 ... 25-28R
Obituary ... 146
Cook, Robin
See Cook, Robert William Arthur
Cook, Robin 1940- ... CANR-109
Brief entry ... 108
Earlier sketches in CA 111, CANR-41, 90
Interview in ... CA-111
See also AAYA 32
See also BEST 90:2
See also BPFB 1
See also CLC 14
See also CPW
See also DA3
See also DAM POP
See also HGG
Cook, Robin (Finlayson) 1946- ... 231
Cook, Roderick 1932-1990 ... 9-12R
Cook, Roger F. 1948- ... 225
Cook, Roy
See Silverberg, Robert
Cook, Stanley 1922-1991 ... 93-96
See also CP 2
Cook, Stephani 1944- ... CANR-23
Earlier sketch in CA 106
Cook, Stephen 1949- ... 118
Cook, Stephen L(loyd) 1962- ... CANR-123
Earlier sketch in CA 161
Cook, Stuart W(ellford) 1913-1993 ... CANR-1
Obituary ... 141
Earlier sketch in CA 1-4R
Cook, Suzanne
See Maril, Nadja
Cook, Sylvia (Carol) 1938- ... 49-52
Cook, T(homas) S(tephen) 1947- ... 128
Cook, Terrence E. 1942- ... 210
Cook, Terry 1942- ... CANR-12
Earlier sketch in CA 73-76
Cook, Thomas H. 1947- ... CANR-98
Earlier sketches in CA 111, CANR-32, 57
See also BYA 12
Cook, Thomas Ira 1907-1976
Obituary ... 111
Cook, Timothy E. 1954- ... 170
Cook, W(illiam) Robert 1928- ... 115
Cook, Warren L. 1925-1989 ... 37-40R
Cook, Wesley
See Abu-Jamal, Mumia
Cook, (George) Whitfield 1909- ... 107
Cook, Will(iam Everett) 1921-1964 ... TCWW 1, 2
Cook, William A. 1944- ... 227
Cook, William H(arleston) 1931- ... 104
Cook, William J(esse), Jr. 1938- ... 29-32R
Cook, William Wallace 1867-1933
Brief entry ... 116
See also TCWW 1, 2
Cooke, (Alfred) Alistair 1908-2004 ... CANR-34
Obituary ... 225
Earlier sketches in CA 57-60, CANR-9
See also AITN 1
Cooke, Ann
See Cole, Joanna
Cooke, Arthur
See Lowndes, Robert A(ugustine) W(ard)
Cooke, Barbara
See Alexander, Anna B(arbara Cooke)
Cooke, Barclay 1912-1981 ... CANR-76
Obituary ... 105
Earlier sketch in CA 97-100
Cooke, Bernard J. 1922- ... CANR-34
Earlier sketches in CA 13-16R, CANR-9
Cooke, Carolyn 1959- ... 203

Cooke, Charles Harris 1904(?)-1977
Obituary ... 73-76
Cooke, Darwyn ... 219
Cooke, David Coxe 1917- ... CANR-2
Earlier sketch in CA 1-4R
See also SATA 2
Cooke, Deryck (Victor) 1919-1976
Obituary ... 115
Cooke, Donald Ewin 1916-1985 ... CANR-76
Obituary ... 117
Earlier sketches in CA 1-4R, CANR-4
See also SATA 2
See also SATA-Obit 45
Cooke, Ebenezer c. 1667-c. 1732 ... RGAL 4
Cooke, Edward F(rancis) 1923- ... 41-44R
Cooke, Elizabeth 1948- ... 129
See also CLC 55
Cooke, Frank E. 1920- ... SATA 87
Cooke, George Willis 1848-1923 ... 178
See also DLB 71
Cooke, Gerald 1925- ... 13-16R
Cooke, Gilbert William 1899-1976 ... CAP-1
Earlier sketch in CA 11-12
Cooke, Greville (Vaughan Turner)
1894-1989 ... 13-16R
Cooke, H. O.
See Hanshew, Thomas W.
Cooke, Hereward Lester 1916-1973 ... CANR-1
Obituary ... 45-48
Earlier sketch in CA 1-4R
Cooke, Hope 1940- ... 108
Cooke, Jacob E(rnest) 1924- ... CANR-82
Earlier sketches in CA 1-4R, CANR-34
Cooke, James Francis 1875-1960
Obituary ... 115
Cooke, Jean (Isobel Esther) 1929- ... SATA 74
Cooke, John Byrne 1940- ... CANR-43
Earlier sketch in CA 119
Cooke, John D(aniel) 1892-1972
Obituary ... 106
Cooke, John Esten 1830-1886 ... DLB 3, 248
See also RGAL 4
Cooke, John Estes
See Baum, L(yman) Frank
Cooke, John Fletcher
See Fletcher-Cooke, John
Cooke, John Peyton 1967- ... 158
Cooke, Joseph R(obinson) 1926- ... 65-68
Cooke, M. E.
See Creasey, John
Cooke, Margaret
See Creasey, John
Cooke, Michael F.R.C.
See Cook, Michael Lewis
Cooke, Michael G(eorge)
1934-1990 ... CANR-75
Obituary ... 132
Earlier sketch in CA 110
Cooke, Miriam 1948- ... 197
Cooke, Nancy
See de Herrera, Nancy Cooke
Cooke, Nathalie 1960- ... 193
Cooke, Philip Pendleton 1816-1850 ... DLB 3, 59, 248
Cooke, Robert (Gordon) 1930-1987 ... CANR-75
Obituary ... 121
Earlier sketch in CA 101
Cooke, Robert William 1935- ... 123
Cooke, Rose Terry 1827-1892 ... DLB 12, 74
Cooke, Terence James 1921-1983
Obituary ... 110
Cooke, Thomas D(arlington) 1933- ... 115
Cooke, Trish 1962- ... 198
See also SATA 129
Cooke, William 1942- ... CANR-14
Earlier sketch in CA 33-36R
Cook-Lynn, Elizabeth 1930- ... 133
See also CLC 93
See also DAM MULT
See also DLB 175
See also NNAL
Cookridge, E. H.
See Spiro, Edward
Cookshaw, Marlene 1953- ... 219
Cookson, Catherine (McMullen)
1906-1998 ... CANR-140
Obituary ... 181
Earlier sketches in CA 13-16R, CANR-9, 28, 68
See also CPW
See also MTCW 2005
See also RHW
See also SATA 9
See also SATA-Obit 116
Cookson, Frank Barton 1912-1977
Obituary ... 69-72
Cookson, Peter (W.) 1913-1990 ... 49-52
Obituary ... 130
Cookson, Peter W., Jr. 1942- ... 121
Cookson, William (George)
1939-2003 ... CANR-30
Obituary ... 212
Earlier sketch in CA 49-52
Cool, Joyce 1938- ... 111
Cool, Ola C. 1890(?)-1977
Obituary ... 69-72
Coolbrith, Ina (Donna) 1841-1928 ... 179
See also DLB 54, 186
Coole, W. W.
See Kulski, Wladyslaw W(szebor)
Cooley, Charles Horton 1864-1929 ... 233
Cooley, Denton A(rthur) 1920- ... CANR-53
Earlier sketch in CA 126
Cooley, John Kent 1927- ... CANR-91
Earlier sketch in CA 13-16R
Cooley, Lee Morrison 1919- ... CANR-3
Earlier sketch in CA 9-12R
Cooley, Leland Frederick 1909-1998 ... CANR-4
Obituary ... 171
Earlier sketch in CA 5-8R
Cooley, Margaret L. 1906(?)-1985
Obituary ... 117
Cooley, Martha S. 1955- ... 172
Cooley, Nicole (Ruth) 1966- ... 154
Cooley, Peter (John) 1940- ... CANR-47
Earlier sketches in CA 69-72, CANR-21
See also DLB 105
Cooley, Richard A(llen) 1925- ... 21-24R
Cooley, Thomas (Winfield) 1942- ... 199
Coolidge, Archibald C(ary), Jr. 1928- ... 37-40R
Coolidge, Clark 1939- ... CANR-117
Earlier sketch in CA 33-36R
See also CP 1, 2, 3, 4, 5, 6, 7
See also DLB 193
See also RGAL 4
Coolidge, Dane 1873-1940 ... TCWW 1, 2
Coolidge, Harold Jefferson 1904-1985
Obituary ... 115
Coolidge, John 1913-1995 ... 144
Coolidge, Martha 1946- ... 201
Coolidge, Olivia E(nsor) 1908- ... CANR-103
Earlier sketches in CA 5-8R, CANR-2
See also BYA 1
See also MAICYA 1, 2
See also SATA 1, 26
Coolidge, Susan
See Woolsey, Sarah Chauncy
Cooling, Benjamin Franklin 1938- ... 53-56
Cooling, Wendy ... 172
See also SATA 111
Coolwater, John
See Conniff, James C(lifford) G(regory)
Coomaraswamy, A. K.
See Coomaraswamy, Ananda K(entish)
Coomaraswamy, Ananda K(entish)
1877-1947 ... 154
Brief entry ... 115
Coombe, Jack D(uncan) 1922- ... CANR-143
Earlier sketch in CA 174
Coombes, B. L. 1894(?)-1974
Obituary ... 53-56
Coombs, Ann
See Pykare, Nina
Coombs, Charles Anthony 1918-1981 ... 109
Obituary ... 105
Coombs, Charles I(ra) 1914-1994 ... CANR-36
Obituary ... 180
Earlier sketches in CA 5-8R, CANR-4, 19
See also MAICYA 1, 2
See also SAAS 15
See also SATA 3, 43
Coombs, Chick
See Coombs, Charles I(ra)
Coombs, Douglas (Stafford) 1924- ... 13-16R
Coombs, H. Samm 1928- ... 93-96
Coombs, Herbert Cole 1906-1997 ... 93-96
Obituary ... 162
Coombs, Murdo
See Davis, Frederick C(lyde)
Coombs, Nina
See Pykare, Nina
Coombs, Orde M. 1939(?)-1984 ... CANR-25
Obituary ... 113
Earlier sketch in CA 73-76
See also BW 1
Coombs, Patricia 1926- ... CANR-103
Earlier sketches in CA 1-4R, CANR-1
See also MAICYA 1, 2
See also SAAS 22
See also SATA 3, 51
Coombs, (Robert) Peter 1913- ... 116
Coombs, Philip H(all) 1915- ... CANR-23
Earlier sketches in CA 17-20R, CANR-8
Coombs, Robert H(olman) 1934- ... CANR-41
Earlier sketch in CA 41-44R
Coomer, Joe 1958- ... 125
Coon, Carl(eton Stevens), (Jr.) 1927- ... 201
Coon, Carleton Stevens 1904-1981 ... CANR-2
Obituary ... 104
Earlier sketch in CA 5-8R
Coon, Gene L(ee) 1924-1973 ... CANR-15
Obituary ... 103
Earlier sketch in CA 1-4R
Coon, Martha Sutherland 1884-1980 ... CAP-2
Earlier sketch in CA 25-28
Coon, Nelson 1895-1988 ... 69-72
Coon, Stephen 1948- ... 57-60
Cooney, Barbara 1917-2000 ... CANR-67
Obituary ... 190
Earlier sketches in CA 5-8R, CANR-3, 37
See also CLR 23
See also CWRI 5
See also MAICYA 1, 2
See also SATA 6, 59, 96
See also SATA-Obit 123
Cooney, Blanche 1917- ... 142
Cooney, Caroline B. 1947- ... CANR-110
Earlier sketches in CA 97-100, CANR-37
See also AAYA 5, 32
See also BYA 10, 11, 13
See also JRDA
See also MAICYA 1, 2
See also SATA 48, 80, 113, 130
See also SATA-Brief 41
See also WYA
See also YAW
Cooney, David M(artin) 1930-1999 ... 17-20R
Cooney, Ellen 1952- ... 217
Cooney, Eugene J(erome) 1931- ... 45-48
Cooney, John 1942- ... 115
Cooney, Michael 1921- ... 25-28R
Cooney, Nancy Evans 1932- ... 105
See also SATA 42
Cooney, Ray ... CBD
See also CLC 62
Cooney, Ray(mond George Alfred) 1932- ... 148
See also CD 5, 6
Cooney, Seamus (Anthony) 1933- ... 53-56
Cooney, Timothy J. 1929- ... 107
Coons, Frederica Bertha (Safley)
1910-1981 ... 17-20R
Coons, William R(ichard) 1934- ... 41-44R
Coonts, Stephen (Paul) 1946- ... CANR-106
Brief entry ... 127
Earlier sketches in CA 133, CANR-59
Interview in ... CA-133
See also BEST 89:2
See also CPW
See also CSW
See also DAM POP
Coontz, Otto 1946- ... 105
See also SATA 33
Coontz, Stephanie ... CANR-72
Earlier sketch in CA 132
Coop, Howard 1928- ... 25-28R
Coope, Rosalys 1921- ... 45-48
Cooper, Alfred Morton 1890-1967 ... CAP-1
Earlier sketch in CA 11-12
Cooper, Alice 1948- ... 106
Cooper, Allan 1954- ... 118
Cooper, Allan D. 1952- ... 121
Cooper, Ann (Catharine) 1939- ... 171
See also SATA 104
Cooper, Anna Julia 1856-1964 ... 219
See also DLB 221
See also FW
Cooper, Anthony Ashley 1671-1713 ... DLB 101
Cooper, Arnold Cook 1933- ... 17-20R
Cooper, Artemis 1953- ... CANR-101
Earlier sketches in CA 127, CANR-54
Cooper, B(rian) Lee 1942- ... CANR-108
Earlier sketches in CA 117, CANR-40
Cooper, Barbara (Ann) 1929- ... 9-12R
Cooper, (Fraser) Barry 1943- ... CANR-94
Earlier sketch in CA 126
Cooper, Barry (Anthony Raymond) 1949- ... 150
Cooper, Bernard 1951- ... CANR-101
Earlier sketch in CA 134
Cooper, Bernarr 1912-1999 ... 41-44R
Cooper, Bev 1936- ... 119
Cooper, Brian (Newman) 1919- ... CANR-45
Earlier sketches in CA 1-4R, CANR-22
Cooper, Bruce M(ichael) 1925- ... CANR-9
Earlier sketch in CA 13-16R
Cooper, Bryan (Robert Wright) 1932- ... 25-28R
Cooper, C(hristopher) D(onald) H(untington)
1942- ... 29-32R
Cooper, C. Everett
See Burgess, Michael (Roy)
Cooper, Carl
See Cooper, Kenneth C(arlton)
Cooper, Carolyn (Joy) 1950- ... CANR-87
Earlier sketch in CA 152
Cooper, Cary L. 1940- ... 203
Cooper, Charles 1936- ... 151
Cooper, Charles M(uhlenberg)
1909-1992 ... 41-44R
Cooper, Charles W(illiam) 1904-1999 ... CAP-2
Earlier sketch in CA 21-22
Cooper, Chester L. 1917- ... 29-32R
Cooper, Christopher (John) 1941- ... 107
Cooper, (Brenda) Clare 1935- ... CANR-41
Earlier sketch in CA 118
Cooper, Clarence L(avaughn), Jr.
1934-1978(?) ... 185
Cooper, Colin Symons 1926- ... 102
Cooper, Courtney Ryley 1886-1940 ... TCWW 1, 2
Cooper, Darien B(rown) 1934- ... CANR-16
Earlier sketches in CA 49-52, 116, CANR-1
Cooper, David (Graham) 1931-1986 ... 97-100
Obituary ... 119
Cooper, David A. 1939- ... 168
Cooper, David D. 1948- ... 137
Cooper, David E(dward) 1942- ... CANR-31
Earlier sketch in CA 49-52
Cooper, Dennis 1953- ... CANR-86
Earlier sketches in CA 133, CANR-72
See also CLC 203
See also GLL 1
See also HGG
Cooper, Derek Macdonald 1925- ... 102
Cooper, Diana (Olivia Winifred Maud Manners)
1892(?)-1986
Obituary ... 119
Cooper, Dominic (Xavier) 1944- ... 65-68
Cooper, Douglas 1911-1984 ... 130
Obituary ... 112
Cooper, Douglas 1960- ... CLC 86
Cooper, Duff 1890-1954 ... 158
Cooper, Edith Emma 1862-1913
See Field, Michael
Cooper, Edmund 1926-1982 ... CANR-31
Earlier sketch in CA 33-36R
See also SFW 4
Cooper, Elisha 1971- ... CANR-134
Earlier sketch in CA 167
See also SATA 99, 157
Cooper, Elizabeth Ann 1927- ... 1-4R
Cooper, Elizabeth Keyser -1992 ... CANR-1
Earlier sketch in CA 1-4R
See also SATA 47
Cooper, Emmanuel 1938- ... CANR-3
Earlier sketch in CA 49-52
Cooper, Esther
See Kellner, Esther
Cooper, Floyd ... CANR-124
Earlier sketch in CA 161
See also CLR 60
See also MAICYA 2
See also MAICYAS 1
See also SATA 96, 144
Cooper, Frank E(dward) 1910-1968 ... CAP-2
Earlier sketch in CA 21-22
Cooper, Gail 1950- ... 205
Cooper, George 1937- ... 144
Cooper, Giles (Stannus) 1918-1966 ... 179
Obituary ... 113
See also DLB 13
Cooper, Gladys 1888-1971
Obituary ... 33-36R
Cooper, Gordon 1932- ... 61-64
See also SATA 23
Cooper, Grace Rogers 1924- ... 41-44R
Cooper, Hannah
See Spence, William John Duncan
Cooper, Harold E(ugene) 1928- ... 45-48
Cooper, Harold H. 1911(?)-1976
Obituary ... 69-72
Cooper, Harold R. 1911(?)-1978
Obituary ... 77-80
Cooper, Helen 1947- ... 129
Cooper, Helen 1963- ... 169
See also MAICYA 2
See also SATA 102
Cooper, Henry S(potswood) F(enimore), Jr.
1933- ... CANR-13
Earlier sketch in CA 69-72
See also SATA 65
Cooper, Henry St. John
See Creasey, John
Cooper, I(rving) S(pencer)
1922-1985 ... CANR-26
Obituary ... 117
Earlier sketch in CA 69-72
Cooper, Ilene 1948- ... CANR-127
Earlier sketch in CA 163
See also SATA 66, 97, 145
Cooper, Irving S(teiger) 1882-1935 ... 219
Cooper, J(ean) C. 1905- ... CANR-54
Earlier sketch in CA 127
Cooper, J(oan) California (?)- ... CANR-55
Earlier sketch in CA 125
See also AAYA 12
See also BW 1
See also CLC 56
See also DAM MULT
See also DLB 212
Cooper, Jackie 1922- ... 133
Cooper, Jacqueline 1924- ... 107
Cooper, James A. ... CANR-26
Earlier sketches in CAP-2, CA 19-20
Cooper, James Fenimore 1789-1851 ... AAYA 22
See also AMW
See also BPFB 1
See also CDALB 1640-1865
See also DA3
See also DLB 3, 183, 250, 254
See also LAIT 1
See also NFS 9
See also RGAL 4
See also SATA 19
See also TUS
See also WCH
Cooper, James L(ouis) 1934- ... 53-56
Cooper, James M. 1939- ... 45-48
Cooper, Jamie Lee ... 9-12R
Cooper, Jane (Marvel) 1924- ... CANR-69
Earlier sketches in CA 25-28R, CANR-17
See also CP 1, 2, 3, 4, 5, 6, 7
See also CWP
Cooper, Jeff 1920- ... 41-44R
Cooper, Jefferson
See Fox, G(ardner) F(rancis)
Cooper, Jennifer Gough
See Gough-Cooper, Jennifer
Cooper, Jeremy (Francis Peter)
1946- ... CANR-89
Earlier sketch in CA 93-96
Cooper, Jilly 1937- ... CANR-30
Earlier sketch in CA 105
See also RHW
Cooper, John 1934-1984
Obituary ... 113
Cooper, John C(harles) 1933- ... CANR-56
Earlier sketches in CA 21-24R, CANR-9, 30
Cooper, John Cobb 1887-1967 ... 5-8R
Cooper, John Dean
See Cooper, Jeff
Cooper, John E(llsworth) 1922- ... 25-28R
Cooper, John Irwin 1905- ... 41-44R
Cooper, John L. 1936- ... CANR-13
Earlier sketch in CA 21-24R
Cooper, John M(iller) 1912- ... 21-24R
Cooper, John Milton, Jr. 1940- ... CANR-112
Brief entry ... 105
Earlier sketch in CA 128
Cooper, John O(wen) 1938- ... 89-92
Cooper, John R. ... CANR-27
Earlier sketches in CAP-2, CA 19-20
See also SATA 1
Cooper, Joseph Bonar 1912- ... 17-20R
Cooper, Joseph D(avid) 1917-1975 ... CANR-4
Obituary ... 57-60
Earlier sketch in CA 5-8R
Cooper, Julian M. 1945- ... CANR-87
Earlier sketch in CA 130
Cooper, Kay 1941- ... CANR-37
Earlier sketches in CA 45-48, CANR-1, 16
See also SATA 11
Cooper, Kenneth C(arlton) 1948- ... 110

Cumulative Index 123 **Corcuff**

Cooper, Kenneth H(ardy) 1931- 134
Brief entry 126
Interview in CA-134
Cooper, Kenneth Schaaf 1918- 9-12R
Cooper, Kent 1880-1965 177
Obituary 89-92
See also DLB 29
Cooper, Lee Pelham 1926- CANR-4
Earlier sketch in CA 5-8R
See also SATA 5
Cooper, Leon N. 1930- 157
Cooper, Leslie M(uir) 1930- 41-44R
Cooper, Lester (Irving) 1919-1985 108
Obituary 116
See also SATA 32
See also SATA-Obit 43
Cooper, Lettice (Ulpha) 1897-1994 .. CANR-68
Obituary 146
Earlier sketches in CA 9-12R, CANR-5
See also CN 1, 2, 3, 4, 5, 6
See also CWRI 5
See also RHW
See also SATA 35
See also SATA-Obit 82
Cooper, Louise 1952- CANR-136
Earlier sketches in CA 107, CANR-53
See also FANT
See also SATA 152
Cooper, Louise Field 1905-1992 .... CANR-4
Obituary 139
Earlier sketch in CA 1-4R
Cooper, Lynda Sue
See Sandoval, Lynda
Cooper, Lynna
See Fox, G(ardner) F(rancis)
Cooper, M. E.
See Lerangis, Peter
Cooper, Mae (Klein) 17-20R
Cooper, Marc 229
Cooper, Mario (Ruben) 1905-1995 .... 21-24R
Obituary 161
Cooper, Martin Du Pre 1910-1986 103
Obituary 118
Cooper, Matthew (Heald) 1952- 85-88
Cooper, Mattie Lula
See Britton, Mattie Lula Cooper
Cooper, Melrose
See Kroll, Virginia L(ouise)
Cooper, Merian C. 1893-1973 .... IDFW 3, 4
Cooper, Michael (John) 1930- 13-16R
Cooper, Michael L. 1950- 189
See also SATA 79, 117
Cooper, Michele F(reda) 1941- 85-88
Cooper, Morley
See Cooper, Alfred Morton
Cooper, Natasha
See Wright, (Idonea) Daphne
Cooper, Neil (Louis) 1930- CANR-44
Earlier sketch in CA 119
Cooper, Parley J(oseph) 1937- CANR-26
Earlier sketches in CA 65-68, CANR-10
Cooper, Patricia J(ean) 1936- 97-100
Cooper, Patrick 1949- 203
See also SATA 134
Cooper, Paul 1926- CANR-34
Earlier sketch in CA 49-52
Cooper, Paul F(enimore) 1900(?)-1970
Obituary 104
Cooper, Paulette 1942- 149
Earlier sketch in CA 37-40R
Cooper, Penny 1918- 137
Cooper, Peter Lee 1949- 111
Cooper, Philip (Jr.) 1926- 33-36R
Cooper, Phyllis 1939- 53-56
Cooper, Polly Wylly 1940- 226
Cooper, R(obert) C(ecil) 1917- 143
Cooper, Richard N(ewell) 1934- CANR-10
Earlier sketch in CA 25-28R
Cooper, Robert G(ravlin) 1943- 110
Cooper, Robert L(eon) 1931- 192
Cooper, Robert St. John 1905(?)-1984
Obituary 111
Cooper, Roger 1935- 172
Cooper, Ron L. 1960- 147
Cooper, Rosaleen 1894-1989
Obituary 129
Cooper, Sandi E. 1936- CANR-29
Earlier sketch in CA 49-52
Cooper, Saul 1934- 1-4R
Cooper, Signe Skott 1921- CANR-4
Earlier sketch in CA 53-56
Cooper, Sister Mary Ursula 1925- 5-8R
Cooper, Sophie
See Amory, Mark
Cooper, Stephen 1949- 215
Cooper, Susan (Mary) 1935- CANR-137
Earlier sketches in CA 29-32R, CANR-15, 37, 63, 103
See also AAYA 13, 41
See also BYA 5
See also CLR 4, 67
See also DLB 161, 261
See also FANT
See also JRDA
See also MAICYA 1, 2
See also MTCW 2
See also MTFW 2005
See also SAAS 6
See also SATA 4, 64, 104, 151
See also SUFW 2
See also YAW
Cooper, Susan Fenimore 1813-1894 .... ANW
See also DLB 239, 254
Cooper, Susan Lewis 1947-2003 172
Cooper, Susan Rogers 1947- CANR-144
Earlier sketches in CA 136, CANR-71
See also CMW 4
Cooper, Sylvia 1903- CAP-2
Earlier sketch in CA 17-18
Cooper, Terry L. 1938- 142
Cooper, Thomas W. 1950- 163
Cooper, Wayne 1938- 93-96
Cooper, Wendy (Lowe) 1919-2004 .... CANR-6
Earlier sketch in CA 13-16R
Cooper, Wilhelmina (Behmenburg) 1939(?)-1980
Obituary 97-100
Cooper, Will 1929- 69-72
Cooper, William
See Hoff, Harry Summerfield
See also CN 1, 2, 3, 4, 5, 6
Cooper, William fl. 1669-1689 .... DLB 170
Cooper, William F(razier) 1932- 69-72
Cooper, William Hurlbert 1924- 49-52
Cooper, William J(ames), Jr. 1940- 69-72
Cooper, William W(ager) 1914- 13-16R
Cooper, Wyatt (Emory) 1927-1978 73-76
Obituary 77-80
See also AITN 2
Cooper-Clark, Diana 1945- 109
Cooper-Klein, Nina
See Cooper, Mae (Klein)
Cooperman, Hasye 1909-1992 .... 37-40R
Cooperman, Stanley 1929-1976 .... CAP-2
Earlier sketch in CA 33-36
See also CP 2
Cooperrider, Allen Y(ale) 1944- 148
Coopersmith, Harry 1903-1975 .... CAP-2
Earlier sketch in CA 21-22
Coopersmith, Jerome 1925- 73-76
Coopersmith, Stanley 1926-1979 .... 21-24R
Obituary 133
Cooperstein, Claire (Louise) 1923- 158
Cooren, Francois 1965- 192
Coote, Cathy 1977- 218
Cooter, Roger James 1948- 123
Cootes, Jim E. 1950- 208
Cootner, Paul H(arold) 1930- 9-12R
Coover, James B(urrell) 1925-2004 ... CANR-23
Obituary 228
Earlier sketches in CA 57-60, CANR-6
Coover, Robert (Lowell) 1932- CANR-115
Earlier sketches in CA 45-48, CANR-3, 37, 58
See also AMWS 5
See also BPFB 1
See also CLC 3, 7, 15, 32, 46, 87, 161
See also CN 1, 2, 3, 4, 5, 6, 7
See also DAM NOV
See also DLB 2, 227
See also DLBY 1981
See also EWL 3
See also MAL 5
See also MTCW 1, 2
See also MTFW 2005
See also RGAL 4
See also RGSF 2
See also SSC 15
Coox, Alvin D(avid) 1924-1999 .... 29-32R
Obituary 186
Copage, Eric V. 228
Copani, Peter 1942- 89-92
Cope, David 1941- 33-36R
Cope, Edward A(llen) 1948- 121
Cope, Jack
See Cope, Robert Knox
See also CN 1, 2, 3, 4, 5, 6
See also CP 1
Cope, Jackson I(rving) 1925- CANR-34
Earlier sketch in CA 103
Cope, Jane U(rsula) 1949- 178
See also SATA 108
Cope, Lewis 1934- 125
Cope, Myron 1929- 57-60
Cope, Oliver 1902-1994 185
Brief entry 109
Cope, Robert Knox 1913-1991 .... 9-12R
See also Cope, Jack
Cope, Stephen 218
Cope, Wendy (Mary) 1945- CANR-120
Earlier sketch in CA 140
See also BRWS 8
See also CP 7
See also CWP
Cope, (Vincent) Zachary 1881-1974 .... CAP-1
Earlier sketch in CA 9-10
Copel, Sidney L(eroy) 1930- 21-24R
Copelan, Rachel 1934- 114
Copeland, Ann
See Furtwangler, Virginia W(alsh)
Copeland, Bill
See Copeland, Paul William
Copeland, Bonnie Chapman 1919- 101
Copeland, Carolyn Faunce 1930- 65-68
Copeland, E(dwin) Luther 1916- CANR-3
Earlier sketch in CA 9-12R
Copeland, Gary A. 1952- 138
Copeland, Helen 1920- 25-28R
See also SATA 4
Copeland, James E(verett) 1937- 125
Copeland, James Isaac 1910- 106
Copeland, Kenneth 1937- 219
Copeland, Lennie 1946- 120
Copeland, Lori 1941- CANR-140
Earlier sketch in CA 142
Copeland, Melvin T. 1884-1975 .... CAP-2
Obituary 57-60
Earlier sketch in CA 21-22
Copeland, Miles 1916(?)-1991 .... 29-32R
Obituary 133
Copeland, Morris A(lbert) 1895-1989 .... CAP-1
Obituary 128
Earlier sketch in CA 17-18
Copeland, Pala 1950- 225
Copeland, Pat
See Bellmon, Patricia
Copeland, Paul W. 105
See also SATA 23
Copeland, Paul William 1917- 25-28R
Copeland, Peter 1957- 139
Copeland, Ray (M.) 1926-1984
Obituary 112
Copeland, Rebecca L. 1956- 163
Copeland, Ross H(ugh) 1930-1980 .... 25-28R
Obituary 133
Copeland, Stewart (Armstrong) 1952- ... CLC 26
Copeland, Thomas Wellsted 1907-1979 ... 5-8R
Copeman, George H(enry) 1922- CANR-8
Earlier sketch in CA 5-8R
Copenhaver, Charles L(eonard) 1915-1982
Obituary 107
Copenhaver, John D., Jr. 1949- 146
Coper, Rudolf 1904-1980 .... CAP-1
Earlier sketch in CA 13-14
Copetas, A. Craig 1951- 121
Copi, Irving M(armer) 1917- CANR-5
Earlier sketch in CA 1-4R
Copic, Branko 1915-1984 .... DLB 181
See also EWL 3
Coplan, David B. 1948- 151
Coplan, Kate M(ildred) 1901-1993 .... 5-8R
Copland, Aaron 1900-1990 .... CANR-83
Obituary 133
Earlier sketch in CA 5-8R
See also MTFW 2005
Copland, Robert 1470(?)-1548 .... DLB 136
Coplans, John (Rivers) 1920-2003 185
Obituary 219
Brief entry 112
Coplans, Peta 1951- .... SATA 84
Copleston, Frederick Charles (John Paul) 1907-1994 .... CANR-7
Earlier sketch in CA 13-16R
Copley, Frederick S.
See Greif, Martin
Copley, Gerald L. C.
See Cole, Lester
Copley (Diana) Heather Pickering 1918- .... SATA 45
Coplin, William D(avid) 1939- CANR-32
Earlier sketches in CA 21-24R, CANR-12
Copman, Louis 1934- 57-60
Copp, Andrew James (III) 1916-1999 .... 25-28R
Copp, DeWitt S(amuel) 1919-1999 199
Copp, Dewitt S(amuel) 1919-1999 204
Copp, E. Anthony 1945- 102
Copp, Jim
See Copp, Andrew James (III)
Copp, (John) Terry 1938- 134
Coppa, Frank John 1937- CANR-55
Earlier sketches in CA 33-36R, CANR-13, 29
Coppard, A(lfred) E(dgar) 1878-1957 167
Brief entry 114
See also BRWS 8
See also DLB 162
See also EWL 3
See also HGG
See also RGEL 2
See also RGSF 2
See also SSC 21
See also SUFW 1
See also TCLC 5
See also YABC 1
Coppard, Audrey 1931- CANR-27
Earlier sketch in CA 29-32R
Coppe, Abiezer
See Taylor, John (Alfred)
Coppee, Francois 1842-1908 170
See also DLB 217
See also TCLC 25
Coppel, Alec 1909(?)-1972
Obituary 33-36R
Coppel, Alfred 1921-2004 .... CANR-10
Earlier sketch in CA 17-20R
See also CAAS 9
See also DLBY 1983
See also SFW 4
Copper, (Robert) Arnold (de Vignier) 1934- 97-100
Copper, Basil 1924- CANR-140
Earlier sketches in CA 133, CANR-72
See also CMW 4
See also HGG
Copper, John Franklin 1940- CANR-11
Earlier sketch in CA 69-72
Copper, Marcia S(nyder) 1934- 53-56
Copperman, Paul 1947- 101
Copperud, Roy H(erman) 1915-1991 .... 9-12R
Obituary 136
Coppin, Fanny (Muriel) J(ackson) 1837-1913 219
Coppin, Levi J(enkins) 1848-1924 219
Coppock, John (Oates) 1914- 13-16R
Coppock, John Terence 1921-2000 102
Coppock, Joseph D(avid) 1909-2000 49-52
Coppola, Francis Ford 1939- CANR-78
Earlier sketches in CA 77-80, CANR-40
See also AAYA 39
See also CLC 16, 126
See also DLB 44
Coppola, Raymond T(homas) 1947- 102
Coppola, Sofia 1971- 221
Copus, Julia 1969- 151
See also CWP
Copway, George 1818-1869 .... DAM MULT
See also DLB 175, 183
See also NNAL
Coquery-Vidrovitch, Catherine 1935- 168
Coquillette, Daniel R(obert) 1944- 195
Coralie
See Anderson, Catherine Corley
Coram, Christopher
See Walker, Peter N.
Coram, Robert 218
Corazzini, Sergio 1886-1907 175
See also DLB 114
Corbalis, Judy 1941- 125
Corballis, Michael C(harles) 1936- 115
Corbally, John (Edward, Jr.) 1924-2004 .... 5-8R
Obituary 230
Corbeil, Carole 1952-2000 198
Corbett, Chan
See Schachner, Nathan(iel)
Corbett, Christopher 1951- 123
Corbett, David 1953- 214
Corbett, Edward P(atrick) J(oseph) 1919-1998 .... CANR-9
Earlier sketch in CA 17-20R
Corbett, Elizabeth (Frances) 1887-1981 .... CANR-2
Obituary 102
Earlier sketch in CA 5-8R
Corbett, Grahame 116
See also SATA 43
See also SATA-Brief 36
Corbett, J(ack) Elliott 1920-2003 .... 29-32R
Obituary 214
Corbett, James A(rthur) 1908-1989 65-68
Corbett, Janice M. 1935- 37-40R
Corbett, John 223
Corbett, Patricia 1951- 227
Corbett, (John) Patrick 1916-1999 .... 17-20R
Corbett, Pearson H(arris) 1900- CAP-1
Earlier sketch in CA 9-10
Corbett, Richard 1582-1635 .... DLB 121
See also RGEL 2
Corbett, Richard (Graham) 1955- 143
Corbett, Richmond McLain 1902-1991 . CAP-1
Earlier sketch in CA 13-16
Corbett, Ruth 1912-1997 .... 29-32R
Corbett, Scott 1913- CANR-23
Earlier sketches in CA 1-4R, CANR-1
See also CLR 1
See also CWRI 5
See also JRDA
See also MAICYA 1, 2
See also SAAS 2
See also SATA 2, 42
Corbett, Thomas H(enry) 1938- 77-80
Corbett, W(illiam) J(esse) 1938- 137
See also CLR 19
See also CWRI 5
See also FANT
See also MAICYA 1, 2
See also SATA 50, 102
See also SATA-Brief 44
Corbett, William 1942- 172
Corbiere, Tristan 1845-1875 .... DLB 217
See also GFL 1789 to the Present
Corbin, Alain 1936- CANR-95
Earlier sketch in CA 146
Corbin, Arnold 1911- 9-12R
Corbin, Charles B. 1940- CANR-14
Earlier sketches in CA 29-32R, CANR-31
Corbin, Claire 1913- 41-44R
Corbin, Donald A(lvin) 1920- 33-36R
Corbin, H(ayman) Dan 1912- 41-44R
Corbin, Iris
See Clinton, Iris A. (Corbin)
Corbin, Jane 1954- CANR-123
Earlier sketch in CA 146
Corbin, John B(oyd) 1935- CANR-22
Earlier sketch in CA 105
Corbin, Michael
See Cartmill, Cleve
Corbin, Richard 1911-1988 .... CANR-3
Obituary 125
Earlier sketch in CA 5-8R
Corbin, Sabra Lee
See Malvern, Gladys
Corbin, Steven 1953- 131
See also BW 2
Corbin, William
See McGraw, William Corbin
Corbishley, Thomas 1903-1976 .... CANR-7
Obituary 65-68
Earlier sketch in CA 13-16R
Corbitt, Helen Lucy 1906-1978 .... CANR-4
Obituary 89-92
Earlier sketch in CA 5-8R
Corby, Dan
See Catherall, Arthur
Corcoran, Barbara (Asenath) 1911- 191
Earlier sketches in CA 21-24R, CANR-11, 28, 48
Autobiographical Essay in 191
See also CAAS 2
See also AAYA 14
See also CLC 17
See also CLR 50
See also DLB 52
See also JRDA
See also MAICYA 2
See also MAICYAS 1
See also RHW
See also SAAS 20
See also SATA 3, 77
See also SATA-Essay 125
Corcoran, Gertrude B(eatty) 1922- 29-32R
Corcoran, Jean (Kennedy) 1926- 1-4R
Corcoran, Neil (Cornelius) 1948- 135
Corcoran, Patrick 1951- 212
Corcoran, Theresa 1928- 228
Corcoran, Tom 1943- 222
Corcos, Lucille 1908-1973 .... 21-24R
Obituary 134
See also SATA 10
Corcuff, Stephane B. 1971- 230

Cord, Barry
See Germano, Peter B.
See also TCWW 1, 2
Cord, Robert L. 1935- 33-36R
Cord, Steven Benson 1928- 21-24R
Cord, William O. 1921- 37-40R
Cordasco, Francesco 1920-2001 ...... CANR-46
Obituary 202
Earlier sketches in CA 13-16R, CANR-6, 21
Cordeiro, Patricia (A.) 1944- 145
Cordelier, John
See Underhill, Evelyn
Cordelier, Maurice
See Giraudoux, Jean(-Hippolyte)
Cordell, Alexander
See Graber, Alexander
Cordell, Alexander
See Graber, (George) Alexander
Cordell, Richard Albert 1896-1986 .... 1-4R
Cordelli, Franco 1943- .... DLB 196
Corden, W(arner) M(ax) 1927- CANR-143
Earlier sketch in CA 33-36R
Corder, Brice W(ood) 1936- 53-56
Corder, Eric
See Mundis, Jerrold
Corder, George Edward 1904-1989 110
Corder, Jim(my Wayne) 1929-1998 .... 17-20R
Corder, Zizou
See Young, Louisa
Cordier, Andrew W(ellington) 1901-1975
Obituary 106
Cordier, Gilbert
See Scherer, Jean-Marie Maurice
Cordier, Ralph Waldo 1902-1990 .... 37-40R
Obituary 161
Cording, Robert 1949- CANR-139
Earlier sketch in CA 173
Cordingley, Patrick 1944- 114
Cordingly, David 1938- CANR-109
Earlier sketch in CA 93-96
Cordis, Lonny
See Donson, Cyril
Cordle, Thomas 1918- 144
Cords, Nicholas J. 1929- 105
Cordtz, Dan 1927- 73-76
Cordwell, Miriam 1908-1986 89-92
Obituary 120
Cordy, Michael 170
Core, George 1939- 232
See also CSW
Corea, Gena
See Corea, Genoveffa
Corea, Genoveffa 1946- 81-84
Corea, Nicholas J. 1943(?)-1999 189
Corella, Joseph
See Odgers, Sally Farrell
Corelli, Marie
See Mackay, Mary
See also DLB 34, 156
See also RGEL 2
See also SUFW 1
See also TCLC 51
Coren, Alan 1938- CANR-54
Earlier sketches in CA 69-72, CANR-29
See also SATA 32
Coren, Michael 1959- 153
Coren, Stanley 1942- 137
Coren, Victoria 1972- 131
Corey, Deborah Joy 1958- CANR-138
Earlier sketch in CA 168
Corey, Dorothy CANR-26
Earlier sketches in CA 69-72, CANR-11
See also SATA 23
Corey, Gerald F(rancis) 1937- 114
Corey, Mary F. 1943- 188
Corey, Melinda (Ann) 1957- CANR-141
Earlier sketch in CA 144
Corey, Paul (Frederick) 1903-1992 ...... CANR-2
Obituary 176
Earlier sketch in CA 5-8R
Corey, Shana 1974- .... SATA 133
Corey, Stephen 1948- CANR-52
Earlier sketch in CA 124
Corfe, Thomas Howell 1928- 103
See also SATA 27
Corfe, Tom
See Corfe, Thomas Howell
Corfield, Conrad Laurence 1893-1980
Obituary 105
Corfield, Robin Bell 1952- .... SATA 74
Corfman, Eunice (Luccock) 1928-1980
Obituary 97-100
Corgan, Billy 1967- 239
Corgan, William Patrick
See Corgan, Billy
Corina, Maurice 1936- 57-60
Corinne, Tee A. 1943- 220
Corio, David 1960- 235
Cork, Patrick
See Cockburn, (Francis) Claud
Cork, Richard (Graham) 1947- CANR-50
Earlier sketches in CA 107, CANR-24
Corke, Helen 1882-1978 .... CAP-1
Earlier sketch in CA 9-10
Corke, Hilary 1921- 97-100
See also CP 1, 2
Corkey, R(obert) 1881-1966 .... CAP-1
Earlier sketch in CA 13-16
Corkran, David Hudson, Jr. 1902-1990 ..... 5-8R
Corkran, Herbert, Jr. 1924- 29-32R
Corle, Edwin 1906-1956 178
See also DLBY 1985
See also TCWW 1, 2
Corless, Roger (Jonathan) 1938- 108
Corlett, Mary Lee 1957- 139
Corlett, William 1938- CANR-88
Earlier sketch in CA 103
See also CWRI 5
See also SATA 46
See also SATA-Brief 39
Corlew, Robert Ewing 1922- 110
Corley, (Thomas) Anthony (Buchanan)
1923- CANR-34
Earlier sketch in CA 1-4R
Corley, Edwin (Raymond)
1931-1981 .... CANR-12
Obituary 105
Earlier sketch in CA 25-28R
Corley, Elizabeth 1956- 205
Corley, Ernest
See Bulmer, (Henry) Kenneth
Corley, Nora T(eresa) 118
Corley, Ray
See Corley, Edwin (Raymond)
Corley, Robert N(eil) 1930- CANR-19
Earlier sketches in CA 9-12R, CANR-3
Corliss, Charlotte N(uzum) 1932- 53-56
Corliss, Richard (Nelson) 1944- 157
Corliss, William R(oger) 1926- CANR-37
Earlier sketches in CA 45-48, CANR-1, 16
Cormack, Alexander James Ross 1942- ... 65-68
Cormack, James Maxwell Ross
1909-1975 .... CAP-1
Earlier sketch in CA 9-10
Cormack, M(argaret) Grant 1913- 1-4R
See also SATA 11
Cormack, Margaret Lawson
1912-1999 .... CANR-35
Earlier sketch in CA 1-4R
Cormack, Maribelle B. 1902-1984 ...... SATA 39
Cormack, Robert J. 1946- 139
Cormack, Sandy
See Cormack, Alexander James Ross
Corman, Avery 1935- 85-88
Corman, Cid
See Corman, Sidney
See also CAAS 2
See also CLC 9
See also CP 1, 2, 3, 4, 5, 6, 7
See also DLB 5, 193
Corman, Roger (William) 1926- 158
Corman, Sidney 1924-2004 .... CANR-44
Obituary 225
Earlier sketch in CA 85-88
See also Corman, Cid
See also DAM POET
Cormany, Michael 1951- 135
Cormick, Craig 1961- 189
Cormier, Bruno M. 1919-
Brief entry 114
Cormier, Frank 1927-1994 .... 21-24R
Obituary 144
Cormier, Gerald
See Rudolph, Alan
Cormier, Ramona 1923- 49-52
Cormier, Raymond J(oseph) 1938- CANR-19
Earlier sketches in CA 53-56, 181, CANR-4
Cormier, Robert (Edmund)
1925-2000 .... CANR-93
Earlier sketches in CA 1-4R, CANR-5, 23, 76
Interview in CANR-23
See also AAYA 3, 19
See also BYA 1, 2, 6, 8, 9
See also CDALB 1968-1988
See also CLC 12, 30
See also CLR 12, 55
See also DA
See also DAB
See also DAC
See also DAM MST, NOV
See also DLB 52
See also EXPN
See also JRDA
See also LAIT 5
See also MAICYA 1, 2
See also MTCW 1, 2
See also MTFW 2005
See also NFS 2, 18
See also SATA 10, 45, 83
See also SATA-Obit 122
See also WYA
See also YAW
Cormillot, Albert E. J. 1938- 69-72
Corn, Alfred (DeWitt III) 1943- 179
Earlier sketch in CANR-44
Autobiographical Essay in 179
See also CAAS 25
See also CLC 33
See also CP 7
See also CSW
See also DLB 120, 282
See also DLBY 1980
Corn, Charles 1936-2001 168
Corn, David 1959- CANR-88
Earlier sketch in CA 149
Corn, Ira George, Jr. 1921-1982 .... CANR-35
Obituary 106
Earlier sketch in CA 85-88
Corn, Joseph J. 1938- 166
Corn, Wanda M. 1940- 191
Cornea, Carol
See Koch, Kurt E(mil)
Cornebise, Alfred E(mile) 1929- CANR-38
Earlier sketch in CA 115
Cornehls, James V(ernon) 1936- 93-96
Corneille, Pierre 1606-1684 .... DAB
See also DAM MST
See also DC 21
See also DFS 21
See also DLB 268
See also EW 3
See also GFL Beginnings to 1789
See also RGWL 2, 3
See also TWA
Corneille, Thomas 1625-1709 .. GFL Beginnings to 1789
See also IDTP
Corneli, Helen McGavran 1926- 235
Cornelisen, Ann 1926-2003 .... CANR-144
Obituary 222
Earlier sketches in CA 25-28R, CANR-17
corneliszavandenheuvel
See van den Heuvel, Cornelisz A.
Cornelius, Carol 1942- CANR-92
Earlier sketch in CA 115
See also SATA 40
Cornelius, Kay 1933- 233
See also SATA 157
Cornelius, Temple H. 1891-1964 .... CAP-1
Earlier sketch in CA 11-12
Cornelius, Wanda Pyle 1936- 105
Cornell, Douglas B. 1906(?)-1982
Obituary 106
Cornell, Drucilla 213
Cornell, Felix M. 1896(?)-1970
Obituary 104
Cornell, Francis Griffith 1906-1979
Obituary 89-92
Cornell, Gary 170
Cornell, George W. 1920-1994 .... 9-12R
Obituary 146
Cornell, J.
See Cornell, Jeffrey
Cornell, James (Clayton, Jr.) 1938- CANR-11
Earlier sketch in CA 69-72
See also SATA 27
Cornell, Jean Gay 1920- CANR-1
Earlier sketch in CA 45-48
See also SATA 23
Cornell, Jeffrey 1945- .... SATA 11
Cornell, Jennifer C 1967- 158
Cornell, Joseph 1903-1972 163
See also AAYA 56
Cornell, Judith 1941- 203
Cornell, Katherine 1898(?)-1974
Obituary 49-52
Cornell, Tim 1946- 115
Cornell, Vincent J(oseph) 1951- 194
Corner, E. J. H.
See Corner, Edred John Henry
Corner, Edred John Henry 1906-
Brief entry 116
Corner, George W(ashington) 1889-1981 ... 102
Obituary 104
Corner, James 1961- 163
Corner, Philip 1933- 21-24R
Cornett, Joe D(elayne) 1935- 53-56
Corney, Estelle 1911- 115
Cornfeld, Betty S. 1944(?)-1988
Obituary 128
Cornfeld, Gaalyah 1902-1989 .... CANR-12
Earlier sketch in CA 73-76
Cornford, A(ndrew) J(ohn) 1942- 112
Cornford, Adam (Francis) 1950- 174
Autobiographical Essay in 174
See also CAAS 28
Cornford, Frances 1886-1960 .... BRWS 8
See also DLB 240
Cornforth, John 1937-2004 202
Cornforth, Maurice 1909-1980 .... CANR-4
Obituary 102
Earlier sketch in CA 5-8R
Corngold, Stanley Alan 1934- CANR-32
Earlier sketches in CA 37-40R, CANR-14
Cornillon, John Raymond Koppleman
1941- 17-20R
Cornish, Dudley T(aylor) 1915- 17-20R
Cornish, Edward (Seymour) 1927- CANR-25
Earlier sketch in CA 108
Cornish, Geoffrey (St. John) 1914- 125
Cornish, John (Buckley) 1914- 25-28R
Cornish, Louis Craig 1870-1950 215
Cornish, Sam(uel James) 1935- CANR-24
Earlier sketch in CA 41-44R
See also BW 1
See also CP 1, 2, 3, 4, 5, 6, 7
See also DLB 41
See also SATA 23
Cornish, W(illiam) R(odolph) 1937- 29-32R
Cornish, William c. 1465-c. 1524 ...... DLB 132
Cornis-Pope, Marcel (H.) 1946- 232
Cornman, James W(elton)
1929-1978 .... CANR-11
Earlier sketch in CA 69-72
Cornock, (John) Stroud 1938- 25-28R
Cornplanter, Jesse J. 1889-1957 219
Corns, T. N.
See Corns, Thomas N.
Corns, Thomas N. 239
Cornthwaite, Robert 1917- CANR-108
Earlier sketch in CA 152
Cornuelle, Richard C. 1927- 17-20R
Cornum, Rhonda (Leah Scott) 1954- 139
Cornwall, E(spie) Judson 1924- CANR-6
Earlier sketch in CA 57-60
Cornwall, I(an) W(olfran) 1909-1994 ...... 9-12R
Cornwall, J. Spencer 1888(?)-1983
Obituary 109
Cornwall, James (Handyside) Marshall
See Marshall-Cornwall, James (Handyside)
Cornwall, Jim
See Rikhoff, James C.
Cornwall, John 1928- CANR-37
Earlier sketch in CA 115
Cornwall, Martin
See Cavendish, Richard
Cornwall, Nellie
See Sloggett, Nellie
Cornwallis the Younger, Sir William c.
1579-1614 .... DLB 151
Cornwell, Anita (R.) 1923- CANR-71
Earlier sketch in CA 142
See also BW 2, 3
See also GLL 2
Cornwell, Anna Christake 1929- 229
Cornwell, Bernard 1944- CANR-82
Earlier sketch in CA 104
See also AAYA 47
See also CPW
See also RHW
Cornwell, David (John Moore)
1931- CANR-132
Earlier sketches in CA 5-8R, CANR-13, 33, 59, 107
See also le Carre, John
See also CLC 9, 15
See also DA3
See also DAM POP
See also MTCW 1, 2
See also MTFW 2005
Cornwell, Elmer E(ckert), Jr. 1924- 180
Brief entry 118
Cornwell, John CANR-89
Earlier sketch in CA 157
Cornwell, Patricia (Daniels) 1956- . CANR-131
Earlier sketches in CA 134, CANR-53
See also AAYA 16, 56
See also BPFB 1
See also CLC 155
See also CMW 4
See also CPW
See also CSW
See also DAM POP
See also DLB 306
See also MSW
See also MTCW 2
See also MTFW 2005
Cornwell, Smith
See Smith, David (Jeddie)
Cornyetz, Nina 234
Coronel, Jorge Icaza
See Icaza (Coronel), Jorge
Coronel Urtecho, Jose 1906-1994 ...... DLB 290
Corp, Edward 1948- CANR-112
Earlier sketch in CA 156
Corpi, Lucha 1945- CANR-80
Earlier sketch in CA 131
See also CWP
See also DLB 82
See also HW 1, 2
See also LLW
Corporal Trim
See Bolger, Philip C(unningham)
Corr, O. Casey 1955- 189
Corradi, Gemma 1939- 21-24R
Corradi, Juan E. 1943- 113
Corrado, Anthony 1957- 143
Corral, Jill M. 205
Corrales, Edwin (G.) 1956- 187
Corrall, Alice Enid 1916- 5-8R
Corran, Mary 1953- 154
See also FANT
Corre, Alan D. 1931- 37-40R
Correa
See Galbraith, Jean
Correa, Gustavo 1914-1995 49-52
Correa, Raul 1961- 237
Correas de Zapata, Celia 1935- 214
Correia-Afonso, John 1924- CANR-13
Earlier sketch in CA 33-36R
Correia da Rocha, Adolfo
See Rocha, Adolfo
Corren, Grace
See Hoskins, Robert (Phillip)
Correnti, Mario
See Togliatti, Palmiro
Correu, Larry M. 1931- 114
Correy, Lee
See Stine, G(eorge) Harry
Corrick, James A. 1945- 143
See also SATA 76
Corrie, Elva
See Clairmont, Elva
Corrigan, (Helen) Adeline 1909- 69-72
See also SATA 23
Corrigan, Barbara 1922- 57-60
See also SATA 8
Corrigan, Eireann 1977- 234
See also SATA 163
Corrigan, Francis Joseph 1919- 5-8R
Corrigan, John D(avitt) 1900-1983 .... 41-44R
Corrigan, John R. 1970- 224
Corrigan, John Thomas 1936- CANR-10
Earlier sketch in CA 65-68
Corrigan, Maureen 1955- 185
Corrigan, Ralph L(awrence), Jr. 1937- ... 33-36R
Corrigan, Robert A(nthony) 1935- 9-12R
Corrigan, Robert W(illoughby)
1927-1993 .... CANR-6
Obituary 142
Earlier sketch in CA 5-8R
Corrigan, Simon 1964- 143
Corrigan, Timothy (J.) 1951- 129
Corrin, Jay P(atrick) 1943- CANR-143
Earlier sketch in CA 125
Corrin, Sara 1918- 120
See also SATA 86
See also SATA-Brief 48

Cumulative Index 125 Cottrell

Corrin, Stephen 121
See also SATA 86
See also SATA-Brief 48
Corrington, John William
1932-1988 .... CANR-143
Obituary 127
Earlier sketches in CA 13-16R, CANR-8
Interview in CANR-8
See also CP 1, 2
See also DLB 6, 244
Corrington, Robert S. 1950- 227
Corris, Peter 1942- 135
See also CMW 4
Corriveau, Monique (Chouinard)
1927-1976 .... CANR-12
Obituary 122
Earlier sketch in CA 61-64
See also DLB 251
Corrothers, James D(avid) 1869-1917 141
See also BW 2
See also DLB 50
Corry, Emmett 1934- 111
Corry, J(ames) A(lexander) 1899-1985
Obituary 120
Corry, John A. 1931- 207
Corsa, Helen Storm 1915- 17-20R
Corsaro, Francesco Andrea 1924- .. CANR-143
Earlier sketch in CA 85-88
Corsaro, Frank
See Corsaro, Francesco Andrea
Corsaro, Maria C(ecelia) 1949- 107
Corsel, Ralph 1920- 25-28R
Corsi, Jerome R(obert) 1946- 89-92
Corsini, Raymond J. 1914- CANR-45
Earlier sketches in CA 1-4R, CANR-3, 21
Corso, (Nunzio) Gregory
1930-2001 .... CANR-132
Obituary 193
Earlier sketches in CA 5-8R, CANR-41, 76
See also AMWS 12
See also BG 1:2
See also CLC 1, 11
See also CP 1, 2, 3, 4, 5, 6, 7
See also DA3
See also DLB 5, 16, 237
See also LMFS 2
See also MAL 5
See also MTCW 1, 2
See also MTFW 2005
See also PC 33
See also WP
Corson, Fred Pierce 1896-1985 .... CAP-2
Obituary 115
Earlier sketch in CA 23-24
Corson, Hazel W. 1906-1990 .... CANR-2
Earlier sketch in CA 1-4R
Corson, John J(ay III) 1905-1990 .... CANR-5
Obituary 132
Earlier sketch in CA 1-4R
Corson, Richard 41-44R
Corson, Trevor 1969- 231
Corson-Finnerty, Adam Daniel
1944- CANR-14
Earlier sketch in CA 81-84
Corstanje, Auspicius van
See van Corstanje, Charles
Corstanje, Charles van
See van Corstanje, Charles
Cort, David 1904-1983 .... 9-12R
Obituary 111
Cort, John C. 1913- 235
Cort, M. C.
See Clifford, Margaret Cort
Cort, Margaret
See Clifford, Margaret Cort
Cort, Ned
See Jagninski, Tom
Cort, Robert (William) 1946- 229
Cort, Van .... TCWW 1, 2
Cortada, James W(illiam) 1946- 133
Brief entry 114
Cortazar, Julio 1914-1984 .... CANR-81
Earlier sketches in CA 21-24R, CANR-12, 32
See also BPFB 1
See also CDWLB 3
See also CLC 2, 3, 5, 10, 13, 15, 33, 34, 92
See also DA3
See also DAM MULT, NOV
See also DLB 113
See also EWL 3
See also EXPS
See also HLC 1
See also HW 1, 2
See also LAW
See also MTCW 1, 2
See also MTFW 2005
See also RGSF 2
See also RGWL 2, 3
See also SSC 7, 76
See also SSFS 3, 20
See also TWA
See also WLIT 1
Cortazzi, (Henry Arthur) Hugh
1924- CANR-39
Earlier sketch in CA 115
Cortazzo, Carman 1936- 109
Corteen, Wes
See Norwood, Victor G(eorge) C(harles)
Corten, Irina H. 1941- 137
Cortes, Carlos E(liseo) 1934- CANR-8
Earlier sketch in CA 61-64
Cortes, Juan B(autista) 1925- 37-40R
Cortese, A(nthony) James 1917- 65-68
Cortese, Peter A. 1928- 149
Cortesi, Lawrence
See Cerri, Lawrence J.
Cortez, Carlos 1923- .... DLB 209
Cortez, Jayne 1936- CANR-126
Earlier sketches in CA 73-76, CANR-13, 31, 68
See also BW 2, 3
See also CWP
See also DLB 41
See also EWL 3
Cortez, Sarah 1950- 192
Cortez, Stanley 1908-1997 .... IDFW 3, 4
Cortez-Villon, Juan
See Herzinger, Kim A(llen)
Corti, Eugenio 1921- 163
Cortina, Rodolfo (Jose) 1946- 179
Cortinez, Carlos 1934- 123
Cortner, Richard C(arroll) 1935- 104
Cortright, Barbara 1927- 112
Cortright, David 1946- CANR-111
Earlier sketch in CA 57-60
Corty, Floyd L(ouis) 1916- 13-16R
Corum, James S(terling) 1953- 139
Corvino, John 1969- 236
Corvinus, Gottlieb Siegmund
1677-1746 .... DLB 168
Corvinus, Jakob
See Raabe, Wilhelm (Karl)
Corwen, Leonard 1921- CANR-15
Earlier sketch in CA 93-96
Corwin, Adele Beatrice Lewis 1922-1990 .. 123
Obituary 131
Corwin, Cecil
See Kornbluth, C(yril) M.
Corwin, Edward S(amuel) 1878-1963 122
Obituary 113
Corwin, Judith H(offman) 1946- CANR-32
Earlier sketch in CA 113
See also SATA 10
Corwin, Norman 1910- CANR-24
Earlier sketches in CA 1-4R, CANR-1
See also AITN 2
Corwin, Ronald G(ary) 1932- CANR-23
Earlier sketches in CA 17-20R, CANR-8
Cory, Annie Sophie
See Cross, Victoria
Cory, Caroline
See Freeman, Kathleen
Cory, Charlotte 1956- 137
Cory, Corrine
See Cory, Irene E.
Cory, Daniel 1904-1972
Obituary 37-40R
Cory, David 1872-1966
Obituary 25-28R
Cory, Desmond
See McCarthy, Shaun (Lloyd)
See also DLB 276
Cory, Howard L.
See Jardine, Jack
Cory, Irene E. 1910-1998 49-52
Cory, Jean-Jacques 1947- 57-60
Cory, Ray
See Marshall, Mel(vin D.)
Cory, Rowena
See Lindquist, Rowena Cory
Cory, William Johnson 1823-1892 .... DLB 35
Corya, I. E.
See Cory, Irene E.
Coryate, Thomas 1577(?)-1617 ... DLB 151, 172
Coryell, Janet L(ee) 1955- 135
Cosby, Bill
See Cosby, William Henry, Jr.
See also BEST 89:4
Cosby, Camille (Olivia Hanks) 1945- 156
Cosby, William Henry, Jr. 1937- CANR-78
Earlier sketches in CA 81-84, CANR-27, 42
See also Cosby, Bill
See also BW 2, 3
See also SATA 66, 110
Cosby, Yvonne Shepard 1886(?)-1980
Obituary 97-100
Coscarelli, Don 1954- 232
Coscarelli, Kate 1927-1999 142
Obituary 183
Cose, Ellis Jonathan 1951- CANR-99
Earlier sketch in CA 119
See also BW 2
Cosell, Howard 1918-1995 108
Obituary 148
Cosentino, Andrew J(oseph) 1931- 120
Cosentino, Donald J(ohn) 1941- 108
Cosentino, Frank 1937- 132
Coser, Lewis A(lfred) 1913-2003 .... CANR-4
Obituary 218
Earlier sketch in CA 1-4R
Coser, Rose Laub 1916- 13-16R
Cosgrave, John O'Hara II 1908-1968 . CANR-1
Earlier sketch in CA 1-4R
See also SATA-Obit 21
Cosgrave, Patrick 1941- 33-36R
Cosgrove, Carol Ann
See Twitchett, Carol Cosgrove
Cosgrove, Denis (Edmund) 1948- ... CANR-115
Earlier sketch in CA 146
Cosgrove, Margaret (Leota) 1926- CANR-6
Earlier sketch in CA 9-12R
See also SATA 47
Cosgrove, Mark P. 1947- 85-88
Cosgrove, Maynard G(iles) 1895-1981 57-60
Cosgrove, Rachel
See Payes, Rachel (Ruth) C(osgrove)
Cosgrove, Richard A(lfred) 1941- 104
Cosgrove, Stephen E(dward) 1945- ... CANR-22
Earlier sketch in CA 69-72
See also AITN 1
See also SATA 53
See also SATA-Brief 40
Cosh, (Ethel Eleanor) Mary 5-8R
Cosic, Dobrica 1921- 138
Brief entry 122
See also CDWLB 4
See also CLC 14
See also CWW 2
See also DLB 181
See also EWL 3
Cosin, Elizabeth M. 221
Cosin, John 1595-1672 .... DLB 151, 213
Cosio Villegas, Daniel
See Cosio Villegas, Daniel
Cosio Villegas, Daniel 1898-1976
Obituary 65-68
Coskey, Evelyn 1932- 41-44R
See also SATA 7
Coskran, Kathleen 1943- 139
Coslow, Sam(son) 1905-1982 .... CANR-29
Obituary 106
Earlier sketch in CA 77-80
Cosman, Carol 104
Cosman, Madeleine Pelner 1937- 127
Brief entry 105
Cosman, Mark 1945- 152
Cosneck, Bernard Joseph 1912-1990 49-52
Cosner, Shaaron 1940- CANR-38
Earlier sketch in CA 116
See also SATA 43
Cosper, Darcy 234
Coss, Thurman L. 1926- 13-16R
Cossa, Roberto 1934- .... DLB 305
Cossart, Theophilus
See Glass, Montague (Marsden)
Cosseboom, Kathy Groehn
See El-Messidi, Kathy Groehn
Cossi, Olga 1921- 81-84
See also SATA 67, 102
Cosslett, Tess 1947- 115
Cossman, E(li) Joseph 1918-2002 .... 17-20R
Obituary 211
Cossolotto, Matthew 1953- 153
Cost, March
See Morrison, Margaret Mackie
Costa, Albert Bernard 1929- 13-16R
Costa, (Elena) Alexandra 1944- 145
Costa, Claudio Manuel da 1729-1789 ...... LAW
Costa, Gustavo 1930- 37-40R
Costa, Horacio (L.) de la 1916-1977
Obituary 112
Costa, Manuel J(oseph) 1933- 161
Costa, Richard Hauer 1921- 21-24R
Costabel, Eva Deutsch 1924- 125
See also SATA 45
Costabel-Deutsch, Eva
See Costabel, Eva Deutsch
Costain, Thomas B(ertram) 1885-1965 ...... 5-8R
Obituary 25-28R
See also BYA 3
See also CLC 30
See also DLB 9
See also RHW
Costantin, M(ary) M(cCaffrey) 1935- 45-48
Costantini, Humberto 1924(?)-1987 131
Obituary 122
See also CLC 49
See also EWL 3
See also HW 1
Costantino, Roselyn 236
Costanza, Mary S(carpone) 1927- 158
Costas, Bob 1952- 237
Costas, Orlando E(nrique)
1942-1987 .... CANR-82
Obituary 124
Earlier sketch in CA 101
Costas, Procope 1900(?)-1974
Obituary 53-56
Coste, Donat 1912-1957 .... DLB 88
Costello, Anne 1937- 102
Costello, Bonnie 1950- 129
Costello, Chris 1947- 107
Costello, David F(rancis) 1904-1990 ..... 33-36R
See also SATA 23
Costello, Donald P(aul) 1931- 17-20R
Costello, Elvis 1954- 204
See also CLC 21
Costello, Elvis 1954(?)- 204
Costello, Gerald M. 1931- 127
Costello, Grace Seymour 1883-1983
Obituary 110
Costello, John E(dward) 1943- 85-88
Costello, Joseph P(atrick) 1924- 115
Costello, Louisa Stuart 1799-1870 ...... DLB 166
Costello, Mark 1962- CANR-112
See also Flood, John
Costello, Matthew J(ohn) 1948- .... BYA 12
See also HGG
Costello, Michael
See Detzer, Karl
Costello, Peter 1946- 93-96
Costello, Sean .... HGG
Costello, William Aloysius 1904-1969 .... 1-4R
Obituary 103
Costelloe, M(artin) Joseph 1914-2000 ... 41-44R
Costenoble, Philostene
See Ghelderode, Michel de
Coster, Graham 1960- 199
Coster, Robert
See Barltrop, Robert
Costigan, Daniel M. 1929- CANR-56
Earlier sketches in CA 33-36R, CANR-14, 31
Costigan, Giovanni 1905-1990 .... CAP-1
Earlier sketch in CA 13-16
Costigan, James 1928- 73-76
Costikyan, Edward N. 1924- 17-20R
Costikyan, Greg 1959- CANR-141
Earlier sketch in CA 112
Costinescu, Tristan
See Gross, Terence
Costis, Harry George 1928- 45-48
Costley, Bill
See Costley, William K(irkwood), Jr.
Costley, William K(irkwood), Jr.
1942- CANR-82
Earlier sketches in CA 81-84, CANR-35, 56
Costonis, John J(oseph) 1937- CANR-4
Earlier sketch in CA 49-52
Cota-Cardenas, Margarita 1941- .... DLB 122
Cote, Denis 1954- .... DLB 251
Cote, Richard G(eorge) 1934- 69-72
Cote, Richard N. 1945- 147
Cotes, Cecil V.
See Duncan, Sara Jeannette
Cotes, Peter 1912-1998 .... CANR-92
Earlier sketches in CA 5-8R, CANR-4, 26
Cothem, Fayly H(ardcastle) 1926- 1-4R
Cothen, Joe H(erbert) 1926- 113
Cothran, J(oseph) Guy 1897-1979 .... CAP-2
Earlier sketch in CA 29-32
Cothran, James R(obert) 1940- 150
Cothran, Jean 1910-1997 93-96
Cotich, Felicia 1926- 115
Cotler, Gordon 1923- 1-4R
Cotler, Sherwin B(arry) 1941- 65-68
Cotlow, Lewis N(athaniel) 1898-1987 65-68
Obituary 122
Cotman, John Walton 1954- 146
Cotner, Robert Crawford 1906-1980 ..... 37-40R
Cotner, Thomas E. 1916- 37-40R
Cott, Hugh B(amford) 1900-1987
Obituary 122
Cott, Jonathan 1942- CANR-139
Earlier sketch in CA 53-56
See also SATA 23
Cott, Nancy F(alik) 1945- CANR-109
Earlier sketches in CA 81-84, CANR-59
See also FW
Cottam, Clarence 1899-1974 97-100
See also SATA 25
Cottam, Francis 1957- 215
Cottam, Keith M. 1941- 81-84
Cottam, Walter P(ace) 1894-1988 .... CAP-1
Earlier sketch in CA 13-16
Cotta Vaz, Mark
See Vaz, Mark Cotta
Cotten, Bruce 1873-1954 202
See also DLB 187
Cotten, Lee 1942- CANR-56
Earlier sketch in CA 127
Cotten, Nell(ie) Wyllie 1908-1997 .... 1-4R
Cotter, Charles H(enry) 1919- 13-16R
Cotter, Cornelius Philip 1924- CANR-1
Earlier sketch in CA 1-4R
Cotter, Edward F(rancis) 1917- CANR-6
Earlier sketch in CA 5-8R
Cotter, James Finn 1929- 33-36R
Cotter, Janet M(errill) 1914-1990 61-64
Cotter, Joseph Seamon Sr. 1861-1949 124
See also BLC 1
See also BW 1
See also DAM MULT
See also DLB 50
See also TCLC 28
Cotter, Joseph Seamon, Jr. 1895-1919 177
See also DLB 50
Cotter, Richard V(ern) 1930- CANR-47
Earlier sketches in CA 41-44R, CANR-14
Cotterell, Geoffrey 1919- 5-8R
Cotterell, (Francis) Peter 1930- CANR-1
Earlier sketch in CA 49-52
Cotterill, Colin 1952- 237
Cotterill, Rodney M(ichael) J(ohn)
1933- CANR-42
Earlier sketch in CA 118
Cotterrell, Roger (B. M.) 1946- 142
Cottin, Sophie 1770-1807 .... DLB 313
Cottingham, John (Graham) 1943- ... CANR-82
Earlier sketches in CA 133, CANR-49
Cottle, Charles
See Anderson, Robert C(harles)
Cottle, Joan 1960- .... SATA 135
Cottle, Thomas J. 1937- CANR-96
Earlier sketches in CA 33-36R, CANR-17
Cottle, William C(ullen) 1913-1992 ...... 41-44R
Cottler, Joseph 1899-1996 .... CAP-2
Earlier sketch in CA 25-28
See also SATA 22
Cotton, Charles 1630-1687 .... DLB 131
See also RGEL 2
Cotton, (Thomas) Henry 1907-1987
Obituary 124
Cotton, John
See Fearn, John Russell
Cotton, John 1584-1652 .... DLB 24
See also TUS
Cotton, John 1925-2003 .... CANR-52
Obituary 218
Earlier sketches in CA 65-68, CANR-11, 27
See also CP 1, 2, 3, 4, 5, 6, 7
Cotton, John W(healdon) 1925- 33-36R
See also TUS
Cotton, Norris 1900-1989 103
Cotton, Sir Robert Bruce 1571-1631 .. DLB 213
Cottonwood, Joe 1947- 156
See also SATA 92
Cottrell, Alan (Howard) 1919- CANR-10
Earlier sketch in CA 65-68
Cottrell, Alan P. 1935-1984 120
Cottrell, Alvin J. 1925(?)-1984
Obituary 112
Cottrell, (William) Fred(erick) 1903-1979 .. 1-4R
Cottrell, Jack (Warren) 1938- CANR-23
Earlier sketch in CA 107
Cottrell, Leonard 1913-1974 .... CANR-4
Earlier sketch in CA 5-8R
See also SATA 24

Cottrell 126 CONTEMPORARY AUTHORS

Cottrell, Leonard S(later), Jr. 1899-1985 107
Obituary 115
Cottrell, Richard 1936- 130
Cottrell, Robert C. 1950- CANR-111
Earlier sketch in CA 142
Cottrell, Robert D(uane) 1930- 53-56
Cottret, Bernard 1951- 143
Cottringer, Anne 1952- CANR-135
Earlier sketch in CA 163
See also SATA 97, 150
Couch, Arthur Thomas Quiller
See Quiller-Couch, Sir Arthur (Thomas)
Couch, Helen F(ox) 1907- CAP-2
Earlier sketch in CA 17-18
Couch, Osma Palmer
See Tod, Osma Gallinger
Couch, William, Jr. 152
See also BW 2, 3
Couch, William T(erry) 1901-1988
Obituary 127
Coudenhove-Kalergi, Richard N(icolas) 1894-1972
Obituary 37-40R
Coudert, Allison P(ierce) 1941- 110
Coudert, Jo 1923- CANR-95
Earlier sketch in CA 17-20R
Coudray, Jean-Marc
See Castoriadis, Cornelius
Couffer, Jack 1924- CANR-1
Earlier sketch in CA 1-4R
Coufoudakis, Van 1938- 197
Couger, J(ames) Daniel 1929- CANR-8
Earlier sketch in CA 53-56
Coughlan, John W. 1927- 21-24R
Coughlan, Margaret N(ourse) 1925- 107
Coughlan, (John) Robert 1914-1992 65-68
Coughlan, William C(arlisle), Jr. 1946- 115
Coughlin, Bernard J. 1922- 13-16R
Coughlin, Charles E(dward) 1891-1979
Obituary 97-100
Coughlin, Con 1955- 218
Coughlin, George G(ordon) 1900-1986 107
Coughlin, Joseph Welter 1919- 1-4R
Coughlin, Patricia (E.) 184
Coughlin, T(homas) Glen 1958- CANR-109
Earlier sketch in CA 136
Coughlin, Violet L(ouise) 73-76
Coughlin, William J(eremiah) 1929-1992 ... 139
Coughran, Larry C. 1925- 21-24R
Coughtry, Jay 1945- 111
Couldery, Fred(erick) A(lan) J(ames) 1928- 9-12R
Coulet du Gard, Rene 1919- CANR-4
Earlier sketch in CA 53-56
Coulette, Henri Anthony 1927-1988 ...... CANR-14
Obituary 125
Earlier sketch in CA 65-68
See also CN 1, 2
Coulling, Mary (Price) 1928- 142
Coulling, Sidney Baxter 1924- 102
Coulman, Valerie 1969- ...... SATA 161
Coulmas, Florian 1949- CANR-89
Earlier sketch in CA 132
Couloumbis, Audrey ...... BYA 15
Couloumbis, Theodore A. 1935- CANR-7
Earlier sketch in CA 17-20R
Coulson, C(harles) A(lfred) 1910-1974 ...... CANR-4
Earlier sketch in CA 5-8R
Coulson, Felicity Carter 1906- 9-12R
Coulson, John H(ubert) A(rthur) 1906- 9-12R
Coulson, Juanita (Ruth) 1933- CANR-83
Earlier sketches in CA 25-28R, CANR-9, 26, 52
See also FANT
See also SFW 4
Coulson, N. J.
See Coulson, Noel J(ames)
Coulson, Noel J(ames) 1928-1986 124
Obituary 120
Coulson, Robert 1924- CANR-83
Earlier sketches in CA 49-52, CANR-36
Coulson, Robert S(tratton) 1928-1999 ...... CANR-24
Earlier sketches in CA 21-24R, CANR-9
Coulson, William D(onald) E(dward) 1942- 89-92
Coulter, Catherine CANR-71
Earlier sketch in CA 139
See also RHW
Coulter, E(llis) Merton 1890-1981 ...... CANR-3
Obituary 104
Earlier sketch in CA 9-12R
Coulter, Edwin M(artin) 1937- 104
Coulter, Harris L. 1932- 136
Coulter, Hope Norman 1961- 129
Coulter, John (William) 1888-1980 ...... CANR-3
Earlier sketch in CA 5-8R
See also DLB 68
Coulter, N(orman) Arthur, Jr. 1920- 65-68
Coulter, Olivia W. 1915(?)-1989
Obituary 129
Coulter, Stephen 1914-
Brief entry 109
Coulton, James
See Hansen, Joseph
Coultrap-McQuin, Susan (M.) 1947- 137
Council, Norman Briggs 1936- 102
Cound, John J(ames) 1928- 37-40R
Counsel, June 1926- 138
See also SATA 70
Counsell, John William 1905-1987 57-60
Obituary 121
Counselman, Mary Elizabeth 1911-1994 ...... CANR-72
Earlier sketch in CA 106
See also HGG
Counsilman, James E(dward) 1920-2004 126
Obituary 223
Count, Earl W(endel) 1899-1996 ...... 37-40R
Obituary 155
Counter, Kenneth (Norman Samuel) 1930- 25-28R
Countess of Athlone
See Alice (Mary Victoria Augusta Pauline), Princess
Countess of Longford
See Longford, Elizabeth (Harmon Pakenham)
Countryman, The
See Whitlock, Ralph
Countryman, Vern 1917-1999 ...... 13-16R
Obituary 179
Counts, Charles Richard 1934- 49-52
Counts, George S(ylvester) 1889-1974 ...... 5-8R
Obituary 53-56
Couper, Heather 1949- 124
Couper, J(ohn) M(ill) 1914- 45-48
See also CP 1
Couper, Stephen
See Gallagher, Stephen
Couperus, Louis (Marie Anne) 1863-1923
Brief entry 115
See also EWL 3
See also RGWL 2, 3
See also TCLC 15
Coupey, Philippe 1937- 104
Coupey, Pierre 1942- ...... CP 1
Coupland, Douglas 1961- CANR-130
Earlier sketches in CA 142, CANR-57, 90
See also AAYA 34
See also CCA 1
See also CLC 85, 133
See also CN 7
See also CPW
See also DAC
See also DAM POP
Coupling, J. J.
See Pierce, John Robinson
Courage, James Francis 1903-1963 77-80
See also RGEL 2
Courant, Curt 1895- ...... IDFW 3, 4
Courant, Richard 1888-1972 157
Obituary 33-36R
Couratin, Arthur Hubert 1902-1988
Obituary 126
Courey, Leigh
See Borrelli, Karen (Troxel)
Courlander, Harold 1908-1996 ...... CANR-40
Obituary 151
Earlier sketches in CA 9-12R, CANR-3, 18
See also SATA 6
See also SATA-Obit 88
Cournand, Andre (Frederic) 1895-1988 157
Cournos, Francine 1945- 199
Cournos, John 1881-1966 ...... CAP-2
Earlier sketch in CA 13-14
See also DLB 54
Couroucli, Jennifer 1922- 29-32R
Course, Alfred George 1895- 9-12R
Course, Edwin 1922- 77-80
Coursen, Herbert R(andolph), Jr. 1932- CANR-41
Earlier sketches in CA 53-56, CANR-4, 19
Coursen, Valerie 1965(?)- ...... SATA 102
Court, Harold
See Swycaffer, Jefferson P(utnam)
Court, Jamie 1967- 203
Court, Margaret Smith 1942- 182
Brief entry 106
Court, Sharon
See Rowland, D(onald) S(ydney)
Court, W(illiam) H(enry) B(assano) 1905(?)-1971
Obituary 104
Court, Wesli
See Turco, Lewis (Putnam)
Court, Wesli 1940- CANR-11
Earlier sketch in CA 69-72
Courtauld, George 1938- 129
Courteline, Georges 1858-1929 ...... DLB 192
Courtenay, Ashley (Reginald) 1888-1986
Obituary 121
Courtenay, Bryce 1933- 138
See also CLC 59
See also CPW
Courtenay, William J(ames) 1935- 9-12R
Courter, Gay 1944- CANR-26
Earlier sketches in CA 57-60, CANR-7
Courthion, Pierre (Barthelemy) 1902-1988 ...... CANR-14
Earlier sketch in CA 81-84
Courtice, Katie 1942- 121
Courtier, S(idney) H(obson) 1904-1970(?) CANR-83
Earlier sketches in CAP-2, CA 25-28
Courtillot, Vincent E(mmanuel) 1948- 182
Courtine, Robert 1910- CANR-14
Earlier sketch in CA 81-84
Courtis, Stuart Appleton 1874-1969
Obituary 105
See also SATA-Obit 29
Courtland, Roberta
See Dern, Erolie Pearl Gaddis
Courtneidge, Cicely 1893-1980
Obituary 105
Courtney, Caroline ...... RHW
Courtney, Dale
See Kimberly, Gail
Courtney, Dayle
See Goldsmith, Howard
Courtney, E(dward) 1932- 129
Courtney, Gwendoline CAP-1
Earlier sketch in CA 9-10
Courtney, James
See Robinson, Frank M(alcolm)
Courtney, John
See Judd, Frederick Charles
Courtney, Nicholas (Piers) 1944- CANR-141
Earlier sketches in CA 113, CANR-32
Courtney, Ragan 1941- 97-100
Courtney, (John) Richard 1927- CANR-48
Earlier sketches in CA 105, CANR-23
Courtney, Richard D. 1925- 187
Courtney, Robert
See Ellison, Harlan (Jay)
Courtney, William J(ohn) 1921- 102
Courtney, Winifred F(isk) 1918- 109
Courtwright, David T(odd) 1952- CANR-93
Earlier sketches in CA 110, CANR-28
Courville, Donovan A(mos) 1901-1996 ... 45-48
Coury, Louise Andree 1895(?)-1983
Obituary 109
See also SATA-Obit 34
Couse, Harold C. 1925- 17-20R
Cousens, Frances Reissman 1913-1985
Obituary 115
Couser, G(riffith) Thomas 1946- 89-92
Cousineau, Phil 1952- 146
Cousins, Albert Newton 1919- 41-44R
Cousins, Geoffrey (Esmond) 1900- 25-28R
Cousins, Linda 1946- CANR-87
Earlier sketch in CA 155
See also SATA 90
Cousins, Margaret 1905-1996 ...... CANR-1
Obituary 152
Earlier sketch in CA 1-4R
See also DLB 137
See also SATA 2
See also SATA-Obit 92
Cousins, Norman 1912-1990 ...... CANR-61
Earlier sketches in CA 17-20R, CANR-13, 33
See also BEST 90:2
See also DLB 137
See also MTCW 1, 2
See also MTFW 2005
Cousins, Peter Edward 1928- 104
Cousse, Raymond 1942- 101
Cousteau, Jacques-Yves 1910-1997 .. CANR-67
Obituary 159
Earlier sketches in CA 65-68, CANR-15
See also CLC 30
See also MTCW 1
See also SATA 38, 98
Cousteau, Philippe Pierre 1940-1979 .... 33-36R
Obituary 89-92
Coustillas, Pierre 1930- 73-76
Coutard, Raoul 1924-1993 ...... IDFW 3, 4
Coutard, Wanda Lundy Hale 1902(?)-1982
Obituary 106
Coutau-Begarie, Herve 1956- 197
Coutinho, Joaquim 1886(?)-1978
Obituary 77-80
Couto, Mia 1955- ...... AFW
Couto, Nancy Vieira 1942- CANR-83
Earlier sketch in CA 136
Couto, Richard A. 1941- CANR-15
Earlier sketch in CA 89-92
Coutts, Frederick Lee 1899-1986 ...... CANR-36
Earlier sketch in CA 109
Couture, Andrea 1943- 85-88
Couture, Christin 1951- ...... SATA 73
Couturier, Louis (Joseph) 1910- 101
Couvreur, Jessie 1848-1897 ...... DLB 230
Couzyn, Jeni 1942- 85-88
See also CP 2, 3, 4, 5, 6, 7
See also CWP
See also WWE 1
Covarrubias, Barbara Faith 1932- 113
Covatta, Anthony Gallo 1944- 53-56
Covell, Alan C(arter) 1952- 118
Covell, Jon Carter 1910-2000 ...... CANR-17
Earlier sketch in CA 97-100
Coven, Brenda 110
Coveney, James 1920- 41-44R
Coveney, Peter (Vivian) 1958- 140
Coventry, Francis 1725-1754 ...... DLB 39
Coventry, John (Joseph Seton) 1915-1998 93-96
Obituary 165
Cover, Arthur Byron 1950- CANR-57
Earlier sketch in CA 107
See also SFW 4
Cover, Robert M. 1943-1986 57-60
Obituary 119
Coverdale, John F(oy) 1940- 73-76
Coverdale, Miles c. 1487-1569 ...... DLB 167
Coverley, Louise Bennett
See Bennett-Coverley, Louise
Covert, James Thayne 1932- 37-40R
Covert, Paul 1941- CANR-20
Earlier sketch in CA 103
Covey, Cyclone 1922- 21-24R
Covey, Stephen R. 1932- CANR-41
Earlier sketches in CA 33-36R, CANR-12
Covici, Pascal, Jr. 1930- 1-4R
Coville, Bruce 1950- CANR-96
Earlier sketches in CA 97-100, CANR-22
See also AAYA 40
See also BYA 14
See also JRDA
See also MAICYA 2
See also MAICYAS 1
See also SATA 32, 77, 118, 155
See also SATA-Essay 155
Coville, Walter J(oseph) 1914-1973 .... CANR-5
Earlier sketch in CA 5-8R
Covin, David L(eroy) 1940- 143
See also BW 2
Covin, Theron Michael 1947- 57-60
Covina, Gina 1952- 101
Covington, Dennis 171
See also SATA 109
Covington, James W. 1917- 33-36R
Covington, Linda
See Windsor, Linda
Covington, Martin Vaden 1936- 37-40R
Covington, Vicki 1952- CANR-144
Earlier sketches in CA 133, CANR-59
See also CSW
Covington, William G., Jr. 1954- 191
Covino, Frank 1931- 57-60
Covino, Joseph, Jr. 1954- 113
Covino, Michael 1950- 132
Covvey, H(arry) Dominic J(oseph) 1944- CANR-28
Earlier sketch in CA 110
Cowan, Alan
See Gilchrist, Alan W.
Cowan, Andrew CANR-130
Earlier sketch in CA 171
Cowan, Catherine ...... SATA 121
Cowan, Charles Donald 1923- 102
Cowan, Edward James 1944- 103
Cowan, G(ordon) 1933- 25-28R
Cowan, G(eorge) H(amilton) 1917- 17-20R
Cowan, Geoffrey 1942- 97-100
Cowan, George McKillop 1916- 102
Cowan, Gregory M(ac) 1935-1979 ...... CANR-9
Earlier sketch in CA 65-68
Cowan, Henry J(acob) 1919- CANR-19
Earlier sketches in CA 53-56, CANR-4
Cowan, Ian Borthwick 1932-1990 ... CANR-24
Obituary 133
Earlier sketches in CA 61-64, CANR-8
Cowan, J(oseph) L(loyd) 1929- 25-28R
Cowan, James (Granville) 1942- CANR-142
Earlier sketch in CA 139
Cowan, James C(ostello) 1927- CANR-29
Earlier sketch in CA 29-32R
Cowan, Janice 1941- 97-100
Cowan, Louise (Shillingburg) 1916- .. CANR-47
Earlier sketch in CA 1-4R
Cowan, Lyn 1942- 116
Cowan, Michael H(eath) 1937- 21-24R
Cowan, Paul 1940-1988
Obituary 126
Cowan, Peter (Walkinshaw) 1914-2002 ...... CANR-83
Earlier sketches in CA 21-24R, CANR-9, 25, 50
See also CN 1, 2, 3, 4, 5, 6, 7
See also DLB 260
See also RGSF 2
See also SSC 28
Cowan, Richard O(lsen) 1934- 53-56
Cowan, Robert G(ranniss) 1895-1993 ... CAP-1
Obituary 174
Earlier sketch in CA 11-12
Cowan, Ruth Schwartz 1941- 115
Cowan, Stuart DuBois 1917- 104
Cowan, Walter G(reaves) 1912- 120
Cowan, Wood (Messick) 1896-1977 69-72
Coward, Barry 1941- CANR-86
Earlier sketch in CA 131
Coward, David 1938- 174
Coward, Noel (Peirce) 1899-1973 .. CANR-132
Obituary 41-44R
Earlier sketches in CAP-2, CA 17-18, CANR-35
See also AITN 1
See also BRWS 2
See also CBD
See also CDBLB 1914-1945
See also CLC 1, 9, 29, 51
See also DA3
See also DAM DRAM
See also DFS 3, 6
See also DLB 10, 245
See also EWL 3
See also IDFW 3, 4
See also MTCW 1, 2
See also MTFW 2005
See also RGEL 2
See also TEA
Cowart, David (Guyland) 1947- CANR-30
Earlier sketch in CA 104
Cowasjee, Saros 1931- CANR-43
Earlier sketches in CA 9-12R, CANR-5, 20
Cowden, Dudley J(ohnstone) 1899-1987 ...... 41-44R
Cowden, Jeanne 1918- 85-88
Cowden, Joanna Dunlap 1933- 53-56
Cowden, Robert H. 1934- 143
Cowdrey, A(lbert) E(dward) 1933- 17-20R
Cowdrey, (Michael) Colin 1932-2000 105
Obituary 190
Cowdrey, H(erbert) E(dward) J(ohn) 1926- .. 129
Cowell, (John) Adrian 1934- 103
Cowell, Cressida 1966- 211
See also SATA 140
Cowell, Cyril 1888- CAP-2
Earlier sketch in CA 21-22
Cowell, Frank A. 135
Cowell, Frank Richard 1897-1978 ...... CANR-8
Earlier sketch in CA 53-56
Cowell, Henry Dixon 1897-1965
Obituary 116
Cowell, Stephanie 1943- CANR-143
Earlier sketch in CA 144
Cowen, David L(aurence) 1909- CANR-47
Earlier sketch in CA 13-16R
Cowen, Emory L(eland) 1926- CANR-51
Earlier sketch in CA 69-72

Cumulative Index 127 Cragg

Cowen, Eve
See Werner, Herma
Cowen, Frances
See Munthe, Frances
Cowen, Ida 1898-1993 45-48
See also SATA 64
Cowen, John (Edwin) 1940- 210
Cowen, Robert Churchill 1927- 13-16R
Cowen, Ron .... CAD
Cowen, Ron(ald) 1944- CANR-67
Earlier sketch in CA 85-88
See also CAD
See also CD 5, 6
Cowen, Roy C(hadwell) 1930- CANR-107
Earlier sketches in CA 33-36R, CANR-12
Cowen, Tyler 1962- CANR-141
Earlier sketch in CA 177
Cowen, Zelman 1919- CANR-1
Earlier sketch in CA 1-4R
Cowgill, Donald O(len) 1911-1987 .... 37-40R
Cowherd, Raymond Gibson 1909-1992 124
Cowie, Alexander 1896-1978 .... 33-36R
Cowie, Colin 1962- 176
Cowie, Donald 1911- 116
Cowie, Evelyn E(lizabeth) 1924- CANR-9
Earlier sketch in CA 13-16R
Cowie, Hamilton Russell 1931- 102
Cowie, Leonard W(allace) 1919- CANR-9
Earlier sketch in CA 13-16R
See also SATA 4
Cowie, Mervyn (Hugh) 1909-1996 .... CAP-1
Obituary 152
Earlier sketch in CA 9-10
Cowie, Peter 1939- CANR-18
Earlier sketches in CA 49-52, CANR-1
Cowle, Jerome Milton 1917- 93-96
Cowle, Jerry
See Cowle, Jerome Milton
Cowler, Rosemary (Elizabeth) 1925- 25-28R
Cowles, Fleur CANR-24
Earlier sketches in CA 9-12R, CANR-4
See also AITN 1
Cowles, Frank, Jr. 1918- 57-60
Cowles, Gardner 1861-1946 .... DLB 29
Cowles, Gardner A., Jr. 1903-1985 178
Obituary 116
See also DLB 127, 137
Cowles, Ginny 1924- 57-60
Cowles, John Sr. 1898-1983
Obituary 109
Cowles, Kathleen
See Krull, Kathleen
Cowles, Lois Thornburg 1909-1980
Obituary 101
Cowles, Mike
See Cowles, Gardner A., Jr.
Cowles, Raymond B(ridgeman) 1896-1975
Obituary 61-64
Cowles, S(amuel) Macon, Jr. 1916- 21-24R
Cowles, Virginia (Spencer)
1912-1983 .... CANR-12
Obituary 110
Earlier sketch in CA 65-68
Cowley, Abraham 1618-1667 .... BRW 2
See also DLB 131, 151
See also PAB
See also RGEL 2
Cowley, Hannah 1743-1809 .... DFS 22
See also DLB 89
See also RGEL 2
Cowley, Joseph (Gilbert) 1923- 106
Cowley, (Cassia) Joy 1936- CANR-124
Earlier sketches in CA 25-28R, CANR-11, 57
See also CLR 55
See also CWRI 5
See also MAICYA 2
See also SAAS 26
See also SATA 4, 90
See also SATA-Essay 118
Cowley, Malcolm 1898-1989 .... CANR-55
Obituary 128
Earlier sketches in CA 5-8R, CANR-3
See also AMWS 2
See also CLC 39
See also CP 1, 2
See also DLB 4, 48
See also DLBY 1981, 1989
See also EWL 3
See also MAL 5
See also MTCW 1, 2
See also MTFW 2005
Cowley, Marjorie 1925- 148
See also SATA 111
Cowley, Robert (William) 1934- 193
Cowlin, Dorothy
See Whalley, Dorothy
Cowling, Elizabeth 1910-
Brief entry 110
Cowling, Ellis 1905-1979 .... CAP-1
Earlier sketch in CA 13-16
Cowling, Maurice John 1926- CANR-3
Earlier sketch in CA 5-8R
Cowlishaw, Ranson 1894- 5-8R
Cowper, Richard
See Middleton-Murry, John, (Jr.)
See also DLB 261
See also SCFW 2
Cowper, William 1731-1800 .... BRW 3
See also DA3
See also DAM POET
See also DLB 104, 109
See also PC 40
See also RGEL 2
Cowser, Bob, Jr. 1971(?)- 239
Cox, A(nthony) B(erkeley)
1893-1971 .... CANR-58
Earlier sketch in CA 97-100
See also Berkeley, Anthony
Cox, Albert W(esley) 1921- 53-56
Cox, Alex 1954- 201
Cox, Allan 1937- 93-96
Cox, Alva Irwin, Jr. 1925- 17-20R
Cox, Archibald 1912-2004 73-76
Obituary 227
Cox, (Christopher) Barry 1931- 103
See also SATA 62
Cox, Bertha Mae (Hill) 1901-1993 .... 17-20R
Cox, Bill 1910-1993 .... 9-12R
Cox, Brad J. 1944- 160
Cox, C. Benjamin 1925- 97-100
Cox, Carol 1946- 117
Cox, Charles B(rian) 1928- 25-28R
Cox, Claire 1919- CANR-2
Earlier sketch in CA 5-8R
Cox, Clinton 1934- 178
See also SATA 74, 108
Cox, Constance 1915-1998 .... CANR-24
Earlier sketches in CA 21-24R, CANR-9
Cox, David (Dundas) 1933- 119
See also SATA 56
Cox, Donald William 1921- CANR-4
Earlier sketch in CA 1-4R
See also SATA 23
Cox, Edith Muriel 102
Cox, Edward Finch 1946- 29-32R
Cox, Edward Franklin 1925- 33-36R
Cox, Edward Locksley 1943- 121
Cox, Edwin B(urk) 1930- 37-40R
Cox, Elizabeth 1942- 130
Cox, Elizabeth 1953- 136
Cox, Erle (Harold) 1873-1950
Brief entry 112
See also SFW 4
Cox, Eugene L. 1931- 21-24R
Cox, Frank D. 1933- 29-32R
Cox, Fred(erick) M(oreland) 1928- CANR-1
Earlier sketch in CA 45-48
Cox, G. William 1949(?)-1988
Obituary 125
Cox, Gary D(uane) 1947- 113
Cox, Gary W(alter) 1955- 139
Cox, Geoffrey Sandford 1910- 103
Cox, George W(yatt) 1935- 115
Cox, Geraldine Vang 1944- 157
Cox, Gertrude (Mary) 1900-1978 169
Cox, Gordon 1942- 146
Cox, Harvey (Gallagher, Jr.) 1929- 77-80
See also AITN 1
Cox, (William) Harvey 1939- 45-48
Cox, Hebe 1909-1994 .... CAP-1
Earlier sketch in CA 13-14
Cox, Howard A. 1958- 192
Cox, Hugh Brandon
See Brandon-Cox, Hugh
Cox, Hugh S(towell) 1874-1969 .... CAP-2
Earlier sketch in CA 21-22
Cox, J(ohn) Gray 1952- 123
Cox, J. Halley 1910-1974
Obituary 112
Cox, Jack
See Cox, John Roberts
Cox, James Anthony 1926- 104
Cox, James M(elville) 1925- 13-16R
Cox, James McMahon 1903-1974 ...... DLB 127
Cox, James Middleton, Jr. 1903-1974
Obituary 89-92
Cox, James Middleton 1870-1957 218
See also DLB 127
Cox, James W(illiam) 1923- 33-36R
Cox, Jeff 1940- CANR-144
Earlier sketch in CA 172
Cox, Jeffrey N. 209
Cox, Jennifer Lloyd 1947- 158
Cox, Jeri
See Kimes, Beverly Rae
Cox, Jim 224
Cox, Joan (Irene) 1942- 101
Cox, John H(enry) 1907-1975
Obituary 115
Cox, John Roberts 1915-1981 .... CANR-14
Earlier sketch in CA 29-32R
See also SATA 9
Cox, John Stuart 1931- 117
Cox, Joseph A. 1896(?)-1980
Obituary 97-100
Cox, Joseph Mason Andrew 1930- CANR-2
Earlier sketch in CA 49-52
See also BW 1
Cox, Joseph W(illiam) 1937- 81-84
Cox, Josephine 1938- 189
See also RHW
Cox, Judy 1954- .... SATA 117, 160
Cox, Julian 226
Cox, Keith (Kohn) 1931- CANR-12
Earlier sketch in CA 69-72
Cox, Kevin R. 1939- 37-40R
Cox, LaWanda Fenlason 1909- 9-12R
Cox, Lee Sheridan 1916- 25-28R
Cox, Leonard c. 1495-c. 1550 .... DLB 281
Cox, Madison 1958- 144
Cox, Marie-Therese Henriette 1925-1991 .. 105
Obituary 136
Cox, Marion Monroe 1898-1983
Obituary 110
See also Monroe, Marion
Cox, Mark 1956- 128
Cox, Martha Heasley 1919- 13-16R
Cox, Mary Elizabeth
See Headapohl, Betty R.
Cox, Maxwell E(vans) 1922-1996 .... 25-28R
Obituary 153
Cox, Michael 1948- 218
Cox, Miriam Stewart 9-12R
Cox, Molly
See Cox, Marie-Therese Henriette
Cox, Oliver Cromwell 1901-1974 .... 1-4R
Obituary 103
Cox, P(atrick) Brian 45-48
Cox, Palmer 1840-1924 185
Brief entry 111
See also CLR 24
See also DLB 42
See also SATA 24
Cox, Patricia Bale 176
See also Cox, Patsi Bale
Cox, Patsi Bale 185
See also Cox, Patricia Bale
Cox, Paul(us) 1940- 143
Cox, R(obert) David 1937- CANR-13
Earlier sketch in CA 29-32R
Cox, R(alph) Merritt 1939- 33-36R
Cox, Rachel Dunaway 1904-1996 .... 33-36R
Cox, Reavis 1900-1992 .... CAP-1
Obituary 139
Earlier sketch in CA 13-16
Cox, Richard 1931- CANR-30
Earlier sketches in CA 21-24R, CANR-11
Cox, Richard 1970- 235
Cox, Richard Howard 1925- CANR-8
Earlier sketch in CA 13-16R
Cox, Robert H(enry) 1961- 147
Cox, Roger L. 1931- 135
Cox, Sebastian 230
Cox, Stephen (LeRoy) 1966- 130
Cox, Steve 1962- 156
Cox, Thomas R(ichard) 1933- 53-56
Cox, Vic 1942- 152
See also SATA 88
Cox, Vicki 1945- 234
See also SATA 158
Cox, Victoria
See Garretson, Victoria Diane
Cox, Wallace (Maynard) 1924-1973 97-100
Obituary 41-44R
See also Cox, Wally
Cox, Wally
See Cox, Wallace (Maynard)
See also SATA 25
Cox, Warren E(arle) 1895-1977 .... CAP-2
Obituary 69-72
Earlier sketch in CA 33-36
Cox, William E(dwin), Jr. 1930- 106
Cox, William R(obert) 1901-1988 .... CANR-59
Obituary 126
Earlier sketches in CA 9-12R, CANR-6, 24
See also Ward, Jonas
See also CMW 4
See also SATA 46
See also SATA-Brief 31
See also SATA-Obit 57
See also TCWW 1, 2
Cox, William Trevor 1928- CANR-139
Earlier sketches in CA 9-12R, CANR-4, 37, 55, 76, 102
Interview in CANR-37
See also Trevor, William
See also DAM NOV
See also MTCW 1, 2
See also MTFW 2005
See also TEA
Coxe, Antony D(acres) Hippisley
See Hippisley Coxe, Antony D(acres)
Coxe, George Harmon 1901-1984 .... CANR-59
Earlier sketch in CA 57-60
See also CMW 4
Coxe, Louis (Osborne) 1918-1993 .... 13-16R
See also CP 1, 2
See also DLB 5
See also TCLE 1:1
Coxe, Molly 1959- 137
See also SATA 69, 101
Coxe, Tench 1755-1824 .... DLB 37
Cox-George, Noah Arthur William
1915- CANR-6
Earlier sketch in CA 13-16R
Coxhead, Elizabeth 1909(?)-1979
Obituary 89-92
Cox-Johnson, Ann
See Saunders, Ann Loreille
Coxon, Michele 1950- .... SATA 76, 158
Coy, Fred E. 1923- 164
Coy, Harold 1902-1986 .... CANR-4
Earlier sketch in CA 5-8R
See also SATA 3
Coy, John 1958- .... SATA 120
Coykendall, Ralf (W.), Jr. 1929- 170
Coyle, Beverly (Jones) 1946- 133
Coyle, David Cushman 1887-1969 .. CANR-15
Obituary 103
Earlier sketch in CA 1-4R
Coyle, Diane 231
Coyle, Harold (W.) 1952- CANR-92
Earlier sketch in CA 140
Coyle, J(ohn) J(ames) 1928- 129
Coyle, Kathleen 1886-1952 171
Coyle, L(eslie) Patrick 1934- 110
Coyle, Lee
See Coyle, Leo (Perry)
Coyle, Leo (Perry) 1925- 41-44R
Coyle, Neva 1943- 138
Coyle, William 1917- CANR-2
Earlier sketch in CA 1-4R
Coyne, James K(itchenman) 1946- 141
Coyne, John (P.) 1940- CANR-90
Earlier sketches in CA 93-96, CANR-12
Interview in CANR-12
See also HGG
Coyne, John R(ichard), Jr. 1935- 37-40R
Coyne, Joseph E. 1918-1978 .... 13-16R
Obituary 134
Coyne, Michael 167
Coyne, P. J.
See Masters, Hilary
Coyne, Tami 1960- 218
Coyote, Peter 1941- 198
Coysh, A(rthur) W(ilfred) 1905- CANR-13
Earlier sketch in CA 73-76
Coysh, Victor 1906- CANR-8
Earlier sketch in CA 61-64
Coze, Paul 1903(?)-1974
Obituary 53-56
Cozzens, Frederic S. 1818-1869 .... DLB 202
Cozzens, James Gould 1903-1978 ... CANR-19
Obituary 81-84
Earlier sketch in CA 9-12R
See also AMW
See also BPFB 1
See also CDALB 1941-1968
See also CLC 1, 4, 11, 92
See also CN 1, 2
See also DLB 9, 294
See also DLBD 2
See also DLBY 1984, 1997
See also EWL 3
See also MAL 5
See also MTCW 1, 2
See also MTFW 2005
See also RGAL 4
Cozzens, Peter 1957- CANR-109
Earlier sketch in CA 140
Craats, Rennay 1973- 200
See also SATA 131
Crabb, Alfred Leland 1884-1979 .... CAP-1
Earlier sketch in CA 13-14
Crabb, Cecil V., Jr. 1924- 13-16R
Crabb, E(dmund) W(illiam) 1912- CAP-1
Earlier sketch in CA 11-12
Crabb, Lawrence J(ames), Jr. 1944- ... CANR-14
Earlier sketches in CA 65-68, CANR-31
Crabb, Richard 1914-1999 .... 21-24R
Crabbe, Buster
See Crabbe, Clarence Linden
Crabbe, Clarence Linden
1908-1983 .... CANR-11
Obituary 109
Earlier sketch in CA 69-72
Crabbe, George 1754-1832 .... BRW 3
See also DLB 93
See also RGEL 2
Crabbe, Katharyn W. 1945- 130
Crabtree, Adam (Gary) 1938- CANR-88
Earlier sketch in CA 146
Crabtree, Arthur B(amford) 1910-1996 .. CAP-2
Earlier sketch in CA 17-18
Crabtree, John 1950- CANR-95
Earlier sketch in CA 145
Crabtree, Judith 1928- CANR-42
Earlier sketch in CA 118
See also SATA 63, 98
Crabtree, Lou V. P. 1913- 167
Crabtree, T(homas) T(avron) 1924- 21-24R
Crace, Jim 1946- CANR-123
Brief entry 128
Earlier sketches in CA 135, CANR-55, 70
Interview in CA-135
See also CLC 157
See also CN 5, 6, 7
See also DLB 231
See also SSC 61
Crackanthorpe, Hubert 1870-1896 ..... DLB 135
Crackel, Theodore J(oseph) 1938- 33-36R
Cracker, Edward E.B.
See Odgers, Sally Farrell
Crackers, Fritz
See Frank, Philip Norman
Cracknell, Basil Edward 1925- 103
Cracraft, James (Edward) 1939- 53-56
Cracroft, Richard Holton 1936- 53-56
Craddock, Charles Egbert
See Murfree, Mary Noailles
Craddock, Curtis 1968- 197
Craddock, Fred B(renning) 1928- 132
Craddock, Patricia (Bland) 1938- CANR-4
Earlier sketch in CA 53-56
Craddock, William J(ames) 1946- 85-88
Cradock, Thomas 1718-1770 .... DLB 31
Craft, Francine 1929- 238
Craft, K. Y.
See Craft, Kinuko Y(amabe)
Craft, Kinuko
See Craft, Kinuko Y(amabe)
Craft, Kinuko Y(amabe) 1940- ..... SATA 65, 127
Craft, Larry L. 1947- 230
Craft, Maurice 1932- CANR-28
Earlier sketches in CA 65-68, CANR-11
Craft, Michael
See Johnson, Michael Craft
Craft, Michael 1928- 25-28R
Craft, Robert 1923- CANR-138
Earlier sketches in CA 9-12R, CANR-7
Craft, Ruth 1935- 133
Brief entry 110
See also SATA 87
See also SATA-Brief 31
Crafton, Donald (Clayton) 1947- 138
Crafts, Glenn Alty 1918- 9-12R
Crafts, Kathy 1952- 109
Crafts, Roger Conant 1911-1987 106
Cragg, D. J.
See Cragg, Dan
Cragg, Dan 1939- CANR-96
Earlier sketches in CA 115, CANR-45
Cragg, Gerald R(obertson) 1906-1976 61-64
Cragg, (Albert) Kenneth 1913- CANR-46
Earlier sketches in CA 17-20R, CANR-7, 22

Craggs, Stewart R. 1943- ... CANR-124
Earlier sketch in CA 164
Craghan, John Francis 1936- ... 53-56
Crago, Hugh 1946- ... 116
Crago, Maureen 1939- ... 116
Crago, T(homas) Howard 1907- ... CAP-1
Earlier sketch in CA 13-16
Crahan, Margaret E(llen) 1939- ... 114
Craib, Ian 1945-2002 ... 69-72
Obituary ... 211
Craib, Ralph G(rant) 1925- ... 136
Craig, A. A.
See Anderson, Poul (William)
Craig, Albert M(orton) 1927- ... 37-40R
Craig, Alec
See Craig, Alexander George
Craig, Alexander 1923- ... CP 1
Craig, Alexander George 1897- ... CAP-1
Earlier sketch in CA 9-10
Craig, Alisa
See MacLeod, Charlotte (Matilda)
Craig, Amanda 1959- ... CANR-117
Earlier sketch in CA 137
Craig, Archibald Campbell 1888-1985
Obituary ... 117
Craig, Barbara Hinkson 1942- ... 135
Craig, Barbara M(ary St. George)
1914-1987 ... 37-40R
Craig, Bill 1930- ... 33-36R
Craig, Brian
See Stableford, Brian (Michael)
Craig, (Robert) Cairns 1949- ... 131
Craig, Charlotte M(arie) 1929- ... 73-76
Craig, Charmaine 1971(?)- ... 207
Craig, Christine (Angela) 1943- ... 120
Craig, Colleen ... 225
Craig, Daniel H. 1811-1895 ... DLB 43
Craig, David
See Tucker, James
Craig, David 1932- ... CANR-37
Earlier sketches in CA 41-44R, CANR-14
Craig, David A. ... 210
Craig, Denys
See Stoll, Dennis G(ray)
Craig, Don(ald) Laurence 1946- ... 73-76
Craig, E(velyn) Quita 1917- ... 103
Craig, Edward Anthony 1905-1998 ... 13-16R
Craig, Edward (Henry) Gordon 1872-1966
Obituary ... 25-28R
Craig, Eleanor 1929- ... 93-96
Craig, Elizabeth (Josephine)
1883-1980 ... CANR-11
Obituary ... 101
Earlier sketch in CA 9-12R
Craig, Emma
See Duncan, Alice
Craig, G(illian) M(ary) 1949- ... 139
Craig, Georgia
See Dern, Erolie Pearl Gaddis
Craig, Gerald M(arquis) 1916- ... 9-12R
Craig, Gordon A(lexander) 1913- ... CANR-120
Earlier sketches in CA 25-28R, CANR-17
Craig, H(enry) A(rmitage) L(lewellyn)
1921-1978 ... 85-88
Obituary ... 81-84
Craig, Hazel Thompson 1904-1994 ... 1-4R
Craig, Helen 1934- ... CANR-68
Earlier sketch in CA 117
See also SATA 46, 49, 94
Craig, James 1930- ... 73-76
Craig, Jasmine
See Cresswell, Jasmine (Rosemary)
Craig, Jean T. 1936- ... 5-8R
Craig, John David 1903-1997 ... CAP-2
Earlier sketch in CA 17-18
Craig, John Eland
See Chipperfield, Joseph Eugene
Craig, John Ernest 1921- ... CANR-84
Earlier sketch in CA 101
See also SATA 23
Craig, John H(erbert) 1885-1977 ... CAP-1
Earlier sketch in CA 9-10
Craig, Jonathan
See Smith, Frank E.
Craig, Kenneth M., Jr. 1960- ... 147
Craig, Kit
See Reed, Kit
Craig, Larry
See Coughran, Larry C.
Craig, Laura
See Sumner, Judith H.
Craig, Lee A(llen) ... 159
See also Sands, Leo G(eorge)
Craig, M. F.
See Craig, Mary (Francis) Shura
Craig, M. Jean ... 73-76
See also SATA 17
Craig, M. S.
See Craig, Mary (Francis) Shura
Craig, Margaret (Maze) 1911-1964 ... 1-4R
See also SATA 9
Craig, Mary
See Craig, Mary (Francis) Shura
Craig, Mary Shura
See Craig, Mary (Francis) Shura
Craig, Mary (Francis) Shura
1923-1991 ... CANR-79
Obituary ... 133
Earlier sketches in CA 1-4R, CANR-4, 26
See also SAAS 7
See also SATA 6, 86
See also SATA-Obit 65
Craig, (Elizabeth) May 1889(?)-1975 ... 101
Obituary ... 89-92
Craig, Nancy
See Maslin, Alice
Craig, Pamela Tudor
See Tudor-Craig, Pamela
Craig, Patricia 1949- ... 128
Craig, Peggy
See Kreig, Margaret B. (Baltzell)
Craig, Peter 1969- ... 229
Craig, Philip R. 1933- ... CANR-101
Earlier sketches in CA 25-28R, CANR-72
Craig, Randolph
See Page, Norvell W(ooten)
Craig, Raymond C. 1928- ... 124
Craig, Richard B(lythe) 1935- ... 53-56
Craig, Robert B(ruce) 1944- ... 49-52
Craig, Robert C(harles) 1921-1990 ... 17-20R
Craig, Robert D(ean) 1934- ... CANR-14
Earlier sketch in CA 81-84
Craig, Robert H. 1942- ... CANR-97
Earlier sketch in CA 140
Craig, Ruth 1922- ... 160
See also SATA 95
Craig, Stephen C. 1948- ... 147
Craig, Vera
See Rowland, D(onald) S(ydney)
Craig, Webster
See Russell, Eric Frank
Craig, William Lane 1949- ... 116
Craige, Betty Jean 1946- ... CANR-40
Earlier sketch in CA 117
Craighead, Frank C(ooper), Jr.
1916-2001 ... 97-100
Obituary ... 200
Craighead, W(ade) Edward 1942-
Brief entry ... 118
Craigie, E(dward) Horne 1894- ... CAP-2
Earlier sketch in CA 25-28
Craigie, Jill 1914-1999 ... 188
Craik, Mrs.
See Craik, Dinah Maria (Mulock)
See also RGEL 2
Craik, Arthur
See Craig, Alexander George
Craik, Dinah Maria (Mulock) 1826-1887
See Craik, Mrs. and
Mulock, Dinah Maria
See also DLB 35, 163
See also MAICYA 1, 2
See also SATA 34
Craik, Elizabeth M(ary) 1939- ... CANR-93
Earlier sketch in CA 131
Craik, Kenneth H(enry) 1936- ... CANR-1
Earlier sketch in CA 45-48
Craik, Thomas Wallace 1927- ... 106
Craik, W(endy) A(nn) 1934- ... 25-28R
Craille, Wesley
See Rowland, D(onald) S(ydney)
Crain, Caleb ... 206
Crain, Jeff
See Meneses, Enrique
Crain, John 1926(?)-1979
Obituary ... 89-92
Crain, Robert L(ee) 1934- ... CANR-13
Earlier sketch in CA 21-24R
Crain, Sharie 1942- ... 77-80
Crain, William C(hristopher) 1943- ... 218
Craine, Eugene R(ichard) 1917-1977 ... 33-36R
Crais, Clifton C(harles) 1960- ... 143
Crais, Robert 1954(?)- ... 187
Craker, Lyle E(ugene) 1941- ... 116
Cram, David L. 1934- ... 193
Cram, Donald J(ames) 1919-2001 ... 157
Obituary ... 198
Cram, Mildred 1889-1985 ... 49-52
Obituary ... 171
Cram, Ralph Adams 1863-1942 ... 160
See also TCLC 45
Cramer, Clarence H(enley)
1905-1982 ... CANR-9
Earlier sketch in CA 13-16R
Cramer, Clayton E. 1956- ... 175
Cramer, Eugene H. 1930- ... 150
Cramer, George H. 1913-1988 ... 21-24R
Cramer, Harold 1927- ... 29-32R
Cramer, J(an) S(olomon) 1928- ... 29-32R
Cramer, James 1915- ... 21-24R
Cramer, James J. 1955- ... 213
Cramer, John F. 1913(?)-1989
Obituary ... 128
Cramer, John Francis 1899-1967 ... CAP-1
Earlier sketch in CA 17-18
Cramer, John G(leason), Jr. 1934- ... 172
Cramer, Kathryn 1943- ... 25-28R
Cramer, Malinda E(lliot) 1844-1906 ... 219
Cramer, Richard Ben 1950- ... CANR-102
Earlier sketches in CA 140, CANR-68
See also DLB 185
Cramer, Richard L(ouis) 1947- ... 102
Cramer, Richard S(eldon) 1928- ... 29-32R
Cramer, Stanley H. 1933- ... 29-32R
Cramer, W. Dale ... 234
Cramp, H(arold) St. G(eorge) 1912- ... 130
Cramp, Rosemary (Jean) 1929- ... 121
Crampton, C(harles) Gregory
1911-1995 ... 21-24R
Crampton, Georgia Ronan 1925- ... 57-60
Crampton, Helen
See Chesney, Marion
Crampton, Luke 1959- ... 139
Crampton, R(ichard) J. 1940- ... 221
Crampton, Roger C. 1929- ... 33-36R
Cranbrook, James L.
See Edwards, William B(ennett)
Cranch, Christopher Pearse 1813-1892 . DLB 1, 42, 243
Crandall, James E(dward) 1930- ... 41-44R
Crandall, Joy
See Martin, Joy
Crandall, Norma 1907- ... 69-72
Crandall, Robert Warren 1940- ... 124
Crandell, Anne (Elizabeth) Shaver
See Shaver-Crandell, Anne (Elizabeth)
Crandell, Rachel 1943- ... 227
See also SATA 152
Crandell, Richard F. 1901-1974
Obituary ... 53-56
Crane, Alex
See Wilkes-Hunter, R(ichard)
Crane, Barbara (Joyce) 1934- ... CANR-29
Earlier sketch in CA 107
See also SATA 31
Crane, Beverley E(ileen) 1943- ... 197
Crane, Bill
See Crane, William B.
Crane, Caroline 1930- ... CANR-41
Earlier sketches in CA 9-12R, CANR-3, 19
See also SATA 11
Crane, Catherine C(owle) 1940- ... 101
Crane, Conrad C(harles) 1952- ... CANR-100
Earlier sketch in CA 147
Crane, Diana 1933- ... 89-92
Crane, Donald P(aul) 1933- ... 61-64
Crane, (Lauren) Edgar 1917- ... 17-20R
Crane, Edna Temple
See Eicher, (Ethel) Elizabeth
Crane, Elaine Forman 1939- ... CANR-119
Earlier sketches in CA 122, CANR-48
Crane, Frances 1896- ... CMW 4
Crane, Frank H. 1912-1991 ... 89-92
Crane, Hamilton
See Mason, Sarah J.
Crane, Harry 1914-1999 ... 226
Crane, (Harold) Hart 1899-1932 ... 127
Brief entry ... 104
See also AMW
See also AMWR 2
See also CDALB 1917-1929
See also DA
See also DA3
See also DAB
See also DAC
See also DAM MST, POET
See also DLB 4, 48
See also EWL 3
See also MAL 5
See also MTCW 1, 2
See also MTFW 2005
See also PC 3
See also RGAL 4
See also TCLC 2, 5, 80
See also TUS
See also WLC
Crane, Hewitt D(avid) 1927- ... 116
Crane, Jacob L(eslie) 1892-1988
Obituary ... 125
Crane, James G(ordon) 1927- ... 13-16R
Crane, Jim
See Crane, James G(ordon)
Crane, Joan St. C(lair) 1927- ... 73-76
Crane, Julia G(orham) 1925- ... 41-44R
Crane, M. A.
See Wartski, Maureen (Ann Crane)
Crane, Megan ... 236
Crane, Milton 1917-1985
Obituary ... 117
Crane, Morley Benjamin 1890-1983
Obituary ... 110
Crane, Nicholas ... 195
Crane, Peter R(obert) 1954- ... 167
Crane, Philip Miller 1930- ... 9-12R
Crane, R(onald) S(almon) 1886-1967 ... 85-88
See also CLC 27
See also DLB 63
Crane, Richard (Arthur) 1944- ... CANR-67
Earlier sketch in CA 77-80
See also CBD
See also CD 5, 6
Crane, Robert
See Glemser, Bernard and
Robertson, Frank C(hester) and
Sellers, Con(nie Leslie, Jr.)
Crane, Robert Dickson 1929- ... 81-84
Crane, Royston Campbell 1901-1977
Obituary ... 89-92
See also SATA-Obit 22
Crane, Stephen (Townley)
1871-1900 ... CANR-84
Brief entry ... 109
Earlier sketch in CA 140
See also AAYA 21
See also AMW
See also AMWC 1
See also BPFB 1
See also BYA 3
See also CDALB 1865-1917
See also DA
See also DA3
See also DAB
See also DAC
See also DAM MST, NOV, POET
See also DLB 12, 54, 78
See also EXPN
See also EXPS
See also LAIT 2
See also LMFS 2
See also MAL 5
See also NFS 4, 20
See also PFS 9
See also RGAL 4
See also RGSF 2
See also SSC 7, 56, 70
See also SSFS 4
See also TCLC 11, 17, 32
See also TUS
See also WLC
See also WYA
See also YABC 2
Crane, Sylvia E(ngel) 1918- ... 33-36R
Crane, Theodore Rawson 1929- ... 97-100
Crane, Verner W(inslow) 1889-1974
Obituary ... 113
Crane, Walter 1845-1915 ... 168
See also CLR 56
See also DLB 163
See also MAICYA 1, 2
See also SATA 18, 100
Crane, Wilder (Willard) 1928- ... 45-48
Crane, William B. 1904-1981 ... 107
Crane, William D(wight) 1892-1976 ... 5-8R
See also SATA 1
Crane, William Earl 1899-1987 ... 103
Cranefield, Paul F. 1925- ... 141
Cranfield, Charles E(rnest) B(urland)
1915- ... CANR-18
Earlier sketches in CA 5-8R, CANR-2
Cranfield, Geoffrey Alan 1920- ... 5-8R
Cranfield, Ingrid 1945- ... 141
See also SATA 74
Cranford, Clarence William 1906-1983 ... 1-4R
Cranford, Robert J(oshua) 1908-1969 ... CAP-2
Earlier sketch in CA 17-18
Cranin, A(braham) Norman 1927- ... 73-76
Cranko, John 1927-1973
Obituary ... 45-48
Crankshaw, Edward 1909-1984 ... CANR-23
Obituary ... 114
Earlier sketch in CA 25-28R
Cranmer, Thomas 1489-1556 ... DLB 132, 213
Cranna, John 1954- ... 233
Cranny, Titus (Francis) 1921-1981 ... CANR-27
Earlier sketch in CA 25-28R
Cranor, Phoebe 1923- ... 112
Cranshaw, Stanley
See Fisher, Dorothy (Frances) Canfield
Cranshaw, Whitney (S.) ... 234
Cranston, Edward
See Fairchild, William
Cranston, Maurice (William)
1920-1993 ... CANR-3
Obituary ... 143
Earlier sketch in CA 5-8R
Cranston, Mechthild ... 53-56
Cranstone, B(ryan) A(llan) L(efevre) 1918-1989
Obituary ... 129
Cranton, Elmer M(itchell) 1932- ... 118
Cranwell, John Philips 1904- ... 61-64
Crapanzano, Vincent 1939- ... CANR-5
Earlier sketch in CA 53-56
Crapol, Edward P(aul) 1936- ... CANR-93
Earlier sketch in CA 45-48
Crapps, Robert W. 1925- ... 53-56
Crapsey, Adelaide 1878-1914 ... 178
See also DLB 54
Crapsey, Algernon Sidney 1847-1927 ... 229
Crary, Catherine S. 1909-1974 ... CAP-1
Earlier sketch in CA 13-16
Crary, Elizabeth (Ann) 1942- ... 158
See also SATA 99
See also SATA-Brief 43
Crary, Margaret (Coleman) 1906-1986 ... 5-8R
See also SATA 9
Crary, Ryland W(esley) 1913-1984
Obituary ... 113
Crase, Douglas 1944- ... 106
See also CLC 58
Crashaw, Richard 1612(?)-1649 ... BRW 2
See also DLB 126
See also PAB
See also RGEL 2
Crassweller, Robert D. 1915- ... 21-24R
Craster, John Montagu 1901-1975
Obituary ... 108
Crates fl. 470B.C.- ... LMFS 1
Crathern, Alice Tarbell 1894-1973
Obituary ... 110
Cratinus c. 519B.C.-c. 422B.C. ... LMFS 1
Craton, Michael (John) 1931- ... 41-44R
Cratty, Bryant J. 1929- ... CANR-11
Earlier sketch in CA 25-28R
Cravath, Lynne W(oodcock) 1951- ... SATA 98, 148
Craveirinha, Jose 1922- ... EWL 3
See also RGWL 3
Craven, Avery (Odelle) 1885(?)-1980 ... 143
Obituary ... 113
See also DLB 17
Craven, David L. 1951- ... 236
Craven, George M(ilton) 1929- ... 61-64
Craven, Margaret 1901-1980 ... 103
See also BYA 2
See also CCA 1
See also CLC 17
See also DAC
See also LAIT 5
Craven, Roy C., Jr. 1924- ... 69-72
Craven, Sara ... RHW
Craven, Thomas 1889-1969 ... 97-100
See also SATA 22
Craven, Wayne 1930- ... 127
Craven, Wes(ley Earl) 1939- ... CANR-70
Earlier sketch in CA 137
See also AAYA 6, 25
Craven, Wesley Frank (Jr.) 1905-1981 ... 61-64
Obituary ... 103
Cravens, Gwyneth ... 85-88
Cravens, Hamilton 1938- ... 162
Craver, Charles B. 1944- ... 237
Craveri, Benedetta 1942- ... 238
Craveri, Marcello 1914- ... 21-24R
Cravey, Pamela J. 1945- ... 224
Crawells, Carl
See Herm, Gerhard

Cumulative Index **129** **Cribb**

Crawford, Alan Pell 1953- CANR-104
  Earlier sketch in CA 101
Crawford, Ann Fears 1932- CANR-9
  Earlier sketch in CA 21-24R
Crawford, Bill
  See Crawford, William Hulfish
Crawford, C(harles) Merle 1924- 45-48
Crawford, Char 1935- 57-60
Crawford, Charles 1752-1815(?) .... DLB 31
Crawford, Charles F. (?)-1983
  Obituary 109
Crawford, Charles O(len) 1934- 37-40R
Crawford, Charles P. 1945- CANR-24
  Earlier sketch in CA 45-48
  See also SATA 28
Crawford, Charles W(ann) 1931- CANR-8
  Earlier sketch in CA 61-64
Crawford, Cheryl 1902-1986
  Obituary 120
  Brief entry 112
Crawford, Christina 1939- 85-88
Crawford, Clan, Jr. 1927- 57-60
Crawford, Daniel J. 1942- 136
Crawford, David
  See Kettelhack, Guy
Crawford, David L. 1890(?)-1974
  Obituary 45-48
Crawford, Dean (Adams) 1949- 127
Crawford, Deborah 1922- 49-52
  See also SATA 6
Crawford, Donald W(esley) 1938- 45-48
Crawford, F(rancis) Marion 1854-1909 168
  Brief entry 107
  See also DLB 71
  See also HGG
  See also RGAL 4
  See also SUFW 1
  See also TCLC 10
Crawford, Fred D. 1947- 117
Crawford, Fred Roberts 1924- CANR-2
  Earlier sketch in CA 45-48
Crawford, Gary W(illiam) 1953- 175
Crawford, Hank
  See Rummel, (Louis) Jack(son)
Crawford, Iain (Padruig) 1922- CANR-23
  Earlier sketch in CA 1-4R
Crawford, Isabel (Alice Hartley)
  1865-1961 225
Crawford, Isabella Valancy 1850-1887 . DLB 92
  See also RGEL 2
Crawford, James M. 1925- 89-92
Crawford, Jean 1907(?)-1976
  Obituary 104
Crawford, Jerry L(eroy) 1934- 106
Crawford, Joan
  See Le Sueur, Lucille
Crawford, Joanna 1941- 9-12R
Crawford, John E(dmund) 1904-1971 .... CAP-2
  Earlier sketch in CA 17-18
  See also SATA 3
Crawford, John R. 1915(?)-1976
  Obituary 65-68
Crawford, John Richard 1932- 106
Crawford, John S(herman) 1928- 106
Crawford, John W(illiam)
  1914-1990 .... CANR-30
  Earlier sketch in CA 1-4R
Crawford, John W(illiam) 1936- CANR-98
  Earlier sketches in CA 53-56, CANR-4
Crawford, Joyce 1931- 25-28R
Crawford, K(aren) Michael 1959- ...... SATA 155
Crawford, Kenneth G(ale) 1902-1983 81-84
  Obituary 108
Crawford, Linda 1938- CANR-23
  Earlier sketch in CA 65-68
Crawford, Marion (Kirk) 1910(?)-1988
  Obituary 124
Crawford, Mark 1954- 170
Crawford, Mary 1942- 144
Crawford, Matsu W(offord) 1902- CAP-2
  Earlier sketch in CA 17-18
Crawford, Max 1938- CANR-139
  Earlier sketch in CA 77-80
Crawford, Mel 1925- .... SATA 44
  See also SATA-Brief 33
Crawford, Oliver 1917- 85-88
Crawford, Patricia 103
Crawford, Phyllis 1899- .... SATA 3
Crawford, Richard (Arthur) 1935- ... CANR-109
  Earlier sketches in CA 57-60, CANR-9
Crawford, Robert
  See Rae, Hugh C(rauford)
  See also CP 7
Crawford, Robert 1959- .... BRWS 11
Crawford, Robert Platt 1893-1970 .... CAP-2
  Earlier sketch in CA 17-18
Crawford, Stanley (Gottlieb) 1937- 69-72
Crawford, T. Hugh 1956- 146
Crawford, T(erence Gordon) S(harman)
  1945- 29-32R
Crawford, Tad 1946- CANR-125
  Brief entry 114
  Earlier sketch in CA 133
Crawford, Terrence Michael 1945- 129
Crawford, Terry
  See Crawford, Terrence Michael
Crawford, Thelmar Wyche 1905-1999 ...... 1-4R
Crawford, Theresa 1956- 110
Crawford, Thomas 1920- CANR-62
  Earlier sketch in CA 128
Crawford, Vaughn Emerson 1917(?)-1981
  Obituary 104
Crawford, Vernon (E.) 1946-1993 136
Crawford, Walter B(yron) 1919- 116
Crawford, William (Elbert) 1929- CANR-4
  Earlier sketch in CA 1-4R
Crawford, William H. 1907(?)-1973
  Obituary 104
Crawford, William Hulfish 1913-1982
  Obituary 105
Crawford, William P(atrick) 1922- 106
Crawley, Aidan Merivale 1908-1993 61-64
  Obituary 143
Crawley, Alan 1887-1975 146
  See also CCA 1
  See also DLB 68
Crawley, C(harles) W(illiam) 1899-1992 109
Crawley, Gerard M(arcus) 1938- 106
Crawley, Harriet 1948- 134
Crawley, Thomas Edward 1920- 111
Crawley, Tony 1938- 129
Cray, David
  See Solomita, Stephen
Cray, Ed(ward) 1933- CANR-37
  Earlier sketches in CA 81-84, CANR-16
Cray, Roberta
  See Emerson, Ru
Craycraft, Kenneth R., Jr. 1962- 221
Crayder, Dorothy 33-36R
  See also SATA 7
Crayder, Teresa
  See Colman, Hila
Crayon, Geoffrey
  See Irving, Washington
Crayon, Porte
  See Strother, David Hunter
Craz, Albert G. 1926- CANR-8
  Earlier sketch in CA 17-20R
  See also SATA 24
Creager, Alfred L(eon) 1910- 17-20R
Creagh, Patrick 1930- CANR-18
  Earlier sketch in CA 25-28R
Creagh-Osborne, Richard 1928- CANR-7
  Earlier sketch in CA 9-12R
Creamer, J. Shane 1929-
  Brief entry 116
Creamer, Robert W. 1922- CANR-63
  Earlier sketch in CA 21-24R
  See also DLB 171
Crean, John Edward, Jr. 1939- 41-44R
Crean, Patrick (G.) 1949- 123
Crean, Susan M. 1945- CANR-123
  Earlier sketch in CA 158
Creasey, John 1908-1973 .... CANR-59
  Obituary 41-44R
  Earlier sketches in CA 5-8R, CANR-8
  See also Marric, J. J.
  See also CLC 11
  See also CMW 4
  See also DLB 77
  See also MTCW 1
Creasy, Robert K(enwood) 1934- 118
Creasy, Rosalind R. CANR-28
  Earlier sketch in CA 110
Creaturo, Barbara 1943-1990 129
  Obituary 132
Crebbin, June 1938- .... SATA 80
Crebillon, Claude Prosper Jolyot de (fils)
  1707-1777 .... DLB 313
  See also GFL Beginnings to 1789
Crebillon, Claude-Prosper Jolyot de (pere)
  1674-1762 .... DLB 313
  See also GFL Beginnings to 1789
Crecelius, Daniel 1937- 139
Crechales, Anthony George 1926- 29-32R
Crechales, Tony
  See Crechales, Anthony George
Crecine, John Patrick 1939- CANR-7
  Earlier sketch in CA 57-60
Crecy, Jeanne
  See Williams, Jeanne
Credland, Peter (Francis) 1946- 69-72
Credle, Ellis 1902-1998 .... CANR-9
  Earlier sketch in CA 13-16R
  See also SATA 1
Credo
  See Creasey, John
Credo, Alvaro J. de
  See Prado (Calvo), Pedro
Creech, Sharon 1945- CANR-113
  Earlier sketch in CA 159
  See also AAYA 21, 52
  See also BYA 9, 11, 12
  See also CLR 42, 89
  See also MAICYA 2
  See also MAICYAS 1
  See also SATA 94, 139
  See also WYAS 1
  See also YAW
Creed, David
  See Guthrie, James Shields
Creed, Joel
  See King, Albert
Creed, William S. 226
Creede, Thomas fl. 1593-1619(?) .... DLB 170
Creeden, Sharon 1938- 155
  See also SATA 91
Creekmore, Betsey B(eeler) 1915- 69-72
Creekmore, Mildred C. 1905(?)-1987
  Obituary 123
Creel, George 1876-1953
  Brief entry 115
  See also DLB 25
Creel, Herrlee G(lessner) 1905-1994 85-88
  Obituary 145
Creel, Stephen Melville 1938- 69-72
Creeley, Robert (White)
  1926-2005 .... CANR-137
  Obituary 237
  Earlier sketches in CA 1-4R, CANR-23, 43, 89
  See also CAAS 10
  See also AMWS 4
  See also CLC 1, 2, 4, 8, 11, 15, 36, 78
  See also CP 1, 2, 3, 4, 5, 6, 7
  See also DA3
  See also DAM POET
  See also DLB 5, 16, 169
  See also DLBD 17
  See also EWL 3
  See also MAL 5
  See also MTCW 1, 2
  See also MTFW 2005
  See also PFS 21
  See also RGAL 4
  See also WP
Creelman, James 1859-1915 178
  See also DLB 23
Creelman, Marjorie B(roer) 1908-1995 .. CAP-2
  Earlier sketch in CA 21-22
Creer, Thomas L(aselle) 1934- CANR-22
  Earlier sketch in CA 69-72
Creese, Bethea CANR-5
  Earlier sketch in CA 9-12R
Creese, Walter L(ittlefield) 1919- 125
Creeth, Edmund Homer 1928- 102
Creevey, Lucy E. 1940- 29-32R
Creevy, Patrick Joseph 1947- 141
Crefeld, Donna Carolyn Anders
  See Anders, Donna Carolyn
Cregan, David (Appleton Quartus)
  1931- CANR-67
  Earlier sketches in CA 45-48, CANR-1
  See also CBD
  See also CD 5, 6
  See also DLB 13
Creger, Ralph (Clinton) 1914- 13-16R
Cregier, Don M(esick) 1930- 69-72
Crehan, Stewart 1942- 118
Crehan, Thomas 1919- CANR-2
  Earlier sketch in CA 5-8R
Creigh, Dorothy (Weyer) 1921- 105
Creighton, Basil 1885-1989
  Obituary 128
Creighton, Don
  See Drury, Maxine Cole
Creighton, Donald Grant 1902-1979 101
  Obituary 93-96
  See also DLB 88
Creighton, (Mary) Helen 1899-1989 ..... 41-44R
  Obituary 130
  See also SATA-Obit 64
Creighton, Helen (Evelyn) 1914- 33-36R
Creighton, Jill 1949- 161
  See also SATA 96
Creighton, Jo Anne
  See Chadwick, Joseph (L.)
Creighton, Joan Scott 232
Creighton, Joanne V(anish) 1942- 69-72
Creighton, John
  See Chadwick, Joseph (L.)
Creighton, Kathleen 1943- 224
Creighton, Linn 1917- 143
Creighton, Luella Bruce 1901- CAP-1
  Earlier sketch in CA 17-18
Creighton, Thomas 1915(?)-1987
  Obituary 123
Creighton, Thomas H(awk)
  1904-1984 .... CANR-6
  Obituary 114
  Earlier sketch in CA 5-8R
Crellin, John 1916- 69-72
Cremazie, Octave 1827-1879 .... DLB 99
Creme, Benjamin 1922- 219
Cremeans, Charles D(avis) 1915- 5-8R
Cremer, Jan 1940- 13-16R
Cremer, Robert Roger 1947- 61-64
Cremer, Robert Wyndham Ketton
  See Ketton-Cremer, Robert Wyndham
Cremer, Victoriano 1909(?)- 175
  See also DLB 108
Cremin, Lawrence A(rthur)
  1925-1990 .... CANR-29
  Obituary 132
  Earlier sketch in CA 33-36R
Cremins, Robert 1968- 207
Cremo, Michael (A.) 1948- 143
Crena de Iongh, Mary (Dows Herter Norton)
  1894(?)-1985
  Obituary 116
Crena de Iongh, Daniel 1888-1970 .... CAP-2
  Obituary 29-32R
  Earlier sketch in CA 25-28
Crenna, C. David 1944- 128
Crennen, Robert Earl 1929-1984
  Obituary 112
Crenner, James 1938- 13-16R
  See also CP 1
Crenshaw, Ben (Daniel) 1952- 203
Crenshaw, Charles A(ndrew) 1933-2001 140
  Obituary 204
Crenshaw, James L. 1934- CANR-34
  Earlier sketches in CA 37-40R, CANR-14
Crenshaw, Marshall (H.) 1953- 149
Crenshaw, Mary Ann CANR-8
  Earlier sketch in CA 57-60
Crenson, Victoria 1952- CANR-143
  Earlier sketch in CA 152
  See also SATA 88, 159
Crepeau, Richard C(harles) 1941- 105
Crerar, Duff (Willis) 1955- 156
Crescas, Hasdai 1340(?)-1412(?) .... DLB 115
Cresp, Gael 1954- 190
  See also SATA 119
Crespo, Angel 1926- .... DLB 134
Crespo, George 1962- .... SATA 82
Cressey, Donald R(ay) 1919-1987 ...... CANR-6
  Obituary 123
  Earlier sketch in CA 13-16R
Cressey, William W. 1939- 33-36R
Cresson, Bruce Collins 1930- 45-48
Cresswell, Helen 1934- CANR-37
  Earlier sketches in CA 17-20R, CANR-8
  See also AAYA 25
  See also CLR 18
  See also CWRI 5
  See also DLB 161
  See also JRDA
  See also MAICYA 1, 2
  See also SAAS 20
  See also SATA 1, 48, 79
Cresswell, Jasmine (Rosemary)
  1941- CANR-113
  Earlier sketches in CA 110, CANR-29
Cresswell, Stephen 1956- 152
Cressy, David 1946- CANR-86
  Earlier sketch in CA 130
Cressy, Michael 1955- .... SATA 124
Cressy, Mike
  See Cressy, Michael
Creston, Dormer
  See Colston-Baynes, Dorothy
Creswell, K(eppel) A(rchibald) C(ameron)
  1879-1974 .... CAP-1
  Earlier sketch in CA 9-10
Cretan, Gladys (Yessayan) 1921- 29-32R
  See also SATA 2
Cretcher, Dorothy 1934- 112
Cretzmeyer, F(rancis) X(avier), Jr.
  1913-2001 .... 13-16R
Cretzmeyer, Stacy (Megan) 1959- ...... SATA 124
Crevecoeur, Hector St. John de
  See Crevecoeur, Michel Guillaume Jean de
  See also ANW
Crevecoeur, Michel Guillaume Jean de
  1735-1813
  See Crevecoeur, Hector St. John de
  See also AMWS 1
  See also DLB 37
Crevel, Rene 1900-1935 .... GLL 2
  See also TCLC 112
Crevier, Daniel 1947- 142
Crew, Danny O(liver) 1947- 200
Crew, Francis Albert Eley 1888-1973 .... CAP-2
  Earlier sketch in CA 17-18
Crew, Gary 1947- CANR-83
  Earlier sketch in CA 142
  See also AAYA 17
  See also CLR 42
  See also HGG
  See also MAICYA 2
  See also SATA 75, 110, 163
  See also YAW
Crew, Helen (Cecilia) Coale 1866-1941 201
  Brief entry 121
  See also YABC 2
Crew, Linda (Jean) 1951- CANR-116
  Earlier sketches in CA 130, CANR-56
  See also AAYA 21
  See also MAICYA 2
  See also MAICYAS 1
  See also SATA 71, 137
  See also YAW
Crew, Louie 1936- CANR-113
  Earlier sketch in CA 81-84
Crewdson, John (Mark) 1945- CANR-120
  Brief entry 128
  Earlier sketch in CA 132
Crewe, Candida 1964- 135
  See also DLB 207
Crewe, Jonathan V(ere) 1941- 116
Crewe, Quentin (Hugh) 1926-1998 144
  Obituary 172
Crews, Clyde F. 1944- CANR-38
  Earlier sketch in CA 116
Crews, Donald 1938- CANR-104
  Earlier sketches in CA 108, CANR-83
  See also CLR 7
  See also CWRI 5
  See also MAICYA 1, 2
  See also SATA 32, 76
  See also SATA-Brief 30
Crews, Frederick C(ampbell)
  1933- CANR-113
  Earlier sketches in CA 1-4R, CANR-1, 44
Crews, Gordon A(rthur) 1964- 175
Crews, Harry (Eugene) 1935- CANR-57
  Earlier sketches in CA 25-28R, CANR-20
  See also AITN 1
  See also AMWS 11
  See also BPFB 1
  See also CLC 6, 23, 49
  See also CN 3, 4, 5, 6, 7
  See also CSW
  See also DA3
  See also DLB 6, 143, 185
  See also MTCW 1, 2
  See also MTFW 2005
  See also RGAL 4
Crews, Judson (Campbell) 1917- CANR-83
  Earlier sketches in CA 13-16R, CANR-7, 24
  See also CAAS 14
  See also CP 1, 2
Crews, Nina 1963- CANR-142
  Earlier sketch in CA 163
  See also SATA 97, 158
Crews, William J. 1931- 25-28R
Creyton, Paul
  See Trowbridge, John Townsend
Cribb, Larry 1934- 109
Cribb, Robert (Bridson) 1957- 137

Cribbet, John E(dward) 1918- 17-20R
Cribbin, James J(oseph) 1915- 121
Crichton, Charles (Ainslie) 1910-1999 163
Obituary 185
Crichton, Elizabeth G. 1946- 211
Crichton, James Dunlop 1907-2001 CANR-5
Obituary 199
Earlier sketch in CA 13-16R
Crichton, Jennifer 1957- 123
Crichton, John 1916- 17-20R
Crichton, Judy 1929- 181
Crichton, Kyle Samuel 1896-1960
Obituary 89-92
Crichton, (John) Michael 1942- CANR-127
Earlier sketches in CA 25-28R, CANR-13, 40, 54, 76
Interview in CANR-13
See also AAYA 10, 49
See also AITN 2
See also BPFB 1
See also CLC 2, 6, 54, 90
See also CMW 4
See also CN 2, 3, 6, 7
See also CPW
See also DA3
See also DAM NOV, POP
See also DLB 292
See also DLBY 1981
See also JRDA
See also MTCW 1, 2
See also MTFW 2005
See also SATA 9, 88
See also SFW 4
See also YAW
Crichton, Robert 1925-1993 CANR-46
Obituary 140
Earlier sketch in CA 17-20R
See also AITN 1
Crichton, Robin 1940- 139
Crichton, Ronald 1913- 128
Crick, Bernard (Rowland) 1929- CANR-141
Earlier sketches in CA 1-4R, CANR-5
Crick, Donald Herbert 1916- 102
Crick, Francis (Harry Compton) 1916-2004 121
Obituary 229
Brief entry 113
Crick, Michael (Lawrence) 1958- CANR-42
Earlier sketch in CA 118
Crickillon, Jacques 1940- 195
Criddle, Byron 1942- 149
Criddle, Joan D(ewey) 1935- 126
Criden, Joseph 1916- 77-80
Criden, Yosef
See Criden, Joseph
Crider, (Allen) Bill(y) 1941- CANR-94
Earlier sketches in CA 112, CANR-30, 56
See also AAYA 32
See also CMW 4
See also SATA 99
See also TCWW 2
Cridge, Edward 1817-1913 219
Cridland, Nancy C. 1932- 111
Crier, Catherine 1954- 214
Crighton, John C(lark) 1903-1997 33-36R
Crighton, Richard E. 1921- 109
Crile, Barney
See Crile, George, Jr.
Crile, George, Jr. 1907-1992 239
Earlier sketch in CA 89-92
Crilley, Mark 1966- 191
See also AAYA 50
See also SATA 120, 148
See also SATA-Essay 148
Crim, Keith R(enn) 1924- CANR-43
Earlier sketch in CA 29-32R
Crim, Mort 1935- 41-44R
Crimmins, G(erald) Garfield 1940- 170
Crimmins, James Custis 1935- CANR-11
Earlier sketch in CA 5-8R
Crimp, Martin (Andrew) 1956- 230
See also CBD
See also CD 5, 6
Crinkley, Richmond (Dillard) 1940-1989 29-32R
Obituary 127
Cripe, Helen 1932- CANR-8
Earlier sketch in CA 61-64
Cripps, (Matthew) Anthony (Leonard) 1913-1997 13-16R
Cripps, L(ouise) L(ilian) 1914-2001 97-100
Cripps, Thomas (Robert) 1932- 97-100
Crisler, Fritz
See Crisler, Herbert Orin
Crisler, Herbert Orin 1899-1982
Obituary 107
Crisler, Lois (Brown) (?)-1971
Obituary 104
Crisman, Ruth 1914- SATA 73
Crisp, Anthony Thomas 1937- 101
Crisp, C(olin) G(odfrey) 1936- 37-40R
Crisp, Frank R(obson) 1915- 9-12R
Crisp, Marta Marie 1947- 198
See also SATA 128
Crisp, Marty
See Crisp, Marta Marie
Crisp, Norman James 1923- 93-96
Crisp, Quentin 1908-1999 CANR-59
Obituary 186
Brief entry 109
Earlier sketch in CA 116
Interview in CA-116
See also GLL 1
Crisp, Robert (James) -1994 1-4R
Crisp, Tony
See Crisp, Anthony Thomas
Crispin, A(nn) C(arol) 1950- CANR-86
Earlier sketches in CA 113, CANR-32
See also AAYA 33
See also SATA 86
Crispin, Edmund
See Montgomery, (Robert) Bruce
See also CLC 22
See also DLB 87
See also MSW
Crispin, John 1936- 53-56
Crispin, Ruth Helen Katz 1940- 93-96
Crispin, Suzy
See Cartwright, Justin
Crispo, John 1933- 37-40R
Crissey, Elwell 1899-1992 CAP-2
Earlier sketch in CA 23-24
Crist, Judith (Klein) 1922- CANR-17
Earlier sketch in CA 81-84
See also AITN 1
Crist, Lyle M(artin) 1924- 53-56
Crist, Raymond E. 1904-1993 73-76
Crist, Steven G(ordon) 1956- 101
Cristabel
See Abrahamsen, Christine Elizabeth
Cristaldi, Franco 1924-1992 IDFW 3, 4
Cristall, Barbara 147
See also SATA 79
Crist-Evans, Craig 1954- 228
See also SATA 153
Cristina, Frank
See Laughlin, Tom
Cristina, Teresa
See Laughlin, Tom
Cristofer, Michael 1945- 152
Brief entry 110
See also CAD
See also CD 5, 6
See also CLC 28
See also DAM DRAM
See also DFS 15
See also DLB 7
Cristol, Vivian 17-20R
Cristy, Ann
See Mittermeyer, Helen (Hayton Monteith)
Cristy, R. J.
See De Cristoforo, R(omeo) J(ohn)
Criswell, Cloyd M. 1908-1989 CAP-1
Earlier sketch in CA 17-18
Criswell, W(allie) A(mos) 1909-2002 17-20R
Obituary 204
Critchfield, Howard J(ohn) 1920- 53-56
Critchfield, Richard (Patrick) 1931-1994 CANR-79
Obituary 147
Earlier sketches in CA 41-44R, CANR-16, 40
Critchley, Edmund M(ichael) R(hys) 1931- 21-24R
Critchley, Julian (Michael Gordon) 1930-2000 85-88
Obituary 189
Critchley, Lynne
See Radford, Richard F(rancis), Jr.
Critchley, T(homas) A(lan) 1919-1991 29-32R
Obituary 134
Critchlow, Donald T. 1948- 156
Crites, Ronald W(ayne) 1945- CANR-18
Earlier sketch in CA 102
Crites, Stephen D(ecatur) 1931- 41-44R
Critic
See Martin, (Basil) Kingsley
Criticus
See Harcourt, Melville and Roe, F(rederic) Gordon
Criton
See Alain
Crittenden, Ann 1937- 201
Crittenden, Danielle Ann 1963- 187
Crittenden, Lindsey 1961- 178
Crittenden, Mabel (Buss) 1917- 103
Crnjanski, Milos 1893-1977 CANR-50
Earlier sketches in CAP-1, CA 9-10
See also CDWLB 4
See also DLB 147
See also EWL 3
Crnobrnja (Tsernobernya), Mihailo 1946- 150
Croall, Jonathan 1941- 130
Crobaugh, Emma AITN 2
Croce, Arlene 1934- CANR-101
Earlier sketch in CA 104
Interview in CA-104
Croce, Benedetto 1866-1952 155
Brief entry 120
See also EW 8
See also EWL 3
See also TCLC 37
See also WLIT 7
Croce, Paul Jerome 1957- 154
Crocetti, Guido M. 1920-1979 85-88
Crock, Stan 1950- 134
Crocker, H(arry) W(illiam) 1960- 198
Crocker, Hannah Mather 1752-1829 DLB 200
Crocker, Helen Bartter 1929- 69-72
Crocker, Lester G(ilbert) 1912-2002 CANR-5
Obituary 211
Earlier sketch in CA 5-8R
Crocker, Lionel (George) 1897-1976 CAP-2
Earlier sketch in CA 25-28
Crocker, Mary Wallace 1941- 93-96
Crocker, Matthew H(allowell) 1962- 214
Crocker, Thomas Dunstan 1936-
Brief entry 108
Crocker, Walter Russell 1902-2002 17-20R
Obituary 212
Crockett, Albert Stevens 1873-1969
Obituary 89-92
Crockett, Bryan 182
Crockett, Christina
See Crockett, Linda and Gray, Linda Crockett
Crockett, David 1786-1836 DLB 3, 11, 183, 248
Crockett, David A. 1963- 235
Crockett, Davy
See Crockett, David
Crockett, G(eorge) Ronald 1906- CAP-1
Earlier sketch in CA 11-12
Crockett, H(arold) Dale 1933- 111
Crockett, James Underwood 1915-1979 CANR-13
Obituary 89-92
Earlier sketch in CA 33-36R
Crockett, Linda 144
See also Crockett, Christina and Gray, Linda Crockett
Crockett, Linda Lea 1962- 155
Crockett, S(amuel) R(utherford) 1860-1914
Brief entry 116
See also CWRI 5
Crocombe, Ronald G(ordon) 1929- 13-16R
Crofford, Emily (Ardell) 1927- 107
See also SATA 61
Crofford, Lena H(enrichson) 1908-1986 CAP-1
Earlier sketch in CA 9-10
Croft, Barbara 1944- CANR-142
Earlier sketch in CA 173
Croft, Charles
See Carr, Dorothy Stevenson Laird
Croft, Julian (Charles Basset) 1941- CANR-55
Earlier sketch in CA 124
Croft, Michael (John) 1922-1986
Obituary 121
Croft, (J.) Pauline 230
Croft, Peter John 1929-1984 122
Obituary 114
Croft, Robert W(ayne) 1957- 175
Croft, Sutton
See Lunn, Arnold
Croft-Cooke, Rupert 1903-1979 CANR-60
Obituary 89-92
Earlier sketches in CA 9-12R, CANR-4
See also Bruce, Leo
See also CMW 4
Croft-Murray, Edward 1907-1980
Obituary 102
Crofton, Denis Hayes 1908-1995 109
Crofts, Freeman Wills 1879-1957 195
Brief entry 115
See also CMW 4
See also DLB 77
See also MSW
See also TCLC 55
Crofts, John E(rnest) V(ictor) 1887-1972 CAP-2
Earlier sketch in CA 25-28
Crofts, William 137
Crofut, William E. III 1934- 25-28R
See also SATA 23
Crohn, Burrill B(ernard) 1884-1983
Obituary 110
Croise, Jacques
See Schakovskoy, Zinaida
Croissant, Michael P. 1971- 205
Croizat, Victor J. 1919- 163
Croizier, Ralph 1935- 61-64
Croker, John Wilson 1780-1857 DLB 110
Croker, Richard 1946- 235
Croll, Carolyn 1945-1994 CANR-101
Earlier sketches in CA 123, CANR-49
See also SATA 56, 102
See also SATA-Brief 52
Croll, (Joan) Elisabeth 1944- 158
Croly, George 1780-1860 DLB 159
Croly, Herbert (David) 1869-1930 178
See also DLB 91
See also NCFS 4
Croly, Jane Cunningham 1829(?)-1901
Brief entry 118
See also DLB 23
Croman, Dorothy Young
See Rosenberg, Dorothy
Crombie, A(listair) C(ameron) 1915-1996 151
Crombie, Deborah 1952- 187
See also AAYA 45
Cromer, Alan (Herbert) 1935- 146
Cromie, Alice Hamilton 1914-2000 CANR-3
Earlier sketch in CA 9-12R
See also SATA 24
Cromie, Robert 1856-1907 SFW 4
Cromie, Robert (Allen) 1909-1999 CANR-83
Earlier sketches in CA 1-4R, CANR-1, 16
Cromie, William J(oseph) 1930- 13-16R
See also SATA 4
Crommelynck, Fernand 1885-1970 189
Obituary 89-92
See also CLC 75
See also EWL 3
Crompton, Anne Eliot 1930- CANR-46
Earlier sketches in CA 33-36R, CANR-13
See also SATA 23, 73
Crompton, John
See Lamburn, John Battersby Crompton
Crompton, Louis (William) 1925- 33-36R
Crompton, Margaret (Norah Mair) 1901- CAP-1
Earlier sketch in CA 13-14
Crompton, Richmal
See Lamburn, Richmal Crompton
See also DLB 160
Cromwell, Chester R. 1925- 89-92
Cromwell, Elsie
See Lee, Elsie
Cromwell, Harvey 1907-1977 17-20R
Obituary 134
Cromwell, James H(enry) R(oberts) 1897(?)-1990
Obituary 131
Cromwell, John 1887-1979
Obituary 89-92
Cromwell, John 1914(?)-1979
Obituary 89-92
Cromwell, Link
See Kaye, Lenny
Cromwell, Richard Sidney 1925- 53-56
Cromwell, Rue L(eVelle) 1928- 149
Cronbach, Abraham 1882-1965 1-4R
See also SATA 11
Cronbach, L. J.
See Cronbach, Lee J(oseph)
Cronbach, Lee J(oseph) 1916-2001 230
Crone, Alla 1923- 113
Crone, G(erald) R(oe) 1899-1982 121
Crone, Moira 1952- CANR-125
Earlier sketches in CA 125, CANR-59
See also CN 6
See also CSW
Crone, Patricia 1945- 197
Crone, (Hans-) Rainer 1942- CANR-14
Earlier sketch in CA 33-36R
Crone, Ruth 1919-2003 9-12R
See also SATA 4
Cronenberg, David 1943- 138
See also CCA 1
See also CLC 143
Croner, Helga 1914- 107
Croner, John A(lton) 1916- 121
Cronin, A(rchibald) J(oseph) 1896-1981 CANR-5
Obituary 102
Earlier sketch in CA 1-4R
See also BPFB 1
See also CLC 32
See also CN 2
See also DLB 191
See also SATA 47
See also SATA-Obit 25
Cronin, Anthony 1926- CANR-81
Earlier sketch in CA 137
See also CP 1, 7
Cronin, Audrey Kurth 1958- 125
Cronin, Doreen (A.) CLR 104
See also SATA 125
Cronin, George 1933- 101
Cronin, James E(mmet) 1908-1985 CANR-24
Earlier sketch in CA 45-48
Cronin, Jeremy 1949- 233
See also CP 7
Cronin, John F(rancis) 1908-1994 37-40R
Obituary 143
Cronin, Joseph M(arr) 1935- CANR-31
Earlier sketch in CA 49-52
Cronin, Justin 210
Cronin, Mary J. 1947- 148
Cronin, Mike 1967- 200
Cronin, Sylvia 1929- 89-92
Cronin, Thomas E(dward) 1940- CANR-42
Earlier sketches in CA 85-88, CANR-20
Cronin, Vincent (Archibald Patrick) 1924- CANR-5
Earlier sketch in CA 9-12R
Cronish, Nettie 1954- 216
Cronjager, Edward 1904-1960 IDFW 3, 4
Cronkhite, Bernice Brown 1893-1983
Obituary 110
Cronkite, Walter (Leland, Jr.) 1916- CANR-112
Earlier sketches in CA 69-72, CANR-37, 62
See also AITN 1, 2
Cronley, Jay 1943- 81-84
Cronne, H(enry) A(lfred) 1904-1990 65-68
Cronon, E(dmund) David 1924- CANR-1
Earlier sketch in CA 1-4R
Cronon, William (John) 1954- 111
Cronus, Diodorus
See Taylor, Richard
Cronyn, Hume 1911-2003 CANR-50
Obituary 217
Earlier sketch in CA 123
Crook, Bette (Jean) 1921- 73-76
Crook, Beverly Courtney 115
See also SATA 38
See also SATA-Brief 35
Crook, Compton Newby 1908-1981 CANR-84
Earlier sketch in CA 121
See also SFW 4
Crook, Connie Brummel
See Crook, Constance
Crook, Constance 166
See also SATA 98
Crook, D(avid) P(aul) 1937- 128
Crook, David 1910- 97-100
Crook, (Mary) Elizabeth 1959- 190
Crook, Howard (Hawthorne) 1937- 107
Crook, Isabel 1915- 97-100
Crook, J(ohn) A(nthony) 1921- 21-24R
Crook, J(oseph) Mordaunt 1937- CANR-99
Earlier sketch in CA 41-44R
Crook, (Peter Michael) John 1946- 195
Crook, Margaret Brackenbury 1886-1972 CAP-1
Earlier sketch in CA 13-16
Crook, Marion 1941- 163
Crook, Roger H(awley) 1921- CANR-4
Earlier sketch in CA 1-4R
Crook, W. Melvin 1912(?)-1984
Obituary 112
Crook, William 1933- 102
Crook, William G. 1917- 129

Cumulative Index 131 Crowley

Crookall, Robert 1890-1981 .... CANR-30
Earlier sketch in CA 33-36R
Crookenden, Napier 1915-2002 .... CANR-11
Obituary 211
Earlier sketch in CA 69-72
Crooker, Constance Emerson 1946- 237
Crooks, James B(enedict) 1933- 25-28R
Cropp, Ben(jamin) 1936- 33-36R
Cropper, Margaret 1886-1980
Obituary 102
Cros, Charles 1842-1888 .... DLB 217
See also GFL 1789 to the Present
Crosbie, John C. 1931- 180
Crosbie, John S(haver) 1920- CANR-12
Earlier sketch in CA 73-76
Crosbie, Lynn 1963- 146
Crosbie, (Hugh) Provan 1912- 9-12R
Crosbie, Sylvia Kowitt 1938- 73-76
Crosby, Alexander L. 1906-1980 .... 29-32R
Obituary 93-96
See also SATA 2
See also SATA-Obit 23
Crosby, Alfred W., Jr. 1931- CANR-68
Earlier sketch in CA 17-20R
Crosby, Bing
See Crosby, Harry Lillis
Crosby, (Mary Jacob) Caresse 1892-1970
Obituary 25-28R
See also DLB 4, 48
Crosby, Caresse 1892-1970 177
Crosby, David (Van Cortlandt) 1941- 200
Crosby, Donald A(llen) 1932- CANR-137
Earlier sketch in CA 53-56
Crosby, Donald F(rancis) 1933- 77-80
Crosby, Donald G(ibson) 1928- 171
Crosby, Elizabeth Caroline 1888-1983 157
Crosby, Fanny J.
See Crosby, Frances J(ane)
Crosby, Faye J. 1947- CANR-98
Earlier sketches in CA 114, CANR-36
Crosby, Floyd 1899-1985 .... IDFW 3, 4
Crosby, Frances J(ane) 1820-1915 219
Crosby, Harry 1898-1929
Brief entry 107
See also DLB 4, 48
See also DLBD 15
Crosby, Harry C., Jr. 161
See also SATA 102
See also SFW 4
Crosby, Harry H(erbert) 1919- CANR-5
Earlier sketch in CA 13-16R
Crosby, Harry Lillis 1904-1977
Obituary 73-76
Crosby, Harry W(illiams) 1926- CANR-101
Earlier sketch in CA 149
Crosby, Henry Grew
See Crosby, Harry
Crosby, Henry Sturgis
See Crosby, Harry
Crosby, Jackie
See Crosby, Jacqueline Garton
Crosby, Jacqueline Garton 1961- 133
Crosby, James O('Hea) 1924- 89-92
Crosby, Jeremiah
See Crosby, Michael (Hugh)
Crosby, John (Campbell) 1912-1991 ... CANR-4
Obituary 135
Earlier sketch in CA 1-4R
Crosby, John F. 1931- CANR-7
Earlier sketch in CA 17-20R
Crosby, Margaret
See Rathmann, Peggy
See also CLR 77
Crosby, Michael (Hugh) 1940- CANR-11
Earlier sketch in CA 17-20R
Crosby, Muriel (Estelle) 1908-1999 ...... 17-20R
Crosby, Philip B(ayard) 1926-2001 73-76
Obituary 199
Crosby, Ruth 1897-1981 49-52
Crosby, Sumner McK(night) 1909-1982 . 13-16R
Obituary 108
Crosby, Theo 1925- 133
Crosher, G. R. 69-72
See also SATA 14
Crosland, Andrew T(ate) 1944- 53-56
Crosland, (Charles) Anthony (Raven)
1918-1977 73-76
Obituary 69-72
Crosland, Camilla Toulmin
1812-1895 .... DLB 240
Crosland, Margaret 1920- CANR-97
Earlier sketches in CA 49-52, CANR-1, 21, 45
Crosland, Mrs. Newton
See Crosland, Camilla Toulmin
Crosley, Reginald O. 1937- 195
Cross, Aleene (Ann) 1922- CANR-26
Earlier sketch in CA 29-32R
Cross, Amanda
See Heilbrun, Carolyn G(old)
See also BPFB 1
See also CMW
See also CPW
See also DLB 306
See also MSW
Cross, Anthony (Glenn) 1936- CANR-17
Earlier sketch in CA 37-40R
Cross, (Alan) Beverley 1931-1998 .... CANR-67
Obituary 166
Earlier sketch in CA 102
See also CBD
See also CD 5, 6
Cross, Charles 174
Cross, Claire 1932- 21-24R
Cross, Colin (John) 1928-1985 .... CANR-7
Obituary 118
Earlier sketch in CA 9-12R
Cross, David
See Chesbro, George C(lark)
Cross, Donna Woolfolk 1947- 97-100
Cross, Frank Moore, Jr. 1921- 65-68
Cross, Gary Scott 1946- 115
Cross, George Lynn 1905-1998 125
Obituary 172
Cross, Gilbert B. 1939- CANR-47
Earlier sketches in CA 105, CANR-23
See also SATA 60
See also SATA-Brief 51
Cross, Gillian (Clare) 1945- CANR-81
Earlier sketches in CA 111, CANR-38
See also AAYA 24
See also BYA 9
See also CLR 28
See also DLB 161
See also JRDA
See also MAICYA 1, 2
See also MAICYAS 1
See also SATA 38, 71, 110
See also YAW
Cross, Helen Reeder
See Broadhead, Helen Cross
Cross, Herbert James 1934- 45-48
Cross, Ian (Robert) 1925- 161
See also CN 1, 2, 3, 4, 5, 6
Cross, Ira Brown 1880-1977
Obituary 106
Cross, James
See Parry, Hugh J(ones)
Cross, Jennifer 1932- 29-32R
Cross, John Keir 1914-1967 .... CANR-72
Earlier sketch in CA 73-76
See also HGG
See also SFW 4
Cross, John R(ay) 1939- 120
Cross, Jonathan (G. E.) 1961- 185
Cross, K(enneth) G(ustav) W(alter)
1927-1967 .... CAP-1
Earlier sketch in CA 13-16
Cross, K(athryn) Patricia 1926- CANR-49
Earlier sketches in CA 33-36R, CANR-13
Cross, Leslie (Frank) 1909-1977 65-68
Obituary 89-92
Cross, M. Claire
See Cross, Claire
Cross, Milton (John) 1897-1975
Obituary 53-56
Cross, Neil 1969- 237
Cross, Nigel 1942- CANR-38
Earlier sketch in CA 116
Cross, Peter 1951- 141
See also SATA 95
Cross, Polton
See Fearn, John Russell
Cross, Poulton
See Fearn, John Russell
Cross, Ralph D(onald) 1931- CANR-17
Earlier sketch in CA 93-96
Cross, Richard 1950(?)-1983
Obituary 110
Cross, Richard K(eith) 1940- CANR-12
Earlier sketch in CA 33-36R
Cross, Robert Brandt 1914-1995 .... 37-40R
Cross, Robert D(ougherty) 1924-2003 .... 1-4R
Obituary 216
Cross, Robert Singlehurst 1925- 5-8R
Cross, (Alfred) Rupert (Neale) 1912-1980 ... 105
Obituary 102
Cross, S. A. M.
See Sherwood, Shirley
Cross, Samuel S(tephen) 1919- 45-48
Cross, Sister Mary Francilda 1902(?)-1984
Obituary 114
Cross, Stewart
See Drago, Harry Sinclair
Cross, T. T.
See da Cruz, Daniel, Jr.
Cross, Theodore L(amont) 1924- CANR-27
Earlier sketch in CA 45-48
Cross, Thomas B. 1949- 123
Cross, Tom 1954- .... SATA 146
Cross, Verda 1914- 142
See also SATA 75
Cross, Victor
See Coffman, Virginia (Edith)
Cross, Victoria 1868-1952 .... DLB 135, 197
Cross, Wilbur Lucius III 1918- CANR-2
Earlier sketch in CA 1-4R
See also SATA 2
Crossan, Darryl
See Smith, Richard Rein
Crossan, John Dominic 178
Crosscountry
See Campbell, Thomas F.
Crossen, Cynthia 199
Crossen, Ken
See Crossen, Kendell Foster
Crossen, Kendell Foster 1910-1981 .. CANR-60
Earlier sketches in CA 1-4R, CANR-4
See also Foster, Richard
See also CMW 4
Crosser, Paul K. 1902-1976 .... CANR-3
Earlier sketch in CA 1-4R
Crossette, Barbara 170
Crossette, George 1910-1984
Obituary 114
Crosskill, W. E. 1904- 129
Crossland, Caroline 1964- .... SATA 83
Crossley, Archibald M(addock) 1896-1985
Obituary 116
Crossley, Pamela Kyle 1955- 154
Crossley, Robert 1945- 127
Crossley-Holland, Kevin (John William)
1941- CANR-102
Earlier sketches in CA 41-44R, CANR-47, 84
See also AAYA 57
See also CLR 47, 84
See also CP 1, 2, 3, 4, 5, 6, 7
See also DLB 40, 161
See also MAICYA 1, 2
See also SAAS 20
See also SATA 5, 74, 120
See also YAW
Crossman, Richard (Howard Stafford)
1907-1974 .... CANR-43
Obituary 49-52
Earlier sketch in CA 61-64
Croswell, Ken 192
Croteau, John T(ougas) 1910- 9-12R
Crothers, George D. 1909-1998 .... CAP-1
Earlier sketch in CA 13-16
Crothers, J(essie) Frances 1913-1984 ..... 33-36R
Crothers, Jessie F.
See Crothers, J(essie) Frances
Crothers, Rachel 1878-1958 194
Brief entry 113
See also CAD
See also CWD
See also DLB 7, 266
See also RGAL 4
See also TCLC 19
Crotty, Shane 1974- 220
Crotty, William J(oseph) 1936- CANR-13
Earlier sketch in CA 21-24R
Crouch, Austin 1870-1957 218
Crouch, Bill, Jr.
See Crouch, William Maxwell, Jr.
Crouch, David 1953- CANR-104
Earlier sketch in CA 129
Crouch, Harold (Arthur) 1940- CANR-15
Earlier sketch in CA 89-92
Crouch, Marcus 1913-1996 .... CANR-23
Earlier sketches in CA 9-12R, CANR-5
See also SATA 4
Crouch, Stanley 1945- CANR-99
Earlier sketch in CA 141
Crouch, Steve 1915-1983 .... CANR-9
Obituary 109
Earlier sketch in CA 53-56
Crouch, Tanja L. 1958- 199
Crouch, Thomas W(illiam) 1932- 73-76
Crouch, Tom D. 1944- CANR-88
Earlier sketch in CA 106
Crouch, W(illiam) George (Alfred)
1903-1970 .... 5-8R
Obituary 89-92
Crouch, William Maxwell, Jr. 1945- 126
Crouch, Winston Winford 1907-
Brief entry 106
Croucher, Michael 1930- 128
Croudace, Glynn 1917- 29-32R
Crouse, Russell M. 1893-1966 77-80
Obituary 25-28R
Crouse, Timothy 1947- 77-80
Crouse, William H(arry) 1907- CANR-6
Earlier sketch in CA 5-8R
Crout, George C(lement) 1917- CANR-11
Earlier sketch in CA 29-32R
See also SATA 11
Crout, Robert Rhodes 1946- 116
Croutier, Alev Lytle 1944- CANR-100
Earlier sketch in CA 142
Crouzet, Francois Marie-Joseph
1922- CANR-42
Earlier sketches in CA 9-12R, CANR-3, 19
Croves, Hal
See Traven, B.
Crovitz, Herbert F(loyd) 1932- 29-32R
Crow, Alice (von Bauer) 1894-1966 ...... CAP-1
Earlier sketch in CA 13-16
Crow, Bill 1927- 140
Crow, C(harles) P(atrick) 1938- 102
Crow, Charles L(loyd) 1940- 112
Crow, Donna Fletcher 1941- CANR-100
Earlier sketches in CA 108, CANR-25, 50
See also SATA 40
Crow, Duncan 1920- 85-88
Crow, Elizabeth (Venture Smith)
1946-2005 103
Obituary 238
Crow, Francis Luther
See Luther, Frank
Crow, Jeffrey J(ay) 1947- CANR-19
Earlier sketch in CA 85-88
Crow, John A(rmstrong) 1906-2001 .... 13-16R
Crow, Lester D(onald) 1897-1983 .... CAP-1
Obituary 110
Earlier sketch in CA 13-16
Crow, Mark (Alan) 1948- 57-60
Crow, Martin M(ichael) 1901-1997 .... CAP-2
Earlier sketch in CA 19-20
Crow, Mary 1933- 138
Crow, Thomas E. 1948- 233
Crow, William Bernard 1895-1976 .... CAP-1
Obituary 65-68
Earlier sketch in CA 13-14
Crowbate, Ophelia Mae
See Smith, C(ora) U.
Crowcroft, Andrew 1923- 21-24R
Crowcroft, Jane
See Crowcroft, Peter
Crowcroft, Peter 1923-1982 101
Crowder, Ashby Bland, (Jr.) 1941- .. CANR-108
Earlier sketch in CA 151
Crowder, Christopher M. D. 1922- 103
Crowder, George 1956- 146
Crowder, Herbert 1925- 127
Crowder, Michael 1934-1988 .... CANR-1
Obituary 126
Earlier sketch in CA 1-4R
Crowder, Richard (Henry) 1909-1989 ... CAP-1
Earlier sketch in CA 17-18
Crowder, Robert G. 1939-2000 138
Obituary 188
Crowder, Stephanie R. Buckhanon 1969- ... 218
Crow Dog, Mary (Ellen) (?)- 154
See also Brave Bird, Mary
See also CLC 93
Crowe, Andrew 182
See also SATA 111
Crowe, C. B.
See Gibson, Walter B(rown)
Crowe, Cameron 1957- CANR-96
Earlier sketch in CA 153
See also AAYA 23, 59
Crowe, Cecily (Teague)
Brief entry 115
Crowe, Charles 1928- 17-20R
Crowe, Charles Monroe 1902-1978 .... 1-4R
Obituary 103
Crowe, David (M.) 1943- 189
Crowe, E. Odell 1925(?)-1983
Obituary 110
Crowe, F. J.
See Johnston, Jill
Crowe, Frederick Ernest 1915- CANR-29
Earlier sketch in CA 111
Crowe, Gregory D(ennis) 1963- 116
Crowe, John
See Lynds, Dennis
Crowe, Kenneth C(harles) 1934- 103
Crowe, Michael (J.) 1936- 203
Crowe, Norman 1938- CANR-110
Earlier sketch in CA 151
Crowe, (Bettina) Peter Lum 1911- 9-12R
See also SATA 6
Crowe, Philip Kingsland 1908-1976 65-68
Obituary 69-72
Crowe, Robert L(ee) 1937- 69-72
Crowe, Sylvia 1901-1997 .... CAP-1
Earlier sketch in CA 9-10
Crowe, Thomas Rain 1949- CANR-139
Earlier sketch in CA 166
Crowe, William J., Jr. 1925- 142
Crowe-Carraco, Carol 1943- 93-96
Crowell, George H. 1931- 25-28R
Crowell, Grace Noll 1877-1969 107
See also SATA 34
Crowell, Jenn(ifer Lindsey) 1978- ... CANR-142
Earlier sketch in CA 159
Crowell, Joan 1921- 57-60
Crowell, Muriel Beyea 1916- 57-60
Crowell, Norton B. 1914-1999 .... 9-12R
Crowell, Pers 1910-1990 .... 29-32R
See also SATA 2
Crowell, Robert Leland 1909-2001 109
Obituary 198
See also SATA 63
Crowfield, Christopher
See Stowe, Harriet (Elizabeth) Beecher
Crowl, Philip A(xtell) 1914-1991 110
Obituary 134
Crowl, Samuel 1940- 142
Crowl, William
See Kennedy, Leo
Crowley, Aleister
See Crowley, Edward Alexander
See also GLL 1
See also TCLC 7
Crowley, Arthur McBlair 1945- 107
See also SATA 38
Crowley, Daniel J(ohn) 1921-1998 ..... CANR-9
Obituary 166
Earlier sketch in CA 21-24R
Crowley, David 1966- 146
Crowley, Diane 1939- 135
Crowley, Edward Alexander 1875-1947
Brief entry 104
See also Abhavananda and
Crowley, Aleister and Perdurabo, Frater and
Therion, Master
See also HGG
Crowley, Ellen T(eresa) 1943- CANR-17
Earlier sketch in CA 97-100
Crowley, Frances G(eyer) 1921- 105
Crowley, George (David) 1913-1987
Obituary 123
Crowley, J(oseph) Donald 1932- 122
Crowley, James B. 1929- 21-24R
Crowley, John 1942- CANR-138
Earlier sketches in CA 61-64, CANR-43, 98
See also AAYA 57
See also BPFB 1
See also CLC 57
See also DLBY 1982
See also FANT
See also MTFW 2005
See also SATA 65, 140
See also SFW 4
See also SUFW 2
Crowley, John Edward 1943- 53-56
Crowley, John W(illiam) 1945- CANR-103
Earlier sketch in CA 69-72
Crowley, Mart 1935- 73-76
See also CAD
See also DFS 14
See also DLB 7, 266
See also GLL 1
Crowley, Mary C. 1915- 97-100
Crowley, Monica 173
Crowley, Raymond 1895-1982
Obituary 106
Crowley, Robert T. 171
Crowley, Robert T(inkham) 1913-1992 161

Crowley, William R. 1946- ... 162
Crowley-Milling, Michael C. 1917- ... 146
Crown, Alan D(avid) 1932- ... 141
Crown, David A. 1928- ... CANR-10
Earlier sketch in CA 25-28R
Crown, Paul 1928- ... 17-20R
Crown, William H. ... 175
Crowne, John 1641-1712 ... DLB 80
See also RGEL 2
Crowner, David 1938- ... 218
Crownfield, Gertrude 1867-1945 ... YABC 1
Crowninshield, Edward Augustus
1817-1859 ... DLB 140
Crowninshield, Francis (Welch)
1872-1947 ... 178
Crowninshield, Frank 1872-1947 ... DLB 91
Crowson, P(aul) S(piller) 1913-2000 ... 53-56
Crowther, Betty 1939- ... 61-64
Crowther, (Francis) Bosley
1905-1981 ... CANR-38
Obituary ... 103
Earlier sketch in CA 65-68
Crowther, Brian
See Grierson, Edward
Crowther, Bruce (Ian) 1933- ... 128
Crowther, Duane S(wofford) 1934- ... CANR-17
Earlier sketch in CA 25-28R
Crowther, Geoffrey 1907-1972
Obituary ... 33-36R
Crowther, Hal 1945- ... 199
Crowther, James Gerald 1899-1983 ... 73-76
See also SATA 14
Crowther, Jean D(ecker) 1937- ... 120
Crowther, Peter 1949- ... CANR-72
Earlier sketch in CA 148
See also HGG
Crowther, Robert 1948- ... 187
See also SATA 163
Crowther, Wilma (Beryl) 1918-1989 ... 5-8R
Obituary ... 128
Crowther-Hunt, Norman Crowther
1920-1987 ... 133
Obituary ... 121
Croxford, Leslie 1944- ... 81-84
Croxton, Anthony H(ugh) 1902- ... 61-64
Croxton, (Charles) Derek 1969- ... 215
Croxton, Frederick E(mory) 1899-1991 ... CAP-2
Obituary ... 133
Earlier sketch in CA 23-24
Croy, Homer 1883-1965 ... 110
Obituary ... 89-92
See also DLB 4
Croyden, Margaret ... 226
Croydon, Michael (Benet) 1931- ... 158
Crozet, Charlotte 1926- ... 25-28R
Crozetti, R(uth G.) Warner
See Warner-Crozetti, R(uth G.)
Crozier, Andrew 1943- ... CANR-84
Earlier sketch in CA 153
See also CP 7
Crozier, Brian (Rossiter) 1918- ... CANR-3
Earlier sketch in CA 9-12R
Crozier, Lorna 1948- ... CANR-68
Earlier sketches in CA 113, CANR-32
See also CP 7
See also CWP
Crozier, Michael (Paul) 1956- ... 161
Crozier, Michel J. 1922- ... 130
Crud
See Crumb, R(obert)
Cruden, Robert 1910- ... 33-36R
Cruger, Melvin J. 1925(?)-1983
Obituary ... 111
Cruickshank, Allan D(udley) 1907-1974
Obituary ... 53-56
Cruickshank, C. G.
See Cruickshank, Charles (Greig)
Cruickshank, Charles (Greig)
1914-1989 ... CANR-25
Obituary ... 128
Earlier sketches in CA 21-24R, CANR-9
Cruickshank, Helen B(urness)
1886-1975 ... CP 1, 2
Cruickshank, Helen Gere 1907- ... CAP-1
Earlier sketch in CA 13-14
Cruickshank, John 1924-1995 ... CANR-20
Earlier sketches in CA 1-4R, CANR-4
Cruickshank, Margrit ... CWRI 5
Cruickshank, Marjorie 1920-1983 ... 122
Obituary ... 111
Cruickshank, William M(ellon)
1915-1992 ... CANR-80
Obituary ... 139
Earlier sketch in CA 89-92
Cruikshank, George 1792-1878 ... CLR 63
See also SATA 22
Cruikshank, Jeffrey L. ... 214
Cruikshank, Margaret (L.) 1940- ... 231
See also GLL 1
Cruise, David 1950- ... CANR-144
Earlier sketch in CA 128
Crum, Laura ... 192
Crum, Shutta ... SATA 134
Crumarums
See Crumb, R(obert)
Crumb, R(obert) 1943- ... CANR-107
Earlier sketch in CA 106
See also CLC 17
Crumbaker, Alice 1911-1989 ... 81-84
Crumbaugh, James C(harles) 1912- ... 37-40R
Crumbley, D(onald) Larry 1941- ... CANR-46
Earlier sketches in CA 29-32R, CANR-12
Crumbley, Paul 1952- ... 168
Crumbum
See Crumb, R(obert)
Crumey, Andrew (David William Bernard)
1961- ... 186
Crumley, James 1939- ... CANR-121
Earlier sketches in CA 69-72, CANR-21, 65
See also CMW 4
See also DLB 226
See also DLBY 1984
See also TCWW 2
Crummel, Susan Stevens 1949- ... SATA 130
Crummey, Donald 1941- ... 205
Crummey, Michael ... 211
Crummey, Robert O(wen) 1936- ... CANR-17
Earlier sketch in CA 25-28R
Crump, Barry (John) 1935-1996 ... CANR-8
Earlier sketch in CA 13-16R
Crump, Fred H., Jr. 1931- ... CANR-41
Earlier sketches in CA 9-12R, CANR-3, 19
See also SATA 11, 76
Crump, Galbraith Miller 1929- ... 57-60
Crump, Geoffrey (Herbert) 1891- ... CAP-1
Earlier sketch in CA 13-14
Crump, J(ames) Irving 1887-1979 ... 73-76
Obituary ... 89-92
See also SATA 57
See also SATA-Obit 21
Crump, Kenneth G(ordon), Jr. 1931- ... 21-24R
Crump, Paul (Orville) 1930(?)- ... BW 2, 3
Crump, Spencer (M., Jr.) 1933- ... CANR-9
Earlier sketch in CA 21-24R
Crump, (Stephen) Thomas 1929- ... CANR-47
Earlier sketch in CA 49-52
Crump, William D(rake) 1949- ... 208
See also SATA 138
Crumpacker, Laurie 1941- ... 118
Crumpet, Peter
See Buckley, Fergus Reid
Crumpler, Frank H(unter) 1935- ... 77-80
Crumpler, Gus H(unt) 1911-1989 ... 69-72
Crumrine, N(orman) Ross II 1934- ... CANR-8
Earlier sketch in CA 13-16R
Crumski
See Crumb, R(obert)
Crum the Bum
See Crumb, R(obert)
Crunden, Reginald
See Cleaver, Hylton Reginald
Crunden, Robert M(orse)
1940-1999 ... CANR-94
Earlier sketches in CA 29-32R, CANR-15
Crunk
See Crumb, R(obert)
Crunk, T.
See Crunk, Tony
Crunk, Tony 1956- ... 199
See also SATA 130
Cruse, Harold (Wright) 1916-2005 ... 77-80
Obituary ... 237
Cruse, Howard 1944- ... 227
Cruse, Mary Anne 1825(?)-1910 ... 207
See also DLB 239
Crush, Jonathan 1953- ... 141
Crusie, Jennifer
See Smith, Jennifer
Crusius, Timothy Wood 1950- ... 193
Cruso, Thalassa 1909-1997 ... 65-68
Obituary ... 158
Crussi, F(rank) Gonzalez
See Gonzalez-Crussi, F(rank)
Crustt
See Crumb, R(obert)
Crutcher, Anne Neilson 1919-1983
Obituary ... 111
Crutcher, Chris(topher C.) 1946- ... CANR-134
Earlier sketches in CA 113, CANR-36, 84
See also AAYA 9, 39
See also BYA 8, 14, 15
See also CLR 28
See also JRDA
See also MAICYA 1, 2
See also MAICYAS 1
See also MTFW 2005
See also NFS 11
See also SATA 52, 99, 153
See also WYA
See also YAW
Crutchfield, Les
See Trumbo, Dalton
Cruver, Brian 1971- ... 214
Cruz, Angie 1972- ... 239
Cruz, Arturo, Jr. 1954(?)- ... 131
See also HW 1, 2
Cruz, Gilbert R(alph) 1929- ... 131
See also HW 1
Cruz, Gilberto Rafael
See Cruz, Gilbert R(alph)
Cruz, Joan Carroll 1931- ... 73-76
Cruz, Migdalia 1958- ... DFS 19
See also DLB 249
Cruz, Nicomedes Santa
See Santa Cruz (Gamarra), Nicomedes
Cruz, Nilo 1961(?)- ... 210
See also DFS 21
Cruz, Ray(mond) 1933- ... SATA 6
Cruz, Ricardo Cortez 1964- ... 175
Earlier sketch in CA 139
See also BW 2, 3
See also HW 2
Cruz, Sor Juana Ines de la
1651-1695 ... DLB 305
See also FL 1:1
Cruz, Victor Hernandez 1949- ... CANR-132
Earlier sketches in CA 65-68, CANR-14, 32, 74
See also CAAS 17
See also BW 2
See also CP 1, 2, 3, 4, 5, 6, 7
See also DAM MULT, POET
See also DLB 41
See also DNFS 1
See also EXPP
See also HLC 1
See also HW 1, 2
See also LLW
See also MTCW 2
See also MTFW 2005
See also PC 37
See also PFS 16
See also WP
Cruz e Sousa, Joao da 1861-1898 ... DLB 307
See also LAW
Cruz Martinez, Alejandro (?)-1987 ... SATA 74
Cruz Monclova, Lidio 1899- ... HW 1
Cryer, Barry 1935- ... 201
Cryer, Gretchen (Kiger) 1935- ... 123
Brief entry ... 114
See also CLC 21
Cryer, Jon 1965- ... 155
Crying Wind
See Stafford, Linda (Crying Wind)
Crystal, Billy 1947- ... CANR-139
Earlier sketch in CA 171
See also SATA 154
Crystal, David 1941- ... CANR-107
Earlier sketches in CA 17-20R, CANR-7, 23, 47
Crystal, John C(urry) 1920- ... 102
Crystal, William ... 171
See also Crystal, Billy
Csaba, Laszlo 1954- ... 154
Csath, Geza 1887-1919
Brief entry ... 111
See also TCLC 13
Csepeli, Gyorgy 1946- ... 145
Csicsery-Ronay, Istvan 1917- ... 21-24R
Csikos-Nagy, Bela 1915- ... 73-76
Csikszentmihalyi, Mihaly 1934- ... CANR-96
Earlier sketch in CA 125
Csokor, Franz Theodor 1885-1969 ... 178
See also DLB 81
See also EWL 3
Csoori, Sandor 1930- ... 154
See also CDWLB 4
See also CWW 2
See also DLB 232
See also EWL 3
Ctvrtek, Vaclav 1911-1976
Obituary ... 107
See also SATA-Obit 27
Cua, Antonio S. 1932- ... CANR-7
Earlier sketch in CA 17-20R
Cuadra, Pablo Antonio 1912-2002 ... 131
Obituary ... 204
See also DLB 290
See also HW 1
Cuaron, Alfonso 1961- ... 220
Cuban, Larry 1934- ... CANR-113
Earlier sketches in CA 29-32R, CANR-12
Cubas, Braz
See Dawes, Robyn M(ason)
Cuber, John F(rank) 1911-1988 ... 9-12R
Cubeta, Paul Marsden 1925- ... 5-8R
Cuciti, Peggy L. 1949- ... 123
Cudahy, Brian J(ames) 1936- ... 41-44R
Cudahy, Sheila 1920- ... 159
Cuddihy, John Murray 1922- ... 85-88
Cuddihy, Michael 1932- ... 172
Cuddon, John Anthony 1928-1996 ... CANR-19
Obituary ... 151
Earlier sketches in CA 5-8R, CANR-3
Cuddy, Don 1925- ... 69-72
Cude, Wilfred ... 221
Cudjoe, Selwyn Reginald 1943- ... CANR-137
Earlier sketch in CA 118
Cudlip, David R(ockwell) 1933- ... 177
See also CLC 34
Cudlipp, Lord
See Cudlipp, Hugh
Cudlipp, Edythe 1929- ... CANR-12
Earlier sketch in CA 33-36R
Cudlipp, Hugh 1913-1998
Obituary ... 167
Brief entry ... 116
Cudmore, Dana (D.) 1954- ... 134
Cudworth, Ralph 1617-1688 ... DLB 252
Cuelho, Art 1943- ... 61-64
Cuervo, Talia
See Vega, Ana Lydia
Cuetara, Mittie 1957- ... CANR-142
Earlier sketch in CA 175
See also SATA 106, 158
Cueva, Juan de la 1543-1612 ... DLB 318
Cuevas, Clara 1933- ... 57-60
Cuevas, Judy
See Ivory, Judith
Cuff, Barry
See Koste, Robert Francis
Cuff, Robert Dennis 1941-2001 ... 235
Brief entry ... 109
Cuffari, Richard 1925-1978 ... MAICYA 1, 2
See also SATA 6, 66
See also SATA-Obit 25
Cugat, Xavier 1900-1990
Obituary ... 132
Cugoano, Quobna Ottabah
1757-(?) ... DLBY 2002
Cuhulain, Kerr
See Ennis, Charles A(lbert)
Cuisenaire, Emile-Georges 1891(?)-1976
Obituary ... 61-64
Cuisenier, Jean 1927- ... CANR-20
Earlier sketch in CA 73-76
Cuklanz, Lisa M. 1963- ... 194
Culbert, David H(olbrook) 1943- ... CANR-31
Earlier sketch in CA 112
Culbert, Samuel Alan 1938- ... 69-72
Culbert, Steven (Tye) 1950- ... 144
Culbert, T(homas) Patrick 1930-
Brief entry ... 107
Culbertson, Don S(tuart) 1927- ... 9-12R
Culbertson, Hugh M. ... 77-80
Culbertson, J(ohn) M(athew) 1921-2001 ... 9-12R
Obituary ... 203
Culbertson, James T(homas) 1911- ... 118
Culbertson, Judi C. 1941- ... CANR-104
Earlier sketches in CA 85-88, CANR-31, 60
Culbertson, Manie 1927- ... 49-52
Culbertson, Margaret ... 221
Culbertson, Paul T(homas) 1905-1993 ... 37-40R
Culbertson, Philip Leroy 1944- ... 209
Culex
See Stanier, Maida Euphemia Kerr
Culhane, Claire 1918- ... 118
Culhane, John (William) 1934- ... CANR-141
Earlier sketch in CA 144
Culhane, Shamus 1908-1996 ... 121
Obituary ... 151
Culican, William 1929(?)-1984
Obituary ... 113
Culkin, Ann Marie 1918- ... 9-12R
Cull, John G(uinn, Jr.) 1934- ... 41-44R
Cullen, Bill 1942- ... 217
Cullen, Charles T(homas) 1940- ... 53-56
Cullen, Countee 1903-1946 ... 124
Brief entry ... 108
See also AFAW 2
See also AMWS 4
See also BLC 1
See also BW 1
See also CDALB 1917-1929
See also DA
See also DA3
See also DAC
See also DAM MST, MULT, POET
See also DLB 4, 48, 51
See also EWL 3
See also EXPP
See also HR 1:2
See also LMFS 2
See also MAL 5
See also MTCW 1, 2
See also MTFW 2005
See also PC 20
See also PFS 3
See also RGAL 4
See also SATA 18
See also TCLC 4, 37
See also WLCS
See also WP
Cullen, Dolores L. 1928- ... 196
Cullen, George Francis 1901-1980
Obituary ... 102
Cullen, Jim 1962- ... 151
Cullen, John 1942- ... 220
Cullen, Joseph P(atrick) 1920- ... 49-52
Cullen, Lee Stowell 1922- ... 103
Cullen, Mark 1956- ... 141
Cullen, Maurice R(aymond), Jr. 1927- ... 73-76
Cullen, Patrick (Colborn) 1940- ... 29-32R
Cullen, Peta
See Pyle, Hilary
Cullen, Robert (B.) 1949- ... 134
Cullen, Seamus ... FANT
Cullen Brown, Joanna 1930- ... 128
Culler, A(rthur) Dwight 1917- ... 17-20R
Culler, Annette Lorena
See Penney, Annette Culler
Culler, Jonathan 1944- ... 104
See also DLB 67, 246
Cullerne Bown, Matthew 1956- ... 132
Cullerton, Brenda ... 229
Culleton, Beatrice 1949- ... CANR-83
Earlier sketch in CA 120
See also DAC
See also NNAL
Culleton, Claire A. ... 238
Culley, Thomas R(obert) 1931- ... 33-36R
Culliford, Pierre 1928-1992 ... 124
Obituary ... 140
See also SATA 40
See also SATA-Obit 74
Culliford, Stanley George 1920- ... 65-68
Culligan, Joe
See Culligan, Matthew J(oseph)
Culligan, Matthew J(oseph)
1918-2002 ... CANR-20
Obituary ... 204
Earlier sketch in CA 81-84
Cullin, Mitch 1968- ... 189
Cullinan, Bernice E(llinger) 1926- ... CANR-113
Earlier sketch in CA 104
See also SATA 135
Cullinan, Elizabeth 1933- ... CANR-11
Earlier sketch in CA 25-28R
See also DLB 234
Cullinan, Gerald 1916- ... 21-24R
Cullinan, Patrick 1932- ... CANR-83
Earlier sketch in CA 153
See also CP 7
Cullinane, Jan ... 235
Cullinane, Leo Patrick 1907(?)-1978
Obituary ... 77-80
Culliney, John L. 1942- ... 65-68

Cumulative Index 133 Curnyn

Cullingford, Cecil H(oward) D(unstan)
1904-1990 .... CANR-7
Obituary 132
Earlier sketch in CA 5-8R
Cullingford, Guy
See Taylor, Constance Lindsay
Cullingworth, J(ohn) Barry
1929-2005 .... CANR-1
Obituary 236
Earlier sketch in CA 1-4R
Cullman, Marguerite Wagner 1908-1999 .. 1-4R
Obituary 185
Cullman, W(illiam) Arthur 1914-1992 113
Brief entry 111
Cullmann, Oscar 1902-1999 106
Cullop, Charles P. 1927- 25-28R
Cullum, John 1930- 222
Cullum, Paul 210
Cullum, Ridgewell 1867-1943 .... TCWW 1, 2
Cully, Iris V(irginia Arnold) 1914- CANR-17
Earlier sketches in CA 1-4R, CANR-1
Cully, Kendig Brubaker 1913-1987 .. CANR-17
Earlier sketches in CA 1-4R, CANR-1
Culme, John 1946- 128
Culotta, Nino
See O'Grady, John (Patrick)
Culp, Delos Poe 1911-2000 .... 17-20R
Culp, John H(ewett, Jr.) 1907- CANR-61
Earlier sketch in CA 29-32R
See also TCWW 1, 2
Culp, Louanna McNary 1901-1965 .... CAP-1
Earlier sketch in CA 13-16
See also SATA 2
Culp, Paula 1941- 57-60
Culp, Stephanie (Anne) 1947- 136
Culpepper, Marilyn Mayer 1922- 238
Culpepper, R(ichard) Alan 1946- 115
Culpepper, Robert H(arrell) 1924- 77-80
Culper, Felix
See McCaughrean, Geraldine
Culross, Michael (Gerard) 1942- 33-36R
Culshaw, John (Royds) 1924-1980 .... CANR-11
Obituary 97-100
Earlier sketch in CA 21-24R
Culver, Dwight W(endell) 1921- 9-12R
Culver, Elsie Thomas 1898-1998 .... CAP-2
Earlier sketch in CA 21-22
Culver, John C. 1932- 191
Culver, Kathryn
See Dresser, Davis
Culver, Kenneth Leon 1903-1991 103
Culver, Robert Duncan 1916- 120
Culver, Roger B(ruce) 1940- 104
Culver, Timothy
See Westlake, Donald E(dwin)
Culverwel, Nathaniel 1619(?)-1651(?) . DLB 252
Cum, R.
See Crumb, R(obert)
Cumali, Necati 1921- .... EWL 3
Cumbaa, Stephen 1947- .... SATA 72
Cumberland, Charles C(urtis)
1914-1970 .... CANR-2
Earlier sketch in CA 1-4R
Cumberland, John H(ammett) 1924- 127
Brief entry 106
Cumberland, Kenneth Brailey 1913- 53-56
Cumberland, Marten 1892-1972 ...... CANR-83
Earlier sketches in CAP-1, CA 11-12
Cumberland, Richard 1732-1811 .... DLB 89
See also RGEL 2
Cumberland, William Henry 1929- 17-20R
Cumberlege, Marcus (Crossley)
1938- CANR-17
Earlier sketch in CA 97-100
See also CP 1, 2, 3, 4, 5, 6, 7
Cumberlege, Vera 1908- 81-84
Cumbler, John T(aylor) 1946- 89-92
Cumes, J(ames) W(illiam) C(rawford)
1922- 73-76
Cuming, Geoffrey John 1917-1988 .. CANR-18
Obituary 125
Earlier sketches in CA 5-8R, CANR-3
Cuming, Pamela 1944- 107
Cumings, Bruce Glenn 1943- CANR-76
Earlier sketch in CA 107
Cumming, Alan 1965- 214
Cumming, Carman 1932- 193
Cumming, Constance Gordon
1837-1924 .... DLB 174
Cumming, Elizabeth (Skeoch) 1948- 137
Cumming, Patricia (Arens) 1932- CANR-11
Earlier sketch in CA 61-64
Cumming, Peter 1951- 129
Cumming, Primrose Amy 1915- CANR-83
Earlier sketch in CA 33-36R
See also SATA 24
Cumming, Robert (Denoon) 1916-2004
Obituary 229
Brief entry 107
Cumming, Robert 1945- CANR-141
Earlier sketches in CA 106, CANR-44
See also MTFW 2005
See also SATA 65
Cumming, William P(atterson)
1900-1989 .... 33-36R
Cummings, Abbott Lowell 1923- 202
Cummings, Ann
See Rudolph, Lee (Norman)
Cummings, Arthur J. 1920(?)-1979
Obituary 89-92
Cummings, Betty Sue 1918- CANR-14
Earlier sketch in CA 73-76
See also SAAS 9
See also SATA 15
Cummings, Bruce F(rederick) 1889-1919
Brief entry 123
See also Barbellion, W. N. P.
Cummings, Charles 1940- 107
Cummings, D(onald) W(ayne) 1935- 101
Cummings, E(dward) E(stlin)
1894-1962 .... CANR-31
Earlier sketch in CA 73-76
See also AAYA 41
See also AMW
See also CDALB 1929-1941
See also CLC 1, 3, 8, 12, 15, 68
See also DA
See also DA3
See also DAB
See also DAC
See also DAM MST, POET
See also DLB 4, 48
See also EWL 3
See also EXPP
See also MAL 5
See also MTCW 1, 2
See also MTFW 2005
See also PAB
See also PC 5
See also PFS 1, 3, 12, 13, 19
See also RGAL 4
See also TCLC 137
See also TUS
See also WLC
See also WP
Cummings, Florence
See Bonime, Florence
Cummings, Gary 1941(?)-1987
Obituary 125
Cummings, Jack 1925- .... TCWW 2
Cummings, Jean 1930- 33-36R
Cummings, Joe 1952- 137
Cummings, John W(illiam), Jr.
1940- CANR-83
Earlier sketches in CA 117, CANR-41
Cummings, Larry L(ee) 1937- 53-56
Cummings, Martha Therese 1958- 185
Cummings, Milton C(urtis), Jr. 1933- 13-16R
Cummings, Monette 1914-1999 .... CANR-40
Earlier sketch in CA 116
Cummings, Parke 1902-1987 .... CAP-1
Obituary 123
Earlier sketch in CA 13-14
See also SATA 2
See also SATA-Obit 53
Cummings, Pat (Marie) 1950- CANR-88
Earlier sketches in CA 122, CANR-44
See also BW 2
See also CLR 48
See also CWRI 5
See also MAICYA 1, 2
See also MAICYAS 1
See also SAAS 13
See also SATA 42, 71, 107
Cummings, Paul 1933-1997 .... CANR-8
Obituary 156
Earlier sketch in CA 21-24R
Cummings, Phil 1957- .... BYA 13
See also SATA 74, 123
Cummings, Priscilla 1951- 198
See also SATA 129
Cummings, Ray(mond King)
1887-1957 .... CANR-83
Brief entry 113
Earlier sketch in CANR-31
See also DLB 8
See also SFW 4
Cummings, Richard
See Gardner, Richard (M.)
Cummings, Richard (Marshall) 1938- 113
Cummings, Richard LeRoy 1933- 45-48
Cummings, Sally (Nikoline) 227
Cummings, Scott 112
Cummings, Thomas G(erald) 1944- .. CANR-16
Earlier sketch in CA 97-100
Cummings, Violet M(ay) 1905-1994 57-60
Cummings, W(alter) T(hies) 1933- 1-4R
Cummins, C. Lyle, Jr. 1930- 149
Cummins, D. Duane 1935- CANR-14
Earlier sketch in CA 37-40R
Cummins, Geraldine Dorothy
1890-1969 .... CAP-1
Earlier sketch in CA 9-10
Cummins, James 1948- 122
Cummins, Jeanine 1975(?)- 235
Cummins, Joseph 218
Cummins, Light Townsend 1946- 141
Cummins, Maria Susanna 1827-1866 ... DLB 42
See also YABC 1
Cummins, Paul F. 1937- 33-36R
Cummins, Robert 1897-1982 219
Cummins, Walter (Merrill) 1936- CANR-15
Earlier sketch in CA 41-44R
Cumper, Patricia 1954- 235
Cumpian, Carlos 1953- 177
See also DLB 209
See also HW 2
Cumyn, Alan 1960- 223
Cunard, (Clara) Nancy 1896-1965 219
See also DLB 240
Cundieff, Rusty 1965(?)- 156
Cundiff, Edward William 1919- CANR-4
Earlier sketch in CA 1-4R
Cundiff, Margaret Joan 1932- CANR-117
Earlier sketches in CA 112, CANR-30, 56
Cundy, Henry Martyn 1913-2005 .... 5-8R
Obituary 236
Cuneo, Ernest (L.) 1905-1988
Obituary 125
Cuneo, Gilbert Anthony 1913-1978
Obituary 77-80
Cuneo, John R(obert) 1911-1984 53-56
Cuneo, Mary Louise -2001 .... SATA 85
Cuney, Waring
See Cuney, William Waring
Cuney, William Waring 1906-1976 125
See also BW 1
See also DLB 51
Cunha, Euclides (Rodrigues Pimenta) da
1866-1909 219
Brief entry 123
See also DLB 307
See also LAW
See also TCLC 24
See also WLIT 1
Cunha, George Daniel Martin
1911-1994 .... 25-28R
Cuninggim, Merrimon 1911-1995 .... 41-44R
Cunliffe, Barrington Windsor 1939- .. CANR-49
Earlier sketches in CA 53-56, CANR-9, 24
Cunliffe, Barry
See Cunliffe, Barrington Windsor
Cunliffe, Elaine 33-36R
Cunliffe, John Arthur 1933- CANR-52
Earlier sketches in CA 61-64, CANR-11
See also CWRI 5
See also SATA 11, 86
Cunliffe, Marcus (Falkner)
1922-1990 .... CANR-10
Obituary 132
Earlier sketch in CA 21-24R
See also SATA 37
See also SATA-Obit 66
Cunliffe, William Gordon 1929- 25-28R
Cunneen, Joseph 1923- 238
Cunningham, Agnes 1909-2004 206
Obituary 228
Cunningham, Aline CANR-9
Earlier sketch in CA 57-60
Cunningham, Allan 1791-1839 .. DLB 116, 144
Cunningham, Barry 1940- 73-76
Cunningham, Bob
See May, Julian
Cunningham, Captain Frank
See Glick, Carl (Cannon)
Cunningham, Cathy
See Cunningham, Chet
Cunningham, Chet 1928- CANR-62
Earlier sketches in CA 49-52, CANR-4, 19
See also SATA 23
See also TCWW 1, 2
Cunningham, Colin 1967- 213
Cunningham, Dale S(peers) 1932- CANR-8
Earlier sketch in CA 13-16R
See also SATA 11
Cunningham, Donald H(ayward)
1935- CANR-20
Earlier sketch in CA 103
Cunningham, Dru 155
See also SATA 91
Cunningham, E. V.
See Fast, Howard (Melvin)
Cunningham, Elaine 1957- 160
Cunningham, Eldon L. 1956- 144
Cunningham, Eugene 1896-1957 .. TCWW 1, 2
Cunningham, Floyd F(ranklin)
1899-1984 .... CAP-1
Earlier sketch in CA 13-16
Cunningham, Frank R. 1937- 137
Cunningham, H(orace) H(erndon)
1913-1969 .... CAP-1
Earlier sketch in CA 11-12
Cunningham, Hugh 1942- CANR-125
Earlier sketch in CA 151
Cunningham, Imogen 1883-1976
Obituary 65-68
See also AAYA 54
Cunningham, J. Morgan
See Westlake, Donald E(dwin)
Cunningham, J(ames) V(incent)
1911-1985 .... CANR-72
Obituary 115
Earlier sketches in CA 1-4R, CANR-1
See also CLC 3, 31
See also CP 1, 2
See also DLB 5
Cunningham, James F. 1901- CAP-2
Earlier sketch in CA 19-20
Cunningham, James V. 1923- 135
Cunningham, Jim
See Cunningham, James V.
Cunningham, John 1729-1773 .... RGEL 2
Cunningham, John D(onovan) 1933- 111
Cunningham, Joseph F. X. 1925- 69-72
Cunningham, Joseph Sandy 1928- 61-64
Cunningham, Julia (Woolfolk)
1916- CANR-36
Earlier sketches in CA 9-12R, CANR-4, 19
See also CLC 12
See also CWRI 5
See also JRDA
See also MAICYA 1, 2
See also SAAS 2
See also SATA 1, 26, 132
Cunningham, Keith 1939- 139
Cunningham, Laura Shaine 1947- .. CANR-106
Earlier sketches in CA 85-88, CANR-23, 47
Cunningham, Lawrence 1935- CANR-15
Earlier sketch in CA 85-88
Cunningham, Lawrence J. 1943- 197
See also SATA 125
Cunningham, Lyda Sue Martin 1938- 17-20R
Cunningham, Marilyn 1927- 125
Cunningham, Mary (Elizabeth) 1951- 114
Cunningham, Michael 1952- CANR-96
Earlier sketch in CA 136
See also AMWS 15
See also CLC 34
See also CN 7
See also DLB 292
See also GLL 2
See also MTFW 2005
Cunningham, Michael A(lan) 1945- 41-44R
Cunningham, Noble E., Jr. 1926- CANR-94
Earlier sketch in CA 81-84
Cunningham, Patricia (A.) 1937- 151
Cunningham, Paul James, Jr. 1917- 73-76
Cunningham, Peter 1947- .... DLB 267
Cunningham, R(onnie) Walter 1932- 103
Cunningham, Richard 1939- 101
Cunningham, Robert Louis 1926- 41-44R
Cunningham, Robert M(aris), Jr.
1909-1992 .... CANR-1
Obituary 137
Earlier sketch in CA 49-52
Cunningham, Robert Stanley 1907- 53-56
Cunningham, Rosemary 1916- 9-12R
Cunningham, Sis
See Cunningham, Agnes
Cunningham, Valentine 1944- 225
Cunningham, Virginia
See Holmgren, Virginia C(unningham)
Cunningham, W(infield) Scott 1899(?)-1986
Obituary 118
Cunninghame Graham, R. B.
See Cunninghame Graham, Robert (Gallnigad) Bontine
Cunninghame Graham, Robert (Gallnigad)
Bontine 1852-1936 184
Brief entry 119
See also Graham, R(obert) B(ontine) Cunninghame
See also TCLC 19
Cunnington, Phillis 1887-1974
Obituary 53-56
Cuno, Kenneth M. 1950- CANR-98
Earlier sketch in CA 147
Cunqueiro, Alvaro 1911-1981 .... DLB 134
See also EWL 3
Cunxin, Li 1961- 238
Cunz, Dieter 1910-1969 .... CAP-2
Earlier sketch in CA 19-20
Cuomo, George (Michael) 1929- CANR-50
Earlier sketches in CA 5-8R, CANR-7
See also DLBY 1980
Cuomo, Mario Matthew 1932- CANR-40
Earlier sketch in CA 103
Cupitt, Don 1934- CANR-89
Earlier sketches in CA 41-44R, CANR-14, 48
Cuppleditch, David 1946- CANR-116
Earlier sketches in CA 116, CANR-38, 56
Cuppy, Will(iam Jacob) 1884-1949
Brief entry 108
See also DLB 11
Cure, Karen 1949- CANR-9
Earlier sketch in CA 65-68
Curiae, Amicus
See Fuller, Edmund (Maybank)
Curie, Eve 1904- CAP-1
Earlier sketch in CA 9-10
See also BYA 2
See also NCFS 2
See also SATA 1
Curie, Marie (Sklodowska) 1867-1934 166
Brief entry 118
Curiel, Barbara Brinson 1956- .... DLB 209
Curl, David H. 1932- 93-96
Curl, Donald Walter 1935- 33-36R
Curl, James Stevens 1937- CANR-135
Earlier sketches in CA 37-40R, CANR-14
Curle, Adam
See Curle, Charles T. W.
Curle, Charles T. W. 1916- 33-36R
Curlee, Lynn 1947- CANR-120
Earlier sketch in CA 165
See also SATA 98, 141
Curler, (Mary) Bernice 1915- 85-88
Curley, Arthur 1938-1998 .... CANR-9
Earlier sketch in CA 21-24R
Curley, Charles 1949- 57-60
Curley, Daniel 1918-1988 .... CANR-18
Obituary 127
Earlier sketches in CA 9-12R, CANR-3
See also SATA 23
See also SATA-Obit 61
Curley, Dorothy Nyren
See Nyren, Dorothy Elizabeth
Curley, Marianne 1959- 200
See also SATA 131
Curley, Michael J. 1900-1972
Obituary 37-40R
Curley, Stephen J. 1947- 188
Curley, Walter J(oseph) P(atrick) 1922- 53-56
Curling, Audrey 61-64
Curling, Bill
See Curling, Bryan William Richard
Curling, Bryan William Richard 1911- 102
Curnow, (Thomas) Allen (Monro)
1911-2001 .... CANR-99
Obituary 202
Earlier sketches in CA 69-72, CANR-48
See also CP 1, 2, 3, 4, 5, 6, 7
See also EWL 3
See also PC 48
See also RGEL 2
Curnow, Frank
See Atkinson, Frank
Curnow, Ray(mond) 1928- 117
Curnow, Wystan 1939- 188
Curnutt, Jordan 1958- 218
Curnyn, Lynda 237

Curran, Bob
See Curran, Robert
Curran, Charles (John) 1921-1980 130
Obituary 105
Curran, Charles A(rthur) 1913-1978 . CANR-29
Earlier sketch in CA 33-36R
Curran, Charles E. 1934- CANR-92
Earlier sketches in CA 21-24R, CANR-14, 48
Curran, Daniel J. 1950- 139
Curran, Dolores 1932- CANR-6
Earlier sketch in CA 57-60
Curran, Donald J. 1926- 45-48
Curran, Francis X. 1914-1993 .... 17-20R
Curran, Jan Goldberg 1937- 101
See also Goldberg, Jan
Curran, Joseph M(aroney) 1932- 103
Curran, Mona (Elisa) 5-8R
Curran, Peter Malcolm 1922- 103
Curran, Phil(ip) R(ead) 1911-1980 73-76
Curran, Robert 1923- 89-92
Curran, Samuel (Crowe) 1912-1998 109
Curran, Stuart (Alan) 1940- 29-32R
Curran, Susan 1952- 113
Curran, Terrie 1942- 127
Curran, Thomas J(oseph) 1929- 45-48
Curran, Ward S(chenk) 1935- 41-44R
Curran, William John 1925- 108
Curren, Polly 1917- CANR-4
Earlier sketch in CA 1-4R
Current, Richard N(elson) 1912- CANR-5
Earlier sketch in CA 1-4R
Current-Garcia, Eugene 1908-1995 .... 17-20R
Currer-Briggs, Noel 1919- CANR-13
Earlier sketch in CA 73-76
Currey, Cecil B(arr) 1932- CANR-51
Earlier sketches in CA 25-28R, CANR-25
Currey, Dave 1953- 140
Currey, R(onald) F(airbridge)
1894-1983 .... CAP-1
Obituary 109
Earlier sketch in CA 9-10
Currey, R(alph) N(ixon) 1907-2001 93-96
Obituary 204
See also CP 1, 2, 3, 4, 5, 6, 7
Currey, Richard 1949- 163
Earlier sketch in CA 117
Curriden, Mark 222
Currie, Ann (Brooke Peterson) 1922(?)-1980
Obituary 102
Currie, Barbara 1942- 219
Currie, Barton Wood 1878-1962
Obituary 116
Currie, David
See Allen, Sydney (Earl), Jr.
Currie, David P(ark) 1936- 134
Brief entry 106
Currie, Dawn 1948- 188
Currie, Donald Glenne 1926-1984
Obituary 111
Currie, Dwight 1953- 199
Currie, Edwina 1946- CANR-98
Earlier sketch in CA 152
Currie, Ellen 19(?)- .... CLC 44
Currie, Elliott (?)-1993(?) 155
Currie, James 1756-1805 .... DLB 142
Currie, Katy
See Kyle, Susan (Spaeth)
Currie, Lauchlin (Bernard)
1902-1993 .... CANR-15
Obituary 143
Earlier sketch in CA 73-76
Currie, Mary Montgomerie Lamb Singleton
1843-1905 176
See also Fane, Violet
Currie, Philip J(ohn) 1949- 168
Currie, Robert 1937- CANR-137
Earlier sketch in CA 112
Currie, Robin 1948- 191
See also SATA 120
Currie, Stephen 1960- CANR-108
Earlier sketch in CA 149
See also SATA 82, 132
Currier, Alvin C. 1932- 21-24R
Currier, Chester S. 1945- 129
Currier, Frederick P(lumer) 1923- 85-88
Currier, Richard L(eon) 1940- 57-60
Curro, Evelyn Malone 1907- 5-8R
Curry, Andrew 1931- 57-60
Curry, Ann (Gabrielle) 1934- .... SATA 72
Curry, Avon
See Bowden, Jean
Curry, Constance (Winifred) 1933- 151
Curry, David 1942- 69-72
Curry, Dean C(onrad) 1952- 118
Curry, Estell H. 1907- CAP-2
Earlier sketch in CA 23-24
Curry, F. Hayden 1940- 108
Curry, G(len) David 1948- 136
Curry, Gene
See McCurtin, Peter
Curry, George E(dward) 1947- 69-72
Curry, Gladys J.
See Washington, Gladys J(oseph)
Curry, Jane L(ouise) 1932- CANR-44
Earlier sketches in CA 17-20R, CANR-7, 24
See also CLR 31
See also CWRI 5
See also MAICYA 1, 2
See also SAAS 6
See also SATA 1, 52, 90, 138
See also SATA-Essay 138
Curry, Jennifer 1934- 77-80
Curry, Kenneth 1910-1999 .... CANR-8
Earlier sketch in CA 17-20R
Curry, Leonard Preston 1929- 29-32R
Curry, Lerond (Loving) 1938- 33-36R
Curry, Martha Mulroy 1926- 61-64
Curry, Neil 1937- 149
Curry, Paul (J.) 1917-1986 49-52
Obituary 118
Curry, Peggy Simson 1911-1987 .... CANR-61
Obituary 121
Earlier sketches in CA 33-36R, CANR-12
See also SATA 8
See also SATA-Obit 50
See also TCWW 1, 2
Curry, Richard Orr 1931- 13-16R
Curry, Thomas Albert 1901(?)-1976
Obituary 69-72
See also TCWW 2
Curry, Windell
See Sujata, Anagarika
Curry-Lindahl, Kai 1917- CANR-19
Earlier sketches in CA 49-52, CANR-2
Curtain, John 1939-1999 189
Curtayne, Alice 1898-1981 53-56
Curteis, Ian Bayley 1935- CANR-36
Earlier sketch in CA 103
Curti, Merle Eugene 1897-1996 .... CANR-4
Obituary 151
Earlier sketch in CA 5-8R
See also DLB 17
Curtin, Dave 1955- 132
Curtin, Deane 1951- 138
Curtin, James R(udd) 1922- 17-20R
Curtin, Mary Ellen 1922- 57-60
Curtin, Patricia Romero
See Romero, Patricia W.
Curtin, Philip
See Lowndes, Marie Adelaide (Belloc)
Curtin, Phillip
See Lowndes, Marie Adelaide (Belloc)
Curtin, Phillip D. 1922- CANR-7
Earlier sketch in CA 13-16R
Curtin, Valerie 130
Curtin, William M(artin) 1927- 53-56
Curtis, Alan R(obert) 1936- 105
Curtis, Anthony 1926- CANR-40
Earlier sketches in CA 101, CANR-18
See also DLB 155
Curtis, (Hubert) Arnold 1917- CANR-29
Earlier sketches in CA 29-32R, CANR-12
Curtis, Brian 1971- 224
Curtis, Bruce (Richard) 1944- .... SATA 30
Curtis, C(hristopher) Michael 1934- 136
Curtis, Carol Edwards 1943- 77-80
Curtis, Chara M(ahar) 1950- .... SATA 78
Curtis, Charles J(ohn) 1921- 21-24R
Curtis, Charles Ralph 1899- 5-8R
Curtis, Charlotte (Murray) 1928-1987 ..... 9-12R
Obituary 122
See also AITN 2
Curtis, Christopher Paul 1954(?)- CANR-119
Earlier sketches in CA 159, CANR-80
See also AAYA 37
See also BW 3
See also BYA 11, 13
See also CLR 68
See also MAICYA 2
See also SATA 93, 140
See also YAW
Curtis, Craig 197
Curtis, Cyrus H(erman) K(otzschmar)
1850-1933 178
See also DLB 91
Curtis, Dan(iel Meyer) 1928- 145
Curtis, David Paul 1942- CANR-13
Earlier sketch in CA 21-24R
Curtis, Donald 1915- CANR-44
Earlier sketches in CA 103, CANR-20
Curtis, Edith Roelker 1893-1977 .... 1-4R
Obituary 103
Curtis, Gavin 1965- .... SATA 107
Curtis, George William 1824-1892 . DLB 1, 43, 223
Curtis, Gerald 1904-1983
Obituary 109
Curtis, Glade B. 1950- 173
Curtis, Howard J(ames) 1906-1972
Obituary 37-40R
Curtis, J(ulie) A. E. 1955- 141
Curtis, J(osiah) Montgomery 1905-1982
Obituary 108
Curtis, Jack
See Harsent, David
Curtis, Jack 1922- 103
Curtis, Jackie
See Holder, John, Jr.
Curtis, James (Richard) 1953- 108
Curtis, James C. 1938-
Brief entry 105
Curtis, James Malcolm 1940- 119
Curtis, Jamie Lee 1958- CANR-124
Earlier sketch in CA 160
See also CLR 88
See also SATA 95, 144
Curtis, Jared Ralph 1936- 101
Curtis, Jean-Louis 1917-1995 221
Curtis, John
See Prebble, John Edward Curtis
Curtis, Lewis Perry 1900-1976 .... CAP-2
Obituary 65-68
Earlier sketch in CA 23-24
Curtis, Lindsay R(aine) 1916- 41-44R
Curtis, Lynn A(lan) 1943- 61-64
Curtis, Marci .... SATA 160
Curtis, Margaret James 1897- 1-4R
Curtis, Marjorie
See Prebble, Marjorie Mary Curtis
Curtis, Mark H(ubert) 1920- 5-8R
Curtis, Michael K. 1942- CANR-120
Earlier sketch in CA 128
Curtis, Michael Raymond 1923- CANR-22
Earlier sketch in CA 103
Curtis, Nancy 1947- 159
Curtis, Norman 1914-2003 45-48
Curtis, Patricia 1921- CANR-18
Earlier sketch in CA 69-72
See also SATA 23, 101
Curtis, Paul
See Czura, R(oman) P(eter)
Curtis, Peter
See Lofts, Norah (Robinson)
Curtis, Philip (Delacourt) 1920- 109
See also SATA 62
Curtis, Price
See Ellison, Harlan (Jay)
Curtis, Richard (Alan) 1937- CANR-25
Earlier sketch in CA 106
See also SATA 29
Curtis, Richard 1956- 157
Curtis, Richard Hale
See Deming, Richard and
Levinson, Leonard and Rothweiler, Paul Roger
Curtis, Richard Kenneth 1924- CANR-47
Earlier sketch in CA 1-4R
Curtis, Rosemary Ann (Stevens) 1935- 9-12R
Curtis, Sharon 1951- CANR-68
Brief entry 116
Earlier sketch in CA 126
See also London, Laura
Curtis, Susan 1956- 145
Curtis, Thomas Bradford 1911-1993 61-64
Obituary 140
Curtis, Thomas Dale 1952- 126
Brief entry 116
See also London, Laura
Curtis, Tom
See Pendower, Jacques
Curtis, Tony 1925- CANR-45
Earlier sketch in CA 73-76
Curtis, Tony 1946- CANR-83
Earlier sketches in CA 106, CANR-22
See also CP 7
Curtis, Wade
See Pournelle, Jerry (Eugene)
Curtis, Will
See Nunn, William Curtis
Curtis, William J(oseph) R. 1948- 110
Curtis Brown, Beatrice 1901-1974 ... CANR-69
Earlier sketches in CAP-2, CA 25-28
Curtiss, A(rlene) B. 1934- CANR-112
Earlier sketch in CA 155
See also SATA 90
Curtiss, Harriette Augusta 1856-1932 209
Curtiss, Huston 1922(?)- 221
Curtiss, John S(helton) 1899-1983 .... CAP-2
Earlier sketch in CA 19-20
Curtiss, Mina (Stein Kirstein) 1896-1985 133
Obituary 118
Curtiss, Thomas Quinn 1915-2000 202
Curtiss, Ursula Reilly 1923-1984 ...... CANR-60
Obituary 114
Earlier sketches in CA 1-4R, CANR-5
See also CMW 4
Curtius, Ernst Robert 1886-1956 154
See also EWL 3
Curtius Rufus, Quintus fl. 35- .... DLB 211
Curtler, Hugh Mercer 1937- CANR-94
Earlier sketches in CA 89-92, CANR-15
Curto, Josephine J. 1927- 17-20R
Curwin, Richard L(eonard) 1944- 77-80
Curwood, James Oliver 1878-1927 .. TCWW 1, 2
Cury, Ivan 1937- 186
Curzon, Clare
See Buchanan, Marie
Curzon, Daniel CANR-108
Earlier sketch in CA 73-76
See also GLL 1
Curzon, David 1941- 137
Curzon, Lucia
See Stevenson, Florence
Curzon, Robert 1810-1873 .... DLB 166
Curzon, Sam
See Krasney, Samuel A.
Curzon, Sarah Anne 1833-1898 .... DLB 99
Curzon, Virginia
See Hawton, Hector
Curzon-Brown, Daniel
See Curzon, Daniel
Cusac, Marian H(ollingsworth) 1932- ... 33-36R
Cusack, (Ellen) Dymphna
1902-1980(?) CANR-11
Earlier sketch in CA 9-12R
See also DLB 260
Cusack, Lawrence X(avier) 1919- 5-8R
Cusack, Margaret 1945- .... SATA 58
Cusack, Michael J(oseph) 1928- 69-72
Cusanus, Nicolaus 1401-1464
See Nicholas of Cusa
Cush, Carol Gregor
See Gregor, Carol
Cushing, Barry E(dwin) 1945- CANR-4
Earlier sketch in CA 53-56
Cushing, Eliza Lanesford 1794-1886 .... DLB 99
Cushing, Harvey 1869-1939 .... DLB 187
Cushing, Jane 1922- 29-32R
Cushing, Mary W(atkins) 1890(?)-1974
Obituary 53-56
Cushing, Peter (Wilton) 1913-1994 .. CANR-83
Obituary 146
Earlier sketch in CA 133
Cushing, Richard Cardinal
See Cushing, Richard James
Cushing, Richard James 1895-1970
Obituary 112
Cushing, Winifred 1907-1990
Obituary 132
Cushion, John P(atrick) 1915- 93-96
Cushman, Clarissa Fairchild 1889-1980
Obituary 93-96
Cushman, Dan 1909-2001 .... CANR-64
Obituary 202
Earlier sketches in CA 5-8R, CANR-3, 18
See also TCWW 1, 2
Cushman, Doug 1953- CANR-136
Earlier sketches in CA 117, CANR-54
See also SATA 65, 101, 157
Cushman, Jerome 1-4R
See also SATA 2
Cushman, Joseph David, Jr. 1925- 111
Cushman, Karen 1941- CANR-130
Earlier sketch in CA 155
See also AAYA 22, 60
See also BYA 9, 13
See also CLR 55
See also MAICYA 2
See also MAICYAS 1
See also SATA 89, 147
See also WYAS 1
See also YAW
Cushman, Keith (Maxwell) 1942- 124
Cushman, Robert F(airchild) 1918- 77-80
Cushman, Stephen B. 1956- CANR-91
Earlier sketches in CA 123, CANR-50
Cusic, Don 1948- 145
Cusick, Heidi Haughy 1946- 150
Cusick, Philip A. 1937- 69-72
Cusick, Richie Tankersley 1952- CANR-119
Earlier sketch in CA 134
See also AAYA 14
See also JRDA
See also SATA 67, 140
See also YAW
Cusk, Rachel 1967- CANR-127
Earlier sketch in CA 175
Cuskelly, Eugene James 1924- 5-8R
Cuskey, (Raymond) Walter 1934- 41-44R
Cuss, (Theodore Patrick) Camerer 1909(?)-1970
Obituary 104
Cussen, Antonio 1952- 144
Cussler, Clive (Eric) 1931- CANR-131
Earlier sketches in CA 45-48, CANR-1, 21, 50, 91
Interview in CANR-21
See also AAYA 19
See also BEST 90:4
See also CMW 4
See also CPW
See also DA3
See also DAM POP
See also MTFW 2005
Cussons, Sheila 1922- 206
Custance, Olive 1874-1944 210
See also DLB 240
Custer, Chester Eugene 1920- 41-44R
Custer, Clint
See Paine, Lauran (Bosworth)
Custer, Robert (Laverne) 1927-1990
Obituary 132
Cusumano, Michael A. 1954- 125
Cutchen, Billye Walker 1930- CANR-13
Earlier sketch in CA 77-80
See also SATA 15
Cutchins, Judy 1947- 127
See also SATA 59
Cutcliffe, Stephen H(osmer) 1947- .. CANR-119
Earlier sketches in CA 116, CANR-48
Cutforth, John Ashlin 1911-1991 .... 9-12R
Cutforth, Rene 1909(?)-1984 123
Obituary 112
Cuthbert, Diana Daphne Holman-Hunt
1913-1993 .... CANR-54
Earlier sketch in CA 1-4R
Cuthbert, Eleonora Isabel (McKenzie)
1902- CAP-1
Earlier sketch in CA 11-12
Cuthbert, John A. 167
Cuthbert, Margaret 172
Cuthbert, Mary
See Hellwig, Monika Konrad
Cuthbert, Neil 1951- 146
Cuthbertson, Gilbert Morris 1937- 57-60
Cuthbertson, Ken 1951- 179
Cuthbertson, Tom 1945- CANR-1
Earlier sketch in CA 45-48
Cuthbertson, Yvonne 1944- 188
Cutler, Alan 1954- 228
Cutler, Bruce 1930-2001 .... CANR-41
Obituary 194
Earlier sketches in CA 1-4R, CANR-2, 18
Cutler, Carl C(uster) 1878-1966 .... 1-4R
Obituary 103
Cutler, Carol 1926- CANR-19
Earlier sketch in CA 103
Cutler, Charles L(ocke, Jr.)
1930-1999 .... CANR-124
Earlier sketch in CA 65-68
Cutler, Daniel S(olomon) 1951- 120
See also SATA 78
Cutler, David 1956- 137
Cutler, David M. 231
Cutler, Donald R. 1930- 21-24R
Cutler, (May) Ebbitt 1923- CANR-4
Earlier sketch in CA 49-52
See also SATA 9
Cutler, Irving H. 1923- CANR-9
Earlier sketch in CA 21-24R
Cutler, Ivor 1923- CANR-9
Earlier sketch in CA 5-8R
See also CP 1
See also SATA 24
Cutler, Jane 1936- CANR-96
Earlier sketch in CA 142
See also SATA 75, 118, 162

Cutler, Judith 1946- ... CANR-108
Earlier sketch in CA 149
Cutler, Katherine Noble 1905- ... CANR-4
Earlier sketch in CA 5-8R
Cutler, Roland 1938- ... CANR-50
Earlier sketches in CA 102, CANR-25
Cutler, Samuel
See Folsom, Franklin (Brewster)
Cutler, Stan 1925- ... 137
Cutler, William W(orcester) III 1941- ... 206
Cutler, Winnifred B(erg) 1944- ... CANR-40
Earlier sketch in CA 117
Cutlip, Kimbra L(eigh-Ann) 1964- ... SATA 128
Cutlip, Scott M. 1915-2000 ... 5-8R
Obituary ... 189
Cutrate, Joe
See Spiegelman, Art
Cutrer, Thomas W(illiam) 1947- ... CANR-97
Earlier sketch in CA 123
Cutright, Paul Russell 1897-1988 ... 65-68
Cutright, Phillips 1930- ... 5-8R
Cutrufelli, Maria Rosa 1364-1431 ... FW
Cutshall, Alden (D.) 1911-1997 ... CANR-3
Obituary ... 162
Earlier sketch in CA 9-12R
Cutsumbis, Michael N(icholas) 1935- ... 45-48
Cutt, W(illiam) Towrie 1898-1981 ... 81-84
Obituary ... 115
See also SATA 16
See also SATA-Obit 85
Cutten, M. J.
See Cutten, Mervyn (James)
Cutten, Mervyn (James) 1916- ... CANR-46
Earlier sketch in CA 120
Cutter, Charles 1936- ... 148
Cutter, Charles R. 1950- ... 127
Cutter, Donald C(olgett) 1922- ... CANR-13
Earlier sketch in CA 33-36R
Cutter, Fred 1924- ... 57-60
Cutter, John
See Shirley, John
Cutter, Leah R. ... 222
Cutter, Martha J. ... 188
Cutter, Robert Arthur 1930- ... CANR-8
Earlier sketch in CA 57-60
Cutter, Tom
See Randisi, Robert J(oseph) and Wallmann, Jeffrey M(iner)
Cutting, Edith E(lsie) 1918- ... 106
Cutting, Linda Katherine 1954(?)- ... 168
Cutting, Pauline 1952- ... 128
Cuttino, G(eorge) P(eddy) 1914-1991 ... 21-24R
Cuttle, Evelyn Roeding ... 57-60
Cuttler, Charles D(avid) 1913- ... 29-32R
Cutts, John P. 1927-1986 ... 45-48
Obituary ... 121
Cutts, Richard 1923- ... 33-36R
Cutul, Ann-Marie 1945- ... 103
Cuyler, Louise E. 1908-1998 ... 21-24R
Cuyler, Margery S(tuyvesant) 1948- ... CANR-127
Earlier sketch in CA 117
See also SATA 39, 99, 156
Cuyler, Stephen
See Bates, Barbara S(nedeker)
Cuyler, Susanna (Stevens) 1946- ... 61-64
Cuza Male, Belkis 1942- ... CANR-87
Earlier sketch in CA 131
See also HW 1
Cykler, Edmund A(lbert) 1903-1988 ... 9-12R
Cylwicki, Albert 1932- ... CANR-38
Earlier sketch in CA 116
Cymbala, Carol Joy 1947- ... 218
Cymbala, Jim 1943- ... 234
Cynan
See Evans-Jones, Albert
Cynewulf c. 770- ... DLB 146
See also RGEL 2
Cynthia
See King, Florence
Cyprien
See Frechette, Louis-Honore
Cyprys, Ruth Altbeker 19(?)-1979 ... 166
Cyr, Arthur 1945- ... 125
Cyr, Don(ald Joseph) 1935- ... 103
Cyr, Gilles 1940- ... 168
Cyr, John Edwin 1915- ... 103
Cyr, Mary 1946- ... 145
Cyrano de Bergerac, Savinien de 1619-1655 ... DLB 268
See also GFL Beginnings to 1789
See also RGWL 2, 3
Cyrill, Christopher 1970- ... 189
Cyrus, Kurt 1954- ... SATA 132
Cytowic, Richard E(dmund) 1952- ... CANR-141
Earlier sketch in CA 144
Czaczkes, Shmuel Yosef Halevi
See Agnon, S(hmuel) Y(osef Halevi)
Czaja, (E.) Michael 1911-1994 ... 57-60
Czajkowski, Chris(tine) 1947- ... 218
Czajkowski, Hania 1949- ... 220
Czaplinski, Suzanne 1943- ... 61-64
Czech, Brian 1960- ... 207
Czechowicz, Jozef 1903-1939 ... EWL 3
Czekanowska, Anna 1929- ... 140
Czepko, Daniel 1605-1660 ... DLB 164
Czerneda, Julie E(lizabeth) 1955- ... CANR-123
Earlier sketch in CA 164
Czerniakow, Adam 1880-1942
Czerniawski, Adam 1934- ... CANR-48
Earlier sketches in CA 37-40R, CANR-14
See also DLB 232
Czerny, Peter G(erd) 1941- ... 65-68
Czestochowski, Joseph S(tephen) 1950- ... 113
Czigany, Lorant (Gyorgy) 1935- ... 130
Czobor, Agnes 1920- ... 37-40R
Czuchlewski, David 1976- ... 223
Czura, R(oman) P(eter) 1913-1982 ... 89-92

D

D, Chuck
See Ridenhour, Carlton
Da, Adi
See Jones, Franklin Albert
Daalder, Hans 1928- ... CANR-85
Earlier sketch in CA 133
Daalder, Ivo H. 1960- ... 204
Daane, Calvin J(ohn) 1925- ... 41-44R
Daane, James 1914-1983 ... 21-24R
Dabberdt, Walter F. 1942- ... CANR-23
Earlier sketch in CA 107
Dabbs, Jack Autrey 1914-1992 ... 17-20R
Dabbs, James McBride 1896-1970 ... CANR-73
Earlier sketches in CAP-1, CA 13-16
Dabcovich, Lydia ... 124
See also SATA 58, 99
See also SATA-Brief 47
Dabit, Eugene 1898-1936 ... 175
See also DLB 65
Dabkin, Edwin Franden 1898(?)-1976
Obituary ... 65-68
Dabney, Dick 1933-1981 ... 69-72
Obituary ... 105
Dabney, Joseph Earl 1929- ... 49-52
Dabney, Ross H. 1934- ... 21-24R
Dabney, Virginia Bell 1919-1997 ... 139
Dabney, Virginius 1901-1995 ... CANR-29
Obituary ... 150
Earlier sketches in CA 45-48, CANR-1
Dabney, William M(inor) 1919-2000 ... 9-12R
Daborne, Robert 1580(?)-1628 ... DLB 58
D'Abreu, Gerald Joseph 1916-(?) ... CAP-2
Earlier sketch in CA 19-20
Dabringhaus, Erhard 1917-1997 ... 115
Dabrowska, Maria (Szumska) 1889-1965 ... 106
See also CDWLB 4
See also CLC 15
See also DLB 215
See also EWL 3
Dabydeen, Cyril 1945- ... CANR-82
Brief entry ... 122
Earlier sketches in CA 133, CANR-48
See also CP 7
Dabydeen, David 1955- ... CANR-92
Earlier sketches in CA 125, CANR-56
See also BW 1
See also CLC 34
See also CN 6, 7
See also CP 7
DaCal, Ernesto Guerra 1911-1994 ... CANR-19
Obituary ... 162
Earlier sketches in CA 5-8R, CANR-4
D'Accone, Frank A(nthony) 1931- ... 177
Dace, Dolores B(oelens) 1929- ... 155
See also SATA 89
Dace, Letitia (Skinner) 1941- ... 106
Dace, Tish
See Dace, Letitia (Skinner)
Dace, (Edwin) Wallace 1920- ... CANR-90
Earlier sketches in CA 61-64, CANR-34
Dacey, Norman F(ranklyn) 1908-1994 ... CANR-2
Obituary ... 144
Earlier sketch in CA 5-8R
Dacey, Philip 1939- ... 231
Earlier sketches in CA 37-40R, CANR-14, 32, 64
Autobiographical Essay in ... 231
See also CAAS 17
See also CLC 51
See also CP 7
See also DLB 105
Dach, Simon 1605-1659 ... DLB 164
Dachman, Ken 1958- ... 110
Dachs, David 1922-1980 ... CANR-11
Earlier sketch in CA 69-72
Dacier, Anne Le Fere 1647-1720 ... DLB 313
Dack, Gail Monroe 1901-1976
Obituary ... 111
da Cruz, Daniel, Jr. 1921-1991 ... CANR-19
Earlier sketches in CA 5-8R, CANR-3
da Cruz, Vera 1910-2002 ... 226
Dacy, Douglas Calvin 1927-
Brief entry ... 104
Dacyczyn, Amy 1955- ... 143
Dadamo, Amadeo F(iliberto), Jr. 1929- ... 168
Dadamo, Peter J. ... 169
Dadey, Debbie 1959- ... 205
See also SATA 73, 136
Dadie, Bernard B(inlin) 1916- ... CANR-17
Earlier sketch in CA 25-28R
See also BW 1
See also CWW 2
See also EWL 3
Dadlez, E(va) M(aria) 1956- ... 167
Daebler, Theodor
See Daubler, Theodor
Daedalus
See Bramesco, Norton J.
Daehlin, Reidar A. 1910-1978 ... CAP-1
Obituary ... 162
Earlier sketch in CA 17-18
Daem, Thelma (Mary) Bannerman 1914- ... 5-8R
Daemer, Will
See Miller, (H.) Bill(y) and Wade, Robert (Allison)
Daemmrich, Horst S. 1930- ... CANR-1
Earlier sketch in CA 45-48
Daen, Daniel
See Abma, G(erben) Willem
Daenzer, Bernard John 1916- ... 53-56
da Fonseca, Eduardo Giannetti 1957- ... 141
Daftary, Farhad 1938- ... 136
Dafydd ap Gwilym c. 1320-c. 1380 ... PC 56
Dagan, Avigdor 1912- ... CANR-30
Earlier sketches in CA 33-36R, CANR-13
Dagenais, James J(oseph) 1928- ... 41-44R
Dager, Edward Z(icca) 1921- ... 61-64
Dagerman, Stig (Halvard) 1923-1954 ... 155
Brief entry ... 117
See also DLB 259
See also EWL 3
See also TCLC 17
Dagg, Anne Innis 1933- ... CANR-28
Earlier sketches in CA 69-72, CANR-11
Daggett, Rollin M(allory) 1831-1901 ... 217
See also DLB 79
Daglarca, Fazil Husnu 1914- ... CWW 2
See also EWL 3
Daglish, Eric Fitch 1892-1966 ... 102
Dagonet
See Sims, George R(obert)
D'Agostino, Albert S. 1893-1970 ... IDFW 3, 4
D'Agostino, Angelo 1926- ... 17-20R
D'Agostino, Anthony 1937- ... 128
D'Agostino, Dennis John 1957- ... 106
D'Agostino, Giovanna P. 1914- ... 57-60
D'Agostino, Joseph David 1929- ... 69-72
Dagover, Lil 1897-1980
Obituary ... 105
D'Aguiar, Fred 1960- ... CANR-101
Earlier sketches in CA 148, CANR-83
See also CLC 145
See also CN 7
See also CP 7
See also DLB 157
See also EWL 3
Dahan, Andre 1935- ... 198
Daheim, Mary 1937- ... CANR-140
Earlier sketches in CA 110, CANR-73
Dahinden, Justus 1925- ... 81-84
Dahl, Arlene (Carol) 1928- ... 140
Brief entry ... 105
Dahl, Borghild (Margarethe) 1890-1984 ... CANR-2
Obituary ... 112
Earlier sketch in CA 1-4R
See also SATA 7
See also SATA-Obit 37
Dahl, Curtis 1920-2004 ... CANR-2
Obituary ... 226
Earlier sketch in CA 1-4R
Dahl, Georg 1905- ... 85-88
Dahl, Gordon J. 1932- ... 49-52
Dahl, John 1956- ... 164
Dahl, Linda 1949- ... CANR-92
Earlier sketch in CA 122
Dahl, Murdoch Edgcumbe 1914-1991 ... CAP-1
Earlier sketch in CA 9-10
Dahl, Nils A(lstrup) 1911-2001 ... 65-68
Dahl, Roald 1916-1990 ... CANR-62
Obituary ... 133
Earlier sketches in CA 1-4R, CANR-6, 32, 37
See also AAYA 15
See also BPFB 1
See also BRWS 4
See also BYA 5
See also CLC 1, 6, 18, 79
See also CLR 1, 7, 41
See also CN 1, 2, 3, 4
See also CPW
See also DA3
See also DAB
See also DAC
See also DAM MST, NOV, POP
See also DLB 139, 255
See also HGG
See also JRDA
See also MAICYA 1, 2
See also MTCW 1, 2
See also MTFW 2005
See also RGSF 2
See also SATA 1, 26, 73
See also SATA-Obit 65
See also SSFS 4
See also TEA
See also YAW
Dahl, Robert A(lan) 1915- ... CANR-114
Earlier sketches in CA 65-68, CANR-30, 56, 87
Dahl, Sophie 1977- ... 228
Dahlberg, Arthur O. 1898(?)-1989 ... 124
Obituary ... 129
Dahlberg, Edward 1900-1977 ... CANR-62
Obituary ... 69-72
Earlier sketches in CA 9-12R, CANR-31
See also CLC 1, 7, 14
See also CN 1, 2
See also DLB 48
See also MAL 5
See also MTCW 1
See also RGAL 4
Dahlberg, Edwin T(heodore) 1892-1986 ... CAP-2
Obituary ... 120
Earlier sketch in CA 17-18
Dahlberg, Jane S. 1923- ... 21-24R
Dahlen, Beverly (Jean) 1934- ... 163
See also CP 7
See also CWP
Dahlhaus, Carl 1928-1989
Obituary ... 128
Dahlie, Hallvard 1925- ... 128
Dahlinger, John Cole 1923-1984
Obituary ... 114
Dahlstedt, Marden (Stewart) 1921-1983 ... CANR-1
Obituary ... 163
Earlier sketch in CA 45-48
See also SATA 8
See also SATA-Obit 110
Dahlsten, Donald L. 1933-2003 ... 132
Obituary ... 220
Dahlstrand, Frederick Charles 1945- ... 111
Dahlstrom, Earl C(arl) 1914-1992 ... 17-20R
Obituary ... 139
Dahlstrom, William Grant 1922- ... 192
Dahl-Wolfe, Louise (Emma Augusta) 1895-1989
Obituary ... 130
Dahm, Charles W(illiam) 1937- ... 107
Dahmer, Lionel (Herbert) 1936- ... 152
Dahms, Alan M(artin) 1937- ... 49-52
Dahmus, Joseph Henry 1909- ... CANR-73
Earlier sketch in CA 21-24R
Dahn, Felix 1834-1912 ... DLB 129
Dahood, Mitchell (Joseph) 1922-1982 ... CANR-20
Obituary ... 106
Earlier sketch in CA 25-28R
Dahrendorf, Ralf 1929- ... CANR-28
Earlier sketches in CA 1-4R, CANR-3
Daiches, David 1912-2005 ... CANR-129
Earlier sketches in CA 5-8R, CANR-7, 29, 54
Daigh, Ralph (Foster) 1907-1986
Obituary ... 121
Daigon, Arthur 1928- ... 33-36R
Daigon, Ruth 1923- ... 159
See also CAAS 25
Daiken, Leslie Herbert 1912-1964 ... 1-4R
Dailey, Charles A(lvin) 1923- ... 89-92
Dailey, Janet (Ann) 1944- ... CANR-117
Earlier sketches in CA 89-92, CANR-17, 39, 63
Interview in ... CANR-17
See also BEST 89:3
See also CPW
See also DAM POP
See also MTCW 1
See also RHW
See also TCWW 1, 2
Daily, Ann 1926- ... CANR-45
Daily, Jay E(lwood) 1923-1995 ... 33-36R
Daims, Diva 1925- ... 113
Dain, Catherine
See Garwood, Judith
Dain, Martin J. 1924-2000 ... 13-16R
See also SATA 35
Dain, Norman 1925- ... 9-12R
Dain, Phyllis 1929- ... 69-72
Dainton, (William) Courtney 1920- ... 9-12R
Daintrey, Adrian (Maurice) 1902-1988
Obituary ... 127
Daise, Benjamin 1942- ... 188
Daisey, Mike 1973- ... 220
Daisne, Johan
See Thiery, Herman
See also EWL 3
Daitch, Susan 1954- ... 161
See also CLC 103
Daiute, Robert James 1926- ... 13-16R
Dajani, M(unther) S(uleiman) 1951- ... 132
Dakers, Elaine Kidner 1905-1978 ... CANR-30
Earlier sketch in CA 85-88
See also RHW
Dakin, Arthur Hazard 1905-
Brief entry ... 106
Dakin, D(avid) Martin 1908- ... 73-76
Dakin, Edwin Franden 1898-1976
Obituary ... 104
Dakin, (David) Julian 1939-1971 ... CAP-2
Earlier sketch in CA 25-28
Dakin, Shaun 1966- ... 162
Dakos, Kalli 1950- ... 186
See also SATA 80, 115
Dakron, Ron 1953- ... 238
Dal', Vladimir Ivanovich 1801-1872 ... DLB 198
Dalai Lama XIV
See Gyatso, Tenzin
Dalal, Nergis 1920-
Brief entry ... 116
Daland, Robert T(heodore) 1919-1994 ... 21-24R
Dalbor, John B(ronislaw) 1929- ... 17-20R
Dalby, Liza Crihfield ... 204
Dalchev, Atanas 1904-1978 ... EWL 3
Dal Co, Francesco 1945- ... CANR-85
Earlier sketch in CA 133
Dalcourt, Gerard J. 1927- ... 33-36R
Dale, (Mary) Alzina Stone 1931- ... CANR-38
Earlier sketch in CA 114
Dale, Antony 1912-1993 ... 107
Dale, Arbie Myron, Jr. 1924- ... 122
Dale, Celia (Marjorie) ... CANR-3
Earlier sketch in CA 5-8R
Dale, Colin
See Lawrence, T(homas) E(dward)
See also TCLC 18
Dale, D(ion) M(urray) C(rosbie) 1930- ... 21-24R
Dale, Doris Cruger 1927- ... 116
Dale, Edgar 1900-1985
Obituary ... 117
Dale, Edward Everett 1879-1972 ... CANR-79
Earlier sketches in CA 5-8R, CANR-4
Dale, Edwin L., (Jr.) 1923-1999 ... 69-72
Obituary ... 179
Dale, Ernest 1917-1996 ... 13-16R
Obituary ... 153
Dale, Gary
See Reece, Colleen L.
Dale, George E.
See Asimov, Isaac
Dale, Henry Hallett 1875-1968 ... 157

Dale, Jack
See Holliday, Joseph
Dale, James 1886-1985 ... CAP-2
Obituary ... 116
Earlier sketch in CA 33-36
Dale, John B. 1905-1972 ... 13-16R
Dale, Kathleen 1895-1984
Obituary ... 112
Dale, Kim 1957- ... SATA 123
Dale, Laura A(bbott) 1919-1983
Obituary ... 113
Dale, Magdalene L(arsen) 1904-1981 ... 13-16R
Dale, Margaret J(essy) Miller 1911- ... CANR-19
Earlier sketches in CA 5-8R, CANR-3
See also SATA 39
Dale, Norman
See Denny, Norman (George)
Dale, Paul W(orthen) 1923- ... 25-28R
Dale, Penny 1954- ... 138
See also CWRI 5
See also SATA 70, 151
Dale, Peter (John) 1938- ... CANR-39
Earlier sketches in CA 45-48, CANR-1, 16
See also CP 1, 2, 3, 4, 5, 6, 7
See also DLB 40
Dale, Peter N(icholas) 1950- ... 126
Dale, Reginald R. 1907- ... 21-24R
Dale, Richard 1932- ... 33-36R
Dale, Robert D(ennis) 1940- ... CANR-33
Earlier sketch in CA 113
Dale, Roman
See Czura, R(oman) P(eter)
d'Alelio, Ellen F. 1938- ... 17-20R
Dales, Douglas S. 1907(?)-1985
Obituary ... 114
Dales, Richard C(lark) 1926- ... CANR-49
Earlier sketches in CA 45-48, CANR-24
Daleski, H(illel) M(atthew) 1926- ... 33-36R
D'Alessandro, Robert (Philip) 1942- ... 61-64
Dalet, Roger (Charles) 1927- ... 107
Daley, Adeline 1922(?)-1984
Obituary ... 112
Daley, Arthur (John) 1904-1974 ... CANR-62
Obituary ... 45-48
Earlier sketches in CAP-2, CA 23-24
See also DLB 171
Daley, Bill
See Appleman, John Alan
Daley, Brian 1947-1996 ... CANR-54
Earlier sketch in CA 126
See also SFW 4
Daley, Eliot A. 1936- ... 97-100
Daley, Harry 1901-1971 ... 134
Daley, Janet 1944- ... 125
Daley, Joseph A(ndrew) 1927- ... 53-56
Daley, Robert 1930- ... CANR-139
Earlier sketches in CA 1-4R, CANR-2, 24
Interview in ... CANR-24
Daley, Sharon
See Barovsky, Sharon Daley
Daley, Stephen Dennis 1948- ... 133
Dalfiume, Richard Myron 1936- ... 25-28R
D'Alfonso, Antonio 1953- ... CANR-137
Earlier sketch in CA 129
D'Alfonso, John 1918- ... 29-32R
Dalgleish, James Corteen 1936-
See Kincaid, J. D.
Dalgleish, Oakley Hedley 1910-1963
Obituary ... 115
Dalgliesh, Alice 1893-1979 ... 73-76
Obituary ... 89-92
See also CLR 62
See also CWRI 5
See also MAICYA 1, 2
See also SATA 17
See also SATA-Obit 21
Dalglish, Edward R(ussell) 1913-2001 ... 37-40R
Dali, Salvador (Domenech Felipe Jacinto)
1904-1989 ... 104
Obituary ... 127
See also AAYA 23
Dalkey, Kara (Mia) 1953- ... CANR-103
Earlier sketch in CA 154
See also AAYA 43
See also FANT
See also SATA 132
Dall, Caroline Wells (Healey) 1822-1912 ... 178
See also DLB 1, 235
See also FW
Dallal, Alberto 1936- ... 195
Dallal, Shaw J. 1934- ... 177
D'Allard, Hunter
See Ballard, (Willis) Todhunter
Dallas, Athena Gianakas
See Dallas-Damis, Athena G(ianakas)
Dallas, E. S. 1828-1879 ... DLB 55
Dallas, Gregor 1948- ... 201
Dallas, John
See Duncan, W(illiam) Murdoch
Dallas, Philip 1921- ... 61-64
Dallas, Roland ... 226
Dallas, Ruth
See Mumford, Ruth
See also CP 1, 2, 3, 4, 5, 6, 7
Dallas, Sandra
See Dallas, Sandra
Dallas, Sandra 1939- ... CANR-118
Earlier sketches in CA 17-20R, CANR-10, 62
Dallas-Damis, Athena G(ianakas) 1925- ... 81-84
Dallek, Robert 1934- ... CANR-143
Earlier sketches in CA 25-28R, CANR-17
Dallemagne-Cookson, Elise 1933- ... 191
D'Allenger, Hugh
See Kershaw, John (Hugh D'Allenger)
Dalley, Jan ... 194
Dallimore, Arnold A(rthur) 1911-1998 ... 112
Dallin, Alexander 1924-2000 ... CANR-79
Obituary ... 188
Earlier sketches in CA 1-4R, CANR-5, 19
Dallin, Leon 1918-1993 ... CANR-1
Earlier sketch in CA 1-4R
Dallmann, Martha (Elsie) 1904-1994 ... 1-4R
Dallmayr, Fred R(einhard) 1928- ... CANR-1
Earlier sketch in CA 49-52
Dally, Ann 1926- ... CANR-21
Earlier sketches in CA 5-8R, CANR-3
Dallyn, Mrs. John
See Meynell, Viola (Mary Gertrude)
Dalmas, John
See Jones, John R(obert)
D'Alonzo, C(onstance) Anthony 1912-1972
Obituary ... 37-40R
Daloz, Laurent A. Parks 1940- ... 158
Dalpadado, J(ames) Kingsley (Evold) 1922- ... 112
Dalphin, John R(obert) 1942- ... 118
Dal Poggetto, Newton Francis 1922- ... 61-64
d'Alpuget, Blanche 1944- ... CANR-134
Earlier sketches in CA 114, CANR-68
See also CN 6, 7
Dalrymple, Byron W(illiam)
1910-1994 ... CANR-6
Obituary ... 163
Earlier sketch in CA 57-60
Dalrymple, Douglas J(esse) 1934- ... 73-76
Dalrymple, G. Brent 1937- ... 157
Dalrymple, Gertrude Bradley 1901(?)-1984
Obituary ... 113
Dalrymple, Ian (Murray) 1903-1989 ... 115
Obituary ... 128
Dalrymple, Jean 1910-1998 ... CANR-5
Obituary ... 172
Earlier sketch in CA 5-8R
Dalrymple, Willard 1921- ... 21-24R
Dalrymple, William ... CANR-136
Earlier sketch in CA 172
Dalsass, Diana 1947- ... 106
Dalsimer, Katherine 1944- ... 239
Dalton, Alene
See Chapin, Alene Olsen Dalton
Dalton, Annie 1948- ... CANR-119
Earlier sketch in CA 156
See also CWRI 5
See also FANT
See also SATA 40, 140
Dalton, Claire
See Burns, Alma
Dalton, Clive
See Clark, F(rederick) Stephen
Dalton, (John) David 1944- ... CANR-72
Earlier sketch in CA 97-100
Dalton, Dennis (Gilmore) 1938- ... 115
Dalton, Dorothy 1915-1987 ... 21-24R
Dalton, Elizabeth 1936- ... 85-88
Dalton, Gene W(ray) 1928- ... 25-28R
Dalton, George 1926-1991 ... 127
Obituary ... 135
Brief entry ... 106
Dalton, Harlon L. ... 231
Dalton, (Edward) Hugh (John Neale)
1887-1962 ... 144
Dalton, Kathleen (M.) 1948- ... 222
Dalton, Kit
See Cunningham, Chet
Dalton, Lord
See Dalton, (Edward) Hugh (John Neale)
D'Alton, Louis (Lynch) 1900-1951
Brief entry ... 110
See also DLB 10
Dalton, Pamela
See Johnson, Pamela
Dalton, Priscilla
See Avallone, Michael (Angelo, Jr.)
Dalton, Quinn ... 223
Dalton, Richard 1930- ... 57-60
Dalton, Roque 1935-1975(?) ... 176
See also DLB 283
See also HLCS 1
See also HW 2
See also PC 36
Dalton, Sean
See Chester, Deborah
Dalton, Sheila 1949- ... 170
See also SATA 108
Dalton, Stephen 1937- ... CANR-88
Earlier sketch in CA 85-88
Daltrey, Roger (Harry) 1944- ... 213
Dalven, Rae 1904-1992 ... 33-36R
Obituary ... 139
Daly, Anne 1896- ... CAP-2
Earlier sketch in CA 29-32
Daly, Augustin 1838-1899 ... RGAL 4
Daly, Brenda 1941- ... 162
Daly, Cahal Brendan 1917- ... CANR-52
Earlier sketches in CA 104, CANR-28
Daly, Carroll John 1889-1958 ... 214
Brief entry ... 112
See also CMW 4
See also DLB 226
See also MSW
Daly, Christopher B. 1954- ... 126
Daly, Donald F(remont) ... 69-72
Daly, Edith Iglauer ... CANR-14
Earlier sketch in CA 77-80
Daly, Elizabeth 1878-1967 ... CANR-60
Obituary ... 25-28R
Earlier sketches in CAP-2, CA 23-24
See also CLC 52
See also CMW 4
Daly, Emily Joseph 1913-1999 ... 9-12R
Daly, Faye Kennedy 1936- ... 97-100
Daly, Gay 1951- ... 131
Daly, Herman E. 1938- ... 89-92
Daly, Ita 1945- ... 136
Daly, Jim
See Stratemeyer, Edward L.
Daly, John Jay 1888(?)-1976
Obituary ... 69-72
Daly, Kathleen N(orah) ... 186
Brief entry ... 115
See also SATA 124
See also SATA-Brief 37
Daly, (Arthur) Leo 1920- ... CANR-50
Earlier sketches in CA 105, CANR-25
Daly, Lowrie John 1914-2000 ... 13-16R
Daly, M(artin) W. 1950- ... 175
Daly, Mary 1928- ... CANR-62
Earlier sketches in CA 25-28R, CANR-30
See also CLC 173
See also FW
See also GLL 1
See also MTCW 1
Daly, Mary Tinley 1904(?)-1979 ... 85-88
Daly, Maureen 1921- ... CANR-108
Earlier sketch in CANR-37, 83
See also AAYA 5, 58
See also BYA 6
See also CLC 17
See also CLR 96
See also JRDA
See also MAICYA 1, 2
See also SAAS 1
See also SATA 2, 129
See also WYA
See also YAW
Daly, Nicholas 1946- ... CANR-123
Earlier sketches in CA 111, CANR-36
See also Daly, Niki
See also CLR 41
See also CWRI 5
See also MAICYA 1, 2
See also SATA 37, 76, 114
Daly, Niki
See Daly, Nicholas
See also SAAS 21
Daly, Padraig J(ohn) 1963- ... 191
Daly, Reginald Aldworth 1871-1957 ... 158
Daly, Robert 1943- ... 104
Daly, Robert Welter 1916-1975 ... CANR-71
Obituary ... 103
Earlier sketch in CA 9-12R
Daly, Saralyn R(uth) 1924- ... 57-60
Daly, Sister Mary Virginia 1925- ... 17-20R
Daly, T(homas) A(ugustine) 1871-1948
Brief entry ... 111
See also DLB 11
Dalyell, Tam 1932- ... 142
Dalzel, Peter
See Dalzel-Job, P(atrick)
Dalzel-Job, P(atrick) 1913-2003 ... 13-16R
Obituary ... 221
Dalzell, Alexander 1925- ... 165
Dalzell, Frederick ... 234
Dalzell, Robert (Fenton), Jr. 1937- ... 81-84
Dam, Hari N(arayan) 1921-1989 ... 57-60
Dam, Kenneth W. 1932- ... CANR-12
Earlier sketch in CA 69-72
Dam, Satyabrata 1965- ... 218
Damachi, (Godwin) Ukandi 1942- ... CANR-2
Earlier sketch in CA 45-48
Damas, David (John) 1926- ... CANR-93
Earlier sketch in CA 132
Damas, Leon-Gontran 1912-1978 ... 125
Obituary ... 73-76
See also BW 1
See also CLC 84
See also EWL 3
Damasio, Antonio R. 1944- ... CANR-98
Earlier sketch in CA 151
Damata, Ted 1909(?)-1988
Obituary ... 125
D'Amato, Alex 1919- ... CANR-18
Earlier sketch in CA 81-84
See also SATA 20
D'Amato, Alfonse 1937- ... 152
D'Amato, Anthony A. 1937- ... 29-32R
D'Amato, Barbara 1938- ... CANR-104
Earlier sketches in CA 69-72, CANR-73
See also CMW 4
D'Amato, Brian ... CANR-86
Earlier sketch in CA 141
D'Amato, Janet (Potter) 1925- ... CANR-18
Earlier sketches in CA 49-52, CANR-1
See also SATA 9
Damaz, Paul F. 1917- ... 5-8R
d'Amboise, Christopher 1960- ... 115
d'Amboise, Jacques Joseph 1934- ... 143
Dambrauskas, Joan Arden 1933- ... 104
D'Ambrosio, Charles 1960- ... 153
D'Ambrosio, Charles A. 1932- ... 21-24R
D'Ambrosio, Richard A(nthony) 1927- ... 102
D'Ambrosio, Vinnie-Marie 1928- ... 45-48
Dame, Enid 1943- ... 198
Dame, Lawrence 1898-1981 ... CAP-1
Obituary ... 163
Earlier sketch in CA 11-12
D'Amelio, Dan 1927- ... 33-36R
Dameron, Chip 1947- ... 207
Dameron, J(ohn) Lasley 1925- ... 53-56
Damerow, Gail (Jane) 1944- ... 150
See also SATA 83
Damerst, William A. 1923- ... 17-20R
Dames, Rob(ert L.) 1944- ... 133
Damiani, Bruno Mario 1942- ... 57-60
D'Amico, Jack (P.) 1939- ... 208
D'Amico, Jack (P.) 1939- ... 209
D'Amico, John Francis 1947(?)-1987
Obituary ... 124
Damis, John 1940- ... 118
Damm, John S. 1926- ... 37-40R
Damm, Kateri
See Akiwenzie-Dam, Kateri (Lorene)
Damman, Gregory C. ... 171
D'Ammassa, Don(ald Eugene) 1946- ... HGG
Damocles
See Benedetti, Mario
Damon, Gene
See Grier, Barbara G(ene Damon)
See also GLL 1
Damon, Matt(hew Paige) 1970- ... CANR-128
Earlier sketch in CA 168
Damon, S(amuel) Foster 1893-1971 ... 101
See also DLB 45
Damon, Virgil Green 1895-1972 ... CAP-1
Obituary ... 37-40R
Earlier sketch in CA 9-10
Damon, William 1944- ... 147
Damor, Hakji
See Lesser, R(oger) H(arold)
D'Amore, Arcangelo R. T. 1920-1986
Obituary ... 118
Damore, Leo J. 1929-1995 ... CANR-35
Obituary ... 149
Earlier sketch in CA 81-84
See also BEST 89:2
See also CCA 1
Damousi, Joy ... 192
Damrell, Liz 1956- ... SATA 77
Damron, Carla 1957- ... 198
Damrosch, Helen
See Tee-Van, Helen Damrosch
Damrosch, Leopold, Jr. 1941- ... 45-48
Dams, Jeanne M(artin) 1941- ... CANR-136
Earlier sketches in CA 155, CANR-73
Damsker, Matt(hew Harry) 1951- ... 108
Damtoft, Walter A(tkinson) 1922- ... 57-60
Dan, Barbara (Griffin) 1934- ... 220
Dan, John 1926- ... 147
Dana, Amber
See Paine, Lauran (Bosworth)
Dana, Barbara 1940- ... CANR-8
Earlier sketch in CA 17-20R
See also SATA 22
Dana, Charles Anderson 1819-1897 ... DLB 3, 23, 250
Dana, E. H.
See Hamel Peifer, Kathleen
Dana, Richard
See Paine, Lauran (Bosworth)
Dana, Richard H(enry) 1927- ... CANR-15
Earlier sketch in CA 85-88
Dana, Richard Henry, Jr. 1815-1882 ... DLB 1, 183, 235
See also LAIT 2
See also RGAL 4
See also SATA 26
Dana, Robert (Patrick) 1929- ... 33-36R
See also CP 1, 2, 3, 4, 5, 6, 7
Dana, Rose
See Ross, W(illiam) E(dward) D(aniel)
Danachair, Caoimhin O
See Danaher, Kevin
Danagher, Edward F. 1919-2001 ... 9-12R
Danaher, Kevin 1913-2002 ... 33-36R
See also SATA 22
Danakas, John 1963- ... 159
See also SATA 94
Danan, Alexis 1889(?)-1979
Obituary ... 89-92
Danby, Hope (Smedley) 1899- ... CAP-1
Earlier sketch in CA 13-14
Danby, John B(lench) 1905-1983
Obituary ... 109
Danby, Mary (Heather) 1941- ... CANR-39
Danby, Miles William 1925- ... 13-16R
Dance, Daryl Cumber 1938- ... CANR-88
Earlier sketch in CA 131
See also BW 2
Dance, E(dward) H(erbert) 1894- ... 37-40R
Dance, F(rancis) E(sburn) X(avier)
1929- ... CANR-16
Earlier sketches in CA 1-4R, CANR-1
Dance, Frank E. X.
See Dance, F(rancis) E(sburn) X(avier)
Dance, Helen Oakley 1913-2001 ... 140
Obituary ... 197
Dance, Jim 1924(?)-1983
Obituary ... 110
Dance, S(tanley) Peter 1932- ... CANR-13
Earlier sketch in CA 69-72
Dance, Stanley (Frank) 1910-1999 ... CANR-8
Obituary ... 177
Earlier sketch in CA 17-20R
Dancer, J. B.
See Harvey, John (Barton) and Wells, Angus
Dancer, J. B.
See Wells, Angus
Dancer, James G.
See Black, Michael A.
Danchin, Antoine 1944- ... 218
Danco, Katharine L(eck) 1929- ... 112
Danco, Katy
See Danco, Katharine L(eck)
Danco, Leon A(ntoine) 1923- ... 112
Dancocks, Daniel G. 1950- ... 120
D'Ancona, Matthew 1968- ... CANR-107
Earlier sketch in CA 154
D'Ancona, Mirella Levi 1919- ... CANR-6
Earlier sketch in CA 53-56
Dancourt, Florent Carton
1661-1725 ... GFL Beginnings to 1789
Dancy, John Christopher 1920- ... 107
Dandamaev, M(uhammad) A. 1928- ... 196
Dandrea, Don(ald E.) 1936- ... 120
D'Andrea, Kate
See Steiner, Barbara A(nnette)

Cumulative Index 137 **Danziger**

D'Andrea, Paul 1939- 120
Dandridge, Ray G.
  See Dandridge, Raymond Garfield
Dandridge, Raymond Garfield 1882-1930 . 125
  See also BW 1
  See also DLB 51
Dandridge, Rita B(ernice) 1940- 141
  See also BW 2
Dandy, James Edgar 1903-1976
  Obituary 104
Dane, Carl
  See Adams, F(rank) Ramsay
Dane, Clemence
  See Ashton, Winifred
  See also DLB 10, 197
  See also RGEL 2
Dane, Les(lie A.) 1925-1990 89-92
Dane, Mark
  See Avallone, Michael (Angelo, Jr.)
Dane, Mary
  See Morland, Nigel
Dane, Nathan II 1916-1980 108
  Obituary 97-100
Dane, Zel
  See Timms, E(dward) V(ivian)
Daneff, Stephen Constantine 1931- 106
Daneke, Gregory A(llen) 1950- 112
Danelski, David J. 1930- 13-16R
Danenberg, Leigh 1893-1976
  Obituary 69-72
Danesh, Abol Hassan 1952- 140
Daneshvar, Simin 1921- 206
  See also Danishvar, Simin
  See also CWW 2
Danford, Howard G(orby) 1904- CAP-1
  Earlier sketch in CA 11-12
Danford, John W. 1947- 220
Danforth, Art(hur Louis) 1913(?)-1987
  Obituary 122
Danforth, John 1660-1730 .... DLB 24
Danforth, John C(laggett) 1936- 148
Danforth, Loring M(andell) 1949- 111
Danforth, Samuel I 1626-1674 .... DLB 24
Danforth, Samuel II 1666-1727 .... DLB 24
Dangaard, Colin (Edward) 1942- 85-88
Dangarembga, Tsitsi 1959- 163
  See also BW 3
  See also WLIT 2
D'angelo, Edward 1932- 37-40R
D'Angelo, Frank J(oseph) 1928- 120
D'Angelo, Lou
  See D'Angelo, Luciano
D'Angelo, Luciano 1932- 33-36R
Dangerfield, Balfour
  See McCloskey, (John) Robert
Dangerfield, Clint
  See Norwood, Victor G(eorge) C(harles)
Dangerfield, George (Bubb)
  1904-1986 .... CANR-81
  Obituary 121
  Earlier sketch in CA 9-12R
Dangerfield, Harlan
  See Padgett, Ron
Dangerfield, Rodney 1921-2004 102
  Obituary 232
Dangor, Achmat 1948- 189
Danhof, Clarence H(enry) 1911- 37-40R
Dani, Ahmad Hasan 1920- 13-16R
Daniel, Alan 1939- .... SATA 76
  See also SATA-Brief 53
Daniel, Anita 1893(?)-1978
  Obituary 77-80
  See also SATA 23
  See also SATA-Obit 24
Daniel, Anne
  See Steiner, Barbara A(nnette)
Daniel, Becky 1947- .... SATA 56
Daniel, Charles 1933- 114
Daniel, Cletus E(dward) 1943- 107
Daniel, (Elbert) Clifton, (Jr.) 1912-2000 142
  Obituary 188
  Brief entry 113
Daniel, Colin
  See Windsor, Patricia
Daniel, Daniel 1890(?)-1981
  Obituary 104
Daniel, Elna Worrell
  See Stone, Elna
Daniel, Emmett Randolph 1935- 102
Daniel, Errol Valentine 111
Daniel, George Bernard, Jr. 1927- 13-16R
Daniel, Glenda 1943- 111
Daniel, Glyn (Edmund) 1914-1986 .. CANR-83
  Obituary 121
  Earlier sketches in CA 57-60, CANR-13, 30
Daniel, Hawthorne 1890- 5-8R
  See also SATA 8
Daniel', Iulii
  See Daniel, Yuli (Markovich)
  See also DLB 302
Daniel, James 1916- 69-72
Daniel, Jerry C(layton) 1937- 33-36R
Daniel, John .... ANW
Daniel, John M. 1825-1865 .... DLB 43
Daniel, John M. 1941- 209
Daniel, Julie Goldsmith 1949- CANR-14
  Earlier sketch in CA 77-80
Daniel, Lee
  See Reid, Daniel P. (Jr.)
Daniel, (Donna) Lee 1944- .... SATA 76
Daniel, Lorne (MacLeod Lyons) 1953- 118
Daniel, Malcolm R. 1956- 150
Daniel, Mark 1954- 133
Daniel, Norman (Alexander)
  1919-1992 .... CANR-6
  Earlier sketch in CA 57-60
Daniel, Pete 1938- CANR-97
  Earlier sketches in CA 37-40R, CANR-14
Daniel, Price, Jr. 1941-1981
  Obituary 103
Daniel, Ralph T(homas) 1921-1985 53-56
Daniel, Rebecca
  See Daniel, Becky
Daniel, Robert L(eslie) 1923- 33-36R
Daniel, Robert W(oodham) 1915- 25-28R
Daniel, Samuel 1562(?)-1619 .... DLB 62
  See also RGEL 2
Daniel, Stephen H(artley) 1950- 119
Daniel, Tony 1963- CANR-118
  Earlier sketch in CA 141
Daniel, Urcel 1908(?)-1984
  Obituary 113
Daniel, Walter C(larence) 1922-1995 110
Daniel, Wayne W. 1929- 135
Daniel, Yuli (Markovich)
  1925-1988 .... CANR-75
  Obituary 127
  Earlier sketch in CA 116
  See also Daniel', Iulii
Daniele, Graciela 1939- 215
Daniele, Joseph William 1927- 89-92
Danielewski, Mark Z. 194
Daniell, Albert Scott 1906-1965 .... CANR-3
  Earlier sketch in CA 5-8R
  See also CWRI 5
Daniell, David Scott
  See Daniell, Albert Scott
Daniell, Jere Rogers 1932- CANR-11
  Earlier sketch in CA 29-32R
Daniell, Rosemary 1935- CANR-44
  Earlier sketch in CA 118
Danielle, Maria 1945- 114
Danielli, James Frederic 1911-1984
  Obituary 113
Daniells, Lorna M(cLean) 1918- CANR-18
  Earlier sketch in CA 89-92
Daniells, Roy 1902-1979 57-60
  See also CCA 1
  See also CP 1, 2
  See also DLB 68
Danielou, Alain 1907-1994 .... CANR-112
  Earlier sketches in CA 73-76, CANR-14, 31, 57
Danielou, Jean 1905-1974 .... CANR-82
  Obituary 49-52
  Earlier sketches in CAP-2, CA 23-24
Daniel-Rops, Henri
  See Petiot, Henri Jules Charles
Daniels, Anna Kleegman 1893-1970
  Obituary 29-32R
Daniels, Anthony 1949- 170
Daniels, Arlene Kaplan 1930- CANR-27
  Earlier sketches in CA 29-32R, CANR-12
Daniels, Brett
  See Adler, Renata
Daniels, Bruce C(olin) 1943- CANR-48
  Earlier sketch in CA 122
Daniels, Charlie 1936- 138
Daniels, David 1933- 53-56
Daniels, Derick (January) 1926(?)-2005 193
  Obituary 236
  Brief entry 112
Daniels, Dewey
  See McKimmey, James
Daniels, Doris Groshen 1931- 131
Daniels, Dorothy 1915- CANR-15
  Earlier sketch in CA 89-92
Daniels, Douglas Henry 1943- CANR-117
  Earlier sketch in CA 125
Daniels, Draper 1913-1983 .... CANR-76
  Obituary 109
  Earlier sketch in CA 53-56
Daniels, Elizabeth Adams 1920- 37-40R
Daniels, Farrington 1889-1972 .... 5-8R
  Obituary 37-40R
Daniels, Frank Arthur 1904-1986
  Obituary 121
Daniels, Frank James 1900(?)-1983
  Obituary 110
Daniels, George H. 1935- CANR-10
  Earlier sketch in CA 25-28R
Daniels, George M(orris) 1927- 29-32R
Daniels, Guy 1919-1989 .... CANR-81
  Obituary 128
  Earlier sketch in CA 21-24R
  See also SATA 11
  See also SATA-Obit 62
Daniels, Harold R(obert) 1919- 17-20R
Daniels, James R(aymond) 1956- CANR-91
  Earlier sketches in CA 121, CANR-47
  See also Daniels, Jim
Daniels, Jeff 1955- 239
Daniels, Jim
  See Daniels, James R(aymond)
  See also DLB 120
Daniels, John Clifford 1915- 13-16R
Daniels, John S.
  See Overholser, Wayne D.
Daniels, Jonathan (Worth)
  1902-1981 .... CANR-29
  Obituary 105
  Earlier sketch in CA 49-52
  See also DLB 127
Daniels, Josephus 1862-1948 193
  Brief entry 122
  See also DLB 29
Daniels, Karen 1957- 211
Daniels, Kate 1953- 124
Daniels, Keith Allen 1956- 175
Daniels, Laura
  See Myers, Amy
Daniels, Les(lie Noel III) 1943- CANR-74
  Earlier sketches in CA 65-68, CANR-9, 24, 49
  See also HGG
Daniels, Lucy
  See Oldfield, Jenny
Daniels, Mark R. 1952- 167
Daniels, Mary 1937- 93-96
Daniels, Max
  See Gellis, Roberta (Leah Jacobs)
Daniels, Norman
  See Lee, Elsie
Daniels, Norman -1995 .... CANR-15
  Earlier sketch in CA 89-92
Daniels, Norman 1942- CANR-22
  Earlier sketch in CA 106
Daniels, Olga
  See Sinclair, Olga
Daniels, Pamela 1937- 101
Daniels, Patricia 1955- .... SATA 93
Daniels, Philip
  See Phillips, D(ennis) J(ohn Andrew)
Daniels, R(obertson) Balfour 1900-1986 . 49-52
Daniels, Randy (Allan) 1949- 81-84
Daniels, Rebecca 1949- 164
Daniels, Robert V(incent) 1926- CANR-70
  Earlier sketches in CA 1-4R, CANR-2
Daniels, Roger 1927- CANR-47
  Earlier sketches in CA 5-8R, CANR-8, 23
Daniels, Sally 1931- 1-4R
Daniels, Sarah 1956(?)- 133
  See also CBD
  See also CD 5, 6
  See also CWD
  See also DLB 245
Daniels, Shouri
  See Ramanujan, Molly
Daniels, Steven Lloyd 1945-1973 .... 33-36R
Daniels, Velma Seawell 1931- 108
Daniels, William H. 1895-1970 .... IDFW 3, 4
Daniels, Zoe
  See Laux, Constance
Danielson, Elena S(chafer) 1947- 116
Danielson, J. D.
  See James, M. R.
Danielson, Michael N(ils) 1934- 33-36R
Danielson, Wayne Allen 1929- 77-80
Danielsson, Bengt (Emmerik) 1921- .. CANR-23
  Earlier sketch in CA 107
Daniere, Andre L(ucien) 1926- 9-12R
D'Anieri, Paul J. D. 1965- 199
Danilevsky, Grigorii Petrovich
  1829-1890 .... DLB 238
Daniloff, Nicholas 1934- 85-88
Danilov, Victor J(oseph) 1924- CANR-45
  Earlier sketches in CA 13-16R, CANR-6, 21
Daninos, Pierre 1913-2005 .... CANR-73
  Obituary 235
  Earlier sketches in CA 77-80, CANR-15
Danish, Barbara 1948- 57-60
Danishvar, Simin
  See Daneshvar, Simin
  See also WLIT 6
Dank, Gloria Rand 1955- CANR-74
  Earlier sketch in CA 114
  See also SATA 56
  See also SATA-Brief 46
Dank, Leonard D(ewey) 1929- .... SATA 44
Dank, Milton 1920- CANR-28
  Earlier sketches in CA 69-72, CANR-11
  See also SATA 31
Danker, Frederick William 1920- CANR-5
  Earlier sketch in CA 13-16R
Danker, W(illiam) John 1914-2001 .... 13-16R
  Obituary 197
Dankleff, Richard E(lden) 1925- 114
Dankner, Laura 142
Danko, William D(avid) 1952- CANR-104
  Earlier sketch in CA 162
Danky, James P(hilip) 1947- CANR-124
  Earlier sketches in CA 69-72, CANR-12
Danley, John R(obert) 1948- 152
Danly, Robert Lyons 1947- 108
Dann, Colin (Michael) 1943- 108
Dann, Jack 1945- CANR-97
  Earlier sketches in CA 49-52, CANR-2, 30
  See also CAAS 20
  See also SFW 4
Dann, John C(hristie) 1944- 126
Dann, John R. 205
Dann, Kevin T. 1956- 218
Dann, Max 1955- 118
  See also SATA 62
Dann, Patty 1953- CANR-138
  Earlier sketch in CA 174
Dann, Uriel 1922- 25-28R
Dannay, Frederic 1905-1982 .... CANR-39
  Obituary 107
  Earlier sketches in CA 1-4R, CANR-1
  See also Queen, Ellery
  See also CLC 11
  See also CMW 4
  See also DAM POP
  See also DLB 137
  See also MTCW 1
Danneberg, Julie 1958- 237
Dannelley, Paul (Edward, Jr.) 1919-1991 122
Dannemiller, Lawrence 1925- 1-4R
Dannen, Fredric 1955- 140
Dannenfeldt, Karl H(enry) 1916- 25-28R
Danner, Margaret (Essie) 1915-1984 ..... 29-32R
  See also BW 1
  See also CP 1
  See also DLB 41
Danner, Mark (David) 1958- 140
Dannett, Sylvia G. L. 1909-1995 .... CANR-4
  Earlier sketch in CA 1-4R
D'Annunzio, Gabriele 1863-1938 155
  Brief entry 104
  See also EW 8
  See also EWL 3
  See also RGWL 2, 3
  See also TCLC 6, 40
  See also TWA
  See also WLIT 7
Dano, Linda 1943- 167
Danoff, I. Michael 1940- 97-100
Danois, N. le
  See Gourmont, Remy(-Marie-Charles) de
Danopoulos, Constantine P. 1948- 175
Danow, David K. 1944- 154
Danowski, T(haddeus) S(tanley)
  1914-1987 .... CANR-75
  Obituary 123
  Earlier sketch in CA 9-12R
Danquah, Meri Nana-Ama 1967- 202
Danska, Herbert 1928- 29-32R
Danson, Lawrence Neil 1942- 85-88
Dante 1265-1321
  See Alighieri, Dante
  See also DA
  See also DA3
  See also DAB
  See also DAC
  See also DAM MST, POET
  See also EFS 1
  See also EW 1
  See also LAIT 1
  See also PC 21
  See also RGWL 2, 3
  See also TWA
  See also WLCS
  See also WP
Dante, Joe 1946- 206
Dante, Nicholas 1941-1991 201
Danter, John fl. 1586-1599 .... DLB 170
d'Antibes, Germain
  See Simenon, Georges (Jacques Christian)
Danticat, Edwidge 1969- 192
  Earlier sketches in CA 152, CANR-73, 129
  Autobiographical Essay in 192
  See also AAYA 29
  See also CLC 94, 139
  See also CN 7
  See also DNFS 1
  See also EXPS
  See also LATS 1:2
  See also MTCW 2
  See also MTFW 2005
  See also SSFS 1
  See also YAW
Dantin, Louis 1865-1945
  See Seers, Eugene
  See also DLB 92
Dantino, Bertuccio
  See Williams, Edward Christopher
Danto, Arthur C(oleman) 1924- CANR-88
  Earlier sketches in CA 17-20R, CANR-56
  See also DLB 279
Danto, Bruce L. 1927- CANR-7
  Earlier sketch in CA 53-56
Danton, J(oseph) Periam
  1908-2002 .... CANR-71
  Obituary 212
  Earlier sketch in CA 9-12R
Danton, Rebecca
  See Roberts, Janet Louise
D'Antonio, Michael 1955- CANR-93
  Earlier sketch in CA 140
D'Antonio, William V. 1926- 222
Dantz, William R.
  See Philbrick, (W.) Rodman
Dantzer, Robert 1944- 149
Dantzic, Cynthia Maris 1933- 101
Dantzig, George Bernard 1914-2005 155
  Obituary 239
  Brief entry 106
Danvers, Dennis 1947- .... CLC 70
Danvers, Jack
  See Caseleyr, Cam(ille Auguste Marie)
Danvers, Pete
  See Henderson, James Maddock
  See also TCWW 2
Danz, Harold P. 1929- 169
Danzell, George
  See Bond, Nelson S(lade)
Danzig, Allan (Peter) 1931- 45-48
Danzig, Allison 1898-1987 .... CANR-62
  Obituary 121
  Earlier sketch in CA 37-40R
  See also DLB 171
Danzig, Fred P(aul) 1925- 65-68
Danziger, Charles 1962- 145
Danziger, Daniel (Guggenheim) 1953- 232
Danziger, Danny
  See Danziger, Daniel (Guggenheim)
Danziger, Edmund J(efferson), Jr. 1938- 102
Danziger, Kurt 1926- 41-44R
Danziger, Marlies K(allmann) 1926- . CANR-18
  Earlier sketch in CA 25-28R
Danziger, Nick 1958- 129

Danziger, Paula 1944-2004 ... CANR-132
Obituary ... 229
Brief entry ... 112
Earlier sketches in CA 115, CANR-37
See also AAYA 4, 36
See also BYA 6, 7, 14
See also CLC 21
See also CLR 20
See also JRDA
See also MAICYA 1, 2
See also MTFW 2005
See also SATA 36, 63, 102, 149
See also SATA-Brief 30
See also SATA-Obit 155
See also WYA
See also YAW
Danziger, Sheldon H. 1948- ... CANR-43
Earlier sketch in CA 119
Daoud, Hassan ... 209
Daoud, Hazim S. 1930-1976 ... 122
Daoudi, M(ohammed) S(uleiman) 1946- ... 132
Daoust, Jean-Paul 1946- ... CANR-138
Earlier sketch in CA 164
Dapper, Gloria 1922-1996 ... 17-20R
Dapping, William Osborne 1880-1969
Obituary ... 115
D'Aprix, Roger M. 1932- ... 33-36R
D'Aquili, Eugene G(uy) 1940-1998 ... 201
Darabont, Frank 1959- ... 199
See also AAYA 46
Darack, Arthur J. 1918- ... CANR-37
Earlier sketch in CA 115
Darbelnet, Jean (Louis) 1904-1990 ... CANR-10
Earlier sketch in CA 25-28R
Darby, Ann ... 233
Darby, Catherine
See Peters, Maureen
Darby, Edwin (Wheeler) 1922-2003 ... 125
Obituary ... 219
Darby, Gene Kegley
See Darby, Jean (Kegley)
Darby, Henry Clifford 1909-1992 ... CANR-81
Earlier sketch in CA 5-8R
Darby, J. N.
See Govan, (Mary) Christine Noble
Darby, Jean (Kegley) 1921- ... CANR-39
See also SATA 68
Darby, John 1940- ... 105
Darby, Mary Ann 1954- ... 225
Darby, Michael 1944- ... CANR-38
Earlier sketch in CA 116
Darby, Patricia (Paulsen) ... 73-76
See also SATA 14
Darby, Ray(mond) 1912-1982 ... 17-20R
See also SATA 7
Darby, William D(uane) 1942- ... 141
D'Arc, Jean
See Wood, Joanna E.
D'Arca-Santa, F. M.
See Lucini, Gian Pietro
d'Arch Smith, Timothy 1936- ... 13-16R
Darcy, Clare ... 102
See also RHW
D'Arcy, Ella c. 1857-1937 ... DLB 135
Darcy, Emma 1940- ... RHW
D'Arcy, G(eorge) Minot 1930- ... 9-12R
Darcy, Jean
See Lepley, Jean Elizabeth
D'Arcy, Jean (Marie) 1913-1983
Obituary ... 109
Darcy, Jenna
See Chastain, Sandra
D'Arcy, Margaretta (Ruth) 1934- ... CANR-58
Earlier sketches in CA 104, CANR-31
See also CBD
See also CWD
D'Arcy, Martin C(yril) 1888-1976 ... CANR-81
Obituary ... 69-72
Earlier sketches in CA 5-8R, CANR-3
D'Arcy, Pamela
See Roby, Mary Linn
D'Arcy, Paul F(rancis) 1921- ... 17-20R
d'Arcy, Willard
See Cox, William R(obert)
Darden, Christopher 1956- ... CANR-102
Earlier sketch in CA 155
See also BW 3
Darden, Lloyd (Nestor) 1931-
Brief entry ... 113
Darden, Norma Jean ... 114
Darden, Robert 1954- ... 152
Darden, William R(aymond) 1936- ... 77-80
Dardess, John W(olfe) 1937- ... 45-48
Dardig, Jill C(arolyn) 1948- ... 69-72
Dardis, Tom 1926-2001 ... CANR-53
Obituary ... 200
Earlier sketches in CA 65-68, CANR-9
Dare, Evelyn
See Everett-Green, Evelyn
Dare, Geena
See McNicoll, Sylvia (Marilyn)
Dare, M(arcus) P(aul) 1902-1962 ... HGG
Dareff, Hal 1920- ... 65-68
Darga, Bert 1931- ... 110
Dargan, Olive (Tilford) 1869-1968
Obituary ... 111
Dargel, Nancy ... 152
Dargo, George 1935- ... 115
d'Argyre, Gilles
See Klein, Gerard
Darian, Shea 1959- ... 163
See also SATA 97
Dariaux, Genevieve Antoine
See Antoine-Dariaux, Genevieve
Darien, Peter
See Bassett, William B. K.
Daring, Mason 1949- ... IDFW 4
Daringer, Helen Fern 1892-1986 ... CANR-81
Earlier sketches in CAP-2, CA 17-18
See also SATA 1
Dario, Ruben 1867-1916 ... CANR-81
Earlier sketch in CA 131
See also DAM MULT
See also DLB 290
See also EWL 3
See also HLC 1
See also HW 1, 2
See also LAW
See also MTCW 1, 2
See also MTFW 2005
See also PC 15
See also RGWL 2, 3
See also TCLC 4
Darion, Joe
See Darion, Joseph
Darion, Joseph 1917-2001 ... 185
Obituary ... 198
Brief entry ... 113
Dark, Alice Elliott ... 190
Dark, Alvin Ralph 1922- ... 105
Dark, Eleanor 1901-1985 ... 202
See also DLB 260
See also RHW
Dark, Harris Edward 1922- ... 57-60
Dark, Johnny
See Norwood, Victor G(eorge) C(harles)
Dark, Larry 1959- ... CANR-107
Earlier sketch in CA 136
Dark, Philip J(ohn) C(rosskey)
1918- ... CANR-18
Earlier sketches in CA 49-52, CANR-2
Darke, James
See James, Laurence
Darke, Marjorie 1929- ... CANR-34
Earlier sketches in CA 81-84, CANR-15
See also CWRI 5
See also SATA 16, 87
Darke, Nick 1948- ... 172
See also CBD
See also CD 5, 6
See also DLB 233
Darkins, Adam William ... 214
Darley, F(elix) O(ctavius) C(arr)
1822-1888 ... DLB 188
See also SATA 35
Darley, George 1795-1846 ... DLB 96
See also RGEL 2
Darley, Gillian ... 218
Darley, John M(cConnon) 1938- ... 93-96
Darling
See Dixie, Florence Douglas
Darling, Arthur Burr 1892-1971 ... 5-8R
Obituary ... 33-36R
Darling, David J. 1953- ... CANR-135
Earlier sketch in CA 138
See also SATA 60
See also SATA-Brief 44
Darling, Diana 1947- ... 142
Darling, Edward 1907-1974 ... CANR-3
Obituary ... 53-56
Earlier sketch in CA 49-52
Darling, Frank Clayton 1925- ... 17-20R
Darling, Frank Fraser
See Fraser Darling, Frank
Darling, Jay Norwood 1876-1962
Obituary ... 93-96
Darling, John R(othburn) 1937- ... 93-96
Darling, Julia 1956-2005 ... 171
Obituary ... 238
Darling, Kathy
See Darling, Mary Kathleen
Darling, Lois (MacIntyre)
1917-1989 ... CANR-38
Obituary ... 130
Earlier sketches in CA 5-8R, CANR-3
See also MAICYA 1, 2
See also SATA 3
See also SATA-Obit 64
Darling, Louis, (Jr.) 1916-1970 ... CANR-38
Obituary ... 89-92
Earlier sketches in CA 5-8R, CANR-3
See also MAICYA 1, 2
See also SATA 3
See also SATA-Obit 23
Darling, Mary Kathleen 1943- ... CANR-4
Earlier sketch in CA 53-56
See also SATA 9, 79, 124
Darling, Richard L(ewis) 1925-2003 ... 21-24R
Obituary ... 213
Darling, Sandra
See Day, Alexandra
Darling, Sharon (Sandling) 1943- ... 128
Darling, T. H.
See Harris, Thomas Walter
Darlington, Alice B(enning) 1906-1973 . CAP-2
Obituary ... 41-44R
Earlier sketch in CA 25-28
Darlington, C(yril) D(ean)
1903-1981 ... CANR-10
Obituary ... 108
Earlier sketch in CA 9-12R
Darlington, Charles F. 1904-1986 ... CANR-76
Obituary ... 119
Earlier sketches in CAP-2, CA 25-28
Darlington, David 1951- ... CANR-61
Earlier sketch in CA 127
Darlington, Joy 1947- ... 89-92
Darlington, Ralph 1954- ... 203
Darlington, Tenaya R. 1971- ... 191
Darlington, William Aubrey (Cecil)
1890-1979 ... CANR-58
Earlier sketches in CAP-1, CA 13-16
See also FANT
Darlow, Michael (George) 1934- ... CANR-102
Earlier sketch in CA 104
Darlton, Clark
See Ernsting, Walter
Darmesteter, Madame James
See Robinson, A(gnes) Mary F(rances)
Darmesteter, Mary
See Robinson, A(gnes) Mary F(rances)
Darmon, Pierre 1939- ... 227
Darmstadter, Joel 1928- ... 121
Darnay, Arsen (Julius) 1936- ... 111
Darnell, K(athryn) L(ynne) 1955- ... SATA 150
Darnley, John
See Drinkwater, John
Darnton, John (Townsend) 1941- ... CANR-87
Brief entry ... 119
Earlier sketches in CA 126, CANR-53
Interview in ... CA-126
Darnton, Robert (Choate) 1939- ... CANR-131
Brief entry ... 113
Earlier sketch in CA 116
Interview in ... CA-116
Darr, Ann 1920- ... CANR-7
Earlier sketch in CA 57-60
Darracott, Joseph C(orbould) 1934- ... 106
Darragh, Tina 1950- ... CWP
Darrah, William C(ulp) 1909-1989 ... 57-60
Darrell, R(obert) D(onaldson) 1903-1988
Obituary ... 125
Darrid, Diana Douglas 1923- ... 181
Darrieussecq, Marie 1970(?)- ... 171
Darroch, James L. 1951- ... 148
Darroch, Maurice A. 1903-1968(?) ... CAP-2
Earlier sketch in CA 19-20
Darroch, Sandra Jobson 1942- ... 89-92
Darroll, Sally
See Odgers, Sally Farrell
Darrow, Clarence (Seward) 1857-1938 ... 164
See also DLB 303
See also TCLC 81
Darrow, Ralph C(arroll) 1918- ... 61-64
Darrow, Richard W(illiam)
1915-1976 ... CANR-75
Obituary ... 120
Earlier sketch in CA 21-24R
Darrow, Siobhan 1960- ... 220
Darrow, Whitney, (Jr.) 1909-1999 ... CANR-71
Obituary ... 183
Earlier sketches in CA 61-64, CANR-14
See also SATA 13
See also SATA-Obit 115
Dart, Gregory ... 194
Dart, Iris Rainer ... CANR-144
Earlier sketch in CA 149
Dart, John 1936- ... 65-68
Dart, Raymond A(rthur) 1893-1988 .. CANR-75
Obituary ... 127
Earlier sketches in CAP-1, CA 13-14
Darton, Eric 1950- ... CANR-120
Earlier sketch in CA 160
Darton, G(erald) C(hristopher) 1913(?)-1987
Obituary ... 122
Daruwalla, Keki N(asserwanji)
1937- ... CANR-141
Earlier sketch in CA 153
See also CP 1, 7
Darvas, Miriam 1926- ... 200
Darvas, Nicolas 1920- ... 61-64
Darveaux, Terry A(lan) 1943- ... 65-68
Darvi, Andrea
See Plate, Andrea
Darvill, Fred T(homas), Jr. 1927- ... CANR-6
Earlier sketch in CA 57-60
Darvill, Timothy (C.) 1957- ... 127
Darville, Helen (Fiona) 1971- ... 168
Darwall, Stephen L(eicester) 1946- ... 113
Darweesh, Mahmoud
See Darwish, Mahmoud
Darwin, Charles 1809-1882 ... BRWS 7
See also DLB 57, 166
See also LATS 1:1
See also RGEL 2
See also TEA
See also WLIT 4
Darwin, Erasmus 1731-1802 ... DLB 93
See also RGEL 2
Darwin, Len
See Darwin, Leonard
Darwin, Leonard 1916- ... SATA 24
Darwin, M. B.
See McDavid, Raven I(oor), Jr.
Darwish, Adel 1945- ... 135
Darwish, Mahmoud 1942- ... CANR-133
Earlier sketch in CA 164
See also Darwish, Mahmud
See also MTCW 2
See also MTFW 2005
Darwish, Mahmud
See Darwish, Mahmoud
See also CWW 2
See also EWL 3
Darwish, Mustafa 1928- ... 209
Dary, David A. 1934- ... CANR-104
Earlier sketches in CA 29-32R, CANR-13, 29, 54
Daryush, Elizabeth 1887-1977 ... CANR-81
Earlier sketches in CA 49-52, CANR-3
See also CLC 6, 19
See also DLB 20
Das, Deb Kumar 1935- ... 102
See also CP 1, 2
Das, Durga 1900-1974 ... CAP-2
Obituary ... 49-52
Earlier sketch in CA 29-32
Das, G. K. 1934- ... 128
Das, Gurcharan 1943- ... CANR-103
Earlier sketch in CA 33-36R
Das, Jagannath Prasad 1931- ... CANR-6
Earlier sketch in CA 57-60
Das, Jibanananda 1899-1954 ... EWL 3
Das, Kamala 1934- ... CANR-59
Earlier sketches in CA 101, CANR-27
See also CLC 191
See also CP 1, 2, 3, 4, 5, 6, 7
See also CWP
See also FW
See also PC 43
Das, Lama Surya 1950- ... CANR-125
Earlier sketch in CA 168
Das, Manmath Nath 1926- ... CANR-8
Earlier sketch in CA 13-16R
Das, Suranjan 1954- ... 139
Dasa, Drutakarma
See Cremo, Michael (A.)
Dasa, Shukavak N. 1953- ... 184
Dascal, Marcelo 1940- ... 140
Dasenbrock, Reed Way 1953- ... CANR-56
Earlier sketch in CA 125
Dasent, Sir George Webbe
1817-1896 ... SATA 62
See also SATA-Brief 29
Das Gupta, Jyotirindra 1933- ... 53-56
Dasgupta, Shamita Das 1949- ... 169
Dasgupta, Subrata 1944- ... CANR-105
Earlier sketch in CA 150
Dasgupta, Surendranath 1887-1952 ... 157
See also TCLC 81
Dash, Irene G(olden) ... 125
Dash, Jack Brien 1907-1989
Obituary ... 128
Dash, Joan 1925- ... CANR-121
Earlier sketches in CA 49-52, CANR-31, 57
See also BYA 11
See also MAICYA 2
See also SATA 142
Dash, Julie 1952- ... 168
See also AAYA 62
Dash, Mike ... 195
Dash, Samuel 1925-2004
Obituary ... 227
Brief entry ... 105
Dash, Tony 1945- ... 33-36R
Dashaway, Lulu
See Blake, Lillie Devereux
Dashiell, Alfred Sheppard 1901-1970
Obituary ... 89-92
Dashing Charley
See Hanshew, Thomas W.
Dashkova, Ekaterina Romanovna
1743-1810 ... DLB 150
Dashner, James ... 236
Dashti, Ali 1894- ... 85-88
Dashwood, Edmee Elizabeth Monica de la
Pasture 1890-1943 ... 154
Brief entry ... 119
See also Delafield, E. M.
Dashwood, Robert Julian 1899- ... CAP-1
Earlier sketch in CA 13-14
da Silva, Howard 1909-1986
Obituary ... 118
DaSilva, Leon
See Wallmann, Jeffrey M(iner)
DaSilva, Zenia Sacks 1925- ... 121
Daskam, Josephine Dodge
See Bacon, Josephine Dodge (Daskam)
Dasmann, Raymond (Frederic)
1919-2002 ... CANR-71
Obituary ... 212
Earlier sketches in CA 5-8R, CANR-2
Dass, Ram
See Alpert, Richard
Dassanowsky, Robert
See Dassanowsky, Robert von
Dassanowsky, Robert von 1960- ... CANR-95
Earlier sketch in CA 150
Dassault, Marcel (Bloch) 1892-1986
Obituary ... 119
Brief entry ... 115
Dassin, Jules 1911- ... 132
Dassonville, Michel A(uguste) 1927- ... 73-76
Daston, Lorraine 1951- ... 128
Datcher, Michael 1967- ... 200
Dater, Henry M. 1909(?)-1974
Obituary ... 49-52
Dates, Jannette L. ... 140
See also BW 2
Datesh, John Nicholas 1950- ... 97-100
D'ath, Justin 1953- ... 175
See also SATA 106
Dathorne, O(scar) R(onald) 1934- ... CANR-67
Earlier sketches in CA 57-60, CANR-26
See also BW 1, 3
See also CN 1, 2, 3, 4, 5, 6
See also CP 1
Dating Doctor, The
See Tessina, Tina B.
Datlow, Ellen (Sue) 1949- ... 192
Datta, Pradip Kumar 1955- ... 190
Dattel, Eugene R. 1944- ... 146
Daube, David 1909-1999 ... CANR-72
Obituary ... 177
Earlier sketches in CA 1-4R, CANR-1
Daubeny, Peter (Lauderdale) 1921-1975 . 61-64
Dauber, Kenneth Marc 1945- ... CANR-37
Earlier sketch in CA 114
Dauber, Philip M. 1942- ... 162
Daudet, (Louis Marie) Alphonse
1840-1897 ... DLB 123
See also GFL 1789 to the Present
See also RGSF 2
Daudet, Alphonse Marie Leon 1867-1942 .. 217
Daudet, Leon 1867-1942
Brief entry ... 121
See also GFL 1789 to the Present

Cumulative Index 139 Davie

Dauenhauer, Richard L(eonard)
1942- CANR-11
Earlier sketch in CA 61-64
Dauer, Dorothea W. 1917- 37-40R
Dauer, Lesley 1965- 165
Dauer, Manning J(ulian) 1909-1987 89-92
Dauer, Rosamond 1934- CANR-10
Earlier sketch in CA 65-68
See also SATA 23
Dauer, Victor Paul 1909- 17-20R
Daugert, Stanley M(atthew) 1918- 17-20R
Daugharty, Janice 1944- CANR-90
Earlier sketch in CA 156
See also CSW
Daughdrill, James H(arold), Jr. 1934- 41-44R
Daughen, Joseph R(obert) 1935- 33-36R
Daugherty, Carroll R(oop) 1900-1988
Obituary 125
Daugherty, Charles Michael 1914- ... CANR-82
Earlier sketch in CA 73-76
See also SATA 16
Daugherty, Greg(ory Ash) 1953- 145
Daugherty, James (Henry)
1889-1974 .... CANR-81
Obituary 49-52
Earlier sketch in CA 73-76
See also BYA 1, 3
See also CLR 78
See also CWRI 5
See also MAICYA 1, 2
See also SATA 13
See also WCH
Daugherty, Richard D(eo) 1922- 108
See also SATA 35
Daugherty, Sarah Bowyer 1949- 106
Daugherty, Sonia Medwedeff (?)-1971
Obituary 104
See also SATA-Obit 27
Daugherty, Tracy 1955- CANR-54
Earlier sketch in CA 127
Daugherty, William J. 1947- 214
Daughtrey, Anne Scott 1920- 17-20R
Daughtry, Herbert D(aniel Sr.) 1931- 204
Daughtry, Susan
See Suntree, Susan
d'Aulaire, Edgar Parin 1898-1986 .... CANR-29
Obituary 119
Earlier sketch in CA 49-52
See also CLR 21
See also CWRI 5
See also DLB 22
See also MAICYA 1, 2
See also SATA 5, 66
See also SATA-Obit 47
d'Aulaire, Ingri (Mortenson Parin)
1904-1980 .... CANR-29
Obituary 102
Earlier sketch in CA 49-52
See also CLR 21
See also CWRI 5
See also DLB 22
See also MAICYA 1, 2
See also SATA 5, 66
See also SATA-Obit 24
Daum, Meghan 1970- 196
Daumal, Rene 1908-1944
Brief entry 114
See also EWL 3
See also TCLC 14
Daunton, M(artin) J(ames) 1949- CANR-127
Earlier sketches in CA 125, CANR-52
Dausset, Jean 1916- 155
Dauster, Frank (Nicholas) 1925- 53-56
Dauten, Carl Anton 1913-1976 .... CANR-3
Earlier sketch in CA 5-8R
Dauw, Dean C(harles) 1933- CANR-6
Earlier sketch in CA 53-56
D'Avanzo, Mario Louis 1931- 41-44R
Davar, Ashok 69-72
Dave, Dave
See Berg, David
Dave, Shyam
See Gantzer, Hugh
Daveluy, Paule Cloutier 1919- 9-12R
See also SATA 11
Davenant, William 1606-1668 ..... DLB 58, 126
See also RGEL 2
D'Aveni, Richard 225
Davenier, Christine 1961- .... SATA 127
Davenport, Doris 1915-1980 .... CANR-87
Earlier sketch in CA 152
See also BW 2
Davenport, Elaine 1946- 102
Davenport, Francine
See Tate, Velma
Davenport, Francis Garvin 1905-1975
Obituary 111
Davenport, Gene L(ooney) 1935- 33-36R
Davenport, Guy (Mattison, Jr.)
1927-2005 .... CANR-73
Obituary 235
Earlier sketches in CA 33-36R, CANR-23
See also CLC 6, 14, 38
See also CN 3, 4, 5, 6
See also CSW
See also DLB 130
See also SSC 16
Davenport, Gwen 1909-2002 .... CANR-82
Obituary 205
Earlier sketch in CA 9-12R
Davenport, John 1905-1987
Obituary 122
Davenport, John 1960- 231
See also SATA 156
Davenport, Kiana 190
Davenport, Marcia 1903-1996 .... CANR-82
Obituary 151
Earlier sketch in CA 9-12R
See also DLBD 17
Davenport, Paul 1946- 132
Davenport, Robert .... DLB 58
Davenport, Roger (Hamilton) 1946- . CANR-86
Earlier sketch in CA 131
Davenport, Spencer CANR-26
Earlier sketches in CAP-2, CA 19-20
Davenport, T(homas) R(odney) H(ope)
1926- 77-80
Davenport, Walter 1889-1971
Obituary 104
Davenport, William H. 1908- CANR-4
Earlier sketch in CA 1-4R
Davenport-Hines, Richard (Peter Treadwell)
1953- 134
Daventry, Leonard John 1915- 17-20R
Daves, Delmer (Lawrence) 1904(?)-1977 181
Obituary 73-76
See also DLB 26
Daves, Francis Marion 1903-1989 45-48
Daves, Jessica 1898(?)-1974
Obituary 53-56
Daves, Michael 1938- 9-12R
See also SATA 40
Davey, Cyril J(ames) 1911- CANR-41
Earlier sketches in CA 5-8R, CANR-2, 18
Davey, Frank 1907(?)-1983
Obituary 109
Davey, Frank(land Wilmot) 1940- 173
Earlier sketches in CA 65-68, CANR-13, 32, 65
Autobiographical Essay in 173
See also CAAS 27
See also CP 1, 7
See also DLB 53
Davey, Gilbert (Walter) 1913- CANR-12
Earlier sketches in CAP-1, CA 9-10
Davey, H. E. 226
Davey, Harold W(illiam) 1915-1986 120
Davey, Jocelyn
See Raphael, Chaim
Davey, John
See Richey, David
Davey, Moyra 1958- 230
Davey, Peter (John) 1940- 135
Davey, Thomas A. 1954- 126
Daviau, Donald G(eorge) 1927- CANR-66
Earlier sketches in CA 81-84, CANR-14, 32
Davico, Oskar 1909- .... EWL 3
David, A. R.
See David, A(nn) Rosalie
David, A(nn) Rosalie 1946- CANR-37
Earlier sketch in CA 114
See also SATA 103
David, Abraham 1943- 196
David, Alfred 1929- 85-88
David, Andrew
See Whittingham, Richard
David, Anne 1924-1987 .... CANR-76
Obituary 122
Earlier sketches in CA 29-32R, CANR-12
David, Anthony 1962- 232
David, Carl 1949- 108
David, Catherine 1949(?)- 168
David, Catherine 1954- 161
David, Ed
See Wohlmuth, Ed
David, Emily
See Alman, David
David, Gerald 1941- 114
David, Heather M(acKinnon) 1937- 37-40R
David, Henry 1907-1984
Obituary 111
David, Henry P. 1923- CANR-6
Earlier sketch in CA 13-16R
David, Hugh (Housdon) 1954- 129
David, Irene 1921-1995 110
David, Jack 1946- CANR-30
Earlier sketch in CA 110
David, James F. 199
David, Jay
See Adler, William
David, Jonah M.
See Jones, David Martin
David, Jonathan
See Ames, Lee J(udah)
David, Joseph Ben
See Ben-David, Joseph
David, Larry 1947- 224
David, Lawrence 1963- 144
See also SATA 111
David, Lester 1914-1997 .... CANR-14
Obituary 162
Earlier sketch in CA 37-40R
David, Marjorie 1950- 112
David, Martin A. 1939- 203
David, Martin H(eidenhain) 1935- 37-40R
David, Michael Robert 1932- 53-56
David, Nicholas
See Morgan, Thomas Bruce
David, Paul A(llan) 1935- 97-100
David, Paul T(heodore) 1906-1994 .. CANR-75
Obituary 146
Earlier sketches in CA 5-8R, CANR-2
David, Peter (Allen) 1956- 214
See also Peters, David
See also SATA 72
David, R. W.
See David, Richard (W.)
David, Richard (W.) 1912-1993 129
David, Robert
See Nezval, Vitezslav
David, Rosalie
See David, A(nn) Rosalie
David, Saul 1921-1996 124
Brief entry 114
David, Stephen M(ark) 1934-1985 .... 33-36R
Obituary 115
David, Thomas 1940- 170
David, William
See Sandman, Peter M(ark)
Davidar, David 1959(?)- 204
David-Neel, Alexandra 1868-1969
Obituary 25-28R
Davidoff, Leonore 1932- 167
Davidow, Michael
See Davidow, Mike
Davidow, Mike 1913-1996 57-60
Obituary 153
Davidow-Goodman, Ann
See Goodman, Ann (Davidow)
Davids, Anthony 1923- 41-44R
Davids, Bob
See Davids, L(eonard) Robert
Davids, Jennifer 1945- .... CP 1
Davids, L(eonard) Robert 1926- 115
Davids, Lewis Edmund 1917- 37-40R
Davids, Richard Carlyle 1913-1984 97-100
Davidsen, Susanna L. 235
Davidsohn, Hans 1887-1942 209
Davidson, Abraham A. 1935- 53-56
Davidson, Alan Eaton 1924-2003 103
Obituary 222
Davidson, Alastair 1939- 29-32R
Davidson, Alice Joyce 1932- 115
See also SATA 54
See also SATA-Brief 45
Davidson, Andrew 1959- 238
Davidson, Angus (Henry Gordon)
1898-1980 .... CANR-71
Obituary 97-100
Earlier sketch in CA 25-28R
Davidson, Arnold E(dward) 1936- 111
Davidson, Avram (James)
1923-1993 .... CANR-26
Obituary 171
Earlier sketch in CA 101
See also Queen, Ellery
See also DLB 8
See also FANT
See also SFW 4
See also SUFW 1, 2
Davidson, Basil 1914- CANR-82
Earlier sketches in CA 1-4R, CANR-1, 17
See also SATA 13
Davidson, Bill
See Davidson, William
Davidson, Bill R.
See Davidson, William R.
Davidson, Caroline 1953- 122
Davidson, Catherine Temma 1963- 172
Davidson, Cathy Notari 1949- CANR-23
Earlier sketch in CA 106
Davidson, Chalmers Gaston
1907-1994 .... CANR-72
Earlier sketch in CA 29-32R
Davidson, Chandler 1936- 45-48
Davidson, Clarissa Start
See Lippert, Clarissa Start
Davidson, Clifford 1932- 45-48
Davidson, Dana H. 1949- 143
Davidson, David 1908-1985 49-52
Obituary 117
Davidson, (Marie) Diane 1924- CANR-57
Earlier sketch in CA 29-32R
See also SATA 91
Davidson, Diane Mott 214
Davidson, Donald (Grady)
1893-1968 .... CANR-84
Obituary 25-28R
Earlier sketches in CA 5-8R, CANR-4
See also CLC 2, 13, 19
See also DLB 45
Davidson, Donald (Herbert)
1917-2003 .... CANR-97
Obituary 219
Earlier sketches in CA 45-48, CANR-2
See also DLB 279
See also RGAL 4
Davidson, E(phraim) E(dward) 1923- 33-36R
Davidson, Ellen Prescott 49-52
Davidson, Eugene (Arthur) 1902- CANR-72
Earlier sketches in CA 1-4R, CANR-3
Davidson, Eva Rucker 1894(?)-1974
Obituary 53-56
Davidson, F(rank) G(eoffrey) 1920- 29-32R
Davidson, Frank P(aul) 1918- CANR-40
Earlier sketch in CA 116
Davidson, Glen W(illiam) 1936- CANR-9
Earlier sketch in CA 61-64
Davidson, Greg (Stuart) 1961- 129
Davidson, Gustav 1895-1971
Obituary 29-32R
Davidson, H(ilda) R(oderick) Ellis
1914- CANR-11
Earlier sketch in CA 17-20R
Davidson, Harold G(ordon) 1912- 65-68
Davidson, Henry A(lexander) 1905-1973
Obituary 45-48
Davidson, Herbert A(lan) 1932- 17-20R
Davidson, Hugh
See Hamilton, Edmond
Davidson, Hugh M(acCullough) 1918- 102
Davidson, Irwin Delmore 1906-1981
Obituary 105
Davidson, James Dale 1947- 107
Davidson, James N. CANR-113
Earlier sketch in CA 172
Davidson, James Norris Goddard 1900- 172
Davidson, James West 1946- CANR-15
Earlier sketch in CA 85-88
Davidson, Jeffrey P(hilip) 1951- CANR-48
Earlier sketches in CA 122, CANR-41
Davidson, Jessica 1915-1986 .... CANR-14
Earlier sketch in CA 41-44R
See also SATA 5
Davidson, John
See Reid, Charles (Stuart)
Davidson, John 1857-1909 217
Brief entry 118
See also DLB 19
See also RGEL 2
See also TCLC 24
Davidson, John 1941- 156
Davidson, John Wells 1903-1986
Obituary 120
Davidson, Jonathan R. T. 1943- 197
Davidson, Judith 1953- 116
See also SATA 40
Davidson, Julian M. 1931- 102
Davidson, Keay 221
Davidson, Lionel 1922- CANR-43
Earlier sketches in CA 1-4R, CANR-1
See also CMW 4
See also CN 4, 5, 6, 7
See also CWRI 5
See also DLB 14, 276
See also SATA 87
Davidson, Margaret 1936- CANR-17
Earlier sketch in CA 25-28R
See also SATA 5
Davidson, Marion
See Garis, Howard R(oger)
Davidson, Mark 1940- 138
Davidson, Marshall B(owman)
1907-1989 .... CANR-42
Obituary 129
Earlier sketch in CA 33-36R
Davidson, Martin 1939- 214
Davidson, Mary R. 1885-1973 .... 5-8R
See also SATA 9
Davidson, Mary S. 1940- 107
See also SATA 61
Davidson, MaryJanice 237
Davidson, Max 1955- 139
Davidson, Max D. 1899(?)-1977
Obituary 73-76
Davidson, Melanie
See Arnold, Madelyn M. a pseudonym
Davidson, Michael
See Rorvik, David M(ichael)
Davidson, Michael 1944- 106
Davidson, Michael Childers 1897- 29-32R
Davidson, Mickie
See Davidson, Margaret
Davidson, Mildred 1935- 93-96
Davidson, Miriam 1960- CANR-101
Earlier sketch in CA 128
Davidson, Morris 1898-1979 .... CANR-72
Earlier sketch in CA 85-88
Davidson, Muriel 1924(?)-1983
Obituary 110
Davidson, Nicole
See Jensen, Kathryn
Davidson, Norman 1933- 119
Davidson, Osha Gray 1954- CANR-93
Earlier sketch in CA 145
Davidson, Pamela 1954- 133
Davidson, Paul 1930- CANR-52
Earlier sketches in CA 13-16R, CANR-6, 28
Davidson, Philip (Grant) 1902-2000 73-76
Obituary 191
Davidson, Phillip B. 1915- 130
Davidson, R.
See Davidson, Raymond
Davidson, Raymond 1926- .... SATA 32
Davidson, Robert F(ranklin) 1902-1985 .. 49-52
Davidson, Robyn 1950- 142
See also DLB 204
Davidson, Roger H(arry) 1936- CANR-49
Earlier sketches in CA 21-24R, CANR-9, 24
Davidson, Rosalie 1921- 69-72
See also SATA 23
Davidson, Sandra Calder 1935- 41-44R
Davidson, Sara 1943- CANR-68
Earlier sketches in CA 81-84, CANR-44
See also CLC 9
See also DLB 185
Davidson, Sol M. 1924- 17-20R
Davidson, Toni 184
Davidson, William 1918-2001 93-96
Obituary 193
Davidson, William H. 1951- 128
Davidson, William R. 1929(?)-1987
Obituary 122
Davidson, William Robert 1919- 17-20R
Davidson-Houston, J(ames) Vivian
1901-1965 .... 5-8R
Davie, Donald (Alfred) 1922-1995 ... CANR-44
Obituary 149
Earlier sketches in CA 1-4R, CANR-1
See also CAAS 3
See also BRWS 6
See also CLC 5, 8, 10, 31
See also CP 1, 2
See also DLB 27
See also MTCW 1
See also PC 29
See also RGEL 2
Davie, Elspeth 1918-1995 .... CANR-141
Obituary 150
Brief entry 120
Earlier sketch in CA 126
See also DLB 139
See also SSC 52
Davie, Helen K(ay) 1952- .... SATA 77, 148
Davie, Ian 1924- 102
Davie, Maurice R(ea) 1893-1964 .... 5-8R

Davie 140 CONTEMPORARY AUTHORS

Davie, Michael 1924- CANR-120
Earlier sketch in CA 57-60
Davie, Peter (Edward Sidney) 1936- 114
Davied, Camille
See Rose, Camille Davied
Davie-Martin, Hugh
See McCutcheon, Hugh Davie-Martin
Davies, A(lfred) Mervyn 1899-1976 .... 17-20R
Obituary 69-72
Davies, A(rthur) Powell 1902-1957 206
Davies, Ada Hilton 1893-1977 .... CAP-2
Earlier sketch in CA 17-18
Davies, Alan T(rewartha) 1933- 33-36R
Davies, Alfred T(homas) 1930- 13-16R
Davies, Andrew (Wynford) 1936- 105
See also CWRI 5
See also SATA 27
Davies, Bettilu D(onna) 1942- CANR-18
Earlier sketch in CA 101
See also SATA 33
Davies, Bronwyn 1945- 212
Davies, Carole Boyce
See Boyce Davies, Carole Elizabeth
Davies, Charles (Michael) 1946- 128
Davies, Charles E. 234
Davies, Christie
See Davies, John Christopher Hughes
Davies, Colin
See Elliot, Ian
Davies, (George) Colliss (Boardman)
1912-1982 .... CAP-1
Earlier sketch in CA 11-12
Davies, D(avid) Jacob 1916-1974 .... 5-8R
Obituary 103
Davies, Daniel R. 1911-1997 .... 37-40R
Davies, David Margerison 1923- 5-8R
Davies, David Michael 1929-
Brief entry 109
Davies, David W(illiam) 1908-1984 .... CANR-3
Earlier sketch in CA 9-12R
Davies, Duncan (Sheppey) 1921-1987 124
Obituary 122
Davies, E(dward) Tegla 1880-1967 217
Davies, Ebenezer Thomas 1903- CAP-1
Earlier sketch in CA 13-14
Davies, Eileen Winifred 1910- CAP-1
Earlier sketch in CA 13-14
Davies, Evelyn 1924- CANR-8
Earlier sketch in CA 61-64
Davies, Evelyn A(dele) 1915- 61-64
Davies, Glyn(dwr) 1919-2003 158
Obituary 212
Davies, Harriet Vaughn 1879(?)-1978
Obituary 77-80
Davies, Horton (Marlais)
1916-2005 .... CANR-79
Obituary 239
Earlier sketches in CA 5-8R, CANR-7
Davies, Hugh Sykes 1909-1984(?)
Obituary 113
Davies, Hunter 1936- CANR-90
Earlier sketches in CA 57-60, CANR-12
See also SATA 55
See also SATA-Brief 45
Davies, (David) Ioan 1936- 21-24R
Davies, Ivor K(evin) 1930- 53-56
Davies, J. Clarence III 1937- CANR-125
Earlier sketches in CA 29-32R, CANR-71
Davies, J(ohn) D(avid) 1957- 139
Davies, J. Kenneth 1925- 57-60
Davies, Jacqueline 1962- 230
See also SATA 155
Davies, James A. 1939- 129
Davies, James Chowning 1918- 45-48
Davies, Jennifer (Eileen) 1950- 139
Davies, Joan 1934- 124
See also SATA 50
See also SATA-Brief 47
Davies, John 1569-1626 .... RGEL 2
Davies, John Christopher Hughes
1941- CANR-106
Earlier sketch in CANR-48
Davies, John Evan Weston
1914-1996 .... CANR-78
Brief entry 111
Earlier sketch in CA 113
Interview in CA-113
Davies, John Gordon 1919-1990 69-72
Davies, John K(enyon) 1937- 120
Davies, John Paton, Jr. 1908-1999 .... CANR-72
Obituary 187
Earlier sketch in CA 9-12R
Davies, Katharine 1968- 239
Davies, Kevin Anthony 1960- 196
Davies, L(eslie) P(urnell) 1914- CANR-59
Earlier sketches in CA 21-24R, CANR-9
See also CMW 4
Davies, Laurence 1926- CANR-72
Earlier sketch in CA 57-60
Davies, Linda 1963- 149
Davies, Loma G. 1934- 137
Davies, Luke 1962- 218
Davies, Mansel Morris 1913-1995 .... 9-12R
Davies, Margaret C(onstance Brown)
1923- 9-12R
Davies, Margaret Lloyd 1935- 106
Davies, Marion
See Douras, Marion Cecilia
Davies, Martin Brett 1936- 102
Davies, Martin L. 1948- 155
Davies, Merton E(dward) 1917-2001 85-88
Obituary 195
Davies, Morton Rees 1939- 37-40R
Davies, Nick 1953- 136
Davies, Nicola 1958- CANR-135
Earlier sketch in CA 167
See also SATA 99, 150
Davies, (Claude) Nigel (Byam)
1920-2004 .... CANR-19
Obituary 232
Earlier sketch in CA 102
Davies, Norman 1939- CANR-92
Earlier sketch in CA 41-44R
Davies, Oliver 1905- CAP-2
Earlier sketch in CA 25-28
Davies, Oliver 1956- 227
Davies, P. C. W.
See Davies, Paul (Charles William)
Davies, Paul (Charles William)
1946- CANR-87
Earlier sketches in CA 106, CANR-31
Davies, (William Thomas) Pennar
1911-1996 .... 13-16R
Obituary 155
Davies, Pete 1959- 195
Davies, Peter Ho 1966- 203
See also SSFS 21
Davies, Peter J(oseph) 1937- CANR-102
Earlier sketch in CA 135
See also SATA 52
Davies, Philip John 1948- 152
Davies, Piers (Anthony David) 1941- 103
Davies, R(onald) E. G. 1921- 17-20R
Davies, R(obert) R(ees) 1938-2005 135
Obituary 239
Davies, R(eginald) T(horne) 1923- 9-12R
Davies, R(obert) W(illiam) 1925- CANR-54
Earlier sketches in CA 33-36R, CANR-13, 29
Davies, Ray(mond Douglas) 1944- CANR-92
Brief entry 116
Earlier sketch in CA 146
See also CLC 21
Davies, Rhys 1901-1978 .... CANR-4
Obituary 81-84
Earlier sketch in CA 9-12R
See also CLC 23
See also CN 1, 2
See also DLB 139, 191
Davies, Richard Llewelyn
See Llewelyn-Davies, Richard
Davies, Richard O. 1937- 17-20R
Davies, (William) Robertson
1913-1995 .... CANR-103
Obituary 150
Earlier sketches in CA 33-36R, CANR-17, 42
Interview in CANR-17
See also Marchbanks, Samuel
See also BEST 89:2
See also BPFB 1
See also CLC 2, 7, 13, 25, 42, 75, 91
See also CN 1, 2, 3, 4, 5, 6
See also CPW
See also DA
See also DA3
See also DAB
See also DAC
See also DAM MST, NOV, POP
See also DLB 68
See also EWL 3
See also HGG
See also MTCW 1, 2
See also MTFW 2005
See also RGEL 2
See also TWA
See also WLC
Davies, Rod 1941- 61-64
Davies, Rosemary Reeves 1925- 49-52
Davies, Rupert Eric 1909-1994 .... CANR-39
Earlier sketches in CA 5-8R, CANR-3, 18
Davies, Ruth A(nn) 1915- CANR-26
Earlier sketch in CA 29-32R
Davies, Sally Kevill
See Kevill-Davies, Sally
Davies, Samuel 1723-1761 .... DLB 31
Davies, Sir John 1569-1626 .... DLB 172
Davies, Stan Gebler 1943-1994 65-68
Obituary 146
Davies, Stanley Powell 1892-1985
Obituary 115
Davies, Stephanie
See Davies, Stevie
Davies, Stevan L(awrence) 1948- 107
Davies, Stevie 1946- CANR-95
Earlier sketch in CA 147
Davies, Sumiko 1942- 126
See also SATA 46
Davies, T(refor) Rendall 1913- CAP-1
Earlier sketch in CA 9-10
Davies, Terence 1945- 156
Davies, Terry
See Davies, J. Clarence III
Davies, Thomas 1712(?)-1785 .... DLB 142
Davies, Thomas 1941- CANR-121
Earlier sketch in CA 115
Davies, Thomas M(ockett), Jr. 1940- CANR-6
Earlier sketch in CA 57-60
Davies, Tom
See Davies, Thomas
Davies, Walter C.
See Kornbluth, C(yril) M.
Davies, William David 1911-2001 .... CANR-1
Obituary 196
Earlier sketch in CA 1-4R
Davies, William Henry 1871-1940 179
Brief entry 104
See also BRWS 11
See also DLB 19, 174
See also EWL 3
See also RGEL 2
See also TCLC 5
Davies, Wyndham (Roy) 1926- 25-28R
Davies of Hereford, John
1565(?)-1618 .... DLB 121
Davila, Angela Maria
See Davila, Angela Maria
Davila, Arlene M.
See Davila, Arlene M.
Davila, Arlene M. 1965- CANR-138
Earlier sketch in CA 169
Davila, Virgilio 1869-1943 131
See also HW 1
Davin, D(aniel) M(arcus)
1913-1990 .... CANR-30
Earlier sketches in CA 9-12R, CANR-3
See also Davin, Dan
See also RGEL 2
Davin, Dan
See Davin, D(aniel) M(arcus)
See also CN 1, 2, 3, 4
See also RGSF 2
Davin, Eric Leif 214
Davin, Nicholas Flood 1840(?)-1901 213
See also DLB 99
Da Vinci, Leonardo 1452-1519 .... AAYA 40
Davinson, Donald E(dward) 1932- CANR-3
Earlier sketch in CA 5-8R
Daviot, Gordon
See Mackintosh, Elizabeth
See also DLB 10
Davis, Ada Romaine
See Romaine-Davis, Ada
Davis, Adelle 1904-1974 .... CANR-30
Obituary 49-52
Earlier sketch in CA 37-40R
Davis, Alan (R.) 1950- CANR-117
Earlier sketch in CA 156
Davis, Albert Belisle 1947- CANR-97
Earlier sketch in CA 138
Davis, Alice Taylor 1903-1989
Obituary 129
Davis, Allen III 1929- 108
Davis, Allen F(reeman) 1931- CANR-50
Earlier sketches in CA 21-24R, CANR-10, 25
Davis, (William) Allison 1902-1983 125
Obituary 111
Brief entry 106
See also BW 1
Davis, Amanda 1971-2003 208
Davis, Amelia 1968- 235
Davis, Andrew 1947- 235
Davis, Andrew Jackson 1826-1910
Brief entry 120
Davis, Andy
See Davis, Andrew
Davis, Angela (Yvonne) 1944- CANR-81
Earlier sketches in CA 57-60, CANR-10
See also BW 2, 3
See also CLC 77
See also CSW
See also DA3
See also DAM MULT
See also FW
Davis, Anita (Grey) P(rice) 1943- 225
Davis, Ann 1946- 137
Davis, Ann E(lizabeth) 1932- 69-72
Davis, Archibald K. 1911-1998 124
Davis, Archie K.
See Davis, Archibald K.
Davis, Arthur G. 1915- 13-16R
Davis, Arthur Hoey 1868-1935
Brief entry 121
See also Rudd, Steele
See also DLB 230
Davis, Arthur Kennard 1910- CAP-1
Earlier sketch in CA 13-14
Davis, Arthur (Shelley) Kennard 1910- .. CAP-1
Earlier sketch in CA 9-10
Davis, Arthur Kyle, Jr. 1897-(?) CAP-2
Earlier sketch in CA 17-18
Davis, Arthur P(aul) 1904-1996 61-64
Obituary 151
See also BW 2
Davis, (A.) Aubrey 1949- .... SATA 153
Davis, Audrey
See Paine, Lauran (Bosworth)
Davis, B. Lynch
See Bioy Casares, Adolfo and Borges, Jorge Luis
Davis, B(enton) Vincent, (Jr.)
1930-2003 .... CANR-23
Obituary 214
Earlier sketches in CA 17-20R, CANR-7
Davis, Barbara Kerr 1946- 104
Davis, Bart 1950- 153
Davis, Ben Reeves 1927- 77-80
Davis, Benjamin J. 1903-1964 .... DLB 303
Davis, Benjamin O(liver), Jr. 1912-2002 134
Obituary 208
See also BW 2
Davis, (Mary) Bernice
See Curler, (Mary) Bernice
Davis, Berrie 1922-1992 101
Davis, Bertram H(ylton) 1918- CANR-1
Earlier sketch in CA 1-4R
Davis, Bette
See Davis, Ruth Elizabeth
Davis, Bette J. 1923- 93-96
See also SATA 15
Davis, Bill C. 1951- 110
Davis, Bob 172
Davis, Brian 1925-1988
Obituary 126
Davis, Burke 1913- CANR-50
Earlier sketches in CA 1-4R, CANR-4, 25
See also SATA 4
Davis, Calvin DeArmond 1927- 5-8R
Davis, Carol Anne 1961- 221
Davis, (Horace) Chandler 1926- .... SFW 4
Davis, Charles 1923- CANR-21
Earlier sketch in CA 5-8R
Davis, Charles A. 1795-1867 .... DLB 11
Davis, Charles R. 1945- 175
Davis, Charles T(witchell) 1918-1981 125
See also BW 1
Davis, Charles T(ill) 1929- 37-40R
Davis, Christopher 1928- CANR-3
Earlier sketch in CA 9-12R
See also CAAS 20
See also SATA 6
Davis, Claire 210
Davis, (Elvis) Clark (III) 1964- 151
Davis, Cliff
See Smith, Richard Rein
Davis, Clive E(dward) 1914-1988 .... CANR-72
Earlier sketch in CA 17-20R
Davis, Clyde Brion 1894-1962 .... 5-8R
See also DLB 9
Davis, Creath 1939-1987 .... CANR-21
Obituary 145
Earlier sketches in CA 57-60, CANR-6
Davis, Curtis Carroll 1916-1997 .... CANR-72
Earlier sketches in CA 9-12R, CANR-6
Davis, Curtis Wheeler 1928-1986 136
Obituary 119
Davis, D(elbert) Dwight 1908-1965
Obituary 111
See also SATA 33
Davis, D(onald) Evan 1923-1979 .... 17-20R
Obituary 122
Davis, Daniel S(heldon) 1936- 45-48
See also SATA 12
Davis, Daphne 65-68
Davis, David Brion 1927- CANR-121
Earlier sketches in CA 17-20R, CANR-9, 26, 51
Davis, David C(harles) L. 1928- 33-36R
Davis, David Howard 1941- 53-56
Davis, David R. 1948- 175
See also SATA 106
Davis, Deane C(handler) 1900-1990 108
Davis, Deborah 1949- 129
Davis, Devra Lee 1946- 223
Davis, Dick 1945- CANR-136
Earlier sketch in CA 155
See also CP 7
See also DLB 40, 282
Davis, Don
See Dresser, Davis
Davis, Donald (D.) 1944- CANR-128
Earlier sketches in CA 146, CANR-68
See also SATA 93
Davis, Donald Gordon, Jr. 1939- CANR-6
Earlier sketch in CA 53-56
Davis, Dorothy Salisbury 1916- CANR-84
Earlier sketches in CA 37-40R, CANR-14, 32
See also CMW 4
See also MSW
Davis, Douglas (Matthew) 1933- 111
Davis, Douglas F(redell) 1935- 105
Davis, E. Adams
See Davis, Edwin Adams
Davis, Earl C(linton) 1938- CANR-46
Earlier sketch in CA 111
Davis, Earle (Rosco) 1905-1991 .... CANR-72
Earlier sketch in CA 65-68
Davis, Edwin Adams 1904-1994 .... CAP-2
Earlier sketch in CA 25-28
Davis, Eleanor Harmon 1909- 106
Davis, Elias 180
Davis, Elise Miller 1915- 69-72
Davis, Elizabeth
See Davis, Lou Ellen
Davis, Elizabeth G. 1910(?)-1974
Obituary 53-56
Davis, Elwood Craig 1896-1985 .... CANR-3
Earlier sketch in CA 1-4R
Davis, F(loyd) James 1920- CANR-4
Earlier sketch in CA 1-4R
Davis, Fitzroy 1912-1980 .... CANR-31
Obituary 102
Earlier sketch in CA 49-52
Davis, Flora 1934- CANR-10
Earlier sketch in CA 65-68
Davis, Forest K(endall) 1918- 41-44R
Davis, Francis (John) 1946- CANR-142
Earlier sketches in CA 123, CANR-50
Davis, Frank (Cecil) 1892-1990
Obituary 131
Davis, Frank G(reene) 1915- 85-88
Davis, Frank Marshall 1905-1987 .... CANR-80
Obituary 123
Earlier sketches in CA 125, CANR-42
See also BLC 1
See also BW 2, 3
See also DAM MULT
See also DLB 51
Davis, Franklin M(ilton), Jr.
1918-1981 .... CANR-4
Earlier sketch in CA 1-4R
Davis, Fred 1925- 13-16R
Davis, Frederick Barton 1909-1975 .. CANR-17
Obituary 116
Earlier sketch in CA 1-4R
Davis, Frederick C(lyde) 1902-1977
Obituary 115
See also CMW 4
Davis, Gail Barbara 1956- 164
Davis, Garold N(eil) 1932- 41-44R
Davis, Gary A(lan) 1938- 106
Davis, Gayle A. 1943- 179
Davis, Genevieve 1928- 65-68
Davis, Genny Wright 1948- 105
Davis, George 1939- CANR-9
Earlier sketch in CA 65-68
See also BW 1
Davis, George L(ittleton) Sr. 1921- 57-60

Cumulative Index 141 Davison

Davis, Gerry 1930-1991
Brief entry 117
Davis, Gibbs 1953- 111
See also SATA 46, 102
See also SATA-Brief 41
Davis, Gil
See Gilmore, Don
Davis, Gilbert 1899-1983
Obituary 109
Davis, Gordon
See Levinson, Leonard
Davis, Gordon
See Hunt, E(verette) Howard, (Jr.)
Davis, Gordon B(itter) 1930- CANR-4
Earlier sketch in CA 53-56
Davis, Graham 1943- 230
Davis, Grania 1943- CANR-84
Earlier sketches in CA 85-88, CANR-16, 39
See also FANT
See also SATA 88
See also SATA-Brief 50
Davis, Grant Miller 1937- CANR-11
Earlier sketch in CA 29-32R
Davis, Gwen 1936- CANR-2
Earlier sketch in CA 1-4R
See also AITN 1
Davis, H(enry) Grady 1890-1975 .... CAP-2
Earlier sketch in CA 21-22
Davis, H(arold) L(enoir) 1896-1960 178
Obituary 89-92
See also ANW
See also CLC 49
See also DLB 9, 206
See also SATA 114
See also TCWW 1, 2
Davis, Hank 1941- 193
Davis, Harley
See Green, Kay
Davis, Harold Eugene 1902-1988 .... CANR-83
Obituary 126
Earlier sketches in CA 1-4R, CANR-1
Davis, Harold S(eaton) 1919- 57-60
Davis, Harriet Eager 1892(?)-1974
Obituary 49-52
Davis, Harry Rex 1921- 1-4R
Davis, Helen Dick 1899-1992 143
Davis, Henry P. 1894(?)-1970
Obituary 104
Davis, Herbert (John) 1893-1967 .... CANR-1
Earlier sketch in CA 1-4R
Davis, Hope Hale 1903(?)-2004 .... 25-28R
Obituary 232
Davis, Hope Harding 1915(?)-1976
Obituary 69-72
Davis, Horace B(ancroft) 1898-1999 .... 21-24R
Davis, Horance G(ibbs), Jr. 1924-2004 65-68
Obituary 230
Davis, Howard V(aughn) 1915- 25-28R
Davis, Hubert J(ackson) 1904-1997 107
See also SATA 31
Davis, I(rene) M(ary) 1926- 61-64
Davis, J(ames) C(olin) 1940- 127
Davis, J(ohn) Cary 1905-2000 .... 41-44R
Davis, J(ames) Madison (Jr.) 1951- CANR-97
Earlier sketch in CA 134
Davis, J. Morton 1929- 124
Davis, J(ames) William 1908-1995 102
Davis, Jack Leonard 1917- 106
See also CD 5, 6
Davis, James Allan 1929- CANR-1
Earlier sketch in CA 1-4R
Davis, James C(urran) 1895-1981
Obituary 108
Davis, James C(ushman) 1931-
Brief entry 117
Davis, James H. 1932- 89-92
Davis, James Kirkpatrick 1939- 127
Davis, James Kotsilibas
See Kotsilibas-Davis, James
Davis, James Richard 1936- 65-68
Davis, James Robert 1945- CANR-41
Earlier sketches in CA 85-88, CANR-16
See also Davis, Jim
See also SATA 32
Davis, James W(arren, Jr.)
1935-1999 .... CANR-72
Earlier sketch in CA 29-32R
Davis, Jan Haddle 1950- 93-96
Davis, Jean Reynolds 1927- 61-64
Davis, Jean Walton 1909- 1-4R
Davis, Jed H(orace, Jr.) 1921- 17-20R
Davis, Jenny 1953- CANR-66
Earlier sketch in CA 128
See also AAYA 21
See also SATA 74
See also YAW
Davis, Jerome 1891-1979 .... CANR-82
Obituary 89-92
Earlier sketches in CA 5-8R, CANR-3
Davis, Jim
Interview in CANR-16
See also Davis, James Robert
See also AAYA 8
Davis, Jim
See Smith, Richard Rein
Davis, Jimmie Dan 1940- 127
Davis, Jinnie Y(eh) 1945- 107
Davis, Jodie 1959- 139
Davis, Joe 1901-1978
Obituary 112
Davis, Joe Lee 1906-1974 .... 5-8R
Obituary 103
Davis, Joel 1948- 146
Davis, Johanna 1937-1974 .... 41-44R
Obituary 53-56
Davis, John 1774-1854 .... DLB 37
Davis, John D(avid) 1937- 29-32R
Davis, John H(erbert) 1904-1988 .... 29-32R
Davis, John H. 1929- CANR-40
Earlier sketches in CA 25-28R, CANR-18
Davis, John J(ames) 1936- 33-36R
Davis, John King 1884-1967 .... CAP-1
Earlier sketch in CA 9-10
Davis, Jon 1952- 151
Davis, Joseph C(ole) 1908-1981 97-100
Davis, Joseph S(tancliffe) 1885-1975 101
Obituary 57-60
Davis, Joyce M. 1953- 237
Davis, Judith 1925-1989 106
Davis, Julia
See Marsh, John
Davis, Julia 1900(?)-1993 .... CANR-81
Obituary 140
Earlier sketches in CA 1-4R, CANR-1
See also SATA 6
See also SATA-Obit 75
Davis, Julian 1902(?)-1974
Obituary 53-56
Davis, K(eith) 1918-1986 .... CANR-20
Earlier sketches in CA 1-4R, CANR-5
Davis, Karen (Elizabeth) 1944- 180
See also SATA 109
Davis, Karen Padgett 1942- 112
Davis, Kathryn 1946- CANR-90
Earlier sketch in CA 149
Davis, Katie 1959(?)- .... SATA 152
Davis, Keith F. 1952- CANR-50
Earlier sketch in CA 123
Davis, Ken(neth Pickett) 1906-1982 49-52
Obituary 135
Davis, Kenneth C. 139
Davis, Kenneth Culp 1908-2003
Obituary 219
Brief entry 115
Davis, Kenneth R(exton) 1921- 17-20R
Davis, Kenneth S(idney)
1912-1999 .... CANR-105
Obituary 181
Earlier sketches in CA 13-16R, CANR-30
Davis, Kingsley 1908-1997 .... CANR-8
Obituary 156
Earlier sketch in CA 13-16R
Davis, L(awrence) J(ames) 1940- CANR-143
Earlier sketches in CA 25-28R, CANR-11, 72
Davis, Lance E(dwin) 1928- 53-56
Davis, Lanny J(esse) 1945- CANR-83
Earlier sketch in CA 57-60
Davis, Lawrence 1932- .... CMW 4
Davis, Lawrence B(ennion) 1939- 45-48
Davis, Leith 1960- 198
Davis, Lennard J. 1949- CANR-93
Earlier sketches in CA 116, CANR-39
Davis, Lenwood G. CANR-86
Earlier sketches in CA 25-28R, CANR-35
Davis, Leslie
See Guccione, Leslie Davis
Davis, Lew A(rter) 1930- 21-24R
Davis, Linda H(onor) 1953- 127
Davis, Linda W. 1945- 146
Davis, Lindsey 1949- CANR-103
Earlier sketch in CA 164
See also CMW 4
See also RHW
Davis, Lloyd (Moore) 1931- 69-72
Davis, Lou Ellen 1936- 81-84
Davis, Louis E(lkin) 1918- 53-56
Davis, Louise Littleton 1921- 103
See also SATA 25
Davis, Loyal Edward 1896-1982
Obituary 107
Davis, Luther 1921- 105
Davis, Lydia 1947- CANR-120
Earlier sketch in CA 139
See also DLB 130
Davis, M(orris) Edward 1899-1978 .... 5-8R
Davis, Mac 1942- 213
Davis, Maggie (Hill) CANR-9
Earlier sketch in CA 13-16R
Davis, Maggie S. 1943- .... SATA 57
Davis, Maralee G.
See Gibson, Maralee G.
Davis, Marc 1934- 29-32R
Davis, Margaret Banfield 1903-1982 .... CAP-1
Earlier sketch in CA 11-12
Davis, Margaret Thomson 1926- 102
See also DLB 14
Davis, Marguerite 1889- .... SATA 34
Davis, Marilyn (Illaine) 1930- 153
Davis, Marilyn K(ornreich) 1928- 5-8R
Davis, Mark H. 1953- 158
Davis, Martha 1942- CANR-4
Earlier sketch in CA 49-52
Davis, Martin 1928- CANR-101
Earlier sketch in CA 148
Davis, Mary Byrd 1936- 158
Davis, Mary Dymond
See Davis, Mary Byrd
Davis, Mary L(ee) 1935- CANR-4
Earlier sketch in CA 49-52
See also SATA 9
Davis, Mary Octavia 1901-1976 .... CAP-2
Earlier sketch in CA 25-28
See also SATA 6
Davis, Maxine
See McHugh, Maxine Davis
Davis, Mel
See Arnold, Madelyn M. a pseudonym
Davis, Melodie M(iller) 1951- CANR-71
Earlier sketches in CA 113, CANR-33
Davis, Melton S(amillow) 1910- 41-44R
Davis, Michael 1936- 185
Davis, (John) Michael 1940- 33-36R
Davis, Michael (S.) 1943- 214
Davis, Michael D(eMond) 1939-2003 141
Obituary 223
See also BW 2
Davis, Michael Justin 1925-1991 102
Davis, Michele Weiner
See Weiner-Davis, Michele
Davis, Mike 1946- 186
Davis, Mildred CANR-84
Earlier sketch in CA 77-80
Davis, Mildred Ann (Campbell) 1916- 5-8R
Davis, Millard C. 1930- 69-72
Davis, Monte 1949- 103
Davis, Morris 1933- CANR-11
Earlier sketch in CA 61-64
Davis, Morton D(avid) 1930- 65-68
Davis, Moshe 1916-1996 .... CANR-20
Earlier sketches in CA 9-12R, CANR-4
Davis, Murray S(tuart) 1940- 53-56
Davis, Myrna (Mushkin) 1936- 69-72
Davis, Nancy Yaw 1936- 200
Davis, Natalie Zemon 1928- CANR-100
Earlier sketches in CA 53-56, CANR-58
See also CLC 204
Davis, Nathaniel 1925- 128
Davis, Neil
See Davis, T(homas) Neil
Davis, Neil 1934(?)-1985
Obituary 117
Davis, Nelle 1958- .... SATA 73
Davis, Nicholas 1965- 136
Davis, Nick
See Davis, Nicholas
Davis, Nolan 1942- CANR-25
Earlier sketch in CA 49-52
See also BW 1
Davis, Norah Deakin 1941- 111
Davis, Norman 1913-1989
Brief entry 106
Davis, Norman Maurice 1936- 69-72
Davis, Nuel Pharr 1915- 29-32R
Davis, Olena Kalytiak 1963- 169
Davis, Olivia (Anne Carr) 1922-2004 81-84
Obituary 225
Davis, Ossie 1917-2005 .... CANR-76
Obituary 236
Earlier sketches in CA 112, CANR-26, 53
See also AAYA 17
See also BW 2, 3
See also CAD
See also CD 5, 6
See also CLR 56
See also CSW
See also DA3
See also DAM DRAM, MULT
See also DLB 7, 38, 249
See also MTCW 2
See also SATA 81
Davis, Owen (Gould) 1874-1956 192
See also DLB 249
Davis, (Mindy) Paige 1970- 222
Davis, Patrick (David Channer) 1925- 93-96
Davis, Patti 1952- 134
Davis, Paul (Benjamin) 1934- 135
Davis, Paxton 1925-1994 .... CANR-3
Obituary 145
Earlier sketch in CA 9-12R
See also DLBY 1994
See also SATA 16
Davis, Peter (Frank) 1937- CANR-54
Earlier sketches in CA 107, CANR-29
Davis, Peter G(raffam) 1936- 165
Davis, Philip E(dward) 1927- 49-52
Davis, Philip J. 1923- CANR-84
Earlier sketches in CA 124, CANR-51
Davis, Polly Ann 1931- 102
Davis, R. G. 1933- 57-60
Davis, R(alph) H(enry) C(arless)
1918-1991 .... CANR-6
Obituary 134
Earlier sketch in CA 5-8R
Davis, R(oland) P(arker) Stephen, Jr. 1951- . 169
Davis, Rachel
See Sizer, Mona Young
Davis, Ralph C(urrier) 1894-1986 .... 33-36R
Davis, Rebecca (Blaine) Harding
1831-1910 179
Brief entry 104
See also DLB 74, 239
See also FW
See also NFS 14
See also RGAL 4
See also SSC 38
See also TCLC 6
See also TUS
Davis, Reuben
See Ship, Reuben
See also CCA 1
Davis, Reuben G. 1889-1966 143
Davis, Rex D. 1924- 9-12R
Davis, Richard CANR-26
Earlier sketches in CA 53-56, CANR-7
Davis, Richard A., (Jr.) 1937- 146
Davis, Richard Beale 1907- CANR-2
Earlier sketch in CA 5-8R
Davis, Richard Harding 1864-1916 179
Brief entry 114
See also DLB 12, 23, 78, 79, 189
See also DLBD 13
See also RGAL 4
See also TCLC 24
Davis, Richard W. 1935- 33-36R
Davis, Robert 1881-1949 .... YABC 1
Davis, Robert Con 1948- CANR-23
Earlier sketch in CA 104
Davis, Robert Hart
See Powell, (Oval) Talmage and
Whittington, Harry (Benjamin)
Davis, Robert Murray 1934- CANR-52
Earlier sketches in CA 33-36R, CANR-12, 28
Davis, Robert P. 1929- CANR-3
Earlier sketch in CA 5-8R
Davis, Robert Ralph, Jr. 1941- 37-40R
Davis, Robert Scott, Jr. 1954- 177
Davis, Robin W(orks) 1962- 151
See also SATA 87
Davis, Rocky 1927- 61-64
Davis, Ronald L(eroy) 1936- CANR-105
Earlier sketches in CA 37-40R, CANR-50
Davis, Rose Parkman 1947- 175
Davis, Rosemary 5-8R
Davis, Rosemary L.
See Davis, Rosemary
Davis, Roy Eugene 1931- CANR-6
Earlier sketch in CA 9-12R
Davis, Rupert (Charles) Hart
See Hart-Davis, Rupert (Charles)
Davis, Russell Gerard 1922- 5-8R
See also BYA 1
See also SATA 3
Davis, Ruth Elizabeth 1908-1989 .... CANR-21
Obituary 129
Earlier sketch in CA 61-64
Davis, Sammy, Jr. 1925-1990 108
Obituary 131
Interview in CA-108
Davis, Samuel 1930- 29-32R
Davis, Samuel Cole 1764-1809 .... DLB 37
Davis, Samuel Post 1850-1918 183
See also DLB 202
Davis, Sandra T. W. 1937- 124
Davis, Sara deSaussure 1943- 125
Davis, Scott C(ampbell) 1948- 230
Davis, Shelley L(orraine) 1956- 161
Davis, Simon J. M. 1950- 128
Davis, Stanley Nelson 1924- 108
Davis, Stephen 1947- CANR-120
Earlier sketch in CA 128
Davis, Stephen M. 1955- 127
Davis, Stephen R(andy) 1956- 159
Davis, Steven Andrew 1947- 112
Davis, Steven J(oseph) 1957- 161
Davis, Stratford
See Bolton, Maisie Sharman
Davis, Suzanne
See Sugar, Bert Randolph
Davis, Sydney Charles Houghton 1887- 5-8R
Davis, Sylvan 1927(?)-1984
Obituary 112
Davis, T. N.
See Davis, T(homas) Neil
Davis, T(homas) Neil 1932- CANR-49
Earlier sketch in CA 123
Davis, Terence 1924- 21-24R
Davis, Terry 1947- .... AAYA 50
Davis, Terry Raymond 1967- .... WYA
See also YAW
Davis, Thomas J(oseph) 1946- CANR-4
Earlier sketch in CA 53-56
Davis, Thulani 182
See also BW 2, 3
Davis, Tim(othy N.) 1957- 159
See also SATA 94
Davis, Timothy Francis Tothill 1941- 81-84
Davis, Timothy G. 1958- 195
Davis, Tom Edward 1929- 85-88
Davis, Townsend 1963- 171
Davis, Troy D. 1962- 191
Davis, Val
See Irvine, Angela
Davis, Verne Theodore 1889-1973 .... 1-4R
See also SATA 6
Davis, W(illiam) Jackson 1942- 107
Davis, W(arren) Jefferson 1885-1973 .... CAP-2
Earlier sketch in CA 29-32
Davis, W(illiam) N(ewell), Jr. 1915- 81-84
Davis, (Edmund) Wade 1953- 131
Davis, Walter A(lbert III) 1942-1998 114
Davis, Walter Richardson 1928- 102
Davis, Wayne A. 1951- 197
Davis, Wayne H(arry) 1930- 33-36R
Davis, Wendi
See Holder, Nancy L.
Davis, Wiley H. 1913-1987 .... 25-28R
Davis, William 1933- CANR-28
Earlier sketches in CA 65-68, CANR-10
Davis, William C(harles) 1946- CANR-120
Earlier sketches in CA 61-64, CANR-8, 23
Davis, William H(atcher) 1939- 33-36R
Davis, William S(terling) 1943- CANR-53
Earlier sketches in CA 111, CANR-28
Davis, William Virgil 1940- CANR-92
Earlier sketches in CA 106, CANR-23, 47
Davis, Winston (Bradley) 1939- 104
Davis, Yvonne 1927- .... SATA 115
Davis-Floyd, Robbie Elizabeth
1951- CANR-142
Earlier sketch in CA 174
Davis-Friedmann, Deborah 1945- CANR-41
Earlier sketch in CA 118
Davis-Gardner, Angela 1942- 110
Davis-Goff, Annabel 1942- 85-88
Davis-Kimball, Jeannine 1929- 227
Davison, Edward 1898-1970
Obituary 29-32R
Davison, Frank Dalby 1893-1970 217
Obituary 116
See also CLC 15
See also DLB 260
Davison, Geoffrey 1927- 110
Davison, Gladys Patton 1905-1982 .... CAP-1
Earlier sketch in CA 13-16
Davison, Jane 1932(?)-1981
Obituary 104

Davison 142 CONTEMPORARY AUTHORS

Davison, Jean 1937- CANR-10
Earlier sketch in CA 65-68
Davison, Kenneth E(dwin) 1924- 9-12R
Davison, Lawrence H.
See Lawrence, D(avid) H(erbert Richards)
Davison, Liam 1957- 161
See also CN 6, 7
Davison, Ned J. 1926- 45-48
Davison, Peter (Hobley) 1926- CANR-143
Earlier sketch in CA 160
Davison, Peter (Hubert) 1928-2004 .. CANR-84
Obituary 234
Earlier sketches in CA 9-12R, CANR-3, 43
See also CAAS 4
See also CLC 28
See also CP 1, 2, 3, 4, 5, 6, 7
See also DLB 5
Davison, Roderic H(ollett) 1916-1996 .. 37-40R
Davison, Verne E(lbert) 1904- 69-72
Davisson, Charles Nelson 1917-1997 ... 25-28R
Davisson, William I. 1929- CANR-11
Earlier sketch in CA 17-20R
Davis-Weyer, Caecilia 1929- 41-44R
Davitt, Thomas E(dward) 1904-1980 ..... 25-28R
Obituary 117
Davitz, J. R.
See Davitz, Joel R(obert)
Davitz, Joel R(obert) 1926- 134
Brief entry 114
Davol, Marguerite W. 1928- .... SATA 82, 146
DaVolls, Andy (P.) 1967- .... SATA 85
DaVolls, Linda 1966- 151
See also SATA 85
d'Avray, David L. CANR-124
Earlier sketch in CA 129
Davy, Francis X(avier) 1916-1988 .... 29-32R
Davy, George Mark Oswald 1898-1983
Obituary 110
Davy, John Charles 1927-1984
Obituary 114
Davydov, Denis Vasil'evich
1784-1839 .... DLB 205
Davydov, Isay
See Davydov, Joseph
Davydov, Joseph 1932- 196
Davys, Mary 1674-1732 .... DLB 39
Davys, Sarah
See Manning, Rosemary (Joy)
See also GLL 2
Dawdy, Doris Ostrander 53-56
Dawe, (Donald) Bruce 1930- CANR-83
Earlier sketches in CA 69-72, CANR-11, 27, 52
See also CP 1, 2, 3, 4, 5, 6, 7
See also DLB 289
See also PFS 10
Dawe, Donald G. 1926- 33-36R
Dawe, Frederick
See Gettings, Fred
Dawe, (Chartres) Gerald 1952- CANR-104
Earlier sketches in CA 114, CANR-36
Dawe, Margaret 1957- 148
Dawe, R(oger) D(avid) 1934- CANR-3
Earlier sketch in CA 146
Dawes, Carol Ann
See Young, Casey
Dawes, Claiborne 1935- 182
See also SATA 111
Dawes, Dorothy
See Cooper, Parley J(oseph)
Dawes, Frank 1933- 69-72
Dawes, Kwame 1962- 195
Dawes, Nathaniel Thomas, Jr. 1937- 49-52
Dawes, Neville 1926- 13-16R
See also CP 1
Dawes, Robyn M(ason) 1936- 37-40R
Dawick, John 1934- 148
Dawid, Annie 1960- CANR-97
Earlier sketch in CA 141
Dawidowicz, Lucy S(childkret)
1915-1990 .... CANR-95
Obituary 133
Earlier sketches in CA 25-28R, CANR-18, 83
Dawisha, Rene V(illaneuva) 1928- 45-48
Dawisha, Adeed Isam 1944- CANR-18
Earlier sketch in CA 102
Dawisha, Karen (Lea) 1949- 120
Dawkins, Cecil 1927- CANR-134
Earlier sketches in CA 5-8R, CANR-36, 73
Dawkins, Louisa a pseudonym 1940- 128
Dawkins, Richard 1941- CANR-79
Earlier sketches in CA 69-72, CANR-26, 51
Dawlatabadi, Mahmud 1940- .... CWW 2
Dawley, Alan (Charles) 1943- CANR-127
Earlier sketch in CA 140
Dawley, David 1941- 45-48
Dawley, Powel Mills 1907-1985 57-60
Dawlish, Peter
See Kerr, James Lennox
Dawn, C(larence) Ernest 1918- 61-64
Dawn, Marva J. 1948- 139
Dawood, N(essim) J(oseph) 1927- CANR-28
Earlier sketch in CA 49-52
Daws, Gavan 1933- 222
Dawson, Alan David 1942- 77-80
Dawson, Beatrice 1908-1976 .... IDFW 4
Dawson, Carl 1938- CANR-1
Earlier sketch in CA 45-48
Dawson, Carol 1951- 141
Dawson, Christopher (Henry)
1889-1970 .... CANR-6
Obituary 29-32R
Earlier sketch in CA 1-4R
Dawson, Clay
See Barrett, Neal, Jr. and
Levinson, Leonard
Dawson, Elizabeth
See Geach, Christine
Dawson, Elmer A. CANR-27
Earlier sketches in CAP-2, CA 19-20
See also SATA 1, 67
Dawson, Ernest 1882-1947 201
See also DLB 140
Dawson, (Guy) Fielding (Lewis)
1930-2002 .... CANR-108
Obituary 202
Earlier sketch in CA 85-88
See also CLC 6
See also DLB 130
See also DLBY 2002
Dawson, Frank G(ates, Jr.) 1925- 69-72
Dawson, George 1898-2001 224
Dawson, George G(lenn) 1925- 37-40R
Dawson, Geralyn 233
Dawson, Giles E(dwin) 1903-1994 .... CAP-2
Obituary 146
Earlier sketch in CA 19-20
Dawson, Grace S(trickler)
1891-1981 .... CANR-94
Earlier sketch in CA 17-20R
Dawson, Howard A. 1895(?)-1979
Obituary 89-92
Dawson, Imogen (Zoe) 1948-
See Dawson, Imogen (Zoe)
Dawson, Imogen (Zoe) 1948- CANR-105
Earlier sketch in CA 155
See also SATA 90, 126
Dawson, James Lee 1949- 127
Dawson, Jan 1939(?)-1980
Obituary 101
Dawson, Janet 1949- CANR-134
Earlier sketch in CA 162
See also CMW 4
Dawson, Janis 1936- 135
Dawson, Jennifer 1929-2000 .... CANR-68
Obituary 192
Earlier sketches in CA 57-60, CANR-10
See also CN 1, 2, 3, 4, 5, 6
Dawson, Jerry F. 1933- 33-36R
Dawson, Jill 1962- 205
Dawson, Jim
See Dawson, James Lee
Dawson, Joseph G(reen) III 1945- 110
Dawson, Joseph M(artin) 1879-1973 205
Dawson, Lorne L. 1954- 185
Dawson, Mary 1919- 21-24R
See also SATA 11
Dawson, Michael C. 1951- 222
Dawson, Mildred A(gnes)
1897-1988 .... CANR-12
Earlier sketch in CA 17-20R
Dawson, Minnie E. 1906-1978 85-88
Dawson, Peter
See Faust, Frederick (Schiller) and
Glidden, Jonathan Hurff
See also TCWW 1, 2
Dawson, (John) Philip 1928- CANR-94
Earlier sketch in CA 21-24R
Dawson, Richard E(vans) 1939- 73-76
Dawson, Robert (Merril) 1941- 21-24R
Dawson, Robert L(ewis) 1943- 105
Dawson, Robert MacGregor 1895-1958 159
Dawson, Roger 1940- 142
Dawson, Roxann (Biggs) 1964- 223
Dawson, Sarah Morgan 1842-1909 .... DLB 239
Dawson, William 1704-1752 .... DLB 31
Dawson-Scott, C(atharine) A(my) 1865-1934
Brief entry 113
See also Scott, Catharine Amy Dawson
Day, A(rthur) Colin 1935- 145
Day, A(rthur) Grove 1904-1994 .... CANR-23
Earlier sketches in CA 21-24R, CANR-8
See also SATA 59
Day, Aidan 1952- 132
Day, Alan 1932- 147
Day, Alan Charles Lynn 1924- 1-4R
Day, Alan J(ohn) 1942- 105
Day, Albert Edward 1884-1973 .... CANR-95
Obituary 45-48
Earlier sketches in CAP-2, CA 23-24
Day, Albert M. 1897-1979 93-96
Obituary 85-88
Day, Alexandra 136
See also CLR 22
See also MAICYA 2
See also MAICYAS 1
See also SAAS 19
See also SATA 67, 97
Day, Alice Taylor 1928- 17-20R
Day, Angel fl. 1586- .... DLB 167, 236
Day, Barry (Leonard) 1934- 206
Day, Benjamin Henry 1810-1889 .... DLB 43
Day, Beth (Feagles) 1924- CANR-40
Earlier sketches in CA 9-12R, CANR-3, 18
See also SATA 33
Day, Bradford M(arshall) 1916-2004 104
Day, Brian 237
Day, Cathy 1968- 233
Day, Clarence (Shepard, Jr.) 1874-1935 199
Brief entry 108
See also DLB 11
See also TCLC 25
Day, Clarence Burton 1889-1987
Obituary 121
Day, David 1944- 93-96
Day, (Stephen) Deforest 1941- 134
Day, Dianne 1938- CANR-91
Earlier sketch in CA 127
See also AAYA 43
Day, Donald
See Harding, Donald Edward
Day, Donna
See Asay, Donna Day
Day, Dorothy 1897-1980 65-68
Obituary 102
See also DLB 29
Day, Douglas (Turner III) 1932-2004 .. CANR-8
Obituary 232
Earlier sketch in CA 9-12R
Day, Edward C. 1932- 133
See also SATA 72
Day, Frank Parker 1881-1950 175
See also DLB 92
Day, Gardiner Mumford 1900-1981
Obituary 104
Day, George 1950- 117
Day, George Harold 1900- CAP-1
Earlier sketch in CA 13-14
Day, Gwynn McLendon 1908-1987 ...... CAP-1
Earlier sketch in CA 11-12
Day, H. Alan 1939- 204
Day, Herbert W.
See Stahl, Jerry
Day, Holliday T. 1936- 137
Day, Houston
See Day, Sam Houston
Day, J(ames) Edward 1914-1996 .... 17-20R
Obituary 154
Day, J(ohn) Laurence 1934- 65-68
Day, James F(rancis) 1917- 33-36R
Day, James Wentworth
1899-1983(?) CANR-10
Obituary 108
Earlier sketch in CA 13-16R
Day, John 1574(?)-1640(?) .... DLB 62, 170
See also RGEL 2
Day, John A(rthur) 1913- 17-20R
Day, John Patrick de Cormelie
1919-1999 .... 5-8R
Obituary 187
Day, John R(obert) 1917- CANR-9
Earlier sketch in CA 5-8R
Day, Jon 1936(?)- .... SATA 79
Day, Kathleen (Mary) 1944- 144
Day, Kenneth 1912- 9-12R
Day, Laura (Globus) 1959- 160
Day, LeRoy Judson 1917-1997 .... 21-24R
Day, Lincoln H(ubert) 1928- 17-20R
Day, Lucille 1947- 110
Day, M(ichael) H(erbert) 1927- 102
Day, Marele 1947- 173
Day, Martin Steele 1917-1984 .... CANR-7
Earlier sketch in CA 5-8R
Day, Maurice 1892- .... SATA-Brief 30
Day, Max
See Cassiday, Bruce (Bingham)
Day, Melvin Norman 1923- 109
Day, Michael
See Dempewolff, Richard F(rederic)
Day, Michael (J.) 219
Day, Nancy 1953- 211
See also SATA 140
Day, Nancy Raines 1951- CANR-129
Earlier sketches in CA 111, CANR-60
See also SATA 93, 148
Day, Neil (Atherton) 1945- 140
Day, (Truman) Owen 1890-1983 69-72
Obituary 163
Day, Paul Woodford 1916- 25-28R
Day, Peter (Morton) 1914-1984 .... 1-4R
Day, Price 1907-1978 85-88
Obituary 81-84
Day, R(oss) H(enry) 1927- 29-32R
Day, Ralph L(ewis) 1926- CANR-7
Earlier sketch in CA 5-8R
Day, Richard 1896-1972 .... IDFW 3, 4
Day, Richard B(ruce) 1942- CANR-27
Earlier sketch in CA 49-52
Day, Richard E. 1929- 33-36R
Day, Richard Hollis 1933- 114
Day, Richard J. F. 1960- 234
Day, Robert 1941- .... TCWW 1, 2
Day, Robert Adams 1924- 53-56
Day, Robin 1923-2000 144
Obituary 189
Day, Sam Houston 1896-1984
Obituary 113
Day, Shirley 1962- 159
See also SATA 94
Day, Sir Robin
See Day, Robin
Day, Stacey B(iswas) 1927- CANR-57
Earlier sketches in CA 33-36R, CANR-29
Day, Thomas 1748-1789 .... DLB 39
See also YABC 1
Day, Trevor 1955- .... SATA 124
Dayal, Rajeshwar 1909-1999 130
Dayan, Moshe 1915-1981 .... CANR-22
Obituary 105
Earlier sketch in CA 21-24R
Dayan, Yael 1939- 89-92
See also Dayan, Yael
See also AITN 1
Dayan, Yael 1939- CANR-98
See also Dayan, Yael
Dayananda, James Yesupriya 1934- 81-84
Daydi-Tolson, Santiago 1943- 127
Day Lewis, C(ecil) 1904-1972 .... CANR-34
Obituary 33-36R
Earlier sketches in CAP-1, CA 13-16
See also Blake, Nicholas and
Lewis, C. Day
See also BRWS 3
See also CLC 1, 6, 10
See also CP 1
See also CWRI 5
See also DAM POET
See also DLB 15, 20
See also EWL 3
See also MTCW 1, 2
See also PC 11
See also RGEL 2
Day-Lewis, Sean (Francis) 1931- 132
Daynes, Byron W(ilford) 1937- 110
Daysh, G(eorge) H(enry) J(ohn) 1901-1987
Obituary 122
Dayton, Arwen Elys 1974- 195
Dayton, Charles (W.) 1943- CANR-91
Earlier sketch in CA 145
Dayton, Donald W(ilber) 1942- CANR-24
Earlier sketch in CA 69-72
Dayton, Edward R(isedorph) 1924- .. CANR-16
Earlier sketch in CA 85-88
Dayton, Eldorous L. 1906-1987
Obituary 122
Dayton, Irene 1922- CANR-6
Earlier sketch in CA 57-60
Dazai Osamu 164
See also Tsushima, Shuji
See also DLB 182
See also EWL 3
See also MJW
See also RGSF 2
See also RGWL 2, 3
See also SSC 41
See also TCLC 11
See also TWA
d'Azevedo, Warren L. 1920- 93-96
Dazey, Agnes J(ohnston) CAP-2
Earlier sketch in CA 23-24
See also SATA 2
Dazey, Frank M. CAP-2
Earlier sketch in CA 23-24
See also SATA 2
de Abreu, Gilda 1905-1979 238
Deacon, Alexis 1978- .... SATA 139
Deacon, Eileen
See Geipel, Eileen
Deacon, George Edward Raven 1906-1984
Obituary 114
Deacon, Joseph John 1920- 69-72
Deacon, Richard
See McCormick, (George) Donald (King)
Deacon, Richard 1922-1984
Obituary 113
Deacon, Ruth E. 1923- 102
Deacon, Terrence W(illiam) 1956(?)- 172
Deacon, William Arthur 1890-1977 89-92
See also CCA
See also DLB 68
Deadman, Ronald 1919-1988(?)
Obituary 125
See also SATA-Obit 56
Deagon, Ann (Fleming) 1930- 57-60
Deak, Edward Joseph, Jr. 1943- 53-56
Deak, Erzsi 1959- 227
See also SATA 152
Deak, Francis 1899-1972
Obituary 33-36R
Deak, Istvan 1926- CANR-119
Earlier sketches in CA 25-28R, CANR-11, 28, 52
Deakin, James 1929- CANR-24
Earlier sketches in CA 21-24R, CANR-8
Deakin, Motley F. 1920-1999 120
Deakin, Roger 1943(?)- 239
Deakin, Rose 1937- 109
Deakin, (Frederick) William (Dampier)
1913-2005 .... CANR-5
Obituary 235
Earlier sketch in CA 5-8R
Deakins, Roger Lee 1933- 61-64
Deal, Babs H(odges) 1929-2004 .... CANR-100
Obituary 223
Earlier sketches in CA 1-4R, CANR-1
Deal, Borden 1922-1985 .... CANR-43
Obituary 114
Earlier sketches in CA 1-4R, CANR-2
See also BW 2
See also DLB 6
Deal, Ernest L(afayette, Jr.) 1918-1984 132
Deal, Terrance E. 1939- 130
Deal, William S(anford) 1910-1992 .... CANR-3
Earlier sketch in CA 5-8R
De Alba, Alicia Gaspar 1958- 180
See also Gaspar de Alba, Alicia
Deale, Kenneth Edwin Lee 1907-(?) ... CANR-4
Earlier sketch in CA 5-8R
Dealey, E(dward) M(usgrove)
1892-1969 .... CAP-2
Earlier sketch in CA 23-24
Dealey, Ted
See Dealey, E(dward) M(usgrove)
de Almeida, Acacio 1938- .... IDFW 3, 4
deAlmeida, Hermione (Beatrice) 1950- 118
Dean, Abner 1910-1982
Obituary 107
Dean, Amber 1902-1985 .... CANR-94
Obituary 116
Earlier sketches in CA 5-8R, CANR-2
Dean, Amy E. 194
Dean, Anabel 1915- CANR-14
Earlier sketch in CA 37-40R
See also SATA 12

Cumulative Index 143 de Chasca

Dean, Barbara 1946- 113
Dean, Basil (Herbert) 1888-1978 ..... CANR-76
 Obituary 134
 Earlier sketch in CA 69-72
 See also IDFW 3, 4
Dean, Beryl 1911-2001 .... 9-12R
 Obituary 194
Dean, Bradley P. 1954- 141
Dean, Burton V(ictor) 1924- CANR-20
 Earlier sketches in CA 45-48, CANR-1
Dean, Carolee 1962- 222
 See also SATA 148
Dean, Christopher G(eorge) 1940- 111
Dean, Cornelia 235
Dean, Dennis R(ichard) 1938- 137
Dean, Dorothy 1932(?)-1987
 Obituary 121
Dean (McGaughy), Dudley .... TCWW 1, 2
Dean, Dwight G(antz) 1918-1989 .... 17-20R
Dean, E. Douglas 1916- 97-100
Dean, Edith M(ae) 1915-1999 111
Dean, Edwin R(obinson) 1933- 17-20R
Dean, Elinor
 See McCann, Helen
Dean, Eric T., Jr. 1950- 170
Dean, Frances Mary 1905(?)-1983
 Obituary 110
Dean, Herbert Morris 1938- 105
Dean, Howard E(dward) 1916-1994 ..... 41-44R
Dean, Ida
 See Grae, Ida
Dean, Jeffrey S. 1939- 37-40R
Dean, (Alfreda) Joan 1925- 101
Dean, Joan FitzPatrick 1949- 118
Dean, Joel 1906-1979 .... 33-36R
Dean, John
 See Bumppo, Nathaniel John Balthazar
Dean, John A(urie) 1921- 53-56
Dean, John R. 1960- 185
Dean, John Wesley III 1938- 105
Dean, Karen Strickler 1923- CANR-26
 Earlier sketch in CA 109
 See also SATA 49
Dean, Leonard Fellows 1909-1999
 Brief entry 105
Dean, Luella Jo 1908(?)-1977
 Obituary 69-72
Dean, Malcolm 1948- CANR-31
 Earlier sketch in CA 105
Dean, Martin 1962- 204
Dean, Morton 1935- 69-72
Dean, Nancy 1930- 65-68
Dean, Nell Marr 1910- 21-24R
Dean (Dyer-Bennett), Pamela (Collins)
 1953- 154
 See also FANT
Dean, Phillip Hayes 230
 See also CAD
 See also CD 5, 6
Dean, Robert George 1904(?)-1989
 Obituary 130
Dean, Roger 1944- 172
 Brief entry 114
Dean, Roy 1925- CANR-6
 Earlier sketch in CA 57-60
Dean, Ruth (Brigham) 1947- 218
 See also SATA 145
Dean, Stanley (Rochelle) 1908-2000 73-76
Dean, Vera Micheles 1903-1972
 Obituary 37-40R
Dean, Warren 1932-1994 .... CANR-76
 Obituary 145
 Earlier sketch in CA 29-32R
Dean, William D(enard) 1937- 37-40R
Dean, William F(rishe) 1899-1981
 Obituary 105
Dean, Winton Basil 1916- CANR-73
 Earlier sketches in CA 65-68, CANR-10
Dean, Yetive H(ornor) 1909-1999 .... CAP-1
 Earlier sketch in CA 9-10
Dean, Zoey
 See Bennett, Cherie
de Andrade, Carlos Drummond
 See Drummond de Andrade, Carlos
de Andrade, Eugenio
 See Fontinhas, Jose
de Andrade, Mario 1892(?)-1945 178
 See also Andrade, Mario de
 See also HW 2
de Andrade, Oswald 1890-1954 176
 See also Andrade, Oswald de
 See also HW 2
DeAndrea, William L(ouis)
 1952-1996 .... CANR-59
 Earlier sketches in CA 81-84, CANR-20
 Interview in CANR-20
 See also CMW 4
Deane, Dee Shirley 1928- 81-84
Deane, Elisabeth
 See Beilenson, Edna
Deane, Herbert Andrew 1921-1991 .... 1-4R
Deane, James G(arner) 1923- 89-92
Deane, Lorna
 See Wilkinson, Lorna Hilda Kathleen
Deane, Nancy H(ilts) 1939- 29-32R
Deane, Norman
 See Creasey, John
Deane, Seamus (Francis) 1940- CANR-42
 Earlier sketch in CA 118
 See also CLC 122
Deane, Shirley Joan 1920- CANR-73
 Earlier sketches in CA 1-4R, CANR-2
de Angeli, Marguerite (Lofft)
 1889-1987 .... CANR-3
 Obituary 122
 Earlier sketch in CA 5-8R
 See also AITN 2
 See also BYA 1
 See also CLR 1
 See also CWRI 5
 See also DLB 22
 See also MAICYA 1, 2
 See also SATA 1, 27, 100
 See also SATA-Obit 51
De Angelis, Barbara (Ann) 1951- CANR-88
 Earlier sketch in CA 139
 See also BEST 90:3
DeAngelis, Lissa G. 1954- 173
De Angelis, Milo 1951- .... DLB 128
DeAngelis, William 1943- 113
Deans, Sis Boulos 1955- CANR-115
 Earlier sketch in CA 146
 See also AAYA 59
 See also SATA 78, 136
de Antonio, Emile 1922-1989 .... CANR-76
 Obituary 130
 Brief entry 113
 Earlier sketch in CA 117
 Interview in CA-117
Dear, John 1959- 200
Dear, Nick 1955- 230
 See also CBD
 See also CD 5, 6
Dear, William (C.) 1937- 125
de Aragon, Ray John 1946- 115
De Araugo, Tess (S.) 1930- 135
De Araugo-O'Mullane, Tess
 See De Araugo, Tess (S.)
Dearborn, Mary V. 1955- CANR-88
 Earlier sketch in CA 142
Dearden, Harold 1882(?)-1962
 Obituary 116
Dearden, James 1949- 136
Dearden, James A(rthur) 1924-1976 ...... 33-36R
Dearden, James S(hackley) 1931- CANR-12
 Earlier sketch in CA 25-28R
Dearden, John 1919-2004 .... 33-36R
 Obituary 222
Dearden, Philip 1952- 179
Deardorff, Robert 1912-1975 61-64
Deardorff, Tom 1940- 89-92
Dearie, John 226
Dearing, James (William) 1959- 114
Dearing, Sarah 234
Dearing, Vinton (Adams) 1920-2005 110
 Obituary 238
Dearlove, John 1944- 97-100
DeArmand, Frances Ullmann
 1904(?)-1984 .... CANR-76
 Obituary 112
 Earlier sketch in CA 5-8R
 See also SATA 10
 See also SATA-Obit 38
De Armas, Frederick A(lfred) 1945- .. CANR-91
 Earlier sketch in CA 37-40R
de Armas, Jose R(afael) 1924- 113
DeArment, Robert K(endall) 1925- 93-96
Dearmer, Geoffrey 1893-1996 .... CAP-2
 Obituary 153
 Earlier sketch in CA 23-24
Dearmin, Jeannie Tarascou 1924- 5-8R
DeArmond, Dale 1914- 138
 See also SATA 70
DeArmond, Dale Burlison
 See DeArmond, Dale
Dearstyne, Howard (Best) 1903-1979 121
 Obituary 85-88
De Arteaga, William 1943- 111
Deary, Terry 1946- 110
 See also SATA 51, 101
 See also SATA-Brief 41
Deason, Hilary J(ohn) 1903-1984 73-76
d'Easum, Cedric (Godfrey)
 1907-1990 .... CANR-12
 Obituary 163
 Earlier sketch in CA 73-76
d'Easum, Dick
 See d'Easum, Cedric (Godfrey)
Deasy, C(ornelius) M(ichael) 1918- 93-96
Deasy, Mary (Margaret) 1914-1978 .... 5-8R
de Athayde, Tristao
 See Amoroso Lima, Alceu
Deathridge, John (William) 1944- 133
Deaton, Charles W. 1942- 93-96
Deaton, John (Graydon) 1939- CANR-11
 Earlier sketch in CA 61-64
Deats, Paul (Kindred), Jr. 1918- 13-16R
Deats, Randy 1954- 93-96
Deats, Richard L(ouis) 1932- 21-24R
D'Eau, Jean
 See Gould, Allan (Mendel)
d'Eaubonne, Jean 1903-1970 .... IDFW 3, 4
Deaux, George (Richard) 1931- CANR-100
 Earlier sketch in CA 5-8R
Deaux, Kay 1941- 114
de Avalle-Arce, Juan Bautista
 See Avalle-Arce, Juan Bautista de
Deaver, Jeff
 See Deaver, Jeffery (Wilds)
Deaver, Jeffery (Wilds) 1950- CANR-105
 Earlier sketch in CA 163
 See also AAYA 41
Deaver, Julie Reece 1953- CANR-135
 Earlier sketches in CA 129, CANR-37
 See also AAYA 52
 See also BYA 8
 See also SATA 68
 See also YAW
Deaver, Michael Keith 1938- 230
Deb, Siddhartha 1970- 222
de Baecque, Antoine 231
DeBakey, Michael E(llis) 1908- 73-76
de Balker, Habakuk II
 See ter Balkt, H(erman) H(endrik)
de Banke, Cecile 1889-1965 .... CAP-1
 Earlier sketch in CA 13-14
 See also SATA 11
Debartolo, Tiffanie 1972- 212
de Bary, Brett
 See Nee, Brett de Bary
deBary, William Theodore 1919- CANR-37
 Earlier sketch in CA 57-60
Debassige, Blake 1956- 212
DeBeaubien, Philip Francis 1913-1979
 Obituary 85-88
de Beauregard, Georges 1920-1984 . IDFW 3, 4
de Beausobre, Iulia
 See Namier, Julia
de Beauvoir, Simone (Lucie Ernestine Marie Bertrand)
 See Beauvoir, Simone (Lucie Ernestine Marie Bertrand) de
de Becker, Gavin CANR-138
 Earlier sketch in CA 166
de Bedts, Ralph F(ortes) 1914-1994 .... 9-12R
De Beer, E(smond) S(amuel)
 1895-1990 .... CANR-76
 Obituary 132
 Earlier sketches in CAP-1, CA 13-14
de Beer, Gavin R(ylands)
 1899-1972 .... CANR-95
 Earlier sketches in CAP-1, CA 13-16
de Beer, P.
 See Bosman, Herman Charles
Debeljak, Ales 1961- .... EWL 3
De Bello, Rosario 1923- .... SATA 89
DeBenedetti, Charles Louis
 1943-1987 .... CANR-77
 Obituary 121
 Earlier sketch in CA 102
DeBerard, Ella 1900-1988 73-76
Deberdt-Malaquais, Elisabeth 1937- 57-60
DeBerg, Betty A. 1953- 199
de Bernieres, Louis 1954- CANR-72
 Earlier sketch in CA 133
 See also Bernieres, Louis de
 See also CN 6, 7
DeBerry, Virginia 180
de Betancourt, Cressy
 See Dobkin De Rios, Marlene
DeBetz, Barbara Holstein 123
de Beus, Jacobus Gysbertus 1909- 102
Debevec Henning, Sylvie Marie 1948- 109
Debi, Anila
 See Chatterje, Sarat Chandra
Debicki, Andrew P(eter) 1934- CANR-37
 Earlier sketch in CA 37-40R
Debicki, Roman 1896-1980 .... 1-4R
 Obituary 163
Debin, David 1942- 150
de Blank, Joost 1908-1968 .... CAP-1
 Earlier sketch in CA 13-14
De Blasis, Celeste (Ninette)
 1946-2001 .... CANR-63
 Earlier sketches in CA 53-56, CANR-4
 See also RHW
 See also TCWW 2
Deblieu, Jan 1955- 146
de Blij, Harm J(an) 1935- CANR-23
 Earlier sketches in CA 13-16R, CANR-8
Debo, Angie 1890-1988 .... CANR-40
 Obituary 124
 Earlier sketch in CA 69-72
De Boe, David C. 1942- 127
DeBoer, John C(harles) 1923- CANR-26
 Earlier sketch in CA 29-32R
DeBoer, John James 1903-1969 .... CANR-3
 Earlier sketch in CA 1-4R
de Bois, Helma
 See de Bois, Wilhelmina J. E.
de Bois, Wilhelmina J. E. 1923- 17-20R
de Boissiere, Ralph (Anthony)
 1907- CANR-67
 Earlier sketch in CA 106
 See also CN 4, 5, 6, 7
DeBold, Richard C. 1927- 21-24R
DeBolt, Margaret Wayt 1930- 115
Debon, Nicolas .... SATA 151
De Bona, Maurice, Jr. 1926- 65-68
De Bondt, Gabe J. 1969- 202
DeBonis, Steven 1949- 150
De Bono, Douglas 1957- 227
de Bono, Edward 1933- CANR-144
 Earlier sketches in CA 21-24R, CANR-10, 43
 See also MTCW 1
 See also SATA 66
De Bonville, Bob 1926- 69-72
De Borchgrave, Arnaud 1926- 73-76
de Borchgrave, Baroness Sheri 1952- 145
Debord, Guy 1931-1994 .... DLB 296
De Borhegyi, Suzanne Sims 1926- 5-8R
de Born, Edith 25-28R
de Boschere, Jean 1878-1953 202
De Botton, Alain 1969- CANR-96
 Earlier sketch in CA 159
 See also CLC 203
De Bow, James Dunwoody Brownson
 1820-1867 .... DLB 3, 79, 248
DeBoy, James J(oseph), Jr. 1942- 113
de Boysson-Bardies, Benedicte 1931- 218
Debray, (Jules) Regis 1940- CANR-117
 Earlier sketches in CA 21-24R, CANR-43
Debre, P(atrice) 1945- 189
de Breadun, Deaglan 204
Debreczeny, Paul 1932- CANR-12
 Earlier sketch in CA 33-36R
De Breffny, Brian (O'Rorke)
 1931(?)-1989 .... CANR-77
 Obituary 127
 Earlier sketch in CA 77-80
Debrett, Hal
 See Dresser, Davis
Debreu, Gerard 1921-2004 .... CANR-23
 Obituary 234
 Earlier sketch in CA 37-40R
de Brissac, Malcolm
 See Dickinson, Peter (Malcolm de Brissac)
Debrix, Francois 1968- 216
de Broca, Philippe (Claude Alex)
 1933-2004 126
 Obituary 233
de Broglie, L.
 See de Broglie, Louis (Victor Pierre Raymond)
de Broglie, Louis (Victor Pierre Raymond)
 1892-1987 155
 Obituary 122
de Brunhoff, Jean
 See Brunhoff, Jean de
De Brunhoff, Laurent
 See Brunhoff, Laurent de
de Bruyn, Guenter 1926- 178
 See also DLB 75
de Bruyn, Monica (Jean) G(rembowicz)
 1952- 65-68
 See also SATA 13
DeBry, Roger K. 1942- 155
 See also SATA 91
Debs, Eugene V. 1855-1926 .... DLB 303
Debs, Victor, Jr. 1949- 164
De Burca, Grainne 1966- 215
de Burgos, Julia 1914-1953 164
 See also Burgos, Julia de
 See also HW 2
DeBuron, Nicole 200
Debus, Allen G(eorge) 1926- CANR-57
 Earlier sketches in CA 37-40R, CANR-14, 31
Debussy, (Achille) Claude 1862-1918
 Brief entry 118
deBuys, William (Eno, Jr.) 1949- 136
Decae, Henri 1915-1987 .... IDFW 3, 4
de Calles, Jane F. Butel 1938- 126
Decalo, Samuel 1937- 121
de Camp, Catherine Crook
 1907-2000 .... CANR-20
 Earlier sketches in CA 21-24R, CANR-9
 See also SATA 12, 83
DeCamp, Graydon 1934- 97-100
de Camp, L(yon) Sprague
 1907-2000 .... CANR-84
 Obituary 191
 Earlier sketches in CA 1-4R, CANR-1, 9, 20
 See also BPFB 1
 See also DLB 8
 See also FANT
 See also SATA 9, 83
 See also SCFW 1, 2
 See also SFW 4
 See also SUFW 1
de Campi, John Webb 1939- 69-72
de Campos, Alvaro
 See Pessoa, Fernando (Antonio Nogueira)
De Campos, L.
 See Dahl, Linda
DeCandido, Keith R. A. 173
 See also SATA 112
De Canio, Stephen J(ohn) 1942- 57-60
De Capite, Raymond Anthony
 1924- CANR-74
 Earlier sketch in CA 1-4R
DeCarava, Roy 1919- .... AAYA 66
Decarie, Therese Gouin 1923- 41-44R
DeCarl, Lennard 1940- 81-84
De Carlo, Andrea 1952- CANR-82
 Earlier sketch in CA 132
 See also DLB 196
de Carvalho, Fernando Jose Cardim 1953- . 143
de Carvalho, Mario 1944- 164
de Carvalho, Ronald 1893-1935 178
 See also HW 2
De Casas, Celso A. .... DLB 209
de Castrique, Mark 1948- 228
de Castro, Fernando J(ose) 1937- 53-56
De Castro, Josue 1908-1973 .... 33-36R
De Caux, Len
 See De Caux, Leonard Howard
De Caux, Leonard Howard 1899-1992 . 29-32R
Decaux, Lucile
 See Bibesco, Marthe Lucie
Decavalles, Andonis (George) 1920- 197
DeCecco, John Paul 1925- 17-20R
de Cervera, Alejo 1919- 21-24R
de Cespedes, Alba 1911-1997 .... DLB 264
 See also WLIT 7
DeCew, Judith (Wagner) 1948- 190
de Chair, Somerset (Struben)
 1911-1995 .... CANR-76
 Obituary 147
 Earlier sketches in CA 45-48, CANR-1
de Chamberet, Georgia 229
DeChancie, John 1946- CANR-41
 Earlier sketch in CA 118
 See also FANT
Dechanet, Jean 1906- 198
Dechant, Emerald V(ictor) 1926- 9-12R
DeChant, John A(loysius) 1917-1974 ..... CAP-2
 Obituary 53-56
 Earlier sketch in CA 23-24
de Chardin, Pierre Teilhard
 See Teilhard de Chardin, (Marie Joseph) Pierre
deCharms, Richard IV 1927- 41-44R
de Chasca, Edmund V(illela) 1903-
 Brief entry 117

de Chatellerault 144 CONTEMPORARY AUTHORS

de Chatellerault, Victor
See Beaudoin, Kenneth Lawrence
Dechausay, Sonia E. 159
See also SATA 94
Dechert, Charles R(ichard) 1927- CANR-10
Earlier sketch in CA 21-24R
Dechert, Robert 1895-1975 .... DLB 187
de Chirico, Giorgio 1888-1978 89-92
Obituary 81-84
De Christoforo, Ron(ald) 1951- 81-84
Deci, Edward L(ewis) 1942- CANR-39
Earlier sketch in CA 53-56
Deck, Allen F.
See Deck, Allen Figueroa
Deck, Allen Figueroa 1945- 150
Decker, Albert 1895-1988
Obituary 127
Decker, Beatrice 1919-1978 61-64
Decker, Donald M(ilton) 1923- 37-40R
Decker, Duane 1910-1964 .... 5-8R
See also SATA 5
Decker, Hannah S(hulman) 1937- 85-88
Decker, Leslie E(dward) 1930- 9-12R
Decker, Peter R(andolph) 1934- 188
Decker, Robert Owen 1927- 65-68
Decker, Thomas (W.) 1927- 216
Decker, William 1926-2000
Obituary 188
Brief entry 115
See also TCWW 1, 2
Deckers, Jeanine 1933(?)-1985
Obituary 115
Deckert, Alice Mae 13-16R
DeClements, Barthe (Faith) 1920- .. CANR-103
Earlier sketches in CA 105, CANR-22, 45
See also CLR 23
See also JRDA
See also MAICYA 2
See also MAICYAS 1
See also SATA 35, 71, 131
De Cock, Liliane 1939- CANR-2
Earlier sketch in CA 45-48
Decoin, Didier 1945- 186
Decolta, Ramon
See Whitfield, Raoul
DeConde, Alexander 1920- CANR-6
Earlier sketch in CA 5-8R
de Conte, Sieur Louis
See Clemens, Samuel Langhorne
De Costa, Elena M. 1949- 144
de Costa, (George) Rene 1939- 102
DeCosta-Willis, Miriam 1934- 142
See also BW 2
deCoste, Fredrik 1910-1977 .... CAP-2
Earlier sketch in CA 21-22
DeCoster, Cyrus C(ole) 1914-1999 ... CANR-29
Earlier sketch in CA 49-52
de Courcy, Anne 221
deCourcy, Lynne Hugo 1946- 196
deCourcy Hinds, Michael 1947- 114
DeCoursey, Virginia 1924- 114
deCoy, Robert H(arold), Jr. 1920-1975 .. 25-28R
DeCredico, Mary A. 1959- 135
De Crescenzo, Luciano 1928- 133
de Crespigny, (Richard) Rafe (Champion)
1936- 57-60
De Cristoforo, R(omeo) J(ohn)
1917-2000 .... CANR-3
Earlier sketch in CA 9-12R
DeCrow, Karen 1937- CANR-37
Earlier sketch in CA 33-36R
Decter, Midge (Rosenthal) 1927- CANR-107
Earlier sketches in CA 45-48, CANR-2
DeCure, John 218
Dedek, John F. 1929- 33-36R
Dederer, John Morgan 1951- 136
Dederick, Robert 1919-
Brief entry 116
See also CP 1
de Dienes, Andre 1913-1985 .... 41-44R
Dedijer, Vladimir 1914-1990 .... CANR-75
Obituary 133
Earlier sketches in CA 1-4R, CANR-4
Dedina, Michel 1933- 33-36R
Dedini, Eldon 1921- 65-68
Dedman, Stephen 166
See also SATA 108
Dedmon, Emmett 1918-1983 .... CANR-76
Obituary 110
Earlier sketches in CA 9-12R, CANR-5
de Duve, Christian (Rene Marie Joseph)
See de Duve, Christian (Rene Marie Joseph)
de Duve, Christian (Rene Marie Joseph)
1917- CANR-134
Earlier sketch in CA 157
Dee, Catherine 1964- 209
See also SATA 138
Dee, Ed(ward J., Jr.) 1940- CANR-72
Earlier sketch in CA 146
Dee, Henry
See Torbett, Harvey Douglas Louis
Dee, John 1527-1608 .... DLB 136, 213
Dee, Johnny
See Krauzer, Steven M(ark)
Dee, Jonathan 204
Dee, Ron(ald David) 1957- .... HGG
Dee, Ruby
See Wallace, Ruby Ann
See also SATA 77
Deeb, Gary (James) 1945- 138
Deedle, R(ussell) J(ohn) .... CP 1
Deedy, John 1923- 33-36R
See also SATA 24
Deegan, Paul Joseph 1937- 102
See also SATA 48
See also SATA-Brief 38
Deeken, Alfons 1932- 77-80
Deeley, Roger 1944- 53-56
Deelman, Christian Felling 1937-1964 .. CAP-1
Earlier sketch in CA 11-12
Deem, James M(organ) 1950- CANR-112
Earlier sketch in CA 142
See also SATA 75, 134
Deemer, Bill 1945- 17-20R
See also CP 1
Deemer, Charles (Robert, Jr.) 1939- 73-76
Deen, Edith Alderman 1905-1994 .... CANR-74
Earlier sketches in CA 5-8R, CANR-2
Deena, Seodial F(rank) H(ubert) 1956- 227
Deener, David R(ussell) 1920-1976 .. CANR-76
Obituary 134
Earlier sketch in CA 17-20R
Deep Chin
See Gould, Allan (Mendel)
Deeping, (George) Warwick 1877-1950
Brief entry 114
See also DLB 153
See also RHW
Deeps, Frederick
See Speed, F(rederick) Maurice
Deep Throat
See Felt, W. Mark
Deer, Irving 1924- 17-20R
Deer, Sandra 1940- 186
See also CLC 45
Deere, Carolyn L. 1973- 235
Deese, Helen 1925- 126
Deese, James (Earle) 1921-1999 .... CANR-5
Earlier sketch in CA 1-4R
Deeter, Allen C. 1931- 45-48
Deeter, Catherine 1947- .... SATA 137
de Extramuros, Quixote
See Espino, Federico (Licsi, Jr.)
DeFalco, Joseph Michael 1931- 13-16R
Defant, Marc J. 1951- CANR-140
Earlier sketch in CA 174
DeFanti, Charles 1942- 89-92
de Faria, Octavio
See Faria, Otavio de
DeFelice, Cynthia (C.) 1951- 192
See also AAYA 36
See also MAICYA 2
See also MAICYAS 1
See also SATA 79, 121
DeFelice, James (V.) 1940- 128
DeFelice, Jim 1956- 142
DeFelice, Louise P(aula) 1945- 61-64
De Felitta, Frank (Paul) 1921- CANR-73
Earlier sketches in CA 61-64, CANR-28
See also HGG
De Felitta, Raymond 1964- 214
De Ferrari, Gabriella 1941- 146
See also CLC 65
Deferrari, Roy J(oseph) 1890-1969 .... CAP-1
Earlier sketch in CA 13-14
DeFerrari, Sister Teresa Mary 1930- 9-12R
Deffaa, Chip 1951- 153
Deffand, Marie de Vichy-Chamrond
1696-1780 .... DLB 313
Deffner, Donald L(ouis) 1924-1997 .. CANR-11
Earlier sketch in CA 17-20R
Deffry, Frank 1938- .... CP 1
DeFilippi, Jim 1943- 200
de Filippo, Eduardo 1900-1984 132
Obituary 114
See also EWL 3
See also MTCW 1
See also RGWL 2, 3
See also TCLC 127
de Flandre, B.
See Ferland, Albert
de Fletin, P.
See Fielden, T(homas) P(erceval)
Defoe, Daniel 1660(?)-1731 .... AAYA 27
See also BRW 3
See also BRWR 1
See also BYA 4
See also CDBLB 1660-1789
See also CLR 61
See also DA
See also DA3
See also DAB
See also DAC
See also DAM MST, NOV
See also DLB 39, 95, 101
See also JRDA
See also LAIT 1
See also LMFS 1
See also MAICYA 1, 2
See also NFS 9, 13
See also RGEL 2
See also SATA 22
See also TEA
See also WCH
See also WLC
See also WLIT 3
de Fontaine, Felix Gregory 1834-1896 . DLB 43
deFontaine, Wade Hampton
1893-1969 .... CANR-77
Obituary 103
Earlier sketch in CA 5-8R
De Forbes
See Forbes, DeLoris (Florine) Stanton
DeFord, Deborah H. CANR-101
Earlier sketch in CA 185
See also SATA 123
Deford, Frank 1938- CANR-113
Earlier sketches in CA 33-36R, CANR-45
See also AAYA 14
deFord, Miriam Allen 1888-1975 .... CANR-4
Earlier sketch in CA 1-4R
See also SFW 4
deFord, Sara (Whitcraft) 1916-1996 .... 25-28R
DeForest, Charlotte B. 1879-1971 .... CAP-2
Earlier sketch in CA 25-28
De Forest, John William 1826-1906 185
Brief entry 119
See also DLB 12, 189
See also RGAL 4
De Forest, Lee 1873-1961 157
Obituary 112
DeForest, Orrin L. 1923- 134
de Forrest, Julie
See DeWitt, Edith Openshaw
de Fossard, R(onald) A(lfred) 1929- 41-44R
de Fox, Lucia Ungaro
See Lockert, Lucia (Alicia Ungaro Fox)
deFrance, Anthony
See DiFranco, Anthony (Mario)
DeFrancis, John Francis 1911- 185
Brief entry 106
DeFrank, Thomas M. 1945- 152
See also DeFrank, Tom
DeFrank, Tom
See DeFrank, Thomas M.
DeFrees, Madeline 1919- CANR-140
Earlier sketches in CA 9-12R, CANR-4
See also CP 1, 7
See also DLB 105
de Funiak, William Q(uinby)
1901-1981 .... 33-36R
de Gamez, Cielo Cayetana Alba
See Alba de Gamez, Cielo Cayetana
de Gamez, Tana
See Alba de Gamez, Cielo Cayetana
Degani, Meir H(ershtenkorn) 1909-1982 102
DeGarmo, Kenneth Scott 1943- 81-84
Degas, Edgar 1834-1917 .... AAYA 56
de Gaulle, Charles (Andre Joseph Marie)
1890-1970 .... CANR-102
Obituary 111
Earlier sketch in CA 130
de Gaulle-Anthonioz, Genevieve
1920-2002 220
de Gaury, Gerald 1897-1984 .... CANR-73
Obituary 112
Earlier sketch in CA 13-16R
Degee, Olivier
See Degee, Olivier
Degen, Bruce 1945- CANR-128
Earlier sketch in CA 124
See also MAICYA 2
See also MAICYAS 1
See also SATA 57, 97, 147
See also SATA-Brief 47
Degeneres, Ellen 1958- 165
Degenhardt, Henry W(illiam) 1910- . CANR-23
Earlier sketch in CA 106
De Gennaro, Angelo Anthony 1919- 13-16R
De Gennes, Pierre-Gilles 1932- 157
Degenshein, George A. 1918(?)-1979
Obituary 93-96
De George, Richard T(homas)
1933- CANR-39
Earlier sketches in CA 5-8R, CANR-2, 17
DeGering, Etta (Belle) Fowler
1898-1996 .... CANR-74
Earlier sketches in CAP-1, CA 9-10
See also SATA 7
Degh, Linda 1920- 85-88
Deghy, Guy (Stephen) 1912-1992 .... CANR-76
Obituary 137
Earlier sketches in CAP-1, CA 9-10
DeGidio, Sandra 1943- 112
Degler, Carl N(eumann) 1921-1998 ... CANR-3
Earlier sketch in CA 5-8R
Degler, Stanley E. 1929- 25-28R
Degli-Esposti, Cristina 231
Degnan, James Philip 1933- 41-44R
De Goldi, Kate
See De Goldi, Kathleen Domenica
De Goldi, Kathleen Domenica 1959- 194
See also MAICYA 2
See also SATA 123
DeGolyer, Everette Lee 1886-1956 199
See also DLB 187
Degonwadonti
See Brant, Beth (E.)
de Gouges, Olympe
See Gouges, Olympe de
de Gourmont, Remy(-Marie-Charles)
See Gourmont, Remy(-Marie-Charles) de
de Gournay, Marie le Jars 1566-1645 .... FW
DeGraaff, Robert M(ark) 1942- 141
de Graca, Jose Vieira Mateus
See Vieira, Jose Luandino
De Graeff, Allen
See Blaustein, Albert Paul
de Graff, Robert F(air) 1895-1981
Obituary 105
See also DLBY 1981
de Graffe, Richard
See St. Clair, Leonard
de Graft, J(oseph) C(oleman)
1924-1978 .... CANR-92
Earlier sketches in CA 73-76, CANR-43
See also DLB 117
de Graft, Joe
See de Graft, J(oseph) C(oleman)
de Graft, John Coleman 1919- 21-24R
See also BW 2
de Graft-Hanson, J(ohn) O(rleans)
1932- .... CWRI 5
de Gramont, Sanche
See Morgan, Ted
De Grave, Kathleen 1950- 152
DeGrave, Philip
See DeAndrea, William L(ouis)
de Grazia, Alfred 1919- CANR-5
Earlier sketch in CA 13-16R
de Grazia, Edward 1927- 129
DeGrazia, Emilio 1941- 140
De Grazia, Ettore 1909-1982 .... CANR-13
Earlier sketch in CA 61-64
See also De Grazia, Ted
De Grazia, Sebastian 1917-2000 .... CANR-43
Obituary 191
Earlier sketch in CA 65-68
De Grazia, Ted
See De Grazia, Ettore
See also SATA 39
DeGre, Muriel (Harris) 1914-1971 .... CAP-1
Earlier sketch in CA 17-18
De Greene, Kenyon B(renton) CANR-14
Earlier sketch in CA 37-40R
De Gregori, Thomas R(oger) 1935- .. CANR-12
Earlier sketch in CA 29-32R
DeGregorio, William A(lfred) 1946- 117
DeGregory, Jerry L(ouis) 1945- 119
de Groat, Diane 1947- CANR-57
Earlier sketch in CA 107
See also SATA 31, 90
de Groen, Alma (Margaret) 1941- 232
See also CD 5, 6
See also CWD
DeGrood, David H. 1937- 33-36R
DeGroot, Alfred Thomas 1903-1992 .. CANR-5
Earlier sketch in CA 5-8R
De Groot, Henri L. F. 1971- 212
de Groot, Roy Andries 1910-1983
Obituary 110
deGros, J. H.
See Villiard, Paul
de Gruchy, John W(esley) 1939- CANR-95
Earlier sketch in CA 131
de Grummond, Lena Young CANR-1
Earlier sketch in CA 1-4R
See also SATA 6, 62
de Grunwald, Anatole 1910-1967 ... IDFW 3, 4
de Grunwald, Constantine 9-12R
de Guadaloupe, Brother Jose
See Mojica, Jose
Deguine, Jean-Claude 1943- 81-84
de Guingand, Francis Wilfred 1900-1979
Obituary 89-92
de Guise, Elizabeth (Mary Teresa) 1934- 126
See also RHW
de Gunzburg, Nicholas
See Gunzburg, Nicholas de
Deguy, Michel 1930- .... CWW 2
deGuzman, Daniel 1911-1987 93-96
DeHaan, M(artin) R(alph) 1891-1965 239
De Haan, Margaret
See Freed, Margaret De Haan
De Haan, Richard W. 1923- 21-24R
De Haas, Elsa 1901-1984 45-48
Obituary 163
de Hamel, Christopher (Frances Rivers)
1950- CANR-134
Earlier sketches in CA 120, CANR-45
de Hamel, Joan Littledale 1924- CANR-84
Earlier sketches in CA 103, CANR-51
See also CWRI 5
See also SATA 86
de Hart, Allen 1926- 119
de Hartmann, Olga 1883(?)-1979
Obituary 89-92
de Hartog, Jan 1914-2002 .... CANR-1
Obituary 210
Earlier sketch in CA 1-4R
See also CLC 19
See also DFS 12
De Haven, Tom 1949- CANR-117
Earlier sketch in CA 133
See also FANT
See also SATA 72
Dehejia, Vidya 1942- CANR-94
Earlier sketch in CA 136
de Herrera, Nancy Cooke 142
de Hevesy, Paul 1883-1988
Obituary 125
Dehmel, Richard 1863-1920 212
Dehn, Olive 1914- 117
Dehn, Paul (Edward) 1912-1976 89-92
See also CN 1, 2
See also IDFW 3
de Hondt, Christine
See Herzberg, Judith (Frieda Lina)
Dehoney, W(illiam) Wayne 1918- 17-20R
de Hostos, E. M.
See Hostos (y Bonilla), Eugenio Maria de
de Hostos, Eugenio M.
See Hostos (y Bonilla), Eugenio Maria de
de Hoyos, Angela
See Hoyos, Angela de
Dehqani-Tafti, H. B. 1920- 106
Dehr, Dorothy 1915- 29-32R
de Hugo, Pierre
See Brackers de Hugo, Pierre
Dei-Anang, Michael 1909-1978 53-56
See also CP 1
Deibler, William E. 1932- 89-92
Deichmann, Ute 1951- CANR-122
Earlier sketch in CA 164
Deighton, Lee C(ecil) 1906-1987 124
Obituary 122
Deighton, Len
See Deighton, Leonard Cyril
See also AAYA 6
See also BEST 89:2
See also BPFB 1
See also CDBLB 1960 to Present
See also CLC 4, 7, 22, 46
See also CMW 4
See also CN 1, 2, 3, 4, 5, 6, 7
See also CPW
See also DLB 87

Cumulative Index 145 Delbanco

Deighton, Leonard Cyril 1929- CANR-68
Earlier sketches in CA 9-12R, CANR-19, 33
See also Deighton, Len
See also AAYA 57
See also DA3
See also DAM NOV, POP
See also MTCW 1, 2
See also MTFW 2005
Deikman, Arthur J(oseph) 1929- 65-68
Deindorfer, Robert Greene
1922-1983 .... CANR-76
Obituary 109
Earlier sketches in CA 9-12R, CANR-3
Deindorfer, Scott 1967- 81-84
Deinzer, Harvey T. 1908-1990 .... 17-20R
de Iongh, Mary (Dows Herter Norton) Crena
See Crena de Iongh, Mary (Dows Herter Norton)
Deisenhofer, Johann 1943- 157
Deiss, Joseph Jay 1915- CANR-100
Earlier sketches in CA 33-36R, CANR-14
See also SATA 12
Deist, Wilhelm 1931- 136
Deitrick, Frances I. 1962- 137
Deitsch, Jeremy Stafford
See Stafford-Deitsch, Jeremy
Deitz, Susan 1934- 110
Deitz, Tom 1952- CANR-126
Earlier sketch in CA 154
See also FANT
De Jaegher, Raymond-Joseph
1905-1980 .... CANR-77
Obituary 93-96
Earlier sketches in CAP-2, CA 21-22
DeJean, Joan (Elizabeth) 1948- CANR-80
Earlier sketch in CA 134
de Jenkins, Lyll Becerra 1925-1997 169
See also AAYA 33
See also HW 2
See also SATA 102
DeJohn, Jacqueline 231
Dejohnson, Shervene 235
De Jong, Arthur J(ay) 1934- 69-72
DeJong, David C(ornel) 1905-1967 .... 5-8R
See also SATA 10
de Jong, Dola 1911-2003 .... 5-8R
Obituary 224
See also de Jong, Dorothea Rosalie
See also SATA 7
See also SATA-Obit 149
de Jong, Dorothea Rosalie
1911-2003 .... CANR-100
See also de Jong, Dola
de Jong, Eveline D(orothea) 1948- 130
De Jong, Gerald Francis 1921- 61-64
de Jong, Gerrit, Jr. 1892-1978 .... 37-40R
De Jong, Gordon F(rederick) 1935- 25-28R
DeJong, Meindert 1906-1991 .... CANR-105
Obituary 134
Earlier sketches in CA 13-16R, CANR-36
See also BYA 2, 3
See also CLR 1, 73
See also CWRI 5
See also DLB 52
See also MAICYA 1, 2
See also SATA 2
See also SATA-Obit 68
De Jong, Peter 1945- 69-72
De Jong, Russell N(elson) 1907-1990
Obituary 132
de Jonge, Alex 1938- CANR-42
Earlier sketches in CA 53-56, CANR-5
DeJonge, Joanne E. 1943- .... SATA 56
De Jonge, Marinus 1925- CANR-105
Earlier sketches in CA 123, CANR-50
de Jongh, James 1942- 85-88
de Journlet, Marie
See Little, Paul H(ugo)
de Jouvenel, Bertrand
See de Jouvenel des Ursins, Edouard Bertrand
de Jouvenel, Hugues Alain 1946- 130
de Jouvenel des Ursins, Edouard Bertrand
1903-1987
Obituary 121
De Jovine, F(elix) Anthony 1927-1976 .. CAP-2
Earlier sketch in CA 29-32
Deju, Raul A(ntonio) 1946- 53-56
Deka, Connie
See Laux, Constance
DeKalb, Lorimer
See Knorr, Marian L(ockwood)
de Kay, James T(ertius) 1930- CANR-10
Earlier sketch in CA 25-28R
de Kay, Ormonde (Jr.) 1923-1998 49-52
Obituary 171
See also SATA 7
See also SATA-Obit 106
de Kerckhove, Derrick 1944- 173
de Kerpely, Theresa 1898-1993 119
deKieffer, Donald (Eulette) 1945- 112
de Kiewiet, Cornelis W(illem) 1902-1986
Obituary 118
de Kiewiet, Cornelius W(illiam)
See de Kiewiet, Cornelis W(illem)
de Kiewit, Cornelis W(illem)
See de Kiewiet, Cornelis W(illem)
de Kiriline, Louise
See Lawrence, Louise de Kiriline
Dekker, Carl
See Laffin, John (Alfred Charles) and Lynds, Dennis
Dekker, George 1934- CANR-74
Earlier sketch in CA 104
Dekker, Rudolf M(ichel) 1951- CANR-93
Earlier sketch in CA 132
Dekker, Thomas 1572(?)-1632 ... CDBLB Before 1660
See also DAM DRAM
See also DC 12
See also DLB 62, 172
See also LMFS 1
See also RGEL 2
Dekkers, Midas 1946- CANR-101
Earlier sketch in CA 153
Dekle, Bernard 1905-1988 .... 17-20R
Dekmejian, Richard Hrair 1933- 37-40R
Deknatel, F(rederick) B(rockway) 1905-1973
Obituary 45-48
Dekobra, Maurice
See Tessier, (Ernst) M(aurice)
De Koenigswerther, Edwin Raymond
1930- 49-52
DeKok, David (Paul) 1953- 124
de Kooning, Elaine (Marie Catherine)
1920-1989 148
de Kooning, Willem 1904-1997 .... AAYA 61
DeKosky, Robert K. 1945- 93-96
DeKoster, Lester Ronald 1915- 13-16R
De Koven, Bernard 1941- 85-88
De Koven, Bernie
See De Koven, Bernard
DeKoven Ezrahi, Sidra 210
Dekovic, Gene 1922- CANR-26
Earlier sketch in CA 108
de Kretser, Michelle 209
deKruif, Paul (Henry) 1890-1971 .... 9-12R
Obituary 29-32R
See also SATA 5, 50
de Kun, Nicolas 1923- 17-20R
de la Barca, Fanny Calderon
1804-1882 .... DLB 183
De La Bedoyere, Michael 1900-1973
Obituary 104
de la Billiere, Peter (Edgar de la Cour)
1934- 143
Delacato, Carl H(enry) 1923- 41-44R
DeLacerda, Fred G. 1937- 236
de Laclos, Pierre Ambroise Franois
See Laclos, Pierre-Ambroise Francois
Delacorta
See Odier, Daniel
Delacorte, George T., Jr. 1894-1991 178
See also DLB 91
Delacorte, Peter 1943- 105
de la Costa, Horacio (L.)
See Costa, Horacio (L.) de la
Delacour, Jean
See Delacour, Jean Theodore
Delacour, Jean Theodore 1890-1985
Obituary 117
Delacre, Lulu 1957- .... SATA 36, 156
de Lacretelle, Jacques 1888-1985 178
DeLaCroix, Alice 1940- 142
See also SATA 75
Delacroix, (Ferdinand-Victor-)Eugene
1798-1863 .... EW 5
de la Cruz, Melissa 1971- 204
DeLacy, Margaret (Eisenstein) 1951- 122
DeLaet, Sigfried J(an) 1914- CANR-18
Earlier sketches in CA 5-8R, CANR-3
Delafield, E. M.
See Dashwood, Edmee Elizabeth Monica de la Pasture
See also DLB 34
See also RHW
See also TCLC 61
de la Fuente, Alejandro M. 1963- 230
de la Fuente, Patricia 179
de la Garza, Rodolfo O(ropea) 1942- 77-80
Delage, Denys 1942- 149
De Lage, Ida 1918- CANR-14
Earlier sketch in CA 41-44R
See also SATA 11
de La Glannege, Roger-Maxe
See Legman, G(ershon)
De La Glannege, Roger-Maxe
See Legman, G(ershon)
Delagny
See Charbonneau, Jean
de la Guardia, Ernesto, Jr. 1904-1983
Obituary 109
de Laguna, Frederica (Annis Lopez de Leo)
1906-2004 .... 37-40R
Obituary 232
de Laguna, Grace Mead A(ndrus)
1878-1978 .... CAP-1
Obituary 77-80
Earlier sketch in CA 11-12
Delahanty, Randolph
See Delehanty, Randolph
Delahay, E(ileen) A(vril) 1915-1982 .. CANR-76
Obituary 117
Earlier sketch in CA 25-28R
Delahaye, Guy 1888-1969
See Lahaise, Francoise-Guillaume
See also CCA 1
See also DLB 92
Delahunt, Meaghan 1961- 204
De La Iglesia, Maria Elena 1936- 29-32R
de la Isla, Jose 1944- 224
Delamaide, Darrell (George) 1949- 146
de la Maraja, Xerex
See Begovic, Milan
de la Mare, Albinia Catherine
1932-2001 .... 33-36R
Obituary 203
de la Mare, Richard (Herbert Ingpen)
1901-1986
Obituary 118
de la Mare, Walter (John) 1873-1956 163
See also CDBLB 1914-1945
See also CLR 23
See also CWRI 5
See also DA3
See also DAB
See also DAC
See also DAM MST, POET
See also DLB 19, 153, 162, 255, 284
See also EWL 3
See also EXPP
See also HGG
See also MAICYA 1, 2
See also MTCW 2
See also MTFW 2005
See also RGEL 2
See also RGSF 2
See also SATA 16
See also SSC 14
See also SUFW 1
See also TCLC 4, 53
See also TEA
See also WCH
See also WLC
DeLamarter, Jeanne
See Bonnette, Jeanne
de Lamartine, Alphonse (Marie Louis Prat)
See Lamartine, Alphonse (Marie Louis Prat) de
DeLamotte, Roy Carroll 1917- CANR-15
Earlier sketch in CA 41-44R
DeLancey, Kiki 1959- 215
DeLancey, Mark W(akeman) 1939- 93-96
de Lancie, John 1948- 223
Deland, Margaret(ta Wade Campbell)
1857-1945
Brief entry 122
See also DLB 78
See also RGAL 4
Delaney, Bud
See Delaney, Francis, Jr.
Delaney, C(ornelius) F. 1938- CANR-16
Earlier sketch in CA 25-28R
Delaney, Carol (Lowery) 1940- 218
Delaney, Daniel J(oseph) 1938- 41-44R
Delaney, Denis
See Green, Peter (Morris)
Delaney, Edmund T. 1914-2000 .... CANR-74
Earlier sketch in CA 13-16R
Delaney, Edward J. 1957- 234
Delaney, Francis, Jr. 1931- 57-60
Delaney, Franey
See O'Hara, John (Henry)
Delaney, Frank 1942- 126
Delaney, Gayle (M. V.) 1949- 142
Delaney, Gina
See Alsobrook, Rosalyn R.
Delaney, Harry 1932- 25-28R
See also SATA 3
Delaney, Jack J(ames) 1921-1988 .... 21-24R
See also Stone, Richard
Delaney, John
See Rowland, D(onald) S(ydney)
Delaney, John Joseph 1910-1985 ..... CANR-76
Obituary 115
Earlier sketches in CA 1-4R, CANR-5
Delaney, Joseph H(enry) 1932-1999 156
See also SFW 4
DeLaney, Joseph Lawrence 1917-1994 102
Delaney, Lolo M(ae) 1937- 57-60
Delaney, Marshall
See Fulford, Robert
Delaney, Mary Murray 1913-1995 53-56
Delaney, Michael 1955- 161
See also SATA 96
Delaney, Ned
See Delaney, Thomas Nicholas III
See also SATA 28
Delaney, Norman Conrad 1932- CANR-92
Earlier sketch in CA 37-40R
Delaney, Robert Finley 1925- CANR-6
Earlier sketch in CA 1-4R
Delaney, Shelagh 1939- CANR-67
Earlier sketches in CA 17-20R, CANR-30
See also CBD
See also CD 5, 6
See also CDBLB 1960 to Present
See also CLC 29
See also CWD
See also DAM DRAM
See also DFS 7
See also DLB 13
See also MTCW 1
Delaney, Steve 1938- 121
Brief entry 110
Interview in CA-121
Delaney, Thomas Nicholas III
1951- CANR-10
Earlier sketch in CA 65-68
See also Delaney, Ned
Delaney, William A(nthony) 1926- 106
de Lange, N. R. M.
See de Lange, Nicholas (Robert Michael)
de Lange, Nicholas (Robert Michael)
1944- CANR-99
Earlier sketches in CA 89-92, CANR-15
de Langiade de la Renta, Francoise
See de la Renta, Francoise de Langiade
Delano, Amasa 1763-1823 .... DLB 183
Delano, Anthony 1930- 102
Delano, Hugh 1933- 65-68
See also SATA 20
Delano, Isaac O. 1904-2000 .... 25-28R
Delano, Kenneth J(oseph) 1934- 57-60
De-la-Noy (Walker), Michael
1934-2002 .... CANR-117
Obituary 206
Earlier sketch in CA 153
de Lantagne, Cecile
See Cloutier-Wojciechowska, Cecile
Delanty, Greg 1958- 190
Delany, A(nnie) Elizabeth 1891-1995 169
See also BW 3
Delany, Bessie
See Delany, A(nnie) Elizabeth
Delany, George (Battle) 1946- 114
Delany, Kevin F(rancis) X(avier) 1927- 73-76
Delany, Martin Robison 1812-1885 ...... DLB 50
See also RGAL 4
Delany, Paul 1937- CANR-41
Earlier sketches in CA 29-32R, CANR-19
Delany, Samuel R(ay), Jr. 1942- CANR-116
Earlier sketches in CA 81-84, CANR-27, 43
See also AAYA 24
See also AFAW 2
See also BLC 1
See also BPFB 1
See also BW 2, 3
See also CLC 8, 14, 38, 141
See also CN 2, 3, 4, 5, 6, 7
See also DAM MULT
See also DLB 8, 33
See also FANT
See also MAL 5
See also MTCW 1, 2
See also RGAL 4
See also SATA 92
See also SCFW 1, 2
See also SFW 4
See also SUFW 2
Delany, Sarah L(ouise) 1889-1999 193
Delany, Sheila 1940- 112
de la Parra, (Ana) Teresa (Sonojo)
1890(?)-1936 178
See also Parra Sanojo, Ana Teresa de la
See also HW 2
De La Pedraja, Rene 1951- CANR-92
Earlier sketch in CA 145
de la Pena, Augustin (Mateo) 1942- 115
de la Pena, (Mary) Terri 1947- 197
See also Pena, Terri de la
Delaplane, Stanton Hill 1907-1988 .. CANR-74
Obituary 125
Earlier sketch in CA 25-28R
Delaporte, Ernest P(ierre) 1924- 97-100
Delaporte, Francois Louis 1941- 137
Delaporte, Theophile
See Green, Julien (Hartridge)
de la Portilla, Marta (Rosa) 1927- 61-64
De Lapp, Ardyce Lucile 1903-1990 97-100
DeLapp, George Leslie 1895-1981 102
deLara, Ellen 1949- 216
De la Ramee, Marie Louise (Ouida)
1839-1908 204
See also Ouida
See also SATA 20
de la Renta, Francoise de Langiade
1921(?)-1983
Obituary 110
de la Roche, Mazo 1879-1961 .... CANR-30
Earlier sketch in CA 85-88
See also CLC 14
See also DLB 68
See also RGEL 2
See also RHW
See also SATA 64
De La Roche Saint Andre, Anne
1950- .... SATA 75
Delarue, Jean
See Dreze, Jean
De La Salle, Innocent
See Hartmann, Sadakichi
Delasanta, Rodney 1932- 33-36R
de las Casas, Walter 1947- CANR-127
Earlier sketch in CA 170
See also HW 2
de las Cuevas, Raymon
See Harrington, Mark Raymond
de las Lunas, Carmencita
See Trocchi, Alexander
de la Torre, Jose 1943- 112
De La Torre, Lillian
See McCue, Lillian Bueno
de la Torre, Victor Raul Haya
See Haya de la Torre, Victor Raul
de la Torre-Bueno, Lillian
See McCue, Lillian Bueno
DeLatte, Carolyn E(lizabeth) 1943- 112
Delattre, Pierre 1930- 105
Delatush, Edith G. 1921- 124
de Laubenfels, David J(ohn) 1925- 53-56
Delaunay, Charles 1911-1988
Obituary 125
de Launay, Jacques F(orment) 1924- ... CANR-3
Earlier sketch in CA 9-12R
Delaunay(-Terk), Sonia 1890-1979 128
Delaune, (Jewel) Lynn (de Grummond) CANR-21
Earlier sketch in CA 1-4R
See also SATA 7
DeLaura, David J(oseph) 1930- 21-24R
de Laureamont, Comte
See Lautreamont
De Laurentiis, Dino 1919- .... IDFW 3, 4
DeLaurentis, Louise Budde 1920- 5-8R
See also SATA 12
Delavigne, Jean-Francois Casimir
1793-1843 .... DLB 192
de la Warr, George Walter 1904-1969 .. CAP-1
Earlier sketch in CA 13-16
Delay(-Tubiana), Claude 1944- CANR-33
Earlier sketches in CA 53-56, CANR-4
Delbanco, Andrew 198
Delbanco, Francesca 233

Delbanco, Nicholas (Franklin) 1942- ... 189
Earlier sketches in CA 17-20R, CANR-29, 55, 116
Autobiographical Essay in ... 189
See also CAAS 2
See also CLC 6, 13, 167
See also CN 7
See also DLB 6, 234
del Barco, Lucy Salamanca 1900(?)-1989 ... CANR-77
Obituary ... 130
Earlier sketch in CA 17-20R
See also SATA-Obit 64
Delblanc, Sven (Axel Herman) 1931-1992 ... CANR-144
Earlier sketch in CA 149
See also DLB 257
See also EWL 3
Delbo, Charlotte 1913-
Del Boca, Angelo 1925- ... 25-28R
Delbridge, Rosemary 1949(?)-1981
Obituary ... 105
del Campo, Estanislao 1834-1880 ... LAW
Del Caro, Adrian 1952- ... CANR-92
Earlier sketch in CA 137
del Castillo, Michel 1933- ... CANR-77
Earlier sketch in CA 109
See also CLC 38
Del Castillo, Ramon 1949- ... DLB 209
del Castillo, Richard Griswold
See Griswold del Castillo, Richard
Delcroix, Carlo 1896-1977
Obituary ... 73-76
Delderfield, Eric R(aymond) 1909-1995 ... CANR-4
Earlier sketch in CA 53-56
See also SATA 14
Delderfield, Ronald Frederick 1912-1972 ... CANR-47
Obituary ... 37-40R
Earlier sketch in CA 73-76
See also DAM POP
See also RHW
See also SATA 20
Delear, Frank J. 1914- ... CANR-9
Earlier sketch in CA 21-24R
Deledda, Grazia (Cosima) 1875(?)-1936 ... 205
Brief entry ... 123
See also DLB 264
See also EWL 3
See also RGWL 2, 3
See also TCLC 23
See also WLIT 7
DeLeeuw, Adele (Louise) 1899-1988 ... CANR-76
Obituary ... 125
Earlier sketches in CA 1-4R, CANR-1
See also SATA 1, 30
See also SATA-Obit 56
DeLeeuw, Cateau 1903-1975 ... CANR-3
Earlier sketch in CA 1-4R
de Leeuw, Hendrik 1891-1977
Obituary ... 73-76
Delehanty, Randolph 1944- ... 123
de Leiris, Alain 1922- ... 73-76
DeLeon, David (Henry) 1947-
Brief entry ... 114
De Leon, Nephtali 1945- ... CANR-79
Earlier sketch in CA 152
See also DLB 82
See also HW 1, 2
See also SATA 97
deLeon, Peter 1943- ... 146
DeLeon, Richard Edward 1942- ... 140
Delerm, Philippe 1950- ... 201
de Lerma, Dominique-Rene 1928- ... CANR-1
Earlier sketch in CA 45-48
Delerue, Georges 1925-1992 ... IDFW 3, 4
Delessert, Etienne 1941- ... CANR-102
Earlier sketches in CA 21-24R, CANR-13, 37
See also CLR 81
See also MAICYA 1, 2
See also SATA 46, 130
See also SATA-Brief 27
Delessert, Jacquine
See Reiter, Victoria (Kelrich)
Deleuze, Gilles 1925-1995 ... DLB 296
See also TCLC 116
DeLey, Herbert (Clemone, Jr.) 1936- ... 21-24R
Delfano, M. M.
See Flammonde, Paris
DelFattore, Joan ... 142
Delfgaauw, Bernard(us Maria Ignatius) 1912- ... 21-24R
Delfini, Antonio 1907-1963 ... DLB 264
Delgado, Abelardo (Lalo) B(arrientos) 1930-2004 ... CANR-90
Obituary ... 230
Earlier sketch in CA 131
See also CAAS 15
See also DAM MST, MULT
See also DLB 82
See also HLC 1
See also HW 1, 2
Delgado, Alan (George) 1909- ... CANR-5
Earlier sketch in CA 9-12R
Delgado, Hector L. 1949- ... 146
Delgado, James P. 1958- ... CANR-88
Earlier sketch in CA 136
See also SATA 122
Delgado, Jose Manuel R(odriguez) 1915- ... 29-32R
Delgado, Maria M. 1965- ... 196
Delgado, Ramon (Louis) 1937- ... CANR-91
Earlier sketches in CA 85-88, CANR-15
Delgado Aparain, Mario 1949- ... 221
Del Giudice, Daniele 1949- ... 196
See also DLB 196
Del Giudice, Filippo 1892-1962 ... IDFW 3
D'Elia, Donald John 1933- ... 57-60
D'Elia, Maria
See Goudiss, Maria Agnes D'Elia
De Libero, Libero 1906-1981 ... DLB 114
Delibes, Miguel
See Delibes Setien, Miguel
See also CLC 8, 18
See also DLB 322
See also EWL 3
Delibes Setien, Miguel 1920- ... CANR-32
Earlier sketches in CA 45-48, CANR-1
See also Delibes, Miguel
See also CWW 2
See also HW 1
See also MTCW 1
Delicado, Francisco c. 1475-c. 1540(?) ... DLB 318
Delicado, Pepe
See Raskin, Jonah (Seth)
Deligiorgis, Stavros (George) 1933- ... 61-64
Deligne, Pierre (R.) 1944- ... 155
DeLillo, Don 1936- ... CANR-133
Earlier sketches in CA 81-84, CANR-21, 76, 92
See also AMWC 2
See also AMWS 6
See also BEST 89:1
See also BPFB 1
See also CLC 8, 10, 13, 27, 39, 54, 76, 143, 210, 213
See also CN 3, 4, 5, 6, 7
See also CPW
See also DA3
See also DAM NOV, POP
See also DLB 6, 173
See also EWL 3
See also MAL 5
See also MTCW 1, 2
See also MTFW 2005
See also RGAL 4
See also TUS
de Lima, Agnes 1887(?)-1974
Obituary ... 53-56
De Lima, Clara Rosa 1922- ... CANR-6
Earlier sketch in CA 57-60
de Lima, Sigrid 1921-1999 ... CANR-74
Obituary ... 185
Earlier sketch in CA 25-28R
Delinsky, Barbara (Ruth Greenberg) 1945- ... CANR-89
Earlier sketches in CA 111, CANR-30
See also RHW
de Lint, Charles (Henri Diederick Hofsmit) 1951- ... CANR-113
Earlier sketch in CA 126
See also AAYA 33
See also BYA 10, 11, 16
See also DLB 251
See also FANT
See also SATA 115, 157
See also SUFW 2
See also YAW
Delisle, Francoise 1886(?)-1974
Obituary ... 53-56
De Lisle, Harold F. 1933- ... 158
de Lisser, H. G.
See De Lisser, H(erbert) G(eorge)
See also DLB 117
De Lisser, H(erbert) G(eorge) 1878-1944 ... 152
Brief entry ... 109
See also de Lisser, H. G.
See also BW 2
See also TCLC 12
Delius, Anthony (Ronald St. Martin) 1916- ... CANR-12
Earlier sketch in CA 17-20R
See also CP 1, 2, 3, 4, 5, 6, 7
Delk, Robert Carlton 1920- ... 45-48
Dell, Belinda
See Bowden, Jean
Dell, Christopher 1927- ... 65-68
Dell, E(dward) T(homas), Jr. 1923- ... 13-16R
Dell, Edmund 1921-1999 ... 103
Obituary ... 186
Dell, Ethel Mary 1881-1939 ... RHW
Dell, Floyd 1887-1969 ... 179
Obituary ... 89-92
See also DLB 9
See also MAL 5
See also RGAL 4
Dell, Jeffrey 1899-1985(?)
Obituary ... 116
Dell, Roberta E(lizabeth) 1946- ... 81-84
Dell, Sidney 1918-1990 ... CANR-17
Earlier sketches in CA 5-8R, CANR-2
Della Femina, Jerry 1936-
Brief entry ... 111
Della-Piana, Gabriel M. 1926- ... 73-76
della Torre, Paolo Filo 1933- ... 197
Delle, James A. 1964- ... 180
delle Grazie, Marie Eugenie 1864-1931 ... 175
See also DLB 81
Deller, John J. 1931- ... 134
delle Stelle, Pier Luigi Bellini
See Bellini delle Stelle, Pier Luigi
Dellheim, Charles (Jay) 1952- ... 128
Delli Colli, Tonino 1923- ... IDFW 3, 4
Dellin, Lubomir A. D. 1920-1980 ... 45-48
Dellinger, David (T.) 1915-2004 ... 65-68
Obituary ... 227
Delloff, Irving Arthur 1920- ... 13-16R
Dellums, Ronald V(ernie) 1935- ... 191
Delman, David 1924-
Brief entry ... 115
del Mar, David Peterson 1957- ... 219
Del Mar, Florentina
See Conde (Abellan), Carmen
Delmar, Ken 1941- ... 121
Del Mar, Marcia 1950- ... 105
Del Mar, Norman (Rene) 1919-1994 ... 149
Delmar, Roy
See Wexler, Jerome (LeRoy)
Delmar, Vina (Croter) 1905-1990 ... 65-68
Obituary ... 130
See also RHW
Del Martia, Astron
See Fearn, John Russell
Delmer, Denis Sefton 1904-1979 ... CANR-73
Earlier sketch in CA 5-8R
Delmonico, Andrea
See Morrison, Eula Atwood
Delo, David Michael 1938- ... 146
De Loach, Allen (Wayne) 1939- ... CANR-16
Earlier sketch in CA 85-88
DeLoach, Charles F. 1927- ... 37-40R
DeLoach, Clarence, Jr. 1936- ... 57-60
Deloire, Pierre
See Peguy, Charles (Pierre)
de Lomellini, C. A.
See Kelley, (Kathleen) Alita
Delon, Floyd G(urney) 1929- ... CANR-21
Earlier sketch in CA 69-72
de Lone, Richard H. 1940- ... 101
DeLone, Ruth
See Rankin, Ruth (DeLone) I(rvine)
Deloney, Thomas 1543(?)-1600 ... DLB 167
See also RGEL 2
Delong, Candice 1952- ... 220
De Long, David G. 1939- ... 139
De Long, Julie
See Hay, Millicent V.
DeLong, Lea Rosson 1947- ... CANR-99
Earlier sketches in CA 119, CANR-48
DeLong, Thomas A(nderton) 1935- ... CANR-25
Earlier sketch in CA 106
de Longchamps, Joanne (Cutten) 1923-1983 ... CANR-3
Earlier sketch in CA 9-12R
De Loo, Tessa 1947- ... 213
De Lora, Joann S.
See Sandlin, Joann S(chepers) De Lora
DeLorean, John Z(achary) 1925-2005 ... 122
Obituary ... 237
DeLorenzo, Lorisa Mernette 1951- ... 117
DeLorenzo, Robert John 1947- ... 117
Deloria, Ella (Cara) 1889-1971(?) ... 152
See also DAM MULT
See also DLB 175
See also NNAL
Deloria, Vine (Victor), Jr. 1933- ... CANR-98
Earlier sketches in CA 53-56, CANR-5, 20, 48
See also CLC 21, 122
See also DAM MULT
See also DLB 175
See also MTCW 1
See also NNAL
See also SATA 21
Delorme, Andre
See Julien, Charles-Andre
DeLorme, Eleanor P. 1922- ... 222
Delorme, Michele
See Cranston, Mechthild
Delort, Robert 1932- ... 102
de los Reyes, Gabriel ... 45-48
de los Rios, Francisco Giner
See Giner de los Rios, Francisco
Deloughery, Grace L. 1933- ... 33-36R
de Loune, Henry
See Popham, Peter (Nicholas Home)
Delp, Michael W(illiam) 1948- ... 77-80
Delpar, Helen 1936- ... 53-56
del Paso, Fernando 1935- ... 217
See also Paso, Fernando del
See also LAWS 1
Delphos, Omar
See Ald, Roy A(llison)
Del Re, Giuseppe 1932- ... 201
del Rey, Judy-Lynn 1943-1986 ... 124
Obituary ... 118
del Rey, Lester 1915-1993 ... CANR-17
Obituary ... 141
Earlier sketch in CA 65-68
See also DLB 8
See also MTCW 1
See also SATA 22
See also SATA-Obit 76
See also SFW 4
Delrio, Martin
See Doyle, Debra and Macdonald, James D.
del Rio, Rikki
See Gordon, Lewis Ricardo
Delsohn, Gary 1952- ... 225
Delta
See Dennett, Herbert Victor
Delton, Jina 1961- ... 106
Delton, Judy 1931-2001 ... CANR-129
Obituary ... 201
Earlier sketches in CA 57-60, CANR-8, 25
See also AAYA 6
See also JRDA
See also SAAS 9
See also SATA 14, 77
See also SATA-Obit 130
Delton, Julie 1959- ... 108
Del Toro, Benicio 1967- ... 172
DeLuca, A(ngelo) Michael 1912-1976 ... CANR-76
Obituary ... 120
Earlier sketch in CA 21-24R
De Luca, Charles J. 1927- ... 73-76
de Luca, Erri 1950- ... 220
De Lucca, John 1920- ... 41-44R
DeLuise, Dom(inick) 1933- ... 231
Delulio, John 1938- ... SATA 15
Delumeau, Jean 1923- ... 97-100
De Luna, Frederick Adolph 1928- ... 65-68
Delupis, Ingrid 1939- ... 103
del Valle, Teresa 1937- ... 149
del Valle-Inclan, Ramon (Maria)
See Valle-Inclan, Ramon (Maria) del
See also DLB 322
Del Vecchio, Deborah 1950- ... 146
Del Vecchio, John M(ichael) 1947- ... 110
See also CLC 29
See also DLBD 9
Delves, Peter J(ohn) 1951- ... CANR-139
Earlier sketch in CA 144
Del'vig, Anton Antonovich 1798-1831 ... DLB 205
Delving, Michael
See Williams, Jay
DeLynn, Jane 1946- ... CANR-142
Earlier sketches in CA 77-80, CANR-72
See also GLL 2
DeLyser, Femmy 1935- ... 110
Delzell, Charles F(loyd) 1920- ... CANR-2
Earlier sketch in CA 1-4R
Demac, Donna A. 1952- ... 121
de Madariaga, Isabel 1919- ... 107
Demaine, Don
See Drinkall, Gordon (Don)
de Man, Paul (Adolph Michel) 1919-1983 ... CANR-61
Obituary ... 111
Earlier sketch in CA 128
See also CLC 55
See also DLB 67
See also MTCW 1, 2
de Mandiargues, Andre Pieyre
See Pieyre de Mandiargues, Andre
de Manio, Jack 1914-1988 ... CANR-76
Obituary ... 127
Earlier sketch in CA 61-64
Demant, Vigo Auguste 1893-1983
Obituary ... 109
de Mar, Esmeralda
See Mellen, Ida M(ay)
Demaratus, DeEtta 1941- ... 230
Demaray, Donald E(ugene) 1926- ... CANR-95
Earlier sketches in CA 1-4R, CANR-1, 16, 37
De Marco, Angelus A. 1916- ... 9-12R
De Marco, Arlene ... AITN 1
DeMarco, Donald 1937- ... CANR-49
Earlier sketches in CA 61-64, CANR-7, 24
DeMarco, Frank 1946- ... 229
DeMarco, Michael ... 207
de Mare, Eric S(amuel) 1910-2002 ... CANR-76
Obituary ... 203
Earlier sketches in CA 9-12R, CANR-6
deMare, George 1912- ... 21-24R
Demarest, Bruce A(lvin) 1935- ... CANR-142
Earlier sketch in CA 118
Demarest, Chris(topher) L(ynn) 1951- ... CANR-107
Earlier sketch in CA 109
See also SATA 45, 82, 128
See also SATA-Brief 44
Demarest, Doug
See Barker, Will
Demarest, Michael 1924(?)-1984
Obituary ... 112
Demarest, Phyllis Gordon 1911-1969
Obituary ... 104
Demarest, Rosemary Regina 1914- ... 116
Demarest, Victoria Booth(-Clibborn) 1890-1982 ... 124
Obituary ... 112
Demaret, James Newton 1910-1983
Obituary ... 111
Demaret, Jimmy
See Demaret, James Newton
Demaret, Pierre 1943- ... CANR-12
Earlier sketch in CA 61-64
De Maria, Robert 1928- ... CANR-5
Earlier sketch in CA 1-4R
De Marinis, Marco 1949- ... 156
DeMarinis, Rick 1934- ... 184
Earlier sketches in CA 57-60, CANR-9, 25, 50
Autobiographical Essay in ... 184
See also CAAS 24
See also CLC 54
See also DLB 218
See also TCWW 2
Demaris, Ovid
See Desmarais, Ovid E.
De Marly, Diana 1939- ... 125
de Marneffe, Daphne 1959- ... 231
de Marquand, Alix
See Skinner, Mike
DeMarr, Mary Jean 1932- ... CANR-93
Earlier sketch in CA 151
DeMartini, Rodney J(ames) 1947- ... 113
De Martino, Manfred F(rank) 1924-
Brief entry ... 117
Demas, Corinne
See Bliss, Corinne Demas
See also SATA 131
Demas, Vida 1927- ... 49-52
See also SATA 9
Demastes, William W. 1956- ... 234
deMatteo, Donna 1941- ... 25-28R
de Mauny, Erik 1920- ... CANR-13
Earlier sketch in CA 33-36R
de Maupassant, (Henri Rene Albert) Guy
See Maupassant, (Henri Rene Albert) Guy de
deMause, Lloyd 1931- ... 65-68
Demb, Ada 1948- ... 138

Cumulative Index 147 Denny

Dembart, Lee 1946- 133
Dembner, Red
See Dembner, S. Arthur
Dembner, S. Arthur 1920-1990
Obituary 131
Dembo, L(awrence) S(anford) 1929- ... CANR-2
Earlier sketch in CA 1-4R
Dembry, R. Emmet
See Murfree, Mary Noailles
Dembski, Stephen (Michael) 1949- 128
Demby, William 1922- CANR-81
Earlier sketch in CA 81-84
See also BLC 1
See also BW 1, 3
See also CLC 53
See also DAM MULT
See also DLB 33
de Medici, Lorenza 1926- 141
de Medici, Marino 1933- 89-92
De Mejo, Oscar 1911-1992 111
See also SATA 40
Dement, William Charles 1928-
Brief entry 105
De Mente, Boye 1928- CANR-8
Earlier sketch in CA 21-24R
de Menton, Francisco
See Chin, Frank (Chew, Jr.)
Demeny, Janos 1915- 118
Demers, David (Pearce) 1953- 162
Demers, James 1942- 97-100
de Mesne, Eugene (Frederick Peter
Cheshire) CANR-25
Earlier sketch in CA 41-44R
de Mesquita, Bruce James Bueno
See Bueno de Mesquita, Bruce James
de Messieres, Nicole 1930- 107
See also SATA 39
Demetillo, Ricaredo 1920- 102
See also CP 1, 2, 3, 4, 5, 6, 7
Demetrakopoulos, Stephanie Anne 1937- ... 111
Demetrescu-Buzau, Demetru Dem. 1883-1923
See Urmuz
Demetrius, James Kleon 1924- CANR-13
Earlier sketch in CA 21-24R
Demetz, Hana 1928-1993 236
Demetz, Peter 1922- CANR-135
Earlier sketches in CA 65-68, CANR-14
Demi
See Hitz, Demi
See also CWRI 5
De Michael, Don(ald Anthony) 1928-1982
Obituary 106
Demidenko, Helen
See Darville, Helen (Fiona)
Demijohn, Thom
See Disch, Thomas M(ichael) and
Sladek, John
de Milan, Sister Jean
See Jean, Gabrielle (Lucille)
D'Emilio, A. Edward 1919(?)-1987
Obituary 122
D'Emilio, John 1948- CANR-97
Earlier sketch in CA 135
de Mille, Agnes
See Prude, Agnes George de Mille
DeMille, Alexandria
See Du Breuil, (Elizabeth) L(or)inda
De Mille, Cecil B(lount) 1881-1959 149
Brief entry 115
De Mille, James 1833-1880 .... DLB 99, 251
De Mille, Nelson
See Levinson, Leonard
DeMille, Nelson (Richard) 1943- CANR-113
Earlier sketches in CA 57-60, CANR-6, 25, 46, 62
See also BEST 90:3
See also CMW 4
See also CPW
See also DAM POP
de Mille, Richard 1922- CANR-13
Earlier sketch in CA 21-24R
de Mille, William 1878-1955 .... DLB 266
De Milly, Walter (A. III) 1953- 189
Deming, Alison Hawthorne 1946- 148
Deming, Barbara 1917-1984 .... CANR-71
Earlier sketches in CA 85-88, CANR-15
See also FW
See also GLL 2
Deming, Kirk
See Drago, Harry Sinclair
Deming, Louise Macpherson 1916-1976
Obituary 61-64
Deming, Philander 1829-1915- 177
See also DLB 74
Deming, Richard 1915-1983 .... CANR-94
Earlier sketches in CA 9-12R, CANR-3
See also Queen, Ellery
See also SATA 24
Deming, Robert H. 1937- 21-24R
Demirguc-Kunt, Asli 1961- 239
DeMirjian, Arto, Jr. 1931- 57-60
Deml, Jakub 1878-1961 .... DLB 215
Demme, Jonathan 1944- .... AAYA 66
De Molen, Richard Lee 1938- 45-48
Demone, Harold W(ellington), Jr.
1924- CANR-9
Earlier sketch in CA 5-8R
De Monfried, Henri 1879(?)-1974
Obituary 53-56
Demong, Phyllis 1920- 106
de Montaigne, Michel (Eyquem)
See Montaigne, Michel (Eyquem) de
de Montalvo, Luis Galvez
See Avalle-Arce, Juan Bautista de
DeMonte, Claudia 1947- 114
de Montebello, Guy-Philippe Lannes
1936- 45-48
de Monteiro, Longteine 1938- 178
de Montfort, Guy
See Johnson, Donald McI(ntosh)
de Montherlant, Henry (Milon)
See Montherlant, Henry (Milon) de
De Montreville Polak, Doris 1904(?)-1974
Obituary 49-52
Demoor, Marysa 1956- 197
De Mordaunt, Walter J(ulius) 1925- 33-36R
Demorest, Jean-Jacques 1920- 5-8R
Demorest, Stephen 1949- CANR-20
Earlier sketch in CA 101
Demorest, William Jennings
1822-1895 .... DLB 79
De Morgan, William (Frend)
1839-1917 .... DLB 153
See also RGEL 2
De Morny, Peter
See Wynne-Tyson, Esme
Demos, John Putnam 1937- CANR-81
Earlier sketch in CA 137
Demos, Paul 1888-1983
Obituary 109
Demosthenes 384B.C.-322B.C. .... AW 1
See also DLB 176
See also RGWL 2, 3
Demotes, Michael
See Burgess, Michael (Roy)
DeMott, Benjamin (Hailer) 1924- ... CANR-103
Earlier sketches in CA 5-8R, CANR-49
De Mott, Donald W(arren) 1928- 61-64
DeMott, Robert (James) 1943- 141
DeMott, Wes 1952- 164
de Mourgues, Odette (Marie Helene Louise)
1914-1988 .... CANR-75
Obituary 126
Earlier sketch in CA 5-8R
Dempewolff, Richard F(rederic)
1914-1997 .... CANR-1
Earlier sketch in CA 1-4R
Dempsey, Charles (Gates) 1937- 217
Dempsey, David Knapp 1914-1999 ... CANR-2
Obituary 173
Earlier sketch in CA 5-8R
Dempsey, Hugh Aylmer 1929- CANR-51
Earlier sketches in CA 69-72, CANR-11, 26
Dempsey, Jack
See Dempsey, William Harrison
Dempsey, James X. 238
Dempsey, Lotta 101
Dempsey, Paul K(enneth) 1935- CANR-19
Earlier sketch in CA 25-28R
Dempsey, Richard A(llen) 1932- 61-64
Dempsey, William Harrison
1895-1983 .... CANR-77
Obituary 109
Earlier sketch in CA 89-92
Dempster, Barry 1952- CANR-32
Earlier sketch in CA 113
Dempster, Chris 1943- 106
Dempster, Derek David 1924- 13-16R
Dempster, Stuart 1936- 104
Demske, James Michael 1922-1994 . CANR-75
Obituary 145
Earlier sketch in CA 29-32R
Demski, Eva 1944- 135
Demski, Joel S. 1940- 148
de Munck, Victor C. 1948- 168
Demura, Fumio 1940- CANR-12
Earlier sketch in CA 61-64
Demus, Otto 1902-1990 144
de Musset, (Louis Charles) Alfred
See Musset, (Louis Charles) Alfred de
Demuth, Norman (Frank) 1898-1968 .... CAP-1
Earlier sketch in CA 13-14
Demuth, Patricia Brennan 1948- 118
See also SATA 84
See also SATA-Brief 51
Demy, Jacques 1931-1990 148
Den, Petr
See Radimsky, Ladislaw
Denali, Peter
See Holm, Don(ald Raymond)
de Natale, Francine
See Malzberg, Barry N(athaniel)
de Navarre, Marguerite 1492-1549
See Marguerite d'Angouleme and
Marguerite de Navarre
See also SSC 85
Denbeaux, Fred J. 1914-1995 .... 5-8R
Denbie, Roger
See Green, Alan (Baer)
Denbigh, Kenneth George 1911-2004 106
Obituary 223
Den Boer, James (Drew) 1937- CANR-10
Earlier sketch in CA 21-24R
See also CP 1, 2
Denby, David 1943(?)- 158
Denby, Edwin (Orr) 1903-1983 138
Obituary 110
See also CLC 48
See also CP 1
Dench, Judi(th Olivia) 1934- 201
Dendel, Esther (Sietmann Warner)
1910-2002 102
Obituary 210
Dender, Jay
See Deindorfer, Robert Greene
Dendinger, Roger E. 1952- 234
See also SATA 158
Dendle, Brian J(ohn) 1936- CANR-42
Earlier sketch in CA 116
Dendy, Marshall C(oleman) 1902-1984 . CAP-2
Earlier sketch in CA 17-18
DeNeef, Arthur Leigh 1942- 102
Deneen, James R. 1928- 45-48
de Nemethy, Bertalan 1911-2002 230
Denenberg, Herbert S(idney) 1929- 37-40R
de Nerval, Gerard
See Nerval, Gerard de
Denes, Magda 1934-1996 158
de Neufville, Richard 1939- 53-56
Denevan, William M(axfield) 1931- 41-44R
de Nevers, Noel (Howard) 1932- 37-40R
DeNevi, Donald P. 1937- 37-40R
Denevi, Marco 1922- .... EWL 3
See also HW 1
See also LAW
Denezhkina, Irina 1981- 238
Denfeld, Duane (Henry) 1939- 41-44R
Deng, Francis Mading 1938- CANR-80
Earlier sketch in CA 157
See also BW 3
Deng, Peng 1948- 188
Deng, William 1929- 13-16R
Deng, Xiao Hua 1953- 139
Dengler, Dieter 1938- 102
Dengler, Marianna (Herron) 1935- 102
See also SATA 103
Dengler, Sandy 1939- CANR-135
Earlier sketches in CA 112, CANR-30, 73
See also SATA 54
See also SATA-Brief 40
Denham, Alice 1933- 21-24R
Denham, Andrew 204
Denham, Avery Strakosch (?)-1970
Obituary 104
Denham, Bertie 1927- 93-96
Denham, H(enry) M(angles)
1897-1993 .... CANR-75
Obituary 142
Earlier sketch in CA 61-64
Denham, Henry fl. 1559-1590(?) .... DLB 170
Denham, James M. 1957- CANR-139
Earlier sketch in CA 172
Denham, John 1615-1669 .... DLB 58, 126
See also RGEL 2
Denham, Laura 1966- 220
Denham, Mary Orr 1918-1983 .... CANR-2
Earlier sketch in CA 1-4R
Denham, Reginald 1894-1983 .... CANR-76
Obituary 109
Earlier sketches in CAP-1, CA 13-16
Denham, Robert D(ayton) 1938- CANR-93
Earlier sketch in CA 53-56
Denham, Sully
See Budd, Mavis
Denhardt, Robert Moorman 1912-1989 101
den Hartog, Kristen 1965- 225
den Heuvel, Albert H(endrik) van
See van den Heuvel, Albert H(endrik)
den Hollander, A(rie) Nicolaas Jan
1906-1976 .... CAP-2
Earlier sketch in CA 29-32
Denholm, Mark
See Fearn, John Russell
Denholm, Therese Mary Zita White
1933- 9-12R
Denholtz, Elaine (Grudin) CANR-13
Earlier sketch in CA 73-76
Denim, Sue
See Pilkey, Dav(id Murray, Jr.)
Dening, Greg 1931- CANR-93
Earlier sketch in CA 107
DeNiord, Chard 1952- 180
Denis, Armand 1896(?)-1971
Obituary 104
Denis, Charlotte
See Plimmer, Charlotte and
Plimmer, Denis
Denis, Julio
See Cortazar, Julio
Denis, Manuel Maldonado
See Maldonado-Denis, Manuel
Denis, Michaela Holdsworth
1914-2003 .... 13-16R
Obituary 216
Denis, Paul 1909-1997 .... 21-24R
Denis, Rafael Cardoso 1964- 226
Denise, Christopher 1968- .... SATA 147
Denisoff, R. Serge 1939-1994 .... 33-36R
Denison, Barbara 1926- 13-16R
Denison, Corrie
See Partridge, Eric (Honeywood)
Denison, Edward F(ulton) 1915-1992 ... 21-24R
Obituary 140
Denison, Merrill 1893-1975 .... CCA 1
See also DLB 92
Denison, (John) Michael (Terence Wellesley)
1915-1998 109
Obituary 169
Denison, Norman 1925- 65-68
Denker, Alfred 1960- 207
Denker, Henry 1912- CANR-57
Earlier sketches in CA 33-36R, CANR-31
See also AITN 1
Denkler, Horst 1935- CANR-19
Earlier sketches in CA 53-56, CANR-4
Denkstein, Vladimir 1906- 103
Denlinger, A(nna) Martha 1931- 113
Denman, D(onald) R(obert)
1911-1999 .... CANR-8
Obituary 185
Earlier sketch in CA 61-64
Denman, Margaret-Love 1940- 180
Denman-West, Margaret W. 1926- 176
Denmark, Florence L. 1932- 85-88
Denmark, Harrison
See Zelazny, Roger (Joseph)
Dennard, Deborah 1953- CANR-115
Earlier sketch in CA 146
See also SATA 78, 126
Dennehy, Raymond L(eo) 1934- 109
Dennery, Adolphe Philippe
1811-1899 .... DLB 192
Dennes, William Ray 1898-1982 73-76
Dennett, Daniel C(lement) 1942- ... CANR-100
Earlier sketches in CA 97-100, CANR-35, 53
Dennett, Herbert Victor 1893- CANR-5
Earlier sketch in CA 5-8R
Dennett, Nolan A. 1950- 147
Dennett, Tyler 1883-1949 220
Denney, Diana 1910-2000 104
Obituary 188
See also SATA 25
See also SATA-Obit 120
Denney, Myron Keith 1930- 102
Denney, Reuel (Nicholas) 1913-1995 . CANR-2
Obituary 148
Earlier sketch in CA 1-4R
See also CP 1
Denney, Robert (Eugene) 1929- 140
Dennie, Joseph 1768-1812 ..... DLB 37, 43, 59, 73
Denning, A. T.
See Denning, Alfred Thompson
Denning, A. T.
See Denning, Alfred Thompson
Denning, Alfred
See Denning, Alfred Thompson
Denning, Alfred Thompson 1899-1999 143
Obituary 177
Brief entry 115
Denning, Basil W. 1928- 33-36R
Denning, Candace 1946- 125
Denning, Melita
See Barcynski, Vivian G(odfrey)
Denning, Patricia
See Willis, Corinne Denneny
Dennis, Arthur
See Edmonds, Arthur Denis
Dennis, Benjamin G. 1929- 45-48
Dennis, C(larence Michael) J(ames)
1876-1938 .... DLB 260
See also RGEL 2
Dennis, Carl 1939- CANR-118
Earlier sketch in CA 77-80
See also PFS 20
Dennis, Charles 1946- CANR-17
Earlier sketch in CA 65-68
Dennis, Deborah Ellis 1950- 116
Dennis, Everette E. 1942- 41-44R
Dennis, Henry C(harles) 1918- 41-44R
Dennis, Ian 1952- 125
See also FANT
Dennis, Jack B(onnell) 1931- 155
Dennis, James M(unn) 1932- 102
Dennis, John 1658-1734 .... DLB 101
See also RGEL 2
Dennis, John V(alue) 1916-2002 107
Obituary 210
Dennis, Landt 1937- 65-68
Dennis, Lane T(imothy) 1943- 93-96
Dennis, Lawrence 1893-1977
Obituary 73-76
Dennis, Morgan 1891(?)-1960 .... SATA 18
Dennis, Nigel (Forbes) 1912-1989 .... 25-28R
Obituary 129
See also CLC 8
See also CN 1, 2, 3, 4
See also DLB 13, 15, 233
See also EWL 3
See also MTCW 1
Dennis, Patrick
See Tanner, Edward Everett III
Dennis, Peggy 1909-1993 .... CANR-76
Obituary 143
Earlier sketch in CA 77-80
Dennis, Peter (John) 1945- 41-44R
Dennis, Ralph .... AITN 1
Dennis, Richard (John) 1949- 118
Dennis, Robert C. 1920-1983 .... CANR-76
Obituary 110
Earlier sketch in CA 101
Dennis, Rutledge M(elvin) 1939- 115
Dennis, Suzanne Easton 1922- 25-28R
Dennis, Wayne 1905-1976 .... 17-20R
Obituary 69-72
Dennis, Wesley 1903-1966 135
See also MAICYA 1, 2
See also SATA 18
Dennis, Yvonne Wakim 238
Dennis-Jones, H(arold) 1915- CANR-8
Earlier sketch in CA 57-60
Dennison, A(lfred) Dudley, Jr.
1914-1988 .... CANR-9
Earlier sketch in CA 57-60
Dennison, George (Harris)
1925-1987 .... CANR-76
Obituary 123
Earlier sketches in CA 101, CANR-44
See also CAAS 6
Dennison, George M(arshel) 1935- 53-56
Dennison, Milo
See Cantwell, Lois and
Ford, John M.
Dennison, Peter (John) 1942- 124
Dennison, Sam 1926- CANR-28
Earlier sketch in CA 109
Dennison, Shane 1933- 73-76
Denniston, Denise 1946- 69-72
Denniston, Elinore 1900-1978
Obituary 81-84
See also SATA-Obit 24
Denniston, Lyle (William) 1931- 65-68
Denniston, Robin 1926- 187
Denny, Alma 1912- 89-92
Denny, Brian
See Doughty, Bradford

Denny, Carol
See Brandt, Carol
Denny, John Howard 1920- CAP-1
Earlier sketch in CA 9-10
Denny, Ludwell 1894-1970
Obituary 29-32R
Denny, M(aurice) Ray 1918- CANR-14
Earlier sketch in CA 41-44R
Denny, Norman (George) 1901-1982 107
See also SATA 43
Denny, Robert 1920- 135
Denny, Roz
See Fox, Rosaline
Denny-Brown, Derek Ernest 1901-1981
Obituary 103
Dennys, Joyce (a pseudonym) 1895-1991 .. 121
Dennys, Rodney Onslow
1911-1993 .... CANR-76
Obituary 142
Earlier sketch in CA 85-88
Denoeu, Francois 1898-1975 53-56
Denomme, Robert T. 1930- 25-28R
Denoon, Donald (John Noble)
1940- CANR-14
Earlier sketch in CA 73-76
de Noronha, Leslie 1926- .... CP 1
DeNovo, John A(ugust) 1916-2000 .... 9-12R
Densen-Gerber, Judianne 1934-2003 .... 37-40R
Obituary 216
Denslow, Sharon Phillips 1947- CANR-121
Earlier sketch in CA 136
See also SATA 68, 142
Denslow, W(illiam) W(allace) 1856-1915 ... 211
See also CLR 15
See also DLB 188
See also SATA 16
Densmore, John 1944- 136
Denson, John Lee 1903-1982
Obituary 108
Dent, Alan (Holmes) 1905-1978 .... CANR-5
Earlier sketch in CA 9-12R
Dent, Anthony Austen 1915- CANR-15
Earlier sketch in CA 25-28R
Dent, Colin 1921- 13-16R
Dent, David J. 226
Dent, Harold (Collett) 1894-1995 .... CANR-76
Obituary 147
Earlier sketches in CA 5-8R, CANR-5
Dent, Harry (Shuler) 1930- 81-84
Dent, Lester 1904-1959 161
Brief entry 112
See also CMW 4
See also DLB 306
See also SFW 4
See also TCLC 72
Dent, Richard J. 1951- 153
Dent, Robert William 1917- 105
Dent, Thomas C(ovington) 1932-1998 125
Obituary 181
Brief entry 122
See also Dent, Tom
See also BW 1
Dent, Tom
See Dent, Thomas C(ovington)
See also DLB 38
Dent, Tory 1958- 220
Dentan, Robert C(laude) 1907-1995 .. CANR-2
Earlier sketch in CA 1-4R
Dentinger, Jane 1951- CANR-56
Earlier sketch in CA 123
See also CMW 4
Dentinger, Stephen
See Hoch, Edward D(entinger)
Dentler, Robert A(rnold) 1928- CANR-17
Earlier sketches in CA 1-4R, CANR-1
Denton, Bradley (Clayton) 1958- 158
Denton, Charles F(rederick) 1942- 37-40R
Denton, D. Keith 1948- 112
Denton, Daniel 1626(?)-1703 .... DLB 24
Denton, H(arry) M. 1882-1970 .... CAP-1
Earlier sketch in CA 11-12
Denton, Herbert H(oward), Jr. 1943-1989
Obituary 128
Denton, J(effrey) H(oward) 1939- CANR-15
Earlier sketch in CA 41-44R
Denton, James A. 1936- 191
Denton, James R. 1972- 209
Denton, Jeremiah A(ndrew), Jr.
1924- CANR-31
Earlier sketch in CA 69-72
Denton, Kady MacDonald 134
See also CLR 71
See also MAICYA 2
See also SATA 66, 110
Denton, Sally 1953- 200
Denton, Wallace 1928- 1-4R
d'Entreves, Alexander (Passerin) 1902-1985
Obituary 118
Dentry, Robert
See White, Osmar (Egmont Dorkin)
Denues, Celia 1915- 41-44R
Den Uyl, Douglas J(ohn) 1950- 117
Denver, Boone
See Rennie, James Alan
Denver, Drake C.
See Nye, Nelson C(oral)
Denver, John 1943-1997 159
Denver, Lee
See Gribble, Leonard (Reginald)
See also TCWW 1
Denver, Rod
See Edson, J(ohn) T(homas)
Denver, Shad
See Meares, Leonard Frank
Denver, Walt
See Redding, Robert Hull and
Sherman, Jory (Tecumseh)
Denvir, Bernard 1917- 115
Denyer, Nicholas (Charles) 1955- 136
Denys, Teresa (a pseudonym) 1947- 105
Denzel, Justin F(rancis) 1917-1999 .. CANR-42
Earlier sketches in CA 53-56, CANR-4
See also SATA 46
See also SATA-Brief 38
Denzer, Ann Wiseman
See Wiseman, Ann (Sayre)
Denzer, Peter W(orthington) 1921- 5-8R
Denzin, Norman K(ent) 1941- CANR-126
Earlier sketches in CA 29-32R, CANR-12, 30, 57
Denzler, Brenda 1953- 205
de Obaldia, Rene
See Obaldia, Rene de
de Oca, Marco Antonio Montes
See Montes de Oca, Marco Antonio
de Oliveira, Paulo C(arlos) 1953- 114
Deon, Michel 1919- CANR-37
Earlier sketches in CA 37-40R, CANR-16
Deorsa, Deorsa Mac Iain 1915-1984
See Hay, George Campbell
de Palchi, Alfredo 1926- CANR-122
Earlier sketch in CA 163
DePalma, Anthony 207
De Palma, Brian (Russell) 1940- 109
See also CLC 20
DePalma, Mary Newell 1961- .... SATA 139
dePaola, Thomas Anthony 1934- ... CANR-130
Earlier sketches in CA 49-52, CANR-2, 37
See also dePaola, Tomie
See also CWRI 5
See also MAICYA 1, 2
See also MTFW 2005
See also SATA 11, 59, 108, 155
dePaola, Tomie
See dePaola, Thomas Anthony
See also CLR 4, 24, 81
See also DLB 61
See also SAAS 15
DePaolo, Charles 1950- 234
de Paor, Louis 1961- 204
de Paor, Risteard
See Power, Richard
Depardieu, Gerard 1948- 156
deParrie, Paul 1949- .... SATA 74
Depas, Spencer 1925- 69-72
DePaul, Edith
See Delatush, Edith G.
DePauw, Linda Grant 1940- CANR-9
Earlier sketch in CA 21-24R
See also SATA 24
de Pedrolo, Manuel
See Pedrolo, Manuel de
Depel, Jim 1936- 73-76
de Pereda, Prudencio 1912-1985 .... CANR-4
Earlier sketch in CA 1-4R
Depestre, Rene 1926- 199
Brief entry 113
See also CWW 2
See also EWL 3
See also RGWL 3
DePew, Alfred (Mansfield) 1952- 141
Depew, Arthur M(c Kinley) 1896-1976 . 41-44R
Depew, Wally
See Depew, Walter Westerfield
Depew, Walter Westerfield 1924- 5-8R
De Pietro, Albert 1913-1989 69-72
de Pillecijn, Filip
See Pillecijn, Filip de
de Pisan, Christine 1364-1431
See de Pizan, Christine
See also FW
de Pizan, Christine
See de Pisan, Christine
See also FL 1:1
de Polman, Willem
See Nichols, Dale (William)
De Polnay, Peter 1906-1984 .... CANR-76
Obituary 114
Earlier sketch in CA 73-76
DePorte, Anton W. 1928- 124
DePorte, Michael V(ital) 1939- 49-52
Depp, Johnny 1963- 173
Depp, Roberta J. 1947- 101
de Pre, Jean-Anne
See Avallone, Michael (Angelo, Jr.)
DePree, Gladis (Lenore) 1933- 101
DePree, Gordon 1930- 101
de Prume, Cathryn 213
Depta, Victor M(arshall) 1939- CANR-107
Earlier sketch in CA 49-52
De Puy, Norman R(obert) 1929- 97-100
Dequasie, Andrew 1929- CANR-82
Earlier sketches in CA 114, CANR-35
de Queiroz, Dinah Silveira 1911-1982 232
de Queiroz, Rachel 1910-2003 ...... CANR-135
Earlier sketch in CA 179
See also Queiroz, Rachel de
De Quille, Dan
See Wright, William
De Quincey, Thomas 1785-1859 .... BRW 4
See also CDBLB 1789-1832
See also DLB 110, 144
See also RGEL 2
DeRan, David 1946- .... SATA 76
D'Erasmo, Martha 1939- 81-84
D'Erasmo, Stacey 1961- 192
Derber, Charles (K.) 1944- 220
Derber, Milton 1915-1997
Brief entry 106
Derby, George Horatio 1823-1861 .... DLB 11
Derby, Pat 1942- 69-72
Derby, Sally 1934- 155
See also SATA 89, 132
Der Derian, James (Arthur) 1955- 152
Derderian, Yeghishe 1910(?)-1990
Obituary 130
de Regniers, Beatrice Schenk (Freedman)
1914-2000 .... CANR-26
Obituary 190
Earlier sketches in CA 13-16R, CANR-6
See also CWRI 5
See also MAICYA 1, 2
See also SAAS 6
See also SATA 2, 68
See also SATA-Obit 123
Dereksen, David
See Stacton, David (Derek)
Deren, Eleanora 1908(?)-1961 192
Obituary 111
See also Deren, Maya
Deren, Maya
See Deren, Eleanora
See also CLC 16, 102
Derenberg, Walter J(ulius) 1903-1975
Obituary 61-64
De Reneville, Mary Margaret Motley Sheridan
1912- 5-8R
Dereske, Jo 1947- 163
See also SATA 72
Deressa, Solomon 1937- .... EWL 3
de Reyna, Rudy 1914-1980 .... CANR-10
Earlier sketch in CA 57-60
Derfler, (Arnold) Leslie 1933- CANR-83
Earlier sketches in CA 5-8R, CANR-9
deRham, Edith 1933- 13-16R
Derham, (Arthur) Morgan 1915- 13-16R
Der Hovanessian, Diana 124
Deriabin, Peter 1921-1992 134
Deric, Arthur J. 1926- 21-24R
de Ricci, Seymour (Montefiore Robert Rosso)
1881-1942 191
See also DLB 201
de Ridder, Alphonsus Josephus
See Elsschot, Willem
Derig, Betty (B.) 1924- 225
de Rijk, Maarten
See Donkersloot, Nicolaas-Anthonie
Dering, Joan (Rosalind Cordelia) 1917- ... 9-12R
De Rios, Marlene Dobkin
See Dobkin De Rios, Marlene
De Risi, William J(oseph) 1938- 53-56
de Rivera, Joseph H(osmer) 1932- 41-44R
Derksen, Jeff 1958- 153
See also CP 7
Derleth, August (William) 1909-1971 . CANR-4
Obituary 29-32R
Earlier sketch in CA 1-4R
See also BPFB 1
See also BYA 9, 10
See also CLC 31
See also CMW 4
See also CN 1
See also DLB 9
See also DLBD 17
See also HGG
See also SATA 5
See also SUFW 1
Derman, Lou 1914(?)-1976
Obituary 65-68
Derman, Martha (Winn) .... SATA 74
Derman, Sarah Audrey 1915- CANR-17
Earlier sketch in CA 1-4R
See also SATA 11
Dermid, Jack 1923- 49-52
Dermout, Maria
See Dermout(-Ingermann), (Helena Antonia) Maria (Elisabeth)
Dermout(-Ingermann), (Helena Antonia) Maria (Elisabeth) 1888-1962
Obituary 114
Dern, Erolie Pearl Gaddis
1895-1966 .... CANR-6
Obituary 25-28R
Earlier sketch in CA 1-4R
Dern, Karl L(udwig) 1894-1989 57-60
Dern, Peggy
See Dern, Erolie Pearl Gaddis
Dernburg, Thomas F(rederick) 1930- .. CANR-2
Earlier sketch in CA 1-4R
Der Nersessian, Sirarpie 1896-1989 102
Der Nister 1884-1950
See Nister, Der
See also TCLC 56
de Robeck, Nesta 1886- CAP-2
Earlier sketch in CA 25-28
DeRoberts, Lyndon
See Silverstein, Robert Alan
de Rochemont, Louis 1899-1978 ..... IDFW 3, 4
De Rochemont, Richard (Guertis) 1903-1982
Obituary 108
de Rocher, Gregory (David) 1943- 114
DeRoin, Nancy 1934- 65-68
de Romaszkan, Gregor 1894- 13-16R
de Romilly, Jacqueline (David)
1913- CANR-144
Earlier sketch in CA 144
de Roo, Anne Louise 1931-1997 ...... CANR-51
Earlier sketch in CA 103
See also CLR 63
See also CWRI 5
See also SATA 25, 84
de Roos, Robert (William) 1912- 9-12R
de Ropp, Robert S(ylvester) 1913-1987 . 17-20R
Deror, Yehezkel
See Dror, Yehezkel
deRosa, Dee .... SATA 70
DeRosa, Peter (Clement) 1932- CANR-9
Earlier sketch in CA 21-24R
DeRosa, Steven 205
DeRose, David J(oseph) 1957- 144
DeRosier, Arthur H(enry), Jr. 1931- 29-32R
De Rosis, Helen A. 1918- 122
Brief entry 107
De Rossi, Claude J(oseph) 1942- 53-56
Derossi, Flavia 1926- 112
De Rosso, H(enry) A(ndrew)
1917-1960 .... TCWW 1, 2
de Rothschild, Edmund (Leopold) 1916- 180
de Rothschild, Guy (Edouard Alphonse Paul)
1909- 129
de Rothschild, Pauline (Fairfax-Potter)
1908(?)-1976
Obituary 65-68
de Rougemont, Denis (Louis) 1906-1985 ... 154
Obituary 118
de Roussan, Jacques 1929- 123
Brief entry 110
See also SATA-Brief 31
de Routisie, Albert
See Aragon, Louis
de Roxas, Juan Bartolome
See Rubia Barcia, Jose
Derr, Mark (Burgess) 1950- CANR-75
Earlier sketch in CA 135
Derr, Richard L(uther) 1930- 53-56
Derr, Thomas Sieger 1931- 53-56
Derrett, J(ohn) Duncan M(artin)
1922- CANR-44
Earlier sketches in CA 13-16R, CANR-6, 21
Derrick, Graham
See Raby, Derek Graham
Derrick, Lionel
See Cunningham, Chet
Derrick, Paul 1916- CAP-1
Earlier sketch in CA 9-10
Derrickson, Jim 1959- 212
See also SATA 141
Derricotte, Toi 1941- CANR-73
Earlier sketches in CA 113, CANR-32
See also BW 2
See also CWP
Derrida, Jacques 1930-2004 .... CANR-133
Obituary 232
Brief entry 124
Earlier sketches in CA 127, CANR-76, 98
See also CLC 24, 87
See also DLB 242
See also EWL 3
See also LMFS 2
See also MTCW 2
See also TWA
Derriman, James Parkyns 1922- 106
Derry, Charles 209
Derry, John W(esley) 1933- CANR-3
Earlier sketch in CA 5-8R
Derry, Margaret E. 1945- 209
Derry, (Thomas) Ramsay 1939- 110
Derry, T(homas) K(ingston)
1905-2001 .... CANR-95
Obituary 199
Earlier sketches in CA 1-4R, CANR-4
Derry Down Derry
See Lear, Edward
Dershowitz, Alan M(orton) 1938- CANR-79
Earlier sketches in CA 25-28R, CANR-11, 44
Dersonnes, Jacques
See Simenon, Georges (Jacques Christian)
Der Stricker c. 1190-c. 1250 .... DLB 138
Dertouzos, Michael L(eonidas)
1936-2001 .... CANR-104
Obituary 201
Earlier sketch in CA 21-24R
Derum, James Patrick 1893-1990 .... CAP-1
Earlier sketch in CA 13-14
De Ruth, Jan 1922-1991 .... 33-36R
Dervaes, Claudine 1954- 167
Dervaux, Isabelle 1961- .... SATA 106
Dervin, Brenda 1938- 29-32R
Dervin, Daniel A(rthur) 1935- 57-60
der Vogelweide, Walther von
See Walther von der Vogelweide
Derwent, Lavinia CANR-27
Earlier sketch in CA 69-72
See also SATA 14
Derwin, Jordan 1931- 13-16R
Dery, Mark 1959- CANR-90
Earlier sketch in CA 153
Dery, Tibor 1894-1977
Obituary 73-76
See also EWL 3
de Rycke, Laurence Joseph 1907-1989
Obituary 129
Derzhavin, Gavriil Romanovich
1743-1816 .... DLB 150
Desai, Anita 1937- CANR-133
Earlier sketches in CA 81-84, CANR-33, 53, 95
See also BRWS 5
See also CLC 19, 37, 97, 175
See also CN 1, 2, 3, 4, 5, 6, 7
See also CWRI 5
See also DA3
See also DAB
See also DAM NOV
See also DLB 271
See also DNFS 2
See also EWL 3
See also FW
See also MTCW 1, 2
See also MTFW 2005
See also SATA 63, 126
Desai, Boman 1950- CANR-128
Earlier sketches in CA 134, CANR-71
See also CN 6, 7
Desai, Kiran 1971- CANR-127
Earlier sketch in CA 171
See also BYA 16
See also CLC 119

Cumulative Index 149 **Deveau**

Desai, Meghnad 1940- CANR-126
Earlier sketch in CA 126
Desai, P(rasannavadan) B(hagwanji)
1924- 29-32R
Desai, Ram 1926- 5-8R
Desai, Rashmi H(arilal) 1928- 13-16R
Desai, Rupin W(alter) 1934- 45-48
Desai Hidier, Tanuja .... AAYA 56
de Ste. Croix, G(eoffrey) E(rnest) M(aurice)
1910-2000 73-76
Obituary 188
de Saint-Gall, Auguste Amedee
See Strich, Christian
de St. Jorre, John 1936- 102
de Saint-Luc, Jean
See Glassco, John
de Saint Phalle, Therese 1930- CANR-21
Earlier sketch in CA 29-32R
de Saint Phalle, Thibaut 1918- 108
de Saint Pierre, Isaure 1944- 197
de Saint Roman, Arnaud
See Aragon, Louis
De Salamanca, Cristina Enriquez
See Enriquez de Salamanca, Cristina
Desalle, Rob 203
DeSalvo, Joseph S(alvatore) 1938- 45-48
DeSalvo, Louise A(nita) 1942- CANR-127
Earlier sketches in CA 102, CANR-23, 62
Desan, Wilfrid 1908-2000 61-64
Obituary 192
Desani, G(ovindas) V(ishnoodas)
1909-2000 .... CANR-70
Earlier sketch in CA 45-48
See also CN 1, 2, 3, 4, 5, 6
See also EWL 3
de Santa Ana, Julio 1934- 132
de Santillana, Giorgio Diaz
1902-1974 .... CANR-100
Earlier sketches in CAP-1, CA 13-14
DeSantis, Mary Allen (Carpe) 1930- 9-12R
De Santis, Vincent P. 1918- CANR-4
Earlier sketch in CA 9-12R
De Santo, Charles P(asquale) 1923- 116
Desarthe, Agnes 1966- 199
De Satge, John (Cosmo) 1928-1984 124
Obituary 113
Desatnick, Robert L(awrence) 1931- 41-44R
De Saulles, Tony 1958- 190
See also SATA 119
Desaulniers, Gonzalve 1863-1934 178
See also DLB 92
de Sausmarez, (Lionel) Maurice
1915-1969 .... CAP-1
Earlier sketch in CA 11-12
de Saussure, Eric 1925- 105
de Saussure, Ferdinand 1857-1913 168
See also DLB 242
Desautels, Denise 1945- 170
Desbarats, Peter 1933- CANR-10
Earlier sketch in CA 17-20R
See also SATA 39
Des Barres, Pamela (Ann) 1948- CANR-57
Earlier sketch in CA 128
Desberry, Lawrence H.
See zur Muhlen, Hermynia
Desbiens, Jean-Paul 1927- 175
See also DLB 53
Desbordes-Valmore, Marceline
1786-1859 .... DLB 217
Desborough, Vincent Robin d'Arba 1914-1978
Obituary 111
Descargues, Pierre 1925- CANR-14
Earlier sketch in CA 37-40R
Descartes, Rene 1596-1650 .... DLB 268
See also EW 3
See also GFL Beginnings to 1789
Deschamps, Emile 1791-1871 .... DLB 217
See also GFL 1789 to the Present
Deschamps, Eustache 1340(?)-1404 ... DLB 208
Deschampsneufs, Henry Pierre Bernard
1911- CANR-6
Earlier sketch in CA 5-8R
de Schanschieff, Juliet Dymoke 1919- 106
See also RHW
Descharnes, Robert (Pierre) 1926- 69-72
De Schauensee, Rodolphe Meyer
1901-1984 155
Deschenaux, Jacques 1945- 61-64
Deschin, Celia Spalter 1903-1983 104
Deschin, Jacob 1900(?)-1983
Obituary 110
Deschler, Lewis 1905-1976
Obituary 65-68
Deschner, Donald (Anthony) 1933- 21-24R
Deschner, (Hans) Guenther 1941- 41-44R
Deschner, (Hans) Gunther
See Deschner, (Hans) Guenther
Deschner, John 1923- 81-84
Deschodt, Eric 229
de Schweinitz, Karl 1887-1975 61-64
Desclos, Anne
See Aury, Dominique
Descola, Philippe 1949- 151
Descombes, Vincent 1943- 136
de Selincourt, Aubrey 1894-1962 ..... CANR-95
Earlier sketch in CA 73-76
See also SATA 14
DeSena, Carmine 1957- CANR-80
Earlier sketch in CA 151
See also HW 2
de Sena, Jorge 1919-1978
Obituary 77-80
See also Sena, Jorge de
De Seversky, Alexander P(rocofieff) 1894-1974
Obituary 53-56
DeSeyn, Donna E. 1933- 21-24R
des Forets, Louis-Rene 1918- 176
See also DLB 83
Desfosses, Helen 1945- 41-44R
Des Gagniers, Jean 1929- CANR-9
Earlier sketch in CA 65-68
Desguin, Guillard
See Humez, Nicholas (David)
DeShazo, Edith K(ind) 1920-1980 61-64
DeShazo, Elmer Anthony 1924-1997 .... 37-40R
DeShell, Jeffrey (George) 1959- 186
Deshen, Shlomo 1935- 57-60
Deshler, G(eorge) Byron 1903-1992 53-56
Deshpande, Chris 1950- 137
See also SATA 69
Deshpande, Gauri 1942- .... CP 1
Deshpande, Shashi 1938- CANR-92
Earlier sketches in CA 128, CANR-60
See also CN 5, 6, 7
See also EWL 3
DeSiano, Francis P(atrick) 1945- CANR-31
Earlier sketch in CA 112
Desiato, Luca 1941- .... DLB 196
De Sica, Vittorio 1901(?)-1974
Obituary 117
See also CLC 20
Desiderato, Otello 1926- 37-40R
de Silva, Alvaro 1949- 138
De Silva, Cara 165
deSilva, David A. 1967- 221
Desimini, Lisa 1964- .... SATA 86, 148
De Simone, Daniel V. 1930- 25-28R
DeSipio, Louis 1959- 187
Desjardins, Marie-Catherine
See Villedieu, Madame de
Desjarlais, John (J.) 1953- CANR-92
Earlier sketch in CA 135
See also SATA 71
Desmangles, Leslie G. 1941- 144
Desmarais, Barbara G.
See Taylor, Barbara G.
Des Marais, Louise M(ercier) 1923- 110
Desmarais, Ovid E. 1919- CANR-23
Earlier sketches in CA 1-4R, CANR-4
Desmarets, Jean 1600-1676 . GFL Beginnings to 1789
Desmoinaux, Christel 1967- 170
See also SATA 103, 149
Desmond, Adrian J(ohn) 1947- CANR-105
Earlier sketches in CA 61-64, CANR-8
See also SATA 51
Desmond, Alice Curtis 1897-1990 ..... CANR-2
Earlier sketch in CA 1-4R
See also SATA 8
Desmond, (Clarice) J(oanne) Patrick (Scholes)
1910- 9-12R
Desmond, John 1909(?)-1977
Obituary 73-76
Desmond, John F(rancis) 1939- 112
Desmond, Ray 1925- 120
Desmond, Robert W(illiam)
1900-1985 .... CANR-12
Earlier sketch in CA 73-76
Desmond, Shaw 1877-1960
Obituary 89-92
Desmonde, William H(erbert) 1921-1971 . 1-4R
Desnica, Vladan 1905-1967 .... DLB 181
See also EWL 3
Desnos, Robert 1900-1945 .... CANR-107
Brief entry 121
Earlier sketch in CA 151
See also DLB 258
See also EWL 3
See also LMFS 2
See also TCLC 22
De Sola, John
See Morland, Nigel
De Sola, Ralph 1908-1993 53-56
de Somogyi, Nick 233
de Sousa, Ronald 1940- 127
de Souza, Eunice 1940- 153
See also CP 7
See also CWP
de Souza, Philip 1964- 197
Desowitz, Robert S. 1926- 126
DeSpain, Pleasant 1943- 151
See also SATA 87
Despalatovic, Elinor Murray 1933- 105
Despert, J(uliette) Louise 1892-1982 69-72
Desplaines, Baroness Julie
See Jennings, Leslie Nelson
Despland, Michel 1936- CANR-29
Earlier sketch in CA 49-52
Desplechin, Marie 1959- 200
Desportes, Philippe
1546-1606 .... GFL Beginnings to 1789
des PrEs, Josquin 1954- 195
Despres, Leo A(rthur) 1932- 25-28R
Despres, Loraine 217
Des Pres, Terrence 1939-1987 .... CANR-76
Obituary 124
Earlier sketch in CA 73-76
Desputeaux, Helene 1959- 160
See also SATA 95
des Rivieres, Jim 1953- 141
DesRochers, Alfred 1901-1978 178
See also CCA 1
See also DLB 68
DesRochers, Diane 1937- 150
Desrosiers, Leo-Paul 1892-1967 148
See also DLB 68
Dess, G. D. 135
Dessaix, Robert 1944- CANR-124
Earlier sketch in CA 161
Dessart, George Baldwin, Jr., Jr. 1925- 172
Dessau, Joanna 1921- CANR-24
Earlier sketch in CA 106
Dessauer, John H(ans) 1905-1993 104
Obituary 142
Dessauer, John P(aul) 1924- 53-56
Dessaulles, Louis-Antoine 1819-1895 .. DLB 99
Dessel, Norman F(rank) 1932- 61-64
Dessen, Alan C(harles) 1935- CANR-94
Earlier sketch in CA 69-72
Dessen, Sarah 1970- 196
See also AAYA 39
See also BYA 12, 16
See also SATA 120
Dessent, Michael H(arold) 1942- 110
Desser, David 1953- 145
Dessi, Giuseppe 1909-1977 65-68
Obituary 126
See also DLB 177
d'Estaing, Valery Giscard
See Giscard d'Estaing, Valery
D'Este, Carlo 1936- CANR-121
Earlier sketch in CA 153
De Steuch, Harriet Henry 1897(?)-1974
Obituary 49-52
Destler, Chester McArthur
1904-1984 .... CANR-16
Obituary 114
Earlier sketch in CA 5-8R
Destler, I. M. 1939- CANR-15
Earlier sketch in CA 89-92
Destouches, Louis-Ferdinand
1894-1961 .... CANR-28
Earlier sketch in CA 85-88
See also Celine, Louis-Ferdinand
See also CLC 9, 15
See also MTCW 1
Destry, Vince
See Norwood, Victor G(eorge) C(harles)
De Sua, William Joseph 1930- 13-16R
des Ursins, Bertrand de Jouvenel
See de Jouvenel des Ursins, Edouard Bertrand
Desurvire, Emmanuel 1955- 237
Desvignes, Lucette 1926- .... DLB 321
de Swaan, Abram 1942- CANR-13
Earlier sketch in CA 69-72
DeSylva, Buddy 1895-1950 .... DLB 265
de Sylva, Donald Perrin 1928- 53-56
de Syon, Guillaume 1966- 208
De Tabley, Lord 1835-1895 .... DLB 35
See also RGEL 2
De Tarr, Francis 1926- 17-20R
Deter, Dean (Allen) 1945- 53-56
de Teran, Lisa St. Aubin
See St. Aubin de Teran, Lisa
Deterline, William A(lexander) 1927- . CANR-8
Earlier sketch in CA 5-8R
de Terra, Helmut 1900-1981
Obituary 104
de Terra, Rhoda Hoff 1901-1999 .... 1-4R
Detherage, May 1908-1983 .... CAP-2
Earlier sketch in CA 23-24
Dethier, Vincent Gaston 1915-1993 ... CANR-9
Obituary 142
Earlier sketch in CA 65-68
Dethlefsen, Merle 1934- 119
Dethloff, Henry C(lay) 1934- 21-24R
De Thomasis, Louis 1940- CANR-49
Earlier sketch in CA 123
Detine, Padre
See Olsen, Ib Spang
de Tirtoff, Romain 1892-1990 69-72
Obituary 131
Detjen, Ervin W(infred) 1909-1993 .... CAP-2
Earlier sketch in CA 19-20
Detjen, Mary (Elizabeth) Ford
1904-1993 .... CAP-1
Earlier sketch in CA 13-14
Detmer, David 1958- 191
de Todany, James
See Beaudoin, Kenneth Lawrence
de Toledano, Ralph
See Toledano, Ralph de
de Tolignac, Gaston
See Griffith, D(avid Lewelyn) W(ark)
De Tolnay, Charles Erich 1899-1981 73-76
de Tonquedec, Jospeh
See Tonquedec, Joseph de
de Toth, Andre 1913(?)-2002 154
Obituary 210
de Trevino, Elizabeth B.
See Trevino, Elizabeth B(orton) de
de Trevino, Elizabeth Borton
See Trevino, Elizabeth B(orton) de
Detrez, Conrad (Jean) 1937-1985 132
Detro, Gene 1935- CANR-12
Earlier sketch in CA 61-64
Detter, Ingrid
See Delupis, Ingrid
Dettmar, Kevin J(ohn) H(offmann) 1958- 145
Detweiler, Robert 1932- 33-36R
Detwiler, Donald S(caife) 1933- 37-40R
Detwiler, Susan Dill 1956- .... SATA 58
Detz, Joan (Marie) 1951- CANR-102
Earlier sketch in CA 118
Detz, Phyllis 1911- CAP-2
Earlier sketch in CA 33-36
Detzer, David (William) 1937- CANR-108
Earlier sketch in CA 93-96
Detzer, Karl 1891-1987 .... CAP-1
Earlier sketch in CA 9-10
Detzler, Jack J. 1922- 33-36R
Detzler, Wayne Alan 1936- 105
Deuchar, Margaret 1952- 113
Deudon, Eric Hollingsworth
See du Plessis, Eric H.
Deuel, Thorne 1890-1984
Obituary 112
Deuker, Carl 1950- CANR-134
Earlier sketch in CA 149
See also AAYA 26
See also BYA 7
See also SATA 82, 150
See also YAW
Deutermann, P(eter) T(homas)
1941- CANR-102
Earlier sketch in CA 142
Deutrich, Mabel E. 1915-1998 .... 5-8R
Deutsch, Adolph 1897-1980 .... IDFW 3, 4
Deutsch, Alfred H(enry) 1914- 116
Deutsch, Arnold R. 1919- 101
Deutsch, Babette 1895-1982 .... CANR-79
Obituary 108
Earlier sketches in CA 1-4R, CANR-4
See also BYA 3
See also CLC 18
See also CP 1, 2
See also DLB 45
See also SATA 1
See also SATA-Obit 33
Deutsch, Bernard Francis 1925- 13-16R
Deutsch, Eberhard Paul 1897-1980
Obituary 93-96
Deutsch, Eliot (Sandler) 1931- CANR-10
Earlier sketch in CA 65-68
Deutsch, Eva Costabel
See Costabel, Eva Deutsch
Deutsch, Harold C(harles)
1904-1995 .... CANR-97
Earlier sketch in CA 21-24R
Deutsch, Helen 1906-1992 .... CANR-78
Obituary 137
Brief entry 108
Earlier sketch in CA 112
Interview in CA-112
See also SATA 76
Deutsch, Helene (Rosenbach) 1884-1982 .. 128
Obituary 106
Deutsch, Herbert A(rnold) 1932- 89-92
Deutsch, Hermann Bacher 1889-1970
Obituary 93-96
Deutsch, John James 1911-1976
Obituary 111
Deutsch, Karl W(olfgang)
1912-1992 .... CANR-46
Obituary 139
Earlier sketch in CA 41-44R
Deutsch, Marilyn Weisberg 1950- 102
Deutsch, Morton 1920-2002 .... 1-4R
Deutsch, Patrizia Giampieri
See Giampieri-Deutsch, Patrizia
Deutsch, Ronald M(artin) 1928- CANR-4
Earlier sketch in CA 1-4R
Deutsch, Sarah (Jane) 1955- 203
Deutsch, Xavier 1965- 195
Deutscher, Irwin 1923- 25-28R
Deutscher, Isaac 1907-1967 .... CANR-4
Obituary 25-28R
Earlier sketch in CA 5-8R
Deutscher, Max 1916(?)-1979
Obituary 93-96
Deutscher, Tamara (Lebenhaft) 1913(?)-1990
Obituary 132
Deutscher, Thomas (Brian) 1949- 124
Deutschkron, Inge 1922- 29-32R
Deutschman, Alan (Barry) 1965- CANR-100
Earlier sketch in CA 116
Devadutt, Vinjamuri E(verett)
1908-1990 .... CAP-2
Earlier sketch in CA 23-24
De Vaere, Ulric Josef 1932- 1-4R
Devahuti, D. 1929- 45-48
Devajee, Ved
See Gool, Reshard
Deval, Gord 1930- 124
Deval, Jacques
See Boularan, Jacques
De Valera, Eamon 1882-1975
Obituary 89-92
De Valera, Sinead 1879(?)-1975
Obituary 53-56
See also SATA-Obit 30
de Vallbona, Rima
See Vallbona, Rima-Gretel Rothe
Devalle, Susana B(eatriz) C(ristina)
1945- CANR-102
Earlier sketch in CA 147
de Valois, Ninette 1898-2001
Obituary 195
Brief entry 115
Devamata, Sister
See Glenn, Laura Franklin
Devaney, John 1926-1994 .... CANR-23
Obituary 145
Earlier sketches in CA 17-20R, CANR-7
See also SATA 12
Devanny, Jean 1894-1962 .... DLB 260
Devaraja, N(and) K(ishore) 1917- 104
de Varona, Frank J. 1943- CANR-87
Earlier sketch in CA 150
See also SATA 83
de Varona, Joanna
See Kerns, Joanna
Devas, Nicolette (Macnamara)
1911-1987(?) 13-16R
Obituary 122
de Vasconcelos, Erika 1965- 172
Devashish, Donald Acosta 1956- 162
DeVault, M(arion) Vere 1922- CANR-20
Earlier sketches in CA 1-4R, CANR-4
Devaux, Claudia 1946- 208
De Vaux, Roland 1903-1971
Obituary 33-36R
Deveau, Sarah L. 1978- 237

De Veaux, Alexis 1948- ... CANR-71
Earlier sketches in CA 65-68, CANR-26
See also BW 1, 3
See also DLB 38
See also GLL 2
de Veaux, Scott Knowles ... 196
De Vecchi, Nicolo 1943- ... 151
D'Evelyn, Katherine E(dith) 1899-1977 . 17-20R
Dever, Joseph 1919-1970 ... CAP-2
Obituary ... 29-32R
Earlier sketch in CA 19-20
Dever, William G(winn) 1933- ... CANR-113
Brief entry ... 109
Earlier sketch in CA 180
Deveraux, Jude
See White, Jude Gilliam
See also BEST 90:1
de Verb, Edouard
See Ficke, Arthur Davison
de Vere, Aubrey 1814-1902 ... 175
See also DLB 35
See also RGEL 2
de Vere, Edward 1550-1604 ... DLB 172
de Vere, Jane
See Watson, Julia
Devereaux, Robert 1947- ... 235
Deverell, Diana 1948- ... 223
Deverell, Rex (Johnson) 1941- ... 132
Deverell, William H(erbert) 1937- ... CANR-43
Earlier sketch in CA 115
Devereux, Frederick L(eonard), Jr.
1914-1993 ... CANR-1
Earlier sketch in CA 49-52
See also SATA 9
Devereux, George 1908-1985 ... 69-72
Devereux, Hilary 1919- ... 13-16R
Devereux, Paul 1965- ... 174
Devereux, Robert 1565-1601 ... DLB 136
Devereux, Robert (Essex) 1922-1999 ... 5-8R
Deverson, Harry 1909(?)-1972
Obituary ... 104
De Vet, Charles V(incent) 1911-1997 ... 102
Obituary ... 163
Devi, Gayatri 1919- ... 159
Devi, Indra 1899-2002 ... CAP-1
Obituary ... 206
Earlier sketch in CA 13-14
Devi, Nila
See Woody, Regina Jones
Devi, Ragini 1894(?)-1982
Obituary ... 110
Deview, Lucille 1920- ... 73-76
De Vilbiss, Philip
See Mebane, John (Harrison)
Deville, Rene
See Kacew, Romain
de Villiers, Gerard 1929- ... 61-64
de Villiers, Marq 1940- ... CANR-127
Earlier sketch in CA 166
de Villiers, Victor
See Hugo, Leon (Hargreaves)
de Vilmorin, Louise Leveque
See Vilmorin, Louise Leveque de
DeVincentes-Hayes, Nan ... 142
de Vinck, Antoine 1924- ... 53-56
de Vinck, Catherine 1922- ... CANR-6
Earlier sketch in CA 57-60
deVinck, Christopher 1951- ... 151
See also SATA 85
de Vinck, (Baron) Jose M. G. A. 1912- .. 17-20R
Devine, Betsy 1946- ... 142
Devine, Bob
See Devine, Robert S.
Devine, D(avid) M(cDonald) 1920- ... CANR-1
Earlier sketch in CA 1-4R
Devine, Dominic
See Devine, D(avid) M(cDonald)
Devine, Donald J. 1937- ... 81-84
Devine, (Mary) Elizabeth 1938- ... CANR-38
Earlier sketch in CA 116
Devine, George 1941- ... CANR-1
Earlier sketch in CA 45-48
Devine, Janice 1909(?)-1973
Obituary ... 41-44R
Devine, (Joseph) Lawrence 1935- ... 73-76
Devine, Robert S. 1951- ... 237
Devine, T(homas) M(artin) 1945- ... 136
Devine, Thomas G. 1928- ... 17-20R
De Vinne, Theodore Low 1828-1914 ... 216
See also DLB 187
DeVinney, Richard 1936- ... 45-48
Devins, Joseph H(erbert), Jr. 1930- ... 21-24R
Devious, B. K.
See Herring, Peggy J.
DeVitis, Angelo A(nthony) 1925- ... 107
DeVito, Basil V., Jr. 1959- ... 200
DeVito, Cara 1956- ... 147
See also SATA 80
De Vito, Joseph Anthony 1938- ... 37-40R
Devkota, Laxmiprasad 1909-1959
Brief entry ... 123
See also TCLC 23
Devletoglou, Nicos E. 1936- ... 41-44R
Devlin, Albert J. ... 204
Devlin, Anne 1951- ... DLB 245
See also SSFS 17
Devlin, Bernadette (Josephine) 1947- ... 105
Devlin, Dean 1962- ... 172
Devlin, Denis 1908-1959 ... RGEL 2
Devlin, Diana (Mary) 1941- ... CANR-37
Earlier sketch in CA 114
Devlin, Gerard M(ichael) 1933- ... 105
Devlin, Harry 1918- ... CANR-103
Earlier sketches in CA 65-68, CANR-8, 37
See also MAICYA 1, 2
See also SATA 11, 74, 136
Devlin, John C. 1911(?)-1984
Obituary ... 113
Devlin, John J(oseph), Jr. 1920- ... 37-40R
Devlin, Judith 1952- ... 207
Devlin, Keith 1947- ... CANR-97
Earlier sketch in CA 141
Devlin, L. Patrick 1939- ... 61-64
Devlin, Paddy
See Devlin, Patrick Joseph
Devlin, Patrick (Arthur) 1905-1992 .. CANR-46
Obituary ... 138
Earlier sketch in CA 69-72
Devlin, Patrick Joseph 1925-1999 ... 189
Devlin, (Dorothy) Wende 1918- ... CANR-103
Earlier sketches in CA 61-64, CANR-8, 37
See also MAICYA 1, 2
See also SATA 11, 74
Devney, Darcy C(ampion) 1960- ... 138
DeVoe, Forrest
See Phillips, Max
DeVoe, Shirley Spaulding 1899-1991 ... 77-80
Obituary ... 163
Devol, Kenneth S(towe) 1929-1997 ... 49-52
Obituary ... 163
Devon, D. G.
See Demorest, Stephen and
Gross, Michael (Robert)
Devon, Gary ... 182
Devon, John Anthony
See Payne, (Pierre Stephen) Robert
Devon, Paddie 1953- ... 156
See also SATA 92
Devons, Sonia 1974- ... SATA 72
Devor, Holly 1951- ... 172
Devor, John W(esley) 1901-1981 ... CAP-1
Earlier sketch in CA 11-12
Devorah-Leah ... 182
See also SATA 111
DeVore, Gary 1941-1997 ... 166
Devore, Irven 1934- ... 21-24R
De Vore, Sheryl (Lynn) 1956- ... 196
DeVorkin, David H(yam) 1944- ... CANR-99
Earlier sketches in CA 108, CANR-26
De Vorsey, Louis, Jr. 1929- ... 21-24R
de Vos, Gail 1949- ... 194
See also SATA 122
DeVos, George A(lphonse) 1922- ... CANR-11
Earlier sketch in CA 21-24R
De Vos, Karen Helder 1939- ... 102
De Vos, Susan 1953- ... 153
de Vosjoli, Philippe L. Thyraud 1920- ... 29-32R
De Voto, Bernard (Augustine) 1897-1955 ... 160
Brief entry ... 113
See also DLB 9, 256
See also MAL 5
See also TCLC 29
See also TCWW 1, 2
de Vries, Abraham H. 1937- ... 206
de Vries, Anne 1904-1964
Obituary ... 116
De Vries, Carrow 1906-1990 ... 53-56
DeVries, Douglas 1933- ... 194
See also SATA 122
deVries, Egbert 1901-1994 ... 61-64
de Vries, Eva
See Herzberg, Judith (Frieda Lina)
de Vries, Herbert A. 1917- ... CANR-13
Earlier sketch in CA 33-36R
De Vries, Hilary ... 228
de Vries, Jan 1943- ... CANR-26
Earlier sketch in CA 69-72
DeVries, Kelly 1956- ... 168
de Vries, Leonard
See Vries, Leonard de
de Vries, Manfred F. R. Kets
See Kets de Vries, Manfred F. R.
de Vries, Marta
See Herzberg, Judith (Frieda Lina)
De Vries, Peter 1910-1993 ... CANR-41
Obituary ... 142
Earlier sketch in CA 17-20R
See also CLC 1, 2, 3, 7, 10, 28, 46
See also CN 1, 2, 3, 4, 5
See also DAM NOV
See also DLB 6
See also DLBY 1982
See also MAL 5
See also MTCW 1, 2
See also MTFW 2005
de Vries, Rachel (Guido) 1947- ... 123
De Vries, Simon J(ohn) 1921- ... 57-60
De Vries, Walter (Dale) 1929- ... 69-72
Dew, Charles B(urgess) 1937- ... CANR-119
Earlier sketches in CA 21-24R, CANR-29
Dew, Donald 1928- ... 106
Dew, Edward MacMillan 1935- ... 81-84
Dew, Joan King 1932- ... 104
Dew, Robb (Reavill) Forman
1946- ... CANR-113
Earlier sketches in CA 104, CANR-29
de Waal, Frans 1948- ... 110
De Waal, Ronald Burt 1932- ... CANR-14
Earlier sketch in CA 37-40R
de Waal, Victor (Alexander) 1929- ... 29-32R
de Waal Malefijt, Annemarie
1914-1982 ... 61-64
Obituary ... 109
De Waard, E(lliott) John 1935- ... CANR-2
Earlier sketch in CA 49-52
See also SATA 7
de Wagenheim, Olga
See Jiminez Wagenheim, Olga
Dewald, Paul A. 1920- ... 17-20R
DeWalt, G. Weston
See DeWalt, Gary W(eston)
DeWalt, Gary W(eston) ... 169
Dewan, Ted 1961- ... CANR-141
Earlier sketch in CA 178
See also SATA 108, 157
Dewar, David R(oss) 1913-1990
Obituary ... 131
Dewar, Deborah 1946(?)-1986
Obituary ... 118
Dewar, Diana Ill 1928(?)-1984
Obituary ... 112
Dewar, Elaine Ruth 1948- ... 206
Dewar, Kenneth C(ameron) 1944- ... 236
Dewar, Margaret
See Quinton, Ann
Dewar, Margaret E(lizabeth) 1948- ... 114
Dewar, Mary (Williamson) 1921-1994 .. 13-16R
Dewart, Edward Hartley 1828-1903 ... 175
See also DLB 99
Dewart, Gilbert 1932- ... 135
Dewart, Leslie 1922- ... 9-12R
de Water, Frederic F(ranklyn) Van
See Van de Water, Frederic F(ranklyn)
Dewberry, Elizabeth 1962- ... CANR-119
Earlier sketch in CA 150
See also CSW
Dewdney, A(lexander) K(eewatin) 1941- ... 142
Dewdney, Christopher 1951- ... CANR-115
Earlier sketches in CA 125, CANR-53
See also CP 7
See also DLB 60
Dewdney, John Christopher 1928- ... 103
Dewdney, Selwyn (Hanington)
1909-1979 ... CANR-27
Earlier sketch in CA 69-72
See also DLB 68
See also SATA 64
DeWeerd, Harvey A. 1902-1979 ... 73-76
DeWeese, Gene
See DeWeese, Thomas Eugene
DeWeese, Jean
See DeWeese, Thomas Eugene
Deweese, Pamela J. 1951- ... 203
DeWeese, Thomas Eugene 1934- ... CANR-24
Earlier sketches in CA 65-68, CANR-9
See also SATA 46
See also SATA-Brief 45
See also SFW 4
De Welt, Don Finch 1919- ... CANR-1
Earlier sketch in CA 1-4R
de Wet, Hugh Oloff 1912(?)-1976(?)
Obituary ... 104
Dewey, Ariane 1937- ... CANR-3
Earlier sketch in CA 49-52
See also SATA 7, 109
Dewey, Barbara I. 1953- ... 221
Dewey, Bradley R. 1934- ... 29-32R
Dewey, Donald O(dell) 1930- ... 37-40R
Dewey, Edward R(ussell) 1895-1978 ... 41-44R
Dewey, Frank L. 1906-1995 ... 122
Dewey, Godfrey 1887-1977 ... CAP-2
Obituary ... 73-76
Earlier sketch in CA 29-32
Dewey, Irene Sargent 1896-1993 ... CAP-2
Earlier sketch in CA 17-18
Dewey, Jennifer (Owings) 1941- ... 126
See also SATA 58, 103
See also SATA-Brief 48
Dewey, John 1859-1952 ... CANR-144
Brief entry ... 114
Earlier sketch in CA 170
See also DLB 246, 270
See also RGAL 4
See also TCLC 95
Dewey, Joseph (Owen) 1957- ... 203
Dewey, Kenneth Francis 1940- ... 112
See also SATA 39
Dewey, Melvil 1851-1931
Brief entry ... 118
Dewey, Melville Louis Kossuth
See Dewey, Melvil
Dewey, Orville 1794-1882 ... DLB 243
Dewey, Robert D(yckman) 1923- ... 9-12R
Dewey, Robert E(ugene) 1923-1979 ... 13-16R
Dewey, Scott Hamilton 1968- ... 232
Dewey, Thomas B(lanchard)
1915-1981 ... CANR-59
Earlier sketches in CA 1-4R, CANR-1
See also CMW 4
See also DLB 226
Dewhirst, Ian 1936- ... 102
Dewhurst, Colleen 1926-1991 ... 158
Dewhurst, Eileen (Mary) 1929- ... CANR-98
Earlier sketches in CA 109, CANR-27
See also CMW 4
Dewhurst, J(ames) Frederic 1895-1967 . CAP-2
Earlier sketch in CA 17-18
Dewhurst, Keith 1931- ... CANR-68
Earlier sketches in CA 61-64, CANR-18
See also CBD
See also CD 5, 6
Dewhurst, Kenneth 1919- ... CANR-2
Earlier sketch in CA 5-8R
deWit, Dorothy (May Knowles)
1916-1980 ... 113
Obituary ... 109
See also SATA 39
See also SATA-Obit 28
de Wit, Wim 1948- ... 128
DeWitt, Addison
See Newman, Kim (James)
DeWitt, Calvin B. 1935- ... 136
DeWitt, Edith Openshaw 1920- ... 111
Dewitt, Helen 1957- ... 199
DeWitt, James
See Lewis, Mildred D.
DeWitt, John 1910(?)-1984
Obituary ... 113
Dewitt, Katherine, Jr. 1943- ... 153
Dewlen, Al 1921- ... CANR-63
Earlier sketches in CA 1-4R, CANR-2
See also TCWW 1, 2
de Wohl, Louis 1903-1961
Obituary ... 111
De Wolf, L. Harold 1905-1986 ... CANR-2
Earlier sketch in CA 1-4R
DeWolf, Rose (Doris) 1934- ... CANR-11
Earlier sketch in CA 29-32R
de Wolfe, Ivor
See Hastings, Hubert de Cronin
de Wolfe, Ivy
See Hastings, Hubert de Cronin
de Worde, Wynkyn 1491-1535 ... DLB 170
Dews, C. L. Barney
See Dews, Carlos L.
Dews, Carlos L. 1963- ... 197
Dewsbury, Donald A(llen) 1939- ... CANR-15
Earlier sketch in CA 89-92
Dexter, Al
See Poindexter, Clarence Albert
Dexter, Alison 1966- ... SATA 125
Dexter, Beverly L(iebherr) 1943- ... 114
Dexter, Byron (Vinson) 1900-1973
Obituary ... 113
Dexter, (Norman) Colin 1930- ... CANR-99
Earlier sketches in CA 65-68, CANR-10, 25, 53, 75
See also CMW 4
See also CPW
See also DAM POP
See also DLB 87
See also MSW
See also MTCW 2
See also MTFW 2005
Dexter, J.B.
See Glasby, John S.
Dexter, John
See Zachary, Hugh
Dexter, John
See Bradley, Marion Zimmer
See also GLL 1
Dexter, Lewis Anthony 1915-1995 ... CANR-4
Obituary ... 148
Earlier sketch in CA 9-12R
Dexter, Martin
See Faust, Frederick (Schiller)
Dexter, N. C.
See Dexter, (Norman) Colin
Dexter, (Ellen) Pat(ricia) Egan ... 81-84
Dexter, Pete 1943- ... CANR-129
Brief entry ... 127
Earlier sketch in CA 131
Interview in ... CA-131
See also BEST 89:2
See also CLC 34, 55
See also CPW
See also DAM POP
See also MAL 5
See also MTCW 1
See also MTFW 2005
Dexter, Peter
See Shaver, Richard S(harpe)
Dexter, Ross
See Stokoe, E(dward) G(eorge)
Dexter, Susan (Elizabeth) 1955- ... CANR-100
Earlier sketches in CA 108, CANR-25, 50
See also FANT
Dey, Frederic (Merrill) Van Rensselaer
1865-1922
Brief entry ... 113
Dey, Joseph C(harles), Jr. 1907-1991 ... CAP-1
Obituary ... 133
Earlier sketch in CA 11-12
Dey, Marmaduke
See Dey, Frederic (Merrill) Van Rensselaer
Deyermond, Alan D(avid) 1932- ... CANR-6
Earlier sketch in CA 13-16R
Deyneka, Anita 1943- ... CANR-26
Earlier sketches in CA 61-64, CANR-11
See also SATA 24
Deyneka, Peter (N. Sr.) 1898-1987
Obituary ... 123
DeYoung, James B. 1941- ... 188
de Young, M(ichael) H(arry) 1849-1925 ... 181
See also DLB 25
DeYoung, Mary 1949- ... 112
Deyrup, Astrith Johnson 1923- ... 65-68
See also SATA 24
Deyssel, Lodewijk van
See Alberdingk Thijm, Karel Joan Lodewijk
See also EWL 3
Deza, Ernest C. 1923- ... 53-56
de Zegher, M. Catherine 1955- ... CANR-136
Earlier sketch in CA 162
Dezenhall, Eric 1962- ... 205
Dhalla, Nariman K. 1925- ... 25-28R
Dhami, Narinder 1958- ... 227
See also SATA 152
Dharker, Imtiaz ... 168
Dharmapala, Anagarika
See Hewavitarne, (Don) David
Dharmi, Santana
See Santana, Dharmi
d'Harnoncourt, Anne (Julie) 1943- ... 120
Dhavamony, Mariasusai 1925- ... 33-36R
Dhiegh, Khigh (Alx) 1910-1991 ... 93-96
Obituary ... 222
Dhlomo, H(erbert) I(saac) E(rnest)
1903-1956 ... 178
See also BW 3
See also DLB 157, 225
Dhofari, Temim
See Djaout, Tahar
Dhokalia, (Ramaa) Prasad 1925- ... 41-44R

Cumulative Index 151 Dickinson

Dhondy, Farrukh 1944- CANR-138
Earlier sketches in CA 132, CANR-81
See also AAYA 24
See also CLR 41
See also MAICYA 1, 2
See also SATA 65, 152
See also YAW
Dhrymes, Phoebus J(ames) 1932- CANR-12
Earlier sketch in CA 29-32R
Dhu al-Rummah c. 696-c. 735 .... DLB 311
Dhuoda c. 803-c. 843 .... DLB 148
Di, Zhu Xiao 1958- 170
Diack, Hunter 1908-1974 .... CAP-2
Earlier sketch in CA 21-22
Dial, Joan 1937- CANR-24
Earlier sketch in CA 81-84
Dial-Driver, Emily 1946- 208
Diallo, Kadiatou 1959- 227
Diallo, Nafissatou (Niang) 1941-1982(?) 116
See also EWL 3
Diallo, Tierno Saidou 1945-
See Monenembo, Tierno
Diaman, N(ikos) A. 1936- 236
Diamano, Silmang
See Senghor, Leopold Sedar
Diamant, Anita 1951- CANR-126
Earlier sketch in CA 145
Diamant, Lincoln 1923- 33-36R
Diamond, Ann
See McLean, Anne (Julia)
Diamond, Arthur 1957- 144
See also SATA 76
Diamond, Arthur Sigismund 1897-1978 .... CAP-1
Earlier sketch in CA 9-10
Diamond, Cora A(nn) 1937- 121
Diamond, David 220
Diamond, Donna 1950- 115
See also MAICYA 1, 2
See also SATA 35, 69
See also SATA-Brief 30
Diamond, Edwin 1925-1997 .... CANR-9
Obituary 159
Earlier sketch in CA 13-16R
Diamond, Ellen 1938- 133
Diamond, Graham 1945- CANR-60
Earlier sketch in CA 85-88
See also FANT
Diamond, Harold J(ames) 1934- 110
Diamond, I(sidore) A. L. 1920-1988 81-84
Obituary 125
See also DLB 26
See also IDFW 3, 4
Diamond, Jacqueline
See Hyman, Jackie (Diamond)
Diamond, Jared (Mason) 1937- CANR-136
Earlier sketches in CA 158, CANR-79
See also MTFW 2005
Diamond, Jay 1934- CANR-33
Earlier sketches in CA 65-68, CANR-14
Diamond, Jed 1943- 216
Diamond, John 1907-2004 109
Obituary 226
Diamond, John 1934-2001 85-88
Diamond, John 1953-2001 239
Diamond, Malcolm L(uria) 1924-1997 .. 25-28R
Diamond, Marc 1944- CANR-44
Earlier sketch in CA 119
Diamond, Martin 1919-1977 77-80
Obituary 73-76
Diamond, Milton 1934- 89-92
Diamond, Neil 1941- 108
See also CLC 30
Diamond, Norma Joyce 1933- 186
Brief entry 108
Diamond, Peter A. 1940- 230
Diamond, Petra
See Sachs, Judith
Diamond, Rebecca
See Sachs, Judith
Diamond, Rickey Gard 1946- 164
Diamond, Robert Mach 1930- CANR-7
Earlier sketch in CA 9-12R
Diamond, Sander A. 1942- CANR-57
Earlier sketch in CA 49-52
Diamond, Sara 1958- CANR-100
Earlier sketch in CA 153
Diamond, Selma 1920-1985
Obituary 116
Diamond, Sigmund 1920-1999 .... 1-4R
Diamond, Solomon 1906-1998 102
Diamond, Stanley 1922-1991 102
Obituary 134
Diamond, Stephen A(rthur) 1946- 89-92
Diamond, William 1917- 65-68
Diamonstein, Barbaralee D. CANR-35
Earlier sketches in CA 85-88, CANR-15
Diaper, William 1685-1717 .... RGEL 2
Diar, Prakash 1956- 137
Diara, Agadem Lumumba 1947- 65-68
Diara, Schavi M.
See Ali, Schavi Mali Oghomaria Meritra
Dias, Earl Joseph 1916- 21-24R
See also SATA 41
Dias, Ron 1937- .... SATA 71
Dias Da Cruz, Eddy
See Rebelo, Marques
Dias Gomes, Alfredo (de Freitas) 1922-1999 179
See also DLB 307
Diawara, Manthia 1953- 178
Diaz, Abby Morton 1821-1904 230
Diaz, David 1959(?)- .... CLR 65
See also MAICYA 2
See also MAICYAS 1
See also SATA 96, 150
Diaz, Henry F(rank) 1948- CANR-87
Earlier sketch in CA 157
Diaz, Janet W(inecoff) 1935- 53-56
Diaz (Gutierrez), Jorge 1930- .... CWW 2
See also HW 1
See also LAW
Diaz, Junot 1968- CANR-119
Earlier sketch in CA 161
See also BYA 12
See also LLW
See also SSFS 20
Diaz, Tony 1968- 203
Diaz-Alejandro, Carlos F(ederico) 1937-1985 131
Obituary 116
See also HW 1
Diaz Alfaro, Abelardo (Milton) 1916(?)-1999 186
Diaz del Castillo, Bernal c. 1496-1584 .... DLB 318
See also HLCS 1
See also LAW
Diaz-Guerrero, Rogelio 1918- 101
Diaz Miron, Salvador 1858-1928 .... HW 1
Diaz Plaja, Guillermo 1909-1984 131
Obituary 113
See also HW 1
Diaz Rodriguez, Manuel 1871(?)-1927 179
See also LAW
Diaz-Stevens, Ana Maria 1942- 144
Diaz Valcarcel, Emilio 1929- 135
See also HW 1
Dib, Mohammed 1920- .... AFW
See also EWL 3
DiBartolomeo, Albert 1952- 141
di Bassetto, Corno
See Shaw, George Bernard
DiBattista, Maria 1947- 113
Dibb, Paul 1939- CANR-1
Earlier sketch in CA 45-48
Dibba, Ebou 1943- 124
Dibbell, Julian 1963- 234
Dibbern, Mary 1951- 204
Dibble, J(ames) Birney 1925- 17-20R
Dibble, L(ucy) Grace 1902-1998 196
See also DLB 204
Dibble, Nancy Ann 1942- 103
Dibble, Vadna Davis 1902(?)-1983
Obituary 110
Dibdin, Charles 1745-1814 .... RGEL 2
Dibdin, Michael 1947- CANR-106
Earlier sketches in CA 77-80, CANR-45, 66
See also CMW 4
Dibdin, Thomas Frognall 1776-1847 .. DLB 184
Dibelius, Otto (Friedrich Karl) 1880-1967
Obituary 114
Dibell, Ansen
See Dibble, Nancy Ann
Di Bella, Anna 1933-
Brief entry 110
di Benedetto, Antonio 1922- .... HW 1
Di Berardino, Angelo 1936- 135
Di Blasi, Debra 1957- CANR-88
Earlier sketch in CA 157
Dible, Donald M(eredith) 1936- 110
Dibner, Andrew Sherman 1926-
Brief entry 110
Dibner, Bern 1897-1988 107
Dibner, Martin 1911-1992 .... CANR-4
Obituary 136
Earlier sketch in CA 1-4R
DiBona, Joseph E. 1927- 185
Brief entry 109
Dicaire, David 1963- 209
Dicaire, David 1963- 208
DiCamillo, Kate 1964- 192
See also AAYA 47
See also BYA 15
See also SATA 121, 163
Di Cavalcanti, Emiliano 1898(?)-1976
Obituary 69-72
Dice, Lee R. 1889(?)-1976
Obituary 69-72
Di Certo, J(oseph) J(ohn) 1933- CANR-139
Earlier sketches in CA 21-24R, CANR-13, 42
See also SATA 60
Di Cesare, Mario A(nthony) 1928- CANR-3
Earlier sketch in CA 5-8R
Dichter, Ernest 1907-1991 .... CANR-44
Earlier sketch in CA 17-20R
Dichter, Harry 1900(?)-1978(?)
Obituary 104
DiCianni, Ron 1952- .... SATA 107
Di Cicco, Pier Giorgio 1949- CANR-137
Earlier sketches in CA 97-100, CANR-17
See also CP 7
See also DLB 60
Dick, Bernard F(rancis) 1935- CANR-93
Earlier sketches in CA 21-24R, CANR-9
Dick, Bruce Allen 1953- 195
Dick, Daniel T. 1946- 61-64
Dick, David 1930- 170
Dick, Everett 1898-1989 .... 25-28R
Dick, Ignace 1926- CANR-12
Earlier sketch in CA 25-28R
Dick, Kay 1915-2001 .... CANR-57
Obituary 200
Earlier sketches in CA 13-16R, CANR-15
Dick, Philip K(indred) 1928-1982 .. CANR-132
Obituary 106
Earlier sketches in CA 49-52, CANR-2, 16
See also AAYA 24
See also BPFB 1
See also BYA 11
See also CLC 10, 30, 72
See also CN 2, 3
See also CPW
See also DA3
See also DAM NOV, POP
See also DLB 8
See also MTCW 1, 2
See also MTFW 2005
See also NFS 5
See also SCFW 1, 2
See also SFW 4
See also SSC 57
Dick, R. A.
See Leslie, Josephine Aimee Campbell
Dick, Robert C. 1938- 37-40R
Dick, Ron 1931- 170
Dick, Susan 1940- CANR-44
Earlier sketch in CA 120
Dick, Trella Lamson 1889-1974 .... 5-8R
See also SATA 9
Dick, Trevor J. O. 1934-
Brief entry 106
Dick, William M(ilner) 1933- 41-44R
Dickason, David Howard 1907-1974 ... CAP-2
Earlier sketch in CA 33-36
Dickason, Olive Patricia 1920- 132
Dick B.
See Burns, Richard Gordon
Dicke, Robert H(enry) 1916-1997 53-56
Obituary 157
Dicke, Thomas S(cott) 1955- 143
Dicken, E(ric) W(illiam) Trueman 1919- .. 9-12R
Dickens, A(rthur) G(eoffrey) 1910-2001 .. 53-56
Obituary 199
Dickens, Charles (John Huffam) 1812-1870 .... AAYA 23
See also BRW 5
See also BRWC 1, 2
See also BYA 1, 2, 3, 13, 14
See also CDBLB 1832-1890
See also CLR 95
See also CMW 4
See also DA
See also DA3
See also DAB
See also DAC
See also DAM MST, NOV
See also DLB 21, 55, 70, 159, 166
See also EXPN
See also GL 2
See also HGG
See also JRDA
See also LAIT 1, 2
See also LATS 1:1
See also LMFS 1
See also MAICYA 1, 2
See also NFS 4, 5, 10, 14, 20
See also RGEL 2
See also RGSF 2
See also SATA 15
See also SSC 17, 49
See also SUFW 1
See also TEA
See also WCH
See also WLC
See also WLIT 4
See also WYA
Dickens, Floyd, Jr. 1940- 111
Dickens, Frank
See Huline-Dickens, Frank William
Dickens, Jacqueline B(ass) 1941- 112
Dickens, Milton 1908-1985 .... 1-4R
Dickens, Monica (Enid) 1915-1992 .. CANR-46
Obituary 140
Earlier sketches in CA 5-8R, CANR-2
See also CN 1, 2, 3, 4, 5
See also SATA 4
See also SATA-Obit 74
Dickens, Norman
See Eisenberg, Lawrence B(enjamin)
Dickens, Peter (Gerald Charles) 1917-1987 124
Obituary 122
Dickens, Roy S(elman), Jr. 1938- CANR-9
Earlier sketch in CA 65-68
Dickenson, Fred 1909-1986
Obituary 119
Dickenson, James R. 1931- CANR-50
Earlier sketch in CA 65-68
Dickenson, Mollie 1935- 129
Dickenson, Reginald 1912- CANR-112
Earlier sketch in CA 155
Dickenson, Victoria J. 1949- 236
Dicker, Davie
See Ritchie, (Harry) Ward
Dicker, Eva Barash 1936- 107
Dicker, Ralph Leslie 1914-2000 65-68
Dickerman, Edmund H. 1935-
Brief entry 110
Dickerson, Dennis C. 1949- 168
Dickerson, Ernest 1952- .... IDFW 4
Dickerson, F(rederick) Reed 1909-1991 .... 17-20R
Dickerson, Grace Leslie 1911-2001 .... 5-8R
Dickerson, James 1945- 186
Dickerson, John 1939- 57-60
Dickerson, Martha Ufford 1922- 81-84
Dickerson, Nancy H(anschman) 1927-1997 69-72
Obituary 162
Dickerson, Oliver M(orton) 1875-1966
Obituary 106
Dickerson, Robert B(radford), Jr. 1955- 106
Dickerson, Roy Ernest 1886-1965 .... 5-8R
Obituary 103
See also SATA-Obit 26
Dickerson, William E(ugene) 1897-1971 .... CAP-2
Earlier sketch in CA 21-22
Dickey, Charley 1920- 69-72
Dickey, Christopher 1951- 146
Dickey, Eleanor 228
Dickey, Eric Jerome 1961- 175
See also DLB 292
Dickey, Franklin M(iller) 1921- 21-24R
Dickey, Glenn (Ernest, Jr.) 1936- CANR-140
Earlier sketches in CA 53-56, CANR-4
Dickey, James (Lafayette) 1923-1997 .... CANR-105
Obituary 156
Earlier sketches in CA 9-12R, CANR-10, 48, 61
Interview in CANR-10
See also CABS 2
See also AAYA 50
See also AITN 1, 2
See also AMWS 4
See also BPFB 1
See also CDALB 1968-1988
See also CLC 1, 2, 4, 7, 10, 15, 47, 109
See also CP 1, 2
See also CPW
See also CSW
See also DA3
See also DAM NOV, POET, POP
See also DLB 5, 193
See also DLBD 7
See also DLBY 1982, 1993, 1996, 1997, 1998
See also EWL 3
See also MAL 5
See also MTCW 1, 2
See also NFS 9
See also PC 40
See also PFS 6, 11
See also RGAL 4
See also TCLC 151
See also TUS
Dickey, Lee
See Bremyer, Jayne Dickey
Dickey, Page 1940- 139
Dickey, R(obert) P(reston) 1936- CANR-44
Earlier sketches in CA 29-32R, CANR-25
See also CP 1, 2
Dickey, William 1928-1994 .... CANR-79
Obituary 145
Earlier sketches in CA 9-12R, CANR-24
See also CLC 3, 28
See also CP 1, 2
See also DLB 5
Dickie, Edgar P(rimrose) 1897-1991 ...... CAP-1
Earlier sketch in CA 11-12
Dickie, George (Thomas) 1926- 33-36R
Dickie, James 1934- 97-100
Dickie, John 1923- 13-16R
Dickie, Margaret (McKenzie) 1935-1999 .... CANR-105
Earlier sketch in CA 162
Dickie, Matthew W(allace) 1941- 216
Dickie-Clark, H(amish) F(indlay) 1922- . 21-24R
Dickins, A. S. M.
See Dickins, Anthony (Stewart Mackay)
Dickins, Anthony (Stewart Mackay) 1914-1987
Obituary 124
Dickins, Barry 1949- 195
See also CD 5, 6
Dickinson, A(lan) E(dgar) F(rederic) 1899-1978 73-76
Dickinson, A(rthur) T(aylor), Jr. 1925-1977 .... 5-8R
Dickinson, Barbara M. 1933- 188
Dickinson, Charles 1951- CANR-141
Earlier sketch in CA 128
See also CLC 49
Dickinson, David 238
Dickinson, Don(ald Percy) 1947- 137
Dickinson, Donald C. 1927- 21-24R
Dickinson, Edward C(live) 1938- 61-64
Dickinson, Eleanor 1931- 65-68
Dickinson, Emily (Elizabeth) 1830-1886 .... AAYA 22
See also AMW
See also AMWR 1
See also CDALB 1865-1917
See also DA
See also DA3
See also DAB
See also DAC
See also DAM MST, POET
See also DLB 1, 243
See also EXPP
See also FL 1:3
See also MAWW
See also PAB
See also PC 1
See also PFS 1, 2, 3, 4, 5, 6, 8, 10, 11, 13, 16
See also RGAL 4
See also SATA 29
See also TUS
See also WLC
See also WP
See also WYA
Dickinson, H(arry) T(homas) 1939- 33-36R
Dickinson, Mrs. Herbert Ward
See Phelps, Elizabeth Stuart
Dickinson, Janice 1955- 217
Dickinson, John 1732-1808 .... DLB 31
Dickinson, John K(ellogg) 1918- 25-28R

Dickinson, Jonathan 1688-1747 ... DLB 24
Dickinson, Leon T. 1912- ... 13-16R
Dickinson, Lois Stice 1898(?)-1970
Obituary ... 104
Dickinson, Margaret
See Muggeson, Margaret Elizabeth
Dickinson, Mary 1949- ... 110
See also SATA 48
See also SATA-Brief 41
Dickinson, Mary-Anne
See Rodda, Emily
Dickinson, Matt ... 203
Dickinson, Mike
See Hutson, Shaun
Dickinson, Patric Thomas
1914-1994 ... CANR-43
Obituary ... 144
Earlier sketches in CA 9-12R, CANR-3
See also CP 1, 2
See also DLB 27
Dickinson, Peter (Malcolm de Brissac)
1927- ... CANR-134
Earlier sketches in CA 41-44R, CANR-31, 58, 88
See also AAYA 9, 49
See also BYA 5
See also CLC 12, 35
See also CLR 29
See also CMW 4
See also DLB 87, 161, 276
See also JRDA
See also MAICYA 1, 2
See also SATA 5, 62, 95, 150
See also SFW 4
See also WYA
See also YAW
Dickinson, Peter A(llen) 1926- ... 102
Dickinson, Richard D(onald) N(ye, Jr.) 1929-
Brief entry ... 109
Dickinson, Robert Eric 1905-1981 ... CANR-3
Earlier sketch in CA 5-8R
Dickinson, Ruth F(rankenstein) 1933- ... 37-40R
Dickinson, (William) Stirling
1909-1998 ... CAP-2
Earlier sketch in CA 33-36
Dickinson, Susan 1931- ... 57-60
See also SATA 8
Dickinson, Terence 1943- ... 160
See also SATA 102
Dickinson, Thorold (Barron) 1903-1984 .. 45-48
Obituary ... 112
Dickinson, W(illiam) Calvin 1938- ... 175
Dickinson, W(illiam) Croft
1897-1963 ... CANR-6
Earlier sketch in CA 1-4R
See also SATA 13
Dickinson, William Boyd 1908-1978 ... 85-88
Obituary ... 81-84
Dick-Lauder, George (Andrew) 1917-1981 . 102
Obituary ... 171
Dickler, Gerald 1912-1999 ... 9-12R
Obituary ... 177
Dickman, James B(ruce) 1949- ... 138
Dickman, Thomas 1955- ... 146
Dickmeyer, Lowell A. 1939- ... 109
See also SATA-Brief 51
Dicks, Henry V(ictor) 1900- ... 102
Dicks, Russell Leslie 1906-1965 ... CAP-1
Earlier sketch in CA 13-16
Dicks, Shirley 1940- ... 138
Dicks, Terrance c. 1939- ... BYA 4
Dickson, Athol 1955- ... CANR-130
Earlier sketch in CA 166
Dickson, Carr
See Carr, John Dickson
Dickson, Carter
See Carr, John Dickson
Dickson, Charles W., Jr. 1926- ... 25-28R
Dickson, Donald R(ichard) 1951- ... 126
Dickson, Franklyn 1941- ... 53-56
Dickson, George E(dmond) 1918-1988 ... 49-52
Dickson, Gordon R(upert)
1923-2001 ... CANR-106
Obituary ... 193
Earlier sketches in CA 9-12R, CANR-6
See also DLB 8
See also FANT
See also SATA 77
See also SCFW 1, 2
See also SFW 4
Dickson, Helen
See Reynolds, Helen Mary Greenwood Campbell
Dickson, K. A.
See Dickson, Kwesi A(botsia)
Dickson, Kwesi A(botsia) 1929- ... 134
Brief entry ... 109
Dickson, (Horatio Henry) Lovat
1902-1987 ... CANR-46
Obituary ... 121
Earlier sketch in CA 13-16R
Dickson, Margaret (Smith) 1947- ... 114
Dickson, (W.) Michael 1968- ... 217
Dickson, Mora (Hope-Robertson)
1918-2001 ... CANR-99
Obituary ... 203
Earlier sketches in CA 13-16R, CANR-5
Dickson, Naida 1916- ... 37-40R
See also SATA 8
Dickson, Paul (Andrew) 1939- ... CANR-112
Earlier sketches in CA 33-36R, CANR-27, 52
Dickson, Peter George Muir 1929- ... 13-16R
Dickson, Robert J(ames) 1919- ... 21-24R
Dickson, Stanley 1927- ... 53-56
Dickstein, Morris 1940- ... CANR-121
Earlier sketch in CA 85-88
Di Cyan, Erwin 1918- ... 37-40R
Didato, Salvatore V. 1926- ... 122
Brief entry ... 107
Diderot, Denis 1713-1784 ... DLB 313
See also EW 4
See also GFL Beginnings to 1789
See also LMFS 1
See also RGWL 2, 3
Didinger, Ray 1946- ... 93-96
Didion, Joan 1934- ... CANR-125
Earlier sketches in CA 5-8R, CANR-14, 52, 76
See also AITN 1
See also AMWS 4
See also CDALB 1968-1988
See also CLC 1, 3, 8, 14, 32, 129
See also CN 2, 3, 4, 5, 6, 7
See also DA3
See also DAM NOV
See also DLB 2, 173, 185
See also DLBY 1981, 1986
See also EWL 3
See also MAL 5
See also MAWW
See also MTCW 1, 2
See also MTFW 2005
See also NFS 3
See also RGAL 4
See also TCLE 1:1
See also TCWW 2
See also TUS
di Donato, Georgia 1932- ... 103
di Donato, Pietro 1911-1992 ... 101
Obituary ... 136
See also DLB 9
See also TCLC 159
Didsbury, Howard F(rancis), Jr. 1924- ... 111
Didsbury, Peter 1946- ... 112
Diebold, Janet
See Sylvester, Janet Hart
Diebold, Janet Oline
See Sylvester, Janet Hart
Diebold, John (Theurer) 1926- ... 53-56
Diebold, William, Jr. 1918-2002 ... CANR-6
Obituary ... 205
Earlier sketch in CA 13-16R
Diebold, William J. 1958- ... 198
Dieckmann, Ed(ward Adolph), Jr.
1920-1994 ... CANR-21
Earlier sketch in CA 102
Dieckmann, Liselotte 1902-1994 ... 97-100
Diederich, Bernard 1926- ... 77-80
Diedrich, Maria 1950- ... 205
Diefendorf, Barbara B(oonstoppel) 1946- ... 124
Diefendorf, Jeffry M(indlin) 1945- ... 104
Diefenthaler, Jon 1943- ... 124
Diego (Cendayo), Gerardo -1987
See Diego Cendoya, Gerardo
See also DLB 134
Diego Cendoya, Gerardo 1896-1987
Obituary ... 123
See also Diego (Cendayo), Gerardo
See also HW 1
Diehl, (Robert) Digby 1940- ... CANR-117
Earlier sketches in CA 53-56, CANR-7
Diehl, Huston 1948- ... 175
Diehl, Jackson 1956- ... 135
Diehl, James M(ichael) 1938- ... 85-88
Diehl, Katharine Smith 1906-1989 ... CAP-1
Earlier sketch in CA 11-12
Diehl, Kemper 1918-2000 ... 118
Obituary ... 188
Diehl, Lorraine B(uscaglia) 1940- ... 119
Diehl, Margaret 1955- ... 237
Diehl, W(illiam) W(ells) 1916-1974 ... 17-20R
Obituary ... 134
Diehl, William (Francis, Jr.) 1924- ... CANR-13
Earlier sketch in CA 101
Interview in ... CANR-13
Diehm, Floyd L(ee) 1925- ... 195
Brief entry ... 110
Diehn, Gwen 1943- ... CANR-116
Earlier sketches in CA 147, CANR-115
See also SATA 80
Diekhoff, John S(iemon) 1905-1976 ... CAP-2
Obituary ... 69-72
Earlier sketch in CA 29-32
Diekman, John R(aymond) 1946- ... 110
Diekmann, Godfrey 1908- ... CANR-2
Earlier sketch in CA 1-4R
Diel, Paul 1893- ... 103
Diem, Max 1947- ... 151
Diener, Royce 1918- ... 176
Brief entry ... 110
Diener, Theodor Otto 1921- ... 157
Dienes, Andre de
See de Dienes, Andre
Dienes, C(harles) Thomas 1940- ... CANR-11
Earlier sketch in CA 69-72
Dienstag, Eleanor 1938- ... 65-68
Dienstein, William 1909- ... CAP-1
Earlier sketch in CA 17-18
Dierenfield, Bruce J(onathan) 1951- ... 145
Dierenfield, Richard B(ruce) 1922- ... 17-20R
Dierickx, C(harles) W(allace) 1921- ... 61-64
Dierker, Larry 1946- ... 227
Dierks, Jack Cameron 1930- ... 29-32R
Diers, Carol Jean 1933- ... 33-36R
Diescho, Joseph 1955- ... 135
Diesing, Paul R. 1922- ... CANR-2
Earlier sketch in CA 1-4R
Dieska, L. Joseph 1913-1995 ... 37-40R
Dieskau, Dietrich Fischer
See Fischer-Dieskau, Dietrich
Dieter, William 1929- ... 114
Dieterich, Michele M. 1962- ... 146
See also SATA 78
Dietl, (Kirsten) Ulla 1940- ... 33-36R
Dietrich, John E(rb) 1913-1990 ... 17-20R
Dietrich, Noah 1889-1982 ... 45-48
Obituary ... 106
Dietrich, R(ichard) F(arr) 1936- ... 21-24R
Dietrich, Richard V(incent) 1924- ... CANR-44
Earlier sketches in CA 53-56, CANR-4, 19
Dietrich, Robert
See Hunt, E(verette) Howard, (Jr.)
Dietrich, Wilfred O. 1924- ... 191
Dietrich, William (S.) 1951- ... CANR-93
Earlier sketch in CA 150
Dietrich, Wilson G. 1916- ... 25-28R
Dietz, Betty Warner
See Dietz, Elisabeth H.
Dietz, David H(enry) 1897-1984 ... CANR-2
Obituary ... 114
Earlier sketch in CA 1-4R
See also SATA 10
See also SATA-Obit 41
Dietz, Elisabeth H. 1908-1989 ... 29-32R
Dietz, Howard 1896-1983 ... 53-56
Obituary ... 110
See also DLB 265
Dietz, Lew 1907-1997 ... CANR-3
Obituary ... 157
Earlier sketch in CA 5-8R
See also SATA 11
See also SATA-Obit 95
Dietz, Marjorie (Priscilla) J(ohnson)
1918- ... CANR-14
Earlier sketch in CA 65-68
Dietz, Norman D. 1930- ... CANR-10
Earlier sketch in CA 21-24R
Dietz, Peter (John) 1924- ... 135
Dietz, Peter O(wen) 1935- ... 33-36R
Dietz, Steven 1958- ... 233
See also CAD
See also CD 5, 6
Dietze, Charles Edgar 1919-1996 ... 69-72
Dietze, Gottfried 1922- ... 21-24R
Dietzel, Paul F(ranklin) 1924- ... 21-24R
Diez, Luis Mateo 1942- ... DLB 322
Diez Del Corral, Luis 1911-1998 ... 13-16R
Diez de Medina, Raul 1909(?)-1985
Obituary ... 117
DiFederico, Frank R. 1933(?)-1987
Obituary ... 125
Diffendorfer, Ralph E(ugene) 1879-1951 ... 234
Diffily, Deborah ... 235
See also SATA 159
Di Filippo, Paul 1954- ... 173
Earlier sketches in CA 157, CANR-134
Autobiographical Essay in ... 173
See also CAAS 29
See also SFW 4
See also SUFW 2
Di Fiori, Larry
See Di Fiori, Lawrence
Di Fiori, Lawrence 1934- ... SATA 130
DiFranco, Anthony (Mario) 1945- .. CANR-105
Earlier sketch in CA 118
See also SATA 42
Di Franco, Fiorenza 1932- ... CANR-17
Earlier sketches in CA 45-48, CANR-1
Difusa, Pati
See Almodovar, Pedro
DiGaetani, John Louis 1943- ... CANR-82
Earlier sketches in CA 114, CANR-35
Digby, Anne 1935- ... SATA 72
Digby, Everard 1550(?)-1605 ... DLB 281
Digby, George (Frederick) Wingfield
See Wingfield Digby, George (Frederick)
Digby, Joan (Hildreth) 1942- ... 126
Digby, John (Michael) 1938- ... 126
Digby-Junger, Richard 1954- ... 176
Digennaro, Joseph 1939- ... 53-56
DiGeronimo, Theresa Foy ... 238
Digges, Deborah Lea 1950- ... CANR-112
Earlier sketch in CA 155
Digges, Jeremiah
See Berger, Josef
Digges, Sister Mary Laurentia
1910-1991 ... CAP-2
Earlier sketch in CA 21-22
Digges, Thomas 1546(?)-1595 ... DLB 136
Diggett, Charles (P.) 1927- ... 128
Diggins, John P(atrick) 1935- ... CANR-97
Earlier sketch in CA 37-40R
Diggle, James 1944- ... CANR-13
Earlier sketch in CA 61-64
Diggory, James C(lark) 1920- ... CANR-9
Earlier sketch in CA 21-24R
Diggory, Terence (Elliott) 1951- ... 112
Diggs, Bernard James 1916-
Brief entry ... 106
Diggs, Elizabeth 1939- ... 109
Diggs, Ellen Irene 1906-1998 ... 114
Diggs, George M(inor), Jr. 1952- ... 198
Diggs, Irene
See Diggs, Ellen Irene
DiGiacomo, James J(oseph) 1924- ... CANR-57
Earlier sketches in CA 112, CANR-30
Di Giacomo, Salvatore 1860-1934 ... EWL 3
Di Girolamo, Vittorio 1928- ... 45-48
D'Ignazio, Fred(erick) 1949- ... 110
See also SATA 39
See also SATA-Brief 35
Di Grazia, Thomas (?)-1983 ... SATA 32
Di Gregorio, Mario A(urelio Umberto)
1950- ... 131
DiGregorio, Mario J. ... 168
di Guisa, Giano
See Praz, Mario
Dihoff, Gretchen 1942- ... 41-44R
Dijkstra, Bram (Abraham Jan) 1938- ... 37-40R
Dijkstra, Edsger W(ybe) 1930-2002 ... 157
Obituary ... 207
Dijon, Jon
See Grant, Pete
Dike, Kenneth Onwuka 1917-1983
Obituary ... 111
Dikshit, R(amesh) D(utta) 1939- ... CANR-10
Earlier sketch in CA 65-68
Diktonius, Elmer 1896-1961 ... 193
See also DLB 259
See also EWL 3
Dikty, Julian May
See May, Julian
Dil, Zakhmi
See Hilton, Richard
di Lampedusa, Giuseppe Tomasi
See Tomasi di Lampedusa, Giuseppe
DiLauro, Stephen 1950- ... 112
Dilcock, Noreen 1907- ... 103
Di Lella, Alexander A. 1929- ... 21-24R
DiLello, Richard 1945- ... 41-44R
DiLeo, John 1961- ... 237
Di Leo, Joseph H. 1902-1994 ... 33-36R
Diles, Dave 1931- ... CANR-8
Earlier sketch in CA 57-60
Diliberto, Gioia 1950- ... 128
Dilke, Annabel (Mary) 1942- ... CAP-1
Earlier sketch in CA 11-12
Dilke, Caroline (Sophia) 1940- ... 102
Dilke, Christopher Wentworth 1913(?)-1987
Obituary ... 125
Dilke, O(swald) A(shton) W(entworth)
1915-1993 ... 69-72
Obituary ... 142
Dilks, David (Neville) 1938- ... CANR-35
Earlier sketches in CA 61-64, CANR-8
Dill, Alonzo T(homas, Jr.) 1914-1993 ... 37-40R
Dill, Clarence C(leveland) 1884-1978
Obituary ... 115
Dill, (George) Marshall, Jr. 1916-2000 ... 1-4R
Dill, W. S.
See Macbeth, Madge (Hamilton)
Dillard, Annie 1945- ... CANR-125
Earlier sketches in CA 49-52, CANR-3, 43, 62, 90
See also AAYA 6, 43
See also AMWS 6
See also ANW
See also CLC 9, 60, 115
See also DA3
See also DAM NOV
See also DLB 275, 278
See also DLBY 1980
See also LAIT 4, 5
See also MAL 5
See also MTCW 1, 2
See also MTFW 2005
See also NCFS 1
See also RGAL 4
See also SATA 10, 140
See also TCLE 1:1
See also TUS
Dillard, Dudley 1913-1991 ... 25-28R
Obituary ... 135
Dillard, Emil L(ee) 1921-1992 ... 57-60
Dillard, Heath (Portmann) 1933- ... 119
Dillard, J(oey) L(ee) 1924- ... CANR-56
Earlier sketches in CA 41-44R, CANR-14, 31
Dillard, J. M. 1954- ... 128
See also HGG
Dillard, James
See Snow, Charles H(orace)
Dillard, Kristine 1964- ... SATA 113
Dillard, Polly Hargis 1916- ... CANR-5
Earlier sketch in CA 9-12R
See also SATA 24
Dillard, R(ichard) H(enry) W(ilde)
1937- ... CANR-10
Earlier sketch in CA 21-24R
See also CAAS 7
See also CLC 5
See also CP 2, 3, 4, 5, 6, 7
See also CSW
See also DLB 5, 244
Dille, John M. 1921(?)-1971
Obituary ... 33-36R
Dille, Robert Crabtree 1924(?)-1983
Obituary ... 109
Dillehay, Ronald C(lifford) 1935- ... 21-24R
Dillen, Frederick G. 1946- ... 222
Dillenbeck, Marsden V. ... CAP-2
Earlier sketch in CA 25-28
Dillenberger, Jane 1916- ... CANR-23
Earlier sketches in CA 17-20R, CANR-7
Dillenberger, John 1918- ... CANR-38
Earlier sketches in CA 1-4R, CANR-2, 17
Diller, Edward 1925-1985 ... 85-88
Diller, Harriett 1953- ... 146
See also SATA 78
Diller, Phyllis (Ada) 1917- ... CANR-22
Earlier sketch in CA 81-84
Dilles, James 1923-1997 ... 1-4R
Dilley, Clyde H(obson) 1939- ... 113
Dilley, Frank B(rown) 1931- ... 13-16R
Dilliard, Irving (Lee) 1904- ... 21-24R
Dilligan, Robert J(ames) 1940- ... 127
Brief entry ... 108
Dilling, Judith
See Rhoades, Judith G(rubman)
Dilling, Yvonne 1955- ... 118
Dillingham, Beth 1927- ... 53-56
Dillingham, William B(yron) 1930- ... 13-16R
Dillistone, Frederick W(illiam)
1903-1993 ... CANR-5
Earlier sketch in CA 1-4R
Dillman, Audrey 1922(?)-1984
Obituary ... 113
Dillman, Bradford 1930- ... 231

Cumulative Index 153 **Ditzler**

Dillman, David D. 1900(?)-1983
  Obituary ... 110
Dillon, Barbara 1927- ... CANR-28
  Earlier sketch in CA 110
  See also SATA 44
  See also SATA-Brief 39
Dillon, Bert 1937- ... 77-80
Dillon, Carmen 1908- ... IDFW 3, 4
Dillon, Conley Hall 1906-1987 ... CANR-17
  Obituary ... 123
  Earlier sketch in CA 1-4R
Dillon, David 1941- ... 69-72
Dillon, Diane (Claire) 1933- ... CLR 44
  See also MAICYA 1, 2
  See also SATA 15, 51, 106
Dillon, Eilis 1920-1994 ... 182
  Obituary ... 147
  Earlier sketches in CA 9-12R, CANR-4, 38, 78
  Autobiographical Essay in ... 182
  See also CAAS 3
  See also CLC 17
  See also CLR 26
  See also MAICYA 1, 2
  See also MAICYAS 1
  See also SATA 2, 74
  See also SATA-Essay 105
  See also SATA-Obit 83
  See also YAW
Dillon, George 1906-1968
  Obituary ... 89-92
Dillon, George Lewis 1944- ... 102
Dillon, J(ames) T(homas) 1940- ... 33-36R
Dillon, Jana (a pseudonym) 1952- ... SATA 117
Dillon, John M(yles) 1939- ... 77-80
Dillon, Katherine V. 1916- ... 145
Dillon, Kathleen M. (Hynek) 1947- ... 146
Dillon, Lawrence S(amuel)
  1910-1999 ... CANR-25
  Earlier sketch in CA 45-48
Dillon, Leo 1933- ... CLR 44
  See also MAICYA 1, 2
  See also SATA 15, 51, 106
Dillon, M(artin) C(onboy) 1938-2005 ... 140
  Obituary ... 237
Dillon, Martin 1949- ... CANR-138
  Earlier sketch in CA 61-64
Dillon, Merton L. 1924- ... 13-16R
Dillon, Millicent (Gerson) 1925- ... CANR-100
  Earlier sketches in CA 65-68, CANR-12
Dillon, Patrick 1945- ... 232
Dillon, Richard H(ugh) 1924- ... CANR-8
  Earlier sketch in CA 17-20R
Dillon, Sam(uel) 1951- ... 233
Dillon, Sharon Saseen
  See Saseen, Sharon (Dillon)
Dillon, Stuart
  See Stuart, Sally E(lizabeth)
Dillon, Wallace Neil 1922- ... 1-4R
Dillon, Wilton S(terling) 1923- ... 37-40R
Dillow, Gordon ... 227
Dillow, Harry C. 1922- ... 123
Dilman, Ilham 1930-2003 ... 205
  Obituary ... 212
Dilmen, Gungr 1930- ... EWL 3
Dilorenzo, Ronald Eugene 1931-
  Brief entry ... 110
DiLorenzo, Thomas J. ... 231
Dils, Tracey E. 1958- ... 150
  See also SATA 83
Dilson, Jesse 1914-1988 ... 25-28R
  See also SATA 24
Dilthey, Wilhelm 1833-1911 ... DLB 129
Diltz, Bert Case 1894- ... CANR-9
  Earlier sketch in CA 65-68
Dilworth, David A. 1934- ... 136
Dilworth, Sharon 1958- ... 135
Dimancescu, Dan 1943- ... 113
di Marco, Gino
  See Weiss, Irving J.
Di Marco, Luis Eugenio 1937- ... CANR-2
  Earlier sketch in CA 45-48
Dimauro, Louis F. 1953- ... 199
Dimberg, Ronald G(ilbert) 1938- ... 61-64
Dimbleby, Jonathan 1944- ... 119
  Brief entry ... 108
Dimbleby, Josceline (Rose) 1943- ... 232
Di Meglio, Clara 1933- ... 97-100
DiMeglio, John E(dward) 1934- ... 77-80
Dimen, Muriel 1942- ... 127
Dimen-Schein, Muriel
  See Dimen, Muriel
DiMento, Joseph F(rank) 1947- ... 69-72
DiMercurio, Michael 1958- ... 140
di Michele, Mary 1949- ... CANR-67
  Earlier sketches in CA 97-100, CANR-17
  See also CWP
Dimick, John M. 1898(?)-1983
  Obituary ... 111
Dimick, Kenneth M. 1937- ... 29-32R
Dimitroff, Pashanko 1924- ... 129
Dimitrova, Blaga 1922- ... 195
  See also CDWLB 4
  See also CWW 2
  See also DLB 181
  See also EWL 3
Dimmette, Celia (Puhr) 1896-1993 ... CAP-2
  Earlier sketch in CA 29-32
Dimmick, Barbara 1954- ... 203
Dimmitt, Richard Bertrand 1925- ... 17-20R
Dimock, Brad 1953- ... 177
Dimock, Edward Cameron, Jr. 1929-2001 .. 102
  Obituary ... 193
Dimock, George E(dward) 1917- ... 133
Dimock, Gladys Ogden 1908-1989 ... 5-8R
Dimock, Hedley G(ardiner) 1928- ... 5-8R
Dimock, Marshall E(dward)
  1903-1991 ... CANR-2
  Obituary ... 136
  Earlier sketch in CA 1-4R
Dimock, Peter 1950- ... 180
DiMona, Joseph 1922(?)-1999 ... 104
  Obituary ... 186
Dimond, E(dmunds) Grey 1918- ... 85-88
Dimond, Mary Clark ... 93-96
Dimond, Peter ... 175
Dimond, Stanley E(llwood) 1905-1989 . 13-16R
  Obituary ... 128
Dimond, Stuart J. 1938-1981 ... CANR-27
  Earlier sketch in CA 33-36R
Dimondstein, Geraldine 1926- ... 33-36R
Dimont, Madelon 1938- ... 41-44R
Dimont, Max I. 1912-1992 ... 17-20R
Dimont, Penelope
  See Mortimer, Penelope (Ruth)
Dimov, Dimitur 1909-1966 ... DLB 181
Dimrecken, B. Grayer
  See de Mille, Richard
Dimsdale, Thomas J. 1831(?)-1866 ... DLB 186
Dimson, Wendy
  See Baron, (Ora) Wendy
Din, Gilbert C. 1932- ... 118
Dinan, Carolyn ... 126
  See also SATA 59
  See also SATA-Brief 47
Dinan, Desmond 1957- ... 232
Dinavo, Jacques V. 1948- ... 174
Dinculeanu, Nicolae 1925- ... 210
Dineley, David Lawrence 1927- ... 101
Dinello, Paul ... 226
Diner, Hasia R(ena) 1946- ... CANR-99
  Earlier sketches in CA 61-64, CANR-9
Diner, Steven J(ay) 1944- ... CANR-29
  Earlier sketch in CA 110
Dinerman, Beatrice 1933- ... 13-16R
Dinerman, Helen Schneider 1921(?)-1974
  Obituary ... 53-56
Dinerstein, Herbert S(amuel) 1919-
  Brief entry ... 108
Dines, (Harry) Glen 1925-1996 ... 9-12R
  See also SATA 7
Dines, Michael 1916- ... 103
Dinescu, Mircea 1950- ... DLB 232
Dinesen, Isak
  See Blixen, Karen (Christentze Dinesen)
  See also CLC 10, 29, 95
  See also EW 10
  See also EWL 3
  See also EXPS
  See also FW
  See also GL 2
  See also HGG
  See also LAIT 3
  See also MTCW 1
  See also NCFS 2
  See also NFS 9
  See also RGSF 2
  See also RGWL 2, 3
  See also SSC 7, 75
  See also SSFS 3, 6, 13
  See also WLIT 2
Dinessi, Alex
  See Schembri, Jim
Ding, J. N.
  See Darling, Jay Norwood
Dingelstedt, Franz von 1814-1881 ... DLB 133
Dinges, John (Charles) 1941- ... 101
Dingle, Derek T. ... 205
Dingle, Graeme 1945- ... 123
Dingle, Herbert 1890-1978 ... 13-16R
  Obituary ... 122
Ding Ling
  See Chiang, Pin-chin
  See also CLC 68
  See also RGWL 3
Dingman, Roger 1938- ... CANR-105
  Earlier sketch in CA 93-96
Dings, John (Garetson) 1939- ... 41-44R
Dingus, Lowell ... 228
Dingwall, E(ric) J(ohn) 1890-1986 ... 89-92
  Obituary ... 120
Dingwall, W(illiam) Orr 1934- ... CANR-13
  Earlier sketch in CA 21-24R
Dinh, Linh 1963- ... 202
Dinhofer, A(lfred) 1929- ... 25-28R
Dini, Paul 1957- ... 230
Dinis, Julio 1839-1871 ... DLB 287
Dinitz, Simon 1926- ... CANR-14
  Earlier sketch in CA 37-40R
Dinkin, Robert J. 1940-
  Brief entry ... 107
Dinkmeyer, Don C. 1924- ... CANR-15
  Earlier sketch in CA 41-44R
Dinman, Bertram David 1925-
  Brief entry ... 109
Dinnan, James A. 1929- ... 69-72
Dinneen, Betty 1929- ... CANR-8
  Earlier sketch in CA 57-60
  See also SATA 61
Dinnerstein, Harvey 1928- ... 112
  See also SATA 42
Dinnerstein, Leonard 1934- ... CANR-24
  Earlier sketches in CA 21-24R, CANR-9
Dino
  See Dinhofer, A(lfred)
Dinov, Todor 1919- ... IDFW 3, 4
Dinsdale, Tim(othy Kay) 1924-1987 ... CANR-2
  Obituary ... 124
  Earlier sketch in CA 1-4R
  See also SATA 11
Dinsky, Lazar 1891(?)-1976
  Obituary ... 69-72
Dinsmore, Charles E(arle) 1947- ... 142
Dinsmore, Herman H. 1900(?)-1980
  Obituary ... 97-100
Dintenfass, Mark 1941- ... CANR-11
  Earlier sketch in CA 25-28R
  Interview in ... CANR-11
  See also DLBY 1984
Dinter, Paul E(dward) ... 218
Dintiman, George B(lough) 1936- ... CANR-42
  Earlier sketches in CA 53-56, CANR-5, 20
Dintrone, Charles V. 1942- ... 162
Dinur, Yehiel
  See Ka-Tzetnik 135633
Dinwiddie, Elza Teresa ... 110
Dinwiddy, J(ohn) R(owland) 1939-1990
  Obituary ... 131
Dinwiddy, John
  See Dinwiddy, J(ohn) R(owland)
Diogenes Laertius c. 200- ... DLB 176
DioGuardi, Joseph J. 1940- ... 140
Diole, Philippe V. 1908- ... 53-56
Diomede, John K.
  See Effinger, George Alec
Dion, Gerard 1912-1990 ... 41-44R
Dion, Mark 1961- ... 194
Dion, Peter
  See Chetwynd, Lionel
Dion, Sister Anita 1918-1998 ... CANR-2
  Earlier sketch in CA 5-8R
Dione, Robert L(ester) 1922-1996 ... 57-60
Dionisopoulos, P(anagiotes) Allan
  1921-1993 ... 29-32R
  Obituary ... 141
Dionne, E(ugene) J., Jr. 1952- ... CANR-112
  Earlier sketch in CA 140
Diop, Birago (Ismael) 1906-1989 ... 125
  Obituary ... 130
  See also BW 2, 3
  See also EWL 3
  See also MTCW 1
  See also SATA-Obit 64
Diop, Cheikh Anta 1923-1986 ... 125
  Obituary ... 118
  Brief entry ... 110
  See also BW 2
Diop, David Mandessi 1927-1960 ... 143
  See also BW 2
Dior, Christian 1905-1957 ... 203
  Brief entry ... 115
DiOrio, Al(bert John) 1950- ... CANR-9
  Earlier sketch in CA 57-60
Diotima
  See Wynne-Tyson, Esme
DiPalma, Ray(mond) 1943- ... CANR-49
  Earlier sketches in CA 29-32R, CANR-24
DiPasquale, Dominic 1932- ... 57-60
DiPego, Gerald F(rancis) 1941- ... CANR-63
  Earlier sketch in CA 85-88
DiPerna, Paula 1949- ... CANR-143
  Earlier sketch in CA 112
DiPersio, Michael S(alvatore) 1934- ... 110
Di Peso, Charles C(orradino) 1920- ... 57-60
Diphusa, Patty
  See Almodovar, Pedro
Di Piero, W(illiam) Simone 1945- .. CANR-118
  Earlier sketch in CA 138
Di Pietro, Robert Joseph 1932-1991 ... CANR-7
  Obituary ... 136
  Earlier sketch in CA 17-20R
Diplomaticus
  See Guerra y Sanchez, Ramiro
Dipoko, Mbella Sonne 1936- ... CANR-80
  Earlier sketch in CA 152
  See also BW 2
  See also CP 1
Dippel, John V(an) H(outen) 1946- ... 154
Dipper, Alan 1922- ... 49-52
Dippie, Brian William 1943- ... CANR-113
  Earlier sketches in CA 108, CANR-25, 50
Dipple, Elizabeth (Dorothea)
  1937-1996 ... 33-36R
  Obituary ... 154
di Prima, Diane 1934- ... CANR-131
  Earlier sketches in CA 17-20R, CANR-13
  See also BG 1:2
  See also CP 1, 2, 3, 4, 5, 6, 7
  See also CWP
  See also DLB 5, 16
  See also WP
Di Prisco, Joseph 1950- ... 215
DiPucchio, Kelly ... SATA 159
Dirac, P. A. M.
  See Dirac, Paul A(drien) M(aurice)
Dirac, Paul A(drien) M(aurice) 1902-1984 .. 133
  Obituary ... 113
Dirda, Michael, (Jr.) 1948- ... 238
DiRenzo, Anthony 1960- ... CANR-120
  Earlier sketch in CA 148
DiRenzo, Gordon J(ames) 1934- ... CANR-4
  Earlier sketch in CA 53-56
Dirie, Waris ... 172
Diringer, David 1900-1975 ... CANR-98
  Obituary ... 57-60
  Earlier sketches in CA 1-4R, CANR-6
Dirk
  See Gringhuis, Richard H.
Dirk, R.
  See Dietrich, Richard V(incent)
Dirks, Raymond L(ouis) 1934- ... 106
Dirks, Rudolph 1877-1968
  Obituary ... 106
  See also SATA-Brief 31
Dirks, Wilhelmina 1916- ... SATA 59
Dirks, Willy
  See Dirks, Wilhelmina
Dirksen, Alvin Joseph 1915-1997 ... 110
Dirksen, Charles J(oseph) 1912-1988 ... 5-8R
Dirksen, Louella Carver 1899-1979 ... 103
  Obituary ... 89-92
Dirlik, Arif 1940- ... 97-100
di Roccaferrera Ferrero, Giuseppe M.
  1912-2000 ... CANR-7
  Earlier sketch in CA 13-16R
Dirr, Michael A(lbert) 1944- ... 237
Dirrim, Allen Wendell 1929- ... 21-24R
Dirscherl, Denis 1934- ... 21-24R
Dirvin, Joseph I. 1917-1993 ... CANR-2
  Obituary ... 141
  Earlier sketch in CA 5-8R
Di Salvatore, Bryan ... 194
DiSalvo, DyAnne 1960- ... SATA 59, 144
DiSalvo, Jacqueline 1943- ... 139
DiSalvo-Ryan, DyAnne
  See DiSalvo, DyAnne
DiScala, Jamie-Lynn 1981- ... 217
Di Scala, Spencer M(ichael) 1941- ... 102
Disch, Thomas M(ichael) 1940- ... CANR-89
  Earlier sketches in CA 21-24R, CANR-17, 36, 54
  See also Disch, Tom
  See also CAAS 4
  See also AAYA 17
  See also BPFB 1
  See also CLC 7, 36
  See also CLR 18
  See also CP 7
  See also DA3
  See also DLB 8
  See also HGG
  See also MAICYA 1, 2
  See also MTCW 1, 2
  See also MTFW 2005
  See also SAAS 15
  See also SATA 92
  See also SCFW 1, 2
  See also SFW 4
  See also SUFW 2
Disch, Tom
  See Disch, Thomas M(ichael)
  See also DLB 282
Dischell, Judy
  See Lalli, Judy
Dischell, Stuart 1954- ... 189
Disher, Garry 1949- ... CANR-104
  Earlier sketches in CA 127, CANR-55
  See also SATA 81, 125
Disher, Maurice Willson
  1893-1969 ... CANR-94
  Earlier sketches in CAP-1, CA 9-10
Dishman, Pat(ricia L.) 1939- ... 17-20R
Diski, Jenny 1947- ... CANR-104
  Earlier sketch in CA 138
  See also DLB 271
d'Isly, Georges
  See Simenon, Georges (Jacques Christian)
Dismukes, Gwynelle
  See Gwynelle (Dismukes)
Disney, Doris Miles 1907-1976 ... CANR-60
  Obituary ... 65-68
  Earlier sketches in CA 5-8R, CANR-3
  See also CMW 4
  See also MSW
Disney, Walt(er Elias) 1901-1966 ... 159
  Obituary ... 107
  See also AAYA 22
  See also DLB 22
  See also IDFW 3, 4
  See also SATA 28
  See also SATA-Brief 27
Dison, Norma 1928- ... 53-56
Dispenza, Joseph Ernest 1942- ... 81-84
Disraeli, Benjamin 1804-1881 ... BRW 4
  See also DLB 21, 55
  See also RGEL 2
D'Israeli, Isaac 1766-1848 ... DLB 107
Disraeli, Robert 1903-1988 ... CAP-1
  Earlier sketch in CA 11-12
Disston, Harry 1899-1989 ... 41-44R
Distel, Peter
  See Koch, Kurt E(mil)
Distler, Ann G.
  See Goethe, Ann
Distler, Paul Francis 1911-1986 ... 5-8R
di Suvero, Victor 1927- ... CAAS 26
Ditchburn, R(obert) W(illiam)
  1903-1987 ... 69-72
  Obituary ... 122
Ditchoff, Pamela J(ane) 1950- ... CANR-124
  Earlier sketch in CA 150
Ditcum, Steve
  See Crumb, R(obert)
DiTerlizzi, Tony 1969- ... 221
  See also SATA 154
Ditko, Steve 1927- ... 224
  See also AAYA 51
Ditlevsen, Tove 1917-1976 ... DLB 214
Dito Und Idem
  See Elisabeth (Ottilie Luise), Queen (Pauline)
Ditsky, John (Michael) 1938- ... CANR-9
  Earlier sketch in CA 65-68
Dittes, James E(dward) 1926- ... 61-64
Dittmer, Lowell 1941- ... 89-92
Ditton, James
  See Clark, Douglas (Malcolm Jackson)
Dittrich, John E(dward) 1931- ... 112
Ditzel, Paul C(alvin) 1926- ... 41-44R
Ditzen, Lowell Russell 1913-1987 ... 17-20R
  Obituary ... 122
Ditzen, Rudolf 1893-1947
  Brief entry ... 123
  See also Fallada, Hans
Ditzion, Sidney 1908-1975 ... 41-44R
  Obituary ... 57-60
Ditzler, James (R.) 1933- ... 135

Ditzler, Jinny S. 194
Divakaruni, Chitra Banerjee 1956- . CANR-127
Earlier sketch in CA 182
See also CN 7
See also SATA 160
See also SSFS 18
Divale, William T(ulio) 1942- 33-36R
Di Valentin, Maria (Amelia) Messuri
1911-1985 .... CANR-5
Earlier sketch in CA 5-8R
See also SATA 7
Di Venanzo, Gianni 1920-1966 .... IDFW 3, 4
Divendal, Joost 1955- 132
Diver, (Katherine Helen) Maud
1867(?)-1945 .... RHW
Diverres, Armel Hugh 1914-1998 .... 9-12R
Divine, Arthur Durham 1904-1987 103
Obituary 122
See also SATA-Obit 52
Divine, David
See Divine, Arthur Durham
Divine, Floy (Sherman) 1881-1986 113
Obituary 118
Divine, Robert A(lexander) 1929- CANR-42
Earlier sketches in CA 5-8R, CANR-3, 20
Divine, Thomas F(rancis) 1900-1979 .... 37-40R
Divinsky, N. J.
See Divinsky, Nathan (Joseph)
Divinsky, Nathan (Joseph) 1925- 132
DiVitto, Barbara A(nn) 1947- 118
Divoky, Diane 1939- 33-36R
Dix, Albert V. 1901(?)-1983
Obituary 109
Dix, Dorothea Lynde 1802-1887 .... DLB 1, 235
Dix, Dorothy
See Gilmer, Elizabeth Meriwether
Dix, Gertrude 1874(?)-(?) .... DLB 197
Dix, Robert H. 1930- 21-24R
Dix, Robin C. 1956- 234
Dix, Shane 1960- 235
Dix, William (Shepherd) 1910-1978
Obituary 77-80
Dixie, Florence Douglas 1857-1905 ... DLB 174
Dixon, A(mzi) C(larence) 1854-1925 205
Dixon, Ann R(enee) 1954- CANR-95
Earlier sketch in CA 145
See also SATA 77, 127
Dixon, Bernard 1938- CANR-51
Earlier sketches in CA 65-68, CANR-10, 26
Dixon, Brenda
See Gottschild, Brenda D(ixon)
Dixon, Christa Klingbeil 1935- 102
Dixon, Colin J. 1933- 105
Dixon, Dougal 1947- CANR-50
Earlier sketches in CA 107, CANR-25
See also SATA 45, 127
Dixon, Ella Hepworth 1855(?)-1932 ... DLB 197
Dixon, Franklin W. CANR-27
Earlier sketch in CA 17-20R
See also Barrett, Neal, Jr. and
Goulart, Ron(ald Joseph) and
Lantz, Francess L(in) and
McFarlane, Leslie (Charles) and
Stanley, George Edward and
Stratemeyer, Edward L.
See also BYA 4
See also CLR 61
See also MAICYA 1, 2
See also SATA 1, 67, 100
Dixon, George
See Willis, Edward Henry
Dixon, Graham (Peter) 1956- 121
Dixon, H(arry) Vernor 1908-1984 .... CAP-1
Earlier sketch in CA 9-10
Dixon, Janice T(horne) 1932- 107
Dixon, Jeane (L.) 1918-1997 .... CANR-21
Obituary 156
Earlier sketch in CA 65-68
Dixon, Jeanne 1936- 105
See also SATA 31
Dixon, Joan DeVee 1963- 142
Dixon, John W(esley), Jr. 1919- CANR-3
Earlier sketch in CA 9-12R
Dixon, Joseph L(awrence) 1896-1984 61-64
Dixon, Kenneth L. 1915(?)-1986
Obituary 119
Dixon, Larry 1966- 193
Dixon, Laurinda S. 1948- 126
Dixon, Marjorie (Mack) 1887- CAP-2
Earlier sketch in CA 23-24
Dixon, Melvin (W.) 1950-1992 132
Obituary 139
See also BW 2
See also GLL 1
Dixon, Michael Bigelow 1953- 192
Dixon, Nancy 1955- 188
Dixon, Norman F(rank) 1922- 130
Dixon, Paige
See Corcoran, Barbara (Asenath)
Dixon, Penelope A(nn) 1948- 113
Dixon, Peter L(ee) 1931- CANR-2
Earlier sketch in CA 45-48
See also SATA 6
Dixon, Pierson (John) 1904-1965 .... CAP-1
Earlier sketch in CA 13-16
Dixon, Rachel 1952- .... SATA 74
Dixon, Richard Watson 1833-1900 173
Brief entry 122
See also DLB 19
See also RGEL 2
Dixon, Robert G(alloway) 1920-1980
Obituary 97-100
Dixon, Roger 1930- 53-56
Dixon, Roger Edmund 1935-1983
Obituary 109
Dixon, Rosie
See Wood, Christopher (Hovelle)
Dixon, Ruth
See Barrows, (Ruth) Marjorie
Dixon, S(ydney) L(awrence) 1930- 69-72
Dixon, Stephen 1936- CANR-91
Earlier sketches in CA 89-92, CANR-17, 40, 54
See also AMWS 12
See also CLC 52
See also CN 4, 5, 6, 7
See also DLB 130
See also MAL 5
See also SSC 16
Dixon, Thomas, Jr. 1864-1946 .... RHW
See also TCLC 163
Dixon, Wheeler Winston 1950- 121
Dixon-Stowell, Brenda
See Gottschild, Brenda D(ixon)
Dizard, Wilson P(aul) 1922- 17-20R
Dizdarevic, Zlatko 1948- 146
Dizenzo, Charles (John) 1938- CANR-67
Earlier sketch in CA 25-28R
See also CAD
See also CD 5, 6
Dizikes, John 1932- CANR-103
Earlier sketch in CA 156
Dizney, Henry (Franklin) 1926- 33-36R
Djaout, Tahar 1954-1993 208
See also EWL 3
Djassi, Abel
See Cabral, Amilcar
Djavakhishvili, Mikheil
See Adamashvili, Mikhail
See also EWL 3
Djebar, Assia 1936- 188
See also CLC 182
See also EWL 3
See also RGWL 3
See also WLIT 2
Djeddah, Eli 1911-1981 .... 37-40R
Djelantik, A(nak) A(gung) M(ade) 1919- 175
Djerassi, Carl 1923- CANR-90
Brief entry 111
Earlier sketch in CA 131
See also CAAS 26
Djian, Philippe 1949- 207
Djilas, Aleksa 1953- 139
Djilas, Milovan 1911-1995 127
Obituary 148
Djoleto, (Solomon Alexander) Amu
1929- CANR-79
Earlier sketch in CA 141
See also BW 2, 3
See also SATA 80
Djonovich, Dusan J. 1920-1995 69-72
DJ Spooky
See Miller, Paul D.
Djwa, Sandra (Ann) 1939- 131
Dluhosch, Eric 1927- 25-28R
Dluznowsky, Moshe 1906-1977
Obituary 73-76
Dmitriev, Andrei Viktorovich 1956- .... DLB 285
Dmitriev, Ivan Ivanovich 1760-1837 .. DLB 150
DMX
See Simmons, Earl
Dmytryshyn, Basil 1925- CANR-26
Earlier sketches in CA 21-24R, CANR-11
Doak, Annie
See Dillard, Annie
Doak, (Dearle) Donn(ell) 1930- 65-68
Doak, Wade Thomas 1940- CANR-6
Earlier sketch in CA 57-60
Doan, Daniel 1914-1993 103
Doan, Eleanor Lloyd CANR-1
Earlier sketch in CA 1-4R
Doan, Laura (L.) 189
Doan, Reece
See King, Albert
Doan, Richard K. 1911(?)-1989
Obituary 128
Doane, Donald P(aul) 1911-1999 77-80
Doane, Gilbert H(arry) 1897-1980 .... CAP-1
Earlier sketch in CA 11-12
Doane, Janice (L.) 1950- CANR-142
Earlier sketch in CA 146
Doane, Marion S.
See Woodward, Grace Steele
Doane, (R.) Michael 1952- CANR-50
Earlier sketch in CA 135
Doane, Pelagie 1906-1966 .... CANR-6
Earlier sketch in CA 1-4R
See also SATA 7
Doane, William H(oward) 1832-1915 220
Doan Van Toai 1946- 145
Dobb, Maurice (Herbert) 1900-1976 .. CANR-4
Obituary 69-72
Earlier sketch in CA 9-12R
Dobbie, Elliott Van Kirk 1907-1970
Obituary 111
Dobbin, John E. 1914-1979 .... 9-12R
Obituary 103
Dobbin, Muriel 1935- 118
Dobbin, Murray 1945- 139
Dobbins, Austin C(harles) 1919- 57-60
Dobbins, Charles G(ordon) 1908-1988 . CAP-1
Obituary 127
Earlier sketch in CA 13-16
Dobbins, Dorothy Wyeth 1929- 69-72
Dobbins, Gaines Stanley 1886-1978 .. CANR-2
Earlier sketch in CA 1-4R
Dobbins, Marybelle King 1900-1990 .... 41-44R
Dobbs, Betty Jo Teeter 1930-1994 69-72
Dobbs, David 1958- 150
Dobbs, Farrell 1907-1983 .... CANR-14
Obituary 111
Earlier sketch in CA 49-52
Dobbs, Greg 1946- 65-68
Dobbs, Kildare (Robert Eric) 1923- ... CANR-19
Earlier sketch in CA 102
Dobbs, Michael 1948- CANR-88
Earlier sketch in CA 147
Dobbs, Michael 1950- 229
Dobbyn, John F(rancis) 1937- 53-56
Dobelis, M(iervaldis) C(hristian) 1929- 116
Dobell, Bertram 1842-1914 .... DLB 184
Dobell, Byron (Maxwell) 1927-
Brief entry 112
Dobell, I(sabel) M(arian) B(arclay)
1909-1998 .... CAP-1
Earlier sketch in CA 17-18
See also SATA 11
Dobell, Sydney Thompson 1824-1874 . DLB 32
See also RGEL 2
Dober, Richard P. 9-12R
Dobie, Ann B(rewster) 1935- 106
Dobie, Bertha McKee 1890(?)-1974
Obituary 53-56
Dobie, Edith 1894-1975 .... CAP-2
Obituary 57-60
Earlier sketch in CA 23-24
Dobie, J(ames) Frank 1888-1964 .... CANR-6
Earlier sketch in CA 1-4R
See also DLB 212
See also SATA 43
Dobie, Kathy 226
Dobin, Abraham 1907-1983 53-56
Dobinson, Charles Henry 1903-1980
Obituary 102
Dobkin, Alexander 1908-1975
Obituary 57-60
See also SATA-Obit 30
Dobkin, Bruce H. 1947- 122
Dobkin, Kathy
See Hamel Peifer, Kathleen
Dobkin, Kaye
See Hamel Peifer, Kathleen
Dobkin, Marjorie Housepian 1923- . CANR-48
Earlier sketches in CA 33-36R, CANR-13
Dobkin De Rios, Marlene 1939- CANR-12
Earlier sketch in CA 61-64
Dobkins, J(ames) Dwight 1943- 49-52
Dobkowski, Michael N. 1947- 215
Dobler, Bruce 1939- CANR-7
Earlier sketch in CA 53-56
Dobler, Lavinia G. 1910- CANR-2
Earlier sketch in CA 1-4R
See also SATA 6
Dobles, Fabian 1918- .... HW 1
Dobles Yzaguirre, Julieta 1943- .... DLB 283
Doblin, Alfred
See Doeblin, Alfred
See also CDWLB 2
See also EWL 3
See also RGWL 2, 3
See also TCLC 13
Dobner, Maeva Park 1918-1984 .... 29-32R
Dobney, Frederick J(ohn) 1943- 53-56
Dobraczynski, Jan 1910-1994 .... CAP-1
Earlier sketch in CA 11-12
Dobree, Bonamy 1891-1974 .... CANR-4
Obituary 53-56
Earlier sketch in CA 5-8R
Dobrez, Patricia 1943- 202
Dobriansky, Lev E. 1918- CANR-2
Earlier sketch in CA 1-4R
Dobrin, Arnold 1928- CANR-11
Earlier sketch in CA 25-28R
See also SATA 4
Dobrin, Arthur 1943- CANR-120
Earlier sketches in CA 61-64, CANR-8
Dobrin, Lyn 1942- 135
Dobrin, Ronald L. 1938- 120
Dobrin, Sidney I. 1967- 218
Dobriner, William M(ann) 1922- 65-68
Dobroliubov, Nikolai Aleksandrovich
See Dobrolyubov, Nikolai Alexandrovich
See also DLB 277
Dobrolyubov, Nikolai Alexandrovich
1836-1861
See Dobroliubov, Nikolai Aleksandrovich
Dobrovolsky, Sergei P(avlovich)
1908-1993 .... CAP-2
Earlier sketch in CA 33-36
Dobrow, Larry 1925- 123
Dobrowolski, Tomasz B. 1914(?)-1976
Obituary 65-68
Dobrynin, Anatoly Fedorovich 1919- 151
Dobschiner, Johanna-Ruth 1925- 97-100
Dobson, Alan P. 1951- 139
Dobson, Andrew (Nicholas Howard)
1957- CANR-95
Earlier sketch in CA 132
Dobson, Austin 1840-1921 .... DLB 35, 144
See also TCLC 79
Dobson, (Henry) Austin 1840-1921 ...... RGEL 2
Dobson, (Richard) Barrie 1931- 33-36R
Dobson, Christopher (Joseph Edward)
1927- CANR-31
Earlier sketch in CA 97-100
Dobson, Dennis 1919(?)-1979(?)
Obituary 104
Dobson, E. Philip 1910- CAP-1
Earlier sketch in CA 13-14
Dobson, Elinore (Lucille) 1934- 114
Dobson, Eric John 1913-1984 .... CANR-5
Obituary 112
Earlier sketch in CA 13-16R
Dobson, Eugene 1936-
Brief entry 113
Dobson, Frank E. 1952- 215
Dobson, James (Clayton, Jr.) 1936- ... CANR-68
Earlier sketches in CA 29-32R, CANR-27
Dobson, Jessie (?)-1984
Obituary 113
Dobson, Jill 1969- 211
See also SATA 140
Dobson, Joanne 1942- CANR-104
Earlier sketch in CA 164
Dobson, John M(cCullough) 1940- 37-40R
Dobson, Julia 1941- 106
See also SATA 48
Dobson, Julia M(argaret) 1937- 73-76
Dobson, Margaret J(une) 1931- 53-56
Dobson, Mary 1954- 189
See also SATA 117
Dobson, Michael 1960- CANR-113
Earlier sketch in CA 142
Dobson, Rosemary 1920- 77-80
See also CP 1, 2, 3, 4, 5, 6, 7
See also CWP
See also DLB 260
See also RGEL 2
Dobson, Terry 1937- 81-84
Dobson, Theodore E(lliott) 1946- CANR-28
Earlier sketch in CA 109
Dobson, William A(rthur) C(harles) H(arvey)
1913- 13-16R
Doby, John T(homas) 1920- 185
Brief entry 114
Doby, Tibor 1914-1998 .... 5-8R
Dobyns, Henry F(armer) 1925- CANR-32
Earlier sketches in CA 37-40R, CANR-15
Dobyns, Lloyd (Allen, Jr.) 1936- 119
Brief entry 110
Interview in CA-119
Dobyns, Stephen 1941- CANR-99
Earlier sketches in CA 45-48, CANR-2, 18
See also AMWS 13
See also CLC 37
See also CMW 4
See also CP 7
See also PFS 23
Dobzhansky, Theodosius 1900-1975 ..... CAP-1
Obituary 61-64
Earlier sketch in CA 13-14
Docherty, James C(airns) 1949- 144
Docherty, James L.
See Raymond, Rene (Brabazon)
Docherty, Jayne Seminare 229
Docherty, Thomas 1955- 120
Dockar-Drysdale, Barbara (Estelle Gordon)
1912-1999 183
Dockeray, J(ames) C(arlton) 1907-1984 ... 45-48
Obituary 114
Dockery, David S. 1952- 223
Dockery, Kevin 233
Dockery, Wallene T. 1941- CANR-22
Earlier sketch in CA 105
See also SATA 27
Dockray, Tracy 1962- .... SATA 139
Dockrell, William Bryan 1929- CANR-32
Earlier sketches in CA 37-40R, CANR-14
Dockrey, Karen 1955- 170
See also SATA 103
Dockstader, Frederick J. 1919-1998 . CANR-99
Earlier sketch in CA 13-16R
Doc Lochard
See Lochard, Metz T(ullus) P(aul)
Doctor, Bernard
See Doctor, Bernard Aquina
Doctor, Bernard Aquina 1950- .... SATA 81
Doctor Baseball
See Bjarkman, Peter C(hristian)
Doctorow, Cory 1971- 221
Doctorow, E(dgar) L(aurence)
1931- CANR-133
Earlier sketches in CA 45-48, CANR-2, 33, 51, 76, 97
See also AAYA 22
See also AITN 2
See also AMWS 4
See also BEST 89:3
See also BPFB 1
See also CDALB 1968-1988
See also CLC 6, 11, 15, 18, 37, 44, 65, 113
See also CN 3, 4, 5, 6, 7
See also CPW
See also DA3
See also DAM NOV, POP
See also DLB 2, 28, 173
See also DLBY 1980
See also EWL 3
See also LAIT 3
See also MAL 5
See also MTCW 1, 2
See also MTFW 2005
See also NFS 6
See also RGAL 4
See also RHW
See also TCLE 1:1
See also TCWW 1, 2
See also TUS
Doctors, Samuel I(saac) 1936- CANR-5
Earlier sketch in CA 53-56
Doctor X
See Nourse, Alan E(dward)
Doczi, George Frederic 1909- 113
Dodd, A(rthur) E(dward) 1913- 9-12R
Dodd, Anne W(escott) 1940- CANR-94
Earlier sketch in CA 93-96
Dodd, Arthur Herbert 1893(?)-1975
Obituary 57-60
Dodd, Bella V.
See Dodd, Maria Assunta Isabella Visono
Dodd, Charles (Harold) 1884-1973
Obituary 45-48
Dodd, Christina 235
Dodd, David (G.) 1957- 189
Dodd, David L(e Fevre) 1895-1988
Obituary 126

Cumulative Index 155 Domin

Dodd, Donald B(radford) 1940- CANR-6
Earlier sketch in CA 57-60
Dodd, Ed(ward Benton) 1902-1991 73-76
Obituary 134
See also SATA 4
See also SATA-Obit 68
Dodd, Edward
See Dodd, Edward Howard, Jr.
Dodd, Edward Howard, Jr.
1905-1988 .... CANR-31
Obituary 127
Earlier sketch in CA 49-52
Dodd, James Harvey 1892-1969 .... 1-4R
Obituary 103
Dodd, Lynley (Stuart) 1941- CANR-51
Earlier sketches in CA 107, CANR-25
See also CLR 62
See also CWRI 5
See also SATA 35, 86, 132
Dodd, Marguerite (Annetta) 1911-1996 ..... 5-8R
Dodd, Maria Assunta Isabella Visono
1904-1969
Obituary 111
Dodd, Martha
See Stern, Martha Eccles Dodd
Dodd, Marty 1921- 213
See also SATA 142
Dodd, Philip W. 1904(?)-1983
Obituary 110
Dodd, Quentin 1972- 207
See also SATA 137
Dodd, Stuart C(arter) 1900-1975 .... 41-44R
Dodd, Susan M. 1946- CANR-114
Earlier sketch in CA 116
See also DLB 244
Dodd, Thomas J. 1907-1971
Obituary 29-32R
Dodd, Valerie A. 1944- 134
Dodd, Wayne (Donald) 1930- CANR-99
Earlier sketch in CA 33-36R
Dodd, William E(dward) 1869-1940 194
See also DLB 17
Dodderidge, Esme 1916- 97-100
Dodds, Bill 1952- 146
See also SATA 78
Dodds, Dayle Ann 1952- 142
See also SATA 75, 150
Dodds, E(ric) R(obertson)
1893-1979 .... CANR-94
Earlier sketch in CA 101
Dodds, Edward Charles 1899-1973
Obituary 115
Dodds, Gordon (Barlow) 1932-2003 .... 5-8R
Obituary 221
Dodds, John W(endell) 1902-1989 .... 5-8R
Dodds, Robert Clyde 1918- 5-8R
Dodds, Robert H(ungerford)
1914-1976 .... CAP-2
Earlier sketch in CA 29-32
Dodds, Tracy 1952- 85-88
Dodek, Miriam (Joyce) Selker 1909-1986
Obituary 118
Doder, Dusko 1937- CANR-90
Earlier sketches in CA 102, CANR-44
Doderer, Heimito von
See von Doderer, Heimito
See also DLB 85
See also EWL 3
See also RGWL 2, 3
Dodge, Bayard 1888-1972
Obituary 111
Dodge, Bertha S(anford) 1902-1995 ... CANR-2
Earlier sketch in CA 5-8R
See also SATA 8
Dodge, Calvert R(enaul) 1931- 61-64
Dodge, Daniel
See Du Breuil, (Elizabeth) L(or)inda
Dodge, David (Francis) 1910-1974 65-68
Dodge, David L(aurence) 1931-
Brief entry 112
Dodge, Dick 1918(?)-1974
Obituary 49-52
Dodge, Dorothy R(ae) 1927- 45-48
Dodge, Emerson .... TCWW 2
Dodge, Ernest Stanley 1913-1980 ...... CANR-2
Obituary 97-100
Earlier sketch in CA 1-4R
Dodge, Fremont
See Grimes, Lee
Dodge, Gil
See Hano, Arnold
Dodge, H(arry) Robert 1929- CANR-27
Earlier sketch in CA 29-32R
Dodge, Jim 1945- 141
Dodge, Langdon
See Wolfson, Victor
Dodge, Lowell 1940- 33-36R
Dodge, Marshall 1935-1982 89-92
Dodge, Mary Abigail 1833-1896 .... DLB 221
Dodge, Mary (Elizabeth) Mapes
1831(?)-1905 137
Brief entry 109
See also BYA 2
See also CLR 62
See also DLB 42, 79
See also DLBD 13
See also MAICYA 1, 2
See also SATA 21, 100
See also WCH
Dodge, Michael J.
See Ford, John M.
Dodge, Nicholas A. 1933- 65-68
Dodge, Norton T(ownshend) 1927- .. CANR-16
Earlier sketch in CA 25-28R
Dodge, Peter 1926- 37-40R
Dodge, Richard H(olmes) 1926-2003 . CANR-8
Obituary 221
Earlier sketch in CA 13-16R
Dodge, Steve
See Becker, Stephen (David)
Dodge, Tom 1939- 154
Dodge, Wendell P(hillips) 1883-1976
Obituary 65-68
Dodgshon, Robert A(ndrew) 1941- 125
Dodgson, Charles L(utwidge) 1832-1898
See Carroll, Lewis
See also CLR 2
See also DA
See also DA3
See also DAB
See also DAC
See also DAM MST, NOV, POET
See also MAICYA 1, 2
See also SATA 100
See also YABC 2
Dodman, Nicholas H. 1946- 227
Dodsley, Robert 1703-1764 .... DLB 95
See also RGEL 2
Dodson, Daniel B(oone) 1918-1991 .. CANR-3
Obituary 133
Earlier sketch in CA 9-12R
Dodson, Fitzhugh (James)
1923-1993 .... CANR-24
Obituary 141
Earlier sketch in CA 29-32R
Dodson, James 1953- 236
Dodson, James L. 1910-1999 53-56
Dodson, James Yarnell 1978- 164
Dodson, Jim
See Dodson, James Yarnell
Dodson, Kenneth MacKenzie 1907-1999 . 1-4R
Obituary 179
See also SATA 11
Dodson, Leonidas 1900-1977
Obituary 111
Dodson, Lisa 190
Dodson, Oscar H(enry) 1905-1996 .... 5-8R
Dodson, Owen (Vincent)
1914-1983 .... CANR-24
Obituary 110
Earlier sketch in CA 65-68
See also BLC 1
See also BW 1
See also CLC 79
See also DAM MULT
See also DLB 76
Dodson, Richard S(licer), Jr.
1896-1980 .... CAP-1
Earlier sketch in CA 11-12
Dodson, Steve(n Yarnell) 1981- 164
Dodson, Susan 1941- 97-100
See also SATA 50
See also SATA-Brief 40
Dodson, Tom 1914- 29-32R
Dodwell, C(harles) R(eginald) 1922-1994 ... 129
Dodwell, Christina 1951- 197
See also DLB 204
Dodwell, Peter C(arpenter) 1930- 29-32R
Dody, Sandford 1918- 129
Doe, John
See Lewin, Leonard C(ase)
Doe, John 1916-1999
See Lewin, Leonard C(ase)
Doe, Mimi 1958- 218
Doebler, Bettie Anne CANR-105
Earlier sketch in CA 150
Doebler, Charles H. 1925- 21-24R
Doebler, John (Willard) 1932- 89-92
Doeblin, Alfred 1878-1957 141
Brief entry 110
See also Doblin, Alfred
See also DLB 66
See also TCLC 13
Doehring, Donald G(ene) 1927- 29-32R
Doell, Charles E(dward) 1894-1983 ...... CAP-1
Earlier sketch in CA 13-16
Doely, Sarah Bentley
See Bentley, Sarah
Doenecke, Justus Drew 1938- CANR-43
Earlier sketches in CA 104, CANR-20
Doenges, Judy 1959- 188
Doenim, Susan
See Effinger, George Alec
Doenitz, Karl 1891-1980
Obituary 103
Doerffler, Alfred 1884-1981 .... 1-4R
Doering, Jeanne
See Zornes, Jeanne Doering
Doeringer, Peter B(rantley) 1941- CANR-12
Earlier sketch in CA 61-64
Doerksen, Nan 1934- CANR-105
Earlier sketches in CA 123, CANR-49
See also SATA-Brief 50
Doerkson, Margaret 1921- 105
Doermann, Humphrey 1930- 25-28R
Doernberg, Myrna 1939- 120
Doerr, Anthony 1973- 204
Doerr, Arthur H(arry) 1924- 41-44R
Doerr, Harriet 1910-2002 .... CANR-47
Obituary 213
Brief entry 117
Earlier sketch in CA 122
Interview in CA-122
See also CLC 34
See also LATS 1:2
Doerr, Juergen C. 1939-2002 171
Doerrie, Doris
See Dorrie, Doris
Doerschuk, Anna Beatrice 1880(?)-1974
Obituary 49-52
Doeser, Linda (Ann) 1950- 81-84
Doesticks, Q. K. Philander P. B.
See Thomson, Mortimer
Doezema, Linda Pegman 1948- 102
Dogan, Mattei 1920- CANR-56
Earlier sketches in CA 25-28R, CANR-12, 30
Dogg, Professor R. L.
See Berman, Ed
Doggett, Frank 1906- CANR-12
Earlier sketches in CAP-2, CA 21-22
Doggett, Rachel H. 1943- 124
Dogniez, Cecile 1953- CANR-119
See also Dogniez, Cecile
Dogniez, Cecile 1953- CANR-119
Earlier sketch in CA 158
See also Dogniez, Cecile
Dogyear, Drew
See Gorey, Edward (St. John)
Dohan, Mary Helen 1914- 85-88
Dohaney, Jean 129
Dohaney, M. T.
See Dohaney, Jean
Dohen, Dorothy M. 1923-1984
Obituary 111
Doheny, Carrie Estelle 1875-1958 ...... DLB 140
Doherty, Barbara 1931- 116
Doherty, Berlie 1943- CANR-126
Earlier sketch in CA 131
See also AAYA 18
See also CLR 21
See also JRDA
See also MAICYA 1, 2
See also SAAS 16
See also SATA 72, 111
See also YAW
Doherty, Catherine de Hueck
1900-1985 .... CANR-12
Earlier sketch in CA 65-68
Doherty, Charles Hugh 1913- 9-12R
See also SATA 6
Doherty, Craig A. 1951- 150
See also SATA 83
Doherty, Dennis J. 1932- 102
Doherty, Eddie
See Doherty, Edward J(oseph)
Doherty, Edward J(oseph) 1890-1975 65-68
Obituary 57-60
Doherty, Herbert J(oseph), Jr. 1926-1993 .. 1-4R
Doherty, Ivy Duffy
See Doherty, Ivy R. Duffy
Doherty, Ivy R. Duffy 1922- CANR-5
Earlier sketch in CA 9-12R
Doherty, John 1798(?)-1854 .... DLB 190
Doherty, Justin (Francis) 1960- 156
Doherty, Katherine M(ann) 1951- 150
See also SATA 83
Doherty, P(aul) C. 1946- 211
Doherty, Paul (Michael) 1948- 199
Doherty, Robert W. 1935- 21-24R
Doherty, Thomas 198
Doherty, William 1911(?)-1984
Obituary 113
Doherty, William Thomas, Jr. 1923- 53-56
Dohme, Alvin R(obert) L(ouis) 1910- 110
Dohrenwend, Barbara Snell
1927-1982 .... CANR-11
Earlier sketch in CA 25-28R
Dohrmann, Wolfgang
See Doroslovac, Milutin
Doig, Desmond 1921-1983 69-72
Obituary 111
Doig, Ivan 1939- CANR-128
Earlier sketches in CA 81-84, CANR-24, 49, 87
See also DLB 206
See also TCWW 2
Doig, Jameson W. 1933- CANR-123
Earlier sketches in CA 37-40R, CANR-15, 32
Doimi di Delupis, Ingrid
See Delupis, Ingrid
Doinas, Stefan Augustin
See Popa, Stefan
See also DLB 232
See also EWL 3
Doisneau, Robert 1912-1994 .... AAYA 60
Dokey, Cameron 1956- CANR-138
Earlier sketch in CA 152
See also SATA 97
Dokmai Sot
See Nimmanhemin, M. L. Buppha Kunjara
See also EWL 3
Dolan, Anthony R(ossi) 1948- 73-76
Dolan, David 1955- 169
Dolan, Edward F(rancis), Jr. 1924- CANR-68
Earlier sketch in CA 33-36R
See also SATA 45, 94
See also SATA-Brief 31
Dolan, Edwin G(eorge) 1943- 123
Dolan, Ellen M(eara) 1929-1998 152
See also SATA 88
Dolan, Frederick Michael 1955- 154
Dolan, Jay P(atrick) 1936- CANR-141
Earlier sketch in CA 81-84
Dolan, John Patrick 1923-1982(?) CANR-2
Obituary 106
Earlier sketch in CA 5-8R
Dolan, John Richard 1893-1996 .... 9-12R
Dolan, Josephine A(loyse) 1913- 49-52
Dolan, Paul 1910-1982 .... 9-12R
Dolan, Sean J. 1958- 141
See also SATA 74
Dolan, Winthrop W(iggin) 1909- 57-60
Dolbeare, Kenneth M(arsh) 1930- 186
Brief entry 113
Dolberg, Alexander 1933- 33-36R
Dolbier, Maurice (Wyman) 1912-1993 65-68
Obituary 143
Dolby, James L(ouis) 1926- 45-48
Dolce, J. Ellen 1948- .... SATA 75
Dolce, Philip C(harles) 1941- 57-60
Dolch, Edward William 1889-1961 ..... SATA 50
Dolch, Marguerite Pierce 1891-1978 .. SATA 50
Dolci, Danilo (Bruno Pietro) 1924-1997 127
Obituary 163
Brief entry 116
Dold, Gaylord 1947- 139
Dold, R(obert) Bruce 1955- 230
Dolden, A(lfred) Stuart 1893- 105
Dole, Gertrude E(velyn) 1915- 41-44R
Dole, Jeremy H(askell) 1932- 17-20R
Dolenz, Micky 1945- 152
Doletzki, Leo
See Ruhmkorf, Peter
Dolezel, Lubomir 1922- 45-48
Dolgoff, Ralph L. 1932- 33-36R
Dolgoff, Sam 1902-1990 102
Obituary 132
Dolgun, Alexander (Michael) 1926-1986 ... 104
Obituary 120
Doliber, Earl L(awrence) 1947- 49-52
Dolim, Mary N(uzum) 1925- 17-20R
Dolin, Anton
See Healey-Kay, (Sydney Francis) Patrick (Chippendall)
Dolin, Edwin 1928- 45-48
Dolin, Eric Jay 226
Dolin, Sharon (Julie) 1956- CANR-125
Earlier sketch in CA 172
Dolinar, Stephen J. 1926- 146
Doliner, Roy 1932- CANR-16
Earlier sketches in CA 1-4R, CANR-1
Dolinger, Jane .... AITN 2
Dolinsky, Meyer 1923-1984 57-60
Obituary 174
Dolinsky, Mike
See Dolinsky, Meyer
Dolit, Alan 1934- 61-64
Doll, Mary A(swell) 1940- CANR-90
Earlier sketch in CA 130
Doll, (William) Richard (Shaboe)
1912-2005 108
Doll, Ronald C. 1913-1998 .... CANR-8
Earlier sketch in CA 13-16R
Doll, Susan Marie 1954- 118
Dollar, Diane (Hills) 1933- .... SATA 57
Dollar, Jim
See Shaginyan, Marietta (Sergeyevna)
Dollar, Truman E. 1937- 97-100
Dollard, John 1900(?)-1980
Obituary 102
Dollar Investor
See D'Ambrosio, Charles A.
Dolle, Raymond F. 1952- 136
Dollen, Charles Joseph 1926- CANR-45
Earlier sketches in CA 5-8R, CANR-6, 21
Dollery, Brian E(dward) 1952- 215
Dolley, Michael 1925-1983 123
Obituary 109
Dollimore, Jonathan 1948- CANR-98
Earlier sketch in CA 132
Dolling-Mann, Patricia May 1939- 217
Dolliver, Barbara Babcock 1927- 5-8R
Dolloff, Eugene Dinsmore 1890-1972 .... 1-4R
Obituary 103
Dolma, Pachen
See Pachen, Ani
Dolmatch, Theodore B(ieley) 1924- 41-44R
Dolmetsch, Carl R(ichard, Jr.) 1924- 21-24R
Dolmetsch, Christopher L(ee) 1950- 111
Dolnick, Barrie 1960- 226
Dolphin, Harry A. 1924- 128
Dolphin, Robert, Jr. 1935- 29-32R
Dols, Michael W(alters) 1942- 69-72
Dolson, Frank(lin Robert) 1933- 112
Dolson, Hildegarde
See Lockridge, Hildegarde (Dolson)
See also SATA 5
Doman, Glenn J(oseph) 1919- 61-64
Domanska, Janina 1913(?)-1995 .... CANR-45
Obituary 147
Earlier sketches in CA 17-20R, CANR-11
See also AITN 1
See also CLR 40
See also MAICYA 1, 2
See also MAICYAS 1
See also SAAS 18
See also SATA 6, 68
See also SATA-Obit 84
Domar, Alice D. 1958- 191
Domaradskij, Igor V. 1925- 235
Domaradzki, Teodor Felix
See Domaradzki, Theodore F(elix)
Domaradzki, Theodore F(elix)
1910-2001 .... CANR-1
Earlier sketch in CA 45-48
Domb, Cyril 1920- 109
Dombrowski, Daniel A. 1953- 142
Dombrowski, James A. 1897-1983
Obituary 109
Domecq, H(onorio Bustos)
See Bioy Casares, Adolfo
Domecq, H(onorio) Bustos
See Bioy Casares, Adolfo and Borges, Jorge Luis
Domencich, Thomas A. 29-32R
Domenico, Roy Palmer 1954- 188
Domergue, Maurice 1907- 25-28R
Domes, Juergen (Otto) 1932- 129
Domett, Alfred 1811-1887 .... RGEL 2
Dom Helder
See Camara, Helder Pessoa
Domhoff, G(eorge) William 1936- CANR-99
Earlier sketch in CA 45-48
Domin, Hilde 1912- 193
See also EWL 3

Dominguez, Angel 1953- ... SATA 76
Dominguez, Jorge Ignacio 1945- ... CANR-70
Earlier sketch in CA 102
Dominguez, Richard H(enry) 1941- ... 102
Dominguez, Sergio D(anilo) Elizondo
See Elizondo (Dominguez), Sergio D(anilo)
Dominguez, Sylvia Maida 1935- ... 179
See also DLB 122
Domini, John 1951- ... 177
Domini, Jon
See LaRusso, Dominic A(nthony)
Domini, Rey
See Lorde, Audre (Geraldine)
See also GLL 1
Dominian, Jack 1929- ... 104
Dominic, Magie 1944- ... 236
Dominic, R. B.
See Hennissart, Martha and
Latsis, Mary J(ane)
Dominic, Sister Mary
See Gallagher, Sister Mary Dominic
Dominick, Andie 1971- ... 174
Dominick, Raymond Hunter III 1945- ... 110
Dominique
See Proust, (Valentin-Louis-George-Eugene) Marcel
Dominique, Meg
See Sanford, Annette
Domino, Edward F(elix) 1924- ... 207
Domino, John
See Averill, Esther (Holden)
Dominowski, Roger L. 1939- ... CANR-1
Earlier sketch in CA 45-48
Dominy, Eric (Norman) 1918- ... 9-12R
Domjan, Joseph (Spiri) 1907-1992 ... CANR-24
Earlier sketches in CA 9-12R, CANR-3
See also SATA 25
Domke, Helmut Georg 1914-1974 ... CAP-1
Earlier sketch in CA 13-14
Domke, Martin 1892-1980 ... CAP-1
Earlier sketch in CA 13-16
Domke, Todd 1952- ... 200
Domm, Jeffrey C. 1958- ... SATA 84
Dommen, Arthur J(ohn) 1934- ... 9-12R
Dommermuth, William P. 1925- ... 17-20R
Dommeyer, Frederick Charles 1909-1988 ... 37-40R
Domnwachukwu, Peter N(lemadim) 1952- ... 213
Domotor, Tekla 1914- ... 132
Domville, Eric 1929- ... 41-44R
Don, A
See Stephen, Sir Leslie
Donabedian, Avedis 1919- ... CANR-12
Earlier sketch in CA 73-76
Donagan, Alan (Harry) 1925- ... 5-8R
Donagan, Barbara (Galley) 1927- ... 17-20R
Donaggio, Pino 1941- ... IDFW 3, 4
Donaghy, Henry J. 1930- ... 53-56
Donaghy, Michael 1954-2004 ... 140
Obituary ... 231
See also CP 7
See also DLB 282
Donaghy, William A. 1910(?)-1975
Obituary ... 53-56
Donahoe, Bernard (Frances) 1932- ... 17-20R
Donahue, Brian 1955- ... 195
Donahue, Don 1942- ... 69-72
Donahue, Francis J. 1917- ... 17-20R
Donahue, George T. 1911-1980 ... 17-20R
Donahue, Jack (Clifford) 1917-1991 . CANR-17
Obituary ... 135
Earlier sketch in CA 97-100
Donahue, June (Geserick) 1918(?)-1984
Obituary ... 111
Donahue, Kenneth 1915-1985 ... 102
Donahue, Leigh Richmond
See Richmond, Leigh (Tucker)
Donahue, Phil(lip John) 1935- ... 107
Donahue, Roy L(uther) 1908-1999 ... CANR-34
Earlier sketches in CA 89-92, CANR-15
Donahue, Thomas John 1943- ... 112
Donald, Aida DiPace 1930- ... 21-24R
Donald, Anabel 1944- ... CANR-142
Earlier sketch in CA 122
Donald, Bruce H(arry) 1935- ... 111
Donald, David Herbert 1920- ... CANR-104
Earlier sketches in CA 9-12R, CANR-4, 54
See also DLB 17
Donald, Diana 1938- ... 157
Donald, Larry W(atson) 1945-2000 ... 93-96
Obituary ... 192
Donald, Maxwell 1897-1978
Obituary ... 89-92
Donald, Merlin W(ilfred) 1939- ... CANR-108
Earlier sketch in CA 137
Donald, Peter (Harry) 1962- ... 137
Donald, R. V.
See Floren, Lee
Donald, Rhonda Lucas 1962- ... 221
See also SATA 147
Donald, Robyn 1940- ... RHW
Donald, Vivian
See Mackinnon, Charles Roy
Donalds, Gordon
See Shirreffs, Gordon D(onald)
Donaldson, Betty 1923-1988 ... 103
Donaldson, Bryna
See Stevens, Bryna
Donaldson, E(thelbert) Talbot 1910-1987 ... CANR-2
Obituary ... 122
Earlier sketch in CA 49-52
Donaldson, Elvin F. 1903-1972 ... 1-4R
Obituary ... 103
Donaldson, Frances (Annesley) 1907-1994 ... CANR-12
Obituary ... 144
Earlier sketch in CA 61-64
Donaldson, Frances (Gertrude) F(laacke) 1892(?)-1987
Obituary ... 122
Donaldson, Gary A. ... 204
Donaldson, Gordon 1913-1993 ... CANR-47
Obituary ... 141
Earlier sketches in CA 13-16R, CANR-5, 22
See also SATA 64
See also SATA-Obit 76
Donaldson, (Charles) Ian (Edward) 1935- ... CANR-35
Earlier sketches in CA 69-72, CANR-12
Donaldson, Islay (Eila) Murray 1921- ... 135
Donaldson, Joan 1953- ... 146
See also SATA 78
Donaldson, John W. 1893(?)-1979
Obituary ... 85-88
Donaldson, Julia 1948- ... CANR-106
Earlier sketch in CA 149
See also SATA 82, 132
Donaldson, Kenneth 1908-1995 ... 73-76
Donaldson, Loraine ... 140
Donaldson, Malcolm 1884-1973 ... CAP-1
Earlier sketch in CA 9-10
Donaldson, Margaret 1926- ... CANR-20
Earlier sketch in CA 103
Donaldson, Molla S(loane) 1944- ... 168
Donaldson, Norman 1922-2000 ... 33-36R
Donaldson, Peter J. ... 232
Donaldson, Robert Herschel 1943- .. CANR-15
Earlier sketch in CA 85-88
Donaldson, S(imon) K. 1957- ... 163
Donaldson, Sam(uel Andrew) 1934- ... 111
Brief entry ... 109
Interview in ... CA-111
Donaldson, Scott 1928- ... CANR-90
Earlier sketches in CA 25-28R, CANR-11, 27
See also DLB 111
Donaldson, Stephen R(eeder) 1947- . CANR-99
Earlier sketches in CA 89-92, CANR-13, 55
Interview in ... CANR-13
See also AAYA 36
See also BPFB 1
See also CLC 46, 138
See also CPW
See also DAM POP
See also FANT
See also SATA 121
See also SFW 4
See also SUFW 1, 2
Donaldson, Thomas 1945- ... 139
Donaldson, (Charles) William 1935- ... 77-80
Donart, Arthur C(harles) 1936- ... 37-40R
Donat, Alexander 1905-1983
Donat, Anton
See Donart, Arthur C(harles)
Donat, John (Annesley) 1933- ... 13-16R
Donati, Danilo 1926- ... IDFW 3, 4
Donati, Sara
See Lippi, Rosina
Donato, Anthony 1909-1990 ... CAP-1
Earlier sketch in CA 13-16
Donavan, John
See Morland, Nigel
Donawerth, Jane (Lynn) 1947- ... 118
Donceel, Joseph F. 1906-1994 ... CANR-1
Earlier sketch in CA 1-4R
Donchess, Barbara (Briggs) 1922- ... 57-60
Donders, Jozef G(erardus) 1929- ... CANR-68
Earlier sketch in CA 129
Dondis, Donis A(snin) 1924-1984 ... 85-88
Donelson, Irene W(itmer) 1913- ... 17-20R
Donelson, Kenneth L(avern) 1927- ... CANR-98
Earlier sketch in CA 69-72
Donelson, Kenneth W(ilber) 1910- ... 17-20R
Donelson, Linda Grace 1943- ... 174
Donem, Sue
See Ross, Stanley Ralph
Doner, Kim 1955- ... SATA 91
Doner, Mary Frances 1893-1985 ... 13-16R
Donetta
See Chester, Tessa Rose
Doney, Todd L. W. 1959- ... SATA 104
Doney, Willis (Frederick, Jr.) 1925- ... 21-24R
Donfried, Karl Paul 1940- ... 108
Dong, Stella ... 228
Dongala, Emmanuel Boundzeki 1941- ... 204
Donham, Jean 1946- ... 196
Donheiser, Alan D. 1936- ... 37-40R
Donhoff, Marion (Hedda Ilse Countess) 1909-2002
Obituary ... 206
Doni, Rodolfo 1919- ... 239
See also DLB 177
Donia, Robert J(ay) 1945- ... 155
Donicht, Mark Allen 1946- ... 93-96
Donigan, Robert L. 1903(?)-1989
Obituary ... 128
Doniger, Lester (Laurence) 1909-1971
Obituary ... 104
Doniger, Wendy (O'Flaherty) 1940- ... 190
Donin, Hayim Halevy 1928- ... 77-80
Donington, Robert 1907-1990 ... CANR-96
Obituary ... 130
Earlier sketches in CA 33-36R, CANR-83
Donis, Miles 1937-1979 ... 29-32R
Obituary ... 93-96
Donker, Anthonie
See Donkersloot, Nicolaas-Anthonie
Donker, Marjorie 1926- ... 145
Donkin, Nance (Clare) 1915- ... CANR-68
Earlier sketches in CA 103, CANR-20, 42
See also SATA 95
Donleavy, J(ames) P(atrick) 1926- ... CANR-124
Earlier sketches in CA 9-12R, CANR-24, 49, 62, 80
Interview in ... CANR-24
See also AITN 2
See also BPFB 1
See also CBD
See also CD 5, 6
See also CLC 1, 4, 6, 10, 45
See also CN 1, 2, 3, 4, 5, 6, 7
See also DLB 6, 173
See also MAL 5
See also MTCW 1, 2
See also MTFW 2005
See also RGAL 4
Donley, Carol C(ram) 1937- ... CANR-48
Earlier sketch in CA 122
Donley, Marshall O(wen), Jr. 1932- .. CANR-14
Earlier sketch in CA 65-68
Donna, Natalie 1934-1979 ... CANR-6
Earlier sketch in CA 9-12R
See also SATA 9
Donnachie, Ian Lowe 1944- ... 105
Donnadieu, Marguerite
See Duras, Marguerite
Donnan, Marcia Jeanne 1932- ... 104
Donne, John 1572-1631 ... AAYA 67
See also BRW 1
See also BRWC 1
See also BRWR 2
See also CDBLB Before 1660
See also DA
See also DAB
See also DAC
See also DAM MST, POET
See also DLB 121, 151
See also EXPP
See also PAB
See also PC 1, 43
See also PFS 2, 11
See also RGEL 3
See also TEA
See also WLC
See also WLIT 3
See also WP
Donne, Maxim
See Duke, Madelaine (Elizabeth)
Donneau de Vise, Jean 1638-1710 ... GFL Beginnings to 1789
Donnell, David 1939(?)- ... 197
See also CLC 34
Donnell, John C(orwin) 1919-2000 ... 41-44R
Donnell, John D(ouglas) 1920- ... CANR-5
Earlier sketch in CA 53-56
Donnell, Susan ... 137
Donnellan, Michael T(homas) 1931- ... 37-40R
Donnelley, Dixon 1915-1982
Obituary ... 105
Donnell-Kotrozo, Carol 1947- ... 113
Donnelly, Alton S(tewart) 1920- ... 21-24R
Donnelly, Austin Stanislaus 1923- ... 112
Donnelly, Deborah ... 204
Donnelly, Denise 1956- ... 184
Donnelly, Desmond L(ouis) 1920- ... 13-16R
Donnelly, Doris (Krimper) 1940- ... 123
Donnelly, Dorothy (Boillotat) 1903-1994 ... CANR-3
Earlier sketch in CA 5-8R
Donnelly, Esmond
See Oberdorf, Charles (Donnell)
Donnelly, Gabrielle (Mary Teresa) 1952- ... 127
Donnelly, Ignatius 1831-1901 ... 162
Brief entry ... 110
See also DLB 12
See also RGAL 4
See also SFW 4
Donnelly, James A. III 1929(?)-1984
Obituary ... 112
Donnelly, James H(oward), Jr. 1941- ... 29-32R
Donnelly, James S(tephen), Jr. 1943- ... CANR-119
Earlier sketch in CA 102
Donnelly, Jane ... RHW
Donnelly, Jennifer 1963- ... 229
See also SATA 154
Donnelly, Joe 1950- ... CANR-73
Earlier sketch in CA 139
See also HGG
Donnelly, John 1941- ... 93-96
Donnelly, John Patrick 1934- ... 81-84
Donnelly, Joseph P(eter) 1905-1982 ... 81-84
Obituary ... 108
Donnelly, Matt 1972- ... 222
See also SATA 148
Donnelly, Michael 1959- ... 184
Donnelly, Sister Gertrude Joseph 1920- ... 13-16R
Donner, Fred McGraw 1945- ... 106
Donner, Joern 1933- ... CANR-9
Earlier sketch in CA 13-16R
See also Donner, Jorn
Donner, Jorn
See Donner, Joern
See also EWL 3
Donner, Rebecca ... 225
Donner, Richard 1930- ... AAYA 34
Donner, Stanley T(emple) 1910- ... 61-64
Donnison, David Vernon 1926- ... 106
Donnison, F(rank) S(iegfried) V(ernon) 1898-1993 ... 1-4R
Donnison, Jean 1925- ... 77-80
Donnithorne, Audrey 1922- ... 17-20R
Donnithorne, Larry 1944- ... 144
Donno, Elizabeth Story 1921- ... CANR-5
Earlier sketch in CA 1-4R
Donoghue, Denis 1928- ... CANR-102
Earlier sketches in CA 17-20R, CANR-16
See also CLC 209
Donoghue, Emma 1969- ... CANR-103
Earlier sketch in CA 155
See also DLB 267
See also GLL 2
See also SATA 101
Donoghue, Mildred R(ansdorf) ... CANR-10
Earlier sketch in CA 25-28R
Donoghue, P. S.
See Hunt, E(verette) Howard, (Jr.)
Donoghue, Quentin 1937- ... 122
Donoghue, William E(lliott) 1941- ... CANR-39
Earlier sketch in CA 116
Donohoe, Thomas 1917- ... 53-56
Donohoe, Tom 1957- ... 123
Donohue, Agnes McNeill 1917-2003 ... 127
Obituary ... 220
Donohue, Gail
See Storey, Gail Donohue
Donohue, James F(itzgerald) 1934- ... 73-76
Donohue, John J. 1926- ... CANR-48
Earlier sketch in CA 122
Donohue, John K. 1909-1978 ... CAP-1
Earlier sketch in CA 11-12
Donohue, John W(aldron) 1917- ... CANR-3
Earlier sketch in CA 5-8R
Donohue, Joseph (Walter, Jr.) 1935- ... 69-72
Donohue, Lynn 1957(?)- ... 207
Donohue, Mark 1937-1975 ... 57-60
Obituary ... 89-92
Donohue, Martin
See Gibson, Walter B(rown)
Donohue, William A. 1947- ... 144
Donoso (Yanez), Jose 1924-1996 ... CANR-73
Obituary ... 155
Earlier sketches in CA 81-84, CANR-32
See also CDWLB 3
See also CLC 4, 8, 11, 32, 99
See also CWW 2
See also DAM MULT
See also DLB 113
See also EWL 3
See also HLC 1
See also HW 1, 2
See also LAW
See also LAWS 1
See also MTCW 1, 2
See also MTFW 2005
See also RGSF 2
See also SSC 34
See also TCLC 133
See also WLIT 1
Donoughue, Bernard 1934- ... 17-20R
Donoughue, Carol 1935- ... 210
See also SATA 139
Donovan, Anne 1956(?)- ... 232
Donovan, Bonita R. 1947- ... 73-76
Donovan, Bonnie
See Donovan, Bonita R.
Donovan, Edward J(oseph) 1904- ... 5-8R
Donovan, Frank (Robert) 1906-1975 .. CANR-6
Obituary ... 61-64
Earlier sketch in CA 1-4R
See also SATA-Obit 30
Donovan, Gregory 1950- ... 198
Donovan, Hedley (Williams) 1914-1990 ... 115
Obituary ... 132
Brief entry ... 110
Interview in ... CA-115
Donovan, James A., Jr. 1917- ... 21-24R
Donovan, James Britt 1916-1970 ... 9-12R
Obituary ... 89-92
Donovan, John 1919- ... CANR-2
Earlier sketch in CA 1-4R
Donovan, John 1928-1992 ... 97-100
Obituary ... 137
See also AAYA 20
See also CLC 35
See also CLR 3
See also MAICYA 1, 2
See also SATA 72
See also SATA-Brief 29
See also YAW
Donovan, John C(hauncey) 1920-1984 . 37-40R
Obituary ... 114
Donovan, Josephine (Campbell) 1941- ... CANR-106
Earlier sketches in CA 106, CANR-24, 49
Donovan, Katie 1962- ... 152
Donovan, Mark ... TCWW 2
Donovan, Mary Lee 1961- ... 151
See also SATA 86
Donovan, Robert Alan 1921- ... 17-20R
Donovan, Robert J(ohn) 1912-2003 . CANR-41
Obituary ... 219
Earlier sketches in CA 1-4R, CANR-2, 18
Donovan, Susan ... 222
Donovan, Timothy Paul 1927- ... 53-56
Donovan, William
See Berkebile, Fred D(onovan)
Donow, Herbert S(tanton) 1936- ... 112
Don Roberto
See Cunninghame Graham, Robert (Gallnigad) Bontine
Donskis, Leonidas 1962- ... 218
Donskoi, Mark Semyonovich 1901-1981
Obituary ... 103
Donson, Cyril 1919-1986 ... CANR-28
Earlier sketches in CA 21-24R, CANR-11
See also TCWW 2
Don-Yehiya, Eliezer 1938- ... 111
Donze, Mary Terese 1911- ... CANR-50
Earlier sketches in CA 108, CANR-25
See also SATA 89
Doob, Anthony N(ewcomb) 1943- ... 33-36R

Cumulative Index 157 Doty

Doob, Leonard W(illiam) 1909-2000 . CANR-2
Earlier sketch in CA 5-8R
See also SATA 8
Doob, Penelope Billings Reed 1943- ... 53-56
Doody, Francis Stephen 1917-1996 ... 13-16R
Doody, Margaret (Anne) 1939- ... CANR-129
Earlier sketches in CA 69-72, CANR-11, 27
Doog, K. Caj
See Good, I(rving) John
Doohan, James (Montgomery) 1920-2005 .. 172
Doohan, Leonard 1941- ... 118
Dooley, Allan C(harles) 1943- ... 138
Dooley, Arch R(ichard) 1925- ... 13-16R
Dooley, Brian J. 1954- ... 217
Dooley, D(avid) J(oseph) 1921- ... CANR-16
Earlier sketch in CA 25-28R
Dooley, David (Allen) 1947- ... 232
See also CP 7
See also CSW
Dooley, Ebon
See Ebon
Dooley, Howard J(ohn) 1944- ... 53-56
Dooley, John 1929(?)-1985
Obituary ... 119
Dooley, Mark 1970- ... 220
Dooley, Maura 1957- ... CANR-127
Earlier sketch in CA 139
Dooley, Norah 1953- ... SATA 74
Dooley, Patrick K(iaran) 1942- ... 53-56
Dooley, Paul 1928- ... 133
Dooley, Peter C(hamberlain) 1937- ... 49-52
Dooley, Roger B(urke) 1920-1993 ... CANR-22
Obituary ... 143
Earlier sketch in CA 1-4R
Dooley, Thomas A(nthony) 1927-1961
Obituary ... 93-96
Dooley, William G(ermain) 1905(?)-1975
Obituary ... 57-60
Doolin, Dennis James 1933- ... 13-16R
Dooling, Dave
See Dooling, David, Jr.
Dooling, David, Jr. 1950- ... 125
Dooling, Michael 1958- ... SATA 105
Dooling, Richard (Patrick) 1954- ... CANR-139
Earlier sketch in CA 139
Doolittle, Hilda 1886-1961 ... CANR-131
Earlier sketches in CA 97-100, CANR-35
See also H. D.
See also AAYA 66
See also AMWS 1
See also CLC 3, 8, 14, 31, 34, 73
See also DA
See also DAC
See also DAM MST, POET
See also DLB 4, 45
See also EWL 3
See also FW
See also GLL 1
See also LMFS 2
See also MAL 5
See also MAWW
See also MTCW 1, 2
See also MTFW 2005
See also PC 5
See also PFS 6
See also RGAL 4
See also WLC
Doolittle, James H(arold) 1896-1993 ... 143
Doolittle, Jerome (Hill) 1933- ... CANR-71
Earlier sketch in CA 53-56
Doolittle, Jimmy
See Doolittle, James H(arold)
Doone, Jice
See Marshall, James Vance
Dooren, Ingrid van
See van Dooren, Ingrid
Doorly, Ruth K. 1919- ... 25-28R
Doorn, A. van
See Greshoff, Jan
Doornkamp, John Charles 1938- ... CANR-7
Earlier sketch in CA 57-60
Doplicher, Fabio 1938- ... DLB 128
Doppo
See Kunikida Doppo
Doppo, Kunikida
See Kunikida Doppo
See also TCLC 99
Dopuch, Nicholas 1929- ... 61-64
Dor, Ana
See Ceder, Georgiana Dorcas
Dor, Carla
See Alia, Valerie
Dor, Milo 1923-
See Doroslovac, Milutin
See also DLB 85
Dor, Moshe 1932- ... 206
Doran, Adelaide L(eMert) 1908-1987 ... 116
Doran, Charles F(rancis) 1943- ... 73-76
Doran, Colleen 1963- ... AAYA 57
Doran, David K. 1929- ... 143
Doran, Madeleine 1905-1996 ... 121
Doran, Robert 1940- ... 150
Dorant, Gene
See Lent, D(ora) Geneva
Dorati, Antal 1906-1988
Obituary ... 127
Doray, Maya 1922- ... 45-48
Dorcey, Mary 1950- ... DLB 319
Dorcy, Sister Mary Jean 1914- ... 9-12R
Dordick, Herbert S(halom) 1925- ... 116
Dore, Anita Wilkes 1914- ... 29-32R
Dore, Claire (Morin) 1934- ... 9-12R
Dore, (Louis Christophe Paul) Gustave
1832-1883 ... SATA 19
Dore, Ronald Philip 1925- ... CANR-103
Earlier sketches in CA 89-92, CANR-15, 34
do Rego, Jose Lins 1901-1957 ... 179
See also Lins do Rego, Jose and
Rego, Jose Lins do
See also HW 2
Doreian, Patrick 1942- ... 45-48
Doremus, Paul N. 1960- ... 203
Doremus, Robert 1913- ... SATA 30
Doremus, Thomas Edmund 1922-1962 ... 1-4R
Doren, Marion (Walker) 1928- ... 125
See also SATA 57
Dorenkamp, Michelle 1957- ... SATA 89
Doreski, William 1946- ... CANR-17
Earlier sketches in CA 45-48, CANR-1
Dorey, T(homas) A(lan) 1921- ... CANR-94
Earlier sketch in CA 17-20R
Dorf, Fran 1953- ... CANR-99
Earlier sketch in CA 138
Dorf, Michael C. 1964- ... 135
Dorf, Richard C. 1933- ... CANR-52
Earlier sketches in CA 110, CANR-28
Dorfer, Ingemar (Nils Hans) 1939- ... 130
Dorff, Elliot N. 1943- ... CANR-51
Earlier sketch in CA 124
Dorflinger, Carolyn 1953- ... 155
See also SATA 91
Dorfman, Ariel 1942- ... CANR-135
Brief entry ... 124
Earlier sketches in CA 130, CANR-67, 70
Interview in ... CA-130
See also CLC 48, 77, 189
See also CWW 2
See also DAM MULT
See also DFS 4
See also EWL 3
See also HLC 1
See also HW 1, 2
See also WLIT 1
Dorfman, Dan 1932- ... 116
Brief entry ... 110
Interview in ... CA-116
Dorfman, Eugene 1917-1974 ... 29-32R
Dorfman, Gerald Allen 1939- ... 118
Dorfman, John 1947- ... CANR-12
Earlier sketch in CA 69-72
Dorfman, Joseph 1904-1991 ... 45-48
Obituary ... 135
Dorfman, Nancy S(chelling) 1922- ... 53-56
Dorfman, Nat N. 1895-1977
Obituary ... 73-76
Dorfman, Robert 1916-2002 ... 17-20R
Obituary ... 206
Dorgan, Charity Anne 1959- ... 134
Dorge, Jeanne Emilie Marie
See Marie-Andre du Sacre-Coeur, Sister
Dorgeles, Roland 1886-1973
See Lecavele, Roland
See also DLB 65
Doria, Charles 1938- ... 73-76
Doria, Vincent Mark 1947- ... 138
Dorian, Edith M(cEwen) 1900-1983 ... CAP-1
Earlier sketch in CA 9-10
See also SATA 5
Dorian, Emil 1893-1956
Dorian, Frederick 1902-1991 ... CAP-1
Earlier sketch in CA 11-12
Dorian, Harry
See Hamilton, Charles (Harold St. John)
Dorian, Marguerite ... 17-20R
See also SATA 7
Dorian, Nancy C(urrier) 1936- ... 104
Doriani, Beth Maclay 1961- ... CANR-128
Earlier sketch in CA 152
Dorin, Patrick C(arberry) 1939- ... CANR-34
Earlier sketches in CA 93-96, CANR-15
See also SATA 59
See also SATA-Brief 52
Dorinson, Joseph 1936- ... 179
Doris, John Lawrence 1923- ... 102
Doris, Lillian 1899-1966 ... 5-8R
Dorkin, Evan ... 225
Dorland, Henry
See Ash, Brian
Dorland, Michael 1948- ... 102
Dorliae, Peter Gondro 1935- ... 29-32R
Dorliae, Saint
See Dorliae, Peter Gondro
Dorman, Daniel ... 233
Dorman, Luke
See Bingley, David Ernest
Dorman, Michael 1932- ... CANR-5
Earlier sketch in CA 13-16R
See also SATA 7
Dorman, N. B. 1927- ... 106
See also SATA 39
Dorman, Sonya 1924-2005 ... 73-76
Dormandy, Clara 1905- ... CAP-1
Earlier sketch in CA 9-10
Dormann, Alexander
See Doroslovac, Milutin
Dorment, Richard 1946- ... 147
d'Ormesson, Jean (Bruno Waldemar
Francois-de-Paule Lefevre) 1925-
Brief entry ... 111
Dormon, James H(unter), Jr. 1936- ... 21-24R
Dorn, Edward (Merton) 1929-1999 .. CANR-79
Obituary ... 187
Earlier sketches in CA 93-96, CANR-42
Interview in ... CA-93-96
See also CLC 10, 18
See also CP 1, 2, 3, 4, 5, 6, 7
See also DLB 5
See also WP
Dorn, Frank 1901-1981 ... CANR-24
Obituary ... 104
Earlier sketch in CA 29-32R
Dorn, Jacob H(enry) 1939- ... 21-24R
Dorn, Phyllis Moore 1910(?)-1978
Obituary ... 77-80
Dorn, Sylvia O'Neill 1918- ... 69-72
Dorn, William S. 1928- ... 65-68
Dornan, James E., Jr. 1938(?)-1979
Obituary ... 85-88
Dornberg, John Robert 1931- ... CANR-1
Earlier sketch in CA 1-4R
Dornbusch, C(harles) E(mil)
1907-1990 ... CAP-1
Earlier sketch in CA 9-10
Dornenburg, Andrew ... 176
Dorner, Marjorie 1942- ... CANR-85
Earlier sketch in CA 133
Dorner, Peter Paul 1925- ... CANR-14
Earlier sketch in CA 37-40R
Dor-Ner, Zvi ... CLC 70
Doro, Edward 1910-1987 ... CANR-99
Earlier sketch in CA 21-24R
Doro, Marion Elizabeth 1928- ... 89-92
Doroch, Efim Yakovlevitch 1908(?)-1972
Obituary ... 37-40R
Doronzo, Emmanuel 1903-1976 ... 21-24R
Doroshkin, Milton 1914-1996 ... 33-36R
Doroslovac, Milutin 1923- ... 203
See also Dor, Milo
Dorothy, R. D.
See Charques, Dorothy (Taylor)
Dorpalen, Andreas 1911-1982 ... 17-20R
Obituary ... 109
Dorpat, Theo(dore) L. 1925- ... 232
Dorr, Donal 1935- ... CANR-44
Earlier sketch in CA 118
Dorr, Lawrence ... 168
Dorr, Rheta (Louise) Childe 1866-1948 ... 236
Brief entry ... 116
See also DLB 25
Dorrell, Linda M. 1962- ... 202
Dorrestein, Renate 1954- ... 202
Dorrie, Doris 1955- ... CANR-136
Earlier sketch in CA 130
Dorrien, Gary J. 1952- ... 135
Dorries, William (Lyle) 1923- ... 37-40R
Dorril, Stephen ... 233
Dorris, Michael (Anthony)
1945-1997 ... CANR-75
Obituary ... 157
Earlier sketches in CA 102, CANR-19, 46
See also AAYA 20
See also BEST 90:1
See also BYA 12
See also CLC 109
See also CLR 58
See also DA3
See also DAM MULT, NOV
See also DLB 175
See also LAIT 5
See also MTCW 2
See also MTFW 2005
See also NFS 3
See also NNAL
See also RGAL 4
See also SATA 75
See also SATA-Obit 94
See also TCWW 2
See also YAW
Dorris, Michael A.
See Dorris, Michael (Anthony)
Dorris, R(obert) T. 1913-1991 ... 29-32R
Dorritt, Susan
See Schlein, Miriam
Dorros, Arthur (M.) 1950- ... CANR-93
Earlier sketch in CA 146
See also CLR 42
See also MAICYA 2
See also MAICYAS 1
See also SAAS 20
See also SATA 78, 122
Dors, Diana
See Fluck, Diana
Dorsan, Luc
See Simenon, Georges (Jacques Christian)
Dorsange, Jean
See Simenon, Georges (Jacques Christian)
Dorsen, Norman 1930- ... 37-40R
Dorset
See Sackville, Thomas
Dorset
See Sackville, Charles
See also RGEL 2
Dorset, Gerald (Harris) 1920-1987 ... 112
Dorset, Phyllis (Flanders) 1924- ... 25-28R
Dorset, Richard
See Shaver, Richard S(harpe)
Dorset, Ruth
See Ross, W(illiam) E(dward) D(aniel)
Dorsett, Danielle
See Daniels, Dorothy
Dorsett, Lyle W(esley) 1938- ... CANR-9
Earlier sketch in CA 21-24R
Dorsey, Candas Jane 1952- ... 216
Earlier sketches in CA 156, CANR-114
Autobiographical Essay in ... 216
See also DLB 251
See also SFW 4
Dorsey, David Frederick, Jr. 1934- ... 115
Dorsey, Hebe 1925-1987
Obituary ... 124
Dorsey, Helen 1928- ... 110
Dorsey, James 1942-2003 ... 227
Dorsey, John M(orris) 1900-1978 ... CANR-4
Earlier sketch in CA 5-8R
Dorsey, John R(ussell) 1938- ... 118
Dorsey, John Thornton, Jr. 1924- ... 111
Dorsey, Thomas A(ndrew) 1899-1993 ... 229
Dorsey, Tim 1961- ... 215
D'Orso, Michael 1953- ... CANR-106
Earlier sketch in CA 154
D'Orso, Mike
See D'Orso, Michael
Dorson, Richard M(ercer) 1916-1981 ... 106
Obituary ... 105
See also SATA 30
Dorsonville, Max 1943- ... 65-68
Dorst, Jean (Pierre) 1924- ... CANR-19
Earlier sketches in CA 5-8R, CANR-3
Dorst, Tankred 1925- ... CANR-30
Earlier sketch in CA 41-44R
See also DLB 75, 124
Dorwart, J(effrey) M(ichael) 1944- ... 97-100
Dorwart, Reinhold August 1911- ... 65-68
Dorworth, Alice Grey 1907-1979 ... 5-8R
Dosa, Marta Leszlei ... 45-48
Doskocilova, Hana 1936- ... CANR-47
Earlier sketches in CA 61-64, CANR-8, 23
Doskow, Minna 1937- ... 118
Dos Passos, John (Roderigo)
1896-1970 ... CANR-3
Obituary ... 29-32R
Earlier sketch in CA 1-4R
See also AMW
See also BPFB 1
See also CDALB 1929-1941
See also CLC 1, 4, 8, 11, 15, 25, 34, 82
See also DA
See also DA3
See also DAB
See also DAC
See also DAM MST, NOV
See also DLB 4, 9, 274, 316
See also DLBD 1, 15
See also DLBY 1996
See also EWL 3
See also MAL 5
See also MTCW 1, 2
See also MTFW 2005
See also NFS 14
See also RGAL 4
See also TUS
See also WLC
Doss, Erika ... 159
Doss, Helen (Grigsby) 1918- ... CANR-6
Earlier sketch in CA 9-12R
See also SATA 20
Doss, James D(aniel) 1939- ... CANR-140
Earlier sketch in CA 163
Doss, Margot Patterson ... CANR-12
Earlier sketch in CA 29-32R
See also SATA 6
Doss, Richard W(eller) 1933-
Brief entry ... 112
Dossage, Jean
See Simenon, Georges (Jacques Christian)
dos Santos, Joyce Audy 1949- ... 136
Brief entry ... 118
See also Zarins, Joyce Audy
See also SATA-Brief 42
Dossey, Larry 1940- ... CANR-139
Earlier sketch in CA 170
Dossick, Philip 1941- ... 81-84
Doster, Stephen M. 1959- ... 213
Doster, William C(lark) 1921- ... 13-16R
Dostoevsky, Fedor Mikhailovich 1821-1881
See Dostoevsky, Fyodor
See also AAYA 40
See also DA
See also DA3
See also DAB
See also DAC
See also DAM MST, NOV
See also EW 7
See also EXPN
See also NFS 3, 8
See also RGSF 2
See also RGWL 2, 3
See also SSC 2, 33, 44
See also SSFS 8
See also TWA
See also WLC
Dostoevsky, Fyodor
See Dostoevsky, Fedor Mikhailovich
See also DLB 238
See also LATS 1:1
See also LMFS 1, 2
Dothard, Robert Loos 1909(?)-1979
Obituary ... 85-88
Dothers, Anne
See Chess, Victoria (Dickerson)
Doti, Lynne Pierson 1948- ... 137
Dotsenko, Paul 1894-1988 ... 117
Obituary ... 140
Dotson, Bob
See Dotson, Robert Charles
Dotson, Floyd 1917- ... 25-28R
Dotson, John L(ouis), Jr. 1937- ... 105
Dotson, Lillian O. 1921- ... 25-28R
Dotson, Robert Charles 1946- ... 134
Brief entry ... 119
Dott, R(obert) H(enry), Jr. 1929- ... 53-56
Dottig
See Grider, Dorothy
Dotto, Lydia 1949- ... 125
Dotts, M. Franklin 1929- ... 57-60
Dotts, Maryann J. 1933- ... CANR-30
Earlier sketches in CA 33-36R, CANR-12
See also SATA 35
Doty, Brant Lee 1921-1998 ... 17-20R
Doty, C(harles) Stewart 1928- ... 65-68
Doty, Carolyn H(ouse) 1941-2003 ... CANR-17
Obituary ... 214
Earlier sketches in CA 105, CANR-23

Doty, Gene Warren 1941- CANR-109
Earlier sketches in CA 49-52, CANR-1
See also Warren, (Francis) Eugene
Doty, Gladys 1908-1985 53-56
Doty, Gresdna Ann 1931- 41-44R
Doty, James Edward 1922- 37-40R
Doty, Jean Slaughter 1929- CANR-2
Earlier sketch in CA 45-48
See also SATA 28
Doty, M. R.
See Doty, Mark (Alan)
Doty, Mark
See Doty, Mark (Alan)
Doty, Mark (Alan) 1953(?)- 183
Earlier sketches in CA 161, CANR-110
Autobiographical Essay in 183
See also AMWS 11
See also CLC 176
See also PC 53
Doty, Mark A.
See Doty, Mark (Alan)
Doty, Richard (George) 1942- 109
Doty, Robert McIntyre 1933- 102
Doty, Roy 1922- CANR-8
Earlier sketch in CA 53-56
See also SATA 28
Doty, William G(uy) 1939- CANR-20
Earlier sketches in CA 53-56, CANR-5
Doty, William Lodewick 1919-1979 .. CANR-1
Earlier sketch in CA 1-4R
Doubiago, Sharon 1946- 112
See also CWP
Doubleday, Neal Frank 1905-1976 .... 41-44R
Doubleday, Veronica 1948- 129
Doubrovsky, Serge 1928- 136
Brief entry 110
See also DLB 299
Doubtfire, Dianne (Abrams) 1918- ... CANR-39
Earlier sketches in CA 1-4R, CANR-1, 17
See also SATA 29
Doucet, Clive 1946- CANR-42
Earlier sketch in CA 118
Doucet, Julie 1965- 224
Doucet, Sharon Arms 1951- ...... SATA 125, 144
See also SATA-Essay 144
Doucette, Leonard E(ugene) 1936- 33-36R
Doud, Laurel (Marian) 1954- 174
Douds, Charles Tucker 1898-1982
Obituary 106
Dougall, Herbert E(dward) 1902-1996 .. CAP-1
Earlier sketch in CA 19-20
Dougall, Lily 1858-1923 175
See also DLB 92
Dougan, Michael B(ruce) 1944- 69-72
Dougherty, Betty 1922- 61-64
Dougherty, Charles 1922- .... SATA 18
Dougherty, Ching-yi (Hsu) 1915- 5-8R
Dougherty, David Mitchell 1903-1985 113
Dougherty, Flavian 1913(?)-1990
Obituary 130
Dougherty, James (Patrick) 1937- 106
Dougherty, James E(dward) 1923- 134
Brief entry 111
Dougherty, Joanna Foster
See Foster, Joanna
Dougherty, John J(oseph) 1907-1986
Obituary 118
Dougherty, Jude P(atrick) 1930- 45-48
Dougherty, Philip H(ugh) 1923-1988
Obituary 126
Dougherty, Richard 1921-1986 .... CANR-2
Obituary 121
Earlier sketch in CA 1-4R
Dougherty, Richard M. 1935- 33-36R
Dougherty, Terri (L.) 1964- 220
See also SATA 146
Doughtie, Edward (Orth) 1935- 45-48
Doughty, Bradford 1921- 65-68
Doughty, Charles M(ontagu) 1843-1926 178
Brief entry 115
See also DLB 19, 57, 174
See also TCLC 27
Doughty, Louise 214
Doughty, Nina Beckett 1911- 53-56
Doughty, Oswald 1889- CAP-1
Earlier sketch in CA 9-10
Doughty, Paul L(arrabee) 1930- 85-88
Doughty, Robin W. 1941- CANR-138
Earlier sketch in CA 122
Douglas, Albert
See Armstrong, Douglas Albert
Douglas, Althea (Cleveland McCoy) 1926- . 124
Douglas, Ann 1942- 149
Douglas, Ann C.
See Welch, Ann Courtenay (Edmonds)
Douglas, Arthur
See Hammond, Gerald (Arthur Douglas)
Douglas, Barbara
See Ovstedal, Barbara
Douglas, Blaise 1960- 168
See also SATA 101
Douglas, Carole Nelson 1944- CANR-93
Earlier sketches in CA 107, CANR-26, 53
See also AAYA 17
See also CMW 4
See also FANT
See also SATA 73
Douglas, Charles H(erbert) 1926- 194
Brief entry 109
Douglas, Christopher
See Neill, Christopher Harry Douglas
Douglas, Claire 1936- 144
Douglas, David C(harles)
1898-1982 .... CANR-28
Obituary 107
Earlier sketch in CA 73-76
Douglas, Ellen
See Haxton, Josephine Ayres and Williamson, Ellen Douglas
See also CLC 73
See also CN 5, 6, 7
See also CSW
See also DLB 292
Douglas, Emily (Taft) 1899-1994 107
Obituary 143
Douglas, Garry
See Kilworth, Garry (D.)
Douglas, Gavin 1475(?)-1522 .... DLB 132
See also RGEL 2
Douglas, George
See Brown, George Douglas
See also RGEL 2
Douglas, George H(alsey) 1934- CANR-14
Earlier sketch in CA 81-84
Douglas, Glenn
See Duckett, Alfred A.
Douglas, Gregory A.
See Cantor, Eli
Douglas, Helen Bee
See Bee, Helen L.
Douglas, Helen Gahagan 1900-1980 161
Obituary 101
Douglas, Ian
See Keith, William H(enry), Jr., Jr.
Douglas, J(ames) D(ixon)
1922-2003 .... CANR-44
Obituary 220
Earlier sketches in CA 13-16R, CANR-6, 21
Douglas, Jack 1909(?)-1989
Obituary 128
Douglas, James McM.
See Butterworth, W(illiam) E(dmund III)
Douglas, Jeff
See Offutt, Andrew J(efferson V)
Douglas, John (Frederick James) 1929- 116
Douglas, John 1947- CANR-107
Earlier sketch in CA 162
Douglas, John 1955- .... HGG
Douglas, Kate
See Douglas, Kathleen
Douglas, Kathleen 1949- 117
Douglas, Kathryn
See Ewing, Kathryn
Douglas, Keith (Castellain) 1920-1944 160
See also BRW 7
See also DLB 27
See also EWL 3
See also PAB
See also RGEL 2
See also TCLC 40
Douglas, Kirk 1916- CANR-114
Earlier sketch in CA 138
See also BEST 90:4
Douglas, L. Warren 1943- CANR-135
Earlier sketch in CA 176
Douglas, Lady Alfred
See Custance, Olive
Douglas, Lauren Wright 1947- CANR-142
Earlier sketch in CA 129
Douglas, Leonard
See Bradbury, Ray (Douglas)
Douglas, Leonard M(arvin) 1910-(?) CAP-2
Earlier sketch in CA 23-24
Douglas, Lloyd C.
See Douglas, Lloyd Cassel
Douglas, Lloyd Cassel 1877-1951
Brief entry 120
See also RHW
Douglas, Louis H(artwell) 1907-1979 ... 21-24R
Obituary 133
Douglas, Mack R. 1922- 21-24R
Douglas, Marcia 1961- 185
Douglas, Marjory Stoneman
1890-1998 .... CANR-72
Obituary 167
Earlier sketches in CA 1-4R, CANR-2
See also AITN 2
See also ANW
See also SATA 10
Douglas, Mary (Tew) 1921- 97-100
Douglas, Melvyn 1901-1981 135
Douglas, Michael
See Crichton, (John) Michael
Douglas, Michael
See Bright, Robert (Douglas Sr.)
Douglas, Mike 1925- CANR-92
Earlier sketch in CA 89-92
Douglas, (George) Norman 1868-1952 157
Brief entry 119
See also BRW 6
See also DLB 34, 195
See also RGEL 2
See also TCLC 68
Douglas, O. -1948 .... RHW
Douglas, Paul Howard 1892-1976 69-72
Douglas, R. M.
See Mason, Douglas R(ankine)
Douglas, Richard
See Whiting, Charles (Henry)
Douglas, Robert
See Andrews, (Charles) Robert Douglas (Hardy)
Douglas, Roy (Ian) 1924- CANR-56
Earlier sketches in CA 73-76, CANR-13, 30
Douglas, Scott
See Smith, William Scott
Douglas, Shane
See Wilkes-Hunter, R(ichard)
Douglas, Susan J(eanne) 1950- 153
Douglas, Thorne
See Haas, Ben(jamin) L(eopold)
See also TCWW 1
Douglas, William
See Brown, George Douglas
Douglas, William A(llison) 1934- 45-48
Douglas, William O(rville)
1898-1980 .... CANR-21
Obituary 93-96
Earlier sketch in CA 9-12R
Douglas-Hamilton, James 1942- CANR-13
Earlier sketch in CA 33-36R
Douglas-Home, Alec
See Home, Alexander Frederick (Douglas-)
Douglas-Home, Charles (Cospatrick)
1937-1985 171
Obituary 117
Douglas-Home, Henry 1907-1980 103
Obituary 101
Douglas-Home, Robin 1932-1968 .... CAP-2
Earlier sketch in CA 25-28
Douglas Home, William
See Home, William Douglas
Douglass, Amanda Hart
See Wallmann, Jeffrey M(iner)
Douglass, Barbara 1930- 114
See also SATA 40
Douglass, Billie
See Delinsky, Barbara (Ruth Greenberg)
Douglass, Donald McNutt 1899-1975 ...... 1-4R
Obituary 103
Douglass, Elisha Peairs 1915- 81-84
Douglass, Frederick 1817(?)-1895 .... AAYA 48
See also AFAW 1, 2
See also AMWC 1
See also AMWS 3
See also BLC 1
See also CDALB 1640-1865
See also DA
See also DA3
See also DAC
See also DAM MST, MULT
See also DLB 1, 43, 50, 79, 243
See also FW
See also LAIT 2
See also NCFS 2
See also RGAL 4
See also SATA 29
See also WLC
Douglass, Harl R(oy) 1892-1972 .... 5-8R
Douglass, Herbert Edgar 1927- CANR-13
Earlier sketch in CA 73-76
Douglass, James W. 1937- CANR-10
Earlier sketch in CA 25-28R
Douglass, Keith
See Keith, William H(enry), Jr., Jr.
Douglass, Malcolm P(aul)
1923-2002 .... CANR-13
Obituary 211
Earlier sketch in CA 73-76
Douglass, Marcia Kent
See Doty, Gladys
Douglass, Paul F(ranklin) 1904-1988 . CANR-3
Earlier sketch in CA 5-8R
Douglass, Robert W. 1934- 57-60
Douglass, Sara
See Warneke, Sara
Douglass, William 1691(?)-1752 .... DLB 24
Douglass, William A(nthony) 1939- 69-72
Douglas-Scott-Montagu, Edward
See Montagu of Beaulieu, Edward John Barrington
Douglas Wood, Ann
See Douglas, Ann
Doulis, Thomas 1931- CANR-11
Earlier sketch in CA 5-8R
Doulos, Jay
See Joyce, Jon L(oyd)
Doumani, Carol 1959- 219
Doumani, George A(lexander) 1929- 187
Doumato, Lamia 1947- 103
Dourado, (Waldomiro Freitas) Autran
1926- CANR-81
Earlier sketches in CA 25-28R, 179, CANR-34
See also CLC 23, 60
See also DLB 145, 307
See also HW 2
Dourado, Waldomiro Freitas Autran
See Dourado, (Waldomiro Freitas) Autran
Douras, Marion Cecilia 1897-1961
Obituary 111
Douskey, Franz 1941- 129
Doutremont, Henri
See Bugnet, Georges (-Charles-Jules)
See also CCA 1
Douty, Esther M(orris) 1909-1978 ..... CANR-94
Obituary 85-88
Earlier sketches in CA 5-8R, CANR-3
See also SATA 8
See also SATA-Obit 23
Douty, Norman F(ranklin)
1899-1993 .... CANR-31
Earlier sketch in CA 49-52
Douvan, Elizabeth (Ann Malcolm)
1926-2002 106
Obituary 206
Douy, Max 1914- .... IDFW 3, 4
Doval (Gimenez), Teresa de la Caridad
1966- 233
Dovalpage, Teresa
See Doval (Gimenez), Teresa de la Caridad
Dove, Arthur G. 1880-1946 .... DLB 188
Dove, Rita (Frances) 1952- CANR-132
Earlier sketches in CA 109, CANR-27, 42, 68, 76, 97
See also CAAS 19
See also AAYA 46
See also AMWS 4
See also BLCS
See also BW 2
See also CDALBS
See also CLC 50, 81
See also CP 7
See also CSW
See also CWP
See also DA3
See also DAM MULT, POET
See also DLB 120
See also EWL 3
See also EXPP
See also MAL 5
See also MTCW 2
See also MTFW 2005
See also PC 6
See also PFS 1, 15
See also RGAL 4
Doveglion
See Villa, Jose Garcia
Dover, C(larence) J(oseph) 1919- 13-16R
Dover, K(enneth) J(ames) 1920- CANR-137
Earlier sketches in CA 25-28R, CANR-12, 29, 56
Dover Wilson, John 1881-1969
Obituary 25-28R
Dovey, Ken 1947- 120
Dovizi da Bibbiena, Bernardo
1470-1520 .... RGWL 2, 3
Dovlatov, Sergei 1941-1990 .... CANR-45
Obituary 132
Earlier sketch in CA 115
See also Dovlatov, Sergei Donatovich and Dovlatov, Sergey (Donatovich)
Dovlatov, Sergei Donatovich
See Dovlatov, Sergei
See also DLB 285
Dovlatov, Sergey (Donatovich)
See Dovlatov, Sergei
See also EWL 3
Dow, Anthony Lee
See Dow, Tony
Dow, Blanche H(innan) 1893-1973
Obituary 41-44R
Dow, Dorothy
See Fitzgerald, Dorothy (Minerva) Dow
Dow, Emily R. 1904-1987 .... CAP-1
Earlier sketch in CA 11-12
See also SATA 10
Dow, George Francis 1868-1936
Brief entry 122
Dow, J(ose) Kamal 1936- 29-32R
Dow, James R(aymond) 1936- 233
Dow, Marguerite R(uth) 1926- 116
Dow, Neal 1906-1994 .... 17-20R
Dow, Sterling 1903-1995 .... CAP-2
Obituary 147
Earlier sketch in CA 21-22
Dow, Tony 1945- CANR-141
Earlier sketch in CA 174
Dow, Vicki
See McVey, Vicki
Dowbiggin, Ian R(obert) 1952- 222
Dowd, Douglas F(itzgerald) 1919- 5-8R
Dowd, Gregory Evans 1956- 218
Dowd, John David 1945- 146
See also SATA 78
Dowd, Laurence P(hillips) 1914-1980 ... 17-20R
Obituary 133
Dowd, Maureen (Brigid) 1952- 238
Dowd, Maxine
See Jensen, Maxine Dowd
Dowd, Merle E(dward) 1918- 85-88
Dowd, Michael Delaney, Jr.
See Douglas, Mike
Dowdell, Dorothy (Florence) Karns
1910- CANR-44
Earlier sketches in CA 9-12R, CANR-5, 20
See also SATA 12
Dowden, Anne Ophelia 1907- CANR-18
Earlier sketches in CA 9-12R, CANR-3
See also SAAS 10
See also SATA 7
Dowden, Edward 1843(?)-1913 181
See also DLB 35, 149
Dowden, George 1932- CANR-22
Earlier sketches in CA 53-56, CANR-4
Dowden, Wilfred S(ellers) 1917- 125
Dowdey, Clifford (Shirley, Jr.)
1904-1979 .... 9-12R
Dowdey, Landon Gerald 1923- 89-92
See also SATA 11
Dowding, Hugh Caswell Tremenheere
1882-1970
Obituary 112
Dowdy, Andrew 1936- 49-52
Dowdy, Cecelia D. 1966- 231
Dowdy, Homer E(arl) 1922- 5-8R
Dowdy, Mrs. Regera
See Gorey, Edward (St. John)
Dowdy, Mrs. Regera
See Gorey, Edward (St. John)
Dowell, Coleman 1925-1985 .... CANR-10
Obituary 117
Earlier sketch in CA 25-28R
See also CLC 60
See also DLB 130
See also GLL 2
Dowell, Frances O'Roark 233
See also SATA 157
Dowell, Jack (Larder) 1908- 57-60

Cumulative Index 159 Drake

Dowell, Richard W(alker) 1931- 116
Dower, J. W.
  See Dower, John W(illiam)
Dower, John W(illiam) 1938- CANR-78
  Brief entry 128
  Earlier sketch in CA 137
  Interview in CA-137
Dower, Penn
  See Pendower, Jacques
Dowie, James Iverne 1911- 41-44R
Dowie, Mark 1939- 85-88
Dowlah, A. F.
  See Dowlah, Caf
Dowlah, Alex F.
  See Dowlah, Caf
Dowlah, Caf 1958- 175
Dowland, John 1563-1626 .... DLB 172
Dowlatabadi, Mahmud
  See Dawlatabadi, Mahmud
Dowler, James R(oss) 1925- CANR-64
  Earlier sketch in CA 29-32R
  See also TCWW 1, 2
Dowley, D. M.
  See Marrison, L(eslie) W(illiam)
Dowley, Timothy Edward 1946- CANR-18
  Earlier sketch in CA 101
Dowling, Allan D. 1903-1983
  Obituary 117
Dowling, Allen 1900-1981 .... 29-32R
Dowling, Basil (Cairns) 1910-2000 97-100
  See also CP 1, 2
Dowling, David (Hurst) 1950- 118
Dowling, Eddie 1894-1976
  Obituary 65-68
Dowling, Harry Filmore 1904-2000 102
Dowling, John E(lliott) 1935- 182
Dowling, Joseph A(lbert) 1926- 37-40R
Dowling, Maria 1955- CANR-105
  Earlier sketch in CA 123
Dowling, Terry 1947- 161
  See also HGG
  See also SATA 101
  See also SFW 4
Dowling, Thomas, Jr. 1921- 85-88
Dowling, Tom
  See Dowling, Thomas, Jr.
Down, Goldie (Malvern) 1918- CANR-51
  Earlier sketches in CA 25-28R, CANR-11, 26
Down, Michael (Graham) 1951- CANR-42
  Earlier sketch in CA 118
Downard, William L. 1940- 49-52
Downer, Alan S(eymour)
  1912-1970 .... CANR-94
  Obituary 33-36R
  Earlier sketches in CAP-1, CA 11-12
Downer, Ann 1960- 230
  See also SATA 155
Downer, Lesley 1949- CANR-95
  Earlier sketch in CA 131
Downer, Marion 1892(?)-1971
  Obituary 33-36R
  See also SATA 25
Downes, Bryan Trevor 1939- 33-36R
Downes, David A(nthony) 1927- 33-36R
Downes, Edward (Olin Davenport)
  1911-2001 105
  Obituary 202
Downes, G. V.
  See Downes, Gwladys (Violet)
Downes, Gwladys (Violet) 1915- CANR-96
  Earlier sketch in CA 147
  See also DLB 88
Downes, Jeremy M. 1961- 235
Downes, Kerry 1930- 119
Downes, Mollie Patricia Panter
  See Panter-Downes, Mollie Patricia
Downes, Quentin
  See Harrison, Michael
Downes, Randolph C(handler)
  1901-1975 49-52
  Obituary 61-64
Downey, Bill
  See Downey, William L(eslie)
Downey, Fairfax D(avis) 1893-1990 ... CANR-1
  Obituary 131
  Earlier sketch in CA 1-4R
  See also SATA 3
  See also SATA-Obit 66
Downey, Glanville 1908-1991 .... CANR-94
  Earlier sketches in CA 1-4R, CANR-1
Downey, Harris 13-16R
Downey, James 1939- 101
Downey, Lawrence William (Lorne)
  1921- 17-20R
Downey, Murray William 1910- CANR-1
  Earlier sketch in CA 1-4R
Downey, Tom 236
Downey, William L(eslie) 1922- 110
Downie, Freda (Christina) 1929-1993 106
Downie, Jill 1938- CANR-25
  Earlier sketch in CA 108
Downie, John 1931- CANR-26
  Earlier sketch in CA 108
  See also SATA 87
Downie, Leonard, Jr. 1942- CANR-1
  Earlier sketch in CA 49-52
Downie, Mary Alice (Dawe) 1934- .. CANR-52
  Earlier sketches in CA 25-28R, CANR-10, 26
  See also CWRI 5
  See also SATA 13, 87
Downie, N(orville) M(organ)
  1910-1994 .... 17-20R
Downing, A(rthur) B(enjamin) 1915- 29-32R
Downing, Andrew Jackson .... DLB 254
Downing, Chris(tine) 1931- 57-60
Downing, David A(lmon) 1950- 150
  See also SATA 84
Downing, David C(laude) 1951- 146
Downing, Douglas 1957- 114
Downing, Graham 1954- 136
Downing, J. Major
  See Davis, Charles A.
Downing, John (Allen) 1922- CANR-20
  Earlier sketches in CA 53-56, CANR-5
Downing, Julie 1956- .... SATA 81, 148
Downing, Lester N. 1914-2002 .... CANR-25
  Earlier sketches in CA 25-28R, CANR-10
Downing, Major Jack
  See Smith, Seba
Downing, Michael (Bernard)
  1958- CANR-120
  Earlier sketch in CA 166
Downing, Noel
  See Shreffler, Philip A.
Downing, Paul B(utler) 1938- 104
Downing, Paula E. 1951- 136
  See also SATA 80
Downing, Taylor 195
Downing, Warwick 1931- CANR-117
  Earlier sketch in CA 53-56
  See also SATA 138
Downing, Wick
  See Downing, Warwick
Downs, Anthony 1930- CANR-28
  Earlier sketch in CA 49-52
Downs, Brian W(esterdale) 1893-1984
  Obituary 112
Downs, Cal W. 1936- 103
Downs, Donald (Alexander) 1948- 119
Downs, Dorothy 1937- 151
Downs, Hugh (Malcolm) 1921- CANR-135
  Earlier sketches in CA 45-48, CANR-2
Downs, Hunton (Leache) 1918- 1-4R
Downs, Jacques M. 1926- 37-40R
Downs, James Francis 1926- 81-84
Downs, Lenthiel H(owell) 1915- 25-28R
Downs, Norton 1918-1985 .... 1-4R
  Obituary 114
Downs, Robert B.
  See Downs, Robert B(ingham)
Downs, Robert B(ingham)
  1903-1991 .... CANR-82
  Obituary 133
  Earlier sketches in CA 1-4R, CANR-2, 17
Downs, Robert C. S. 1937- CANR-91
  Earlier sketches in CA 45-48, CANR-1
Downs, William Randall, Jr. 1914-1978 .. 81-84
  Obituary 77-80
Dowpreeth, Hughbridge
  See Kay, Jeremy
Dowriche, Anne 1560-1613(?) .... DLB 172
Dowse, Robert E. 1933- 21-24R
Dowse, (Dale) Sara 1938- 119
  See also CN 7
Dowsey-Magog, Paul 1950- 105
Dowson, Ernest (Christopher) 1867-1900 ... 150
  Brief entry 105
  See also DLB 19, 135
  See also RGEL 2
  See also TCLC 4
Dowst, Somerby R(ohrer) 1926-1990 .... 33-36R
  Obituary 133
Dowty, Alan K. 1940- 122
Doxey, Roy W(atkins) 1908-1992 .... 41-44R
Doxey, William S(anford, Jr.) 1935- .. CANR-25
  Earlier sketches in CA 65-68, CANR-9
Doxiadis, Apostolos (C.) 1953- 195
Doxiadis, Constantinos Apostolos
  1913-1975 .... 41-44R
  Obituary 57-60
Doy, Gen 1948- 191
Doyle, A. Conan
  See Doyle, Sir Arthur Conan
Doyle, Adrian M. C.
  See Conan Doyle, Adrian Malcolm
Doyle, Sir Arthur Conan
  1859-1930 .... CANR-131
  Brief entry 104
  Earlier sketch in CA 122
  See also Conan Doyle, Arthur
  See also AAYA 14
  See also BRWS 2
  See also CDBLB 1890-1914
  See also CMW 4
  See also DA
  See also DA3
  See also DAB
  See also DAC
  See also DAM MST, NOV
  See also DLB 18, 70, 156, 178
  See also EXPS
  See also HGG
  See also LAIT 2
  See also MSW
  See also MTCW 1, 2
  See also MTFW 2005
  See also RGEL 2
  See also RGSF 2
  See also RHW
  See also SATA 24
  See also SCFW 1, 2
  See also SFW 4
  See also SSC 12, 83
  See also SSFS 2
  See also TCLC 7
  See also TEA
  See also WCH
  See also WLC
  See also WLIT 4
  See also WYA
  See also YAW
Doyle, Brian 1930- 53-56
Doyle, Brian 1935- CANR-140
  Earlier sketches in CA 135, CANR-55
  See also AAYA 16
  See also CCA 1
  See also CLR 22
  See also JRDA
  See also MAICYA 1, 2
  See also SAAS 16
  See also SATA 67, 104, 156
  See also YAW
Doyle, Charles (Desmond) 1928- CANR-51
  Earlier sketches in CA 25-28R, CANR-11, 26
  See also CP 1, 2, 3, 4, 5, 6, 7
Doyle, Charlotte (Lackner) 1937- ... CANR-129
  Earlier sketches in CA 81-84, CANR-65
  See also SATA 94
Doyle, Conan
  See Doyle, Sir Arthur Conan
Doyle, David
  See Carter, David C(harles)
Doyle, Debra 1952- CANR-137
  Earlier sketch in CA 165
  See also Appleton, Victor
  See also SATA 105
Doyle, Denis P. 1940- CANR-26
  Earlier sketch in CA 109
Doyle, Dennis M(ichael) 1952- 225
Doyle, Don H(arrison) 1946- CANR-14
  Earlier sketch in CA 81-84
Doyle, Donovan
  See Boegehold, Betty (Doyle)
Doyle, Edward (Gerard) 1949- 118
Doyle, Edward Park 1907-1985
  Obituary 115
Doyle, Esther M. 1910- 45-48
Doyle, Frank D. 1909(?)-1983
  Obituary 109
Doyle, Gerald A. 1898(?)-1986
  Obituary 119
Doyle, Gerald O.
  See Beckett, Ralph L(awrence) (Sr.)
Doyle, Harold Edmund
  See Stearns, Harold Edmund
Doyle, James (Stephen) 1935- 73-76
Doyle, Jeff (C.) 1952- 239
Doyle, Jerry
  See Doyle, Gerald A.
Doyle, John
  See Graves, Robert (von Ranke)
Doyle, John Robert, Jr. 1910-1998 .... 25-28R
Doyle, Kirby 1932- 177
  See also DLB 16
Doyle, Laura 1967- 211
Doyle, Malachy 1954- 191
  See also CLR 83
  See also SATA 120
Doyle, Mary Ellen 1932- 114
Doyle, Mary K. 1954- 213
Doyle, Michael W. 1948- 120
Doyle, Mike
  See Doyle, Charles (Desmond)
Doyle, Noreen 237
Doyle, Paul A. 1925- CANR-92
  Earlier sketches in CA 13-16R, CANR-7, 22
Doyle, Paul E. 1946- 234
Doyle, Paul I(gnatius) 1959- 143
Doyle, Richard 1824-1883 .... SATA 21
Doyle, Richard 1948- 85-88
Doyle, Richard Edward 1929-1987 113
Doyle, Richard J(ames) 1923- 65-68
Doyle, Robert C(harles) 1946- CANR-91
  Earlier sketch in CA 145
Doyle, Robert J. 1931- 143
Doyle, Robert V(aughn) 1916- CANR-9
  Earlier sketch in CA 65-68
Doyle, Roddy 1958- CANR-128
  Earlier sketches in CA 143, CANR-73
  See also AAYA 14
  See also BRWS 5
  See also CLC 81, 178
  See also CN 6, 7
  See also DA3
  See also DLB 194
  See also MTCW 2
  See also MTFW 2005
Doyle, Sir A. Conan
  See Doyle, Sir Arthur Conan
Doyle, William 1942- CANR-86
  Earlier sketch in CA 130
Doyno, Victor A(nthony) 1937- 37-40R
Dozer, Donald Marquand
  1905-1980 .... CANR-1
  Earlier sketch in CA 1-4R
Dozier, Craig Lanier 1920- 41-44R
Dozier, Edward P. 1916-1971
  Obituary 29-32R
Dozier, Robert R. 1932- 120
Dozier, Zoe
  See Browning, Dixie (Burrus)
Dozois, Gardner R(aymond)
  1947- CANR-124
  Earlier sketches in CA 108, CANR-27
  See also SFW 4
Dr. A
  See Asimov, Isaac and
  Silverstein, Alvin and
  Silverstein, Virginia B(arbara Opshelor)
Dr. Alphabet
  See Morice, Dave
Dr. Fred
  See Bortz, Alfred B(enjamin)
Dr. Guano
  See Gootenberg, Paul
Dr. Hip
  See Schoenfeld, Eugene
Dr. Hippocrates
  See Schoenfeld, Eugene
Dr. Judy
  See Kuriansky, Judith (Anne Brodsky)
Dr. Laura
  See Schlessinger, Laura (Catherine)
Dr. Loon
  See Martien, Jerry
Dr. NO
  See Many, Seth E(dward)
Dr. Paula
  See Elbirt, Paula M.
Dr. Rock
  See Bordowitz, Hank
Dr. Romance
  See Tessina, Tina B.
Dr. Ruth
  See Westheimer, Ruth K(arola)
Dr. Science
  See Coffey, Daniel
Dr. Seuss
  See Geisel, Theodor Seuss and
  LeSieg, Theo. and Seuss, Dr. and
  Stone, Rosetta
  See also AAYA 48
  See also CLR 1, 9, 53, 100
Dr. Spektor
  See Glut, Donald F(rank)
Dr. Zed
  See Penrose, Gordon
Drabble, Margaret 1939- CANR-131
  Earlier sketches in CA 13-16R, CANR-18, 35, 63, 112
  See also BRWS 4
  See also CDBLB 1960 to Present
  See also CLC 2, 3, 5, 8, 10, 22, 53, 129
  See also CN 1, 2, 3, 4, 5, 6, 7
  See also CPW
  See also DA3
  See also DAB
  See also DAC
  See also DAM MST, NOV, POP
  See also DLB 14, 155, 231
  See also EWL 3
  See also FW
  See also MTCW 1, 2
  See also MTFW 2005
  See also RGEL 2
  See also SATA 48
  See also TEA
Drabble, Phil 1914- 102
Drabeck, Bernard A. 1932- 129
Drabek, Jan 1935- 93-96
Drabek, Thomas E(dward) 1940- CANR-37
  Earlier sketches in CA 45-48, CANR-1, 16
Drach, Albert 1902-1995 180
  See also DLB 85
Drache, Sharon (Abron) 1943- CANR-47
  Earlier sketch in CA 118
Drachkovitch, Milorad M. 1921-1996 .. 17-20R
Drachler, Jacob 1909-1998 61-64
Drachler, Rose 1911-1982 .... CANR-4
  Earlier sketch in CA 53-56
Drachman, Bernard 1861-1945 229
Drachman, Edward Ralph 1940- 29-32R
Drachman, Julian M(oses) 1894-1983 61-64
Drachman, Theodore S(olomon)
  1904-1988 81-84
Drachmann, Holger 1846-1908 .... DLB 300
Drackett, Phil(ip Arthur) 1922- CANR-3
  Earlier sketch in CA 9-12R
  See also SATA 53
Draco, F.
  See Davis, Julia
Dracup, Angela 1943- 141
  See also SATA 74
Drage, Charles H(ardinge) 1897- CANR-2
  Earlier sketch in CA 5-8R
Drager, Marvin 1920- 81-84
Dragisic, Patricia 188
  See also SATA 116
Dragland, Stan L(ouis) 1942- CANR-52
  Earlier sketch in CA 125
Dragnich, Alex N. 1912- CANR-15
  Earlier sketch in CA 89-92
Drago, Edmund Leon 1942- 109
Drago, Harry Sinclair 1888-1979 ..... CANR-63
  Obituary 89-92
  Earlier sketch in CA 113
  See also TCWW 1, 2
Drago, Sinclair
  See Drago, Harry Sinclair
Dragojevic, Danijel 1934- .... DLB 181
Dragon, Caroline
  See Du Breuil, (Elizabeth) L(or)inda
Dragonette, Jessica 1910(?)-1980
  Obituary 97-100
Dragonwagon, Crescent 1952- CANR-111
  Earlier sketches in CA 65-68, CANR-12, 36, 89
  See also BYA 8
  See also JRDA
  See also MAICYA 1, 2
  See also SAAS 14
  See also SATA 11, 41, 75, 133
Dragun, Osvaldo 1929-1999 .... DLB 305
  See also EWL 3
  See also HW 1
  See also LAW
Drahos, Mary 1927- 116
Drainie, Bronwyn 1945- 129
Draitser, Emil 1937- CANR-18
  Earlier sketch in CA 89-92
Drakakis, John 1944- 120
Drake, Albert (Dee) 1935- CANR-43
  Earlier sketches in CA 33-36R, CANR-13
Drake, Alice Hutchins 1889(?)-1975
  Obituary 61-64

Drake, Alison
See Janeshutz, Patricia M(arie)
Drake, Asa (a pseudonym) ... 113
Drake, Barbara (Ann Robertson) 1939- ... CANR-97
Earlier sketches in CA 33-36R, CANR-13
See also CWP
Drake, Bonnie
See Delinsky, Barbara (Ruth Greenberg)
Drake, Charles D(ominic) 1924- ... 116
Drake, Connie
See Feddersen, Connie
Drake, David (Allen) 1945- ... CANR-88
Earlier sketches in CA 93-96, CANR-17, 38
See also AAYA 38
See also SATA 85
See also SFW 4
Drake, Donald C(harles) 1935- ... 85-88
Drake, Earl G. 1928- ... 230
Drake, Elizabeth 1948- ... 109
Drake, Francis Vivian 1894-1971
Obituary ... 104
Drake, Frank
See Hamilton, Charles (Harold St. John)
Drake, Frank D(onald) 1930- ... 17-20R
Drake, Frederick Charles 1937- ... 119
Drake, George Randolph 1938- ... CANR-11
Earlier sketch in CA 69-72
Drake, H(enry) B(urgess) 1894-1963 ... HGG
Drake, Harold Allen 1942- ... 97-100
Drake, James A. 1944- ... 130
Drake, Jane 1954- ... 149
See also SATA 82
Drake, Joan H(oward) ... CANR-24
Earlier sketch in CA 13-16R
Drake, Joseph Rodman 1795-1820 ... RGAL 4
Drake, Kimbal
See Gallagher, Rachel
Drake, Lisl
See Beer, Eloise C. S.
Drake, Michael 1935- ... CANR-16
Earlier sketch in CA 25-28R
Drake, Paul Winter 1944- ... 106
Drake, Richard Bryant 1925- ... CANR-109
Earlier sketch in CA 37-40R
Drake, Robert (Young, Jr.) 1930- ... 17-20R
Drake, (John Gibbs) St. Clair (Jr.) 1911-1990 ... CANR-75
Obituary ... 131
Earlier sketch in CA 65-68
Drake, Samuel Gardner 1798-1875 ... DLB 187
Drake, Shannon
See Pozzessere, Heather Graham
Drake, (Bryant) Stillman 1910- ... CANR-40
Earlier sketches in CA 41-44R, CANR-18
Drake, Timothy A. 1967- ... 211
Drake, W. Anders
See Eshbach, Lloyd Arthur
Drake, W(inbourne) Magruder 1914- ... 41-44R
Drake, W(alter) Raymond 1913-1989 ... CANR-5
Earlier sketch in CA 53-56
Drake, William D(onovan) 1922- ... 21-24R
Drake, William Daniel 1941- ... 69-72
Drake, William E(arle) 1903-1989 ... CAP-1
Earlier sketch in CA 17-18
Drake-Brockman, David 1933- ... 114
Drakeford, Dale B(enjamin) 1952- ... 185
See also SATA 113
Drakeford, John W. 1914- ... CANR-5
Earlier sketch in CA 1-4R
Drakulic, Slavenka 1949- ... CANR-92
Earlier sketch in CA 144
See also CLC 173
Drakulic-Ilic, Slavenka
See Drakulic, Slavenka
Dralle, Elizabeth (Mary) 1910-1993 ... 1-4R
Drane, James F. 1930- ... CANR-7
Earlier sketch in CA 13-16R
Drane, John (William) 1946- ... CANR-15
Earlier sketch in CA 93-96
Drange, Theodore M. 1934- ... 37-40R
Dranoff, Linda Silver ... CANR-64
Earlier sketch in CA 129
Dranow, John (Theodore) 1948- ... 140
Dransfield, Michael (John Pender) 1948-1973 ... CANR-30
Earlier sketch in CA 37-40R
Drant, Thomas 1540(?)-1578(?) ... DLB 167
Drape, Joe ... 200
Draper, Alfred 1924- ... CANR-53
Earlier sketches in CA 33-36R, CANR-13, 29
Draper, Cena C(hristopher) 1907- ... CANR-10
Earlier sketch in CA 17-20R
Draper, Charles Stark 1901-1987 ... 157
Draper, Edgar 1926- ... 13-16R
Draper, (Ellinor) Elizabeth (Nancy) 1915- ... 17-20R
Draper, Ellen Dooling 1944- ... 195
Draper, Hal 1914-1990 ... CANR-76
Obituary ... 130
Earlier sketches in CA 17-20R, CANR-7, 24
Draper, Hastings
See Jeffries, Roderic (Graeme)
Draper, James P(atrick) 1959- ... 143
Draper, James T(homas), Jr. 1935- ... 89-92
Draper, Jo 1949- ... CANR-43
Earlier sketch in CA 119
Draper, John W. 1811-1882 ... DLB 30
Draper, John William 1893-1976 ... CANR-16
Obituary ... 69-72
Earlier sketches in CAP-1, CA 9-10
Draper, Lydia
See Gershgoren Novak, Estelle
Draper, Lyman C. 1815-1891 ... DLB 30
Draper, Maureen McCarthy 1941- ... 204
Draper, Norman R(ichard) 1931- ... 53-56
Draper, Polly 1956- ... 232
Draper, Robert 1959(?)- ... 204
Draper, Ronald Philip 1928- ... 69-72
Draper, Sharon M(ills) ... CANR-124
Earlier sketch in CA 170
See also AAYA 28
See also CLR 57
See also MAICYA 2
See also SATA 98, 146
See also SATA-Essay 146
See also YAW
Draper, Theodore 1912- ... 13-16R
Draper, Thomas 1928- ... 108
Drapier, M. B.
See Swift, Jonathan
Drapkin, Herbert 1916- ... 33-36R
Drapkin, Israel 1906-1990 ... 57-60
Draskovich, Slobodan M. 1910-1982 ... CANR-75
Obituary ... 108
Earlier sketch in CA 93-96
Drath, Viola Herms 1926- ... CANR-14
Earlier sketch in CA 65-68
Draugsvold, Ottar G. 1946- ... 198
Drawbell, James Wedgwood 1899-1979 . 65-68
Drawe, D. Lynn 1942- ... CANR-93
Earlier sketch in CA 146
Drawson, Blair 1943- ... CANR-105
Earlier sketch in CA 85-88
See also SATA 17, 126
Dray, Philip ... 204
Dray, William H(erbert) 1921- ... CANR-13
Earlier sketch in CA 33-36R
Drayer, Adam Matthew 1913-1995 ... 9-12R
Drayham, James
See Mencken, H(enry) L(ouis)
Drayne, George
See McCulley, Johnston
Drayson, Nicholas 1954- ... 215
Drayton, Michael 1563-1631 ... DAM POET
See also DLB 121
See also RGEL 2
Drazan, Joseph Gerald 1943- ... 110
Drazin, Charles 1960- ... 222
Drazin, Israel 1935- ... 151
Dre, Dr. 1965(?)- ... 156
Dreadstone, Carl
See Campbell, (John) Ramsey
Drebinger, John 1891(?)-1979
Obituary ... 89-92
Drefus, Jean-Paul Etienne 1909-1985
Obituary ... 117
Dreger, Georgia 1918- ... 115
Dreger, Ralph Mason 1913- ... 73-76
Dregni, Michael 1961- ... 238
Dreher, Carl 1896-1976 ... 73-76
Dreher, Diane Elizabeth 1946- ... CANR-115
Earlier sketch in CA 119
Dreher, Henry 1955- ... 149
Dreher, Melanie (Creagan) 1943- ... 114
Dreher, Sarah 1937- ... GLL 2
Dreier, Hans 1885-1966 ... IDFW 3, 4
Dreifort, John E. 1943- ... 45-48
Dreifus, Claudia 1944- ... CANR-1
Earlier sketch in CA 45-48
Dreifuss, Kurt 1897-1991 ... CANR-16
Obituary ... 171
Earlier sketches in CA 1-4R, CANR-1
Dreikurs, Rudolf 1897-1972 ... CANR-6
Obituary ... 33-36R
Earlier sketch in CA 1-4R
Dreiser, Theodore (Herman Albert) 1871-1945 ... 132
Brief entry ... 106
See also AMW
See also AMWC 2
See also AMWR 2
See also BYA 15, 16
See also CDALB 1865-1917
See also DA
See also DA3
See also DAC
See also DAM MST, NOV
See also DLB 9, 12, 102, 137
See also DLBD 1
See also EWL 3
See also LAIT 2
See also LMFS 2
See also MAL 5
See also MTCW 1, 2
See also MTFW 2005
See also NFS 8, 17
See also RGAL 4
See also SSC 30
See also TCLC 10, 18, 35, 83
See also TUS
See also WLC
Dreiser, Vera -1998 ... 69-72
Dreiss, Joseph G. 1949- ... 125
Dreiss-Tarasovic, Marcia M(argaret) 1943- ... 65-68
Dreitzel, Hans Peter 1935- ... 41-44R
Drekmeier, Charles 1927- ... 1-4R
Drennen, D(onald) A(rthur) 1925- ... CANR-17
Earlier sketches in CA 1-4R, CANR-2
Dresang, Eliza (Carolyn Timberlake) 1941- ... 69-72
See also SATA 19
Dresbach, Glen Ward 1889-1968 ... 5-8R
Drescher, Fran 1957- ... CANR-115
Earlier sketch in CA 155
Drescher, Henrik 1955- ... 135
See also CLR 20
See also MAICYA 1, 2
See also SATA 67, 105
Drescher, Joan E(lizabeth) 1939- ... 106
See also SATA 30, 137
Drescher, John 1960- ... 228
Drescher, John M(ummau) 1928- ... CANR-16
Earlier sketches in CA 49-52, CANR-1
Drescher, Sandra 1957- ... CANR-16
Earlier sketch in CA 85-88
Drescher, Seymour 1934- ... CANR-94
Earlier sketches in CA 9-12R, CANR-4
Drescher-Lehman, Sandra
See Drescher, Sandra
Dresner, Hal 1937- ... 13-16R
Dresner, Samuel H(ayim) 1923- ... CANR-9
Earlier sketch in CA 5-8R
Dressel, Paul L(eroy) 1910-1989 ... CANR-3
Earlier sketch in CA 9-12R
Dresselhaus, Mildred S. 1930- ... 157
Dresser, Davis 1904-1977 ... CANR-49
Obituary ... 69-72
Earlier sketch in CA 77-80
See also Halliday, Brett
See also CMW 4
See also DLB 226
See also TCWW 1, 2
Dresser, Helen
See McCloy, Helen (Worrell Clarkson)
Dresser, Norine 1931- ... 132
Dressler, Alan (Michael) 1948- ... 147
Dressler, Joshua 1947- ... 199
Dressler, Mylene 1963- ... 231
Dressman, Dennis L(ee) 1945- ... 106
Dressman, Denny
See Dressman, Dennis L(ee)
Dressman, John 1947- ... 122
Dretske, Frederick I(rwin) 1932- ... CANR-10
Earlier sketch in CA 25-28R
Dreux, William B(ehan) 1911-1983 ... 89-92
Dreves, Veronica R. 1927-1986
Obituary ... 121
See also SATA-Obit 50
Drevet, Patrick (Francois Antoine) 1948- ... 236
Drew, Bernard 1926(?)-1984
Obituary ... 111
Drew, Bettina 1956- ... CANR-109
Earlier sketch in CA 151
Drew, Donald J. 1920- ... 57-60
Drew, Eileen 1957- ... 143
Drew, Elizabeth 1887-1965 ... 5-8R
Drew, Elizabeth 1935- ... CANR-142
Earlier sketch in CA 104
Interview in ... CA-104
Drew, Fraser Bragg Robert 1913- ... 13-16R
Drew, George A(lexander) 1894-1973
Obituary ... 113
Drew, Horace R. III 1955- ... 169
Drew, Katherine Fischer 1923- ... 9-12R
Drew, Kenneth
See Cockburn, (Francis) Claud
Drew, Mary Anne
See Cassiday, Bruce (Bingham)
Drew, Morgan
See Price, Robert
Drew, Patricia (Mary) 1938- ... 77-80
See also SATA 15
Drew, Philip 1943- ... 107
Drew, Simon 1952- ... 171
Drew, Wayland 1932-1998 ... 154
See also FANT
See also SFW 4
Drew-Bear, Robert 1901-1991 ... CAP-2
Earlier sketch in CA 33-36
Drewe, Robert (Duncan) 1943- ... CANR-99
Earlier sketch in CA 138
See also CN 4, 5, 6, 7
Drewery, Mary 1918- ... 25-28R
See also SATA 6
Drewes, Athena A. 1948- ... 146
Drewitz, Ingeborg 1923-1986 ... 178
See also DLB 75
Drewnowski, Jan 1908- ... CANR-68
Earlier sketch in CA 129
Drewry, Guy Carleton 1901-1991 ... CANR-75
Obituary ... 135
Earlier sketch in CA 5-8R
Drewry, Henry N(athaniel) 1924- ... CANR-117
Earlier sketch in CA 97-100
See also SATA 138
Drewry, John E(ldridge) 1902-1983
Obituary ... 109
Drexel, Jay B.
See Bixby, Jerome Lewis
Drexelius, J.
See Gourmont, Remy(-Marie-Charles) de
Drexler, Arthur 1925-1987 ... CANR-76
Obituary ... 121
Earlier sketch in CA 97-100
Drexler, J. F.
See Paine, Lauran (Bosworth)
Drexler, K(im) Eric 1955- ... CANR-48
Earlier sketch in CA 121
Drexler, Rosalyn 1926- ... CANR-124
Earlier sketches in CA 81-84, CANR-68
See also CAD
See also CD 5, 6
See also CLC 2, 6
See also CWD
See also MAL 5
Dreyer, Carl Theodor 1889-1968
Obituary ... 116
See also CLC 16
Dreyer, Edward C. 1937- ... 21-24R
Dreyer, Eileen 1952- ... 224
Dreyer, Frederick 1932- ... 111
Dreyer, Peter (Richard) 1939- ... 81-84
Dreyfack, Raymond ... CANR-24
Earlier sketches in CA 65-68, CANR-9
Dreyfus, Edward A(lbert) 1937- ... 37-40R
Dreyfus, Fred
See Rosenblatt, Fred
Dreyfus, Hubert L(ederer) 1929- ... CANR-143
Earlier sketches in CA 33-36R, CANR-28
Dreyfus, Kay 1942- ... 124
Dreyfuss, Henry 1904-1972 ... 45-48
Obituary ... 37-40R
Dreyfuss, Joel 1945- ... 97-100
Dreyfuss, Larry 1928- ... 65-68
Dreyfuss, Randolph (Lowell) 1956- ... 97-100
Drez, Ronald J(oseph) 1940- ... CANR-120
Earlier sketch in CA 146
Dreze, Jean 1959- ... CANR-82
Earlier sketch in CA 133
Drial, J. E.
See Laird, Jean E(louise)
Dribben, Judith Strick 1923- ... 37-40R
Driberg, Thomas Edward Neil 1905-1976 ... 65-68
Obituary ... 104
Driberg, Tom
See Driberg, Thomas Edward Neil
Driedger, Leo ... CANR-93
Earlier sketch in CA 146
Driesen, David M. 1958- ... 235
Driessen, Paul 1940- ... IDFW 3, 4
Drieu la Rochelle, Pierre(-Eugene) 1893-1945
Brief entry ... 117
See also DLB 72
See also EWL 3
See also GFL 1789 to the Present
See also TCLC 21
Driftwood, Penelope
See De Lima, Clara Rosa
Drimmer, Frederick 1916-2000 ... CANR-23
Obituary ... 190
Earlier sketches in CA 61-64, CANR-7
See also SATA 60
See also SATA-Obit 124
Drinan, Adam
See Macleod, Joseph (Todd Gordon)
See also CP 1
Drinan, Robert F(rederick) 1920- ... CANR-3
Earlier sketch in CA 9-12R
Dring, Nathaniel
See McBroom, R. Curtis
Drinkall, Gordon (Don) 1927- ... 9-12R
Drinker, Elizabeth 1735-1807 ... DLB 200
Drinkle, Ruth Wolfley 1903-1993 ... 93-96
Drinkrow, John
See Hardwick, (John) Michael (Drinkrow)
Drinkwater, Carol 1948- ... 207
Drinkwater, Francis Harold 1886- ... CANR-1
Earlier sketch in CA 1-4R
Drinkwater, John 1882-1937 ... 149
Brief entry ... 109
See also DLB 10, 19, 149
See also RGEL 2
See also TCLC 57
Drinkwater, Terry 1936-1989 ... 69-72
Obituary ... 128
Drinnon, Richard 1925- ... CANR-6
Earlier sketch in CA 13-16R
Driscoll, Eli
See King, Albert
Driscoll, Gertrude 1898(?)-1975
Obituary ... 61-64
Driscoll, Jack 1946- ... 188
Driscoll, James P. 1946- ... 146
Driscoll, Jeanne Watson ... 220
Driscoll, Peter (John) 1942- ... CANR-2
Earlier sketch in CA 49-52
See also CMW 4
Driscoll, R(obert) E(ugene) 1949- ... 85-88
Driscoll, Richard
See Gorman, Edward
Driskell, David Clyde 1931- ... 102
Driskill, Frank A. 1912-1987 ... 130
Driskill, J. Lawrence 1920- ... 155
See also SATA 90
Driskill, Larry
See Driskill, J. Lawrence
Driver, C(harles) J(onathan) 1939- ... CANR-57
Earlier sketches in CA 29-32R, CANR-30
See also CN 2, 3, 4, 5, 6, 7
See also CP 1
Driver, Christopher (Prout) 1932-1997 ... 57-60
Obituary ... 156
Driver, Cynthia C.
See Lovin, Roger Robert
Driver, David E. 1955- ... CANR-80
Earlier sketch in CA 155
See also BW 3
Driver, Donald 1922-1988
Obituary ... 125
Driver, Edwin D(ouglas) 1925- ... 114
Driver, Felix ... 229
Driver, Godfrey Rolles 1892-1975 ... CAP-2
Obituary ... 57-60
Earlier sketch in CA 21-22
Driver, Harold Edson 1907- ... CANR-6
Earlier sketch in CA 1-4R
Driver, Tom F(aw) 1925- ... CANR-1
Earlier sketch in CA 1-4R
Driving Hawk, Virginia
See Sneve, Virginia Driving Hawk
Drlica, Karl 1943- ... 151
Drobot, Eve 1951- ... 131
Droege, Thomas Arthur 1931- ... 113
Droescher, Vitus B(ernward) 1925- ... 33-36R
Drogheda, Earl of
See Moore, Charles Garrett Ponsonby
Drogin, Karen ... 236
Droit, Michel (Arnould Arthur) 1923-2000 ... CANR-32
Obituary ... 188
Earlier sketches in CA 5-8R, CANR-11
Drooker, Eric 1958- ... 196
Droppers, Carl Hyink 1918- ... 5-8R

Drop Shot
See Cable, George Washington
Dror, Yehezkel 1928- CANR-13
Earlier sketch in CA 21-24R
Drosnin, Michael 1946- 163
Drossaart Lulofs, H(endrik) J(oan) 1906- 13-16R
Droste-Hulshoff, Annette Freiin von 1797-1848 .... CDWLB 2
See also DLB 133
See also RGSF 2
See also RGWL 2, 3
Drotar, David Lee 1952- 112
Drotning, Phillip T(homas) 1920- CANR-10
Earlier sketch in CA 25-28R
Drought, James (William) 1931-1983 .... CANR-20
Obituary 110
Earlier sketch in CA 5-8R
Drouin, Francis M. 1901-1985 .... 37-40R
Drouin, Marie-Josee 1949- 116
Drowatzky, John N(elson) 1936- 89-92
Drower, E(thel) S(tefana May) 1879-1972 .... CAP-1
Earlier sketch in CA 11-12
Drower, G(eorge) M(atthew) F(rederick) 1954- 131
Drown, Harold J(ames) 1904-1991 49-52
Drown, Merle 1943- CANR-91
Earlier sketch in CA 109
Drowne, Tatiana B(alkoff) 1913-1994 ... 17-20R
Droz, Eugenie 1893(?)-1976
Obituary 104
Droz, Vanessa 1952- 195
Droze, Wilmon H(enry) 1924- CANR-10
Earlier sketch in CA 17-20R
Drubert, John H. 1925- 45-48
Druce, Christopher
See Pulling, Christopher Robert Druce
Drucker, Daniel Charles 1918-2001 157
Obituary 199
Drucker, Doris 1910(?)- 235
Drucker, H. M.
See Drucker, Henry M(atthew)
Drucker, Henry M(atthew) 1942-2002 .... CANR-29
Obituary 211
Earlier sketch in CA 106
Drucker, Johanna 1952- CANR-138
Earlier sketch in CA 151
See also CP 7
Drucker, Malka 1945- CANR-31
Earlier sketches in CA 81-84, CANR-14
See also SATA 39, 111
See also SATA-Brief 29
Drucker, Mark L(ewis) 1947- 107
Drucker, Mort 1929- 133
Drucker, Olga Levy 1927- 147
See also SATA 79
Drucker, Peter 1958- 147
Drucker, Peter F(erdinand) 1909- CANR-96
Earlier sketches in CA 61-64, CANR-46
Druett, Joan 1939- 218
Earlier sketches in CA 140, CANR-100
Autobiographical Essay in 218
Druffel, Ann 1926- 218
Drukker, J.
See Presser, (Gerrit) Jacob
Druks, Herbert 1937- CANR-9
Earlier sketch in CA 21-24R
Drum, Alice 1935- 154
Drum, Bob
See Drum, Robert F.
Drum, Robert F. 1918- 5-8R
Drumheller, Sidney J(ohn) 1923- 53-56
Drumm, D. B.
See Naha, Ed and Shirley, John
Drummond, Alison 1903-1984 112
Drummond, Donald F(rasier) 1914-1983 .... CANR-4
Earlier sketch in CA 1-4R
Drummond, Dorothy W(eitz) 1928- 41-44R
Drummond, Edith Marie Dulce Carman 1883-1970 .... CAP-1
Earlier sketch in CA 9-10
Drummond, Edward H. 1953- 211
Drummond, Ellen Lane 1897-1981 .... 1-4R
Drummond, Emma .... RHW
Drummond, Harold D. 1916- CANR-12
Earlier sketch in CA 33-36R
Drummond, Ian (Macdonald) 1933- 37-40R
Drummond, Ivor
See Longrigg, Roger (Erskine)
Drummond, Jack 1923(?)-1978
Obituary 81-84
Drummond, John
See Chance, John Newton
Drummond, John 1900-1982
Obituary 106
Drummond, John (Dodds) 1944- CANR-87
Earlier sketch in CA 102
Drummond, June 1923- CANR-72
Earlier sketches in CA 13-16R, CANR-7
See also CMW 4
Drummond, Kenneth H(erbert) 1922- ... 17-20R
Drummond, Maldwin Andrew Cyril 1932- CANR-14
Earlier sketch in CA 73-76
Drummond, Michael 1964- 232
Drummond, Richard H(enry) 1916- 41-44R
Drummond, (James) Roscoe 1902-1983 104
Obituary 110
Drummond, V(iolet) H(ilda) 1911-2000 .... 13-16R
See also CWRI 5
See also SATA 6
Drummond, Walter
See Silverberg, Robert
Drummond, William
See Calder-Marshall, Arthur
Drummond, William Henry 1854-1907 160
See also DLB 92
See also TCLC 25
Drummond, William Joe 1944- 77-80
See also BW 1
Drummond de Andrade, Carlos 1902-1987 132
Obituary 123
See also Andrade, Carlos Drummond de
See also CLC 18
See also DLB 307
See also LAW
See also TCLC 139
Drummond of Hawthornden, William 1585-1649 .... DLB 121, 213
See also RGEL 2
Drummy, Michael F. 1956- 212
Druon, Maurice (Samuel Roger Charles) 1918- CANR-12
Earlier sketch in CA 13-16R
Drury, Alan 1949- 106
Drury, Allen (Stuart) 1918-1998 .... CANR-52
Obituary 170
Earlier sketches in CA 57-60, CANR-18
Interview in CANR-18
See also CLC 37
See also CN 1, 2, 3, 4, 5, 6
Drury, Clare Marie
See Hoskyns-Abrahall, Clare (Constance Drury)
Drury, Clifford Merrill 1897-1984 ...... CANR-3
Earlier sketch in CA 9-12R
Drury, George H(erbert) 1940- CANR-47
Earlier sketch in CA 121
Drury, James Westbrook 1919- 5-8R
Drury, Joan M. 1945- 189
Drury, John 1898-1972 .... 5-8R
Obituary 33-36R
Drury, John 1936- CANR-85
Earlier sketch in CA 133
Drury, Margaret Josephine 1937- 53-56
Drury, Maxine Cole 1914- 5-8R
Drury, Michael CANR-27
Earlier sketch in CA 49-52
Drury, Rebecca
See Barrett, Neal, Jr.
Drury, Roger W(olcott) 1914-1996 65-68
See also SATA 15
Drury, S(hadia) B(asilious) 1950- CANR-91
Earlier sketch in CA 116
Drury, Sally 1960- 139
Drury, Tom 199
Drury, Treesa Way 1937- 53-56
Drury, William 1918-1993 125
Druse, Eleanor
See King, Stephen (Edwin)
Drutman, Irving 1910-1978 85-88
Obituary 81-84
Druxman, Michael Barnett 1941- CANR-37
Earlier sketches in CA 49-52, CANR-1, 16
Druzhinin, Aleksandr Vasil'evich 1824-1864 .... DLB 238
Druzhnikov, Yuri 1933- 188
See also DLB 317
Drvota, Mojmir 1923- 57-60
Dryansky, G. Y. 49-52
Dryden, Cecil P(earl) 1887-1977 .... 25-28R
Dryden, Charles 1860(?)-1931 201
See also DLB 171
Dryden, Edgar A. 1937- 89-92
Dryden, John
See Rowland, D(onald) S(ydney)
Dryden, John 1631-1700 .... BRW 2
See also CDBLB 1660-1789
See also DA
See also DAB
See also DAC
See also DAM DRAM, MST, POET
See also DC 3
See also DLB 80, 101, 131
See also EXPP
See also IDTP
See also LMFS 1
See also PC 25
See also RGEL 2
See also TEA
See also WLC
See also WLIT 3
Dryden, Ken(neth Wayne) 1947- 105
Dryden, Lennox
See Steen, Marguerite
Dryden, Pamela
See St. John, Nicole
Dryfoos, Joy G. 1925- CANR-143
Earlier sketch in CA 172
Dryhurst, Edward
See Roberts, Edward Dryhurst
Drysdale, Frank R(eiff) 1943- 89-92
Drysdale, George Russell 1912-1981
Obituary 108
Drysdale, Helena 1960- CANR-127
Earlier sketch in CA 125
Drysdale, Vera Louise 1923- 115
Drzazga, John 1907- CAP-1
Earlier sketch in CA 11-12
Drzemczewski, Andrew (Zbigniew) 1951- .. 116
Drzic, Marin c. 1508-1567 .... CDWLB 4
See also DLB 147
D'Souza, Dinesh 1961- CANR-76
Earlier sketches in CA 118, CANR-54
See also DA3
See also MTCW 2
D.T., Hughes
See Hughes, Dean
Du, Ding-Zhu 1948- 229
Dua, R(am) P(arkash) 1930- 25-28R
Duan, Le
See Le, Duan
Duane, Daniel 1967- CANR-101
Earlier sketch in CA 159
Duane, Daniel King
See Duane, Daniel
Duane, Diane (Elizabeth) 1952- CANR-126
Earlier sketches in CA 139, CANR-66
See also AAYA 30
See also BYA 6, 10, 11
See also FANT
See also SATA 58, 95, 145
See also SATA-Brief 46
See also SFW 4
See also YAW
Duane, Jim
See Hurley, Vic
Duane, William 1760-1835 .... DLB 43
Duarte (Fuentes), Jose Napoleon 1925-1990 137
Obituary 131
Duarte, Joseph S(imon) 1913- 57-60
Dubal, David 1944- CANR-144
Earlier sketch in CA 118
Duball, Michael
See Ald, Roy A(llison)
Duban, James 1951- 125
Dubanevich, Arlene 1950- CANR-40
Earlier sketch in CA 116
See also SATA 56
Dubay, Robert W. 1943- 65-68
DuBay, Sandra 1954- CANR-47
Earlier sketches in CA 107, CANR-23
Dubay, Thomas Edward 1921- CANR-6
Earlier sketch in CA 1-4R
DuBay, William H. 1934- 17-20R
Dubber, Markus Dirk 227
Dube, Marcel 1930- 129
Brief entry 117
See also CCA 1
See also DLB 53
Dube, Pierre Herbert 1943- CANR-10
Earlier sketch in CA 65-68
Dube, Rodolphe
See Hertel, Francois
Dube, Saurabh 1960- 230
Dube, Siddharth 1961- 223
Dubelaar, Thea 1947- .... SATA 60
du Bellay, Joachim 1524-1560 . GFL Beginnings to 1789
See also RGWL 2, 3
Dubens, Eugene (M.) 1957- 217
Duberman, Lucile 1926- 69-72
Duberman, Martin (Bauml) 1930- .. CANR-137
Earlier sketches in CA 1-4R, CANR-2, 63
See also CAD
See also CD 5, 6
See also CLC 8
Duberstein, Helen 1926- CANR-44
Earlier sketches in CA 45-48, CANR-1
Duberstein, Larry 1944- 135
Dubh, Cathal O
See Duff, Charles (St. Lawrence)
Dubie, Norman (Evans) 1945- CANR-115
Earlier sketches in CA 69-72, CANR-12
See also CLC 36
See also CP 7
See also DLB 120
See also PFS 12
Dubin, Al 1891-1945 .... DLB 265
Dubin, Michael J. 1938- 137
Dubin, Robert 1916- CANR-1
Earlier sketch in CA 45-48
Dubin, Samuel Sanford 1914-1992 .... 37-40R
Dubinsky, David 1892-1982
Obituary 107
Dubinsky, Rostislav (D.) 1923- 133
Dubitsky, Cora Marie 1933- 124
Dubkin, Lois (V.) Knudson 1911- 5-8R
du Blane, Daphne
See Groom, Arthur William
Dublin, Jack 1915- 21-24R
Dublin, Thomas Louis 1946- 101
Dubner, Stephen J. 1963- CANR-130
Earlier sketch in CA 184
Dubnick, Mel(vin Jay) 1946- CANR-30
Earlier sketch in CA 112
Dubnick, Randa Kay 1948- 112
Du Boccage, Anne-Marie 1710-1802 . DLB 313
Dubofsky, Melvyn 1934- CANR-102
Earlier sketches in CA 49-52, CANR-1, 16, 37
Dubois, Brendan 212
Dubois, Charles
See Counselman, Mary Elizabeth
Du Bois, David G(raham) 1925-2005 65-68
Obituary 236
See also BW 1
Dubois, Elfrieda T(heresia Pichler) 1916- 9-12R
DuBois, Ellen Carol 1947- CANR-89
Brief entry 113
Earlier sketch in CA 136
DuBois, Josiah Ellis, Jr. 1912-1983
Obituary 114
Dubois, M.
See Kent, Arthur William Charles
duBois, Page 222
DuBois, Paul M(artin) 1945- 102
DuBois, Paul Z(inkhan) 1936- 111
DuBois, Rochelle (Lynn) Holt 1946- ... CANR-7
Earlier sketch in CA 57-60
See also Holt, Rochelle L.
DuBois, Rosemary
See Durrant, Rita D(elores)
Du Bois, Shirley Graham 1907(?)-1977 ... 77-80
Obituary 69-72
See also Graham, Shirley
See also BW 1
See also SATA 24
Dubois, Silvia 1788(?)-1889 .... DLB 239
Du Bois, W(illiam) E(dward) B(urghardt) 1868-1963 .... CANR-132
Earlier sketches in CA 85-88, CANR-34, 82
See also AAYA 40
See also AFAW 1, 2
See also AMWC 1
See also AMWS 2
See also BLC 1
See also BW 1, 3
See also CDALB 1865-1917
See also CLC 1, 2, 13, 64, 96
See also DA
See also DA3
See also DAC
See also DAM MST, MULT, NOV
See also DLB 47, 50, 91, 246, 284
See also EWL 3
See also EXPP
See also HR 1:2
See also LAIT 2
See also LMFS 2
See also MAL 5
See also MTCW 1, 2
See also MTFW 2005
See also NCFS 1
See also PFS 13
See also RGAL 4
See also SATA 42
See also TCLC 169
See also WLC
du Bois, William Pene
See Pene du Bois, William (Sherman)
Duboise, Novella 1911-1999 152
See also SATA 88
Dubos, Jean (Porter) 1918(?)-1988
Obituary 126
Dubos, Rene (Jules) 1901-1982 .... CANR-80
Obituary 106
Earlier sketches in CA 5-8R, CANR-48
Dubosarsky, Ursula (Bridget) 1961- 221
See also SATA 107, 147
See also YAW
DuBose, Fred 1945- 118
DuBose, LaRocque (Russ) 1926- 21-24R
See also SATA 2
Dubose, Lou(is H.) 1948- 226
DuBose, Louise Jones 1901-1985 .... CAP-1
Earlier sketch in CA 13-14
Dubost, Thierry 1958- CANR-122
Earlier sketch in CA 164
du Bouchet, Andre 1924- 206
Du Boulay, F(rancis) R(obin) H(oussemayne) 1920- 131
du Boulay, Shirley 1933- CANR-65
Earlier sketch in CA 129
Dubout, C(harles) A(lbert) 1905-1976
Obituary 65-68
Dubov, Gwen Bagni -2001 97-100
Obituary 196
Dubov, Paul (?)-1979 97-100
Obituary 89-92
DuBow, Fredric L(ee) 1944- 25-28R
Du Breuil, (Elizabeth) L(or)inda 1924-1980 104
Interview in CA-104
DuBrin, Andrew J(ohn) 1935- CANR-33
Earlier sketches in CA 41-44R, CANR-15
Dubro, Alec 1944- 133
Dubro, James (Richard) 1946- 129
Du Broff, Nedra 1931- 110
Du Broff, Sidney 1929- CANR-9
Earlier sketch in CA 21-24R
Dubrovin, Vivian 1931- CANR-118
Earlier sketches in CA 57-60, CANR-9, 40, 71
See also SATA 65, 139
Dubrovina, Ekaterina Oskarovna 1846-1913 204
See also DLB 238
DuBruck, Alfred J(oseph) 1922- 37-40R
DuBruck, Edelgard (Conradt) 1925- 17-20R
Du Brul, Jack B. 1968- 225
Du Brul, Paul 1938(?)-1987
Obituary 125
Dubs, Homer H(asenpflug) 1892-1969 . CAP-1
Earlier sketch in CA 13-16
Dubus, Andre III 1959- CANR-125
Earlier sketch in CA 132
See also DLB 292
See also MTFW 2005
Dubus, Andre 1936-1999 .... CANR-17
Obituary 177
Earlier sketch in CA 21-24R
Interview in CANR-17
See also AMWS 7
See also CLC 13, 36, 97
See also CN 5, 6
See also CSW
See also DLB 130
See also RGAL 4
See also SSC 15
See also SSFS 10
See also TCLE 1:1
Dubus, Elizabeth Nell 1933- 110
Duby, Georges (Michel Claude) 1919-1996 .... CANR-48
Obituary 154
Earlier sketches in CA 104, CANR-22
Duca Minimo
See D'Annunzio, Gabriele

Du Camp, Maxime 1822-1894 ..... GFL 1789 to the Present
Du Cane, Peter 1901-1984
Obituary 114
Ducange, Victor 1783-1833 .... DLB 192
du Cann, Charles Garfield Lott 1889(?)-1983
Obituary 109
Ducas, Dorothy 1905-1987 .... CANR-27
Earlier sketch in CA 5-8R
Ducasse, C(urt) J(ohn) 1881-1969 .... CANR-6
Earlier sketch in CA 1-4R
Duce, Ivy Oneita 1895-1981 232
Duce, Robert 1908- 5-8R
Ducey, Jean Sparks 1915- 158
See also SATA 93
Duchac, Joseph 1932- 144
Duchacek, Ivo D(uka) 1913-1988 .... CANR-1
Obituary 124
Earlier sketch in CA 1-4R
See also SATA-Obit 55
Du Chaillu, Paul (Belloni) 1835(?)-1903
Brief entry 112
See also DLB 189
See also SATA 26
Duchamp, (Henri-Robert) Marcel 1887-1968 116
Obituary 110
See also AAYA 47
Ducharme, Dede Fox
See Ducharme, Lilian Fox
Ducharme, Lilian Fox 1950- 194
See also SATA 122
Ducharme, Rejean 1941-
Obituary 165
See also CLC 74
See also DLB 60
du Chatelet, Emilie 1706-1749
See Chatelet, Gabrielle-Emilie Du
Duche, Jean 1915- CANR-9
Earlier sketch in CA 9-12R
Duchein, Michel 1926- 135
Duchen, Claire .... CLC 65
Duchene, Louis-Francois 1927-2005 105
Duchesne, Antoinette
See Paine, Lauran (Bosworth)
Duchesne, Jacques
See Saint-Denis, Michel Jacques
Duchesne, Janet 1930-
Brief entry 111
See also SATA-Brief 32
Duchess of Marlborough
See Spencer-Churchill, Laura
Duchess of Windsor
See Windsor, (Bessie) Wallis Warfield (Spencer) Simpson
Duchin, Faye 1944- 125
Duchin, Peter (Oelrichs) 1937- 217
Ducic, Jovan 1871-1943 .... CDWLB 4
See also DLB 147
See also EWL 3
Duck, Stephen 1705(?)-1756 .... DLB 95
See also RGEL 2
Duckat, Walter Benjamin 1911-1983 .... 29-32R
Ducker, Bruce 1938- CANR-91
Earlier sketch in CA 65-68
Ducker, James H. 1950- 130
Duckert, Mary 1929- 53-56
Duckett, Alfred A. 1917(?)-1984 45-48
Obituary 114
Duckett, Eleanor Shipley 1880(?)-1976
Obituary 69-72
Duckham, A(lec) N(arraway) 1903-1988 . 73-76
Obituary 126
Duckham, Baron Frederick 1933- 103
Duckworth, Alistair M(cKay) 1936- 41-44R
Duckworth, Eleanor 1935- 142
Duckworth, F(rancis) R(obinson) G(ladstone) 1881-1964
Obituary 113
Duckworth, George E(ckel) 1903-1972 .... CANR-1
Obituary 33-36R
Earlier sketch in CA 1-4R
Duckworth, Leslie Blakey 1904- 105
Duckworth, Marilyn (Rose Adcock) 1935- CANR-129
Earlier sketch in CA 163
See also CN 6, 7
Duckworth, William (Ervin) 1943- 151
Duclaux, Madame
See Robinson, A(gnes) Mary F(rances)
Duclaux, Madame Mary
See Robinson, A(gnes) Mary F(rances)
Duclaux, Mary
See Robinson, A(gnes) Mary F(rances)
Duclos, Charles Pinot- 1704-1772 .... GFL Beginnings to 1789
Ducornet, Erica 1943- CANR-82
Earlier sketches in CA 37-40R, CANR-14, 34, 54
See also SATA 7
Ducornet, Rikki
See Ducornet, Erica
Duda, Margaret B(arbalich) 1941- 65-68
Dudarew-Ossetynski, Leonidas 1911(?)-1989
Obituary 128
Dudden, Arthur P(ower) 1921- CANR-3
Earlier sketch in CA 5-8R
Dudek, Louis 1918-2001 .... CANR-1
Obituary 215
Earlier sketch in CA 45-48
See also CAAS 14
See also CLC 11, 19
See also CP 1, 2, 3, 4, 5, 6, 7
See also DLB 88
Duden, Jane 1947- 205
See also SATA 136
Duder, Tessa 1940- CANR-96
Earlier sketch in CA 147
See also CLR 43
See also MAICYA 2
See also MAICYAS 1
See also SAAS 23
See also SATA 80, 117
See also YAW
Dudintsev, Vladimir 1918-1998
See Dudintsev, Vladimir Dmitrievich
Dudintsev, Vladimir Dmitrievich
See Dudintsev, Vladimir
See also DLB 302
Dudley, B(illy) J(oseph) 1931- 25-28R
Dudley, Barbara Hudson 1921- 65-68
Dudley, Carl Safford 1932- CANR-44
Earlier sketch in CA 116
Dudley, Donald Reynolds 1910-1972 .... CANR-99
Earlier sketches in CA 5-8R, CANR-4
Dudley, Edward 1926- 45-48
Dudley, Ellen 182
Dudley, Ellen 1938- 171
Dudley, Ernest 1908- 13-16R
Dudley, Geoffrey A(rthur) 1917-1992 . CANR-6
Earlier sketch in CA 13-16R
Dudley, Guilford, Jr. 1907-2002 .... CAP-2
Obituary 206
Earlier sketch in CA 19-20
Dudley, Guilford A(llerton) 1921-1972 . 41-44R
Dudley, Helen
See Hope Simpson, Jacynth
Dudley, James F. 1942- 130
Dudley, Jay
See Chapman, J. Dudley
Dudley, Lavinia P(ratt) 1891(?)-1984
Obituary 113
Dudley, Louise 1884-1975 73-76
Dudley, Martha Ward 1909(?)-1985
Obituary 117
See also SATA-Obit 45
Dudley, Nancy
See Cole, Lois Dwight
Dudley, Robert
See Baldwin, James
Dudley, Ruth H(ubbell) 1905-2001 61-64
See also SATA 11
Dudley Edwards, Ruth 1944- 107
Dudley-Gordon, Tom
See Barker, Dudley
Dudley-Smith, T.
See Trevor, Elleston
Dudley-Smith, Timothy 1926- 103
Dudman, Clare 229
Dudman, Martha Tod 1952- 207
Dudman, Richard (Beebe) 1918- 45-48
Due, Linnea A. 1948- CANR-139
Earlier sketch in CA 105
See also MTFW 2005
See also SATA 64
Due, Tananarive 1966- CANR-123
Earlier sketch in CA 170
See also MTFW 2005
See also SUFW 2
Dueck, Adele 1955- 163
See also SATA 97
Dueker, Christopher W(ayne) 1939- 57-60
Dueker, Joyce S(utherlin) 1942- 57-60
Dueland, Joy V(ivian) 106
See also SATA 27
Duell, Charles Halliwell 1905-1970
Obituary 104
Duerig, Alfred W. 1926- 129
Duerr, Edwin 1904-1985 73-76
Duerr, Gisela 1968- .... SATA 89
Duerrenmatt, Friedrich 1921-1990 .... CANR-33
Earlier sketch in CA 17-20R
See also Durrenmatt, Friedrich
See also CLC 1, 4, 8, 11, 15, 43, 102
See also CMW 4
See also DAM DRAM
See also DLB 69, 124
See also MTCW 1, 2
Duettmann, Martina (Friederike) 1938- 142
Duey, Kathleen 1950- 201
See also SATA 132
Dufallo, Richard 1933-2000 133
Obituary 188
Dufault, Joseph Ernest Nephtali
See James, Will(iam Roderick)
Dufault, Peter Kane 1923- CANR-123
Earlier sketch in CA 33-36R
Dufault, Roseanna Lewis 1954- 138
Duff, Alan 1950- 147
See also CN 6, 7
See also EWL 3
Duff, Annis (James) 1904(?)-1986
Obituary 120
See also SATA-Obit 49
Duff, Carolyn S. 1941- 189
Duff, Charles (St. Lawrence) 1894-1966 .... CANR-95
Earlier sketches in CA 1-4R, CANR-2
Duff, David Skene 1912- 128
Brief entry 118
Duff, Ernest A(rthur) 1929- 25-28R
Duff, Gerald (Aldine) 1938- CANR-118
Earlier sketch in CA 45-48
Duff, John B. 1931- CANR-1
Earlier sketch in CA 45-48
Duff, Maggie
See Duff, Margaret K(app)
Duff, Margaret K(app) 1916-2003 .... CANR-14
Obituary 217
Earlier sketch in CA 37-40R
See also SATA 37
See also SATA-Obit 144
Duff, Raymond S(tanley) 1923- 21-24R
Duffee, David E(ugene) 1946- 104
Dufferin, Lady Helen 1807-1867 .... DLB 199
Duffett, Michael 1943- 212
Duffey, Bernard I. 1917- 114
Duffey, Betsy (Byars) 1953- 200
See also SATA 80, 131
Duffey, Margery 1926- 73-76
Duff Gordon, Lucie 1821-1869 .... DLB 166
Duffie, Charles 1960- 217
See also SATA 144
Duffield, Anne (Tate) 1893-1976 .... CAP-1
Earlier sketch in CA 13-16
See also RHW
Duffield, Katy S. 1961- .... SATA 147
Duffield, Wendell A. 1941- 234
Duffin, Henry Charles 1884- CAP-1
Earlier sketch in CA 9-10
Duffus, R(obert) L(uther) 1888-1972 101
Obituary 37-40R
Duffy, Ben
See Duffy, Bernard C.
Duffy, Bernard C. 1902-1972
Obituary 37-40R
Duffy, Bernard K. 1948- 187
Duffy, Brian 1954- 143
Duffy, Bruce 1953(?)- 172
See also CLC 50
Duffy, Carol Ann 1955- CANR-120
Earlier sketches in CA 119, CANR-70
See also CP 7
See also CWP
See also SATA 95
Duffy, Charles 1940- 104
Duffy, Clinton T(ruman) 1898-1982
Obituary 108
Duffy, Dennis 1938- 113
Duffy, Eamon CANR-141
Earlier sketch in CA 166
Duffy, Edmund 1899-1962
Obituary 93-96
Duffy, Edward (Thomas) 1942- 229
Duffy, Elizabeth 1904-1970(?) CAP-2
Earlier sketch in CA 19-20
Duffy, Francis R(amon) 1915- CANR-30
Earlier sketch in CA 49-52
Duffy, Helene (Krainovich) 1926- 17-20R
Duffy, James (Edward) 1923- 129
Duffy, James H(enry) 1934- 131
Duffy, James P(atrick) 1941- 237
Duffy, Jean H. 1955- 190
Duffy, John 1915- CANR-8
Earlier sketch in CA 17-20R
Duffy, John 1963- 223
Duffy, John J(oseph) 1934- 57-60
Duffy, Kevin 1929- 147
Duffy, Margaret 1942- CANR-73
Earlier sketch in CA 139
Duffy, Maureen (Patricia) 1933- CANR-68
Earlier sketches in CA 25-28R, CANR-33
See also CBD
See also CLC 37
See also CN 1, 2, 3, 4, 5, 6, 7
See also CP 7
See also CWD
See also CWP
See also DFS 15
See also DLB 14, 310
See also FW
See also MTCW 1
Duffy, Patricia Lynne 1952- 220
Duffy, Peter 1969- 225
Duffy, Regis Anthony 1934- 110
Duffy, Susan 1951- 199
Dufief, Nicholas Gouin 1776-1834 .... DLB 187
Dufner, Max 1920- 145
Dufrechou, Carole
See Monroe, Carole
Dufresne, Isabelle 1935- 136
DuFresne, Jim 1955- 154
Dufresne, John (Louis) 1948- 202
Earlier sketches in CA 139, CANR-61, 97
Autobiographical Essay in 202
See also CSW
See also DLB 292
Dufty, William (F.) 1916-2002 65-68
Obituary 208
Du Fu
See Tu Fu
See also RGWL 2, 3
Dugan, Alan 1923-2003 .... CANR-119
Obituary 220
Earlier sketch in CA 81-84
See also CLC 2, 6
See also CP 1, 2, 3, 4, 5, 6, 7
See also DLB 5
See also MAL 5
See also PFS 10
Dugan, George 1909-1982
Obituary 107
Dugan, J(ohn) Raymond 1935- 121
Dugan, Jack
See Butterworth, W(illiam) E(dmund III)
Dugan, James (Thomas) 1912-1967 .... CANR-4
Earlier sketch in CA 5-8R
Dugan, Michael (Gray) 1947- CANR-64
Earlier sketches in CA 77-80, CANR-14, 32
See also SATA 15
Dugard, C. J(ohn) R. 1936- 85-88
Dugard, Martin 184
du Gard, Roger Martin
See Martin du Gard, Roger
Dugard, William 1606-1662 .... DLB 170, 281
Dugas, Marcel 1883-1947 177
See also DLB 92
Dugaw, Dianne (M.) 1948- 239
Dugdale, Robert
See Hardy, Henry
Duggan, Alfred Leo 1903-1964 73-76
See also RHW
See also SATA 25
Duggan, Christopher 1957- 155
Duggan, Eileen (May) 1894-1972 .... CP 1
See also RGEL 2
Duggan, George Henry 1912- 17-20R
Duggan, Joseph J(ohn) 1938- CANR-140
Earlier sketch in CA 29-32R
Duggan, Laurence James 1949- 153
See also CP 7
Duggan, Laurie
See Duggan, Laurence James
Duggan, Mary M. 1921- 25-28R
Duggan, Maurice (Noel) 1922-1974 .... CANR-17
Obituary 53-56
Earlier sketch in CA 73-76
See also CN 1, 2
See also CWRI 5
See also RGEL 2
See also RGSF 2
See also SATA 40
See also SATA-Obit 30
Duggan, P(atrick) G. 1945- 213
Duggan, William 1952- 122
Duggan, William Redman 1915- 69-72
Duggans, Pat
See Connolly, Robert D(uggan, Jr.)
Dugger, Ronnie 1930- CANR-12
Earlier sketch in CA 21-24R
Duggins, James (Harry), Jr. 1933- 37-40R
Duggleby, John 1952- 159
See also SATA 94
Dughi, Nancy -1993 .... 1-4R
Dugin, Andrej 1955- .... SATA 77
Dugina, Olga 1964- .... SATA 77
Dugmore, Clifford W(illiam) 1909-1990 .... 13-16R
Obituary 132
Duguid, Charles 1884- 109
Duguid, John Bright 1895-1980
Obituary 102
Duguid, Naomi 174
Duguid, Robert
See Pring-Mill, Robert D(uguid) F(orrest)
Duguid, Stephen 1943- 212
Duhamel, Denise 1961- 207
Duhamel, Georges 1884-1966 .... CANR-35
Obituary 25-28R
Earlier sketch in CA 81-84
See also CLC 8
See also DLB 65
See also EWL 3
See also GFL 1789 to the Present
See also MTCW 1
Duhamel, Marcel 1900(?)-1977
Obituary 104
Duhamel, P(ierre) Albert 1920- 5-8R
du Hault, Jean
See Grindel, Eugene
Duhl, Leonard J. 1926- 13-16R
Duhon, Christine
See Orban, Christine
Duigan, John 1949- 164
Duignan, Peter 1926- CANR-11
Earlier sketch in CA 13-16R
Duijker, Hubrecht 1942- 183
Duiker, K. Sello 1974- 233
Duiker, William J(ohn) 1932- CANR-100
Earlier sketches in CA 85-88, CANR-16
Duina, Francesco G. 1969- 201
Duinkerken, Anton van
See Asselbergs, Wilhelmus Johannes Maria Antonius
Duis, Perry R. 1943- 124
Dujardin, Edouard (Emile Louis) 1861-1949
Brief entry 109
See also DLB 123
See also TCLC 13
du Jardin, Rosamond Neal 1902-1963 .... 1-4R
Obituary 103
See also SATA 2
Dujarric, Robert 1961(?)- 236
Duka, Ivo
See Duchacek, Ivo D(uka)
Duka, John 1949-1989
Obituary 127
Dukakis, Katharine 1937(?)- 135
Dukakis, Kitty
See Dukakis, Katharine
Dukakis, Olympia 1931- 227
Duke, Alvah (Carter) 1908-1984 45-48
Duke, Anna Marie 1946- 130
Duke, Benjamin 1931- 49-52
Duke, Charles (Richard) 1940- CANR-28
Earlier sketches in CA 69-72, CANR-11
Duke, David C. 1940- 112
Duke, Donald Norman 1929- CANR-7
Earlier sketch in CA 17-20R
Duke, Forrest R(eagan) 1918- 77-80
Duke, James A. 1929- 135
Duke, James T(aylor) 1933- 65-68
Duke, Jim
See Duke, James A.
Duke, John
See Chalmers, Floyd S(herman)
Duke, Judith S(ilverman) 1934- 118
Duke, Kate 1956- 188
See also CLR 51
See also MAICYA 2
See also SATA 90, 148
Duke, Madelaine (Elizabeth) 1925- CANR-9
Earlier sketch in CA 57-60
Duke, Martin 1930- 138

Cumulative Index 163 Dundes

Duke, Maurice 1934- 112
Duke, Michael Geoffrey Hare
See Hare Duke, Michael Geoffrey
Duke, Michael S. 1940- 136
Duke, Patty
See Duke, Anna Marie
Duke, Raoul
See Thompson, Hunter S(tockton)
Duke, Richard DeLaBarre 1930- 57-60
Duke, Robin (Antony Hare) 1916-1984
Obituary 115
Duke, Simon (William) 1959- 127
Duke, Steven B. 1934- 144
Duke, Vernon 1903-1969 .... CAP-2
Earlier sketch in CA 29-32
Duke, Will
See Gault, William Campbell
Duke-Elder, Stewart 1896-1978
Obituary 77-80
Dukelsky, Vladimir
See Duke, Vernon
Duke of Beaufort
See Somerset, Henry Hugh Arthur FitzRoy
Duke of Brunswick-Luneburg
See Ulrich, Anton
Duker, Abraham G(ordon) 1907-1987 53-56
Obituary 164
Duker, Sam 1905-1978 .... 13-16R
Obituary 77-80
Dukert, Joseph M(ichael) 1929- CANR-3
Earlier sketch in CA 5-8R
Dukes, Ashley 1885-1959 183
Brief entry 110
See also DLB 10
Dukes, Paul 1889-1967
Obituary 112
Dukes, Paul 1934- CANR-9
Earlier sketch in CA 21-24R
Dukes, Philip
See Bickers, Richard (Leslie) Townshend
Dukes, Tyrone 1946(?)-1983
Obituary 110
Dukore, Bernard F. 1931- CANR-53
Earlier sketches in CA 25-28R, CANR-12, 29
Dukore, Margaret Mitchell 1950- CANR-23
Earlier sketch in CA 106
Dukthas, Ann
See Doherty, P(aul) C.
Dulac, Edmund 1882-1953 .... SATA 19
Dulack, Thomas 1935- 25-28R
Dulaney, W. Marvin 1950- 156
Dulany, Don E., Jr. 1928- 69-72
Dulany, Harris 1940- 33-36R
Dulbecco, Renato 1914- 157
Dulieu, Jean
See van Oort, Jan
Dull, Jonathan R(omer) 1942- 69-72
Dulles, Allen W(elsh) 1893-1969 .... CAP-2
Earlier sketch in CA 23-24
Dulles, Avery (Robert) 1918- CANR-21
Earlier sketches in CA 9-12R, CANR-3
Dulles, Eleanor Lansing 1895-1996 .... 9-12R
Obituary 154
Dulles, Foster Rhea 1900-1970 .... CAP-1
Obituary 29-32R
Earlier sketch in CA 13-14
Dulles, John Foster 1888-1959 149
Brief entry 115
See also TCLC 72
Dulles, John W(atson) F(oster)
1913- CANR-107
Earlier sketches in CA 1-4R, CANR-1
Duloup, Victor
See Volkoff, Vladimir
Dulsey, Bernard M. 1914-1992 .... 9-12R
Duman, Daniel 1948- 129
Dumarchais, Pierre 1882-1970
Obituary 29-32R
Dumarchey, Pierre
See Dumarchais, Pierre
Dumas, Alexandre (pere) 1802-1870 .. AAYA 22
See also BYA 3
See also DA
See also DA3
See also DAB
See also DAC
See also DAM MST, NOV
See also DLB 119, 192
See also EW 6
See also GFL 1789 to the Present
See also LAIT 1, 2
See also NFS 14, 19
See also RGWL 2, 3
See also SATA 18
See also TWA
See also WCH
See also WLC
Dumas, Alexandre (fils) 1824-1895 .... DC 1
See also DLB 192
See also GFL 1789 to the Present
See also RGWL 2, 3
Dumas, Andre 1918- CANR-29
Earlier sketches in CA 73-76, CANR-13
Dumas, Claire
See Van Weddingen, Marthe
Dumas, Claudine
See Malzberg, Barry N(athaniel)
du Mas, Frank (Maurice) 1918- 106
Dumas, Frederic 1913- 69-72
Dumas, Gerald J. 1930- 25-28R
Dumas, Henry L. 1934-1968 85-88
See also BW 1
See also CLC 6, 62
See also DLB 41
See also RGAL 4
Dumas, Jacqueline 1946- 123
See also SATA 55
Dumas, James 1929- 184
Dumas, Jim
See Dumas, James
Dumas, Philippe 1940- CANR-97
Earlier sketch in CA 107
See also SATA 52, 119
Dumas, Spider
See Dumas, James
Dumas, Timothy 184
du Maurier, Daphne 1907-1989 .... CANR-55
Obituary 128
Earlier sketches in CA 5-8R, CANR-6
See also AAYA 37
See also BPFB 1
See also BRWS 3
See also CLC 6, 11, 59
See also CMW 4
See also CN 1, 2, 3, 4
See also CPW
See also DA3
See also DAB
See also DAC
See also DAM MST, POP
See also DLB 191
See also GL 2
See also HGG
See also LAIT 3
See also MSW
See also MTCW 1, 2
See also NFS 12
See also RGEL 2
See also RGSF 2
See also RHW
See also SATA 27
See also SATA-Obit 60
See also SSC 18
See also SSFS 14, 16
See also TEA
Du Maurier, George 1834-1896 . DLB 153, 178
See also RGEL 2
Dumbauld, Edward 1905-1997 129
Dumbleton, Mike 1948- .... SATA 73, 124
Dumbleton, William A(lbert) 1927- 37-40R
Dumbraveanu, Anghel 1933- .... EWL 3
Dumbrell, John 1950- 151
Dumenil, Lynn 1950- 125
Dumery, Henry 1920 101
Dumezil, Georges (Edmond Raoul)
1898-1986 165
Obituary 120
Dumitriu, Petru 1924-2002 155
Brief entry 116
Dumke, Edward J. 1946- 124
Dumke, Glenn S. 1917-1989 .... CANR-31
Obituary 129
Earlier sketch in CA 112
Dummett, (Agnes Margaret) Ann 1930- 135
Dummett, Michael Anthony Eardley
1925- 102
See also DLB 262
Dumond, Dwight Lowell 1895-1976 69-72
Obituary 65-68
Dumont, Jean-Paul 1940- CANR-12
Earlier sketch in CA 73-76
Dumoulin, Heinrich 1905-1995 .... CANR-4
Earlier sketch in CA 5-8R
Dumper, Michael (Ricardo Thomas) 1956- . 222
Dumpleton, John Le F(evre) 1924- 13-16R
Dumpty, Humpty S.
See Denenberg, Herbert S(idney)
Dun, Angus 1892-1971
Obituary 33-36R
Dun, Mao
See Yen-Ping, Shen
See also RGSF 2
Dunant, Sarah 1950- CANR-91
Earlier sketch in CA 131
Dunas, Joseph C. 1900-1987 .... 17-20R
Dunathan, Arni T(homas) 1936- 53-56
Dunaway, David King 1948- 107
Dunaway, Faye 1941- 155
Dunaway, John M(arson) 1945- 89-92
Dunayevskaya, Raya 1910-1987 130
Obituary 122
Dunbabin, J(ohn) P(aul) D(elacour)
1938- 69-72
Dunbabin, Jean 1939- 119
Dunbar, Alice
See Nelson, Alice Ruth Moore Dunbar
Dunbar, Alice Moore
See Nelson, Alice Ruth Moore Dunbar
Dunbar, Andrea 1961(?)-1990 231
See also CBD
See also CD 5
See also CWD
Dunbar, Anthony P. 1949- CANR-71
Earlier sketch in CA 33-36R
Dunbar, Charles Stuart 1900-1992 107
Dunbar, David
See Baxter, Craig
Dunbar, Dorothy 1923- 9-12R
Dunbar, Edward
See Smith, David MacLeod
Dunbar, Ernest 1927- 25-28R
Dunbar, Gary S(eamans) 1931- 144
Dunbar, Janet 1901-1989 .... CANR-97
Obituary 129
Earlier sketches in CA 9-12R, CANR-6
Dunbar, John Greenwell 1930- 21-24R
Dunbar, Joyce 1944- CANR-137
Earlier sketch in CA 144
See also SATA 76, 112, 162
Dunbar, Leslie W(allace) 1921- CANR-52
Earlier sketch in CA 125
Dunbar, Maxwell John 1914-1995 103
Dunbar, Paul Laurence 1872-1906 ... CANR-79
Brief entry 104
Earlier sketch in CA 124
See also AFAW 1, 2
See also AMWS 2
See also BLC 1
See also BW 1, 3
See also CDALB 1865-1917
See also DA
See also DA3
See also DAC
See also DAM MST, MULT, POET
See also DLB 50, 54, 78
See also EXPP
See also MAL 5
See also PC 5
See also RGAL 4
See also SATA 34
See also SSC 8
See also TCLC 2, 12
See also WLC
Dunbar, Polly 1980(?)- 237
Dunbar, Robert E(verett) 1926- CANR-34
Earlier sketches in CA 85-88, CANR-15
See also SATA 32
Dunbar, Robert George 1907- 114
Dunbar, Sophie 1946-2001 199
Dunbar, Tony
See Dunbar, Anthony P.
Dunbar, William 1460(?)-1520(?) .... BRWS 8
See also DLB 132, 146
See also PC 67
See also RGEL 2
Dunbar, Willis F(rederick)
1902-1970 .... CANR-4
Earlier sketch in CA 5-8R
Dunbar, Wylene (Wisby) 1949- 229
Dunbar-Nelson, Alice
See Nelson, Alice Ruth Moore Dunbar
See also HR 1:2
Dunbar-Nelson, Alice Moore
See Nelson, Alice Ruth Moore Dunbar
Dunbaugh, Frank Montgomery
1895-1976 45-48
Duncan, A(nthony) D(ouglas) 1930- 33-36R
Duncan, Alastair 1942- CANR-40
Earlier sketch in CA 117
Duncan, Alex
See Duke, Madelaine (Elizabeth)
Duncan, Alexandra
See Moore, Ishbel (Lindsay)
Duncan, Alice 1945- 215
See also Sharpe, Jon
Duncan, Alice Faye 1967- 160
See also SATA 95
Duncan, Alistair (Charteris) 1927- 61-64
Duncan, Andy 1964- 227
Duncan, Archibald A(lexander) M(cBeth)
1926- 81-84
Duncan, Ardinelle Bean 1913-2002 .... 1-4R
Duncan, Bill 1953- 212
Duncan, (Reid) Bingham 1911-1979 85-88
Duncan, Bowie 1941- 33-36R
Duncan, C(yril) J(ohn) 1916- 25-28R
Duncan, Carl P(orter) 1921-1999
Brief entry 115
Duncan, Carol Greene 1936- 145
Duncan, Charles T(homas) 1914-1997 .. 17-20R
Duncan, Chester 1913-2002 93-96
Duncan, Christine H. 225
Duncan, Clyde H. 1903-1986 .... 17-20R
Duncan, Colin A(drien) M(acKinley)
1954- 162
Duncan, Cynthia M. 199
Duncan, Dave 1933- CANR-88
Earlier sketch in CA 143
See also BYA 13
See also DLB 251
See also FANT
See also SFW 4
See also SUFW 2
Duncan, David 1913-1999 .... 5-8R
See also SFW 4
Duncan, David Douglas 1916- CANR-92
Brief entry 112
Earlier sketch in CA 145
See also AITN 1
Duncan, David James 1952- CANR-112
Earlier sketch in CA 169
See also DLB 256
Duncan, Dayton 1949- CANR-144
Earlier sketch in CA 127
Duncan, Delbert J(ames) 1895-1980 ..... 41-44R
Duncan, Denis (Macdonald) 1920- .. CANR-23
Earlier sketch in CA 107
Duncan, Dora Angela
See Duncan, Isadora
Duncan, Dougal 1921- 102
Duncan, Duke
See Rathborne, St. George (Henry)
Duncan, Elmer H(ubert) 1933- 69-72
Duncan, Florence Belle 1917(?)-1980
Obituary 97-100
Duncan, (Sandy) Frances (Mary)
1942- CANR-37
Earlier sketches in CA 97-100, CANR-17
See also SATA-Brief 48
Duncan, George
See Davison, Geoffrey
Duncan, Glen 1965- 239
Duncan, Gregory
See McClintock, Marshall
Duncan, Harry (Alvin) 1916-1997 162
Duncan, Helen (Harger Bodwell) 1902- 125
Duncan, Hugh Dalziel 1909-1970 .... CAP-2
Earlier sketch in CA 23-24
Duncan, Irma 1897-1977 49-52
Obituary 73-76
Duncan, Isadora 1877(?)-1927 149
Brief entry 118
See also TCLC 68
Duncan, Jane
See Cameron, Elizabeth Jane
Duncan, Jennifer 1967- 229
Duncan, Jennifer Ann 1940-1989
Obituary 128
Duncan, Joseph E(llis) 1921- 5-8R
Duncan, Julia Coley
See Sather, Julia Coley Duncan
Duncan, Julia K. CANR-27
Earlier sketches in CAP-2, CA 19-20
See also Benson, Mildred (Augustine Wirt)
See also SATA 1
Duncan, Kenneth S(andilands) 1912- 9-12R
Duncan, Kunigunde 1886-1971 .... 5-8R
Duncan, Lois 1934- CANR-111
Earlier sketches in CA 1-4R, CANR-2, 23, 36
See also AAYA 4, 34
See also BYA 6, 8
See also CLC 26
See also CLR 29
See also JRDA
See also MAICYA 1, 2
See also MAICYAS 1
See also MTFW 2005
See also SAAS 2
See also SATA 1, 36, 75, 133, 141
See also SATA-Essay 141
See also WYA
See also YAW
Duncan, Marion Moncure 1913-1978
Obituary 77-80
Duncan, Mark (Winchester) 1952- 130
Duncan, Norman 1871-1916
Brief entry 117
See also CWRI 5
See also DLB 92
See also YABC 1
Duncan, Otis Dudley 1921-2004 ..... CANR-22
Obituary 233
Earlier sketches in CA 13-16R, CANR-6
Duncan, Pam 1938- 37-40R
Duncan, Patrick Sheane CANR-122
Earlier sketch in CA 169
Duncan, Philip D. 1957- 158
Duncan, Pope A(lexander) 1920-2003 .. 13-16R
Obituary 222
Duncan, Quince 1940- 178
See also DLB 145
See also HW 1
Duncan, Robert (Edward)
1919-1988 .... CANR-62
Obituary 124
Earlier sketches in CA 9-12R, CANR-28
See also BG 1:2
See also CLC 1, 2, 4, 7, 15, 41, 55
See also CP 1, 2
See also DAM POET
See also DLB 5, 16, 193
See also EWL 3
See also MAL 5
See also MTCW 1, 2
See also MTFW 2005
See also PC 2
See also PFS 13
See also RGAL 4
See also WP
Duncan, Robert 1942-1988 .... GLL 1
Duncan, Robert F. 1890(?)-1974
Obituary 53-56
Duncan, Robert L(ipscomb) 1927-1999 106
Obituary 173
See also CAAS 2
Duncan, Roger F. 1916- 216
Duncan, Ronald 1914-1982 .... CANR-4
Obituary 107
Earlier sketch in CA 5-8R
See also CP 1, 2
See also DLB 13
See also RGEL 2
Duncan, Sara Jeannette 1861-1922 157
See also DLB 92
See also TCLC 60
Duncan, T. Bentley 1929- 77-80
Duncan, Terence
See Nolan, William F(rancis)
Duncan, Theodore G(arfield) 1928- 128
Duncan, Thomas (William)
1905-1987 .... CANR-1
Earlier sketch in CA 1-4R
Duncan, W(illiam) Murdoch
1909-1976 .... CANR-6
Earlier sketch in CA 13-16R
Duncan, W. R.
See Duncan, Robert L(ipscomb)
Duncan, W. Raymond 1936- 41-44R
Duncan, Wilbur H(oward) 1910- 116
Duncan, William (Robert) 1944- 115
Duncanson, Michael E(dward) 1948- 57-60
Duncker, Patricia 1951- CANR-124
Earlier sketch in CA 163
Duncombe, David C(ameron) 1928- 29-32R
Duncombe, Frances (Riker)
1900-1994 .... CANR-96
Obituary 146
Earlier sketch in CA 25-28R
See also SATA 25
See also SATA-Obit 82
Dundee, Robert
See Kirsch, Robert R.
Dundes, Alan 1934-2005 .... CANR-52
Obituary 237
Earlier sketches in CA 21-24R, CANR-9, 26

Dundy, Elaine 1927- CANR-143
Earlier sketches in CA 97-100, CANR-67
See also CN 2, 3, 4, 5, 6, 7
Duneier, Mitchell 1961(?)- CANR-103
Earlier sketch in CA 144
Dunford, Judith 1933- 107
Dunford, Warren 1963- 220
Dung, Van Tien 1917-2002 144
Obituary 205
Dungan, David L(aird) 1936- 123
Dunham, Arthur 1893-1980 33-36R
Dunham, Barrows 1905-1995 5-8R
Dunham, Bob
See Dunham, Robert
Dunham, Donald Carl 1908-2000 CANR-17
Earlier sketch in CA 1-4R
Dunham, H(enry) Warren
1906-1985 CANR-8
Obituary 118
Earlier sketch in CA 13-16R
Dunham, John L. 1939- 29-32R
Dunham, Katherine 1910- CANR-17
Earlier sketch in CA 65-68
See also BW 1
Dunham, Lowell 1910- 37-40R
Dunham, (Bertha) Mabel 1881-1957
Brief entry 114
Dunham, Mikel 1948- 138
Dunham, Montrew (Goetz) 1919- 17-20R
See also SATA 162
Dunham, Robert 1931- 69-72
Dunham, William 1947- 133
Dunham, William Huse, Jr. 1901-1982 49-52
Dunhill, Alfred H(enry) 1896(?)-1971
Obituary 104
Dunhill, Mary 1907(?)-1988
Obituary 124
Duning, George 1908- IDFW 3, 4
Dunk, Thomas W. 1955- 139
Dunkel, Elizabeth 1951- 142
Dunkel, Harold Baker 1912-1990 5-8R
Dunkel, Richard H(adley) 1933- 73-76
Dunkell, Samuel (V.) 1919-
Brief entry 115
Dunkelman, Ben(jamin) 1913-1997
Brief entry 111
Dunker, Marilee (Pierce) 1950- 171
Dunkerley, Elsie Jeanette (?)-1960
Obituary 116
Dunkerley, James 1953- CANR-118
Earlier sketch in CA 131
Dunkerley, Roderic 1884- CAP-1
Earlier sketch in CA 13-14
Dunkin, Paul S(haner) 1905-1975 CAP-2
Earlier sketch in CA 33-36
Dunkle, Clare B. 1964- 237
See also SATA 155
Dunkle, William F(rederick), Jr.
1911-1984 53-56
Dunkley, Christopher 1944- 121
Dunkley, Graham (Royce) 1946- 171
Dunkling, Leslie Alan 1935- CANR-14
Earlier sketch in CA 81-84
Dunkman, William E(dward)
1903-1987 CAP-2
Earlier sketch in CA 25-28
Dunlap, Anna
See Higgins, Anna Dunlap
Dunlap, Aurie N(ichols) 1907-1977 37-40R
Dunlap, David W. 157
Dunlap, G(eorge) D(ale) 1923- 49-52
Dunlap, Jan 65-68
Dunlap, Jane
See Davis, Adelle
Dunlap, John 1747-1812 DLB 43
Dunlap, Joseph R(iggs) 1913- 85-88
Dunlap, Julie 1958- 150
See also SATA 84
Dunlap, Leslie W(hittaker) 1911- 37-40R
Dunlap, Lon
See McCormick, Wilfred
Dunlap, Orrin E(lmer), Jr. 1896-1970 CAP-1
Earlier sketch in CA 11-12
Dunlap, Pat
See Dunlap, Patricia Riley
Dunlap, Patricia Riley 1943- 162
Dunlap, Susan 1943- CANR-115
Earlier sketch in CA 165
See also CMW 4
Dunlap, Thomas R(ichard) 1943- 126
Dunlap, William 1766-1839 DLB 30, 37, 59
See also RGAL 4
Dunlay, Thomas W. 1944- 112
Dunleavy, Deborah 1951- 202
See also SATA 133
Dunleavy, Gareth W(inthrop) 1923- 33-36R
Dunleavy, Janet Egleson 1928- CANR-21
Earlier sketches in CA 57-60, CANR-6
Dunleavy, Patrick 1952- 123
Dunlop, Agnes M. R. (?)-1982 CANR-9
Earlier sketch in CA 13-16R
See also Kyle, Elisabeth
See also SATA 87
Dunlop, Derrick Melville 1902-1980
Obituary 101
Dunlop, Douglas Morton 1909-1987
Obituary 123
Dunlop, Eileen (Rhona) 1938- CANR-73
Earlier sketches in CA 73-76, CANR-14, 32
See also JRDA
See also MAICYA 1, 2
See also SAAS 12
See also SATA 24, 76
See also YAW
Dunlop, Ian G(eoffrey) D(avid)
1925- CANR-103
Earlier sketches in CA 9-12R, CANR-5, 24
Dunlop, John (Thomas) 1914-2003 CANR-5
Obituary 221
Earlier sketch in CA 13-16R
Dunlop, John B. 1942- 57-60
Dunlop, M(ary) H(elen) 1941- 229
Dunlop, Richard (B.) 1921- CANR-25
Earlier sketches in CA 17-20R, CANR-7
Dunlop, Robert 1953- 116
Dunlop, Tiger
See Dunlop, William
Dunlop, William 1792-1848 DLB 99
Dunlop MacTavish, Shona 1920- 205
Dunmore, Helen 1952- CANR-93
Earlier sketch in CA 153
See also CP 7
See also CWP
See also DLB 267
Dunmore, John 1923- CANR-47
Earlier sketches in CA 106, CANR-23
Dunmore, Spencer (Sambrook)
1928- CANR-13
Earlier sketch in CA 33-36R
Dunmore, Timothy 1948- 129
Dunn, Alan (Cantwell) 1900-1974 CAP-2
Obituary 49-52
Earlier sketch in CA 33-36
Dunn, Anne M. 1940- SATA 107
Dunn, Carola 1946- CANR-90
Earlier sketch in CA 118
Dunn, Catherine M(ary) 1930- 37-40R
Dunn, Charles W(illiam) 1915- 49-52
Dunn, Delmer D(elano) 1941- 25-28R
Dunn, Dennis J(ohn) 1942- 129
Dunn, Donald H(arley) 1929- 33-36R
Dunn, Douglas (Eaglesham) 1942- . CANR-126
Earlier sketches in CA 45-48, CANR-2, 33
See also BRWS 10
See also CLC 6, 40
See also CP 1, 2, 3, 4, 5, 6, 7
See also DLB 40
See also MTCW 1
Dunn, Durwood 1943- 166
Dunn, Edgar S(treeter), Jr. 1921- 9-12R
Dunn, Edward D. 1883(?)-1978
Obituary 77-80
Dunn, Esther Cloudman 1891-1977
Obituary 73-76
Dunn, Ethel (Deikman) 1932- 21-24R
Dunn, Frederick Sherwood 1893-1962
Obituary 113
Dunn, Halbert Louis 1896-1975
Obituary 61-64
Dunn, (Henry) Hampton 1916- 57-60
Dunn, Harold 1929- 9-12R
Dunn, Harris
See Doerffler, Alfred
Dunn, Harvey T(homas) 1884-1952 177
See also DLB 188
See also SATA 34
Dunn, Herb
See Gutman, Dan
Dunn, Hugh Patrick 1916-1998 CANR-48
Earlier sketch in CA 122
Dunn, J. R. 180
Dunn, James
See Wilkes-Hunter, R(ichard)
Dunn, James D(ouglas Grant) 1939- 73-76
Dunn, James Taylor 1912- CANR-43
Earlier sketches in CA 5-8R, CANR-4, 20
Dunn, Jane 187
Dunn, Jean 1921- 109
Dunn, Jerry G. 1916- CANR-11
Earlier sketch in CA 21-24R
Dunn, John (Montfort) 1940- CANR-11
Earlier sketch in CA 69-72
Dunn, John M. (III) 1949- CANR-116
Earlier sketch in CA 159
See also SATA 93
Dunn, Joseph (Willcox, Jr.) 1937- 122
Dunn, Judith F.
See Bernal, Judith F.
Dunn, Judy
See Spangenberg, Judith Dunn
Dunn, Kate 1958- 171
Dunn, Katherine (Karen) 1945- CANR-72
Earlier sketch in CA 33-36R
See also CLC 71
See also HGG
See also MTCW 2
See also MTFW 2005
Dunn, Kaye
See Dunham, Katherine
Dunn, Linwood 1904-1998 IDFW 3, 4
Dunn, Lloyd W. 1906-1991 CANR-78
Obituary 134
Earlier sketch in CA 57-60
Dunn, Marion Herndon 1920- 29-32R
Dunn, Mark (Rodney) 1956- 203
Dunn, Mary Lois 1930- CANR-12
Earlier sketch in CA 61-64
See also SATA 6
Dunn, Mary Maples 1931- 114
Dunn, Nell (Mary) CANR-66
See also Sandford, Nell Mary
See also CBD
See also CD 5, 6
See also CN 2, 3, 4, 5, 6
See also CWD
Dunn, Olav 1876-1939 DLB 297
Dunn, Patience (Louise Ralli) 1922- 5-8R
Dunn, Peter N(orman) 1926- 122
Dunn, Richard S(lator) 1928- 134
Brief entry 112
Dunn, Ronald (Louis) 1936-
Brief entry 120
Dunn, S. P.
See Dunn, Stephen P(orter)
Dunn, Samantha 1966(?)- 212
Dunn, Samuel Watson 1918-1997 CANR-5
Earlier sketch in CA 1-4R
Dunn, Si 1944- 77-80
Dunn, Stephen (Elliott) 1939- CANR-105
Earlier sketches in CA 33-36R, CANR-12, 48, 53
See also AMWS 11
See also CLC 36, 206
See also CP 7
See also DLB 105
See also PFS 21
Dunn, Stephen P(orter) 1928- 124
Dunn, Stuart (James) 1900-1980 57-60
Dunn, Susan 1945- 189
Dunn, Suzannah 1963- 176
Dunn, Thomas G(eorge) 1950- CANR-44
Earlier sketch in CA 119
Dunn, Thomas Tinsley 1901-1998 107
Dunn, Waldo H(ilary) 1882-1969 CAP-2
Earlier sketch in CA 21-22
Dunn, Walter Scott, Jr. 1928- CANR-143
Earlier sketch in CA 101
Dunn, William J. 1906-1992 CANR-78
Obituary 139
Earlier sketch in CA 33-36R
Dunn, William L(awrence, Jr.) 1924- 37-40R
Dunn, William Robert 1916- 113
Dunnage, Jonathan (Michael) 1963- 175
Dunnahoo, Terry Janson 1927- CANR-57
Earlier sketches in CA 41-44R, CANR-14, 31
See also SATA 7
Dunnam, Maxie D(enton) 1934- 73-76
Dunnan, Nancy 1941- 112
Dunne, Colin 1937- 123
Dunne, Dominick 1925- CANR-88
Earlier sketches in CA 121, CANR-46
See also BEST 89:1, 90:4
See also CPW
See also DA3
See also DAM POP
See also DLB 306
Dunne, Finley Peter 1867-1936 178
Brief entry 108
See also DLB 11, 23
See also RGAL 4
See also TCLC 28
Dunne, George H(arold) 1905-1998 CANR-5
Obituary 181
Earlier sketch in CA 1-4R
Dunne, Gerald T. 1919- CANR-1
Earlier sketch in CA 45-48
Dunne, Gillian A(nne) 1956- 168
Dunne, Jeanette 1952- SATA 72
Dunne, John Gregory 1932-2003 CANR-50
Obituary 222
Earlier sketches in CA 25-28R, CANR-14
See also CLC 28
See also CN 5, 6, 7
See also DLBY 1980
Dunne, John S(cribner) 1929- 13-16R
Dunne, Kathleen 1933- SATA 126
Dunne, (Christopher) Lee 1934- 120
Dunne, Marie
See Clark, Ann Nolan
Dunne, Mary Collins 1914- CANR-14
Earlier sketch in CA 41-44R
See also SATA 11
Dunne, Mary Jo
See Dunne, Mary Collins
Dunne, Pete 1951- 176
Dunne, Peter
See Dunne, Pete
Dunne, Philip 1908-1992 CANR-11
Earlier sketches in CAP-1, CA 9-10
See also DLB 26
See also IDFW 3, 4
Dunne, Phillip 1908-1992
Obituary 137
Dunne, Robert Williams 1895-1977
Obituary 69-72
Dunnell, Robert C(hester) 1942- 89-92
Dunner, Joseph 1908-1978 CANR-14
Earlier sketch in CA 21-24R
Dunnett, Alastair M(acTavish)
1908-1998 65-68
Obituary 170
Dunnett, Sir Alistair MacTavish
See Dunnett, Alastair M(acTavish)
Dunnett, Dorothy 1923-2001 CANR-101
Obituary 203
Earlier sketches in CA 1-4R, CANR-3, 43, 65
See also CMW 4
See also CN 5, 6, 7
See also RHW
Dunnett, Margaret (Rosalind) 1909-1977 108
See also SATA 42
Dunnett, Nigel (P.) 1962(?)- 237
Dunnigan, Alice Allison 1906-1983 125
Obituary 109
See also BW 1
Dunnigan, Brian Leigh 1949- 212
Dunnigan, James F(rancis) 1943- 145
Dunning, Brad 1957- 102
Dunning, Bruce 1940- 77-80
Dunning, Chester S(idney) L(arson)
1949- CANR-123
Earlier sketch in CA 116
Dunning, Edward
See Gilbert, R(obert) A(ndrew)
Dunning, Eric (Geoffrey) 1936- 116
Dunning, George 1920-1979 IDFW 3, 4
Dunning, John 1942- CANR-92
Earlier sketches in CA 93-96, CANR-16
Dunning, John H(arry) 1927- CANR-106
Earlier sketches in CA 104, CANR-21, 49
Dunning, Lawrence 1931- 77-80
Dunning, Ralph Cheever 1878-1930 228
Brief entry 107
See also DLB 4
Dunning, Robert William 1938- CANR-42
Earlier sketches in CA 53-56, CANR-5, 20
Dunning, (Arthur) Stephen (Jr.)
1924- CANR-12
Earlier sketch in CA 25-28R
Dunning, William Archibald 1857-1922 178
See also DLB 17
Dunnington, Hazel Brain 1912-1989 21-24R
du Nouey, Pierre (-Andre-Leon) Lecomte
See Lecomte du Nouey, Pierre(-Andre-Leon)
Dunoyer, Maurice
See Domergue, Maurice
Dunoyer De Segonzac, Andre 1884-1974
Obituary 53-56
Dunphy, Jack 1914-1992 CANR-78
Obituary 137
Earlier sketch in CA 25-28R
Dunqul, Amal 1940-1983 EWL 3
Dunrea, Olivier (Jean-Paul Dominique)
1953- CANR-143
Earlier sketch in CA 124
See also SATA 59, 118, 160
See also SATA-Brief 46
Dunsany, Lord
See Dunsany, Edward John Moreton Drax Plunkett
See also DLB 77, 153, 156, 255
See also FANT
See also IDTP
See also RGEL 2
See also SFW 4
See also SUFW 1
See also TCLC 2, 59
Dunsany, Edward John Moreton Drax Plunkett
1878-1957 148
Brief entry 104
See also Dunsany, Lord
See also DLB 10
See also MTCW 2
Dunsheath, Joyce (Houchen) 1902-1976 5-8R
Dunsheath, Percy 1886-1979 107
Dunsmore, Roger 1938- 110
Dunson, Josh 1941- 25-28R
Duns Scotus, John 1266(?)-1308 DLB 115
Dunstan, Andrew
See Chandler, A(rthur) Bertram
Dunstan, Don(ald Allan) 1926-1999 110
Obituary 177
Dunstan, G(ordon) R(eginald)
1917- CANR-93
Earlier sketch in CA 130
Dunstan, Reginald (Ernest) 1914- 21-24R
Dunster, Julian A. 1954- 160
Dunster, Katherine (Jane) 1955- 177
Dunster, Mark 1927- 85-88
Dunsterville, G(alfrid) C. K.
1905-1988 CANR-78
Obituary 127
Earlier sketches in CAP-1, CA 9-10
Dunston, Arthur John 1922- 109
Duntemann, Jeff 1952- 224
Dunthorn, David J. 1943- 213
Dunton, (Arnold) Davidson 1912-1987
Obituary 121
Dunton, Dorothy 1912- 156
See also SATA 92
Dunton, John 1659-1732 DLB 170
Dunton, Samuel Cady 1910(?)-1975
Obituary 61-64
Dunton, W. Herbert 1878-1936 DLB 188
Dunwoodie, Peter 1946- 192
Dunye, Cheryl 1966- GLL 2
Duong, Thu Huong 1947- CANR-106
Earlier sketch in CA 152
Dupasquier, Philippe 1955- CANR-136
Earlier sketch in CA 130
See also SATA 86, 151
Dupea, Bobby
See Crawley, Tony
Dupee, F(rederick) W(ilcox)
1904-1979 CANR-78
Obituary 85-88
Earlier sketches in CAP-1, CA 13-14
du Perron, Edgar 1899-1940
See Perron, Edgar du
du Perry, Jean
See Simenon, Georges (Jacques Christian)
Dupin, August Dupont
See Taylor, John (Alfred)
Dupin, Jacques 1927- 187
Brief entry 119
See also CWW 2
Duplechan, Larry 1956- CANR-81
Earlier sketch in CA 141
See also BW 2, 3
See also DAM MULT
See also GLL 2
Du Plessis, David J(ohannes) 1905-1987 230
du Plessis, Eric H. 1950- 187
DuPlessis, Rachel Blau 1941- CANR-94
Earlier sketch in CA 139
See also CWP
Duplessis, Yves
See Duplessis, Yvonne
Duplessis, Yvonne 1912- CANR-3
Earlier sketch in CA 9-12R
Dupont, Jacques 1915- 130
Dupont, Judith (Eva Maria) 1925- 136
Dupont, Paul
See Frewin, Leslie Ronald
DuPont, Robert L(ouis) 1936- CANR-52
Earlier sketch in CA 125
Du Pont de Nemours, Pierre Samuel
1739-1817 DLB 313

DuPrau, Jeanne 1944- 217
See also SATA 144
Dupre, Catherine CANR-16
Earlier sketch in CA 25-28R
Dupre, J(osef) Stefan 1936- 102
Dupre, Judith 1956- 221
Dupre, Louis (K.) 1925- CANR-39
Earlier sketches in CA 9-12R, CANR-3, 18
Dupree, A(nderson) Hunter 1921- 9-12R
Dupree, Louis 1925-1989 .... CANR-28
Earlier sketch in CA 41-44R
Dupree, Nathalie 1939- 154
Dupree, Robert S(cott) 1940- 125
DuPree, Sherry Sherrod 1946- 153
Dupres, Henri
See Fawcett, F(rank) Dubrez
Duprey, Richard A(llen) 1929- CANR-6
Earlier sketch in CA 5-8R
Dupuis, Adrian M(aurice) 1919- 9-12R
Dupuis, Robert 1926- 141
Dupuy, Arnold C. 1962- 135
Dupuy, Eliza Ann 1814-1880 .... DLB 248
Dupuy, R(ichard) Ernest 1887-1975 .... CANR-6
Obituary 57-60
Earlier sketch in CA 1-4R
Dupuy, T(revor) N(evitt) 1916-1995 . CANR-40
Obituary 149
Earlier sketches in CA 1-4R, CANR-2, 18
See also SATA 4
See also SATA-Obit 86
Duquette, David A. 1949- 233
DuQuette, Keith 1960- .... SATA 90, 155
Durac, Jack
See Rachman, Stanley Jack
Durack, Mary 1913-1994 .... CANR-17
Earlier sketch in CA 97-100
See also CWRI 5
See also DLB 260
Duram, James C(arl) 1939- CANR-4
Earlier sketch in CA 53-56
Duran, Gloria Diana Bradley 1924- 107
Duran, Jane 1947- 170
See also CWP
Duran, Manuel E. 1925- CANR-11
Earlier sketch in CA 25-28R
Duran, Richard (Paul) 1943- 114
Duran, Roberto (Tinoco) 1953- CANR-81
Earlier sketch in CA 131
See also HW 1, 2
Duranceau, Suzanne 1952- .... SATA 162
Durand, G. Forbes
See Burgess, Michael (Roy)
Durand, John Dana 1913-1981 .... CANR-9
Earlier sketch in CA 61-64
Durand, Loup 1933- 124
Durand, Loyal, Jr. 1902-1970 .... CAP-2
Earlier sketch in CA 21-22
Durand, Lucile
See Bersianik, Louky
Durand, Robert 1944- 57-60
Durand, William F. 1859-1958 157
Durandeaux, Jacques 1926- 25-28R
Durang, Christopher (Ferdinand)
1949- CANR-130
Earlier sketches in CA 105, CANR-50, 76
See also CAD
See also CD 5, 6
See also CLC 27, 38
See also MTCW 2
See also MTFW 2005
Durant, Alan 1958- 192
See also SATA 121
Durant, Ariel K(aufman) 1898-1981 ... CANR-4
Obituary 105
Earlier sketch in CA 9-12R
Durant, David N(orton) 1925- CANR-99
Earlier sketch in CA 77-80
Durant, Frederick C(lark) III 1916- 113
Durant, Henry 1902-1982
Obituary 107
Durant, John 1902- CANR-5
Earlier sketch in CA 9-12R
See also SATA 27
Durant, Michael J. 1961- 239
Durant, Stuart 1932- 104
Durant, Will(iam James)
1885-1981 .... CANR-117
Obituary 105
Earlier sketches in CA 9-12R, CANR-4, 61
See also MTCW 1, 2
See also MTFW 2005
Durante, James Francis 1893-1980
Obituary 93-96
Durante, Jimmy
See Durante, James Francis
Duranti (Rossi), (Maria) Francesca
1935- CANR-103
Earlier sketch in CA 133
See also DLB 196
See also EWL 3
See also RGWL 3
Duranty, Walter 1884-1957 178
See also DLB 29
Duras, Marguerite 1914-1996 .... CANR-50
Obituary 151
Earlier sketch in CA 25-28R
See also BPFB 1
See also CLC 3, 6, 11, 20, 34, 40, 68, 100
See also CWW 2
See also DFS 21
See also DLB 83, 321
See also EWL 3
See also FL 1:5
See also GFL 1789 to the Present
See also IDFW 4
See also MTCW 1, 2
See also RGWL 2, 3
See also SSC 40
See also TWA
Duratschek, (Mary) Claudia
1894-1988 .... 37-40R
Duratschek, Sister Mary Claudia
See Duratschek, (Mary) Claudia
Durbahn, Walter E. 1895(?)-1981
Obituary 102
Durban, (Rosa) Pam 1947- CANR-98
Earlier sketch in CA 123
See also CLC 39
See also CSW
Durband, Alan 1927-1993 .... CANR-20
Earlier sketches in CA 5-8R, CANR-2
Durbin, Brice 1899(?)-1983
Obituary 111
Durbin, Frederic S. 1966- 185
Durbin, Kathie 1944- 192
Durbin, Mary Lou 1927- 21-24R
Durbin, Richard Louis 1928- CANR-7
Earlier sketch in CA 53-56
Durbin, William 1951- 215
See also SATA 143
Durbridge, Francis (Henry)
1912-1998 .... CANR-24
Obituary 166
Earlier sketches in CA 77-80, CANR-6
See also CMW 4
Durcan, Paul 1944- CANR-123
Earlier sketch in CA 134
See also CLC 43, 70
See also CP 1, 7
See also DAM POET
See also EWL 3
Durden, Robert Franklin 1925- 9-12R
Durell, Ann 1930- 136
See also SATA 66
Durer, Albrecht 1471-1528 .... AAYA 58
See also DLB 179
Durey, Michael (John) 1947- 107
d'Urfe, Honore
See Urfe, Honore d'
Durfee, David A(rthur) 1929- 29-32R
Durfee, Mary 1951- 154
Durfey, Thomas 1653-1723 .... DLB 80
See also RGEL 2
Durgin, Doranna 1960- 193
Durgnat, Raymond (Eric) 1932-2002 ..... 17-20R
Obituary 208
Durham, David
See Vickers, Roy C.
Durham, David Anthony 1969- 198
Durham, Frank (Edington) 1935- 114
Durham, Jennifer L. 1972- 218
Durham, Jerry D. 1946- 146
Durham, John
See Paine, Lauran (Bosworth)
Durham, John I 1933- CANR-13
Earlier sketch in CA 29-32R
Durham, John 1925- 107
Durham, Mae
See Roger, Mae Durham
Durham, Marilyn 1930- CANR-63
Earlier sketch in CA 49-52
See also TCWW 1, 2
Durham, Philip 1912-1977 .... CANR-7
Earlier sketch in CA 9-12R
Durham, Walter T. 1924- CANR-124
Earlier sketch in CA 168
During, Simon 1950- 210
Durka, Gloria 1939- CANR-45
Earlier sketches in CA 65-68, CANR-14
Durkee, Mary C. 1921- 13-16R
Durkheim, Emile 1858-1917 .... TCLC 55
Durkin, Barbara W(ernecke) 1944- ... CANR-49
Earlier sketch in CA 123
Durkin, Henry P(aul) 1940- 53-56
Durkin, Joseph T(homas) 1903-2003 ..... CAP-1
Obituary 216
Earlier sketch in CA 11-12
Durkin, Mary G(reeley) 1934- 221
Durlacher, Gerhard (Leopold) 1928-1996
Durland, Frances Caldwell 1892-1986 113
Durland, William R(eginald) 1931- CANR-7
Earlier sketch in CA 57-60
Durnbaugh, Donald F. 1927- CANR-8
Earlier sketch in CA 21-24R
Durnin, Richard G(erry) 1920- 110
Durning, Addis
See Ranzini, Addis Durning
Duro, Paul 1953- 143
Duroche, Leonard L(eRoy) 1933- 37-40R
DuRocher, Richard J(ames) 1955- 118
Duroselle, Jean-Baptiste (Marie Lucien Charles)
1917- CANR-45
Earlier sketches in CA 9-12R, CANR-3, 18
Durova, Nadezhda Andreevna
1783-1866 .... DLB 198
Durr, Bob 237
Durr, Fred
See Durr, Frederick R(oland) E(ugene)
Durr, Frederick R(oland) E(ugene)
1921-1978 .... 37-40R
Durr, R(obert) A(llen)
See Durr, Bob
Durr, Virginia Foster 1903-1999 185
Durr, William Kirtley 1924- 13-16R
Durrani, Mahmood Khan 1914- CAP-1
Earlier sketch in CA 13-14
Durrant, Digby 1926- CANR-13
Earlier sketch in CA 21-24R
Durrant, Lynda 1954- CANR-130
Earlier sketch in CA 161
See also SATA 96, 148
Durrant, Rita D(elores) 108
Durrant, Theo
See Teilhet, Darwin L(eOra)
Durrell, Donald D(e Witt) 1903- CANR-8
Earlier sketch in CA 17-20R
Durrell, Gerald (Malcolm)
1925-1995 .... CANR-59
Obituary 147
Earlier sketches in CA 5-8R, CANR-4, 25
See also MTCW 1
See also SATA 8
See also SATA-Obit 84
Durrell, Jacqueline Sonia Rasen 1929- .. 21-24R
Durrell, Jacquie
See Durrell, Jacqueline Sonia Rasen
Durrell, Julie 1955- 150
See also SATA 94
Durrell, Lawrence (George)
1912-1990 .... CANR-77
Obituary 132
Earlier sketches in CA 9-12R, CANR-40
See also BPFB 1
See also BRWS 1
See also CDBLB 1945-1960
See also CLC 1, 4, 6, 8, 13, 27, 41
See also CN 1, 2, 3, 4
See also CP 1, 2
See also DAM NOV
See also DLB 15, 27, 204
See also DLBY 1990
See also EWL 3
See also MTCW 1, 2
See also RGEL 2
See also SFW 4
See also TEA
Durrell, Zoe C(ompton) 1910- 89-92
Durrenberger, E. Paul 1943- 152
Durrenberger, Robert Warren 1918- . CANR-10
Earlier sketch in CA 21-24R
Durrenmatt, Friedrich
See Duerrenmatt, Friedrich
See also CDWLB 2
See also EW 13
See also EWL 3
See also RGWL 2, 3
Durrett, Deanne 1940- CANR-124
Earlier sketch in CA 156
See also SATA 92, 144
Durschmied, Erik 1930- 140
Durslag, Melvin 1921- 101
Durst, Paul 1921-1986 .... CANR-63
Earlier sketch in CA 21-24R
See also TCWW 1, 2
d'Urstelle, Pierre
See Dorst, Jean (Pierre)
Durstewitz, Jeff 1951- 189
Durston, Christopher 238
Durville, Hector 1849-1923
Brief entry 117
Dury, George H(arry) 1916- 113
Durych, Jaroslav 1886-1962 .... EWL 3
Duryee, Mary Ballard 1896-1988
Obituary 125
Durzak, Manfred 1938- CANR-1
Earlier sketch in CA 49-52
DuSablon, Mary Anna 1939- 187
du Sautoy, Peter (Francis De Courcy)
1921- 5-8R
Dusay, Katherine M(ulholland) 1943- 118
Duscha, Julius (Carl) 1924- 73-76
Dusenberry, William Howard
1908-1979 .... CAP-1
Earlier sketch in CA 19-20
Dusenbery, Gail 1939- .... CP 1
Dusenbury, Winifred L.
See Frazer, Winifred L(oesch)
Dushkin, Alexander M(ordecai) 1890-1976
Obituary 65-68
Dushnitzky-Shner, Sara 1913- 29-32R
Dusic, Stanko
See Begovic, Milan
Duska, Ronald 1937- 97-100
Duskin, Ruthie
See Feldman, Ruth Duskin
Dusky, Lorraine 1942- 85-88
Du Soe, Robert C. 1892-1958 .... YABC 2
d'Usseau, Arnaud 1916-1990
Obituary 130
Dussel, Enrique D. 1934- 89-92
Dussel Peters, Enrique 1965- 204
Dussere, Carol
See Dussere, Carolyn T(homas)
Dussere, Carolyn T(homas) 1942- 103
Dussinger, John A(ndrew) 1935- CANR-44
Earlier sketch in CA 113
Dussling, Jennifer 1970- CANR-122
Earlier sketch in CA 161
See also SATA 96, 143
Duster, Alfreda Barnett 1904-1983
Obituary 109
Duster, Troy 1936- 29-32R
Dustin, Charles
See Giesy, J(ohn) U(lrich)
Duston, Hannah 1657-1737 .... DLB 200
DuTemple, Lesley A. 1952- .... SATA 113
Duthie, Charles S. 1911- CAP-2
Earlier sketch in CA 29-32
Duthie, Niall 1947- 191
Dutile, Fernand N(eville) 1940- 107
Dutka, June 1943- 215
Dutkina, Galina (Borisovna) 1952- 154
See also Annikova, Galina
Dutoit, Ulysse 1944- 199
Dutourd, Jean (Hubert) 1920- CANR-31
Earlier sketch in CA 65-68
Dutt, R(ajani) Palme 1896-1974 .... CANR-95
Obituary 53-56
Earlier sketches in CAP-1, CA 11-12
Dutt, Toru 1856-1877 .... DLB 240
Dutta, Dulal 1925- .... IDFW 3, 4
Dutta, Reginald 1914-1989(?) 61-64
Dutta, Rex
See Dutta, Reginald
Dutter, Barry 1974- 223
Duttman, Martina
See Duettmann, Martina (Friederike)
Dutton, Bertha P(auline) 1903-1994 122
Brief entry 117
Dutton, Diana B. 1943- 129
Dutton, Frederick G(ary) 1923-2005
Brief entry 111
Dutton, Geoffrey (Piers Henry)
1922-1998 .... CANR-98
Obituary 170
Earlier sketches in CA 45-48, CANR-1, 17, 68
See also CN 1, 2, 3, 4, 5, 6
See also CP 1, 2
See also RGEL 2
Dutton, H(arold) I. (?)-1984
Obituary 116
Dutton, Joan Parry 1908-1998 .... 9-12R
Dutton, John M(ason) 1926- 41-44R
Dutton, Mary 1922- 33-36R
Dutton, Michael R. 1967- CANR-92
Earlier sketch in CA 145
Dutton, Paul 1943- CANR-128
Earlier sketches in CA 112, CANR-31
Dutton, Paul Edward 1952- CANR-99
Earlier sketch in CA 148
Dutton, Ralph (Stawell) 1898-1985 .. CANR-96
Obituary 116
Earlier sketch in CA 13-16R
Dutton, Richard Edward 1929-
Brief entry 106
Duty, Michael (W.) 1951- 222
Dutz
See Davis, Mary Octavia
Duun, Olav 1876-1939 190
Brief entry 121
See also EWL 3
Duus, Masayo 1938- 89-92
Duus, Peter 1933- 25-28R
du Vair, Guillaume
1556-1621 .... GFL Beginnings to 1789
DuVal, F(rancis) Alan 1916- 33-36R
Duval, Jean-Jacques 1930- 69-72
DuVal, John 1940- 120
Duval, Katherine
See James, Elizabeth
Duval, Margaret
See Robinson, Patricia Colbert
DuVal, Miles P(ercy), Jr. 1896-1989
Obituary 130
Duval, Pete(r) 238
Duvall, Aimee
See Thurlo, Aimee and
Thurlo, David
Duvall, Evelyn Millis 1906- CANR-1
Earlier sketch in CA 1-4R
See also SATA 9
Duvall, Jill D(onovan) 1932- 169
See also SATA 102
Duvall, Richard M. 1934- 45-48
Duvall, Robert (Selden) 1931- 146
Brief entry 116
Duvall, Shelley (Alexis) 1949- 230
Duvall, W(illiam) Clyde (Jr.) 1917- 17-20R
DuVaul, Virginia C.
See Coffman, Virginia (Edith)
Duveen, Geoffrey 1883-1975
Obituary 61-64
Duveneck, Josephine Whitney 1891-1978 .. 114
Duverger, Maurice 1917- CANR-27
Earlier sketch in CA 65-68
Duvergier de Hauranne, Jean
See Saint-Cyran, Jean Duvergier de Hauranne
Duvoisin, Roger (Antoine)
1904-1980 .... CANR-11
Obituary 101
Earlier sketch in CA 13-16R
See also CLR 23
See also CWRI 5
See also DLB 61
See also MAICYA 1, 2
See also SATA 2, 30
See also SATA-Obit 23
Duvoisin, Roger C(lair) 1927- 132
Duwlat-Uli, Mir Jaqib 1885-1937(?) .... EWL 3
DuWors, Richard E(dward) 1914-1979 45-48
Duy, Pham 1927- 61-64
Duyckinck, Evert Augustus 1816-1878 .. DLB 3, 64, 250
Duyckinck, George Long 1823-1863 .... DLB 3, 250
Duyfhuizen, Bernard 1953- 145
Dvoretsky, Edward 1930- CANR-31
Earlier sketches in CA 37-40R, CANR-14
Dvorkin, Daniel 1969- 236
Dvorkin, David 1943- 118
Dvornik, Francis 1893-1975 .... CANR-6
Obituary 61-64
Earlier sketch in CA 1-4R

Dwaraki, Leela 1942- 106
Dweck, Susan 1943- 33-36R
Dwiggins, Don(ald J.) 1913-1988 ..... CANR-23
Obituary 127
Earlier sketches in CA 17-20R, CANR-8
See also SATA 4
See also SATA-Obit 60
Dwight, Allan
See Cole, Lois Dwight
Dwight, Jeffry 1958- 234
Dwight, John Sullivan 1813-1893 .. DLB 1, 235
Dwight, Olivia
See Hazzard, Mary
Dwight, Timothy 1752-1817 .... DLB 37
See also RGAL 4
Dwinger, Edwin Erich 1898-1981 202
Dwork, Deborah 223
Dworkin, Andrea 1946-2005 .... CANR-96
Obituary 238
Earlier sketches in CA 77-80, CANR-16, 39, 76
Interview in CANR-16
See also CAAS 21
See also CLC 43, 123
See also FL 1:5
See also FW
See also GLL 1
See also MTCW 1, 2
See also MTFW 2005
Dworkin, Gerald 1937- 53-56
Dworkin, James B(arnet) 1948- 112
Dworkin, R. M.
See Dworkin, Ronald M(yles)
Dworkin, Rita 1928- 21-24R
Dworkin, Ronald
See Dworkin, Ronald M(yles)
Dworkin, Ronald M(yles) 1931- CANR-102
Brief entry 123
Earlier sketch in CA 127
Interview in CA-127
Dwoskin, Charles 1922(?)-1980
Obituary 102
Dwoskin, Stephen 1939- 89-92
Dwyer, Augusta (Maria) 1956- 133
Dwyer, Deanna
See Koontz, Dean R(ay)
Dwyer, James Francis 1874-1952 154
See also FANT
Dwyer, Jim 1949- CANR-116
Earlier sketch in CA 159
Dwyer, John C. 1930- CANR-32
Earlier sketch in CA 113
Dwyer, Judith A(nne) 1948- 117
Dwyer, K. R.
See Koontz, Dean R(ay)
Dwyer, Kelly 1964- 180
Dwyer, Michael J(oseph) 1953- 215
Dwyer, Richard A. 1934- 135
Dwyer, T. Ryle 1944- 105
Dwyer, Thomas A. 1923- 115
Dwyer, Vincent Michael 1912-1987
Obituary 123
Dwyer-Joyce, Alice 1913-1986 .... CANR-4
Earlier sketch in CA 53-56
See also RHW
Dyal, Donald H(enriques) 1947- 156
Dyal, James A. 1928- CANR-10
Earlier sketch in CA 5-8R
Dyal, William M., Jr. 1928- 21-24R
Dyall, Valentine 1908-1985
Obituary 117
Dybek, Stuart 1942- CANR-39
Earlier sketch in CA 97-100
See also CLC 114
See also DLB 130
See also SSC 55
Dychtwald, Ken 1950- 189
Dychtwald, Maddy Kent 1952- 225
Dyck, Anni 1931- 25-28R
Dyck, Cornelius J(ohn) 1921- 89-92
Dyck, Harvey L(eonard) 1934- 69-72
Dyck, Ian 1954- 143
Dyck, J. William 1918- 57-60
Dyck, Martin 1927- 41-44R
Dyck, Peter J. 1914- 142
See also SATA 75
Dyckman, John William 1922-1987 ... CANR-2
Obituary 123
Earlier sketch in CA 1-4R
Dyckman, Thomas Richard 1932- CANR-13
Earlier sketch in CA 33-36R
Dye, Anne G.
See Phillips, Anne G(arvey)
Dye, Charles
See MacLean, Katherine
Dye, David L. 1925- 21-24R
Dye, Dwight L(atimer) 1931- 118
Dye, Frank Charles 1930- 103
Dye, H(ershel) Allan 1931- 93-96
Dye, Harold E(ldon) 1907- CANR-24
Earlier sketch in CA 29-32R
Dye, James W(ayne) 1934- 21-24R
Dye, Margaret 1932- 81-84
Dye, Richard
See De Voto, Bernard (Augustine)
Dye, Thomas R(oy) 1935- CANR-52
Earlier sketches in CA 33-36R, CANR-12, 28
Dyen, Isidore 1913- 53-56
Dyer, Beverly 1921- 61-64
Dyer, Braven 1900(?)-1983
Obituary 110
Dyer, Brian
See Petrocelli, Orlando R(alph) and Rothery, Brian
Dyer, C. Raymond
See Dyer, Charles (Raymond)
Dyer, Charles (Raymond) 1928- CANR-44
Earlier sketch in CA 21-24R
See also CBD
See also CD 5, 6
See also DLB 13
Dyer, Christopher (Charles) 1944- 223
Dyer, Daniel .... BYA 13
Dyer, Davis 232
Dyer, Donald R(ay) 1918- 140
Dyer, Sir Edward 1543-1607 .... DLB 136
Dyer, Elinor Mary Brent
See Brent-Dyer, Elinor Mary
Dyer, Esther R(uth) 1950- 102
Dyer, Frederick C. 1918- 17-20R
Dyer, Geoff 1958- CANR-88
Earlier sketch in CA 125
See also CLC 149
Dyer, George 1755-1841 .... DLB 93
Dyer, George Bell 1903-1978 85-88
Obituary 81-84
Dyer, George E(dward) 1928-1974 .... 37-40R
Dyer, George J(ohn) 1927- 13-16R
Dyer, James (Frederick) 1934- 102
See also SATA 37
Dyer, Jane .... SATA 147
Dyer, Joel 1958- 164
Dyer, John 1699-1757 .... DLB 95
See also RGEL 2
Dyer, John M. 1920- 13-16R
Dyer, John Percy 1902-1975 .... 1-4R
Obituary 103
Dyer, Joyce 1947- CANR-91
Earlier sketch in CA 146
Dyer, Judith Clements 1947- 112
Dyer, K(enneth) F(rank) 1939- 114
Dyer, Lucinda 1947- 105
Dyer, T(homas) A(llan) 1947- 101
Dyer, Thomas G(eorge) 1943- CANR-25
Earlier sketch in CA 107
Dyer, Wayne W(alter) 1940- CANR-115
Earlier sketches in CA 69-72, CANR-25
Dyer, William G(ibb) 1925- CANR-14
Earlier sketch in CA 41-44R
Dyess, John (Foster) 1939- .... SATA 76
Dygard, Thomas J. 1931-1996 .... CANR-15
Obituary 153
Earlier sketch in CA 85-88
See also AAYA 7
See also JRDA
See also MAICYA 2
See also MAICYAS 1
See also SAAS 15
See also SATA 24, 97
See also SATA-Obit 92
Dygat, Stanislaw 1914-1978
Obituary 111
See also EWL 3
Dygert, James H(erbert) 1934- CANR-10
Earlier sketch in CA 65-68
Dyja, Thomas 1962- CANR-122
Earlier sketch in CA 162
Dyja, Tom
See Dyja, Thomas
Dyk, Viktor 1877-1931 .... DLB 215
Dyk, Walter 1899-1972
Obituary 37-40R
Dyke, John 1935- CANR-12
Earlier sketch in CA 25-28R
See also SATA 35
Dykema, Karl W(ashburn) 1906-1970 ... CAP-2
Earlier sketch in CA 25-28
Dykeman, Richard M(ills) 1943- 93-96
Dykeman, Therese B(oos) 1936- 149
Dykeman, Wilma 1920- CANR-1
Earlier sketch in CA 1-4R
See also CN 7
Dykes, Archie R(eece) 1931- CANR-7
Earlier sketch in CA 17-20R
Dykes, Jack
See Owen, Jack
Dykes, Jeff(erson) C(henowth) 1900-1989 .... CANR-17
Earlier sketches in CA 5-8R, CANR-2
Dykewomon, Elana 1949- .... GLL 2
Dykhuizen, George 1899-1987 49-52
Dykstra, Craig Richard 1947- 112
Dykstra, Gerald 1922- 45-48
Dykstra, John 1947- .... IDFW 3, 4
Dykstra, Monique 1964- 218
Dykstra, Robert R. 1930- 25-28R
Dylan, Bob 1941- CANR-108
Earlier sketch in CA 41-44R
See also CLC 3, 4, 6, 12, 77
See also CP 1, 2, 3, 4, 5, 6, 7
See also DLB 16
See also PC 37
Dymally, Mervyn M(alcolm) 1926- 41-44R
Dyment, Clifford (Henry) 1914-1971 .... CAP-1
Obituary 33-36R
Earlier sketch in CA 9-10
See also CP 1
Dymoke, Juliet
See de Schanschieff, Juliet Dymoke
Dymond, Dorothy 1891-1985
Obituary 117
Dymond, Rosalind
See Cartwright, Rosalind Dymond
Dymski, Gary A(rthur) 1953- 198
Dymsza, William A(lexander) 1920- .. CANR-2
Earlier sketch in CA 49-52
Dyne, Michael Bradley 1918-1989
Obituary 128
Dynes, Russell R(owe) 1923- CANR-23
Earlier sketches in CA 9-12R, CANR-6
Dynes, Wayne R. 1934- 226
Dyott, George (Miller) 1883-1972
Obituary 37-40R
Dyrness, William A(rthur) 1943- CANR-35
Earlier sketches in CA 33-36R, CANR-13
Dyroff, Jan Michael 1942- 61-64
Dyson, A(nthony) E(dward) 1928-2002 ... 57-60
Obituary 207
Dyson, Anne Jane 1912- 21-24R
Dyson, Esther 1951- 170
Dyson, Freeman J(ohn) 1923- CANR-17
Earlier sketch in CA 89-92
Dyson, Geoffrey Harry George 1914-1981
Obituary 114
Dyson, George (Bernard) 1953- CANR-115
Earlier sketch in CA 126
Dyson, John 1943- 144
See also CLC 70
Dyson, Lowell Keith 1929- 107
Dyson, Michael Eric 1958- CANR-80
Earlier sketch in CA 154
See also BW 3
Dyson, R(obert) W(illiam) 1949- CANR-49
Earlier sketch in CA 123
Dywasuk, Colette Taube 1941- 45-48
Dziech, Billie Wright 1941- CANR-43
Earlier sketch in CA 113
Dzielska, Maria 1942- 152
Dziewanowski, M(arian) Kamil 1913- ... 29-32R
Dzuback, Mary Ann 1950- 138
Dzung Wong, Baoswan 1949- 146
Dzwonkoski, Peter 1940- 123
Dzyubin, Eduard Georgievich 1895-1934 .. 170
See also Bagritsky, Eduard and Bagritsky, Edvard

E

E. A. H. O.
See Ogilvy, Eliza (Anne Harris)
E. R.
See Ross, W. W. E(ustace)
E. V. L.
See Lucas, E(dward) V(errall)
Eade, Alfred Thompson 1891-1988
Obituary 125
Eadie, Betty J(ean) 1942- 230
Eadie, Donald 1919-1981 .... 33-36R
Eadie, John W(illiam) 1935- 104
Eadie, Thomas Michael 1941- .... CP 1
Eady, Cornelius 1954- 204
Eagan, Andrea Boroff 1943-1993 ..... CANR-46
Obituary 140
Earlier sketch in CA 73-76
Eagan, Barbara Tiritilli 1935(?)-1986
Obituary 118
Eagar, Frances (Elisabeth Stuart) 1940-1978 61-64
Obituary 120
See also SATA 11
See also SATA-Obit 55
Eager, Edward (McMaken) 1911-1964 .... CANR-87
Earlier sketch in CA 73-76
See also CLR 43
See also CWRI 5
See also DLB 22
See also FANT
See also MAICYA 1, 2
See also SATA 17
Eager, George B. 1921- .... SATA 56
Eager, Mary Ann 1905(?)-1984
Obituary 111
Eager, Molly
See Eager, Mary Ann
Eagle, Chester (Arthur) 1933- 57-60
Eagle, Dorothy 1912- CANR-9
Earlier sketch in CA 21-24R
Eagle, Ellen 1953- .... SATA 61
Eagle, Joanna 1934- 25-28R
Eagle, Kathleen 1947- 209
Eagle, Kin
See Adlerman, Daniel (Ezra) and Adlerman, Kimberly M(arie)
Eagle, Mike 1942- .... SATA 11
Eagle, Robert H(arold) 1921-1969 .... CAP-2
Earlier sketch in CA 21-22
Eagles, Charles W. 1946- 138
Eagles, Douglas Alan 1943- 110
Eaglesfield, Francis
See Guirdham, Arthur
Eagleson, John 1941- 53-56
Eagleton, Terence (Francis) 1943- ... CANR-115
Earlier sketches in CA 57-60, CANR-7, 23, 68
See also CLC 63, 132
See also DLB 242
See also LMFS 2
See also MTCW 1, 2
See also MTFW 2005
Eagleton, Terry
See Eagleton, Terence (Francis)
Eagleton, Thomas Francis 1929- 187
Brief entry 105
Eagly, Robert V(ictor) 1933- 49-52
Eaker, Ira
See Eaker, Ira C(larence)
Eaker, Ira C(larence) 1896-1987
Obituary 123
Eakin, Frank Edwin, Jr. 1936- 53-56
Eakin, Mary K(atherine) 1917- CANR-1
Earlier sketch in CA 1-4R
Eakin, Mary Mulford 1914-1980 126
Brief entry 106
Eakin, Paul John 1938- CANR-91
Earlier sketches in CA 120, CANR-45
Eakin, Richard M(arshall) 1910-1999 61-64
Obituary 186
Eakin, Sue 1918- 69-72
Eakins, David W(alter) 1923- 49-52
Eakins, Pamela 1953- 117
Eakins, Patricia 1942- 225
Eales, John R(ay) 1910-1983 .... 9-12R
Ealy, Lawrence O(rr) 1915-1998 .... 33-36R
Eames, Alexandra 1942- 105
Eames, Andrew (John) 1958- 124
Eames, Anne 1945- 239
Eames, David 1934- 77-80
Eames, Edwin 1930- CANR-14
Earlier sketch in CA 41-44R
Eames, Elizabeth Ramsden 1921- 125
Eames, Hugh 1917- 45-48
Eames, John Douglas 1915- 69-72
Eames, Ray (Kaiser) 1916(?)-1988 162
Eames, S(amuel) Morris 1916- 57-60
Eames, Wilberforce 1855-1937 186
See also DLB 140
Ear, The
See McLellan, Diana
Eardley, George C(harles) 1926- 57-60
Earhart, H(arry) Byron 1935- CANR-14
Earlier sketch in CA 37-40R
Earl, David M(agarey) 1911-1996 .... 13-16R
Earl, Donald (Charles) 1931-1996 57-60
Obituary 153
Earl, Johnrae 1919(?)-1978
Obituary 77-80
Earl, Lawrence 1915- 9-12R
Earl, Maureen 1944- 137
Earl, Paul Hunter 1945- CANR-2
Earlier sketch in CA 49-52
Earl, Riggins R., Jr. 1942- 204
Earle, (Mary) Alice Morse 1853(?)-1911
Brief entry 117
See also DLB 221
Earle, Garet W.
See Earle-Hall, Wilton
Earle, Jean
See Burge, Doris
Earle, John 1600(?)-1665 .... DLB 151
Earle, Marilee
See Zdenek, Marilee
Earle, (Karl Mc)Neil 1947- CANR-98
Earlier sketch in CA 147
Earle, Olive L(ydia) 1888-1982 .... 21-24R
See also SATA 7
Earle, Peter G. 1923- 17-20R
Earle, Ralph 1907-1995 .... CANR-4
Earlier sketch in CA 1-4R
Earle, Sylvia A(lice) 1935- CANR-106
Earlier sketch in CA 157
Earle, Timothy K. 1946- 125
Earle, William
See Johns, W(illiam) E(arle)
Earle, William (Alexander) 1919-1988 85-88
Obituary 127
Earle, Wilton
See Earle-Hall, Wilton
Earle-Hall, Wilton 1930- 229
Earley, Charity (Edna) Adams 1918-2002 132
Obituary 201
Earley, Martha
See Westwater, Agnes Martha
Earley, Pete CANR-127
Earlier sketch in CA 163
Earley, Tom 1911-1998 .... CAP-2
Earlier sketch in CA 33-36
See also CP 1
Earley, Tony (L.) 1961- CANR-95
Earlier sketch in CA 156
See also CSW
Earling, Debra Magpie 1957- 229
Earll, Tony
See Buckland, Raymond
Earl Mountbatten of Burma
See Mountbatten, Louis (Francis Albert Victor Nicholas)
Earl of Arran
See Gore, Arthur Kattendyke S(trange) D(avid) A(rchibald)
Earl of Carnarvon
See Herbert, Henry George Alfred Marius Victor Francis
Earl of Longford
See Pakenham, Edward Arthur Henry and Pakenham, Francis Aungier
Earl of Orrey
See Boyle, Roger
Earls, Irene 175
Earls, Nick 1963- CANR-115
Earlier sketch in CA 160
See also SATA 95, 156
Earlson, Ian Malcolm
See Dorn, William S.
Early, Gerald 1952- 133
Early, H(enry) C(lay) 1855-1941 206
Early, Jack
See Scoppettone, Sandra
See also GLL 1
Early, James 1923- 45-48
Early, John D. 1949- 187
Early, Jon
See Johns, W(illiam) E(arle)
Early, Margaret 1951- .... SATA 72
Early, Martha
See Westwater, Agnes Martha
Early, Richard E(lliott) 1908- 102
Early, Robert 1940- 49-52
Early, Tom
See Kelton, Elmer
Earnest, Ernest (Penney) 1901-1981 ...... 33-36R
Obituary 164
Earney, Fillmore C(hristy) F(idelis) 1931- . 57-60
Earnshaw, Anthony (Sydney) 1924-2001 . 53-56
Obituary 197

Cumulative Index 167 **Eckhardt**

Earnshaw, Brian 1929- CANR-27
Earlier sketches in CA 25-28R, CANR-11
See also SATA 17
Earnshaw, Micky
See Earnshaw, Spencer Wright
Earnshaw, Spencer Wright 1939- 152
See also SATA 88
Earnshaw, Steven 1962- 227
Earp, Virgil
See Keevill, Henry J(ohn)
Easley, MaryAnn 159
See also SATA 94
Easmon, R(aymond) Sarif 1913- .... CD 5, 6
Eason, Ruth P. 1898(?)-1978
Obituary 81-84
Easson, James 1895-1979 .... 5-8R
Obituary 103
Easson, Roger R(alph) 1945- 112
Easson, William M(cAlpine) 1931- 65-68
East, Ben 1898-1990 .... CANR-27
Earlier sketch in CA 33-36R
East, Bob 1920(?)-1985
Obituary 115
East, Charles 1924- 17-20R
See also CSW
East, Churchill
See Harner, Stephen M.
East, Fred
See West, Tom
East, John (Marlborough) 1936-2003 ..... 21-24R
Obituary 217
East, John Porter 1931-1986 .... 17-20R
Obituary 119
East, June
See Pearce, Ellen
East, Michael
See West, Morris L(anglo)
East, P. D. 1921-1971 .... 1-4R
Obituary 103
East, W(illiam) Gordon 1902-1998 69-72
Eastaugh, Kenneth 1929- 106
Eastaway, Edward
See Thomas, (Philip) Edward
Eastaway, Robert 1962- 139
Easter, Junior
See Easter, Willie, Jr.
Easter, Willie, Jr. 1963- 166
Easterbrook, Frank H. 1948- 138
Easterbrook, Gregg 1953- CANR-136
Earlier sketch in CA 140
Easterlin, Richard A(inley) 1926- 109
Easterling, Keller 1959- 142
Easterman, Alexander Levvey 1890-1983
Obituary 110
Easterman, Daniel
See MacEoin, Denis
Eastham, Thomas 1923- 77-80
Easthope, Antony 1939-1999 .... CANR-86
Earlier sketch in CA 130
Easthope, Gary 1945- 69-72
Eastin, Roy B(randon) 1917- 41-44R
Eastlake, William (Derry)
1917-1997 .... CANR-63
Obituary 158
Earlier sketches in CA 5-8R, CANR-5
Interview in CANR-5
See also CAAS 1
See also CLC 8
See also CN 1, 2, 3, 4, 5, 6
See also DLB 6, 206
See also MAL 5
See also TCWW 1, 2
Eastland, Terry 1950- 97-100
Eastlick, John Taylor 1912-1990 106
Eastman, Addison J. 1918- 85-88
Eastman, Ann Heidbreder 1933- CANR-14
Earlier sketch in CA 37-40R
Eastman, Arthur M(orse) 1918- 21-24R
Eastman, Carol 116
See also DLB 44
Eastman, Charles 116
Eastman, Charles A(lexander)
1858-1939 .... CANR-91
Earlier sketch in CA 179
See also DAM MULT
See also DLB 175
See also NNAL
See also TCLC 55
See also YABC 1
Eastman, Edward Roe 1885-1970 .... CAP-1
Earlier sketch in CA 13-14
Eastman, Frances W(hittier) 1915- CANR-28
Earlier sketch in CA 1-4R
Eastman, G. Don
See Oosterman, Gordon
Eastman, Harry Claude MacColl 1923-
Brief entry 105
Eastman, Joel Webb 1939- 13-16R
Eastman, John 1935- CANR-41
Earlier sketch in CA 117
Eastman, Lloyd E. 1929- 126
Brief entry 112
Eastman, Max (Forrester) 1883-1969 .... 9-12R
Obituary 25-28R
See also DLB 91
Eastman, P(hilip) D(ey) 1909-1986 107
Obituary 118
See also MAICYA 2
See also SATA 33
See also SATA-Obit 46
Eastman, Richard M(orse) 1916- 17-20R
Eastman, Robert E. 1913-1999 93-96
Eastman, Roger (Herbert) 1931- 53-56
Easton, Allan 1916- CANR-20
Earlier sketches in CA 49-52, CANR-2
Easton, Anthony Terrence 1947- 127
Easton, Carol 1932- CANR-39
Earlier sketch in CA 65-68
Easton, David 1917- 33-36R
Easton, Edward
See Malerich, Edward P.
Easton, Elizabeth Wynne 1956- 134
Easton, Jane 1918-2003 138
Easton, Kelly 1960- 212
See also SATA 141
Easton, Laird M. 1956- 234
Easton, Loyd D(avid) 1915- 21-24R
Easton, M(alcolm) Coleman 1942- 239
See also FANT
Easton, Nina J(ane) 1958- 232
Easton, Robert (Olney) 1915-1999 ... CANR-27
Earlier sketches in CA 13-16R, CANR-7
See also CAAS 14
See also TCWW 1, 2
Easton, Stewart Copinger
1907-1989 .... CANR-18
Earlier sketches in CA 1-4R, CANR-2
Easton, Thomas A(twood) 1944- CANR-135
Earlier sketches in CA 114, CANR-45
Eastwick, Ivy (Ethel) O(live) CANR-2
Earlier sketch in CA 5-8R
See also SATA 3
Eastwood, C(harles) Cyril 1916- 5-8R
Eastwood, Clint(on, Jr.) 1930- 237
See also AAYA 18, 59
Eastwood, Cyril
See Eastwood, C(harles) Cyril
Easum, Bill
See Easum, William M.
Easum, William M. 1939- 167
Easwaran, Eknath 1911-1999 205
Eatock, Marjorie 1927- 89-92
Eaton, Anne T(haxter) 1881-1971
Obituary 111
See also SATA 32
Eaton, Charles Edward 1916- 193
Earlier sketches in CA 5-8R, CANR-2, 20, 44
Autobiographical Essay in 193
See also CAAS 20
See also CP 1, 2, 3, 4, 5, 6, 7
See also CSW
Eaton, Clement 1898-1980 .... CANR-4
Obituary 118
Earlier sketch in CA 1-4R
Eaton, Daniel Isaac 1753-1814 .... DLB 158
Eaton, Edith Maude 1865-1914 154
See also Far, Sui Sin
See also AAL
See also DLB 221, 312
See also FW
Eaton, Evelyn (Sybil Mary) 1902-1983 53-56
Obituary 171
See also RHW
Eaton, Faith (Sybil) 1927- 103
Eaton, George L.
See Verral, Charles Spain
Eaton, J(ohn) H(erbert) 1927- CANR-19
Earlier sketches in CA 1-4R, CANR-4
Eaton, Jack 1947- 208
Eaton, Janet
See Givens, Janet E(aton)
Eaton, Jeanette 1886-1968 73-76
See also MAICYA 1, 2
See also SATA 24
Eaton, John
See Bodington, Stephen
Eaton, John P. 126
Eaton, Joseph W. 1919- CANR-4
Earlier sketch in CA 1-4R
Eaton, Leonard K. 1922- 21-24R
Eaton, Marcia M(uelder) 1938- 113
Eaton, Richard M. 1940- 148
Eaton, Theodore H(ildreth), Jr. 1907- 53-56
Eaton, Tom 1940- CANR-15
Earlier sketch in CA 41-44R
See also SATA 22
Eaton, Trevor 1934- 21-24R
Eaton, William Edward 1943- 69-72
Eaton, (Lillie) Winnifred 1875-1954 217
See also AAL
See also DLB 221, 312
See also RGAL 4
Eatwell, Roger 1949- 152
Eauclaire, Sally 1950- 118
Eaves, Elisabeth 1971- 214
Eaves, James Clifton 1912-2002 .... 13-16R
Eaves, Morris (Emery) 1944- CANR-45
Earlier sketch in CA 120
Eaves, T(homas) C(ary) Duncan 1918- 77-80
Eavey, Charles B(enton) 1889-1974 .... 5-8R
Obituary 164
Eavey, Louise Bone 1900-1971 .... 5-8R
Obituary 164
Eayrs, James George 1926-
Brief entry 106
Eban, Abba (Solomon) 1915-2002 .... CANR-92
Obituary 213
Earlier sketches in CA 57-60, CANR-26
Eban, Aubrey
See Eban, Abba (Solomon)
Ebaugh, Helen Rose (Fuchs) 1942- 204
Ebb, Fred 1933(?)-2004 .... CANR-127
Obituary 231
Earlier sketches in CA 69-72, CANR-24
Ebbesen, Ebbe B(ruce) 1944- CANR-2
Earlier sketch in CA 49-52
Ebbett, (Frances) Eva 1925- 103
Ebbett, Eve
See Ebbett, (Frances) Eva
Ebejer, Francis 1925- CANR-40
Earlier sketches in CA 29-32R, CANR-16
See also EWL 3
Ebel, Alex 1927- .... SATA 11
Ebel, Henry 1938- 53-56
Ebel, Robert L(ouis) 1910-1982 89-92
Ebel, Roland H. 1928- 140
Ebel, Suzanne
See Goodwin, Suzanne
Ebeling, Gerhard 1912-2001 .... CANR-5
Earlier sketch in CA 9-12R
Ebeling, Walter 1907- 119
Ebenstein, Ronnie Sue 1946- 103
Ebenstein, William 1910-1976 .... CANR-6
Obituary 65-68
Earlier sketch in CA 1-4R
Eber, Dorothy (Margaret) Harley 1930- . 41-44R
See also SATA 27
Eber, Irene 1929- 102
Eberhard, Wolfram 1909-1989 .... CANR-2
Earlier sketch in CA 49-52
Eberhardt, Newman Charles 1912-1995 ... 1-4R
Eberhardt, Peter
See Adams, (Franklin) Robert
Eberhart, Dikkon 1946- 93-96
Eberhart, George M(artin) 1950- CANR-134
Earlier sketch in CA 105
Eberhart, Mignon G(ood)
1899-1996 .... CANR-60
Obituary 154
Earlier sketch in CA 73-76
See also AITN 2
See also CMW 4
See also MSW
Eberhart, (Wilfred) Perry 1924- 17-20R
Eberhart, Richard (Ghormley)
1904-2005 .... CANR-125
Earlier sketches in CA 1-4R, CANR-2
See also AMW
See also CDALB 1941-1968
See also CLC 3, 11, 19, 56
See also CP 1, 2, 3, 4, 5, 6, 7
See also DAM POET
See also DLB 48
See also MAL 5
See also MTCW 1
See also RGAL 4
Eberle, Gary 1951- CANR-72
Earlier sketch in CA 150
Eberle, Irmengarde 1898-1979 .... CANR-2
Obituary 85-88
Earlier sketch in CA 1-4R
See also SATA 2
See also SATA-Obit 23
Eberle, Nancy (Oates) 1935(?)-1988
Obituary 125
Eberle, Paul 1928- 101
Eberle, Shirley 1929- 142
Eberman, (Gilbert) Willis 1917- 9-12R
Ebershoff, David 1969- 219
Ebershoff-Coles, Susan Vaughan 1941- 102
Ebersohn, Wessel (Schalk) 1940- 97-100
Ebersole, A(lva) V(ernon), Jr. 1919- ... CANR-31
Earlier sketches in CA 37-40R, CANR-14
Ebersole, Lucinda 1956- 142
Eberstadt, Charles F. 1914(?)-1974
Obituary 53-56
Eberstadt, Fernanda 1960- CANR-128
Earlier sketches in CA 136, CANR-69
See also CLC 39
Eberstadt, Isabel 1933- 126
Eberstadt, Lindley E. 1910(?)-1985
Obituary 115
Eberstadt, Nicholas (Nash) 1955- CANR-91
Earlier sketch in CA 150
Ebert, Alan 1935- CANR-16
Earlier sketch in CA 85-88
Ebert, Arthur Frank 1902-1984 .... 5-8R
Obituary 114
Ebert, James I(an) 1948- 145
Ebert, John E(dward) 1922- 106
Ebert, Katherine 1921- 107
Ebert, Roger (Joseph) 1942- CANR-115
Earlier sketches in CA 69-72, CANR-22, 45
Ebert-Schifferer, Sybille 1955- 190
Eberwein, Jane Donahue 1943- 111
Eberwein, Robert Thomas 1940- 111
Eblana, Sister 1907- CAP-1
Earlier sketch in CA 11-12
Eble, Connie 1942- 161
Eble, Diane 1956- .... SATA 74
Eble, Kenneth Eugene 1923- CANR-19
Earlier sketches in CA 1-4R, CANR-4
Eblen, Jack Ericson 1936- 33-36R
Eblis, J. Philip
See Phillips, James W.
Ebner, Jeannie 1918- 178
See also DLB 85
Ebner, Mark 237
Ebner-Eschenbach, Marie von 1830-1916 .. 179
See also DLB 81
Eboch, Chris 185
See also SATA 113
Ebon 1942- 177
See also DLB 41
Ebon, Martin 1917- CANR-29
Earlier sketches in CA 21-24R, CANR-10
Ebsen, Buddy
See Ebsen, Christian (Rudolf, Jr.)
Ebsen, Christian (Rudolf, Jr.) 1908-2003 103
Obituary 218
Ebsworth, (George Arthur) Raymond
1911- 1-4R
Eby, Cecil D(eGrotte) 1927- CANR-43
Earlier sketches in CA 1-4R, CANR-4
Eby, Richard E(ngle) 1912- 112
Eca de Queiros, Jose Maria de
See Eca de Queiroz, Jose Maria
See also RGWL 2, 3
Eca de Queiroz, Jose Maria 1845-1900
See Eca de Queiros, Jose Maria de
See also EW 7
Eccles, David (McAdam) 1904-1999 53-56
Obituary 177
Eccles, Frank 1923- 103
Eccles, Henry E. 1898-1986 .... CAP-1
Earlier sketch in CA 13-16
Eccles, John Carew 1903-1997 .... CANR-9
Obituary 158
Earlier sketch in CA 65-68
Eccles, Marjorie 1927- 191
Eccles, Mary Hyde
See Hyde, Mary (Morley Crapo)
Eccles, W(illiam) J(ohn) 1917- 9-12R
Ecclestone, Giles 1936-1990
Obituary 132
Eccles Williams, Ferelith 1920- CANR-21
Earlier sketch in CA 105
See also Williams, Ferelith Eccles
Eccli, Sandra Fulton 1936- 102
Echegaray (y Eizaguirre), Jose (Maria Waldo)
1832-1916 .... CANR-32
Brief entry 104
See also EWL 3
See also HLCS 1
See also HW 1
See also MTCW 1
See also TCLC 4
Echenoz, Jean 1947- CANR-95
Earlier sketch in CA 147
Echeruo, Michael J(oseph) C(hukwudalu)
1937- CANR-8
Earlier sketch in CA 57-60
See also BW 2
See also CP 1, 2, 3, 4, 5, 6, 7
Echevarria, Jana 1956- 226
Echevarria, Roberto Gonzalez
See Gonzalez Echevarria, Roberto
Echeverria, Durand 1913-2001 .... 9-12R
Echeverria, (Jose) Esteban (Antonino)
1805-1851 .... LAW
Echewa, T(homas) Obinkaram 1940- 73-76
Echikson, William 1959- 134
Echlin, Edward P. 1930- 21-24R
Echlin, Kim 194
Echo
See Proust, (Valentin-Louis-George-Eugene) Marcel
Echols, Alice 1951- 190
Echols, Allan K. .... TCWW 2
Echols, Barbara E(llen) 1934- 106
Echols, John M(inor) 1913-1982 .... CANR-2
Obituary 107
Earlier sketch in CA 5-8R
Echols, Margit 1944- 97-100
Eck, Diana L. 1945- CANR-143
Earlier sketch in CA 107
Eckard, Paula G. 1950- 234
Eckardt, A(rthur) Roy 1918-1998 ...... CANR-42
Obituary 167
Earlier sketches in CA 37-40R, CANR-14, 31
Eckardt, Alice L(yons) 1923- CANR-42
Earlier sketches in CA 37-40R, CANR-14
Eckardt, Arthur Roy
See Eckardt, A(rthur) Roy
Eckart, Gabriele 1954- 142
Eckaus, Richard S(amuel) 1926- 45-48
Eckblad, Edith Berven 1923- 17-20R
See also SATA 23
Eckbo, Garrett 1910-2000 .... 25-28R
Obituary 188
Ecke, Betty Tseng Yu-ho 1924- CANR-6
Earlier sketch in CA 5-8R
Ecke, Wolfgang 1927-1983
Obituary 111
See also SATA-Obit 37
Eckel, Malcolm W(illiam) 1912-2000 61-64
Eckel, Paul E(dward) 1908-1986
Obituary 119
Eckelberry, Grace Kathryn 1902-1996 ... CAP-2
Earlier sketch in CA 33-36
Eckels, Jon CANR-3
Earlier sketch in CA 49-52
Ecker, Beverly A. 1938- 116
Ecker, H(erman) Paul 1922-1976 .... CAP-2
Earlier sketch in CA 29-32
Ecker-Racz, L. Laszlo 1906- 49-52
Eckerson, Olive Taylor 1901-1985 .... 1-4R
Eckert, Allan W. 1931- CANR-45
Earlier sketches in CA 13-16R, CANR-14
Interview in CANR-14
See also AAYA 18
See also BYA 2
See also CLC 17
See also MAICYA 2
See also MAICYAS 1
See also SAAS 21
See also SATA 29, 91
See also SATA-Brief 27
Eckert, Edward K(yle) 1943- 77-80
Eckert, Horst 1931- CANR-38
Earlier sketch in CA 37-40R
See also Janosch
See also MAICYA 1, 2
See also SATA 8, 72
Eckert, Kathryn Bishop 1935- 147
Eckert, Lorie K(leiner) 1952- 200
Eckert, Martina 1960- 145
Eckert, Ruth E(lizabeth) 1905-1987 .... 13-16R
Eckes, Alfred Edward, Jr. 1942- CANR-9
Earlier sketch in CA 61-64
Eckhardt, Bob
See Eckhardt, Robert Christian
Eckhardt, C(harles) F(rederick) 1940- 205
Eckhardt, Celia Morris
See Morris, Celia

Eckhardt, Robert Christian 1913-2001 85-88
Obituary 200
Eckhardt, Tibor 1888-1972
Obituary 37-40R
Eckhart, Meister 1260(?)-1327(?) .... DLB 115
See also LMFS 1
Eckholm, Erik P(eter) 1949- CANR-6
Earlier sketch in CA 57-60
Ecklar, Julia (Marie) 1964- 173
See also SATA 112
Eckley, Grace 1932- CANR-28
Earlier sketch in CA 45-48
Eckley, Mary M. 102
Eckley, Wilton Earl, Jr. 1929- CANR-28
Earlier sketch in CA 49-52
Eckman, Frederick (Willis) 1924- 33-36R
Eckman, Lester S(amuel) 1937- CANR-2
Earlier sketch in CA 49-52
Eckmar, F. R.
See de Hartog, Jan
Eckroate, Norma 1951- 188
Eckstein, Alexander 1915-1976 .... CANR-6
Obituary 69-72
Earlier sketch in CA 1-4R
Eckstein, Gustav 1890-1981 57-60
Obituary 104
Eckstein, Harry 1924-1999 .... CANR-1
Obituary 181
Earlier sketch in CA 1-4R
Eckstein, Jerome 1925- CANR-36
Earlier sketch in CA 114
Eckstein, Otto 1927-1984 .... CANR-14
Obituary 112
Earlier sketch in CA 13-16R
Eckstein, Rick 1960- 165
Eclov, Shirley
See Pfoutz, Shirley Eclov
Eco, Umberto 1932- CANR-131
Earlier sketches in CA 77-80, CANR-12, 33, 55, 110
See also BEST 90:1
See also BPFB 1
See also CLC 28, 60, 142
See also CPW
See also CWW 2
See also DA3
See also DAM NOV, POP
See also DLB 196, 242
See also EWL 3
See also MSW
See also MTCW 1, 2
See also MTFW 2005
See also NFS 22
See also RGWL 3
See also WLIT 7
Economou, George 1934- CANR-119
Earlier sketches in CA 25-28R, CANR-38
See also CP 1, 2
Ecott, Tim 220
Ecroyd, Donald H(owarth) 1923- CANR-4
Earlier sketch in CA 1-4R
Edari, Ronald S(amuel) 1943- 65-68
Edberg, Rolf 1912- CANR-54
Earlier sketches in CA 69-72, CANR-11, 26
Eddenden, A(rthur) E(dward) 1928- .. CANR-54
Earlier sketch in CA 127
Eddie, David 1961- 193
Eddings, David (Carroll) 1931- CANR-107
Earlier sketches in CA 110, CANR-35, 53
See also AAYA 17
See also BEST 90:2
See also CPW
See also DAM POP
See also FANT
See also SATA 91
See also SFW 4
See also SUFW 2
See also YAW
Eddings, Leigh 1937- CANR-104
Earlier sketch in CA 164
Eddington, Arthur Stanley 1882-1944 157
Eddins, Dwight L. 1939- 33-36R
Eddison, E(ric) R(ucker) 1882-1945 156
Brief entry 109
See also DLB 255
See also FANT
See also SFW 4
See also SUFW 1
See also TCLC 15
Eddison, John 1916- CANR-48
Earlier sketches in CA 61-64, CANR-8, 23
Eddison, Roger (Tatham) 1916- CAP-1
Earlier sketch in CA 11-12
Eddleman, H(enry) Leo 1911-1995 ..... CANR-9
Earlier sketch in CA 13-16R
Eddy, C. M., Jr.
See Eddy, Clifford Martin, Jr.
Eddy, Clifford Martin, Jr. 1896-1967
Obituary 113
Eddy, Edward D(anforth, Jr.) 1921-1998 .. 73-76
Obituary 181
Eddy, Elizabeth M. 1926- 21-24R
Eddy, John J(ude) 1933- 73-76
Eddy, John P(aul) 1932- CANR-9
Earlier sketch in CA 61-64
Eddy, John Percy 1881-1975
Obituary 61-64
Eddy, Mary (Ann Morse) Baker 1821-1910 . 174
Brief entry 113
See also TCLC 71
Eddy, Pamela 1956- 214
Eddy, Paul 1944- CANR-98
Earlier sketches in CA 73-76, CANR-15
Eddy, Roger (Whittlesey) 1920-2003 ..... 17-20R
Obituary 214
Eddy, Samuel K(ennedy) 1926- CANR-17
Earlier sketch in CA 1-4R
Ede, H(arold) S(tanley) 1895-1990 131
Ede, Janina 1937- .... SATA 33
Ede, Jim
See Ede, H(arold) S(tanley)
Ede, Lisa S. 1947- 123
Edeiken, Louise 1956- 140
Edel, Abraham 1908- 1-4R
Edel, (Joseph) Leon 1907-1997 .... CANR-112
Obituary 161
Earlier sketches in CA 1-4R, CANR-1, 22
Interview in CANR-22
See also CLC 29, 34
See also DLB 103
Edel, Marjorie
See Sinclair, Marjorie (Jane)
Edel, Matthew (David) 1941-1990 .... 29-32R
Obituary 133
Edel, Wilbur 1915- 138
Edelberg, Cynthia Dubin 1940- 89-92
Edelen, Georges 1924- 93-96
Edelhart, Michael 1951- 129
Edelhart, Mike
See Edelhart, Michael
Edelheit, Abraham J. 1958- 134
Edelheit, Hershel 1926-1995 134
Edell, Celeste 1-4R
See also SATA 12
Edelman, Alice Fisher 1940- 112
Edelman, Bernard 1946- CANR-136
Earlier sketch in CA 126
Edelman, Elaine 113
See also SATA-Brief 50
Edelman, Gerald Maurice 1929- 112
Edelman, John W(alter) 1893-1971
Obituary 113
Edelman, Lily (Judith) 1915-1981 61-64
Obituary 102
See also SATA 22
Edelman, Marek 1922-
Edelman, Marian Wright 1939- CANR-137
Earlier sketches in CA 124, CANR-61
See also BW 2, 3
See also MTFW 2005
Edelman, Maurice 1911-1975 65-68
Obituary 61-64
See also CN 1, 2
Edelman, Murray J. 1919-2000 .... 33-36R
Obituary 192
Edelman, Nathan 1911-1971
Obituary 113
Edelman, Paul S. 1926- 9-12R
Edelman, Rob 1949- 219
Edelman, Scott 1955- 237
Edelsberg, Herman 1909-1986
Obituary 120
Edelson, Edward 1932- CANR-13
Earlier sketch in CA 17-20R
See also SATA 51
Edelson, Julie 1949- CANR-108
Earlier sketches in CA 122, CANR-48
Edelson, Marshall 1928-2005 153
Obituary 235
Brief entry 111
Edelstein, Alan 237
Edelstein, Alex S. 1920(?)- 133
Edelstein, Arthur CANR-9
Earlier sketch in CA 65-68
Edelstein, David S(imeon) 1913- 61-64
Edelstein, J(erome) M(elvin) 1924-1996 ... 53-56
Obituary 152
Edelstein, Morton A. 1925- 69-72
Edelstein, Robert 1960- 239
Edelstein, Scott 1954- CANR-49
Earlier sketch in CA 122
Edelstein, Stuart J. 1941- 122
Edelstein, Terese 1950- 135
Eden, Alvin N(oam) 1926- CANR-9
Earlier sketch in CA 61-64
Eden, (Robert) Anthony 1897-1977 77-80
Obituary 69-72
Eden, Dorothy (Enid) 1912-1982 ...... CANR-46
Obituary 106
Earlier sketch in CA 81-84
See also RHW
Eden, Laura
See Harrison, Claire (E.)
Eden, Marc
See Eden, Marcus
Eden, Marcus 1935- 147
Eden, Mark
See Eden, Marcus
Eden, Robert 1942- 113
Edens, Cooper 1945- 184
See also SATA 49, 112
Edens, (Bishop) David 1926- 108
See also SATA 39
Edens, Roger 1905-1970 .... IDFW 3, 4
Eder, George Jackson 1900-1998 85-88
Obituary 172
Eder, Richard (Gray) 1932- 130
Brief entry 123
Interview in CA-130
Edes, Benjamin 1732-1803 .... DLB 43
Edeson, Arthur 1891-1970 .... IDFW 3, 4
Edey, Maitland A(rmstrong)
1910-1992 .... CANR-6
Obituary 137
Earlier sketch in CA 57-60
See also SATA 25
See also SATA-Obit 71
Edgar, David 1948- CANR-112
Earlier sketches in CA 57-60, CANR-12, 61
See also CBD
See also CD 5, 6
See also CLC 42
See also DAM DRAM
See also DFS 15
See also DLB 13, 233
See also MTCW 1
Edgar, Donald 1916- 121
Edgar, Frank Terrell Rhoades 1932- 69-72
Edgar, Josephine
See Mussi, Mary
Edgar, Ken(neth Frank) 1925- CANR-27
Earlier sketch in CA 49-52
Edgar, Neal Lowndes 1927-1983 ...... CANR-27
Obituary 110
Earlier sketch in CA 69-72
Edgar, Stacey L. 1940- 147
Edgar, Walter B. 1943- 192
Edge, Arabella 220
Edge, David O(wen) 1932- 73-76
Edge, Findley B(artow) 1916-2002 .... 5-8R
Edge, Laura B(ufano) 1953- 238
Edgecombe, David 1952- 232
See also CD 5, 6
Edgell, Zee
See Edgell, Zelma Inez
Edgell, Zelma Inez 1940- CANR-143
Earlier sketch in CA 135
See also EWL 3
Edgerton, Clyde (Carlyle) 1944- CANR-125
Brief entry 118
Earlier sketches in CA 134, CANR-64
Interview in CA-134
See also AAYA 17
See also CLC 39
See also CN 7
See also CSW
See also DLB 278
See also TCLE 1:1
See also YAW
Edgerton, David 1959- 138
Edgerton, Franklin 1885-1963
Obituary 110
Edgerton, Gary Richard 1952- 111
Edgerton, Harold E(ugene)
1903-1990 .... CANR-80
Obituary 130
Earlier sketches in CA 53-56, CANR-5
Edgerton, James Arthur 1869-1938 204
Edgerton, Joseph S. 1900(?)-1983
Obituary 109
Edgerton, Leslie H. 1943- 153
Edgerton, Lucile Selk 1896-1987
Obituary 122
Edgerton, Robert B(reckenridge)
1931- CANR-103
Earlier sketch in CA 53-56
Edgerton, Teresa (Ann) 1949- CANR-117
Earlier sketch in CA 154
See also FANT
Edgerton, William B(enbow)
1914-2004 .... 29-32R
Edgette, Janet Sasson 1956- 234
Edgeworth, Maria 1768-1849 .... BRWS 3
See also DLB 116, 159, 163
See also FL 1:3
See also FW
See also RGEL 2
See also SATA 21
See also TEA
See also WLIT 3
Edghill, India 238
Edghill, Rosemary
See bes-Shahar, Eluki
Edgington, Eugene S(inclair) 1924- 25-28R
Edgley, Charles K(enneth) 1943- 57-60
Edgley, Roy 1925- 29-32R
Edgren, Gretchen (Grondahl) 1931- 178
Edgren, Harry D(aniel) 1899-1978 .... CAP-2
Earlier sketch in CA 33-36
Edgy, Wardore
See Gorey, Edward (St. John)
Edholm, O(tto) G(ustav) 1909-1985
Obituary 115
Edie, James M. 1927- 9-12R
Ediger, Peter J. 1926- 33-36R
Edinborough, Arnold 1922- 73-76
Edinger, Edward F(erdinand) 1922-1998 162
Obituary 169
Edington, Andrew 1914-1998 73-76
Edison, Judith
See Paul, Judith Edison
Edison, Michael (G.) 1937-
Brief entry 110
Edison, Theodore
See Stratemeyer, Edward L.
Edkardt, Roy
See Eckardt, A(rthur) Roy
Edkins, Anthony 1927- 97-100
Edkins, Diana M(aria) 1947- 41-44R
Edler, Peter 1934- 107
Edler, Richard (Bruce) 1943-2002 215
Edler, Tim(othy) 1948- .... SATA 56
Edlin, Herbert Leeson 1913-1976 .... CANR-9
Obituary 69-72
Earlier sketch in CA 61-64
Edlin, Rosabelle Alpern 1914- 9-12R
Edlow, Jonathan A. 1952- 225
Edlund, Richard 1940- .... IDFW 3, 4
Edman, David 1930- 37-40R
Edman, Marion (Louise) 1901-1996 ...... CAP-1
Earlier sketch in CA 17-18
Edman, Victor Raymond 1900-1967 .. CANR-6
Earlier sketch in CA 1-4R
Edmands, Allan 1942- 117
Edmands, Dodie 1947- 116
Edmisten, Patricia Taylor 1939- 132
Edmiston, (Helen) Jean (Mary) 1913- 13-16R
Edmiston, Jim 1948- .... SATA 80
Edmiston, Susan 1940- 65-68
Edmond, Jay
See Jones, Jack
Edmond, Lauris (Dorothy) 1924-2000 153
Obituary 188
See also CP 7
See also CWP
Edmond, Mary 1916- 121
Edmond, Murray (Donald) 1949- 153
See also CP 7
Edmond, Rod 1946- 188
Edmonds, Alan
See Edmonds, Arthur Denis
Edmonds, Ann C.
See Welch, Ann Courtenay (Edmonds)
Edmonds, Arthur Denis 1932- 73-76
Edmonds, C(ecil) J(ohn) 1889-1979 .... CAP-1
Earlier sketch in CA 13-14
Edmonds, Charles
See Carrington, Charles Edmund
Edmonds, David 1964- 230
Edmonds, Helen G(rey) 1911-1995 65-68
Edmonds, I(vy) G(ordon) 1917- CANR-30
Earlier sketches in CA 33-36R, CANR-13
See also SATA 8
Edmonds, Jae
See Edmonds, James A.
Edmonds, James A. 1947- 118
Edmonds, Margaret Hammett 101
Edmonds, Margot
See Edmonds, Margaret Hammett
Edmonds, Paul
See Kuttner, Henry
Edmonds, R(obert) H(umphrey) G(ordon)
1920- 69-72
Edmonds, (Sheppard) Randolph
1900-1983 125
See also BW 1
See also DLB 51
Edmonds, Robert 1913-1990 112
Obituary 132
Edmonds, Robin
See Edmonds, R(obert) H(umphrey) G(ordon)
Edmonds, Ronald R. 1935-1983
Obituary 110
Edmonds, Vernon H. 1927- 37-40R
Edmonds, Walter D(umaux)
1903-1998 .... CANR-2
Earlier sketch in CA 5-8R
See also BYA 2
See also CLC 35
See also CWRI 5
See also DLB 9
See also LAIT 1
See also MAICYA 1, 2
See also MAL 5
See also RHW
See also SAAS 4
See also SATA 1, 27
See also SATA-Obit 99
Edmondson, Clifton Earl 1937- 102
Edmondson, G(arry) C(otton)
1922-1995 .... CANR-89
Obituary 171
Earlier sketches in CA 57-60, CANR-11, 26
See also SFW 4
Edmondson, Garry C.
See Edmondson, G(arry) C(otton)
Edmondson, Wallace
See Ellison, Harlan (Jay)
Edmonson, Harold A(rthur) 1937- 41-44R
Edmonson, Munro Sterling 1924- CANR-28
Earlier sketch in CA 33-36R
Edmund, Sean
See Pringle, Laurence P(atrick)
Edmunds, H(enry) Tudor 1897- 106
Edmunds, (Arthur) Lowell 1938- 185
Edmunds, Malcolm 1938- 73-76
Edmunds, (Thomas) Murrell
1898-1981 .... CANR-4
Earlier sketch in CA 1-4R
Edmunds, R(ussell) David 1939- 149
Edmunds, Simeon 1917- 17-20R
Edmunds, Stahrl W(illiam) 1917-1999 69-72
Edmundson, Bruce 1952- 126
Edmundson, Mark 1952- 212
Edney, Matthew H(enry) 1962- 162
Edom, Clifton C. 1907-1991 105
Edouart, Farciot 1895-1980 .... IDFW 3, 4
Edric, Robert
See Armitage, G(ary) E(dric)
Edrich, William J(ohn) 1916-1986
Obituary 120
Edsall, Florence S(mall) 1898(?)-1986
Obituary 119
Edsall, Marian (Stickney) 1920- CANR-27
Earlier sketch in CA 49-52
See also SATA 8
Edsall, Mary D(eutsch) 1943- 142
Edsall, Thomas Byrne 1941- 126
Edschmid, Kasimir 1890-1966 177
See also Schmid, Eduard
See also DLB 56
Edson, Harold
See Hall, Asa Zadel
Edson, J(ohn) T(homas) 1928- CANR-55
Earlier sketches in CA 29-32R, CANR-12, 30
See also TCWW 1, 2
Edson, Margaret 1961- 190
See also CLC 199
See also DC 24
See also DFS 13
See also DLB 266

Cumulative Index 169 Egginton

Edson, Peter 1896-1977
  Obituary 73-76
Edson, Russell 1935- CANR-115
  Earlier sketch in CA 33-36R
  See also CLC 13
  See also CP 2, 3, 4, 5, 6, 7
  See also DLB 244
  See also WP
Eduardi, Guillermo
  See Edwards, William B(ennett)
Edvardson, Cordelia (Maria Sara) 1929-
Edwa
  See Edwards, Bill
Edward VIII 1894-1972 220
  Obituary 33-36R
Edward, John 215
Edwardes, Allen
  See Kinsley, D(aniel) A(llan)
Edwardes, Michael (F. H.) 1923- CANR-10
  Earlier sketch in CA 57-60
Edwards, A. W. F. 1935- 73-76
Edwards, Al
  See Nourse, Alan E(dward)
Edwards, Alexander
  See Fleischer, Leonore
Edwards, Allen J(ack) 1926- 33-36R
Edwards, Allen L. 1914-1994 ..... CANR-10
  Earlier sketch in CA 25-28R
Edwards, Amelia Anne Blandford
  1831-1892 ..... DLB 174
  See also SUFW
Edwards, Andie
  See Edwards, Audrey
Edwards, Anne 1927- CANR-89
  Earlier sketches in CA 61-64, CANR-13, 33, 73
  Interview in CANR-33
  See also SATA 35
Edwards, Anne K.
  See Emmons, Mary L.
Edwards, Anne-Marie 1932- CANR-38
  Earlier sketches in CA 85-88, CANR-16
Edwards, Anthony David 1936- 13-16R
Edwards, Audrey 1929- 175
Edwards, Audrey 1947- 81-84
  See also SATA 52
  See also SATA-Brief 31
Edwards, Becky (Jane) 1966- ..... SATA 125
Edwards, Bertram
  See Edwards, Herbert Charles
Edwards, Betty 1926- 105
Edwards, Bill 1929(?)-1987
  Obituary 121
Edwards, Blake 1922- CANR-32
  Earlier sketch in CA 81-84
Edwards, Bob
  See Edwards, Robert Alan
Edwards, Bronwen Elizabeth
  See Rose, Wendy
Edwards, Carl N(ormand) 1943- 57-60
Edwards, Carolyn McVickar 1954- 196
Edwards, Cecile Hoover 1926- 180
  Earlier sketch in CA 157
Edwards, Cecile Pepin 1916- 5-8R
  See also SATA 25
Edwards, Charles Edward 1930- 17-20R
Edwards, Charles Mundy, Jr. 1903-1985 .. 45-48
  Obituary 117
Edwards, Charlotte 1907-1987 ..... CANR-35
  Earlier sketch in CA 29-32R
Edwards, Christine 1902- CAP-1
  Earlier sketch in CA 19-20
Edwards, Claudia J(ane) 1943- 154
  See also FANT
Edwards, Clifford D(uane) 1934- 61-64
Edwards, Clive D. 1947- CANR-122
  Earlier sketch in CA 164
Edwards, Corwin D. 1901-1979 ..... CANR-10
  Obituary 85-88
  Earlier sketch in CA 17-20R
Edwards, David C(harles) 1937- 41-44R
Edwards, David L(awrence) 1929- CANR-54
  Earlier sketches in CA 5-8R, CANR-12, 29
Edwards, David V(andeusen) 1941- 126
  Brief entry 105
Edwards, Deborah R. 1945- 166
  See also BW 3
Edwards, Dic 1953- ..... DLB 245
Edwards, Donald (Isaac) 1904-1991 65-68
Edwards, Donald Earl
  See Harding, Donald Edward
Edwards, Dorothy 1903(?)-1934
  Brief entry 122
Edwards, Dorothy 1914-1982 ..... CANR-84
  Obituary 107
  Earlier sketches in CA 25-28R, CANR-12
  See also CWRI 5
  See also SATA 4, 88
  See also SATA-Obit 31
Edwards, Douglas 1917-1990 ..... CANR-80
  Obituary 132
  Brief entry 110
  Earlier sketch in CA 118
  Interview in CA-118
Edwards, Edgar O(wen) 1919- CANR-6
  Earlier sketch in CA 1-4R
Edwards, Edward 1812-1886 ..... DLB 184
Edwards, Eli
  See McKay, Festus Claudius
Edwards, Elizabeth
  See Inderlied, Mary Elizabeth
Edwards, Elwyn Hartley 1927- CANR-8
  Earlier sketch in CA 61-64
Edwards, F. E.
  See Nolan, William F(rancis)
Edwards, Francis
  See Brandon, Johnny
Edwards, Frank Allyn 1908-1967 ..... CANR-1
  Earlier sketch in CA 1-4R
Edwards, Frank B. 1952- 158
  See also SATA 93
Edwards, G(erald) B(asil) 1899-1976 201
  Obituary 110
  See also CLC 25
Edwards, Gawain
  See Pendray, George Edward
Edwards, George 1914-1995 53-56
Edwards, George Charles III 1947- . CANR-100
  Earlier sketches in CA 107, CANR-24, 49
Edwards, Gerald (Kenneth Savery) Hamilton
  See Hamilton-Edwards, Gerald (Kenneth Savery)
Edwards, Gillian (Mary) 1918- 25-28R
Edwards, Grace F. 180
  See also BYA 12
Edwards, Graham 1965- 154
  See also FANT
Edwards, Gunvor 107
  See also SATA 32
Edwards, Gus 1939- 108
  Interview in CA-108
  See also CLC 43
Edwards, Gwynne 215
Edwards, Hank
  See Broomall, Robert W(alter)
Edwards, Harry
  See Edwards, Henry James
Edwards, Harry (Jr.) 1942- 111
  Brief entry 109
  Interview in CA-111
Edwards, Harvey 1929- 25-28R
  See also SATA 5
Edwards, Hazel (Eileen) 1945- CANR-113
  Earlier sketch in CA 124
  See also SATA 135
Edwards, Henry James 1893-1976 ..... 13-16R
  Obituary 122
Edwards, Herbert Charles 1912- 9-12R
  See also SATA 12
Edwards, Hilton 1903-1982 65-68
Edwards, I(orwerth) E(iddon) S(tephen)
  1909-1996 ..... CANR-7
  Obituary 153
  Earlier sketch in CA 13-16R
Edwards, India 1896(?)-1990
  Obituary 130
Edwards, James Don(ald) 1926- CANR-4
  Earlier sketch in CA 9-12R
Edwards, James Keith O'Neill 1920-1988
  Obituary 126
Edwards, Jane Campbell 1932- 13-16R
  See also SATA 10
Edwards, Jaroldeen 1932- 102
Edwards, Jerome E(arl) 1937- 37-40R
Edwards, Jimmy
  See Edwards, James Keith O'Neill
Edwards, John 1943- 118
Edwards, John Carver 1939- 181
Edwards, John Milton
  See Cook, William Wallace
Edwards, Jonathan, Jr. 1745-1801 ..... DLB 37
Edwards, Jonathan 1703-1758 ..... AMW
  See also DA
  See also DAC
  See also DAM MST
  See also DLB 24, 270
  See also RGAL 4
  See also TUS
Edwards, Jorge 1931- 191
  See also EWL 3
  See also LAW
Edwards, Josephine Cunnington
  1904-1993 ..... 13-16R
Edwards, Josh
  See Levinson, Leonard
Edwards, Julia
  See Stratemeyer, Edward L.
Edwards, Julia Spalding 1920- 37-40R
Edwards, Julie
  See Andrews, Julie
Edwards, Julie Andrews
  See Andrews, Julie
Edwards, June CANR-45
  See also Bhatia, Jamunadevi
Edwards, Junius 1929- 142
  See also BW 2
  See also DLB 33
Edwards, K(enneth) Morgan 1912-2003 .... 5-8R
  Obituary 216
Edwards, Kate F(lournoy) 1877-1980 107
Edwards, Kim 1958- 219
  See also SSFS 18
Edwards, Larry 1957- 160
Edwards, Lee 1932- CANR-10
  Earlier sketch in CA 25-28R
Edwards, Lee R. 1942- 124
Edwards, Leo
  See Lee, Edward Edson
Edwards, Linda Strauss 1948- 126
  See also SATA 49
  See also SATA-Brief 42
Edwards, Louis 1962- CANR-140
  Earlier sketch in CA 168
Edwards, Lyford Paterson 1882-1984
  Obituary 113
Edwards, Lynne 1943- 73-76
Edwards, Margaret (Alexander)
  1902-1988 ..... CAP-2
  Obituary 125
  Earlier sketch in CA 29-32
  See also SATA-Obit 56
Edwards, Marie Babare 57-60
Edwards, Mark U(lin), Jr. 1946- CANR-10
  Earlier sketch in CA 65-68
Edwards, (Kenneth) Martin 1955- 137
Edwards, Marvin L(ouis) 1915- 13-16R
Edwards, Max
  See Benjamin, Claude (Max Edward Pohlman)
Edwards, Michael 1932- 85-88
Edwards, Michael 1938- CANR-22
  Earlier sketch in CA 106
Edwards, Michelle 1955- 138
  See also SATA 70, 152
Edwards, Monica le Doux Newton
  1912-1998 ..... 9-12R
  Obituary 164
  See also CWRI 5
  See also SATA 12
Edwards, Nicky 1958- 122
Edwards, Norman
  See Carr, Terry (Gene) and
  White, Theodore Edwin
Edwards, Norman
  See Carr, Terry (Gene)
Edwards, O(tis) C(arl), Jr. 1928- 53-56
Edwards, Oliver
  See Haley, William (John)
Edwards, Olwen
  See Gater, Dilys
Edwards, Owen Dudley 1938- CANR-7
  Earlier sketch in CA 57-60
Edwards, P(rior) Max(imilian) H(emsley)
  1914- 37-40R
Edwards, Page (Lawrence, Jr.)
  1941-1999 ..... CANR-27
  Earlier sketches in CA 45-48, CANR-1
  See also SATA 59
Edwards, Paul 1923-2004 85-88
  Obituary 234
Edwards, Paul 1940- 123
Edwards, Paul Geoffrey 1926-1992 57-60
  Obituary 137
Edwards, Paul M(adison) 1933- 41-44R
Edwards, P.D. 1931- 170
Edwards, Peter (William) 1934- 109
Edwards, Philip 1923- CANR-55
  Earlier sketches in CA 25-28R, CANR-12, 29
Edwards, Phoebe
  See Bloch, Barbara
Edwards, Phyllis Irene 1916-1984
  Obituary 114
Edwards, R. M.
  See Edwards, Roselyn
Edwards, R. T.
  See Goulart, Ron(ald Joseph)
Edwards, (H. C.) Ralph 1894-1977 ..... CAP-1
  Earlier sketch in CA 13-16
Edwards, Raoul D(urant) 1928-1987
  Obituary 125
Edwards, Rem B(lanchard, Jr.) 1934- 37-40R
Edwards, Richard 1524-1566 ..... DLB 62
Edwards, Richard Alan 1934- 69-72
Edwards, Richard C. 1944- CANR-2
  Earlier sketch in CA 45-48
Edwards, Robert (John) 1925- 129
Edwards, Robert Alan 1947- 121
  Interview in CA-121
Edwards, Ron(ald George) 1930- 105
Edwards, Roselyn 1929- 25-28R
Edwards, Ruth Dudley
  See Dudley Edwards, Ruth
Edwards, S. W.
  See Sublette, Walter (Edwards)
Edwards, Sally (Cary) 1929- 25-28R
  See also SATA 7
Edwards, Samuel
  See Gerson, Noel Bertram
Edwards, Sarah (Anne) 1943- 201
Edwards, Sarah Pierpont 1710-1758 ... DLB 200
Edwards, Sean J(ames) A(lexander) 1964- ... 195
Edwards, Stephen
  See Palestrant, Simon S.
Edwards, Susan 228
Edwards, Susan 1947- CANR-138
  Earlier sketch in CA 151
Edwards, T(homas) Bentley 1906- CAP-2
  Earlier sketch in CA 23-24
Edwards, Thomas R(obert), Jr. 1928- 5-8R
Edwards, Thomas S. 1959- 207
Edwards, Tilden Hampton, Jr. 1935- . CANR-18
  Earlier sketch in CA 102
Edwards, Verne E(rvie), Jr. 1924- 33-36R
Edwards, Vince 1928-1996 159
Edwards, Ward 1927-2005 ..... 21-24R
  Obituary 236
Edwards, William 1896- CAP-1
  Earlier sketch in CA 13-14
Edwards, William B(ennett) 1927- 5-8R
Edwards Bello, Joaquin 1886(?)-1968 178
  See also HW 2
Edwin, Brother B.
  See Arnandez, Richard
Edzard, Christine 1945- 164
Eeden, Frederik Willem van 1860-1932 . EWL 3
Eekelaar, John M(ichael) 1942- 116
Eekman, Thomas 1923- 81-84
Eells, George 1922-1995 ..... CANR-14
  Earlier sketch in CA 21-24R
Eells, Richard S(edric) F(ox) 1917- 132
Eells, Robert J(ames) 1944- 102
Ee Tiang Hong 1933- ..... CP 1
Eeuwens, Adam 238
Efemey, Raymond (Frederick) 1928- 21-24R
Effinger, George Alec 1947-2002 ..... CANR-23
  Obituary 206
  Earlier sketch in CA 37-40R
  See also DLB 8
  See also SFW 4
Efimova, Alla 1961- 162
Efird, James M(ichael) 1932- CANR-31
  Earlier sketches in CA 37-40R, CANR-14
Efremov, Ivan (Antonovich)
  See Yefremov, Ivan (Antonovich)
Efron, Alexander 1897-1981 ..... CAP-2
  Earlier sketch in CA 29-32
Efron, Arthur 1931- CANR-21
  Earlier sketch in CA 69-72
Efron, Benjamin 1908-1991 ..... CANR-5
  Earlier sketch in CA 5-8R
Efron, Edith Carol 1922- 102
Efron, Marina Ivanovna Tsvetaeva
  See Tsvetaeva (Efron), Marina (Ivanovna)
Efron, Marshall 1938(?)- 126
  Brief entry 112
Efros, Israel (Isaac) 1891-1981 ..... 21-24R
  Obituary 102
Efros, Susan Elyse 1947- 104
Efrot
  See Efros, Israel (Isaac)
Egami, Tomi 1899- 61-64
Egan, Beresford Patrick 1905-1984
  Obituary 111
Egan, Catherine 1943- 146
Egan, David R(onald) 1943- 102
Egan, Desmond 1936- CANR-102
  Earlier sketch in CA 149
Egan, E(dward) W(elstead) 1922- CANR-9
  Earlier sketch in CA 21-24R
  See also SATA 35
Egan, Ferol 1923- 29-32R
Egan, Fred(erick Julian) 1905(?)-1986
  Obituary 118
Egan, Gerard 1930- CANR-52
  Earlier sketches in CA 29-32R, CANR-12, 28
Egan, Greg 1961- CANR-109
  Earlier sketch in CA 165
  See also SFW 4
Egan, Harvey Daniel 1937- 113
Egan, James F. 191
Egan, Jennifer 1962- CANR-112
  Earlier sketch in CA 154
Egan, Jim
  See Egan, James F.
Egan, John P. 1934- 110
Egan, Kathleen
  See Chamberlain, Kathleen P.
Egan, Kieran 1942- 161
Egan, Lesley
  See Linington, (Barbara) Elizabeth
Egan, Linda 1945- 208
Egan, Lorraine Hopping 1960- CANR-109
  Earlier sketch in CA 155
  See also SATA 91, 134
Egan, Melinda A(nne) 1950- 102
Egan, Michael 1941- 45-48
Egan, Philip S(idney) 1920- 1-4R
Egan, Pierce 1772-1849 ..... RGEL 2
Egan, Robert 1945- 77-80
Egan, Tim 1957- 149
  See also SATA 89, 155
Egan, Timothy 1954- 141
Egawa, Keith 1966- 189
Egbert, Donald Drew 1902-1973 ..... CAP-2
  Obituary 37-40R
  Earlier sketch in CA 23-24
Egbert, Kathlyn Whitsitt 1950- 150
Egbert, Virginia Wylie
  See Kilborne, Virginia Wylie
Egbuna, Obi B(enue Joseph) 1938- 102
  See also AFW
  See also CD 5, 6
Ege, Arvia MacKaye 1903(?)-1989
  Obituary 128
Egejuru, Phanuel Akubueze 106
Egelhof, Joseph (Baird) 1919(?)-1980
  Obituary 97-100
Eger, Jeffrey 1946- 125
Egermeier, Elsie E(milie) 1890-1986 ..... 5-8R
  See also SATA 65
Egerton, Frank N(icholas) III 1936- 110
Egerton, George 1859-1945 ..... DLB 135
Egerton, George W(illiam) 1942- 85-88
Egerton, John (Walden) 1935- CANR-47
  Earlier sketch in CA 85-88
Egerton, Judy 178
Egerton, Lucy
  See Malleson, Lucy Beatrice
Egg, Maria 1910- 29-32R
Egg-Benes, Maria
  See Egg, Maria
Eggeling, Hans Friedrich 1878-1977 ..... 1-4R
  Obituary 73-76
Eggenberger, David 1918- 9-12R
  See also SATA 6
Eggenschwiler, David 1936- 37-40R
Egger, Andrea (A.) 1967- 209
Egger, M(aurice) David 1936- 57-60
Egger, Rowland (Andrews)
  1908-1979 ..... CANR-4
  Earlier sketch in CA 5-8R
Egger-Bovet, Howard W. 1956- 221
Eggers, Dave 1971(?)- CANR-138
  Earlier sketch in CA 198
  See also AAYA 56
  See also MTFW 2005
Eggers, J(ohn) Philip 1940- 33-36R
Eggers, Kerry 1953- 137
Eggers, Paul 1953- 222
Eggers, William T. 1912-1993 ..... 29-32R
Eggert, Gerald G(ordon) 1926- 21-24R
Eggert, James (Edward) 1943- CANR-47
  Earlier sketches in CA 107, CANR-23
Eggert, Jim
  See Eggert, James (Edward)
Egginton, Joyce 142

Eggleston, Edward 1837-1902
Brief entry 111
See also DLB 12
See also RGAL 4
See also SATA 27
Eggleston, George T(eeple) 1906-1990
Obituary 132
Eggleston, Wilfrid 1901-1986 .... CANR-8
Obituary 119
Earlier sketch in CA 21-24R
See also DLB 92
Eggum, Arne 1936- 134
Egharevba, Jacob U(wadiae)
1920(?)- CANR-87
Earlier sketch in CA 152
See also BW 2
Egielski, Richard 1952- 175
See also MAICYA 1, 2
See also SATA 11, 49, 106, 163
Egler, Claudio A(ntonio) G(oncalves)
1951- 144
Egler, Frank E(dwin) 1911-1996 .... 29-32R
Obituary 155
Egleson, Janet F.
See Dunleavy, Janet Egleson
Egleton, Clive (Frederick) 1927- CANR-121
Earlier sketches in CA 103, CANR-22
See also CMW 4
Egli, Ida Rae 1946- 137
Eglin, Anthony 238
Eglington, Charles 1918- .... CP 1
Eglitis, Anslavs 1906-1993 .... DLB 220
Egoff, Sheila A. 1918- CANR-86
Brief entry 116
Earlier sketch in CA 132
Egolf, Tristan 1971-2005 217
Obituary 239
Egoyan, Atom 1960- 157
See also AAYA 63
See also CLC 151
Egremont, Max 1948- CANR-82
Earlier sketches in CA 93-96, CANR-35
Egremont, Michael
See Harrison, Michael
Eguchi, Shinichi 1914-1979
Obituary 85-88
Egudu, R. N.
See Egudu, Romanus N(nagbo)
Egudu, Romanus N(nagbo) 1940- 143
See also BW 2
Eguren, Jose Maria 1874-1942 .... DLB 290
See also LAW
Egypt, Ophelia Settle 1903-1984 81-84
Obituary 112
See also SATA 16
See also SATA-Obit 38
Ehle, John (Marsden, Jr.) 1925- 9-12R
See also CLC 27
See also CSW
Ehler, R(ichard) L. 1930- 137
Ehlers, Henry James 1907-1995 .... 13-16R
Ehlert, Lois (Jane) 1934- CANR-107
Earlier sketch in CA 137
See also CLR 28
See also CWRI 5
See also MAICYA 1, 2
See also SATA 35, 69, 128
Ehling, Katalin Olah 1941- .... SATA 93
Ehmann, James 1948- 109
Ehninger, Douglas W(agner)
1913-1979 .... CANR-4
Earlier sketch in CA 5-8R
Ehre, Edward 1905-1990 .... 9-12R
Ehre, Milton 1933- 53-56
Ehrenberg, John 1944- 159
Ehrenberg, Miriam 124
Ehrenberg, Otto 1926- 124
Ehrenberg, Victor (Leopold)
1891-1976 .... CANR-4
Obituary 65-68
Earlier sketch in CA 5-8R
Ehrenbourg, Ilya (Grigoryevich)
See Ehrenburg, Ilya (Grigoryevich)
Ehrenburg, Ilya (Grigoryevich) 1891-1967 .. 102
Obituary 25-28R
See also Erenburg, Il'ia Grigor'evich
See also CLC 18, 34, 62
See also EWL 3
Ehrenburg, Ilyo (Grigoryevich)
See Ehrenburg, Ilya (Grigoryevich)
Ehrenfeld, David W(illiam) 1938- 81-84
Ehrenfest, Paul 1880-1933 157
Ehrenfreund, Norbert 1921- 151
See also SATA 86
Ehrenhalt, Alan 1947- 112
Ehrenpreis, Anne Henry 1927-1978 53-56
Ehrenpreis, Irvin 1920-1985 121
Obituary 116
Brief entry 110
Ehrenreich, Barbara 1941- CANR-117
Earlier sketches in CA 73-76, CANR-16, 37, 62
See also BEST 90:4
See also CLC 110
See also DLB 246
See also FW
See also MTCW 1, 2
See also MTFW 2005
Ehrenreich, Herman 1900(?)-1970
Obituary 104
Ehrenreich, John H. 1943- 125
Ehrenstein, Albert 1886-1950 177
See also DLB 81
Ehrensvaerd, Goesta (Carl Henrik)
1910- CANR-2
Earlier sketch in CA 49-52
Ehrenwald, Jan 1900-1988 .... CANR-2
Obituary 125
Earlier sketch in CA 49-52
Ehrenzweig, Albert A(rmin) 1906-1974 . CAP-2
Earlier sketch in CA 29-32
Ehresmann, Donald L(ouis) 1937- 69-72
Ehresmann, Julia M. 1939- 33-36R
Ehresnvard, Gosta Carl Henrik
See Ehrensvaerd, Goesta (Carl Henrik)
Ehret, Christopher 1941- 37-40R
Ehret, Terry 1955- CANR-97
Earlier sketch in CA 143
Ehrhardt, Reinhold 1900- 29-32R
Ehrhart, W(illiam) D(aniel) 1948- CANR-90
Earlier sketches in CA 61-64, CANR-7, 52
See also DLBD 9
Ehricke, Krafft A(rnold) 1917-1984
Obituary 114
Ehrler, Brenda 1953- 175
Ehrlich, Amy 1942- CANR-121
Earlier sketches in CA 37-40R, CANR-14, 32, 67
See also MAICYA 2
See also MAICYAS 1
See also SATA 25, 65, 96, 132
See also YAW
Ehrlich, Anne (Fitzhugh) Howland
1933- CANR-8
Earlier sketch in CA 61-64
Ehrlich, Arnold 1923-1989 .... 33-36R
Obituary 129
Ehrlich, Bettina Bauer 1903-1985 .... CAP-1
Earlier sketch in CA 13-14
See also CWRI 5
See also SATA 1
Ehrlich, Carol H. 1927- 165
Ehrlich, Cyril 1925-2004 103
Obituary 227
Ehrlich, David 1941- CANR-112
Earlier sketches in CA 127, CANR-55
Ehrlich, Eugene H. 1922- CANR-5
Earlier sketch in CA 1-4R
Ehrlich, Ev(erett M.) 1950- CANR-108
Earlier sketch in CA 112, 190
Ehrlich, Gretel 1946- CANR-74
Earlier sketch in CA 140
See also ANW
See also DLB 212, 275
See also TCWW 2
Ehrlich, H. M.
See Ziefert, Harriet
Ehrlich, Howard J. 1932- 17-20R
Ehrlich, Isaac 1938- 118
Ehrlich, Jack
See Ehrlich, John Gunther
See also TCWW 2
Ehrlich, Jacob Wilburn 1900-1971
Obituary 33-36R
Ehrlich, Jake
See Ehrlich, Jacob Wilburn
Ehrlich, John Gunther 1930- CANR-63
Earlier sketches in CA 1-4R, CANR-4
See also Ehrlich, Jack
Ehrlich, Leonard Harry 1924- 102
Ehrlich, Linda C. 1952- 201
Ehrlich, Max 1909-1983 .... CANR-72
Obituary 115
Earlier sketches in CA 1-4R, CANR-1
See also HGG
Ehrlich, Nathaniel J(oseph) 1940- 53-56
Ehrlich, Otto Hild 1892-1979
Obituary 85-88
Ehrlich, Paul R(alph) 1932- CANR-135
Earlier sketches in CA 65-68, CANR-8, 28
Ehrlich, Robert S. 1935- 21-24R
Ehrlich, Thomas 1934- 113
Ehrlich, Walter 1921- 53-56
Ehrlichman, John Daniel
1925-1999 .... CANR-45
Obituary 177
Earlier sketch in CA 65-68
Ehrman, Bart D. 203
Ehrman, John (Patrick William)
1920- CANR-26
Earlier sketches in CA 5-8R, CANR-4
Ehrman, John 1959- 149
Ehrman, Kit 1956- 214
Ehrman, Lee 1935- 69-72
Ehrmann, Herbert B(rutus) 1891-1970 ... CAP-2
Earlier sketch in CA 25-28
Ehrsam, Theodore George 1909- 45-48
Eibel, Deborah 1940- 151
Eibl-Eibesfeldt, Irenaeus 1928- CANR-3
Earlier sketch in CA 9-12R
Eibling, Harold Henry 1905-1976 .... CANR-29
Earlier sketch in CA 37-40R
Eiby, George 1918- 53-56
Eich, Gunter
See Eich, Gunter
See also RGWL 2, 3
Eich, Gunter 1907-1972 111
Obituary 93-96
See also Eich, Gunter
See also CLC 15
See also DLB 69, 124
See also EWL 3
Eichelbaum, Samuel 1894-1967 .... LAW
Eichelbaum, Stanley 1926- 73-76
Eichelberger, Clark M(ell) 1896-1980
Obituary 93-96
Eichelberger, Clayton L. 1925- 41-44R
Eichelberger, Ethyl 1945-1990
Obituary 132
Eichelberger, Rosa Kohler 1896-1982 102
Eichenbaum, Luise 1952- 126
Eichenberg, Fritz 1901-1990 .... CANR-57
Obituary 133
Earlier sketches in CA 57-60, CANR-6
See also AAYA 54
See also MAICYA 1, 2
See also SATA 9, 50
Eichendorff, Joseph 1788-1857 .... DLB 90
See also RGWL 2, 3
Eichengreen, Lucille 1925- 190
Eichenlaub, John Ellis 1922- CANR-4
Earlier sketch in CA 1-4R
Eichenwald, Kurt 1962(?)- 229
Eicher, David J(ohn) 1961- CANR-111
Earlier sketch in CA 113
Eicher, (Ethel) Elizabeth 17-20R
Eicher, Joanne B(ubolz) 1930- CANR-28
Earlier sketch in CA 49-52
Eichhorn, David Max 1906-1986 .... CAP-1
Earlier sketch in CA 11-12
Eichhorn, Werner 1899-1991 .... 29-32R
Eichler, Margrit 1942- 107
See also SATA 35
Eichler, Ned 1930- 132
Eichman, Mark 1949- 109
Eichner, Alfred S. 1937-1988 .... CANR-5
Obituary 124
Earlier sketch in CA 13-16R
Eichner, Hans 1921- CANR-41
Earlier sketches in CA 5-8R, CANR-4, 19
Eichner, James A. 1927- 13-16R
See also SATA 4
Eichner, Maura 1915- CANR-14
Earlier sketch in CA 37-40R
Eichorn, Dorothy H(ansen) 1924- CANR-27
Earlier sketch in CA 49-52
Eichorn, Rosemary D. 1943- 202
Eick, Gretchen Cassel 1942- 209
Eickhoff, Andrew R(obert) 1924- 21-24R
Eickhoff, R. L.
See Eickhoff, Randy Lee
Eickhoff, Randy Lee 204
Eicoff, Alvin M(aurey) 1921-2002 112
Obituary 208
Eid, Leif 1908(?)-1976
Obituary 65-68
Eidam, Klaus 1926- 231
Eidelberg, Ludwig 1898-1970 .... CAP-1
Obituary 29-32R
Earlier sketch in CA 19-20
Eidelberg, Paul 1928- CANR-129
Earlier sketches in CA 21-24R, CANR-27
Eidem, Odd 1913-1988 190
See also EWL 3
Eidenberg, Eugene 1939- 81-84
Eidesheim, Julie 1884-1972
Obituary 104
Eidinow, John 231
Eidse, Faith 1955- 234
Eidsmoe, John 1945- CANR-40
Earlier sketch in CA 114
Eidson, Thomas 1944- 173
See also SATA 112
Eidson, William 1956- 190
Eidsvik, Charles Vernon 1943- 101
Eidt, Robert C. 1923- 33-36R
Eidus, Janice 1951- 186
Eiduson, Bernice T(abackman)
1921-1985 .... CANR-27
Earlier sketch in CA 1-4R
Eiesland, Nancy L. 1964- 222
Eifert, Virginia (Louise) S(nider)
1911-1966 .... CANR-15
Earlier sketch in CA 1-4R
See also ANW
See also SATA 2
Eifukumon'in, Empress 1271-1342 ..... DLB 203
Eige, (Elizabeth) Lillian 1915- CANR-127
Earlier sketch in CA 136
See also SATA 65
Eigen, Manfred 1927- 108
Eigen, Michael 1936- CANR-39
Earlier sketch in CA 115
Eighner, Lars 1948- 143
Eigner, Edwin M(oss) 1931- 21-24R
Eigner, Larry
See Eigner, Laurence (Joel)
See also CAAS 23
See also CLC 9
See also CP 1, 2
See also DLB 5
See also WP
Eigner, Laurence (Joel) 1927-1996 .... CANR-84
Obituary 151
Earlier sketches in CA 9-12R, CANR-6
See also Eigner, Larry
See also CP 7
See also DLB 193
Eiken, J. Melia 1967- .... SATA 125
Eikerenkoetter, Frederick J(oseph) II 1935- .. 226
Eiland, Howard 1948- CANR-95
Earlier sketch in CA 111
Eiland, Murray L(ee) 1936- CANR-144
Earlier sketch in CA 85-88
Eilberg-Schwartz, Howard 1956- 147
Eilert, Richard E. 1947- 129
Eilert, Rick
See Eilert, Richard E.
Eilhart von Oberge c. 1140-c. 1195 .... DLB 148
Eilon, Samuel 1923- CANR-4
Earlier sketch in CA 5-8R
Eimer, D(ean) Robert 1927- 13-16R
Eimerl, Sarel (Henry) 1925- 21-24R
Einbond, Bernard Lionel 1937- 37-40R
Einhard c. 770-840 .... DLB 148
Einhorn, Barbara 1942- 156
Einhorn, Virginia Hilu
See Hilu, Virginia
Einsel, Mary E. 1929- 29-32R
Einsel, Naiad .... SATA 10
Einsel, Walter 1926- .... SATA 10
Einstein, Albert
See Brooks, Albert
Einstein, Albert 1879-1955 133
Brief entry 121
See also MTCW 1, 2
See also TCLC 65
Einstein, Charles 1926- CANR-96
Earlier sketches in CA 65-68, CANR-29
Einstein, Elizabeth (Ann) 1939- CANR-27
Earlier sketch in CA 109
Einstein, Stanley 1934- CANR-4
Earlier sketch in CA 53-56
Einstoss, Ron 1930(?)-1977
Obituary 69-72
Einzig, Paul 1897-1973 .... CANR-5
Obituary 89-92
Earlier sketch in CA 9-12R
Einzig, Susan 1922- .... SATA 43
Eire, Carlos M(ario) N(ieto) 1950- .. CANR-134
Earlier sketch in CA 127
Eirelin, Glenn
See Evans, Glen
Eisdorfer, Carl 1930- 41-44R
Eisele, Albert A(lois) 1936- 41-44R
Eisele, Robert H. 1948- CANR-25
Earlier sketch in CA 108
Eiseley, Loren
See Eiseley, Loren Corey
See also DLB 275
Eiseley, Loren Corey 1907-1977 .... CANR-6
Obituary 73-76
Earlier sketch in CA 1-4R
See also Eiseley, Loren
See also AAYA 5
See also ANW
See also CLC 7
See also DLBD 17
Eiseman, Alberta 1925- 77-80
See also SATA 15
Eiseman, Alvord L. 1916-1991 112
Eisen, Arnold M. 1951- 189
Eisen, Carol G.
See Rinzler, Carol Eisen (Gene)
Eisen, Jack 1925-1996 73-76
Eisen, Sydney 1929- 135
Eisenach, Eldon J(ohn) 1938- 106
Eisenberg, Arlene 1934-2001 139
Obituary 193
Eisenberg, Azriel (Louis) 1903-1985 . CANR-10
Obituary 164
Earlier sketch in CA 49-52
See also SATA 12
Eisenberg, Benjamin 1916-1984
Obituary 112
Eisenberg, Daniel Bruce 1946- CANR-6
Earlier sketch in CA 57-60
Eisenberg, Deborah 1945- CANR-143
Earlier sketch in CA 158
See also DLB 244
Eisenberg, Dennis (Harold) 1929- CANR-28
Earlier sketch in CA 25-28R
Eisenberg, Ellen M. 1962- 154
Eisenberg, Evan 1955(?)- 192
Eisenberg, Gerson G. 1909-1999 81-84
Eisenberg, Hershey H. 1927- 104
Eisenberg, Howard 1946- 101
Eisenberg, John S. 1956- 225
Eisenberg, Larry 1919- 33-36R
Eisenberg, Lawrence B(enjamin) 77-80
Eisenberg, Lee 1946- CANR-9
Earlier sketch in CA 61-64
Eisenberg, Lisa 1949- CANR-139
Earlier sketch in CA 110
See also SATA 57, 155
See also SATA-Brief 50
Eisenberg, Maurice 1902-1972
Obituary 37-40R
Eisenberg, Phyllis Rose 1924- 111
See also SATA 41
Eisenberg, Ralph 1930-1973 .... CANR-3
Obituary 45-48
Earlier sketch in CA 5-8R
Eisenberg, Robert 1956- 161
Eisenberg, Ronald L(ee) 1945- CANR-53
Earlier sketches in CA 73-76, CANR-13, 28
Eisenberg, Susan 1950- 209
Eisenberger, Kenneth 1948- 81-84
Eisenbud, Jule 1908-1999 .... CANR-27
Obituary 177
Earlier sketch in CA 49-52
Eisendrath, Craig R. 1936- CANR-112
Earlier sketch in CA 49-52
Eisendrath, Maurice N(athan) 1902-1973 ... 234
Eisendrath, Polly Young
See Young-Eisendrath, Polly
Eisenhart, Margaret A. 1950- 190
Eisenhower, Dwight D(avid)
1890-1969 .... CANR-24
Earlier sketch in CA 65-68
Eisenhower, John S(heldon) D(oud)
1922- CANR-127
Earlier sketches in CA 33-36R, CANR-14, 32
Eisenhower, Julie Nixon 1948- 114
Eisenhower, Milton S(tover) 1899-1985 ... 73-76
Obituary 116
Eisenhower, Susan (Elaine) 1951- 162
Eisenman, Peter D(avid) 1932- 108
Eisenman, Stephen F. 1956- CANR-71
Earlier sketch in CA 140
Eisenmenger, Robert Waltz 1926- 37-40R
Eisenreich, Herbert 1925-1986 176
See also DLB 85
Eisenschiml, Otto 1880-1963 .... 1-4R

Cumulative Index 171 **Eliot**

Eisenson, Jon 1907-2001 .... 17-20R
  Obituary 197
Eisenson, Marc 1943- 171
Eisenstadt, Abraham S(eldin) 1920- .. CANR-94
  Earlier sketches in CA 9-12R, CANR-4
Eisenstadt, Jill 1963- 140
  See also CLC 50
Eisenstadt, Shmuel N(oah) 1923- 25-28R
Eisenstaedt, Alfred 1898-1995 108
  Obituary 149
  See also AAYA 45
Eisenstat, Jane Sperry 1920- 1-4R
Eisenstein, Elizabeth L(ewisohn) 1923- 89-92
Eisenstein, Hester 1940- 137
Eisenstein, Ira 1906-2001 .... 21-24R
  Obituary 196, 197
Eisenstein, James 1940- 180
  Brief entry 111
Eisenstein, Linda 1950- 221
Eisenstein, Phyllis 1946- CANR-83
  Earlier sketches in CA 85-88, CANR-16, 36
  See also FANT
  See also SFW 4
Eisenstein, Sam(uel Abraham)
  1932- CANR-16
  Earlier sketch in CA 61-64
Eisenstein, Sergei (Mikhailovich)
  1898-1948 149
  Brief entry 114
  See also TCLC 57
Eiserer, Leonard Arnold 1948- 73-76
Eisgruber, Christopher L(udwig) 1961- 227
Eisiminger, Sterling, (Jr.) 1941- 141
Eisinger, Chester E(manuel) 1915- 21-24R
Eisinger, Josef 1924- 167
Eisinger, Peter K(endall) 1942- 69-72
Eisler, Barry 1964- 225
Eisler, Benita 1937- CANR-89
  Earlier sketch in CA 136
Eisler, Colin (Tobias) 1931- 85-88
Eisler, Frieda Goldman
  See Goldman-Eisler, Frieda
Eisler, Georg 1928-1998
  Brief entry 106
Eisler, George B. 1892(?)-1983
  Obituary 111
Eisler, Hanns 1898-1962
  Obituary 116
  See also IDFW 3, 4
Eisler, Lawrence 1920- 122
Eisler, Paul (Erich) 1922-1978 .... CANR-76
  Obituary 125
  Earlier sketch in CA 61-64
Eisler, Riane Tennenhaus 1931- CANR-94
  Earlier sketch in CA 73-76
Eisman, Hy 1927- 65-68
Eisman, Mark 1948- 108
Eismann, Bernard N(orman) 1933- 1-4R
Eisner, Betty Grover 1915- 29-32R
Eisner, Elliot W(ayne) 1933- CANR-136
  Brief entry 118
  Earlier sketch in CA 123
Eisner, Gisela (Spanglet) 1925- CAP-1
  Earlier sketch in CA 9-10
Eisner, Kurt 1867-1919 176
  See also DLB 66
Eisner, Lotte (Henriette) 1896-1983 .. CANR-14
  Obituary 111
  Earlier sketch in CA 45-48
Eisner, Michael (Dammann) 1942- 176
Eisner, Michael Alexander 203
Eisner, Peter (Norman) 1950- 232
Eisner, Robert 1922-1998 .... CANR-92
  Obituary 172
  Earlier sketch in CA 107
Eisner, Sigmund 1920- 124
Eisner, Simon
  See Kornbluth, C(yril) M.
Eisner, Thomas 1929- 157
Eisner, Victor 1921- 53-56
Eisner, Vivienne
  See Margolis, Vivienne
Eisner, Will(iam Erwin) 1917-2005 . CANR-140
  Obituary 235
  Earlier sketches in CA 108, CANR-114
  See also AAYA 52
  See also MTFW 2005
  See also SATA 31
Eiss, Harry Edwin 1950- CANR-52
  Earlier sketch in CA 124
Eissenstat, Bernard W. 1927- 45-48
Eissler, Kurt (Robert) 1908-1999 199
Eister, Allan W(ardell) 1915-1979 .... CANR-2
  Earlier sketch in CA 45-48
Eiteman, David (Kurt) 1930- 45-48
Eiteman, Wilford J(ohn) 1902-1986 .... CANR-4
  Earlier sketch in CA 1-4R
Eitinger, Leo S(hua) 1912-1996 .... CANR-16
  Earlier sketch in CA 89-92
Eitington, Julius E. 1918- 120
Eitner, Lorenz E. A. 1919- CANR-5
  Earlier sketch in CA 1-4R
Eitzen, Allan 1928- .... SATA 9
Eitzen, D(avid) Stanley 1934- CANR-41
  Earlier sketches in CA 53-56, CANR-4, 19
Eitzen, Ruth (Carper) 1924- 41-44R
  See also SATA 9
Ekbatani, Glayol 187
Ekblaw, Robert 1964- 178
Ekblaw, Sidney E(verette) 1903-1990 .... 37-40R
  Obituary 164
Ekdahl, Janis (Kay) 1946-
  Brief entry 112
Ekeblad, Frederick A(lfred) 1917- 5-8R
Ekeh, Peter P(almer) 1937- 102
Ekeloef, (Bengt) Gunnar 1907-1968 123
  Obituary 25-28R
  See also Ekelof, (Bengt) Gunnar
  See also CLC 27
  See also DAM POET
  See also PC 23
Ekelof, (Bengt) Gunnar 1907-1968
  See Ekeloef, (Bengt) Gunnar
  See also DLB 259
  See also EW 12
  See also EWL 3
Ekelund, Vilhelm 1880-1949 189
  See also EWL 3
  See also TCLC 75
Ekert-Rotholz, Alice Maria (Augusta)
  1900-1995 129
Ekins, Paul (Whitfield) 1950- CANR-50
  Earlier sketch in CA 123
Ekirch, A(rthur) Roger 1950- 109
Ekirch, Arthur A., Jr. 1915- CANR-2
  Earlier sketch in CA 5-8R
Ekker, Charles 1930- 37-40R
Ekland, Britt(-Marie) 1942- 172
Eklund, Gordon (Stewart) 1945- CANR-83
  Earlier sketches in CA 33-36R, CANR-24
  See also DLBY 1983
  See also SFW 4
Eklund, Jane Mary
  See Ball, Jane Eklund
Ekman, Kerstin (Lillemor) 1933- CANR-124
  Earlier sketch in CA 154
  See also DLB 257
  See also EWL 3
Ekman, Paul 1934- CANR-143
  Earlier sketches in CA 37-40R, CANR-14
Ekman, Rosalind 1933- 33-36R
Ekola, Giles C(hester) 1927- 17-20R
Ekstein, Rudolf 1912-2005 .... CANR-4
  Obituary 237
  Earlier sketch in CA 5-8R
Eksteins, Modris 1943- CANR-90
  Earlier sketches in CA 77-80, CANR-34
Ekstroem, (Sigrid) Margareta 1930- 135
Ekstrom, Margareta
  See Ekstroem, (Sigrid) Margareta
Ekstrom, Parmenia Migel 1908-1989
  Obituary 130
Ekuan, Kenji 1929- 188
Ekvall, Robert B(rainerd) 1898-1983 .. CANR-5
  Obituary 164
  Earlier sketch in CA 1-4R
Ekwall, Eldon E(dward) 1933- CANR-12
  Earlier sketch in CA 29-32R
Ekwensi, C. O. D.
  See Ekwensi, Cyprian (Odiatu Duaka)
Ekwensi, Cyprian (Odiatu Duaka)
  1921- CANR-125
  Earlier sketches in CA 29-32R, CANR-18, 42, 74
  See also AFW
  See also BLC 1
  See also BW 2, 3
  See also CDWLB 3
  See also CLC 4
  See also CN 1, 2, 3, 4, 5, 6
  See also CWRI 5
  See also DAM MULT
  See also DLB 117
  See also EWL 3
  See also MTCW 1, 2
  See also RGEL 2
  See also SATA 66
  See also WLIT 2
Ela, Jonathan P(ell) 1945- 81-84
Elad, Amikam 1946- 152
Elaine
  See Leverson, Ada Esther
  See also TCLC 18
Elaine, Monika
  See Jackson, Monica
Elam, Richard M(ace, Jr.) 1920- 61-64
  See also SATA 9
El-Aref, Aref (?)-1973
  Obituary 41-44R
Elashoff, Janet Dixon 1942- 61-64
Elath, Eliahu 1903-1990 .... CANR-75
  Obituary 132
  Earlier sketch in CA 13-16R
Elaw, Zilpha 1790(?)-(?) .... DLB 239
El-Ayouty, Yassin 1928- CANR-14
  Earlier sketch in CA 29-32R
Elazar, Daniel J(udah) 1934- CANR-13
  Earlier sketch in CA 21-24R
El-Baz, Farouk 1938- CANR-51
  Earlier sketches in CA 25-28R, CANR-10, 26
Elbert, Edmund J(oseph) 1923- 37-40R
Elbert, George A. 1911-1995 .... CANR-35
  Obituary 149
  Earlier sketch in CA 61-64
Elbert, Samuel H(oyt) 1907-1997 .... CANR-5
  Earlier sketch in CA 1-4R
Elbert, Sarah 1937- 135
Elbert, Virginie Fowler 1912- CANR-35
  Earlier sketches in CA 61-64, CANR-8
Elbertus, Fra
  See Hubbard, Elbert
Elbin, Paul Nowell 1905-1985 .... CANR-35
  Earlier sketch in CA 69-72
Elbing, Alvar O(liver), Jr. 1928- 21-24R
Elbing, Carol J(eppson) 1930- 21-24R
Elbirt, Paula M. 1954- 200
El-Bisatie, Mohamed 1937-
  See Al-Bisatie, Mohamed
  See also SSFS 17
Elbogen, Paul 1894-1987 .... 5-8R
  Obituary 164
Elbom, Gilad 1968- 237
Elborn, Andrew
  See Clements, Andrew and Clements, Andrew
Elborn, Geoffrey 1950- 109
Elbow, Peter (Henry) 1935- CANR-28
  Earlier sketches in CA 65-68, CANR-12
Elboz, Stephen 1956- 227
  See also SATA 152
Elbrecht, Paul G. 1921- 17-20R
El Bundukhari
  See Dent, Anthony Austen
Elchamo, Jason
  See Caballero, Manuel
Elchamo, Sebastian
  See Caballero, Manuel
Elcock, Howard J(ames) 1942- CANR-117
  Earlier sketches in CA 29-32R, CANR-12, 29, 56
El Conde de Pepe
  See Mihura, Miguel
El Crummo
  See Crumb, R(obert)
Eld, George fl. 1603-1624 .... DLB 170
Eldefonso, Edward 1933- CANR-14
  Earlier sketch in CA 21-24R
Elder, Betty Doak 1938- 112
Elder, Ellen Rozanne 1940- 111
Elder, Gary 1939-2000 .... CANR-94
  Earlier sketch in CA 73-76
Elder, George Colman the 1732-1794 .. DLB 89
Elder, Glen(nard) H(oll), Jr. 1934- CANR-3
  Earlier sketch in CA 49-52
Elder, Jo-Anne 239
Elder, John 1947- CANR-82
  Earlier sketch in CA 133
Elder, John William 1933- 111
Elder, Karl 1948- CANR-97
  Earlier sketch in CA 77-80
Elder, Larry (A.) 1952- 219
Elder, Leon
  See Young, Noel (B.)
Elder, Lonne III 1931-1996 .... CANR-25
  Obituary 152
  Earlier sketch in CA 81-84
  See also BLC 1
  See also BW 1, 3
  See also CAD
  See also DAM MULT
  See also DC 8
  See also DLB 7, 38, 44
  See also MAL 5
Elder, Mark 1935- CANR-2
  Earlier sketch in CA 49-52
Elder, Michael (Aiken) 1931-2004 .... 33-36R
  Obituary 229
Elder, R(ichard) Bruce 1947- 214
Elder, Rob(ert Laurie) 1938- 125
Elder, Robert E(llsworth) 1915- 1-4R
Elder, Shirley (A.) 1931- 132
  Brief entry 118
Elderfield, John 1943- 132
Elderkin, Susan 1968- 219
Elders, (Minnie) Joycelyn 1933- 156
Eldershaw, Flora Sydney Patricia
  1897-1956 156
  See also Eldershaw, M. Barnard
  See also DLB 260
  See also SFW 4
Eldershaw, M. Barnard
  See Eldershaw, Flora Sydney Patricia
  See also SFW 4
Eldersveld, Samuel James 1917- 111
Eldin, Peter 1939- 229
  See also SATA 154
Eldin, Raymond
  See Morton, James (Severs)
Eldjarn, Kristjan (Thorarinsson) 1916-1982
  Obituary 110
Eldjarn, Thorarinn 1949- .... DLB 293
Eldon, Kathy 1946- 169
  See also SATA 107
Eldred, Vince 1924- 69-72
Eldredge, Dirk Chase 1932- 181
Eldredge, H(anford) Wentworth
  1909-1991 .... CANR-75
  Obituary 133
  Earlier sketch in CA 41-44R
Eldredge, Laurence H(oward)
  1902-1982 .... CAP-2
  Earlier sketch in CA 25-28
Eldredge, Niles 1943- CANR-142
  Earlier sketch in CA 157
Eldred-Grigg, Stevan (Treleaven)
  1952- CANR-136
  Earlier sketch in CA 162
  See also CN 6, 7
Eldridge, Colin Clifford 1942- 107
Eldridge, Frank R. 1889(?)-1976
  Obituary 69-72
Eldridge, J(ohn) E. T. 1936- CANR-11
  Earlier sketch in CA 25-28R
Eldridge, Marian (Favel Clair)
  1936-1997 .... CANR-42
  Earlier sketch in CA 118
Eldridge, Paul 1888-1982 .... 9-12R
  Obituary 171
Eldridge, Retha Hazel (Giles)
  1910-1990 .... CAP-1
  Earlier sketch in CA 13-14
Eleanor, Sister Joseph 25-28R
Eleb, Monique 1945- 226
Elegant, Robert (Sampson) 1928- CANR-73
  Earlier sketches in CA 1-4R, CANR-1, 30
Elegant, Simon 171
Elek, Paul 1906(?)-1976
  Obituary 69-72
el-Erian, Abdullah Ali 1920-1981
  Obituary 108
Elethea, Abba
  See Thompson, James W.
Eleveld, Mark 226
Elevitch, M(orton) D. 1925- CANR-117
  Earlier sketches in CA 49-52, CANR-2
Eley, Beverley 167
Eley, Geoff(rey Howard) 1949- CANR-141
  Earlier sketch in CA 129
Eley, Lynn W. 1925- CANR-16
  Earlier sketch in CA 25-28R
Elfenbein, Julien 1897-1983 .... CANR-75
  Obituary 109
  Earlier sketches in CA 1-4R, CANR-5
Elfers, James E. 1963- 234
Elffers, Joost 184
Elfman, Blossom 1925- CANR-39
  Earlier sketches in CA 45-48, CANR-2, 17
  See also SATA 8
Elfman, Danny 1953- CANR-71
  Earlier sketch in CA 148
  See also AAYA 14
  See also IDFW 4
Elford, Homer J. R. 1912-1995 .... CANR-9
  Earlier sketch in CA 21-24R
Elfstrom, Gerard 1945- CANR-91
  Earlier sketch in CA 145
Elgar, Edward (William) 1857-1934
  Brief entry 116
Elgar, Frank 1899- 102
Elgin, Kathleen 1923- 25-28R
  See also SATA 39
Elgin, Mary
  See Stewart, Dorothy Mary
Elgin, (Patricia Anne) Suzette Haden
  1936- CANR-83
  Earlier sketches in CA 61-64, CANR-8
  See also SFW 4
Elgood, Robert (Francis Willard) 1948- 125
El Greco 1541-1614 .... AAYA 64
el Hajjam, Mohammed ben Chaib
  1940- CANR-38
  Earlier sketches in CA 97-100, CANR-17
El Huitlacoche
  See Keller, Gary D.
Elia
  See Lamb, Charles
Eliach, Yaffa 1935- CANR-144
  Earlier sketch in CA 110
Eliade, Mircea 1907-1986 .... CANR-62
  Obituary 119
  Earlier sketches in CA 65-68, CANR-30
  See also CDWLB 4
  See also CLC 19
  See also DLB 220
  See also EWL 3
  See also MTCW 1
  See also RGWL 3
  See also SFW 4
Elias, Albert J. 1920- 81-84
Elias, C(laude) E(dward), Jr. 1924- 13-16R
Elias, Christopher 1925- 33-36R
Elias, Eileen
  See Davies, Eileen Winifred
Elias, Horace J(ay) 1910-1989 .... CANR-16
  Earlier sketch in CA 89-92
Elias, Jason 1947- CANR-143
  Earlier sketch in CA 150
Elias, John L(awrence) 1933- CANR-51
  Earlier sketches in CA 69-72, CANR-25
Elias, Norbert 1897-1990
  Obituary 132
Elias, Robert H(enry) 1914- 61-64
Elias, Ruth 1922- 172
Elias, Scott A. 1953- 148
Elias, Taslim Olawale 1914-1991 ..... CANR-75
  Obituary 145
  Earlier sketches in CA 13-16R, CANR-6, 21
Elias, Thomas S. 1942- CANR-35
  Earlier sketch in CA 114
Elias, Victor J. 1937- 146
Eliason, Joyce 1934- 77-80
Eliasson, Gyrdir 1961- .... DLB 293
Eliav, Arie L(ova) 1921- CANR-28
  Earlier sketches in CA 69-72, CANR-11
Elicker, Charles W. 1951-1978
  Obituary 115
Elie, Lolis Eric 1963- CANR-87
  Earlier sketch in CA 159
Elie, Paul 1965- 225
Elie, Robert 1915-1973 148
  See also CCA 1
  See also DLB 88
Elieff, Deanne D(esmond) 1926- 113
Elin Pelin
  See Stoyanov, Dimitur Ivanov
  See also CDWLB 4
  See also DLB 147
  See also EWL 3
Elinson, Jack 1917- CANR-20
  Earlier sketches in CA 45-48, CANR-2
Elinwood, Ellae 219
Elioseff, Lee Andrew 1933- 17-20R
Eliot, A. D.
  See Jewett, (Theodora) Sarah Orne
Eliot, Alexander 1919- CANR-1
  Earlier sketch in CA 49-52
Eliot, Alice
  See Jewett, (Theodora) Sarah Orne
Eliot, Anne
  See Cole, Lois Dwight
Eliot, Dan
  See Silverberg, Robert
Eliot, Frederick M(ay) 1889-1958 230

Eliot, George 1819-1880
See Evans, Mary Ann
See also BRW 5
See also BRWC 1, 2
See also BRWR 2
See also CDBLB 1832-1890
See also CN 7
See also CPW
See also DA
See also DA3
See also DAB
See also DAC
See also DAM MST, NOV
See also DLB 21, 35, 55
See also FL 1:3
See also LATS 1:1
See also LMFS 1
See also NFS 17, 20
See also PC 20
See also RGEL 2
See also RGSF 2
See also SSC 72
See also SSFS 8
See also TEA
See also WLC
See also WLIT 3
Eliot, George Fielding 1894-1971
Obituary 29-32R
Eliot, John 1604-1690 .... DLB 24
Eliot, Karen
See Home, Stewart
Eliot, Marc 189
Eliot, Nathan
See Kramer, Edward (E.)
Eliot, Sonny 1926- 81-84
Eliot, T(homas) S(tearns) 1888-1965 . CANR-41
Obituary 25-28R
Earlier sketch in CA 5-8R
See also AAYA 28
See also AMW
See also AMWC 1
See also AMWR 1
See also BRW 7
See also BRWR 2
See also CBD
See also CDALB 1929-1941
See also CLC 1, 2, 3, 6, 9, 10, 13, 15, 24, 34, 41, 55, 57, 113
See also DA
See also DA3
See also DAB
See also DAC
See also DAM DRAM, MST, POET
See also DFS 4, 13
See also DLB 7, 10, 45, 63, 245
See also DLBY 1988
See also EWL 3
See also EXPP
See also LAIT 3
See also LATS 1:1
See also LMFS 2
See also MAL 5
See also MTCW 1, 2
See also MTFW 2005
See also NCFS 5
See also PAB
See also PC 5, 31
See also PFS 1, 7, 20
See also RGAL 4
See also RGEL 2
See also TUS
See also WLC
See also WLIT 4
See also WP
Eliot, Thomas H(opkinson) 1907-1991 89-92
Obituary 135
Eliot Hurst, M(ichael) E(liot) 1938- 57-60
Eliovson, Sima (Benveniste) 1919- CANR-20
Earlier sketches in CA 13-16R, CANR-5
Elis, Islwyn Ffowc 1924-2004 93-96
Obituary 223
Elisabeth (Ottilie Luise), Queen (Pauline) 1843-1916
Brief entry 123
Elisabeth von Nassau-Saarbrucken c. 1393-1456 .... DLB 179
Eliscu, Frank 1912-1996 57-60
Obituary 152
Elish, Dan 1960- 136
See also SATA 68, 129
Elisha, Ron 1951- CANR-126
Earlier sketch in CA 171
See also CD 6
See also SATA 104
Elisofon, Eliot 1911-1973
Obituary 41-44R
See also SATA-Obit 21
Elison, George 1937- 53-56
Elium, Don 1954- 139
Elium, Jeanne (Ann) 1947- 138
Elizabeth
See Russell, Mary Annette Beauchamp
Elizabeth 1866-1941 .... TCLC 41
Elizabeth I 1533-1603 .... DLB 136
Elizabeth Marie, Sister 1914- 9-12R
Elizondo, Salvador 1932- 179
See also DLB 145
See also EWL 3
See also HW 2
Elizondo, Sergio
See Elizondo (Dominguez), Sergio D(anilo)
Elizondo (Dominguez), Sergio D(anilo) 1930- 131
See also DLB 82
See also HW 1
Elizondo, Virgil P. 1935- 226
Elizur, Joel 1952- 135
Elkann, Alain 1950- 127
Elkhadem, Saad (Eldin Amin) 1932- . CANR-86
Earlier sketch in CA 131
El Khazen, Farid 1960- 191
Elkholy, Abdo A. 1925- 21-24R
Elkin, Benjamin 1911-1995 .... CANR-4
Earlier sketch in CA 1-4R
See also SATA 3
Elkin, Frederick 1918- 41-44R
Elkin, H. V.
See Hinkle, Vernon
Elkin, Judith Laikin 1928- CANR-41
Earlier sketches in CA 53-56, CANR-4, 19
Elkin, Stanley L(awrence) 1930-1995 .... CANR-46
Obituary 148
Earlier sketches in CA 9-12R, CANR-8
Interview in CANR-8
See also AMWS 6
See also BPFB 1
See also CLC 4, 6, 9, 14, 27, 51, 91
See also CN 1, 2, 3, 4, 5, 6
See also CPW
See also DAM NOV, POP
See also DLB 2, 28, 218, 278
See also DLBY 1980
See also EWL 3
See also MAL 5
See also MTCW 1, 2
See also MTFW 2005
See also RGAL 4
See also SSC 12
See also TCLE 1:1
Elkin, Stephen L(loyd) 1941- 93-96
Elkind, David 1931- CANR-1
Earlier sketch in CA 45-48
Elkins, Aaron 1935- 233
Earlier sketches in CA 126, CANR-121
Autobiographical Essay in 233
See also CAAS 18
See also BEST 89:1
See also CMW 4
Elkins, Caroline 238
Elkins, Charlotte 1948- 167
Elkins, Dov Peretz 1937- CANR-30
Earlier sketches in CA 29-32R, CANR-12
See also SATA 5
Elkins, Ella Ruth 1929- 25-28R
Elkins, James P. 1955- CANR-102
Earlier sketch in CA 162
Elkins, Stanley Maurice 1925- 102
Elkins, T(homas) H(enry) 1926-
Brief entry 111
Elkins, William R. 1926- 33-36R
Elkon, Jon 1949- 134
Elkon, Juliette
See Elkon-Hamelecourt, Juliette
Elkon-Hamelecourt, Juliette 1912-2002 ... 57-60
Elkouri, Frank 1921- 69-72
Elkus, Jonathan Britton 1931- 111
Ellacott, S(amuel) E(rnest) 1911- CANR-3
Earlier sketch in CA 5-8R
See also SATA 19
Elledge, Jim 1950- CANR-39
Earlier sketches in CA 102, CANR-19
Elledge, Scott .... CLC 34
Elledge, Scott (Bowen) 1914-1997 145
Elledge, W(aymon) Paul 1938- 25-28R
Elleman, Barbara 1934- 221
See also SATA 147
Ellen, Barbara 1938- 5-8R
Ellen, Jaye
See Nixon, Joan Lowery
Ellenbecker, Todd S. 1962- CANR-125
Earlier sketch in CA 171
Ellenberg, Jordan S. 1971- 226
Ellenberger, Allan R. 1956- 221
Ellenberger, Henri F(rederic) 1905- CAP-2
Earlier sketch in CA 29-32
Ellenbogen, Eileen 1917- 104
Ellender, Raphael 1906-1972
Obituary 37-40R
Ellenius, Allan M. 1927- 192
Ellens, J(ay) Harold 1932- CANR-58
Earlier sketches in CA 57-60, CANR-7, 31
Ellenshaw, Peter 1913- .... IDFW 3, 4
Ellenson, Gene 1921- 57-60
Eller, John 1935- 105
Eller, Ronald D. 1948- CANR-92
Earlier sketch in CA 110
Eller, Scott
See Holinger, William (Jacques) and Shepard, Jim
Eller, Vernard (Marion) 1927- CANR-24
Earlier sketches in CA 21-24R, CANR-9
Eller, William 1921- 77-80
Ellerbeck, Rosemary (Anne L'Estrange) CANR-83
Earlier sketches in CA 106, CANR-24
Ellerbee, Linda (Jane) 1944- CANR-110
Brief entry 110
Earlier sketches in CA 115, CANR-54
Interview in CA-115
See also AAYA 16
Ellerman, Annie Winifred
See Bryher
See also MTCW 2
Ellery, John Blaise 1920- 9-12R
Elles, Dora Amy 1878-1961 197
See also Wentworth, Patricia
See also DLB 77
Ellestad, Myrvin H. 1921- 191
See also SATA 120
Ellet, Elizabeth F. 1818(?)-1877 .... DLB 30
Ellett, Marcella H. 1931- 21-24R
Ellfeldt, Lois 1910-1998 .... 33-36R
Ellice, Jane
See Hopkins, Ellice (Jane)
Ellicott, V. L.
See Ellicott, Valcoulon MeMoyne
Ellicott, Valcoulon MeMoyne 1893-1983
Obituary 109
Ellin, E(lizabeth) M(uriel) 1905- CANR-83
Earlier sketches in CAP-2, CA 29-32
See also CWRI 5
Ellin, Stanley (Bernard) 1916-1986 ... CANR-28
Obituary 119
Earlier sketches in CA 1-4R, CANR-4
See also CMW 4
See also DAM POP
See also DLB 306
See also MSW
See also MTCW 1
Elling, Karl A(lwin) 1935- 25-28R
Elling, Ray H. 1929- 33-36R
Ellingham, Lewis 1933- 167
Ellingsen, Mark 1949- 184
Ellingsworth, Huber W. 1928- CANR-10
Earlier sketch in CA 21-24R
Ellington, Duke
See Ellington, Edward Kennedy
Ellington, Edward Kennedy 1899-1974 . 97-100
Obituary 49-52
Ellington, James W(esley) 1927- 37-40R
Ellington, Mercer (Kennedy) 1919-1996
Obituary 151
Brief entry 113
Ellington, Richard 1915(?)-1980
Obituary 102
Ellingwood, Ken 234
Ellinwood, Leonard Webster 1905-1994 ... 1-4R
Elliot, Alistair 1932- CANR-126
Earlier sketches in CA 129, CANR-64
See also CP 7
Elliot, Asa
See Blinder, Elliot
Elliot, Daniel
See Feldman, Leonard
Elliot, David 1952- .... SATA 122
Elliot, Edith M(arie Farmer) 1912-1998 . 21-24R
Elliot, Elisabeth (Howard) 1926- CANR-100
Earlier sketches in CA 5-8R, CANR-6
Elliot, Frances Minto (Dickinson) 1820-1898 .... DLB 166
Elliot, Geraldine
See Bingham, Evangeline M(arguerite) L(adys) (Elliot)
Elliot, Ian 1925- 69-72
Elliot, Jason 1965- 188
Elliot, Jeffrey M. 1947- CANR-24
Earlier sketch in CA 106
Elliot, John 1898-1988
Obituary 126
Elliot, Kate
See Rubinsky, Holley
Elliott, Alan C(urtis) 1952- CANR-18
Earlier sketch in CA 102
Elliott, Allan
See Elliott, K(enneth) A(llan) C(aldwell)
Elliott, Anthony 1964- 187
Elliott, Aubrey (George) 1917- 93-96
Elliott, Ben
See Haas, Ben(jamin) L(eopold)
Elliott, Bill 1945- 179
Elliott, Bob
See Elliott, Robert B.
Elliott, Brian (Robinson) 1910-1991 ...... 25-28R
Elliott, Bruce
See Field, Edward
Elliott, Bruce (Walter Gardner Lively Stacy) 1915(?)-1973
Obituary 41-44R
Elliott, C(larence) Orville 1913-1987 .... 33-36R
Elliott, Charles 1951- 138
Elliott, Charlotte 1789-1871 .... DLB 199
Elliott, Chip
See Elliott, E(scalus) E(mmert) III
Elliott, Chris 1960- 147
Elliott, Clark A. 1941- 137
Elliott, David 1952- 239
See also SATA 163
Elliott, David W. 1939- 45-48
Elliott, Don
See Silverberg, Robert
Elliott, Donald 1928- 69-72
Elliott, Douglas B(yron) 1947- 113
Elliott, E(scalus) E(mmert) III 1945- 29-32R
Elliott, Ebenezer 1781-1849 .... DLB 96, 190
See also RGEL 2
Elliott, Elaine M. 1931- 166
Elliott, Elizabeth Shippen Green
See Green, Elizabeth Shippen
Elliott, Emory 1942- CANR-23
Earlier sketch in CA 69-72
Elliott, Errol T(homas) 1894-1992 69-72
Obituary 164
Elliott, Gary E(ugene) 1941- 151
Elliott, George 1923- 174
See also DLB 68
Elliott, George P(aul) 1918-1980 .... CANR-2
Obituary 97-100
Earlier sketch in CA 1-4R
See also CLC 2
See also CN 1, 2
See also DLB 244
See also MAL 5
Elliott, Harley 1940- CANR-4
Earlier sketch in CA 49-52
Elliott, Hugh (Francis Ivo) 1913-1989
Brief entry 112
Elliott, Inger McCabe 1933- 127
Elliott, James Francis 1914-1981
Obituary 110
Elliott, Jan Walter 1939- 37-40R
Elliott, Janice 1931-1995 .... CANR-84
Earlier sketches in CA 13-16R, CANR-8, 29
See also CLC 47
See also CN 5, 6, 7
See also DLB 14
See also SATA 119
Elliott, Joey
See Houk, Randy
Elliott, John 1938- 25-28R
Elliott, John E(d) 1931- CANR-5
Earlier sketch in CA 1-4R
Elliott, John H(uxtable) 1930- CANR-3
Earlier sketch in CA 5-8R
Elliott, John H(all) 1935- 126
Brief entry 113
Elliott, John Michael
See Haas, Ben(jamin) L(eopold)
Elliott, John R., Jr. 1937- 25-28R
Elliott, Jumbo
See Elliott, James Francis
Elliott, K(enneth) A(llan) C(aldwell) 1903-1986 108
Obituary 119
Elliott, Kate
See Rasmussen, Alis A.
Elliott, Kit 1936- 29-32R
Elliott, Larry 178
Elliott, Lawrence 1924- CANR-21
Earlier sketches in CA 5-8R, CANR-3
Elliott, Leonard M. 1902-1978 .... CAP-1
Earlier sketch in CA 13-14
Elliott, Lesley 1905- CANR-14
Earlier sketch in CA 77-80
Elliott, Louise 182
See also SATA 111
Elliott, Malissa Childs 1929(?)-1979 101
Obituary 85-88
Elliott, Marianne 1948- CANR-108
Earlier sketch in CA 132
Elliott, Mark Rowe 1947- CANR-24
Earlier sketch in CA 107
Elliott, Maud Howe 1854-1948 204
Elliott, Melinda 1947- 157
Elliott, Neil 1939- 25-28R
Elliott, Odette 1939- 142
See also SATA 75
Elliott, Osborn 1924- CANR-12
Earlier sketch in CA 69-72
Elliott, P(hilip) R(oss) C(ourtney) 1943(?)-1983
Obituary 110
Elliott, Ralph H. 1925- CANR-2
Earlier sketch in CA 1-4R
Elliott, Ralph W(arren) V(ictor) 1921- 127
Elliott, Raymond Pruitt 1904- 17-20R
Elliott, Richard V. 1934- 33-36R
Elliott, Robert
See Garfinkel, Bernard Max
Elliott, Robert B. 1923- 134
Brief entry 109
Elliott, Robert C(arl) 1914-1981 .... CANR-21
Earlier sketch in CA 1-4R
Elliott, Roberta 97-100
Elliott, Russell Richard 1912-1998 69-72
Elliott, Sam Davis 1956- 188
Elliott, Sarah Barnwell 1848-1928 ...... DLB 221
Elliott, Sarah M(cCarn) 1930- 41-44R
See also SATA 14
Elliott, (Robert) Scott 1970- 228
See also SATA 153
Elliott, Sheldon D(ouglass) 1906-1972
Obituary 33-36R
Elliott, Spencer H(ayward) 1883-1967 ... CAP-1
Earlier sketch in CA 11-12
Elliott, Stephen 1971- 220
Elliott, Sumner Locke 1917-1991 .... CANR-21
Obituary 134
Earlier sketches in CA 5-8R, CANR-2
See also CLC 38
See also DLB 289
Elliott, Susan (Anthony) 1947- 104
Elliott, Thomas Joseph 1941- 49-52
Elliott, Ward E(dward) Y(andell) 1937- 85-88
Elliott, William
See Bradbury, Ray (Douglas)
Elliott, William III 1788-1863 .... DLB 3, 248
Elliott, William Douglas 1938- CANR-9
Earlier sketch in CA 65-68
Elliott, William M(arion), Jr. 1903-1990 . CAP-1
Earlier sketch in CA 9-10
Elliott, William Yandell 1896-1979
Obituary 85-88
Ellis, A. E. .... CLC 7
Ellis, Albert 1913- CANR-40
Earlier sketches in CA 1-4R, CANR-2, 17
Ellis, Alec (Charles Owen) 1932- CANR-1
Earlier sketch in CA 45-48
Ellis, Alice Marie 1932- .... CN 7
Ellis, Alice Thomas
See Haycraft, Anna (Margaret)
See also CLC 40
See also CN 4, 5, 6
See also DLB 194
Ellis, (Mary) Amabel (Nassau Strachey) Williams
See Williams-Ellis, (Mary) Amabel (Nassau Strachey)
Ellis, Amanda M. 1898-1969 .... CAP-2
Earlier sketch in CA 23-24
Ellis, Anyon
See Rowland-Entwistle, (Arthur) Theodore (Henry)
Ellis, Audrey CANR-10
Earlier sketch in CA 65-68
Ellis, B(yron) Robert 1940- 53-56
Ellis, Barbara W. 1953- 139
Ellis, Bill 1950- 195

Cumulative Index 173 Elson

Ellis, Bret Easton 1964- CANR-126
Brief entry 118
Earlier sketches in CA 123, CANR-51, 74
Interview in CA-123
See also AAYA 2, 43
See also CLC 39, 71, 117
See also CN 6, 7
See also CPW
See also DA3
See also DAM POP
See also DLB 292
See also HGG
See also MTCW 2
See also MTFW 2005
See also NFS 11
Ellis, Brooks (Fleming) 1897-1976
Obituary 65-68
Ellis, C(uthbert) Hamilton 1909- 13-16R
Ellis, Carl F., Jr. 1946- 121
Ellis, Carolyn Sue 1950- CANR-48
Earlier sketch in CA 122
Ellis, Charles D(aniel) 1937-
Brief entry 115
Ellis, Charles Drummond 1895-1980
Obituary 105
Ellis, Charles Howard 1895-1975 CAP-1
Earlier sketch in CA 13-14
Ellis, Clyde 1958- CANR-97
Earlier sketch in CA 162
Ellis, Clyde T(aylor) 1908-1980 CAP-2
Earlier sketch in CA 23-24
Ellis, Dan C. 1949- 125
Ellis, David 212
Ellis, David Maldwyn 1914-1999 9-12R
Ellis, Deborah 1961- 198
See also AAYA 48
See also MAICYA 2
See also SATA 129
Ellis, Dock (Phillip, Jr.) 1945-
Brief entry 111
Ellis, Donald G. 1947- 231
Ellis, E. S.
See Ellis, Edward S(ylvester)
Ellis, Edward Robb 1911-1998 CANR-53
Obituary 170
Earlier sketch in CA 25-28R
Ellis, Edward S(ylvester) 1840-1916
Brief entry 122
See also DLB 42
See also YABC 1
Ellis, Ella Thorp 1928- CANR-106
Earlier sketches in CA 49-52, CANR-2
See also SAAS 9
See also SATA 7, 127
Ellis, Elma I(srael) 1918- 33-36R
Ellis, Erika 1965- 186
Ellis, Evelyn 1948- 138
Ellis, Florence Hawley 1906- 61-64
Ellis, (J.) Frank(lyn) 1904(?)-1976
Obituary 65-68
Ellis, Frank Hale 1916- 73-76
Ellis, Frank K. 1933- 25-28R
Ellis, George F(rancis) R(ayner) 1939- 222
Ellis, Gwen 1938- 203
Ellis, Harry Bearse 1921-2004 CANR-2
Earlier sketch in CA 1-4R
See also SATA 9
Ellis, (Henry) Havelock 1859-1939 169
Brief entry 109
See also DLB 190
See also TCLC 14
Ellis, Helen E. (Oickle) 1926- CANR-96
Earlier sketches in CA 120, CANR-45
Ellis, Henry C(arlton) 1927- CANR-17
Earlier sketch in CA 97-100
Ellis, Herbert
See Wilson, Lionel
Ellis, Hilda Roderick
See Davidson, H(ilda) R(oderick) Ellis
Ellis, Howard S(ylvester) 1898-1992 CANR-28
Obituary 137
Earlier sketch in CA 49-52
Ellis, Howard W(oodrow)
1914-1998 CANR-38
Earlier sketches in CA 1-4R, CANR-17
Ellis, Humphry F(rancis) 1907- 5-8R
Ellis, J(ames) H(ervey) S(tewart) 1893- CAP-2
Earlier sketch in CA 23-24
Ellis, J(ohn) R(ichard) 1938- 85-88
Ellis, Jack C(lare) 1922- CANR-92
Earlier sketch in CA 89-92
Ellis, Jack D. 1941- 121
Ellis, Jamellah 227
Ellis, James 1935- 37-40R
Ellis, Jerry 1947- CANR-136
Earlier sketch in CA 153
Ellis, Jody 1925- 57-60
Ellis, John H. 1931- CANR-52
Earlier sketch in CA 125
Ellis, John M(artin) 1936- CANR-66
Earlier sketches in CA 49-52, CANR-3
Ellis, John Marion 1917- 49-52
Ellis, John O(liver) 1917- 85-88
Ellis, John Tracy 1905-1992 CANR-46
Obituary 139
Earlier sketches in CA 1-4R, CANR-5
Ellis, Joseph J(ohn) 1943- CANR-103
Earlier sketch in CA 53-56
Ellis, Joyce K. (Eileen) 1950- 116
Ellis, Julie 1933- CANR-84
Brief entry 111
Earlier sketch in CA 142
See also RHW
Ellis, Kail C. 1940- 127
Ellis, Kate 1953- 204
Ellis, Kathleen Lignell 1942- 205
Ellis, Kathy
See Bentley, Margaret
Ellis, Keith Stanley 1927- 102
Ellis, L(ewis) Ethan 1898-1977 CANR-4
Earlier sketch in CA 5-8R
Ellis, Landon
See Ellison, Harlan (Jay)
Ellis, Leigh 1959- 105
Ellis, Leo R(oy) 1909-1995 9-12R
Ellis, M(adeleine) B(lanche) 1915- 69-72
Ellis, M(arion) LeRoy 1928- 37-40R
Ellis, Marc H. 1952- CANR-24
Earlier sketch in CA 107
Ellis, Mark Karl 1945- 103
Ellis, Mary Jackson 1916- CANR-17
Earlier sketch in CA 1-4R
Ellis, Mary Leith 1921- 21-24R
Ellis, Mary Relindes 1960- 233
Ellis, Mel(vin Richard) 1912-1984 13-16R
Obituary 113
See also SATA 7
See also SATA-Obit 39
Ellis, Norman R. 1924- 13-16R
Ellis, Olivia
See Wintle, Anne
Ellis, Peter Berresford 1943- CANR-95
Earlier sketches in CA 81-84, CANR-21, 56
See also HGG
Ellis, Peter F(rancis) 1921- 115
Ellis, Publius
See Washington, Ellis
Ellis, Ralph D. 204
Ellis, Ray C(lifton) 1898-1995 CAP-2
Earlier sketch in CA 21-22
Ellis, Reuben 1955- 211
Ellis, Richard 1938- CANR-79
Earlier sketch in CA 104
See also SATA 130
Ellis, Richard E(manuel) 1937- 61-64
Ellis, Richard J. 1960- CANR-120
Earlier sketch in CA 135
Ellis, Richard N(athaniel) 1939- 33-36R
Ellis, Richard White Bernard 1902- CAP-1
Earlier sketch in CA 13-16
Ellis, Roger (Melville) 1943- 126
Ellis, Ron(ald Walter) 1941- CANR-121
Earlier sketch in CA 77-80
Ellis, (Christopher) Royston (George)
1941- 5-8R
Ellis, Sarah 1952- CANR-84
Earlier sketches in CA 123, CANR-50
See also AAYA 57
See also CLR 42
See also JRDA
See also MAICYA 2
See also MAICYAS 1
See also SATA 68, 131
See also YAW
Ellis, Scott
See Schorr, Mark
Ellis, Stephen 1953- 215
Ellis, Steven G. 1950- 158
Ellis, Trey 1962- CANR-92
Earlier sketch in CA 146
See also CLC 55
See also CN 7
Ellis, Ulrich Ruegg 1904-1981
Obituary 108
Ellis, Walter M. 1943- 137
Ellis, Wesley
See Barrett, Neal, Jr. and
Wallmann, Jeffrey M(iner)
Ellis, William Donahue 1918- CANR-29
Earlier sketch in CA 49-52
Ellis, William E(lliott) 1940- CANR-101
Earlier sketch in CA 163
Ellis, William S. 1927- 182
Ellisen, Stanley A(rthur) 1922- 133
Ellison, Alfred 1916- 1-4R
Ellison, Anthony P. 1943- 221
Ellison, Craig W(illiam) 1944- CANR-6
Earlier sketch in CA 57-60
Ellison, Emily 180
See also SATA 114
Ellison, Fred P(ittman) 1922-
Brief entry 113
Ellison, George R. 1907(?)-1983
Obituary 110
Ellison, Gerald Alexander 1910-1992 CAP-1
Obituary 139
Earlier sketch in CA 13-14
Ellison, Glenn (Curtiss) 1911-1990 89-92
Ellison, Glenn "Tiger"
See Ellison, Glenn (Curtiss)
Ellison, H(enry) L(eopold) 1903- CANR-6
Earlier sketch in CA 5-8R
Ellison, Harlan (Jay) 1934- CANR-115
Earlier sketches in CA 5-8R, CANR-5, 46
Interview in CANR-5
See also AAYA 29
See also BPFB 1
See also BYA 14
See also CLC 1, 13, 42, 139
See also CPW
See also DAM POP
See also DLB 8
See also HGG
See also MTCW 1, 2
See also MTFW 2005
See also SCFW 2
See also SFW 4
See also SSC 14
See also SSFS 13, 14, 15, 21
See also SUFW 1, 2
Ellison, Henry 1931-1965 5-8R
Ellison, Herbert J(ay) 1929- 13-16R
Ellison, James E. 1927- 13-16R
Ellison, James Whitfield 1929- CANR-1
Earlier sketch in CA 1-4R
Ellison, Jerome 1907-1981 CANR-75
Obituary 104
Earlier sketch in CA 29-32R
Ellison, Joan Jarvis 1948- 158
Ellison, John Malcus 1889-1979 CANR-25
Earlier sketch in CA 1-4R
Ellison, Katherine (White) 1941- 101
Ellison, Katherine (Esther) 1957- CANR-137
Earlier sketch in CA 127
Ellison, Katherine W.
See Ellison, Katherine (Esther)
Ellison, Lucile Watkins 1907(?)-1979 109
Obituary 93-96
See also SATA 50
See also SATA-Obit 22
Ellison, Max 1914-1985 CANR-76
Obituary 116
Earlier sketch in CA 57-60
See also AITN 1
Ellison, Peter T(horpe) 200
Ellison, Ralph (Waldo) 1914-1994 CANR-53
Obituary 145
Earlier sketches in CA 9-12R, CANR-24
See also AAYA 19
See also AFAW 1, 2
See also AMWC 2
See also AMWR 2
See also AMWS 2
See also BLC 1
See also BPFB 1
See also BW 1, 3
See also BYA 2
See also CDALB 1941-1968
See also CLC 1, 3, 11, 54, 86, 114
See also CN 1, 2, 3, 4, 5
See also CSW
See also DA
See also DA3
See also DAB
See also DAC
See also DAM MST, MULT, NOV
See also DLB 2, 76, 227
See also DLBY 1994
See also EWL 3
See also EXPN
See also EXPS
See also LAIT 4
See also MAL 5
See also MTCW 1, 2
See also MTFW 2005
See also NCFS 3
See also NFS 2, 21
See also RGAL 4
See also RGSF 2
See also SSC 26, 79
See also SSFS 1, 11
See also WLC
See also YAW
Ellison, Randall Erskine 1904-1984
Obituary 113
Ellison, Reuben Young 1907-1991 13-16R
Ellison, Robert H. 1967- 188
Ellison, Virginia H(owell) 1910- 33-36R
See also SATA 4
Ellison, William McLaren 1919(?)-1978
Obituary 81-84
Elliston, Frederick Allen 1944- 105
Elliston, Thomas R(alph) 1919-1977
Obituary 73-76
Elliston, Valerie Mae (Watkinson) 1929- 9-12R
Ellithorpe, Harold (Earle) 1925- 77-80
Ellman, Michael 1942- 45-48
Ellmann, Lucy (Elizabeth) 1956- 128
See also CLC 61
Ellmann, Richard (David)
1918-1987 CANR-61
Obituary 122
Earlier sketches in CA 1-4R, CANR-2, 28
See also BEST 89:2
See also CLC 50
See also DLB 103
See also DLBY 1987
See also MTCW 1, 2
See also MTFW 2005
Elroy, James 1948- CANR-133
Earlier sketches in CA 138, CANR-74
See also BEST 90:4
See also CMW 4
See also CN 6, 7
See also DA3
See also DLB 226
See also MTCW 2
See also MTFW 2005
Ellsberg, Daniel 1931- CANR-135
Earlier sketch in CA 69-72
Ellsberg, Edward 1891-1983 5-8R
See also SATA 7
Ellsworth, L(ida) E(lizabeth) 1948- 118
Ellsworth, Mary Ellen (Tressel) 1940- 220
See also SATA 146
Ellsworth, P(aul) T(heodore)
1897-1991 17-20R
Ellsworth, Ralph Eugene 1907-2000 CANR-2
Obituary 190
Earlier sketch in CA 1-4R
Ellsworth, S(amuel) George 1916-1997 45-48
Ellsworth, Scott 1954- 109
Ellul, Jacques 1912-1994 CANR-75
Obituary 145
Earlier sketch in CA 81-84
Ellvinger, Barbara Anne Price
See Price, Barbara Anne Ellvinger
Ellwood, Edith E(lizabeth)
See Muesing-Ellwood, Edith E(lizabeth)
Ellwood, Gracia-Fay 1938- 29-32R
Ellwood, Robert S(cott), Jr. 1933- CANR-14
Earlier sketch in CA 41-44R
Ellwood, Sheelagh (Margaret) 1949- 146
Ellyard, David 147
El Mahdy, Christine 199
El Mallakh, Ragaei (William) 1925- 112
Elman, Richard (Martin) 1934-1997 CANR-47
Obituary 163
Earlier sketch in CA 17-20R
See also CAAS 3
See also CLC 19
See also TCLE 1:1
Elman, Robert 1930- CANR-3
Earlier sketch in CA 45-48
Elmandjra, Mahdi 1933- 89-92
Elmanovich, Tatiana 1934- 174
Elmblad, Mary (B.) 1927-1990 108
El-Meligi, A(bdel) Moneim 1923- 17-20R
Elmen, Paul H. 1913-1999 89-92
Elmendorf, Mary Lindsay 1917- 57-60
Elmer, Carlos Hall 1920- 102
Elmer, Gary W. 1941- 122
Elmer, Irene (Elizabeth) 1937- 1-4R
Elmer, Peter 1954- 197
Elmer, Robert 1958- CANR-128
Earlier sketch in CA 167
See also SATA 99, 154
El-Messidi, Kathy Groehn 1946- 57-60
Elmhirst, Leonard Knight 1893-1974
Obituary 115
Elmore, Ernest Carpenter 1901-1957
Brief entry 114
Elmore, (Carolyn) Patricia 1933- 114
See also SATA 38
See also SATA-Brief 35
Elmore, Phyllis Pearson 1954- 196
El-Moslimany, Ann P(axton) 1937- 155
See also SATA 90
Elms, Alan C(linton) 1938- 69-72
Elmslie, Kenward 1929- CANR-84
Earlier sketches in CA 21-24R, CANR-9, 25, 50
See also CP 1, 2, 3, 4, 5, 6, 7
Elmslie, William Alexander Leslie
1885-1965 CAP-1
Earlier sketch in CA 13-14
Elmstrom, George P. 1925- 5-8R
El Muhajir 1944- CANR-26
Earlier sketch in CA 49-52
See also Marvin X
See also BW 1
el-Nawawy, Mohammed 1968- 221
Elon, Amos 1926- CANR-73
Brief entry 121
Earlier sketch in CA 128
Interview in CA-128
El-Or, Tamar 1955- 239
Elovitz, Mark H(arvey) 1938- 69-72
Elphick, Richard Hall 1943- CANR-48
Earlier sketch in CA 112
Elphinstone, Francis
See Powell-Smith, Vincent (Walter Francis)
Elphinstone, Murgatroyd
See Kahler, Hugh (Torbert) MacNair
Elrick, George S(eefurth) 1921-1997 112
Obituary 163
Elrod, P(atricia) N(ead) 149
See also AAYA 60
See also HGG
Elron
See Hubbard, L(afayette) Ron(ald)
el Ropo, Smokestack
See Perry, Charles
El Saadawi, Nawal 1931- CANR-92
Earlier sketches in CA 118, CANR-44
See also al'Sadaawi, Nawal and
Sa'adawi, al- Nawal and
Saadawi, Nawal El and
Sa'dawi, Nawal al-
See also CAAS 11
See also CLC 196
El Saffar, Ruth (Ann) 1941- 69-72
Elsasser, Albert B(ertrand) 1918- CANR-22
Earlier sketch in CA 69-72
Elsasser, Glen Robert 1935- 65-68
Elsberry, Terence 1943- 45-48
Elsbree, Langdon 1929- 33-36R
Else, Barbara 1947- 232
Else, Gerald Frank 1908-1982 CANR-77
Obituary 107
Earlier sketch in CA 61-64
Elsea, Janet G(ayle) 1942- 119
Elsen, Albert E(dward) 1927-1995 CANR-85
Obituary 147
Earlier sketches in CA 5-8R, CANR-11, 26
El-Shabazz, El-Hajj Malik
See Little, Malcolm
El-Shazly, Nadia El-Sayed 1936- 175
Elshtain, Jean Bethke 1941- CANR-99
Earlier sketch in CA 106
Elsmere, Jane Shaffer 1932- 37-40R
Elsner, Gisela 1937- 9-12R
Elsner, Henry, Jr. 1930- 21-24R
Elsom, John Edward 1934- 65-68
Elson, Edward L(ee) R(oy)
1906-1993 CANR-75
Obituary 142
Earlier sketches in CA 5-8R, CANR-3
Elson, Jean 236
Elson, Lawrence M(cClellan) 1935- 53-56
Elson, R. N.
See Nelson, R(adell) Faraday
Elson, Rebecca (Ann Wood) 1960-1999 216
Elson, Robert T(ruscott) 1906-1987 CANR-76
Obituary 121
Earlier sketch in CA 77-80
Elson, Ruth Miller 1917- 13-16R

Elspeth
See Bragdon, Elspeth MacDuffie
Elsschot, Willem 1882-1960 ... 217
See also EWL 3
Elstar, Dow
See Gallun, Raymond Z(inke)
Elster, Jean Alicia 1953- ... SATA 150
Elster, Jon 1940- ... 192
Elstob, Peter 1915-2002 ... CANR-1
Obituary ... 208
Earlier sketch in CA 1-4R
Elston, Allan Vaughan 1887-1976 ... CANR-63
Earlier sketches in CA 1-4R, CANR-3
See also TCWW 1, 2
Elston, Gene 1922- ... 33-36R
Elston, Robert 1934-1987
Obituary ... 124
Elston, Wilbur E(vans) 1913-
Brief entry ... 112
Elstun, Esther N(ies) 1935- ... 117
Elsy, (Winifred) Mary ... 93-96
El-Tahri, Jihan ... 231
Elting, John R(obert) 1911-2000 ... CANR-57
Earlier sketches in CA 112, CANR-31
Elting, Mary 1906- ... CANR-19
Earlier sketches in CA 9-12R, CANR-4
See also SAAS 20
See also SATA 2, 88
Eltis, David 1940- ... 127
Eltis, Walter (Alfred) 1933- ... 131
Elton, Ben(jamin Charles) 1959- ... 192
Elton, Edwin J(oel) 1939- ... 53-56
Elton, G(eoffrey) R(udolph)
1921-1994 ... CANR-30
Earlier sketches in CA 9-12R, CANR-3
Elton, Hugh 1964- ... 153
Elton, John
See Marsh, John
Elton, W(illiam) R. 1921- ... 185
Brief entry ... 111
el-Toure, Askia Muhammad Abu Bakr
See Toure, Askia Muhammad Abu Bakr el
Eltringham, S(tewart) K(eith) 1929- ... 110
Eluard, Paul
See Grindel, Eugene
See also EWL 3
See also GFL 1789 to the Present
See also PC 38
See also RGWL 2, 3
See also TCLC 7, 41
Eluard, Paul
See Grindel, Eugene
See also DLB 258
El Uqsor
See Borgmann, Dmitri A(lfred)
Elvenstar, Diane C.
See Medved, Diane
Elvin, Drake
See Beha, Ernest
Elvin, Harold 1909-1985 ... CANR-75
Obituary ... 115
Earlier sketches in CA 5-8R, CANR-4
Elvin, (Herbert) Lionel 1905- ... CAP-1
Earlier sketch in CA 13-14
Elvin, Mark 1938- ... 73-76
Elward, James (Joseph) 1928-1996 ... CANR-12
Obituary ... 153
Earlier sketch in CA 29-32R
Elwart, Joan Potter 1927- ... 25-28R
See also SATA 2
Elwell, Brenda ... 223
Elwell, Fayette Herbert 1885-1980 ... 5-8R
Elwell, Jerry MacElroy 1922- ... 57-60
Elwell, Stillman J. 1894-1977
Obituary ... 110
Elwell, Walter A(lexander) 1937- ... 119
Elwell-Sutton, L(aurence) P(aul)
1912-1984 ... CANR-76
Obituary ... 114
Earlier sketch in CA 5-8R
Elwin, Malcolm 1903-1973
Obituary ... 89-92
Elwin, William
See Ebenstein, William
Elwood, Ann 1931- ... 125
See also SATA 55
See also SATA-Brief 52
Elwood, Catharyn 1903(?)-1975
Obituary ... 61-64
Elwood, Douglas J(ames) 1924- ... 116
Elwood, Muriel 1902-1976 ... CAP-1
Earlier sketch in CA 9-10
Elwood, Roger 1943- ... CANR-10
Earlier sketch in CA 57-60
See also SATA 58
Elwyn-Jones, Pearl Binder 1904-1990 ... 107
Ely, David 1927- ... CANR-85
Earlier sketch in CA 53-56
See also CN 1, 2, 3, 4, 5, 6, 7
Ely, Donald P(aul) 1930- ... 29-32R
Ely, James W(allace), Jr. 1938- ... 73-76
Ely, John Hart 1938-2003 ... 103
Obituary ... 220
Ely, John Wilton
See Wilton-Ely, John
Ely, Melvin Patrick 1952- ... 140
Ely, Paul (Henri) 1897-1975
Obituary ... 53-56
Ely, Scott 1944- ... 127
Ely, Virginia (Shackelford)
1899-1984 ... CANR-24
Earlier sketch in CA 1-4R
Elya, Susan M(iddleton) 1955- ... CANR-144
Earlier sketch in CA 176
See also SATA 106, 159
Elyot, Amanda
See Carroll, Leslie (Sara)
Elyot, Kevin 1951- ... 230
See also CD 5
Elyot, Thomas 1490(?)-1546 ... DLB 136
See also RGEL 2
Elytis, Odysseus 1911-1996 ... CANR-94
Obituary ... 151
Earlier sketch in CA 102
See also Alepoudelis, Odysseus
See also CLC 15, 49, 100
See also CWW 2
See also DAM POET
See also EW 13
See also EWL 3
See also MTCW 1, 2
See also PC 21
See also RGWL 2, 3
El-Zayyat, Latifa
See al-Zayyat, Latifa
Elzbieta ... SATA 88
Elzinga, Kenneth G(erald) 1941- ... CANR-13
Earlier sketches in CA 49-52, CANR-1
Emans, Robert 1934- ... 53-56
Emanuel, Ezekiel J(onathan) 1957- ... 139
Emanuel, James A(ndrew Sr.) 1921- ... CANR-85
Earlier sketches in CA 29-32R, 153, CANR-12
See also CAAS 18
See also BW 1
See also CP 2, 3, 4, 5, 6, 7
See also DLB 41
Emanuel, Lynn (Collins) 1949- ... 188
Ember, Carol R(uchlis) 1943- ... 77-80
Emberley, Barbara A(nne) 1932- ... CANR-129
Earlier sketches in CA 5-8R, CANR-5
See also CLR 5
See also MAICYA 1, 2
See also SATA 8, 70, 146
Emberley, Ed(ward Randolph)
1931- ... CANR-129
Earlier sketches in CA 5-8R, CANR-5, 36, 82
See also CLR 5, 81
See also MAICYA 1, 2
See also SATA 8, 70, 146
Emberley, Michael 1960- ... CANR-97
Earlier sketch in CA 104
See also SATA 34, 80, 119
Emberley, Peter C. 1956- ... CANR-112
Earlier sketch in CA 151
Embey, Philip
See Philipp, Elliot Elias
Emblen, D(onald) L(ewis) 1918- ... 33-36R
Embling, John 1952- ... 111
Emboden, William A(llen), Jr. 1935- ... CANR-34
Earlier sketches in CA 41-44R, CANR-14
Embree, Ainslie Thomas 1921- ... CANR-2
Earlier sketch in CA 1-4R
Embry, Margaret Jacob 1919-1975 ... CANR-3
Earlier sketch in CA 1-4R
See also SATA 5
Emecheta, (Florence Onye) Buchi
1944- ... CANR-126
Earlier sketches in CA 81-84, CANR-27, 81
See also AAYA 67
See also AFW
See also BLC 2
See also BW 2, 3
See also CDWLB 3
See also CLC 14, 48, 128
See also CN 4, 5, 6, 7
See also CWRI 5
See also DA3
See also DAM MULT
See also DLB 117
See also EWL 3
See also FL 1:5
See also FW
See also MTCW 1, 2
See also MTFW 2005
See also NFS 12, 14
See also SATA 66
See also WLIT 2
Emeneau, Murray Barnson 1904- ... CANR-5
Earlier sketch in CA 1-4R
Emenegger, Bob
See Emenegger, Robert
Emenegger, Robert 1933- ... 102
Emenhiser, JeDon A(llen) 1933- ... 37-40R
Emenyonu, Ernest Nneji 1939- ... 197
Emerick, Kenneth F(red) 1925- ... 53-56
Emerson, Alice B. ... CANR-27
Earlier sketches in CAP-2, CA 19-20
See also Benson, Mildred (Augustine Wirt)
See also SATA 1, 67
Emerson, Caroline D. 1891-1973 ... CAP-1
Obituary ... 45-48
Earlier sketch in CA 17-18
Emerson, Caryl (Geppert) 1944- ... CANR-91
Earlier sketch in CA 123
Emerson, Claudia 1957- ... 234
See also Andrews, Claudia Emerson
Emerson, Connie 1930- ... 109
Emerson, (Alan) David 1900- ... CANR-2
Earlier sketch in CA 5-8R
Emerson, Donald (Conger) 1913-1998 .. 21-24R
Emerson, Earl W. 1948- ... CANR-122
Earlier sketches in CA 123, CANR-51, 66
See also CMW 4
Emerson, Everett Harvey 1925- ... CANR-90
Earlier sketches in CA 13-16R, CANR-5, 22
Emerson, Frank C(reighton) 1936- ... 53-56
Emerson, Gloria 1930(?)-2004 ... 221
Obituary ... 231
Emerson, H(enry) O(liver) 1893- ... CAP-2
Earlier sketch in CA 23-24
Emerson, James G(ordon), Jr. 1926- ... 17-20R
Emerson, Kathy Lynn 1947- ... CANR-98
Earlier sketches in CA 127, CANR-54
See also SATA 63
Emerson, Ken 1948- ... CANR-122
Earlier sketch in CA 170
Emerson, Laura S(alome) 1907- ... CAP-1
Earlier sketch in CA 13-16
Emerson, Mary Lee
See Kennedy, Mary
Emerson, O. B. 1922- ... CANR-16
Earlier sketch in CA 25-28R
Emerson, Ralph Waldo 1803-1882 ... AAYA 60
See also AMW
See also ANW
See also CDALB 1640-1865
See also DA
See also DA3
See also DAB
See also DAC
See also DAM MST, POET
See also DLB 1, 59, 73, 183, 223, 270
See also EXPP
See also LAIT 2
See also LMFS 1
See also NCFS 3
See also PC 18
See also PFS 4, 17
See also RGAL 4
See also TUS
See also WLC
See also WP
Emerson, Ronald
See Scotland, James
Emerson, Ru 1944- ... CANR-85
Earlier sketches in CA 121, CANR-44
See also FANT
See also SATA 70, 107
See also SFW 4
Emerson, Rupert 1899-1979 ... CANR-2
Obituary ... 85-88
Earlier sketch in CA 1-4R
Emerson, Sally 1952- ... 172
See also SATA 111
Emerson, Steven A. 1954- ... CANR-127
Earlier sketch in CA 140
Emerson, Thomas E. 1945- ... 165
Emerson, Thomas I(rwin)
1907-1991 ... CANR-76
Obituary ... 134
Earlier sketch in CA 21-24R
Emerson, William 1769-1811 ... DLB 37
Emerson, William K(eith) 1925- ... 41-44R
See also SATA 25
Emerson, William R. 1923-1997 ... DLBY 1997
Emert, Phyllis R(aybin) 1947- ... 159
See also SATA 93
Emery, Alan E(glin) H(eathcote) 1928- ... 69-72
Emery, Allan C(omstock), Jr. 1919- ... 104
Emery, Anne (McGuigan) 1907- ... CANR-2
Earlier sketch in CA 1-4R
See also SATA 1, 33
Emery, Clayton 1953- ... 156
Emery, David A(mos) 1920- ... 29-32R
Emery, Edwin 1914-1993 ... CANR-11
Obituary ... 142
Earlier sketch in CA 69-72
Emery, Fred 1933- ... 65-68
Emery, Gary 1942- ... CANR-29
Earlier sketch in CA 110
Emery, Glenn D. 1954- ... 135
Emery, Kenneth Orris 1914-1998 ... 107
Obituary ... 165
Emery, Marc 1932- ... 132
Emery, Marcia R. 1937- ... 222
Emery, Michael 1940-1995 ... 73-76
Obituary ... 150
Emery, Pierre-Yves 1929- ... 101
Emery, (Walter) Ralph 1932(?)- ... CANR-117
Earlier sketch in CA 142
Emery, Robert F(irestone) 1927- ... 37-40R
Emery, Robert J. 1941- ... 227
Emery, Tom 1971- ... CANR-122
Earlier sketch in CA 164
Emery, Walter Byron 1907-1973 ... CANR-22
Earlier sketch in CA 1-4R
Emett, Rowland 1906-1990 ... 102
Obituary ... 133
Emig, Janet Ann ... 73-76
Emiliani, Cesare 1922-1995 ... 144
Emin, Fedor Aleksandrovich c.
1735-1770 ... DLB 150
Emlen, Robert P. 1946- ... 135
Emma, Ronald David 1920-1988 ... 25-28R
Emmanuel, Philip D. 1909-1991 ... CAP-1
Earlier sketch in CA 13-16
Emmanuel, Pierre
See Mathieu, Noel Jean
See also DLB 258
See also EWL 3
Emme, Eugene M(orlock) 1919-1985 . CANR-8
Obituary ... 116
Earlier sketch in CA 13-16R
Emmel, Thomas C. 1941- ... 185
Brief entry ... 111
Emmens, Carol Ann 1944- ... 106
See also SATA 39
Emmerich, Andre 1924- ... 9-12R
Emmerich, Roland 1955- ... 187
See also AAYA 53
Emmerick, R(onald) E(ric) 1937- ... CANR-11
Earlier sketch in CA 25-28R
Emmerij, L. J.
See Emmerij, Louis (Johan)
Emmerij, Louis (Johan) 1934- ... 169
Emmerson, Donald K(enneth)
1940- ... CANR-32
Earlier sketches in CA 65-68, CANR-14
Emmerson, Henry Russell 1899-1989 ... 5-8R
Emmerson, John K(enneth)
1908-1984 ... CANR-14
Obituary ... 112
Earlier sketch in CA 57-60
Emmerson, Richard Kenneth 1948- ... 106
Emmet, Alan 1927- ... CANR-115
Earlier sketch in CA 158
Emmet, Dorothy (Mary) 1904-2000 .. CANR-92
Obituary ... 189
Earlier sketch in CA 9-12R
Emmet, E(ric) R(evell) 1909- ... 107
Emmet, Herman LeRoy 1943- ... 141
Emmet, Olivia (Lily) 1933- ... 146
Emmett, Ayala 1935- ... 163
Emmett, Bruce 1949- ... 57-60
Emmett, Jonathan 1965- ... 209
See also SATA 138
Emmett, R. T.
See Hanshew, Thomas W.
Emmett, Rita ... 215
Emmis, Yetta
See Mekler, Eva
Emmitt, Robert (P.) 1925- ... 29-32R
Emmons, Cai 1951- ... 223
Emmons, Charles F(rank) 1942- ... 110
Emmons, Della (Florence) Gould 1890-1983
Obituary ... 111
See also SATA-Obit 39
Emmons, Didi 1963- ... 233
Emmons, Mary L. 1940- ... 217
Emmons, Michael 1938- ... 107
Emmons, Nuel 1927- ... 125
Emmons, Phillip
See Little, Bentley
Emmons, Shirlee 1923- ... CANR-98
Earlier sketch in CA 147
Emmott, Bill
See Emmott, William John
Emmott, William John 1956- ... 136
Emmrich, Curt 1897-1975 ... CAP-2
Earlier sketch in CA 29-32
Emmrich, Kurt
See Emmrich, Curt
Emorey, N.
See Ellison, Jerome
Emory, Alan (Steuer) 1922-2000 ... CANR-12
Obituary ... 192
Earlier sketch in CA 69-72
Emory, Jerry 1957- ... 161
See also SATA 96
Empedocles 5th cent. B.C.- ... DLB 176
Empey, Arthur Guy 1883-1963
Obituary ... 107
Empey, LaMar T(aylor) 1923- ... CANR-30
Earlier sketch in CA 29-32R
Employee X
See Fautsko, Timothy F(rank)
Empringham, Antoinette F(leur) 1939- ... 124
Empringham, Toni
See Empringham, Antoinette F(leur)
Empson, William 1906-1984 ... CANR-61
Obituary ... 112
Earlier sketches in CA 17-20R, CANR-31
See also BRWS 2
See also CLC 3, 8, 19, 33, 34
See also CP 1, 2
See also DLB 20
See also EWL 3
See also MTCW 1, 2
See also RGEL 2
Emrich, Duncan (Black Macdonald)
1908-1970(?) ... CANR-9
Earlier sketch in CA 61-64
See also SATA 11
Emshwiller, Carol (Fries) 1921- ... 231
Earlier sketches in CA 53-56, CANR-52, 103
Autobiographical Essay in ... 231
See also AAYA 67
See also FANT
See also FW
See also SFW 4
Emsley, Clare
See Plummer, Clare (Emsley)
Emsley, John 1938- ... CANR-94
Earlier sketch in CA 142
Emsley, Michael Gordon 1930- ... 97-100
Emslie, M. L.
See Simpson, Myrtle L(illias)
Emswiler, Sharon Neufer 1944- ... 119
Emy, Hugh (Vincent) 1944- ... 77-80
Enamorado Cuesta, Jose 1892- ... HW 1
Encausse, Gerard (Anaclet Vincent) 1865-1916
Brief entry ... 113
Encel, Sol
See Encel, Solomon
Encel, Solomon 1925- ... CANR-37
Earlier sketch in CA 115
Enchi, Fumiko (Ueda) 1905-1986 ... 129
Obituary ... 121
See also Enchi Fumiko
See also CLC 31
See also FW
See also MJW
Enchi Fumiko
See Enchi, Fumiko (Ueda)
See also DLB 182
See also EWL 3
Encinias, Miguel 1923- ... 144
Enckell, Rabbe 1903-1974 ... 189
See also EWL 3
Endacott, G(eorge) B(eer) 1901- ... 5-8R
Endacott, M(arie) Violet 1915- ... 9-12R
Ende, Jean 1947- ... 53-56

Cumulative Index 175 Entwistle

Ende, Michael (Andreas Helmuth)
1929-1995 ... CANR-110
Obituary ... 149
Brief entry ... 118
Earlier sketches in CA 124, CANR-36
See also BYA 5
See also CLC 31
See also CLR 14
See also DLB 75
See also MAICYA 1, 2
See also MAICYAS 1
See also SATA 61, 130
See also SATA-Brief 42
See also SATA-Obit 86
Ende, Richard Chaffey von
See von Ende, Richard Chaffey
Endelman, Todd M(ichael) 1946- ... CANR-135
Earlier sketch in CA 125
Enderle, Dotti 1954- ... 218
See also SATA 145
Enderle, Georges 1943- ... 188
Enderle, Judith (Ann) Ross 1941- ... CANR-104
Earlier sketches in CA 106, CANR-22, 49
See also SAAS 26
See also SATA 38, 89
See also SATA-Essay 114
Enderlin, Charles 1945- ... 224
Enders, Richard
See Fenster, Robert
Endersby, Clive 1944- ... 133
Endfield, Mercedes
See von Block, Bela W(illiam)
Endicott, Frank S(impson) 1904-1990
Obituary ... 131
Endicott, Marina 1958- ... 212
Endicott, Ruth Belmore ... CANR-26
Earlier sketches in CAP-2, CA 19-20
Endicott, Stephen (Lyon) 1928- ... 184
Earlier sketch in CA 107
Endleman, Robert ... 152
Endler, Norman S(olomon) 1931- ... CANR-9
Earlier sketch in CA 21-24R
Endo, Mitsuko 1942- ... 65-68
Endo, Shusaku 1923-1996 ... CANR-131
Obituary ... 153
Earlier sketches in CA 29-32R, CANR-21, 54
See also Endo Shusaku
See also CLC 7, 14, 19, 54, 99
See also DA3
See also DAM NOV
See also MTCW 1, 2
See also MTFW 2005
See also RGSF 2
See also RGWL 2, 3
See also SSC 48
See also TCLC 152
Endore, (Samuel) Guy 1900-1970 ... CANR-72
Obituary ... 25-28R
Earlier sketches in CA 1-4R, CANR-6
See also HGG
Endo Shusaku
See Endo, Shusaku
See also CWW 2
See also DLB 182
See also EWL 3
Endres, Clifford 1941- ... 108
Endrezze, Anita 1952- ... 214
Endy, Melvin B(ecker), Jr. 1938- ... 81-84
Enei, Yevgeni 1890-1971 ... IDFW 3, 4
Enell, Trinka (Gochenour) 1951- ... SATA 79
Enelow, Allen J(ay) 1922- ... CANR-7
Earlier sketch in CA 17-20R
Enelow, H(illel Hyman) G(erson)
1877-1934 ... 229
Ener, Guener 1935- ... 146
Ener, Guner
See Ener, Guener
Enfield, Carrie
See Smith, Susan Vernon
Enfield, Harry 1961- ... 206
Eng, David L. ... 226
Eng--, Tom
See Engelhardt, Thomas Alexander
Engberg, Edward 1928- ... 21-24R
Engberg, Holger L(aessoe) 1930- ... 37-40R
Engberg, (Johanna) Susan 1940- ... CANR-41
Earlier sketch in CA 117
Engdahl, Sylvia Louise 1933- ... 195
Earlier sketches in CA 29-32R, CANR-14, 85, 95
Autobiographical Essay in ... 195
See also AAYA 36
See also BYA 4
See also CLR 2
See also JRDA
See also MAICYA 1, 2
See also SAAS 5
See also SATA 4
See also SATA-Essay 122
See also SFW 4
See also YAW
Engebrecht, P(atricia) A(nn) 1935- ... 57-60
Engel, A. J.
See Engel, Arthur (Jason)
Engel, Alan
See Engelberg, Alan (D.)
Engel, Alan S(tuart) 1932- ... 37-40R
Engel, Arthur (Jason) 1944- ... 129
Engel, Bernard F. 1921- ... 13-16R
Engel, Cindy ... 204
Engel, Diana 1947- ... 138
See also SATA 70
Engel, Herbert M. 1918- ... CANR-43
Earlier sketch in CA 120
Engel, Howard 1931- ... CANR-119
Earlier sketches in CA 112, CANR-44, 66
See also CMW 4
Engel, J. Ronald 1936- ... CANR-51
Earlier sketch in CA 124
Engel, James F. 1934- ... CANR-13
Earlier sketch in CA 21-24R
Engel, Joel 1952- ... 217
Engel, (Aaron) Lehman 1910-1982 ... CANR-31
Obituary ... 107
Earlier sketch in CA 41-44R
Engel, Louis (Henry, Jr.) 1909-1982 ... 21-24R
Obituary ... 108
Engel, Lyle Kenyon 1915-1986 ... 85-88
Obituary ... 120
Engel, Madeline H(elena) 1941- ... 85-88
Engel, Margorie L(ouise) 1943- ... 147
Engel, Marian 1933-1985 ... CANR-12
Earlier sketch in CA 25-28R
Interview in ... CANR-12
See also CLC 36
See also CN 2, 3
See also DLB 53
See also FW
See also TCLC 137
Engel, Mary June Montgomery 1920(?)-1985
Obituary ... 117
Engel, Matthew (Lewis) 1951- ... CANR-125
Earlier sketch in CA 146
Engel, Michael 1944- ... 207
Engel, Monroe 1921- ... 5-8R
Engel, Pauline Newton 1918- ... 17-20R
Engel, Peter H. 1935- ... CANR-15
Earlier sketch in CA 81-84
Engel, Richard 1974(?)- ... 232
Engel, S(rul) Morris (von) 1931- ... CANR-14
Earlier sketch in CA 37-40R
Engel, Salo 1908-1972 ... CAP-2
Earlier sketch in CA 33-36
Engel, Samuel G. 1904-1984
Obituary ... 112
Engelbach, David (Charles) 1946- ... 133
Engelberg, Alan (D.) 1941- ... 132
Engelberg, Edward 1929- ... 37-40R
Engelberg, Stephen 1958- ... 215
Engel'gardt, Sof'ia Vladimirovna
1828-1894 ... DLB 277
Engelhard, Jack 1940- ... 132
Engelhardt, Frederick
See Hubbard, L(afayette) Ron(ald)
Engelhardt, H(ugo) Tristram, Jr. 1941- ... 139
Engelhardt, Thomas Alexander 1930- ... 133
Engelhardt, Tom
See Engelhardt, Thomas Alexander
Engelhart, Margaret S. 1924- ... 122
See also SATA 59
Engelking, L. L. 1903(?)-1980
Obituary ... 102
Engell, James 1951- ... 135
Engelman, Rose C. 1919(?)-1979
Obituary ... 89-92
Engelmann, Hugo O(tto) 1917- ... 41-44R
Engelmann, Kim (V.) 1959- ... 151
See also SATA 87
Engelmann, Larry 1941- ... CANR-88
Earlier sketch in CA 101
Engelmann, Ruth 1919- ... 106
Engelmann, Siegfried E. 1931- ... CANR-13
Earlier sketch in CA 21-24R
Engelmayer, Sheldon David 1945- ... 114
Engels, Donald (W.) 1946- ... CANR-90
Earlier sketch in CA 102
Engels, Friedrich 1820-1895 ... DLB 129
See also LATS 1:1
Engels, John David 1931- ... CANR-6
Earlier sketch in CA 13-16R
See also CP 1, 7
Engels, Norbert (Anthony) 1903-1983 ... CAP-2
Earlier sketch in CA 17-18
Engeman, Thomas S(ledge) 1944- ... 109
Engen, Rodney K(ent) 1948- ... CANR-15
Earlier sketch in CA 65-68
Enger, L. L.
See Enger, Leif
Enger, Leif 1961- ... 204
Enger, Norman L. 1937- ... CANR-10
Earlier sketch in CA 25-28R
Engerman, Stanley L(ewis) 1936- ... 53-56
Enggass, Robert 1921- ... CANR-9
Earlier sketch in CA 13-16R
Engh, M(ary) J(ane) 1933- ... CANR-58
Earlier sketch in CA 69-72
See also SFW 4
Engh, Rohn 1938- ... 69-72
Engholm, Eva 1909- ... 93-96
Engl, Lieselotte 1918- ... 49-52
Engl, Theodor 1925- ... 49-52
Englade, Ken(neth Francis) 1938- ... 157
England, Anthony Bertram 1939- ... 85-88
England, Barry 1932- ... 25-28R
See also CBD
England, Chris 1961- ... 208
England, Colin
See Jeans, Michael
England, E. M.
See Anders, Edith (Mary) England
England, E Squires
See Ball, Sylvia Patricia
England, George Allan 1877-1936 ... 161
Brief entry ... 112
See also SATA 102
See also SFW 4
England, George W(illiam) 1927- ... 104
England, John C(arol) 1930- ... 116
England, Martha Winburn 1909-1989 ... CAP-1
Earlier sketch in CA 11-12
England, Maurice Derrick 1908-1980 ... 104
England, Piers
See Kersh, Gerald
England, Rodney Charles Bennett
See Bennett-England, Rodney Charles
England, Wilbur Birch 1903-1991 ... 1-4R
Englander, Nathan 1970- ... 218
Englart, Mindi Rose 1965- ... 220
See also SATA 146
Engle, Eloise
See Paananen, Eloise (Katherine)
See also SATA 9
Engle, Jeff(rey) 1947- ... 103
Engle, John D(avid), Jr. 1922- ... CANR-25
Earlier sketches in CA 57-60, CANR-7
Engle, Louise Boardman Proctor 1897(?)-1987
Obituary ... 121
Engle, Margarita 1951- ... 152
See also LLW
Engle, Parke F. 1900(?)-1984
Obituary ... 111
Engle, Paul (Hamilton) 1908-1991 ... CANR-82
Obituary ... 134
Earlier sketches in CA 1-4R, CANR-5
See also CP 1, 2
See also DLB 48
Engle, Stephen D(ouglas) 1962- ... 192
Engle, T(helburn) L(aRoy) 1901-1994 ... 13-16R
Englebert, Victor 1933- ... 57-60
See also SATA 8
Englefield, Ronald 1891-1975
Obituary ... 105
Englehart, Bob
See Englehart, Robert (Wayne), Jr.
Englehart, Robert (Wayne), Jr. 1945- ... 133
Englekirk, John E(ugene) 1905-1983
Obituary ... 112
Engleman, Finis E(wing) 1895-1978 ... 9-12R
Obituary ... 134
Engleman, Paul 1953- ... 131
Engler, Larry 1949- ... 53-56
Engler, Richard E(mil), Jr. 1925- ... 37-40R
Engler, Robert 1922- ... CANR-2
Earlier sketch in CA 1-4R
Englert, Clement Cyril 1910-1987 ... CANR-5
Earlier sketch in CA 1-4R
English, Adrian J(oseph) 1939- ... 118
English, Arnold
See Hershman, Morris
English, Barbara (Anne) 1933- ... CANR-13
Earlier sketch in CA 33-36R
English, Charles
See Nuetzel, Charles (Alexander)
English, David 1931-1998 ... 69-72
Obituary ... 181
English, Deirdre (Elena) 1948- ... 85-88
English, E(ugene) Schuyler 1899-1981 ... 107
Obituary ... 103
English, Earl (Franklin) 1905-2000 ... 37-40R
Obituary ... 190
English, Edward (H.) 19(?)-1973
Obituary ... 41-44R
English, Fenwick Walter 1939- ... CANR-1
Earlier sketch in CA 45-48
English, Isobel 1925-1994 ... CANR-84
Obituary ... 145
Earlier sketch in CA 53-56
See also CN 2, 3, 4, 5, 6
English, James W(ilson) 1915- ... 21-24R
See also SATA 37
English, (Emma) Jean M(artin) 1937- ... 29-32R
English, John A(lan) 1940- ... 175
English, John W(esley) 1940- ... 69-72
English, Lyn D. 1953- ... 154
English, Maurice 1909-1983 ... CANR-12
Obituary ... 111
Earlier sketch in CA 9-12R
See also CP 1, 2
English, O(liver) Spurgeon 1901-1993 ... CAP-2
Obituary ... 143
Earlier sketch in CA 33-36
English, Peter (C.) 1947- ... 189
English, Richard
See Shaver, Richard S(harpe)
English, Ronald (Frederick) 1913- ... CAP-1
Earlier sketch in CA 9-10
English, Sharon 1965- ... 233
English, Thomas Dunn 1819-1902 ... 201
See also DLB 202
English, Thomas H(opkins)
1895-1992 ... CANR-2
Earlier sketch in CA 5-8R
English, Thomas Saunders 1928-
Brief entry ... 105
Englizian, H. Crosby 1923- ... 21-24R
Engquist, Richard 1933- ... 29-32R
Engren, Edith
See McCaig, Robert Jesse
Engs, Robert Francis 1943- ... 101
Engs, Ruth C(lifford) 1939- ... 160
Engster, Daniel (Albert) 1965- ... 208
Engstrand, Iris (H.) Wilson 1935- ... 107
Engstroem, Albert
See Engstrom, Albert (Laurentius Johannes)
Engstrom, Elizabeth 1951- ... CANR-127
Earlier sketch in CA 172
See also SATA 110
Engstrom, Ted W.
See Engstrom, Theodore W(ilhelm)
Engstrom, Theodore W(ilhelm)
1916- ... CANR-25
Earlier sketches in CA 65-68, CANR-9
Engstrom, W(infred) A(ndrew) 1925- ... 57-60
Enis, Ben M(elvin) 1942- ... CANR-22
Earlier sketches in CA 57-60, CANR-7
Enke, Stephen 1916-1974 ... 65-68
Obituary ... 53-56
Enkelis, Liane 1948- ... 215
Enloe, Cynthia H(olden) 1938- ... CANR-39
Earlier sketches in CA 37-40R, CANR-17
Enlow, David R(oland) 1916- ... CANR-10
Earlier sketch in CA 5-8R
Ennals, Peter 1943- ... 202
Ennes, James M(arquis), Jr. 1933- ... CANR-34
Earlier sketch in CA 102
Ennis, Bruce J(ames) 1940-2000
Obituary ... 188
Brief entry ... 110
Ennis, Charles A(lbert) 1954- ... 195
Ennis, Garth 1970- ... 234
Ennis, Robert H(ugh) 1927- ... CANR-10
Earlier sketch in CA 25-28R
Ennius 239B.C.-169B.C. ... DLB 211
See also RGWL 2, 3
Ennulat, Egbert M. 1929- ... 142
Eno, Susan ... 101
Enoch, Kurt 1895-1982
Obituary ... 106
Enoch, Suzanne ... 230
Enockson, Paul G(eorge) 1938- ... 110
Enomiya-Lassalle, Hugo M(akibi)
1898-1990 ... 21-24R
Enquist, Per Olov 1934- ... 193
Brief entry ... 109
See also CWW 2
See also DLB 257
See also EWL 3
Enrick, Norbert Lloyd 1920-1991 ... CANR-43
Earlier sketches in CA 13-16R, CANR-6
Enright, Anne 1962- ... 185
See also DLB 267
Enright, D(ennis) J(oseph)
1920-2002 ... CANR-83
Obituary ... 211
Earlier sketches in CA 1-4R, CANR-1, 42
See also CLC 4, 8, 31
See also CN 1, 2
See also CP 1, 2, 3, 4, 5, 6, 7
See also DLB 27
See also EWL 3
See also SATA 25
See also SATA-Obit 140
Enright, Elizabeth (Wright)
1909-1968 ... CANR-83
Obituary ... 25-28R
Earlier sketch in CA 61-64
See also BYA 3
See also CLR 4
See also CWRI 5
See also DLB 22
See also MAICYA 1, 2
See also SATA 9
See also WCH
Enright, Maureen Patricia Ford 1908(?)-1983
Obituary ... 111
Enright, Michael J(ohn) 1958- ... 139
Enright, Nicholas (Paul) 1950-2003 ... 233
See also CD 5, 6
Enright, Nick
See Enright, Nicholas (Paul)
Enriquez de Salamanca, Cristina 1952- ... 158
See also HW 2
Enroth, Clyde A(dolph) 1926- ... 37-40R
Enscoe, Gerald (Eugene) 1926- ... CANR-10
Earlier sketch in CA 5-8R
Ense, Wolfgang
See Frank, Rudolf
Ensign, Thomas 1940- ... 101
Ensign, Tod
See Ensign, Thomas
Ensler, Eve 1953- ... CANR-126
Earlier sketch in CA 172
See also CLC 212
Ensley, Eddie ... 208
Ensley, Evangeline 1907-1996 ... CANR-83
Brief entry ... 114
Earlier sketch in CA 122
Interview in ... CA-122
See also FANT
Ensley, Francis Gerald 1907- ... CAP-1
Earlier sketch in CA 13-16
Enslin, Morton S(cott) 1897-1980 ... 17-20R
Obituary ... 134
Enslin, Theodore (Vernon) 1925- ... CANR-83
Earlier sketches in CA 53-56, CANR-4, 19, 41
See also CAAS 3
See also CP 1, 2, 3, 4, 5, 6, 7
Enslow, Sam 1946- ... 136
Ensminger, Audrey H(elen) 1919- ... 149
Ensminger, Marion Eugene
1908-1998 ... CANR-16
Earlier sketches in CA 49-52, CANR-1
Ensminger, Peter A. 1957- ... 200
Ensor, Allison (Rash) 1935- ... 25-28R
Ensor, (Alick Charles) David(son) 1906-1987
Obituary ... 121
Ensor, Robert (T.) 1922- ... 158
See also SATA 93
Enstice, Wayne 1943- ... 139
Enstrom, Robert (William) 1946- ... 104
Enteman, Willard F(inley) 1936- ... 33-36R
Entenza, John Dymock 1905-1984
Obituary ... 112
Enterline, James Robert 1932- ... 41-44R
Enters, Angna 1907-1989
Obituary ... 128
Enthoven, Alain C(harles) 1930- ... CANR-27
Earlier sketch in CA 49-52
Entine, Alan D(avid) 1936- ... 21-24R
Entman, Robert M(athew) 1949- ... CANR-102
Earlier sketch in CA 130
Entwisle, Doris R(oberts) 1924- ... 5-8R
Entwistle, Florence Vivienne 1889(?)-1982
Obituary ... 105
Entwistle, Harold 1923- ... 29-32R
Entwistle, Noel (James) 1936- ... CANR-39
Earlier sketches in CA 93-96, CANR-16

Entwistle 176 CONTEMPORARY AUTHORS

Entwistle, (Arthur) Theodore (Henry) Rowland
See Rowland-Entwistle, (Arthur) Theodore (Henry)
Envall, Markku Sakari 1944- 194
Enyeart, James L(yle) 1943- 113
Enys, Sarah L.
See Sloggett, Nellie
Enz, Jacob J(ohn) 1919- 41-44R
Enzensberger, Hans Magnus 1929- . CANR-103
Brief entry 116
Earlier sketch in CA 119
See also CLC 43
See also CWW 2
See also EWL 3
See also PC 28
Enzler, Clarence J. 1910(?)-1976
Obituary 69-72
Enzweiler, Joseph A. 1950- 151
Eotvos, Jozsef 1813-1871 .... RGWL 2, 3
Eoyang, Eugene Chen 1939- 140
Epafrodito
See Wagner, C(harles) Peter
Epand, Len 1950- 85-88
Epanomitis, Fotini 1969- 169
Epanya, Christian A(rthur Kingue)
1956- .... SATA 91
Epernay, Mark
See Galbraith, John Kenneth
See also CCA 1
Ephraim, Gavriel Ben
See Ben-Ephraim, Gavriel
Ephraim, Shelly S(chonebaum) 1952- .. SATA 97
Ephron, Amy 1955- CANR-88
Earlier sketch in CA 138
Ephron, Delia 1944- CANR-97
Earlier sketches in CA 97-100, CANR-12, 52
See also SATA 65
See also SATA-Brief 50
Ephron, G. H.
See Ephron, Hallie
Ephron, Hallie 1948- 223
Ephron, Henry 1911(?)-1992 73-76
Obituary 139
Ephron, Nora 1941- CANR-83
Earlier sketches in CA 65-68, CANR-12, 39
See also AAYA 35
See also AITN 2
See also CLC 17, 31
See also DFS 22
Ephron, Phoebe (Wolkind) 1916-1971
Obituary 33-36R
Epicharmus c. 530B.C.-c. 440B.C. .... LMFS 1
Epictetus c. 55-c. 125 .... AW 2
See also DLB 176
Epicurus 341B.C.-270B.C. .... DLB 176
Epinay, Louise d' 1726-1783 .... DLB 313
Epler, Doris M. 1928- .... SATA 73
Epler, Percy H. 1872-1975
Obituary 57-60
Epp, Eldon Jay 1930- CANR-7
Earlier sketch in CA 17-20R
Epp, Frank H(enry) 1929-1986 .... CANR-29
Earlier sketch in CA 29-32R
Epp, Margaret A(gnes) 1913- CANR-3
Earlier sketch in CA 9-12R
See also SATA 20
Eppard, Philip B(lair) 1945- 112
Eppenbach, Sarah 1947- 114
Eppenstein, Louise (Kohn) 1892-1987
Obituary 123
See also SATA-Obit 54
Epperly, Elizabeth Rollins 1951- 106
Epperson, Gordon 1921- 25-28R
Eppie
See Naismith, Helen
Eppinga, Jacob D. 1917- 33-36R
Eppinga, Jane 1939- 230
Eppinger, Josh 1940- 89-92
Eppink, Norman R(oland) 1906-1985 53-56
Epple, Anne Orth 1927- 33-36R
See also SATA 20
Epps, Bernard 1936- 177
See also DLB 53
Epps, Bradley S. 1958- 166
Epps, Edgar G(ustavas) 1929- 49-52
Epps, Garrett 1950- 69-72
Epps, Jack, Jr. 1949- 133
Epps, Preston H(erschel) 1888-1982 .... 37-40R
Obituary 133
Epps, Robert L(ee) 1932- 17-20R
Eppstein, John 1895-1988
Obituary 125
Eprile, Tony 1955(?)- 232
Epshtein, Mikhail Naumovich
See Epstein, Mikhail N(aumovich)
See also DLB 285
Epsilon
See Betjeman, John
Epstein, Alan 1949- 200
Epstein, Ann Wharton
See Wharton, Annabel (Jane)
Epstein, Anne Merrick 1931- 69-72
See also SATA 20
Epstein, Barbara 1928-
Brief entry 110
Epstein, Benjamin Robert 1912-1983 45-48
Obituary 109
Epstein, Beryl (M. Williams) 1910- ... CANR-39
Earlier sketches in CA 5-8R, CANR-2, 18
See also CLR 26
See also SAAS 17
See also SATA 1, 31
Epstein, Charlotte 1921- CANR-8
Earlier sketch in CA 61-64
Epstein, Cy(ril Robert) 1942-
Brief entry 108
Epstein, Cynthia Fuchs 1933- CANR-14
Earlier sketch in CA 29-32R
Epstein, Daniel Mark 1948- CANR-90
Earlier sketches in CA 49-52, CANR-2, 53
See also CLC 7
Epstein, David G(eorge) 1943- 69-72
Epstein, Dena J. 1916- 41-44R
Epstein, Edmund L(loyd) 1931- 118
Epstein, Edward Jay 1935- CANR-71
Earlier sketches in CA 17-20R, CANR-13
Epstein, Edwin M(ichael) 1937- 25-28R
Epstein, Ellen Robinson 1947- 115
Epstein, Eric Joseph 1959- 176
Epstein, Erwin H(oward) 1939- 29-32R
Epstein, Eugene 1944- 69-72
Epstein, Fritz T(heodor) 1898-1979 .. CANR-22
Earlier sketch in CA 69-72
Epstein, Helen 1947- CANR-144
Earlier sketch in CA 89-92
Epstein, Howard M(ichael) 1927- 21-24R
Epstein, Jacob 1880-1959 163
Brief entry 120
Epstein, Jacob 1956- 114
See also CLC 19
Epstein, Jason 1928- CANR-110
Earlier sketch in CA 57-60
Epstein, Jean 1897-1953 .... TCLC 92
Epstein, Joseph 1937- CANR-117
Brief entry 112
Earlier sketches in CA 119, CANR-50, 65
See also AMWS 14
See also CLC 39, 204
Epstein, Judith Sue 1947- 69-72
Epstein, Julia 205
Epstein, Julius 1901-1975
Obituary 57-60
Epstein, Julius J. 1909-2000 124
Obituary 190
Brief entry 113
See also DLB 26
See also IDFW 3, 4
Epstein, June CANR-57
Earlier sketches in CA 73-76, CANR-13, 30
Epstein, Lawrence J(effrey) 1946- CANR-89
Earlier sketch in CA 132
Epstein, Lee 1958- 119
Epstein, Leon D. 1919- 13-16R
Epstein, Leslie 1938- 215
Earlier sketches in CA 73-76, CANR-23, 69
Autobiographical Essay in 215
See also CAAS 12
See also AMWS 12
See also CLC 27
See also DLB 299
Epstein, Louis M. 1887-1949 205
Epstein, Mark 1953- 209
Epstein, Melech (Michael) 1889(?)-1979
Obituary 89-92
Epstein, Mikhail N(aumovich)
1950- CANR-94
Earlier sketch in CA 156
See also Epshtein, Mikhail Naumovich
Epstein, Morris 1921-1973 .... CAP-1
Obituary 45-48
Earlier sketch in CA 13-16
Epstein, Perle
See Besserman, Perle
Epstein, Perle S.
See Besserman, Perle
Epstein, Perle S(herry) 1938- CANR-9
Earlier sketch in CA 65-68
See also SATA 27
Epstein, Philip G. 1909-1952
Brief entry 117
See also DLB 26
See also IDFW 3, 4
Epstein, Rachel S. 1941- CANR-129
Earlier sketch in CA 169
See also SATA 102
Epstein, Richard A(llen) 1943- CANR-115
Earlier sketch in CA 158
Epstein, Robert M(orris) 1948- 149
Epstein, Samuel 1909-2000 .... CANR-39
Earlier sketches in CA 9-12R, CANR-4, 18
See also CLR 26
See also SAAS 17
See also SATA 1, 31
Epstein, Samuel S(tanley) 1926- 115
Epstein, Seymour 1917- CANR-25
Earlier sketches in CA 1-4R, CANR-5
Epstein, Stephan R. 1960- 144
Epstein, William 1912-2001 .... CANR-11
Obituary 193
Earlier sketch in CA 69-72
Epstein, William H(enry) 1944- 61-64
Epstein, William M(aurice) 1944- 188
Epton, Nina C(onsuelo) CANR-11
Earlier sketch in CA 5-8R
Equiano, Olaudah 1745(?)-1797 .... AFAW 1, 2
See also BLC 2
See also CDWLB 3
See also DAM MULT
See also DLB 37, 50
See also WLIT 2
Eramus, M. Nott
See Stuber, Stanley I(rving)
Erasmus, Charles J(ohn) 1921- 1-4R
Erasmus, Desiderius 1469(?)-1536 .... DLB 136
See also EW 2
See also LMFS 1
See also RGWL 2, 3
See also TWA
Erasmus, M. Nott
See Stuber, Stanley I(rving)
Erazmus, Edward T. 1920- 187
Brief entry 106
Erb, Alta Mae 1891-1995 .... CAP-1
Earlier sketch in CA 9-10
Erb, Paul 1894-1984 .... 9-12R
Erb, Peter C. 1943- CANR-73
Earlier sketches in CA 113, CANR-32
Erba, Luciano 1922- 182
See also CWW 2
See also DLB 128
Erbsen, Claude E. 1938- 89-92
Erce
See Campert, Remco Wouter
Ercilla y Zuniga, Don Alonso de
1533-1594 .... LAW
Ercoli, Ercole
See Togliatti, Palmiro
Erdahl, Carol Syvertsen 1932- 108
Erdahl, Lowell O. 1931- 109
Erdman, Charles R(osenbury) 1866-1960 233
Erdman, David V(orse) 1911-2001 ... CANR-17
Earlier sketches in CA 1-4R, CANR-1
Erdman, Harley 1962- 162
Erdman, Howard Loyd 1935- 21-24R
Erdman, Loula Grace 1905(?)-1976 .. CANR-63
Earlier sketches in CA 5-8R, CANR-10
See also SATA 1
See also TCWW 1, 2
Erdman, Nikolai R(obertovich) 1900-1970
Obituary 29-32R
See also DLB 272
Erdman, Paul E(mil) 1932- CANR-84
Earlier sketches in CA 61-64, CANR-13, 43
See also AITN 1
See also CLC 25
Erdmann, Jack 1931(?)- 205
Erdmans, Mary Patrice 1959- 177
Erdoes, Richard 1912- 77-80
See also SATA 33
See also SATA-Brief 28
Erdos, Paul L(ouis) 1914-2000 188
Erdrich, (Karen) Louise 1954- CANR-138
Earlier sketches in CA 114, CANR-41, 62, 118
See also AAYA 10, 47
See also AMWS 4
See also BEST 89:1
See also BPFB 1
See also CDALBS
See also CLC 39, 54, 120, 176
See also CN 5, 6, 7
See also CP 7
See also CPW
See also CWP
See also DA3
See also DAM MULT, NOV, POP
See also DLB 152, 175, 206
See also EWL 3
See also EXPP
See also FL 1:5
See also LAIT 5
See also LATS 1:2
See also MAL 5
See also MTCW 1, 2
See also MTFW 2005
See also NFS 5
See also NNAL
See also PC 52
See also PFS 14
See also RGAL 4
See also SATA 94, 141
See also SSFS 14
See also TCWW 2
Erdt, Terrence 1942- 106
Ereira, Alan 1943- 137
Erenberg, Arthur 1909(?)-1980
Obituary 114
Erenberg, Lewis A. 1944- CANR-89
Earlier sketch in CA 125
Erenburg, Il'ia Grigor'evich
See Erenburg, Ilya (Grigoryevich)
See also DLB 272
Erenburg, Ilya (Grigoryevich)
See Ehrenburg, Ilya (Grigoryevich)
Erens, Patricia 1938- 93-96
E-Rex
See Hilbert, Richard A.
Erhard, Ludwig 1897-1977
Obituary 112
Erhard, Thomas A. 1923- CANR-29
Earlier sketches in CA 33-36R, CANR-13
Erhard, Walter 1920- .... SATA-Brief 30
Erhart, Margaret 1953- 127
Eri, Vincent Serei 1936-1993 233
See also CN 4, 5
Erian, Alicia 200
Eribon, Didier 1953- 138
Eric, Kenneth
See Henley, Arthur
Ericcson, Volter Adalbert
See Kilpi, Volter Adalbert
Erich, Otto
See Hartleben, Otto Erich
Erichsen, Heino R(ichard) 1924- 110
Erichsen-Brown, Gwethalyn Graham
See Graham, Gwethalyn
Erichsen-Nelson, Jean 1934- 109
Ericksen, Ephraim Gordon 1917- 5-8R
Ericksen, Gerald L(awrence) 1931- 29-32R
Ericksen, Julia A(nn) 188
Ericksen, Kenneth J(errold) 1939- 37-40R
Ericksen, Stanford Clark 1911-2000
Brief entry 108
Erickson, Aake
See Gripenberg, Bertel (Johan Sebastian)
Erickson, Ake
See Gripenberg, Bertel (Johan Sebastian)
Erickson, Ann 1943- .... CAAS 29
Erickson, Arthur (Charles) 1924- 89-92
Erickson, Arvel Benjamin 1905-1974 .... CAP-2
Earlier sketch in CA 21-22
Erickson, Ben 1952- 198
Erickson, Betty J(ean) ' 1923- 163
See also SATA 97
Erickson, Bonnie H(eather) 1944- 112
Erickson, Carolly 1943- CANR-112
Earlier sketches in CA 69-72, CANR-11
Erickson, Darlene (E.) Williams 1941- 143
Erickson, Don 1932- 110
Erickson, Donald A(rthur) 1925- 29-32R
Erickson, E(rnst) Walfred 1911-1996 ... CANR-5
Earlier sketch in CA 5-8R
Erickson, Edsel L(ee) 1928- 53-56
Erickson, Erling Arthur 1934- 33-36R
Erickson, Hal 1950- 142
Erickson, John 1929-2002 101
Obituary 205
Erickson, John R. 1943- CANR-115
Earlier sketch in CA 138
See also SATA 70, 136
Erickson, Jon 1948- 212
See also SATA 141
Erickson, Keith V. 1943- 29-32R
Erickson, Lynn
See Swanton, Molly (Butler)
Erickson, Lynn
See Peltonen, Carla
Erickson, M(elvin) E(ddy) 1918-(?) 9-12R
Erickson, Marilyn T. 1936- 73-76
Erickson, Marion J. 1913-1997 .... 17-20R
Erickson, Millard J. 1932- 93-96
Erickson, Milton H(yland) 1901-1980 106
Obituary 97-100
Erickson, Peter (Brown) 1945- CANR-99
Earlier sketch in CA 126
Erickson, Phoebe CANR-3
Earlier sketch in CA 1-4R
See also SATA 59
Erickson, Raymond (F.) 1941- 169
Erickson, Robert 1917-1997
Obituary 157
Brief entry 109
Erickson, Russell E(verett) 1932- 93-96
See also SATA 27
Erickson, Sabra Rollins 1912-1995 .... CANR-5
Earlier sketch in CA 5-8R
See also SATA 35
Erickson, Stephen A(nthony) 1940- 85-88
Erickson, Stephen Michael 1950- 129
See also Erickson, Steve
See also SFW 4
Erickson, Steve CANR-136
Earlier sketch in CANR-60, 68
See also Erickson, Stephen Michael
See also CLC 64
See also MTFW 2005
See also SUFW 2
Erickson, Tyler 171
Erickson, W(alter) Bruce 1938- 49-52
Erickson, Walter
See Fast, Howard (Melvin)
Erickson, Winston P(erry) 1943- 151
Ericson, David F. 1950- 142
Ericson, Edward E(inar) 1939- 69-72
Ericson, Joe Ellis 1925- 41-44R
Ericson, Julia
See Leisy, James (Franklin)
Ericson, Maria 1965- 239
Ericson, Richard V(ictor) 1948- CANR-124
Earlier sketch in CA 168
Ericson, Walter
See Fast, Howard (Melvin)
Ericsson, Emily (Alice) 1904-1976
Obituary 65-68
Ericsson, Mary Kentra 1910-1995 .... CANR-20
Earlier sketches in CA 1-4R, CANR-5
Ericsson, Ronald James 1935- 110
Erikson, Erik H(omburger)
1902-1994 .... CANR-80
Obituary 145
Earlier sketches in CA 25-28R, CANR-33
See also MTCW 1, 2
Erikson, Kai T(heodor) 1931- 142
Brief entry 107
Erikson, Mel 1937- .... SATA 31
Erikson, Robert 1938- 161
Erikson, Roy L. 1939(?)-1985
Obituary 116
Erikson, Stanley 1906- 37-40R
Erikson, Steven
See Lundin, Steve (Rune)
Eriksson, Buntel
See Bergman, (Ernst) Ingmar and Josephson, Erland
Eriksson, Edward 1941- 77-80
Eriksson, Marguerite A. 1911-1984 .... 13-16R
Eriksson, Ulf (Nils Erik) 1958- 195
Erim, Kenan Tevfik 1929-1990
Obituary 132
Eringer, Robert 1954- 114
Erisman, Fred (Raymond) 1937- CANR-29
Earlier sketch in CA 110
Eriugena, John Scottus c. 810-877 .... DLB 115
Erkkila, Betsy 1944- 140
Erlander, Tage Fritiof 1901-1985
Obituary 116
Erlanger, Baba
See Trahey, Jane
Erlanger, Ellen (Louise) 1950- CANR-32
Earlier sketches in CA 85-88, CANR-15
See also SATA-Brief 52
Erlanger, Joseph 1874-1965 157
Erlanger, Philippe 1903- CANR-20
Earlier sketches in CA 5-8R, CANR-5
Erlanger, Steven Jay 1952- 133

Cumulative Index 177 **Estes**

Erlbach, Arlene 1948- 146
See also SATA 78, 115, 160
Erlewine, Michael 1941- 145
Erlich, Alexander 1912-1985
Obituary 114
Erlich, Gloria C. 125
Erlich, Lillian (Feldman) 1910-1983 ... CANR-5
Earlier sketch in CA 1-4R
See also SATA 10
Erlich, Victor 1914- CANR-3
Earlier sketch in CA 9-12R
Erline, N. T.
See Ragen, Naomi
Erlmann, Veit 1951- 139
Ermarth, Elizabeth 1939- 117
Ermelino, Louisa 194
Ermine, Will
See Drago, Harry Sinclair
Ermolaev, Herman Sergei 1924- 107
Ernaux, Annie 1940- CANR-93
Earlier sketch in CA 147
See also CLC 88, 184
See also MTFW 2005
See also NCFS 3, 5
Erne, Lukas (Christian) 1968- 215
Ernenwein, Leslie c. 1900-1961 .... TCWW 1, 2
Ernest, Victor (Hugo) 1911-1989 .... CAP-2
Earlier sketch in CA 33-36
Ernest, William
See Berkebile, Fred D(onovan)
Ernharth, Ronald Louis 1936- 45-48
Erno, Richard B. 1923- 13-16R
Ernotte, Andre (Gilbert) 1943-1999 164
Obituary 177
Ernst, Barbara 1945- 65-68
Ernst, Carl Henry 1938- 45-48
Ernst, Carl W. 1950- 163
Ernst, Clara
See Barnes, Clara Ernst
Ernst, Earle 1911-1994 .... 5-8R
Ernst, Eldon G(ilbert) 1939- 85-88
Ernst, Jimmy 1920-1984
Obituary 112
Ernst, (Lyman) John 1940- 45-48
See also SATA 39
Ernst, Joseph Albert 1931-
Brief entry 109
Ernst, Kathleen A. 1959- 238
See also SATA 162
Ernst, Kathryn (Fitzgerald) 1942- CANR-12
Earlier sketch in CA 61-64
See also SATA 25
Ernst, Lisa Campbell 1957- CANR-139
Earlier sketches in CA 114, CANR-67
See also SATA 55, 95, 154
See also SATA-Brief 44
Ernst, Margaret Samuels 1894-1964 ...... CAP-1
Earlier sketch in CA 13-14
Ernst, Margot Klebe 1939- 21-24R
Ernst, Max(imillian) 1891-1976 152
Obituary 65-68
Ernst, Morris L(eopold) 1888-1976 ..... CANR-7
Obituary 65-68
Earlier sketch in CA 5-8R
Interview in CANR-7
Ernst, Paul (Carl Friedrich) 1866-1933 179
See also DLB 66, 118
Ernst, Richard R(obert) 1933- 158
Ernst, Robert 1915-1999 .... 21-24R
Ernst, Sheila 1941- 109
Ernsting, Walter 1920-2005 .... 37-40R
Obituary 235
Erny, Pierre Jean Paul 1933- CANR-13
Earlier sketch in CA 73-76
Erofeev, Venedikt Vasil'evich
1938-1990 .... DLB 285
Erofeev, Viktor Vladimirovich
See Erofeyev, Victor
See also DLB 285
Erofeyev, Victor 1947- 140
See also Erofeev, Viktor Vladimirovich
Eron, Carol (Lehman) 1945- 112
Eron, Leonard D(avid) 1920-
Brief entry 110
Errington, Frederick (Karl) 1940- 104
Errington, (Elizabeth) Jane 1951- CANR-60
Earlier sketch in CA 128
Ershov, Petr Pavlovich 1815-1869 ...... DLB 205
Erskine, Albert 1911-1993 .... DLBY 1993, 2000
Erskine, Barbara 1944- CANR-50
Earlier sketch in CA 123
Erskine, Beatrice Caroline (?)-1948
See Erskine, Mrs. Steuart
Erskine, Carl 1926- 195
Erskine, Chester 1904(?)-1986
Obituary 121
Erskine, Jim 1956- 107
Erskine, John 1879-1951 159
Brief entry 112
See also DLB 9, 102
See also FANT
See also TCLC 84
Erskine, Laurie York 1894(?)-1976
Obituary 69-72
Erskine, Margaret
See Williams, (Margaret) Wetherby
Erskine, Mrs. Steuart (?)-1948
See Erskine, Beatrice Caroline
See also DLB 195
Erskine, Noel Leo 116
Erskine, Rosalind
See Longrigg, Roger (Erskine)
Erskine, Thomas L(eonard) 1939- 65-68
Erskine, Wilson Fiske 1911-1972(?) 1-4R
Obituary 134
Erskine-Hill, (Henry) Howard 1936- 189
Erskine-Lindop, Audrey (Beatrice Noel)
1920-1986 69-72
Obituary 121
See also RHW
Erspamer, Peter R(oy) 1959- 165
Erte
See de Tirtoff, Romain
Ertel', Aleksandr Ivanovich
1855-1908 .... DLB 238
Ertel, (Richard) James 1922-1985 .... 9-12R
Obituary 117
Ertelt, Justin P. 1978- 202
Ertz, Susan 1894-1985 .... CANR-63
Obituary 116
Earlier sketch in CA 5-8R
See also RHW
See also TCWW 1, 2
Ervin, Janet Halliday 1923- 29-32R
See also SATA 4
Ervin, Sam(uel) J(ames), Jr. 1896-1985 119
Obituary 115
Brief entry 113
Ervin, Susan
See Ervin-Tripp, Susan Moore
Ervin, Theodore Robert 1928- 13-16R
Ervine, (John) St. John Greer 1883-1971 179
Obituary 29-32R
See also DLB 10
See also RGEL 2
Ervin-Tripp, Susan Moore 1927- 53-56
Erwin, Annabel
See Barron, Ann Forman
Erwin, Douglas H. 1958- 165
Erwin, Edward (James) 1937- 29-32R
Erwin, John D(raper) 1883-1983
Obituary 109
Erwin, John Seymour 1911- 105
Erwin, Will
See Eisner, Will(iam Erwin)
Erzinclioglu, Zakaria 1951-2002 222
Esau, Helmut 1941- 57-60
Esau, Katherine 1898-1997 158
Esbensen, Barbara J(uster) 1925-1996 134
See also MAICYA 2
See also MAICYAS 1
See also SATA 62, 97
See also SATA-Brief 53
Escandon, Maria Amparo 185
Escandon, Ralph 1928- CANR-33
Earlier sketches in CA 37-40R, CANR-14
Escarpenter, Claudio 1922-1977 .... 17-20R
Obituary 120
Escarraz, Donald Ray 1932- 21-24R
Eschbacher, Roger 236
See also SATA 160
Eschelbach, Claire John 1929- 1-4R
Eschenbach, Wolfram von
See Wolfram von Eschenbach
See also RGWL 3
Eschenburg, Johann Joachim
1743-1820 .... DLB 97
Escher, Franklin (Jr.) 1915-1998 .... 9-12R
Escher, M(aurits) C(ornelis) 1898-1972 164
See also AAYA 16
Escherich, Elsa Falk 1888-1977 .... 5-8R
Eschholz, Paul A(nderson) 1942- CANR-14
Earlier sketch in CA 37-40R
Eschmeyer, R(einhart) E(rnst) 1898-1989 105
See also Eshmeyer, R. E.
Eschmeyer, William N(eil) 1939- 112
Escofet, Cristina 1945- .... DLB 305
Escoto, Julio 1944- 178
See also DLB 145
See also HW 2
Escott, Colin 1949- CANR-123
Earlier sketch in CA 107
Escott, Jonathan 1922- CANR-84
Earlier sketches in CA 65-68, CANR-20
Escott, Paul David 1947- 93-96
Escritor
See Cole, Cornelius
Escriva, Josemaria
See Escriva de Balaguer, Josemaria
Escriva de Balaguer, Josemaria 1902-1975
Obituary 57-60
Esdaile, Arundell (James Kennedy)
1880-1956 210
See also DLB 201
Esdaile, E. A.
See Esdaile, Arundell (James Kennedy)
Esdaile, Leslie
See Banks, Leslie Esdaile
Eseki, Bruno
See Mphahlele, Ezekiel
Esenin, Sergei (Alexandrovich) 1895-1925
Brief entry 104
See also Yesenin, Sergey
See also RGWL 2, 3
See also TCLC 4
Eseoghene
See Barrett, (Eseoghene) Lindsay
Esfandiary, F. M.
See FM-2030
Eshbach, Lloyd Arthur 1910-2003 .... CANR-42
Earlier sketch in CA 118
See also FANT
See also SFW 4
Eshelman, Byron E(lias) 1915-1989 .... 1-4R
Esherick, Joseph W(harton) 1942- 65-68
Eshleman, Clayton 1935- 212
Earlier sketches in CA 33-36R, CANR-93
Autobiographical Essay in 212
See also CAAS 6
See also CLC 7
See also CP 1, 2, 3, 4, 5, 6, 7
See also DLB 5
Eshleman, Edwin D(uing) 1920-1985
Obituary 114
Eshleman, J. Ross 1936- 101
Eshmeyer, R. E.
See Eschmeyer, R(einhart) E(rnst)
See also SATA 29
Eskelin, Neil J(oyner) 1938- 33-36R
Eskelund, Karl 1918-1972 .... CAP-2
Earlier sketch in CA 23-24
Eskenazi, Gerald 1936- CANR-7
Earlier sketch in CA 61-64
Eskew, Glenn T. 1962- 166
Eskey, Kenneth 1930- 77-80
Eskin, Blake 1970- 215
Eskin, Frada 1936- 37-40R
Eskow, John 1949- 105
Eskow, Seymour 1924- 9-12R
Eskridge, Ann E. 1949- CANR-80
Earlier sketch in CA 150
See also BW 3
See also SATA 84
Eskridge, Kelley 1960- 216
Eskridge, William N(ichol), Jr. 1951- 204
Esler, Anthony (James) 1934- CANR-26
Earlier sketches in CA 21-24R, CANR-8
Esler, Carol Clemeau 1935- 108
Esler, William K. 1930- CANR-5
Earlier sketch in CA 53-56
Esman, Aaron H(irsh) 1924- CANR-11
Earlier sketch in CA 61-64
Esman, Milton J. 1918- 81-84
Esmein, Jean 1923- CANR-57
Earlier sketches in CA 49-52, CANR-31
Esmond, Harriet
See Burke, John (Frederick)
Esohg, Lama
See Ghose, Amal
Eson, Morris E. 1921- 13-16R
Espada, Martin 1957- CANR-80
Earlier sketch in CA 159
See also EXPP
See also LLW
See also MAL 5
See also PFS 13, 16
Espaillat, Rhina P. 1932- 170
See also DLB 282
See also HW 2
Espanca, Florbela 1894-1930 .... DLB 287
Espeland, Pamela (Lee) 1951- CANR-107
Earlier sketch in CA 107
See also SATA 52, 128
See also SATA-Brief 38
Espenshade, Edward B(owman), Jr. 1910- . 1-4R
Esper, Erwin A(llen) 1895-1972(?) CAP-1
Earlier sketch in CA 13-16
Espey, John (Jenkins) 1913-2000 .... CANR-50
Obituary 189
Earlier sketches in CA 5-8R, CANR-4, 25
See also CN 1, 2
Espina, Concha 1869-1955 208
Espinasse, Albert 1903-1972
Obituary 37-40R
'Espinasse, Margaret 1903(?)-1980
Obituary 114
Espino, Federico (Licsi, Jr.) 1939- 93-96
See also CP 1, 2
Espinosa, Aurelio M(acedonio), Jr. 1907- 131
See also HW 1
Espinosa, Aurelio M(acedonio) 1880-1958 . 131
See also HW 1
Espinosa, Jose E(dmundo) 1900-1967 .... CAP-2
Earlier sketch in CA 25-28
Espinosa, Maria 1939- 174
Earlier sketch in CANR-138
Autobiographical Essay in 174
See also CAAS 30
Espinosa, Rudy
See Espinoza, Rudolph Louis
Espinoza, Guillermo
See Robinson, William I.
Espinoza, Rudolph Louis 1933- 73-76
Esposito, John C(abrino) 1940- 33-36R
Esposito, John L(ouis) 1940- CANR-124
Earlier sketch in CA 116
Esposito, Joseph L(ouis) 1941- CANR-35
Earlier sketch in CA 114
Esposito, Mary Ann 1942- CANR-130
Earlier sketch in CA 153
Esposito, Phil(ip Anthony) 1942- 227
Brief entry 108
Espriella, Don Manuel Alvarez
See Southey, Robert
Espriu, Salvador 1913-1985 154
Obituary 115
See also CLC 9
See also DLB 134
See also EWL 3
Espy, Richard 1952- 105
Espy, Willard R(ichardson)
1910-1999 .... CANR-2
Obituary 177
Earlier sketch in CA 49-52
See also SATA 38
See also SATA-Obit 113
Esquenazi-Mayo, Roberto 1920-2004 45-48
Obituary 234
Esquith, Rafe 1954- 226
Esquivel, Laura 1951(?)- CANR-113
Earlier sketches in CA 143, CANR-68
See also AAYA 29
See also CLC 141
See also DA3
See also DNFS 2
See also HLCS 1
See also LAIT 3
See also LMFS 2
See also MTCW 2
See also MTFW 2005
See also NFS 5
See also WLIT 1
Essame, Hubert 1896-1976 .... CANR-28
Obituary 65-68
Earlier sketch in CA 49-52
Essbaum, Jill Alexander 196
Esse, James
See Stephens, James
Essed, Philomena 1955- 172
Esser, Robin 1933- 29-32R
Esses, Michael (Isaiah) 1923-
Brief entry 110
Essex
See Essex
Essex, Andrew 235
Essex, Frances
See French, Alice
Essex, Harry J. 1910(?)-1997 .... 33-36R
Obituary 156
Essex, Karen 204
Essex, Mary
See Bloom, Ursula (Harvey)
Essex, Rosamund (Sibyl) 1900-1985 107
Obituary 116
Essex, Saran 1948- .... TCWW 2
Essick, Robert N(ewman) 1942- CANR-41
Earlier sketches in CA 53-56, CANR-5, 19
Esslin, Martin (Julius) 1918-2002 ...... CANR-74
Obituary 204
Earlier sketches in CA 85-88, CANR-27
See also MTCW 1, 2
See also MTFW 2005
Esslinger, Dean R(obert) 1942- CANR-92
Earlier sketch in CA 61-64
Esslinger, Pat M.
See Carr, Pat
Essoe, Gabe (Attila) 1944- 25-28R
Esson, (Thomas) Louis (Buvelot)
1878-1943 .... DLB 260
Essop, Ahmed 1931- CANR-84
Earlier sketches in CA 123, CANR-50
See also CN 4, 5, 6, 7
See also DLB 225
Essrig, Harry 1912- 108
See also SATA 66
Esstman, Barbara 1947- 237
Estabrook, Robert Harley 1918- 69-72
Estabrooks, George H. 1896(?)-1973
Obituary 45-48
Estang, Luc 1911-1992 61-64
Obituary 139
Estarellas, Juan 1918- CANR-2
Earlier sketch in CA 45-48
Estavan, Lawrence (L.) 1903-1988 212
Estaver, Marguerite M. 1893-1984 97-100
Estelle, Sister Mary 1907- CAP-1
Earlier sketch in CA 11-12
Estensen, Miriam 220
Estenssoro, Hugo 1946- 69-72
Estep, Irene Compton 1-4R
See also SATA 5
Estep, Maggie 1962(?)- CANR-92
Earlier sketch in CA 159
Estep, W(illiam) R(oscoe), Jr.
1920-2000 .... CANR-51
Earlier sketches in CA 13-16R, CANR-9, 25
Esterberg, Kristin G. 1960- 172
Esterbrook, Tom
See Hubbard, L(afayette) Ron(ald)
Estergreen, M. Morgan
See Estergreen, Marian Morgan
Estergreen, Marian Morgan 1910-1984 . 17-20R
Esterhammer, Angela 1961- CANR-93
Earlier sketch in CA 146
Esterhazy, Peter 1950- CANR-137
Earlier sketch in CA 140
See also CDWLB 4
See also CWW 2
See also DLB 232
See also EWL 3
See also RGWL 3
Esterl, Arnica 1933- .... SATA 77
Esterly, Glenn 1942- 33-36R
Estermann, Carlos (?)-1976
Obituary 105
Esterow, Milton 1928- 17-20R
Estes, Bill 1941- 107
Estes, Clarissa Pinkola 1943- CANR-67
Earlier sketch in CA 143
Estes, Daniel J. 170
Estes, Eleanor (Ruth) 1906-1988 .... CANR-84
Obituary 126
Earlier sketches in CA 1-4R, CANR-5, 20
See also BYA 1
See also CLR 2, 70
See also CWRI 5
See also DLB 22
See also JRDA
See also MAICYA 1, 2
See also SATA 7, 91
See also SATA-Obit 56
Estes, J(oseph) Worth 1934- 104
Estes, John E(dward) 1939- 57-60
Estes, Rice 1907- CAP-1
Earlier sketch in CA 11-12

Estes, Richard J. 1942- CANR-41
Earlier sketch in CA 118
Estes, Rose FANT
Estes, Steve(n Douglas) 1952- 97-100
Estes, Winston M(arvin) 1917-1982 29-32R
Obituary 126
Estess, Jenifer 1963-2003 232
Estess, Sybil P. 1942- 129
Estess, Ted L(ynn) 1942- 114
Esteven, John
See Shellabarger, Samuel
Esteves, Sandra Maria 1948- LLW
Estevez, Emilio 1962- 159
Estey, George F. 1924- 33-36R
Estey, Ralph H(oward) 1916- 148
Esthus, Raymond Arthur 1925- 13-16R
Estleman, Loren D. 1952- CANR-139
Earlier sketches in CA 85-88, CANR-27, 74
Interview in CANR-27
See also AAYA 27
See also CLC 48
See also CMW 4
See also CPW
See also DA3
See also DAM NOV, POP
See also DLB 226
See also MTCW 1, 2
See also MTFW 2005
See also TCWW 1, 2
Estner, Lois J(ane) 1947- 114
Estock, Anne (Martin) 1923- 1-4R
Estoril, Jean
See Allan, Mabel Esther
Estow, Clara 1945- 154
Estrada, Doris (Perkins) 1923- 17-20R
Estrada, Jacquelyn (Ann) 1946- 29-32R
Estrada, Pau 1961- SATA 74
Estrada, Rita Clay CANR-135
Earlier sketch in CA 164
Estragon, Vladimir
See Stokes, Geoffrey
Estrich, Susan Rachel 1952- 187
Estridge, Robin 1920- 226
See also CMW 4
Estrin, Herman A. 1915-1999 CANR-7
Earlier sketch in CA 17-20R
Estrin, Marc 236
Estrin, Saul 1952- 212
Estroff, Sue E. 1950- 105
Estupinan Bass, Nelson 1915- HW 1
Esty, Daniel C. 1959- CANR-125
Earlier sketch in CA 170
Esty, John Cushing, Jr. 1928-
Brief entry 106
Eszterhas, Joe
See Eszterhas, Joseph A(nthony)
See also IDFW 4
Eszterhas, Joseph A(nthony) 1944- CANR-128
Brief entry 124
Earlier sketches in CA 130, CANR-68
See also Eszterhas, Joe
See also DLB 185
Etchebaster, Pierre 1894-1980 102
Obituary 97-100
Etchemendy, Nancy (Elise Howell)
1952- ... CANR-128****kEarlier sketch in CA 106SATA 38
Etcheson Craig Carlyle1955-117
Etcheson, Warren W(ade) 1920- 41-44R
Etchison, Birdie L(ee) 1937- 106
See also SATA 38
Etchison, Craig 1945- CANR-111
Earlier sketch in CA 188
See also SATA 133
Etchison, Dennis (William) 1943- CANR-100
Brief entry 115
Earlier sketch in CA 118
Interview in CA-118
See also HGG
See also SUFW 2
Etcoff, Nancy 1955- 228
Eterovich, Adam S(lav) 1930- CANR-27
Earlier sketch in CA 49-52
Eterovich, Francis Hyacinth
1913-1980 CANR-28
Earlier sketch in CA 37-40R
Ethell, Jeffrey L(ance) 1947-1997 CANR-39
Obituary 158
Earlier sketches in CA 101, CANR-18
Etherege, Sir George 1636-1692 BRW 2
See also DAM DRAM
See also DC 23
See also DLB 80
See also PAB
See also RGEL 2
Etheridge, Eugene Wesley 1925- 5-8R
Etherington, Charles Leslie 1903- 5-8R
Etherington, Frank 1945- SATA 58
Etherington, Wendy 1967- 222
Etherton, Michael (James) 1939- 121
Ethridge, James M(erritt) 1921- 114
Ethridge, Mark (Foster) 1896-1981 177
Obituary 103
See also DLB 127
Ethridge, Mark Foster, Jr. 1924-1985
Obituary 115
Ethridge, Willie Snow 1900-1983(?) 17-20R
Obituary 108
See also AITN 1
Etienne
See King-Hall, (William) Stephen (Richard)
Etkin, Anne (Dunwody Little) 1923- 73-76
Etlin, Richard A. 1947- CANR-109
Earlier sketch in CA 155
Etmekjian, James 1915- CANR-3
Earlier sketch in CA 5-8R
Eton, Robert
See Meynell, Laurence Walter
Etra, Jonathan 1952-1991 102
Obituary 133
Ets, Marie Hall 1893-1984 CANR-83
Earlier sketches in CA 1-4R, CANR-4
See also CLR 33
See also CWRI 5
See also DLB 22
See also MAICYA 1, 2
See also SATA 2
Ets-Hokin, Judith Diane 1938- 61-64
Etteldorf, Raimondo
See Etteldorf, Raymond P(hilip)
Etteldorf, Raymond P(hilip) 1911-1986 9-12R
Ettelson, Trudy (G.) 1947- 219
Etter, Dave 1928- CANR-101
Earlier sketches in CA 17-20R, CANR-8, 24, 49
See also CP 1
See also DLB 105
Etter, Les(ter Frederick) 1904-1983 25-28R
Etter, Patricia A. 1932- CANR-56
Earlier sketch in CA 120
Ettin, Andrew V(ogel) 1943- 124
Ettinger, Elzbieta 1925-2005 CANR-52
Obituary 237
Earlier sketch in CA 29-32R
Ettinger, Richard Prentice 1893-1971
Obituary 29-32R
Ettinger, Robert C(hester) W(ilson)
1918- 13-16R
Ettinghausen, Maurice Leon 1883-1974
Obituary 116
Ettinghausen, Richard 1906-1979 CANR-9
Obituary 85-88
Earlier sketch in CA 65-68
Ettleson, Abraham 1897-1971 CAP-2
Earlier sketch in CA 23-24
Ettling, John 1944- 125
Ettlinger, Gerard H(erman) 1935- 61-64
Ettlinger, L. D.
See Ettlinger, Leopold D(avid)
Ettlinger, Leopold D(avid) 1913-1989 184
Obituary 129
Brief entry 111
Ettner, Johann Christoph 1654-1724 DLB 168
Etulain, Richard W(ayne) 1938- CANR-16
Earlier sketches in CA 45-48, CANR-1
Etzioni, Amitai (Werner) 1929- CANR-22
Earlier sketches in CA 1-4R, CANR-5
Etzioni, Minerva M(orales) 1938(?)-1985
Obituary 118
Etzioni-Halevy, Eva 1934- CANR-115
Earlier sketches in CA 127, CANR-58
Etzkorn, K(laus) Peter 1932- 49-52
Etzkowitz, Henry 1940- CANR-120
Earlier sketch in CA 25-28R
Etzold, Thomas H(erman) 1945- CANR-14
Earlier sketch in CA 81-84
Euba, Femi 1941- CANR-135
Earlier sketch in CA 141
See also BW 2
Eubank, (Weaver) Keith (Jr.) 1920- CANR-2
Earlier sketch in CA 5-8R
Eubank, Nancy 1934- 41-44R
Eubanks, Ralph T(ravis) 1920- 17-20R
Euchner, Charles C. 1960- 164
Eucken, Rudolf (Christof) 1846-1926
Brief entry 119
Eugenides, Jeffrey 1960(?)- CANR-120
Earlier sketch in CA 144
See also AAYA 51
See also CLC 81, 212
See also MTFW 2005
Eula, Michael J(ames) 1957- CANR-100
Earlier sketch in CA 150
Eulau, Heinz 1915-2004
Obituary 222
Brief entry 107
Eulenspiegel, Alexander
See Shea, Robert (Joseph)
Eulert, Don(ald Dean) 1935- CANR-40
Earlier sketches in CA 49-52, CANR-2, 18
Euller, John E(lmer) 1926- 9-12R
Eulo, Ken 1939- CANR-72
Brief entry 109
Earlier sketch in CA 126
See also HGG
Eunson, (John) Dale 1904-2002 41-44R
Obituary 202
See also SATA 5
See also SATA-Obit 132
Eunson, Robert C(harles) 1912-1975 13-16R
Obituary 61-64
Euphan
See Todd, Barbara Euphan
Euphemides, Aristos
See von Koerber, Hans Nordewin
Eupolemius fl. c. 1095- DLB 148
Eupolis fl. 429B.C.-411B.C. LMFS 1
Eurich, Alvin C(hristian) 1902-1987 CANR-83
Obituary 123
Earlier sketch in CA 17-20R
Eurich, Nell 1919- CANR-12
Earlier sketch in CA 73-76
Euripides c. 484B.C.-406B.C. AW 1
See also CDWLB 1
See also DA
See also DA3
See also DAB
See also DAC
See also DAM DRAM, MST
See also DC 4
See also DFS 1, 4, 6
See also DLB 176
See also LAIT 1
See also LMFS 1
See also RGWL 2, 3
See also WLCS
European
See Mosley, Oswald (Ernald)
Europicus
See Coser, Lewis A(lfred)
Eusden, John (Dykstra) 1922- 45-48
Eustace, Cecil John 1903-1992 49-52
Eustace, May (Corcoran) 1904- 5-8R
Eustace, Robert
See Barton, Eustace Robert
Eustis, Alvin Allen, Jr. 1917-1994 102
Eustis, Helen (White) 1916- 190
Eustis, Laurette
See Murdock, Laurette P.
Eustis, O. B.
See Eustis, Orville B.
Eustis, Orville B. 1913-1986 124
Euwe, Machgielis 1901-1981
Obituary 105
Euwe, Max
See Euwe, Machgielis
Evain, Elaine 1931- 57-60
Evan, Carol
See Goldsmith, Carol Evan
Evan, Evin
See Faust, Frederick (Schiller)
Evan, Paul
See Lehman, Paul Evan
Evan, William (Martin) 1922- CANR-2
Earlier sketch in CA 1-4R
Evang, Karl 1902-1981 65-68
Evanier, David 183
Brief entry 108
Evanier, Mark 1952- 217
See also AAYA 58
Evanoff, Vlad 1916- CANR-6
Earlier sketch in CA 5-8R
See also SATA 59
Evanovich, Janet CANR-115
Earlier sketch in CA 167
See also AAYA 52
Evans, A(lfred) Alexander 1905-2002 CAP-1
Obituary 207
Earlier sketch in CA 9-10
Evans, A(nthony) G. 236
Evans, Abbie Huston 1881-1983 57-60
See also CP 1, 2
Evans, Alan
See Stoker, Alan
Evans, Albert 1917- 85-88
Evans, Alice Frazer 1939- CANR-58
Earlier sketches in CA 112, CANR-30
Evans, Arthur Bruce 1948- CANR-97
Earlier sketch in CA 61-64
Evans, Augusta J. 1835-1909
See Wilson, Augusta Jane Evans
See also DLB 239
Evans, Augusta Jane 1835-1909
See Wilson, Augusta Jane Evans
See also DLB 239
Evans, Barbara Lloyd
See Lloyd Evans, Barbara
Evans, Benjamin Ifor 1899-1982
Obituary 107
Evans, Bennett
See Berger, Ivan (Bennett)
Evans, Bergen (Baldwin) 1904-1978 CANR-4
Obituary 77-80
Earlier sketch in CA 5-8R
Evans, Brendan 1944- CANR-116
Earlier sketch in CA 158
Evans, Bruce A. 1946- 134
Evans, C(harles) Stephen 1948- CANR-127
Earlier sketches in CA 33-36R, CANR-13, 29
Evans, C. Stephen 1948- 162
Evans, Calvin (Donald) 1931- 146
Evans, Caradoc 1878-1945 DLB 162
See also SSC 43
See also TCLC 85
Evans, Chad (Arthur) 1951- 131
Evans, Charles 1850-1935 200
See also DLB 187
Evans, (Jean) Cherry (Drummond)
1928-2005 CAP-1
Obituary 237
Earlier sketch in CA 9-10
Evans, Christopher (Riche) 1931-1979 102
Evans, Christopher H. 1959- 214
Evans, Clifford 1916(?)-1983
Obituary 110
Evans, Constance May 1890- 9-12R
Evans, Craig A. 1952- CANR-66
Earlier sketch in CA 129
Evans, D(avid) Ellis 1930- CANR-16
Earlier sketch in CA 25-28R
Evans, Dale
See Rogers, Dale Evans
Evans, David Allan 1940- CANR-57
Earlier sketches in CA 49-52, CANR-31
Evans, David Beecher 1928-
Brief entry 105
Evans, David C(hristian) 1940-1999 170
Evans, David Huhn, Jr. 1944- 110
Evans, David R(ussell) 1937- CANR-17
Earlier sketch in CA 33-36R
Evans, David R(ichard) 1940- CANR-39
Earlier sketch in CA 116
Evans, David S(tanley) 1916-2004 41-44R
Evans, Debra 1953- 122
Evans, Don 1938-2003 111
Obituary 220
Evans, Donald 1884-1921
Brief entry 123
See also DLB 54
Evans, Donald (Dwight) 1927- 41-44R
Evans, Donald P(aul) 1930-1992 CANR-46
Obituary 140
Earlier sketches in CA 57-60, CANR-7
Evans, Dorinda 1944- 121
Evans, Douglas 1953- CANR-116
Earlier sketch in CA 159
See also SATA 93, 144
Evans, Dwight Landis 1947- 169
Evans, E(myr) Estyn 1905-1989 CANR-5
Obituary 129
Earlier sketch in CA 5-8R
Evans, E(dward) Everett 1893-1958 160
Brief entry 113
See also SFW 4
Evans, Earlene Green 1938- 200
Evans, Edward G(ordon), Jr. 1916- 45-48
Evans, Eli N. 1936- 45-48
See also AITN 1
Evans, Elizabeth 1932- 53-56
Evans, Elizabeth (J.) 1935- 191
Evans, Ellen
See Du Breuil, (Elizabeth) L(or)inda
Evans, Ellen Lovell 1930- 235
Evans, Emerald
See Du Breuil, (Elizabeth) L(or)inda
Evans, Eric J(ohn) 1945- 108
Evans, Eva (Knox) 1905-1998 73-76
See also SATA 27
Evans, Evan
See Faust, Frederick (Schiller)
Evans, (Francis) Fallon 1925-1996 1-4R
Evans, Fanny-Maude 1914-1997 117
Evans, F.M.G.
See Higham, Florence May Grier
Evans, Frances Monet Carter
See Carter, Frances Monet
Evans, Frank Bernard 1927- CANR-36
Earlier sketch in CA 114
Evans, Freddi Williams 1957- SATA 134
Evans, G. B.
See Evans, Gwynne Blakemore
Evans, G. Blakemore
See Evans, Gwynne Blakemore
Evans, G(ayle) Edward 1937- 33-36R
Evans, G(eraint) N(antglyn) D(avies)
1935-1971 CAP-2
Earlier sketch in CA 33-36
Evans, G. R.
See Evans, Gillian (Rosemary)
Evans, Gareth Lloyd
See Lloyd Evans, Gareth
Evans, Gary P. 1942- 233
Evans, Gavin 1960- 167
Evans, Geoffrey (Charles) 1901-1987 17-20R
Obituary 121
Evans, George Bird 1906- CANR-2
Earlier sketch in CA 1-4R
Evans, George Brinley 1925- 200
Evans, George Ewart 1909-1988(?) 61-64
Obituary 124
Evans, George Henry 1805-1856 DLB 43
Evans, George W(illiam) II 1920- 21-24R
Evans, Geraldine 1953- 224
Evans, Giles (Edwin) 1949-1988 141
Evans, Gillian (Rosemary) 1944- CANR-111
Earlier sketches in CA 126, CANR-53
Evans, Glen 1921- 85-88
Evans, Gordon H(eyd) 1930- 13-16R
Evans, Greg 1947- CANR-122
Earlier sketch in CA 160
See also AAYA 23
See also SATA 73, 143
Evans, (Richard) Gwynfor 1912-2005 61-64
Obituary 238
Evans, Gwynne B.
See Evans, Gwynne Blakemore
Evans, Gwynne Blakemore 1912- 125
Evans, Harold 1911-1983 129
Obituary 109
Evans, Harold Matthew 1928- 41-44R
Evans, Harris
See Evans, George Bird and
Evans, Kay Harris
Evans, Harry 1896(?)-1988
Obituary 126
Evans, Helen C. 235
Evans, Herndon J. 1895-1976 69-72
Evans, Hilary 1929- CANR-42
Earlier sketches in CA 1-4R, CANR-5, 20
Evans, Howard Ensign 1919-2002 CANR-52
Earlier sketch in CA 5-8R
Evans, Hubert John Filmer 1904-1989
Obituary 129
Evans, Hubert Reginald 1892-1986 CANR-84
Obituary 119
Earlier sketch in CA 103
See also CWRI 5
See also DLB 92
See also SATA 118
See also SATA-Obit 48
Evans, Humphrey (Marshall, Jr.)
1914-1982 29-32R
Evans, I(drisyn) O(liver) 1894-1977 CANR-15
Earlier sketch in CA 13-16R

Cumulative Index 179 Exley

Evans, Ian
See Wells, Angus
Evans, Idella M(arie Crowe) 1924- 29-32R
Evans, Ilona 1918(?)-1980
Obituary 102
Evans, J(ames) A(llan) S(tewart) 1931- 37-40R
Evans, J(ohn) D(avid) G(emmill) 1942- 127
Evans, J. Martin 1935- 85-88
Evans, J(ack) N(aunton) 1920- 25-28R
Evans, J(ohn) Robert 1942- CANR-7
Earlier sketch in CA 57-60
Evans, Jacob A. 1920- 25-28R
Evans, James Allen 1926(?)-1983
Obituary 110
Evans, James H., Jr. 145
Evans, James R(ichard) 1908-1995 141
Evans, Jay 1925- 61-64
Evans, Jean 1939- 102
Evans, Jessica
See Lottman, Eileen
Evans, Joan 1893-1977 13-16R
Obituary 73-76
Evans, John
See Browne, Howard
Evans, John Davies 1925- 127
Evans, John Lewis 1930- 85-88
Evans, John W(alker) 1904-1985 33-36R
Evans, John X(avier) 1933- 37-40R
Evans, Jonathan
See Freemantle, Brian (Harry)
Evans, Joseph S., Jr. 1909(?)-1978 85-88
Obituary 81-84
Evans, Joseph W(illiam) 1921- 21-24R
Evans, Juanita Blick 1943- 188
Evans, Julia (Rendel) 1913- 13-16R
Evans, K(athleen) M(arianne) 1911- 9-12R
Evans, Karin NCFS 5
Evans, Katherine (Floyd) 1901-1964 5-8R
See also SATA 5
Evans, Kay Harris 1906- CANR-2
Earlier sketch in CA 1-4R
Evans, (Cyril) Kenneth 1917- 53-56
Evans, Kenneth R. 1938- 134
Brief entry 110
Evans, Larry
See Evans, Laurence Chubb
Evans, Larry (Melvyn) 1932- 129
Evans, Laura 1949(?)-2000 158
Evans, Laurence 1923- 37-40R
Evans, Laurence Chubb 1939- 152
See also SATA 88
Evans, Lawrence Watt
See Watt-Evans, Lawrence
See also FANT
See also SATA 75
See also SFW 4
Evans, Lee
See Forrest, Richard (Stockton)
Evans, Lloyd (Lloyd Thomas) 1927- 69-72
Evans, Louis Hadley Sr. 1897-1981 116
Evans, Luther Harris 1902-1981 CANR-9
Obituary 106
Earlier sketch in CA 17-20R
Evans, M(edford) Stanton 1934- 65-68
Evans, Mari 1923- CANR-80
Earlier sketches in CA 49-52, CANR-2, 27
See also BW 1
See also CP 2, 3, 4, 5, 6, 7
See also DLB 41
See also SATA 10
Evans, Marian
See Eliot, George
Evans, Mark 65-68
See also SATA 19
Evans, Marvin R(ussell) 1915- 49-52
Evans, Mary 1946- CANR-107
Earlier sketches in CA 122, CANR-48
Evans, Mary Ann
See Eliot, George
See also NFS 20
Evans, Mary Anna 226
Evans, Mary Lowe
See Lowe-Evans, Mary
Evans, Max 1925(?)-1992 CANR-134
Earlier sketches in CA 1-4R, CANR-1, 64
See also TCWW 1, 2
Evans, Medford (Bryon) 1907-1989 25-28R
Evans, Mel 1912(?)-1984
Obituary 112
Evans, Melbourne G(riffith) 1912-2001 CAP-2
Earlier sketch in CA 33-36
Evans, Michael K(aye) 1938- 132
Evans, Morgan
See Davies, L(eslie) P(urnell)
Evans, N(orman) Dean 1925- CANR-13
Earlier sketch in CA 21-24R
Evans, Nancy 1950- CANR-34
Earlier sketch in CA 77-80
See also SATA 65
Evans, Nathaniel 1742-1767 DLB 31
Evans, Nicholas 1950- 182
Evans, Oliver 1915- 17-20R
Evans, Olwen (Elizabeth) Carey
See Carey Evans, Olwen (Elizabeth)
Evans, Patricia Healy
See Carpenter, Patricia (Healy Evans)
Evans, Paul 1945- CP 1
Evans, Paul Richer 1925-2000 187
Brief entry 106
Evans, (Alice) Pearl 1927- SATA 83
Evans, Penelope 1959- 178
Evans, Peter (Andrew) 131
Evans, Philip 1944-
Brief entry 110
Evans, Rand B(oyd) 1942-
Brief entry 107
Evans, Ray 1915- DLB 265
Evans, Richard 217
Evans, Richard 1939- 106
Evans, Richard Evan 1898-1983
Obituary 109
Evans, Richard I(sadore) 1922- 131
Brief entry 108
Evans, Richard J(ohn) 1947- CANR-111
Earlier sketch in CA 138
Evans, Richard L(ouis) 1906-1971 9-12R
Obituary 103
Evans, Richard Paul 212
Evans, Robert, Jr. 1932- 17-20R
Evans, Robert 1930- 147
Evans, Robert Allen 1937- 112
Evans, Robert C. 1955- CANR-98
Earlier sketch in CA 148
Evans, Robert F(ranklin) 1930-1974 CAP-2
Earlier sketch in CA 23-24
Evans, Robert Henry 1937- 21-24R
Evans, Robert L(eonard) 1917- CANR-32
Earlier sketch in CA 49-52
Evans, Robert Owen 1919- 13-16R
Evans, Robert P. 1918- 13-16R
Evans, Rodney E(arl) 1939- 49-52
Evans, Rowland, Jr. 1921-2001 CANR-15
Obituary 194
Earlier sketch in CA 21-24R
Evans, Rupert N. 1921- 37-40R
Evans, Sara 1943- 93-96
Evans, Sebastian 1830-1909 176
See also DLB 35
Evans, Shirlee 1931- 61-64
See also SATA 58
Evans, Stanley G(eorge) 1912-1965 CAP-1
Earlier sketch in CA 9-10
Evans, Stephen S(tewart) 1954- 168
Evans, Stuart 1934-1994 CANR-79
Evans, (Edwin) Stuart (Gomer) 1934-1994 124
Obituary 147
Brief entry 118
Interview in CA-124
Evans, Susan H(ope) 1951- 115
Evans, Tabor
See Cameron, Lou and
Knott, William C(ecil, Jr.) and
Wallmann, Jeffrey M(iner) and
Whittington, Harry (Benjamin)
Evans, Thomas W(illiam) 1930- 45-48
Evans, Travers Moncure 1938- 57-60
Evans, Virginia Moran 1909-1990 CANR-5
Earlier sketch in CA 5-8R
Evans, W(illiam) Glyn 1918- 89-92
Evans, W(illiam) McKee 1923- 21-24R
Evans, Walker (III) 1903-1975 CANR-130
Obituary 89-92
See also AAYA 44
See also LATS 1:2
Evans, (William Edis) Webster
1908-1982 41-44R
Obituary 133
Evans, Wick TCWW 2
Evans, Wilbur 1913- 97-100
Evans, William 1895-1988 81-84
Obituary 126
Evans, William David 1912-1985
Obituary 117
Evans, William Howard 1924- 21-24R
Evans, William R. 1938- 105
Evans Davies, Gloria 1932- 5-8R
See also CP 1, 2
Evansen, Virginia Besaw 1921- 13-16R
Evans-Jones, Albert 1895-1970 5-8R
Evans-Pritchard, Edward Evan
1902-1973 65-68
Evanzz, Karl 1953- CANR-92
Earlier sketch in CA 140
See also BW 2
Evaristi, Marcella 1953- 237
See also CBD
See also CD 5, 6
See also CWD
See also DLB 233
Evaristo, Bernardine 1959- 212
Evarts, Esther
See Benson, Sally
Evarts, Hal G(eorge) 1887-1934
Brief entry 121
See also TCWW 1, 2
Evarts, Hal G., (Jr.) 1915-1989 CANR-63
Earlier sketches in CA 49-52, CANR-2
See also SATA 6
See also TCWW 1, 2
Evdokimov, Paul 1901-1970 172
Eve, Barbara
See Reiss, Barbara Eve
Eve, Nomi 1968- 191
Evein, Bernard 1929- IDFW 3, 4
Eveland, Bill
See Eveland, Wilbur Crane
Eveland, Wilbur Crane 1918-1990 101
Evelegh, Tessa 236
Eveling, (Harry) Stanley 1925- 61-64
See also CBD
See also CD 5, 6
Evely, Louis 1910- 85-88
Evelyn, Anthony
See Ward-Thomas, Evelyn Bridget Patricia Stephens
Evelyn, John 1620-1706 BRW 2
See also RGEL 2
Evelyn, (John) Michael
1916-1992(?) CANR-69
Obituary 140
Earlier sketches in CA 5-8R, CANR-6, 22, 46
See also CMW 4
Evenbach, Anton
See Steiner, Evgeny
Evenhuis, Gertie 1932- 107
Evenson, Brian 1966- 148
Everage, Dame Edna
See Humphries, Barry
Everdell, William R(omeyn) 1941- 164
Evered, James F(letcher) 1928- 107
Everest, Allan S(eymour) 1913-1997 CANR-51
Earlier sketches in CA 29-32R, CANR-11, 26
Everett, Alexander Hill 1790-1847 DLB 59
Everett, Arthur (W., Jr.) 1914- 103
Everett, Barbara 1949- 223
Everett, Donald E(dward) 1920- 9-12R
Everett, Edward 1794-1865 DLB 1, 59, 235
Everett, Gail
See Hale, Arlene
Everett, Glenn D. 1921- 69-72
Everett, Kathleen
See Wood, Edward D(avis), Jr.
Everett, Percival
See Everett, Percival L.
See also CSW
Everett, Percival L. 1956- CANR-134
Earlier sketches in CA 129, CANR-94
See also Everett, Percival
See also BW 2
See also CLC 57
See also CN 7
See also MTFW 2005
Everett, Peter 1931-1999 CANR-31
Earlier sketch in CA 69-72
See also CN 1, 2, 3
Everett, Peter W(illiam) 1924- 13-16R
Everett, Rupert 1960(?)- 142
Everett, Susanne
See Keegan, Susanne
Everett, T(homas) H(enry) 1903(?)-1986 133
Obituary 120
Everett, Wade
See Cook, Will(iam Everett) and
Lutz, Giles A(lfred)
Everett, Walter 1936- 93-96
Everett, Walter T. 1954- 194
Everett-Green, Evelyn 1856-1932
Brief entry 114
Evergood, Philip 1901-1973
Obituary 41-44R
Everhart, James W(illiam), Jr. 1924- 89-92
Everhart, Jim
See Everhart, James W(illiam), Jr.
Everitt, Alan (Milner) 1926- CANR-11
Earlier sketch in CA 21-24R
Everitt, Anthony (Michael) 1940- 221
Everitt, Arva Graham Johnson 1916(?)-1982
Obituary 107
Everitt, Bridget Mary 1924- 45-48
Everitt, C(harles) W(illiam) F(rancis)
1934- 65-68
Everitt, David (Samuel) 1952- CANR-111
Earlier sketch in CA 110
Everitt, James H. 199
Everman, Welch D(uane) 1946- 57-60
Evernden, Margery 1916- 5-8R
See also SATA 5
Evers, (James) Charles 1923(?)-
Brief entry 111
Evers, Christopher 1940- 122
Evers, Larry 1946- 135
Eversley, D(avid) E(dward) C(harles)
1921-1995 CANR-1
Earlier sketch in CA 1-4R
Eversole, Finley T. 1933- 9-12R
Eversole, Robyn Harbert 1971- SATA 74
Everson, Dale Millar 1928- 17-20R
Everson, David H. 1941-1999 124
Everson, Ida Gertrude 1898-1976 37-40R
Everson, R(onald) G(ilmour)
1903-1992 17-20R
See also CLC 27
See also CP 1, 2
See also DLB 88
Everson, William (Oliver)
1912-1994 CANR-20
Obituary 145
Earlier sketch in CA 9-12R
See also Antoninus, Brother
See also BG 1:2
See also CLC 1, 5, 14
See also CP 2
See also DLB 5, 16, 212
See also MTCW 1
Everson, William Keith 1929-1996 CANR-2
Obituary 151
Earlier sketch in CA 1-4R
Eversz, Robert (McLeod) 1954- 204
Eversz, Robert McLeod 1954- 127
Everton, Frank
See Meares, Leonard Frank
Everton, Macduff 1947- 104
Evertts, Eldonna L(ouise) 1917-1992 21-24R
Everwine, Peter Paul 1930- 73-76
See also AMWS 15
See also CP 7
Every, George 1909-2003 CANR-6
Obituary 220
Earlier sketch in CA 13-16R
Eves, Douglas 1922- 119
Evetts, Julia 1944- 69-72
Evinger, William R. 1943- 150
Evins, Joseph Landon 1910-1984 61-64
Eviota, Elizabeth Uy 1946- CANR-94
Earlier sketch in CA 146
Evitts, William J(oseph) 1942- 121
Brief entry 112
EVOE
See Knox, Edmund George Valpy
Evold, Beth 1936- 129
Evoy, John J(oseph) 1911-2001 5-8R
Evreinov, Nikolai (Nickolaevich)
1879-1953 DLB 317
Evslin, Bernard 1922-1993 CANR-48
Obituary 142
Earlier sketches in CA 21-24R, CANR-9
See also SATA 45, 83
See also SATA-Brief 28
See also SATA-Obit 77
Evslin, Dorothy 1923- 57-60
Evtushenko, Evgenii Aleksandrovich
See Yevtushenko, Yevgeny (Alexandrovich)
See also CWW 2
See also RGWL 2, 3
Ewald, Johannes 1743-1781 DLB 300
Ewald, Mary (Thediek) 1922-1997 229
Ewald, Wendy Taylor 1951- 120
Ewald, William Bragg, Jr. 1925- CANR-27
Earlier sketch in CA 107
Ewans, Michael (Christopher) 1946- 129
Ewart, Andrew 1911- 17-20R
Ewart, Charles
See Lyte, Charles
Ewart, Claire 1958- CANR-139
Earlier sketch in CA 144
See also SATA 76, 145
Ewart, Gavin (Buchanan)
1916-1995 CANR-46
Obituary 150
Earlier sketches in CA 89-92, CANR-17
See also BRWS 7
See also CLC 13, 46
See also CP 1, 2
See also DLB 40
See also MTCW 1
Ewart, Simon
See Herd, Michael
Ewbank, Henry L(ee), Jr. 1924- 73-76
Ewbank, Walter F(rederick) 1918- CANR-38
Earlier sketches in CA 25-28R, CANR-17
Ewell, Barbara C(laire) 1947- CANR-82
Earlier sketches in CA 114, CANR-35
Ewell, Judith 1943- 107
Ewen, David 1907-1985 CANR-79
Obituary 118
Earlier sketches in CA 1-4R, CANR-2
See also SATA 4
See also SATA-Obit 47
Ewen, Elizabeth 1943- CANR-92
Earlier sketch in CA 124
Ewen, Frederic 1899-1988 73-76
Obituary 126
Ewen, Robert B. 1940- CANR-15
Earlier sketch in CA 37-40R
Ewen, Stuart 1945- CANR-12
Earlier sketch in CA 69-72
Ewens, James 1939- 116
Ewers, Hanns Heinz 1871-1943 149
Brief entry 109
See also TCLC 12
Ewers, John C(anfield) 1909-1997 CANR-22
Obituary 158
Earlier sketches in CA 17-20R, CANR-7
Ewert, David 1922- 105
Ewing, Alfred Cyril 1899-1973 CANR-4
Earlier sketch in CA 5-8R
Ewing, Alice Randall 1960(?)- 192
See also AAYA 64
Ewing, Barbara 184
Ewing, David Walkley 1923- CANR-5
Earlier sketch in CA 1-4R
Ewing, Donald M. 1895(?)-1978
Obituary 81-84
Ewing, Elizabeth 1904- 41-44R
Ewing, Frederick R.
See Sturgeon, Theodore (Hamilton)
Ewing, George W(ilmeth) 1923- 45-48
Ewing, John A(lexander) 1923- 125
Brief entry 105
Ewing, John Melvin 1925- 53-56
Ewing, John S(inclair) 1916- 13-16R
Ewing, Juliana (Horatia Gatty)
1841-1885 CLR 78
See also DLB 21, 163
See also SATA 16
See also WCH
Ewing, Kathryn 1921- CANR-7
Earlier sketch in CA 61-64
See also SATA 20
Ewing, Lynne 235
Ewing, Sherman 1901-1975
Obituary 57-60
Ewing, Steve 1941- 160
Ewton, Ralph W(aldo), Jr. 1938- 81-84
Ewy, Donna 1934- CANR-14
Earlier sketch in CA 33-36R
Ewy, Rodger 1931- CANR-14
Earlier sketch in CA 33-36R
Exall, Barry
See Nugent, John Peer
Exander, Max
See Reed, Paul
Excellent, Matilda
See Farson, Daniel (Negley)
Exell, Frank Kingsley 1902- 5-8R
Exetastes
See Harakas, Stanley Samuel
Exley, Frederick (Earl) 1929-1992 CANR-117
Obituary 138
Earlier sketch in CA 81-84
See also AITN 2
See also BPFB 1
See also CLC 6, 11
See also DLB 143
See also DLBY 1981
Exley, Jo Ella Powell 1940- 122

Exman, Eugene 1900-1975 .... CAP-1
Obituary 61-64
Earlier sketch in CA 17-18
Exner, Judith (Cambell) 1934-1999 188
Ex-R. S. M.
See Lindsay, Harold Arthur
Exton, Clive (Jack Montague) 1930- 61-64
Exton, William, Jr. 1907-1988 45-48
Obituary 127
Eyck, Frank 1921- CANR-11
Earlier sketch in CA 25-28R
Eye, Glen G(ordon) 1904-1997 .... CANR-2
Earlier sketch in CA 49-52
Eyen, Jerome
See Eyen, Tom
Eyen, Tom 1941-1991 .... CANR-126
Obituary 134
Earlier sketches in CA 25-28R, CANR-22
Eyer, Diane E(lizabeth) 1944- 143
Eyerly, Jeannette (Hyde) 1908- CANR-51
Earlier sketches in CA 1-4R, CANR-4, 19
See also SAAS 10
See also SATA 4, 86
See also WYA
See also YAW
Eyestone, Robert 1942- 41-44R
Eykman, Christoph 1937- 41-44R
Eyles, Wilfred Charles 1891-1968 .... CAP-2
Earlier sketch in CA 17-18
Eyman, Scott 1951- 222
Eynhardt, Guillermo
See Quiroga, Horacio (Sylvestre)
Eynon, Robert 1941- .... TCWW 2
Eyre, Annette
See Worboys, Anne(tte Isobel) Eyre
Eyre, Dorothy
See McGuire, Leslie (Sarah)
Eyre, Frank 1910-1988 .... SATA-Obit 62
Eyre, Katherine Wigmore 1901-1970
Obituary 104
See also SATA 26
Eyre, Linda 178
Eyre, Peter 1942- 140
Eyre, Richard M(elvin) 1944- CANR-143
Earlier sketches in CA 61-64, CANR-13
Eyre, Ronald 1929-1992 104
Eyre, S(amuel) R(obert) 1922- 21-24R
Eysenck, Hans J(urgen) 1916-1997 ... CANR-50
Obituary 161
Earlier sketches in CA 9-12R, CANR-4, 25
Eysenck, Michael (William) 1944- CANR-86
Earlier sketch in CA 131
Eysman, Harvey (Allen) 1939- 104
Eyster, C(harles) William 1917-1982 ..... 29-32R
Eyvindson, Peter (Knowles) 1946- 124
See also SATA-Brief 52
Ezekiel, Mordecai J(oseph) B(rill)
1899-1974 65-68
Obituary 53-56
Ezekiel, Nissim (Moses) 1924-2004 61-64
Obituary 223
See also CLC 61
See also CP 1, 2, 3, 4, 5, 6, 7
See also EWL 3
Ezekiel, Raphael S. 1931- 53-56
Ezekiel, Tish O'Dowd 1943- 129
See also CLC 34
Ezell, Edward C(linton) 1939-1993 ... CANR-79
Obituary 143
Earlier sketch in CA 128
Ezell, Harry E(ugene) 1918-1974 .... 1-4R
Obituary 103
Ezell, John Samuel 1917- 1-4R
Ezell, Lee 203
Ezell, Macel D. 1934- 77-80
Ezell, Margaret J. M. 1955- 146
Ezenwa-Ohaeto 1959- 178
Ezera, Kalu 1925- 13-16R
Ezera, Regina
See Samreto, Regina
See also DLB 232
See also EWL 3
Ezergailis, Andrew 1930- 89-92
Ezorsky, Gertrude 89-92
Ezrahi, Sidra Dekoven
See DeKoven Ezrahi, Sidra
Ezrahi, Yaron 172
Ezrati, Milton (Joseph) 1947- 190
Ezzell, Marilyn 1937- 109
See also SATA 42
See also SATA-Brief 38
Ezzo (?)-c. 1065 .... DLB 148

F

F. P. A.
See Adams, Franklin P(ierce)
Faas, (K.) Ekbert 1938- CANR-82
Earlier sketch in CA 130
Faas, Horst 1933- 228
Faas, Larry A(ndrew) 1936- 29-32R
Fabbri, Diego 1911-1980 206
Obituary 105
Fabe, Maxene 1943- 77-80
See also SATA 15
Faber, Adele 1928- CANR-37
Earlier sketch in CA 77-80
Faber, Charles F(ranklin) 1926- CANR-12
Earlier sketch in CA 29-32R
Faber, Doris (Greenberg) 1924- CANR-56
Earlier sketches in CA 17-20R, CANR-8, 30
See also SATA 3, 78
Faber, Frederick William 1814-1863 .... DLB 32
Faber, Harold 1919- CANR-55
Earlier sketches in CA 13-16R, CANR-8, 29
See also SATA 5
Faber, Heije 1907- 139
Faber, John Henry 1918- 13-16R
Faber, Nancy W(eingarten) 1909-1976 ..... 5-8R
Obituary 65-68
Faber, Richard Stanley 1924- 61-64
Faber-Kaiser, Andreas 1944- 73-76
Fabian, Ann 1949- 207
Fabian, Donald L(eroy) 1919- 21-24R
Fabian, Johannes 197
Fabian, Josephine C(unningham)
1903-1984 .... CAP-1
Obituary 114
Earlier sketch in CA 9-10
Fabian, Robert (Honey) 1901-1978 81-84
Obituary 77-80
Fabian, Ruth
See Quigley, Aileen
Fabian, Warner
See Adams, Samuel Hopkins
Fabiani, (Marie) Louise 1957- 189
Fabijancic, Tony 1966- 226
Fabilli, Mary 1914- 172
Earlier sketch in CANR-142
Autobiographical Essay in 172
See also CAAS 29
See also CP 1
Fabinyi, Andrew 1908-1978
Obituary 108
Fabio, Sarah Webster 1928-1979 ..... CANR-22
Earlier sketch in CA 69-72
See also BW 1
Fabisch, Judith Patricia 1938- CANR-19
Earlier sketch in CA 103
Fabos, Julius Gy(ula) 1932- 97-100
Fabre, Genevieve E. 1936- 109
Fabre, Jean Henri (Casimir)
1823-1915 .... SATA 22
Fabre, Michel J(acques) 1933- CANR-37
Earlier sketches in CA 45-48, CANR-1, 16
Fabrega, Horacio, Jr. 1934- 73-76
Fabri, Ralph 1894-1975 .... CAP-2
Obituary 57-60
Earlier sketch in CA 19-20
Fabricand, Burton Paul 1923- 93-96
Fabricant, Carole 1944- 113
Fabricant, Michael B. 1948- 143
Fabricant, Solomon 1906-1989
Obituary 129
Fabricius, Johan (Johannes)
1899-1981 .... CANR-5
Earlier sketch in CA 53-56
Fabricius, Sara (Cecilie Margarete Gjorwell)
1880-1974
See Sandel, Cora
Fabrizio, Ray 1930- 33-36R
Fabrizio, Timothy C(harles) 1948- .. CANR-126
Earlier sketch in CA 165
Fabrizius, Peter
See Fabry, Joseph B(enedikt) and
Knight, Max
Fabry, Joseph B(enedikt) 1909-1999 ...... 25-28R
Fabrycky, Wolter Joseph 1932- 21-24R
Fabun, Don 1920- 45-48
Faccio, Rina Pierangeli
See Aleramo, Sibilla
Facey-Crowther, David R. 1938- 235
Fackenheim, Emil L(udwig) 1916-2003 . 21-24R
Obituary 220
Facklam, Margery (Metz) 1927- CANR-48
Earlier sketches in CA 5-8R, CANR-6, 21
See also SATA 20, 85, 132
Fackler, Eli
See Fackler, Elizabeth
Fackler, Elizabeth 1947- 118
Fackre, Gabriel Joseph 1926- CANR-7
Earlier sketch in CA 17-20R
Facos, James F(rancis) 1924- 41-44R
Factor, Regis A(nthony) 1937- 118
Fadeev, Aleksandr Aleksandrovich
See Bulgya, Alexander Alexandrovich
See also DLB 272
Fadeev, Alexandr Alexandrovich
See Bulgya, Alexander Alexandrovich
See also EWL 3
Fader, Daniel 1930- 33-36R
Fader, Shirley Sloan 1931- CANR-14
Earlier sketch in CA 77-80
Faderman, Lillian 1940- 218
Earlier sketches in CA 33-36R, CANR-16, 37,
93
Autobiographical Essay in 218
See also FW
See also GLL 1
Fadeyev, A.
See Bulgya, Alexander Alexandrovich
Fadeyev, Alexander
See Bulgya, Alexander Alexandrovich
See also TCLC 53
Fadiman, Anne 1953- CANR-139
Earlier sketch in CA 169
Fadiman, Clifton (Paul) 1904-1999 .. CANR-44
Obituary 181
Earlier sketches in CA 61-64, CANR-9
See also SATA 11
See also SATA-Obit 115
Fadiman, Edwin, Jr. 1925-1994 .... 29-32R
Fadiman, James 1939- 33-36R
Fadiman, Jeffrey A(ndrew) 1936- 116
Fadner, Frank (Leslie) 1910-1987 .... 9-12R
Obituary 123
Faegre, Torvald 1941- 89-92
Faelten, Sharon 1950- CANR-23
Earlier sketch in CA 106
Faessler, Shirley 1921(?)- 106
Fagan, Brian M(urray) 1936- CANR-104
Earlier sketches in CA 41-44R, CANR-14, 31,
56
Fagan, Cary 1957- 136
Fagan, Edward R(ichard) 1924- CANR-20
Earlier sketches in CA 9-12R, CANR-5
Fagan, Louis J. 1971- 170
Fagan, Patrick 1922- 228
Fagan, Thomas K(evin) 1943- 175
Fagan, Tom
See Fagan, Thomas K(evin)
Fage, John Donnelly 1921-2002 .... CANR-7
Obituary 208
Earlier sketch in CA 5-8R
Fagen, Donald 1948- .... CLC 26
Fagen, Richard R. 1933- CANR-22
Earlier sketches in CA 17-20R, CANR-7
Fagen, Stanley Alan 1936- 102
Fager, Charles E(ugene) 1942- 21-24R
Fagerberg, Sven (Gustaf) 1918- 191
Fagerholm, Monika 1961- 183
Fagerstrom, Stan 1923- 57-60
Fagg, Elizabeth
See Olds, Elizabeth Fagg
Fagg, John (Edwin) 1916-1998 81-84
Obituary 171
Fagg, William Buller 1914-1992 102
Faggen, Robert 170
Fagles, Robert 1933- 165
Brief entry 104
Fagley, Richard M(artin) 1910-1993 .... 1-4R
Fagon, Alfred 1937-1986
Obituary 120
Fagothey, Austin 1901-1975 .... CAP-1
Earlier sketch in CA 11-12
Fague, William Robert 1927- 109
Fagundes Telles, Lygia
See Telles, Lygia Fagundes
See also LAW
Fagundo, Ana Maria 1938- 37-40R
See also DLB 134
Fagunwa, D(aniel) O(lorunfemi) 1910(?)-1963
Obituary 116
Fagyas, Maria -1999 .... 33-36R
Faherty, Terence (P.) 197
Faherty, William B(arnaby) 1914- CANR-5
Earlier sketch in CA 5-8R
Fahey, Curtis 1951- 230
Fahey, David (Allen) 1948- 131
Fahey, David M(ichael) 1937- 169
Fahey, Frank M(ichael) 1917- 101
Fahey, James C(harles) 1903-1974
Obituary 53-56
Fahlman, Clyde 1931- 161
Fahlstrom, Oyvind (Axel Christian) 1928-1976
Obituary 69-72
Fahmy, Ismail 1922-1997 133
Obituary 162
Fahnestock, Beatrice Beck 1899(?)-1980
Obituary 97-100
Fahs, Ivan J(oel) 1932-2003 45-48
Obituary 212
Fahs, Sophia Blanche Lyon 1876-1978 164
Obituary 77-80
See also SATA 102
Fahy, Christopher 1937- CANR-55
Earlier sketches in CA 69-72, CANR-11, 29
Faig, Kenneth W(alter), Jr. 1948- CANR-109
Earlier sketch in CA 154
Faigley, Lester 1947- 146
Faigman, David L(aurence) 231
Failing, Patricia 1944- 151
Fain, Gordon L. 1946- 195
Fain, Haskell 1926- 33-36R
Fain, Michael 1937- 139
Fain, Tyrus Gerard 1933- 104
Fainaru, Steve 232
Fainlight, Harry .... CP 1
Fainlight, Ruth (Esther) 1931- 191
Earlier sketches in CA 17-20R, CANR-8, 26,
51, 84
Autobiographical Essay in 191
See also CP 1, 2, 3, 4, 5, 6, 7
See also CWP
Fainsod, Merle 1907-1972 .... CAP-1
Obituary 33-36R
Earlier sketch in CA 13-16
Fainstein, Norman Ira 1944- 102
Fainstein, Susan S. 1938- 93-96
Fainzil'berg, Il'ia Arnol'dovich
See Fainzilberg, Ilya Arnoldovich
Fainzilberg, Ilya Arnoldovich 1897-1937 ... 165
Brief entry 120
See also Il'f, Il'ia and
Ilf, Ilya
Fair, A. A.
See Gardner, Erle Stanley
Fair, C. A. 1923- .... CP 1
Fair, Charles M. 1916- CANR-10
Earlier sketch in CA 13-16R
Fair, David 1952- 161
See also SATA 96
Fair, Harold L(loyd) 1924- 89-92
Fair, James 1898(?)-1984
Obituary 112
Fair, James R(utherford), Jr. 1920- CANR-86
Earlier sketches in CA 29-32R, CANR-34
Fair, Marvin L(uke) 1897(?)-1983
Obituary 110
Fair, Ray C(larence) 1942- 29-32R
Fair, Ronald L. 1932- CANR-25
Earlier sketch in CA 69-72
See also BW 1
See also CLC 18
See also DLB 33
Fair, Sylvia 1933- 69-72
See also SATA 13
Fairbairn, Ann
See Tait, Dorothy
Fairbairn, Brett 1959- CANR-125
Earlier sketch in CA 169
Fairbairn, Douglas 1926- 33-36R
Fairbairn, Garry L. 1947- 77-80
Fairbairn, Helen
See Southard, Helen Fairbairn
Fairbairn, Ian J(ohn) 1933- 53-56
Fairbairn, Roger
See Carr, John Dickson
Fairbairns, Zoe (Ann) 1948- CANR-85
Earlier sketches in CA 103, CANR-21
See also CLC 32
See also CN 4, 5, 6, 7
Fairbank, Alfred John 1895-1982 .... CANR-6
Obituary 106
Earlier sketch in CA 5-8R
Fairbank, John K(ing) 1907-1991 ...... CANR-80
Obituary 135
Earlier sketches in CA 1-4R, CANR-3
Fairbanks, Carol 1935- 69-72
Fairbanks, Henry G(eorge) 1914-1987
Brief entry 112
Fairbanks, Nancy
See Herndon, Nancy
Fairbrother, Nan 1913-1971 .... CANR-3
Obituary 33-36R
Earlier sketch in CA 5-8R
Fairburn, A(rthur) R(ex) D(ugard)
1904-1957 .... RGEL 2
Fairburn, Eleanor 1928- CANR-8
Earlier sketch in CA 61-64
Fairchild, B(ertram) H., Jr. 1942- 170
Fairchild, Hoxie Neale 1894-1973 .... 5-8R
Obituary 45-48
Fairchild, John B(urr) 1927-
Brief entry 117
Fairchild, Louis W. 1901-1981
Obituary 105
Fairchild, William 1918-2000 73-76
Obituary 188
Fairclough, Adam 1952- CANR-120
Earlier sketches in CA 127, CANR-54
Fairclough, Chris 1951- 112
Faire, Zabrina
See Stevenson, Florence
Fairfax, Ann
See Chesney, Marion
Fairfax, Beatrice
See Manning, Marie and
McCarroll, Marion C(lyde)
Fairfax, Beatrice
See Scarberry, Alma Sioux
Fairfax, Di
See Blake, Lillie Devereux
Fairfax, Felix
See Gibson, Walter B(rown)
Fairfax, John 1930- 97-100
See also CP 1, 2
Fairfax, John 1937- 49-52
Fairfax, Warwick (Oswald) 1901-1987
Obituary 121
Fairfax-Blakeborough, Jack
See Fairfax-Blakeborough, John Freeman
Fairfax-Blakeborough, John Freeman
1883-1978(?) 102
Fairfax-Lucy, Brian (Fulke Cameron-Ramsay)
1898-1974 .... CAP-2
Earlier sketch in CA 29-32
See also SATA 6
See also SATA-Obit 26
Fairfield, Darrell
See Larkin, Rochelle
Fairfield, Flora
See Alcott, Louisa May
Fairfield, James G(lencairn) T(homson)
1926- 126
Fairfield, John
See Livingstone, Harrison Edward
Fairfield, John D. 1955- 148
Fairfield, Lesley 1949- 130
Fairfield, Leslie P(arke) 1941- 186
Brief entry 107
Fairfield, Paul 1066- 208
Fairfield, Richard 1937- 41-44R
Fairfield, Roy P(hillip) 1918- 33-36R
Fairhall, David Keir 1934- 103
Fairholm, Gil
See Fairholm, Gilbert W(ayne)
Fairholm, Gilbert W(ayne) 1932- ... CANR-138
Earlier sketch in CA 174
Fairholme, Elizabeth 1910- 97-100
Fairless, Caroline S. 1947- 105
Fairley, Barker 1887-1986 .... 1-4R
Obituary 121
Fairley, Irene R. 1940- 73-76
Fairley, James Stewart 1940- 102
Fairley, John (Alexander) 1939- 131
Fairley, M(ichael) C(harles) 1937- CANR-14
Earlier sketch in CA 37-40R
Fairley, Peter 1930-1998 .... CANR-24
Obituary 169
Earlier sketch in CA 29-32R
Fairlie, Gerard 1899-1983 179
Obituary 109
See also DLB 77
See also SATA-Obit 34
Fairlie, Henry (Jones) 1924-1990 104
Obituary 131
Fairman, Charles 1897-1988 45-48
Fairman, Herbert Walter 1907-1982 111
Obituary 108
Fairman, Honora C. 1927(?)-1978
Obituary 81-84
Fairman, Joan A(lexandra) 1935- 33-36R
See also SATA 10

Cumulative Index **181** **Farhi**

Fairman, Paul W. 1916-1977
  Obituary ... 114
  See also Queen, Ellery
  See also SFW 4
Fairn, (Richard) Duncan 1906-1986
  Obituary ... 119
Fairstein, Linda A. 1947(?)- ... CANR-127
  Earlier sketches in CA 154, CANR-88
Fairweather, Digby 1946- ... CANR-58
  Earlier sketch in CA 127
Fairweather, Eileen 1954- ... 125
Fairweather, Eugene Rathbone 1920-
  Brief entry ... 108
Fairweather, George W. 1921- ... 13-16R
Fairweather, Janet (Anne) 1945- ... 124
Fairweather, Peter G. 1949- ... 179
Fairweather, Sally (Hallberg) 1917- ... 112
Fairweather, Virginia 1922- ... 29-32R
Faison, S(amson) Lane, Jr. 1907- ... 89-92
Faison, Seth 1959(?)- ... 237
Faissler, Margareta (A.) 1902-1990 ... 5-8R
  Obituary ... 170
Fait, Hollis F. 1918- ... CANR-5
  Earlier sketch in CA 1-4R
Faith, Barbara
  See Covarrubias, Barbara Faith
Faith, (Richard) Mack 1944- ... 125
Faith, Nicholas 1933- ... 204
Faith, William Robert
  See Fague, William Robert
Faithfull, Emily 1835-1895 ... FW
Faithfull, Gail 1936- ... 57-60
  See also SATA 8
Faithfull, Marianne 1946- ... CANR-134
  Earlier sketch in CA 148
Faiz, Faiz Ahmad 1912(?)-1984
  Obituary ... 115
  See also Faiz, Faiz Ahmed
Faiz, Faiz Ahmed
  See Faiz, Faiz Ahmad
  See also EWL 3
Fakhry, Majid 1923- ... 29-32R
Fakinos, Aris 1935- ... 81-84
Falassi, Alessandro 1945- ... 105
Falb, Lewis W(illiam) 1935- ... 102
Falck, (Adrian) Colin 1934- ... CANR-122
  Earlier sketch in CA 65-68
  See also CP 2
Falco, Edward 1948- ... CANR-114
  Earlier sketch in CA 134
Falco, Gian
  See Papini, Giovanni
Falco, Maria J(osephine) 1932- ... CANR-12
  Earlier sketch in CA 61-64
Falcoff, Mark 1941- ... 65-68
Falcon
  See Nestle, John Francis
Falcon, Debra
  See Feddersen, Connie
Falcon, Mark 1940- ... TCWW 2
Falcon, Richard
  See Shapiro, Samuel
Falcon, Walter P(hillip) 1936- ... 126
  Brief entry ... 109
Falcon, William D(yche) 1932- ... 17-20R
Falcon-Barker, Ted 1923- ... 25-28R
Falcone, L(ucy) M. 1951- ... 230
  See also SATA 155
Falconer, A. F.
  See Falconer, Alexander Frederick
Falconer, Alexander Frederick 1908-1987
  Obituary ... 122
Falconer, Alun (?)-1973
  Obituary ... 104
Falconer, Colin 1953- ... 192
Falconer, Delia 1966- ... 176
Falconer, Ian 1959- ... 197
  See also CLR 90
  See also SATA 125
Falconer, James
  See Kirkup, James
Falconer, Kenneth
  See Kornbluth, C(yril) M.
Falconer, Lee N.
  See May, Julian
Falconer, William 1732-1769 ... RGEL 2
Falconieri, John V(incent) 1920- ... 130
Faldbakken, Knut 1941- ... CWW 2
  See also DLB 297
Falero, Frank, Jr. 1937- ... 37-40R
Fales, Dean Abner, Jr. 1925-
  Brief entry ... 110
Fales, Edward (Daniel, Jr.) 1906- ... 97-100
Fales-Hill, Susan 1962- ... 227
Falk, Avner 1943- ... 163
Falk, Candace 1947- ... 136
Falk, Charles J(ohn) 1899-1971 ... CAP-2
  Earlier sketch in CA 23-24
Falk, Doris Virginia 1919- ... 186
  Brief entry ... 111
Falk, Elsa
  See Escherich, Elsa Falk
Falk, Eugene H(annes) 1913-2000 ... 116
Falk, Gerhard 1924- ... CANR-137
  Earlier sketches in CA 117, CANR-39, 40, 55
Falk, Harvey 1932- ... 127
  Brief entry ... 112
Falk, I(sidore) S(ydney) 1899-1984
  Obituary ... 114
Falk, Irving A. 1921- ... 21-24R
Falk, John ... 237
Falk, Kathryn 1940- ... CANR-20
  Earlier sketch in CA 97-100
  Interview in ... CANR-20
Falk, Lee
  See Copper, Basil and
  Goulart, Ron(ald Joseph)
Falk, Lee Harrison 1915-1999 ... 97-100
  Obituary ... 177
Falk, Leslie A. 1915- ... 9-12R
Falk, Louis A. 1896(?)-1979
  Obituary ... 85-88
Falk, Marvin W. 1943- ... 122
Falk, Minna Regina 1900-1983
  Obituary ... 109
Falk, Pamela S. 1953- ... 122
Falk, Peter H(astings) 1950- ... 139
Falk, Quentin 1948- ... CANR-48
  Earlier sketch in CA 122
Falk, Richard A(nderson) 1930- ... CANR-112
  Earlier sketches in CA 5-8R, CANR-12
Falk, Robert 1914-1996 ... 89-92
Falk, Roger (Salis) 1910-1997 ... 65-68
Falk, S(tephen) J(ohn) 1942-1997 ... 124
  Obituary ... 156
Falk, Signi Lenea 1906- ... 5-8R
Falk, Stanley L(awrence) 1927- ... CANR-2
  Earlier sketch in CA 1-4R
Falk, Susan Meyers 1942- ... 117
Falk, Thomas H(einrich) 1935- ... 145
Falk, Toby
  See Falk, S(tephen) J(ohn)
Falk, Ursula Adler ... 114
Falk, Ze'ev W(ilhelm) 1923-1998 ... CANR-42
  Earlier sketches in CA 21-24R, CANR-15
Falkberget, Johan 1879-1967 ... DLB 297
  See also EWL 3
Falkender, Baroness Marcia
  See Williams, Marcia
Falkingham, Jane (Cecelia) 1963- ... 144
Falkirk, Richard
  See Lambert, Derek
Falkland, Samuel
  See Heijermans, Herman
Falkner, J(ohn) Meade 1858-1932 ... HGG
Falkner, Jack
  See Falkner, Murry (Charles)
Falkner, Leonard 1900-1977 ... 21-24R
  See also SATA 12
Falkner, Murry (Charles) 1899-1975 ... CAP-2
  Obituary ... 171
  Earlier sketch in CA 23-24
Falk-Roenne, Arne 1920- ... CANR-14
  Earlier sketch in CA 21-24R
Falkus, Hugh Edward Lance 1917-1996 ... 111
  Obituary ... 151
Fall, Aminata Sow
  See Sow Fall, Aminata
  See also CWW 2
Fall, Andrew
  See Arthur, Robert, (Jr.)
Fall, Bernard B. 1926-1967 ... CANR-6
  Obituary ... 25-28R
  Earlier sketch in CA 1-4R
Fall, Frieda Kay 1913- ... 41-44R
Fall, Thomas
  See Snow, Donald Clifford
Falla, Jack 1944- ... 205
Fallaci, Oriana 1930- ... CANR-134
  Earlier sketches in CA 77-80, CANR-15, 58
  See also CLC 11, 110
  See also FW
  See also MTCW 1
Fallada, Hans
  See Ditzen, Rudolf
  See also DLB 56
Fallaw, Wesner 1907- ... 1-4R
Faller, Kevin 1920- ... CANR-4
  Earlier sketch in CA 53-56
  See also CP 1
Fallers, Lloyd A(shton, Jr.) 1925-1974 . CANR-4
  Obituary ... 49-52
  Earlier sketch in CA 9-12R
Falley, Margaret Dickson 1898-1983
  Obituary ... 110
Fallis, Greg(ory S.) 1951- ... 223
Fallon, Brian A(nthony) 1955- ... 188
Fallon, Carlos 1909-1989 ... 41-44R
  Obituary ... 176
Fallon, Eileen Brydon 1954- ... 118
Fallon, Frederic (Michael) 1944-1970 ... 41-44R
Fallon, George
  See Bingley, David Ernest
Fallon, Ivan (Gregory) 1944- ... 137
Fallon, Jack
  See Fallon, John W(illiam)
Fallon, Jennifer ... 233
Fallon, John W(illiam) 1924- ... 77-80
Fallon, Martin
  See Patterson, Harry
Fallon, Padraic 1905-1974 ... 103
  Obituary ... 89-92
  See also CP 1, 2
Fallon, Peter 1951- ... CANR-84
  Brief entry ... 106
  Earlier sketch in CA 133
  See also CP 7
Fallon, Robert Thomas 1927- ... CANR-143
  Earlier sketch in CA 121
Fallowell, Duncan (Richard) 1948- ... 137
Fallows, James M(ackenzie) 1949- .. CANR-111
  Earlier sketches in CA 45-48, CANR-2, 43
Falls, C(harles) B(uckles) 1874-1960
  Obituary ... 116
  See also SATA 38
  See also SATA-Brief 27
Falls, Cyril Bentham 1888-1971 ... CAP-1
  Earlier sketch in CA 13-14
Falls, Joe 1928-2004 ... 77-80
  Obituary ... 229
Fallwell, Marshall Leigh, Jr. 1943- ... 69-72
Falola, Toyin 1953- ... CANR-104
  Earlier sketch in CA 151
Falorp, Nelson P.
  See Jones, Stephen (Phillip)
Falstein, Louis 1909-1995 ... 97-100
  See also SATA 37
Faltas Youssef, Edwar Kolta
  See al-Kharrat, Edwar
Falter-Barns, Suzanne 1958- ... 141
Faludi, Susan 1959- ... CANR-126
  Earlier sketch in CA 138
  See also CLC 140
  See also FW
  See also MTCW 2
  See also MTFW 2005
  See also NCFS 3
Faludy, George 1913- ... 21-24R
  See also CLC 42
Faludy, Gyoergy
  See Faludy, George
Falvey, Jack 1938- ... 122
Falwell, Jerry 1933- ... 102
Falzeder, Ernst 1955- ... 146
Fama, Eugene F. 1939- ... 186
  Brief entry ... 113
Famiglietti, Eugene Paul 1931(?)-1980
  Obituary ... 97-100
Famularo, Joseph John 1922- ... CANR-4
  Earlier sketch in CA 1-4R
Fan, Kuang Huan 1932- ... 21-24R
Fanburg, Walter H. 1936- ... 186
  Brief entry ... 114
Fancher, Betsy 1928- ... 143
  See also DLBY 1983
Fancher, Ewilda 1928- ... 61-64
Fancher, Jane S(uzanne) 1952- ... 172
Fancher, Raymond E(lwood), Jr. 1940- 69-72
Fancher, Robert T. 1954- ... 135
Fanchi, John R(ichard) 1952- ... CANR-122
  Earlier sketch in CA 169
Fanchon, Lisa
  See Floren, Lee
Fancutt, Walter 1911- ... CANR-12
  Earlier sketches in CAP-1, CA 9-10
Fandel, John 1925- ... CANR-23
  Earlier sketch in CA 69-72
Fane, Bron
  See Fanthorpe, R(obert) Lionel
Fane, Julian Charles 1927- ... CANR-6
  Earlier sketch in CA 13-16R
Fane, Violet
  See Currie, Mary Montgomerie Lamb Singleton
  See also DLB 35
Fanelli, Sara 1969- ... SATA 89, 126
Fang, Chaoying 1908(?)-1985
  Obituary ... 116
Fang, Irving E. 1929- ... CANR-31
  Earlier sketch in CA 49-52
Fang, Josephine (Maria) Riss 1922- ... 69-72
Fang, L. Z.
  See Fang, Lizhi
Fang, Lizhi 1936- ... 135
Fangen, Ronald (August) 1895-1946 ... 195
  See also EWL 3
Fanger, Donald (Lee) 1929- ... 13-16R
Fang Fang 1955- ... RGSF 2
Fann, K(uang) T(ih) 1937- ... 61-64
Fann, William E(dwin) 1930- ... CANR-2
  Earlier sketch in CA 49-52
Fannin, Allen 1939- ... 69-72
Fanning, Buckner 1926- ... 69-72
Fanning, Charles (Frederick, Jr.)
  1942- ... CANR-108
  Earlier sketch in CA 81-84
Fanning, Katherine (Woodruff) 1927-2000 . 182
  Obituary ... 191
  See also DLB 127
Fanning, Leonard M(ulliken) 1888-1967 ... 5-8R
  See also SATA 5
Fanning, Louis A(lbert) 1927- ... 69-72
Fanning, Michael 1942- ... 89-92
Fanning, Odom 1920- ... 53-56
Fanning, Richard (Ward) 1953- ... 152
Fanning, Robbie 1947- ... CANR-31
  Earlier sketches in CA 77-80, CANR-14
Fanon, Frantz 1925-1961 ... 116
  Obituary ... 89-92
  See also BLC 2
  See also BW 1
  See also CLC 74
  See also DAM MULT
  See also DLB 296
  See also LMFS 2
  See also WLIT 2
Fanshawe, David 1942- ... 97-100
Fanshawe, Richard 1608-1666 ... DLB 126
Fant, Joseph Lewis III 1928- ... 13-16R
Fant, Louis J(udson), Jr. 1931-2001 ... 37-40R
  Obituary ... 198
Fanta, J. Julius 1907- ... 33-36R
Fante, John (Thomas) 1911-1983 .... CANR-104
  Obituary ... 109
  Earlier sketches in CA 69-72, CANR-23
  See also AMWS 11
  See also CLC 60
  See also DLB 130
  See also DLBY 1983
  See also SSC 65
Fantel, Hans 1922- ... CANR-31
  Earlier sketch in CA 49-52
Fanthorpe, Patricia Alice 1938- ... CANR-14
  Earlier sketch in CA 89-92
Fanthorpe, R(obert) Lionel 1935- ... CANR-84
  Earlier sketches in CA 73-76, CANR-14, 32
  See also SFW 4
Fanthorpe, U(rsula) A(skham)
  1929- ... CANR-110
  Earlier sketch in CA 156
  See also CP 7
  See also CWP
Fantini, Mario D. 1927(?)-1989 ... CANR-83
  Obituary ... 129
  Earlier sketch in CA 77-80
Fantoni, Barry (Ernest) 1940- ... 129
Faqih, Ahmed 1942- ... 154
Faqiri, Amin 1944- ... EWL 3
Far, Sui Sin
  See Eaton, Edith Maude
  See also SSC 62
  See also SSFS 4
Farabee, Barbara 1944- ... 57-60
Farabough, Laura 1949- ... DLB 228
Farace, Joe 1941- ... CANR-123
  Earlier sketch in CA 162
Faraday, Ann 1935- ... 77-80
Faraday, M. M.
  See Rorvik, David M(ichael)
Faraday, Robert
  See Cassiday, Bruce (Bingham)
Faragher, John Mack 1945- ... CANR-92
  Brief entry ... 111
  Earlier sketch in CA 147
Farago, Ladislas 1906-1980 ... CANR-10
  Obituary ... 102
  Earlier sketch in CA 65-68
Farah, Caesar Elie 1929- ... 41-44R
Farah, Madelain 1934- ... 73-76
Farah, Nuruddin 1945- ... CANR-81
  Earlier sketch in CA 106
  See also AFW
  See also BLC 2
  See also BW 2, 3
  See also CDWLB 3
  See also CLC 53, 137
  See also CN 4, 5, 6, 7
  See also DAM MULT
  See also DLB 125
  See also EWL 3
  See also WLIT 2
Faraj, Alfred 1929- ... EWL 3
Faralla, Dana 1909- ... 49-52
  See also SATA 9
Faralla, Dorothy W.
  See Faralla, Dana
Faramelli, Norman Joseph 1932- ... 188
  Brief entry ... 109
Farau, Alfred 1904-1972
  Obituary ... 37-40R
Farb, Peter 1929-1980 ... CANR-12
  Obituary ... 97-100
  Earlier sketch in CA 13-16R
  See also SATA 12
  See also SATA-Obit 22
Farber, Barry J. 1959- ... 175
Farber, Bernard 1922-2000 ... 21-24R
Farber, Daniel A. 1950- ... 128
Farber, Donald C. ... CANR-30
  Earlier sketches in CA 29-32R, CANR-13
Farber, Edward (Rolke) 1914-1982
  Obituary ... 110
Farber, Joseph C. 1903-1994 ... 33-36R
Farber, Leslie Hillel 1912-1981 ... 110
  Obituary ... 103
Farber, Marvin 1901-1980 ... CANR-42
  Earlier sketch in CA 49-52
Farber, Norma 1909-1984 ... CANR-84
  Obituary ... 112
  Earlier sketch in CA 102
  See also BYA 7
  See also DLB 61
  See also MAICYA 1, 2
  See also SATA 25, 75
  See also SATA-Obit 38
Farber, Paul Lawrence 1944- ... 112
Farber, Seymour M(organ) 1912-1995 57-60
  Obituary ... 150
Farber, Stephen E. 1943- ... CANR-19
  Earlier sketch in CA 103
Farber, Susan L. 1945- ... 106
Farber, Thomas (David) 1944- ... CANR-130
  Earlier sketch in CA 103
Farberman, Harvey A(lan) 1939- ... CANR-35
  Earlier sketch in CA 45-48
Farberow, Norman L(ouis) 1918- ... CANR-7
  Earlier sketch in CA 17-20R
Farbman, Albert I. 1934- ... 145
Farca, Marie C. 1935- ... 37-40R
Farcau, Bruce W. 1951- ... CANR-92
  Earlier sketch in CA 138
Farel, Conrad
  See Bardens, Dennis (Conrad)
Farely, Alison
  See Poland, Dorothy (Elizabeth Hayward)
Farer, Tom J. 1935- ... CANR-8
  Earlier sketch in CA 17-20R
Farewell, Nina
  See Cooper, Mae (Klein)
Fargis, Paul (McKenna) 1939- ... CANR-13
  Earlier sketch in CA 21-24R
Fargo, Doone
  See Norwood, Victor G(eorge) C(harles)
Fargo, Joe
  See Rikhoff, James C.
Fargue, Leon-Paul 1876(?)-1947 ..... CANR-107
  Brief entry ... 109
  See also DLB 258
  See also EWL 3
  See also TCLC 11
Fargus, Fredrick John
  See Conway, Hugh
Farhi, Moris 1935- ... CANR-13
  Earlier sketch in CA 77-80

Faria, A(nthony) J(ohn) 1944- CANR-40
Earlier sketches in CA 102, CANR-19
Faria, Almeida 1943- .... EWL 3
Faria, Otavio de 1908-1984 221
Farias, Victor 1940- 135
Faricy, Robert L(eo) 1926- CANR-34
Earlier sketches in CA 37-40R, CANR-15
Farid, 'Umar Ibn al-
See Ibn al-Farid, 'Umar
Faridi, S. N.
See Faridi, Shah Nasiruddin Mohammad
Faridi, Shah Nasiruddin Mohammad
1929- 29-32R
Faries, Clyde J. 1928- 37-40R
Faries, David A(llan) 1938- 112
Farigoule, Louis
See Romains, Jules
Farina, John 1950- 114
Farina, Richard 1936(?)-1966 81-84
Obituary 25-28R
See also CLC 9
Faris, (Earl) Barry 1889-1966
Obituary 114
Faris, Robert E. L(ee) 1907- 17-20R
Faris, Wendy B(ush) 1945- 115
Farisani, Tshenuwani Simon 1947- 134
See also BW 2
Farish, Donald J(ames) 1942- 106
Farish, Margaret Kennedy 1918- 5-8R
Farish, Terry 1947- CANR-127
Earlier sketches in CA 137, CANR-104
See also SATA 82, 146
Farjeon, (Eve) Annabel 1919-2004 53-56
Obituary 223
See also SATA 11
See also SATA-Obit 153
Farjeon, Eleanor 1881-1965 .... CAP-1
Earlier sketch in CA 11-12
See also CLR 34
See also CWRI 5
See also DLB 160
See also MAICYA 1, 2
See also SATA 2
See also WCH
Farkas, Emil 1946- CANR-32
Earlier sketch in CA 69-72
Farkas, George 1946- 163
Farkas, Philip (Francis) 1914-1992 ... CANR-31
Earlier sketch in CA 49-52
Farland, David
See Wolverton, Dave
Farley, Carol (J.) 1936- CANR-116
Earlier sketches in CA 21-24R, CANR-10, 25, 50
See also SATA 4, 137
Farley, (William) Edward 1929- 61-64
Farley, Eugene J. 1916- CANR-12
Earlier sketch in CA 33-36R
Farley, Harriet 1812-1907 .... DLB 239
Farley, James A(loysius) 1888-1976
Obituary 65-68
Farley, Jean 1928- 21-24R
Farley, Jennie (Tiffany Towle) 1932- 132
Farley, John E. 1949- 178
Farley, Miriam Southwell 1907(?)-1975
Obituary 57-60
Farley, Paul 1965- 222
Farley, Rawle 1922- 45-48
Farley, Walter (Lorimer) 1915-1989 .. CANR-84
Earlier sketches in CA 17-20R, CANR-8, 29
See also AAYA 58
See also BYA 14
See also CLC 17
See also DLB 22
See also JRDA
See also MAICYA 1, 2
See also SATA 2, 43, 132
See also YAW
Farley-Hills, David 1931- 73-76
Farlie, Barbara L(eitzow) 1936- 65-68
Farlow, James O(rville, Jr.) 1951- 142
See also SATA 75
Farlow, John King
See King-Farlow, John
Farmacevten
See Holm, Sven (Aage)
Farman, Gha'ib Tu'ma 1927(?)-1990 ...... EWL 3
Farman Farmaian, Sattareh 1921- 142
Farmar, Hugh William 1908-1987
Obituary 123
Farmborough, Florence 1887-1978 207
See also DLB 204
Farmer, Albert J(ohn) 1894-1976 .... 21-24R
Obituary 120
Farmer, Bernard James 1902- 5-8R
Farmer, Bertram Hughes 1916-1996 104
Farmer, Beverley 1941- 189
See also CN 6, 7
Farmer, Charles J(oseph) 1943- CANR-10
Earlier sketch in CA 57-60
Farmer, David Hugh 1923- CANR-54
Earlier sketch in CA 125
Farmer, Don 1938- 65-68
Farmer, Gary R(ay) 1923- 57-60
Farmer, Gene 1919-1972
Obituary 37-40R
Farmer, Herbert Henry 1892-1981(?)
Obituary 102
Farmer, Kathleen 1946- CANR-10
Earlier sketch in CA 65-68
Farmer, Laurence 1895(?)-1976
Obituary 65-68
Farmer, Lesley S. J. 1949- 205
Farmer, Martha L(ouise) 1912- 21-24R
Farmer, Nancy 1941- CANR-94
Earlier sketch in CA 167
See also AAYA 26, 53
See also BYA 11
See also MAICYA 2
See also MAICYAS 1
See also SATA 79, 117, 161
See also YAW
Farmer, Norman K(ittrell, Jr.) 1934- 123
Farmer, Patti 1948- .... SATA 79
Farmer, Penelope (Jane) 1939- CANR-84
Earlier sketches in CA 13-16R, CANR-9, 37
See also CLR 8
See also DLB 161
See also FANT
See also JRDA
See also MAICYA 1, 2
See also SAAS 22
See also SATA 40, 105
See also SATA-Brief 39
See also YAW
Farmer, Peter 1950- .... SATA 38
Farmer, Philip Jose 1918- CANR-111
Earlier sketches in CA 1-4R, CANR-4, 35
See also AAYA 28
See also BPFB 1
See also CLC 1, 19
See also DLB 8
See also MTCW 1
See also SATA 93
See also SCFW 1, 2
See also SFW 4
Farmer, R. L.
See Lamont, Rosette C(lementine)
Farmer, Richard Neil 1928- CANR-8
Earlier sketch in CA 17-20R
Farmer, Robert Allen 1938- 21-24R
Farmer, Rod(ney Bruce) 1947- 209
Farmer, Rod(ney Bruce) 1947- 208
Farmer, Sarah Bennett 185
Farmer, William R(euben) 1921- CANR-49
Brief entry 109
Earlier sketch in CA 123
Farmer Jones
See Jones, Bryan L.
Farmiloe, Dorothy Alicia 1920- CANR-8
Earlier sketch in CA 61-64
Farnaby, Thomas 1575(?)-1647 .... DLB 236
Farnan, D(orothy) J(eanne-Therese)
1919-2003 130
Farnash, Hugh
See Luff, S(tanley) G(eorge) A(nthony)
Farndale, W(illiam) A(rthur) J(ames)
1916- CANR-11
Earlier sketch in CA 25-28R
Farner, Donald S(ankey) 1915- 53-56
Farnes, Maria Aurelia Capmany
See Capmany (Farnes), Maria Aurelia
Farnham, Burt
See Clifford, Harold B(urton)
Farnham, Emily 1912- 69-72
Farnham, Marynia F. 1900(?)-1979
Obituary 85-88
Farnham, Thomas J(avery) 1938- CANR-4
Earlier sketch in CA 53-56
Farnie, D(ouglas) A(ntony) 1926- CANR-12
Earlier sketch in CA 73-76
Farningham, Marianne
See Hearn, Mary Anne
Farnol, (John) Jeffery 1878-1952 199
See also RHW
Farnsworth, Bill 1958- .... SATA 84, 135
Farnsworth, Clyde 1931- 203
Farnsworth, Clyde A. 1908(?)-1984
Obituary 112
Farnsworth, Dana (Lyda)
1905-1986 .... CANR-75
Obituary 119
Earlier sketch in CA 61-64
Farnsworth, E(dward) Allan 1928-2005 . 13-16R
Obituary 235
Farnsworth, James
See Pohle, Robert W(arren), Jr.
Farnsworth, Jerry 1895-1982 .... CAP-1
Earlier sketch in CA 13-16
Farnsworth, Kahanah 1946- 193
Farnsworth, Lee W(infield) 1932- 33-36R
Farnsworth, Paul Randolph 1899-1978 . CAP-2
Earlier sketch in CA 29-32
Farnsworth, Robert M. 1929- 53-56
Farnsworth, Stephen J(ames) 1961- 224
Farnum, K. T.
See Rips, Ervine M(ilton)
Farnworth, Warren 1935- 93-96
Farny, Michael H(olt) 1934- 65-68
Faroghi, Suraiya 1941- 199
Faron, Fay 1949- 157
Faron, Louis C. 1923- 9-12R
Farquhar, Francis P(eloubet)
1887-1975 .... CAP-1
Obituary 57-60
Earlier sketch in CA 19-20
Farquhar, George 1677-1707 .... BRW 2
See also DAM DRAM
See also DLB 84
See also RGEL 2
Farquhar, Margaret C(utting) 1905-1988 .. 69-72
See also SATA 13
Farquhar, Mary Ann 1949- 199
Farquharson, Alexander 1944- .... SATA 46
Farquharson, Charlie
See Harron, Don(ald)
Farquharson, Martha
See Finley, Martha
Farr, Bill
See Farr, William T.
Farr, David M. L. 1922- 37-40R
Farr, Dennis (Larry Ashwell) 1929- 187
Farr, Diana (Pullein-Thompson) CANR-84
Earlier sketches in CA 13-16R, CANR-7, 20
See also Pullein-Thompson, Diana
See also CWRI 5
See also SATA 82
Farr, Diane 226
Farr, Dorothy M(ary) 1905- 77-80
Farr, Douglas
See Gilford, C(harles) B(ernard)
Farr, Finis (King) 1904-1982 .... CANR-76
Obituary 105
Earlier sketches in CA 1-4R, CANR-1
See also SATA 10
Farr, Hilary
See Foster, Jeannette Howard
See also GLL 1
Farr, John
See Webb, Jack (Randolph)
Farr, Jory 1952- 146
Farr, Judith 1937- CANR-12
Earlier sketch in CA 29-32R
Farr, Kenneth R(aymond) 1942- 73-76
Farr, Michael 1924- 29-32R
Farr, Moira 1958- 207
Farr, Roger C. 33-36R
Farr, Sidney Saylor 1932- 114
Farr, Walter Greene, Jr. 1925-
Brief entry 106
Farr, William T. 1934-1987
Obituary 121
Farra, Madame E.
See Fawcett, F(rank) Dubrez
Farrakhan, Louis (Abdul) 1933- 179
Farrand, Phil 1958- 148
Farrant, Leda 1927- 21-24R
Farrant, M(arion) A(lice) C(oburn) 1947- 189
Farrar, Frederic William 1831-1903 186
See also DLB 163
Farrar, John C(hipman) 1896-1974 65-68
Obituary 53-56
Farrar, Lancelot Leighton, Jr. 1932- CANR-4
Earlier sketch in CA 53-56
Farrar, Larston Dawn 1915-1970 .... 1-4R
Obituary 29-32R
Farrar, Margaret Petherbridge 1897-1984
Obituary 113
Farrar, Richard B(artlett), Jr. 1939- 65-68
Farrar, Ronald T(ruman) 1935- 33-36R
Farrar, Rowena Rutherford 1903-1999 108
Farrar, Susan Clement 1917- 101
See also SATA 33
Farrar-Hockley, Anthony Heritage 1924- . 69-72
Farrell, Alan 1920- 13-16R
Farrell, Anne A. 1916- 25-28R
Farrell, B. A.
See Farrell, Brian Anthony
Farrell, Barry 1935(?)-1984
Obituary 114
Farrell, Ben
See Cebulash, Mel
Farrell, Brian
See Farrell, Brian Anthony
Farrell, Brian 1929- 135
Farrell, Brian Anthony 1912- 130
Farrell, Bryan (Henry) 1923- CANR-2
Earlier sketch in CA 49-52
Farrell, C(larence) Frederick, Jr.
1934- CANR-48
Earlier sketch in CA 122
Farrell, Catharine
See O'Connor, Sister Mary Catharine
Farrell, Cliff 1899-1977 .... CANR-64
Obituary 125
Earlier sketch in CA 65-68
See also TCWW 1, 2
Farrell, David
See Smith, Frederick E(screet)
Farrell, David M. 1960- 203
Farrell, Desmond
See Organ, John
Farrell, Edith R(odgers) 1933- CANR-48
Earlier sketch in CA 122
Farrell, Edmund J(ames) 1927- 120
Farrell, Fiona 1947- 195
Farrell, Francis (Thomas) 1912-1983
Obituary 109
Farrell, Frank
See Farrell, Francis (Thomas)
Farrell, Gillian B. 1955(?)- CANR-142
Earlier sketch in CA 140
Farrell, Harry (Guy) 1924- 139
Farrell, J(ames) G(ordon)
1935-1979 .... CANR-36
Obituary 89-92
Earlier sketch in CA 73-76
See also CLC 6
See also CN 1, 2
See also DLB 14, 271
See also MTCW 1
See also RGEL 2
See also RHW
See also WLIT 4
Farrell, James T(homas) 1904-1979 .. CANR-61
Obituary 89-92
Earlier sketches in CA 5-8R, CANR-9
See also AMW
See also BPFB 1
See also CLC 1, 4, 8, 11, 66
See also CN 1, 2
See also DLB 4, 9, 86
See also DLBD 2
See also EWL 3
See also MAL 5
See also MTCW 1, 2
See also MTFW 2005
See also RGAL 4
See also SSC 28
Farrell, John A(loysius) 1953- 205
Farrell, John J(oseph) 1934-
Brief entry 110
Farrell, John Philip 1939- 102
Farrell, Kathleen (Amy) 1912-1999 .... 5-8R
Farrell, Kirby 1942- 33-36R
Farrell, M. J.
See Keane, Mary Nesta (Skrine)
Farrell, Matthew Charles 1921- 49-52
Farrell, Melvin L(loyd) 1930- CANR-5
Earlier sketch in CA 13-16R
Farrell, Michael 1944- CANR-23
Earlier sketch in CA 69-72
Farrell, Patricia
See Zelver, Patricia (Farrell)
Farrell, Patrick
See Odgers, Sally Farrell
Farrell, Robert T(homas) 1938- 93-96
Farrell, Sally
See Odgers, Sally Farrell
Farrell, Susan Caust 1944- 112
Farrell, Suzanne 1945(?)- 141
Farrell, Trace 1959- 185
Farrell, Warren (Thomas) 1943- CANR-120
Earlier sketch in CA 146
See also CLC 70
Farrell, William E. 1936(?)-1985
Obituary 115
Farrell-Beck, Jane 204
Farrelly, Bobby 1957- 173
See also AAYA 29
Farrelly, M(ark) John 1927- 13-16R
Farrelly, Peter (John) 1956- CANR-89
Earlier sketch in CA 127
See also AAYA 29
Farrelly, Robert
See Farrelly, Bobby
Farren, David
See McFerran, Douglass David
Farren, Mick 1943- CANR-88
Earlier sketch in CA 156
See also SFW 4
Farren, Richard J.
See Betjeman, John
Farren, Richard M.
See Betjeman, John
Farren, Robert 1909- .... CP 1
Farrer, Claire R(afferty) 1936- CANR-51
Earlier sketches in CA 65-68, CANR-10, 26
Farrer, (Bryan) David 1906-1983 ...... CANR-75
Obituary 109
Earlier sketch in CA 25-28R
Farrer, Katharine Dorothy (Newton)
1911- CANR-85
Earlier sketch in CA 5-8R
Farrer, Keith Thomas Henry 1916- 110
Farrer-Halls, Gill 1958- 170
Farrimond, John 1913- 102
Farrington, Benjamin 1891-1974 65-68
Obituary 53-56
See also SATA-Obit 20
Farrington, D. P.
See Farrington, David P.
Farrington, David P. 1944- CANR-86
Earlier sketch in CA 130
Farrington, (Mary) Elizabeth Pruett 1898-1984
Obituary 113
Farrington, (Roland) Gene 1931- 130
Farrington, Lisa E(dith) 1956- 238
Farrington, S(elwyn) Kip, Jr.
1904-1983 .... CANR-77
Obituary 109
Earlier sketch in CA 73-76
See also SATA 20
Farrington, Tim 184
Farris, Jack 1921-1998 129
Farris, John 1936- CANR-135
Earlier sketches in CA 101, CANR-72
See also HGG
Farris, Martin T(heodore) 1925- CANR-11
Earlier sketch in CA 21-24R
Farris, Paul L(eonard) 1919- 9-12R
Farris, William Wayne 1951- 150
Farrison, William Edward 1902-1985 .... 29-32R
Farriss, N(ancy) M(arguerite) 1938- 25-28R
Farrokhzad, Forugh
See Farrukhzad, Furugh
Farrokhzad, Forugh 1935-1967 .... EWL 3
See also PFS 21
Farrow, G(eorge) E(dward) 1862-1920 . CWRI 5
Farrow, J.
See Fonarow, Jerry
Farrow, James S.
See Tubb, E(dwin) C(harles)
Farrow, John
See Ferguson, Trevor
Farrow, Mia 1946- 166
Farrukhzad, Furugh 1935- .... WLIT 6
Farshtey, Greg(ory T.) 1965- 222
See also SATA 148

Cumulative Index 183 **Feder**

Farson, Daniel (Negley) 1927-1997 . CANR-89
Obituary ... 162
Earlier sketches in CA 93-96, CANR-16, 37
Farson, (James Scott) Negley 1890-1960
Obituary ... 93-96
Farstad, Arthur L(eonard) 1935- ... 109
Farthing, Alison 1936- ... 117
See also SATA 45
See also SATA-Brief 36
Farthing-Knight, Catherine 1933- ... 156
See also SATA 92
Faruque, Cathleen Jo ... 234
Farwell, Byron E. 1921-1999 ... CANR-47
Obituary ... 183
Earlier sketches in CA 13-16R, CANR-9
Farwell, Edie
See Farwell, Edith F.
Farwell, Edith F. 1960- ... 175
Farwell, George Michell 1911-1976 ... 21-24R
Obituary ... 69-72
Farwell, Loring C(hapman) 1915-
Brief entry ... 111
Farzan, Massud 1936- ... 53-56
Fasana, Paul James 1933- ... CANR-14
Earlier sketch in CA 37-40R
Fasching, Darrell J. 1944- ... CANR-94
Earlier sketch in CA 145
Faschinger, Lilian 1950- ... 166
Fasel, George W(illiam) 1938- ... 21-24R
Fasick, Adele M(ongan) 1930- ... CANR-54
Earlier sketch in CA 125
Fasold, Ralph W(illiam August) 1940- ... 29-32R
Fasolt, Constantin 1951- ... 139
Fass, Paula S. 1947- ... CANR-122
Brief entry ... 112
Earlier sketches in CA 129, CANR-66
Fassbinder, Rainer Werner
1946-1982 ... CANR-31
Obituary ... 106
Earlier sketch in CA 93-96
See also CLC 20
Fassett, James 1904-1986 ... CANR-75
Obituary ... 121
Earlier sketch in CA 49-52
Fassett, John D. 1926- ... 157
Fassler, Joan (Grace) 1931- ... 61-64
See also SATA 11
Fassmann, Heinz 1955- ... CANR-109
Earlier sketch in CA 151
Fast, Barbara 1924- ... 104
Fast, Howard (Melvin) 1914-2003 ... 181
Obituary ... 214
Earlier sketches in CA 1-4R, CANR-1, 33, 54, 75, 98, 140
Interview in ... CANR-33
Autobiographical Essay in ... 181
See also CAAS 18
See also AAYA 16
See also BPFB 1
See also CLC 23, 131
See also CMW 4
See also CN 1, 2, 3, 4, 5, 6, 7
See also CPW
See also DAM NOV
See also DLB 9
See also LATS 1:1
See also MAL 5
See also MTCW 2
See also MTFW 2005
See also RHW
See also SATA 7
See also SATA-Essay 107
See also TCWW 1, 2
See also YAW
Fast, Jonathan (David) 1948- ... CANR-34
Earlier sketch in CA 77-80
Fast, Julius 1919- ... CANR-27
Earlier sketches in CA 25-28R, CANR-11
Fastlife
See Grogan, Emmett
Fasulo, Michael 1963- ... 150
See also SATA 83
Fatchen, Max 1920- ... CANR-83
Earlier sketches in CA 25-28R, CANR-11, 28, 53
See also CWRI 5
See also SAAS 20
See also SATA 20, 84
Fate, Marilyn
See Collins, Paul
Fate, Terry 1949- ... 116
Fatemi, Nasrollah S(aifpour) 1910-1990 .. 77-80
Obituary ... 131
Father Goose
See Ghigna, Charles
Fathy, Hassan 1900-1989
Obituary ... 130
Fatigati, (Frances) Evelyn 1948- ... 77-80
See also SATA 24
Fatio, Louise 1904-1993 ... CANR-83
Earlier sketch in CA 37-40R
See also CWRI 5
See also SATA 6
Fatjo, Thomas Joseph, Jr. 1940- ... 107
Fatouros, A(rghyrios) A. 1932- ... 13-16R
Fatout, Paul 1897-1982 ... 21-24R
Fatt, Amelia 1943- ... 118
Fauber, Fernand
See Auberjonois, Fernand
Faucher, Real 1940- ... 101
Faucher, W. Thomas 1945- ... 57-60
Fauconnier, Gilles Raymond 1944- ... 212
Faught, C. Brad 1963- ... 236
Faulcon, Robert
See Holdstock, Robert P.
Faulhaber, Charles Bailey 1941- ... 53-56
Faulhaber, Martha 1926- ... 33-36R
See also SATA 7
Faulk, Anne O. ... 188
Faulk, Charles Johnson, Jr. 1916(?)-1990
Obituary ... 131
Faulk, John Henry 1913-1990 ... 102
Obituary ... 131
Faulk, Odie B. 1933- ... CANR-14
Earlier sketch in CA 25-28R
Faulkenburg, Marilyn T. 1943- ... 191
Faulkes, Anthony 1937- ... 138
Faulkner, Alex 1905(?)-1983
Obituary ... 109
Faulkner, Anne Irvin 1906- ... CANR-2
Earlier sketch in CA 1-4R
See also SATA 23
Faulkner, Charles H. 1937- ... 25-28R
Faulkner, Christopher G(raham) 1942- ... 125
Faulkner, Edwin J. 1900(?)-1987
Obituary ... 121
Faulkner, Elsie 1905-1995 ... 65-68
Faulkner, Frank
See Ellis, Edward S(ylvester)
Faulkner, Harold Underwood 1890-1968 . 1-4R
Obituary ... 103
Faulkner, Howard J. 1945- ... 135
Faulkner, John 1901-1963 ... CANR-1
Earlier sketch in CA 1-4R
Faulkner, Joseph E. 1928- ... 45-48
Faulkner, Nancy
See Faulkner, Anne Irvin
Faulkner, Peter 1933- ... CANR-20
Earlier sketches in CA 5-8R, CANR-3
Faulkner, Ray (Nelson) 1906- ... 5-8R
Faulkner, Trader 1930- ... 102
Faulkner, Virginia (Louise)
1913-1980 ... CANR-11
Earlier sketch in CA 65-68
Faulkner, (Herbert Winthrop) Waldron
1898-1979 ... 93-96
Obituary ... 85-88
Faulkner, William (Cuthbert)
1897-1962 ... CANR-33
Earlier sketch in CA 81-84
See also AAYA 7
See also AMW
See also AMWR 1
See also BPFB 1
See also BYA 5, 15
See also CDALB 1929-1941
See also CLC 1, 3, 6, 8, 9, 11, 14, 18, 28, 52, 68
See also DA
See also DA3
See also DAB
See also DAC
See also DAM MST, NOV
See also DLB 9, 11, 44, 102, 316
See also DLBD 2
See also DLBY 1986, 1997
See also EWL 3
See also EXPN
See also EXPS
See also GL 2
See also LAIT 2
See also LATS 1:1
See also LMFS 2
See also MAL 5
See also MTCW 1, 2
See also MTFW 2005
See also NFS 4, 8, 13
See also RGAL 4
See also RGSF 2
See also SSC 1, 35, 42
See also SSFS 2, 5, 6, 12
See also TCLC 141
See also TUS
See also WLC
Faulknor, Cliff(ord Vernon) 1913- ... CANR-83
Earlier sketches in CA 17-20R, CANR-8, 51
See also SATA 86
Faulks, Neville 1908-1985
Obituary ... 118
Faulks, Sebastian 1953- ... CANR-89
Earlier sketches in CA 131, CANR-58
See also CN 6, 7
See also DLB 207
Faunce, Roland Cleo 1905-1983 ... 1-4R
Faunce, William A(lden) 1928- ... 25-28R
Faunce-Brown, Daphne (Bridget) 1938- ... 115
Faupel, John F(rancis) 1906- ... 5-8R
Faure, Bernard ... 182
Faure, Lucie 1908-1977
Obituary ... 73-76
Faure, William C(aldwell), Jr. 1949- ... 109
Faurot, Albert 1914-1990 ... 77-80
Faurot, Jean H(iatt) 1911-1996 ... 29-32R
Faurot, Jeannette 1943- ... 106
Faurot, Ruth Marie 1916- ... 85-88
Fauset, Arthur Huff 1899-1983 ... 25-28R
Fauset, Jessie Redmon
1882(?)-1961 ... CANR-83
Earlier sketch in CA 109
See also AFAW 2
See also BLC 2
See also BW 1
See also CLC 19, 54
See also DAM MULT
See also DLB 51
See also FW
See also HR 1:2
See also LMFS 2
See also MAL 5
See also MAWW
Fausett, David 1950- ... 130
Fausold, Martin L. 1921- ... 21-24R
Fausset, Hugh I'Anson 1895-1965
Obituary ... 93-96
Faust, Barbie
See Burana, Lily
Faust, Christa 1969- ... 234
Faust, Clarence H(enry) 1901-1975
Obituary ... 57-60
Faust, Drew Gilpin 1947- ... 110
Faust, Frederick (Schiller)
1892-1944 ... CANR-143
Brief entry ... 108
Earlier sketch in CA 152
See also Brand, Max and
Dawson, Peter and
Frederick, John
See also DAM POP
See also DLB 256
See also TCLC 49
See also TUS
Faust, Irvin 1924- ... CANR-67
Earlier sketches in CA 33-36R, CANR-28
See also CLC 8
See also CN 1, 2, 3, 4, 5, 6, 7
See also DLB 2, 28, 218, 278
See also DLBY 1980
Faust, Jeff 1966- ... 167
Faust, John R. 1930- ... 151
Faust, Minister
See Azania, Malcolm
Faust, Naomi F(lowe) ... 61-64
Fausti, Remo P(hilip) 1917- ... 41-44R
Fausto-Sterling, Anne 1944- ... CANR-92
Earlier sketch in CA 137
Fauth, Robert T. 1916- ... 1-4R
Fautsko, Timothy F(rank) 1945- ... 85-88
Faux, Marian 1945- ... CANR-14
Earlier sketch in CA 81-84
Fava, Sylvia Fleis 1927- ... 115
Faverty, Frederic Everett 1902-1981 ... 45-48
Obituary ... 104
Favilla, Candice Lynn 1949- ... 139
Faville, David Ernest 1899-1970 ... 1-4R
Obituary ... 103
Favole, Robert J(ames) 1950- ... 196
See also SATA 125
Favreau, John
See Favreau, Jon
Favreau, Jon 1966- ... 226
Favret, Andrew G. 1925- ... 17-20R
Favretti, Rudy J(ohn) 1932- ... CANR-4
Earlier sketch in CA 53-56
Fawcett, Brian 1906- ... 102
Fawcett, Chris 1950- ... 107
Fawcett, Clara Hallard 1887-1983 ... CAP-1
Earlier sketch in CA 13-16
Fawcett, Claude W(eldon) 1911-1998 ... 49-52
Fawcett, Edgar 1847-1904 ... 183
See also DLB 202
Fawcett, F(rank) Dubrez 1891-1968 ... CAP-1
Earlier sketch in CA 9-10
Fawcett, J(ames) E(dmund) S(anford)
1913-1991 ... 97-100
Fawcett, Jan Alan 1934- ... 212
Fawcett, Ken(neth Richard) 1944- ... 104
Fawcett, Marion
See Sanderson, Sabina W(arren)
Fawcett, Millicent Garrett 1847-1929 ... 188
See also DLB 190
Fawcett, Quinn
See Yarbro, Chelsea Quinn
Fawcett, Robin P(owell) 1937- ... 119
Fawcett, Roger Knowlton 1909-1979
Obituary ... 89-92
Fawcett, Ron
See Harrison, M(ichael) John
Fawcett, Webster
See Albert, Harold A.
Fawdry, Marguerite 1912-1995 ... 135
Fawkes, Guy
See Benchley, Robert (Charles)
Fawkes, Richard (Brian) 1944- ... CANR-103
Earlier sketches in CA 103, CANR-20
Fax, Elton Clay 1909-1993 ... CANR-43
Earlier sketches in CA 13-16R, CANR-15
See also BW 2
See also SATA 25
Faxon, Alicia Craig 1931- ... CANR-53
Earlier sketches in CA 69-72, CANR-29
Faxon, Arba D. 1895(?)-1975
Obituary ... 61-64
Faxon, Lavinia
See Russ, Lavinia (Faxon)
Fay, Allen 1934- ... 123
Brief entry ... 118
Fay, Erica
See Stopes, Marie (Charlotte) Carmichael
Fay, Frederic L(eighton) 1890-1973 ... CAP-2
Earlier sketch in CA 21-22
Fay, Gerard (Francis Arthur)
1913-1968 ... CAP-1
Earlier sketch in CA 13-16
Fay, Gordon S(haw) 1912- ... 53-56
Fay, Jim 1934- ... 145
Fay, John 1921- ... 57-60
Fay, Julie 1951- ... 185
Fay, Laurel E. ... 218
Fay, Leo (Charles) 1920- ... 13-16R
Fay, Mary Helen
See Fagyas, Maria
Fay, Peter Ward 1924-2004 ... 57-60
Obituary ... 222
Fay, S(amuel) P(rescott), Jr. 1926- ... 89-92
Fay, Stanley
See Shulman, Fay Grissom Stanley
Fay, Stephen (Francis John) 1938- ... CANR-61
Earlier sketches in CA 25-28R, CANR-31
Fay, Terence J. 1932- ... 219
Fay, Theodore Sedgwick 1807-1898 ... DLB 202
Fay, Thomas A(rthur) 1927- ... 102
Faye, Jean-Pierre 1925- ... 102
See also EWL 3
Fayer, Mischa Harry 1902-1977 ... CANR-6
Earlier sketch in CA 1-4R
Fayer, Steve 1935- ... CANR-89
Earlier sketch in CA 132
Fayerweather, John 1922- ... CANR-1
Earlier sketch in CA 1-4R
Fazakas, Ray 1932- ... 101
Fazakerley, George Raymond 1921- ... 13-16R
Fazal, M(uhammad) A(bul) 1939- ... 29-32R
Fazio, James R. 1943- ... 230
Fazzano, Joseph E. 1929- ... 5-8R
Feagans, Lynne 1945- ... 117
Feagans, Raymond (John) 1953- ... 57-60
Feagin, Joe R(ichard) 1938- ... CANR-105
Earlier sketches in CA 37-40R, CANR-13, 46, 55
Feagles, Anita M(acRae) 1927- ... CANR-4
Earlier sketch in CA 1-4R
See also SATA 9
Feagles, Elizabeth
See Day, Beth (Feagles)
Feague, Mildred H. 1915- ... 29-32R
See also SATA 14
Feal-Deibe, Carlos 1935- ... 37-40R
Fear, David E. 1941- ... 53-56
Fear, Richard Arthur 1909- ... 125
Fear, Ypk fan der
See Post-Beukens, L(ipkje)
Fear, Ypk van der
See Post-Beukens, L(ipkje)
Fear Chanaidh
See Campbell, John Lorne
Fearing, Kenneth (Flexner)
1902-1961 ... CANR-59
Earlier sketch in CA 93-96
See also CLC 51
See also CMW 4
See also DLB 9
See also MAL 5
See also RGAL 4
Fearn, John Russell 1908-1960 ... 162
See also SFW 4
See also TCWW 1, 2
Fearnley, Jan 1965- ... SATA 153
Fearnley-Whittingstall, Jane 1939- ... CANR-90
Earlier sketch in CA 139
Fearon, George Edward 1901- ... CAP-1
Earlier sketch in CA 9-10
Fearon, John D(aniel) 1920- ... 37-40R
Fearon, Peter (Shaun) 1942- ... 29-32R
Fearrington, Ann (Peyton) 1945- ... 220
See also SATA 146
Fears, Gerald ... 81-84
Feather, John 1947- ... CANR-48
Earlier sketch in CA 122
Feather, Leonard G(eoffrey) 1914-1994 ... 61-64
Obituary ... 146
Feather, Norman 1904-1978
Obituary ... 111
Feather, Norman T(homas) 1930- ... 73-76
Featherstone, D.
See Warren, David
Featherstone, Helen 1944- ... 102
Featherstone, Joseph (Luke) 1940- ... 33-36R
Featherstonehaugh, Francis
See MacGregor, Alasdair Alpin (Douglas)
Feaver, George (Arthur) 1937- ... 29-32R
Feaver, J(ohn) Clayton 1911-1995 ... CAP-2
Earlier sketch in CA 25-28
Feaver, Vicki 1943- ... 129
See also CWP
Feaver, William Andrew 1942- ... 103
February, Vernie A.
See February, Vernon Alexander
February, Vernon Alexander 1938- ... 129
Fecamps, Elise
See Creasey, John
Fecher, Charles A(dam) 1917- ... 81-84
Fecher, Constance
See Heaven, Constance (Christina)
Fechter, Alyce Shinn 1909-1983 ... CAP-1
Earlier sketch in CA 13-16
Fecit
See Barclay, Robert
Feck, Luke 1935- ... 69-72
Fedde, Norman A(ndreas) 1914-1989 ... 5-8R
Fedden, Henry (Romilly) 1908-1977 ... 9-12R
See also CP 1
Fedden, Robin
See Fedden, Henry (Romilly)
Fedder, Edwin H(ersh) 1929- ... 37-40R
Fedder, Norman J(oseph) 1934- ... CANR-104
Earlier sketches in CA 21-24R, CANR-9, 25, 50
Fedder, Ruth 1907- ... CANR-2
Earlier sketch in CA 5-8R
Feddersen, Connie 1948- ... 198
See also Finch, Carol
Feder, Bernard 1924- ... CANR-15
Earlier sketch in CA 33-36R
Feder, Chris Welles 1938- ... 149
See also SATA 81
Feder, Ernest 1913-1984 ... 37-40R
Feder, Fritz
See Soyfer, Jura
Feder, Harriet K. 1928- ... SATA 73
Feder, Jane 1940- ... 93-96
Feder, Jose 1917- ... 105
Feder, Karah (Tal) 1920- ... 17-20R
Feder, Lillian ... CANR-110
Earlier sketch in CA 41-44R
Feder, Martin E(lliott) 1951- ... 145

Feder, Paula (Kurzband) 1935- ... 105
See also SATA 26
Federbusch, Simon
See Federbush, Simon
Federbush, Arnold 1935- ... 104
Federbush, Simon 1892(?)-1969
Obituary ... 115
Federico, Ronald Charles 1941- ... 89-92
Federman, Raymond 1928- ... 208
Earlier sketches in CA 17-20R, CANR-10, 43, 83, 108
Autobiographical Essay in ... 208
See also CAAS 8
See also CLC 6, 47
See also CN 3, 4, 5, 6
See also DLBY 1980
Federoff, Alexander 1927(?)-1979
Obituary ... 89-92
Federspiel, J(uerg) F. 1931- ... 146
See also CLC 42
Fedin, Konstantin A(lexandrovich)
1892-1977 ... CANR-28
Obituary ... 73-76
Earlier sketch in CA 81-84
See also Fedin, Konstantin Aleksandrovich
Fedin, Konstantin Aleksandrovich
See Fedin, Konstantin A(lexandrovich)
See also DLB 272
See also EWL 3
Fedler, Fred 1940- ... 97-100
Fedoroff, Alexander 1927-1979 ... CANR-5
Earlier sketch in CA 1-4R
Fedoroff, Nina (V.) 1942- ... 143
Fedorov, Innokentii Vasil'evich
See Omulevsky, Innokentii Vasil'evich
Fedorov, Yevgeny Konstantinovich 1910-1981
Obituary ... 106
Fedorowicz, J(an) K(rzysztof) 1949- ... 130
Feduccia, (John) Alan 1943- ... 124
Fedullo, Mick 1949- ... 230
Fedyshyn, Oleh S(ylvester) 1928- ... 49-52
Fee, Elizabeth 1946- ... 126
Fee, Gordon D(onald) 1934- ... 117
Feegel, John R(ichard) 1932-2003 ... CANR-9
Obituary ... 220
Earlier sketch in CA 57-60
Feehan, Christine ... 237
Feeley, Gregory 1955- ... 135
Feeley, Kathleen 1929- ... 33-36R
Feeley, Malcolm M(cCollum) 1942- ... 142
Brief entry ... 105
Feeley, Pat(ricia Falk) 1941- ... 81-84
Feelings, Muriel (Lavita Grey) 1938- ... 93-96
See also BW 1
See also CLR 5
See also MAICYA 1, 2
See also SAAS 8
See also SATA 16
Feelings, Thomas 1933-2003 ... CANR-25
Obituary ... 222
Earlier sketch in CA 49-52
See also Feelings, Tom
See also BW 1
See also MAICYA 1, 2
See also MAICYAS 1
See also SATA 8
See also SATA-Obit 148
See also YAW
Feelings, Tom
See Feelings, Thomas
See also AAYA 25
See also CLR 5, 58
See also SAAS 19
See also SATA 69
Feely, Terence (John) 1928-2000 ... CANR-25
Obituary ... 189
Earlier sketch in CA 106
Feenberg, Eugene 1906-1977
Obituary ... 73-76
Feeney, Don J(oseph), Jr. 1948- ... 204
Feeney, Leonard 1897-1978 ... 81-84
Obituary ... 77-80
Feeney, Stephanie S(inger) 1939- ... 118
Feenstra, Henry John 1936- ... 37-40R
Feerick, John D(avid) 1936- ... 69-72
Fegan, Camilla 1939- ... 21-24R
Fegan, Patrick W. 1947- ... 111
Fegely, Thomas D(avid) 1941- ... 97-100
Feherty, David 1958- ... 212
Fehl, Philipp P(inhas) 1920- ... 33-36R
Fehler, Gene 1940- ... SATA 74
Fehr, Howard Franklin 1901-1982
Obituary ... 106
Fehr, Richard 1920- ... 147
Fehren, Henry 1920- ... CANR-9
Earlier sketch in CA 21-24R
Fehrenbach, T(heodore) R(eed, Jr.)
1925- ... CANR-1
Earlier sketch in CA 1-4R
See also SATA 33
Fehrenbacher, Don E. 1920-1997 ... CANR-2
Obituary ... 163
Earlier sketch in CA 1-4R
Fehrman, Carl (Abraham Daniel)
1915- ... CANR-82
Brief entry ... 113
Earlier sketch in CA 133
Feibes, Walter 1928- ... 53-56
Feibleman, James K(ern) 1904-1987 . CANR-22
Earlier sketches in CA 5-8R, CANR-7
See also AITN 2
Feibleman, Peter S(teinam) 1930- ... 110
Brief entry ... 108
Interview in ... CA-110
Feiden, Karyn L. 1954- ... 140
Feider, Paul 1951- ... CANR-35
Earlier sketch in CA 114
Feied, Frederick (James) 1925- ... 13-16R
Feierman, Steven 1940- ... 53-56
Feifel, Herman 1915-2003 ... 101
Obituary ... 212
Feifer, George 1934- ... CANR-105
Earlier sketch in CA 148
Feiffer, Jules (Ralph) 1929- ... CANR-129
Earlier sketches in CA 17-20R, CANR-30, 59
Interview in ... CANR-30
See also AAYA 3, 62
See also CAD
See also CD 5, 6
See also CLC 2, 8, 64
See also DAM DRAM
See also DLB 7, 44
See also MTCW 1
See also SATA 8, 61, 111, 157
Feig, Barbara Krane 1937- ... 104
See also SATA 34
Feig, Barry 1948- ... 162
Feig, Douglas 1946- ... 114
Feig, Paul ... 213
Feige, Hermann Albert Otto Maximilian
See Traven, B.
Feigelson, Naomi
See Chase, Naomi Feigelson
Feigen, Brenda 1944- ... 190
Feigen, Richard 1930- ... 197
Feigenbaum, Edward A(lbert) 1936- ... 134
Feigenbaum, Lawrence H. 1918- ... 25-28R
Feigert, Frank B(rook) 1937- ... CANR-19
Earlier sketches in CA 53-56, CANR-4
Feigl, Herbert 1902-1988 ... CAP-1
Earlier sketch in CA 13-14
Feigon, Lee (Nathan) 1945- ... 117
Fei-Kan, Li
See Li Fei-kan
Feikema, Feike
See Manfred, Frederick (Feikema)
Feil, Hila 1942- ... 37-40R
See also SATA 12
Feild, Reshad 1934- ... CANR-25
Earlier sketch in CA 69-72
Feilding, Charles (Rudolph) 1902- ... CAP-2
Earlier sketch in CA 25-28
Feilen, John
See May, Julian
Feiler, Bruce 1964- ... CANR-103
Earlier sketch in CA 145
Feiler, Seymour 1919- ... 41-44R
Fein, Albert 1930-1989 ... CANR-80
Obituary ... 128
Earlier sketch in CA 115
Fein, Ellen ... CANR-118
Earlier sketch in CA 159
Fein, Helen 1934- ... 110
Fein, Irving A(shley) 1911- ... 69-72
Fein, John M(orton) 1922- ... 120
Fein, Judith 1941- ... 107
Fein, Leah Gold ... 49-52
Fein, Leonard J. 1934- ... 13-16R
Fein, Rashi 1926- ... 122
Fein, Richard J(acob) 1929- ... 45-48
Feinberg, Abraham L. 1899-1986 ... 9-12R
Obituary ... 120
Feinberg, Barbara ... 231
Feinberg, Barbara Jane 1938- ... CANR-45
Earlier sketches in CA 106, CANR-22
See also Feinberg, Barbara Silberdick
See also SATA 58
Feinberg, Barbara Silberdick ... CANR-101
See also Feinberg, Barbara Jane
See also SATA 123
Feinberg, Barry (Vincent) 1938- ... 29-32R
Feinberg, Beatrice Cynthia Freeman
1915(?)-1988 ... CANR-29
Obituary ... 126
Earlier sketch in CA 81-84
See also RHW
Feinberg, Charles E. 1899-1988 ... 176
See also DLB 187
See also DLBY 1988
Feinberg, David B. 1956-1994 ... 135
Obituary ... 147
See also CLC 59
Feinberg, Gerald 1933-1992 ... CANR-12
Earlier sketch in CA 25-28R
Feinberg, Gloria (Granditer) 1923-
Brief entry ... 109
Feinberg, Hilda ... 49-52
Feinberg, Joel 1926-2004 ... CANR-45
Obituary ... 225
Earlier sketches in CA 17-20R, CANR-22
Feinberg, Lawrence B(ernard) 1940- ... 73-76
Feinberg, Leonard 1914- ... CANR-2
Earlier sketch in CA 5-8R
Feinberg, Leslie 1949- ... 159
See also GLL 2
Feinberg, Mortimer R(obert) 1922- ... 102
Feinberg, Renee 1940- ... CANR-42
Earlier sketch in CA 112
Feinberg, Richard 1947- ... CANR-116
Earlier sketch in CA 158
Feinberg, Rosa Castro 1939- ... 225
Feinberg, Walter 1937- ... 57-60
Feinbloom, Deborah Heller 1940- ... 65-68
Feinbloom, Richard I. 1935- ... 135
Feind, Barthold 1678-1721 ... DLB 168
Feiner, Yechiel
See Ka-Tzetnik 135633
Feingold, Ben(jamin) F(ranklin)
1900-1982 ... 97-100
Obituary ... 106
Feingold, Eugene (Neil) 1931-2002 .. CANR-22
Earlier sketch in CA 17-20R
Feingold, Henry L(eo) 1931- ... CANR-56
Earlier sketches in CA 29-32R, CANR-31
Feingold, Jessica 1910- ... CAP-2
Earlier sketch in CA 25-28
Feingold, Michael 1945- ... 89-92
Feingold, S. Norman 1914-2005 ... CANR-56
Obituary ... 236
Earlier sketches in CA 13-16R, CANR-13, 30
Feininger, Andreas (Bernhard Lyonel)
1906-1999 ... CANR-20
Earlier sketch in CA 85-88
Feininger, Lyonel 1871-1956 ... 149
Feinman, Jay (M.) 1951- ... 191
Feinman, Jeffrey 1943- ... CANR-10
Earlier sketch in CA 65-68
Feinsilver, Alexander 1910-1987 ... 13-16R
Feinsilver, Lillian Mermin 1917- ... 29-32R
Feinsinger, Nathan Paul 1902-1983
Obituary ... 111
Feinstein, Alan (Shawn) 1931- ... 25-28R
Feinstein, David 1946- ... 135
Feinstein, Edward 1954- ... 225
Feinstein, Elaine 1930- ... CANR-121
Earlier sketches in CA 69-72, CANR-31, 68
See also CAAS 1
See also CLC 36
See also CN 3, 4, 5, 6, 7
See also CP 2, 3, 4, 5, 6, 7
See also CWP
See also DLB 14, 40
See also MTCW 1
Feinstein, George W(illiamson) 1913- ... 73-76
Feinstein, John 1956- ... CANR-108
Earlier sketch in CA 133
See also AAYA 31
See also SATA 163
Feinstein, Lloyd L(eonard) 1941- ... 113
Feinstein, Moshe 1895-1986
Obituary ... 118
Feinstein, Otto 1930- ... 104
Feinstein, Roni 1954- ... 134
Feinstein, Sascha 1963- ... CANR-137
Earlier sketch in CA 165
Feinstein, Sherman C. 1923- ... CANR-7
Earlier sketch in CA 57-60
Feintuch, Burt H. 1949- ... 124
Feirstein, Bruce 1953- ... 108
Feirstein, Frederick 1940- ... CANR-1
Earlier sketch in CA 45-48
See also CAAS 11
See also DLB 282
Feis, Herbert 1893-1972 ... CAP-1
Obituary ... 33-36R
Earlier sketch in CA 9-10
Feis, Ruth (Stanley-Brown) 1892-1981 .. CAP-2
Earlier sketch in CA 19-20
Feis, William B. 1963- ... 239
Feise, Ernst 1884-1966 ... CAP-2
Earlier sketch in CA 17-18
Feiss, Hugh (Bernard) 1939- ... 209
Feiss, Paul Louis 1875-1952 ... 204
See also DLB 187
Feist, Aubrey (Noel Lydston) 1903- ... 41-44R
Feist, Gene 1930- ... 129
Feist, Raymond E(lias) 1945- ... CANR-104
Earlier sketch in CA 154
See also FANT
See also SFW 4
See also SUFW 2
Feit, E(wald) Edward 1924- ... CANR-10
Earlier sketch in CA 5-8R
Feitel, Donald G. 1925(?)-1976
Obituary ... 65-68
Feith, Herbert 1930- ... CANR-47
Earlier sketch in CA 1-4R
Feitlowitz, Marguerite ... 205
Feiwel, George R(ichard) 1929- ... CANR-23
Earlier sketches in CA 17-20R, CANR-8
Feiwel, Raphael Joseph 1907-1985 ... 129
Obituary ... 117
Fejes, Claire 1920- ... CANR-13
Earlier sketch in CA 21-24R
Fejes, Endre 1923- ... 25-28R
Fejto, Francois (Philippe) 1909- ... 29-32R
Feke, Gilbert David ... CLC 65
Fekete, John 1946- ... CANR-72
Earlier sketch in CA 129
Fekrat, M. Ali 1937- ... 45-48
Felber, Lynette ... 228
Felber, Ron ... 236
Felber, Stanley B. 1932- ... 77-80
Feld, Bernard (David III) 1947- ... 125
Feld, Bernard T(aub) 1919-1993 ... 104
Feld, Ellen F. 1961- ... 239
Feld, Michael 1938- ... 33-36R
Feld, Rose Caroline 1895-1981
Obituary ... 105
Feld, Ross 1947-2001 ... CANR-88
Obituary ... 197
Earlier sketches in CA 33-36R, CANR-16
Feld, Werner (Joachim) 1910-1998 .. CANR-24
Earlier sketches in CA 21-24R, CANR-8
Feldbaum, Eleanor G. 1935- ... 117
Feldberg, Michael 1943- ... 113
Feldenkrais, Moshe (Pinchas)
1904-1984 ... 73-76
Felder, David W. 1945- ... 136
Felder, Paul
See Wellen, Edward (Paul)
Felder, Raoul Lionel 1934- ... 33-36R
Felderman, Eric 1944- ... CANR-46
Earlier sketch in CA 69-72
Feldherr, Andrew 1963- ... 193
Feldhusen, John F. 1926- ... 141
Feldkamp, Fred 1915(?)-1981
Obituary ... 105
Feldkamp, Phyllis ... 102
Feldman, Abraham J(ehiel) 1893-1977 ... 81-84
Obituary ... 73-76
Feldman, Alan 1945- ... CANR-13
Earlier sketch in CA 73-76
Feldman, Alfred 1923- ... 208
Feldman, Anne (Rodgers) 1939- ... 73-76
See also SATA 19
Feldman, Annette (Gerber)
1913-1980(?) ... CANR-34
Earlier sketch in CA 69-72
Feldman, Burton E. 1926-2003 ... CANR-107
Obituary ... 212
Earlier sketch in CA 33-36R
Feldman, Daniel L(ee) 1949- ... 131
Feldman, David Lewis 1951- ... 140
Feldman, Edmund Burke 1924- ... 33-36R
Feldman, Edwin B(arry) 1925- ... CANR-2
Earlier sketch in CA 5-8R
Feldman, Egal 1925- ... CANR-130
Earlier sketches in CA 125, CANR-111
Feldman, Elane ... 147
See also SATA 79
Feldman, Ellen (Bette) 1941- ... CANR-142
Earlier sketches in CA 97-100, CANR-18, 39
Feldman, Elliot S. 1946- ... 221
Feldman, Gayle 1951- ... 146
Feldman, George J(ay) 1904-1994 ... CAP-1
Earlier sketch in CA 13-14
Feldman, Gerald D(onald) 1937- ... CANR-52
Earlier sketches in CA 21-24R, CANR-9, 27
Feldman, Herbert (H. S.) 1910- ... 29-32R
Feldman, Irving (Mordecai) 1928- ... CANR-1
Earlier sketch in CA 1-4R
See also CLC 7
See also CP 1, 2, 3, 4, 5, 6, 7
See also DLB 169
See also TCLE 1:1
Feldman, Kenneth A. 1937- ... 29-32R
Feldman, Lawrence H. 1942- ... 218
Feldman, Leon A(ryeh) 1921- ... CANR-16
Earlier sketch in CA 97-100
Feldman, Leonard 1927- ... 69-72
Feldman, Leslie ... AITN 1
Feldman, Louis H(arry) 1926- ... 53-56
Feldman, Lynne B. 1956- ... 138
Feldman, M(aurice) P(hilip) 1933- ... 41-44R
Feldman, Marty 1934(?)-1982 ... 110
Obituary ... 108
Feldman, Noah (R.) 1970- ... 227
Feldman, Paula R. 1948- ... CANR-109
Earlier sketch in CA 128
Feldman, Richard 1949- ... 128
Feldman, Robert A.
See Feldman, Robert Alan
Feldman, Robert Alan 1953- ... 123
Feldman, Ruth 1911- ... CANR-57
Earlier sketches in CA 106, CANR-31
Feldman, Ruth Duskin 1934- ... CANR-43
Earlier sketch in CA 119
Feldman, Samuel Nathan 1931- ... 25-28R
Feldman, Sandor S. 1891(?)-1973
Obituary ... 41-44R
Feldman, Saul D(aniel) 1943- ... 41-44R
Feldman, Sidney 1902(?)-1986
Obituary ... 121
Feldman, Silvia (Dash) 1928- ... 97-100
Feldman, Sol(omon) E. 1933- ... 25-28R
Feldman, Sophie 1930-1978
Obituary ... 108
Feldman, Stephen L. 1946-1990
Obituary ... 132
Feldmann, Susan Judith 1928-1969
Obituary ... 104
Feldmeir, Daryle M(atthew) 1923-1987 ... 73-76
Obituary ... 122
Feldon, Leah 1944- ... 97-100
Feldstein, Martin S(tuart) 1939- ... 73-76
Feldstein, Paul J(oseph) 1933- ... 89-92
Feldstein, Stuart A(lan) 1948- ... 113
Feldt, Allan Gunnar 1932- ... 41-44R
Felдzamen, A(lvin) N(orman) 1931- ... 25-28R
Felheim, Marvin 1914-1979 ... 1-4R
Felice, Cynthia 1942- ... CANR-56
Earlier sketch in CA 107
See also SFW 4
Feliciano, Hector 1952(?)- ... 172
See also HW 2
Felinto (Barbosa de Lima), Marilene 1957- . 146
Felipe, Carlos 1911-1975 ... DLB 305
Felipe, Leon 1884-1968 ... 174
See also DLB 108
See also HW 2
Felix
See Vincent, Felix
Felix, Antonia ... 200
Felix, Charles Reis 1923- ... 210
Felix, Christopher
See McCargar, James (Goodrich)
Felix, David 1921- ... CANR-94
Earlier sketch in CA 45-48
Felix, Jennie
See Saxton, Judith
Felix-Tchicaya, Gerald
See Tchicaya, Gerald Felix
Felkenes, George T(heodore) 1930- ... CANR-8
Earlier sketch in CA 57-60
Felker, Clay S(chuette) 1925- ... 73-76
Felker, Evelyn H. 1933- ... 57-60
Felker, Jere L. 1934- ... 21-24R
Felknor, Bruce L(ester) 1921- ... 21-24R
Fell, Alison 1944- ... CANR-112
Earlier sketch in CA 156
See also CWP
Fell, Barry
See Fell, H(oward) Barraclough
Fell, Derek (John) 1939- ... CANR-50
Earlier sketches in CA 108, CANR-25
Fell, H(oward) Barraclough 1917-1994 . 33-36R
Obituary ... 164

Cumulative Index **185** **Fergusson**

Fell, H. Barry
See Fell, H(oward) Barraclough
Fell, James E(dward), Jr. 1944- 107
Fell, John L(ouis) 1927- 53-56
Fell, Joseph P(hineas) III 1931- CANR-6
Earlier sketch in CA 13-16R
Fell, Peter John 1941- 214
Fellig, Arthur H.
See Weegee
Fellig, Usher H.
See Weegee
Fellini, Federico 1920-1993 .... CANR-33
Obituary 143
Earlier sketch in CA 65-68
See also CLC 16, 85
Fellman, Gordon 1934- 53-56
Fellman, Michael (Dinion) 1943- ... CANR-105
Earlier sketch in CA 45-48
Fellmeth, Robert C(harles) 1945- CANR-2
Earlier sketch in CA 49-52
Fellner, William John 1905-1983 .... CANR-2
Obituary 110
Earlier sketch in CA 1-4R
Fellowes, Anne
See Mantle, Winifred (Langford)
Fellowes, Julian 1950- 214
Fellowes-Gordon, Ian (Douglas)
1921- CANR-10
Earlier sketch in CA 5-8R
Fellows, Brian John 1936- 25-28R
Fellows, Catherine .... RHW
Fellows, Donald Keith 1920- 41-44R
Fellows, Hugh P. 1915- 37-40R
Fellows, Jay 1940- CANR-11
Earlier sketch in CA 61-64
Fellows, Lawrence (Perry) 1924-2000 49-52
Obituary 189
Fellows, Malcolm Stuart 1924- 9-12R
Fellows, Muriel H. 53-56
See also SATA 10
Fellows, Oscar L. 1943- CANR-138
Earlier sketch in CA 174
Fellows, Otis (Edward) 1908-1993 ..... CANR-1
Obituary 141
Earlier sketch in CA 1-4R
Fellows, Richard A(stley) 1947- CANR-102
Earlier sketches in CA 121, CANR-47
Fellows, Warren 1953- 238
Fellows, Will 229
Felltham, Owen 1602(?)-1668 .... DLB 126, 151
Felman, Shoshana 1942- CANR-144
Earlier sketch in CA 162
See also DLB 246
Felmly, Lloyd McPherson 1894-1984
Obituary 112
Felperin, Howard (Michael) 1941- 136
Fels, Ludwig 1946- 177
See also DLB 75
Fels, Rendigs 1917- 37-40R
Felsen, Henry Gregor 1916-1995 .... CANR-1
Obituary 180
Earlier sketch in CA 1-4R
See also CLC 17
See also SAAS 2
See also SATA 1
Felsenfeld, Daniel 238
Felsenstein, Walter 1901-1975
Obituary 111
Felsenthal, Carol 1949- CANR-90
Earlier sketch in CA 108
Felsher, Howard D. 1927- 17-20R
Felske, Coerte V. W. 1960- 166
Felski, Rita .... CLC 65
Felstein, Ivor 1933- 41-44R
Felstiner, L(ouis) John, Jr. 1936- CANR-93
Earlier sketch in CA 45-48
Felstiner, Mary Lowenthal 1941- 159
Felt, Jeremy P(ollard) 1930- 21-24R
Felt, Margaret Elley 1917- 9-12R
Feltenstein, Arlene (H.) 1934- 190
See also SATA 119
Felter, Emma K. (Schroeder)
1896-1986 .... CAP-1
Earlier sketch in CA 13-16
Felton, Bruce 1946- 65-68
Felton, Cornelius Conway 1807-1862 ... DLB 1, 235
Felton, D(ebbie) 1964- 191
Felton, Harold William 1902-1991 .... CANR-1
Earlier sketch in CA 1-4R
See also SATA 1
Felton, John Richard 1917- 89-92
Felton, Keith Spencer 1942- 181
Felton, Ronald Oliver 1909- CANR-85
Earlier sketches in CA 9-12R, CANR-3
See also CWRI 5
See also SATA 3
Felton, Sandra 1935- CANR-96
Earlier sketches in CA 120, CANR-45
Feltrinelli, Carlo 1962- 237
Felts, Shirley 1934- .... SATA 33
Feltskog, E(lmer) N. 1935- 37-40R
Feltwell, John 1948- 142
Felver, Charles S(tanley) 1916- 33-36R
Felver, Chris 1946- 164
Fel'zen, Iurii
See Freidenshtein, Nikolai Berngardovich
See also DLB 317
Femiano, Samuel D. 1932- 21-24R
Femina, Jerry Della
See Della Femina, Jerry
Fen, Elisaveta
See Jackson, Lydia
Fenady, Andrew J. 1928- CANR-13
Earlier sketch in CA 77-80
Fenander, Elliot W(atkins) 1938- 21-24R
Fenberg, Matilda 1888(?)-1977
Obituary 73-76
Fenby, Eric (William) 1906-1997 .... 25-28R
Fenby, Jonathan 1942- 173
Fendell, Bob 1925- 57-60
Fendelman, Helaine (Woll) 1942- .. CANR-143
Earlier sketch in CA 69-72
Fenderson, Lewis H., Jr. 1907-1983 106
Obituary 111
See also SATA 47
See also SATA-Obit 37
Fendrich, James Max 1938- 155
Fenelon, Fania 1918-1983 77-80
Obituary 111
Fenelon, Francois de Pons de Salignac de la
Mothe- 1651-1715 .... DLB 268
See also EW 3
See also GFL Beginnings to 1789
Fenelon, Kevin G(erard) 1898-1983 73-76
Obituary 109
Feng, Chin
See Liu, Sydney (Chieh)
Feng, Jicai 1942- 164
See also Feng Jicai
Fenger, Henning Johannes Hauch 1921- . 73-76
Feng Jicai
See Feng, Jicai
See also CWW 2
Fenical, Marlin Edward 1907-1983
Obituary 110
Fenichel, Carol Hansen 1935- 119
Fenichell, Stephen 1956- CANR-120
Earlier sketch in CA 108
Fenick, Barbara 1951- 118
Fenik, Bernard Carl 1934- 122
Fenin, George N(icolaievich) 1916- 9-12R
Fenlon, Dick 1930- 89-92
Fenlon, Paul Edward 1921- 13-16R
Fenn, Charles (Henry) 1907- 9-12R
Fenn, Dan H(untington), Jr. 1923- CANR-1
Earlier sketch in CA 1-4R
Fenn, Elizabeth A. 1959- CANR-115
Earlier sketch in CA 115
Fenn, Harry 1837-1911 .... DLB 188
Fenn, Henry Courtenay 1894-1978
Obituary 81-84
Fenn, Lionel
See Grant, Charles L(ewis)
Fennario, David 1947- 181
See also CD 5, 6
See also DLB 60
Fennell, Francis L(e Roy), Jr. 1942- ... CANR-39
Earlier sketch in CA 116
Fennell, John (Lister Illingworth)
1918-1992 .... CANR-19
Obituary 139
Earlier sketches in CA 1-4R, CANR-1
Fennell, William Oscar 1916- 101
Fennelly, Beth Ann 1971- 233
Fennelly, Catherine 1918- 37-40R
Fennelly, John F(auntleroy) 1899-1974
Obituary 53-56
Fennelly, Parker W. 1891-1988
Obituary 125
Fennelly, Tony 1945- CANR-111
Earlier sketches in CA 119, CANR-43
Fennema, Owen Richard 1929- CANR-3
Earlier sketch in CA 49-52
Fenner, Carol (Elizabeth)
1929-2002 .... CANR-57
Obituary 204
Earlier sketches in CA 5-8R, CANR-3
See also BYA 11
See also SAAS 24
See also SATA 7, 89
See also SATA-Obit 132
Fenner, Dudley 1558-1587(?) .... DLB 236
Fenner, H(arry) Wolcott 1911-1972 .... CAP-2
Obituary 37-40R
Earlier sketch in CA 33-36
Fenner, James 1923- 37-40R
Fenner, James R.
See Tubb, E(dwin) C(harles)
Fenner, Kay Toy CAP-1
Earlier sketch in CA 9-10
Fenner, Mildred Sandison 1910-1985 ... 33-36R
Fenner, Phyllis R(eid) 1899-1982 .... CANR-2
Obituary 106
Earlier sketch in CA 5-8R
See also SATA 1
See also SATA-Obit 29
Fenner, Theodore (Lincoln) 1919- 37-40R
Fennimore, Keith John 1917- 57-60
Fenno, Jack
See Calisher, Hortense
Fenno, Jenny 1765(?)-1803(?) .... DLB 200
Fenno, John 1751-1798 .... DLB 43
Fenno, R(ichard) Francis, Jr. 1926- 5-8R
Fenoglio, Beppe 1922-1963 .... DLB 177
See also EWL 3
Fenollosa, Ernest (Francisco)
1853-1908 .... TCLC 91
Fensch, Edwin A. 1903-1995 .... CAP-1
Earlier sketch in CA 13-16
Fensch, Thomas 1943- CANR-114
Earlier sketches in CA 25-28R, CANR-11, 29
Fenster, Robert 1946- CANR-32
Earlier sketch in CA 113
Fenster, Valmai (Ruth) Kirkham 1939-1984 . 110
Obituary 114
Fensterheim, Herbert 1921- 112
Fenstermaker, J(oseph) Van 1933- 29-32R
Fenten, Barbara D(oris) 1935- CANR-5
Earlier sketch in CA 33-36
See also SATA 26
Fenten, D(onald) X. 1932- CANR-5
Earlier sketch in CA 33-36R
See also SATA 4
Fenton, Alexander 1929- 131
Fenton, Carroll Lane 1900-1969 .... CANR-6
Obituary 29-32R
Earlier sketch in CA 1-4R
See also SATA 5
Fenton, Clyde 1901-1982
Obituary 106
Fenton, Edward 1917-1995 .... CANR-85
Obituary 151
Earlier sketches in CA 9-12R, CANR-13, 34
See also BYA 13
See also CWRI 5
See also SATA 7
See also SATA-Obit 89
Fenton, Frank 1903-1971
Obituary 33-36R
Fenton, Freda
See Rowland, D(onald) S(ydney)
Fenton, Geoffrey 1539(?)-1608 .... DLB 136
Fenton, James Martin 1949- CANR-108
Earlier sketch in CA 102
See also CLC 32, 209
See also CP 2, 3, 4, 5, 6, 7
See also DLB 40
See also PFS 11
Fenton, John C(harles) 1921- CAP-1
Earlier sketch in CA 9-10
Fenton, John H(arold) 1921- 37-40R
Fenton, John Y(oung) 1933- 53-56
Fenton, Joseph Clifford 1906- 5-8R
Fenton, Julia
See Fenton, Robert L.
Fenton, Kate 1954- 141
Fenton, M(elville) Brockett 1943- ... CANR-142
Earlier sketch in CA 144
Fenton, Mildred Adams 1899-1995 77-80
See also SATA 21
Fenton, Robert L. 1929- 135
Fenton, Shane
See Stardust, Alvin
Fenton, Sophia Harvati 1914- 33-36R
Fenton, Thomas Patrick 1943- 89-92
Fenton, Thomas Trail 1930- 102
Fenton, William N(elson) 1908- 93-96
Fentress, John Simmons 1925(?)-1981
Obituary 104
Fenvessy, Stanley J(ohn) 1918- 106
Fenwick, Charles G(hequiere) 1880-1973
Obituary 41-44R
Fenwick, Gillian 182
Fenwick, Kay
See Bean, Keith F(enwick)
Fenwick, (Ian Graham) Keith 1941- 102
Fenwick, Millicent Hammond
1910-1992 .... CANR-80
Obituary 139
Earlier sketch in CA 112
Fenwick, Patti
See Grider, Dorothy
Fenwick, Sheridan 1942- 69-72
Fenwick-Owen, Roderic (Franklin Rawnsley)
1921- 129
Brief entry 111
Fenyvesi, Charles 1937- 102
Feofanov, Dmitry N. 1957- 189
Feola, Jose (Maria) 1926- 69-72
Feraca, Stephen E. 1934-1999 213
Feraoun, Mouloud 1913-1962 .... EWL 3
Feravolo, Rocco Vincent 1922- CANR-1
Earlier sketch in CA 1-4R
See also SATA 10
Ferazani, Larry 1938- 61-64
Ferber, Andrew 1935- 53-56
Ferber, Edna 1887-1968 .... CANR-105
Obituary 25-28R
Earlier sketches in CA 5-8R, CANR-68
See also AITN 1
See also CLC 18, 93
See also DLB 9, 28, 86, 266
See also MAL 5
See also MTCW 1, 2
See also MTFW 2005
See also RGAL 4
See also RHW
See also SATA 7
See also TCWW 1, 2
Ferber, Elizabeth 1967- 228
Ferber, Ellen 1939- 102
Ferber, Robert 1922- 37-40R
Ferder, Fran 217
Ferderber-Salz, Bertha 1902-
Ferdinand, Theodore N(ichols)
1929-1992 .... 21-24R
Ferdinand, Vallery III
See Salaam, Kalamu ya
Ferdon, Edwin N(elson), Jr. 1913-2002 . 21-24R
Ferdowsi, Abu'l Qasem 940-1020(?)
See Firdawsi, Abu al-Qasim
See also RGWL 2, 3
Ferejohn, John A(rthur) 1944- 53-56
Ferencz, Benjamin B(erell) 1920- CANR-19
Earlier sketch in CA 97-100
Fergus, Charles 180
See also SATA 114
Fergus, Jan 1943- 125
Fergus, Jim 190
Fergus, Patricia M(arguerita) 1918- 53-56
Ferguson, Alane 1957- CANR-129
Earlier sketch in CA 151
See also SATA 85
Ferguson, Alfred R(iggs) 1915-1974 .... CANR-6
Obituary 49-52
Earlier sketch in CA 1-4R
Ferguson, Annabelle Evelyn 1923-2001 102
Obituary 199
Ferguson, Arthur B(owles) 1913-1999 .... 5-8R
Ferguson, Bird
See Engh, M(ary) J(ane)
Ferguson, Bob
See Ferguson, Robert Bruce
Ferguson, Brad 1953- 166
Ferguson, C(harles) E(lmo) 1928-1972 ... 17-20R
Obituary 134
Ferguson, Cecil 1931- .... SATA 45
Ferguson, Charles Albert
1921-1998 .... CANR-46
Obituary 170
Earlier sketch in CA 69-72
Ferguson, Charles Austin 1937- 121
Ferguson, Charles H. 1957- 189
Ferguson, Charles W. 1901-1987 .... 13-16R
Obituary 124
Ferguson, Chris(topher Wilson) 1944- 57-60
Ferguson, Clarence Clyde, Jr.
1924-1983 .... CANR-6
Obituary 111
Earlier sketch in CA 5-8R
Ferguson, Craig 1962- 207
Ferguson, David L. 1930- 73-76
Ferguson, Donald N(ivison) 1882-1985 .... 5-8R
Obituary 116
Ferguson, E(lmer) James 1917- 61-64
Ferguson, Emily
See Murphy, Emily (Gowan Ferguson)
Ferguson, Everett 1933- 33-36R
Ferguson, Franklin C(ole) 1934- 69-72
Ferguson, Gary 217
Ferguson, Harry 1903-1980
Obituary 97-100
Ferguson, Helen
See Kavan, Anna
Ferguson, Howard 1908-1999 .... CAP-1
Obituary 186
Earlier sketch in CA 11-12
Ferguson, J. A.
See Ferguson, Jo Ann
Ferguson, J(ohn) Halcro 1920-1968 .... 1-4R
Obituary 103
Ferguson, James M(ilton) 1936- 21-24R
Ferguson, Jo Ann 1953- 205
Ferguson, John 1921- CANR-25
Earlier sketches in CA 5-8R, CANR-8
Ferguson, John Henry 1907-1997 .... 13-16R
Obituary 180
Ferguson, Kathy E. 1950- 143
Ferguson, M(ilton) Carr, Jr. 1931- CANR-30
Earlier sketch in CA 49-52
Ferguson, M. J.
See Engh, M(ary) J(ane)
Ferguson, Margaret W(illiams) 1948- 112
Ferguson, Marilyn 1938- 114
Brief entry 110
Interview in CA-114
Ferguson, Mark W. J. 1955- 144
Ferguson, Mary Anne 1918- 77-80
Ferguson, Niall 1964- 190
See also CLC 134
Ferguson, Nicola 1949- 179
Ferguson, Oliver W(atkins) 1924- 5-8R
Ferguson, Pamela 1943- 101
Ferguson, Peter R(oderick) I(nnes)
1933- CANR-3
Earlier sketch in CA 5-8R
Ferguson, R. Brian 1951- 155
Ferguson, Robert (Thomas) 1948- 135
Ferguson, Robert A. 1942- 131
Ferguson, Robert Bruce 1927-2001 69-72
Obituary 200
See also SATA 13
Ferguson, Robert D(ouglas) 1921- 17-20R
Ferguson, Robert W(illiam) 1940- CANR-12
Earlier sketch in CA 61-64
Ferguson, Ronald 1939- 134
Ferguson, Rowena 1904-1988 85-88
Ferguson, Russell 197
Ferguson, Samuel 1810-1886 .... DLB 32
See also RGEL 2
Ferguson, Sarah (Margaret) 1959- 135
See also SATA 66, 110
Ferguson, Suzanne 1939- 57-60
Ferguson, Sybil (Rae) 1934- 129
Ferguson, Ted 1936- 65-68
Ferguson, Tom 1943- 107
Ferguson, Trevor 1947- CANR-99
Earlier sketches in CA 116, CANR-40
Ferguson, Walter (W.) 1930- 107
See also SATA 34
Ferguson, Will 171
Ferguson, William (Rotch) 1943- CANR-33
Earlier sketch in CA 49-52
Ferguson, William M. 171
Ferguson, William M(cDonald)
1917- CANR-41
Earlier sketch in CA 117
Ferguson, William Scott 1875-1954 177
See also DLB 47
Fergusson, Adam 1932-
Brief entry 112
Fergusson, Bernard Edward
1911-1980 .... CANR-7
Obituary 102
Earlier sketch in CA 9-12R
Fergusson, Bruce (Chandler) 1951- 154
See also FANT
Fergusson, Erna 1888-1964 .... CAP-1
Earlier sketch in CA 13-14
See also SATA 5

Fergusson, Francis (De Liesseline) 1904-1986 ... CANR-3
Obituary ... 121
Earlier sketch in CA 9-12R
Fergusson, Harvey 1890-1971
Obituary ... 33-36R
See also TCWW 1, 2
Fergusson, James 1904-1973
Obituary ... 104
Fergusson, Lorna 1957- ... 187
Fergusson, Peter (J.) ... 210
Fergusson, Robert 1750-1774 ... DLB 109
See also RGEL 2
Fergusson, Rosalind (Joyce) 1953- ... 117
Fergusson Hannay, Doris 1902(?)-1982 ... CANR-85
Obituary ... 107
Earlier sketches in CA 9-12R, CANR-6
See also DLB 191
See also RHW
Fericano, Paul 1951- ... CANR-29
Earlier sketches in CA 69-72, CANR-12
Ferkiss, Victor C(hristopher) 1925- ... 21-24R
Ferland, Albert 1872-1943 ... 177
See also DLB 92
Ferland, Carol 1936- ... 102
Ferlin, Nils 1898-1961 ... EWL 3
Ferling, John E. 1940- ... CANR-95
Earlier sketch in CA 143
Ferling, Lawrence
See Ferlinghetti, Lawrence (Monsanto)
Ferlinghetti, Lawrence (Monsanto) 1919(?)- ... CANR-125
Earlier sketches in CA 5-8R, CANR-3, 41, 73
See also BG 1:2
See also CAD
See also CDALB 1941-1968
See also CLC 2, 6, 10, 27, 111
See also CP 1, 2, 3, 4, 5, 6, 7
See also DA3
See also DAM POET
See also DLB 5, 16
See also MAL 5
See also MTCW 1, 2
See also MTFW 2005
See also PC 1
See also RGAL 4
See also WP
Ferlita, Ernest (Charles) 1927- ... CANR-112
Earlier sketches in CA 29-32R, CANR-11, 26, 54
Ferllini, Roxana
See Ferllini Timms, Roxana
Ferlosio, Rafael Sanchez 1927- ... DLB 322
Ferm, Betty 1926- ... 21-24R
Ferm, Deane William 1927- ... CANR-13
Earlier sketch in CA 33-36R
Ferm, Max A(rnold) 1929- ... 116
Ferm, Robert Livingston 1931- ... 13-16R
Ferm, Vergilius (Ture Anselm) 1896-1974 ... 9-12R
Obituary ... 49-52
Ferman, Edward L(ewis) 1937- ... 106
Ferman, Joseph W(olfe) 1906-1975
Obituary ... 104
Fermi, Enrico 1901-1954 ... 157
Brief entry ... 115
Fermi, Laura 1907-1977 ... CANR-6
Earlier sketch in CA 1-4R
See also SATA 6
See also SATA-Obit 28
Fermi, Rachel 1964- ... 151
Fermine, Maxence 1968- ... 224
Fermor, Patrick Leigh
See Leigh Fermor, Patrick (Michael)
See also DLB 204
Fern, Alan M(axwell) 1930- ... CANR-12
Earlier sketch in CA 33-36R
Fern, Eugene A. 1919-1987 ... CANR-76
Obituary ... 123
Earlier sketches in CA 1-4R, CANR-16
See also SATA 10
See also SATA-Obit 54
Fern, Fanny
See Parton, Sara Payson Willis
Fernald, John (Bailey) 1905-1985 ... CANR-76
Obituary ... 115
Earlier sketches in CAP-2, CA 23-24
Fernandes, Eugenie 1943- ... SATA 77, 139
Fernandes, Florestan 1922- ... 187
Fernandez (Revuelta), Alina 1956- ... 193
Fernandez, Benedict J. (III) 1936- ... 85-88
Fernandez, Gladys Craven 1939- ... 106
Fernandez, Happy Craven
See Fernandez, Gladys Craven
Fernandez, James D. 1961- ... 139
Fernandez, James William 1930- ... CANR-23
Earlier sketch in CA 107
Fernandez, John P(eter) 1941- ... CANR-10
Earlier sketch in CA 65-68
Fernandez, Jose S(alvador) 1893-1967
Obituary ... 113
Fernandez, Joseph A. 1921- ... 37-40R
Fernandez, Julio A. 1936- ... 33-36R
Fernandez, Macedonio 1874-1952 ... LAW
Fernandez, Peter 1927- ... AAYA 67
Fernandez, Roberto G. 1951- ... CANR-68
Earlier sketch in CA 131
See also DAM MULT
See also HW 1, 2
See also LLW
Fernandez, Vicente Garcia Huidobro
See Huidobro Fernandez, Vicente Garcia
Fernandez-Armesto, Felipe ... CLC 70
Fernandez-Armesto, Felipe (Fermin Ricardo) 1950- ... CANR-93
Earlier sketch in CA 142
Fernandez Cubas, Cristina 1945- ... 211
See also EWL 3
Fernandez de la Reguera, Ricardo 1914-2000 ... CANR-3
Earlier sketch in CA 5-8R
Fernandez de Lizardi, Jose Joaquin
See Lizardi, Jose Joaquin Fernandez de
Fernandez Florez, Wenceslao 1885-1964 ... 211
Fernandez-Marina, R(amon) 1909- ... 41-44R
Fernandez Mendez, E.
See Fernandez Mendez, Eugenio
Fernandez Mendez, Eugenio 1924- ... HW 1
Fernandez Moreno, Baldomero 1886-1950 ... HW 1
Fernandez Moreno, Cesar 1919- ... 131
See also HW 1
Fernandez-Morera, Dario 1944- ... 178
Fernandez Olmos, Margarite 1949- ... 179
Fernandez Retamar, Roberto 1930- ... 131
See also HW 1
Fernandez-Shaw, Carlos M(anuel) 1924- ... 140
Fernando, Ajith 1948- ... 122
Fernando, Lloyd 1926- ... 77-80
Fernando, Patrick 1931- ... CP 1
Fernan Gomez, Fernando 1921- ... 207
Fernea, Elizabeth Warnock 1927- ... CANR-29
Earlier sketches in CA 13-16R, CANR-12
Fernea, Robert Alan 1932- ... CANR-29
Earlier sketch in CA 33-36R
Fernett, Gene 1924- ... 49-52
Ferngren, Gary B(urt) 1942- ... 218
Fernie, Eric (Campbell) 1939- ... CANR-126
Earlier sketch in CA 119
Ferns, H(enry) S(tanley) 1913-1992 ... CANR-76
Obituary ... 137
Earlier sketches in CA 5-8R, CANR-4, 19
Fernsworth, Lawrence 1893(?)-1977(?)
Obituary ... 89-92
Ferone, Joseph 1942- ... 197
Ferracuti, Franco 1927- ... CANR-30
Earlier sketches in CA 25-28R, CANR-11
Ferrante, Don
See Gerbi, Antonello
Ferrante, Joan M(arguerite Aida) 1936- ... 85-88
Ferrar, Harold 1935-
Brief entry ... 116
Ferrara, Abel 1952(?)- ... 239
Ferrara, V(ernon) Peter 1912-1988
Obituary ... 127
Ferrari, Enzo 1898-1988
Obituary ... 126
Ferrari, Maria ... SATA 123
Ferrari, R(onald) L(eslie) 1930- ... 135
Ferrarini, Elizabeth M. 1948- ... 124
Ferraro, Barbara 1943- ... 143
Ferraro, Gary P(aul) 1940- ... CANR-116
Earlier sketch in CA 89-92
Ferraro, Geraldine 1935- ... 190
Ferraro, Susan (Lyons) 1946- ... 148
Ferrars, E. X.
See Brown, Morna Doris
Ferrars, Elizabeth
See Brown, Morna Doris
See also DLB 87
Ferrat, Jacques Jean
See Merwin, (W.) Sam(uel Kimball), Jr.
Ferrater-Mora, Jose 1912-1991 ... CANR-29
Earlier sketch in CA 1-4R
See also HW 1
Ferrato, Donna 1949- ... 147
Ferre, Frederick (Pond) 1933- ... CANR-113
Earlier sketch in CA 13-16R
Ferre, Gustave A. 1918- ... 1-4R
Ferre, John P. 1956- ... 139
Ferre, Nels F(redrik) S(olomon) 1908-1971 ... CAP-2
Earlier sketch in CA 29-32
Ferre, Rosario 1938- ... CANR-134
Earlier sketches in CA 131, CANR-55, 81
See also CLC 139
See also CWW 2
See also DLB 145
See also EWL 3
See also HLCS 1
See also HW 1, 2
See also LAWS 1
See also MTCW 2
See also MTFW 2005
See also SSC 36
See also WLIT 1
Ferree, Myra Marx 1949- ... CANR-113
Earlier sketch in CA 154
Ferreira, Vergilio 1916-1996 ... DLB 287
Ferreira de Castro, Jose Maria 1898-1974 ... 102
Obituary ... 49-52
See also Castro, Jose Maria Ferreira de
See also EW 11
Ferreiro, Carmen 1958- ... 234
See also SATA 158
Ferrell, Anderson ... 236
Ferrell, Carolyn ... 170
Ferrell, Frank 1940- ... 136
Ferrell, Jeannette Y(vonne) 1947- ... 220
Ferrell, Jeff ... 204
Ferrell, Mallory Hope 1935- ... CANR-116
Earlier sketches in CA 33-36R, CANR-13, 30, 56
Ferrell, Nancy Warren 1932- ... 138
See also SATA 70
Ferrell, Robert H(ugh) 1921- ... CANR-102
Earlier sketches in CA 5-8R, CANR-6, 22
Ferrell, Robert W(illingham) 1913-1995 ... 13-16R
Ferreol, Marcel Auguste 1899-1974 ... 97-100
Obituary ... 53-56
See also Achard, Marcel
Ferrer, Aldo 1927- ... CANR-28
Earlier sketches in CA 25-28R, CANR-11
Ferrer, Elizabeth 1955- ... 172
Ferrer, Gabriel (Francisco Victor) Miro
See Miro (Ferrer), Gabriel (Francisco Victor)
Ferrer, Gloria M. Pagan
See Pagan Ferrer, Gloria M.
Ferrer, Sister Vincent
See Doherty, Barbara
Ferreras, Francisco 1962- ... 237
Ferreri, Marco 1928-1997 ... 126
Obituary ... 158
Ferres, John H(oward) 1932- ... 41-44R
Ferridge, Philippa 1933- ... CANR-59
Earlier sketches in CA 102, CANR-18
See also RHW
Ferrier, Janet Mackay 1919- ... 9-12R
Ferrier, Lucy
See Penzler, Otto
Ferrier, Susan (Edmonstone) 1782-1854 ... DLB 116
See also RGEL 2
Ferrigno, Lou 1952- ... 213
Ferrigno, Robert 1948(?)- ... CANR-125
Earlier sketch in CA 140
See also CLC 65
Ferril, Thomas Hornsby 1896-1988 ... CANR-77
Obituary ... 127
Earlier sketch in CA 65-68
See also CP 1, 2
See also DLB 206
Ferrill, Arther 1938- ... 129
Ferrini, Vincent 1913- ... 158
See also CAAS 24
See also DLB 48
Ferris, David 1960- ... 207
Ferris, David S. 1954- ... 230
Ferris, Helen Josephine 1890-1969 ... 77-80
See also SATA 21
Ferris, James Cody ... CANR-27
Earlier sketches in CAP-2, CA 19-20
See also McFarlane, Leslie (Charles)
See also SATA 1
Ferris, Jean 1939- ... CANR-38
Earlier sketch in CA 116
See also AAYA 38
See also SATA 56, 105, 149
See also SATA-Brief 50
See also YAW
Ferris, Jeri Chase 1937- ... 150
See also SATA 84
Ferris, John (Stephen) 1937- ... 146
Ferris, Norman (Bernard) 1931- ... 81-84
Ferris, Paul (Frederick) 1929- ... CANR-22
Earlier sketches in CA 5-8R, CANR-3
Ferris, Scott R. 1956- ... 181
Ferris, Theodore P(arker) 1908-1972
Obituary ... 37-40R
Ferris, Timothy 1944- ... CANR-73
Earlier sketches in CA 69-72, CANR-11, 30
Interview in ... CANR-30
Ferris, Tom
See Walker, Peter N.
Ferris, William (R.) 1942- ... 136
See also CSW
Ferriss, Abbott Lamoyne 1915- ... 29-32R
Ferriter, Diarmaid 1972- ... 234
Ferritor, Daniel Edward 1939- ... CANR-35
Earlier sketch in CA 49-52
Ferro, Marc 1924- ... 77-80
Ferro, Robert (Michael) 1941-1988 ... CANR-76
Obituary ... 126
Earlier sketch in CA 29-32R
Ferron, Jacques 1921-1985 ... 129
Brief entry ... 117
See also CCA 1
See also CLC 94
See also DAC
See also DLB 60
See also EWL 3
Ferron, Madeleine 1922- ... 182
See also DLB 53
Ferrone, John 1924- ... 173
Ferrous, Vincent
See Ferrini, Vincent
Ferrucci, Franco 1936- ... 205
See also DLB 196
Ferruolo, Stephen C(arl) 1949- ... 120
Ferry, Anne Davidson 1930- ... 17-20R
Ferry, Charles 1927- ... CANR-57
Earlier sketches in CA 97-100, CANR-16
See also AAYA 29
See also CLR 34
See also SAAS 20
See also SATA 43, 92
Ferry, David (Russell) 1924- ... CANR-88
Earlier sketch in CA 13-16R
See also CP 1
Ferry, Luc 1951- ... 198
Ferry, W(illiam) Hawkins 1914(?)-1988 ... CANR-76
Obituary ... 124
Earlier sketch in CA 61-64
Fersh, Seymour H. 1926-1999 ... CANR-14
Earlier sketch in CA 37-40R
Ferster, C(harles) B(ohris) 1922-1981 ... CANR-75
Obituary ... 102
Earlier sketch in CA 97-100
Ferster, Dorothy C(oben) 1922- ... 111
Ferster, Marilyn B(ender)
See Gilbert, Marilyn B(ender)
Ferullo, Dan 1948- ... 106
Feshbach, Murray 1929- ... 140
Feshbach, Norma Deitch 1926- ... CANR-8
Earlier sketch in CA 61-64
Feshbach, Seymour 1925- ... CANR-8
Earlier sketch in CA 37-40R
Fesler, James W(illiam) 1911- ... 21-24R
Fesperman, John (Thomas, Jr.) 1925- ... CANR-2
Earlier sketch in CA 5-8R
Fess, Philip E. 1931- ... 33-36R
Fessel, Murray 1927- ... 21-24R
Fessenden, Katherine 1896(?)-1974
Obituary ... 53-56
Fessenden, Seth A(rthur) 1903-1976 ... CANR-10
Earlier sketch in CA 17-20R
Fessenko, Tatiana (Sviatenko) 1915- ... 13-16R
Fessier, Michael 1905(?)-1988
Obituary ... 126
Fessler, Loren W. 1923- ... 9-12R
Fest, Joachim C. 1926- ... CANR-128
Earlier sketches in CA 49-52, CANR-47
Fest, Thorrel B(rooks) 1910-1996 ... CAP-1
Earlier sketch in CA 13-16
Festa Campanile, Pasquale 1927-1986 ... 162
Obituary ... 118
Festa-McCormick, Diana ... 117
Festinger, Leon 1919-1989 ... CANR-31
Obituary ... 127
Earlier sketch in CA 1-4R
Fet, Afanasii Afanas'evich 1820(?)-1892 ... DLB 277
Fetherling, Dale 1941- ... 77-80
Fetherling, Douglas
See Fetherling, (Douglas) George
See also CP 2
Fetherling, (Douglas) George 1949- ... 203
Autobiographical Essay in ... 203
See also Fetherling, Douglas
Fetherston, Drew ... 172
Fetler, Andrew 1925- ... 13-16R
Fetridge, William Harrison 1906-1989 ... CANR-75
Obituary ... 129
Earlier sketch in CA 73-76
Fetros, John G. 1932- ... 57-60
Fetscher, Iring 1922- ... CANR-12
Earlier sketch in CA 69-72
Fettamen, Ann
See Hoffman, Anita
Fetter, Elizabeth Head 1904-1973 ... 5-8R
Obituary ... 41-44R
Fetter, Frank Whitson 1899-1991 ... CANR-76
Obituary ... 135
Earlier sketch in CA 106
Fetter, Richard (Leland) 1943- ... CANR-15
Earlier sketch in CA 89-92
Fetterley, Judith 1938- ... 188
Brief entry ... 113
Fetterman, Elsie 1927- ... 97-100
Fetterman, John (Davis) 1920-1975 ... 93-96
Obituary ... 61-64
Fetters, Thomas T. 1938- ... 227
Fettig, Art(hur John) 1929- ... CANR-53
Earlier sketches in CA 73-76, CANR-13, 29
Fetz, Ingrid 1915- ... SATA 30
Fetzer, John F(rancis) 1931- ... 61-64
Feucht, Oscar E(mil) 1895-1982 ... 103
Feuchtersleben, Ernst Freiherr von 1797-1848 ... DLB 133
Feuchtwanger, E(dgar) J(oseph) 1924- ... CANR-11
Earlier sketch in CA 69-72
Feuchtwanger, Lion 1884-1958 ... 187
Brief entry ... 104
See also DLB 66
See also EWL 3
See also TCLC 3
Feuer, Avrohom Chaim 1946- ... CANR-32
Earlier sketch in CA 113
Feuer, Kathryn Beliveau 1926-1992 ... CANR-76
Obituary ... 137
Earlier sketch in CA 102
Feuer, Lewis S(amuel) 1912-2002 ... CANR-3
Obituary ... 210
Earlier sketch in CA 5-8R
Feuerbach, Ludwig 1804-1872 ... DLB 133
Feuerlicht, Ignace ... CAP-2
Earlier sketch in CA 33-36
Feuerlicht, Roberta Strauss 1931-1991 ... CANR-77
Obituary ... 135
Earlier sketch in CA 17-20R
Feuerman, Ruchama King
See King, Ruchama
Feuerstein, Georg 1947- ... CANR-96
Earlier sketches in CA 123, CANR-49
Feuerstein, Phyllis A. 1930- ... 105
Feuerwerger, Marvin C(harles) 1950- ... 104
Feuerwerker, Albert 1927- ... CANR-8
Earlier sketch in CA 21-24R
Feuillet, Octave 1821-1890 ... DLB 192
Feulner, Edwin J(ohn), Jr. 1941- ... 115
Feulner, Patricia N(ancy) 1946- ... 105
Feur, D. C.
See Stahl, Fred Alan
Feurey, Benita S. 1940(?)-1989
Obituary ... 129
Fewster, Kevin (John) 1953- ... 125
Fey, Harold E(dward) 1898-1990 ... CANR-75
Obituary ... 130
Earlier sketch in CA 17-20R
Feydeau, Georges (Leon Jules Marie) 1862-1921 ... CANR-84
Brief entry ... 113
Earlier sketch in CA 152
See also DAM DRAM
See also DLB 192
See also EWL 3
See also GFL 1789 to the Present
See also RGWL 2, 3
See also TCLC 22

Cumulative Index **187** **Figueroa**

Feydy, Anne Lindbergh
See Sapieyevski, Anne Lindbergh
See also SATA-Brief 32
Feyerabend, Paul K(arl) 1924-1994 .. CANR-95
Earlier sketch in CA 150
Feynman, R. P.
See Feynman, Richard Phillips
Feynman, Richard
See Feynman, Richard Phillips
Feynman, Richard P.
See Feynman, Richard Phillips
See also BEST 89:3
Feynman, Richard Phillips 1918-1988 ... 129
Obituary ... 125
Brief entry ... 119
See also Feynman, Richard P.
See also MTCW 1
See also MTFW 2005
Fezler, William 1945- ... CANR-48
Earlier sketch in CA 122
Ffinch, Michael 1934-1999 ... 137
ffolkes
See Davis, Brian
Ffolkes, Michael
See Davis, Brian
ffolliott, Rosemary 1934- ... 97-100
Fforde, Jasper 1961- ... 204
Fforde, Katie ... 182
ffrench-Beytagh, Gonville (Aubie) 1912-1991 ... 103
ffrench Blake, Neil (St. John) 1940- ... 69-72
ffrench Blake, Robert L(ifford) V(alentine) 1913- ... 61-64
Fiacc, Padraic
See O'Connor, Patrick Joseph
Fialka, John J. 1938- ... CANR-138
Earlier sketches in CA 139, CANR-60
Fialkowski, Barbara 1946- ... 77-80
Fiamengo, Marya 1926- ... 197
Fiammenghi, Gioia 1929- ... SATA 9, 66
Fiandt, Mary K. 1914-1999 ... 89-92
Fiarotta, Noel
See Ficarotta, Noel
See also SATA 15
Fiarotta, Phyllis
See Ficarotta, Phyllis
See also SATA 15
Fiber, Alan ... 102
Fibiger, Mathilde 1830-1872 ... DLB 300
Fibkins, William L. 1934- ... 235
Ficarotta, Noel 1944- ... CANR-11
Earlier sketch in CA 69-72
See also Fiarotta, Noel
Ficarotta, Phyllis 1942- ... CANR-11
Earlier sketch in CA 69-72
See also Fiarotta, Phyllis
Ficera, Kim (M.) 1959- ... 232
Fichte, Johann Gottlieb 1762-1814 ... DLB 90
Fichtelius, Karl-Erik 1924- ... 53-56
Fichtenau, Heinrich 1912-2000 ... 187
Fichter, Andrew J(ohn) 1945- ... 117
Fichter, George S. 1922-1993 ... CANR-23
Earlier sketches in CA 17-20R, CANR-7
See also SATA 7
Fichter, Joseph (H.) 1908-1994 ... CANR-76
Obituary ... 144
Earlier sketches in CA 1-4R, CANR-4, 19, 41
Ficino, Marsilio 1433-1499 ... LMFS 1
Fick, Carl 1918- ... 167
Ficke, Arthur Davison 1883-1945 ... 176
See also DLB 54
Ficken, Frederick A(rthur) 1910-1978
Obituary ... 81-84
Ficker, Victor B. 1937- ... CANR-13
Earlier sketch in CA 33-36R
Fickert, Kurt J(on) 1920- ... CANR-57
Earlier sketches in CA 37-40R, CANR-14, 31
Fickett, Harold L., Jr. 1918-2000 ... 13-16R
Fickett, Lewis P., Jr. 1926- ... 21-24R
Fickle, James Edward 1939- ... 106
Fickling, Forrest E. 1925-1998 ... 5-8R
Obituary ... 166
Fickling, G. G.
See Fickling, Forrest E.
Ficowski, Jerzy 1924- ... CANR-114
Earlier sketch in CA 154
Fidelio
See Hunt, Edgar H(ubert)
Fidler, James M. 1900-1988
Obituary ... 126
Fidler, Jimmie
See Fidler, James M.
Fidler, Kathleen (Annie) 1899-1980 .. CANR-83
Obituary ... 117
Earlier sketches in CA 25-28R, CANR-20
See also CWRI 5
See also SATA 3, 87
See also SATA-Obit 45
Fido, Martin (Austin) 1939- ... 159
Fidrych, Mark 1954-
Brief entry ... 112
Fie, Jacquelyn Joyce 1937- ... 57-60
Fiechter, J. J.
See Fiechter, Jean-Jacques
Fiechter, Jean-Jacques 1927- ... 189
Fiedel, Stuart J(ay) 1952- ... 128
Fiedeler, Hans
See Doeblin, Alfred
Fiedler, Fred E(dward) 1922- ... 21-24R
Fiedler, Jean(nette Feldman) ... CANR-11
Earlier sketch in CA 29-32R
See also SATA 4
Fiedler, Johanna 1946- ... CANR-113
Earlier sketch in CA 133
Fiedler, Joseph Daniel ... SATA 159
Fiedler, Leslie A(aron) 1917-2003 ... CANR-63
Obituary ... 212
Earlier sketches in CA 9-12R, CANR-7
See also AMWS 13
See also CLC 4, 13, 24
See also CN 1, 2, 3, 4, 5, 6
See also DLB 28, 67
See also EWL 3
See also MAL 5
See also MTCW 1, 2
See also RGAL 4
See also TUS
Fiedler, Lois (Wagner) 1928- ... 17-20R
Fieg, Victor P. 1924- ... 106
Field, Adelaide (Anderson) 1916- ... 106
Field, Andrew 1938- ... CANR-25
Earlier sketch in CA 97-100
See also CLC 44
Field, Arthur J(ordan) 1927-1975 ... 33-36R
Field, Barbara 1935- ... 110
Field, Barron 1789-1846 ... DLB 230
Field, Carol (Hart) 1940- ... CANR-110
Earlier sketch in CA 113
Field, Charles
See Rowland, D(onald) S(ydney)
Field, Daniel 1938- ... 65-68
Field, David (McLucas) 1944- ... CANR-82
Earlier sketch in CA 133
Field, David D(udley) 1918- ... 73-76
Field, Dawn Stewart 1940- ... 57-60
Field, Dick 1912- ... 57-60
Field, Dorothy 1944- ... 163
See also SATA 97
Field, Edward 1924- ... 176
Earlier sketches in CA 13-16R, CANR-10
Autobiographical Essay in ... 176
See also CAAS 27
See also CP 1, 2, 3, 4, 5, 6, 7
See also DLB 105
See also SATA 8, 109
Field, Eleanor S. 1932- ... 122
Field, Elinor Whitney 1889-1980
Obituary ... 109
See also SATA-Obit 28
Field, Ernest R. 1925- ... 5-8R
Field, Eugene 1850-1895 ... DLB 23, 42, 140
See also DLBD 13
See also MAICYA 1, 2
See also RGAL 4
See also SATA 16
Field, Fern
See Brooks, Fern Field
Field, Frances Fox 1913(?)-1977
Obituary ... 69-72
Field, Frank 1936- ... 21-24R
Field, Frank Chester
See Robertson, Frank C(hester)
Field, Frank McCoy 1887-1978 ... CANR-75
Obituary ... 103
Earlier sketch in CA 45-48
Field, Frederick V.
See Field, Frederick Vanderbilt
Field, Frederick Vanderbilt 1905-2000 ... 130
Obituary ... 188
Field, G(eorge) W(allis) 1914-2003 ... 37-40R
Field, Gans T.
See Wellman, Manly Wade
Field, Genevieve 1970- ... 173
Field, George B(rooks) 1929- ... 101
Field, Gordon Lawrence 1939- ... 17-20R
Field, Harry
See Field, Henry
Field, Hartry H(amlin) 1946- ... CANR-127
Earlier sketches in CA 124, CANR-52
Field, Hazel E(lizabeth) 1891-1969(?) ... CAP-1
Earlier sketch in CA 19-20
Field, Henry 1902-1986 ... CANR-76
Obituary ... 118
Earlier sketch in CA 69-72
Field, Hermann H(aviland) 1910-2001 ... CANR-93
Obituary ... 193
Earlier sketch in CA 135
Field, Irving M(edcraft) 1934- ... 25-28R
Field, J. V. 1943- ... 173
Field, James 1959- ... SATA 113
Field, James A(lfred), Jr. 1916-1996 ... 25-28R
Obituary ... 152
Field, Ioanna
See Milner, Marion (Blackett)
Field, John 1545(?)-1588 ... DLB 167
Field, John (Leslie) 1910-1987 ... 33-36R
Field, John P(aul) 1936- ... 37-40R
Field, Joseph M. 1810-1856 ... DLB 248
Field, Joyce W(olf) 1932- ... 29-32R
Field, Kate (Margaret) 1912- ... 200
Field, Les W. ... 194
Field, Leslie A. 1926- ... 29-32R
Field, Mark G(eorge) 1923- ... 37-40R
Field, Marshall III 1893-1956 ... 181
See also DLB 127
Field, Marshall IV 1916-1965 ... DLB 127
Field, Marshall V 1941- ... 182
See also DLB 127
Field, Michael ... 205
See also Bradley, Katherine Harris and Cooper, Edith Emma
See also DLB 240
Field, Michael 1915-1971
Obituary ... 29-32R
See also TCLC 43
Field, Minna (Kagan) ... 25-28R
Field, Nathan 1587-1620(?) ... DLB 58
See also RGEL 2
Field, Ophelia ... 225
Field, Penelope
See Giberson, Dorothy (Dodds)
Field, Peter
See Drago, Harry Sinclair and Dresser, Davis and Mann, E(dward) B(everly)
Field, Phyllis Frances 1946- ... 107
Field, Rachel (Lyman) 1894-1942 ... CANR-79
Brief entry ... 109
Earlier sketch in CA 137
See also BYA 5
See also CLR 21
See also CWRI 5
See also DLB 9, 22
See also MAICYA 1, 2
See also RHW
See also SATA 15
See also WCH
Field, Sally (Margaret) 1946- ... 171
Field, Stanley 1911-1998 ... CANR-9
Earlier sketch in CA 21-24R
Field, Syd ... 222
Field, Thalia ... 204
Field, Thomas P(arry) 1914-1990 ... 9-12R
Field, Tiffany (Martini) 1942- ... 209
Field, (William) Todd 1964- ... 215
Field, Walter S(herman) 1899-1981 ... 49-52
Fielden, Charlotte ... 93-96
Fielden, Ned L. 1954- ... 220
Fielden, T(homas) P(erceval) 1882-1974 ... 5-8R
Fielder, Mildred (Craig) 1913-2000 .. CANR-10
Earlier sketch in CA 13-16R
Fieldhouse, David Kenneth 1925- ... 196
Fieldhouse, W. L.
See Fieldhouse, William
Fieldhouse, William ... TCWW 2
Fielding, A. W.
See Wallace, Alexander Fielding
Fielding, Daphne Winifred Louise 1904-1997 ... 9-12R
Obituary ... 163
Fielding, G(ordon) J. 1934- ... 97-100
Fielding, Gabriel
See Barnsley, Alan Gabriel
See also CN 1, 2, 3, 4
Fielding, Helen 1958- ... CANR-127
Earlier sketch in CA 172
See also AAYA 65
See also CLC 146
See also DLB 231
See also MTFW 2005
Fielding, Henry 1707-1754 ... BRW 3
See also BRWR 1
See also CDBLB 1660-1789
See also DA
See also DA3
See also DAB
See also DAC
See also DAM DRAM, MST, NOV
See also DLB 39, 84, 101
See also NFS 18
See also RGEL 2
See also TEA
See also WLC
See also WLIT 3
Fielding, Hubert
See Schonfield, Hugh J(oseph)
Fielding, Joy 1945- ... CANR-100
Earlier sketches in CA 49-52, CANR-2, 43
Fielding, Kate
See Oldfield, Jenny
Fielding, Nancy (Parker) 1913-1983 ... 176
Obituary ... 111
Brief entry ... 108
Fielding, Nigel G(oodwin) 1950- ... CANR-86
Earlier sketch in CA 131
Fielding, Raymond E. 1931- ... CANR-8
Earlier sketch in CA 17-20R
Fielding, Sarah 1710-1768 ... DLB 39
See also RGEL 2
See also TEA
Fielding, Temple (Hornaday) 1913-1983 ... CANR-14
Obituary ... 109
Earlier sketch in CA 21-24R
Fielding, Waldo L. 1921- ... 45-48
Fielding, William H.
See Teilhet, Darwin L(eOra)
Fielding, William J(ohn) 1886-1973 . CANR-76
Obituary ... 134
Earlier sketch in CA 13-16R
Fielding, Xan
See Wallace, Alexander Fielding
Fields, Alan
See Duprey, Richard A(llen)
Fields, Annie Adams 1834-1915 ... DLB 221
Fields, Arthur C. 1926(?)-1974
Obituary ... 49-52
Fields, Beverly 1917-2003 ... 49-52
Obituary ... 220
Fields, Debbi
See Fields, Debra J.
Fields, Debra J. 1956- ... 140
Fields, Dorothy 1905-1974 ... 93-96
Obituary ... 49-52
See also DLB 265
Fields, Frank ... TCWW 2
Fields, Gracie 1898-1979
Obituary ... 112
Fields, Hillary ... 204
Fields, Howard K(enneth) 1938- ... 81-84
Fields, James Thomas 1817-1881 ... DLB 1, 235
Fields, Jeff ... AITN 2
Fields, Jennie 1953- ... CANR-137
Earlier sketch in CA 147
Fields, Joseph 1895-1966
Obituary ... 25-28R
Fields, Julia 1938- ... CANR-26
Earlier sketch in CA 73-76
See also BW 1
See also DLB 41
Fields, Karen E. 1945- ... 221
Fields, Kenneth (Wayne) 1939-
Brief entry ... 110
Fields, L. Marc 1955- ... 146
Fields, Morgan
See Morgan, J(ill) M(eredith)
Fields, Nora ... 49-52
Fields, Polly S(tevens) ... 190
Fields, Rick 1942-1999 ... CANR-27
Obituary ... 181
Earlier sketches in CA 65-68, CANR-9
Fields, Rona M(arcia) 1934- ... 69-72
Fields, Ronald J. ... 218
Fields, Scott (Gary) 1956- ... 134
Fields, Suzanne 1936- ... 129
Fields, Totie
See Feldman, Sophie
Fields, Verna -1982 ... IDFW 3, 4
Fields, Victor A(lexander) 1901-1992 ... 5-8R
Fields, W. C. 1880-1946 ... DLB 44
See also TCLC 80
Fields, Wayne 1942- ... 134
Fields, Wilbert J. 1917- ... 13-16R
Fields, Wilmer Clemont 1922-
Brief entry ... 106
Fieler, Frank B(ernard) 1933- ... 41-44R
Fienberg, Anna 1956- ... 184
See also CWRI 5
See also SATA 112
Fiene, Donald M(ark) 1930- ... 69-72
Fiene, Ernest 1894-1965 ... CAP-1
Earlier sketch in CA 13-14
Fiennes, Jini
See Lash, Jennifer
Fiennes, Ranulph (Twisleton-Wykeham) 1944- ... CANR-123
Earlier sketches in CA 45-48, CANR-3, 20, 48
Fiennes, Richard
See Twisleton-Wykeham-Fiennes, Richard Nathaniel
Fiennes, William 1971- ... 206
Fienup-Riordan, Ann 1948- ... CANR-119
Earlier sketch in CA 148
Fiering, Norman Sanford 1935- ... 105
Fierro, Robert Daniel 1945- ... 109
Fierstein, Harvey (Forbes) 1954- ... 129
Brief entry ... 123
See also CAD
See also CD 5, 6
See also CLC 33
See also CPW
See also DA3
See also DAM DRAM, POP
See also DFS 6
See also DLB 266
See also GLL
See also MAL 5
Fieser, Louis F(rederick) 1899-1977 ... 157
Obituary ... 73-76
Fieser, Max E(ugene) 1930- ... 13-16R
Fiester, Mark (Lafayette) 1907- ... 65-68
Fieve, Ronald R(obert) 1930-
Brief entry ... 107
Fife, Austin E(dwin) 1909-1986 ... 53-56
Fife, Dale (Odile Hollerbach) 1901- . CANR-19
Earlier sketch in CA 85-88
See also SATA 18
Fife, Robert Oldham 1918- ... 37-40R
Fifer, Elizabeth 1944- ... 139
Fifer, Ken 1947- ... 104
Fifield, Christopher G(eorge) 1945- .. CANR-86
Earlier sketch in CA 130
Fifield, William 1916-1987 ... CANR-77
Obituary ... 124
Earlier sketches in CA 13-16R, CANR-9
Fifo, Ray
See Glazar, Bob
Fifoot, Cecil Herbert Stuart 1899-1975
Obituary ... 107
Figes, Eva 1932- ... CANR-83
Earlier sketches in CA 53-56, CANR-4, 44
See also CLC 31
See also CN 2, 3, 4, 5, 6, 7
See also DLB 14, 271
See also FW
Figes, Kate ... 199
Figes, Orlando (Guy) 1959- ... CANR-136
Earlier sketch in CA 163
Figgie, Harry E., Jr. 1923- ... 143
Figgins, Ross 1936- ... CANR-11
Earlier sketch in CA 69-72
Figh, Margaret Gillis 1896-1984 ... CAP-2
Earlier sketch in CA 29-32
Fighter Pilot, A
See Johnston, H(ugh) A(nthony) S(tephen)
Figiel, Sia 1967- ... 202
Figler, Howard Elliot 1939- ... 127
Brief entry ... 109
Figler, Jeanie 1949- ... 194
See also SATA 123
Figler, Stephen K(enneth) 1942- ... 117
Figley, Marty Rhodes 1948- ... CANR-143
Earlier sketch in CA 152
See also SATA 88, 158
Figueira, Thomas J. 1948- ... CANR-122
Earlier sketch in CA 142
Figuera, Angela 1902-1984 ... 174
See also DLB 108
See also HW 2
Figueredo, D(anilo) H. 1951- ... 230
See also SATA 155
Figueroa, Gabriel 1907- ... IDFW 3, 4

Figueroa, John
See Figueroa, John J(oseph Maria)
See also CP 1, 2
Figueroa, John J(oseph Maria)
1920-1999 ... CANR-83
Brief entry ... 108
Earlier sketch in CA 125
See also Figueroa, John
See also BW 2
Figueroa, John L(ewis) 1936- ... 65-68
Figueroa (Mercado), Loida
See Figueroa-Mercado, Loida
See also HW 1
Figueroa, Pablo 1938- ... 61-64
See also HW 1
See also SATA 9
Figueroa-Chapel, Ramon 1935- ... 45-48
Figueroa-Mercado, Loida 1917- ... CANR-28
Earlier sketches in CA 57-60, CANR-9
See also Figueroa (Mercado), Loida
Figuli, Margita 1909-1995 ... EWL 3
Figurito, Joseph 1922- ... 29-32R
Fijan, Carol 1918- ... 53-56
See also SATA 12
Fikes, Jay C(ourtney) 1951- ... 152
Fikkens, J.
See Brunclair, Victor
Fikky
See Brunclair, Victor
Fiksman, David Mironovich 1900-1955
See Knut, Dovid
Fikso, Eunice Cleland 1927- ... 5-8R
Filas, Francis L(ad) 1915-1985 ... CANR-76
Obituary ... 115
Earlier sketches in CA 5-8R, CANR-2
Filby, P(ercy) William 1911-2002 ... CANR-27
Obituary ... 210
Earlier sketches in CA 9-12R, CANR-3
Filderman, Diane E(lizabeth) 1959- ... 151
See also SATA 87
Filene, Benjamin 1965- ... 207
Filene, Peter G. 1940- ... 21-24R
Filep, Robert Thomas 1931- ... CANR-19
Earlier sketches in CA 45-48, CANR-1
Files, Lolita ... 179
Files, Meg 1946- ... CANR-126
Earlier sketch in CA 169
See also SATA 107
Filey, Mike ... 166
Filho, Adonias 1915-1990 ... 178
See also DLB 145, 307
See also HW 2
Filho, Adonias Aguiar
See Filho, Adonias
Filicchia, Ralph 1935- ... 103
Filip, Raymond 1950- ... 113
Filipacchi, Amanda 1967- ... 150
Filipovic, Zlata 1980- ... 148
Filipovitch, Anthony J(oseph) 1947- ... 102
Filippo, Eduardo de
See de Filippo, Eduardo
Filkins, Peter 1958- ... 169
Fill, Joseph Herbert 1924-2001
Obituary ... 203
Brief entry ... 112
Filler, Louis 1912-1998 ... CANR-2
Earlier sketch in CA 1-4R
Fillmer, Henry Thompson 1932- ... 21-24R
Fillmore, Lowell 1882-1985 ... CAP-1
Earlier sketch in CA 9-10
Fillmore, Parker H(oysted) 1878-1944 .. YABC 1
Fillmore, Roscoe Alfred 1887-1968 ... 5-8R
Filmer, Henry
See Childs, J(ames) Rives
Filmer, Sir Robert c. 1586-1653 ... DLB 151
Filosa, Gary Fairmont Randolph de Marco II
1931- ... CANR-54
Earlier sketch in CA 65-68
Filreis, Alan 1956- ... 125
Filson, Floyd V(ivian) 1896-1980 ... 61-64
Filson, John 1753(?)-1788 ... DLB 37
Filstrup, Chris
See Filstrup, E(dward) Christian
Filstrup, E(dward) Christian 1942- ... 113
See also SATA 43
Filstrup, Jane (Merrill) 1946- ... 110
Filstrup, Janie
See Filstrup, Jane (Merrill)
Filtzer, Donald (Arthur) 1948- ... CANR-124
Earlier sketches in CA 126, CANR-53
Finan, John J(oseph) 1925- ... 117
Finberg, H(erbert) P(atrick) R(eginald)
1900-1974 ... CAP-1
Obituary ... 53-56
Earlier sketch in CA 13-16
Finch, A. R. C.
See Finch, Annie (Ridley Crane)
Finch, Anne 1661-1720 ... BRWS 9
See also DLB 95
See also PC 21
Finch, Annie (Ridley Crane) 1956- ... CANR-94
Earlier sketch in CA 146
See also DLB 282
Finch, Caleb E(llicott) 1939- ... 139
Finch, Carol 1948-
See Feddersen, Connie
See also RHW
Finch, Christopher (Robin) 1939- ... CANR-126
Brief entry ... 112
Earlier sketch in CA 138
Finch, Donald George 1937- ... 53-56
Finch, Henry LeRoy 1918- ... CANR-100
Earlier sketch in CA 41-44R
Finch, Matthew
See Fink, Merton
Finch, Peter 1947- ... 219
See also CP 1
Finch, Robert (Duer Claydon)
1900-1995 ... CANR-49
Earlier sketches in CA 57-60, CANR-9, 24
See also CLC 18
See also CP 1, 2
See also DLB 88
Finch, Robert (Charles) 1943- ... CANR-83
Earlier sketch in CA 137
See also ANW
Finch, Roger 1937- ... 140
Finch, Sheila 1935- ... CANR-46
Earlier sketch in CA 121
Fincham, A(nthony) A(rthur) 1943- ... 117
Fincham, Francis D. 1954- ... 140
Fincham, Frank D.
See Fincham, Francis D.
Fincher, Cameron Lane 1926- ... 41-44R
Fincher, David 1963- ... AAYA 36
Fincher, Ernest B(arksdale)
1910-1985 ... CANR-76
Obituary ... 115
Earlier sketches in CA 53-56, CANR-9
Finchler, Judy 1943- ... 158
See also SATA 93
Finck, Furman J(oseph) 1900-1997 ... CAP-2
Earlier sketch in CA 33-36
Fincke, Gary (William) 1945- ... CANR-102
Earlier sketches in CA 57-60, CANR-50
Finckenauer, James O(liver) 1939- ... 108
Finder, Joseph 1958- ... CANR-62
Earlier sketch in CA 113
Finder, Martin
See Salzmann, Siegmund
Findlater, Richard
See Bain, Kenneth Bruce Findlater
Findlay, Bill 1947- ... 188
Findlay, Bruce Allyn 1895-1972 ... CAP-1
Earlier sketch in CA 13-14
Findlay, David K. 1901- ... CAP-1
Earlier sketch in CA 13-14
Findlay, James Arthur 1883-1964
Obituary ... 111
Findlay, James F(ranklin), Jr. 1930- ... 49-52
Findlay, John N(iemeyer)
1903-1987 ... CANR-76
Obituary ... 123
Earlier sketches in CA 5-8R, CANR-5
Findlay, Robert R. 1932- ... 45-48
Findley, Carter Vaughn 1941- ... 102
Findley, Paul 1921- ... 29-32R
Findley, Timothy (Irving Frederick)
1930-2002 ... CANR-109
Obituary ... 206
Earlier sketches in CA 25-28R, CANR-12, 42, 69
See also CCA 1
See also CLC 27, 102
See also CN 4, 5, 6, 7
See also DAC
See also DAM MST
See also DLB 53
See also FANT
See also RHW
Findling, John Ellis 1941- ... 102
Findon, Joanne 1957- ... 237
See also SATA 161
Fine, Anne 1947- ... CANR-105
Earlier sketches in CA 105, CANR-38, 83
See also AAYA 20
See also CLR 25
See also CWRI 5
See also JRDA
See also MAICYA 1, 2
See also MAICYAS 1
See also SAAS 15
See also SATA 29, 72, 111, 160
Fine, Benjamin 1905-1975 ... CANR-4
Obituary ... 57-60
Earlier sketch in CA 5-8R
Fine, Bob
See Fine, Robert (David)
Fine, Carla 1946- ... CANR-129
Earlier sketch in CA 112
Fine, Doris Landau 1949- ... 153
Fine, Elsa Honig 1930- ... CANR-28
Earlier sketch in CA 49-52
Fine, Estelle
See Jelinek, Estelle C.
Fine, Gary Alan 1950- ... CANR-120
Earlier sketches in CA 111, CANR-46
Fine, I(sadore) V. 1918- ... 17-20R
Fine, Jane
See Ziefert, Harriet
Fine, John (Van Antwerp), Jr. 1939- ... 117
Fine, John Van Antwerp (Sr.) 1903-1987 ... 160
Fine, Jonathan 1949- ... 149
Fine, Judylaine 1948- ... 117
Fine, Marshall 1950- ... 137
Fine, Nathan 1893(?)-1979
Obituary ... 89-92
Fine, Ralph Adam 1941- ... 29-32R
Fine, Reuben 1914-1993 ... CANR-12
Earlier sketch in CA 17-20R
Fine, Richard 1951- ... 146
Fine, Robert (David) 1948(?)- ... 229
Fine, S(eymour) Morton 1930- ... 104
Fine, Seymour H(oward) 1925- ... CANR-30
Earlier sketch in CA 111
Fine, Sidney 1920- ... CANR-123
Earlier sketches in CA 1-4R, CANR-1
Fine, Warren 1943- ... 21-24R
Fine, William Michael 1924- ... 13-16R
Fineberg, Robert Gene 1940- ... 107
Finegan, Jack 1908-2000 ... CANR-1
Earlier sketch in CA 1-4R
Finegan, T(homas) Aldrich 1929-
Brief entry ... 108
Finello, Dominick 1944- ... 149
Fineman, Howard (David) 1948- ... 133
Fineman, Irving 1893-1976 ... 5-8R
Fineman, Joel 1947-1989 ... 127
Obituary ... 128
Fineman, Martha Albertson 1943- ... 172
Finer, Leslie 1921- ... 13-16R
Finer, S(amuel) E(dward) 1915-1993 . CANR-48
Obituary ... 141
Earlier sketch in CA 41-44R
Finerty, Catherine Palmer 1908- ... 198
Finestone, Harold 1920-
Brief entry ... 110
Finestone, Harry 1920-2003 ... 45-48
Obituary ... 220
Fingarette, Herbert 1921- ... 77-80
Finger, Charles J(oseph) 1869(?)-1941
Brief entry ... 119
See also BYA 4
See also SATA 42
Finger, J(oseph) Michael 1939- ... 222
Finger, Seymour Maxwell 1915-2005 ... 104
Finger, Stanley 1943- ... 191
Finger, William R(atliff) 1947- ... 111
Fingerhut, Eugene R. 1932- ... 111
Fingesten, Peter 1916-1987 ... CANR-77
Obituary ... 123
Earlier sketch in CA 13-16R
Fingleton, Eamonn 1948- ... 200
Finifter, Ada W(eintraub) 1938- ... CANR-21
Earlier sketch in CA 104
Fink, Arthur Emil 1903- ... 1-4R
Fink, Augusta 1916- ... CANR-13
Earlier sketch in CA 33-36R
Fink, Carole 1940- ... 135
Fink, Deborah 1944- ... 144
Fink, Edith 1918- ... 61-64
Fink, Eli E. 1908(?)-1979
Obituary ... 85-88
Fink, Gary M. 1936- ... 53-56
Fink, George ... 230
Fink, Ida 1921- ... CANR-71
Earlier sketch in CA 136
Fink, Joanne 1954- ... 123
Fink, John (Philip) 1926-1995 ... CANR-71
Earlier sketch in CA 139
Fink, Joseph 1915- ... 57-60
Fink, Karl J. 1942- ... 138
Fink, Lawrence Alfred 1930- ... 97-100
Fink, Leon 1948- ... 135
Fink, Merton 1921- ... 9-12R
Fink, Paul Jay 1933- ... 53-56
Fink, Stevanne Auerbach
See Auerbach, Stevanne
Fink, Steven (B.) 1948- ... CANR-141
Earlier sketch in CA 147
Fink, William
See Mencken, H(enry) L(ouis)
Fink, William B(ertrand) 1916- ... 41-44R
See also SATA 22
Fink, Z(era) S(ilver) 1902-1979 ... CAP-1
Earlier sketch in CA 9-10
Fink Cline, Beverly 1951- ... 113
Finke, Blythe Foote 1922- ... 65-68
See also SATA 26
Finke, Jack A. 1918(?)-1979
Obituary ... 89-92
Finke, Ronald A. 1950- ... 143
Finkel, Alvin 1949- ... CANR-75
Earlier sketch in CA 131
Finkel, Donald 1929- ... CANR-59
Earlier sketches in CA 21-24R, CANR-9, 29
See also CP 1, 2, 3, 4, 5, 6, 7
Finkel, George (Irvine) 1909-1975 ... CANR-85
Earlier sketches in CAP-2, CA 17-18
See also CWRI 5
See also SATA 8
Finkel, Lawrence S. 1925- ... 13-16R
Finkel, LeRoy 1939- ... 105
Finkelhor, David 1947- ... 118
Finkelhor, Dorothy Cimberg 1902-1988 ... 110
Finkell, Max
See Catto, Max(well Jeffrey)
Finkelman, Paul 1949- ... CANR-22
Earlier sketch in CA 105
Finkelstein, Bonnie B(lumenthal) 1946- ... 85-88
Finkelstein, Israel 1949- ... 197
Finkelstein, Jacob Joel 1922-1974
Obituary ... 53-56
Finkelstein, Leonid Vladimirovitch
1924- ... 21-24R
Finkelstein, Louis 1895-1991 ... CANR-76
Obituary ... 136
Earlier sketch in CA 13-16R
Finkelstein, Marina S. 1921(?)-1972
Obituary ... 33-36R
Finkelstein, Milton 1920- ... 89-92
Finkelstein, Miriam 1928- ... 108
Finkelstein, Norman 1954- ... 208
Finkelstein, Norman G. 1953- ... 162
Finkelstein, Norman H. 1941- ... CANR-116
Earlier sketch in CA 177, 185
See also SATA 73, 137
Finkelstein, Sidney 1910(?)-1974
Obituary ... 45-48
Finkenstaedt, Rose L. H. 1927- ... 147
Finkielkraut, Alain 1949- ... 238
Finkle, Derek ... 175
Finkle, Jason L(eonard) 1926- ... 21-24R
Finklehoffe, Fred F. 1910-1977
Obituary ... 73-76
Finkler, Kaja 1935- ... 114
Finklestone, Joseph 1924-2002 ... 212
Finlander, Alexander
See Alkio, Santeri
Finlander, Santeri
See Alkio, Santeri
Finlator, John Haywood 1911-1990 ... 102
Finlay, Alice Sullivan 1946- ... SATA 82
Finlay, Campbell K(irkman) 1909- ... 5-8R
Finlay, David J(ames) 1934- ... CANR-16
Earlier sketch in CA 25-28R
Finlay, Fiona
See Stuart, (Violet) Vivian (Finlay)
Finlay, Ian Hamilton 1925- ... 81-84
See also CP 1, 2, 3, 4, 5, 6, 7
See also DLB 40
Finlay, John 1941-1991 ... CSW
Finlay, Matthew Henderson 1916- ... 13-16R
Finlay, Peter (Warren) 1961- ... 217
Finlay, Richard J(ason) 1962- ... 146
Finlay, Roger (Anthony Peter) 1952- ... 132
Finlay, William
See Mackay, James (Alexander)
Finlay, Winifred Lindsay Crawford (McKissack)
1910-1989 ... CANR-84
Earlier sketch in CA 9-12R
See also CWRI 5
See also SATA 23
Finlayson, Ann 1925- ... 29-32R
See also SATA 8
Finlayson, Geoffrey B(eauchamp) A(listair)
M(oubray) 1934- ... 131
Finlayson, Iain (Thorburn) 1945- ... 144
Finlayson, Michael G(eorge) 1938- ... 128
Finlayson, Roderick (David) 1904-1992 .. 81-84
See also CN 2, 3, 4, 5
See also RGEL 2
Finler, Joel W(aldo) 1938- ... CANR-32
Earlier sketch in CA 77-80
Finletter, Thomas K(night) 1893-1980
Obituary ... 101
Finley, Gerald Eric 1931- ... 105
Finley, Glenna
See Witte, Glenna Finley
Finley, Guy 1949- ... 209
Finley, Harold Marshall 1916-1999 ... 17-20R
Obituary ... 187
Finley, James 1943- ... 97-100
Finley, Joseph E(dwin) 1919-1997 ... 69-72
Obituary ... 159
Finley, Karen 1956- ... CANR-108
Earlier sketch in CA 154
Finley, Lewis M(erren) 1929- ... 61-64
Finley, M(oses) I. 1912-1986 ... CANR-76
Obituary ... 119
Earlier sketches in CA 5-8R, CANR-10
Finley, Martha 1828-1909
Brief entry ... 118
See also DLB 42
See also SATA 43
Finley, Mary Peace 1942- ... SATA 83
Finley, Michael 1950- ... CANR-125
Earlier sketch in CA 166
Finley, Mitch 1945- ... CANR-88
Earlier sketch in CA 142
Finley, Randy 1954- ... 158
Finley, Robert 1957- ... 201
Finman, Ted 1931-
Brief entry ... 110
Finn, David 1921- ... CANR-99
Earlier sketch in CA 73-76
Finn, Doug(las Arthur) 1946- ... 118
Finn, Edward E(rnest) 1908-1992 ... 115
Finn, Elizabeth Anne (McCaul) 1825-1921 . 185
See also DLB 166
Finn, Geraldine 1947- ... 118
Finn, Hugh Lauder 1925- ... CP 1
Finn, James 1924-
Brief entry ... 108
Finn, Jerry 1946- ... 196
Finn, Jonathan 1884(?)-1971
Obituary ... 29-32R
Finn, Margot C. 1960- ... 146
Finn, Michael R(aeburn) 1941- ... 185
Finn, R. Welldon
See Finn, Reginald Patrick Arthur Welldon
Finn, Ralph L(eslie) 1912- ... CANR-9
Earlier sketch in CA 5-8R
Finn, Reginald Patrick Arthur Welldon
1900-1971 ... CANR-10
Earlier sketch in CA 13-16R
Finn, Rex Welldon
See Finn, Reginald Patrick Arthur Welldon
Finn, Susan C(alvert) ... 140
Finn, (Patrick) Timothy 1938- ... 129
Finnegan, Marianne Gilbert 1931- ... 227
Finnegan, Mary Jeremy 1907- ... 135
Finnegan, Robert
See Ryan, Paul William
Finnegan, Ruth H(ilary) 1933- ... CANR-12
Earlier sketch in CA 25-28R
Finnegan, Seamus 1949- ... DLB 245
Finnegan, William (Patrick) 1952- ... CANR-88
Earlier sketch in CA 136
Finneran, Kathleen 1958(?)- ... 229
Finneran, Richard J(ohn) 1943- ... CANR-29
Earlier sketches in CA 29-32R, CANR-12
Finnerty, Adam Daniel
See Corson-Finnerty, Adam Daniel
Finnerty, Daniel John
See Corson-Finnerty, Adam Daniel
Finney, Ben R(udolph) 1933- ... CANR-1
Earlier sketch in CA 45-48
Finney, Brian (Hubert) 1935- ... 201
Finney, Charles G(randison)
1905-1984 ... CANR-58
Obituary ... 112
Earlier sketches in CAP-2, CA 29-32
See also FANT
See also SUFW 1
Finney, Ernest J. ... 134

Cumulative Index 189 Fisher

Finney, Gertrude Elva (Bridgeman)
1892-1977 .... CAP-1
Earlier sketch in CA 13-16
Finney, Gretchen Ludke 1901- 9-12R
Finney, Humphrey S. 1902-1984 97-100
Finney, Jack
See Finney, Walter Braden
See also AAYA 30
See also BPFB 1
See also CMW
See also DLB 8
See also FANT
See also SATA 109
See also SFW 4
Finney, Jarlath (John) 1930-1999 186
Finney, Nathaniel Solon 1903-1982
Obituary 108
Finney, Patricia 1958- 97-100
See also SATA 163
Finney, Paul B(urnham) 1929- 73-76
Finney, Paul Corby 1939- 195
Finney, Shan 1944- 111
See also SATA 65
Finney, Theodore M(itchell) 1902-1978 .. 61-64
Finney, Walter Braden 1911-1995 .... CANR-84
Obituary 150
Brief entry 110
Earlier sketch in CA 133
See also Finney, Jack
Finnigan, Joan (MacKenzie) 1925- ... CANR-85
Earlier sketches in CA 17-20R, CANR-13, 29, 53
See also CP 1, 2, 3, 4, 5, 6, 7
See also CWP
Finnin, (Olive) Mary 106
See also CP 1
Finnis, John M(itchell) 1940- 136
Finocchiaro, Mary (Bonomo)
1913-1996 .... CANR-27
Earlier sketch in CA 29-32R
Finocchiaro, Maurice (A.) 1942- 189
Fins, Alice 1944- 110
Finson, Jon W(illiam) 1950- 125
Finstad, Suzanne 1955- CANR-141
Earlier sketch in CA 131
Finstein, Max .... CP 1
Finucane, Ronald C(harles) 135
Finz, Steven R. 1943- 180
Fiore, Edith 1930- 85-88
Fiore, Michael V. 1934- 45-48
Fiore, Peter Amadeus 1927- 33-36R
Fiore, Robert Louis 1935- 73-76
Fiore, Silvestro 1921- 17-20R
Fiorenza, Elisabeth Schussler
1938- CANR-108
Earlier sketches in CA 106, CANR-39
Fiorenza, Francis S(chuessler) 1941- . CANR-39
Earlier sketch in CA 115
Fiori, Pamela A. 1944- 89-92
Fiorina, Morris Paul, Jr. 1946- 85-88
Fiorino, A(ngelo) John 1926- 29-32R
Fiorio, Franco Emilio 1912-1975
Obituary 61-64
Firbank, Louis 1942-
Brief entry 117
See also Reed, Lou
Firbank, (Arthur Annesley) Ronald
1886-1926 177
Brief entry 104
See also BRWS 2
See also DLB 36
See also EWL 3
See also RGEL 2
See also TCLC 1
Firchow, Evelyn Scherabon 1932- CANR-11
Earlier sketch in CA 21-24R
Firchow, Peter (Edgerly) 1937- 37-40R
Firda, Richard Arthur 1931- 144
Firdawsi, Abu al-Qasim
See Ferdowsi, Abu'l Qasem
See also WLIT 6
Firebrace, Aylmer (Newton George)
1886-1972 .... 5-8R
Firer, Ben Zion
See Firer, Benzion
Firer, Benzion 1914- 131
See also SATA 64
Fires, Alicia
See Oglesby, Joseph
Fireside, Bryna J. 1932- .... SATA 73
Fireside, Harvey 1929- 29-32R
Firestone, Harvey S(amuel), Jr. 1898-1973
Obituary 41-44R
Firestone, O(tto) J(ohn) 1913-1993 .... 41-44R
Firestone, Robert W. 1930- 130
Firestone, Roy 1953- 222
Firestone, Shulamith 1945- 154
See also FW
Firestone, Tom
See Newcomb, Duane G(raham)
Firey, Walter Irving (Jr.) 1916- 1-4R
Firkatian, Mari A. 1959- 155
Firkins, Peter (Charles) 1926- 107
Firmage, George J(ames) 1928- 9-12R
Firmat, Gustavo (Francisco) Perez
See Perez-Firmat, Gustavo (Francisco)
Firmin, Charlotte 1954- CANR-47
Earlier sketches in CA 106, CANR-23
See also SATA 29
Firmin, Giles 1615-1697 .... DLB 24
Firmin, Peter 1928- CANR-40
Earlier sketches in CA 81-84, CANR-17
See also SATA 15, 58
Firor, John (W.) 1927- 136
Firouz, Anahita (Homa) 1953- 234
Firschling, F. Henry 1923- 183
Firsoff, V(aldemar) Axel 1910-1982 93-96
First, Philip
See Williamson, Philip G.
First, Ruth 1925-1982 .... CANR-10
Obituary 107
Earlier sketch in CA 53-56
Firstbrook, Peter 1951(?)- 221
Firth, (Frederick) Anson 1902- 117
Firth, Grace (Ushler) 1922-2004 73-76
Obituary 229
Firth, J. R.
See Firth, John Rupert
Firth, John Rupert 1890-1960
Obituary 116
Firth, Raymond (William) 1901-2002 65-68
Obituary 202
Firth, Robert E. 1921- 77-80
Firth, Tony 1937(?)-1980
Obituary 97-100
Fisch, Edith L. 1923- 77-80
Fisch, Gerald G(rant) 1922- 13-16R
Fisch, Harold 1923- CANR-90
Earlier sketch in CA 37-40R
Fisch, Martin L. 1924- 109
Fisch, Max H.
See Fisch, Max Harold
Fisch, Max Harold 1900-1995 .... 33-36R
Fisch, Richard 1926-
Brief entry 106
Fischart, Johann c. 1546-c. 1590 .... DLB 179
Fischbach, Julius 1894-1988 .... CANR-2
Earlier sketch in CA 5-8R
See also SATA 10
Fischel, Walter J(oseph) 1902-1973 .... CAP-2
Obituary 41-44R
Earlier sketch in CA 23-24
Fischel, William A. 1945- CANR-113
Earlier sketch in CA 156
Fischell, Jack R. 1937- 175
Fischer, Alfred (George) 1920- 73-76
Fischer, Ann 1919-1971 .... CAP-2
Earlier sketch in CA 25-28
Fischer, Arlene 1934- 111
Fischer, Bernd Jurgen 1952- 221
Fischer, Bobby
See Fischer, Robert James
Fischer, Bruno 1908-1992 .... CANR-59
Earlier sketch in CA 77-80
See also CMW 4
Fischer, Carl H(ahn) 1903-1988 .... 17-20R
Fischer, Catherine Hoffpauir 1947(?)- 203
Fischer, Claude S(erge) 1948- 107
Fischer, David Hackett 1935- 17-20R
Fischer, Dennis 1960- 140
Fischer, Dietrich 1941- 117
Fischer, Donald E(dward) 1935- 41-44R
Fischer, Edward (Adam) 1914-1992 .. CANR-37
Earlier sketches in CA 1-4R, CANR-1, 16
Fischer, Ernst 1899-1972
Obituary 37-40R
Fischer, Ernst Otto 1918- 157
Fischer, Fritz 1908-1999 .... CANR-9
Obituary 187
Earlier sketch in CA 65-68
Fischer, George 1923- CANR-9
Earlier sketch in CA 53-56
Fischer, George 1932- 25-28R
Fischer, Gerald C(harles) 1928- CANR-9
Earlier sketch in CA 21-24R
Fischer, Gretl Keren 1919- 211
Fischer, Gretl Kraus
See Fischer, Gretl Keren
Fischer, Gunnar 1910- .... IDFW 3, 4
Fischer, J(ohn) L(yle) 1923- 17-20R
Fischer, Joel 1939- CANR-40
Earlier sketches in CA 53-56, CANR-4, 19
Fischer, John
See Fluke, Joanne
Fischer, John 1910-1978 .... CANR-4
Obituary 81-84
Earlier sketch in CA 9-12R
Fischer, John F. 182
Fischer, John Irwin 1940- 129
Fischer, John Martin 1952- CANR-51
Earlier sketch in CA 124
Fischer, Karoline Auguste Fernandine
1764-1842 .... DLB 94
Fischer, Klaus P. 1942- CANR-86
Earlier sketch in CA 150
Fischer, LeRoy H(enry) 1917- CANR-8
Earlier sketch in CA 17-20R
Fischer, Louis 1896-1970 .... CAP-1
Obituary 25-28R
Earlier sketch in CA 11-12
Fischer, Lucy Rose 1944- 138
Fischer, Lynn 1943- 150
Fischer, Maribeth 200
Fischer, Michael R(obert) 1949- 118
Fischer, R. J.
See Fluke, Joanne
Fischer, Robert H. 1918- 37-40R
Fischer, Robert James 1943- 103
Fischer, Roger Adrian 1939-
Brief entry 109
Fischer, Tibor 1959- CANR-95
Earlier sketch in CA 157
See also CN 6, 7
See also DLB 231
Fischer, Vera Kistiakowsky
See Kistiakowsky, Vera
Fischer, Victor 1924-
Brief entry 110
Fischer, William F(rank) 1934-
Brief entry 111
Fischer, Wolfgang Georg 1933- 33-36R
Fischer-Dieskau, Dietrich 1925- 97-100
Fischer-Fabian, S(iegfried) 1922- CANR-90
Earlier sketch in CA 130
Fischer-Galati, Stephen A(lexander) 1924- .. 127
Brief entry 117
Fischer-Nagel, Andreas 1951- 123
See also SATA 56
Fischer-Nagel, Heiderose 1956- 123
See also SATA 56
Fischerova, Daniela 1948- 232
Fischerova, Sylva 1963- 197
Fischetti, John 1916-1980
Obituary 102
Fischetti, Mark 225
Fischinger, Oskar 1900-1967 .... IDFW 3, 4
Fischl, Viktor
See Dagan, Avigdor
Fischler, Alan 1952- 137
Fischler, Shirley (Walton) 136
See also SATA 66
Fischler, Stan(ley I.) 128
Brief entry 116
See also SATA 66
See also SATA-Brief 36
Fischlin, Daniel 213
Fischman, Dennis 1958- 140
Fischman, Harve 1930- 185
Brief entry 113
Fischman, Leonard L(ipman) 1919- .. CANR-10
Earlier sketch in CA 13-16R
Fischtrom, Harvey 1933-1974 .... CAP-2
Obituary 53-56
Earlier sketch in CA 25-28
See also Zemach, Harve
Fisdel, Steven A. 163
Fish, Byron 1908-1996 45-48
Fish, Charles (K.) 1936- 149
Fish, Joe
See Williamson, Philip G.
Fish, Julian
See Campbell, Blanche
Fish, Kenneth L(loyd) 1926- 29-32R
Fish, Margery (Townshend)
1892-1969 .... CANR-4
Earlier sketch in CA 5-8R
Fish, Peter Graham 1937- 69-72
Fish, Robert L(loyd) 1912-1981 .... CANR-61
Obituary 103
Earlier sketches in CA 13-16R, CANR-13
See also CMW 4
Fish, Roy J(ason) 1930- 123
Brief entry 118
Fish, Stanley
See Fish, Stanley Eugene
Fish, Stanley E.
See Fish, Stanley Eugene
Fish, Stanley Eugene 1938- CANR-90
Brief entry 112
Earlier sketch in CA 132
See also CLC 142
See also DLB 67
Fishacre, Richard 1205(?)-1248 .... DLB 115
Fishback, Margaret
See Antolini, Margaret Fishback
Fishback, Mary 1954- 225
Fishback, Price V(anmeter) 1955- 138
Fishbane, Michael A(lton) 1943- 113
Fishbein, Harold D(ennis) 1938- CANR-53
Brief entry 105
Earlier sketch in CA 126
Fishbein, Meyer H(arry) 1916- 41-44R
Fishbein, Morris 1889-1976 .... CANR-4
Obituary 69-72
Earlier sketch in CA 5-8R
Fishburn, Hummel 1901-1976 .... CAP-1
Earlier sketch in CA 19-20
Fishburn, Janet Forsythe 1937- 108
Fishburn, Peter C(lingerman) 1936- 45-48
Fishel, Edwin C. 1914-1999 162
Obituary 177
Fishel, Elizabeth 1950- CANR-94
Earlier sketch in CA 103
Fishel, Leslie H(enry), Jr. 1921- 21-24R
Fishel, Wesley R(obert) 1919-1977 73-76
Obituary 69-72
Fisher, A(rnold) Garth 1933- 104
Fisher, A(rthur) Stanley T(heodore)
1906- 93-96
Fisher, Aileen (Lucia) 1906-2002 ...... CANR-84
Obituary 216
Earlier sketches in CA 5-8R, CANR-2, 17, 37
See also CLR 49
See also CWRI 5
See also MAICYA 1, 2
See also SATA 1, 25, 73
See also SATA-Obit 143
Fisher, Alan (E.) 1929- CANR-48
Earlier sketch in CA 121
Fisher, Alan W(ashburn) 1939- 53-56
Fisher, Alden L(owell) 1928-1970 .... CAP-2
Earlier sketch in CA 25-28
Fisher, Allan C(arroll), Jr. 1919- 112
Fisher, Allan G(eorge) B(arnard)
1895-1976 .... 33-36R
Fisher, Allen J. 1907(?)-1980
Obituary 102
Fisher, Ameel J(oseph) 1909-1985 104
Fisher, Angela 1947- CANR-91
Earlier sketch in CA 145
Fisher, Anne B. 1957- 135
Fisher, Antwone Quenton 1959- 206
Fisher, Arthur 1931- 110
Fisher, Barbara 1940- CANR-56
Earlier sketches in CA 104, CANR-30
See also SATA 44
See also SATA-Brief 34
Fisher, Bart (Steven) 1943- 45-48
Fisher, Benjamin Franklin IV 1940- .. CANR-58
Earlier sketches in CA 112, CANR-30
Fisher, Bob
See Fisher, Robert Percival
Fisher, Bruce 1931- 118
Fisher, C(harles) William 1916- CANR-6
Earlier sketch in CA 5-8R
Fisher, Carolyn 1968- .... SATA 154
Fisher, Carrie (Frances) 1956- 135
See also BEST 90:4
See also CPW
See also DA3
See also DAM POP
Fisher, Catherine 1957- 233
See also SATA 155
Fisher, Charles Alfred 1916-1982(?)
Obituary 105
Fisher, Chris 1958- .... SATA 80
Fisher, Clavin C(argill) 1912- 65-68
See also SATA 24
Fisher, Clay
See Allen, Henry Wilson
Fisher, Cyrus
See Teilhet, Darwin L(eOra)
Fisher, David 1946- CANR-111
Earlier sketch in CA 143
Fisher, David E(limelech) 1932- CANR-45
Earlier sketches in CA 53-56, CANR-4, 22
Fisher, Dominic (Mayne Maitland) 1953- ... 124
Fisher, Don 1933(?)-1983
Obituary 111
Fisher, Dorothy (Frances) Canfield
1879-1958 .... CANR-80
Brief entry 114
Earlier sketch in CA 136
See also CLR 71
See also CWRI 5
See also DLB 9, 102, 284
See also MAICYA 1, 2
See also MAL 5
See also TCLC 87
See also YABC 1
Fisher, Douglas 1934- 102
Fisher, Douglas 1954- 118
Fisher, Douglas Mason 1919- 89-92
Fisher, Eddie
See Fisher, Edwin Jack
Fisher, Edward 1902- 1-4R
Fisher, Edwin Jack 1928- 198
Fisher, Elizabeth 1941- 117
Fisher, Ernest Arthur 1887- 13-16R
Fisher, Ernest F., Jr. 1918- 150
Fisher, Esther Oshiver 1910-1988 85-88
Fisher, Eugene J(oseph) 1943- CANR-22
Earlier sketch in CA 105
Fisher, Florence (Anna) 1928-
Brief entry 112
Fisher, Franklin M(arvin) 1934- 17-20R
Fisher, Fred L(ewis) 1911-1990 .... CANR-5
Earlier sketch in CA 1-4R
Fisher, (Donald) Gary 1938- 103
Fisher, Gary L. 1949- 151
See also SATA 86
Fisher, Gene H. 1922- 41-44R
Fisher, Gene L(ouis) 1947- 81-84
Fisher, George E(dward) 1923- 127
Fisher, George W. 1910(?)-1987
Obituary 124
Fisher, Gerry 1926- .... IDFW 3, 4
Fisher, Glen H(arry) 1922-
Brief entry 111
Fisher, Glenn W(illiam) 1924- 53-56
Fisher, Gordon N(eil) 1928-1985
Obituary 117
Fisher, Harold H. 1890-1975
Obituary 61-64
Fisher, Harry 1911-2003 236
Fisher, Harvey Irvin 1916- 69-72
Fisher, Helen E(lizabeth) 1945- CANR-88
Earlier sketch in CA 108
Fisher, Humphrey J(ohn) 1933- CANR-138
Earlier sketch in CA 33-36R
Fisher, J(ohn) R(obert) 1943- CANR-1
Earlier sketch in CA 45-48
Fisher, J(oseph) Thomas 1936- 33-36R
Fisher, James (Maxwell McConnell)
1912-1970 126
Obituary 89-92
Fisher, James R(aymond), Jr. 1937- 81-84
Fisher, Jerry M. 1940- 187
Fisher, Joe 1947-2001 .... CANR-128
Earlier sketch in CA 103
Fisher, Johanna 1922- 93-96
Fisher, John (Oswald Hamilton) 1909- 81-84
See also SATA 15
Fisher, John C(harles) 1927- 41-44R
Fisher, John H(urt) 1919- CANR-11
Earlier sketch in CA 21-24R
Fisher, John J(acob) III 1951(?)-1990
Obituary 131
Fisher, Joseph C. 1948- 182
Fisher, Kenneth L(awrence) 1950- 118
Fisher, Kim N. 1948- 121
Fisher, Laine
See Howard, James A(rch)
Fisher, Laura Harrison 1934- 13-16R
See also SATA 5
Fisher, Lawrence V. 1923- 17-20R
Fisher, Lee 1908-1999 .... 33-36R
Fisher, Leonard Everett 1924- CANR-98
Earlier sketches in CA 1-4R, CANR-2, 37, 77
See also CLR 18
See also CWRI 5
See also DLB 61
See also MAICYA 1, 2
See also SAAS 1
See also SATA 4, 34, 73, 120
See also SATA-Essay 122

Fisher, Lillian Estelle 1891-1988 ... CAP-1
Earlier sketch in CA 13-16
Fisher, Lois H(amilton) 1936- ... 113
Fisher, Lois I. 1948- ... 113
See also SATA 38
See also SATA-Brief 35
Fisher, Lois Jeannette 1909-1988 ... 5-8R
Fisher, Louis 1934- ... CANR-136
Earlier sketch in CA 37-40R
Fisher, M(ary) F(rances) K(ennedy) 1908-1992 ... CANR-44
Obituary ... 138
Earlier sketch in CA 77-80
See also CLC 76, 87
See also MTCW 2
Fisher, Malcolm R(obertson) 1923-
Brief entry ... 110
Fisher, Margaret B(arrow) 1918- ... 17-20R
Fisher, Margery (Turner) 1913-1992 .. CANR-46
Obituary ... 140
Earlier sketch in CA 73-76
See also SATA 20
See also SATA-Obit 74
Fisher, Margot
See Paine, Lauran (Bosworth)
Fisher, Marshall Jon 1963- ... 175
See also SATA 113
Fisher, Marvin 1927- ... 21-24R
Fisher, Mary 1948- ... 148
Fisher, Mary L. 1928- ... 33-36R
Fisher, Michael John 1933- ... CANR-92
Earlier sketches in CA 1-4R, CANR-3
Fisher, Miles Mark 1899-1970 ... CAP-1
Earlier sketch in CA 13-16
Fisher, Milton 1917- ... 182
Fisher, Miriam Louise (Scharfe) 1939- ... 13-16R
Fisher, Morris 1922- ... 21-24R
Fisher, Neal F(loyd) 1936- ... 106
Fisher, Nigel 1913-1996 ... 102
Fisher, Nikki
See Strachan, Ian
Fisher, Norman George 1910-1972
Obituary ... 107
Fisher, Peter Jack 1930- ... 69-72
Fisher, Philip 1941- ... CANR-72
Earlier sketches in CA 113, CANR-33
Fisher, Philip A(rthur) 1907-2004 ... 61-64
Obituary ... 225
Fisher, R. A.
See Fisher, Ronald A(ylmer)
Fisher, Ralph Talcott, Jr. 1920- ... 41-44R
Fisher, Rhoda Lee 1924-2004 ... 65-68
Obituary ... 226
Fisher, Richard 1936- ... 17-20R
Fisher, Richard B(ernard) 1919- ... 77-80
Fisher, Robert (Tempest) 1943- ... CANR-52
Earlier sketches in CA 109, CANR-26
See also SATA 47
Fisher, Robert C(harles) 1930- ... CANR-49
Earlier sketch in CA 53-56
Fisher, Robert E. 1940- ... 169
Fisher, Robert J(ay) 1924- ... 61-64
Fisher, Robert Percival 1935- ... 93-96
Fisher, Roger (Dummer) 1922- ... 37-40R
Fisher, Ronald A(ylmer) 1890-1962 ... 157
Obituary ... 112
Fisher, Roy 1930- ... CANR-16
Earlier sketch in CA 81-84
See also CAAS 10
See also CLC 25
See also CP 1, 2, 3, 4, 5, 6, 7
See also DLB 40
Fisher, Rudolph 1897-1934 ... CANR-80
Brief entry ... 107
Earlier sketch in CA 124
See also BLC 2
See also BW 1, 3
See also DAM MULT
See also DLB 51, 102
See also HR 1:2
See also SSC 25
See also TCLC 11
Fisher, Seymour 1922-1996 ... CANR-12
Obituary ... 155
Earlier sketch in CA 33-36R
Fisher, Shelton 1911-1985
Obituary ... 115
Fisher, Sidney Thomson 1908-1992 ... 124
Fisher, Stephen (Gould) 1913-1980 ... 238
See also Fisher, Steve
Fisher, Stephen L(ynn) 1944- ... 139
Fisher, Sterling Wesley 1899(?)-1978 ... 85-88
Obituary ... 81-84
Fisher, Steve
See Fisher, Stephen (Gould)
See also CMW 4
See also DLB 226
Fisher, Susan M(ichal) 1937- ... 119
Fisher, Suzanne
See Staples, Suzanne Fisher
Fisher, Sydney G.
See Fisher, Sydney George
Fisher, Sydney George 1856-1927
Brief entry ... 122
See also DLB 47
Fisher, Vardis (Alvero) 1895-1968 ... CANR-68
Obituary ... 25-28R
Earlier sketch in CA 5-8R
See also CLC 7
See also DLB 9, 206
See also MAL 5
See also RGAL 4
See also TCLC 140
See also TCWW 1, 2
Fisher, Wade
See Norwood, Victor G(eorge) C(harles)
Fisher, Wallace E. 1918- ... CANR-10
Earlier sketch in CA 21-24R
Fisher, Walter R. 1931- ... 13-16R
Fisher, Welthy Honsinger 1879-1980 ... CANR-76
Obituary ... 102
Earlier sketches in CA 1-4R, CANR-2
Fisher, Wesley Andrew 1944- ... 104
Fisher, William Bayne 1916-1984 ... CANR-76
Obituary ... 113
Earlier sketch in CA 65-68
Fishkin, Shelley Fisher 1950- ... 145
Fishler, Mary Shiverick 1920- ... 5-8R
Fishlock, David (Jocelyn) 1932- ... 130
Fishlock, Trevor 1941- ... 161
Fishman, Aryei 1922- ... 142
Fishman, Betty G(oldstein) 1918- ... 5-8R
Fishman, Burton J(ohn) 1942- ... 45-48
Fishman, Cathy Goldberg 1951- ... 176
See also SATA 106
Fishman, Charles 1942- ... CANR-7
Earlier sketch in CA 57-60
Fishman, George Samuel 1937- ... 25-28R
Fishman, Jack 1920- ... CANR-7
Earlier sketch in CA 9-12R
Fishman, Joshua A(aron) 1926- ... CANR-93
Earlier sketches in CA 41-44R, CANR-15, 34
Fishman, Katherine Davis 1937- ... 130
Fishman, Ken 1950- ... 105
Fishman, Leo 1914-1975 ... CANR-77
Obituary ... 120
Earlier sketch in CA 17-20R
Fishman, Lew 1939- ... CANR-11
Earlier sketch in CA 61-64
Fishman, Lisa 1966- ... 166
Fishman, Robert (Lawrence) 1946- ... 112
Fishman, Solomon
See Rolfe, Edwin
Fishman, Sterling 1932- ... 45-48
Fishman, Steve 1955- ... 226
Fishman, Sylvia Barack 1942- ... 231
Fishof, David 1956- ... 115
Fishta, Gjergj 1871-1940 ... EWL 3
Fishwick, Marshall William 1923- ... CANR-6
Earlier sketch in CA 5-8R
Fisk, E(rnest) K(elvin) 1917- ... 17-20R
Fisk, Erma J(onnie) 1905(?)-1990
Obituary ... 130
See also ANW
Fisk, McKee 1900-1978 ... CAP-2
Earlier sketch in CA 21-22
Fisk, Milton 1932- ... 201
Fisk, Nicholas ... CANR-28
Earlier sketches in CA 65-68, CANR-11
See also Higginbottom, David
See also SATA 25
See also SFW 4
See also YAW
Fisk, Pauline 1948- ... CANR-124
Earlier sketch in CA 136
See also FANT
See also SATA 66, 160
Fisk, Robert 1946(?)- ... 140
Fisk, Samuel 1907- ... 57-60
Fiske, Edward B(ogardus) 1937- ... CANR-41
Earlier sketches in CA 85-88, CANR-16
Fiske, Irene ... GLL 1
Fiske, John 1608-1677 ... DLB 24
Fiske, John 1842-1901 ... 179
See also DLB 47, 64
Fiske, Marjorie ... CANR-1
Earlier sketch in CA 45-48
Fiske, Robert H(artwell) 1948- ... 163
Fiske, Roger E(lwyn) 1910-1987 ... 13-16R
Fiske, Sharon
See Hill, Pamela
Fiske, Tarleton
See Bloch, Robert (Albert)
Fisketjon, Gary 1954- ... 129
Brief entry ... 123
Interview in ... CA-129
Fiskin, A(bram) M. I. 1916-1975 ... CAP-2
Earlier sketch in CA 23-24
Fison, Joseph Edward 1906-1972
Obituary ... 114
Fiss, Owen M(itchell) 1938- ... 112
Fisscher, Catharina G. M. 1958- ... 213
See also SATA 142
Fisscher, Tiny
See Fisscher, Catharina G. M.
Fiszel, Henryk 1910- ... 29-32R
Fiszman, Joseph R. 1921- ... 41-44R
Fitch, Alger Morton, Jr. 1919- ... 53-56
Fitch, Bob
See Fitch, Robert Beck
Fitch, Clarke
See Sinclair, Upton (Beall)
Fitch, (William) Clyde 1865-1909 ... 179
Brief entry ... 110
See also DLB 7
See also MAL 5
See also RGAL 4
Fitch, Donald S(heldon) 1949- ... 106
Fitch, Edwin M(edbery) 1902-1986 ... CAP-2
Earlier sketch in CA 25-28
Fitch, George Ashmore 1883-1979
Obituary ... 85-88
Fitch, Geraldine T(ownsend) 1892(?)-1976
Obituary ... 69-72
Fitch, James Marston 1909-2000 ... 89-92
Obituary ... 190
Fitch, Janet ... 185
Fitch, John IV
See Cormier, Robert (Edmund)
Fitch, Kenneth (Leonard) 1929- ... 49-52
Fitch, Lyle C(raig) 1913-1996 ... 13-16R
Obituary ... 155
Fitch, Marina 1957- ... 222
Fitch, Noel Riley 1937- ... CANR-140
Earlier sketches in CA 144, CANR-73
Fitch, Raymond E(dward) 1930- ... 110
Fitch, Robert Beck 1938- ... 21-24R
Fitch, Sheree 1956- ... 169
See also CWRI 5
See also SATA 108
Fitch, Stanley K. 1920- ... 29-32R
Fitch, Thomas 1700(?)-1774 ... DLB 31
Fitch, Willis Stetson 1896(?)-1978
Obituary ... 81-84
Fite, Gilbert C(ourtland) 1918- ... 33-36R
Fite, James David 1933- ... 107
Fite, Mack
See Schneck, Stephen
Fites, Philip 1946- ... 141
Fitler, Mary Biddle 1878(?)-1966
Obituary ... 25-28R
Fitrat, Abdalrauf 1886-1937 ... EWL 3
Fitschen, Dale 1937- ... 77-80
See also SATA 20
Fitt, Mary
See Freeman, Kathleen
Fitter, Chris 1955- ... 150
Fitter, Richard Sidney Richmond 1913- ... CANR-49
Earlier sketches in CA 65-68, CANR-11
Fitting, Greer A. 1943- ... 81-84
Fitting, James E. 1939- ... 45-48
Fitting, Melvin (Chris) 1942- ... CANR-11
Earlier sketch in CA 29-32R
Fitton, James 1899-1982
Obituary ... 106
Fitts, Dudley 1903-1968 ... 93-96
Obituary ... 25-28R
See also MAL 5
Fitts, Henry (King) 1914-1999 ... 113
Fitts, William Howard 1918- ... 21-24R
Fittslaiion, Kirill Zinov'ev
See Fitzlyon, Kyril
Fitz, Jean DeWitt 1912-1982 ... 29-32R
Fitzalan, Roger
See Trevor, Elleston
Fitzball, Edward 1793-1873 ... RGEL 2
Fitzell, John 1922- ... 13-16R
Fitzgerald, Arlene J. -1980 ... CANR-8
Earlier sketch in CA 21-24R
Fitzgerald, Astrid 1938- ... CANR-113
Earlier sketch in CA 154
Fitzgerald, Barbara
See Newman, Mona Alice Jean and Value, Barbara Ann
Fitzgerald, Barry Charles 1939- ... 37-40R
FitzGerald, Brian Seymour Vesey
See Vesey-FitzGerald, Brian Seymour
FitzGerald, C(harles) P(atrick) 1902-1992 ... CANR-76
Obituary ... 137
Earlier sketches in CA 17-20R, CANR-11
Fitzgerald, Captain Hugh
See Baum, L(yman) Frank
Fitzgerald, Carol 1942- ... 226
Fitz-Gerald, Carolyn 1932- ... 41-44R
FitzGerald, Cathleen 1932-1987 ... CANR-76
Obituary ... 121
Earlier sketch in CA 33-36R
See also SATA-Obit 50
Fitzgerald, Cathy ... 232
Fitzgerald, Dorothy (Minerva) Dow 1903(?)-1989
Obituary ... 128
Fitzgerald, E(dmund) V(alpy) K(nox) 1947- ... 73-76
FitzGerald, Edward 1809-1883 ... BRW 4
See also DLB 32
See also RGEL 2
Fitzgerald, Edward 1898(?)-1982
Obituary ... 108
Fitzgerald, Edward Earl 1919-2001 ... 73-76
Obituary ... 193
See also SATA 20
Fitzgerald, Ellen
See Stevenson, Florence
Fitzgerald, Eric
See Brewer, Gil
Fitzgerald, Ernest A. 1925- ... CANR-12
Earlier sketch in CA 29-32R
Fitzgerald, F(rancis) A(nthony) 1940- ... SATA 15
Fitzgerald, F(rancis) Scott (Key) 1896-1940 ... 123
Brief entry ... 110
See also AAYA 24
See also AITN 1
See also AMW
See also AMWC 2
See also AMWR 1
See also BPFB 1
See also CDALB 1917-1929
See also DA
See also DA3
See also DAB
See also DAC
See also DAM MST, NOV
See also DLB 4, 9, 86, 219, 273
See also DLBD 1, 15, 16
See also DLBY 1981, 1996
See also EWL 3
See also EXPN
See also EXPS
See also LAIT 3
See also MAL 5
See also MTCW 1, 2
See also MTFW 2005
See also NFS 2, 19, 20
See also RGAL 4
See also RGSF 2
See also SSC 6, 31, 75
See also SSFS 4, 15, 21
See also TCLC 1, 6, 14, 28, 55, 157
See also TUS
See also WLC
FitzGerald, Frances 1940- ... CANR-78
Earlier sketches in CA 41-44R, CANR-32
Interview in ... CANR-32
FitzGerald, Garret 1926- ... 109
Fitzgerald, George R. 1932- ... CANR-17
Earlier sketch in CA 97-100
Fitzgerald, Gerald (Pierce) 1930- ... 37-40R
Fitzgerald, Gerald (Norman) 1932-1990
Obituary ... 131
Fitzgerald, Gerald E(dward) 1920- ... 25-28R
Fitz Gerald, Gregory 1923- ... CANR-1
Earlier sketch in CA 49-52
Fitzgerald, Hal
See Johnson, Joseph E(arl)
Fitzgerald, Harold Alvin 1896-1984
Obituary ... 114
Fitzgerald, Hiram E(arl) 1940- ... CANR-16
Earlier sketch in CA 77-80
Fitzgerald, Jack
See Shea, John Gerald
Fitzgerald, James A(ugustine) 1892-1965 ... CANR-1
Earlier sketch in CA 1-4R
Fitzgerald, James V. 1889(?)-1976
Obituary ... 69-72
Fitzgerald, John
See Fazzano, Joseph E.
Fitzgerald, John D(ennis) 1907(?)-1988 ... CANR-84
Obituary ... 126
Earlier sketch in CA 93-96
See also CLR 1
See also CWRI 5
See also MAICYA 1, 2
See also SATA 20
See also SATA-Obit 56
Fitzgerald, John Joseph 1928- ... 37-40R
Fitzgerald, Judith 1952- ... CANR-62
Earlier sketches in CA 113, CANR-32
Fitzgerald, Julia
See Watson, Julia
FitzGerald, Kathleen Whalen 1938- ... 109
Fitzgerald, Kitty 1946- ... 129
Fitzgerald, Laurine Elisabeth 1930- ... 37-40R
Fitzgerald, Lawrence
See Dwight, Jeffry
Fitzgerald, Lawrence P(ennybaker) 1906-1976 ... CANR-2
Earlier sketch in CA 1-4R
Fitzgerald, Liv 1950- ... 215
Fitzgerald, Mary Anne ... 175
Fitzgerald, Maury 1906(?)-1986
Obituary ... 121
Fitzgerald, Merni Ingrassia 1955- ... 124
See also SATA 53
Fitzgerald, Michael G(arrett) 1950- ... 77-80
Fitzgerald, Michael W(illiam) 1956- ... 235
Fitzgerald, Nancy 1951- ... 85-88
Fitzgerald, Patrick (John) 1928- ... 9-12R
Fitzgerald, Penelope 1916-2000 ... CANR-131
Obituary ... 190
Earlier sketches in CA 85-88, CANR-56, 86
See also CAAS 10
See also BRWS 5
See also CLC 19, 51, 61, 143
See also CN 3, 4, 5, 6, 7
See also DLB 14, 194
See also EWL 3
See also MTCW 2
See also MTFW 2005
Fitzgerald, Randall 1950- ... 118
Fitzgerald, Richard (Ambrose) 1938- ... 45-48
Fitzgerald, Robert (Stuart) 1910-1985 . CANR-1
Obituary ... 114
Earlier sketch in CA 1-4R
See also CLC 39
See also CP 1, 2
See also DLBY 1980
See also MAL 5
FitzGerald, Robert D(avid) 1902-1987 .. 17-20R
See also CLC 19
See also CP 1, 2
See also DLB 260
See also RGEL 2
FitzGerald, Stephen (Arthur) 1938- ... 97-100
Fitzgerald, Tamsin 1950- ... 97-100
Fitzgerald, Thomas 1819-1891 ... DLB 23
Fitzgerald, Valerie 1927- ... 165
See also RHW
Fitzgerald, Zelda (Sayre) 1900-1948 ... 126
Brief entry ... 117
See also AMWS 9
See also DLBY 1984
See also TCLC 52
FitzGibbon, (Robert Louis) Constantine (Lee-Dillon) 1919-1983 ... CANR-2
Obituary ... 109
Earlier sketch in CA 1-4R
Fitzgibbon, Russell H(umke) 1902-1979 ... CANR-14
Earlier sketch in CA 65-68
Fitzgibbon, Terry 1948- ... SATA 121
FitzGibbon, Theodora (Joanne Eileen Winifred) Rosling 1916- ... CANR-3
Earlier sketch in CA 5-8R
Fitzgibbons, James P. 1912(?)-1983
Obituary ... 110
Fitzhardinge, Joan Margaret 1912- ... CANR-36
Earlier sketches in CA 13-16R, CANR-6, 23
See also Phipson, Joan
See also MAICYA 1, 2

Cumulative Index 191 Fleming

See also SATA 2, 73
See also YAW
Fitzhenry, Robert Irvine 1918- 110
FitzHerbert, Katrin 1936- 190
FitzHerbert, Margaret 1942-1986 130
Fitzhugh, Louise (Perkins)
1928-1974 .... CANR-84
Obituary 53-56
Earlier sketches in CAP-2, CA 29-32, CANR-34
See also AAYA 18
See also CLR 1, 72
See also CWRI 5
See also DLB 52
See also JRDA
See also MAICYA 1, 2
See also SATA 1, 45
See also SATA-Obit 24
Fitzhugh, Percy Keese 1876-1950 133
See also SATA 65
Fitzhugh, Robert Tyson 1906-1981
Obituary 104
Fitzhugh, William 1651(?)-1701 .... DLB 24
Fitzlyon, (Cecily) April (Mead) 1920- 5-8R
Fitzlyon, Kyril 1910- 93-96
Fitzmaurice, Gabriel 1952- CANR-138
Earlier sketch in CA 137
Fitzmaurice, George 1877-1963
Obituary 93-96
See also RGEL 2
Fitzmyer, Joseph A(ugustine) 1920- CANR-5
Earlier sketch in CA 9-12R
Fitzpatrick, Billie 175
Fitzpatrick, Christina 1973- 207
Fitzpatrick, Daniel Robert 1891-1969
Obituary 89-92
Fitzpatrick, David 1948- 156
Fitzpatrick, Deanne 211
Fitzpatrick, James
See Fitzpatrick, Jim
Fitzpatrick, James K(evin) 1942- 65-68
Fitzpatrick, Jim 222
Fitzpatrick, Jimmy
See Fitzpatrick, Jim
Fitzpatrick, Joseph P(atrick) 1913-1995 . 17-20R
Fitzpatrick, Kathryn 1934- 113
Fitzpatrick, Marie-Louise 1962- CANR-104
Earlier sketch in CA 186
See also SATA 125
Fitzpatrick, Mary Anne 1949- 145
Fitzpatrick, Nina
See Witoszek, Nina
FitzPatrick, Paul Joseph 1894-1984
Obituary 111
Fitzpatrick, Tom 1927-2002
Obituary 206
Brief entry 111
Fitzpatrick, Tony 1949- CANR-93
Earlier sketch in CA 140
Fitzpatrick, Vincent (dePaul III) 1950- 131
FitzRalph, Matthew
See McInerny, Ralph (Matthew)
Fitz-Randolph, Jane (Currens) 1915- 103
See also SATA 51
FitzRoy, Charles (Patrick Hugh) 1957- 136
Fitzroy, Rosamond
See Briggs, Desmond Lawther
Fitzsimmons, Cleo 1900-1998 .... 1-4R
Fitzsimmons, Michael P. 1949- 129
Fitzsimmons, Thomas 1926- CANR-15
Earlier sketch in CA 33-36R
Fitz-Simon, Christopher 1934- CANR-102
Earlier sketches in CA 113, CANR-48
Fitzsimons, Cecilia (A. L.) 1952- 163
See also SATA 97
Fitzsimons, Louise 1932- 61-64
Fitzsimons, M(athew) A(nthony)
1912-1992 .... 13-16R
FitzSimons, Maureen 1920(?)- 234
FitzSimons, Neal 1928-2000 .... 33-36R
Obituary 190
Fitzsimons, Peter 206
FitzSimons, Raymund CANR-15
Earlier sketch in CA 33-36R
FitzSimons, Ruth M(arie Mangan) 53-56
Fitzwilliam, Michael
See Lyons, J. B.
Five, Billy
See Obrecht, Jas
Five, U.S.
See Stanton, Robert J.
Fivelson, Scott 1954- 117
Fix, Michael 1950- 147
Fix, Paul
See Morrison, Paul Fix
Fix, William R. 1941- CANR-15
Earlier sketch in CA 85-88
Fixel, Lawrence 1917-2003 .... CANR-116
Earlier sketches in CA 137, CANR-115
See also CAAS 28
Fixico, Fus 1873-1908
See Posey, Alexander (Lawrence)
Fixler, Michael 1927- 13-16R
Fixx, James F(uller) 1932-1984 .... CANR-13
Earlier sketch in CA 73-76
Fixx, Jim
See Fixx, James F(uller)
Fizer, John 1925- 53-56
Fjalldal, Magnus 189
Fjelde, Rolf (Gerhard) 1926-2002 .... 17-20R
Obituary 210
Flach, Frederic F(rancis) 1927- 81-84
Flachmann, Michael 1942- CANR-40
Earlier sketch in CA 117
Flack, Audrey L. 1931- CANR-26
Earlier sketch in CA 106
Flack, Dora D(utson) 1919- CANR-45
Earlier sketches in CA 57-60, CANR-6, 21
Flack, Elmer Ellsworth 1894-1976 .... 17-20R
Flack, Harley E. 1943-1998 145
Flack, Jerry D(avid) 1943- 131
Flack, Marjorie 1897-1958 .... CANR-84
Brief entry 112
Earlier sketch in CA 136
See also CLR 28
See also CWRI 5
See also MAICYA 1, 2
See also SATA 100
See also YABC 2
Flack, Naomi John White -1999 .... CANR-1
Earlier sketch in CA 1-4R
See also SATA 40
See also SATA-Brief 35
Flacks, Niki 1943- 110
Flacks, Richard 1938- 49-52
Fladeland, Betty 1919- 45-48
Flader, Susan L. 1941- 81-84
Fladmark, Knut R. 1946- 162
Flage, Daniel E(rvin) 1951- 127
Flagg, Fannie 1941- CANR-40
Earlier sketch in CA 111
See also CPW
See also CSW
See also DA3
See also DAM POP
See also NFS 7
Flagg, James Montgomery 1877-1960 186
See also DLB 188
Flagg, Kenneth
See Ayvazian, L. Fred
Flagstad, Kirsten 1895-1962
Obituary 112
Flaherty, Daniel Leo 1929- 89-92
Flaherty, David H(arris) 1940- 25-28R
Flaherty, Doug(las Ernest) 1939- 33-36R
See also CP 1
Flaherty, Gloria 1938- 85-88
Flaherty, Joe 1936(?)-1983 141
Obituary 111
Flaherty, Joe 1940- 213
Flaherty, Liz 1950- 227
Flaherty, Mary Pat 1955- 132
Brief entry 127
Interview in CA-132
Flaherty, Michael G. 1952- CANR-91
Earlier sketch in CA 145
Flaherty, Regis J. 1953- 191
Flaherty, Robert J(oseph) 1884-1951
Brief entry 115
Flaherty, Robert Joseph 1933- 73-76
Flaherty, Vincent X. 1908(?)-1977
Obituary 73-76
Flaiano, Ennio 1910-1972
Obituary 37-40R
See also IDFW 3, 4
Flake, Chad J(ohn) 1929- 29-32R
Flake, Sharon G. 236
Flam, Jack D(onald) 1940- CANR-139
Earlier sketch in CA 144
Flambeau, Blossom
See Stocking, Kathleen
Flamhaft, Ziva 1944- 162
Flamholtz, Eric 1943- 57-60
Flamini, Roland 170
Flamm, Dudley 1931- 25-28R
Flamm, Gerald R(obert) 1916- 77-80
Flamm, Jerry
See Flamm, Gerald R(obert)
Flammarion, (Nicolas) Camille 1842-1925
Brief entry 120
Flammarion, Henri (Claude) 1910-1985
Obituary 117
Flammer, Philip M(eynard) 1928- 45-48
Flammonde, Paris 17-20R
Flanagan, Brenda A. 1948- 158
Flanagan, Cynthia
See Goss, Cynthia Flanagan
Flanagan, David 168
Flanagan, (Richard) Dennis 1919-2005 128
Obituary 235
Flanagan, Dorothy Belle
See Hughes, Dorothy B(elle)
Flanagan, John C(lemans) 1906- CANR-1
Earlier sketch in CA 1-4R
Flanagan, John T(heodore) 1906- 17-20R
Flanagan, Joseph David Stanislaus
1903-1990 .... 13-16R
Flanagan, Mary 1943- CANR-54
Earlier sketch in CA 125
Flanagan, Michael 1943- 148
Flanagan, Mike 1950- 133
Flanagan, Neal M. 1920-1985 .... 17-20R
Obituary 117
Flanagan, Owen J. 1949- CANR-115
Earlier sketch in CA 125
Flanagan, Richard 1961- 195
Flanagan, Robert (James) 1941- 33-36R
See also CAAS 17
Flanagan, Thomas (James Bonner)
1923-2002 .... CANR-55
Obituary 206
Earlier sketch in CA 108
Interview in CA-108
See also CLC 25, 52
See also CN 3, 4, 5, 6, 7
See also DLBY 1980
See also MTCW 1
See also RHW
See also TCLE 1:1
Flanagan, William G(eorge) 1940- CANR-15
Earlier sketch in CA 93-96
Flanagan, William G(eorge) 1942- 119
Flanagan, William I. 1916(?)-1986
Obituary 118
Flanders, Helen Hartness 1890-1972 .... CAP-1
Obituary 33-36R
Earlier sketch in CA 13-16
Flanders, Henry Jackson, Jr. 1921- 33-36R
Flanders, James P(rescott) 1942- 69-72
Flanders, Jane (Hess) 1940- 110
Flanders, John
See Kremer, Raymond Jean Marie de
Flanders, Judith 235
Flanders, Laura 231
Flanders, Michael (Henry)
1922-1975 .... CANR-4
Obituary 57-60
Earlier sketch in CA 5-8R
Flanders, Ned A. 1918- 37-40R
Flanders, Ralph Edward 1880-1970 ...... CAP-1
Earlier sketch in CA 11-12
Flanders, Rebecca
See Ball, Donna
Flanders, Robert Bruce 1930- 17-20R
Flanery, E(dward) B(oyd) 1932- 61-64
Flanigan, James 1936- 134
Flanigan, Lloyd A(llen) 1933- 33-36R
Flanner, Hildegarde 147
See also Monhoff, June Hildegarde Flanner
See also DLB 48
Flanner, Janet 1892-1978 .... CANR-13
Obituary 81-84
Earlier sketch in CA 65-68
See also DLB 4
See also GLL 1
Flannery, Edward H(ugh) 1912-1998 ..... 13-16R
Flannery, Harry W. 1900-1975 .... CAP-1
Obituary 57-60
Earlier sketch in CA 9-10
Flannery, James W(illiam) 1936-
Brief entry 110
Flannery, Kate
See De Goldi, Kathleen Domenica
Flannery, Peter 1951- 104
See also CBD
See also CD 5, 6
See also DLB 233
Flannery, Sean
See Hagberg, David J(ames)
Flannery, Tim(othy Fridtjof) 1956- CANR-88
Earlier sketch in CA 154
Flasch, Joy 1932- 37-40R
Flaste, Richard (Alfred) 1942- 158
Flaster, Donald J(ohn) 1932- 115
Flath, Arnold W(illiam) J. 1929- 65-68
Flath, Carol Apollonio 1955- 146
Flato, Charles 1908(?)-1984
Obituary 111
Flatt, Lizann
See Brunskill, Elizabeth Ann Flatt
Flattau, Edward 1937- 65-68
Flaubert, Gustave 1821-1880 .... DA
See also DA3
See also DAB
See also DAC
See also DAM MST, NOV
See also DLB 119, 301
See also EW 7
See also EXPS
See also GFL 1789 to the Present
See also LAIT 2
See also LMFS 1
See also NFS 14
See also RGSF 2
See also RGWL 2, 3
See also SSC 11, 60
See also SSFS 6
See also TWA
See also WLC
Flavell, Carol Willsey Bell 1939- 73-76
Flavell, John H(urley) 1928- CANR-85
Earlier sketches in CA 17-20R, CANR-11
Flavin, Martin 1883-1967 .... 5-8R
Obituary 25-28R
See also DLB 9
Flavius, Brother
See Ellison, James E.
Flavius Josephus
See Josephus, Flavius
Flaxman, Traudl 1942- 25-28R
Flayderman, Phillip C(harles)
1930-1969 .... CAP-2
Earlier sketch in CA 23-24
Flayhart, William Henry (III) 1944- 146
Fleagle, Gail S(hatto) 1940- .... SATA 117
Fleck, Betty
See Paine, Lauran (Bosworth)
Fleck, Henrietta 1903-1991 77-80
Fleck, Konrad fl. c. 1220- .... DLB 138
Fleck, Richard Francis 1937- CANR-40
Earlier sketches in CA 102, CANR-18
Flecker, Herman Elroy
See Flecker, (Herman) James Elroy
Flecker, (Herman) James Elroy 1884-1915 .. 150
Brief entry 109
See also DLB 10, 19
See also RGEL 2
See also TCLC 43
Fleece, Jeffrey (Atkinson) 1920- 17-20R
Fleege, Urban H(erman) 1908-2000 ... CANR-1
Earlier sketch in CA 45-48
Fleenor, Juliann (Evans) 1942- 219
Fleer, Jack D(avid) 1937- 25-28R
Fleeson, Doris 1901-1970 177
Obituary 93-96
See also DLB 29
Fleet, Michael 1941- 131
Fleetwood, Frances 1902- CANR-17
Earlier sketches in CA 45-48, CANR-1
Fleetwood, Frank
See Fleetwood, Frances
Fleetwood, Hugh (Nigel) 1944- 144
Brief entry 112
Fleetwood, Jenni 1947- .... SATA 80
Fleetwood, Mick 1947- 143
Fleetwood-Hesketh, (Charles) Peter (Fleetwood)
1905-1985
Obituary 115
Flegg, (Henry) Graham 1924- 114
Fleischacker, Samuel 1961- 194
Fleischbein, Sister M. Catherine Frederic
1902- 5-8R
Fleischer, Cornell H(ugh) 1950- 128
Fleischer, Dave 1894-1979 .... IDFW 3, 4
Fleischer, Jane
See Oppenheim, Joanne
Fleischer, Leonore
Brief entry 109
See also SATA-Brief 47
Fleischer, Manfred P(aul) 1928- 29-32R
Fleischer, Max 1883-1972
Obituary 109
See also IDFW 3, 4
See also SATA-Brief 30
Fleischer, Nathaniel S. 1887(?)-1972
Obituary 37-40R
See also DLB 241
Fleischhauer-Hardt, Helga 1936- 102
See also SATA 30
Fleischman, Harry 1914-2004 .... CANR-3
Obituary 233
Earlier sketch in CA 5-8R
Fleischman, John 1948- 218
See also SATA 145
Fleischman, Paul 1952- CANR-105
Earlier sketches in CA 113, CANR-37, 84
See also AAYA 11, 35
See also BYA 5, 6, 8, 11, 12, 16
See also CLR 20, 66
See also JRDA
See also MAICYA 1, 2
See also MAICYAS 1
See also SAAS 20
See also SATA 39, 72, 110, 156
See also SATA-Brief 32
See also WYAS 1
See also YAW
Fleischman, Paul R. 1945- 160
Fleischman, (Albert) Sid(ney)
1920- CANR-131
Earlier sketches in CA 1-4R, CANR-5, 37, 67
See also BYA 4, 11
See also CLR 1, 15
See also CWRI 5
See also JRDA
See also MAICYA 1, 2
See also SATA 8, 59, 96, 148
Fleischmann, Glen H(arvey)
1909-1985 .... 33-36R
Fleischmann, Harriet 1904-1999 .... CAP-2
Earlier sketch in CA 21-22
Fleischmann, Raoul H(erbert) 1885-1969
Obituary 115
Fleischmann, Wolfgang Bernard 1928- 116
Fleischner, Jennifer 1956- 158
See also SATA 93
Fleisher, Belton Mendel 1935- 69-72
Fleisher, Frederic 1933- 21-24R
Fleisher, Martin 1925- 45-48
Fleisher, Michael (Lawrence) 1942- 25-28R
Fleisher, Paul 1948- CANR-113
Earlier sketches in CA 137, CANR-55
See also SATA 81, 132
Fleisher, Robbin 1951-1977 .... SATA 52
See also SATA-Brief 49
Fleisher, Wilfried 1897(?)-1976
Obituary 65-68
Fleishman, Avrom (Hirsch) 1933- 21-24R
Fleishman, Edwin A(lan) 1927- CANR-11
Earlier sketch in CA 21-24R
Fleishman, Lazar 1944- CANR-82
Earlier sketch in CA 133
Fleishman, Seymour 1918- 133
Brief entry 111
See also SATA 66
See also SATA-Brief 32
Fleiss, Paul M. 1933- 229
Fleisser, Marieluise 191
See also Fleißer, Marieluise
See also EWL 3
Fleißer, Marieluise 1901-1974
Obituary 49-52
See also Fleisser, Marieluise and
Haindl, Marieluise
See also DLB 56, 124
Fleissner, Robert F. 1932- 168
Flem, Lydia 171
Flem-Ath, Rand 200
Flem-Ath, Rose 1948- 192
Flemer, William III 1922- 61-64
Fleming, A. A.
See Arthur, Robert, (Jr.)
Fleming, Abraham 1552(?)-1607 .... DLB 236
Fleming, Alice Mulcahey 1928- CANR-2
Earlier sketch in CA 1-4R
See also SATA 9
Fleming, Amalia 1912-1986
Obituary 118
Fleming, Anne 1928- 151
Fleming, Anne Taylor 1950- 233
Fleming, Berry 1899-1989 .... CANR-18
Obituary 129
Earlier sketches in CA 1-4R, CANR-2
Fleming, C(harlotte) M(ary) 1894- 5-8R

Fleming 192 CONTEMPORARY AUTHORS

Fleming, Candace 1962- CANR-117
Earlier sketch in CA 159
See also SATA 94, 143
Fleming, Charles 182
Fleming, D(enna) F(rank) 1893-1980 .. CANR-1
Earlier sketch in CA 1-4R
Fleming, Daniel B(arry), Jr. 1931- 226
Fleming, David A(rnold) 1939- 93-96
Fleming, Deborah (Diane) 1950- 145
Fleming, Denise 1950- .... SATA 81, 126
Fleming, Donald M(ethuen) 1905-1986 130
Obituary 121
Fleming, Elizabeth P. 1888-1985
Obituary 119
See also SATA-Obit 48
Fleming, Fergus 1959- 237
Fleming, G(ordon) H(oward) 228
Fleming, George J(oseph) 1917- 37-40R
Fleming, George James 1904(?)-1990
Obituary 132
Fleming, Gerald 1921- 53-56
Fleming, Guy
See Masur, Harold Q.
Fleming, H(orace) K(ingston)
1901-2000 .... 33-36R
Fleming, Harold (Lee) 1927- 17-20R
Fleming, Harold M(anchester)
1900-1971(?) CAP-2
Earlier sketch in CA 21-22
Fleming, Ian (Lancaster) 1908-1964 . CANR-59
Earlier sketch in CA 5-8R
See also AAYA 26
See also BPFB 1
See also CDBLB 1945-1960
See also CLC 3, 30
See also CMW 4
See also CPW
See also DA3
See also DAM POP
See also DLB 87, 201
See also MSW
See also MTCW 1, 2
See also MTFW 2005
See also RGEL 2
See also SATA 9
See also TEA
See also YAW
Fleming, Irene 1923(?)-1979
Obituary 89-92
Fleming, Jacky 1955- 142
Fleming, James Rodger 1949- CANR-100
Earlier sketch in CA 150
Fleming, Jennifer Baker 1943- 77-80
Fleming, Jim
See Fleming, James Rodger
Fleming, Joan Margaret 1908-1980 .. CANR-60
Obituary 102
Earlier sketch in CA 81-84
See also CMW 4
See also DLB 276
Fleming, John 1919-2001 129
Obituary 197
Fleming, John Henry 1964- 198
Fleming, John V(incent) 1936- 139
Fleming, June 1935- 110
Fleming, Justin 1953- 225
Fleming, Kate 1946- 137
Fleming, Keith 1960(?)- 226
Fleming, Lady Amalia
See Fleming, Amalia
Fleming, Laurence (William Howie) 1929- . 107
Fleming, Macklin 1911- 77-80
Fleming, May Agnes 1840-1880 .... DLB 99
Fleming, Miles 1919-1978 .... 29-32R
Obituary 134
Fleming, Oliver
See MacDonald, Philip
Fleming, Paul 1609-1640 .... DLB 164
Fleming, Peggy (Gale) 1948- 187
Fleming, (Robert) Peter 1907-1971 179
Obituary 33-36R
See also DLB 195
Fleming, Ray(mond) 1945- 115
See also BW 1
Fleming, Reid
See Obrecht, Jas
Fleming, Robert E. 1936- 146
Fleming, Robert H(enry) 1912-1984
Obituary 114
Fleming, Ronald Lee 1941- 108
See also SATA 56
Fleming, Sally
See Walker, Sally M(acArt)
Fleming, Sandford 1888-1974 .... CAP-1
Earlier sketch in CA 9-10
Fleming, Stuart
See Knight, Damon (Francis)
Fleming, Susan 1932- CANR-14
Earlier sketch in CA 81-84
See also SATA 32
Fleming, Theodore B(owman), Jr. 1917- .. 45-48
Fleming, Thomas (James) 1927- CANR-102
Earlier sketches in CA 5-8R, CANR-10
Interview in CANR-10
See also CLC 37
See also SATA 8
Fleming, Thomas J. 1945- 193
Fleming, Virginia (Edwards) 1923- 150
See also SATA 84
Fleming, William (Coleman)
1909-2001 .... 17-20R
Flemming, Nicholas Coit 1936- 97-100
Flemmons, Jerry 1936-1999 124
Flender, Harold 1924-1975 49-52
Obituary 135
Flenley, John (Roger) 231
Flesch, Janos Laszlo 1933(?)-1983
Obituary 111
Flesch, Rudolf (Franz) 1911-1986 .... CANR-3
Obituary 120
Earlier sketch in CA 9-12R
Flesch, Y.
See Flesch, Yolande (Catarina)
Flesch, Yolande (Catarina) 1950- 122
See also SATA 55
Flescher, Irwin 1926- 37-40R
Flescher, Joachim 1906(?)-1976
Obituary 65-68
Fletcher, Adele (Whitely) 1898-1979 ..... CAP-1
Earlier sketch in CA 17-18
Fletcher, Alan Mark 1928- 73-76
Fletcher, Angus (John Stewart) 1930- 104
Fletcher, Anthony John 1941- 73-76
Fletcher, Arnold Charles 1917- 17-20R
Fletcher, Banister F.
See Fletcher, Banister Flight
Fletcher, Banister Flight 1866-1953
Brief entry 123
Fletcher, Barbara (Helen) 1935- 110
Fletcher, Basil Alais 1900-1983 65-68
Obituary 109
Fletcher, Bramwell 1904(?)-1988
Obituary 125
Fletcher, Charlie May Hogue
1897-1977 .... 9-12R
See also SATA 3
Fletcher, Charlotte Goldsborough 1915- 233
Fletcher, Colin 1922- CANR-121
Earlier sketches in CA 13-16R, CANR-11
See also AITN 1
See also SATA 28
Fletcher, David
See Barber, D(ulan) F(riar Whilberton)
Fletcher, Dirk
See Cunningham, Chet
Fletcher, Donna 212
Fletcher, Geoffrey Scowcroft 1923- 103
Fletcher, George U.
See Pratt, (Murray) Fletcher
Fletcher, Giles, the Elder 1546-1611 ... DLB 136
See also RGEL 2
Fletcher, Giles, the Younger c.
1585-1623 .... RGEL 2
Fletcher, Gordon A(lan) 1942- 127
Fletcher, Grace Nies 1895-1991 .... 5-8R
Fletcher, H(arry) L(utf) V(erne)
1902-1970(?) CANR-4
Earlier sketch in CA 9-12R
Fletcher, Harold Roy 1907-1978
Obituary 111
Fletcher, Harris Francis 1892-1979 .... 1-4R
Obituary 103
Fletcher, Harvey 1884-1981
Obituary 108
Fletcher, Helen Jill 1910- 9-12R
See also SATA 13
Fletcher, Henry Lancelot Aubrey
See Aubrey-Fletcher, Henry Lancelot
Fletcher, Ian 1920-1988
Obituary 127
Brief entry 124
See also CP 1, 2
Fletcher, (Minna) Inglis 1888-1969 .... 5-8R
See also AITN 1
See also RHW
Fletcher, J(oseph) S(mith) 1863-1935 219
Brief entry 109
See also CMW 4
See also DLB 70
Fletcher, Jesse C. 1931- CANR-4
Earlier sketch in CA 9-12R
Fletcher, John 1579-1625 .... BRW 2
See also CDBLB Before 1660
See also DC 6
See also DLB 58
See also RGEL 2
See also TEA
Fletcher, John (Walter James) 1937- .. CANR-15
Earlier sketch in CA 81-84
Fletcher, John C(aldwell) 1931-2004 124
Obituary 227
Fletcher, John Gould 1886-1950 167
Brief entry 107
See also DLB 4, 45
See also LMFS 2
See also MAL 5
See also RGAL 4
See also TCLC 35
Fletcher, Joseph (Francis III)
1905-1991 .... CANR-11
Obituary 135
Earlier sketch in CA 21-24R
Fletcher, Joyce K(ubiac) 1946- 190
Fletcher, Katharine 1952- 180
Fletcher, Leon 1921- CANR-33
Earlier sketch in CA 49-52
Fletcher, Lucille
See Wallop, Lucille Fletcher
Fletcher, Marilyn P(endleton) 1940- 106
Fletcher, Marjorie 1941- 189
Brief entry 113
Fletcher, Mary .... AITN 1
Fletcher, (William) Miles (III) 1946- 114
Fletcher, Phineas 1582-1650 .... DLB 121
See also RGEL 2
Fletcher, Ralph (J.) 1953- CANR-132
Earlier sketch in CA 173
See also SATA 105, 149
Fletcher, Richard (Alexander) 1944-2005 ... 176
Obituary 236
Fletcher, Richard E. 1917(?)-1983
Obituary 109
See also SATA-Obit 34
Fletcher, Rick
See Fletcher, Richard E.
Fletcher, Robert H. 1885(?)-1972
Obituary 37-40R
Fletcher, Roger A(nthony) 1942- 121
Fletcher, Ronald 1921-1992 .... CANR-42
Earlier sketches in CA 33-36R, CANR-13
Fletcher, Sir Banister
See Fletcher, Banister Flight
Fletcher, Susan (Clemens) 1951- CANR-129
Earlier sketches in CA 138, CANR-71
See also AAYA 37
See also SATA 70, 110
Fletcher, Tony 1964- 205
Fletcher, William C(atherwood) 1932- .. 21-24R
Fletcher, William W(higham) 1918- . CANR-15
Earlier sketch in CA 81-84
Fletcher, Winston 1937- CANR-42
Earlier sketch in CA 118
Fletcher-Cooke, John 1911-1989 102
Fletcher the Younger, Giles
1585(?)-1623 .... DLB 121
Flett, Una (Leonie) 1932- 137
Fleur, Anne 1901- .... SATA-Brief 31
Fleur, Paul
See Pohl, Frederik
Fleurant, Gerdes 1939- 175
Fleure, H. J.
See Fleure, Herbert John
Fleure, Herbert John 1877-1969
Obituary 115
Fleuridas, Ellie Rae
See Sherman, Eleanor Rae
Fleury, Delphine
See Amatora, Sister Mary
Flew, Antony G(arrard) N(ewton)
1923- CANR-140
Earlier sketches in CA 5-8R, CANR-3, 18, 40
Flewelling, Lynn 1958- 198
Flexner, Eleanor 1908-1995 45-48
Flexner, James Thomas 1908-2003 ... CANR-78
Obituary 213
Earlier sketches in CA 1-4R, CANR-2, 37
See also SATA 9
Flexner, Simon 1863-1946 156
Flexner, Stuart Berg 1928-1990 .... CANR-11
Obituary 133
Earlier sketch in CA 13-16R
Flick, Carlos Thomas 1927- 89-92
Flickenger, Rob 227
Flieg, Helmut
See Heym, Stefan
Fliegel, Frederick C(hristian) 1925- 49-52
Flieger, Verlyn 1933- 168
Flieger, Wilhelm 1931- 25-28R
Flier, Michael S(tephen) 1941- CANR-32
Earlier sketches in CA 37-40R, CANR-14
Fliess, Peter J(oachim) 1915-1993 .... 21-24R
Fligstein, Neil 1951- 135
Flinders, Carol Lee 1943- 213
Flinders, Neil J. 1934- 21-24R
Flink, James J(ohn) 1932-
Brief entry 112
Flink, Salomon J. 1906-1983 .... CANR-17
Earlier sketch in CA 1-4R
Flinker, Moshe (Zev) 1926-1944
Flinn, Alex 1966- 235
See also AAYA 50
See also SATA 159
Flinn, Elaine 236
Flinn, Kelly 1971- 169
Flinn, M(ichael) W(alter)
1917-1983 .... CANR-13
Obituary 110
Earlier sketch in CA 17-20R
Flint, Betty M. 1920- 21-24R
Flint, Carol 182
Flint, Cort R(ay) 1915-1983 .... CANR-47
Obituary 169, 180
Earlier sketch in CA 49-52
Flint, E. de P.
See Fielden, T(homas) P(erceval)
Flint, Eric 1947- 182
Flint, F(rank) S(tuart) 1885-1960 177
Obituary 113
See also DLB 19
Flint, Helen 1952- 128
See also SATA 102
Flint, Homer Eon 1892-1924 160
Brief entry 114
Flint, James (Bragg) 1968- 175
Flint, Jeremy 1928(?)-1989
Obituary 130
Flint, Jerry 1931- 127
Flint, John E(dgar) 1930- 37-40R
Flint, Kenneth C(ovey), Jr. 1947- CANR-85
Earlier sketch in CA 140
See also FANT
Flint, Lucy
See Flint-Gohlke, Lucy
Flint, Roland (Henry) 1934-2000 153
Obituary 193
See also CP 7
Flint, Russ 1944- .... SATA 74
Flint, Timothy 1780-1840 .... DLB 73, 186
Flint-Gohlke, Lucy 1954- CANR-37
Flippo, Chet 1943- 89-92
Flippo, Edwin B(ly) 1925- CANR-13
Earlier sketch in CA 33-36R
Flitner, David P(erkins), Jr. 1949- ...., CANR-1
Earlier sketch in CA 45-48
See also SATA 7
Flitter, Marc 172
Floan, Howard R(ussell) 1918- 17-20R
Floca, Brian .... SATA 155
Flock, Elizabeth 239
Floegstad, Kjartan 1944- 166
Floethe, Louise Lee 1913-1988 .... CANR-2
Earlier sketch in CA 1-4R
See also SATA 4
Floethe, Richard 1901-1998 .... 33-36R
Obituary 169, 180
See also SATA 4
Flogstad, Kjartan 1944- 192
See also Floegstad, Kjartan
See also CWW 2
See also DLB 297
See also EWL 3
Floherty, John Joseph 1882-1964 .... SATA 25
Flohr, Paul R.
See Mendes-Flohr, Paul R(obert)
Floinn, Criostoir O
See O'Flynn, Criostoir
Flokos, Nicholas 175
Flood, Bo
See Flood, Nancy Bo
Flood, Charles Bracelen 1929- 41-44R
Flood, Christopher 1936- .... TCWW 2
Flood, Curt(is Charles) 1938-1997
Obituary 156
Brief entry 115
Flood, E(dward) Thadeus 1932-1977 49-52
Obituary 133
Flood, John 182
See also Costello, Mark
Flood, John A(nthony) 1949- 129
Flood, John M(ichael) 1947- 115
Flood, Josephine 1936- 191
Flood, Kenneth Urban 1925- 9-12R
Flood, Lynn .... GLL 2
Flood, Nancy Bo 1945- 199
See also SATA 130
Flood, Norman 1935- 134
Flood, Pansie Hart 1964- 211
See also SATA 140
Flood, Patrick James 178
Flood, Robert G. 1935- CANR-22
Earlier sketch in CA 106
Flood, William 1942- 198
See also SATA 129
Flooglebuckle, Al
See Spiegelman, Art
Flook, Maria 1952- CANR-61
Earlier sketch in CA 110
Flora, Fletcher 1914-1969 .... CANR-85
Earlier sketches in CA 1-4R, CANR-3
See also Queen, Ellery
Flora, James (Royer) 1914-1998 .... CANR-3
Obituary 169
Earlier sketch in CA 5-8R
See also CWRI 5
See also SAAS 6
See also SATA 1, 30
See also SATA-Obit 103
Flora, Joseph M(artin) 1934- CANR-137
Earlier sketches in CA 13-16R, CANR-5, 21, 44
Flora, Kate Clark 206
Flora, Paul 1922-
Brief entry 113
Floren, Lee 1910-1995 .... CANR-64
Earlier sketches in CA 5-8R, CANR-3, 18
See also TCWW 2
Floren, Myron (Howard) 1919-2005 129
Florence, Philip Sargant 1890-1982
Obituary 106
Florence, Ronald 1942- CANR-15
Earlier sketch in CA 33-36R
Florensky, Pavel Aleksandrovich
1882-1937 .... DLB 295
Florentin, Eddy 1923- 49-52
Florentin, Ovidiu
See Smarandache, Florentin
Flores, Angel 1900-1992 .... CANR-40
Earlier sketches in CA 103, CANR-19, 32
See also HW 1
Flores, Dan Louie 1948- CANR-106
Earlier sketches in CA 121, CANR-47
Flores, Ivan 1923- CANR-22
Earlier sketches in CA 17-20R, CANR-7
Flores, Janis 1946- CANR-51
Earlier sketches in CA 65-68, CANR-10, 26
Flores, John 1943- 77-80
Flores, Juan de fl. 1470-1500 .... DLB 286
Flores, Lauro H. 1950- 196
Florescu, Radu R. 1925- 41-44R
Flores-Williams, Jason 1969- .... DLB 209
Florey, Howard Walter 1898-1968 158
Florey, Kitty B.
See Florey, Kitty Burns
Florey, Kitty Burns 1943- CANR-111
Earlier sketch in CA 149
Florez, Pablo de Azcarate y
See Azcarate y Florez, Pablo de
Florian, Douglas 1950- CANR-101
Earlier sketches in CA 123, CANR-49
See also SATA 19, 83, 125
Florian, Tibor 1908-1986 73-76
Obituary 180
Florida, Richard (L.) 1957- CANR-122
Earlier sketch in CA 139
Florin, Lambert F. 1905-1993 .... CANR-7
Earlier sketch in CA 17-20R
Florinsky, Michael T(imothy)
1894-1981 .... CANR-15
Obituary 105
Earlier sketch in CA 1-4R
Florio, John 1553(?)-1625 .... DLB 172
Floriot, Rene 1902-1975
Obituary 61-64
Florit (y Sanchez de Fuentes), Eugenio
1903-1999 .... CANR-32
Earlier sketch in CA 104
See also HW 1

Cumulative Index 193 Foner

Florman, Samuel C(harles) 1925- ... CANR-129
Earlier sketch in CA 102
Florovsky, Georges (Vasilievich) 1893-1979
Obituary ... 111
Flory, Charles D(avid) 1902-1994 ... 41-44R
Flory, David A. 1939- ... 227
Flory, Harry R. 1899-1976
Obituary ... 69-72
Flory, Jane Trescott 1917- ... CANR-3
Earlier sketch in CA 9-12R
See also SATA 22
Flory, Julia McCune 1882-1971 ... CAP-2
Obituary ... 29-32R
Earlier sketch in CA 21-22
Flory, Paul (John) 1910-1985 ... 156
Obituary ... 117
Flory, Wendy Stallard 1943- ... 132
Floud, Roderick 1942- ... CANR-1
Earlier sketch in CA 45-48
Flournoy, Don Michael 1937- ... 126
Flournoy, Valerie (Rose) 1952- ... CANR-79
Earlier sketch in CA 142
See also BW 2, 3
See also SATA 95
Flower, Dean S. 1938- ... 21-24R
Flower, Desmond (John Newman)
1907-1997 ... 9-12R
Obituary ... 156
Flower, Elizabeth Farquhar 1914-1995 ... 103
Obituary ... 149
Flower, Harry A(lfred) 1901- ... CAP-1
Earlier sketch in CA 11-12
Flower, Joe
See Flower, Joseph Edward
Flower, (Harry) John 1936- ... 37-40R
Flower, Joseph Edward 1950- ... 130
Flower, Margaret Cameron Coss ... 61-64
Flower, Milton E(mbick) 1910-1996 ... 129
Flower, (Walter) Newman 1879-1964
Obituary ... 109
Flower, Pat 1914-1977 ... 213
Flower, Raymond (Charles) 1921- ... 108
Flowerdew, Phyllis -1994 ... 103
See also SATA 33
Flowers, Ann Moore 1923- ... 9-12R
Flowers, Arthur ... 180
Flowers, Betty S(ue) 1947- ... 65-68
Flowers, Charles 1942- ... 29-32R
Flowers, Charles E(ly, Jr.) 1920-1999 ... 93-96
Flowers, Charles V., Jr. 1926(?)-1990
Obituary ... 130
Flowers, John V(ictor) 1938- ... 106
Flowers, Pam 1946- ... 231
See also SATA 136
Flowers, Paul Abbott 1905-1984
Obituary ... 112
Flowers, R(onald) Barri ... 218
Flowers, Ronald B(ruce) 1935- ... CANR-116
Earlier sketch in CA 151
Flowers, Sarah 1952- ... 166
See also SATA 98
Floyd, Barry Neil 1925- ... 33-36R
Floyd, Charity
See Blake, Lillie Devereux
Floyd, Gareth 1940- ... SATA 62
See also SATA-Brief 31
Floyd, Harriet 1925- ... 69-72
Floyd, John E(arl) 1937- ... 145
Floyd, Lois Gray 1910(?)-1978 ... 85-88
Obituary ... 81-84
Floyd, Samuel A(lexander), Jr.
1937- ... CANR-39
Earlier sketch in CA 115
See also BW 2
Floyd, Troy S(mith) 1920- ... 37-40R
Floyd, W(illiam) E(dward) G(regory)
1939- ... 33-36R
Floyd, William Anderson 1928- ... 29-32R
Fluchere, Henri (Auguste) 1898-1987
Obituary ... 123
Fluchere, Henri 1914-1991 ... 77-80
See also SATA 40
Fluck, Diana 1931-1984
Obituary ... 113
Fluck, Reginald Alan Paul 1928- ... 9-12R
Fludd, Robert 1574-1637 ... DLB 281
Fluehr-Lobban, Carolyn 1945- ... CANR-137
Earlier sketch in CA 144
Flugge-Lotz, Irmgard 1903-1974 ... 164
Fluke, Joanne ... CANR-101
Fluke, Joanne ... CANR-101
Earlier sketch in CA 152
See also SATA 88
Flume, Violet S(igoloff) ... 116
Flumiani, Carlo M(aria) 1911- ... CANR-9
Earlier sketch in CA 13-16R
Fluno, Robert Y(ounger) 1916- ... 33-36R
Flusberg, Helen Tager
See Tager-Flusberg, Helen
Flusfeder, David (L.) 1960- ... 227
Flusser, Martin 1947- ... 73-76
Flute, Molly
See Lottman, Eileen
Fly, Claude L(ee) 1905-1991 ... 97-100
Obituary ... 169, 180
Flyat, Sten G(unnar) 1911-1978 ... 9-12R
Flying Officer X
See Bates, H(erbert) E(rnest)
Flynn, Barbara 1928- ... SATA 9
Flynn, Bernice (Lydia Carlson) 1922- ... 114
Flynn, Carol Houlihan 1945- ... 112
Flynn, Casey
See Flint, Kenneth C(ovey), Jr.
Flynn, Charles F(rederick) 1949- ... 57-60
Flynn, David H(oughton) 1953- ... 115
Flynn, Don
See Flynn, Donald R(obert)
Flynn, Donald R(obert) 1928- ... CANR-90
Earlier sketches in CA 29-32R, CANR-12, 30
Flynn, Elizabeth A. 1944- ... 235
Flynn, Elizabeth Gurley 1890-1964
Obituary ... 111
See also DLB 303
Flynn, Fahey 1916-1983
Obituary ... 110
Flynn, George
See Paine, Lauran (Bosworth)
Flynn, George L. 1931- ... CANR-90
Earlier sketches in CA 65-68, CANR-9, 24
Flynn, George Q(uitman) 1937- ... 25-28R
Flynn, Gerard (Cox) 1924- ... 41-44R
Flynn, Jackson
See Bensen, Donald R. and
Shirreffs, Gordon D(onald)
Flynn, James Joseph 1911-1977 ... 21-24R
Flynn, James R. 1934- ... 21-24R
Flynn, John Joseph 1936- ... 17-20R
Flynn, John L. 1954- ... 174
Flynn, John Thomas 1882-1964
Obituary ... 89-92
Flynn, Joseph ... 225
Flynn, Leslie Bruce 1918- ... CANR-37
Earlier sketches in CA 1-4R, CANR-2, 17
Flynn, Nancy L. 1956- ... 227
Flynn, Nicholas
See Odgers, Sally Farrell
Flynn, Nick 1960- ... 222
Flynn, Paul P(atrick) 1942- ... 37-40R
Flynn, Rachel 1953- ... 180
See also SATA 109
Flynn, Raymond (Leo) 1939- ... 197
Flynn, Robert (Lopez) 1932- ... CANR-83
Earlier sketches in CA 29-32R, CANR-55
See also TCWW 1, 2
Flynn, T(homas) T(heodore, Jr.) 1902-1978 . 162
See also TCWW 1, 2
Flynn, Vince ... 182
Flynn, Warren (G.) 1950- ... 229
See also SATA 154
Flynt, Candace 1947- ... 102
Flynt, Larry ... AITN 2
Flynt, Wayne 1940- ... CANR-48
Earlier sketches in CA 37-40R, CANR-13
Flythe, Starkey S(harp), Jr. 1935- ... 69-72
Flyvbjerg, Bent 1952- ... 227
FM-2030 1930-2000 ... CANR-31
Obituary ... 189
Fo, Dario 1926- ... CANR-134
Brief entry ... 116
Earlier sketches in CA 128, CANR-68, 114
See also CLC 32, 109
See also CWW 2
See also DA3
See also DAM DRAM
See also DC 10
See also DLBY 1997
See also EWL 3
See also MTCW 1, 2
See also MTFW 2005
See also WLIT 7
Foat Tugay, Emine 1897- ... CAP-1
Earlier sketch in CA 13-14
Fobel, James M. 1946- ... 129
Fobel, Jim
See Fobel, James M.
Fobes, Tracy ... 238
Foda, Aun
See Foxe, Arthur N(orman)
Fodaski-Black, Martha 1929- ... 73-76
Fodden, Simon R. 1944- ... 131
Foden, Giles 1967- ... DLB 267
See also NFS 15
Fodi, Lee E(dward) 1970- ... 236
Fodor, Eugene 1905-1991 ... CANR-14
Obituary ... 133
Earlier sketch in CA 21-24R
Fodor, M. W. 1890(?)-1977
Obituary ... 69-72
Fodor, Nandor 1895-1964
Obituary ... 112
Fodor, R(onald) V(ictor) 1944- ... CANR-15
Earlier sketch in CA 65-68
See also SATA 25
Foell, Earl W(illiam) 1929-1999 ... 69-72
Obituary ... 185
Foelsing, Albrecht 1940- ... 168
Foer, Franklin ... 239
Foer, Jonathan Safran 1977- ... 204
See also AAYA 57
See also MTFW 2005
Foerstel, Herbert N. 1933- ... CANR-134
Earlier sketch in CA 175
Foerstel, Karen 1965- ... 175
Foerstel, Lenora 1929- ... 144
Foerster, Eberhard
See Weisenborn, Guenther
Foerster, Leona M(itchell) 1930- ... 89-92
Foerster, Lotte B(rand) 1910-1986 ... 77-80
Obituary ... 119
Foerster, Norman 1887-1972 ... 5-8R
Foerster, Richard 1949- ... 188
Fofanov, Konstantin Mikhailovich
1862-1911 ... DLB 277
Foff, Arthur R(aymond) 1925-1973 ... CAP-2
Earlier sketch in CA 33-36
Fogarty, John J. 1931- ... 128
Fogarty, Jonathan Titulescu Esq.
See Farrell, James T(homas)
Fogarty, Michael P(atrick) 1916-2001 . CANR-9
Obituary ... 195
Earlier sketch in CA 21-24R
Fogarty, Robert S(tephen) 1938- ... CANR-108
Earlier sketches in CA 65-68, CANR-9
Fogel, Daniel
See Kahn-Fogel, Daniel (Mark)
Fogel, Daniel (Mark) Kahn
See Kahn-Fogel, Daniel (Mark)
Fogel, Ephim G(regory) 1920-1992 ... 120
Obituary ... 139
Fogel, Robert W(illiam) 1926- ... CANR-103
Earlier sketches in CA 77-80, CANR-13, 48
Fogel, Ruby ... 17-20R
Fogelin, Adrian 1951- ... 198
See also AAYA 67
See also SATA 129
Fogelmark, Staffan 1939- ... 139
Fogelquist, Donald Frederick
1906-1980 ... 69-72
Obituary ... 171, 180
Fogelson, Robert M(ichael) 1937- ... CANR-115
Earlier sketch in CA 81-84
Fogelstroem, Per Anders
See Fogelstrom, Per Anders
Fogg, Sam R. 1917(?)-1987
Obituary ... 123
Fogle, Bruce 1944- ... CANR-144
Earlier sketch in CA 106
Fogle, French R(owe) 1912- ... 37-40R
Fogle, James 1936- ... 134
Fogle, Jeanne M. 1949- ... CANR-94
Earlier sketch in CA 145
Fogle, Richard Harter 1911-1995 ... CANR-5
Earlier sketch in CA 5-8R
Fogler, Michael 1953- ... 185
Foglia, Leonard ... 230
Foglio, Frank 1921- ... 57-60
Foiles, Keith Andrew 1926-1983
Obituary ... 109
Foin, Theodore C(hin) 1940- ... 93-96
Foisie, Jack 1919-2001 ... 104
Obituary ... 198
Foix, J(osep) V(icenc) 1893-1987 ... DLB 134
See also EWL 3
Fokkema, D(ouwe) W(essel) 1931- ... CANR-23
Earlier sketches in CA 17-20R, CANR-7
Fol, Alexander 1933-
Brief entry ... 111
Foladare, Joseph 1909-1997 ... 102
Folb, Edith A(rlene) 1938- ... 102
Folbre, Nancy ... 199
Folch-Ribas, Jacques 1928- ... 69-72
Folda, Jaroslav (Thayer III) 1940- ... 127
Foldessy, Edward P(atrick) 1941- ... 126
Folds, Thomas M. ... 93-96
Foldvary, Fred E. 1946- ... 147
Folejewski, Zbigniew 1910-1999 ... CANR-7
Earlier sketch in CA 17-20R
Foley, Allen Richard 1898-1978 ... 45-48
Obituary ... 77-80
Foley, (Anna) Bernice Williams
1902-1987 ... CANR-12
Earlier sketch in CA 29-32R
See also SATA 28
Foley, Charles 1908-1995 ... CAP-1
Obituary ... 148
Earlier sketch in CA 13-16
Foley, Daniel J(oseph) 1913-1999 ... CANR-5
Earlier sketch in CA 5-8R
Foley, Denise (M.) 1950- ... 146
Foley, Doug 1942- ... 57-60
Foley, Duncan K(arl) 1942- ... 93-96
Foley, Gaelen ... 204
Foley, Gerald (Patrick) 1936- ... CANR-11
Earlier sketch in CA 69-72
Foley, Helen
See Fowler, Helen Rosa Huxley
Foley, Jack 1940- ... CANR-115
Earlier sketch in CA 160
See also CAAS 24
Foley, (Cedric) John 1917-1974 ... CANR-4
Obituary ... 53-56
Earlier sketch in CA 9-12R
Foley, John Miles 1947- ... CANR-96
Earlier sketches in CA 111, CANR-45
Foley, June 1944- ... CANR-85
Earlier sketch in CA 109
See also SATA 44
See also YAW
Foley, Leonard 1913-1994 ... 89-92
Foley, (Mary) Louise Munro 1933- ... 37-40R
See also SATA 54, 106
See also SATA-Brief 40
Foley, Martha 1897(?)-1977 ... 117
Obituary ... 73-76
See also DLB 137
Foley, Mary Mix 1918- ... 102
Foley, Michael 1947- ... 188
Foley, Michael F(rancis) 1940-1984
Obituary ... 113
Foley, Mick 1965- ... 225
Foley, Paul 1914-1983
Obituary ... 111
Foley, Rae
See Denniston, Elinore
Foley, Richard 1947- ... 126
Foley, Richard N. 1910(?)-1980
Obituary ... 102
Foley, Sallie 1950- ... 214
Foley, Scott
See Dareff, Hal
Foley, Thomas W. 1931- ... 237
Foley, Vincent D. 1933- ... 57-60
Foley, William E. 1938- ... 33-36R
Foley, Winifred 1914- ... 102
Folgarait, Leonard ... 193
Folger, Henry Clay 1857-1930 ... 211
See also DLB 140
Folk, Jerry ... 114
Folk, Thomas C. 1955- ... 168
Folkard, Charles James 1878-1963
Obituary ... 109
See also SATA-Brief 28
Folke, Will
See Bloch, Robert (Albert)
Folkenflik, Robert 1939- ... 162
Brief entry ... 111
Folkers, George Fulton 1929- ... 49-52
Folkerts, George W(illiam) 1938- ... 53-56
Folkman, Jerome (Daniel) 1907- ... CAP-2
Earlier sketch in CA 29-32
Folks, Jeffrey Jay 1948- ... 145
Follain, Jean (Rene) 1903-1971 ... 130
See also DLB 258
Follain, John ... 182
Folland, H(arold) F(reeze) 1906- ... 49-52
Follen, Charles 1796-1840 ... DLB 235
Follen, Eliza Lee (Cabot) 1787-1860 ... DLB 1, 235
Follen, Mrs.
See Homer, Winslow
Follett, Beth ... 210
Follett, C. B. 1936- ... CANR-108
Earlier sketch in CA 171
Follett, Helen Thomas 1884(?)-1970
Obituary ... 107
See also SATA-Obit 27
Follett, James 1939- ... CANR-95
Brief entry ... 112
Earlier sketch in CA 134
Follett, Ken(neth Martin) 1949- ... CANR-102
Earlier sketches in CA 81-84, CANR-13, 33, 54
Interview in ... CANR-33
See also AAYA 6, 50
See also BEST 89:4
See also BPFB 1
See also CLC 18
See also CMW 4
See also CPW
See also DA3
See also DAM NOV, POP
See also DLB 87
See also DLBY 1981
See also MTCW 1
Follett, Robert J(ohn) R(ichard)
1928- ... CANR-47
Earlier sketches in CA 21-24R, CANR-8, 23
Folley, Terence T. 1931- ... 21-24R
Folley, Vern L(eRoy) 1936- ... 49-52
Folliard, Edward T(homas) 1899-1976
Obituary ... 69-72
Follis, Anne Bowen 1947- ... 106
Follmann, J(oseph) F(rancis), Jr.
1908-1989 ... CANR-7
Obituary ... 128
Earlier sketch in CA 17-20R
Folly, Martin H(arold) 1957- ... 225
Folmar, J. Kent
See Folmar, John Kent
Folmar, John Kent 1932- ... 116
Folmsbee, Stanley J(ohn) 1899-1974 ... CAP-2
Earlier sketch in CA 29-32
Folsey, George 1898-1988 ... IDFW 3
Folsom, Allan (R.) 1941- ... CANR-106
Earlier sketch in CA 148
Folsom, Anne (Ferril) 1922- ... 185
Brief entry ... 114
Folsom, Burton W(hitmore), Jr. 1947- ... 118
Folsom, Franklin (Brewster)
1907-1995 ... CANR-2
Obituary ... 150
Earlier sketch in CA 1-4R
See also SATA 5
See also SATA-Obit 88
Folsom, Jack
See Folsom, John B(entley)
Folsom, John B(entley) 1931- ... 45-48
Folsom, Kenneth E(verett) 1921- ... 21-24R
Folsom, Marcia McClintock 1940- ... 188
Folsom, Marion Bayard 1893-1976 ... CAP-2
Earlier sketch in CA 17-18
Folsom, Marvin Hugh 1929- ... 57-60
Folsom, Michael (Brewster) 1938-1990 ... 112
Obituary ... 150
See also SATA 40
See also SATA-Obit 88
Folsom, Robert S(lade) 1915- ... 77-80
Folster, David 1937- ... 134
Folta, Jeannette R. 1934- ... 25-28R
Foltin, Lore (Barbara) 1913-1974(?) ... CAP-2
Obituary ... 169, 180
Earlier sketch in CA 25-28
Foltz, Richard C. 1961- ... 230
Foltz, William J(ay) 1936- ... 9-12R
Folz, Hans c. 1435-1513 ... DLB 179
Fombona, Rufino Blanco
See Blanco Fombona, Rufino
Fombrun, Charles J. 1954- ... 144
Fomin
See Golomstock, Igor (Naumovitch)
Fomon, Samuel J(oseph) 1923- ... 53-56
Fonagy, Peter 1952- ... 146
Fonarow, Jerry 1935- ... CANR-4
Earlier sketch in CA 53-56
Fonda, Henry (Jaynes) 1905-1982
Obituary ... 107
Fonda, Jane (Seymour) 1937- ... 138
Fonda, Peter 1939(?)- ... 169
Brief entry ... 112
Fondane, Benjamin 1898-1944 ... TCLC 159
Fone, Byrne (Reginald Spencer) 1936- ... 171
Fon Eisen, Anthony T. 1917- ... 13-16R
Foner, Eric 1943- ... CANR-104
Earlier sketches in CA 29-32R, CANR-12, 49
Foner, Jack D(onald) 1910-1999 ... 77-80
Obituary ... 187

Foner, Nancy 1945- CANR-105
Earlier sketch in CA 53-56
Foner, Naomi CANR-126
Earlier sketch in CA 166
Foner, Philip (Sheldon) 1910-1994 CANR-47
Earlier sketches in CA 9-12R, CANR-3
Fong, Bobby 1950- 169
Fong, C. K.
See Cassiday, Bruce (Bingham)
Fong, Leo 1928- 127
Fong, Wen Chih 1930- 103
Fong-Torres, Ben 1945- 93-96
Fonrobert, Charlotte Elisheva 1965- 201
Fonseca, Aloysius Joseph 1915-1991 CANR-9
Earlier sketch in CA 13-16R
Fonseca, James W(illiam) 1947- 146
Fonseca, John R. 1925- CANR-8
Earlier sketch in CA 17-20R
Fonseca, Manuel da 1911-1993 DLB 287
Fonseca, Rubem 1925- 189
See also DLB 307
See also EWL 3
Fonstad, Karen Wynn 1945-2005 104
Fontaine, Andre 1910-1994 65-68
Fontaine, Andre (Lucien Georges)
1921- CANR-12
Earlier sketch in CA 25-28R
Fontaine, Felix Gregory de
See de Fontaine, Felix Gregory
Fontaine, Joan 1917- 81-84
Fontana, Bernard L(ee) 1931- CANR-7
Earlier sketch in CA 17-20R
Fontana, Biancamaria 1952- CANR-51
Earlier sketch in CA 124
Fontana, Thomas M(ichael) 1951- 130
Brief entry 113
Fontana, Vincent James 1923-2005 13-16R
Fontane, Theodor 1819-1898 CDWLB 2
See also DLB 129
See also EW 6
See also RGWL 2, 3
See also TWA
Fontanel, Beatrice 1957- 168
Fontanet, Joseph 1921-1980
Obituary 105
Fontara, Johannes
See Ruhmkorf, Peter
Fontcreuse, Marquis de
See Jaeger, Cyril Karel Stuart
Fontenay, Charles L(ouis) 1917- 25-28R
Fontenelle, Bernard Le Bovier de
1657-1757 DLB 268, 313
See also GFL Beginnings to 1789
Fontenelle, Don H(arris) 1946- 106
Fontenot, Chester CLC 65
Fontenot, Chester J. 1950- CANR-43
Earlier sketch in CA 112
Fontenot, Mary Alice 1910- CANR-57
Earlier sketches in CA 37-40R, CANR-14, 31
See also SATA 34, 91
Fontenrose, Joseph (Eddy) 1903-1986 5-8R
Obituary 180
Fontes, Manuel D(a Costa) 1945- 200
Fontes, Montserrat 1940- 136
See also DLB 209
Fonteyn, Margot
See Fonteyn de Arias, Margot
Fonteyn de Arias, Margot 1919-1991 117
Obituary 133
Brief entry 110
Fontinhas, Jose 1923-
See Andrade, Eugénio de
Fonvizin, Denis Ivanovich
1744(?)-1792 DLB 150
See also RGWL 2, 3
Fonzi, Bruno 1913(?)-1976
Obituary 65-68
Foon, Dennis 1951- CANR-84
Earlier sketches in CA 111, CANR-28
See also CWRI 5
See also SATA 119
Fooner, Michael 81-84
See also SATA 22
Foord, Archibald Smith 1914-1969 CAP-1
Earlier sketch in CA 11-12
Foos, Laurie 1966- CANR-88
Earlier sketch in CA 150
Foosaner, Samuel J. 1907(?)-1988
Obituary 125
Foot, David 1929- CANR-84
Earlier sketch in CA 136
Foot, Hugh Mackintosh 1907-1990 9-12R
Foot, M(ichael) R(ichard) D(aniell)
1919- CANR-123
Earlier sketches in CA 5-8R, CANR-3, 48
Foot, Michael 1913- 108
Foot, Mirjam M(ichaela) 1941- 139
Foot, Paul (Mackintosh) 1937-2004 17-20R
Obituary 230
Foot, Philippa Ruth 1920- CANR-113
Earlier sketch in CA 101
Foote, A(von) Edward 1937- CANR-13
Earlier sketch in CA 73-76
Foote, Arthur 1911-1999 114
Foote, Darby Mozelle 1942- 61-64
Foote, Dorothy Norris (McBride) 1908- CAP-2
Earlier sketch in CA 21-22
Foote, Geoffrey 1950- 123
Foote, Horton 1916- CANR-110
Earlier sketches in CA 73-76, CANR-34, 51
Interview in CANR-34
See also CAD
See also CD 5, 6
See also CLC 51, 91
See also CSW
See also DA3
See also DAM DRAM
See also DFS 20
See also DLB 26, 266
See also EWL 3
See also MTFW 2005
Foote, Mary Anna Hallock 1847-1938 197
Foote, Mary Hallock 1847-1938 DLB 186,
188, 202, 221
See also TCLC 108
See also TCWW 2
Foote, Patricia 165
Foote, Samuel 1721-1777 DLB 89
See also RGEL 2
Foote, Shelby 1916-2005 CANR-131
Earlier sketches in CA 5-8R, CANR-3, 45, 74
See also AAYA 40
See also CLC 75
See also CN 1, 2, 3, 4, 5, 6, 7
See also CPW
See also CSW
See also DA3
See also DAM NOV, POP
See also DLB 2, 17
See also MAL 5
See also MTCW 2
See also MTFW 2005
See also RHW
Foote, Timothy (Gilson) 1926- 93-96
See also SATA 52
Foote, Tom 1935- 177
Foote, Victoria 1954- 118
Foote, Wilder 1905-1975
Obituary 57-60
Foote-Smith, Elizabeth 1913- 69-72
Footitt, Hilary 1948- 132
Footman, David (John) 1895-1983 97-100
Obituary 111
Footman, Robert 1916-1995 126
Footner, (William) Hulbert 1879-1944
Brief entry 114
Foran, Donald J. 1943- 33-36R
Forattini, Giorgio 1931(?)- 237
Forberg, Ati
See Forberg, Beate Gropius
See also SATA 22
Forberg, Beate Gropius 1925- 105
See also Forberg, Ati
Forbes, Aleck
See Rathborne, St. George (Henry)
Forbes, Anna 1954- 168
See also SATA 101
Forbes, Bryan 1926- CANR-44
Earlier sketch in CA 69-72
See also SATA 37
Forbes, Cabot L.
See Hoyt, Edwin P(almer), Jr.
Forbes, Calvin 1945- CANR-97
Earlier sketches in CA 49-52, CANR-26
See also CAAS 16
See also BW 1
See also DLB 41
Forbes, Clarence A(llen) 1901- 77-80
Forbes, Colin CANR-62
Earlier sketch in CA 103
See also Sawkins, Raymond H(arold)
See also CMW 4
Forbes, Cosmo
See Lewton, Val
Forbes, Daniel
See Kenyon, Michael
Forbes, DeLoris (Florine) Stanton
1923- CANR-84
Earlier sketches in CA 9-12R, CANR-5
Forbes, Donald (Galen) 1918-1987
Obituary 122
Forbes, Edith 1954- CANR-104
Earlier sketch in CA 159
Forbes, Elliot 1917- 9-12R
Forbes, Eric Gray 1933-1984 CANR-10
Obituary 114
Earlier sketch in CA 65-68
Forbes, Esther 1891-1967 CAP-1
Obituary 25-28R
Earlier sketch in CA 13-14
See also AAYA 17
See also BYA 2
See also CLC 12
See also CLR 27
See also DLB 22
See also JRDA
See also MAICYA 1, 2
See also RHW
See also SATA 2, 100
See also YAW
Forbes, Graham B. CANR-27
Earlier sketches in CAP-2, CA 19-20
See also SATA 1
Forbes, Henry W(illiam) 1918- 1-4R
Forbes, J(ohn) V(an) G(elder) 1916- 9-12R
Forbes, Jack D. 1934- CANR-4
Earlier sketch in CA 1-4R
Forbes, Jan
See Keltz, Martha
Forbes, Joanne R. (Triebel) 1930- 37-40R
Forbes, John 1950- CP 7
See also WWE 1
Forbes, John Douglas 1910- 53-56
Forbes, Kathryn
See McLean, Kathryn (Anderson)
Forbes, Malcolm S(tevenson)
1919-1990 CANR-28
Obituary 131
Earlier sketch in CA 69-72
Forbes, Murray (M.) 1906-1987
Obituary 121
Forbes, (Christopher) Patrick 1925- 25-28R
Forbes, Peter 1947- 186
Forbes, Robert
See Arthur, Robert, (Jr.)
Forbes, Rosita 196
See also McGrath, Joan Rosita (Torr)
See also DLB 195
Forbes, Stanton
See Forbes, DeLoris (Florine) Stanton
Forbes, Thomas Rogers 1911-1988 41-44R
Forbes-Boyd, Eric 1897-1979 13-16R
Obituary 125
Forbes-Dennis, Phyllis 1884-1963
Obituary 93-96
See also Bottome, Phyllis
Forbes-Robertson, Diana
See Sheean, Diana
Forbis, Judith 1934- 101
Forbis, William H. 1918- CANR-15
Earlier sketch in CA 37-40R
Forbus, Ina B(ell) -1994 1-4R
Forcade, Robert J. 1935- 125
Force, Peter 1790-1868 DLB 30
Force, Roland W(ynfield) 1924-1996 41-44R
Obituary 152
Force, William M. 1916- 21-24R
Forcey, Charles B(udd) 1925- CANR-1
Earlier sketch in CA 1-4R
Forche, Carolyn (Louise) 1950- CANR-138
Brief entry 109
Earlier sketches in CA 117, CANR-50, 74
Interview in CA-117
See also CLC 25, 83, 86
See also CP 7
See also CWP
See also DA3
See also DAM POET
See also DLB 5, 193
See also MAL 5
See also MTCW 2
See also MTFW 2005
See also PC 10
See also PFS 18
See also RGAL 4
Forchheimer, Paul 1913- 53-56
Forcione, Alban Keith 1938- CANR-13
Earlier sketch in CA 33-36R
Ford, A(lec) G(eorge) 1926- 5-8R
Ford, Adam 1940- 111
Ford, Agnes Gibbs 1902-1997 CAP-2
Earlier sketch in CA 21-22
Ford, Albert Lee
See Stratemeyer, Edward L.
Ford, Alice 1906- CAP-1
Earlier sketch in CA 19-20
Ford, Amasa B. 1922- 21-24R
Ford, Arielle 218
Ford, Arthur A. 1897-1971
Obituary 112
Ford, Arthur L(ewis) 1937- 57-60
Ford, Barbara 134
Brief entry 112
See also SATA 56
See also SATA-Brief 34
Ford, Betty
See Ford, Elizabeth Anne Bloomer
Ford, Boris 1917-1998 CANR-46
Obituary 167
Earlier sketch in CA 112
Ford, Brian J(ohn) 1939- CANR-94
Earlier sketches in CA 41-44R, CANR-15, 34
See also SATA 49
Ford, Carin T. 237
Ford, Carolyn (Mott) 1938- 165
See also SATA 98
Ford, Catherine 1961- 218
Ford, Cathy Diane 1952- 105
Ford, Charles Henri 1908-2002 CANR-13
Obituary 211
Earlier sketch in CA 25-28R
See also CP 2, 3, 4, 5, 6, 7
See also DLB 4, 48
Ford, Colin John 1934- 85-88
Ford, Collier
See Ford, James L(awrence) C(ollier)
Ford, Corey 1902-1969 177
Obituary 25-28R
See also DLB 11
Ford, D(ouglas) W(illiam) Cleverley
See Cleverley Ford, D(ouglas) W(illiam)
Ford, Daniel (Francis) 1931- CANR-11
Earlier sketch in CA 17-20R
Ford, David
See Harknett, Terry (Williams)
Ford, Donald (Frank William) 1924- 5-8R
Ford, Donald H(erbert) 1926- 41-44R
Ford, Edmund Brisco 1901-1988 CANR-47
Obituary 124
Earlier sketch in CA 85-88
Ford, Edsel 1928-1970 CAP-1
Obituary 29-32R
Earlier sketch in CA 13-16
Ford, Edward (Charles) 1928- 89-92
Ford, Eileen (Otte) 1922- 120
Ford, Elaine 1938- CANR-19
Earlier sketch in CA 102
Ford, Elbur
See Hibbert, Eleanor Alice Burford
Ford, Elizabeth
See Bidwell, Marjory Elizabeth Sarah
Ford, Elizabeth Anne Bloomer
1918- CANR-144
Earlier sketches in CA 105, CANR-23
Ford, Ellen 1949- SATA 89
Ford, Florence
See Novelli, Florence
Ford, Ford Madox 1873-1939 CANR-74
Brief entry 104
Earlier sketch in CA 132
See also Chaucer, Daniel
See also BRW 6
See also CDBLB 1914-1945
See also DA3
See also DAM NOV
See also DLB 34, 98, 162
See also EWL 3
See also MTCW 1, 2
See also RGEL 2
See also TCLC 1, 15, 39, 57
See also TEA
Ford, Frank B(ernard) 1932- 85-88
Ford, Franklin L(ewis) 1920-2003 17-20R
Obituary 219
Ford, Fred
See Doerffler, Alfred
Ford, G. M. 1945- CANR-72
Earlier sketch in CA 154
Ford, George (Jr.) 107
See also SATA 31
Ford, George Barry 1885-1978
Obituary 81-84
Ford, George D. 1880(?)-1974
Obituary 53-56
Ford, George H(arry) 1914-1994 CANR-2
Obituary 147
Earlier sketch in CA 1-4R
Ford, George L(onnie) 1914-1993 5-8R
Ford, Gerald R(udolph, Jr.) 1913- 114
Brief entry 110
Ford, Glenn 1916- 167
Ford, Gordon B(uell), Jr. 1937- CANR-13
Earlier sketch in CA 21-24R
Ford, Guy B(arrett) 1922- 5-8R
Ford, Harry 1938- 194
Ford, Harvey Seabury 1905(?)-1978
Obituary 73-76
Ford, Henry II 1863-1947 148
Obituary 123
Brief entry 111
Ford, Henry 1863-1947 148
Brief entry 115
See also TCLC 73
Ford, Herbert Paul 1927- 17-20R
Ford, Hilary
See Youd, (Christopher) Samuel
Ford, Hildegarde
See Morrison, Velma Ford
Ford, Hugh D. 1925-
Brief entry 114
Ford, J. Massingberd
See Ford, Josephine Massyngbaerde
Ford, Jack
See Ford, John
Ford, James Allan 1920- CAP-1
Earlier sketch in CA 9-10
Ford, James L(awrence) C(ollier) 1907- 29-32R
Ford, Jeffrey 1955- 194
See also AAYA 57
Ford, Jennifer 176
Ford, Jerome W. 1949- 146
See also SATA 78
Ford, Jerry
See Ford, Jerome W.
Ford, Jesse Hill (Jr.) 1928-1996 CANR-67
Obituary 152
Earlier sketches in CA 1-4R, CANR-1
See also CAAS 21
See also CN 1, 2, 3, 4, 5, 6
See also CSW
See also DLB 6
Ford, John 1586-1639 BRW 2
See also CDBLB Before 1660
See also DA3
See also DAM DRAM
See also DC 8
See also DFS 7
See also DLB 58
See also IDTP
See also RGEL 2
Ford, John 1895-1973 187
Obituary 45-48
See also CLC 16
Ford, John M. 1957- 198
See also FANT
See also SFW 4
Ford, Josephine Massyngbaerde 41-44R
Ford, Judy 1944- CANR-124
Earlier sketch in CA 171
Ford, Juwanda G(ertrude) 1967- 169
See also SATA 102
Ford, Kathleen 1932- 25-28R
Ford, Katie 1975- 232
Ford, Kenneth W(illiam) 1926- 229
Ford, Kirk
See Spence, William John Duncan
Ford, Larry R. 223
Ford, Lee 1936- 25-28R
Ford, Leighton F. S. 1931- 17-20R
Ford, LeRoy 1922- 9-12R
Ford, Leslie
See Brown, Zenith Jones
Ford, Lewis
See Patten, Lewis B(yford)
Ford, Lewis S. 1933- 137
Ford, Marcia
See Radford, Ruby L(orraine)
Ford, Marcus Peter 1950- 108

Cumulative Index 195 Forsythe

Ford, Margaret Patricia 1925- 9-12R
Ford, Marjorie Leet 1947- 203
Ford, Mark 1962- 196
Ford, Mary Forker 1905-1973 .... 9-12R
Ford, Michael Curtis 203
Ford, Michael Thomas .... MTFW 2005
Ford, Murray J(ohn) S(tanley) 1923- 93-96
Ford, Nancy K(effer) 1906-1961
Obituary 109
See also SATA-Obit 29
Ford, Nick Aaron 1904-1982 .... CANR-11
Earlier sketch in CA 25-28R
See also BW 1
Ford, Norman D(ennis) 1921- CANR-10
Earlier sketch in CA 21-24R
Ford, Norrey
See Dilcock, Noreen
Ford, Patrick 1914- 21-24R
Ford, Paul F(rancis X.) 1947- CANR-22
Earlier sketch in CA 105
Ford, Percy 1894-1983
Obituary 110
Ford, Peter 1936- 126
See also SATA 59
Ford, Philip J(ohn) 1949- 115
Ford, Phyllis M(arjorie) 1928- CANR-30
Earlier sketches in CA 33-36R, CANR-13
Ford, R(obert) A(rthur) D(ouglass)
1915- CANR-83
Earlier sketches in CA 97-100, CANR-19, 41
See also CP 1, 2
See also DLB 88
Ford, R(ichard) Clyde 1870-1951
Brief entry 121
Ford, Richard 1944- CANR-128
Earlier sketches in CA 69-72, CANR-11, 47, 86
See also AMWS 5
See also CLC 46, 99, 205
See also CN 5, 6, 7
See also CSW
See also DLB 227
See also EWL 3
See also MAL 5
See also MTCW 2
See also MTFW 2005
See also RGAL 4
See also RGSF 2
Ford, Richard Brice 1935- 37-40R
Ford, Robert A. D.
See Ford, R(obert) A(rthur) D(ouglass)
Ford, Robert E. 1913-1975 .... CAP-2
Earlier sketch in CA 29-32
Ford, Robert N(icholas) 1909- 33-36R
Ford, Ronnie E. 1961- 151
Ford, S. M.
See Uhlig, Susan
Ford, Stephen 1949- 77-80
Ford, Susan 1957- 226
Ford, Thomas R(obert) 1923- CANR-47
Earlier sketch in CA 49-52
Ford, Thomas W(ellborn) 1924- 21-24R
Ford, W(illiam) Clay(ton, Jr.) 1946- 93-96
Ford, W(illiam) Herschel 1900-1976 .. CANR-5
Earlier sketch in CA 9-12R
Ford, Wallace
See King, Albert
Ford, Webster
See Masters, Edgar Lee
Ford, Whitey
See Ford, Edward (Charles)
Ford, Worthington C(hauncey) 1858-1941 . 178
See also DLB 47
Forde, A.N. 1923- .... CP 1
Forde, Gerhard O(laf) 1927- 89-92
Forde-Johnston, James (Leo) 1927- CANR-3
Earlier sketch in CA 9-12R
Fordham, Benjamin O. 1966- 185
Fordham, Frieda 1903-1988
Obituary 124
Fordham, Peta 1905- 106
Fordin, Hugh 1935- 57-60
Fordyce, Rachel (Poole) 1942- 121
Brief entry 118
Fore, William Frank 1928- 5-8R
Forell, George W(olfgang) 1919- CANR-16
Earlier sketches in CA 1-4R, CANR-1
Foreman, Amanda 1968- 173
Foreman, Carl 1914-1984 .... 41-44R
Obituary 113
See also DLB 26
See also IDFW 3, 4
Foreman, Clark H(owell) 1902-1977
Obituary 69-72
Foreman, Dave 1946- 139
Foreman, Gene 1934- 77-80
Foreman, George 1949- 233
Foreman, Harry 1915- 33-36R
Foreman, Jennifer 1949- 214
Foreman, Kenneth Joseph 1891-1967 ... CAP-2
Earlier sketch in CA 33-36
Foreman, L(eonard) L(ondon)
1901-1967(?) CANR-63
Obituary 180
Earlier sketches in CA 5-8R, CANR-5
See also TCWW 1, 2
Foreman, Laura 1936-2001 205
Foreman, Lawton Durant 1913-1984 ...... 9-12R
Obituary 180
Foreman, Lee
See King, Albert
Foreman, Lelia M. 1952- 150
Foreman, Lelia Rose
See Foreman, Lelia M.
Foreman, Michael 1938- CANR-108
Earlier sketches in CA 21-24R, CANR-10, 38, 68
See also CLR 32
See also CWRI 5
See also MAICYA 1, 2
See also MAICYAS 1
See also SAAS 21
See also SATA 2, 73, 129, 135
Foreman, Richard 1937- CANR-143
Earlier sketches in CA 65-68, CANR-32, 63
See also CAD
See also CD 5, 6
See also CLC 50
Foreman, Russell 1921- 77-80
Foreman, Wilmoth 1939- 228
See also SATA 153
Foreman-Peck, James S. 1948- 195
Forer, Lois G(oldstein) 1914-1994 .... 29-32R
Obituary 145
Forer, Lucille K(remith) 37-40R
Forer, Mort 1922- 97-100
Fores, John 1914- 25-28R
Forest, Antonia 1915-2003 .... CANR-83
Earlier sketch in CA 103
See also Rubinstein, Patricia (Giulia Caulfield Kate)
Forest, Dial
See Gault, William Campbell
Forest, Heather 1948- 191
See also SATA 120
Forest, Ilse 1896- CAP-2
Earlier sketch in CA 19-20
Forest, James H. 1941- 136
Forest, Jim
See Forest, James H.
Forest, Lee
See Woods, Clee
Forester, Bruce (Michael) 1939- CANR-108
Earlier sketches in CA 107, CANR-25
Forester, C(ecil) S(cott) 1899-1966 .... CANR-83
Obituary 25-28R
Earlier sketch in CA 73-76
See also CLC 35
See also DLB 191
See also RGEL 2
See also RHW
See also SATA 13
See also TCLC 152
Forester, Frank
See Herbert, Henry William
Forester, S.
See Snell, William R(obert)
Forester, Tom 1949- 127
Foreyt, John P(aul) 1943- CANR-127
Earlier sketches in CA 118, CANR-41
Forez
See Mauriac, Francois (Charles)
Forgie, George B(arnard) 1941- 89-92
Forgus, Ronald (Henry) 1928- 41-44R
Forhan, Chris 1959- 196
Forio, Robert
See Weiss, Irving J.
Forisha, Barbara L.
See Kovach, Barbara (Ellen) L(usk)
Forker, Charles R(ush) 1927- 136
Forkosch, Morris D(avid) 1908-1989 .... 41-44R
Form, William H. 1917- 65-68
Forma, Warren 1923- 45-48
Forman, Brenda 1936- CANR-6
Earlier sketch in CA 9-12R
See also SATA 4
Forman, Celia Adler 1890(?)-1979
Obituary 85-88
Forman, Charles William 1916- 13-16R
Forman, Harrison 1904-1978 .... 5-8R
Obituary 77-80
Forman, Harry Buxton
See Forman, Harry (Henry) Buxton
Forman, Harry (Henry) Buxton
1842-1917 .... DLB 184
Forman, Henry James 1879-1966 .... 5-8R
Forman, James
See Forman, James D(ouglas)
Forman, James D(ouglas) 1932- CANR-42
Earlier sketches in CA 9-12R, CANR-4, 19
See also AAYA 17
See also CLC 21
See also JRDA
See also MAICYA 1, 2
See also SATA 8, 70
See also YAW
Forman, Joan 102
Forman, Jonathan 1887-1974 .... CAP-2
Earlier sketch in CA 23-24
Forman, Leona S. 1940- 25-28R
Forman, Marc A(llan) 1935- 57-60
Forman, Max Leon 1909-1990 112
Forman, Milos 1932- 109
See also AAYA 63
See also CLC 164
Forman, Richard T. T. 235
Forman, Robert E(dgar) 1924- 9-12R
Forman, Robert K. C. 1947- CANR-91
Earlier sketch in CA 145
Forman, Shepard (Lewis) 1938-
Brief entry 112
Forman, (James Adam) Sholto 1915- 25-28R
Formby, William A(rthur) 1943- 109
Formento, Dan 1954- 112
Formhals, Robert W(illard) Y(ates) S(arguszko)
1919- 53-56
Formisano, Ronald P. 1939- 154
Brief entry 115
Formwalt, Lee W(illiam) 1949- 119
Fornara, Charles William 1935- 130
Fornari, Franco 1921- CANR-12
Earlier sketch in CA 29-32R
Fornari, Harry D(avid) 1919- 69-72
Fornell, Earl Wesley 1915-1969 .... 1-4R
Obituary 103
Fornes, Maria Irene 1930- CANR-81
Earlier sketches in CA 25-28R, CANR-28
Interview in CANR-28
See also CAD
See also CD 5, 6
See also CLC 39, 61, 187
See also CWD
See also DC 10
See also DLB 7
See also HLCS 1
See also HW 1, 2
See also LLW
See also MAL 5
See also MTCW 1
See also RGAL 4
Forney, Ellen 1968- 197
Forni, P(ier) M(assimo) 1951- CANR-129
Earlier sketch in CA 167
Forno, Lawrence J(oseph) 1943- 37-40R
Forrest, A(lfred) C(linton)
1916-1978 .... CANR-27
Obituary 103
Earlier sketch in CA 49-52
Forrest, Allen
See Snow, Charles H(orace)
Forrest, Anthony
See MacKenzie, Norman (Ian)
Forrest, Brett 222
Forrest, Caleb
See Telfer, Dariel (Doris)
Forrest, David
See Forrest-Webb, Robert and Maddow, Ben
Forrest, Derek W(illiam) 1926- 77-80
Forrest, Earle Robert 1883-1969 .... 1-4R
Obituary 103
Forrest, Elizabeth
See Salsitz, Rhondi Vilott
Forrest, Felix C.
See Linebarger, Paul M(yron) A(nthony)
Forrest, Gary Gran 1943- CANR-32
Earlier sketch in CA 113
Forrest, James Taylor 1921- 115
Forrest, John Galbraith 1898-1982
Obituary 107
Forrest, Julian
See Wagenknecht, Edward (Charles)
Forrest, Julie de
See DeWitt, Edith Openshaw
Forrest, Katherine V(irginia) 1939- CANR-83
Earlier sketch in CA 131
See also CMW 4
Forrest, Leon (Richard) 1937-1997 ... CANR-87
Obituary 162
Earlier sketches in CA 89-92, CANR-25, 52
See also CAAS 7
See also AFAW 2
See also BLCS
See also BW 2
See also CLC 4
See also CN 4, 5, 6
See also DLB 33
Forrest, Norman
See Morland, Nigel
Forrest, Richard (Stockton) 1932- CANR-83
Earlier sketches in CA 57-60, CANR-9, 25, 50
Forrest, Sybil
See Markun, Patricia Maloney
Forrest, W(illiam) G(eorge) 1925- 25-28R
Forrest, Wilbur S. 1887-1977
Obituary 69-72
Forrestal, Dan J(oseph), Jr. 1912-1991 77-80
Forrestal, Elaine 1941- 189
See also SATA 117
Forrester, Anouchka Grose 1970- 221
Forrester, Duncan B(aillie) 1933- CANR-93
Earlier sketch in CA 131
Forrester, Frank H. 1919(?)-1986
Obituary 119
See also SATA-Obit 52
Forrester, Helen
See Bhatia, Jamunadevi
See also SATA 48
Forrester, Jay W(right) 1918- CANR-1
Earlier sketch in CA 45-48
Forrester, John 1949- 141
Forrester, Larry 1924- 25-28R
Forrester, Leland S. 1905(?)-1978
Obituary 81-84
Forrester, Leo
See Lee, Edward Edson
Forrester, Marian
See Schachtel, Roger (Bernard)
Forrester, Martyn (John) 1952- 129
Forrester, Mary
See Humphries, Mary
Forrester, Michael A. 1953- CANR-91
Earlier sketch in CA 146
Forrester, (William) Ray 1911-2001 .... 21-24R
Forrester, Rex Desmond 1928- 103
Forrester, Sandra 1949- 155
See also SATA 90
Forrester, Sibelan 1961- 161
Forrester, Victoria 1940- CANR-25
Earlier sketch in CA 108
See also SATA 40
See also SATA-Brief 35
Forrest-Webb, Robert 1929- CANR-4
Earlier sketch in CA 49-52
Forsberg, (Charles) Gerald 1912-2000 102
Forsberg, Malcolm I(ver) 1908-1991 ..... 21-24R
Obituary 176, 180
Forsberg, Roberta Jean 1914-1986
Brief entry 105
Forsee, (Frances) Aylesa -1986 .... CANR-1
Earlier sketch in CA 1-4R
See also SATA 1
Forsey, Chris 1950- .... SATA 59
Forsh, Ol'ga Dmitrievna 1873-1961 ... DLB 272
Forshay-Lunsford, Cin 1965- 119
See also SATA 60
Forshee, Jill 220
Forssell, Lars 1928- .... EWL 3
Forssmann, Werner Theodor Otto 1904-1979
Obituary 111
Forstchen, William R. 1950- 165
See also SFW 4
Forstenzer, Thomas R. 1944- 154
Forstenzer, Tom
See Forstenzer, Thomas R.
Forster, Arnold 1912- 13-16R
Forster, E(dward) M(organ)
1879-1970 .... CANR-45
Obituary 25-28R
Earlier sketches in CAP-1, CA 13-14
See also AAYA 2, 37
See also BRW 6
See also BRWR 2
See also BYA 12
See also CDBLB 1914-1945
See also CLC 1, 2, 3, 4, 9, 10, 13, 15, 22, 45, 77
See also DA
See also DA3
See also DAB
See also DAC
See also DAM MST, NOV
See also DLB 34, 98, 162, 178, 195
See also DLBD 10
See also EWL 3
See also EXPN
See also LAIT 3
See also LMFS 1
See also MTCW 1, 2
See also MTFW 2005
See also NCFS 1
See also NFS 3, 10, 11
See also RGEL 2
See also RGSF 2
See also SATA 57
See also SSC 27
See also SUFW 1
See also TCLC 125
See also TEA
See also WLC
See also WLIT 4
Forster, Georg 1754-1794 .... DLB 94
Forster, Gwynne
See Johnson-Acsadi, Gwendolyn
Forster, John 1812-1876 .... DLB 144, 184
Forster, Kent 1916-1981 .... 21-24R
Obituary 125
Forster, Klaus 1945- 131
Forster, Marc R. 1959- 138
Forster, Margaret 1938- CANR-115
Earlier sketches in CA 133, CANR-62
See also CLC 149
See also CN 4, 5, 6, 7
See also DLB 155, 271
Forster, Mark Arnold
See Arnold-Forster, Mark
Forster, Merlin H(enry) 1928- 41-44R
Forster, Michelanne 1953- 231
See also CD 5, 6
Forster, Peter 1926(?)-1982
Obituary 107
Forster, Robert 1926- 41-44R
Forstman, H(enry) Jackson 1929- 13-16R
Forsyth, Alison 1961- 220
Forsyth (Outram), Anne 1933- CANR-29
Earlier sketches in CA 29-32R, CANR-12
Forsyth, Bill 1948- 122
Forsyth, David J(ames) C(ameron)
1940- 41-44R
Forsyth, David P(ond) 1930- 9-12R
Forsyth, Frederick 1938- CANR-137
Earlier sketches in CA 85-88, CANR-38, 62, 115
See also BEST 89:4
See also CLC 2, 5, 36
See also CMW 4
See also CN 3, 4, 5, 6, 7
See also CPW
See also DAM NOV, POP
See also DLB 87
See also MTCW 1, 2
See also MTFW 2005
Forsyth, George H(oward), Jr.
1901-1991 .... 37-40R
Obituary 133
Forsyth, Ilene (Haering) 1928- 37-40R
Forsyth, James (Law) 1913- 73-76
See also CBD
See also CD 5, 6
Forsyth, Jean
See McIlwraith, Jean Newton
Forsyth, Kate 1966- 216
See also SATA 154
Forsyth, Michael (de Jong) 1951- CANR-82
Earlier sketch in CA 133
Forsyth, Moira 207
Forsyth, Phyllis Young 1944- 169
Forsyth, Richard S(andes) 1948- 116
Forsythe, Elizabeth 1927- 93-96
Forsythe, Irene
See Hanson, Irene (Forsythe)
Forsythe, Malcolm
See Hutton, Malcolm

Forsythe, Robert
See Crichton, Kyle Samuel
Forsythe, Sidney A. 1920- ... 41-44R
Fort, Charles Hoy 1874-1932 ... 205
Fort, Ilene Susan 1949- ... 140
Fort, John 1942- ... 77-80
Fort, Paul
See Stockton, Francis Richard
Fort, Paul 1872-1960
Obituary ... 114
See also GFL 1789 to the Present
Fort, Williams Edwards, Jr. 1905-1988 .. 37-40R
Fortas, Abe 1910-1982
Obituary ... 106
Forte, Allen 1926- ... CANR-88
Earlier sketch in CA 41-44R
Forte, Dan 1935- ... 65-68
Forte, David F. 1941- ... 53-56
Forte, Dieter 1935-
Forte, James A. 1951- ... 214
Forte, Maurizio 1961- ... 172
See also SATA 110
Fortebraccia, Donato
See Forte, Dan
Forten, Charlotte
See Grimke, Charlotte L(ottie) Forten
Forten, Charlotte L. 1837-1914
See Grimke, Charlotte L(ottie) Forten
See also BLC 2
See also DLB 50, 239
See also TCLC 16
Fortenbaugh, William W. 1936- ... 230
Fortes (De Leff), Jacqueline 1952- ... 148
Fortes, Meyer 1906-1983 ... 129
Obituary ... 109
Fortescue, William (Archer Irvine)
1945- ... CANR-48
Earlier sketch in CA 122
Fortey, Richard (Alan) 1946- ... CANR-128
Earlier sketch in CA 171
See also SATA 109
Forth, Melissa D(eal) ... 161
See also SATA 96
Forti, Simone 1935- ... 205
Fortin, Noonie 1947- ... 152
Fortinbras
See Grieg, (Johan) Nordahl (Brun)
Fortini, Franco 1917- ... DLB 128
Fortman, Edmund J. 1901-1990 ... CANR-28
Obituary ... 130
Earlier sketches in CA 21-24R, CANR-11
Fortney, Steven D. 1937- ... 209
Fortnum, Peggy
See Nuttall-Smith, Margaret Emily Noel
See also SATA 26
Fortune, Dion 1890-1946 ... HGG
See also SUFW
Fortune, Mary 1833-1910 ... DLB 230
Fortune, T(imothy) Thomas 1856-1928
Brief entry ... 112
See also DLB 23
Forty, Adrian 1948- ... CANR-101
Earlier sketch in CA 123
Forty, George 1927- ... CANR-34
Earlier sketches in CA 89-92, CANR-15
Forward, Luke
See Patrick, Johnstone G(illespie)
Forward, Robert L(ull) 1932-2002 ... CANR-84
Obituary ... 211
Earlier sketches in CA 103, CANR-20
See also SATA 82
See also SFW 4
Forward, Susan ... 130
See also BEST 90:1
Forzano, Giovacchino 1884-1970
Obituary ... 104
Fosburgh, Hugh (Whitney) 1916-1976
Obituary ... 69-72
Fosburgh, Lacey 1942-1993 ... CANR-22
Obituary ... 140
Earlier sketch in CA 85-88
Fosburgh, Liza 1930- ... CANR-30
Earlier sketch in CA 112
Fosburgh, Pieter Whitney 1914(?)-1978
Obituary ... 77-80
Foscolo, Ugo 1778-1827 ... EW 5
See also WLIT 7
Foscue, Edwin Jay 1899-1972 ... 1-4R
Obituary ... 103
Fosdick, Charles Austin 1842-1915
Brief entry ... 119
See also DLB 42
Fosdick, Harry Emerson 1878-1969
Obituary ... 25-28R
Fosdick, Raymond B(laine) 1883-1972
Obituary ... 37-40R
Foshay, Toby (Avard) 1950- ... 119
Foshee, John (Hugh) 1931- ... 69-72
Foskett, D(ouglas) J(ohn) 1918-2004 .. CANR-5
Obituary ... 227
Earlier sketch in CA 1-4R
Foskett, Daphne 1911-1998 ... 102
Foskett, Reginald 1909-1973 ... CAP-2
Earlier sketch in CA 21-22
Foss, Christopher F(rank) 1946- ... CANR-128
Earlier sketch in CA 93-96
Foss, Clive (Frank Wilson) 1939- ... CANR-135
Earlier sketch in CA 132
Foss, Dennis C(arleton) 1947- ... 104
Foss, Karen A. 1950- ... 187
Foss, P. M.
See Foss, P. Maureen
Foss, P. Maureen 1941- ... 220
Foss, Phillip Oliver ... 13-16R
Foss, Rene 1962- ... 213
Foss, William O(tto) 1918- ... 17-20R
Fosse, Alfred
See Jelly, George Oliver
Fosse, Bob
See Fosse, Robert Louis
See also CLC 20
Fosse, Jon 1959- ... DLB 297
Fosse, Robert Louis 1927-1987
Obituary ... 123
Brief entry ... 110
See also Fosse, Bob
Fossedal, Gregory
See Fossedal, Gregory A.
Fossedal, Gregory A. 1959- ... 125
Fossey, Dian 1932-1985 ... CANR-34
Obituary ... 118
Earlier sketch in CA 113
See also MTCW 1
Fossum, Karin 1954- ... 230
Fossum, Robert H. 1923- ... 25-28R
Foster, Alan Dean 1946- ... CANR-105
Earlier sketches in CA 53-56, CANR-5, 22, 56
See also AAYA 16
See also CPW
See also DAM POP
See also FANT
See also SATA 70
See also SFW 4
Foster, Barbara (M.) ... 169
Foster, Brad W. 1955- ... SATA 34
Foster, Brian 1920-
Brief entry ... 112
Foster, Carno A(ugustus) 1916- ... 41-44R
Foster, Catharine Osgood 1907- ... 65-68
Foster, Cecil (A.) 1954- ... 154
See also BW 3
Foster, Cedric 1900-1975
Obituary ... 89-92
Foster, Charles Howell 1913-1995 ... 17-20R
Foster, Charles I(rving) 1898-1970(?) ... 1-4R
Obituary ... 134
Foster, Charles R(obert) 1927- ... 110
Foster, Charles William 1939- ... 57-60
Foster, Chris(topher Joseph) 1932- ... 139
Foster, Daniel W(illet) 1930- ... 108
Foster, David
See Foster, David Manning
See also DLB 289
Foster, David 1908- ... CANR-84
Earlier sketch in CA 97-100
Foster, David Manning 1944- ... CANR-39
Earlier sketches in CA 97-100, CANR-18
See also CN 2, 3, 4, 5, 6, 7
Foster, David William (Anthony)
1940- ... CANR-97
Earlier sketches in CA 21-24R, CANR-8, 22, 50
Foster, Don
See Foster, Donald W(ayne)
Foster, Don(ald) 1948- ... 33-36R
See also CP 1
Foster, Donald (LeRoy) 1928- ... 53-56
Foster, Donald W(ayne) 1950- ... CANR-127
Earlier sketch in CA 132
Foster, Doris Van Liew 1899-1993 ... 102
See also SATA 10
Foster, Dorothy 1936-2001 ... 93-96
Foster, E(lizabeth) C(onnell) 1902- ... 53-56
See also SATA 9
Foster, Earl M(asters) 1940- ... 57-60
Foster, Edward Halsey 1942- ... 178
Earlier sketches in CA 49-52, CANR-2, 18, 40
Autobiographical Essay in ... 178
See also CAAS 26
Foster, Elizabeth 1902- ... 85-88
See also SATA 12
Foster, Elizabeth 1905-1963 ... 1-4R
See also SATA 10
Foster, Elizabeth Read 1912-1999 ... 106
Foster, Evan
See King, Albert
Foster, F. Blanche 1919- ... 61-64
See also SATA 11
Foster, Frances Smith 1944- ... 135
Foster, (Reginald) Francis 1896-1975 ... 109
Obituary ... 107
Foster, Frederick
See Godwin, John (Frederick)
Foster, G(eorge) Allen 1907-1969 ... 9-12R
See also SATA 26
Foster, Genevieve (Stump)
1893-1979 ... CANR-4
Obituary ... 89-92
Earlier sketch in CA 5-8R
See also CLR 7
See also DLB 61
See also MAICYA 1, 2
See also SATA 2
See also SATA-Obit 23
Foster, Genevieve W(akeman)
1902-1992 ... 69-72
Foster, George
See Haswell, Chetwynd John Drake
Foster, George M(cClelland, Jr.) 1913-
Brief entry ... 113
Foster, Gwendolyn Audrey 1960- ... 190
Foster, H. Lincoln 1906-1989 ... CAP-1
Obituary ... 128
Earlier sketch in CA 19-20
Foster, Hal
See Foster, Harold (Rudolf)
See also AAYA 51
See also AITN 2
Foster, Hannah Webster 1758-1840 .... DLB 37, 200
See also RGAL 4
Foster, Harold (Rudolf) 1892-1982
Obituary ... 107
See also Foster, Hal
See also SATA 31
Foster, Harold D(ouglas) 1943- ... 111
Foster, Harry
See Paine, Lauran (Bosworth)
Foster, Henry H(ubbard), Jr.
1911-1988 ... CANR-2
Obituary ... 125
Earlier sketch in CA 1-4R
Foster, Herbert L(awrence) 1928- ... 57-60
Foster, Herbert W. 1920(?)-1979
Obituary ... 89-92
Foster, Idris Llywelyn 1911-1984
Obituary ... 113
Foster, Iris
See Posner, Richard
Foster, J(ames) A(nthony) 1932- ... 130
Foster, Jack Donald 1930- ... 29-32R
Foster, Jake
See Gorman, Edward
Foster, James C(aldwell) 1943- ... CANR-7
Earlier sketch in CA 57-60
Foster, Jeanne
See Williams, Jeanne
Foster, Jeanne Robert (Ollivier) 1884-1970
Obituary ... 104
Foster, Jeannette Howard 1895-1981 ... 148
See also Addison, Jan and
Farr, Hilary and
Sanford, Abigail
Foster, Joanna 1928- ... CANR-8
Earlier sketch in CA 5-8R
Foster, Joanne Reckler 1941- ... 173
Foster, Jodie 1962- ... AAYA 24
Foster, John
See Foster, John L(ouis) and
Furcolo, Foster
Foster, John 1648-1681 ... DLB 24
Foster, John 1915- ... 5-8R
Foster, John (Thomas) 1925- ... 33-36R
See also SATA 8
Foster, John (Andrew) 1941- ... 126
Foster, John Bellamy 1953- ... 148
Foster, John Burt, Jr. 1945- ... 106
Foster, John L(awrence) 1930- ... 53-56
Foster, John L(ouis) 1941- ... 161
See also SATA 102
Foster, John Wilson 1944- ... 227
Foster, Joseph O'Kane 1898-1985 ... 49-52
Foster, Julian F(rancis) S(herwood)
1926- ... 29-32R
Foster, K(enneth) Neill 1935- ... CANR-4
Earlier sketch in CA 53-56
Foster, Ken ... 234
Foster, Laura Louise (James) 1918- ... 17-20R
See also SATA 6
Foster, (William) Lawrence 1947- ... 131
Foster, Lee 1923(?)-1977
Obituary ... 69-72
Foster, Lee Edwin 1943- ... 33-36R
Foster, Leila Merrell 1929- ... SATA 73
Foster, Linda Nemec 1950- ... 232
Foster, Lynn 1952- ... CANR-32
Earlier sketch in CA 113
Foster, Lynne 1937- ... SATA 74
Foster, M(ichael) A(nthony) 1939- ... CANR-84
Earlier sketches in CA 57-60, CANR-9, 25
See also SFW 4
Foster, Malcolm (Burton) 1931- ... 109
Foster, Margaret Lesser 1899(?)-1979
Obituary ... 89-92
See also SATA-Obit 21
Foster, Margery S(omers) 1914- ... 5-8R
Foster, Marguerite H. 1909-1981 ... CAP-2
Earlier sketch in CA 21-22
Foster, Marian Curtis 1909-1978 ... 73-76
Obituary ... 85-88
See also SATA 23
Foster, Marilee 1971- ... 212
Foster, Marion
See Shea, Shirley
Foster, Mark Stewart 1939- ... CANR-92
Earlier sketch in CA 106
Foster, Martha S(tanding) ... 5-8R
Foster, Michael 1904-1956
Brief entry ... 110
See also DLB 9
Foster, Michael S(immler) 1942- ... 117
Foster, Myles Birket 1825-1899 ... DLB 184
Foster, Nancy Haston ... 122
Foster, Nora R(akestraw) 1947- ... 140
Foster, O'Kane
See Foster, Joseph O'Kane
Foster, Paul 1931- ... CANR-26
Earlier sketches in CA 21-24R, CANR-9
See also CAD
See also CD 5, 6
Foster, Peter 1947- ... CANR-25
Earlier sketch in CA 108
Foster, Philip (John) 1927- ... 69-72
Foster, Raymond Keith 1945-
See Giles, Jack
Foster, Richard ... 137
See also Crossen, Kendell Foster
Foster, Richard J(ames) 1942- ... CANR-127
Earlier sketches in CA 85-88, CANR-15, 34
Foster, Robert A(lfred) 1949- ... 81-84
Foster, Ruel Elton 1916- ... 33-36R
Foster, Russell G. ... 236
Foster, Sally ... SATA 58
Foster, Shirley 1943- ... 122
Foster, Stephen C. 1941- ... 174
Foster, Stephen Collins 1826-1864 ... RGAL 4
Foster, Steven 1957- ... CANR-127
Earlier sketch in CA 135
Foster, Suzy
See Foster-Fritts, Suzy
Foster, Timothy R(ichard) V(ernon) 1938- ... 112
Foster, Tony
See Foster, J(ames) A(nthony)
Foster, Virginia Ramos ... 29-32R
Foster, W(alter) Bert(ram)
1869-1929 ... TCWW 1, 2
Foster, Walter Roland 1925-
Brief entry ... 116
Foster, William Z. 1881-1961 ... DLB 303
Foster-Fritts, Suzy 1967- ... 164
Foster-Harris, William 1903(?)-1978
Obituary ... 104
Fothergill, (Arthur) Brian 1921-1990 ... 17-20R
Obituary ... 132
Fothergill, Philip G(ilbert) 1908- ... 5-8R
Fotheringham, Nick 1943- ... 121
Foti, Veronique M. 1938- ... 141
Fotopoulos, Takis 1940- ... CANR-124
Earlier sketch in CA 171
Fottler, Myron David 1941- ... CANR-14
Earlier sketch in CA 37-40R
Foucault, Michel 1926-1984 ... CANR-34
Obituary ... 113
Earlier sketch in CA 105
See also CLC 31, 34, 69
See also DLB 242
See also EW 13
See also EWL 3
See also GFL 1789 to the Present
See also GLL 1
See also LMFS 2
See also MTCW 1, 2
See also TWA
Fougasse
See Bird, (Cyril) Kenneth
Fought, John G(uy) 1938- ... 189
Brief entry ... 113
Fouhy, Ed(ward Michael) 1934- ... 69-72
Foulds, E. V.
See Foulds, Elfrida Vipont
Foulds, Elfrida Vipont 1902-1992 ... CANR-84
Earlier sketches in CA 53-56, CANR-4, 38
See also Vipont, Elfrida
See also CWRI 5
See also MAICYA 1, 2
See also SATA 52
Foulis, Hugh
See Munro, Neil
Foulke, Adrienne 1915- ... 65-68
Foulke, Robert (Dana) 1930- ... 45-48
Foulke, Roy Anderson 1896-1994 ... CANR-1
Earlier sketch in CA 1-4R
Foulkes, A(lbert) Peter 1936- ... 37-40R
Foulkes, (William) David 1935-
Brief entry ... 107
Foulkes, Fred K. 1941- ... CANR-12
Earlier sketch in CA 33-36R
Foulkes, Paul 1923- ... 153
Foulkes, Richard (George) 1944- ... 141
Fountain, Charles (Francis) 1950- ... 118
Fountain, Leatrice 1924- ... 21-24R
Fountain, Richard
See Sproat, Iain (MacDonald)
Fouque, Caroline de la Motte
1774-1831 ... DLB 90
See also RGWL 2, 3
Fouque, Friedrich (Heinrich Karl) de la Motte
1777-1843 ... DLB 90
See also RGWL 2, 3
See also SUFW 1
Fouraker, Lawrence Edward 1923- ... 1-4R
Four Arrows
See Jacobs, Donald Trent
Four Arrows-Jacobs, Donald
See Jacobs, Donald Trent
Fourastie, Jean Joseph Hubert 1907-1990
Obituary ... 132
Fourcade, Marie-Madeleine 1909-1989
Obituary ... 129
Four Corners, George
See Viereck, George S(ylvester)
Fourest, Henry-Pierre 1911- ... 136
Brief entry ... 109
Fourest, Michel
See Wynne-Tyson, (Timothy) Jon (Lyden)
Fourie, Corlia 1944- ... 155
See also SATA 91
Fournet, Jean-Claude 1932- ... 124
Fournier, Frank
See Chapman, Frank M(onroe)
Fournier, Henri-Alban 1886-1914 ... 179
Brief entry ... 104
See also Alain-Fournier
Fournier, Pierre 1916-1997 ... CANR-40
Earlier sketches in CA 89-92, CANR-16
See also Gascar, Pierre
See also CLC 11
Fourth, Clifton
See Morse, H(enry) Clifton IV
Fourth Brother, The
See Aung, (Maung) Htin
Fourth Earl of Chesterfield
See Stanhope, Philip Dormer
Foust, Jeff 1971- ... 202
Foust, Paul J(ohn) 1920- ... 49-52
Fouste, E(thel) Bonita Rutledge 1926- ... 13-16R
Fout, John C(alvin) 1937- ... 57-60
Foveaux, Jessie Lee Brown 1899-1999 ... 163
Fowells, Robert M. 1921- ... 209
Fowers, Blaine J. 1956- ... 193
Fowke, Edith (Margaret) 1913-1996 ... 37-40R
See also SATA 14
Fowkes, Robert Allen 1913-1998
Brief entry ... 106

Cumulative Index 197 Fraenkel-Conrat

Fowle, Eleanor Cranston
See Cameron, Eleanor Cranston
Fowler, Alastair (David Shaw)
1930- CANR-39
Earlier sketch in CA 13-16R
Fowler, Austin 1928- 21-24R
Fowler, Bo 1971- 187
Fowler, Brenda 1963- 207
Fowler, Carolyn 117
Fowler, Charles B(runer) 1931- CANR-49
Earlier sketches in CA 57-60, CANR-8, 24
Fowler, Christopher 1953- CANR-139
Earlier sketches in CA 137, CANR-74
See also DLB 267
See also HGG
Fowler, Connie May 1959- CANR-127
Earlier sketches in CA 156, CANR-90
See also CSW
See also DLB 292
Fowler, David Covington 1921- CANR-58
Earlier sketches in CA 1-4R, CANR-28
Fowler, David Henry 1924-
Brief entry 112
Fowler, Don 1955-1999 203
Fowler, Don D. 1936- CANR-45
Earlier sketches in CA 33-36R, CANR-15
Fowler, Doreen (Angela) 1948- 119
Fowler, Douglas 1940- 57-60
Fowler, Earlene 1954- CANR-96
Earlier sketch in CA 146
Fowler, Elaine W(ootten) 1914- 93-96
Fowler, Elizabeth Millspaugh 1921- 102
Fowler, Eugene Devlan 1890-1960 97-100
Obituary 89-92
Fowler, Frank 1900-1971 .... CANR-64
Obituary 113
See also Chase, Borden
Fowler, Gene
See Fowler, Eugene Devlan
Fowler, Gene 1931- CANR-20
Earlier sketches in CA 53-56, CANR-5
See also CP 1, 2, 3, 4, 5, 6, 7
Fowler, George P(almer) 1909-1991 ..... 41-44R
Fowler, Guy 1893(?)-1966
Obituary 25-28R
Fowler, Harry (Jr.) 1934- CANR-1
Earlier sketch in CA 45-48
Fowler, Heather T.
See Remoff, Heather T(rexler)
Fowler, Helen Rosa Huxley 1917- CAP-1
Earlier sketch in CA 9-10
Fowler, James W(iley) III 1940- 104
Fowler, Jim
See Fowler, James W(iley) III
Fowler, John M(ajor) 1926- 103
Fowler, Karen Joy 1950- CANR-84
Earlier sketch in CA 143
See also AAYA 64
See also SFW 4
Fowler, Kenneth A(brams)
1900-1987 .... CANR-63
Obituary 122
Earlier sketch in CA 5-8R
See also TCWW 1, 2
Fowler, Marian (Elizabeth) 1929- CANR-123
Earlier sketches in CA 114, CANR-48
Fowler, Mark 1949- 65-68
Fowler, Mary Elizabeth 1911- CAP-2
Earlier sketch in CA 29-32
Fowler, Mary Jane
See Wheeler, Mary Jane
Fowler, (Edward) Michael (Coulson) 1929- . 109
Fowler, Raymond Dalton, Jr. 1930- 185
Brief entry 110
Fowler, Raymond E(veleth) 1933- 85-88
Fowler, Richard A(lan) 1948- CANR-36
Earlier sketch in CA 113
Fowler, Richard Hindle 1910-1996 130
Fowler, Robert H(oward) 1926- 73-76
Fowler, Roger 1938- 65-68
Fowler, Sandra (Lynn) 1937- 106
Fowler, Sydney
See Wright, S(ydney) Fowler
Fowler, Virginia C. 1948- CANR-95
Earlier sketch in CA 145
Fowler, Virginie
See Elbert, Virginie Fowler
Fowler, Wilfred 1907- CAP-1
Earlier sketch in CA 13-14
Fowler, Will 1922-2004 .... 5-8R
Obituary 226
Fowler, William A(lfred) 1911-1995 156
Fowler, William Morgan, Jr. 1944- CANR-57
Earlier sketches in CA 45-48, CANR-1, 31
Fowler, Wilton B(onham) 1936- 53-56
Fowles, Jib 1940- 69-72
Fowles, John (Robert) 1926- CANR-103
Earlier sketches in CA 5-8R, CANR-25, 71
See also BPFB 1
See also BRWS 1
See also CDBLB 1960 to Present
See also CLC 1, 2, 3, 4, 6, 9, 10, 15, 33, 87
See also CN 1, 2, 3, 4, 5, 6, 7
See also DA3
See also DAB
See also DAC
See also DAM MST
See also DLB 14, 139, 207
See also EWL 3
See also HGG
See also MTCW 1, 2
See also MTFW 2005
See also NFS 21
See also RGEL 2
See also RHW
See also SATA 22
See also SSC 33
See also TEA
See also WLIT 4
Fowlie, Wallace 1908-1998 .... CANR-5
Obituary 169
Earlier sketch in CA 5-8R
See also MAL 5
Fowlkes, Diane L(owe) 1939- 143
Fox, Adam 229
Fox, Adam 1883-1977 .... CANR-10
Earlier sketches in CAP-1, CA 13-14
Fox, Aileen 1907- CANR-5
Earlier sketch in CA 5-8R
See also SATA 58
Fox, Alan John 13-16R
Fox, Alistair 1948- CANR-39
Earlier sketch in CA 116
Fox, Allan M(ark) 1948- 41-44R
Fox, Andrew Jay 1964- 227
Fox, Angela 1912-1999 186
Fox, Annette Baker 1912-
Brief entry 109
Fox, Anthony
See Fullerton, Alexander (Fergus)
Fox, Barry 225
Fox, Bill
See Fox, William
Fox, Brian
See Ballard, (Willis) Todhunter
Fox, C(arol) Lynn 1948- CANR-29
Earlier sketch in CA 110
Fox, Charles Elliot 1878-1974 .... CAP-1
Earlier sketch in CA 9-10
Fox, Charles Philip 1913-2003 .... CANR-1
Obituary 224
Earlier sketch in CA 1-4R
See also SATA 12
See also SATA-Obit 150
Fox, Col. Victor J.
See Winston, R(obert) A(lexander)
Fox, Connie
See Fox, Hugh (Bernard, Jr.)
Fox, Daniel
See Brenchley, Chaz
Fox, Daniel Michael 1938- 112
Fox, David J(oseph) 1927- 13-16R
Fox, Dorothea Warren 1914-1999 61-64
Fox, Douglas A(llan) 1927- CANR-17
Earlier sketch in CA 41-44R
Fox, Douglas McMurray 1940- CANR-15
Earlier sketch in CA 33-36R
Fox, E(dward) Inman 1933- 17-20R
Fox, Edward J(ackson) 1913-1987 .... 1-4R
Fox, Edward L. 1938-1983 134
Brief entry 110
Fox, Edward Whiting 1911-1996 200
Brief entry 106
Fox, Eleanor
See St. John, Wylly Folk
Fox, Faulkner 231
Fox, Fontaine Talbot, Jr. 1884-1964
Obituary 89-92
See also SATA-Obit 23
Fox, Frances Margaret
See Field, Frances Fox
Fox, Frank 1923- CANR-115
Earlier sketch in CA 159
Fox, Frank W(ayne) 1940- 109
Fox, Fred 1903(?)-1981
Obituary 104
See also SATA-Obit 27
Fox, Frederic Ewing 1917-1981 .... 1-4R
Obituary 103
Fox, Freeman
See Hamilton, Charles (Harold St. John)
Fox, G(ardner) F(rancis) 1911-1986 .. CANR-58
Earlier sketches in CA 5-8R, CANR-5
See also FANT
See also SFW 4
Fox, G(eoffrey) P. 1938- CANR-11
Earlier sketch in CA 21-24R
Fox, Gail 1942- CANR-19
Earlier sketch in CA 103
Fox, Geoffrey 1941- .... SATA 73
Fox, George (Richard) 1934- 37-40R
Fox, Gilbert T(heodore) 1915-2004 69-72
Obituary 227
Fox, Gill
See Fox, Gilbert T(heodore)
Fox, Grace
See Anderson, Grace Fox
Fox, Grace (Estelle) 1899-1984 .... 37-40R
Obituary 111
Fox, Grace Imogene 1907- 1-4R
Fox, H(enry) B(enjamin) 1910-1989 57-60
Fox, Harrison W(illiam), Jr. 1944- 126
Fox, Helen Morgenthau 1885(?)-1974
Obituary 45-48
Fox, Hugh (Bernard, Jr.) 1932- CANR-54
Earlier sketches in CA 25-28R, CANR-11, 29
Fox, J. N.
See Janeczko, Paul B(ryan)
Fox, Jack C(urtis) 1925-1987 .... 21-24R
Obituary 122
Fox, Jack Vernon 1918-1982
Obituary 106
Fox, James (Lyttleton) 1945- CANR-100
Earlier sketch in CA 120
Fox, James M. 1908(?)-1989 .... CANR-85
Obituary 128
Earlier sketch in CA 102
Fox, Jeffrey J. 1945- 190
Fox, Jimmy 1955- 228
Fox, John
See Todd, John M(urray)
Fox, John (William), Jr. 1862(?)-1919
Brief entry 108
See also DLB 9
See also DLBD 13
Fox, John 1906-1984
Obituary 114
Fox, John 1939- .... DLB 245
Fox, John 1952-1990
Obituary 132
Fox, John H(oward) 1925- CANR-8
Earlier sketch in CA 5-8R
Fox, John O. 1938- 211
Fox, John Roger 1896-1987
Obituary 125
Fox, Joseph M(ichael) 1934- 106
Fox, Karen A. 1956- 229
Fox, Karl A(ugust) 1917- CANR-7
Earlier sketch in CA 17-20R
Fox, Kenneth 1944- 125
Fox, Larry 106
See also SATA 30
Fox, Laurie (Anne) 208
Fox, Les 173
Fox, Levi 1914- CANR-57
Earlier sketches in CA 77-80, CANR-14, 31
Fox, Logan J(ordan) 1922- 53-56
Fox, Loren 1967- 228
Fox, Lorraine 1922-1976 .... SATA 11, 27
Fox, Louisa
See Kroll, Virginia L(ouise)
Fox, Lucia
See Lockert, Lucia (Alicia Ungaro Fox)
Fox, Marcia R(ose) 1942- 105
Fox, Mary Virginia 1919- CANR-136
Earlier sketches in CA 29-32R, CANR-12, 44
See also SATA 44, 88, 152
See also SATA-Brief 39
Fox, Matthew (Timothy) 1940- CANR-79
Brief entry 109
Earlier sketch in CA 126
Fox, Mem
See Fox, Merrion Frances
See also CLR 23
See also MAICYA 1
See also SATA 103
Fox, Merrion Frances 1946- CANR-84
Earlier sketch in CA 127
See also Fox, Mem
See also CLR 80
See also CWRI 5
See also MAICYA 2
See also SATA 51, 155
Fox, Michael A(llen) 1940- CANR-19
Earlier sketch in CA 103
Fox, Michael J. 1961- 218
Fox, Michael V. 1940- 190
Fox, Michael W(ilson) 1937- CANR-88
Earlier sketches in CA 73-76, CANR-14
See also SATA 15
Fox, Milton S. 1904-1971
Obituary 33-36R
Fox, Nancy L. 1917- 122
Fox, Norman A(rnold) 1911-1960
Obituary 114
See also TCWW 1, 2
Fox, Owen
See Farmer, Bernard James
Fox, Paula 1923- CANR-105
Earlier sketches in CA 73-76, CANR-20, 36, 62
See also AAYA 3, 37
See also BYA 3, 8
See also CLC 2, 8, 121
See also CLR 1, 44, 96
See also DLB 52
See also JRDA
See also MAICYA 1, 2
See also MTCW 1
See also NFS 12
See also SATA 17, 60, 120
See also WYA
See also YAW
Fox, Peter (Kendrew) 1949- 185
Fox, Ralph H(artzler) 1913-1973
Obituary 49-52
Fox, Ray Errol 1941- 85-88
Fox, Renee C(laire) 1928- CANR-65
Earlier sketches in CA 49-52, CANR-47
Fox, Richard Allan, Jr. 1943- 147
Fox, Richard G(abriel) 1939- 41-44R
Fox, Richard Kyle 1846-1922 176
See also DLB 79
Fox, Richard Wightman 1945- CANR-84
Earlier sketches in CA 93-96, CANR-27
Fox, Robert 1943- 77-80
Fox, Robert Barlow 1930- 13-16R
Fox, Robert J. 1927- CANR-40
Earlier sketches in CA 45-48, CANR-1, 17
See also SATA 33
Fox, Robin 1934- 135
Fox, Rosaline 1939- 221
Fox, Roy F. 1948- 175
Fox, Roz Denny
See Fox, Rosaline
Fox, Ruth 1895-1989 73-76
Obituary 128
Fox, Samuel 1905-1993 .... CAP-2
Obituary 143
Earlier sketch in CA 21-22
Fox, Samuel J. 1919- 53-56
Fox, Sharon E(lizabeth) 1938- 45-48
Fox, Sidney W(alter) 1912-1998 156
Obituary 169
Fox, Siv Cedering
See Cedering, Siv
Fox, Sonny 1925- 41-44R
Fox, Stephen
See Furthmann, Julius Grinnell
Fox, Stephen R. 1945- CANR-12
Earlier sketch in CA 29-32R
Fox, Sue 1949- 189
Fox, Ted
See Fox, Gilbert T(heodore) and
Fox, Theodore J.
Fox, Terry Curtis 1948- 117
Fox, Theodore J. 1954- 123
Fox, Uffa 1898-1972
Obituary 37-40R
Fox, V. Helen
See Couch, Helen F(ox)
Fox, Vernon (Brittain) 1916- CANR-35
Earlier sketch in CA 37-40R
Fox, Willard 1919- 21-24R
Fox, William 1919(?)-1952
Obituary 116
See also IDFW 3, 4
Fox, William L(yman) 1949- 220
Fox, William L. 1953- CANR-126
Earlier sketch in CA 167
Fox, William Lloyd 1921- 17-20R
Fox, William McNair 1924- 5-8R
Fox, William Price (Jr.) 1926- CANR-142
Earlier sketches in CA 17-20R, CANR-11
See also CAAS 19
See also CLC 22
See also CSW
See also DLB 2
See also DLBY 1981
Fox, William Thornton Rickert 1912-1988
Brief entry 108
Fox, William W(ellington) 1909-1981 .... 1-4R
Foxall, Raymond (Jehoiada Campbell)
1916- CANR-5
Earlier sketch in CA 9-12R
Foxe, Arthur N(orman) 1902-1982 ..... CANR-4
Obituary 108
Earlier sketch in CA 9-12R
Foxe, John 1517(?)-1587 .... DLB 132
Foxell, Nigel 1931- 97-100
Fox-Genovese, Elizabeth 1941- CANR-55
Earlier sketches in CA 65-68, CANR-10, 26
See also FW
Foxley, William M(cLachlan) 1926-1978 . 77-80
Foxley-Norris, Christopher Neil
1917-2003 109
Obituary 220
Fox-Lockert, Lucia
See Lockert, Lucia (Alicia Ungaro Fox)
Foxman, Sherri 1950- 112
Fox-Martin, Milton 1914(?)-1977
Obituary 69-72
Foxon, A(ndrew David) 1956- 121
Foxon, David Fairweather 1923- 102
Fox-Sheinwold, Patricia 102
Foxwell, Elizabeth (M.) 1963- 222
Foxworth, Thomas G(ordon) 1937-1994 114
Obituary 146
Foxworthy, Jeff 1958- 155
Foxx, Jack
See Pronzini, Bill
Foxx, Redd 1922-1991 89-92
Obituary 135
Foxx, Richard M(ichael) 1944- CANR-17
Earlier sketches in CA 45-48, CANR-1
Foxx, Rosalind
See Haydon, June and
Simpson, Judith H(olroyd)
Foxx, Teralene S. 1939- 122
Foy, George 1952- CANR-98
Earlier sketch in CA 116
Foy, Kenneth R(ussell) 1922- 25-28R
Foy, Nancy 1934- CANR-2
Earlier sketch in CA 45-48
Fozdar, Jamshed K(hodadad) 1926- 49-52
Fraber, Daniel A. 1950- 128
Fracchia, Charles A(nthony) 1937- 89-92
Fracis, Sohrab Homi 1958- 232
Frackenpohl, Arthur R(oland) 1924- 17-20R
Frackman, Nathaline 1903(?)-1977
Obituary 69-72
Fraddle, Farragut
See Mearns, David Chambers
Fradenburg, Louise Olga 1953- 142
Fradetal, Marcel 1908- .... IDFW 3, 4
Fradin, Dennis
See Fradin, Dennis Brindell
Fradin, Dennis Brindell 1945- CANR-100
Earlier sketches in CA 69-72, CANR-50
See also AAYA 49
See also SATA 29, 90, 135
Fradin, Judith (Bernette) Bloom 1945- 227
See also SATA 90, 152
Fradkin, Elvira (Thekla) Kush 1890(?)-1972
Obituary 37-40R
Fradkin, Philip L(awrence) 1935- 107
Frady, Marshall (Bolton)
1940-2004 .... CANR-120
Obituary 225
Earlier sketch in CA 147
Fraelich, Richard O(ddly) 1924- 5-8R
Fraenkel, Abraham Adolf 1891-1965 159
Fraenkel, Gerd 1919-1970 .... CAP-1
Earlier sketch in CA 11-12
Fraenkel, Gottfried S(amuel) 1901-1984
Obituary 114
Fraenkel, Heinrich 1897-1986 .... 13-16R
Fraenkel, Jack R(unnels) 1932- 29-32R
Fraenkel, Michael 1896-1957
Brief entry 107
See also DLB 4
Fraenkel, Osmond K. 1888-1983 .... CAP-2
Obituary 109
Earlier sketch in CA 23-24
Fraenkel-Conrat, Heinz (Ludwig)
1910-1999 156

Obituary 177
Frager, Robert 1940- 81-84
Fragoulis, Tess 210
Frahm, Anne B. Schwerdt 1927- 9-12R
fra Hvitadal, Stefan
See Sigurdsson, Stefan
Fraiberg, Louis Benjamin 1913-1994 .... 1-4R
Fraiberg, Selma 1918-1981 97-100
Obituary 105
Frailey, Paige (Menefee) 1965- .... SATA 82
Frain, Betty 1947- 179
Fraine, Harold G(eorge) 1900-1990 .... 1-4R
Frair, Wayne Franklin 1926- 113
Fraistat, Neil (Richard) 1952- CANR-123
Earlier sketch in CA 122
Fraistat, Rose Ann C. 1952- 123
Frajlich(-Zajac), Anna 1942- 201
Frake, Warner
See Musciano, Walter A.
Fraker, William A. 1923- .... IDFW 3, 4
Frakes, George Edward 1932- 29-32R
Frakes, Jonathan 1952- 207
Frakes, Jonathan Scott
See Frakes, Jonathan
Frakes, William B. 1952- 141
Fraley, Oscar (B.) 1914-1994
Brief entry 109
Fraley, Tobin 1951- 226
Fram, Eugene Harry 1929- 17-20R
Frame, Donald M(urdoch) 1911-1991 ... 17-20R
Obituary 133
Frame, J. Davidson 1947- 203
Frame, Janet
See Clutha, Janet Paterson Frame
See also CLC 2, 3, 6, 22, 66, 96
See also CN 1, 2, 3, 4, 5, 6, 7
See also CP 2
See also CWP
See also EWL 3
See also RGEL 2
See also RGSF 2
See also SSC 29
See also TWA
Frame, Paul 1913-1994
Obituary 147
Brief entry 111
See also SATA 60
See also SATA-Brief 33
See also SATA-Obit 83
Frame, Ronald (William Sutherland)
1953- CANR-84
Earlier sketch in CA 143
See also CN 5, 6, 7
See also DLB 319
Frame, T. R.
See Frame, Thomas R.
Framo, James L(awrence)
1922-2001 .... CANR-15
Obituary 201
Earlier sketch in CA 41-44R
Frampton, Hollis 1936-1984 141
Obituary 112
Frampton, Kenneth Brian 1930- CANR-103
Earlier sketch in CA 105
Frampton, Merle E(lbert) 1903-1998 .... CAP-2
Obituary 172
Earlier sketch in CA 25-28
Frampton, Paul H. 1943- 205
Frampton, Peter (Kenneth) 1950- 186
Brief entry 117
Franc, Helen M. 1908- 103
Franca, Celia 1921- 89-92
Franca, Jose-Augusto 1922- CANR-19
Earlier sketch in CA 102
Franca Junior, Oswaldo 1936-1989 217
France, Anatole
See Thibault, Jacques Anatole Francois
See also DLB 123
See also EWL 3
See also GFL 1789 to the Present
See also RGWL 2, 3
See also SUFW 1
See also TCLC 9
France, Anna Kay 1940- 103
France, Beulah Sanford 1891-1971
Obituary 33-36R
France, Claire
See Dore, Claire (Morin)
France, David 1959- 140
France, Evangeline
See France-Hayhurst, Evangeline (Chaworth-Musters)
France, Harold L(eroy) 1930- 49-52
France, Linda 1958- 141
France, Malcolm 1928- 21-24R
France, Miranda 1966- CANR-142
Earlier sketch in CA 168
France, Pierre Mendes
See Mendes France, Pierre
France, R(ichard) T(homas) 1938- .. CANR-137
Earlier sketch in CA 162
See also DLB 7
France-Hayhurst, Evangeline
(Chaworth-Musters) 1904- CAP-1
Earlier sketch in CA 9-10
Frances, Miss
See Horwich, Frances R(appaport)
Francesca, Rosina
See Brookman, Rosina Francesca
Franceschini, Remo 1932- 144
Franchere, Ruth 73-76
See also SATA 18
Franchi, Eda
See Vickers, Antoinette L.
Francis, Anne
See Bird, Florence (Bayard) and Wintle, Anne
Francis, Arlene 1912-2001 89-92
Obituary 197
Francis, Arthur
See Gershwin, Ira
Francis, Basil (Hoskins) 1906- CAP-1
Earlier sketch in CA 13-14
Francis, C. D. E.
See Howarth, Patrick (John Fielding)
Francis, Cat
See Francis, Emile (Percy)
Francis, Charles
See Holme, Bryan
Francis, Clare 1946- CANR-86
Earlier sketches in CA 77-80, CANR-15, 34
Francis, Claude 192
See also CLC 50
Francis, Convers 1795-1863 .... DLB 1, 235
Francis, Daniel
See Cranny, Titus (Francis)
Francis, Daniel 1947- 111
Francis, (Alan) David 1900-1987 .... 21-24R
Francis, David Noel 1904- 5-8R
Francis, David R(ichard) 1933- 133
Francis, Dee
See Haas, Dorothy F.
Francis, Dennis S. 1943(?)-1980
Obituary 102
Francis, Devon (Earl) 1901-1986 61-64
Obituary 118
Francis, Diane (Marie) 1946- CANR-128
Earlier sketch in CA 169
Francis, Dick
See Francis, Richard Stanley
See also CN 2, 3, 4, 5, 6
Francis, Dorothy Brenner 1926- CANR-100
Earlier sketches in CA 21-24R, CANR-9, 24, 49
See also SATA 10, 127
Francis, Emile (Percy) 1926-
Brief entry 112
Francis, Sir Frank Chalton 1901-1988 65-68
Obituary 126
See also DLB 201
Francis, Freddie 1917- .... IDFW 3, 4
Francis, Gloria A(ileen) 1930-1988
Obituary 125
Brief entry 113
Francis, H(erbert) E(dward, Jr.)
1924- CANR-10
Earlier sketch in CA 25-28R
Francis, Helen Dannefer 1915- 13-16R
Francis, J. Alcuin
See Francis, James A.
Francis, James A. 1954- 151
See also Francis, James A.
Francis, John M(ichael) 1939- 118
Francis, Lesley Lee 1931- 151
Francis, Marilyn 1920- CANR-3
Earlier sketch in CA 5-8R
Francis, Matthew (Charles) 1956- 132
Francis, Michael J(ackson) 1938- 89-92
Francis, Michel
See Cattaui, Georges
Francis, Mother Mary
See Aschmann, Alberta
Francis, Nelle (Trew) 1914- 37-40R
Francis, Pamela (Mary) 1926- 29-32R
See also SATA 11
Francis, Paul
See Engleman, Paul
Francis, Philip
See Lockyer, Roger
Francis, Philip S(heridan) 1918- 17-20R
Francis, R(ichard) A. 232
Francis, R. Mabel 1880-1975(?) CAP-2
Earlier sketch in CA 25-28
Francis, Richard (H.) 1945- CANR-111
Earlier sketches in CA 102, CANR-24, 49
Francis, Richard Stanley 1920- CANR-141
Earlier sketches in CA 5-8R, CANR-9, 42, 68, 100
Interview in CANR-9
See also Francis, Dick
See also AAYA 5, 21
See also BEST 89:3
See also BPFB 1
See also CDBLB 1960 to Present
See also CLC 2, 22, 42, 102
See also CMW 4
See also CN 7
See also DA3
See also DAM POP
See also DLB 87
See also MSW
See also MTCW 1, 2
See also MTFW 2005
Francis, Robert (Churchill)
1901-1987 .... CANR-1
Obituary 123
Earlier sketch in CA 1-4R
See also AMWS 9
See also CLC 15
See also CP 1, 2
See also EXPP
See also PC 34
See also PFS 12
See also TCLE 1:1
Francis, Roy G. 1919- CANR-47
Earlier sketch in CA 1-4R
Francis, Samuel 1947- 144
Francis, Wayne L(ouis) 1935- 41-44R
Francisco, Charles 1930- 109
Francisco, Clyde Taylor 1916- 186
Brief entry 106
Francisco, Nia 1952- 145
Francisco, Patricia Weaver 1951- 221
Francis, Lord Jeffrey
See Jeffrey, Francis
See also DLB 107
Francis-Williams, Lord
See Williams, Edward Francis
Franck, Dan 1952- CANR-125
Earlier sketch in CA 163
Franck, Eddie
See Cooke, Frank E.
Franck, Frederick 1909- CANR-96
Earlier sketches in CA 1-4R, CANR-5
Franck, Harry Alverson 1881-1962
Obituary 110
Franck, Irene M(ary) 1941- CANR-21
Earlier sketch in CA 104
Franck, Michael S. 1957- 214
Franck, Phyllis 1928- 53-56
Franck, Sebastian
See Jacoby, Henry
Franck, Sebastian 1499-1542 .... DLB 179
Franck, Thomas M. 1931- 33-36R
Franck, Violet M. 1949- 140
Francke, Donald Eugene 1910-1978
Obituary 81-84
Francke, Herbert W(erner) 1927- 156
Francke, Kuno 1855-1930 176
See also DLB 71
Francke, Linda Bird 1939- CANR-73
Earlier sketches in CA 85-88, CANR-15
Franco, Betsy 225
See also SATA 150
Franco, Eloise (Bauder) 1910- .... SATA 62
Franco, Jean 1914-1971 .... CAP-2
Earlier sketch in CA 25-28
Franco, Jean 1924- CANR-122
Earlier sketches in CA 21-24R, CANR-9
Franco, Johan (Henri Gustave)
1908-1988 97-100
See also SATA 62
Franco, Jorge
See Franco Ramos, Jorge
Franco, Marjorie 114
See also SATA 38
Franco, Veronica 1546-1591 .... WLIT 7
Francoeur, Anna K(otlarchyk) 1940- 53-56
Francoeur, Robert T(homas) 1931- ... CANR-57
Earlier sketches in CA 37-40R, CANR-14, 31
Francois, Andre 1915-2005 93-96
Obituary 238
See also SATA 25
Francois, Louise von 1817-1893 .... DLB 129
Francois, Pierre 1932- 17-20R
Francois, William E. 1924- CANR-5
Earlier sketch in CA 13-16R
Francois de Sales
See Sales, Francois de
Francoise
See Seignobosc, Francoise
Francoise 1863-1910 .... DLB 92
Francois-Poncet, Andre 1887-1978
Obituary 73-76
Franco Ramos, Jorge 1962- 230
Franda, Marcus F. 1937- CANR-9
Earlier sketch in CA 21-24R
Frandsen, Arden N. 1902- 1-4R
Frandsen, Julius 1907-1976
Obituary 69-72
Franey, Pierre 1921-1996 .... CANR-15
Obituary 154
Earlier sketch in CA 89-92
Frangsmyr, Tore (Lennart) 1938- 129
Frank, A. Scott
See Frank, (A.) Scott
Frank, Adolph F(rederick) 1918- 106
Frank, Andre Gunder 1929-2005 ... CANR-130
Obituary 238
Earlier sketches in CA 21-24R, CANR-28
Frank, Anne(lies Marie) 1929-1945 .. CANR-68
Brief entry 113
Earlier sketch in CA 133
See also AAYA 12
See also BYA 1
See also CLR 101
See also DA
See also DA3
See also DAB
See also DAC
See also DAM MST
See also LAIT 4
See also MAICYA 2
See also MAICYAS 1
See also MTCW 1, 2
See also MTFW 2005
See also NCFS 2
See also SATA 87
See also SATA-Brief 42
See also TCLC 17
See also WLC
See also WYA
See also YAW
Frank, Benis M. 1925- 37-40R
Frank, Benjamin 1902-1984
Obituary 113
Frank, Bernhard 1931- 105
Frank, Bruno 1887-1945 189
See also DLB 118
See also EWL 3
See also TCLC 81
Frank, Charles E(dward) 1911- 21-24R
Frank, Charles Paul 1935-
Brief entry 112
Frank, Charles Raphael (Jr.) 1937- 37-40R
Frank, Daniel B. 1956- 117
See also SATA 55
Frank, Dorothea Benton 227
Frank, E(mily) R. 1967- 233
See also AAYA 60
See also SATA 157
Frank, Elizabeth 1945- CANR-78
Brief entry 121
Earlier sketch in CA 126
Interview in CA-126
See also CLC 39
Frank, Florence Kiper 1885(?)-1976
Obituary 65-68
Frank, Frederick S. 1935- 138
Frank, Gerold 1907-1998
Obituary 170
Brief entry 109
Frank, Goldalie 1908-1986 .... CAP-1
Earlier sketch in CA 17-18
Frank, H(ans) Eric 1921- 49-52
Frank, Harry Thomas 1933-1980 53-56
Obituary 103
Frank, Helene
See Vautier, Ghislaine
Frank, Helmut J(ack) 1922- CANR-7
Earlier sketch in CA 17-20R
Frank, Hillary 1976- 222
See also SATA 148
Frank, Irving 1910-1998 .... CAP-2
Earlier sketch in CA 21-22
Frank, Isaiah 1917- CANR-1
Earlier sketch in CA 1-4R
Frank, J. Suzanne 1967- 172
Frank, Jacqueline (?)-1982
Obituary 114
Frank, Janet
See Dunleavy, Janet Egleson
Frank, Jeffrey 1942- 21-24R
Frank, Jerome (New) 1889-1957
Brief entry 121
Frank, Jerome D(avid) 1909-2005 .... CANR-3
Obituary 237
Earlier sketch in CA 5-8R
Frank, Joan 200
Frank, John G. 1896(?)-1978
Obituary 81-84
Frank, Joseph (Nathaniel) 1918- CANR-79
Earlier sketches in CA 77-80, CANR-32
Interview in CANR-32
Frank, Joseph 1918-1993 .... CANR-1
Obituary 174
Earlier sketch in CA 1-4R
Frank, Joseph Allan 236
Frank, Josette 1893-1989 .... CAP-1
Obituary 129
Earlier sketch in CA 19-20
See also SATA 10
See also SATA-Obit 63
Frank, Judith M. 127
Frank, Katherine CANR-117
Earlier sketches in CA 124, CANR-49
Frank, Larry 1926- CANR-141
Earlier sketch in CA 170
Frank, Lawrence K(elso) 1890-1968 .... 1-4R
Obituary 103
Frank, Lee
See Griffin, Arthur J.
Frank, Leonard
See King, Roger (Frank Graham)
Frank, Leonhard 1882-1961 183
Obituary 116
See also DLB 56, 118
Frank, Lucy 1947- 159
See also SATA 94
Frank, Mark W. 1971- 221
Frank, Mary 1933- .... SATA 34
Frank, Melvin 1913(?)-1988
Obituary 126
See also DLB 26
Frank, Morton 1912-1989 102
Frank, Murray 1908-1977 .... 37-40R
Obituary 73-76
Frank, Nathalie D. 1918- 9-12R
Frank, Pat (Harry Hart) 1907-1964 ... CANR-80
Earlier sketch in CA 5-8R
See also SFW 4
Frank, Peter (Solomon) 1950- CANR-15
Earlier sketch in CA 81-84
Frank, Philip Norman 1943- 113
Frank, Philipp (G.) 1884-1966
Obituary 25-28R
Frank, R., Jr.
See Ross, Frank (Xavier), Jr.
Frank, Reuven 1920- 81-84
Frank, Richard B. 1947- 222
Frank, Robert 1924- .... AAYA 67
Frank, Robert G(regg), Jr. 1943- 134
Brief entry 113
Frank, Robert J(oseph) 1939- 65-68
Frank, Robert Worth, Jr. 1914- 13-16R
Frank, Roberta 1941- 115
Frank, Ronald E(dward) 1933- CANR-18
Earlier sketches in CA 5-8R, CANR-3
Frank, Rudolf 1886-1979 121
Frank, (A.) Scott 1960(?)- 170
Frank, Sheldon 1943- 77-80
Frank, Stanley B. 1908-1979 .... 5-8R
Obituary 85-88
Frank, T. C.
See Laughlin, Tom
Frank, Thaisa 1943- 117
Frank, Thomas (C.) 1965(?)- 184
Earlier sketch in CA 182
Frank, Tom
See Frank, Thomas (C.)
Frank, Waldo (David) 1889-1967 93-96
Obituary 25-28R
See also DLB 9, 63
See also MAL 5
See also RGAL 4

Cumulative Index 199 Fraser

Frank, William G.
See Frank, Rudolf
Frank, William L(uke) 1929- 106
Frankau, Gilbert 1884-1952 .... RHW
Frankau, Mary Evelyn Atkinson 1899-1974 .... CAP-1
Earlier sketch in CA 9-10
See also SATA 4
Frankau, Pamela 1908-1967
Obituary 25-28R
Frank-Baron, Elizabeth 1911(?)-1982
Obituary 108
Franke, C(arl) W(ilfred) 1928- 21-24R
Franke, Christopher 1941- 77-80
Franke, David 1938- 49-52
Franke, Herbert W(erner) 1927- CANR-113
Brief entry 110
Earlier sketch in CA 156
See also SFW 4
Franke, Holly L(ambro) 1943- 49-52
Franke, William 1956- 155
Frankel, A(rthur) Steven 1942- 53-56
Frankel, Alona 1937- CANR-128
Earlier sketch in CA 135
See also SATA 66
Frankel, Bernice 61-64
See also SATA 9
Frankel, Charles 1917-1979 .... CANR-4
Obituary 89-92
Earlier sketch in CA 5-8R
Frankel, Edward 1910- 85-88
See also SATA 44
Frankel, Eliot 1922-1990 77-80
Obituary 130
Frankel, Ellen 1951- CANR-87
Earlier sketch in CA 135
See also SATA 78
Frankel, Felice 1945- 222
Frankel, Flo 1923- 105
Frankel, Glenn 1949- 150
Frankel, Hans H(ermann) 1916- 61-64
Frankel, Haskel 1926-1999 89-92
Obituary 186
Frankel, Hermann F. 1899(?)-1977
Obituary 69-72
Frankel, J(oseph) 1913-1989 .... CANR-3
Earlier sketch in CA 5-8R
Frankel, Julie 1947- CANR-36
Earlier sketch in CA 113
See also SATA 40
See also SATA-Brief 34
Frankel, Marvin E(arl) 1920-2002 154
Obituary 205
Frankel, Max 1930- 65-68
Frankel, Otto (Herzberg) 1900-1998 108
Obituary 172
Frankel, Sandor 1943- 33-36R
Frankel, Tobia (Brown) 1935(?)-1987
Obituary 122
Frankel, Valerie 1965- CANR-137
Earlier sketch in CA 138
Frankel, William 1917- 106
Frankel, Zygmunt 1929- 41-44R
Franken, Al 1951(?)- 173
Franken, Rose D(orothy Lewin) 1895(?)-1988 179
Obituary 125
See also DLB 228
See also DLBY 1984
See also RHW
Frankena, William K(laas) 1908-1994 .... CANR-10
Obituary 147
Earlier sketch in CA 17-20R
Frankenberg, Celestine Gilligan 9-12R
Frankenberg, Dirk 1937-2000 160
Frankenberg, Lloyd 1907-1975 .... CANR-6
Obituary 57-60
Earlier sketch in CA 1-4R
Frankenberg, Robert 1911- .... SATA 22
Frankenberg, Ruth 230
Frankenheimer, John (Michael) 1930-2002 . 237
Frankenstein, Alfred Victor 1906-1981 .... CANR-2
Obituary 104
Earlier sketch in CA 1-4R
Frankenstein, Carl 1905-1990 .... 9-12R
Frankenthal, Kate 1889-1976
Obituary 65-68
Frankenthaler, Helen 1928- .... AAYA 62
Frankfort, Ellen 1936-1987 .... CANR-44
Obituary 122
Earlier sketch in CA 29-32R
Frankforter, A(lbertus) Daniel (III) 1939- .. 81-84
Frankfurt, Harry Gordon 1929- 41-44R
Frankfurter, Felix 1882-1965 168
Brief entry 124
Frankl, Razelle 1932- 133
Frankl, Viktor E(mil) 1905-1997 65-68
Obituary 161
See also CLC 93
Frankland, Mark 1934- CANR-43
Earlier sketch in CA 69-72
Frankland, (Anthony) Noble 1922- CANR-92
Earlier sketches in CA 65-68, CANR-14, 49
Franklet, Duane 1963- 162
Franklin, A.
See Arnold, Adlai F(ranklin)
Franklin, Ada C(rogman) (?)-1983
Obituary 111
Franklin, Adele 1887(?)-1977
Obituary 69-72
Franklin, Alexander (John) 1921- 13-16R
Franklin, Alfred White 1905-1984 .... CANR-7
Earlier sketch in CA 57-60
Franklin, Allan (David) 1938- 226
Franklin, Aretha 1942- 186
Franklin, Ben(jamin) A. 1927- 89-92
Franklin, Benjamin
See Hasek, Jaroslav (Matej Frantisek)
Franklin, Benjamin V 1939- CANR-39
Earlier sketch in CA 115
Franklin, Benjamin 1706-1790 .... AMW
See also CDALB 1640-1865
See also DA
See also DA3
See also DAB
See also DAC
See also DAM MST
See also DLB 24, 43, 73, 183
See also LAIT 1
See also RGAL 4
See also TUS
See also WLCS
Franklin, Billy J(oe) 1940- 33-36R
Franklin, Bob 1949- 124
Franklin, Buck Colbert 1879-1960 171
Franklin, Burt 1903-1972 .... CAP-1
Earlier sketch in CA 13-16
Franklin, Carl (Mikal) 1949- 157
Franklin, Caroline 1949- CANR-102
Earlier sketch in CA 145
Franklin, Charles
See Usher, Frank (Hugh)
Franklin, Cheryl J. 1955- 138
See also SATA 70
Franklin, Colin 1923- 77-80
Franklin, Daniel P. 1954- 144
Franklin, David 1961- 229
Franklin, David B. 1951- 151
Franklin, Denson Nauls 1914- 1-4R
Franklin, Edward Herbert 1930- 13-16R
Franklin, Elizabeth
See Campbell, Hannah
Franklin, Eugene
See Bandy, (Eugene) Franklin
Franklin, George E. 1890-1971 .... CAP-1
Earlier sketch in CA 19-20
Franklin, H. Bruce 1934- CANR-9
Earlier sketch in CA 5-8R
Franklin, Harold 1926- 29-32R
See also SATA 13
Franklin, Harold L(eroy) 1934- 57-60
Franklin, Harry 1906- CANR-12
Earlier sketches in CAP-1, CA 13-14
Franklin, Harry S. 1911(?)-1999 183
Franklin, J(ennie) E(lizabeth) 1937- 61-64
See also BW 1
Franklin, J. Jeffrey 194
Franklin, James 1697-1735 .... DLB 43
Franklin, James L(ee), Jr. 1947- 234
Franklin, Jane (Morgan) 1934- 161
Franklin, Jay
See Carter, John Franklin
Franklin, Jeffrey P. 1951- 168
Franklin, Jerome L(ee) 1943- 102
Franklin, Jill (Leslie) 1928-1988
Obituary 125
Franklin, Jimmie Lewis 1939- 126
Brief entry 106
Franklin, Joe 1926- 134
Brief entry 108
Franklin, John 1786-1847 .... DLB 99
Franklin, John Hope 1915- CANR-84
Earlier sketches in CA 5-8R, CANR-3, 26
See also BW 2
See also CSW
Franklin, Jon (Daniel) 1942- CANR-27
Earlier sketch in CA 104
Franklin, Kay 1933-1996 118
Obituary 154
Franklin, Keith
See Foy, Kenneth R(ussell)
Franklin, Kerry
See Caldwell, Stratton F(ranklin)
Franklin, Kristine L. 1958- .... SATA 80, 124
Franklin, Lance
See Lantz, Francess L(in)
Franklin, Linda Campbell 1941- CANR-26
Earlier sketch in CA 105
Franklin, Lynn C. 205
Franklin, Marc A. 1932- 29-32R
Franklin, Marshall 1929- 53-56
Franklin, Max
See Deming, Richard
Franklin, Michael J(ohn) 1949- 159
Franklin, (Stella Maria Sarah) Miles (Lampe) 1879-1954 164
Brief entry 104
See also DLB 230
See also FW
See also MTCW 2
See also RGEL 2
See also TCLC 7
See also TWA
Franklin, Nat
See Bauer, Erwin A(dam)
Franklin, Olga 1912-1985 102
Obituary 115
Franklin, Pat
See Cady, Jack A(ndrew)
Franklin, Penelope (Florence) 1948- 125
Franklin, R(alph) W(illiam) 1937- CANR-9
Earlier sketch in CA 21-24R
Franklin, Richard 1918- 21-24R
Franklin, Robert M(ichael) 1954- 135
Franklin, S. D.
See Macklin, F. Anthony
Franklin, S(amuel) Harvey 1928- CANR-26
Earlier sketch in CA 105
Franklin, Sarah 1960- 212
Franklin, Sidney 1903-1976
Obituary 65-68
Franklin, Steve
See Stevens, Franklin
Franklin, Tom 194
Franklin, Ursula 1929- 112
Franklin, Wayne S(teven) 1945- 125
Franklin, Yelena 1945- 173
Franklyn, Charles Aubrey Hamilton 1896-1982 .... 9-12R
Franklyn, Charlotte
See Haldane, Charlotte (Franken)
Franklyn, Julian 1899-1970
Obituary 112
Franklyn, Robert Alan 1918- 89-92
Franklyn, Ross
See Hardy, Francis Joseph
Franko, Ivan 1856-1916 .... EWL 3
Franko, Lawrence G. 1942- 37-40R
Frankowski, Leo 1943- 120
Franks, C(harles) E(dward) S(elwyn) 1936- 77-80
Franks, Claudia Stillman 1947- 117
Franks, Clyda (Ruth) 1946- 213
Franks, Cyril Maurice 1923- 13-16R
Franks, Don(ald Richard) 1945- 160
Franks, Ed
See Brandon, Johnny
Franks, Felix 1926- 125
Franks, Helen 1934- 133
Franks, Kenny Arthur 1945- CANR-100
Earlier sketches in CA 123, CANR-50
Franks, Lucinda 1946- 53-56
Franks, Marlene Strong 1955- 125
Franks, Maurice R(udolph) 1942- 112
Franks, Robert S(leightholme) 1871-1963 . 5-8R
Fransella, Fay CANR-13
Earlier sketch in CA 25-28R
Franson, Leanne R. 1963- .... SATA 111
Frantz, Charles 1925- CANR-3
Earlier sketch in CA 5-8R
Frantz, Douglas 1949- 126
Frantz, Harry Warner 1891-1982
Obituary 106
Frantz, Joe B. 1917-1993 .... CANR-1
Obituary 143
Earlier sketch in CA 1-4R
Frantz, Klaus 1948- 187
Frantz, Ralph Jules 1902-1979 77-80
Obituary 89-92
See also DLB 4
Frantzen, Allen J. 1947- 121
Frantzich, Stephen E. 1944- 164
Franz, Barbara E(van) 1946- 110
Franz, Carl 1944- 107
Franz, William S(trasser) 1945- 110
Franzblau, Abraham N(orman) 1901-1982 .... 29-32R
Obituary 108
Franzblau, Rose N(adler) 1905-1979 .... 29-32R
Obituary 89-92
Franzen, Gosta Knut 1906- 41-44R
Franzen, Jonathan 1959- CANR-105
Earlier sketch in CA 129
See also AAYA 65
See also CLC 202
Franzen, Lavern G(erhardt) 1926- CANR-7
Earlier sketch in CA 61-64
Franzen, Nils-Olof 1916- CANR-25
Earlier sketch in CA 29-32R
See also SATA 10
Franzen, William Edward 1952- 129
Franzero, Carlo Maria 1892-1986 .... CANR-5
Obituary 120
Earlier sketch in CA 1-4R
Franzero, Charles Marie
See Franzero, Carlo Maria
Franzius, Enno 1901-1976 .... 25-28R
Franzke, Andreas 1938- CANR-134
Earlier sketches in CA 129, CANR-68
Franzmann, Martin H. 1907-1976 .... CANR-3
Earlier sketch in CA 1-4R
Franzoni, David (H.) 171
Franzos, Karl Emil 1848-1904 .... DLB 129
Franzwa, Gregory M. 1926- CANR-9
Earlier sketch in CA 21-24R
Frappier-Mazur, Lucienne 1932- 158
Frary, Michael 1918- 77-80
Frasca, John (Anthony) 1916-1979 .... CANR-3
Obituary 93-96
Earlier sketch in CA 49-52
Frascatoro, Gerald
See Hornback, Bert G(erald)
Frascino, Edward CANR-37
Brief entry 111
Earlier sketch in CA 114
See also MAICYA 1, 2
See also SAAS 9
See also SATA 48
See also SATA-Brief 33
Frascona, Joseph Lohengrin 1910-2000 .... 17-20R
Frasconi, Antonio 1919- CANR-48
Earlier sketches in CA 1-4R, CANR-1
See also AAYA 58
See also MAICYA 1, 2
See also SAAS 11
See also SATA 6, 53, 131
Frase, Larry E. 1945- 41-44R
Frase, Robert W(illiam) 1912-2003 .... 33-36R
Obituary 222
Fraser, Alex
See Brinton, Henry
Fraser, Allan 1900- 57-60
Fraser, Amy Stewart 1892- CANR-9
Earlier sketch in CA 49-52
Fraser, Anthea CANR-101
Earlier sketches in CA 65-68, CANR-10, 25, 50, 66
Fraser, (Lady) Antonia
See Fraser, Antonia (Pakenham)
Fraser, Antonia (Pakenham) 1932- CANR-119
Earlier sketches in CA 85-88, CANR-44, 65
See also AAYA 57
See also CLC 32, 107
See also CMW
See also DLB 276
See also MTCW 1, 2
See also MTFW 2005
See also SATA-Brief 32
Fraser, Arthur Ronald 1888-1974
Obituary 53-56
See also FANT
Fraser, Arvonne S. 1925- 33-36R
Fraser, B. Kay 1941- 69-72
Fraser, Betty
See Fraser, Elizabeth Marr
Fraser, Blair 1909-1968 .... CAP-2
Earlier sketch in CA 23-24
Fraser, Brad 1959- 230
See also CD 5, 6
Fraser, Bruce (Donald) 1910-1993 109
Obituary 142
Fraser, Caroline 1961- 190
Fraser, Christine Marion
See Ashfield, Christian Marion
See also RHW
Fraser, Colin 1935- 21-24R
Fraser, Conon 1930- CAP-1
Earlier sketch in CA 9-10
Fraser, D(onald) M(urray) 1946-1985 117
Fraser, David (William) 1920- CANR-65
Earlier sketch in CA 129
Fraser, Dawn 1937- 206
Fraser, (William) Dean 1916- 45-48
Fraser, Diane Lynch
See Lynch-Fraser, Diane
Fraser, Dorothy May 1903(?)-1980
Obituary 102
Fraser, Douglas 1910- 102
Fraser, Douglas Ferrar 1929- CANR-4
Earlier sketch in CA 1-4R
Fraser, Edith Emily Rose Oram 1903- CAP-1
Earlier sketch in CA 11-12
Fraser, Elise Parker 1903-1988 .... 1-4R
Fraser, Elizabeth Marr 1928- .... SATA 31
Fraser, Eric (George) 1902-1983 .... SATA 38
Fraser, Flora 1958- CANR-73
Earlier sketch in CA 124
Fraser, G(eorge) S(utherland) 1915-1980 .... CANR-45
Obituary 105
Earlier sketch in CA 85-88
See also CP 1, 2
See also DLB 27
Fraser, George (C.) 1945- CANR-93
Earlier sketch in CA 146
Fraser, George MacDonald 1925- 180
Earlier sketches in CA 45-48, CANR-2, 48, 74
Autobiographical Essay in 180
See also AAYA 48
See also CLC 7
See also MTCW 2
See also RHW
Fraser, Gordon 1943- CANR-126
Earlier sketch in CA 168
Fraser, Gordon Holmes 1898-1990 .... CAP-1
Earlier sketch in CA 13-16
Fraser, Hamish 1913-1986
Obituary 120
Fraser, (William Jocelyn) Ian 1897-1974
Obituary 53-56
Fraser, Ian 1901(?)-1999 186
Fraser, J(ulius) T(homas) 1923- CANR-53
Earlier sketches in CA 61-64, CANR-8, 27
Fraser, James
See White, Alan
See also CMW 4
Fraser, Jane
See Pilcher, Rosamunde
Fraser, Janet Hobhouse
See Hobhouse, Janet
Fraser, Joelle 1966- 213
Fraser, John 1931- 29-32R
Fraser, Kathleen 1937- 106
See also CP 1, 7
See also CWP
See also DLB 169
Fraser, Keath 1944- 125
Fraser, Kennedy 163
Fraser, Laura (Jane) 1961- 204
Fraser, Margot 1936- 135
Fraser, Marian Botsford 1948- 215
Fraser, Mary
See James, Laurence
Fraser, Mary Ann 1959- CANR-116
Earlier sketch in CA 144
See also SAAS 23
See also SATA 76, 137
Fraser, Maxwell
See Fraser, Dorothy May
Fraser, Morris 1941- 102
Fraser, Neil McCormick 1902-1974 .... 5-8R
Fraser, Nicholas C(ampbell) 1958- 151
Fraser, Peter (Malcolm) 1928-1987 107
Obituary 121
Fraser, Peter (Shaw) 1932- 33-36R
Fraser, Ray
See Fraser, Raymond (Joseph)
Fraser, Raymond (Joseph) 1941- 130
Brief entry 107
Fraser, Robert (H.) 1947- CANR-122
Earlier sketch in CA 134
Fraser, Ronald
See Fraser, Arthur Ronald

Fraser, Ronald
See Tiltman, Ronald Frank
Fraser, Ronald (Angus) 1930- ... CANR-83
Earlier sketch in CA 131
Fraser, Russell A(lfred) 1927- ... 37-40R
Fraser, Steven 1945- ... 238
Fraser, Stewart Erskine 1929- ... CANR-32
Earlier sketches in CA 13-16R, CANR-10
Fraser, Stuart
See Wood, James (Alexander Fraser)
Fraser, Sylvia 1935- ... CANR-60
Earlier sketches in CA 45-48, CANR-1, 16
See also CCA 1
See also CLC 64
Fraser, W(aller) B(rown) 1905- ... CAP-2
Earlier sketch in CA 25-28
Fraser, W(illiam) Hamish 1941- ... 103
Fraser, W(illiam) Lionel 18(?)-1965 ... CAP-1
Earlier sketch in CA 9-10
Fraser, Wynnette (McFaddin) 1925- ... 155
See also SATA 90
Fraser Darling, Frank 1903-1979 ... CANR-89
Obituary ... 89-92
Earlier sketch in CA 61-64
Fraser Harrison, Brian 1918- ... CAP-1
Earlier sketch in CA 9-10
Fraser Roberts, J(ohn) A(lexander)
See Roberts, J(ohn) A(lexander) Fraser
Frasier, Anne
See Weir, Theresa
Frasier, Arthur
See James, Laurence
Frasier, David K. 1951- ... 220
Frasier, Debra 1953- ... 137
See also MAICYA 2
See also SATA 69, 112
Frasier, James E(dwin) 1923- ... 17-20R
Frassanito, William A(llen) 1946- ... CANR-9
Earlier sketch in CA 57-60
Frassetto, Michael 1961- ... 234
Frasure, David W(illiam) 1942- ... 113
Fratcher, William F(ranklin)
1913-1992 ... CANR-3
Earlier sketch in CA 5-8R
Frater, Alexander 1937- ... 140
Frater Perdurabo
See Crowley, Edward Alexander
Fratianni, Michele (Ugo) 1941- ... CANR-140
Earlier sketch in CA 144
Fraticelli, Marco 1945- ... 118
Fratkin, Elliot 1948- ... 144
Frattaroli, Elio ... 207
Fratti, Mario 1927- ... 77-80
See also CAD
See also CD 5, 6
Frattini, Alberto 1922- ... DLB 128
Frau Ava (?)-1127 ... DLB 148
Frauenglass, Harvey 1929- ... 207
Fraunce, Abraham 1560(?)-1592(?) ... DLB 236
Fraustino, Lisa Rowe 1961- ... 150
See also SATA 84, 146
See also SATA-Essay 146
Frautschi, R(ichard) L(ane) 1926- ... 17-20R
Frawley, Ernest D(avid) 1920-1984
Obituary ... 114
Frawley, William John 1953- ... CANR-137
Earlier sketch in CA 114
Fraydas, Stan 1918- ... 57-60
Frayling, Christopher 1946- ... CANR-95
Earlier sketch in CA 110
Frayn, Michael 1933- ... CANR-133
Earlier sketches in CA 5-8R, CANR-30, 69, 114
See also BRWC 2
See also BRWS 7
See also CBD
See also CD 5, 6
See also CLC 3, 7, 31, 47, 176
See also CN 1, 2, 3, 4, 5, 6, 7
See also DAM DRAM, NOV
See also DFS 22
See also DLB 13, 14, 194, 245
See also FANT
See also MTCW 1, 2
See also MTFW 2005
See also SFW 4
Frayser, Suzanne G. 1943- ... 127
Fraze, Candida (Merrill) 1945- ... 126
See also CLC 50
Frazee, Charles A(aron) 1929- ... CANR-143
Earlier sketch in CA 37-40R
Frazee, Charles Stephen 1909-1992 . CANR-70
Obituary ... 171
Earlier sketches in CA 5-8R, CANR-5
See also Frazee, Steve
Frazee, Marla 1958- ... SATA 105, 151
Frazee, Randy 1961- ... 200
Frazee, Steve
See Frazee, Charles Stephen
See also TCWW 1, 2
Frazen, Bill
See Franzen, William Edward
Frazer, Andrew
See Marlowe, Stephen
Frazer, Fred
See Avallone, Michael (Angelo, Jr.)
Frazer, Gail 1946- ... 232
Frazer, J(ames) G(eorge) 1854-1941
Brief entry ... 118
See also BRWS 3
See also NCFS 5
See also TCLC 32
Frazer, Margaret
See Frazer, Gail
Frazer, Mark Petrovich
See Maclean, Donald Duart
Frazer, Robert Caine
See Creasey, John
Frazer, Robert W(alter) 1911- ... 17-20R
Frazer, Sir James George
See Frazer, J(ames) G(eorge)
Frazer, Timothy C. 1941- ... 147
Frazer, William J(ohnson), Jr. 1924- ... 17-20R
Frazer, Winifred Dusenbury
See Frazer, Winifred L(oesch)
Frazer, Winifred L(oesch) ... 25-28R
Frazer-Hurst, Douglas 1883- ... CAP-1
Earlier sketch in CA 9-10
Frazetta, Frank 1928- ... CANR-119
Earlier sketches in CA 104, CANR-46
See also AAYA 14
See also SATA 58
Frazier, Allie M. 1932-2002
Obituary ... 206
Brief entry ... 110
Frazier, Anitra 1937- ... 113
Frazier, Arthur
See Bulmer, (Henry) Kenneth
Frazier, Charles 1950- ... CANR-126
Earlier sketch in CA 161
See also AAYA 34
See also CLC 109
See also CSW
See also DLB 292
See also MTFW 2005
Frazier, Claude A(lbee) 1920-2005 ... CANR-32
Earlier sketch in CA 29-32R
Frazier, Cliff(ord) 1934-
Brief entry ... 109
Frazier, Donald S(haw) 1965- ... 151
Frazier, Edward Franklin 1894-1962 ... 213
Obituary ... 108
Frazier, George 1911-1974 ... CAP-2
Obituary ... 49-52
Earlier sketch in CA 25-28
Frazier, Harriet C. 1934- ... 214
Frazier, Ian 1951- ... CANR-93
Earlier sketches in CA 130, CANR-54
See also CLC 46
Frazier, Kendrick (Crosby) 1942- ... CANR-39
Earlier sketches in CA 101, CANR-17
Frazier, Mansfield B. 1943- ... CANR-87
Earlier sketch in CA 150
Frazier, Neta (Osborn) Lohnes
1890-1990 ... CANR-1
Obituary ... 131
Earlier sketch in CA 1-4R
See also SATA 7
Frazier, Sarah
See Wirt, Winola Wells
Frazier, Shervert Hughes 1921- ... 85-88
Frazier, Shirley George 1957- ... 164
Frazier, Thomas R(ichard) 1931- ... 33-36R
Frazier, Walt(er) 1945- ... 103
Frears, J(ohn) R(ussell) 1936- ... 107
Freas, Frank Kelly 1922-2005 ... CANR-21
Obituary ... 235
Earlier sketch in CA 102
Freburger, William J. 1940- ... 115
Frech, Frances 1923- ... 97-100
Frechet, (Rene) Maurice 1878-1973 ... 156
Frechette, Louis-Honore 1839-1908 ... 176
See also DLB 99
Freda, Joseph 1951- ... CANR-137
Earlier sketch in CA 152
Freddi, Cris 1955- ... 106
Frede, Richard 1934- ... CANR-32
Earlier sketch in CA 69-72
Fredeman, William E(van) 1928-1999 ... 33-36R
Fredenburgh, Franz A(lvah) 1906- ... 33-36R
Frederic, Harold 1856-1898 ... AMW
See also DLB 12, 23
See also DLBD 13
See also MAL 5
See also NFS 22
See also RGAL 4
Frederic, Mike
See Cox, William R(obert)
Frederic, Sister M. Catherine
See Fleischbein, Sister M. Catherine Frederic
Frederick, Carl Louis 1942- ... 65-68
Frederick, David C. 1961- ... 156
Frederick, Dick
See Dempewolff, Richard F(rederic)
Frederick, John
See Faust, Frederick (Schiller)
See also TCWW 2
Frederick, John H(utchinson) 1896-1981 .. 1-4R
Frederick, John Towner 1893-1975
Obituary ... 111
Frederick, K. C. 1935- ... 205
Frederick, Lee
See Nussbaum, Al(bert F.)
Frederick, Oswald
See Snelling, O(swald) F(rederick)
Frederick, Pauline 1908-1990 ... 102
Obituary ... 131
Frederick, Robert Allen 1928- ... CANR-3
Earlier sketch in CA 45-48
Fredericks, Anthony D. 1947- ... 185
See also SATA 113
Fredericks, Carlton 1910-1987 ... CANR-7
Obituary ... 123
Earlier sketch in CA 53-56
See also AITN 1
Fredericks, Emmi
See Fredericks, Mariah
Fredericks, Frohm
See Kerner, Fred
See also CCA 1
Fredericks, Mariah ... 230
Fredericks, Pierce Griffin 1920-1985 ... 13-16R
Obituary ... 117
Fredericks, Vic
See Majeski, William
Frederics, Jocko
See Frede, Richard
Frederics, Macdowell
See Frede, Richard
Frederika (Louise), Queen 1917-1981
Obituary ... 108
Frederiksen, Alan Ryle 1935- ... 113
Frederiksen, Martin W. 1930-1980
Obituary ... 101
Frederikson, Edna 1904-1998 ... 49-52
Fredge, Frederique 1906- ... CAP-2
Earlier sketch in CA 21-22
Fredman, Alice G(reen) 1924-1993 ... 102
Obituary ... 141
Fredman, Henry John 1927- ... 29-32R
Fredman, John
See Fredman, Henry John
Fredman, Ruth Gruber 1934- ... 106
Fredricks, Edgar J(ohn) 1942- ... 25-28R
Fredrickson, George M(arsh)
1934- ... CANR-122
Earlier sketches in CA 17-20R, CANR-8, 24, 49
Fredrickson, Michael 1945(?)- ... 238
Fredrickson, Olive A(lta) 1901- ... 49-52
Fredriksen, John C(onrad) 1953- ... 220
Fredriksen, Paula 1951- ... 198
Fredriksson, Don 1926- ... 110
Fredriksson, Kristine 1940- ... 122
Fredston, Jill A. 1958(?)- ... 207
Free
See Hoffman, Abbie
Free, Ann Cottrell 1916-2004 ... 9-12R
Obituary ... 232
Free, James S(tillman) 1908-1996 ... 77-80
Obituary ... 151
Free, Lloyd A. 1908-1996 ... 13-16R
Obituary ... 154
Free, William Joseph 1933- ... 9-12R
Free, William Norris 1933- ... 25-28R
Freeberg, Ernest ... 208
Freeborn, Brian (James) 1939- ... 65-68
Freeborn, Richard H. 1926- ... CANR-1
Earlier sketch in CA 1-4R
Freed, Alvyn M. 1913-1993 ... CANR-8
Earlier sketch in CA 61-64
See also SATA 22
Freed, Anne O. 1917- ... 145
Freed, Arthur 1894-1973
Obituary ... 41-44R
See also DLB 265
See also IDFW 3, 4
Freed, Barry
See Hoffman, Abbie
Freed, Curt R(ichard) 1943- ... 216
Freed, Donald 1932- ... 85-88
Freed, Louis Franklin 1903-1981 ... 5-8R
Freed, Lynn (Ruth) 1945- ... CANR-124
Earlier sketches in CA 108, CANR-27, 56
Freed, Margaret De Haan 1917- ... 73-76
Freed, Melvyn N. 1937- ... 239
Freed, Ray 1939- ... CANR-40
Earlier sketch in CA 117
Freedberg, S(ydney) J(oseph)
1914-1997 ... CANR-17
Obituary ... 158
Earlier sketches in CA 1-4R, CANR-1
Freedeman, Charles E(ldon) 1926- ... 102
Freeden, Michael S(tephen) 1944- ... 127
Freedgood, Lillian (Fischel) 1911- ... 13-16R
Freedgood, Morton 1912- ... 128
Brief entry ... 108
See also AITN 1
See also CMW 4
Freedland, Jonathan ... 183
Freedland, Michael 1934- ... CANR-29
Earlier sketches in CA 65-68, CANR-11
Freedland, Nat(haniel) 1936- ... 65-68
Freedley, George (Reynolds)
1904-1967 ... CANR-4
Earlier sketch in CA 5-8R
Freedman, Alfred M(ordecai) 1917- ... CANR-4
Earlier sketch in CA 49-52
Freedman, Anne (E.) 1938- ... 150
Freedman, Arthur M(erton) 1916- ... 41-44R
Freedman, Benedict 1919- ... 69-72
See also SATA 27
Freedman, Bryn ... 218
Freedman, Dan 1952- ... 126
Freedman, Daniel X. 1921-1993 ... 41-44R
Obituary ... 141
Freedman, David A(sa) 1918- ... 167
Freedman, David M(ichael) 1949- ... 112
Freedman, David Noel 1922- ... CANR-1
Earlier sketch in CA 1-4R
Freedman, Diane P. 1955- ... 194
Freedman, Eric 1949- ... CANR-136
Earlier sketch in CA 144
Freedman, Estelle B(renda) 1947- ... 212
Freedman, Hy 1914- ... 85-88
Freedman, J. F. ... CANR-111
Earlier sketch in CA 161
Freedman, James O. 1935- ... 152
Freedman, Jeff 1953- ... 155
See also SATA 90
Freedman, Jeffrey E. 1957- ... 223
Freedman, Jessica B(lackman)
1954(?)-2002 ... 233
Freedman, Jonathan (Borwick) 1950- ... 157
Freedman, Lawrence (David) 1948- ... 170
Freedman, Leonard 1924- ... CANR-1
Earlier sketch in CA 1-4R
Freedman, Luba 1953- ... CANR-110
Earlier sketch in CA 152
Freedman, M(orris) David 1938- ... CANR-16
Earlier sketch in CA 41-44R
Freedman, Marc ... 192
Freedman, Marcia K(ohl) 1922- ... CANR-10
Earlier sketch in CA 25-28R
Freedman, Maurice 1920-1975 ... CAP-2
Obituary ... 61-64
Earlier sketch in CA 25-28
Freedman, Mervin B. 1920- ... 29-32R
Freedman, Michael H(artley) 1951- ... 161
Freedman, Michael R. 1952- ... 169
Freedman, Monroe H(enry) 1928-
Brief entry ... 107
Freedman, Morris 1920- ... CANR-3
Earlier sketch in CA 5-8R
Freedman, Nancy 1920- ... CANR-19
Earlier sketches in CA 45-48, CANR-1
Interview in ... CANR-19
See also SATA 27
Freedman, Paul H(arris) 1949- ... CANR-88
Earlier sketch in CA 122
Freedman, Ralph (William Bernard) 1920- . 128
Brief entry ... 117
Freedman, Richard 1932-1991 ... 77-80
Obituary ... 134
Freedman, Robert Owen 1941- ... CANR-13
Earlier sketch in CA 33-36R
Freedman, Ronald 1917- ... CANR-6
Earlier sketch in CA 9-12R
Freedman, Russell (Bruce) 1929- ... CANR-101
Earlier sketches in CA 17-20R, CANR-7, 23, 46, 81
See also AAYA 4, 24
See also BYA 2, 11, 14
See also CLR 20, 71
See also JRDA
See also MAICYA 1, 2
See also MAICYAS 1
See also SATA 16, 71, 123
See also WYA
See also YAW
Freedman, Samuel G. 1955- ... 219
See also MTFW 2005
Freedman, Samuel Sumner 1927- ... 112
Freedman, Sarah Warshauer 1946- ... 160
Freedman, Warren 1921- ... 17-20R
Freedman, Wiliam 1938- ... 178
Freehill, Maurice F(rancis) 1915- ... 5-8R
Freehling, Alison Goodyear 1941- ... 112
Freehling, William W(ilhartz) 1935- ... 226
Freehof, Solomon B(ennett) 1892-1990 ... 93-96
Obituary ... 131
Freeland, Cynthia A(nne) 1951- ... 177
Freeland, Jay
See McLeod, John F(reeland)
Freeland, John Maxwell 1920- ... 13-16R
Freeland, Richard M. 1941- ... 81-84
Freeland, Stephen L. 1911(?)-1977
Obituary ... 69-72
Freeley, Austin J. 1922-2005 ... 5-8R
Obituary ... 235
Freeling, Nicolas 1927-2003 ... CANR-84
Obituary ... 218
Earlier sketches in CA 49-52, CANR-1, 17, 50
See also CAAS 12
See also CLC 38
See also CMW 4
See also CN 1, 2, 3, 4, 5, 6
See also DLB 87
Freely, John 1926- ... 213
Freely, Maureen 1952- ... CANR-92
Earlier sketch in CA 97-100
Freeman, A. Myrick III 1936- ... 85-88
Freeman, Anne Frances 1936- ... 1-4R
Freeman, Anne Hobson 1934- ... 154
Freeman, Arthur 1938- ... CANR-1
Earlier sketch in CA 1-4R
Freeman, Barbara C(onstance)
1906- ... CANR-84
Earlier sketch in CA 73-76
See also CWRI 5
See also SATA 28
Freeman, Barbara M. 1947- ... CANR-82
Earlier sketch in CA 132
Freeman, Bill
See Freeman, William Bradford
Freeman, Bjorn
See Pratney, William Alfred
Freeman, C(lifford) Wade 1906- ... 5-8R
Freeman, Castle (William), Jr.
1944- ... CANR-125
Earlier sketch in CA 153
Freeman, Charles K. 1900-1980
Obituary ... 97-100
Freeman, Charles Wellman, Jr. 1943- ... 150
Freeman, Chas W.
See Freeman, Charles Wellman, Jr.
Freeman, Chris 1965- ... 192
Freeman, Cynthia
See Feinberg, Beatrice Cynthia Freeman
Freeman, Daniel E(van) 1959- ... 144
Freeman, Darlene 1934- ... 29-32R
Freeman, Dave
See Freeman, David
Freeman, David 1922-2005 ... CANR-84
Obituary ... 237
Earlier sketch in CA 102
See also CD 5
Freeman, David E(dgar) 1945- ... 131
Brief entry ... 108
See also CD 6
Freeman, David Hugh 1924- ... CANR-17
Earlier sketch in CA 1-4R
Freeman, Davis
See Friedman, David F.
Freeman, Derek J(ohn) 1916- ... 190

Cumulative Index 201 **Freund**

Freeman, Don 1908-1978 ... CANR-44
Earlier sketch in CA 77-80
See also CLR 30, 90
See also CWRI 5
See also MAICYA 1, 2
See also SATA 17
Freeman, Donald Cary 1938- ... 53-56
Freeman, Donald McKinley 1931- ... CANR-15
Earlier sketch in CA 37-40R
Freeman, Douglas Southall 1886-1953 ... 195
Brief entry ... 109
See also DLB 17
See also DLBD 17
See also TCLC 11
Freeman, Eugene 1906- ... CANR-26
Earlier sketch in CA 41-44R
Freeman, G(raydon) L(a Verne)
1904-1995 ... CANR-13
Earlier sketch in CA 13-16R
Freeman, Garry 1955- ... 234
Freeman, Gary 1945- ... 93-96
Freeman, Gillian 1929- ... CANR-84
Earlier sketches in CA 5-8R, CANR-3, 43
See also CN 1, 2, 3, 4, 5, 6, 7
Freeman, Gregory A. ... 219
Freeman, Harrop A(rthur) 1907- ... 13-16R
Freeman, Harry 1906-1978 ... 77-80
Freeman, Harry M. 1943- ... 154
Freeman, Howard E(dgar)
1929-1992 ... CANR-23
Obituary ... 139
Earlier sketches in CA 5-8R, CANR-6
Freeman, Ira Henry 1906-1997 ... CAP-1
Obituary ... 156
Earlier sketch in CA 13-16
Freeman, Ira Maximilian 1905-1987 ... 73-76
See also SATA 21
Freeman, James Andrew 1956- ... 188
Freeman, James Dillet 1912- ... 17-20R
Freeman, James Montague 1936- ... 102
Freeman, Jean Kenny 1929- ... 115
Freeman, Jean Todd 1929- ... 25-28R
Freeman, Jo 1945- ... CANR-92
Earlier sketches in CA 61-64, CANR-8, 45
Freeman, John Crosby 1941- ... 13-16R
Freeman, Joseph 1897-1965
Obituary ... 89-92
See also DLB 303
Freeman, Joshua B. 1949- ... CANR-95
Earlier sketch in CA 139
Freeman, Judith 1946- ... CANR-120
Earlier sketch in CA 148
See also CLC 55
See also DLB 256
Freeman, Kathleen 1897-1959
Brief entry ... 112
See also CMW 4
Freeman, Larry
See Freeman, G(raydon) L(a Verne)
Freeman, Lea David 1887(?)-1976
Obituary ... 69-72
Freeman, Legh Richmond 1842-1915 ... 181
See also DLB 23
Freeman, Leslie J(ane) 1944- ... 106
Freeman, Linton C(larke) 1927- ... 69-72
Freeman, Lucy (Greenbaum)
1916-2004 ... CANR-3
Obituary ... 234
Earlier sketch in CA 5-8R
See also SATA 24
Freeman, Mae (Blacker) 1907- ... 73-76
See also SATA 25
Freeman, Marcia S. 1937- ... 169
See also SATA 102
Freeman, Margaret B. 1899-1980 ... 109
Obituary ... 97-100
Freeman, Margaret C(ooper) 1913- ... 57-60
Freeman, Margaret N(adgwick) 1915- ... 9-12R
Freeman, Martha 1956- ... CANR-136
Earlier sketch in CA 168
See also SATA 101, 152
Freeman, Mary E(leanor) Wilkins
1852-1930 ... 177
Brief entry ... 106
See also DLB 12, 78, 221
See also EXPS
See also FW
See also HGG
See also MAWW
See also RGAL 4
See also RGSF 2
See also SSC 1, 47
See also SSFS 4, 8
See also SUFW 1
See also TCLC 9
See also TUS
Freeman, Max Herbert 1907-
Brief entry ... 109
Freeman, Michael 1945- ... 229
Freeman, Morton S(igmund) 1912-2001 ... 118
Freeman, Nancy 1932- ... SATA 61
Freeman, Paul 1929(?)-1980
Obituary ... 101
Freeman, Peter J.
See Calvert, Patricia
Freeman, Philip 1961- ... 232
Freeman, R(ichard) Austin
1862-1943 ... CANR-84
Brief entry ... 113
See also CMW 4
See also DLB 70
See also TCLC 21
Freeman, R(ichard) B(roke) 1915-1986 ... 133
Obituary ... 120
Freeman, Rich 1949- ... 184
Freeman, Richard B(arry) 1944- ... CANR-15
Earlier sketch in CA 85-88
Freeman, Richard Borden
1908-1986 ... CANR-17
Earlier sketch in CA 1-4R
Freeman, Roger A(dolph) 1904-1991 ... 25-28R
Obituary ... 136
Freeman, Roger A(nthony Wilson)
1928- ... CANR-51
Earlier sketches in CA 65-68, CANR-10, 26
Freeman, Roger Anthony
See Freeman, Roger A(nthony Wilson)
Freeman, Roger K. 1935- ... 127
Freeman, Roger L(ouis) 1928- ... CANR-12
Earlier sketch in CA 69-72
Freeman, Ruth B(enson) 1906- ... 41-44R
Freeman, Ruth (Lazear) S(underlin)
1907- ... CANR-13
Earlier sketches in CAP-1, CA 13-16
Freeman, Sarah (Caroline) 1940- ... CANR-86
Earlier sketch in CA 133
See also SATA 66
Freeman, Simon (David) 1952- ... 133
Freeman, Sue
See Freeman, Susan J.
Freeman, Susan J. 1953- ... 184
Freeman, Susan Tax 1938- ... 85-88
Freeman, T(homas) W(alter) 1908-1988 ... 5-8R
Obituary ... 125
Freeman, Thomas 1919-2002 ... 93-96
Obituary ... 206
Freeman, Tony ... 134
See also SATA-Brief 44
Freeman, Walter (Jackson, Jr.)
1895-1972 ... CAP-1
Obituary ... 33-36R
Earlier sketch in CA 17-18
Freeman, Warren S(amuel) 1911-1986 ... 5-8R
Freeman, William Bradford 1938- ... CWRI 5
See also SATA 58
See also SATA-Brief 48
Freeman, William M. 1913-1990
Obituary ... 130
Freeman, Yvette ... 213
Freeman-Grenville, Greville Stewart Parker
1918-2005 ... CANR-3
Obituary ... 236
Earlier sketch in CA 5-8R
Freeman-Ishill, Rose 1895-1977 ... CAP-1
Earlier sketch in CA 9-10
Freemantle, Brian (Harry) 1936- ... CANR-112
Earlier sketches in CA 65-68, CANR-16, 43, 66
See also CMW 4
Freemon, Frank R(eed) 1938- ... 45-48
Freer, Coburn 1939- ... 125
Brief entry ... 105
Freer, Harold Wiley 1906- ... CAP-2
Earlier sketch in CA 21-22
Freese, Arthur S. 1917- ... 77-80
Freese, Barbara 1960- ... 224
Freese, Gene Scott 1969- ... 170
Freese, Mathias B(alogh) 1940- ... 164
Freestrom, Hubert J. 1928- ... 37-40R
Freeth, Zahra 1925- ... 121
Freeze, Gregory L. 1945- ... 168
Frega, Donnalee 1956- ... 170
Fregault, Guy 1918-1977 ... 101
Frege, (Friedrich Ludwig) Gottlob 1848-1925
Brief entry ... 120
Fregly, Bert 1922- ... CANR-8
Earlier sketch in CA 57-60
Fregosi, Claudia (Anne Marie) 1946- ... 69-72
See also SATA 24
Fregosi, Paul ... 235
Frei, Eduardo
See Frei Montalva, Eduardo
Frei, Hans W(ilhelm) 1922-1988 ... 204
Obituary ... 126
Brief entry ... 111
Frei, Terry 1955- ... 219
Freiberg, Stanley K(enneth) 1923- ... CANR-31
Earlier sketch in CA 112
Freiberger, Steven Z. 1950- ... 138
Freid, Jacob L. 1913-2000 ... CANR-17
Earlier sketch in CA 1-4R
Freidank c. 1170-c. 1233 ... DLB 138
Freidel, Frank (Burt, Jr.) 1916-1993 ... CANR-46
Obituary ... 140
Earlier sketches in CA 1-4R, CANR-5
Freidenreich, Harriet Pass 1947- ... 114
Freidenshtein, Nikolai Berngardovich
1894-1943
See Fel'zen, Iurii
Freides, Thelma K(atz) 1930- ... 49-52
Freidin, Seymour K(enneth)
1917-1991 ... CANR-2
Obituary ... 134
Earlier sketch in CA 1-4R
Freidson, Eliot 1923- ... CANR-8
Earlier sketch in CA 5-8R
Freihofer, Lois Diane 1933- ... 13-16R
Freilich, Ariel Segal
See Segal (Freilich), Ariel
Freilich, Joan S(herman) 1941- ... 57-60
Freilich, Morris 1928- ... 37-40R
Freiligrath, Ferdinand 1810-1876 ... DLB 133
Frei Montalva, Eduardo 1911-1982
Obituary ... 110
Freire, P.
See Freire, Paulo
Freire, P.
See Freire, Paulo
Freire, Paulo 1921-1997 ... 132
Obituary ... 158
Brief entry ... 116
Freireich, Valerie J. 1952- ... 156
Freire-Maia, Newton 1918- ... 29-32R
Freitas, Margarete Elisabeth 1927- ... 45-48
Freivalds, John 1944- ... 69-72
Freixedo, Salvador 1923- ... CANR-46
Earlier sketch in CA 29-32R
Freke, Timothy 1959- ... 203
Freleng, Friz 1906-1995 ... IDFW 3
Frelinghuysen, Joseph S(herman)
1912-2005 ... 134
Obituary ... 235
Fremantle, Anne(-Marie Huth)
1910-2002 ... 13-16R
Obituary ... 212
Fremedon, Ellen
See Meagher, John C(arney)
Fremes, Ruth 1930- ... 237
Fremgen, James Morgan 1933- ... 17-20R
Fremlin, Celia
See Goller, Celia (Fremlin)
See also DLB 276
Fremont, Jessie Benton 1813-1902 ... 194
See also DLB 183
Fremont, John Charles 1813-1890 ... DLB 183, 186
Fremont, W. B.
See Bowers, Warner Fremont
Fremont-Smith, Eliot 1929- ... 105
Frenaud, Andre 1907- ... CWW 2
Frenay, Henri 1905-1988
Obituary ... 126
French, Albert 1943- ... 167
See also BW 3
See also CLC 86
French, Alfred 1916-1997 ... 102
French, Alice 1850-1934 ... 176
See also DLB 74
See also DLBD 13
French, Allen 1870-1946
Brief entry ... 122
See also BYA 4
See also YABC 1
French, Anne 1956- ... 153
See also CP 7
See also CWP
French, Antonia
See Kureishi, Hanif
French, Ashley
See Robins, Denise (Naomi)
French, Bevan M(eredith) 1937- ... 97-100
French, Brandon 1944- ... 89-92
French, Calvin L(eonard) 1934- ... 53-56
French, Charles E(zra) 1923- ... CANR-1
Earlier sketch in CA 45-48
French, Christopher W. 1940(?)-1989
Obituary ... 129
French, David 1939- ... CANR-138
Earlier sketch in CA 101
See also CD 5, 6
See also DAC
See also DLB 53
French, Doris
See Shackleton, Doris (Cavell)
French, Dorothy Kayser 1926- ... CANR-3
Earlier sketch in CA 9-12R
See also SATA 5
French, Edward L(ivingstone)
1916-1969 ... CAP-2
Earlier sketch in CA 21-22
French, Evangeline 1869-1960 ... DLB 195
French, Fiona 1944- ... CANR-40
Earlier sketch in CA 29-32R
See also CLR 37
See also CWRI 5
See also MAICYA 1, 2
See also SAAS 21
See also SATA 6, 75, 132
French, Francesca 1874-1960 ... DLB 195
French, Herbert E(liot) 1912-1991 ... 45-48
French, Howard W. 1957- ... 231
French, Jackie ... 178
See also French, Jacqueline Anne
See also SATA 108, 139
See also SATA-Essay 139
French, Jacqueline Anne 1953-
See French, Jackie
See also MAICYA 2
French, Kathryn
See Mosesson, Gloria R(ubin)
French, Marilyn 1929- ... CANR-134
Earlier sketches in CA 69-72, CANR-3, 31
Interview in ... CANR-31
See also BPFB 1
See also CLC 10, 18, 60, 177
See also CN 5, 6, 7
See also CPW
See also DAM DRAM, NOV, POP
See also FL 1:5
See also FW
See also MTCW 1, 2
See also MTFW 2005
French, Michael 1944- ... 89-92
Interview in ... CA-89-92
See also BYA 6
See also SATA 49
See also SATA-Brief 38
See also WYA
French, Nicci
See French, Sean
French, Patrick 1966- ... CANR-143
Earlier sketch in CA 172
French, Paul
See Asimov, Isaac
French, Peter 1918- ... 1-4R
French, Peter A(ndrew) 1942- ... CANR-30
Earlier sketches in CA 45-48, CANR-1, 17
French, Philip (Neville) 1933- ... 103
French, R(obert) B(utler) D(igby)
1904-1981 ... CAP-2
Obituary ... 104
Earlier sketch in CA 25-28
French, R(oger) K(enneth)
1938-2002 ... CANR-42
Obituary ... 205
Earlier sketch in CA 118
French, Richard (De Land) 1947- ... CANR-11
Earlier sketch in CA 69-72
French, Ruth M. 1921(?)-1987
Obituary ... 122
French, Scot ... 231
French, Scott Robert 1948- ... 57-60
French, Sean 1959- ... CANR-95
Earlier sketch in CA 160
French, Simon 1957- ... CANR-128
Earlier sketches in CA 105, CANR-22, 49, 117
See also SATA 86, 147
See also YAW
French, Warren G(raham) 1922- ... CANR-46
Earlier sketches in CA 1-4R, CANR-1, 16
French, Wendell L(owell) 1923- ... 116
French, Will 1890(?)-1979
Obituary ... 89-92
French, William (Harold) 1926- ... 69-72
French, William Marshall 1907- ... CAP-1
Earlier sketch in CA 13-16
Frend, A.
See Cleveland, Philip Jerome
Frend, W(illiam) H(ugh) C(lifford)
1916- ... CANR-9
Earlier sketch in CA 21-24R
Freneau, Philip Morin 1752-1832 ... AMWS 2
See also DLB 37, 43
See also RGAL 4
Frenette, Liza ... SATA 126
Freni, Melo 1934- ... DLB 128
Frenkel, Jacob A(haron) 1943- ... 89-92
Frenkel, Richard E(ugene) 1924- ... 21-24R
Frentzen, Jeffrey 1956- ... 109
Frenz, Horst 1912-1990 ... 29-32R
Frenzel, Louis (Earl), Jr. 1938- ... 112
Frere, A. S.
See Frere-Reeves, Alexander Stuart
Frere, Emile (George) 1917-1974 ... 41-44R
Frere, James Arnold 1920-1994 ... 5-8R
Frere, John Hookham 1769-1846 ... RGEL 2
Frere, Maud
See Frere, Maud
Frere, Paul 1917- ... CANR-14
Earlier sketch in CA 5-8R
Frere, Sheppard (Sunderland) 1916- ... 21-24R
Frere-Cook, Gervis 1928-
Brief entry ... 111
Frere-Reeves, Alexander Stuart 1892-1984
Obituary ... 114
Frere Untel
See Desbiens, Jean-Paul
Frerichs, A(lbert) C(hristian) 1910-1984 . CAP-2
Earlier sketch in CA 25-28
Freron, Elie-Catherine 1718-1776 ... DLB 313
See also GFL Beginnings to 1789
Freschet, Berniece (Louise Speck)
1927- ... CANR-11
Earlier sketch in CA 17-20R
Freschet, Gina 1960- ... 210
See also SATA 139
Frese, Dolores Warwick 1936- ... CANR-9
Earlier sketch in CA 5-8R
Freshfield, Douglas W. 1845-1934 ... DLB 174
Fretheim, Terence E(rling) 1936- ... CANR-11
Earlier sketch in CA 25-28R
Fretter, T. W.
See Andre, (Kenneth) Michael
Fretter, William Bache 1916- ... 113
Fretwell, Stephen DeWitt 1942- ... 53-56
Freuchen, (Lorence) Peter (Elfred) 1886-1957
Brief entry ... 114
Freuchen, Pipaluk 1918- ... BYA 1
Freud, Anna 1895-1982 ... CANR-34
Obituary ... 108
Earlier sketch in CA 112
See also MTCW 1
Freud, Clement (Raphael) 1924- ... 102
Freud, Ernst L. 1892-1970 ... 160
Freud, Esther 1963- ... 144
Freud, Sigmund 1856-1939 ... CANR-69
Brief entry ... 115
Earlier sketch in CA 133
See also DLB 296
See also EW 8
See also EWL 3
See also LATS 1:1
See also MTCW 1, 2
See also MTFW 2005
See also NCFS 3
See also TCLC 52
See also TWA
Freud, Sophie 1924- ... 134
Freudberg, Frank 1953- ... 118
Freudenberger, C(arlton) Dean 1930- ... 135
Freudenberger, Herman 1922- ... 13-16R
Freudenheim, Leslie Ann Mandelson
1941- ... 69-72
Freudenheim, Yehoshua (Oskar)
1894-1975 ... CAP-2
Earlier sketch in CA 21-22
Freudenthal, Gad 1944- ... 153
Freudenthal, Hans 1905-1990 ... CANR-27
Earlier sketches in CA 25-28R, CANR-11
Freund, Diane ... 203
Freund, E(rnest) Hans 1905-1994 ... 1-4R
Freund, Edith 1931- ... 118
Freund, Gerald 1930-1997 ... CANR-1
Obituary ... 158
Earlier sketch in CA 1-4R

Freund, Gisele 1912-2000 49-52
Obituary 190
Freund, John E(rnst) 1921- 13-16R
Freund, Karl 1890-1969 .... IDFW 3, 4
Freund, Otto Kahn
See Kahn-Freund, Otto
Freund, Paul A(braham) 1908-1992 . CANR-47
Obituary 136
Earlier sketch in CA 1-4R
Freund, Philip (Herbert) 1909- CANR-12
Earlier sketch in CA 13-16R
Freund, Rudolf 1915-1969 .... SATA-Brief 28
Freund, Thatcher 1955- 146
Freundlich, August L(udwig) 1924- ... CANR-49
Earlier sketch in CA 49-52
Frevert, Peter 1938- 81-84
Frew, David R(ichard) 1943- 77-80
Frewer, Glyn (M.) 1931- CANR-10
Earlier sketch in CA 13-16R
See also SATA 11
Frewin, Leslie Ronald 1917-1997 ..... CANR-48
Obituary 160
Earlier sketches in CA 5-8R, CANR-11
Frey, Andrew 1905(?)-1983
Obituary 109
Frey, Bruno S. 1941- 166
Frey, Darcy 157
See also SATA 98
Frey, Erich A. 1931- 45-48
Frey, Frederick Ward 1929- 53-56
Frey, Henry A. 1923- 33-36R
Frey, James N. 233
Frey, John Andrew 1929- 89-92
Frey, Julia (Bloch) 1943- 149
Frey, Leonard H(amilton) 1927- 29-32R
Frey, Linda (Sue) 176
Frey, Louise I.
See Ireland-Frey, Louise
Frey, Marlys
See Mayfield, Marlys
Frey, Marsha L. 175
Frey, Richard L(incoln) 1905-1988 89-92
Obituary 126
Frey, Robert Seitz 1955- 128
Frey, Stephen W. CANR-102
Earlier sketch in CA 157
Freyberg, Paul (Richard) 1923-1993 135
Obituary 141
Freyd, Jennifer J. 1957- 158
Freyddnt, Shelley 1949- 204
Freyer, Frederic
See Ballinger, William Sanborn
Freyer, Tony (Allan) 1947- 143
Freyfogle, Eric T. 1952- 196
Freymann-Weyr, (Rhoda) Garret (Michaela)
1965- 218
See also AAYA 52
See also SATA 145
Freyre, Gilberto (de Mello)
1900-1987 .... CANR-84
Brief entry 116
Earlier sketch in CA 126
See also EWL 3
See also RGWL 2, 3
Freyre, Ricardo Jaimes
See Jaimes Freyre, Ricardo
Freytag, Gustav 1816-1895 .... DLB 129
Freytag, Joseph
See Cooper, Parley J(oseph)
Freytag, Josephine
See Cooper, Parley J(oseph)
Frezza, Robert (A.) 1956- 154
Friar, Kimon 1911-1993 85-88
Obituary 141
Friar Tuck
See Tucker, Irwin St. John
Fribourg, Marjorie G. 1920- CANR-4
Earlier sketch in CA 1-4R
Frick, C. H.
See Irwin, Constance (H.) Frick
Frick, Constance
See Irwin, Constance (H.) Frick
Frick, Ford Christopher 1894-1978
Obituary 89-92
Frick, George F(rederick) 1925- 13-16R
Fricke, Aaron 1962- 155
See also GLL 2
See also SATA 89
Fricke, Cedric V. 1928- 13-16R
Fricker, E(dward) G(eorge) 1910- 125
Fricker, Mary 1940- 134
Friday, Jo
See Druett, Joan
Friday, Nancy 1937- CANR-70
Earlier sketches in CA 77-80, CANR-28
See also MTCW 1
Friday, Peter
See Harris, Herbert
Friddle, Mindy 238
Fridegard, Jan 1897-1968 .... DLB 259
Fridell, Ron 1943- .... SATA 124
Fridenson, Patrick 1944- 129
Frideres, James S(tephen) 1943- 113
Fridy, (William) Wallace 1910-1998 . CANR-17
Earlier sketch in CA 1-4R
Friebert, Stuart (Alyn) 1931- 65-68
Fried, Barbara 1924- 45-48
Fried, Charles 1935- CANR-12
Earlier sketch in CA 29-32R
Fried, Dennis F. 1946- 202
Fried, Eleanor L.
See Furman, Eleanor L.
Fried, Emanuel 1913- 73-76
Fried, Erich 1921-1988 126
Obituary 127
Brief entry 114
See also DLB 85
Fried, Eunice 124
Fried, Frederick 1908-1994 77-80
Fried, John J(ames) 1940- CANR-12
Earlier sketch in CA 33-36R
Fried, Jonathan L(ester) 1955- 113
Fried, Joseph P. 1939- 37-40R
Fried, Lawrence 1926-1983
Obituary 110
Fried, Marc (Allen) 1922- 77-80
Fried, Marc B(ernard) 1944- 77-80
Fried, Mary McKenzie Hill 1914- 93-96
Fried, Morton H(erbert) 1923-1986 .... 21-24R
Obituary 121
Fried, Peter A(lexander) 1943- 108
Fried, Richard M(ayer) 1941- 73-76
Fried, Robert L. 231
Fried, Stephen (Marc) 1958- CANR-136
Earlier sketch in CA 144
Fried, William 1945- 57-60
Frieda, Leonie 1957(?)- 238
Friedan, Betty (Naomi) 1921- CANR-74
Earlier sketches in CA 65-68, CANR-18, 45
See also CLC 74
See also DLB 246
See also FW
See also MTCW 1, 2
See also MTFW 2005
See also NCFS 5
Friedberg, Aaron L. 1956- 190
Friedberg, Ardy 1935- 108
Friedberg, Gertrude (Tonkonogy)
1908(?)-1989 .... CANR-83
Obituary 129
Earlier sketch in CA 21-24R
See also SFW 4
Friedberg, Joan Brest 1927- 124
Friedberg, Maurice 1929- CANR-5
Earlier sketch in CA 1-4R
Friedberg, Ruth C(rane) 1928- 236
Friede, Eleanor Kask 1920- 101
Friedeberg-Seeley, Frank (J. B.) 1912- 138
Friedelbaum, Stanley H(erman) 1927- ... 37-40R
Friedell, Aaron 1890(?)-1985
Obituary 116
Frieden, Bernard J. 1930- CANR-10
Earlier sketch in CA 13-16R
Frieden, Jeffry Alan 1953- 201
Frieden, Ken(neth) 1955- CANR-42
Earlier sketch in CA 118
Friedenberg, Edgar Zodiag 1921- CANR-29
Earlier sketch in CA 65-68
Friedenberg, Robert V. 1943- 175
Friedenberg, Walter Drew 1928- 89-92
Friedenreich, Harriet Pass
See Freidenreich, Harriet Pass
Friedenthal, Richard 1896-1979 103
Obituary 89-92
Frieder, Emma 1891-1973 .... CAP-2
Earlier sketch in CA 33-36
Friederich, Werner P(aul) 1905-1993 .... 13-16R
Friederichsen, Kathleen (Hockman)
1910-1988 .... 17-20R
Friederichsen, Kay
See Friederichsen, Kathleen (Hockman)
Friedgut, Theodore H. 1931- 89-92
Friedheim, Robert L(yle) 1934-2001 . CANR-12
Obituary 194
Earlier sketch in CA 21-24R
Friedhofer, Hugo 1902-1981 .... IDFW 3, 4
Friedkin, William 1939- 107
Friedl, Erika (Loeffler) 1940- 147
Friedl, Ernestine 1920- 37-40R
Friedl, John 1945- CANR-4
Earlier sketch in CA 53-56
Friedlaender, Walter (Ferdinand) 1873-1966
Obituary 115
Friedland, David Lionel 1936- .... CP 1
Friedland, Martin L(awrence) 1932- . CANR-94
Earlier sketch in CA 146
Friedland, Michael B(rooks) 1963- 171
Friedland, Ronald Lloyd 1937-1975 ...... CAP-2
Obituary 57-60
Earlier sketch in CA 33-36
Friedland, Ronnie 1945- 106
Friedland, Seymour 1928- CANR-17
Earlier sketch in CA 25-28R
Friedland, William H. 1923- 13-16R
Friedlander, Albert H(oschander)
1927-2004 .... CANR-51
Obituary 230
Earlier sketches in CA 21-24R, CANR-9, 25
Friedlander, Benjamin 177
Friedlander, Edward Jay 1945- 196
Friedlander, Henry (Egon) 1930- 153
Friedlander, Howard 1941- 105
Friedlander, Joanne K(ohn) 1930- 61-64
See also SATA 9
Friedlander, Lee (Norman) 1934- 219
Friedlander, Michael W(ulf) 1928- .. CANR-102
Earlier sketch in CA 150
Friedlander, Saul 1932- CANR-72
Brief entry 117
Earlier sketch in CA 130
See also CLC 90
Friedlander, Shems 226
Friedlander, Stanley Lawrence 1938- 17-20R
Friedlander, Walter A(ndreas)
1891-1984 .... 37-40R
Friedman, Alan 144
See also Horowitz, Shel Alan
Friedman, Alan J(acob) 1942- 125
Friedman, Alan Warren 1939- 25-28R
Friedman, Albert B(arron) 1920- CANR-17
Earlier sketch in CA 1-4R
Friedman, Alice R. 1900-1980 .... 41-44R
Friedman, Amy 1952- 133
Friedman, Andrew 1967- 233
Friedman, Arnold D'Arcy 1900-1981
Obituary 109
Friedman, Arnold P(hineas)
1909-1990 .... CANR-1
Earlier sketch in CA 45-48
Friedman, Avi 1952- 232
Friedman, Avner 1932- 53-56
Friedman, B(ernard) H(arper) 1926- .. CANR-48
Earlier sketches in CA 1-4R, CANR-3
See also CLC 7
Friedman, Benjamin M. 1944- 139
Friedman, Bernard 1896-1983
Obituary 110
Friedman, Bonnie 1958- 204
Friedman, Bruce Jay 1930- CANR-101
Earlier sketches in CA 9-12R, CANR-25, 52
Interview in CANR-25
See also CAD
See also CD 5, 6
See also CLC 3, 5, 56
See also CN 1, 2, 3, 4, 5, 6, 7
See also DLB 2, 28, 244
See also MAL 5
See also SSFS 18
Friedman, C(elia) S. 1957- 204
Friedman, Carl 1952- 183
See also DLB 299
Friedman, Charles 1902-1984
Obituary 113
Friedman, David 1945- CANR-123
Earlier sketch in CA 89-92
Friedman, David F. 1923- 134
Friedman, Debra 1955- 225
See also SATA 150
Friedman, Donald 1943- 221
Friedman, Edward H. 1948- 127
Friedman, Edward Ludwig 1903- 1-4R
Friedman, Elizabeth 1893(?)-1980
Obituary 102
Friedman, Estelle (Ehrenwald) 1920- 5-8R
See also SATA 7
Friedman, Francine 1948- 153
Friedman, Frieda 1905- .... SATA 43
Friedman, George 1949- 235
Friedman, Hal
See Friedman, Harold
Friedman, Harold 1942- 89-92
Friedman, Herbert 1916-2000
Obituary 192
Brief entry 112
Friedman, Ina R(osen) 1926- 53-56
Obituary 205
See also BYA 15
See also SATA 49, 136
See also SATA-Brief 41
Friedman, Irving S(igmund)
1915-1989 .... CANR-3
Obituary 130
Earlier sketch in CA 45-48
Friedman, Isaiah 1921- 53-56
Friedman, Jerrold David
See Gerrold, David
Friedman, John 1916-
See Pater, Elias
Friedman, John Block 1934- 125
Friedman, John S(aul) 1942- 118
Friedman, Josephine Troth 1928- 77-80
Friedman, Josh(ua M.) 1941- 140
Brief entry 126
Friedman, Josh Alan 1956- CANR-136
Earlier sketch in CA 122
Friedman, Joy Troth
See Friedman, Josephine Troth
Friedman, Judi 1935- 65-68
See also AITN 2
See also SATA 59
Friedman, Julian R. 1920(?)-1983
Obituary 111
Friedman, Kathy V(allone) 1943- CANR-38
Earlier sketch in CA 114
Friedman, Ken(neth Scott) 65-68
Friedman, Ken(neth) 1939- CANR-48
Earlier sketch in CA 25-28R
Friedman, Kinky 1944- CANR-89
Earlier sketch in CA 147
See also CMW 4
See also CN 7
See also DLB 292
Friedman, Laurie 1964- 209
See also SATA 138
Friedman, Lawrence J. 1940- 53-56
Friedman, Lawrence M(eir) 1930- .. CANR-129
Earlier sketches in CA 13-16R, CANR-5, 43
Friedman, Lawrence S(amuel) 1936- 160
Friedman, Lenemaja 1924- 61-64
Friedman, Leon 1933- 81-84
Friedman, Lester David 1945- 108
Friedman, Marcia 1925- 57-60
Friedman, Marvin 1930- .... SATA 42
See also SATA-Brief 33
Friedman, Matthew 172
Friedman, Maurice S(tanley) 1921- 13-16R
Friedman, Max Motel 1899(?)-1988
Obituary 125
Friedman, Melvin J(ack) 1928-1996 ...... 21-24R
Friedman, Meyer 1910-2001 127
Obituary 195
Brief entry 113
Friedman, Michael H(enry) 1945- 101
Friedman, Michael J(an) 1955- 119
Friedman, Michaele Thompson
1944- CANR-137
Earlier sketches in CA 111, CANR-44
Friedman, Mickey
See Friedman, Michaele Thompson
Friedman, Milton 1912- CANR-69
Earlier sketches in CA 1-4R, CANR-1, 22
See also MTCW 1, 2
Friedman, Murray 1926- 57-60
Friedman, Myles I(van) 1924- CANR-6
Earlier sketch in CA 57-60
Friedman, Nancy 1950- 107
Friedman, Norman 1925- CANR-1
Earlier sketch in CA 1-4R
Friedman, Paul 1899-1972
Obituary 37-40R
Friedman, Paul 1937- 122
Friedman, Paul Belais 1953- 110
Friedman, Philip (J.) 141
Friedman, Ralph 1916- 69-72
Friedman, Richard Elliot 185
Friedman, Robert I. 1950-2002 215
Friedman, Robin 1968- 238
See also SATA 162
Friedman, Rochelle (Rame) 1942- 112
Friedman, Ron 1943- 151
Friedman, Ronald S(amuel) 1962- .. CANR-141
Earlier sketch in CA 172
Friedman, Rose D(irector) CANR-22
Earlier sketch in CA 101
Friedman, (Eve) Rosemary (Tibber)
1929- CANR-44
Earlier sketches in CA 5-8R, CANR-3, 21
Friedman, Roslyn Berger 1924- 17-20R
Friedman, Roy 1934- 25-28R
Friedman, Sanford 1928- 73-76
Friedman, Sara Ann 1935- 77-80
Friedman, Saul S. 1937- 57-60
Friedman, Stuart 1913-1993 .... 1-4R
Friedman, Susan Stanford 1943- CANR-128
Earlier sketch in CA 109
Friedman, Thomas L(oren) 1953- ... CANR-122
Earlier sketches in CA 109, CANR-38
See also BEST 90:1
Friedman, Warner G(eorge) 1934- 97-100
Friedman, Winifred 1923(?)-1975
Obituary 61-64
Friedman, Yona 1923- 130
Friedmann, Arnold 1925- 41-44R
Friedmann, Daniel 1936- 234
Friedmann, Deborah Davis
See Davis-Friedmann, Deborah
Friedmann, Elizabeth 1941- 142
Friedmann, Georges 1902(?)-1977
Obituary 104
Friedmann, Herbert 1900-1987 106
Obituary 122
Friedmann, John 1926- CANR-41
Earlier sketches in CA 85-88, CANR-15
Friedmann, Patty 1946- 200
Friedmann, Stan 1953- .... SATA 80
Friedmann, Thomas 1947- 118
Friedmann, Wolfgang (Gaston)
1907-1972 .... CANR-6
Earlier sketch in CA 1-4R
Friedmann, Yohanan 1936- 33-36R
Friedrich, Anton
See Strich, Christian
Friedrich, Carl Joachim 1901-1984 .. CANR-30
Obituary 113
Earlier sketch in CA 69-72
Friedrich, Dick
See Friedrich, Richard
Friedrich, Gustav W(illiam) 1941-
Brief entry 111
Friedrich, Otto (Alva) 1929-1995 .... CANR-3
Obituary 148
Earlier sketch in CA 5-8R
See also SATA 33
Friedrich, Paul 1927- CANR-12
Earlier sketch in CA 29-32R
Friedrich, Priscilla 1927- 113
See also SATA 39
Friedrich, Richard 1936- 103
Friedrichs, Christopher R(ichard) 1947- ... 89-92
Friedrichs, David O. 1944- 206
Friedrichs, Robert W(inslow) 1923- 49-52
Friedrich von Hausen c. 1171-1190 ... DLB 138
Friedson, Anthony M(artin) 1924- 108
Friedwald, Will 1961- 189
Friel, Brian 1929- CANR-131
Earlier sketches in CA 21-24R, CANR-33, 69
See also BRWS 5
See also CBD
See also CD 5, 6
See also CLC 5, 42, 59, 115
See also DC 8
See also DFS 11
See also DLB 13, 319
See also EWL 3
See also MTCW 1
See also RGEL 2
See also SSC 76
See also TEA
Friel, George 1910-1975 189
Friel, James 1958- 139
Friel, Maeve 1950- .... CWRI 5
Frielink, A(braham) Barend 1917- 21-24R
Frieman, Jerome 1942- 148
Friend, Dorie
See Friend, Theodore (Wood III)
Friend, Ed
See Wormser, Richard (Edward)
Friend, Joseph H(arold) 1909-1972 .... CAP-2
Earlier sketch in CA 25-28
Friend, Julius W(eis) 1926- 230
Friend, Krebs 1895(?)-1967(?) .... DLB 4
Friend, (Harold) Krebs 1896-1967(?) 202
Friend, Oscar 1897-1963
See Smith, Ford
See also TCWW 2

Cumulative Index 203 Fry

Friend, Robert 1913-1998 ... CANR-7
Obituary ... 163
Earlier sketch in CA 13-16R
Friend, Theodore (Wood III) 1931- ... 138
Friendlich, Dick
See Friendlich, Richard J.
Friendlich, Richard J. 1909- ... CAP-1
Earlier sketch in CA 13-16
See also SATA 11
Friendly, Alfred, Jr. 1938- ... 152
Friendly, Alfred 1911-1983 ... 101
Obituary ... 111
Friendly, Fred W. 1915-1998 ... CANR-14
Obituary ... 165
Earlier sketch in CA 21-24R
Friendly, Henry Jacob 1903-1986 ... 103
Obituary ... 118
Friends, Jalynn
See Alsobrook, Rosalyn R.
Frier, Bruce W(oodward) 1943- ... 125
Friermood, Elisabeth Hamilton
1903-1992 ... CANR-1
Earlier sketch in CA 1-4R
See also SATA 5
Fries, Albert Charles 1908-1999 ... CANR-4
Earlier sketch in CA 1-4R
Fries, Fritz Rudolf 1935- ... CANR-11
Earlier sketch in CA 25-28R
See also DLB 75
Fries, James Franklin 1938- ... 89-92
Fries, Robert Francis 1911-2003 ... 106
Obituary ... 219
Friesel, Evyatar 1930- ... 135
Friesen, Bernice (Sarah Anne) 1966- ... 166
See also SATA 105
Friesen, Garry 1947- ... 114
Friesen, Gayle 1960- ... 180
See also SATA 109
Friesen, Gerald 1943- ... 120
Friesen, Patrick 1945- ... CANR-32
Earlier sketch in CA 113
Friesner, Esther M. 1951- ... CANR-83
Earlier sketch in CANR-41
See also AAYA 10
See also FANT
See also SATA 71
See also SUFW 2
Friess, Horace L(eland) 1900-1975 ... 65-68
Obituary ... 61-64
Friggens, Arthur (Henry) 1920- ... 103
Friggieri, Oliver 1947- ... EWL 3
Frigstad, David B. 1954- ... 150
Friis, Erik J(ohan) 1913-1999 ... 69-72
Obituary ... 177
Friis, Harald T(rap) 1893-1976
Obituary ... 65-68
Friis-Baastad, Babbis Ellinor
1921-1970 ... 17-20R
Obituary ... 134
See also CLC 12
See also SATA 7
Frijling-Schreuder, E(lisabeth) C. M.
1908- ... 61-64
Frillmann, Paul W. 1911-1972 ... CAP-2
Obituary ... 37-40R
Earlier sketch in CA 25-28
Friman, Alice 1933- ... CANR-98
Earlier sketches in CA 129, CANR-65
Friman, H. Richard 1956- ... 190
Frimbo, E. M.
See Whitaker, Rogers E(rnest) M(alcolm)
Friml, Rudolf 1879-1972
Obituary ... 37-40R
Frimmer, Steven 1928- ... 33-36R
See also SATA 31
Frimoth, Lenore B(eck) 1927- ... 5-8R
Frindall, Bill
See Frindall, William Howard
Frindall, William Howard 1939- ... 135
Frings, Ketti 1915-1981 ... 101
Obituary ... 103
Frings, Manfred S. 1925- ... CANR-51
Earlier sketches in CA 17-20R, CANR-8, 26
Frink, Helen H. 1947- ... 187
Frink, Maurice 1895-1972 ... CAP-2
Earlier sketch in CA 25-28
Frinta, Mojmir S(vatopluk) 1922- ... 25-28R
Fripp, Patricia 1945- ... 93-96
Frisbie, Charlotte J(ohnson) 1940- ... 226
Frisbie, Louise K(elley) 1913-1989 ... 61-64
Frisbie, Margery (Rowbottom) 1923- ... 5-8R
Frisbie, Richard P(atrick) 1926- ... CANR-38
Earlier sketches in CA 5-8R, CANR-2, 17
Frisby, Terence (Peter Michael) 1932- ... 65-68
See also CBD
See also CD 5, 6
Frisch, Karl (Ritter) von 1886-1982 ... CANR-42
Obituary ... 115
Earlier sketch in CA 85-88
Frisch, Max (Rudolf) 1911-1991 ... CANR-74
Obituary ... 134
Earlier sketches in CA 85-88, CANR-32
See also CDWLB 2
See also CLC 3, 9, 14, 18, 32, 44
See also DAM DRAM, NOV
See also DLB 69, 124
See also EW 13
See also EWL 3
See also MTCW 1, 2
See also MTFW 2005
See also RGWL 2, 3
See also TCLC 121
Frisch, Michael H(erbert) 1942- ... 126
Frisch, Morton J. 1923- ... 33-36R
Frisch, O(tto) R(obert) 1904-1979 ... 9-12R
Frisch, Paul Z. 1926(?)-1977
Obituary ... 73-76
Frisch, Ragnar Anton Kittil 1895-1973
Obituary ... 115
Frisch, Walter 1951- ... 225
Frischauer, Willi 1906- ... CANR-7
Earlier sketch in CA 5-8R
Frischer, Bernard D(avid) 1949- ... 113
Frischlin, Nicodemus 1547-1590 ... DLB 179
Frischmuth, Barbara 1941- ... 178
See also DLB 85
See also SATA 114
Frischwasser-Ra'Anan, H. F.
See Ra'Anan, Uri
Friskey, Margaret (Richards)
1901-1995 ... CANR-55
Earlier sketches in CA 5-8R, CANR-2
See also SATA 5
Frison, George C(arr) 1924- ... 93-96
Frist, Bill
See Frist, William H.
Frist, William H. 1952- ... CANR-122
Earlier sketch in CA 136
Frister, Roman ... 192
Fritchley, Alma 1954- ... 203
Fritchman, Stephen Hole 1902-
Brief entry ... 105
Frith, David (Edward John) 1937- ... 138
Frith, H(arold) J(ames) 1921- ... 102
Frith, Katherine Toland 1946- ... 170
Frith, Nigel (Andrew Silver) 1941- ... CANR-64
Earlier sketch in CA 69-72
See also FANT
Fritsch, Albert Joseph 1933- ... 102
Fritsch, Bruno 1926- ... CANR-41
Earlier sketches in CA 69-72, CANR-11
Fritsch, Charles Theodore 1912-1989 ... 112
Fritschler, A. Lee 1937- ... 33-36R
Fritts, Mary Bahr
See Bahr, Mary (Madelyn)
Fritz
See Whitehall, Harold
Fritz, Henry E(ugene) 1927- ... 17-20R
Fritz, Jean (Guttery) 1915- ... CANR-97
Earlier sketches in CA 1-4R, CANR-5, 16, 37
Interview in ... CANR-16
See also BYA 2, 3, 14, 16
See also CLR 2, 14, 96
See also DLB 52
See also JRDA
See also MAICYA 1, 2
See also SAAS 2
See also SATA 1, 29, 72, 119, 163
See also SATA-Essay 122
Fritz, Leah 1931- ... 93-96
Fritz, Marianne 1948- ... 195
Fritz, Sara 1944- ... 183
Fritze, Julius Arnold 1918-1999 ... 103
Fritze, Ronald H. 1951- ... 175
Fritzell, Peter A(lgren) 1940- ... CANR-86
Earlier sketch in CA 133
Fritzer, Penelope Joan 1949- ... 175
Fritzsch, Harald 1943- ... 113
Fritzsche, Peter 1959- ... 139
Frobish, Nestle J(ohn) 1930- ... 101
Froboess, Harry (August) 1899-1985 ... CAP-2
Earlier sketch in CA 17-18
Froehlich, Gustav 1902-1987
Obituary ... 124
Froehlich, Margaret W(alden) 1930- ... 115
See also SATA 56
Froelich, Robert E. 1929- ... CANR-3
Earlier sketch in CA 45-48
Froes, Joao 1965- ... 213
Froese, Deborah ... 213
Froetschel, Susan 1956- ... 227
Frohlich, Gustav
See Froehlich, Gustav
Frohlich, Norman 1941- ... 77-80
Frohman, Charles E(ugene) 1901-1976 ... CAP-2
Earlier sketch in CA 29-32
Frohnen, Bruce (P.) 1962- ... CANR-137
Earlier sketch in CA 139
Frohnmayer, John 1942- ... 143
Frohock, Fred M(anuel) 1937- ... CANR-101
Earlier sketch in CA 163
See also HW 2
Frohock, W(ilbur) M(errill) 1908-1984 ... 73-76
Obituary ... 113
Frois, Jeanne 1953- ... SATA 73
Froissard, Lily Powell ... CANR-25
Earlier sketch in CA 45-48
Froissart, Jean 1338(?)-1410(?) ... DLB 208
See also RGWL 2, 3
See also SATA 28
Froman, Elizabeth Hull 1920-1975 ... CAP-1
Obituary ... 53-56
Earlier sketch in CA 13-16
See also SATA 10
Froman, Lewis A(crelius), Jr. 1935- ... 5-8R
Froman, Robert (Winslow) 1917- ... CANR-1
Earlier sketch in CA 1-4R
See also SATA 8
Frome, David
See Brown, Zenith Jones
Frome, Frieda
See Krieger, Frieda Frome
Frome, Michael 1920- ... CANR-16
Earlier sketches in CA 1-4R, CANR-1
Fromentin, Eugene (Samuel Auguste)
1820-1876 ... DLB 123
See also GFL 1789 to the Present
Fromer, Margot J(oan) 1939- ... 110
Fromkin, David (Henry) 1932- ... CANR-88
Earlier sketch in CA 109
Fromkin, Howard L(arry) 1939- ... 121
Brief entry ... 118
Fromkin, Victoria A(lexandria)
1923-2000 ... 89-92
Obituary ... 188
Fromm, Erich 1900-1980 ... CANR-29
Obituary ... 97-100
Earlier sketch in CA 73-76
See also DLB 296
See also MTCW 1
Fromm, Erika 1910-2003 ... 9-12R
Obituary ... 216
Fromm, Gary 1933- ... CANR-7
Earlier sketch in CA 17-20R
Fromm, Gloria G(likin) 1931-
Brief entry ... 112
Fromm, Harold 1933- ... 21-24R
Fromm, Herbert 1905-1995 ... CANR-1
Earlier sketch in CA 49-52
Fromm, Lilo 1928- ... 81-84
See also SATA 29
Fromm, Pete 1958- ... CANR-93
Earlier sketch in CA 139
Fromme, Babbette Brandt 1925- ... 106
Frommel, Christoph Lvitpold 1933- ... 158
Frommer, Harvey 1937- ... CANR-137
Earlier sketches in CA 103, CANR-26, 51
See also SATA 41
Frommer, Myrna (Katz) 1941- ... CANR-135
Earlier sketch in CA 111
Frommer, Sara Hoskinson 1938- ... 187
Froncek, Thomas (Walter) 1942- ... 81-84
Frondizi, Risieri 1910-1983 ... 41-44R
Frontier, Tex
See Miller, J(ames) P(inckney)
Frontinus c. 35-c. 104 ... DLB 211
Frooks, Dorothy 1899-1997 ... 57-60
Obituary ... 157
Froomkin, Joseph 1927- ... CANR-13
Earlier sketch in CA 21-24R
Frosch, John 1909-1999 ... 183
Frosch, Thomas Richard 1943- ... 69-72
Froscher, Wingate 1918- ... 1-4R
Frost, A(rthur) B(urdett) 1851-1928 ... 136
See also DLB 188
See also DLBD 13
See also MAICYA 1, 2
See also SATA 19
Frost, Carol 1948- ... CANR-112
Earlier sketches in CA 69-72, CANR-11
See also AMWS 15
Frost, David (Paradine) 1939- ... CANR-31
Earlier sketch in CA 69-72
Frost, Diane 1962- ... 204
Frost, Elizabeth
See Frost-Knappman, Elizabeth
Frost, Erica
See Supraner, Robyn
Frost, Ernest 1918- ... 9-12R
Frost, Everett L(loyd) 1942- ... 65-68
Frost, Frank (Jasper) 1929- ... 89-92
Frost, Frederick
See Faust, Frederick (Schiller)
Frost, Gavin 1930- ... CANR-1
Earlier sketch in CA 45-48
Frost, Gerhard Emanuel 1909-1987 ... CAP-1
Earlier sketch in CA 9-10
Frost, Gregory 1951- ... CANR-138
Earlier sketch in CA 118
Frost, Helen 1898-1998 ... CAP-1
Earlier sketch in CA 13-14
Frost, Helen 1949- ... 233
See also SATA 157
Frost, James A(rthur) 1918- ... 37-40R
Frost, Jason
See Obstfeld, Raymond
Frost, Joe L. 1933- ... 25-28R
Frost, Jonathan 1949- ... 228
Frost, Joni
See Paine, Lauran (Bosworth)
Frost, Lawrence A(ugust)
1907-1990 ... CANR-26
Obituary ... 132
Earlier sketches in CA 69-72, CANR-11
Frost, Lesley 1899-1983 ... 21-24R
Obituary ... 110
See also SATA 14
See also SATA-Obit 34
Frost, Leslie Miscampbell 1895-1973
Obituary ... 41-44R
Frost, M(ax) Gilbert 1908- ... CAP-1
Earlier sketch in CA 13-14
Frost, Marjorie 1914- ... 25-28R
Frost, Mark 1953- ... CANR-139
Earlier sketch in CA 168
See also HGG
Frost, O(rcutt) W(illiam) 1926- ... 136
Frost, Paul
See Castle, Anthony (Percy)
Frost, Peter Kip 1936- ... 33-36R
Frost, Richard 1929- ... CANR-95
Earlier sketch in CA 33-36R
Frost, Richard H(indman) 1930- ... 25-28R
Frost, Richard T. 1926-1972 ... CAP-1
Obituary ... 37-40R
Earlier sketch in CA 13-16
Frost, Robert (Lee) 1874-1963 ... CANR-33
Earlier sketch in CA 89-92
See also AAYA 21
See also AMW
See also AMWR 1
See also CDALB 1917-1929
See also CLC 1, 3, 4, 9, 10, 13, 15, 26, 34, 44
See also CLR 67
See also DA
See also DA3
See also DAB
See also DAC
See also DAM MST, POET
See also DLB 54, 284
See also DLBD 7
See also EWL 3
See also EXPP
See also MAL 5
See also MTCW 1, 2
See also MTFW 2005
See also PAB
See also PC 1, 39
See also PFS 1, 2, 3, 4, 5, 6, 7, 10, 13
See also RGAL 4
See also SATA 14
See also TUS
See also WLC
See also WP
See also WYA
Frost, Robert Carlton 1926- ... 53-56
Frost, Roon 1943- ... 126
Frost, Ryker
See Foster, Raymond Keith
Frost, S. E., Jr. 1899- ... CAP-2
Earlier sketch in CA 19-20
Frost, Scott ... 239
Frost, Shelley 1960- ... 208
See also SATA 138
Frost, Stanley Brice 1913- ... 61-64
Frost, William 1917- ... 41-44R
Frostenson, Katarina 1953- ... 192
See also DLB 257
Frostic, Gwen 1906- ... 17-20R
Frostick, Michael 1917- ... 9-12R
Frost-Knappman, Elizabeth 1943- ... 149
Frothingham, Octavius Brooks
1822-1895 ... DLB 1, 243
Froud, Brian 1947- ... 225
See also SATA 150
Froude, James Anthony 1818-1894 ... DLB 18, 57, 144
Frow, John 1948- ... 120
Frowen, Stephen F(rancis) 1923- ... 180
Froy, Herald
See Deghy, Guy (Stephen) and Waterhouse, Keith (Spencer)
Frucht, Abby 1957- ... CANR-92
Earlier sketch in CA 127
See also CN 7
Frucht, Phyllis 1936- ... 57-60
Fruchtenbaum, Arnold G(enekovich)
1943- ... CANR-11
Earlier sketch in CA 61-64
Fruchter, Benjamin 1914- ... 1-4R
Fruchter, Norman D. ... 81-84
Frude, Neil 1946- ... 114
Fruehling, Rosemary T(herese)
1933- ... CANR-82
Earlier sketches in CA 33-36R, CANR-13, 35
Frug, Gerald E(llison) 1939- ... 190
Frugoni, Cesare 1881-1978
Obituary ... 73-76
Fruhan, William E(dward), Jr. 1943- ... 41-44R
Fruin, W. Mark 1943- ... 140
Frum, Barbara 1937-1992 ... 101
Obituary ... 137
Interview in ... CA-101
Frum, David 1960- ... CANR-92
Earlier sketch in CA 148
Fruman, Norman 1923- ... 37-40R
Frumkes, Lewis Burke 1939- ... CANR-36
Earlier sketch in CA 114
Frumkin, Gene 1928- ... CANR-4
Earlier sketch in CA 9-12R
Frumkin, Robert M. 1928- ... CANR-9
Earlier sketch in CA 21-24R
Frump, Robert (R.) 1947- ... 212
Frushell, Richard C(layton) 1935- ... 185
Frutkin, Mark J. 1948- ... 213
Fruton, Joseph S(tewart) 1912- ... CANR-34
Earlier sketch in CA 49-52
Fruzzetti, Lina M(aria) 1942- ... 113
Fry, Alan 1931- ... CANR-1
Earlier sketch in CA 45-48
Fry, Andrew C. 1956- ... 173
Fry, Annette R(iley) ... SATA 89
Fry, Barbara 1932- ... 25-28R
Fry, C(harles) George 1936- ... CANR-57
Earlier sketches in CA 37-40R, CANR-14, 31
Fry, Christine 1943- ... 107
Fry, Christopher 1907- ... CANR-132
Earlier sketches in CA 17-20R, CANR-9, 30, 74
See also CAAS 23
See also BRWS 3
See also CBD
See also CD 5, 6
See also CLC 2, 10, 14
See also CP 1, 2, 3, 4, 5, 6, 7
See also DAM DRAM
See also DLB 13
See also EWL 3
See also MTCW 1, 2
See also MTFW 2005
See also RGEL 2
See also SATA 66
See also TEA
Fry, David
See Roper, William L(eon)
Fry, Dennis Butler 1907-1983 ... 109
Obituary ... 110
Fry, Donald K(lein, Jr.) 1937- ... 25-28R
Fry, E(dwin) Maxwell 1899-1987 ... 65-68
Obituary ... 123
Fry, Earl H(oward) 1947- ... 102
Fry, Edward Bernard 1925- ... CANR-5
Earlier sketch in CA 9-12R
See also SATA 35
Fry, Hilary G. 1922- ... 17-20R

Fry, Howard T(yrrell) 1919- ... 37-40R
Fry, John 1930- ... 93-96
Fry, Maggie Culver 1900- ... AITN 1
Fry, Maxwell
See Fry, E(dwin) Maxwell
Fry, Michael G(raham) 1934- ... CANR-48
Earlier sketches in CA 69-72, CANR-23
Fry, P(atricia) Eileen 1947- ... 104
Fry, Paul H. 1944- ... 129
Fry, Plantagenet Somerset
See Somerset Fry, (Peter George Robin) Plantagenet
Fry, Roger (Eliot) 1866-1934
Brief entry ... 115
See also DLBD 10
Fry, Ronald W(illiam) 1949- ... CANR-142
Earlier sketch in CA 57-60
Fry, Rosalie Kingsmill 1911-1992 ... CANR-83
Earlier sketch in CA 9-12R
See also SAAS 11
See also SATA 3
Fry, Stephen 1957- ... 210
See also DLB 207
Fry, Thomas Frederick 1919- ... 118
Fry, Tom
See Fry, Thomas Frederick
Fry, Virginia Lynn 1952- ... 160
See also SATA 95
Fry, William F(inley, Jr.) 1924- ... 5-8R
Fry, Ying Ying ... 210
Fryatt, Norma R. ... 57-60
Fryburger, Vernon R(ay), Jr. 1918- ... 1-4R
Fryd, Norbert 1913-1976
Obituary ... 65-68
Fryd, Vivien Green 1952- ... 144
Frydman, Szajko 1911-1978 ... CANR-48
Earlier sketch in CA 25-28R
Frye, (Charles) Alton 1936- ... 21-24R
Frye, Charles A(nthony) 1946-1994 ... 153
See also BW 2, 3
Frye, Ellen 1940- ... 49-52
Frye, John 1910- ... CANR-28
Earlier sketch in CA 49-52
Frye, Keith 1935- ... 53-56
Frye, Marilyn 1941- ... 154
See also FW
See also GLL 2
Frye, (Herman) Northrop
1912-1991 ... CANR-37
Obituary ... 133
Earlier sketches in CA 5-8R, CANR-8
See also CLC 24, 70
See also DLB 67, 68, 246
See also EWL 3
See also MTCW 1, 2
See also MTFW 2005
See also RGAL 4
See also TCLC 165
See also TWA
Frye, Richard N(elson) 1920- ... CANR-3
Earlier sketch in CA 5-8R
Frye, Roland Mushat 1921- ... 9-12R
Frye, Sally
See Moore, Elaine
Frye, William R(uggles) 1918- ... 73-76
Fryer, Donald S.
See Sidney-Fryer, Donald
Fryer, Holly C(laire) 1908- ... CAP-1
Earlier sketch in CA 19-20
Fryer, Jonathan 1950- ... 85-88
Fryer, Judith 1939- ... 69-72
Fryer, Mary Beacock 1929- ... 97-100
Fryer, William T. 1900(?)-1980
Obituary ... 93-96
Frykenberg, Robert Eric 1930- ... 25-28R
Fryklund, Verne C(harles) 1896-1980 ... 13-16R
Obituary ... 126
Frykman, John H(arvey) 1932- ... CANR-43
Earlier sketch in CA 33-36R
Frym, Gloria 1947- ... CANR-88
Earlier sketch in CA 105
Frymer-Kensky, Tikva ... 222
Frymier, Jack R(immel) 1925- ... 17-20R
Fryscak, Milan 1932- ... 53-56
Fu, Limin
See Freeman, Charles Wellman, Jr.
Fubini, Riccardo 1934- ... 239
Fuchida, Mitsuo 1902(?)-1976
Obituary ... 65-68
Fuchs, Bernie 1932- ... SATA 95, 162
Fuchs, Daniel 1909-1993 ... CANR-40
Obituary ... 142
Earlier sketch in CA 81-84
See also CAAS 5
See also CLC 8, 22
See also CN 1, 2, 3, 4, 5
See also DLB 9, 26, 28
See also DLBY 1993
See also MAL 5
Fuchs, Daniel 1934- ... CANR-48
Earlier sketches in CA 37-40R, CANR-14
See also CLC 34
Fuchs, Elinor 1933- ... 105
Fuchs, Erich 1916- ... 29-32R
See also SATA 6
Fuchs, Estelle ... 57-60
Fuchs, Guenter Bruno 1928-1977
Obituary ... 114
Fuchs, Jacob 1939- ... 21-24R
Fuchs, Jerome H(erbert) 1922- ... 69-72
Fuchs, Josef 1912- ... 21-24R
Fuchs, Juergen 1950(?)-1999 ... 186
Fuchs, Lawrence H. 1927- ... CANR-5
Earlier sketch in CA 1-4R
Fuchs, Lucy 1935- ... CANR-30
Earlier sketches in CA 73-76, CANR-12
See also SATA-Brief 52
Fuchs, Miriam 1949- ... 147
Fuchs, Rachel G(innis) 1939- ... 144
Fuchs, Robert S. 1912- ... 169
Fuchs, Roland J(ohn) 1933- ... CANR-14
Earlier sketch in CA 81-84
Fuchs, Victor R(obert) 1924- ... CANR-41
Earlier sketches in CA 1-4R, CANR-2, 18
Fuchs, Vivian (Ernest) 1908-1999 ... CANR-21
Obituary ... 186
Earlier sketch in CA 104
Fuchshuber, Annegert 1940- ... 112
See also SATA 43
Fuchssteiner, Benno 1941- ... 149
Fucilla, Joseph G(uerin) 1897-1981 ... 89-92
Fucini, Joseph J(ames) 1951- ... 120
Fucini, Suzy 1951- ... 120
Fudge, William Kingston 1904-1985
Obituary ... 116
Fuegi, John 1936- ... 37-40R
Fueloep-Miller, Rene 1891-1963
Obituary ... 110
Fuente, Patricia de la
See de la Fuente, Patricia
Fuentes, Carlos 1928- ... CANR-138
Earlier sketches in CA 69-72, CANR-10, 32, 68, 104
See also AAYA 4, 45
See also AITN 2
See also BPFB 1
See also CDWLB 3
See also CLC 3, 8, 10, 13, 22, 41, 60, 113
See also CWW 2
See also DA
See also DA3
See also DAB
See also DAC
See also DAM MST, MULT, NOV
See also DLB 113
See also DNFS 2
See also EWL 3
See also HLC 1
See also HW 1, 2
See also LAIT 3
See also LATS 1:2
See also LAW
See also LAWS 1
See also LMFS 2
See also MTCW 1, 2
See also MTFW 2005
See also NFS 8
See also RGSF 2
See also RGWL 2, 3
See also SSC 24
See also TWA
See also WLC
See also WLIT 1
Fuentes, Gregorio Lopez y
See Lopez y Fuentes, Gregorio
Fuentes, Martha Ayers 1923- ... 73-76
Fuentes, Roberto 1934- ... 57-60
Fuentes Mohr, Alberto 1928(?)-1979
Obituary ... 85-88
Fueredi, Frank
See Furedi, Frank
Fuerer-Haimendorf, Christoph von
1909-1995 ... CANR-13
Earlier sketch in CA 13-16R
Fuermann, George Melvin 1918- ... 103
Fuerst, Jeffrey B. 1956- ... 215
See also SATA 143
Fuertes, Gloria 1918-1998 ... 180
Earlier sketch in CA 178
See also DLB 108
See also HW 2
See also PC 27
See also SATA 115
Fufuka, Karama
See Morgan, Sharon A(ntonia)
Fugard, (Harold) Athol 1932- ... CANR-118
Earlier sketches in CA 85-88, CANR-32, 54
See also AAYA 17
See also AFW
See also CD 5, 6
See also CLC 5, 9, 14, 25, 40, 80, 211
See also DAM DRAM
See also DC 3
See also DFS 3, 6, 10
See also DLB 225
See also DNFS 1, 2
See also EWL 3
See also LATS 1:2
See also MTCW 1
See also MTFW 2005
See also RGEL 2
See also WLIT 2
Fugard, Sheila 1932- ... 125
See also CLC 48
Fugate, Bryan I(rven) 1943- ... 120
Fugate, Francis L(yle) 1915- ... 25-28R
Fugate, Joe K. 1931- ... 21-24R
Fugate, Roberta B(auslin) 1917- ... 111
Fugate, Terence (McCuddy) 1930- ... 5-8R
Fuge, Charles 1966- ... SATA 74, 144
Fugitt, Eva D(raper) 1929- ... 110
Fuguet, Alberto 1964- ... CANR-144
Earlier sketch in CA 170
Fuhrman, Chris 1960-1991 ... 151
Fuhrman, Ellsworth R(aymond) 1946- ... 112
Fuhrman, Joanna 1972- ... 214
Fuhrman, Lee 1903(?)-1977
Obituary ... 73-76
Fuhrman, Mark 1952(?)- ... 161
Fuhrmann, Joseph T(heodore) 1940- ... 73-76
Fuhro, Wilbur J. 1914- ... 9-12R
Fujikawa, Gyo 1908-1998 ... CANR-46
Obituary ... 172
Earlier sketch in CA 113
See also CLR 25
See also CWRI 5
See also MAICYA 1, 2
See also SAAS 16
See also SATA 39, 76
See also SATA-Brief 30
See also SATA-Obit 110
Fujimura, Joan H. ... 168
Fujishima, Kosuke 1964- ... 220
Fujita, Marty 1954- ... 221
Fujita, Tamao 1905-1999 ... 37-40R
See also SATA 7
Fujiwara, Iwaichi 1908-1986 ... 132
Fujiwara, Kim 1957- ... SATA 81
Fujiwara, Michiko 1946- ... 77-80
See also SATA 15
Fujiwara, Yoichi 1909- ... CANR-22
Earlier sketch in CA 105
Fujiwara no Shunzei 1114-1204 ... DLB 203
Fujiwara no Tameaki 1230(?)-1290(?) . DLB 203
Fujiwara no Tameie 1198-1275 ... DLB 203
Fujiwara no Teika 1162-1241 ... DLB 203
Fuka, Vladimir 1926-1977
Obituary ... 104
See also SATA-Obit 27
Fukei, Gladys Arlene (Harper) 1920- ... 13-16R
Fuks, Ladislav 1923-1994 ... 118
See also DLB 299
See also EWL 3
Fukuda, Haruko 1946- ... 109
Fukuda, Tsutomu 1905- ... 103
See also CP 1
Fukui, Haruhiro 1935- ... 29-32R
Fukui, Kenichi 1918-1998 ... 156
Obituary ... 163
Fukutake, Tadashi 1917- ... CANR-5
Earlier sketch in CA 13-16R
Fukuyama, Francis 1952- ... CANR-125
Earlier sketches in CA 140, CANR-72
See also CLC 131
Fukuyama, Yoshio 1921- ... 41-44R
Fulani, Lenora (Branch) 1950- ... 155
See also BW 3
Fulbecke, William 1560-1603(?) ... DLB 172
Fulbright, J(ames) William 1905-1995 ... 9-12R
Obituary ... 147
Fulbrook, Mary (Jean Alexandra)
1951- ... CANR-47
Earlier sketch in CA 121
Fulcher, James 1942- ... 139
Fulcher, Jane F. ... 190
Fulco, William J(ames) 1936- ... 49-52
Fuld, James J. 1916- ... 21-24R
Fuld, Leonard M. 1953- ... 120
Fulda, Carl H. 1909-1975 ... CAP-2
Earlier sketch in CA 33-36
Fulda, Joseph S. 1958- ... 206
Fuldauer, Ivan 1927- ... 69-72
Fuldheim, Dorothy (Violet Snell)
1893-1989 ... CANR-29
Obituary ... 130
Earlier sketch in CA 49-52
Fulford, Robert 1932- ... 89-92
Fulford, Roger (Thomas Baldwin)
1902-1983 ... 65-68
Obituary ... 109
Fulford, Tim(othy John) 1962- ... 223
Fulghum, Robert (L.) 1937- ... CANR-62
Earlier sketch in CA 139
See also BEST 89:2
See also CPW 1
See also CSW
See also DAM POP
Fulks, Bryan 1897-1980 ... 97-100
Full, Harold 1919- ... 17-20R
Fullbrook, Kate 1950-2003 ... CANR-102
Earlier sketch in CA 148
Fuller, Alexandra 1969- ... 212
Fuller, Alfred C(arl) 1885-1973
Obituary ... 45-48
Fuller, Beverley 1927- ... 69-72
Fuller, Blair 1927- ... 9-12R
Fuller, Buckminster
See Fuller, R(ichard) Buckminster (Jr.)
Fuller, Catherine Leuthold 1916- ... 29-32R
See also SATA 9
Fuller, Charles (H.), (Jr.) 1939- ... CANR-87
Brief entry ... 108
Earlier sketch in CA 112
Interview in ... CA-112
See also BLC 2
See also BW 2
See also CAD
See also CD 5, 6
See also CLC 25
See also DAM DRAM, MULT
See also DC 1
See also DFS 8
See also DLB 38, 266
See also EWL 3
See also MAL 5
See also MTCW 1
Fuller, Curtis G. 1912-1991
Brief entry ... 120
Fuller, Daniel P(ayton) 1925- ... 127
Brief entry ... 112
Fuller, David O(tis) 1903-1988 ... 53-56
Fuller, Dorothy Mason 1898-1993 ... 101
Fuller, Edgar 1904-1973
Obituary ... 45-48
Fuller, Edmund (Maybank) 1914- ... 77-80
See also CN 1, 2
See also SATA 21
Fuller, Edward C. 1907- ... 53-56
Fuller, Elizabeth 1946- ... CANR-33
Earlier sketch in CA 113
Fuller, Graham E. 1937- ... 228
Fuller, Harold 1940- ... 65-68
Fuller, Helen 1914(?)-1972
Obituary ... 37-40R
Fuller, Henry Blake 1857-1929 ... 177
Brief entry ... 108
See also DLB 12
See also RGAL 4
See also TCLC 103
Fuller, Hoyt (William) 1927-1981 ... 53-56
Obituary ... 103
See also BW 1
Fuller, Iola
See McCoy, Iola Fuller
Fuller, Jack (William) 1946- ... CANR-77
Brief entry ... 125
Earlier sketch in CA 130
Interview in ... CA-130
Fuller, Jean (Violet) Overton 1915- ... CANR-42
Earlier sketches in CA 5-8R, CANR-4, 19
Fuller, John (Harold) ... CAP-1
Earlier sketch in CA 9-10
Fuller, John (Leopold) 1937- ... CANR-44
Earlier sketches in CA 21-24R, CANR-9
See also CLC 62
See also CP 1, 2, 3, 4, 5, 6, 7
See also DLB 40
Fuller, John Frederick Charles
1878-1966 ... CAP-1
Earlier sketch in CA 13-16
Fuller, John G(rant, Jr.) 1913-1990 ... CANR-2
Obituary ... 133
Earlier sketch in CA 1-4R
See also SATA 65
Fuller, Kathleen
See Gottfried, Theodore Mark
Fuller, Ken 1946- ... 125
Fuller, Loie 1862-1928 ... 205
Fuller, Lois Hamilton 1915- ... CANR-29
Earlier sketch in CA 1-4R
See also SATA 11
Fuller, Lon (Luvois) 1902-1978 ... CAP-2
Obituary ... 77-80
Earlier sketch in CA 33-36
Fuller, Margaret
See Ossoli, Sarah Margaret (Fuller)
See also AMWS 2
See also DLB 183, 223, 239
See also FL 1:3
Fuller, Mary Lou 1929- ... CANR-130
Earlier sketch in CA 164
Fuller, Maud
See Petersham, Maud (Sylvia Fuller)
Fuller, Miriam Morris 1933- ... 37-40R
Fuller, Paul E(ugene) 1932- ... 73-76
Fuller, Peter (Michael) 1947- ... 97-100
Fuller, R(ichard) Buckminster (Jr.)
1895-1983 ... CANR-12
Obituary ... 109
Earlier sketch in CA 9-12R
See also MAL 5
See also MTCW 1, 2
Fuller, Reginald H(orace) 1915- ... CANR-39
Earlier sketches in CA 5-8R, CANR-3, 18
Fuller, Robert C(harles) 1952- ... CANR-117
Earlier sketches in CA 116, CANR-38
Fuller, Roger
See Tracy, Don(ald Fiske)
Fuller, Roy (Broadbent) 1912-1991 ... CANR-83
Obituary ... 135
Earlier sketches in CA 5-8R, CANR-53
See also CAAS 10
See also BRWS 7
See also CLC 4, 28
See also CN 1, 2, 3, 4, 5
See also CP 1, 2
See also CWRI 5
See also DLB 15, 20
See also EWL 3
See also RGEL 2
See also SATA 87
Fuller, Ruth
See Perry, Ruth (Fuller)
Fuller, Sam
See Fuller, Samuel (Michael)
Fuller, Samuel (Michael) 1912-1997 . CANR-84
Brief entry ... 112
Earlier sketch in CA 129
See also DLB 26
Fuller, Sarah Margaret
See Ossoli, Sarah Margaret (Fuller)
Fuller, Sarah Margaret
See Ossoli, Sarah Margaret (Fuller)
See also DLB 1, 59, 73
Fuller, Sophie 1961- ... 234
Fuller, Steve William 1959- ... CANR-111
Earlier sketch in CA 137
Fuller, Thomas 1608-1661 ... DLB 151
Fuller, Thomas C(harles) 1918- ... 126
Fuller, Wayne E(dison) 1919- ... 13-16R
Fuller, William A(lbert) 1924- ... 41-44R
Fullerton, Alexander (Fergus)
1924- ... CANR-114
Earlier sketches in CA 17-20R, CANR-7, 23, 48
Fullerton, Gail Jackson 1927- ... 37-40R
Fullerton, Gail Putney
See Fullerton, Gail Jackson
Fullerton, Hugh 1873-1945 ... 201
See also DLB 171
Fullilove, Mindy Thompson 1950- ... 229
Fullinwider, Robert King 1942- ... 108
Fullinwider, S. P(endleton) 1933- ... 127
Brief entry ... 109

Fullmer, Daniel W(arren) 1922- CANR-29
Earlier sketches in CA 33-36R, CANR-13
Fullmer, June Z(immerman) 1920- 25-28R
Fullwood, William ..... DLB 236
Fulmer, David 1950- 205
Fulmer, Robert M(arion) 1939- CANR-10
Earlier sketch in CA 57-60
Fulop-Miller, Rene
See Fueloep-Miller, Rene
Fulsom, Lowell
See Fulson, Lowell
Fulson, Lowell 1921-1999 183
Fulton, A(lbert) R(ondthaler) 1902- 1-4R
Fulton, Alice 1952- CANR-88
Earlier sketches in CA 116, CANR-57
See also CLC 52
See also CP 7
See also CWP
See also DLB 193
Fulton, Gere (Burke) 1939- 53-56
Fulton, John 1902-1966 ..... IDFW 3
Fulton, Len 1934- 57-60
See also DLBY 1986
Fulton, Norman 1927- 37-40R
Fulton, Paul C(edric) 1901-1985 ..... CAP-1
Obituary 118
Earlier sketch in CA 13-16
Fulton, Robert Lester 1926-
Brief entry 105
Fulton, Robin 1937- CANR-84
Earlier sketches in CA 33-36R, CANR-16, 38
See also CP 1, 2, 3, 4, 5, 6, 7
See also DLB 40
Fults, John Lee 1932- 53-56
See also SATA 33
Fultz, Jay 1936- 170
Fultz, Walter J. 1924(?)-1971
Obituary 104
Fulweiler, Howard Wells 1932- 77-80
Fumaroli, Marc 1932- 225
Fumento, Michael (Aaron) 1960- 139
Fumento, Rocco 1923- 1-4R
Fumerton, Patricia 140
Funabashi, Seiichi 1904(?)-1976
Obituary 65-68
Funai, Mamoru (Rolland) 1932- .. SATA-Brief 46
Funakawa, Atsushi 1956- 171
Fundaburk, Emma Lila 1922- 41-44R
Funder, Anna 1966- 228
Funderburk, Guy B(ernard) 1902-1982 ... 45-48
Funderburk, Thomas R(ay) 1928- 17-20R
Fundi
See Baraka, Amiri
Fung, Gong
See Goon, Fook Mun
Fung, Raymond (Wai Man) 1940- 123
Funiciello, Theresa 1947- 143
Funigiello, Philip J. 1939- 65-68
Funk, Arthur Layton 1914- 21-24R
Funk, Charles Earle, Jr. 1913-1993 122
Funk, David G. 1938- 237
Funk, Mary Margaret 1943- 187
Funk, Peter V(an) K(euren) 1921- CANR-13
Earlier sketch in CA 21-24R
Funk, Rainer 1943- 109
Funk, Robert W(alter) 1926-2005 ..... 33-36R
Funk, Thompson 1911- CANR-2
Earlier sketch in CA 49-52
See also SATA 7
Funk, Tom
See Funk, Thompson
Funk, Wilfred (John) 1883-1965
Obituary 89-92
Funke, Cornelia (Caroline) 1958- 221
See also SATA 154
Funke, Lewis 1912-1992 49-52
See also SATA 11
Funkhouser, Erica 1949- CANR-121
Earlier sketch in CA 135
See also CWP
Funston, Richard Y(ork) 1943- 123
Brief entry 118
Funt, Allen 1914-1999 146
Obituary 185
Funt, Julian 1907(?)-1980
Obituary 97-100
Funt, Marilyn 1937- 102
Fuoss, Robert Martin 1912-1980
Obituary 93-96
Fuqua, Jonathon Scott 1966- 212
See also SATA 141
Furbank, P(hilip) N(icholas) 1920- .. CANR-123
Earlier sketches in CA 21-24R, CANR-18, 40, 63
See also DLB 155
Furbee, Leonard J. 1896(?)-1975
Obituary 61-64
Furbee, Mary R.
See Furbee, Mary Rodd
Furbee, Mary Rodd 1954- 209
See also SATA 138
Furchgott, Terry 1948- 105
See also SATA 29
Furcolo, Foster 1911(?)-1995 117
Obituary 149
Furdyna, Anna M. 1938- 143
Furedi, Frank 1947- 191
Furer, Howard B(ernard) 1934- 33-36R
Furer-Haimendorf, Christoph von
See Fuerer-Haimendorf, Christoph von
Furet, Francois 1927-1997 187
Furetiere, Antoine 1619-1688 ..... DLB 268
See also GFL Beginnings to 1789
Furey, Maggie CANR-137
Earlier sketch in CA 165
Furey, Michael
See Ward, Arthur Henry Sarsfield
Furfey, Paul Hanly 1896-1992 ..... CAP-2
Earlier sketch in CA 23-24
Furgurson, Ernest B(aker, Jr.) 1929- 73-76
Furgurson, Pat
See Furgurson, Ernest B(aker, Jr.)
Furia, Philip (G.) 1943- 136
Furino, Antonio 1931- 144
Furley, David John 1922- 108
Furlong, Monica (Mavis)
1930-2003 ..... CANR-84
Obituary 212
Brief entry 117
Earlier sketch in CA 151
See also AAYA 45
See also SATA 86
See also SATA-Obit 142
See also YAW
Furlonge, Geoffrey (Warren) 1903-1984
Obituary 114
Furman, Bess 1894-1969
Obituary 115
Furman, Eleanor L. 1913- CANR-12
Earlier sketch in CA 29-32R
Furman, Erna 1926(?)-2002 217
Furman, Gertrude Lerner Kerman
1909- CANR-31
Earlier sketch in CA 5-8R
See also SATA 21
Furman, Laura (J.) 1945- 236
Earlier sketches in CA 104, CANR-30, 118
Autobiographical Essay in 236
See also CAAS 18
See also DLBY 1986
Furman, Roger 1924(?)-1983
Obituary 111
Furmanov, Dmitrii Andreevich
1891-1926 ..... DLB 272
Furnas, J(oseph) C(hamberlain)
1905-2001 77-80
Obituary 196
Furneaux, Robin
See Smith, Frederick William Robin
Furneaux, Rupert 1908- CANR-1
Earlier sketch in CA 1-4R
Furness, Edna L(ue) 1906- 37-40R
Furness, Horace Howard 1833-1912 175
See also DLB 64
Furness, William Henry 1802-1896 ..... DLB 1, 235
Furnier, Vincent Damon
See Cooper, Alice
Furnish, Dorothy Jean 1921- 106
Furnish, Victor Paul 1931- CANR-94
Earlier sketches in CA 21-24R, CANR-10, 25
Furniss, Edgar S(tephenson) 1890-1972
Obituary 37-40R
Furniss, Graham (Lytton) 1949- 156
Furniss, Norman Francis 1922- 1-4R
Furniss, Tim 1948- CANR-29
Earlier sketch in CA 109
See also SATA 49
Furniss, W(arren) Todd 1921- 57-60
Furnivall, Frederick James 1825-1910 188
See also DLB 184
Furphy, Joseph 1843-1912 163
See also Collins, Tom
See also DLB 230
See also EWL 3
See also RGEL 2
See also TCLC 25
Furrer, Juerg 1939- 69-72
Furry, Elda 1890-1966 113
Furse, John 1932- 109
Fursenko, Aleksandr (A.) 165
Furst, Alan 1941- CANR-102
Earlier sketches in CA 69-72, CANR-12, 34, 59
See also DLBY 01
Furst, Lilian Renee 1931- CANR-93
Earlier sketches in CA 102, CANR-18, 40
Furstinger, Nancy 213
Furtado, Celso (Monteiro)
1920-2004 ..... CANR-107
Obituary 233
Earlier sketches in CA 17-20R, CANR-9, 25, 50
Furth, Alex
See Sasuly, Richard
Furth, George 1932- CANR-144
Earlier sketch in CA 73-76
See also CAD
See also CD 5, 6
Furth, Hans G. 1920-1999 45-48
Obituary 186
Furthman, Jules 178
See also Furthmann, Julius Grinnell
See also DLB 26
See also IDFW 3, 4
Furthmann, Julius Grinnell 1888-1966
Obituary 113
See also Furthman, Jules
Furtwangler, Albert (J.) 1942- CANR-41
Earlier sketch in CA 118
Furtwangler, Virginia W(alsh) 1932- . CANR-41
Earlier sketch in CA 118
Furubotn, Eirik G. 1923- 137
Furui, Yoshikichi 1937- 194
See also Furui Yoshikichi
Furui Yoshikichi
See Furui, Yoshikichi
See also DLB 182
See also EWL 3
Furukawa, Toshi 1924- CANR-2
Earlier sketch in CA 45-48
See also SATA 24
Furutani, Dale 1946- CANR-130
Earlier sketch in CA 164
Fury, David (A.) 1950- 222
Fusaro, Peter C. 1950- 228
Fusco, Giovanni 1906-1968 ..... IDFW 3
Fusco, Margie 1949- 85-88
Fusero, Clemente 1913-1975 81-84
Fusfeld, Daniel R(oland) 1922- 45-48
Fushimi, Emperor 1265-1317 ..... DLB 203
Fusi (Aizpurua), Juan Pablo 1945- CANR-87
Earlier sketch in CA 131
See also HW 1
Fusilli, Jim 231
Fusillo, Archimede 1962- 207
See also SATA 137
Fuson, Benjamin Willis 1911-1994 ..... 37-40R
Fuson, Robert H(enderson) 1927- ... CANR-103
Earlier sketch in CA 89-92
See also CLC 70
Fuss, Peter 1932- CANR-9
Earlier sketch in CA 21-24R
Fussel, Stephan 1952- 226
Fussell, Betty Harper 1927- 121
Fussell, E. Robert 1942- 201
Fussell, Edwin 1922- 53-56
Fussell, G(eorge) E(dwin) 1889- CANR-3
Earlier sketch in CA 5-8R
Fussell, Paul 1924- CANR-135
Earlier sketches in CA 17-20R, CANR-8, 21, 35, 69
Interview in CANR-21
See also BEST 90:1
See also CLC 74
See also MTCW 1, 2
See also MTFW 2005
Fussner, F(rank) Smith 1920- CANR-5
Earlier sketch in CA 1-4R
Futabatei, Shimei 1864-1909 162
See also Futabatei Shimei
See also MJW
See also TCLC 44
Futabatei Shimei
See Futabatei, Shimei
See also DLB 180
See also EWL 3
Futcher, Jane P. 1947- 144
See also SATA 76
Futrell, Allan W. 1952- 123
Futrell, Gene Allen 1928- 107
Futrelle, Jacques 1875-1912 155
Brief entry 113
See also CMW 4
See also TCLC 19
Futterman, Enid (Susan) 1943- 169
Futuyma, Douglas Joel 1942- 108
Fuzuli
See Sulayman, Muhammad ibn
See also WLIT 6
Fye, W(allace) Bruce (III) 1946- 126
Fyfe, Christopher 223
Fyffe, Don(ald Lewis) 1925- 25-28R
Fyfield, Frances
See Hegarty, Frances
Fyleman, Rose (Amy) 1877-1957 205
Brief entry 111
See also CWRI 5
See also DLB 160
See also SATA 21
Fyler, John (Morgan) 1943- 89-92
Fyodorov, Yevgeny Konstantinovich
See Fedorov, Yevgeny Konstantinovich
Fysh, Wilmot Hudson 1895-1974 ..... 17-20R
Obituary 134
Fyson, J(enny) G(race) 1904- CAP-2
Earlier sketch in CA 21-22
See also CWRI 5
See also SATA 42
Fyvel, T. R.
See Feiwel, Raphael Joseph
Fyvel, Tosco Raphael
See Feiwel, Raphael Joseph

G

Gaa, Charles J(ohn) 1911-1991 ..... 17-20R
Gaan, Margaret 1914- 81-84
See also SATA 65
Gaar, Gillian G. 1959- 142
Gaard, David 1945- 25-28R
Gaard, Greta 1960- 140
Gaarder, Jostein 1952- CANR-139
Earlier sketch in CA 153
See also DLB 297
See also MTFW 2005
Gaastra, F(emme) S(imon) 1945- 132
Gaathon, A(ryeh) L(udwig) 1898-1985 49-52
GAB
See Russell, George William
Gabaldon, Diana 1952(?)- CANR-125
Earlier sketches in CA 149, CANR-72
Gabbard, Glen O(wens) 1949- CANR-137
Earlier sketches in CA 126, CANR-53
Gabbard, Krin 1948- 126
Gabbard, Lucina P(aquet) 1922- 110
Gabbett, Harry 1910(?)-1985
Obituary 116
Gabeira, Fernando (Nagle) 1943- 220
Gabel, (W.) Creighton 1931- 184
Brief entry 106
Gabel, Gernot Uwe 1941- CANR-123
Earlier sketch in CA 169
Gabel, Joseph 1912- 101
Gabel, Margaret 1938- 33-36R
Gabel, Medard 1946- CANR-11
Earlier sketch in CA 65-68
Gabel, Shainee 1969(?)- 171
Gaber, Susan 1956- 186
See also SATA 115
Gaberman, Judie Angell 1937- CANR-49
Earlier sketch in CA 77-80
See also AAYA 11
See also CLR 33
See also JRDA
See also SATA 22, 78
See also YAW
Gabhart, Ann 1947- 142
See also SATA 75
Gabin, Sanford B(yron) 1936- 114
Gable, Tom 1944- 93-96
Gablehouse, Charles 1928- 21-24R
Gabler, Hans Walter 1938- 173
Gabler, Mirko 1951- ..... SATA 77
Gabler, Neal 1950(?)- 153
Gabler-Hover, Janet A. 1953- CANR-109
Earlier sketch in CA 135
Gablik, Suzi 1934- 33-36R
Gabo, Naum 1890-1977 ..... CAP-2
Obituary 73-76
Earlier sketch in CA 33-36
Gabor, Andrea (Anna Gisela) 193
Gabor, Dennis 1900-1979 ..... CANR-76
Obituary 120
Earlier sketch in CA 17-20R
Gabor, Georgia M. 1930- 108
Gabor, Mark 1939- 81-84
Gabor, Thomas 1952- 149
Gabori, Susan 1947- 210
Gaboriau, Emile 1835-1873 ..... CMW 4
See also MSW
Gaboury, Antonio 1919- CANR-2
Earlier sketch in CA 45-48
Gabre-Medhin, Tsegaye (Kawessa) 1936- ... 101
See also BW 2
See also CD 5, 6
Gabre-Tsadick, Marta 1932- 115
Gabrial, Jan 1912- 201
Gabriel, A(strik) L. 1907- CANR-6
Earlier sketch in CA 5-8R
Gabriel, Adriana
See Rojany, Lisa
Gabriel, Gwendolyn D. 1966- 219
Gabriel, H(enry) 1922- 77-80
Gabriel, Joyce 1949- 97-100
Gabriel, Jueri (Evald) 1940- 93-96
Gabriel, Kathryn (Ann) 1955- 140
Gabriel, Mabel McAfee 1884(?)-1976
Obituary 65-68
Gabriel, Mari Cruz 1926- ..... CP 1
Gabriel, Marius 1954- 221
Gabriel, Michael P. 1962- 233
Gabriel, Philip L(ouis) 1918-1993 .... CANR-76
Obituary 141
Earlier sketch in CA 93-96
Gabriel, Ralph Henry 1890-1987 ..... CANR-76
Obituary 122
Earlier sketch in CA 13-16R
Gabriel, Richard A(lan) 1942- 147
Brief entry 104
Gabriel, Roman 1940-
Brief entry 107
Gabriel-Robinet, Louis 1909-1975
Obituary 61-64
Gabrielson, Frank 1911(?)-1980
Obituary 93-96
Gabrielson, Ira N(oel) 1889-1977 ..... CAP-1
Obituary 73-76
Earlier sketch in CA 9-10
Gabrielson, James B. 1917- 29-32R
Gabrys, Ingrid Schubert
See Schubert-Gabrys, Ingrid
Gach, Gary 1947- 77-80
Gach, Michael Reed 1952- CANR-128
Earlier sketches in CA 110, CANR-29
Gackenbach, Dick 1927- CANR-38
Earlier sketch in CA 115
See also MAICYA 1, 2
See also SATA 48, 79
See also SATA-Brief 30
Gackenbach, Jayne 1946- 193
Gadalla, Moustafa 1944- 178
Gadallah, Leslie 1939- ..... DLB 251
See also SFW 4
Gadamer, Hans-Georg 1900-2002 85-88
Obituary 206
See also DLB 296
Gadbow, Kate 221
Gadd, David 1912- 57-60
Gadd, Jeremy 1949- 188
See also SATA 116
Gadd, Maxine 1940- 116
Gadda, Carlo Emilio 1893-1973 89-92
See also CLC 11
See also DLB 177
See also EWL 3
See also TCLC 144
See also WLIT 7
Gaddes, Peter
See Sheldon, Peter
Gaddis, J. Wilson 1910(?)-1975
Obituary 57-60
Gaddis, John Lewis 1941- CANR-139
Earlier sketches in CA 45-48, CANR-30, 56
Gaddis, Peggy
See Dern, Erolie Pearl Gaddis
Gaddis, Sarah 1955(?)- 142
Gaddis, Thomas E(ugene)
1908-1984 ..... CANR-16
Obituary 114
Earlier sketch in CA 29-32R
Gaddis, Vincent H. 1913-1997 ..... 13-16R
See also SATA 35

Gaddis, William 1922-1998 .... CANR-48
Obituary 172
Earlier sketches in CA 17-20R, CANR-21
See also AMWS 4
See also BPFB 1
See also CLC 1, 3, 6, 8, 10, 19, 43, 86
See also CN 1, 2, 3, 4, 5, 6
See also DLB 2, 278
See also EWL 3
See also MAL 5
See also MTCW 1, 2
See also MTFW 2005
See also RGAL 4
Gaddy, C(urtis) Welton 1941- 61-64
Gaddy, David Winfred 1932- 129
Gade, Daniel W. 1936- 220
Gadgil, Gangadhar (Gopal) 1923- .... RGSF 2
Gadler, Steve J. 1905-1985 97-100
See also SATA 36
Gadney, Reg 1941- CANR-50
Earlier sketches in CA 49-52, CANR-3, 18
See also CMW 4
Gado, Frank 1936- CANR-31
Earlier sketch in CA 49-52
Gadol, Peter 1964- CANR-93
Earlier sketch in CA 134
Gadpaille, Warren J(oseph) 1924- 61-64
Gaebelein, Frank Ely 1899-1983 .... CANR-2
Earlier sketch in CA 13-16R
Gaeddert, Lou Ann (Bigge) 1931- CANR-29
Earlier sketches in CA 73-76, CANR-13
See also SATA 20, 103
Gaeddert, Louann
See Gaeddert, Lou Ann (Bigge)
Gaedeke, Ralph M(ortimer) 1941- CANR-24
Earlier sketches in CA 65-68, CANR-9
Gaelique, Moruen le
See Jacob, (Cyprien-)Max
Gaeng, Paul A. 1924- 37-40R
Gaenzl, Kurt (Friedrich) 1946- 134
Gaer, Joseph 1897-1969 .... CANR-76
Obituary 122
Earlier sketch in CA 9-12R
See also SATA 118
Gaer, Yossef
See Gaer, Joseph
Gaess, Roger 1943- 104
Gaetz, Dayle Campbell 1947- 208
See also SATA 138
Gaff, Jerry G(ene) 1936- 85-88
Gaffaney, Timothy J. 1966- 210
Gaffen, Fred 1944- 127
Gaffney, Edward McGlynn, Jr. 1941- 114
Gaffney, Elizabeth M(allory) 1966- 237
Gaffney, James 1931- CANR-6
Earlier sketch in CA 57-60
Gaffney, (Merrill) Mason 1923- CANR-3
Earlier sketch in CA 49-52
Gaffney, Patricia 215
Gaffney, Timothy R. 1951- 137
See also SATA 69
Gaffron, Norma (Bondeson) 1931- 163
See also SATA 97
Gag, Flavia 1907-1979 .... CANR-76
Obituary 104
Earlier sketch in CA 5-8R
See also SATA-Obit 24
Gag, Wanda (Hazel) 1893-1946 137
Brief entry 113
See also CLR 4
See also CWRI 5
See also DLB 22
See also MAICYA 1, 2
See also SATA 100
See also WCH
See also YABC 1
Gagan, Bernard 1915-1984
Obituary 112
Gagan, Jeannette M. 1936- 180
Gagarin, Ivan Sergeevich 1814-1882 .. DLB 198
Gagarin, Michael 1942- 89-92
Gagarin, Yuri A(lekseevich) 1934-1968 157
Obituary 112
Gage, Brian .... SATA 162
Gage, Diane 1954- 116
Gage, Edwin 1943- 85-88
Gage, Elizabeth
See Libertson, Joseph
Gage, Joy P. 1930- CANR-35
Earlier sketch in CA 114
Gage, Matilda Joslyn 1826-1898 .... FW
Gage, Nathaniel Lees 1917- 69-72
Gage, Nicholas
See Ngagoyeanes, Nicholas
Gage, S. R. 1945- 134
Gage, Stephen
See Michaud, Stephen G(age)
Gage, Walter
See Inge, William (Motter)
Gage, William 1915-1973 .... CAP-2
Earlier sketch in CA 25-28
Gage, William W(hitney) 1925- 13-16R
Gage, Wilson
See Steele, Mary Q(uintard Govan)
Gager, John Goodrich, Jr. 1937-
Brief entry 104
Gager, Nancy Land 1932(?)-1980
Obituary 93-96
Gagliani, William D. 233
Gagliano, Eugene M. 1946- 225
See also SATA 150
Gagliano, Frank 1931- CANR-1
Earlier sketch in CA 45-48
See also CAD
See also CD 5, 6
Gagliardo, John G(arver) 1933- 21-24R
Gagliardo, Ruth Garver 1895(?)-1980
Obituary 104
See also SATA-Obit 22
Gagne, Cole 1954- 112
Gagne, Robert M(ills) 1916- 121
Brief entry 116
Gagnier, Ed 1936- 65-68
Gagnier, Regenia (A.) 1953- CANR-118
Earlier sketches in CA 126, CANR-53
Gagnon, Cecile 1936- .... SATA 58
Gagnon, Jean-Louis 1913- 21-24R
Gagnon, John H(enry) 1931- CANR-128
Earlier sketch in CA 33-36R
Gagnon, Madeleine 1938- 160
See also DLB 60
Gagnon, Paul A(delard) 1925-2005
Obituary 238
Brief entry 104
Gahagan, Helen
See Douglas, Helen Gahagan
Gahagan, Jayne D. 1929(?)-1983
Obituary 110
Gaherty, Sherry 1951- 57-60
Gaidar, Yegor Timurovich 1956- 191
Gaiduk, Ilya V(alerievich) 1961- 154
Gail, Marzieh CANR-11
Earlier sketch in CA 69-72
Gail, Otto 1896-1956 160
See also SFW 4
Gailey, Harry A(lfred) 1926-2004 ..... CANR-16
Obituary 232
Earlier sketches in CA 45-48, CANR-1
Gailey, James H(erbert), Jr. 1916- 5-8R
Gaillard, Frye 1946- 144
Gailmor, William S. 1910(?)-1970
Obituary 104
Gaiman, Neil (Richard) 1960- CANR-129
Earlier sketches in CA 133, CANR-81
See also AAYA 19, 42
See also CLC 195
See also DLB 261
See also HGG
See also MTFW 2005
See also SATA 85, 146
See also SFW 4
See also SUFW 2
Gaine, Hugh 1726-1807 .... DLB 43
Gainer, Bernard 1944-
Brief entry 109
Gainer, Cindy 1962- .... SATA 74
Gaines, Ann-Janine Morey
See Morey, Ann-Janine
Gaines, Bill
See Gaines, William Maxwell
Gaines, Charles (Latham, Jr.) 1942- 119
Gaines, Diana 1912-2002 .... 1-4R
Obituary 205
Gaines, Donna 1951- CANR-134
Earlier sketch in CA 136
Gaines, Ernest J(ames) 1933- CANR-126
Earlier sketches in CA 9-12R, CANR-6, 24, 42, 75
See also AAYA 18
See also AFAW 1, 2
See also AITN 1
See also BLC 2
See also BPFB 2
See also BW 2, 3
See also BYA 6
See also CDALB 1968-1988
See also CLC 3, 11, 18, 86, 181
See also CLR 62
See also CN 1, 2, 3, 4, 5, 6, 7
See also CSW
See also DA3
See also DAM MULT
See also DLB 2, 33, 152
See also DLBY 1980
See also EWL 3
See also EXPN
See also LAIT 5
See also LATS 1:2
See also MAL 5
See also MTCW 1, 2
See also MTFW 2005
See also NFS 5, 7, 16
See also RGAL 4
See also RGSF 2
See also RHW
See also SATA 86
See also SSC 68
See also SSFS 5
See also YAW
Gaines, Jack
See Gaines, Jacob
Gaines, Jacob 1918- 101
Gaines, Jane (Marie) 1946- 199
Gaines, Patrice 162
Gaines, Pierce Welch 1905-1977 .... 13-16R
Gaines, Richard L. 1925- 49-52
Gaines, Thomas A. 1923- 139
Gaines, William Maxwell 1922-1992
Brief entry 108
Gainham, Sarah
See Ames, Rachel
Gains, Larry 1900-1983
Obituary 110
Gainsbrugh, Glen M. 1949- 25-28R
Gainsbrugh, Martin R(euben) 1907-1977
Obituary 69-72
Gainsburg, Joseph (Charles) 1894-1970 .... 5-8R
Gainza Paz, Alberto 1899-1977 77-80
Obituary 73-76
Gaiser, Gerhard 1908-1976 175
See also DLB 69
Gaita, Raimond 1946- 197
Gaitan Duran, Jorge 1924-1962 .... EWL 3
Gaitano, Nick
See Izzi, Eugene
Gaite, Carmen Martin 1925-2000 ...... DLB 322
Gaite, Francis
See Coles, Cyril Henry
Gaither, Carl C. 1944- CANR-123
Earlier sketch in CA 165
Gaither, Gant 1917-2004 .... 9-12R
Obituary 223
Gaither, Gloria 1942- 197
See also SATA 127
Gaither, Norman 1937- 112
Gaitskell, Charles D(udley) 1908- 29-32R
Gaitskell, H. T. N.
See Gaitskell, Hugh (Todd Naylor)
Gaitskell, Hugh (Todd Naylor) 1906-1963
Obituary 112
Gaitskill, Mary (Lawrence) 1954- CANR-61
Earlier sketch in CA 128
See also CLC 69
See also DLB 244
See also TCLE 1:1
Gaius Suetonius Tranquillus
See Suetonius
Gajdusek, Robert Elemer 1925- 102
Gajdusek, Robin
See Gajdusek, Robert Elemer
Gakwandi, Shatto Arthur 1943- 131
Gal, Allon 1934- CANR-1
Earlier sketch in CA 45-48
Gal, Hans 1890-1987 .... 5-8R
Gal, Istvan 1912-1982
Obituary 107
Gal, Laszlo 1933- 161
See also CLR 61
See also CWRI 5
See also MAICYA 2
See also MAICYAS 1
See also SATA 52, 96
See also SATA-Brief 32
Gala (y Velasco), Antonio (Angel Custodio) 1936- 211
See also CWW 2
Galai, Shmuel 1933- 107
Galambos, Louis (Paul) 1931- 81-84
Galamian, Ivan (Alexandrovitch) 1903-1981
Obituary 108
Galand, Rene 1923- CANR-49
Earlier sketches in CA 45-48, CANR-24
Galanes, Philip 1963- 231
Galang, M. Evelina 1961- 155
Galanoy, Terry 1927- CANR-4
Earlier sketch in CA 45-48
Galanskov, Yuri 1939(?)-1972
Obituary 37-40R
Galantay, Ervin Yvan 1930- 101
Galante, Jane Hohfeld 1924- CANR-90
Earlier sketch in CA 132
Galante, Pierre 1909-1998 .... 13-16R
Galanter, Eugene 1924- 1-4R
Galanter, Marc 1931- 122
Galantin, I(gnatius) J(oseph) 1910- 154
Galarza, Ernest
See Galarza, Ernesto
Galarza, Ernesto 1905-1984 .... CANR-84
Obituary 113
Earlier sketch in CA 131
See also DLB 122
See also HW 1
See also LAIT 3
Galassi, Jonathan (White) 1949- CANR-88
Earlier sketch in CA 101
Galati, Stephen A(lexander) Fischer
See Fischer-Galati, Stephen A(lexander)
Galatopoulos, Stelios (Emille) 1932- 232
Brief entry 110
Galay, Ted 1941- 122
Galbraith, Clare K(earney) 1919- 33-36R
Galbraith, Georgie Starbuck
1909-1980 .... CANR-76
Obituary 97-100
Earlier sketches in CAP-1, CA 9-10
Galbraith, James K. 1952- 130
Galbraith, Jean 1906- 37-40R
Galbraith, John Kenneth 1908- CANR-139
Earlier sketches in CA 21-24R, CANR-34, 68
Interview in CANR-34
See also Epernay, Mark and McLandress, Herschel
See also MTCW 1, 2
See also MTFW 2005
See also NCFS 3
Galbraith, John S. 1916-2003 .... CANR-6
Obituary 217
Earlier sketch in CA 5-8R
Galbraith, Kathryn O(sebold) 1945- 151
See also SATA 85
Galbraith, Madelyn 1897-1976 .... CAP-2
Earlier sketch in CA 33-36
Galbraith, Robert c. 1483-1544 .... DLB 281
Galbraith, Stuart IV 1965- CANR-122
Earlier sketch in CA 159
Galbraith, Vivian Hunter
1889-1976 .... CANR-29
Obituary 69-72
Earlier sketch in CA 73-76
Galbreath, Robert (Carroll) 1938- 41-44R
Galczynski, Konstanty Ildefons
1905-1953 .... EWL 3
Galdone, Paul 1907(?)-1986 .... CANR-76
Obituary 121
Earlier sketches in CA 73-76, CANR-13
See also CLR 16
See also MAICYA 1, 2
See also SATA 17, 66
See also SATA-Obit 49
Galdorisi, George V(ictor) 176
Galdos, Benito Perez
See Perez Galdos, Benito
See also EW 7
Gale, Barry 1935- 110
Gale, Bill
See Gale, William
Gale, Bob
See Gale, Michael Robert
Gale, Elliot N(yman) 1938-
Brief entry 110
Gale, Fredric G. 1933- 150
Gale, Herbert M(orrison) 1907-1992 ..... CAP-1
Earlier sketch in CA 13-16
Gale, John
See Gaze, Richard
Gale, Linda A(nn) 1939- 112
Gale, Michael Robert 1951- 133
Gale, Monica R(achel) 1966- 151
Gale, Patrick (Evelyn Hugh Sadler) 1962- .. 124
Gale, Raymond F(loyd) 1918- 25-28R
Gale, Richard M. 1932- 25-28R
Gale, Richard Nelson 1896-1982
Obituary 107
Gale, Robert L(ee) 1919- CANR-99
Earlier sketches in CA 9-12R, CANR-3, 18, 40
Gale, Vi 33-36R
See also CP 1, 2
Gale, William 1925- 97-100
Gale, William C.
See Giles, Carl H(oward)
Gale, William Daniel 1906- 107
Gale, Zona 1874-1938 .... CANR-84
Brief entry 105
Earlier sketch in CA 153
See also DAM DRAM
See also DFS 17
See also DLB 9, 78, 228
See also RGAL 4
See also TCLC 7
Galeano, Eduardo (Hughes) 1940- . CANR-100
Earlier sketches in CA 29-32R, CANR-13, 32
See also CLC 72
See also HLCS 1
See also HW 1
Galeen, Henrik 1882-1949 .... IDFW 3, 4
Galef, David 1959- 145
Galella, Ron 1931- CANR-14
Earlier sketch in CA 53-56
Interview in CANR-14
See also AITN 1
Galen of Pergamon c. 129-c. 210 ...... DLB 176
Galenson, Walter 1914-1999 .... CANR-51
Obituary 188
Earlier sketches in CA 25-28R, CANR-11, 27
Galeotti, Mark 1965- 151
Gales, Barbara J. 1940- CANR-14
Earlier sketch in CA 81-84
Gales, Winifred Marshall 1761-1839 .. DLB 200
Galewitz, Herb 1928- CANR-14
Earlier sketch in CA 41-44R
Galfo, Armand J. 1924- 17-20R
Galford, Ellen 1947- 163
See also GLL 2
Galgut, Damon 1963- 229
Galiano, Juan Valera y Alcala
See Valera y Alcala-Galiano, Juan
Galich, Alexander 1918(?)-1977
Obituary 73-76
See also DLB 317
Galilea, Segundo 1928- 105
Galindo, P.
See Hinojosa(-Smith), Rolando (R.)
Galindo, Sergio 1926-1993 190
Galinsky, Ellen 1942- CANR-127
Earlier sketches in CA 65-68, CANR-9
See also SATA 23
Galinsky, G(otthard) Karl 1942- 33-36R
Galison, Peter (Louis) 1955- 200
Galkin, Elliott W(ashington) 1921-1990
Obituary 131
Gall, Auguste Amedee de Saint
See Strich, Christian
Gall, Lothar 1936- 157
Gall, Louise von 1815-1855 .... DLB 133
Gall, Meredith D(amien) 1942- CANR-44
Earlier sketches in CA 53-56, CANR-6, 21
Gall, Morris 1907- 45-48
Gall, Sally M(oore) 1941- 110
Gall, Sandy 1927- CANR-87
Earlier sketch in CA 130
Gallacher, Tom 1934- .... CBD
See also CD 5, 6
Gallafent, Edward 228
Gallager, Gale
See Oursler, Will(iam Charles)
Gallagher, Buell Gordon
1904-1978 .... CANR-76
Obituary 133
Earlier sketch in CA 65-68
Gallagher, Carole 1950- 142
Gallagher, Charles A(ugustus) 1927- ... CANR-9
Earlier sketch in CA 61-64
Gallagher, David P. 1944- 45-48
Gallagher, Diana G. 1946- 228
See also SATA 153
Gallagher, Dorothy 1935- CANR-105
Earlier sketch in CA 65-68
Gallagher, Edward J. 1892(?)-1978
Obituary 81-84
Gallagher, Fred 1968- .... AAYA 67
Gallagher, Gary W(illiam) 1950- CANR-130
Earlier sketch in CA 136
Gallagher, Hugh (Gregory) 1932-2004 185
Obituary 230
Gallagher, Idella J(ane Smith) 1917-
Brief entry 108
Gallagher, J(ames) Roswell 1903-1995 57-60

Cumulative Index 207 **Gangloff**

Gallagher, James J(ohn) 1926- 114
Gallagher, Jock 1938- 129
Gallagher, John (Andrew) 1919-1980 133
Gallagher, John F(redrick) 1936- 17-20R
Gallagher, (John) Joseph 1929- 122
Gallagher, Kathleen 1965- 200
Gallagher, Kent G(rey) 1933- 33-36R
Gallagher, Louis J(oseph) 1885-1972
Obituary 37-40R
Gallagher, Lurlene Nora
See McDaniel, Lurlene
Gallagher, (Joseph) Mark 1953- 123
Gallagher, Marsha V. 1943- 117
Gallagher, Mary 1947- 97-100
Gallagher, Matthew P(hilip) 1919-1999 .... 5-8R
Obituary 186
Gallagher, Maureen 1938- 118
Gallagher, Neil 1941- 114
Gallagher, Nora 1949- 209
Gallagher, Patricia CANR-83
Earlier sketches in CA 65-68, CANR-11, 27
Gallagher, Patricia C. 1957- 138
See also RHW
Gallagher, Patrick (Francis) 1930- 45-48
Gallagher, Rachel 89-92
Gallagher, Richard
See Levinson, Leonard
Gallagher, Richard (Farrington)
1926- CANR-6
Earlier sketch in CA 1-4R
Gallagher, Robert E(mmett) 1922- 13-16R
Gallagher, Sister Mary Dominic 1917- .. 17-20R
Gallagher, Stephen 1954- 138
See also HGG
Gallagher, Susan VanZanten 1955- 137
Gallagher, Tag 236
Gallagher, Tess 1943- 106
See also CLC 18, 63
See also CP 7
See also CWP
See also DAM POET
See also DLB 120, 212, 244
See also PC 9
See also PFS 16
Gallagher, Thomas (Michael)
1918-1992 .... CANR-76
Obituary 140
Earlier sketches in CA 1-4R, CANR-5
Gallagher, Vera 1917- CANR-38
Earlier sketch in CA 115
Gallagher, (James) Wes(ley) 1911-1997 147
Obituary 162
See also DLB 127
Gallagher, William Davis 1808-1894 ... DLB 73
Gallagher, William M. 1923-1975
Obituary 89-92
Gallagher, Winifred 231
Gallaher, Art, Jr. 1925- CANR-3
Earlier sketch in CA 1-4R
Gallaher, Cynthia 1953- 198
Gallaher, John G(erard) 1928- 126
Brief entry 112
Gallaher, (William) Rhea, Jr. 1945- 136
Gallahue, David L(ee) 1943- CANR-57
Earlier sketches in CA 77-80, CANR-13, 30
Gallahue, John (Jeremiah) 1930- 186
Brief entry 110
Gallant, Christine C. 1940-
Brief entry 106
Gallant, Felicia
See Dano, Linda
Gallant, Jennie
See Smith, Joan Gerarda
Gallant, Mavis 1922- CANR-117
Earlier sketches in CA 69-72, CANR-29, 69
See also CCA 1
See also CLC 7, 18, 38, 172
See also CN 1, 2, 3, 4, 5, 6, 7
See also DAC
See also DAM MST
See also DLB 53
See also EWL 3
See also MTCW 1, 2
See also MTFW 2005
See also RGEL 2
See also RGSF 2
See also SSC 5, 78
Gallant, Roy A(rthur) 1924- CANR-117
Earlier sketches in CA 5-8R, CANR-4, 29, 54
See also CLC 17
See also CLR 30
See also MAICYA 1, 2
See also SATA 4, 68, 110
Gallant, Stephen I. 1946- 145
Gallant, T(homas) Grady 1920- 5-8R
Gallardo, Edward 131
See also HW 1
Gallardo, Evelyn 1948- 146
See also SATA 78
Gallas, John (Edward) 1950- 143
Gallas, Karen 1949- 149
Gallati, Mary Ernestine 5-8R
Gallati, Robert R. J. 1913-1996 .... CANR-1
Earlier sketch in CA 1-4R
Gallaz, Christophe 1948- 238
See also SATA 162
Galle, F(rederick) C(harles) 1919- 61-64
Galle, William 1938- 93-96
Gallegly, J(oseph) S(tephen) 1898-1982 ..... 5-8R
Gallego, Laura (Matilde) 1924- .... HW 1
Gallegos, Maria Magdalena 1935- ..... DLB 209
Gallegos (Freire), Romulo 1884-1969 131
See also EWL 3
See also HW 1
See also LAW
See also MTCW 1
See also WLIT 1
Gallen, John (J.) 1932- 186
Brief entry 113
Gallenberger, Joseph (M.) 1950- 218
Gallenkamp, Charles (Benton)
1930- CANR-111
Earlier sketch in CA 131
Galler, David 1929- 25-28R
See also CP 1
Galler, Meyer 1914- 89-92
Gallerite, The
See Bason, Frederick (Thomas)
Gallery, Dan
See Gallery, Daniel V.
Gallery, Daniel V. 1901-1977 .... 13-16R
Obituary 69-72
Gallhofer, Irmtraud N(ora) 1945- 175
Gallico, Paul (William) 1897-1976 ... CANR-23
Obituary 69-72
Earlier sketch in CA 5-8R
See also AITN 1
See also CLC 2
See also CN 1, 2
See also DLB 9, 171
See also FANT
See also MAICYA 1, 2
See also SATA 13
Gallie, Duncan (Ian Dunbar) 1946- 123
Gallie, Menna (Patricia Humphreys)
1920- CANR-1
Earlier sketch in CA 1-4R
Gallie, W(alter) B(ryce) 1912-1998 85-88
Obituary 169
Galligan, Edward L(awrence) 1926- 126
Galligan, Thomas C., Jr. 1955- 189
Gallimard, Gaston 1881-1975
Obituary 61-64
Gallimore, Ronald 1938- 65-68
Gallin, Sister Mary Alice 1921- 13-16R
Gallinger, Osma Couch
See Tod, Osma Gallinger
Gallison, Kate
See Gallison, Kathleen
Gallison, Kathleen 1939- CANR-129
Earlier sketch in CA 120
Gallistel, C(harles) R(ansom) 1941- 119
Gallix, Francois 1939- CANR-26
Earlier sketch in CA 109
Gallman, Waldemar J(ohn)
1899-1980 .... CANR-76
Obituary 101
Earlier sketches in CAP-1, CA 11-12
Gallmann, Kuki 145
Gallner, Sheldon M(ark) 1949- 53-56
Gallo, Donald R(obert) 1938- 184
Autobiographical Essay in 184
See also AAYA 39
See also SATA 112
See also SATA-Essay 104
Gallo, Gina 1954- 202
Gallo, Max Louis 1932- 85-88
See also CLC 95
Gallo, Patrick J. 1937- 139
Gallo, Robert C(harles) 1937- 143
Gallo, Rose Adrienne 1938- 185
Brief entry 107
Gallois, Claire 1938- CANR-18
Earlier sketch in CA 85-88
Gallois, Lucien
See Desnos, Robert
Gallon, Arthur J(ames) 1915-1992 57-60
Gallop, David 1928- 65-68
Gallop, Jane 1952- CANR-144
Earlier sketch in CA 107
See also DLB 246
Galloping Gourmet
See Kerr, Graham
Galloway, A(llan) D(ouglas) 1920- 25-28R
Galloway, David D(arryl) 1937- CANR-37
Earlier sketches in CA 21-24R, CANR-16
Galloway, George Barnes
1898-1967 .... CANR-77
Obituary 103
Earlier sketch in CA 1-4R
Galloway, Grace Growden
1727-1782 .... DLB 200
Galloway, Janice 1956- CANR-115
Earlier sketches in CA 137, CANR-67
See also CN 6, 7
See also DLB 319
Galloway, John C. 1915-1970 .... CAP-2
Earlier sketch in CA 25-28
Galloway, Jonathan F(uller) 1939- 77-80
Galloway, Joseph L(ee) 1941- CANR-12
Earlier sketch in CA 73-76
Galloway, Kara
See Cail, Carol
Galloway, Margaret C(ecilia) 1915- 13-16R
Galloway, Owateka (S.) 1981- 192
See also SATA 121
Galloway, Patricia Kay 1945- CANR-30
Earlier sketch in CA 112
Galloway, Priscilla 1930- CANR-132
Earlier sketch in CA 112
See also SATA 66, 112
Gallu, Samuel 85-88
See also AITN 2
Gallucci, Robert L(ovis) 1946- 61-64
Galluccio, Michael 1963(?)- 219
Gallun, Raymond Z(inke)
1911-1994 .... CANR-57
Earlier sketches in CA 65-68, CANR-9
See also SFW 4
Gallup, Dick 1941- .... CANR 110
Earlier sketch in CA 33-36R
Gallup, Donald (Clifford)
1913-2000 .... CANR-58
Obituary 189
Earlier sketches in CA 25-28R, CANR-11, 27
See also DLB 187
Gallup, George, Jr. 1930- 192
Gallup, George (Horace)
1901-1984 .... CANR-13
Earlier sketch in CA 13-16R
Gallup, Joan 1957- .... SATA 128
Gallup, Ralph
See Whitemore, Hugh (John)
Gallwey, W. Timothy 1938- CANR-4
Earlier sketch in CA 53-56
Gallwitz, Klaus 1930- 131
Brief entry 109
Galouchko, Annouchka Gravel 1960- 160
See also SATA 95
Galouye, Daniel Francis
1920-1976 .... CANR-76
Obituary 134
Earlier sketch in CA 9-12R
See also SFW 4
Galper, Harvey 1937- 119
Galster, George C(harles) 1948- 126
Galston, Arthur William 1920- 102
Galsworthy, John 1867-1933 .... CANR-75
Brief entry 104
Earlier sketch in CA 141
See also BRW 6
See also CDBLB 1890-1914
See also DA
See also DA3
See also DAB
See also DAC
See also DAM DRAM, MST, NOV
See also DLB 10, 34, 98, 162
See also DLBD 16
See also EWL 3
See also MTCW 2
See also RGEL 2
See also SSC 22
See also SSFS 3
See also TCLC 1, 45
See also TEA
See also WLC
Galt, Alfreda Sill 114
Galt, Anthony H(oward) 1944- 137
Galt, George 1948- 169
Galt, John 1779-1839 .... DLB 99, 116, 159
See also RGEL 2
See also RGSF 2
Galt, Serena
See Donald, Anabel
Galt, Thomas Franklin, Jr. 1908-1989 ...... 5-8R
See also SATA 5
Galt, Tom
See Galt, Thomas Franklin, Jr.
Galt, Walter
See Mundy, Talbot
Galton, Sir Francis 1822-1911 183
Brief entry 121
See also DLB 166
Galton, Lawrence 1913-1996 .... CANR-6
Earlier sketch in CA 57-60
Galub, Jack 1915- 85-88
Galus, Henry S(tanley) 1923- 5-8R
Galvez (Baluzera), Manuel 1882-1962 ... EWL 3
See also HW 1
See also LAW
Galvez de Montalvo, Luis
See Avalle-Arce, Juan Bautista de
Galvin, Brendan 1938- CANR-83
Earlier sketches in CA 45-48, CANR-1, 24, 49
See also CAAS 13
See also CP 7
See also DLB 5
Galvin, James 1951- CANR-26
Earlier sketch in CA 108
See also CLC 38
Galvin, John R(ogers) 1929- CANR-13
Earlier sketch in CA 21-24R
Galvin, Matthew R(eppert) 1950- 159
See also SATA 93
Galvin, Patrick Joseph 1927- CANR-18
Earlier sketch in CA 102
See also CP 1, 7
Galvin, Thomas J(ohn) 1932-2004 ... CANR-10
Obituary 224
Earlier sketch in CA 13-16R
Galway, James 1939- 189
Brief entry 105
Gam, Rita (Elenore) 1927- 45-48
Gamarra, Eduardo (A.) 1957- CANR-87
Earlier sketch in CA 131
See also HW 1
Gambaccini, Peter 1950- 105
Gambaro, Griselda 1928- 131
See also CWW 2
See also DLB 305
See also EWL 3
See also HW 1
See also LAW
Gamba-Stonehouse, Virginia (Silvia Isabel)
1954- 134
Gambetta, Diego 1952- 144
Gambill, Edward Lee 1936- 112
Gambino, Richard 1939(?)- 160
Gambino, Thomas D(ominic) 1942- 101
Gamble, Andrew (Michael) 1947- CANR-12
Earlier sketch in CA 69-72
Gamble, Ed 1943- CANR-86
Earlier sketch in CA 133
Gamble, Frederick (John) 1904- CAP-1
Earlier sketch in CA 9-10
Gamble, Kim 1952- .... SATA 81, 124
Gamble, Mary
See Murry, Mary Middleton
Gamble, Michael (Wesley) 1943- 110
Gamble, Sidney David 1890-1968 .... CAP-1
Earlier sketch in CA 11-12
Gamble, Teri (Susan) Kwal 1947- 110
Gamble, Terry 227
Gamboa, Federico 1864-1939 167
See also HW 2
See also LAW
See also TCLC 36
Gamboa (T., Jr.), Harry, Jr. 1951- 177
See also HW 1, 2
Gamboa, Reymundo 1948- 175
See also DLB 122
See also HW 2
Gambone, Philip 1948- 198
Gambrell, Herbert (Pickens) 1898-1982 .... 1-4R
Gambrell, Jamey CANR-130
Earlier sketch in CA 149
See also SATA 82
Gambrill, Eileen 1934- CANR-93
Earlier sketches in CA 89-92, CANR-15, 34
Gambs, John S(ake) 1899-1986 .... 13-16R
Obituary 171
Gamer, Robert E(manuel) 1938- 65-68
Gamerman, Martha 1941- 77-80
See also SATA 15
Games, Alexander 1963- 221
Gamez, Cielo Cayetana Alba de
See Alba de Gamez, Cielo Cayetana
Gamm, David B(ernard) 1948- 69-72
Gamm, Gerald 1964- 188
Gammage, Allen Z. 1917-1980 .... CANR-11
Earlier sketch in CA 5-8R
Gammage, Bill
See Gammage, William Leonard
Gammage, William Leonard 1942- .. CANR-10
Earlier sketch in CA 57-60
Gammel, Irene 1959- 211
Gammelgaard, Lene 1961- 190
Gammell, Stephen 1943- CANR-107
Earlier sketches in CA 135, CANR-55
See also CLR 83
See also MAICYA 1, 2
See also SATA 53, 81, 128
Gammell, Susanna Valentine Mitchell
1897(?)-1979
Obituary 85-88
Gammer, Moshe 1950- CANR-92
Earlier sketch in CA 146
Gammie, John G(lenn) 1929- 121
Gammon, Roland I. 1920-1981 49-52
Obituary 103
Gammon, Samuel Rhea (III) 1924-
Brief entry 112
Gammond, Peter 1925- CANR-31
Earlier sketches in CA 81-84, CANR-14
Gamoran, Mamie (Goldsmith)
1900-1984 .... CANR-3
Obituary 171
Earlier sketch in CA 5-8R
Gamow, George 1904-1968 102
Obituary 93-96
Gamsakhurdia, Konstantine 1891-1975 . EWL 3
Gamson, Joshua (Paul) 1962- CANR-100
Earlier sketch in CA 150
Gamson, William A. 1934- CANR-13
Earlier sketch in CA 33-36R
Gamst, Frederick C(harles) 1936- CANR-11
Earlier sketch in CA 29-32R
Gan, Elena Andreevna 1814-1842 ...... DLB 198
Gance, Abel 1889-1981
Obituary 108
Ganci, Dave 1937- 115
Gandalac, Lennard
See Berne, Eric (Lennard)
See also CCA 1
Gandee, Lee R(auss) 1917-1998 .... 33-36R
Gander, Forrest 1956- CANR-83
Earlier sketch in CA 145
See also CP 7
Gandevia, Bryan Harle 1925- CANR-45
Earlier sketches in CA 106, CANR-22
Gandhi, Indira (Priyadarshini Nehru)
1917-1984 128
Obituary 113
Gandhi, M. K.
See Gandhi, Mohandas Karamchand
Gandhi, Mahatma
See Gandhi, Mohandas Karamchand
Gandhi, Mohandas Karamchand
1869-1948 132
Brief entry 121
See also DA3
See also DAM MULT
See also MTCW 1, 2
See also TCLC 59
Gandlevsky, Sergei Markovich 1952- . DLB 285
Gandley, Kenneth Royce 1920- CANR-64
Earlier sketches in CA 69-72, CANR-12
See also CMW 4
Gandolfo, Joe M. 1936- 105
Gandossy, Robert P. 1951- 120
Gandt, Robert 234
Gandy, Matthew 1965- 214
Ganesan, Indira 169
Ganey, Terry 1948- 144
Gangel, Kenneth O(tto) 1935- CANR-39
Earlier sketches in CA 25-28R, CANR-17
Gangemi, Joseph 1970- 233
Gangemi, Kenneth 1937- CANR-67
Earlier sketch in CA 29-32R
See also CN 5, 6, 7
Gangewere, Robert J(ay) 1936- 89-92
Gangloff, Deborah 1952- 130

Gangopadyay, Surendranath
See Chatterje, Sarat Chandra
Ganguly, Sumit 1954- ... 177
Ganley, Albert Charles 1918- ... 13-16R
Ganley, Gladys Dickens 1929- ... CANR-41
Earlier sketch in CA 113
Ganley, Oswald Harold 1929- ... CANR-41
Earlier sketch in CA 112
Ganly, Helen (Mary) 1940- ... 125
See also SATA 56
Gann, Ernest Kellogg 1910-1991 ... CANR-83
Obituary ... 136
Earlier sketches in CA 1-4R, CANR-1
See also AITN 1
See also BPFB 2
See also CLC 23
See also RHW
Gann, L(ewis) H(enry) 1924-1997 ... CANR-31
Obituary ... 156
Earlier sketches in CA 5-8R, CANR-3
Gann, Walter ... TCWW 1, 2
Gannett, Frank E(rnest) 1876-1957
Brief entry ... 117
See also DLB 29
Gannett, Lewis Stiles 1891-1966
Obituary ... 89-92
Gannett, Ruth Chrisman (Arens)
1896-1979 ... SATA 33
Gannett, Ruth Stiles 1923- ... CANR-83
Earlier sketch in CA 21-24R
See also CWRI 5
See also SATA 3
Gannon, Frank 1952- ... CANR-53
Earlier sketch in CA 126
Gannon, Martin John 1934- ... 145
Gannon, Robert Haines 1931- ... CANR-4
Earlier sketch in CA 9-12R
See also SATA 8
Gannon, Robert I(gnatius) 1893-1978 ... CAP-1
Obituary ... 77-80
Earlier sketch in CA 13-16
Gannon, Steve 1944- ... 162
Gannon, Thomas M(ichael) 1936- ... CANR-26
Earlier sketch in CA 109
Gano, Lila 1949- ... 144
See also SATA 76
Ganong, Lawrence H. ... 222
Gans, Bruce Michael 1951- ... CANR-95
Earlier sketch in CA 81-84
Gans, Chaim 1948- ... 145
Gans, Eric L. 1941- ... 33-36R
Gans, Herbert J. 1927- ... CANR-141
Earlier sketches in CA 1-4R, CANR-6, 63
Gans, Roma 1894-1996 ... CANR-32
Obituary ... 154
Earlier sketch in CA 77-80
See also SATA 45
See also SATA-Obit 93
Gansberg, Judith M. 1947- ... 85-88
Ganshof, Francois-Louis 1895-1980 ... CAP-2
Earlier sketch in CA 19-20
Gansky, Alton 1953- ... 200
Gansler, Jacques Singleton 1934- ... 135
Gans-Ruedin, E(rwin) 1915- ... 65-68
Ganss, George Edward 1905-2000 ... CANR-31
Earlier sketch in CA 49-52
Gant, Chuck
See Galub, Jack
Gant, Jonathan
See Adams, Clifton
Gant, Matthew
See Hano, Arnold
Gant, Phyllis 1922- ... 57-60
Gant, Richard
See Freemantle, Brian (Harry)
Gantner, Neilma 1922- ... 104
Gantner, Susan (Verble) 1939- ... SATA 63
Gantos, Jack
See Gantos, John (Bryan), Jr.
See also AAYA 40
See also CLR 18, 85
Gantos, John (Bryan), Jr. 1951- ... CANR-97
Earlier sketches in CA 65-68, CANR-15, 56
See also Gantos, Jack
See also SATA 20, 81, 119
Gantry, Susan Nadler 1947- ... 61-64
Gantschev, Ivan 1925- ... 159
Gantt, Fred, Jr. 1922-1970(?) ... CANR-3
Earlier sketch in CA 9-12R
Gantt, William Andrew Horsley
1893-1980 ... 102
Obituary ... 97-100
Gantz, Charlotte Orr 1909- ... 49-52
Gantz, Joe
See Gantz, Joseph S.
Gantz, Joseph S. 1954- ... 168
Gantzer, Hugh 1931- ... 61-64
Ganz, Arthur (Frederick) 1928- ... CANR-46
Earlier sketch in CA 49-52
Ganz, David L(awrence) 1951- ... 105
Ganz, Lowell 1948- ... 154
Ganz, Margaret 1927- ... 45-48
Ganz, Yaffa 1938- ... 115
See also SATA 61
See also SATA-Brief 52
Ganzalass, Martin Richard 1941- ... 33-36R
Ganzel, Dewey Alvin, Jr. 1927- ... 25-28R
Ganzl, Kurt
See Gaenzl, Kurt (Friedrich)
Gao, Xiaosheng 1928- ... 168
See also Kao Hsiao-sheng
Gao, (Sonya) Xiongya 1955- ... 206
Gaos (Gonzalez-Pola), Vicente
1919-1980 ... DLB 134
Gao Xingjian 1940-
See Xingjian, Gao
See also CLC 167
See also MTFW 2005
Gapanov, Boris 1934(?)-1972
Obituary ... 37-40R
Gapper, Patience 1928- ... 139
Gar, The
See Garfinkel, Charles H.
Gara, Larry 1922- ... 53-56
Garab, Arra M. 1930- ... 81-84
Garafano, Marie 1942- ... SATA 84
Garafola, Lynn 1946- ... CANR-91
Earlier sketch in CA 135
Garagiola, Joe
See Garagiola, Joseph Henry
Garagiola, Joseph Henry 1926- ... 126
Garant, Andre J. 1968- ... 194
See also SATA 123
Garard, Ira D(ufresne) 1888-1980 ... 73-76
Obituary ... 176, 180
Garaudy, Roger 1913- ... 149
Garavaglia, Louis A(ubrey) 1940- ... 119
Garb, Howard N. 1955- ... 177
Garb, Solomon 1920-1982 ... CANR-9
Earlier sketch in CA 13-16R
Garb, Tamar 1956- ... 153
Garbarino, James 1947- ... 213
Garbarino, Joseph W. 1919- ... 53-56
Garbarino, Merwyn S(tephens) ... 77-80
Garbe, Ruth Moore
See Moore, Ruth (Ellen)
Garber, Anne (Theresa) 1946- ... 138
Garber, Emil 1901(?)-1985
Obituary ... 115
Garber, Eric 1943(?)- ... CANR-89
See also Holleran, Andrew
Garber, Eugene K. 1932- ... CANR-6
Earlier sketch in CA 57-60
Garber, Frederick 1929- ... 53-56
Garber, Joseph R(ene) 1943- ... CANR-89
Earlier sketch in CA 132
Garber, Lawrence (Arnold) 1937- ... 122
Garber, Lee O(rville) 1900-1986 ... 37-40R
Garber, Marjorie 1944- ... CANR-117
Earlier sketch in CA 170
See also GLL 2
Garber, Steven D(aniel) 1954- ... 128
Garber, Zev (Warren) 1941- ... CANR-127
Earlier sketch in CA 154
Garbett, Colin (Campbell) 1881-1972 ... CAP-1
Earlier sketch in CA 9-10
Garbini, Giovanni 1931- ... CANR-51
Earlier sketches in CA 21-24R, CANR-9, 25
Garbo, Norman 1919- ... CANR-9
Earlier sketch in CA 17-20R
Garborg, Arne 1851-1924 ... 209
Garbus, Cassandra 1966- ... 169
Garbus, Martin 1934- ... CANR-126
Earlier sketch in CA 133
Garbutt, Bernard 1900-1975
Brief entry ... 110
See also SATA-Brief 31
Garbutt, Janice (D.) Lovoos ... 124
Garceau, Dee 1955- ... CANR-130
Earlier sketch in CA 169
Garceau, Oliver 1911-1987 ... CAP-2
Earlier sketch in CA 29-32
Garchik, Leah (Lieberman) 1945- ... 133
Garchik, Morton (Lloyd) 1929- ... 119
Garcia, Alfredo 1952- ... 143
Garcia, Andrew 1854(?)-1943 ... DLB 209
Garcia, Ann O'Neal 1939- ... 108
Garcia, C(elso-) R(amon) 1921-2004 ... 118
Obituary ... 225
Garcia, Cristina 1958- ... CANR-130
Earlier sketches in CA 141, CANR-73
See also AMWS 11
See also CLC 76
See also CN 7
See also DLB 292
See also DNFS 1
See also EWL 3
See also HW 2
See also LLW
See also MTFW 2005
Garcia, Diana 1960- ... 204
Garcia, Eric 1972- ... 209
Garcia, F(laviano) Chris 1940- ... CANR-4
Earlier sketch in CA 53-56
Garcia, George Haddad
See Haddad-Garcia, George
Garcia, Guy D. 1955- ... 177
See also HW 2
Garcia, Ignacio M. 1950- ... 205
Garcia, Jerry 1942-1995 ... 211
Garcia, Lionel G. 1935- ... 131
See also DLB 82
See also HW 1
Garcia, Mario R(amon) 1947- ... 77-80
Garcia, Nasario 1936- ... 134
Garcia, Richard A(mado) 1941- ... 178
See also DLB 209
See also HW 1, 2
Garcia, Sam(uel), Jr. 1957- ... 179
See also HW 1
Garcia, Santiago 1928- ... DLB 305
Garcia, Yolanda P(acheco) 1952- ... 185
See also SATA 113
Garcia-Aguilera, Carolina 1949- ... CANR-138
Earlier sketch in CA 172
See also HW 2
Garcia Alvarez, Alejandro 1932- ... 214
Garcia-Camarillo, Cecilio 1943- ... DLB 209
Garcia Castaneda, Salvador 1932- ... 61-64
Garcia-Castanon, Santiago 1959- ... 199
Garcia-Johnson, Ronie 1968- ... 200
Garcia Lorca, Federico 1898-1936 ... CANR-81
Brief entry ... 104
Earlier sketch in CA 131
See also Lorca, Federico Garcia
See also AAYA 46
See also DA
See also DA3
See also DAB
See also DAC
See also DAM DRAM, MST, MULT, POET
See also DC 2
See also DFS 4, 10
See also DLB 108
See also EWL 3
See also HLC 2
See also HW 1, 2
See also LATS 1:2
See also MTCW 1, 2
See also MTFW 2005
See also PC 3
See also TCLC 1, 7, 49
See also TWA
See also WLC
Garcia Marquez, Gabriel (Jose)
1928- ... CANR-128
Earlier sketches in CA 33-36R, CANR-10, 28, 50, 75, 82
See also AAYA 3, 33
See also BEST 89:1, 90:4
See also BPFB 2
See also BYA 12, 16
See also CDWLB 3
See also CLC 2, 3, 8, 10, 15, 27, 47, 55, 68, 170
See also CPW
See also CWW 2
See also DA
See also DA3
See also DAB
See also DAC
See also DAM MST, MULT, NOV, POP
See also DLB 113
See also DNFS 1, 2
See also EWL 3
See also EXPN
See also EXPS
See also HLC 1
See also HW 1, 2
See also LAIT 2
See also LATS 1:2
See also LAW
See also LAWS 1
See also LMFS 2
See also MTCW 1, 2
See also MTFW 2005
See also NCFS 3
See also NFS 1, 5, 10
See also RGSF 2
See also RGWL 2, 3
See also SSC 8, 83
See also SSFS 1, 6, 16, 21
See also TWA
See also WLC
See also WLIT 1
Garcia-Marquez, Vicente 1953- ... 134
Garcia Marruz, Fina 1923- ... DLB 283
Garcia Morales, Adelaida 1946- ... 190
Garcia Ponce, Juan 1932-2003 ... 131
Obituary ... 223
See also HW 1
Garcia Rocha, Rina 1954- ... CANR-87
Earlier sketch in CA 153
See also HW 1
Garcia Sanchez, Javier 1955- ... CANR-144
Earlier sketch in CA 136
Garcia y Robertson, R(odrigo)
1949- ... CANR-117
Earlier sketch in CA 165
See also FANT
Garcilaso de la Vega 1499(?)-1536 ... DLB 318
Garcilaso de la Vega, El Inca
1539-1616 ... DLB 318
See also HLCS 1
See also LAW
Gard, Janice
See Latham, Jean Lee
Gard, Joyce
See Reeves, Joyce
Gard, Richard A(bbott) 1914- ... CANR-1
Earlier sketch in CA 1-4R
Gard, Robert Edward 1910-1992 ... CANR-83
Obituary ... 140
Earlier sketch in CA 85-88
See also SATA 18
See also SATA-Obit 74
Gard, Roger Martin du
See Martin du Gard, Roger
Gard, (Sanford) Wayne 1899-1986 ... CANR-43
Obituary ... 120
Earlier sketch in CA 1-4R
See also SATA-Obit 49
Gardam, Jane (Mary) 1928- ... CANR-106
Earlier sketches in CA 49-52, CANR-2, 18, 33, 54
See also CLC 43
See also CLR 12
See also DLB 14, 161, 231
See also MAICYA 1, 2
See also MTCW 1
See also SAAS 9
See also SATA 39, 76, 130
See also SATA-Brief 28
See also YAW
Gardaphe, Fred L(ouis) 1952- ... 136
Gardea, Jesus 1939- ... 172
See also HW 2
Gardell, Jonas 1963- ... DLB 257
Gardell, Mattias ... 225
Gardella, Robert (P.) 1943- ... 150
Gardella, Tricia 1944- ... 161
See also SATA 96
Garden, Alexander 1685(?)-1756 ... DLB 31
Garden, Bruce
See Mackay, James (Alexander)
Garden, Edward J(ames) C(larke)
1930- ... 25-28R
Garden, Graeme 1943- ... 107
Garden, John
See Fletcher, H(arry) L(utf) V(erne)
Garden, Nancy 1938- ... CANR-84
Earlier sketches in CA 33-36R, CANR-13, 30
See also AAYA 18, 55
See also BYA 7
See also CLR 51
See also JRDA
See also MAICYA 2
See also MAICYAS 1
See also SAAS 8
See also SATA 12, 77, 114, 147
See also SATA-Essay 147
See also WYAS 1
See also YAW
Garden, Robert Hal 1937- ... 69-72
Gardiner, C(linton) Harvey
1913-2000 ... CANR-16
Earlier sketches in CA 1-4R, CANR-1
Gardiner, Charles Wrey 1901-1981
Obituary ... 103
Gardiner, Dorothy 1894-1979
Obituary ... 93-96
See also TCWW 1, 2
Gardiner, George (Arthur) 1935-2002 ... 193
Obituary ... 210
Gardiner, Glenn Lion 1896-1962 ... 1-4R
Gardiner, Jeremy 1957- ... 145
Gardiner, John Reynolds 1944- ... 127
See also SATA 64
Gardiner, John Rolfe 1936- ... 223
See also DLB 244
Gardiner, Judith Kegan 1941- ... 138
Gardiner, Judy 1922- ... CANR-9
Earlier sketch in CA 21-24R
Gardiner, Lindsey 1971- ... SATA 144
Gardiner, Margaret Power Farmer
See Blessington, Marguerite
Gardiner, Mary Summerfield 1896-1982
Obituary ... 106
Gardiner, Muriel
See Buttinger, Muriel Gardiner
Gardiner, Patrick (Lancaster)
1922-1997 ... CANR-5
Obituary ... 158
Earlier sketch in CA 1-4R
Gardiner, Robert K. A. 1914- ... 21-24R
Gardiner, Robert W(orthington) 1932- ... 53-56
Gardiner, Stephen 1925- ... CANR-142
Earlier sketch in CA 97-100
Gardinier, David E(lmer) 1932- ... 112
Gardiol, Rita M(azzetti) ... 81-84
Gardner, Alan (Harold) 1925- ... 21-24R
Gardner, Angela Davis
See Davis-Gardner, Angela
Gardner, Anne
See Shultz, Gladys Denny
Gardner, Ava (Lavinia) 1922-1990 ... 139
Gardner, Beau ... SATA-Brief 50
Gardner, (Robert) Brian 1931- ... 13-16R
Gardner, Carl 1931- ... 107
Gardner, Craig Shaw 1949- ... 157
See also FANT
See also SATA 99
See also SFW 4
Gardner, D(avid) Bruce 1924- ... 49-52
Gardner, David P(ierpont) 1933- ... 21-24R
Gardner, Dic
See Gardner, Richard (M.)
Gardner, Donald Robert Hugh 1938- ... CP 1
Gardner, Dorothy E. M. 1900-1972 ... CAP-2
Earlier sketch in CA 23-24
Gardner, E(dward) Clinton 1920- ... 13-16R
Gardner, Eldon J(ohn) 1909-1989 ... 41-44R
Gardner, Erle Stanley 1889-1970 ... 5-8R
Obituary ... 25-28R
See also BPFB 2
See also CMW 4
See also MSW
See also MTCW 1, 2
See also RGAL 4
Gardner, Frank Matthias 1908-1980
Obituary ... 109
Gardner, G(erald) B(rosseau) 1884-1964
Obituary ... 112
Gardner, Gerald 1929- ... CANR-5
Earlier sketch in CA 1-4R
Gardner, Graham ... 236
See also SATA 159
Gardner, Helen (Louise) 1908-1986 ... 97-100
Gardner, Herb(ert George)
1934-2003 ... CANR-119
Obituary ... 220
Earlier sketch in CA 149
See also CAD
See also CD 5, 6
See also CLC 44
See also DFS 18, 20
Gardner, Howard 1943- ... CANR-89
Earlier sketches in CA 65-68, CANR-9, 48
Gardner, Hugh 1910-1986
Obituary ... 120
See also SATA-Obit 49
Gardner, Hy 1908-1989 ... 101
Obituary ... 128

Cumulative Index 209 Garrett

Gardner, Isabella 1915-1981 97-100
Obituary 104
See also CP 1, 2
See also MAL 5
Gardner, Jack Irving 1934- 102
Gardner, Jane Mylum 1946- 150
See also SATA 83
Gardner, Jani 1943- 25-28R
Gardner, Jeanne LeMonnier 1925- 17-20R
See also SATA 5
Gardner, Jeffrey
See Fox, G(ardner) F(rancis)
Gardner, Jeremy
See Gardner, Jerome
Gardner, Jerome 1932- .... TCWW 2
Gardner, John (Champlin), Jr.
1933-1982 .... CANR-73
Obituary 107
Earlier sketches in CA 65-68, CANR-33
See also AAYA 45
See also AITN 1
See also AMWS 6
See also BPFB 2
See also CDALBS
See also CLC 2, 3, 5, 7, 8, 10, 18, 28, 34
See also CN 2, 3
See also CPW
See also DA3
See also DAM NOV, POP
See also DLB 2
See also DLBY 1982
See also EWL 3
See also FANT
See also LATS 1:2
See also MAL 5
See also MTCW 1, 2
See also MTFW 2005
See also NFS 3
See also RGAL 4
See also RGSF 2
See also SATA 40
See also SATA-Obit 31
See also SSC 7
See also SSFS 8
Gardner, John (Edmund) 1926- CANR-127
Earlier sketches in CA 103, CANR-15, 69
See also CLC 30
See also CMW 4
See also CPW
See also DAM POP
See also MTCW 1
Gardner, John E(dward) 1917- 17-20R
Gardner, John W(illiam) 1912-2002 ... CANR-4
Obituary 206
Earlier sketch in CA 1-4R
Gardner, Joseph L(awrence) 1933- ... CANR-30
Earlier sketch in CA 29-32R
Gardner, Lawrence
See Brannon, William T.
Gardner, Leonard 1934- 226
Brief entry 111
Gardner, Lewis 1943- 65-68
Gardner, Lloyd C(alvin) 1934- CANR-3
Earlier sketch in CA 9-12R
Gardner, (Alice) Lucille 1913-1989 69-72
Gardner, Marilyn 101
Gardner, Mark L(ee) 1960- 149
Gardner, Martin 1914- CANR-121
Earlier sketches in CA 73-76, CANR-46, 84
See also SATA 16, 142
Gardner, Mary 1936- 124
Gardner, Mary A(delaide) 1920-2004 .... 21-24R
Obituary 222
Gardner, Michael R. 1942- 226
Gardner, Miriam
See Bradley, Marion Zimmer
See also GLL 1
Gardner, Nancy Bruff 1915- CANR-70
Earlier sketch in CA 13-16R
Gardner, Noel
See Kuttner, Henry
Gardner, Paul 69-72
Gardner, R(ufus) H(allette III)
1918-1995 .... 33-36R
Gardner, Ralph D(avid) 1923-2005 .... CANR-6
Obituary 237
Earlier sketch in CA 13-16R
Gardner, Richard (M.) 1931- CANR-10
Earlier sketch in CA 21-24R
See also SATA 24
Gardner, Richard A(lan) 1931-2003 . CANR-56
Obituary 217
Earlier sketches in CA 33-36R, CANR-34
See also SATA 13
See also SATA-Obit 144
Gardner, Richard Kent 1928- CANR-27
Earlier sketch in CA 69-72
Gardner, Richard N(ewton) 1927- 89-92
Gardner, Riley W(etherell) 1921- 13-16R
Gardner, Robert 1911- 61-64
Gardner, Robert 1929- 147
See also SATA-Brief 43
Gardner, Robert W(ayne) 1940- 144
Gardner, Sandra 1940- 138
See also SATA 70
Gardner, Scot 1968- 215
See also SATA 143
Gardner, Sheldon 1934- 104
See also SATA 33
Gardner, Stanley (?)-1996 179
Gardner, Ted
See Gardner, Theodore Roosevelt II
Gardner, Theodore Roosevelt II
1934- CANR-98
Earlier sketch in CA 150
See also SATA 81
Gardner, Thomas 1952- 222
Gardner, Tim A. 1959- 220
Gardner, Tom 1968- 169
Gardner, Virginia (Marberry)
1904-1992 .... CANR-83
Obituary 136
Earlier sketch in CA 112
See also Adams, Barbara
Gardner, Wanda Kirby 1914-2000 73-76
Gardner, Wayland Downing 1928- 73-76
Gardner, William Earl 1928- CANR-18
Earlier sketches in CA 5-8R, CANR-3
Gardner, William Henry 1902-1969 ...... CAP-1
Earlier sketch in CA 13-16
Gardner, Wynelle B. 1918- 65-68
Gardner-Smith, Percival 1888-1985 ...... CAP-2
Obituary 116
Earlier sketch in CA 17-18
Gardon, Anne 1948- 201
Gardons, S. S.
See Snodgrass, W(illiam) D(e Witt)
Garduk, Harry David 1910(?)-1985
Obituary 116
Gare, Fran
See Mandell, Fran Gare
Gareau, Etienne 1915-1988 .... CANR-54
Earlier sketch in CA 45-48
Gareau, Frederick H(enry) 1923- 5-8R
Garebian, Keith 1943- CANR-119
Earlier sketch in CA 129
Gareffa, Peter M(ichael) 1952- CANR-43
Earlier sketch in CA 118
Garelick, May 1910-1989 73-76
Obituary 130
See also SATA 19
Garelli, Jacques .... CWW 2
Garetz, Mark 1953- 112
Garfield, Brian (Francis Wynne)
1939- CANR-63
Earlier sketches in CA 1-4R, CANR-6
See also Ward, Jonas
See also CMW 4
See also TCWW 1, 2
Garfield, Eugene 1925- 114
Garfield, Evelyn Picon 1940- CANR-25
Earlier sketches in CA 57-60, CANR-9
Garfield, James B. 1881-1984
Obituary 112
See also SATA 6
See also SATA-Obit 38
Garfield, Leon 1921-1996 .... CANR-78
Obituary 152
Earlier sketches in CA 17-20R, CANR-38, 41
See also AAYA 8
See also BYA 1, 3
See also CLC 12
See also CLR 21
See also DLB 161
See also JRDA
See also MAICYA 1, 2
See also MAICYAS 1
See also SATA 1, 32, 76
See also SATA-Obit 90
See also TEA
See also WYA
See also YAW
Garfield, Patricia L(ee) 1934- CANR-111
Earlier sketch in CA 85-88
Garfield, Simon 1960- 209
Garfield, Sol L(ouis) 1918- CANR-12
Earlier sketch in CA 29-32R
Garfield, Sydney 1916(?)-1988
Obituary 124
Garfinkel, Alan 1941- CANR-21
Earlier sketch in CA 105
Garfinkel, Bernard Max 1929- CANR-17
Earlier sketch in CA 25-28R
Garfinkel, Charles H. 1939- 112
Garfinkel, Charlie
See Garfinkel, Charles H.
Garfinkel, Herbert 1920- 1-4R
Garfinkel, Perry 1948- 121
Garfinkle, Adam M. 1951- CANR-58
Earlier sketch in CA 112
Garfinkle, Louis (Alan) 1928- 185
Brief entry 112
Garfinkle, Richard 222
Garfitt, Roger 1944- CANR-13
Earlier sketch in CA 33-36R
See also CP 7
Garforth, Francis William 1917- 9-12R
Garfunkel, Louis X. 1897(?)-1972
Obituary 37-40R
Garfunkel, Trudy 1944- 154
See also MTFW 2005
Garg, Anu 1967- 223
Gargan, Edward A. 1950- 211
Gargan, Edward T(homas) 1922-1995
Brief entry 111
Gargan, William (Michael) 1950- 111
Gargan, William Dennis 1905-1979
Obituary 106
Garibaldi, Gerald 1951- 108
Gariepy, Henry 1930- CANR-2
Earlier sketch in CA 49-52
Garioch, Robert Sutherland 1909-1981 103
See also CP 1, 2
Garis, Howard R(oger) 1873-1962 ... CANR-27
Earlier sketch in CA 73-76
See also DLB 22
See also SATA 13
Garis, Robert (Erwin) 1925-2001 .... 17-20R
Obituary 192
Garitano, Rita 1939- 118
Garlan, Patricia Wallace 1926- 120
Garland, Alex 1970- 167
See also CN 7
Garland, Ardella
See Joe, Yolanda
Garland, Bennett
See Garfield, Brian (Francis Wynne)
Garland, Charles T(albot) 1910(?)-1976
Obituary 69-72
Garland, George
See Roark, Garland
See also TCWW 1, 2
Garland, (Hannibal) Hamlin 1860-1940
Brief entry 104
See also DLB 12, 71, 78, 186
See also MAL 5
See also RGAL 4
See also RGSF 2
See also SSC 18
See also TCLC 3
See also TCWW 1, 2
Garland, Hazel (Barbara) 1913-1988
Obituary 125
Garland, Madge 1900(?)-1990 .... 25-28R
Obituary 132
Garland, Mark (A.) 1953- 147
See also SATA 79
Garland, Mary 1922- 89-92
Garland, Max 1950- 150
Garland, Michael 1952- 213
Garland, Phyl(lis T.) 1935- 69-72
Garland, Robert (Sandford John) 1947- 120
Garland, Sarah 1944- .... SATA 62, 135
Garland, Sherry 1948- CANR-126
Earlier sketch in CA 186
See also SATA 73, 114, 145
See also SATA-Essay 145
Garlick, Peter C(yril) 1923- 41-44R
Garlick, Raymond 1926- CANR-4
Earlier sketch in CA 53-56
See also CP 1, 2, 3, 4, 5, 6, 7
Garlington, Phil 1943- 81-84
Garlington, Warren K(ing) 1923- 9-12R
Garlinski, Jozef 1914- 108
Garlock, Dorothy CANR-105
Earlier sketch in CA 160
Garmaise, Freda 1928- 134
Garmendia, Joseba Irazu 1951- CANR-120
Earlier sketch in CA 164
Garment, Grace R. 1927(?)-1976
Obituary 104
Garment, Leonard CANR-100
Earlier sketch in CA 158
Garment, Suzanne 1946- 142
Garmes, Lee 1898-1978 .... IDFW 3, 4
Garmey, Jane 1942- 114
Garmon, William S. 1926- 21-24R
Garms, Walter I(rving, Jr.) 1925- 120
Garn, Edwin Jacob 1932- 107
Garn, Jake
See Garn, Edwin Jacob
Garneau, Francois-Xavier 1809-1866 ... DLB 99
Garneau, Michel 1939- 165
See also DLB 53
Garneau, (Hector de) Saint-Denys 1912-1943
Brief entry 111
See also DLB 88
See also TCLC 13
Garner, Abigail 230
Garner, Alan 1934- 178
Earlier sketches in CA 73-76, CANR-15, 64, 134
Autobiographical Essay in 178
See also AAYA 18
See also BYA 3, 5
See also CLC 17
See also CLR 20
See also CPW
See also DAB
See also DAM POP
See also DLB 161, 261
See also FANT
See also MAICYA 1, 2
See also MTCW 1, 2
See also MTFW 2005
See also SATA 18, 69
See also SATA-Essay 108
See also SUFW 1, 2
See also YAW
Garner, Alan (Francis) 1950- CANR-89
Earlier sketch in CA 132
Garner, Claud (Wilton) 1891-1978 .... 9-12R
Obituary 169, 180
Garner, David 1958- .... SATA 78
Garner, Dwight L. 1913-1999 .... 25-28R
Garner, Eleanor Ramrath 1930- 194
See also SATA 122
Garner, Graham
See Rowland, D(onald) S(ydney)
Garner, H(essle) F(ilmore) 1926- 73-76
Garner, Harry Hyman 1910-1973 .... 17-20R
Obituary 134
Garner, Helen 1942- CANR-71
Brief entry 124
Earlier sketch in CA 127
See also CN 4, 5, 6, 7
See also GLL 2
See also RGSF 2
Garner, Hugh 1913-1979 .... CANR-31
Earlier sketch in CA 69-72
See also Warwick, Jarvis
See also CCA 1
See also CLC 13
See also CN 1, 2
See also DLB 68
Garner, James Finn 1960(?)- CANR-135
Earlier sketch in CA 153
See also SATA 92
Garner, Joe 228
Garner, John S. 1945- 146
Garner, Joseph John Saville 1908-1983
Obituary 111
Garner, (Samuel) Paul 1910-1996 .... 37-40R
Garner, Roberta 1943- 85-88
Garner, Rolf
See Berry, Bryan
Garner, (Lafayette) Ross 1914- 33-36R
Garner, Sharon K. 228
Garner, Wendell R(ichard) 1921- CANR-11
Earlier sketch in CA 5-8R
Garner, William 1920- CANR-12
Earlier sketch in CA 29-32R
Garner, William R(obin) 1936- 21-24R
Garnet, A. H.
See Slote, Alfred
Garnet, Eldon 1946- CANR-9
Earlier sketch in CA 61-64
Garnett, A(rthur) Campbell
1894-1970 .... CANR-2
Earlier sketch in CA 1-4R
Garnett, Angelica 1918- 136
Garnett, Bill
See Garnett, William John
Garnett, Christopher Browne 1906-1975
Obituary 61-64
Garnett, Cliff
See Zlotchew, Clark M.
Garnett, David 1892-1981 .... CANR-79
Obituary 103
Earlier sketches in CA 5-8R, CANR-17
See also CLC 3
See also CN 1, 2
See also DLB 34
See also FANT
See also MTCW 2
See also RGEL 2
See also SFW 4
See also SUFW 1
Garnett, Eve C. R. 1900-1991 .... CANR-85
Obituary 134
Earlier sketches in CA 1-4R, CANR-2
See also DLB 160
See also SATA 3
See also SATA-Obit 70
See also YAW
Garnett, Gale Zoe 200
Garnett, Henrietta (Catherine Vanessa)
1945- 125
Garnett, Isobel
See Waddington, Patrick (Haynes)
Garnett, Lynne 1942- 138
Garnett, Mark 1963- 230
Garnett, Richard 1835-1906 .... DLB 184
See also FANT
See also SUFW
Garnett, Richard (Duncan Carey)
1923- CANR-84
Earlier sketch in CA 5-8R
Garnett, Roger
See Morland, Nigel
Garnett, Tay 1894(?)-1977
Obituary 73-76
Garnett, William John 1941- 102
Garnham, Nicholas 1937- 33-36R
Garnham, Trevor 1947- 162
Garnier, Robert c. 1545-1590 .. GFL Beginnings to 1789
Garofalo, Janeane 1964- 184
Garofalo, Reebee
See Garofalo, Robert L.
Garofalo, Robert L. 1944- 77-80
Garoogian, Andrew 1928-
Brief entry 113
Garoogian, Rhoda 1933- CANR-19
Earlier sketch in CA 102
Garos, Stephanie
See Katz, Steve and
Krentz, Jayne Ann
Garou, Louis P.
See Bowkett, Stephen
Garoyan, Leon 1925- CANR-5
Earlier sketch in CA 1-4R
Garr, Doug(las) 190
Garrad, Larch S(ylvia) 1936- 61-64
Garrard, Gene
See Garrard, Jeanne Sue
Garrard, J. G.
See Garrard, John (Gordon)
Garrard, Jeanne Sue 81-84
Garrard, John (Gordon) 1934- 151
Brief entry 114
Garrard, Lancelot Austin
1904-1993 .... CANR-46
Obituary 140
Earlier sketches in CAP-1, CA 9-10
Garrard, Lewis H. 1829-1887 .... DLB 186
Garrard, Mary D(ubose) 1937- 125
Garrard, Timothy F(rancis) 1943- 131
Garratt, James E. 1954- 211
Garraty, John A(rthur) 1920- CANR-36
Earlier sketches in CA 1-4R, CANR-2
See also DLB 17
See also SATA 23
Garreau, Joel 1948- 101
Garren, Christine (Elizabeth) 1957- 207
Garren, Devorah-Leah
See Devorah-Leah
Garret, Maxwell R. 1917- 106
See also SATA 39
Garretson, Lucy Reed 1936- 97-100
Garretson, Robert L. 1920- 17-20R
Garretson, Victoria Diane 1945- 108
See also SATA 44
Garrett, Albert Charles 1915-1983
Obituary 109
Garrett, Alfred B. 1906-1996 .... 5-8R
Garrett, Almeida 1799-1854 .... DLB 287

Garrett, Charles 1925-1977
Obituary ... 73-76
Garrett, Charles C.
See James, Laurence and Wells, Angus
Garrett, Clarke 1935- ... 73-76
Garrett, Eileen J(eanette) 1893-1970 ... CAP-2
Earlier sketch in CA 25-28
Garrett, Elizabeth 1963- ... CWP
Garrett, Franklin M(iller) 1906-2000 ... 57-60
Garrett, Garet 1878-1954
Brief entry ... 122
Garrett, George (Palmer, Jr.) 1929- ... 202
Earlier sketches in CA 1-4R, CANR-1, 42, 67, 109
Autobiographical Essay in ... 202
See also CAAS 5
See also AMWS 7
See also BPFB 2
See also CLC 3, 11, 51
See also CN 1, 2, 3, 4, 5, 6, 7
See also CP 1, 2, 3, 4, 5, 6, 7
See also CSW
See also DLB 2, 5, 130, 152
See also DLBY 1983
See also SSC 30
Garrett, Gerald R. 1940- ... CANR-53
Earlier sketches in CA 73-76, CANR-12, 28
Garrett, Gerard 1928- ... 73-76
Garrett, Greg ... 210
Garrett, Helen 1895- ... SATA 21
Garrett, Howard 1931- ... 61-64
Garrett, James Leo, Jr. 1925- ... CANR-103
Earlier sketches in CA 33-36R, CANR-13, 92
Garrett, (Ruth) Jane 1914- ... 105
Garrett, Jennifer 1960- ... 122
Garrett, John (Allen) 1920- ... CANR-16
Earlier sketch in CA 33-36R
Garrett, John Work 1872-1942 ... DLB 187
Garrett, Laurie 1951- ... CANR-98
Earlier sketch in CA 148
Garrett, Leonard J(oseph) 1926- ... 17-20R
Garrett, Leslie 1931- ... 17-20R
Garrett, Leslie 1964- ... 239
Garrett, Lillian ... 29-32R
Garrett, Martin ... 235
Garrett, Peter K. 1940- ... 25-28R
Garrett, (Gordon) Randall (Phillip) 1927-1987 ... CANR-85
Earlier sketch in CA 130
See also BPFB 2
See also FANT
See also SFW 4
Garrett, Richard 1920- ... CANR-37
Earlier sketches in CA 81-84, CANR-16
See also SATA 82
Garrett, Romeo Benjamin 1910-2000 ... 37-40R
Garrett, Stephen A(rmour) 1939- ... 111
Garrett, Susan 1931- ... 146
Garrett, Thomas M(ichael) 1924- ... CANR-5
Earlier sketch in CA 1-4R
Garrett, Thomas S(amuel) 1913-1980 ... CANR-3
Earlier sketch in CA 1-4R
Garrett, Tom
See Garrett, Thomas S(amuel)
Garrett, Truman
See Judd, Margaret Haddican
Garrett, Wendell D(ouglas) 1929- ... 9-12R
Garrett, William 1890-1967 ... CAP-1
Earlier sketch in CA 11-12
Garrettson, Charles Lloyd (III) 1953- ... 144
Garrick, David 1717-1779 ... DAM DRAM
See also DLB 84, 213
See also RGEL 2
Garrigan, Owen (Walter) 1928- ... 21-24R
Garrigue, Jean 1914-1972 ... CANR-20
Obituary ... 37-40R
Earlier sketch in CA 5-8R
See also CLC 2, 8
See also CP 1
See also MAL 5
Garrigue, Sheila 1931- ... 69-72
See also SATA 21
Garrigus, Charles B(yford) 1914-2000 ... 136
Obituary ... 191
Garris, Mick ... CANR-105
Earlier sketch in CA 165
Garrison, Barbara 1931- ... SATA 19, 163
Garrison, Bruce 1950- ... 141
Garrison, Cal 1948- ... 210
Garrison, Christian (Bascom) 1942- ... 65-68
Garrison, Daniel H. 1937- ... 136
Garrison, David Lee 1945- ... 200
Garrison, Deborah (Gottlieb) 1965- ... 169
Garrison, Dee 1934- ... 125
Garrison, Ervan G. 1943- ... 172
Garrison, Frederick
See Sinclair, Upton (Beall)
Garrison, J. Ritchie 1951- ... 137
Garrison, James (Dale) 1943- ... 61-64
Garrison, Jim (C.) 1921-1992 ... 132
Obituary ... 139
Brief entry ... 111
Garrison, Joan
See Neubauer, William Arthur
Garrison, Karl C(laudius) 1900-1980 ... CANR-31
Earlier sketch in CA 37-40R
Garrison, Mary 1952- ... 220
See also SATA 146
Garrison, Omar V. 1913-1997 ... 33-36R
Garrison, Paul 1918-1997 ... CANR-48
Earlier sketch in CA 122
Garrison, Phil
See Brandner, Gary (Phil)
Garrison, R. Benjamin 1926- ... CANR-5
Earlier sketch in CA 13-16R
Garrison, Webb B(lack) 1919-2000 ... CANR-122
Earlier sketches in CA 1-4R, CANR-2, 18
See also SATA 25
Garrison, William Lloyd 1805-1879 ... CDALB 1640-1865
See also DLB 1, 43, 235
Garrison, Winfred Ernest 1874-1969 ... CANR-6
Earlier sketch in CA 1-4R
Garrity
See Gerrity, David James
Garrity, Dave
See Gerrity, David James
Garrity, Devin Adair 1905-1981 ... 107
Obituary ... 103
Garrity, Jennifer Johnson 1961- ... SATA 124
Garrity, Joan Terry 1940- ... 69-72
See also AITN 1
Garrity, Linda K. 1947- ... 198
See also SATA 128
Garrity, Richard (George) 1903-1992 ... 77-80
Garrity, Terry
See Garrity, Joan Terry
Garro, Elena 1920(?)-1998 ... 131
Obituary ... 169
See also CWW 2
See also DLB 145
See also EWL 3
See also HLCS 1
See also HW 1
See also LAWS 1
See also TCLC 153
See also WLIT 1
Garrod, Rene J(eannette) 1954- ... CANR-49
Earlier sketch in CA 120
Garrow, David J(effries) 1953- ... 93-96
Garroway, Dave
See Garroway, David Cunningham
Garroway, David Cunningham 1913-1982
Obituary ... 107
Garry, Charles R. 1909-1991 ... 73-76
Garshin, Vsevolod Mikhailovich 1855-1888 ... DLB 277
Garside, Charles, Jr. 1927-1987
Obituary ... 122
Garside, (Clifford) Jack 1924- ... 127
Garside, Roger R(amsay) 1938- ... 107
Garskof, Michele Hoffnung
See Hoffnung, Michele
Garson, Barbara ... CANR-110
Earlier sketch in CA 33-36R
Garson, Clee
See Fairman, Paul W.
Garson, G(eorge) David 1943- ... CANR-4
Earlier sketch in CA 53-56
Garson, Helen Sylvia 1925- ... 107
Garson, Noel George 1931- ... 29-32R
Garson, Paul 1946- ... CANR-143
Earlier sketch in CA 49-52
Garst, Doris Shannon 1894-1981 ... 1-4R
Obituary ... 180
See also BYA 1
See also SATA 1
Garst, John Fredric 1932- ... 45-48
Garst, Robert E(dward) 1900-1980 ... 108
Obituary ... 97-100
Garst, Shannon
See Garst, Doris Shannon
Garstang, Jack
See Garstang, James Gordon
Garstang, James Gordon 1927- ... 13-16R
Garstein, Oskar Bernhard 1924- ... 13-16R
Gart, Murray Joseph 1924-2004 ... 103
Obituary ... 225
Garten, Helen A. 1953- ... 201
Garten, Hugh F(rederick) 1904-1975 ... CANR-3
Earlier sketch in CA 5-8R
Garten, Jeffrey E. 1946- ... CANR-142
Earlier sketch in CA 166
Gartenberg, Egon 1911-1982 ... 57-60
Obituary ... 180
Gartenberg, Leo 1906-1990 ... 9-12R
Obituary ... 171, 180
Garth, Samuel 1661-1719 ... DLB 95
See also RGEL 2
Garth, Will
See Hamilton, Edmond and Kuttner, Henry
Garthoff, Raymond L(eonard) 1929- ... 5-8R
Garthwaite, Malaby
See Dent, Anthony Austen
Garthwaite, Marion H(ook) 1893-1981 ... 5-8R
See also SATA 7
Gartland, Robert Aldrich 1927- ... 17-20R
Gartman, Louise 1920- ... 17-20R
Gartner, Alan 1935- ... CANR-86
Earlier sketches in CA 33-36R, CANR-15, 34
Gartner, Carol B(licker) 1935- ... 114
Gartner, Chloe (Maria) 1916- ... CANR-20
Earlier sketches in CA 1-4R, CANR-5
Gartner, Lloyd P. 1927- ... CANR-2
Earlier sketch in CA 1-4R
Gartner, Michael G(ay) 1938- ... 77-80
Gartner, Scott Sigmund 1963- ... 169
Garton, Charles 1926- ... CANR-45
Earlier sketches in CA 45-48, CANR-21
Garton, Janet 1944- ... CANR-36
Earlier sketch in CA 114
Garton, Jean Staker 1929- ... 114
Garton, Malinda D(ean) (?)-1976 ... 1-4R
Obituary ... 103
See also SATA-Obit 26
Garton, Nancy Wells 1908- ... 5-8R
Garton, Nina R. 1905-1987 ... CAP-2
Earlier sketch in CA 21-22
Garton, Ray 1962- ... 185
See also HGG
See also SUFW 2
Garton Ash, Timothy 1955- ... 166
Garton Ash, Timothy 1955- ... 166
Garve, Andrew
See Winterton, Paul
See also DLB 87
Garver, Newton 1928- ... 142
Garver, Richard B(ennett) 1934- ... 33-36R
Garverick, Linda M. 1959- ... 152
Garvey, Amy Jacques 1896(?)-1973
Obituary ... 45-48
Garvey, Edward B. 1914-1999 ... 41-44R
Obituary ... 185
Garvey, Gerald (Thomas) 1935-2000
Brief entry ... 112
Garvey, John 1944- ... CANR-14
Earlier sketch in CA 65-68
Garvey, John H. 1948- ... 168
Garvey, Marcus (Moziah, Jr.) 1887-1940 ... CANR-79
Brief entry ... 120
Earlier sketch in CA 124
See also BLC 2
See also BW 1
See also DAM MULT
See also HR 1:2
See also TCLC 41
Garvey, Mark 1959- ... 147
Garvey, Mona C. 1934- ... CANR-34
Earlier sketch in CA 29-32R
Garvey, Robert 1908-1983 ... CANR-78
Obituary ... 109
Earlier sketch in CA 107
Garvey, Steve(n Patrick) 1948- ... 133
Garvey, Terence Willcocks 1915- ... 103
Garvice, Charles 1833-1920 ... RHW
Garvie, A(lexander) F(emister) 1934- ... 73-76
Garvin, Charles D. 1929- ... CANR-6
Earlier sketch in CA 57-60
Garvin, Glenn 1954- ... 136
Garvin, (Hilda) Katharine 1904- ... 5-8R
Garvin, Lawrence 1945- ... 53-56
Garvin, Paul L(ucian) 1919-1994 ... CANR-5
Earlier sketch in CA 13-16R
Garvin, Philip 1947- ... 73-76
Garvin, Richard M(cClellan) 1934-1980 ... 49-52
Obituary ... 180
Garvin, Thomas Christopher 1943- ... 113
Garvin, Tom
See Garvin, Thomas Christopher
Garvin, William 1922-1998 ... 25-28R
Garwood, Darrell (Nelson) 1909-1988 ... 29-32R
Garwood, Judith 1941- ... CANR-92
Earlier sketch in CA 144
Garwood, Julie 1946- ... CANR-96
Earlier sketch in CA 138
Gary, Dorothy
See Page, Myra
Gary, Dorothy Page
See Page, Myra
Gary, Romain
See Kacew, Romain
See also CLC 25
See also DLB 83, 299
Garza, Roberto J(esus) 1934- ... 104
See also HW 1
Garza, Rodolfo O(ropea) de la
See de la Garza, Rodolfo O(ropea)
Garzilli, Enrico 1937- ... 41-44R
Gasaway, Laura N. 1945- ... 169
Gasca, Philip D. Ortego
See Ortego y Gasca, Philip D.
Gascar, Pierre
See Fournier, Pierre
See also CLC 11
See also EWL 3
Gasche, Rodolphe 1938- ... 135
Gaschnitz, Michael K. ... 168
Gasco, Elyse 1971(?)- ... 194
Gascoigne, Bamber 1935- ... CANR-28
Earlier sketches in CA 25-28R, CANR-10
See also SATA 62
Gascoigne, George 1539-1577 ... DLB 136
See also RGEL 2
Gascoigne, John 1951- ... CANR-82
Earlier sketch in CA 133
Gascoigne, Marguerite
See Lazarus, Marguerite
Gascon, The
See Miller, F(rederick) W(alter) G(ascoyne)
Gascoyne, David (Emery) 1916-2001 ... CANR-54
Obituary ... 200
Earlier sketches in CA 65-68, CANR-10, 28
See also CLC 45
See also CP 1, 2, 3, 4, 5, 6, 7
See also DLB 20
See also MTCW 1
See also RGEL 2
Gash, Joe
See Granger, Bill
Gash, Jonathan
See Grant, John
See also DLB 276
Gash, Norman 1912- ... CANR-1
Earlier sketch in CA 1-4R
Gaskell, Elizabeth Cleghorn 1810-1865 ... BRW 5
See also CDBLB 1832-1890
See also DAB
See also DAM MST
See also DLB 21, 144, 159
See also RGEL 2
See also RGSF 2
See also SSC 25
See also TEA
Gaskell, Ivan 1955- ... 143
Gaskell, Jane 1941- ... CANR-58
Earlier sketches in CA 5-8R, CANR-11
See also DLB 261
See also FANT
Gaskell, (John) Philip (Wellesley) 1926-2001 ... CANR-3
Obituary ... 199
Earlier sketch in CA 5-8R
Gaskell, Thomas F. 1916- ... 17-20R
Gaskill, Harold V. 1905-1975
Obituary ... 57-60
Gaskin, Catherine 1929- ... CANR-83
Earlier sketches in CA 65-68, CANR-10
See also RHW
Gaskin, David Edward 1939- ... 69-72
Gaskin, Ina May 1940- ... 129
Gaskin, J(ohn) C(harles) A(ddison) 1936- ... CANR-141
Earlier sketches in CA 131, CANR-73
Gaskin, Stephen (F.) 1935- ... 129
Gaskins, Pearl Fuyo 1957- ... 197
See also SATA 134
Gaskins, Richard H. 1946- ... 145
Gasnick, Roy M(ichael) 1933- ... 117
Gaspar, Frank X. ... 190
Gaspar de Alba, Alicia
See De Alba, Alicia Gaspar
See also LLW
Gasparini, Graziano 1926- ... 41-44R
Gasparotti, Elizabeth Seifert 1897-1983 ... CANR-68
Obituary ... 110
Earlier sketches in CA 1-4R, CANR-2
See also RHW
Gasper, Louis 1911- ... 13-16R
Gasperetti, David 1952- ... 181
Gasperini, Jim 1952- ... 122
See also SATA 54
See also SATA-Brief 49
Gaspey, Thomas 1788-1871 ... DLB 116
Gasque, W(oodrow) Ward 1939- ... CANR-15
Earlier sketch in CA 65-68
Gass, Thomas Edward ... 234
Gass, William H(oward) 1924- ... CANR-100
Earlier sketches in CA 17-20R, CANR-30, 71
See also AMWS 6
See also CLC 1, 2, 8, 11, 15, 39, 132
See also CN 1, 2, 3, 4, 5, 6, 7
See also DLB 2, 227
See also EWL 3
See also MAL 5
See also MTCW 1, 2
See also MTFW 2005
See also RGAL 4
See also SSC 12
Gassan, Arnold 1930- ... 73-76
Gassegg, Mumle
See Borgen, Johan
Gassendi, Pierre 1592-1655 ... GFL Beginnings to 1789
Gassenheimer, Linda 1942- ... 137
Gassert, Robert G(eorge) 1921-1993 ... 17-20R
Gasset, Jose Ortega y
See Ortega y Gasset, Jose
Gassier, Pierre 1915- ... CANR-34
Earlier sketch in CA 49-52
Gassner, John Waldhorn 1903-1967 ... CANR-3
Obituary ... 25-28R
Earlier sketch in CA 1-4R
Gassner, Julius S(tephen) 1915- ... 37-40R
Gast, Kelly P.
See Edmondson, G(arry) C(otton)
Gaster, T(heodor) Herzl 1906-1992 ... CANR-78
Obituary ... 136
Earlier sketch in CA 73-76
Gastil, John (Webster) 1967- ... 147
Gastil, Raymond D(uncan) 1931- ... 29-32R
Gastmann, Albert (Lodewijk) 1921- ... 97-100
Gaston, Bill 1953- ... 197
Gaston, Edwin W(illmer), Jr. 1925- ... CANR-2
Earlier sketch in CA 1-4R
Gaston, Georg M(eri-) A(kri) 1938- ... 109
Gaston, Jerry (Collins) 1940- ... CANR-1
Earlier sketch in CA 45-48
Gaston, Patricia S. 1946- ... 144
Gaston, Wilber
See Gibson, Walter B(rown)
Gat, Azar 1959- ... 143
Gat, Dimitri V(sevolod) 1936- ... CANR-31
Earlier sketch in CA 29-32R
Gatch, Jean 1924-1991 ... 127
Gatch, Milton McC(ormick, Jr.) 1932- ... CANR-27
Earlier sketch in CA 29-32R
Gatell, Frank Otto 1931- ... 9-12R
Gatenby, Greg 1950- ... CANR-102
Earlier sketch in CA 97-100
See also CP 7
Gatenby, Rosemary 1918- ... CANR-9
Earlier sketch in CA 21-24R
Gater, Dilys 1944- ... 112
See also SATA 41
Gater, Hubert 1913(?)-1980
Obituary ... 101
Gates, Albert
See Glotzer, Albert

Cumulative Index 211 **Gebler**

Gates, Arthur Irving 1890-1972
Obituary ... 37-40R
Gates, Barbara T. 1936- ... 201
Gates, Bea
See Gates, Beatrix
Gates, Beatrix ... 210
Gates, Bill
See Gates, William Henry III
Gates, David 1947(?)- ... CANR-88
Earlier sketch in CA 140
Gates, David Murray 1921- ... 81-84
Gates, Doris 1901-1987 ... CANR-46
Obituary ... 124
Earlier sketches in CA 1-4R, CANR-1
See also DLB 22
See also MAICYA 1, 2
See also SAAS 1
See also SATA 1, 34
See also SATA-Obit 54
Gates, Frieda 1933- ... 93-96
See also SATA 26
Gates, Henry Louis, Jr. 1950- ... CANR-125
Earlier sketches in CA 109, CANR-25, 53, 75
See also BLCS
See also BW 2, 3
See also CLC 65
See also CSW
See also DA3
See also DAM MULT
See also DLB 67
See also EWL 3
See also MAL 5
See also MTCW 2
See also MTFW 2005
See also RGAL 4
Gates, Hill ... 221
Gates, J(eannette) M(cPherson) 1924- . CANR-7
Earlier sketch in CA 57-60
Gates, Jean Key 1911- ... 33-36R
Gates, John A(lexander) 1898-1979 ... 5-8R
Gates, John D. 1939- ... 89-92
Gates, John Floyd 1915- ... 1-4R
Gates, Lewis E. 1860-1924 ... 176
See also DLB 71
Gates, Lillian Francis 1901-1990 ... CAP-2
Earlier sketch in CA 25-28
Gates, Marilyn 1944- ... 145
Gates, Natalie ... 21-24R
Gates, Norman T(immins) 1914- ... 77-80
Gates, Paul W(allace) 1901-1999 ... CANR-2
Earlier sketch in CA 1-4R
Gates, Philomene (A.) 1918- ... 134
Gates, Robbins L(adew) 1922- ... 13-16R
Gates, Ronda 1940- ... 161
Gates, Susan 1950- ... 228
See also SATA 153
Gates, Viola R. 1931- ... 168
See also SATA 101
Gates, William Byram 1917-1975
Obituary ... 61-64
Gates, William Henry III 1955- ... 154
Gateward, Frances 1963- ... 206
Gatewood, Robert (Payne) 1974- ... 213
Gatewood, Willard B., Jr. 1931- ... 17-20R
Gathercole, Adrienne Lois
See Kaeppler, Adrienne Lois
Gatheridge, R. Edward
See Wilson, Robert (Edward)
Gathorne-Hardy, Jonathan G. 1933- . CANR-95
Earlier sketches in CA 104, CANR-39
See also SATA 26, 124
Gati, Charles 1934- ... 146
Gatley, Jimmy 1931(?)-1985
Obituary ... 115
Gatley, Richard Harry 1936- ... 101
Gatlin, Douglas S. 1928- ... 21-24R
Gatlin, Lila L(ee) 1928- ... 101
Gatner, Elliott S(herman) M(ozian)
1914- ... CANR-3
Earlier sketch in CA 9-12R
Gato, J. A.
See Keller, John E(sten)
Gattegno, Caleb 1911-1988
Obituary ... 126
Gattey, Charles Neilson 1921- ... CANR-20
Earlier sketches in CA 13-16R, CANR-5
Gatti, Anne 1952- ... 170
See also SATA 103
Gatti, Armand
See Gatti, Daute
See also CWW 2
Gatti, Arthur Gerard 1942- ... 65-68
Gatti, Daniel Jon 1946- ... 45-48
Gatti, Daute 1924-
See Gatti, Armand
Gatti, Enzo
See Gatti, Vincenzo
Gatti, Richard DeY 1947- ... 45-48
Gatti, Vincenzo 1942- ... CANR-8
Earlier sketch in CA 61-64
Gattmann, Eric 1925- ... 49-52
Gatto, Alfonso 1909-1976 ... 176
See also DLB 114
See also EWL 3
Gatto, Katherine (Gyekenyesi) 1945- ... 189
Gatty, Juliana Horatia
See Ewing, Juliana (Horatia Gatty)
Gatty, Margaret Scott
1809-1873 ... SATA-Brief 27
Gatty, Ronald 1929- ... 85-88
Gatzke, Hans W(ilhelm) 1915-1987 . CANR-78
Obituary ... 123
Earlier sketches in CA 1-4R, CANR-5
Gau, Colleen ... 232
Gaubatz, Kathlyn Taylor 1957- ... 154
Gaubatz, Kurt Taylor 1957- ... 201
Gauch, Patricia Lee 1934- ... CANR-9
Earlier sketch in CA 57-60
See also CLR 56
See also CWRI 5
See also MAICYA 2
See also MAICYAS 1
See also SAAS 21
See also SATA 26, 80
Gauch, Sigfrid 1945- ... 222
Gauchat, Dorothy 1921- ... 97-100
Gauchet, Marcel ... 183
Gaudet, Frederick J(oseph) 1902-1977 ... 5-8R
Obituary ... 73-76
Gaudio, Tony 1885-1951 ... IDFW 3, 4
Gaudiose, Dorothy M(arie) 1920- ... 89-92
Gauer, Harold 1914- ... 13-16R
Gaugh, Harry F. ... 116
Gaugin, Paul 1848-1903 ... AAYA 52
Gaul, Randy 1959- ... SATA 63
Gauld, Alan (Ogilvie) 1932- ... 144
Gauld, Charles A(nderson) 1911-1977 .. 13-16R
Gauld, Joseph W(arren) 1927- ... 144
Gaulden, Albert Clayton 1938- ... 160
Gaulden, Ray 1914-(?) ... CANR-64
Earlier sketches in CA 17-20R, CANR-8
See also TCWW 1, 2
Gauldie, Enid 1928- ... CANR-14
Earlier sketch in CA 77-80
Gauldie, (William) Sinclair 1918- ... 33-36R
Gaulle, Charles (Andre Joseph Marie) de
See de Gaulle, Charles (Andre Joseph Marie)
Gault, Clare 1925- ... 97-100
See also SATA 36
Gault, Frank 1926-1982 ... CANR-11
Earlier sketch in CA 69-72
See also SATA 36
See also SATA-Brief 30
Gault, Henri (Andre Paul Victor)
1929-2000 ... 130
Obituary ... 188
Gault, Mark
See Cournos, John
Gault, Peter 1958- ... 138
Gault, William Campbell
1910-1995 ... CANR-84
Earlier sketches in CA 49-52, CANR-1, 16, 37
See also CMW 4
See also DLB 226
See also SATA 8
Gaumnitz, Jack E(rwin) 1935- ... 120
Gaumnitz, Walter Herbert 1891-1979
Obituary ... 89-92
Gaumont, Leon 1864-1946 ... IDFW 3, 4
Gaunt, Graham
See Grant, John
Gaunt, Kenneth
See Spillman, Ken
Gaunt, Leonard 1921- ... CANR-3
Earlier sketch in CA 5-8R
Gaunt, Mary 1861-1942 ... 184
See also DLB 174, 230
Gaunt, Michael
See Robertshaw, (James) Denis
Gaunt, Peter
See Eshbach, Lloyd Arthur
Gaunt, William 1900-1980 ... CANR-6
Obituary ... 97-100
Earlier sketch in CA 9-12R
Gauquelin, Michel (Roland) 1928- ... CANR-31
Earlier sketch in CA 57-60
Gaur, Albertine 1932- ... CANR-47
Earlier sketch in CA 121
Gaus, Gerald F. 1952- ... 112
Gaus, Paul L(ouis) 1949- ... 185
Gause, Damon J. 1915(?)-1944 ... 211
Gaustad, Edwin Scott 1923- ... CANR-1
Earlier sketch in CA 1-4R
Gauthier, Gail 1953- ... 184
See also SATA 118, 160
Gautier, Theophile 1811-1872 ... DAM POET
See also DLB 119
See also EW 6
See also GFL 1789 to the Present
See also PC 18
See also RGWL 2, 3
See also SSC 20
See also SUFW
See also TWA
Gautreaux, Tim 1947- ... 187
See also CSW
See also DLB 292
Gauvreau, Claude 1925-1971 ... 148
See also DLB 88
Gavaskar, Sunil 1949- ... 131
Gavell, Mary Ladd 1919-1967 ... 204
Gaver, Becky
See Gaver, Rebecca
Gaver, Jack 1906-1974 ... 97-100
Obituary ... 53-56
Gaver, Jessyca (Russell) 1915-1996 ... CANR-9
Earlier sketch in CA 53-56
Gaver, Mary Virginia 1906-1991 ... CANR-34
Obituary ... 136
Earlier sketch in CA 1-4R
Gaver, Rebecca 1952- ... SATA 20
Gaverick, Linda M. 1959- ... 152
Gavett, J(oseph) William 1921- ... 25-28R
Gavett, Thomas W(illiam) 1932- ... 13-16R
Gavin
See Frost, Gavin
Gavin, Amanda
See Gibson-Jarvie, Clodagh
Gavin, Bill
See Gavin, William S.
Gavin, Catherine (Irvine)
1907-1999 ... CANR-85
Earlier sketches in CA 1-4R, CANR-1
See also RHW
Gavin, Claire (E.) 1944- ... 150
Gavin, Eileen A. 1931- ... 45-48
Gavin, James M(aurice) 1907-1990 .. CANR-78
Obituary ... 131
Earlier sketches in CAP-1, CA 13-16
Gavin, Jamila 1941- ... CANR-110
Earlier sketches in CA 110, CANR-68
See also BYA 15
See also MAICYA 2
See also SATA 96, 125
Gavin, Lettie 1922- ... 166
Gavin, Thomas 1941- ... 85-88
Gavin, Thomas F. 1910-1983 ... 108
Gavin, William
See Houston, Douglas (Norman)
Gavin, William S. 1907(?)-1985
Obituary ... 114
Gavin-Brown, Wilfred A(rthur) 1904- ... CAP-1
Earlier sketch in CA 9-10
Gavron, Daniel 1935- ... CANR-99
Earlier sketches in CA 29-32R, CANR-12
Gavron, Susan J. 1947- ... 152
Gavronsky, Serge 1932- ... CANR-108
Earlier sketches in CA 65-68, CANR-9
See also CP 1
Gavshon, Arthur L(eslie) 1916- ... 5-8R
Gaw, Walter A. 1904- ... 1-4R
Gawain, Shakti 1948- ... 93-96
Gawaine, John
See Hamilton-Hill, Donald
Gawain Poet, The 14th cent. - ... BRWS 7
See also RGEL 2
Gawande, Atul A. 1965- ... 210
Gawron, Jean Mark 1953- ... 103
Gawsworth, John
See Armstrong, Terence Ian Fytton
See also CP 1
See also DLB 255
Gawthrop, Louis C. 1930- ... 81-84
Gaxotte, Pierre 1895-1982 ... 111
Obituary ... 108
Gay, A. Nolder
See Koelsch, William Alvin
Gay, Amelia
See Hogarth, Grace (Weston Allen)
Gay, Carlo T(eofilo) E(berhard)
1913-1998 ... CANR-51
Earlier sketches in CA 49-52, CANR-27
Gay, Ebenezer 1696-1787 ... DLB 24
Gay, Francis
See Gee, H(erbert) L(eslie)
Gay, John 1685-1732 ... BRW 3
See also DAM DRAM
See also DLB 84, 95
See also RGEL 2
See also WLIT 3
Gay, John E(dward) 1942- ... 81-84
Gay, John H. 1928- ... 143
See also BW 2
Gay, Kathlyn 1930- ... CANR-124
Earlier sketches in CA 21-24R, CANR-8, 25, 50
See also SATA 9, 144
Gay, Marie-Louise 1952- ... CANR-105
Earlier sketch in CA 135
See also CLR 27
See also CWRI 5
See also MAICYA 2
See also MAICYAS 1
See also SAAS 21
See also SATA 68, 126
Gay, Michel 1947- ... SATA 162
Gay, Oliver
See Gogarty, Oliver St. John
Gay, Peter (Jack) 1923- ... CANR-77
Earlier sketches in CA 13-16R, CANR-18, 41
Interview in ... CANR-18
See also CLC 158
Gay, Ruth 1922- ... CANR-142
Earlier sketch in CA 139
Gay, Volney P(atrick) 1948- ... CANR-40
Earlier sketch in CA 117
Gay, William 1943(?)- ... 209
See also CN 7
Gay, Zhenya 1906-1978 ... 73-76
See also SATA 19
Gaya-Nuno, Juan Antonio
1913-1975 ... CANR-31
Earlier sketch in CA 81-84
Gayarre, Charles E. A. 1805-1895 ... DLB 30
Gay-Crosier, Raymond 1937- ... CANR-15
Earlier sketch in CA 41-44R
Gaydos, Michael J. 1940- ... 53-56
Gaye, Carol
See Shann, Renee
Gaye, Marvin (Pentz, Jr.) 1939-1984 ... 195
Obituary ... 112
See also CLC 26
Gay-Kelly, Doreen 1952- ... 61-64
Gayle, Addison, Jr. 1932-1991 ... CANR-78
Obituary ... 135
Earlier sketches in CA 25-28R, CANR-13
See also BW 1
Gayle, Emma
See Fairburn, Eleanor
Gayle, Marilyn
See Hoff, Marilyn
Gayle, Mike 1970- ... 238
Gayle, Stephen H. 1948(?)-1982
Obituary ... 107
Gayles, Anne Richardson 1923- ... 53-56
Gaylin, Willard (M.) 1925- ... CANR-97
Earlier sketches in CA 21-24R, CANR-13, 44
Gaylord, Billy
See Gaylord, William (Gilbert)
Gaylord, Edward King 1873-1974 ... 175
Obituary ... 89-92
See also DLB 127
Gaylord, Edward Lewis 1919-2003 ... 182
Obituary ... 215
See also DLB 127
Gaylord, Sherwood Boyd 1914-2000
Brief entry ... 105
Gaylord, William (Gilbert) 1945-1985 ... 69-72
Obituary ... 118
Gayn, Mark J. 1909-1981
Obituary ... 105
Gaynor, Gloria 1949(?)- ... 168
Gaynor, Harry J. 1921-2003 ... 134
Obituary ... 213
Gayre, G(eorge) R(obert) 1907-1996 .. CANR-4
Earlier sketch in CA 5-8R
Gayre of Gayre, R.
See Gayre, G(eorge) R(obert)
Gayre of Gayre and
Nigg, Robert
Nigg
See Gayre, G(eorge) R(obert)
Gazaway, Rena 1910-1985 ... CAP-2
Earlier sketch in CA 29-32
Gazda, George M(ichael) 1931- ... CANR-29
Earlier sketches in CA 61-64, CANR-13
Gazdanov, Gaito 1903-1971
Obituary ... 104
See also DLB 317
Gazdanov, Georgii
See Gazdanov, Gaito
Gazdar, Mushtaq 1937- ... 190
Gaze, Gillian
See Barklem, Jill
Gaze, Richard 1917- ... 1-4R
Gazell, James A(lbert) 1942- ... 49-52
Gazetas, Aristides 1930- ... 193
Gazi, Stephen 1914-1978 ... 45-48
Obituary ... 103
Gazis, Denos C(onstantinos) 1930- ... 57-60
Gazley, John G(erow) 1895-1991 ... 61-64
Gazzaniga, Michael S(aunders) 1939- ... 121
Gdanski, Marek
See Thee, Marek
Geach, Christine 1930- ... CANR-10
Earlier sketch in CA 25-28R
Geach, Patricia Sullivan 1916-1983 ... 29-32R
Geach, Peter Thomas 1916- ... 103
Gealt, Adelheid (M. Medicus)
1946- ... CANR-82
Earlier sketches in CA 114, CANR-36
Geanakoplos, Deno John 1916- ... CANR-2
Earlier sketch in CA 1-4R
Geaney, Dennis J(oseph)
1914-1992 ... CANR-20
Obituary ... 140
Earlier sketches in CA 5-8R, CANR-5
Gear, C. William 1935- ... 53-56
Gear, Kathleen (M.) O'Neal 1954- ... 229
See also SATA 71
Gear, Sheila 1942- ... 114
Gear, W. Michael 1955- ... 203
See also SATA 71
Geare, Michael 1919- ... 117
Geare, Mildred Mahler 1888(?)-1977
Obituary ... 73-76
Gearey, John 1926-1997 ... CANR-23
Earlier sketch in CA 45-48
Gearhart, Sally Miller 1931- ... CANR-59
Earlier sketch in CA 57-60
See also FW
Gearheart, B(ill) R. 1928- ... CANR-9
Earlier sketch in CA 21-24R
Gearing, Catherine 1916- ... 103
Gearing, Fred(erick) O(smond) 1922- ... 29-32R
Gearing-Thomas, G.
See Norwood, Victor G(eorge) C(harles)
Gearin-Tosh, Michael 1940(?)- ... 210
Geary, David 1963- ... CD 5, 6
Geary, David C(yril) 1957- ... 232
Geary, Douglas 1931- ... 13-16R
Geary, Frederick Charles 1886(?)-1975(?)
Obituary ... 104
Geary, Herbert Valentine (Rupert)
1894-1965 ... CAP-1
Earlier sketch in CA 9-10
Geary, Joseph ... 225
Geary, Nancy 1967- ... 236
Geary, Patricia (Carol) 1951- ... CANR-85
Earlier sketch in CA 134
See also FANT
Geary, Patrick J(oseph) 1948- ... 104
Geary, Rick 1946- ... 213
See also SATA 142
Geary, Roger 1950- ... CANR-49
Earlier sketch in CA 123
Geasland, Jack
See Geasland, John Buchanan, Jr.
Geasland, John Buchanan, Jr. 1944- ... 81-84
Geason, Susan 1946- ... 194
See also SATA 122
Gebhard, Anna Laura Munro 1914- ... 5-8R
Gebhard, Bruno (Frederic) 1901-1985 ... 73-76
Gebhard, Paul H(enry) 1917- ... CANR-70
Earlier sketch in CA 5-8R
Gebhardt, James F(rederick) 1948- ... 147
Gebhart, Benjamin 1923- ... 53-56
Gebler, Carlo (Ernest) 1954- ... CANR-96
Brief entry ... 119
Earlier sketch in CA 133
See also CLC 39
See also DLB 271

Gebler, Ernest 1915-1998 ... CANR-3
Obituary ... 164
Earlier sketch in CA 5-8R
Gecan, Michael ... 224
Gece
See Gimenez Caballero, Ernesto
Geck, Francis J(oseph) 1900- ... 73-76
Geckle, George L. 1939- ... 77-80
Gecys, Casimir C. 1904- ... CAP-2
Earlier sketch in CA 19-20
Geda, Sigitas 1943- ... DLB 232
Gedalecia, David 1942- ... 191
Gedalof, Robin
See McGrath, Robin
Gedda, George 1941- ... 77-80
Geddes, Charles L(ynn) 1928- ... CANR-2
Earlier sketch in CA 49-52
Geddes, Gary 1940- ... 140
See also CCA 1
See also CP 7
See also DLB 60
Geddes, Joan Bel 1916- ... 57-60
Geddes, Paul 1922- ... 136
Geddes, Virgil 1897-1989(?) ... 148
See also DLB 4
Geddie, John 1937- ... 69-72
Gedeon c. 1730-1763 ... DLB 150
Gedge, Pauline (Alice) 1945- ... 161
See also SATA 101
Gediman, Helen K. 1931- ... 150
Gedmin, Jeffrey (N.) 1958- ... 143
Gedo, John E. 1927- ... CANR-101
Earlier sketches in CA 121, CANR-47
Gedo, Mary M(athews) 1925- ... 104
Geduld, Harry M(aurice) 1931- ... 239
Earlier sketches in CA 9-12R, CANR-5, 20, 42
Autobiographical Essay in ... 239
See also CAAS 21
Gedye, George Eric Rowe 1890-1970
Obituary ... 93-96
Gee, H(erbert) L(eslie) 1901-1977 ... 9-12R
Obituary ... 103
See also SATA-Obit 26
Gee, Helen (Charlotte) 1919-2004 ... 174
Obituary ... 232
Gee, Henry ... 192
Gee, Maggie (Mary) 1948- ... CANR-125
Earlier sketch in CA 130
See also CLC 57
See also CN 4, 5, 6, 7
See also DLB 207
See also MTFW 2005
Gee, Maurice (Gough) 1931- ... CANR-123
Earlier sketches in CA 97-100, CANR-67
See also AAYA 42
See also CLC 29
See also CLR 56
See also CN 2, 3, 4, 5, 6, 7
See also CWRI 5
See also EWL 3
See also MAICYA 2
See also RGSF 2
See also SATA 46, 101
Gee, Shirley 1932- ... 156
See also CBD
See also CWD
See also DLB 245
Geehan, Wayne (E.) 1947- ... SATA 107
Geehr, Richard S. 1938- ... 136
Geelhoed, Glenn W. 1942- ... 182
Geemis, Joseph (Stephen) 1935- ... 69-72
Geen, Russell Glenn 1932- ... CANR-22
Earlier sketch in CA 104
Geer, Charles 1922- ... 108
See also SATA 42
See also SATA-Brief 32
Geer, Emily A(pt) 1912-1998 ... 127
Geer, Stephen (DuBois) 1930- ... 69-72
Geer, William D. 1906(?)-1976
Obituary ... 104
Geering, R(onald) G(eorge) 1918- ... CANR-86
Earlier sketch in CA 133
Geertz, Clifford (James) 1926- ... CANR-82
Earlier sketches in CA 33-36R, CANR-36
Interview in ... CANR-36
Geertz, Hildred 1927- ... 77-80
Geeslin, Campbell 1925- ... 102
See also SATA 107, 163
Gefen, Nan Fink ... 230
Geffen, Maxwell Myles 1896-1980
Obituary ... 102
Geffen, Roger 1919- ... 17-20R
Gefvert, Constance J(oanna) 1941- ... 53-56
Gega, Peter C(hristopher) 1924- ... 73-76
Gegauff, Paul 1922-1983 ... IDFW 3, 4
Geggus, David Patrick 1949- ... CANR-37
Earlier sketch in CA 114
Geha, Joseph (A.) 1944- ... 134
Geherin, David J(ohn) 1943- ... CANR-39
Earlier sketches in CA 101, CANR-17
Gehlbach, Frederick Renner 1935- ... 106
Gehlek, Rimpoche Nawang
See Rimpoche, (Nawang) Gelek
Gehlen, Reinhard 1902-1979
Obituary ... 89-92
Gehman, Betsy Holland 1932- ... 17-20R
Gehman, Christian 1948- ... 119
Gehman, Henry Snyder 1888-1981 ... 13-16R
Gehman, Mary W. 1923- ... 151
See also SATA 86
Gehman, Richard (Boyd)
1921-1972 ... CANR-16
Obituary ... 33-36R
Earlier sketch in CA 1-4R
Gehr, Mary 1910(?)-1997 ... SATA 32
See also SATA-Obit 99
Gehrels, Franz 1922- ... 101
Gehri, Alfred 1896(?)-1972
Obituary ... 33-36R
Gehrig, Klaus 1946- ... 137
Gehring, Wes D(avid) 1950- ... CANR-143
Earlier sketch in CA 137
Gehris, Paul 1934- ... 45-48
Gehry, Frank (Owen) 1929- ... 198
See also AAYA 48
Geibel, Emanuel 1815-1884 ... DLB 129
Geier, Arnold 1926- ... 1-4R
Geier, Woodrow A. 1914-1994 ... 21-24R
Geigel Polanco, Vicente 1904-1979
Obituary ... 85-88
See also HW 1
Geiger, Don(ald) Jesse 1923- ... 5-8R
Geiger, H(omer) Kent 1922- ... CANR-5
Earlier sketch in CA 1-4R
Geiger, John (Grigsby) 1960- ... CANR-139
Earlier sketch in CA 129
Geiger, Louis G. 1913-2002 ... 13-16R
Geiger, Ray(mond Aloysius) 1910-1994 ... 118
Obituary ... 145
See also AITN 1
Geiger, Theodore 1915-2004
Obituary ... 223
Brief entry ... 114
Geiogamah, Hanay 1945- ... 153
See also DAM MULT
See also DLB 175
See also NNAL
Geipel, Eileen 1932- ... 107
See also SATA 30
Geipel, John 1937- ... CANR-13
Earlier sketch in CA 73-76
Geiringer, Hilda 1893-1973 ... 170
Geiringer, Irene (Steckel) 1899-1983
Obituary ... 111
Geiringer, Karl (Johannes) 1899-1989 ... 13-16R
Obituary ... 127
Geis, Darlene Stern 1918(?)-1999 ... CANR-5
Obituary ... 177
Earlier sketch in CA 1-4R
See also SATA 7
See also SATA-Obit 111
Geis, Florence L(indauer) 1933- ... CANR-8
Earlier sketch in CA 57-60
Geis, Gilbert 1925- ... CANR-6
Earlier sketch in CA 9-12R
Geis, Richard E(rwin) 1927- ... 101
Interview in ... CA-101
Geisel, Helen 1898-1967
Obituary ... 107
See also SATA 26
Geisel, Theodor Seuss 1904-1991 ... CANR-132
Obituary ... 135
Earlier sketches in CA 13-16R, CANR-13, 32
See also Dr. Seuss
See also CLR 1, 9, 53, 100
See also DA3
See also DLB 61
See also DLBY 1991
See also MAICYA 1, 2
See also MTCW 1, 2
See also MTFW 2005
See also SATA 1, 28, 75, 100
See also SATA-Obit 67
See also TUS
Geiser, Robert L(ee) 1931- ... 97-100
Geisert, Arthur (Frederick) 1941- ... CANR-111
Earlier sketches in CA 120, CANR-44, 57
See also CLR 87
See also MAICYA 2
See also MAICYAS 1
See also SAAS 23
See also SATA 56, 92, 133
See also SATA-Brief 52
Geisert, Bonnie 1942- ... SATA 92
Geisinger, David L. 1938- ... 110
Geisler, Norman L(eo) 1932- ... CANR-51
Earlier sketches in CA 25-28R, CANR-10, 27
Geismar, Ludwig L(eo) 1921- ... CANR-53
Earlier sketches in CA 25-28R, CANR-11, 29
Geismar, Maxwell (David)
1909-1979 ... CANR-33
Obituary ... 104
Earlier sketch in CA 1-4R
Geissman, Erwin William 1920-1980
Obituary ... 101
Geissman, Grant 1953- ... 210
Geisst, Charles R. 1946- ... 210
Geist, Bill
See Geist, William E.
Geist, Harold 1916-1994 ... CANR-22
Earlier sketches in CA 17-20R, CANR-7
Geist, Kenneth L(ee) 1936- ... 81-84
Geist, Robert John 1912-1985 ... 41-44R
Geist, Roland C. 1896-1992 ... 89-92
Geist, Sidney 1914- ... 184
Brief entry ... 112
Geist, Valerius 1938- ... CANR-8
Earlier sketch in CA 61-64
Geist, William E. 1945(?)- ... 140
Geitgey, Doris A. 1920- ... 53-56
Geiwitz, P(eter) James 1938- ... CANR-11
Earlier sketch in CA 29-32R
Gekoski, R. A.
See Gekoski, Rick (A.)
Gekoski, Rick (A.) ... 231
Gelatt, Roland 1920-1986 ... 13-16R
Obituary ... 121
Gelb, Alan
See Gelb, Alan Lloyd
Gelb, Alan Lloyd 1950- ... 126
Gelb, Arthur 1924- ... CANR-103
Earlier sketches in CA 1-4R, CANR-21
See also DLB 103
Gelb, Barbara (Stone) 1926- ... CANR-21
Earlier sketch in CA 1-4R
See also DLB 103
Gelb, Ignace J(ay) 1907-1985 ... 9-12R
Obituary ... 118
Gelb, Joyce 1940- ... 61-64
Gelb, Leslie H(oward) 1937- ... CANR-19
Earlier sketch in CA 103
Gelb, Michael J. 1952- ... CANR-115
Earlier sketch in CA 147
Gelb, Norman 1929- ... CANR-30
Earlier sketch in CA 108
Gelbart, Larry
See Gelbart, Larry (Simon)
See also CAD
See also CD 5, 6
Gelbart, Larry (Simon) 1928- ... CANR-94
Earlier sketches in CA 73-76, CANR-45
See also Gelbart, Larry
See also CLC 21, 61
Gelbart, Nina Rattner ... 181
Gelber, Harry G. 1926- ... 25-28R
Gelber, Jack 1932-2003 ... CANR-2
Obituary ... 216
Earlier sketch in CA 1-4R
See also CAD
See also CLC 1, 6, 14, 79
See also DLB 7, 228
See also MAL 5
Gelber, Lionel (Morris) 1907-1989 ... 13-16R
Obituary ... 129
Gelber, Steven M(ichael) 1943- ... 53-56
Gelbert, Doug 1956- ... 237
Gelbspan, Ross 1939(?)- ... CANR-142
Earlier sketch in CA 172
Geld, Ellen Bromfield 1932- ... 37-40R
Geldard, Frank A(rthur) 1904-1984 ... 41-44R
Obituary ... 114
Geldard, Richard G. 1935- ... 202
Geldart, William 1936- ... SATA 15
Geldenhuys, Deon 1950- ... 139
Gelder, Ken (D.) 1955- ... 182
Gelderman, Carol Wettlaufer
1939- ... CANR-104
Earlier sketch in CA 105
Gelernt, Jules 1928- ... 21-24R
Gelernter, David (Hillel) 1955(?)- ... CANR-65
Earlier sketch in CA 149
Gelfand, Elissa D(eborah) 1949- ... 114
Gelfand, Lawrence Emerson 1926- ... CANR-3
Earlier sketch in CA 5-8R
Gelfand, Mark I. ... 181
Gelfand, Morris Arthur 1908-1998 ... 49-52
Gelfman, Dick 1947- ... 122
Gelfman, Judith S(chlein) 1937- ... 65-68
Gelfond, Rhoda 1946- ... CANR-12
Earlier sketch in CA 49-52
Gelinas, Gratien 1909-1999 ... 175
See also DLB 88
Gelinas, Paul J. 1904-1996 ... 41-44R
See also SATA 10
Gell, Frank
See Kowet, Don
Gell, Paul (Frederick William) 1928- ... 116
Gellatly, Peter 1923-1999
Brief entry ... 111
Geller, Allen 1941- ... 25-28R
Geller, Bruce 1930-1978
Obituary ... 77-80
Geller, Evelyn
See Gottesfeld, Evelyn
Geller, Jaclyn 1963- ... 202
Geller, Uri 1946- ... 69-72
Gellerman, Saul W(illiam)
1929-2003 ... CANR-8
Obituary ... 215
Earlier sketch in CA 5-8R
Gellert, Christian Furchtegott
1715-1769 ... DLB 97
Gellert, Judith 1925- ... 33-36R
Gellert, Lew
See Wellen, Edward (Paul)
Gelles, Richard J(ames) 1946- ... CANR-72
Earlier sketches in CA 61-64, CANR-8, 22, 45
Gelles, Sandi
See Gelles-Cole, Sandi
Gelles-Cole, Sandi 1949- ... 121
Gelley, Alexander 1933- ... 127
Brief entry ... 108
Gellhorn, Ernst 1893-1973 ... CAP-2
Earlier sketch in CA 21-22
Gellhorn, Martha (Ellis) 1908-1998 ... CANR-44
Obituary ... 164
Earlier sketch in CA 77-80
See also CLC 14, 60
See also CN 1, 2, 3, 4, 5, 6 7
See also DLBY 1982, 1998
Gellhorn, Walter 1906-1995 ... 13-16R
Obituary ... 150
Gellinek, Christian 1930- ... CANR-9
Earlier sketch in CA 21-24R
Gellinek, Janis Little
See Solomon, Janis Little
Gellis, Roberta (Leah Jacobs)
1927- ... CANR-107
Earlier sketches in CA 5-8R, CANR-3, 22, 45, 70
See also RHW
See also SATA 128
Gellman, Estelle Sheila 1941- ... 53-56
Gellman, Irwin F(rederick) 1942- ... CANR-87
Earlier sketches in CA 45-48, CANR-1
Gellman, Marc ... 173
See also SATA 112
Gell-Mann, Murray 1929- ... 156
Gellman-Waxner, Libby
See Rudnick, Paul
Gellner, Ernest (Andre) 1925-1995 ... CANR-94
Obituary ... 150
Earlier sketches in CA 5-8R, CANR-4, 22
Gellner, John 1907- ... 29-32R
Gellrich, Jesse M. 1942- ... 118
Gelman, Amy 1961- ... SATA 72
Gelman, David Graham 1926- ... 103
Gelman, Jan 1963- ... SATA 58
Gelman, Juan 1930- ... HW 1
Gelman, Milton S. 1920(?)-1990
Obituary ... 131
Gelman, Mitch(ell Barry) 1962- ... CANR-51
Earlier sketch in CA 124
Gelman, Rita Golden 1937- ... CANR-111
Earlier sketches in CA 81-84, CANR-16
See also SATA 84, 131
See also SATA-Brief 51
Gelman, Steve 1934- ... CANR-16
Earlier sketch in CA 25-28R
See also SATA 3
Gelman, Woodrow 1915(?)-1978
Obituary ... 104
Gelman, Woody
See Gelman, Woodrow
Gelmis, Joseph S(tephan) 1935- ... 45-48
Gelperin, L.
See Halpern, Leivick
Gelpi, Albert 1931- ... 33-36R
Gelpi, Barbara Charlesworth 1933- ... 112
Gelpi, Donald L. 1934- ... CANR-7
Earlier sketch in CA 17-20R
Geltmaker, Ty 1952- ... 211
Geltman, Max 1906(?)-1984
Obituary ... 112
Gelula, Abner Joseph 1906-1985
Obituary ... 116
Gelven, (Charles) Michael 1937- ... 29-32R
Gelzer, Matthias 1886-1974 ... CAP-2
Earlier sketch in CA 25-28
Gemme, Francis Robert 1934- ... 21-24R
Gemme, Leila Boyle 1942- ... 81-84
Gemmell, Alan Robertson 1913-1986 ... 114
Gemmell, David A(ndrew) 1948- ... CANR-117
Earlier sketch in CA 154
See also FANT
See also SFW 4
Gemmell, Nikki 1967- ... 190
Gemmett, Robert J(ames) 1936- ... CANR-140
Earlier sketch in CA 33-36R
Gemmill, Jane Brown 1898-1994 ... 1-4R
Gemmill, Paul F. 1890(?)-1976
Obituary ... 69-72
Gemming, Elizabeth 1932- ... CANR-9
Earlier sketch in CA 65-68
See also SATA 11
Gemming, Mary 1941- ... 182
Gems, Gerald (Robert) 1947- ... 197
Gems, Jonathan (Malcolm Frederick)
1952- ... 230
See also CBD
See also CD 5, 6
Gems, (Iris) Pam(ela) 1925- ... CANR-110
Earlier sketches in CA 107, CANR-58
See also CBD
See also CD 5, 6
See also CWD
See also DLB 13
See also FW
Gemuenden, Gerd
See Gemunden, Gerd
Gemunden, Gerd 1959- ... 166
Genasi, Chris 1962- ... 227
Genauer, Emily 1911-2002 ... 106
Obituary ... 206
Interview in ... CA-106
Gendel, Evelyn W. 1916(?)-1977
Obituary ... 104
See also SATA-Obit 27
Gendell, Murray 1924- ... CANR-5
Earlier sketch in CA 9-12R
Gendlin, Eugene T. 1926- ... 1-4R
Gendron, George M. 1949- ... 93-96
Gendzier, Irene Lefel 1936- ... 21-24R
Gendzier, Stephen J(ules) 1930- ... 33-36R
General, David 1950- ... 211
General, Lloyd 1924(?)-1986
Obituary ... 119
Genet
See Flanner, Janet
Genet, Jean 1910-1986 ... CANR-18
Earlier sketch in CA 13-16R
See also CLC 1, 2, 5, 10, 14, 44, 46
See also DA3
See also DAM DRAM
See also DC 25
See also DFS 10
See also DLB 72, 321
See also DLBY 1986
See also EW 13
See also EWL 3
See also GFL 1789 to the Present
See also GLL 1
See also LMFS 2
See also MTCW 1, 2
See also MTFW 2005
See also RGWL 2, 3
See also TCLC 128
See also TWA
Genette, Gerard (Raymond) 1930- ... 238
See also DLB 242
Genevoix, Maurice Charles Louis
1890-1980 ... 175
Obituary ... 102
See also DLB 65

Cumulative Index 213 Gerould

Geng, Veronica 1941-1997 .... CANR-51
Obituary 163
Brief entry 119
Earlier sketch in CA 124
Geniesse, Jane Fletcher 193
Genini, Ronald 1946- 162
Genis, Aleksandr Aleksandrovich
1953- .... DLB 285
Genizi, Haim 1934- 233
Genlis, Stephanie-Felicite Ducrest
1746-1830 .... DLB 313
Genn, Calder
See Gillie, Christopher
Gennaro, Angelo Anthony De
See De Gennaro, Angelo Anthony
Gennaro, Joseph F(rancis), Jr. 1924- 101
See also SATA 53
Genne, Elizabeth Steel 1911- 186
Brief entry 108
Genne, William H. 1910-1997 .... 17-20R
Obituary 156
Gennes, Pierre-Gilles De
See De Gennes, Pierre-Gilles
Genoa, Catherine of 1447-1510 .... LMFS 1
Genovese, Eugene D(ominick)
1930- CANR-10
Earlier sketch in CA 69-72
See also DLB 17
Genovese, Vincent J. 1945- 206
Genoves Tarazaga, Santiago 1923- 127
Brief entry 107
Gensemer, Robert Eugene 1936-
Brief entry 110
Genser, Cynthia 1950- 69-72
Gensler, Kinereth 1922- CANR-108
Earlier sketch in CA 116
Genszler, G(eorge) William II 1915- ... CANR-9
Earlier sketch in CA 65-68
Gent, Peter 1942- 89-92
See also AITN 1
See also CLC 29
See also DLBY 1982
Genthe, Charles V(incent) 1937- 29-32R
Gentil, Richard 1917- 102
Gentile, Gennaro L. 1946- 115
Gentile, Giovanni 1875-1944
Brief entry 119
See also TCLC 96
Gentile, John S(amuel) 1956- 132
Gentile, Petrina 1969- .... SATA 91
Gentle, Mary 1956- CANR-137
Earlier sketches in CA 106, CANR-56
See also FANT
See also SATA 48
See also SFW 4
Gentleman, A
See Sophia
Gentleman, David (William) 1930- .. CANR-15
Earlier sketch in CA 25-28R
See also SATA 7
Gentles, Frederick (Ray) 1912-2001 ...... 29-32R
Gentlewoman in New England, A
See Bradstreet, Anne
Gentlewoman in Those Parts, A
See Bradstreet, Anne
Gentry, Byron B. 1913-1992 .... 13-16R
Gentry, Curt 1931- CANR-5
Earlier sketch in CA 9-12R
Gentry, Diane Koos 1943- 128
Gentry, Dwight L. 1919- 1-4R
Gentry, Marshall Bruce 1953- CANR-119
Earlier sketches in CA 121, CANR-47
Gentry, Peter
See Newcomb, Kerry and
Schaefer, Frank
Gentz, William Howard 1918- 107
Gentzler, J(ennings) Mason 1930- 93-96
Genya, Monica 168
Geoff
See Dyson, Geoffrey Harry George
Geoffrey, J. Iqbal
See Jafree, Mohammed Jawaid Iqbal
Geoffrey, Theodate
See Wayman, Dorothy G.
Geoffrey of Monmouth c. 1100-1155 . DLB 146
See also TEA
Geoghegan, Adrienne 1962- 215
See also SATA 143
Geoghegan, Sister Barbara 1902-1981 .. CAP-1
Earlier sketch in CA 11-12
Geoghegan, Thomas Dolan 1917(?)-1987
Obituary 121
Georgakas, Dan 1938- CANR-45
Earlier sketches in CA 45-48, CANR-1, 22
George III 1738-1820 .... DLB 213
George, A(lfred) Raymond 1912-1998 108
George, Alexander Lawrence 1920- 13-16R
George, Alice Rose 1944- 193
George, Anne Carroll 1927-2001 ... CANR-130
Earlier sketch in CA 181
George, Barbara
See Katz, Bobbi
George, Charles H(illes) 1922- 9-12R
George, Chief Dan 1899-1981 110
Obituary 108
George, Claude Swanson, Jr.
1920-1995 .... 13-16R
George, Collins Crusor 1909-1980 77-80
Obituary 133
George, Dan
See George, Chief Dan
George, David
See Vogenitz, David George
George, David (John) 1948- 146
George, E(dgar) Madison 1907-1975 .... 1-4R
Obituary 103
George, Edward
See Vardeman, Robert E(dward)
George, Eliot
See Freeman, Gillian
George, (Susan) Elizabeth 1949- CANR-112
Earlier sketches in CA 137, CANR-62
See also CMW 4
See also CPW
See also DLB 306
George, Emery E(dward) 1933- CANR-122
Earlier sketches in CA 41-44R, CANR-16, 36
George, Emily
See Katz, Bobbi
George, Eugene
See Chevalier, Paul Eugene George
George, Gail
See Katz, Bobbi
George, Henry 1839-1897 .... DLB 23
George, Hermon, Jr. 1945- 126
George, Jay
See Strachan, J(ohn) George
George, Jean
See George, Jean Craighead
George, Jean Craighead 1919- CANR-25
Earlier sketch in CA 5-8R
See also AAYA 8
See also BYA 2, 4
See also CLC 35
See also CLR 1; 80
See also DLB 52
See also JRDA
See also MAICYA 1, 2
See also SATA 2, 68, 124
See also WYA
See also YAW
George, John 1936- CANR-89
Earlier sketch in CA 132
George, John E(dwin) 1936- 53-56
George, John L(othar) 1916- 5-8R
See also SATA 2
George, Jonathan
See Burke, John (Frederick) and
Theiner, George (Fredric)
George, Judith W(ordsworth) 1940- 143
George, Kathleen Elizabeth 1943- 193
George, Kristine O'Connell 1954- .. CANR-140
Earlier sketch in CA 180
See also SATA 110, 156
George, Lindsay Barrett 1952- 160
See also SATA 95, 155
George, M(ary) Dorothy CAP-1
Earlier sketch in CA 13-16
George, Malcom F(arris) 1930- 57-60
George, Margaret 1943- CANR-123
Earlier sketch in CA 143
George, Marion
See Benjamin, Claude (Max Edward Pohlman)
George, Mary Carolyn Hollers Jutson
1930- CANR-12
Earlier sketch in CA 73-76
George, Mary Yanaga 1940- 29-32R
George, Melanie 213
George, N(orvil) L(ester) 1902-1979 ...... CAP-2
Earlier sketch in CA 29-32
George, Nelson 1957- CANR-100
Earlier sketch in CA 119
George, Peter 1924-1966
Obituary 25-28R
See also SFW 4
George, Phyllis 1949- 222
George, Richard R(obert) 1943- 104
George, Robert Esmonde Gordon
1890-1969 .... CAP-1
Earlier sketch in CA 11-12
George, Rolf 1930- 110
George, Roy E(dwin) 1923- CANR-14
Earlier sketch in CA 37-40R
George, S(idney) C(harles) 1898- 53-56
See also SATA 11
George, Sally
See Orr, Wendy
George, Sally 1945- 105
George, Sara 1947- 65-68
George, Stefan (Anton) 1868-1933 193
Brief entry 104
See also EW 8
See also EWL 3
See also TCLC 2, 14
George, Stephen (Alan) 1949- 139
George, Susan Akers 1934- 77-80
George, Susanne K. 1947- 141
George, Timothy S. 1955- 214
George, Twig C. 1950- 186
See also SATA 114
George, W(alter) L(ionel) 1882-1926 .. DLB 197
George, W(illiam) Lloyd 1900(?)-1975
Obituary 53-56
See also SATA-Obit 30
George, W(illiam) R(ichard) P(hilip)
1912- 69-72
George, Wilfred R(aymond) 1928- 111
George, Wilma
See Crowther, Wilma (Beryl)
George-Brown, George Alfred 1914-1985 .. 170
Obituary 116
Brief entry 110
Georges, Georges Martin
See Simenon, Georges (Jacques Christian)
Georges, Robert A(ugustus) 1933- 111
Georgescu, Vlad 1937(?)-1988
Obituary 127
Georgescu-Roegen, Nicholas
1906-1994 .... CANR-80
Obituary 147
Earlier sketches in CA 21-24R, CANR-9
Georges-Michel, Michel 1883-1985
Obituary 116
Georgi, Charlotte CANR-17
Earlier sketches in CA 1-4R, CANR-2
Georgiana, Sister
See Terstegge, Mabel Alice
Georgi-Findlay, Brigitte 1956- 157
Georgiou, Constantine 1927- 13-16R
See also SATA 7
Georgiou, Steven Demetre 1948- 101
Georgiou, Theo
See Odgers, Sally Farrell
Georgopoulos, Basil S(pyros) 1926- 73-76
Gephart, William J(ay) 1928- 69-72
Geraci, Philip C. 1929- 77-80
Geraghty, Paul 1959- 199
See also SATA 130
Geraghty, Tony 186
Gerald, J(ames) Edward 1906-2001 .... 5-8R
Obituary 197
Gerald, John Bart 1940- CANR-45
Earlier sketches in CA 5-8R, CANR-7, 22
Gerald, Ziggy
See Zeigerman, Gerald
Gerard, Albert S(tanislas) 1920- CANR-13
Earlier sketch in CA 29-32R
Gerard, Andrew
See Gatti, Arthur Gerard
Gerard, Charles (Franklin) 1914-1998 ... 29-32R
Gerard, Charley 1950- 175
Gerard, Dave 1909- 53-56
Gerard, David 1923- 77-80
Gerard, Elaine
See Ryder, Eileen
Gerard, H(arold) B(enjamin) 1923-2003
Obituary 212
Brief entry 110
Gerard, Jane 1930- 1-4R
Gerard, Jean Ignace Isidore
1803-1847 .... SATA 45
Gerard, Jules B(ernard) 1929- 110
Gerard, Karen (Nina) 1932- 120
Gerard, Louise 1878(?)-1970
Obituary 104
Gerard, Philip 1955- CANR-122
Earlier sketch in CA 148
Gerard, Ralph W(aldo) 1900-1974
Obituary 49-52
Gerard-Libois, Jules C. 1923- 33-36R
Geras, Adele (Daphne Weston)
1944- CANR-119
Earlier sketch in CA 97-100
Interview in CANR-19
See also Geras, Adele (Daphne Weston)
See also AAYA 48
See also SAAS 21
See also SATA 23, 87, 129
See also YAW
Geras, Adele (Daphne Weston)
1944- CANR-119
See also Geras, Adele (Daphne Weston)
Geras, Norman (Myron) 1943- CANR-19
Earlier sketch in CA 102
Gerasimov, Gennadi (Ivanovitch)
1930- CANR-32
Earlier sketch in CA 69-72
Gerasimov, Innokentii Petrovich 1905-1985
Obituary 115
Gerasimov, Mikhail Mikhaylovich 1907-1970
Obituary 107
Gerassi, John 1931- CANR-8
Earlier sketch in CA 5-8R
Geraud, (Charles Joseph) Andre
1882-1974 69-72
Obituary 53-56
Gerber, Albert B(enjamin) 1913-2001 ... 17-20R
Gerber, Barbara (Lin) 1942- 117
Gerber, Bobbie
See Gerber, Barbara (Lin)
Gerber, Dan(iel Frank) 1940- CANR-101
Earlier sketches in CA 33-36R, CANR-41
Gerber, David A(llison) 1944- 77-80
Gerber, Douglas E(arl) 1933- CANR-15
Earlier sketch in CA 29-32R
Gerber, Ellen W. 1936- 193
Brief entry 107
Gerber, Helmut E. 1920-1981 .... CANR-10
Earlier sketch in CA 21-24R
Gerber, Israel J(oshua) 1918- 77-80
Gerber, John 1907(?)-1981
Obituary 103
Gerber, John C(hristian) 1908- 102
Gerber, Merrill Joan 1938- 234
Earlier sketches in CA 13-16R, CANR-10, 26, 51, 97
Autobiographical Essay in 234
See also CAAS 20
See also DLB 218
See also SATA 64, 127
Gerber, Michael E. 1936- 204
Gerber, Perren 1933- .... SATA 104
Gerber, Philip Leslie 1923-2005
Obituary 235
Brief entry 108
Gerber, Rudolph Joseph 1938- 105
Gerber, Sanford E(dwin) 1933- CANR-1
Earlier sketch in CA 49-52
Gerber, William 1908-1999 .... 37-40R
Obituary 185
Gerberding, Richard A. 1945- 128
Gerberg, Mort 1931- .... SATA 64
Gerbers, Teresa 1933- 53-56
Gerbi, Antonello 1904-1976 77-80
Gerbner, George 1919- CANR-1
Earlier sketch in CA 45-48
Gerboth, Walter W(illiam) 1925-1984 .. 13-16R
Obituary 112
Gerchunoff, Alberto 1883-1950 .... HW 1
Gerdes, Eckhard 1959- 147
Gerdes, Florence Marie 1919- 25-28R
Gerdts, William H. 1929- CANR-136
Earlier sketches in CA 13-16R, CANR-10
Gerdy, John R. 1957- CANR-138
Earlier sketch in CA 169
Gere, Richard 1949- 172
Gergely, Tibor 1900-1978 107
Obituary 106
See also SATA 54
See also SATA-Obit 20
Gergen, Kenneth J(ay) 1934- 33-36R
Gerhan, David R. 1945- 182
Gerhard, Anselm 1958- 197
Gerhard, Happy 1920- 57-60
Gerhardi, William Alexander
See Gerhardie, William Alexander
Gerhardie, William Alexander
1895-1977 .... CANR-18
Obituary 73-76
Earlier sketch in CA 25-28R
See also CLC 5
See also CN 1, 2
See also DLB 36
See also RGEL 2
Gerhardt, Lydia A(nn) 1934- CANR-10
Earlier sketch in CA 61-64
Gerhardt, Michael E. 1947- 175
Gerhardt, Paul 1607-1676 .... DLB 164
Gerhart, Ann 234
Gerhart, Gail M. 1943- 85-88
Gerhart, Genevra 1930- 57-60
Gerig, Reginald R(oth) 1919- 57-60
Gerin, Winifred 1901(?)-1981 .... CANR-20
Obituary 104
Earlier sketch in CA 25-28R
See also DLB 155
Geringer, Laura 1948- CANR-68
Earlier sketch in CA 107
See also SATA 29, 94
Gerken, Arthur E. 1934- 212
Gerken, Ted
See Gerken, Arthur E.
Gerlach, Barbara A(nn) 1946- 114
Gerlach, Don R(alph) 1932- 9-12R
Gerlach, Douglas 1963- 217
Gerlach, John 1941- 101
Gerlach, Larry R(euben) 1941- CANR-86
Brief entry 109
Earlier sketch in CA 133
Gerlach, Luther P(aul) 1930- 41-44R
Gerlach, Russel L(ee) 1939- 89-92
Gerlach, Vernon S(amuel) 1922- 61-64
Gerlach, Wolfgang 1933- 198
Gerler, William R(obert) 1917-1996 65-68
See also SATA 47
Germain, Edward B. 1937- 89-92
Germain, Sylvie 1954- 191
Germain, Walter 1889-1962
Obituary 112
German, Donald R(obert)
1931-1986 .... CANR-22
Obituary 119
Earlier sketches in CA 57-60, CANR-7
German, Gene Arlin 1933- 45-48
German, Joan
See German-Grapes, Joan
German, Tony 1924- 97-100
Germane, Gayton E. 1920- CANR-18
Earlier sketches in CA 1-4R, CANR-2
German-Grapes, Joan 1933- CANR-96
Earlier sketch in CANR-45
Germani, Gino 1911-1979 .... CANR-7
Earlier sketch in CA 53-56
Germanicus
See Dunner, Joseph
Germann, A(lbert) C(arl) 1921- 1-4R
Germann, Richard Wolf 1930- 104
Germano, Peter B. 1913-1983 186
Brief entry 116
See also Cord, Barry
Germany, (Vera) Jo(sephine) CANR-9
Earlier sketch in CA 65-68
Germar, Herb
See Germar, William H(erbert)
Germar, William H(erbert) 1911- 21-24R
Germeshausen, Anna Louise 1906-1968
Obituary 108
Germino, Dante (Lee) 1931-2002 53-56
Obituary 206
Germond, Jack W. 1928- CANR-91
Brief entry 108
Earlier sketch in CA 112
Interview in CA-112
Gernert, Eleanor Towles 1928- 37-40R
Gernes, Sonia 1942- 107
Gernet, Jacques 1921- 163
Gernsback, Hugo 1884-1967 181
Obituary 93-96
See also DLB 8, 137
See also SFW 4
Gernsheim, Helmut (Erich Robert)
1913-1995 .... CANR-45
Obituary 149
Earlier sketches in CA 5-8R, CANR-5, 22
Geroely, Kalman
See Gabel, Joseph
Gerold, Karl 1906-1973
Obituary 41-44R
Gerold, William 1932- 17-20R
Geroly, Kalman
See Gabel, Joseph
Gerome
See Thibault, Jacques Anatole Francois
Gerosa, Guido 1933- 73-76
Gerould, Daniel C(harles) 1928- CANR-33
Earlier sketch in CA 29-32R

Gerould, Katharine (Fullerton) 1879-1944 .. 175
See also DLB 78
Gerow, Edwin 1931- ... 53-56
Gerow, Josh(ua R.) 1941- ... 103
Gerrard, A. J.
See Gerrard, John
Gerrard, Gary 1952- ... 220
Gerrard, Jean 1933- ... 115
See also SATA 51
Gerrard, John 1944- ... 135
Gerrard, Michael B. 1951- ... 147
Gerrard, Roy 1935-1997 ... CANR-57
Obituary ... 160
Earlier sketch in CA 110
See also CLR 23
See also MAICYA 2
See also MAICYAS 1
See also SATA 47, 90
See also SATA-Brief 45
See also SATA-Obit 99
Gerrietts, John 1912-1992 ... 77-80
Obituary ... 136
Gerrig, Richard J. 1959- ... 147
Gerring, Ray H. 1926- ... 13-16R
Gerrish, B(rian) A(lbert) 1931- ... CANR-4
Earlier sketch in CA 5-8R
Gerritsen, Terry
See Gerritsen, Tess
Gerritsen, Tess 1953- ... CANR-116
Earlier sketch in CA 159
See also AAYA 42
Gerrity, David James 1923-1984 ... CANR-4
Earlier sketch in CA 1-4R
Gerrold, David 1944- ... CANR-124
Earlier sketches in CA 93-96, CANR-78
Interview in ... CA-93-96
See also DLB 8
See also SATA 66, 144
See also SFW 4
Gersao, Teolinda 1940- ... DLB 287
Gerschenkron, Alexander (Pavlovich)
1904-1978 ... CANR-1
Earlier sketch in CA 45-48
Gersh, Harry 1912-2001 ... CANR-1
Earlier sketch in CA 1-4R
Gershator, David 1937- ... 115
Gershator, Phillis 1942- ... CANR-137
Earlier sketches in CA 102, CANR-57
See also SATA 90, 158
Gershen, Martin 1924-1985 ... 33-36R
Obituary ... 114
Gershenson, Daniel E(noch) 1935- ... 5-8R
Gershgoren Novak, Estelle 1940- ... 237
Gershman, Herbert S. 1926-1971 ... CAP-2
Obituary ... 33-36R
Earlier sketch in CA 25-28
Gershman, Michael ... 171
Gershon, Karen
See Tripp, Karen
See also CP 1, 2
See also DLB 299
Gershoni, Israel 1946- ... 150
Gershoy, Leo 1897-1975 ... CAP-1
Obituary ... 57-60
Earlier sketch in CA 13-14
Gershtein, E(mma)
See Gerstein, Emma
Gershtein, E(mma) G.
See Gerstein, Emma
Gershten, Donna M. 1953- ... 203
Gershuny, Grace 1950- ... 144
Gershwin, George 1898-1937 ... AAYA 62
Gershwin, Ira 1896-1983 ... 164
Obituary ... 110
Brief entry ... 108
See also DLB 265
See also DLBY 1996
Gerson, Corinne 1927- ... CANR-25
Earlier sketch in CA 93-96
See also SATA 37
Gerson, Jean 1363-1429 ... DLB 208
Gerson, Kathleen 1947- ... 147
Gerson, Louis Leib 1921- ... 17-20R
Gerson, Mary-Joan ... 205
See also SATA 79, 136
Gerson, Noel Bertram 1914-1988 ... CANR-82
Obituary ... 127
Earlier sketch in CA 81-84
See also SATA 22
See also SATA-Obit 60
Gerson, Walter (Max) 1935- ... 41-44R
Gerson, Wolfgang 1916- ... 33-36R
Gersoni, Diane 1947- ... 53-56
Gersonides 1288-1344 ... DLB 115
Gersoni-Stavn, Diane
See Gersoni, Diane
Gerstad, John (Leif) 1924-1981 ... 103
Obituary ... 105
Gerstaecker, Friedrich 1816-1872 ... DLB 129
Gerstein, Arnold A. 1940- ... 124
Gerstein, Emma 1903-2002 ... 237
Gerstein, Linda (Groves) 1938-
Brief entry ... 110
Gerstein, Mordicai 1935- ... CANR-121
Brief entry ... 117
Earlier sketches in CA 127, CANR-36, 56, 82
See also CLR 102
See also MAICYA 1, 2
See also SATA 47, 81, 142
See also SATA-Brief 36
Gerstenberg, Alice 1885-1972 ... DFS 17
Gerstenberg, Heinrich Wilhelm von
1737-1823 ... DLB 97
Gerstenberger, Donna Lorine 1929- ... CANR-4
Earlier sketch in CA 5-8R
Gerstenberger, Erhard S. 1932- ... 164
Gerstenfeld, Phyllis B. 1967- ... 238
Gersten-Vassilaros, Alexandra ... 235
Gerster, Georg (Anton) 1928- ... 37-40R
Gerster, Patrick G(eorge) 1942- ... 57-60
Gerstine, Jack
See Gerstine, John
Gerstine, John 1915- ... 5-8R
Gerstl, Joel E. 1932- ... 21-24R
Gerstle, Kurt H(erman) 1923- ... 53-56
Gerstler, Amy 1956- ... CANR-99
Earlier sketch in CA 146
See also CLC 70
Gerstmann, Evan ... 226
Gerstner, Edna Suckau 1914-1999 ... 1-4R
Gerstner, John H(enry) 1914-1996 ... CANR-2
Earlier sketch in CA 1-4R
Gert, Bernard 1934- ... 29-32R
Gerteiny, Alfred G(eorges) 1930- ... 21-24R
Gerteis, Louis S(axton) 1942- ... 45-48
Gerth, Donald Rogers 1928- ... 45-48
Gerth, Hans Heinrich 1908-1978
Obituary ... 81-84
Gertler, Menard M. 1919- ... 9-12R
Gertler, Stephanie (Jocelyn) ... 207
Gertler, T. ... 121
Brief entry ... 116
See also CLC 34
Gertman, Samuel 1915-1968 ... 1-4R
Gertridge, Allison 1967- ... 201
See also SATA 132
Gertsen, Aleksandr Ivanovich
See Herzen, Aleksandr Ivanovich
Gertz, Bill 1952(?)- ... 228
Gertz, Elmer 1906-2000 ... CANR-42
Obituary ... 190
Earlier sketches in CA 13-16R, CANR-11
Gertz, Theodore G(erson) 1936- ... 115
Gertzog, Irwin N(orman) 1933- ... 29-32R
Gerulaitis, Leonardas Vytautas 1928- ... 77-80
Geruson, Richard J. 1957- ... 140
Gervais, Bernadette 1959- ... SATA 80
Gervais, C(harles) H(enry) 1946- ... 97-100
See also CP 7
Gervais, Marty
See Gervais, C(harles) H(enry)
Gervais, (George) Paul 1946- ... CANR-117
Earlier sketch in CA 145
Gervasi, Eugene Michael 1937-1989
Obituary ... 127
Gervasi, Frank H(enry) 1908-1990 ... CAP-1
Obituary ... 130
Earlier sketch in CA 13-16
Gervasi, Tom
See Gervasi, Eugene Michael
Gervinus, Georg Gottfried
1805-1871 ... DLB 133
Gerwig, Anna Mary (Gerwig)
1907-1981 ... CAP-2
Earlier sketch in CA 17-18
Gerwin, Donald 1937- ... 25-28R
Gery, John (Roy Octavius) 1953- ... 151
See also DLB 282
Gerzina, Gretchen (Aletha) Holbrook
1950- ... 140
Gerzon, Mark ... 81-84
Gerzon, Robert 1946- ... 164
Gesch, Dorothy K(atherine) 1923- ... 29-32R
Gesch, Roy G(eorge) 1920- ... 21-24R
Geschickter, Charles F(reeborn) 1901-1987
Obituary ... 123
Geschwender, James A(rthur) 1933- ... 41-44R
Gesell, Arnold Lucius 1880-1961
Obituary ... 116
Geserick, June
See Donahue, June (Geserick)
Gesler, Wilbert M. 1941- ... 138
Gesner, Carol 1922- ... 29-32R
Gesner, Clark 1938-2002 ... 109
Obituary ... 216
See also SATA 40
See also SATA-Obit 143
Gesner, Elsie Miller 1919- ... 17-20R
Gess, Denise 1952- ... CANR-141
Earlier sketch in CA 135
Gessel, Van C(raig) 1950- ... CANR-94
Earlier sketch in CA 145
Gessert, Kate Rogers 1948- ... 113
Gessner, Lynne 1919- ... CANR-10
Earlier sketch in CA 25-28R
See also SATA 16
Gessner, Michael (G.) 1944- ... 182
Geßner, Salomon 1730-1788 ... DLB 97
Geston, Mark S(ymington) 1946- ... CANR-58
Earlier sketch in CA 102
See also DLB 8
See also SFW 4
Geter, Tyrone ... SATA 150
Gethers, Peter 1953- ... CANR-117
Earlier sketches in CA 103, CANR-31, 57
Gethers, Steven 1922(?)-1989
Obituary ... 130
Gething, Thomas W(ilson) 1939- ... 41-44R
Gethner, Perry (J.) 1947- ... 151
Getis, Victoria 1966- ... 203
Getlein, Dorothy Woolen 1921- ... 9-12R
Getlein, Frank 1921-2000 ... CANR-6
Obituary ... 188
Earlier sketch in CA 9-12R
Getman, Gerald Nathan 1914(?)-1990
Obituary ... 131
Getman, Julius (G.) 1931- ... 140
Gettel, Ronald 1931- ... 112
Gettens, Rutherford John 1900(?)-1974
Obituary ... 49-52
Gettings, Eunice J. 1901(?)-1978
Obituary ... 81-84
Gettings, Fred 1937- ... 123
Gettleman, Marvin E. 1933- ... 37-40R
Gettleman, Susan
See Braiman, Susan
Gettlin, Robert ... 160
Getty, Gerald W(inkler) 1913-2004 ... 57-60
Obituary ... 224
Getty, Hilda F. 1938- ... 61-64
Getty, J(ean) Paul 1882-1976 ... 69-72
Obituary ... 65-68
Getty, Mary Ann 1943- ... 114
Getz, David 1957- ... 155
See also SATA 91
Getz, Gene A(rnold) 1932- ... CANR-54
Earlier sketches in CA 29-32R, CANR-12, 29
Getz, Malcolm 1945- ... CANR-18
Earlier sketch in CA 101
Getz, Marshall J(ay) 1957- ... 224
Getz, Oscar 1897-1983
Obituary ... 110
Getzels, Jacob Warren 1912-2001 ... CANR-30
Obituary ... 194
Earlier sketch in CA 45-48
Getzinger, Donna 1968- ... 198
See also SATA 128
Getzoff, Carole 1943- ... 61-64
Geubtner, Virginia Reidel
See Reidel-Geubtner, Virginia
Geuna, Aldo 1965- ... 196
Geve, Thomas 1929- ... 127
Gevirtz, Don L(ee) 1928-2001 ... 121
Obituary ... 195
Gevirtz, Eliezer 1950- ... 121
See also SATA 49
Gevirtz, Stanley 1929-1988
Obituary ... 126
Brief entry ... 109
Gewe, Raddory
See Gorey, Edward (St. John)
Gewecke, Clifford George, Jr. 1932- ... 21-24R
Gewehr, Wolf M(ax) 1939- ... CANR-1
Earlier sketch in CA 45-48
Gewertz, Deborah B. 1948- ... 143
Gewirth, Alan 1912-2004
Obituary ... 227
Brief entry ... 107
Gewirtz, Jacob L(eon) 1924- ... 45-48
Gewirtz, Leonard Benjamin 1918- ... 1-4R
Geyer, Alan (Francis) 1931- ... 9-12R
Geyer, Georgie Anne 1935- ... CANR-17
Earlier sketch in CA 29-32R
Interview in ... CANR-17
Geyl, Pieter (Catharinus Arie) 1887-1966 ... 103
Obituary ... 89-92
Geyman, John P. 1931- ... CANR-14
Earlier sketch in CA 37-40R
Gezelle, Guido 1803-1899 ... RGWL 2, 3
Gezi, Kal
See Gezi, Kalil I(smail)
Gezi, Kalil I(smail) 1930- ... CANR-17
Earlier sketch in CA 25-28R
Ghad Gaja
See Kishon, Ephraim
Ghadimi, Hossein 1922- ... 61-64
Ghai, Dharam P. 1936- ... CANR-93
Earlier sketches in CA 21-24R, CANR-15, 34
Ghalib
See Ghalib, Asadullah Khan
Ghalib, Asadullah Khan 1797-1869
See Ghalib
See also DAM POET
See also RGWL 2, 3
Ghallab, Abd al-Karim 1919- ... EWL 3
Ghan, Linda (R.) 1947- ... 145
See also SATA 77
Ghani, Cyrus 1929- ... 186
Ghazarian, Barouyr Raphael 1924-1971
See Sevag, Barouyr
Ghazi, Suhaib Hamid ... 196
Gheddo, Piero 1929- ... CANR-15
Earlier sketch in CA 73-76
Ghelardi, Robert (Anthony) 1939- ... 69-72
Ghelderode, Michel de 1898-1962 .. CANR-77
Earlier sketches in CA 85-88, CANR-40
See also CLC 6, 11
See also DAM DRAM
See also DC 15
See also DLB 321
See also EW 11
See also EWL 3
See also TWA
Ghent, Natale 1962- ... 222
See also SATA 148
Gheorghiu, (Constantin) Virgil
1916-1992 ... CANR-76
Obituary ... 138
Earlier sketches in CA 33-36R, CANR-30
Gherardi, Piero 1909-1971 ... IDFW 3, 4
Gherity, James Arthur 1929- ... 17-20R
Gherman, Beverly 1934- ... CANR-101
Earlier sketch in CA 136
See also SATA 68, 123
Ghezzi, Bert (Bertil W.) 1941- ... CANR-86
Earlier sketch in CA 133
Ghigna, Charles 1946- ... CANR-137
Earlier sketch in CA 77-80
See also SATA 108, 153
Ghilarducci, Teresa 1957- ... 144
Ghine, Wunnakyawhtin U Ohn
See Maurice, David (John Kerr)
Ghiotto, Renato 1923- ... 49-52
Ghiradella, Robert 1934- ... 114
Ghiselin, Brewster 1903-2001 ... CANR-13
Earlier sketch in CA 13-16R
See also CAAS 10
See also CLC 23
See also CP 1, 2, 3, 4, 5, 6, 7
Ghiselin, Michael T(enant) 1939- ... 49-52
Ghiselli, Edwin E(rnest) 1907-1980 ... 37-40R
Ghitani, Jamal al- 1945- ... EWL 3
Ghnassia, Maurice (Jean-Henri)
1920- ... CANR-34
Earlier sketch in CA 49-52
Ghose, Amal 1929- ... CANR-28
Earlier sketch in CA 106
Ghose, Aurabinda 1872-1950 ... 163
See also Ghose, Aurobindo
See also TCLC 63
Ghose, Aurobindo
See Ghose, Aurabinda
See also EWL 3
Ghose, Indira ... 233
Ghose, Manmohan 1869-1924 ... RGEL 2
Ghose, Sri Chinmoy Kumar
See Chinmoy, Sri
Ghose, Sudhin(dra) N(ath) 1899- ... 5-8R
Ghose, Zulfikar 1935- ... CANR-67
Earlier sketch in CA 65-68
See also CLC 42, 200
See also CN 1, 2, 3, 4, 5, 6, 7
See also CP 1, 2, 3, 4, 5, 6, 7
See also EWL 3
Ghosh, Amitav 1956- ... CANR-80
Earlier sketch in CA 147
See also CLC 44, 153
See also CN 6, 7
See also WWE 1
Ghosh, Arun Kumar 1930- ... CANR-26
Earlier sketches in CA 21-24R, CANR-10
Ghosh, Dipali 1945- ... CANR-51
Earlier sketch in CA 124
Ghosh, Jyotis Chandra 1904(?)-1975
Obituary ... 57-60
Ghosh, Tapan 1928- ... 53-56
Ghougassian, Joseph P(eter) 1944- ... 49-52
Ghurye, G(ovind) S(adashiv)
1893-1983 ... CANR-3
Earlier sketch in CA 5-8R
Ghymn, Esther Mikyung ... 196
Giacconi, Riccardo 1931- ... 156
Giacosa, Giuseppe 1847-1906
Brief entry ... 104
See also TCLC 7
Giacumakis, George, Jr. 1937- ... 41-44R
Giallombardo, Rose (Mary) 1925- ... 61-64
Giamatti, A(ngelo) Bartlett
1938-1989 ... CANR-77
Obituary ... 129
Earlier sketch in CA 97-100
Giamatti, Valentine 1911-1982
Obituary ... 106
Giambastiani, Kurt R. A. 1958- ... 212
See also SATA 141
Giamo, Benedict 1954- ... 204
Giampieri-Deutsch, Patrizia ... 148
Gianakaris, C(onstantine) J(ohn) 1934- .. 25-28R
Gianaris, Nicholas V. 1929- ... 175
Giangreco, D. M. 1952- ... 231
Giannaris, George (B.) 1936- ... CANR-45
Earlier sketches in CA 45-48, CANR-2, 22
Giannestras, Nicholas James 1909-1978
Obituary ... 105
Giannetti, Louis D. 1937- ... 33-36R
Giannini, Enzo 1946- ... SATA 68
Giannone, Richard 1934- ... CANR-95
Earlier sketch in CA 21-24R
Giannoni, Carlo Borromeo 1939- ... 41-44R
Giap Vo Nguyen
See Vo Nguyen, Giap
Giard, Robert 1939-2002 ... 170
Obituary ... 206
Giardina, Anthony 1950- ... CANR-108
Earlier sketch in CA 118
Giardina, Denise 1951- ... CANR-72
Earlier sketch in CA 119
Giardinelli, Mempo 1947- ... 176
See also EWL 3
Giardino, Vittorio 1946- ... 214
Giauque, William Francis 1895-1982
Obituary ... 106
Gibaldi, Joseph 1942- ... CANR-15
Earlier sketch in CA 89-92
Gibans, Nina Freedlander 1932- ... 116
Gibb, Hamilton (Alexander Rosskeen)
1895-1971 ... CANR-6
Obituary ... 33-36R
Earlier sketch in CA 1-4R
Gibb, Jack (Rex) 1914- ... 17-20R
Gibb, Lee
See Deghy, Guy (Stephen) and
Waterhouse, Keith (Spencer)
Gibb, Robert 1946- ... 169
Gibbard, Allan (Fletcher) 1942- ... 136
Gibbard, Graham S(tewart) 1942- ... 53-56
Gibbens, T(revor) C(harles) N(oel) 1912-1983
Obituary ... 111
Gibberd, Frederick 1908-1984
Obituary ... 111
Gibbings, Robert 1889-1958 ... DLB 195
Gibbins, Peter 1947- ... 127
Gibble, Kenneth L(ee) 1941- ... 130
Gibbon, Edward 1737-1794 ... BRW 3
See also DLB 104
See also RGEL 2
Gibbon, John Murray 1875-1952 ... 163
See also DLB 92
Gibbon, Lewis Grassic
See Mitchell, James Leslie
See also RGEL 2
See also TCLC 4
Gibbon, (William) Monk
1896-1987 ... CANR-76
Obituary ... 124
Earlier sketch in CA 69-72
See also CP 1, 2
Gibbon, Peter H(azen) 1942- ... 212

Cumulative Index 215 Gifford

Gibbon, Sean ... 231
Gibbon, Vivian 1917- ... 103
Gibbons, Alan 1953- ... SATA 124
Gibbons, Anne R(obert) 1947- ... 168
Gibbons, Barbara (Halloran) 1934- .. CANR-10
Earlier sketch in CA 61-64
Gibbons, Bob
See Gibbons, Robert
Gibbons, Brian 1938- ... CANR-11
Earlier sketch in CA 25-28R
Gibbons, Cedric 1893-1960 ... IDFW 3, 4
Gibbons, Don C(ary) 1926- ... 184
Brief entry ... 110
Gibbons, Euell (Theophilus)
1911-1975 ... CAP-2
Obituary ... 61-64
Earlier sketch in CA 23-24
See also AITN 1
Gibbons, Faye 1938- ... 109
See also SATA 65, 103
Gibbons, Felton L(ewis) 1929-1990 . CANR-75
Obituary ... 131
Earlier sketch in CA 124
Gibbons, (Raphael) Floyd (Phillips) 1887-1939
Brief entry ... 113
See also DLB 25
Gibbons, Gail (Gretchen) 1944- CANR-129
Earlier sketches in CA 69-72, CANR-12
See also CLR 8
See also CWRI 5
See also MAICYA 1, 2
See also SAAS 12
See also SATA 23, 72, 104, 160
Gibbons, Helen Bay 1921- ... 17-20R
Gibbons, J. Whitfield 1939- ... CANR-82
Earlier sketches in CA 114, CANR-35
Gibbons, John H(oward) 1929- ... 127
Gibbons, John William 1907-1983
Obituary ... 109
Gibbons, Kaye 1960- ... CANR-127
Earlier sketches in CA 151, CANR-75
See also AAYA 34
See also AMWS 10
See also CLC 50, 88, 145
See also CN 7
See also CSW
See also DA3
See also DAM POP
See also DLB 292
See also MTCW 2
See also MTFW 2005
See also NFS 3
See also RGAL 4
See also SATA 117
Gibbons, Maurice 1931- ... 89-92
Gibbons, Reginald 1947- ... 199
Earlier sketches in CA 97-100, CANR-18
Autobiographical Essay in ... 199
See also CAAS 24
See also CP 7
See also DLB 120
Gibbons, Robert 1949- ... CANR-39
Earlier sketch in CA 116
Gibbons, Stella (Dorothea)
1902-1989 ... CANR-76
Obituary ... 130
Earlier sketch in CA 13-16R
See also CN 1, 2, 3, 4
Gibbons, Whit
See Gibbons, J. Whitfield
Gibbons, William ... DLB 73
Gibbs, A(twood) James 1922- ... 17-20R
Gibbs, A(nthony) M(atthews) 1933- ... 33-36R
Gibbs, Adrea 1960- ... SATA 126
Gibbs, Alonzo (Lawrence)
1915-1992 ... CANR-5
Earlier sketch in CA 5-8R
See also SATA 5
Gibbs, Anthony 1902-1975 ... CAP-2
Earlier sketch in CA 29-32
Gibbs, Barbara 1912-1993 ... 25-28R
See also CP 1
Gibbs, C. Earl 1935- ... 69-72
Gibbs, David N. 1958- ... 139
Gibbs, Esther 1904-1990 ... 57-60
Gibbs, George (Fort) 1870-1942 ... 201
Brief entry ... 120
Gibbs, Henry
See Rumbold-Gibbs, Henry St. John Clair
Gibbs, Jack P(orter) 1927- ... 122
Brief entry ... 118
Gibbs, James A.
See Gibbs, James Atwood
Gibbs, James Atwood 1922- ... CANR-29
Earlier sketches in CA 69-72, CANR-11
Gibbs, Jim
See Gibbs, James Atwood
Gibbs, Joanifer 1947- ... 57-60
Gibbs, John G(amble) 1930- ... 41-44R
Gibbs, Mark 1920- ... 5-8R
Gibbs, Mary Ann
See Bidwell, Marjory Elizabeth Sarah
Gibbs, (Cecilia) May 1877-1969
Obituary ... 104
See also CWRI 5
See also SATA-Obit 27
Gibbs, Norman Henry 1910-1990
Obituary ... 131
Gibbs, Paul T(homas) 1897-1977 ... 9-12R
Gibbs, Peter Bawtree 1903- ... 1-4R
Gibbs, Philip (Hamilton) 1877-1962
Obituary ... 89-92
Gibbs, Rafe
See Gibbs, Raphael Sanford
Gibbs, Raphael Sanford 1912-1998 ... 5-8R
Gibbs, Tony
See Gibbs, Wolcott, Jr.
Gibbs, Tyson ... 175
Gibbs, William E. 1936-(?) ... CAP-2
Earlier sketch in CA 21-22
Gibbs, Wolcott, Jr. 1935- ... CANR-72
Earlier sketch in CA 85-88
See also SATA 40
Gibbs-Smith, Charles Harvard
1909-1981 ... CANR-4
Obituary ... 108
Earlier sketch in CA 9-12R
Gibbs-Wilson, Kathryn (Beatrice)
1930- ... CANR-10
Earlier sketch in CA 65-68
Gibby, Robert Gwyn 1916-1987 ... 13-16R
Giberson, Dorothy (Dodds) -1990 ... CANR-2
Earlier sketch in CA 1-4R
Giberson, Karl 1957- ... 187
Gibian, George 1924-1999 ... CANR-19
Earlier sketches in CA 1-4R, CANR-5
Gibilisco, Stan 1953- ... 147
Giblin, Charles Homer 1928-2002 ... 41-44R
Obituary ... 203
Giblin, James Cross 1933- ... CANR-100
Earlier sketches in CA 106, CANR-24
See also AAYA 39
See also BYA 9, 10
See also CLR 29
See also MAICYA 1, 2
See also SAAS 12
See also SATA 33, 75, 122
Giblon, Shirley T(enhouse) 1935- ... 131
Gibney, Frank (Bray) 1924- ... CANR-11
Earlier sketch in CA 69-72
Gibney, Harriet
See Harvey, Harriet
Gibney, Sheridan 1904(?)-1988
Obituary ... 125
Giboire, Clive (John) 1945- ... 118
Gibran, Daniel K. 1945- ... 208
Gibran, Jean 1933- ... 69-72
Gibran, Kahlil 1883-1931 ... 150
Brief entry ... 104
See also DA3
See also DAM POET, POP
See also EWL 3
See also MTCW 2
See also PC 9
See also TCLC 1, 9
See also WLIT 6
Gibran, Khalil
See Gibran, Kahlil
Gibson, A(lex) J. S. 1958- ... 150
Gibson, Alexander Cameron 1926- ... 134
Gibson, Alexander Dunnett 1901-1978
Obituary ... 77-80
Gibson, Andrew (William) 1949- ... SATA 72
Gibson, Ann Eden 1944- ... 169
Gibson, Anne (E.) 1954- ... 125
Gibson, Arrell Morgan 1921-1987 ... 41-44R
Gibson, Arthur 1943- ... 130
Gibson, Betty 1911- ... SATA 75
Gibson, Charles (Edmund) 1916-1997(?) ... 5-8R
Gibson, Charles 1920- ... 21-24R
Gibson, Charles Dana 1867-1944 ... 184
See also DLB 188
See also DLBD 13
Gibson, Charline 1937- ... 69-72
Gibson, D. Parke 1930-1979 ... 93-96
Obituary ... 85-88
Gibson, Derlyne 1936- ... 21-24R
Gibson, Donald B. 1933- ... 25-28R
See also BW 1
Gibson, E(rnest) Dana 1906-2000 ... 29-32R
Gibson, E(dward) Lawrence 1935- ... 93-96
Gibson, Eleanor Jack 1910-2002 ... 226
Gibson, Elizabeth 1949- ... 118
Gibson, Elsie (Edith) 1907- ... 61-64
Gibson, Eva 1939- ... CANR-35
Earlier sketch in CA 114
Gibson, Evan K(eith) 1909-1994 ... 105
Gibson, Frank K. 1924- ... 37-40R
Gibson, George H(orner) 1932-
Brief entry ... 114
Gibson, Gerald Don 1938- ... 104
Gibson, Gertrude Hevener 1906-1999 ... 5-8R
Gibson, Gifford Guy 1943- ... 77-80
Gibson, Graeme 1934- ... CANR-69
Earlier sketch in CA 130
See also CCA 1
See also CN 6, 7
See also DLB 53
Gibson, Gregory 1945- ... 214
Gibson, H(amilton) B(ertie) 1914-2001 ... 102
Obituary ... 194
Gibson, Harry Clark
See Hubler, Richard Gibson
Gibson, Henry 1935- ... 207
Gibson, Ian 1939- ... CANR-89
Earlier sketch in CA 145
Gibson, James (Charles) 1919-2005 . CANR-41
Obituary ... 238
Earlier sketch in CA 117
Gibson, James C.
See Gibson, James (Charles)
Gibson, James J(erome) 1904-1979 ... 85-88
Gibson, James L(awrence) 1935- ... CANR-8
Earlier sketch in CA 5-8R
Gibson, James W(illiam) 1932- ... 41-44R
Gibson, Janice T(horne) 1934- ... 41-44R
Gibson, Jo
See Fluke, Joanne
Gibson, John 1907- ... 33-36R
Gibson, John M(endinghall) 1899-1966(?) . 1-4R
Obituary ... 134
Gibson, John Michael ... 168
Gibson, Jon L. 1943- ... 223
Gibson, Josephine
See Hine, Al(fred Blakelee) and
Hine, Sesyle Joslin
Gibson, Karon Rose (White) 1946- ... 105
Gibson, Maralee G. 1924- ... 17-20R
Gibson, Margaret 1944- ... CANR-139
Earlier sketch in CA 77-80
See also CSW
See also DLB 120
Gibson, Margaret 1948- ... 103
Gibson, Margaret Dunlop 1843-1920 . DLB 174
Gibson, Mary Ellis 1952- ... 167
Gibson, Miles 1947- ... CANR-18
Earlier sketch in CA 102
Gibson, Morgan 1929- ... CANR-14
Earlier sketch in CA 25-28R
Gibson, (William) Morris(on) 1916- ... 117
Gibson, Nevin H(erman) 1915- ... 49-52
Gibson, P(atricia) J(oann) ... 142
See also BW 2
Gibson, Paul 1936- ... 144
Gibson, Raymond E(ugene) 1924- ... 21-24R
Gibson, Reginald Walter 1901- ... CAP-1
Earlier sketch in CA 13-14
Gibson, Richard (Thomas) 1931- ... 41-44R
See also BW 2
Gibson, Richard G. 1953- ... 159
Gibson, Robert (Donald Davidson)
1927- ... 65-68
Gibson, Robert L(ewis) 1927- ... 121
Gibson, Robert William, Jr. 1923- ... 107
Gibson, Ronald George 1909- ... 109
Gibson, Rosemary
See Newell, Rosemary
Gibson, Shirley 1927- ... 103
Gibson, Tony
See Gibson, H(amilton) B(ertie)
Gibson, (William) Walker 1919- ... CANR-1
Earlier sketch in CA 1-4R
Gibson, Walter B(rown) 1897-1985 . CANR-63
Obituary ... 118
Brief entry ... 108
Earlier sketch in CA 110
Interview in ... CA-110
See also CMW 4
Gibson, Walter Samuel 1932- ... 102
Gibson, Wilfrid Wilson 1878-1962 ... 176
Obituary ... 113
See also DLB 19
Gibson, William 1914- ... CANR-125
Earlier sketches in CA 9-12R, CANR-9, 42, 75
See also CAD
See also CD 5, 6
See also CLC 23
See also DA
See also DAB
See also DAC
See also DAM DRAM, MST
See also DFS 2
See also DLB 7
See also LAIT 2
See also MAL 5
See also MTCW 2
See also MTFW 2005
See also SATA 66
See also YAW
Gibson, William (Ford) 1948- ... CANR-106
Brief entry ... 126
Earlier sketches in CA 133, CANR-52, 90
See also AAYA 12, 59
See also BPFB 2
See also CLC 39, 63, 186, 192
See also CN 6, 7
See also CPW
See also DA3
See also DAM POP
See also DLB 251
See also MTCW 2
See also MTFW 2005
See also SCFW 2
See also SFW 4
See also SSC 52
Gibson, William Carleton 1913- ... 17-20R
Gibson, William E(dward) 1944- ... 33-36R
Gibson, William M(erriam) 1912-1987 ... 121
Obituary ... 146
Gibson-Jarvie, Clodagh 1923- ... 105
Gichon, Mordechai 1922- ... 89-92
Gicovate, Bernard 1922- ... 37-40R
Gidal, Nachum
See Gidal, Tim Nachum
Gidal, Peter 1946- ... 103
Gidal, Sonia (Epstein) 1922- ... CANR-14
Earlier sketch in CA 5-8R
See also SATA 2
Gidal, Tim Nachum 1909-1996 ... CANR-44
Obituary ... 154
Earlier sketches in CA 5-8R, CANR-14, 20
See also SATA 2
Gidalewitsch, Nachum
See Gidal, Tim Nachum
Giddens, Anthony 1938- ... CANR-114
Earlier sketch in CA 175
Gidding, Nelson 1919-2004 ... 142
Obituary ... 227
Giddings, Franklin Henry 1855-1931 ... 212
Giddings, James Louis 1909-1964 ... CAP-1
Earlier sketch in CA 11-12
Giddings, John Calvin 1930-1996 ... 109
Giddings, Paula 1948- ... CANR-80
Earlier sketch in CA 125
See also BW 1
Giddings, Robert (Lindsay) 1935- ... CANR-9
Earlier sketch in CA 21-24R
Giddins, Gary 1948- ... CANR-66
Earlier sketches in CA 77-80, CANR-13, 32
Giddy, Ian H. 1948- ... 114
Gide, Andre (Paul Guillaume) 1869-1951 .. 124
Brief entry ... 104
See also DA
See also DA3
See also DAB
See also DAC
See also DAM MST, NOV
See also DLB 65, 321
See also EW 8
See also EWL 3
See also GFL 1789 to the Present
See also MTCW 1, 2
See also MTFW 2005
See also NFS 21
See also RGSF 2
See also RGWL 2, 3
See also SSC 13
See also TCLC 5, 12, 36
See also TWA
See also WLC
Gideonse, Harry David 1901-1985
Obituary ... 115
Gidley, Charles
See Wheeler, (Charles) Gidley
Gidley, (Gustavus) M(ick) 1941- ... 102
Gidlow, Elsa 1898-1986 ... 77-80
Obituary ... 119
See also GLL 1
Gidney, James B. 1914- ... 45-48
Giedion, Sigfried 1888(?)-1968
Obituary ... 116
Giegling, John A(llan) 1935- ... 29-32R
See also SATA 17
Giele, Janet Z(ollinger) 1934- ... CANR-36
Earlier sketch in CA 114
Gielgud, Gwen Bagni
See Dubov, Gwen Bagni
Gielgud, (Arthur) John 1904-2000 ... 147
Obituary ... 188
Brief entry ... 111
Gielgud, Val (Henry) 1900-1981 ... CANR-80
Earlier sketches in CA 9-12R, CANR-5
Gien, Pamela ... 222
Gienow-Hecht, Jessica C. E. 1964- ... 225
Gier, Scott G. ... 167
Gierach, John 1946- ... 177
Giere, Ronald N(elson) 1938- ... CANR-4
Earlier sketch in CA 49-52
Giergielewicz, Mieczyslaw F.
1901-1983 ... CAP-2
Obituary ... 113
Earlier sketch in CA 25-28
Gierow, Karl Ragnar (Knut) 1904-1982
Obituary ... 108
Giersch, Herbert 1921- ... 147
Giersch, Julius
See Arnade, Charles W(olfgang)
Giertz, Bo H(arald) 1905-1998 ... CANR-9
Earlier sketch in CA 21-24R
Gies, David T(hatcher) 1945- ... 151
Gies, Frances 1915- ... CANR-9
Earlier sketch in CA 25-28R
Gies, Joseph (Cornelius) 1916- ... CANR-9
Earlier sketch in CA 5-8R
Gies, Thomas G(eorge) 1921- ... 33-36R
Giesbrecht, Martin Gerhard 1933- ... CANR-4
Earlier sketch in CA 53-56
Gieseking, Hal E. 1932- ... 131
Giesen, Rolf 1953- ... 238
Giesey, Ralph E(dwin) 1923- ... 25-28R
Giessler, Phillip Bruce 1938- ... CANR-8
Earlier sketch in CA 61-64
Giesy, J(ohn) U(lrich) 1877-1947
Brief entry ... 112
Gifaldi, David 1950- ... 143
See also SATA 76
Giff, Patricia Reilly 1935- ... CANR-99
Earlier sketches in CA 101, CANR-18, 41, 79
See also AAYA 54
See also JRDA
See also MAICYA 1, 2
See also SATA 33, 70, 121, 160
Giffard, Hannah 1962- ... SATA 83
Giffen, Daniel H. 1938- ... 107
Giffin, Frederick Charles 1938- ... 41-44R
Giffin, James Manning 1935- ... 105
Giffin, Mary (Elizabeth) 1919-2002 ... 130
Obituary ... 210
Giffin, Sidney F. 1907-1977
Obituary ... 73-76
Gifford, Barry (Colby) 1946- ... CANR-90
Earlier sketches in CA 65-68, CANR-9, 30, 40
See also CLC 34
Gifford, Denis 1927-2000 ... CANR-18
Obituary ... 188
Earlier sketch in CA 101
Gifford, Don (Creighton) 1919-2000 ... 53-56
Obituary ... 188
Gifford, Edward S(tewart), Jr. 1907- ... CAP-2
Earlier sketch in CA 19-20
Gifford, Francis Newton
See Gifford, Frank
Gifford, Frank 1930-
Brief entry ... 109
Gifford, Griselda 1931- ... CANR-24
Earlier sketch in CA 107
See also SATA 42
Gifford, (Charles) Henry 1913-2003 ... 17-20R
Obituary ... 221
Gifford, James Fergus, Jr. 1940- ... 57-60
Gifford, James J. 1946- ... 160
Gifford, Kathie Lee 1953- ... CANR-80
Earlier sketch in CA 142
Gifford, Kerri 1961- ... SATA 91
Gifford, Matt
See King, Albert
Gifford, Paul 1944- ... 209

Gifford, Prosser 1929- ... CANR-39
Earlier sketches in CA 101, CANR-18
Gifford, Terry 1946- ... CANR-24
Earlier sketch in CA 106
Gifford, Thomas (Eugene)
1937-2000 ... CANR-80
Obituary ... 191
Earlier sketch in CA 77-80
See also CMW 4
Gifford-Jones, W.
See Walker, Kenneth Francis
Gigerenzer, Gerd 1947- ... CANR-106
Earlier sketch in CA 135
Giggal, Kenneth 1927- ... CANR-80
Earlier sketches in CA 104, CANR-20, 44
Giggans, Patricia O(cchiuzzo) ... 168
Giglio, Ernest D(avid) 1931- ... 33-36R
Giglio, James N. 1939- ... CANR-104
Earlier sketch in CA 138
Giguere, Diane 1937- ... 25-28R
See also DLB 53
Giguere, Roland 1929- ... 175
See also DLB 60
Gih, Andrew 1901-1985 ... 21-24R
Gijsen, Marnix
See Goris, Jan-Albert
See also EWL 3
Gikandi, Simon ... 182
Gikow, Jacqueline 1947- ... 239
Gil, David G(eorg) 1924- ... CANR-12
Earlier sketch in CA 29-32R
Gil, Federico Guillermo 1915-2000 ... CANR-2
Earlier sketch in CA 1-4R
Gil, Moshe 1921- ... 143
Gil-Albert, Juan 1906-1994 ... DLB 134
Gilb, Corinne Lathrop 1925- ... 17-20R
Gilb, Dagoberto 1950- ... CANR-107
Earlier sketch in CA 159
Gilbar, Steven 1941- ... CANR-139
Earlier sketch in CA 106
Gilberg, Gail H(osking) 1950- ... 162
Gilbert
See Harrisse, Henry
Gilbert, Alan Graham 1944- ... 112
Gilbert, Allan H. 1888-1987 ... 9-12R
Gilbert, Alma M. 1937- ... 172
Gilbert, Amy M(argaret) 1895-1980 ... 49-52
Obituary ... 133
Gilbert, Ann
See Taylor, Ann
Gilbert, Anna
See Lazarus, Marguerite
Gilbert, Anne 1927- ... CANR-7
Earlier sketch in CA 57-60
Gilbert, Anne Yvonne 1951- ... SATA 128
Gilbert, Anthony
See Malleson, Lucy Beatrice
See also DLB 77
Gilbert, Arlene E(lsie) 1934- ... 49-52
Gilbert, Arthur 1926-1976 ... CANR-9
Earlier sketch in CA 17-20R
Gilbert, Barbara Snow 1954- ... CANR-141
Earlier sketch in CA 163
See also SATA 97
Gilbert, Ben W(illiam) 1918- ... 45-48
Gilbert, Benjamin Franklin
1918-1992 ... CANR-22
Earlier sketches in CA 17-20R, CANR-7
Gilbert, Bentley B(rinkerhoff) 1924- ... 25-28R
Gilbert, Bil 1927- ... CANR-78
Brief entry ... 129
Earlier sketch in CA 134
Interview in ... CA-134
Gilbert, Bill 1931- ... 105
Gilbert, Celia 1932- ... 115
Gilbert, Charles 1913- ... 41-44R
Gilbert, Christine B(ell) 1909- ... 103
Gilbert, Christopher 1949- ... 120
See also BW 2
Gilbert, Creighton (Eddy) 1924- ... CANR-15
Earlier sketch in CA 33-36R
Gilbert, David 1913-2002 ... 137
Gilbert, David T(hompson) 1953- ... 106
Gilbert, Doris Wilcox ... 17-20R
Gilbert, Doug 1938-1979
Obituary ... 104
Gilbert, Douglas 1942- ... 53-56
Gilbert, Douglas L. 1925- ... 13-16R
Gilbert, Edmund W(illiam) 1900-1973 ... 65-68
Gilbert, Edwin 1907-1976 ... 77-80
Obituary ... 69-72
Gilbert, Elizabeth 1969- ... CANR-137
Earlier sketch in CA 173
See also DLB 292
Gilbert, Elizabeth Rees ... 184
Gilbert, Elizabeth Stepp ... 184
Gilbert, Elliot L(ewis) 1930-1991 ... 147
Gilbert, Fabiola Cabeza de Baca
1898-1993 ... 177
See also Cabeza de Baca Gilbert, Fabiola
See also HW 2
Gilbert, Felix 1905-1991 ... 132
Brief entry ... 106
Gilbert, Frances
See Collings, Gillian
Gilbert, Frank
See De Voto, Bernard (Augustine)
Gilbert, George 1922- ... 69-72
Gilbert, Glenn Gordon 1936- ... CANR-13
Earlier sketch in CA 33-36R
Gilbert, Gordon Allan 1942- ... 103
Gilbert, Gorman 1943- ... 114
Gilbert, Gustave M. 1911-1977
Obituary ... 69-72
Gilbert, Harriett 1948- ... CANR-9
Earlier sketch in CA 57-60
See also SATA 30
Gilbert, Harry 1946- ... 106
Gilbert, Herman Cromwell
1923-1997 ... CANR-12
Earlier sketch in CA 29-32R
See also BW 2
Gilbert, Sir Humphrey 1537-1583 ... DLB 136
Gilbert, Jack 1925- ... CANR-80
Brief entry ... 116
Earlier sketch in CA 123
See also CP 1
See also TCLE 1:1
Gilbert, Jack G(lenn) 1934- ... 25-28R
Gilbert, James 1935- ... 29-32R
Gilbert, James B(urkhart) 1939- ... CANR-65
Earlier sketch in CA 129
Gilbert, Jarvey 1917-2000 ... 33-36R
Gilbert, (Agnes) Joan (Sewell) 1931- ... 21-24R
See also SATA 10
Gilbert, John (Raphael) 1926- ... 107
See also SATA 36
Gilbert, Julie Goldsmith
See Daniel, Julie Goldsmith
Gilbert, Kevin 1933-1993 ... 188
Gilbert, Lewis 1920- ... 237
Gilbert, Manu
See West, Joyce (Tarlton)
Gilbert, Marilyn B(ender) 1926- ... CANR-1
Earlier sketch in CA 1-4R
Gilbert, Martin (John) 1936- ... CANR-81
Earlier sketches in CA 9-12R, CANR-31
Gilbert, Michael (Francis) 1912- ... CANR-80
Earlier sketch in CA 1-4R
See also CAAS 15
See also CMW 4
See also DLB 87
See also MSW
Gilbert, Milton 1909(?)-1979
Obituary ... 93-96
Gilbert, Miriam
See Presberg, Miriam Goldstein
Gilbert, Nan
See Gilbertson, Mildred Geiger
Gilbert, Neil 1940- ... 77-80
Gilbert, R(obert) A(ndrew) 1942- ... 124
Gilbert, Robert E(mile) 1939- ... 53-56
Gilbert, Roby Goodale 1966- ... SATA 90
Gilbert, Rod(rigue Gabriel) 1941-
Brief entry ... 109
Gilbert, Ronnie 1926- ... 174
Gilbert, Russell Wieder 1905-1985 ... CANR-27
Obituary ... 115
Earlier sketch in CA 45-48
Gilbert, (Florence) Ruth 1917-
See Mackay, Florence Ruth
See also CP 2
Gilbert, Ruth Gallard Ainsworth
See Ainsworth, Ruth (Gallard)
Gilbert, S(tuart) R(eid) 1948- ... 101
Gilbert, Sandra M(ortola) 1936- ... CANR-106
Earlier sketches in CA 41-44R, CANR-14, 33, 69
See also CWP
See also DLB 120, 246
See also FW 1
See also MTCW 1
See also RGAL 4
Gilbert, Sara (Dulaney) 1943- ... CANR-6
Earlier sketch in CA 57-60
See also SATA 11, 82
Gilbert, Sarah 1959- ... 139
Gilbert, Sheri L. ... 233
See also SATA 157
Gilbert, Sister Mary
See DeFrees, Madeline
Gilbert, Stephen 1912- ... 25-28R
Gilbert, Steven E(dward) 1943-1999 ... 164
Gilbert, Suzie 1956- ... 164
See also SATA 97
Gilbert, Tom 1955- ... 142
Gilbert, Virginia 1946- ... 195
Gilbert, W(illiam) S(chwenck) 1836-1911 ... 173
Brief entry ... 104
See also DAM DRAM, POET
See also RGEL 2
See also SATA 36
See also TCLC 3
Gilbert, W(illiam) Stephen 1947- ... 155
Gilbert, Willie 1916-1980 ... CANR-37
Earlier sketch in CA 45-48
Gilbert, Yvonne
See Gilbert, Anne Yvonne
Gilbert, (Lerman) Zack 1925- ... 65-68
Gilberts, Helen 1909- ... 29-32R
Gilbertson, Merrill Thomas 1911-1988 ... 9-12R
Gilbertson, Mildred Geiger
1908-1988 ... CANR-2
Earlier sketch in CA 5-8R
See also SATA 2
Gilbey, John F.
See Smith, Robert W(illiam)
Gilbo, Patrick F(rancis) 1937- ... 107
Gilboa, Amir 1917-1984
Obituary ... 114
Gilboa, Yehoshua A. 1918-1981 ... CANR-35
Earlier sketch in CA 29-32R
Gilborn, Alice 1936- ... 69-72
Gilbreath, Alice 1921- ... CANR-25
Earlier sketches in CA 25-28R, CANR-10
See also SATA 12
Gilbreath, (Larry) Kent 1945- ... 45-48
Gilbreth, Frank B(unker), Jr. 1911-2001 ... 9-12R
See also CLC 17
See also SATA 2
Gilbreth, Lillian (Evelyn) Moller
1878-1972 ... 158
Obituary ... 33-36R
Gilcher, Edwin L. 1909- ... 29-32R
Gilchrist, Agnes A(ddison) 1907-1976
Obituary ... 65-68
Gilchrist, Alan W. 1913- ... 21-24R
Gilchrist, Alexander 1828-1861 ... DLB 144
Gilchrist, Andrew (Graham)
1910-1993 ... CANR-46
Obituary ... 140
Earlier sketches in CA 109, CANR-26
Gilchrist, Ellen (Louise) 1935- ... CANR-104
Brief entry ... 113
Earlier sketches in CA 116, CANR-41, 61
See also BPFB 2
See also CLC 34, 48, 143
See also CN 4, 5, 6, 7
See also CPW
See also CSW
See also DAM POP
See also DLB 130
See also EWL 3
See also EXPS
See also MTCW 1, 2
See also MTFW 2005
See also RGAL 4
See also RGSF 2
See also SSC 14, 63
See also SSFS 9
Gilchrist, J(ohn Thomas) 1927- ... 25-28R
Gilchrist, Jan Spivey 1949- ... MAICYA 2
See also MAICYAS 1
See also SATA 72, 130
Gilchrist, John
See Gardner, Jerome
Gilchrist, R(obert) Murray 1868-1917 ... HGG
Gilday, Robert M. 1925(?)-1980
Obituary ... 101
Gildea, Robert 1952- ... CANR-124
Earlier sketch in CA 154
Gildea, William 1939- ... 164
Gil de Biedma, Jaime 1929-1990 ... 174
See also DLB 108
See also HW 2
Gilden, Bert 1915(?)-1971 ... CAP-1
Obituary ... 29-32R
Earlier sketch in CA 11-12
Gilden, K. B.
See Gilden, Bert and
Gilden, Katya Alpert
Gilden, Katya Alpert 1919(?)-1991 ... 9-12R
Obituary ... 134
Gilden, Mel 1947- ... 153
See also SATA 97
Gilder, Eric 1911-2000 ... CANR-46
Earlier sketches in CA 89-92, CANR-15
Gilder, George F. 1939- ... CANR-102
Earlier sketches in CA 17-20R, CANR-9, 26
See also AITN 1
Gilder, Jeannette L. 1849-1916 ... 176
See also DLB 79
Gilder, Joshua 1954- ... 221
Gilder, Richard Watson 1844-1909 ... 176
See also DLB 64, 79
Gilder, Rosamond de Kay 1891-1986 ... 1-4R
Obituary ... 120
Gildersleeve, Basil Lanneau 1831-1924 ... 175
See also DLB 71
Gildersleeve, Thomas R(obert) 1927- ... 29-32R
Gildiner, Catherine 1948- ... 197
Gildner, Gary 1938- ... CANR-12
Earlier sketch in CA 33-36R
See also CP 7
Gildner, Judith 1943- ... 89-92
Gildrie, Richard P(eter) 1945- ... 73-76
Gildzen, Alex 1943- ... 41-44R
Gilead, Zerubavel 1912-1988 ... 123
Gilens, Martin ... 193
Giles, C(harles) W(ilfred) Scott
See Scott-Giles, C(harles) W(ilfred)
Giles, Carl H(oward) 1935- ... CANR-39
Earlier sketch in CA 29-32R
Giles, Elizabeth
See Holt, John (Robert)
Giles, Fiona ... 212
Giles, Frank (Thomas Robertson)
1919- ... CANR-82
Earlier sketch in CA 133
Giles, Frederick John 1928- ... 93-96
Giles, Gail ... 227
See also SATA 152
Giles, Geoffrey J(ohn) 1947- ... 122
Giles, Gordon A.
See Binder, Otto O(scar)
Giles, Henry 1809-1882 ... DLB 64
Giles, Jack
See Foster, Raymond Keith
See also TCWW 2
Giles, James R(ichard) 1937- ... 73-76
Giles, Janice Holt 1909-1979 ... CANR-3
Earlier sketch in CA 1-4R
See also RHW
Giles, Jeff 1965- ... 137
Giles, John (Richard) 1921-1991 ... 104
Giles, Kris
See Nielsen, Helen Berniece
Giles, Mary E(lizabeth) 1934- ... 108
Giles, Molly 1942- ... CANR-98
Earlier sketch in CA 126
See also CLC 39
Giles, Paul 1957- ... 145
Giles, Raymond
See Holt, John (Robert)
Giles, Robert Hartmann 1933- ... 141
Giles of Rome 1243(?)-1316 ... DLB 115
Gilfillan, Edward S(mith), Jr. 1906-1977 ... 57-60
Gilfillan, George 1813-1878 ... DLB 144
Gilfillan, Merrill (C.) 1945(?)- ... CANR-119
Obituary ... 152
Earlier sketch in CA 138
Gilfillan, Ross 1956- ... 180
Gilfond, Henry ... CANR-24
Earlier sketches in CA 21-24R, CANR-9
See also SATA 2
Gilford, C(harles) B(ernard) 1920- ... 17-20R
Gilford, Madeline Lee 1923- ... 85-88
Gilfoyle, Keren ... FANT
Gilge, Jeanette 1924- ... 61-64
See also SATA 22
Gilgen, Albert R(udolph) 1930- ... 37-40R
Gilgoff, Alice 1946- ... 85-88
Gilgun, John F(rancis) 1935- ... CANR-41
Earlier sketch in CA 117
Gilhooley, Jack
See Gilhooley, John
Gilhooley, John 1940- ... CANR-31
Earlier sketch in CA 85-88
Gilhooley, Leonard 1921- ... 37-40R
Gili, Phillida 1944- ... SATA 70
Gilien, Sasha 1925(?)-1971
Obituary ... 33-36R
Giliomee, Hermann (Buhr) 1938- ... 102
Gilison, Jerome Martin 1935- ... 103
Gilkerson, William 1936- ... 127
Gilkes, A(ntony) N(ewcombe) 1900- ... 5-8R
Gilkes, Cheryl Townsend 1947- ... 208
Gilkey, Langdon (Brown)
1919-2004 ... CANR-115
Obituary ... 233
Earlier sketches in CA 17-20R, CANR-7
Gilkyson, Bernice Kenyon 1898(?)-1982
Obituary ... 106
Gill, Alan
See Gillespie, Alfred
Gill, Anton 1948- ... CANR-86
Earlier sketch in CA 130
Gill, B. M.
See Trimble, Barbara Margaret
Gill, Bartholomew
See McGarrity, Mark
Gill, Bob 1931- ... CANR-48
Earlier sketch in CA 1-4R
Gill, Brendan 1914-1997 ... CANR-37
Obituary ... 163
Earlier sketch in CA 73-76
See also CN 1, 2, 3, 4, 5, 6
See also MTCW 1, 2
See also MTFW 2005
Gill, Christopher 1946- ... 209
Gill, (Ronald) Crispin 1916- ... CANR-12
Earlier sketch in CA 21-24R
Gill, David (Lawrence William)
1934- ... CANR-12
Earlier sketch in CA 29-32R
See also CP 1, 2
Gill, Derek (Lewis Theodore)
1919-1997 ... CANR-19
Earlier sketches in CA 49-52, CANR-4
See also SATA 9
Gill, Dominic 1941- ... 106
Gill, Elizabeth
See Hankin, Elizabeth Rosemary
Gill, Eric
See Gill, (Arthur) Eric (Rowton Peter Joseph)
See also TCLC 85
Gill, (Arthur) Eric (Rowton Peter Joseph)
1882-1940
Brief entry ... 120
See also Gill, Eric
See also DLB 98
Gill, Evan Robertson 1892- ... 9-12R
Gill, Frances McLaughlin 1919- ... 223
Gill, Frederick (Cyril) 1898- ... 5-8R
Gill, Gillian
See Gill, Gillian C(atherine)
Gill, Gillian C(atherine) 1942- ... 134
Gill, Glenda E. 1939- ... 192
Gill, Graeme 1947- ... 144
Gill, Harold B. 1933- ... 179
Gill, I(nayat) K(hera) 1924- ... 61-64
Gill, Jerry H. 1933- ... CANR-28
Earlier sketches in CA 33-36R, CANR-12
Gill, John Edward 1938- ... 106
Gill, Joseph 1901- ... CANR-3
Earlier sketch in CA 9-12R
Gill, Kay 1944- ... 111
Gill, Lakshmi 1943- ... 199
See also CP 1
Gill, LaVerne McCain 1947- ... CANR-130
Earlier sketch in CA 164
Gill, Margery Jean 1925- ... SATA 22
Gill, Mary Louise G(lanville) 1950- ... 209
Gill, Merton M(ax) 1914-1994 ... 122
Obituary ... 147
Gill, Patrick
See Creasey, John
Gill, Peter 1939- ... CANR-22
Earlier sketch in CA 103
See also CBD
See also CD 5, 6
Gill, Richard 1922-1989 ... CANR-75
Obituary ... 128
Earlier sketch in CA 41-44R
Gill, Richard T(homas) 1927- ... CANR-13
Earlier sketch in CA 21-24R
Gill, Sam D. 1943- ... 130
Gill, Sarah Prince 1728-1771 ... DLB 200
Gill, Stephen 1932- ... SATA 63
Gill, Suzanne L(utz) 1941- ... 136
Gill, Traviss 1891- ... CAP-1
Earlier sketch in CA 13-14
Gill, Walter 1937- ... 146
Gillan, Garth J. 1939- ... 102
Gillan, Maria (Mazziotti) 1940- ... 189
Gillan, Patricia Wagstaff 1936- ... 102
Gilland, Steve(n E.) 1953- ... 212
Gillchrest, Muriel Noyes 1905-1989 ... 25-28R

Cumulative Index **217** **Gingerich**

Gillelan, G(eorge) Howard 1917-1998 ... CANR-6
  Obituary ... 164
  Earlier sketch in CA 1-4R, 164
Gillen, Lucy
  See Stratton, Rebecca
Gillen, Mollie 1908- ... 41-44R
Gillen, Robert L(eonard) 1946- ... 114
Gillenson, Lewis William 1918-1992 ... 5-8R
  Obituary ... 139
Giller, Robert M(aynard) 1942-1996 ... 124
  Obituary ... 154
Gilles, Albert S(imeon) Sr. 1888-1979 ... 57-60
Gilles, Anthony E(ugene) 1945- ... 114
Gilles, Daniel 1917- ... 103
Gillese, John Patrick 1920- ... 13-16R
Gillespie, A(braham) Lincoln, Jr. 1895-1950
  Brief entry ... 115
  See also DLB 4
Gillespie, Alfred 1924- ... 77-80
Gillespie, Angus Kress 1942- ... CANR-90
  Earlier sketch in CA 132
Gillespie, Arnold 1899-1978 ... IDFW 3, 4
Gillespie, C. Kevin ... 212
Gillespie, Carol Ann 1951- ... 234
  See also SATA 158
Gillespie, Curtis 1960- ... 236
Gillespie, Cynthia K. 1941-1993 ... 133
  Obituary ... 140
Gillespie, Diane Filby 1943- ... 130
Gillespie, Dizzy
  See Gillespie, John Birks
Gillespie, Gerald 1933- ... CANR-10
  Earlier sketch in CA 25-28R
Gillespie, Haven 1888-1975 ... DLB 265
Gillespie, I(ris) S(ylvia) 1923- ... 65-68
Gillespie, J(ohn) David 1944- ... 144
Gillespie, James E(rnest), Jr. 1940- ... 53-56
Gillespie, Janet Wicks 1913- ... 5-8R
Gillespie, John Birks 1917-1993 ... 104
Gillespie, John E. 1921- ... 17-20R
Gillespie, John T(homas) 1928- ... CANR-57
  Earlier sketches in CA 73-76, CANR-13, 31
Gillespie, Kingsley 1895-1984
  Obituary ... 112
Gillespie, Link
  See Gillespie, A(braham) Lincoln, Jr.
Gillespie, Marcia Ann 1944- ... 134
  See also AITN 2
Gillespie, Michael Patrick 1946- ... 127
Gillespie, Neal C(ephas) 1933- ... 33-36R
Gillespie, Robert B(yrne) 1917- ... CANR-29
  Earlier sketch in CA 110
Gillespie, Robert W. 1922(?)-1983
  Obituary ... 110
Gillespie, Susan
  See Turton-Jones, Edith Constance (Bradshaw)
Gillet, Lev 1892(?)-1980
  Obituary ... 97-100
Gillett, Charlie 1942- ... 33-36R
Gillett, Edward 1915- ... 131
Gillett, Eric (Walkey) 1893-1978 ... CANR-3
  Earlier sketch in CA 5-8R
Gillett, Grant (Randall) 1950- ... 143
Gillett, J(ohn) D(avid) 1913-1995 ... 49-52
Gillett, Margaret 1930- ... CANR-82
  Earlier sketches in CA 1-4R, CANR-2, 17, 39
Gillett, Mary (Bledsoe) ... CAP-2
  Earlier sketch in CA 25-28
  See also SATA 7
Gillette, Arnold S(impson) 1904-1989 ... CANR-2
  Earlier sketch in CA 1-4R
Gillette, Douglas ... CLC 70
Gillette, Henry Sampson 1915- ... 5-8R
  See also SATA 14
Gillette, J(an) Lynett 1946- ... 170
  See also SATA 103
Gillette, J(ay) Michael 1939- ... 113
Gillette, Michael
  See Gillette, J(ay) Michael
Gillette, Paul 1938-1996 ... 53-56
  Obituary ... 151
Gillette, Virginia M(ary) 1920-1995 ... 57-60
Gillette, William 1933- ... 108
  See also RGAL 4
Gilley, Bruce 1966- ... 209
Gilley, Kay 1949- ... 212
Gilley, Sheridan (Wayne) 1945- ... CANR-86
  Earlier sketch in CA 133
Gillham, Bill
  See Gillham, W(illiam) E(dwin) C(harles)
Gillham, D. G. 1921- ... 21-24R
Gillham, Nicholas Wright 1932- ... 209
Gillham, W(illiam) E(dwin) C(harles) 1936- ... 113
  See also SATA 42
Gilliam, Dorothy B(utler) 1936- ... 97-100
Gilliam, Florence (Edna) ... 177
  See also DLB 4
Gilliam, Stan 1946- ... SATA 39
  See also SATA-Brief 35
Gilliam, Terry (Vance) 1940- ... CANR-35
  Brief entry ... 108
  Earlier sketch in CA 113
  Interview in ... CA-113
  See also Monty Python
  See also AAYA 19, 59
  See also CLC 21, 141
Gillian, Jerry
  See Gilliam, Terry (Vance)
Gillian, Kay
  See Smith, Kay Nolte
Gilliatt, Mary ... 237
Gilliatt, Penelope (Ann Douglass) 1932-1993 ... CANR-49
  Obituary ... 141
  Earlier sketch in CA 13-16R
  See also AITN 2
  See also CLC 2, 10, 13, 53
  See also CN 1, 2, 3, 4, 5
  See also DLB 14
Gillie, Christopher 1914- ... 102
Gillie, Oliver (John) 1937- ... CANR-12
  Earlier sketch in CA 65-68
Gillies, Archibald L. ... 127
Gillies, David 1952- ... 164
Gillies, John 1925- ... CANR-28
  Earlier sketches in CA 73-76, CANR-12
Gillies, Malcolm 1954- ... 137
Gillies, Mary Davis 1900-1993 ... CAP-2
  Earlier sketch in CA 25-28
Gillies, Valerie 1948- ... 188
Gilligan, Carol 1936- ... CANR-121
  Earlier sketch in CA 142
  See also CLC 208
  See also FW
Gilligan, Edmund 1898-1973
  Obituary ... 45-48
Gilligan, James F. 1935- ... 164
Gilligan, Sonja Carl 1936- ... 57-60
Gilliland, Alexis A(rnaldus) 1931- ... CANR-50
  Earlier sketches in CA 108, CANR-25
  See also FANT
  See also SATA 72
  See also SFW 4
Gilliland, C. Herbert 1942- ... 207
Gilliland, Charles
  See Muller, Charles G(eorge Geoffrey)
Gilliland, Charles Edward, Jr. 1916-1975
  Obituary ... 110
Gilliland, (Cleburne) Hap 1918- ... CANR-57
  Earlier sketches in CA 53-56, CANR-5
  See also SATA 92
Gillin, Caroline J(ulia) 1932- ... 45-48
Gillin, Donald George 1930- ... 33-36R
Gillin, John P(hilip) 1907-1973 ... 41-44R
  Obituary ... 45-48
Gilling, Tom ... 222
Gillingham, John (Bennett) 1940- ... CANR-18
  Earlier sketch in CA 97-100
Gillings, Richard John 1902-1987 ... 77-80
Gillion, Kenneth Lowell (Oliver) 1929- ... 93-96
Gillis, Chester 1951- ... 136
Gillis, Daniel 1935- ... 106
Gillis, Everett A(lden) 1914-1989 ... CANR-47
  Earlier sketches in CA 41-44R, CANR-15
Gillis, John R. 1939- ... 33-36R
Gillis, Patricia Ingle 1932-
  Brief entry ... 108
Gillis, Phyllis 1945- ... 116
Gillison, Samantha 1967- ... 174
Gillispie, Charles C(oulston) 1918- ... 13-16R
Gillman, Olga Marjorie 1894- ... 5-8R
Gillman, Peter (Charles) 1942- ... CANR-100
  Earlier sketch in CA 131
Gillman, Richard 1929- ... 17-20R
Gillmeister, Heiner 1939- ... 203
Gillmer, Thomas C(harles) 1911- ... CANR-45
  Earlier sketches in CA 57-60, CANR-6
Gillmer, Tom
  See Gillmer, Thomas C(harles)
Gillmor, C(harles) Stewart 1938- ... 45-48
Gillmor, Daniel S. 1917(?)-1975
  Obituary ... 61-64
Gillmor, Don 1954- ... 197
  See also SATA 127
Gillmor, Donald M(iles) 1926- ... 41-44R
Gillmor, Frances 1903-1993 ... CAP-2
  Earlier sketch in CA 17-18
Gillmore, David (Howe) 1934-1999 ... 21-24R
  Obituary ... 177
  See also Allamand, Pascale
Gillmore, Margalo 1897-1986
  Obituary ... 119
Gillon, Adam 1921- ... CANR-8
  Earlier sketch in CA 5-8R
Gillon, Diana (Pleasance Case) 1915- ... 13-16R
Gillon, Meir Selig 1907-1999 ... 13-16R
Gillon, Steven M. ... 231
Gillon, Werner 1905-1996 ... 126
Gillott, Jacky 1939-1980 ... 102
  See also DLB 14
Gillquist, Peter E. 1938- ... CANR-12
  Earlier sketch in CA 29-32R
Gilluly, James 1896-1980
  Obituary ... 102
Gilluly, Sheila ... 178
Gillum, Helen L(ouise) 1909- ... 69-72
Gilman, Andrew D. 1951- ... 137
Gilman, C(harles) Malcolm B(rookfield) 1898-1981 ... 107
Gilman, Caroline (Howard) 1794-1888 . DLB 3, 73
Gilman, Charlotte (Anna) Perkins (Stetson) 1860-1935 ... 150
  Brief entry ... 106
  See also AMWS 11
  See also BYA 11
  See also DLB 221
  See also EXPS
  See also FL 1:5
  See also FW
  See also HGG
  See also LAIT 2
  See also MAWW
  See also MTCW 2
  See also MTFW 2005
  See also RGAL 4
  See also RGSF 2
  See also SFW 4
  See also SSC 13, 62
  See also SSFS 1, 18
  See also TCLC 9, 37, 117
Gilman, Dorothy 1923- ... CANR-129
  Earlier sketch in CANR-30, 80
  Interview in ... CANR-30
  See also Butters, Dorothy Gilman
  See also CMW 4
Gilman, Esther 1925- ... SATA 15
Gilman, George G.
  See Harknett, Terry (Williams)
  See also TCWW 1, 2
Gilman, J. D.
  See Fishman, Jack and Orgill, Douglas
Gilman, James
  See Gilmore, Joseph L(ee)
Gilman, Owen W(inslow), Jr. 1947- ... 144
Gilman, Peter 1927-1999 ... 186
Gilman, Phoebe 1940-2002 ... CANR-128
  Obituary ... 210
  Earlier sketch in CA 171
  See also CWRI 5
  See also SATA 58, 104
  See also SATA-Obit 141
Gilman, Rebecca (Claire) 1965- ... 210
Gilman, Richard (Joan Thomas) 1925- ... CANR-74
  Earlier sketches in CA 53-56, CANR-5
Gilman, Robert Cham
  See Coppel, Alfred
Gilman, Sander L(awrence) 1944- ... CANR-5
  Earlier sketch in CA 53-56
Gilman, Stephen 1917-1986 ... 107
Gilman, Susan Jane 1964- ... 238
Gilman, William 1909-1978 ... 1-4R
Gilman, William H(enry) 1911-1976 ... 17-20R
  Obituary ... 65-68
Gilmer, Ann
  See Ross, W(illiam) E(dward) D(aniel)
Gilmer, B(everley) von Haller 1909- ... CANR-5
  Earlier sketch in CA 5-8R
Gilmer, Elizabeth Meriwether 1861(?)-1951
  Brief entry ... 114
  See also DLB 29
Gilmer, Francis Walker 1790-1826 ... DLB 37
Gilmer, (Frank) Walker 1935- ... 33-36R
Gilmer, Wesley, Jr. 1928- ... 115
Gil-Montero, Martha 1940- ... 153
  See also HW 1, 2
Gilmore, Alec 1928- ... 93-96
Gilmore, Al-Tony 1946- ... CANR-7
  Earlier sketch in CA 57-60
Gilmore, Anthony
  See Bates, Harry
Gilmore, Cecile
  See MacMillan, Cecile
Gilmore, Charles L(ee) ... 33-36R
Gilmore, Christopher Cook 1940- ... CANR-17
  Earlier sketch in CA 101
Gilmore, Daniel F(rancis) 1922-1988 ... CANR-76
  Obituary ... 126
  Earlier sketch in CA 65-68
Gilmore, David D. 1943- ... 133
Gilmore, Don 1930- ... 29-32R
Gilmore, Eddy (Lanier King) 1907-1967 ... 5-8R
Gilmore, Edith Spacil 1920- ... 1-4R
Gilmore, Gene 1920- ... 33-36R
Gilmore, Grant 1910-1982
  Obituary ... 111
Gilmore, Harold L(awrence) 1931- ... 53-56
Gilmore, Haydn 1928- ... 85-88
Gilmore, Iris 1900-1982 ... 97-100
  See also SATA 22
Gilmore, J(on) Barnard 1937- ... 195
Gilmore, J. Herbert, Jr. 1925- ... 33-36R
Gilmore, Jene Carlton 1933- ... 33-36R
Gilmore, John 1935- ... 180
  Earlier sketch in CA 25-28R
  Autobiographical Essay in ... 180
Gilmore, John (Norman) 1951- ... 133
Gilmore, Joseph L(ee) 1929- ... 81-84
Gilmore, Kate 1931- ... 151
  See also SATA 87
Gilmore, Maeve (?)-1983 ... CANR-76
  Obituary ... 110
  Earlier sketch in CA 102
Gilmore, Mary (Jean Cameron) 1865-1962 . 114
  See also DLB 260
  See also RGEL 2
  See also SATA 49
Gilmore, Mikal (George) 1951- ... CANR-117
  Earlier sketch in CA 149
Gilmore, Rachna 1953- ... 200
  See also MAICYA 2
Gilmore, Richard 1943- ... 107
Gilmore, Susan 1954- ... SATA 59
Gilmore, Thomas B(arry, Jr.) 1932- ... 73-76
Gilmore, William J(ames) 1945- ... 120
Gilmour, Barbara
  See Trimble, Barbara Margaret
Gilmour, David 1946- ... CLC 35
Gilmour, David 1949- ... CANR-115
  Earlier sketch in CA 138
Gilmour, David 1952- ... 147
Gilmour, Garth (Hamilton) 1925- ... CAP-1
  Earlier sketch in CA 9-10
Gilmour, H. B. 1939- ... 81-84
Gilmour, John C. 1939- ... 136
Gilmour, Robert S(cott) 1940- ... 69-72
Gilmour, Robin 1943- ... 124
Gilner, Elias 1888(?)-1976
  Obituary ... 65-68
Gilot, Francoise 1921- ... 108
Gilpatrick, Eleanor G(ottesfocht) 1930- ... CANR-9
  Earlier sketch in CA 21-24R
Gilpin, Alan 1924- ... CANR-28
  Earlier sketches in CA 25-28R, CANR-11
Gilpin, Alec Richard 1920-2000 ... 45-48
Gilpin, Andrea A. 1969- ... 198
Gilpin, John 1930-1983
  Obituary ... 114
Gilpin, Laura 1891-1979
  Obituary ... 111
Gilpin, Robert G., Jr. 1930- ... CANR-94
  Earlier sketch in CA 5-8R
Gilray, J. D.
  See Mencken, H(enry) L(ouis)
Gilray, James
  See Madsen, (Mark) Hunter
Gilroy, Beryl (Agatha) 1924- ... CANR-90
  Earlier sketch in CA 135
  See also BW 2
  See also EWL 3
  See also SATA 80
Gilroy, Frank D(aniel) 1925- ... CANR-86
  Earlier sketches in CA 81-84, CANR-32, 64
  See also CAD
  See also CD 5, 6
  See also CLC 2
  See also DFS 17
  See also DLB 7
Gilroy, Harry 1908(?)-1981
  Obituary ... 104
Gilroy, Thomas Laurence 1951- ... 103
Gilroy, Tom
  See Gilroy, Thomas Laurence
Gilson, Barbara
  See Gilson, Charles James Louis
Gilson, Charles James Louis 1878-1943 ... YABC 2
Gilson, Chris
  See Gilson, Christopher C.
Gilson, Christopher C. ... 204
Gilson, Estelle 1926- ... CANR-101
  Earlier sketch in CA 148
Gilson, Etienne Henry 1884-1978 ... 102
  Obituary ... 81-84
Gilson, Goodwin Woodrow 1918-1991 ... 17-20R
Gilson, Jamie 1933- ... CANR-135
  Earlier sketches in CA 111, CANR-57
  See also MAICYA 2
  See also MAICYAS 1
  See also SATA 37, 91
  See also SATA-Brief 34
Gilson, Thomas Q(uinleven) 1916- ... 5-8R
Gilstrap, John 1957(?)- ... CANR-101
  Earlier sketch in CA 160
  See also AAYA 67
  See also CLC 99
Gilstrap, Robert L(awrence) 1933- ... 9-12R
Gilyard, Keith 1952- ... 196
Gilzean, Elizabeth Houghton Blanchet 1913- ... 9-12R
Gimbel, John 1922-1992 ... CANR-2
  Earlier sketch in CA 1-4R
Gimbel, Wendy ... 182
Gimbutas, Marija (Alseika) 1921-1994 ... CANR-75
  Obituary ... 144
  Earlier sketch in CA 13-16R
Gimenez Caballero, Ernesto 1899-1988 ... 208
Gimferrer, Pere (Pedro) 1945- ... DLB 134
Gimlette, John 1963- ... 229
Gimmestad, Victor E(dward) 1912-1982 ... CANR-75
  Obituary ... 109
  Earlier sketch in CA 57-60
Gimpel, Erich 1910-1996 ... 225
Gimpel, Herbert J. 1915-1998 ... 17-20R
Gimpel, Jean (Victor) 1918-1996 ... 69-72
  Obituary ... 152
Gimson, Alfred Charles 1917-1985 ... CANR-77
  Obituary ... 116
  Earlier sketch in CA 5-8R
Ginandes, Shepard 1928- ... 41-44R
Ginat, Joseph ... 172
Ginder, Richard 1914-1984 ... 65-68
Gindin, James 1926-1994 ... CANR-2
  Earlier sketch in CA 5-8R
Gindorf, Rolf 1939- ... 171
Giner de los Rios, Francisco 1839-1915 ... 211
  Brief entry ... 105
Gines, Montserrat 1951- ... 212
Gingell, Benjamin Broughton 1924- ... 104
  See also CP 1
Ginger, Aleksandr 1897-1965 ... DLB 317
Ginger, Ann Fagan 1925- ... CANR-44
  Earlier sketches in CA 53-56, CANR-4, 19
Ginger, Helen 1916-1988 ... 17-20R
Ginger, John 1933- ... 25-28R
Gingerich, Martin E(llsworth) 1933- ... 118
Gingerich, Melvin 1902-1975 ... CAP-2
  Earlier sketch in CA 25-28

Gingerich, Owen (Jay) 1930- ... CANR-48
Earlier sketches in CA 53-56, CANR-5, 22
Gingher, Marianne 1947- ... 138
Gingher, Robert (S.) 1945- ... 141
Ginglend, David R. 1913-1989 ... 17-20R
Gingold, Hermione (Ferdinanda) 1887-1987 ... CANR-76
Obituary ... 122
Earlier sketch in CA 5-8R
Gingrich, Arnold 1903-1976 ... 13-16R
Obituary ... 69-72
See also DLB 137
Gingrich, F(elix) Wilbur 1901-1993 ... CAP-2
Earlier sketch in CA 17-18
Gingrich, Newt(on Leroy) 1943- ... CANR-129
Earlier sketches in CA 131, CANR-62
Giniger, Carol Virginia Wilkins 1929(?)-1985
Obituary ... 117
Giniger, Kenneth Seeman 1919- ... CANR-3
Earlier sketch in CA 5-8R
Ginn, Robert Jay, Jr. 1946- ... 107
Ginna, Robert Emmett, Jr. 1927(?)- ... 226
Ginnings, Harriett W.
See Harriett
Ginns, Patsy (Lee) M(oore) 1937- ... 69-72
Ginns, Ronald 1896-1976 ... CAP-1
Earlier sketch in CA 11-12
Ginori Lisci, Leonardo 1908-1987
Obituary ... 122
Ginott, Haim G. 1922-1973
Obituary ... 45-48
Ginsberg, Allen 1926-1997 ... CANR-95
Obituary ... 157
Earlier sketches in CA 1-4R, CANR-2, 41, 63
See also AAYA 33
See also AITN 1
See also AMWC 1
See also AMWS 2
See also BG 1:2
See also CDALB 1941-1968
See also CLC 1, 2, 3, 4, 6, 13, 36, 69, 109
See also CP 1, 2, 3, 4, 5, 6
See also DA
See also DA3
See also DAB
See also DAC
See also DAM MST, POET
See also DLB 5, 16, 169, 237
See also EWL 3
See also GLL 1
See also LMFS 2
See also MAL 5
See also MTCW 1, 2
See also MTFW 2005
See also PAB
See also PC 4, 47
See also PFS 5
See also RGAL 4
See also TCLC 120
See also TUS
See also WLC
See also WP
Ginsberg, Benjamin 1947- ... CANR-101
Earlier sketches in CA 121, CANR-48
Ginsberg, Debra 1962- ... 214
Ginsberg, Harold Louis 1903-1990
Obituary ... 132
Ginsberg, Joanne
See Summerfield, Joanne
Ginsberg, Leon H(erman) 1936- ... 105
Ginsberg, Louis 1895-1976 ... CANR-119
Obituary ... 65-68
Earlier sketch in CA 13-16R
See also CP 1
Ginsberg, Morris 1889-1970
Obituary ... 116
Ginsberg, Robert 1937- ... CANR-101
Earlier sketch in CA 25-28R
Ginsberg, Ruta
See Colombo, John Robert
Ginsborg, Paul (Anthony) 1945- ... 224
Ginsburg, Faye D(iana) 1952- ... 133
Ginsburg, Herbert (Paul) 1939- ... CANR-12
Earlier sketch in CA 73-76
Ginsburg, Mark B. 1949- ... CANR-102
Earlier sketch in CA 147
Ginsburg, Mirra 1909-2000 ... CANR-54
Obituary ... 193
Earlier sketches in CA 17-20R, CANR-11, 28
See also CLR 45
See also MAICYA 2
See also MAICYAS 1
See also SATA 6, 92
Ginsburg, (Joan) Ruth Bader 1933- ... CANR-124
Earlier sketch in CA 53-56
Ginsburg, Seymour 1927- ... CANR-13
Earlier sketch in CA 21-24R
Ginsburgh, Robert N(eville) 1923-1992 ... 13-16R
Ginsburgs, George 1932- ... CANR-4
Earlier sketch in CA 53-56
Ginsbury, Norman 1902-1991 ... 5-8R
Ginter, Maria 1922- ... 105
Ginther, John R(obert) 1922-1988 ... 185
Brief entry ... 107
Gintis, Herbert 1940- ... 57-60
Ginty, Robert 1948- ... CANR-144
Earlier sketch in CA 174
Ginzberg, Eli 1911-2002 ... CANR-52
Obituary ... 213
Earlier sketches in CA 5-8R, CANR-8, 27
Ginzberg, Yevgeniya 1906(?)-1977
Obituary ... 69-72
Ginzburg, Aleksandr (Ilich) 1936-2002 ... 239
Ginzburg, Alexander
See Ginzburg, Aleksandr (Ilich)
Ginzburg, Carlo 1939- ... CANR-101
Earlier sketch in CA 147
Ginzburg, Eugenia
See Ginzburg, Evgeniia
See also CLC 59
Ginzburg, Evgeniia 1904-1977
See Ginzburg, Eugenia
See also DLB 302
Ginzburg, Lidiia Iakovlevna 1902-1990 ... DLB 302
Ginzburg, Natalia 1916-1991 ... CANR-33
Obituary ... 135
Earlier sketch in CA 85-88
See also CLC 5, 11, 54, 70
See also DFS 14
See also DLB 177
See also EW 13
See also EWL 3
See also MTCW 1, 2
See also MTFW 2005
See also RGWL 2, 3
See also SSC 65
See also TCLC 156
Ginzburg, Ralph 1929- ... 21-24R
Ginzkey, Franz Karl 1871-1963 ... 175
See also DLB 81
Gioia, (Michael) Dana 1950- ... CANR-88
Earlier sketches in CA 130, CANR-70
See also AMWS 15
See also CP 7
See also DLB 120, 282
Gioia, Ted 1957- ... CANR-86
Earlier sketch in CA 127
Giono, Jean 1895-1970 ... CANR-35
Obituary ... 29-32R
Earlier sketches in CA 45-48, CANR-2
See also CLC 4, 11
See also DLB 72, 321
See also EWL 3
See also GFL 1789 to the Present
See also MTCW 1
See also RGWL 2, 3
See also TCLC 124
Giordan, Alma Roberts 1917- ... 57-60
Giordan, Marion (?)-1983
Obituary ... 110
Giordanetti, Elmo 1925-1984
Obituary ... 113
Giorno, John 1936- ... 33-36R
See also CP 1
Gioseffi, Daniela 1941- ... CANR-108
Earlier sketches in CA 45-48, CANR-3
Giotti, Virgilio 1885-1957 ... 175
See also DLB 114
Giovacchini, Peter L(ouis) 1922- ... 101
Giovagnoli, Melissa (E.) 1955- ... 193
Giovannetti, Alberto 1913- ... 9-12R
Giovanni, Nikki 1943- ... CANR-130
Earlier sketches in CA 29-32R, CANR-18, 41, 60, 91
Interview in ... CANR-18
See also CAAS 6
See also AAYA 22
See also AITN 1
See also BLC 2
See also BW 2, 3
See also CDALBS
See also CLC 2, 4, 19, 64, 117
See also CLR 6, 73
See also CP 2, 3, 4, 5, 6, 7
See also CSW
See also CWP
See also CWRI 5
See also DA
See also DA3
See also DAB
See also DAC
See also DAM MST, MULT, POET
See also DLB 5, 41
See also EWL 3
See also EXPP
See also MAICYA 1, 2
See also MAL 5
See also MTCW 1, 2
See also MTFW 2005
See also PC 19
See also PFS 17
See also RGAL 4
See also SATA 24, 107
See also TUS
See also WLCS
See also YAW
Giovannitti, Arturo 1884-1959 ... DLB 303
Giovannitti, Len 1920-1992 ... CANR-75
Obituary ... 137
Earlier sketch in CA 13-16R
Giovanopoulos, Paul (Arthur) 1939- ... SATA 7
Giovene, Andrea 1904-1998 ... 85-88
See also CLC 7
Giovino, Andrea ... 235
Gipe, George 1933-1986 ... CANR-75
Obituary ... 120
Earlier sketch in CA 77-80
Gippius, Zinaida (Nikolaevna) 1869-1945 . 212
Brief entry ... 106
See also Hippius, Zinaida (Nikolaevna)
Gipson, Carolyn R. 1944- ... 147
Gipson, Fred(erick Benjamin) 1908-1973 ... CANR-63
Obituary ... 45-48
Earlier sketches in CA 1-4R, CANR-3
See also BYA 2
See also JRDA
See also MAICYA 1, 2
See also SATA 2
See also SATA-Obit 24
See also TCWW 1, 2
See also YAW
Gipson, John (Durwood) 1932- ... 61-64
Gipson, Lawrence Henry 1880-1971 . CANR-3
Obituary ... 33-36R
Earlier sketch in CA 5-8R
See also DLB 17
Giragosian, Newman H. 1922- ... 93-96
Girard, Danielle ... 210
Girard, Hazel Batten 1901-1989 ... CANR-48
Earlier sketch in CA 112
Girard, Henri Georges Charles Achille 1917-1987
Obituary ... 121
Girard, James P(reston) 1944- ... 69-72
Girard, Joe 1928- ... CANR-129
Earlier sketches in CA 77-80, CANR-9
Girard, John
See Messerly, John G.
Girard, Linda (Walvoord) 1942- ... 114
See also SATA 41
Girard, Marvin Eugene 1924- ... 112
Girard, Mustang Marve
See Girard, Marvin Eugene
Girard, Rene N(oel) 1923- ... CANR-28
Earlier sketches in CA 9-12R, CANR-4
Girard, Robert C(olby) 1932- ... 101
Girard, Rodolphe 1879-1956 ... 175
See also DLB 92
Girardi, Joe
See Girard, Joe
Girardi, Robert 1962(?)- ... 230
Girardot, Norman J(ohn) 1943- ... 110
Giraud, Marcel 1900- ... 77-80
Giraudoux, Jean(-Hippolyte) 1882-1944 ... 196
Brief entry ... 104
See also DAM DRAM
See also DLB 65, 321
See also EW 9
See also EWL 3
See also GFL 1789 to the Present
See also RGWL 2, 3
See also TCLC 2, 7
See also TWA
Girdlestone, Cuthbert Morton 1895-1975 ... CANR-3
Obituary ... 65-68
Earlier sketch in CA 5-8R
Girgus, Sam B. 1941- ... 127
Girion, Barbara 1937- ... CANR-15
Earlier sketch in CA 85-88
See also SAAS 14
See also SATA 26, 78
Girling, John L(awrence) S(cott) 1926- ... 106
Girling, Richard 1945- ... CANR-129
Earlier sketch in CA 108
Girod, Gerald R(alph) 1939- ... 53-56
Girod, Gordon H. 1920-1992 ... 1-4R
Girodias, Maurice 1919-1990 ... CANR-72
Obituary ... 132
Brief entry ... 112
Earlier sketch in CA 129
Girodo, Michel 1945- ... 81-84
Giron, Manuel Buendia Tellez 1926(?)-1984
Obituary ... 112
See also HW 1
Girondo, Oliverio 1891-1967 ... DLB 283
See also HW 1
Gironella, Jose Maria
See Gironella, Jose Maria (Pous)
Gironella, Jose Maria (Pous) 1917-2003 ... 101
Obituary ... 212
See also CLC 11
See also EWL 3
See also RGWL 2, 3
Girouard, Mark 1931- ... CANR-101
Earlier sketch in CA 147
Girouard, Patrick 1957- ... SATA 155
Giroud, Francoise 1916-2003
See Giroud, Francoise
Giroud, Francoise 1916-2003 ... CANR-135
Obituary ... 212
Earlier sketches in CA 81-84, CANR-17, 39
See also AITN 1
Giroux, Andre 1916-1977 ... 166
Giroux, E. X.
See Shannon, Doris
Giroux, Henry A(rmand) 1943- ... CANR-141
Earlier sketches in CA 112, CANR-30
Giroux, Joan 1922- ... 93-96
Giroux, Robert 1914- ... CANR-52
Earlier sketches in CA 107, CANR-28
Girri, A.
See Girri, Alberto
Girri, Alberto 1919- ... EWL 3
See also HW 1
See also LAWS 1
Girsh, Myers L. 1906-1999 ... 166
Girshick, Lori B. 1953- ... 191
Girson, Rochelle ... 21-24R
Girtin, Thomas 1913-1994 ... 9-12R
Obituary ... 145
Girtin, Tom
See Girtin, Thomas
Girty, Simon
See King, Albert
Girvan, Helen (Masterman) 1891-1990 ... 73-76
Girvetz, Harry K(enneth) 1910-1974
Obituary ... 111
Girzaitis, Loretta 1920- ... CANR-2
Earlier sketch in CA 49-52
Girzone, Joseph F(rancis) 1930- ... CANR-115
Earlier sketches in CA 130, CANR-69
See also BEST 90:1
See also DAM POP
See also SATA 76
Giscard, Valery
See Giscard d'Estaing, Valery
Giscard d'Estaing, Valery 1926- ... 172
Brief entry ... 111
Gischler, Victor 1969- ... 230
Giscombe, C. S. 1950- ... CANR-99
Earlier sketch in CA 127
Gise, Joanne
See Mattern, Joanne
Gish, Arthur G. 1939- ... 29-32R
Gish, Lillian (Diana) 1893(?)-1993 ... 128
Obituary ... 140
Gish, Nancy K. 1942- ... 132
Gish, Robert F(ranklin) 1940- ... CANR-86
Earlier sketches in CA 133, CANR-50
Gishford, Anthony (Joseph) 1908-1975
Obituary ... 53-56
Gislason Hagalin, Gudmundur
See Hagalin, Gudmundur Gislason
Gisolfi, Anthony M. 1909-1992 ... CAP-2
Earlier sketch in CA 17-18
Gisselquist, David 1947- ... 112
Gissen, Max 1909(?)-1984
Obituary ... 114
Gissing, George (Robert) 1857-1903 ... 167
Brief entry ... 105
See also BRW 5
See also DLB 18, 135, 184
See also RGEL 2
See also SSC 37
See also TCLC 3, 24, 47
See also TEA
Gissler, Sig(vard Gunnar, Jr.) 1935- ... 134
Gist, John 1963- ... 181
Gist, Noel P(itts) 1899-1983 ... CANR-1
Earlier sketch in CA 1-4R
Gist, Ronald R. 1932- ... 21-24R
Gitchoff, G(eorge) Thomas 1938- ... 53-56
Gitchoff, Tom
See Gitchoff, G(eorge) Thomas
Gitelman, Zvi Y(echiel) 1940- ... 128
Brief entry ... 112
Githens, Suzanne B.
See Blanc, Suzanne
Gitin, David (Daniel) 1941- ... CANR-92
Earlier sketches in CA 49-52, CANR-2
Gitin, Maria (Brians) 1946- ... CANR-8
Earlier sketch in CA 61-64
Gitisetan, Dariush ... 118
Gitisetan, Darrin Dariush
See Gitisetan, Dariush
Gitlin, Murray 1903-1994 ... 1-4R
Gitlin, Todd 1943- ... CANR-88
Earlier sketches in CA 29-32R, CANR-25, 50
See also CLC 201
Gitlow, A(braham) Leo 1918- ... 1-4R
Gitlow, Benjamin 1891-1965
Obituary ... 89-92
Gittell, Marilyn 1931- ... CANR-55
Earlier sketches in CA 21-24R, CANR-9, 29
Gittelsohn, Roland B(ertram) 1910-1995 ... CANR-2
Earlier sketch in CA 5-8R
Gittelson, Celia ... 105
Gitter, A. George 1926- ... 102
Gitter, Elizabeth 1945- ... 204
Gittinger, J(ames) Price ... 41-44R
Gittings, Clare (St. Quentin) 1954- ... 130
Gittings, Jo (Grenville) Manton 1919- ... CANR-3
Earlier sketch in CA 5-8R
See also SATA 3
Gittings, John 1938- ... CANR-9
Earlier sketch in CA 21-24R
Gittings, Robert (William Victor) 1911-1992 ... CANR-43
Obituary ... 136
Earlier sketch in CA 25-28R
See also CP 1, 2
See also SATA 6
See also SATA-Obit 70
Gittins, Diana 1946- ... 113
Gittleman, Edwin 1929- ... 21-24R
Gittleman, Sol 1934- ... 65-68
Gittler, Joseph B(ertram) 1912- ... 37-40R
Giudici, Ann Couper 1929- ... 73-76
Giudici, Giovanni 1924- ... DLB 128
Giuliani, Alfredo 1924- ... 238
See also DLB 128
Giuliani, George A. 1938- ... 120
Giuliani, Rudolph W(illiam) 1944- ... 223
Giuliani, Rudy
See Giuliani, Rudolph W(illiam)
Giunti, Renato 1905-1983
Obituary ... 109
Giurlani, Aldo
See Palazzeschi, Aldo
Giuseppi, John (Anthony) 1900- ... CAP-2
Earlier sketch in CA 23-24
Giussani, Luigi 1922- ... 239
Giuttari, Theodore Richard 1931- ... 29-32R
Given, David R(oger) 1943- ... 157
Givens, Bill ... 222
Givens, Charles J. 1942(?)-1998 ... 140
Obituary ... 169
See also BEST 90:3
Givens, David B(radley) 1944- ... 119

Cumulative Index 219 Glendinning

Givens, Douglas R. 1944- CANR-96
Earlier sketch in CA 145
Givens, Janet E(aton) 1932- 111
See also SATA 60
Givens, John 1943- 77-80
Givens, Kathleen 1950- 209
Givner, Abraham 1944- 89-92
Givner, Joan Mary 1936- CANR-101
Earlier sketches in CA 108, CANR-25, 50
Giziowski, Richard (John) 1946- 171
Gizycka, Eleanor M.
See Patterson, Eleanor Medill
Gizzi, Michael 1949- CANR-117
Earlier sketch in CA 117
Gizzi, Peter 1959- 234
Gjellerup, Karl Adolf 1857-1919 .... DLB 300
Gjertsen, Derek 1933- 125
Gkoll, Yban
See Goll, Yvan
Glaab, Charles N(elson) 1927- CANR-8
Earlier sketch in CA 5-8R
Glaberman, Martin 1918- 187
Glackens, William J. 1870-1938 .... DLB 188
Glad, Betty 1929- 21-24R
Glad, Donald 1915-1978 .... 13-16R
Glad, John 1941- 133
Glad, Paul W(ilbur) 1926- 73-76
Gladden, E(dgar) Norman 1897- 21-24R
Gladden, Vivianne Cervantes 1927- 102
Gladding, Samuel T. 1945- 222
Glade, William P(atton), Jr. 1929- 41-44R
Gladilin, Anatolii Tikhonovich
See Gladilin, Anatoly (Tikhonovich)
See also DLB 302
Gladilin, Anatoly (Tikhonovich)
1935- CANR-44
Earlier sketches in CA 101, CANR-18
See also Gladilin, Anatolii Tikhonovich
Gladish, David F(rancis) 1928- 41-44R
Gladkov, Fedor Vasil'evich
See Gladkov, Fyodor (Vasilyevich)
See also DLB 272
Gladkov, Fyodor (Vasilyevich) 1883-1958 .. 170
See also Gladkov, Fedor Vasil'evich
See also EWL 3
See also TCLC 27
Gladney, Heather 1957- 127
Gladney, Margaret Rose 1945- 156
Gladney Glasserow, Marion 1925- 118
Gladstein, Mimi Reisel 1936- 187
Gladstone, Arthur M. 1921- 97-100
See also RHW
Gladstone, Eve
See Werner, Herma
Gladstone, Gary 1935- 29-32R
See also SATA 12
Gladstone, Josephine 1938- 21-24R
Gladstone, M(yron) J. 1923- 53-56
See also SATA 37
Gladstone, Maggie
See Gladstone, Arthur M.
Gladstone, Meredith 1939- 69-72
Gladstone, William Ewart 1809-1898 .. DLB 57, 184
Gladwin, William Zachary
See Zollinger, Gulielma
Gladych, B. Michael 1910- 5-8R
Glaeser, Ernst 1902-1963 178
See also DLB 69
Glaettli, Walter E(ric) 1920- 21-24R
Glahe, Fred R(ufus) 1934- CANR-14
Earlier sketch in CA 37-40R
Glain, Stephen 237
Glaister, John 1892-1971
Obituary 104
Glaister, Lesley (G.) 1956- CANR-127
Earlier sketch in CA 134
Glamis, Walter
See Schachner, Nathan(iel)
Glancy, Diane 1941- 225
Earlier sketches in CA 136, CANR-87
Autobiographical Essay in 225
See also CAAS 24
See also CLC 210
See also DLB 175
See also NNAL
Glancy, Ruth F(ergusson) 1948- 141
Glantz, David M. 1942- CANR-93
Earlier sketch in CA 135
Glantz, Kalman 1937- 132
Glanvill, Joseph 1636-1680 .... DLB 252
Glanville, Brian (Lester) 1931- CANR-70
Earlier sketches in CA 5-8R, CANR-3
See also CAAS 9
See also CLC 6
See also CN 1, 2, 3, 4, 5, 6, 7
See also DLB 15, 139
See also SATA 42
Glanville, Maxwell 1918-1992 85-88
Glanville, Ranulph 1946- 114
Glanz, Edward C(oleman) 1924-1986 .... 1-4R
Glanz, Karen 1953- 135
Glanz, Rudolf 1892-1978 .... CANR-3
Earlier sketch in CA 49-52
Glanzman, Louis S. 1922- .... SATA 36
Glapthorne, Henry 1610-1643(?) .... DLB 58
See also RGEL 2
Glasberg, Davita Silfen 1951- 165
Glasby, John S. 1928- 224
Glasco, Michael 1945- 153
Glaser, Byron 1954- .... SATA 154
Glaser, Daniel 1918- 61-64
Glaser, Dianne E(lizabeth) 1937- 77-80
See also SATA 50
See also SATA-Brief 31
Glaser, E(ric) M(ichael) 1913-1992 .... 21-24R
Glaser, Edward 1918-1972
Obituary 37-40R
Glaser, Eleanor Dorothy
See Zonik, Eleanor Dorothy
Glaser, Elizabeth 1947-1994 .... CANR-80
Obituary 147
Earlier sketch in CA 138
Glaser, Elton 1945- CANR-93
Earlier sketch in CA 111
Glaser, Eva Schocken 1918-1982
Obituary 105
Glaser, Hermann 1928- 180
Glaser, Isabel Joshlin 1929- CANR-65
Earlier sketch in CA 77-80
See also SATA 94
Glaser, James M. 1960- 163
Glaser, Kurt (Comstock) 1914-1993 .... CANR-5
Earlier sketch in CA 1-4R
Glaser, Lynn 1943- 21-24R
Glaser, Milton 1929- CANR-135
Earlier sketches in CA 17-20R, CANR-11
See also SATA 11, 151
Glaser, Robert 1921- CANR-7
Earlier sketch in CA 17-20R
Glaser, Rollin Oliver 1932- CANR-10
Earlier sketch in CA 25-28R
Glaser, Shirley .... SATA 151
Glaser, William A(rnold) 1925- CANR-45
Earlier sketch in CA 1-4R
Glasgow, Douglas G. 108
Glasgow, Ellen (Anderson Gholson)
1873-1945 164
Brief entry 104
See also AMW
See also DLB 9, 12
See also MAL 5
See also MAWW
See also MTCW 2
See also MTFW 2005
See also RGAL 4
See also RHW
See also SSC 34
See also SSFS 9
See also TCLC 2, 7
See also TUS
Glasgow, Eric 1924- 69-72
Glasgow, Gordon H(enry) H(arper)
1926- 29-32R
Glasgow, Jack
See Larson, Doran
Glasgow, Mary Cecilia 1905-1983
Obituary 111
Glasheen, Adaline 1920-1993 101
Glasheen, Patrick 1897- CAP-1
Earlier sketch in CA 13-14
Glasier, Katharine Bruce 1867-1950 ... DLB 190
Glaskin, G(erald) M(arcus) 1923- CANR-46
Earlier sketches in CA 53-56, CANR-5
Glaskowsky, Nicholas A(lexander), Jr.
1928- CANR-3
Earlier sketch in CA 5-8R
Glasmeier, Amy (K.) 1955- 199
Glaspell, Susan 1882(?)-1948 154
Brief entry 110
See also AMWS 3
See also DC 10
See also DFS 8, 18
See also DLB 7, 9, 78, 228
See also MAWW
See also RGAL 4
See also SSC 41
See also SSFS 3
See also TCLC 55
See also TCWW 2
See also TUS
See also YABC 2
Glasrud, Bruce (Alden) 1940- 41-44R
Glass, Albert J(ulius) 1908-1983
Obituary 109
Glass, Amanda
See Krentz, Jayne Ann
Glass, Andrew 1949- CANR-123
Earlier sketches in CA 134, CANR-57
See also SATA 90, 150
See also SATA-Brief 46
Glass, Andrew J(ames) 1935- 65-68
Glass, Bill 1935- CANR-13
Earlier sketch in CA 73-76
Glass, Charles 1951- 139
Glass, David Victor 1911-1978 85-88
Obituary 81-84
Glass, Dee Dee 1948- CANR-100
Earlier sketch in CA 149
Glass, Ian Cameron 1926-1997 77-80
Glass, James C. 1937- 183
Glass, Joanna (McClelland) 1936- CANR-43
Earlier sketch in CA 81-84
Glass, John F(ranklin) 1936- 53-56
Glass, Jospeh
See Libertson, Joseph
Glass, Julia 1956- 222
Glass, Justine C.
See Corrall, Alice Enid
Glass, Leopold
See Pascoe, Bruce
Glass, Leslie CANR-98
Earlier sketch in CA 168
Glass, Malcolm (Sanford) 1936- CANR-20
Earlier sketch in CA 104
Glass, Montague (Marsden) 1877-1934 173
Brief entry 117
See also DLB 11
Glass, Philip 1937- CANR-131
Earlier sketch in CA 171
Glass, Ruth 1912-1990
Obituary 131
Glass, Sandra
See Shea, Robert (Joseph)
Glass, Stanley T(homas) 1932- 21-24R
Glassberg, B(ertrand) Y(ounker)
1902-1971(?) CAP-1
Earlier sketch in CA 13-16
Glassberg, David 199
Glassburner, Bruce 1920- 33-36R
Glassco, John 1909-1981 .... CANR-15
Obituary 102
Earlier sketch in CA 13-16R
See also CLC 9
See also CN 1, 2
See also CP 1, 2
See also DLB 68
Glasscock, Amnesia
See Steinbeck, John (Ernst)
Glasscock, Anne Bonner 1924- 1-4R
See also Bonner, Michael
Glasscock, Sarah (Jean) 1952- 130
Glasse, Robert Marshall 1929-1993 ...... 29-32R
Obituary 140
Glasser, Allen 1918- 9-12R
Glasser, Ira 1938- 137
Glasser, Paul H(arold) 1929- CANR-15
Earlier sketch in CA 29-32R
Glasser, Perry 1948- 127
Glasser, Ronald J. 1940(?)- 209
See also CLC 37
Glasser, Selma 110
Glasser, Stephen A(ndrew) 1943- 53-56
Glasser, William 1925- CANR-93
Earlier sketch in CA 73-76
Glasserow, Mario N.
See Gladney Glasserow, Marion
Glasserow, Marion Gladney
See Gladney Glasserow, Marion
Glassford, Wilfred
See McNeilly, Wilfred (Glassford)
Glassgold, Peter 1939- 103
Glassie, Henry 1941- 148
Glassie, Henry H(aywood) 1914-1987
Obituary 124
Glassman, Bernard Tetsugen
1939- CANR-122
Earlier sketch in CA 112
Glassman, Bernie
See Glassman, Bernard Tetsugen
Glassman, Bruce 1961- 143
See also SATA 76
Glassman, James K(enneth) 1947- CANR-88
Earlier sketch in CA 127
Glassman, Jon David 1944- 69-72
Glassman, Jonathon P. 1956- 151
Glassman, Joyce
See Johnson, Joyce
Glassman, Maxine 181
Glassman, Michael 1899-1982 .... 13-16R
Glassman, Peter Joel 1945- 113
Glassman, Ronald M. 1937- 134
Brief entry 111
Glassman, Steve 1946- 191
Glassner, Barry 1952- 135
Glassner, Lester 1939- 107
Glassner, Martin Ira 1932- CANR-90
Earlier sketches in CA 41-44R, CANR-15, 34
Glasson, Thomas Francis 1906- CAP-1
Earlier sketch in CA 9-10
Glassop, (Jack) Lawson 1913-1966 .... CAP-1
Earlier sketch in CA 9-10
Glasstone, Victor 1924- CANR-10
Earlier sketch in CA 65-68
Glaston, W. B.
See Lazenby, Norman
Glatstein, Jacob 1896-1971
Obituary 33-36R
See also EWL 3
Glatt, John 1952- 155
Glatt, Lisa 1963- 231
Glatthaar, Joseph T(homas) 1957- 142
Glatthorn, Allan A. 1924- 13-16R
Glattstein, Judy 1942- 137
Glatzer, Hal 1946- CANR-122
Earlier sketch in CA 57-60
Glatzer, Nahum Norbert
1903-1990 .... CANR-83
Obituary 131
Earlier sketches in CA 13-16R, CANR-7
Glauber, Uta (Heil) 1936- 29-32R
See also SATA 17
Glaus, Marlene 1933- 21-24R
Glauser, Friedrich 1896-1938 175
See also DLB 56
Glave, Thomas 1964- 223
Glavin, Anthony 1946- .... DLB 319
Glavin, John P(atrick) 1933- 57-60
Glazar, Bob 1954- 115
Glazar, Richard 1920-1998
Glaze, Andrew (Louis III) 1920- CANR-108
Earlier sketches in CA 17-20R, CANR-8, 24
Glaze, Eleanor 1930- 49-52
Glaze, Thomas E(dward) 1914- 1-4R
Glazebrook, G(eorge) P(arkin) de T(wenebrokes)
1899-1989 102
Glazebrook, Philip (Kirkland)
1937- CANR-113
Earlier sketch in CA 29-32R
Glazener, Mary U(nderwood) 1921- 17-20R
Glazer, Amihai 1950- 215
Glazer, Benjamin 1887-1956 .... IDFW 3
Glazer, Daphne (Fae) 1938- CANR-92
Earlier sketches in CA 119, CANR-45
Glazer, Ellen Sarasohn 1947- CANR-101
Earlier sketch in CA 148
Glazer, Nathan 1923- CANR-64
Earlier sketch in CA 5-8R
Glazer, Nona Y.
See Glazer-Malbin, Nona
Glazer, Sidney 1905-1983 .... 1-4R
Obituary 111
Glazer, Thomas (Zachariah)
1914-2003 .... CANR-8
Obituary 213
Earlier sketch in CA 61-64
See also SATA 9
Glazer, Tom
See Glazer, Thomas (Zachariah)
Glazer-Malbin, Nona 1932- 33-36R
Glazier, Kenneth MacLean 1912- 9-12R
Glazier, Loss P(equeno) 228
Glazier, Lyle (Edward) 1911- 37-40R
See also CAAS 24
Glazier, Stephen 1947- 108
Glazier, Stephen D. 1949- 175
Glazner, Greg(ory Allen) 1958- 142
Glazner, Joseph Mark 1945- 104
Gleadow, Rupert Seeley 1909-1974 . CANR-82
Obituary 103
Earlier sketch in CA 9-12R
Gleasner, Diana (Cottle) 1936- CANR-86
Earlier sketches in CA 65-68, CANR-15, 33
See also SATA 29
Gleason, Abbott 1938- CANR-21
Earlier sketch in CA 104
Gleason, Eugene Franklin 1914-1987 .... 1-4R
Gleason, Gene
See Gleason, Eugene Franklin
Gleason, Harold 1892-1980 .... CAP-1
Earlier sketch in CA 9-10
Gleason, John (Marquis) 1942- 107
Gleason, John J(ames), Jr. 1934- 120
Gleason, Judith 1929- CANR-9
Earlier sketch in CA 61-64
See also SATA 24
Gleason, Katherine (A.) 1960- CANR-132
Earlier sketch in CA 171
See also SATA 104
Gleason, Madeline 1913- .... CP 1
Gleason, Ralph J(oseph) 1917-1975 65-68
Obituary 61-64
Gleason, Robert 1945- 118
Gleason, Robert J(ames) 1906- 73-76
Gleason, Robert Walter 1917-1982 .... CANR-4
Earlier sketch in CA 1-4R
Gleason, S(arel) Everett 1905-1974
Obituary 53-56
Gleave, T(homas) P(ercy) 1908-1993 127
Obituary 141
Gleaves, Robert M(ilnor) 1938- 53-56
Gleaves, Suzanne 1904-1991 .... 9-12R
Gleckner, Robert Francis
1925-2001 .... CANR-17
Earlier sketches in CA 1-4R, CANR-2
Gledhill, Alan 1895-1983 .... CAP-1
Obituary 110
Earlier sketch in CA 9-10
Gledhill, John 1949- 151
Gleditsch, Kristian Skrede 1971- 236
Glees, Anthony 1948- 134
Gleeson, Janet 221
Gleeson, Kathleen 1964- 174
Gleeson, Libby 1950- CANR-121
Earlier sketches in CA 149, CANR-96
See also CWRI 5
See also SATA 82, 118, 142
See also SATA-Essay 142
Gleeson, Ruth (Ryall) 1925- 9-12R
Gleick, James (W.) 1954- CANR-97
Brief entry 131
Earlier sketch in CA 137
Interview in CA-137
See also CLC 147
Gleick, Peter H. 1956- 201
Gleim, Johann Wilhelm Ludwig
1719-1803 .... DLB 97
Gleiman, Lubomir 1923- 41-44R
Gleisser, Marcus D(avid) 1923- 17-20R
Gleiter, Jan 1947- 172
See also SATA 111
Gleitman, Lila R. 1929- 114
Gleitzman, Morris 1953- CANR-140
Earlier sketch in CA 131
See also CLR 88
See also CWRI 5
See also SATA 88, 156
Glemser, Bernard 1908-1990
Obituary 131
Glen, Duncan (Munro) 1933- CANR-12
Earlier sketch in CA 21-24R
See also CP 2, 3, 4, 5, 6, 7
Glen, Eugene
See Fawcett, F(rank) Dubrez
Glen, Frank Grenfell 1933- 106
Glen, J(ohn) Stanley 1907-1986 .... CAP-1
Obituary 118
Earlier sketch in CA 9-10
Glen, Maggie 1944- .... SATA 88
Glen, Paul (Michael) 1965- 225
Glen, Robert S. 1925- 29-32R
Glenday, Alice 1920- 57-60
Glendenning, Donn
See Paine, Lauran (Bosworth)
Glendenning, Raymond Carl 1907-1974
Obituary 114
Glendinning, Chellis 230
Glendinning, Miles CANR-105
See also Horsey, Miles G.
Glendinning, Richard 1917-1988 .... 21-24R
See also SATA 24
Glendinning, Robin 1938- .... DLB 310
Glendinning, Sally
See Glendinning, Sara W(ilson)

Glendinning 220 CONTEMPORARY AUTHORS

Glendinning, Sara W(ilson)
1913-1993 .... CANR-2
Earlier sketch in CA 49-52
See also SATA 24
Glendinning, Victoria 1937- CANR-89
Brief entry 120
Earlier sketches in CA 127, CANR-59
See also CLC 50
See also DLB 155
Glendon, Mary Ann 1938- CANR-105
Earlier sketch in CA 41-44R
Glener, Doug 226
Glenn, Armon 1912-1992 107
Glenn, Cheryl 162
Glenn, Christine Genevieve 1947- 115
Glenn, Constance W(hite) 1933- 128
Glenn, Dorothy
See Garlock, Dorothy
Glenn, Edmund S(tanislas) 1915-1987 113
Glenn, Evelyn Nakano 1940- 233
Glenn, Frank 1901-1982
Obituary 106
Glenn, Harold T(heodore)
1910-1977 .... CANR-5
Earlier sketch in CA 5-8R
Glenn, Jack 1936- 194
Glenn, Jacob B. 1905-1974 .... CANR-4
Obituary 49-52
Earlier sketch in CA 9-12R
Glenn, James
See Paine, Lauran (Bosworth)
Glenn, Jerry (Hesmer, Jr.) 1938- 45-48
Glenn, John H(erschel), Jr. 1921- 156
Glenn, Laura Franklin 1867-1942 204
Glenn, Lois (Ruth) 1941- 61-64
Glenn, Mel 1943- CANR-127
Earlier sketches in CA 123, CANR-49, 68
See also AAYA 25
See also CLR 51
See also MAICYA 2
See also MAICYAS 1
See also SATA 51, 93
See also SATA-Brief 45
See also WYAS 1
See also YAW
Glenn, Morton B(ernard) 1922- 61-64
Glenn, Norval Dwight 1933- 17-20R
Glenn, Patricia Brown 1953- 151
See also SATA 86
Glenn, Russell W(illiam) 1953- 195
Glenn, Sharlee 235
See also SATA 159
Glenn, Sharlee Mullins
See Glenn, Sharlee
Glenn, Susan A(nita) 1950- 215
Glennon, Bert 1893-1967 .... IDFW 3, 4
Glennon, James 1900- 25-28R
Glennon, Karen M. 1946- 151
See also SATA 85
Glennon, Maurade 1926- 25-28R
Glenny, Lyman A(lbert) 1918-2001 .... CANR-7
Obituary 199
Earlier sketch in CA 17-20R
Glenny, Michael Valentine 1927-1990 102
Obituary 132
Glenny, Misha 1958- 192
Gles, Margaret Breitmaier 1940- 57-60
See also SATA 22
Gleser, Goldine C(ohnberg) 1915- 17-20R
Gless, Darryl James 1945- 102
Glessing, Robert J(ohn) 1930- 29-32R
Gleysteen, William 1926-2002 228
Gliauda, Jurgis 1906- CANR-3
Earlier sketch in CA 5-8R
Glick, Bernard R. 1945- 150
Glick, Carl (Cannon) 1890-1971 .... 5-8R
Obituary 103
See also SATA 14
Glick, Edward Bernard 1929- CANR-8
Earlier sketch in CA 21-24R
Glick, G(arland) Wayne 1921- 25-28R
Glick, Paul C(harles) 1910- 5-8R
Glick, Paula Brown
See Brown, Paula
Glick, Ruth (Burtnick) 1942- CANR-92
Earlier sketches in CA 89-92, CANR-16
See also SATA 125
Glick, Thomas F(rederick) 1939- CANR-34
Earlier sketches in CA 29-32R, CANR-15
Glick, Virginia Kirkus 1893-1980 .... CAP-2
Obituary 101
Earlier sketch in CA 21-22
See also SATA-Obit 23
Glick, Wendell 1916- 111
Glick, William H. 1952- 146
Glickman, Albert S(eymour) 1923- 53-56
Glickman, Arthur P. 1940- 61-64
Glickman, Beatrice Marden 1919- 102
Glickman, Gary 1959- CANR-74
Earlier sketch in CA 128
See also GLL 2
Glickman, James (A.) 1948- 157
Glickman, Norman J. 1942- 135
Glickman, Rose L. 1933- 196
Glickman, S(teyen) Craig 1947- 116
Glickman, Susan 1953- CANR-38
Earlier sketch in CA 116
Glicksberg, Charles Irving
1900-1998 .... CANR-2
Earlier sketch in CA 1-4R
Glicksman, Abraham M(orton)
1911-1999 .... 5-8R
Glidden, F. D.
See Glidden, Frederick D(illey)
Glidden, Frederick D(illey)
1908-1975 .... CANR-71
Obituary 61-64
Earlier sketches in CAP-2, CA 21-22
See also Short, Luke
See also DLB 256
Glidden, Horace Knight 1901-1987 ...... CAP-1
Earlier sketch in CA 13-16
Glidden, Jonathan Hurff 1907-1957
See Dawson, Peter
Glidden, Laraine Masters 1943- 236
Gliddend, Fred
See Glidden, Frederick D(illey)
Glidewell, John Calvin 1919- CANR-48
Earlier sketches in CA 13-16R, CANR-7, 23
Glieberman, Herbert A(llen) 1930- 112
Gliewe, Unada (Grace) 1927- CANR-12
Earlier sketch in CA 29-32R
See also SATA 3
Glik, Hirsh 1922-1944
Glikberg, Aleksandr Mikhailovich 1880-1932
See Cherny, Sasha
Glikes, Erwin (Arno) 1937-1994 .... 13-16R
Obituary 145
Glimcher, Arnold B. 1938- 81-84
Glimm, James Y(ork) 1942- 132
Glimmerveen, Ulco 1958- 132
See also SATA 85
Glines, Carroll V(ane), Jr. 1920- CANR-2
Earlier sketch in CA 1-4R
See also SATA 19
Glinka, Fedor Nikolaevich
1786-1880 .... DLB 205
Gliori, Debi 1959- 209
See also SATA 72, 138
Gliozzo, Charles 1932- 45-48
Gliserman, Martin 1945- 157
Glissant, Edouard (Mathieu) 1928- .. CANR-111
Earlier sketch in CA 153
See also CLC 10, 68
See also CWW 2
See also DAM MULT
See also EWL 3
See also RGWL 3
Glisson, J(ake) T. 1927- 143
Glisson, Jerry (Lee) 1923- 113
Gloag, John (Edwards) 1896-1981 .... CANR-10
Obituary 104
Earlier sketch in CA 65-68
Gloag, Julian 1930- CANR-70
Earlier sketches in CA 65-68, CANR-10
See also AITN 1
See also CLC 40
See also CN 1, 2, 3, 4, 5, 6
Glob, Peter Vilhelm 1911-1985 97-100
Obituary 117
Globe, Leah Ain 1900- 107
See also SATA 41
Globus, Yoram c. 1943- .... IDFW 3
Glock, Allison 226
Glock, Charles Y(oung) 1919- CANR-5
Earlier sketch in CA 53-56
Glock, Marvin D(avid) 1912-2000 .... 21-24R
Gloer, (William) Hulitt 1950- CANR-53
Earlier sketch in CA 126
Glogau, Art(hur H.) 1922-1974 53-56
Glogau, Lillian Flatow Fleischer 1925- 85-88
Glogowski, Maryruth F(rancine) P(helps)
1950- 120
Glorfeld, Louis E(arl) 1916-1979 53-56
Glori Ann
See Blakely, Gloria
Glos, Raymond E(ugene) 1903-1988 ..... 21-24R
Gloss, Molly 1944- CANR-90
Earlier sketch in CA 132
Glossop, Ronald J. 1933- 144
Glotzer, Albert 1908-1999 133
Glovach, Linda 1947- CANR-31
Earlier sketches in CA 37-40R, CANR-14
See also SATA 7, 105
Glover, Albert Gould 1942- 89-92
Glover, Bob
See Glover, Robert H.
Glover, Crispin (Hellion) 1964- 201
Glover, Denis (James Matthews)
1912-1980 .... CANR-30
Obituary 101
Earlier sketch in CA 77-80
See also CP 1, 2
See also RGEL 2
See also SATA 7
Glover, Donald E(llsworth) 1933- 116
Glover, Douglas (Herschel) 1948- 182
Earlier sketches in CA 137, CANR-80
Autobiographical Essay in 182
See also CAAS 23
See also CN 6, 7
Glover, Harry 1912- 77-80
Glover, Janice 1919-2000 .... 17-20R
Glover, John D(esmond) 1915- CANR-2
Earlier sketch in CA 5-8R
Glover, Jon(athan Martin) 1943- 133
See also CP 7
Glover, Judith 1943- CANR-22
Earlier sketch in CA 106
See also RHW
Glover, Keith 1966- .... DLB 249
Glover, Leland E(llis) 1917-1966 .... 9-12R
Glover, Michael 1922- CANR-23
Earlier sketches in CA 17-20R, CANR-8
Glover, Richard 1712-1785 .... DLB 95
Glover, Robert H. 1946- 116
Glover, Ruth 237
Glover, Stephen (Charles Morton)
1952- CANR-128
Earlier sketch in CA 164
Glover, Sue 1943- .... DLB 310
Glover, (David) Tony "Harp Dog"
1939- CANR-125
Earlier sketch in CA 13-16R
Gloversmith, Frank 1936- 127
Glowacki, Aleksander
See Prus, Boleslaw
Glowacki, Janusz 1938- 116
Glubb, John Bagot 1897-1986 .... CANR-83
Obituary 118
Earlier sketches in CA 9-12R, CANR-5
Glubb Pasha
See Glubb, John Bagot
Glubok, Shirley (Astor) CANR-43
Earlier sketches in CA 5-8R, CANR-4
See also CLR 1
See also MAICYA 1, 2
See also SAAS 7
See also SATA 6, 68, 146
See also SATA-Essay 146
Gluck, Carol 1941- CANR-53
Earlier sketch in CA 126
Gluck, Felix 1923-1981
Obituary 103
See also SATA-Obit 25
Gluck, Herb 1925- CANR-31
Earlier sketches in CA 45-48, CANR-2
Gluck, Jay 1927- CANR-12
Earlier sketch in CA 21-24R
Gluck, Louise (Elisabeth) 1943- CANR-133
Earlier sketches in CA 33-36R, CANR-40, 69, 108
See also AMWS 5
See also CLC 7, 22, 44, 81, 160
See also CP 1, 2, 3, 4, 5, 6, 7
See also CWP
See also DA3
See also DAM POET
See also DLB 5
See also MAL 5
See also MTCW 2
See also MTFW 2005
See also PC 16
See also PFS 5, 15
See also RGAL 4
See also TCLE 1:1
Gluck, Mary 1947- 127
Gluck, Robert 1947- CANR-68
Earlier sketches in CA 113, CANR-32
Gluckin, Doreen Sandra 1949- 108
Gluckman, Janet
See Berliner, Janet
Gluckman, Max 1911-1975 .... 9-12R
Obituary 57-60
Glucksberg, Harold 1939- 105
Glueck, Eleanor T(ouroff) 1898-1972 . CANR-9
Obituary 37-40R
Earlier sketches in CAP-2, CA 17-18
Glueck, Nelson 1900-1971 .... CAP-2
Earlier sketch in CA 17-18
Glueck, Sheldon 1896-1980 .... CANR-9
Obituary 97-100
Earlier sketch in CA 5-8R
Glueck, William F(rank) 1934-1980 . CANR-27
Earlier sketch in CA 33-36R
Glueckauf, Eugen 1906-1981
Obituary 108
Gluss, Brian 1930- 104
Glustrom, Simon W. 1924- 21-24R
Glut, Donald F(rank) 1944- CANR-139
Earlier sketches in CA 33-36R, CANR-13
Gluyas, Constance (J.) 1920-1983 136
Brief entry 115
Gluzman, Brian
See Gluss, Brian
Glyman, Caroline A. 1967- 170
See also SATA 103
Glyn, Anthony 1922-1998 53-56
Obituary 164
Glyn, Caroline 1947- CANR-5
Earlier sketch in CA 9-12R
Glyn, Elinor 1864-1943 .... DLB 153
See also RHW
See also TCLC 72
Glyn, Richard Hamilton 1907-1980 105
Obituary 102
Glynn, Alan 1960- 235
Glynn, James A. 1941- 57-60
Glynn, Jeanne Davis 1932- 29-32R
Glynn, Jenifer 1929- 128
Glynn, Leonard M. 1948- 130
Glynn, Prudence (Loveday) 1935-1986 129
Obituary 120
Glynn, Thomas P(eter) 1935- 93-96
Glynne-Jones, M(arjorie) L(ilian) 1936- 186
Brief entry 111
Glynne-Jones, William 1907-1977 .... 5-8R
See also SATA 11
Gmelch, George 1944- 103
Gmelch, Sharon Bohn 1947- 103
Gmelch, Walter H(oward) 1947- 112
Gnaegy, Charles 1938- 89-92
Gnagey, Thomas D(avid) 1938- CANR-46
Earlier sketch in CA 49-52
Gnagy, Jon
See Gnagy, Michael Jacques
Gnagy, Michael Jacques 1907(?)-1981
Obituary 103
Gnarowski, Michael 1934- 41-44R
See also CP 1, 2
Gnedich, Nikolai Ivanovich
1784-1833 .... DLB 205
Gneuss, Helmut (Walter Georg) 1927- 141
Gniffke, Rudolf
See Hartmann, Rudolf A.
Gnosticus
See Weschcke, Carl L(ouis)
Gnuse, Robert K(arl) 1947- 121
Go, Janet G. 1930- 166
Go, Puan Seng 1904-1994 .... CAP-2
Earlier sketch in CA 29-32
Goacher, Denis (John) 1925-1998 104
See also CP 2
Goaman, Muriel
See Cox, Edith Muriel
Goane, Thomas
See James, Laurence
Gobar, Ash 1930- 41-44R
Gobbato, Imero 1923- .... SATA 39
Gobbell, John J. 1937- CANR-127
Earlier sketch in CA 154
Gobbi, Tito 1915-1984 129
Obituary 112
Brief entry 105
Gobbletree, Richard
See Quackenbush, Robert M(ead)
Gobineau, Joseph-Arthur 1816-1882 .. DLB 123
See also GFL 1789 to the Present
Goble, Alan 1938- 143
Goble, Danney 1946- 136
Goble, Dorothy 93-96
See also SATA 26
Goble, Frank G(ordon) 1917-2000 112
Goble, (Lloyd) Neil 1933- 29-32R
Goble, Paul 1933- CANR-16
Earlier sketch in CA 93-96
See also CLR 21
See also CWRI 5
See also MAICYA 1, 2
See also SATA 25, 69, 131
Goble, Warwick (?)-1943 .... SATA 46
Gobodo-Madikizela, Pumla 225
Gocek, Matilda A(rkenbout) 1923- CANR-1
Earlier sketch in CA 49-52
Gochfeld, Michael 1940- 137
Gockel, Herman W. 1906-1996 .... CANR-1
Earlier sketch in CA 1-4R
Godard, Jean-Luc 1930- 93-96
See also CLC 20
Godbeer, Richard 213
Godber, John (Harry) 1956- 205
See also CBD
See also CD 5, 6
See also DLB 233
Godbert, Geoffrey Harold 1937- .... CP 1
Godbold, E(dward) Stanly, Jr. 1942- 37-40R
Godbolt, Jim 1922- 129
Godbout, Jacques 1933- 142
Brief entry 125
See also CCA 1
See also DLB 53
See also EWL 3
Goddard, Alfred
See Harper, Carol Ely
Goddard, Beatrice Romaine
See Brooks, Romaine
Goddard, Burton L(eslie) 1910- 21-24R
Goddard, Donald 1934- CANR-28
Earlier sketches in CA 17-20R, CANR-11
Goddard, Gladys Benjamin 1881(?)-1976
Obituary 61-64
Goddard, Hugh (P.) 1953- 216
Goddard, J(ack) R. 1930- 29-32R
Goddard, Kenneth (William) 1946- .. CANR-72
Earlier sketch in CA 110
Goddard, Morrill 1865-1937 181
See also DLB 25
Goddard, Robert (William) 1954- CANR-72
Earlier sketch in CA 134
Goddard, Robert H(utchings) 1882-1945 ... 156
Brief entry 118
Goddard, Tariq 1975- 226
Goddard, William 1740-1817 .... DLB 43
Godden, Geoffrey 1929- 102
Godden, Jon 1906-1984 .... CANR-27
Obituary 112
Earlier sketch in CA 77-80
Godden, (Margaret) Rumer
1907-1998 .... CANR-80
Obituary 172
Earlier sketches in CA 5-8R, CANR-4, 27, 36, 55
See also AAYA 6
See also BPFB 2
See also BYA 2, 5
See also CLC 53
See also CLR 20
See also CN 1, 2, 3, 4, 5, 6
See also CWRI 5
See also DLB 161
See also MAICYA 1, 2
See also RHW
See also SAAS 12
See also SATA 3, 36
See also SATA-Obit 109
See also TEA
Gode, Alexander
See Gode von Aesch, Alexander (Gottfried Friedrich)
Godechot, Jacques Leon
1907-1989 .... CANR-25
Earlier sketches in CA 65-68, CANR-9
Godefroy, Vincent 1912-1978 69-72
Godel, Kurt
See Godel, Kurt Friedrich
Godel, Kurt Friedrich 1906-1978 157
Obituary 108
Gode von Aesch, Alexander (Gottfried Friedrich) 1906-1970 .... CAP-1
Earlier sketch in CA 9-10
See also SATA 14
Godey, John
See Freedgood, Morton
Godey, Louis A. 1804-1878 .... DLB 73
Godfrey, Bob 1921- .... IDFW 3, 4

Cumulative Index 221 **Goldberg**

Godfrey, Cuthbert John 5-8R
Godfrey, (William) Dave 1938- CANR-70
Earlier sketches in CA 69-72, CANR-11
See also CN 1, 2, 3, 4, 5, 6
See also DLB 60
Godfrey, Donald G. 140
Godfrey, Eleanor S(mith) 1914-2002 69-72
Godfrey, Ellen (Rachel) 1942- CANR-134
Earlier sketch in CA 113
Godfrey, Frederick M. 1901-1974 .... CAP-1
Earlier sketch in CA 13-14
Godfrey, Henry F. 1906-1975 .... CAP-2
Earlier sketch in CA 25-28
Godfrey, Jane
See Bowden, Joan Chase
Godfrey, Joline 1950- 220
Godfrey, Laurie R(ohde) 1945- 113
Godfrey, Lionel (Robert Holcombe)
1932- 81-84
Godfrey, Martyn
See Godfrey, Martyn N. and
Godfrey, Martyn N.
See also CWRI 5
Godfrey, Martyn N. 1949-2000 .... CANR-68
Earlier sketch in CA 126
See also Godfrey, Martyn
See also CLR 57
See also SATA 95
Godfrey, Michael A. 1940- CANR-14
Earlier sketch in CA 81-84
Godfrey, Neale S. 1951- 149
Godfrey, Peter 1917-1992 .... CANR-122
Earlier sketch in CA 124
Godfrey, R. H.
See Tubb, E(dwin) C(harles)
Godfrey, Thomas 1736-1763 .... DLB 31
Godfrey, Vincent H. 1895(?)-1975
Obituary 57-60
Godfrey, William
See Youd, (Christopher) Samuel
Godin, Gabriel 1929- 73-76
Godine, David R(ichard) 1944- 101
Godkin, Celia (Marilyn) 1948- CANR-126
Earlier sketches in CA 133, CANR-82
See also SATA 66, 145
Godkin, E(dwin) L(awrence) 1831-1902 210
See also DLB 79
Godley, John
See Kilbracken, John (Raymond Godley)
Godly, J. P.
See Plawin, Paul
Godman, Arthur 1916-2004 .... CANR-24
Earlier sketch in CA 106
Godolphin, Francis R(ichard) B(orroum)
1903-1974 65-68
Obituary 53-56
Godolphin, Sidney 1610-1643 .... DLB 126
See also RGEL 2
Godown, Marian Bailey 103
Godoy Alcayaga, Lucila 1899-1957 . CANR-81
Brief entry 104
Earlier sketch in CA 131
See also Mistral, Gabriela
See also BW 2
See also DAM MULT
See also DNFS
See also HLC 2
See also HW 1, 2
See also MTCW 1, 2
See also MTFW 2005
See also PC 32
See also TCLC 2
Godsey, John Drew 1922- 13-16R
Godshalk, C. S. 170
Godshalk, William Leigh 1937- 41-44R
Godson, John 1937- 77-80
Godson, Joseph 1913-1986 142
Obituary 120
Godson, Roy (S.) 1942- CANR-109
Brief entry 111
Earlier sketch in CA 155
Godwin, Anthony Richard James Wylie
1920(?)-1976
Obituary 104
Godwin, Gail (Kathleen) 1937- CANR-132
Earlier sketches in CA 29-32R, CANR-15, 43, 69
Interview in CANR-15
See also BPFB 2
See also CLC 5, 8, 22, 31, 69, 125
See also CN 3, 4, 5, 6, 7
See also CPW
See also CSW
See also DA3
See also DAM POP
See also DLB 6, 234
See also MAL 5
See also MTCW 1, 2
See also MTFW 2005
Godwin, Gaylord 1906(?)-1979
Obituary 85-88
Godwin, George (Stanley) 1889-1974 .... 5-8R
Godwin, Harry 1901-1985 109
Obituary 117
Godwin, John (Frederick) 1922- CANR-41
Earlier sketches in CA 102, CANR-19
Godwin, John 1929- CANR-89
Earlier sketches in CA 1-4R, CANR-1, 16
Godwin, Joscelyn 1945- CANR-96
Earlier sketches in CA 69-72, CANR-12, 29, 55, 91
Godwin, Larry 1942- 187
Godwin, Mary Jane 1766-1841 .... DLB 163
Godwin, Mike 1956- 185
Godwin, Parke 1816-1904
Brief entry 119
See also DLB 3, 64, 250
Godwin, Parke 1929- CANR-136
Earlier sketch in CA 157
See also FANT
Godwin, Peter (Christopher) 1957- . CANR-103
Earlier sketch in CA 143
Godwin, Phillip E(arl) 1954-1989
Obituary 130
Godwin, Rebecca T. 1950- 139
Godwin, Tom 1915-1980 156
See also SFW 4
Godwin, Tony
See Godwin, Anthony Richard James Wylie
Godwin, William
1756-1836 .... CDBLB 1789-1832
See also CMW 4
See also DLB 39, 104, 142, 158, 163, 262
See also GL 2
See also HGG
See also RGEL 2
Godwin-Jones, Robert 1949- 137
Goebbels, Josef
See Goebbels, (Paul) Joseph
Goebbels, (Paul) Joseph 1897-1945 148
Brief entry 115
See also TCLC 68
Goebbels, Joseph Paul
See Goebbels, (Paul) Joseph
Goebel, Dorothy (Burne) 1898-1976 69-72
Obituary 65-68
Goebel, Julius, Jr. 1893(?)-1973
Obituary 45-48
Goedecke, Christopher (John) 1951- 149
See also SATA 81
Goedecke, W(alter) Robert 1928- 29-32R
Goedertier, Joseph M. 1907- CAP-2
Earlier sketch in CA 25-28
Goedicke, Hans 1926- CANR-19
Earlier sketches in CA 45-48, CANR-1
Goedicke, Patricia (McKenna)
1931- CANR-53
Earlier sketches in CA 25-28R, CANR-11, 27
See also CP 1, 2, 3, 4, 5, 6, 7
See also CWP
Goedicke, Victor (Alfred) 1912-1996 .... 17-20R
Goehlert, Robert 1948- 157
Goehr, Lydia 194
Goekler, Susan
See Wooley, Susan Frelick
Goel, M(adan) Lal 1936- 53-56
Goeldner, Charles R. 1932- CANR-62
Earlier sketch in CA 128
Goele, Dhruv 198
Goeller, Carl 1930- 21-24R
Goelz, Paul Cornelius 1914- 109
Goemans, Camille (Constant Ghislain)
1900-1960 209
Goemans, Hein E.
See Goemans, Henk E.
Goemans, Henk E. 1957- 200
Goen, Clarence C(urtis), Jr. 1924-1990 ..... 1-4R
Obituary 133
Goen, Rayburne Wyndham, Jr. 1942- 107
Goen, Tex, Jr.
See Goen, Rayburne Wyndham, Jr.
Goeney, William M(orton) 1914-1989 ...... 5-8R
Goeppert-Mayer, Maria 1906-1972 156
Goerdt, Arthur L(inus) 1912-1995 .... 41-44R
Goergen, Donald 1943- 61-64
Goering, Helga
See Wallmann, Jeffrey M(iner)
Goering, Reinhard 1887-1936 185
See also DLB 118
Goerlach, Manfred 1937- 140
Goerler, Raimund E. 1948- 167
Goerling, Lars 1931-1966 .... CAP-2
Earlier sketch in CA 21-22
Goerner, E(dward) A(lfred) 1929- 49-52
Goerner, S. J.
See Goerner, Sally J.
Goerner, Sally J. 1952- 148
Goerres, Joseph 1776-1848 .... DLB 90
Goertz, Donald C(harles) 1939- 53-56
Goertzel, Ted George 1942- 69-72
Goes, Albrecht 1908-2000 176
See also DLB 69
See also EWL 3
Goetchius, Eugene Van Ness 1921- 118
Goetel, Ferdynand 1890-1960 .... EWL 3
Goethals, George W. 1920-1995 .... 13-16R
Goethe, Ann 1945- 143
Goethe, Johann Wolfgang von
1749-1832 .... CDWLB 2
See also DA
See also DA3
See also DAB
See also DAC
See also DAM DRAM, MST, POET
See also DC 20
See also DLB 94
See also EW 5
See also GL 2
See also LATS 1
See also LMFS 1:1
See also PC 5
See also RGWL 2, 3
See also SSC 38
See also TWA
See also WLC
Goethe, Staffan
See Gothe, Staffan
Goetsch-Trevelyan, Katherine
See Trevelyan, Katharine
Goette, Ann
See Goethe, Ann
Goettel, Elinor 1930 .... 29-32R
See also SATA 12
Goetz, Billy E. 1904-1985 .... CAP-1
Earlier sketch in CA 13-14
Goetz, Curt 1888-1960 183
See also DLB 124
Goetz, Delia 1898-1996 73-76
Obituary 152
See also SATA 22
See also SATA-Obit 91
Goetz, George 1900-1940
See Calverton, V. F.
Goetz, Ignacio L. 1933- CANR-91
Earlier sketch in CA 37-40R
Goetz, Johann Nikolaus 1721-1781 ..... DLB 97
Goetz, Joseph (William) 1933- 118
Goetz, Lee Garrett 1932- 25-28R
Goetz, Rainald 1954- 195
Goetz, Ruth G(oodman) 1912-2001 218
Goetze, Albrecht E. R. 1897-1971
Obituary 33-36R
Goetzmann, William H. 1930- 21-24R
Goetz-Stankiewicz, Marketa 122
Goff, Charles Ray 1889-1984
Obituary 114
Goff, Frederick Richmond
1916-1982 .... CANR-7
Obituary 108
Earlier sketch in CA 17-20R
Goff, Ivan 1910-1999 188
Goff, James R., Jr. 1957- 126
Goff, M(adison) Lee 1944- 199
Goff, Martyn 1923- CANR-2
Earlier sketch in CA 5-8R
Goffart, Walter (Andre) 1934- CANR-38
Earlier sketches in CA 37-40R, CANR-16
Goffe, Thomas 1592(?)-1629 .... DLB 58
Goffe, Toni 1936- .... SATA 61
Goffee, Robert (Edward) 1952- 181
Goffen, Rona 1944-2004 .... CANR-139
Obituary 231
Earlier sketch in CA 121
Goffin, Raymond C. 1890(?)-1976
Obituary 65-68
Goffin, Robert 1898-1984 195
Goffman, Erving 1922-1982 .... CANR-9
Obituary 108
Earlier sketch in CA 21-24R
Goffman, Ken 1952- 238
Goffstein, Brooke
See Goffstein, M(arilyn) B(rooke)
Goffstein, M(arilyn) B(rooke) 1940- .. CANR-28
Earlier sketches in CA 21-24R, CANR-9
See also CLR 3
See also DLB 61
See also MAICYA 1, 2
See also SATA 8, 70
Gofman, John W(illiam) 1918- 65-68
Goforth, Ellen
See Francis, Dorothy Brenner
Goga, Octavian 1881-1938 .... EWL 3
Gogarty, Oliver St. John 1878-1957 150
Brief entry 109
See also DLB 15, 19
See also RGEL 2
See also TCLC 15
Goggin, Dan 1943- 126
Goggin, Terrence P(atrick) 1941- 103
Gogisgi
See Arnett, Carroll
Gogol, Nikolai (Vasilyevich) 1809-1852 ...... DA
See also DAB
See also DAC
See also DAM DRAM, MST
See also DC 1
See also DFS 12
See also DLB 198
See also EW 6
See also EXPS
See also RGSF 2
See also RGWL 2, 3
See also SSC 4, 29, 52
See also SSFS 7
See also TWA
See also WLC
Gogol, Sara 1948-2004 .... CANR-126
Earlier sketch in CA 147
See also SATA 80
Goh, Chan Hon 1969- 218
See also SATA 145
Goh, Cheng-Teik 1943- 41-44R
Goh, Poh Seng 1936- 194
Gohdes, Clarence Louis Frank
1901-1997 .... 13-16R
Gohman, Fred Joseph 1918- 5-8R
Goines, David Lance 1945- 147
Goines, Donald 1937(?)-1974 .... CANR-82
Obituary 114
Earlier sketch in CA 124
See also AITN 1
See also BLC 2
See also BW 1, 3
See also CLC 80
See also CMW 4
See also DA3
See also DAM MULT, POP
See also DLB 33
Going, K(elly) L. 231
See also SATA 156
Goingback, Owl 1959- CANR-141
Earlier sketch in CA 154
Goins, Ellen H(aynes) 1927-1979 ..... CANR-26
Earlier sketch in CA 33-36R
Goist, Park Dixon 1936- 37-40R
Goitein, S(helomo) D(ov)
1900-1985 .... CANR-83
Obituary 115
Earlier sketches in CA 61-64, CANR-8
Goitein, Solomon Dob Fritz
See Goitein, S(helomo) D(ov)
Gokak, Vinayak Krishna 1909- 69-72
Gokhale, Balkrishna Govind 1919- CANR-4
Earlier sketch in CA 1-4R
Gokhale, Namita 1956- 123
Golan, Aviezer 1922- 104
Golan, Matti 1936- 101
Golan, Menahem 1929- 216
See also IDFW 3, 4
Golann, Cecil Paige 1921-1995 .... 33-36R
See also SATA 11
Golann, Stuart E(ugene) 1936- 57-60
Golant, Stephen M(yles) 1945- 145
Golant, William 1937- 65-68
Golany, Gideon S. 1928-1999 143
Golay, Frank H(indman) 1915-1990 ... CANR-1
Earlier sketch in CA 1-4R
Golay, Michael 1951- CANR-88
Earlier sketch in CA 147
Golbin, Andree 1923- .... SATA 15
Golburgh, Stephen J. 1935- 21-24R
Golby, J(ohn) M(ichael) 1935- 127
Golczewski, James A. 1945- 175
Gold, Aaron 1937-1983 101
Obituary 109
Gold, Alan R(obert) 1948- 45-48
Gold, Alison Leslie 1945- 136
See also SATA 104
Gold, Arthur 1917-1990 132
Gold, Artie 1947- 114
Gold, Barbara K(irk) 1945- CANR-29
Earlier sketch in CA 110
Gold, Bernice 225
See also SATA 150
Gold, Don 1931- CANR-9
Earlier sketch in CA 61-64
Gold, Doris B. 1919- CANR-9
Earlier sketch in CA 21-24R
Gold, Douglas 1894-1985 .... CAP-1
Earlier sketch in CA 11-12
Gold, Ellen .... GLL 2
Gold, Glen David 1964- 208
Gold, H(orace) L(eonard) 1914-1996 167
Gold, Hazel 1953- 145
Gold, Herbert 1924- CANR-125
Earlier sketches in CA 9-12R, CANR-17, 45
See also CLC 4, 7, 14, 42, 152
See also CN 1, 2, 3, 4, 5, 6, 7
See also DLB 2
See also DLBY 1981
See also MAL 5
Gold, Ivan 1932- CANR-93
Earlier sketches in CA 5-8R, CANR-3
See also CN 1, 2
Gold, Janet N(owakowski) 1948- 149
Gold, Jerome 1943- CANR-87
Earlier sketch in CA 154
Gold, Joseph 1933- CANR-137
Earlier sketch in CA 21-24R
Gold, Kenneth M. 1966- 210
Gold, Lee 1919(?)-1985
Obituary 116
Gold, Martin 1931- 29-32R
Gold, Michael
See Granich, Irving
Gold, Michael 1894-1967 139
Gold, Michael Evan 1943- 138
Gold, Milton J. 1917- 17-20R
Gold, Nora 1953(?)- 172
Gold, Phyllis
See Goldberg, Phyllis
See also SATA 21
Gold, Robert S(tanley) 1924- 53-56
See also SATA 63
Gold, Seymour M(urray) 1933- CANR-21
Earlier sketch in CA 41-44R
Gold, Sharlya CANR-8
Earlier sketch in CA 61-64
See also SATA 9
Gold, Steven J(ames) 1955- CANR-107
Earlier sketch in CA 141
Gold, Susan
See Gold, Susan Dudley
Gold, Susan Dudley 1949- CANR-128
Earlier sketch in CANR-48
See also SATA 147
Gold, Thomas 1920-2004 156
Obituary 228
Gold, Todd 1958- CANR-115
Earlier sketch in CA 136
Gold, Victor Roland 1924- 53-56
Gold, William E. 1912-1997 69-72
Obituary 156
Goldbach, Joseph V. 1930- 178
Goldbarth, Albert 1948- CANR-40
Earlier sketches in CA 53-56, CANR-6
See also AMWS 12
See also CLC 5, 38
See also CP 7
See also DLB 120
Goldbeck, David M. 1942- CANR-30
Earlier sketch in CA 49-52
Goldbeck, Frederick E(rnest) 1902- 102
Goldbeck, Nikki 1947- CANR-30
Earlier sketch in CA 49-52
Goldbeck, Willis 1899(?)-1979
Obituary 89-92
Goldberg, Adele (E.) 1945- 156
Goldberg, Albert (Levi) 1898-1990
Obituary 130
Goldberg, Alvin Arnold 1931- 41-44R
Goldberg, Anatol 1910-1982 131
Obituary 117
See also CLC 34
Goldberg, Arnold I(rving) 1929- CANR-19
Earlier sketch in CA 103

Goldberg, Arthur J(oseph) 1908-1990 ... 65-68
Obituary ... 130
Goldberg, Barney 1918-1969 ... 21-24R
Goldberg, Benjamin 1915-1994 ... 120
Goldberg, Bernard 1945- ... 199
Goldberg, Bruce (Edward) 1948- ... CANR-134
Earlier sketch in CA 163
Goldberg, Carl 1938- ... CANR-18
Earlier sketches in CA 49-52, CANR-3
Goldberg, Danny ... 225
Goldberg, David J. 1939- ... CANR-55
Earlier sketch in CA 127
Goldberg, Dick 1947- ... 97-100
Interview in ... CA-97-100
See also DLB 7
Goldberg, Dorothy K(urgans)
1909(?)-1988 ... 103
Obituary ... 124
Goldberg, E(lliott) Marshall 1930- ... CANR-26
Earlier sketches in CA 69-72, CANR-11
Goldberg, Edward M(orris) 1931-2000 ... 53-56
Goldberg, Fats
See Goldberg, Larry
Goldberg, George 1935- ... 69-72
Goldberg, Gerald Jay 1929- ... 49-52
Goldberg, Grace 1956- ... SATA 78
Goldberg, Harold ... 233
Goldberg, Harvey E(llis) 1939- ... CANR-25
Earlier sketch in CA 45-48
Goldberg, Herb 1937- ... CANR-9
Earlier sketch in CA 61-64
Goldberg, Herbert S. 1926- ... 5-8R
See also SATA 25
Goldberg, Herman Raphael
1915-1997 ... CANR-5
Earlier sketch in CA 9-12R
Goldberg, Hillel 1946- ... 116
Goldberg, Hyman 1908(?)-1970
Obituary ... 104
Goldberg, Jacob 1943- ... CANR-65
Earlier sketch in CA 159
See also SATA 94
Goldberg, Jacob 1948- ... 120
Goldberg, Jake
See Goldberg, Jacob
Goldberg, Jan ... 194
See also Curran, Jan Goldberg
See also SATA 123
Goldberg, Jane G. 1946- ... 138
Goldberg, Joan Rachel 1955- ... 110
Goldberg, Jonathan 1943- ... 122
Goldberg, Joseph P(hilip) 1918-2002 ... 37-40R
Obituary ... 212
Goldberg, Kenneth P(hilip) 1945- ... 116
Goldberg, Larry 1934-2003 ... 113
Obituary ... 212
Goldberg, Leah 1911-1970
Obituary ... 25-28R
Goldberg, Lee 1962- ... CANR-72
Earlier sketch in CA 156
Goldberg, Leonard S. 1936- ... CANR-130
Earlier sketches in CA 153, CANR-71
Goldberg, Lester 1924-2000 ... 126
Goldberg, Louis
See Grant, Louis T(heodore)
Goldberg, Louis 1908-1997 ... 13-16R
Goldberg, Lucianne Cummings 1935- ... 85-88
Goldberg, M(ilton) A(llan) 1919-1970 ... CAP-2
Earlier sketch in CA 25-28
Goldberg, M(elvyn) Hirsh 1942- ... 73-76
Goldberg, Marie Waife
See Waife-Goldberg, Marie
Goldberg, Maxwell Henry 1907- ... CANR-24
Earlier sketch in CA 103
Goldberg, Miriam Levin 1914(?)-1996 .. 41-44R
Obituary ... 154
Goldberg, Moses H(aym) 1940- ... CANR-15
Earlier sketch in CA 93-96
Goldberg, Myla 1972(?)- ... 210
Goldberg, Natalie ... CANR-99
Earlier sketch in CA 154
Goldberg, Nathan 1903(?)-1979
Obituary ... 85-88
Goldberg, Norman L(ewis) 1906-1982 ... 81-84
Obituary ... 133
Goldberg, P(ercy) Selvin 1917- ... 5-8R
Goldberg, Paul (Boris) 1959- ... 135
Goldberg, Philip 1944- ... CANR-141
Earlier sketches in CA 85-88, CANR-15
Goldberg, Phyllis 1941- ... 57-60
See also Gold, Phyllis
Goldberg, Ray A(llan) 1926- ... CANR-48
Earlier sketch in CA 49-52
Goldberg, Reuben L(ucius)
1883-1970 ... CANR-9
Earlier sketch in CA 5-8R
Goldberg, Robert Alan 1949- ... CANR-119
Earlier sketches in CA 105, CANR-55
Goldberg, RoseLee 1947- ... 120
Goldberg, Rube
See Goldberg, Reuben L(ucius)
Goldberg, Samuel Louis 1925-1991 ... 112
Goldberg, Sidney 1931- ... 77-80
Goldberg, Stan J. 1939- ... 49-52
See also SATA 26
Goldberg, Steven 1941- ... CANR-75
Earlier sketch in CA 53-56
Goldberg, Susan 1948- ... SATA 71
Goldberg, Tod 1973(?)- ... 210
Goldberg, Vicki ... 192
See also MTFW 2005
Goldberg, Whoopi 1955- ... 165
See also SATA 119
Goldberger, Arthur Stanley 1930- ... 9-12R
Goldberger, Avriel H(orwitz)
1928- ... CANR-108
Earlier sketch in CA 140
Goldberger, Judith M. 1948- ... 112
See also Mathews, Judith
Goldberger, Leo 1930- ... 127
Goldberger, Nancy Rule 1937- ... 124
Goldberger, Paul (Jesse) 1950- ... 129
Brief entry ... 122
Goldblatt, Mark (Meyer) 1957- ... 210
Golde, Peggy 1930- ... 37-40R
Golde, Roger A(lan) 1934- ... 69-72
Goldemberg, Isaac 1945- ... CANR-32
Earlier sketches in CA 69-72, CANR-11
See also CAAS 12
See also CLC 52
See also EWL 3
See also HW 1
See also WLIT 1
Goldemberg, Rose Leiman ... CANR-2
Earlier sketch in CA 49-52
Golden, Arthur 1924- ... CANR-72
Earlier sketch in CA 33-36R
Golden, Arthur 1956- ... CANR-125
Earlier sketch in CA 171
See also NFS 19
Golden, Christie 1963- ... 181
See also SATA 116
Golden, Christopher 1967- ... CANR-106
Earlier sketch in CA 150
Golden, Eve 1957- ... CANR-94
Earlier sketch in CA 136
Golden, Harry, Jr. 1928(?)-1988
Obituary ... 125
Golden, Harry (Lewis) 1902-1981 ... CANR-2
Obituary ... 104
Earlier sketch in CA 1-4R
Golden, James L. 1919-
Brief entry ... 109
Golden, Jeffrey S. 1950- ... 33-36R
Golden, L(ouis) L(awrence) L(ionel)
1909(?)-1983 ... 21-24R
Obituary ... 111
Golden, Leon 1930- ... 17-20R
Golden, Marita 1950- ... CANR-82
Earlier sketches in CA 111, CANR-42
See also BW 2, 3
Golden, Mark 1948- ... CANR-88
Earlier sketch in CA 135
Golden, Morris 1926-1994 ... 1-4R
Golden, Renny 1937- ... 142
Golden, Richard M(artin) 1947- ... 138
Golden, Robert Edward 1945- ... 65-68
Golden, Ruth I(sbell) 1910-1986 ... CAP-2
Earlier sketch in CA 17-18
Golden, Samuel A(dler) 1909-
Brief entry ... 110
Golden, Sean V(alentine) 1948- ... 107
Golden, Sherry (Lazar) 1945- ... 123
Golden, Stephanie 1946- ... 186
Goldenbaum, Sally 1941- ... 124
Goldenberg, Edie N. 1945- ... 69-72
Goldenberg, Herbert 1926- ... 41-44R
Goldenberg, I(sidore) Ira 1936- ... 110
Goldenberg, Robert 1942- ... 109
Goldenberg, Susan 1944- ... 134
Goldensohn, Barry 1937- ... CANR-93
Earlier sketch in CA 77-80
Goldenson, Daniel R. 1944- ... 25-28R
Goldenson, Robert M(yar) 1908-1999 ... 29-32R
Goldenthal, Allan Benarria 1920-1985 . 17-20R
Goldenthal, Edgar J. 1917- ... 169
Goldenthal, Peter 1948- ... 210
Goldentyer, Debra 1960- ... 150
See also SATA 84
Golder, Herbert (Alan) 1952- ... 186
Goldfader, Edward H. 1930- ... 29-32R
Goldfarb, Clare R(osett) 1934- ... 113
Goldfarb, Nathan 1913-1989 ... 13-16R
Goldfarb, Ronald L. 1933- ... CANR-40
Earlier sketches in CA 21-24R, CANR-9
Goldfarb, Russell M. 1934- ... 37-40R
Goldfarb, Sally F(ay) 1957- ... 104
Goldfeder, Cheryl
See Pahz, (Anne) Cheryl Suzanne
Goldfeder, James
See Pahz, James Alon
Goldfeder, Jim
See Pahz, James Alon
Goldfein, Donna 1933- ... 116
Goldfield, David (R.) 1944- ... 223
Goldfinch, Shaun 1967- ... 210
Goldfrank, David M. ... 118
Goldfrank, Esther S(chiff) 1896-1997 ... 61-64
Obituary ... 157
Goldfrank, Helen Colodny 1912- ... CANR-3
Earlier sketch in CA 1-4R
See also SATA 6
Goldfrank, Lewis 1941- ... 127
Goldfried, Marvin R(obert) 1936- ... 37-40R
Goldgar, Bertrand A(lvin) 1927- ... 65-68
Goldhaber, Gerald Martin 1944- ... CANR-9
Earlier sketch in CA 57-60
Goldhamer, Douglas (Hirsch) 1945- ... 187
Goldhamer, Herbert 1907-1977 ... CANR-2
Earlier sketch in CA 45-48
Goldhammer, Arthur 1946- ... CANR-95
Earlier sketch in CA 139
Goldhill, Simon (D.) ... 229
Goldhurst, Richard 1927- ... 57-60
Goldhurst, William 1929- ... 5-8R
Goldie, Frederick 1914-1980
Obituary ... 105
Goldie, Terrence William 1950- ... CANR-32
Earlier sketch in CA 113
Goldie, Terry
See Goldie, Terrence William
Goldin, Augusta 1906-1999 ... CANR-7
Earlier sketch in CA 17-20R
See also SATA 13
Goldin, Barbara Diamond 1946- ... CANR-114
Earlier sketches in CA 132, CANR-57
See also SAAS 26
See also SATA 92, 129
See also SATA-Essay 129
Goldin, Claudia 1946- ... 142
Goldin, David 1963- ... SATA 101
Goldin, Grace 1916-1995 ... 115
Goldin, Judah 1914-1998 ... 33-36R
Goldin, Kathleen Mckinney 1943- ... 133
Brief entry ... 118
Goldin, Milton 1927- ... 61-64
Goldin, Owen 1957- ... 158
Goldin, Stephen 1947- ... 77-80
See also SFW 4
Golding, Alan 1952- ... 154
Golding, Arthur 1536-1606 ... DLB 136
Golding, Lawrence A(rthur) 1926- ... 61-64
Golding, Louis 1885-1958 ... DLB 195
Golding, Louis 1907- ... CAP-1
Earlier sketch in CA 9-10
Golding, Martin Philip 1930- ... 101
Golding, Michael 1958- ... 187
Golding, Morton J(ay) 1925- ... 21-24R
Golding, Peter 1947- ... 103
Golding, Theresa Martin 1960- ... 225
See also SATA 150
Golding, William (Gerald)
1911-1993 ... CANR-54
Obituary ... 141
Earlier sketches in CA 5-8R, CANR-13, 33
See also AAYA 5, 44
See also BPFB 2
See also BRWR 1
See also BRWS 1
See also BYA 2
See also CD 5
See also CDBLB 1945-1960
See also CLC 1, 2, 3, 8, 10, 17, 27, 58, 81
See also CLR 94
See also CN 1, 2, 3, 4
See also DA
See also DA3
See also DAB
See also DAC
See also DAM MST, NOV
See also DLB 15, 100, 255
See also EWL 3
See also EXPN
See also HGG
See also LAIT 4
See also MTCW 1, 2
See also MTFW 2005
See also NFS 2
See also RGEL 2
See also RHW
See also SFW 4
See also TEA
See also WLC
See also WLIT 4
See also YAW
Goldingay, John (Edgar) 1942- ... 215
Goldknopf, David 1918- ... 53-56
Goldman, A(ndrew) E. O. 1947- ... 57-60
Goldman, Alan H(arris) 1945- ... 93-96
Goldman, Albert 1927-1994 ... CANR-48
Obituary ... 144
Earlier sketches in CA 17-20R, CANR-9
See also BEST 89:2
Goldman, Alex J. 1917- ... 49-52
See also SATA 65
Goldman, Alvin I(ra) 1938- ... 77-80
Goldman, Alvin L. 1938- ... CANR-1
Earlier sketch in CA 45-48
Goldman, Ari L. 1949- ... CANR-101
Earlier sketch in CA 140
Goldman, Arnold (Melvyn) 1936- ... 17-20R
Goldman, Bernard 1922- ... 53-56
Goldman, Bo 1932- ... CANR-125
Brief entry ... 109
Earlier sketch in CA 112
Interview in ... CA-112
Goldman, Bruce (Eliot) 1942- ... 61-64
Goldman, Carl A(lexander) 1942- ... 101
Goldman, Charles R(emington) 1930- ... 53-56
Goldman, Dave 1927- ... 107
Goldman, E(leanor) M(aureen) 1943- ... 170
See also SATA 103
Goldman, E. S. 1913- ... CANR-66
Earlier sketch in CA 128
Goldman, Elizabeth 1949- ... 155
See also SATA 90
Goldman, Emma 1869-1940 ... 150
Brief entry ... 110
See also DLB 221
See also FW
See also RGAL 4
See also TCLC 13
See also TUS
Goldman, Eric (Frederick) 1915-1989 ... 5-8R
Obituary ... 127
Goldman, Francisco 1954- ... 162
See also CLC 76
Goldman, Frederick 1921-1976 ... 81-84
Goldman, George D(avid) 1923- ... 101
Goldman, Howard H(irsch) 1949- ... 112
Goldman, Irving 1911- ... 29-32R
Goldman, Ivan G. 1942- ... 143
Goldman, Jacquelin (Roberta) 1934- ... 69-72
Goldman, James A. 1927-1998 ... CANR-1
Obituary ... 171
Earlier sketch in CA 45-48
See also CAD
See also CD 5, 6
See also DFS 20
Goldman, Jane 1970- ... 209
Goldman, Joel ... 237
Goldman, Judy (Ann) 1942- ... 186
Goldman, Karla 1960- ... 199
Goldman, Katherine (Wyse) 1951- ... 143
Goldman, Katie 1960- ... BYA 7
Goldman, Lee A. 1946- ... 25-28R
Goldman, Leo 1920-1999 ... 85-88
Goldman, Lorraine 1940- ... 111
Goldman, Louis 1925- ... 125
Goldman, Marcus Selden 1894-1984 ... 41-44R
Goldman, Marshall I(rwin) 1930- ... 9-12R
Goldman, Martin (Raymond Rubin)
1920- ... 69-72
Goldman, Martin 1950(?)-1984
Obituary ... 113
Goldman, Merle 1931- ... 33-36R
Goldman, Michael (Paul) 1936- ... CANR-8
Earlier sketch in CA 17-20R
See also CP 1
Goldman, Minton F. ... 199
Goldman, Molly Rose 1988(?)- ... 229
Goldman, Norma Wynick 1922- ... CANR-56
Earlier sketch in CA 110
Goldman, Paul (Henry Joseph)
1950- ... CANR-135
Earlier sketches in CA 129, CANR-65
Goldman, Peter (Louis) 1933- ... CANR-49
Earlier sketches in CA 21-24R, CANR-8, 24
Goldman, Phyllis W. 1927- ... 29-32R
Goldman, Ralph M(orris) 1920- ... 89-92
Goldman, Richard Franko
1910-1980 ... CANR-5
Obituary ... 93-96
Earlier sketch in CA 9-12R
Goldman, Roger L. 1941- ... 142
Goldman, Ronald ... 21-24R
Goldman, Sheldon 1939- ... 21-24R
Goldman, Sherli E(vens) 1930- ... 25-28R
Goldman, Shifra M(eyerowitz)
1926- ... CANR-25
Earlier sketch in CA 106
Goldman, Susan 1939- ... 65-68
Goldman, William (W.) 1931- ... CANR-106
Earlier sketches in CA 9-12R, CANR-29, 69
See also BPFB 2
See also CLC 1, 48
See also CN 1, 2, 3, 4, 5, 6, 7
See also DLB 44
See also FANT
See also IDFW 3, 4
Goldman-Eisler, Frieda 1909(?)-1982
Obituary ... 105
Goldmann, Lucien 1913-1970 ... CAP-2
Earlier sketch in CA 25-28
See also CLC 24
Goldmann, Nahum 1895-1982
Obituary ... 107
Goldmark, Peter C(arl) 1906-1977 ... 77-80
Obituary ... 73-76
Goldner, Bernard (Burton) 1919-1990 ... 5-8R
Goldner, Jack 1900-1999 ... CAP-2
Earlier sketch in CA 25-28
Goldner, Nancy 1943- ... 57-60
Goldner, Orville (Charles) 1906-1985 ... 53-56
Goldoni, Carlo 1707-1793 ... DAM DRAM
See also EW 4
See also RGWL 2, 3
See also WLIT 7
Goldovsky, Boris 1908-2001 ... CANR-16
Obituary ... 194
Earlier sketch in CA 81-84
Goldring, Ann 1937- ... 223
See also SATA 149
Goldring, Douglas 1887-1960 ... 176
Obituary ... 93-96
See also DLB 197
Goldring, Patrick (Thomas Zachary)
1921- ... 29-32R
Goldsberry, Steven 1949- ... 131
See also CLC 34
Goldsborough, James Oliver 1936- ... 142
Goldsborough, June 1923- ... SATA 19
Goldsborough, Robert (Gerald) 1937- ... 138
Goldscheider, Calvin 1941- ... 122
Brief entry ... 108
Goldscheider, Ludwig 1896-1973 ... 5-8R
Goldschmidt, Arthur (Eduard), Jr.
1938- ... CANR-122
Earlier sketch in CA 162
Goldschmidt, Clara Malraux
See Malraux, Clara (Goldschmidt)
Goldschmidt, Meir 1819-1887 ... DLB 300
Goldschmidt, Paul W. 1967- ... 212
Goldschmidt, Tijs ... 168
Goldschmidt, Victor (Moritz) 1888-1947 ... 156
Goldschmidt, Walter Rochs 1913- ... 9-12R
Goldschmidt, Yaagov 1927- ... 29-32R
Goldschneider, Gary 1939- ... 227
Goldsen, Rose Kohn 1918- ... CANR-33
Earlier sketch in CA 1-4R
Goldsman, Akiva ... 167
Goldsmith
See Miller, Lynne (Ellen)
Goldsmith, Arnold L(ouis) 1928- ... 41-44R
Goldsmith, Arthur (A., Jr.) 1926- ... CANR-5
Earlier sketch in CA 13-16R
Goldsmith, Barbara 1931- ... CANR-5
Earlier sketch in CA 53-56
Goldsmith, Carol Evan 1930- ... 29-32R
Goldsmith, Connie 1945- ... 221
See also SATA 147
Goldsmith, David H(irsh) 1933- ... 117
Goldsmith, Donald 1943- ... CANR-81
Earlier sketch in CA 77-80
Goldsmith, Edward ... 104
Goldsmith, Emanuel S(idney) 1935-
Brief entry ... 109

Cumulative Index 223 **Gonzalez**

Goldsmith, Howard 1943- CANR-40
Earlier sketches in CA 101, CANR-21
See also SATA 24, 108
Goldsmith, Ilse Sondra (Weinberg)
1933- 37-40R
Goldsmith, Jack 1931- 57-60
Goldsmith, Jerry 1929-2004 .... IDFW 3, 4
Goldsmith, Joel S. 1892(?)-1964
Obituary 109
Goldsmith, John 1947- 125
Goldsmith, John Herman Thorburn 1903-1987
Obituary 122
See also SATA-Obit 52
Goldsmith, Lynn 1948- 142
Goldsmith, Martin 1952- 229
Goldsmith, Oliver 1730-1774 .... BRW 3
See also CDBLB 1660-1789
See also DA
See also DAB
See also DAC
See also DAM DRAM, MST, NOV, POET
See also DC 8
See also DFS 1
See also DLB 39, 89, 104, 109, 142
See also IDTP
See also RGEL 2
See also SATA 26
See also TEA
See also WLC
See also WLIT 3
Goldsmith, Oliver 1794-1861 .... DLB 99
Goldsmith, Olivia
See Rendal, Justine
Goldsmith, Peter
See Priestley, J(ohn) B(oynton)
Goldsmith, Peter D(avid) 1952-2004 174
Obituary 227
Goldsmith, Raymond W(illiam)
1904-1988 115
Obituary 126
Goldsmith, Robert Hillis 1911-1992 49-52
Goldsmith, Ruth M. 1919- .... SATA 62
Goldsmith, Sharon S(weeney) 1948- 57-60
Goldsmith, Walter (Kenneth) 1938- 120
Goldson, Rae L(illian) Segalowitz
1893-1987 .... 5-8R
Goldstein, Abraham 1903(?)-1982
Obituary 106
Goldstein, Abraham S(amuel)
1925-2005 .... CANR-29
Earlier sketch in CA 33-36R
Goldstein, Alvin H. Sr. 1902-1972
Obituary 33-36R
Goldstein, Arthur D(avid) 1937- 73-76
Goldstein, Avram 1919- 156
Goldstein, Bernard R. 1938- 57-60
Goldstein, Carl 1938- 130
Goldstein, David 1933- CANR-11
Earlier sketch in CA 17-20R
Goldstein, David I. 1924-1987(?) 130
Goldstein, Donald M(aurice) 1932- .. CANR-26
Earlier sketch in CA 108
Goldstein, E. Ernest 1918- 9-12R
Goldstein, Edward 1923-1989 .... 9-12R
Goldstein, Ernest A. 1933- 110
See also SATA-Brief 52
Goldstein, Gersham 1938-
Brief entry 108
Goldstein, Howard 1922- 93-96
Goldstein, Imre 1938- 140
Goldstein, Irwin L. 1937- 41-44R
Goldstein, Israel 1896-1986 .... CANR-83
Obituary 119
Earlier sketch in CA 53-56
Goldstein, Jack 1930- 73-76
Goldstein, Jeffrey H(askell) 1942- CANR-32
Earlier sketches in CA 81-84, CANR-14
Goldstein, Jerome 1931- 101
Goldstein, Joan 1932- CANR-35
Earlier sketch in CA 114
Goldstein, Jonathan A(mos)
1929-2004 .... CANR-142
Obituary 234
Earlier sketch in CA 25-28R
Goldstein, Joseph 1923-2000 .... 17-20R
Obituary 190
Goldstein, Joshua S. 1952- 216
Goldstein, Judy
See Botello, Judy Goldstein
Goldstein, Kenneth M(ichael) 1940- 33-36R
Goldstein, Kenneth S. 1927-1995
Obituary 150
Brief entry 107
Goldstein, Larry Joel 1944- 139
Goldstein, Laurence 1937(?)-1972
Obituary 33-36R
Goldstein, Laurence 1943- 93-96
Goldstein, Leo S. 1924- 13-16R
Goldstein, Leon J. 1927-2002 69-72
Obituary 211
Goldstein, Lisa 1953- CANR-25
Earlier sketch in CA 108
See also FANT
See also SFW 4
Goldstein, Malcolm 1925- CANR-127
Earlier sketches in CA 49-52, CANR-32
Goldstein, Marc 1948- 109
Goldstein, Martin E(ugene) 1939- 41-44R
Goldstein, Melissa Anne 1969- 188
Goldstein, Melvyn C. 1938- CANR-102
Earlier sketches in CA 121, CANR-47
Goldstein, Michael J(oseph) 1930- 103
Goldstein, Michael S. 1944- 143
Goldstein, Milton 1915- CANR-24
Earlier sketch in CA 45-48
Goldstein, Naama 1969(?)- 235
Goldstein, Nathan 1927- CANR-16
Earlier sketches in CA 45-48, CANR-1
See also SATA 47
Goldstein, Philip 1910-1997 53-56
See also SATA 23
Goldstein, Rebecca 1950- CANR-99
Earlier sketch in CA 144
See also TCLE 1:1
Goldstein, Rhoda L.
See Blumberg, Rhoda L(ois Goldstein)
Goldstein, Richard 1944- CANR-68
Earlier sketch in CA 25-28R
See also DLB 185
Goldstein, Robert Justin 1947- CANR-93
Earlier sketch in CA 131
Goldstein, Roberta Butterfield 1917- 9-12R
Goldstein, Robin 1952- 133
Goldstein, Robin 1955(?)-1989
Obituary 129
Goldstein, Ruth M(artha) 1913-1992 113
Goldstein, Ruth Tessler 1924- 69-72
Goldstein, Sidney 1927- CANR-25
Earlier sketches in CA 21-24R, CANR-9
Goldstein, Stanley 1922- 103
Goldstein, Stephen R(obert) 1938- ... CANR-30
Earlier sketches in CA 61-64, CANR-13
Goldstein, Stewart 1941- 65-68
Goldstein, Thomas Eugene 1913-1997
Brief entry 108
Goldstein, William Isaac 1932- 13-16R
Goldstein-Jackson, Kevin 1946- 106
Goldstine, Herman Heine 1913-2004 110
Goldston, Robert (Conroy) 1927- CANR-13
Earlier sketch in CA 17-20R
See also SATA 6
Goldstone, Aline L(ewis) 1878(?)-1976
Obituary 65-68
Goldstone, Harmon H(endricks)
1911-2001 77-80
Obituary 193
Goldstone, Herbert 1921- 77-80
Goldstone, Lawrence A.
See Treat, Lawrence
Goldstone, Nancy Bazelon
1957(?)- CANR-111
Earlier sketch in CA 158
Goldstone, Richard H. 1921- 33-36R
Goldstone, Richard J. 1938- 215
Goldsworthy, David 1938- 33-36R
Goldsworthy, Graeme 1934- CANR-35
Earlier sketch in CA 114
Goldsworthy, Peter 1951- 118
See also CP 7
Goldsworthy, Vesna 1961- 197
Goldszmit, Henryk 1878-1942 133
See also Korczak, Janusz
Goldthorpe, J(ohn) E(rnest) 1921- CANR-33
Earlier sketch in CA 49-52
Goldthorpe, Rhiannon 1934- 126
Goldthwait, Bob 1962- 164
Goldthwait, Bobcat
See Goldthwait, Bob
Goldthwaite, Eaton K. 1907-1994 .... 25-28R
Goldthwaite, Richard A(llen) 1933- 136
Brief entry 108
Goldwasser, Thomas 1939- 135
Goldwater, Barry (Morris) 1909-1998 .... 41-44R
Obituary 167
Goldwater, Eleanor Lowenstein 1909(?)-1980
Obituary 102
Goldwater, John L(eonard) 1916-1999 131
Obituary 177
See also AITN 1
Goldwater, Robert 1907-1973
Obituary 41-44R
Goldwater, Walter Delmar 1907-1985
Obituary 116
Goldwin, Robert Allen 1922- 102
Goldwyn, Robert M(alcolm) 1930- 122
Goldwyn, Samuel 1884-1974 .... IDFW 3, 4
Gole, Victor Leslie 1903- CANR-23
Earlier sketch in CA 107
Goleman, Daniel 1946- CANR-118
Earlier sketch in CA 111
Golembe, Carla 1951- .... SATA 79
Golembiewski, Robert T(homas)
1932- CANR-45
Earlier sketches in CA 5-8R, CANR-6, 21
Golenbock, Peter 1946- CANR-101
Earlier sketches in CA 57-60, CANR-8, 92
See also SATA 99
Golenpaul, Ann 1907(?)-1986
Obituary 119
Golf, Loyal E.
See Golv, Loyal E(ugene)
Golffing, Francis (Charles) 1910- CANR-5
Earlier sketch in CA 5-8R
Golffing, Franz Karl
See Golffing, Francis (Charles)
Goliard, Roy
See Shipley, Joseph T(wadell)
Golightly, Bonnie H(elen) 1919-1998 .... 1-4R
Golinski, Jan 1957- 139
Goll, Ivan
See Goll, Yvan
See also RGWL 2, 3
Goll, Iwan
See Goll, Yvan
Goll, Reinhold W(eimar) 1897-1993 .... 5-8R
Obituary 176
See also SATA 26
Goll, Yvan 1891-1950 196
See also Goll, Ivan
Gollaher, David L. 1949- 149
Gollan, [illegible] 1917- 13-16R
Gollancz, Sir Israel 1864-1930 .... DLB 201
Gollancz, Victor 1893-1967
Obituary 116
Golledge, Reginald G(eorge) 1937- 41-44R
Goller, Celia (Fremlin) 1914- CANR-5
Earlier sketch in CA 13-16R
See also Fremlin, Celia
See also CMW 4
Golley, Frank Benjamin 1930-
Brief entry 106
Gollin, Gillian Lindt
See Lindt, Gillian
Gollin, James (M.) 1932- 237
Gollin, Rita K. 1928- 140
Gollings, Franklin O. A. 1919- 21-24R
Gollmar, Robert H. 1903(?)-1987
Obituary 123
Gollob, Herman 1930- 217
Gollub, Matthew 1960- CANR-112
Earlier sketch in CA 150
See also SATA 83, 134
Gollwitzer, Heinz 1917- 25-28R
Gologor, Ethan 1940- 101
Golomb, Claire 1928- 103
Golomb, Jacob 1947- 232
Golomb, Louis 1943- CANR-16
Earlier sketch in CA 85-88
Golombek, Harry 1911-1995 103
Golomstock, Igor (Naumovitch) 1929- 134
Golon, Serge(anne) 1903-1972
Obituary 37-40R
Golovine, Michael N(icholas) 1903-1965 . 5-8R
Golovnya, Anatoli 1900-1982 .... IDFW 3, 4
Golsan, Richard J(oseph) 1952- 223
Golson, G(eorge) Barry 1944- CANR-33
Earlier sketch in CA 69-72
Goltz, Thomas (Caufield) 184
Golubitsky, Martin 1945- 140
Golv, Loyal E(ugene) 1926- CANR-1
Earlier sketch in CA 1-4R
Golway, Terry 1955- 174
Golz, R(einhardt) Lud 1936- CANR-5
Earlier sketch in CA 13-16R
Gom, Leona 1946- CANR-137
Earlier sketch in CA 116
Gombault, Charles Henri 1907-1983
Obituary 110
Gomberg, Adeline Wishengrad
1915-1998 .... 17-20R
Gomberg, William 1911-1985 .... 17-20R
Obituary 118
Gomberville, Marin Le Roy
1599-1674 .... DLB 268
See also GFL Beginnings to 1789
Gombocz, Istvan 1956- 188
Gombossy, Zoltan
See Gabel, Joseph
Gombrich, E(rnst) H(ans Josef)
1909-2001 .... CANR-142
Obituary 202
Earlier sketches in CA 53-56, CANR-5, 32, 71
See also MTFW 2005
See also NCFS 5
Gombrich, Richard Francis 1937- 138
Gombrowicz, Witold 1904-1969 ... CANR-105
Obituary 25-28R
Earlier sketches in CAP-2, CA 19-20
See also CDWLB 4
See also CLC 4, 7, 11, 49
See also DAM DRAM
See also DLB 215
See also EW 12
See also EWL 3
See also RGWL 2, 3
See also TWA
Gomery, Douglas 1945- CANR-29
Earlier sketch in CA 110
Gomes, Paulo Emilio Salles 1916-1977 171
Gomes, Peter J(ohn) 1942- CANR-122
Earlier sketch in CA 162
Gomes Coelho, Joaquim Guilherme
See Dinis, Julio
Gomez, Alberto Perez
See Perez-Gomez, Alberto
Gomez, Carlos F. 1958- 129
Gomez, David F(ederico) 1940- 49-52
Gomez, Elizabeth .... SATA 133
Gomez, Jeff 1970- 222
Gomez, Jewelle 1948- 142
See also BW 2
See also FW
See also GLL 1
Gomez, Joseph A(nthony) 1942- 104
Gomez, Madeleine-Angelique Poisson de
1684-1770 .... DLB 313
Gomez, Raul R. 1953- 192
Gomez, Rudolph 1930- 53-56
Gomez Carrillo, Enrique 1873-1927 .... LAW
Gomez de Avellaneda, Gertrudis
1814-1873 .... LAW
Gomez de Ciudad Real, Alvar c.
1488-1538 .... DLB 318
Gomez de Guadalajara, Alvar
See Gomez de Ciudad Real, Alvar
Gomez de la Serna, Ramon
1888-1963 .... CANR-79
Obituary 116
Earlier sketch in CA 153
See also CLC 9
See also EWL 3
See also HW 1, 2
Gomez-Freer, Elizabeth
See Gomez, Elizabeth
Gomez-Gil, Alfredo 1936- CANR-49
Earlier sketch in CA 41-44R
See also AITN 1
Gomez-Jefferson, Annetta L(ouise) 1927- 178
Gomez-Pena, Guillermo 1955- CANR-117
Earlier sketch in CA 147
Gomez-Quinones, Juan (H.) 1942- 131
See also DLB 122
See also HW 1
Gomez Rosa, Alexis 1950- 153
See also Rosa, Alexis Gomez
See also HW 1, 2
Gomez-Vega, Ibis (del Carmen) 1952- 180
Gomi, Taro 1945- 162
See also CLR 57
See also MAICYA 2
See also SATA 64, 103
Gommans, Jos J. L. 1963- 151
Gomori, George 1934- CANR-112
Earlier sketches in CA 21-24R, CANR-9
Gompers, Samuel 1850-1924 .... DLB 303
Gompertz, Rolf 1927- CANR-11
Earlier sketch in CA 69-72
Gomringer, Eugen 1925- 195
See also EWL 3
Goncalves, Olga 1929- .... EWL 3
Goncalves Dias, Antonio 1823-1864 .. DLB 307
See also LAW
Goncharov, Ivan Alexandrovich
1812-1891 .... DLB 238
See also EW 6
See also RGWL 2, 3
Goncourt, Edmond (Louis Antoine Huot) de
1822-1896 .... DLB 123
See also EW 7
See also GFL 1789 to the Present
See also RGWL 2, 3
Goncourt, Jules (Alfred Huot) de
1830-1870 .... DLB 123
See also EW 7
See also GFL 1789 to the Present
See also RGWL 2, 3
Goncz, Arpad 1922- .... CWW 2
Gondosch, Linda 1944- 127
See also SATA 58
Gonen, Jay Y. 1934- 200
Gongora (y Argote), Luis de
1561-1627 .... RGWL 2, 3
Gongora, Maria Eugenia 1948- 104
Gonick, Jean 1950- 121
Gonick, Larry 1946- CANR-123
Earlier sketch in CA 127
Gonnerman, Jennifer 1971- 230
Gontarski, S(tanley) E. 1942- CANR-76
Earlier sketches in CA 114, CANR-74
Gontier, Fernande 19(?)- .... CLC 50
Gonzales, (Elizabeth) Anne H. 1944- 138
Gonzales, Corky
See Gonzales, Rodolfo
Gonzales, John
See Terrall, Robert
Gonzales, Manuel G(arcia) 1943- .. CANR-108
Earlier sketch in CA 111
Gonzales, Pancho
See Gonzales, Richard Alonzo
Gonzales, Phillip B. 1946- 202
Gonzales, Rebecca 1946- 180
Earlier sketch in CA 177
See also HW 2
Gonzales, Richard Alonzo 1928-1995
Brief entry 105
Gonzales, Rodolfo 1928-2005 181
Obituary 238
See also DLB 122
Gonzales, Sylvia Alicia 1943- 77-80
See also HW 1
Gonzales-Berry, Erlinda (V.) 1942- 220
See also DLB 209
Gonzalez, Alexander G. 1952- .... HW 2
Gonzalez, Alexander G. 1952- 175
Gonzalez, Alfonso 1927- 41-44R
Gonzalez, Angel 1925- CANR-15
Earlier sketch in CA 85-88
See also DLB 108
Gonzalez, Anibal 1956- CANR-99
Earlier sketch in CA 148
Gonzalez, Arturo 1928- 77-80
Gonzalez, Catherine Gunsalus 1934- 136
Gonzalez, Catherine Troxell 1917-2000 151
See also SATA 87
Gonzalez, Cesar A.
See Gonzalez T(rujillo), Cesar A.
See also DLB 82
Gonzalez, Christina
See Gonzalez, Maya Christina
Gonzalez, Edward 1933-
Brief entry 109
Gonzalez (Mandri), Flora 1948- 151
See also HW 2
Gonzalez, Francisco J. 237
Gonzalez, Genaro 1949- CANR-79
Earlier sketch in CA 148
See also AAYA 15
See also DLB 122
See also HW 2
Gonzalez, Gloria 1940- CANR-49
Earlier sketches in CA 65-68, CANR-24
See also SATA 23
Gonzalez, Jaime Jose 1925-1992 103
Gonzalez, Jose Luis 1926- 131
See also HW 1
Gonzalez, Justo L(uis) 1937- CANR-109
Earlier sketches in CA 29-32R, CANR-16, 54
Gonzalez, Justo L(uis) 1937-
See Gonzalez, Justo L(uis)
Gonzalez, Maya
See Gonzalez, Maya Christina
Gonzalez, Maya Christina 1964- 186
See also SATA 115

Gonzalez, N(estor) V(icente) M(adali)
1915-1999 .... CANR-2
Obituary 186
Earlier sketch in CA 1-4R
See also DLB 312
See also EWL 3
Gonzalez, Nancie L(oudon) 1929- 103
Gonzalez, Otto-Raul 1921- .... DLB 290
Gonzalez, Ray 1952- 175
See also DLB 122
See also HW 2
Gonzalez, Richard F(lorentz) 1927- 114
Gonzalez, Rigoberto 1970- 221
See also SATA 147
Gonzalez, Sergio A(ntonio) Torres
See Torres Gonzalez, Sergio A(ntonio)
Gonzalez, Victor Hugo 1953- 170
See also HW 2
Gonzalez, Victoria 1969- 228
Gonzalez-Aller, Faustino 1922- 81-84
Gonzalez-Balado, Jose Luis 1933- 162
Gonzalez-Crussi, F(rank) 1936- CANR-54
Brief entry 121
Earlier sketch in CA 126
Interview in CA-126
See also HW 1, 2
Gonzalez de Eslava, Fernan
1534-1601(?) .... LAW
Gonzalez de Mireles, Jovita
1899-1983 .... DLB 122
Gonzalez De Mireles, Jovita 1899-1983 202
Gonzalez Echevarria, Roberto
1943- CANR-144
Earlier sketch in CA 106
Gonzalez-Gerth, Miguel 1926- 69-72
Gonzalez Lopez, Emilio 1903-1991 ... CANR-2
Earlier sketch in CA 49-52
Gonzalez Martinez, Enrique
See Gonzalez Martinez, Enrique
See also DLB 290
Gonzalez Martinez, Enrique
1871-1952 .... CANR-81
Earlier sketch in CA 166
See also Gonzalez Martinez, Enrique
See also EWL 3
See also HW 1, 2
See also TCLC 72
Gonzalez-Mena, Janet 1937- 111
Gonzalez-Paz, Elsie E. 1913-1999 45-48
Gonzalez Prada, Manuel 1848-1918 .... EWL 3
See also HW 1
See also LAW
Gonzalez T(rujillo), Cesar A. 1931- 153
See also Gonzalez, Cesar A.
See also HW 1
Gonzalez-Wippler, Migene 1936- 109
Goobie, Beth 1959- 194
See also SATA 128
Gooby, Peter Taylor
See Taylor-Gooby, Peter
Gooch, Bob
See Gooch, Robert M(iletus)
Gooch, Brad 1952- CANR-143
Earlier sketches in CA 132, CANR-74
See also GLL 2
Gooch, Brison D(owling) 1925- 13-16R
Gooch, Bryan Niel Shirley 1937- 93-96
Gooch, George Peabody 1873-1968 .... 5-8R
Gooch, John 1945- 126
Gooch, Paul W(illiam) 1941- 172
Gooch, Robert M(iletus) 1919- CANR-55
Earlier sketches in CA 77-80, CANR-13, 29
Gooch, Stan(ley Alfred) 1932- CANR-46
Earlier sketches in CA 77-80, CANR-14
Gooch, Steve 1945- CANR-43
Earlier sketches in CA 101, CANR-20
See also CBD
See also CD 5, 6
Gooche, Terry, Jr. 1927- 145
Good, Alice 1950- .... SATA 73
Good, Carter V(ictor) 1897-1997 .... 5-8R
Good, Clare
See Romano, Clare
Good, David F(ranklin) 1943- 125
Good, David L. 1942- 218
Good, Edwin M(arshall) 1928- CANR-11
Earlier sketch in CA 17-20R
Good, H(arry) G(ehman) 1880-1971 .... 1-4R
Obituary 103
Good, Howard 1951- CANR-98
Earlier sketch in CA 147
Good, I(rving) John 1916- CANR-3
Earlier sketch in CA 5-8R
Good, Kenneth 1942- 134
Good, Lawrence R. 1924- 13-16R
Good, Mary L(owe) 1931- 156
Good, Paul (Joseph), (Jr.) 1929-2005 85-88
Obituary 235
Good, Robert Crocker 1924- 73-76
Good, Thomas L(indall) 1943- CANR-22
Earlier sketches in CA 57-60, CANR-8
Goodacre, Elizabeth Jane 1929- 102
Goodall, Daphne Machin
See Machin Goodall, Daphne (Edith)
Goodall, Harold Lloyd, (Jr.) 1952- .. CANR-101
Earlier sketch in CA 132
Goodall, Jane 1934- CANR-109
Earlier sketches in CA 45-48, CANR-2, 43, 69
See also MTCW 1
See also SATA 111
Goodall, John S(trickland) 1908-1996 ... 33-36R
Obituary 152
See also CLR 25
See also MAICYA 1, 2
See also MAICYAS 1
See also SATA 4, 66
See also SATA-Obit 91
Goodall, Leonard E. 1937- 85-88
Goodall, Marcus C(ampbell) 1914- 33-36R
Goodall, Melanie
See Drachman, Julian M(oses)
Goodall, Nigel 1950- 222
Goodall, Norman 1896-1985
Obituary 115
Goodall, Vanne Morris
See Morris-Goodall, Vanne
Goodavage, Joseph F. 1925-1989 .... 25-28R
Goodavage, Maria 1962- 225
Goodbody, Slim
See Burstein, John
Goodchild, Peter 1939- 106
Goode, Barry 1938- 118
Goode, Diane (Capuozzo) 1949- 186
See also SATA 15, 84, 114
Goode, Erica 166
Goode, Erich 1938- CANR-37
Earlier sketches in CA 49-52, CANR-1, 16
Goode, Gerald 1899(?)-1983
Obituary 111
Goode, James (Arthur) 1924-1992 123
Obituary 140
Goode, James M. 1939- 93-96
Goode, John 1927- 103
Goode, Kenneth G. 1932- 49-52
Goode, Richard (Benjamin) 1916- 17-20R
Goode, Ruth 1905-1997 77-80
Obituary 162
Goode, Stephen H(ogue) 1924- CANR-2
Earlier sketch in CA 45-48
Goode, Stephen Ray 1943- CANR-18
Earlier sketch in CA 57-60
See also SATA 55
See also SATA-Brief 40
Goode, William Josiah 1917-2003 102
Obituary 216
Goodell, Charles E(llsworth) 1926-1987 .. 81-84
Obituary 121
Goodell, Donald (James) 1938- 45-48
Goodell, Jeff 160
Goodell, John S. 1939- 73-76
Goodell, Rae 1944- 77-80
Gooden, Arthur Henry .... TCWW 1, 2
Gooden, Philip 238
Goodenough, Erwin R(amsdell)
1893-1965 .... 5-8R
Goodenough, Evelyn
See Pitcher, Evelyn G(oodenough)
Goodenough, Ursula (Wiltshire) 1943- 181
Goodenough, Ward Hunt 1919- CANR-2
Earlier sketch in CA 1-4R
Goodenow, Earle 1913- .... SATA 40
Gooders, John 1937- CANR-6
Earlier sketch in CA 57-60
Goodfellow, Peter 1935- 115
Goodfellow, Samuel Huston 1957- 195
Goodfield, (Gwyneth) June 1927- 9-12R
Goodfriend, Arthur 1907-1998 .... 5-8R
Goodgold, Edwin 1944- CANR-23
Earlier sketch in CA 21-24R
Goodhart, A. L.
See Goodhart, Arthur Lehman
Goodhart, Arthur Lehman
1891-1978 .... CANR-31
Obituary 81-84
Earlier sketch in CA 85-88
Goodhart, Pippa 1958- .... SATA 153
Goodhart, Robert S(tanley) 1909-1992 89-92
Goodheart, Barbara 1934- 33-36R
Goodheart, Eugene 1931- CANR-39
Earlier sketches in CA 5-8R, CANR-3, 18
Goodheart, Lawrence B. 1944- 135
Goodhue, Thomas W. 1949- CANR-124
Earlier sketch in CA 142
See also SATA 143
Goodin, Gayle 1938- 33-36R
Goodin, Robert E(dward) 1950- CANR-45
Earlier sketches in CA 105, CANR-22
Goodin, Sallie (Brown) 1953- .... SATA 74
Gooding, Cynthia 1924-1988 .... 33-36R
Gooding, John (Ervine) 1940- 21-24R
Gooding, Judson 1926- 73-76
Gooding, Kathleen (Tinney) 116
Gooding, Mel 1941- 235
Goodis, David 1917-1967 .... CANR-60
Earlier sketch in CA 1-4R
See also CMW 4
See also DLB 226
Goodison, Lorna 1947- CANR-88
Earlier sketch in CA 142
See also CP 7
See also CWP
See also DLB 157
See also EWL 3
See also PC 36
Goodkin, Richard E. 1953- 141
Goodkin, Sanford R(onald) 1929- 104
Goodkind, Henry M. 1904(?)-1970
Obituary 104
Goodkind, Terry 1948- CANR-113
Earlier sketch in CA 165
See also AAYA 27
See also FANT
Goodlad, John I. 1920- CANR-43
Earlier sketches in CA 5-8R, CANR-3, 19
Goodman, A(lvin) Harold 1924- 103
Goodman, A(dolph) W(inkler) 1915- 57-60
Goodman, Alison 1966- 182
See also SATA 111
Goodman, Allegra 1967- 204
See also DLB 244
Goodman, Ann (Davidow) 1932- 107
Goodman, Anthony (Eric) 1936- 220
Goodman, Arnold Abraham 1913-1995 109
Obituary 148
Goodman, Aviel 1955- 178
Goodman, Benjamin David 1909(?)-1986
Obituary 119
Goodman, Benny
See Goodman, Benjamin David
Goodman, Carol 239
Goodman, Celia (Mary) 1916-2002 123
Obituary 219
Goodman, Charles S(chaffner) 1916- 33-36R
Goodman, Charlotte Margolis 1934- 134
Goodman, David (Allen) 1941- 119
Goodman, David Michael 1936- 17-20R
Goodman, David S. 1917- 29-32R
Goodman, Deborah Lerme 1956- 121
See also SATA 50
See also SATA-Brief 49
Goodman, Edward J(ulius) 1916- 111
Goodman, Elaine 1930- 37-40R
See also SATA 9
Goodman, Elizabeth B. 1912-1991 .... 25-28R
Goodman, Ellen (Holtz) 1941- CANR-101
Earlier sketch in CA 104
Interview in CA-104
Goodman, Elliot R(aymond) 1923- 1-4R
Goodman, Emily Jane 1940- 65-68
Goodman, Eric 1953- 141
Goodman, Eugene B(enedict) 1922- 113
Goodman, Felicitas D(aniels) 1914- . CANR-46
Earlier sketches in CA 53-56, CANR-4, 23
Goodman, Fred 1950(?)- 160
Goodman, George J(erome) W(aldo)
1930- CANR-68
Earlier sketches in CA 21-24R, CANR-31
Interview in CANR-31
See also Smith, Adam
Goodman, Grant K(ohn) 1924- CANR-15
Earlier sketch in CA 41-44R
Goodman, Hannah Grad
See Sverdlin, Hannah Grad
Goodman, Harriet Wilinsky 111
Goodman, Herman 1894-1971
Obituary 105
Goodman, James 1956- 146
Goodman, James M(arion) 1929- 117
Goodman, Jay S. 1940- 37-40R
Goodman, Joan Elizabeth 1950- CANR-143
Earlier sketches in CA 126, CANR-67
See also SATA 50, 94, 162
Goodman, John 1952- 146
Goodman, Jon 1969- 195
Goodman, Jonathan 1931- CANR-13
Earlier sketch in CA 33-36R
Goodman, Jordan E. 1954- 147
Goodman, Joseph Irving 1908-1998 102
Goodman, Kenneth S. 1927- 25-28R
Goodman, Lenn Evan 1944- 53-56
Goodman, Leonard H(enry) 1941- 103
Goodman, Linda 1925-1995 .... CANR-52
Obituary 150
Earlier sketch in CA 89-92
Goodman, Lizbeth (L.) 1964- CANR-102
Earlier sketch in CA 163
Goodman, Louis Wolf 1942- 25-28R
Goodman, Mark 1939- 126
Goodman, Martin (David) 1953- 172
Goodman, Melinda 1957- .... GLL 2
Goodman, Melvin A. 1938- CANR-111
Earlier sketch in CA 138
Goodman, Michael B(arry) 1949- CANR-97
Earlier sketch in CA 107
Goodman, Mitchell 1923-1997 .... CANR-4
Obituary 156
Earlier sketch in CA 1-4R
Goodman, Nan 1957- 177
Goodman, (Henry) Nelson 1906-1998 45-48
See also DLB 279
Goodman, Norman 1934- CANR-17
Earlier sketches in CA 49-52, CANR-1
Goodman, Paul 1911-1972 .... CANR-34
Obituary 37-40R
Earlier sketches in CAP-2, CA 19-20
See also CAD
See also CLC 1, 2, 4, 7
See also CN 1
See also DLB 130, 246
See also MAL 5
See also MTCW 1
See also RGAL 4
Goodman, Percival 1904-1989 .... 1-4R
Obituary 129
Goodman, Philip 1911- 33-36R
Goodman, Randolph 1908- CANR-2
Earlier sketch in CA 5-8R
Goodman, Rebecca Gruver 1931- 77-80
Goodman, Richard 1945- 136
Goodman, Richard Merle
1932-1989 .... CANR-40
Earlier sketches in CA 102, CANR-18
Goodman, Roger B. 1919- CANR-9
Earlier sketch in CA 21-24R
Goodman, Ronald A. 1938- 73-76
Goodman, Rubin Robert 1913-1978
Obituary 81-84
Goodman, Saul 1919- 103
Goodman, Seymour S. 1931- CANR-22
Earlier sketch in CA 45-48
Goodman, Sonya
See Arcone, Sonya
Goodman, Stanley J(oshua) 1910-1992 110
Goodman, Steve 1948-1984
Obituary 113
Goodman, Steven M(ichael) 1957- 126
Goodman, Susan 1951- CANR-91
Earlier sketch in CA 146
Goodman, Susan E. 1952- 235
Goodman, Walter 1927-2002 .... CANR-7
Obituary 207
Earlier sketch in CA 9-12R
See also SATA 9
Goodnough, David L. 1930- 93-96
Goodnow, Henry F(rank) 1917- 13-16R
Goodnow, Jacqueline (Jarrett) 1924- ... CANR-5
Earlier sketch in CA 13-16R
Goodovitch, I(srael) M(eir) 1934- 25-28R
Gooaster, Andrew J(ackson), (Jr.)
1915-2005 109
Obituary 239
Gooaster, Kenneth E(dwin) 1944- CANR-17
Earlier sketch in CA 97-100
Gooasture, H(enry) McKennie 1929-2000 .. 134
Goodreau, William Joseph, Jr. 1931- 1-4R
Goodrich, Chris 1956- 134
Goodrich, David L(loyd) 1930- 85-88
Goodrich, Donna Clark 1938- 117
Goodrich, Foster E(dward) 1908-1972
Obituary 37-40R
Goodrich, Frances 1890(?)-1984 169
Obituary 111
See also DFS 15
See also DLB 26
See also IDFW 3, 4
Goodrich, Frances C. 1933- 21-24R
Goodrich, L(uther) Carrington
1894-1986 .... CANR-2
Obituary 120
Earlier sketch in CA 5-8R
Goodrich, Leland Matthew 1899-1990 ... 81-84
Goodrich, Lloyd 1897-1987 .... CANR-31
Obituary 122
Earlier sketch in CA 69-72
Goodrich, Norma Lorre 1917- 53-56
Goodrich, Robert E(dward), Jr.
1909-1985 .... 33-36R
Goodrich, Samuel Griswold
1793-1860 .... DLB 1, 42, 73, 243
See also SATA 23
Goodrich, William Lloyd 1910(?)-1975
Obituary 61-64
Goodrick, Edward W(illiam)
1913-1992 .... CANR-29
Earlier sketch in CA 111
Goodrick-Clarke, Nicholas 1953- ... CANR-115
Earlier sketch in CA 123
Goodrum, Charles A(lvin) 1923- CANR-57
Earlier sketches in CA 25-28R, CANR-12, 27
Goodsall, Robert Harold 1891-(?) CANR-4
Earlier sketch in CA 5-8R
Goodsell, Charles T(rue) 1932- CANR-8
Earlier sketch in CA 61-64
Goodsell, Fred Field 1880-1976 .... 1-4R
Obituary 69-72
Goodsell, Jane Neuberger 1921(?)-1988
Obituary 126
See also SATA-Obit 56
Goodson, Felix E(mmett) 1922- 49-52
Goodson, Larry P. 217
Goodspeed, Donald J(ames) 1919- 5-8R
Goodspeed, Edgar Johnson 1871-1962
Obituary 93-96
Goodspeed, Peter 1944- 110
Goodstein, David B. 1932(?)-1985
Obituary 116
Goodstein, Leonard D(avid) 1927- ... CANR-13
Earlier sketch in CA 33-36R
Goodstein, Marvin (Elias) 1927- 125
Goodstein, Phil(lip) 1952- CANR-123
Earlier sketch in CA 171
Goodstein, R(euben) L(ouis) 1912-1985 .. 53-56
Obituary 116
GoodWeather, Harley
See King, Thomas
Goodwin, Albert 1906-1995 .... 5-8R
Goodwin, Archie 1937-1998 227
Goodwin, Bennie Eugene II 1933- 112
Goodwin, Craufurd D(avid) W(ycliffe)
1934- CANR-14
Earlier sketch in CA 37-40R
Goodwin, Dave 1926- 113
Goodwin, Derek 1920- 93-96
Goodwin, Donald W(illiam) 1931-1999 . 65-68
Goodwin, Doris (Helen) Kearns
1943- CANR-53
Earlier sketch in CANR-23
Goodwin, Eugene D.
See Kaye, Marvin (Nathan)
Goodwin, Frederick K(ing) 1936- 148
Goodwin, Geoffrey (Lawrence)
1916-1995 106
Obituary 148
Goodwin, H(arry) Eugene 1922-1987 126
Goodwin, Hal
See Goodwin, Harold L(eland)
Goodwin, Harold 1919- 57-60
Goodwin, Harold L(eland)
1914-1990 .... CANR-29
Obituary 131
Earlier sketches in CA 1-4R, CANR-2
See also SATA 13, 51
See also SATA-Obit 65
Goodwin, Jan 1944- 154
Goodwin, Jason 1964- 209
Goodwin, Joan W. 1926- 209
Goodwin, Joanne L. 1949- 167
Goodwin, John (Lonnen) 1921- CANR-93
Earlier sketch in CA 108
Goodwin, John R(obert) 1929- 77-80
Goodwin, Karin 181
Goodwin, Ken(neth Leslie) 1934- CANR-92
Earlier sketch in CA 131
Goodwin, Leonard 1929- 41-44R
Goodwin, Mark
See Matthews, Stanley G(oodwin)

Goodwin, Michael 1949- 141
Goodwin, Neil 1940- 204
Goodwin, (Trevor) Noel 1927- 124
Goodwin, R(ichard) M(urphey)
1913-1996 .... CANR-29
Obituary 153
Earlier sketches in CA 29-32R, CANR-12
Goodwin, Richard N(aradhof) 1931- 146
Brief entry 111
Goodwin, Robert L. 1928(?)-1983
Obituary 109
Goodwin, Ruby Berkley 1903- 153
See also BW 2
Goodwin, Stephen 1943- CANR-8
Earlier sketch in CA 57-60
See also DLBY 1982
Goodwin, Suzanne CANR-31
Earlier sketches in CA 77-80, CANR-14
See also RHW
Goodwin, William 1943- 184
See also SATA 117
Goodwyn, Floyd L(owell) 1940- 113
Goodwyn, Lawrence 1928- 21-24R
Goody, Joan Edelman 1935- 17-20R
Goodyear, Frank H., Jr. 1944- 122
Goodyear, John H(enry) III 1941- CANR-41
Earlier sketch in CA 111
Goody-Jones
See Janko, (Kathleen) Susan
Googe, Barnabe 1540-1594 .... DLB 132
See also RGEL 2
Gookin, Daniel 1612-1687 .... DLB 24
Gool, Reshard 1931- 97-100
Goolagong, Evonne 1951- 89-92
Goold-Adams, Richard (John Moreton)
1916-1995 .... 13-16R
Obituary 148
Goon, Fook Mun 1917(?)-1984
Obituary 113
Gooneratne, (Malini) Yasmine
1935- CANR-41
Earlier sketches in CA 29-32R, CANR-18
See also CP 1
Goonetilleke, D(evapriya) C(hitra) R(anjan)
A(lwis) 1938- CANR-86
Earlier sketch in CA 130
Goor, Nancy (Ruth Miller) 1944- CANR-139
Earlier sketches in CA 113, CANR-32
See also SATA 39
See also SATA-Brief 34
Goor, Ron(ald Stephen) 1940- CANR-137
Earlier sketches in CA 113, CANR-32
See also SATA 39
See also SATA-Brief 34
Goossen, Agnes
See Epp, Margaret A(gnes)
Goossen, Irvy W. 37-40R
Goossen, Rachel Waltner 1960- 167
Goosson, Stephen 1893-1973 .... IDFW 3, 4
Goot, Mary Vander
See Vander Goot, Mary
Gootenberg, Paul 1954- CANR-105
Earlier sketch in CA 149
Gopal, Sarvepalli 1923-2002 104
Gopalakrishnan, Chennat 1936- CANR-30
Earlier sketch in CA 112
Gopegui, Belen 1963- .... DLB 322
Gopen, George D(avid) 1945- 113
Gopher, Euell
See Moss, Kay K.
Gopiah
See Keys, Kerry Shawn
Gopnik, Adam 1956- CANR-102
Earlier sketch in CA 165
Gopnik, Alison 1955- 192
Gorak, Jan 1952- CANR-124
Earlier sketches in CA 126, CANR-58
Goralski, Robert 1928-1988 105
Obituary 125
Goran, Abdulla 1904-1962 .... EWL 3
See also RGWL 3
Goran, Lester 1928- CANR-144
Earlier sketches in CA 45-48, CANR-48
See also DLB 244
Goran, Morris (Herbert) 1918-1987 ... CANR-2
Earlier sketch in CA 1-4R
Gorbachev, Mikhail (Sergeyevich)
1931- CANR-117
Earlier sketches in CA 132, CANR-69
See also MTCW 1
Gorbachev, Raisa (Maksimovna)
1932-1999 141
Obituary 185
Gorbachev, Valeri 1944- CANR-117
Earlier sketch in CA 166
See also SATA 98, 143
See also SATA-Essay 143
Gorbanevskaia, Natalia (Evgen'evna)
See Gorbanevskaya, Natalya
See also CWW 2
Gorbanevskaya, Natalya 1936- 111
See also Gorbanevskaia, Natalia (Evgen'evna)
Gorbatov, Alexander V. 1891(?)-1973
Obituary 45-48
Gordeeva, Ekaterina 1971- CANR-127
Earlier sketch in CA 158
Gorden, Raymond L(owell) 1919-1995 ... 53-56
Gordenker, Leon 1923- 21-24R
Gordett, Marea (Beth) 1949- 117
Gordh, George (Rudolph) 1912-1999 ... 13-16R
Gordievsky, Oleg 1938- 140
Gordimer, Nadine 1923- CANR-131
Earlier sketches in CA 5-8R, CANR-3, 28, 56, 88
Interview in CANR-28
See also AAYA 39
See also AFW
See also BRWS 2
See also CLC 3, 5, 7, 10, 18, 33, 51, 70, 123, 160, 161
See also CN 1, 2, 3, 4, 5, 6, 7
See also DA
See also DA3
See also DAB
See also DAC
See also DAM MST, NOV
See also DLB 225
See also EWL 3
See also EXPS
See also LATS 1:2
See also MTCW 1, 2
See also MTFW 2005
See also NFS 4
See also RGEL 2
See also RGSF 2
See also SSC 17, 80
See also SSFS 2, 14, 19
See also TWA
See also WLCS
See also WLIT 2
See also YAW
Gordin, Michael D. 232
Gordin, Richard Davis 1928- 53-56
Gordion, Mark
See Turtledove, Harry (Norman)
Gordis, Daniel H. 1959- 197
Gordis, Robert 1908-1992 .... CANR-9
Earlier sketch in CA 13-16R
Gordon, Ad
See Hano, Arnold
Gordon, Adam Lindsay 1833-1870 .... DLB 230
Gordon, Alan F. 1947- 102
Gordon, Albert I(saac) 1903-1968 .... CAP-1
Earlier sketch in CA 11-12
Gordon, Alex
See Cotler, Gordon
Gordon, Alison (Ruth) 1943- CANR-127
Earlier sketch in CA 121
Gordon, Alvin J. 1912-1989 .... 33-36R
Obituary 130
Gordon, Ambrose, Jr. 1920-1987 .... 33-36R
Obituary 122
Gordon, Amy 1949- CANR-140
Earlier sketch in CA 186
See also SATA 115, 156
Gordon, Andrew (Mark) 1945- 115
Gordon, Andrew D. 1952- 217
Gordon, Angela
See Paine, Lauran (Bosworth)
Gordon, Anne Wolrige
See Wolrige Gordon, Anne
Gordon, Antoinette K. 1892(?)-1975
Obituary 57-60
Gordon, April A. 1947- 162
Gordon, Archibald Victor Dudley 1913-1984
Obituary 114
Gordon, Archie
See Gordon, Archibald Victor Dudley
Gordon, Arthur 1912-2002 .... 5-8R
Obituary 203
Gordon, Barbara 1935- CANR-78
Earlier sketches in CA 89-92, CANR-17
Interview in CANR-17
Gordon, Barry (Lewis John) 1934-1994 102
Gordon, Beate Sirota 1923- 194
Gordon, Bernard 1918- 193
Gordon, Bernard K. 1932- 85-88
Gordon, Bernard Ludwig 1931- 29-32R
See also SATA 27
Gordon, Bertram M(artin) 1943- 101
Gordon, Beverly 1948- 93-96
Gordon, Bill
See Athanas, (William) Verne
Gordon, Burton L(e Roy) 1920- 114
Gordon, Caroline 1895-1981 .... CANR-36
Obituary 103
Earlier sketches in CAP-1, CA 11-12
See also AMW
See also CLC 6, 13, 29, 83
See also CN 1, 2
See also DLB 4, 9, 102
See also DLBD 17
See also DLBY 1981
See also EWL 3
See also MAL 5
See also MTCW 1, 2
See also MTFW 2005
See also RGAL 4
See also RGSF 2
See also SSC 15
Gordon, Charles C. 1944- .... CD 5
Gordon, Charles F. 1943- 232
See also OyamO
Gordon, Charles William 1860-1937
Brief entry 109
See also Connor, Ralph
Gordon, Colin 1962- 150
Gordon, Colonel H. R.
See Ellis, Edward S(ylvester)
Gordon, Cyrus H(erzl) 1908-2001 ...... CANR-5
Obituary 201
Earlier sketch in CA 1-4R
Gordon, Dane R. 1925- 33-36R
Gordon, David
See Garrett, (Gordon) Randall (Phillip)
Gordon, David Cole 1922- 25-28R
Gordon, David J. 1929-
Brief entry 105
Gordon, David M(ichael) 1944-1996 128
Obituary 151
Gordon, Deborah Hannes 1946- 130
See also RHW
Gordon, Diana
See Andrews, Lucilla (Mathew)
Gordon, Diana R(ussell) 1938- CANR-28
Earlier sketch in CA 49-52
Gordon, Donald
See Payne, Donald Gordon
Gordon, Donald Craigie 1911-2003 ...... 17-20R
Obituary 212
Gordon, Donald E(dward) 1931-1984
Obituary 112
Gordon, Donald Ramsay 1929- CANR-31
Earlier sketches in CA 37-40R, CANR-14
Gordon, Doreen
See Chard, Judy
Gordon, Dorothy 1893-1970 73-76
See also SATA 20
Gordon, Edmund Wyatt 1921- 37-40R
Gordon, Edwin 1927- CANR-10
Earlier sketch in CA 17-20R
Gordon, Eric A(rthur) 1945- 132
Gordon, Ernest 1916-2002 .... CANR-2
Obituary 204
Earlier sketch in CA 1-4R
Gordon, (Alexander) Esme 1910-1993 108
Gordon, Esther S(aranga) 1935- CANR-7
Earlier sketch in CA 53-56
See also SATA 10
Gordon, Ethel Edison 1915- 53-56
See also RHW
Gordon, Felice 1939- 97-100
Gordon, Fran 222
Gordon, Frances
See Wood, Bridget
Gordon, Frederick CANR-26
Earlier sketches in CAP-2, CA 19-20
See also SATA 1
Gordon, Fritz
See Jarvis, Fred(erick) G(ordon, Jr.)
Gordon, Gaelyn 1939-1997 .... CLR 75
See also CWRI 5
Gordon, Garrett
See Garrett, (Gordon) Randall (Phillip)
Gordon, Gary
See Edmonds, I(vy) G(ordon)
Gordon, George
See Hasford, (Jerry) Gustav
Gordon, George Byron 1911-1993 .... 33-36R
Gordon, George J(acob) 1943- 111
Gordon, George N(ewton) 1926- CANR-5
Earlier sketch in CA 1-4R
Gordon, Gerald 1909- CAP-1
Earlier sketch in CA 13-14
Gordon, Giles (Alexander Esme)
1940-2003 .... CANR-69
Obituary 221
Earlier sketches in CA 41-44R, CANR-43
See also CN 3, 4, 5, 6, 7
See also CP 1, 2
See also DLB 14, 139, 207
Gordon, Gordon 1912-2002 .... CANR-7
Earlier sketch in CA 5-8R
See also CMW 4
Gordon, Graeme 1966- 151
Gordon, Guanetta Stewart 37-40R
Gordon, Haim 1936- 175
Gordon, Hal
See Goodwin, Harold L(eland)
Gordon, Harold J(ackson), Jr.
1919-1980 .... 33-36R
Gordon, Harry 137
Gordon, Harry
See Gordon, Henry Alfred
Gordon, (Charles) Harry (Clinton) Pirie
See Pirie-Gordon, (Charles) Harry (Clinton)
Gordon, Helen Cameron 1867-1949 .. DLB 195
Gordon, Henry Alfred 1925- CANR-5
Earlier sketch in CA 53-56
Gordon, I(an) R(obert) F(raser) 1939- 69-72
Gordon, Ian
See Fellowes-Gordon, Ian (Douglas)
Gordon, Ian A(listair) 1908-2004 ...... CANR-11
Obituary 231
Earlier sketch in CA 25-28R
Gordon, Ida L. 1907- CAP-2
Earlier sketch in CA 33-36
Gordon, Ira J(ay) 1923-1978 .... CANR-26
Earlier sketch in CA 69-72
Gordon, Jacob U. 1939- 147
Gordon, Jaimy 1944- CANR-87
Earlier sketch in CA 140
Gordon, (Gilbert) James 1918- 61-64
Gordon, James S(amuel) 1941- 158
Gordon, Jane
See Lee, Elsie
Gordon, Jay 1948- 218
Gordon, Jeffie Ross
See Enderle, Judith (Ann) Ross and Gordon, Stephanie Jacob
Gordon, Joanne J(oy) 1956- 108
Gordon, Joe
See Gordon, Marvin (Joseph), Jr.
Gordon, John
See Gesner, Clark
Gordon, John (Rutherford) 1890-1974
Obituary 104
Gordon, John (William) 1925- CANR-60
Earlier sketches in CA 103, CANR-11, 27, 51
See also CWRI 5
See also HGG
See also SATA 84
Gordon, John Fraser 1916- CANR-45
Earlier sketches in CA 105, CANR-22
Gordon, John Steele 1944- CANR-119
Earlier sketch in CA 57-60
Gordon, Kermit 1916-1976
Obituary 65-68
Gordon, Kurtz
See Kurtz, C(larence) Gordon
Gordon, Leland J(ames) 1897-1982 ...... 41-44R
Obituary 133
Gordon, Leonard 1935- 53-56
Gordon, Leonard A. 1938- 37-40R
Gordon, Leonard H. D. 1928- 29-32R
Gordon, Lesley
See Elliott, Lesley
Gordon, Lew
See Baldwin, Gordon C(ortis)
Gordon, Lewis Ricardo 1962- 158
See also BW 3
Gordon, Lillian L. 1925-1977 .... 29-32R
Gordon, Lincoln 1913-1996 117
Gordon, (Irene) Linda 1940- CANR-50
Earlier sketches in CA 65-68, CANR-10, 25
See also FW
Gordon, Lois G. 1938- CANR-110
Earlier sketches in CA 33-36R, CANR-13, 29, 55
Gordon, Lou 1917(?)-1977
Obituary 69-72
Gordon, Lyndall (Felicity) 1941- CANR-97
Earlier sketch in CA 141
See also DLB 155
Gordon, M. Joseph, Jr.
See Gordon, Marvin (Joseph), Jr.
Gordon, Mack 1904-1959 .... DLB 265
Gordon, Margaret (Anna) 1939- .... SATA 9
Gordon, Margaret T(aber) 1939- 81-84
Gordon, Mark 1942- 118
Gordon, Marvin (Joseph), Jr. 1938- 238
Gordon, Mary (Catherine) 1949- CANR-92
Earlier sketches in CA 102, CANR-44
Interview in CA-102
See also AMWS 4
See also BPFB 2
See also CLC 13, 22, 128
See also CN 4, 5, 6, 7
See also DLB 6
See also DLBY 1981
See also FW
See also MAL 5
See also MTCW 1
See also SSC 59
Gordon, Mary Ebbitt
See Winters, Catherine (Mary)
Gordon, Mary McDougall 1929- 130
Gordon, Matthew S. 1957- 212
Gordon, Michael 1940- 41-44R
Gordon, Michael (David) 1952- 123
Gordon, Mike 1948- CANR-126
Earlier sketch in CA 168
See also SATA 101
Gordon, Mildred 1912-1979 .... CANR-7
Obituary 85-88
Earlier sketch in CA 5-8R
See also CMW 4
See also SATA-Obit 24
Gordon, Milton Myron 1918- 190
Gordon, Mitchell 1925- 5-8R
Gordon, Mordechai 1961- 219
Gordon, Myron J(ules) 1920- CANR-6
Earlier sketch in CA 5-8R
Gordon, N. J.
See Bosman, Herman Charles
Gordon, Nancy
See Heinl, Nancy G(ordon)
Gordon, Neil 1958- CANR-144
Earlier sketch in CA 174
Gordon, Noah 1926- CANR-123
Earlier sketches in CA 17-20R, CANR-62
Gordon, Oliver
See Emerson, H(enry) O(liver)
Gordon, Patricia 1909- 21-24R
Gordon, Percival Hector 1884-1975 ..... 41-44R
Gordon, Peter
See Wilkes-Hunter, R(ichard)
Gordon, Peter H. 1948- 130
Gordon, R(ichard) L(aurence) 1920-
Brief entry 114
Gordon, Ray
See Wainwright, Gordon Ray
Gordon, Rex
See Hough, S(tanley) B(ennett)
Gordon, Richard
See Ostlere, Gordon (Stanley)
Gordon, Richard 1947- 160
Gordon, Richard L(ewis) 1934- 29-32R
Gordon, Rivca 1945- 175
Gordon, Robert 1961- 239
Gordon, Robert A(aron) 1908-1978 .... CANR-4
Obituary 77-80
Earlier sketch in CA 5-8R
Gordon, Robert C(oningsby) 1921- 5-8R
Gordon, Robert Ellis 1954- CANR-122
Earlier sketch in CA 146
Gordon, Robert J. 1947- 121
Gordon, Ruth 1896-1985 .... CANR-31
Obituary 117
Earlier sketch in CA 81-84
Gordon, Samuel 1907(?)-1984
Obituary 114
Gordon, Sanford D(aniel) 1924- 33-36R
Gordon, Sarah (Ann) 1944- 132
Gordon, Selma
See Lanes, Selma Gordon
Gordon, Sheila 1927- 132
See also CLR 27
See also SATA 88

Gordon, Shirley 1921- 97-100
See also SATA 48
See also SATA-Brief 41
Gordon, Sol 1923- CANR-4
Earlier sketch in CA 53-56
See also CLC 26
See also SATA 11
Gordon, Spike
See Fearn, John Russell
Gordon, Stephanie Jacob 1940- CANR-118
Earlier sketches in CA 124, CANR-59
See also SAAS 26
See also SATA 64, 89
See also SATA-Essay 114
Gordon, Steve 1938(?)-1982
Obituary 108
Gordon, Stewart
See Shirreffs, Gordon D(onald)
Gordon, Strathearn 1902-1983
Obituary 109
Gordon, Stuart 1947- .... SFW 4
Gordon, Suzanne 1945- CANR-70
Earlier sketches in CA 49-52, CANR-4
Gordon, Sydney 1914- 29-32R
Gordon, Theodore J. 1930- 17-20R
Gordon, Thomas 1918-2002 .... 29-32R
Obituary 208
Gordon, Vivian V(erdell)
1934-1995 .... CANR-83
Obituary 147
Earlier sketch in CA 143
See also BW 2
Gordon, W. Terrence 1942- 162
Gordon, Walter Kelly 1930- 33-36R
Gordon, Walter L(ockhart) 1906-1987 .. 97-100
Obituary 122
Gordon, Wendell (Chaffee) 1916-1997 . 17-20R
Gordon, William A. 1950- 135
Gordone, Charles 1925-1995 180
Obituary 150
Earlier sketches in CA 93-96, CANR-55
Interview in CA-93-96
Autobiographical Essay in 180
See also BW 1, 3
See also CAD
See also CLC 1, 4
See also DAM DRAM
See also DC 8
See also DLB 7
See also MTCW 1
Gordon-Reed, Annette 212
Gordons, The
See Gordon, Gordon and
Gordon, Mildred
Gordon Walker, Patrick (Chrestien)
1907-1980 .... 29-32R
Gordon-Watson, Mary 1948- CANR-37
Earlier sketch in CA 112
Gordy, Berry Sr. 1888-1978 102
Gordy, Berry, Jr. 1929- CANR-127
Earlier sketch in CA 148
Gore, Al(bert, Jr.) 1948- CANR-110
Earlier sketch in CA 142
Gore, Albert (Arnold), Sr. 1907-1998
Obituary 172
Brief entry 112
Gore, Ariel 1971- 167
Gore, Arthur Kattendyke S(trange) D(avid)
A(rchibald) 1910-1983
Obituary 109
Gore, Catherine 1800-1861 .... DLB 116
See also RGEL 2
Gore, Christopher 1946(?)-1988
Obituary 125
Gore, John Francis 1885-1983
Obituary 110
Gore, Mary Elizabeth 1948- CANR-130
Earlier sketch in CA 142
Gore, Patrick Wilson 1938- 233
Gore, Robert Hayes 1886-1972
Obituary 89-92
Gore, Tipper
See Gore, Mary Elizabeth
Gore, William Jay 1924- 9-12R
Goreau, Angeline 1951- 102
Gore-Booth, Eva (Selena) 1870-1926 218
See also DLB 240
Gore-Booth, Paul Henry 1909-1984
Obituary 113
Gorecki, Jan 1926- 57-60
Goreham, Gary A. 1953- 172
Gorelick, Bryna Siegel
See Siegel-Gorelick, Bryna
Gorelick, Molly C(hernow) 1920-2003 . 21-24R
Obituary 224
See also SATA 9
See also SATA-Obit 153
Gorelik, Mordecai 1909-1990 .... CAP-2
Obituary 131
Earlier sketch in CA 23-24
Goren, Arthur A(ryeh) 1926- 127
Brief entry 111
Goren, Charles H(enry) 1901-1991 .. CANR-48
Obituary 134
Earlier sketch in CA 69-72
Goren, Judith 1933- 61-64
Goren, Roberta C. 1943-1983 135
Gorenko, Anna Andreevna
See Akhmatova, Anna
Gorenstein, Paul 1934- 114
Gorenstein, Shirley 1928- 73-76
Gorer, Geoffrey (Edgar) 1905-1985 69-72
Obituary 116
Gores, Joe
See Gores, Joseph N(icholas)
See also CMW
See also DLB 226
See also DLBY 2002
Gores, Joseph N(icholas) 1931- CANR-105
Earlier sketches in CA 25-28R, CANR-10, 28, 54
See also Gores, Joe
Gorey, Edward (St. John)
1925-2000 .... CANR-78
Obituary 187
Earlier sketches in CA 5-8R, CANR-9, 30
Interview in CANR-30
See also AAYA 40
See also CLR 36
See also CWRI 5
See also DLB 61
See also MAICYA 1, 2
See also SATA 29, 70
See also SATA-Brief 27
See also SATA-Obit 118
Gorey, Hays 57-60
Gorga, Carmine 1935- 223
Gorgias of Leontini c.
485B.C.-376B.C. .... DLB 176
Gorham, Charles Orson 1868-1936 ... CANR-6
Obituary 61-64
Earlier sketch in CA 1-4R
See also SATA 36
Gorham, Deborah 1937- 216
Gorham, J(eanne) U(rich) 1920- 53-56
Gorham, Maurice Anthony Coneys
1902-1975 .... 9-12R
Gorham, Michael
See Folsom, Franklin (Brewster)
Gorin, Natalio 1940- 215
Goris, Jan-Albert 1899-1984
See Gijsen, Marnix
Gorkiano
See Salvat-Papasseit, Joan
Gor'kii, Maksim
See Peshkov, Alexei Maximovich
See also RGSF 2
See also RGWL 2, 3
Gorkin, Jess 1913-1985
Obituary 115
Gorky, Maxim
See Peshkov, Alexei Maximovich
See also DAB
See also DFS 9
See also DLB 295
See also EW 8
See also EWL 3
See also SSC 28
See also TCLC 8
See also TWA
See also WLC
Gorlach, Manfred
See Goerlach, Manfred
Gorling, Lars
See Goerling, Lars
Gorman, Beth
See Paine, Lauran (Bosworth)
Gorman, Burton W(illiam) 1907-1999 .. 29-32R
Gorman, Carol 225
See also SATA 150
Gorman, Clem 1942- .... CD 5, 6
Gorman, E. J.
See Gorman, Edward
Gorman, Ed
See Gorman, Edward
See also TCWW 2
Gorman, Edward 1941- CANR-100
Earlier sketch in CA 138
See also Gorman, Ed
See also CMW 4
See also HGG
Gorman, George H. 1916-1982
Obituary 106
Gorman, Ginny
See Zachary, Hugh
Gorman, Jacqueline Laks 1955- 222
See also SATA 148
Gorman, James 1949- 152
Gorman, John Andrew 1938- 41-44R
Gorman, Katherine (?)-1972 .... CAP-2
Earlier sketch in CA 29-32
Gorman, Lyn 1947- 231
Gorman, Martha 1953- 147
Gorman, Michael E. 1952- 139
Gorman, R(udolph) C(arl) 1931- 210
Gorman, Ralph 1897-1972
Obituary 37-40R
Gorman, T. Walter 1916(?)-1972
Obituary 37-40R
Gorman, Thomas David 1919-1986 123
Obituary 120
Gorman, Tom
See Gorman, Thomas David
Gormley, Beatrice 1942- CANR-106
Earlier sketch in CA 113
See also SATA 39, 127
See also SATA-Brief 35
Gormley, Gerard (Joseph) 1931- CANR-14
Earlier sketch in CA 81-84
Gormley, Mike 1945- 69-72
Gorn, Elliott (J.) 1951- 200
Gorn, Janice L(eonora) 1915- 53-56
Gorn, Michael H. 1950- 139
Gorn, Mordechai Martin 1890-1986
Obituary 119
Gorney, Roderic 1924- 73-76
Gorney, Sondra 1918- 45-48
Gorni, Yosef
See Gorny, Yosef
Gornick, Vivian 1935- CANR-92
Earlier sketch in CA 101
Gorny, Joseph
See Gorny, Yosef
Gorny, Yosef 1933- 130
Goro, Fritz 1901-1986
Obituary 121
Gorodetsky, Gabriel 1945- CANR-89
Earlier sketch in CA 69-72
Gorodetsky, Sergei Mitrofanovich
1884-1967 .... DLB 295
Gorog, Judith (Katharine Allen)
1938- CANR-45
Earlier sketch in CA 114
See also SATA 39, 75
Gorostiza, Carlos 1920- 210
Gorostiza, Celestino 1904-1967 191
See also HW 1
Gorostiza, Jose 1901-1973 131
See also DLB 290
See also EWL 3
See also HW 1
See also LAW
Gorovitz, Samuel 1938- 140
Gorra, Michael (Edward) 1957- 216
Gorrell, Lorraine 146
Gorrell, Robert Mark 1914- CANR-5
Earlier sketch in CA 1-4R
Gorriti (Ellenbogen), Gustavo 235
Gorse, Brendan
See Benson, Gerard
Gorsky, Susan Rubinow 1944- 144
Gorsline, Douglas (Warner)
1913-1985 .... CANR-9
Obituary 116
Earlier sketch in CA 61-64
See also SATA 11
See also SATA-Obit 43
Gorsline, (Sally) Marie 1928- 106
See also SATA 28
Gorsline, S. M.
See Gorsline, (Sally) Marie
Gorst, Elliot Marcet 1885-1973
Obituary 104
Gort, Sam
See Barrett, Geoffrey John
Gortner, Ross A(iken), Jr. 1912-1988 .... 5-8R
Gortner, Willis Alway 1913-1993 108
Gorton, Kaitlyn
See Emerson, Kathy Lynn
Gorton, Richard A. 1932- CANR-7
Earlier sketch in CA 57-60
Gorup, Radmilla J(ovanovic) 170
Goryan, Sirak
See Saroyan, William
Goscilo, Helena 1945- 118
Goscinny, Rene 1926-1977 117
Obituary 113
See also CLR 37
See also SATA 47
See also SATA-Brief 39
Gosden, Freeman F(isher) 1899-1982
Obituary 108
Gosden, Peter Henry John Heather
1927- 93-96
Gosden, Roger 1948- CANR-122
Earlier sketch in CA 165
Gosdin, Rex 1938(?)-1983
Obituary 109
Gose, Elliott B(ickley), Jr. 1926- 33-36R
Gose, Peter 1955- 150
Goshay, Robert C. 1931- 13-16R
Goshen, Charles E(rnest)
1916-1989 .... CANR-13
Earlier sketch in CA 21-24R
Goshen-Gottstein, Esther 1928- 137
Goshgarian, Gary 1942- 112
Goshorn, Elizabeth 1953- 61-64
Goslar, Lotte 1907-1997 205
Goslin, David A. 1936- 9-12R
Gosling, J(ustin) C(yril) B(ertrand) 1930- .. 77-80
Gosling, John Neville 1905- 5-8R
Gosling, Nigel 1909-1982 129
Obituary 106
Gosling, Paula 1939- CANR-57
Earlier sketches in CA 111, CANR-30
See also CMW 4
Gosling, William Flower 1901- 5-8R
Goslovich, Marianne
See Brown, Morris Cecil
Gosnell, Betty
See Gosnell, Elizabeth Duke Tucker
Gosnell, Elizabeth Duke Tucker
1921-1984 .... 29-32R
Gosnell, Harold F(oote) 1896-1997 ...... 41-44R
Obituary 156
Gosoon, Stephen 1554-1624 .... DLB 172
Goss, Clay(ton E.) 1946- CANR-79
Earlier sketches in CA 57-60, CANR-42
See also BW 2, 3
See also SATA 82
Goss, Cynthia Flanagan 1957- 149
Goss, Gary 1947- .... SATA 124
Goss, Glenda Dawn 1947- 151
Goss, Pete 1962(?)- 234
Gosse, Edmund (William) 1849-1928
Brief entry 117
See also DLB 57, 144, 184
See also RGEL 2
See also TCLC 28
Gosse, Joanna M. 1948- 220
Gosselin, Chris(topher C.) 1929- 110
Gosselin, Peter G. 1951- CANR-141
Earlier sketch in CA 133
Gosset, W(illiam) P(atrick) 1946- 126
Gossett, Philip 1941- CANR-15
Earlier sketch in CA 89-92
Gossett, Thomas F. 1916- 13-16R
Gossman, Lionel 1929- CANR-7
Earlier sketch in CA 17-20R
Gossop, Michael 1948- 127
Gostelow, Mary 1943- CANR-8
Earlier sketch in CA 61-64
Goswami, Amit 1936- 129
Goswami, Maggie 1937- 117
Gotanda, Philip Kan 1949(?)- 163
See also CAD
See also CD 5, 6
See also DLB 266
Gotchi, Iris 1933- 132
Gotesky, Rubin 1906-1997 45-48
Gotfryd, Bernard 1924- 133
Gotfurt, Frederick 1902(?)-1973
Obituary 104
Gothard, Jan 210
Gotlieb, Phyllis (Fay Bloom)
1926- CANR-135
Earlier sketches in CA 13-16R, CANR-7
See also CLC 18
See also CN 7
See also CP 1, 2
See also DLB 88, 251
See also SFW 4
Gotlieb, Sondra 1936- CANR-137
Brief entry 111
Earlier sketch in CA 144
Goto, Hiromi 1966- CANR-142
Earlier sketch in CA 165
Goto, Junichi 1951- 141
Go-Toba 1180-1239 .... DLB 203
Gotoff, Harold C(harles) 1936-
Brief entry 112
Gots, Ronald E(ric) 1943- 65-68
Gotschalk, Felix C. 1929- 161
See also SFW 4
Gotshalk, D(ilman) W(alter)
1901-1973 .... CANR-6
Earlier sketch in CA 1-4R
Gotshalk, Richard 1931- 203
Gott, J. Richard III 1947- 220
Gott, K(enneth) D(avidson) 1923- 81-84
Gott, Richard (Willoughby) 1938- ... CANR-111
Earlier sketch in CA 81-84
Gottehrer, Barry H. 1935- 13-16R
Gotterer, Malcolm H(arold) 1924- 37-40R
Gottesfeld, Evelyn 1948- 104
Gottesfeld, Mary L. 1926(?)-1984
Obituary 113
Gottesman, Irving I(sadore) 1930- 37-40R
Gottesman, Ronald 1933- CANR-13
Earlier sketch in CA 33-36R
Gottesman, S. D.
See Kornbluth, C(yril) M. and
Lowndes, Robert A(ugustine) W(ard) and
Pohl, Frederik
Gottfried, Alex 1919- 1-4R
Gottfried, Manfred 1900-1985
Obituary 117
Gottfried, Martin 1933- CANR-136
Earlier sketches in CA 21-24R, CANR-14, 63
Gottfried, Robert R(ichard) 1948- 154
Gottfried, Robert Steven 1949- 111
Gottfried, Ted
See Gottfried, Theodore Mark
Gottfried, Theodore Mark 1928- CANR-134
Earlier sketches in CA 33-36R, CANR-18
See also SATA 85, 150
Gottfried von Strassburg fl. c.
1170-1215 .... CDWLB 2
See also DLB 138
See also EW 1
See also RGWL 2, 3
Gotthelf, Jeremias 1797-1854 .... DLB 133
See also RGWL 2, 3
Gottlieb, Adolph 1903-1974
Obituary 49-52
Gottlieb, Alan M(erril) 1947- CANR-115
Earlier sketches in CA 125, CANR-57
Gottlieb, Alex 1906-1988
Obituary 126
Gottlieb, Alma 1954- 138
Gottlieb, Andrew R. 1952- 198
Gottlieb, Annie 1946- 135
Gottlieb, Arthur 1929- 137
Gottlieb, Beatrice 1925- 144
Gottlieb, Beatrice M. 1889(?)-1979
Obituary 89-92
Gottlieb, Bernhardt Stanley 1898-1991 ..... 1-4R
Gottlieb, Carl 143
Gottlieb, Carla 1912- 119
Gottlieb, Daphne 232
Gottlieb, Darcy 1922- 77-80
Gottlieb, Elaine 61-64
Gottlieb, Erika (Simon) 1938- CANR-102
Earlier sketch in CA 148
Gottlieb, Freema (Peninah) 1946- 137
Gottlieb, Gerald 1923- 5-8R
See also SATA 7
Gottlieb, Gilbert 1929- 138
Gottlieb, Lois Davidson 1926- 17-20R
Gottlieb, Moshe R(aphael) 1931-1993 113
Gottlieb, Naomi R(uth) 1925-1995 57-60
Gottlieb, Paul 1936- 93-96
Gottlieb, Robert A(dams) 1931- CANR-95
Brief entry 125
Earlier sketch in CA 129
Gottlieb, Robin (Grossman) 1928- CANR-2
Earlier sketch in CA 1-4R
Gottlieb, Sherry Gershon 1948- 193
Gottlieb, Stephen E. 1941- 138
Gottlieb, Steven 1946- 228
Gottlieb, (Anne Ruth) Vera 1945- ... CANR-104
Earlier sketches in CA 117, CANR-49

Cumulative Index 227 Grabhorn

Gottlieb, William P(aul) 1917- 101
  See also SATA 24
Gottman, John M(ordechai) 1942- CANR-12
  Earlier sketch in CA 69-72
Gottschalk c. 804-c. 866 .... DLB 148
Gottschalk, Elin Toona
  See Toona, Elin(-Kai)
Gottschalk, Laura Riding
  See Jackson, Laura (Riding)
Gottschalk, Louis (Reichenthal)
  1899-1975 .... CANR-9
  Obituary 57-60
  Earlier sketch in CA 13-16R
Gottschalk, Louis A(ugust) 1916- CANR-41
  Earlier sketches in CA 53-56, CANR-5, 19
Gottschalk, Paul A. 1939- 61-64
Gottschalk, Shimon S. 1929- 89-92
Gottschalk, Stephen 1940- 77-80
Gottschall, Edward M(aurice) 1915- 133
Gottsched, Johann Christoph
  1700-1766 .... DLB 97
Gottschild, Brenda D(ixon) 1942- 180
Gottsegen, Abby J. 1956- 105
Gottsegen, Gloria Behar 1930- 77-80
Gottshall, Franklin Henry 1902-1992 . CANR-2
  Earlier sketch in CA 5-8R
Gottstein, Esther Goshen
  See Goshen-Gottstein, Esther
Gottwald, Norman K(arol) 1926- CANR-137
  Earlier sketch in CA 108
Gotwals, Vernon (Detwiler, Jr.) 1924- 5-8R
Gotz, Ignacio L.
  See Goetz, Ignacio L.
Gotze, Heinz 1912-2001 177
Gotzsche, Anne-Lise 1939- 97-100
Goubert, Pierre 1915- 136
Goud, Anne 1917- 61-64
Goudeket, Maurice 1889-1977
  Obituary 69-72
Goudey, Alice E(dwards) 1898-1993 73-76
  See also SATA 20
Goudge, Eileen 1950- CANR-115
  Earlier sketches in CA 126, CANR-77
  See also AAYA 6
  See also CPW
  See also DAM POP
  See also SATA 88
Goudge, Elizabeth (de Beauchamp)
  1900-1984 .... CANR-5
  Obituary 112
  Earlier sketch in CA 5-8R
  See also CLR 94
  See also CWRI 5
  See also DLB 191
  See also MAICYA 1, 2
  See also RHW
  See also SATA 2
  See also SATA-Obit 38
Goudie, Andrew S(haw) 1945- CANR-38
  Earlier sketches in CA 49-52, CANR-1, 17
Goudinoff, Peter Alexis 1941- 112
Goudiss, Maria Agnes D'Elia 1941- 114
Goudsmit, Samuel A(braham) 1902-1978 ... 157
  Obituary 81-84
Goudsouzian, Aram 1973- 234
Goudzwaard, Bob 1934- 207
Gouge, Orson
  See Larner, Jeremy
Gougeon, Len (G.) 1947- 135
Gouges, Olympe de 1748-1793 .... DLB 313
Gough, Barry Morton 1938- CANR-58
  Earlier sketches in CA 61-64, CANR-11, 30
Gough, Bill
  See Gough, William (John)
Gough, Catherine
  See Mulgan, Catherine
  See also SATA 24
Gough, John B. 1817-1886 .... DLB 243
Gough, John W(iedhofft) 1900- 13-16R
Gough, Julian 1966- 210
Gough, Kathleen
  See Aberle, Kathleen Gough
Gough, Laurence 168
Gough, Laurie 1964- 193
Gough, Michael 1939- 147
Gough, Philip 1908- .... SATA 45
Gough, Sue 1940- 176
  See also SATA 106
Gough, Vera 25-28R
Gough, William (John) 1945- 131
Gough-Cooper, Jennifer 1942- 146
Gougov, Nikola Delchev 1914- CANR-37
  Earlier sketch in CA 45-48
Gouk, Penelope 221
Goulart, Frances Sheridan 1938- CANR-25
  Earlier sketches in CA 57-60, CANR-7
Goulart, Ron(ald Joseph) 1933- CANR-117
  Earlier sketches in CA 25-28R, CANR-7, 79
  See also Dixon, Franklin W. and
  Keene, Carolyn
  See also CMW 4
  See also SATA 6, 138
  See also SFW 4
Goulbourne, Harry 1948- 137
Gould, Alan
  See Canning, Victor
Gould, Alan (David) 1949- .... CP 7
Gould, Alberta 1945- 161
  See also SATA 96
Gould, Alfred Ernest 1909- 5-8R
Gould, Allan (Mendel) 1944- 132
Gould, Beatrice Blackmar 1898-1989 ... CAP-2
  Obituary 127
  Earlier sketch in CA 25-28
Gould, (Charles) Bruce 1898-1989
  Obituary 129
Gould, Bruce Grant 1942- CANR-22
  Earlier sketch in CA 45-48
Gould, Bryan 1939- 136
Gould, Carol C. 1946- 103
Gould, Cecil (Hilton Monk)
  1918-1994 .... CANR-9
  Obituary 145
  Earlier sketch in CA 21-24R
Gould, Chester 1900-1985 .... CANR-30
  Obituary 116
  Earlier sketch in CA 77-80
  See also AAYA 7
  See also SATA 49
  See also SATA-Obit 43
Gould, Douglas Parsons 1919- 1-4R
Gould, Ed(win Orrin) 1936- CANR-16
  Earlier sketch in CA 93-96
Gould, Felix CAP-1
  Earlier sketch in CA 11-12
Gould, James A(dams) 1922-2001 .... 33-36R
Gould, James L. 1945- CANR-90
  Earlier sketch in CA 130
Gould, James Warren 1924- CANR-2
  Earlier sketch in CA 5-8R
Gould, Janice 1949- CANR-101
  Earlier sketch in CA 147
Gould, Jay R(eid) 1906-1999 .... CANR-24
  Earlier sketch in CA 45-48
Gould, Jean R(osalind) 1909-1993 ... CANR-83
  Obituary 142
  Earlier sketches in CA 5-8R, CANR-3, 21
  See also SATA 11
  See also SATA-Obit 77
Gould, Joan 1927- 107
Gould, John (Thomas) 1908-2003 65-68
  Obituary 219
Gould, John A(llen) 1944- 57-60
Gould, Joseph E(dmund) 1912-2001 .... 9-12R
Gould, Josiah B(ancroft) 1928- 45-48
Gould, Joy
  See Boyum, Joy Gould
Gould, Judith
  See Bienes, Nicholas Peter
Gould, K. Lance 1938- 173
Gould, Leroy C. 1937- 93-96
Gould, Leslie 1902-1977
  Obituary 73-76
Gould, Lettie
  See Paxson, Ethel
Gould, Lewis L(udlow) 1939- CANR-138
  Earlier sketch in CA 41-44R
Gould, Lilian CANR-2
  Earlier sketch in CA 49-52
  See also SATA 6
Gould, Lois 1932(?)-2002 .... CANR-29
  Obituary 208
  Earlier sketch in CA 77-80
  See also CLC 4, 10
  See also MTCW 1
Gould, Marilyn 1928- .... SATA 15, 76
Gould, Mary Earle 1885-1972 .... 5-8R
Gould, Maurice M. 1909-1975 .... CANR-5
  Earlier sketch in CA 5-8R
Gould, Michael
  See Girsh, Myers L.
Gould, Milton Samuel 1909-1999 93-96
  Obituary 177
Gould, Peter R(obin) 1932-2000 .... CANR-51
  Earlier sketches in CA 1-4R, CANR-27
Gould, Philip 1925- CANR-89
  Earlier sketch in CA 124
Gould, Randall 1898(?)-1979
  Obituary 89-92
Gould, Richard A(llan) 1939- CANR-7
  Earlier sketch in CA 53-56
Gould, Robert .... SATA 154
Gould, Roger L(ouis) 1935-
  Brief entry 110
Gould, Ronald 1904-1986 102
Gould, Shirley (Goldman) 81-84
Gould, Stephen
  See Fisher, Stephen (Gould)
Gould, Stephen Jay 1941-2002 ...... CANR-125
  Obituary 205
  Earlier sketches in CA 77-80, CANR-10, 27, 56, 75
  Interview in CANR-27
  See also AAYA 26
  See also BEST 90:2
  See also CLC 163
  See also CPW
  See also MTCW 1, 2
  See also MTFW 2005
Gould, Steven (Charles) 1955- 140
  See also BYA 11
  See also SATA 95
Gould, Terry 1949- 235
Gould, Wallace 1882-1940 204
  See also DLB 54
Gould, Warwick 1947- 110
Gould, Wesley Larson 1917- CANR-2
  Earlier sketch in CA 1-4R
Gould, William B(enjamin) IV
  1936- CANR-107
  Brief entry 118
  Earlier sketch in CA 132
Goulden, Joseph C. (Jr.) 1934- CANR-31
  Earlier sketches in CA 17-20R, CANR-8
Goulden, Mark 1896(?)-1980
  Obituary 101
Goulder, Grace
  See Izant, Grace Goulder
Goulding, Brian 1933- 103
Goulding, Dorothy Jane 1923- 65-68
Goulding, Edwin (John) 1938- 163
Goulding, Peter Geoffrey 1920- 106
Goulding, Ray(mond Walter)
  1922-1990 .... CANR-36
  Obituary 131
  Earlier sketch in CA 85-88
Gouldner, Alvin W(ard) 1920-1980 .. CANR-17
  Obituary 102
  Earlier sketch in CA 13-16R
  See also MTCW 1
Gouled, Vivian G(loria) 1911- 41-44R
Goulet, Denis A. 1931- CANR-15
  Earlier sketch in CA 41-44R
Goulet, John 1942- 85-88
Goulet, Robert (Joseph) 1924- 1-4R
Goulet, Rosalina Morales 1930- 119
Goulett, Harlan M(ador) 1927-1969 ...... CAP-2
  Earlier sketch in CA 21-22
Goulianos, Joan Rodman 1939- 49-52
Gouliashki, (Stoianov) Andrei 1914- . CANR-19
  Earlier sketch in CA 101
Goullart, Peter 1902- CANR-136
  Earlier sketches in CAP-1, CA 13-14
Goulson, Carlyn Floyd 1922- 113
Goulson, Cary F.
  See Goulson, Carlyn Floyd
Goulston, Mark 200
Goulter, Barbara 141
Gouma-Peterson, Thalia 1933- CANR-95
  Earlier sketch in CA 140
Gourdie, Thomas 1913- CANR-1
  Earlier sketch in CA 1-4R
Gourdin, Amalia
  See Lindal, Amalia
Gourevitch, Doris-Jeanne 17-20R
Gourevitch, Peter A(lexis) 1943- 112
Gourevitch, Philip 1961- CANR-125
  Earlier sketch in CA 179
Gourgouris, Stathis 1958- CANR-143
  Earlier sketch in CA 172
Gourhan, Andre (Georges Leandre) Leroi
  See Leroi-Gourhan, Andre (Georges Leandre)
Gouri, Haim 1923(?)- 103
  See also Guri, Haim
Gourlay, Elizabeth 1917-1996 .... CANR-30
  Earlier sketch in CA 112
Gourley, Catherine 1950- CANR-115
  Earlier sketch in CA 160
  See also SATA 95
Gourley, G(erald) Douglas 1911- 1-4R
Gourley, Jay 1947- 73-76
Gourlie, Norah Dundas CAP-1
  Earlier sketch in CA 9-10
Gourmont, Remy(-Marie-Charles) de
  1858-1915 150
  Brief entry 109
  See also GFL 1789 to the Present
  See also MTCW 2
  See also TCLC 17
Gournay, Marie le Jars de
  See de Gournay, Marie le Jars
Gourse, (Roberta) Leslie 1939-2004 . CANR-96
  Obituary 234
  Earlier sketches in CA 1-4R, CANR-57
  See also SATA 89
Gourvish, T(erry) R. 1943- 125
Gouzenko, Igor 1919-1982
  Obituary 107
Govan, (Mary) Christine Noble
  1898-1985 .... CANR-2
  Earlier sketch in CA 1-4R
  See also SATA 9
Govan, Thomas P(ayne) 1907-1979 ... CANR-2
  Earlier sketch in CA 45-48
Gove, Doris 1944- .... SATA 72
Gove, Michael 1967- 214
Gove, Philip Babcock 1902-1972 .... CAP-1
  Obituary 37-40R
  Earlier sketch in CA 13-14
Gove, Samuel K(imball) 1923- 33-36R
Gove, Walter R(oberts) 1938- 118
Goveia, Elsa V(esta) 1925- 21-24R
Govenar, Alan B(ruce) 1952- 109
Gover, (John) Robert 1929- CANR-70
  Earlier sketch in CA 9-12R
  See also CN 3, 4, 5, 6, 7
Govern, Elaine 1939- 53-56
  See also SATA 26
Govi, O.
  See Gover, (John) Robert
Govier, Katherine 1948- CANR-128
  Earlier sketches in CA 101, CANR-18, 40
  See also CCA 1
  See also CLC 51
Govier, Trudy 1944- CANR-128
  Earlier sketch in CA 170
Govinda, Anagarika Brahmacari
  1898-1985 .... CANR-14
  Earlier sketch in CA 21-24R
  See also Hoffman, Ernst
Govinda, Lama Anagarika Brahmacari
  See Govinda, Anagarika Brahmacari
Govoni, Albert P(eter) 1914-1982 53-56
  Obituary 108
Govoni, Corrado 1884-1965 .... DLB 114
Govoni, Laura E. 1914- 33-36R
Govorchin, Gerald Gilbert 1912-1999 .. 13-16R
Govrin, Michal 1950- .... DLB 299
Gow, Andrew Colin 1962- 154
Gow, Donald 1920- 41-44R
Gow, James 181
Gow, Michael 1955- 232
  See also CD 5, 6
Gow, Ronald 1897-1993 .... CANR-13
  Obituary 141
  Earlier sketches in CAP-2, CA 25-28
  See also CBD
Gowan, Donald E(lmer) 1929- 69-72
Gowan, John Curtis 1912-1986 .... CANR-5
  Obituary 121
  Earlier sketch in CA 13-16R
Gowan, Lee 1961- 204
Gowans, Alan 1923-2001 .... CANR-40
  Obituary 200
  Earlier sketches in CA 1-4R, CANR-2, 18
Gowar, Antonia
  See Dunford, Judith and
  Margolis, Susanna
Gowar, Michael Robert 1951- 127
Gowar, Mick
  See Gowar, Michael Robert
Gowen, (Samuel) Emmett 1902-1973 .... CAP-1
  Earlier sketch in CA 11-12
Gowen, James A(nthony) 1928-1981 .... 17-20R
  Obituary 134
Gowen, Kenneth K. 1924- 166
Gowen, L. Kris 1968- 231
  See also SATA 156
Gower, Herschel 1919- 5-8R
Gower, Iris 1939- .... RHW
Gower, John c. 1330-1408 .... BRW 1
  See also DLB 146
  See also PC 59
  See also RGEL 2
Gowers, Ernest (Arthur) 1880-1966
  Obituary 89-92
Gowin, D(ixie) Bob 1925- CANR-26
  Earlier sketch in CA 108
Gowing, Lawrence (Burnett) 1918-1991 . 9-12R
  Obituary 133
Gowing, Margaret Mary 1921-1998 81-84
  Obituary 172
Gowing, Peter Gordon 1930- 53-56
Gowland, Mariano E(zequiel) 1933- 5-8R
Goy, Richard J(ohn) 1947- CANR-142
  Earlier sketch in CA 118
Goya, Francisco 1746-1828 .... AAYA 55
Goyder, George Armin 1908-1997 105
  Obituary 156
Goyen, (Charles) William
  1915-1983 .... CANR-71
  Obituary 110
  Earlier sketches in CA 5-8R, CANR-6
  Interview in CANR-6
  See also AITN 2
  See also CLC 5, 8, 14, 40
  See also CN 1, 2, 3
  See also DLB 2, 218
  See also DLBY 1983
  See also EWL 3
  See also MAL 5
Goyeneche, Gabriel
  See Avalle-Arce, Juan Bautista de
Goyer, David S. 1966- 226
Goyer, Robert S(tanton) 1923- CANR-16
  Earlier sketch in CA 41-44R
  See also CN 1, 2
Goytisolo (Gay), Jose Agustin 1928- ... DLB 134
Goytisolo, Juan 1931- CANR-131
  Earlier sketches in CA 85-88, CANR-32, 61
  See also CLC 5, 10, 23, 133
  See also CWW 2
  See also DAM MULT
  See also DLB 322
  See also EWL 3
  See also GLL 2
  See also HLC 1
  See also HW 1, 2
  See also MTCW 1, 2
  See also MTFW 2005
Goytisolo (Gay), Luis 1935- .... CWW 2
  See also DLB 322
Gozzano, Guido 1883-1916 154
  See also DLB 114
  See also EWL 3
  See also PC 10
Gozzi, (Conte) Carlo 1720-1806
Gozzi, Raymond D(ante) 1920- 116
Graaf, Peter
  See Youd, (Christopher) Samuel
Graas, Ulrik
  See Gras, Ulrik
Grabar, Andre 1896-1990 111
Grabar, Andrei (Nikolaevich)
  See Grabar, Andre
Grabar, Oleg 1929- CANR-108
  Earlier sketches in CA 124, CANR-51
Grabau, Warren E(dward) 1919- 205
Grabbe, Christian Dietrich
  1801-1836 .... DLB 133
  See also RGWL 2, 3
Grabbe, Crockett L(ane) 1951- 138
Grabbe, Paul (Alexandrovich)
  1902-1999 93-96
Graber, Alexander 1914-1997 .... CANR-1
  Obituary 159
  Earlier sketch in CA 1-4R
  See also SATA 7, 98
Graber, (George) Alexander 1914-1997 159
  See also RHW
  See also SATA 98
Graber, Doris A. 1923- CANR-13
  Earlier sketch in CA 33-36R
Graber, G(erald) S(amuel) 1928-2000 81-84
Graber, Julia A. 1961- 161
Graber, Richard (Fredrick) 1927- 85-88
  See also SATA 26
Graber, Valerie
  See Alia, Valerie
Graber Miller, Keith Allen 1959- 164
Grabes, Herbert 1936- CANR-89
  Earlier sketch in CA 130
Grabhorn, Lynn 1931- 197

Grabianski, Janusz 1928-1976 ... CANR-2
Earlier sketch in CA 45-48
See also SATA 39
See also SATA-Obit 30
Grabien, Deborah ... FANT
Grabill, Joseph L. 1931- ... 29-32R
Grabner-Haider, Anton 1940- ... 73-76
Grabo, Norman Stanley 1930- ... CANR-49
Earlier sketch in CA 1-4R
Graboff, Abner 1919-1986 ... 107
See also SATA 35
Grabois, Aryeh 1930- ... 105
Grabosky, Peter Nils 1945- ... 85-88
Grabow, Stephen (Harris) 1943- ... 121
Grabowski, Z(bigniew) Anthony 1903- ... 5-8R
Graburn, Nelson H(ayes) H(enry)
1936- ... CANR-1
Earlier sketch in CA 45-48
Grace, Alexander M.
See Farcau, Bruce W.
Grace, C. L.
See Doherty, P(aul) C.
Grace, Carol
See Matthau, Carol (Grace Marcus)
Grace, Deborah
See Winer, Deborah Grace
Grace, Edward
See de Grazia, Edward
Grace, Fran(ces Jane) ... CANR-141
Earlier sketch in CA 111
See also SATA 45
Grace, Gerald R(upert) 1936- ... CANR-22
Earlier sketch in CA 45-48
Grace, Helen K(ennedy) 1935- ... 53-56
Grace, J. Peter 1913-1995 ... 126
Obituary ... 148
Grace, Joan C(arroll) 1921- ... 61-64
Grace, John
See Hoskins, Robert (Phillip)
Grace, John Patrick 1942- ... CANR-31
Earlier sketch in CA 112
Grace, Joseph
See Hornby, John (Wilkinson)
Grace, Nancy McCampbell 1952- ... 151
Grace, Patricia Frances 1937- ... CANR-118
Earlier sketch in CA 176
See also CLC 56
See also CN 4, 5, 6, 7
See also EWL 3
See also RGSF 2
Grace, Sherrill E(lizabeth) 1944- ... CANR-129
Earlier sketch in CA 110
Grace, Susan Andrews 1949- ... 218
Grace, Theresa
See Mattern, Joanne
Grace, Tom ... 209
Grace, William J(oseph), Jr. 1948- ... CANR-38
Earlier sketch in CA 111
Grace, William Joseph 1910-1979 ... CAP-1
Earlier sketch in CA 13-14
Gracey, Harry L(ewis) 1933- ... 41-44R
Gracia, Jorge J(esus) E(miliano)
1942- ... CANR-81
Earlier sketches in CA 109, CANR-30, 56
See also HW 1, 2
Gracie, Archibald 1859-1912
Brief entry ... 122
Gracq, Julien
See Poirier, Louis
See also CLC 11, 48
See also CWW 2
See also DLB 83
See also GFL 1789 to the Present
Gracy, David B(ergen) II 1941- ... CANR-16
Earlier sketch in CA 25-28R
Gracza, Margaret Young 1928- ... 13-16R
See also SATA 56
Grad, Bonnie L(ee) 1949- ... 117
Grad, Eli 1928- ... 115
Grad, Frank P. 1924- ... 33-36R
Grad, Laurie Burrows 1944- ... 168
Grade, Arnold (Edward) 1928- ... 29-32R
Grade, Chaim 1910-1982 ... 93-96
Obituary ... 107
See also CLC 10
See also EWL 3
Gradidge, (John) Roderick (Warlow)
1929-2000 ... CANR-41
Obituary ... 190
Earlier sketch in CA 117
Gradon, Pamela O(live) E(lizabeth)
1915- ... 97-100
Graduate of Oxford, A
See Ruskin, John
Gradwohl, David M(ayer) 1934- ... CANR-51
Earlier sketch in CA 125
Grady, Don(ald Wyndham) 1929- ... 115
Grady, Henry W. 1850-1889 ... DLB 23
Grady, James (Thomas) 1949- ... CANR-22
Earlier sketch in CA 104
Grady, Liz
See Coughlin, Patricia (E.)
Grady, Ronan Calistus, Jr. 1921-1992 ... 49-52
Grady, Tex
See Webb, Jack (Randolph)
Grae, Ida 1918- ... 97-100
Graeber, Charlotte Towner ... 134
See also SATA 56, 106
See also SATA-Brief 44
Graebner, Alan 1938- ... 61-64
Graebner, Norman A. 1915- ... CANR-49
Earlier sketches in CA 13-16R, CANR-7, 24
Graebner, Walter 1909-1976 ... CAP-1
Earlier sketch in CA 13-16
Graebner, William Sievers 1943- ... 104
Graedon, Joe (David) 1945- ... CANR-135
Earlier sketch in CA 77-80
Graedon, Teresa 1947- ... 127
Graef, Hilda C(harlotte) 1907- ... 5-8R
Graeff, Grace M. 1918-1996 ... 21-24R
Graeme, Bruce
See Jeffries, Graham Montague
Graeme, David
See Jeffries, Graham Montague
Graeme, Roderic
See Jeffries, Roderic (Graeme)
Graeme, Sheila 1944- ... 25-28R
Graeub, Ralph 1921- ... 144
Graf, L. A.
See Cercone, Karen Rose
Graf, Le Roy Philip 1915- ... 41-44R
Graf, Oskar Maria 1894-1967 ... 179
Obituary ... 115
See also DLB 56
See also EWL 3
Graf, Rudolf F. 1926- ... 9-12R
Graf, William L. 1947- ... 156
Graff, Dale E(dward) 1934- ... 168
Graff, E. J. 1958- ... 186
Graff, George 1886-1973
Obituary ... 41-44R
Graff, Gerald (Edward) 1937- ... CANR-126
Earlier sketches in CA 29-32R, CANR-31
See also DLB 246
Graff, Harvey J. 1949- ... CANR-55
Earlier sketch in CA 127
Graff, Henry F(ranklin) 1921- ... CANR-143
Earlier sketches in CA 1-4R, CANR-1, 17
Graff, Polly Anne Colver
See Colver, Anne
Graff, (S.) Stewart 1908- ... CANR-29
Earlier sketch in CA 49-52
See also SATA 9
Graffigny, Francoise d'Issembourg de
1695-1758 ... DLB 313
Grafftey, Heward 1928- ... 127
Grafftey-Smith, Laurence Barton 1892-1989
Obituary ... 128
Grafton, Ann
See Owens, Thelma
Grafton, Anthony T(homas) 1950- ... CANR-96
Earlier sketch in CA 166
Grafton, C(ornelius) W(arren) 1909-1982 ... 237
See also CMW 4
Grafton, Carl 1942- ... 53-56
Grafton, David 1930- ... 126
Grafton, Garth
See Duncan, Sara Jeannette
Grafton, Richard fl. 1534-1573 ... DLB 170
Grafton, Sue 1940- ... CANR-134
Earlier sketches in CA 108, CANR-31, 55, 111
See also AAYA 11, 49
See also BEST 90:3
See also CLC 163
See also CMW 4
See also CPW
See also CSW
See also DA3
See also DAM POP
See also DLB 226
See also FW
See also MSW
See also MTFW 2005
Gragg, Rod 1950- ... CANR-100
Earlier sketch in CA 134
Graglia, Lino A(nthony) 1930- ... 69-72
Graham, A(lexander) John 1930- ... CANR-8
Earlier sketch in CA 13-16R
Graham, A(lexander) S(teel) 1917- ... 104
Graham, Ada 1931- ... CANR-4
Earlier sketch in CA 29-32R
See also SATA 11
Graham, Aelred 1907-1984 ... CANR-5
Obituary ... 114
Earlier sketch in CA 5-8R
Graham, Alastair 1945- ... 141
See also SATA 74
Graham, Alice Walworth 1905-1994 ... CANR-5
Earlier sketch in CA 1-4R
Graham, Alistair (Dundas) 1938- ... CANR-46
Earlier sketch in CA 49-52
Graham, Andrew Guillemard 1913-1981
Obituary ... 103
Graham, Angus (Charles) 1919-1991 ... 17-20R
Obituary ... 134
Graham, Arthur Kennon
See Harrison, David L(ee)
Graham, Billy
See Graham, William Franklin
Graham, Bob 1942- ... CANR-123
Earlier sketch in CA 165
See also CLR 31
See also CWRI 5
See also MAICYA 2
See also SATA 63, 101, 151
Graham, Bradley ... 236
Graham, Brenda Knight 1942- ... 103
See also SATA 32
Graham, Carlotta
See Wallmann, Jeffrey M(iner)
Graham, Carol (Lee) 1962- ... 234
Graham, Caroline 1931- ... 119
See also CMW 4
Graham, Charles S.
See Tubb, E(dwin) C(harles)
Graham, Charlotte
See Bowden, Joan Chase
Graham, Chinelo
See Mitchell, Mozella G.
Graham, Clarence H. 1906-1971
Obituary ... 33-36R
Graham, Cooper C(arrington) 1938- ... 228
Graham, Cosmo 1956- ... 138
Graham, Daniel O., Jr. 1952- ... CANR-124
Earlier sketch in CA 151
Graham, Daniel O(rrin) 1925- ... 132
Graham, David (Duane) 1927- ... 69-72
Graham, Desmond 1940- ... 73-76
Graham, Dominick S(tuart) 1920- ... 233
Graham, Don(ald R.) 1947- ... 133
Graham, Don B(allew) 1940- ... CANR-129
Earlier sketches in CA 102, CANR-18, 39
Graham, Donald W(ilkinson)
1903-1976 ... CAP-2
Earlier sketch in CA 29-32
Graham, Edward M(ontgomery) 1944- ... 141
Graham, Eleanor 1896-1984 ... 73-76
Obituary ... 112
See also CWRI 5
See also SATA 18
See also SATA-Obit 38
Graham, Elizabeth
See Edmonds, Arthur Denis
Graham, Ennis
See Molesworth, Mary Louisa
Graham, Frank, Jr. 1925- ... CANR-4
Earlier sketch in CA 9-12R
See also SATA 11
Graham, Frank 1893-1965 ... 201
See also DLB 241
Graham, Fred P(atterson) 1931- ... 37-40R
Graham, Gene S(wann) 1924-1982 ... 41-44R
Graham, George J(ackson), Jr.
1938- ... CANR-48
Earlier sketch in CA 45-48
Graham, George Rex 1813-1894 ... DLB 73
Graham, Gerald (Sandford) 1903-1988 ... 102
Obituary ... 126
Graham, Grace 1910-1989 ... CAP-1
Earlier sketch in CA 13-14
Graham, Gwethalyn 1913-1965 ... 148
See also CCA 1
See also DLB 88
Graham, Harriet 1935- ... 127
Graham, Harry
See Jons, Hal
Graham, Harry (Jocelyn Clive)
1874-1936 ... CWRI 5
Graham, Harry Edward 1940- ... 29-32R
Graham, Heather
See Pozzessere, Heather Graham
See also AAYA 50
Graham, Henry 1930- ... 103
See also CP 1, 2, 3, 4, 5, 6, 7
Graham, Howard Jay 1905-1986 ... CAP-2
Earlier sketch in CA 33-36
Graham, Hugh
See Barrows, (Ruth) Marjorie
Graham, Hugh Davis 1936-2002 ... CANR-13
Obituary ... 205
Earlier sketch in CA 21-24R
Graham, Ian (James Alastair) 1923- ... CANR-2
Earlier sketch in CA 45-48
Graham, Ian 1953- ... 184
See also SATA 112
Graham, Ilse 1914-1988 ... CANR-8
Obituary ... 127
Earlier sketch in CA 57-60
Graham, J. W. 1925- ... 93-96
Graham, J(ames) Walter 1906- ... 1-4R
Graham, James
See Patterson, Harry
Graham, Janice ... 205
Graham, Jefferson 1956- ... 145
Graham, John
See Phillips, David Graham
Graham, John 1926- ... 33-36R
See also SATA 11
Graham, John Alexander 1941- ... 25-28R
Graham, John D. 1956- ... 168
Graham, John Remington 1940- ... 33-36R
Graham, John Thomas 1928- ... 53-56
Graham, Jorie 1950- ... CANR-118
Earlier sketches in CA 111, CANR-63
See also AAYA 67
See also CLC 48, 118
See also CP 7
See also CWP
See also DLB 120
See also EWL 3
See also MTFW 2005
See also PC 59
See also PFS 10, 17
See also TCLE 1:1
Graham, Jory 1925-1983 ... CANR-13
Obituary ... 109
Earlier sketch in CA 29-32R
Graham, Joseph M. 1911(?)-1971
Obituary ... 104
Graham, Katharine (Meyer)
1917-2001 ... CANR-71
Obituary ... 197
Earlier sketch in CA 105
See also AITN 1
See also DLB 127
Graham, (George) Kenneth 1936- ... 77-80
Graham, Kennon
See Harrison, David L(ee)
Graham, Larry
See Graham, Lawrence (Otis)
Graham, Laurie 1941- ... 188
Graham, Lawrence (Otis) 1962- ... CANR-93
Earlier sketch in CA 116
See also SATA 63
Graham, Lawrence S(herman)
1936- ... CANR-47
Earlier sketch in CA 45-48
Graham, Lee E. 1913(?)-1977
Obituary ... 73-76
Graham, Lew
See Paine, Lauran (Bosworth)
Graham, Linda
See Graham-Barber, Lynda
Graham, Lloyd M. 1889-1985 ... 97-100
Graham, Lola Bell
See Graham, Shirley
Graham, Loren R. 1933- ... CANR-13
Earlier sketch in CA 21-24R
Graham, Lorenz (Bell) 1902-1989 ... CANR-25
Obituary ... 129
Earlier sketch in CA 9-12R
See also BW 1
See also CLR 10
See also DLB 76
See also MAICYA 1, 2
See also SAAS 5
See also SATA 2, 74
See also SATA-Obit 63
See also YAW
Graham, Malcolm 1923- ... 53-56
Graham, Margaret Althea 1924- ... 9-12R
Graham, Margaret Bloy 1920- ... 77-80
See also SATA 11
Graham, Mark 1950- ... 183
Graham, Martha 1894-1991 ... 129
Obituary ... 134
Graham, Matthew
See Arnold, Peter
Graham, Michael 1898-1972
Obituary ... 104
Graham, Michael Angelo 1921-1985
Obituary ... 117
Graham, Milton D(uke) 1916-1977 ... 45-48
Graham, Neile 1958- ... 113
Graham, Neill
See Duncan, W(illiam) Murdoch
Graham, (Roger) Neill 1941- ... CANR-26
Earlier sketch in CA 109
Graham, Otis L., Jr. 1935- ... CANR-11
Earlier sketch in CA 21-24R
Graham, Patricia Albjerg 1935- ... 25-28R
Graham, Peter W(illiam) 1951- ... CANR-98
Earlier sketches in CA 121, CANR-47
Graham, Philip Leslie 1915-1963 ... 175
Obituary ... 89-92
See also DLB 127
Graham, R(obert) B(ontine) Cunninghame
See Cunninghame Graham, Robert (Gallnigad)
Bontine
See also DLB 98, 135, 174
See also RGEL 2
See also RGSF 2
Graham, Rachel (Metcalf) 1895- ... CAP-1
Earlier sketch in CA 13-16
Graham, Ramona
See Cook, Ramona Graham
Graham, Richard 1934- ... CANR-89
Earlier sketches in CA 29-32R, CANR-15, 34
Graham, Robert
See Haldeman, Joe (William)
Graham, Robert G. 1925- ... CANR-12
Earlier sketch in CA 25-28R
Graham, Robin Lee 1949- ... 49-52
See also SATA 7
Graham, Ron 1948- ... 133
Graham, Ruth
See Evans, Jean
Graham, Sean 1920- ... 21-24R
Graham, Sheilah 1908(?)-1988 ... CANR-83
Obituary ... 127
Earlier sketch in CA 108
See also AITN 1
Graham, Shirley 1896(?)-1977 ... 176
See also Du Bois, Shirley Graham
See also DLB 76
Graham, Sonia
See Sinclair, Sonia
Graham, Stephen 1884-1975 ... 179
Obituary ... 93-96
See also DLB 195
Graham, (Maude Fitzgerald) Susan
1912- ... 17-20R
Graham, Thomas F(rancis) 1923- ... 21-24R
Graham, Tom
See Lewis, (Harry) Sinclair
Graham, Toni 1945- ... 180
Graham, Vanessa
See Fraser, Anthea
Graham, Victor E(rnest) 1920- ... 93-96
Graham, Virginia
See Guttenberg, Virginia
Graham, W(illiam) Fred 1930- ... 33-36R
Graham, W(illiam) S(idney) 1918-1986 ... 73-76
Obituary ... 118
See also BRWS 7
See also CLC 29
See also CP 1, 2
See also DLB 20
See also RGEL 2
Graham, William Franklin 1918- ... CANR-71
Earlier sketches in CA 9-12R, CANR-20, 42
Graham, Winston (Mawdsley)
1910-2003 ... CANR-66
Obituary ... 218
Earlier sketches in CA 49-52, CANR-2, 22, 45
See also CLC 23
See also CMW 4
See also CN 1, 2, 3, 4, 5, 6, 7
See also DLB 77
See also RHW
Graham, Ysenda Maxtone
See Maxtone Graham, Ysenda (May)
Graham-Barber, Lynda 1944- ... 113
See also SATA 42, 159
Graham-Cameron, M.
See Graham-Cameron, M(alcolm) G(ordon)

Cumulative Index 229 Grass

Graham-Cameron, M(alcolm) G(ordon) 1931- ... 123
See also SATA 53
See also SATA-Brief 45
Graham-Cameron, Mike
See Graham-Cameron, M(alcolm) G(ordon)
Graham-Campbell, David (John) 1912-1994 ... 113
Grahame, Kenneth 1859-1932 ... CANR-80
Brief entry ... 108
Earlier sketch in CA 136
See also BYA 5
See also CLR 5
See also CWRI 5
See also DA3
See also DAB
See also DLB 34, 141, 178
See also FANT
See also MAICYA 1, 2
See also MTCW 2
See also NFS 20
See also RGEL 2
See also SATA 100
See also TCLC 64, 136
See also TEA
See also WCH
See also YABC 1
Graham Scott, Peter 1923- ... 108
Graham-White, Anthony 1940- ... 61-64
Graham-Yooll, Andrew M(ichael) 1944- ... CANR-28
Earlier sketch in CA 108
Grahn, Judith L. 1940- ... CANR-78
Brief entry ... 116
Earlier sketch in CA 122
Interview in ... CA-122
See also Grahn, Judy
See also CAAS 29
See also CWP
Grahn, Judy
See Grahn, Judith L.
See also GLL 1
Grainger, A(nthony) J(ohn) 1929- ... 33-36R
Grainger, J(ohn) H(erbert) 1917- ... 77-80
Grainger, James c. 1721-1766 ... RGEL 2
Grainger, John D(ownie) 1939- ... CANR-136
Earlier sketch in CA 144
Grainger, Margaret 1936- ... 116
Grainger, Martin Allerdale 1874-1941 ... 175
See also DLB 92
Grainville, Patrick 1947- ... 184
Gralapp, Leland Wilson 1921-1998 ... 13-16R
Gralla, Cynthia ... 225
Gram, Harold A(lbert) 1927- ... 25-28R
Gram, Moltke (Stefanus) 1938- ... CANR-13
Earlier sketch in CA 69-72
Gramatky, Hardie 1907-1979 ... CANR-3
Obituary ... 85-88
Earlier sketch in CA 1-4R
See also AITN 1
See also CLR 22
See also CWRI 5
See also DLB 22
See also MAICYA 1, 2
See also SATA 1, 30
See also SATA-Obit 23
Grambling, Lois G. 1927- ... 222
See also SATA 71, 148
Grambo, Rebecca L(ynn) 1963- ... 171
See also SATA 109
Grambs, David (Lawrence) 1938- ... 146
Grambs, Jean D(resden) 1919-1989 ... CANR-7
Obituary ... 129
Earlier sketch in CA 17-20R
Gramcko, Ida 1924-1994 ... DLB 290
Gramer, Rod 1953- ... 147
Gramet, Charles -1978 ... 1-4R
Gramick, Jeannine 1942- ... 113
Gramlich, Edward M(artin) 1939- ... CANR-144
Earlier sketch in CA 172
Gramling, Lea Gene, Jr. 1942- ... 194
Gramling, Lee
See Gramling, Lea Gene, Jr.
Grammatico, Maria 1941- ... 225
Grammaticus
See Blaiklock, Edward Musgrave
Grammer, June Amos 1927- ... SATA 58
Grampp, William D(yer) 1914- ... 33-36R
Grams, Armin 1924- ... 45-48
Gramsci, Antonio 1891-1937 ... DLB 296
See also WLIT 7
Gran, Peter 1941- ... 156
Gran, Sara 1971- ... 204
Granada, Fray Luis de 1504-1588 ... DLB 318
Granado, Alberto 1922- ... 239
Granados, Paul
See Kent, Arthur William Charles
Granat, Robert 1925- ... CANR-2
Earlier sketch in CA 1-4R
Granatstein, J(ack) L(awrence) 1939- ... CANR-139
Earlier sketches in CA 25-28R, CANR-10
Granbeck, Marilyn
See Henderson, M(arilyn) R(uth)
Granberg, W(ilbur) J(ohn) 1906-1979 ... 5-8R
Granberry, Edwin 1897-1988 ... CAP-2
Earlier sketch in CA 21-22
Granby, Milton
See Wallmann, Jeffrey M(iner)
Grand, David 1968- ... 209
Grand, Samuel 1912-1988 ... 107
See also SATA 42
Grand, Sarah 1854-1943 ... DLB 135, 197
Granda, Chabuca
See Larco, Isabel Granda
Grandbois, Alain 1900-1975 ... 148
See also CCA 1
See also DLB 92
Grande, Luke M. 1922- ... CANR-2
Earlier sketch in CA 5-8R
Grande Vitesse
See Walkerley, Rodney Lewis (de Burgh)
Grandfield, Raymond J(oseph) 1931- ... 53-56
Grandin, Temple 1947- ... CANR-138
Earlier sketch in CA 154
Grandinetti, Fred M. 1961- ... CANR-120
Earlier sketch in CA 148
Grandower, Elissa
See Waugh, Hillary Baldwin
Grandson, Oton de c. 1345-1397 ... DLB 208
Grandville, J. J.
See Gerard, Jean Ignace Isidore
Grandville, Jean Ignace Isidore Gerard
See Gerard, Jean Ignace Isidore
Grandy, Richard (Edward) 1942- ... 77-80
Granelli, Roger 1950- ... 151
Granfield, Linda 1950- ... CANR-114
Earlier sketches in CA 128, CANR-60
See also MAICYA 2
See also SATA 96, 160
Grange, Chris
See Gnaegy, Charles
Grange, Cyril 1900- ... CAP-1
Earlier sketch in CA 13-16
Grange, Jean-Christophe 1961- ... 210
Grange, John 1556-(?) ... DLB 136
Grange, Peter
See Nicole, Christopher (Robin)
Grange, William M(arshall) 1947- ... 175
Granger, (Patricia) Ann 1939- ... CANR-111
Earlier sketch in CA 143
Granger, Bill 1941- ... CANR-80
Brief entry ... 127
Earlier sketch in CA 131
See also CMW 4
Granger, Bruce Ingham 1920- ... CANR-47
Earlier sketch in CA 1-4R
Granger, Byrd Howell 1912-1991 ... 107
Granger, Clive W(illiam) J(ohn) 1934- ... CANR-8
Earlier sketch in CA 9-12R
Granger, Darius John
See Marlowe, Stephen
Granger, Guy
See Green, Kay
Granger, Margaret Jane 1925(?)-1977
Obituary ... 104
See also SATA-Obit 27
Granger, Michele 1949- ... 152
See also SATA 88
Granger, Peggy
See Granger, Margaret Jane
Granger, Percy 1945-1997 ... 136
Obituary ... 157
Granger, Pip 1947- ... 237
Granger, Thomas 1578-1627 ... DLB 281
Granich, Irving 1894-1967 ... 97-100
Obituary ... 45-48
See also DLB 9, 28
Granich, Reuben ... 209
Granick, David 1926- ... 1-4R
Granick, Harry 1898-1998 ... CANR-48
Earlier sketch in CA 85-88
Granik, (S.) Theodore 1906-1970
Obituary ... 89-92
Granin, Daniil 1918- ... CLC 59
See also DLB 302
Granit, Arthur 1917- ... 120
Granite, Harvey R. 1927- ... CANR-15
Earlier sketch in CA 33-36R
Granite, Tony
See Politella, Dario
Grannis, Chandler B(rinkerhoff) 1912-
Brief entry ... 111
Granovetter, Mark S. 1943- ... 85-88
Granovsky, Anatoli 1922-1974
Obituary ... 53-56
Granovsky, Timofei Nikolaevich 1813-1855 ... DLB 198
Granowsky, Alvin 1936- ... 21-24R
See also SATA 101
Gransden, Antonia 1928- ... CANR-30
Earlier sketch in CA 77-80
Gransden, K(arl) W(atts) 1925- ... CP 1
Granstaff, Bill 1925- ... SATA 10
Granstroem, Brita 1969- ... 182
See also SATA 111
Granstrom, Brita
See Granstroem, Brita
Grant, Alan
See Kennington, (Gilbert) Alan
Grant, Alexander T(homas) K(ingdom) 1906- ... 53-56
Grant, Ambrose
See Raymond, Rene (Brabazon)
Grant, Anne MacVicar 1755-1838 ... DLB 200
Grant, Anne Underwood 1946- ... CANR-124
Earlier sketch in CA 168
Grant, Anthony
See Pares, Marion (Stapylton)
Grant, Barbara L.
See Lachman, Barbara
Grant, Barbara M(oll) 1932- ... 53-56
Grant, Barry Keith 1947- ... 138
Grant, Ben
See Henderson, M(arilyn) R(uth)
Grant, Brian W. 1939- ... CANR-7
Earlier sketch in CA 57-60
Grant, Bruce 1893-1977 ... CANR-6
Obituary ... 69-72
Earlier sketch in CA 1-4R
See also SATA 5
See also SATA-Obit 25
Grant, Bruce Alexander 1925- ... 107
Grant, C. B. S.
See Haga, Enoch J.
Grant, Charles L(ewis) 1942- ... CANR-73
Earlier sketch in CA 85-88
See also HGG
See also SFW 4
See also SUFW 2
Grant, Cynthia D. 1950- ... CANR-130
Earlier sketches in CA 104, CANR-20, 42
See also AAYA 23
See also BYA 7
See also SATA 33, 77, 147
See also YAW
Grant, Daniel 1954- ... CANR-118
Earlier sketch in CA 150
Grant, David
See Thomas, Craig (David)
Grant, Don
See Glut, Donald F(rank)
Grant, Donald J. 1939-1984
Obituary ... 113
Grant, Donna ... 222
Grant, Dorothy 1927- ... 114
Grant, Dorothy Fremont 1900-1976 ... CAP-2
Earlier sketch in CA 23-24
Grant, Duncan (James Corrowr) 1885-1978 ... 148
See also DLBD 10
Grant, Elliott Mansfield 1895-1969 ... CANR-5
Earlier sketch in CA 5-8R
Grant, Ellsworth Strong 1917- ... 57-60
Grant, Eva 1907-1996 ... CANR-49
Earlier sketch in CA 49-52
See also SATA 7
Grant, Evva H. 1913-1977
Obituary ... 104
See also SATA-Obit 27
Grant, Frederick C(lifton) 1891-1974 ... CANR-47
Obituary ... 49-52
Earlier sketch in CA 1-4R
Grant, George (Parkin) 1918-1988
Obituary ... 126
See also DLB 88
Grant, George Monro 1835-1902 ... 175
See also DLB 99
Grant, Gerald 1938- ... 81-84
Grant, Gordon 1875-1962 ... 102
See also SATA 25
Grant, Graeme 1961- ... 151
Grant, Gwen(doline Ellen) 1940- ... CANR-22
Earlier sketch in CA 106
See also SATA 47
Grant, H. Roger 1943- ... 89-92
Grant, Harry J(ohnston) 1881-1963 ... 175
Obituary ... 114
See also DLB 29
Grant, Hilda Kay 1910-1996 ... 1-4R
Grant, Isabel F(rances) 1887-1983
Obituary ... 110
Grant, J(ohn) B(arnard) 1940- ... CANR-28
Earlier sketches in CA 57-60, CANR-6
Grant, Jack
See Grant, J(ohn) B(arnard)
Grant, James
See Crowther, Bruce (Ian)
Grant, James Edward 1905-1966 ... 175
Obituary ... 113
See also DLB 26
Grant, James G. 1926(?)-1979
Obituary ... 89-92
Grant, James Russell 1924- ... CANR-17
Earlier sketch in CA 101
Grant, Jane
See Leader, (Evelyn) Barbara (Blackburn)
Grant, Jane (Cole) 1895-1972 ... CAP-2
Obituary ... 33-36R
Earlier sketch in CA 25-28
Grant, Jill 1951- ... 148
Grant, Joan
See Kelsey, Joan Marshall
Grant, Joanne B(enzel) 1940- ... 106
Grant, John 1933- ... CANR-98
Earlier sketches in CA 77-80, CANR-45
See also Gash, Jonathan
See also CMW 4
See also FANT
Grant, John E(rnest) 1925- ... CANR-47
Earlier sketch in CA 41-44R
Grant, John J. 1932- ... 53-56
Grant, John Webster 1919- ... CANR-6
Earlier sketch in CA 5-8R
Grant, Jonathan
See Grant, John
Grant, Judith 1929- ... 21-24R
Grant, Kay ... 21-24R
Grant, Kerry S. 1945- ... 121
Grant, Landon
See Gribble, Leonard (Reginald)
Grant, Lee 1931- ... 173
Grant, (Alice) Leigh 1947- ... SATA 10
Grant, Linda 1951- ... 205
Grant, Louis T(heodore) 1943- ... 53-56
Grant, Madeleine Parker 1895-1974 ... 73-76
Grant, Margaret
See Franken, Rose D(orothy Lewin)
Grant, Mark N. 1952- ... 209
Grant, Mary A(melia) 1890-1987 ... CAP-2
Earlier sketch in CA 25-28
Grant, Mary Kathryn 1941- ... 81-84
Grant, Matthew G.
See May, Julian
Grant, Maxwell
See Gibson, Walter B(rown) and Lynds, Dennis
Grant, Michael 1914-2004 ... CANR-50
Obituary ... 232
Earlier sketches in CA 1-4R, CANR-4, 25
Grant, Michael Johnston 1961- ... 233
Grant, Myrna (Lois) 1934- ... CANR-4
Earlier sketch in CA 53-56
See also SATA 21
Grant, Neil 1938- ... CANR-138
Earlier sketches in CA 33-36R, CANR-15, 34, 90
See also SATA 14, 154
Grant, Nicholas
See Nicole, Christopher (Robin)
Grant, Nigel (Duncan Cameron) 1932- ... CANR-7
Earlier sketch in CA 17-20R
Grant, Ozro F. 1908-1977 ... CAP-2
Earlier sketch in CA 21-22
Grant, Patrick 1941- ... CANR-100
Earlier sketch in CA 132
Grant, Pete ... 225
Grant, Richard 1936-
See Freemantle, Brian (Harry)
Grant, Richard 1948- ... 147
See also SATA 80
Grant, Richard 1952- ... SFW 4
Grant, Richard B(abson) 1925- ... CANR-4
Earlier sketch in CA 1-4R
Grant, Richard E. 1957- ... 197
Grant, Robert B(ruce) 1933- ... 180
Earlier sketch in CA 45-48
Grant, Robert M(cQueen) 1917- ... 65-68
Grant, Roderick 1941-
Brief entry ... 112
Grant, Roger
See Ferrell, Mallory Hope
Grant, Skeeter
See Spiegelman, Art
Grant, Stephanie ... 160
Grant, Susan ... 235
Grant, Susan-Mary C. 1962- ... 202
Grant, Ulysses S. III 1881-1968
Obituary ... 111
Grant, Vanessa ... 202
Grant, Verne E(dwin) 1917- ... 53-56
Grant, Vernon W(esley) 1904-1979 ... 17-20R
Grant, W(illiam) Leonard 1914- ... 17-20R
Grant, William
See Reasoner, James M(orris)
Grant, Wilson Wayne 1941- ... 97-100
Grant, Wyn(ford) 1947- ... CANR-75
Earlier sketches in CA 114, CANR-35
Grant, Zalin (Belton) 1941- ... 73-76
Grant-Adamson, Lesley 1942- ... CANR-66
Earlier sketches in CA 121, CANR-47
See also CMW 4
Grant Duff, Shiela 1913-2004 ... 159
Obituary ... 225
Grantham, Alexander (William George Herder) 1899-1978 ... CAP-2
Earlier sketch in CA 19-20
Grantham, Dewey Wesley 1921- ... CANR-1
Earlier sketch in CA 1-4R
Grantland, Keith
See Beaumont, Charles
Granton, Ester Fannie 1914(?)-1980
Obituary ... 101
Grant Wallace, Lewis
See Wallace, Lewis Grant
Granville, Evelyn Boyd 1924- ... 161
Granville, Joseph E(nsign) 1923- ... 65-68
Granville, W. Wilfred 1905- ... CAP-1
Earlier sketch in CA 9-10
Granville-Barker, Harley 1877-1946 ... 204
Brief entry ... 104
See also Barker, Harley Granville
See also DAM DRAM
See also RGEL 2
See also TCLC 2
Granzotto, Gianni
See Granzotto, Giovanni Battista
Granzotto, Giovanni Battista 1914-1985 ... 166
See also CLC 70
Grape, Oliver
See Wood, Christopher (Hovelle)
Grapho
See Oakley, Eric Gilbert
Gras, Ulrik 1940- ... 207
Grass, Guenter (Wilhelm) 1927- ... CANR-133
Earlier sketches in CA 13-16R, CANR-20, 75, 93
See also Grass, Gunter (Wilhelm)
See also BPFB 2
See also CDWLB 2
See also CLC 1, 2, 4, 6, 11, 15, 22, 32, 49, 88, 207
See also DA
See also DA3
See also DAB
See also DAC
See also DAM MST, NOV
See also DLB 75, 124
See also EW 13
See also EWL 3
See also MTCW 1, 2
See also MTFW 2005
See also RGWL 2, 3
See also TWA
See also WLC
Grass, Gunter (Wilhelm)
See Grass, Guenter (Wilhelm)
See also CWW 2

Grassi, Joseph A(ugustus) 1922- CANR-41
Earlier sketches in CA 103, CANR-19
Grassi, Maggi Lidchi
See Lidchi Grassi, Maggi
Grassian, Esther S. 1946- 221
Grasso, Domenico 1917- 73-76
Grasty, Charles H. 1863-1924 175
See also DLB 25
Grater, Michael 1923- .... SATA 57
Grathwohl, Larry D(avid) 1947- 65-68
Grattan, C(linton) Hartley 1902-1980 . CANR-1
Obituary 101
Earlier sketch in CA 1-4R
Grattan, Virginia L(ee) 1932- 115
Grattan-Guinness, I. 1941- 73-76
Gratton, Thomas
See Hulme, T(homas) E(rnest)
Gratus, Jack 1935- CANR-48
Earlier sketch in CA 93-96
Grau (Delgado), Jacinto 1877-1958 .... EWL 3
Grau, Joseph A(ugust) 1921-1991 65-68
Grau, Shirley Ann 1929- CANR-69
Earlier sketches in CA 89-92, CANR-22
Interview in CA-89-92; CANR-22
See also CLC 4, 9, 146
See also CN 1, 2, 3, 4, 5, 6, 7
See also CSW
See also DLB 2, 218
See also MTCW 1
See also SSC 15
Graubard, Mark A(aron) 1904-1992 ... CANR-5
Earlier sketch in CA 1-4R
Graubard, Paul S. 1932- 103
Graubard, S. R.
See Graubard, Stephen R(ichards)
Graubard, Stephen R(ichards) 1924- 161
Brief entry 113
Graubart, David 1907(?)-1984
Obituary 112
Grauer, Ben(jamin Franklin) 1908-1977
Obituary 69-72
Grauer, Neil A(lbert) 1947- 122
Grauerholz, James 230
Graulich, Melody 1951- 128
Grauman, Lawrence, Jr. 1935- 33-36R
Graupe, Daniel 1934- 41-44R
Graupera, Carlos M(anuel) 1915- 49-52
Grava, Sigurd 1934- 77-80
Gravagnuolo, Benedetto 1949- 112
Grave, S(elwyn) A(lfred) 1916- 5-8R
Gravel, Fern
See Hall, James Norman
Gravel, Francois 1951- 215
Gravel, Mike 1930- 41-44R
Gravelle, Jane G(ibson) 1947- 150
Gravelle, Karen 1942- 135
See also SATA 78
Gravely, William B(ernard) 1939- 49-52
Graver, Elizabeth 1964- CANR-129
Earlier sketches in CA 135, CANR-71
See also CLC 70
Graver, Jane (Ann) 1931- 117
Graver, Lawrence 1931- CANR-92
Earlier sketch in CA 25-28R
Graver, Suzanne 1936- 117
Graversen, Pat 1935-2000 109
Graves, Allen W(illis) 1915-1991 .... 17-20R
Graves, Barbara Farris 1938- 41-44R
Graves, Charles Parlin 1911-1972 ...... CANR-4
Obituary 37-40R
Earlier sketch in CA 5-8R
See also SATA 4
Graves, Edgar B(aldwin) 1898-1983
Obituary 109
Graves, Eleanor MacKenzie 1926- 102
Graves, Ida Affleck 1902-1999 189
Graves, John (Alexander III) 1920- . CANR-138
Earlier sketches in CA 13-16R, CANR-9, 68
See also ANW
See also DLBY 1983
See also TCWW 2
Graves, Joseph L(ewis), Jr. 1955- 239
Graves, Keith .... SATA 156
Graves, Keller
See Rogers, Evelyn
Graves, Leon B(erneil) 1946- 29-32R
Graves, Lucia 1943- 189
Graves, Michael A(rthur) R(oy) 1933- 131
Graves, Neil
See Graves, Roy Neil
Graves, Nora Calhoun 1914- 73-76
Graves, Phillip E(arl) 1945- 115
Graves, Ralph (Augustus) 1924- 138
Graves, Richard 1715-1804 .... DLB 39
See also RGEL 2
Graves, Richard L(atshaw) 1928- 57-60
Graves, Richard L(ayton) 1931- 53-56
Graves, Richard Perceval
1895-1985 .... CANR-51
Earlier sketches in CA 65-68, CANR-9, 26
See also CLC 44
Graves, Robert (von Ranke)
1895-1985 .... CANR-36
Obituary 117
Earlier sketches in CA 5-8R, CANR-5
See also BPFB 2
See also BRW 7
See also BYA 4
See also CDBLB 1914-1945
See also CLC 1, 2, 6, 11, 39, 44, 45
See also CN 1, 2, 3
See also CP 1, 2
See also DA3
See also DAB
See also DAC
See also DAM MST, POET
See also DLB 20, 100, 191
See also DLBD 18
See also DLBY 1985
See also EWL 3
See also LATS 1:1
See also MTCW 1, 2
See also MTFW 2005
See also NCFS 2
See also NFS 21
See also PC 6
See also RGEL 2
See also RHW
See also SATA 45
See also TEA
Graves, Roy Neil 1939- 188
Graves, Russell A. 1969- 225
Graves, Sarah 1951- 234
Graves, Susan B(ernard) 1933- 41-44R
Graves, Tricia
See Graversen, Pat
Graves, Valerie
See Bradley, Marion Zimmer
Graves, W(illiam) Brooke 1899-1973 .... CAP-1
Earlier sketch in CA 9-10
Graves, Wallace 1922-1999 .... 33-36R
Graves, Warren 1933- 128
Graveson, R(onald) H(arry) 1911-1991 122
Gravitz, Herbert L. 1942- 171
Grawbarger, Josephine (Clara) 1908- 121
Grawoig, Sheila
See Raeschild, Sheila
Gray, A(lbert) W(illiam) 1940- CANR-71
Earlier sketch in CA 127
Gray, Alasdair (James) 1934- CANR-140
Earlier sketches in CA 126, CANR-47, 69, 106
Interview in CA-126
See also BRWS 9
See also CLC 41
See also CN 4, 5, 6, 7
See also DLB 194, 261, 319
See also HGG
See also MTCW 1, 2
See also MTFW 2005
See also RGSF 2
See also SUFW 2
Gray, Alexander 1882-1968 .... 5-8R
Gray, Alfred 1939-1998 146
Gray, Alfred O(rren) 1914- CANR-7
Earlier sketch in CA 17-20R
Gray, Amlin 1946- 138
See also CLC 29
Gray, Angela
See Daniels, Dorothy
Gray, Anne 1931- CANR-9
Earlier sketch in CA 65-68
Gray, Asa 1810-1888 .... DLB 1, 235, 254
Gray, Barry 1916-1996 155
Gray, Basil 1904-1989 .... CAP-1
Obituary 128
Earlier sketch in CA 9-10
Gray, Betsy
See Poole, Gray Johnson
Gray, Bettyanne 1934- 81-84
Gray, Bradford H(itch) 1942- 57-60
Gray, Captain Bill
See Gray, William Bittle
Gray, Caroline
See Nicole, Christopher (Robin)
Gray, Charles A(ugustus) 1938- 17-20R
Gray, Charlotte 1928(?)- 173
Gray, Chris Hables 1953- CANR-134
Earlier sketch in CA 164
Gray, Christopher 1950- 225
Gray, Clifford F. 1930- 25-28R
Gray, Darrell 1945- 65-68
Gray, David 1838-1861 .... DLB 32
Gray, David 1927-1983
Obituary 110
Gray, Deborah D. 1951- 225
Gray, Dorothea Helen Forbes (?)-1983
Obituary 110
Gray, Dorothy (Kamer) 1936- 69-72
Gray, Dorothy Kate 1918- 102
Gray, Douglas 1930- 117
Gray, Dulcie CANR-24
Earlier sketches in CA 5-8R, CANR-3
Gray, Dwight E(lder) 1903-1996 .... CAP-2
Earlier sketch in CA 23-24
Gray, Ed(ward Emmet) 1945- 210
Gray, Eden 1907-1999 93-96
Gray, Edna Redmond 1905(?)-1983
Obituary 110
Gray, Edwyn 1927- 41-44R
Gray, Elizabeth Janet
See Vining, Elizabeth Gray
See also BYA 1, 3
Gray, Ellington
See Jacob, Naomi (Ellington)
Gray, Ernest
See Gray, Ernest Alfred
Gray, Ernest A.
See Gray, Ernest Alfred
Gray, Ernest Alfred 1908- 118
Gray, Farnum 1940- 49-52
Gray, Floyd (Francis) 1926- CANR-10
Earlier sketch in CA 25-28R
Gray, Francine du Plessix 1930- CANR-81
Earlier sketches in CA 61-64, CANR-11, 33, 75
Interview in CANR-11
See also CAAS 2
See also BEST 90:3
See also CLC 22, 153
See also DAM NOV
See also MTCW 1, 2
See also MTFW 2005
Gray, Genevieve S(tuck) 1920-1995 ...... 33-36R
See also SATA 4
Gray, George Hugh 1922- CANR-7
Earlier sketch in CA 17-20R
Gray, Gibson 1922- 33-36R
Gray, Giles Wilkeson 1889-1972 .... 5-8R
Gray, Ginna 1938- 195
Gray, Gordon 1909-1982
Obituary 109
Gray, H(enry) Peter 1924- 184
Brief entry 111
Gray, Harold (Lincoln) 1894-1968 107
See also SATA 33
See also SATA-Brief 32
Gray, Harold James 1907-1998 107
Gray, Harriet
See Robins, Denise (Naomi)
Gray, Ian 1951- 142
Gray, J(esse) Glenn 1913-1977 .... 37-40R
Obituary 73-76
Gray, J(ames) M(artin) 1930- 53-56
Gray, J(ohn) Richard 1929- CANR-5
Earlier sketch in CA 1-4R
Gray, J(ohn) Stanley 1894-1968 .... CAP-2
Earlier sketch in CA 17-18
Gray, Jack 1927- 103
See also CD 5, 6
Gray, James 1899-1984 .... 13-16R
Gray, James H(enry) 1906- 97-100
Gray, James P. 1945- 210
Gray, James R(obert) 1921- 33-36R
Gray, Jane
See Evans, Constance May
Gray, Jeffrey A(lan) 1934-2004 104
Obituary 227
Gray, Jenny
See Gray, Genevieve S(tuck)
Gray, John (Henry) 1866-1934 162
Brief entry 119
See also RGEL 2
See also TCLC 19
Gray, John (MacLachlan) 1946- .... CD 5, 6
Gray, John 1951- CANR-123
Earlier sketches in CA 145, CANR-66
Gray, John E(dmund) 1922- 65-68
Gray, John Lee
See Jakes, John (William)
Gray, John Milner 1889-1970
Obituary 29-32R
Gray, John Morgan 1907-1978 103
Gray, John Rodger 1913-1984
Obituary 113
Gray, John S(tephens) 1910-1991 73-76
Gray, John W(ylie) 1935- 17-20R
Gray, Juanita R(uth) 1918- 61-64
Gray, Judith A(nne) 1949- 158
See also SATA 93
Gray, Keith 214
See also SATA 151
Gray, Kes 1960- .... SATA 153
Gray, Lee Learner 1924- 73-76
Gray, Les 1929- .... SATA 82
Gray, Libba Moore 1937- .... SATA 83
Gray, Linda Crockett 1943- 109
See also Crockett, Linda
Gray, Luli 1945- CANR-132
Earlier sketch in CA 151
See also SATA 90, 149
Gray, Malcolm
See Stuart, Ian
Gray, Margaret E(lla) 1956- 141
Gray, Margaret K. 1949- 123
Gray, Marian
See Pierce, Edith Gray
Gray, Marianne 1947- 110
Gray, Martin 1926- CANR-14
Earlier sketch in CA 77-80
See also AITN 1
Gray, Mary Taylor
See Young, Mary Taylor
Gray, Mayo Loiseau 1938- 104
Gray, Michael H(aslam) 1946- 103
Gray, Muriel 153
Gray, Nicholas Stuart 1922-1981 ..... CANR-11
Obituary 103
Earlier sketch in CA 21-24R
See also BYA 5
See also CWRI 5
See also SATA 4
See also SATA-Obit 27
Gray, Nicolete (Mary) 1911-1997 103
Gray, Nigel 1941- 85-88
See also SATA 33, 104
Gray, (Lucy) Noel (Clervaux) 1898-1983 . 65-68
See also SATA 47
Gray, Oscar S(halom) 1926- 29-32R
Gray, Parke H. 1936(?)-1987
Obituary 121
Gray, Pat 1953- 181
Gray, Patience (Jean Stanham) 1917-2005 .. 142
Obituary 237
Gray, Patricia (Clark) 29-32R
See also SATA 7
Gray, Patsey
See Gray, Patricia (Clark)
Gray, Paul 1918-2002 218
Gray, Penny 1957- 210
Gray, Peter 1908-1981 .... 41-44R
Gray, Philip
See Perlman, Jess
Gray, Piers 1947-1996 224
Gray, Ralph D(ale) 1933- CANR-49
Earlier sketches in CA 21-24R, CANR-8, 24
Gray, Richard
See Gray, J(ohn) Richard
Gray, Richard A. 1927- 154
Gray, Richard B(utler) 1922- CANR-2
Earlier sketch in CA 1-4R
Gray, Richard G(eorge) 1932-1984
Obituary 114
Gray, Richard J(ohn) 1944- 232
Gray, Robert (Archibald Speir) 1942- 134
Gray, Robert (Curtis) 1945- 233
Gray, Robert Curtis 1946- .... CP 7
Gray, Robert F(red) 1912-1999 .... 17-20R
Gray, Robert Keith 1923- 1-4R
Gray, Robert Mack 1922- 13-16R
Gray, Rod
See Fox, G(ardner) F(rancis)
Gray, Ronald (Douglas) 1919- CANR-22
Earlier sketches in CA 17-20R, CANR-7
Gray, Ronald Francis 1918- 5-8R
Gray, (Clemency Anne) Rose(mary) 1939- .. 231
Gray, Russell
See Fischer, Bruno
Gray, Seymour Jerome 1911-2001 130
Gray, Simon (James Holliday)
1936- CANR-69
Earlier sketches in CA 21-24R, CANR-32
See also CAAS 3
See also AITN 1
See also CBD
See also CD 5, 6
See also CLC 9, 14, 36
See also CN 1, 2, 3
See also DLB 13
See also EWL 3
See also MTCW 1
See also RGEL 2
Gray, Spalding 1941-2004 .... CANR-138
Obituary 225
Earlier sketches in CA 128, CANR-74
See also AAYA 62
See also CAD
See also CD 5, 6
See also CLC 49, 112
See also CPW
See also DAM POP
See also DC 7
See also MTCW 2
See also MTFW 2005
Gray, Stephen E. 1925- 73-76
Gray, Stephen Richard 1941- .... CN 6, 7
See also CP 7
Gray, Thomas 1716-1771 .... BRW 3
See also CDBLB 1660-1789
See also DA
See also DA3
See also DAB
See also DAC
See also DAM MST
See also DLB 109
See also EXPP
See also PAB
See also PC 2
See also PFS 9
See also RGEL 2
See also TEA
See also WLC
See also WP
Gray, Tony
See Gray, George Hugh
Gray, Vanessa
See Aeby, Jacquelyn
Gray, Victor
See Conquest, (George) Robert (Acworth)
Gray, Wallace 1927-2001 219
Gray, Wellington Burbank 1919-1977 .... 1-4R
Obituary 103
Gray, William Bittle 1891-1974 .... CANR-11
Earlier sketch in CA 13-16R
Gray, William R(alph) 1946- 97-100
Gray, Wood 1905(?)-1977
Obituary 69-72
Graybar, Lloyd J(oseph) 1938- 57-60
Graybeal, David M(cConnell) 1921- 17-20R
Graybill, Florence Curtis
1898-1987 .... CANR-107
Earlier sketch in CA 97-100
Graybill, Ron(ald D.) 1944- 33-36R
Graydon, Shari 1958- 234
See also SATA 158
Grayeff, Felix 1906- 77-80
Grayland, Eugene C(harles)
1916-1976 .... CANR-11
Earlier sketches in CAP-1, CA 9-10
Grayland, V. Merle
See Grayland, Valerie (Merle Spanner)
Grayland, Valerie (Merle Spanner) CANR-11
Earlier sketch in CA 9-12R
See also SATA 7
Graymont, Barbara 81-84
Graymore, Clive (Norman) 1930-1999 186
Graysmith, Robert 1942- CANR-122
Earlier sketches in CA 117, CANR-41
Grayson, A(lbert) K(irk) 1935- 41-44R
Grayson, Alice Barr
See Grossman, Jean Schick
Grayson, Benson Lee 1932- 93-96
Grayson, C(harles) Jackson, Jr. 1923- 106

Cumulative Index 231 **Green**

Grayson, Cary Travers, Jr. 1919- CANR-10
Earlier sketch in CA 17-20R
Grayson, Cecil 1920-1998 .... 13-16R
Obituary 166
Grayson, Charles 1905-1973
Obituary 41-44R
Grayson, David
See Baker, Ray Stannard
Grayson, Devin (Kalile) 1970- .... SATA 119
Grayson, Donald K. 1945- 146
Grayson, Elizabeth
See Witmer-Gow, Karen
Grayson, Emily 232
Grayson, Henry (Wesley) 1910-1985 .... 41-44R
Grayson, Janet 1934- 53-56
Grayson, Kristine
See Rusch, Kristine Kathryn
Grayson, L(inda) M(ary) 1947- 89-92
Grayson, Marion F. 1906-1976 .... CANR-4
Obituary 69-72
Earlier sketch in CA 5-8R
Grayson, Melvin J(ay) 1924- 45-48
Grayson, Paul 1946- 147
See also SATA 79
Grayson, Richard
See Grindal, Richard
Grayson, Richard (A.) 1951- 210
Earlier sketches in CA 85-88, CANR-14, 31, 57
Autobiographical Essay in 210
See also CLC 38
See also DLB 234
Grayson, Robert A. 1927- 33-36R
Grayson, Ruth (King) 1926- 73-76
Grayson, William John 1788-1863 .. DLB 3, 64, 248
Graystone, Lynn
See Brennan, Joseph Lomas
Grayzel, Solomon 1896-1980 .... CANR-4
Earlier sketch in CA 1-4R
Grazer, Brian 1951(?)- 181
Grazer, Gigi Levangie 227
Grazhdanin, Misha
See Burgess, Michael (Roy)
Graziano, Anthony M(ichael) 1932- 93-96
Greacen, Lavinia 224
Grealey, Thomas Louis 1916- 81-84
Grealis, Walt(er) 1929- 77-80
Grealy, Desmond 1923(?)-1979
Obituary 85-88
Grealy, Lucinda (Margaret)
1963-2002 .... CANR-99
Obituary 212
Earlier sketch in CA 147
Grealy, Lucy
See Grealy, Lucinda (Margaret)
Grean, Stanley 1920-1996 .... 29-32R
Greanias, George C. 1948- 126
Grearson, Jessie Carroll 234
Greatbatch, Wilson 1919- 208
Earlier sketch in CA 207
Great Comte, The
See Hawkesworth, Eric
Great Merlini, The
See Rawson, Clayton
Greatorex, Wilfred 1921(?)-2002 103
Obituary 211
Greatrex, Joan (Gertrude) 1926- 180
Greaves, Bettina Herbert Bien
1917- CANR-136
Earlier sketch in CA 144
Greaves, H(arold) R(ichard) G(oring)
1907-1981 .... 5-8R
Greaves, (Brian) John 1898- 103
Greaves, M(elvyn) F. 1941- 192
Greaves, Margaret 1914-1995 .... CANR-53
Earlier sketches in CA 25-28R, CANR-18
See also CWRI 5
See also SATA 7, 87
Greaves, Mel
See Greaves, M(elvyn) F.
Greaves, Nick 1955- 145
See also SATA 77
Greaves, Percy L(aurie), Jr.
1906-1984 .... CANR-48
Earlier sketch in CA 49-52
Greaves, Richard L(ee) 1938-2004 ... CANR-97
Obituary 230
Earlier sketches in CA 33-36R, CANR-16, 39
Greaves, William 1926- 125
See also BW 1
Grebanier, Bernard (David N.)
1903-1977 .... CANR-10
Earlier sketch in CA 21-24R
Grebe, Maria Ester 1928- 25-28R
Greben, Stanley E(dward) 1927- CANR-45
Earlier sketch in CA 120
Greber, Judith 1939- CANR-144
Earlier sketch in CA 116
Grebstein, Lawrence C(harles) 1937- 29-32R
Grebstein, Sheldon Norman 1928- CANR-5
Earlier sketch in CA 1-4R
Grech, Nikolai Ivanovich 1787-1867 . DLB 198
Greco, Jose
See Greco, (Constanzo) Jose
Greco, (Constanzo) Jose 1918-2000 85-88
Obituary 190
Greco, Margaret
See Fry, Barbara
Greco, Sal 1947- 237
Gree, Alain 1936- 89-92
See also SATA 28
Greeley, Andrew M(oran) 1928- CANR-136
Earlier sketches in CA 5-8R, CANR-7, 43, 69, 104
See also CAAS 7
See also BPFB 2
See also CLC 28
See also CMW 4
See also CPW
See also DA3
See also DAM POP
See also MTCW 1, 2
See also MTFW 2005
Greeley, Dana McLean 1908-1986
Obituary 119
Greeley, Horace 1811-1872 .... DLB 3, 43, 189, 250
Greeley, Valerie 1953- CANR-43
Earlier sketch in CA 118
Green, A(dwin) Wigfall 1900-1971(?) CAP-1
Earlier sketch in CA 9-10
Green, Abel 1900-1973
Obituary 41-44R
Green, Adam
See Weisgard, Leonard (Joseph)
Green, Adolph 1915-2002 130
Obituary 213
Brief entry 110
See also DLB 44, 265
See also IDFW 3, 4
Green, Alan (Baer) 1906-1975 53-56
Obituary 57-60
Green, Alan 1950- 209
Green, Alan Singer 1907-1989 85-88
Green, Andrew (Malcolm)
1927-2004 .... CANR-12
Obituary 227
Earlier sketch in CA 73-76
Green, Angela 1949(?)- 226
Green, Anita Jane 1940- 85-88
Green, Anna Katharine 1846-1935 159
Brief entry 112
See also CMW 4
See also DLB 202, 221
See also MSW
See also TCLC 63
Green, Anne (Mitchell) 1947- 120
Green, Anne Canevari 1943- .... SATA 62
Green, Anne M. 1922- 1-4R
Green, Arnold W(ilfred) 1914-1995 .... 5-8R
Green, Arthur 1941- CANR-92
Earlier sketch in CA 145
Green, Arthur S(amuel) 1927- 5-8R
Green, Ben 1951- 186
Green, Ben K. 1911(?)-1974
Obituary 115
See also AITN 1
Green, Benny
See Green, Bernard
Green, Bernard 1927-1998 .... 25-28R
Obituary 169
Green, Betty Radley 1926-1978
Obituary 111
Green, Brian
See Card, Orson Scott
Green, Bryan S(tuart) W(estmacott)
1901-1993 .... CAP-1
Obituary 140
Earlier sketch in CA 13-14
Green, Celia (Elizabeth) 1935- 65-68
Green, Charles H. 1950- 224
Green, Christine 211
Green, Cliff(ord) 1934- CANR-90
Earlier sketch in CA 131
See also SATA 126
Green, Connie Jordan 1938- 147
See also SATA 80
Green, Constance McLaughlin
1897-1975 .... 9-12R
Obituary 61-64
Green, Cynthia R(achel) 1961- 197
Green, D.
See Casewit, Curtis W(erner)
Green, Daniel W(illiam) E(dward) 1958- 121
Green, Daryl D. 1966- CANR-125
Earlier sketch in CA 169
See also BW 3
Green, David 1942- 77-80
Green, David Bronte 1910- 13-16R
Green, David M(arvin) 1932- 41-44R
Green, Deborah 1948- 104
Green, December 1961- 144
Green, Dennis Howard 1922- 110
Green, Dewayne
See Green, Daryl D.
Green, Donald E(dward) 1936- CANR-1
Earlier sketch in CA 45-48
Green, Donald Ross 1924- 37-40R
Green, Dorothy (Auchterlonie) 1915-1991 . 112
See also Auchterlonie, Dorothy
Green, Duff 1791-1875 .... DLB 43
Green, Duncan 1958- 154
Green, Edith Pinero 1929- CANR-15
Earlier sketch in CA 77-80
Green, Edward 1920- 13-16R
Green, Edwin 1948- CANR-38
Earlier sketch in CA 116
Green, Elisabeth Sara 1940- CANR-42
Green, Elizabeth A(dine) H(erkimer)
1906-1995 .... 21-24R
Green, Elizabeth Shippen 1871-1954 . DLB 188
See also SATA 139
Green, Elmer Ellsworth 1917- 103
Green, Elna C. 1959- 166
Green, Ernestene L(averne) 1939- 57-60
Green, Evelyn Everett
See Everett-Green, Evelyn
Green, F(rederick) C(harles) 1891-1964
Obituary 89-92
Green, Fitzhugh 1917-1990 77-80
Obituary 132
Green, Fletcher Melvin 1895-1978 .... CANR-6
Earlier sketch in CA 1-4R
Green, Frederick Pratt 1903-2000 102
Obituary 191
See also CP 1
Green, G. Dorsey 1949(?)- 231
Green, Galen 1949- 57-60
Green, George D(avid) 1938-
Brief entry 114
Green, George Dawes 1954- 196
Green, George MacEwan 1931- 81-84
Green, George S(herman) 1930- 97-100
Green, Georgia M. 1944- 93-96
Green, Gerald 1922- CANR-8
Earlier sketch in CA 13-16R
See also DLB 28
Green, Gil(bert) 1906-1997 73-76
Obituary 158
Green, H(enry) Gordon 1912-1991 110
Green, Hannah
See Greenberg, Joanne (Goldenberg)
Green, Hannah 1927(?)-1996 .... CANR-93
Earlier sketches in CA 73-76, CANR-59
See also CLC 3
See also NFS 10
Green, Harold P(aul) 1922- 13-16R
Green, Harvey 1946- CANR-37
Earlier sketch in CA 115
Green, Henry 175
See also Yorke, Henry Vincent
See also BRWS 2
See also CLC 2, 13, 97
See also DLB 15
See also EWL 3
See also RGEL 2
Green, Hollis Lynn 1933- 103
Green, J(ames) C. R. 1949- 104
Green, J. Paul 1929- 141
Green, James L(eroy) 1919- 17-20R
Green, James R(obert) 1944- 130
Green, (Charles Stuart) Jamison 1948- 232
Green, Jane 1937- 61-64
See also SATA 9
Green, Jane 1968- 232
Green, Jane Nugent 1918- 61-64
Green, Janet 1939- CANR-30
Earlier sketch in CA 112
Green, Jeffrey M. 1944- 140
Green, Jeffrey P(hillip) 1944- 111
Green, Jerome Frederic 1928- 125
Green, Jerry
See Green, Jerome Frederic
Green, Jesse 1958- CANR-88
Earlier sketch in CA 139
Green, Jim 1941- 114
Green, Joann 1938- 115
Green, Joey 1958- 182
Green, John Alden 1925- CANR-3
Earlier sketch in CA 5-8R
Green, John F. 1943- 126
Green, John L(afayette), Jr. 1929- CANR-22
Earlier sketch in CA 45-48
Green, Johnny 1908-1989 .... IDFW 3, 4
Green, Jonas 1712-1767 .... DLB 31
Green, Jonathan (William) 1939- CANR-9
Earlier sketch in CA 61-64
Green, Jonathan David 1964- 220
Green, Jonathon 1948- 134
Green, Joseph 1706-1780 .... DLB 31
Green, Joseph 1931- 29-32R
See also SFW 4
Green, Joseph F(ranklin), Jr. 1924- 13-16R
Green, Judith
See Galbraith, Jean and Rodriguez, Judith Green
Green, Julian
See Green, Julien (Hartridge)
See also CLC 3, 11, 77
See also EWL 3
See also GFL 1789 to the Present
See also MTCW 2
Green, Julien (Hartridge)
1900-1998 .... CANR-87
Obituary 169
Earlier sketches in CA 21-24R, CANR-33
See also Green, Julian
See also CWW 2
See also DLB 4, 72
See also MTCW 1, 2
See also MTFW 2005
Green, K. Gordon 1934- 210
Green, Kay 1927- CANR-41
Earlier sketch in CA 117
See also CAAS 11
Green, Kenneth Hart 1953- 162
Green, Landis K(night) 1940- 57-60
Green, Lawrence W(inter) 1940- CANR-42
Earlier sketches in CA 69-72, CANR-12
Green, Leslie Claude 1920- 13-16R
Green, Lewis 1946- 125
Green, Lewis W(allace) 1932- 119
Green, Louis 1929- 45-48
Green, Marc Edward 1943- CANR-42
Earlier sketch in CA 117
Green, Margaret (Murphy) 1926- CANR-1
Earlier sketch in CA 1-4R
Green, Maria A. 1922- 144
Green, Maria del Rosario
See Rosario Green (de Heller), Maria del
Green, Marilyn 1948- 187
Green, Mark J(oseph) 1945- 41-44R
Green, Martin (Burgess) 1927- CANR-125
Earlier sketches in CA 17-20R, CANR-9, 29, 56
Green, Martyn 1899-1975
Obituary 57-60
Green, Mary McBurney 1896-1985 ...... CAP-2
Earlier sketch in CA 29-32
Green, Mary Moore 1906- CAP-1
Earlier sketch in CA 13-14
See also SATA 11
Green, Matthew 1696-1737 .... RGEL 2
Green, Maureen Patricia 1933- 101
Green, (James) Maurice (Spurgeon) 1906-1987
Obituary 123
Green, Maurice B(erkeley) 1920- 77-80
Green, Maurice R(ichard) 1922- 13-16R
Green, Maury 1916-1996 155
Green, Michael Foster 1956- 223
Green, Michael Frederick 1927- CANR-41
Earlier sketches in CA 102, CANR-19
Green, Michelle 1953- 140
Green, Milton D(ouglas) 1903-1990 ..... 41-44R
Green, Miranda J(ane Aldhouse) 1947- 139
Green, Morton 1937- 57-60
See also SATA 8
Green, Norma B(erger) 1925- 41-44R
See also SATA 11
Green, Norman 1954- 227
Green, O. O.
See Durgnat, Raymond (Eric)
Green, Otis H(oward) 1898-1978 .... 9-12R
Green, Paul (Eliot) 1894-1981 .... CANR-3
Obituary 103
Earlier sketch in CA 5-8R
See also AITN 1
See also CAD
See also CLC 25
See also DAM DRAM
See also DLB 7, 9, 249
See also DLBY 1981
See also MAL 5
See also RGAL 4
Green, Paul E(dgar) 1927- CANR-51
Earlier sketches in CA 69-72, CANR-11, 27
Green, Peter
See Bulmer, (Henry) Kenneth
Green, Peter (Morris) 1924- CANR-4
Earlier sketch in CA 5-8R
See also CN 1, 2
See also RHW
Green, Phyllis 1932- CANR-17
Earlier sketches in CA 45-48, CANR-1
See also SATA 20
Green, R. P. H. 1943- 138
Green, Rayna (Diane) 1942- 114
Green, Reginald Herbold 1935- CANR-17
Earlier sketch in CA 25-28R
Green, Richard 1936-1989 159
Brief entry 111
See also AITN 1
Green, Richard Firth 1943- 186
Green, Richard Lancelyn (Gordon)
1953-2004 160
Obituary 226
Green, Ricky K(enneth) 1958- 211
Green, River
See Joyner, Stephen Christopher
Green, Robert
See Smith, Richard Rein
Green, Robert D(avid) 1942- 77-80
Green, Robert L(ee) 1933- CANR-15
Earlier sketch in CA 65-68
Green, Roger C(urtis) 1932- CANR-49
Earlier sketches in CA 45-48, CANR-24
Green, Roger James 1944- 123
See also SATA-Brief 52
Green, Roger (Gilbert) Lancelyn
1918-1987 .... CANR-2
Obituary 123
Earlier sketch in CA 1-4R
See also BYA 4
See also CWRI 5
See also SATA 2
See also SATA-Obit 53
Green, Roland (James) 1944- CANR-100
Earlier sketches in CA 77-80, CANR-58
See also FANT
Green, Ronald Michael 1942- 85-88
Green, Rosalie B(eth) 1917- 1-4R
Green, Rose Basile 1914- CANR-39
Earlier sketches in CA 41-44R, CANR-15
Green, (James Le)Roy 1948- .... SATA 89
Green, Samuel 1921(?)-1983
Obituary 111
Green, Samuel 1948- 77-80
Green, Scott E. 1951- CANR-91
Earlier sketch in CA 132
Green, Sharon 1942- CANR-136
Earlier sketches in CA 120, CANR-45
See also FANT
Green, Sharony Andrews 1967(?)- 168
Green, Sheila Ellen 1934- CANR-131
Earlier sketches in CA 1-4R, CANR-2, 17, 39, 53
See also SATA 8, 87, 148
See also YAW
Green, Sid(ney Charles) 1928-1999 183
Green, Simon
See Green, Simon R(ichard)
Green, Simon R(ichard) 1955- CANR-123
Earlier sketch in CA 164
See also FANT
Green, Smith Wendell 1917(?)-1987
Obituary 124
Green, Stanley 1923-1990 .... CANR-17
Obituary 133
Earlier sketches in CA 1-4R, CANR-1

Green, Stephen J(ohn) 1940- 131
Green, Susan 1941- 81-84
Green, Terence M(ichael) 1947- 215
Earlier sketch in CA 157
Autobiographical Essay in 215
See also DLB 251
See also SFW 4
Green, Thomas Andrew 1940- 125
Green, Thomas F. 1927- 57-60
Green, Thomas Hill 1836-1882 . DLB 190, 262
Green, Thomas J(ohn) 1946- 113
Green, Tim 1963- 192
Green, Timothy (Seton) 1936- CANR-22
Earlier sketches in CA 49-52, CANR-5
Green, Timothy 1953- 155
See also SATA 91
Green, Toby 1974- 231
Green, Vincent S(cott) 1953- 140
Green, Vivian (Hubert Howard)
1915-2005 .... 9-12R
Obituary 235
Green, Walon 1936- 237
Green, William 1926- 53-56
Green, William A., Jr. 1935- 85-88
Green, William Baillie 1927- 118
Green, William M(ark) 1929- CANR-35
Earlier sketch in CA 45-48
Greenacre, Phyllis 1894-1989 .... 5-8R
Greenall, Jack 1905-1983
Obituary 110
Greenawalt, R(obert) Kent 1936- 33-36R
Greenaway, George W(illiam) 1903- 118
Greenaway, Gladys 1901- 93-96
Greenaway, Kate 1846-1901 137
See also AAYA 56
See also CLR 6
See also DLB 141
See also MAICYA 1, 2
See also SATA 100
See also YABC 2
Greenaway, Peter 1942- 127
See also CLC 159
Greenbank, Anthony Hunt 1933- CANR-19
Earlier sketches in CA 49-52, CANR-4
See also SATA 39
Greenbaum, Beth Aviv 1951- 236
Greenbaum, Everett 1919-1999 186
Greenbaum, Fred 1930- 37-40R
Greenbaum, Leonard 1930- 21-24R
Greenbaum, Sidney 1929-1996 ...... CANR-33
Obituary 152
Earlier sketches in CA 33-36R, CANR-15
Greenberg, Alfred Henry 1924-1990
Obituary 131
Greenberg, Alvin (David) 1932- 183
Earlier sketch in CA 33-36R
Greenberg, Arthur
See Granit, Arthur
Greenberg, Barbara L(evenson) 1932- 53-56
Greenberg, Bernard 1922- 69-72
Greenberg, Bernard L(ouis) 1917-1997 . 41-44R
Greenberg, Bradley S(ander) 1934- 104
Greenberg, Carl 1908-1984
Obituary 114
Greenberg, Cheryl Lynn 1958- 140
Greenberg, Clement 1909-1994 .... CANR-93
Obituary 145
Earlier sketches in CA 1-4R, CANR-2
Greenberg, Daniel A. 1934- 5-8R
Greenberg, Daniel S. 1931- CANR-117
Earlier sketch in CA 29-32R
Greenberg, Dolores 1934- 112
Greenberg, Douglas 1947- 117
Greenberg, Edward (Seymour) 1942- 53-56
Greenberg, Eliezer 1897(?)-1977
Obituary 69-72
Greenberg, Elinor Miller 1932- 143
Greenberg, Eric Rolfe 1945- 114
Greenberg, Gerald S. 1946- 175
Greenberg, Harvey R. 1935- 33-36R
See also SATA 5
Greenberg, Herbert 1935- 25-28R
Greenberg, Ira A(rthur) 1924- CANR-2
Earlier sketch in CA 49-52
Greenberg, Ivan 1908-1973 85-88
See also Rahv, Philip
Greenberg, Jae W. 1894(?)-1974
Obituary 104
Greenberg, James B(rian) 1945- 105
Greenberg, Jan 1942- 196
See also JRDA
See also SATA 61, 125
Greenberg, Jan W(eingarten) 1943- 118
Greenberg, Jay (R.) 1942- 137
Greenberg, Joanne (Goldenberg)
1932- CANR-69
Earlier sketches in CA 5-8R, CANR-14, 32
See also AAYA 12, 67
See also CLC 7, 30
See also CN 6, 7
See also SATA 25
See also YAW
Greenberg, Jonathan D. 1958- 133
Greenberg, Joseph Harold 1915-2001 102
Obituary 196
Greenberg, Judith Anne
See Azrael, Judith Anne
Greenberg, Kenneth R(ay) 1930- 57-60
Greenberg, Kenneth S. 1947- CANR-142
Earlier sketch in CA 124
Greenberg, Louis M. 1933-
Brief entry 112
Greenberg, Martin 1918- 140
Greenberg, Martin Harry 1941- CANR-121
Earlier sketch in CA 49-52
Greenberg, Martin J. 1945- 131
Greenberg, Melanie Hope 1954- .... SATA 72
Greenberg, Milton 1927- 25-28R
Greenberg, Morrie
See Greenberg, Morris S.
Greenberg, Morris S. 1924- 33-36R
Greenberg, Moshe 1928- 13-16R
Greenberg, Norman 1945- 129
Greenberg, Paul 1937- CANR-123
Earlier sketch in CA 69-72
Greenberg, Paul 1967- 214
Greenberg, Pearl 1927- 93-96
Greenberg, Peter 232
Greenberg, Polly 1932- 85-88
See also SATA 52
See also SATA-Brief 43
Greenberg, Richard 1959(?)- 138
See also CAD
See also CD 5, 6
See also CLC 57
Greenberg, Robert Arthur 1930-1989 . CANR-4
Obituary 129
Earlier sketch in CA 1-4R
Greenberg, Roger P(aul) 1941- CANR-90
Earlier sketch in CA 131
Greenberg, Selig 1904-1988 49-52
Greenberg, Selma (Weintraub)
1930-1997 .... 29-32R
Obituary 158
Greenberg, Sidney 1917- CANR-3
Earlier sketch in CA 9-12R
Greenberg, Simon 1901-1993 .... CANR-14
Obituary 142
Earlier sketch in CA 77-80
Greenberg, Stan 1931- 119
Greenberg, Stanley Bernard 1945- 53-56
Greenberg, Uri Zvi 1896-1981
Obituary 103
See also EWL 3
Greenberger, Allen J(ay) 1937- 41-44R
Greenberger, Evelyn Barish
See Barish, Evelyn
Greenberger, Howard 1924- 45-48
Greenberger, Martin 1931- CANR-8
Earlier sketch in CA 61-64
Greenbie, Barrie B(arstow) 1920-1998 107
Greenbie, Marjorie Barstow 1889(?)-1976
Obituary 61-64
Greenblat, Cathy S(tein) 1940- 133
Brief entry 118
Greenblat, Rodney Alan 1960- 176
See also SATA 106
Greenblatt, Augusta 1912-1994 .... CANR-6
Earlier sketch in CA 57-60
Greenblatt, Edwin 1920- 49-52
Greenblatt, M(anuel) H(arry)
1922-1972 .... CAP-2
Earlier sketch in CA 17-18
Greenblatt, Richard 1952- 130
Greenblatt, Robert Benjamin
1906-1987 .... CAP-1
Obituary 123
Earlier sketch in CA 11-12
Greenblatt, Stephen J(ay) 1943- CANR-115
Earlier sketch in CA 49-52
See also CLC 70
Greenblum, Joseph 1925- 21-24R
Greenburg, Dan 1936- CANR-25
Earlier sketches in CA 13-16R, CANR-9
See also SATA 102
Greenburger, Francis 1949- 85-88
Greenburger, Ingrid Elisabeth 1913-2001 ... 104
Greene, Adam
See Scott, Peter Dale
Greene, Alvin Carl 1923-2002 .... CANR-92
Obituary 205
Earlier sketches in CA 37-40R, CANR-14
Greene, Anthony Hamilton Millard Kirk
See Kirk-Greene, Anthony (Hamilton Millard)
Greene, Asa 1789-1838 .... DLB 11
Greene, Belle da Costa 1883-1950 .... DLB 187
Greene, Bert 1923-1988 .... CANR-27
Obituary 125
Earlier sketches in CA 57-60, CANR-6
Greene, Bette 1934- CANR-4
Earlier sketch in CA 53-56
See also AAYA 7
See also BYA 3
See also CLC 30
See also CLR 2
See also CWRI 5
See also JRDA
See also LAIT 4
See also MAICYA 1, 2
See also NFS 10
See also SAAS 16
See also SATA 8, 102, 161
See also WYA
See also YAW
Greene, Bob
See Greene, Robert Bernard, Jr.
Greene, Bob (W.) 238
Greene, Carla 1916- CANR-1
Earlier sketch in CA 1-4R
See also SATA 1, 67
Greene, Carol 134
See also SATA 66, 102
See also SATA-Brief 44
Greene, Charles Jerome 1910-1983
Obituary 110
Greene, Constance C(larke) 1924- ... CANR-38
Earlier sketches in CA 61-64, CANR-8
See also AAYA 7
See also CLR 62
See also CWRI 5
See also JRDA
See also MAICYA 1, 2
See also SAAS 11
See also SATA 11, 72
Greene, David B(eckwith) 1939- 117
Greene, David H. 1913- 21-24R
Greene, David L(ouis) 1944-
Brief entry 114
Greene, David M(ason) 1920- 118
Greene, Don 201
Greene, Donald J(ohnson)
1916-1997 .... CANR-2
Obituary 158
Earlier sketch in CA 1-4R
Greene, Douglas G. 1944- CANR-132
Earlier sketch in CA 164
Greene, Ellin 1927- 77-80
See also SATA 23
Greene, Felix 1909-1985 .... CANR-83
Obituary 116
Earlier sketches in CA 1-4R, CANR-6
Greene, Fred
See Cadet, John
Greene, Gael CANR-10
Earlier sketch in CA 13-16R
See also CLC 8
Greene, Gayle (Jacoba) 1943- CANR-93
Earlier sketch in CA 137
Greene, Gloria
See Johnson, Doris
Greene, Graham (Henry)
1904-1991 .... CANR-131
Obituary 133
Earlier sketches in CA 13-16R, CANR-35, 61
See also AAYA 61
See also AITN 2
See also BPFB 2
See also BRWR 2
See also BRWS 1
See also BYA 3
See also CBD
See also CDBLB 1945-1960
See also CLC 1, 3, 6, 9, 14, 18, 27, 37, 70, 72, 125
See also CMW 4
See also CN 1, 2, 3, 4
See also DA
See also DA3
See also DAB
See also DAC
See also DAM MST, NOV
See also DLB 13, 15, 77, 100, 162, 201, 204
See also DLBY 1991
See also EWL 3
See also MSW
See also MTCW 1, 2
See also MTFW 2005
See also NFS 16
See also RGEL 2
See also SATA 20
See also SSC 29
See also SSFS 14
See also TEA
See also WLC
See also WLIT 4
Greene, Harlan 1953- 137
See also GLL 1
Greene, Harris 1921- 13-16R
Greene, Harry A. 1889-1974 .... CAP-2
Earlier sketch in CA 17-18
Greene, Harry J(oseph) 1906-1995 57-60
Greene, Herbert 1898- CAP-1
Earlier sketch in CA 9-10
Greene, Howard R. 1937- 61-64
Greene, Hugh (Carleton)
1910-1987 .... CANR-82
Obituary 121
Earlier sketch in CA 102
Greene, Jack P(hillip) 1931- CANR-40
Earlier sketches in CA 9-12R, CANR-3, 18
Greene, Jacqueline Dembar 1946- 144
See also SATA 76, 131
Greene, James H. 1915- 17-20R
Greene, Janet (Churchill) 1917- 5-8R
Greene, Janice Presser
See Presser, Janice
Greene, Jay E(lihu) 1914- CANR-5
Earlier sketch in CA 5-8R
Greene, Jerry
See Greene, Charles Jerome
Greene, John C(olton) 1917- CANR-88
Earlier sketch in CA 89-92
Greene, John Robert 1955- 191
Greene, John William, Jr. 1946- 89-92
Greene, Johnny
See Greene, John William, Jr.
Greene, Jonathan Edward 1943- CANR-12
Earlier sketch in CA 33-36R
See also CP 1, 2, 3, 4, 5, 6, 7
Greene, Laura Offenhartz 1935- CANR-47
Earlier sketches in CA 107, CANR-23
See also SATA 38
Greene, Lawrence J. 1943- CANR-141
Earlier sketch in CA 113
Greene, Lee S(eifert) 1905-1986 .... CANR-5
Earlier sketch in CA 13-16R
Greene, Leonard M(ichael) 1918- 109
Greene, Lorenzo Johnston 1899-1988
Obituary 124
Greene, Lyn 1954(?)- 171
Greene, Mabel
See Bean, Mabel Greene
Greene, Mark R. 1923- CANR-5
Earlier sketch in CA 1-4R
Greene, Maxine 1917- CANR-13
Earlier sketch in CA 21-24R
Greene, Meg
See Malvasi, Meg Greene
Greene, Melissa Fay 1952- CANR-127
Earlier sketch in CA 138
See also CSW
Greene, Mott T(uthill) 1945- CANR-28
Earlier sketch in CA 110
Greene, Naomi 1942- CANR-91
Earlier sketch in CA 45-48
Greene, Nathanael 1935- 25-28R
Greene, Owen (John) 1954- 124
Greene, Pamela
See Forman, Joan
Greene, Philip L(eon) 1924-1993 219
Brief entry 113
Greene, Reynolds W(illiam), Jr.
1924- CANR-2
Earlier sketch in CA 5-8R
Greene, Rhonda Gowler 1955- CANR-135
Earlier sketch in CA 168
See also SATA 101, 160
Greene, Richard (Thomas) 1961- 144
Greene, Richard C. 1941- 111
Greene, Richard Leighton
1904-1983 .... CANR-2
Obituary 111
Earlier sketch in CA 5-8R
Greene, Robert
See Deindorfer, Robert Greene
Greene, Robert 1558-1592 .... BRWS 8
See also DLB 62, 167
See also IDTP
See also RGEL 2
See also TEA
Greene, Robert Bernard, Jr. 1947- CANR-77
Earlier sketches in CA 107, CANR-27
Interview in CANR-27
See also DLB 185
Greene, Robert W. 1929- 104
Greene, Robert W(illiam) 1933-
Brief entry 111
Greene, Ruth Altman 1896-1986 73-76
Greene, Sara
See Strong, June
Greene, Sheldon L. 1934- 132
Greene, Shirley E(dward) 1911-1996 .... 1-4R
Greene, Stanley A. 1929- CANR-122
Earlier sketch in CA 170
Greene, Stephanie 1953- 61-64
See also SATA 127
Greene, Stephen 1914-1979
Obituary 89-92
Greene, Thomas M(cLernon) 1926- 9-12R
Greene, Victor R(obert) 1933- 25-28R
Greene, Virginia A. 1959- 222
Greene, Vivian .... AITN 2
Greene, Wade 1933- .... SATA 11
Greene, Walter E. 1929- 25-28R
Greene, Wilda 1911- CANR-9
Earlier sketch in CA 21-24R
Greene, William C. 1933- 13-16R
Greene, Yvonne
See Flesch, Yolande (Catarina)
Greenebaum, Louise G(uggenheim)
1919-2004 69-72
Obituary 223
Greener, Leslie 1900-1974 .... CAP-2
Earlier sketch in CA 21-22
Greener, Michael (John) 1931- 25-28R
Greenewalt, Crawford Hallock
1902-1993 .... CANR-2
Obituary 142
Earlier sketch in CA 1-4R
Greenfeder, Paul 1925(?)-1983
Obituary 109
Greenfeld, Howard (Scheinman)
1928- CANR-119
Earlier sketches in CA 81-84, CANR-19
See also SATA 19, 140
Greenfeld, Josh(ua Joseph) 1928- 140
Brief entry 116
See also SATA 62
Greenfeld, Karl Taro 1964(?)- CANR-134
Earlier sketch in CA 149
Greenfeld, Liah 1954- CANR-120
Earlier sketch in CA 138
Greenfield, Darby
See Ward, Philip
Greenfield, Edward 1928-
Brief entry 110
Greenfield, Eloise 1929- CANR-127
Earlier sketches in CA 49-52, CANR-1, 19, 43
Interview in CANR-19
See also BW 2
See also CLR 4, 38
See also CWRI 5
See also JRDA
See also MAICYA 1, 2
See also SAAS 16
See also SATA 19, 61, 105, 155
Greenfield, Gerald Michael 1943- 114
Greenfield, Harry I. 1922- 127
Brief entry 109
Greenfield, Howard 1937(?)-1986
Obituary 118
Greenfield, Irving A. 1928- 33-36R
Greenfield, James Lloyd 1924- 73-76
Greenfield, Jeanette 134
Greenfield, Jeff 1943- CANR-71
Earlier sketches in CA 37-40R, CANR-24
Greenfield, Jerome 1923- 5-8R
Greenfield, Jerry
See Greenfield, Jerome
Greenfield, Jonas Carl 1926-
Brief entry 110
Greenfield, Meg 1930-1999 128
Obituary 179
Brief entry 123
Greenfield, Norman S(amuel) 1923- 41-44R
Greenfield, Patricia Marks 1940- CANR-24
Earlier sketches in CA 21-24R, CANR-9
Greenfield, Sidney M(artin) 1932- 21-24R

Cumulative Index 233 Greinke

Greenfield, Stanley B(rian) 1922-1987 .... 9-12R
Greenfield, Thelma N. 1922- 25-28R
Greengold, Jane
  See Stevens, Jane Greengold
Greengrass, Mark 1949- 118
Greengroin, Artie
  See Brown, Harry (Peter McNab, Jr.)
Greenhalgh, P(eter) A(ndrew) L(ivsey) 1945- CANR-1
  Earlier sketch in CA 49-52
Greenhalgh, Paul 1955- CANR-113
  Earlier sketch in CA 130
Greenhall, Ken 1928- CANR-139
  Earlier sketch in CA 173
Greenhaus, Thelma Nurenberg 1903-1984 .... CANR-42
  Obituary 113
  See also SATA-Obit 45
Greenhaw, H(arold) Wayne 1940- CANR-24
  Earlier sketches in CA 21-24R, CANR-9
Greenhill, Basil (Jack) 1920-2003 ..... CANR-38
  Obituary 215
  Earlier sketches in CA 5-8R, CANR-2, 17
Greenhill, Pauline 1955- CANR-101
  Earlier sketch in CA 149
Greenhood, (Clarence) David 1895-1983 . 1-4R
  Obituary 109
Greenhouse, Carol J(ane) 1950- 163
Greenhouse, Linda 1947- 77-80
Greenhow, Robert 1800-1854 .... DLB 30
Greenhut, Melvin L. 1921- 13-16R
Greening, Hamilton
  See Hamilton, Charles (Harold St. John)
Greening, John 1954- 226
Greenland, Colin 1954- CANR-56
  Earlier sketch in CA 117
  See also FANT
  See also SFW 4
Greenlaw, Jean-Pierre 1910- 69-72
Greenlaw, Lavinia (Elaine) 1962- CANR-118
  Earlier sketch in CA 153
  See also CP 7
  See also CWP
Greenlaw, Linda 1960- 189
  See also AAYA 47
Greenlaw, M. Jean 1941- .... SATA 107
Greenlaw, Paul S(tephen) 1930- CANR-5
  Earlier sketch in CA 1-4R
Greenleaf, Barbara Kaye 1942- 29-32R
  See also SATA 6
Greenleaf, Peter 1910-1997 85-88
  See also SATA 33
Greenleaf, Richard Edward 1930- 25-28R
Greenleaf, Robert Kiefner 1904-1990 125
Greenleaf, Stephen (Howell) 1942- .. CANR-95
  Earlier sketch in CA 102
  See also CMW 4
Greenleaf, William 1917-1975 .... 9-12R
  See also SFW 4
Greenlee, Douglas 1935-1979 45-48
  Obituary 103
Greenlee, J(acob) Harold 1918- 17-20R
Greenlee, James W(allace) 1933- CANR-11
  Earlier sketch in CA 69-72
Greenlee, Sam 1930- 69-72
  See also BW 1
Greenlee, Sharon 1935- 145
  See also SATA 77
Greenlee, William B. 1872-1953 .... DLB 187
Greenlee, William Brooks 1872-1953 200
Greenlick, Merwyn R(onald) 1935- 41-44R
Greenman, Robert 1939- CANR-38
  Earlier sketch in CA 115
Greenman, Russell Lester 1904-1983
  Obituary 111
Greeno, Gayle 1949- 149
  See also SATA 81
Greenough, Horatio 1805-1852 ..... DLB 1, 235
Greenough, Malcolm W(helen), Jr. 1926- ... 128
Greenough, Sarah 1951- CANR-136
  Earlier sketch in CA 126
Greenough, William Croan 1914-1989 . 13-16R
  Obituary 130
Greenseid, Diane 1948- .... SATA 93
Greenside, Mark 1944- 159
Greenslade, Roy 1946- 146
Greenslade, S(tanley) L(awrence) 1905-1977
  Obituary 111
Greenson, Ralph R(omeo) 1911-1979
  Brief entry 114
Greenspan, Bud 1927- 103
Greenspan, Cappy Petrash
  See Greenspan, Constance Anne Petrash
Greenspan, Charlotte L. 1921-1988 ...... 33-36R
Greenspan, Constance Anne Petrash 1932(?)-1983
  Obituary 110
Greenspan, David 1956- .... CAD
  See also CD 5, 6
Greenspan, Elaine 1929- 110
Greenspan, Emily
  See Shapiro, Ann R.
Greenspan, Emily 1953- 124
Greenspan, Sophie 1906-1990 97-100
Greenspan, Stanley I(ra) 1941- CANR-119
  Earlier sketch in CA 154
Greenspoon, Leonard J(ay) 1945- CANR-30
  Earlier sketch in CA 111
Greenspun, Adele Aron 1938- .... SATA 76, 142
Greenspun, H(erman) M(ilton) 1909-1989 .... CAP-2
  Obituary 129
  Earlier sketch in CA 21-22
  See also AITN 2
Greenspun, Hank
  See Greenspun, H(erman) M(ilton)
Greenspun, Roger (Austin) 1929- 102
Greenstein, Elaine 1959- .... SATA 82, 150
Greenstein, Fred I(rwin) 1930- CANR-4
  Earlier sketch in CA 49-52
Greenstein, George 1940- CANR-92
  Earlier sketch in CA 130
Greenstein, Jack 1915- 130
Greenstock, David Lionel 1912-1990 ..... 9-12R
Greenstone, J. David 1937- 25-28R
Greentree, Leslie 1966- 229
Greenup, Ruth (Robinson) 1912(?)-1984
  Obituary 113
Greenwald, G. Jonathan 1943- 142
Greenwald, Harold 1910-1999 .... CANR-4
  Obituary 177
  Earlier sketch in CA 1-4R
Greenwald, Jeff 1954- CANR-111
  Earlier sketch in CA 153
Greenwald, Jerry 1923- 57-60
Greenwald, Marilyn S. 1954- 233
Greenwald, Ricky 1958- 239
Greenwald, Sheila
  See Green, Sheila Ellen
Green-Wanstall, Kenneth 1918- 13-16R
Greenway, Hugh D(avids) S(cott) 1935- .. 73-76
Greenway, John 1919-1991 .... 9-12R
Greenway, Roger S(elles) 1934- CANR-4
  Earlier sketch in CA 53-56
Greenwell, Dora 1821-1882 .... DLB 35, 199
Greenwood, (Arthur) Alexander 1920- 180
Greenwood, Barbara 1940- CANR-118
  Earlier sketch in CA 134
  See also SATA 90, 129
Greenwood, David Charles 1927-1984 ... 61-64
  Obituary 112
Greenwood, Duncan 1919- 21-24R
Greenwood, Ed 1959- 192
Greenwood, Edward Alister 1930- ... CANR-30
  Earlier sketches in CA 29-32R, CANR-12
  See also CWRI 5
Greenwood, Frank 1924- CANR-10
  Earlier sketch in CA 25-28R
Greenwood, Gordon 1913- CANR-9
  Earlier sketch in CA 21-24R
Greenwood, Gordon E(dward) 1935- 37-40R
Greenwood, Grace
  See Lippincott, Sara Jane Clarke
Greenwood, Judith Goodwin 1941- 144
Greenwood, Julia Eileen Courtney 1910- CAP-1
  Earlier sketch in CA 13-14
Greenwood, Kathryn Moore 1922- 93-96
Greenwood, Kerry 1954- 221
Greenwood, Leigh 1942- 225
Greenwood, Lillian Bethel 1932- 104
Greenwood, Marianne (Hederstrom) 1926- CANR-6
  Earlier sketch in CA 9-12R
Greenwood, Ned H. 1932-
  Brief entry 110
Greenwood, Pamela D. 1944- 186
  See also SATA 115
Greenwood, Pippa 209
Greenwood, Ted
  See Greenwood, Edward Alister
Greenwood, Theresa 1936- 29-32R
Greenwood, Val D(avid) 1937- 73-76
Greenwood, Walter 1903-1974 93-96
  Obituary 53-56
  See also CBD
  See also DLB 10, 191
  See also RGEL 2
Greer, Andrew Sean 1970- 235
Greer, Ann Lennarson 1944- CANR-43
  Earlier sketch in CA 53-56
Greer, Art(hur Ellis, Jr.) 1929- 81-84
Greer, Ben 1948- 102
  See also DLB 6
Greer, Carlotta C(herryholmes) 1879-1965 .... CAP-1
  Earlier sketch in CA 13-16
Greer, Francesca
  See Janas, Frankie-Lee
Greer, Georgeanna H(errmann) 1922-1992 .... CANR-6
  Earlier sketch in CA 57-60
Greer, Germaine 1939- CANR-133
  Earlier sketches in CA 81-84, CANR-33, 70, 115
  See also AITN 1
  See also CLC 131
  See also FW
  See also MTCW 1, 2
  See also MTFW 2005
Greer, Herb 1929- CANR-8
  Earlier sketch in CA 5-8R
Greer, Jack
  See Barrett, Geoffrey John
Greer, Jane 1951- 199
Greer, Louise 1899-1966 .... CAP-1
  Earlier sketch in CA 13-16
Greer, Pedro Jose, Jr. 1956- 192
Greer, Philip 1930-1985
  Obituary 116
Greer, Rebecca Ellen 1935- 103
Greer, Richard
  See Garrett, (Gordon) Randall (Phillip) and Silverberg, Robert
Greer, Rita 1942- 97-100
Greer, Robert O. 172
Greer, Scott (Allen) 1922-1996 .... CANR-43
  Earlier sketch in CA 45-48
Greer, Steven (Crawford) 1956- CANR-102
  Earlier sketch in CA 149
Greer, Thomas H(oag) 1914- 21-24R
Greeson, Janet 1952- 121
Greet, Brian Aubrey 1922- 105
Greet, Kenneth (Gerald) 1918- CANR-25
  Earlier sketches in CA 5-8R, CANR-6
Greet, T(homas) Y(oung) 1923-1990 ..... 13-16R
Greet, William Cabell 1901-1972
  Obituary 37-40R
Greetham, D(avid) C. 1941- 176
Greever, William S(t. Clair) 1916- 5-8R
Greeves, Frederic 1903-1985
  Obituary 115
Greevy, David U(pton) 1953- 112
Greflinger, Georg 1620(?)-1677 .... DLB 164
Greg, W. R. 1809-1881 .... DLB 55
Greg, W(alter) W(ilson) 1875-1959 183
  See also DLB 201
Greger, Debora 1949- CANR-31
  Earlier sketch in CA 112
Gregersen, Edgar (Alstrup) 1937- 120
Gregersen, Era 219
Gregerson, Linda (K.) 1950- CANR-108
  Earlier sketch in CA 149
Gregg, Andrew K. 1929- CANR-15
  Earlier sketch in CA 29-32R
  See also SATA 81
Gregg, Charles T(hornton) 1927- CANR-40
  Earlier sketches in CA 81-84, CANR-14
  See also SATA 65
Gregg, Clark 1962- 234
Gregg, Davis W(einert) 1918-1993 .... 17-20R
  Obituary 143
Gregg, Hubert (Robert Harry) 1914-2004 ... 102
  Obituary 226
Gregg, James E(rwin) 1927- 21-24R
Gregg, James R. 1914- 21-24R
Gregg, Jess 1926- 61-64
Gregg, John E(dwin) 1925- 45-48
Gregg, Josiah 1806-1850 .... DLB 183, 186
Gregg, Larry
  See Leighton, Lauren G(ray)
Gregg, Linda (Alouise) 1942- CANR-88
  Earlier sketch in CA 113
  See also PFS 20
Gregg, Martin
  See McNeilly, Wilfred (Glassford)
Gregg, Pauline 5-8R
Gregg, Richard A(lexander) 1927- 13-16R
Gregg, Robert J(ohn) 1912-
  Brief entry 110
Gregg, Walter H(arold) 1919- 73-76
  See also SATA 20
Gregg, William H. 1904(?)-1983
  Obituary 109
Gregor, A(nthony) James 1929- CANR-99
  Earlier sketch in CA 57-60
Gregor, Arthur 1923- CANR-11
  Earlier sketch in CA 25-28R
  See also CAAS 10
  See also CLC 9
  See also CP 1, 2, 3, 4, 5, 6, 7
  See also SATA 36
Gregor, Carol 1943- 117
Gregor, Howard F(rank) 1920-2000 ... CANR-2
  Earlier sketch in CA 5-8R
Gregor, Lee
  See Pohl, Frederik
Gregor, Neil 169
Gregor, Rex H. 1922- 13-16R
Gregor-Dellin, Martin 1926- 157
Gregori, Leon 1919- .... SATA 15
Gregorian, Joyce Ballou 1946-1991 . CANR-24
  Obituary 147
  Earlier sketch in CA 107
  See also FANT
  See also SATA 30
  See also SATA-Obit 83
Gregorian, Vartan 1934- CANR-131
  Earlier sketch in CA 29-32R
Gregorich, Barbara 1943- CANR-42
  Earlier sketch in CA 117
  See also SATA 66
Gregorios, Paulos Mar 1922- CANR-11
  Earlier sketch in CA 25-28R
Gregorowski, Christopher 1940- CANR-15
  Earlier sketch in CA 89-92
  See also SATA 30
Gregory, Andre 1934- 207
Gregory, Bettina 1946- 69-72
Gregory, Chuck
  See Gnaegy, Charles
Gregory, Desmond 1916- 205
Gregory, Diana (Jean) 1933- 97-100
  See also SATA 49
  See also SATA-Brief 42
Gregory, Dick 1932- CANR-7
  Earlier sketch in CA 45-48
  Interview in CANR-7
  See also BW 1
Gregory, Elizabeth
  See Gilford, C(harles) B(ernard)
Gregory, Frederick 1942- 138
Gregory, Freida 1938- 69-72
Gregory, George H(arland) 1913-1996 214
Gregory, H(ollingsworth) F(ranklin) 1906-1978 69-72
Gregory, Harry
  See Gottfried, Theodore Mark
Gregory, Hilton
  See Ferguson, Charles W.
Gregory, Horace (Victor) 1898-1982 .... CANR-22
  Obituary 106
  Earlier sketches in CA 5-8R, CANR-3
  See also CP 1, 2
  See also DLB 18
  See also MAL 5
  See also RGAL 4
Gregory, Lady Isabella Augusta (Persse) 1852-1932 184
  Brief entry 104
  See also BRW 6
  See also DLB 10
  See also IDTP
  See also RGEL 2
  See also TCLC 1
Gregory, J. Dennis
  See Williams, John A(lfred)
Gregory, J. S.
  See Gregory, James S(tothert)
Gregory, Jackson 1882-1943 .... TCWW 1, 2
Gregory, James S(tothert) 1912-1983 77-80
  Obituary 133
Gregory, Jean
  See Ure, Jean
Gregory, Jill
  See Camp, Candace (Pauline)
Gregory, Jill 215
Gregory, John
  See Hoskins, Robert (Phillip)
Gregory, K(enneth) J(ohn) 1938- 107
Gregory, Kenneth (Malcolm) 1921-2001 . 73-76
  Obituary 193
Gregory, Kristiana 1951- CANR-115
  Earlier sketch in CA 141
  See also SATA 74, 136
Gregory, Lester
  See Gribble, Leonard (Reginald)
Gregory, Lisa
  See Camp, Candace (Pauline)
Gregory, Lydia
  See Carey, Diane
Gregory, Mark
  See Burch, Monte G.
Gregory, Nan 1944- .... MAICYA 2
  See also SATA 148
Gregory, Patrick 239
Gregory, Paul Roderick 1941- 53-56
Gregory, Peter 1924- 41-44R
Gregory, Philippa 1954- CANR-88
  Earlier sketch in CA 131
  See also RHW
  See also SATA 122
Gregory, R(ichard) L(angton) 1923- 57-60
Gregory, Raymond F. 1927- 197
Gregory, Richard Claxton
  See Gregory, Dick
Gregory, Robert G(ranville) 1924- 41-44R
Gregory, Robert Lloyd 1892-1983 .... 29-32R
Gregory, Roberta 1953- 228
Gregory, Ross 1933- 29-32R
Gregory, Roy 1935- 37-40R
Gregory, Ruth W(ilhelmine) 1910-2001 .. 77-80
Gregory, Sara
  See Gray, A(lbert) W(illiam)
Gregory, Sean
  See Hossent, Harry
Gregory, Sinda 1947- 115
Gregory, Stephan
  See Pendleton, Don(ald Eugene)
Gregory, Stephen
  See Penzler, Otto
Gregory, Stephen 1952- 136
Gregory, Steven
  See Jones, Stephen
Gregory, Susan 1945- 108
Gregory, Thomas B(ernard) 1940- 45-48
Gregory, Timothy E(dmund) 1943- 111
Gregory, Vahan 1927- 69-72
Gregory, Valiska 1940- CANR-138
  Earlier sketch in CA 149
  See also SATA 82
Gregory, Vicki L. 1950- 202
Gregory, Violet L(efler) 1907-1991 ..... CANR-8
  Earlier sketch in CA 57-60
Gregory, William King 1876-1970
  Obituary 29-32R
Gregory, Yvonne 1919(?)-1979
  Obituary 89-92
Gregory of Rimini 1300(?)-1358 .... DLB 115
Gregson, Lee F. .... TCWW 2
Gregson, Paul
  See Oakley, Eric Gilbert
Gregston, Gene 1925- 81-84
Grehan, Ida 1916- CANR-93
  Earlier sketch in CA 146
Greider, William (Harold) 1936- CANR-143
  Earlier sketches in CA 117, CANR-41, 71
  Interview in CA-117
Greif, E(dwin) Charles 1915- 1-4R
Greif, Geoffrey L. 1949- 140
Greif, Martin 1938-1996 .... CANR-25
  Earlier sketches in CA 65-68, CANR-10
Greiff, Barrie S(anford) 1935- 134
  Brief entry 114
Greiff, Leon de 1895-1976 .... DLB 283
Greiffenberg, Catharina Regina von 1633-1694 .... DLB 168
Greig, Andrew 1951- 187
Greig, Cicely (?)-1983
  Obituary 116
Greig, Maysie 1902-1971 102
  Obituary 104
  See also RHW
Greig, Noel 1944- .... DLB 245
Greig, Solveig Fredriksen
  See Grieg, Solveig Christov
Greil, Arthur L(awrence) 1949- 139
Greimas, A. J.
  See Greimas, Algirdas Julien
Greimas, Algirdas Julien 1917- 132
Greiner, Donald J(ames) 1940- CANR-37
  Earlier sketches in CA 45-48, CANR-1, 16
Greiner, Hoard W. 1923- 177
Greinke, (Lawrence) Eric 1948- 41-44R

Greisman, Joan Ruth 1937- ... 103
See also SATA 31
Grekova, I.
See Ventsel, Elena Sergeevna
See also CLC 59
See also CWW 2
Grekova, Irina
See Ventsel, Elena Sergeevna
See also DLB 302
Grele, Ronald J(ohn) 1934- ... 73-76
Grell, Mike 1947- ... 199
Grelsamer, Ronald P. 1953- ... 227
Gremillion, Joseph 1919- ... 102
Gremmels, Marion Louise Chapman
1924-1987 ... 111
Obituary ... 142
Grenander, M(ary) E(lizabeth)
1918-1998 ... CANR-4
Obituary ... 167
Earlier sketch in CA 53-56
Grendahl, J(ay) Spencer 1943- ... 29-32R
Grendler, Paul F(rederick) 1936- ... 41-44R
Grendon, Edward
See LeShan, Lawrence L(ee)
Grendon, Stephen
See Derleth, August (William)
Grene, Marjorie (Glicksman) 1910- .. CANR-25
Earlier sketches in CA 13-16R, CANR-8
Grenelle, Lisa
See Munroe, Elizabeth L(ee)
Grenfell, Joyce (Irene) 1910-1979 ... CANR-20
Obituary ... 89-92
Earlier sketch in CA 81-84
Grenfell, Wilfred Thomason 1865-1940 ... 178
See also DLB 92
Grenham, John 1954- ... 146
Grenier, Judson A(chille) 1930- ... 89-92
Grenier, Mildred 1917- ... CANR-12
Earlier sketch in CA 29-32R
Grenier, Roger 1919- ... 204
Grennan, Eamon 1941- ... CANR-86
Earlier sketches in CA 133, CANR-54
See also PFS 21
Grennan, Margaret R(ose) ... 41-44R
Grenville, Bryan P(eter) 1955- ... 117
Grenville, J(ohn) A(shley) S(oames)
1928- ... CANR-5
Earlier sketch in CA 9-12R
Grenville, Kate 1950- ... CANR-93
Earlier sketches in CA 118, CANR-53
See also CLC 61
See also CN 7
Grenville, Pelham
See Wodehouse, P(elham) G(renville)
Grenyer, Norman 1913-1983
Obituary ... 110
Grenz, Stanley J. 1950- ... 163
Grescoe, Paul 1939- ... 165
Greshake, Gisbert 1933- ... 158
Gresham, Anthony
See Russell, Roy
Gresham, Claude Hamilton, Jr.
1922- ... CANR-8
Earlier sketch in CA 5-8R
Gresham, Elizabeth (Fenner) 1904-1985 . 81-84
Gresham, Grits
See Gresham, Claude Hamilton, Jr.
Gresham, Perry E(pler) 1907-1994 ... CANR-42
Earlier sketch in CA 45-48
Gresham, Stephen (Leroy) 1947- ... HGG
Greskovic, Robert ... 173
Gress, Elsa 1919-1988 ... DLB 214
Gresser, Seymour 1926- ... 29-32R
Gresser, Sy
See Gresser, Seymour
Gressley, Gene M(aurice) 1931- ... CANR-10
Earlier sketch in CA 17-20R
Greteman, James 1933- ... 112
Greteman, Jim
See Greteman, James
Gretz, Susanna 1937- ... CANR-28
Earlier sketch in CA 29-32R
See also SATA 7
Gretzer, John ... SATA 18
Gretzky, Walter 1938- ... 120
Greulach, Victor A(ugust) 1906-1984 ... 49-52
Grevatt, Wallace 1925- ... 129
Greve, Felix Paul (Berthold Friedrich)
1879-1948 ... CANR-79
Brief entry ... 104
Earlier sketch in CA 141, 175
See also Grove, Frederick Philip
See also DAC
See also DAM MST
Grever, Carol 1940- ... 214
Greville, Fulke 1554-1628 ... BRWS 11
See also DLB 62, 172
See also RGEL 2
Grew, James Hooper 1906-1992 ... 103
Grew, Raymond 1930- ... 13-16R
Grewdead, Roy
See Gorey, Edward (St. John)
Grewer, Eira M(ary) 1931- ... 21-24R
Grex, Leo
See Gribble, Leonard (Reginald)
Grey, Abby (Bartlett) Weed 1903(?)-1983
Obituary ... 110
Grey, Anthony 1938- ... CANR-55
Earlier sketches in CA 29-32R, CANR-29
Grey, Belinda
See Peters, Maureen
Grey, Beryl (Elizabeth) 1927- ... 109
Grey, Brenda
See Mackinlay, Leila Antoinette Sterling
Grey, Carenna Jane
See Kalpakian, Laura Anne
Grey, Carol
See Lowndes, Robert A(ugustine) W(ard)
Grey, Charles
See Tubb, E(dwin) C(harles)
Grey, David Lennox 1935- ... 93-96
Grey, Dorothy 1913- ... 120
Grey, Elizabeth
See Hogg, Elizabeth (Tootill)
Grey, Sir George 1812-1898 ... DLB 184
Grey, Georgina
See Roby, Mary Linn
Grey, Ian 1918-1996 ... CANR-2
Earlier sketch in CA 5-8R
Grey, J. David 1935-1993 ... CANR-76
Obituary ... 140
Earlier sketch in CA 133
Grey, Lady Jane 1537-1554 ... DLB 132
Grey, Jeffrey ... 187
Grey, Jerry 1926- ... CANR-43
Earlier sketches in CA 53-56, CANR-5, 20
See also SATA 11
Grey, Johnny ... 237
Grey, Lindsey
See Peel, Colin D(udley)
Grey, Louis
See Gribble, Leonard (Reginald)
Grey, Marian Powys 1883(?)-1972
Obituary ... 104
Grey, Robert Waters 1943- ... 49-52
Grey, Robin
See Gresham, Elizabeth (Fenner)
Grey, Romer Zane
See Curry, Thomas Albert
Grey, Rudolph ... 171
Grey, Vivian (Hoffman) ... 17-20R
Grey, Zane 1872-1939 ... 132
Brief entry ... 104
See also BPFB 2
See also DA3
See also DAM POP
See also DLB 9, 212
See also MTCW 1, 2
See also MTFW 2005
See also RGAL 4
See also TCLC 6
See also TCWW 1, 2
See also TUS
Greybeard the Pirate
See Macintosh, Brownie
Grey Owl
See Belaney, Archibald Stansfeld
See also CLR 32
See also DLB 92
Greyser, Stephen A. 1935- ... 33-36R
Gri
See Denney, Diana
Gribben, Alan 1941- ... 191
Gribbin, John (R.) 1946- ... CANR-95
Earlier sketch in CA 113
See also SATA 159
Gribbin, Lenore S. 1922- ... 33-36R
Gribbin, Mary ... 236
Gribbin, William James 1943- ... CANR-17
Earlier sketches in CA 45-48, CANR-1
Gribble, Charles E(dward) 1936- ... 41-44R
Gribble, Harry Wagstaff (Graham) 1896(?)-1981
Obituary ... 102
Gribble, James 1938- ... 29-32R
Gribble, Jennifer 1937- ... 116
Gribble, Leonard (Reginald)
1908-1985 ... CANR-60
Earlier sketches in CA 53-56, CANR-7
See also Cody, Stetson and
Denver, Lee
See also CMW 4
See also TCWW 2
Gribbons, Warren D(avid) 1921-1990 ... 29-32R
Griboedov, Aleksandr Sergeevich
1795(?)-1829 ... DLB 205
See also RGWL 2, 3
Grice, Frederick 1910-1983 ... CANR-3
Earlier sketch in CA 9-12R
See also CWRI 5
See also SATA 6
Grice, Gordon 1965- ... 176
Grice, Grimes
See Kamp, Irene Kittle
Grice, Julia (Haughey) 1940- ... CANR-16
Earlier sketch in CA 77-80
Grice, Paul 1913-1988 ... DLB 279
Gridban, Volsted
See Fearn, John Russell and
Tubb, E(dwin) C(harles)
Grider, Dorothy 1915- ... SATA 31
Grider, Jay
See Miller, John Grider
Gridley, Marion E(leanor) 1906-1974 ... 45-48
Obituary ... 103
See also SATA 35
See also SATA-Obit 26
Gridley, Roy E. 1935- ... 127
Brief entry ... 109
Gridzewski, Mieczylawski 1895(?)-1970
Obituary ... 104
Grieb, Kenneth J. 1939- ... CANR-12
Earlier sketch in CA 29-32R
Grieb, Lyndal 1940- ... 61-64
Grieco-Tiso, Pina 1954- ... 178
See also SATA 108
Grieder, Jerome B. 1932- ... 130
Grieder, Josephine 1939- ... 53-56
Grieder, Terence 1931- ... CANR-35
Earlier sketch in CA 114
Grieder, Theodore 1926- ... 45-48
Grieder, Walter 1924- ... 41-44R
See also SATA 9
Grieg, Michael 1922-1989 ... 17-20R
Grieg, (Johan) Nordahl (Brun) 1902-1943 .. 189
Brief entry ... 107
See also EWL 3
See also TCLC 10
Grieg, Solveig Christov 1918-1984
See Christov, Solveig
Griego, Tony A. 1955- ... SATA 77
Grier, B. R. 1913- ... 25-28R
Grier, Barbara G(ene Damon) 1933- ... 107
See also Casey, Gladys and
Damon, Gene and
Niven, Vern and
Strong, Lennox
Grier, Edward F(rancis) 1917- ... 121
Grier, Eldon 1917- ... 113
See also CP 1
See also DLB 88
Grier, Frances Belle Powner 1886(?)-1980(?)
Obituary ... 104
Grier, Katherine C. 1953- ... 132
Grier, Roosevelt 1932- ... 113
Grier, Rosey
See Grier, Roosevelt
Grierson, Edward 1914-1975 ... CANR-59
Earlier sketches in CA 1-4R, CANR-4
See also CMW 4
Grierson, Francis Durham 1888-1972
Obituary ... 104
Grierson, Herbert John Clifford 1886-1960
Obituary ... 93-96
Grierson, John 1898-1972
Obituary ... 116
Grierson, John 1909-1977 ... CAP-2
Obituary ... 69-72
Earlier sketch in CA 19-20
Grierson, (Monica) Linden 1914- ... CAP-1
Earlier sketch in CA 9-10
Grierson, Philip 1910- ... CANR-122
Earlier sketches in CA 129, CANR-71
Gries, Tom 1923(?)-1977
Obituary ... 69-72
Griese, Arnold A(lfred) 1921- ... CANR-1
Earlier sketch in CA 49-52
See also SATA 9
Griesemer, John 1947- ... 204
Griesemer, Lynn (M.) 1962- ... 193
Grieson, Ronald Edward 1943- ... CANR-1
Earlier sketch in CA 49-52
Griesse, Carolyn 1941- ... 107
Griessman, Annette 1962- ... 188
See also SATA 116
Griessman, Benjamin Eugene 1934- ... 41-44R
Griest, Guinevere L(indley) 1924- ... 65-68
Griest, Stephanie Elizondo 1974- ... 233
Grieve, Andrew W. 1925-1982 ... 9-12R
Grieve, C(hristopher) M(urray)
1892-1978 ... CANR-107
Obituary ... 85-88
Earlier sketches in CA 5-8R, CANR-33
See also MacDiarmid, Hugh and
Pteleon
See also CLC 11, 19
See also DAM POET
See also MTCW 1
See also RGEL 2
Grieve, James 1934- ... 220
See also SATA 146
Grieves, Forest L(eslie) 1938- ... 53-56
Grieves, R.
See Hill, Janet Muirhead
Grifalconi, Ann 1929- ... CANR-111
Earlier sketches in CA 5-8R, CANR-9, 35
See also CLR 35
See also MAICYA 1, 2
See also SAAS 16
See also SATA 2, 66, 133
Griff
See Fawcett, F(rank) Dubrez and
Fearn, John Russell and
McKeag, Ernest L(ionel)
Griffen, Edmund
See Du Breuil, (Elizabeth) L(or)inda
Griffen, (James) Jeff(erds) 1923- ... 13-16R
Griffin, A(rthur) H(arold) 1911- ... CANR-9
Earlier sketch in CA 21-24R
Griffin, A(rthur) Harry
See Griffin, A(rthur) H(arold)
Griffin, Adele 1970- ... CANR-138
Earlier sketch in CA 173
See also AAYA 37
See also SATA 105, 153
See also WYAS 1
Griffin, Al 1919-1977 ... 33-36R
Griffin, Alice ... 163
Griffin, Andrew
See Heckelmann, Charles N(ewman)
Griffin, Anne J.
See Griffin, Arthur J.
Griffin, Arthur J. 1921- ... CANR-1
Earlier sketch in CA 49-52
Griffin, Barbara C(ook) 1945- ... 53-56
Griffin, Bartholomew fl. 1596- ... DLB 172
Griffin, Bryan F(rederick) ... 120
Brief entry ... 113
Interview in ... CA-120
Griffin, C. F.
See Fikso, Eunice Cleland
Griffin, C. S.
See Griffin, Clifford S(tephen)
Griffin, C(harles) W(illiam) 1925- ... 53-56
Griffin, Charles C(arroll) 1902-1976
Obituary ... 65-68
Griffin, Charles Henry 1922- ... 17-20R
Griffin, Clifford S(tephen) 1929-
Brief entry ... 111
Griffin, (George) Dan(iel) 1937-1984
Obituary ... 112
Griffin, David Ray 1939- ... 77-80
Griffin, Donald (Redfield)
1915-2003 ... CANR-15
Obituary ... 221
Earlier sketch in CA 37-40R
Griffin, Dustin H(adley) 1943- ... 120
Griffin, Eddie 1968- ... 214
Griffin, Edward M(ichael) 1937- ... 89-92
Griffin, Elizabeth May 1985- ... 155
See also SATA 89
Griffin, Emilie Russell Dietrich
1936- ... CANR-21
Earlier sketch in CA 103
Griffin, Ernest G(eorge) 1916- ... 25-28R
Griffin, Farah Jasmine 1963- ... CANR-111
Earlier sketch in CA 172
Griffin, Gerald 1803-1840 ... DLB 159
See also RGEL 2
Griffin, Gerald G(ehrig) 1933-1978 ... CANR-9
Earlier sketch in CA 57-60
Griffin, Gillett Good 1928- ... SATA 26
Griffin, Glen C. 1934- ... CANR-17
Earlier sketch in CA 29-32R
Griffin, (Arthur) Gwyn 1922(?)-1967
Obituary ... 89-92
Griffin, Jack
See Axelrod, Alan
Griffin, Jacqueline P. 1927- ... 33-36R
Griffin, James A. 1934- ... 29-32R
Griffin, Jasper 1937- ... 161
Griffin, Jill 1955- ... CANR-125
Earlier sketch in CA 164
Griffin, John Howard 1920-1980 ... CANR-2
Obituary ... 101
Earlier sketch in CA 1-4R
See also AITN 1
See also CLC 68
Griffin, John Q(uealy) 1948- ... 77-80
Griffin, Jonathan
See Griffin, Robert John Thurlow
Griffin, Judith Berry ... 108
See also SATA 34
Griffin, Keith B(roadwell) 1938- ... CANR-7
Earlier sketch in CA 57-60
Griffin, Kitty 1951- ... 207
See also SATA 137
Griffin, Larry D. 1951- ... 191
Griffin, (Samuel) Marvin 1907-1982
Obituary ... 108
Griffin, Mary 1916-1998 ... 61-64
Obituary ... 166
Griffin, Mary Claire 1924- ... 17-20R
Griffin, Merv(yn) Edward, Jr.) 1925- ... 130
Griffin, Nicholas 1971- ... 222
Griffin, P(auline) M. 1947- ... 140
Griffin, Peni R(ae Robinson) 1961- ... 134
See also SATA 67, 99
Griffin, Peter 1942- ... 136
See also CLC 39
Griffin, Robert 1936- ... 53-56
Griffin, Robert John Thurlow 1906- ... 129
Griffin, Rod L. 1966- ... 218
Griffin, Russell M(organ) 1943-1986 ... 114
See also SFW 4
Griffin, Steven A(rthur) 1953- ... 155
See also SATA 89
Griffin, Stuart 1917- ... 5-8R
Griffin, Susan 1943- ... CANR-50
Earlier sketches in CA 49-52, CANR-3, 27
See also CWP
See also FW
Griffin, Thomas E., Jr. 1946- ... 131
Griffin, Tom
See Griffin, Thomas E., Jr.
Griffin, W. E. B.
See Butterworth, W(illiam) E(dmund III)
See also BPFB 2
Griffin, Walter 1937- ... 73-76
Griffin, (Henry) William 1935- ... 93-96
Griffin, William D(enis) 1936- ... 122
Griffin, William Lloyd 1938- ... 21-24R
Griffin-Beale, Christopher 1947-1998 ... 118
Obituary ... 167
Griffin-Pierce, Trudy 1949- ... 233
Griffis, Dale 1936- ... 214
Griffiss, James E(dward) 1928- ... 132
Brief entry ... 118
Griffith, A. Kinney 1897-1981 ... CANR-17
Earlier sketch in CA 1-4R
Griffith, A(rthur) Leonard 1920- ... CANR-5
Earlier sketch in CA 9-12R
Griffith, Albert J(oseph, Jr.) 1932- ... 37-40R
Griffith, Benjamin Woodward, Jr.
1922- ... CANR-42
Earlier sketches in CA 1-4R, CANR-5, 20
Griffith, Bill
See Granger, Bill
Griffith, Bill 1944- ... 129
Griffith, Connie 1946- ... 155
See also SATA 89
Griffith, Corinne 1898(?)-1979
Obituary ... 89-92
Griffith, D(avid Lewelyn) W(ark)
1875(?)-1948 ... CANR-80
Brief entry ... 119
Earlier sketch in CA 150
See also TCLC 68
Griffith, Elisabeth 1947- ... 166
Griffith, Elizabeth 1727(?)-1793 ... DLB 39, 89
Griffith, Ernest S(tacey) 1896-1997 ... 13-16R
Obituary ... 156
Griffith, Francis 1906- ... 106
Griffith, G(uy) T(hompson) 1908-1985
Obituary ... 117

Griffith(-Jones), George (Chetwynd)
1857-1906 ... 188
Brief entry ... 112
See also DLB 178
See also SFW 4
Griffith, Gershom 1960- ... SATA 85
Griffith, Helen V(irginia) 1934- ... CANR-45
Earlier sketches in CA 105, CANR-22
See also CWRI 5
See also SATA 39, 87
See also SATA-Essay 107
Griffith, Ivelaw L(loyd) 1955- ... 162
Griffith, Jeannette
See Eyerly, Jeannette (Hyde)
Griffith, Jerry 1932- ... 53-56
Griffith, Jim ... 225
Griffith, Kathryn 1923- ... 73-76
Griffith, Kenneth 1921- ... CANR-44
Earlier sketches in CA 69-72, CANR-21
Griffith, Lawrence
See Griffith, D(avid Lewelyn) W(ark)
Griffith, Leon Odell 1921-1984 ... CANR-2
Earlier sketch in CA 1-4R
Griffith, Lucille B(lanche) 1905-1993 ... 17-20R
Griffith, Mark ... 182
Griffith, Marlene 1928- ... 151
Griffith, Michael ... 207
Griffith, Nicola 1960- ... CANR-107
Earlier sketch in CA 154
See also SFW 4
Griffith, Patricia Browning 1935- ... CANR-35
Earlier sketches in CA 77-80, CANR-13
Griffith, Paul 1921-1983 ... CANR-76
Obituary ... 109
Earlier sketch in CA 21-24R
Griffith, Richard (Edward)
1912-1969 ... CANR-6
Earlier sketch in CA 1-4R
Griffith, Robert 1940- ... 45-48
Griffith, Samuel Blair II 1906-1983
Obituary ... 109
Griffith, Thomas 1915-2002 ... 21-24R
Obituary ... 208
Griffith, Thomas Gwynfor 1926- ... 103
Griffith, William E(dgar) 1920-1998 ... 61-64
Obituary ... 170
Griffith, Winthrop 1931- ... 9-12R
Griffith-Jones, Robin 1956- ... 195
Griffith-Jones, Stephany 1947- ... CANR-110
Earlier sketches in CA 126, CANR-53
Griffiths, A(lan) Bede 1906-1993 ... CANR-7
Earlier sketch in CA 13-16R
Griffiths, Alison 1953- ... 128
Griffiths, Andy 1961- ... 206
See also SATA 152
Griffiths, Anne M(arjorie) O(rd) 1953- ... 181
Griffiths, Bill
See Griffiths, William G.
Griffiths, Brian 1941- ... 120
Griffiths, Bryn(lyn) David 1933- ... 101
See also CP 1, 2
Griffiths, Daniel E(dward) 1917-1999 ... 25-28R
Griffiths, G. D.
See Griffiths, (Edith) Grace (Chalmers)
Griffiths, G(ordon) D(ouglas)
1910-1973 ... CAP-2
Earlier sketch in CA 21-22
See also CWRI 5
See also SATA-Obit 20
Griffiths, (Edith) Grace (Chalmers)
1921- ... CANR-22
Earlier sketch in CA 106
Griffiths, Helen 1939- ... CANR-51
Earlier sketches in CA 17-20R, CANR-7, 25
See also CLR 75
See also CWRI 5
See also SAAS 5
See also SATA 5, 86
Griffiths, John C(harles) 1934- ... 108
Griffiths, John Gwyn 1911-2004 ... 106
Griffiths, Kitty Anna ... 105
Griffiths, Linda 1956- ... 132
Griffiths, Louise Benckenstein
1907-1988 ... CANR-47
Earlier sketch in CA 1-4R
Griffiths, Mark (Dennis) 1963- ... 174
Griffiths, (Thomas) Mel(vin) 1910-1989 ... 85-88
Griffiths, Michael C(ompton) 1928- ... CANR-60
Earlier sketches in CA 37-40R, CANR-14, 31
Griffiths, Naomi 1934- ... 101
Griffiths, Niall 1966- ... 239
Griffiths, Paul (Anthony) 1947- ... 107
Griffiths, Paul E(dmund) 1962- ... 232
Griffiths, Percival Joseph 1899-1992 ... 103
Griffiths, Ralph A(lan) 1937- ... CANR-92
Earlier sketches in CA 105, CANR-22, 45
Griffiths, Reginald 1912- ... CP 1
Griffiths, Rhys Adrian 1928-1990 ... 176
See also Adrian, Rhys
Griffiths, Richard M(athias) 1935- ... CANR-8
Earlier sketch in CA 17-20R
Griffiths, Robert David 1952- ... 118
Griffiths, Sally 1934- ... 25-28R
Griffiths, Stephen Gareth 1949- ... 131
Griffiths, Steve
See Griffiths, Stephen Gareth
Griffiths, Tom 1957- ... 160
Griffiths, Trevor 1935- ... CANR-45
Earlier sketch in CA 97-100
See also CBD
See also CD 5, 6
See also CLC 13, 52
See also DLB 13, 245
Griffiths, Vincent Llewellyn 190?(?)-1984
Obituary ... 113
Griffiths, William G. ... 227
Griffy
See Griffith, Bill
Grigg, Charles M(eade) 1918-1992 ... 13-16R
Grigg, John (Edward Poynder) 1924-2001 ... 104
Obituary ... 201
Grigg, Ray 1938- ... 149
Griggs, Barbara
See van der Zee, Barbara (Blanche)
Griggs, Charles Irwin 1902-1994 ... 1-4R
Griggs, Earl Leslie 1899-1975 ... 73-76
Griggs, Gary B(ruce) 1943- ... 118
Griggs, Lee 1928- ... 69-72
Griggs, Mary
See Phillips, Bluebell Stewart
Griggs, Sutton (Elbert) 1872-1930 ... 186
Brief entry ... 123
See also DLB 50
See also TCLC 77
Griggs, Tamar 1941- ... 77-80
Griggs, Terry 1951- ... CANR-141
Earlier sketch in CA 140
Griggs, Vanessa Davis ... 239
Grignon, Claude-Henri 1894-1976 ... 148
See also Bacle, Claude
See also DLB 68
Grigoli, Valorie 1955- ... 122
Grigorenko, P. G.
See Grigorenko, Petro Grigorevich
Grigorenko, Petr Grigorevich
See Grigorenko, Petro Grigorevich
Grigorenko, Petro Grigorevich 1907-1987 ... 144
Grigorenko, Piotr Grigorevich
See Grigorenko, Petro Grigorevich
Grigor'ev, Apollon Aleksandrovich
1822-1864 ... DLB 277
Grigorovich, Dmitrii Vasil'evich
1822-1899 ... DLB 238
Grigorovich, Yuri Nikolayevich 1927- ... 126
Grigsby, Gordon 1927- ... CANR-19
Earlier sketch in CA 97-100
Grigson, Geoffrey (Edward Harvey)
1905-1985 ... CANR-33
Obituary ... 118
Earlier sketches in CA 25-28R, CANR-20
See also CLC 7, 39
See also CP 1, 2
See also DLB 27
See also MTCW 1, 2
Grigson, Jane (McIntire) 1928-1990 ... CANR-76
Obituary ... 131
Earlier sketches in CA 49-52, CANR-1, 20
See also SATA 63
Grihm, Amanda 1952- ... 217
Grile, Dod
See Bierce, Ambrose (Gwinett)
Grill, Johnpeter Horst 1943- ... 112
Grill, Nannette L. 1935- ... 65-68
Grilley, Robert (L.) 1920- ... 233
Grilli, Peter M. 1942- ... 120
Grilliot, Harold J(ohn) 1937- ... 107
Grillo, John 1942-
Brief entry ... 117
See also CBD
Grillo, Laura S. 1956- ... 144
Grillo, Ralph David 1940- ... CANR-102
Earlier sketches in CA 49-52, CANR-48
Grillo, Virgil 1938- ... 53-56
Grillparzer, Franz 1791-1872 ... CDWLB 2
See also DC 14
See also DLB 133
See also EW 5
See also RGWL 2, 3
See also SSC 37
See also TWA
Grim, John A(llen) 1946- ... 117
Grim, Patrick 1950- ... CANR-37
Earlier sketch in CA 115
Grim, Ronald E(ugene) 1946- ... 118
Grimal, Pierre Antoine 1912-1996 ... CANR-7
Earlier sketch in CA 13-16R
Grimald, Nicholas 1519(?)-1562(?) ... DLB 136
Grimaldi, J(ohn) V. 1916- ... CANR-19
Earlier sketches in CA 5-8R, CANR-3
Grimaldi, Janette Pienkny 1938- ... 139
Grimassi, Raven 1951- ... 223
Grimaud, Michel (Robert)
1945-1993 ... CANR-77
Obituary ... 142
Earlier sketch in CA 129
Grimault, Berthe 1940- ... 13-16R
Grimault, Paul 1905- ... IDFW 3, 4
Grimble, Ian (Naughton)
1921-1995 ... CANR-39
Earlier sketches in CA 5-8R, CANR-2, 18
Grimble, Reverend Charles James
See Eliot, T(homas) S(tearns)
Grime, Harol (Riley) 1896-1984
Obituary ... 114
Grimes, Alan P. 1919- ... CANR-48
Earlier sketches in CA 1-4R, CANR-1
Grimes, (Lewis) Howard 1915-1989 ... 25-28R
Grimes, Johnnie Marie ... 103
Grimes, Joseph E(vans) 1928- ... 37-40R
Grimes, Lee 1920- ... CANR-37
Earlier sketch in CA 61-64
See also SATA 68
Grimes, Martha ... CANR-109
Brief entry ... 113
Earlier sketch in CA 117
See also BEST 90:1
See also BPFB 2
See also BYA 11
See also DAM POP
See also MTCW 1
Grimes, Michael D. 1942- ... 175
Grimes, Nikki 1950- ... CANR-115
Earlier sketches in CA 77-80, CANR-60
See also AAYA 53
See also CLR 42
See also CWRI 5
See also MAICYA 2
See also MAICYAS 1
See also SATA 93, 136
Grimes, Orville F(rank), Jr. 1943- ... 106
Grimes, Paul 1924-2002 ... 77-80
Obituary ... 207
Grimes, Ronald L. 1943- ... CANR-17
Earlier sketches in CA 45-48, CANR-1
Grimes, Terris McMahan ... 196
Grimes, Thomas J. 1954- ... CANR-88
Earlier sketch in CA 140
Grimes, Tom 1954-
See Grimes, Thomas J.
Grimes, W(illiam) H(enry) 1892-1972
Obituary ... 33-36R
Grimke, Angelina (Emily) Weld
1880-1958 ... 124
See also Weld, Angelina (Emily) Grimke
See also BW 1
See also DAM POET
See also DLB 50, 54
See also HR 1:2
Grimke, Charlotte L(ottie) Forten
1837(?)-1914 ... 124
Brief entry ... 117
See also Forten, Charlotte L.
See also BW 1
See also DAM MULT, POET
Grimke, Sarah Moore 1792-1873 ... DLB 239
See also FW
Grimley, Mildred H(ess) 1919- ... 5-8R
Grimm, Charles John 1898(?)-1983
Obituary ... 111
Grimm, Charlie
See Grimm, Charles John
Grimm, Cherry Barbara 1930-2002 ... 101
See also FANT
See also SATA-Brief 43
See also SFW 4
Grimm, Fredeic Melchior
See Grimm, Friedrich Melchior
See also DLB 313
Grimm, Friedrich Melchior 1723-1807
See Grimm, Fredeic Melchior
See also GFL Beginnings to 1789
Grimm, Hans 1875-1959 ... 177
See also DLB 66
Grimm, Harold J(ohn) 1901-1983 ... 13-16R
Grimm, Jacob Ludwig Karl 1785-1863 ... DLB 90
See also MAICYA 1, 2
See also RGSF 2
See also RGWL 2, 3
See also SATA 22
See also SSC 36
See also WCH
Grimm, Reinhold 1931- ... CANR-47
Earlier sketches in CA 61-64, CANR-8, 23
Grimm, Wilhelm Karl 1786-1859 ... CDWLB 2
See also DLB 90
See also MAICYA 1, 2
See also RGSF 2
See also RGWL 2, 3
See also SATA 22
See also SSC 36
See also WCH
Grimm, William C(arey) 1907-1992 ... CANR-34
Earlier sketch in CA 49-52
See also SATA 14
Grimmelshausen, Hans Jakob Christoffel von
See Grimmelshausen, Johann Jakob Christoffel von
See also RGWL 2, 3
Grimmelshausen, Johann Jakob Christoffel von
1621-1676
See Grimmelshausen, Hans Jakob Christoffel von
See also CDWLB 2
See also DLB 168
Grimond, Joseph 1913-1993 ... CANR-76
Obituary ... 143
Earlier sketch in CA 108
Grimsdell, Jeremy 1942- ... SATA 83
Grimsditch, Herbert Borthwick 1898-1971
Obituary ... 104
Grimshaw, Allen Day 1929- ... CANR-9
Earlier sketch in CA 65-68
Grimshaw, Beatrice Ethel 1871-1953 ... DLB 174
Grimshaw, James A(lbert), Jr. 1940- ... CANR-98
Earlier sketch in CA 109
Grimshaw, Mark
See McKeag, Ernest L(ionel)
Grimshaw, Nigel (Gilroy) 1925- ... CANR-17
Earlier sketch in CA 101
See also SATA 23
Grimsley, Gordon
See Groom, Arthur William
Grimsley, Jim 1955- ... CANR-88
Earlier sketch in CA 148
See also CSW
See also GLL 2
Grimsley, Linda 1940- ... 81-84
Grimsley, Mark 1959- ... 189
Grimsley, Ronald 1915-2003 ... CANR-3
Obituary ... 219
Earlier sketch in CA 5-8R
Grimsley, Will (Henry) 1914-2002 ... 33-36R
Obituary ... 211
Grimson, Todd 1952- ... CANR-72
Earlier sketch in CA 129
Grimsson, Stefan Hordur
1919(?)-2002 ... DLB 293
See also EWL 3
Grimstead, Hettie 1903-1986
Brief entry ... 115
Grimsted, David Allen 1935- ... 25-28R
Grimsted, Patricia Kennedy 1935- ... 77-80
Grimwood, Ken(neth Milton) 1944-2003 ... 198
Obituary ... 217
See also FANT
Grin, Aleksandr Stepanovich
1880-1932 ... DLB 272
Grinberg, Michel
See Vinaver, Michel
Grinberg, Uri Tsevi
See Greenberg, Uri Zvi
Grindal, Bruce T. 1940- ... 41-44R
Grindal, Edmund 1519(?)-1583 ... DLB 132
Grindal, Gracia (Marie) 1943- ... 116
Grindal, Richard 1922- ... 167
Grinde, Donald A(ndrew), Jr. 1946- ... 141
Grindea, Miron 1909-1995 ... CANR-5
Obituary ... 150
Earlier sketch in CA 5-8R
Grindel, Carl W(illiam) 1905-1982 ... 85-88
Grindel, Eugene 1895-1952 ... 193
Brief entry ... 104
See also Eluard, Paul and
Eluard, Paul
See also LMFS 2
Grindel, John Anthony 1937- ... 65-68
Grindell, Robert M(aclean) 1933- ... 13-16R
Grinder, Michael 1942- ... 61-64
Grindle, Carleton
See Page, Gerald W(ilburn)
Grindley, John (Thomas Ellam) 1926- ... 25-28R
Grindley, (Jane) Sally 1953- ... 121
See also SATA 148
Grindrod, Muriel (Kathleen) 1902-1994 ... 5-8R
Grindstaff, Laura ... 214
Gringhuis, Dirk
See Gringhuis, Richard H.
Gringhuis, Richard H. 1918-1974 ... CANR-5
Earlier sketch in CA 1-4R
See also SATA 6
See also SATA-Obit 25
Grinker, Roy Richard 1961- ... 196
Grinnell, David
See Wollheim, Donald A(llen)
Grinnell, George Bird 1849-1938 ... SATA 16
Grinnell, Isabel Hoopes 1899(?)-1988
Obituary ... 124
Grinsell, Leslie Valentine 1907-1995 ... CANR-3
Earlier sketch in CA 9-12R
Grinspoon, David H. 1959- ... SATA 156
Grinspoon, Lester 1928- ... 81-84
Grinstead, David 1939- ... 105
Grinstein, Alexander 1918- ... CANR-5
Earlier sketch in CA 13-16R
Grinstein, Louise S. 1929- ... 175
Gripari, Pierre 1925- ... CANR-31
Earlier sketch in CA 29-32R
Gripe, Maria (Kristina) 1923- ... CANR-39
Earlier sketches in CA 29-32R, CANR-17
See also CLR 5
See also DLB 257
See also MAICYA 1, 2
See also SATA 2, 74
Grippando, James M. 1958- ... 181
Grippo, Charles ... 235
Griscom, Richard 1956- ... 228
Griscom, Rufus 1968(?)- ... 172
Grise, Jeannette
See Thomas, Jeannette Grise
Grisewood, Harman (Joseph Gerard)
1906- ... CAP-2
Earlier sketch in CA 29-32
Grisez, Germain G. 1929- ... CANR-45
Earlier sketches in CA 13-16R, CANR-6, 21
Grisham, John 1955- ... CANR-133
Earlier sketches in CA 138, CANR-47, 69, 114
See also AAYA 14, 47
See also BPFB 2
See also CLC 84
See also CMW 4
See also CN 6, 7
See also CPW
See also CSW
See also DA3
See also DAM POP
See also MSW
See also MTCW 2
See also MTFW 2005
Grisham, Noel 1916- ... CANR-10
Earlier sketch in CA 25-28R
Grispino, Joseph Aloysius 1922- ... 17-20R
Grissim, John 1941- ... 113
Grissom, Fay
See Shulman, Fay Grissom Stanley
Grissom, Ken 1945- ... 135
Griswold, Charles L., Jr. 1951- ... 123
Griswold, Erwin N(athaniel)
1904-1994 ... CANR-76
Obituary ... 147
Earlier sketches in CAP-1, CA 13-16
Griswold, George
See Dean, Robert George
Griswold, Jerome 1947- ... CANR-89
Earlier sketch in CA 130
Griswold, Jerry
See Griswold, Jerome
Griswold, Lawrence T. 1904(?)-1984
Obituary ... 113
Griswold, Rufus Wilmot 1815-1857 ... DLB 3, 59, 250
Griswold, Wesley S(outhmayd)
1909-1996 ... 1-4R
Griswold del Castillo, Richard 1942- ... 101
Gritsch, Eric W. 1931- ... CANR-10
Earlier sketch in CA 21-24R

Grivas, Theodore 1922- 9-12R
Grizzard, Lewis (M., Jr.) 1946-1994 129
Obituary 144
Brief entry 123
Interview in CA-129
See also CPW
See also CSW
See also DAM POP
See also MTCW 1
Grizzle, Ralph 1957- 199
Grmek, M. D.
See Grmek, Mirko D(razen)
Grmek, M. Drazen
See Grmek, Mirko D(razen)
Grmek, Mirko D(razen) 1924-2000 231
Grmek, Mirko Drazen
See Grmek, Mirko D(razen)
Grob, Alan 1932- 184
Brief entry 113
Grob, Gerald N. 1931- CANR-141
Earlier sketches in CA 1-4R, CANR-5, 20, 42
Grobel, Lawrence 1947- CANR-120
Earlier sketch in CA 131
Grobman, Alex 1946- 116
Grobsmith, Elizabeth S. 1946- 147
Grobsmith, Liz
See Grobsmith, Elizabeth S.
Grobstein, Clifford 1916-1998 130
Obituary 170
Groch, Judith (Goldstein) 1929- 9-12R
See also SATA 25
Grode, Redway
See Gorey, Edward (St. John)
Groden, Michael (Lewis) 1947- CANR-86
Earlier sketch in CA 131
Grodin, Charles 1935- CANR-115
Earlier sketch in CA 157
Grodnick, Susan 1951- 122
Grodstein, Lauren P. 1975- 220
Groemer, Gerald 1957- 139
Groemping, Franz A(lbert) 1909(?)-1987
Obituary 123
Groenbjerg, Kirsten A(ndersen)
1946- CANR-46
Earlier sketches in CA 85-88, CANR-15
Groene, Bertram Hawthorne 1923- 45-48
Groene, Janet 1936- 37-40R
Groener, Carl
See Lowndes, Robert A(ugustine) W(ard)
Groenewegen, Peter 1939- 151
Groenhoff, Edwin L. 1924- 57-60
Groening, Matt 1954- CANR-94
Earlier sketches in CA 138, CANR-56
See also AAYA 8, 34
See also SATA 81, 116
Groennings, Sven O(le) 1934-1998 45-48
Obituary 169
Groenoset, Dagfinn 1920- 93-96
Groeschel, Benedict J(oseph) 1933- CANR-37
Earlier sketch in CA 115
Grof, Stanislav 1931- 73-76
Groff, Patrick J(ohn) 1924- 41-44R
Groff, Warren F(rederick) 1924- 53-56
Grofman, Bernard (N.) 1944- 221
Grogan, Emmett 1942-1978 41-44R
Groh, Ed(win Charles) 1910-1985 49-52
Groh, George W. 1922-1984 CANR-47
Obituary 114
Earlier sketch in CA 85-88
Grohman, Joann Sills 1928- 107
Grohmann, Susan 1948- SATA 84
Grohskopf, Bernice CANR-3
Earlier sketch in CA 5-8R
See also SATA 7
Groia, Phil(ip) 1941- 53-56
Grol, Lini R(icharda) 1913- CANR-25
Earlier sketches in CA 61-64, CANR-8
See also SATA 9
Grollman, Earl A. 1925- 21-24R
See also SATA 22
Grollman, Sharon Hya 1954- CANR-15
Earlier sketch in CA 81-84
Grollmes, Eugene E. 1931- 29-32R
Gromacki, Robert Glenn 1933- CANR-19
Earlier sketches in CA 53-56, CANR-4
Gromada, Thaddeus V(ladimir) 1929- 45-48
Groman, George L. 1928- 21-24R
Grombach, John V(alentin) 1901-1982 103
Gromov, Dmitry E. 1963- 230
Gromyko, Andrei (Andreevich) 1909-1989 134
Gronbeck, Bruce E(lliot) 1941- 132
Brief entry 118
Gronbjerg, Kirsten A(ndersen)
See Groenbjerg, Kirsten A(ndersen)
Grondahl, Jens Christian 1959- CANR-136
Earlier sketch in CA 195
See also MTFW 2005
Grondahl, Paul 1959- 233
Grondal, Benedikt
See Grondal (Sveinbjarnarson), Benedikt
Grondal (Sveinbjarnarson), Benedikt
1826-1907 DLB 293
Grondal, Jens Christian 1959-
See Grondahl, Jens Christian
Grondona, L(eo) St. Clare
1890-1982 CANR-76
Obituary 108
Earlier sketch in CA 103
Groneman, Carol 1943- 199
Groneman, Chris Harold 1906-1992 CANR-1
Earlier sketch in CA 1-4R
Gronert, Bernard G(eorge) 1920-1985
Obituary 116
Gronewold, Sue Ellen
See Gronewold, Susan Ellen
Gronewold, Susan Ellen 1947- 115
Groninger, William C. 1928(?)-1983
Obituary 111
Gronlund, Laurence 1846-1899 DLB 303
Gronowicz, Antoni 1913-1985 CANR-45
Obituary 117
Earlier sketch in CA 25-28R
Groocock, J(ohn) M(ichael) 1929- 57-60
Groom, Arthur William 1898-1964 CANR-1
Earlier sketch in CA 1-4R
See also SATA 10
Groom, Bernard 1892- CAP-2
Earlier sketch in CA 21-22
Groom, Gloria 151
Groom, Nick 1966- 215
Groom, Nigel 1924- 117
Groom, Winston 1943- CANR-121
Earlier sketches in CA 85-88, CANR-34, 50
See also CN 7
See also CSW
See also DLBY 2001
Groome, Thomas H(enry) 1945- 110
Grooms, Anthony
See Grooms, Tony (M.)
Grooms, Tony (M.) 1955- 189
Groopman, Jerome E. 168
Gropius, Walter 1883-1969 231
Obituary 25-28R
Gropman, Donald S(heldon) 1936- 101
Gropp, Louis (Oliver) 1935- 120
Gropper, William 1897-1977 102
Obituary 89-92
Grosart, Alexander Balloch
1827-1899 DLB 184
Grosbard, Ulu 1929- 25-28R
Grose, B(url) Donald 1943- CANR-22
Earlier sketch in CA 45-48
Grose, Christopher (Waldo) 1939-
Brief entry 114
Grose, Peter (Bolton) 1934- CANR-99
Brief entry 119
Earlier sketch in CA 149
Groseclose, Barbara 1944- 152
Groseclose, Elgin E. 1899-1983 CANR-76
Obituary 109
Earlier sketches in CAP-2, CA 21-22
Groseclose, Kel(vin) 1940- CANR-66
Earlier sketches in CA 113, CANR-32
Grosholz, Emily 1950- DLB 282
Grosman, Brian A(llen) 1935- 73-76
Grosman, Ladislav 1921- 102
Grosman, Tatyana 1904-1982
Obituary 107
Grosofsky, Leslie
See Gross, Leslie
Gross, Alan 1947- CANR-24
Earlier sketch in CA 89-92
See also SATA 54
See also SATA-Brief 43
Gross, Albert C. 1947- 125
Gross, Anthony 1905-1984
Obituary 114
Gross, Beatrice 1935- 77-80
Gross, Ben Samuel 1891-1979 97-100
Obituary 89-92
Gross, Bertram M(yron) 1912-1997 CANR-9
Obituary 157
Earlier sketch in CA 13-16R
Gross, Beverly 1938- 29-32R
Gross, Carl H. 1911-1994 13-16R
Gross, Charles G. 1936- 185
Gross, Daniel R(ussell) 1942- 53-56
Gross, David 1940- 140
Gross, David C(harles) 1923- 102
Gross, Ernest A(rnold) 1906-1999 5-8R
Obituary 179
Gross, Ernie 1913- 136
See also SATA 67
Gross, Feliks 1906- CANR-12
Earlier sketch in CA 29-32R
Gross, Franz B(runo) 1919-1988 29-32R
Gross, Gerald 1932- 9-12R
Gross, Gwendolen -1967 200
Gross, Hanns 1928- 41-44R
Gross, Harvey S(eymour) 1922-1996 CANR-8
Earlier sketch in CA 13-16R
Gross, Helen Shimota 1931- 9-12R
Gross, Irma H(annah) 1892-1980 CAP-1
Earlier sketch in CA 13-16
Gross, James A. 1933- 57-60
Gross, Jan Tomasz 1947- 205
Gross, Joel 1951- CANR-57
Earlier sketches in CA 29-32R, CANR-14, 31
Gross, Johannes Heinrich 1916- CANR-43
Earlier sketch in CA 29-32R
Gross, John (Jacob) 1935- CANR-39
Earlier sketch in CA 29-32R
Gross, John J. 1912-1970 CAP-2
Earlier sketch in CA 25-28
Gross, John Owen 1894-1971 CAP-2
Earlier sketch in CA 17-18
Gross, Jonathan David 1962- CANR-137
Earlier sketch in CA 170
Gross, Kenneth 1954- 118
Gross, Kenneth G. 1939- 25-28R
Gross, Leonard 1928- 118
Brief entry 112
Interview in CA-118
Gross, Leslie 1927- 5-8R
Gross, Llewellyn (Zwicker) 1914- 25-28R
Gross, Martha 1931- 143
Gross, Martin (Arnold) 1934- CANR-11
Earlier sketch in CA 13-16R
Gross, Martin L(ouis) 1925- CANR-53
Earlier sketches in CA 9-12R, CANR-7
Gross, Mary Anne 1943- 49-52
Gross, Michael 1891(?)-1979
Obituary 97-100
Gross, Michael (Robert) 1952- CANR-93
Earlier sketches in CA 93-96, CANR-20, 50
Gross, Milt 1895-1953 175
See also DLB 11
Gross, Milton 1912(?)-1973
Obituary 41-44R
See also AITN 1
Gross, Nancy Lammers 1956- 218
Gross, Neal 1920-1981
Obituary 108
Gross, Philip (John) 1952- CANR-82
Earlier sketch in CA 131
See also CP 7
See also SATA 84
Gross, Phyllis P(ennebaker) 1915- 93-96
Gross, Polly 1952- 128
Gross, Richard Edmund 1920- CANR-1
Earlier sketch in CA 1-4R
Gross, Ronald 1935- CANR-5
Earlier sketch in CA 5-8R
Interview in CANR-5
Gross, Ruth Belov 1929- SATA 33
Gross, S(amuel Harry) 1933- CANR-51
Earlier sketches in CA 45-48, CANR-27
Gross, Sarah Chokla 1906-1976 61-64
Obituary 65-68
See also SATA 9
See also SATA-Obit 26
Gross, Seymour L. 1926- CANR-3
Earlier sketch in CA 1-4R
Gross, Sheldon H(arvey) 1921- 81-84
Gross, Shelley 1938- 21-24R
Gross, Shelly
See Gross, Sheldon H(arvey)
Gross, Stuart D. 1914-1996 57-60
Gross, Suzanne 1933- 17-20R
Gross, Terence 1947- 101
Gross, Terry 1951- 238
Gross, Theodore L(awrence) 1930- CANR-14
Earlier sketch in CA 41-44R
Gross, Walter 1923- 21-24R
Gross, William Joseph 1894-1970 CAP-1
Earlier sketch in CA 11-12
Gross, Zenith Henkin 1925- 196
Grossack, Irvin Millman 1927- 97-100
Grossack, Martin Myer 1928- CANR-6
Earlier sketch in CA 9-12R
Grossbach, Robert 1941- CANR-140
Earlier sketches in CA 33-36R, CANR-13
Grossbart, Ted A. 1946- 126
Grossberg, Irving
See Grossberg, Yitzroch Loiza
Grossberg, Yitzroch Loiza 1923-2002 124
Obituary 214
Brief entry 117
See also Rivers, Larry
Grossberger, Lewis 1940(?)-
Brief entry 121
Grosscup, Beau 171
Grosse, W. Jack 1923- 143
Grossen, Neal E. 1943- 93-96
Grosser, Alfred 1925- CANR-44
Earlier sketches in CA 45-48, CANR-2, 20
Grosser, Arthur E(dward) 1934- 116
Grosser, Morton 1931- CANR-17
Earlier sketch in CA 97-100
See also SATA 74
Grosser, Vicky 1958- SATA 83
Grosseteste, Robert 1175(?)-1253 DLB 115
Grossfeld, Stan 1951- 136
Grosshans, Henry 1921- 29-32R
Grossholtz, Jean 1929- 13-16R
Grossinger, Harvey L. 1948- 163
Grossinger, Richard (Selig) 1944- CANR-42
Earlier sketches in CA 103, CANR-19
Grossinger, Tania 1937- CANR-4
Earlier sketch in CA 53-56
Grosskurth, Phyllis 1924- CANR-42
Earlier sketches in CA 13-16R, CANR-9
Grossman, Alfred 1927- 5-8R
See also CN 1, 2, 3, 4
Grossman, Allen (Richard) 1932- CANR-111
Earlier sketches in CA 1-4R, CANR-1, 16, 38
See also DLB 193
Grossman, Bill 1948- SATA 72, 126
Grossman, David 1954- CANR-114
Earlier sketch in CA 138
See also CLC 67
See also CWW 2
See also DLB 299
See also EWL 3
See also WLIT 6
Grossman, Edith Marian 1936- 108
Grossman, Edith (Howitt) Searle
1863-1931 RGEL 2
Grossman, Ellie 110
Grossman, Frances Kaplan 1939- 57-60
Grossman, Gary H(oward) 1948- 69-72
Grossman, Herbert 1934- 17-20R
Grossman, Jean Schick 1894-1972
Obituary 37-40R
Grossman, Jo 238
Grossman, Joan (Adess) 1940- 120
Grossman, Joan Delaney 1928- 111
Grossman, Judith 1937- 190
Grossman, Julian 1931- 53-56
Grossman, Karl (H.) 1942- CANR-82
Earlier sketch in CA 130
Grossman, Kurt R. 1897-1972
Obituary 33-36R
Grossman, Lawrence 1945- 65-68
Grossman, Lee 1931- 69-72
Grossman, Lev (Thomas) 1969(?)- 234
Grossman, Louis Irwin 1901-1988
Obituary 125
Grossman, Manuel Lester 1939-
Brief entry 106
Grossman, Mark 1967- 147
Grossman, Martin (Allen) 1943- CANR-13
Earlier sketch in CA 77-80
Grossman, Martin A. 1951- 102
Grossman, Mary Louise 1930- 77-80
Grossman, Morton Charles
1919-1981 CANR-2
Earlier sketch in CA 1-4R
Grossman, Nancy 1940- SATA 29
Grossman, Patricia 1951- SATA 73
Grossman, Richard 1943- 169
Grossman, Richard L(ee) 1921- 97-100
Interview in CA-97-100
Grossman, Robert 1940- SATA 11
Grossman, Ronald P(hilip) 1934- 21-24R
Grossman, Samuel 1897-1992 53-56
Grossman, Sebastian P. 1934- 21-24R
Grossman, Shelly 1928(?)-1975
Obituary 57-60
Grossman, Vasilii Semenovich
See Grossman, Vasily (Semenovich)
See also DLB 272
Grossman, Vasily (Semenovich)
1905-1964 130
Brief entry 124
See also Grossman, Vasilii Semenovich
See also CLC 41
See also MTCW 1
Grossman, Wendy 168
Grossman, William L(eonard)
1906-1980 CANR-76
Obituary 97-100
Earlier sketches in CAP-2, CA 23-24
Grossmann, Reinhardt S. 1931- CANR-42
Earlier sketches in CA 33-36R, CANR-20
Grossmith, George 1847-1912 RGEL 2
Grossmith, Robert (Anthony) 1954- 134
Grossu, Sergiu 1920- CANR-8
Earlier sketch in CA 57-60
Grossvogel, David I. 1925- CANR-4
Earlier sketch in CA 1-4R
Grosswirth, Marvin 1931-1984 CANR-77
Obituary 112
Earlier sketch in CA 33-36R
Grosvenor, Donna K(erkam) 1938- 109
Grosvenor, Gilbert (Hovey) 1875-1966 175
Obituary 93-96
See also DLB 91
Grosvenor, Kali Diana 1960- 69-72
Grosvenor, Melville Bell 1901-1982 CANR-34
Obituary 106
Earlier sketch in CA 69-72
Grosvenor, Verta Mae 1938- CANR-42
Earlier sketch in CA 69-72
See also BW 2
Grosz, George (Ehrenfried) 1893-1959 147
Grosz, Terry 235
Grot, Anton 1884-1974 IDFW 3, 4
Grote, David (G.) 1945- 130
Grote, JoAnn A. 1951- 185
See also SATA 113
Groten, Dallas 1951- CANR-38
Earlier sketch in CA 115
See also SATA 64
Groth, A(loysius) Nicholas 1937- CANR-125
Earlier sketch in CA 171
Groth, Alexander J(acob) 1932- CANR-14
Earlier sketch in CA 41-44R
Groth, Janet 1936- CANR-143
Earlier sketch in CA 151
Groth, Jeanette L(ue) 1947- 111
Groth, John (August) 1908-1988 CANR-76
Obituary 125
Earlier sketch in CA 101
See also SATA 21
See also SATA-Obit 56
Groth, Klaus 1819-1899 DLB 129
Groth, Paul 1949- 229
Grothendieck, Alexander 1928- 164
Groth-Fleming, Candace
See Fleming, Candace
Grotjahn, Martin 1904-1990 CANR-76
Obituary 132
Earlier sketches in CA 41-44R, CANR-15
Grotowski, Jerzy 1933-1999
Obituary 173
Brief entry 105
Grotpeter, John J. 1938-1993 150
Groult, Benoite 1920- 142
Groulx, Lionel (Adolphe) 1878-1967 153
See also DLB 68
Grounds, Roger (Ransford Paterson)
1938- 97-100
Grounds, Vernon C(arl) 1914- 122
Groundwater, William 1906(?)-1982
Obituary 106
Groupe, Darryl R.
See Bunch, David R(oosevelt)
Groussard, Serge 1921- 108
Grout, Donald Jay 1902-1987 CANR-76
Obituary 121
Earlier sketch in CA 102
Grout, Jack 1910-1989 69-72
Grout, Ruth E(llen) 1901-1998 CAP-2
Earlier sketch in CA 17-18
Grove, Andrew S. 1936- CANR-119
Earlier sketch in CA 130
Grove, Fred(erick Herridge) 1913- CANR-121
Earlier sketches in CA 1-4R, CANR-2, 17, 37
See also TCWW 1, 2
Grove, Frederick Philip
See Greve, Felix Paul (Berthold Friedrich)
See also DLB 92
See also RGEL 2
See also TCLC 4
See also TCWW 1, 2
Grove, Jack William 1920- 5-8R

Cumulative Index 237 Guernsey

Grove, Lee E(dmonds) (?)-1971
Obituary ... 104
Grove, Pearce S(eymour) 1930- ... 73-76
Grove, Richard H(ugh) 1955- ... 149
Grove, Valerie 1946- ... 194
Grove, Vicki 1948- ... 195
See also AAYA 38
See also BYA 9, 10
See also SATA 122, 151
See also SATA-Essay 151
Grove, Will O.
See Brister, Richard
Grovelands, Sarah
See Schneider, Myra
Grover, Chris 1934- ... 216
Grover, David H(ubert) 1925- ... 13-16R
Grover, David S(teele) 1939- ... 89-92
Grover, Jan Zita ... 165
Grover, Janice Zita
See Grover, Jan Zita
Grover, John W(agner) 1927- ... 77-80
Grover, Kathryn 1953- ... 190
Grover, Linda 1934- ... 29-32R
Grover, Lorie Ann ... 238
Grover, Marshall
See Meares, Leonard Frank
See also TCWW 1, 2
Grover, Max 1953- ... 187
Grover, Philip 1929- ... 104
Grover, Ralph Scott 1917- ... 145
Grover, Wayne 1934- ... 137
See also SATA 69
Groves, Colin Peter 1942- ... 61-64
Groves, Don(ald) George ... 106
Groves, Francis Richard 1889- ... CAP-1
Earlier sketch in CA 13-14
Groves, Georgina
See Symons, (Dorothy) Geraldine
Groves, H(arry) E(dward) 1921- ... 5-8R
Groves, Harold M(artin) 1897-1969 . CANR-76
Obituary ... 134
Earlier sketch in CA 5-8R
Groves, Maketa 1950- ... SATA 107
Groves, Naomi Jackson 1910- ... CANR-40
Earlier sketch in CA 117
Groves, Paul 1930- ... CANR-17
Earlier sketch in CA 93-96
Groves, Reg(inald) 1908-1988 ... 13-16R
Groves, Ruth Clouse 1902-1996 ... CAP-2
Earlier sketch in CA 17-18
Groves, Seli ... 145
See also SATA 77
Grow, L(ynn) M(erle) ... 193
Grow, Lawrence 1939- ... CANR-25
Earlier sketches in CA 73-76, CANR-10
Growe, Sarah Jane 1939- ... 134
Groys, Boris Efimovich 1947- ... DLB 285
Grozny, I. L.
See Berger, Ivan (Bennett)
Gruault, Jean (Valery) 1924- ... 169
Grub, Phillip D. 1932- ... CANR-32
Earlier sketches in CA 25-28R, CANR-14
Grubar, Francis S(tanley) 1924-1992 ... 33-36R
Grubb
See Crumb, R(obert)
Grubb, Davis Alexander 1919-1980 ... CANR-4
Obituary ... 101
Earlier sketch in CA 1-4R
See also DLB 6
Grubb, Frederick (Crichton-Stuart) 1930- ... 101
See also CP 1, 2
Grubb, Jeff 1957- ... 239
Grubb, Kenneth George 1900-1980 . CANR-76
Obituary ... 97-100
Earlier sketches in CAP-1, CA 9-10
Grubb, Lisa ... SATA 160
Grubb, Michael (J.) 1960- ... 143
Grubb, Norman (Percy) 1895-1993 .. CANR-13
Earlier sketches in CAP-1, CA 13-16
Grubb, W. Norton 1948- ... 110
Grubbs, David H(arold) 1929- ... 117
Grubbs, Donald H. 1936- ... 81-84
Grubbs, Frank Leslie, Jr. 1931- ... 29-32R
Grubbs, Robert L(owell) 1919-1998 ... CANR-2
Earlier sketch in CA 1-4R
Grube, Georges M(aximilien) A(ntoine)
1899- ... CAP-1
Earlier sketch in CA 13-14
Grube, John Deen 1930- ... CP 1
Grubel, Herbert G(unter) 1934- ... CANR-5
Earlier sketch in CA 9-12R
Gruber, Frank 1904-1969 ... CANR-60
Obituary ... 25-28R
Earlier sketches in CAP-1, CA 13-14
See also CMW 4
See also TCWW 1, 2
Gruber, Frederick C(harles) 1903-1981 ... 49-52
Gruber, Gary R. 1940- ... CANR-135
Earlier sketches in CA 53-56, CANR-9, 24, 49
Gruber, Helmut 1928- ... 103
Gruber, Howard E(rnest) 1922-2005 ... 119
Obituary ... 236
Brief entry ... 113
Interview in ... CA-119
Gruber, Ira D(empsey) 1934-
Brief entry ... 110
Gruber, Jacob W(illiam) 1921- ... 1-4R
Gruber, Joseph John, Jr. 1930- ... CANR-6
Earlier sketch in CA 5-8R
Gruber, Katherine 1952- ... 123
Gruber, Loren (C.) 1941- ... 203
Gruber, Martin Jay 1937- ... CANR-8
Earlier sketch in CA 53-56
Gruber, Michael 1940- ... 237
Gruber, Ruth ... CANR-12
Earlier sketch in CA 25-28R
Gruber, Terry (deRoy) 1953- ... 97-100
See also SATA 66
Gruber, William E. 1943- ... CANR-122
Earlier sketch in CA 150
Gruberg, Martin 1935- ... 33-36R
Grubian, Motel 1909(?)-1972
Obituary ... 104
Grudin, Louis 1898-1993 ... 1-4R
Grudin, Robert 1938- ... 144
Grue, Lee Meitzen ... 180
Gruelle, John (Barton) 1880-1938 ... 175
Brief entry ... 115
See also Gruelle, Johnny
See also CWRI 5
See also MAICYA 2
See also MAICYAS 1
See also SATA 35
See also SATA-Brief 32
Gruelle, Johnny
See Gruelle, John (Barton)
See also CLR 34
See also DLB 22
Gruelle, Worth ... AITN 2
Gruen, Erich S(tephen) 1935- ... CANR-138
Earlier sketches in CA 131, CANR-73
Gruen, John 1926- ... CANR-8
Earlier sketch in CA 17-20R
Gruen, Sara ... 236
Gruen, Victor (David) 1903-1980 ... CANR-10
Obituary ... 97-100
Earlier sketch in CA 13-16R
Gruen, Yetta Fisher ... 125
Gruenbaum, Adolf 1923- ... CANR-43
Earlier sketches in CA 9-12R, CANR-5, 20
Gruenbaum, Ludwig
See Gaathon, A(ryeh) L(udwig)
Gruenberg, Benj(amin) C(harles)
1875-1965 ... CAP-1
Earlier sketch in CA 13-14
Gruenberg, Sidonie Matsner
1881-1974 ... CAP-1
Obituary ... 49-52
Earlier sketch in CA 13-16
See also SATA 2
See also SATA-Obit 27
Gruenberger, Fred J(oseph) 1918- ... 118
Grueneberg, Hans 1907-1982
Obituary ... 108
Gruenfeld, Lee 1950- ... CANR-104
Earlier sketch in CA 142
Gruenhagen, Robert W. 1932- ... 29-32R
Gruening, Ernest (Henry)
1887-1974 ... CANR-34
Earlier sketch in CA 49-52
Gruenstein, Peter 1947- ... 77-80
Gruenther, Alfred M(aximilian) 1899-1983
Obituary ... 109
Gruesser, John Cullen 1959- ... CANR-139
Earlier sketch in CA 144
Gruffydd, Peter 1935- ... 104
See also CP 1, 2
Gruhn, Carrie (E.) Myers 1907-1990 ... CAP-1
Obituary ... 174
Earlier sketch in CA 11-12
Gruhn, George 1945- ... 150
Gruhzit-Hoyt, Olga (Margaret)
1922- ... CANR-94
Earlier sketch in CA 25-28R
See also SATA 16, 127
Gruits, Patricia Beall 1923- ... 105
Gruliow, Leo 1913-1997 ... 5-8R
Obituary ... 159
Grumbach, Doris (Isaac) 1918- ... CANR-127
Earlier sketches in CA 5-8R, CANR-9, 42, 70
Interview in ... CANR-9
See also CAAS 2
See also CLC 13, 22, 64
See also CN 6, 7
See also MTCW 2
See also MTFW 2005
Grumbine, R. Edward 1953- ... 140
Grumbling Gourmet, The
See Chapman, Frank M(onroe)
Grumelli, Antonio 1928- ... 37-40R
Grumet, Robert Steven 1949- ... 102
Grumich, Charles A. 1905(?)-1981
Obituary ... 104
Grumley, Michael 1941-1988 ... CANR-77
Obituary ... 125
Earlier sketch in CA 29-32R
Grumman, Bob 1941- ... 217
See also CAAS 25
Grumme, Marguerite (Evelyn) ... 5-8R
Grummer, Arnold E(dward) 1923- ... 106
See also SATA 49
Grun, Bernard 1901-1972
Obituary ... 37-40R
Grunbaum, Adolf
See Gruenbaum, Adolf
Grunberg, Arnon 1971- ... 195
Grund, Josef Carl 1920- ... 73-76
Grundberg, Andy
See Grundberg, John Andrew
Grundberg, John Andrew 1947- ... 103
Grundlehner, Philip 1945- ... 115
Grundstein, Nathan D(avid)
1913-2000 ... CANR-15
Earlier sketch in CA 37-40R
Grundt, Leonard 1936- ... 57-60
Grundtvig, Nikolai Frederik Severin
1783-1872 ... DLB 300
Grundy, Isobel 1938- ... 186
Grundy, J(ohn) B(rownsdon) C(lowes)
1902-1987
Obituary ... 123
Grundy, J(ohn) Owen 1911-1985
Obituary ... 114
Grundy, Joan 1920- ... 109
Grundy, Kenneth W(illiam) 1936- ... CANR-12
Earlier sketch in CA 73-76
Grundy, Lester H. 1914(?)-1985
Obituary ... 116
Grundy, Mabel (Sarah) Barnes ... RHW
Grundy, Pamela C. 1962- ... 140
Grundy, Stephan 1967- ... CANR-101
Earlier sketch in CA 154
See also FANT
Gruneau, Richard S(teven) 1948- ... CANR-30
Earlier sketch in CA 110
Gruneberg, Hans
See Grueneberg, Hans
Gruner, Charles R. 1931- ... 167
Grunewalt, Pine
See Kunhardt, Edith
Grunfeld, Frederic V(olker)
1929-1987 ... CANR-76
Obituary ... 124
Earlier sketches in CA 73-76, CANR-18
Grunge
See Crumb, R(obert)
Grunlan, Stephen Arthur 1942- ... CANR-39
Earlier sketches in CA 101, CANR-18
Grunwald, Constantine de
See de Grunwald, Constantine
Grunwald, Henry (Anatole)
1922-2005 ... CANR-94
Obituary ... 236
Earlier sketch in CA 107
Grunwald, Joseph 1920-1997 ... 115
Obituary ... 158
Grunwald, Lisa 1959- ... 120
See also CLC 44
Grunwald, Stefan 1933- ... 29-32R
Grunwell, Jeanne Marie 1971- ... 221
See also SATA 147
Grupp, Stanley E(ugene) 1927- ... 53-56
Grupper, Jonathan ... SATA 137
Grusa, Jiri 1938- ... 117
Grusas, Juozas 1901-1986 ... EWL 3
Grusd, Edward Elihu 1904-1988 ... CAP-2
Earlier sketch in CA 19-20
Grushkin, Paul D(avid) 1951- ... 142
Grushow, Ira 1933- ... 128
Grusin, Dave 1934- ... IDFW 4
Gruskin, Alan D(aniel) 1904-1970 ... CAP-1
Obituary ... 29-32R
Earlier sketch in CA 11-12
Grusky, Scott T. 1961- ... 175
Gruson, Edward S. 1929- ... 45-48
Gruss, Edmond C(harles) 1933- ... 53-56
Grutz, Mariellen Procopio 1946- ... 93-96
Grutzmacher, Harold M(artin), Jr.
1930- ... CANR-43
Earlier sketch in CA 29-32R
Gruver, Rebecca
See Goodman, Rebecca Gruver
Gruver, William R. II 1929- ... 45-48
Gruzen, Lee Ferguson 1945- ... 128
Grylls, Bear
See Grylls, Edward
Grylls, David (Stanway) 1947- ... 85-88
Grylls, Edward 1974- ... 200
Grylls, (Mary) Rosalie Glynn
1905(?)-1988 ... CANR-76
Obituary ... 127
Earlier sketch in CA 65-68
Grymeston, Elizabeth
1563(?)-1604(?) ... DLB 136
Grynberg, Henryk 1936- ... CANR-137
Earlier sketches in CA 29-32R, CANR-34
See also DLB 299
Gryphius, Andreas 1616-1664 ... CDWLB 2
See also DLB 164
See also RGWL 2, 3
Gryphius, Christian 1649-1706 ... DLB 168
Gryski, Camilla 1948- ... SATA 72
Gryst, Edward (George) 1911- ... 1-4R
Grzimek, Bernhard (Klemens Maria H. P.)
1909-1987 ... 133
Obituary ... 121
Guadaloupe, Brother Jose de
See Mojica, Jose
Guado, Sergio
See Gerosa, Guido
Guandagnolo, Joseph F(rancis)
1912-1998 ... 5-8R
Guandolo, John 1919-1996 ... 21-24R
Guano, Dr.
See Gootenberg, Paul
Guaragna, Salvatore 1893-1981
Obituary ... 105
Guard, Dave
See Guard, David
Guard, David 1934-1991 ... CANR-76
Obituary ... 134
Earlier sketch in CA 77-80
Guardia, Ernesto de la, Jr.
See de la Guardia, Ernesto, Jr.
Guardini, Romano 1885-1968 ... 167
Guardo, Carol Joan 1939- ... 103
Guare, John 1938- ... CANR-118
Earlier sketches in CA 73-76, CANR-21, 69
See also CAD
See also CD 5, 6
See also CLC 8, 14, 29, 67
See also DAM DRAM
See also DC 20
See also DFS 8, 13
See also DLB 7, 249
See also EWL 3
See also MAL 5
See also MTCW 1, 2
See also RGAL 4
Guarendi, Raymond N(icholas) 1952- ... 120
Guareschi, Giovanni 1908-1968 ... 105
Obituary ... 25-28R
Guarino, Dagmar
See Guarino, Deborah
Guarino, Deborah 1954- ... 136
See also SATA 68
Guarino, M(artin) Vincent 1939- ... 41-44R
Guarnieri, Gianfrancesco 1934- ... DLB 307
Guarnieri, Patrizia 1954- ... 151
Guaspari, John ... 199
Guattari, Felix 1930-1992 ... 206
Guay, Georgette (Marie Jeanne) 1952- ... 132
See also SATA 54
Guback, Georgia ... SATA 88
Guback, Thomas H(enry) 1937- ... 25-28R
Gubar, Susan (David) 1944- ... CANR-139
Earlier sketches in CA 108, CANR-45, 70
See also CLC 145
See also FW
See also MTCW 1
See also RGAL 4
Guberman, Igor' Mironovich 1936- ... DLB 285
Gubern, Santiago (Garriga-Nogues)
1933- ... CANR-2
Earlier sketch in CA 45-48
Gubernick, Lisa Rebecca 1955-2004 ... 140
Obituary ... 225
Gubert, Betty Kaplan 1934- ... 112
Gubrium, Jaber F(andy) 1943- ... CANR-4
Earlier sketch in CA 53-56
Gubser, Nicholas J. 1938- ... 17-20R
Guccione, Leslie Davis 1946- ... 182
See also SATA 72, 111
Guccione, Robert, Jr. ... AITN 2
Guches, Richard (Clement) 1938- ... 115
Guck, Dorothy 1913-2002 ... 49-52
See also SATA 27
Gudde, Erwin G(ustav) 1889-1969 ... CANR-4
Earlier sketch in CA 5-8R
Gudenian, Haig (Krikor) 1918-1985(?)
Obituary ... 115
Guder, Darrell L(ikens) 1939- ... 221
Guder, Eileen (Likens) 1919- ... 17-20R
Gudiol, Jose
See Gudiol i Ricart, Josep
Gudiol i Ricart, Josep 1904-1985 ... 81-84
Gudiol Ricart, Jose M.
See Gudiol i Ricart, Josep
Gudiol Ricart, Josep
See Gudiol i Ricart, Josep
Gudjonsson, Halldor Kiljan 1902-1998 ... 103
Obituary ... 164
See also Halldor Laxness and
Laxness, Halldor (Kiljan)
Gudmundsson, Bodvar 1939- ... DLB 293
Gudmundsson, Einar Mar 1954- ... DLB 293
Gudmundsson, Stefan 1853-1927
See Stephansson, Stephan G.
Gudmundsson, Sveinn Vidar 1962- ... 191
Gudmundsson, Tomas
See Gudmundsson, Tomas
See also DLB 293
Gudmundsson, Tomas 1901-1983
See Gudmundsson, Tomas
See also EWL 3
Gudorf, Christine E. 1949- ... 150
Gudschinsky, Sarah C(aroline)
1919-1975 ... CAP-2
Earlier sketch in CA 33-36
Guede, Norina (Maria Esterina) Lami
1913- ... 9-12R
Guedj, Denis 1940- ... 224
Guehenne, Jean
See Guehenno, Jean (Marcel Jules Marie)
Guehenno, Jean (Marcel Jules Marie)
1890-1978
Obituary ... 104
Guelbenzu, Jose Maria 1944- ... 211
Guelich, Robert A(llison) 1939- ... CANR-17
Earlier sketches in CA 45-48, CANR-2
Guelke, Adrian ... 227
Guelzo, Allen C(arl) 1953- ... 190
Guemple, Lee 1930- ... 41-44R
Guenderrode, Caroline von
1780-1806 ... DLB 90
Guenette, Robert (Homer) 1935-2003 ... 25-28R
Obituary ... 220
Guenter, Erich
See Eich, Gunter
Guenther, Charles (John) 1920- ... CANR-45
Earlier sketch in CA 29-32R
Guenther, Herbert V. 1917- ... 73-76
Guenther, John (Lewis) ... CANR-9
Earlier sketch in CA 5-8R
Guenther, (Robert) Wallace 1929- ... 65-68
Guerard, Albert Joseph 1914-2000 ... CANR-69
Obituary ... 191
Earlier sketches in CA 1-4R, CANR-2
See also CAAS 2
See also CN 1, 2, 3, 4, 5, 6, 7
Guerif, Francois 1944- ... 170
Guerin, Daniel 1904-1988 ... 195
Guerin, (Georges-Pierre-)Maurice De
1810-1839 ... GFL 1789 to the Present
Guerin, Wilfred L(ouis) 1929- ... 17-20R
Guerlac, Henry (Edward) 1910-1985
Obituary ... 116
Guerlac, Rita 1916- ... 116
Guerney, Bernard G(uilbert), Jr. 1930- ... 93-96
Guerney, Bernard Guilbert 1894-1979
Obituary ... 85-88
Guernsey, Bruce H(ubbard) 1944- ... 108
Guernsey, James Lee 1923- ... 37-40R
Guernsey, Otis L(ove), Jr. 1918-2001 ... 89-92
Obituary ... 196
Guernsey, Thomas F. 1951- ... 146

Guerny, Gene
See Gurney, Gene
Guerra, Antonio
See Guerra, Tonino
Guerra, Emilio Louis 1909-1980
Obituary ... 97-100
Guerra, Tonino 1920- ... 181
See also DLB 128
See also IDFW 3, 4
Guerrant, Edward Owings 1911- ... 21-24R
Guerra y Sanchez, Ramiro 1880-1970
Obituary ... 104
Guerrero, Eduardo, Jr. 1916-2005 ... 224
Obituary ... 237
Guerrero, Lalo
See Guerrero, Eduardo, Jr.
Guerrero, Rogelio Diaz
See Diaz-Guerrero, Rogelio
Guerrette, Richard H(ector) 1930- ... 49-52
Guerrier, Dennis 1923- ... 29-32R
Guers-Villate, Yvonne 1924- ... 41-44R
Guesclin, Du
See Witting, Amy
Guess, Carol (A.) 1968- ... CANR-141
Earlier sketch in CA 174
Guess, Edward Preston 1925-1993 ... 73-76
Guest, A(nthony) G(ordon) 1930- ... CANR-1
Earlier sketch in CA 1-4R
Guest, Barbara 1920- ... CANR-84
Earlier sketches in CA 25-28R, CANR-11, 44
See also BG 1:2
See also CLC 34
See also CP 1, 2, 3, 4, 5, 6, 7
See also CWP
See also DLB 5, 193
See also PC 55
Guest, Christopher 1948- ... 157
Guest, Edgar A(lbert) 1881-1959 ... 168
Brief entry ... 112
See also TCLC 95
Guest, Elissa Haden 1953- ... 196
See also SATA 125
Guest, Harry
See Guest, Henry Bayly
See also CP 1, 2, 3, 4, 5, 6, 7
Guest, Henry Bayly 1932- ... CANR-9
Earlier sketch in CA 65-68
See also Guest, Harry
Guest, Ivor (Forbes) 1920- ... CANR-42
Earlier sketches in CA 5-8R, CANR-2, 20
Guest, Jacqueline 1952- ... 204
See also SATA 135
Guest, Judith (Ann) 1936- ... CANR-138
Earlier sketches in CA 77-80, CANR-15, 75
Interview in ... CANR-15
See also AAYA 7, 66
See also CLC 8, 30
See also DA3
See also DAM NOV, POP
See also EXPN
See also LAIT 5
See also MTCW 1, 2
See also MTFW 2005
See also NFS 1
Guest, Lynn 1939- ... 131
Guest, Tim 1975- ... 232
Guetersloh, Albert Paris 1887-1973 ... 177
See also Allamand, Pascale and Gutersloh, Albert Paris
See also DLB 81
Guett, Dieter 1924- ... 65-68
Gueulette, David G(eorge) 1941- ... 111
Guevara, Che
See Guevara (Serna), Ernesto
See also CLC 87
See also HLC 1
Guevara (Serna), Ernesto
1928-1967 ... CANR-56
Obituary ... 111
Earlier sketch in CA 127
See also Guevara, Che
See also CLC 87
See also DAM MULT
See also HLC 1
See also HW 1
Guevara, Fray Antonio de
1480(?)-1545 ... DLB 318
Guevara, Susan ... SATA 97
Guevremont, (Marianne) Germaine
1893-1968 ... 148
See also DLB 68
Guffey, Burnett 1905-1983 ... IDFW 3, 4
Guffey, George
See Guffey, George Robert
Guffey, George R.
See Guffey, George Robert
Guffey, George Robert 1932- ... 132
Brief entry ... 118
Guffin, Gilbert L(ee) 1906-1992 ... 17-20R
Gugas, Chris 1921- ... 97-100
Gugelyk, M(yron) Ted 1938- ... 120
Guggenbuhl, Allan 1952- ... 170
Guggenheim, Edward Armand 1901-1970
Obituary ... 104
Guggenheim, Hans Georg 1927- ... 125
Guggenheim, Harry Frank 1890-1971
Obituary ... 89-92
Guggenheim, Marguerite 1898-1979
Obituary ... 105
Guggenheim, Martin 1946- ... 129
Guggenheim, Peggy
See Guggenheim, Marguerite
Guggenheimer, Richard 1906-1977 ... 41-44R
Obituary ... 69-72
Guggenmos, Josef 1922- ... 81-84
Guggisberg, C(harles) A(lbert) W(alter)
1913- ... 81-84
Gugler, Laurel Dee ... 160
See also SATA 95
Guglielminetti, Amalia 1881-1941 ... DLB 264
Gugliotta, Bobette 1918-1994 ... CANR-31
Earlier sketches in CA 41-44R, CANR-14
See also SATA 7
Guha, Ramachandra 1958- ... 230
Guhin, Michael A(lan) 1940- ... 41-44R
Gui, Ming Chao 1946- ... 219
Guianan, Eve 1965- ... SATA 102
Guiberson, Brenda Z. 1946- ... SATA 71, 124
Guibert, Herve 1955-1991 ... 155
See also GLL 2
Guice, John D(avid) W(ynne) 1931- ... 41-44R
Guicharnaud, June 1922-1989 ... CANR-76
Obituary ... 129
Earlier sketch in CA 93-96
Guidacci, Margherita 1921-1992 ... DLB 128
Guido, Beatriz 1924-1988 ... 153
See also EWL 3
See also HW 1
Guido, (Cecily) Margaret 1912- ... 65-68
Guignon, Charles B(urke) 1944- ... CANR-93
Earlier sketch in CA 145
Guild, Lurelle Van Arsdale 1898-1985 .. CAP-2
Earlier sketch in CA 29-32
Guild, Nicholas M. 1944- ... 93-96
See also CLC 33
Guild, Thelma S(croggs) 1911-1996 ... 118
Guild, Vera Palmer 1906-1981
Brief entry ... 106
Guilds, John C(aldwell, Jr.) 1924- ... 77-80
Guile, Melanie 1949- ... CANR-135
Earlier sketch in CA 171
See also SATA 104, 152
Guiles, Fred Lawrence 1920-2000 ... CANR-12
Obituary ... 189
Earlier sketch in CA 25-28R
Guilford, J(oy) Paul 1897-1987 ... CANR-4
Earlier sketch in CA 1-4R
Guilford, Joan S. 1928- ... 29-32R
Guillaume, Alfred 1888-1965(?) ... CAP-1
Earlier sketch in CA 13-16
Guillaume, Bernice F(orrest) 1950- ... 145
Guillaume, Jeanette G. Flierl 1899-1990 .. 1-4R
See also SATA 8
Guillaume, Robert 1927(?)- ... 214
Guillaume de Machaut c.
1300-1377 ... RGWL 2, 3
Guillaumin, Colette 1934- ... 154
See also FW
Guille, Frances V(ernor) 1908-1975 ... 45-48
Obituary ... 61-64
Guillemin, Henri 1903-1992 ... 81-84
Guillemin, Jacques
See Sartre, Jean-Paul
Guillemin, Jeanne (Harley) 1943- ... 193
Guillemot, Agnes 1931- ... IDFW 3, 4
Guillen, Jorge 1893-1984 ... 89-92
Obituary ... 112
See also CLC 11
See also DAM MULT, POET
See also DLB 108
See also EWL 3
See also HLCS 1
See also HW 1
See also PC 35
See also RGWL 2, 3
Guillen, Mauro (Federico) 1964- ... 134
Guillen, Michael (Arthur) 1940- ... 158
Guillen, Nicolas (Cristobal)
1902-1989 ... CANR-84
Obituary ... 129
Brief entry ... 116
Earlier sketch in CA 125
See also BLC 2
See also BW 2
See also CLC 48, 79
See also DAM MST, MULT, POET
See also DLB 283
See also EWL 3
See also HLC 1
See also HW 1
See also LAW
See also PC 23
See also RGWL 2, 3
See also WP
Guillen, Tomas 1949- ... 134
Guillen Cuervo, Fernando ... 202
Guillen y Alvarez, Jorge
See Guillen, Jorge
Guilleragues, Gabriel-Joseph de Lavergne
1628-1685 ... GFL Beginnings to 1789
Guillermoprieto, Alma 1949- ... 202
Guillet, Edwin C(larence) 1898-1975 ... 107
Guillet, Jacques 1910- ... 102
Guillevic, (Eugene) 1907-1997 ... 93-96
See also CLC 33
See also CWW 2
Guillois
See Desnos, Robert
Guillois, Valentin
See Desnos, Robert
Guillory, Dan 1944- ... 144
Guillot, Rene 1900-1969 ... CANR-39
Earlier sketch in CA 49-52
See also CLR 22
See also SATA 7
Guillou, Jan 1944- ... 143
Guilloux, Louis 1899-1980 ... 177
Obituary ... 104
See also DLB 72
See also EWL 3
Guilmartin, John Francis, Jr. 1940- ... 53-56
Guilpin, Everard 1572(?)-1608(?) ... DLB 136
Guimaraes, Dona 1926(?)-1989
Obituary ... 129
Guimaraes Rosa, Joao 1908-1967 ... 175
See also Rosa, Joao Guimaraes
See also HLCS 2
See also LAW
See also RGSF 2
See also RGWL 2, 3
See also SFW 4
Guimary, Donald L(ee) 1932- ... 73-76
Guimond, James K. 1936- ... 25-28R
Guin, Wyman (Woods) 1915-1989 ... 102
Obituary ... 171
See also SFW 4
Guinagh, Kevin (Joseph) 1897-1995 ... 17-20R
Guinan, Michael D(amon) 1939- ... 117
Guindey, Guillaume Louis 1909-1989
Obituary ... 128
Guinee, Kathleen K. 1902(?)-1982
Obituary ... 109
Guiney, Louise Imogen 1861-1920 ... 160
See also DLB 54
See also RGAL 4
See also TCLC 41
Guiney, Mortimer 1930- ... 53-56
Guinier, (Carol) Lani 1950- ... CANR-92
Earlier sketch in CA 158
Guinizelli, Guido c. 1230-1276
See Guinizzelli, Guido
Guinizzelli, Guido
See Guinizelli, Guido
See also WLIT 7
Guinn, Paul (Spencer, Jr.) 1928- ... 13-16R
Guinness (de Cuffe), Alec 1914-2000 ... 183
Obituary ... 189
Guinness, Bryan (Walter)
1905-1992 ... CANR-46
Obituary ... 139
Earlier sketch in CA 102
Guinness, Desmond 1931- ... 141
Guinness, Jonathan (Bryan) 1930- ... 159
Guinness, (Ian) Os(wald) 1941- ... CANR-94
Earlier sketch in CA 65-68
Guinther, John 1927- ... CANR-56
Earlier sketches in CA 69-72, CANR-11, 28
Guion, Robert M(organ) 1924- ... CANR-7
Earlier sketch in CA 17-20R
Guiraldes, Ricardo (Guillermo)
1886-1927 ... 131
See also EWL 3
See also HW 1
See also LAW
See also MTCW 1
See also TCLC 39
Guirdham, Arthur 1905-1992 ... 103
Guisewite, Cathy (Lee) 1950- ... 113
Brief entry ... 111
Interview in ... CA-113
See also AAYA 2, 45
See also SATA 57
Guisinger, Stephen Edward 1941- ... 103
Guitar, Mary Anne 1922-
Brief entry ... 113
Guiterman, Arthur 1871-1943
Brief entry ... 120
See also DLB 11
Guither, Harold D. 1927- ... 29-32R
Guiver, Patricia ... 170
Gul', Roman (Borisovich) 1896-1986 . DLB 317
Gula, Richard M(ichael) 1947- ... 109
Gula, Robert J(ohn) 1941- ... 97-100
Gulbis, Stephen 1959- ... 213
See also SATA 142
Gulick, Bill
Interview in ... CANR-17
See also Gulick, Grover C.
See also TCWW 1, 2
Gulick, Edward Vose 1915-2000 ... 113
Gulick, Grover C. 1916- ... CANR-77
Earlier sketches in CA 33-36R, CANR-17, 39
See also Gulick, Bill
Gulick, Robert Lee, Jr. 1912-1987
Obituary ... 122
Gulik, Robert H(ans) van
See van Gulik, Robert Hans
Gulker, Virgil G. 1947- ... 65-68
Gullace, Gino 1925- ... CANR-17
Earlier sketch in CA 69-72
Gullan, Harold I(ves) 1931- ... 189
Gullans, Charles (Bennett)
1929-1993 ... CANR-77
Obituary ... 141
Earlier sketches in CA 1-4R, CANR-4, 18, 39
See also CP 1, 2
Gullason, Thomas A(rthur) 1924- ... CANR-8
Earlier sketch in CA 21-24R
Gullberg, Hjalmar 1898-1961 ... 202
See also EWL 3
Gulley, Halbert E(dison) 1919- ... CANR-6
Earlier sketch in CA 5-8R
Gulley, Judie 1942- ... SATA 58
Gulley, Norman 1920- ... 33-36R
Gulley, Philip 1961- ... 237
Gullick, Charles Francis William Rowley
1907- ... 5-8R
Gullick, Charlotte ... 213
Gullick, Etta 1916- ... 89-92
Gullick, John M(ichael) 1916- ... 13-16R
Gulliford, Andrew 1953- ... 120
Gulliford, Ronald 1920-1997 ... 13-16R
Gulliver, Harold S. 1935- ... 97-100
Gulliver, Lemuel
See Hastings, Macdonald
Gullotta, Thomas P. 1948- ... CANR-136
Earlier sketch in CA 144
Gulston, Charles 1913-1981 ... 122
Gumilev, Nikolai (Stepanovich)
1886-1921 ... 165
See also Gumilyov, Nikolay Stepanovich
See also DLB 295
See also TCLC 60
Gumilyov, Nikolay Stepanovich
See Gumilev, Nikolai (Stepanovich)
See also EWL 3
Gummer, Selwyn 1907-1999 ... 183
Gummere, Richard M(ott), Jr. 1912- ... 45-48
Gump, P. Q.
See Card, Orson Scott
Gump, Richard (Benjamin) 1906-1989 . CAP-1
Earlier sketch in CA 9-10
Gump, Sally
See Stanford, Sally
Gumpert, David E. ... 236
Gumpertz, Robert 1925- ... 69-72
Gumperz, John J(oseph) 1922- ... 132
Gumplowicz, Ludwig 1838-1909 ... 217
Gumprecht, Blake 1959- ... 184
Gunders, Henry 1924- ... 29-32R
Gundersheimer, Karen 1939- ... 133
See also SATA-Brief 44
Gundersheimer, Werner L. 1937- ... 53-56
Gunderson, Doris V. ... 29-32R
Gunderson, Frank L(ester) 1902-1983
Obituary ... 110
Gunderson, Keith (Robert) 1935- ... 33-36R
Gunderson, Robert Gray 1915-1996 ... 1-4R
Gundle, Stephen 1956- ... 215
Gundolf, Friedrich
See Gundelfinger, Friederich
Gundrey, Elizabeth 1924- ... CANR-6
Earlier sketch in CA 13-16R
See also SATA 23
Gundry, Robert H(orton) 1932- ... 29-32R
Gundry, Stanley Norman 1937- ... 114
Gundulic, Ivan 1589-1638 ... CDWLB 4
See also DLB 147
Gundy, Elizabeth ... CANR-45
Earlier sketch in CA 112
Gundy, H(enry) Pearson) 1905- ... 45-48
Gundy, Jeff(rey Gene) 1952- ... CANR-112
Earlier sketch in CA 154
Gunesekera, Romesh 1954- ... CANR-140
Earlier sketch in CA 159
See also BRWS 10
See also CLC 91
See also CN 6, 7
See also DLB 267
Gunetti, Daniele 1963- ... 159
Guney, Yilmaz 1937(?)-1984
Obituary ... 113
Gunji, Masakatsu 1913-1998 ... 29-32R
Gunlicks, Arthur B. 1936- ... CANR-53
Earlier sketch in CA 126
Gunn, Bill
See Gunn, William Harrison
See also CLC 5
See also DLB 38
Gunn, Brooke
See Brooks-Gunn, Jeanne
Gunn, Christopher Eaton 1944- ... 117
Gunn, Diana Maureen 1926- ... CANR-18
Earlier sketch in CA 97-100
Gunn, Douglas 1950- ... 151
Gunn, Drewey Wayne 1939- ... 57-60
Gunn, Elizabeth
See Gunn, Diana Maureen
Gunn, Giles B(uckingham) 1938- ... 57-60
Gunn, Helen Montgomery 1900(?)-1987
Obituary ... 122
Gunn, J(ohn) A(lexander) W(ilson)
1937- ... CANR-20
Earlier sketch in CA 25-28R
Gunn, James E(dwin) 1923- ... 199
Earlier sketches in CA 9-12R, CANR-5, 22
Autobiographical Essay in ... 199
See also CAAS 2
See also DLB 8
See also SATA 35
See also SFW 4
Gunn, John (Charles) 1937- ... CANR-29
Earlier sketch in CA 49-52
Gunn, Kirsty 1960- ... CANR-117
Earlier sketch in CA 166
Gunn, Mrs. Aneas 1870-1961
Obituary ... 115
Gunn, Neil M(iller) 1891-1973 ... 175
Obituary ... 37-40R
See also CN 1
See also DLB 15
See also FANT
See also RGEL 2
Gunn, Peter (Nicholson)
1914-1995 ... CANR-18
Obituary ... 150
Earlier sketches in CA 25-28R, CANR-10
Gunn, Robin Jones 1955- ... CANR-101
Earlier sketch in CA 150
See also SATA 84
Gunn, S(teven) J(ohn) 1960- ... 128
Gunn, Sister Agnes Marie 1928- ... 17-20R

Gunn, Thom(son William)
1929-2004 .... CANR-116
Obituary 227
Earlier sketches in CA 17-20R, CANR-9, 33
Interview in CANR-33
See also BRWS 4
See also CDBLB 1960 to Present
See also CLC 3, 6, 18, 32, 81
See also CP 1, 2, 3, 4, 5, 6, 7
See also DAM POET
See also DLB 27
See also MTCW 1
See also PC 26
See also PFS 9
See also RGEL 2
Gunn, William Harrison
1934(?)-1989 .... CANR-76
Obituary 128
Earlier sketches in CA 13-16R, CANR-12, 25
See also Gunn, Bill
See also AITN 1
See also BW 1, 3
Gunn Allen, Paula
See Allen, Paula Gunn
Gunnars, Kristjana 1948- 113
See also CCA 1
See also CLC 69
See also CP 7
See also CWP
See also DLB 60
Gunnarsson, Gunnar
See Gunnarsson, Gunnar
Gunnarsson, Gunnar 1889-1975
Obituary 61-64
See also DLB 293
See also EW 10
See also EWL 3
Gunnarsson, Petur 1947- .... DLB 293
Gunnell, Bryn 1933- 103
Gunnell, John G. 1933- 25-28R
Gunneweg, Antonius H. J. 1922- CANR-16
Earlier sketch in CA 89-92
Gunning, Monica Olwen 1930- 65-68
See also SATA 161
Gunning, Robert 1908-1980 .... CANR-76
Obituary 97-100
Earlier sketches in CAP-2, CA 25-28
Gunning, Sally (Carlson) 1951- 140
Gunsalus Gonzalez, Catherine
See Gonzalez, Catherine Gunsalus
Gunston, Bill
See Gunston, William Tudor
Gunston, William Tudor 1927- CANR-42
Earlier sketches in CA 49-52, CANR-3, 19
See also SATA 9
Gunstone, A(ntony) J. H. 1937(?)-1984
Obituary 112
Gunter, (J.) Bradley (Hunt) 1940- 29-32R
Gunter, Erich
See Eich, Gunter
Gunter, Pete A(ddison) Y(ancey)
1936- CANR-90
Earlier sketches in CA 33-36R, CANR-15, 34
Gunterman, Bertha Lisette 1886(?)-1975
Obituary 104
See also SATA-Obit 27
Gunther, A(lbert) E(verard) 1903- 29-32R
Gunther, Bernard 1929- CANR-2
Earlier sketch in CA 45-48
Gunther, Gerald 1927-2002 .... CANR-13
Obituary 213
Earlier sketch in CA 33-36R
Gunther, Johann Christian
1695-1723 .... DLB 168
Gunther, John 1901-1970 .... CANR-85
Obituary 25-28R
Earlier sketch in CA 9-12R
Gunther, Marc 1951- 129
Gunther, Max 1927- 13-16R
Gunther, Peter F. 1920-1992 .... 9-12R
Gunther, Richard (Paul) 1946- 103
Gunther, Robert E. 1960- 234
Gunton, Colin E(wart) 1941-2003 192
Obituary 216
Gunton, Sharon R(ose) 1952- 102
Guntrip, Harry
See Guntrip, Henry James Samuel
Guntrip, Henry James Samuel
1901-1975 .... CANR-5
Earlier sketch in CA 5-8R
Gunzberg, Lynn M(arian) 1944-2002 143
Obituary 213
Gunzburg, Nicholas de 1904-1981
Obituary 103
Gup, Ted (S.) 1950- 202
Guppy, Nicholas (Gareth Lechmere)
1925- CANR-6
Earlier sketch in CA 5-8R
Guppy, Shusha 1938- 128
Guppy, Stephen (Anthony) 1951- CANR-133
Earlier sketch in CA 166
Gupta, Anil K. 1949- CANR-97
Earlier sketch in CA 144
Gupta, Brijen K(ishore) 1929- CANR-16
Earlier sketches in CA 45-48, CANR-1
Gupta, Marie (Jacqueline) 1946- 57-60
Gupta, Pranati Sen
See Sen Gupta, Pranati
Gupta, Ram Chandra 1927- CANR-13
Earlier sketch in CA 21-24R
Gupta, S(ushil) (Kumar) 1927- 57-60
Gupta, Shiv K(umar) 1930- 57-60
Gupta, Sulekh Chandra 1928- 13-16R
Gupta, Sunetra 1965- CANR-88
Earlier sketch in CA 137
See also CN 7
Gupta, U. S. 1940- 147
Guptara, Prabhu S(iddhartha) 1949- 81-84
Guptill, Nathanael M(ann) 1917- 45-48
Gur, Batya 1947-2005 209
Obituary 239
Gura, Philip F(rancis) 1950- CANR-98
Earlier sketches in CA 111, CANR-47
Guralnick, Peter 1943(?)- CANR-91
Earlier sketch in CA 147
Guravich, Dan 1918- .... SATA 74
Gurdjieff, G(eorgei) I(vanovich)
1877(?)-1949 157
See also TCLC 71
Gurdus, Luba Krugman 1914- 120
Gurevich, Aaron 1924- 144
Gurevich, David 1951- 140
Gurewitsch, Edna P. 204
Gurganus, Allan 1947- CANR-114
Earlier sketch in CA 135
See also BEST 90:1
See also CLC 70
See also CN 6, 7
See also CPW
See also CSW
See also DAM POP
See also GLL 1
Guri, Haim
See Gouri, Haim
See also CWW 2
Gurian, Michael W. 1958- 223
Gurik, Robert 1932- CANR-71
Earlier sketch in CA 129
See also CAAS 23
See also DLB 60
Gurin, Joel 1953- 108
Gurko, Leo 1914- CANR-5
Earlier sketch in CA 5-8R
See also SATA 9
Gurko, Miriam 1910(?)-1988 .... CANR-76
Obituary 126
Earlier sketch in CA 1-4R
See also SATA 9
See also SATA-Obit 58
Gurman, Alan S(tephen) 1945- CANR-5
Earlier sketch in CA 53-56
Gurnah, Abdulrazak (S.) 1948- 179
See also CN 7
See also EWL 3
Gurnee, Jeanne 1926- 93-96
Gurnee, Russell H(ampton) 1922-1995 107
Gurney, A. R.
See Gurney, A(lbert) R(amsdell), Jr.
See also DLB 266
Gurney, A(lbert) R(amsdell), Jr.
1930- CANR-121
Earlier sketches in CA 77-80, CANR-32, 64
See also Gurney, A. R.
See also AMWS 5
See also CAD
See also CD 5, 6
See also CLC 32, 50, 54
See also DAM DRAM
See also EWL 3
Gurney, Alan 235
Gurney, Gene 1924- CANR-9
Earlier sketch in CA 5-8R
See also SATA 65
Gurney, George 1939- 119
Gurney, Ivor (Bertie) 1890-1937 167
See also BRW 6
See also DLBY 2002
See also PAB
See also RGEL 2
See also TCLC 33
Gurney, J. Eric -1992 .... CANR-2
Earlier sketch in CA 1-4R
Gurney, James 1958- 191
See also SATA 76, 120
Gurney, John Steven 1962- .... SATA 75, 143
Gurney, Nancy Jack 1915(?)-1973
Obituary 45-48
Gurney, Peter
See Gurney, A(lbert) R(amsdell), Jr.
Guro, Elena (Genrikhovna)
1877-1913 .... DLB 295
See also TCLC 56
Gurr, Andrew (John) 1936- CANR-106
Earlier sketch in CA 33-36R
Gurr, David 1936- CANR-105
Brief entry 125
Earlier sketch in CA 132
Interview in CA-132
Gurr, Michael 1961- 232
See also CD 5, 6
Gurr, Ted Robert 1936- CANR-124
Earlier sketches in CA 41-44R, CANR-16
Gurrey, Percival 1890-1980
Obituary 97-100
Gursky, Andreas 1955- .... AAYA 58
Gurtov, Melvin 1941- CANR-126
Brief entry 112
Earlier sketch in CA 164
Gurval, Robert Alan 1958- 156
Gurvis, Sandra J. 1951- 202
Gurwitsch, Aron 1901-1973 .... CAP-1
Obituary 41-44R
Earlier sketch in CA 13-16
Guschov, Stephen D. 1965- 169
Guse, Ernst-Gerhard 234
Gusfield, Joseph R. 1923- 53-56
Gusikoff, Lynne
See Hawes, Lynne Gusikoff Salop
Guss, Donald L(eroy) 1929- 17-20R
Guss, Jeffrey R. 1953- 218
Guss, John Walker 1964- 229
Guss, Leonard M. 1926- 21-24R
Gussman, Boris (William) 1914- 5-8R
Gussow, Adam 1958- 181
Gussow, Alan 1931-1997 183
Brief entry 111
Gussow, Don 1907-1992 .... CANR-76
Obituary 136
Earlier sketch in CA 132
Gussow, Joan Dye 1928- CANR-140
Earlier sketch in CA 29-32R
Gussow, Mel 1933-2005 .... CANR-88
Obituary 239
Earlier sketch in CA 107
Gustafson, Alrik 1903-1970 .... CANR-76
Obituary 103
Earlier sketch in CA 1-4R
Gustafson, Anita
See Larsen, Anita
Gustafson, Anita 1942- 112
See also SATA-Brief 45
Gustafson, Chris(tine) 1950- 239
Gustafson, David A(rthur) 1946- 141
Gustafson, Donald F. 1934- CANR-36
Earlier sketch in CA 9-12R
Gustafson, James 1949- 125
Gustafson, James M(oody) 1925- CANR-37
Earlier sketch in CA 25-28R
See also CLC 100
Gustafson, Jim
See Gustafson, James
Gustafson, Paula Catherine 1941- 106
Gustafson, Ralph (Barker)
1909-1995 .... CANR-84
Earlier sketches in CA 21-24R, CANR-8, 45
See also CLC 36
See also CP 1, 2
See also DLB 88
See also RGEL 2
Gustafson, Richard C(larence) 1933-1977
Obituary 111
Gustafson, Richard F(olke) 1934- 17-20R
Gustafson, Sarah R.
See Riedman, Sarah R(egal)
Gustafson, Scott 1956- .... SATA 34
Gustafson, Sid 1954- 227
Gustafson, Susan E(lizabeth)
1959- CANR-126
Earlier sketch in CA 152
Gustafson, W(illiam) Eric 1933- 57-60
Gustafsson, Lars (Erik Einar) 1936- CANR-119
Earlier sketch in CA 85-88
See also CWW 2
See also DLB 257
See also EWL 3
Gustaf VI, Adolf, King of Sweden 1882-1973
Obituary 45-48
Gustaitis, Rasa 1934- 25-28R
Gustavson, Carl G(ustav) 1915-1999 .... 17-20R
Gustav-Wrathall, John (Donald) 1963- 235
Guste, Roy F(rancis), Jr. 1951- 162
Gustin, Lawrence Robert 1937- CANR-37
Earlier sketch in CA 57-60
Gustkey, Earl 1940- 57-60
Gut, Gom
See Simenon, Georges (Jacques Christian)
Gutch, John 1905-1988
Obituary 124
Gutcheon, Beth R(ichardson) 1945- CANR-99
Earlier sketches in CA 49-52, CANR-2
Gutek, Gerald L(ee) 1935- CANR-40
Earlier sketches in CA 81-84, CANR-17
Gutenberg, Arthur W(illiam)
1920-2001 .... 37-40R
Gutenberg, Beno 1889-1960 157
Guterl, Matthew Pratt 1970- 206
Guterman, Norbert 1900-1984
Obituary 113
Guterman, Simeon L(eonard)
1907-1997 .... 41-44R
Guterman, Stanley S(anford) 1934- 29-32R
Gutersloh, Albert Paris
See Guetersloh, Albert Paris
See also EWL 3
Guterson, David 1956- CANR-126
Earlier sketches in CA 132, CANR-73
See also CLC 91
See also CN 7
See also DLB 292
See also MTCW 2
See also MTFW 2005
See also NFS 13
Guth, Alan (Harvey) 1947- 158
Guth, DeLloyd J. 1938- 129
Gutheim, Frederick 1908-1993 .... CANR-76
Obituary 142
Earlier sketches in CA 21-24R, CANR-9
Guthke, Karl S(iegfried) 1933- CANR-88
Earlier sketches in CA 41-44R, CANR-15, 37
Guthman, Edwin 1919- 33-36R
Guthman, William H(arold) 1924- CANR-37
Earlier sketch in CA 57-60
Guthmann, Harry G. 1896-1981 .... 1-4R
Guthridge, George L(loyd) 1948- 174
Guthrie, A(lfred) B(ertram), Jr.
1901-1991 .... CANR-24
Obituary 134
Earlier sketch in CA 57-60
See also CLC 23
See also CN 1, 2, 3
See also DLB 6, 212
See also MAL 5
See also SATA 62
See also SATA-Obit 67
See also TCWW 1, 2
Guthrie, Alan
See Tubb, E(dwin) C(harles)
Guthrie, Anne 1890-1979 .... CANR-77
Obituary 134
Earlier sketch in CA 5-8R
See also SATA 28
Guthrie, Arlo (Davy) 1947- CANR-53
Earlier sketch in CA 113
Guthrie, David
See Allen, H(ubert) R(aymond)
Guthrie, Donald 1916- CANR-23
Earlier sketches in CA 13-16R, CANR-7
Guthrie, Donna W. 1946- CANR-141
Earlier sketch in CA 173
See also SATA 63, 105
Guthrie, Gwen 1957(?)-1999 185
Guthrie, Harvey Henry, Jr. 1924- 13-16R
Guthrie, Hugh
See Freeman, John Crosby
Guthrie, Hunter 1901-1974 65-68
Obituary 53-56
Guthrie, Isobel
See Grieve, C(hristopher) M(urray)
Guthrie, James Shields 1931- CANR-15
Earlier sketch in CA 33-36R
Guthrie, James W. 1936- 41-44R
Guthrie, John 1908-1980 106
Guthrie, John A(lexander) 1908-1980 .... 1-4R
Guthrie, Judith Bretherton 1905(?)-1972
Obituary 37-40R
Guthrie, Marjorie (Greenblatt Mazia)
1917-1983
Obituary 117
Guthrie, Ramon 1896-1973 .... CANR-85
Obituary 45-48
Earlier sketch in CA 5-8R
See also CP 1, 2
See also DLB 4
See also RGAL 4
Guthrie, Randolph H. 1934- 146
Guthrie, Robert V(al) 1930- 53-56
Guthrie, Russell Dale 1936-
Brief entry 106
Guthrie, T.
See Guthrie, (William) Tyrone
Guthrie, Thomas Anstey 1856-1934 173
Brief entry 113
See also Anstey, F.
See also BW 3
See also FANT
Guthrie, (William) Tyrone 1900-1971 123
Obituary 29-32R
Guthrie, William Keith Chambers
1906-1981 .... CANR-11
Obituary 103
Earlier sketch in CA 65-68
Guthrie, Woodrow Wilson 1912-1967 113
Obituary 93-96
See also Guthrie, Woody
Guthrie, Woody
See Guthrie, Woodrow Wilson
See also CLC 35
See also DLB 303
See also LAIT 3
Gutierrez, Donald 1932- CANR-36
Earlier sketch in CA 109
Gutierrez, Gustavo
See Gutierrez Merino, Gustavo
Gutierrez, Pedro Juan 1950- 215
Gutierrez, Stephen (D.) 1959- 214
Gutierrez M., Gustavo
See Gutierrez Merino, Gustavo
Gutierrez Merino, Gustavo 1928- 130
See also HW 1
Gutierrez Najera, Manuel
1859-1895 .... DLB 290
See also HLCS 2
See also LAW
Gutierrez-Vega, Zenaida 1924- CANR-19
Earlier sketch in CA 41-44R
Gutin, Bernard 1934- 112
Gutjahr, Paul C. 1962- 192
Gutkin, Harry 1915- 101
Gutkind, Erwin A(nton) 1886-1968 .... CANR-8
Earlier sketch in CA 5-8R
Gutkind, Lee 1943- CANR-106
Earlier sketches in CA 53-56, CANR-5, 20
Gutkind, Peter C(laus) W(olfgang)
1925-2001 116
Gutman, Bill CANR-97
Earlier sketch in CA 135
See also BYA 14
See also SATA 67, 128
See also SATA-Brief 43
Gutman, Dan 1955- CANR-135
Earlier sketch in CA 133
See also AAYA 47
See also SATA 77, 139
Gutman, David 1957- 127
Gutman, Herbert G(eorge)
1928-1985 .... CANR-36
Obituary 116
Earlier sketch in CA 65-68
Gutman, Judith Mara 1928- 21-24R
Gutman, Kellie O. 1952- 124
Gutman, Naham 1899(?)-1981
Obituary 102
See also SATA-Obit 25
Gutman, Richard J(ay) S(tephen) 1949- 101
Gutman, Robert 1926- 45-48
Gutman, Robert W. 1925- 25-28R
Gutman, Roy (W.) 1944- 131
Gutman, Stanley T. 1943- 127
Gutman, Walter
See Gutman, Walter Knowlton
Gutman, Walter Knowlton 1903-1986
Obituary 119
Gutmann, Amy 1949- CANR-120
Earlier sketches in CA 120, CANR-64
Gutmann, Bessie Pease 1876-1960 .... SATA 73
Gutmann, David L(eo) 1925- 135

Gutmann, James 1897-1988 ... CANR-76
Obituary ... 127
Earlier sketches in CAP-2, CA 21-22
Gutmann, Joseph 1923- ... CANR-37
Earlier sketches in CA 49-52, CANR-1, 17
Gutmann, Myron P. 1949- ... 127
Brief entry ... 105
Gutmann, Stephanie ... 206
Gutnik, Martin J(erome) 1942- ... CANR-3
Earlier sketch in CA 49-52
Gutowski, Armin (Ferdinand) 1930-1987 ... 136
Gutsche, Thelma 1915- ... 21-24R
Gutstein, Morris A(aron) 1905-1987
Obituary ... 122
Gutt, Dieter
See Guett, Dieter
Guttenberg, Barnett ... 89-92
Guttenberg, Virginia 1912-1998 ... 81-84
Obituary ... 172
Guttenplan, D. D. 1957- ... 204
Guttenplan, Samuel 1944- ... 215
Guttentag, Marcia 1932-1977 ... CANR-8
Earlier sketch in CA 57-60
Gutteridge, Anne C(hristine) 1943- ... 108
Gutteridge, Bernard 1916-1985
Obituary ... 117
See also CP 1
Gutteridge, Don(ald George) 1937- .. CANR-82
Earlier sketches in CA 65-68, CANR-9, 36
See also CP 2, 3, 4, 5, 6, 7
Gutteridge, Lindsay 1923- ... 49-52
See also SFW 4
Gutteridge, Rene ... 236
Gutteridge, Richard (Joseph Cooke) 1911- .. 122
Gutteridge, Thomas G. 1942- ... 147
Gutteridge, William F(rank) 1919- ... 13-16R
Gutterson, Herbert (Lindsley, Jr.) 1915- ... 9-12R
Guttery, Ben R. 1965- ... 178
Gutting, Gary (Michael) 1942- ... CANR-37
Earlier sketch in CA 103
Guttmacher, Alan F(rank) 1898-1974 . CANR-6
Obituary ... 49-52
Earlier sketch in CA 1-4R
Guttmacher, Manfred S(chanfarber)
1898-1966 ... CAP-1
Earlier sketch in CA 11-12
Guttmann, Alexander ... 29-32R
Guttmann, Allen 1932- ... CANR-93
Earlier sketches in CA 1-4R, CANR-1, 16, 39
Guttmann, Hadassah 1952- ... 143
Guttmann, Joseph 1946- ... 144
Guttmann, Melinda Given 1944- ... 222
Guttormsson, Guttormur J(onsson)
1878-1966 ... DLB 293
Guttridge, Leonard F(rancis) 1918- ... CANR-99
Earlier sketch in CA 85-88
Guttsman, Wilhelm Leo 1920-1998 ... 9-12R
Gutwirth, Samuel William 1903-1983
Obituary ... 111
Gutzke, Manford G(eorge) 1896-1993 .. 17-20R
Gutzkow, Karl 1811-1878 ... DLB 133
Gutzwiller, Kathryn J(arrell) 1948- ... 185
Guy, Anne W(elsh) 1898-1995 ... 5-8R
Guy, Bill ... 229
Guy, David 1948- ... CANR-108
Earlier sketch in CA 105
Guy, Geoffrey 1942- ... SATA 153
Guy, Harold A. 1904- ... 17-20R
Guy, J. A.
See Guy, John (Alexander)
Guy, John (Alexander) 1949- ... 230
Guy, Mary E. 1947- ... 138
Guy, Ray 1939- ... 147
See also CCA 1
See also DLB 60
Guy, Rosa (Cuthbert) 1925- ... CANR-83
Earlier sketches in CA 17-20R, CANR-14, 34
See also AAYA 4, 37
See also BW 2
See also CLC 26
See also CLR 13
See also DLB 33
See also DNFS 1
See also JRDA
See also MAICYA 1, 2
See also SATA 14, 62, 122
See also YAW
Guy, Susan 1948- ... SATA 149
Guyer, Paul 1948- ... CANR-24
Earlier sketch in CA 105
Guymer, (Wilhelmina) Mary 1909- ... SATA 50
Guyot, Arnold 1807-1884 ... DLBD 13
Guyot, Gabriele
See Wohmann, Gabriele
Guyot, James F(ranklin) 1932- ... 53-56
Guy-Sheftall, Beverly 1946- ... 142
See also BW 2
Guyton, Arthur C(lifton) 1919-2003 ... CANR-7
Obituary ... 215
Earlier sketch in CA 17-20R
Guzie, Tad W(alter) 1934- ... CANR-5
Earlier sketch in CA 13-16R
Guzman (Franco), Martin Luis 1887-1976 .. 153
See also EWL 3
See also HW 1
See also LAW
Guzman, Nicomedes 1915-1964 ... EWL 3
Guzman, Ralph C. 1924-1985
Obituary ... 117
Guzzetti, Alfred F. 1942- ... 136
Guzzo, Lou(is Richard) 1919- ... 135
Guzzo, Sandra E(lizabeth) 1941- ... CANR-45
Earlier sketch in CA 120
Guzzwell, John 1930- ... 13-16R
Gwaltney, Francis Irby 1921-1981 ... CANR-2
Earlier sketch in CA 1-4R
Gwaltney, John Langston 1928-1998 ... 77-80
Gwendolyn
See Bennett, (Enoch) Arnold
Gwilliam, Kenneth M(ason) 1937- ... 17-20R
Gwin, Lucy 1943- ... 109
Gwin, Minrose C(layton) ... 228
Gwinup, Thomas 1932- ... 73-76
Gwirtzman, Milton S. 1933- ... 29-32R
Gwisdek, Michael 1942- ... 201
Gwyn, Aaron 1972- ... 231
Gwyn, Julian 1937- ... 57-60
Gwyn, Richard J. 1934- ... CANR-17
Earlier sketch in CA 25-28R
Gwyn, W(illiam) B(rent) 1927- ... CANR-82
Earlier sketches in CA 13-16R, CANR-5, 36
Gwynelle (Dismukes) 1952- ... 147
Gwynn, Denis (Rolleston) 1893-1971 ... CAP-1
Earlier sketch in CA 13-14
Gwynn, Mary 1952- ... 111
Gwynn, R(obert) S(amuel) 1948- ... CANR-127
Earlier sketch in CA 161
See also DLB 282
See also TCLE 1:1
Gwynn, Robin D(avid) 1942- ... CANR-99
Earlier sketches in CA 121, CANR-47
Gwynne, Erskine 1898-1948
Brief entry ... 107
See also DLB 4
Gwynne, Fred(erick Hubbard)
1926-1993 ... CANR-76
Obituary ... 141
Earlier sketch in CA 113
See also SATA 41
See also SATA-Brief 27
See also SATA-Obit 75
Gwynne, Oscar A.
See Ellis, Edward S(ylvester)
Gwynne, Oswald A.
See Ellis, Edward S(ylvester)
Gwynne, Peter 1941- ... 89-92
Gwynne-Jones, Allan 1892-1982
Obituary ... 107
Gwynne-Thomas, E(ric) H(ubert) 1917- ... 120
Gyani, Gabor
See Gyani, Gabor
Gyani, Gabor 1950- ... 236
Gyanranjan 1936- ... CWW 2
Gyatso, Palden 1933- ... 172
Gyatso, Tenzin 1935- ... CANR-102
Earlier sketch in CA 141
Gyftopoulos, Elias Panayiotis 1927- . CANR-82
Earlier sketches in CA 104, CANR-36
Gygax, (Ernest) Gary 1938- ... AAYA 65
See also FANT
Gyldenvand, Lily M. 1917-1994 ... CANR-6
Earlier sketch in CA 13-16R
Gyles, John 1680-1755 ... DLB 99
Gylfason, Thorvaldur 1951- ... CANR-95
Earlier sketch in CA 145
Gyllembourg, Thomasine 1773-1856 . DLB 300
Gyllenhammar, Pehr G(ustaf) 1935- . CANR-13
Earlier sketch in CA 73-76
Gyllensten, Lars (Johan Wictor) 1921- ... 194
See also DLB 257
See also EWL 3
Gyoergyi, Albert (von Nagyrapolt) Szent
See Szent-Gyoergyi, Albert (von Nagyrapolt)
Gyohten, Toyoo 1931- ... 140
Gyorgy, Andrew 1917-1993 ... 122
Gyorgyey, Clara 1936- ... 77-80
Gyorgyi, Albert (von Nagyrapolt) Szent
See Szent-Gyoergyi, Albert (von Nagyrapolt)
Gysbers, Norman C(harles) 1932- ... 61-64
Gysi, Klaus 1912-1999 ... 183
Gysin, Brion 1916-1986 ... CANR-77
Obituary ... 120
Brief entry ... 113
Earlier sketch in CA 117
Interview in ... CA-117
See also DLB 16
Gzowski, Peter 1934-2002 ... CANR-40
Obituary ... 203
Earlier sketch in CA 106
Interview in ... CA-106

H

H. D.
See Doolittle, Hilda
See also CLC 3, 8, 14, 31, 34, 73
See also FL 1:5
See also PC 5
H. D. P.
See Dickey, Christopher
H. de V.
See Buchan, John
H. M. S.
See Kirk-Greene, Anthony (Hamilton Millard)
Haab, Sherri 1964- ... SATA 91
Haaby, Lawrence O. 1915-1992 ... 33-36R
Obituary ... 171
Haac, Oscar A(lfred) 1918- ... 33-36R
Haack, Susan 1945- ... 61-64
Haaf, Beverly T(erhune) 1936- ... 97-100
Haaften, Julia Van
See Van Haaften, Julia
Haag, Herbert 1915-2001 ... 206
Haag, Jessie Helen 1917- ... CANR-5
Earlier sketch in CA 13-16R
Haagensen, Cushman D(avis) 1900-1990
Obituary ... 132
Haak, Bob 1926- ... 144
Haaken, Janice (Kay) 1947- ... 228
Haaker, Ann M. ... 25-28R
Haakonssen, Knud 1947- ... CANR-109
Earlier sketches in CA 124, CANR-51
Haan, Aubrey Edwin 1908-1988 ... 1-4R
Obituary ... 174
Haanpaa, Pentti 1905-1955 ... EWL 3
Haanpaeae, Pentti
See Haanpaa, Pentti
Haar, Charles M(onroe) 1920- ... 33-36R
Haar, Francis 1908-1997 ... 53-56
Obituary ... 176
Haar, Franklin B(laine) 1906-1990 ... CAP-1
Obituary ... 180
Earlier sketch in CA 11-12
Haar, Jaap ter
See ter Haar, Jaap
See also CLR 15
Haar, James 1929- ... CANR-101
Earlier sketch in CA 21-24R
Haarer, Alec Ernest 1894-1970 ... CANR-4
Earlier sketch in CA 5-8R
Haarhoff, Theodore Johannes
1892-1971 ... CAP-1
Earlier sketch in CA 13-14
Haarsager, Sandra (L.) 1946- ... 146
Haas, Albert E. 1917- ... 21-24R
Haas, Antonio 1923- ... 131
Haas, Ben(jamin) L(eopold)
1926-1977 ... CANR-63
Obituary ... 73-76
Earlier sketches in CA 9-12R, CANR-8
See also Douglas, Thorne
See also TCWW 2
Haas, Carol 1949- ... 146
Haas, Carolyn Buhai 1926- ... CANR-9
Earlier sketch in CA 65-68
See also SATA 43
Haas, Charles A. 1947- ... 125
Haas, Charlie 1952- ... 73-76
Haas, Dan 1957- ... 173
See also SATA 105
Haas, Dorothy F. ... CANR-44
Earlier sketches in CA 5-8R, CANR-3, 20
See also SAAS 17
See also SATA 46
See also SATA-Brief 43
Haas, Ernst 1921-1986
Obituary ... 120
Haas, Ernst B(ernard) 1924-2003 ... 81-84
Obituary ... 215
Haas, Gerda (Schild) 1922- ... 110
Haas, Harold I(rwin) 1925- ... 29-32R
Haas, Irene 1929- ... CANR-65
Earlier sketch in CA 97-100
See also SATA 17, 96
Haas, Irvin 1916- ... 41-44R
Haas, J(ohn) Eugene 1926- ... 41-44R
Haas, James E(dward) 1943- ... CANR-7
Earlier sketch in CA 61-64
See also SATA 40
Haas, (Katherine) Jessie 1959- ... CANR-144
Earlier sketch in CA 114
See also MAICYA 2
See also SATA 98, 135
See also SATA-Essay 135
Haas, Kenneth B(rooks) Sr.
1898-1988 ... CANR-6
Obituary ... 180
Earlier sketch in CA 57-60
Haas, Kurt ... 53-56
Haas, LaVerne 1942- ... 49-52
Haas, Lawrence J. 1956- ... 147
Haas, Lynne 1939- ... 65-68
Haas, Marilyn L(oomis) 1931- ... 117
Haas, Mary Odin 1910-1995 ... CAP-1
Earlier sketch in CA 13-14
Haas, Mary R(osamond) 1910-1996 ... 9-12R
Obituary ... 152
Haas, Merle S. 1896(?)-1985
Obituary ... 114
See also SATA-Obit 41
Haas, Michael 1938- ... 53-56
Haas, Raymond Michael 1935- ... 37-40R
Haas, Robert Bartlett 1916-
Brief entry ... 108
Haas, Robert Lewis 1936- ... 101
Haase, Ann Marie Bernazza 1942- ... 33-36R
Haase, Donald 1950- ... CANR-101
Earlier sketch in CA 148
Haase, John 1923- ... CANR-14
Earlier sketch in CA 5-8R
Haasler, Sue
See Haasler, Susan
Haass, Richard Nathan 1951- ... 192
Haasse, Helene Serafia
See Haasse, Hella
Haasse, Hella 1918- ... 193
See also EWL 3
Haataja, Lance
See Drake, Timothy A.
Haavikko, Paavo Juhani 1931- ... 106
See also CLC 18, 34
See also CWW 2
See also EWL 3
Habakkuk, (Hrothgar) John 1915-2002 ... 151
Obituary ... 213
Habbema, Koos
See Heijermans, Herman
Habe, Hans 1911-1977 ... CANR-2
Obituary ... 73-76
Earlier sketch in CA 45-48
Habegger, Alfred (Carl) 1941- ... CANR-86
Earlier sketch in CA 131
Habel, Janette
See Grimaldi, Janette Pienkny
Habel, Norman C. 1932- ... 17-20R
Habenstreit, Barbara 1937- ... 29-32R
See also SATA 5
Haber, Audrey 1940- ... CANR-13
Earlier sketch in CA 33-36R
Haber, Barbara (Lubotsky) 1934- ... 210
Haber, Carole R. 1951- ... 124
Haber, Eitan 1940- ... 104
Haber, Francis Colin 1920-1990
Obituary ... 131
Haber, Fritz 1868-1934 ... 156
Haber, Heinz 1913-1990 ... 73-76
Haber, Jack 1939-1984 ... CANR-76
Obituary ... 114
Earlier sketch in CA 69-72
Haber, Joyce 1932-1993 ... CANR-76
Obituary ... 142
Earlier sketch in CA 65-68
Haber, Karen 1955- ... CANR-128
Earlier sketch in CA 146
See also SATA 78
Haber, Louis 1910-1988 ... 29-32R
See also SATA 12
Haber, Ralph Norman 1932- ... 33-36R
Haber, Samuel 1928- ... 9-12R
Haber, Tom Burns 1900-1976 ... CAP-2
Earlier sketch in CA 17-18
Haber, William 1899-1988 ... CAP-2
Earlier sketch in CA 21-22
Haberer, Joseph 1929- ... 65-68
Haberler, Gottfried (von) 1900-1995 ... 103
Obituary ... 180
Haberly, David T(ristram) 1942- ... 106
Haberly, Loyd 1896-1981 ... 105
Obituary ... 103
Haberman, Daniel 1933-1991 ... CANR-76
Obituary ... 135
Earlier sketch in CA 110
Haberman, David A. 1928- ... 126
Haberman, Donald (Charles) 1933- ... 21-24R
Haberman, Jacob 1932- ... 231
Haberman, Martin 1932- ... 57-60
Haberman, Shelby J(oel) 1947- ... 103
Habermann, Helen M(argaret) 1927- ... 53-56
Habermas, Juergen 1929- ... CANR-85
Earlier sketch in CA 109
See also CLC 104
See also DLB 242
Habermas, Jurgen
See Habermas, Juergen
Habermas, Ronald Thomas 1951- ... 195
Habers, Walther A(drianus) 1926- .. CANR-120
Earlier sketch in CA 147
Haberstroh, Chadwick John 1927- ... 41-44R
Habgood, John Stapylton 1927- ... CANR-45
Earlier sketches in CA 13-16R, CANR-5, 22
Habibi, Emile
See Habibi, Imil
Habibi, Imil 1919(?)-1996
See Habiby, Emile
See also CWW 2
Habiby, Emile
See Habibi, Imil
See also WLIT 6
Habig, Marion A(lphonse)
1901-1984 ... CANR-20
Obituary ... 114
Earlier sketches in CA 5-8R, CANR-5
Habila, Helon 1967- ... 217
Habinek, Thomas N. 1953- ... 172
Habington, William 1605-1654 ... DLB 126
See also RGEL 2
Hablutzel, Philip 1935- ... 37-40R
Habsburg-Lothringen, Geza Louis Eusebius
Gebhard Ralphael Albert Maria
See von Habsburg(-Lothringen), Geza Louis
Eusebius Gebhard Ralphael Albert Maria
Hach, Clarence Woodrow 1917- ... 13-16R
Hachey, Thomas E(ugene) 1938- ... 37-40R
Hachten, Harva ... 108
Hachten, William Andrews 1924- ... 107
Hacikyan, A(gop) J. 1931- ... 33-36R
Hack, Richard 1947- ... 189
Hack, Walter G. 1925- ... 29-32R
Hackady, Hal
Brief entry ... 105
Hackbarth, Steven (L.) 1945- ... 159
Hackelsberger, Christoph 1931- ... 167
Hacker, Andrew 1929- ... CANR-41
Earlier sketches in CA 1-4R, CANR-1
Hacker, Barton C(lyde) 1935- ... 150
Hacker, Carlotta 1931- ... 118
Hacker, Frederick J. 1914-1989
Obituary ... 129
Brief entry ... 104
Hacker, Jeffrey H. 1954- ... 125
Hacker, Kenneth L. 1951- ... 175
Hacker, Leonard
See Hackett, Buddy
Hacker, Louis M(orton) 1899-1987 ... CANR-77
Obituary ... 122
Earlier sketch in CA 17-20R
Hacker, Marilyn 1942- ... CANR-129
Earlier sketches in CA 77-80, CANR-68
See also CLC 5, 9, 23, 72, 91
See also CP 7
See also CWP
See also DAM POET
See also DLB 120, 282
See also FW
See also GLL 2
See also MAL 5
See also PC 47
See also PFS 19
Hacker, Mary Louise 1908- ... CAP-2
Earlier sketch in CA 17-18
Hacker, P(eter) M(ichael) S(tephen)
1939- ... CANR-118
Earlier sketch in CA 158
Hacker, Rose (Goldbloom) 1906- ... 13-16R
Hacker, Shyrle 1910-2000 ... 101

Cumulative Index 241 **Hagstrum**

Hackes, Peter Sidney 1924-1994 ..... CANR-76
Obituary 145
Earlier sketch in CA 102
Hackett, Albert (Maurice) 1900-1995 166
See also DFS 15
See also DLB 26
See also IDFW 3, 4
Hackett, Blanche Ann 1924- 73-76
Hackett, Bob
See Hackett, Robert A(nthony)
Hackett, Buddy 1924-2003
Obituary 217
Brief entry 108
Hackett, Cecil Arthur 1908-2000 ..... 13-16R
Obituary 189
Hackett, Charles J(oseph) 1915- 73-76
Hackett, Donald F. 1918- 29-32R
Hackett, Francis 1883-1962 108
Obituary 89-92
Hackett, Herbert L(ewis) 1917-1964 ..... 1-4R
Hackett, Jan Michele 1952-1996 ..... CANR-71
Obituary 152
Earlier sketch in CA 105
See also Kerouac, Jan
Hackett, John W. 1924- 17-20R
Hackett, John Winthrop 1910-1997 . CANR-49
Obituary 161
Earlier sketch in CA 89-92
See also SATA 65
Hackett, Laura Lyman 1916- 17-20R
Hackett, Lee
See Arkley, Arthur J(ames)
Hackett, Marie G. 1923- 37-40R
Hackett, Pat 105
Hackett, Paul 1920- 29-32R
Hackett, Peter 1940-
Brief entry 108
Hackett, Philip 1941- 77-80
Hackett, Robert A(nthony) 1952- 170
Hackett, Roger F(leming) 1922- 77-80
Hackett, William H. Y., Jr. 1921(?)-1986
Obituary 118
Hackford, Robert 1921(?)-1983
Obituary 111
Hackforth-Jones, (Frank) Gilbert 1900- .. 13-16R
Hacking, Ian 1936- CANR-70
Earlier sketch in CA 69-72
Hackl, Erich 1954- 137
Hackleman, Michael A(lan) 1946- 106
Hackler, George 1948- 208
Hackler, James C(ourtland) 1930- 112
Hackman, Eugene Alden 1930- 198
Hackman, Gene
See Hackman, Eugene Alden
Hackman, J(ohn) Richard 1940- CANR-1
Earlier sketch in CA 49-52
Hackman, Martha L. 1912- 29-32R
Hackney, Alan 1924- 5-8R
Hackney, Rod(erick Peter) 1942- 135
Hackney, Sheldon 1933- 41-44R
Hackney, Vivian 1914-1992 ..... 21-24R
Hacks, Peter 1928-2003 192
Obituary 224
See also CWW 2
See also DLB 124
See also EWL 3
See also SATA-Obit 151
Hackwell, W. John 1942- 126
Hackworth, David H(askell)
1931-2005 ..... CANR-88
Obituary 239
Earlier sketch in CA 130
See also BEST 89:4
Hadamard, Jacques (Salomon) 1865-1963 . 158
Hadas, Moses 1900-1966 ..... CANR-6
Obituary 25-28R
Earlier sketch in CA 1-4R
Hadas, Pamela White 1946- CANR-16
Earlier sketch in CA 93-96
Hadas, Rachel 1948- CANR-85
Earlier sketches in CA 111, CANR-29, 55
See also CAAS 23
See also CP 7
See also CWP
See also DLB 120, 282
Hadawi, Sami 1904- CANR-13
Earlier sketch in CA 21-24R
Hadda, Janet (Ruth) 1945- 128
Haddad, Bill
See Haddad, William F(rederick)
Haddad, George M(eri) 1910-2000 ..... 17-20R
Haddad, Gladys 1930- CANR-99
Earlier sketch in CA 138
Haddad, Jurj Mari
See Haddad, George M(eri)
Haddad, Robert M(itchell) 1930- 69-72
Haddad, William
See Haddad, William F(rederick)
Haddad, William F(rederick) 1928- 159
Brief entry 108
Haddad, Yvonne Y(azbeck) 1935- CANR-50
Earlier sketches in CA 108, CANR-25
Haddad-Garcia, George 1954- 107
Haddam, Jane
See Papazoglou, Orania
Haddan, Eugene E. 1918-
Brief entry 108
Hadden, Briton 1898-1929 174
See also DLB 91
Hadden, Jeffrey K(eith) 1936-2003 106
Obituary 213
Hadden, Maude Miner 1880-1967 ..... CAP-2
Earlier sketch in CA 17-18
Hadden, Sally E. 200
Haddix, Cecille
See Haddix-Kontos, Cecille P.
Haddix, Margaret Peterson 1964- ... CANR-102
Earlier sketch in CA 159
See also AAYA 42
See also BYA 16
See also MAICYA 2
See also SATA 94, 125
Haddix-Kontos, Cecille P. 1937- 69-72
Haddo, Oliver
See Puechner, Ray
Haddock, Doris 1910- 221
Haddock, K(eith) S(tanford) 1967- 145
Haddock, Lisa (Robyn) 1960- 146
Haddock, Sally 1954- 121
Haddon, A(lfred) C(ort) 1855-1940 190
Haddon, Celia 1944- 130
Haddon, Christopher
See Palmer, John (Leslie)
Haddon, Mark 1962- 222
See also SATA 155
Haddox, John H(erbert) 1929- 45-48
Hader, Berta (Hoerner)
1891(?)-1976 ..... CANR-85
Obituary 65-68
Earlier sketch in CA 73-76
See also CWRI 5
See also MAICYA 1, 2
See also SATA 16
Hader, Elmer (Stanley) 1889-1973 .... CANR-84
Earlier sketch in CA 73-76
See also CWRI 5
See also MAICYA 1, 2
See also SATA 16
Hadewijch of Antwerp fl. 1250- ..... RGWL 3
Hadfield, Alice M(ary) 1908- CANR-26
Earlier sketch in CA 108
Hadfield, Andrew 1962- 187
Hadfield, (Ellis) Charles (Raymond)
1909-1996 ..... CANR-51
Earlier sketches in CA 13-16R, CANR-7, 26
Hadfield, E. C. R.
See Hadfield, (Ellis) Charles (Raymond)
Hadfield, John (Charles Heywood)
1907-1999 128
Hadfield, Miles H(eywood)
1903-1982 ..... CANR-76
Obituary 106
Earlier sketches in CAP-1, CA 13-16
Hadfield, Vic(tor Edward) 1940- 209
Brief entry 106
Hadham, John
See Parkes, James William
Hadik, Laszlo 1932(?)-1973
Obituary 45-48
Hadingham, Evan 1951- 102
Hadithi, Mwenye
See Hobson, Bruce
Hadjiandreas, Yannis 1911-1980
See Tsirkas, Stratis
Hadleigh, Boze 1954- 195
Hadley, Arthur T. 1924- 89-92
Hadley, Charles D(avid), Jr. 1942- CANR-93
Earlier sketches in CA 110, CANR-31
Hadley, Eleanor M(artha) 1916- 29-32R
Hadley, Franklin
See Winterbotham, R(ussell) R(obert)
Hadley, Hamilton 1896-1975 ..... CAP-1
Obituary 180
Earlier sketch in CA 9-10
Hadley, Jay 1947- 114
Hadley, Joan
See Hess, Joan
Hadley, Lee 1934-1995 ..... CANR-83
Obituary 149
Earlier sketches in CA 101, CANR-19, 36
See also Irwin, Hadley
See also CLR 40
See also MAICYA 1, 2
See also MAICYAS 1
See also SATA 47, 89
See also SATA-Brief 38
See also SATA-Obit 86
See also WYA
See also YAW
Hadley, Leila 1925- CANR-86
Earlier sketches in CA 41-44R, CANR-14
Hadley, Michael L(lewellyn) 1936- 118
Hadley, Morris 1894-1979
Obituary 85-88
Hadley, Rollin van N. 1927- 127
Hadley, Tessa 1956- 212
Hadley Chase, James
See Raymond, Rene (Brabazon)
Hadlich, Roger L(ee) 1930- 209
Brief entry 108
Hadlow, Leonard Harold 1908- CAP-1
Earlier sketch in CA 13-14
Hadot, Pierre 1922- 210
Hadrill, Andrew (Frederic) Wallace
See Wallace-Hadrill, Andrew (Frederic)
Hadrill, John Michael Wallace
See Wallace-Hadrill, John Michael
Haduqa, 'Abd al-Hamid Ibn 1925- ..... EWL 3
Hadwiger, Don F. 1930- 21-24R
Haeberle, Erwin J(akob) 1936- CANR-29
Earlier sketch in CA 29-32R
Haebich, Kathryn A. 1899-1980 ..... 5-8R
Obituary 180
Haeckel, Ernst Heinrich (Philipp August)
1834-1919 157
See also TCLC 83
Haedrich, Marcel 1913- CANR-44
Earlier sketch in CA 85-88
Haefele, John W(illiam) 1913- 1-4R
Haefeli, Evan 1969- 238
Haefele, Deborah 1954- ..... SATA 76
Haefner, Richard 1929- 108
Haeger, John Denis 1942- 137
Haegg, Goeran
See Hagg, Goran
Haegg, Tomas 1938- 111
Haegglund, Bengt 1920- CANR-10
Earlier sketch in CA 25-28R
Haekkerup, Per 1915-1979
Obituary 85-88
Haenel, Wolfram 1956- 155
See also CLR 64
See also SATA 89
Haenicke, Diether H. 1935- 33-36R
Haentzschel, Adolph T(heodore)
1881-1971 ..... CANR-77
Obituary 103
Earlier sketch in CA 1-4R
Haeri, Niloofar 230
Haeri, Shahla 224
Haering, Bernhard 1912-1998 ..... CANR-9
Obituary 169
Earlier sketch in CA 5-8R
Haering, Georg Wilhelm Heinrich
See Alexis, Willibald
Haertig, Evelyn 1919- 198
Haes, Frans De
See De Haes, Frans
Haessler, Herbert A(lfred) 1926- 125
Haessly, Jacqueline 1937- 120
Haestrup, Jorgen 1909-1998 199
Hafemeister, David W(alter) 1934- ... CANR-51
Earlier sketch in CA 124
Hafen, Ann Woodbury 1893-1970
Obituary 111
Hafen, Brent Q(ue) 1940- CANR-40
Earlier sketch in CA 112
Hafen, LeRoy R(euben) 1893- 65-68
Obituary 196
Hafer, W(illiam) Keith 108
Hafertepe, Kenneth 1955- CANR-101
Earlier sketch in CA 137
Hafez, Mohammed M. 1970- 238
Haffar, Rif K. 1955- 220
Haffenden, Philip Spencer 1926- 61-64
Haffner, J. Lilliwhite
See Speed, F(rederick) Maurice
Haffner, Robert C(hristian) G(ert) 1970- 158
Haffner, Sebastian 1907-1999 217
Hafiz c. 1326-1389(?) ..... RGWL 2, 3
See also WLIT 6
Hafley, James 1928- 17-20R
Hafner, Katie 1957- 204
See also MTFW 2005
Hafner, Lawrence E. 1924- CANR-10
Earlier sketch in CA 25-28R
Hafner, Marylin 1925- ..... SATA 7, 121
Hafrey, Leigh 1951- 142
Hafstein, Hannes 1861-1922 ..... DLB 293
Haftmann, Werner 1912-1999 188
Haga, Enoch J. 1931- 25-28R
Hagalin, Gudmundur Gislason
1898-1985 ..... DLB 293
Hagan, Arthur Peter 1912-1987 107
Hagan, Charles B(anner) 1905-1991 ..... 37-40R
Hagan, Chet 1922- CANR-25
Earlier sketch in CA 107
Hagan, John T(homas) 1926- 25-28R
Hagan, Kenneth J(ames) 1936- 41-44R
Hagan, Patricia
See Howell, Patricia Hagan
Hagan, William T(homas) 1918- CANR-8
Earlier sketch in CA 5-8R
Hagar, George
See Maria Del Rey, Sister
Hagarty, (Daniel) Britt 1949-1999 110
Hagberg, David J(ames) 1942- CANR-143
Earlier sketch in CA 106
Hagbrink, Bodil 1936- 104
Hage, Jerald 1932- 37-40R
Hagedorn, Friedrich von 1708-1754 .. DLB 168
Hagedorn, Hermann 1882-1964
Obituary 116
Hagedorn, Jessica T(arahata) 1949- .. CANR-69
Earlier sketch in CA 139
See also CLC 185
See also CWP
See also DLB 312
See also RGAL 4
Hagedorn, John M. 1947- 152
Hagedorn, Robert (Bruce) 1925- CANR-28
Earlier sketch in CA 49-52
Hagee, John C(harles) 1940- CANR-3
Earlier sketch in CA 45-48
Hagelin, Aiban 1934- 145
Hagelman, Charles W(illiam), Jr. 1920-. 21-24R
Hagelstange, Rudolf 1912-1984 81-84
See also DLB 69
Hageman, Howard G(arberich)
1921-1992 ..... CANR-46
Obituary 140
Earlier sketches in CA 1-4R, CANR-5
Hagen, Clifford (Warren, Jr.) 1943- 29-32R
Hagen, Elizabeth Pauline 1915- 13-16R
Hagen, Everett E(inar) 1906- CANR-1
Earlier sketch in CA 1-4R
Hagen, George 1958- 234
Hagen, John Milton 1902-1977 57-60
Hagen, John William 1940- 61-64
Hagen, Lorinda
See Du Breuil, (Elizabeth) L(or)inda
Hagen, Richard L(ionel) 1935- 93-96
Hagen, Uta (Thyra) 1919-2004 77-80
Obituary 222
Hager, Alan 1940- 175
Hager, Alice Rogers 1894-1969 ..... CANR-76
Obituary 103
Earlier sketch in CA 5-8R
See also SATA-Obit 26
Hager, Betty 1923- 155
See also SATA 89
Hager, Henry B. 1926- 17-20R
Hager, Jean 1932- CANR-84
Earlier sketch in CA 101
See also CMW 4
Hager, Judith
See Polley, Judith (Anne)
Hager, Robert M. 1938- 65-68
Hager, Thomas Arthur 1953- 126
Hager, Tom 1953- 190
See also SATA 119
Hagerman, Edward 1939- CANR-82
Earlier sketch in CA 130
Hagerman, Paul Stirling 1949- 106
Hagerstrand, (Stig) Torsten (Erik) 1916-2004
See Hagerstrand, (Stig) Torsten (Erik)
Hagerstrand, (Stig) Torsten (Erik) 1916-2004
Obituary 227
Brief entry 116
Hagerty, James C(ampbell) 1909-1981 129
Obituary 103
Hagerty, Nancy K. 1935- 33-36R
Hagerty, Sheward 1930-1983
Obituary 109
Hagerup, Inger (Halsor) 1905-1985 .... DLB 297
Hagg, G. Eric 1908(?)-1979
Obituary 85-88
Hagg, Goran 1947- 190
Hagg, Tomas
See Haegg, Tomas
Haggai, Thomas Stephens 1931- 93-96
Haggar, R. G.
See Haggar, Reginald George
Haggar, Reginald G.
See Haggar, Reginald George
Haggar, Reginald George 1905-1988
Obituary 128
Haggard, H(enry) Rider
1856-1925 ..... CANR-112
Brief entry 108
Earlier sketch in CA 148
See also BRWS 3
See also BYA 4, 5
See also DLB 70, 156, 174, 178
See also FANT
See also LMFS 1
See also MTCW 2
See also RGEL 2
See also RHW
See also SATA 16
See also SCFW 1, 2
See also SFW 4
See also SUFW 1
See also TCLC 11
See also WLIT 4
Haggard, Howard W. 1902-1959 121
Haggard, Merle (Ronald) 1937- 156
Brief entry 112
Haggard, Paul
See Longstreet, Stephen
Haggard, Raymond (Gordon Rider) 1921-
Brief entry 109
Haggard, Virginia 1915- 122
Haggard, William
See Clayton, Richard Henry Michael
See also CN 1, 2, 3, 4, 5
See also DLB 276
See also DLBY 1993
Hagger, Nicholas 1939- CANR-104
Earlier sketch in CA 149
Haggerson, Nelson L. 1927- 41-44R
Haggerty, Brian A(rthur) 1943- CANR-32
Earlier sketch in CA 113
Haggerty, James J(oseph) 1920- 41-44R
See also SATA 5
Haggerty, Kevin D. 1965- 222
Haggerty, P(atrick) E(ugene) 1914-1980
Obituary 105
Haggett, Peter 1933- 73-76
Haggie, Paul 1949- 124
Haggin, B(ernard) H. 1900-1987 ..... CANR-76
Obituary 122
Earlier sketches in CA 102, CANR-18
Haggren, Maria Gustava
See Haggren, Maria Gustava
Hagiosy, L.
See Larbaud, Valery (Nicolas)
Hagiwara, Michio Peter 1932- CANR-13
Earlier sketch in CA 73-76
Hagiwara, Sakutaro 1886-1942 154
See also Hagiwara Sakutaro
See also PC 18
See also RGWL 3
See also TCLC 60
Hagiwara Sakutaro
See Hagiwara, Sakutaro
See also EWL 3
Hagler, Erwin Harrison 1947- 120
Hagler, Skeeter
See Hagler, Erwin Harrison
Haglund, Elaine J(ean) 1937- 109
Hagman, Bette 1922- 53-56
Hagman, Donald Gerald 1932-1982
Obituary 114
Hagner, Donald A(lfred) 1936- CANR-142
Earlier sketch in CA 110
Hagon, Priscilla
See Allan, Mabel Esther
Hagopian, John V. 1923- 41-44R
Hagopian, Mark N. 1940- CANR-28
Earlier sketch in CA 49-52
Hagstrom, Jerry 1947- CANR-34
Earlier sketch in CA 111
Hagstrom, Julie 1930- 111
Hagstrom, Warren Olaf 1930- 21-24R
Hagstrum, Jean (Howard) 1913-1995 .... 17-20R

Hague, Douglas Chalmers 1926- CANR-20
Earlier sketch in CA 69-72
Hague, G(raeme) M(alcolm) 1959- .... HGG
Hague, Harlan 1932- CANR-40
Earlier sketch in CA 116
Hague, (Susan) Kathleen 1949- 125
See also SATA 49
See also SATA-Brief 45
Hague, Michael R. 1948- CANR-36
Brief entry 111
Earlier sketch in CA 123
See also AAYA 18
See also MAICYA 1, 2
See also SATA 48, 80, 129
See also SATA-Brief 32
Hague, Nora 215
Hague, Richard 1947- CANR-122
Earlier sketches in CA 126, CANR-54
Hague, William Edward, Jr. 1919- 85-88
Hagy, Alyson 1960- CANR-97
Earlier sketch in CA 137
See also CSW
See also DLB 244
Hagy, James William 1936- 143
Hagy, Ruth Geri
See Brod, Ruth Hagy
Hahm, Sung Deuk 1963- 167
Hahn, Cynthia T. 1961- CANR-123
Earlier sketch in CA 162
Hahn, Emily 1905-1997 .... CANR-27
Obituary 156
Earlier sketches in CA 1-4R, CANR-1
Interview in CANR-27
See also CAAS 11
See also SATA 3
See also SATA-Obit 96
Hahn, F. E.
See Hahn, Friedrich Ernest
Hahn, Fred 1906- 45-48
Hahn, Fred E.
See Hahn, Friedrich Ernest
Hahn, Fred Ernest
See Hahn, Friedrich Ernest
Hahn, Friedrich Ernest 1916-1989
Obituary 129
Hahn, Gloria 1926-1987
Obituary 123
Hahn, H. George 1942- 107
Hahn, Hannelore CANR-3
Earlier sketch in CA 5-8R
See also SATA 8
Hahn, Harlan 1939- 33-36R
Hahn, James (Sage) 1947- CANR-17
Earlier sketches in CA 49-52, CANR-2
See also SATA 9
Hahn, Kimiko 1955- 190
See also PFS 23
Hahn, Lewis E(dwin) 1908- 143
Hahn, (Mona) Lynn 1949- CANR-17
Earlier sketches in CA 49-52, CANR-2
See also SATA 9
Hahn, Mary Downing 1937- CANR-117
Earlier sketches in CA 122, CANR-48
See also AAYA 23
See also JRDA
See also MAICYA 1, 2
See also MAICYAS 1
See also SAAS 12
See also SATA 50, 81, 138, 157
See also SATA-Brief 44
See also SATA-Essay 157
Hahn, Michael T. 1953- 156
See also SATA 92
Hahn (Garces), Oscar (Arturo)
1938- CANR-98
Earlier sketch in CA 131
See also HW 1
Hahn, Otto 1879-1968 158
Obituary 112
Hahn, Paul H. 1932- 117
Hahn, Robert H. 1920- 123
Hahn, Robert O(scar) 1916- 69-72
Hahn, Roger 1932- 33-36R
Hahn, Scott (Walker) 1957- 189
Hahn, Steven 1951- 123
Hahn, Ulla 1946- 195
Hahnel, Robin (Eric) 1946- 209
Hahner, June E(dith) 1940- CANR-11
Earlier sketch in CA 25-28R
Hahn-Hahn, Ida Graefin von
1805-1875 .... DLB 133
Hahon, James
See Swift, Patrick
Hai, Lan
See Gao, Yuan
Haiblum, Isidore 1935- CANR-84
Earlier sketches in CA 53-56, CANR-4, 19
See also SFW 4
Haidar, Qurratulain 1927- .... CWW 2
Haidu, Peter 1931- 37-40R
Haig, Alexander M(eigs), Jr. 1924- 138
Brief entry 124
Haig, Brian 220
Haig, Fenil
See Ford, Ford Madox
Haig, Kathryn 1947- 172
Haig, (Irvine Reid) Stirling 1936- 33-36R
Haigaz, Aram
See Chekenian, Aram Haigaz
Haig-Brown, Roderick (Langmere)
1908-1976 .... CANR-83
Obituary 69-72
Earlier sketches in CA 5-8R, CANR-4, 38
See also CLC 21
See also CLR 31
See also CWRI 5
See also DLB 88
See also MAICYA 1, 2
See also SATA 12
See also TCWW 2
Haigerty, Leo James 1924- 1-4R
Haigh, Christopher 1944- 126
Haigh, Jennifer 1968- 221
Haigh, Richard
See James, Laurence
Haight, Amanda 1939- 77-80
Haight, Anne Lyon 1895-1977 .... CAP-2
Obituary 73-76
Earlier sketch in CA 33-36
See also SATA-Obit 30
Haight, Gordon S(herman)
1901-1985 .... CANR-76
Obituary 118
Earlier sketches in CAP-2, CA 25-28
See also DLB 103
Haight, John McVickar, Jr. 1917- 29-32R
Haight, M. R. 1938- 124
Haight, Mabel V. Jackson
See Jackson-Haight, Mabel V.
Haight, Mary Ellen Jordan
See Jordan Haight, Mary Ellen
Haight, Rip
See Carpenter, John (Howard)
Haight, Robert 1955- 191
Haight, Sandy 1949- .... SATA 79
Haij, Vera
See Jansson, Tove (Marika)
Haiken, Elizabeth CANR-138
Earlier sketch in CA 172
Hail, Marshall 1905- 5-8R
Haile, H(arry) G(erald) 1931- 65-68
Hailes, Julia 1961- 130
Hailey, Arthur 1920-2004 .... CANR-75
Obituary 233
Earlier sketches in CA 1-4R, CANR-2, 36
See also AITN 2
See also BEST 90:3
See also BPFB 2
See also CCA 1
See also CLC 5
See also CN 1, 2, 3, 4, 5, 6, 7
See also CPW
See also DAM NOV, POP
See also DLB 88
See also DLBY 1982
See also MTCW 1, 2
See also MTFW 2005
Hailey, Elizabeth Forsythe 1938- 188
Earlier sketches in CA 93-96, CANR-15, 48
Interview in CANR-15
Autobiographical Essay in 188
See also CAAS 1
See also CLC 40
Hailey, J. P.
See Hall, Parnell
Hailey, Johanna
See Howl, Marcia (Yvonne Hurt)
Hailey, Johanna
See Jarvis, Sharon
Hailey, (Elizabeth) Kendall 1966- 136
Hailey, Oliver 1932-1993 .... CANR-83
Obituary 140
Earlier sketches in CA 41-44R, CANR-15, 46
See also CAD
Hailey, Sheila 1927- 85-88
Hailperin, Herman 1899-1973 .... CANR-77
Obituary 103
Earlier sketch in CA 5-8R
Hailstock, Shirley 180
Hailstones, Thomas J(ohn) 1919- 41-44R
Hailwood, Mike
See Hailwood, Stanley Michael Bailey
Hailwood, Stanley Michael Bailey 1940-1981
Obituary 108
Haiman, Franklyn S(aul) 1921- 37-40R
Haiman, Robert James 1936- 133
Haimann, Theo 1911-1991 .... CANR-2
Earlier sketch in CA 5-8R
Haime, Agnes Irvine Constance (Adams)
1884- CAP-1
Earlier sketch in CA 9-10
Haimes, Norma 53-56
Haimo, Ethan 1950- 128
Haimowitz, Morris (Loeb) 1918- 37-40R
Haimowitz, Natalie Reader 1923- 53-56
Haimson, Leopold Henri 1917- 126
Brief entry 109
Hain, Peter 1950- 131
Hainaux, Rene 1918- 73-76
Haindl, Marieluise
Obituary 49-52
See also Fleißer, Marieluise
Haine, Edgar A. 1908- 97-100
Haines, Carolyn 1953- CANR-115
Earlier sketch in CA 163
Haines, Catharine M(anya) C(olton) 1939- . 232
Haines, Charles 1928- 41-44R
Haines, Charles G(rove) 1906-1976
Obituary 65-68
Haines, David W. 1947- 175
Haines, Edward Burdette 1910-1984
Obituary 112
Haines, Francis 1899-1988 .... 5-8R
Haines, Francis D., Jr. 1923- 53-56
Haines, Gail Kay 1943- CANR-31
Earlier sketches in CA 37-40R, CANR-14
See also SATA 11
Haines, George H(enry), Jr. 1937- 33-36R
Haines, Harry B. 1949(?)-1984
Obituary 112
Haines, John
See Richardson, Gladwell
Haines, John (Meade) 1924- CANR-34
Earlier sketches in CA 17-20R, CANR-13
See also AMWS 12
See also CLC 58
See also CP 1, 2
See also CSW
See also DLB 5, 212
See also TCLE 1:1
Haines, Max 1931- CANR-15
Earlier sketch in CA 85-88
Haines, Pamela Mary 1929-1991 ..... CANR-83
Earlier sketches in CA 106, CANR-24
See also RHW
Haines, Perry Franklin 1889-1968 .... 5-8R
Haines, Richard W. 1957- 146
Haines, Walter W(ells) 1918- 1-4R
Haines, William Wister 1908-1989 .. CANR-76
Obituary 130
Earlier sketches in CAP-1, CA 9-10
Haining, Peter (Alexander) 1940- ... CANR-142
Earlier sketches in CA 45-48, CANR-1
See also SATA 14
Hains, Harriet
See Watson, Carol
Hainsworth, D(avid) R(oger) 1931- 141
Hainsworth, Peter (R. J.) 226
Hainworth, Henry Charles 1914-2005 109
Obituary 236
Hair, Donald S(herman) 1937- 69-72
Hair, P(aul) E(dward) H(edley)
1926-2001 .... 25-28R
Obituary 202
Hair, William Ivy 1930- 29-32R
Haire, Wilson John 1932- 101
See also CBD
See also CD 5, 6
Haire-Sargeant, Lin 1946- 139
Hairston, William (Russell, Jr.) 1928- 143
See also BW 2
Haislip, Harvey (Shadle)
1889-1978 .... CANR-76
Obituary 103
Earlier sketch in CA 1-4R
Haislip, John 1925- 33-36R
Haislip, Martha Pratt 1889(?)-1984
Obituary 112
Haithcox, John Patrick 1933- 29-32R
Haizlip, Harold C(ornelius) 1935- 192
Haizlip, Shirlee Taylor 1937- 146
Haj, Fareed 1935- 29-32R
Hajdin, Mane 1959- 192
Hajdu, David 1955- 166
Hajdusiewicz, Babs Bell 239
See also SATA 163
Hajj, Unsi Luwis al- 1937- .... EWL 3
Hakala, Dee 1958- 226
Hakanson, Bjoern Gunnar
See Hakanson, Bjorn Gunnar
Hake, Edward 1566-1604 .... DLB 136
Hake, Thomas Gordon 1809-1895 .... DLB 32
Hakeda, Yoshito S. 1924(?)-1983
Obituary 110
Hakeem, Brother Wali
See Gill, Walter
Hakes, Joseph Edward 1916- 9-12R
Hakim, Catherine 1948- CANR-130
Earlier sketch in CA 170
Hakim, Joy 1931- 222
See also SATA 83
Hakim, Raymond 1909-1980 .... IDFW 3, 4
Hakim, Robert 1907- .... IDFW 3, 4
Hakim, Seymour 1933- 65-68
Hakim, Tawfiq al- 1902-1987
See Tawfiq al-Hakim
See also AFW
See also EWL 3
See also RGWL 3
See also WLIT 2
Hakluyt, Richard 1552-1616 .... DLB 136
See also RGEL 2
Hakutani, Yoshinobu 1935- 101
Halabi, Rafik 1946- 127
Halaby, Najeeb E(lias) 1915-2003 183
Obituary 218
Brief entry 107
Halacy, D(aniel) S(tephen), Jr.
1919-2002 .... CANR-9
Earlier sketch in CA 5-8R
See also Halacy, Dan
See also SATA 36
Halacy, Dan
See Halacy, D(aniel) S(tephen), Jr.
See also SAAS 8
Halal, William E. 1933- 123
Halam, Ann
See Jones, Gwyneth A(nn)
Hal'amova, Masa 1908-1995 .... EWL 3
Halas, Celia (Mary) 1922- 103
Halas, Frantisek 1901-1949 .... DLB 215
See also EWL 3
Halas, George Stanley 1895-1983
Obituary 111
Halas, John 1912-1995 108
See also IDFW 3, 4
Halasz, Gyula 1899-1984 .... CANR-58
Obituary 113
Earlier sketch in CA 126
Halasz, Janos
See Halas, John
Halasz, Nicholas 1895-1985 .... CANR-76
Obituary 116
Earlier sketch in CA 17-20R
Halbach, Edward C(hristian), Jr. 1931- 93-96
Halbe, Max 1865-1944 196
See also DLB 118
Halberg, Arvo Kusta
See Hall, Gus
Halberstadt, John 1941- 49-52
Halberstadt, William Harold 1930- 1-4R
Halberstam, David 1934- CANR-134
Earlier sketches in CA 69-72, CANR-10, 45, 69, 107
See also BEST 89:4
See also DLB 241
See also MTCW 2
See also MTFW 2005
Halberstam, Michael J(oseph)
1932-1980 .... CANR-10
Obituary 102
Earlier sketch in CA 65-68
Halbert, Frederic (Leslie) 1945- 122
Brief entry 118
Halbert, Sandra (Edith) 1943- 123
Halbrook, Stephen P. CANR-47
Earlier sketch in CA 121
Halcomb, Ruth 1936- 97-100
Halcrow, Harold Graham 1911- 17-20R
Haldane, A(rchibald) R(ichard) B(urdon)
1900-1982 120
Obituary 108
Haldane, Charlotte (Franken)
1894-1969 .... DLB 191
Haldane, J(ohn) B(urdon) S(anderson)
1892-1964 101
See also CWRI 5
See also DLB 160
Haldane, R(obert) A(ylmer) 1907- 69-72
Haldane, Roger John 1945- .... SATA 13
Haldar, Achintya 1945- 199
Haldeman, Charles (Heuss) 1931- 5-8R
Haldeman, H(arry) R(obbins)
1926-1993 .... CANR-75
Obituary 143
Earlier sketch in CA 81-84
Haldeman, Jack C(arroll) II 1941- CANR-83
Brief entry 119
Earlier sketch in CA 148
See also SFW 4
Haldeman, Joe (William) 1943- 179
Earlier sketches in CA 53-56, CANR-6, 70, 72, 130
Interview in CANR-6
Autobiographical Essay in 179
See also Graham, Robert
See also CAAS 25
See also AAYA 38
See also CLC 61
See also DLB 8
See also SCFW 2
See also SFW 4
Haldeman, Linda (Wilson) 1935-1988 85-88
Halder, Ras Mohun 1905(?)-1990
Obituary 131
Haldon, John F. 208
Hale, Agnes Burke 1890-1981
Obituary 103
Hale, Allean Lemmon 1914- CANR-30
Earlier sketch in CA 33-36R
Hale, Antoinette
See Stockenberg, Antoinette
Hale, Arlene 1924-1982 .... CANR-1
Earlier sketch in CA 1-4R
See also SATA 49
Hale, Barbara N. 1938- 197
Hale, Bob
See Hale, Robert D(avid)
Hale, Bruce 1957- 194
See also SATA 123
Hale, Charles A(dams) 1930- 25-28R
Hale, Charlotte
See Allen, Charlotte Hale
Hale, Christy
See Apostolou, Christine Hale
Hale, Clarence B(enjamin) 1905-1992 69-72
Hale, Daniel J. 1960(?)- 229
Hale, David G(eorge) 1938- 45-48
Hale, Deborah 212
Hale, Dennis 1944- 25-28R
Hale, Douglas 1929- 140
Hale, Edward Everett 1822-1909 160
Brief entry 119
See also DLB 1, 42, 74, 235
See also SATA 16
See also SFW 4
Hale, Francesca
See Halpern, Frances J(oy)
Hale, Francis Joseph 1922- 53-56
Hale, Frank (Wilbur), Jr. 1927- 65-68
Hale, Glenn
See Walker, Robert W(ayne)
Hale, Helen
See Mulcahy, Lucille Burnett
Hale, Irina 1932- 105
See also SATA 26
Hale, J. Russell 1918- 101
Hale, Jade
See Hyatt, Betty H(ale)
Hale, Janet Campbell 1947- CANR-75
Earlier sketches in CA 49-52, CANR-45
See also DAM MULT
See also DLB 175
See also MTCW 2
See also MTFW 2005
See also NNAL
Hale, Janice E(llen) 1948- 208
Hale, John (Barry) 1926- CANR-130
Earlier sketch in CA 102
See also CBD
See also CD 5, 6
Hale, Sir John Rigby 1923-1999 .... CANR-19
Obituary 183
Earlier sketch in CA 102
Hale, Judson (Drake) 1933- 69-72
Hale, Julian A(nthony) S(tuart) 1940- 41-44R
Hale, Kathleen 1898-2000 .... CANR-83
Obituary 188

Cumulative Index 243 Hall

Earlier sketch in CA 73-76
See also CWRI 5
See also DLB 160
See also SATA 17, 66
See also SATA-Obit 121
Hale, Keith 1955- CANR-102
Earlier sketch in CA 126
Hale, Kenneth L(ocke) 1934-2001 213
Hale, Leo Thomas
See Ebon
Hale, Leo Thomas
See Ebon
Hale, Leon 1921- CANR-10
Earlier sketch in CA 17-20R
Hale, (Charles) Leslie 1902-1985 ..... CANR-76
Obituary 116
Earlier sketches in CAP-1, CA 13-16
Hale, Linda (Howe) 1929- 5-8R
See also SATA 6
Hale, Lionel Ramsay 1909-1977
Obituary 107
Hale, Lucretia P.
See Hale, Lucretia Peabody
Hale, Lucretia Peabody 1820-1900 136
Brief entry 122
See also DLB 42
See also MAICYA 1, 2
See also SATA 26
See also WCH
Hale, Margaret
See Higonnet, Margaret R(andolph)
Hale, Mason E(llsworth, Jr.) 1928-1990
Obituary 131
Hale, Michael
See Bullock, Michael
Hale, Nancy 1908-1988 .... 5-8R
Obituary 126
See also CN 1, 2, 3, 4
See also DLB 86
See also DLBD 17
See also DLBY 1980, 1988
See also SATA 31
See also SATA-Obit 57
Hale, Nathan Cabot 1925- 53-56
Hale, Nathan G., Jr. 1922- 154
Hale, Oron James 1902-1991 .... 13-16R
Obituary 135
Hale, Patricia Whitaker 1922- 53-56
Hale, Philip
See Eastwood, C(harles) Cyril
Hale, Richard W(alden) 1909-1976
Obituary 65-68
Hale, Robert Beverly 1901-1985 141
Obituary 117
Hale, Robert D(avid) 1928- 134
Hale, Robert William 1937- 114
Hale, Sarah Josepha (Buell) 1788-1879 . DLB 1, 42, 73, 243
Hale, Shannon 234
See also SATA 158
Hale, Susan 1833-1910 .... DLB 221
Hale, Wanda
See Coutard, Wanda Lundy Hale
Hale, William 1940- 125
Hale, William Harlan 1910-1974 93-96
Obituary 49-52
Hales, Ann
See Hales-Tooke, Ann (Mary Margaret)
Hales, E(dward) E(lton) Y(oung)
1908-1986 85-88
Hales, Edward John 1927- 106
Hales, John 1584-1656 .... DLB 151
Hales, Loyde (Wesley) 1933- 89-92
Hales, Norman
See Young, Vernon
Hales, Peter Bacon 1950- 132
Hales, Shelley 1971- 236
Hales, Steven D(ouglas) 1966- 193
Hales-Tooke, Ann (Mary Margaret) 1926- ... 123
Brief entry 116
Halevi, Judah c. 1070-1141 .... WLIT 6
Halevi, Yossi Klein 1953- CANR-119
Earlier sketch in CA 154
Halevi, Z'ev ben Shimon
See Kenton, Warren
Halevy, Daniel 1872-1962 ...... GFL 1789 to the Present
Halevy, Elie 1870-1937 .... TCLC 104
Halevy, Eva Etzioni
See Etzioni-Halevy, Eva
Halevy, Ludovic 1834-1908 182
See also DLB 192
Haley, Alex(ander Murray Palmer)
1921-1992 .... CANR-61
Obituary 136
Earlier sketch in CA 77-80
See also AAYA 26
See also BLC 2
See also BPFB 2
See also BW 2, 3
See also CDALBS
See also CLC 8, 12, 76
See also CPW
See also CSW
See also DA
See also DA3
See also DAB
See also DAC
See also DAM MST, MULT, POP
See also DLB 38
See also LAIT 5
See also MTCW 1, 2
See also NFS 9
See also TCLC 147
Haley, Andrew G(allagher) 1904-1966 .. CAP-1
Earlier sketch in CA 13-16
Haley, Bruce Everts 1933- 186
Brief entry 108
Haley, Earl. J. 1898(?)-1987
Obituary 122
Haley, Gail E(inhart) 1939- CANR-115
Earlier sketches in CA 21-24R, CANR-14, 35, 82
See also CLR 21
See also MAICYA 1, 2
See also SAAS 13
See also SATA 43, 78, 136, 161
See also SATA-Brief 28
See also SATA-Essay 161
Haley, Jack, Jr.
See Haley, John J., Jr.
Haley, James L(ewis) 1951- CANR-115
Earlier sketch in CA 77-80
Haley, Jay 1923- CANR-9
Earlier sketch in CA 21-24R
Haley, John J., Jr. 1933-2001 135
Obituary 194
Haley, Joseph E. 1915- 13-16R
Haley, Ken(neth) H(arold) D(obson)
1920-1997 159
Haley, Margaret Angela 1861-1939
Brief entry 112
Haley, Michael 1952- 109
Haley, Neale 41-44R
See also SATA 52
Haley, P. Edward 130
Haley, (Harry) Russell 1934- CANR-70
Earlier sketch in CA 118
See also CN 6, 7
Haley, William (John) 1901-1987
Obituary 123
Half, Robert 1918-2001 107
Obituary 200
Halford, Graeme S(ydney) 1937- 154
Haliburton, Hugh
See Robertson, James Logie
Haliburton, Thomas Chandler
1796-1865 .... DLB 11, 99
See also RGEL 2
See also RGSF 2
Halifax, Joan (Squire) 1942- 85-88
Halio, Jay L(eon) 1928- CANR-10
Earlier sketch in CA 25-28R
Halivni, David
See Halivni, David Weiss
Halivni, David Weiss 1928- CANR-49
Halkett, John G(eorge) 1933- 57-60
Halkin, Abraham S. 1903-1990
Obituary 131
Halkin, Ariela 1942- 175
Halkin, Hillel 1939- 215
Halkin, Shimon 1899-1987 53-56
Halkin, Simon
See Halkin, Shimon
Hall, Adam
See Trevor, Elleston
See also DLB 276
Hall, Adele 1910- 1-4R
See also SATA 7
Hall, Adrian 1927- CANR-22
Earlier sketch in CA 106
Hall, Al(fred) Rupert 1920- 9-12R
Hall, Alice Clay 1900-1983 73-76
Hall, Andrew 1935- 21-24R
Hall, Angus 1932- CANR-13
Earlier sketch in CA 21-24R
Hall, Ann
See Duckert, Mary
Hall, Ann C. 1959- CANR-104
Earlier sketch in CA 149
Hall, Anna Gertrude 1882-1967 .... CAP-1
Earlier sketch in CA 11-12
See also SATA 8
Hall, Anna Maria 1800-1881 .... DLB 159
Hall, Anthony Stewart 1945- 102
Hall, Ariel Perry 1906- 69-72
Hall, Arlene Stevens 1923- 17-20R
Hall, Asa Zadel 1875-1965 .... CANR-4
Earlier sketch in CA 1-4R
Hall, Austin 1882(?)-1933 160
Brief entry 114
See also SFW 4
Hall, Aylmer
See Hall, Norah E. L.
Hall, B(axter) C(larence) 1936- CANR-9
Earlier sketch in CA 57-60
Hall, Barbara 1960- CANR-84
Earlier sketch in CA 135
See also AAYA 21
See also SATA 68
See also YAW
Hall, Bennie Caroline (Humble) 1-4R
Hall, Bert S(tewart) 1945- 167
Hall, Beverly B. 1918- 160
See also SATA 95
Hall, Blaine H(ill) 1932- 140
Hall, Borden
See Yates, Raymond F(rancis)
Hall, Brian (Jonathan) 1959- CANR-139
Earlier sketch in CA 137
Hall, Brian P(atrick) 1935- CANR-9
Earlier sketch in CA 61-64
See also SATA 31
Hall, C(onstance) Margaret 1937- CANR-12
Earlier sketch in CA 73-76
Hall, Calvin (Springer) 1909- 13-16R
Hall, Cameron
See del Rey, Lester
Hall, Cameron P(arker) 1898-1987 49-52
Hall, Carl W. 1924- 135
Hall, Carolyn Vorburg 1937- 61-64
Hall, Caryl
See Hansen, Caryl (Hall)
Hall, Catherine 230
Hall, Challis A(lva), Jr. 1917-1968 .... 1-4R
Obituary 103
Hall, Charles A(rthur) M(ann) 1924-
Brief entry 107
Hall, Clarence W(ilbur) 1902-1985
Obituary 114
Hall, Claudia
See Floren, Lee
Hall, Clifton L. 1898-1987 .... CAP-1
Earlier sketch in CA 11-12
Hall, Conrad 1926- .... IDFW 3, 4
Hall, Constance
See Koslow, Connie H.
Hall, D(onald) J(ohn) 1903- 13-16R
Hall, Daniel 1952- 163
Hall, Daniel George Edward 1891-1979 103
Hall, David C. 1943- 140
Hall, David D(risko) 1936- 125
Brief entry 108
Hall, David Locke 1955- 140
Hall, Don 1929- 110
Hall, Don Alan 1938- 108
Hall, Donald (Andrew, Jr.) 1928- CANR-133
Earlier sketches in CA 5-8R, CANR-2, 44, 64, 106
See also CAAS 7
See also AAYA 63
See also CLC 1, 13, 37, 59, 151
See also CP 1, 2, 3, 4, 5, 6, 7
See also DAM POET
See also DLB 5
See also MAL 5
See also MTCW 2
See also MTFW 2005
See also RGAL 4
See also SATA 23, 97
Hall, Donald Ray 1933- 33-36R
Hall, Dorothy Judd 122
Hall, Douglas 1931- .... SATA 43
Hall, Douglas C. 234
Hall, Douglas John 1928- CANR-14
Earlier sketch in CA 69-72
Hall, Douglas Kent 1938- 33-36R
Hall, Edward 1497-1547 .... DLB 132
Hall, Edward Twitchell, (Jr.) 1914- 65-68
Hall, Elizabeth 1929- CANR-60
Earlier sketches in CA 65-68, CANR-14, 31
See also SATA 77
Hall, Elizabeth Cornelia 1898-1989 ...... 37-40R
Hall, Elvajean 1910-1984 .... CANR-8
Earlier sketch in CA 13-16R
See also SATA 6
Hall, Eric B(rinn) 1963- 149
Hall, Eric J(ohn) 1933- 97-100
Hall, Evan
See Halleran, E(ugene) E(dward)
Hall, F. H. 1926- 77-80
Hall, Fernau 102
Hall, Florence (Marion) Howe 1845-1922 . 209
Hall, Frederic Sauser
See Sauser-Hall, Frederic
Hall, Gene E(rwin) 1941- 93-96
Hall, Geoffrey Fowler 1888-1970 .... CAP-1
Earlier sketch in CA 13-14
Hall, George 1941- CANR-15
Earlier sketch in CA 85-88
Hall, George F(ridolph) 1908-2000 .. CANR-22
Earlier sketch in CA 45-48
Hall, George R. 1930- 123
Hall, Georgette Brockman 1915- 57-60
Hall, Geraldine M(arion) 1935- 33-36R
Hall, Gimone 1940- CANR-33
Earlier sketches in CA 29-32R, CANR-15
Hall, Gladys 1891(?)-1977
Obituary 73-76
Hall, Gordon Langley
See Simmons, Dawn Langley
Hall, Gregory 1948- 165
Hall, Gus 1910-2000 137
Obituary 191
Brief entry 108
Hall, Gwendolyn Midlo 1929- 41-44R
Hall, H(essel) Duncan 1891-1976 .... CAP-2
Obituary 65-68
Earlier sketch in CA 29-32
Hall, H(ugh) Gaston 1931- CANR-86
Earlier sketch in CA 131
Hall, Halbert Weldon 1941- 53-56
Hall, Halsey 1898-1977 217
See also DLB 241
Hall, Haywood 1898-1985 77-80
Hall, Helen 1892-1982 104
Hall, Henry M(arion) 1877-1963 .... 5-8R
Hall, Ivan P(arker) 1932- 172
Hall, J(ohn) C(live) 1920- 101
See also CP 1, 2, 3, 4, 5, 6, 7
Hall, J(ames) Curtis 1926- 53-56
Hall, J. De P.
See McKelway, St. Clair
Hall, J. Tillman 1916- CANR-6
Earlier sketch in CA 1-4R
Hall, Jacquelyn (Dowd) 1943- 97-100
Hall, James
See Kuttner, Henry
Hall, James 1793-1868 .... DLB 73, 74
Hall, James 1918- 102
Hall, James (Herrick, Jr.) 1933- 53-56
Hall, James Andrew 1935- CANR-42
Earlier sketch in CA 118
Hall, James B(yron) 1918- CANR-42
Earlier sketches in CA 1-4R, CANR-1
See also CAAS 12
See also CN 1, 2, 3, 4, 6, 7
Hall, James Baker 1935- 116
See also CSW
Hall, James Norman 1887-1951 173
Brief entry 123
See also LAIT 1
See also RHW 1
See also SATA 21
See also TCLC 23
Hall, James W(illiam) 1937- CANR-47
Earlier sketches in CA 45-48, CANR-22
Hall, James W(ilson) 1947- 207
Hall, Jay 1932- CANR-56
Earlier sketch in CA 127
Hall, Jay C.
See Hall, John C.
Hall, Jean R(ogers) 1941- 105
Hall, Jerome 1901-1992 .... CAP-1
Obituary 137
Earlier sketch in CA 11-12
Hall, Jesse
See Boesen, Victor
Hall, Joan Wylie 1947- 154
Hall, John 1937- 93-96
Hall, John C. 1915- 57-60
Hall, John F. 1919- CANR-17
Earlier sketch in CA 1-4R
Hall, John O(rland) P(hilip) 1911-1978 ... 9-12R
Hall, John Ryder
See Rotsler, (Charles) William
Hall, John Whitney 1916-1997 .... 25-28R
Obituary 162
Hall, Josef Washington 1894-1960
Obituary 89-92
Hall, Joseph 1574-1656 .... DLB 121, 151
See also RGEL 2
Hall, Joseph (Sargent) 1906- 41-44R
Hall, Judith 169
Hall, Julie (Ann) 1943- 184
Brief entry 110
Hall, Kathleen M(ary) 1924- CANR-3
Earlier sketch in CA 5-8R
Hall, Katy
See McMullan, Kate (Hall)
Hall, Kendall
See Heath, Harry E(ugene), Jr.
Hall, Kenneth E(stes) 1954- 187
Hall, Kenneth F(ranklin) 1926- 17-20R
Hall, Kermit L(ance) 1944- 101
Hall, Kirsten Marie 1974- 135
See also SATA 67
Hall, Laurence James 1940- 97-100
Hall, Lawrence Sargent 1915- 1-4R
Hall, Lee 1934- CANR-136
Earlier sketch in CA 159
Hall, (Frederick) Leonard
1899-1992 .... CANR-27
Earlier sketch in CA 65-68
Hall, Lesley A(nn) 1949- 142
Hall, Leslie 1948- 126
Hall, Linda B(iesele) 1939- CANR-23
Earlier sketch in CA 106
Hall, Livingston 1903-1995 .... CAP-2
Earlier sketch in CA 21-22
Hall, Louis Brewer 1920- 110
Hall, Luella J(emima) 1890-1973 45-48
Obituary 103
Hall, Lynn 1937- CANR-78
Earlier sketches in CA 21-24R, CANR-9, 25, 37
See also AAYA 4, 49
See also BYA 6, 7, 8, 9
See also JRDA
See also MAICYA 1, 2
See also SAAS 4
See also SATA 2, 47, 79
See also WYA
See also YAW
Hall, Maggi Smith
See Hall, Margaret Smith
Hall, Malcolm 1945- CANR-4
Earlier sketch in CA 49-52
See also SATA 7
Hall, Manly Palmer 1901-1990 93-96
Obituary 132
Hall, Marcia B. 1939- 192
Hall, Margaret Smith 1945- 221
Hall, Marie Boas 1919- 9-12R
Hall, Marie-Beth 1933- 145
Hall, Marjory
See Yeakley, Marjory Hall
Hall, Mark David 1966- 186
Hall, Mark W. 1943- 33-36R
Hall, Martha Lacy 1923- 162
Hall, Martin Hardwick
1925-1979(?) CANR-35
Earlier sketch in CA 33-36R
Hall, Mary Ann 1942- 116
Hall, Mary Bowen 1932- 21-24R
Hall, MaryAnne 1934- CANR-25
Earlier sketch in CA 29-32R
Hall, Matthew 1958- 167
Hall, Melanie 1949- .... SATA 78, 116
Hall, Michael Garibaldi 1926- 13-16R
Hall, Monty 1924- 184
Brief entry 108
Hall, N(orman) John 1933- CANR-144
Earlier sketches in CA 61-64, CANR-12, 31, 57
Hall, Nancy Lee 1923- 57-60
Hall, Natalie Watson 1923- 5-8R
Hall, Neal (Gordon) 1952- 134
Hall, Noel (Frederick) 1902-1983
Obituary 109
Hall, Norah E. L. 1914- CANR-83
Earlier sketch in CA 97-100
Hall, O. M.
See Hall, Oakley (Maxwell)

Hall, Oakley (Maxwell) 1920- CANR-83
Earlier sketches in CA 9-12R, CANR-3, 46
See also TCWW 1, 2
Hall, Parnell 1944- CANR-99
Earlier sketch in CA 166
See also CMW 4
Hall, Patricia 181
See also SATA 136
Hall, Patrick 1932- 21-24R
Hall, Penelope C(oker) 1933- 17-20R
Hall, Peter (Reginald Frederick) 1930- 133
Hall, Peter (Geoffrey) 1932- CANR-24
Earlier sketches in CA 17-20R, CANR-8
Hall, Phil 1953- 102
Hall, R(obert) Cargill 1937- CANR-1
Earlier sketch in CA 49-52
Hall, (Marguerite) Radclyffe
1880-1943 .... CANR-83
Brief entry 110
Earlier sketch in CA 150
See also BRWS 6
See also DLB 191
See also MTCW 2
See also MTFW 2005
See also RGEL 2
See also RHW
See also TCLC 12
Hall, Richard
See Bickers, Richard (Leslie) Townshend
Hall, Richard (Seymour) 1925-1997 ... CANR-9
Obituary 162
Earlier sketch in CA 17-20R
Hall, (Patrick) Richard Compton
See Compton-Hall, (Patrick) Richard
Hall, Richard H(ammond) 1934- CANR-13
Earlier sketch in CA 77-80
Hall, Richard W(alter) 1926-1992 148
See also Hirshfeld, Richard
Hall, Robert
See Wubbels, Lance
Hall, Robert A(nderson), Jr.
1911-1997 .... CANR-5
Earlier sketch in CA 13-16R
Hall, Robert Benjamin 1918- 57-60
Hall, Robert Burnett, Jr. 1923-
Brief entry 109
Hall, Robert E(lliott) 1924- CANR-13
Earlier sketch in CA 17-20R
Hall, Robert E(rnest) 1943- 114
Hall, Robert Lee 1941- 73-76
Hall, Robert T(om) 1938-
Brief entry 110
Hall, Rodney 1935- CANR-69
Earlier sketch in CA 109
See also CLC 51
See also CN 6, 7
See also CP 1, 2, 3, 4, 5, 6, 7
See also DLB 289
Hall, Roger (Wolcott) 1919- 29-32R
Hall, Roger (Leighton) 1939- CANR-83
Earlier sketch in CA 134
See also CD 5, 6
Hall, Roger 1945- 112
Hall, Rosalys Haskell 1914- 9-12R
See also SATA 7
Hall, Ross H(ume) 1926- 61-64
Hall, Rubylea (Ray) 1910- CAP-2
Earlier sketch in CA 17-18
Hall, Ruth 1933(?)-1981
Obituary 104
Hall, Sam 1936- 137
Hall, Sarah 1974- 226
Hall, Sarah Ewing 1761-1830 .... DLB 200
Hall, Stacey A. 1957- 208
Hall, Steffie
See Evanovich, Janet
Hall, Stephen S. 1951- CANR-72
Earlier sketch in CA 141
Hall, Steven (Leonard) 1960- 93-96
Hall, Stuart 1932- .... DLB 242
Hall, Susan 1940- 57-60
Hall, Susan Bard 1954- 173
Hall, Susan G(rove) 1941- 192
Hall, T(homas) William 1921- 118
Hall, Tarquin 1969- 210
Hall, Ted Byron 1902-1986 .... CAP-2
Earlier sketch in CA 33-36
Hall, Thor 1927- 37-40R
Hall, Timothy L. 1955- CANR-123
Earlier sketch in CA 170
Hall, Tom T. 1936- 102
Interview in CA-102
Hall, Tony
See Hall, Anthony Stewart
Hall, Tord (Erik Martin) 1910- 29-32R
Hall, Trevor H(enry) 1910-1991 .... CANR-82
Obituary 134
Earlier sketches in CA 29-32R, CANR-16
Hall, Van Beck 1934- 45-48
Hall, Vernon, Jr. 1913-1987 .... CANR-3
Earlier sketch in CA 5-8R
Hall, Wade H. 1934- CANR-123
Earlier sketches in CA 5-8R, CANR-6
Hall, Walter (Earl, Jr.) 1940- CANR-13
Earlier sketch in CA 21-24R
Hall, Wayne E(dward) 1947- 105
Hall, William N(orman) 1915-1974
Obituary 53-56
Hall, Willis 1929-2005 .... CANR-82
Obituary 237
Earlier sketches in CA 101, CANR-36, 70
See also CBD
See also CD 5, 6
See also MTCW 1
See also SATA 66
Hall, Wilson (Dudley) 1922-1991 69-72
Obituary 133
Halla, (Robert) Chris(tian) 1949- CANR-18
Earlier sketch in CA 77-80
Hallahan, William H(enry) 204
Brief entry 109
Hallahmi, Benjamin Beit
See Beit-Hallahmi, Benjamin
Hallaj, al- 857-922 .... DLB 311
Hallam, Arthur Henry 1811-1833 .... DLB 32
Hallam, (Samuel Benoni) Atlantis
1915-1987 .... 5-8R
Obituary 196
Hallam, Elizabeth M. 1950- CANR-106
Earlier sketches in CA 123, CANR-50
Hallam, H(erbert) E(noch) 1923- 21-24R
Hallam, J(ohn) Harvey 1917- 13-16R
Hallam, Kerry 1937- 219
Hallard, Peter
See Catherall, Arthur
Hallas, James H(enry) 1952- 176
Hallas, Richard
See Knight, Eric (Mowbray)
Hallberg, Charles William 1899-1985 ... CAP-1
Earlier sketch in CA 17-18
Hallberg, Edmond C. 1931-
Brief entry 111
Hallberg, Peter 1916- CANR-4
Earlier sketch in CA 53-56
Hall-Clarke, James
See Rowland-Entwistle, (Arthur) Theodore (Henry)
Halldor Laxness
See Gudjonsson, Halldor Kiljan
See also CLC 25
See also DLB 293
See also EW 12
See also EWL 3
See also RGWL 2, 3
Halle, Francis 1938- 239
Halle, Jean-Claude 1939- CANR-17
Earlier sketch in CA 93-96
Halle, Katherine Murphy 1904(?)-1997 . 41-44R
Obituary 160
Halle, Kay
See Halle, Katherine Murphy
Halle, Louis J(oseph) 1910-1998 .... CANR-2
Obituary 169
Earlier sketch in CA 1-4R
See also ANW
Halleck, Fitz-Greene 1790-1867 .... DLB 3, 250
See also RGAL 4
Halleck, Seymour L(eon) 1929- CANR-13
Earlier sketch in CA 21-24R
Hallendy, Norman 1932- 202
Haller, Albrecht von 1708-1777 .... DLB 168
Haller, Archibald O(rben), Jr. 1926- 45-48
Haller, Bill
See Bechko, P(eggy) A(nne)
Haller, Dorcas Woodbury 1946- 117
See also SATA 46
Haller, Ellis M(etcalf) 1915-1981
Obituary 103
Haller, Ernest 1896-1970 .... IDFW 3, 4
Haller, Hermann W. 1945- 217
Haller, John Samuel, Jr. 1940- 61-64
Haller, Mark H(ughlin) 1928- CANR-5
Earlier sketch in CA 9-12R
Haller, Mike 1945- 110
Haller, Robert S(pencer) 1933- CANR-2
Earlier sketch in CA 1-4R
Haller, Robin Meredith 1944- 65-68
Haller, William 1885-1974
Obituary 49-52
Halleran, E(ugene) E(dward)
1905-1994 .... CANR-63
Earlier sketch in CA 1-4R
See also TCWW 1, 2
Hallet, Jean-Pierre 1927- 17-20R
Hallett, Charles A(rthur) 141
Hallett, Ellen Kathleen 1899- CAP-1
Earlier sketch in CA 13-16
Hallett, Garth L(ie) 1927- CANR-13
Earlier sketch in CA 69-72
Hallett, George H(ervey), Jr. 1895-1985
Obituary 116
Hallett, Graham 1929- CANR-16
Earlier sketch in CA 25-28R
Hallett, Judith Peller 1944- CANR-51
Earlier sketch in CA 124
Hallett, Kathryn J(osephine) 1937- 57-60
Hallett, Mark 1947- .... SATA 83
Hallett, Robin 1926- 103
Halley, Anne 1928- 121
Halley, Laurence
See O'Keeffe, (Peter) Laurence
Hallgarten, George W(olfgang) F(elix)
1901-1975 65-68
Obituary 57-60
Hallgarten, Peter A(lexander) 1931- 97-100
Hallgarten, Siegfried Fritz
1902-1991 .... CANR-18
Earlier sketches in CA 5-8R, CANR-3
Hallgren, Chris 1947- 115
Hallgrimsson, Jonas 1807-1845 .... DLB 293
Halliburton, David (Garland) 1933- 159
Brief entry 116
Halliburton, Lloyd 1934- 191
Halliburton, Richard 1900-1939(?) 135
Brief entry 114
See also SATA 81
Halliburton, Rudia, Jr. 1929- 81-84
Halliburton, Warren J. 1924- CANR-24
Earlier sketch in CA 33-36R
See also BW 2
See also SATA 19
Halliday, Brett
See Dresser, Davis and Johnson, (Walter) Ryerson and Terrall, Robert
See also BPFB 2
Halliday, David 1948- 113
Halliday, Dorothy
See Dunnett, Dorothy
Halliday, E(rnest) M(ilton) 1913- CANR-104
Earlier sketch in CA 1-4R
Halliday, Ena
See Baumgarten, Sylvia
Halliday, F(rank) E(rnest) 1903-1982 .. CANR-2
Obituary 106
Earlier sketch in CA 1-4R
Halliday, Fred 1937- 53-56
Halliday, James
See Symington, David
Halliday, Jerry 1949- 69-72
Halliday, Jon 1939- 97-100
Halliday, M(ichael) A(lexander) K(irkwood)
1925- 126
Brief entry 112
Halliday, Michael
See Creasey, John
Halliday, Nigel Vaux 1956- 140
Halliday, Pat 1930- 232
Halliday, Richard 1905-1973
Obituary 41-44R
Halliday, Tim (Richard) 1945- 112
Halliday, William R(oss) 1926- 49-52
See also SATA 52
Hallie, Philip P(aul) 1922-1994 .... CANR-9
Obituary 146
Earlier sketch in CA 13-16R
Hallier, Amedee 1913- 73-76
Halligan, Marion (Mildred Crothall)
1940- CANR-128
Earlier sketch in CA 160
See also CN 6, 7
Halligan, Nicholas 1917- CANR-5
Earlier sketch in CA 13-16R
Hallin, Emily Watson CANR-26
Earlier sketches in CA 25-28R, CANR-10
See also SATA 6
Hallinan, Hazel Hunkins 1891(?)-1982
Obituary 106
Hallinan, Nancy 1921- CANR-3
Earlier sketch in CA 9-12R
Hallinan, P(atrick) K(enneth) 1944- ... CANR-11
Earlier sketch in CA 69-72
See also SATA 39
See also SATA-Brief 37
Hallinan, Vincent 1896-1992 .... 1-4R
Hallion, Richard P(aul, Jr.) 1948- CANR-142
Earlier sketch in CA 41-44R
Hallissy, Margaret 1945- 175
Halliwell, David (William) 1936- CANR-57
Earlier sketches in CA 65-68, CANR-11, 31
See also CBD
See also CD 5, 6
Halliwell, Geraldine Estelle 1972- 190
Halliwell, Geri
See Halliwell, Geraldine Estelle
Halliwell, Leslie 1929-1989 .... CANR-16
Obituary 127
Earlier sketches in CA 49-52, CANR-1
Halliwell, Ruth 181
Halliwell-Phillipps, James Orchard
1820-1889 .... DLB 184
Hall-Jones, Frederick George 1891-1982
Obituary 108
Hallman, Frank Curtis 1943(?)-1975
Obituary 104
Hallman, G(eorge) Victor III 1930- 101
Hallman, Howard W(esley) 1928- 116
Hallman, Ralph J(efferson) 1911-1985 ... 13-16R
Hallman, Ruth 1929- CANR-15
Earlier sketch in CA 85-88
See also SATA 43
See also SATA-Brief 28
Hallmann, Johann Christian c.
1640-1704(?) .... DLB 168
Hallo, William W. 1928- CANR-15
Earlier sketch in CA 37-40R
Hallock, Daniel W. 1960- 177
Hallock, G. B. F.
See Hallock, Gerard B(enjamin) F(leet)
Hallock, Gerard B(enjamin) F(leet) 1856-1953
Brief entry 122
Hallock, John W(esley) M(atthew) 1959- 201
Hallock, Robert Lay 1898(?)-1986
Obituary 120
Halloran, Richard (Colby) 1930- 29-32R
Halloway, Vance 1916- 53-56
Hallowell, A(lfred) Irving 1892-1974 .... 5-8R
Obituary 53-56
Hallowell, Christopher (L.) 1945- CANR-111
Earlier sketch in CA 93-96
Hallowell, Edward M(cKey) CANR-141
Earlier sketch in CA 173
Hallowell, Janis 231
Hallowell, John H(amilton)
1913-1991 .... CANR-5
Earlier sketch in CA 13-16R
Hallowell, Tommy
See Hill, Thomas
Hallpike, C. R. 1938- 41-44R
Hall-Quest, (Edna) Olga W(ilbourne)
1899-1986 .... 5-8R
Obituary 118
See also SATA 11
See also SATA-Obit 47
Halls, Geraldine (Mary) 1919-1996 .. CANR-60
Earlier sketch in CA 103
See also CMW 4
Halls, Kelly Milner 1957- 200
See also SATA 131
Halls, W(ilfred) D(ouglas) 1918- CANR-5
Earlier sketch in CA 1-4R
Hallstead, William F(inn III) 1924- ... CANR-21
Earlier sketches in CA 5-8R, CANR-6
See also SATA 11
Hallstein, Walter 1901-1982
Obituary 106
Hallstroem, Lasse 1946- 165
Hallstroem, Per
See Hallstrom, Per (August Leonard)
Hallstrom, Lasse
See Hallstroem, Lasse
Hallstrom, Per (August Leonard) 1866-1960
Obituary 116
Hallus, Tak
See Robinett, Stephen (Allen)
Hallward, Michael 1889-1982 49-52
Obituary 196
See also SATA 12
Hallwas, John E(dward) 1945- CANR-124
Earlier sketch in CA 154
Hallwood, Jan 172
Halm, Ben B. 1957- 151
Halm, George N(ikolaus) 1901-1984 .... 21-24R
Halman, Talat Sait 1931- CANR-4
Earlier sketch in CA 53-56
Halme, Kathleen 1955- 180
Halmi, Katherine A. 1939- 144
Halmos, Paul 1911-1977 .... CANR-8
Earlier sketch in CA 17-20R
Halo, Thea 221
Halpe, Ashley 1933- .... CP 1
Halper
See Halpern, Leivick
Halper, Albert 1904-1984 .... CANR-3
Obituary 111
Earlier sketch in CA 5-8R
See also DLB 9
Halper, Nathan 1908(?)-1983
Obituary 110
Halper, Sam 1916-1989
Obituary 128
Halper, Thomas 1942- 41-44R
Halperin, David M(artin) 1952- CANR-41
Earlier sketch in CA 117
Halperin, Don A(kiba) 1925- 57-60
Halperin, Edwin G. 1935(?)-1987
Obituary 123
Halperin, Irving 1922- 29-32R
Halperin, James L(ewis) 1952- 157
Halperin, Joan Ungersma 1932- 137
Halperin, John (William) 1941- CANR-92
Earlier sketches in CA 53-56, CANR-6, 57
See also DLB 111
Halperin, Jonathan L. 1949- CANR-90
Earlier sketch in CA 132
Halperin, Mark (Warren) 1940- CANR-102
Earlier sketches in CA 65-68, CANR-9
Halperin, Maurice (H.) 1906-1995 73-76
Obituary 147
Halperin, Michael 231
See also SATA 156
Halperin, Morton H. 1938- CANR-3
Earlier sketch in CA 9-12R
Halperin, S(amuel) William 1905-1979 . 97-100
Obituary 85-88
Halperin, Samuel 1930- CANR-1
Earlier sketch in CA 1-4R
Halperin, Wendy Anderson 1952- ...... SATA 80, 125
Halpern, A(braham) M(eyer)
1914-1985 .... 17-20R
Halpern, Barbara Kerewsky
See Kerewsky-Halpern, Barbara
Halpern, Barbara Strachey 1912-1999 106
Obituary 187
Halpern, Ben(jamin) 1912-1990 203
Obituary 131
Brief entry 115
Halpern, Cynthia Leone 1952- 147
Halpern, Daniel 1945- CANR-93
Earlier sketch in CA 33-36R
See also CLC 14
See also CP 7
Halpern, Frances J(oy) 114
Halpern, Howard Marvin 1929- 93-96
Halpern, Jake 1975- 234
Halpern, Joel M. 1929- CANR-3
Earlier sketch in CA 5-8R
Halpern, L.
See Halpern, Leivick
Halpern, Leivick 1888-1962
Obituary 114
Halpern, Lucy
See Wang, Lucy
Halpern, Manfred 1924- 9-12R
Halpern, Martin 1929- CANR-7
Earlier sketch in CA 5-8R
Halpern, Moyshe Leyb 1886-1932 .... EWL 3
Halpern, Oscar Saul 1912-1994 97-100
Obituary 145
Halpern, Paul 1961- 141
Halpern, Paul G. 1937- 45-48
Halpern, Paul J(oseph) 1942- CANR-7
Earlier sketch in CA 57-60
Halpern, Rick 1959- 189
Halpern, Stephen Mark 1940- 57-60
Halpern, Sue 139
Halpert, Inge D. 1926- 21-24R
Halpert, Sam 1920- 181
Halpert, Stephen 1941- 37-40R
Halpin, Andrew W(illiams) 1911-1992 .. 17-20R
Halpin, Marlene 1927- 152
See also SATA 88
Halprin, Anna Schuman 1920- 85-88

Cumulative Index 245 Hamilton

Halprin, Lawrence 1916- 41-44R
Hals, Ronald M. 1926- 33-36R
Halsall, Elizabeth 1916- 33-36R
Halsall, Eric 1920-1996 107
Halsband, Robert 1914-1989 .... CANR-8
Obituary 130
Earlier sketch in CA 17-20R
Halsell, Grace (Eleanor) 1923-2000 . CANR-13
Obituary 189
Earlier sketch in CA 21-24R
See also AITN 1
See also SATA 13
Halsey, A(lbert) H(enry) 1923- CANR-7
Earlier sketch in CA 17-20R
Halsey, Elizabeth 1890-1974 .... CAP-2
Earlier sketch in CA 17-18
Halsey, Elizabeth Tower 1903(?)-1976
Obituary 65-68
Halsey, George Dawson 1889-1970 .... 1-4R
Obituary 103
Halsey, Margaret (Frances) 1910-1997 81-84
Obituary 156
Halsey, Martha T. 1932- CANR-14
Earlier sketch in CA 37-40R
Halsey, William D(arrach) 1918-
Brief entry 117
Halsman, Philippe 1906-1979 .... CANR-10
Obituary 89-92
Earlier sketch in CA 21-24R
Halstead, Dirck S. 1936- 133
Halstead, Murat 1829-1908 175
See also DLB 23
Halstead, Ted 1968- 204
Halstead, William Perdue 1906-1982
Obituary 109
Halsted, Anna Roosevelt 1906-1975
Obituary 61-64
See also SATA-Obit 30
Halstock, Max
See Caulfield, Malachy Francis
Halter, Carl 1915- 17-20R
Halter, Jon C(harles) 1941- CANR-13
Earlier sketch in CA 61-64
See also SATA 22
Halter, Marek 1936- 140
Halterman, H. Lee 1935- 209
Halton, David 1940- 73-76
Halton, Eugene Rochberg
See Rochberg-Halton, Eugene
Haltrecht, Montague 1932- 29-32R
Halttunen, Karen (L.) 1951- 179
Halverson, Alton C. O. 1922- 61-64
Halverson, Richard C(hristian)
1916-1995 .... CANR-3
Obituary 150
Earlier sketch in CA 1-4R
Halverson, Richard P(aul) 1941- 109
Halverson, William H(agen) 1930- ... CANR-98
Earlier sketches in CA 37-40R, CANR-47
Halvorson, Arndt L(eroy) 1915- CANR-3
Earlier sketch in CA 5-8R
Halvorson, Marilyn 1948- CANR-93
Earlier sketch in CA 132
See also SATA 123
See also YAW
Halward, Leslie G. 1904(?)-1976
Obituary 65-68
Ham, Debra Newman 1948- CANR-98
Earlier sketch in CA 148
Ham, Wayne 1938- CANR-11
Earlier sketch in CA 21-24R
Hamachek, Don E. 1933- 17-20R
Hamada, Hirosuke 1893- 45-48
Hamadhani, al- (Badi' al-Zaman)
967-1007 .... WLIT 6
Hamady, Walter .... AITN 1
Hamalainen, Pekka Kalevi 1938- 97-100
Hamalainen, Pertti (Olavi) 1952- 138
Hamalian, Leo 1920- CANR-2
Earlier sketch in CA 5-8R
See also SATA 41
Hamamoto, Darrell Y. 1953- 151
Hamanaka, Sheila 228
Hamann, Johann Georg 1730-1788 ...... DLB 97
Hamberg, Daniel 1924- 1-4R
Hamberger, John 1934- 69-72
See also SATA 14
Hambleton, Ronald 1917- .... CP 1
Hambletonian
See Fairfax-Blakeborough, John Freeman
Hamblett, Theora 1895(?)-1977
Obituary 69-72
Hamblin, C(harles) L(eonard) 1922- 25-28R
Hamblin, Dora Jane 1920- 37-40R
See also SATA 36
Hamblin, Douglas H. 1923- 115
Hamblin, Robert L(ee) 1927- 97-100
Hamblin, Robert W(ayne) 1938- 131
Hamblin, W. K. 1928- 53-56
Hambling, Gerry 1926- .... IDFW 4
Hambly, Barbara 1951- CANR-122
Earlier sketch in CA 170
See also AAYA 28
See also FANT
See also SATA 108
Hambourg, Maria Morris 1949- 130
Hambrey, Michael (John) 1948- 143
Hambrick-Stowe, Charles E(dwin) 1948- 125
Hamburg, Carl H(einz) 1915- 37-40R
Hamburg, David A(llen) 1925-
Brief entry 109
Hamburg, Morris 1922- 194
Brief entry 114
Hamburger, Aaron 232
Hamburger, Ernest 1891(?)-1980
Obituary 97-100
Hamburger, Estelle 1898(?)-1983
Obituary 110
Hamburger, Joseph 1922-1997 204
Hamburger, Kaete 1896-1992 .... CANR-14
Earlier sketch in CA 29-32R
Hamburger, Max 1897-1970 .... CAP-2
Earlier sketch in CA 17-18
Hamburger, Michael (Peter Leopold)
1924- 196
Earlier sketches in CA 5-8R, CANR-2, 47
Autobiographical Essay in 196
See also CAAS 4
See also CLC 5, 14
See also CP 1, 2, 3, 4, 5, 6, 7
See also DLB 27
Hamburger, Michael J(ay) 1938- CANR-3
Earlier sketch in CA 45-48
Hamburger, Philip (Paul)
1914-2004 .... CANR-86
Obituary 227
Earlier sketch in CA 5-8R
Hamburger, Robert (A., Jr.) 1943- CANR-8
Earlier sketch in CA 61-64
Hamburger, Viktor 1900-2001 156
Obituary 196
Hamburgh, Max 1922- 61-64
Hamby, Alonzo L. 1940- CANR-66
Earlier sketches in CA 37-40R, CANR-15
Hameiri, Avigdor 1890(?)-1970 206
Hamel, Peter Michael 1947- 97-100
Hamel Dobkin, Kathleen
See Hamel Peifer, Kathleen
Hamelin, Louis-Edmond 1923- 110
Hamell, Patrick Joseph 1910-1998 .... CAP-1
Earlier sketch in CA 13-16
Hamelman, Paul W(illiam) 1930-1976 . 41-44R
Hamel Peifer, Kathleen 1945- CANR-28
Earlier sketch in CA 110
Hamer, David Allan 1938- CANR-35
Earlier sketch in CA 45-48
Hamer, Forrest 1956- 152
Hamer, Frank 1929- 105
Hamer, Martyn
See Eldin, Peter
Hamer, Mick 1946- 109
Hamer, Philip (May) 1891-1971
Obituary 104
Hamermesh, Daniel S(elim) 1943-
Brief entry 110
Hamermesh, Morton 1915-2003 .... 5-8R
Obituary 222
Hamerow, Theodore S(tephen)
1920- CANR-28
Earlier sketch in CA 49-52
Hamerstrom, Frances 1907-1998 69-72
Obituary 169
See also SATA 24
Hames, (Alice) Inez 1892- 29-32R
Hamey, J(ohn) A(nthony) 1956- 109
Hamey, L(eonard) A(rnold) 1918- 109
Hamid, Ahmad A. 1948- 146
Hamid, Mohsin 1971- 199
Hamil, Sharon Hide 1939- 122
Hamil, Thomas Arthur 1928- 73-76
See also SATA 14
Hamill, Denis 1951- 110
Hamill, Ethel
See Webb, Jean Francis (III)
Hamill, Janet 1945- 203
Hamill, Pete 1935- CANR-127
Earlier sketches in CA 25-28R, CANR-18, 71
See also CLC 10
Hamill, Robert H(offman) 1912-1975 .... CAP-2
Earlier sketch in CA 33-36
Hamill, Sam P(atrick) 1943(?)- CANR-114
Earlier sketch in CA 161
See also CAAS 15
Hamilton, A(lbert) C(harles) 1921- 133
Hamilton, Adam
See Henderson, M(arilyn) R(uth)
Hamilton, (John) Alan 1943- CANR-36
Earlier sketch in CA 115
See also SATA 66
Hamilton, Alastair 1941- CANR-129
Earlier sketch in CA 144
Hamilton, Alex John 1939- 103
See also HGG
Hamilton, Alexander 1712-1756 .... DLB 31
Hamilton, Alexander 1755(?)-1804 .... DLB 37
Hamilton, Alfred Starr 1914- 53-56
See also CP 1
Hamilton, Alice
See Cromie, Alice Hamilton
Hamilton, Alice 1869-1970 156
Hamilton, Anita 1919- 156
See also SATA 92
Hamilton, B(ertram) L(awson) St. John
1914- 13-16R
Hamilton, Beth Alleman 1927- 110
Hamilton, (Arthur Douglas) Bruce 1900-1974
Obituary 109
Hamilton, Buzz
See Hemming, Roy G.
Hamilton, Carl 1914-1991 53-56
Hamilton, Carl 1956- 216
Hamilton, Carlos D. 1908-1988 69-72
Hamilton, Carol (Jean Barber) 1935- 159
See also SATA 94
Hamilton, Charles (Harold St. John)
1876-1961 .... CANR-29
Earlier sketch in CA 73-76
See also CWRI 5
See also SATA 13
Hamilton, Charles 1913-1996 .... CANR-49
Obituary 155
Earlier sketches in CA 5-8R, CANR-3, 20
See also SATA 65
See also SATA-Obit 93
Hamilton, Charles D(aniel) 1940-
Brief entry 112
Hamilton, Charles F(ranklin) 1915- 89-92
Hamilton, Charles Granville
1905-1984 .... CANR-15
Earlier sketch in CA 41-44R
Hamilton, Charles V(ernon) 1929- ... CANR-42
Earlier sketch in CA 77-80
See also BW 2
Hamilton, Charles W(alter) 1890-1972 ..... 5-8R
Hamilton, Cicely (Mary) 1872-1952 192
Brief entry 113
See also DLB 10, 197
See also FW
Hamilton, Clare
See Lawless, Bettyclare Hamilton
Hamilton, Clive
See Lewis, C(live) S(taples)
Hamilton, Dakota 181
Hamilton, Dave
See Troyer, Byron L(eRoy)
Hamilton, David (Boyce, Jr.) 1918- 29-32R
Hamilton, David (Peter) 1935- 119
Hamilton, David 1939- CANR-109
Earlier sketches in CA 126, CANR-54
Hamilton, (Charles) Denis 1918-1988 109
Obituary 125
Hamilton, Denise 215
Hamilton, Donald (Bengtsson)
1916- CANR-59
Earlier sketches in CA 1-4R, CANR-2, 18, 39
See also CMW 4
See also TCWW 1, 2
Hamilton, Dorothy (Drumm)
1906-1983 .... 33-36R
Obituary 110
See also SATA 12
See also SATA-Obit 35
Hamilton, Earl J(efferson) 1899-1989 .... CAP-1
Obituary 128
Earlier sketch in CA 9-10
Hamilton, Edith 1867-1963 .... CANR-85
Earlier sketch in CA 77-80
See also MTFW 2005
See also SATA 20
Hamilton, Edmond 1904-1977 .... CANR-84
Earlier sketches in CA 1-4R, CANR-3
See also CLC 1
See also DLB 8
See also SATA 118
See also SFW 4
Hamilton, Edward G. 1897-1972 .... CAP-1
Earlier sketch in CA 11-12
Hamilton, Eleanor Poorman 1909- CANR-2
Earlier sketch in CA 1-4R
Hamilton, Elizabeth 1758-1816 .. DLB 116, 158
Hamilton, (Muriel) Elizabeth (Mollie)
1906- CAP-1
Earlier sketch in CA 9-10
See also SATA 23
Hamilton, Elizabeth 1928- 97-100
Hamilton, Ernest
See Merril, Judith
Hamilton, Eugene (Jacob) Lee
See Lee-Hamilton, Eugene (Jacob)
Hamilton, Floyd (Garland) 1908(?)-1984
Obituary 113
Hamilton, Franklin
See Silverberg, Robert
Hamilton, Franklin Willard 1923- 33-36R
Hamilton, Gail
See Corcoran, Barbara (Asenath) and
Dodge, Mary Abigail
Hamilton, Gene 1943- 120
Hamilton, George Baillie
See Baillie-Hamilton, George
Hamilton, George Rostrevor 1888-1967
Obituary 93-96
Hamilton, Hamish 1900-1988
Obituary 125
Hamilton, Henry W. 1898-1984 .... 33-36R
Hamilton, Hervey
See Robins, Denise (Naomi)
Hamilton, Holman 1910-1980 .... CANR-10
Obituary 97-100
Earlier sketch in CA 13-16R
Hamilton, Horace E(rnst) 1911- 21-24R
Hamilton, Howard Devon 1920- 13-16R
Hamilton, Hugo 1953- 138
See also CN 7
See also DLB 267
Hamilton, Iain (Bertram)
1920-1986 .... CANR-117
Earlier sketch in CA 130
Hamilton, (Robert) Ian 1938-2001 ... CANR-67
Obituary 203
Earlier sketches in CA 106, CANR-41
See also CLC 191
See also CP 1, 2, 3, 4, 5, 6, 7
See also DLB 40, 155
Hamilton, J(ames) A(lan) B(ousfield) 1899-1971
Obituary 116
Hamilton, J(ames) Scott 1956- 163
Hamilton, J(ames) Wallace 1900-1968 .. CAP-1
Earlier sketch in CA 13-14
Hamilton, Jack
See Brannon, William T.
Hamilton, James 1948- 239
Hamilton, James Robertson 1921-1999 103
Hamilton, James T. 192
Hamilton, Jane 1957- CANR-128
Earlier sketches in CA 147, CANR-85
See also CLC 179
See also CN 7
See also MTFW 2005
Hamilton, Janet 1795-1873 .... DLB 199
Hamilton, Janet 1951-1998 114
Hamilton, Jean Tyree 1909- 33-36R
Hamilton, Jessica
See Greenhall, Ken
Hamilton, Joan Lesley 1942- 102
Hamilton, John
See Hayden, Sterling
Hamilton, John Maxwell 1947- CANR-47
Earlier sketch in CA 121
Hamilton, Julia
See Watson, Julia
Hamilton, Katie 1945- 118
Hamilton, Kay
See DeLeeuw, Cateau
Hamilton, Kelly 1945- 220
Hamilton, Kenneth (Morrison) 1917- 17-20R
Hamilton, Kersten 1958- 203
See also SATA 134
Hamilton, Kirk .... TCWW 2
Hamilton, Laurell K. 181
See also AAYA 46
Hamilton, Lyn 209
Hamilton, Marshall Lee 1937- 37-40R
Hamilton, Martha 1953- .... SATA 123
Hamilton, Mary (E.) 1927- 123
See also SATA 55
Hamilton, Mary Agnes 1884-1962 ..... DLB 197
Hamilton, Masha 207
Hamilton, Michael (Pollock) 1927- .. CANR-30
Earlier sketch in CA 29-32R
Hamilton, Milton W(heaton)
1901-1989 .... CAP-1
Obituary 128
Earlier sketch in CA 13-16
Hamilton, Mollie
See Kaye, M(ary) M(argaret)
Hamilton, Molly
See Hamilton, Mary Agnes
Hamilton, Morse 1943-1998 108
See also SATA 35, 101
Hamilton, Nancy 1908-1985
Obituary 115
Hamilton, Neil (W.) 1945- CANR-112
Earlier sketch in CA 154
Hamilton, Neill Q. 1925- 61-64
Hamilton, (Charles) Nigel 1944- CANR-135
Earlier sketches in CA 101, CANR-41
Hamilton, (Anthony Walter) Patrick
1904-1962 176
Obituary 113
See also CLC 51
See also DLB 10, 191
Hamilton, Patrick Macfarlan 1892-1977
Obituary 108
Hamilton, Paul
See Dennis-Jones, H(arold)
Hamilton, Peter (Edward) 1947- 73-76
Hamilton, Peter F. 1960- CANR-116
Earlier sketch in CA 162
See also SATA 109
Hamilton, Peter N(apier) 1925(?)-1989
Obituary 128
Hamilton, Priscilla
See Gellis, Roberta (Leah Jacobs)
Hamilton, Ralph
See Stratemeyer, Edward L.
Hamilton, Raphael N(oteware)
1892-1980 .... CAP-2
Earlier sketch in CA 29-32
Hamilton, Richard 1922- 159
Brief entry 116
Hamilton, Richard 1943- 233
Hamilton, Richard F(rederick)
1930- CANR-26
Earlier sketch in CA 108
Hamilton, Robert W. CANR-26
Earlier sketches in CAP-2, CA 19-20
Hamilton, Ron 1948- 215
Hamilton, Ronald 1909- 13-16R
Hamilton, Russell G(eorge) 1934- 61-64
Hamilton, Saskia 1967- 200
Hamilton, Scott (Scovell) 1958- 187
Hamilton, Seena M. 1926- 17-20R
Hamilton, Sharon Jean 1944- 151
Hamilton, Steve 1961- CANR-128
Earlier sketch in CA 174
Hamilton, Virginia (Esther)
1936-2002 .... CANR-126
Obituary 206
Earlier sketches in CA 25-28R, CANR-20, 37, 73
Interview in CANR-20
See also AAYA 2, 21
See also BW 2, 3
See also BYA 1, 2, 8
See also CLC 26
See also CLR 1, 11, 40
See also DAM MULT
See also DLB 33, 52
See also DLBY 2001
See also JRDA
See also LAIT 5
See also MAICYA 1, 2
See also MAICYAS 1
See also MTCW 1, 2
See also MTFW 2005
See also SATA 4, 56, 79, 123
See also SATA-Obit 132
See also WYA
See also YAW

Hamilton, W(illiam) B(askerville)
1908-1972 ... CAP-1
Obituary ... 37-40R
Earlier sketch in CA 17-18
Hamilton, W(illis) D(avid) 1936- ... 105
Hamilton, Wade
See Floren, Lee
Hamilton, Wallace 1919-1983 ... CANR-15
Obituary ... 110
Earlier sketch in CA 85-88
Hamilton, Walter 1908-1988 ... 109
Obituary ... 124
Hamilton, William, Jr. 1924- ... 53-56
Hamilton, William 1939- ... CANR-15
Earlier sketch in CA 69-72
Hamilton, Sir William 1788-1856 ... DLB 262
Hamilton, William B(aillie) 1930- ... 102
Hamilton-Edwards, Gerald (Kenneth Savery)
1906- ... CANR-14
Earlier sketch in CA 21-24R
Hamilton-Hill, Donald 1915-1985
Obituary ... 117
Hamilton-Paterson, James 1941- ... CANR-89
Earlier sketch in CA 137
Interview in ... CA-137
See also DLB 267
See also SATA 82
Hamizrachi, Yoram 1942- ... 107
Hamlet, Ova
See Lupoff, Richard A(llen)
Hamlet, Sybil E. 1913(?)-1989
Obituary ... 129
Hamley, Dennis 1935- ... CANR-26
Earlier sketches in CA 57-60, CANR-11
See also CLR 47
See also SAAS 22
See also SATA 39, 69
Hamlin, Catherine 1925- ... 210
Hamlin, Charles Hughes 1907-1984 ... 69-72
Hamlin, Dallas
See Schulze, Dallas
Hamlin, Gladys E(va) ... 37-40R
Hamlin, Griffith Askew 1919- ... 37-40R
Hamlin, Marjorie (Day) 1921- ... 105
Hamlin, Peter J. 1970- ... SATA 84
Hamlin, Talbot (Faulkner) 1889-1956 ... 183
Hamlin, Wilfrid G(ardiner) 1918- ... 93-96
Hamlisch, Marvin 1944- ... IDFW 3, 4
Hamlyn, D(avid) W(alter) 1924- ... CANR-89
Earlier sketch in CA 132
Hamm, Charles Edward 1925- ... CANR-72
Earlier sketch in CA 103
Hamm, Cleve 1927(?)-1984
Obituary ... 112
Hamm, Dale C. 1916- ... 172
Hamm, Diane Johnston 1949- ... 146
See also SATA 78
Hamm, Edward Frederick, Jr. 1908-1985
Obituary ... 115
Hamm, Glenn B(ruce) 1936-1980 ... 53-56
Obituary ... 125
Hamm, Jack 1916- ... CANR-9
Earlier sketch in CA 5-8R
Hamm, Marie Roberson 1917- ... 65-68
Hamm, Mark S. ... 210
Hamm, Michael Franklin 1943- ... 89-92
Hamm, Robert M(acGowan) 1950- ... 116
Hamm, Russell Leroy 1926- ... CANR-2
Earlier sketch in CA 5-8R
Hamm, Thomas D. 1957- ... 137
Hammack, David C(onrad) 1941- ... 115
Hammack, James W., Jr. 1937- ... 81-84
Hamman, Henry (Longley) 1946- ... 119
Hamman, Ray T(racy) 1945- ... 69-72
Hammar, Russell A(lfred) 1920- ... 104
Hammarskjoeld, Dag (Hjalmar Agne Carl)
1905-1961 ... 77-80
Hammarskjold, Dag
See Hammarskjoeld, Dag (Hjalmar Agne Carl)
Hammel, Eric M(axwell) 1946- ... CANR-35
Earlier sketch in CA 107
Hammel, Faye 1929- ... CANR-5
Earlier sketch in CA 1-4R
Hammell, Ian
See Emery, Clayton
Hammen, Carl Schlee 1923- ... 53-56
Hammen, Oscar J(ohn) 1907-1993 ... CAP-2
Obituary ... 197
Earlier sketch in CA 25-28
Hammer, Armand 1898-1990
Obituary ... 134
Hammer, Carl, Jr. 1910-1990 ... 53-56
Hammer, Charles 1934- ... SATA 58
Hammer, David Harry 1893(?)-1978
Obituary ... 81-84
Hammer, Emanuel F(rederick) 1926- ... 29-32R
Hammer, Jacob
See Oppenheimer, Joel (Lester)
Hammer, Jeanne-Ruth 1912- ... 9-12R
Hammer, Jefferson J(oseph) 1933- ... 41-44R
Hammer, Joshua 1957- ... 209
Hammer, Kenneth M. 1918- ... 85-88
Hammer, Louis (Zelig) 1931- ... 139
Hammer, Michael 1948- ... 210
Hammer, Reuven 1933- ... CANR-56
Earlier sketch in CA 127
Hammer, Richard 1928- ... CANR-11
Earlier sketch in CA 25-28R
See also SATA 6
Hammer, Signe ... 102
Hammerman, Donald R. 1925- ... 13-16R
Hammerman, Gay M(orenus) 1926- ... 33-36R
See also SATA 9
Hammerman, Joshua 1957- ... 192
Hammerschlag, Carl A(llen) 1939- ... 128
Hammerslough, Jane ... 203
Hammerstein, Oscar (Greeley Glendenning) II
1895-1960 ... 101
See also AAYA 52
See also DFS 1
See also DLB 265
Hammes, John A(nthony) 1924- ... 13-16R
Hammes, Tobi Gillian Sanders 1948(?)-1987
Obituary ... 122
Hammett, (Samuel) Dashiell
1894-1961 ... CANR-42
Earlier sketch in CA 81-84
See also AAYA 59
See also AITN 1
See also AMWS 4
See also BPFB 2
See also CDALB 1929-1941
See also CLC 3, 5, 10, 19, 47
See also CMW 4
See also DA3
See also DLB 226, 280
See also DLBD 6
See also DLBY 1996
See also EWL 3
See also LAIT 3
See also MAL 5
See also MSW
See also MTCW 1, 2
See also MTFW 2005
See also NFS 21
See also RGAL 4
See also RGSF 2
See also SSC 17
See also TUS
Hammett, Jo(sephine) ... 210
Hammick, Georgina 1939- ... CANR-134
Earlier sketch in CA 126
Hammil, Joel 1909- ... 114
Hamming, Richard W(esley) 1915-1998 . 57-60
Obituary ... 164
Hammon, Jupiter 1720(?)-1800(?) ... BLC 2
See also DAM MULT, POET
See also DLB 31, 50
See also PC 16
Hammond, Albert L(anphier) 1892-1970 .. 1-4R
Obituary ... 103
Hammond, Antony Derek 1938- ... 114
Hammond, Brad
See King, Albert
Hammond, Bray 1886-1968 ... 186
Hammond, Brean S(imon) 1951- ... 119
Hammond, Charles Montgomery, Jr.
1922- ... 106
Hammond, Dorothy 1924- ... 69-72
Hammond, Edwin Hughes 1919- ... 13-16R
Hammond, Gerald (Arthur Douglas)
1926- ... CANR-128
Earlier sketches in CA 107, CANR-62
See also CMW 4
Hammond, Guyton B(owers) 1930- ... 17-20R
Hammond, Herb(ert L.) 1945- ... 140
Hammond, J(ames) D(illard) 1933- ... CANR-22
Earlier sketch in CA 45-48
Hammond, J(ohn) R. 1933- ... 130
Hammond, Jane
See Poland, Dorothy (Elizabeth Hayward)
Hammond, John (?)-1663 ... DLB 24
Hammond, John (Henry, Jr.) 1910-1987 ... 106
Obituary ... 123
Hammond, Keith
See Kuttner, Henry
Hammond, Laurence ... 104
Hammond, Lawrence 1925- ... 81-84
Hammond, Mac (Sawyer) 1926-1997 ... 17-20R
See also CP 1
Hammond, Mason 1903-2002 ... 65-68
Obituary ... 211
Hammond, Michelle McKinney 1957- ... 210
Hammond, N(icholas) G(eoffrey) L(empriere)
1907-2001 ... CANR-44
Obituary ... 195
Earlier sketches in CA 13-16R, CANR-5, 21
Hammond, Norman 1944- ... CANR-19
Earlier sketches in CA 49-52, CANR-3
Hammond, Paul 1947- ... CANR-88
Earlier sketch in CA 57-60
Hammond, Paul Y(oung) 1929- ... CANR-2
Earlier sketch in CA 1-4R
Hammond, Peter B(oyd) 1928- ... 69-72
Hammond, Philip C. 1924- ... 5-8R
Hammond, Phillip E(verett) 1931- ... CANR-7
Earlier sketch in CA 17-20R
Hammond, Ralph
See Hammond Innes, Ralph
Hammond, Richard J(ames) 1911-1982 ... 61-64
Obituary ... 122
Hammond, Ross W(illiam) 1918- ... 33-36R
Hammond, Susan ... 174
Hammond, Thomas T(aylor)
1920-1993 ... CANR-46
Obituary ... 140
Earlier sketch in CA 9-12R
Hammond, W(illiam) Rogers 1920- ... 45-48
Hammond, Wayne G(ordon)
1953- ... CANR-102
Earlier sketch in CA 145
Hammond, William M. 1943- ... 186
Hammond, Winifred G(raham) 1899-1992 . 107
Obituary ... 171
See also SATA 29
See also SATA-Obit 107
Hammond Innes, Ralph 1913-1998 . CANR-80
Earlier sketches in CA 5-8R, CANR-4, 26, 52
See also Innes, (Ralph) Hammond
See also CMW 4
See also CN 6
See also SATA 116
Hammonds, Michael (Galen) 1942- ... 45-48
Hammontree, Marie (Gertrude) 1913- ... 5-8R
See also SATA 13
Hamner, Earl (Henry), Jr. 1923- ... 73-76
See also AITN 2
See also CLC 12
See also DLB 6
Hamner, Robert D(aniel) 1941- ... CANR-94
Earlier sketch in CA 106
Hamod, (Hamode) Sam(uel) 1936- ... CANR-22
Earlier sketch in CA 45-48
Hamori, Laszlo Dezso 1911- ... 9-12R
Hamovitch, Mitzi Berger 1924-1992 ... 112
Obituary ... 140
Hamp, Eric P(ratt) 1920- ... 17-20R
Hampden, John 1898-1974 ... 109
Hampden-Turner, Charles M. 1934- ... 33-36R
Hamper, Ben 1956(?)- ... 138
Hampl, Patricia 1946- ... CANR-88
Earlier sketches in CA 104, CANR-21
Hample, Stuart 1926- ... 108
Hample, Zack 1977- ... 237
See also SATA 161
Hampsch, George H(arold) 1927- ... 13-16R
Hampshire, Joyce Gregorian
See Gregorian, Joyce Ballou
Hampshire, Stuart (Newton)
1914-2004 ... CANR-117
Obituary ... 228
Brief entry ... 116
Earlier sketch in CA 143
Hampshire, Susan 1942- ... CANR-65
Brief entry ... 112
Earlier sketch in CA 129
See also SATA 98
Hampson, Anne ... CANR-84
Brief entry ... 111
Earlier sketch in CA 117
Interview in ... CA-117
See also RHW
Hampson, (Margaret) Daphne
1944- ... CANR-126
Earlier sketch in CA 165
Hampson, (Richard) Denman 1929- ... SATA 15
Hampson, Frank 1918(?)-1985
Obituary ... 117
See also SATA-Obit 46
Hampson, John 1901-1955 ... 201
See also DLB 191
Hampson, Norman 1922- ... CANR-138
Earlier sketch in CA 25-28R
Hampson, Robert (Gavin) 1948- ... 135
Hampton, Angeline A.
See Kelly, A(ngeline) A(gnes)
Hampton, Brenda ... AAYA 62
Hampton, Charles
See Martin, (Roy) Peter
Hampton, Christopher 1929- ... CANR-4
Earlier sketch in CA 53-56
See also CBD
See also CP 2
Hampton, Christopher (James) 1946- ... 25-28R
See also CD 5, 6
See also CLC 4
See also DLB 13
See also MTCW 1
Hampton, David
See Fairclough, Chris
Hampton, David R(ichard) 1933- ... 81-84
Hampton, H(arold) Duane 1932- ... 33-36R
Hampton, Henry (Eugene, Jr.) 1940-1998 ... 139
Obituary ... 172
See also BW 2
Hampton, James 1936- ... 213
Hampton, Jim
See Hampton, John Lewis
Hampton, Jimmy
See Hampton, James
Hampton, Joanna
See Ferguson, Jo Ann
Hampton, John Lewis 1935- ... 133
Hampton, Kathleen 1923- ... 1-4R
Hampton, Mark
See Norwood, Victor G(eorge) C(harles)
Hampton, Robert E. 1924- ... 33-36R
Hampton, Wilborn ... CANR-140
Earlier sketch in CA 171
See also SATA 156
Hampton, William (Albert) 1929- ... CANR-13
Earlier sketch in CA 33-36R
Hampton-Jones, Hollis ... 225
Hamre, Leif 1914- ... CANR-4
Earlier sketch in CA 5-8R
See also SATA 5
Hamrick, Samuel J., Jr. 1929- ... 120
Brief entry ... 115
Interview in ... CA-120
Hamrin, Robert 1946- ... 155
Hamsa, Bobbie 1944- ... 106
See also SATA 52
See also SATA-Brief 38
Hamscher, Albert N(elson) 1946- ... 73-76
Hamsher, J. Herbert 1938- ... 57-60
Hamshere, Cyril (Eric) 1912- ... 41-44R
Hamson, C. J.
See Hamson, Charles John
Hamson, Charles John 1905-1987
Obituary ... 124
Hamsun, Knut
See Pedersen, Knut
See also DLB 297
See also EW 8
See also EWL 3
See also RGWL 2, 3
See also TCLC 2, 14, 49, 151
Hamsund, Knut Pedersen
See Pedersen, Knut
Hamza, Khidhir (Abdul Abbas) ... 196
Han, Henry H. 1932- ... 125
Han, Lu
See Stickler, Soma Han
Han, Seung Soo 1936- ... CANR-2
Earlier sketch in CA 45-48
Han, Soma
See Stickler, Soma Han
Han, Sungjoo 1940- ... 53-56
Han, Suzanne Crowder 1953- ... 155
See also SATA 89
Hanafi, Rhoda
See Hanafi, Zakiya (Asha Jenan)
Hanafi, Zakiya (Asha Jenan) 1959- ... 222
Hanagan, Eva (Helen) 1923- ... 101
Hanagan, Michael Patrick 1947- ... 109
Hanaghan, Jonathan 1887-1967 ... 65-68
Hanami, Tadashi (Akamatsu) 1930- ... 89-92
Hanan, Patrick Dewes 1927- ... 106
Hanan, Stephen Mo 1947(?)- ... 210
Hanania, Tony 1964- ... 190
Hanau, Laia 1916- ... 89-92
Hanawalt, Barbara A(nn) 1941- ... 101
Hanbury, Victor
See Losey, Joseph (Walton)
Hanbury-Tenison, Marika 1938-1982 ... 104
Obituary ... 108
Hanbury-Tenison, (Airling) Robin 1936- .. 57-60
Hance, Kenneth G(ordon) 1903-1986 ... 85-88
Hance, William A(dams) 1916- ... 9-12R
Hanchett, William 1922- ... 33-36R
Hancock, Alice Van Fossen 1890-1984 ... 1-4R
Hancock, Carla ... 89-92
Hancock, Carol Helen Brooks
See Hancock, Morgan
Hancock, Edward L(eslie) 1930- ... CANR-1
Earlier sketch in CA 45-48
Hancock, Geoffrey 1946- ... CANR-19
Earlier sketch in CA 101
Hancock, Graham 1950(?)- ... 156
Hancock, Harold B(ell) 1913-1987 ... 53-56
Hancock, Herbert Jeffrey 1940- ... 172
Hancock, Herbie
See Hancock, Herbert Jeffrey
Hancock, Ian (Robert) 1940- ... 142
Hancock, James (A.) 1921- ... 141
Hancock, John Lee 1956- ... 178
Hancock, Joy Bright 1898-1986
Obituary ... 120
Hancock, Karen 1953- ... 215
Hancock, Keith
See Hancock, W(illiam) K(eith)
Hancock, Leslie 1941- ... 21-24R
Hancock, Lyn 1938- ... 77-80
Hancock, M. Donald 1939- ... 33-36R
Hancock, Malcolm Cyril 1936-1993 ... 25-28R
Obituary ... 140
Hancock, Mary A. 1923- ... 37-40R
See also SATA 31
Hancock, Maxine 1942- ... CANR-8
Earlier sketch in CA 61-64
Hancock, Morgan 1941- ... 103
Hancock, Niel (Anderson) 1941- ... CANR-58
Earlier sketches in CA 97-100, CANR-21
See also FANT
Hancock, Ralph Lowell 1903-1987 ... CAP-1
Earlier sketch in CA 9-10
Hancock, Roger Nelson 1929- ... 97-100
Hancock, Sheila 1942- ... 49-52
Hancock, Sibyl 1940- ... CANR-16
Earlier sketches in CA 49-52, CANR-1
See also SATA 9
Hancock, Taylor 1920-2000 ... 97-100
Hancock, W(illiam) K(eith)
1898-1988 ... CANR-5
Obituary ... 126
Earlier sketch in CA 5-8R
Hancocks, David 1941- ... 207
Hand, David J. 1950- ... 222
Hand, Elizabeth 1957- ... CANR-92
Earlier sketches in CA 136, CANR-84
See also AAYA 67
See also SATA 118
See also SFW 4
See also SUFW 2
Hand, G(eoffrey) J(oseph Philip Macaulay)
1931- ... 25-28R
Hand, J(oan) C(arole) 1943- ... 57-60
Hand, (Andrus) Jackson 1913-1982 .. CANR-10
Earlier sketch in CA 61-64
Hand, John
See Pierson, John H(erman) G(roesbeck)
Hand, Richard A(llen) 1941- ... 149
Hand, Thomas A(lypius) 1915- ... 13-16R
Hand, Wayland D(ebs) 1907-1986 ... 41-44R
Obituary ... 120
Handel, Gerald 1924- ... CANR-11
Earlier sketch in CA 21-24R
Handel, Michael I. 1942-2001 ... 131
Obituary ... 199
Handelman, Howard 1943- ... 57-60
Handelman, John R(obert) 1948- ... 77-80
Handelman, Stephen 1947- ... 152
Handelman, Susan A. 1949- ... 137
Handel-Mazzetti, Enrica von
1871-1955 ... DLB 81
Handelsman, Judith Florence 1948- ... 61-64
Handey, Jack 1949- ... 141
Handford, Martin (John) 1956- ... 137
See also CLR 22
See also MAICYA 1, 2
See also SATA 64
Handforth, Thomas (Schofield) 1897-1948 . 183
Brief entry ... 120
See also SATA 42

Cumulative Index 247 Hansen

Handke, Peter 1942- CANR-133
Earlier sketches in CA 77-80, CANR-33, 75, 104
See also CLC 5, 8, 10, 15, 38, 134
See also CWW 2
See also DAM DRAM, NOV
See also DC 17
See also DLB 85, 124
See also EWL 3
See also MTCW 1, 2
See also MTFW 2005
See also TWA
Handl, Irene 1902(?)-1987 103
Obituary 124
Handler, Daniel
See Snicket, Lemony
See also CLR 79
Handler, David 1952- CANR-138
Earlier sketches in CA 141, CANR-72
Handler, Evan 1961- 153
Handler, Jerome S(idney) 1933- 53-56
Handler, Joel F. 1932-
Brief entry 113
Handler, Julian Harris 1922- 21-24R
Handler, Meyer Srednick 1905-1978
Obituary 77-80
Handler, Milton 1903-1998 61-64
Obituary 172
Handler, Philip 1917-1981 .... 33-36R
Obituary 105
Handler, Ruth 1916-2002 237
Handley, Arnold 217
Handley, Graham Roderick 1926- CANR-24
Earlier sketch in CA 105
Handley-Taylor, Geoffrey 1920-2005 . CANR-7
Obituary 239
Earlier sketch in CA 5-8R
Handlin, Mary (Flug) 1913-1976 .... CAP-2
Obituary 65-68
Earlier sketch in CA 33-36
Handlin, Oscar 1915- CANR-23
Earlier sketches in CA 1-4R, CANR-5
See also DLB 17
Handman, Herbert Ira 1932- 89-92
Handover, P(hyllis) M(argaret) 1923(?)-1974 .... 9-12R
Obituary 53-56
Hands, D(ouglas) Wade 1951- CANR-93
Earlier sketch in CA 145
Hands, Jeremy 1951-1999 183
Handscombe, Richard 1935- 37-40R
Handville, Robert (Tompkins) 1924- .... SATA 45
Handy, Charles 1932- 210
Handy, D(orothy) Antoinette 1930- 198
Handy, Edward Smith Craighill 1893(?)-1980
Obituary 102
Handy, Lowell K. 1949- 150
Handy, Robert T(heodore) 1918- CANR-2
Earlier sketch in CA 5-8R
Handy, Rollo 1927- 9-12R
Handy, Toni 1930- 97-100
Handy, W(illiam) C(hristopher) 1873-1958 . 167
Brief entry 121
See also BW 3
See also TCLC 97
Handy, William J. 1918- 45-48
Hane, Mikiso 1922-2003 .... CANR-15
Obituary 222
Earlier sketch in CA 81-84
Hane, Roger 1940-1974 .... SATA-Obit 20
Hanel, Wolfram
See Haenel, Wolfram
Hanenkrat, Frank (Thomas) 1939- 93-96
Haner, F(rederick) T(heodore) 1929- 53-56
Hanes, Bailey C(ass) 1915- 77-80
Hanes, Elizabeth Sill 1-4R
Hanes, Frank Borden 1920- CANR-28
Earlier sketch in CA 1-4R
Hanes, Mary (a pseudonym) 1940(?)-
Brief entry 117
Haney, David P. 1938- CANR-21
Earlier sketches in CA 57-60, CANR-6
Haney, David P. 1952- 219
Haney, Eleanor H(umes) 1931-1999
Brief entry 114
Haney, John B. 1931- 29-32R
Haney, Lauren
See Winkelman, Betty J.
Haney, Lynn 1941- CANR-1
Earlier sketch in CA 49-52
See also SATA 23
Haney, Thomas K. 1936- 13-16R
Haney, Thomas R. 45-48
Haney, William V. 1925- 17-20R
Hanff, Helene 1916-1997 .... CANR-3
Obituary 157
Earlier sketch in CA 5-8R
See also DFS 17
See also SATA 11, 97
Hanfmann, George M(axim) A(nossov) 1911-1986
Obituary 118
Brief entry 117
Hanford, Lloyd D(avid) 1901-1979 ... CANR-11
Earlier sketch in CA 13-16R
Hanford, S. A. 1898-1978
Obituary 81-84
Hang, T(ing-)Y(ung) 1908(?)-1987
Obituary 122
Hangen, (Putnam) Welles 1930- 9-12R
Hanh, Thich Nhat 1926- CANR-111
Earlier sketch in CA 167
See also CP 1
Hanifi, M(ohammed) Jamil 1935- 61-64
Hanigan, James Patrick 1938- 125
Haning, Bob
See Haning, James R(obert)
Haning, James R(obert) 1928- CANR-2
Earlier sketch in CA 45-48
Hanke, Howard August 1911-1996 .... 1-4R
Hanke, Lewis (Ulysses) 1905-1993 65-68
Hankey, Cyril Patrick 1886-1973 .... 1-4R
Obituary 103
Hankey, Rosalie A.
See Wax, Rosalie (Amelia) H.
Hankey, Roy 1932- 108
Hankin, C(herry) A(nne) 1937- 131
Hankin, Elizabeth Rosemary 1950- 156
Hankin, (Edward Charles) St. John (Emile Clavering) 1869-1909
Brief entry 110
See also DLB 10
See also RGEL 2
Hankins, Clabe
See McDonald, Erwin L(awrence)
Hankins, Frank Hamilton 1877-1970
Obituary 104
Hankins, John Erskine 1905-1996 49-52
Hankins, Norman E(lijah) 1935- CANR-11
Earlier sketch in CA 61-64
Hankins, Thomas Leroy 1933- 108
Hankinson, Alan 1926- 130
Hankinson, Cyril (Francis James) 1895-1984 .... CAP-1
Earlier sketch in CA 9-10
Hankla, Cathryn 1958- CANR-113
Earlier sketches in CA 116, CANR-39
Hanks, Lucien M(ason) 1910-1988 .... 37-40R
Obituary 197
Hanks, Patrick 1940- 186
Hanks, Stedman Shumway 1889-1979
Obituary 85-88
Hanle, Dorothea Zack 1917-1999 .... 13-16R
Obituary 177
Hanle, Mrs. Frank L.
See Hanle, Dorothea Zack
Hanley, Boniface Francis 1924- 9-12R
See also SATA 65
Hanley, Brent 1970- 227
Hanley, Christine A.
See Adams(-Butch), Christine A(nn)
Hanley, Clifford (Leonard Clark) 1922-1999 .... CANR-69
Obituary 183
Earlier sketches in CA 9-12R, CANR-3, 23
See also CN 1, 2, 3, 4, 5, 6, 7
See also DLB 14
Hanley, Elizabeth
See Du Breuil, (Elizabeth) L(or)inda
Hanley, Evelyn A(lice) 1916-1980 .... 41-44R
Obituary 97-100
Hanley, Gerald (Anthony) 1916-1992 .... CANR-6
Obituary 139
Earlier sketch in CA 1-4R
See also CN 1, 2, 3, 4, 5
Hanley, Hope Anthony 1926- CANR-5
Earlier sketch in CA 9-12R
Hanley, James 1901-1985 .... CANR-36
Obituary 117
Earlier sketch in CA 73-76
See also CBD
See also CLC 3, 5, 8, 13
See also CN 1, 2, 3
See also DLB 191
See also EWL 3
See also MTCW 1
See also RGEL 2
Hanley, Katharine Rose 1932- 37-40R
Hanley, Michael F. IV 1941- 65-68
Hanley, Mike
See Hanley, Michael F. IV
Hanley, Theodore Dean 1917- 5-8R
Hanley, Thomas O'Brien 1918- CANR-1
Earlier sketch in CA 1-4R
Hanley, William 1931- 41-44R
See also CAD
See also CD 5, 6
Hanlon, Emily 1945- 77-80
See also SATA 15
Hanlon, Gregory 1953- CANR-93
Earlier sketch in CA 146
Hanlon, John J(oseph) 1912-1988 57-60
Hanlon, Joseph 210
Hanmer, Davina
See Courtney, Nicholas (Piers)
Hann, C. M. 1953- CANR-47
Earlier sketch in CA 121
Hann, Jacquie 1951- CANR-13
Earlier sketch in CA 73-76
See also SATA 19
Hann, Judith 1942- 145
See also SATA 77
Hanna, Alfred Jackson 1893-1978 ...... CANR-2
Earlier sketch in CA 45-48
Hanna, Bill
See Hanna, William (Denby)
Hanna, Cheryl 1951- .... SATA 84
Hanna, David 1917-1993 .... CANR-6
Earlier sketch in CA 57-60
Hanna, Edward B. 1935- 226
Hanna, Frank A(llan) 1907-1978
Obituary 111
Hanna, J. Marshall 1907-1997 .... CANR-24
Earlier sketch in CA 1-4R
Hanna, Jack (Bushnell) 1947- 141
See also SATA 74
Hanna, John Paul 1932- CANR-1
Earlier sketch in CA 45-48
Hanna, Lavone Agnes 1896-1982 .... 13-16R
Obituary 201
Hanna, Mary Carr 1905-1991 45-48
Hanna, Mary T. 1935- 97-100
Hanna, Nell(ie L.) 1908- .... SATA 55
Hanna, Paul R(obert) 1902-1988 ...... CANR-48
Earlier sketch in CA 45-48
See also SATA 9
Hanna, S(uhail) S(alim) 1943- CANR-92
Earlier sketch in CA 126
Hanna, Thomas 1928- CANR-1
Earlier sketch in CA 1-4R
Hanna, Warren L(eonard) 1898-1987 130
Hanna, William (Denby) 1910-2001 171
Obituary 194
See also IDFW 3, 4
See also SATA 51
See also SATA-Obit 126
Hanna, William John 1931- CANR-8
Earlier sketch in CA 61-64
Hannaford, John 1918- 45-48
Hannaford, Peter (Dor) 1932- 130
Hannah, (Juliel) Barbara 1891-1986 97-100
Hannah, Barry 1942- CANR-113
Brief entry 108
Earlier sketches in CA 110, CANR-43, 68
Interview in CA-110
See also BPFB 2
See also CLC 23, 38, 90
See also CN 4, 5, 6, 7
See also CSW
See also DLB 6, 234
See also MTCW 1
See also RGSF 2
Hannah, James 1951- 145
Hannah, Kristin 1960- 141
Hannah, Leslie 1947- 215
Hannah, Norman B(ritton) 1919-2002 127
Obituary 205
Hannah, Sophie 1971- .... CWP
Hannak, Johann Jacques 1892- CAP-1
Earlier sketch in CA 9-10
Hannam, Charles 1925- CANR-11
Earlier sketch in CA 61-64
See also SATA 50
Hannam, June 1947- 161
Hannan, Chris(topher John) 1958- 234
See also CBD
See also CD 5, 6
Hannan, Joseph F(rancis) 1923- CANR-3
Earlier sketch in CA 9-12R
Hannan, Maggie 1962- 229
Hannant, Larry 171
Hannas, Linda 1913- 113
Hannau, Hans W(alter) 1904- CANR-10
Earlier sketch in CA 21-24R
Hannavy, John Michael 1946- CANR-11
Earlier sketch in CA 69-72
Hannaway, Patricia H(inman) 1929- 61-64
Hannaway, Patti
See Hannaway, Patricia H(inman)
Hannay, Alastair 1932- CANR-89
Earlier sketch in CA 130
Hannay, Allen 1946- 109
Hannay, Doris Fergusson
See Fergusson Hannay, Doris
Hannay, James 1827-1873 .... DLB 21
Hannay, Margaret Patterson 1944- ... CANR-44
Earlier sketches in CA 104, CANR-21
Hannelle, Pirkko
See Vainio, Pirkko
Hanneman, Audre (Louise) 1926- 21-24R
Hanney, Peter 1930-1976
Obituary 105
Hannibal
See Alexander, Stanley Walter
Hannibal, Edward 1936- CANR-28
Earlier sketch in CA 29-32R
Hannifin, Jerry (Bernard) 1917- 77-80
Hanning, Hugh 1925-2000 .... 25-28R
Obituary 188
Hanning, Robert William 1938- 93-96
Hannity, Sean 1961- 211
Hannon, Ezra
See Hunter, Evan
Hann-Syme, Marguerite 197
See also SATA 127
Hannula, Reino 1918- 105
Hannum, Alberta Pierson 1906-1985 65-68
Obituary 115
Hannum, Hurst 1945- 161
Hano, Arnold 1922- CANR-5
Earlier sketch in CA 9-12R
See also DLB 241
See also SATA 12
Hano, Renee Roth
See Roth-Hano, Renee
Hanover, Terri
See Huff, Tanya (Sue)
Hanrahan, Barbara 1939-1991 127
Brief entry 121
See also CN 4, 5
See also DLB 289
Hanrahan, John D(avid) 1938- CANR-15
Earlier sketch in CA 77-80
Hanrieder, Wolfram F. 1931- CANR-23
Earlier sketches in CA 21-24R, CANR-8
Hans, Valerie P(atricia) 1951- 126
Hansberry, Lorraine (Vivian) 1930-1965 .... CANR-58
Obituary 25-28R
Earlier sketch in CA 109
See also CABS 3
See also AAYA 25
See also AFAW 1, 2
See also AMWS 4
See also BLC 2
See also BW 1, 3
See also CAD
See also CDALB 1941-1968
See also CLC 17, 62
See also CWD
See also DA
See also DA3
See also DAB
See also DAC
See also DAM DRAM, MST, MULT
See also DC 2
See also DFS 2
See also DLB 7, 38
See also EWL 3
See also FL 1:6
See also FW
See also LAIT 4
See also MAL 5
See also MTCW 1, 2
See also MTFW 2005
See also RGAL 4
See also TUS
Hansberry, William Leo 1894-1965 155
See also BW 3
Hanscom, Leslie Rutherford 1924- 135
Hanscombe, Gillian E. 1945- 144
Hansel, C(harles) E(dward) M(ark) 1917-
Brief entry 115
Hansel, Robert R(aymond) 1936- 186
Brief entry 110
Hansell, Antonina
See Looker, Antonina (Hansell)
Hansen, Al(fred Earl) 1927- 17-20R
Hansen, Alvin H(arvey) 1887-1975 .... CAP-1
Obituary 57-60
Earlier sketch in CA 13-16
Hansen, Ann Larkin 1958- 161
See also SATA 96
Hansen, Anton
See Tammsaare, A(nton) H(ansen)
Hansen, Arlen J. 1936- 133
Hansen, Barbara (Louise) 1935- 190
Hansen, Bertrand Lyle 1922- 9-12R
Hansen, Brooks 1965- CANR-89
Earlier sketches in CA 132, CANR-56
See also SATA 104
Hansen, Carl (Francis) 1906-1983 ...... CANR-2
Obituary 110
Earlier sketch in CA 5-8R
Hansen, Carol
See Fenichel, Carol Hansen
Hansen, Caryl (Hall) 1929- 108
See also SATA 39
Hansen, Cecil
See Huffaker, Clair
Hansen, Cecil Dan
See Huffaker, Clair
Hansen, Chadwick (Clarke) 1926- 29-32R
Hansen, David James 1953- 196
Hansen, Debra Gold 1953- 146
Hansen, Donald A(ndrew) 1933- 73-76
Hansen, Donald Charles 1935- 33-36R
Hansen, Drew D. 1964(?)- 226
Hansen, Emmanuel 1937- 104
Hansen, Flemming 1938- 93-96
Hansen, Forest Warnyr 1931- 45-48
Hansen, G. Eric 1938- 226
Hansen, Gary B(arker) 1935- CANR-21
Earlier sketches in CA 9-12R, CANR-3
Hansen, Gunnar 1947- 144
Hansen, Hardy 1941- 139
Hansen, Harry 1884-1977 73-76
Obituary 69-72
Hansen, Ian V. 1929- 185
See also SATA 113
Hansen, Jennifer 1972- 231
See also SATA 156
Hansen, Joseph 1923-2004 .... CANR-125
Obituary 233
Earlier sketches in CA 29-32R, CANR-16, 44, 66
Interview in CANR-16
See also Brock, Rose and Colton, James
See also CAAS 17
See also BPFB 2
See also CLC 38
See also CMW 4
See also DLB 226
See also GLL 1
Hansen, Joyce (Viola) 1942- CANR-143
Earlier sketches in CA 105, CANR-43, 87
See also AAYA 41
See also BW 2
See also CLR 21
See also CWRI 5
See also JRDA
See also MAICYA 1, 2
See also SAAS 15
See also SATA 46, 101, 158
See also SATA-Brief 39
Hansen, Karen V. 1955- CANR-102
Earlier sketch in CA 149
Hansen, Kenneth H(arvey) 1917- 13-16R
Hansen, Klaus J(uergen) 1931- 21-24R
Hansen, Leroy John 1922-1990
Obituary 132
Hansen, Marcus Lee 1892-1938 177

Hansen 248 CONTEMPORARY AUTHORS

Hansen, Maren Tonder 1952- ... 167
Hansen, Mark Victor ... 173
See also SATA 112
Hansen, Martin A(lfred) 1909-1955 ... 167
See also DLB 214
See also EWL 3
See also TCLC 32
Hansen, Mary Lewis (Patterson) 1933- .. 17-20R
Hansen, Matthew Scott 1953- ... 227
Hansen, Niles M(aurice) 1937- ... CANR-30
Earlier sketches in CA 25-28R, CANR-13
Hansen, Norman J. 1918- ... 29-32R
Hansen, Poul Einer 1939- ... 141
Hansen, R. C. 1926- ... 169
Hansen, Richard H(erbert) 1929- ... 1-4R
Hansen, Rodney Thor 1940- ... 53-56
Hansen, Roger D(ennis) 1935-1991 ... 105
Obituary ... 133
Hansen, Ron(ald Thomas) 1947- CANR-104
Earlier sketches in CA 89-92, CANR-17, 63
See also CN 5, 6
See also SATA 56
See also TCWW 2
Hansen, Rosanna 1947- ... 105
Hansen, Terrence Leslie 1920-1974 ... 37-40R
Hansen, Thorkild 1927-1989 ... 184
See also DLB 214
See also EWL 3
Hansen, Vern
See Hanson, Vic(tor) J(oseph)
Hansen, W(illiam) Lee 1928- ... 29-32R
Hansen, William F(reeman) 1941- CANR-30
Earlier sketch in CA 49-52
Hansen and
Philipson eds.
Philipson ... CLC 65
Hansen-Hill, N. D. ... 217
Hanser, Richard (Frederick)
1909-1981 ... CANR-8
Earlier sketch in CA 5-8R
See also SATA 13
Han Shaogong 1953- ... 206
Hanshew, Thomas W. 1857-1914 ... 228
Brief entry ... 113
See also CMW 4
Hansi
See Hirschmann, Maria Anne
Hanson, A(lbert) H(enry) 1913-1971 .. CANR-4
Obituary ... 89-92
Earlier sketch in CA 5-8R
Hanson, Agnes O(lin) 1905-1999 ... 107
Hanson, Anne Coffin 1921-2004 ... 21-24R
Obituary ... 231
Hanson, Anthony Tyrrell
1916-1991 ... CANR-24
Obituary ... 134
Earlier sketches in CA 21-24R, CANR-9
Hanson, Charles G(oring) 1934- ... 138
Hanson, Curtis (Lee) 1945- ... 207
See also AAYA 52
Hanson, David J. 1941- ... 180
Hanson, Dirk 1950- ... 111
Hanson, Duane 1925-1996 ... AAYA 39
Hanson, E(ugene) Kenneth 1930- ... 13-16R
Hanson, Earl D(orchester)
1927-1993 ... CANR-12
Obituary ... 143
Earlier sketch in CA 73-76
Hanson, Earl Parker 1899-1978 ... 41-44R
Hanson, Elizabeth 1684-1737 ... DLB 200
Hanson, Eric O. 1942- ... 125
Hanson, F(ridolf) Allan 1939- ... 41-44R
Hanson, Harvey 1941- ... 65-68
Hanson, Howard (Harold) 1896-1981
Obituary ... 103
Hanson, Howard Gordon 1931- ... 21-24R
Hanson, Irene (Forsythe) 1898-1994 ... 49-52
Hanson, Isabel 1929- ... 106
Hanson, James Arthur 1940- ... CANR-30
Earlier sketch in CA 49-52
Hanson, Jim 1953- ... 97-100
Hanson, Joan 1938- ... CANR-15
Earlier sketch in CA 33-36R
See also SATA 8
Hanson, Joseph E. 1894(?)-1971
Obituary ... 104
See also SATA-Obit 27
Hanson, June Andrea 1941- ... 97-100
Hanson, Kenneth O(stlin) 1922- ... CANR-7
Earlier sketch in CA 53-56
See also CLC 13
See also CP 1, 2
Hanson, Kristine 1958- ... 123
Hanson, Michael James 1942- ... 61-64
Hanson, Neil 1948- ... CANR-94
Earlier sketch in CA 150
Hanson, Norwood Russell
1924-1967 ... CANR-8
Earlier sketch in CA 5-8R
Hanson, Paul D(avid) 1939- ... 61-64
Hanson, Paul R. 1952- ... 134
Hanson, Pauline ... 45-48
See also CP 1, 2
Hanson, Peggy 1934- ... CANR-12
Earlier sketch in CA 29-32R
Hanson, Peter G. 1947- ... 145
Hanson, Philip 1936- ... 103
Hanson, R(ichard) P(atrick) C(rosland)
1916-1988 ... CANR-9
Obituary ... 127
Earlier sketch in CA 21-24R
Hanson, Richard S(imon) 1931- ... 37-40R
Hanson, Robert Carl 1926- ... 37-40R
Hanson, Robert P(aul) 1918- ... 9-12R
Hanson, Roy (Francis) 1934-1989
Obituary ... 128
Hanson, Ruth Katie 1900-1977 ... 5-8R
Hanson, Simon
See Hanson, Richard S(imon)
Hanson, Susan F. 1955- ... 239
Hanson, V. Joseph
See Hanson, Vic(tor) J(oseph)
Hanson, Vern
See Hanson, Vic(tor) J(oseph)
Hanson, Vern ... TCWW 2
Hanson, Vic(tor) J(oseph)
1920(?)-2001 ... TCWW 2
Hanson, Victor Davis 1953- ... 187
Hanson, Warren 1949- ... SATA 155
Hanson, William S(tewart) 1950- ... 123
Hansson, Gunilla 1939- ... SATA 64
Hansten, Philip D. 1943- ... 33-36R
Han Suyin 1917- ... 17-20R
Hanushek, Eric Alan 1943- ... 41-44R
Hanut, Eryk 1967- ... 222
Hanzlicek, C(harles) G(eorge)
1942- ... CANR-118
Earlier sketches in CA 73-76, CANR-12
Hanzo, L(ajos) 1952- ... 226
Hao, Qian
See Qian Hao
Hao, Yen-ping 1934- ... 53-56
Hao Ran
See Liang Jinguang
See also CWW 2
Hapgood, Charles Hutchins
1904-1982 ... 17-20R
Hapgood, David 1926- ... 13-16R
Hapgood, Fred 1942- ... 93-96
Hapgood, Hutchins 1869-1944 ... DLB 303
Hapgood, Norman 1868-1937 ... 175
See also DLB 91
Hapgood, Ruth K(nott) 1920- ... 49-52
Hapke, Laura 1946- ... CANR-110
Earlier sketch in CA 138
Happe, Peter 1932- ... CANR-28
Earlier sketch in CA 45-48
Happel, Eberhard Werner 1647-1690 . DLB 168
Happel, Robert A. 1916- ... 1-4R
Happel, Stephen (Paul) 1944-2003 ... 114
Obituary ... 220
Happenstance, Aurelia
See Furdyna, Anna M.
Happold, F(rederick) C(rossfield) 1893- ... 101
Haq, Mahbub ul 1934-1998 ... 13-16R
Obituary ... 169
Haqqi, Yahya 1905- ... EWL 3
Harada, Masako 1939- ... 161
Harakas, Stanley Samuel 1932- ... 134
Harald, Eric
See Boesen, Victor
Haraldsson, Erlendur 1931- ... 101
Haran, Maeve 1950- ... 136
Harap, Henry 1893-1981
Obituary ... 104
Harap, Louis 1904-1998 ... 57-60
Harari, Ehud 1935- ... 65-68
Harari, Oren 1949- ... 193
Harary, Keith 1953- ... CANR-102
Earlier sketches in CA 120, CANR-48
Harary, Stuart Blue
See Harary, Keith
Harasymiw, Bohdan 1936- ... 124
Hara Tamiki 1905-1951 ... MJW
Haraway, Donna Jeanne 1944- ... 73-76
Harayda, Janice 1949- ... 187
Harbach, Otto (Abels) 1873-1963
Obituary ... 112
See also DLB 265
Harbage, Alfred (Bennett)
1901-1976 ... CANR-58
Obituary ... 65-68
Earlier sketches in CA 5-8R, CANR-5
See also CMW 4
Harbaugh, John W(arvelle) 1926- ... CANR-30
Earlier sketch in CA 49-52
Harbaugh, William Henry 1920-2005 ... 1-4R
Obituary ... 239
Harberger, Arnold C. 1924- ... CANR-6
Earlier sketch in CA 13-16R
Harbert, Earl N(orman) 1934- ... CANR-29
Earlier sketches in CA 33-36R, CANR-13
Harbert, Mary Ann 1945- ... 61-64
Harbeson, Georgiana Brown 1894(?)-1980
Obituary ... 101
Harbeson, Gladys Evans ... 21-24R
Harbeson, John Willis 1938- ... 57-60
Harbin, Calvin E(dward) 1916- ... 21-24R
Harbin, Robert
See Williams, Ned
Harbinson, Allen
See Harbinson, W(illiam) A(llen)
Harbinson, Robert
See Bryans, Robert Harbinson
Harbinson, W(illiam) A(llen) 1941- .. CANR-72
Earlier sketches in CA 61-64, CANR-9, 25
See also HGG
Harbison, Frederick Harris 1912-1976
Obituary ... 65-68
Harbison, Peter 1939- ... 65-68
Harbison, Robert 1940- ... 102
Harbottle, Michael (Neale)
1917-1997 ... CANR-45
Obituary ... 157
Earlier sketch in CA 29-32R
Harbron, John D(avison) 1924- ... 9-12R
Harburg, E(dgar) Y(ipsel) 1896-1981 ... 85-88
Obituary ... 103
See also DLB 265
Harburg, Ernest 1926- ... 145
Harburg, Ernie
See Harburg, Ernest
Harburg, Yip
See Harburg, E(dgar) Y(ipsel)
Harbury, Colin (Desmond) 1922- ... 102
Harcave, Sidney S(amuel) 1916- ... 17-20R
Harcleroad, Fred F(arley) 1918- ... CANR-23
Earlier sketches in CA 17-20R, CANR-8
Harclerode, Peter 1947- ... 199
Harcourt, Ellen Knowles 1890(?)-1984
Obituary ... 111
See also SATA-Obit 36
Harcourt, G(eoffrey) C(olin) 1931- CANR-16
Earlier sketch in CA 25-28R
Harcourt, Melville 1909- ... 5-8R
Harcourt, Palma -1999 ... CANR-31
Earlier sketches in CA 77-80, CANR-14
Harcourt, Peter 1931- ... 81-84
Harcourt, Wendy ... 181
Hard, Charlotte (Ann) 1969- ... 166
See also SATA 98
Hard, Edward W(ilhelm), Jr. 1939- ... 85-88
Hard, Frederick 1897-1981 ... CAP-2
Earlier sketch in CA 25-28
Hard, Margaret (Steel) 1888(?)-1974
Obituary ... 49-52
Hard, T. W.
See Hard, Edward W(ilhelm), Jr.
Hard, Walter (Rice) 1882-1966
Obituary ... 116
Hardach, Gerd 1941- ... 105
Hardach, Karl 1936- ... 130
Hardaway, Francine 1941- ... 81-84
Hardcastle, Michael 1933- ... CANR-85
Earlier sketches in CA 25-28R, CANR-12
See also CWRI 5
See also SATA 47
See also SATA-Brief 38
Hardcastle, Robert B. 1940- ... 145
Hardeman, Martin J. 1946- ... 218
Harden, Arthur 1865-1940 ... 158
Harden, Blaine 1952- ... CANR-128
Earlier sketch in CA 135
Harden, Donald B(enjamin) 1901-1994 .... 5-8R
Harden, Edgar F(rederick) 1932- ... CANR-49
Earlier sketch in CA 123
Harden, Ian (John) 1954- ... 126
Harden, Oleta Elizabeth (McWhorter)
1935- ... 37-40R
Harden, (John) William 1903-1985 ... 93-96
Harder, Eleanor (Loraine) 1925- ... 37-40R
Harder, Geraldine Gross 1926- ... 53-56
Harder, Kelsie B(rown) 1922- ... 139
Harder, Leland 1926- ... 143
Harder, Raymond Wymbs, Jr. 1920- ... 85-88
Hardesty, Larry (Lynn) 1947- ... CANR-109
Earlier sketch in CA 151
Hardesty, Nancy A(nn) 1941- ... CANR-99
Earlier sketches in CA 57-60, CANR-8, 23
Hardesty, Sarah 1951- ... 126
Hardesty, Von 1939- ... CANR-91
Earlier sketches in CA 112, CANR-46
Hardgrave, Robert L(ewis), Jr. 1939- . CANR-11
Earlier sketch in CA 25-28R
Hardie, Frank 1911-1989 ... 33-36R
Obituary ... 127
Hardie, Kerry 1951- ... 220
Hardie, Philip Russell 1952- ... 222
Hardie, Sean 1947- ... 135
Hardie, William Francis Ross 1902-1990
Obituary ... 132
Hardiman, James W. 1919- ... 33-36R
Hardin, Charles M(eyer) 1908-1997 . CANR-30
Obituary ... 158
Earlier sketch in CA 49-52
Hardin, Clement
See Newton, D(wight) B(ennett)
Hardin, Dave
See Holmes, L(lewellyn) P(erry)
Hardin, Garrett James 1915-2003 ... CANR-9
Obituary ... 220
Earlier sketch in CA 17-20R
Hardin, J. D.
See Barrett, Neal, Jr. and
Riefe, Alan and
Sheldon, Walter J(ames)
Hardin, James (Neal) 1939- ... CANR-82
Earlier sketches in CA 114, CANR-35
Hardin, John A. 1948- ... 169
Hardin, Paul III 1931- ... 25-28R
Hardin, Peter
See Vaczek, Louis
Hardin, Richard F(rancis) 1937- ... 45-48
Hardin, Robert 1934- ... 77-80
Hardin, Tim 1941(?)-1981
Obituary ... 102
Hardin, Tom
See Bauer, Erwin A(dam)
Harding, A(nthony) F(ilmer) 1946- ... 77-80
Harding, Barbara 1926- ... 41-44R
Harding, Bertita (Leonarz de) 1902-1971 .. 5-8R
Harding, Carl B.
See Barker, Elver A.
Harding, D(ouglas) E(dison) 1909-
Brief entry ... 116
Harding, D(enys Clement) W(yatt)
1906-1993 ... CANR-16
Obituary ... 141
Earlier sketches in CAP-1, CA 13-16
Harding, D(ennis) W(illiam) 1940- ... 41-44R
Harding, Davis P. 1915(?)-1970
Obituary ... 104
Harding, Donald Edward 1916- ... CANR-4
Earlier sketch in CA 53-56
Harding, Duncan
See Whiting, Charles (Henry)
Harding, Georgina 1955- ... 133
Harding, Harold F(riend) 1903-1986 ... 37-40R
Harding, Harry (Jr.) 1946- ... CANR-28
Earlier sketch in CA 109
Harding, Ian
See Whiting, Charles (Henry)
Harding, Jack 1914- ... 29-32R
Harding, James 1929- ... CANR-65
Earlier sketches in CA 33-36R, CANR-14, 32
Harding, John 1948- ... 97-100
See also CBD
See also CD 5, 6
Harding, Kenneth
See Little, Paul H(ugo)
Harding, Lee 1937- ... CANR-85
Earlier sketch in CA 106
See also CWRI 5
See also SATA 32
See also SATA-Brief 31
See also SFW 4
Harding, Les 1950- ... 176
Harding, Maria
See Goudiss, Maria Agnes D'Elia
Harding, Matt
See Floren, Lee
Harding, Matthew Whitman
See Floren, Lee
Harding, Mildred Davis 1916- ... CANR-121
Earlier sketch in CA 157
Harding, Neil 1942- ... 125
Harding, Paul
See Doherty, P(aul) C.
Harding, Peter
See Burgess, Michael (Roy)
Harding, Rose
See Gemmell, David A(ndrew)
Harding, Sandra G. 1935- ... CANR-44
Earlier sketch in CA 120
See also FW
Harding, Susan Friend 1946- ... CANR-144
Earlier sketch in CA 126
Harding, T(imothy) D. 1948- ... 85-88
Harding, Thomas G(rayson) 1937- ... 21-24R
Harding, Todd
See Reynolds, Dallas McCord
Harding, Virginia Hamlet 1909- ... 45-48
Harding, Walter Roy 1917-1996 ... CANR-17
Obituary ... 151
Earlier sketches in CA 1-4R, CANR-1
See also DLB 111
Harding, Warren G. III 1941- ... 238
Harding, Wes
See Keevill, Henry J(ohn)
Harding, William Harry 1945- ... 93-96
Hardinge, Helen (Mary Cecil)
1901-1979 ... CAP-2
Earlier sketch in CA 29-32
Hardingham, John (Frederick Watson)
1916- ... CAP-1
Earlier sketch in CA 11-12
Hardison, O(sborne) B(ennett, Jr.)
1928-1990 ... CANR-40
Obituary ... 132
Earlier sketches in CA 5-8R, CANR-6
See also BEST 90:2
Hardisty, Jean V. ... 229
Hardman, John (David) 1944- ... 45-48
Hardman, Keith (Jordan) 1931- ... 116
Hardman, Richards Lynden 1924- ... 13-16R
Hardon, John A(nthony) 1914-2000 ... CANR-2
Earlier sketch in CA 1-4R
Hardoy, Jorge Enrique 1926- ... 33-36R
Hardt, Helga Fleischhauer
See Fleischhauer-Hardt, Helga
Hardt, J(ohn) Pearce 1922- ... CANR-3
Earlier sketch in CA 5-8R
Hardt, Michael 1960- ... 235
Hardwick, Adam
See Connor, John Anthony
Hardwick, Clyde T(homas) 1915- ... 5-8R
Hardwick, Elizabeth (Bruce) 1916- . CANR-139
Earlier sketches in CA 5-8R, CANR-3, 32, 70, 100
See also AMWS 3
See also CLC 13
See also CN 4, 5, 6
See also CSW
See also DA3
See also DAM NOV
See also DLB 6
See also MAWW
See also MTCW 1, 2
See also MTFW 2005
See also TCLE 1:1
Hardwick, Gary (Clifford) 1960- ... 180
Hardwick, Homer
See Rogers, Paul (Patrick)
Hardwick, J. M. D.
See Hardwick, (John) Michael (Drinkrow)
Hardwick, Joan 1940- ... 135
Hardwick, Mary Atkinson
1915-2003 ... CANR-42
Obituary ... 222
Earlier sketches in CA 49-52, CANR-2
Hardwick, (John) Michael (Drinkrow)
1924-1991 ... CANR-42
Obituary ... 134
Earlier sketches in CA 49-52, CANR-2
Hardwick, Mollie
See Hardwick, Mary Atkinson
Hardwick, Phil 1948- ... 225
Hardwick, Richard Holmes, Jr. 1923- . CANR-9
Earlier sketch in CA 5-8R
See also SATA 12
Hardwick, Sylvia
See Doherty, Ivy R. Duffy
Hardy, Adam
See Bulmer, (Henry) Kenneth
Hardy, Alan 1932- ... 73-76
Hardy, Alexander G(eorge) 1920-1973
Obituary ... 45-48

Cumulative Index 249 Harmon

Hardy, Alexandre 1570(?)-1632 ... DLB 268
See also GFL Beginnings to 1789
See also IDTP
Hardy, Alice Dale ... CANR-26
Earlier sketches in CAP-2, CA 19-20
See also SATA 1, 67
Hardy, Alister C(lavering) 1896-1985 ... 85-88
Obituary ... 116
Hardy, Antoinette
See Stockenberg, Antoinette
Hardy, B. Carmon 1934- ... 144
Hardy, Barbara (Gladys) ... 85-88
Hardy, C. Colburn 1910-1998 ... CANR-47
Earlier sketches in CA 53-56, CANR-6, 21
Hardy, David A(ndrews) 1936- ... CANR-8
Earlier sketch in CA 61-64
See also SATA 9
Hardy, Dennis 1941- ... 124
Hardy, Douglas
See Andrews, (Charles) Robert Douglas (Hardy)
Hardy, Edward R(ochie) 1908-1981 ... CAP-1
Earlier sketch in CA 13-16
Hardy, Eric ... 61-64
Hardy, Evelyn 1902- ... 21-24R
Hardy, Francis Joseph 1917-1994 ... CANR-83
Earlier sketch in CA 154
See also Hardy, Frank
Hardy, Frank
See Hardy, Francis Joseph
See also CN 4, 5, 6
See also DLB 260
Hardy, Frank J.
See Hardy, Francis Joseph
Hardy, G(odfrey) H(arold) 1877-1947 ... 163
See also NCFS 5
Hardy, Gayle J. 1942- ... CANR-93
Earlier sketch in CA 151
Hardy, Henry 1949- ... CANR-47
Earlier sketch in CA 113
Hardy, J(ohn) P(hillips) 1933- ... 25-28R
Hardy, Jason
See Oxley, William
Hardy, John Edward 1922- ... 13-16R
Hardy, Jon 1958- ... 123
See also SATA 53
Hardy, Jules 1958- ... 223
Hardy, Laura
See Holland, Sheila
Hardy, LeAnne 1951- ... 229
See also SATA 154
Hardy, Leroy C(lyde) 1927- ... 29-32R
Hardy, Lyndon (Maurice) 1941- ... CANR-83
Earlier sketch in CA 154
See also FANT
Hardy, Melissa 1952- ... CANR-142
Earlier sketch in CA 102
Hardy, Michael (James Langley) 1933- .. 25-28R
Hardy, Peter 1931-2003 ... 65-68
Obituary ... 222
Hardy, Richard E(arl) 1938- ... 37-40R
Hardy, Richard P(eter) 1940- ... 117
Hardy, Robert (Charles) 1925- ... 207
Hardy, Ronald Harold 1919- ... 5-8R
Hardy, Russ
See Snow, Charles H(orace)
Hardy, Stuart
See Schisgall, Oscar
Hardy, Thomas 1840-1928 ... 123
Brief entry ... 104
See also BRW 6
See also BRWC 1, 2
See also BRWR 1
See also CDBLB 1890-1914
See also DA
See also DA3
See also DAB
See also DAC
See also DAM MST, NOV, POET
See also DLB 18, 19, 135, 284
See also EWL 3
See also EXPN
See also EXPP
See also LAIT 2
See also MTCW 1, 2
See also MTFW 2005
See also NFS 3, 11, 15, 19
See also PC 8
See also PFS 3, 4, 18
See also RGEL 2
See also RGSF 2
See also SSC 2, 60
See also TCLC 4, 10, 18, 32, 48, 53, 72, 143, 153
See also TEA
See also WLC
See also WLIT 4
Hardy, Tom 1943- ... 116
Hardy, W(illiam) G(eorge) 1895-1979 ... CANR-83
Earlier sketches in CA 5-8R, CANR-5
See also RHW
Hardy, Willene S(chaefer) 1937- ... 112
Hardy, William M(arion) 1922- ... CANR-2
Earlier sketch in CA 1-4R
Hardyck, Curtis D(ale) 1929- ... 29-32R
Hare, A(lexander) Paul 1923- ... CANR-2
Earlier sketch in CA 1-4R
Hare, Bill
See Hare, William Moorman
Hare, Cyril
See Clark, Alfred Alexander Gordon
See also DLB 77
Hare, Darrell T. 1930- ... 155
Hare, David 1947- ... CANR-91
Earlier sketches in CA 97-100, CANR-39
See also BRWS 4
See also CBD
See also CD 5, 6
See also CLC 29, 58, 136
See also DC 26
See also DFS 4, 7, 16
See also DLB 13, 310
See also MTCW 1
See also TEA
Hare, Douglas Robert Adams 1929- ... 45-48
Hare, Eric B. 1894-1982 ... CAP-1
Earlier sketch in CA 13-16
Hare, F(rederick) Kenneth 1919- ... CANR-14
Earlier sketch in CA 37-40R
Hare, John 1935- ... CANR-110
Earlier sketch in CA 21-24R
Hare, Nathan 1934- ... CANR-24
Earlier sketch in CA 41-44R
See also BW 2
Hare, Norma Q(uarles) 1924- ... 101
See also SATA 46
See also SATA-Brief 41
Hare, Peter H. 1935- ... 33-36R
Hare, R(ichard) M(ervyn) 1919-2002 ... CANR-57
Obituary ... 204
Earlier sketches in CA 5-8R, CANR-2, 31
See also DLB 262
Hare, Richard (Gilbert) 1907-1966 ... CAP-1
Earlier sketch in CA 13-14
Hare, Ronald 1899- ... 77-80
Hare, Steve 1950- ... 151
Hare, Thomas Blenman
See Hare, Thomas William
Hare, Thomas William 1952- ... 122
Hare, Van Court, Jr. 1929- ... 25-28R
Hare, William 1944- ... CANR-95
Earlier sketches in CA 111, CANR-28
Hare, William Moorman 1934- ... 101
Hare Duke, Michael Geoffrey 1925- ... 111
Harel, Isser 1912-2003 ... CANR-10
Obituary ... 213
Earlier sketch in CA 65-68
Harel, Nira 1936- ... SATA 154
Harer, John B. 1948- ... 143
Haresnape, Geoffrey Laurence 1939- ... CP 1
Hareven, Shulamith 1931- ... 159
Brief entry ... 117
Hareven, Tamara K(ern) 1937-2002 . CANR-30
Obituary ... 211
Earlier sketches in CA 25-28R, CANR-13
Harewood, George Henry Hubert Lascelles 1923- ... 125
Harewood, John
See Van Druten, John (William)
Harford, David K(ennedy) 1947- ... 49-52
Harford, Henry
See Hudson, W(illiam) H(enry)
Harford, James J(oseph) 1924- ... 172
Earlier sketch in CA 169
Hargarten, Stephen W. 1949- ... 162
Harger, Rolla N(eil) 1890-1983
Obituary ... 114
Harger, William Henderson 1936- ... 57-60
Hargrave, John Gordon 1894-1982
Obituary ... 110
Hargrave, Leonie
See Disch, Thomas M(ichael)
Hargrave, O. T. 1936- ... 33-36R
Hargrave, Rowena 1906- ... CANR-40
Earlier sketch in CA 33-36R
Hargrave, W. Lee 1943- ... 212
Hargraves, Orin (Knight) 1953- ... 223
Hargraves, Thomas
See Ainsworth, Thomas Hargraves, Jr.
Hargreaves, Alec G(ordon) 1948- ... 131
Hargreaves, Harry 1922-2004 ... 5-8R
Obituary ... 233
Hargreaves, John D(esmond) 1924- ... 9-12R
Hargreaves, Mary W(ilma) M(assey) 1914- ... CANR-14
Earlier sketch in CA 37-40R
Hargreaves, Reginald (Charles) 1888- ... CAP-1
Earlier sketch in CA 9-10
Hargreaves, (Charles) Roger 1935-1988
Obituary ... 126
See also SATA-Obit 56
Hargreaves-Mawdsley, W(illiam) Norman 1921-1980 ... CANR-7
Earlier sketch in CA 9-12R
Hargroder, Charles M(erlin) 1926- ... 73-76
Hargrove, Barbara Watts 1924- ... 33-36R
Hargrove, Erwin C. 1930- ... CANR-96
Brief entry ... 111
Earlier sketch in CA 146
Hargrove, James 1947- ... 120
See also SATA 57
See also SATA-Brief 50
Hargrove, Jim
See Hargrove, James
Hargrove, Katharine T. ... 33-36R
Hargrove, (Edward Thomas) Marion (Lawton, Jr.) 1919-2003 ... 175
Obituary ... 219
See also DLB 11
Hargrove, Merwin Matthew 1910-1986 .. 9-12R
Hargrove, Nancy Duvall 1941- ... 97-100
Hargrove, Richard J(ohn), Jr. 1941- ... 116
Hariharan, Githa 1954- ... 192
Harik, Iliya F. 1934- ... CANR-16
Earlier sketch in CA 25-28R
Haring, Bernard
See Haering, Bernhard
Haring, Bruce ... 231
Haring, Firth 1937- ... 25-28R
Haring, Jo 1934- ... 116
Haring, Joseph E(merick) 1931-1994 ... 33-36R
Haring, Keith 1958-1990 ... 158
See also AAYA 21
Haring, Lee 1930- ... 143
Haring, Norris G. 1923- ... CANR-2
Earlier sketch in CA 1-4R
Haring, Philip S(myth) 1915- ... 37-40R
Harington, Donald 1935- ... CANR-109
Earlier sketches in CA 13-16R, CANR-7, 55
See also BPFB 2
See also DLB 152
Harington, John 1560-1612 ... DLB 136
See also RGEL 2
Hariri, Al- al-Qasim ibn 'Ali Abu Muhammad al-Basri
See al-Hariri, al-Qasim ibn 'Ali Abu Muhammad al-Basri
Haris, Petros
See Marmariadis, Yiannis
See also EWL 3
Hariton, Anca I. 1955- ... SATA 79
Harizi, al- Judah 1166(?)-1225 ... WLIT 6
Harjo, Chinnubbie 1873-1908
See Posey, Alexander (Lawrence)
Harjo, Chinnubie
See Posey, Alexander (Lawrence)
Harjo, Joe
See Posey, Alexander (Lawrence)
Harjo, Joy 1951- ... CANR-129
Earlier sketches in CA 114, CANR-35, 67, 91
See also AMWS 12
See also CLC 83
See also CP 7
See also CWP
See also DAM MULT
See also DLB 120, 175
See also EWL 3
See also MTCW 2
See also MTFW 2005
See also NNAL
See also PC 27
See also PFS 15
See also RGAL 4
Hark, Mildred
See McQueen, Mildred Hark
Harkabi, Yehoshafat 1921-1994 ... CANR-27
Obituary ... 146
Earlier sketch in CA 73-76
Harkavy, Robert E(dward) 1936- ... CANR-30
Earlier sketch in CA 111
Harkaway, Hal
See Stratemeyer, Edward L.
Harker, Kenneth 1927- ... 97-100
Harker, Michael P. 1950- ... 235
Harker, Ronald 1909-1999 ... 77-80
Harkey, Ira B(rown), Jr. 1918- ... 57-60
Harkey, William G. 1914- ... 25-28R
Harkins, Anthony ... 234
Harkins, Arthur M(artin) 1936- ... 97-100
Harkins, Paul W(illiam) 1911-1992 ... 116
Harkins, Philip 1912-1997 ... 29-32R
Obituary ... 198
See also SATA 6
See also SATA-Obit 129
Harkins, William E(dward) 1921- ... 33-36R
Harkness, Bruce 1923- ... 13-16R
Harkness, D(avid) W(illiam) 1937- ... CANR-15
Earlier sketch in CA 29-32R
Harkness, David J(ames) 1913- ... CANR-3
Earlier sketch in CA 9-12R
Harkness, Edward 1947- ... 77-80
Harkness, Georgia (Elma) 1891-1974 . CANR-6
Obituary ... 53-56
Earlier sketch in CA 1-4R
Harkness, Gladys Estelle Suiter 1908(?)-1973
Obituary ... 41-44R
Harkness, Jack
See Harkness, John Leigh
Harkness, Joan ... 210
Harkness, John Leigh 1918-1994 ... 120
Obituary ... 145
Harkness, Margaret (Elise) 1854-1923 ... 215
See also DLB 197
Harkness, Marjory Gane 1880-1974(?) .. CAP-2
Earlier sketch in CA 23-24
Harkness, Peter (William) 1929- ... 237
Harknett, Terry (Williams) 1936- ... CANR-21
Earlier sketches in CA 57-60, CANR-6
See also Gilman, George G.
Harlan
See Shaw, William Harlan
Harlan, Elizabeth 1945- ... 111
See also SATA 41
See also SATA-Brief 35
Harlan, Glen
See Cebulash, Mel
Harlan, John Marshall 1899-1971
Obituary ... 33-36R
Harlan, Judith 1949- ... 204
See also CLR 81
See also SATA 74, 135
Harlan, Louis R(udolph) 1922- ... CANR-80
Earlier sketches in CA 21-24R, CANR-25, 55
See also CLC 34
Harlan, Malvina Shanklin 1838-1916 ... 224
Harlan, Rex
See Buslik, Gary
Harlan, Ross
See King, Albert
Harlan, Russell 1903-1974 ... IDFW 3, 4
Harlan, Thomas 1964- ... 228
Harlan, William K(eith) 1938- ... 45-48
Harland, Marion
See Terhune, Mary Virginia
Harland, Richard 1947- ... 227
See also SATA 152
Harle, Elizabeth
See Roberts, Irene
Harlee, J. V.
See Leese, Jennifer L.B.
Harleman, Ann 1945- ... CANR-91
Earlier sketch in CA 145
Harlequin
See Reed, A(lexander) W(yclif)
Harler, Ann
See Van Steenwyk, Elizabeth (Ann)
Harley, Bill
See Harley, Willard F., Jr.
Harley, Bill 1954- ... 151
See also SATA 87
Harley, Edward 1689-1741 ... DLB 213
Harley, Ethel Brilliana
See Tweedie, Ethel Brilliana
Harley, John
See Marsh, John
Harley, Robert 1661-1724 ... DLB 213
Harley, Sharon ... 222
Harley, Willard F., Jr. 1941- ... CANR-137
Earlier sketch in CA 167
Harling, Robert 1951(?)- ... 147
See also CLC 53
Harling, Thomas
See Eastham, Thomas
Harlow, Enid 1939- ... 102
Harlow, Francis H(arvey) 1928- ... 57-60
Harlow, Harry F(rederick) 1905-1981 ... 97-100
Harlow, Joan Hiatt 1932- ... CANR-128
Earlier sketch in CA 89-92
See also SATA 157
Harlow, LeRoy F(rancis) 1913-1995 ... 85-88
Harlow, Lewis A(ugustus) 1901- ... CAP-1
Earlier sketch in CA 13-14
Harlow, Neal 1908-2000 ... 109
Obituary ... 188
Harlow, Robert 1923- ... 128
See also CCA 1
See also DLB 60
Harlow, Rosie 1961- ... 149
Harlow, Samuel Ralph 1885-1972 ... 1-4R
Obituary ... 37-40R
Harlow, W(illiam) M(orehouse) 1900-1986 ... 13-16R
Obituary ... 119
Harman, Alec
See Harman, Richard Alexander
Harman, Andrew ... FANT
Harman, Barbara Leah 1946- ... 126
Harman, Claire
See Schmidt, Claire Harman
Harman, David 1944- ... 105
Harman, Fred 1902(?)-1982
Obituary ... 106
See also SATA-Obit 30
Harman, Gilbert H(elms) 1938- ... 73-76
Harman, Harry E. III 1917- ... CANR-39
Earlier sketch in CA 116
Harman, Hugh 1903-1982
Obituary ... 108
See also SATA-Obit 33
Harman, Jane
See Harknett, Terry (Williams)
Harman, Jeanne Perkins 1919- ... CANR-39
Earlier sketches in CA 69-72, CANR-11
Harman, Mark 1951- ... CANR-105
Earlier sketches in CA 118, CANR-49
Harman, Nicholas 1933- ... 101
Harman, P(eter) M(ichael) 1943- ... 110
Harman, R. Alec
See Harman, Richard Alexander
Harman, Richard Alexander 1917- ... CANR-5
Earlier sketch in CA 9-12R
Harman, Thomas 1566-1573 ... DLB 136
Harman, Willis W(alter) 1918-1997 ... 5-8R
Obituary ... 156
Harmel, Robert 1950- ... 110
Harmelink, Barbara (Mary) ... 61-64
See also SATA 9
Harmer, Mabel 1894-1992 ... 9-12R
See also SATA 45
Harmer, Ruth Mulvey 1919- ... 9-12R
Harmetz, Aljean ... 139
Harmin, Merrill 1928- ... 89-92
Harmon, A(llen) J(ackson) 1926- ... 21-24R
Harmon, Christopher C. 1954- ... 201
Harmon, Dan
See Harmon, Daniel E(lton)
Harmon, Daniel E(lton) 1949- ... 233
See also SATA 157
Harmon, Frederick G(ardner) 1932- ... 119
Harmon, Gary L. 1935- ... 37-40R
Harmon, Gil
See King, Albert
Harmon, Glynn 1933- ... 45-48
Harmon, H. H.
See Williams, Robert Moore
Harmon, James Judson 1933- ... 21-24R
Harmon, Jim
See Harmon, James Judson
Harmon, Lily 1912-1998 ... 105
Obituary ... 166
Harmon, Louise ... 172
Harmon, Lyn S. 1930- ... 21-24R
Harmon, Margaret 1906- ... 69-72
See also SATA 20
Harmon, Maurice 1930- ... CANR-123
Earlier sketches in CA 21-24R, CANR-9
Harmon, Nolan B(ailey) 1892-1993 ... 89-92
Harmon, (Norman) Paul 1942- ... 122
Harmon, Robert Bartlett 1932- ... CANR-48
Earlier sketches in CA 17-20R, CANR-8, 23
Harmon, Sandra ... 171
Harmon, Susanna M(arie) 1940- ... 57-60

Harmon, William (Ruth) 1938- CANR-35
Earlier sketches in CA 33-36R, CANR-14, 32
See also CLC 38
See also SATA 65
Harms, Ernest 1895-1974 CAP-1
Obituary 49-52
Earlier sketch in CA 13-14
Harms, John 1900-1975 17-20R
Harms, Leroy Stanley 1928- CANR-8
Earlier sketch in CA 53-56
Harms, Robert T(homas) 1932- 37-40R
Harms, Valerie 1940- CANR-101
Earlier sketches in CA 49-52, CANR-2
Harmsel, Henrietta Ten
See Ten Harmsel, Henrietta
Harmsen, Dorothy B. Bahneman 103
Harmsen, Frieda 1931- 107
Harmston, Olivia
See Weber, Nancy
Harmsworth, Esmond Cecil 1898-1978
Obituary 89-92
Harnack, Curtis (Arthur) 1927- CANR-22
Earlier sketches in CA 1-4R, CANR-2
Harnack, R(obert) Victor 1927- 13-16R
Harnack, William J. 1953- 125
Harnan, Terry 1920- 45-48
See also SATA 12
Harnden, Ruth Peabody 73-76
Harned, David Baily 1932- 135
Brief entry 112
Harner, James L(owell) 1946- CANR-103
Earlier sketch in CA 110
Harner, Michael J(ames) 1929- 134
Brief entry 114
Harner, Stephen M. 1949- 151
Harness, Charles L(eonard) 1915- CANR-136
Brief entry 113
Earlier sketch in CA 158
See also DLB 8
See also SFW 4
Harness, Cheryl 1951- SATA 131
Harnett, Bertram 1923- 119
Harnett, Cynthia (Mary) 1893-1981 CANR-85
Obituary 111
Earlier sketches in CAP-1, CA 9-10
See also DLB 161
See also SATA 5
See also SATA-Obit 32
See also YAW
Harnetty, Peter 1927- 37-40R
Harnick, Sheldon 1924- DLB 265
Harnik, Bernard 1910- 93-96
Harnois, Albert J. 1945- 151
Harnsberger, Caroline Thomas
1902-1991 61-64
Obituary 134
Harnum, Robert 204
Harnwell, Gaylord Probasco 1903-1982
Obituary 106
Haro, Robert P(eter) 1936- 33-36R
Haroian-Guerin, Gil 1957- 163
Harold, Clive
See Hutson, Shaun
Harold, Fred(erick) G(ordon) 1937- 118
Haroldson, William
See King, Harold
Haroutunian, Joseph 1904-1968
Obituary 111
Harp, Gillis J(ohn) 1956- 150
Harp, Stephen L. 1964- 197
Harpaz, Beth J. 234
Harper, Anita 1943- 114
See also SATA 41
Harper, Annette
See Harper, M(eredith) A(nnette)
Harper, Betty 1946- SATA 126
Harper, Bill
See Harper, William A(rthur)
Harper, Carol Ely -2000 61-64
Harper, Christopher 181
Harper, Daniel
See Brossard, Chandler
Harper, David
See Corley, Edwin (Raymond)
Harper, Donna Akiba Sullivan
See Sullivan Harper, Donna Akiba
Harper, Douglas A(lbert) 1948- 117
Harper, Edith Alice Mary
See Wickham, Anna
Harper, Elaine
See Hallin, Emily Watson
Harper, Ellen
See Noble, Marty
Harper, F. E. W.
See Harper, Frances Ellen Watkins
Harper, Fletcher 1806-1877 DLB 79
Harper, Floyd H(enry) 1899-1978
Obituary 77-80
Harper, Frances E. W.
See Harper, Frances Ellen Watkins
Harper, Frances E. Watkins
See Harper, Frances Ellen Watkins
Harper, Frances Ellen
See Harper, Frances Ellen Watkins
Harper, Frances Ellen Watkins
1825-1911 CANR-79
Brief entry 111
Earlier sketch in CA 125
See also AFAW 1, 2
See also BLC 2
See also BW 1, 3
See also DAM MULT, POET
See also DLB 50, 221
See also MAWW
See also PC 21
See also RGAL 4
See also TCLC 14
Harper, George Mills 1914- 136
Brief entry 114
Harper, George W(illiam) 1927- 113
Harper, Harold W. 89-92
Harper, Harry H(alsted), Jr. 1910-1983
Obituary 110
Harper, Howard (V.) 1904-1978 17-20R
Obituary 133
Harper, Howard M(orrall), Jr. 1930- CANR-22
Earlier sketch in CA 21-24R
Harper, J(ohn) Russell 1914-1983 CANR-13
Earlier sketch in CA 33-36R
Harper, James E(dwin) 1927- 41-44R
Harper, Jessica (R.) 1949- SATA 148
Harper, Jo 1932- 163
See also SATA 97
Harper, Joan (Marie) 1932- 101
Harper, John C(arsten) 1924-2002 103
Obituary 211
Harper, John Dickson 1910-1985 103
Harper, Karen 1945- CANR-92
Earlier sketches in CA 114, CANR-42, 45
Harper, Kate
See Harper, Katherine E(rna)
Harper, Katherine E(rna) 1946- 103
Harper, Kenn 1945- 191
Harper, Kenneth
See Miles, Keith
Harper, Lila Marz 1955- 226
Harper, Linda
See Lloyd, Linda Marie
Harper, Linda Lee 181
Harper, M(eredith) A(nnette) 1949- 141
Harper, M(ichael) J(ohn) K(ennedy) 1935- 116
Harper, Marjory(-Ann Denoon)
1956- CANR-66
Earlier sketch in CA 129
Harper, Marvin Henry 1901-1997 49-52
Harper, Mary Wood
See Dixon, Jeanne
Harper, Michael 1931- CANR-15
Earlier sketch in CA 65-68
Harper, Michael S(teven) 1938- 224
Earlier sketches in CA 33-36R, CANR-24, 108
Autobiographical Essay in 224
See also AFAW 2
See also BW 1
See also CLC 7, 22
See also CP 2, 3, 4, 5, 6, 7
See also DLB 41
See also RGAL 4
See also TCLE 1:1
Harper, Mrs. F. E. W.
See Harper, Frances Ellen Watkins
Harper, Paula (Hays) 1938- 105
Harper, Piers 1966- 173
See also SATA 105, 161
Harper, Robert A(lexander) 1924- 17-20R
Harper, Robert J(ohnston) C(raig)
1927- 13-16R
Harper, Stephen (Dennis) 1924- 97-100
Harper, Steven
See Piziks, Steven
Harper, Susan (Rice) 1943- 142
Harper, T(imothy) N(orman) 1965- 209
Harper, Tara K. 1961- 141
Harper, Tom 1923(?)-1983
Obituary 110
Harper, Valerie 1940- 201
Harper, Wilhelmina 1884-1973 CAP-1
Earlier sketch in CA 17-18
See also SATA 4
See also SATA-Obit 26
Harper, William A(rthur) 1944- 77-80
Harpham, Geoffrey Galt 1946- CANR-101
Earlier sketch in CA 111
Harpham, Wendy S(chlessel) 1954- 226
Harpole, Charles H(enry) 1943- 111
Harpole, Patricia Chayne 1933- 37-40R
Harpur, Charles 1813-1868 DLB 230
See also RGEL 2
Harpur, Patrick 1950- CANR-143
Earlier sketch in CA 114
Harpur, Thomas William 1929- CANR-139
Earlier sketch in CA 137
Harpur, Tom
See Harpur, Thomas William
Harr, John Ensor 1926- 189
Harr, Wilber C. 1908-1971 1-4R
Obituary 103
Harra, Carmen 222
Harraden, Beatrice 1864-1936 DLB 153
Harragan, Betty Lehan 1921-1998 CANR-17
Obituary 169
Earlier sketch in CA 77-80
Harrah, Barbara K. 1938- 107
Harrah, David 1926- 5-8R
Harrah, David Fletcher 1949- 65-68
Harrah, Madge 1931- 229
See also SATA 154
Harrah, Michael 1940- 115
See also SATA 41
Harrah, Monique
See Harrah, Madge
Harral, Stewart 1906-1964 5-8R
Harrar, E(llwood) S(cott) 1905-1975 CAP-1
Earlier sketch in CA 11-12
Harrar, George E. 1949- 188
See also SATA 124
Harrar, J(acob) George 1906-1982
Obituary 110
Harre, John 1931- 21-24R
Harre, (Horace) Rom(ano) 1927- CANR-21
Earlier sketches in CA 5-8R, CANR-2
Harrell, Allen W(aylan) 1922- 29-32R
Harrell, Anne
See Neggers, Carla A(malia)
Harrell, Beatrice Orcutt 1943- 159
See also SATA 93
Harrell, Costen J(ordan) 1885-1971 5-8R
Harrell, David Edwin, Jr. 1930- CANR-143
Earlier sketches in CA 37-40R, CANR-15, 34
Harrell, (Mildred) Irene B(urk)
1927-1992 CANR-25
Earlier sketches in CA 21-24R, CANR-9
Harrell, Janice 1945- 138
See also SATA 70
Harrell, John G(rinnell) 1922- CANR-18
Earlier sketches in CA 9-12R, CANR-3
Harrell, Sara (Jeanne) Gordon 1940- 105
See also Banks, Sara (Jeanne Gordon Harrell)
Harrell, (Clyde) Stevan 1947- 106
Harrell, Thomas Willard 1911-2002 1-4R
Obituary 206
Harrelson, Walter (Joseph) 1919- 9-12R
Harrer, Heinrich 1912- CANR-31
Earlier sketches in CA 17-20R, CANR-7
Harrier, Richard C(harles) 1923- 122
Brief entry 117
Harries, Ann 1942- 187
Harries, Elizabeth Wanning 1938- 212
Harries, Joan 1922- 107
See also SATA 39
Harries, Karsten 1937- CANR-117
Earlier sketch in CA 165
Harries, Owen 1930- 127
Harries, Richard (Douglas) 1936- 116
Harriett 1905-1987 77-80
Harrigan, Anthony (Hart) 1925- 21-24R
Harrigan, Edward 1844-1911 RGAL 4
Harrigan, Kathryn Rudie 1951- CANR-26
Earlier sketch in CA 109
Harrigan, Lana M. 182
Harrigan, Patrick J. 1941- 142
Harrigan, Stephen 1948- CANR-93
Earlier sketches in CA 122, CANR-48
Harriger, Katy J(ean) 1957- 143
Harrill, Ronald 1950- 155
See also SATA 90
Harriman, Ann 1932- 111
Harriman, Averell
See Harriman, W(illiam) Averell
Harriman, Edward 1922- 114
Harriman, Margaret 1928- 21-24R
Harriman, Richard L(evet) 1944- 33-36R
Harriman, Sarah 1942- 57-60
Harriman, W(illiam) Averell 1891-1986
Obituary 119
Brief entry 111
Harrington, Alan 1919-1997 73-76
Obituary 158
Harrington, Alexis 226
Harrington, Charles (Christopher)
1942- CANR-9
Earlier sketch in CA 65-68
Harrington, Curtis 1928- 103
Harrington, Denis J(ames) 1932- 69-72
See also SATA 88
Harrington, Donald Szantho 1914- 21-24R
Harrington, Elbert W(ellington)
1901-1987 37-40R
Harrington, Evelyn Davis 1911- CANR-4
Earlier sketch in CA 5-8R
See also Harrington, Lyn
Harrington, Gary 1953- 135
Harrington, Geri CANR-44
Earlier sketches in CA 57-60, CANR-6, 21
Harrington, Harold David
1903-1981 CANR-11
Earlier sketch in CA 25-28R
Harrington, Jack 1918- 57-60
Harrington, Jeremy 1932- 41-44R
Harrington, John P. 1952- 138
Harrington, John W(ilbur)
1918-1986 CANR-83
Earlier sketch in CA 132
Harrington, Joseph 1941- 179
Harrington, Joseph Daniel 1923- CANR-83
Earlier sketch in CA 89-92
Harrington, Joyce 1931- CMW 4
Harrington, K.
See Bean, Keith F(enwick)
Harrington, Kathleen 160
Harrington, Kent (Michael) 1945- CANR-122
Earlier sketch in CA 141
Harrington, Kent (A.) 1952- 229
Harrington, Lyn
See Harrington, Evelyn Davis
See also SATA 5
Harrington, Mark Raymond
1882-1971 CAP-2
Earlier sketch in CA 17-18
Harrington, (Edward) Michael
1928-1989 CANR-80
Obituary 129
Earlier sketches in CA 17-20R, CANR-19
Harrington, Mona 1936- 188
Harrington, Norman W. 1922(?)-1987
Obituary 123
Harrington, Philip S(tuart) 1956- 167
Harrington, (Peter) Ty(rus) 1951- 102
Harrington, William 1931-2000 CANR-70
Earlier sketches in CA 9-12R, CANR-4, 19, 42
Harriot, Thomas 1560-1621 DLB 136
Harriott, Edwin Thomas 1933- 117
Harriott, Peter 1927- CANR-136
Earlier sketch in CA 144
Harriott, Ted
See Harriott, Edwin Thomas
Harris, Alan 1928- 5-8R
Harris, Alan 1944- 139
See also SATA 71
Harris, Albert J(osiah) 1908-1990 CANR-5
Obituary 132
Earlier sketch in CA 1-4R
Harris, Alex(ander Eisemann) 1949- 124
Harris, Alexander 1805-1874 DLB 230
Harris, Alf(red) 1928- 53-56
Harris, Andrea
See Connolly, Vivian and
Walker, Irma Ruth (Roden)
Harris, Andrew
See Poole, Frederick King
Harris, Anita M(arie) 1948- 152
Harris, Ann Sutherland 1937- 126
Harris, Anne L. 1964- 176
Harris, Aurand 1915-1996 CANR-83
Obituary 152
Earlier sketches in CA 93-96, CANR-16, 36
See also CWRI 5
See also SATA 37
See also SATA-Obit 91
Harris, Barbara J. 1942- 115
Harris, Barbara S(eger) 1927- 49-52
Harris, Ben(jamin) Charles 1907-1978 57-60
Obituary 89-92
Harris, Ben(jamin) M(axwell) 1923- CANR-2
Earlier sketch in CA 5-8R
Harris, Benjamin (?)-1720(?) DLB 42, 43
Harris, Bernice K(elly) 1892-1973 5-8R
Obituary 45-48
Harris, Bertha 1937- CANR-71
Earlier sketch in CA 29-32R
See also GLL 2
Harris, Beulah (?)-1970
Obituary 104
Harris, Bill
See Harris, William F., Jr.
Harris, Bill 1933- 180
Harris, Bill 1941- 180
Harris, Brayton
See Harris, (Frank) Brayton
Harris, (Frank) Brayton 1932- CANR-139
Earlier sketch in CA 21-24R
Harris, Brian
See King, Harold
Harris, Brownie 1949- 107
Harris, C. Nelson 1964- 232
Harris, Carl V(ernon) 1937- 97-100
Harris, Carol Flynn 1933- SATA 135
Harris, Catherine
See Ainsworth, Catherine Harris
Harris, Charlaine 1951- CANR-99
Earlier sketch in CA 105
Harris, Charles 1923- 102
Harris, Charles B(urt) 1940- 53-56
Harris, Charles H(ouston) III 1937- 13-16R
Harris, Charles Wesley 1929- 150
Harris, Chauncy D(ennison)
1914-2003 29-32R
Obituary 223
Harris, Chester W(illiam) 1910-1994 CAP-1
Earlier sketch in CA 11-12
Harris, Chris 1951- 210
Harris, Christie
See Harris, Christie (Lucy) Irwin
Harris, Christie (Lucy) Irwin
1907-2002 CANR-83
Earlier sketches in CA 5-8R, CANR-6
See also CLC 12
See also CLR 47
See also DLB 88
See also JRDA
See also MAICYA 1, 2
See also SAAS 10
See also SATA 6, 74
See also SATA-Essay 116
Harris, Christine 1955- CANR-138
Earlier sketch in CA 173
See also SATA 105
Harris, Claire (Kathleen Patricia) 1937- 171
See also CWP
Harris, Clyde E., Jr. 21-24R
Harris, Colver
See Colver, Anne
Harris, Curtis C(lark), Jr. 1930- 53-56
Harris, Cyril 1891-1968 CAP-1
Earlier sketch in CA 11-12
Harris, Dale B(enner) 1914- 13-16R
Harris, Daniel A(rthur) 1942- 89-92
Harris, David (William) 1942- 190
See also SATA 118
Harris, David (Victor) 1946- CANR-57
Earlier sketch in CA 69-72
Harris, David A. 1957- 209
Harris, David W. 1948-
Brief entry 107
Harris, Deborah Turner 1951- 135
Harris, Del(mer William) 1937- CANR-8
Earlier sketch in CA 61-64
Harris, Donald 1931- 126
Harris, Dorothy Joan 1931- CANR-137
Earlier sketches in CA 45-48, CANR-1
See also SATA 13, 153
Harris, Douglas H(ershel, Jr.) 1930- 25-28R
Harris, E. Lynn 1957- CANR-111
Earlier sketch in CA 164
See also MTFW 2005
Harris, Edward Arnold 1910-1976
Obituary 65-68
Harris, Elizabeth 1944- 136
Harris, Elliot 1932- 25-28R
Harris, Ernest E(dward) 1914-1981 33-36R
Harris, Errol E(ustace) 1908- CANR-41
Earlier sketches in CA 49-52, CANR-2, 18
See also DLB 279
Harris, Francis 1957- 130

Cumulative Index 251 Harrison

Harris, Frank 1856-1931 .... CANR-80
Brief entry 109
Earlier sketch in CA 150
See also DLB 156, 197
See also RGEL 2
See also TCLC 24
Harris, Fred (Roy) 1930- 193
Earlier sketches in CA 77-80, CANR-26, 52
Autobiographical Essay in 193
Harris, Frederick John 1943- 57-60
Harris, Gene Gray 1929- 17-20R
Harris, George A. 1950- 130
Harris, George Washington 1814-1869 . DLB 3, 11, 248
See also RGAL 4
Harris, Geraldine (Rachel) 1951- CANR-59
Earlier sketch in CA 116
See also CWRI 5
See also FANT
See also SATA 54
Harris, Gertrude (Margaret) 1916- 57-60
Harris, H(arold) A(rthur) 1902-1974 . CANR-30
Earlier sketch in CA 49-52
Harris, H(enry) S(ilton) 1926- 130
Harris, Harold (Morris) 1915-1993 132
Obituary 142
Harris, Helen(a Barbara Mary) 1927- 61-64
Harris, Herbert 1911- CANR-85
Earlier sketch in CA 102
Harris, Herbert 1914(?)-1974
Obituary 49-52
Harris, Hyde
See Harris, Timothy Hyde
Harris, Ian (Anthony) 1937- 107
Harris, Irving David 1914- 13-16R
Harris, Jacqueline L. 1929- 126
See also SATA 62
Harris, James E(dward) 1928- 126
Brief entry 110
Harris, James F. 1941- 146
Harris, Jana 1947- CANR-129
Earlier sketch in CA 105
Harris, Jane Allen 1918- 1-4R
Harris, Jane Gary 111
Harris, Janet 1932-1979 .... CANR-28
Obituary 93-96
Earlier sketch in CA 33-36R
See also SATA 4
See also SATA-Obit 23
Harris, Janice Hubbard 1943- 118
Harris, Jay S(tephen) 1938- 85-88
Harris, Jean (S.) 1923- 137
Harris, Jed
See Horowitz, Jacob
Harris, Jesse
See Standiford, Natalie
Harris, Jessica L.
See Milstead, Jessica L(ee)
Harris, Joan 1946- 220
See also SATA 146
Harris, Joanne 1964- 185
See also DLB 271
See also HGG
Harris, Jocelyn 1939- 128
Harris, Joel Chandler 1848-1908 ...... CANR-80
Brief entry 104
Earlier sketch in CA 137
See also CLR 49
See also DLB 11, 23, 42, 78, 91
See also LAIT 2
See also MAICYA 1, 2
See also RGSF 2
See also SATA 100
See also SSC 19
See also TCLC 2
See also WCH
See also YABC 1
Harris, John (Roy) 1915- CANR-2
Earlier sketch in CA 5-8R
Harris, John 1916-1991 .... CANR-89
Obituary 134
Earlier sketch in CA 93-96
See also CMW 4
Harris, John (Wyndham Parkes Lucas) Beynon
1903-1969 .... CANR-84
Obituary 89-92
Earlier sketch in CA 102
See also Wyndham, John
See also SATA 118
See also SFW 4
Harris, John S(harp) 1917- 29-32R
Harris, John S(terling) 1929- 65-68
Harris, Johnson
See Harris, John (Wyndham Parkes Lucas) Beynon
Harris, Jonathan 1921-1997 .... CANR-48
Earlier sketch in CA 121
See also SATA 52
Harris, Jose 147
Harris, Joseph E(arl) 1929- 122
Brief entry 117
Harris, Joseph Pratt 1896-1985 .... 1-4R
Obituary 115
Harris, Judith (Lynn) 1955- 210
Harris, Judith Rich 1938- 174
Harris, Julian (Earle) 1896-1988 .... CANR-31
Earlier sketch in CA 1-4R
Harris, Julie 1925- 103
Harris, Karen H(arriman) 1934- CANR-22
Earlier sketch in CA 103
Harris, Katherine 1957- 221
Harris, Kathleen
See Humphries, Adelaide M.
Harris, Kathryn Gibbs
See Gibbs-Wilson, Kathryn (Beatrice)
Harris, Kenn 1947- 116
Harris, Kenneth 1904-1983
Obituary 109
Harris, Kenneth 1919- 129
Harris, Larry M.
See Janifer, Laurence M(ark)
Harris, Larry Vincent 1939- .... SATA 59
Harris, Lavinia
See St. John, Nicole
Harris, Leon A., Jr. 1926-2000 .... CANR-3
Obituary 189
Earlier sketch in CA 9-12R
See also SATA 4
Harris, Leonard 1929- CANR-9
Earlier sketch in CA 65-68
Harris, Lloyd J(ohn) 1947- 61-64
Harris, Lorle K(empe) 1912-2001 97-100
See also SATA 22
Harris, Louis 1921- 13-16R
Harris, Louise 1903-1993 .... CANR-7
Earlier sketch in CA 17-20R
Harris, Lynn CANR-134
Earlier sketch in CA 170
Harris, M(iddleton) A. 1908-1977
Obituary 111
Harris, MacDonald
See Heiney, Donald (William)
See also CLC 9
Harris, Madalene 1925- 105
Harris, Marcia Lee 1951- 109
Harris, Margaret 1951- 202
Harris, Marguerite 1899- .... CP 1
Harris, Marie 1943- CANR-120
Earlier sketches in CA 104, CANR-20
Harris, Marilyn
See Springer, Marilyn Harris
Harris, Marion Rose (Young) 1925- .. CANR-57
Earlier sketches in CAP-1, CA 9-10, CANR-12, 30
Harris, Marjorie Silliman 1890-1976 ..... CAP-1
Earlier sketch in CA 13-14
Harris, Mark 1922- CANR-83
Earlier sketches in CA 5-8R, CANR-2, 55
See also CAAS 3
See also CLC 19
See also CN 1, 2, 3, 4, 5, 6, 7
See also DLB 2
See also DLBY 1980
Harris, Mark C(harles) 1955- 113
Harris, Mark Jonathan 1941- CANR-21
Earlier sketch in CA 104
See also SATA 32, 84
Harris, Marshall (Dees) 1903-1976 .... CANR-1
Earlier sketch in CA 1-4R
Harris, Martyn 1952-1996 132
Obituary 154
Harris, Marvin 1927-2001 124
Obituary 203
Brief entry 110
Harris, Mary (Emma) 1943- 135
Harris, Mary B(ierman) 1943- 53-56
Harris, Mary Imogene 49-52
Harris, Mary K(athleen) 1905-1966 .. CANR-84
Earlier sketches in CAP-1, CA 13-16
See also CWRI 5
See also SATA 119
Harris, Mary Law 1892(?)-1980
Obituary 102
Harris, Max 1921- .... CP 1
Harris, Max 1949- 222
Harris, Maynard L(awrence) 1902-1974
Obituary 116
Harris, Michael (Terry) 1948- 125
Harris, Michael H(ope) 1941- 57-60
Harris, Michael R(ichard) 1936- 29-32R
Harris, Miles F(itzgerald) 1913- CANR-6
Earlier sketch in CA 5-8R
Harris, Neil 1938- 142
Harris, Norman .... CLC 65
Harris, P(eter) B(ernard) 1929- 104
Harris, Patricia 57-60
Harris, Paul 1948- 156
Harris, Philip R(obert) 1926- CANR-25
Earlier sketches in CA 17-20R, CANR-8
Harris, R(ansom) Baine 1927- 73-76
Harris, R(obert) J(ohn) C(ecil)
1922-1980 .... CANR-15
Earlier sketch in CA 65-68
Harris, R(obert) Laird 1911- CANR-1
Earlier sketch in CA 1-4R
Harris, Radie 1905-2001 65-68
Obituary 193
Harris, Randy Allen 1956- 142
Harris, Raymond 1919-1989
Obituary 129
Harris, Rex 1904-1985
Obituary 118
Harris, Richard (Frederick James)
1914-1999 186
Harris, Richard (S.) 1928(?)-1987 129
Obituary 123
Harris, Richard 1930-2002 107
Obituary 212
See also CBD
See also CD 5
Harris, Richard 1955- 126
Harris, Richard Colebrook 1936- 97-100
Harris, Richard H. 1942- 103
Harris, Richard J(ohn) 1948- 115
Harris, Richard N(elson) 1942- 77-80
Harris, Ricky 1922- 103
Harris, Robert (Jennings) 1907-1992 .... 5-8R
Harris, Robert (Dennis) 1957- CANR-124
Earlier sketch in CA 143
See also MTFW 2005
Harris, Robert Dalton 1921- 93-96
Harris, Robert Harry 1941- 108
Harris, Robert Samuel 1904-1983
Obituary 111
Harris, Robert T(aylor) 1912-1987 .... 5-8R
Harris, Robie H. 1940- 155
See also SATA 90, 147
See also SATA-Brief 53
Harris, Robin
See Shine, Deborah
Harris, Robin S(utton) 1919- 21-24R
Harris, Roger
See Wilson, R(oger) H(arris) L(ebus)
Harris, Ronald W(alter) 1916-1999 .... 5-8R
Obituary 181
Harris, Rosemary (Jeanne) CANR-84
Earlier sketches in CA 33-36R, CANR-13, 30
See also CLR 30
See also CWRI 5
See also SAAS 7
See also SATA 4, 82
Harris, Roy J. 1903(?)-1980
Obituary 93-96
Harris, Ruth Elwin 1935- 146
Harris, Ruth Roy 1927- 170
Harris, S(eymour) E(dwin) 1897-1974 65-68
Obituary 53-56
Harris, Sandra 1946- 239
Harris, Sara Lee
See Stadelman, S(ara) L(ee)
Harris, Sheila
See Harte, Kelly E.
Harris, Sheldon H(oward) 1928-2002 ... 37-40R
Obituary 207
Harris, Sherwood 1932- 97-100
See also SATA 25
Harris, Stacy 1952- 142
Harris, Stephen E. 1943-
Brief entry 111
Harris, Stephen L(eRoy) 1937-1995 ...... 29-32R
Harris, Steve 1950- 168
Harris, Steve 1954- 165
Harris, Steven Michael 1957- 121
See also HGG
See also SATA 55
Harris, (William) Stewart 1922-1994 104
Obituary 147
Harris, Stuart
See Fantoni, Barry (Ernest)
Harris, Styron 1936- 112
Harris, Sydney J(ustin) 1917-1986 .... CANR-11
Obituary 120
Earlier sketch in CA 61-64
Interview in CANR-11
Harris, T George 1924- CANR-47
Earlier sketch in CA 69-72
Harris, Thistle Y.
See Stead, Thistle Yolette
Harris, Thomas 1940(?)- CANR-106
Earlier sketches in CA 113, CANR-35, 73
See also AAYA 34
See also BPFB 2
See also CMW 4
See also CPW
See also CSW
See also DAM POP
See also HGG
See also MTFW 2005
Harris, Thomas (E.) 1944- 193
Harris, Thomas A(nthony) 1910-1995 93-96
Obituary 148
Harris, Thomas Cunningham 1908-1985
Obituary 114
Harris, Thomas Harold 1933- 125
Harris, Thomas J. 1892(?)-1983
Obituary 109
Harris, Thomas O(rville) 1935- 73-76
Harris, Thomas Walter 1930- 141
See also BW 2
Harris, Timothy Hyde 1946- CANR-83
Earlier sketch in CA 101
Harris, (Jonathan) Toby 1953- 118
Harris, Tom
See Harris, Thomas Cunningham and Harris, Thomas Walter
Harris, Trudier 1948- CANR-139
Earlier sketches in CA 115, CANR-40
Harris, Trudy 1949- 198
See also SATA 128
Harris, Valentina 1957- 128
Harris, Walter A. 1929- 29-32R
Harris, Warren G(ene) 1936- CANR-115
Earlier sketches in CA 77-80, CANR-26
Harris, Wayne T. (Sr.) 1954- 146
Harris, Wendell V. 1932- 111
Harris, William Bliss 1901(?)-1981
Obituary 104
Harris, William Charles 1933- 188
Harris, William F., Jr. 1933- CANR-30
Earlier sketch in CA 109
Harris, William Foster
See Foster-Harris, William
Harris, William Hamilton 1944- 111
Harris, William J(oseph) 1942- CANR-19
Earlier sketches in CA 53-56, CANR-5
Harris, William McKinley Sr. 1941- 126
Harris, William Torrey 1835-1909 ...... DLB 270
Harris, William V. 1938- 226
Harris, (Theodore) Wilson 1921- CANR-114
Earlier sketches in CA 65-68, CANR-11, 27, 69
See also CAAS 16
See also BRWS 5
See also BW 2, 3
See also CDWLB 3
See also CLC 25, 159
See also CN 1, 2, 3, 4, 5, 6, 7
See also CP 1, 2, 3, 4, 5, 6, 7
See also DLB 117
See also EWL 3
See also MTCW 1
See also RGEL 2
Harris, Y. L.
See Harris, Yvonne L.
Harris, Yvonne L. 138
Harris-Filderman, Diane
See Filderman, Diane E(lizabeth)
Harris-Lopez, Trudier
See Harris, Trudier
Harrison, A(llie) Cleveland 1924- 194
Harrison, Allan E(ugene) 1925- CANR-6
Earlier sketch in CA 57-60
Harrison, Ann Tukey 1938- 149
Harrison, Antony H. 1948- CANR-82
Earlier sketch in CA 132
Harrison, Barbara 1936- .... BYA 13
Harrison, Barbara 1941- CANR-53
Earlier sketches in CA 29-32R, CANR-12, 28
Harrison, Barbara Grizzuti
1934-2002 .... CANR-48
Obituary 205
Earlier sketches in CA 77-80, CANR-15
Interview in CANR-15
See also CLC 144
Harrison, Barry (Joseph Douglas) 1935- 129
Harrison, Bennett 1942-1999 53-56
Obituary 173
Harrison, Bernard 1933- 93-96
Harrison, Beverly Wildung 1932- 111
Harrison, Bill
See Harrison, William C.
Harrison, Billy R. 1937- 121
Harrison, Brian (Howard) 1937- 149
Harrison, Brian Fraser
See Fraser Harrison, Brian
Harrison, Mrs. Burton
See Harrison, Constance Cary
Harrison, C(hester) William
1913-1994 .... CANR-64
Earlier sketch in CA 107
See also SATA 35
See also TCWW 2
Harrison, Carey 1944- 61-64
Harrison, Carol
See Harrison, Carol Thompson
Harrison, Carol Thompson 185
See also SATA 113
Harrison, Charles Yale 1898-1954 175
See also DLB 68
Harrison, Chip
See Block, Lawrence
Harrison, Chip 1952- 29-32R
Harrison, Claire (E.) 1946- CANR-28
Earlier sketch in CA 111
Harrison, Colin 1960- CANR-94
Earlier sketches in CA 138, CANR-56
Harrison, Constance Cary
1843-1920 .... DLB 221
Harrison, Cynthia Ellen 1946- 57-60
Harrison, David L(akin) 1926- 117
Harrison, David L(ee) 1937- CANR-121
Earlier sketches in CA 93-96, CANR-57
See also SATA 26, 92, 150
Harrison, Deloris 1938- 61-64
See also SATA 9
Harrison, Don(ald Dean) 1941- 112
Harrison, Edward Hardy 1926- CANR-39
Earlier sketch in CA 116
See also SATA 56
Harrison, Eliza Cope 1936- 202
Harrison, Elizabeth (Francourt) .... RHW
Harrison, Elizabeth (Allen) Cavanna
1909-2001 .... CANR-121
Obituary 200
Earlier sketches in CA 9-12R, CANR-6, 27, 85, 104
See also Cavanna, Betty
See also MAICYA 2
See also SATA 142
See also YAW
Harrison, Eric George William Warde
1893-1987
Obituary 124
Harrison, Everett F(alconer) 1902-1999 . CAP-1
Earlier sketch in CA 11-12
Harrison, Francis Llewelyn 1905-1987
Obituary 124
Harrison, Frank Llewelyn
See Harrison, Francis Llewelyn
Harrison, Frank R(ussell) III 1935- 53-56
Harrison, Fred
See Paine, Lauran (Bosworth)
Harrison, Fred 1917- 29-32R
Harrison, Frederic 1831-1923 175
See also DLB 57, 190
Harrison, G(eorge) B(agshawe)
1894-1991 .... CANR-3
Obituary 136
Earlier sketch in CA 1-4R
Harrison, Gary 1949- 150
Harrison, George 1943-2001 192
Obituary 203
Harrison, George Russell
1898-1979 .... CANR-27
Earlier sketches in CAP-2, CA 19-20

Harrison, Hank 1940- 41-44R
Harrison, Harry (Max) 1925- CANR-84
Earlier sketches in CA 1-4R, CANR-5, 21
See also CLC 42
See also DLB 8
See also SATA 4
See also SCFW 2
See also SFW 4
Harrison, Helen A(my) 1943- CANR-122
Earlier sketch in CA 114
Harrison, Helen P(atricia) 1935- 102
Harrison, Howard 1930- 5-8R
Harrison, J(ohn) F(letcher) C(lews)
1921- CANR-10
Earlier sketch in CA 25-28R
Harrison, James (Ernest) 1927- 140
Harrison, James (Thomas) 1937- CANR-142
Earlier sketches in CA 13-16R, CANR-8, 51, 79
Interview in CANR-8
See also Harrison, Jim
See also CLC 6, 14, 33, 66, 143
See also DLBY 1982
See also SSC 19
Harrison, James Pinckney 1932- CANR-48
Earlier sketch in CA 77-80
Harrison, Jamie (Louise) CANR-97
Earlier sketch in CA 156
Harrison, Jay S(molens) 1927-1974
Obituary 53-56
Harrison, Jeffrey (Woods) 1957- CANR-141
Earlier sketches in CA 127, CANR-58
Harrison, Jennifer 1955- 223
Harrison, Jim
See Harrison, James (Thomas)
See also AMWS 8
See also CN 5, 6
See also CP 1, 2, 3, 4, 5, 6, 7
See also RGAL 4
See also TCWW 2
See also TUS
Harrison, Joan (Mary) 1909-1994 104
Obituary 146
See also IDFW 3, 4
Harrison, John 1924- CANR-65
Earlier sketch in CA 129
Harrison, John A(rmstrong) 1915-
Brief entry 111
Harrison, John Baugham 1907-1985 .... 1-4R
Harrison, John M(arshall) 1914-1999 .... 25-28R
Harrison, John R(aymond) 1933- 101
See also AITN 2
Harrison, K(enneth) C(ecil) 1915- CANR-3
Earlier sketch in CA 9-12R
Harrison, Kathryn 1961- CANR-122
Earlier sketches in CA 144, CANR-68
See also CLC 70, 151
Harrison, Keith 1945- 222
Harrison, Keith Edward 1932- 73-76
See also CP 1, 2
Harrison, Kyle 1970- 234
Harrison, Lawrence E. 1932- CANR-114
Earlier sketch in CA 127
Harrison, Louise C(ollbran) 1908-1978 . CAP-1
Earlier sketch in CA 11-12
Harrison, Lowell H(ayes) 1922- CANR-121
Earlier sketch in CA 162
Harrison, M(ichael) John 1945- CANR-101
Earlier sketches in CA 53-56, CANR-59
See also FANT
See also HGG
See also SFW 4
See also SUFW 2
Harrison, Marcus 1924- 102
Harrison, Marshall 1933- 138
Harrison, Martin 1930- 49-52
Harrison, Mary
See Rash, Nancy
Harrison, Max 69-72
Harrison, Mette Ivie 1970- 223
See also SATA 149
Harrison, Michael 1907-1991 .... CANR-61
Earlier sketch in CA 97-100
See also CMW 4
See also FANT
Harrison, Michael 1939- 176
See also SATA 106
Harrison, Michael A. 1936- 126
See also DLB 261
Harrison, Michelle Jessica 1942- 109
Harrison, Molly (Hodgett) 1909-2002 108
Obituary 206
See also SATA 41
Harrison, Nancy 1923- 142
Harrison, Nicolas 1937(?)-1984
Obituary 114
Harrison, Paul Carter 1936- 125
Brief entry 117
Interview in CA-125
See also BW 2
See also DLB 38
Harrison, Paul M. 1923- 53-56
Harrison, Payne 1949- 139
Harrison, Randall P(aul) 1929- CANR-11
Earlier sketch in CA 69-72
Harrison, Ray(mond Vincent) 1928- . CANR-84
Earlier sketch in CA 126
See also CMW 4
Harrison, Raymond H(enry)
1911-1985 .... 17-20R
Harrison, Reginald Carey 1908-1990
Obituary 131
Harrison, Rex
See Harrison, Reginald Carey
Harrison, Richard A(rnold) 1945- 107
Harrison, Richard John 1920-1999 109
Harrison, Robert (Ligon) 1932- 25-28R
Harrison, Robert Pogue 1954- 138
Harrison, Roland Kenneth 1920- CANR-48
Earlier sketch in CA 49-52
Harrison, Rosina 1899- 102
Harrison, (Thomas) Ross 1943- CANR-9
Earlier sketch in CA 61-64
Harrison, Roy M(ichael) 1948- 140
Harrison, Royden John 1927-2002 .... 17-20R
Obituary 206
Harrison, Russell (T.) 1944- 149
Harrison, S(ydney) Gerald 1924- 13-16R
Harrison, S(tanley) L. 1930- 186
Harrison, Sarah 1946- CANR-84
Earlier sketch in CA 102
See also RHW
See also SATA 63
Harrison, Saul I. 1925- CANR-10
Earlier sketch in CA 21-24R
Harrison, Selig S(eidenman) 1927- 85-88
Harrison, Stanley R. 1927- 41-44R
Harrison, Stuart 1958- 184
Harrison, Sue 1950- 135
Interview in CA-135
Harrison, Susan Frances (Riley)
1859-1935 174
See also DLB 99
Harrison, Suzan 1956- 166
Harrison, Ted
See Harrison, Edward Hardy
Harrison, Tony 1937- CANR-98
Earlier sketches in CA 65-68, CANR-44
See also BRWS 5
See also CBD
See also CD 5, 6
See also CLC 43, 129
See also CP 2, 3, 4, 5, 6, 7
See also DLB 40, 245
See also MTCW 1
See also RGEL 2
Harrison, Trevor (W.) 1952- 152
Harrison, Wallace (Kirkman) 1895-1981
Obituary 108
Harrison, Whit
See Whittington, Harry (Benjamin)
Harrison, Wilfrid 1909- CAP-1
Earlier sketch in CA 11-12
Harrison, William 1535-1593 .... DLB 136
Harrison, William (Neal) 1933- CANR-98
Earlier sketches in CA 17-20R, CANR-9
See also DLB 234
Harrison, William C. 1919- 25-28R
Harrison-Church, Ronald James
1915-1998 .... CANR-99
Obituary 172
Earlier sketch in CA 13-16R
Harriss, C(lement) Lowell 1912- CANR-2
Earlier sketch in CA 1-4R
Harriss, Clarinda 1939- 218
Harriss, Joseph 1936- 57-60
Harriss, R(obert) P(reston) 1902-1989 73-76
Obituary 129
Harriss, Will(ard Irvin) 1922- 111
See also CLC 34
Harrisse, Henry 1829-1910 174
See also DLB 47
Harrity, Richard 1907-1973
Obituary 41-44R
Harrod, Leonard Montague 1905- 13-16R
Harrod, Roy Forbes 1900-1978 .... 9-12R
Obituary 103
Harrod, Tanya 234
Harrod-Eagles, Cynthia 1948- CANR-85
Earlier sketch in CA 144
See also RHW
Harrold, Stanley 1946- CANR-95
Earlier sketch in CA 128
Harrold, William E(ugene) 1936- CANR-92
Earlier sketch in CA 41-44R
Harron, Don(ald) 1924- 104
Harrop-Allin, Clinton 1936- 107
Harroun, Catherine 1907-1986 109
Harrow, Benjamin 1888-1970
Obituary 104
Harrow, Judy 1945- 231
Harrow, Kenneth W. 1943- 148
Harrowe, Fiona
See Hurd, Florence
Harrower, Elizabeth 1928- CANR-70
Earlier sketch in CA 101
See also CN 1, 2, 3, 4, 5, 6, 7
Harrower, Molly 1906-1999 .... 5-8R
Obituary 177
Harry, Deborah Ann 1945- 129
Harry, J. S. 1939- CANR-85
Earlier sketch in CA 153
See also CP 7
See also CWP
Harry, M.
See Lewis, Sasha Gregory
Harryhausen, Ray 1920- 231
See also IDFW 3, 4
Harryman, Carla 1952- 187
See also DLB 193
Harsany, Peter 1913- CANR-56
Earlier sketch in CA 111
Harsch, Ernest 1951- 69-72
Harsch, Hilya
See Jelly, George Oliver
Harsch, Joseph C(lose) 1905-1998 102
Obituary 181
Harsch, Rick 1959- CANR-126
Earlier sketch in CA 169
Harsdoerffer, Georg Philipp
1607-1658 .... DLB 164
Harsent, David 1942- CANR-142
Earlier sketch in CA 93-96
See also CP 1, 2, 3, 4, 5, 6, 7
See also DLB 40
Harsh, Fred (T.) 1925- .... SATA 72
Harsh, George 1908(?)-1980
Obituary 93-96
Harsh, Wayne C. 1924- CANR-15
Earlier sketch in CA 29-32R
Harshav, Barbara 1940- CANR-135
Earlier sketch in CA 157
Harshaw, Ruth H(etzel) 1890-1968
Obituary 107
See also SATA 27
Harshbarger, David Dwight 1938- 53-56
Harshman, Marc 1950- .... SATA 71, 109
Harshman, Marc 1950- 180
Harsin, Jill 1951- 212
Harson, Sley
See Slesar, Henry
Harss, Luis 1936- 17-20R
Harstad, Donald 181
Harstad, Peter Tjernagel 1935- 37-40R
Harston, Ruth 1944- 41-44R
Hart, A(rthur) Tindal 1908-1993 .... 9-12R
Hart, Albert Bushnell 1854-1943
Brief entry 116
See also DLB 17
Hart, Albert Gailord 1909-1997 .... CAP-2
Obituary 161
Earlier sketch in CA 23-24
Hart, Alexandra 1939- CANR-6
Earlier sketch in CA 57-60
See also Jacopetti, Alexandra
Hart, Alison
See Leonhardt, Alice
Hart, Allan H(untley) 1935- 106
Hart, (Margaret Eleanor) Anne 141
Hart, Anne 1768-1834 .... DLB 200
Hart, Archibald D(aniel) 1932- CANR-15
Earlier sketch in CA 93-96
Hart, Barry
See Bloom, Herman Irving
Hart, Basil Henry Liddell
See Liddell Hart, Basil Henry
Hart, Benjamin 1958- 126
Brief entry 118
Hart, Bruce 1938- 107
See also SATA 57
See also SATA-Brief 39
Hart, Carol 1944- 65-68
Hart, Carole 1943- 107
See also SATA 57
See also SATA-Brief 39
Hart, Carolyn G(impel) 1936- CANR-126
Earlier sketches in CA 13-16R, CANR-25, 41, 58
See also CMW 4
See also SATA 74
Hart, Catherine 1948- 139
Hart, Charles (A.) 1940- 133
Hart, Christopher 1957- CANR-142
Earlier sketch in CA 169
Hart, David 1944- 128
Hart, David K(irkwood) 1933- 123
Brief entry 117
Hart, David M(ontgomery) 1927- 136
Hart, Donald J(ohn) 1917- 9-12R
Hart, Douglas C. 1950- 101
Hart, E. Richard 1945- 152
Hart, Edward J(ack) 1941- 53-56
Hart, Edward L. 1916- CANR-14
Earlier sketch in CA 37-40R
Hart, Elizabeth 1771-1833 .... DLB 200
Hart, Ellen 1949- CANR-90
Earlier sketch in CA 154
Hart, Ellis
See Ellison, Harlan (Jay)
Hart, Ernest H(untley) 1910-1985 102
Hart, Frances (Newbold) Noyes 1890-1943
Brief entry 112
See also CMW 4
Hart, Francis
See Paine, Lauran (Bosworth)
Hart, Francis Dudley 1909- CANR-25
Earlier sketch in CA 108
Hart, Gary (Warren) 1936(?)- 124
Brief entry 114
Hart, Gavin 1939- 106
Hart, George L. III 1942- 93-96
Hart, Gordon
See Hensley, Sophie Almon
Hart, H(erbert) L(ionel) A(dolphus)
1907-1992 .... CANR-46
Obituary 140
Earlier sketches in CA 1-4R, CANR-2
Hart, Henry (W.) 1954- CANR-93
Earlier sketch in CA 128
Hart, Henry C(owles) 1916- 1-4R
Hart, Henry Hersch 1886-1968 .... CAP-1
Earlier sketch in CA 9-10
Hart, Herbert Michael 1928- 9-12R
Hart, Hornell (Norris) 1888-1967
Obituary 111
Hart, James
See Hough, Harold
Hart, James D(avid) 1911-1990 .... CANR-1
Obituary 132
Earlier sketch in CA 1-4R
Hart, Jan Siegel 1940- 147
See also SATA 79
Hart, Jane (Meyers) 1922- 107
Hart, Jeanne
See Schrager, Jeanne Hart
Hart, Jeffrey Allen 1947- 109
Hart, Jenifer (Fischer) 1914-2005 138
Obituary 237
Hart, Jennifer B.
See Hough, Harold
Hart, Jim Allee 1914-1986 .... 13-16R
Hart, John 1942- 109
Hart, John 1948- CANR-11
Earlier sketch in CA 65-68
Hart, John E(dward) 1917- 33-36R
Hart, John Fraser 1924- 37-40R
Hart, John Lewis 1931- CANR-4
Earlier sketch in CA 49-52
See also Hart, Johnny
Hart, John Mason 1935- 132
Hart, Johnny
See Hart, John Lewis
See also AITN 1
Hart, Jon
See Harvey, John (Barton)
Hart, Jonathan (Locke) 1956- 142
Hart, Joseph 1945- 85-88
Hart, Josephine 1942(?)- CANR-70
Earlier sketch in CA 138
See also CLC 70
See also CPW
See also DAM POP
Hart, Joyce 1954- 222
See also SATA 148
Hart, Judith (Constance Mary) 1924-1991 .. 109
Hart, Julia Catherine 1796-1867 .... DLB 99
Hart, Kate
See Kramer, Roberta
Hart, Kevin 1954- CANR-85
Earlier sketch in CA 135
See also BRWS 11
See also CP 7
Hart, Kitty 1926- 117
Hart, Larry 1920- 33-36R
Hart, Lizzie
See Haines, Carolyn
Hart, Lois B(orland) 1941- 117
Hart, Lorenz 1895-1943 .... DLB 265
Hart, Lynda 1953- 146
Hart, Marie 1932- 41-44R
Hart, Marilyn M(cGuire) 1926- 45-48
Hart, Marion Rice 1892(?)-1990
Obituary 132
Hart, Martin 1944- 129
See also 't Hart, Maarten
Hart, Matthew 1945- CANR-113
Earlier sketch in CA 125
Hart, Maxwell
See Skipp, John (Mason)
Hart, Megan E. 1971- 217
Hart, Milton R. 1896(?)-1983
Obituary 109
Hart, Moss 1904-1961 .... CANR-84
Obituary 89-92
Earlier sketch in CA 109
See also CLC 66
See also DAM DRAM
See also DFS 1
See also DLB 7, 266
See also RGAL 4
Hart, Oliver 1723-1795 .... DLB 31
Hart, Patricia Susan 1950- 118
Hart, Patrick 1925- 53-56
Hart, Peter 184
Hart, Peter 1963- 184
Hart, Ray L(ee) 1929- 29-32R
Hart, Richard (Harry) 1908- CAP-1
Earlier sketch in CA 9-10
Hart, Robert A(llan) 1929-
Brief entry 117
Hart, Roderick P(atrick) 1945- CANR-93
Earlier sketches in CA 106, CANR-45
Hart, Sandra Lynn Housby 1948- CANR-50
Earlier sketches in CA 108, CANR-25
Hart, Sarah
See Child, Maureen
Hart, Stan 1929- 118
Hart, Stephanie 1949- 97-100
Hart, Sue
See Hart, Susanne
Hart, Susanne 1927- CANR-20
Earlier sketch in CA 102
Hart, V(orhis) Donn 1918- 13-16R
Hart, Vaughan 1960- 189
Hart, Virginia 1949- 150
See also SATA 83
Hart, W. D. 1943- 157
Hart, Walter 1906(?)-1973
Obituary 45-48
Hart, William 1945- 210
Hart, Winston Scott 1903(?)-1979
Obituary 89-92
Hartcup, Adeline 1918- 116
Hartcup, Guy 1919- 29-32R
Hart-Davis, Duff 1936- CANR-27
Earlier sketch in CA 29-32R
Hart-Davis, Phyllida
See Barstow, Phyllida
Hart-Davis, Rupert (Charles)
1907-1999 .... CANR-105
Obituary 188
Brief entry 115
Earlier sketch in CA 134
Hartdegen, Stephen J. 1907-1989
Obituary 130
Harte, Amanda 225

Cumulative Index 253 **Harwell**

Harte, (Francis) Bret(t) 1836(?)-1902 . CANR-80
Brief entry 104
Earlier sketch in CA 140
See also AMWS 2
See also CDALB 1865-1917
See also DA
See also DA3
See also DAC
See also DAM MST
See also DLB 12, 64, 74, 79, 186
See also EXPS
See also LAIT 2
See also RGAL 4
See also RGSF 2
See also SATA 26
See also SSC 8, 59
See also SSFS 3
See also TCLC 1, 25
See also TUS
See also WLC
Harte, Edward Holmead 1922- 151
See also DLB 127
Harte, Houston Harriman 1927- 155
See also DLB 127
Harte, Jack 1944- .... DLB 319
Harte, Kelly E. 1949- 238
Harte, Lara 1975- 202
Harte, Marjorie
See McEvoy, Marjorie Harte
Harte, Samantha
See Hart, Sandra Lynn Housby
Harte, Thomas Joseph 1914-1974
Obituary 53-56
Harteis, Richard 1946- 203
See also CAAS 26
Hartel, Klaus Dieter
See Vandenberg, Philipp
Hartendorp, A(bram) V(an) H(eyningen)
1893- CAP-1
Earlier sketch in CA 13-16
Harter, Debbie 1963- .... SATA 107
Harter, Eugene C(laudius) 1926- CANR-43
Earlier sketch in CA 119
Harter, H(arman) Leon 1919- 157
Harter, Helen (O'Connor) 1905-1990 .... 5-8R
Harter, Hugh A(nthony) 1922- 110
Harter, Kenneth W. 1912(?)-1984
Obituary 112
Harter, Lafayette George, Jr. 1918- 9-12R
Harter, Penny 1940- 172
Earlier sketch in CA 77-80
Autobiographical Essay in 172
See also CAAS 28
Hartfeld, Hermann 1942- 136
Hartfield, Claire 1957- 221
See also SATA 147
Hartfield, Ronne 1936- 236
Hartford, Claire 1913- 29-32R
Hartford, Ellis F(ord) 1905-1980 .... CAP-1
Earlier sketch in CA 13-14
Hartford, (George) Huntington II 1911- . 17-20R
Hartford, Margaret E(lizabeth) 1917- 41-44R
Hartford, Vin
See Donson, Cyril
Harth, Erica CANR-118
Earlier sketch in CA 116
Harth, Erich 1919- 107
Harth, (John) Phillip 1926- 193
Brief entry 116
Harth, Robert 1940- 33-36R
Harthan, John Plant 1916-2002 102
Obituary 204
Harthoorn, A(ntonie) M(arinus) 1923- 53-56
Hartich, Alice 1888-1967 .... CAP-2
Earlier sketch in CA 17-18
Hartig, John H. 1952- 143
Hartigan, Francis 223
Hartill, Rosemary (Jane) 1949- CANR-55
Earlier sketch in CA 127
Harting, Emilie Clothier 1942- 73-76
Hartinger, Brent 1964- 218
See also SATA 145
Hartje, Robert G(eorge) 1922- 25-28R
Hartje, Tod D(ale) 1968- 139
Hartjen, Clayton A(lfred) 1943- 69-72
Hartke, Vance (Rupert) 1919-2003 .... 25-28R
Obituary 218
Hartland, Michael 1941- 110
Hartlaub, Felix 1913(?)-1945 174
See also DLB 56
Hartlaub, G(ustav) F(riedrich) 1884-1963
Obituary 112
Hartle, Anthony E. 1942- 137
Hartleben, Otto Erich 1864-1905 179
See also DLB 118
Hartley, Aidan 1965- 225
Hartley, Cathy J. 1965- 143
Hartley, David 1705-1757 .... DLB 252
Hartley, Dorothy 1893-1985 105
Obituary 118
Hartley, Ellen (Raphael) 1915-1980 .... CANR-4
Earlier sketch in CA 5-8R
See also SATA 23
Hartley, Fred Allan III 1953- 106
See also SATA 41
Hartley, Hal 1959- CANR-141
Earlier sketch in CA 144
Hartley, Jean 1933- 135
Hartley, John I(rvin) 1921- 5-8R
Hartley, Keith 1940- CANR-37
Earlier sketch in CA 115
Hartley, L(eslie) P(oles) 1895-1972 ... CANR-33
Obituary 37-40R
Earlier sketch in CA 45-48
See also BRWS 7
See also CLC 2, 22
See also CN 1
See also DLB 15, 139
See also EWL 3
See also HGG
See also MTCW 1, 2
See also MTFW 2005
See also RGEL 2
See also RGSF 2
See also SUFW 1
Hartley, Livingston 1900- 61-64
Hartley, Lodwick (Charles)
1906-1979 .... CANR-1
Earlier sketch in CA 1-4R
Hartley, Margaret L(ohlker) 1909-1983 .. 97-100
Obituary 110
Hartley, Marie 1905- 9-12R
Hartley, Mariette 1940- 207
Hartley, Marsden 1877-1943 171
Brief entry 123
See also AAYA 63
See also DLB 54
See also GLL 2
Hartley, Mary Loretta
See Hartley, Mariette
Hartley, Peter (Roy) 1933- 103
Hartley, Rachel M. 1895-1983 .... 5-8R
Hartley, Robert E. 1936- 130
Hartley, Robert F(rank) 1927- CANR-57
Earlier sketches in CA 69-72, CANR-11, 28
Hartley, Shirley Foster 1928- CANR-13
Earlier sketch in CA 73-76
Hartley, Steven W. 1956- 139
Hartley, Travis
See Paine, Lauran (Bosworth)
Hartley, William B(rown) 1913-1980 . CANR-4
Earlier sketch in CA 5-8R
See also SATA 23
Hartling, Peter
See Hartling, Peter
See also CLR 29
See also DLB 75
Hartling, Peter 1933- CANR-48
Earlier sketches in CA 101, CANR-22
See also Hartling, Peter
See also DLB 75
See also MAICYA 1, 2
See also SATA 66
Hartman, Berl
See Hartman, Berl Mendelson
Hartman, Berl Mendelson 1938- 122
Hartman, (Howard) Carl 1917- 122
Hartman, Carl 1928- 104
Hartman, Charles O(ssian) 1949- 108
Hartman, Chester W(arren) 1936- 57-60
Hartman, David 1931- 210
Hartman, David N. 1921- 13-16R
Hartman, Donald K. 1959- CANR-123
Earlier sketch in CA 163
Hartman, Evert 1937- 113
See also SATA 38
See also SATA-Brief 35
Hartman, Geoffrey H. 1929- CANR-79
Brief entry 117
Earlier sketch in CA 125
See also CLC 27
See also DLB 67
Hartman, George E(dward) 1926- 41-44R
Hartman, Hermene D(emaris) 1948- 122
Hartman, James D. 1949- 218
Hartman, Jan 1938- 65-68
Hartman, Jane E(vangeline) 1928- CANR-22
Earlier sketch in CA 105
See also SATA 47
Hartman, John J(acob) 1942- CANR-48
Earlier sketch in CA 49-52
Hartman, Louis F(rancis) 1901-1970 ..... CAP-2
Earlier sketch in CA 23-24
See also SATA 22
Hartman, Mary S(usan) 1941- 81-84
Hartman, Nancy Carol 1942- 53-56
Hartman, Olov 1906-1982 .... CANR-14
Earlier sketch in CA 29-32R
Hartman, Patience
See Zawadsky, Patience
Hartman, Phil(ip Edward) 1948-1998 163
Hartman, Rachel (Frieda) 1920-1972 .... 5-8R
Obituary 33-36R
Hartman, Rhondda Evans 1934- 61-64
Hartman, Robert K(intz) 1940- 41-44R
Hartman, Robert S. 1910-1973 .... CAP-2
Obituary 45-48
Earlier sketch in CA 17-18
Hartman, Roger
See Mehta, Rustam Jehangir
Hartman, Shirley 1929- 57-60
Hartman, Victoria 1942- 155
See also SATA 91
Hartman, Virginia 1959- 169
Hartman, William E(llis) 1919-1997 69-72
Obituary 161
Hartman, William T(aylor) 1942- 117
Hartmann, Betsy
See Hartmann, Elizabeth
Hartmann, Dennis L. 1949- 148
Hartmann, Edward George 1912-1995 . 41-44R
Hartmann, Elizabeth 1951- CANR-143
Earlier sketch in CA 126
Hartmann, Ernest 1934- 21-24R
Hartmann, Franz 1838-1912
Brief entry 115
Hartmann, Frederick Howard 1922- . CANR-38
Earlier sketches in CA 1-4R, CANR-1, 16
Hartmann, Heinz 1894-1970
Obituary 104
Hartmann, Helmut Henry 1931- 105
Hartmann, Klaus 1925- 21-24R
Hartmann, Michael 1944- 97-100
Hartmann, Rudolf A. 1937- 186
Brief entry 111
Hartmann, Sadakichi 1869-1944 157
See also DLB 54
See also TCLC 73
Hartmann, Susan M(arie) 1940- CANR-109
Earlier sketch in CA 41-44R
Hartmann, William K(enneth)
1939- CANR-140
Earlier sketch in CA 69-72
Hartmann von Aue c. 1170-c. 1210 . CDWLB 2
See also DLB 138
See also RGWL 2, 3
Hartnack, Justus 1912- 41-44R
Hartnell, Agnes Peg 1925- 174
Hartnett, D(avid) W(illiam) 1952- CANR-48
Earlier sketch in CA 122
Hartnett, Geraldine
See Evans, Geraldine
Hartnett, Ken(neth Owen) 1934- 118
Hartnett, Michael 1941-1999 .... CANR-85
Earlier sketch in CA 130
See also CP 1, 2
See also PFS 10
Hartnett, Sonya 1968- CANR-110
Earlier sketch in CA 158
See also AAYA 35
See also SATA 93, 130
See also YAW
Hartnett, Stephen J. 1963- 222
Hartnoll, Phyllis (Mary) 1906-1997 81-84
Obituary 156
Hartocollis, Peter 1922- CANR-1
Earlier sketch in CA 45-48
Hartog, Diana 1942- 123
Hartog, Jan de
See de Hartog, Jan
Hartog, Joseph 1933- 102
Hartoonian, Gevork 1947- 167
Hartshorn, Ruth M. 1928- .... SATA 11
Hartshorne, Charles 1897-2000 .... CANR-29
Obituary 191
Earlier sketches in CA 9-12R, CANR-4
See also DLB 270
Hartshorne, Richard 1899-1992 .... 5-8R
Hartshorne, Thomas L(lewellyn) 1935- . 37-40R
Hart-Smith, William 1911-1990 .... CANR-11
Earlier sketch in CA 21-24R
See also CP 1, 2
Hartsock, John (C.) 1951- 189
Hartsoe, Colleen Ivey 1925- 109
Hartston, W(illiam) R(oland) 1947- 116
Hartsuch, Paul Jackson 1902-1982 57-60
Hartswick, Kim J(ay) 236
Hartt, Julian 1916(?)-1984
Obituary 113
Hartt, Julian N(orris) 1911- 132
Hartung, Albert Edward 1923- 103
Hartung, Hans (Heinrich Ernst) 1904-1989
Obituary 130
Hartung, Susan Kathleen .... SATA 150
Hartup, Willard W(ert) 1927- 25-28R
Hartwell, David G(eddes) 1941- CANR-123
Earlier sketch in CA 162
Hartwell, Dickson Jay 1906-1981 .... CAP-1
Obituary 103
Earlier sketch in CA 11-12
Hartwell, (William) Michael Berry
1911-2001 142
Obituary 195
Hartwell, Nancy
See Callahan, Claire Wallis
Hartwell, Ronald Max 1921- 25-28R
Hartwick, Sylvia
See Doherty, Ivy R. Duffy
Hartwig, Manfred 1950- 149
See also SATA 81
Hartwig, Marie (Dorothy) 1906- 1-4R
Hartwig, Michael J. 1953- 201
Hartwig, Richard E(ric) 1942- 118
Harty, (Fredric) Russell 1934-1988
Obituary 125
Hartz, Fred R. 1933- 122
Hartz, Jim .... AITN 2
Hartz, Louis 1919-1986
Obituary 118
Hartzell, Scott Taylor 1951- 228
Hartzler, Daniel David 1941- 61-64
Hartzmark, Gini 167
Haruf, Kent 1943- CANR-131
Earlier sketches in CA 149, CANR-91
See also AAYA 44
See also CLC 34
Harvard, Andrew Carson 1949- 69-72
Harvard, Charles
See Gibbs-Smith, Charles Harvard
Harvard, Jane
See Adiele, Faith (E.)
Harvard, Stephen 1948- 57-60
Harvester, Simon
See Rumbold-Gibbs, Henry St. John Clair
Harvey, Andrew 1952- CANR-118
Brief entry 126
Earlier sketch in CA 132
Harvey, Anne 1933- CANR-48
Earlier sketch in CA 121
Harvey, Anthony Peter 1940- 106
Harvey, Barbara (Fitzgerald) 1928- 116
Harvey, Brett 1936- CANR-53
Earlier sketch in CA 126
See also SATA 61
Harvey, C(harles) J(ohn) D(errick) 1922- .. 9-12R
See also CP 1
Harvey, Caroline
See Trollope, Joanna
Harvey, Clay 165
Harvey, David 1935- 145
Earlier sketch in CA 123
Harvey, David Dow 1931- 65-68
Harvey, Donald J(oseph) 1922- 41-44R
Harvey, Earle (Sherburn) 1906- CANR-29
Earlier sketch in CA 109
Harvey, Edith 1908(?)-1972
Obituary 104
See also SATA-Obit 27
Harvey, Edward Burns 1939- 41-44R
Harvey, Frank 1912-1981
Obituary 105
Harvey, Frank (Laird) 1913-1982 .... 5-8R
Obituary 199
Harvey, Gabriel 1550(?)-1631 ... DLB 167, 213, 281
Harvey, Geoffrey 1943- 126
Harvey, Gina Cantoni 1922- CANR-33
Earlier sketch in CA 45-48
Harvey, Harriet 1924- 109
Harvey, Hazel (Mary) 1936- CANR-91
Earlier sketch in CA 145
Harvey, Ian Douglas 1914-1987 .... CAP-1
Obituary 121
Earlier sketch in CA 9-10
Harvey, Jack
See Rankin, Ian (James)
Harvey, James 1929- CANR-141
Earlier sketch in CA 135
Harvey, James C(ardwell) 1925- 45-48
Harvey, James O. 1926- 17-20R
Harvey, Jean-Charles 1891-1967 148
See also DLB 88
Harvey, Joan C. 1948- 132
Harvey, Joan M(argaret) 1918- 102
Harvey, John (Barton) 1938- CANR-56
Earlier sketch in CA 125
See also CMW 4
See also TCWW 1, 2
Harvey, John (Robert) 1942- CANR-58
Earlier sketch in CA 93-96
Harvey, John B.
See Harvey, John (Barton)
Harvey, John F(rederick) 1921- CANR-23
Earlier sketches in CA 13-16R, CANR-8
Harvey, John Hooper 1911-1997 ...... CANR-44
Earlier sketches in CA 5-8R, CANR-6, 21
Harvey, Jonathan 1939- 61-64
Harvey, Karen D. 1935- 152
See also SATA 88
Harvey, Karen (E.) G(iddens) 1944- 117
Harvey, Kathryn
See Wood, Barbara
Harvey, Kenneth 1919(?)-1979
Obituary 89-92
Harvey, Lashley Grey 1900-1982 .... 37-40R
Harvey, Maria Luisa Alvarez 1938- 53-56
Harvey, Marian 1927- 89-92
Harvey, Matthea 1973- 207
Harvey, Michael G. 1944- 110
Harvey, Mose Lofley 1910-1985
Obituary 115
Harvey, Nancy Lenz 1935- 65-68
Harvey, Nigel 1916- CANR-57
Earlier sketches in CA 73-76, CANR-13, 30
Harvey, O. J. 1927- 37-40R
Harvey, P(aul) D(ean) A(dshead) 1930- 112
Harvey, Paul
See Aurandt, Paul Harvey
Harvey, Paulett
See Tumay, Paulett
Harvey, (Brian) Peter 1951- 135
Harvey, R. C.
See Harvey, Robert C.
Harvey, Rachel
See Bloom, Ursula (Harvey)
Harvey, Richard B(lake) 1930- 49-52
Harvey, Robert 1884- 5-8R
Harvey, Robert C. 1937- CANR-109
Earlier sketch in CA 151
Harvey, Roland 1945- .... SATA 71, 123
Harvey, Ruth C(harlotte) 1918-1980 .... 1-4R
Obituary 102
Harvey, Stephen 1949-1993 134
Obituary 140
Harvey, Steven 1949- CANR-130
Earlier sketch in CA 163
Harvey, Thomas 1956- 224
Harvey, Van A(ustin) 1926- 33-36R
Harvey, Virginia I(sham) 1917- 57-60
Harvey, William Burnett 1922-1999 ..... 41-44R
Harvey, William Fryer 1885-1937 .... HGG
See also SUFW
Harvey-Jones, John (Henry) 1924- 140
Harvey Wood, (Elizabeth) Harriet 1934- 123
Harvie, Christopher (Thomas) 1944- 154
Harvie-Watt, George Steven 1903-1989 109
Harvor, Beth
See Harvor, (Erica) Elisabeth (Arendt Deichmann)
Harvor, (Erica) Elisabeth (Arendt Deichmann)
1936- CANR-124
Earlier sketch in CA 134
Harward, Donald W. 1939- 93-96
Harward, Timothy Blake 1932- 25-28R
Harwell, Ann (Manning) J. 1936- 57-60
Harwell, Ernie
See Harwell, William Earnest
Harwell, Richard Barksdale 1915- CANR-17
Earlier sketches in CA 1-4R, CANR-2

Harwell, William Earnest 1918- ... CANR-130
Brief entry ... 116
Earlier sketches in CA 128, CANR-66
Harwick, B. L.
See Keller, Beverly L(ou)
Harwin, Brian
See Henderson, LeGrand
Harwit, Martin Otto 1931- ... 105
Harwood, Alan 1935- ... 113
Harwood, Alice (Mary) -1985 ... CANR-84
Earlier sketch in CA 5-8R
See also RHW
Harwood, (Henry) David 1938- ... 104
Harwood, Edwin 1939- ... 29-32R
Harwood, Gina
See Battiscombe, E(sther) Georgina (Harwood)
Harwood, Gwen(doline Nessie)
1920-1995 ... 97-100
See also CP 1, 2
See also DLB 289
Harwood, John 1946- ... 232
Harwood, Jonathan 1943- ... 103
Harwood, Lee 1939- ... CANR-9
Earlier sketch in CA 21-24R
See also CAAS 19
See also CP 1, 2, 3, 4, 5, 6, 7
See also DLB 40
Harwood, Michael 1934(?)-1989
Obituary ... 130
Harwood, Pearl Augusta (Bragdon)
1903-1998 ... 13-16R
See also SATA 9
Harwood, Raymond C(harles) 1906-1987
Obituary ... 122
Harwood, Ronald 1934- ... CANR-55
Earlier sketches in CA 1-4R, CANR-4
See also CBD
See also CD 5, 6
See also CLC 32
See also DAM DRAM, MST
See also DLB 13
Hary c. 1440-c. 1495 ... RGEL 2
Harzfeld, Lois 1932- ... 107
Hasan, Ruqaiya ... 232
Hasan, Saiyid Zafar 1930- ... 73-76
Hasan, Sana ... 128
Hasan al-Basri, al- 642-728 ... DLB 311
Hasbrouck, Kenneth E(dward) Sr.
1916-1996 ... CANR-31
Obituary ... 152
Earlier sketch in CA 49-52
Hasegawa, Nyozekan 1875-1969
Obituary ... 111
Hasegawa, Tsuyoshi 1941- ... 109
Hasegawa Tatsunosuke
See Futabatei, Shimei
Hasek, Jaroslav (Matej Frantisek)
1883-1923 ... 129
Brief entry ... 104
See also CDWLB 4
See also DLB 215
See also EW 9
See also EWL 3
See also MTCW 1, 2
See also RGSF 2
See also RGWL 2, 3
See also SSC 69
See also TCLC 4
Hasel, Gerhard F(ranz) 1935- ... CANR-15
Earlier sketch in CA 41-44R
Haselden, John
See Forrester, Martyn (John)
Haselden, Kyle (Emerson) 1913-1968 ... 5-8R
Haseler, Stephen Michael Alan 1942- ... 85-88
Haseley, Dennis 1950- ... CANR-141
Earlier sketch in CA 162
See also SATA 57, 105, 157
See also SATA-Brief 44
Haseman, John B. 1942- ... 228
Hasenclever, Herbert Frederick 1924-1978
Obituary ... 81-84
Hasenclever, Walter 1890-1940
Hasford, (Jerry) Gustav 1947-1993 ... 85-88
Obituary ... 140
Hashimoto, Sharon 1953- ... PFS 22
Hashmi, Aurangzeb Alamgir 1951- ... CANR-84
Earlier sketches in CA 77-80, CANR-16, 48
See also CP 7
Hashmi, Kerri 1955- ... 178
See also SATA 108
Hashway, Robert M. 1946- ... 219
Haskel, Frank
See Frankel, Haskel
Haskell, Arnold L(ionel)
1903-1981(?) ... CANR-7
Obituary ... 102
Earlier sketch in CA 5-8R
See also SATA 6
Haskell, Douglas 1899-1979
Obituary ... 89-92
Haskell, Edward Froehlich 1906- ... 186
Brief entry ... 105
Haskell, Francis (James Herbert)
1928-2000 ... CANR-6
Obituary ... 187
Earlier sketch in CA 9-12R
Haskell, Guy H. 1956- ... 150
Haskell, Harry 1954- ... CANR-65
Earlier sketch in CA 129
Haskell, John Duncan, Jr. 1941- ... CANR-50
Earlier sketches in CA 107, CANR-25
Haskell, Martin R(oy) 1912-1980 ... 41-44R
Haskell, Molly 1939- ... 135
Haskett, Edythe Rance 1915- ... 21-24R
Haskin, Byron 1899-1984 ... IDFW 3, 4
Haskin, Dorothy C(lark) 1905-1995 ... 5-8R
Haskin, Gretchen 1936- ... 103
Haskins, Barbara
See Stone, Barbara Haskins
Haskins, Caryl P(arker) 1908-2001 ... 206
Haskins, Charles Homer 1870-1937 ... 201
See also DLB 47
Haskins, George Lee 1915-1991 ... CANR-1
Obituary ... 135
Earlier sketch in CA 1-4R
Haskins, Ilma 1919- ... 45-48
Haskins, James
See Haskins, James S.
Haskins, James S. 1941-2005 ... CANR-79
Earlier sketches in CA 33-36R, CANR-25, 48
See also Haskins, Jim
See also AAYA 14
See also BW 2, 3
See also CLR 3, 39
See also JRDA
See also MAICYA 1, 2
See also MAICYAS 1
See also SATA 9, 69, 105, 132
See also SATA-Essay 132
See also YAW
Haskins, Jim
See Haskins, James S.
See also SAAS 4
See also WYAS 1
Haskins, Lola 1943- ... 209
Haskins, Sam(uel Joseph) 1926- ... 103
Haskins, Scott (M.) 1953- ... 153
Haslam, Gerald W. 1937- ... 197
Earlier sketches in CA 29-32R, CANR-11, 27, 58, 97
Autobiographical Essay in ... 197
See also DLB 212
See also TCWW 2
Hasler, Eveline 1937- ... 106
Hasler, Joan 1931- ... 29-32R
See also SATA 28
Hasler, Julie 1963- ... 170
Haslerud, George M(artin) 1906- ... 45-48
Haslett, Adam 1970- ... 216
Hasley, Louis (Leonard) 1906- ... 37-40R
Hasley, Lucile (Charlotte Hardman)
1909- ... CAP-1
Earlier sketch in CA 11-12
Hasling, John 1928- ... 33-36R
Haslip, Joan 1912-1994 ... 107
Obituary ... 145
Hasluck, Nicholas (Paul) 1942- ... CANR-130
Earlier sketches in CA 137, CANR-69
See also CN 4, 5, 6, 7
Hasluck, Paul (Meernaa Caedwalla)
1905-1993 ... CANR-46
Obituary ... 140
Earlier sketch in CA 109
Haspel, Eleanor C. 1944- ... 69-72
Haspiel, Dean 1968(?)- ... 202
Hass, Amira 1956- ... 210
Hass, C(harles) Glen 1915- ... 17-20R
Hass, Eric 1905(?)-1980
Obituary ... 102
Hass, Hans 1919- ... 108
Hass, Robert 1941- ... CANR-71
Earlier sketches in CA 111, CANR-30, 50
See also AMWS 6
See also CLC 18, 39, 99
See also CP 7
See also DLB 105, 206
See also EWL 3
See also MAL 5
See also MTFW 2005
See also PC 16
See also RGAL 4
See also SATA 94
See also TCLE 1:1
Hassall, Anthony J. 1939- ... 126
Hassall, Christopher (Vernon) 1912-1963
Obituary ... 89-92
Hassall, Joan 1906-1988 ... SATA 43
See also SATA-Obit 56
Hassall, Mark (William Cory) 1940- ... CANR-13
Earlier sketch in CA 73-76
Hassall, William Owen 1912-1994 ... 13-16R
Obituary ... 146
Hassam, Andrew ... 181
Hassam, Nick
See Crowther, Peter
Hassan, Aftab Syed 1952- ... 148
Hassan, Ihab Habib 1925- ... CANR-41
Earlier sketches in CA 5-8R, CANR-3, 19
See also CAAS 12
Hassan, Richard
See Hassan, Aftab Syed
Hassan, William Ephraim, Jr. 1923- ... 33-36R
Hasse, John Edward 1948- ... 119
Hassel, David John 1923- ... CANR-32
Earlier sketch in CA 113
Hassel, Odd 1897-1981 ... 157
Obituary ... 108
Hassel, R. Chris, Jr. 1939- ... 129
Hassel, Sven 1917- ... 93-96
Hasselbach, Ingo 1967- ... 154
Hasselstrom, Linda (Michele) 1943- ... 222
Earlier sketches in CA 153, CANR-110
Autobiographical Essay in ... 222
See also ANW
See also DLB 256
Hassen, Philip Charles 1943- ... 147
Hassenger, Robert (Leo) 1937- ... 21-24R
Hassett, Ann 1936- ... 186
See also SATA 162
Hassett, John ... SATA 162
Hassing, Per 1916- ... 37-40R
Hassinger, Edward W(esley) 1925- ... 125
Hassler, Donald M. (II) 1937- ... CANR-57
Earlier sketches in CA 41-44R, CANR-14, 31
Hassler, Jon (Francis) 1933- ... CANR-80
Earlier sketches in CA 73-76, CANR-21
Interview in ... CANR-21
See also CN 6, 7
See also SATA 19
Hassler, Warren W., Jr. 1926- ... 9-12R
Hassler, William T(homas) 1954- ... 104
Hassrick, Peter H(eyl) 1941- ... CANR-140
Earlier sketches in CA 49-52, CANR-1, 16
Hast, Adele 1931- ... 119
Hastedt, Glenn Peter 1950- ... 239
Hastings, Adrian 1929-2001 ... CANR-47
Obituary ... 197
Earlier sketches in CA 17-20R, CANR-7, 23
Hastings, Alan
See Williamson, Geoffrey
Hastings, Arthur Claude 1935- ... 37-40R
Hastings, Beverly
See Barkin, Carol and
James, Elizabeth
Hastings, Brooke
See Gordon, Deborah Hannes
Hastings, Cecily Mary Eleanor 1924- ... 5-8R
Hastings, Graham
See Jeffries, Roderic (Graeme)
Hastings, Harrington
See Marsh, John
Hastings, Hubert de Cronin 1902-1986 ... 109
Obituary ... 121
Hastings, Hudson
See Kuttner, Henry
Hastings, Ian 1912- ... 45-48
See also SATA 62
Hastings, Macdonald 1909-1982 ... CANR-85
Earlier sketches in CA 53-56, CANR-9
Hastings, March
See Levinson, Leonard
Hastings, Margaret 1910-1979 ... 41-44R
Hastings, (Macdonald) Max 1945- ... CANR-48
Earlier sketch in CA 81-84
Hastings, Michael
See Bar-Zohar, Michael
Hastings, Michael (Gerald) 1938- ... CANR-45
Earlier sketch in CA 97-100
See also CBD
See also CD 5, 6
See also DLB 233
Hastings, Paul G(uiler) 1914-1995 ... CANR-24
Earlier sketch in CA 1-4R
Hastings, Philip Kay 1922- ... 102
Hastings, Phyllis (Dora Hodge) ... CANR-84
Earlier sketches in CA 9-12R, CANR-8
Hastings, Robert J. 1924- ... CANR-48
Earlier sketch in CA 122
Hastings, Robert Paul 1933- ... 73-76
Hastings, Robin Hood William Stewart
1917-1990
Obituary ... 131
Hastings, Roderic
See Jeffries, Graham Montague
Hastings, Selina ... CLC 44
Hastings, Susan 1942- ... 128
Hastings, William T(homson) 1881-1969 ... 5-8R
Haston, Dougal 1940-1977
Obituary ... 105
Hastorf, Albert H(erman) 1920- ... 97-100
Hastorf, Christine Ann 1950- ... 146
Hasty, Olga Peters 1951- ... 128
Hasty, Ronald W. 1941- ... CANR-4
Earlier sketch in CA 53-56
Hasty, Will ... 193
Haswell, Chetwynd John Drake 1919- ... 41-44R
Haswell, Harold Alanson, Jr. 1912- ... 45-48
Haswell, Janis Tedesco 1950- ... CANR-121
Earlier sketch in CA 168
Haswell, Jock
See Haswell, Chetwynd John Drake
Haswell, Richard H(enry) 1940- ... CANR-124
Earlier sketch in CA 168
Haszard, Patricia Moyes
1923-2000 ... CANR-83
Obituary ... 189
Earlier sketches in CA 17-20R, CANR-13, 29, 54
See also Moyes, Patricia
See also CMW 4
See also YAW
Hatab, Lawrence J. 1946- ... 160
Hatar, Gyozo 1914- ... CWW 2
See also DLB 215
Hatch, Alden 1898-1975 ... 65-68
Obituary ... 57-60
Hatch, (Alden) Denison 1935- ... 33-36R
Hatch, Elvin (James) 1937- ... 45-48
Hatch, Eric S(towe) 1902(?)-1973
Obituary ... 41-44R
Hatch, James V(ernon) 1928- ... 41-44R
Hatch, John (Charles) 1917-1992 ... 9-12R
Hatch, Lynda S. 1950- ... 155
See also SATA 90
Hatch, Mary Cottam 1912-1970
Obituary ... 109
See also SATA-Brief 28
Hatch, Michael F. 1947- ... 162
Hatch, Mike
See Hatch, Michael F.
Hatch, Nathan O(rr) 1946- ... 129
Brief entry ... 109
Hatch, Orrin G(rant) 1934- ... 221
Hatch, Preble D(elloss) K(ellogg)
1898-1977 ... CAP-2
Earlier sketch in CA 23-24
Hatch, Raymond N(orris) 1911-1997 ... 21-24R
Hatch, Richard A(llen) 1940- ... CANR-9
Earlier sketch in CA 21-24R
Hatch, Robert McConnell 1910- ... 93-96
Hatch, Thom 1946- ... 220
Hatch, William H(enry) P(aine) 1875-1972
Obituary ... 37-40R
Hatcher, George W. 1906(?)-1983
Obituary ... 110
Hatcher, Harlan (Henthorne)
1898-1998 ... CAP-2
Obituary ... 165
Earlier sketch in CA 19-20
Hatcher, John 1942- ... 33-36R
Hatcher, John S(outhall) 1940- ... 97-100
Hatcher, Larry (L.) 1956- ... 151
Hatcher, Nat(han) B(razzell) 1897-1969 ... 1-4R
Hatcher, Robert Anthony 1937- ... 93-96
Hatcher, Robin Lee 1951- ... CANR-105
Earlier sketch in CA 154
Hatcher, William S(pottswood) 1935- ... 123
Hatem, Mohamed Abdel-Kader
See Hatim, Muhammad 'Abd al-Qadir
Hatfield, Antoinette Kuzmanich 1929- ... 85-88
Hatfield, Dorothy B(lackmon) 1921- ... 53-56
Hatfield, Elaine (Catherine) 1937- ... CANR-38
Earlier sketches in CA 25-28R, CANR-10, 17
Hatfield, Henry Caraway 1912-1995 ... 65-68
Hatfield, Julie (Stockwell) 1940- ... 126
Hatfield, Kate
See Wright, (Idonea) Daphne
Hatfield, Mark O(dom) 1922- ... 77-80
Hatfield, Michael (Vernon) 1935- ... 119
Hatfield, Phyllis 1944- ... 146
Hatfield, Shelley Bowen 1947- ... 174
Hathaway, Baxter L. 1909- ... CANR-5
Earlier sketch in CA 1-4R
Hathaway, Bo 1942- ... 106
Hathaway, Dale E(rnest) 1925- ... 9-12R
Hathaway, Jan
See Neubauer, William Arthur
Hathaway, Katharine Butler 1890-1942 ... 199
Hathaway, Lulu (Bailey) 1903-1982 ... 13-16R
Hathaway, Mavis
See Avery, Ira
Hathaway, Nancy 1946- ... 108
Hathaway, Richard Dean 1927- ... 125
Hathaway, Robin 1934- ... 225
Hathaway, Sibyl Collings 1884-1974 ... 1-4R
Obituary ... 103
Hathaway, Starke R(osecrans) 1903-1984 ... 5-8R
Obituary ... 113
Hathaway, William 1944- ... 73-76
See also DLB 120
Hathcock, Louise -1966 ... 1-4R
Hatherly, Ana 1929- ... DLB 287
Hathorn, Elizabeth Helen 1943- ... 191
See also Hathorn, Libby
Hathorn, Libby
See Hathorn, Elizabeth Helen
See also AAYA 37
See also CWRI 5
See also SATA 74, 120, 156
See also SATA-Essay 156
Hathorn, Richmond Y(ancey) 1917- ... CANR-1
Earlier sketch in CA 1-4R
Hatim, Muhammad 'Abd al-Qadir
1918- ... 89-92
Hatkoff, Amy ... 141
Hatlen, Burton (Norval) 1936- ... 109
Hatley, Allen G., Jr. 1930- ... 200
Hatley, George B(erton) 1924- ... 106
Hatlo, Jimmy 1898-1963
Obituary ... 93-96
See also SATA-Obit 23
Hatmon, Paul W. 1921- ... 106
Hatoum, Milton 1952- ... CANR-135
Earlier sketch in CA 156
Hatt, Harold E(rnest) 1932- ... 21-24R
Hatta, Kayo 1958(?)- ... 234
Hatta, Mari ... 234
Hatta, Mohammed 1902-1980
Obituary ... 97-100
Hattaway, Herman (Morell) 1938- ... CANR-117
Earlier sketch in CA 65-68
Hattaway, Michael 1941- ... CANR-39
Earlier sketch in CA 116
Hattendorf, John B(rewster) 1941- ... 135
Hatteras, Amelia
See Mencken, H(enry) L(ouis)
Hatteras, Owen
See Mencken, H(enry) L(ouis) and
Nathan, George Jean
See also TCLC 18
Hatteras, Owen III
See McDavid, Raven I(oor), Jr.
Hatterer, Lawrence J(ohn) 1925-
Brief entry ... 118
Hattersley, Ralph (Marshall, Jr.) 1921- ... 103
Hattersley, Roy (Sydney George)
1932- ... CANR-102
Earlier sketch in CA 103
Hattersley-Smith, Geoffrey (Francis) 1923- ... 118
Hattery, Lowell H(arold) 1916- ... 17-20R
Hatton, G. Noel
See Caird, Alice Mona
Hatton, Ragnhild Marie 1913-1995 ... CANR-12
Obituary ... 148
Earlier sketch in CA 25-28R
Hatton, Robert Wayland 1934- ... 37-40R
Hatton, Thomas J(enison) 1935- ... 114
Hattwick, Richard E(arl) 1938- ... 73-76
Hatvary, George Egon ... 53-56
Hatzenbuehler, Ronald L(ee) 1945- ... 117
Hatzfeld, Helmut A(nthony)
1892-1979 ... 97-100
Obituary ... 85-88
Hauberg, Clifford A(lvin) 1906- ... 37-40R
Hauch, Carsten 1790-1872 ... DLB 300
Hauck, Allan 1925- ... 1-4R
Hauck, Charles ... 178

Cumulative Index 255 Hawkins

Hauck, Charlie
See Hauck, Charles
Hauck, Paul A(nthony) 1924- CANR-14
Earlier sketch in CA 41-44R
Hauck, Richard Boyd 1936- 53-56
Haueisen, Kathryn M. 1946- 128
Haueisen, Kathy
See Haueisen, Kathryn M.
Hauerwas, Stanley Martin 1940- CANR-107
Earlier sketch in CA 57-60
Hauff, Wilhelm 1802-1827 DLB 90
See also SUFW 1
Haug, C(harles) James 1946- CANR-38
Earlier sketch in CA 116
Haug, James 1954- 202
Haugaard, Erik Christian 1923- CANR-38
Earlier sketches in CA 5-8R, CANR-3
See also AAYA 36
See also BYA 1
See also CLR 11
See also CWRI 5
See also JRDA
See also MAICYA 1, 2
See also SAAS 12
See also SATA 4, 68
Haugaard, Kay 189
See also SATA 117
Haugaard, William Paul 1929- 25-28R
Hauge, Alfred 1915-1986 190
Hauge, Olav H(akonson) 1908-1994 205
See also CWW 2
See also DLB 297
See also EWL 3
Hauge, Ron 1955- 151
Hauge, Sharon K(aye) 1943- 116
Haugeland, John (Christian) 1945- CANR-140
Earlier sketch in CA 133
Haugen, Edmund Bennett 1913-1970 17-20R
Haugen, Einar (Ingvald) 1906-1994 CANR-25
Obituary 145
Earlier sketches in CA 21-24R, CANR-9
Haugen, Paal-Helge 1945- DLB 297
Haugen, Tormod 1945- 135
See also SATA 66
Haugh, Richard (Stanley) 1942- CANR-9
Earlier sketch in CA 57-60
Haugh, Robert F(ulton) 1910-1994 61-64
Haughey, John C. 1930- 77-80
Haughey, Thomas Brace 1943- 113
Haught, James A(lbert, Jr.) 1932- 140
Brief entry 122
Haught, John F(rancis) 1942- CANR-118
Earlier sketch in CA 85-88
Haughton, Claire Shaver 1901-1993 85-88
Haughton, Rosemary (Luling) 1927- CANR-35
Earlier sketch in CA 5-8R
Haughton, Sidney Henry 1888-1982
Obituary 107
Haughton-James, Jean Rosemary 1924-1981
Obituary 105
Haugland, Vern(on Arnold) 1908-1984 93-96
Obituary 113
Haugwitz, August Adolph von
1647-1706 DLB 168
Hauk, Maung
See Hobbs, Cecil (Carlton)
Haule, James M(ark) 1945- CANR-27
Earlier sketch in CA 109
Hauman, Doris 1898-1984 SATA 32
Hauman, George 1890-1961 SATA 32
Haun, Paul 1906-1969 CAP-2
Earlier sketch in CA 17-18
Hau'Ofa, Epeli 1939- CANR-70
Earlier sketch in CA 124
See also CN 4, 5, 6
Haupt, Christopher (Charles Herbert) Lehmann
See Lehmann-Haupt, Christopher (Charles Herbert)
Haupt, Zygmunt 1907(?)-1975
Obituary 61-64
Hauptly, Denis J(ames) 1945- 118
See also SATA 57
Hauptman, Don 1947- 138
Hauptman, Jodi 198
Hauptman, Laurence Marc 1945- 139
Hauptman, Robert 1941- 143
Hauptman, Terry 1947- 111
Hauptman, William (Thornton)
1942- CANR-85
Earlier sketch in CA 128
Interview in CA-128
See also CAD
See also CD 5, 6
Hauptmann, Carl 1858-1921 DLB 66, 118
Hauptmann, Gerhart (Johann Robert)
1862-1946 153
Brief entry 104
See also CDWLB 2
See also DAM DRAM
See also DLB 66, 118
See also EW 8
See also EWL 3
See also RGSF 2
See also RGWL 2, 3
See also SSC 37
See also TCLC 4
See also TWA
Haury, Emil W(alter) 1904-1992 CANR-49
Obituary 140
Earlier sketch in CA 65-68
Hausdorff, Don 1927- 45-48
Hausdorff, Felix 1868-1942 159
Hause, Steven C. 1942- 127
Hauser, Bengamin Gayelord 1895-1984 183
Obituary 114
Brief entry 111
Hauser, Carl Maria 1895-1985
Obituary 117
Hauser, Charles McCorkle (Newland)
1929-2005 69-72
Obituary 238
Hauser, Frank
See Wiemer, Rudolf Otto
Hauser, Gayelord
See Hauser, Bengamin Gayelord
Hauser, Gerald Dwight 208
See also Hauser, Wings
Hauser, Gerard A. 1943- 195
Hauser, Hillary 1944- CANR-56
Earlier sketches in CA 69-72, CANR-11, 30
Hauser, J. D.
See Hauser, Wings
Hauser, Jill Frankel 1950- 197
See also SATA 127
Hauser, Kaspar
See Tucholsky, Kurt
Hauser, Margaret L(ouise) 1909- CAP-1
Earlier sketch in CA 11-12
See also SATA 10
Hauser, Marianne 1909- CANR-70
Earlier sketches in CAP-1, CA 11-12, CANR-13
See also CAAS 11
See also CN 6, 7
See also DLBY 1983
Hauser, Melanie 200
Hauser, Philip M(orris) 1909-1994 17-20R
Hauser, Robert Mason 1942- 109
Hauser, Susan Carol 1942- 201
Hauser, Thomas 1946- CANR-88
Earlier sketches in CA 85-88, CANR-45
Hauser, William B(arry) 1939- 69-72
Hauser, Wings 1947- 208
See also Hauser, Gerald Dwight
Hausherr, Rosmarie 1943- SATA 86
Hausknecht, Murray 1925- 37-40R
Hausknecht, Richard 1929- 121
Hausman, Gerald 1945- CANR-108
Earlier sketches in CA 45-48, CANR-2, 17, 38
See also CLR 89
See also SATA 13, 90, 132
Hausman, Gerry
See Hausman, Gerald
Hausman, Patricia 1953- CANR-52
Earlier sketches in CA 107, CANR-26
Hausman, Warren H. 1939- 17-20R
Hausmann, Bernard A(ndrew)
1899-1992 CAP-2
Earlier sketch in CA 23-24
Hausmann, Manfred 1898-1986
Obituary 120
Hausmann, Winifred 1922- CANR-26
Earlier sketches in CA 21-24R, CANR-11
Hausrath, Alfred Hartmann 1901-1986 41-44R
Haussig, Hans Wilhelm 1916- 29-32R
Hausvater, Alexander 1948- 130
Hautala, Rick 1949- 180
Hauth, Katherine B. 1940- 167
See also SATA 99
Hauther, Brenda 1951- 113
Hautman, Pete(r Murray) 1952- CANR-107
Earlier sketches in CA 144, CANR-72
See also AAYA 49
See also SATA 82, 128
Hautzig, Deborah 1956- 89-92
See also BYA 8
See also SATA 31, 106
Hautzig, Esther Rudomin 1930- CANR-132
Earlier sketches in CA 1-4R, CANR-5, 20, 46, 85
See also BYA 1
See also CLR 22
See also JRDA
See also LAIT 4
See also MAICYA 1, 2
See also SAAS 15
See also SATA 4, 68, 148
See also YAW
Hauxwell, Hannah 1926- 140
Havard, William C(lyde), Jr. 1923- CANR-5
Earlier sketch in CA 1-4R
Havazelet, Ehud 1956- 199
Havel, Geoff 1955- 227
See also SATA 152
Havel, Harvey 1971- 173
Havel, J(ean) E(ugene Martial) 1928- 41-44R
Havel, Jennifer
See Havill, Juanita
Havel, Vaclav 1936- CANR-124
Earlier sketches in CA 104, CANR-36, 63
See also CDWLB 4
See also CLC 25, 58, 65, 123
See also CWW 2
See also DA3
See also DAM DRAM
See also DC 6
See also DFS 10
See also DLB 232
See also EWL 3
See also LMFS 2
See also MTCW 1, 2
See also MTFW 2005
See also RGWL 3
Havelin, Kate 1961- 215
See also SATA 143
Havelock, Christine Mitchell 1924- 85-88
Havelock, Eric A(lfred) 1903-1988 CAP-1
Obituary 125
Earlier sketch in CA 13-16
Havelock, Ronald G(eoffrey) 1935- 85-88
Havelock-Allan, Anthony 1904-2003 IDFW 3, 4
Haveman, Robert H. 1936- 17-20R
Havemann, Ernest (Carl) 1912-1995 1-4R
Obituary 148
Havemann, Ernst 1918- 135
Havemann, Joel 1943- 85-88
Havemann, Robert (Hans Gunther) 1910-1982
Obituary 110
Havemeyer, Loomis 1886-1971
Obituary 33-36R
Haven, Alice B. Neal 1827-1863 DLB 250
Haven, Kendall F. 1946- 187
Haven, Richard 1924-1999 25-28R
Havens, Daniel F(rederick) 1931- 69-72
Havens, George R(emington)
1890-1977 CANR-4
Obituary 73-76
Earlier sketch in CA 5-8R
Havens, Gordon 1903-1983
Obituary 111
Havens, Leston Laycock 1924- CANR-43
Earlier sketch in CA 119
Havens, Murray Clark 1932- 41-44R
Havens, Richard Pierce 1941- 185
Havens, Richie
See Havens, Richard Pierce
Havens, Shirley E(lise) 1925-2000 89-92
Obituary 189
Havens, Thomas R. H. 1939- CANR-34
Earlier sketches in CA 41-44R, CANR-15
Haver, Ronald D. 1939- 109
Havergal, Frances Ridley 1836-1879 DLB 199
Haverkamp-Begemann, Egbert
1923- CANR-11
Earlier sketch in CA 17-20R
Haverstick, John (Mitchell) 1919- 25-28R
Haverstock, Mary Sayre 1932- 81-84
Haverstock, Nathan Alfred 1931- 53-56
Haverty, Anne CANR-139
Earlier sketch in CA 163
Havet, Jose (L.) 1937- 137
Haviaras, Stratis
See Chaviaras, Strates
See also CLC 33
Havighurst, Alfred F(reeman)
1904-1991 33-36R
Obituary 133
Havighurst, Marion (M.) 1894-1974 CANR-29
Obituary 49-52
Earlier sketches in CAP-1, CA 13-14
Havighurst, Robert J(ames) 1900-1991 21-24R
Obituary 133
Havighurst, Walter (Edwin)
1901-1994 CANR-29
Obituary 144
Earlier sketches in CA 1-4R, CANR-1
See also SATA 1
See also SATA-Obit 79
Haviland, Virginia 1911-1988 CANR-12
Obituary 124
Earlier sketch in CA 17-20R
See also SATA 6
See also SATA-Obit 54
Havill, Adrian 203
Havill, Juanita 1949- 230
See also SATA 74, 155
Havill, Steven 1945- CANR-72
Earlier sketches in CA 108, CANR-25
Havis, Allan 1951- CANR-83
Earlier sketches in CA 108, CANR-28, 53
See also CAD
See also CD 5, 6
Havlice, Patricia Pate 1943- CANR-12
Earlier sketch in CA 29-32R
Havlik, John F(ranklin) 1917-1984 CANR-24
Earlier sketch in CA 45-48
Havoc, June 1916- 107
Havran, Martin J. 1929- CANR-1
Earlier sketch in CA 1-4R
Havrevold, Finn 1905-1988 109
Havrilesky, Thomas M(ichael)
1939- CANR-19
Earlier sketches in CA 53-56, CANR-4
Haw, Richard Claude 1913- CAP-1
Earlier sketch in CA 9-10
Hawass, Zahi A. 1947- 210
Hawcroft, Michael 1961- 205
Hawdon, Robin 1939- 231
Hawes, Charles Boardman 1889-1923 213
See also BYA 4
See also CWRI 5
Hawes, Evelyn (Johnson) 13-16R
See also AITN 1
Hawes, Frances Cooper (Richmond)
1897- CAP-1
Earlier sketch in CA 9-10
Hawes, Gene R(obert) 1922-2004 CANR-39
Obituary 231
Earlier sketches in CA 5-8R, CANR-3, 18
Hawes, Grace M. 1926- 69-72
Hawes, Hampton 1929(?)-1977
Obituary 69-72
Hawes, J. M.
See Hawes, J(ames) M.
Hawes, J(ames) M. 1960(?)- 178
Hawes, John T. 1906(?)-1983
Obituary 109
Hawes, Joseph M(ilton) 1938- 53-56
Hawes, Judy 1913- 33-36R
See also SATA 4
Hawes, Louis 1931- 114
Hawes, Louise 1943- SATA 60
Hawes, Lynne Gusikoff Salop
1931- CANR-22
Earlier sketch in CA 106
Hawes, Stephen 1475(?)-1529(?) DLB 132
See also RGEL 2
Hawes, William (Kenneth) 1931- 77-80
Hawgood, John Arkas 1905-1971
Obituary 104
Hawi, Khalil 1925- EWL 3
Hawk, Alex
See Garfield, Brian (Francis Wynne) and Kelton, Elmer and Lutz, Giles A(lfred)
Hawk, Grace E. 1905-1983
Obituary 110
Hawk, Philip B(ovier) 1874-1966
Obituary 116
Hawke, Bob
See Hawke, Robert James Lee
Hawke, David Freeman 1923-1999 CANR-18
Obituary 181
Earlier sketch in CA 102
Hawke, Ethan 1970- CANR-117
Earlier sketch in CA 165
See also AAYA 64
Hawke, Gary Richard 1942- 102
Hawke, Nancy
See Nugent, Nancy
Hawke, Robert James Lee 1929- 152
Hawke, Rosanne (Joy) 1953- SATA 124
Hawke, Simon
See Yermakov, Nicholas
Hawken, Paul G(erard) 1946- 223
Hawken, William R. 1917- CANR-5
Earlier sketch in CA 9-12R
Hawker, Robert Stephen 1803-1875 DLB 32
See also RGEL 2
Hawkes, (Charles Francis) Christopher 1905-
Brief entry 105
Hawkes, David 1964- 221
Hawkes, Delmar
See Elman, Richard (Martin)
Hawkes, G(ary) W(arren) 1953- CANR-94
Earlier sketch in CA 138
Hawkes, Glenn R(ogers) 1919- 17-20R
Hawkes, J(ohn) G(regory) 1915- 135
Hawkes, (Jessie) Jacquetta (Hopkins)
1910-1996 CANR-15
Obituary 151
Earlier sketch in CA 69-72
Hawkes, John (Clendennin Burne, Jr.)
1925-1998 CANR-64
Obituary 167
Earlier sketches in CA 1-4R, CANR-2, 47
See also BPFB 2
See also CLC 1, 2, 3, 4, 7, 9, 14, 15, 27, 49
See also CN 1, 2, 3, 4, 5, 6
See also DLB 2, 7, 227
See also DLBY 1980, 1998
See also EWL 3
See also MAL 5
See also MTCW 1, 2
See also MTFW 2005
See also RGAL 4
Hawkes, Judith 1949- 132
Hawkes, Kevin (Cliff) 1959- CANR-123
Earlier sketch in CA 135
See also MAICYA 2
See also MAICYAS 1
See also SATA 78, 150
Hawkes, Nigel 1943- 190
See also MAICYA 2
See also SATA 119
Hawkes, Robert E(rnest) 1930- 113
Hawkes, Terence 1932- 17-20R
Hawkesworth, (Elizabeth) Celia 1942- 121
Hawkesworth, Eric 1921- 29-32R
See also SATA 13
Hawkesworth, John 1720-1773 DLB 142
Hawking, S. W.
See Hawking, Stephen W(illiam)
Hawking, Stephen W(illiam) 1942- CANR-115
Brief entry 126
Earlier sketches in CA 129, CANR-48
See also AAYA 13
See also BEST 89:1
See also CLC 63, 105
See also CPW
See also DA3
See also MTCW 2
See also MTFW 2005
Hawkins, Alexander Desmond
See Hawkins, (Alec) Desmond
Hawkins, Angus 1953- 126
Hawkins, Anne Hunsaker 1944- CANR-96
Earlier sketch in CA 142
Hawkins, Anthony Hope
See Hope, Anthony
Hawkins, Arthur 1903-1985 CANR-8
Earlier sketch in CA 21-24R
See also SATA 19
Hawkins, Bradford A(lan) 1952- 151
Hawkins, Brett W(illiam) 1937- CANR-11
Earlier sketch in CA 21-24R
Hawkins, Colin 1945- 184
See also SATA 112, 162
Hawkins, (Alec) Desmond
1908-1999 CANR-9
Obituary 179
Earlier sketch in CA 65-68
Hawkins, Edward H. 1934- 85-88
Hawkins, Erick 1909-1994 205
Hawkins, Frances P(ockman) 1913- 105
Hawkins, Gary J(ames) 1937- 115
Hawkins, Gerald S(tanley) 1928-2003 17-20R
Obituary 217
Hawkins, Gordon 1919- 41-44R
Hawkins, Harriett B(loker) 1934-1995 184
Brief entry 112
Hawkins, Hugh (Dodge) 1929- CANR-57
Earlier sketches in CA 1-4R, CANR-31
Hawkins, Hunt 1943- 148

Hawkins, Jack
See Hawkins, John Edward
Hawkins, Jacqui 184
See also SATA 112, 162
Hawkins, Jim 1944- 73-76
Hawkins, John 1719-1789 .... DLB 104, 142
Hawkins, John C(harles) 1948- 106
Hawkins, John Edward 1910-1973 120
Obituary 111
Hawkins, John Noel 1944- CANR-8
Earlier sketch in CA 61-64
Hawkins, John P. 1946- 120
Hawkins, Joyce M(ary) 1928- 128
Hawkins, Laura 1951- .... SATA 74
Hawkins, Odie 1937- 57-60
Hawkins, Peter S(tephen) 1945- CANR-116
Earlier sketch in CA 110
Hawkins, (Helena Ann) Quail
1905-2002 .... 17-20R
Obituary 212
See also SATA 6
See also SATA-Obit 141
Hawkins, Regina Trice 1938- 165
Hawkins, Richard (Anthony James) 1938- .. 129
Hawkins, Robert 1923- CANR-14
Earlier sketch in CA 21-24R
Hawkins, Robert O(usley), Jr. 1938- 117
Hawkins, W(alter) Lincoln 1911-1992 159
See also BW 3
Hawkins, Walter Everette 1883-(?) 174
See also BW 3
See also DLB 50
Hawkins, William (Waller) 1912- 1-4R
Hawkinson, John (Samuel) 1912-1994 .. 21-24R
See also SATA 4
Hawkinson, Lucy (Ozone) 1924-1971 103
See also SATA 21
Hawks, Howard (Winchester) 1896-1977 ... 161
Obituary 73-76
See also AAYA 67
Hawks, Kate
See Godwin, Parke
Hawks, Robert 1961- 151
See also BYA 8
See also SATA 85
Hawksworth, Henry D. 1933- 73-76
Hawkwood, Allan
See Bedford-Jones, H(enry James O'Brien)
Hawley, Amos H(enry) 1910- 37-40R
Hawley, Beatrice
See Jagel, Beatrice Hawley
Hawley, Cameron 1905-1969 .... 1-4R
Obituary 25-28R
Hawley, Donald Frederick 1921- 108
Hawley, Donald Thomas 1923- CANR-11
Earlier sketch in CA 65-68
Hawley, Ellen 1947- 171
Hawley, Ellis W. 1929- CANR-7
Earlier sketch in CA 17-20R
Hawley, Florence M.
See Ellis, Florence Hawley
Hawley, Gessner G. 1906(?)-1983
Obituary 110
Hawley, Henrietta Ripperger 1890(?)-1974
Obituary 49-52
Hawley, Isabel (Allen) L(ockwood)
1935- CANR-7
Earlier sketch in CA 57-60
Hawley, Jane Stouder 1936- 21-24R
Hawley, John C(harles) 1947- 167
Hawley, John Stratton 1941- CANR-58
Earlier sketch in CA 110
Hawley, Mabel C. CANR-26
Earlier sketches in CAP-2, CA 19-20
See also SATA 1, 67
Hawley, Noah 1967(?)- 235
Hawley, Richard A. 1945- 123
Hawley, Robert C(oit) 1933- CANR-46
Earlier sketches in CA 57-60, CANR-7, 22
Hawley, T. M. 1953- 140
Hawley, Willis D(avid) 1938- 114
Haworth, Don 1924- CANR-60
Earlier sketch in CA 128
Haworth, Lawrence 1926- 5-8R
Haworth, Mary
See Young, Mary Elizabeth Reardon
Haworth, Walter (Norman) 1883-1950 159
Haworth-Booth, Mark 1944- CANR-112
Earlier sketches in CA 124, CANR-52
Haworth-Booth, Michael 1896-1999 .... 5-8R
Haws, Duncan 1921- 97-100
Hawthorn, Jeremy 1942- 97-100
Hawthorne, Captain R. M.
See Ellis, Edward S(ylvester)
Hawthorne, Douglas B(ruce) 1948- 143
Hawthorne, (Ivy Ellen) Jennie Crawley
1916- CAP-1
Earlier sketch in CA 9-10
Hawthorne, Julian 1846-1934 165
See also HGG
See also TCLC 25
Hawthorne, Nathaniel 1804-1864 ...... AAYA 18
See also AMW
See also AMWC 1
See also AMWR 1
See also BPFB 2
See also BYA 3
See also CDALB 1640-1865
See also CLR 103
See also DA
See also DA3
See also DAB
See also DAC
See also DAM MST, NOV
See also DLB 1, 74, 183, 223, 269
See also EXPN
See also EXPS
See also GL 2
See also HGG
See also LAIT 1
See also NFS 1, 20
See also RGAL 4
See also RGSF 2
See also SSC 3, 29, 39
See also SSFS 1, 7, 11, 15
See also SUFW 1
See also TUS
See also WCH
See also WLC
See also YABC 2
Hawthorne, Rainey
See Riddell, Charlotte
Hawthorne, Sophia Peabody
1809-1871 ....DLB 183, 239
Hawton, Hector 1901-1975 .... 13-16R
Haxton, Brooks 1950- 217
Haxton, Josephine Ayres 1921- CANR-83
Earlier sketches in CA 115, CANR-41
See also Douglas, Ellen
Hay, Ashley 1971- 207
Hay, David M(cKechnie) 1935- 53-56
Hay, Deborah 1941- 205
Hay, Dennis 1952- 105
Hay, Denys 1915-1994 .... 13-16R
Obituary 146
Hay, Elizabeth (Jean) 1936- 131
Hay, Elizabeth 1951- 219
Hay, Eloise K(napp) 1926- 9-12R
Hay, George Campbell 1915-1984 .... CP 1
Hay, Jacob 1920-1976 .... 25-28R
Hay, James G(ordon) 1936- CANR-4
Earlier sketch in CA 53-56
Hay, Jeff T. 229
See also SATA 154
Hay, John (Milton) 1838-1905 179
Brief entry 108
See also DLB 12, 47, 189
Hay, John 1915- CANR-9
Earlier sketch in CA 65-68
See also ANW
See also DLB 275
See also RGAL 4
See also SATA 13
Hay, Leon Edwards 25-28R
Hay, Melba Porter 1949- 133
Hay, Millicent V. 1945- CANR-97
Earlier sketch in CA 128
Hay, Peter 1935- 21-24R
Hay, Robert D(ean) 1921- CANR-8
Earlier sketch in CA 61-64
Hay, Samuel A. 1937- 193
Hay, Sara Henderson 1906-1987 .... CAP-1
Obituary 123
Earlier sketch in CA 13-16
See also AMWS 14
Hay, Stephen N(orthup) 1925- 5-8R
Hay, Thomas Robson 1888-1974
Obituary 49-52
Hay, Timothy
See Brown, Margaret Wise
Hay, Vicky
See Hay, Millicent V.
Hay, Victoria
See Hay, Millicent V.
Haya de la Torre, Victor Raul 1895-1979
Obituary 89-92
Hayakawa, S(amuel) I(chiye)
1906-1992 .... CANR-83
Obituary 137
Earlier sketches in CA 13-16R, CANR-20
Hayami, Yujiro 1932- 77-80
Hayano, David M(amoru) 1942- 115
Hayasaka, Fumio 1914-1955 .... IDFW 3, 4
Hayaseca y Eizaguirre, Jorge
See Echegaray (y Eizaguirre), Jose (Maria Waldo)
Hayashi, Chikio 1918- 175
Hayashi, Fumiko 1904-1951 161
See also Hayashi Fumiko
See also TCLC 27
Hayashi, Kyoko 1930- .... MJW
Hayashi, Leslie Ann 1954- 186
See also SATA 115
Hayashi, Nancy 1939- 147
See also SATA 80
Hayashi, Tetsumaro 1929- CANR-14
Earlier sketch in CA 37-40R
Hayashi Fumiko
See Hayashi, Fumiko
See also DLB 180
See also EWL 3
Haycock, Kate 1962- 145
See also SATA 77
Haycock, Ken(neth) Roy 1948- 104
Haycock, Ronald G. 1942- 123
Haycox, Ernest 1899-1950 .... BPFB 2
See also DLB 206
See also TCWW 1, 2
Haycraft, Anna (Margaret)
1932-2005 .... CANR-141
Obituary 237
Earlier sketches in CA 122, CANR-90
See also Ellis, Alice Thomas
See also MTCW 2
See also MTFW 2005
Haycraft, Howard 1905-1991 .... 21-24R
Obituary 136
See also SATA 6
See also SATA-Obit 70
Haycraft, John (Stacpoole) 1926-1996 133
Obituary 152
Haycraft, Molly Costain 1911- 13-16R
See also SATA 6
Haydari, Buland al- 1926- .... CWW 2
Hayden, Albert A(rthur) 1923- 33-36R
Hayden, Barbara
See Carleton, Barbara
Hayden, Brian (Douglas) 1946- CANR-91
Earlier sketch in CA 145
Hayden, C. Gervin
See Wicker, Randolfe Hayden
Hayden, C. J. 1956- 216
Hayden, Carl T(rumbull) 1877-1972
Obituary 33-36R
Hayden, Dolores 1945- CANR-108
Earlier sketches in CA 65-68, CANR-9
Hayden, Donald E(ugene) 1915- CANR-10
Earlier sketch in CA 25-28R
Hayden, Elsie 1949- 229
Hayden, Eric W(illiam) 1919- CANR-2
Earlier sketch in CA 5-8R
Hayden, G. Miki 1944- 215
Hayden, Gwendolen Lampshire
1904- .... SATA 35
Hayden, Howard K. 1930- 17-20R
Hayden, Jay
See Paine, Lauran (Bosworth)
Hayden, Jay G. 1884-1971
Obituary 89-92
Hayden, John O(lin) 1932- CANR-10
Earlier sketch in CA 25-28R
Hayden, Julia Elizabeth 1939(?)-1981
Obituary 104
Hayden, Julie
See Hayden, Julia Elizabeth
Hayden, L. C.
See Hayden, Elsie
Hayden, Martin S(choll) 1912-1991 69-72
Hayden, (Holden) Mike 1920-1984 120
Hayden, Naura 1942- CANR-12
Earlier sketch in CA 73-76
Hayden, Patrick Nielsen
See Nielsen Hayden, Patrick (James)
Hayden, Robert C(arter), Jr. 1937- CANR-24
Earlier sketch in CA 69-72
See also BW 1
See also SATA 47
See also SATA-Brief 28
Hayden, Robert E(arl) 1913-1980 ..... CANR-82
Obituary 97-100
Earlier sketches in CA 69-72, CANR-24, 75
See also CABS 2
See also AFAW 1, 2
See also AMWS 2
See also BLC 2
See also BW 1, 3
See also CDALB 1941-1968
See also CLC 5, 9, 14, 37
See also CP 1, 2
See also DA
See also DAC
See also DAM MST, MULT, POET
See also DLB 5, 76
See also EWL 3
See also EXPP
See also MAL 5
See also MTCW 1, 2
See also PC 6
See also PFS 1
See also RGAL 4
See also SATA 19
See also SATA-Obit 26
See also WP
Hayden, Sterling 1916-1986 111
Obituary 119
Hayden, Stirling
See Hayden, Sterling
Hayden, Thomas E(mmet) 1939- CANR-113
Earlier sketches in CA 107, CANR-41
Hayden, Tom
See Hayden, Thomas E(mmet)
Hayden, Torey L(ynn) 1951- CANR-82
Earlier sketches in CA 103, CANR-35
See also SATA 65, 163
Haydn, Hiram 1907-1973 .... CAP-1
Obituary 45-48
Earlier sketch in CA 9-10
See also CN 1
Haydn, Richard 1905-1985
Obituary 115
Haydon, A(lbert) Eustace 1880-1975
Obituary 61-64
Haydon, Benjamin Robert
1786-1846 .... DLB 110
Haydon, Elizabeth 199
See also AAYA 46
Haydon, Glen 1896-1966 .... CAP-1
Earlier sketch in CA 9-10
Haydon, June 1932- 109
Haydon, Roger (Malcolm) 1950- 118
Hayek, F(riedrich) A(ugust von)
1899-1992 .... CANR-20
Obituary 137
Earlier sketch in CA 93-96
See also MTCW 1, 2
See also TCLC 109
Hayes, Alden C(ary) 1916- 57-60
Hayes, Alfred 1911-1985 106
Obituary 117
Interview in CA-106
See also MAL 5
Hayes, Ann L(ouise) 1924- 25-28R
Hayes, Anna Hansen 1886-1987 .... 1-4R
Hayes, Bartlett (Harding, Jr.) 1904-1988 .. 77-80
Obituary 124
Hayes, Billy 97-100
Hayes, Carlton J(oseph) H(untley)
1882-1964 .... CANR-3
Earlier sketch in CA 1-4R
See also SATA 11
Hayes, Christopher L. 1958- 142
Hayes, Dade 238
Hayes, Daniel 1952- CANR-128
Earlier sketch in CA 173
See also AAYA 29
See also SATA 73, 109
Hayes, Denis A(llen) 1944- 132
Hayes, (Robert) Dennis 1952- 130
Hayes, Dorsha 1897(?)-1990 77-80
Obituary 133
Hayes, Douglas A(nderson) 1918- CANR-18
Earlier sketch in CA 1-4R
Hayes, E(ugene) Nelson 1920- 29-32R
Hayes, Edward C(ary) 1937- CANR-35
Earlier sketch in CA 45-48
Hayes, Edward L(ee) 1931- 29-32R
Hayes, Elizabeth T. 181
Hayes, Ellen (Amanda) 1851-1930 170
Hayes, Elvin 1945- 209
Brief entry 111
Hayes, Evelyn
See Bethell, Mary Ursula
Hayes, Francis Clement 1904-1990 ...... CAP-2
Earlier sketch in CA 21-22
Hayes, Geoffrey 1947- CANR-57
Earlier sketches in CA 65-68, CANR-9, 25
See also SATA 26, 91
Hayes, Grace Person 1919- 33-36R
Hayes, Harold T(homas) P(ace)
1926-1989 .... CANR-22
Obituary 128
Earlier sketch in CA 69-72
Hayes, Helen 1900-1993 138
Obituary 140
Hayes, Hunter 1970- 220
Hayes, J. (M.) 1944- 198
Hayes, James T(homas) 1923- 29-32R
Hayes, Joe 1945- 152
See also SATA 88, 131
Hayes, John F. 1904-1980 .... CANR-84
Earlier sketches in CAP-1, CA 13-14
See also CWRI 5
See also SATA 11
Hayes, John H(aralson) 1934- CANR-21
Earlier sketch in CA 69-72
Hayes, John Michael 1919- 108
Interview in CA-108
See also DLB 26
See also IDFW 3, 4
Hayes, John P(hillip) 1949- CANR-100
Earlier sketches in CA 93-96, CANR-15
Hayes, John R(ichard) 1929- 108
Hayes, John S. 1910-1981
Obituary 108
Hayes, Joseph 1918- CANR-84
Earlier sketches in CA 17-20R, CANR-7, 30
See also CN 1, 2
See also DFS 20
Hayes, Judith 1945- 194
Hayes, Kevin J(on) 1959- 192
Hayes, Louis D. 1940- 29-32R
Hayes, Margaret 1925- 21-24R
Hayes, Mary Anne 1956- 105
Hayes, Mary-Rose 1939- 102
Hayes, N.
See DeVincentes-Hayes, Nan
Hayes, Nan
See DeVincentes-Hayes, Nan
Hayes, Nelson (Taylor) 1903-1971 .... 1-4R
Obituary 33-36R
Hayes, Paul J(ames) 1922- 57-60
Hayes, Paul Martin 1942- 77-80
Hayes, Penny 1940- CANR-98
Earlier sketches in CA 121, CANR-47
Hayes, Ralph E(ugene) 1927- CANR-15
Earlier sketch in CA 21-24R
Hayes, Robert M(ayo) 1926- 9-12R
Hayes, Roger S(tanley) 1947- 195
Hayes, Rosemary 234
See also SATA 158
Hayes, Samuel P(erkins) 1910- CANR-3
Earlier sketch in CA 5-8R
Hayes, Sheila 1937- CANR-45
Earlier sketches in CA 106, CANR-22
See also SATA 51
See also SATA-Brief 50
Hayes, Steven C(harles) 1948- CANR-31
Earlier sketch in CA 112
Hayes, Terrance 1971- 197
Hayes, Timothy
See Rubel, James Lyon
Hayes, W. Woodrow
See Hayes, Wayne Woodrow
Hayes, Wayland J(ackson) 1893-1972 ... CAP-1
Earlier sketch in CA 13-14
Hayes, Wayne Woodrow 1913-1987
Obituary 121

Cumulative Index 257 **Healey**

Hayes, Will ... 5-8R
See also SATA 7
Hayes, William D(imitt) 1913-1976 ... 5-8R
See also SATA 8
Hayes, Wilson
See Gibbs-Wilson, Kathryn (Beatrice)
Hayes, Woody
See Hayes, Wayne Woodrow
Hayes, Zachary (Jerome) 1932- ... CANR-39
Earlier sketch in CA 115
Hayflick, Leonard 1928- ... 148
Hayford, Charles W. 1941- ... 136
Hayford, Fred Kwesi 1937- ... 45-48
Hayford, Harrison (Mosher) 1916-2001 ... 118
Obituary ... 203
Hayford, J(oseph) E(phraim) Casely
See Casely-Hayford, J(oseph) E(phraim)
Hayford, Jack W. 1934- ... 206
Hayford, Taria
See Haydon, June
Haygood, Johnnie 1924- ... 167
See also BW 3
Haygood, Wil 1954- ... CANR-137
Earlier sketch in CA 142
See also BW 2
Hayles, Marsha ... 174
Hayles, N. Katherine 1943- ... 197
Hayley, Barbara 1938- ... 131
Hayley, William 1745-1820 ... DLB 93, 142
Hayley Bell, Mary ... 25-28R
Haylock, John (Mervyn) 1918- ... CANR-82
Earlier sketch in CA 133
Haym, Rudolf 1821-1901 ... DLB 129
Hayman
See Peel, H(azel) M(ary)
Hayman, Carol Bessent 1927- ... 53-56
Hayman, David 1927- ... CANR-7
Earlier sketch in CA 17-20R
Hayman, John L(uther), Jr. 1929- ... 25-28R
Hayman, LeRoy 1916- ... 85-88
Hayman, Max 1908-2000 ... 17-20R
Hayman, Richard 1959- ... 165
Hayman, Robert 1575-1629 ... DLB 99
Hayman, Ronald 1932- ... CANR-88
Earlier sketches in CA 25-28R, CANR-18, 50
See also CD 5, 6
See also CLC 44
See also DLB 155
Haymes, Robert C. 1931- ... 33-36R
Haymon, S. T.
See Haymon, Sylvia (Theresa)
Haymon, Sylvia (Theresa)
1918(?)-1995 ... CANR-62
Brief entry ... 127
Earlier sketch in CA 131
See also CMW 4
Hayn, Annette 1922- ... 65-68
Haynal, Andre (Emeric) 1930- ... 120
Hayne, Paul Hamilton 1830-1886 .. DLB 3, 64, 79, 248
See also RGAL 4
Haynes, Alfred H(enry) 1910- ... 5-8R
Haynes, Anne
See Madlee, Dorothy (Haynes)
Haynes, Betsy 1937- ... CANR-67
Earlier sketches in CA 57-60, CANR-8
See also CLR 90
See also SATA 48, 94
See also SATA-Brief 37
Haynes, Brian 1939- ... 111
Haynes, C. Rayfield 1943- ... 145
Haynes, Cynthia 1952- ... 184
Haynes, David 1955- ... 154
See also SATA 97
Haynes, Duncan H(arold) 1945- ... 216
Haynes, Gary (Anthony) 1948- ... 143
Haynes, Glynn W(alker) 1936- ... 65-68
Haynes, James 1932- ... 110
Haynes, James Almand 1933- ... 131
Haynes, Jim
See Haynes, James Almand
Haynes, John Earl 1944- ... CANR-125
Earlier sketches in CA 143, CANR-70
Haynes, Jonathan 1952- ... 146
Haynes, Lincoln 1924- ... 116
Haynes, Linda
See Swinford, Betty (June Wells)
Haynes, Maria S(chnee) 1912-1998 ... 25-28R
Haynes, Mary 1938- ... CANR-35
Earlier sketch in CA 111
See also SATA 65
Haynes, Max 1956- ... SATA 72
Haynes, Melinda 1955- ... 203
Haynes, Pat
See McKeag, Ernest L(ionel)
Haynes, Renee (Oriana Tickell)
1906-1992 ... CANR-34
Obituary ... 139
Earlier sketch in CA 49-52
Haynes, Richard F(rederick) 1935- ... 49-52
Haynes, Robert Talmadge, Jr. 1926- ... 1-4R
Haynes, Robert Vaughn 1929- ... 41-44R
Haynes, Sybille 1926- ... 57-60
Haynes, Todd 1961- ... 220
Haynes, W. P.
See Waddington, Patrick (Haynes)
Haynes, William Warren 1921- ... CANR-8
Earlier sketch in CA 5-8R
Haynie, Barbara 1947- ... 227
Haynie, Hugh 1927-1999 ... 121
Obituary ... 186
Haynie, Sandra (B.) 1943- ... 186
Brief entry ... 121
Haynsworth, Leslie 1966- ... 170
Hays, (Lawrence) Brooks 1898-1981 ... CAP-1
Obituary ... 105
Earlier sketch in CA 11-12
Hays, Clark 1966- ... 182
Hays, Constance L. ... 232
Hays, Daniel 1960- ... CANR-139
Earlier sketch in CA 154
Hays, David G(lenn) 1928-1995 ... CANR-14
Obituary ... 149
Earlier sketch in CA 21-24R
Hays, Donald 1947- ... 132
Hays, Elinor Rice -1994 ... 1-4R
Obituary ... 144
Hays, H(offmann) R(eynolds)
1904-1980 ... CANR-31
Obituary ... 105
Earlier sketch in CA 81-84
See also CP 1, 2
See also SATA 26
Hays, Helen Ireland 1903- ... 61-64
Hays, Kelley Ann 1960- ... 142
Hays, Mary 1760-1843 ... DLB 142, 158
See also RGEL 2
Hays, Paul R. 1903-1980 ... CAP-2
Obituary ... 93-96
Earlier sketch in CA 19-20
Hays, Peter L. 1938- ... CANR-138
Earlier sketches in CA 33-36R, CANR-72
Hays, R. Vernon 1902-1985 ... 89-92
Hays, Richard D. 1942- ... 37-40R
Hays, Robert Glenn 1935- ... 53-56
Hays, Samuel Pfrimmer 1921- ... 103
Hays, Terence E(ugene) 1942- ... 69-72
Hays, Thomas Anthony 1957- ... CANR-117
Earlier sketch in CA 150
See also SATA 84
Hays, Tommy ... 227
Hays, Tony
See Hays, Thomas Anthony
Hays, Wilma Pitchford 1909- ... CANR-45
Earlier sketches in CA 1-4R, CANR-5
See also CLR 59
See also MAICYA 1, 2
See also SAAS 3
See also SATA 1, 28
Hayslip, Le Ly 1949- ... 145
See also DLB 312
Haystead, Wes
See Haystead, Wesley
Haystead, Wesley 1942- ... CANR-45
Earlier sketches in CA 57-60, CANR-6, 22
Hayter, Adrian (Goodenough) 1914-1990
Obituary ... 131
Hayter, Alethea (Catharine) 1911- ... 29-32R
Hayter, Earl W(iley) 1901-1994 ... 41-44R
Obituary ... 145
Hayter, Sparkle (Lynnette) 1958- ... 186
Hayter, Stanley William 1901-1988
Obituary ... 125
Hayter, William Goodenough
1906-1995 ... CANR-9
Obituary ... 148
Earlier sketch in CA 21-24R
Haythe, Justin 1973- ... 228
Haythornthwaite, Philip John 1951- . CANR-42
Earlier sketches in CA 103, CANR-19
Hayton, Richard Neil 1916- ... 57-60
Hayward, Brooke 1937- ... 81-84
Hayward, Charles H(arold) 1898- ... CANR-7
Earlier sketch in CA 9-12R
Hayward, Douglas J. J. 1940- ... 195
Hayward, Jack 1931- ... CANR-44
Earlier sketches in CA 57-60, CANR-6, 21
Hayward, Jennifer (Poole) 1961- ... 168
Hayward, Joel S. A. ... 209
Hayward, John (Davy) 1905-1965 ... 181
See also DLB 201
Hayward, John F(orrest) 1916-1983 ... 9-12R
Obituary ... 109
Hayward, John F(rank) 1918- ... 5-8R
Hayward, Linda 1943- ... 112
See also SATA 101
See also SATA-Brief 39
Hayward, Max 1925(?)-1979 ... 93-96
Obituary ... 85-88
Hayward, Philip 1956- ... 146
Hayward, Richard
See Kendrick, Baynard H(ardwick)
Hayward, Richard 1893-1964 ... CAP-1
Earlier sketch in CA 9-10
Hayward, Stephen 1954- ... 133
Hayward, Steven F(redric) 1958- ... 212
Haywood, C. Robert 1921- ... 137
Haywood, Carolyn 1898-1990 ... CANR-83
Obituary ... 130
Earlier sketches in CA 5-8R, CANR-5, 20
See also CLR 22
See also CWRI 5
See also MAICYA 1, 2
See also SATA 1, 29, 75
See also SATA-Obit 64
Haywood, Charles 1904-2000 ... CANR-22
Earlier sketch in CA 1-4R
Haywood, Dixie 1933- ... CANR-142
Earlier sketch in CA 105
Haywood, Eliza (Fowler) 1693(?)-1756 . DLB 39
See also RGEL 2
Haywood, Gar Anthony 1954- ... 167
See also BW 3
Haywood, H(erbert) Carl(ton) 1931- ... CANR-3
Earlier sketch in CA 49-52
Haywood, Harry
See Hall, Haywood
Haywood, John Alfred 1913- ... 17-20R
Haywood, Kathleen M. 1950- ... 216
Haywood, Melanio
See Murphey, Cecil B(laine)
Haywood, Richard Mansfield
1905-1977 ... CAP-2
Obituary ... 69-72
Earlier sketch in CA 33-36
Haywood, Richard Mowbray 1933- ... 25-28R
Haywood, Stephen Patrick 1949- ... 138
Haywood, Steve
See Haywood, Stephen Patrick
Haywood, William D(udley)
1869-1928 ... DLB 303
Hazam, Louis J. 1911-1983
Obituary ... 110
Hazan, Marcella (Maddalena)
1924- ... CANR-71
Brief entry ... 116
Earlier sketch in CA 128
Hazan, Victor 1928- ... 114
Hazard, Ann 1952- ... 163
Hazard, David 1955- ... 116
Hazard, Harry W(illiams) 1918- ... 122
Hazard, Jack
See Booth, Edwin
Hazard, John N(ewbold)
1909-1995 ... CANR-31
Obituary ... 148
Earlier sketch in CA 1-4R
Hazard, Leland 1893-1980 ... 17-20R
Obituary ... 133
Hazard, Mary E. ... 198
Hazard, Patrick D. 1927- ... 13-16R
Hazareesingh, Sudhir ... 209
Hazel, Dann 1954- ... 194
Hazel, (E.) Paul 1944- ... CANR-84
Earlier sketch in CA 114
See also FANT
Hazelden, John
See Ade, George
Hazelgrove, William E(lliot III) 1959- ... 138
Hazell, Rebecca (Eileen) 1947- ... 212
See also SATA 141
Hazelrigg, Meredith K(ent) 1942- ... 33-36R
Hazelton, Alexander
See Armstrong, William A(lexander)
Hazelton, Fran 1947- ... 150
Hazelton, Roger 1909-1988 ... CANR-16
Earlier sketches in CA 1-4R, CANR-1
Hazelwood, Robert R. ... 225
Hazelwood, Roy
See Hazelwood, Robert R.
Hazen, Allen T(racy) 1904-1977 ... CAP-1
Earlier sketch in CA 13-14
Hazen, Barbara Shook 1930- ... CANR-46
Earlier sketches in CA 105, CANR-22
See also SATA 27, 90
Hazen, Helen 1943- ... 116
Hazen, Margaret Hindle 1948- ... 126
Hazen, Robert M(iller) 1948- ... 112
Hazlehurst, Cameron 1941- ... 103
Hazleton, Lesley 1945- ... 128
Brief entry ... 126
Hazlett, Bill
See Hazlett, William Scott
Hazlett, William Scott 1931-1983
Obituary ... 110
Hazlitt, Henry 1894-1993 ... CANR-48
Obituary ... 141
Earlier sketches in CA 5-8R, CANR-3
Hazlitt, Joseph
See Strage, Mark
Hazlitt, William 1778-1830 ... BRW 4
See also DLB 110, 158
See also RGEL 2
See also TEA
Hazo, Robert G. 1931- ... 21-24R
Hazo, Samuel (John) 1928- ... CANR-58
Earlier sketches in CA 5-8R, CANR-8, 31
See also CAAS 11
See also CP 1, 2, 3, 4, 5, 6, 7
Hazuka, Tom 1956- ... 235
Hazzard, Dorothy M. 1935- ... 179
Hazzard, Lowell B(restel) 1898-1978
Obituary ... 77-80
Hazzard, Mary 1928- ... CANR-96
Earlier sketches in CA 105, CANR-46
Hazzard, Shirley 1931- ... CANR-127
Earlier sketches in CA 9-12R, CANR-4, 70
See also CLC 18
See also CN 1, 2, 3, 4, 5, 6, 7
See also DLB 289
See also DLBY 1982
See also MTCW 1
H'Doubler, Margaret (Newell) 1889-1982 .. 206
Heacox, Cecil E. 1903-1992 ... 101
Heacox, Kim 1951- ... 137
Head, Alice Maud 1886-1981
Obituary ... 116
Head, Ann
See Morse, Anne Christensen
Head, Bessie 1937-1986 ... CANR-82
Obituary ... 119
Earlier sketches in CA 29-32R, CANR-25
See also AFW
See also BLC 2
See also BW 2, 3
See also CDWLB 3
See also CLC 25, 67
See also CN 1, 2, 3, 4
See also DA3
See also DAM MULT
See also DLB 117, 225
See also EWL 3
See also EXPS
See also FL 1:6
See also FW
See also MTCW 1, 2
See also MTFW 2005
See also RGSF 2
See also SSC 52
See also SSFS 5, 13
See also WLIT 2
See also WWE 1
Head, Constance 1939- ... 37-40R
Head, David M. 1951- ... 158
Head, Dominic 1962- ... CANR-92
Earlier sketch in CA 145
Head, Edith 1898(?)-1981
Obituary ... 105
See also IDFW 3, 4
Head, Gay
See Hauser, Margaret L(ouise)
Head, Gwen 1940- ... 89-92
Head, K(enneth) Maynard 1938- ... 110
Head, (Joanne) Lee 1931-1983 ... 65-68
Obituary ... 110
Head, Matthew
See Canaday, John E(dwin)
Head, Raymond (Victor) 1948- ... 136
Head, Richard G(lenn) 1938- ... CANR-35
Earlier sketch in CA 53-56
Head, Robert V. 1929-2003 ... CANR-15
Obituary ... 213
Earlier sketch in CA 41-44R
Head, Sydney W(arren) 1913-1991 ... CANR-9
Earlier sketch in CA 65-68
Head, Timothy E. 1934- ... 13-16R
Head, William P(ace) 1949- ... 181
Headapohl, B. R.
See Headapohl, Betty R.
Headapohl, Betty R. 1940- ... 122
Headings, Mildred J(ean) 1908-1982 ... 37-40R
Headington, Bonnie Jay 1940- ... 114
Headington, Christopher (John Magenis)
1930-1996 ... 165
Obituary ... 151
Brief entry ... 106
Headlam, Catherine 1960- ... 139
Headley, Bernard D. ... 231
Headley, Elizabeth
See Harrison, Elizabeth (Allen) Cavanna
Headley, Gwyn 1946- ... 125
Headley, J. T.
See Headley, Joel Tyler
See also DLBD 13
Headley, Joel T.
See Headley, Joel Tyler
See also DLB 30
Headley, Joel Tyler 1813-1897
See Headley, Joel T.
See also DLB 183
Headley, John M. 1929- ... CANR-89
Earlier sketch in CA 130
Headley, Victor 1960- ... 146
Headmess, Violet ... 175
Headon, (Nicky) Topper 1956(?)- ... CLC 30
Headrick, Daniel R. 1941- ... CANR-91
Earlier sketch in CA 145
Headstrom, (Birger) Richard
1902-1985 ... CANR-13
Earlier sketches in CA 1-4R, CANR-2
See also SATA 8
Heady, Earl O(rel) 1916-1987 ... CANR-8
Earlier sketch in CA 17-20R
Heady, Eleanor B(utler) 1917-1979 .. CANR-31
Earlier sketch in CA 41-44R
See also SATA 8
Heady, Harold F(ranklin) 1916- ... CANR-31
Earlier sketch in CA 53-56
Heagle, John L. ... 218
Heagney, Anne 1901-1987 ... 5-8R
Heagy, William D. 1964- ... SATA 76
Heal, Edith 1903-1995 ... CANR-2
Earlier sketch in CA 1-4R
See also SATA 7
Heal, Geoffrey (M.) 1944- ... 189
Heal, Gillian 1934- ... 149
See also SATA 89
Heal, Jane 1946- ... 132
Heal, Jeanne (Bennett) 1917- ... CAP-1
Earlier sketch in CA 9-10
Heald, Charles Brehmer 1882-1974
Obituary ... 49-52
Heald, Edward Thornton 1885-1967 ... 17-20R
Heald, Gordon 1941- ... 128
Heald, Morrell 1922-
Brief entry ... 111
Heald, Suzette 1943- ... 132
Heald, Tim(othy Villiers) 1944- ... CANR-57
Earlier sketches in CA 49-52, CANR-2, 30
See also CMW 4
Heale, Jay (Jeremy Peter Wingfield)
1937- ... SATA 84
Healey, B. J.
See Healey, Ben (James)
Healey, Ben (James) 1908- ... CANR-85
Earlier sketches in CA 77-80, CANR-17

Healey, Brooks
See Albert, Burton
Healey, Denis Winston 1917- ... 110
Healey, Dorothy (Ray) 1914- ... 138
Healey, F(rancis) G(eorge) 1903-1992 ... CAP-2
Earlier sketch in CA 21-22
Healey, James 1936- ... 53-56
Healey, James Stewart 1931- ... 57-60
Healey, Joseph G(raham) 1938- ... CANR-40
Earlier sketch in CA 116
Healey, Judith Koll ... 234
Healey, Larry 1927- ... 101
See also SATA 44
See also SATA-Brief 42
Healey, Robert (Mathieu) 1921- ... 61-64
Healey-Kay, (Sydney Francis) Patrick (Chippendall) 1904-1983
Obituary ... 111
Healy, Ann Marie 1974- ... 228
Healy, David ... 223
Healy, David F(rank) 1926- ... 17-20R
Healy, Dermot 1947- ... CANR-88
Earlier sketches in CA 114, CANR-53
See also BRWS 9
See also CN 7
Healy, Fleming 1911- ... 5-8R
Healy, George Robert 1923- ... 17-20R
Healy, George W(illiam), Jr. 1905-1980 .. 69-72
Obituary ... 125
Healy, Jeremiah (F. III) 1948- ... 137
See also CMW 4
Healy, John D(elaware) 1921- ... 93-96
Healy, Kent T(enney) 1902-1985
Obituary ... 114
Healy, Patrick III 1910-
Brief entry ... 110
Healy, Paul F(rancis) 1915-1984 ... 17-20R
Obituary ... 114
Healy, Richard J. 1916- ... 25-28R
Healy, Sean D(esmond) 1927- ... CANR-11
Earlier sketch in CA 25-28R
Healy, Sister Kathleen ... 61-64
Healy, Sophia (Warner) 1938- ... 136
Healy, Timothy S(tafford)
1923-1992 ... CANR-46
Obituary ... 140
Earlier sketch in CA 41-44R
Heaney, John J. 1925- ... CANR-5
Earlier sketch in CA 9-12R
Heaney, Marie 1940- ... CANR-144
Earlier sketch in CA 153
Heaney, Seamus (Justin) 1939- ... CANR-128
Earlier sketches in CA 85-88, CANR-25, 48, 75, 91
See also AAYA 61
See also BRWR 1
See also BRWS 2
See also CDBLB 1960 to Present
See also CLC 5, 7, 14, 25, 37, 74, 91, 171
See also CP 1, 2, 3, 4, 5, 6, 7
See also DA3
See also DAB
See also DAM POET
See also DLB 40
See also DLBY 1995
See also EWL 3
See also EXPP
See also MTCW 1, 2
See also MTFW 2005
See also PAB
See also PC 18
See also PFS 2, 5, 8, 17
See also RGEL 2
See also TEA
See also WLCS
See also WLIT 4
Heany, Donald Francis 1918-1990
Obituary ... 132
Heap, Desmond 1907-1998 ... CANR-15
Obituary ... 181
Earlier sketches in CAP-1, CA 9-10
Heap, Sue 1954- ... MAICYA 2
See also SATA 150
Heaps, Willard A(llison) 1908-1987 ... 85-88
See also SATA 26
Heard, (George) Alexander 1917- ... 17-20R
Heard, Anthony Hazlitt 1937- ... 134
Heard, (Henry Fitz) Gerald
1889-1971 ... CANR-72
Obituary ... 29-32R
Earlier sketches in CAP-2, CA 21-22
See also HGG
See also SFW 4
Heard, H. F.
See Heard, (Henry Fitz) Gerald
Heard, J(oseph) Norman 1922- ... 9-12R
Heard, Nathan C(liff) 1936-2004 ... CANR-25
Obituary ... 225
Earlier sketch in CA 53-56
See also BW 1
See also DLB 33
Hearden, Patrick J. 1942- ... 138
Hearder, Harry 1924- ... 5-8R
Hearn, Charles R(alph) 1937- ... 77-80
Hearn, Chester G. 1932- ... CANR-107
Earlier sketch in CA 151
Hearn, Diane Dawson 1952- ... SATA 79
Hearn, Emily
See Valleau, Emily
Hearn, Janice W. 1938- ... 65-68
Hearn, John 1920- ... 97-100
Hearn, Julie ... 227
See also SATA 152
Hearn, (Patricio) Lafcadio (Tessima Carlos)
1850-1904 ... 166
Brief entry ... 105
See also DLB 12, 78, 189
See also HGG
See also MAL 5
See also RGAL 4
See also TCLC 9
Hearn, Lian
See Rubinstein, Gillian (Margaret)
Hearn, M(illard) F(illmore, Jr.) 1938- ... 115
Hearn, Mary Anne 1834-1909 ... 200
See also DLB 240
Hearn, Sneed
See Gregg, Andrew K.
Hearnden, Arthur (George) 1931- ... 65-68
Hearne, Betsy Gould 1942- ... CANR-127
Earlier sketches in CA 114, CANR-35, 68
See also SATA 38, 95, 146
Hearne, John (Edgar Caulwell)
1926-1995 ... CANR-81
Brief entry ... 116
Earlier sketch in CA 125
See also BW 1, 3
See also CN 1, 2, 3, 4, 5
See also DLB 117
See also EWL 3
See also MTCW 1
Hearne, Samuel 1745-1792 ... DLB 99
Hearne, Thomas 1678(?)-1735 ... DLB 213
Hearne, Vicki 1946-2001 ... 139
Obituary ... 201
See also CLC 56
Hearnshaw, Leslie Spencer 1907-1991 ... 89-92
Hearon, Shelby 1931- ... CANR-103
Earlier sketches in CA 25-28R, CANR-18, 48
See also AITN 2
See also AMWS 8
See also CLC 63
See also CSW
Hearsey, John E(dward) N(icholl)
1928- ... CANR-8
Earlier sketch in CA 5-8R
Hearst, David Whitmire 1915-1986
Obituary ... 119
Hearst, George Randolph 1904-1972
Obituary ... 89-92
Hearst, James 1900-1983 ... CANR-15
Earlier sketch in CA 85-88
Hearst, Patricia Campbell 1954- ... 136
Hearst, Patty
See Hearst, Patricia Campbell
Hearst, William Randolph, Jr. 1908-1993 ... 139
See also DLB 127
Hearst, William Randolph 1863-1951 ... 169
Brief entry ... 118
See also DLB 25
Heartman, Charles F(rederick)
1883-1953 ... DLB 187
Heartman, Harold
See Mebane, John (Harrison)
Heasman, Kathleen Joan 1913- ... CAP-1
Earlier sketch in CA 9-10
Heater, Derek (Benjamin) 1931- ... CANR-6
Earlier sketch in CA 57-60
Heath, Catherine 1924-1991 ... CANR-30
Obituary ... 136
Earlier sketch in CA 93-96
See also DLB 14
Heath, Charles C(hastain) 1921- ... 69-72
Heath, Charles D(ickinson) 1941- ... 121
See also SATA 46
Heath, Douglas H(amilton) 1925- ... 17-20R
Heath, Dwight B(raley) 1930- ... CANR-7
Earlier sketch in CA 17-20R
Heath, Edward Richard George
1916-2005 ... 33-36R
Heath, G. Louis 1944- ... 37-40R
Heath, Harry E(ugene), Jr. 1919- ... CANR-28
Earlier sketch in CA 85-88
Heath, (Ernest) James 1920- ... 17-20R
Heath, James Ewell 1792-1862 ... DLB 248
Heath, Jennifer ... 171
Heath, Jim F(rank) 1931- ... 29-32R
Heath, Lester
See Cassiday, Bruce (Bingham)
Heath, Lorraine 1954- ... CANR-123
Earlier sketch in CA 153
Heath, Malcolm (Frederick) 1957- ... 130
Heath, Mary Ellen 1928- ... 115
Heath, Monica
See Fitzgerald, Arlene J.
Heath, (Charles) Monro 1899-1966 ... CAP-1
Earlier sketch in CA 9-10
Heath, Peter (Lauchlan) 1922- ... 41-44R
Heath, Robert L. 1941- ... CANR-53
Earlier sketch in CA 126
Heath, Robert W. 1931- ... 13-16R
Heath, Roy 1917- ... 9-12R
Heath, Roy A(ubrey) K(elvin) 1926- .. CANR-82
Earlier sketches in CA 106, CANR-33, 53
See also BW 2, 3
See also CN 3, 4, 5, 6, 7
See also DLB 117
See also MTCW 1
Heath, Royton E(dward) 1907- ... 9-12R
Heath, Sandra
See Wilson, Sandra
Heath, Sebastian E. 1955- ... 173
Heath, Terrence (George) 1936- ... CANR-36
Earlier sketch in CA 97-100
Heath, Veronica
See Blackett, Veronica Heath
Heath, William (Webster) 1929- ... CANR-31
Earlier sketch in CA 1-4R
Heath, William 1942- ... 234
Heathcott, Mary
See Keegan, Mary Heathcott
Heather
See MacKay, Isabel Ecclestone (Macpherson)
Heath-Stubbs, John (Francis Alexander)
1918- ... CANR-85
Earlier sketches in CA 13-16R, CANR-49
See also CAAS 21
See also CP 1, 2, 3, 4, 5, 6, 7
See also DLB 27
Heat-Moon, William Least
See Trogdon, William (Lewis)
See also AAYA 9
See also CLC 29
Heaton, Charles Huddleston 1928- .. CANR-20
Earlier sketch in CA 1-4R
Heaton, Eric William 1920- ... 61-64
Heaton, Herbert 1890-1973 ... 5-8R
Obituary ... 41-44R
Heaton, Herbert 1919- ... 163
Heaton, Patricia 1958- ... 215
Heaton, Peter 1919- ... 104
Heaton, Rose Henniker 1884-1975
Obituary ... 61-64
Heaton, Thomas Peter Starke 1928- ... 134
Heaton, Tom
See Heaton, Thomas Peter Starke
Heaton-Ward, William Alan 1919- ... 102
Heatter, Gabriel 1890-1972
Obituary ... 89-92
Heaven, Constance (Christina)
1911- ... CANR-84
Earlier sketches in CA 49-52, CANR-2, 18, 40
See also RHW
See also SATA 7
Heavin, Gary 1956(?)- ... 229
Heavysege, Charles 1816-1876 ... DLB 99
Hebald, Carol 1934- ... 200
Hebard, Edna L(aura Henriksen)
1913-1996 ... 9-12R
Hebb, D(onald) O(lding) 1904-1985 .. CANR-2
Obituary ... 118
Earlier sketch in CA 1-4R
Hebbel, Friedrich 1813-1863 ... CDWLB 2
See also DAM DRAM
See also DC 21
See also DLB 129
See also EW 6
See also RGWL 2, 3
Hebbert, Michael 1947- ... 229
Hebblethwaite, Brian Leslie 1939- ... CANR-27
Earlier sketch in CA 109
Hebblethwaite, Margaret 1951- ... CANR-68
Earlier sketch in CA 129
Hebblethwaite, Peter 1930-1994 ... CANR-44
Obituary ... 147
Earlier sketch in CA 69-72
Hebborn, Eric 1934-1996 ... 144
Obituary ... 151
Hebden, Mark
See Harris, John
Hebel, Johann Peter 1760-1826 ... DLB 90
Heber, Richard 1774-1833 ... DLB 184
Heberer, Thomas 1947- ... 135
Hebert, Anne 1916-2000 ... CANR-126
Obituary ... 187
Earlier sketches in CA 85-88, CANR-69
See also CCA 1
See also CLC 4, 13, 29
See also CWP
See also CWW 2
See also DA3
See also DAC
See also DAM MST, POET
See also DLB 68
See also EWL 3
See also GFL 1789 to the Present
See also MTCW 1, 2
See also MTFW 2005
See also PFS 20
Hebert, Ernest 1941- ... CANR-110
Earlier sketch in CA 102
See also CAAS 24
Hebert, F(elix) Edward 1901-1979 ... 110
Obituary ... 106
Hebert, (Arthur) Gabriel 1886-1963 ... 1-4R
Hebert, Jacques 1923- ... CANR-52
Earlier sketches in CA 25-28R, CANR-11, 27
See also DLB 53
Hebert, Tom 1938- ... 69-72
Hebert-Collins, Sheila 1948- ... 182
See also SATA 111
Hebreo, Leon c. 1460-1520 ... DLB 318
Hebson, Ann (Hellebusch) 1925- ... 17-20R
Hechinger, Fred M(ichael) 1920-1995 ... 77-80
Obituary ... 150
Hechinger, Grace (Bernstein) 1931- ... 166
Hechler, David (S.) 1950- ... 127
Hechler, Ken 1914- ... 109
Hecht, Anthony (Evan) 1923-2004 . CANR-108
Obituary ... 232
Earlier sketches in CA 9-12R, CANR-6
See also AMWS 10
See also CLC 8, 13, 19
See also CP 1, 2, 3, 4, 5, 6, 7
See also DAM POET
See also DLB 5, 169
See also EWL 3
See also PFS 6
See also WP
Hecht, Ben 1894-1964 ... 85-88
See also CLC 8
See also DFS 9
See also DLB 7, 9, 25, 26, 28, 86
See also FANT
See also IDFW 3, 4
See also RGAL 4
See also TCLC 101
Hecht, Daniel ... 181
Hecht, George J(oseph) 1895-1980
Obituary ... 97-100
See also SATA-Obit 22
Hecht, Henri Joseph 1922- ... 29-32R
See also SATA 9
Hecht, James L(ee) 1926- ... 33-36R
Hecht, Jeff(rey Charles) 1947- ... CANR-94
Earlier sketches in CA 131, CANR-89
Hecht, Jennifer Michael 1965- ... 227
Hecht, Joseph C. 1924- ... 29-32R
Hecht, Marie B(ergenfeld) 1918- ... 21-24R
Hecht, Michael L. 1949- ... CANR-99
Earlier sketch in CA 145
Hecht, Robert A(nthony) 1929- ... 114
Hecht, Roger 1926- ... 17-20R
Hecht, Warren Jay 1946- ... 103
Hechter, Iosif 1907-1945
See Sebastian, Mihail
Hechter, Michael 1943- ... CANR-108
Earlier sketch in CA 69-72
Hechtkopf, Henryk 1910- ... SATA 17
Hechtlinger, Adelaide 1914-1981 ... 29-32R
Heck, Alfons 1928-2005 ... CANR-130
Obituary ... 238
Earlier sketch in CA 131
Heck, Bessie (Mildred) Holland
1911-1995 ... 5-8R
See also SATA 26
Heck, Frank H(opkins) 1904-1983 ... 69-72
Obituary ... 126
Heck, Harold J(oseph) 1906- ... 41-44R
Heck, Peter J(ewell) ... CANR-137
Earlier sketch in CA 165
Heck, Peter M. 1937- ... 53-56
Heck, Suzanne Wright 1939- ... 53-56
Heckart, Barbara Hooper 1937- ... 118
Heckart, Beverly Anne 1938- ... 103
Heckel, Robert V. 1925- ... 9-12R
Heckelmann, Charles N(ewman)
1913- ... CANR-30
Earlier sketch in CA 49-52
See also TCWW 1, 2
Hecker, Isaac Thomas 1819-1888 .. DLB 1, 243
Heckerling, Amy 1954- ... 139
See also AAYA 22
Heckert, Connie K(aye Delp) 1948- ... 149
See also SATA 82
Heckert, J(osiah) Brooks 1893-1990 ... 5-8R
Heckler, Jonellen (Beth) 1943- ... CANR-41
Earlier sketch in CA 109
Heckman, Hazel 1904- ... 21-24R
Heckman, Robert A. 1965- ... 239
Heckman, William O(scar) 1921- ... 21-24R
Heckmann, Wolf 1929- ... 114
Heckroth, Hein 1897-1970 ... IDFW 3, 4
Heckscher, August 1913-1997 ... CANR-35
Obituary ... 157
Earlier sketch in CA 1-4R
Heckscher, Charles 1949- ... 149
Hedayat, Sadeq 1903-1951
Brief entry ... 120
See also EWL 3
See also RGSF 2
See also TCLC 21
Hedberg, Nancy 1944- ... 122
Hedde, Wilhelmina G(enevava)
1895-1988 ... 5-8R
Hedden, Walter Page 1898(?)-1976
Obituary ... 65-68
Hedden, Worth Tuttle 1896-1985 ... CAP-2
Obituary ... 117
Earlier sketch in CA 21-22
Hedderwick, Mairi 1939- ... CANR-125
Earlier sketches in CA 137, CANR-84
See also CWRI 5
See also MAICYA 1, 2
See also SATA 30, 77, 145
Hederman, Thomas M(artin), Jr. 1911-1985
Obituary ... 114
Hedge, Frederic Henry 1805-1890 .. DLB 1, 59, 243
Hedge, Leslie (Joseph) 1922- ... 9-12R
Hedgecoe, John 1937- ... 159
Hedge Coke, Allison Adelle
See Coke, Allison Adelle Hedge
Hedgeman, Anna Arnold 1899-1990 ... CAP-1
Obituary ... 130
Earlier sketch in CA 13-16
Hedges, Bob A(tkinson) 1919- ... 45-48
Hedges, Chris(topher Lynn) ... 218
Hedges, David (Paget) 1930- ... 45-48
Hedges, Elaine R(yan) 1927-1997 ... CANR-7
Obituary ... 158
Earlier sketch in CA 57-60
Hedges, Inez (Kathleen) 1947- ... 116
Hedges, Joseph
See Harknett, Terry (Williams)
Hedges, Richard (Houston) 1952- ... 214
Hedges, Sid(ney) G(eorge)
1897-1974 ... CANR-4
Earlier sketch in CA 9-12R
See also SATA 28
Hedges, Trimble R(aymond)
1906-1982 ... CAP-2
Earlier sketch in CA 21-22
Hedges, Ursula M. 1940- ... CANR-47
Earlier sketch in CA 29-32R

Cumulative Index 259 Heintz

Hedges, William L(eonard) 1923-2005 ... 37-40R
Obituary ... 239
Hedin, Mary ... 103
Hedin, Raymond (William) 1943- ... 228
Hedin, Robert (Alexander) 1949- ... CANR-93
Earlier sketch in CA 146
Hedley, George (Percy) 1899-1971 ... CAP-2
Earlier sketch in CA 19-20
Hedley, (Gladys) Olwen 1912- ... CANR-9
Earlier sketch in CA 61-64
Hedlund, Ronald D(avid) 1941- ... 33-36R
Hedren, Paul L(eslie) 1949- ... CANR-37
Earlier sketch in CA 114
Hedrick, Addie M(ae) 1903-1986 ... CAP-2
Earlier sketch in CA 25-28
Hedrick, Basil C(alvin) 1932- ... CANR-21
Earlier sketch in CA 33-36R
Hedrick, Floyd D(udley) 1927-2003 ... 33-36R
Obituary ... 218
Hedrick, Joan D(oran) 1944- ... CANR-52
Earlier sketch in CA 107
Hedrick, Travis K. 1904(?)-1977
Obituary ... 69-72
Heefner, Wilson A. 1931- ... 150
Heelan, Jamee Riggio 1965- ... 220
See also SATA 146
Heeley, D(avid) A. 1971- ... 154
Heenan, David A. 1940- ... 215
Heeney, Brian 1933- ... 89-92
Heer, David M(acAlpine) 1930- ... 162
Heer, John E(dward), Jr. 1921-(?)
Obituary ... 113
Heer, Nancy Whittier ... 33-36R
Heerboth, Sharon
See Leon, Sharon
Heeresma, Heere 1932- ... CANR-48
Earlier sketch in CA 25-28R
Heeresma Inc.
See Heeresma, Heere
Heermance, J. Noel 1939- ... 25-28R
Heertje, Arnold 1934- ... CANR-86
Earlier sketch in CA 131
Heerwagen, Paul K(illian) 1895-1991 ... 29-32R
Heesterman, J(ohannes) C(ornelis) 1925- ... 128
Heezen, Bruce C(harles)
1924-1977 ... CANR-29
Obituary ... 69-72
Earlier sketch in CA 49-52
Hefer, Hayim (Baruch) 1925- ... 226
Heffer, Eric S(amuel) 1922-1991 ... 123
Heffer, Simon (James) 1960- ... 172
Heffern, Richard 1950- ... 61-64
Heffernan, Deborah Daw 1952- ... 215
Heffernan, James A(nthony) W(alsh)
1939- ... 25-28R
Heffernan, John 1949- ... 192
See also SATA 121
Heffernan, Michael 1942- ... CANR-40
Earlier sketches in CA 77-80, CANR-18
Heffernan, Nancy Coffey 1936- ... 146
Heffernan, Patrick
See O'Heffernan, Patrick
Heffernan, Paul 1905(?)-1983
Obituary ... 110
Heffernan, Thomas (Patrick Carroll)
1939- ... 81-84
Heffernan, Thomas Farel 1933- ... CANR-140
Earlier sketch in CA 107
Heffernan, Thomas J(ohn Andrew) 1944- ... 125
Heffernan, William A. 1937- ... CANR-103
Earlier sketch in CA 25-28R
Heffley, Wayne 1927- ... 9-12R
Heffner, Richard D(ouglas) 1925- ... 69-72
Heffron, Dorris 1944- ... CANR-82
Earlier sketches in CA 49-52, CANR-36
See also SATA 68
Heffron, Mary J. 1935- ... 135
Hefley, James C(arl) 1930- ... CANR-7
Earlier sketch in CA 13-16R
Heflin, Donald
See Wallmann, Jeffrey M(iner)
Heflin, Ruth J. 1963- ... 195
Hefner, Hugh (Marston) 1926- ... 148
Brief entry ... 110
See also AITN 1
See also DLB 137
Hefner, Paul
See Tabori, Paul
Hefner, Robert W(illiam) 1952- ... CANR-111
Earlier sketch in CA 119
Hefter, Richard 1942- ... CANR-47
Earlier sketches in CA 107, CANR-23
See also SATA 31
Hegarty, Edward J. 1891-1984 ... CANR-5
Earlier sketch in CA 1-4R
Hegarty, Ellen 1918- ... 37-40R
Hegarty, Frances 1948- ... CANR-84
Earlier sketch in CA 135
See also CMW 4
Hegarty, Reginald Beaton 1906-1973 ... CAP-1
Obituary ... 41-44R
Earlier sketch in CA 13-16
See also SATA 10
Hegarty, Sister M(ary) Loyola
See Hegarty, Ellen
Hegarty, Walter 1922- ... 65-68
Hegel, Claudette 1959- ... 196
Hegel, Georg Wilhelm Friedrich
1770-1831 ... DLB 90
See also TWA
Hegel, Richard 1927- ... CANR-6
Earlier sketch in CA 57-60
Hegel, Robert Earl 1943- ... 108
Hegeler, Sten 1923- ... 107
Hegeman, Elizabeth Blair 1942- ... 61-64
Hegeman, Susan 1964- ... 209
Hegenberger, John 1947- ... 135
Hegener, Mark Paul 1919-1988
Obituary ... 125
Heger, Theodore Ernest 1907-1979 ... 33-36R
Hegesippus
See Schonfield, Hugh J(oseph)
Heggan, Christiane ... 209
Heggen, Thomas 1918-1949 ... DFS 20
Heggie, Iain 1953- ... 230
See also CD 5, 6
Heggie, John Hamilton
See Heggie, Iain
Heggoy, Alf Andrew 1938- ... CANR-14
Earlier sketch in CA 37-40R
Hegi, Ursula 1946- ... CANR-134
Earlier sketches in CA 104, CANR-93
See also CN 7
See also MTFW 2005
Heginbotham, Stanley J. 1938-
Brief entry ... 106
Hegland, Jean (Alma) 1957(?)- ... 228
Heglar, Mary Schnall 1934- ... 49-52
Hegner, William 1928- ... 93-96
Hegre, Theodore A. 1908-1984
Obituary ... 115
Hegstad, Roland R(ex) 1926- ... 57-60
Hegwood, Martin 1951- ... 219
Hehenberger, Shelly 1968- ... SATA 126
Hehn, Paul N. 1927- ... 226
Heiber, Helmut 1924- ... 49-52
Heiberg, Johan Ludvig 1791-1860 ... DLB 300
Heiberg, Johanne Luise 1812-1890 ... DLB 300
Heiby, Walter A(lbert) 1918- ... 21-24R
Heichberger, Robert Lee 1930- ... 53-56
Heichelheim, Fritz M(oritz) 1901-1968
Obituary ... 116
Heicher, Merlo K. W. 1882-1967 ... CAP-1
Earlier sketch in CA 13-14
Heidar, Knut (Martin) 1949- ... 200
Heidbreder, Margaret Ann
See Eastman, Ann Heidbreder
Heidbreder, Robert K. 1947- ... 199
See also SATA 130
Heide, Florence Parry 1919- ... CANR-84
Earlier sketch in CA 93-96
See also CLR 60
See also CWRI 5
See also JRDA
See also MAICYA 1, 2
See also SAAS 6
See also SATA 32, 69, 118
Heide, Kathleen M. 1954- ... 145
Heide, Robert 1939- ... CANR-20
Earlier sketch in CA 103
See also DLB 249
Heidegger, Martin 1889-1976 ... CANR-34
Obituary ... 65-68
Earlier sketch in CA 81-84
See also CLC 24
See also DLB 296
See also MTCW 1, 2
See also MTFW 2005
Heidel, R. Andrew 1969- ... 173
Heidelberger, Michael (Johannes) 1947- ... 130
Heideman, Eugene P. 1929- ... 69-72
Heiden, Carol A. 1939- ... 57-60
Heiden, David 1946- ... 139
Heiden, Konrad 1901-1966
Obituary ... 116
Heidenreich, Charles A(lbert) 1917- ... 25-28R
Heidenry, John 1939- ... CANR-86
Earlier sketch in CA 142
Heidenstam, (Carl Gustaf) Verner von
1859-1940
Brief entry ... 104
See also TCLC 5
Heider, Karl G(ustav) 1935- ... 132
Heiderstadt, Dorothy 1907-2001 ... CANR-1
Earlier sketch in CA 1-4R
See also SATA 6
Heidi, Gloria ... 69-72
Heidi Louise
See Erdrich, (Karen) Louise
Heidingsfield, Myron S(amuel)
1914-1969 ... CANR-31
Obituary ... 103
Earlier sketch in CA 1-4R
Heidish, Marcy Moran 1947- ... 101
See also DLBY 1982
Heidler, David S(tephen) 1955- ... 172
See also SATA 132
Heidler, Jeanne T(wiggs) 1956- ... 172
Heidler, Jeanne T. 1956- ... SATA 132
Heidmann, Jean 1923- ... CANR-89
Earlier sketch in CA 130
Heiferman, Ronald Ian 1941- ... 61-64
Heifetz, Harold 1919- ... CANR-10
Earlier sketch in CA 25-28R
Heifetz, Milton D. 1921- ... 57-60
Heifner, Jack 1946- ... CANR-47
Earlier sketch in CA 105
See also CLC 11
Heiges, P. Myers 1887-1968 ... CAP-1
Earlier sketch in CA 13-16
Heighton, Steven 1961- ... 210
Heijermans, Herman 1864-1924
Brief entry ... 123
See also EWL 3
See also TCLC 24
Heijke, John 1927- ... 21-24R
Heikal, M. Hassanein
See Heikal, Mohamed Hassanein
Heikal, Mohamed
See Heikal, Mohamed Hassanein
Heikal, Mohamed H.
See Heikal, Mohamed Hassanein
Heikal, Mohamed Hassanein 1923- ... CANR-86
Brief entry ... 112
Earlier sketch in CA 127
Heikin, Nancy 1948- ... 172
Heikin-Pepin, Nancy
See Heikin, Nancy
Heil, John ... 112
Heil, Ruth 1947- ... 112
Heilbron, J(ohn) L(ewis) 1934- ... CANR-90
Earlier sketches in CA 53-56, CANR-4, 19, 41
Heilbroner, Joan Knapp 1922- ... 1-4R
See also SATA 63
Heilbroner, Robert L(ouis)
1919-2005 ... CANR-47
Obituary ... 235
Earlier sketches in CA 1-4R, CANR-4, 21
Heilbronner, Walter L(eo) 1924- ... 25-28R
Heilbrun, Carolyn G(old)
1926-2003 ... CANR-94
Obituary ... 220
Earlier sketches in CA 45-48, CANR-1, 28, 58
See also Cross, Amanda
See also CLC 25, 173
See also FW
Heilbrun, Lois Hussey 1922(?)-1987
Obituary ... 123
See also SATA-Obit 54
Heilbrunn, Otto 1906-1969 ... CAP-1
Earlier sketch in CA 13-16
Heilig, Matthias R. 1881-1971(?) ... CAP-2
Earlier sketch in CA 23-24
Heiliger, Edward Martin 1909- ... 13-16R
Heiligman, Deborah 1958- ... CANR-124
Earlier sketch in CA 155
See also SATA 90, 144
Heilman, Arthur (William) 1914- ... CANR-5
Earlier sketch in CA 5-8R
Heilman, Grant 1919- ... 53-56
Heilman, Joan Rattner ... CANR-44
Earlier sketches in CA 57-60, CANR-6, 21
See also SATA 50
Heilman, Robert Bechtold 1906- ... CANR-52
Earlier sketches in CA 13-16R, CANR-9, 27
Heilman, Robert Leo 1952- ... 151
Heilman, Samuel C(hiel) 1946- ... CANR-108
Earlier sketch in CA 69-72
Heilner, Van Campen 1899-1970
Obituary ... 29-32R
Heim, Alice (Winifred) 1913-1992 ... CANR-14
Earlier sketch in CA 33-36R
Heim, Bruno Bernhard 1911-2003 ... 89-92
Obituary ... 215
Heim, Joseph A(rthur) 1949- ... 142
Heim, Kathleen M(cEntee) ... CANR-105
Earlier sketches in CA 111, CANR-49
Heim, Michael Henry 1943- ... 159
Heim, Ralph D(aniel) 1895-1983 ... 73-76
Obituary ... 133
Heim, Scott 1966- ... 158
Heiman, Ernest J(ean) 1930- ... CANR-4
Earlier sketch in CA 53-56
Heiman, Grover G(eorge, Jr.) 1920- ... CANR-6
Earlier sketch in CA 5-8R
Heiman, Judith 1935- ... 1-4R
Heiman, Marcel 1909-1976
Obituary ... 65-68
Heimann, Judith M(oscow) 1936- ... 193
Heimann, Robert Karl 1918-1990
Obituary ... 130
Heimann, Rolf 1940- ... 191
See also SATA 120
Heimann, Susan 1940- ... 33-36R
Heimarck, Theodore 1906- ... 5-8R
Heimbeck, Raeburne S(eeley) 1930- ... 29-32R
Heimberg, Marilyn Markham
See Ross, Marilyn (Ann) Heimberg
Heimdahl, Ralph 1909- ... 69-72
Heimer, Mel(vin Lytton) 1915-1971 ... CANR-4
Obituary ... 29-32R
Earlier sketch in CA 1-4R
Heimert, Alan (Edward) 1928-1999 ... 5-8R
Obituary ... 186
Heimler, Eugene 1922- ... CANR-8
Earlier sketch in CA 13-16R
Heimlich, Henry Jay 1920- ... CANR-143
Earlier sketch in CA 102
Heims, Steve J(oshua) 1926- ... 131
Heims, Steve Paul
See Heims, Steve J(oshua)
Heimsath, Charles H. 1928- ... 17-20R
Hein, Christoph 1944- ... CANR-108
Earlier sketch in CA 158
See also CDWLB 2
See also CLC 154
See also CWW 2
See also DLB 124
Hein, David 1954- ... 188
Hein, Eleanor C(harlotte) 1933- ... 61-64
Hein, John 1921- ... CANR-16
Earlier sketches in CA 45-48, CANR-1
Hein, Leonard William 1916- ... 53-56
Hein, Lucille Eleanor 1915-1994 ... CANR-2
Earlier sketch in CA 5-8R
See also SATA 20
Hein, Marvin Lester 1925- ... 125
Hein, Norvin 1914- ... 61-64
Hein, Piet 1905-1996 ... CANR-4
Earlier sketch in CA 49-52
See also CWW 2
See also DLB 214
Hein, Rolland Neal 1932- ... CANR-89
Earlier sketch in CA 112
Heinberg, Paul (Julius) 1924- ... CANR-23
Earlier sketch in CA 45-48
Heinbuch, Jean (M.) 1953- ... 142
Heindel, Richard Heathcote 1912-1979
Obituary ... 89-92
Heine, Arthur J. 1940- ... 138
Heine, Carl 1936- ... 57-60
Heine, Heinrich 1797-1856 ... CDWLB 2
See also DLB 90
See also EW 5
See also PC 25
See also RGWL 2, 3
See also TWA
Heine, Helme 1941- ... 135
See also CLR 18
See also MAICYA 1, 2
See also SATA 67, 135
Heine, Irwin (Millard) 1909-2002 ... 213
Heine, Lala Koehn
See Koehn-Heine, Lala
Heine, Ralph W(illiam) 1914- ... 41-44R
Heine, William C(olbourne) 1919- ... 97-100
Heineman, Benjamin Walter, Jr.
1944- ... CANR-28
Earlier sketch in CA 105
Heineman, Helen 1936- ... 125
Heineman, Kenneth J. 1962- ... CANR-116
Earlier sketch in CA 144
Heineman, Toni Vaughn 1947- ... 178
Heinemann, George Alfred
1918- ... SATA-Brief 31
Heinemann, Katherine 1918- ... 77-80
Heinemann, Larry (Curtiss) 1944- ... CANR-81
Earlier sketches in CA 110, CANR-31
Interview in ... CANR-31
See also CAAS 21
See also CLC 50
See also DLBD 9
Heinemann, Ronald L(ynton) 1939- ... 112
Heinemann, Steven
See Bach, Steven
Heinen, Hubert (Plummer) 1937- ... 41-44R
Heinerman, John 1946- ... 128
Heinesen, Jens Pauli 1932- ... CWW 2
Heinesen, (Andreas) William 1900-1991 ... 230
See also DLB 214
See also RGWL 2, 3
Heiney, Donald (William)
1921-1993 ... CANR-58
Obituary ... 142
Earlier sketches in CA 1-4R, CANR-3
See also Harris, MacDonald
See also FANT
Heinke, Clarence H. 1912-1994 ... 53-56
Heinl, Nancy G(ordon) 1916- ... 81-84
Heinl, Robert Debs, Jr. 1916-1979 ... CANR-4
Obituary ... 85-88
Earlier sketch in CA 5-8R
Heinlein, Robert A(nson)
1907-1988 ... CANR-53
Obituary ... 125
Earlier sketches in CA 1-4R, CANR-1, 20
See also AAYA 17
See also BPFB 2
See also BYA 4, 13
See also CLC 1, 3, 8, 14, 26, 55
See also CLR 75
See also CN 1, 2, 3, 4
See also CPW
See also DA3
See also DAM POP
See also DLB 8
See also EXPS
See also JRDA
See also LAIT 5
See also LMFS 2
See also MAICYA 1, 2
See also MTCW 1, 2
See also MTFW 2005
See also RGAL 4
See also SATA 9, 69
See also SATA-Obit 56
See also SCFW 1, 2
See also SFW 4
See also SSC 55
See also SSFS 7
See also YAW
Heinrich, Bernd 1940- ... CANR-88
Earlier sketch in CA 109
Heinrich, Will 1978(?)- ... 225
Heinrich, Willi 1920- ... CANR-15
Earlier sketch in CA 93-96
See also DLB 75
Heinrichs, Waldo H(untley), Jr.
1925- ... CANR-48
Earlier sketch in CA 122
Heinrich von dem Tuerlin fl. c.
1230- ... DLB 138
Heinrich von Melk fl. 1160- ... DLB 148
Heinrich von Veldeke c. 1145-c.
1190 ... DLB 138
Heins, A(rthur) James 1931- ... 5-8R
Heins, Ethel L(eah) 1918-1997 ... 102
Obituary ... 158
See also SATA 101
Heins, Marjorie 1946- ... 69-72
Heins, Paul 1909- ... 69-72
See also SATA 13
Heinse, Wilhelm 1746-1803 ... DLB 94
Heinsohn, A(ugereau) G(ray), Jr.
1896-1980 ... CAP-1
Earlier sketch in CA 11-12
Heinsohn, Thomas William 1934-
Brief entry ... 118
Heinsohn, Tommy
See Heinsohn, Thomas William
Heintz, Ann Christine 1930-1989 ... CANR-8
Obituary ... 127
Earlier sketch in CA 61-64
Heintz, Bonnie L(ee) 1924- ... 69-72
Heintz, John 1936- ... 45-48

Heintze, Carl 1922- ... 57-60
See also SATA 26
Heintzelman, Donald S(haffer) 1938- ... CANR-16
Earlier sketch in CA 93-96
Heinz, Brian J(ames) 1946- ... 160
See also SATA 95
Heinz, G.
See Gerard-Libois, Jules C.
Heinz, Thomas A(rthur) 1949- ... 237
Heinz, W(ilfred) C(harles) 1915- ... CANR-113
Earlier sketches in CA 5-8R, CANR-4, 62
See also DLB 171
See also SATA 26
Heinz, William Frederick 1899-1976 ... CANR-12
Earlier sketch in CA 61-64
Heinze, Robert H(arold) 1920-1984
Obituary ... 113
Heinzelman, Kurt 1947- ... 101
Heinzen, Mildred
See Masters, Mildred
Heinzerling, Larry E(dward) 1945- ... 73-76
Heinzerling, Lynn Louis 1906-1983
Obituary ... 111
Heinzman(n), George (Melville) 1916- ... 1-4R
Heiremans, Luis Alberto 1928-1964 ... LAW
Heirich, Max 1931- ... 29-32R
Heise, David R(euben) 1937- ... 89-92
Heise, Edward Tyler 1912- ... 1-4R
Heise, Hans-Juergen
See Heise, Hans-Jurgen
Heise, Hans-Jurgen 1930- ... 197
Heise, Kenan 1933- ... 57-60
Heisel, Sharon E(laine) 1941- ... CANR-104
Earlier sketch in CA 150
See also SATA 84, 125
Heisenberg, Werner 1901-1976
Obituary ... 65-68
Heiser, Charles B(ixler), Jr. 1920- ... CANR-142
Earlier sketch in CA 45-48
Heiser, Victor George 1893-1972
Obituary ... 33-36R
Heiserman, Arthur Ray 1929-1975 ... CANR-15
Obituary ... 103
Earlier sketch in CA 1-4R
Heiserman, David L(ee) 1940- ... CANR-8
Earlier sketch in CA 61-64
Heisey, Alan Milliken 1928- ... 57-60
Heising, Willetta L. 1947- ... 167
Heiskell, Andrew 1915-2003 ... 184
Obituary ... 218
Heiskell, John Netherland 1872-1972 ... 182
Obituary ... 89-92
See also DLB 127
Heisler, Martin O. 1938- ... CANR-23
Earlier sketch in CA 45-48
Heisler, Philip Samuel 1915-1988
Obituary ... 127
Heisner, Beverly F. 1937- ... 165
Heiss, Jerold (Sheldon) 1930- ... 126
Brief entry ... 111
Heissenbuettel, Helmut 1921-1996 ... 81-84
Obituary ... 154
See also Heissenbuttel, Helmut
See also DLB 75
Heissenbuttel, Helmut
See Heissenbuettel, Helmut
Heissenbuttel, Helmut
See Heissenbuettel, Helmut
See also EWL 3
Heisserer, Andrew Jackson 1935- ... 111
Heitler, Walter (Heinrich) 1904-1981 ... CANR-8
Earlier sketch in CA 13-16R
Heitlinger, Alena 1950- ... 214
Heitman, Sidney 1924- ... 9-12R
Heitmiller, David A. 1945- ... 163
Heitner, Robert R. 1920- ... 5-8R
Heitschmidt, Rodney K. 1944- ... 142
Heitzmann, Kristen ... 231
Heitzmann, William Ray 1948- ... CANR-92
Earlier sketches in CA 97-100, CANR-17, 49
See also SATA 73
Heitzmann, Wm. Ray
See Heitzmann, William Ray
Heizer, Robert Fleming 1915-1979 ... 102
Hejinian, Lyn 1941- ... CANR-85
Earlier sketch in CA 153
See also CP 7
See also CWP
See also DLB 165
See also RGAL 4
Heker, Liliana 1943- ... 215
Hekker, Terry 1932- ... 97-100
Hekman, Susan J(ean) 1949- ... 114
Helberg, Shirley Adelaide Holden 1919- ... 209
See also SATA 138
Helbich, Wolfgang J(ohannes) 1935- ... 160
Helbig, Alethea K. 1928- ... CANR-37
Earlier sketches in CA 97-100, CANR-17
Helbing, Terry 1951- ... 89-92
Helbling, Robert E(ugene) 1923- ... CANR-48
Earlier sketch in CA 49-52
Helck, C. Peter 1893-1988 ... CANR-1
Earlier sketch in CA 1-4R
Held, David 1951- ... CANR-143
Earlier sketch in CA 110
Held, Jack Preston 1926- ... 33-36R
Held, Jacqueline 1936- ... CANR-14
Earlier sketch in CA 73-76
Held, Joseph 1930- ... 45-48
Held, Julius S(amuel) 1905-2002 ... CANR-45
Obituary ... 212
Earlier sketch in CA 103
Held, Peter
See Vance, John Holbrook
Held, R(over) Burnell 1921- ... 33-36R
Held, Ray E(ldred) 1918- ... 45-48
Held, Richard 1922- ... 41-44R
Held, Virginia (Potter) 1929- ... CANR-16
Earlier sketches in CA 1-4R, CANR-1
Helder, Dom
See Camara, Helder Pessoa
Helder, Herberto 1930- ... DLB 287
Heldman, Dan C(hristopher) 1943- ... 110
Heldman, Gladys M(edalie) 1922-2003
Obituary ... 217
Brief entry ... 111
Heldman, Robert Keith 1938- ... 144
Heldmann, Richard Bernard 1857-1915 ... 215
See also Marsh, Richard
Heldrich, Philip 1965- ... 239
Heleniak, Kathryn Moore ... 110
Heley, Veronica 1933- ... 192
Helfand, Jessica ... 219
Helfen, Otto J. Maenchen
See Maenchen, Otto John
Helfert, Erich A(nton) 1931- ... 9-12R
Helfgott, Daniel (Andrew) 1952- ... CANR-46
Earlier sketches in CA 106, CANR-22
Helfgott, Gillian ... 169
Helfgott, Roy B. 1925- ... 81-84
Helfman, Elizabeth S(eaver) 1911-2001 ... CANR-5
Earlier sketch in CA 5-8R
See also SATA 3
Helfman, Harry Carmozin 1910-1995 ... 25-28R
See also SATA 3
Helforth, John
See Doolittle, Hilda
Helfritz, Hans 1902-1995 ... 41-44R
Helgason, Hallgrimur 1959- ... 221
Helgeland, Brian 1961- ... 235
Helgerson, Richard 1940- ... 116
Helgesen, Geir 1950- ... 185
Helgesen, Sally 1948- ... CANR-111
Earlier sketches in CA 115, CANR-50
Helion, Jean 1904-1987
Obituary ... 124
Helitzer, Florence (Saperstein) 1928-1995 ... 17-20R
Hell, Richard 1949- ... 219
Hellaakoski, Aaro 1893-1952 ... 191
Hellberg, Hans-Eric 1927- ... CANR-18
Earlier sketch in CA 101
See also SATA 38
Helldorfer, M(ary) C(laire) 1954- ... CANR-144
Earlier sketch in CA 129
Hellegers, Andre E. 1926-1979
Obituary ... 85-88
Helleiner, Gerald K(arl) 1936- ... 140
Hellen, J(ohn) A(nthony) 1935- ... 61-64
Hellenga, Robert 1941- ... 154
See also CN 6
Hellenhofferu, Vojtech Kapristian z
See Hasek, Jaroslav (Matej Frantisek)
Heller
See Iranek-Osmecki, Kazimierz
Heller, Abraham M. 1898-1975
Obituary ... 57-60
Heller, Agnes 1929- ... 160
Heller, Bernard 1896-1976
Obituary ... 65-68
Heller, Celia S(topnicka) ... 37-40R
Heller, David (A.) 1922-1968 ... CAP-1
Earlier sketch in CA 9-10
Heller, David 1957- ... CANR-52
Earlier sketch in CA 124
Heller, Dawn Hansen 1932- ... 125
Heller, Deane Fons 1924- ... 9-12R
Heller, Erich 1911-1990 ... CANR-8
Obituary ... 132
Earlier sketch in CA 13-16R
Heller, Francis H(oward) 1917- ... CANR-57
Earlier sketches in CA 1-4R, CANR-31
Heller, H(einz) Robert 1940- ... CANR-22
Earlier sketch in CA 69-72
Heller, Herbert L. 1908-1983 ... 21-24R
Heller, Jane ... 200
Heller, Janet Ruth 1949- ... 195
Heller, Jean 1942- ... 73-76
Heller, John 1896(?)-1987
Obituary ... 124
Heller, John H(erbert) 1921- ... 114
Heller, Joseph 1923-1999 ... CANR-126
Obituary ... 187
Earlier sketches in CA 5-8R, CANR-8, 42, 66
Interview in ... CANR-8
See also CABS 1
See also AAYA 24
See also AITN 1
See also AMWS 4
See also BPFB 2
See also BYA 1
See also CLC 1, 3, 5, 8, 11, 36, 63
See also CN 1, 2, 3, 4, 5, 6
See also CPW
See also DA
See also DA3
See also DAB
See also DAC
See also DAM MST, NOV, POP
See also DLB 2, 28, 227
See also DLBY 1980, 2002
See also EWL 3
See also EXPN
See also LAIT 4
See also MAL 5
See also MTCW 1, 2
See also MTFW 2005
See also NFS 1
See also RGAL 4
See also TCLC 131, 151
See also TUS
See also WLC
See also YAW
Heller, Keith 1949- ... 119
Heller, Linda 1944- ... 108
See also SATA 46
See also SATA-Brief 40
Heller, Mark (Francis) 1914-1998 ... CANR-10
Earlier sketch in CA 61-64
Heller, Marvin J. 1940- ... 167
Heller, Michael (David) 1937- ... 210
Earlier sketches in CA 45-48, CANR-26, 52, 85
Autobiographical Essay in ... 210
See also CP 7
See also DLB 165
Heller, Mike
See Hano, Arnold
Heller, Otto 1896-1970 ... IDFW 3, 4
Heller, Peter 1920-1998 ... CANR-32
Earlier sketches in CA 41-44R, CANR-14
Heller, Rachelle S(ara) 1943- ... 111
Heller, Reinhold (August Friedrich) 1940- ... 77-80
Heller, Robert 1899(?)-1973
Obituary ... 41-44R
Heller, Robert (Gordon Barry) 1932- ... CANR-108
Earlier sketch in CA 132
Heller, Robert W(illiam) 1933- ... 25-28R
Heller, Ruth M. 1924- ... CANR-88
Earlier sketch in CA 130
See also SATA 66, 112
Heller, Shelly
See Heller, Rachelle S(ara)
Heller, Sipa 1897(?)-1980
Obituary ... 97-100
Heller, Steven 1950- ... CANR-109
Earlier sketch in CA 160
Heller, Ted
See Heller, Theodore Michael
Heller, Theodore Michael 1956- ... 222
Heller, Trudy (Marie) 1944- ... 115
Heller, Walter W(olfgang) 1915-1987 ... 21-24R
Obituary ... 122
Heller, Wilson Battin 1893-1983
Obituary ... 110
Hellerman, Herbert 1927- ... 53-56
Hellerstein, David (Joel) 1953- ... CANR-95
Earlier sketches in CA 120, CANR-46
Hellerstein, Jerome R. 1907-2000 ... CAP-1
Earlier sketch in CA 13-14
Hellerstein, Kathryn (Ann) 1952- ... CANR-105
Earlier sketch in CA 114
Hellie, Ann 1925- ... CANR-15
Earlier sketch in CA 77-80
Hellie, Richard 1937- ... CANR-82
Earlier sketches in CA 33-36R, CANR-14, 36
Hellinga, Lotte 1932- ... CANR-105
Earlier sketch in CA 129
Hellinga, Wytze (Gs) 1908-1985
Obituary ... 116
Hellinger, Douglas A(lan) 1948- ... CANR-21
Earlier sketch in CA 69-72
Hellinger, Stephen H(enry) 1948- ... CANR-21
Earlier sketch in CA 69-72
Hellison, Donald R(aymond) 1938- ... 53-56
Hellman, Arthur D(avid) 1942- ... 69-72
Hellman, C(larisse) Doris 1910-1973
Obituary ... 41-44R
Hellman, Geoffrey T(heodore) 1907-1977 ... CANR-30
Obituary ... 73-76
Earlier sketch in CA 69-72
Hellman, Hal
See Hellman, Harold
Hellman, Harold 1927- ... CANR-116
Earlier sketches in CA 25-28R, CANR-10
See also SATA 4
Hellman, Hugo E. 1908-1975 ... CAP-2
Earlier sketch in CA 19-20
Hellman, John 1940- ... 129
Hellman, Judith Adler 1945- ... 113
Hellman, Lillian (Florence) 1906-1984 ... CANR-33
Obituary ... 112
Earlier sketch in CA 13-16R
See also AAYA 47
See also AITN 1, 2
See also AMWS 1
See also CAD
See also CLC 2, 4, 8, 14, 18, 34, 44, 52
See also CWD
See also DA3
See also DAM DRAM
See also DC 1
See also DFS 1, 3, 14
See also DLB 7, 228
See also DLBY 1984
See also EWL 3
See also FL 1:6
See also FW
See also LAIT 3
See also MAL 5
See also MAWW
See also MTCW 1, 2
See also MTFW 2005
See also RGAL 4
See also TCLC 119
See also TUS
Hellman, Peter 1943- ... 107
Hellman, Robert 1919-1984 ... 17-20R
Obituary ... 113
Hellman, Stephen 1943- ... 144
Hellmann, Anna 1902(?)-1972
Obituary ... 33-36R
Hellmann, Donald C(harles) 1933- ... CANR-28
Earlier sketch in CA 45-48
Hellmann, Ellen 1908-1982 ... 106
Hellmann, John 1948- ... CANR-24
Earlier sketch in CA 105
Hellmann, Libby Fischer ... 231
Hellmuth, Jerome (A.) 1911-1990 ... 13-16R
Hellmuth, William Frederick, Jr. 1920- ... CANR-4
Earlier sketch in CA 1-4R
Hellstroem, Gustaf
See Hellstrom, (Erik) Gustaf
Hellstrom, Ward 1930- ... 33-36R
Hellwig, Johann 1609-1674 ... DLB 164
Hellwig, Monika Konrad 1929-2005 ... 37-40R
Helly, Dorothy O. 1931- ... 122
Hellyer, A(rthur) G(eorge) L(ee) 1902-1993 ... CANR-19
Obituary ... 140
Earlier sketches in CA 9-12R, CANR-4
Hellyer, Arthur
See Hellyer, A(rthur) G(eorge) L(ee)
Hellyer, Clement David 1914-2001 ... 118
Hellyer, David Tirrell 1913- ... 17-20R
Hellyer, Jill 1925- ... 118
Hellyer, Paul (Theodore) 1923- ... CANR-48
Earlier sketches in CA 69-72, CANR-14
Helm, Bertrand P. 1929- ... 37-40R
Helm, Ernest Eugene 1928- ... CANR-2
Earlier sketch in CA 1-4R
Helm, Everett 1913-1999 ... 49-52
Helm, Levon 1940- ... 146
Helm, P(eter) J(ames) 1916- ... CANR-3
Earlier sketch in CA 9-12R
Helm, Robert Meredith 1917- ... 17-20R
Helm, Thomas (William) 1919- ... 5-8R
Helman, Andrea (Jean) 1946- ... SATA 107, 160
Helman, Andy
See Helman, Andrea (Jean)
Helmer, Diana Star 1962- ... 151
See also SATA 86
Helmer, John 1946- ... 41-44R
Helmer, Marilyn ... CANR-141
Earlier sketch in CA 173
See also SATA 112, 160
Helmer, William F. 1926- ... 33-36R
Helmer, William J(oseph) 1936- ... 73-76
Helmericks, Bud
See Helmericks, Harmon R.
Helmericks, Constance (Chittenden) 1918-1987 ... 9-12R
Obituary ... 122
Helmericks, Harmon R. 1917- ... 29-32R
Helmering, Doris Wild 1942- ... 65-68
Helmers, George Dow 1906- ... 61-64
Helmes, Scott 1945- ... 213
Helmholz, R(ichard) H(enry) 1940- ... CANR-29
Earlier sketch in CA 61-64
Helmi, Jack
See Sands, Leo G(eorge)
Helming, Ann 1924-(?) ... CANR-2
Earlier sketch in CA 1-4R
Helminiak, Daniel A. 1942- ... 126
Helminski, Camille Adams 1951- ... 140
Helmker, Judith Anne 1940- ... 33-36R
Helmlinger, (Benita) Trudy 1943- ... 69-72
Helmore, G(eoffrey) A(nthony) 1922- ... 29-32R
Helm-Pirgo, Marian 1897-1995 ... 77-80
Helmreich, Ernst C(hristian) 1902-1997 ... CANR-46
Earlier sketch in CA 1-4R
Helmreich, Jonathan Ernst 1936-
Brief entry ... 105
Helmreich, Paul C(hristian) 1933- ... 53-56
Helmreich, Robert Louis 1937- ... 65-68
Helmreich, William B. 1945- ... 105
Helms, Alan 1937- ... 151
Helms, Christine Moss ... 129
Helms, Jesse (Alexander, Jr.) 1921- ... 152
Brief entry ... 124
Helms, Mary W. 1938- ... CANR-108
Earlier sketch in CA 151
Helms, Randel 1942- ... CANR-48
Earlier sketch in CA 49-52
Helms, Robert B(rake) 1940- ... 148
Helms, Roland Thomas, Jr. 1940- ... 102
Helms, Tom
See Helms, Roland Thomas, Jr.
Helmstadter, Gerald C. 1925- ... 13-16R
Heloise
See Reese, Heloise (Bowles)
Helou, Anissa 1952- ... 213
Helper, Rose ... 77-80
Helpern, Milton 1902-1977 ... 73-76
Obituary ... 69-72
Helprin, Mark 1947- ... CANR-124
Earlier sketches in CA 81-84, CANR-47, 64
See also CDALBS
See also CLC 7, 10, 22, 32
See also CN 7
See also CPW
See also DA3
See also DAM NOV, POP
See also DLBY 1985
See also FANT
See also MAL 5
See also MTCW 1, 2
See also MTFW 2005
See also SUFW 2
Helps, Racey 1913-1971 ... CAP-2
Obituary ... 29-32R
Earlier sketch in CA 23-24
See also SATA 2
See also SATA-Obit 25
Helquist, Brett ... SATA 146
Helson, Harry 1898-1977 ... CAP-1
Earlier sketch in CA 11-12
Helterman, Jeffrey A. 1942- ... 103
Helton, David (Kirby) 1940- ... 25-28R

Cumulative Index 261 Hendrie

Helton, Tinsley 1915- ... 1-4R
Helvarg, David 1951- ... CANR-128
Earlier sketch in CA 146
Helvetius, Claude-Adrien 1715-1771 . DLB 313
Helvick, James
See Cockburn, (Francis) Claud
Helweg, Hans H. 1917- ... 126
See also SATA 50
See also SATA-Brief 33
Helwig, David (Gordon) 1938- ... CANR-85
Earlier sketches in CA 33-36R, CANR-43
See also CN 4, 5, 6
See also CP 1, 2, 3, 4, 5, 6, 7
See also DLB 60
Helwig, Maggie
See Helwig, Sarah Magdalen
Helwig, Sarah Magdalen 1961- ... 130
Hely, Sara ... 224
Helyar, Jane Penelope Josephine
1933- ... CANR-26
Earlier sketches in CA 21-24R, CANR-10
See also Poole, Josephine
See also CWRI 5
See also SATA 82, 138
See also SATA-Essay 138
Helyar, John 1951- ... 140
See also BEST 90:3
Hemans, Donna 1970(?)- ... 220
Hemans, Felicia 1793-1835 ... DLB 96
See also RGEL 2
Hembree, Charles R. 1938- ... 33-36R
Hembry, Phyllis (May) 1916- ... 136
Hemdahl, Reuel Gustaf 1903-1977 ... 37-40R
Hemel Dobkin, Kathleen
See Hamel Peifer, Kathleen
Hemenway, Abby Maria 1828-1890 ... DLB 243
Hemenway, Robert 1921- ... 33-36R
Hemenway, Ruby 1884(?)-1987
Obituary ... 123
Hemery, Eric 1914- ... 111
Hemesath, Caroline 1899-1996 ... 61-64
Hemeze
See Caballero, Manuel
Hemeze, Sebastian
See Caballero, Manuel
Hemings, T. J.
See Reiter, Victoria (Kelrich)
Hemington, Judith 1949- ... 129
Hemingway, Amanda
See Askew, Amanda Jane
Hemingway, Ernest (Miller)
1899-1961 ... CANR-34
Earlier sketch in CA 77-80
See also AAYA 19
See also AMW
See also AMWC 1
See also AMWR 1
See also BPFB 2
See also BYA 2, 3, 13, 15
See also CDALB 1917-1929
See also CLC 1, 3, 6, 8, 10, 13, 19, 30, 34, 39, 41, 44, 50, 61, 80
See also DA
See also DA3
See also DAB
See also DAC
See also DAM MST, NOV
See also DLB 4, 9, 102, 210, 308, 316
See also DLBD 1, 15, 16
See also DLBY 1981, 1987, 1996, 1998
See also EWL 3
See also EXPN
See also EXPS
See also LAIT 3, 4
See also LATS 1:1
See also MAL 5
See also MTCW 1, 2
See also MTFW 2005
See also NFS 1, 5, 6, 14
See also RGAL 4
See also RGSF 2
See also SSC 1, 25, 36, 40, 63
See also SSFS 17
See also TCLC 115
See also TUS
See also WLC
See also WYA
Hemingway, Gregory H. 1931(?)-2001
Obituary ... 202
Brief entry ... 112
Hemingway, Hilary 1961(?)- ... 225
Hemingway, Jack
See Hemingway, John Hadley Nicanor
Hemingway, John Hadley Nicanor
1923-2000 ... 199
Hemingway, Leicester C. 1915-1982
Obituary ... 107
Hemingway, Lorian 1951- ... CANR-135
Earlier sketch in CA 141
Hemingway, Maggie 1946-1993 ... CANR-47
Obituary ... 141
Earlier sketch in CA 125
Hemingway, Mariel 1961- ... 229
Hemingway, Mary Welsh 1908-1986 ... 73-76
Obituary ... 121
Hemingway, Patricia Drake 1926-1978 ... 69-72
Obituary ... 73-76
Hemingway, Taylor
See Rywell, Martin
Heminway, John (H., Jr.) 1944- ... 25-28R
Hemleben, Sylvester John 1902-1991 ... CAP-2
Earlier sketch in CA 25-28
Hemley, Cecil Herbert 1914-1966 ... CANR-1
Obituary ... 25-28R
Earlier sketch in CA 1-4R
Hemley, Elaine Gottlieb
See Gottlieb, Elaine
Hemley, Robin 1958- ... 130
Hemlin, Tim ... 238
Hemlow, Joyce 1906-2001 ... 5-8R
Obituary ... 202
Hemmant, Lynette 1938- ... SATA 69
Hemmer, Joseph J., Jr. 1939- ... 198
Hemmerechts, Kristien 1955- ... 133
Hemming, (Laurence) Charles 1950- ... 132
Hemming, John (Henry) 1935- ... CANR-12
Earlier sketch in CA 29-32R
Hemming, Roy G. 1928-1995 ... 61-64
Obituary ... 149
See also SATA 11
See also SATA-Obit 86
Hemmings, F(rederic) W(illiam) J(ohn)
1920- ... CANR-58
Earlier sketches in CA 97-100, CANR-27
Hemmings, Susan 1941- ... 118
Hemon, Aleksandar 1964- ... 210
See also MTFW 2005
Hemon, Louis 1880-1913 ... CANR-85
Earlier sketch in CA 150
See also CCA 1
See also DAC
See also DLB 92
Hempel, Amy 1951- ... CANR-70
Brief entry ... 118
Earlier sketch in CA 137
See also CLC 39
See also DA3
See also DLB 218
See also EXPS
See also MTCW 2
See also MTFW 2005
See also SSFS 2
Hempel, Carl G.
See Hempel, Carl Gustav
See also DLB 279
Hempel, Carl Gustav 1905-1998
Obituary ... 162
Brief entry ... 116
See also Hempel, Carl G.
Hemphill, A. Marcus 1930(?)-1986
Obituary ... 120
Hemphill, Betty
See Hemphill, Elizabeth Anne
Hemphill, Charles F., Jr. 1917- ... 101
Hemphill, Christopher (Glenn) 1950-1987
Obituary ... 122
Hemphill, Elizabeth Anne 1920- ... 115
Hemphill, Essex 1956(?)-1995 ... 153
See also BW 2, 3
See also GLL 1
Hemphill, George 1922- ... 13-16R
Hemphill, Herbert Waide, Jr. 1929-1998 ... 116
Obituary ... 167
Hemphill, Ian ... 210
Hemphill, John K(nox) 1919- ... 53-56
Hemphill, Kenneth S. 1948- ... 134
Hemphill, Kris (Harrison) 1963- ... SATA 118
Hemphill, Martha Locke 1904-1973 ... 37-40R
See also SATA 37
Hemphill, Paul 1936- ... CANR-102
Earlier sketches in CA 49-52, CANR-12, 29, 55
See also AITN 2
See also DLBY 1987
Hemphill, W(illiam) Edwin 1912-1983 . 21-24R
Hempstone, Smith 1929- ... CANR-1
Earlier sketch in CA 1-4R
Hempton, David 1952- ... 125
Hemry, John G. ... 229
Hemschemeyer, Judith 1935- ... 49-52
Hen, Yitzhak 1963- ... CANR-113
Earlier sketch in CA 154
Henaghan, Jim 1919- ... 102
Henahan, Donal 1921-
Brief entry ... 111
Henault, (Joseph-Paul-)Gilles(-Robert)
1920- ... 178
See also DLB 88
Henault, Marie (Josephine) 1921-1989 . 33-36R
Henba, Bobbie 1926- ... SATA 87
Henbest, Nigel 1951- ... CANR-113
Earlier sketches in CA 124, CANR-53
See also SATA 55
See also SATA-Brief 52
Henbos
See Bosch, Henry G(erard)
Hench, John B(ixler) 1943- ... 131
Henchman, Daniel 1689-1761 ... DLB 24
Hencken, Hugh O'Neill 1902-1981
Obituary ... 104
Hendee, John C(lare) 1938- ... 93-96
Hendel, Charles William
1890-1982 ... CANR-13
Obituary ... 108
Earlier sketches in CAP-1, CA 13-16
Hendel, Samuel 1909-1984 ... CANR-1
Obituary ... 113
Earlier sketch in CA 1-4R
Hendel, Yehudit ... 210
See also SSFS 14
Hendelson, William H. 1904-1975
Obituary ... 104
Henderley, Brooks ... CANR-26
Earlier sketches in CAP-2, CA 19-20
See also SATA 1
Henderlite, Rachel 1905-1991 ... 1-4R
Hendershot, Cyndy
See Hendershot, Cynthia
Hendershot, Cynthia ... 186
Hendershot, Ralph 1896(?)-1979
Obituary ... 89-92
Henderson, Alexander (John) 1910- ... CAP-1
Earlier sketch in CA 13-16
Henderson, Algo D(onmyer)
1897-1988 ... CANR-1
Obituary ... 126
Earlier sketch in CA 1-4R
Henderson, Alice Corbin 1881-1949 ... 176
See also DLB 54
Henderson, Archibald 1877-1963 ... 183
Obituary ... 93-96
See also DLB 103
Henderson, Archibald 1916- ... 53-56
Henderson, Bert C. 1904-1974 ... CAP-1
Earlier sketch in CA 9-10
Henderson, Bill
See Henderson, William Charles
Henderson, Brian 1941- ... 112
Henderson, Bruce B. 1946- ... 139
Henderson, C(rispin) A(listair) P(oland)
1955- ... 119
Henderson, C(elia) Nell 1959- ... 135
Henderson, C(harles) William 1925- ... 65-68
Henderson, Charles, Jr. 1923- ... CANR-101
Earlier sketch in CA 45-48
Henderson, Charles P(ackard), Jr.
1941- ... 41-44R
Henderson, Charles W(illiam) 1948- ... 135
Henderson, Dan Fenno 1921-2001 ... 17-20R
Henderson, David 1927- ... 206
Henderson, David 1942- ... CANR-10
Earlier sketch in CA 25-28R
See also BW 1
See also CP 1
See also DLB 41
Henderson, Dion (Winslow)
1921-1984 ... CANR-5
Obituary ... 114
Earlier sketch in CA 9-12R
Henderson, Donald
See Laughlin, Tom
Henderson, Dwight F. 1937- ... 41-44R
Henderson, Edwin Bancroft 1883-1977
Obituary ... 116
Henderson, Eva Pendleton 1890-1986 ... 115
Henderson, F. C.
See Mencken, H(enry) L(ouis)
Henderson, Florence (Agnes) 1934- ... 230
Henderson, G. D. S.
See Henderson, George (David Smith)
Henderson, G(eorge) P(atrick) 1915- ... 29-32R
Henderson, G(eorge) P(oland)
1920-2003 ... 37-40R
Obituary ... 224
Henderson, George (David Smith)
1931- ... CANR-27
Earlier sketch in CA 25-28R
Henderson, George 1932- ... 183
Henderson, George L(eslie) 1925- ... 69-72
Henderson, George Wylie 1904-1965 ... 125
See also BW 1
See also DLB 51
Henderson, Gordon 1950- ... SATA 53
Henderson, Hamish 1919-2002 ... CANR-85
Obituary ... 206
Earlier sketch in CA 153
See also CP 1, 2, 3, 4, 5, 6, 7
Henderson, Harold 1948- ... 148
Henderson, Harold G(ould) 1889-1974
Obituary ... 53-56
Henderson, Harold H(ale) 1928-1996 ... 114
Henderson, Harry B(rinton), Jr. 1914-2003
Obituary ... 220
Brief entry ... 109
Henderson, Hazel 1933- ... 129
Henderson, Ian 1910-1969 ... CAP-2
Earlier sketch in CA 17-18
Henderson, Isabel 1933- ... 25-28R
Henderson, James 1934- ... CANR-13
Earlier sketch in CA 33-36R
Henderson, James D. 1942- ... 205
Henderson, James Maddock
See Danvers, Pete
Henderson, James Youngblood 1944- ... 110
Henderson, Jean Carolyn Glidden 1916- ... 102
Henderson, Jennifer 1929- ... 107
Henderson, John 1906(?)-1982
Obituary ... 108
Henderson, John 1915- ... 5-8R
Henderson, John S(teele) 1919- ... 5-8R
Henderson, John W(illiam) 1910-1994 . 25-28R
Henderson, K(enneth) D(avid) D(ruitt)
1903-1988 ... CAP-1
Earlier sketch in CA 13-16
Henderson, Katherine Usher 1937- ... 126
Henderson, Kathy 1949- ... CANR-132
Earlier sketches in CA 123, CANR-67
See also SATA 55, 95, 155
See also SATA-Brief 53
Henderson, (Alan) Keith 1883-1982 ... 107
Obituary ... 106
Henderson, Keith M. 1934- ... 21-24R
Henderson, Laurance G. 1924(?)-1977
Obituary ... 73-76
Henderson, Laurence 1928- ... 53-56
Henderson, Lawrence W. 1921- ... 103
Henderson, LeGrand 1901-1965 ... 5-8R
See also SATA 9
Henderson, Linda Dalrymple 1948- ... 124
Henderson, Lois T(hompson) 1918- ... 81-84
Henderson, M(arilyn) R(uth) 1927- ... CANR-27
Henderson, Mary
See Mavor, Osborne Henry
Henderson, Mary C. 1928- ... CANR-111
Earlier sketch in CA 77-80
Henderson, (Andrew) Maxwell 1908-1997 . 132
Henderson, Meg 1948- ... 204
Henderson, Michael (Douglas)
1932- ... CANR-52
Earlier sketches in CA 110, CANR-27
Henderson, Monika 1954- ... 129
Henderson, Nancy 1943- ... 41-44R
Henderson, Nancy Wallace 1916- ... 97-100
See also SATA 22
Henderson, (John) Nicholas 1919- . CANR-127
Earlier sketch in CA 132
Henderson, Norman S. 1960- ... 212
Henderson, Paul III 1939- ... 144
Brief entry ... 122
Henderson, Peter 1904-1983 ... 108
Obituary ... 111
Henderson, Peter V. N. 1947- ... 213
Henderson, Philip (Prichard)
1906-1977 ... CANR-14
Obituary ... 104
Earlier sketches in CAP-1, CA 9-10
Henderson, Randall 1888- ... CAP-1
Earlier sketch in CA 13-14
Henderson, Richard 1924- ... CANR-20
Earlier sketches in CA 13-16R, CANR-5
Henderson, Richard B(eveir) 1921- ... 77-80
Henderson, Richard I(van) 1926- ... CANR-11
Earlier sketch in CA 69-72
Henderson, Robert 1906- ... 106
Henderson, Robert M. 1926- ... 33-36R
Henderson, Robert W(augh) 1920- ... 1-4R
Henderson, Robert William 1888-1985
Obituary ... 117
Henderson, S(hirley) P(rudence) A(nn)
1929- ... 37-40R
Henderson, Stephen E. 1925-1997 ... 29-32R
See also BW 1
Henderson, Sylvia
See Ashton-Warner, Sylvia (Constance)
Henderson, Thomas W(alter) 1949- ... 73-76
Henderson, Vivian (Wilson) 1923-1976 .. 65-68
Obituary ... 61-64
Henderson, W(illiam) O(tto) 1904- ... CANR-4
Earlier sketch in CA 1-4R
Henderson, William III 1922- ... 17-20R
Henderson, William Charles 1941- .. CANR-96
Earlier sketch in CANR-48
Henderson, William Darryl 1938- ... 140
Henderson, William L(eroy) 1927- ... 33-36R
Henderson, William McCranor
1943- ... CANR-72
Earlier sketch in CA 143
Henderson, Zenna (Chlarson)
1917-1983 ... CANR-84
Obituary ... 133
Earlier sketches in CA 1-4R, CANR-1
See also DLB 8
See also SATA 5
See also SFW 4
See also SSC 29
Henderson-Howat, Gerald
See Howat, Gerald Malcolm David
Hendin, David (Bruce) 1945- ... 41-44R
Hendin, Herbert (Martin) 1926- ... 129
Brief entry ... 117
Hendin, Josephine 1946- ... 102
Hendley, Coit (Taylor), Jr. 1920-1985
Obituary ... 116
Hendon, William S(cott) 1933- ... CANR-35
Earlier sketch in CA 45-48
Hendra, Tony 1941(?)- ... CANR-44
Earlier sketch in CA 102
Hendren, Ron 1945- ... 77-80
Hendrich, Paula Griffith 1928- ... CANR-1
Earlier sketch in CA 1-4R
Hendrick, Burton Jesse 1870-1949 ... 189
Hendrick, George 1929- ... CANR-23
Earlier sketches in CA 13-16R, CANR-8
Hendrick, Irving G(uilford) 1936- ... 81-84
Hendrick, Ives 1898-1972 ... CAP-1
Obituary ... 33-36R
Earlier sketch in CA 11-12
Hendrick, T(homas) W(illiam) 1909- ... 108
Hendricks, Faye N(eidhold) 1913-1997 .. 69-72
Hendricks, Frances Wade Kellam
1900-1994 ... 37-40R
Hendricks, Gay 1945- ... CANR-136
Earlier sketch in CA 73-76
Hendricks, George D(avid) 1913-1993 ... 5-8R
Hendricks, J(ames) Edwin 1935- ... CANR-34
Earlier sketches in CA 41-44R, CANR-15
Hendricks, Obery M(ack), Jr. 1953- ... 227
Hendricks, Robert J(oseph) 1944- ... 45-48
Hendricks, Vicki (Due) 1951- ... CANR-88
Earlier sketch in CA 154
Hendricks, Walter 1892-1979
Obituary ... 103
Hendricks, William Lawrence
1929- ... CANR-17
Earlier sketches in CA 49-52, CANR-2
Hendrickson, David C. 1953- ... 126
Hendrickson, Donald E(ugene) 1941- ... 93-96
Hendrickson, James E. 1932- ... 21-24R
Hendrickson, Paul 1944- ... CANR-66
Earlier sketch in CA 108
Hendrickson, R. J.
See Jensen, Ruby Jean
Hendrickson, Robert 1933- ... CANR-144
Earlier sketches in CA 49-52, CANR-1
Hendrickson, Robert A(ugustus)
1923-1996 ... CANR-12
Obituary ... 155
Earlier sketch in CA 29-32R
Hendrickson, Walter Brookfield, Jr.
1936- ... CANR-1
Earlier sketch in CA 1-4R
See also SATA 9
Hendrie, Don(ald Franz), Jr. 1942- ... CANR-18
Earlier sketches in CA 49-52, CANR-3
Hendrie, Laura 1954- ... 196

Hendriks, A(rthur) L(emiere) 1922-1992 ... 97-100
See also CP 1, 2
Hendriksen, Eldon Sende 1917- ... 13-16R
Hendrix, Harville 1935- ... 130
Hendrix, Howard V. 1959- ... 222
Hendry, Allan 1950- ... 106
Hendry, Diana 1941- ... CANR-143
Earlier sketch in CA 136
See also SATA 68, 106
Hendry, Frances Mary 1941- ... 180
See also SATA 110
Hendry, J(ames) F(indlay) 1912-1986 ... 29-32R
Hendry, John (Lovat) 1952- ... 136
Hendry, Joy (McLaggan) 1953- ... 133
Hendry, Linda (Gail) 1961- ... SATA 83
Hendry, Thomas 1929- ... 69-72
See also Hendry, Tom
See also CD 5
Hendry, Tom
See Hendry, Thomas
See also CD 6
Hendryx, James B(eardsley) 1880-1963 ... TCWW 1, 2
Hendy, M(ichael) F(rank) 1942- ... 137
Hendy, Philip (Anstiss) 1900-1980
Obituary ... 102
Henegan, Lucius Herbert, Jr. 1902(?)-1979
Obituary ... 85-88
Heneghan, James 1930- ... CANR-123
Earlier sketch in CA 129
See also AAYA 54
See also SATA 53, 97, 160
Henehan, Mary Pat 1942- ... 234
Heneman, Herbert Gerhard, Jr. 1916- ... CANR-1
Earlier sketch in CA 1-4R
Henfil
See Souza Filho, Henrique de
Henfrey, Colin (Vere Fleetwood) 1941- ... 13-16R
Henfrey, Norman 1929- ... 25-28R
Heng, Liu 1954- ... 171
Henggeler, Paul R. 1955- ... 149
Henggeler, Scott Walter 1950- ... CANR-144
Earlier sketch in CA 144
Henig, Gerald S(heldon) 1942- ... 57-60
Henig, Martin (Edward) 1942- ... 114
Henig, Robin Marantz 1953- ... CANR-111
Earlier sketch in CA 108
Henig, Ruth B(eatrice) 1943- ... 49-52
Henig, Suzanne 1936- ... CANR-2
Earlier sketch in CA 45-48
Henige, David 1938- ... CANR-39
Earlier sketch in CA 103
Henigham, Stephen (P. G.) ... 186
Henighan, Tom 1934- ... DLB 251
Heninger, S(imeon) K(ahn), Jr. 1922- ... CANR-1
Earlier sketch in CA 1-4R
Henisch, Bridget Ann 1932- ... CANR-56
Earlier sketch in CA 127
Henisch, Heinz K. 1922- ... CANR-125
Earlier sketches in CA 73-76, CANR-70
Henisch, Peter 1943- ... 177
See also DLB 85
Henissart, Martha ... CMW 4
Henissart, Paul 1923- ... 29-32R
Henke, Dan (Ferdinand) 1924- ... 53-56
Henke, Emerson O(verbeck) 1916- ... CANR-12
Earlier sketch in CA 17-20R
Henke, Roxanne (Sayler) 1954(?)- ... 238
Henke, Roxy
See Henke, Roxanne (Sayler)
Henke, Shirl ... CANR-128
Earlier sketch in CA 170
Henkel, Barbara Osborn 1921- ... 9-12R
Henkel, Stephen C. 1933- ... 37-40R
Henkels, Robert M(acAllister), Jr. 1936- ... 57-60
Henkes, Kevin 1960- ... CANR-139
Earlier sketches in CA 114, CANR-38
See also AAYA 59
See also CLR 23
See also MAICYA 1, 2
See also SATA 43, 76, 108, 154
Henkes, Robert 1922- ... CANR-113
Earlier sketches in CA 33-36R, CANR-13, 29, 54
Henkin, Harmon 1940(?)-1980
Obituary ... 101
Henkin, Joshua ... 161
See also CLC 119
Henkin, Louis 1917- ... CANR-13
Earlier sketch in CA 33-36R
Henkle, Roger B. 1935- ... 129
Henle, Faye (?)-1972
Obituary ... 37-40R
Henle, Fritz 1909-1993 ... 73-76
Obituary ... 140
Henle, James 1891(?)-1973
Obituary ... 37-40R
Henle, Jane 1913- ... 77-80
Henle, Mary 1913- ... 33-36R
Henle, Robert John 1909-2000 ... 110
Obituary ... 187
Henle, Theda O(strander) 1918-2005 ... 33-36R
Obituary ... 238
Henley, Arthur 1921- ... 21-24R
Henley, Beth
See Henley, Elizabeth Becker
See also CABS 3
See also CAD
See also CD 5, 6
See also CLC 23
See also CSW
See also CWD
See also DC 6, 14
See also DFS 2
See also DLBY 1986
See also FW
Henley, Elizabeth Becker 1952- ... CANR-140
Earlier sketches in CA 107, CANR-32, 73
See also Henley, Beth
See also DA3
See also DAM DRAM, MST
See also DFS 21
See also MTCW 1, 2
See also MTFW 2005
Henley, Gail 1952- ... CANR-21
Earlier sketch in CA 89-92
Henley, Helen 1952- ... 217
Henley, Jan (S.) 1956- ... 219
Henley, Karyn 1952- ... 102
Henley, Nancy Eloise Main 1934-
Brief entry ... 106
Henley, Norman 1915- ... 17-20R
Henley, Patricia 1947- ... 200
Henley, Virginia 1935- ... CANR-98
Earlier sketches in CA 109, CANR-41
Henley, W(illiam) Ballentine 1905-1988 ... 61-64
Henley, Wallace (Boynton) 1941- ... CANR-14
Earlier sketch in CA 65-68
Henley, William Ernest 1849-1903 ... 234
Brief entry ... 105
See also DLB 19
See also RGEL 2
See also TCLC 8
Henn, Harry George 1919-1994 ... CANR-36
Obituary ... 147
Earlier sketch in CA 45-48
Henn, Henry
See Henn, Harry George
Henn, Martin J. 1968- ... 238
Henn, Thomas Rice 1901-1974 ... CANR-4
Earlier sketch in CA 5-8R
Hennacy, Ammon 1893-1970
Obituary ... 104
Henne, Frances E. 1906-1985
Obituary ... 118
Hennedy, Hugh L(ouis) 1929- ... 41-44R
Henneman, John Bell, Jr. 1935-1998 ... CANR-57
Earlier sketches in CA 45-48, CANR-31
Henner, Marilu 1952- ... CANR-129
Earlier sketch in CA 172
Hennesey, James J. 1926- ... 33-36R
Hennessee, Judith Adler 1932- ... 199
Hennessey, Caroline
See von Block, Bela W(illiam) and von Block, Sylvia
Hennessey, R(oger) A(nthony) S(ean) 1937- ... 29-32R
Hennessey, Thomas W. ... 233
Hennessy, Bernard C. 1924- ... 13-16R
Hennessy, David James George 1932- ... CANR-22
Earlier sketch in CA 106
Hennessy, James Pope
See Pope-Hennessy, James
Hennessy, John J(oseph) 1958- ... 141
Hennessy, Joseph (K.) 1932- ... 213
Hennessy, Jossleyn (Michael Stephen Philip) 1903- ... 9-12R
Hennessy, Mary L. 1927- ... 21-24R
Hennessy, Max
See Harris, John
Hennessy, Peter 1947- ... CANR-103
Earlier sketch in CA 123
Hennessy, Thomas C(hristopher) 1916- ... 115
Henney, Carolee Wells 1928- ... 169
See also SATA 102
Hennig, Margaret (Marie) 1940- ... 81-84
Henniker, Florence 1855-1923 ... DLB 135
Henning, Ann
See Jocelyn, Ann Henning
Henning, Basil Duke 1910-1990
Obituary ... 130
Henning, Charles N(athaniel) 1915- ... CANR-49
Earlier sketch in CA 1-4R
Henning, Daniel H(oward) 1931- ... CANR-2
Earlier sketch in CA 45-48
Henning, Edward B(urk) 1922-1993 ... CANR-49
Obituary ... 141
Earlier sketch in CA 17-20R
Henning, Rachel 1826-1914 ... DLB 230
Henning, Standish 1932-
Brief entry ... 107
Henning, Sylvie Marie Debevec
See Debevec Henning, Sylvie Marie
Henninger, G. Ross 1898-1984
Obituary ... 112
Hennings, Dorothy Grant 1935- ... CANR-4
Earlier sketch in CA 53-56
Hennings, Josephine Silva 1899(?)-1985
Obituary ... 117
Henningsen, Agnes 1868-1962 ... DLB 214
Hennissart, Martha 1929- ... CANR-64
Earlier sketch in CA 85-88
See also Lathen, Emma
Henrey, Madeleine 1906-2004 ... CANR-6
Obituary ... 226
Earlier sketch in CA 13-16R
Henrey, Mrs. Robert
See Henrey, Madeleine
Henrey, Robert
See Henrey, Madeleine
Henri, Adrian (Maurice) 1932-2000 ... CANR-34
Obituary ... 190
Earlier sketches in CA 25-28R, CANR-15
See also CP 1, 2, 3, 4, 5, 6, 7
See also MTCW 1
Henri, Florette 1908-1985 ... 73-76
Obituary ... 117
Henri, G.
See Clement, George H.
Henri, Noble
See Wynorski, Jim
Henrichsen, Walt(er Arlie), Jr. 1934- ... 89-92
Henricks, Kaw
See Wolfe, Charles Keith
Henricks, Mark ... 223
Henricksson, John 1926- ... 163
Henries, A. Doris Banks 1913(?)-1981 ... 125
Obituary ... 103
See also BW 1
Henries, Doris
See Henries, A. Doris Banks
Henriksen, Louise Levitas 1917- ... 128
Henriksen, Margot A. ... 172
Henriksen, Thomas H(ollinger) 1939- ... 112
Henrikson, Arthur A. 1921- ... 130
Henriod, Lorraine 1925- ... CANR-47
Earlier sketch in CA 45-48
See also SATA 26
Henriot, Christian ... 227
Henriques, Veronica 1931- ... 102
Henriquez, Emile F. 1937- ... SATA 89
Henriquez Urena, Pedro 1884-1946 ... LAW
Henry VIII 1491-1547 ... DLB 132
Henry, Alexander 1739-1824 ... DLB 99
Henry, April 1959- ... 191
Henry, Avril (Kay) 1935- ... 123
Henry, Bessie Walker 1921- ... 9-12R
Henry, Bill
See Henry, William Mellors
Henry, Buck 1930- ... 77-80
See also DLB 26
See also IDFW 3, 4
Henry, Carl F(erdinand) H(oward) 1913-2003 ... CANR-46
Obituary ... 222
Earlier sketches in CA 13-16R, CANR-6, 21
Henry, Chad 1946- ... 224
Henry, (William) Claud 1914-1984 ... 45-48
Henry, Daniel
See Kahnweiler, Daniel-Henry
Henry, David Dodds 1905-1995 ... 106
Obituary ... 149
Henry, David Lee
See Hill, R. Lance
Henry, Desmond Paul 1921- ... CANR-90
Earlier sketch in CA 132
Henry, DeWitt (Pawling II) 1941- ... CANR-104
Earlier sketch in CA 131
Henry, Edgar
See Tourgee, Albion W.
Henry, Elyssa
See Lavene, Jim and Lavene, Joyce
Henry, Eric P(utnam) 1943- ... 108
Henry, Ernest 1948- ... SATA 107
Henry, Faith
See Levine, Nancy D.
Henry, Fran Worden 1948- ... 111
Henry, Frances 1931- ... 77-80
Henry, Francoise 1902-1982
Obituary ... 106
Henry, Gordon D., Jr. 1955- ... 146
Henry, Harold Wilkinson 1926- ... 37-40R
Henry, Harriet
See De Steuch, Harriet Henry
Henry, James P(aget) 1914-1996 ... 104
Henry, James S(helburne) 1950- ... 49-52
Henry, Janet Cope 1925(?)-1986
Obituary ... 118
Henry, Jeanne Heffernan 1940- ... 105
Henry, Joanne Landers 1927- ... 17-20R
See also SATA 6
Henry, John Case 1905-1990
Obituary ... 132
Henry, Joseph B. 1901-1982 ... CAP-2
Earlier sketch in CA 17-18
Henry, Jules 1904-1969
Obituary ... 109
Henry, Kenneth 1920- ... 57-60
Henry, Laurin L(uther) 1921- ... CANR-43
Earlier sketch in CA 1-4R
Henry, Maeve 1960- ... 142
See also SATA 75
Henry, Marcel
See Dugas, Marcel
Henry, Marguerite 1902-1997 ... CANR-9
Obituary ... 162
Earlier sketch in CA 17-20R
See also BYA 2
See also CLR 4
See also CWRI 5
See also DLB 22
See also JRDA
See also MAICYA 1, 2
See also SAAS 7
See also SATA 100
See also SATA-Obit 99
Henry, Marie H. 1935- ... SATA 65
Henry, Marilyn 1939- ... SATA 117
Henry, Marion
See del Rey, Lester
Henry, Neil 1954- ... 200
Henry, Noble
See Wynorski, Jim
Henry, O.
See Porter, William Sydney
See also AAYA 41
See also AMWS 2
See also EXPS
See also RGAL 4
See also RGSF 2
See also SSC 5, 49
See also SSFS 2, 18
See also TCLC 1, 19
See also TCWW 1, 2
See also WLC
Henry, Oliver
See Porter, William Sydney
Henry, Patrick 1736-1799 ... LAIT 1
Henry, Patrick 1940- ... 145
Henry, Paul 1959- ... 235
Henry, Peter 1926- ... 109
Henry, Rene A. 1933- ... 187
Henry, Robert
See Powell, (Oval) Talmage
Henry, Robert Selph 1889-1970 ... CANR-17
Obituary ... 103
Earlier sketch in CA 1-4R
See also DLB 17
Henry, Shirley 1925(?)-1972
Obituary ... 33-36R
Henry, Sondra 1930- ... CANR-49
Earlier sketch in CA 119
Henry, Stuart (Dennis) 1949- ... 143
Henry, Sue 1940- ... 199
Henry, T. E.
See Rowland-Entwistle, (Arthur) Theodore (Henry)
Henry, Vera 1909(?)-1987 ... CAP-2
Obituary ... 123
Earlier sketch in CA 21-22
Henry, W. P. 1929- ... 17-20R
Henry, Will
See Allen, Henry Wilson
Henry, William A(lfred) III 1950-1994 ... CANR-65
Obituary ... 146
Brief entry ... 116
Earlier sketch in CA 130
Henry, William Earl 1917-
Brief entry ... 108
Henry, William Mellors 1890-1970
Obituary ... 89-92
Henry of Ghent 1217(?)-1293 ... DLB 115
Henryson, Robert 1430(?)-1506(?) ... BRWS 7
See also DLB 146
See also PC 65
See also RGEL 2
Henry the Minstrel
See Hary
Henschel, Elizabeth Georgie ... 107
See also SATA 56
Henschke, Alfred
See Klabund
Henseler, Christine 1969- ... 236
Hensey, Frederick G(erald) 1931- ... 89-92
Hensey, Fritz
See Hensey, Frederick G(erald)
Henshall, A(udrey) S(hore) 1927- ... 9-12R
Henshaw, James Ene 1924- ... 101
See also BW 2
See also CD 5, 6
Henshaw, Richard 1945- ... 101
Henshaw, Tom 1924- ... 103
Henshel, Richard L(ee) 1939- ... 57-60
Hensher, Philip 1965- ... 195
See also DLB 267
Hensley, Almon
See Hensley, Sophie Almon
Hensley, Charles S(tanley) 1919- ... 41-44R
Hensley, Christopher 1972- ... 225
Hensley, Dennis 1964- ... 171
Hensley, Jeff (Lane) 1947- ... 117
Hensley, Joe L.
See Hensley, Joseph Louis
Hensley, Joseph Louis 1926- ... CANR-107
Earlier sketches in CA 33-36R, CANR-14, 31, 57, 62
See also CMW 4
See also SFW 4
Hensley, Sophie Almon 1866-1946 ... 176
See also DLB 99
Hensley, (Malcolm) Stewart 1914(?)-1976
Obituary ... 65-68
Henslin, James M(arvin) 1937- ... CANR-86
Earlier sketches in CA 41-44R, CANR-15, 34
Henson, Beth 1950- ... 148
Henson, Clyde E(ugene) 1914-1984 ... 5-8R
Henson, James Maury 1936-1990 ... 124
Obituary ... 131
Brief entry ... 106
See also Henson, Jim
See also SATA 43
See also SATA-Obit 65
Henson, Jim -1990
See Henson, James Maury
See also IDFW 3, 4
Henson, Lance 1944- ... 146
See also DLB 175
See also NNAL
Henson, Margaret Swett 1924- ... CANR-50
Earlier sketch in CA 122
Henstell, Bruce 1945- ... 131
Henstell, Diana
See Silber, Diana
Henstra, Friso 1928- ... SAAS 14
See also SATA 8, 73
Henthorn, William E(llsworth) 1928- ... 41-44R

Hentoff, Nat(han Irving) 1925- CANR-114
Earlier sketches in CA 1-4R, CANR-5, 25, 77
Interview in CANR-25
See also CAAS 6
See also AAYA 4, 42
See also BYA 6
See also CLC 26
See also CLR 1, 52
See also JRDA
See also MAICYA 1, 2
See also SATA 42, 69, 133
See also SATA-Brief 27
See also WYA
See also YAW
Henty, G(eorge) A(lfred) 1832-1902 177
Brief entry 112
See also CLR 76
See also DLB 18, 141
See also RGEL 2
See also SATA 64
Hentz, Caroline Lee (Whiting) 1800-1856 .... DLB 3, 248
Henwood, James N. J. 1932- 29-32R
Henze, Donald F(rank) 1928- 21-24R
Henze, Hans Werner 1926- 183
Henze, Paul B(ernard) 1924- 206
Heo, Yumi 1964- 159
See also SATA 94, 146
Hepburn, Andrew H. 1899(?)-1975
Obituary 57-60
Hepburn, James Gordon 1922- CANR-29
Earlier sketch in CA 85-88
Hepburn, Katharine (Houghton) 1909-2003 .... CANR-78
Obituary 217
Earlier sketch in CA 139
Hepburn, Ronald W(illiam) 1927- 13-16R
Heper, Metin 1940- 156
Hepinstall, Kathy 200
Hepner, Harry W(alker) 1893-1984 .... 29-32R
Obituary 114
Hepner, James O(rville) 1933- 57-60
Hepner, Lisa Ann 1969- 213
Heppenheimer, T(homas) A(dolph) 1947- CANR-140
Earlier sketches in CA 93-96, CANR-16
Heppenstall, Margit Strom 1913-1995 .. 21-24R
Heppenstall, (John) Rayner 1911-1981 .... CANR-29
Obituary 103
Earlier sketch in CA 1-4R
See also CLC 10
See also CN 1, 2
See also CP 1, 2
See also EWL 3
Hepple, Alex 1904(?)-1983
Obituary 111
Hepple, Bob (Alexander) 1934- CANR-12
Earlier sketch in CA 29-32R
Hepple, Peter 1927- 81-84
Heppner, Cheryl M. 1951- 142
Heppner, Ernest G. 1921- 149
Heppner, Mike 1972- 221
Heppner, P(uncky) Paul 1951- 141
Heppner, Sam(uel) 1913-1983 .... 25-28R
Obituary 109
Hepworth, James B. 1910-1993 .... 1-4R
Hepworth, James Michael 1938- CANR-13
Earlier sketch in CA 73-76
Hepworth, Mike
See Hepworth, James Michael
Hepworth, (Charles) Philip 1912- 17-20R
Her
See Deal, Borden
Heraclitus c. 540B.C.-c. 450B.C. .... DLB 176
Herail, Rene James 1939- 118
Herald, Earl Stannard 1914-1973
Obituary 112
Herald, George William 1911- 73-76
Herald, Kathleen
See Peyton, Kathleen Wendy (Herald)
Heraud, Brian J(eremy) 1934- 73-76
Heraud, Javier 1942-1963 131
See also HW 1
Heravi, Mehdi 1940- 29-32R
Herb, Angela M. 1970- 156
See also SATA 92
Herber, Bernard P. 1929- 21-24R
Herber, Harold L. 1929- 108
Herber, Lewis
See Bookchin, Murray
Herberg, Will 1909-1977 73-76
Obituary 69-72
Herberger, Charles F. 1920- CANR-91
Earlier sketch in CA 41-44R
Herbers, John N. 1923- 33-36R
Herbert, A(lan) P(atrick) 1890-1971 97-100
Obituary 33-36R
See also CN 1
See also DLB 10, 191
Herbert, Agnes c. 1880(?)-1960 .... DLB 174
Herbert, Anthony B(ernard) 1930- 77-80
Herbert, Arthur
See Shappiro, Herbert (Arthur)
Herbert, Brian 1947- CANR-103
Earlier sketch in CA 133
Herbert, Cecil
See Hamilton, Charles (Harold St. John)
Herbert, Cecil L. 1926- .... CP 1
Herbert, Cynthia Ridgeway 1943- 118
Herbert, David (Alexander Reginald) 1908-1995 141
Obituary 148
Herbert, David T(homas) 1935- CANR-10
Earlier sketches in CA 49-52, CANR-2, 18
Herbert, Don(ald Jeffrey) 1917- CANR-30
Earlier sketch in CA 29-32R
See also SATA 2
Herbert, Edward 1583-1648
See Herbert of Cherbury, Lord
See also DLB 121, 151, 252
Herbert, Eugenia W(arren) 1929- CANR-86
Earlier sketches in CA 93-96, CANR-35
Herbert, Frank (Patrick) 1920-1986 .. CANR-43
Obituary 118
Earlier sketches in CA 53-56, CANR-5
Interview in CANR-5
See also AAYA 21
See also BPFB 2
See also BYA 4, 14
See also CDALBS
See also CLC 12, 23, 35, 44, 85
See also CPW
See also DAM POP
See also DLB 8
See also LAIT 5
See also MTCW 1, 2
See also MTFW 2005
See also NFS 17
See also SATA 9, 37
See also SATA-Obit 47
See also SCFW 1, 2
See also SFW 4
See also YAW
Herbert, Gary B. 1941- 237
Herbert, George 1593-1633 .... BRW 2
See also BRWR 2
See also CDBLB Before 1660
See also DAB
See also DAM POET
See also DLB 126
See also EXPP
See also PC 4
See also RGEL 2
See also TEA
See also WP
Herbert, Gilbert 1924- CANR-47
Earlier sketches in CA 107, CANR-23
Herbert, Helen (Jean) 1947- .... SATA 57
Herbert, Henry George Alfred Marius Victor Francis 1898-1987
Obituary 123
Herbert, Henry K.
See Knibbs, H(enry) H(erbert)
Herbert, Henry William 1807-1858 . DLB 3, 73
Herbert, Ian 1939- 111
Herbert, (Edward) Ivor (Montgomery) 1925- CANR-19
Earlier sketches in CA 53-56, CANR-4
Herbert, James 1943- CANR-81
Earlier sketch in CA 81-84
See also HGG
See also SFW 4
Herbert, Janis 1956- 210
See also SATA 139
Herbert, Jean (Daniel Fernand) 1897-1980 .... CANR-9
Earlier sketch in CA 17-20R
Herbert, John
See Brundage, John Herbert
See also CD 6
See also DLB 53
Herbert, John (David) 1924- CANR-13
Earlier sketch in CA 21-24R
Herbert, Kevin (Barry John) 1921- 17-20R
Herbert, Marie 1941- 69-72
Herbert, Martin 1933- 103
Herbert, Nick 1936- 128
Herbert, Robert L(ouis) 1929- CANR-82
Earlier sketches in CA 9-12R, CANR-5, 36
Herbert, Sandra (Swanson) 1942- 130
Herbert, Stephen 1951- 153
Herbert, Theodore T(erence) 1942- .. CANR-15
Earlier sketch in CA 65-68
Herbert, Thomas Walter, Jr. 1938- .. CANR-137
Earlier sketch in CA 104
Herbert, Victor (Daniel) 1927-2002 112
Obituary 210
Herbert, W. N. 1961- 206
Herbert, Wally
See Herbert, Walter William
Herbert, Walter William 1934- CANR-15
Earlier sketch in CA 69-72
See also SATA 23
Herbert, William
See Croly, Herbert (David)
Herbert, William 1580-1630 .... DLB 121
Herbert, (Alfred Francis) Xavier 1901-1984 .... CANR-46
Obituary 114
Earlier sketch in CA 69-72
See also CN 1, 2, 3
See also DLB 260
See also EWL 3
See also RGEL 2
Herbert, Zbigniew 1924-1998 .... CANR-74
Obituary 169
Earlier sketches in CA 89-92, CANR-36
See also CDWLB 4
See also CLC 9, 43
See also CWW 2
See also DAM POET
See also DLB 232
See also EWL 3
See also MTCW 1
See also PC 50
See also PFS 22
See also TCLC 168
Herbert of Cherbury, Lord
See Herbert, Edward
See also RGEL 2
Herbertson, Gary J. 1938- 25-28R
Herblock
See Block, Herbert (Lawrence)
Herbrand, Jan(ice M.) 1931- 49-52
Herbruck, Christine Comstock
See Comstock, Christine
Herbst, Anthony F(rancis) 1941- CANR-35
Earlier sketch in CA 114
Herbst, Josephine (Frey) 1897-1969 .... 5-8R
Obituary 25-28R
See also CLC 34
See also DLB 9
Herbst, Judith 1947- .... SATA 74
Herbst, Jurgen (F. H.) 1928- 37-40R
Herbst, Phil(ip H.) 1944- 160
Herbst, Robert L(eroy) 1935- 61-64
Herburger, Gunter 1932- 190
See also DLB 75, 124
Herculano, Alexandre 1810-1877 .... DLB 287
Hercules, Frank (E. M.) 1911-1996 .... CANR-2
Obituary 152
Earlier sketch in CA 1-4R
See also BW 1
See also DLB 33
Herd, Dale 1940- 61-64
Herd, David 210
Herd, Michael 1937- 128
Herda, D. J. 1948- 147
See also SATA 80
Herdan, Gustav 1897- 1-4R
Herdan, Innes 1911- 142
Herdeck, Donald E(lmer) 1924-2005 53-56
Obituary 238
Herdeg, Klaus 1937- 130
Herder, Johann Gottfried von 1744-1803 .... DLB 97
See also EW 4
See also TWA
Herding, Klaus 1939- 140
Herdt, Gilbert H(enry) 1949- 105
Herdt, Sheryll (Enette) Patterson 1941- 57-60
Heredia, Jose Maria 1803-1839 .... HLCS 2
See also LAW
Heredia, Jose-Maria de 1842-1905 ... GFL 1789 to the Present
Heredia, Jose-Maria de 1842-1905 .... DLB 217
Hereford, John
See Fletcher, H(arry) L(utf) V(erne)
Heren, Louis (Philip) 1919-1995 .... CANR-12
Obituary 147
Earlier sketch in CA 25-28R
Hert, Jeffrey 1947- 168
Herfindahl, Orris C(lemens) 1918-1972 .... 41-44R
Obituary 37-40R
Herford, C(harles) H(arold) 1853-1931 183
See also DLB 149
Herford, C(harles) H(arold) 1853-1931 183
Herge
See Remi, Georges
See also AAYA 55
See also CLR 6
Hergenhahn, B(aldwin) R(oss) 1934- 123
Brief entry 118
Hergenhan, L(aurence) T(homas) 1931- CANR-121
Earlier sketches in CA 127, CANR-56
Hergenhan, Laurie
See Hergenhan, L(aurence) T(homas)
Hergesheimer, Joseph 1880-1954 194
Brief entry 109
See also DLB 102, 9
See also RGAL 4
See also TCLC 11
Herget, Paul 1908(?)-1981
Obituary 105
Herian, V.
See Gregorian, Vartan
Heriat, Philippe
See Payelle, Raymond-Gerard
Herilany, Dorthea Rosa 1963- .... RGWL 3
Hering, Doris (Minnie) 1920- 128
Herington, C. J(ohn) 1924- CANR-15
Earlier sketch in CA 29-32R
Heriot, Angus 1927- 5-8R
Heritage, John 1953- 205
Heritage, Martin
See Horler, Sydney
Heriteau, Jacqueline 1925- CANR-37
Earlier sketches in CA 45-48, CANR-1, 16
Herity, Michael 1929- 49-52
Herivel, Tara 227
Herken, Gregg (Franklin) 1947- CANR-123
Earlier sketches in CA 104, CANR-20
Herkimer, L(awrence) R(ussell) 1925(?)- 110
See also SATA 42
Herlihy, David (Joseph) 1930-1991 .... 41-44R
Obituary 133
Herlihy, Dirlie Anne 1935- .... SATA 73
Herlihy, James Leo 1927-1993 .... CANR-2
Obituary 143
Earlier sketch in CA 1-4R
See also CAD
See also CLC 6
See also CN 1, 2, 3, 4, 5
Herlin, Hans 1925-1994 77-80
Obituary 147
Herling, Gustaw 1919-2000 158
Obituary 188
Herling, John 1907-
Brief entry 112
Herling-Grudzinski, Gustaw
See Herling, Gustaw
Herlth, Robert 1893-1962 .... IDFW 3, 4
Herm, Gerhard 1931- CANR-45
Earlier sketches in CA 104, CANR-22
Hermalyn, Gary 1952- CANR-50
Earlier sketch in CA 123
Herman, A(rthur) L(udwig) 1930- 65-68
Herman, Arthur 192
Herman, Barbara 1945- CANR-99
Earlier sketch in CA 145
Herman, Ben 1927- 104
Herman, Bernard L. 1951- 140
Herman, Charlotte 1937- CANR-86
Earlier sketches in CA 41-44R, CANR-15, 34
See also SATA 20, 99
Herman, Didi 1961- CANR-125
Earlier sketch in CA 164
Herman, Donald L. 1928- CANR-29
Earlier sketches in CA 53-56, CANR-4
Herman, Ellen 1957- 149
Herman, Esther 1935- 102
Herman, George E(dward) 1920-2005 69-72
Obituary 236
Herman, George R(ichard) 1925- 5-8R
Herman, Jan (Jacob) 1942- CANR-60
Earlier sketch in CA 45-48
Herman, John R(ufus) 1928- 119
Herman, Judith 1943- 49-52
Herman, Judith Lewis 1942- 142
Herman, Justin B. 1907(?)-1983
Obituary 111
Herman, Kenneth Neil 1954- 77-80
Herman, Louis Jay 1925-1996 53-56
Obituary 152
Herman, Marguerite Shalett 1914-1977 .... 41-44R
Herman, Masako 103
Herman, Melvin (Jerome) 1922-1983
Brief entry 111
Herman, Melvin 1922(?)-1983
Obituary 109
Herman, Michael 1929- 169
Herman, Michelle 1955- CANR-90
Earlier sketch in CA 136
Herman, Pee-Wee
See Reubens, Paul
Herman, Richard, Jr. 1939- 137
Herman, Roger E. 1943- 128
Herman, Simon N(athan) 1912-1995 .... 29-32R
Herman, Sondra R(enee) 1932- 25-28R
Herman, Stanley M. 1928- 25-28R
Herman, Stephen L. 1946- 225
Herman, Vic(tor J.) 1919- 107
Herman, Victor 1916(?)-1985
Obituary 115
Herman, Walter
See Wager, Walter H(erman)
Herman, William
See Bierce, Ambrose (Gwinett)
Herman, William 1926- 126
Hermand, Jost 1930- CANR-57
Earlier sketches in CA 41-44R, CANR-14, 31
Hermann, Donald H(arold) J(ames) 1943- CANR-17
Earlier sketches in CA 45-48, CANR-2
Hermann, Edward J(ulius) 1919- 17-20R
Hermann, John 1917- 49-52
Hermann, L. William
See Licht, H. William
Hermann, Philip J(ay) 1916- CANR-41
Earlier sketch in CA 117
Hermann, (Theodore) Placid 1909-(?) CAP-1
Earlier sketch in CA 13-16
Hermanns, Peter
See Brannon, William T.
Hermanns, William 1895-1990 .... CANR-15
Earlier sketch in CA 37-40R
Hermann the Lame 1013-1054 .... DLB 148
Hermans, Hubert J. M. 1937- 146
Hermans, Willem Frederik 1921-1995 .. CAP-1
Earlier sketch in CA 9-10
See also CWW 2
See also EWL 3
Hermansen, Gustav 1909- 117
Hermansen, John 1918- 45-48
Hermanson, Dennis (Everett) 1947- .... SATA 10
Hermeren, Goeran A. 1938- CANR-15
Earlier sketch in CA 89-92
Hermes
See Flammarion, (Nicolas) Camille
Hermes, Johann Timotheus 1738-1821 .... DLB 97
Hermes, Jules 1962- 156
See also SATA 92
Hermes, Patricia (Mary) 1936- CANR-130
Earlier sketches in CA 104, CANR-22, 50
See also AAYA 15, 60
See also SATA 31, 78, 141
See also YAW
Hermlin, Stephan 1915- 153
See also DLB 69
See also EWL 3
Hermodsson, Elisabet (Hermine) 1927- 189
Hern, (George) Anthony 1916- 21-24R
Hern, Katie 1969- 188
Hern, Nicholas 1944- 115
Hernadi, Paul 1936- CANR-92
Earlier sketches in CA 41-44R, CANR-15, 42
Hernandez, Al 1909- CAP-2
Earlier sketch in CA 21-22
Hernandez, Alfonso C. 1938- .... DLB 122
Hernandez, Amado V. 1903-1970
Obituary 112
Hernandez, Felisberto 1902-1964 213
See also EWL 3
See also LAWS 1
Hernandez, Frances 1926- 37-40R
Hernandez, Gilbert 1957(?)- CANR-134
Earlier sketch in CA 171
Hernandez, Ines
See Hernandez-Avila, Ines
Hernandez, Jaime 1959(?)- 224

Hernandez, Jo(anne) Farb 1952- ... CANR-143
Earlier sketch in CA 172
Hernandez, Joel
See Turnipseed, Joel
Hernandez, Jose 1834-1886 ... LAW
See also RGWL 2, 3
See also WLIT 1
Hernandez, Juana Amelia ... 45-48
Hernandez, Lea ... AAYA 57
Hernandez, Luis F. 1923- ... 61-64
Hernandez, Luisa Josefina 1928- ... CWW 2
See also EWL 3
Hernandez, Miguel 1910-1942 ... DLB 134
See also EWL 3
Hernandez, Natalie Nelson 1929- ... SATA 123
Hernandez, Pedro F(elix) 1925- ... 45-48
Hernandez Aquino, Luis 1907-(?) ... HW 1
Hernandez-Avila, Ines 1947- ... 190
See also DLB 122
See also HW 2
Herndl, Carl G(eorge) 1956- ... 158
Herndl, George C. 1927- ... 33-36R
Herndon, Booton 1915- ... CANR-4
Earlier sketch in CA 9-12R
Herndon, Ernest ... CANR-113
Earlier sketch in CA 155
See also SATA 91
Herndon, James 1926- ... 89-92
Interview in ... CA-89-92
Herndon, John 1954- ... 194
Herndon, Nancy 1934- ... CANR-128
Earlier sketch in CA 169
Herndon, Terry (Eugene) 1939- ... 130
Herndon, Ursule Molinaro
See Molinaro, Ursule
Herndon, Venable 1927-1999 ... CANR-32
Obituary ... 188
Earlier sketch in CA 109
Herne, Brian 1938- ... 190
Herne, Huxley
See Brooker, Bertram (Richard)
Herne, James A. 1839-1901 ... RGAL 4
Herner, Charles H. 1930- ... 29-32R
Hernes, Helga Maria 1938- ... CANR-20
Earlier sketch in CA 103
Hernon, Peter 1944- ... CANR-8
Earlier sketch in CA 61-64
Hernton, Calvin C(oolidge)
1932-2001 ... CANR-26
Obituary ... 203
Earlier sketches in CA 9-12R, CANR-3
See also BW 1
See also CP 2
See also DLB 38
Hero, Alfred O(livier), Jr. 1924- ... 21-24R
Herodotus c. 484B.C.-c. 420B.C. ... AW 1
See also CDWLB 1
See also DLB 176
See also RGWL 2, 3
See also TWA
Heroet, Antoine 1492-1568 . GFL Beginnings to 1789
Herold, Ann Bixby 1937- ... SATA 72
Herold, Brenda 1948- ... 33-36R
Herold, J(ean) Christopher 1919-1964 ... CAP-1
Earlier sketch in CA 9-10
Heron, Alasdair I(ain) C(ampbell) 1942- ... 115
Heron, Ann 1954- ... 147
Heron, David Winston 1920- ... 112
Heron, Laurence Tunstall 1902-1991 ... 49-52
Heron, Patrick 1920-1999 ... 109
Obituary ... 177
Heron, Robert 1764-1807 ... DLB 142
Heron-Allen, Edward 1861-1943
Brief entry ... 113
See also HGG
See also SFW 4
Herpel, George L(loyd) 1921- ... CANR-15
Earlier sketch in CA 41-44R
Herr, Dan(iel J.) 1917-1990 ... 1-4R
Obituary ... 132
Herr, Edwin L. 1933- ... 37-40R
Herr, Ethel 1936- ... 112
Herr, Michael 1940(?)- ... CANR-142
Earlier sketches in CA 89-92, CANR-68
See also DLB 185
See also MTCW 1
Herr, Pamela (Staley) 1939- ... 126
Herr, Richard 1922- ... 1-4R
Herrera, (C.) Andrea O'Reilly 1959- ... 193
Herrera, Dario 1870-1914 ... DLB 290
Herrera, Fernando de 1534(?)-1597 ... DLB 318
3
Herrera, Jorge -1981 ... IDFW 3, 4
Herrera, Juan Felipe 1948- ... CANR-96
Earlier sketch in CA 131
See also AAYA 44
See also DLB 122
See also HW 1
See also LLW
See also SATA 127
Herrera, Robert A. 1930- ... 207
Herrera-Sobek, Maria ... 131
See also HW 1
Herrera y Reissig, Julio 1875-1910 ... EWL 3
See also HW 1
See also LAW
Herrero, Stephen M(atthew) 1939- ... 118
Herreshoff, David 1921- ... 21-24R
Herreshoff, L. Francis 1890-1972 ... CAP-1
Obituary ... 37-40R
Earlier sketch in CA 13-14
Herreweghen, Hubert van
See van Herreweghen, Hubert
Herrick, Bruce Hale 1936- ... CANR-7
Earlier sketch in CA 17-20R
Herrick, James A. 1954- ... 225
Herrick, Joy Field 1930- ... 101
Herrick, Marvin Theodore
1899-1966 ... CANR-1
Earlier sketch in CA 1-4R
Herrick, Neal Q(uentin) 1927- ... CANR-43
Earlier sketch in CA 49-52
Herrick, Robert 1591-1674 ... BRW 2
See also BRWC 2
See also DA
See also DAB
See also DAC
See also DAM MST, POP
See also DLB 126
See also EXPP
See also PC 9
See also PFS 13
See also RGAL 4
See also RGEL 2
See also TEA
See also WP
Herrick, Robert (Welch) 1868-1938
Brief entry ... 119
See also DLB 9, 12, 78
Herrick, Robert L(ee) 1930- ... 61-64
Herrick, Steven 1958- ... CANR-141
Earlier sketch in CA 170
See also SATA 103, 156
Herrick, Tracy Grant 1933- ... CANR-42
Earlier sketch in CA 112
Herrick, Walter R(ussell), Jr. 1918- ... 21-24R
Herrick, William 1915-2004 ... CANR-9
Obituary ... 225
Earlier sketch in CA 21-24R
See also DLBY 1983, 2001
Herridge, Robert 1914(?)-1981
Obituary ... 104
Herriges, Greg C. 1950- ... 213
Herriman, George (Joseph)
1880-1944 ... CANR-119
Earlier sketch in CA 174
See also AAYA 43
See also SATA 140
Herrin, Lamar 1940- ... 142
Herring, Dale-Marie 1968- ... 213
Herring, George (C.) 1936- ... CANR-98
Earlier sketches in CA 41-44R, CANR-14
Herring, Guilles
See Somerville, Edith Oenone
Herring, Hubert Clinton 1889-1967
Obituary ... 105
Herring, Jack W(illiam) 1925- ... 115
Herring, Peggy J. 1953- ... 162
Herring, Phillip F. 1936- ... 151
Herring, Ralph A(lderman)
1901-1972(?) ... CAP-2
Earlier sketch in CA 21-22
Herring, Reuben 1922-1993 ... CANR-7
Earlier sketch in CA 17-20R
Herring, Robert H(erschel) 1938- ... CANR-21
Earlier sketch in CA 105
Herrington, Anne J. 1948- ... 145
Herrington, James L(awrence) 1928- ... 73-76
Herrington, Pat
See Herrington, Patricia (Murphy)
Herrington, Patricia (Murphy) 1927- ... 114
Herrington, Stuart A. 1941- ... 109
Herrington, Terri
See Blackstock, Terri
Herriot, James 1916-1995 ... CANR-40
Obituary ... 148
See also Wight, James Alfred
See also AAYA 1, 54
See also BPFB 2
See also CLC 12
See also CLR 80
See also CPW
See also DAM POP
See also LAIT 3
See also MAICYA 2
See also MAICYAS 1
See also MTCW 2
See also SATA 86, 135
See also TEA
See also YAW
Herriot, Peter 1939- ... CANR-25
Earlier sketch in CA 29-32R
Herriott, Robert E. 1929- ... CANR-7
Earlier sketch in CA 17-20R
Herris, Violet
See Hunt, Violet
Herrmann, Bernard 1911-1975 ... IDFW 3, 4
Herrmann, Dorothy 1941- ... 107
See also CLC 44
Herrmann, Frank 1927- ... CANR-10
Earlier sketch in CA 21-24R
Herrmann, Heinz 1911- ... 178
Herrmann, John 1900-1959
Brief entry ... 107
See also DLB 4
Herrmann, Klaus J(acob) 1929- ... 37-40R
Herrmann, Luke John 1932- ... 103
Herrmann, Nina 1943- ... 77-80
Herrmann, R(obert) L(awrence) 1928- ... 109
Herrmann, Richard K. 1952- ... 124
Herrmann, Robert O(mer) 1932- ... 41-44R
Herrmann, Taffy
See Herrmann, Dorothy
Herrmann, Wolfgang 1899-1994 ... 202
Herrmanns, Ralph 1933- ... CANR-18
Earlier sketches in CA 9-12R, CANR-3
See also SATA 11
Herrnstadt, Richard L. 1926- ... 33-36R
Herrnstein, Barbara
See Smith, Barbara Herrnstein
Herrnstein, Richard J(ulius) 1930-1994 ... 153
Brief entry ... 107
Herrold, Tracey
See Dils, Tracey E.
Herron, Carolivia 1947- ... 141
See also BW 2
Herron, Don 1952- ... CANR-54
Earlier sketches in CA 111, CANR-29
Herron, Edward A(lbert) 1912- ... 5-8R
See also SATA 4
Herron, Ima Honaker 1899-1997 ... CAP-2
Earlier sketch in CA 25-28
Herron, Lowell William 1916- ... 1-4R
Herron, Nancy L. 1942- ... 151
Herron, Orley R., Jr. 1933- ... CANR-12
Earlier sketch in CA 25-28R
Herron, Shaun 1912-1989 ... CANR-44
Earlier sketch in CA 29-32R
Herron, William George 1933- ... 37-40R
Herschberger, Ruth (Margaret) 1917- ... 33-36R
See also CP 1
Herschensohn, Bruce 1932- ... 69-72
Herscher, Uri David 1941- ... 107
Herschfield, Harry
See Gibson, Walter B(rown)
Herschlag, Rich
See Herschlag, Richard
Herschlag, Richard 1962- ... 173
Herschler, Mildred Barger ... 199
See also SATA 130
Herscovici, Alan 1948- ... 138
Hersey, George Leonard 1927- ... CANR-120
Earlier sketch in CA 41-44R
Hersey, Jean 1902-1997 ... CANR-3
Earlier sketch in CA 9-12R
Hersey, John (Richard) 1914-1993 ... CANR-33
Obituary ... 140
Earlier sketch in CA 17-20R
See also AAYA 29
See also BPFB 2
See also CDALBS
See also CLC 1, 2, 7, 9, 40, 81, 97
See also CN 1, 2, 3, 4, 5
See also CPW
See also DAM POP
See also DLB 6, 185, 278, 299
See also MAL 5
See also MTCW 1, 2
See also MTFW 2005
See also SATA 25
See also SATA-Obit 76
See also TUS
Hersey, William Dearborn 1910- ... CAP-1
Earlier sketch in CA 11-12
Hersh, Burton 1933- ... 73-76
Hersh, Jacques 1935- ... 103
Hersh, Reuben 1927- ... CANR-85
Earlier sketch in CA 125
Hersh, Seymour M. 1937- ... CANR-99
Earlier sketches in CA 73-76, CANR-15
See also AITN 1
Hersha, Cheryl ... 236
Hersha, Lynn ... 204
Hershan, Stella K. 1915- ... 33-36R
Hershatter, Richard Lawrence 1923- ... 81-84
Hershberg, David 1935- ... 45-48
Hershberger, Hazel Kuhns ... 5-8R
Hershberger, Priscilla (Gorman)
1951- ... SATA 81
Hershenhorn, Esther 1945- ... 226
See also SATA 151
Hershenson, David Bert 1933- ... 41-44R
Hershenson, Maurice (Eugene) 1933- ... 41-44R
Hersher, Leonard 1925- ... 41-44R
Hershey, Burnet 1896-1971 ... CAP-2
Obituary ... 33-36R
Earlier sketch in CA 25-28
Hershey, Daniel 1931- ... CANR-16
Earlier sketch in CA 89-92
Hershey, Ed
See Hershey, Edward (Norman)
Hershey, Edward (Norman) 1944-
Brief entry ... 118
Hershey, Gerald L. 1931- ... 53-56
Hershey, Kathleen M. 1934- ... 147
See also SATA 80
Hershey, Lenore 1919(?)-1997 ... 104
Obituary ... 156
Hershey, Nathan 1930- ... 117
Hershey, Olive ... 130
Hershey, Robert Delp 1909- ... 69-72
Hershfield, Harry 1885-1974
Obituary ... 53-56
Hershhorn, Bernard S(eymour) 1928- ... 119
Hershkowitz, Allen (J.) 1955- ... 237
Hershkowitz, Leo 1924- ... 25-28R
Hershman, Marcie 1951- ... CANR-106
Earlier sketch in CA 141
Hershman, Morris 1926- ... CANR-5
Earlier sketch in CA 53-56
Hershon, Joanna (Brett) ... 233
Hershon, Robert (Myles) 1936- ... CANR-111
Earlier sketches in CA 33-36R, CANR-13
Hershorn, Michael 1956- ... 236
Herskovits, Frances Shapiro 1897-1972
Obituary ... 33-36R
Herskowitz, Herbert Bennett 1925- ... 17-20R
Herskowitz, Mickey ... 81-84
Hersom, Kathleen 1911- ... SATA 73
Herspring, Dale R(oy) 1940- ... CANR-123
Earlier sketch in CA 164
Herst, Herman, Jr. 1909-1999 ... CANR-2
Obituary ... 173
Earlier sketch in CA 1-4R
Herstein, I(srael) N(athan) 1923-1988
Obituary ... 125
Herstein, Sheila R. 1942- ... 119
Hertel, Francois 1905-1985 ... CCA 1
See also DLB 68
Herter, Christian A(rchibald) 1895-1966
Obituary ... 116
Herter, David ... 213
Hertling, G(unter) H. 1930- ... 41-44R
Hertling, James E. 1935- ... 93-96
Hertog, Susan ... 198
Hertsens, Marcel 1918- ... 9-12R
Hertweck, Alma Louise 1937- ... 122
Hertz, Aleksander 1895-1983
Obituary ... 109
Hertz, David Michael 1954- ... CANR-103
Earlier sketches in CA 125, CANR-52
Hertz, Grete Janus 1915- ... 101
See also SATA 23
Hertz, Jackoline G. 1920- ... 69-72
Hertz, Jacky
See Hertz, Jackoline G.
Hertz, K(enneth) V(ictor) 1945- ... CP 1
Hertz, Karl H(erbert) 1917- ... 73-76
Hertz, Leah 1937-1988
Obituary ... 126
Hertz, Noreena ... 213
Hertz, Peter Donald 1933- ... 37-40R
Hertz, Richard C(ornell) 1916- ... 21-24R
Hertz, Solange (Strong) 1920- ... 5-8R
Hertzberg, Arthur 1921- ... CANR-136
Earlier sketch in CA 17-20R
Hertzberg, Hazel W(hitman) 1918-1988 . 73-76
Obituary ... 126
Hertzberg, Hendrik 1943- ... 126
Hertzberg, Sidney 1910-1984
Obituary ... 114
Hertzke, Allen D. 1950- ... 141
Hertzler, Daniel 1925- ... 115
Hertzler, Joyce O(ramel) 1895-1975 ... 1-4R
Obituary ... 103
Hertzler, Lois Shank 1927- ... 57-60
Hertzman, Lewis 1927- ... 9-12R
Herubel, Jean-Pierre V. M. 1949- ... 174
Herum, John (Maurice) 1931- ... 61-64
Herve, Jean-Luc
See Humbaraci, D(emir) Arslan
Herve-Bazin, Jean Pierre Marie
1911-1996 ... 81-84
Obituary ... 151
See also Bazin, Herve
Hervent, Maurice
See Grindel, Eugene
Hervey, Evelyn
See Keating, H(enry) R(eymond) F(itzwalter)
Hervey, Jane
See McGaw, Naomi Blanche Thoburn
Hervey, John 1696-1743 ... DLB 101
Hervey, Michael 1920-1979 ... 9-12R
Herwarth, Johnnie
See Herwarth Von Bittenfeld, Hans (Heinrich)
Herwarth Von Bittenfeld, Hans (Heinrich)
1904-1999 ... 188
Herwegh, Georg 1817-1875 ... DLB 133
Herwig, Holger H(einrich) 1941- ... CANR-117
Earlier sketches in CA 61-64, CANR-7
Herz, Irene 1948- ... 93-96
Herz, Jerome Spencer ... 45-48
Herz, Jerry
See Herz, Jerome Spencer
Herz, John H(ermann) 1908- ... 41-44R
Herz, Martin F(lorian) 1917-1983 ... CANR-9
Obituary ... 111
Earlier sketch in CA 21-24R
Herz, Norman 1923- ... 172
Herz, Peggy 1936- ... 37-40R
Herz, Stephanie M(argarette) 1900-1997 ... 101
Herzberg, Donald Gabriel 1925-1980
Obituary ... 101
Herzberg, Gerhard 1904-1999 ... 188
Herzberg, Joseph Gabriel 1907-1976
Obituary ... 65-68
Herzberg, Judith (Frieda Lina) 1934- ... CWP
See also CWW 2
Herzberg, Nancy K. 1951- ... 150
Herzberger, Maximillian Jacob 1899-1982
Obituary ... 106
Herzel, Catherine (Williams) 1908-1999 ... 5-8R
Herzen, Aleksandr Ivanovich 1812-1870
See Herzen, Alexander
Herzen, Alexander
See Herzen, Aleksandr Ivanovich
See also DLB 277
Herzfeld, Michael (F.) 1947- ... 202
Herzfeld, Thomas J. 1945- ... 107
Herzig, Alison Cragin 1935- ... 151
See also SATA 87
Herzinger, Kim A(llen) 1946- ... 114
Herzka, Heinz (Stefan) 1935- ... 37-40R
Herzl, Theodor 1860-1904 ... 168
See also TCLC 36
Herzog, Arthur (III) 1927- ... CANR-30
Earlier sketches in CA 17-20R, CANR-9
Herzog, Brad 1968- ... 200
See also SATA 131
Herzog, Chaim 1918-1997 ... CANR-42
Obituary ... 157
Earlier sketch in CA 103
Herzog, E.
See Maurois, Andre
Herzog, Frederick 1925- ... 116
Herzog, Gerard 1920- ... 104
Herzog, John P(hillip) 1931- ... 29-32R
Herzog, Kristin (K. H.) 1929- ... 114
Herzog, Peter Emilius 1925- ... 125
Herzog, Stephen J(oel) 1938- ... 33-36R
Herzog, Tobey C. 1946- ... 144
Herzog, Werner 1942- ... 89-92
See also CLC 16
Herzog, Whitey 1931- ... 206
Herzstein, Robert Edwin 1940- ... CANR-95
Earlier sketches in CA 57-60, CANR-7

Cumulative Index 265 Heyward

Hesburgh, Theodore M(artin) 1917- 13-16R
Heschel, Abraham Joshua
1907-1972 .... CANR-4
Obituary 37-40R
Earlier sketch in CA 5-8R
Heseltine, George Coulehan 1895-1980
Obituary 97-100
Heseltine, Nigel 1916- 9-12R
See also CN 1
See also CP 1
Hesiod c. 8th cent. B.C.- .... AW 1
See also DLB 176
See also RGWL 2, 3
Heskes, Irene 1928-1999 93-96
Hesketh, (Charles) Peter (Fleetwood) Fleetwood
See Fleetwood-Hesketh, (Charles) Peter (Fleetwood)
Hesketh, Phoebe (Rayner)
1909-2005 .... CANR-14
Obituary 236
Earlier sketches in CAP-1, CA 9-10
See also CP 7
Heskett, J(ames) L(ee) 1933- CANR-141
Earlier sketches in CA 13-16R, CANR-8
Hesky, Olga (?)-1974 .... CAP-2
Obituary 53-56
Earlier sketch in CA 25-28
Hesla, David H(eimarck) 1929- 33-36R
Heslam, Peter S. 1963- 176
Heslep, Robert D(urham) 1930- 37-40R
Heslewood, Juliet 1951- 149
See also SATA 82
Heslin, Jo-Ann 1946- CANR-16
Earlier sketch in CA 93-96
Heslin, Richard 1936- 37-40R
Heslop, J. Malan 1923- 37-40R
Hespro, Herbert
See Robinson, Herbert Spencer
Hess, Alan 239
Hess, Albert G(unter) 1909- CAP-1
Earlier sketch in CA 19-20
Hess, Alexander 1898(?)-1981
Obituary 105
Hess, Bartlett L(eonard) 1910-1999 .. CANR-21
Earlier sketch in CA 61-64
Hess, Beth B(owman) CANR-50
Earlier sketches in CA 65-68, CANR-9, 24
Hess, Bill 234
Hess, David J. 1956- 173
Hess, Earl J(ohn) 1955- 118
Hess, Eckhard H(einrich) 1916-1986 57-60
Obituary 118
Hess, Elizabeth 172
Hess, Gary R(ay) 1937- 21-24R
Hess, Hannah S(pier) 1934- 45-48
Hess, Hans 1908-1975
Obituary 53-56
Hess, J(ohn) Daniel 1937- 116
Hess, Joan 1949- CANR-85
Earlier sketch in CA 134
See also CMW 4
Hess, John L. 1917-2005 102
Obituary 235
Hess, John M(ilton) 1929- 21-24R
Hess, Karen 1918- 105
Hess, Karl 1923-1994 81-84
Obituary 145
Hess, Lilo 1916- CANR-12
Earlier sketch in CA 33-36R
See also SATA 4
Hess, Margaret Johnston 1915- CANR-21
Earlier sketches in CA 57-60, CANR-6
Hess, Paul 1961- .... SATA 134
Hess, Robert D(aniel) 1920- CANR-13
Earlier sketch in CA 21-24R
Hess, Robert L(ee) 1932-1992 .... 29-32R
Obituary 136
Hess, (Walther Richard) Rudolf 1894-1987
Obituary 123
Hess, Stephen 1933- CANR-30
Earlier sketches in CA 17-20R, CANR-10
Hess, Thomas B(aer) 1920-1978 ...... CANR-45
Obituary 77-80
Earlier sketch in CA 81-84
Hess, William N. 1925- 29-32R
Hesse, Hermann 1877-1962 .... CAP-2
Earlier sketch in CA 17-18
See also AAYA 43
See also BPFB 2
See also CDWLB 2
See also CLC 1, 2, 3, 6, 11, 17, 25, 69
See also DA
See also DA3
See also DAB
See also DAC
See also DAM MST, NOV
See also DLB 66
See also EW 9
See also EWL 3
See also EXPN
See also LAIT 1
See also MTCW 1, 2
See also MTFW 2005
See also NFS 6, 15
See also RGWL 2, 3
See also SATA 50
See also SSC 9, 49
See also TCLC 148
See also TWA
See also WLC
Hesse, Karen 1952- CANR-118
Earlier sketch in CA 168
See also AAYA 27, 52
See also BYA 9
See also CLR 54
See also MAICYA 2
See also SAAS 25
See also SATA 74, 103, 158
See also SATA-Essay 113
See also WYAS 1
See also YAW
Hesse, Mary (Brenda) 1924- CANR-12
Earlier sketch in CA 17-20R
Hesselgesser, Debra 1939- 69-72
Hesselgrave, David J(ohn) 1924- 81-84
Hessell Tiltman, Marjorie (Hand)
1900-1999 204
Hesseltine, William Best 1902-1963 .... 1-4R
Hesser, Amanda (Lea) 1971- 227
Hessert, Paul 1925- 33-36R
Hessing, Dennis
See Dennis-Jones, H(arold)
Hession, Charles H(enry) 1911- 33-36R
Hession, Roy 1908-1992 81-84
Hessler, Gene 1928- 73-76
Hessler, Peter 1970- 204
Hessler-Key, Mary 219
Hesslink, George K. 1940-1980 .... 21-24R
Obituary 120
Hessus, Eobanus 1488-1540 .... DLB 179
Hest, Amy 1950- CANR-109
Earlier sketches in CA 115, CANR-56
See also MAICYA 2
See also SATA 55, 82, 129
Hester, Elliott 220
Hester, Hubert Inman 1895-1983 .... CANR-5
Earlier sketch in CA 5-8R
Hester, Hugh Bryan 1895-1983
Obituary 111
Hester, James J. 1931- 37-40R
Hester, Katherine L. 1964- 163
Hester, Kathleen B. 1905- CAP-2
Earlier sketch in CA 19-20
Hester, M(arvin) Thomas 1941- 131
Hester, Marcus B. 1937- 33-36R
Hester, Randolph Thompson, Jr.
1944- CANR-34
Earlier sketch in CA 113
Hester, Thomas R(oy) 1946- CANR-32
Earlier sketch in CA 113
Hester, William
See Hester, William C.
Hester, William C. 1934- 129
Hesterman, Vicki 1951- 112
Heston, Alan (Wiley) 1934- 97-100
Heston, Charlton 1924- CANR-57
Brief entry 108
Earlier sketch in CA 110
Interview in CA-110
Heston, Edward 1908(?)-1973
Obituary 45-48
Heston, Leonard L(ancaster) 1930- 101
Heth, Meir 1932- 21-24R
Hetherington, (Hector) Alastair 1919-1999 . 109
Hetherington, Eileen Mavis (Plenderleith)
1926- 115
Hetherington, Hugh W(illiam)
1903-1981 .... 5-8R
Hetherington, John (Aikman) 1907-1974 . 93-96
Obituary 53-56
Hetherington, Norriss Swigart
1942- CANR-55
Earlier sketch in CA 126
Hetherington, Stephen Cade 1959- 158
Hethmon, Robert H(enry) 1925- 13-16R
Hetley, James A. 1947- 220
Hettche, Thomas 1964- 231
Hettich, Michael 1953- 191
Hettinger, Herman Strecker 1902-1972
Obituary 37-40R
Hettlinger, Richard F(rederick) 1920- .. CANR-7
Earlier sketch in CA 17-20R
Hetzell, Margaret Carol 1917-1978 85-88
Obituary 81-84
Hetzler, Florence M(ary) 1926- CANR-25
Earlier sketch in CA 107
Hetzler, Stanley Arthur 1919- 37-40R
Hetzron, Robert 1937- 33-36R
Heuer, John (Michael) 1941- CANR-14
Earlier sketch in CA 69-72
Heuer, Kenneth John 1927- CANR-30
Earlier sketch in CA 110
See also SATA 44
Heuman, William 1912-1971 .... CANR-64
Earlier sketches in CA 5-8R, CANR-7
See also SATA 21
See also TCWW 1, 2
Heumann, Milton 1947- 110
Heuscher, Julius E(rnst) 1918- 9-12R
Heuser, Beatrice 1961- CANR-141
Earlier sketch in CA 138
Heusler, Marianna C. 1948- 228
Heuss, John 1908-1966 .... CAP-1
Earlier sketch in CA 9-10
Heussler, Robert 1924- CANR-8
Earlier sketch in CA 5-8R
Heussner, Ralph C(lyde), Jr. 1949- 119
Heuterman, Thomas H(enry) 1934- 101
Heuvel, Albert H(endrik) van den
See van den Heuvel, Albert H(endrik)
Heuvelmans, Bernard (Joseph Pierre)
1916-2001 97-100
Obituary 199
Heuvelmans, Martin 1903-1976 49-52
Heuving, Jeanne 1951- 138
Heuyer, Georges 1884-1977
Obituary 73-76
Hevener, John W(atts) 1933- 103
Hevia, James L. 1947- 151
Heward, Constance 1884-1968 .... CWRI 5
Heward, Edmund (Rawlings) 1912- 93-96
Heward, William L(ee) 1949- CANR-4
Earlier sketch in CA 53-56
Hewat, Alexander 1743(?)-1824 .... DLB 30
Hewavitarne, (Don) David 1864-1933 237
Hewens, Frank Edgar 1912- 45-48
Hewer, Humphrey Robert 1903-1974
Obituary 105
Hewes, Agnes Danforth 1874-1963
Obituary 113
See also SATA 35
Hewes, Cady
See De Voto, Bernard (Augustine)
Hewes, Dorothy W. 1922- 37-40R
Hewes, Hayden 1943- 85-88
Hewes, Henry 1917- 13-16R
Hewes, Jeremy Joan 1944- 77-80
Hewes, Laurence (Ilsley) 1902-1989 105
Hewes, Leslie 1906-1999 .... 41-44R
Hewett, Anita 1918-1989 .... 21-24R
See also CWRI 5
See also SATA 13
Hewett, Dorothy (Coade)
1923-2002 .... CANR-69
Obituary 212
Earlier sketch in CA 97-100
See also CD 5, 6
See also CP 1, 7
See also CWD
See also CWP
See also DLB 289
See also FW
Hewett, Joan 1930- CANR-119
Earlier sketch in CA 149
See also SATA 81, 140
Hewett, John H(arris) 1952- 115
Hewett, Richard 1929- .... SATA 81
Hewett, William S. 1924- 21-24R
Hewins, Geoffrey Shaw 1889- CAP-1
Earlier sketch in CA 9-10
Hewins, Ralph Anthony 1909-1984(?) ... CAP-1
Obituary 112
Earlier sketch in CA 9-10
Hewison, Robert 1943- CANR-100
Earlier sketches in CA 81-84, CANR-50
Hewitson, Jennifer 1961- .... SATA 97
Hewitson, John Nelson 1917- 29-32R
Hewitt, Arthur Wentworth 1883-1971 69-72
Hewitt, Bernard (Wolcott) 1906- 13-16R
Hewitt, Cecil Rolph 1901-1994 .... CANR-18
Obituary 144
Earlier sketch in CA 102
Hewitt, David (Sword) 1942- 118
Hewitt, Don (S.) 1922- CANR-121
Brief entry 119
Earlier sketches in CA 146, CANR-120
Hewitt, Emily Clark 1944- CANR-2
Earlier sketch in CA 45-48
Hewitt, Foster (William) 1903(?)-1985
Obituary 115
Hewitt, Garnet (William) 1939- 110
Hewitt, Geof (George F.) 1943- 33-36R
See also CP 1, 2
Hewitt, H(erbert) J(ames) 1890- 13-16R
Hewitt, James 1928- CANR-21
Earlier sketches in CA 57-60, CANR-6
Hewitt, Jean D(aphne) 1925-1997 77-80
Obituary 156
Hewitt, John (Harold) 1907-1987 ..... CANR-16
Obituary 123
Earlier sketch in CA 97-100
See also CP 1, 2
See also DLB 27
Hewitt, John P(aul) 1941- 53-56
Hewitt, Margaret 1961- .... SATA 84
Hewitt, Nicholas 1945- 132
Hewitt, Philip Nigel 1945- 81-84
Hewitt, Richard 1950- 235
Hewitt, Robert L. 1917(?)-1983
Obituary 111
Hewitt, Sally 1949- .... SATA 127
Hewitt, Sue Whitsett 1919(?)-1984
Obituary 111
Hewitt, W(arren) E(dward) 1954- 139
Hewitt, William Henry 1936- 17-20R
Hewivitarne, David
See Hewavitarne, (Don) David
Hewlett, Dorothy (?)-1979
Obituary 85-88
Hewlett, Frank West 1909(?)-1983
Obituary 110
Hewlett, Maurice (Henry) 1861-1923
Brief entry 121
See also DLB 34, 156
See also RHW
Hewlett, Richard Greening 1923- 9-12R
Hewlett, Roger S. 1911(?)-1977
Obituary 73-76
Hewlett, Sylvia Ann 1946- CANR-125
Brief entry 118
Earlier sketch in CA 123
Hewlett, Virginia B. 1912(?)-1979
Obituary 85-88
Hewson, David 1953- 229
Hewson, John 1930- 37-40R
Hewton, Eric 1934- 126
Hexham, Irving (Roger) 1943- CANR-113
Earlier sketches in CA 125, CANR-52
Hexner, Ervin Paul 1893-1968 .... 5-8R
Obituary 103
Hext, Harrington
See Phillpotts, Eden
Hextall, David
See Phillips-Birt, Douglas Hextall Chedzey
Hexter, J(ack) H. 1910-1996 .... 13-16R
Obituary 155
Hey, Jeanne A. K. 1963- 154
Hey, John D(enis) 1944- 106
Hey, Nigel S(tewart) 1936- 33-36R
See also SATA 20
Hey, Robert P(ierpont) 1935- 133
Heyck, Denis Lynn Daly 1943- 229
Heyd, David 1945- 118
Heydenburg, Harry E. 1891(?)-1979
Obituary 89-92
Heydenreich, Ludwig Heinrich 1903-
Brief entry 105
Heydon, Peter Richard 1913-1971 .... CAP-1
Earlier sketch in CA 19-20
Heydron, Vicki Ann 1945- 131
Heyduck-Huth, Hilde 1929- 57-60
See also SATA 8
Heyel, Carl 1908-2000 .... CANR-22
Earlier sketches in CA 17-20R, CANR-7
Heyen, William 1940- 220
Earlier sketches in CA 33-36R, CANR-98
Autobiographical Essay in 220
See also CAAS 9
See also CLC 13, 18
See also CP 7
See also DLB 5
Heyer, Carol 1950- CANR-89
Earlier sketch in CA 130
See also SATA 74, 130
Heyer, Georgette 1902-1974 .... CANR-58
Obituary 49-52
Earlier sketch in CA 93-96
See also CMW 4
See also CPW
See also DA3
See also DAM POP
See also DLB 77, 191
See also MTCW 1, 2
See also RHW
Heyer, Marilee 1942- CANR-52
Earlier sketch in CA 125
See also SATA 64, 102
Heyer, Paul 1946- 177
Heyerdahl, Thor 1914-2002 .... CANR-73
Obituary 207
Earlier sketches in CA 5-8R, CANR-5, 22, 66
See also CLC 26
See also LAIT 4
See also MTCW 1, 2
See also MTFW 2005
See also SATA 2, 52
Heyes, (Nancy) Eileen 1956- CANR-135
Earlier sketches in CA 147, CANR-99
See also SATA 80, 150
Heyler, David B. Sr. 1905(?)-1983
Obituary 110
Heyliger, William 1884-1955 .... YABC 1
Heylin, Clinton (M.) 1960- CANR-122
Earlier sketch in CA 135
Heym, Georg (Theodor Franz Arthur)
1887-1912 181
Brief entry 106
See also TCLC 9
Heym, Stefan 1913-2001 .... CANR-4
Obituary 203
Earlier sketch in CA 9-12R
See also CLC 41
See also CWW 2
See also DLB 69
See also EWL 3
Heyman, Abigail 1942- 57-60
Heyman, Eva 1931-1944
Heyman, Josiah McC(onnell) 1958- 140
Heyman, Ken(neth Louis) 1930- 112
See also SATA 34, 114
Heyman, Neil Michael 1937- 113
Heymann, C. David
See Heymann, Clemens Claude
See also BEST 89:4
Heymann, Clemens Claude 1945- . CANR-137
Earlier sketches in CA 129, CANR-66
See also Heymann, C. David
Heymann, Frederick Gotthold 1900-1983
Obituary 111
Heymann, Thomas N. 1958- 135
Heymann, Tom
See Heymann, Thomas N.
Heymanns, Betty 1932- 85-88
Heymanson, Randal 1903-1984
Obituary 113
Heymsfield, Steven B. 1944- 162
Heyn, Ernest V(ictor) 1904-1995 134
Obituary 149
Brief entry 111
Heyne, Paul 1931-2000 89-92
Heyneman, Martha (Tarpey) 1927- 142
Heynen, Jim 1940- CANR-109
Earlier sketches in CA 77-80, CANR-63
See also TCWW 2
Heyns, Barbara 1943- 85-88
Heyrman, Christine Leigh 1950- CANR-66
Earlier sketch in CA 115
Heyse, Paul (Johann Ludwig von)
1830-1914 209
Brief entry 104
See also DLB 129
See also TCLC 8
Heyst, Axel
See Grabowski, Z(bigniew) Anthony
Heytesbury, William 1310(?)-1372(?) .. DLB 115
Heyward, Carter 1945- 65-68
Heyward, Dorothy (Hartzell Kuhns)
1890-1961 103
Obituary 112
See also DLB 7, 249

Heyward, (Edwin) DuBose 1885-1940 ... 157
Brief entry ... 108
See also DLB 7, 9, 45, 249
See also HR 1:2
See also MAL 5
See also SATA 21
See also TCLC 59
Heyward, Vivian H. 1947- ... 161
Heywood, Andrew 1952- ... CANR-103
Earlier sketch in CA 147
Heywood, Christopher 1928- ... 41-44R
Heywood, Colin 1947- ... 130
Heywood, Hugh Christopher Lempriere 1896-1987
Obituary ... 122
Heywood, Ian 1948- ... 178
Heywood, Joe T.
See Heywood, Joseph (T.)
Heywood, John 1497(?)-1580(?) ... DLB 136
See also RGEL 2
Heywood, Joseph (T.) 1943- ... CANR-98
Brief entry ... 128
Earlier sketch in CA 134
Interview in ... CA-134
Heywood, Karen 1946- ... SATA 48
Heywood, Lorimer D. 1899(?)-1977
Obituary ... 73-76
Heywood, Philip 1938- ... 69-72
Heywood, Rosalind 1895-1980 ... 89-92
Heywood, Terence ... CAP-1
Earlier sketch in CA 9-10
See also CP 1
Heywood, Thomas 1573(?)-1641 . DAM DRAM
See also DLB 62
See also LMFS 1
See also RGEL 2
See also TEA
Heyworth, Gregory ... 213
Heyworth, Laurence 1955- ... 134
Heyworth, Peter (Lawrence Frederick) 1921-1991 ... 65-68
Obituary ... 135
Heyworth-Dunne, James (?)-1974
Obituary ... 53-56
Hezel, Francis X(avier) 1939- ... CANR-42
Earlier sketch in CA 118
Hezlep, William (Earl) 1936- ... 152
See also SATA 88
Hiaasen, Carl 1953- ... CANR-133
Earlier sketches in CA 105, CANR-22, 45, 65, 113
See also CMW 4
See also CPW
See also CSW
See also DA3
See also DLB 292
See also MTCW 2
See also MTFW 2005
Hiam, Alexander 1957- ... 176
Hian
See Higginson, William J(ohn)
Hiat, Elchik
See Katz, Menke
Hiatt, Brenda ... 229
Hiatt, Howard H(aym) 1925- ... CANR-94
Earlier sketch in CA 133
Hibbard, George Richard 1915- ... 85-88
Hibbard, Howard 1928-1984 ... CANR-9
Obituary ... 114
Earlier sketch in CA 53-56
Hibben, Frank Cummings 1910-2002 ... CANR-2
Obituary ... 208
Earlier sketch in CA 1-4R
Hibberd, Andrew Stuart 1893-1983(?)
Obituary ... 111
Hibberd, Jack 1940- ... CANR-83
Earlier sketches in CA 103, CANR-47
See also CD 5, 6
See also DLB 289
Hibbert, Alun 1949- ... 130
Hibbert, Christopher 1924- ... CANR-121
Earlier sketches in CA 1-4R, CANR-2
See also SATA 4
Hibbert, Eleanor Alice Burford 1906-1993 ... CANR-59
Obituary ... 140
Earlier sketches in CA 17-20R, CANR-9, 28
See also Holt, Victoria
See also BEST 90:4
See also CLC 7
See also CMW 4
See also CPW
See also DAM POP
See also MTCW 2
See also MTFW 2005
See also RHW
See also SATA 2
See also SATA-Obit 74
Hibbett, Howard (Scott) 1920- ... 106
Hibbing, John R. 1953- ... 140
Hibbs, Ben 1901-1975 ... 65-68
Obituary ... 104
See also DLB 137
Hibbs, Douglas A(lbert), Jr. 1944- ... CANR-3
Earlier sketch in CA 49-52
Hibbs, Euthymia D. 1937- ... 141
Hibbs, John 1925- ... CANR-41
Earlier sketches in CA 103, CANR-19
Hibbs, Paul 1906- ... CAP-1
Earlier sketch in CA 13-16
Hibdon, James E(dward) 1924- ... 25-28R
Hibler, Jane (Franke) ... 230
Hibler, Janie
See Hibler, Jane (Franke)
Hichens, Robert (Smythe) 1864-1950 ... 162
See also DLB 153
See also HGG
See also RHW
See also SUFW
See also TCLC 64
Hichwa, John S. 1938- ... 171
Hick, John (Harwood) 1922- ... CANR-22
Earlier sketches in CA 9-12R, CANR-6
Hickam, Homer H(adley), Jr. 1943- ... 187
Hickel, Walter J(oseph) 1919- ... 41-44R
Hicken, Mandy
See Hicken, Marilyn E.
Hicken, Marilyn E. 1937- ... 135
Hicken, Victor 1921- ... 21-24R
Hickerson, J(ohn) Mel(ancthon) 1897-1992 ... 25-28R
Hickey, Edward Shelby 1928(?)-1978 ... 85-88
Obituary ... 81-84
Hickey, Emily 1845-1924 ... DLB 199
Hickey, Joseph J(ames) 1907-1993 ... 41-44R
Hickey, Michael 1929- ... CANR-101
Earlier sketch in CA 102
Hickey, Neil 1931- ... 1-4R
Hickey, Raymond 1936- ... CANR-37
Earlier sketch in CA 114
Hickey, William
See Driberg, Thomas Edward Neil
Hickford, Jessie 1911- ... 53-56
Hickin, Norman E(rnest) 1910-1990 . CANR-15
Earlier sketch in CA 85-88
Hickinbotham, Tom 1903-1983
Obituary ... 111
Hickler, Holly 1923- ... 117
Hickling, C(harles) F(rederick) 1902-1977
Obituary ... 117
Hickman, (William) Albert 1877-1957 ... 183
See also DLB 92
Hickman, Bert G(eorge), Jr. 1924- ... 108
Hickman, C(harles) Addison 1916- ... 103
Hickman, Charles 1905-1983
Obituary ... 109
Hickman, Estella (Lee) 1942- ... SATA 111
Hickman, (Gertrud) Hannah 1928- ... 123
Hickman, Hoyt L(eon) 1927- ... CANR-47
Earlier sketch in CA 121
Hickman, Janet 1940- ... CANR-106
Earlier sketches in CA 65-68, CANR-10
See also AAYA 62
See also SATA 12, 127
Hickman, John (Kyrle) 1927-2001 ... 225
Hickman, Katie 1960- ... 128
Hickman, Martha Whitmore 1925- ... CANR-135
Earlier sketches in CA 25-28R, CANR-10, 26, 52
See also SATA 26
Hickman, Martin B(erkeley) 1925- ... 65-68
Hickman, Pamela M. 1958- ... 198
See also SATA 128
Hickman, Patricia ... 213
Hickman, Peggy 1906- ... 73-76
Hickman, Tracy Raye 1955- ... CANR-100
Earlier sketch in CA 126
Hickock, Will
See Harrison, C(hester) William
Hickok, Dorothy Jane 1912-1999 ... 73-76
Hickok, Lorena A. 1893-1968 ... CANR-44
Earlier sketch in CA 73-76
See also SATA 20
Hickok, Ralph 1938- ... 141
Hickok, Robert (Blair) 1927- ... 61-64
Hickox, Rebecca (Ayres) ... 181
See also SATA 116
Hicks, Brian 1966- ... 235
Hicks, Carola 1941- ... 208
Hicks, Charles B(alch) 1916- ... 5-8R
Hicks, Clifford B. 1920- ... CANR-24
Earlier sketches in CA 5-8R, CANR-9
See also SATA 50
Hicks, Darryl E(dwin) 1948- ... 120
Hicks, David E. 1931- ... CANR-7
Earlier sketch in CA 9-12R
Hicks, Donald A(lbert) 1947- ... 111
Hicks, Eleanor B.
See Coerr, Eleanor (Beatrice)
Hicks, George L(eon) 1935- ... 65-68
Hicks, Granville 1901-1982 ... CANR-117
Obituary ... 107
Earlier sketches in CA 9-12R, CANR-13
See also CN 1, 2, 3
See also DLB 246
Hicks, Harvey
See Stratemeyer, Edward L.
Hicks, J. L.
See Hicks, Jim(my Lyn)
Hicks, Jack 1942- ... 97-100
Hicks, James L. 1915(?)-1986
Obituary ... 118
Hicks, Jim(my Lyn) 1937- ... 107
Hicks, John (Richard) 1904-1989 ... CANR-13
Obituary ... 128
Earlier sketch in CA 65-68
Hicks, John (Kenneth) 1918- ... 25-28R
Hicks, John D(onald) 1890-1972 ... CANR-2
Earlier sketch in CA 1-4R
Hicks, John Edward 1890(?)-1971
Obituary ... 104
Hicks, John H(arland) 1919- ... 45-48
Hicks, John V(ictor) 1907-1999 ... CANR-56
Earlier sketches in CA 110, CANR-30
Hicks, L. Edward 1949- ... 150
Hicks, Michael 1956- ... 187
Hicks, Peter 1952- ... 182
See also SATA 111
Hicks, Raymond L. 1926- ... 61-64
Hicks, Robert E(lden) 1920-
Brief entry ... 109
Hicks, Roger W(illiam) 1950- ... 124
Hicks, Ronald G(raydon) 1934- ... 73-76
Hicks, Thomas 1936- ... 129
Hicks, Tyler Gregory 1921- ... 103
Hicks, Ursula Kathleen (Webb) 1896-1985 ... 103
Obituary ... 117
Hicks, Warren B(raukman) 1921- ... 33-36R
Hicks, Wilson 1897-1970
Obituary ... 29-32R
Hickson, Joyce (Horton) ... 175
Hicky, Daniel Whitehead 1902- ... AITN 1
Hicok, Bob 1960- ... 211
Hicyilmaz, Gaye 1947- ... CANR-121
Earlier sketch in CA 133
See also SATA 77, 157
Hidalgo, Jose Luis 1919-1947 ... DLB 108
Hidayat, Sadiq 1903-1951 ... WLIT 6
Hidden, (Frederick) Norman 1913- ... 77-80
See also CP 1, 2
Hidore, John J. 1932- ... CANR-44
Earlier sketches in CA 57-60, CANR-6, 21
Hidy, Muriel E(mmie) 1906- ... 97-100
Hidy, Ralph W(illard) 1905-1977 ... 5-8R
Hieatt, A(llen) Kent 1921- ... 21-24R
Hieatt, Constance B(artlett) 1928- ... CANR-23
Earlier sketches in CA 5-8R, CANR-8
See also SATA 4
Hiebel, Friedrich 1903-1989 ... CANR-11
Earlier sketch in CA 65-68
Hiebert, Clarence 1927- ... 61-64
Hiebert, D(avid) Edmond 1910-1995 ... 17-20R
Hiebert, Paul (Gerhardt) 1892-1987 . CANR-17
Earlier sketches in CAP-2, CA 23-24
See also DLB 68
Hiebert, Ray Eldon 1932- ... CANR-7
Earlier sketch in CA 17-20R
See also SATA 13
Hiemstra, Marvin R. 1939- ... CAAS 26
Hieng, Andrej 1925- ... DLB 181
Hiernaux, Jean 1921- ... 57-60
Hieronymous, J.
See Kay, Jeremy
Hieronymus, Clara (Booth) 1913- ... 73-76
Hierro, Jose 1922- ... DLB 108
Hiers, John Turner 1945- ... 102
Hiers, Richard H(yde) 1932- ... 53-56
Hiesberger, Jean Marie 1941- ... 41-44R
Hiesinger, Kathryn B(loom) 1943- ... 119
Hiestand, Dale L(eroy) 1925- ... 41-44R
Hiestand, Emily (L.) 1947- ... 134
Hifler, Joyce Sequichie 1925- ... CANR-109
Earlier sketch in CA 21-24R
Higashiuchi, Yoshio 1915(?)-1987
Obituary ... 122
Higbe, (Walter) Kirby 1915-1985
Obituary ... 116
Higbee, Edward (Counselman) 1910-1999 ... 13-16R
Higbee, Kenneth Leo 1941- ... 101
Higby, Mary Jane ... 25-28R
Higdon, David Leon 1939- ... 77-80
Higdon, Hal 1931- ... CANR-3
Earlier sketch in CA 9-12R
See also SATA 4
Higenbottam, Frank 1910-1982 ... 25-28R
Obituary ... 117
Higgie, Lincoln William 1938- ... 5-8R
Higginbotham, A(loysius) Leon, Jr., Jr. 1928-1998 ... 110
Obituary ... 172
Higginbotham, Elizabeth 1948- ... 216
Higginbotham, (Prieur) Jay 1937- ... CANR-37
Earlier sketches in CA 93-96, CANR-17
Higginbotham, John E. 1933- ... 29-32R
Higginbotham, R(obert) Don 1931- ... 17-20R
Higginbotham, Sanford Wilson 1913-1997(?)
Brief entry ... 105
Higginbotham, Sylvia 1945- ... 196
Higginbotham, Virginia 1935- ... 115
Brief entry ... 110
Higginbottom, David 1923- ... CANR-52
See also Fisk, Nicholas
See also SATA 87
Higginbottom, J(effrey) Winslow 1945- ... SATA 29
Higgins, A(lbert) C(orbin) 1930- ... 37-40R
Higgins, A(ngus) J(ohn) B(rockhurst) 1911- ... 13-16R
Higgins, Aidan 1927- ... CANR-115
Earlier sketches in CA 9-12R, CANR-70
See also CN 1, 2, 3, 4, 5, 6, 7
See also DLB 14
See also SSC 68
Higgins, Alice 1924(?)-1974
Obituary ... 53-56
Higgins, Anna Dunlap 1962- ... 147
Higgins, Chester (Archer, Jr.) 1946- ... 73-76
Higgins, Colin 1941-1988 ... CANR-30
Obituary ... 126
Earlier sketch in CA 33-36R
See also DLB 26
Higgins, D. S(ydney) 1938- ... 132
Higgins, Dick
See Higgins, Richard C(arter)
See also CAAS 8
See also CD 5, 6
Higgins, Don 1928- ... CANR-14
Earlier sketch in CA 25-28R
Higgins, George V(incent) 1939-1999 ... CANR-96
Obituary ... 186
Earlier sketches in CA 77-80, CANR-17, 51, 89
Interview in ... CANR-17
See also CAAS 5
See also BPFB 2
See also CLC 4, 7, 10, 18
See also CMW 4
See also CN 2, 3, 4, 5, 6
See also DLB 2
See also DLBY 1981, 1998
See also MSW
See also MTCW 1
Higgins, Gina O'Connell 1950- ... 151
Higgins, Ian (Kevin) 1959- ... 149
Higgins, Ink
See Weiss, Morris S(amuel)
Higgins, Jack
See Patterson, Harry
See also BEST 89:3
Higgins, James E(dward) 1926- ... 73-76
Higgins, Jean C. 1932- ... 29-32R
Higgins, Joan 1948- ... 125
Higgins, Joanna 1945- ... CANR-89
Earlier sketch in CA 141
See also SATA 125
Higgins, John 1934-1999 ... 138
Obituary ... 183
Higgins, John A(loysius) 1931- ... CANR-13
Earlier sketch in CA 77-80
Higgins, John C(layborn) 1934- ... 132
Higgins, John J(oseph) 1935- ... 45-48
Higgins, John Joseph 1959- ... CWRI 5
Higgins, Judith Holden 1930- ... 102
Higgins, Kathleen M(arie) 1954- ... CANR-98
Earlier sketch in CA 138
Higgins, Lionel G(eorge) 1891-1985 ... 123
Higgins, Marguerite 1920-1966 ... 5-8R
Obituary ... 25-28R
Higgins, Michael James 1946- ... 146
Higgins, Paul C. 1950- ... 106
Higgins, Paul Lambourne 1916- ... CANR-17
Earlier sketches in CA 1-4R, CANR-2
Higgins, Reynold Alleyne 1916-1993 ... CANR-50
Obituary ... 141
Earlier sketch in CA 25-28R
Higgins, Richard C(arter) 1938-1998 ... CANR-56
Obituary ... 171
Earlier sketches in CA 13-16R, CANR-8, 29
See also Higgins, Dick
Higgins, Ronald 1929- ... 81-84
Higgins, Rosalyn (Cohen) 1937- ... CANR-3
Earlier sketch in CA 9-12R
Higgins, Simon (Richard) 1958- ... CANR-142
Earlier sketch in CA 173
See also SATA 105
Higgins, Thomas J(oseph) 1899-1993 ... CANR-49
Earlier sketches in CA 1-4R, CANR-5
Higgins, Trumbull 1919-1990 ... 17-20R
Obituary ... 131
Higgins, W(illiam) Robert 1938- ... 37-40R
Higgins, William R(eynolds) 1935- ... 128
Higginsen, Vy ... 147
See also SATA 79
Higginson, Fred H(all) 1921- ... 1-4R
Higginson, Joanne M. 1960- ... 228
Higginson, Margaret V(alliant) 1923- ... 105
Higginson, Thomas Wentworth 1823-1911 ... 162
See also DLB 1, 64, 243
See also TCLC 36
Higginson, William J(ohn) 1938- ... 123
Higgonet, Margaret ed. ... CLC 65
Higgs, David (Clive) 1939- ... 61-64
Higgs, E(ric) S(idney) 1908-1976 ... 9-12R
Obituary ... 69-72
Higgs, Gerald B. 1921- ... 106
Higgs, Gertrude Monro
See Monro-Higgs, Gertrude
Higgs, Liz Curtis 1956(?)- ... 235
Higgs, Robert J(ackson) 1932- ... 115
High, Dallas M. 1931- ... 21-24R
High, Jack 1942- ... 230
High, Jack C.
See High, Jack
High, John Alexander 1957- ... 194
High, Linda Oatman 1958- ... CANR-127
Earlier sketch in CA 159
See also SATA 94, 145
High, Monique Raphel 1949- ... CANR-21
Earlier sketch in CA 102
High, Philip E(mpson) 1914- ... CANR-84
Earlier sketch in CA 97-100
See also SATA 119
See also SFW 4
High, Stanley (Hoflund) 1895-1961
Obituary ... 89-92
Higham, Charles 1931- ... CANR-17
Earlier sketch in CA 33-36R
See also BEST 89:1
See also CP 1, 2
Higham, David 1895-1978 ... CANR-2
Earlier sketch in CA 1-4R
Higham, David (Michael) 1949- ... 126
See also SATA 50
Higham, Florence May Grier 1896-1980
Obituary ... 97-100
Higham, John 1920-2003 ... CANR-134
Obituary ... 218
Earlier sketches in CA 1-4R, CANR-6
Higham, Jon Atlas
See Higham, Jonathan Huw

Cumulative Index 267 Hill

Higham, Jonathan Huw 1960- 127
See also SATA 59
Higham, N(icholas) J(ohn) 237
Higham, Nicholas
See Higham, N(icholas) J(ohn)
Higham, Robin (David Stewart)
1925- CANR-141
Earlier sketches in CA 1-4R, CANR-1, 31
Higham, Roger 1935- 33-36R
Higham, T. F.
See Higham, Thomas Farrant
Higham, Thomas Farrant 1890-1975
Obituary 116
Highberger, Ruth 1917- 65-68
Highet, Gilbert (Arthur) 1906-1978 .... CANR-6
Obituary 73-76
Earlier sketch in CA 1-4R
Highet, Helen
See MacInnes, Helen (Clark)
Highfield, (John) Roger (Loxdale) 1922- 130
Highland, Dora
See Avallone, Michael (Angelo, Jr.)
Highland, Monica
See Espey, John (Jenkins) and
Kendall, Lisa See and
See, Carolyn (Penelope)
Highsmith, (Mary) Patricia
1921-1995 .... CANR-108
Obituary 147
Earlier sketches in CA 1-4R, CANR-1, 20, 48, 62
See also Morgan, Claire
See also AAYA 48
See also BRWS 5
See also CLC 2, 4, 14, 42, 102
See also CMW 4
See also CN 1, 2, 3, 4, 5
See also CPW
See also DA3
See also DAM NOV, POP
See also DLB 306
See also MSW
See also MTCW 1, 2
See also MTFW 2005
Highsmith, Richard M(organ), Jr. 1920- . 37-40R
Hightower, Florence Cole
1916-1981 .... CANR-85
Obituary 103
Earlier sketches in CA 1-4R, CANR-35
See also CWRI 5
See also SATA 4
See also SATA-Obit 27
Hightower, John M(urmann) 1909-1987
Obituary 121
Hightower, Lynn S. CANR-123
Earlier sketch in CA 140
Hightower, Paul
See Collins, Thomas Hightower
Hightower, Scott 1952- 226
Highwater, Jamake (Mamake)
1942(?)-2001 .... CANR-84
Obituary 199
Earlier sketches in CA 65-68, CANR-10, 34
See also CAAS 7
See also AAYA 7
See also BPFB 2
See also BYA 4
See also CLC 12
See also CLR 17
See also CWRI 5
See also DLB 52
See also DLBY 1985
See also JRDA
See also MAICYA 1, 2
See also SATA 32, 69
See also SATA-Brief 30
Highway, Tomson 1951- CANR-75
Earlier sketch in CA 151
See also CCA 1
See also CD 5, 6
See also CLC 92
See also CN 7
See also DAC
See also DAM MULT
See also DFS 2
See also MTCW 2
See also NNAL
Higley, John (Clark) 1938-
Brief entry 116
Higman, B(arry) W(illiam) 1943- CANR-143
Earlier sketch in CA 81-84
Higman, Francis M(ontgomery)
1935- CANR-12
Earlier sketch in CA 25-28R
Hignett, Sean 1934- CANR-44
Earlier sketch in CA 49-52
Higon, Albert
See Jeury, Michel
Higonnet, Anne 1959- 139
Higonnet, Margaret R(andolph)
1941- CANR-107
Earlier sketch in CA 61-64
Higonnet, Patrice Louis-Rene 1938- . CANR-86
Earlier sketch in CA 65-68
Higson, Charles 142
Higson, James D(oran) 1925- 49-52
Hijazi, Ahmad 'Abd al-Mu'ti 1935- .... EWL 3
Hijirida, Kyoko 1937- 126
Hijuelos, Oscar 1951- CANR-125
Earlier sketches in CA 123, CANR-50, 75
See also AAYA 25
See also AMWS 8
See also BEST 90:1
See also CLC 65
See also CPW
See also DA3
See also DAM MULT, POP
See also DLB 145
See also HLC 1
See also HW 1, 2
See also LLW
See also MAL 5
See also MTCW 2
See also MTFW 2005
See also NFS 17
See also RGAL 4
See also WLIT 1
Hikmet, Nazim 1902-1963 141
Obituary 93-96
See also Nizami of Ganja
See also CLC 40
See also EWL 3
See also WLIT 6
Hilary, Christopher 1927(?)-1979
Obituary 89-92
Hilberg, Raul 1926- CANR-119
Earlier sketch in CA 33-36R
Hilberry, Conrad (Arthur) 1928- CANR-136
Earlier sketches in CA 25-28R, CANR-10
See also DLB 120
Hilbert, David 1862-1943 162
Hilbert, Richard A. 1947- 142
Hilbert, Robert G. 1939-1993 144
Hilborn, Ann 1942- 109
Hilborn, Harry (Warren) 1900-1978 ...... CAP-2
Earlier sketch in CA 33-36
Hilborn, Robert C. 1943- CANR-103
Earlier sketch in CA 149
Hild, Jack
See Garside, (Clifford) Jack
Hild, Jack
See Preston, John
See also GLL 1
Hildebidle, John 1946- CANR-95
Earlier sketch in CA 114
Hildebrand, Ann Meinzen 1933- 144
Hildebrand, George H(erbert) 1913- .. CANR-8
Earlier sketch in CA 17-20R
Hildebrand, Grant 1934- CANR-105
Earlier sketch in CA 57-60
Hildebrand, Joel H(enry) 1881-1983 ..... CAP-1
Obituary 109
Earlier sketch in CA 11-12
Hildebrand, John 1949- 131
Hildebrand, Klaus 1941- 158
Hildebrand, Verna 1924- CANR-52
Earlier sketches in CA 33-36R, CANR-13, 28
Hildebrandt, Erik A(lan) 1966- 171
Hildebrandt, Franz 1909-1985 118
Hildebrandt, Greg 1939- 104
See also AAYA 12
See also SATA 55
See also SATA-Brief 33
Hildebrandt, Tim(othy) 1939- 122
Brief entry 111
See also AAYA 12
See also SATA 55
See also SATA-Brief 33
Hildebrandts, The
See Hildebrandt, Greg and
Hildebrandt, Tim(othy)
Hildegard von Bingen 1098-1179 .... DLB 148
Hilden, Joanne (M.) 1957- 235
Hilder, Rowland 1905-1993 .... SATA 36
See also SATA-Obit 77
Hilderbrand, Robert Clinton 1947- 105
Hildesheimer, Wolfgang 1916-1991 101
Obituary 135
See also CLC 49
See also DLB 69, 124
See also EWL 3
Hildick, E. W.
See Hildick, (Edmund) Wallace
See also SAAS 6
Hildick, (Edmund) Wallace
1925-2001 .... CANR-80
Earlier sketches in CA 25-28R, CANR-49
See also Hildick, E. W.
See also CWRI 5
See also MAICYA 1, 2
See also SATA 2, 68
Hildreth, Gertrude Howell 1898-1984
Obituary 112
Hildreth, Margaret Holbrook 1927- 89-92
Hildreth, Richard 1807-1865 .... DLB 1, 30, 59, 235
Hildt, Elisabeth 1966- 171
Hildum, Donald C(layton) 1930- 21-24R
Hildyard, Nicholas 1955- 122
Hildyard, Robin 212
Hilfer, Anthony Channell 1936- 73-76
Hilfiker, David 1945- CANR-137
Earlier sketches in CA 123, CANR-49
Hilgard, Ernest R(opiequet)
1904-2001 .... CANR-32
Obituary 202
Earlier sketch in CA 113
Hilgard, Jack
See Hilgard, Ernest R(opiequet)
Hilgartner, Beth 1957- .... SATA 58
Hilgartner, Stephen 1956- 111
Hilger, Sister Mary Inez 1891-1977 73-76
Hilgert, Ronald J(oseph) 1934-2002 219
Hilken, Glen A. 1936-1976 61-64
Obituary 134
Hill, A. J. 1946- 221
Hill, Aaron 1685-1750 .... DLB 84
See also RGEL 2
Hill, Ab
See Hill, Abram (Barrington)
Hill, Abram (Barrington) 1910(?)-1986
Obituary 120
Hill, Adrian Keith Graham
1895-1977 .... CANR-29
Earlier sketch in CA 77-80
Hill, Alexis
See Craig, Mary (Francis) Shura and
Glick, Ruth (Burtnick)
Hill, Alfred T(uxbury) 1908-1980 .... 21-24R
Hill, Andrew 1950- 201
Hill, Anita Faye 1956- 153
Hill, Anthony (Robert) 1942- CANR-93
Earlier sketch in CA 151
See also SATA 91
Hill, Archibald A(nderson) 1902- CANR-47
Earlier sketch in CA 49-52
Hill, Arthur Norman 1920(?)-1988
Obituary 125
Hill, Barrington Julian Warren
1915-1985 .... 5-8R
Hill, Barry 1943- 239
Hill, Bennett D(avid) 1934-2005 111
Obituary 236
Hill, Bob
See Hill, Robert C(ecil)
Hill, Brian (Merrikin) 1896-1979 .... CAP-1
Earlier sketch in CA 9-10
Hill, Brian W. 1932- 145
Hill, Carol (Dechellis) 1942- CANR-69
Earlier sketch in CA 77-80
See also CN 2, 3, 4, 5, 6, 7
Hill, Charles 1904-1989
Obituary 129
Hill, Charles William, Jr. 1940- 125
Hill, (John Edward) Christopher
1912-2003 .... CANR-22
Obituary 213
Earlier sketches in CA 9-12R, CANR-4
Hill, Christopher R. 1935- CANR-66
Earlier sketch in CA 128
Hill, Claude 1911-1991 .... 21-24R
Obituary 136
Hill, Clifford S. 1927- CANR-27
Earlier sketches in CA 13-16R, CANR-7
Hill, Crag 1957- 174
Autobiographical Essay in 174
See also CAAS 29
Hill, Craig C. 1957- 220
Hill, D. W. R.
See Tubb, E(dwin) C(harles)
Hill, Daniel G., Jr. 1896(?)-1979
Obituary 89-92
Hill, Dave
See Hill, David Charles
Hill, Dave
See Hill, David John
Hill, David 1942- CANR-139
Earlier sketch in CA 170
See also CWRI 5
See also SATA 103, 152
Hill, David Charles 1936- CANR-11
Earlier sketch in CA 17-20R
Hill, David John 1958- 132
Hill, Deborah 1936- 108
Hill, Dee
See Zucker, Dolores Mae Bolton
Hill, Denise 1919- CANR-23
Earlier sketch in CA 106
Hill, Denise Nicholas
See Nicholas, Denise
Hill, (Richard) Desmond 1920-1984 .... 5-8R
Obituary 114
Hill, Devra Z.
See Zucker, Dolores Mae Bolton
Hill, Dilys M(ary) 1935- 61-64
Hill, Donald (Routledge) 1922- 122
Hill, Donald Hamilton
See Hamilton-Hill, Donald
Hill, Donna 238
Hill, Donna (Marie) 1921- CANR-100
Earlier sketches in CA 13-16R, CANR-7, 25, 50
See also MAICYA 2
See also SATA 24, 124
Hill, Douglas (Arthur) 1935- CANR-83
Earlier sketches in CA 53-56, CANR-4
See also BYA 6, 7
See also CP 1
See also SATA 39, 78
See also YAW
Hill, Draper
See Hill, L(eroy) Draper, Jr.
Hill, Earle 1941- 33-36R
Hill, Edmund 1923- 146
Hill, Eileen
See Stack, Nicolete Meredith
Hill, Elizabeth Ann 1952- 209
Hill, Elizabeth Starr 1925- CANR-122
Earlier sketches in CA 17-20R, CANR-31, 45, 90
See also SATA 24, 143
Hill, Ellen Wise 1942- 77-80
Hill, Eric 1927- CANR-111
Earlier sketch in CA 134
See also CLR 13
See also MAICYA 1, 2
See also SATA 66, 133
See also SATA-Brief 53
Hill, Ernest 1915- 53-56
Hill, Ernest 1961(?)- 237
Hill, Errol Gaston 1921-2003 .... CANR-84
Obituary 220
Earlier sketches in CA 45-48, CANR-26
See also BW 2
See also CAD
See also CD 5, 6
Hill, Evan 1919- CANR-5
Earlier sketch in CA 9-12R
Hill, Fiona
See Pall, Ellen Jane
Hill, (Charles) Fowler 1901(?)-1973
Obituary 37-40R
Hill, (James William) Francis 1899-1980
Obituary 108
Hill, Frank Ernest 1888-1969 73-76
Hill, Gene (Atkins) 1928-1997 97-100
Obituary 158
Hill, Geoffrey (William) 1932- CANR-89
Earlier sketches in CA 81-84, CANR-21
See also BRWS 5
See also CDBLB 1960 to Present
See also CLC 5, 8, 18, 45
See also CP 1, 2, 3, 4, 5, 6, 7
See also DAM POET
See also DLB 40
See also EWL 3
See also MTCW 1
See also RGEL 2
Hill, George E(dward) 1907- CAP-1
Earlier sketch in CA 17-18
Hill, George Roy 1921-2002 122
Obituary 213
Brief entry 110
See also CLC 26
Hill, Gerald N. 1929- 148
Hill, Gladwin 1914-1992 .... 25-28R
Hill, Gordon
See Eldin, Peter
Hill, Grace Brooks CANR-26
Earlier sketches in CAP-2, CA 19-20
See also SATA 1, 67
Hill, Grace Livingston 1865-1947 .... YABC 2
Hill, (Norman) Graham 1929-1975
Obituary 108
Hill, H. D. N.
See Disston, Harry
Hill, Hamlin (Lewis) 1932-2002 .... CANR-18
Obituary 208
Earlier sketches in CA 9-12R, CANR-3
Hill, Harold E(verett) 1905-1987 ...... CANR-11
Earlier sketch in CA 69-72
Hill, Harvey 1965- 234
Hill, Helen
See Miller, Helen Hill
Hill, Helen M(orey) 1915- 57-60
See also SATA 27
Hill, Henry Bertram 1907-1990 .... 1-4R
Hill, Herbert 1924-2004 65-68
Obituary 229
Hill, Hyacinthe
See Anderson, Virginia (R. Cronin)
Hill, I(saac) William 1908-1993 65-68
Hill, Ingrid 233
Hill, J(ohn) C(ampbell) 1888- 37-40R
Hill, James
See Jameson, (Margaret) Storm
Hill, James N(ewlin) 1934-1997 .... 33-36R
Obituary 160
Hill, Jane Bowers 1950- 126
Hill, Janet Muirhead 1942- 204
Hill, Jim Dan 1897-1983 .... CAP-1
Earlier sketch in CA 11-12
Hill, Joe 1879-1915 .... DLB 303
Hill, John
See Koontz, Dean R(ay)
Hill, Sir John 1714(?)-1775 .... DLB 39
Hill, John Hugh 1905-1992 .... CANR-5
Earlier sketch in CA 1-4R
Hill, John L. 1960- 124
Hill, John P(aul) 1936- 29-32R
Hill, John S(tanley) 1929- 37-40R
Hill, John Spencer 1943-1998 .... CANR-71
Earlier sketch in CA 150
Hill, John Wiley 1890-1977
Obituary 69-72
Hill, Johnson
See Kunhardt, Edith
Hill, Jonathan D. 1954- 147
Hill, Judith 1945- 187
Hill, Judy I. R.
See Roberts, Judy I.
Hill, Justin 1971- 217
Hill, Kathleen 188
Hill, Kathleen Louise 1917- CANR-3
Earlier sketch in CA 9-12R
See also SATA 4
Hill, Kathleen Thompson 1941- 148
Hill, Kay
See Hill, Kathleen Louise
Hill, Ken(neth) 1937-1995 108
Obituary 147
Hill, King
See Robertson, Frank C(hester)
Hill, Kirkpatrick 1938- 196
See also SATA 72, 126
Hill, Knox C(alvin) 1910-2005 .... CAP-1
Obituary 236
Earlier sketch in CA 19-20
Hill, L(eslie) A(lexander) 1918- CANR-101
Earlier sketches in CA 21-24R, CANR-48
Hill, L(eroy) Draper, Jr. 1935- CANR-12
Earlier sketch in CA 17-20R
Hill, Larry D(ean) 1935- 73-76
Hill, Lawrence 1957- 212
Obituary 125
Hill, Lawson (Traphagen) 1927- 118

Hill 268 CONTEMPORARY AUTHORS

Hill, Lee H(alsey) 1899-1974 ... 37-40R
  Obituary ... 45-48
Hill, Lee Sullivan 1958- ... CANR-68
  Earlier sketch in CA 162
  See also SATA 96
Hill, Leslie Pinckney 1880-1960 ... 125
  See also BW 1
  See also DLB 51
Hill, Lew
  See Skene-Melvin, (Lewis) David (St. Columb)
Hill, Lloyd E(rnest) 1938- ... 141
Hill, Lois
  See Sternau, Cynthia
Hill, Lorna 1902-1991 ... CANR-85
  Earlier sketches in CAP-1, CA 9-10, CANR-14
  See also CWRI 5
  See also SATA 12
Hill, Lowell Dean 1930- ... 114
Hill, M(elba) Anne 1953- ... CANR-50
  Earlier sketch in CA 123
Hill, Malcolm R(onald) 1942- ... 130
Hill, Margaret (Ohler) 1915- ... CANR-16
  Earlier sketches in CA 1-4R, CANR-1
  See also SATA 36
Hill, Marnesba D. 1913- ... 101
Hill, Marvin S(idney) 1928- ... 61-64
Hill, Mary A. 1939- ... 102
Hill, Mary Raymond 1923- ... CANR-6
  Earlier sketch in CA 57-60
Hill, Mary V. 1941- ... 102
Hill, Meg
  See Hill, Margaret (Ohler)
Hill, Meredith
  See Craig, Mary (Francis) Shura
Hill, Mike 1944- ... 122
Hill, Monica
  See Watson, Jane Werner
Hill, Nancy Klenk 1936- ... 108
Hill, Napoleon 1883(?)-1970
  Obituary ... 104
Hill, Nellie
  See Hill, Ellen Wise
Hill, Norman Llewellyn 1895-1976 ... 5-8R
Hill, Pamela 1920- ... CANR-84
  Earlier sketches in CA 49-52, CANR-1, 16, 37
  See also RHW
Hill, Pamela Smith 1954- ... 184
  See also BYA 12
  See also SATA 112
Hill, Pati ... 69-72
Hill, Patricia Liggins 1942- ... 184
Hill, Peter Proal 1926- ... 33-36R
Hill, Philip G(eorge) 1934- ... 33-36R
Hill, Polly
  See Humphreys, Mary Eglantyne Hill
Hill, R(ufus) Carter 1945- ... 110
Hill, R. Lance 1943- ... CANR-11
  Earlier sketch in CA 65-68
Hill, Ralph Nading 1917-1987 ... CANR-1
  Obituary ... 124
  Earlier sketch in CA 1-4R
  See also SATA 65
Hill, Rebecca 1944- ... 111
Hill, Reginald (Charles) 1936- ... CANR-122
  Earlier sketches in CA 73-76, CANR-32, 64
  See also BRWS 9
  See also CMW 4
  See also DLB 276
Hill, Reuben (Lorenzo, Jr.) 1912-1985 ... 131
  Obituary ... 117
Hill, Richard (Leslie) 1901-1996 ... CANR-1
  Obituary ... 151
  Earlier sketch in CA 1-4R
Hill, Richard (Fontaine) 1941- ... 33-36R
Hill, Richard E. 1920- ... 33-36R
Hill, Richard Johnson 1925- ... CANR-4
  Earlier sketch in CA 9-12R
Hill, Richard W. Sr. 1950- ... 211
Hill, Rick
  See Hill, Richard W. Sr.
Hill, Robert A. 1943- ... 132
Hill, Robert C(ecil) 1929- ... CANR-42
  Earlier sketch in CA 118
Hill, Robert S. 1954- ... 162
Hill, Robert W(hite) 1919-1982 ... 9-12R
  Obituary ... 107
  See also SATA 12
  See also SATA-Obit 31
Hill, Roger
  See Paine, Lauran (Bosworth)
Hill, Ronald C. 1937- ... 211
Hill, Rosalind M(ary) T(heodosia)
  1908-1997 ... CAP-1
  Obituary ... 156
  Earlier sketch in CA 11-12
Hill, Roscoe E(arl) 1936- ... 37-40R
Hill, Rowland
  See Wallace-Clarke, George
Hill, Roy Gerald 1926- ... 111
Hill, Russell 1935- ... 141
Hill, Ruth A.
  See Viguers, Ruth Hill
Hill, Ruth Beebe 1913- ... 89-92
Hill, Ruth Livingston
  See Munce, Ruth Hill
Hill, Sam(uel Ivey) 1953- ... 219
Hill, Samuel E(rvin) 1913-1994 ... 17-20R
Hill, Samuel S(mythe, Jr.) 1927- ... CANR-98
  Earlier sketches in CA 9-12R, CANR-5
Hill, Sandra ... 229
Hill, Sarah H. ... 163
Hill, Selima 1945- ... CANR-127
  Earlier sketch in CA 117
  See also CP 7
  See also CWP
Hill, Stephen 1946- ... 111
Hill, Susan (Elizabeth) 1942- ... CANR-129
  Earlier sketches in CA 33-36R, CANR-29, 69
  See also CLC 4, 113
  See also CN 2, 3, 4, 5, 6, 7
  See also DAB
  See also DAM MST, NOV
  See also DLB 14, 139
  See also HGG
  See also MTCW 1
  See also RHW
Hill, Thomas 1960- ... 135
  See also SATA 82
Hill, Thomas E(nglish), Jr. 1937- ... 137
Hill, Thomas English 1909- ... 13-16R
Hill, Tobias 1970- ... CANR-122
  Earlier sketch in CA 168
Hill, W. M.
  See Dodd, Edward Howard, Jr.
Hill, W(illiam) Speed 1935- ... 41-44R
Hill, Walter 1942- ... 140
  Brief entry ... 109
  See also DLB 44
Hill, Weldon
  See Scott, William R(alph)
Hill, West T(hompson), Jr. 1915- ... 37-40R
Hill, Wilhelmina 1902-1979 ... 57-60
Hill, William 1959- ... 176
Hill, William Joseph 1924-2001 ... 37-40R
  Obituary ... 202
Hill, Winfred F(arrington) 1929- ... 29-32R
Hillaby, John (D.) 1917-1996
  Obituary ... 154
  Brief entry ... 109
Hillam, Ray C. 1928- ... 203
  Brief entry ... 107
Hillard, Asa G. III ... CLC 70
Hillard, Darla 1946- ... 135
Hillard, James M(ilton) 1920- ... 73-76
Hillary, Edmund (Percival) 1919- ... 112
Hillary, Peter 1954- ... 123
Hillas, Julian
  See Dashwood, Robert Julian
Hillbrand, Marc 1957- ... 165
Hillbruner, Anthony 1914- ... 41-44R
Hillcourt, William 1900-1992 ... CANR-46
  Obituary ... 139
  Earlier sketch in CA 93-96
  See also SATA 27
Hillegas, Mark R(obert) 1926- ... 33-36R
Hillel, Yehoshua Bar
  See Bar-Hillel, Yehoshua
Hillenbrand, Barry R. 1941- ... 73-76
Hillenbrand, Laura 1967- ... 206
Hillenbrand, Martin J(oseph) 1915-2005 ... 108
  Obituary ... 236
Hillenbrand, Will 1960- ... SATA 84, 147
Hillenburg, Steven 1962- ... AAYA 53
Hiller, Catherine 1946- ... 106
Hiller, Doris
  See Nussbaum, Al(bert F.)
Hiller, Flora
  See Hurd, Florence
Hiller, Herbert L. 1931- ... 125
Hiller, Ilo (Ann) 1938- ... 121
  See also SATA 59
Hiller, Lejaren A(rthur), Jr. 1924-1994 ... 1-4R
  Obituary ... 144
Hillerbrand, Hans J(oachim) 1931- ... 134
  Brief entry ... 111
Hillerich, Robert L(ee) 1927- ... 112
Hillerman, Anne 1949- ... 118
Hillerman, Tony 1925- ... CANR-134
  Earlier sketches in CA 29-32R, CANR-21, 42, 65, 97
  See also AAYA 40
  See also BEST 89:1
  See also BPFB 2
  See also CLC 62, 170
  See also CMW 4
  See also CPW
  See also DA3
  See also DAM POP
  See also DLB 206, 306
  See also MAL 5
  See also MSW
  See also MTCW 2
  See also MTFW 2005
  See also RGAL 4
  See also SATA 6
  See also TCWW 2
  See also YAW
Hillers, Delbert R(oy) 1932-1999 ... 77-80
Hillers, H(erman) W(illiam) 1925- ... 73-76
Hillert, Margaret 1920- ... CANR-40
  Earlier sketches in CA 49-52, CANR-1, 17
  See also AITN 1
  See also SATA 8, 91
Hillery, George A(nthony), Jr. 1927- ... 25-28R
Hilles, Frederick W(hiley) 1900-1975 ... 5-8R
  Obituary ... 61-64
Hilles, Robert ... 165
Hillesum, Etty 1914-1943 ... 137
  See also TCLC 49
Hillgarth, J(ocelyn) N(igel) 1929- ... CANR-127
  Earlier sketch in CA 37-40R
Hillgruber, Andreas (Fritz)
  1925-1989 ... CANR-48
  Obituary ... 128
  Earlier sketch in CA 106
Hillhouse, Raelynn (J.) ... 237
Hilliard, Asa G(rant) III 1933- ... CANR-87
  Earlier sketch in CA 153
  See also BW 2
Hilliard, David 1942- ... 142
  See also BW 2
Hilliard, Jan
  See Grant, Kay
Hilliard, Noel (Harvey) 1929-1996 ... CANR-69
  Earlier sketches in CA 9-12R, CANR-7
  See also CLC 15
  See also CN 1, 2, 3, 4, 5, 6
Hilliard, Robert L. 1925- ... 107
Hilliard, Sam B(owers) 1930- ... 61-64
Hillier, Bevis 1940- ... CANR-137
  Earlier sketch in CA 29-32R
Hillier, Jack R(onald) 1912-1995 ... CANR-3
  Obituary ... 147
  Earlier sketch in CA 5-8R
Hillier, James Martin 1941- ... 113
Hillier, Jim
  See Hillier, James Martin
Hillier, Mary 1917-1999 ... 187
Hillier, Tristram (Paul) 1905-1983
  Obituary ... 114
Hilliker, Grant 1921- ... 33-36R
Hilling, David 1935- ... CANR-12
  Earlier sketch in CA 29-32R
Hillinger, Brad 1952- ... 73-76
Hillis, Bryan V. 1956- ... 141
Hillis, Charles Richard 1913- ... 13-16R
Hillis, Dave 1945- ... 57-60
Hillis, Dick
  See Hillis, Charles Richard
Hillis, Rick 1956- ... 134
  See also CLC 66
Hillis, W. Daniel 1956- ... 230
Hillix, W(illiam) A(llen) 1927- ... 89-92
Hillkirk, John ... 188
Hillman, Arthur 1909-1985
  Obituary ... 115
Hillman, Barry L(eslie) 1942- ... 102
Hillman, Brenda 1951- ... CANR-112
  Earlier sketch in CA 129
  See also PFS 20
Hillman, David (A.) ... 234
Hillman, Elizabeth 1942- ... 142
  See also SATA 75
Hillman, Howard 1934- ... CANR-20
  Earlier sketch in CA 41-44R
Hillman, James 1926- ... CANR-48
  Earlier sketch in CA 89-92
Hillman, John 1952- ... 191
  See also SATA 120
Hillman, Libby 1919-2002 ... 146
  Obituary ... 208
Hillman, Martin
  See Hill, Douglas (Arthur)
Hillman, Priscilla 1940- ... 108
  See also SATA 48
  See also SATA-Brief 39
Hillman, Richard S. 1943- ... 151
Hillman, Ruth Estelyn 1925- ... 53-56
Hill-Miller, Katherine C(ecelia) 1949- ... 139
Hillocks, George, Jr. 1934- ... 53-56
Hill-Reid, William Scott 1890- ... 5-8R
Hills, Argentina Schifano 1921- ... 136
  See also Hills, Tina
Hills, C(harles) A(lbert) R(eis) 1955- ... CANR-23
  Earlier sketch in CA 106
  See also SATA 39
Hills, Christopher B. 1926- ... 114
Hills, Denis (Cecil) 1913-2004 ... CANR-10
  Obituary ... 226
  Earlier sketch in CA 65-68
Hills, George 1918-2002 ... 25-28R
  Obituary ... 210
Hills, L(awrence) Rust 1924- ... 25-28R
Hills, Lawrence Donegan 1911-1990
  Obituary ... 132
Hills, Lee 1906-2000 ... 101
  Obituary ... 188
  See also AITN 2
  See also DLB 127
Hills, P. J.
  See Hills, Philip J(ames)
Hills, Patricia Gorton Schulze 1936- ... 103
Hills, Philip
  See Hills, Philip J(ames)
Hills, Philip J(ames) 1933- ... 129
  Brief entry ... 117
Hills, Stuart Lee 1932- ... 33-36R
Hills, Theo(dore) L(ewis) 1925- ... 5-8R
Hills, Tina
  See Hills, Argentina Schifano
  See also AITN 2
Hillsbery, Kief
  See Hillsbery, Thom Kief
Hillsborough, Romulus (a pseudonym)
  1953- ... CANR-115
  Earlier sketch in CA 168
Hillson, Maurie 1925- ... 17-20R
Hillstrom, Kevin 1963- ... 179
Hillstrom, Tom 1943- ... 102
Hillus, Wilhelm
  See Hillers, H(erman) W(illiam)
Hillway, Tyrus 1912-1998 ... CANR-4
  Earlier sketch in CA 1-4R
Hillyard, Brian P. 1949- ... 111
Hillyer, Barbara 1934- ... 146
Hillyer, Robert (Silliman) 1895-1961 ... 193
  Obituary ... 89-92
  See also DLB 54
Hilmes, Michele 1953- ... 136
Hilscher, Herb(ert H.) 1902-1987
  Obituary ... 122
Hilsdale, (Eric) Paul 1922- ... 9-12R
Hilsenrath, Edgar 1926- ... 49-52
  See also DLB 299
Hilsman, Roger 1919- ... 5-8R
Hilt, Douglas Richard 1932- ... 65-68
Hiltebeital, Alf 1942- ... 103
Hiltner, Seward 1909-1984 ... CANR-1
  Obituary ... 114
  Earlier sketch in CA 1-4R
Hilton, Alec
  See Chesser, Eustace and
  Fullerton, Alexander (Fergus)
Hilton, Alice Mary 1924- ... 29-32R
Hilton, Bruce 1930- ... CANR-8
  Earlier sketch in CA 5-8R
Hilton, Conrad N(icholson) 1887-1979
  Obituary ... 81-84
Hilton, Della (Marion) 1934- ... 69-72
Hilton, Earl (Raymond) 1914-2002 ... 21-24R
Hilton, George W(oodman) 1925- ... CANR-4
  Earlier sketch in CA 1-4R
Hilton, Howard H(oyt, Jr.) 1926- ... 105
Hilton, Irene Pothus -1979 ... 1-4R
  See also SATA 7
Hilton, Isabel 1947- ... 191
Hilton, James 1900-1954 ... 169
  Brief entry ... 108
  See also DLB 34, 77
  See also FANT
  See also SATA 34
  See also TCLC 21
Hilton, John Buxton 1921-1986 ... CANR-58
  Earlier sketches in CA 53-56, CANR-5
  See also CMW 4
Hilton, Joni 1956- ... 211
Hilton, Lewis B. 1920- ... CANR-8
  Earlier sketch in CA 57-60
Hilton, Lisa 1974- ... 219
Hilton, Margaret Lynette 1946- ... CANR-105
  Earlier sketch in CA 136
  See also Hilton, Nette
  See also SATA 68, 105
Hilton, Margery ... RHW
Hilton, (Howard) Nelson 1950- ... 110
Hilton, Nette
  See Hilton, Margaret Lynette
  See also CLR 25
  See also SAAS 21
Hilton, Peter 1913-1974 ... 69-72
Hilton, R. H.
  See Hilton, Rodney (Howard)
Hilton, Ralph 1907-1982 ... 29-32R
  See also SATA 8
Hilton, Richard 1894- ... CAP-1
  Earlier sketch in CA 9-10
Hilton, Rodney (Howard) 1916-2002 ... 134
  Obituary ... 207
  Brief entry ... 112
Hilton, Ronald 1911- ... 29-32R
Hilton, Suzanne 1922- ... CANR-30
  Earlier sketches in CA 29-32R, CANR-12
  See also SATA 4
Hilton, Thomas Leonard 1924- ... 13-16R
Hilton, Walter (?)-1396 ... DLB 146
  See also RGEL 2
Hilton-Bruce, Anne
  See Hilton, Margaret Lynette
Hilton Smith, Robert D(ennis) (?)-1974
  Obituary ... 53-56
Hilts, Philip J(ames) 1947- ... CANR-138
  Earlier sketch in CA 110
Hilty, James W. 1939- ... 163
Hilu, Virginia 1929(?)-1976
  Obituary ... 104
Hilvert, John (Peter Paul) 1945- ... 124
Him
  See Deal, Borden
Him, Chanrithy 1965- ... 201
Him, George 1937-1982
  Obituary ... 106
  See also SATA-Obit 30
Himber, Jacob 1907-1984 ... 105
Hime, James 1954- ... 224
Himelblau, Jack J. 1935- ... 195
Himelfarb, Richard 1963- ... 151
Himelick, (James) Raymond
  1910-1979 ... 33-36R
Himelstein, Morgan Y(ale) 1926- ... 5-8R
Himelstein, Shmuel 1940- ... 150
  See also SATA 83
Himes, Chester (Bomar) 1909-1984 ... CANR-89
  Obituary ... 114
  Earlier sketches in CA 25-28R, CANR-22
  See also AFAW 2
  See also BLC 2
  See also BPFB 2
  See also BW 2
  See also CLC 2, 4, 7, 18, 58, 108
  See also CMW 4
  See also CN 1, 2, 3
  See also DAM MULT
  See also DLB 2, 76, 143, 226
  See also EWL 3
  See also MAL 5
  See also MSW
  See also MTCW 1, 2
  See also MTFW 2005
  See also RGAL 4
  See also TCLC 139
Himes, Joseph S(andy) 1908-1992 ... 25-28R
Himler, Ann 1946- ... 53-56
  See also SATA 8
Himler, Ronald (Norbert) 1937- ... CANR-57
  Earlier sketches in CA 53-56, CANR-5
  See also SATA 6, 92, 137
Himmel, Richard L. 1950- ... 149
Himmelfarb, Gertrude 1922- ... CANR-102
  Earlier sketches in CA 49-52, CANR-28, 66
  See also CLC 202
Himmelfarb, Milton 1918- ... 101
Himmelheber, Diana Martin 1938- ... 17-20R
Himmelman, John C(arl) 1959- ... CANR-143
  Earlier sketches in CA 114, CANR-68
  See also SATA 47, 94, 159
Himmelstein, Jerome L(ionel) 1948- ... CANR-47
  Earlier sketch in CA 113

Cumulative Index 269 Hirshman

Himstreet, William Charles 1923- CANR-16
Earlier sketches in CA 1-4R, CANR-1
Hinchliff, Peter Bingham 1929-1995 102
Obituary 150
Hinchliffe, Arnold P. 1930- CANR-14
Earlier sketch in CA 77-80
Hinchman, Lewis P(atrick) 1946- ... CANR-107
Earlier sketch in CA 150
Hinchman, Sandra K(uracina) 1950- 149
Hinckle, Warren James III 1938- 89-92
Hinckley, Barbara 1937-1995 57-60
Hinckley, Gordon B(itner) 1910- 217
Hinckley, Helen
See Jones, Helen Hinckley
Hinckley, Ted C(harles) 1925- CANR-40
Earlier sketch in CA 57-60
Hind, Dolores (Ellen) 1931- 129
See also SATA 53
See also SATA-Brief 49
Hind, Robert James 1931- 45-48
Hinde, Richard Standish Elphinstone
1912-1995 .... CAP-1
Earlier sketch in CA 9-10
Hinde, Robert A(ubrey) 1923- CANR-57
Earlier sketches in CA 109, CANR-30
Hinde, Thomas
See Chitty, Thomas Willes
See also CLC 6, 11
See also CN 1, 2, 3, 4, 5, 6
See also EWL 3
Hinde, Wendy 1919- 103
Hindemith, Paul 1895-1963
Obituary 112
Hinden, Michael C(harles) 1941- 109
Hinderer, Walter (Hermann) 1934- CANR-1
Earlier sketch in CA 45-48
Hindess, Barry 1939- 153
Hindin, Nathan
See Bloch, Robert (Albert)
Hindin, Philip 1916- 166
Hinding, Andrea 1942- 126
Hindle, Brooke 1918-2001 .... CANR-23
Obituary 199
Earlier sketches in CA 13-16R, CANR-7
Hindle, Lee J(ohn) 1965- 117
Hindle, W(ilfred) H(ope) 1903-1967 ..... CAP-2
Earlier sketch in CA 23-24
Hindley, Geoffrey 1935- CANR-109
Earlier sketch in CA 109
Hindley, Judy 1940- 191
See also SATA 120
Hindman, Hugh D. 219
Hindman, Jane F(erguson)
1905-1996 .... CANR-10
Earlier sketch in CA 25-28R
Hindman, Jo(sephine Long) 1910-1989 . 97-100
Hindmarch, Gladys 1940- 128
Hindmarsh, Joseph fl. 1678-1696 .... DLB 170
Hinds, Dudley S. 1926- 115
Hinds, E. M.
See Hinds, (Evelyn) Margery
Hinds, (Evelyn) Margery 9-12R
Hinds, Michael deCourcy
See deCourcy Hinds, Michael
Hinds, P(atricia) Mignon 165
See also SATA 98
Hindus, Maurice (Gerschon) 1891-1969
Obituary 25-28R
Hindus, Michael S(tephen) 1946- 105
Hindus, Milton Henry 1916-1998 ...... CANR-7
Obituary 167
Earlier sketch in CA 17-20R
Hine, Al(fred Blakelee) 1915-1974 ..... CANR-2
Obituary 200
Earlier sketch in CA 1-4R
Hine, Darlene Clark 1947- 143
Hine, (William) Daryl 1936- CANR-20
Earlier sketches in CA 1-4R, CANR-1
See also CAAS 15
See also CLC 15
See also CP 1, 2, 3, 4, 5, 6, 7
See also DLB 60
Hine, Frederick R. 1925- 37-40R
Hine, James R. 1909- CANR-17
Earlier sketches in CA 45-48, CANR-2
Hine, Robert Van Norden, Jr. 1921- ... CANR-1
Earlier sketch in CA 1-4R
Hine, Sesyle Joslin 1929- 13-16R
See also Joslin, Sesyle
Hine, Thomas 1947- CANR-88
Earlier sketch in CA 123
Hine, Virginia H(aglin) 1920- 97-100
Hiner, Louis C(hase) 1919- 73-76
Hiner, N. Ray, Jr. 1937- 127
Hines, Alan 1951- 220
Hines, Anna Grossnickle 1946- CANR-122
Earlier sketches in CA 114, CANR-36, 67
See also SAAS 16
See also SATA 51, 95, 141
See also SATA-Brief 45
Hines, Barry (Melvin) 1939- CANR-70
Earlier sketch in CA 102
See also CN 4, 5, 6, 7
Hines, Bede F(rancis) 1918- 45-48
Hines, Donald M. 1931-1998 136
Hines, Earl Kenneth 1905-1983
Obituary 109
Hines, Fatha
See Hines, Earl Kenneth
Hines, Gary (Roger) 1944- .... SATA 74, 136
Hines, Jeanne 1922- 140
See also RHW
Hines, Jerome (Albert Link) 1921-2003 130
Obituary 212
Hines, Joanna 1949- 154
Hines, John 1956- 145
Hines, Neal O(ldfield) 1908-1993 ...... CANR-2
Earlier sketch in CA 5-8R
Hines, Paul (David) 1934- 29-32R
Hines, Robert Stephan 1926- CANR-3
Earlier sketch in CA 9-12R
Hines, Terence (Michael) 1951- 128
Hines, Thomas S(pight) 1936- CANR-73
Earlier sketches in CA 53-56, CANR-5, 72
Hines, William H. 1909(?)-1976
Obituary 65-68
Hiney, Tom 1970- 232
Hinger, Charlotte 1940- 123
Hingley, Ronald F(rancis) 1920- CANR-48
Earlier sketch in CA 5-8R
See also DLB 155
Hingorani, R(up) C. 1925- CANR-26
Earlier sketch in CA 29-32R
Hinkel, John V.
See Hinkel, John Vincent
Hinkel, John Vincent 1906-1986
Obituary 121
Hinkemeyer, Michael T(homas)
1940- CANR-34
Earlier sketches in CA 69-72, CANR-11
Hinkle, Douglas P(addock) 1923- 69-72
Hinkle, Gerald H(ahn) 1931- 89-92
Hinkle, Olin Ethmer 1902-1982 .... 1-4R
Hinkle, Vernon 1935- CANR-30
Earlier sketch in CA 109
Hinkson, James 1943- 69-72
Hinkson, Katharine Tynan
See Tynan, Katharine
Hinkson, Pamela 1900(?)-1982
Obituary 107
Hin-Mah-Too-Yah-Lat-Kekt
See Chief Joseph
Hinman, Charlton (Joseph Kadio)
1911-1977 .... CANR-3
Obituary 89-92
Earlier sketch in CA 5-8R
Hinman, George W., Jr. 1891-1977
Obituary 73-76
Hinman, Robert B(enedict) 1920- 5-8R
Hinn, Benny 1952- 142
Hinnant, Charles H(askell) 213
Hinnebusch, Paul (Gerard) 1917- CANR-35
Earlier sketch in CA 114
Hinnebusch, Raymond A. 1946- 136
Hinnebusch, William A(quinas)
1908-1981 .... 37-40R
Hinnefeld, Joyce 1961- 193
Hinnells, John R(ussell) 1941- CANR-48
Earlier sketch in CA 49-52
Hinojosa, Gilberto Miguel 1942- 151
See also HW 2
Hinojosa, Maria (de Lourdes) 1961- . CANR-93
Earlier sketch in CA 152
See also SATA 88
Hinojosa(-Smith), Rolando (R.)
1929- CANR-62
Earlier sketch in CA 131
See also Hinojosa-Smith, Rolando
See also CAAS 16
See also DAM MULT
See also DLB 82
See also HLC 1
See also HW 1, 2
See also LLW
See also MTCW 2
See also MTFW 2005
See also RGAL 4
Hinojosa-S., Rolando R.
See Hinojosa(-Smith), Rolando (R.)
Hinojosa-Smith, Rolando
See Hinojosa(-Smith), Rolando (R.)
See also EWL 3
Hinrichs, Bruce H. 1945- 219
Hinrichs, Ernest H(enry) 1922- 155
Hinrichsen, Max (Henry) 1901-1965 ..... CAP-1
Earlier sketch in CA 13-14
Hinshaw, Cecil E(ugene) 1911-1982 ..... 13-16R
Hinshaw, H(orton) Corwin 1902-2000 104
Obituary 191
Hinshaw, Randall (Weston)
1915-1997 .... CANR-15
Obituary 160
Earlier sketch in CA 41-44R
Hinshaw, Robert E(ugene) 1933- 57-60
Hinshaw, Seth B(ennett) 1908-1998 112
Hinshelwood, Cyril (Norman) 1897-1967
Obituary 116
Hinsley, F(rancis) H(arry) 1918-1998 ..... 17-20R
Obituary 166
Hinsley, Sir Francis Harry
See Hinsley, F(rancis) H(arry)
Hinson, E(dward) Glenn 1931- CANR-8
Earlier sketch in CA 21-24R
Hinson, (Grady) Maurice 1930- CANR-38
Earlier sketches in CA 45-48, CANR-2, 17
Hinterhoff, Eugene 1895- CAP-1
Earlier sketch in CA 9-10
Hintikka, (Kaarlo) Jaakko (Juhani)
1929- CANR-2
Earlier sketch in CA 1-4R
Hinton, Ann Pearlman 1941- 108
Hinton, Bernard L. 1937- 33-36R
Hinton, Harold C(lendenin)
1924-1993 .... 17-20R
Obituary 142
Hinton, John (Mark) 1926- CANR-48
Earlier sketch in CA 49-52
Hinton, Michael 1927- 149
Hinton, Milt
See Hinton, Milton John
Hinton, Milton John 1910-2000 134
Obituary 191
Hinton, Nigel 1941- 85-88
Hinton, Richard W.
See Angoff, Charles
Hinton, S(usan) E(loise) 1950- CANR-133
Earlier sketches in CA 81-84, CANR-32, 62, 92
See also AAYA 2, 33
See also BPFB 2
See also BYA 2, 3
See also CDALBS
See also CLC 30, 111
See also CLR 3, 23
See also CPW
See also DA
See also DA3
See also DAB
See also DAC
See also DAM MST, NOV
See also JRDA
See also LAIT 5
See also MAICYA 1, 2
See also MTCW 1, 2
See also MTFW 2005 !**
See also NFS 5, 9, 15, 16
See also SATA 19, 58, 115, 160
See also WYA
See also YAW
Hinton, Sam 1917- 73-76
See also SATA 43
Hinton, Ted C. 1904(?)-1977
Obituary 73-76
Hinton, William H(oward)
1919-2004 .... CANR-40
Obituary 227
Earlier sketches in CA 25-28R, CANR-18
Hintz, Martin 1945- CANR-107
Earlier sketches in CA 65-68, CANR-12, 30
See also SATA 47, 128
See also SATA-Brief 39
Hintz, Stephen V. 1975- 198
See also SATA 129
Hintze, Guenther 1906- CAP-2
Earlier sketch in CA 21-22
Hintze, Naomi A(gans) 1909-1997 ..... CANR-1
Earlier sketch in CA 45-48
Hinxman, Margaret 1924- 124
Hinz, Evelyn J. 1938- CANR-10
Earlier sketch in CA 65-68
Hipp, George
See Abrams, George J(oseph)
Hippel, Theodor Gottlieb von
1741-1796 .... DLB 97
Hippisley Coxe, Antony D(acres)
1912-1988 103
Obituary 124
Hippius, Zinaida (Nikolaevna)
See Gippius, Zinaida (Nikolaevna)
See also DLB 295
See also EWL 3
See also TCLC 9
Hipple, Theodore W(allace) 1935- ... CANR-10
Earlier sketch in CA 65-68
Hipple, Walter J(ohn), Jr. 1921- 41-44R
Hippler, Arthur E(dwin) 1935- 57-60
Hippocrates of Cos fl. c.
460B.C.-377B.C. .... CDWLB 1
See also DLB 176
Hippopotamus, Eugene H.
See Kraus, (Herman) Robert
Hipps, Juanita Redmond 1913(?)-1979
Obituary 85-88
Hipskind, Judith 1945- 97-100
Hipskind, Verne K(enneth) 1925-1975 .. CAP-2
Earlier sketch in CA 21-22
Hirabayashi, Lane Ryo 1952- 152
Hirabayashi, Taiko 1905-1972
See Hirabayashi Taiko
Hirabayashi Taiko
See Hirabayashi, Taiko
See also DLB 180
Hirano, Cathy 1957- .... SATA 68
Hirano, Marsha
See Hirano-Nakanishi, Marsha J(oyce)
Hirano-Nakanishi, Marsha J(oyce) 1949- 119
Hiraoka, Kimitake 1925-1970 97-100
Obituary 29-32R
See also Mishima, Yukio and
Mishima Yukio
See also DA3
See also DAM DRAM
See also GLL 1
See also MTCW 1, 2
Hirleby, Ashley
See Earle-Hall, Wilton
Hiro, Dilip CANR-119
Earlier sketches in CA 77-80, CANR-14, 32, 64
Hirsal, Josef 1920- 192
Hirsch, Abby 1946- 45-48
Hirsch, Alan 181
Hirsch, Barbara B. 1938- 73-76
Hirsch, Charles S. 1942- 105
Hirsch, David H. 1930-1999 97-100
Hirsch, E(ric) D(onald), Jr. 1928- CANR-51
Earlier sketches in CA 25-28R, CANR-27
Interview in CANR-27
See also CLC 79
See also DLB 67
See also MTCW 1
Hirsch, Edward 1950- CANR-102
Earlier sketches in CA 104, CANR-20, 42
See also CLC 31, 50
See also CP 7
See also DLB 120
See also PFS 22
Hirsch, Ernest A(lbert) 1924-1977 ..... CANR-11
Earlier sketch in CA 25-28R
Hirsch, Foster (Lance) 1943- CANR-120
Earlier sketches in CA 45-48, CANR-2, 17, 39
Hirsch, Fred 1931-1978 .... CANR-28
Obituary 77-80
Earlier sketch in CA 25-28R
Hirsch, Herbert 1941- CANR-15
Earlier sketch in CA 41-44R
Hirsch, James (S.) 1962- 201
Hirsch, Karen 1941- 105
See also SATA 61
Hirsch, Kathleen 1953- 220
Hirsch, Lester M. 1925- 17-20R
Hirsch, Linda 1949- 105
Hirsch, Marianne 1949- CANR-86
Earlier sketches in CA 113, CANR-46
Hirsch, Mark David 1910-1989 89-92
Obituary 128
Hirsch, Miriam F. 1927- 106
Hirsch, Monroe J(erome)
1917-1982 .... CANR-48
Earlier sketch in CA 41-44R
Hirsch, Morris Isaac 1915- 103
Hirsch, Odo CANR-141
Earlier sketch in CA 182
See also SATA 111, 157
Hirsch, Pam 1947- 176
Hirsch, Phil 1926- 102
See also SATA 35
Hirsch, Robin 1942- 154
Hirsch, S. Carl 1913-1990 .... CANR-2
Earlier sketch in CA 5-8R
See also SAAS 7
See also SATA 2
Hirsch, Seev 1931- 33-36R
Hirsch, Steven R(ichard) 1937- CANR-32
Earlier sketch in CA 113
Hirsch, Thomas L. 1931- 49-52
Hirsch, Walter 1919- 13-16R
Hirsch, Werner Z. 1920- CANR-7
Earlier sketch in CA 17-20R
Hirsch, William Randolph
See Kitman, Marvin and
Lingeman, Richard R(oberts)
Hirschberg, Cornelius 1901-1995 .... CAP-2
Earlier sketch in CA 17-18
Hirschberg, Stuart 1942- 187
Hirschfeld, Al(bert) 1903-2003 .... CANR-2
Obituary 212
Earlier sketch in CA 1-4R
Hirschfeld, Burt 1923- 134
Brief entry 111
Hirschfeld, Charles 1913-1975 127
Brief entry 105
Hirschfeld, Fritz 1924- 167
Hirschfeld, Herman 1905-1986 .... CAP-1
Earlier sketch in CA 13-16
Hirschfeld, Lawrence A. 1947- 158
Hirschfeld, Magnus 1868-1935 148
See also GLL 1
Hirschfeld, Yizhar 1950- 143
Hirschfelder, Arlene B. 1943- CANR-107
Earlier sketch in CA 147
See also SATA 80, 138
Hirschfelder, Joseph Oakland 1911-1990
Obituary 131
Hirschfield, Robert S(idney) 1928-1995 .. 45-48
Obituary 149
Hirschhorn, Clive 1940- CANR-9
Earlier sketch in CA 57-60
Hirschhorn, Howard H(arvey)
1931- CANR-42
Earlier sketches in CA 93-96, CANR-16
Hirschhorn, Joel 1937- 159
Hirschhorn, Richard Clark 1933- 69-72
Hirschi, Ron 1948- CANR-141
Earlier sketches in CA 120, CANR-68
See also SATA 56, 95
Hirschi, Travis 1935- CANR-13
Earlier sketch in CA 77-80
Hirschman, A. O.
See Hirschman, Albert O.
Hirschman, Albert O. 1915- CANR-37
Earlier sketches in CA 1-4R, CANR-1, 16
Hirschman, Jack 1933- CANR-128
Earlier sketches in CA 105, CANR-22
See also CP 1, 2, 3, 4, 5, 6, 7
Hirschmann, Linda (Ann) 1941- 106
See also SATA 40
Hirschmann, Maria Anne 85-88
Hirschmeier, Johannes 1921- CANR-5
Earlier sketch in CA 13-16R
Hirsh, James E(ric) 1946- 109
Hirsh, M(ary) E(lizabeth) 1947- 125
Hirsh, Marilyn 1944-1988 .... CANR-16
Obituary 126
Earlier sketches in CA 49-52, CANR-1
See also SATA 7
See also SATA-Obit 58
Hirsh, Michael 1957- 239
Hirsh, Richard F. 213
Hirshberg, Al(bert Simon) 1909-1973 . CANR-4
Obituary 41-44R
Earlier sketch in CA 1-4R
See also SATA 38
Hirshberg, Glen 1966- 229
Hirshfeld, Alan 1951- 141
Hirshfeld, Richard
See Hall, Richard W(alter)
See also GLL 1
Hirshfield, Daniel S. 1942- 29-32R
Hirshfield, Jane 1953- CANR-108
Earlier sketches in CA 149, CANR-70
See also CP 7
See also CWP
See also PFS 16
Hirshman, Linda R. 1944- 175

Hirsh-Pasek, Kathy 1953- CANR-121
Earlier sketch in CA 163
Hirshson, Stanley Philip 1928- CANR-119
Earlier sketch in CA 1-4R
Hirst, David W(ayne) 1920- 37-40R
Hirst, John Bradley 1942- 213
Hirst, Paul H(eywood) 1927- 65-68
Hirst, Paul Quentin 1946-2003 104
Obituary 217
Hirst, Rodney Julian 1920-1999 .... 9-12R
Hirst, Stephen M(ichael) 1939- 53-56
Hirst, Wilma E(llis) 1914- 13-16R
Hirt, Howard (Franklin) 1924-1987 131
Hirt, Michael L(eonard) 1934- 9-12R
Hisamatsu, (Hoseki) Shin'ichi
1889-1980 81-84
Hischak, Thomas S. 1951- 175
Hiscock, Bruce 1940- CANR-135
Earlier sketches in CA 122, CANR-49
See also SATA 57, 137
Hiscock, Eric 1899-1989(?) 109
Obituary 127
Hiscock, Eric C(harles) 1908-1986 107
Obituary 120
Hiscock, Geoff 1947- 212
Hiscocks, C(harles) Richard 1907-1998 .. 53-56
Obituary 169
Hiscoe, Helen B. 1919- 137
Hise, Greg 1953- 201
Hise, Phaedra 1964- 239
Hiser, Constance 1950- .... SATA 71
Hiser, Iona Seibert -1998 .... CANR-2
Earlier sketch in CA 1-4R
See also SATA 4
Hiskett, Mervyn 1920- 61-64
Hislop, Codman 1906- CAP-2
Earlier sketch in CA 33-36
Hislop, Julia Rose Catherine 1962- 141
See also SATA 74
Hisrich, Robert D(ale) 1944- 112
Hiss, Alger 1904-1996 .... 33-36R
Obituary 154
Hiss, Tony 1941- CANR-89
Earlier sketch in CA 77-80
Hissey, Jane (Elizabeth) 1952- 124
See also SATA 58, 103, 130
See also SATA-Essay 130
Hitch
See Hitchcock, Raymond (John)
Hitchcock, Alfred (Joseph) 1899-1980 159
Obituary 97-100
See also AAYA 22
See also CLC 16
See also SATA 27
See also SATA-Obit 24
Hitchcock, Alma Reville 1899-1982
Obituary 107
Hitchcock, Deborah J.
See Jessup, Deborah Hitchcock
Hitchcock, George 1914- CANR-13
Earlier sketch in CA 33-36R
See also CAAS 12
See also CP 1, 2
Hitchcock, H(ugh) Wiley 1923- CANR-17
Earlier sketches in CA 45-48, CANR-1
Hitchcock, Henry-Russell 1903-1987 125
Obituary 122
Hitchcock, James 1938- 33-36R
Hitchcock, Jane Stanton 1946- 212
Hitchcock, Michael 1954- 184
Hitchcock, Raymond (John) 1922-1992 .. 85-88
Hitchcock, Susan Tyler 1950- CANR-18
Earlier sketch in CA 102
Hitchcock, William I. 222
Hitchcott, Nicki 1965- CANR-135
Earlier sketch in CA 156
Hitchens, Christopher (Eric) 1949- ... CANR-89
Earlier sketch in CA 152
See also CLC 157
Hitchens, Dolores 1908(?)-1973
Obituary 45-48
Hitchens, Neal 1957-2000 141
Hitchin, Martin Mewburn 1917- 13-16R
Hitching, (John) Francis 1933- 103
Hitchins, Keith 1931- CANR-98
Earlier sketch in CA 147
Hitchman, James H. 1932- 37-40R
Hitchman, Janet 1916-1980 .... 21-24R
Obituary 97-100
Hite, James (Cleveland) 1941- 53-56
Hite, Molly 1947- CANR-51
Earlier sketch in CA 124
Hite, Shere 1942- CANR-31
Earlier sketch in CA 81-84
See also CPW
See also MTCW 1
Hite, Sid 1954- CANR-115
Earlier sketch in CA 142
See also SATA 75, 136
Hitiris, Theodore 1938- 41-44R
Hitler, Adolf 1889-1945 147
Brief entry 117
See also TCLC 53
Hitrec, Joseph George 1912-1972 .... CAP-2
Earlier sketch in CA 17-18
Hitsman, J(ohn) Mackay 1917-1970 ...... CAP-1
Earlier sketch in CA 17-18
Hitt, Russell T(rovillo) 1905-1992 .... 1-4R
Hitt, William D(ee) 1929- 49-52
Hitte, Kathryn 1919- 21-24R
See also SATA 16
Hitti, Philip K(huri) 1886-1978 .... CANR-6
Obituary 81-84
Earlier sketch in CA 1-4R
Hittinger, (F.) Russell 1949- 145
Hitz, Demi 1942- CANR-35
Earlier sketches in CA 61-64, CANR-8
See also Demi
See also CLR 58
See also MAICYA 1, 2
See also SATA 11, 66, 102, 152
Hitz, Frederick P(orter) 1939- 232
Hitz, Mary Buford 1941- 197
Hitzeroth, Deborah L. 1961- 146
See also SATA 78
Hitz-Holman, Betsy
See Holman, Betsy Hitz
Hively, Pete (Chester) 1934- 69-72
Hivnor, Robert 1916- CANR-28
Earlier sketch in CA 65-68
See also CAD
See also CD 5, 6
Hix, Charles (Arthur) 1942- CANR-21
Earlier sketch in CA 102
Hixon, Don L(ee) 1942- 73-76
Hixson, Joseph R(andolph) 1927- 65-68
Hixson, Richard F. 1932- 21-24R
Hixson, William B(utler), Jr. 1940- 37-40R
Hixson, William F. 181
Hjartarson, Snorri 1906-1986 .... DLB 293
See also EWL 3
Hjelte, George 1893-1979 .... CANR-23
Earlier sketch in CA 29-32R
Hjortoe, Knud Anders
See Hjorto, Knud Anders
Hjortsberg, William (Reinhold)
1941- CANR-141
Earlier sketches in CA 33-36R, CANR-72
See also HGG
Hlasko, Marek 1933(?)-1969
Obituary 25-28R
See also EWL 3
Hlybinny, Uladzimer
See Seduro, Vladimir
Hlybinny, Vladimir
See Seduro, Vladimir
Hnizdovsky, Jacques 1915- .... SATA 32
Ho, Alfred K(uo-liang) 1919- CANR-75
Earlier sketches in CA 25-28R, CANR-35
Ho, Allan 1955- 187
Ho, Anh Thai 1960- 181
Ho, Chi Minh 1890(?)-1969
Obituary 112
Ho, Ch'i-fang
See Ho Ch'i-fang
Ho, Minfong 1951- CANR-67
Earlier sketch in CA 77-80
See also AAYA 29
See also CLR 28
See also MAICYA 2
See also MAICYAS 1
See also SATA 15, 94, 151
See also YAW
Ho, Ping-ti 1917- CANR-11
Earlier sketch in CA 5-8R
Ho, Xuan Huong
See Ho Xuan Huong
Hoa, Nguyen-Dinh
See Nguyen, Dinh Hoa
Hoadley, Irene Braden 1938- 29-32R
Hoadley, Walter E(vans) 1916- 102
Hoag, Edwin 1926- 13-16R
Hoag, Tami 1959- CANR-136
Earlier sketches in CA 138, CANR-72
Hoagland, Anthony Dey 1953- 153
See also CP 7
See also PFS 19
Hoagland, Edward (Morley) 1932- . CANR-107
Earlier sketches in CA 1-4R, CANR-2, 31, 57
See also ANW
See also CLC 28
See also CN 1, 2, 3, 4, 5, 6, 7
See also DLB 6
See also SATA 51
See also TCWW 2
Hoagland, Everett (III) 1942- CANR-25
Earlier sketch in CA 33-36R
See also BW 1
See also DLB 41
Hoagland, Jimmie Lee 1940- 101
Hoagland, John 1947(?)-1984
Obituary 112
Hoagland, Kathleen M(ary) Dooher
1909(?)-1984 .... 5-8R
Obituary 112
Hoagland, Mahlon B(ush) 1921- 85-88
Hoagland, Tony
See Hoagland, Anthony Dey
Hoak, Dale 1941- 209
Hoang Van Chi 1915- CANR-7
Earlier sketch in CA 13-16R
Hoar, Jere (Richmond) 1929- 163
Hoar, Roger Sherman 1887-1963 160
See also SFW 4
Hoar, Stuart (Murray) 1957- .... CD 5, 6
Hoare, Merval Hannah 1914-2001 103
See also Connelly, Merval Hannah
Hoare, Philip 1958- 134
Hoare, Robert J(ohn) 1921-1975 .... CANR-6
Earlier sketch in CA 9-12R
See also SATA 38
Hoare, Wilber W., Jr. 1921-1976
Obituary 65-68
Hobaek Haff, Bergljot
See Haff, Bergljot Hobaek
Hoban, Lillian 1925-1998 .... CANR-23
Obituary 169
Earlier sketch in CA 69-72
See also CLR 67
See also MAICYA 1, 2
See also SATA 22, 69
See also SATA-Obit 104
Hoban, Russell (Conwell) 1925- CANR-138
Earlier sketches in CA 5-8R, CANR-23, 37, 66, 114
See also BPFB 2
See also CLC 7, 25
See also CLR 3, 69
See also CN 4, 5, 6, 7
See also CWRI 5
See also DAM NOV
See also DLB 52
See also FANT
See also MAICYA 1, 2
See also MTCW 1, 2
See also MTFW 2005
See also SATA 1, 40, 78, 136
See also SFW 4
See also SUFW 2
See also TCLE 1:1
Hoban, Tana 1917(?)- CANR-141
Earlier sketches in CA 93-96, CANR-23
See also CLR 13, 76
See also MAICYA 1, 2
See also SAAS 12
See also SATA 22, 70, 104
Hobart, Alice Nourse 1882-1967 .... 5-8R
Obituary 25-28R
Hobart, Alice Tisdale
See Hobart, Alice Nourse
Hobart, Billie 1935- 49-52
Hobart, Donald Bayne .... TCWW 1, 2
Hobart, Lois (Elaine) CANR-139
Earlier sketch in CA 5-8R
See also SATA 7
Hobb, Robin
See Ogden, Margaret (Astrid) Lindholm
Hobbes, Thomas 1588-1679 ..... DLB 151, 252, 281
See also RGEL 2
Hobbie, Holly 1944- .... CLR 88
Hobbing, Enno 1920- 89-92
Hobbs, Albert Hoyt 1940- 125
Hobbs, Anne
See Purdy, Anne S.
Hobbs, Anne Stevenson 1942- 133
Hobbs, Aspasia
See Hubbard, Elbert
Hobbs, Cecil (Carlton) 1907-1991 .... 21-24R
Hobbs, Charles R(ene) 1931- 13-16R
Hobbs, (Carl) Fredric 1931- 81-84
Hobbs, Herschel Harold 1907-1995 .. CANR-2
Earlier sketch in CA 5-8R
Hobbs, J. Kline 1928- 108
Hobbs, John Leslie 1916-1964 .... 5-8R
Hobbs, Mary 1923- 153
Hobbs, Michael 1934- 111
Hobbs, Perry
See Blackmur, R(ichard) P(almer)
Hobbs, Peter V(ictor) 1936- 53-56
Hobbs, Richard (Wright) 1931- 123
Brief entry 118
Hobbs, Robert C(arleton) 1946- CANR-24
Earlier sketch in CA 106
Hobbs, Valerie 1941- CANR-127
Earlier sketch in CA 159
See also AAYA 28
See also SATA 93, 145
See also SATA-Essay 145
Hobbs, Will(iam Carl) 1947- CANR-124
Earlier sketch in CA 180
See also AAYA 14, 39
See also BYA 6
See also CLR 59
See also MAICYA 2
See also MAICYAS 1
See also SATA 72, 110
See also SATA-Essay 127
See also WYA
See also YAW
Hobbs, William (Beresford) 1939- 21-24R
Hobbs, Williston C. 1925(?)-1978
Obituary 81-84
Hobby, Bertram Maurice 1905-1983
Obituary 110
Hobby, Elaine (Ann) 1956- 130
Hobby, Gladys L(ounsbury) 1910-1993 119
Obituary 141
Hobby, Oveta Culp 1905-1995 81-84
See also DLB 127
Hobby, William 1878-1964 .... DLB 127
Hobby, William P. 1932- 85-88
Hobday, Charles (Henry)
1917-2005 .... CANR-75
Obituary 237
Earlier sketch in CA 132
Hobday, Jose 181
Hobday, Sister Jose
See Hobday, Jose
Hobday, Victor C(arr) 1914-2002 97-100
Hobel, Phil
See Fanthorpe, R(obert) Lionel
Hoben, John B. 1908-1994 .... 37-40R
Hoberecht, Earnest 1918-1999 .... 21-24R
Obituary 185
Hoberman, Gerald 1943- 111
Hoberman, Mary Ann 1930- CANR-124
Earlier sketch in CA 41-44R
See also CLR 22
See also CWRI 5
See also MAICYA 1, 2
See also SAAS 18
See also SATA 5, 72, 111, 158
Hobfoll, Stevan E(arl) 1951- CANR-49
Earlier sketch in CA 123
Hobgood, Burnet M(cLean) 1922-2000 101
Obituary 190
Hobhouse, Christina 1941- 25-28R
Hobhouse, Hermione 1934- CANR-15
Earlier sketch in CA 41-44R
Hobhouse, Janet 1948-1991 57-60
Obituary 133
Hobhouse, Penelope
See Malins, Penelope
Hobkirk, Michael D(algliesh) 1924- 119
Hobley, Leonard Frank 1903- CANR-5
Earlier sketch in CA 13-16R
Hobsbaum, Philip (Dennis) 1932- CANR-56
Earlier sketches in CA 9-12R, CANR-3, 29
See also CP 1, 2, 3, 4, 5, 6, 7
See also DLB 40
Hobsbawm, Eric J(ohn Ernest)
1917- CANR-56
Earlier sketches in CA 5-8R, CANR-3
See also DLB 296
Hobson, Anthony (Robert Alwyn)
1921- 33-36R
Hobson, Bruce 1950- CANR-54
Earlier sketch in CA 127
See also SATA 62
Hobson, Burton (Harold) 1933- CANR-2
Earlier sketch in CA 5-8R
See also SATA 28
Hobson, Charles F. 1943- 164
Hobson, Charlotte 1971(?)- 203
Hobson, Christine
See El Mahdy, Christine
Hobson, Edmund (Schofield) 1931- 45-48
Hobson, Fred (Colby, Jr.) 1943- CANR-105
Earlier sketches in CA 53-56, CANR-5
Hobson, Geary 1941- 122
Hobson, Hank
See Hobson, Harry
Hobson, Harold 1904-1992 81-84
Obituary 137
Hobson, Harry 1908- CAP-1
Earlier sketch in CA 9-10
Hobson, J(ohn) Allan 1933- CANR-110
Earlier sketch in CA 140
Hobson, Julius W(ilson) 1922(?)-1977 102
See also BW 1
Hobson, Laura Z(ametkin)
1900-1986 .... CANR-55
Obituary 118
Earlier sketch in CA 17-20R
See also BPFB 2
See also CLC 7, 25
See also CN 1, 2, 3, 4
See also DLB 28
See also SATA 52
Hobson, Mary 1926- 106
Hobson, Polly
See Evans, Julia (Rendel)
Hobson, Sally 1967- .... SATA 84
Hobson, Sarah 1947- 197
See also DLB 204
Hobson, William 1911- 103
Hoby, Thomas 1530-1566 .... DLB 132
Hobzek, Mildred J(ane) 1919- 101
Hoccleve, Thomas c. 1368-c. 1437 ... DLB 146
See also RGEL 2
Hoch, Edward D(entinger) 1930- CANR-97
Earlier sketches in CA 29-32R, CANR-11, 27, 51
See also Queen, Ellery
See also CMW 4
See also DLB 306
See also SFW 4
Hoch, Paul L(awrence) 1942- CANR-27
Earlier sketch in CA 65-68
Hoch, Winton C. 1907-1979 .... IDFW 3, 4
Hochbaum, H(ans) Albert 1911- 103
Hochfield, George 1926- 1-4R
Hochhuth, Rolf 1931- CANR-136
Earlier sketches in CA 5-8R, CANR-33, 75
See also CLC 4, 11, 18
See also CWW 2
See also DAM DRAM
See also DLB 124
See also EWL 3
See also MTCW 1, 2
See also MTFW 2005
Ho Ch'i-fang 1912-1977 .... EWL 3
Hochman, Baruch 1930- 128
Hochman, Elaine S(chwartz) 166
Hochman, Gloria 1943- 141
Hochman, Harold M(arvin) 1936- 108
Hochman, Jiri 1926- 141
Hochman, Sandra 1936- 5-8R
See also CLC 3, 8
See also CP 1, 2
See also DLB 5
Hochman, Shel 1944- 69-72
Hochman, Shirley D(ean) 1917- 61-64
Hochman, Stanley Richard 1928- CANR-48
Earlier sketch in CA 103
Hochschild, Adam 1942- CANR-86
Brief entry 121
Earlier sketches in CA 125, CANR-53
Interview in CA-125
Hochschild, Arlie Russell 1940- CANR-72
Earlier sketches in CA 57-60, CANR-45
See also BEST 89:4
See also SATA 11
Hochschild, Harold K. 1892-1981
Obituary 103
Hochstein, Rolaine CANR-23
Earlier sketch in CA 45-48
Hochstetter, Leo D. 1911(?)-1987
Obituary 122

Cumulative Index 271 Hoffman

Hochwaelder, Fritz 1911-1986 ... CANR-42
Obituary ... 120
Earlier sketch in CA 29-32R
See also Hochwalder, Fritz
See also CLC 36
See also DAM DRAM
See also MTCW 1
See also RGWL 3
Hochwald, Werner 1910-1989 ... 17-20R
Hochwalder, Fritz
See Hochwaelder, Fritz
See also EWL 3
See also RGWL 2
Hock, Randolph 1944- ... 231
Hockaby, Stephen
See Mitchell, Gladys (Maude Winifred)
Hocke, Martin 1938- ... 154
See also FANT
Hocken, Thomas Morland
1836-1910 ... DLB 184
Hockenberry, Hope
See Newell, Hope Hockenberry
Hockenberry, John 1956(?)- ... CANR-107
Earlier sketch in CA 155
See also AAYA 48
See also MTFW 2005
Hockensmith, Sean M. 1972- ... 164
Hocker, Karla
See Hoecker, Karla
Hockett, Charles F(rancis) 1916-2000 ... 17-20R
Obituary ... 192
Hocking, Anthony 1938- ... 102
Hocking, Brian 1914-1974 ... CAP-2
Earlier sketch in CA 17-18
Hocking, Mary (Eunice) 1921- ... CANR-40
Earlier sketches in CA 101, CANR-18
See also CLC 13
Hocking, William Ernest 1873-1966 ... CAP-1
Earlier sketch in CA 13-14
See also DLB 270
Hockley, Allen ... 228
Hockley, G(raham) C(harles) 1931- ... 29-32R
Hockney, David 1937- ... CANR-98
Brief entry ... 116
Earlier sketch in CA 150
See also AAYA 17
Hocks, Richard A(llen) 1936- ... 81-84
Hocquenghem, Guy 1946-1988 ... 148
See also GLL 1
Hodder-Williams, (John) Christopher
(Glazebrook) 1926-1995 ... CANR-1
Obituary ... 148
Earlier sketch in CA 1-4R
See also SFW 4
Hoddeson, Lillian 1940- ... 213
Hoddinott, Ralph Field 1913- ... 127
Hoddle, Glenn 1957- ... 191
Hodeir, Andre 1921- ... CANR-86
Earlier sketches in CA 85-88, CANR-15, 34
Hodel, Steve 1941- ... 234
Hodemart, Peter
See Audemars, Pierre
Hodes, Aubrey 1927- ... 33-36R
Hodes, Scott 1937- ... 49-52
Hodgart, Matthew (John Caldwell)
1916-1996 ... CANR-9
Obituary ... 151
Earlier sketch in CA 5-8R
Hodge, A(lfred) Trevor 1930- ... 190
Hodge, Alan 1915-1979
Obituary ... 89-92
Hodge, David W(ayne) 1935- ... 61-64
Hodge, Deborah 1954- ... 195
See also SATA 122, 163
Hodge, Francis (Richard) 1915- ... CANR-12
Earlier sketch in CA 33-36R
Hodge, Gene (Meany) 1898-1989 ... 45-48
Hodge, James L(ee) 1935- ... 41-44R
Hodge, Jane Aiken 1917- ... CANR-96
Earlier sketches in CA 5-8R, CANR-3, 45
See also RHW
Hodge, Marshall Bryant 1925-(?) ... CAP-2
Earlier sketch in CA 23-24
Hodge, Merle 1944- ... EWL 3
Hodge, P. W.
See Hodge, Paul W(illiam)
Hodge, Paul W(illiam) 1934- ... CANR-42
Earlier sketches in CA 33-36R, CANR-14
See also SATA 12
Hodge, Robert 1940- ... 128
Hodge, Susie 1960- ... 239
Hodge, William H(oward) 1932- ... CANR-15
Earlier sketch in CA 65-68
Hodgell, P(atricia) C(hristine)
1951- ... CANR-142
Earlier sketches in CA 109, CANR-60
See also FANT
See also SATA 42
Hodges, C(yril) Walter 1909-2004 ... CANR-5
Obituary ... 233
Earlier sketch in CA 13-16R
See also CWRI 5
See also SATA 2
See also SATA-Obit 158
Hodges, Carl G. 1902-1964 ... 5-8R
See also SATA 10
Hodges, Cyril 1915- ... CP 1
Hodges, Devon Leigh 1950- ... CANR-113
Earlier sketches in CA 125, CANR-51
Hodges, Donald Clark 1923- ... CANR-100
Earlier sketches in CA 53-56, CANR-6, 24, 49
Hodges, Doris M(arjorie) 1915- ... CANR-11
Earlier sketch in CA 25-28R
Hodges, Elizabeth Jamison ... 9-12R
See also SATA 1
Hodges, Gil(bert Ray) 1924-1972
Obituary ... 109
Hodges, Graham R(ushing) 1915- ... 5-8R
Hodges, Graham Russell 1946- ... 188
Hodges, H(erbert) A(rthur)
1905-1976 ... CANR-48
Obituary ... 69-72
Earlier sketch in CA 73-76
Hodges, Harold Mellor 1922- ... 17-20R
Hodges, Henry (Woolmington MacKenzie)
1920- ... 37-40R
Hodges, Henry G. 1888-1971 ... 5-8R
Hodges, John C(unyus) 1892-1967 ... 5-8R
Obituary ... 103
Hodges, Louis W. 1933- ... 81-84
Hodges, Luther (Hartwell) 1898-1974
Obituary ... 53-56
Hodges, Margaret Moore 1911- ... CANR-95
Earlier sketches in CA 1-4R, CANR-2, 30
See also CWRI 5
See also MAICYA 1, 2
See also SAAS 9
See also SATA 1, 33, 75, 117
Hodges, Michael P. 1941- ... 136
Hodges, Richard E(dwin) 1928- ... CANR-15
Earlier sketch in CA 41-44R
Hodges, Turner
See Morehead, Albert H(odges)
Hodges, Zane Clark 1932- ... CANR-15
Earlier sketch in CA 41-44R
Hodgetts, A(lfred) Birnie 1911-1987 ... 101
Hodgetts, Blake Christopher 1967- ... 114
See also SATA 43
Hodgetts, J(ohn) E(dwin) 1917- ... 13-16R
Hodgetts, Richard M(ichael)
1942-2001 ... CANR-23
Earlier sketches in CA 57-60, CANR-8
Hodgins, Bruce W(illard) 1931- ... CANR-98
Earlier sketch in CA 37-40R
Hodgins, Eric 1899-1971 ... 104
Obituary ... 29-32R
Hodgins, Jack 1938- ... 93-96
See also CLC 23
See also CN 4, 5, 6, 7
See also DLB 60
Hodgins, (Ian) Philip 1959- ... 153
See also CP 7
Hodgkin, Alan (Lloyd) 1914-1998 ... 140
Obituary ... 172
Hodgkin, Robert Allason 1916-2003 ... 102
Obituary ... 219
Hodgkin, Robin A.
See Hodgkin, Robert Allason
Hodgkin, Thomas Lionel 1910-1982
Obituary ... 115
Hodgkinson, Anthony 1916-1983 ... 126
Hodgkinson, Christopher 1928- ... 115
Hodgkinson, Edith 1959- ... 117
Hodgkinson, Liz 1943- ... 124
Hodgkinson, Marie Elisabeth 1921(?)-1983
Obituary ... 110
Hodgkiss, A(lan) G(eoffrey) 1921- ... 124
Hodgman, Helen 1945- ... 131
Brief entry ... 117
See also DLB 14
Hodgskin, Thomas 1787-1869 ... DLB 158
Hodgson, Barbara (L.) 1955- ... 233
Hodgson, D(avid) H(argraves) 1939- ... 25-28R
Hodgson, David
See Lewis, David
Hodgson, Derek 1929- ... 118
Hodgson, Geoffrey M. 1946- ... CANR-120
Earlier sketch in CA 146
Hodgson, Godfrey (Michael Talbot)
1934- ... CANR-95
Earlier sketch in CA 25-28R
Hodgson, Harriet (W.) 1935- ... CANR-100
Earlier sketch in CA 150
See also SATA 84
Hodgson, John A(lfred) 1945- ... 125
Hodgson, Leonard 1889-1969 ... CAP-1
Earlier sketch in CA 9-10
Hodgson, Margaret
See Ballinger, (Violet) Margaret (Livingstone)
Hodgson, Marshall G. S. 1922-1968 ... CAP-2
Earlier sketch in CA 21-22
Hodgson, Martha (Keeling) 1906- ... 57-60
Hodgson, Norma
See Russell, Norma Hull Lewis
Hodgson, Pat 1928- ... CANR-7
Earlier sketch in CA 57-60
Hodgson, Peter Crafts 1934- ... CANR-15
Earlier sketch in CA 29-32R
Hodgson, Peter E(dward) 1928- ... 9-12R
Hodgson, Phyllis 1909-2000 ... CAP-1
Earlier sketch in CA 13-14
Hodgson, Ralph 1871-1962 ... 102
See also DLB 19
See also RGEL 2
Hodgson, Richard Sargeant 1924- ... CANR-7
Earlier sketch in CA 13-16R
Hodgson, Robert D(avid) 1923- ... 5-8R
Hodgson, William Hope 1877(?)-1918 ... 164
Brief entry ... 111
See also CMW 4
See also DLB 70, 153, 156, 178
See also HGG
See also MTCW 2
See also SFW 4
See also SUFW 1
See also TCLC 13
Hodin, J(osef) P(aul) 1905-1995 ... 41-44R
Obituary ... 150
Hodnett, Edward 1901-1984 ... CANR-5
Obituary ... 114
Earlier sketch in CA 13-16R
Hodsdon, Nicholas E(dward) 1941- ... 49-52
Hodsdon, Nick
See Hodsdon, Nicholas E(dward)
Hodson, Arthur
See Nickson, Arthur
Hodson, Henry V(incent) 1906-1999 ... CANR-3
Obituary ... 177
Earlier sketch in CA 5-8R
Hodson, Peregrine ... 128
Hoe, Robert III 1839-1909 ... 183
See also DLB 187
Hoebel, Edward Adamson
1906-1993 ... CANR-1
Obituary ... 142
Earlier sketch in CA 1-4R
Hoeck, Klaus
See Hoeck, Klaus
Hoeck, Klaus 1938- ... 193
See also EWL 3
Hoecker, Karla 1901- ... CANR-2
Earlier sketch in CA 49-52
Hoedemaker, Bert 1935- ... 175
Hoeflich, Michael H. 1952- ... 213
Hoeg, Peter 1957- ... CANR-75
Earlier sketch in CA 151
See also CLC 95, 156
See also CMW 4
See also DA3
See also DLB 214
See also EWL 3
See also MTCW 2
See also MTFW 2005
See also NFS 17
See also RGWL 3
See also SSFS 18
Hoehling, A(dolph) A(ugust)
1915-2004 ... CANR-1
Obituary ... 234
Earlier sketch in CA 1-4R
Hoehling, Mary (Duprey) 1914-2004 ... 93-96
Obituary ... 234
Hoehn, Richard A(lbert) 1936- ... 116
Hoehne, Horst Karl Heinrich
See Hohne, Horst (Karl Heinrich)
Hoehne, Marcia 1951- ... 155
See also SATA 89
Hoehner, Harold W. 1935- ... 37-40R
Hoekema, Anthony A(ndrew)
1913-1988 ... 9-12R
Hoeksema, Gertrude 1921- ... 106
Hoel, Robert F(loyd) 1942- ... 53-56
Hoel, Sigurd 1890-1960 ... DLB 297
See also EWL 3
Hoelldobler, Bert(hold Karl) 1936- ... 134
Hoellerer, Walter (Friedrich)
See Hollerer, Walter (Friedrich)
Hoellwarth, Cathryn Clinton 1957- ... 205
See also SATA 136
Hoelterhoff, Manuela (Vali) 1949- ... 120
Brief entry ... 114
Interview in ... CA-120
Hoelzel, Alfred 1934- ... 41-44R
Hoelzer, Max
See Holzer, Max
Hoem, Edvard 1949- ... 195
See also DLB 297
Hoenig, J(ulius) 1916- ... 29-32R
Hoenig, Sidney B(enjamin)
1907-1979 ... CANR-2
Earlier sketch in CA 45-48
Hoeniger, F(rederick) David 1921- ... 41-44R
Hoenigswald, Henry M(ax)
1915-2003 ... CANR-39
Obituary ... 217
Earlier sketch in CA 13-16R
Hoepffner, Bernard 1946- ... 145
Hoepfl, Harro (Maximilian) 1943- ... 129
Hoeppner, Edward Haworth 1951- ... 150
Hoequist, Charles Ernest, Jr. 1954- ... 108
Hoerder, Dirk 1943- ... 193
Hoerr, John P. (III) 1930- ... 135
Hoest, Bill
See Hoest, William P.
Hoest, William P. 1926-1988 ... CANR-23
Obituary ... 127
Earlier sketch in CA 69-72
Hoestlandt, Jo(celyne) 1948- ... 159
See also SATA 94
Hoetink, H(armannus) 1931- ... 21-24R
Hoeveler, Diane Long 1949- ... CANR-90
Earlier sketch in CA 102
Hoeveler, J. David, Jr. 1943- ... CANR-141
Earlier sketch in CA 129
Hoexter, Corinne K. 1927- ... CANR-27
Earlier sketch in CA 49-52
See also SATA 6
Hoey, Joanne Nobes 1936- ... 106
Hoeye, Michael 1947- ... 213
See also SATA 136
Hoezee, Scott E. 1964- ... 168
Hofer, Peter
See Kortner, Peter
Hofer, Philip 1898-1984
Obituary ... 114
Hoff, Al 1964- ... 171
Hoff, B. J. 1940- ... CANR-121
Earlier sketch in CA 162
Hoff, Benjamin 1946- ... CANR-143
Earlier sketch in CA 142
Hoff, Carol 1900-1979 ... CAP-2
Earlier sketch in CA 21-22
See also SATA 11
Hoff, Ebbe Curtis 1906- ... 57-60
Hoff, H. S.
See Hoff, Harry Summerfield
Hoff, Harry Summerfield
1910-2002 ... CANR-94
Obituary ... 211
Earlier sketches in CA 1-4R, CANR-2, 20, 42
See also Cooper, William
See also CN 7
Hoff, Joan ... CANR-99
See also Wilson, Joan Hoff
Hoff, Marilyn 1942- ... CANR-7
Earlier sketch in CA 17-20R
Hoff, Mary (King) 1956- ... 233
See also SATA 74, 157
Hoff, Syd(ney) 1912-2004 ... CANR-117
Obituary ... 227
Earlier sketches in CA 5-8R, CANR-4, 38
See also CLR 83
See also CWRI 5
See also MAICYA 1, 2
See also SAAS 4
See also SATA 9, 72, 138
See also SATA-Obit 154
Hoffa, James R(iddle) 1913-1975(?)
Obituary ... 109
Hoffecker, Carol E(leanor) 1938- ... 85-88
Hoffecker, (John) Savin 1908-1981 ... 5-8R
Hoffeld, Donald R(aymond) 1933- ... 29-32R
Hoffeld, Laura 1946(?)-1982
Obituary ... 106
Hoffenberg, Jack 1906-1977 ... 81-84
Hoffenberg, Mason 1922(?)-1986
Obituary ... 119
Hoffenstein, Samuel Goodman 1890-1947
Brief entry ... 111
See also DLB 11
See also IDFW 3, 4
Hoffer, Charles R(ussell) 1929- ... CANR-22
Earlier sketches in CA 13-16R, CANR-7
Hoffer, Eric 1902-1983 ... CANR-18
Obituary ... 109
Earlier sketch in CA 13-16R
Hoffer, Peter T(homas) 1942- ... 145
Hoffer, Thomas William 1938- ... 118
Hoffer, William 1943- ... CANR-27
Earlier sketch in CA 65-68
Hofferbert, Richard I(ra) 1937- ... 29-32R
Hoffheimer, Michael H. 1954- ... 195
Hoffine, Lyla 1897-1984 ... 1-4R
Hoffman, Abbie 1936-1989 ... CANR-63
Obituary ... 128
Earlier sketches in CA 21-24R, CANR-8, 35
See also MTCW 1
See also NCFS 5
Hoffman, Abraham 1938- ... 106
Hoffman, Adeline M(ildred)
1908-1979 ... CANR-23
Earlier sketch in CA 29-32R
Hoffman, Alice 1952- ... CANR-138
Earlier sketches in CA 77-80, CANR-34, 66, 100
See also AAYA 37
See also AMWS 10
See also CLC 51
See also CN 4, 5, 6, 7
See also CPW
See also DAM NOV
See also DLB 292
See also MAL 5
See also MTCW 1, 2
See also MTFW 2005
See also TCLE 1:1
Hoffman, Allan M. 1948- ... 175
Hoffman, Andrew (Jay) 1956- ... 162
Hoffman, Andy
See Hoffman, Andrew (Jay)
Hoffman, Anita 1942-1998 ... 69-72
Obituary ... 172
Hoffman, Art
See King, Albert
Hoffman, Arthur S. 1926- ... CANR-10
Earlier sketch in CA 25-28R
Hoffman, Arthur W(olf) 1921- ... 5-8R
Hoffman, Bengt R(uno) 1913-1997 ... 69-72
Hoffman, Bernard G(ilbert) 1925- ... 41-44R
Hoffman, Betty Hannah 1918- ... 9-12R
Hoffman, Bruce 1954- ... 172
Hoffman, Calvin 1908(?)-1986
Obituary ... 118
Hoffman, Carl 1960- ... 202
Hoffman, Charles Fenno 1806-1884 ... DLB 3, 250
See also RGAL 4
Hoffman, Daniel (Gerard) 1923- ... CANR-142
Earlier sketches in CA 1-4R, CANR-4
See also CLC 6, 13, 23
See also CP 1, 2, 3, 4, 5, 6, 7
See also DLB 5
See also TCLE 1:1
Hoffman, David Herbert 1932(?)-1985
Obituary ... 115
Hoffman, Dominic M. 1913- ... 116
Hoffman, Donald D(avid) 1955- ... 186
Hoffman, Donald S(tone) 1936- ... 57-60
Hoffman, Edward ... 106
Hoffman, Edwin D. ... 101
See also SATA 49
Hoffman, Elizabeth P(arkinson)
1921-2003 ... 77-80
Obituary ... 218
See also SATA-Obit 153
Hoffman, Ernst
See Govinda, Anagarika Brahmacari
See also WP
Hoffman, Eva 1945- ... 132
See also CLC 182
Hoffman, Frank B. 1888-1958 ... 195
See also DLB 188

Hoffman, Frederick J(ohn)
1909-1967 ... CANR-6
Earlier sketch in CA 1-4R
Hoffman, Gail 1896-1977 ... 5-8R
Hoffman, George W(alter) 1914-1990 ... 13-16R
Hoffman, Harry G. 1911(?)-1977
Obituary ... 69-72
Hoffman, Helmut 1912-1992 ... CANR-17
Earlier sketch in CA 1-4R
Hoffman, Herbert H(einz) 1928- ... CANR-40
Earlier sketch in CA 117
Hoffman, Hester R(osalyn) 1895-1965 .. CAP-1
Earlier sketch in CA 9-10
Hoffman, Jilliane 1967- ... 228
Hoffman, Jo Ann S. 1942- ... 81-84
Hoffman, Jon T. 1955- ... CANR-118
Earlier sketch in CA 146
Hoffman, Joseph G(ilbert) 1909-1974 ... 65-68
Obituary ... 53-56
Hoffman, Joy 1954- ... 108
Hoffman, Julius Jennings 1895-1983
Obituary ... 110
Hoffman, L. Richard 1930- ... 13-16R
Hoffman, Lee 1932- ... CANR-68
Earlier sketches in CA 25-28R, CANR-18
Interview in ... CANR-18
See also CAAS 10
See also SFW 4
See also TCWW 1, 2
Hoffman, Lisa 1919- ... 29-32R
Hoffman, Lois Wladis 1929- ... 13-16R
Hoffman, Mark S. 1952- ... 125
Hoffman, Marshall 1942- ... 106
Hoffman, Mary (Margaret) 1945- ... CANR-122
Earlier sketches in CA 131, CANR-68
See also Lassiter, Mary
See also AAYA 59
See also CWRI 5
See also SAAS 24
See also SATA 59, 97, 144
Hoffman, Mat 1972- ... 225
See also SATA 150
Hoffman, Michael Allen 1944-1990 ... 106
Obituary ... 131
Hoffman, Michael J(erome) 1939- ... 29-32R
Hoffman, Nancy Jo 1942- ... 107
Hoffman, Nina Kiriki 1955- ... CANR-107
Earlier sketch in CA 166
See also AAYA 52
See also SATA 160
Hoffman, Paul 1934-1984 ... CANR-28
Obituary ... 112
Earlier sketches in CA 45-48, CANR-1
Hoffman, Paul 1956- ... 235
Hoffman, Philip T(homas) 1947- ... 119
Hoffman, Phyllis M(iriam) 1944- ... CANR-28
Earlier sketches in CA 29-32R, CANR-12
See also SATA 4
Hoffman, Richard L(ester)
1937-1981 ... CANR-23
Earlier sketch in CA 29-32R
Hoffman, Robert C. 1899(?)-1985
Obituary ... 116
Hoffman, Robert L. 1937- ... 37-40R
Hoffman, Ronald 1941- ... CANR-86
Brief entry ... 112
Earlier sketch in CA 133
Hoffman, Rosekrans 1926- ... CANR-15
Earlier sketch in CA 89-92
See also SATA 15
Hoffman, Ross John Swartz 1902-1979 ... 65-68
Hoffman, Stanley 1944- ... 77-80
See also CLC 5
Hoffman, Valerie J. 1954- ... 165
Hoffman, Willa M(athews) 1914- ... 61-64
Hoffman, William 1925- ... CANR-103
Earlier sketches in CA 21-24R, CANR-9
See also CLC 141
See also CSW
See also DLB 234
See also TCLE 1:1
Hoffman, William M.
See Hoffman, William M(oses)
See also CAD
See also CD 5, 6
Hoffman, William M(oses) 1939- ... CANR-71
Earlier sketches in CA 57-60, CANR-11
See also Hoffman, William M.
See also CLC 40
Hoffman, Yoel ... 210
Hoffmann, Ann (Marie) 1930- ... 37-40R
Hoffmann, Banesh 1906-1986 ... CANR-3
Obituary ... 119
Earlier sketch in CA 5-8R
Hoffmann, Carl 1881-1947 ... IDFW 3, 4
Hoffmann, Charles 1921-1999 ... 106
Hoffmann, Charles G. 1921-1999 ... 13-16R
Hoffmann, Donald 1933- ... 25-28R
Hoffmann, E(rnst) T(heodor) A(madeus)
1776-1822 ... CDWLB 2
See also DLB 90
See also EW 5
See also GL 2
See also RGSF 2
See also RGWL 2, 3
See also SATA 27
See also SSC 13
See also SUFW 1
See also WCH
Hoffmann, Eleanor 1895-1990 ... CAP-1
Earlier sketch in CA 13-16
Hoffmann, Erik P(eter) 1939- ... CANR-29
Earlier sketches in CA 33-36R, CANR-13
Hoffmann, Felix 1911-1975 ... CAP-2
Obituary ... 57-60
Earlier sketch in CA 29-32
See also SATA 9
Hoffmann, Frank W(illiam) 1949- ... 106
Hoffmann, George 1960- ... 190
Hoffmann, Heinrich 1809-1894 ... CLR 70
See also WCH
Hoffmann, Henryk 1949- ... 228
Hoffmann, Hilde 1927- ... 25-28R
Hoffmann, Leon-Francois 1932- ... CANR-96
Earlier sketches in CA 49-52, CANR-46
Hoffmann, Malcolm A(rthur) 1912-1997 . 65-68
Obituary ... 158
Hoffmann, Margaret Jones 1910- ... CANR-2
Earlier sketch in CA 5-8R
See also SATA 48
Hoffmann, Peggy
See Hoffmann, Margaret Jones
Hoffmann, Peter (Conrad Werner)
1930- ... CANR-14
Earlier sketch in CA 81-84
Hoffmann, Peter R. 1935- ... CANR-136
Earlier sketch in CA 108
Hoffmann, Roald 1937- ... 142
Hoffmann, Stanley (H.) 1928- ... CANR-14
Earlier sketches in CA 81-84, CANR-1
Hoffmann, Yoel 1937- ... 97-100
Hoffmannswaldau, Christian Hoffmann von
1616-1679 ... DLB 168
Hoffmeister, Adolf 1903-1973
Obituary ... 41-44R
Hoffmeister, Donald F(rederick) 1916- ... 53-56
Hoffmeister, Gerhart 1936- ... 130
Hoffnung, Michele 1944- ... 81-84
Hoff-Wilson, Joan
See Wilson, Joan Hoff
Hofheinz, Roy Mark, Jr. 1935- ... 110
Hofher, Catherine Baxley 1954- ... SATA 130
Hofher, Cathy
See Hofher, Catherine Baxley
Hofinger, Johannes 1905-1984 ... CAP-1
Earlier sketch in CA 19-20
Hofling, Charles K(reimer)
1920-1980 ... CANR-34
Earlier sketch in CA 41-44R
Hofman, Anton
See Hollo, Anselm
Hofmann, Adele Dellenbaugh
1926-2001 ... 97-100
Obituary ... 196
Hofmann, George F. ... 231
Hofmann, Gert 1931-1993 ... 128
See also CLC 54
See also EWL 3
Hofmann, Hans 1923- ... CANR-4
Earlier sketch in CA 1-4R
Hofmann, Melita C(ecelia) (?)-1976 ... 5-8R
Obituary ... 69-72
Hofmann, Michael 1957- ... CANR-103
Earlier sketch in CA 160
See also CP 7
See also DLB 40
Hofmann, Paul Leopold 1912- ... CANR-130
Earlier sketch in CA 107
Hofmann, William J(ohn) 1931- ... 114
Hofmannsthal, Hugo von 1874-1929 ... 153
Brief entry ... 106
See also CDWLB 2
See also DAM DRAM
See also DC 4
See also DFS 17
See also DLB 81, 118
See also EW 9
See also EWL 3
See also RGWL 2, 3
See also TCLC 11
Hofmeyr, Dianne (Louise) ... 194
See also SATA 138
Hofmo, Gunvor 1921-1995 ... DLB 297
Hofschroer, Peter ... 235
Hofsepian, Sylvia A. 1932- ... SATA 74
Hofsinde, Robert 1902-1973 ... 73-76
Obituary ... 45-48
See also SATA 21
Hofsommer, Don(ovan) L(owell)
1938- ... CANR-49
Earlier sketches in CA 65-68, CANR-9, 24
Hofstadter, Albert 1910-1989 ... 33-36R
Hofstadter, Douglas R(ichard) 1945- ... 105
Interview in ... CA-105
See also MTCW 1
Hofstadter, Richard 1916-1970 ... CANR-117
Obituary ... 29-32R
Earlier sketches in CA 1-4R, CANR-4
See also DLB 17, 246
Hofstede, Geert
See Hofstede, Gerard H(endrik)
Hofstede, Geert H.
See Hofstede, Gerard H(endrik)
Hofstede, Gerard H(endrik) 1928- ... CANR-35
Earlier sketches in CA 41-44R, CANR-15
Hofstetter, Richard R(yan) 1956- ... 117
Hofvendahl, Russ(ell Lloyd) 1921- ... 116
Hogan, Bernice Harris 1929- ... CANR-7
Earlier sketch in CA 13-16R
See also SATA 12
Hogan, Chuck 1967- ... 156
Hogan, David Gerard 1959- ... 165
Hogan, Dennis P. 1950- ... 110
Hogan, Desmond 1950- ... CANR-44
Earlier sketch in CA 102
See also CN 4, 5, 6, 7
See also DLB 14, 319
Hogan, Inez 1895-1973 ... CANR-1
Earlier sketch in CA 1-4R
See also SATA 2
Hogan, J(ames) Michael 1953- ... 151
Hogan, James P(atrick) 1941- ... CANR-103
Earlier sketches in CA 81-84, CANR-15, 58
See also SATA 81
See also SFW 4
Hogan, John Charles 1919- ... 17-20R
Hogan, John D. 1927- ... 45-48
Hogan, Judy 1937- ... CANR-39
Earlier sketches in CA 77-80, CANR-16
Hogan, Lawrence D(aniel) 1944- ... 124
Hogan, Linda 1947- ... 226
Earlier sketches in CA 120, CANR-45, 73, 129
Autobiographical Essay in ... 226
See also AMWS 4
See also ANW
See also BYA 12
See also CLC 73
See also CWP
See also DAM MULT
See also DLB 175
See also NNAL
See also PC 35
See also SATA 132
See also TCWW 2
Hogan, Michael 1943- ... CANR-34
Earlier sketches in CA 77-80, CANR-14
Hogan, Patrick Colm 1957- ... 134
Hogan, Paul 1927- ... 61-64
Hogan, (Eugene) Pendleton 1907-1993 ... 127
Hogan, (Robert) Ray 1908-1998 ... CANR-64
Earlier sketches in CA 9-12R, CANR-4
See also TCWW 1, 2
Hogan, Robert (Goode) 1930-1999 .. CANR-86
Earlier sketches in CA 1-4R, CANR-1, 19, 41
Hogan, Robert F(rancis) 1927- ... 41-44R
Hogan, Thom(as Eugene, Jr.) 1952- ... 103
Hogan, Ursula 1899-1987 ... 5-8R
Hogan, Willard N(ewton) 1909- ... CAP-2
Earlier sketch in CA 21-22
Hogan, William Francis 1930- ... 25-28R
Hogan, William T. 1919- ... 97-100
Hogarth, Burne 1911-1996 ... 93-96
Obituary ... 151
See also SATA 63, 89
Hogarth, Charles
See Bowen, (Ivor) Ian and
Creasey, John
Hogarth, Douglas
See Phillips-Birt, Douglas Hextall Chedzey
Hogarth, Emmett
See Polonsky, Abraham (Lincoln)
Hogarth, Grace (Weston Allen)
1905-1995 ... 89-92
Obituary ... 150
See also CWRI 5
See also SATA 91
Hogarth, John
See Finnin, (Olive) Mary
Hogarth, Jr.
See Kent, Rockwell
Hogarth, (Arthur) Paul 1917-2001 ... CANR-51
Obituary ... 203
Earlier sketches in CA 49-52, CANR-27
See also SATA 41
Hogarth, William 1697-1764 ... AAYA 56
Hogarty, Richard A(nthony) 1933- ... 235
Hogben, Lancelot T. 1895-1975 ... 73-76
Obituary ... 61-64
Hogbin, H(erbert) Ian 1904-1989 ... 9-12R
Hogbotel, Sebastian
See Gott, K(enneth) D(avidson)
Hoge, Cecil C(unningham) Sr. 1913-1999 .. 116
Hoge, Dean R(ichard) 1937- ... CANR-57
Earlier sketches in CA 53-56, CANR-27
Hoge, Hilary 1954- ... 239
Hoge, James F(ulton), Jr. 1935- ... 166
Hoge, James O(tey) 1944- ... 89-92
Hoge, Phyllis
See Thompson, Phyllis Hoge
Hoge, Warren McClamroch 1941- ... 102
Hogendorn, Jan S(tafford) 1937- ... CANR-43
Earlier sketches in CA 37-40R, CANR-14
Hogg, Beth
See Hogg, Elizabeth (Tootill)
Hogg, Clayton L(eRoy) 1924- ... 104
Hogg, Elizabeth (Tootill) 1917- ... CANR-10
Earlier sketch in CA 5-8R
Hogg, Enderby
See Meades, Jonathan (Turner)
Hogg, Garry 1902-1976 ... CANR-10
Earlier sketch in CA 21-24R
See also SATA 2
Hogg, Gary 1957- ... SATA 105
Hogg, Helen (Battles) Sawyer
1905-1993 ... 69-72
Hogg, Ian V(ernon) 1926- ... CANR-12
Earlier sketch in CA 29-32R
Hogg, James 1770-1835 ... BRWS 10
See also DLB 93, 116, 159
See also GL 2
See also HGG
See also RGEL 2
See also SUFW 1
Hogg, James (Dalby) 1937- ... 137
Hogg, Oliver Frederick Gillilan
1887-1979 ... 93-96
Obituary ... 85-88
Hogg, Patrick Scott 1961(?)- ... 216
Hogg, Quintin McGarel 1907-2001 . CANR-14
Obituary ... 204
Earlier sketches in CAP-1, CA 11-12
Hogg, Robert (Lawrence) 1942- ... 53-56
See also CP 1
Hogg, W(illiam) Richey 1921- ... 1-4R
Hoggard, James 1941- ... 187
Hoggart, Richard 1918- ... CANR-93
Earlier sketch in CA 9-12R
Hogins, James Burl 1936- ... 53-56
Hogner, Dorothy Childs ... 33-36R
See also SATA 4
Hogner, Nils 1893-1970 ... 77-80
See also SATA 25
Hogrefe, Pearl ... CAP-1
Earlier sketch in CA 13-16
Hogrogian, Nonny 1932- ... CANR-49
Earlier sketches in CA 45-48, CANR-2
See also CLR 2, 95
See also MAICYA 1, 2
See also SAAS 1
See also SATA 7, 74
See also SATA-Essay 127
Hogshire, Jim 1958- ... 223
Hogue, Arthur R(eed) 1906-1986 ... 37-40R
Obituary ... 118
Hogue, C(harles) B(illy) 1928- ... 69-72
Hogue, Charles Leonard 1935- ... 105
Hogue, Richard 1946- ... 49-52
Hogue, W. Lawrence 1951- ... 126
Hoguet, Susan Ramsay 1945- ... 119
Hogwood, Brian W(alter) 1950- ... CANR-66
Earlier sketch in CA 128
Hogwood, Christopher (Jarvis Haley)
1941- ... CANR-56
Brief entry ... 120
Earlier sketch in CA 127
Interview in ... CA-127
Hoh, Diane 1937- ... 120
See also SATA 52, 102
See also SATA-Brief 48
Hohberg, Wolfgang Freiherr von
1612-1688 ... DLB 168
Hohenberg, Dorothy Lannuier 1905(?)-1977
Obituary ... 73-76
Hohenberg, John 1906-2000 ... CANR-6
Obituary ... 189
Earlier sketch in CA 13-16R
Hohenberg, Paul M(arcel) 1933- ... 25-28R
Hohendahl, Peter Uwe 1936- ... CANR-40
Earlier sketches in CA 45-48, CANR-2, 17
Hohenstein, C(harles) Louis 1930- ... 116
Hohenstein, Henry J(ohn) 1931- ... 53-56
Hohenzollern, Friedrich Wilhelm (Victor Albert)
1859-1941
Brief entry ... 120
Hohimer, Frank 1928- ... 57-60
Hohl, Ludwig 1904(?)-1980 ... 181
See also DLB 56
Hohler, Robert T(illman) 1951- ... 123
Hohlfelder, Robert Lane 1938- ... CANR-45
Earlier sketch in CA 45-48
Hohlwein, Kathryn Joyce 1930- ... 125
Hohn, Hazel (Stamper) ... 5-8R
Hohne, Horst (Karl Heinrich) 1927- ... 199
Hohnen, David 1925- ... 21-24R
Hohoff, Tay
See Torrey, Therese von Hohoff
Hoig, Stan(ley Warlick) 1924- ... CANR-1
Earlier sketch in CA 1-4R
Hoijer, Harry 1904-1976 ... 73-76
Obituary ... 65-68
Hoisington, Harland 1896(?)-1973
Obituary ... 45-48
Hojholt, Per
See Hojholt, Per
Hojholt, Per 1928- ... 192
See also DLB 214
See also EWL 3
Hojman, David E(nrique) 1946- ... 141
Hokanson, (Anthony) Drake 1951- ... 162
Hoke, Helen
See Watts, Helen L. Hoke
See also SATA-Obit 65
Hoke, Helen L.
See Watts, Helen L. Hoke
Hoke, John (Lindsay) 1925- ... 41-44R
See also SATA 7
Hol, Coby 1943- ... SATA 126
Holabird, Katharine 1948- ... 121
See also SATA 62, 135
Holaday, Allan Gibson 1916- ... 37-40R
Holaday, Bobbie 1922- ... 228
See also SATA 153
Holahan, Susan 1940- ... 171
Holan, Vladimir 1905-1980 ... 162
Obituary ... 114
See also DLB 215
See also EWL 3
Holappa, Pentti 1927- ... 192
Holbach, Paul-Henri Thiry
1723-1789 ... DLB 313
Holbeach, Henry
See Rands, William Brighty
Holbeche, Philippa Jack 1919- ... CAP-1
Earlier sketch in CA 9-10
Holberg, Ludvig 1684-1754 ... DLB 300
See also RGWL 2, 3
Holberg, Ruth L(angland) 1889-1984 ... 5-8R
See also SATA 1
Holbik, Karel 1920- ... 37-40R
Holbo, Paul Sothe 1929- ... 25-28R
Holborn, Hajo 1902-1969 ... CAP-2
Earlier sketch in CA 25-28
Holborn, Louise W(ilhelmine)
1898-1975(?) ... CAP-2
Earlier sketch in CA 25-28
Holborn, Mark 1949- ... 104
Holbrook, Belinda 1953- ... 236
Holbrook, Bill 1921- ... 61-64
Holbrook, Clyde A(mos) 1911-1989
Obituary ... 130
Holbrook, David (Kenneth) 1923- ... CANR-43
Earlier sketches in CA 5-8R, CANR-3
See also CN 1
See also CP 1, 2, 3, 4, 5, 6, 7
See also DLB 14, 40

Cumulative Index 273 **Hollis**

Holbrook, Jennifer Kearns 1931- ... 102
Holbrook, John
  See Vance, John Holbrook
Holbrook, Kathy 1963- ... SATA 107
Holbrook, Peter
  See Glick, Carl (Cannon)
Holbrook, Sabra
  See Erickson, Sabra Rollins
Holbrook, Sara ... 200
  See also SATA 131
Holbrook, Stewart Hall 1893-1964 ... CAP-1
  Earlier sketch in CA 9-10
  See also SATA 2
Holbrook, Teri ... 170
Holbrooke, Richard 1941- ... 135
Holburn, James 1900-1988
  Obituary ... 124
Holck, Manfred, Jr. 1930- ... 17-20R
Holcomb, Adele M(ansfield) 1930- ... 113
Holcomb, Brent H. 1950- ... 165
Holcomb, Donald F(rank) 1925- ... 97-100
Holcomb, George L. 1911- ... 45-48
Holcomb, Jerry (Leona) Kimble 1927- ... 25-28R
  See also SATA 113
Holcomb, Nan
  See McPhee, Norma H.
Holcombe, Arthur N(orman)
  1884-1977 ... CAP-2
  Obituary ... 73-76
  Earlier sketch in CA 29-32
Holcombe, Randall G(regory)
  1950- ... CANR-53
  Earlier sketches in CA 111, CANR-29
Holcroft, Thomas 1745-1809 . DLB 39, 89, 158
  See also RGEL 2
Holdefer, Charles 1959- ... 169
Holden, Anthony (Ivan) 1947- ... CANR-135
  Earlier sketches in CA 101, CANR-68
Holden, Anton 1934- ... 108
Holden, Clare
  See Loden, Rachel
Holden, Curry
  See Holden, William Curry
Holden, Dalby
  See Hammond, Gerald (Arthur Douglas)
Holden, David (Shipley) 1924-1977 ... 41-44R
Holden, Donald 1931- ... CANR-43
  Earlier sketches in CA 45-48, CANR-2, 18
Holden, Edith 1871-1920
  Brief entry ... 113
Holden, Elizabeth Rhoda
  See Lawrence, Louise
Holden, Genevieve
  See Pou, Genevieve Long
Holden, George S(cott) 1926- ... 106
Holden, Inez 1906-1974
  Obituary ... 53-56
Holden, Joan 1939- ... 230
  See also CAD
  See also CD 5, 6
  See also CWD
Holden, Jonathan 1941- ... 238
  Earlier sketches in CA 45-48, CANR-1, 16, 37, 90
  Autobiographical Essay in ... 238
  See also CAAS 22
  See also DLB 105
Holden, Matthew
  See Parkinson, Roger
Holden, Matthew, Jr. 1931- ... 57-60
Holden, Molly 1927-1981 ... 25-28R
  Obituary ... 133
  See also CP 1, 2
  See also DLB 40
Holden, Paul E. 1894(?)-1976
  Obituary ... 65-68
Holden, Peter 1948- ... 151
Holden, Philip (Joseph) 1962- ... 175
Holden, Raymond (Peckham)
  1894-1972 ... CANR-4
  Obituary ... 37-40R
  Earlier sketch in CA 5-8R
Holden, Ursula 1921- ... CANR-22
  Earlier sketch in CA 101
  See also CAAS 8
  See also CLC 18
Holden, Vincent F. 1911-1972
  Obituary ... 37-40R
Holden, W. C.
  See Holden, William Curry
Holden, W(illis) Sprague 1909-1973 ... 1-4R
  Obituary ... 45-48
Holden, Wendy 1965- ... 207
Holden, William Curry 1898(?)-
  Brief entry ... 117
Holder, Glenn 1906- ... 41-44R
Holder, Gwynneth 1943- ... 119
Holder, John, Jr. 1947-1985 ... CANR-77
  Obituary ... 116
  Earlier sketch in CANR-42
Holder, Nancy L. 1953- ... CANR-107
  Earlier sketch in CA 164
  See also HGG
Holder, Ray 1913- ... 102
Holder, William G. 1937- ... CANR-10
  Earlier sketch in CA 25-28R
Holderlin, (Johann Christian) Friedrich
  1770-1843 ... CDWLB 2
  See also DLB 90
  See also EW 5
  See also PC 4
  See also RGWL 2, 3
Holdgate, Martin Wyatt 1931- ... 109
Holdheim, William Wolfgang 1926- .. CANR-2
  Earlier sketch in CA 1-4R
Holding, Charles H. 1897-1973 ... CAP-1
  Earlier sketch in CA 11-12
Holding, Elizabeth Sanxay 1889-1955
  Brief entry ... 111
  See also CMW 4
Holding, James (Clark Carlisle, Jr.)
  1907-1997 ... 25-28R
  See also SATA 3
Holding, Vera Zumwalt 1894-1984
  Obituary ... 114
Holditch, W(illiam) Kenneth 1933- .. CANR-45
  Earlier sketch in CA 119
Holdren, Bob R. 1922- ... 37-40R
Holdren, John P(aul) 1944- ... 33-36R
Holdsclaw, Chamique 1977- ... 196
Holdstock, Pauline 1948- ... 184
Holdstock, Robert
  See Holdstock, Robert P.
Holdstock, Robert P. 1948- ... CANR-81
  Earlier sketch in CA 131
  See also CLC 39
  See also DLB 261
  See also FANT
  See also HGG
  See also SFW 4
  See also SUFW 2
Holdsworth, Christopher (John)
  1931- ... CANR-54
  Earlier sketch in CA 124
Holdsworth, Irene ... CAP-1
  Earlier sketch in CA 9-10
Holdsworth, Mary (Zvegintzov) 1908- ... CAP-1
  Earlier sketch in CA 13-16
Hole, Christina 1896-1985 ... 165
  Obituary ... 118
Hole, Dorothy (Henrietta Field) ... 135
Hole, Tahu Ronald Charles Pearce 1908-1985
  Obituary ... 118
Holechek, Jerry L. 1948- ... 197
Holeman, Linda 1949- ... CANR-142
  Earlier sketch in CA 160
  See also BYA 16
  See also MAICYA 2
  See also SATA 102, 136
  See also SATA-Essay 136
  See also YAW
Holenstein, Elmar 1937- ... CANR-28
  Earlier sketches in CA 65-68, CANR-11
Holford, Ingrid 1920- ... 102
Holford, William Graham 1907-1975
  Obituary ... 108
Holiday, F(rederick) W(illiam)
  1921-1979 ... 25-28R
Holiday, Homer
  See DeBeaubien, Philip Francis
Holinger, William (Jacques) 1944- ... CANR-57
  Earlier sketch in CA 123
  See also SATA 90
Holinshed, Raphael fl. 1580- ... DLB 167
  See also RGEL 2
Holisher, Desider 1901-1972 ... CAP-2
  Obituary ... 37-40R
  Earlier sketch in CA 19-20
  See also SATA 6
Holl, Adelaide Hinkle 1910- ... CANR-2
  Earlier sketch in CA 1-4R
  See also SATA 8
Holl, Adolf 1930- ... 101
Holl, Jack M. 1937- ... 57-60
Holl, Kristi D(iane) 1951- ... CANR-48
  Earlier sketch in CA 114
  See also SATA 51
Holladay, Sylvia A(gnes) 1936- ... 57-60
Holladay, William L(ee) 1926- ... 53-56
Holland, Ada Morehead 1911-2002 ... 122
Holland, Agnieszka 1948- ... 144
Holland, Alma Boice ... 29-32R
Holland, Barbara A(dams)
  1925-1988 ... CANR-113
  Earlier sketch in CA 57-60
Holland, Brud
  See Holland, Jerome H(eartwell)
Holland, Cecelia (Anastasia)
  1943- ... CANR-141
  Earlier sketches in CA 17-20R, CANR-9, 68
  See also RHW
Holland, Cecil Fletcher 1907-1978
  Obituary ... 77-80
Holland, D(eborah) K(atherine)
  1947- ... CANR-136
  Earlier sketch in CA 57-60
Holland, DeWitte T(almage) 1923- ... 45-48
Holland, Edward John 1947-2004 ... CANR-88
  Obituary ... 227
  Earlier sketch in CA 105
Holland, Elizabeth (Anne) 1928- ... 124
Holland, Endesha Ida Mae 1944- ... 220
Holland, Flournoy C.
  See Holland, Noy
Holland, Francis Ross, Jr. 1927- ... 33-36R
Holland, Gail Bernice 1940- ... 126
Holland, Gay W. 1941- ... SATA 128
Holland, Glen A. 1920- ... 37-40R
Holland, Harrison M(elsher) 1921- ... CANR-43
  Earlier sketch in CA 117
Holland, Hilda 1901(?)-1973
  Obituary ... 57-60
Holland, Isabelle (Christian)
  1920-2002 ... 21-24R
  Obituary ... 205
  Earlier sketch in CANR-10, 25, 47
  Autobiographical Essay in ... 181
  See also AAYA 11, 64
  See also CLC 21
  See also CLR 57
  See also CWRI 5
  See also JRDA
  See also LAIT 4
  See also MAICYA 1, 2
  See also SATA 8, 70
  See also SATA-Essay 103
  See also SATA-Obit 132
  See also WYA
Holland, J. G. 1819-1881 ... DLBD 13
Holland, Jack
  See Holland, Edward John
Holland, Jack H. 1922- ... 81-84
Holland, James C(larence) 1935- ... 112
Holland, James Gordon 1927- ... 1-4R
Holland, James R. 1944- ... 37-40R
Holland, Janice 1913-1962 ... 73-76
  See also SATA 18
Holland, Jerome H(eartwell) 1916-1985
  Obituary ... 114
Holland, Jimmie C. 1928- ... 194
Holland, John H(enry) 1929- ... 188
Holland, John L(ewis) 1919- ... CANR-17
  Earlier sketch in CA 25-28R
  See also SATA 20
Holland, Joyce
  See Morice, Dave
Holland, Joyce (Flint) 1921- ... 5-8R
Holland, Julia 1954- ... 176
  See also SATA 106
Holland, Kel
  See Whittington, Harry (Benjamin)
Holland, Kenneth 1948- ... 118
Holland, Kenneth J(ohn) 1918- ... 33-36R
Holland, Laurence B(edwell)
  1920-1980 ... 17-20R
  Obituary ... 102
Holland, Louise Adams 1893-1990 ... 89-92
Holland, Lynda (H.) 1959- ... 145
  See also SATA 77
Holland, Lynwood M. 1905-1993 ... 41-44R
Holland, Lys
  See Gater, Dilys
Holland, Marcus
  See Caldwell, (Janet Miriam) Taylor (Holland)
Holland, Marion 1908-1989 ... 61-64
  Obituary ... 128
  See also SATA 6
  See also SATA-Obit 61
Holland, Max (Mendel) 1950- ... 135
Holland, Merlin ... 210
Holland, Norman N(orwood) 1927- ... 17-20R
  See also DLB 67
Holland, Noy 1960- ... 149
Holland, Patricia G. 1940- ... 115
Holland, Philip Welsby 1917- ... 109
Holland, Richard c. 1420-1480 ... RGEL 2
Holland, Robert 1940- ... 33-36R
Holland, Sheila 1937-2000 ... CANR-15
  Obituary ... 192
  Earlier sketch in CA 85-88
  See also Lamb, Charlotte
Holland, Thomas E(dward) 1934- ... 53-56
Holland, Tim 1931- ... 57-60
Holland, Tom
  See King, Albert
Holland, Tom 1947- ... 126
  See also HGG
Holland, Vyvyan (Beresford)
  1886-1967 ... 97-100
  Obituary ... 25-28R
Holland, William E. 1940- ... 124
Hollander, A(rie) Nicolaas Jan den
  See den Hollander, A(rie) Nicolaas Jan
Hollander, Anne 1930- ... CANR-88
  Earlier sketch in CA 131
Hollander, David ... 203
Hollander, Eric 1957- ... 187
Hollander, Evan
  See van Belkom, Edo
Hollander, Hans 1899-1986 ... 103
  Obituary ... 120
Hollander, Herbert S. 1904(?)-1976
  Obituary ... 69-72
Hollander, John 1929- ... CANR-136
  Earlier sketches in CA 1-4R, CANR-1, 52
  See also CLC 2, 5, 8, 14
  See also CP 1, 2, 3, 4, 5, 6, 7
  See also DLB 5
  See also MAL 5
  See also SATA 13
Hollander, Lee M(ilton) 1880-1972 ... 1-4R
Hollander, Nicole 1940(?)- ... 162
  See also SATA 101
Hollander, Paul
  See Silverberg, Robert
Hollander, Paul 1932- ... CANR-13
  Earlier sketch in CA 37-40R
Hollander, Phyllis 1928- ... CANR-18
  Earlier sketch in CA 97-100
  See also SATA 39
Hollander, Richard Isaac 1912-1985
  Obituary ... 117
Hollander, Robert 1933- ... CANR-110
  Earlier sketches in CA 13-16R, CANR-5
Hollander, Sophie Smith 1911-1987 ... 13-16R
Hollander, Stanley C(harles)
  1919-2004 ... 37-40R
Hollander, Xaviera 1943- ... 215
Hollander, Zander 1923- ... CANR-18
  Earlier sketch in CA 65-68
  See also SATA 63
Hollands, Roy (Derrick) 1924- ... CANR-37
  Earlier sketch in CA 114
Hollandsworth, James G., Jr.
  1944- ... CANR-121
  Earlier sketch in CA 135
Hollar, David W(ason, Jr.) 1960- ... 144
Hollaway, Otto 1903- ... 69-72
Hollberg, John
  See Hall, Gus
Holldobler, Bert
  See Hoelldobler, Bert(hold Karl)
Holldobler, Turid 1939- ... SATA 26
Holleb, Arthur Irving 1921- ... 103
Holleman, Gary L. 1947- ... 150
Hollenberg, Donna Krolik 1942- ... CANR-101
  Earlier sketch in CA 142
Hollender, Edward A. 1899-1996 ... 105
Hollenweger, Walter J(acob) 1927- ... CANR-19
  Earlier sketches in CA 53-56, CANR-4
Holler, Frederick L. 1921- ... 97-100
Holler, Ronald F. 1938- ... 53-56
Holleran, Andrew ... 144
  See also Garber, Eric
  See also CLC 38
  See also GLL 1
Hollerer, Walter (Friedrich) 1922- ... EWL 3
Holles, Everett R. 1904(?)-1978
  Obituary ... 77-80
Holles, Robert Owen 1926-1999 ... CANR-18
  Earlier sketches in CA 5-8R, CANR-3
Holley, Bobbie Lee 1927- ... 33-36R
Holley, Edward Gailon 1927- ... CANR-6
  Earlier sketch in CA 5-8R
Holley, Frederick S. 1924- ... 109
Holley, I(rving) B(rinton), Jr. 1919- ... CANR-14
  Earlier sketch in CA 37-40R
Holley, Margaret 1944- ... 202
Holley, Marietta 1836(?)-1926
  Brief entry ... 118
  See also DLB 11
  See also FL 1:3
  See also TCLC 99
Holli, Betsy B. 1933- ... 171
Holli, Melvin G(eorge) 1933- ... CANR-107
  Earlier sketches in CA 25-28R, CANR-11, 26
Hollick, Ann L(orraine) 1941- ... 57-60
Holliday, Barbara Gregg 1917- ... 73-76
Holliday, Joe
  See Holliday, Joseph
Holliday, Joseph 1910- ... CAP-2
  Earlier sketch in CA 29-32
  See also SATA 11
Hollifield, James F. 1954- ... 139
Hollindale, Peter 1936- ... 103
Holling, Holling C(lancy) 1900-1973
  Obituary ... 106
  See also CLR 50
  See also CWRI 5
  See also MAICYA 1, 2
  See also SATA 15
  See also SATA-Obit 26
Hollingdale, R(eginald) J(ohn) 1930-2001 .. 102
  Obituary ... 204
Hollinghurst, Alan 1954- ... 114
  See also BRWS 10
  See also CLC 55, 91
  See also CN 5, 6, 7
  See also DLB 207
  See also GLL 1
Hollings, Michael (Richard) 1921-1997 .. 81-84
  Obituary ... 156
Hollings, Robert L. 1953- ... 175
Hollingshead, August deBelmont
  1907-1980 ... 13-16R
  Obituary ... 120
Hollingshead, Greg 1947- ... CANR-123
  Earlier sketch in CA 162
Hollingshead, (Ronald) Kyle 1941- ... CANR-11
  Earlier sketch in CA 21-24R
Hollingsworth, A(lan) B. 1949- ... 231
Hollingsworth, Alvin C(arl) 1930- ... SATA 39
Hollingsworth, Brian 1923-2001 ... 130
Hollingsworth, Dorothy Frances
  1916-1994 ... 85-88
Hollingsworth, Harold M(arvin) 1932- ... 53-56
Hollingsworth, J(oseph) Rogers
  1932- ... CANR-22
  Earlier sketches in CA 13-16R, CANR-7
Hollingsworth, Kent 1929-1999 ... 81-84
  Obituary ... 178
Hollingsworth, Lyman B(urgess) 1919- ... 45-48
Hollingsworth, Margaret 1942- ... 123
  See also CD 5, 6
  See also CWD
  See also DLB 60
Hollingsworth, Mary 1947- ... CANR-113
  Earlier sketch in CA 155
  See also SATA 91
Hollingsworth, Mary H(ead) 1910- ... 69-72
Hollingsworth, Michael 1950- ... 144
Hollingsworth, Paul M. 1932- ... 29-32R
Hollingworth, Clare 1911- ... 121
Hollinrake, Roger (Barker) 1929- ... 115
Hollins, Etta R(uth) ... 167
  See also BW 3
Hollis, C(harles) Carroll 1911- ... 125
Hollis, (Maurice) Christopher
  1902-1977 ... 73-76
  Obituary ... 69-72
Hollis, Daniel W(ebster) III 1942- ... 118
Hollis, Daniel W(alker) 1922- ... 5-8R
Hollis, Florence 1907-1987
  Obituary ... 123
Hollis, Harry Newcombe, Jr. 1938- ... 57-60

Hollis, Helen Rice 1908-1994 ... 61-64
Hollis, James R(ussell) 1940- ... 41-44R
Hollis, Jim
See Summers, Hollis (Spurgeon, Jr.)
Hollis, Joseph W(illiam) 1922- ... 25-28R
Hollis, Lucile U(ssery) 1921- ... 25-28R
Hollis, Marcia 1937- ... 114
Hollis, Stephanie 1946- ... 141
Hollis, Tim 1963- ... 201
Hollister, Bernard C(laiborne) 1938- ... CANR-3
Earlier sketch in CA 49-52
Hollister, C(harles) Warren
1930-1997 ... CANR-122
Earlier sketches in CA 1-4R, CANR-1, 25
Hollister, Charles A(mmon) 1918- ... 17-20R
Hollister, George E(rwin) 1905-1996 ... CAP-2
Earlier sketch in CA 17-18
Hollister, Herbert A(llen) 1933- ... 104
Hollister, Leo E. 1920- ... CANR-14
Earlier sketch in CA 21-24R
Hollister, William G(ray) 1915- ... 122
Hollmann, Clide John 1896-1966 ... 5-8R
Hollo, Anselm 1934- ... CANR-113
Earlier sketches in CA 21-24R, CANR-9
See also CAAS 19
See also CP 1, 2, 3, 4, 5, 6, 7
See also DLB 40
Hollom, Philip Arthur Dominic 1912- ... 13-16R
Hollon, Frank Turner 1963- ... 210
Hollon, W. Eugene 1913- ... CANR-2
Earlier sketch in CA 1-4R
See also AITN 1
Hollos, Marida 1940- ... 139
Hollow, John Walter 1939- ... 111
Holloway, Brenda W(ilmar) 1908- ... CAP-1
Earlier sketch in CA 9-10
Holloway, David (Richard) 1924-1995 ... 107
Holloway, Diane 1937- ... 189
Holloway, (Rufus) Emory 1885-1977 ... 49-52
Obituary ... 73-76
See also DLB 103
Holloway, (Percival) Geoffrey
1918- ... CANR-27
Earlier sketch in CA 49-52
See also CP 7
Holloway, George (Edward Talbot)
1921- ... 25-28R
Holloway, Harry (Albert) 1925- ... 9-12R
Holloway, James Y(oung) 1927- ... 53-56
Holloway, Jean
See Tobin, Jean Holloway
Holloway, John 1920- ... CANR-3
Earlier sketch in CA 5-8R
See also CP 1, 2
See also DLB 27
Holloway, Jonathan S(cott) 1967- ... 228
Holloway, Joseph E(dward) 1948- ... 111
Holloway, Karla F. C. 1949- ... CANR-92
Earlier sketch in CA 141
Holloway, Marcella M(arie) 1913- ... 89-92
Holloway, Mark 1917-2004 ... 21-24R
Obituary ... 223
Holloway, Maurice 1920- ... 9-12R
Holloway, Nigel 1953- ... 135
Holloway, Richard (Frederick) 1933- ... 204
Holloway, Robert J. 1921- ... 13-16R
Holloway, Robin (Grenville) 1943- ... 165
Holloway, Stanley 1890-1982
Obituary ... 106
Holloway, Sue (A.) 1944- ... 193
Holloway, Teresa (Bragunier) 1906- ... 17-20R
See also SATA 26
Holloway, Thomas H(alsey) 1944- ... 106
Holloway, W(illiam) V(ernon)
1903-1986 ... CANR-2
Earlier sketch in CA 1-4R
Holloway, Watson L(ee) 1943- ... 213
Hollowell, John 1945- ... 102
Hollowood, Albert Bernard 1910-1981 ... 9-12R
Obituary ... 103
Holly, Buddy 1936-1959 ... 213
See also TCLC 65
Holly, David C. 1915- ... 142
Holly, Ellen (Virginia) 1931- ... 159
See also BW 3
Holly, J(ohn) Fred 1915- ... CANR-6
Earlier sketch in CA 5-8R
Holly, J. Hunter
See Holly, Joan C(arol)
Holly, Joan C(arol) 1932-1982 ... CANR-1
Obituary ... 176
Earlier sketch in CA 1-4R
Holly, Joan Hunter
See Holly, Joan C(arol)
Holly, Michael Ann 1944- ... CANR-47
Earlier sketch in CA 121
Hollyday, Frederic B(lackmar) M(umford)
1928- ... 45-48
Holm, (Else) Anne (Lise) 1922-1998 ... 17-20R
See also CLR 75
See also MAICYA 1, 2
See also SAAS 7
See also SATA 1
See also YAW
Holm, Bill
See Holm, Oscar William
Holm, Don(ald Raymond) 1918- ... 33-36R
Holm, Jeanne M(arjorie) 1921- ... 130
Holm, Jennifer L. 1968(?)- ... 191
See also SATA 120, 163
Holm, John Cecil 1904-1981
Obituary ... 116
Holm, Lillemor
See Evander, Per Gunnar (Henning)
Holm, Marilyn D. (Franzen) 1944- ... 17-20R
Holm, Oscar William 1925- ... 234
Brief entry ... 117
Holm, Sharon Lane 1955- ... SATA 78, 114
Holm, Sven (Aage) 1902- ... CAP-1
Earlier sketch in CA 11-12
Holm, Sven 1940- ... 189
Holman, Betsy Hitz 1951- ... 119
Holman, Bob
See Holman, Robert
Holman, C(larence) Hugh
1914-1981 ... CANR-21
Earlier sketch in CA 5-8R
Holman, Dennis (Idris) 1915- ... 9-12R
Holman, Felice 1919- ... CANR-40
Earlier sketches in CA 5-8R, CANR-3, 18
See also AAYA 17
See also SAAS 17
See also SATA 7, 82
See also YAW
Holman, Harriet R. 1912-1992 ... 37-40R
Holman, J. Alan 1931- ... 208
Holman, John (William) 1951- ... 133
Holman, L(loyd) Bruce 1939- ... 61-64
Holman, Mary A(lida) 1933- ... 93-96
Holman, Portia Grenfell 1903-1983
Obituary ... 109
Holman, Robert 1936- ... 116
See also CD 5
Holman, Robert 1952- ... CBD
See also CD 5, 6
Holman, Sheri ... CANR-135
Earlier sketch in CA 169
Holman, Virginia 1966- ... 230
Holman, William R(oger) 1926- ... 49-52
Holm and
Hamel
Hamel
See Holm, Jennifer L.
Holman-Hunt, Diana
See Cuthbert, Diana Daphne Holman-Hunt
Holmans, Alan Edward 1934- ... 1-4R
Holmberg, Anne ... 177
Holmberg, Arthur 1921- ... 188
Holme, Bryan 1913-1990 ... 103
Obituary ... 132
See also SATA 26
See also SATA-Obit 66
Holme, (Edith) Constance 1880(?)-1955
Brief entry ... 118
See also DLB 34
Holme, K. E.
See Hill, (John Edward) Christopher
Holme, Thea 1903-1980 ... 41-44R
Holme, Timothy 19(?)-1987 ... 158
Holmelund, Paul 1890-1978 ... 5-8R
Holmer, Paul L(eroy) 1916- ... 37-40R
Holmes, A. R.
See Bates, Harry
Holmes, Abraham S. 1821(?)-1908 ... 213
See also DLB 99
Holmes, Ann 1936(?)-1985
Obituary ... 114
Holmes, Arthur 1890-1965
Obituary ... 116
Holmes, Arthur F. 1924- ... 33-36R
Holmes, B(ryan) J(ohn) 1939- ... TCWW 2
Holmes, Barbara Ware 1945- ... CANR-106
Earlier sketch in CA 120
See also SATA 65, 127
Holmes, Burnham 1942- ... 97-100
Holmes, C. Raymond 1929- ... 57-60
Holmes, Charles M(ason) 1923- ... 29-32R
Holmes, Charles S(hiveley) 1916-1976 ... 41-44R
Obituary ... 61-64
Holmes, Charles Warfield 1931-1984
Obituary ... 112
Holmes, Charlotte (Amalie) 1956- ... 174
Holmes, Colin 1938- ... CANR-11
Earlier sketch in CA 25-28R
Holmes, David Charles 1919-2004 ... 9-12R
Obituary ... 228
Holmes, David M(orton) 1929- ... 33-36R
Holmes, Diana 1949- ... 157
Holmes, Donald J. 1924- ... 170
Holmes, Douglas 1933- ... 41-44R
Holmes, Edward M(orris) 1910- ... CANR-14
Earlier sketch in CA 37-40R
Holmes, Efner Tudor 1949- ... 65-68
Holmes, Eric M(ills) 1943- ... 121
Holmes, Frank Wakefield 1924- ... 109
Holmes, Frederic L(awrence)
1932-2003 ... CANR-120
Obituary ... 215
Earlier sketch in CA 93-96
Holmes, Geoffrey (Shorter) 1928-1993 ... 25-28R
Obituary ... 143
Holmes, George (Arthur) 1927- ... CANR-65
Earlier sketch in CA 128
Holmes, Gordon
See Shiel, M(atthew) P(hipps)
Holmes, Grant
See Fox, James M.
Holmes, H. H.
See White, William A(nthony) P(arker)
Holmes, Jack D(avid) L(azarus)
1930- ... CANR-24
Earlier sketch in CA 41-44R
Holmes, Jay
See Holmes, Joseph Everett
Holmes, Jeffrey 1934- ... CANR-47
Earlier sketch in CA 120
Holmes, John
See Souster, (Holmes) Raymond
Holmes, John (Albert) 1904-1962
Obituary ... 115
Holmes, John 1913-2000 ... 104
Holmes, John Clellon 1926-1988 ... CANR-4
Obituary ... 125
Earlier sketch in CA 9-12R
See also BG 1:2
See also CLC 56
See also CN 1, 2, 3, 4
See also DLB 16, 237
Holmes, John Haynes 1879-1964
Obituary ... 89-92
Holmes, John L. 1925- ... 115
Holmes, John W(endell) 1910-1989 ... 134
Brief entry ... 109
Holmes, Jon 1948- ... 114
Holmes, Joseph Everett 1922- ... CANR-1
Earlier sketch in CA 1-4R
Holmes, Joseph R. 1928(?)-1983
Obituary ... 109
Holmes, Katie ... 171
Holmes, Kenneth L(loyd) 1915- ... CANR-27
Earlier sketch in CA 37-40R
Holmes, Kim R(ene) 1952- ... 111
Holmes, L(lewellyn) P(erry)
1895-1988 ... TCWW 2
Holmes, Larry 1949- ... 181
Holmes, Leslie (Templeman) 1948- ... CANR-95
Earlier sketch in CA 146
Holmes, Lowell D(on) 1925- ... 33-36R
Holmes, Marjorie (Rose)
1910-2002 ... CANR-23
Obituary ... 206
Earlier sketches in CA 1-4R, CANR-5
See also AITN 1
See also SATA 43
Holmes, Martha 1961- ... SATA 72
Holmes, Martin (Rivington)
1905-1997 ... CANR-1
Earlier sketch in CA 49-52
Holmes, Mary Jane 1825-1907 ... 182
See also DLB 202, 221
Holmes, Mary Tavener 1954- ... 141
Holmes, Mary Z(astrow) 1943- ... 147
See also SATA 80
Holmes, Melody Moore 1972- ... 168
Holmes, (John) Michael (Aleister)
1931- ... 25-28R
Holmes, Michael Stephan 1942- ... 77-80
Holmes, Nancy 1921- ... 69-72
Holmes, Olive 1911- ... 115
Holmes, Oliver Wendell, Jr. 1841-1935 ... 186
Brief entry ... 114
See also TCLC 77
Holmes, Oliver Wendell 1809-1894 ... AMWS 1
See also CDALB 1640-1865
See also DLB 1, 189, 235
See also EXPP
See also RGAL 4
See also SATA 34
Holmes, Olivia 1958- ... 237
Holmes, Parker Manfred 1895-1982 ... CAP-1
Earlier sketch in CA 13-14
Holmes, Paul Allen 1901-1985 ... CAP-2
Obituary ... 114
Earlier sketch in CA 19-20
Holmes, Paul Carter 1926- ... CANR-11
Earlier sketch in CA 21-24R
Holmes, Peggy 1898- ... 121
See also SATA 60
Holmes, Rachel ... 220
Holmes, Raymond
See Souster, (Holmes) Raymond
Holmes, Richard 1945- ... CANR-78
Brief entry ... 126
Earlier sketch in CA 133
Interview in ... CA-133
See also DLB 155
Holmes, (Edward) Richard 1946- ... CANR-51
Earlier sketches in CA 106, CANR-25
Holmes, Rick
See Hardwick, Richard Holmes, Jr.
Holmes, Robert A(lexander) 1943- ... 57-60
Holmes, Robert L(awrence) 1935- ... 41-44R
Holmes, Robert Merrill 1925- ... 89-92
Holmes, Theodore 1928- ... CP 1
Holmes, Thomas James 1874-1959 ... 194
See also DLB 187
Holmes, Thomas K. ... CANR-26
Earlier sketches in CAP-2, CA 19-20
Holmes, Tiffany 1944- ... 97-100
Holmes, Tommy 1903-1975
Obituary ... 57-60
Holmes, Urban T(igner) 1900-1972 ... CAP-2
Earlier sketch in CA 21-22
Holmes, Victoria ... 236
Holmes, W(ilfred) J(ay) 1900-1986 ... 29-32R
Holmes, William Kersley 1882- ... CAP-1
Earlier sketch in CA 9-10
Holmes Norton, Eleanor 1937- ... 221
Holmevik, Jan Rune 1966- ... 186
Holmgren, Fredrick Carlson 1926- ... 219
Holmgren, Helen Jean 1930- ... 97-100
See also SATA 45
Holmgren, Norah 1939- ... 102
Holmgren, Sister George Ellen
See Holmgren, Helen Jean
Holmgren, Virginia C(unningham) 1909- ... 107
See also SATA 26
Holmquist, Anders 1933- ... 29-32R
Holmquist, Eve 1921- ... 53-56
See also SATA 11
Holmsen, Bjarne P.
See Holz, Arno
Holmstrand, Marie Juline (Gunderson)
1908- ... 5-8R
Holmstrom, (John) Edwin 1898- ... CAP-1
Earlier sketch in CA 11-12
Holmstrom, Lynda Lytle 1939- ... 33-36R
Holmvik, Oyvind 1914- ... 17-20R
Holoch, Naomi ... 181
Holod, Renata O. 1942- ... 119
Holohan, Maureen 1972- ... 177
Holoien, Martin O. 1928- ... 112
Holquist, (James) Michael 1935- ... CANR-17
Earlier sketches in CA 45-48, CANR-2
Holquist, Peter (Isaac) 1964- ... 236
Holroyd, Michael (de Courcy Fraser)
1935- ... CANR-95
Earlier sketches in CA 53-56, CANR-4, 18, 35, 63
See also DLB 155
See also MTCW 1, 2
See also MTFW 2005
Holroyd, Sam
See Burton, S(amuel) H(olroyd)
Holroyd, Stuart 1933- ... 93-96
Holsaert, Eunice (?)-1974
Obituary ... 53-56
Holsinger, Jane Lumley ... 17-20R
Holske, Katherine (?)-1973
Obituary ... 104
Holsopple, Barbara 1943- ... 73-76
Holst, Hermann E(duard) von 1841-1904 ... 213
See also DLB 47
Holst, Imogen (Clare) 1907-1984
Obituary ... 112
Holst, Johan J(oergen) 1937-1994 ... CANR-11
Obituary ... 143
Earlier sketch in CA 25-28R
Holst, Lawrence E(berhardt) 1929- ... 61-64
Holst, Spencer 1925(?)-2001 ... 236
Holstad, Scott Cameron 1966- ... CANR-117
Earlier sketch in CA 156
Holsti, Kalevi J(acque) 1935- ... 21-24R
Holsti, Ole R(udolf) 1933- ... CANR-52
Earlier sketches in CA 25-28R, CANR-11, 28
Holst-Warhaft, Gail 1941- ... 217
Holt, Andrew
See Anhalt, Edward
Holt, Conrad G.
See Fearn, John Russell
Holt, Constance Wall 1932- ... 147
Holt, Edgar Crawshaw 1900-1975 ... CANR-6
Obituary ... 61-64
Earlier sketch in CA 1-4R
Holt, Elizabeth B(asye) G(ilmore)
1906(?)-1987 ... 124
Holt, Frank (L.) 1954- ... 214
Holt, Gavin
See Rodda, Charles
Holt, George
See Tubb, E(dwin) C(harles)
Holt, Georgia 1927- ... 129
Holt, (Wilma) Geraldene ... 137
Holt, Hazel 1928- ... CANR-137
Earlier sketch in CA 160
Holt, Helen
See Paine, Lauran (Bosworth)
Holt, (Laurence) James 1939- ... 25-28R
Holt, John 1721-1784 ... DLB 43
Holt, John (Caldwell) 1923-1985 ... CANR-32
Obituary ... 117
Earlier sketch in CA 69-72
Holt, John (Robert) 1926- ... CANR-11
Earlier sketch in CA 25-28R
Holt, John Agee 1920- ... 1-4R
Holt, Judd 1941- ... 141
Holt, Kaare 1917-
Brief entry ... 111
See also Holt, Kare
Holt, Kare
See Holt, Kaare
See also EWL 3
Holt, Kimberly Willis 1960- ... 195
See also AAYA 38
See also BYA 15
See also MAICYA 2
See also SATA 122
Holt, L. Emmett, Jr. 1895-1974
Obituary ... 53-56
Holt, Lee E(lbert) 1912- ... 13-16R
Holt, Margaret 1937- ... 17-20R
See also SATA 4
Holt, Margaret Van Vechten (Saunders)
1899-1963
Obituary ... 111
See also SATA 32
Holt, Marilyn Irvin 1949- ... CANR-109
Earlier sketch in CA 144
Holt, Michael (Paul) 1929- ... CANR-5
Earlier sketch in CA 53-56
See also SATA 13
Holt, Michael F(itzgibbon) 1940- ... 81-84
Holt, Pat Mayo 1920- ... 111
Holt, Rackham
See Holt, Margaret Van Vechten (Saunders)
Holt, Robert R(utherford) 1917- ... CANR-75
Earlier sketches in CA 41-44R, CANR-15, 35
Holt, Robert T. 1928- ... 37-40R
Holt, Rochelle L.
See DuBois, Rochelle (Lynn) Holt
See also SATA 41
Holt, Stephen
See Thompson, Harlan (Howard)
Holt, Stephen 1949- ... 202
Holt, Tex
See Joscelyn, Archie L(ynn)
Holt, Thaddeus 1929- ... 235
Holt, Thelma Jewett 1913-2000 ... 29-32R
Holt, Thomas Charles Louis 1961- ... 135
See also FANT
See also SUFW 2
Holt, Thomas J(ung) 1928- ... 102
Holt, Tom
See Holt, Thomas Charles Louis

Holt, Victoria
  See Hibbert, Eleanor Alice Burford
  See also BPFB 2
Holt, Will 1929- ... 105
Holt, William 1897-1977 ... CAP-1
  Obituary ... 69-72
  Earlier sketch in CA 17-18
Holtan, Orley I. 1933- ... 33-36R
Holtby, Robert Tinsley 1921-2003 ... 108
  Obituary ... 215
Holtby, Winifred 1898-1935 ... 212
  See also DLB 191
  See also FW
  See also RGEL 2
  See also RHW
Holte, James Craig 1949- ... CANR-140
  Earlier sketch in CA 144
Holter, Don W. 1905-1999 ... 37-40R
Holter, Knut 1958- ... 224
Holthe, Tess Uriza 1966- ... 202
Holthusen, Hans Egon 1913-1997 ... 45-48
  See also DLB 69
Holtje, Herbert F(ranklin) 1931- ... CANR-8
  Earlier sketch in CA 61-64
Holton, Felicia Antonelli 1921- ... 69-72
Holton, Gerald (James) 1922- ... 13-16R
Holton, Hugh -2001 ... 180
  Obituary ... 196
Holton, Leonard
  See Wibberley, Leonard (Patrick O'Connor)
  See also MSW
Holton, (William) Milne 1931- ... 41-44R
Holton, Richard H(enry) 1926-
  Brief entry ... 107
Holtrop, William Frans 1908-1994 ... 57-60
Holty, Ludwig Christoph Heinrich
  1748-1776 ... DLB 94
Holtz, Avraham 1934- ... 29-32R
Holtz, Barry W(illiam) 1947- ... 109
Holtz, Herman R(alph) 1919- ... 105
Holtze, Sally Holmes 1952- ... 123
  See also SATA 64
Holtzman, Abraham 1921- ... CANR-2
  Earlier sketch in CA 1-4R
Holtzman, Elizabeth 1941- ... 157
Holtzman, Harry 1912-1987
  Obituary ... 123
Holtzman, Jerome 1926- ... CANR-4
  Earlier sketch in CA 53-56
  See also SATA 57
Holtzman, Paul D(ouglas) 1918-2002 ... 33-36R
Holtzman, Wayne H(arold) 1923- ... CANR-34
  Earlier sketches in CA 37-40R, CANR-15
Holtzman, Will 1951- ... 102
Holub, Joan 1956- ... CANR-132
  Earlier sketch in CA 167
  See also SATA 99, 149
Holub, Miroslav 1923-1998 ... CANR-10
  Obituary ... 169
  Earlier sketch in CA 21-24R
  See also CDWLB 4
  See also CLC 4
  See also CWW 2
  See also DLB 232
  See also EWL 3
  See also RGWL 3
Holub, Robert C(harles) 1949- ... CANR-82
  Earlier sketches in CA 114, CANR-35
Holubitsky, Katherine 1955- ... 192
  See also MAICYA 2
  See also SATA 121
Holum, Dianne 1951- ... 123
Holway, John 1929- ... 57-60
  See also BYA 9, 14
Holy, Ladislav 1933- ... 141
Holyer, Erna Maria 1925- ... CANR-12
  Earlier sketch in CA 29-32R
  See also SATA 22
Holyer, Ernie
  See Holyer, Erna Maria
Holz, Arno 1863-1929 ... 190
  See also DLB 118
Holz, Cynthia 1950- ... 225
Holz, Detlev
  See Benjamin, Walter
Holz, Loretta (Marie) 1943- ... CANR-10
  Earlier sketch in CA 65-68
  See also SATA 17
Holz, Robert K(enneth) 1930- ... 53-56
Holzapfel, Kathleen G. 1956- ... 230
Holzapfel, Rudolf Patrick 1938- ... CAP-1
  Earlier sketch in CA 11-12
  See also CP 1
Holzberger, William George 1932- ... 53-56
Holzel, Thomas Martin 1940- ... 126
Holzel, Tom
  See Holzel, Thomas Martin
Holzer, Erika 1935- ... 141
Holzer, Hans 1920- ... CANR-22
  Earlier sketches in CA 13-16R, CANR-7
Holzer, Harold 1949- ... CANR-39
  Earlier sketch in CA 116
Holzer, Jenny 1950- ... AAYA 50
Holzer, Max 1915-1984 ... 239
Holzman, Franklyn Dunn 1918- ... 61-64
  Obituary ... 211
Holzman, Philip Seidman 1922-2004 ... 37-40R
  Obituary ... 228
Holzman, Red
  See Holzman, William
Holzman, Robert S(tuart) 1907-1998 .. CANR-2
  Earlier sketch in CA 1-4R
Holzman, William 1920-1998 ... CANR-91
  Obituary ... 172
  Earlier sketch in CA 101
Holzman, Winnie ... 169
Holzner, Burkart 1931- ... 93-96
Hom, Ken 1949- ... CANR-26
  Earlier sketch in CA 109
Hom, Marlon Kau 1947- ... 131
Homan, Lynn M. ... 238
Homan, Madeleine ... 234
Homan, Robert Anthony 1929- ... 5-8R
Homan, Sidney 1938- ... 146
Homans, Abigail Adams 1879-1974
  Obituary ... 104
Homans, George Caspar 1910-1989 ... 107
  Obituary ... 128
Homans, Margaret 1952- ... 185
Homans, Peter 1930- ... CANR-94
  Earlier sketches in CA 21-24R, CANR-11, 28, 57
Homberger, Eric (Ross) 1942- ... CANR-141
  Earlier sketches in CA 106, CANR-23, 47
Homburger, Erik
  See Erikson, Erik H(omburger)
Home, Alexander Frederick (Douglas-)
  1903-1995 ... 102
  Obituary ... 150
Home, Charles (Cospatrick) Douglas
  See Douglas-Home, Charles (Cospatrick)
Home, Henry 1696-1782 ... DLB 31,104
Home, Henry Douglas
  See Douglas-Home, Henry
Home, John 1722-1808 ... DLB 84
  See also RGEL 2
Home, Michael
  See Bush, Charlie Christmas
Home, Stewart 1962- ... 154
Home, William Douglas
  1912-1992 ... CANR-71
  Obituary ... 139
  Earlier sketch in CA 102
  See also DLB 13
Homel, David 1952- ... CANR-90
  Earlier sketch in CA 149
  See also SATA 97
Homel, Michael W. 1944- ... 126
Homer c. 8th cent. B.C.- ... AW 1
  See also CDWLB 1
  See also DA
  See also DA3
  See also DAB
  See also DAC
  See also DAM MST, POET
  See also DLB 176
  See also EFS 1
  See also LAIT 1
  See also LMFS 1
  See also PC 23
  See also RGWL 2, 3
  See also TWA
  See also WLCS
  See also WP
Homer, Frank X. J. 1941- ... 127
Homer, Frederic D(onald) 1939- ... 65-68
Homer, Sidney 1902-1983
  Obituary ... 110
Homer, William Innes 1929- ... CANR-136
  Earlier sketch in CA 13-16R
Homer, Winslow 1836-1910 ... 193
  See also DLB 188
Homes, A(my) M(ichael) 1961- ... CANR-127
  Earlier sketches in CA 136, CANR-66
  See also MTFW 2005
Homes, Geoffrey
  See Mainwaring, Daniel
Homewood, Charles H. 1914(?)-1984
  Obituary ... 112
Homewood, Harry
  See Homewood, Charles H.
Homola, Priscilla 1947- ... 116
Homola, Samuel 1929- ... 97-100
Homolya, Istvan 1940- ... 131
Homosap
  See Nuttall, Jeff
Homrighausen, Elmer George
  1900-1982 ... 45-48
Homsher, Deborah 1952- ... 201
Homsher, Lola Mae 1913-1986 ... 1-4R
Homze, Alma C. 1932- ... 29-32R
  See also SATA 17
Homze, Edward L. 1930- ... 33-36R
Honan, Park 1928- ... CANR-100
  Earlier sketches in CA 77-80, CANR-14
  See also DLB 111
Honan, William H(olmes) 1930- ... CANR-79
  Earlier sketches in CA 123, CANR-49
Honce, Charles E. 1895-1975
  Obituary ... 61-64
Honchar, Oles 1918- ... EWL 3
Hond, Paul ... 171
Honderich, John A. 1946- ... 128
Honderich, Ted 1933- ... CANR-99
  Earlier sketches in CA 33-36R, CANR-14, 35
Hone, Joseph 1937- ... CANR-35
  Earlier sketches in CA 65-68, CANR-14
Hone, Ralph E(merson) 1913-1999 ... CANR-9
  Earlier sketch in CA 21-24R
Hone, William 1780-1842 ... DLB 110, 158
Honegger, Arthur 1892-1955 ... IDFW 3, 4
Honerkamp, Nicholas 1950- ... 138
Honey, Elizabeth 1947- ... 184
  See also MAICYA 2
  See also SATA 112, 137
  See also SATA-Essay 137
Honey, Martha S(pencer) 1945- ... CANR-31
  Earlier sketch in CA 112
Honey, Maureen 1945- ... 190
Honey, P(atrick) J(ames) 1922- ... 13-16R
Honey, William (Houghton) 1910- ... 33-36R
Honeycombe, Gordon 1936- ... CANR-72
  Earlier sketches in CA 77-80, CANR-13, 34
  See also HGG
Honeycutt, Ann 1902(?)-1989
  Obituary ... 129
Honeycutt, Benjamin L(awrence) 1938- .. 57-60
Honeycutt, Natalie 1945- ... 163
  See also SATA 97
Honeycutt, Roy L(ee), Jr. 1926- ... 41-44R
Honeygosky, Stephen R(aymond) 1948- ... 144
Honeyman, Brenda
  See Clarke, Brenda (Margaret Lilian)
Hong, Cathy Park 1976- ... 220
Hong, Edna H. 1913- ... CANR-9
  Earlier sketch in CA 21-24R
Hong, Howard V(incent) 1912- ... CANR-9
  Earlier sketch in CA 21-24R
Hong, James 1929(?)- ... 220
Hong, Jane Fay 1954- ... 93-96
Hong, Lily Toy 1958- ... 144
  See also SATA 76
Hong, Yong Ki 1929(?)-1979
  Obituary ... 85-88
Hongo, Garrett Kaoru 1951- ... 133
  See also CAAS 22
  See also CP 7
  See also DLB 120, 312
  See also EWL 3
  See also EXPP
  See also PC 23
  See also RGAL 4
Honhart, Frederick L(ewis III) 1943- ... 112
Honig, Alice S(terling) 1929- ... 214
Honig, Donald 1931- ... CANR-71
  Earlier sketches in CA 17-20R, CANR-9, 24
  See also SATA 18
Honig, Edwin 1919- ... CANR-144
  Earlier sketches in CA 5-8R, CANR-4, 45
  See also CAAS 8
  See also CLC 33
  See also CP 1, 2, 3, 4, 5, 6, 7
  See also DLB 5
Honig, Louis 1911-1977 ... 77-80
  Obituary ... 73-76
Honig, Lucy 1948- ... 191
Honigfeld, Gilbert
  See Howard, Gilbert
Honigmann, E(rnst) A(nselm) J(oachim)
  1927- ... CANR-9
  Earlier sketch in CA 21-24R
Honigmann, John J(oseph)
  1914-1977 ... CANR-2
  Earlier sketch in CA 1-4R
Honigsbaum, Mark ... 217
Honnalgere, Gopal 1944- ... 73-76
Honnef, Klaus 1939- ... 142
Honness, Elizabeth H. 1904- ... 25-28R
  See also SATA 2
Honnold, John Otis, Jr. 1915- ... CANR-8
  Earlier sketch in CA 13-16R
Honnold, RoseMary 1954- ... 232
Honore, Antony Maurice 1921- ... CANR-1
  Earlier sketch in CA 1-4R
Honore, Carl 1967- ... 235
Honour, Hugh 1927- ... 103
Honourable Member for X
  See de Chair, Somerset (Struben)
Honri, Peter 1929- ... 103
Honwana, Luis (Augusto) Bernardo (Manuel)
  1942- ... AFW
  See also WLIT 2
Hoobler, Dorothy 1941- ... CANR-139
  Earlier sketches in CA 69-72, CANR-11, 27
  See also SATA 28, 109, 161
Hoobler, Thomas ... CANR-53
  Earlier sketches in CA 69-72, CANR-11, 27
  See also SATA 28, 109, 161
Hood, Ann 1956- ... CANR-86
  Earlier sketch in CA 136
Hood, Bruce 1936- ... 130
Hood, Buck 1907(?)-1983
  Obituary ... 110
Hood, Charles (Wayne) 1959- ... 214
Hood, Daniel 1967- ... 168
Hood, David Crockett 1937- ... 37-40R
Hood, Donald W(ilbur) 1918- ... 37-40R
Hood, Dora (Ridout) 1885- ... CAP-2
  Earlier sketch in CA 17-18
Hood, Edward Waters 1954- ... 180
Hood, F(rancis) C(ampbell) 1895-1971 . CAP-1
  Earlier sketch in CA 13-14
Hood, Flora M(ae) 1898-1974 ... 5-8R
Hood, Graham 1936- ... 77-80
Hood, Hugh (John Blagdon) 1928- ... CANR-87
  Earlier sketches in CA 49-52, CANR-1, 33
  See also CAAS 17
  See also CLC 15, 28
  See also CN 1, 2, 3, 4, 5, 6, 7
  See also DLB 53
  See also RGSF 2
  See also SSC 42
Hood, James W. 1957- ... 214
Hood, Joseph F. 1925- ... 33-36R
  See also SATA 4
Hood, Lynley (Jane) 1942- ... CANR-138
  Earlier sketch in CA 135
Hood, Margaret Page 1892-1983 ... 1-4R
Hood, Mary 1946- ... CANR-126
  Earlier sketch in CA 128
  See also CSW
  See also DLB 234
Hood, Robert (Maxwell) 1951- ... HGG
Hood, Robert E. 1926- ... 21-24R
  See also SATA 21
Hood, Roger (Grahame) 1936- ... CANR-124
  Earlier sketches in CA 128, CANR-67
Hood, Sarah
  See Killough, (Karen) Lee
Hood, (Martin) Sinclair (Frankland)
  1917- ... CANR-9
  Earlier sketch in CA 21-24R
Hood, Stuart (Clink) 1915- ... 152
Hood, Thomas 1799-1845 ... BRW 4
  See also DLB 96
  See also RGEL 2
Hood, William (Joseph) 1920- ... CANR-141
  Earlier sketches in CA 109, CANR-26
Hoodbhoy, Pervez 1950- ... 143
Hoofnagle, Keith Lundy 1941- ... 13-16R
Hooft, Hendrik (G. A.) 1939- ... 200
Hooft, Pieter Corneliszoon
  1581-1647 ... RGWL 2, 3
Hoog, Michel 1932- ... 230
Hoogasian-Villa, Susie 1921-1978 ... 17-20R
  Obituary ... 114
Hoogenboom, Ari (Arthur) 1927- ... CANR-50
  Earlier sketch in CA 45-48
Hoogenboom, Olive 1927- ... 21-24R
Hoogestraat, Wayne E. ... 5-8R
Hook, Andrew 1932- ... CANR-139
  Earlier sketch in CA 53-56
Hook, Brendan 1963- ... 173
  See also SATA 105
Hook, Brian ... 204
Hook, Diana ffarington 1918- ... 61-64
Hook, Donald D(wight) 1928- ... CANR-4
  Earlier sketch in CA 53-56
Hook, Frances 1912-1983 ... 105
  See also SATA 27
Hook, Frank S(cott) 1922- ... 21-24R
Hook, Geoffrey R(aynor) 1928- ... 170
  See also SATA 103
Hook, Hilary 1917-1990
  Obituary ... 132
Hook, J(ulius) N(icholas) 1913- ... CANR-38
  Earlier sketches in CA 5-8R, CANR-2, 17
Hook, Jeff
  See Hook, Geoffrey R(aynor)
Hook, Jonathan B(yron) 1953- ... 169
Hook, Judith 1941(?)-1984
  Obituary ... 113
Hook, Martha 1936- ... 105
  See also SATA 27
Hook, Sidney 1902-1989 ... CANR-7
  Obituary ... 129
  Earlier sketch in CA 9-12R
  Interview in ... CANR-7
  See also DLB 279
Hook, Theodore 1788-1841 ... DLB 116
  See also RGEL 2
Hooke, Nina Warner 1907-1994 ... 73-76
Hooke, Sylvia Denys
  See Malleson, Lucy Beatrice
Hooker, C(lifford) A(lan) 1942- ... CANR-19
  Earlier sketches in CA 49-52, CANR-4
Hooker, Craig Michael 1951- ... 57-60
Hooker, Frances
  See Horovitz, Frances Margaret
Hooker, James Ralph 1929- ... 21-24R
Hooker, (Peter) Jeremy 1941- ... CANR-22
  Earlier sketch in CA 77-80
  See also CLC 43
  See also CP 2, 3, 4, 5, 6, 7
  See also DLB 40
Hooker, Mark T(roy) 1948- ... 175
Hooker, Richard
  See Heinz, W(ilfred) C(harles)
Hooker, Richard 1554-1600 ... BRW 1
  See also DLB 132
  See also RGEL 2
Hooker, Richard D., Jr. 1957- ... 145
Hooker, Richard J(ames) 1912-1986 ... 122
Hooker, Ruth 1920-1998 ... 69-72
  Obituary ... 169
  See also SATA 21
Hooker, Stanley (George) 1907-1984
  Obituary ... 112
Hooker, Thomas 1586-1647 ... DLB 24
Hookham, Hilda Henriette (Kuttner)
  1915- ... 9-12R
hooks, bell
  See Watkins, Gloria Jean
Hooks, G(aylor) Eugene 1927- ... 1-4R
Hooks, Gene
  See Hooks, G(aylor) Eugene
Hooks, Gregory M. 1953- ... 141
Hooks, William H(arris) 1921- ... CANR-67
  Earlier sketches in CA 81-84, CANR-19
  See also CWRI 5
  See also SATA 16, 94
Hool, Lance (Winston) 1948- ... 201
Hoole, Daryl Van Dam 1934- ... 21-24R
Hoole, W(illiam) Stanley 1903-1990 .. CANR-7
  Earlier sketch in CA 17-20R
Hooley, D(aniel) M. 1950- ... 169
Hoon, Patricia Easterly 1954- ... SATA 90
Hooper, Biff
  See Obrecht, Jas
Hooper, Byrd
  See St. Clair, Byrd Hooper
Hooper, Chloe 1973- ... 201
Hooper, David (Vincent) 1915- ... 85-88
Hooper, Douglas 1927- ... CANR-18
  Earlier sketch in CA 25-28R
Hooper, Edward Jonathan ... 223
Hooper, Finley (Allison) 1922- ... 123
Hooper, Hedley Colwill 1919-1991 ... 124
  See also Hooper, Peter
Hooper, John W(illiam) 1926- ... 29-32R
Hooper, Johnson Jones 1815-1862 .. DLB 3, 11, 248
  See also RGAL 4
Hooper, Judith 1949- ... CANR-143
  Earlier sketch in CA 136

Hooper, Kay 1957- CANR-109
Earlier sketches in CA 122, CANR-66
See also RHW
Hooper, Mary 1944- 236
See also SATA 160
Hooper, Maureen Brett 1927- 143
See also SATA 76
Hooper, Meredith (Jean) 1939- CANR-139
Earlier sketches in CA 106, CANR-22, 47
See also SATA 28, 101, 159
Hooper, Patricia 1941- CANR-129
Earlier sketches in CA 127, CANR-69
See also SATA 95
Hooper, Paul F(ranklin) 1938- CANR-92
Earlier sketches in CA 101, CANR-18
Hooper, Peter
See Hooper, Hedley Colwill
See also CN 4
Hooper, Tobe 1943- 237
Hooper, Walter (McGehee) 1931- CANR-50
Earlier sketches in CA 17-20R, CANR-7, 22
Hooper, William Loyd 1931- CANR-19
Earlier sketches in CA 5-8R, CANR-3
Hoopes, Clement R. 1906-1979 73-76
Obituary 89-92
Hoopes, David S. 1928- CANR-42
Earlier sketch in CA 118
Hoopes, Donelson F(arquhar) 1932- 33-36R
Hoopes, James 1944- CANR-10
Earlier sketch in CA 65-68
Hoopes, John W. 1958- 163
Hoopes, Lyn Littlefield 1953- 120
See also SATA 49
See also SATA-Brief 44
Hoopes, Ned E(dward) 1932- 17-20R
See also SATA 21
Hoopes, Robert (Griffith) 1920- CANR-1
Earlier sketch in CA 1-4R
Hoopes, Roy 1922- CANR-125
Earlier sketches in CA 21-24R, CANR-15
See also SATA 11
Hoopes, Townsend (Walter) II
1922-2004 97-100
Obituary 231
Interview in CA-97-100
Hoople, Cheryl G.
Brief entry 111
See also SATA-Brief 32
Hoops, Richard A(llen) 1933- 41-44R
Hoornik, Ed(uard Jozef Antonie Marie)
1910-1970
Obituary 104
Hoos, Ida Russakoff 1912- 17-20R
Hoose, Phillip M. 1947- 202
See also SATA 137
Hooson, David J. M. 1926- 17-20R
Hooten, William J(arvis) 1900-1991 61-64
Hooton, Charles
See Rowe, Vivian C(laud)
Hooton, Joy 1935- CANR-98
Earlier sketch in CA 127
Hoover, Calvin Bryce 1897-1974 .... CAP-1
Obituary 49-52
Earlier sketch in CA 13-14
Hoover, Carol Faith 1921- 188
Hoover, D(onald) B(runton) 1930- 144
Hoover, Dorothy Estheryne 1918- 49-52
Hoover, Dwight W(esley) 1926- 33-36R
Hoover, Edgar M. 1907-1992 .... 13-16R
Hoover, F(rancis) Louis 1913- 41-44R
Hoover, H(elen) M(ary) 1935- CANR-36
Earlier sketches in CA 105, CANR-22
See also AAYA 11
See also BYA 8
See also JRDA
See also MAICYA 1, 2
See also SAAS 8
See also SATA 44, 83, 132
See also SATA-Brief 33
See also SFW 4
See also YAW
Hoover, Hardy 1902-1990 .... 29-32R
Hoover, Helen (Drusilla Blackburn)
1910-1984 .... 21-24R
Obituary 113
See also ANW
See also SATA 12
See also SATA-Obit 39
Hoover, Herbert (Clark) 1874-1964 108
Obituary 89-92
Hoover, Herbert Theodore 1930- 106
Hoover, J(ohn) Edgar 1895-1972 .... CANR-2
Obituary 33-36R
Earlier sketch in CA 1-4R
Hoover, John P(age) 1910-1998 53-56
Hoover, Kenneth H(arding) 1920- CANR-7
Earlier sketch in CA 57-60
Hoover, Kenneth R(ay) 1940- CANR-75
Earlier sketch in CA 132
Hoover, Marjorie L(awson) 1910-1999 .. 41-44R
Hoover, Mary B(idgood) 1917- 93-96
Hoover, Paul 1946- CANR-95
Earlier sketch in CA 141
Hoover, Thomas 1941- 102
Hopcke, Robert H(enry) 1958- 154
Hopcraft, Arthur 1932-2004 .... CANR-82
Obituary 233
Earlier sketches in CA 25-28R, CANR-14, 35
Hope, A(lec) D(erwent) 1907-2000 .. CANR-74
Obituary 188
Earlier sketches in CA 21-24R, CANR-33
See also BRWS 7
See also CLC 3, 51
See also CP 1, 2
See also DLB 289
See also EWL 3
See also MTCW 1, 2
See also MTFW 2005
See also PC 56
See also PFS 8
See also RGEL 2
Hope, A(shley) Guy 1914-1982 .... 25-28R
Obituary 133
Hope, Amanda
See Lewis, Judith Mary
Hope, Andrew
See Hern, (George) Anthony
Hope, Anthony 1863-1933 157
See also DLB 153, 156
See also RGEL 2
See also RHW
See also TCLC 83
Hope, Bob 1903-2003 .... CANR-43
Obituary 218
Earlier sketch in CA 101
See also BEST 90:4
Hope, Brian
See Creasey, John
Hope, C(harles) E(velyn) G(raham)
1900-1971 .... CAP-1
Earlier sketch in CA 13-16
Hope, Charlie
See Miles, Keith
Hope, Christopher (David Tully)
1944- CANR-101
Earlier sketches in CA 106, CANR-47
See also AFW
See also CLC 52
See also CN 4, 5, 6, 7
See also DLB 225
See also SATA 62
Hope, David
See Fraser, Douglas
Hope, Eva
See Hearn, Mary Anne
Hope, F. T. L.
See Farrar, Frederic William
Hope, Felix
See Williamson, Claude C(harles) H.
Hope, Francis 1938- .... CP 1
Hope, Jack 1940- 81-84
Hope, Jane 1938- 110
Hope, Judith Richards 1940- 219
Hope, Karol 93-96
Hope, Laura Lee CANR-80
Earlier sketches in CA 17-20R, CANR-27
See also Goulart, Ron(ald Joseph) and
Stanley, George Edward
See also SATA 1, 67
Hope, Laurence
See Nicolson, Adela Florence Cory
See also DLB 240
Hope, Margaret
See Knight, Alanna
Hope, Marjorie (Cecelia) 1923- 29-32R
Hope, Norman Victor 1908-1983
Obituary 110
Hope, Quentin M(anning) 1923- 13-16R
Hope, Ronald (Sidney) 1921- CANR-3
Earlier sketch in CA 9-12R
Hope, Welborn 1903-1988 .... 29-32R
Hope-Jones, Arthur 1911-1984
Obituary 112
Hopes, David Brendan 1953- CANR-26
Earlier sketch in CA 109
Hope Simpson, Jacynth 1930- CANR-7
Earlier sketch in CA 13-16R
See also CWRI 5
See also SATA 12
Hope-Wallace, Philip (Adrian) 1911-1979
Obituary 93-96
Hopewell, S(ydney) 1924- 25-28R
Hopf, Alice (Martha) L(ightner)
1904-1988 .... CANR-9
Obituary 124
Earlier sketch in CA 17-20R
See also SATA 5
See also SATA-Obit 55
See also SFW 4
Hopke, William E. 1918- 21-24R
Hopkin, Alannah 1949- CANR-27
Earlier sketch in CA 109
Hopkins, A. T.
See Turngren, Annette
Hopkins, Andrew 1965- 229
Hopkins, Anne (Marie) 1946- 238
Hopkins, Antony 1921- CANR-17
Earlier sketch in CA 101
Hopkins, Bill 1928- 9-12R
Hopkins, Brian A. 1960- 181
Hopkins, Bruce R. 1941- 150
Hopkins, C(harles) Howard 1905-2000 123
Hopkins, Clark 1895-1976 129
Obituary 109
See also SATA-Obit 34
Hopkins, David 1948- CANR-98
Earlier sketches in CA 122, CANR-48
Hopkins, Donald R(oswell) 1941- 123
Hopkins, Dwight N. 1953- 193
Hopkins, Ellen L. 1955- 198
See also SATA 128
Hopkins, Ellice (Jane) 1836-1904 188
See also DLB 190
Hopkins, Fred W(right), Jr. 1935- 69-72
Hopkins, George E(mil) 1937- 33-36R
Hopkins, Gerard Manley 1844-1889 ..... BRW 5
See also BRWR 2
See also CDBLB 1890-1914
See also DA
See also DA3
See also DAB
See also DAC
See also DAM MST, POET
See also DLB 35, 57
See also EXPP
See also PAB
See also PC 15
See also RGEL 2
See also TEA
See also WLC
See also WP
Hopkins, Harry 1913-1998 .... 29-32R
Hopkins, Hiram
See Seltzer, Charles Alden
Hopkins, J(ohn) F(eely) 1922- 102
Hopkins, Jack W(alker) 1930- 25-28R
Hopkins, Jackie (Mims) 1952- CANR-139
Earlier sketch in CA 156
See also SATA 92
Hopkins, James Franklin 1909- 1-4R
Hopkins, Jasper (Stephen, Jr.) 1936- . CANR-57
Earlier sketches in CA 37-40R, CANR-14, 31
Hopkins, (Paul) Jeffrey 1940- 207
Hopkins, Jerry 1935- CANR-128
Earlier sketches in CA 25-28R, CANR-18
Hopkins, John (?)-1570 .... DLB 132
Hopkins, John (Richard) 1931-1998 85-88
Obituary 169
See also CBD
See also CD 5, 6
See also CLC 4
Hopkins, John 1938- 165
Hopkins, Joseph G(erard) E(dward)
1909- CANR-5
Earlier sketch in CA 1-4R
See also SATA 11
Hopkins, Joseph Martin 1919- 49-52
Hopkins, Judy 1941- 172
Hopkins, (Morris) Keith 1934-2004 .. CANR-99
Obituary 226
Earlier sketch in CA 130
Hopkins, (Hector) Kenneth
1914-1988 .... CANR-1
Obituary 125
Earlier sketch in CA 1-4R
See also SATA-Obit 58
Hopkins, Lee (Wallace) 57-60
Hopkins, Lee Bennett 1938- CANR-104
Earlier sketches in CA 25-28R, CANR-29, 55
See also AAYA 18
See also CLR 44
See also JRDA
See also MAICYA 1, 2
See also MAICYAS 1
See also SAAS 4
See also SATA 3, 68, 125
Hopkins, Lemuel 1750-1801 .... DLB 37
Hopkins, Lightnin'
See Hopkins, Sam
Hopkins, Lyman
See Folsom, Franklin (Brewster)
Hopkins, Marjorie 1911-1999 .... 21-24R
See also SATA 9
Hopkins, Mark W(yatt) 1931- 29-32R
Hopkins, Mary R(ice) 1956- 164
See also SATA 97
Hopkins, Milton 1906-1983
Obituary 109
Hopkins, Nalo 1960- .... DLB 251
Hopkins, Nicholas S(nowden) 1939- 77-80
Hopkins, Pauline Elizabeth
1859-1930 .... CANR-82
Earlier sketch in CA 141
See also AFAW 2
See also BLC 2
See also BW 2, 3
See also DAM MULT
See also DLB 50
See also TCLC 28
Hopkins, Prynce (C.) 1885-1970 .... CAP-2
Earlier sketch in CA 21-22
Hopkins, Pryns
See Hopkins, Prynce (C.)
Hopkins, Raymond F(rederick)
1939- CANR-28
Earlier sketch in CA 49-52
Hopkins, Robert A. 1923- 89-92
Hopkins, Robert S(ydney) CANR-38
Earlier sketch in CA 115
Hopkins, Sam 1912-1982
Obituary 106
Hopkins, Samuel 1721-1803 .... DLB 31
Hopkins, Terence K(ilbourne) 1928- 9-12R
Hopkins, Thomas H(ollis) 1945- 116
Hopkins, Thomas J(ohns) 1930- 37-40R
Hopkins, Viola
See Winner, Viola Hopkins
Hopkins, Vivian C. 1909- CAP-2
Earlier sketch in CA 33-36
Hopkinson, Amanda 1948- 150
See also SATA 84
Hopkinson, Clement Allan Slade 1934- .... CP 1
Hopkinson, Deborah 1952- CANR-72
Earlier sketch in CA 143
See also SATA 76, 108, 159
Hopkinson, Diana 1912- 29-32R
Hopkinson, Francis 1737-1791 .... DLB 31
See also RGAL 4
Hopkinson, Henry Thomas 1905-1990 . 17-20R
Obituary 132
See also Hopkinson, Tom
Hopkinson, Nalo 1960- 219
Earlier sketch in CA 196
Autobiographical Essay in 219
See also AAYA 40
See also DLB 251
Hopkinson, Tom
See Hopkinson, Henry Thomas
See also CN 1, 2
Hopkirk, Peter 1930- 107
Hopley, George
See Hopley-Woolrich, Cornell George
Hopley-Woolrich, Cornell George
1903-1968 .... CANR-58
Earlier sketches in CAP-1, CA 13-14
See also Woolrich, Cornell
See also CMW 4
See also DLB 226
See also MTCW 2
Hoppe, Art(hur Watterson)
1925-2000 .... CANR-3
Obituary 188
Earlier sketch in CA 5-8R
Hoppe, Eleanor Sellers 1933- 73-76
Hoppe, Emil Otho 1878-1972 .... 9-12R
Hoppe, Joanne 1932- 81-84
See also SATA 42
Hoppe, Matthias 1952- 143
See also SATA 76
Hoppe, Ronald A. 1931- 45-48
Hoppen, K(arl) Theodore 1941- CANR-89
Earlier sketch in CA 119
Hoppenstedt, Elbert M. 1917- 1-4R
Hopper, Carolyn Hinton 1945- 214
Hopper, Columbus B(urwell) 1931- 33-36R
Hopper, David H. 1927- 21-24R
Hopper, Dennis 1936- 114
Hopper, Edward 1882-1967 .... AAYA 33
Hopper, Grace (Brewster) Murray
1906-1992 164
Hopper, Hedda
See Furry, Elda
Hopper, John 1934- 17-20R
Hopper, Kim 226
Hopper, Nancy J. 1937- CANR-38
Earlier sketch in CA 115
See also SATA 38
See also SATA-Brief 35
Hopper, Nora 1871-1906 203
See also DLB 240
Hopper, R(obert) J(ohn) 1910-1987 123
Hopper, Robert 1945-1998 .... CANR-9
Earlier sketch in CA 65-68
Hopper, Vincent Foster 1906-1976 ..... CANR-6
Obituary 61-64
Earlier sketch in CA 1-4R
Hoppin, Augustus 1828-1896 .... DLB 188
Hoppin, Richard H(allowell)
1913-1991 .... 41-44R
Hopping, Lorraine Jean
See Egan, Lorraine Hopping
Hoppock, Robert 1901-1995 .... 1-4R
Hopson, Dan, Jr. 1930- 21-24R
Hopson, Janet L(ouise) 1950- 89-92
Hopson, William (L.) 1907- .... TCWW 1, 2
Hopwood, Robert R. 1910- CAP-1
Earlier sketch in CA 13-14
Hora, F. Bayard 1909(?)-1984
Obituary 112
Hora, Josef 1891-1945 .... CDWLB 4
See also DLB 215
See also EWL 3
Horace 65B.C.-8B.C. .... AW 2
See also CDWLB 1
See also DLB 211
See also PC 46
See also RGWL 2, 3
Horacek, Petr .... SATA 163
Horak, Jan-Christopher 1951- 153
Horak, M. Stephan 1920- 9-12R
Horan, Elizabeth (Rosa) 1956- 146
Horan, Francis Harding 1900-1978
Obituary 81-84
Horan, James David 1914-1981 .... CANR-9
Obituary 105
Earlier sketch in CA 13-16R
Horan, (Harold) Joseph Taaffe 1898(?)-1985
Obituary 117
Horan, Patrick M. 1958- 166
Horan, Richard (Vincent), (Jr.)
1957- CANR-115
Earlier sketch in CA 153
Horan, William D. 1933- 25-28R
Horat, Heinz 1948- 141
Horatio
See Proust, (Valentin-Louis-George-Eugene)
Marcel
Horatio, Algernon 89-92
Horatio, Jane
See Cudlipp, Edythe
Horbach, Michael 1924-1986 .... CANR-25
Obituary 120
Earlier sketch in CA 29-32R
Horch, Daniel 223
Horchler, Richard (Thomas) 1925- 5-8R
Horchow, (Samuel) Roger 1928- 106
Hord, Frederick (Lee) 1941- CANR-100
Earlier sketch in CA 143
See also BW 2
Horder, John (Rearson Peter) 1936- .... CP 1
Horder, (Thomas) Mervyn 1910-1997 104
Obituary 158
Hordern, William (Edward) 1920- 13-16R
Hordon, Harris E(ugene) 1942- 53-56
Horecky, Paul Louis 1913-1999 .... CANR-2
Earlier sketch in CA 5-8R
Horelick, Arnold L(awrence) 1928- CANR-8
Earlier sketch in CA 17-20R

Cumulative Index 277 Hoskens

Horenstein, Henry 1947- 178
See also SATA 108
Horgan, Denis E. 1941- 101
Horgan, Edward R. 1934- 109
Horgan, John 1953- CANR-139
Earlier sketch in CA 162
Horgan, John J(oseph) 1910- 61-64
Horgan, John Joseph 1881-1967
Obituary 116
Horgan, Paul (George Vincent O'Shaughnessy)
1903-1995 .... CANR-35
Obituary 147
Earlier sketches in CA 13-16R, CANR-9
Interview in CANR-9
See also BPFB 2
See also CLC 9, 53
See also CN 1, 2, 3, 4, 5
See also DAM NOV
See also DLB 102, 212
See also DLBY 1985
See also MTCW 1, 2
See also MTFW 2005
See also SATA 13
See also SATA-Obit 84
See also TCWW 1, 2
Hori, Ichiro 1910-1974 .... CAP-2
Earlier sketch in CA 25-28
Horie, Shigeo 1903- CAP-1
Earlier sketch in CA 13-14
Horikoshi, Jiro 1904(?)-1982
Obituary 110
Horka-Follick, Lorayne Ann 1940- 29-32R
Horkheimer, Max 1895-1973 216
Obituary 41-44R
See also DLB 296
See also TCLC 132
Horlak, E. E.
See Tepper, Sheri S.
Horler, Sydney 1888-1954 157
See also CMW 4
See also SATA 102
Horlick, Allan S. 1941- 151
Horman, Richard E. 1945- 29-32R
Horn, Bernd 1959- 222
Horn, D(avid) B(ayne) 1901-1969 ...... CANR-6
Earlier sketch in CA 1-4R
Horn, Daniel 1934-1991 .... 21-24R
Obituary 134
Horn, Edward Newman 1903(?)-1976
Obituary 65-68
Horn, Francis H(enry) 1908-1999 53-56
Horn, George F(rancis) 1917- CANR-8
Earlier sketch in CA 5-8R
Horn, Henry Eyster 1913- 21-24R
Horn, Jeanne P. 1925- 5-8R
Horn, John L(eonard) 1928- CANR-14
Earlier sketch in CA 37-40R
Horn, Linda L(ouise) 1947- 101
Horn, Maurice 1931- CANR-22
Earlier sketch in CA 89-92
Horn, Michiel 1939- CANR-134
Earlier sketch in CA 169
Horn, Miriam 233
Horn, Pamela (Lucy Ray) 1936- CANR-30
Earlier sketch in CA 69-72
Horn, Peter
See Kuttner, Henry
Horn, Peter (Rudolf Gisela) 1934- 103
Horn, Pierre L(aurence) 1942- CANR-44
Earlier sketch in CA 119
Horn, Richard 1954-1989 105
Obituary 128
Horn, Robert M. 1933- 29-32R
Horn, Sandra Ann 1944- .... SATA 154
Horn, Shifra 228
Horn, Siegfried H(erbert) 1908-1993 ..... 37-40R
Horn, Stacy 1956- CANR-124
Earlier sketch in CA 169
Horn, Stefan F. 1900-1996 .... CAP-1
Earlier sketch in CA 13-16
Horn, (John) Stephen 1931- 13-16R
Horn, Stephen (McCaffrey Moore)
1931- CANR-126
Earlier sketch in CA 45-48
Horn, Thomas D. 1918- 13-16R
Horn, Vivi 1878(?)-1971
Obituary 104
Horn, Walter (William) 1908-1995 .... 21-24R
Hornbacher, Marya 1974- 172
Hornback, Bert G(erald) 1935- CANR-22
Earlier sketch in CA 29-32R
Hornbaker, Alice 1927- 77-80
Hornbeck, William 1901-1983 .... IDFW 3, 4
Hornbein, Thomas Frederic 1930- 53-56
Hornberger, H. Richard 1923(?)-1997 105
Obituary 162
Hornberger, Theodore 1906-1975 ...... CANR-3
Earlier sketch in CA 5-8R
Hornblow, Arthur, Jr. 1893-1976 89-92
Obituary 65-68
See also SATA 15
Hornblow, Leonora (Schinasi) 1920- 73-76
See also SATA 18
Hornblower, Harry C.
See Shriver, Harry C(lair)
Hornblum, Allen Michael 1947- 174
Hornbostel, Lloyd 1934- 159
Hornbruch, Frederick William, Jr.
1913-2001 109
Hornby, C(harles) H(arry) St. John
1867-1946 182
See also DLB 201
Hornby, John (Wilkinson) 1913-1978 ...... 9-12R
Hornby, Leslie 1949- 103
Hornby, Nick 1958- CANR-104
Earlier sketch in CA 151
See also CN 7
See also DLB 207
Hornby, Richard 1938- 89-92
Hornby, William H(arry) 1923- 106
Horne, A(lexander) D(ouglas) 1932- 109
Horne, Aaron 1940- 138
See also BW 2
Horne, Alistair (Allan) 1925- CANR-9
Earlier sketch in CA 5-8R
Horne, Bernard Shea 1905-1970
Obituary 104
Horne, Chevis Ferber 1914-1998 ..... CANR-16
Earlier sketch in CA 97-100
Horne, Constance 1927- 223
See also SATA 149
Horne, Cynthia Miriam 1939- 5-8R
Horne, Donald (Richmond)
1921-2005 .... CANR-42
Earlier sketches in CA 103, CANR-20
Horne, Elliott 1922(?)-1989
Obituary 129
Horne, Fiona 1966- 202
Horne, Frank (Smith) 1899-1974 125
Obituary 53-56
See also BW 1
See also DLB 51
See also HR 1:2
See also WP
Horne, Geoffrey 1916- CANR-64
Earlier sketch in CA 9-12R
See also CMW 4
Horne, Gerald 1949- CANR-99
Earlier sketch in CA 140
See also BW 2
Horne, Howard
See Payne, (Pierre Stephen) Robert
Horne, Hugh Robert 1915- 5-8R
Horne, Kenneth 1900-1975
Obituary 115
Horne, Lewis 1932- 110
Horne, Marilyn 1934- 133
Horne, Peter 1947- 69-72
Horne, Philip 1958- 196
Horne, R(alph) A(lbert) 1929- 106
Horne, Richard (George Anthony) 1960- 182
See also SATA 111
Horne, Richard Henry Hengist
1802(?)-1884 .... DLB 32
See also SATA 29
Horne, Roman L(emuel) 1901-1987
Obituary 121
Horne, Shirley (Faith) 1919- 49-52
Horne, Thomas 1608-1654 .... DLB 281
Hornem, Horace Esq.
See Byron, George Gordon (Noel)
Horner, Althea (Jane) 1926- 81-84
See also SATA 36
Horner, Dave 1934- 17-20R
See also SATA 12
Horner, David 1948- 231
Horner, David Stuart 1900(?)-1983(?)
Obituary 111
Horner, George F(rederick) 1899-1974 .. CAP-2
Earlier sketch in CA 33-36
Horner, Harry 1910-1994 .... IDFW 3, 4
Horner, J. C.
See Horner, John Curwen
Horner, Jack
See Horner, John R(obert)
Horner, John Curwen 1922- 103
Horner, John R(obert) 1946- 168
See also SATA 106
Horner, Joyce Mary 1903-1980
Obituary 112
Horner, Kenric Lancaster 1902-1973
Obituary 111
See also Horner, Lance
Horner, Lance
See Horner, Kenric Lancaster
See also RHW 1
Horner, Thomas Marland 1927- 37-40R
Horner, Tom (Julian) 1913- 121
Horner, Winifred Bryan 1922- CANR-41
Earlier sketch in CA 118
Horney, Karen (Clementine Theodore
Danielsen) 1885-1952 165
Brief entry 114
See also DLB 246
See also FW
See also TCLC 71
Horngren, Charles T(homas) 1926- 57-60
Hornig, Doug 1943- CANR-66
Earlier sketches in CA 117, CANR-40
See also CMW 4
Hornik, Edith Lynn
See Beer, Edith Lynn
Hornik, Laurie Miller .... SATA 159
Hornik-Beer, Edith Lynn
See Beer, Edith Lynn
Horniman, Joanne 1951- 166
See also SATA 98
Horning, Alice S. 1950- 137
Hornman, Wim 1920-
Brief entry 106
Hornos, Axel 1907-1994 .... CAP-2
Earlier sketch in CA 29-32
See also SATA 20
Hornsblow, Doreen -2001 237
See also Wentworth, Sally
Hornsby, Albert Sidney 1898(?)-1978
Obituary 104
Hornsby, Alton, Jr. 1940- 37-40R
Hornsby, Ken 1934- 105
Hornsby, Roger A. 1926- 21-24R
Hornsby, Wendy (Nelson) 1947- 232
See also CMW 4
Hornsby-Smith, Michael P(eter) 1932- 126
Hornschemeier, Paul 1977- 233
Hornstein, Gail A. 1951- 204
Hornstein, Harvey A. 1938- 53-56
Hornstein, Lillian Herlands 1909- 45-48
Hornstein, Reuben Aaron 1912- 106
See also SATA 64
Hornung, Clarence Pearson
1899-1997 .... CANR-9
Earlier sketch in CA 17-20R
Hornung, E(rnest) W(illiam) 1866-1921 160
Brief entry 108
See also CMW 4
See also DLB 70
See also TCLC 59
Hornung, Erik 1933- 117
Hornung, Maximilian 1942- 107
Horobin, Ian M. 1899-1976
Obituary 69-72
Horovitz, David (Phillip) 229
Horovitz, Frances Margaret 1938-1983
Obituary 111
Horovitz, Israel (Arthur) 1939- CANR-59
Earlier sketches in CA 33-36R, CANR-46
See also CAD
See also CD 5, 6
See also CLC 56
See also DAM DRAM
See also DLB 7
See also MAL 5
Horovitz, Michael 1935- 81-84
See also CP 1, 2
Horowitz, Al
See Horowitz, I(srael) A.
Horowitz, Anthony 1955- 207
See also SATA 137
Horowitz, Daniel 1938- CANR-86
Earlier sketch in CA 145
Horowitz, David 1903-2002 69-72
Obituary 209
Horowitz, David (Joel) 1939- CANR-138
Earlier sketches in CA 13-16R, CANR-68
Horowitz, David A. 1941- 89-92
Horowitz, David Charles 1937- 89-92
Horowitz, Donald L(eonard) 1939- 126
Horowitz, Edward 1904-1986 .... CANR-4
Earlier sketch in CA 1-4R
Horowitz, Esther 1920- 49-52
Horowitz, Eve 1963- 139
Horowitz, Gene 1930- 77-80
Horowitz, Helen Lefkowitz 1942- CANR-58
Earlier sketch in CA 125
Horowitz, I(srael) A. 1907-1973
Obituary 41-44R
Horowitz, Ira 1934- 41-44R
Horowitz, Irving Louis 1929- CANR-95
Earlier sketches in CA 41-44R, CANR-50
Horowitz, Jacob 1900-1979
Obituary 89-92
Horowitz, Joseph 1948- CANR-27
Earlier sketch in CA 109
Horowitz, Laura (Godofsky) 1943-1983
Obituary 110
Horowitz, Leonard M(artin) 1937- 37-40R
Horowitz, Lois 1940- 119
Horowitz, Mardi J(on) 1934- 33-36R
Horowitz, Michael M. 1933- CANR-49
Earlier sketches in CA 41-44R, CANR-15
Horowitz, Morris A(aron) 1919- CANR-9
Earlier sketch in CA 65-68
Horowitz, Renee B(arbara) 1932- 159
Horowitz, Robert S. 1924- 9-12R
Horowitz, Ruth 1957- .... SATA 136
Horowitz, Shel Alan 1956- CANR-96
Earlier sketches in CA 120, CANR-46
See also Friedman, Alan
Horrell, C. William 1918- CANR-13
Earlier sketch in CA 61-64
Horricks, Raymond (Anthony)
1933- CANR-136
Earlier sketches in CA 129, CANR-64
Horrie, Chris(topher) 1956- 150
Horrock, Berta Crone 1896(?)-1983
Obituary 110
Horrock, Nicholas (Morton) 1936- 49-52
Horrocks, Brian (Gwynne) 1895-1985
Obituary 114
Horrocks, Edna M. 1908-1982 .... CAP-2
Earlier sketch in CA 17-18
Horrocks, John E(dwin) 1913-2002 .... 5-8R
Horsbrugh, Ian 1941- 111
Horsburgh, David Michael 1923-1984
Obituary 114
Horsburgh, H(oward) J(ohn) N(eate)
1918- 25-28R
Horse, Harry
See Horne, Richard (George Anthony)
Horsefield, J(ohn) Keith 1901-1997 .... 5-8R
Obituary 157
Horsely, Ramsbottom
See Berne, Eric (Lennard)
See also CCA 1
Horseman, Elaine Hall 1925- 13-16R
Horsey, Dave
See Horsey, David
Horsey, David 1951- 224
Horsey, Miles G. 1956- 149
Horsfield, Alan 1939- 228
See also SATA 153
Horsfield, Debbie 1955- 231
See also CBD
See also CD 5, 6
See also CWD
Horsford, Howard C(larke) 1921- 136
Horsley, David
See Bingley, David Ernest
Horsley, James (Allen) 1938- 45-48
Horsley, Kate 1952- 210
Horsley, (Beresford) Peter (Torrington)
1921-2001 219
Horsley, Richard A. 173
Horsman, Reginald 1931- CANR-17
Earlier sketches in CA 1-4R, CANR-2
Horst, Irvin B(uckwalter) 1915- 41-44R
Horst, Louis 1884-1964 208
Horst, Samuel (Levi) 1919- 21-24R
Horstman, Allen (Henry) 1943- 122
Horton, Andrew 1944- 190
Horton, Arthur MacNeill, Jr. 1947- ... CANR-75
Earlier sketches in CA 114, CANR-35
Horton, David (Edward) 1931- 164
Horton, Felix Lee
See Floren, Lee
Horton, Frank E. 1939- 29-32R
Horton, George Moses
1797(?)-1883(?) .... DLB 50
Horton, H. Mack 1952- 238
Horton, J(ames) Wright (Jr.) 1950- 138
Horton, James O(liver) 1943- CANR-136
Earlier sketches in CA 114, CANR-35
Horton, John (William) 1905- CANR-18
Earlier sketches in CA 9-12R, CANR-3
Horton, Lois E. 236
Horton, Louise (Walthall) 1916- CANR-40
Earlier sketches in CA 49-52, CANR-2
Horton, Lowell 1936- 53-56
Horton, Madelyn (Stacey) 1962- 145
See also SATA 77
Horton, Michael Scott 1964- 135
Horton, Myles 1905-1990 140
Horton, Patricia Campbell 1943- 89-92
Horton, Paul Burleigh 1916- CANR-20
Earlier sketch in CA 1-4R
Horton, Paul Chester 1942- 106
Horton, Philip C. 1911(?)-1989
Obituary 129
Horton, Rod W(illiam) 1910-2000 49-52
Horton, Russell M. 1946- 97-100
Horton, Stanley M(onroe) 1916- CANR-6
Earlier sketch in CA 57-60
Horton, Susan R. 1941- 109
Horton, Thomas R. 1926- 144
Horvat, Branko 1928- 53-56
Horvath, Agnes 1957- 147
Horvath, Betty 1927- 17-20R
See also SATA 4
Horvath, Janos 1921- 41-44R
Horvath, Joan 1944- 81-84
Horvath, John, Jr. 1948- 216
Horvath, odon von 1901-1938
See von Horvath, Odon
See also EWL 3
Horvath, Oedoen von -1938
See von Horvath, Odon
Horvath, Polly 1957- 132
See also CLR 90
See also SATA 85, 140
Horvath, Violet M. 1924- 29-32R
Horwich, Frances R(appaport)
1908-2001 .... CAP-1
Obituary 199
Earlier sketch in CA 13-16
See also SATA 11
See also SATA-Obit 130
Horwitt, Sanford D. 1943- 159
Horwitz, Elinor Lander CANR-13
Earlier sketch in CA 77-80
See also SATA 45
See also SATA-Brief 33
Horwitz, Joshua 236
Horwitz, Julius 1920-1986 .... CANR-12
Obituary 119
Earlier sketch in CA 9-12R
See also CLC 14
Horwitz, Richard P(aul) 1949- CANR-98
Earlier sketches in CA 122, CANR-48
Horwitz, Simi L(ouise) 1949- 103
Horwitz, Sylvia L(aibman) 1911-1995 61-64
Horwitz, Tony 1958- CANR-123
Earlier sketch in CA 140
Horwood, Harold (Andrew) 1923- 229
Earlier sketches in CA 21-24R, CANR-9, 25
Autobiographical Essay in 229
See also CAAS 15
See also DLB 60
Horwood, William 1944- 141
See also FANT
See also SATA 85
Hosek, Chaviva (Milada) 1946- 127
Hoselitz, Bert(hold) F(rank)
1913-1995 .... CANR-1
Earlier sketch in CA 1-4R
Hosford, Bowen I. 1916- CANR-24
Earlier sketch in CA 107
Hosford, Dorothy (Grant) 1900-1952 .. SATA 22
Hosford, Jessie 1892-1990 .... 41-44R
See also SATA 5
Hosford, Philip L(ewis) 1926- 57-60
Hosford, Ray E. 1933- 85-88
Hoshi, Shin'ichi 1926- 162
See also SATA 101
See also SFW 4
Hoshizaki, Barbara Joe 1928- 200
Hosie, Stanley W(illiam) 1922- 25-28R
Hosier, Helen Kooiman 1928- CANR-8
Earlier sketch in CA 61-64
Hosier, Peter
See Clark, Douglas (Malcolm Jackson)
Hosken, Fran(ziska) P(orges) 1919- CANR-6
Earlier sketch in CA 57-60
Hoskens, Jane Fenn 1693-1770(?) ...... DLB 200

Hoskin 278 CONTEMPORARY AUTHORS

Hoskin, Cyril Henry 1911(?)-1981
 Obituary 102
Hosking, Eric (John) 1909-1991 .... CANR-17
 Earlier sketch in CA 101
Hosking, Geoffrey A(lan) 1942- CANR-120
 Earlier sketches in CA 85-88, CANR-19, 71
Hoskins, Katharine Bail 1924- 65-68
Hoskins, Katherine (de Montalant) 1909- CAP-2
 Earlier sketch in CA 25-28
 See also CP 1, 2
Hoskins, Percy 1904-1989
 Obituary 127
Hoskins, Phillip
 See Hoskins, Robert (Phillip)
Hoskins, Robert (Phillip) 1933-1993 .... CANR-56
 Obituary 174
 Earlier sketch in CA 29-32R
 See also SFW 4
Hoskins, William George 1908-1992 .... 13-16R
 Obituary 136
Hoskyns, John c. 1566-1638 ...... DLB 121, 281
Hoskyns, Tam 1961- 164
Hoskyns-Abrahall, Clare (Constance Drury) 29-32R
 See also SATA 13
Hosle, Vittorio
 See Hosle, Vittorio
Hosle, Vittorio 1960- 195
Hosley, Richard 1921- CANR-8
 Earlier sketch in CA 5-8R
Hosmer, Charles B(ridgham), Jr. 1932- .. 13-16R
Hosmon, Robert Stahr 1943- 45-48
Hosokawa, Bill
 See Hosokawa, William K.
Hosokawa, William K. 1915- CANR-143
 Earlier sketches in CA 29-32R, CANR-11
Hosokawa Yusai 1534-1610 .... DLB 203
Hosozawa-Nagano, Elaine 1954- 165
Hospers, John, Jr. 1918- CANR-2
 Earlier sketch in CA 1-4R
 See also DLB 279
Hospital, Janette Turner 1942- CANR-48
 Earlier sketch in CA 108
 See also CLC 42, 145
 See also CN 5, 6, 7
 See also DLBY 2002
 See also RGSF 2
Hoss, Marvin Allen 1929- 29-32R
Hoss, Norman 1923(?)-1983
 Obituary 111
Hossack, Joei Carlton 1944- 157
Hossack, Sylvia 1939- .... SATA 83
Hossack, Sylvie Adams
 See Hossack, Sylvia
Hosseini, Khaled 1965- 225
 See also SATA 156
Hossell, Karen Price
 See Price, Karen
Hossent, Harry 1916- CAP-1
 Earlier sketch in CA 9-10
Hostetler, Beulah Stauffer 1926- 126
Hostetler, John Andrew 1918-2001 205
Hostetler, Marian 1932- CANR-49
 Earlier sketches in CA 65-68, CANR-9, 24
 See also SATA 91
Hostetter, B(enjamin) Charles 1916- ... CANR-1
 Earlier sketch in CA 1-4R
Hostler, Charles W(arren) 1919- 21-24R
Hostos, Adolfo de 1887-1982 131
 See also HW 1
Hostos, E. M. de
 See Hostos (y Bonilla), Eugenio Maria de
Hostos, Eugenio M. de
 See Hostos (y Bonilla), Eugenio Maria de
Hostos, Eugenio Maria
 See Hostos (y Bonilla), Eugenio Maria de
Hostos (y Bonilla), Eugenio Maria de 1839-1903 131
 Brief entry 123
 See also HW 1
 See also TCLC 24
Hostovsky, Egon 1908-1973
 Obituary 89-92
 See also DLB 215
 See also EWL 3
Hostrop, Richard Winfred 1925- 25-28R
Hotaling, Edward 1937- 77-80
Hotchkiss, Bill 1936- CANR-110
 Earlier sketch in CA 104
Hotchkiss, Jeanette 1901-1994 .... 21-24R
Hotchkiss, Ralf D. 1947- 33-36R
Hotchner, A(aron) E(dward) 1920- .. CANR-123
 Earlier sketches in CA 69-72, CANR-27, 56
Hotchner, Tracy 1950- 102
Hothem, Lar(ry Lee) 1938- 106
Hothersall, David 1940- 111
Hotschnig, Alois 1959- 211
Hotson, John H(argrove) 1930- 25-28R
Hotspur
 See Curling, Bryan William Richard
Hottois, James W. 1943- 77-80
Hotz, Robert B(ergmann) 1914- 101
Hou, Chi-ming 1924- 21-24R
Hou, Fu-Wu
 See Houn, Franklin W.
Houarner, Gerard Daniel 1955- CANR-139
 Earlier sketch in CA 175
Houblon, Doreen (Lindsay) Archer
 See Archer Houblon, Doreen (Lindsay)
Houchin, Thomas D(ouglas) 1925- 77-80
Houck, Carter 1924- CANR-14
 Earlier sketch in CA 77-80
 See also SATA 22
Houck, John W(illiam) 1931- CANR-11
 Earlier sketch in CA 29-32R
Houdar de la Motte, Antoine-Charles de 1672-1731 .... GFL Beginnings to 1789
Houde, John 1956- 187
Houdini
 See Lovecraft, H(oward) P(hillips)
Houdini, Merlin X.
 See Borgmann, Dmitri A(lfred)
Houedard, Dom Sylvester 1924-1992 103
 See also CP 1, 2
Houedard, Pierre Thomas Paul Jean
 See Houedard, Dom Sylvester
Houellebecq, Michel 1958- CANR-140
 Earlier sketch in CA 185
 See also CLC 179
 See also MTFW 2005
Houfe, Simon (Richard) 1942- CANR-19
 Earlier sketch in CA 103
Hougan, Carolyn 1943- 139
 See also CLC 34
Hougan, James Richard 1942- CANR-94
 Earlier sketch in CA 77-80
Hougan, Jim
 See Hougan, James Richard
Hough, (Helen) Charlotte 1924- CANR-5
 Earlier sketch in CA 9-12R
 See also CWRI 5
 See also SATA 9
Hough, Denny C. 1925(?)-1983
 Obituary 111
Hough, Emerson 1857-1923
 Brief entry 120
 See also DLB 9, 212
 See also TCWW 1, 2
Hough, George A(nthony) III 1920- 121
 Brief entry 117
Hough, Graham (Goulder) 1908-1990 .... CANR-25
 Obituary 132
 Earlier sketch in CA 69-72
 See also CP 1
Hough, Harold 1952- 144
Hough, Henry Beetle 1896-1985 .... CANR-2
 Obituary 116
 Earlier sketch in CA 1-4R
Hough, Henry W(ade) 1906-1970(?) 25-28R
 Obituary 122
Hough, Hugh 1924-1986 73-76
 Obituary 119
Hough, Jerry F(incher) 1935- 137
 Brief entry 114
Hough, John T., Jr. 1946- CANR-138
 Earlier sketch in CA 33-36R
Hough, Joseph C(arl), Jr. 1933- 21-24R
Hough, Judy Taylor 1932- 124
 See also SATA 56, 63
 See also SATA-Brief 51
Hough, Lindy Downer 1944- CANR-8
 Earlier sketch in CA 61-64
Hough, Louis 1914-1985 .... 37-40R
Hough, Michael 1928- 133
Hough, Peter A. 1954- 142
Hough, Richard (Alexander) 1922-1999 .... CANR-18
 Earlier sketches in CA 5-8R, CANR-3
 See also CWRI 5
 See also SATA 17
Hough, S(tanley) B(ennett) 1917- CANR-3
 Earlier sketch in CA 5-8R
 See also SFW 4
Hough, Susan Elizabeth 1961- 223
Houghteling, James L(awrence), Jr. 1920- .. 5-8R
Houghton, Bernard 1935- 77-80
Houghton, Diane 1940- 123
Houghton, Elizabeth
 See Gilzean, Elizabeth Houghton Blanchet
Houghton, Eric 1930- CANR-2
 Earlier sketch in CA 1-4R
 See also SATA 7
Houghton, George William 1905-1993 . 13-16R
Houghton, Gordon 1965- 199
Houghton, J. T.
 See Houghton, John T(heodore)
Houghton, Sir John
 See Houghton, John T(heodore)
Houghton, John T(heodore) 1931- 168
Houghton, Katharine 1945- CANR-91
 Earlier sketch in CA 130
Houghton, Neal D(oyle) 1895-1985 ...... CAP-2
 Earlier sketch in CA 25-28
Houghton, (Charles) Norris 1909-2001 . 21-24R
 Obituary 202
Houghton, Peter 1938- 119
Houghton, R(alph) E(dward) C(unliffe) 1896-1990
 Obituary 132
Houghton, Samuel G(ilbert) 1902-1975 .. 65-68
Houghton, (William) Stanley 1881-1913 178
 Brief entry 110
 See also DLB 10
 See also RGEL 2
Houghton, Walter Edwards 1904-1983 . CAP-1
 Obituary 109
 Earlier sketch in CA 9-10
Houk, Randy 1944- 151
 See also SATA 97
Houlbrooke, Ralph (A.) 1944- 132
Houlden, J(ames) L(eslie) 1929- 77-80
Houle, Cyril O(rvin) 1913-1998 .... CANR-3
 Obituary 167
 Earlier sketch in CA 5-8R
Houlehen, Robert J. 1918- 49-52
 See also SATA 18
Houlgate, Deke 1930- 61-64
Houlgate, Stephen (Glynn) 1954- 127
Hoult, Norah 1898-1984
 Obituary 112
Hoult, Thomas Ford 1920-
 Brief entry 116
Houlton, Peggy Mann 1925(?)-1990 . CANR-35
 See also Mann, Peggy
Houn, Franklin W. 1920- 21-24R
Hounshell, David A. 1950- 129
Hounsome, Terry 1944- 109
Houppert, Karen 1956- 230
Houpt, Katherine Albro 1939- 105
Hourani, A. H.
 See Hourani, Albert (Habib)
Hourani, Albert (Habib) 1916(?)-1993 140
Hourani, Cecil 1917- 129
Hourani, George F(adlo) 1913-1984 .... CANR-23
 Earlier sketch in CA 45-48
Hours, Madeleine 1915- CANR-28
 Earlier sketch in CA 49-52
Hours-Miedan, Madeleine
 See Hours, Madeleine
Hours-Miedan, Magdeleine
 See Hours, Madeleine
Housden, Roger 223
House, Adrian 209
House, Anne W.
 See McCauley, Elfrieda B(abnick)
House, Charles (Albert) 1916- 25-28R
House, Ernest R(obert) 1937- CANR-23
 Earlier sketch in CA 45-48
House, Gloria 1941- CANR-41
 Earlier sketch in CA 117
 See also BW 2
House, H(ershel) Wayne 1948- 119
House, James S. 1944- 143
House, John William 1919-1984 106
 Obituary 112
House, Karen Elliott 1947- 130
 Brief entry 125
 Interview in CA-130
House, Kurt D(uane) 1947- 104
House, R(ichard) C(alvin) 1927-2004 142
 Obituary 223
House, Robert Burton 1892-1987 .... CAP-1
 Earlier sketch in CA 11-12
House, Robert J. 1932- 101
House, Robert W(illiam) 1920- 53-56
House, Ruth Sizemore 1946- 116
House, Silas D. 1971- 202
House, Tom 1962- 225
House, Victor 1893-1983
 Obituary 109
Household, Geoffrey (Edward West) 1900-1988 .... CANR-58
 Obituary 126
 Earlier sketch in CA 77-80
 See also CLC 11
 See also CMW 4
 See also CN 1, 2, 3, 4
 See also DLB 87
 See also SATA 14
 See also SATA-Obit 59
Houselander, (Frances) Caryll 1901-1954
 Brief entry 110
 See also SATA-Brief 31
Houseman, Barton L(eroy) 1933- 61-64
Houseman, Gerald L. 1935- 108
Houseman, John 1902-1988 163
 Obituary 127
 Brief entry 110
 See also IDFW 3, 4
Housepian, Marjorie
 See Dobkin, Marjorie Housepian
Houser, Caroline 115
Houser, Lynn Raymond 1951(?)- 167
Housewright, David 1955- 166
Housewright, Wiley L. 1913- 140
Housley, Norman (James) 1952- 108
Housman, A(lfred) E(dward) 1859-1936 125
 Brief entry 104
 See also AAYA 66
 See also BRW 6
 See also DA
 See also DA3
 See also DAB
 See also DAC
 See also DAM MST, POET
 See also DLB 19, 284
 See also EWL 3
 See also EXPP
 See also MTCW 1, 2
 See also MTFW 2005
 See also PAB
 See also PC 2, 43
 See also PFS 4, 7
 See also RGEL 2
 See also TCLC 1, 10
 See also TEA
 See also WLCS
 See also WP
Housman, Clemence 1861-1955 .... HGG
Housman, Laurence 1865-1959 155
 Brief entry 106
 See also DLB 10
 See also FANT
 See also RGEL 2
 See also SATA 25
 See also TCLC 7
Houston, Beverle (Ann) 1936-1988 89-92
 Obituary 124
Houston, C(larence) Stuart 1927- 119
Houston, Cecil J(ames) 1943- 135
Houston, David 1938- 118
Houston, Dick 1943- .... SATA 74
Houston, Douglas (Norman) 1947- .. CANR-50
 Earlier sketch in CA 123
Houston, Gloria CANR-86
 Earlier sketch in CA 149
 See also SATA 81, 138
 See also SATA-Essay 138
Houston, James A(rchibald) 1921-2005 .... CANR-108
 Obituary 238
 Earlier sketches in CA 65-68, CANR-38, 60
 See also AAYA 18
 See also CLR 3
 See also DAC
 See also DAM MST
 See also JRDA
 See also MAICYA 1, 2
 See also SAAS 17
 See also SATA 13, 74
 See also SATA-Obit 163
 See also YAW
Houston, James D. 1933- 204
 Earlier sketches in CA 25-28R, CANR-29, 55
 Autobiographical Essay in 204
 See also CAAS 16
 See also LAIT 4
 See also SATA 78
Houston, James M(ackintosh) 1922- 13-16R
Houston, Jean
 Brief entry 115
Houston, Jeanne (Toyo) Wakatsuki 1934- ... 232
 Earlier sketches in CA 103, CANR-29, 123
 Autobiographical Essay in 232
 See also CAAS 16
 See also AAL
 See also AAYA 49
 See also LAIT 4
 See also SATA 78
Houston, Joan 1928- 17-20R
Houston, John Porter 1933-1987 .... CANR-3
 Obituary 123
 Earlier sketch in CA 9-12R
Houston, Juanita C. 1921- .... SATA 129
Houston, Neal B. 1928- 41-44R
Houston, Pam(ela Lynne) 1962(?)- .. CANR-118
 Earlier sketch in CA 143
 See also DLB 244
 See also SSFS 17
Houston, Peyton (Hoge) 1910-1994 ... CANR-1
 Obituary 144
 Earlier sketch in CA 49-52
Houston, R. B.
 See Rae, Hugh C(rauford)
Houston, Robert 1935- 37-40R
Houston, Tex .... TCWW 1, 2
Houston, Velina Hasu 1957- 144
Houston, W(illiam) Robert, Jr. 1928- CANR-40
 Earlier sketches in CA 5-8R, CANR-3, 18
Houston, Will
 See Paine, Lauran (Bosworth)
Houston, William Neil 1948- 123
Houtart, Francois 1925- 13-16R
Houthakker, Hendrik S(amuel) 1924- 17-20R
Houton, Kathleen
 See Kilgore, Kathleen
Houts, Marshall (Wilson) 1919-1993 .... CANR-13
 Obituary 143
 Earlier sketch in CA 21-24R
Houts, Peter S. 1933- CANR-49
 Earlier sketch in CA 49-52
Houwald, Ernst von 1778-1845 .... DLB 90
Hovannisian, Richard G. 1932- CANR-101
 Earlier sketch in CA 21-24R
Hovda, Robert W(alker) 1920-1992 ... CANR-3
 Obituary 136
 Earlier sketch in CA 9-12R
Hovde, A(nnis) J(orgen) 1917- 112
Hovde, Christian A(rneson) 1922- 5-8R
Hovde, David M. 1952- 236
Hovde, Howard 1928- 25-28R
Hovell, Lucille A. (Peterson) 1916- 5-8R
Hovell, Lucy A.
 See Hovell, Lucille A. (Peterson)
Hoverland, H. Arthur 1928- 45-48
Hoversten, Chester E. 1922- 5-8R
Hovey, E(lwyn) Paul 1908-1996 .... CANR-1
 Earlier sketch in CA 1-4R
Hovey, Kate 234
 See also SATA 158
Hovey, Richard 1864-1900 183
 See also DLB 54
 See also RGAL 4
Hovey, Richard B(ennett) 1917-1995 .... 25-28R
Hovey, Sonya 1888-1960
 Obituary 113
 See also Levien, Sonya
Hoveyda, Fereydoun 1924- 101
 See also EWL 3
Hovick, Rose Louise 1914(?)-1970
 Obituary 113
Hoving, Thomas (Pearsall Field) 1931- CANR-124
 Earlier sketches in CA 101, CANR-72
 Interview in CA-101
Hovre, Roll
 See Jacobsen, Rolf
Howald, Reed Anderson 1930- 57-60
Howar, Barbara 1934- 89-92
 See also AITN 1, 2
Howard, A(rthur) E(llsworth) Dick 1933- 13-16R
Howard, Alan 1922- .... SATA 45
Howard, Alan 1934- CANR-20
 Earlier sketch in CA 37-40R
Howard, Alvin Wendell 1922-1975 ...... 33-36R

Cumulative Index **279** **Howells**

Howard, Alyssa
See Buckholtz, Eileen (Garber) and Glick, Ruth (Burtnick) and Titchener, Louise
Howard, Anthony (Michell) 1934- ... 109
Howard, Audrey 1929- ... 163
See also RHW
Howard, Barbara 1930- ... 53-56
Howard, Ben(jamin Willis) 1944- ... 73-76
Howard, Bill
See Shannon, Mike
Howard, Bion B(radbury) 1912-1994 ... 13-16R
Obituary ... 144
Howard, Blanche 1923- ... 101
Howard, Bronson 1842-1908 ... RGAL 4
Howard, C(hester) Jeriel 1939- ... CANR-31
Earlier sketches in CA 29-32R, CANR-14
Howard, Carleton
See Howe, Charles H(orace)
Howard, Cecil
See Smith, Cecil (Howard III)
Howard, Charles Frederick 1904-1990 . 17-20R
Howard, Christopher 1913- ... 21-24R
Howard, Clark ... 122
See also CMW 4
Howard, Clive (?)-1974
Obituary ... 53-56
Howard, Constance (Mildred) 1910-2000 ... CANR-11
Earlier sketch in CA 69-72
Howard, Coralie
See Cogswell, Coralie (Norris)
Howard, D(erek) L(ionel) 1930- ... CANR-8
Earlier sketch in CA 5-8R
Howard, Daniel F(rancis) 1928- ... 41-44R
Howard, David A. 1942- ... 165
Howard, David M(orris) 1928- ... CANR-10
Earlier sketch in CA 25-28R
Howard, Deborah (Janet) 1946- ... CANR-108
Earlier sketch in CA 124
Howard, Dick 1943- ... 77-80
Howard, Don (Marcel) 1940- ... CANR-22
Earlier sketch in CA 106
Howard, Donald R(oy) 1927-1987 ... CANR-1
Obituary ... 121
Earlier sketch in CA 1-4R
See also DLB 111
Howard, Donald R. 1927-1987 ... 197
Howard, Dorothy (Arlynne) 1912- ... 65-68
Howard, Dorothy Gray 1902-1996 ... 93-96
Howard, Edmund (Bernard Carlo) 1909- . 85-88
Howard, Edward G(arfield) 1918(?)-1972
Obituary ... 104
Howard, Edwin 1924- ... 65-68
Howard, Edwin J(ohnston) 1901-1971 .. CAP-1
Earlier sketch in CA 11-12
Howard, Elizabeth
See Paine, Lauran (Bosworth)
Howard, Elizabeth Fitzgerald 1927- . CANR-97
Earlier sketches in CA 128, CANR-60
See also BW 2
See also SATA 74, 119
Howard, Elizabeth Jane 1923- ... CANR-62
Earlier sketches in CA 5-8R, CANR-8
See also BRWS 11
See also CLC 7, 29
See also CN 1, 2, 3, 4, 5, 6, 7
Howard, Ellen 1943- ... CANR-137
Earlier sketch in CA 130
See also SATA 67, 99
Howard, Evan B. 1955- ... 214
Howard, Frances Minturn
Brief entry ... 111
Howard, Fred D(avid) 1919- ... CANR-19
Earlier sketches in CA 1-4R, CANR-4
Howard, Frederick James 1904-1984 ... 109
Howard, Gerald J(ohn) 1950- ... 108
Howard, Gilbert 1934- ... 49-52
Howard, Harold P. 1905-1990 ... CAP-2
Earlier sketch in CA 33-36
Howard, Harry Nicholas 1902-1987 ... CANR-34
Obituary ... 123
Earlier sketch in CA 49-52
Howard, Hartley
See Ognall, Leopold Horace
Howard, Helen Addison 1904-1989 .. CANR-3
Earlier sketch in CA 5-8R
Howard, Ian P. 1927- ... 21-24R
Howard, J. Grant 1929- ... 125
Howard, J. Woodford, Jr. 1931- ... 33-36R
Howard, James A(rch) 1922- ... CANR-8
Earlier sketch in CA 13-16R
Howard, James H(enri) 1925- ... 41-44R
Howard, James K(enton) 1943- ... 85-88
Howard, James T(homas) 1934- ... 101
Howard, Jane (Temple) 1935-1996 ... CANR-13
Obituary ... 152
Earlier sketch in CA 29-32R
Howard, Jane (Mary) 1959- ... 222
Howard, Jane R(uble) 1924- ... 151
See also SATA 87
Howard, Jean
See MacGibbon, Jean
Howard, Jessica
See Schere, Monroe
Howard, Joan E. 1951- ... 141
Howard, John
See Hewitt, John (Harold)
Howard, John (Arnold) 1916- ... 41-44R
Howard, John R(obert) 1933- ... 53-56
Howard, John Tasker 1890-1964
Obituary ... 89-92
Howard, Joseph
See Rudnick, Paul
Howard, Joseph Leon 1917- ... CANR-1
Earlier sketch in CA 1-4R
Howard, Josephine
See Saxton, Josephine (Mary)
Howard, Joy
See Gorsky, Susan Rubinow
Howard, Joyce 1922- ... 5-8R
Howard, Kathleen L. 1942- ... 176
Howard, Ken(neth Joseph, Jr.) 1944- ... 201
Howard, Kenneth I(rwin) 1932-2000 ... 115
Obituary ... 192
Howard, Kenneth Samuel 1882-1972 ... 9-12R
Obituary ... 103
Howard, Kez
See Houston, David
Howard, Lee M(ilton) 1922- ... 108
Howard, Leigh
See Lee Howard, Leon Alexander
Howard, Leon 1903-1982 ... 109
Howard, Leon Alexander Lee
See Lee Howard, Leon Alexander
Howard, Leslie G(raham) 1947- ... 114
Howard, Linda 1950- ... CANR-135
Earlier sketch in CA 170
See also RHW
Howard, Lowell B(ennett) 1925- ... 13-16R
Howard, M(ichael) C. 1945- ... 142
Howard, Marie
See Lena, Marie H(oward)
Howard, Mark
See Rigsby, Howard
Howard, Mary
See Mussi, Mary
Howard, Maureen 1930- ... CANR-140
Earlier sketches in CA 53-56, CANR-31, 75
Interview in ... CANR-31
See also CLC 5, 14, 46, 151
See also CN 4, 5, 6, 7
See also DLBY 1983
See also MTCW 1, 2
See also MTFW 2005
Howard, Michael (Eliot) 1922- ... CANR-122
Earlier sketches in CA 1-4R, CANR-2
Howard, Michael S. 1922-1974
Obituary ... 53-56
Howard, Moses L(eon) 1928- ... 109
Howard, Munroe 1913-1974 ... CAP-2
Earlier sketch in CA 23-24
Howard, Nona
See Luxton, Leonora Kathrine
Howard, Norman Barry 1949- ... 155
See also SATA 90
Howard, Oliver Otis 1830-1909
Brief entry ... 109
Howard, P. M.
See Howard, Pauline Rodriguez
Howard, Patricia (Lowe) 1937- ... CANR-7
Earlier sketch in CA 17-20R
Howard, Paul 1967- ... SATA 118
Howard, Paul Jack 1908-1984
Obituary ... 113
Howard, Pauline Rodriguez 1951- ... SATA 124
Howard, Peter
See Koch, Howard
Howard, Peter D(unsmore) 1908-1965 . CAP-1
Earlier sketch in CA 11-12
Howard, Philip 1933- ... 65-68
Howard, Philip K. 1948- ... CANR-110
Earlier sketch in CA 153
Howard, Prosper
See Hamilton, Charles (Harold St. John)
Howard, Richard 1929- ... CANR-80
Earlier sketches in CA 85-88, CANR-25
Interview in ... CANR-25
See also AITN 1
See also CLC 7, 10, 47
See also CP 1, 2, 3, 4, 5, 6, 7
See also DLB 5
See also MAL 5
Howard, Richard C. 1929- ... 53-56
Howard, Robert 1626-1698 ... RGEL 2
Howard, Robert 1926- ... 41-44R
Howard, Robert E(rvin) 1906-1936 ... 157
Brief entry ... 105
See also BPFB 2
See also BYA 5
See also FANT
See also SUFW 1
See also TCLC 8
See also TCWW 1, 2
Howard, Robert West 1908-1988 ... CANR-1
Earlier sketch in CA 1-4R
See also SATA 5
Howard, Roger 1938- ... CANR-39
Earlier sketches in CA 93-96, CANR-17
See also CBD
Howard, Ron 1954- ... AAYA 8, 48
Howard, Ronnalie Roper
See Roper, Ronnalie J.
Howard, Ross 1946- ... 120
Howard, Roy Joseph 1925- ... 112
Howard, Roy W(ilson) 1883-1964 ... 235
Obituary ... 89-92
See also DLB 29
Howard, Sidney (Coe) 1891-1939 ... 198
See also DLB 7, 26, 249
See also IDFW 3, 4
See also MAL 5
See also RGAL 4
Howard, Stanley E. 1888(?)-1980
Obituary ... 102
Howard, Ted
See Howard, Theodore Korner
Howard, Theodore Korner 1915- ... 103
Howard, Thomas 1585-1646 ... DLB 213
Howard, Thomas 1930- ... 37-40R
Howard, Thomas T(rumbull) 1935- ... 111
Howard, Todd 1964- ... 204
See also SATA 135
Howard, Tristan
See Currie, Stephen
Howard, Troy
See Paine, Lauran (Bosworth)
Howard, Vanessa 1955- ... 153
See also BW 2, 3
Howard, Vechel
See Rigsby, Howard
Howard, Vernon (Linwood) 1918-1992 ... 108
Obituary ... 139
See also SATA 40
See also SATA-Obit 73
Howard, Walter T. 1951- ... 152
Howard, Warren F.
See Pohl, Frederik
Howard, Warren Starkie 1930- ... 5-8R
Howard-Hassmann, Rhoda E. 1948- ... 157
Howard-Hill, Trevor Howard 1933- ... 85-88
Howard-Williams, Jeremy (Napier) 1922-1995 ... CANR-22
Earlier sketch in CA 106
Howarth, David (Armine) 1912-1991 ... CANR-25
Obituary ... 134
Earlier sketches in CA 13-16R, CANR-9
See also SATA 6
See also SATA-Obit 68
Howarth, Donald 1931- ... 25-28R
See also CBD
See also CD 5, 6
Howarth, Lesley 1952- ... CANR-125
Earlier sketch in CA 153
See also AAYA 29
See also SATA 94
Howarth, Pamela 1954- ... 102
Howarth, Patrick (John Fielding) 1916-2004 ... 77-80
Obituary ... 233
Howarth, Stephen (William Russell) 1953- ... CANR-25
Earlier sketch in CA 107
Howarth, T(homas) E(dward) B(rodie) 1914-1988 ... 141
Obituary ... 125
Howarth, W(illiam) D(river) 1922- ... CANR-82
Earlier sketches in CA 45-48, CANR-35
Howarth, William Louis 1940- ... CANR-134
Earlier sketches in CA 37-40R, CANR-20
Howat, Gerald Malcolm David 1928- ... CANR-16
Earlier sketch in CA 93-96
Howat, John K(eith) 1937- ... CANR-107
Earlier sketch in CA 49-52
Howatch, Joseph 1935- ... 65-68
Howatch, Susan 1940- ... CANR-95
Earlier sketches in CA 45-48, CANR-24, 55
See also AITN 1
See also CPW
See also DAM POP
See also RHW
Howd Machan, Katharyn 1952- ... 207
Howe, C.
See Howe, Christina A.
Howe, Charles H(orace) 1912-1975 ... 53-56
Howe, Charles L. 1932- ... 17-20R
Howe, Christina A. 1974- ... 188
Howe, Christine J. 1948- ... CANR-92
Earlier sketch in CA 146
Howe, Christopher (Barry) 1937- ... 121
Howe, Christy
See Howe, Christina A.
Howe, Christy Filek
See Howe, Christina A.
Howe, Daniel Walker 1937- ... 29-32R
Howe, Deborah 1946-1978 ... 105
See also SATA 29
Howe, Doris Kathleen ... CANR-3
Earlier sketch in CA 49-52
Howe, E(dgar) W(atson) 1853-1937 ... 183
See also DLB 12, 25
See also RGAL 4
Howe, Ellic (Paul) 1910-1991 ... 25-28R
Obituary ... 135
Howe, Fanny (Quincy) 1940- ... 187
Earlier sketches in CA 117, CANR-70, 116
Autobiographical Essay in ... 187
See also CAAS 27
See also CLC 47
See also CP 7
See also CWP
See also SATA-Brief 52
Howe, Florence 1929- ... CANR-136
Brief entry ... 109
Earlier sketch in CA 124
Interview in ... CA-124
Howe, G(eorge) Melvyn 1920- ... 101
Howe, (Richard Edward) Geoffrey 1926- ... 150
Howe, George Frederick 1901-1988
Obituary ... 124
Howe, George Locke 1898(?)-1977
Obituary ... 69-72
Howe, Helen 1905-1975 ... CAP-2
Obituary ... 57-60
Earlier sketch in CA 23-24
Howe, Henry 1816-1893 ... DLB 30
Howe, Hubert S(hattuck), Jr. 1942- ... 57-60
Howe, Irving 1920-1993 ... CANR-50
Obituary ... 141
Earlier sketches in CA 9-12R, CANR-21
See also AMWS 6
See also CLC 85
See also DLB 67
See also EWL 3
See also MAL 5
See also MTCW 1, 2
See also MTFW 2005
Howe, James 1946- ... CANR-71
Earlier sketches in CA 105, CANR-22, 46
See also CLR 9
See also CWRI 5
See also JRDA
See also MAICYA 1, 2
See also SATA 29, 71, 111, 161
Howe, James Robinson 1935- ... 69-72
Howe, James Wong 1899-1976 ... IDFW 3, 4
Howe, John F. 1957- ... SATA 79
Howe, Jonathan Trumbull 1935- ... 29-32R
Howe, Joseph 1804-1873 ... DLB 99
Howe, Josephine (Mary) O'Connor
See O'Connor Howe, Josephine (Mary)
Howe, Julia Ward 1819-1910 ... 191
Brief entry ... 117
See also DLB 1, 189, 235
See also FW
See also TCLC 21
Howe, LeAnne 1951- ... 234
Howe, Leland W(right) 1940- ... 123
Brief entry ... 118
Howe, Louise Kapp 1934-1984
Obituary ... 111
Howe, Marie 1950- ... 165
See also PFS 15
Howe, Mark Anthony DeWolfe 1864-1960
Obituary ... 89-92
Howe, Melodie Johnson ... 169
Howe, Neil 1951- ... CANR-69
Earlier sketch in CA 132
Howe, Nelson 1935- ... 33-36R
Howe, Norma 1930- ... 194
See also AAYA 41
See also SATA 126
Howe, P(ercival) P(resland) 1886-1944 ... 183
See also DLB 149
Howe, Quincy 1900-1977 ... 49-52
Obituary ... 69-72
Howe, R. Brian 1947- ... 214
Howe, Reuel L(anphier) 1905-1985 ... 21-24R
Howe, Richard J. 1937- ... 77-80
Howe, Russell Warren 1925- ... CANR-109
Earlier sketches in CA 49-52, CANR-27
Howe, Stephen 1958- ... 176
Howe, Susan 1937- ... 160
See also AMWS 4
See also CLC 72, 152
See also CP 7
See also CWP
See also DLB 120
See also FW
See also PC 54
See also RGAL 4
Howe, Tina 1937- ... CANR-125
Earlier sketch in CA 109
See also CAD
See also CD 5, 6
See also CLC 48
See also CWD
Howe, W(arren) Asquith 1910-1988 ... 29-32R
Howe, William Hugh 1928- ... 65-68
Howell, Anthony 1945- ... 128
See also CP 2
Howell, Barbara 1937-1994 ... 49-52
Obituary ... 145
Howell, Benjamin Franklin 1890-1976
Obituary ... 65-68
Howell, Bette 1920- ... 130
Howell, Christopher 1945- ... 239
Howell, Clark Sr. 1863-1936 ... 200
See also DLB 25
Howell, Clinton T(almage) 1913-1981 .. 29-32R
Obituary ... 133
Howell, David
See Wynne, John (Stewart)
Howell, David Arthur Russell 1936- ... 109
Howell, Dorothy J(ulia) 1940- ... 142
Howell, Elsworth Seaman 1915-1987
Obituary ... 122
Howell, Evan P(ark) 1839-1905
Brief entry ... 119
See also DLB 23
Howell, Helen (Jane) 1934- ... 57-60
Howell, James 1594(?)-1666 ... DLB 151
Howell, James Edwin 1928- ... CANR-20
Earlier sketch in CA 1-4R
Howell, John
See Hall, Gus
Howell, John C(hristian) 1924- ... CANR-9
Earlier sketch in CA 21-24R
Howell, John M(ichael) 1933- ... 33-36R
Howell, Joseph T(oy III) 1942- ... CANR-24
Earlier sketch in CA 45-48
Howell, Leon 1936- ... 25-28R
Howell, Michael J. 1932(?)-1986
Obituary ... 118
Howell, Pat 1947- ... SATA 15
Howell, Patricia Hagan 1939- ... 81-84
Howell, Paul (Philip) 1917-1994 ... 135
Howell, Peter (Adrian) 1941- ... 128
Howell, Reet 1945- ... 110
Howell, Richard W(esley) 1926- ... 57-60
Howell, Robert Lee 1928- ... 25-28R
Howell, Roger (Jr.) 1936- ... CANR-11
Earlier sketch in CA 21-24R
Howell, S.
See Styles, (Frank) Showell
Howell, Thomas 1944- ... 73-76
Howell, Virginia
See Ellison, Virginia H(owell)
Howell, Warren Richardson 1912-1984 ... DLB 140
Howell, Wilbur Samuel 1904-1992 ... 33-36R
Obituary ... 137
Howell, William C(arl) 1932- ... 93-96
Howells, Coral Ann 1939- ... 197

Howells, J(ames) Harvey 1912-1983 ... 97-100
Howells, John G(wilym) 1918- ... CANR-65
Earlier sketches in CA 21-24R, CANR-9, 24
Howells, Roscoe 1919- ... 104
Howells, W. D.
See Howells, William Dean
Howells, William D.
See Howells, William Dean
Howells, William Dean 1837-1920 ... 134
Brief entry ... 104
See also AMW
See also CDALB 1865-1917
See also DLB 12, 64, 74, 79, 189
See also LMFS 1
See also MAL 5
See also MTCW 2
See also RGAL 4
See also SSC 36
See also TCLC 7, 17, 41
See also TUS
Howells, William White 1908- ... CANR-19
Earlier sketches in CA 1-4R, CANR-2
Hower, Edward 1941- ... 106
Hower, Ralph M(erle) 1903-1973 ... 1-4R
Obituary ... 45-48
Howes, Alan B(arber) 1920-
Brief entry ... 112
Howes, Barbara 1914-1996 ... CANR-53
Obituary ... 151
Earlier sketch in CA 9-12R
See also CAAS 3
See also CLC 15
See also CP 1, 2
See also SATA 5
See also TCLE 1:1
Howes, Connie B. 1933- ... 89-92
Howes, Craig 1955- ... 148
Howes, Edith (Annie) 1874-1954 ... CWRI 5
Howes, Frank Stewart 1891-1974
Obituary ... 115
Howes, Laura L(ouise) 1956- ... 168
Howes, Michael 1904- ... 61-64
Howes, Paul Griswold 1892-1984 ... 29-32R
Obituary ... 113
Howes, Raymond F(loyd) 1903-1986 ... CAP-1
Earlier sketch in CA 17-18
Howes, Robert Gerard 1919- ... CANR-4
Earlier sketch in CA 1-4R
Howes, Royce (Bucknam) 1901-1973 ... CAP-2
Obituary ... 41-44R
Earlier sketch in CA 19-20
Howes, Ruth H. 1944- ... 198
Howes, Wright 1882-1978
Obituary ... 104
Howey, John 1933- ... CANR-110
Earlier sketch in CA 154
Howick, William Henry 1924- ... 33-36R
Howie, Betsy ... 181
Howie, Carl G(ordon) 1920- ... 13-16R
Howie, Diana (Melson) 1945- ... 194
See also SATA 122
Howie, John 1929- ... 189
Howington, Linda S.
See Howard, Linda
Howith, Harry 1934- ... 25-28R
See also CP 1, 2
Howitt, Mary 1799-1888 ... DLB 110, 199
Howitt, William 1792-1879 ... DLB 110
Howitzer, Bronson
See Hardman, Richards Lynden
Howker, Janni 1957- ... 137
See also AAYA 9
See also CLR 14
See also JRDA
See also MAICYA 1, 2
See also SAAS 13
See also SATA 72
See also SATA-Brief 46
See also YAW
Howkins, Heidi 1968(?)- ... 220
Howkins, John 1945- ... CANR-32
Earlier sketches in CA 65-68, CANR-14
Howl, Marcia (Yvonne Hurt) 1947- ... 121
Howland, Bette 1937- ... 85-88
Howland, Ethan 1963- ... 200
See also SATA 131
Howland, Harold Edward 1913-1980
Obituary ... 102
Howlett, D(onald) Roger 1945- ... 135
Howlett, David Robert 1944- ... 210
Howlett, Duncan 1906-2003 ... 107
Obituary ... 216
Howlett, John (Reginald) 1940- ... CANR-12
Earlier sketch in CA 69-72
Howorth, Beckett 1902-1986 ... 114
Howorth, M. K.
See Black, Margaret K(atherine)
Howorth, Muriel ... CAP-1
Earlier sketch in CA 9-10
Howse, Ernest Marshall (Frazer)
1902-1993 ... CANR-43
Earlier sketch in CA 49-52
Howson, Gerald 1925- ... 189
Howson, Susan 1945- ... 113
Howton, F(rank) William 1925- ... 29-32R
Hoxha, Enver 1908-1985 ... 228
Hoxie, Frederick E(ugene) 1947- ... 117
Hoxie, R(alph) Gordon 1919-2002 ... 103
Obituary ... 213
Ho Xuan Huong c. 1775-c. 1820 ... PFS 18
Hoy, Claire 1940- ... CANR-93
Earlier sketch in CA 140
Hoy, Cyrus H. 1926- ... 21-24R
Hoy, David 1930- ... 17-20R
Hoy, Elizabeth ... RHW
Hoy, Helen E. 1949- ... 220
Hoy, James F(ranklin) 1939- ... 57-60
Hoy, John C. 1933- ... CANR-9
Earlier sketch in CA 21-24R
Hoy, Linda 1946- ... CANR-89
Earlier sketch in CA 130
See also SATA 65
See also YAW
Hoy, Nina
See Roth, Arthur J(oseph)
Hoye, Anna Scott 1915- ... 13-16R
Hoyem, Andrew 1935- ... 9-12R
See also CP 1, 2
See also DLB 5
Hoyer, George W. 1919- ... CANR-4
Earlier sketch in CA 1-4R
Hoyer, H(arvey) Conrad 1907-1996 ... 33-36R
Hoyer, Mildred N(aeher) ... 57-60
Hoyers, Anna Ovena 1584-1655 ... DLB 164
Hoyland, Michael 1925- ... 21-24R
Hoyle, Carolyn ... 231
Hoyle, Fred 1915-2001 ... CANR-110
Obituary ... 201
Earlier sketches in CA 5-8R, CANR-3, 29, 55
See also CN 1
See also DLB 261
See also MTCW 1, 2
See also MTFW 2005
See also SCFW 1, 2
See also SFW 4
Hoyle, Geoffrey 1942- ... CANR-29
Earlier sketches in CA 53-56, CANR-6
See also SATA 18
See also SFW 4
Hoyle, Martha Byrd
See Byrd, Martha
Hoyle, Peter 1939- ... 124
Hoyle, Trevor 1940- ... 142
See also SFW 4
Hoyles, J(ames) Arthur 1908-1999 ... 5-8R
Hoyningen-Huene, Paul 1946- ... 145
Hoyos, Angela de 1940(?)- ... 131
See also DLB 82
See also HW 1
Hoyos Salcedo, Pedro (Pablo) 1947- ... 219
Hoyt, Charles 1860-1900 ... RGAL 4
Hoyt, Charles Alva 1931- ... 33-36R
Hoyt, Charles K(ing) 1938- ... 110
Hoyt, Clark 1942- ... 69-72
Hoyt, Edwin P(almer), Jr. 1923- ... CANR-66
Earlier sketches in CA 1-4R, CANR-1
See also SATA 28
Hoyt, Elizabeth E(llis) 1893-1980 ... 37-40R
Hoyt, Erich 1950- ... CANR-142
Earlier sketches in CA 106, CANR-69
See also AAYA 58
See also SATA 65, 140
Hoyt, Herman A(rthur) 1909-2000 ... 29-32R
Hoyt, Homer 1896-1984 ... CANR-1
Obituary ... 114
Earlier sketch in CA 1-4R
Hoyt, Jo Wasson 1927- ... 21-24R
Hoyt, Joseph B(ixby) 1913-1994 ... 5-8R
Hoyt, Kenneth B(oyd) 1924- ... CANR-1
Earlier sketch in CA 45-48
Hoyt, Mary Finch 1924(?)- ... 107
Hoyt, Murray 1904-2001 ... 9-12R
Hoyt, Nelson
See King, Albert
Hoyt, Olga
See Gruhzit-Hoyt, Olga (Margaret)
Hoyt, (Edwin) Palmer 1897-1979
Obituary ... 89-92
See also DLB 127
Hoyt, Richard (Duane) 1941- ... CANR-122
Earlier sketch in CA 129
See also CMW 4
Hoyt, Robert S(tuart) 1918-1971
Obituary ... 111
Hoyt, Sarah (de) A(lmeida) ... 237
Hoyt, Waite (Charles) 1899-1984
Obituary ... 113
Hozeny, Tony 1946- ... 61-64
Hozic, Aida (A.) 1963- ... 233
Hozjusz
See Dobraczynski, Jan
Hrabal, Bohumil 1914-1997 ... CANR-57
Obituary ... 156
Earlier sketch in CA 106
See also CAAS 12
See also CLC 13, 67
See also CWW 2
See also DLB 232
See also EWL 3
See also RGSF 2
See also TCLC 155
Hrabanus Maurus 776(?)-856 ... DLB 148
Hrbek, Greg 1969- ... 198
Hrdlitschka, Shelley 1956- ... 182
See also SATA 111
Hrdy, Sarah Blaffer 1946- ... CANR-86
Earlier sketches in CA 107, CANR-35
Hrebejk, Jan 1967- ... 215
Hribal, C. J. ... 204
Hromadka, Josef L(ukl) 1889-1971 ... CAP-1
Earlier sketch in CA 9-10
Hromic, Alma A. 1963- ... 233
Hronsky, Jozef Ciger 1896-1960 ... DLB 215
See also EWL 3
Hrotsvit of Gandersheim c. 935-c.
1000 ... DLB 148
Hruska-Cortes, Elias 1943- ... 45-48
Hruza, Zdenek 1926- ... 61-64
Hrycej, Tomas 1954- ... 167
Hsia, Adrian (Rue Chun) 1938- ... 77-80
Hsia, C(hih)-T(sing) 1921- ... CANR-17
Earlier sketches in CA 1-4R, CANR-2
Hsia, David Yi-Yung 1925-1972
Obituary ... 33-36R
Hsia, Hsiao
See Liu, Wu-chi
Hsia, Tsi-an 1916-1965 ... CAP-2
Earlier sketch in CA 25-28
Hsiang, Yeh
See Liu, Sydney (Chieh)
Hsiao, Katharine H(uei-Ying Huang)
1923- ... 77-80
Hsiao, Kung-Chuan 1897-1981 ... 1-4R
Hsiao, Li-hung ... 239
Hsiao, Tso-liang 1910- ... 1-4R
Hsi Hsi
See Zhang Yan
Hsiung, James Chieh 1935- ... 37-40R
Hsu, Benedict (Pei-Hsiung) 1933- ... 69-72
Hsu, Chih-mo
See Hsu Chih-mo
Hsu, Cho-yun 1930- ... CANR-9
Earlier sketch in CA 17-20R
Hsu, Feng-Hsiung 1959- ... 215
Hsu, Francis L(ang) K(wang)
1909-1999 ... CANR-16
Obituary ... 188
Earlier sketches in CA 1-4R, CANR-1
Hsu, Immanuel C. Y. 1923- ... 1-4R
Hsu, K.
See Hsu, Kenneth J(inghwa)
Hsu, K. J.
See Hsu, Kenneth J(inghwa)
Hsu, K. Jinghwa
See Hsu, Kenneth J(inghwa)
Hsu, Kai-yu 1922-1982 ... CANR-14
Earlier sketch in CA 21-24R
Hsu, Kenneth J(inghwa) 1929- ... 135
Hsu, Kylie 1957- ... 192
Hsu, Madeleine (DeMory) 1938- ... 157
Hsu, Robert C. 1937- ... 141
Hsu Chih-mo 1897-1931 ... EWL 3
Hsueh, Chun-tu 1922- ... CANR-34
Earlier sketches in CA 41-44R, CANR-15
Hsueh, Tien-tung 1939- ... CANR-92
Earlier sketch in CA 146
Hsun, Lu
See Lu Hsun and
Shu-Jen, Chou
Hsu Ying 1935- ... 124
Htin Aung, U.
See Aung, (Maung) Htin
Hu, Hua-ling 1938- ... 195
Hu, Hung-hsing
See Hu Shih
Hu, Shi Ming
See Hu, Shu Ming
Hu, Shih
See Hu Shih
Hu, Shizhang 1954- ... 177
Hu, Shu Ming 1927- ... 85-88
Hu, Sze-Tsen 1914-1999 ... 41-44R
Hu, Xu-wei 1928- ... 143
Hua, Gu 1942- ... 162
Hua, Jinma
See Ruan, Fang-fu
Huaco, George A. 1927- ... 17-20R
Huang, Alfred 1921- ... CANR-139
Earlier sketch in CA 172
Huang, Benrei 1959- ... SATA 86
Huang, Chun-chieh 1946- ... 151
Huang, Ch'un-ming 1939- ... 193
See also EWL 3
See also RGWL 3
Huang, David S(hih-Li) 1930- ... 9-12R
Huang, Parker (Po-fei) 1914- ... CANR-2
Earlier sketch in CA 45-48
Huang, Philip C(hung-Chih) 1940- ... 127
Obituary ... 105
Huang, Philip C(hung-chih) 1940- ... 194
Huang, Po-fei
See Huang, Parker (Po-fei)
Huang, Ray (Jen-yu) 1918- ... CANR-43
Earlier sketches in CA 61-64, CANR-8
Huang, Stanley S(hang) C(hien) 1923- ... 77-80
Huan Yue
See Shen, Congwen
Hubach, Robert R(ogers) 1916- ... 1-4R
Hubalek, Linda K. 1954- ... 182
See also SATA 111
Huband, Mark 1963- ... CANR-118
Earlier sketch in CA 174
Hubartt, Paul L(eroy) 1919- ... 5-8R
Hubback, David 1916- ... CANR-66
Earlier sketch in CA 128
Hubback, Judith 1917- ... 230
Hubbard, Barbara Marx 1929- ... 103
Hubbard, Bill
See Hubbard, William
Hubbard, Charles M. 1939- ... 171
Hubbard, D(onald) L(ee) 1929- ... 21-24R
Hubbard, David Allan 1928-1996 ... CANR-40
Obituary ... 152
Earlier sketches in CA 33-36R, CANR-16
Hubbard, David G(raham) 1920- ... 33-36R
Hubbard, Dolan 1949- ... CANR-129
Earlier sketch in CA 166
See also BW 3
Hubbard, Don 1926- ... 109
Hubbard, Edward (Horton) 1937-1989 ... 124
Obituary ... 128
Hubbard, Elbert 1856-1915 ... 198
See also DLB 91
Hubbard, Frank T. 1921(?)-1976
Obituary ... 65-68
Hubbard, Freeman (Henry) 1894-1981 ... 5-8R
Hubbard, George (Barron) 1884-1958
Brief entry ... 122
See also Moore, Amos
Hubbard, J(ake) T(imothy) W(illiam)
1935- ... CANR-51
Earlier sketch in CA 124
Hubbard, (Frank Mc)Kin(ney) 1868-1930
Brief entry ... 113
See also DLB 11
Hubbard, L(afayette) Ron(ald)
1911-1986 ... CANR-52
Obituary ... 118
Earlier sketch in CA 77-80
See also AAYA 64
See also CLC 43
See also CPW
See also DA3
See also DAM POP
See also FANT
See also MTCW 2
See also MTFW 2005
See also SFW 4
Hubbard, Lucien 1889(?)-1971
Obituary ... 33-36R
Hubbard, Margaret Ann
See Priley, Margaret (Ann) Hubbard
Hubbard, Michelle Calabro 1953- ... 194
See also SATA 122
Hubbard, P(hilip) M(aitland)
1910-1980 ... CANR-61
Obituary ... 97-100
Earlier sketch in CA 85-88
See also CMW 4
Hubbard, Patricia 1945- ... SATA 124
Hubbard, Paul H. 1900(?)-1983
Obituary ... 109
Hubbard, Preston John 1918- ... 5-8R
Hubbard, (Andrew) Ray 1924-1999 ... 103
Obituary ... 188
Hubbard, Robert Hamilton 1916- ... CANR-21
Earlier sketch in CA 1-4R
Hubbard, Ruth 1924-1991 ... CANR-41
Earlier sketch in CA 116
Hubbard, S. W. ... 238
Hubbard, Steve (Albert) 1957- ... CANR-121
Earlier sketch in CA 163
Hubbard, Susan (Mary) 1951- ... CANR-98
Earlier sketch in CA 138
Hubbard, Thomas K. 1956- ... 136
Hubbard, Thomas Leslie Wallan 1905- . CAP-1
Earlier sketch in CA 13-14
Hubbard, Tom 1950- ... 190
Hubbard, William 1621(?)-1704 ... DLB 24
Hubbard, William 1954- ... 170
Hubbard, Woodleigh Marx ... 165
See also SATA 98, 160
Hubbell, Harriet Weed 1909- ... 5-8R
Hubbell, Harry M. 1881-1971
Obituary ... 29-32R
Hubbell, Helene Johnson
See Johnson, Helene
Hubbell, Jay B(roadus) 1885-1979 ... CANR-17
Obituary ... 116
Earlier sketch in CA 1-4R
Hubbell, John G(erard) 1927- ... 65-68
Hubbell, Lindley Williams 1901-1994 .. CAP-1
Earlier sketch in CA 13-16
Hubbell, Patricia 1928- ... CANR-139
Earlier sketch in CA 17-20R
See also SATA 8, 132
Hubbell, Richard Whittaker
1914-1990 ... 13-16R
Hubbell, Sue 1935- ... CANR-138
Earlier sketches in CA 120, CANR-47
See also ANW
See also MTFW 2005
Hubber, Therese 1764-1829 ... DLB 90
Hubbs, Carl Leavitt 1894-1979
Obituary ... 89-92
Hubbs, G(uy) Ward 1952- ... 114
Hubenka, Lloyd J(ohn) 1931-1982 ... CANR-47
Earlier sketch in CA 49-52
Huber, Evelyne
See Stephens, Evelyne Huber
Huber, Jack T(ravis) 1918- ... 21-24R
Huber, Jeffrey T(odd) 1960- ... CANR-140
Earlier sketch in CA 144
Huber, Joan 1925- ... CANR-13
Earlier sketch in CA 77-80
Huber, Leonard Victor 1903-1984 ... CANR-6
Earlier sketch in CA 57-60
Huber, Morton Wesley 1923- ... 17-20R
Huber, Peter W(illiam) 1952- ... CANR-96
Earlier sketch in CA 128
Huber, Richard M(iller) 1922- ... 33-36R
Huber, Thomas 1937- ... 29-32R
Huber, Thomas Michael 1944- ... 112
Huberman, Edward 1910-1994 ... 13-16R
Huberman, Elizabeth Duncan Lyle
1915- ... 13-16R
Huberman, Leo 1903-1968 ... CANR-4
Earlier sketch in CA 1-4R
Hubert, Cam
See Cameron, (Barbara) Anne
Hubert, James Lee 1947- ... 73-76
Hubert, Jim
See Hubert, James Lee
Hubert, Renee Riese 1916-2005 ... 61-64
Obituary ... 239
Hubin, Allen J. 1936- ... 33-36R
Hubka, Betty (Josephine Morgan)
1924- ... 13-16R
Hubka, Thomas C. 1946- ... 126
Hubler, Clark
See Hubler, H(erbert) C(lark)
Hubler, David 1941- ... 110
Hubler, Edward L(orenzo) 1902-1965 ... CAP-1
Earlier sketch in CA 13-14
Hubler, H(erbert) C(lark) 1910-1998 ... 85-88

Hubler, Richard Gibson 1912-1998 ... CANR-2
Earlier sketch in CA 1-4R
Hubley, Faith Elliot 1924-2001 .... CANR-29
Obituary 204
Earlier sketch in CA 81-84
See also SATA 48
See also SATA-Obit 133
Hubley, John 1914-1977 .... IDFW 3, 4
See also SATA 48
See also SATA-Obit 24
Huby, Pamela M(argaret Clark) 1922- ... 21-24R
Huch, Friedrich (Georg Edmund)
1873-1913 .... DLB 66
Huch, Ricarda (Octavia) 1864-1947 189
Brief entry 111
See also Hugo, Richard
See also DLB 66
See also EWL 3
See also TCLC 13
Huchel, Peter 1903-1981 .... CANR-43
Earlier sketch in CA 81-84
See also EWL 3
Huchthausen, Peter 1939- 225
Huck, Charlotte S. 1922- .... SATA 82, 136
Huck, Gabe (Donald Joseph) 1941- . CANR-30
Earlier sketch in CA 112
Huckaby, Elizabeth (Paisley) 1905-1999 106
Obituary 177
Huckaby, Gerald 1933- 33-36R
Hucker, Charles O(scar) 1919- 69-72
Hucker, Hazel 1937- 149
Huckins, Wesley C. 1918- 21-24R
Huckleberry, E(vermont) R(obbins)
1894-1996 .... CANR-11
Earlier sketch in CA 61-64
Huckshorn, Robert J(ack) 1928- 97-100
Hudak, Michal 1956- 216
See also SATA 143
Hudd, Roy 1936- 105
Huddle, David 1942- CANR-89
Earlier sketch in CA 57-60
See also CAAS 20
See also CLC 49
See also DLB 130
Huddle, Frank, Jr. 1943- 37-40R
Huddleston, Eugene L(ee) 1931- CANR-41
Earlier sketches in CA 102, CANR-19
Huddleston, Lee Eldridge 1935- 21-24R
Huddleston, Mark W. 1950- 154
Huddleston, Rodney D(esmond)
1937- CANR-141
Earlier sketch in CA 33-36R
Huddleston, (Ernest Urban) Trevor
1913-1998 188
Huddy, Delia 1934- CANR-19
Earlier sketch in CA 25-28R
Hudgens, A(lice) Gayle 1941- 37-40R
Hudgins, Andrew (Leon, Jr.) 1951- ... CANR-90
Earlier sketch in CA 132
See also CAAS 21
See also CSW
See also DLB 120, 282
See also PFS 14
Hudgins, H(erbert) C(ornelius), Jr.
1932- 33-36R
Hudgins, Sharon 229
Hudler, Ad 1965(?)- 211
Hudnut, Robert K(ilborne) 1934- CANR-38
Earlier sketches in CA 25-28R, CANR-17
Hudoba, Michael 1913-1984
Obituary 113
Hudon, Edward Gerard 1915- 5-8R
Hudson, Alec
See Holmes, W(ilfred) J(ay)
Hudson, Arthur Palmer 1892(?)-1978
Obituary 111
Hudson, Charles M(elvin, Jr.) 1932- 33-36R
Hudson, Cheryl Willis 1948- .... SATA 81, 160
Hudson, Danny L. 1940- 122
Hudson, Darril 1931- 45-48
Hudson, Derek (Rommel) 1911-2003 ...... 9-12R
Obituary 220
Hudson, Geoffrey Francis 1903-1974
Obituary 49-52
Hudson, Gladys W(atts) 1926- 33-36R
Hudson, Gossie Harold 1930- 93-96
Hudson, Harriet
See Myers, Amy
Hudson, Helen
See Lane, Helen
Hudson, Henry Norman 1814-1886 ..... DLB 64
Hudson, Henry T(homas) 1932- CANR-41
Earlier sketch in CA 118
Hudson, Herman 1923- 97-100
Hudson, James A(lbert) 1924- 33-36R
Hudson, James J(ackson) 1919- 25-28R
Hudson, James R. 1933- 124
Hudson, Jan 1954-1990 136
See also AAYA 22
See also BYA 15
See also CLR 40
See also CWRI 5
See also JRDA
See also MAICYA 2
See also MAICYAS 1
See also SATA 77
Hudson, Jean B(arlow) 1915- 93-96
Hudson, Jeffrey
See Crichton, (John) Michael
Hudson, John A(llen) 1927- 25-28R
Hudson, John B. 1934- 142
Hudson, Kenneth 1916-1999 128
Obituary 188
Brief entry 117
Hudson, (Margaret) Kirsty 1947- 107
See also SATA 32
Hudson, Liam 1933-2005 .... CANR-12
Obituary 236
Earlier sketch in CA 29-32R
Hudson, Lois Phillips 1927- CANR-64
Earlier sketch in CA 1-4R
See also TCWW 2
Hudson, Marc 1947- 116
Hudson, Margaret
See Shuter, Jane (Margaret)
Hudson, Mark 1957- 132
Hudson, Meg
See Koehler, Margaret (Hudson)
Hudson, Michael
See Kube-McDowell, Michael P(aul)
Hudson, Michael C(raig) 1938- 37-40R
Hudson, Michael Huckleberry
1939- CANR-13
Earlier sketch in CA 33-36R
Hudson, Miles (Matthew Lee)
1925- CANR-137
Earlier sketch in CA 132
Hudson, (Arthur) Palmer 1892-1978 ..... CAP-2
Earlier sketch in CA 19-20
Hudson, Peggy
See Herz, Peggy
Hudson, R(obert) Lofton 1910-2002 ...... 13-16R
Hudson, Randolph H(oyt) 1927- 17-20R
Hudson, Richard (McLain, Jr.) 1925- 65-68
Hudson, Robert
See Oleksy, Walter
Hudson, Robert P(aul) 1926- 116
Hudson, Robert Vernon 1932- 109
Hudson, Stephen 1868(?)-1944 203
See also Schiff, Sydney (Alfred)
See also DLB 197
Hudson, Theodore R. 45-48
Hudson, W(illiam) H(enry) 1841-1922 190
Brief entry 115
See also DLB 98, 153, 174
See also RGEL 2
See also SATA 35
See also TCLC 29
Hudson, Wade 1946- CANR-79
Earlier sketch in CA 142
See also BW 2, 3
See also SATA 74, 162
Hudson, Wilma J(ones) 1916- 33-36R
Hudson, Wilson Mathis 1907- 102
Hudson, Winthrop Still 1911-2001 ..... CANR-2
Earlier sketch in CA 1-4R
Hudspeth, Robert N. 1936- 103
Huebel, Harry Russell 1943- 77-80
Huebener, Theodore 1895-1983
Obituary 111
Huebner, Anna (Ismelda Mathews)
1877(?)-1974
Obituary 53-56
Huebner, Fredrick D. 1955- CANR-140
Earlier sketch in CA 133
Huebner, Klaus H(ermann) 1916- 126
Huebner, Kurt 1921- 132
Huebner, Timothy S. 1966- 207
Hueffer, Ford Madox
See Ford, Ford Madox
Hueffer, Oliver Franz
See Hueffer, Oliver Madox
Hueffer, Oliver Madox 1876-1931 ..... DLB 197
Huegli, A(lbert) G(eorge) 1913-1998 ..... 13-16R
Huelden, Lars
See Hulden, Lars
Huelsman, Richard J(oseph) 1921- 111
Huelsmann, Carl (H.) 1914- CANR-86
Earlier sketch in CA 130
Huelsmann, Eva 1928- .... SATA 16
Huene, Paul Hoyningen
See Hoyningen-Huene, Paul
Huerlimann, Bettina 1909-1983 109
Obituary 110
See also Hurlimann, Bettina
See also MAICYA 1, 2
Huerlimann, Ruth 1939- 107
See also Hurlimann, Ruth
Huerta, Jorge
See Huerta, Jorge A(lfonso)
Huerta, Jorge A(lfonso) 1942- 131
See also HW 1
Huessy, Hans R. 1921- 21-24R
Hueston, Frederick M. 1953- 153
Hueston, Marie Proeller 237
Huet, Pierre-Daniel
1630-1721 .... GFL Beginnings to 1789
Hueter, John E(dwin) 1918- 114
Huether, Anne Frances
See Freeman, Anne Frances
Huey, F. B., Jr. 1925- CANR-47
Earlier sketches in CA 106, CANR-23
Huey, John (Wesley, Jr.) 1948- 144
Huey, Lynda 1947- 65-68
Hufana, A(lejandrino) G. 1926- 77-80
See also CP 1, 2, 3, 4, 5, 6, 7
Hufbauer, Karl (George) 1937- 109
Huff, Afton (A.) W(alker) 1928- 65-68
Huff, Barbara A. 1929- 135
See also SATA 67
Huff, Betty Tracy 25-28R
Huff, Brent 1961- 226
Huff, Darrell 1913-2001 .... CANR-5
Earlier sketch in CA 1-4R
Huff, Richard (M.) 1962- CANR-136
Earlier sketch in CA 139
Huff, Robert 1924- CANR-6
Earlier sketch in CA 13-16R
See also CP 1, 2
Huff, T(om) E. 1938(?)- 93-96
See also AITN 2
Huff, T. S.
See Huff, Tanya (Sue)
Huff, Tanya (Sue) 1957- CANR-136
Earlier sketches in CA 128, CANR-58
See also AAYA 38
See also FANT
See also SATA 85
Huff, Toby E. 1942- CANR-107
Earlier sketch in CA 149
Huff, Vaughn E(dward) 1935- 29-32R
Huff, Vivian 1948- .... SATA 59
Huffaker, Clair 1926(?)-1990 .... CANR-63
Obituary 131
Earlier sketch in CA 113
See also TCWW 1, 2
Huffaker, Sandy 1943- .... SATA 10
Huffard, Grace Thompson 1892-1989 .. CAP-1
Earlier sketch in CA 11-12
Huffer, Lynne 1960- 143
Huffert, Anton M. 1912-1982 .... 13-16R
Huffey, Rhoda 1948- 210
Huffington, Arianna Stassinopoulos
1950- CANR-95
Earlier sketch in CA 129
Huffman, Carolyn 1928- 69-72
Huffman, Claire (De Cesare Licari) 116
Huffman, Franklin E(ugene) 1934- CANR-12
Earlier sketch in CA 29-32R
Huffman, James Lamar 1941- 102
Huffman, Jennifer Lee 1950- 170
Huffman, Laurie 1916- 45-48
Huffman, Suzanne 1951- 220
Huffman, Tom .... SATA 24
Hufford, Susan 1940- CANR-9
Earlier sketch in CA 57-60
See also RHW
Hufschmidt, Maynard Michael
1912- CANR-47
Earlier sketches in CA 41-44R, CANR-15
Hufstader, Jonathan 1939- 210
Hufton, Olwen H. 1938- 21-24R
Hug, Bernal D(ean) 1896-1987 57-60
Hugdahl, Kenneth 1948- 163
Huggan, Isabel 1943- 119
Huggett, Frank E(dward) 1924- CANR-19
Earlier sketches in CA 9-12R, CANR-3
Huggett, Joyce 1937- 126
Huggett, Richard 1929- CANR-89
Earlier sketch in CA 53-56
Huggett, William Turner 1939(?)-2004 53-56
Huggins, Alice Margaret 1891-1971 ...... CAP-1
Earlier sketch in CA 17-18
Huggins, Charles B(renton) 1901-1997
Obituary 156
Brief entry 115
Huggins, James Byron 1959- 170
Huggins, Nathan Irvin 1927-1989 .... CANR-25
Obituary 130
Earlier sketch in CA 29-32R
See also BW 1
See also SATA 63
Hughart, Barry 1934- 137
See also CLC 39
See also FANT
See also SFW 4
See also SUFW 2
Hughes, Agatha C(hipley) 1924-1997 145
Hughes, Alan 1935- 97-100
Hughes, Albert 1972- .... AAYA 51
Hughes, Alice 1899(?)-1977
Obituary 104
Hughes, Allen 1972- .... AAYA 51
Hughes, Andrew 1937- 61-64
Hughes, Angela 1926- 192
Hughes, Anthony John 1933- 9-12R
Hughes, Arthur Joseph 1928- 17-20R
Hughes, Arthur Montague D'Urban 1873-1974
Obituary 49-52
Hughes, B(asil) P(erronet) 1903-1989 61-64
Hughes, Babette 1927- CANR-101
Earlier sketch in CA 29-32R
Hughes, C(hristopher) J(ohn) 1918- 17-20R
Hughes, C. J. Pennethorne
See Hughes, (Charles James) Pennethorne
Hughes, Carol 1955- 178
See also SATA 108
Hughes, Catharine R(achel)
1935-1987 .... CANR-27
Obituary 123
Earlier sketch in CA 41-44R
Hughes, Charles C(ampbell) 1929- 41-44R
Hughes, Charles L(loyd) 1933- CANR-11
Earlier sketch in CA 17-20R
Hughes, Cheri Lynn 1957- .... SFW 4
Hughes, (John) Cledwyn 1920-1978 ..... 13-16R
Obituary 126
Hughes, Colin
See Creasey, John
Hughes, Colin A(nfield) 1930- CANR-50
Earlier sketches in CA 21-24R, CANR-9, 25
Hughes, D. T.
See Hughes, Dean
Hughes, Daniel 1929- 33-36R
Hughes, Daniel T(homas) 1930- 89-92
Hughes, David (John) 1930-2005 129
Obituary 238
Brief entry 116
See also CLC 48
See also CN 4, 5, 6, 7
See also DLB 14
Hughes, Dean 1943- CANR-22
Earlier sketch in CA 106
See also AAYA 53
See also CLR 76
See also SATA 33, 77, 139
See also YAW
Hughes, Dean Aubrey 1908(?)-1987
Obituary 122
Hughes, Dorothy (Berry) 1910-1980 ..... CAP-2
Earlier sketch in CA 33-36
Hughes, Dorothy B(elle) 1904-1993 . CANR-60
Obituary 141
Earlier sketch in CA 104
See also CMW 4
Hughes, Douglas A(llan) 1938- 29-32R
Hughes, Dusty
See Hughes, Richard Holland
See also CBD
See also CD 5, 6
See also DLB 233
Hughes, Eden
See Butterworth, W(illiam) E(dmund III)
Hughes, Edward James
See Hughes, Ted
See also DA3
See also DAM MST, POET
Hughes, Elizabeth
See Zachary, Hugh
Hughes, Emmet John 1920-1982 69-72
Obituary 107
Hughes, Erica 1931- CANR-28
Earlier sketch in CA 109
Hughes, Everett Cherrington 1897-1983 103
Obituary 108
Hughes, Felicity 1938- 33-36R
Hughes, Frieda 1960- 187
Hughes, G(eorge) E(dward) 1918- 21-24R
Hughes, Gerald (Thomas) 1930- 117
Hughes, Gerard J. 227
Hughes, Gervase 1905- 9-12R
Hughes, Glenn 1951- 143
Hughes, Glyn 1935- CANR-35
Earlier sketches in CA 33-36R, CANR-13
See also CP 2, 3, 4, 5, 6, 7
Hughes, Graham 1928- 57-60
Hughes, Gwilym Fielden 1899- 97-100
Hughes, H(enry) Stuart 1916-1999 ..... CANR-2
Earlier sketch in CA 1-4R
Hughes, Harold K(enneth) 1911-1993 ..... 9-12R
Hughes, (Harvey) Hatcher 1881-1945 227
See also DLB 249
Hughes, Heather 1954- 133
Hughes, Helen (Gintz) 1928- 13-16R
Hughes, Holly 1955- .... GLL 2
Hughes, Howard (Robard) 1905-1976
Obituary 112
Hughes, Howard C. 222
Hughes, Irene Finger 103
Hughes, J(ohnson) Donald 1932- CANR-10
Earlier sketch in CA 65-68
Hughes, James Monroe 1890-1971 .... 1-4R
Obituary 103
Hughes, James Pennethorne
See Hughes, (Charles James) Pennethorne
Hughes, James W(ilfred) 1934- 77-80
Hughes, John 1677-1720 .... DLB 84
See also RGEL 2
Hughes, (Robert) John 1930- CANR-4
Earlier sketch in CA 1-4R
Hughes, John 1950(?)- 129
Brief entry 124
See also AAYA 7
Hughes, John A(nthony) 1941- 41-44R
Hughes, John Jay 1928- 57-60
Hughes, John L(ewis) 1938- 77-80
Hughes, John Paul 1920-1974 .... 1-4R
Obituary 53-56
Hughes, Jonathan R(oberts) T(yson)
1928-1992 81-84
Obituary 137
Hughes, Judith M(arkham) 1941- 33-36R
Hughes, Judy 1943- 69-72
Hughes, Kathleen W. 1927(?)-1977
Obituary 69-72
Hughes, Kathryn 1959- 191
Hughes, Ken(neth Graham)
1922-2001 .... CANR-39
Obituary 194
Earlier sketches in CA 5-8R, CANR-16
Hughes, (James Mercer) Langston
1902-1967 .... CANR-82
Obituary 25-28R
Earlier sketches in CA 1-4R, CANR-1, 34
See also AAYA 12
See also AFAW 1, 2
See also AMWR 1
See also AMWS 1
See also BLC 2
See also BW 1, 3
See also CDALB 1929-1941
See also CLC 1, 5, 10, 15, 35, 44, 108
See also CLR 17
See also DA
See also DA3
See also DAB
See also DAC
See also DAM DRAM, MST, MULT, POET
See also DC 3
See also DFS 6, 18
See also DLB 4, 7, 48, 51, 86, 228, 315
See also EWL 3
See also EXPP
See also EXPS
See also HR 1:2
See also JRDA
See also LAIT 3
See also LMFS 2
See also MAICYA 1, 2
See also MAL 5
See also MTCW 1, 2
See also MTFW 2005
See also NFS 21
See also PAB
See also PC 1, 53
See also PFS 1, 3, 6, 10, 15

See also RGAL 4
See also RGSF 2
See also SATA 4, 33
See also SSC 6
See also SSFS 4, 7
See also TUS
See also WCH
See also WLC
See also WP
See also YAW
Hughes, Leo 1908-1995 .... 41-44R
Hughes, Libby .... SATA 71
Hughes, Lindsey 1949- CANR-144
Earlier sketch in CA 174
Hughes, Louis 1832-(?) 229
Hughes, Margaret Kelly 1894(?)-1980
Obituary 101
Hughes, Marija Matich 97-100
Hughes, Mary 1951- 122
Hughes, Mary Gray 1930-1999 61-64
Obituary 185
Hughes, Mary Louise 1910-1996 .... 29-32R
Hughes, Matilda
See MacLeod, Charlotte (Matilda)
Hughes, Matthew 1965- 210
Hughes, Merrit Y(erkes) 1893-1970 .... CAP-1
Earlier sketch in CA 17-18
Hughes, Monica (Ince) 1925-2003 . CANR-110
Earlier sketches in CA 77-80, CANR-23, 46
See also AAYA 19
See also BYA 6, 14, 15
See also CLR 9, 60
See also JRDA
See also MAICYA 1, 2
See also SAAS 11
See also SATA 15, 70, 119, 162
See also WYA
See also YAW
Hughes, Nathaniel Cheairs, Jr. 1930- 17-20R
Hughes, Owain (Gardner Collingwood)
1943- 21-24R
Hughes, Patrick 1939- 61-64
Hughes, Paul L(ester) 1915- 9-12R
Hughes, (Charles James) Pennethorne
1907-1967 .... CAP-2
Earlier sketch in CA 21-22
Hughes, Philip 1895-1967 .... CAP-2
Earlier sketch in CA 17-18
Hughes, Philip Edgcumbe 1915- CANR-18
Earlier sketches in CA 9-12R, CANR-3
Hughes, (James) Quentin 1920-2004 . CANR-6
Obituary 227
Earlier sketch in CA 13-16R, 29-31R
Hughes, R(ichard) E(dward) 1927- CANR-6
Earlier sketch in CA 5-8R
Hughes, Rhys H(enry) 1966- 172
See also SUFW 2
Hughes, Richard (Arthur Warren)
1900-1976 .... CANR-4
Obituary 65-68
Earlier sketch in CA 5-8R
See also CLC 1, 11
See also CN 1, 2
See also DAM NOV
See also DLB 15, 161
See also EWL 3
See also MTCW 1
See also RGEL 2
See also SATA 8
See also SATA-Obit 25
Hughes, Richard 1906-1984
Obituary 111
Hughes, Richard 1941- 107
Hughes, Richard (Edward) 1950- 156
Hughes, Richard Holland 1947- 131
See also Hughes, Dusty
Hughes, Richard T(homas) 1943- ... CANR-115
Earlier sketch in CA 154
Hughes, Riley 1914-1981 107
Obituary 103
Hughes, Robert 1929(?)-1972
Obituary 37-40R
Hughes, Robert (Studley Forrest) 1938(?)- ... 112
Brief entry 110
Hughes, Russell C. 1893(?)-1982
Obituary 108
Hughes, Russell Meriwether 1898(?)-1988
Obituary 124
Hughes, Sam
See Wilks, Brian
Hughes, Sara
See Saunders, Susan
Hughes, Sean 1965- 162
Hughes, Shirley 1927- CANR-144
Earlier sketches in CA 85-88, CANR-24, 47
See also CLR 15
See also CWRI 5
See also MAICYA 1, 2
See also SATA 16, 70, 110, 159
Hughes, Stella 1916- 127
Hughes, Stephen Ormsby 1924- 61-64
Hughes, Ted 1930-1998 .... CANR-108
Obituary 171
Earlier sketches in CA 1-4R, CANR-1, 33, 66
See also Hughes, Edward James
See also BRWC 2
See also BRWR 2
See also BRWS 1
See also CLC 2, 4, 9, 14, 37, 119
See also CLR 3
See also CP 1, 2, 3, 4, 5, 6
See also DAB
See also DAC
See also DLB 40, 161
See also EWL 3
See also EXPP
See also MAICYA 1, 2
See also MTCW 1, 2
See also MTFW 2005
See also PAB
See also PC 7
See also PFS 4, 19
See also RGEL 2
See also SATA 49
See also SATA-Brief 27
See also SATA-Obit 107
See also TEA
See also YAW
Hughes, Terry A. 1933- 65-68
Hughes, Theodore E(rmond) 1942- .. CANR-40
Earlier sketch in CA 116
Hughes, Thomas 1822-1896 .... BYA 3
See also DLB 18, 163
See also LAIT 2
See also RGEL 2
See also SATA 31
Hughes, Thomas M(ears) 1927- 65-68
Hughes, Thomas P(arke) 1923- CANR-96
Earlier sketches in CA 29-32R, CANR-47
Hughes, Tracy
See Blackstock, Terri
Hughes, Virginia
See Campbell, Hope
Hughes, Walter (Llewellyn)
1910-1993 .... CANR-1
Earlier sketch in CA 1-4R
See also SATA 26
Hughes, William J., Jr. 1897(?)-1974
Obituary 45-48
Hughes, William W(auters) 1918- 126
Hughes, Zach
See Zachary, Hugh
Hughes, Zachary
See Zachary, Hugh
Hughes-Hallett, Lucy 1951- 138
Hughey, Roberta 1942- .... SATA 61
Hughey, Ruth Willard 1899-1980 .... 1-4R
Hugh of St. Victor c. 1096-1141 .... DLB 208
Hugill, Stan(ley) James 1906-1992 .... CAP-2
Earlier sketch in CA 23-24
Hugo, Etienne
See Hugo, Leon (Hargreaves)
Hugo, Grant
See Cable, James (Eric)
Hugo, Herbert W. 1930(?)-1979
Obituary 89-92
Hugo, Leon (Hargreaves) 1931- 192
Hugo, Lynne
See deCourcy, Lynne Hugo
Hugo, Pierre Brackers de
See Brackers de Hugo, Pierre
Hugo, Richard
See Huch, Ricarda (Octavia)
See also MAL 5
Hugo, Richard F(ranklin) 1923-1982 .. CANR-3
Obituary 108
Earlier sketch in CA 49-52
See also AMWS 6
See also CLC 6, 18, 32
See also CP 1, 2
See also DAM POET
See also DLB 5, 206
See also EWL 3
See also PC 68
See also PFS 17
See also RGAL 4
Hugo, Victor (Marie) 1802-1885 .... AAYA 28
See also DA
See also DA3
See also DAB
See also DAC
See also DAM DRAM, MST, NOV, POET
See also DLB 119, 192, 217
See also EFS 2
See also EW 6
See also EXPN
See also GFL 1789 to the Present
See also LAIT 1, 2
See also NFS 5, 20
See also PC 17
See also RGWL 2, 3
See also SATA 47
See also TWA
See also WLC
Hugon, Anne 1965- 145
Huhne, Christopher 1954- CANR-86
Earlier sketch in CA 133
Huhta, James K(enneth) 1937- 37-40R
Hu Hung-hsing
See Hu Shih
Huidobro, Vicente
See Huidobro Fernandez, Vicente Garcia
See also DLB 283
See also EWL 3
See also LAW
Huidobro Fernandez, Vicente Garcia
1893-1948 131
See also Huidobro, Vicente
See also HW 1
See also TCLC 31
Huie, William Bradford 1910-1986 .... CANR-7
Obituary 121
Earlier sketch in CA 9-12R
See also AITN 1
See also CN 1, 2, 3, 4
Huie, William O(rr) 1911-1999 .... 21-24R
Huisken, Ronald H(erman) 1946- 93-96
Huizenga, John R(obert) 1921- 144
Huizinga, Johan 1872-1945 161
Hukanovic, Rezak 1950- 192
Hula, Harold L. 1930- 25-28R
Hulbert, Ann 1956- 138
Hulbert, Jack 1892-1978
Obituary 115
Hulda
See Bjarklind, Unnur Benekiktsdottir
See also DLB 293
Hulden, Lars 1926- 192
See also EWL 3
Huler, Scott 237
Hulet, Claude Lyle 1920- CANR-9
Earlier sketch in CA 53-56
Hulicka, Irene M(ackintosh) 1927- 37-40R
Hulicka, Karel 1913- 41-44R
Huline-Dickens, Frank William 1931- 107
See also SATA 34
Hulke, Malcolm 1924-1979 81-84
Obituary 171
Hull, Cary Schuler 1946- 106
Hull, Charles
See Charles, Gordon H(ull)
Hull, David L(ee) 1935- 77-80
Hull, David Stewart 1938-(?) 25-28R
Hull, Denison Bingham 1897-1988 ...... 37-40R
Hull, E(dith) M(aude) .... RHW
Hull, Eleanor (Means) 1913- CANR-19
Earlier sketches in CA 9-12R, CANR-4
See also SATA 21
Hull, Eric Traviss
See Harnan, Terry
Hull, Eugene L(eslie) 1928- 37-40R
Hull, George F. 1909(?)-1974
Obituary 53-56
Hull, Gloria T(heresa Thompson)
1944- CANR-25
Earlier sketch in CA 108
See also BW 2
Hull, H. Braxton
See Jacobs, Helen Hull
Hull, Helen (Rose) 1888(?)-1971 .... CAP-1
Obituary 29-32R
Earlier sketch in CA 9-10
Hull, Isabel V. 1949- 156
Hull, J(ohn) H(owarth) E(ric) 1923- 25-28R
Hull, Jesse Redding
See Hull, Jessie Redding
Hull, Jessie Redding 1932- 109
See also SATA 51
Hull, John M. 1935- 137
Hull, Jonathan 232
Hull, Katharine 1921-1977 .... 29-32R
See also CWRI 5
See also SATA 23
Hull, Lise (E.) 1954- 222
See also SATA 148
Hull, Lynda (K.) 1954-1994 126
Obituary 145
Hull, Marion A(da) 1911- 105
Hull, Maureen 1949- 213
See also SATA 142
Hull, Opal
See Lehnus, Opal (Hull)
Hull, Oswald 1919- 25-28R
Hull, R(ichard) F(rancis) C(arrington)
1913(?)-1974
Obituary 53-56
Hull, Raymona E. 1907-1997 116
Hull, Raymond 1919-1985 .... CANR-11
Obituary 116
Earlier sketch in CA 25-28R
Hull, Richard 1896-1973
See Sampson, Richard Henry
See also CMW 4
See also DLB 77
Hull, Richard W. 1940- CANR-25
Earlier sketch in CA 45-48
Hull, Roger H. 1942- 25-28R
Hull, Suzanne W(hite) 1921- 125
Hull, William (Doyle) 1918- CANR-5
Earlier sketch in CA 13-16R
Hull, William E(dward) 1930- CANR-24
Earlier sketches in CA 17-20R, CANR-7
Hulland, J(ennifer) R(osemary) 1936- 122
Hulley, Clarence C(harles) 1905-1981 .. 41-44R
Hulme, Ann
See Granger, (Patricia) Ann
Hulme, Derek C(rawshaw) 1924- 239
Hulme, George 1930- 215
Hulme, Hilda Mary 1914- 77-80
Hulme, Joy N. 1922- 184
See also SATA 74, 112, 161
Hulme, Kathryn 1900-1981 .... CAP-1
Obituary 104
Earlier sketch in CA 9-10
Hulme, Keri 1947- CANR-69
Earlier sketch in CA 125
Interview in CA-125
See also CLC 39, 130
See also CN 4, 5, 6, 7
See also CP 7
See also CWP
See also EWL 3
See also FW
Hulme, Peter 228
Hulme, T(homas) E(rnest) 1883-1917 203
Brief entry 117
See also BRWS 6
See also DLB 19
See also TCLC 21
Hulme, William E(dward) 1920- CANR-5
Earlier sketch in CA 13-16R
Hulse, Clark 1947- 106
Hulse, Erroll 1931- CANR-21
Earlier sketch in CA 104
Hulse, James Warren 1930- 9-12R
Hulse, (Herman) LaWayne 1922- 29-32R
Hulse, Michael (William) 1955- CANR-97
Earlier sketches in CA 118, CANR-43
See also CP 7
Hulse, Stewart H(arding), Jr. 1931- ... CANR-14
Earlier sketch in CA 33-36R
Hulsey, Byron C. 1967- 214
Hulsker, Jan 1907-2002 144
Hult, Karen M(arie) 1956- 151
Hult, Ruby El 1912- 57-60
Hultberg, Peer 1935- 195
See also EWL 3
Hulteng, John L. 1921- CANR-13
Earlier sketch in CA 33-36R
Hultgren, Arland J(ohn) 1939- 215
Hultgren, Thor 1902-1975 .... CAP-1
Earlier sketch in CA 17-18
Hultkrantz, Aake G. B. 1920- 130
Hultkrantz, Ake G. B.
See Hultkrantz, Aake G. B.
Hultman, Charles W(illiam) 1930- CANR-1
Earlier sketch in CA 1-4R
Hulton, Anne (?)-1779(?) .... DLB 200
Hults, Dorothy Niebrugge 1898-2000 ... CAP-1
Earlier sketch in CA 9-10
See also SATA 6
Humbaraci, D(emir) Arslan 1923- 49-52
Humbard, (Alpha) Rex (Emmanuel) 1919-
Brief entry 111
Humber, William 1949- CANR-51
Earlier sketch in CA 124
Humbert, Marie-Therese 1940- .... EWL 3
Humble, Richard 1945- CANR-17
Earlier sketches in CA 45-48, CANR-2
See also SATA 60
Humble, William F(rank) 1948- 21-24R
Humboldt, Alexander von 1769-1859 .. DLB 90
Humboldt, Wilhelm von 1767-1835 .... DLB 90
Hume, Alexander c. 1560-1609 .... RGEL 2
Hume, Arthur W. J. G. Ord
See Ord-Hume, Arthur W. J. G.
Hume, Basil
See Hume, George Haliburton
Hume, (Alexander) Brit(ton) 1943- 126
Brief entry 119
Interview in CA-126
Hume, Christine 1968- 215
Hume, David 1711-1776 .... BRWS 3
See also DLB 104, 252
See also LMFS 1
See also TEA
Hume, Fergus(on Wright) 1859-1932
Brief entry 109
See also CMW 4
See also DLB 70
Hume, George Haliburton 1923-1999 126
Obituary 181
Hume, John E. N., Jr. 1915-1986
Obituary 118
Hume, John Robert 1939- 106
Hume, Kathryn 1945- 57-60
Hume, L(eonard) J(ohn) 1926-1993 135
Hume, Lotta Carswell CAP-1
Earlier sketch in CA 9-10
See also SATA 7
Hume, Mark 179
Hume, Martha 1947- 112
Hume, Paul Chandler 1915-2001 102
Obituary 204
Hume, Robert D. 1944- CANR-135
Earlier sketches in CA 29-32R, CANR-12
Hume, Ruth Fox 1922-1980
Obituary 97-100
See also SATA 26
See also SATA-Obit 22
Hume, Sophia 1702-1774 .... DLB 200
Hume, Stephen Eaton 1947- CANR-115
Earlier sketch in CA 125
See also SATA 136
Hume-Rothery, Mary Catherine
1824-1885 .... DLB 240
Humes, D(ollena) Joy 1921- 1-4R
Humes, Edward 203
See also MTFW 2005
Humes, H(arold) L. 1926-1992 .... 5-8R
Humes, Harry 1935- 187
Humes, James C. 1934- CANR-1
Earlier sketch in CA 45-48
Humes, John Portner 1921-1985
Obituary 117
Humes, Samuel 1930- 5-8R
Humez, Jean McMahon 1944- 124
Humez, Nicholas (David) 1948- 145
Humez, Nick
See Humez, Nicholas (David)

Cumulative Index 283 Hunter

Humfrey, C.
See Osborne, C(harles) H(umfrey) C(aulfeild)
Humfrey, (James) Michael 1936- 127
Hum-Ishu-Ma
See Mourning Dove
Hummel, Berta 1909-1946 .... SATA 43
Hummel, Charles E. 1923- 17-20R
Hummel, Jeffrey Rogers 1949- 156
Hummel, Madeline
See Moore, Madeline (Roberta)
Hummel, Monte 1946- 135
Hummel, Ray O(rvin), Jr. 1909- 33-36R
Hummel, Ruth Stevenson 1929- 5-8R
Hummel, Sister Maria Innocentia
See Hummel, Berta
Hummer, T(erry) R. 1950- 128
See also CP 7
See also CSW
See also DLB 120
Humphreville, Frances Tibbetts 1909- 9-12R
Humphrey 1391-1447 .... DLB 213
Humphrey, Carol Sue 1956- 142
Humphrey, David C(hurchill) 1937- 85-88
Humphrey, Doris 1895-1958 208
Humphrey, Henry (III) 1930- 77-80
See also SATA 16
Humphrey, Hubert H(oratio)
1911-1978 .... CANR-43
Obituary 73-76
Earlier sketch in CA 69-72
Humphrey, J(ames) Edward 1918- 93-96
Humphrey, James (Earl) 1939- CANR-47
Earlier sketch in CA 45-48
Humphrey, James H(arry) 1911- CANR-48
Earlier sketches in CA 61-64, CANR-8, 23
Humphrey, Kate
See Forsyth, Kate
Humphrey, Mary Ann 1943- 134
Humphrey, Michael (Edward) 1926- 29-32R
Humphrey, Paul 1915- 110
Humphrey, Phyllis
See Ashworth, Phyll
Humphrey, Robert (W.) 1947- 198
Humphrey, Robert L. 1923- 57-60
Humphrey, Sandra McLeod 1936- .. CANR-137
Earlier sketch in CA 160
See also SATA 95
Humphrey, William 1924-1997 .... CANR-68
Obituary 160
Earlier sketch in CA 77-80
See also AMWS 9
See also CLC 45
See also CN 1, 2, 3, 4, 5, 6
See also CSW
See also DLB 6, 212, 234, 278
See also TCWW 1, 2
Humphreys, A(rthur) R(aleigh) 1911-1988
Obituary 126
Humphreys, Alexander J(eremiah)
1913-1991 .... 33-36R
Humphreys, Alice Lee 1893-1976 .... 5-8R
Humphreys, (Travers) Christmas
1901-1983 77-80
Obituary 109
Humphreys, David 1752-1818 .... DLB 37
Humphreys, Emyr Owen 1919- CANR-24
Earlier sketches in CA 5-8R, CANR-3
See also CLC 47
See also CN 1, 2, 3, 4, 5, 6, 7
See also DLB 15
Humphreys, George G(ary) 1949- 138
Humphreys, Graham 1945- .... SATA-Brief 32
Humphreys, Helen (Caroline) 1961- 201
Humphreys, J(ohn) R(ichard Adams)
1918-2003 .... CANR-50
Obituary 219
Earlier sketches in CA 1-4R, CANR-22
Humphreys, Josephine 1945- CANR-97
Brief entry 121
Earlier sketch in CA 127
Interview in CA-127
See also CLC 34, 57
See also CSW
See also DLB 292
Humphreys, (Robert Allan) Laud
1930-1988 .... 29-32R
Obituary 126
Humphreys, Margaret 1955- CANR-93
Earlier sketch in CA 146
Humphreys, Martha 1943- .... SATA 71
Humphreys, Mary Eglantyne Hill
1914- CANR-6
Earlier sketch in CA 5-8R
Humphreys, R(obert) A(rthur) 1907-1999 ... 129
Obituary 179
Humphreys, Richard Stephen 1942- 195
Humphreys, Robin
See Humphreys, R(obert) A(rthur)
Humphreys, Susan L.
See Lowell, Susan
Humphreyville, Theresa R. 1918- 13-16R
Humphries, Adelaide M. 1898- CAP-1
Earlier sketch in CA 13-16
Humphries, Barry 1934- 129
Humphries, Helen Speirs Dickie 1915- . CAP-1
Earlier sketch in CA 9-10
Humphries, (John) Jefferson 1955- CANR-36
Earlier sketch in CA 114
Humphries, Mary 1905- 53-56
Humphries, Patrick 184
Humphries, (George) Rolfe
1894-1969 .... CANR-3
Obituary 25-28R
Earlier sketch in CA 5-8R
Humphries, Sydney Vernon 1907- 103
Humphry, Derek 1930- CANR-105
Earlier sketches in CA 41-44R, CANR-41
Humphrys, Geoffrey
See Humphrys, Leslie George
Humphrys, Leslie George 1921- 107
Humpstone, Charles Cheney 1931- 49-52
Hunayn ibn Ishaq 809-873(?) .... DLB 311
Huncke, Herbert E(dwin)
1915-1996 .... CANR-61
Obituary 153
Earlier sketch in CA 130
See also AMWS 14
See also BG 1:2
See also DLB 16
Hundal, Nancy 1957- .... SATA 128
Hundert, E(dward) J. 1940- 149
Hundert, Edward M. 1956- 156
Hundert, Gershon David 1946- 146
Hundley, Joan Martin 1921- 45-48
Hundley, Norris (Cecil), Jr. 1935- CANR-8
Earlier sketch in CA 17-20R
Huneck, Stephen 1949- .... SATA 129
Huneker, James Gibbons 1860-1921 193
See also DLB 71
See also RGAL 4
See also TCLC 65
Huneryager, S(herwood) G(eorge) 1933- ... 1-4R
Huneven, Michelle CANR-88
Earlier sketch in CA 181
Hung, Chang-tai 1949- 148
Hungerford, Cy(rus Cotton) 1889(?)-1983
Obituary 109
Hungerford, Edward Buell 1900-1988 .. 37-40R
Hungerford, Harold R(alph) 1928- 33-36R
Hungerford, Hesba Fay
See Brinsmead, H(esba) F(ay)
Hungerford, Mary Jane 1913-1998 77-80
Hungerford, Pixie
See Brinsmead, H(esba) F(ay)
Hungerford, Rachael A. 145
Hungry Wolf, Adolf 1944- CANR-38
Earlier sketch in CA 115
Hungry Wolf, Beverly 1950- CANR-38
Earlier sketch in CA 117
Hunker, Henry L. 1924- 13-16R
Hunkin, Timothy Mark Trelawney 1950- 102
See also SATA 53
Hunkins, Francis P(eter) 1938- 57-60
Hunkins, Lee(cynth) 1930- 108
Hunnex, Milton D(eVerne) 1917- 29-32R
Hunnicutt, Benjamin Kline 1943- 130
Hunnings, Neville March 1929- CANR-12
Earlier sketch in CA 25-28R
Hunnings, Vicky 1947- 215
Hunnisett, Basil 1923- 119
Hunold, Christian Friedrich
1681-1721 .... DLB 168
Hunsaker, David M(alcolm) 1944- 33-36R
Hunsaker, Steven V. 1965- 191
Hunsberger, Edith Mae 1927- 109
Hunsberger, Warren S(eabury)
1911-1997 .... 41-44R
Obituary 163
Hunsehe, Raymond W. 1891(?)-1983
Obituary 111
Hunsinger, George 1945- 65-68
Hunsinger, Paul 1919- 33-36R
Hunsinger, Walter (William) 1923- 122
Hunt, Abby Campbell 1933(?)-1985 135
Obituary 116
Hunt, Angela Elwell 1957- CANR-123
Earlier sketch in CA 142
See also SATA 75, 159
Hunt, Barbara
See Watters, Barbara H(unt)
Hunt, Bernice (Kohn) 1920- CANR-21
Earlier sketch in CA 9-12R
See also Kohn, Bernice
Hunt, Bob
See Kouf, M(arvin) James, Jr.
Hunt, Bruce J. 1956- 136
Hunt, Charles Butler 1906- 110
Hunt, Charlotte
See Hodges, Doris M(arjorie)
Hunt, Chester L. 1912-1994 .... CANR-5
Earlier sketch in CA 13-16R
Hunt, Clarence
See Holman, C(larence) Hugh
Hunt, Dave
See Hunt, David C(harles Hadden)
Hunt, David (Wathen Stather) 1913-1998 .. 102
Hunt, David 1942- 33-36R
Hunt, David C(harles Hadden) 1926- . CANR-9
Earlier sketch in CA 57-60
Hunt, David C(urtis) 1935- CANR-38
Earlier sketches in CA 89-92, CANR-16
Hunt, Douglas 1918- 13-16R
Hunt, E(verette) Howard, (Jr.)
1918- CANR-103
Earlier sketches in CA 45-48, CANR-2, 47
See also AITN 1
See also CLC 3
See also CMW 4
Hunt, E. K. 1937- 77-80
Hunt, Earl B. 1933- 93-96
Hunt, Earl W(ilbur) 1926- 85-88
Hunt, Edgar H(ubert) 1909- CAP-1
Earlier sketch in CA 9-10
Hunt, Elgin F(raser) 1895-1978 .... 1-4R
Hunt, Everett C. 1928- 237
Hunt, Everett Lee 1890(?)-1984
Obituary 112
Hunt, F(lorence) V(ance) 132
Hunt, Florine E(lizabeth) 1928- 13-16R
Hunt, Francesca
See Holland, Isabelle (Christian)
Hunt, Francis CANR-26
Earlier sketches in CAP-2, CA 19-20
Hunt, Frazier 1885-1967
Obituary 93-96
Hunt, Garry Edward 1942- 115
Hunt, Geoffrey 1915(?)-1974
Obituary 104
Hunt, George Laird 1918- 49-52
Hunt, George W(illiam) 1937- 120
Hunt, Gill
See Tubb, E(dwin) C(harles)
Hunt, Gladys M. 1926- CANR-13
Earlier sketch in CA 29-32R
Hunt, (Leslie) Gordon 1906-1970 .... CAP-2
Earlier sketch in CA 29-32
Hunt, H(arry) Draper 1935- 37-40R
Hunt, Harrison
See Ballard, (Willis) Todhunter
Hunt, Herbert James 1899-1973
Obituary 89-92
Hunt, Howard
See Hunt, E(verette) Howard, (Jr.)
Hunt, Hugh 1911-1993 .... CANR-3
Obituary 141
Earlier sketch in CA 5-8R
Hunt, Ignatius 1920- 17-20R
Hunt, Inez Whitaker 1899-1983 .... CAP-1
Earlier sketch in CA 17-18
Hunt, Irene 1907-2001 .... CANR-57
Earlier sketches in CA 17-20R, CANR-8
See also AAYA 18
See also BYA 1, 3
See also CLR 1
See also DLB 52
See also JRDA
See also LAIT 2
See also MAICYA 1, 2
See also SATA 2, 91
See also YAW
Hunt, J(oseph) McVicker 1906-1991 ..... 37-40R
Obituary 133
Hunt, J. Roy 1884- .... IDFW 3
Hunt, J. William, Jr. 1930- 53-56
Hunt, James Gerald 1932- CANR-60
Earlier sketches in CA 65-68, CANR-14, 31
Hunt, Janie Louise 1963- 169
See also SATA 102
Hunt, John
See Paine, Lauran (Bosworth)
Hunt, (Henry Cecil) John 1910-1998 109
Obituary 172
Hunt, John Dixon 1936- CANR-17
Earlier sketch in CA 85-88
Hunt, John J. 1929- 33-36R
Hunt, John P(aul) 1915-1988 .... 33-36R
Obituary 124
Hunt, John W(esley) 1927- 21-24R
Hunt, Jonathan 1966- .... SATA 84
Hunt, Joyce 1927- CANR-45
Earlier sketches in CA 106, CANR-22
See also SATA 31
Hunt, June 1944- 103
Hunt, Kari (Eleanor B.) 1920- 41-44R
Hunt, Kellogg W(esley) 1912-1998 .... 5-8R
Hunt, Kenneth E(dward) 1917(?)-1978
Obituary 104
Hunt, Kyle
See Creasey, John
Hunt, Lawrence J. 1920- 5-8R
Hunt, (James Henry) Leigh
1784-1859 .... DAM POET
See also DLB 96, 110, 144
See also RGEL 2
See also TEA
Hunt, Leon (Gibson) 1931- 65-68
Hunt, Linda 1940- 106
See also SATA 39
Hunt, Lisa B(ehnke) 1967- .... SATA 84
Hunt, Lynn (Avery) 1945- CANR-87
Earlier sketch in CA 131
Hunt, Mabel Leigh 1892-1971 .... CAP-1
Obituary 106
Earlier sketch in CA 9-10
See also CWRI 5
See also SATA 1
See also SATA-Obit 26
Hunt, Marjorie 1954- 203
Hunt, Marsha 1946- CANR-79
Earlier sketch in CA 143
See also BW 2, 3
See also CLC 70
Hunt, Maurice P. 1915- 25-28R
Hunt, Michael H. 1942- CANR-58
Earlier sketch in CA 127
Hunt, Morton M(agill) 1920- CANR-21
Earlier sketch in CA 5-8R
See also SATA 22
Hunt, Nan
See Ray, N(ancy) L(ouise)
Hunt, Nancy (Ridgely) 1927- 103
Hunt, Nigel
See Greenbank, Anthony Hunt
Hunt, Noel Aubrey Bonavia
See Bonavia-Hunt, Noel Aubrey
Hunt, Noreen 1931- 103
Hunt, Norman C.
See Crowther-Hunt, Norman Crowther
Hunt, Norman Crowther Crowther
See Crowther-Hunt, Norman Crowther
Hunt, Patricia 1922(?)-1983
Obituary 120
Hunt, Patricia Joan CANR-44
Earlier sketches in CA 103, CANR-21
Hunt, Penelope
See Napier, Priscilla
Hunt, Peter 1922- 5-8R
Hunt, Peter (Leonard) 1945- CANR-127
Earlier sketches in CA 113, CANR-32, 65
See also CWRI 5
See also SATA 76
Hunt, R(ichard) W(illiam) 1908-1979 141
Hunt, Ray(mond) C(hamp), Jr. 1919- 122
Hunt, Raymond G(eorge) 1928- CANR-3
Earlier sketch in CA 9-12R
Hunt, Richard (Paul) 1921-1992 73-76
Obituary 139
Hunt, Richard (Patrick) 1938- CANR-71
Earlier sketch in CA 137
Hunt, Richard N(orman) 1931- 9-12R
Hunt, Robert C(ushman) 1934- CANR-9
Earlier sketch in CA 21-24R
Hunt, Sam 1946- 110
See also CP 2, 3, 4, 5, 6, 7
Hunt, Samantha (J.) 239
Hunt, Stoker
See Piotrowski, Andrew
Hunt, Tim(othy A.) 1949- CANR-112
Earlier sketch in CA 121
Hunt, Todd T. 1938- 13-16R
Hunt, Tony 1944- 160
Hunt, Tristram 1974- 224
Hunt, V. Daniel 1939- 111
Hunt, (Isobel) Violet 1866-1942 .... HGG
Hunt, Violet 1866(?)-1942 184
See also DLB 162, 197
See also TCLC 53
Hunt, Virginia Lloyd 1888(?)-1977
Obituary 73-76
Hunt, Walter H. 1959- 204
Hunt, Wayne Henry
See Hunt, Wolf Robe
Hunt, William 1934- CANR-3
Earlier sketch in CA 49-52
Hunt, William A(lvin) 1903-1986
Obituary 118
Hunt, William Dudley, Jr.
1922-1987 .... CANR-14
Obituary 122
Earlier sketch in CA 33-36R
Hunt, William Gibbes 1791-1833 .... DLB 73
Hunt, William R(aymond) 1929- 93-96
Hunt, Wolf Robe 1905-1977 215
Hunte, Otto -1960 .... IDFW 3, 4
Hunter, A(rchibald) M(acbride)
1906-1991 .... CANR-6
Earlier sketch in CA 9-12R
Hunter, Alan (James Herbert) 1922- . CANR-66
Earlier sketches in CA 9-12R, CANR-3, 18, 40
See also CMW 4
Hunter, Allan A(rmstrong) 1893-1982 .... 5-8R
Hunter, Allan G. 1955- 187
Hunter, Anne B. 1966- .... SATA 118
Hunter, Anson
See Orrmont, Arthur
Hunter, Archie 1929- 222
Hunter, Beatrice Trum 1918- CANR-50
Earlier sketches in CA 17-20R, CANR-7, 22
Hunter, Bernice Thurman 1922- CANR-52
Earlier sketch in CA 119
See also CWRI 5
See also SATA 85
See also SATA-Brief 45
Hunter, Bill R. 1932(?)-1990
Obituary 131
Hunter, Bobbi Dooley 1945- .... SATA 89
Hunter, Bruce (William) 1952- CANR-58
Earlier sketch in CA 123
Hunter, C. Bruce 1917- 61-64
Hunter, Captain Marcy
See Ellis, Edward S(ylvester)
Hunter, Catherine (Rose) 1957- 236
Hunter, Chris
See Fluke, Joanne
Hunter, Christine
See Hunter, Maud L(ily)
Hunter, Clark 124
Hunter, Clingham M.D.
See Adams, William Taylor
Hunter, Damion
See Cockrell, Amanda
Hunter, Dard 1883-1966 .... CAP-1
Obituary 25-28R
Earlier sketch in CA 13-16
Hunter, Dawe
See Downie, Mary Alice (Dawe)
Hunter, Dia
See Pace, DeWanna
Hunter, Doris A. 1929- 37-40R
Hunter, E. Waldo
See Sturgeon, Theodore (Hamilton)
Hunter, Edith Fisher 1919- 107
See also SATA 31
Hunter, Edward 1902-1978 .... 5-8R
Obituary 77-80
Hunter, Elizabeth
See de Guise, Elizabeth (Mary Teresa)
Hunter, Evan 1926-2005 .... CANR-97
Earlier sketches in CA 5-8R, CANR-5, 38, 62
Interview in CANR-5
See also McBain, Ed
See also AAYA 39
See also BPFB 2
See also CLC 11, 31
See also CMW 4
See also CN 1, 2, 3, 4, 5, 6, 7
See also CPW
See also DAM POP
See also DLB 306
See also DLBY 1982
See also MSW
See also MTCW 1
See also SATA 25
See also SFW 4

Hunter, Fred (W.) 1954- ... 227
Hunter, Frederick J(ames) 1916- ... 33-36R
Hunter, Gary
See Hunter, Gwen
Hunter, Geoffrey (Basil Bailey) 1925- ... 33-36R
Hunter, George
See Ballard, (Willis) Todhunter
Hunter, George E.
See Ellis, Edward S(ylvester)
Hunter, Gordon C. 1924- ... 106
Hunter, (James) Graham ... 136
Hunter, Gwen 1956- ... 147
Hunter, Hall
See Marshall, Edison
Hunter, Henry MacGregor 1929-
Brief entry ... 109
Hunter, Hilda 1921- ... 49-52
See also SATA 7
Hunter, Howard Eugene 1929- ... 41-44R
Hunter, J(ames) A(lston) H(ope) 1902-1986 ... CANR-14
Earlier sketches in CAP-1, CA 9-10
Hunter, J(ohn) F(letcher) M(acGregor) 1924- ... 37-40R
Hunter, J(ames) Paul 1934- ... CANR-49
Earlier sketches in CA 21-24R, CANR-9, 24
Hunter, Jack D(ayton) 1921- ... CANR-29
Earlier sketches in CA 5-8R, CANR-6
Hunter, James H(ogg) 1890- ... 85-88
Hunter, Jane (Harlow) 1949- ... 125
Hunter, Jessie Prichard 1957(?)- ... 168
Hunter, Jim 1939- ... CANR-7
Earlier sketch in CA 9-12R
See also CN 1, 2
See also DLB 14
See also SATA 65
Hunter, Joan
See Yarde, Jeanne Betty Frances
Hunter, Joe
See McNeilly, Wilfred (Glassford)
Hunter, John
See Ballard, (Willis) Todhunter and Hunter, Maud L(ily)
Hunter, John M(erlin) 1921- ... 13-16R
Hunter, Karen 1945- ... 215
Hunter, Kim 1922-2002 ... 61-64
Obituary ... 211
Hunter, Kristin
See Lattany, Kristin (Elaine Eggleston) Hunter
See also CN 1, 2, 3, 4, 5, 6
Hunter, Leigh
See Etchison, Birdie L(ee)
Hunter, Leona Wesley
See Greif, Martin
Hunter, Leslie S(tannard) 1890-1983 ... CAP-1
Obituary ... 110
Earlier sketch in CA 19-20
Hunter, Lieutenant Ned
See Ellis, Edward S(ylvester)
Hunter, Louis C. 1898(?)-1984
Obituary ... 112
Hunter, Louise H(arris) ... 41-44R
Hunter, Mac
See Hunter, Henry MacGregor
Hunter, Maddy ... 237
Hunter, Madeline 1952- ... 196
Hunter, Marjorie 1922-2001 ... 69-72
Obituary ... 195
Hunter, Mark 1952- ... 128
Hunter, Marvin H(erbert) 1930-
Brief entry ... 111
Hunter, Mary
See Austin, Mary (Hunter)
Hunter, Mary Vann 1937- ... 107
Hunter, Matthew
See Stone, Rodney
Hunter, Maud L(ily) 1910- ... CANR-4
Earlier sketch in CA 9-12R
Hunter, Mel 1927-2004 ... 93-96
See also SATA 39
Hunter, Michael (Cyril William) 1949- ... 104
Hunter, Milton R(eed) 1902-1975
Obituary ... 104
Hunter, Mollie 1922- ... CANR-78
Earlier sketch in CANR-37
See also McIlwraith, Maureen Mollie Hunter
See also AAYA 13
See also BYA 6
See also CLC 21
See also CLR 25
See also DLB 161
See also JRDA
See also MAICYA 1, 2
See also SAAS 7
See also SATA 54, 106, 139
See also SATA-Essay 139
See also WYA
See also YAW
Hunter, Ned
See Ellis, Edward S(ylvester)
Hunter, Neil
See Linaker, Mike
Hunter, Norman (George Lorimer) 1899-1995 ... CANR-15
Obituary ... 147
Earlier sketch in CA 93-96
See also CWRI 5
See also SATA 26, 84
Hunter, Norman Charles 1908-1971
Obituary ... 29-32R
See also DLB 10
See also RGEL 2
Hunter, R(ichard) L(awrence) 1953- ... 144
Hunter, Richard 1923-1981
Obituary ... 105
Hunter, Robert 1874-1942 ... DLB 303
Hunter, Robert (Christie) 1941- ... 156
Hunter, Robert E(dwards) 1940- ... CANR-33
Earlier sketches in CA 41-44R, CANR-15
Hunter, Robert Grams 1927- ... 93-96
Hunter, Rodello
See Calkins, Rodello
Hunter, Ross 1916-1996 ... IDFW 3, 4
Hunter, Ryan Ann
See Greenwood, Pamela D. and Macalaster, Elizabeth G.
Hunter, Sam 1923- ... CANR-8
Earlier sketch in CA 13-16R
Hunter, Sara Hoagland 1954- ... 165
See also SATA 98
Hunter, Seb 1971- ... 235
Hunter, Stephen 1946- ... CANR-143
Earlier sketches in CA 102, CANR-19, 70
Hunter, T. Willard 1915- ... 143
Hunter, Thomas 1932- ... 108
Hunter, Tim 1947- ... 85-88
Hunter, Valancy
See Meaker, Eloise
Hunter, Vickie
See Hunter, Victoria Alberta
Hunter, Victoria Alberta 1929- ... 5-8R
Hunter, William A(lbert) 1908-1985 ... 13-16R
Hunter, William B(ridges), Jr. 1915- ... 77-80
Hunter Blair, Pauline
See Clarke, Pauline
See also SATA 3
Hunter Blair, Peter 1912-1982
Obituary ... 108
Brief entry ... 107
Hunter-Duvar, John 1821-1899 ... DLB 99
Hunter-Gault, Charlayne 1942- ... CANR-101
Earlier sketch in CA 141
See also BW 2
Huntford, Roland 1927- ... 142
Hunting, Constance 1925- ... CANR-23
Earlier sketch in CA 45-48
Huntingdon, Eugenia 1910- ... 127
Huntington, Amy 1956- ... SATA 138
Huntington, Anna Hyatt 1876-1973
Obituary ... 45-48
Huntington, (E.) Gale 1902-1993 ... 9-12R
Huntington, Geoffrey ... SATA 145
Huntington, Harriet E(lizabeth) 1909- ... CANR-5
Earlier sketch in CA 5-8R
See also SATA 1
Huntington, Henry E. 1850-1927 ... DLB 140
Huntington, Henry S., Jr. 1882-1981
Obituary ... 103
Huntington, John (Willard) 1940- ... 112
Huntington, Madge 1937- ... 126
Huntington, Roy P. 1934- ... 166
Huntington, Samuel P(hillips) 1927- ... CANR-120
Earlier sketches in CA 1-4R, CANR-1
Huntington, Susan Mansfield 1791-1823 ... DLB 200
Huntington, Thomas W(aterman) 1893-1973
Obituary ... 45-48
Huntington, Vince
See Huntington, Roy P.
Huntington, Virginia 1889-1983 ... 21-24R
Huntley, Chester Robert 1911-1974 ... 97-100
Obituary ... 49-52
See also AITN 1
Huntley, Chet
See Huntley, Chester Robert
Huntley, Frances E.
See Mayne, Ethel(ind Frances) Colburn
Huntley, Frank Livingstone 1902-1998 ... 33-36R
Huntley, H(erbert) E(dwin) 1892- ... CAP-1
Earlier sketch in CA 13-14
Huntley, James L(ewis) 1914-1996 ... 101
Huntley, James Robert 1923- ... CANR-12
Earlier sketch in CA 29-32R
Huntley, Paula (Bowlin) 1944- ... 225
Huntley, Timothy Wade 1939- ... 102
Huntly, Moira 1932- ... 175
Hunton, Mary
See Gilzean, Elizabeth Houghton Blanchet
Hunton, Richard E(dwin) 1924- ... 21-24R
Huntress, Keith G(ibson) 1913-1990 ... 5-8R
Huntsberger, John (Paul) 1931- ... 5-8R
Huntsberry, William E(mery) 1916- ... CANR-2
Earlier sketch in CA 1-4R
See also SATA 5
Hunzicker, Beatrice Plumb 1886-1981 ... 5-8R
Huo, T. C. ... 181
Huot-Vickery, Jim dale ... 238
Hupchick, Dennis P(aul) 1948- ... CANR-142
Earlier sketch in CA 151
Hupka, Robert 1919-2001 ... 61-64
Obituary ... 201
Huppe, Bernard Felix 1911-1989 ... CANR-3
Earlier sketch in CA 5-8R
Huppert, George 1934- ... CANR-89
Earlier sketch in CA 29-32R
Hurd, Barbara 1949- ... 209
Hurd, Charles (Wesley Bolick) 1903-1968 ... CAP-1
Earlier sketch in CA 11-12
Hurd, Clement (G.) 1908-1988 ... CANR-24
Obituary ... 124
Earlier sketches in CA 29-32R, CANR-9
See also CLR 49
See also MAICYA 1, 2
See also SATA 2, 64
See also SATA-Obit 54
Hurd, Douglas (Richard) 1930- ... CANR-10
Earlier sketch in CA 25-28R
Hurd, Edith Thacher 1910-1997 ... CANR-24
Obituary ... 156
Earlier sketches in CA 13-16R, CANR-9
See also CLR 49
See also MAICYA 1, 2
See also MAICYAS 1
See also SAAS 13
See also SATA 2, 64
See also SATA-Obit 95
Hurd, Florence 1918- ... CANR-19
Earlier sketch in CA 103
Hurd, Gale Ann 1955- ... 150
See also AAYA 17
Hurd, John C(oolidge), Jr. 1928- ... 17-20R
Hurd, Michael John 1928- ... CANR-12
Earlier sketch in CA 65-68
Hurd, Paul DeHart 1905- ... 181
Hurd, (John) Thacher 1949- ... CANR-82
Earlier sketches in CA 106, CANR-24, 36, 68
See also CWRI 5
See also MAICYA 1, 2
See also SATA 46, 94
See also SATA-Brief 45
See also SATA-Essay 123
Hure, Anne 1918- ... 9-12R
Hureau, Jean (Emile Pierre) 1915-
Brief entry ... 110
Hurewitz, J(acob) C(oleman) 1914- ... CANR-2
Earlier sketch in CA 1-4R
Hurka, Joseph 1960- ... 230
Hurka, Thomas 1952- ... CANR-116
Earlier sketch in CA 147
hurkey, rooan
See Holzapfel, Rudolf Patrick
Hurkos, Peter 1911-1988
Obituary ... 125
Hurlbut, Allen F. 1910-1983
Obituary ... 110
Hurlbut, Cornelius S(earle), Jr. 1906- ... CANR-11
Earlier sketch in CA 25-28R
Hurlbutt, Robert H(arris) III 1924- ... 13-16R
Hurley, Alfred F(rancis) 1928- ... 97-100
Hurley, Andrew 1944- ... 176
Hurley, Ann 1947- ... 154
Hurley, Doran 1900-1964 ... 5-8R
Hurley, F(orrest) Jack 1940- ... CANR-50
Earlier sketches in CA 45-48, CANR-25
Hurley, Graham ... 181
Hurley, Jane (Hezel) 1928- ... 13-16R
Hurley, John 1928- ... CANR-13
Earlier sketch in CA 33-36R
Hurley, John J(erome) 1930- ... 104
Hurley, Kathy 1947- ... 109
Hurley, Leslie J(ohn) 1911-1983 ... 49-52
Hurley, Mark J(oseph, Jr.) 1919- ... 53-56
Hurley, Neil 1925- ... 29-32R
Hurley, Valerie 1943- ... 234
Hurley, Vic 1898-1978 ... 1-4R
Obituary ... 103
Hurley, W(illiam) Maurice 1916- ... 37-40R
Hurley, Wilfred G(eoffrey) 1895-1973 ... CAP-2
Obituary ... 45-48
Earlier sketch in CA 17-18
Hurley, William James, Jr. 1924- ... 9-12R
Hurlimann, Bettina
See Huerlimann, Bettina
See also SATA 39
See also SATA-Obit 34
Hurlimann, Ruth
See Huerlimann, Ruth
See also SATA 32
See also SATA-Brief 31
Hurlock, Elizabeth B(ergner) 1898-1988 ... 41-44R
Hurlow, (Wilma) Janet 1939- ... 118
Hurlow, Marcia L. 1952- ... 217
Hurm, Ken 1934- ... 106
Hurmence, Belinda 1921- ... 145
See also AAYA 17
See also CLR 25
See also JRDA
See also MAICYA 2
See also MAICYAS 1
See also SAAS 20
See also SATA 77
Hurne, Ralph 1932- ... 21-24R
Hurok, Sol(omon) 1888-1974
Obituary ... 49-52
Hursch, Carolyn J(udge) ... 41-44R
Hurst, A(lexander) A(nthony) 1917- ... 5-8R
Hurst, Carol Otis 1933- ... SATA 130
Hurst, Charles G., Jr. 1928- ... 37-40R
Hurst, Christopher 1929- ... 223
Hurst, Fannie 1889-1968 ... CAP-1
Obituary ... 25-28R
Earlier sketch in CA 13-16
See also DLB 86
See also FW
See also RHW
Hurst, G(eorge) Cameron III 1941- ... 85-88
Hurst, James M(arshall) 1924- ... 29-32R
Hurst, James Willard 1910-1997 ... 130
Obituary ... 158
Hurst, M(ichael) E(liot) Eliot
See Eliot Hurst, M(ichael) E(liot)
Hurst, Michael (Charles) 1931- ... 21-24R
Hurst, Norman 1944- ... 53-56
Hurst, Richard Maurice 1938- ... 101
Hurst, Virginia Radcliffe 1914(?)-1976
Obituary ... 69-72
Hurstfield, Joel 1911-1980 ... CANR-6
Obituary ... 102
Earlier sketch in CA 53-56
Hurston, Zora Neale 1891-1960 ... CANR-61
Earlier sketch in CA 85-88
See also AAYA 15
See also AFAW 1, 2
See also AMWS 6
See also BLC 2
See also BW 1, 3
See also BYA 12
See also CDALBS
See also CLC 7, 30, 61
See also DA
See also DA3
See also DAC
See also DAM MST, MULT, NOV
See also DC 12
See also DFS 6
See also DLB 51, 86
See also EWL 3
See also EXPN
See also EXPS
See also FL 1:6
See also FW
See also HR 1:2
See also LAIT 3
See also LATS 1:1
See also LMFS 2
See also MAL 5
See also MAWW
See also MTCW 1, 2
See also MTFW 2005
See also NFS 3
See also RGAL 4
See also RGSF 2
See also SSC 4, 80
See also SSFS 1, 6, 11, 19, 21
See also TCLC 121, 131
See also TUS
See also WLCS
See also YAW
Hurt, C(harlie) D(euel III) 1950- ... 127
Hurt, Freda M(ary) E(lizabeth) 1911- ... 103
Hurt, Harry III 1951- ... CANR-100
Earlier sketch in CA 143
Hurt, Henry 1942- ... 106
Hurt, James (Riggins) 1934- ... CANR-47
Earlier sketches in CA 45-48, CANR-23
Hurt, Ray Douglas 1946- ... CANR-53
Earlier sketch in CA 125
Hurtado, Albert L. 1946- ... CANR-86
Earlier sketch in CA 130
Hurtado, Larry W. 1943- ... 217
Hurtgen, Andre O(scar) 1932- ... 81-84
Hurtig, Mel ... CANR-110
Earlier sketch in CA 137
Hurt-Newton, Tania 1968- ... SATA 84
Hurvitz, Leon Nahum 1923- ... 106
Hurvitz, Yair 1941-1988 ... 233
Hurwitz, Abraham B. 1905-1981 ... 29-32R
Obituary ... 133
Hurwitz, Edith F(arber) 1941- ... 108
Hurwitz, Gregg (Andrew) 1973- ... 220
Hurwitz, Howard L(awrence) 1916- ... 37-40R
Hurwitz, Johanna 1937- ... CANR-114
Earlier sketches in CA 65-68, CANR-10, 25, 44, 50
See also CWRI 5
See also JRDA
See also MAICYA 1, 2
See also SAAS 18
See also SATA 20, 71, 113
See also YAW
Hurwitz, Ken 1948- ... 33-36R
Hurwitz, Samuel J(ustin) 1912-1972 ... CAP-2
Earlier sketch in CA 25-28
Hurwitz, Stephan 1901-1981
Obituary ... 103
Hurwood, Bernhardt J. 1926-1987 ... CANR-43
Obituary ... 121
Earlier sketch in CA 25-28R
See also SATA 12
See also SATA-Obit 50
Husain, Adrian 1942- ... CP 1
Husain, Shahrukh 1950- ... CANR-110
Earlier sketch in CA 168
See also SATA 108
Husar, John 1937- ... 81-84
Husayn, Taha
See Hussein, Taha
See also EWL 3
See also WLIT 2
Husband, William Hollow 1899(?)-1978
Obituary ... 81-84
Huse, Dennis P(aul) 1944- ... 115
Huseman, Richard C. 1939- ... 127
Brief entry ... 109
Husen, Torsten 1916- ... CANR-53
Earlier sketches in CA 21-24R, CANR-9, 27
Huser, Glen 1943- ... 226
See also SATA 151
Huser, (La)Verne (Carl) 1931- ... CANR-22
Earlier sketch in CA 106
Hu Shih 1891-1962 ... EWL 3
Huskey, Eugene 1952- ... CANR-91
Earlier sketch in CA 145
Huson, Paul (Anthony) 1942- ... CANR-12
Earlier sketch in CA 29-32R
Huss, Roy 1927- ... CANR-47
Earlier sketch in CA 25-28R
Huss, Sally 1940- ... 195
Huss, Sandy 1953- ... 138
Hussein, Abdullah
See Khan, Muhammad
See also CWW 2
Hussein, Nadir 1939- ... CP 1

Cumulative Index 285 Hyde

Hussein, Taha 1889-1973
Obituary 45-48
See also Husayn, Taha and Taha Husayn
Husserl, E. G.
See Husserl, Edmund (Gustav Albrecht)
Husserl, Edmund (Gustav Albrecht) 1859-1938 133
Brief entry 116
See also DLB 296
See also TCLC 100
Hussey, David Edward 1934- CANR-9
Earlier sketch in CA 57-60
Hussey, Gemma 1938- 145
Hussey, John A(dam) 1913-1994 61-64
Hussey, Mark 1956- 135
Hussey, Maurice Percival 1925- 9-12R
Hussey, Patricia (Ann) 1949- 143
Hussey, (John) Walter (Atherton) 1909-1985 133
Hussman, Lawrence Eugene, Jr. 1932- CANR-99
Earlier sketch in CA 115
Hussmann, Mary (Margaret) 1953- 147
Husson, Jules-Francois-Felix
See Champfleury
Hustak, Alan (Joseph) 1944- 128
Huste, Annemarie 1943- 57-60
Husted, Darrell 1931- 81-84
Hustle, Charlie
See Rose, Pete(r Edward)
Huston, Anne Marshall CANR-40
Earlier sketch in CA 116
Huston, Fran
See Miller, R. S.
Huston, James A(lvin) 1918- CANR-33
Earlier sketches in CA 41-44R, CANR-15
Huston, James E(dward) 1930- 171
Huston, James W(ebb) 1953- 172
Huston, John (Marcellus) 1906-1987 .... CANR-34
Obituary 123
Earlier sketch in CA 73-76
See also CLC 20
See also DLB 26
Huston, Luther A. 1888-1975 .... CAP-2
Earlier sketch in CA 21-22
Huston, Mervyn James 1912-2001 .... CANR-8
Earlier sketch in CA 61-64
Huston, Nancy 1953- CANR-102
Earlier sketch in CA 145
Huston, Paula 1952- 188
Huston, Perdita (Constance) 1936-2001 218
Huston, Tony
See Huston, Walter Anthony
Huston, Walter Anthony 1950- 166
Hustvedt, Lloyd (Merlyn) 1922- 21-24R
Hustvedt, Siri 1955- 137
See also CLC 76
Huszar, George B(ernard) de 1919-(?) CAP-2
Earlier sketch in CA 19-20
Hutchcroft, Vera 1923- 102
Hutchens, Eleanor Newman 1919- 13-16R
Hutchens, John Kennedy 1905-1995 65-68
Hutchens, Paul 1902-1977 61-64
See also SATA 31
Hutcheon, Linda (Ann) 1947- 131
Hutcheon, Michael 1945- CANR-130
Earlier sketch in CA 158
Hutcherson, Hilda 1955- 216
Hutcheson, Francis 1694-1746 .... DLB 252
Hutcheson, Richard G(ordon), Jr. 1921- 107
Hutchin, Kenneth Charles 1908-1993 110
Hutchings, Alan Eric 1910- 1-4R
Hutchings, Arthur (James Bramwell) 1906- CANR-6
Earlier sketch in CA 5-8R
Hutchings, Bill
See Hutchings, William Bruce
Hutchings, Edward, Jr. 1912- 126
Hutchings, Margaret (Joscelyne) 1918- CANR-3
Earlier sketch in CA 9-12R
Hutchings, Monica Mary 1917- 9-12R
Hutchings, Patrick A(elfred) 1929- CANR-4
Earlier sketch in CA 53-56
Hutchings, Raymond 1924-1998 .... CANR-12
Earlier sketch in CA 33-36R
Hutchings, William Bruce 1948- 111
Hutchins, Carleen Maley 1911- 17-20R
See also SATA 9
Hutchins, Charles R. 1928- 123
Hutchins, Francis Gilman 1939- 21-24R
Hutchins, Hazel J. 1952- CANR-137
Earlier sketches in CA 123, CANR-50
See also CWRI 5
See also SAAS 24
See also SATA 81, 135
See also SATA-Brief 51
Hutchins, Maude (Phelps McVeigh) 61-64
See also CN 1, 2, 3
Hutchins, Myldred Flanigan 1910-1999 112
Hutchins, Nigel 1945- CANR-136
Earlier sketch in CA 170
Hutchins, Pat 1942- CANR-125
Earlier sketches in CA 81-84, CANR-15, 32, 64
See also CLR 20
See also CWRI 5
See also MAICYA 1, 2
See also SAAS 16
See also SATA 15, 70, 111
Hutchins, Robert Maynard 1899-1977 69-72
Hutchins, Ross Elliott 1906- CANR-5
Earlier sketch in CA 9-12R
See also SATA 4
Hutchins, William Maynard 1944- 233
Hutchinson, Allan C. 1951- 154
Hutchinson, Arthur Stuart Menteth 1879-1971
Obituary 29-32R
See also BPFB 2
Hutchinson, Bill 1947- 170
Hutchinson, C(ecil) Alan 1914-1981 .... 29-32R
Obituary 133
Hutchinson, D(ouglas) S(tanley) 1955- 128
Hutchinson, David (Christopher) 1960- 119
Hutchinson, Dennis J(ames) 1946- 185
Hutchinson, Earl Ofari 1945- CANR-87
Earlier sketch in CA 138
See also BW 2
Hutchinson, Eliot Dole 1900-1979 61-64
Hutchinson, G(eorge) Evelyn 1903-1991 .... CANR-14
Obituary 134
Earlier sketches in CAP-1, CA 13-14
Hutchinson, G(regory) O(wen) 1957- CANR-107
Earlier sketch in CA 148
Hutchinson, George 1920-1980
Obituary 97-100
Hutchinson, Gloria 1939- 195
Hutchinson, H(ugh) Lester 1904- 17-20R
Hutchinson, John 1921- 45-48
Hutchinson, John F(ranklin) 1938- 158
Hutchinson, Joseph (Burtt) 1902-1988 109
Obituary 124
Hutchinson, Margaret Massey 1904- CAP-1
Earlier sketch in CA 13-16
Hutchinson, Mary Jane 1924- 106
Hutchinson, Michael E. 1925- 17-20R
Hutchinson, (William Patrick Henry) Pearse 1927- 103
See also CP 1, 2, 3, 4, 5, 6, 7
Hutchinson, Peter 1943- CANR-8
Earlier sketch in CA 61-64
Hutchinson, Ray Coryton 1907-1975 .... CANR-3
Obituary 61-64
Earlier sketch in CA 1-4R
See also CN 1, 2
See also DLB 191
Hutchinson, Richard Wyatt 1894-1970 .... 5-8R
Obituary 89-92
Hutchinson, Robert 1924- 13-16R
Hutchinson, Roger 1949- 156
Hutchinson, Ron 1947- 233
See also CBD
See also CD 5, 6
See also DLB 245
Hutchinson, Samuel 1965- 232
Hutchinson, Thomas 1711-1780 .... DLB 30, 31
Hutchinson, Timothy A. 1960- 226
Hutchinson, Vernal 1922- 49-52
Hutchinson, Veronica S(omerville) 1895-1961
Obituary 111
Hutchinson, Warner Alton, Jr. 1929- 110
Hutchinson, William K(enneth) 1945- 102
Hutchinson, William M(iller) 1916- 112
Hutchison, (William) Bruce 1901-1992 103
Hutchison, Chester Smith 1902-1985 .... CAP-2
Earlier sketch in CA 17-18
Hutchison, (Dorothy) Dwight 1890(?)-1975
Obituary 57-60
Hutchison, E(arl) R. 1926- CANR-10
Earlier sketch in CA 25-28R
Hutchison, Emery 1919(?)-1985
Obituary 116
Hutchison, Harold Frederick 1900- CANR-4
Earlier sketch in CA 1-4R
Hutchison, Jane Campbell 1932- 37-40R
Hutchison, John Alexander 1912-2000 69-72
Hutchison, Linda 1942- 227
See also SATA 152
Hutchison, Sidney C(harles) 1912-2000 .... 25-28R
Hutchison, T(erence) W(ilmot) 1912- 129
Hutchison, William Robert 1930- 21-24R
Hutchisson, James M. 1961- 156
Huth, Angela 1938- CANR-88
Earlier sketches in CA 85-88, CANR-20
See also BYA 9
See also DLB 271
Huth, Marta 1898-
Brief entry 106
Huth, Mary Jo(sephine) 1929- 103
Huth, Tom 1941- 97-100
Huthmacher, J. Joseph 1929- 21-24R
See also SATA 5
Hutin, Magdeleine 1898-1989
Obituary 130
Hutmacher (MacLean), Barbara Anne 1926- 112
Hutman, Norma Louise 1935- 25-28R
Hutschnecker, Arnold A. 1898-2000 81-84
Obituary 191
Hutslar, Donald Andrew 1931- 127
Hutson, Anthony Brian Austen 1934- 93-96
Hutson, James H(oward) 1937- 85-88
Hutson, Jan 1932- 106
Hutson, Joan 1929- 89-92
Hutson, Lorna 1958- CANR-127
Earlier sketch in CA 146
Hutson, Shaun
See Bishop, Samuel P.
Hutson, Shaun 1958- 239
See also Bishop, Samuel P.
See also HGG
Hutt, Maurice George 1928- 13-16R
Hutt, Max L. 1908-1985 57-60
Hutt, W(illiam) H(arold) 1899-1988 57-60
Obituary 125
Hutten 1874-1957 .... RHW
Hutten, Ulrich von 1488-1523 .... DLB 179
Huttenback, Robert A. 1928- 25-28R
Hutter, Albert David 1941- 130
Huttig, Jack W(ilfred) 1919- 53-56
Huttner, Harry J. M. 1938- 175
Huttner, Matthew 1915-1975
Obituary 104
Hutto, Nelson (Allen) 1904-1985 .... CAP-1
Earlier sketch in CA 9-10
See also SATA 20
Hutton, Ann 1929- 108
Hutton, Barbara (Audrey) 1920- 132
Hutton, Clarke 1898- 107
Hutton, Drew 1947- 204
Hutton, Frankie 161
Hutton, Geoffrey (William) 1909-1985 130
Hutton, Geoffrey 1928- 41-44R
Hutton, Ginger
See Hutton, Virginia Carol
Hutton, Harold 1912-2001 102
Hutton, J(oseph) Bernard 1911-(?) CANR-14
Earlier sketch in CA 21-24R
Hutton, J(ohn) H(enry) 1885-1968 .... CAP-1
Earlier sketch in CA 13-14
Hutton, James 1902-1980 .... CANR-27
Earlier sketch in CA 77-80
Hutton, John (Harwood) 1928- 107
Hutton, Kathryn 1915- .... SATA 89
Hutton, Malcolm 1921- CANR-24
Earlier sketch in CA 107
See also Ward, Graham
Hutton, Paul Andrew 1949- CANR-134
Earlier sketch in CA 133
Hutton, Richard 1949- 109
Hutton, Richard Holt 1826-1897 .... DLB 57
Hutton, Ronald 1953- CANR-90
Earlier sketch in CA 131
Hutton, Virginia Carol 1940- 77-80
Hutton, Warwick 1939-1994 .... CANR-9
Obituary 147
Earlier sketch in CA 61-64
See also SAAS 17
See also SATA 20
See also SATA-Obit 83
Hutton, Will(iam Nicholas) 1950- CANR-96
Earlier sketch in CA 130
Huus, Helen 1913- CANR-1
Earlier sketch in CA 1-4R
Huvos, Kornel 1913-1998 49-52
Huws, Daniel 1932- 81-84
See also CP 2
Huws Jones, Enid (Mary) 1911- 49-52
Huxhold, Harry N(orman) 1922- 61-64
Huxley, Aldous (Leonard) 1894-1963 .... CANR-99
Earlier sketches in CA 85-88, CANR-44
See also AAYA 11
See also BPFB 2
See also BRW 7
See also CDBLB 1914-1945
See also CLC 1, 3, 4, 5, 8, 11, 18, 35, 79
See also DA
See also DA3
See also DAB
See also DAC
See also DAM MST, NOV
See also DLB 36, 100, 162, 195, 255
See also EWL 3
See also EXPN
See also LAIT 5
See also LMFS 2
See also MTCW 1, 2
See also MTFW 2005
See also NFS 6
See also RGEL 2
See also SATA 63
See also SCFW 1, 2
See also SFW 4
See also SSC 39
See also TEA
See also WLC
See also YAW
Huxley, Anthony J(ulian) 1920-1992 .... CANR-49
Obituary 140
Earlier sketches in CA 9-12R, CANR-7, 22
Huxley, Elspeth (Josceline Grant) 1907-1997 .... CANR-58
Obituary 156
Earlier sketches in CA 77-80, CANR-28
See also CMW 4
See also DLB 77, 204
See also SATA 62
See also SATA-Obit 95
Huxley, George 1932- 21-24R
Huxley, Herbert H(enry) 1916- 5-8R
Huxley, Judith 1927(?)-1983
Obituary 111
Huxley, Julian (Sorell) 1887-1975 .... CANR-7
Obituary 57-60
Earlier sketch in CA 9-12R
See also MTCW 1
Huxley, Laura Archera 1911- CANR-44
Earlier sketch in CA 13-16R
Huxley, T(homas) H(enry) 1825-1895 .... DLB 57
See also TEA
Huxley-Blythe, Peter J(ames) 1925- 17-20R
Huxtable, Ada Louise (Landman) 1921- 120
Huxtable, (William) John (Fairchild) 1912-1990 .... 13-16R
Huy, Nguyen Ngoc
See Nguyen, Ngoc Huy
Huyck, Dorothy Boyle 1925(?)-1979
Obituary 89-92
Huyck, Margaret Hellie 1939- 49-52
Huyck, Peter H(azelwood) 1940- 107
Huyck, Willard 1945(?)- 128
Brief entry 111
Huygen, Wil(librord Joseph) 1922- CANR-15
Earlier sketch in CA 81-84
Huygens, Constantijn 1596-1687 .... RGWL 2, 3
Huyghe, Patrick 1952- 135
Huyghe, Rene (Louis) 1906- CANR-20
Earlier sketch in CA 81-84
Huyghue, Douglas Smith 1816-1891 .... DLB 99
Huyler, Frank 1964- 233
Huyler, Jean Wiley 1935- CANR-35
Earlier sketches in CA 69-72, CANR-13
Huynh, Quang Nhuong 1946- 107
Huyser, Robert E(rnest) 1924- 139
Huysmans, Charles Marie Georges
See Huysmans, Joris-Karl
Huysmans, J.-K.
See Huysmans, Joris-Karl
Huysmans, Joris-Karl 1848-1907 165
Brief entry 104
See also DLB 123
See also EW 7
See also GFL 1789 to the Present
See also LMFS 2
See also RGWL 2, 3
See also TCLC 7, 69
Huzar, Eleanor G(oltz) 1922- 85-88
Hvidt, Kristian 1929- CANR-86
Earlier sketch in CA 130
Hvitadal, Stefan fra
See Sigurdsson, Stefan
See also DLB 293
Hwang, David Henry 1957- CANR-124
Brief entry 127
Earlier sketches in CA 132, CANR-76
Interview in CA-132
See also CAD
See also CD 5, 6
See also CLC 55, 196
See also DA3
See also DAM DRAM
See also DC 4, 23
See also DFS 11, 18
See also DLB 212, 228, 312
See also MAL 5
See also MTCW 2
See also MTFW 2005
See also RGAL 4
Hy, Ronald John 1942- 115
Hyam, Ronald 1936- 97-100
Hyams, Barry 1911-1989 .... 13-16R
Obituary 129
Hyams, Edward (Solomon) 1910-1975 .... CANR-8
Obituary 61-64
Earlier sketch in CA 5-8R
Hyams, Joe
See Hyams, Joseph
Hyams, Joseph 1923- CANR-45
Earlier sketches in CA 17-20R, CANR-7, 22
Hyams, Philip 1954- 217
Hyatt, Betty H(ale) 1927- 125
Hyatt, Carole S. 1935- 93-96
Hyatt, Daniel
See James, Daniel (Lewis)
Hyatt, I. Ralph 1927- 115
Hyatt, J(ames) Philip 1909-1972 .... 9-12R
Obituary 134
Hyatt, Richard Herschel 1944- 101
Hybels, Bill 1951- 126
Hybels, Saundra 1938- 57-60
Hyde, Anthony 1946- 136
See also Chase, Nicholas
See also CCA 1
See also CLC 42
Hyde, Catherine R(yan) 1955- 196
See also SATA 141
Hyde, Charles K(eith) 1945- 116
Hyde, Christopher 1949- 211
See also HGG
Hyde, Cynthia
See Skinner, Mike
Hyde, Dayton O(gden) 25-28R
See also SATA 9
Hyde, Donald 1909-1966 199
See also DLB 187
Hyde, Douglas 1860-1949 190
Hyde, Douglas Arnold 1911-1996 156
Obituary 153
Brief entry 109
Hyde, Edward 1609-1674 .... DLB 101
Hyde, Eleanor (M.) 154
Hyde, Elisabeth 1953- 122
Hyde, Fillmore 1896(?)-1970
Obituary 104
Hyde, George E. 1882-1968 .... 5-8R
Obituary 133
Hyde, H(arford) Montgomery 1907-1989 .... 5-8R
Obituary 129
Hyde, Hawk
See Hyde, Dayton O(gden)
Hyde, Janet Shibley 1948- CANR-10
Earlier sketch in CA 65-68
Hyde, Jennifer
See Eccles, Marjorie
Hyde, L(ouis) K(epler, Jr.) 1901-1979 .... CAP-1
Earlier sketch in CA 13-14
Hyde, Laurence 1914-1987 .... 17-20R
Hyde, (W.) Lewis 1945- CANR-143
Earlier sketch in CA 144
Hyde, Margaret O(ldroyd) 1917- CANR-137
Earlier sketches in CA 1-4R, CANR-1, 36
See also CLC 21
See also CLR 23
See also JRDA
See also MAICYA 1, 2
See also SAAS 8
See also SATA 1, 42, 76, 139

Hyde, Mary (Morley Crapo)
1912-2003 .... CANR-27
Obituary 219
Earlier sketch in CA 49-52, 172
See also DLB 187
Hyde, Nina Solomon 1932-1990
Obituary 131
Hyde, Robin
See Wilkinson, Iris Guiver
See also RGEL 2
Hyde, Samuel C., Jr. 1958- CANR-121
Earlier sketch in CA 168
Hyde, Shelley
See Reed, Kit
Hyde, Simeon, Jr. 1919- 21-24R
Hyde, Stuart W(allace) 1923- 61-64
Hyde, Tracy Elliot
See Venning, Corey
Hyde, Wayne Frederick 1922- 1-4R
See also SATA 7
Hyden, (Sten Gustav Vilhelm) Goeran
1938- CANR-20
Earlier sketch in CA 103
Hyde-Price, Adrian 1957- 140
Hyder, Clyde Kenneth 1902-1992 .... 33-36R
Hyder, O(liver) Quentin 1930- 127
Brief entry 105
Hyder, Qurratulain 1927- 186
See also CWW 2
See also RGWL 3
Hyer, James Edgar 1923- 77-80
Hyer, Paul Van 1926- 104
Hyers, M. Conrad 1933- 33-36R
Hyett, Barbara Helfgott 1945- CANR-46
Earlier sketch in CA 120
Hygen, Johan B(ernitz) 1911- 21-24R
Hyink, Bernard L(ynn) 1913-2004 .... CANR-49
Obituary 228
Earlier sketch in CA 45-48
Hyland, Douglas K(irk) S(amuel) 1949- 124
Hyland, Drew A(lan) 1939- CANR-15
Earlier sketch in CA 89-92
Hyland, Jean Scammon 1926- 49-52
Hyland, Paul 1947- 121
Hyland, Peter 1943- 236
Hyland, (Henry) Stanley 1914- 9-12R
Hyland, William G. 1929- 148
Hylander, Clarence J(ohn) 1897-1964 .... 5-8R
See also SATA 7
Hylton, Delmer P(aul) 1920- 17-20R
Hyma, Albert 1893-1978 .... 17-20R
Hyman, Alan 1910- 102
Hyman, Ann 1936- 53-56
Hyman, (Robert) Anthony 1928- 132
Hyman, B(arbara) D(avis) 1947- 125
Hyman, David N(eil) 1943- CANR-22
Earlier sketches in CA 57-60, CANR-7
Hyman, Dick 1904- CANR-7
Earlier sketch in CA 17-20R
Hyman, Frieda Clark 1913-2001 .... 5-8R
Hyman, Harold M(elvin) 1924- CANR-29
Earlier sketch in CA 5-8R
Hyman, Helen Kandel 1920- 105
Hyman, Herbert H(iram) 1918-1985 .... 21-24R
Obituary 118
Hyman, Irwin A(braham Meltzer)
1935-2005 93-96
Obituary 236
Hyman, Jackie (Diamond) 1949- CANR-28
Earlier sketch in CA 108
Hyman, Jeremy (A.) 125
Hyman, Lawrence W. 1919- 41-44R
Hyman, Meryl 1950- 169
Hyman, Miranda
See Miller, Miranda
Hyman, Paula 1946- 89-92
Hyman, Paula (E.) 1946- CANR-134
Hyman, Peter (D.) 1968(?)- 236
Hyman, Richard J(oseph) 1921- CANR-1
Earlier sketch in CA 45-48
Hyman, Robin P(hilip) 1931- CANR-15
Earlier sketch in CA 41-44R
See also SATA 12
Hyman, Ronald T. 1933- CANR-50
Earlier sketches in CA 21-24R, CANR-9, 25
Hyman, Sidney 1917- 102
Hyman, Stanley Edgar 1919-1970 85-88
Obituary 25-28R
Hyman, Steven E(dward) 1952- 145
Hyman, Timothy 1946- CANR-122
Earlier sketch in CA 170
Hyman, Trina Schart 1939-2004 .... CANR-70
Obituary 233
Earlier sketches in CA 49-52, CANR-2, 36
See also CLR 50
See also CWRI 5
See also DLB 61
See also MAICYA 1, 2
See also MAICYAS 1
See also SATA 7, 46, 95
See also SATA-Obit 158
Hymans, Jacques Louis 1937- 57-60
Hymes, Dell H(athaway) 1927- 13-16R
Hymes, Lucia M(anley) 1907-1998 .... 5-8R
See also SATA 7
Hymoff, Edward 1924- 17-20R
Hymowitz, Kay S. 1948- 229
Hynam, John Charles 1915-1974 158
See also SFW 4
Hynd, Alan 1904(?)-1974
Obituary 45-48
Hyndman, Donald W(illiam) 1936- CANR-51
Earlier sketches in CA 57-60, CANR-27
Hyndman, Jane Andrews Lee
1912-1978 .... CANR-5
Obituary 89-92
Earlier sketch in CA 5-8R
See also SATA 1, 46
See also SATA-Obit 23
Hyndman, Robert Utley 1906-1973 97-100
See also SATA 18
Hynds, Frances Jane 1929- 77-80
Hyne, C(harles) J(ohn) Cutcliffe (Wright)
1865-1944
Brief entry 111
See also SFW 4
Hynek, J(osef) Allen 1910-1986 81-84
Obituary 119
Hyneman, Charles S(hang) 1900-1985 .... CAP-1
Obituary 114
Earlier sketch in CA 13-14
Hynes, James 1956(?)- CANR-105
Earlier sketch in CA 164
See also CLC 65
Hynes, Pat 166
See also SATA 98
Hynes, Samuel (Lynn) 1924- CANR-32
Earlier sketch in CA 105
Hyppolite, Joanne .... DNFS 2
Hyry, Antti Kalevi 1931- 189
Hyslop, Beatrice F. 1900(?)-1973
Obituary 45-48
Hyslop, James H(ervey) 1854-1920
Brief entry 123
Hyslop, Lois Boe 1908- 41-44R
Hysom, John L(eland, Jr.) 1934- 115
Hyson, Marion C. 1942- 148
Hytier, Jean (Pierre) 1899-1983
Obituary 109
Hyun, Peter 1906-1993 136
Obituary 142
Hyvrard, Jeanne .... CWW 2
Hyzy, Julie A. 235

I

Iaccino, James F(rancis) 1955- 146
Iaccino, Jim
See Iaccino, James F(rancis)
Iacocca, Lee
See Iacocca, Lido Anthony
See also BEST 89:1
Iacocca, Lido Anthony 1924- 125
See also Iacocca, Lee
Iacone, Salvatore J(oseph) 1945- CANR-15
Earlier sketch in CA 85-88
Iacovou, Judy 227
Iacuzzi, Alfred 1896-1977
Obituary 73-76
Iagnemma, Karl 1972- 226
Iakovou, Takis 227
Iams, Jack
See Iams, Samuel Harvey, Jr.
Iams, Samuel Harvey, Jr. 1910-1990
Obituary 130
Ian, Janis 1951- 187
Brief entry 105
See also CLC 21
Iannelli, Richard 1949- 118
Ianni, Francis A(nthony) J(ames)
1926- CANR-28
Earlier sketch in CA 45-48
Ianniello, Lynne Young 1925- 17-20R
Iannone, Abel Pablo 1940- 187
Iannone, Jeanne
See Balzano, Jeanne (Koppel)
See also SATA 7
Iannone, Ron(ald Vincent) 1940- 53-56
Iannuzzi, John Nicholas 1935- 93-96
Iannuzzi, Joseph 1931- 170
Ianuzzi, "Joe Dogs"
See Iannuzzi, Joseph
Iatrides, John O(restes) 1932- CANR-10
Earlier sketch in CA 25-28R
Iavorsky, Stefan 1658-1722 .... DLB 150
Iazykov, Nikolai Mikhailovich
1803-1846 .... DLB 205
Ibanez, Armando P. 1949- .... DLB 209
Ibanez, Carlos G. Velez
See Velez-Ibanez, Carlos G(uillermo)
Ibanez, Sara de 1909-1971 .... DLB 290
Ibanez, Vicente Blasco
See Blasco Ibanez, Vicente
See also DLB 322
Ibarbourou, Juana de 1895(?)-1979 .... DLB 290
See also HLCS 2
See also HW 1
See also LAW
Ibarguengoitia, Jorge 1928-1983 124
Obituary 113
See also CLC 37
See also EWL 3
See also HW 1
See also TCLC 148
Ibarra, Crisostomo
See Yabes, Leopoldo Y(abes)
Ibarra, Herminia 1961- 222
Ibbitson, John Perrie 1955- 160
See also SATA 102
Ibbotson, Eva 1925- CANR-140
Earlier sketches in CA 81-84, CANR-15, 43
See also AAYA 53
See also RHW
See also SATA 13, 103, 156
Ibbotson, M. C(hristine) 1930- 25-28R
See also SATA 5
Ibbotson, Roger G. 1943- 145
Ibele, Oscar H(erman) 1917- 184
Brief entry 106
Iber, Jorge 1961- 200
Ibert, Jacques 1890-1962 .... IDFW 3, 4
Ibingira, G(race) S(tuart) K(atebarirwe)
1932- 103
Iblacker, Reinhold A. 1930- 130
Ibn Abi Tahir Tayfur 820-893 .... DLB 311
Ibn al-Arabi, Muhyi al-Din
1165-1240 .... RGWL 3
Ibn al-Farid, 'Umar 1811(?)-1235 .... RGWL 3
Ibn al-Muqaffa', Abd Allah c. 720-c.
756 .... DLB 311
See also WLIT 6
Ibn al-Mu'tazz 861-908 .... DLB 311
Ibn al-Rumi 836-896 .... DLB 311
Ibn Bajja 1077(?)-1138 .... DLB 115
Ibn Battuta, Abu Abdalla 1304-1368(?) .... WLIT 2
Ibn Gabirol, Solomon
1021(?)-1058(?) .... DLB 115
Ibn Haduqa, 'Abd al-Hamid
See Haduqa, 'Abd al-Hamid Ibn
Ibn Khafajah, Ibrahim ibn Abi al-Fath Abu Ishaq
1058(?)-1139 .... RGWL 3
Ibn Qutaybah 828-889 .... DLB 311
Ibn Sa'd 784-845 .... DLB 311
Ibn Tufayl, (Abu Bakr) c. 1116-1185 .... WLIT 6
Ibrahim, Abdel-Sattar 1939- CANR-109
Earlier sketch in CA 69-72
Ibrahim, Ibrahim Abdelkader 1923- 13-16R
Ibrahim, Sami
See Moreh, Shmuel
Ibrahim al-Mawsili c. 742-c. 803 .... DLB 311
Ibsen, Henrik (Johan) 1828-1906 141
Brief entry 104
See also AAYA 46
See also DA
See also DA3
See also DAB
See also DAC
See also DAM DRAM, MST
See also DC 2
See also DFS 1, 6, 8, 10, 11, 15, 16
See also EW 7
See also LAIT 2
See also LATS 1:1
See also MTFW 2005
See also RGWL 2, 3
See also TCLC 2, 8, 16, 37, 52
See also WLC
Ibuka, Masaru 1908-1997 102
Obituary 163
Ibuse, Masuji 1898-1993 127
Obituary 141
See also Ibuse Masuji
See also CLC 22
See also MJW
See also RGWL 3
Ibuse Masuji
See Ibuse, Masuji
See also CWW 2
See also DLB 180
See also EWL 3
Icaza (Coronel), Jorge 1906-1978 89-92
Obituary 85-88
See also EWL 3
See also HW 1
See also LAW
Ice, Jackson Lee 1925- 25-28R
Icenhower, Joseph Bryan 1913-1995 .... CANR-5
Obituary 171
Earlier sketch in CA 5-8R
Ichijo Kanera 1402-1481
See Ichijo Kaneyoshi
Ichijo Kaneyoshi 1402-1481 .... DLB 203
Ichikawa, Kon 1915- 121
See also CLC 20
Ichikawa, Satomi 1949- CANR-129
Brief entry 116
Earlier sketch in CA 126
See also CLR 62
See also MAICYA 2
See also MAICYAS 1
See also SATA 47, 78, 146
See also SATA-Brief 36
Ichimura, Shinichi 1925- CANR-64
Earlier sketch in CA 129
Ichioka, Yuji 1936-2002 128
Obituary 210
Ichiyo, Higuchi 1872-1896 .... MJW
Icks, Robert J(oseph) 1900- 41-44R
Obituary 174
Icolari, Daniel Leonardo 1942- 17-20R
Iconoclast
See Hamilton, Mary Agnes
Iddon, Don 1913(?)-1979
Obituary 89-92
Ide, Richard S(myth) 1943-1998 120
Idel, Moshe 1947- 192
Idelsohn, Abraham Zevi 1882-1938
Brief entry 109
Iden, William
See Green, William M(ark)
Idinopulos, Thomas A. 1935- 141
Idle, Eric 1943- CANR-91
Earlier sketches in CA 116, CANR-35
See also Monty Python
See also CLC 21
Idol, John L(ane), Jr. 1932- 140
Idone, Christopher 1937- 122
Idriess, Ion L. 1891(?)-1979
Obituary 89-92
See also RHW
Idris, Yusuf 1927-1991 .... AFW
See also EWL 3
See also RGSF 2, 3
See also RGWL 3
See also SSC 74
See also WLIT 2
Iduarte, Andres (Foucher) 1907-1984 .... 33-36R
Obituary 176
Idyll, C(larence) P(urvis) 1916- CANR-8
Earlier sketch in CA 9-12R
Ierardi, Francis B. 1886-1970
Obituary 104
Iffland, August Wilhelm 1759-1814 .... DLB 94
Ifft, James B(rown) 1935-1982 53-56
Ifkovic, Edward 1943- CANR-87
Earlier sketches in CA 61-64, CANR-8, 33
Iggers, Georg G(erson) 1926- CANR-87
Earlier sketches in CA 25-28R, CANR-33
Iggers, Wilma Abeles 1921- 25-28R
Iggulden, Conn 1971- 219
Iggulden, John
See Iggulden, John Manners
See also DLB 289
Iggulden, John Manners 1917- 9-12R
See also DLBY 01
Iglauer, Edith
See Daly, Edith Iglauer
Iglehart, Alfreda P(aulette) 1950- 109
Iglehart, Louis Tillman 1915-1981
Obituary 104
Iglesia, Maria Elena De La
See De La Iglesia, Maria Elena
Iglesias, Mario 1924- CANR-50
Earlier sketches in CA 45-48, CANR-25
Iglicka, Krystyna
See Iglicka, Krystyna
Iglicka, Krystyna 1964- 207
Iglitzin, Lynne 1931- 41-44R
Ignatieff, George 1913-1989 119
Ignatieff, Michael 1947- CANR-88
Earlier sketch in CA 144
See also CN 6, 7
See also DLB 267
Ignatiev, Noel 1940- CANR-114
Earlier sketch in CA 153
Ignatius, David 1950- CANR-74
Earlier sketches in CA 128, CANR-71
Ignatow, David 1914-1997 .... CANR-96
Obituary 162
Earlier sketches in CA 9-12R, CANR-31, 57
See also CAAS 3
See also CLC 4, 7, 14, 40
See also CP 1, 2, 3, 4, 5, 6
See also DLB 5
See also EWL 3
See also MAL 5
See also PC 34
Ignoffo, Matthew 1945- 156
See also SATA 92
Ignotus
See Strachey, (Giles) Lytton
Ignotus, Paul 1901-1978 .... CANR-8
Obituary 77-80
Earlier sketch in CA 5-8R
Igo, John N., Jr. 1927- CANR-33
Earlier sketch in CA 13-16R
Igoe, James (Thomas) 1935- 108
Igoe, (Lesly) Lynn Moody 1937- 108
Igus, Toyomi 1953- CANR-92
Earlier sketch in CA 143
See also SATA 76, 112
Ihara, Saikaku 1642-1693 .... RGWL 3
Ihara Saikaku
See Ihara, Saikaku
Ihde, Don 1934- CANR-13
Earlier sketch in CA 33-36R
Ihimaera, Witi (Tame) 1944- CANR-130
Earlier sketch in CA 77-80
See also CLC 46
See also CN 2, 3, 4, 5, 6, 7
See also RGSF 2
See also SATA 148
Ihnat, Steve 1935(?)-1972
Obituary 33-36R
Iiams, Thomas M(arion), Jr.
1928-1989 .... CANR-35
Obituary 196
Earlier sketch in CA 9-12R
Iida, Deborah 1956- 156
Iino, (David) Norimoto 1918- 61-64
Iizuka, Naomi 1965- .... DFS 21
Ike, (Vincent) Chukwuemeka
1931- CANR-130
Earlier sketch in CA 168
See also BW 3
See also DLB 157
Ike, Nobutaka 1916- 21-24R
Ike, Rev.
See Eikerenkoetter, Frederick J(oseph) II
Ike, Reverend
See Eikerenkoetter, Frederick J(oseph) II
Ikeda, Daisaku 1928- 85-88
See also SATA 77
Ikeda, Kiyoshi 1928- 184
Brief entry 104
Ikejiani, Okechukwu 1917- 17-20R
Ikenberry, Oliver Samuel 1908-1978 53-56
Obituary 134
Ikerman, Ruth C. (Percival) 1910-1990 .... 13-16R
Obituary 198
Ikezawa, Natsuki 177
Ikkyu Sojun 1394-1481 .... DLB 203
Ikle, Fred Charles 1924- 45-48
Iko, Momoko 1940- CANR-14
Earlier sketch in CA 77-80
Ikor, Roger 1912-1986 184
Ilardi, Vincent 1925- 29-32R

Ilardo, Joseph A(nthony) 1944- CANR-114
Earlier sketch in CA 89-92
Ilchman, Warren Frederick 1934- CANR-1
Earlier sketch in CA 1-4R
Iles, Bert
See Ross, Zola Helen
Iles, Francis
See Cox, A(nthony) B(erkeley)
Iles, Greg CANR-109
Earlier sketch in CA 161
Iles, Jane 1954- 135
Il'f, Il'ia
See Fainzilberg, Ilya Arnoldovich
See also DLB 272
Ilf, Ilya
See Fainzilberg, Ilya Arnoldovich
See also EWL 3
See also TCLC 21
Ilg, Frances L(illian) 1902-1981 107
Obituary 104
Ilgen, Thomas
See Ilgen, Thomas L.
Ilgen, Thomas L. 1946- 120
Ilhan, Attila 1925- .... EWL 3
Ilich, John 1933- 106
Ilie, Paul 1932- CANR-10
Earlier sketch in CA 25-28R
Ilkanic Butler, Julie 1956- 177
Illan, Jose M(anuel) 1924- 45-48
Illes, Robert E(noch) 1914-1999 103
Illiano, Antonio 1934- CANR-120
Earlier sketch in CA 41-44R
Illich, Ivan 1926-2002 .... CANR-35
Obituary 213
Earlier sketches in CA 53-56, CANR-10
See also AITN 2
See also DLB 242
See also MTCW 1
Illick, Joseph E. 1934- CANR-138
Earlier sketch in CA 17-20R
Illingworth, Frank (M. B.) 1908- CANR-5
Earlier sketch in CA 5-8R
Illingworth, John 1904(?)-1980
Obituary 97-100
Illingworth, Neil 1934- 13-16R
Illingworth, Ronald Stanley
1909-1990(?) CANR-3
Obituary 131
Earlier sketch in CA 9-12R
Illwitzer, Elinor G. 1934- 29-32R
Illyes, Gyula 1902-1983 114
Obituary 109
See also CDWLB 4
See also DLB 215
See also EWL 3
See also PC 16
See also RGWL 2, 3
Ilma, Viola 1911(?)-1989
Obituary 129
Ilowite, Sheldon A. 1931- 106
See also SATA 27
Ilsey, Dent
See Chapman, John Stanton Higham
Ilsley, Dent
See Chapman, John Stanton Higham
Ilsley, Velma (Elizabeth) 1918- CANR-3
Earlier sketch in CA 9-12R
See also SATA 12
Ilson, Robert (Frederick) 1937- 124
Ilton, Phil 1948- 189
Ilyin, Mikhail Andreyevich 1878-1942
Brief entry 119
See also Osorgin, M. A.
Imai, Masaaki 1930- 129
Imai, Miko 1963- .... SATA 90
Imalayen, Fatima-Zohra
See Djebar, Assia
Imamura, Anne E(lizabeth Sommers)
1946- 126
Imamura, Shigeo 1922-1998 77-80
Imber, Gerald 1941- 89-92
Imbert, Enrique (Eduardo) Anderson
See Anderson Imbert, Enrique (Eduardo)
Imbrie, John 1925-
Brief entry 107
Imbrie, Katherine P(almer) 1952- 104
Imbs, Bravig (Wilbur Eugene) 1904-1946
Brief entry 107
See also DLB 4
Imbuga, Francis D. 1947- 186
See also DLB 157
See also EWL 3
Imel, Dorothy Myers 1934- 149
Imershein, Betsy 1953- .... SATA 62
Imerti, Arthur D(ante) 1915-1994 .... 37-40R
Obituary 197
Imes, Birney 1951- 151
Imfeld, Al 1935- CANR-29
Earlier sketches in CA 69-72, CANR-13
Imhof, Arthur E(rwin) 181
Imhoof, Maurice Lee 1930- 191
Brief entry 108
Imlah, Mick 1956- 153
See also CP 7
Immaculata, Sister
See Maxwell, Sister Mary
Immel, Erich 1926- 171
Immel, Mary Blair 1930- CANR-6
Earlier sketch in CA 13-16R
See also SATA 28
Immell, Myra H. 1941- 156
See also SATA 92
Immerman, Leon Andrew 1952- 103
Immerman, Richard H. 1949- 129
Immermann, Karl (Lebrecht)
1796-1840 .... DLB 133
Immerwahr, Sara Anderson 1914-
Brief entry 108
Immoos, Thomas 1918- CANR-82
Earlier sketches in CA 85-88, CANR-15, 35
Immroth, John Phillip 1936-1976 .... CAP-2
Earlier sketch in CA 33-36
Imperato, Pascal James 1937- CANR-56
Brief entry 106
Earlier sketch in CA 127
Imperato, Robert 1945- 228
Impey, Oliver (Richard) 1936- 108
Impey, Rose 1947- 137
See also SATA 69, 152
Impola, Richard A(arre) 1923- 139
Imrich, Jozef 1958- 218
Imrie, Richard
See Pressburger, Emeric
Imru al-Qays
See al-Qays, Imru
See also DLB 311
See also WLIT 6
Imus, (John) Don(ald) 1940- 156
Inada, Lawson Fusao 1938- CANR-126
Earlier sketches in CA 33-36R, CANR-59
See also EXPP
Inalcik, Halil 1916- CANR-28
Earlier sketch in CA 49-52
Inayat-Khan, Vilayat 1916-2004 93-96
Obituary 228
Inbar, Efraim 1947- 195
Inbau, Fred E(dward) 1909-1998 .... CANR-1
Obituary 167
Earlier sketch in CA 1-4R
Inber, Vera Mikhailovna 1893-1972
Obituary 37-40R
Ince, Basil A(ndre) 1933- 57-60
Ince, Martin (Jeffrey) 1952- 110
Ince, Thomas H. 1882-1924 .... IDFW 3, 4
See also TCLC 89
Ince, W(alter) N(ewcombe) 1927(?)-1988
Obituary 126
Inch, Morris Alton 1925- CANR-11
Earlier sketch in CA 29-32R
Inchbald, Elizabeth 1753-1821 ...... DLB 39, 89
See also RGEL 2
Inchbald, Peter 1919- 130
Inciardi, James A(nthony) 1939- CANR-8
Earlier sketch in CA 61-64
Inclan, Jessica Barksdale 214
Inclan, Ramon (Maria) del Valle
See Valle-Inclan, Ramon (Maria) del
Incogniteau, Jean-Louis
See Kerouac, Jean-Louis Lebris de
Ind, Allison 1903-1974 .... CAP-1
Earlier sketch in CA 13-16
Indelman, Elchanan Chonon 1908(?)-1983
Obituary 109
Indelman-Yinnon, Moshe 1895(?)-1977
Obituary 73-76
Inderlied, Mary Elizabeth 1945- 49-52
Indiana, Gary 1950- 171
Indik, Bernard P(aul) 1932- 33-36R
Inez, Colette 1931- 221
Earlier sketch in CA 37-40R
Autobiographical Essay in 221
See also CAAS 10
Infante, G(uillermo) Cabrera
See Cabrera Infante, G(uillermo)
Infeld, Leopold 1898-1968 201
Infield, Glenn (Berton) 1920-1981 ..... CANR-5
Obituary 103
Earlier sketch in CA 5-8R
Ing, Dean 1931- CANR-100
Earlier sketches in CA 106, CANR-23, 60
See also SFW 4
Ingalls, Daniel H(enry) H(olmes)
1916-1999 .... 17-20R
Obituary 185
Ingalls, David Sinton 1899-1985
Obituary 116
Ingalls, (Mildred Dodge) Jeremy
1911-2000 .... CANR-27
Obituary 189
Earlier sketch in CA 1-4R
Ingalls, Rachel (Holmes) 1940- 127
Brief entry 123
See also CLC 42
Ingalls, Robert Paul 1941- 110
Brief entry 107
Ingamells, John (Anderson Stuart) 1934- 187
Ingamells, Reginald Charles
See Ingamells, Rex
Ingamells, Rex 1913-1955 167
See also DLB 260
See also TCLC 35
Ingard, K(arl) Uno 1921- 33-36R
Ingarden, Roman Witold 1893-1970
Obituary 113
Ingate, Mary 1912- 73-76
Ingbar, Mary Lee 1926- 41-44R
Ingberman, Sima 1947- 150
Inge, M(ilton) Thomas 1936- CANR-51
Earlier sketches in CA 17-20R, CANR-9, 25
Inge, W. R.
See Inge, William Ralph
Inge, William (Motter) 1913-1973 .... 9-12R
See also CAD
See also CDALB 1941-1968
See also CLC 1, 8, 19
See also DA3
See also DAM DRAM
See also DFS 1, 3, 5, 8
See also DLB 7, 249
See also EWL 3
See also MAL 5
See also MTCW 1, 2
See also MTFW 2005
See also RGAL 4
See also TUS
Inge, William Ralph 1860-1954
Brief entry 116
Ingelfinger, Franz Joseph 1910-1980
Obituary 97-100
Ingelow, Jean 1820-1897 .... DLB 35, 163
See also FANT
See also SATA 33
Ingemann, B. S. 1789-1862 .... DLB 300
Ingerman, Sandra 196
Ingermann, Helena Antonia Maria Elisabeth
Dermout
See Dermout(-Ingermann), (Helena Antonia)
Maria (Elisabeth)
Ingermanson, Randall (Scott) 1958- 203
See also SATA 134
Ingersol, Jared
See Paine, Lauran (Bosworth)
Ingersoll, David E(dward) 1939- 41-44R
Ingersoll, Earl G(eorge) 1938- CANR-134
Earlier sketch in CA 159
Ingersoll, John H. 1925- 73-76
Ingersoll, Norman 1928- .... SATA 79
Ingersoll, Ralph (McAllister)
1900-1985 .... CAP-1
Obituary 115
Earlier sketch in CA 13-14
See also DLB 127
Ingersoll, Robert Franklin 1933- 104
Ingham, Colonel Frederic
See Hale, Edward Everett
Ingham, Daniel
See Lambot, Isobel
Ingham, Henry Lloyd
See Allen, Chester
Ingham, Jennie 1944- 108
Ingham, John N. 1939- 138
Ingham, Kenneth 1921- 110
Brief entry 108
Ingham, (Ann) Mary 1947- 120
Ingham, Richard Arnison 1935- 104
Ingham, Robert E(dward) 1934- 108
Inghirami, Isabel
See Leon, Maria Teresa
Ingilby, Joan Alicia 1911-2000 .... 9-12R
Obituary 192
Ingle, Clifford 1915-1977 .... 29-32R
Obituary 134
Ingle, Dwight Joyce 1907-1978 .... CAP-1
Obituary 199
Earlier sketch in CA 9-10
Ingle, Joseph B. 1946- 136
Ingle, Stephen (James) 1940- 127
Ingleby, Terry 1901- 106
Ingles, G(lenn) Lloyd 1901-1981 .... CAP-1
Obituary 200
Earlier sketch in CA 19-20
Inglis, Brian (St. John) 1916-1993 ..... CANR-47
Obituary 140
Earlier sketches in CA 17-20R, CANR-7, 23
Inglis, David Rittenhouse 1905-1995 . CANR-5
Obituary 171
Earlier sketch in CA 5-8R
Inglis, James 1927- 21-24R
Inglis, Janet 1946- 152
Inglis, John K(enneth) 1933- 106
Inglis, K. S.
See Inglis, Kenneth Stanley
Inglis, Kenneth Stanley 1929- 199
Inglis, R(obert) M(orton) G(all)
1910-1975 .... CANR-8
Earlier sketch in CA 13-16R
Inglis, Ruth Langdon 1927- CANR-1
Earlier sketch in CA 49-52
Inglis, Stuart J(ohn) 1923- 41-44R
Ingman, Bruce 1963- .... SATA 134
Ingman, Nicholas 1948- 134
See also SATA 52
Ingold, Gerard (Antoine Hubert)
1922- CANR-23
Earlier sketch in CA 106
Ingold, Jeanette 198
See also AAYA 43
See also SATA 128
Ingold, Klara (Schmid) 1913-1980 61-64
Obituary 134
Ingoldby, Grace 181
Ingpen, Robert Roger 1936- 180
See also MAICYA 2
See also SATA 109
Ingraham, Barton L(ee) 1930- CANR-43
Earlier sketch in CA 119
Ingraham, Chrys 1947- 191
Ingraham, Erick 1950- .... SATA 145
Ingraham, Joseph Holt 1809-1860 . DLB 3, 248
See also RGAL 4
Ingraham, Leonard W(illiam)
1913-2003 .... 25-28R
See also SATA 4
Ingraham, Mark H(oyt) 1896-1982 61-64
Obituary 109
Ingraham, Vernon L. 1924- 33-36R
Ingram, Allan 229
Ingram, Anne (Whitten) Bower 1937- 102
Ingram, (Mildred Rebecca) Bowen
(Prewett) 37-40R
Ingram, Collingwood 1880-1981 61-64
Obituary 103
Ingram, Derek (Thynne) 1925- 9-12R
Ingram, Forrest L(eo) 1938- 53-56
Ingram, Gregory Keith 1944- 77-80
Ingram, Heather E(lizabeth) 1969- 226
Ingram, Helen Moyer 1937- CANR-22
Earlier sketch in CA 105
Ingram, Hunter
See Lutz, Giles A(lfred)
Ingram, James C(arlton) 1922- 5-8R
Ingram, (Archibald) Kenneth
1882-1965 .... CAP-1
Earlier sketch in CA 13-14
Ingram, Martha R(obinson) 1935- 210
Ingram, Paul O. 1939- 168
Ingram, R(eginald) W(illiam) 1930-1989 129
Ingram, Scott 1948- 156
See also SATA 92
Ingram, Thomas Henry 1924- CANR-2
Earlier sketch in CA 49-52
Ingram, Tom
See Ingram, Thomas Henry
Ingram, William 1930- 41-44R
Ingram, Willis J.
See Harris, Mark
Ingrams, Doreen 1906-1997 .... CANR-12
Obituary 159
Earlier sketch in CA 33-36R
See also SATA 20, 97
Ingrams, Richard (Reid) 1937- 103
Ingrao, Charles W(illiam) 1948- 101
Ingrid, Charles
See Salsitz, Rhondi Vilott
Ingstad, Helge (Marcus) 1899-2001 65-68
Obituary 194
Ingves, Gunilla (Anna Maria Folkesdotter)
1939- 161
See also SATA 101
Ingwersen, Faith 1934- CANR-15
Earlier sketch in CA 69-72
Ingwersen, Niels 1935- CANR-15
Earlier sketch in CA 69-72
Ingwersen, Will (Alfred Theodore) 1905-1990
Obituary 132
Inigo, Martin
See Miles, Keith
Inkeles, Alex 1920- CANR-1
Earlier sketch in CA 1-4R
Inkiow, (Janakiev) Dimiter 1932- 101
Inkpen, Mick 1952- CANR-138
Earlier sketch in CA 167
See also MAICYA 2
See also SATA 99, 154
Inkster, Ian 1949- 113
Inkster, Tim 1949- 163
Inlow, Gail M(aurice) 1910-1996 .... CANR-4
Earlier sketch in CA 5-8R
Inman, Arthur Crew 1895-1963 122
Inman, Billie (Jo) Andrew 1929- CANR-28
Earlier sketches in CA 29-32R, CANR-12
Inman, Jack (Ingles) 1919-1998 .... 25-28R
Obituary 200
Inman, John 1805-1850 .... DLB 73
Inman, Robert 1943- 17-20R
Inman, Will 1923- CANR-12
Earlier sketch in CA 25-28R
Inmerito
See Javitch, Daniel Gilbert
Inmon, W(illiam) H(arvey) 1945- 110
Innaurato, Albert (F.) 1948(?)- CANR-78
Brief entry 115
Earlier sketch in CA 122
Interview in CA-122
See also CAD
See also CD 5, 6
See also CLC 21, 60
Innerhofer, Franz 1944- 101
See also DLB 85
Innes, Alan
See Tubb, E(dwin) C(harles)
Innes, Brian 1928- CANR-14
Earlier sketch in CA 21-24R
Innes, C(atherine) L(ynette) 1940- 123
Innes, Christopher David 1941- 107
Innes, Clive 1909-1999 155
Obituary 177
Innes, Frank C. 1934- 45-48
Innes, (Ralph) Hammond
See Hammond Innes, Ralph
See also CN 1, 2, 3, 4, 5
Innes, Jean
See Saunders, Jean
Innes, Michael
See Stewart, J(ohn) I(nnes) M(ackintosh)
See also DLB 276
See also MSW
Innes, Ralph Hammond
See Hammond Innes, Ralph
Innes, Rosemary E(lizabeth Jackson) 25-28R
Innes, Stephen 1946- 116
Inness, Sherrie A. 1965- CANR-107
Earlier sketch in CA 161
Inness-Brown, Elizabeth (Ann)
1954- CANR-142
Earlier sketch in CA 156
Innis, Donald Quayle 1924- 41-44R
Innis, Harold Adams 1894-1952 181
See also DLB 88
See also TCLC 77
Innis, Mary Quayle 1899-1972 201
See also DLB 88
Innis, Pauline B. (Coleman) 1918- CANR-4
Earlier sketch in CA 1-4R
Innis, Robert E(dward) 1941- 130

Innis 288 CONTEMPORARY AUTHORS

Innis, W. Joe 1937- 234
Innocenti, Roberto 1940- .... CLR 56
See also MAICYA 2
See also MAICYAS 1
See also SATA 96, 159
Inoguchi, Takashi 1944- CANR-95
Earlier sketch in CA 131
Ino Sogi 1421-1502 .... DLB 203
Inoue, Hisashi 1934- 212
Inoue, Yasushi 1907-1991 192
See also Inoue Yasushi
Inoue, Yukitoshi 1945- 25-28R
Inoue Yasushi
See Inoue, Yasushi
See also DLB 182
See also EWL 3
Inouye, Daniel K(en) 1924- 25-28R
Insall, Donald W(illiam) 1926- 61-64
Insana, Tino 1948- 123
Insel, Deborah (June) 1949- 110
Insight, James
See Coleman, Robert William Alfred
Insignares, Harriette Bias 1943- 197
Insingel, Mark 1935- CANR-87
Brief entry 110
Earlier sketch in CA 131
Insluis, Alanus de
See Alain de Lille
Insolia, Anthony Edward 1926- 120
Insoll, Timothy (Alexander) 1967- 222
Intriligator, Michael D(avid) 1938- 53-56
Invernizzi, Marcia 1950- 185
Inwood, Christiane Sourvinou
See Sourvinou-Inwood, Christiane
Inwood, M(ichael) J(ames) 1944- 117
Inwood, Stephen 1947- 186
Inyart, Gene
See Namovicz, Gene Inyart
See also SATA 6
Inzana, Ryan (J.) 228
Ioanid, Radu 237
Ioannou, Susan 1944- 194
Ioffe, Grigory 1951- CANR-121
Earlier sketch in CA 167
Iola
See Wells-Barnett, Ida B(ell)
Ionazzi, Daniel A. 145
Ione
See Ione, Carole
Ione, Carole 1937- 137
See also BW 2
Ionesco, Eugene 1912-1994 .... CANR-132
Obituary 144
Earlier sketches in CA 9-12R, CANR-55
See also CLC 1, 4, 6, 9, 11, 15, 41, 86
See also CWW 2
See also DA
See also DA3
See also DAB
See also DAC
See also DAM DRAM, MST
See also DC 12
See also DFS 4, 9
See also DLB 321
See also EW 13
See also EWL 3
See also GFL 1789 to the Present
See also LMFS 2
See also MTCW 1, 2
See also MTFW 2005
See also RGWL 2, 3
See also SATA 7
See also SATA-Obit 79
See also TWA
See also WLC
Ionescu, Ghita G. 1913-1996 103
Iongh, Mary (Dows Herter Norton) Crena de
See Crena de Iongh, Mary (Dows Herter Norton)
Iorio, James 1921- 61-64
Iorio, John 1925- 49-52
Iorizzo, Luciano J(ohn) 1930- 73-76
Ipcar, Dahlov (Zorach) 1917- CANR-45
Earlier sketches in CA 17-20R, CANR-9
See also MAICYA 1, 2
See also SAAS 8
See also SATA 1, 49, 147
See also SATA-Essay 147
Ippolito, Donna 1945- 104
Ipse, Henrik
See Hartleben, Otto Erich
Ipsen, D(avid) C(arl) 1921- 33-36R
Iqbal, Afzal 1919- CANR-53
Earlier sketches in CA 61-64, CANR-10, 26
Iqbal, Muhammad 1877-1938 215
See also EWL 3
See also TCLC 28
Iqbal, Sabiha 1950- 111
Iranek-Osmecki, Kazimierz 1897-1984 ... 49-52
Obituary 113
Irby, Kenneth (Lee) 1936- CANR-22
Earlier sketch in CA 69-72
See also CP 1, 2
Iredale, Robyn Rae 1944- 221
Ireland, Alan Stuart 1940- .... CP 1
Ireland, Ann 1953- CANR-139
Earlier sketches in CA 127, CANR-58
Ireland, David 1927- CANR-29
Earlier sketch in CA 25-28R
See also CN 2, 3, 4, 5, 6, 7
See also DLB 289
Ireland, Earl (Crowell) 1928- 5-8R
Ireland, Jill (Dorothy) 1936-1990 135
Ireland, Joe C. 1936- 73-76
Ireland, Karin CANR-128
Earlier sketch in CA 168
See also SATA 101, 151
Ireland, Kathy 1963- 214
Ireland, Kevin (Mark) 1933- 73-76
See also CP 1, 2, 3, 4, 5, 6, 7
Ireland, Norma Olin 1907- CANR-3
Earlier sketch in CA 9-12R
Ireland, Patricia 1945- 156
Ireland, Patrick
See O'Doherty, Brian
Ireland, Patrick R(ichard) 1961- 148
Ireland, Perrin 221
Ireland, Robert M(ichael) 1937- CANR-92
Earlier sketches in CA 45-48, CANR-25
Ireland, Sandra L(eora) Jones 1942- 137
Ireland-Frey, Louise 1912- 219
Iremonger, Lucille (d'Oyen)
1915-1989(?) CANR-6
Obituary 127
Earlier sketch in CA 9-12R
Iremonger, Valentin 1918- 101
See also CP 1, 2
Ireson, Barbara (Francis) 1927- CANR-21
Earlier sketch in CA 5-8R
Ireton, Rollo
See Shirley, Ralph
Irfani, Suroosh 1947- 118
Irgang, Jacob 1930-1995 85-88
Obituary 176
Iribarne, Louis 1940- CANR-78
Earlier sketch in CA 123
Interview in CA-123
Irigaray, Luce 1930- CANR-121
Earlier sketch in CA 154
See also CLC 164
See also FW
Irion, Mary Jean 1922- 21-24R
Irion, Paul E(rnst) 1922- 21-24R
Irion, Ruth (Hershey) 1921- 65-68
Irish, Donald P(aul) 1919- 49-52
Irish, Jerry 125
Irish, Marian D(oris) 1909-2001 .... 9-12R
Obituary 201
Irish, Richard K. 1932- 65-68
Irish, William
See Hopley-Woolrich, Cornell George
Iriye, Akira 1934- CANR-11
Earlier sketch in CA 25-28R
Irizarry, Estelle 1937- 187
Irland, David
See Green, Julien (Hartridge)
Irmscher, Christoph 1962- 201
Iroh, Eddie 170
See also BW 3
Iron, Ralph
See Schreiner, Olive (Emilie Albertina)
Irons, Peter
See Irons, Peter H(anlon)
Irons, Peter H(anlon) 1940- CANR-113
Earlier sketch in CA 128
Ironside, Henry Allan 1876-1951
Brief entry 115
Ironside, Jetske 1940- .... SATA 60
Ironside, Virginia 1944- 120
Iron Thunderhorse
See Sekaxsu, Petakwonexnajunkis
Irsfeld, John H(enry) 1937- 65-68
Irvin, Bob
See Irvin, Robert W.
Irvin, Candace 228
Irvin, Dona L. 1917- 138
Irvin, Eric 1908- .... CP 1
Irvin, Fred 1914- .... SATA 15
Irvin, Margaret Elizabeth 1916- .... CP 1
Irvin, Rea 1881-1972
Obituary 93-96
Irvin, Robert W. 1933-1980
Obituary 103
Irvine, Alexander C. 214
Irvine, Angela 235
Irvine, Betty Jo 1943- 77-80
Irvine, Demar (Buel) 1908-1995 .... 33-36R
Obituary 196
Irvine, Georgeanne 1955- .... SATA 72
Irvine, Janice M. 1951- CANR-126
Earlier sketch in CA 135
Irvine, Joan 1951- .... SATA 80
Irvine, John Henry 1951- 119
Irvine, Leslie 1958- 188
Irvine, Lucy 1956- CANR-126
Earlier sketch in CA 118
Irvine, M. Keith 1924-1994 .... 29-32R
Obituary 145
Irvine, R. R.
See Irvine, Robert (Ralstone)
Irvine, Reed (John) 1922-2004 128
Obituary 233
Irvine, Robert (Ralstone) 1936- CANR-57
Earlier sketches in CA 81-84, CANR-15
See also CMW 4
Irvine, Sidney H(erbert) 1931-
Brief entry 106
Irvine, William 1906-1964
Obituary 106
Irvine, William (Burriss III) 1958- 144
Irving, Alexander
See Hume, Ruth Fox
Irving, Blanche M(cDaniel) 1904-1985 114
Obituary 199
Irving, Brian William 1932- 53-56
Irving, Clifford Michael 1930- CANR-2
Earlier sketch in CA 1-4R
See also AITN 1
Irving, Clive 1933- CANR-22
Earlier sketch in CA 85-88
Irving, David (John Cawdell) 1938- .. CANR-25
Earlier sketch in CA 13-16R
Irving, Edward B(urroughs), Jr. 1923-
Brief entry 112
Irving, Gordon 1918- 25-28R
Irving, Henry
See Kanter, Hal
Irving, John (Winslow) 1942- CANR-133
Earlier sketches in CA 25-28R, CANR-28, 73, 112
See also AAYA 8, 62
See also AMWS 6
See also BEST 89:3
See also BPFB 2
See also CLC 13, 23, 38, 112, 175
See also CN 3, 4, 5, 6, 7
See also CPW
See also DA3
See also DAM NOV, POP
See also DLB 6, 278
See also DLBY 1982
See also EWL 3
See also MAL 5
See also MTCW 1, 2
See also MTFW 2005
See also NFS 12, 14
See also RGAL 4
See also TUS
Irving, Karen D. 1957- 220
Irving, R(obert) L(ock) Graham
1877-1969 .... CAP-1
Earlier sketch in CA 13-16
Irving, Robert
See Adler, Irving
Irving, Shae (Lyn) 1966- 173
Irving, Stephanie (Jean) 1962- 139
Irving, T(homas) B(allantine)
1914-2002 .... 37-40R
Irving, Washington 1783-1859 .... AAYA 56
See also AMW
See also CDALB 1640-1865
See also CLR 97
See also DA
See also DA3
See also DAB
See also DAC
See also DAM MST
See also DLB 3, 11, 30, 59, 73, 74, 183, 186, 250, 254
See also EXPS
See also GL 2
See also LAIT 1
See also RGAL 4
See also RGSF 2
See also SSC 2, 37
See also SSFS 1, 8, 16
See also SUFW 1
See also TUS
See also WCH
See also WLC
See also YABC 2
Irwin, Ann(abelle Bowen)
1915-1998 .... CANR-36
Obituary 170
Earlier sketches in CA 101, CANR-19
See also Irwin, Hadley
See also CLR 40
See also MAICYA 1, 2
See also SATA 44, 89
See also SATA-Brief 38
See also SATA-Obit 106
See also WYA
See also YAW
Irwin, Bill 1950- 213
Irwin, Constance (H.) Frick
1913-1995 .... CANR-5
Obituary 197
Earlier sketch in CA 1-4R
See also SATA 6
Irwin, Cynthia C.
See Irwin-Williams, Cynthia (Cora)
Irwin, David 1933- 53-56
Irwin, Francis William 1905-1985 189
Brief entry 105
Irwin, G. H.
See Palmer, Raymond A.
Irwin, George 1910-1971 .... 41-44R
Irwin, Grace (Lilian) 1907- 17-20R
See also DLB 68
Irwin, Graham W(ilkie) 1920-1991 121
Obituary 135
Brief entry 118
Irwin, Hadley
See Hadley, Lee and Irwin, Ann(abelle Bowen)
See also AAYA 13
See also BYA 8
See also CLR 40
See also SAAS 14
See also WYA
See also YAW
Irwin, Inez Haynes 1873-1970 102
Irwin, James W. 1891(?)-1977
Obituary 73-76
Irwin, John P. 1926- 214
Irwin, John T(homas) 1940- 53-56
Irwin, John V(aleur) 1915- CANR-1
Earlier sketch in CA 45-48
Irwin, Keith Gordon 1885-1964 .... 5-8R
See also SATA 11
Irwin, Margaret 1889-1967
Obituary 93-96
See also FANT
See also RHW
Irwin, Mark 1953- 219
Irwin, P. K.
See Page, P(atricia) K(athleen)
Irwin, (Joseph) Paul 1940- 107
Irwin, Raymond 1902-1976 .... CAP-1
Earlier sketch in CA 9-10
Irwin, Robert (Graham) 1946- CANR-81
Earlier sketches in CA 121, CANR-48
See also FANT
See also SUFW 2
Irwin, Ruth Beckey 1906- 29-32R
Irwin, Theodore 1907-1997 65-68
Irwin, Vera Rushforth 1913-1995 .... 33-36R
Obituary 197
Irwin, W(illiam) R(obert) 1915- 65-68
Irwin, Will(iam Henry) 1873-1948
Brief entry 117
See also DLB 25
Irwin-Williams, Cynthia (Cora) 1936- . CANR-1
Earlier sketch in CA 45-48
Isaac, Erich 1928- 45-48
Isaac, Glynn Llewelyn 1937-1985
Obituary 117
Isaac, Joanne 1934- 25-28R
See also SATA 21
Isaac, Joseph Ezra 1922- 115
Isaac, Megan (Lynn) 1966- 195
Isaac, Paul E(dward) 1926- 17-20R
Isaac, Rael Jean (Isaacs) 1933- 17-20R
Isaac, Rhys L(lywelyn) 1937- 113
Isaac, Stephen 1925- 33-36R
Isaacs, Alan 1925- CANR-3
Earlier sketch in CA 9-12R
Isaacs, Anne 1949- CANR-120
Earlier sketch in CA 155
See also BYA 16
See also SATA 90
Isaacs, Arnold R. 1941- CANR-79
Earlier sketch in CA 143
Isaacs, Bernard 1924-1995 107
Obituary 148
Isaacs, E. Elizabeth 1917- 5-8R
Isaacs, Edith Somborn 1884-1970
Obituary 77-80
Isaacs, Harold Robert 1910-1986 .... CANR-2
Obituary 119
Earlier sketch in CA 1-4R
Isaacs, Jacob
See Kranzler, George G(ershon)
Isaacs, Jeremy (Israel) 1932- 195
Isaacs, Jorge Ricardo 1837-1895 .... LAW
Isaacs, Neil D(avid) 1931- CANR-89
Earlier sketches in CA 5-8R, CANR-9
Isaacs, Norman Ellis 1908-1999 81-84
Obituary 165
Isaacs, Ronald (Howard) 1947- CANR-129
Earlier sketch in CA 162
Isaacs, Stan 1929- 13-16R
Isaacs, Stephen D(avid) 1937- 81-84
Isaacs, Susan (Sutherland Fairhurst) 1885-1948
Brief entry 120
Isaacs, Susan 1943- CANR-134
Earlier sketches in CA 89-92, CANR-20, 41, 65, 112
Interview in CANR-20
See also BEST 89:1
See also BPFB 2
See also CLC 32
See also CPW
See also DA3
See also DAM POP
See also MTCW 1, 2
See also MTFW 2005
Isaacson, Joel 1930-
Brief entry 114
Isaacson, Judith Magyar 1925- 133
Isaacson, Philip M(arshal) 1924- 128
See also SATA 87
Isaacson, Robert L. 1928- CANR-7
Earlier sketch in CA 17-20R
Isaacson, Walter (Seff) 1952- CANR-43
Earlier sketch in CA 112
Isaak, Robert A(llen) 1945- CANR-13
Earlier sketch in CA 61-64
Isacoff, Stuart (Michael) 1949- 214
Isadora, Rachel 1953(?)- CANR-99
Brief entry 111
Earlier sketch in CA 137
See also CLR 7
See also CWRI 5
See also MAICYA 1, 2
See also SATA 54, 79, 121
See also SATA-Brief 32
Isai
See Ishikawa, Jun
Isais, Juan M. 1926- 29-32R
Isakovsky, Mikhail Vasilyevich 1900-1973
Obituary 41-44R
Isaksson, Folke 1927- 194
Isaksson, Ulla (Margareta Lundberg) 1916-2000
Obituary 189
Brief entry 109
See also DLB 257
Isard, Walter 1919- 114
Brief entry 112
Isban, Samuel 1905-1995 .... CANR-2
Obituary 176
Earlier sketch in CA 49-52
See also Izban, Samuel
Isbell, Rebecca T(emple) 1942- 196
See also SATA 125
Isbister, Clair
See Isbister, Jean Sinclair
Isbister, Jean Sinclair 1915- CANR-39
Earlier sketches in CA 1-4R, CANR-1, 18
Isbister, John 1942- 139
Ise, John 1885-1960(?) CAP-1
Earlier sketch in CA 13-14
Isegawa, Moses 1963- 232
Isely, Flora Kunigunde Duncan
See Duncan, Kunigunde
Isely, Helen Sue (Pearson) 1917-1978 .... 5-8R
Obituary 120

Cumulative Index 289 Jack

Iseminger, Gary 1937- 37-40R
Isenberg, Andrew C(hristian) 231
Isenberg, Barbara CANR-121
Earlier sketch in CA 171
Isenberg, Irwin M. 1931-1979 .... CANR-11
Earlier sketch in CA 17-20R
See also BYA 1
Isenberg, Jane Frances 1940- 215
Isenberg, Joan P. 1941- 166
Isenberg, Noah 191
Isenberg, Seymour 1930- 33-36R
Isenberg, Sheila 1943- CANR-109
Earlier sketch in CA 149
Isenhour, Thomas Lee 1939- 57-60
Iser, Wolfgang 1926- 57-60
See also DLB 242
Isernhagen, Hartwig Wolf Ernst 1940- 186
Iserson, Kenneth Victor 1949- CANR-127
Earlier sketch in CA 157
Ishak, Fayek (Matta) 1922- 41-44R
Ishak, Yusof bin 1910(?)-1970
Obituary 104
Isham, Charlotte H(ickock) 1912- 73-76
See also SATA 21
Isham, Linda (Rose) 1938-
Brief entry 107
Ishee, John A. 1934- CANR-18
Earlier sketch in CA 25-28R
Isherwood, Charles 1964- 163
Isherwood, Christopher (William Bradshaw)
1904-1986 .... CANR-133
Obituary 117
Earlier sketches in CA 13-16R, CANR-35, 97
See also AMWS 14
See also BRW 7
See also CLC 1, 9, 11, 14, 44
See also CN 1, 2, 3
See also DA3
See also DAM DRAM, NOV
See also DLB 15, 195
See also DLBY 1986
See also EWL 3
See also IDTP
See also MTCW 1, 2
See also MTFW 2005
See also RGAL 4
See also RGEL 2
See also SSC 56
See also TUS
See also WLIT 4
Isherwood, Robert M. 1935- 126
Ishida, Hakyo
See Ishida, Tetsuo
Ishida, Takeshi 1923- CANR-38
Earlier sketches in CA 97-100, CANR-16
Ishigaki, Rin 1920- .... RGWL 3
Ishigaki Rin
See Ishigaki, Rin
Ishigo, Estelle 1899-1990 61-64
Ishiguro, Kazuo 1954- CANR-133
Earlier sketches in CA 120, CANR-49, 95
See also AAYA 58
See also BEST 90:2
See also BPFB 2
See also BRWS 4
See also CLC 27, 56, 59, 110
See also CN 5, 6, 7
See also DA3
See also DAM NOV
See also DLB 194
See also EWL 3
See also MTCW 1, 2
See also MTFW 2005
See also NFS 13
See also WLIT 4
See also WWE 1
Ishihara, Shintaro 1932- 139
Ishii, Sogo 1957- 215
Ishikawa, Hakuhin
See Ishikawa, Takuboku
Ishikawa, Jun 1899-1987 193
See also Ishikawa Jun
Ishikawa, Takuboku 1886(?)-1912 153
Brief entry 113
See also Ishikawa Takuboku
See also DAM POET
See also PC 10
See also TCLC 15
Ishikawa Jun
See Ishikawa, Jun
See also DLB 182
See also EWL 3
Ishikawa Takuboku .... EWL 3
Ishino, Iwao 1921- 17-20R
Ish-Kishor, Judith 1892-1972 .... 1-4R
Obituary 103
See also SATA 11
Ish-Kishor, Sulamith 1896-1977 73-76
Obituary 69-72
See also BYA 2
See also CWRI 5
See also SATA 17
Ishlon, Deborah 1925- 1-4R
Ishmael, Woodi 1914-1995 .... SATA 31
See also SATA-Obit 109
Ishmole, Jack 1924- 49-52
Ishwaran, K(arigoudar) 1922- 49-52
Isichei, Elizabeth 1939- CANR-5
Earlier sketch in CA 53-56
Isikoff, Michael 1952- 192
Isis
See Torbett, Harvey Douglas Louis
Isitt, Debbie 1966- 197
See also CBD
See also CP 5, 6
See also CWD
See also DLB 233
Isitt, Larry R. 1945- 231
Iskander, Fazil (Abdulovich) 1929- 102
See also Iskander, Fazil' Abdulevich
See also CLC 47
See also EWL 3
Iskander, Fazil' Abdulevich
See Iskander, Fazil (Abdulovich)
See also DLB 302
Iskander, Sylvia Patterson 1940- 198
Iskander, Sylvia W.
See Iskander, Sylvia Patterson
Islam, A(bul) K(hair) M(uhammed) Aminul
1933- 41-44R
Islam, Kazi Nazrul 1899(?)-1976
Obituary 69-72
See also Nazrul Islam
Island, David 141
Islas, Arturo 1938-1991 131
Obituary 140
See also DLB 122
See also HW 1
Isle, Sue 1963- 173
See also SATA 105
Isle, Walter (Whitfield) 1933- 25-28R
Isler, Alan (David) 1934- CANR-105
Earlier sketch in CA 156
See also CLC 91
Isler, Betty
See Isler, Elizabeth
Isler, Elizabeth 1915-1994 114
Obituary 171
Ismach, Arnold H(arvey) 1930- 85-88
Ismael, Tareq Y. 125
Ismail, A. H. 1923- 25-28R
Isma'il, Isma'il Fahd 1940- .... EWL 3
Isocrates c. 436B.C.-338B.C. .... AW 1
Isogai, Hiroshi 1940- 102
Isola, Frank 1964- 201
Isom, Joan Shaddox 1932- 174
Ison, Graham 236
Isozaki, Arata 1931- 194
Ispahani, Mirza Abol Hassan 1902-1981
Obituary 108
Israel, Abby 1942- 107
Israel, Betsy 1958- 227
Israel, Charles E(dward) 1920-1999 .... 1-4R
See also CN 1, 2, 3
Israel, Elaine 1945- CANR-9
Earlier sketch in CA 53-56
See also SATA 12
Israel, Fred L. 1934- CANR-12
Earlier sketch in CA 17-20R
Israel, Gerard 1928- 81-84
Israel, Jerry (Michael) 1941- 29-32R
Israel, John (Warren) 1935- 21-24R
Israel, Jonathan I. 1946- 109
Israel, Lee 1939- 143
Israel, Marion Louise 1882-1973 .... 1-4R
Obituary 103
See also SATA-Obit 26
Israel, Martin 1927- 109
Israel, Paul (B.) 179
Israel, Peter 1933- CANR-126
Earlier sketch in CA 128
Israel, Philip 1935- 133
Israel, Saul 1910-1990 .... CAP-1
Obituary 131
Earlier sketch in CA 13-16
Israel-Curley, Marcia 1930-2004 215
Obituary 229
Israeloff, Roberta 1952- 118
Israelowitz, Oscar 1949- CANR-32
Earlier sketch in CA 113
Israelyan, Victor (Levonov) 1919- 151
Issachar
See Stanford, J(ohn) K(eith)
Issakson, C. Benjamin
See Bordowitz, Hank
Issawi, Charles (Philip) 1916-2000 ... CANR-89
Obituary 190
Earlier sketches in CA 5-8R, CANR-4, 20, 42
Isser, Natalie 1927- 53-56
Isserman, Maurice 1951- 192
Issler, Anne Roller 1892-1975 49-52
Istrati, Panait 1884-1935 .... GFL 1789 to the Present
Iswolsky, Helene 1896-1975 .... 5-8R
Obituary 61-64
Italiaander, Rolf (Bruno Maximilian)
1913-1991 .... CANR-23
Earlier sketches in CA 5-8R, CANR-6
Itani, Frances (Susan) 1942- 138
Iterson, S(iny) R(ose) Van
See Van Iterson, S(iny) R(ose)
Itim, Talang
See Lapena-Bonifacio, Amelia
Itse, Elizabeth M(yers) 1930- CANR-1
Earlier sketch in CA 49-52
Itule, Bruce D. 1947- 125
Itwaru, Arnold (Harrichand) 1942- 134
Itzin, Catherine 1944- CANR-14
Earlier sketch in CA 77-80
Itzkoff, Seymour W(illiam) 1928- 33-36R
Iurenen, Sergey
See Yuryenen, Sergey
Ivan, Martha Miller Pfaff 1909-1990 ..... CAP-2
Earlier sketch in CA 19-20
Ivancevich, John M(ichael) 1939- CANR-25
Earlier sketch in CA 29-32R
Ivanisevic, Drago 1907-1981 .... DLB 181
Ivanko, John D(uane) 1966- 182
See also SATA 111
Ivanov, Georgii 1894-1958 .... DLB 317
Ivanov, Miroslav 1929- 81-84
Ivanov, Viacheslav Ivanovich
1866-1949 .... DLB 295
Ivanov, Vsevolod Viacheslavovich
See Ivanov, Vsevolod Vyacheslavovich
See also DLB 272
Ivanov, Vsevolod Vyacheslavovich 1895-1963
Obituary 93-96
See also Ivanov, Vsevolod Viacheslavovich
Ivanov, Vyacheslav Ivanovich 1866-1949
Brief entry 122
See also EWL 3
See also TCLC 33
Ivanova, T(atiana) G(rigoryevna) 232
Ivanova, Tatyana
See Ivanova, T(atiana) G(rigoryevna)
Ivanov-Vano, Ivan 1900-1987 .... IDFW 3, 4
Ivask, George
Obituary 118
See also Ivask, Iurii
Ivask, Iurii 1907-1986
See Ivask, George
See also DLB 317
Ivask, Ivar Vidrik 1927-1992 .... CANR-24
Obituary 139
Earlier sketch in CA 37-40R
See also CLC 14
Ivaska, Astride 1926- .... DLB 232
Ivens, Georg Henri Anton 1898(?)-1989
Obituary 129
Ivens, Joris
See Ivens, Georg Henri Anton
Ivens, Michael 1924-2001 .... 5-8R
Obituary 200
See also CP 1
Ivens, Virginia R(uth) 1922- 105
Ivers, Larry E(dward) 1936- 77-80
Iversen, Gudmund R(agnvaldsson)
1934- CANR-4
Earlier sketch in CA 53-56
Iversen, Leslie 1937- 199
Iversen, Nick 1951- 73-76
Iverson, Carol (L.) 1941- 218
See also SATA 145
Iverson, Diane 1950- 194
See also SATA 122
Iverson, Eric G.
See Turtledove, Harry (Norman)
Iverson, Genie 1942- CANR-9
Earlier sketch in CA 65-68
See also SATA-Brief 52
Iverson, Jeffrey (James) 1934- 105
Iverson, Lucille K(arin) 1925- 61-64
Iverson, Peter James 1944- 106
Ivery, Martha M. 1948- .... SATA 124
Ives, Burl (Icle Ivanhoe) 1909-1995 103
Obituary 148
Ives, Charles Edward 1874-1954 149
Brief entry 113
Ives, Colta Feller 1943- CANR-137
Earlier sketch in CA 118
Ives, David 1951- 207
Ives, Edward D(awson) 1925- 25-28R
Ives, John
See Garfield, Brian (Francis Wynne)
Ives, Lawrence
See Woods, Frederick
Ives, Morgan
See Bradley, Marion Zimmer
See also GLL 1
Ives, Sandy
See Ives, Edward D(awson)
Ives, Sumner 1911-1984 .... 9-12R
Ivey, Allen E(ugene) 1933- CANR-2
Earlier sketch in CA 49-52
Ivey, Donald 1918- 89-92
Ivey, James Burnett 1925- 119
Ivey, Jim
See Ivey, James Burnett
Ivey, Monteria (Henry) 1960-2001 205
Ivie, Robert L(ynn) 1945- 115
Ivie, Robert M. 1930- 9-12R
Ivins, Mary Tyler 1944- CANR-98
See also Ivins, Molly
Ivins, Molly 1944(?)- 138
See also Ivins, Mary Tyler
See also CSW
Ivnev, Riurik
See Kovalev, Mikhail A(leksandrovich)
Ivo, Ledo 1924- CANR-134
Earlier sketches in CA 129, CANR-65
See also LAWS 1
Ivory, James (Francis) 1928- 139
Brief entry 109
Ivory, Judith 163
Ivry, Alfred Lyon 1935- CANR-1
Earlier sketch in CA 45-48
Ivry, Benjamin 1958- CANR-100
Earlier sketch in CA 144
Ivy, Ralph 1938- 120
Iwajin, Antony
See Evenbach, Anton
Iwamatsu, Jun Atsushi 1908-1994 .... CANR-45
Obituary 146
Earlier sketch in CA 73-76
See also Yashima, Taro
See also CWRI 5
See also MAICYA 1, 2
See also MAICYAS 1
See also SATA 14, 81
Iwamura, Kazuo 1939- 129
Iwaniuk, Waclaw 1915- 130
See also DLB 215
See also EWL 3
Iwano, Homei 1873-1920
See Iwano Homei
Iwano Homei
See Iwano, Homei
See also DLB 180
Iwao, Sumiko 1935- 141
Iwasaki (Matsumoto), Chihiro 1918-1974 ... 233
See also CLR 18
Iwasaki, Mineko 1949- 215
Iwaszkiewicz, Jaroslaw 1894-1980
Obituary 97-100
See also DLB 215
See also EWL 3
Iwata, Masakazu 1917- 17-20R
Iwerks, Ub 1901-1971 .... IDFW 3, 4
Iyasere, Solomon O(gbede) 1940- 179
Iyayi, Festus 1947- 161
See also AFW
See also CN 5, 6, 7
See also DLB 157
See also EWL 3
Iyengar, B(ellur) K(rishnamachar) S(undararaja)
1918- 97-100
Iyengar, K(odaganallur) R(amaswami) Srinivasa
1908-1999 .... CANR-8
Earlier sketch in CA 5-8R
Iyengar, S. Kesava 1894- 17-20R
Iyer, C. Subramania 1882-1921
See Bharati, Subramania
Iyer, Pico 1957- CANR-95
Earlier sketch in CA 144
Iyer, Raghavan (Narasimhan)
1930-1995 .... CANR-22
Obituary 149
Earlier sketches in CA 57-60, CANR-6
Izant, Grace Goulder 1893-1984 .... CAP-1
Earlier sketch in CA 9-10
Izard, Barbara 1926- 29-32R
Izard, Carroll E(llis) 1923- CANR-4
Earlier sketch in CA 49-52
Izban, Samuel 176
See also Isban, Samuel
Izban, Shmuel
See Isban, Samuel
Izenberg, Gerald N(athan) 1939- 105
Izenour, George Charles 1912- 93-96
Izetbegovic, Alija Ali 1925-2003 197
Obituary 220
Izumi, Kyoka 1873-1939 191
See also Izumi Kyoka and Kyoka
Izumi Kyoka
See Izumi, Kyoka
See also DLB 180
See also EWL 3
Izzi, Eugene 1953(?)-1996 144
Obituary 155
See also Izzi, Eugene
Izzidien, Mawil 1948- 203
Izzo, Herbert J(ohn) 1928- 41-44R
Izzo, Jean-Claude 1945-2000 224

J

J 232
See also AAYA 63
J. L.-M.
See Lees-Milne, James
J. R. S.
See Gogarty, Oliver St. John
Jaanus, Maire 1940- CANR-45
Earlier sketch in CA 120
Jabavu, Davidson Don Tengo 1885-1959 ... 153
See also BW 2
Jabay, Earl 1925- 21-24R
Jabbar, Kareem Abdul
See Abdul-Jabbar, Kareem
Jabber, Fuad (Amin)
See Jabber, Paul
Jabber, Paul 1943- CANR-27
Earlier sketch in CA 113
Jaber, Diana Abu
See Abu-Jaber, Diana
Jabes, Edmond 1912-1991 127
Obituary 133
See also EWL 3
Jabez
See Nicol, Eric (Patrick)
Jabine, Thomas B(oyd) 1925- 141
Jablokov, Alexander 1956- 142
See also SFW 4
Jablon, Howard 1939- 116
Jablon, Madelyn 1956- 190
Jablonski, Edward 1922-2004 .... CANR-18
Obituary 224
Earlier sketches in CA 1-4R, CANR-2
Jablonski, Ronald E. 1929-
Brief entry 104
Jablonsky, David 1938- 133
Jablow, Martha M(oraghan) 1944- CANR-43
Earlier sketch in CA 112
Jabra, Jabra Ibrahim 1920-1994 .... CWW 2
See also EWL 3
Jabran, Kahlil
See Gibran, Kahlil
Jabran, Khalil
See Gibran, Kahlil
Jabs, Carolyn 1950- 110
Jac, Cherlyn
See Biggs, Cheryl
Jac, Lee
See Morton, Lee Jack, Jr.
Jaccard, Mark (Kenneth) 1955- 239
Jaccottet, Philippe 1925- 129
Brief entry 116
See also CWW 2
See also GFL 1789 to the Present
Jach, Antoni 1958- 188
Jack, Andrew (John) 1967- 234
Jack, Belinda E(lizabeth) 195

Jack, Coyote
See Bowen, Peter
Jack, Dana Crowley 1945- ... 141
Jack, Daniel Thomson 1901-1984
Obituary ... 115
Jack, Donald Lamont 1924- ... CANR-3
Earlier sketch in CA 1-4R
Jack, Homer A(lexander)
1916-1993 ... CANR-14
Obituary ... 142
Earlier sketch in CA 41-44R
Jack, Ian 1923- ... 57-60
Jack, Malcolm Roy 1946- ... 226
Jack, R. D. S.
See Jack, Ronald D(yce) S(adler)
Jack, R(obert) Ian 1935- ... CANR-3
Earlier sketch in CA 49-52
Jack, Ronald D(yce) S(adler) 1941- ... 120
Jacka, Judy 1938- ... 219
Jacka, Martin 1943- ... SATA 72
Jackall, Robert ... CANR-79
Earlier sketch in CA 135
Jackendoff, Ray (Saul) 1945- ... CANR-127
Earlier sketches in CA 53-56, CANR-6
Jackendoff, Ray S.
See Jackendoff, Ray (Saul)
Jacker, Corinne L(itvin) 1933- ... CANR-45
Earlier sketch in CA 17-20R
Jackins, Harvey 1916- ... CANR-37
Earlier sketches in CA 49-52, CANR-1, 17
Jackley, John L. 1955- ... 158
Jacklin, Anthony 1944- ... 85-88
Jacklin, Tony
See Jacklin, Anthony
Jackman, E(dwin) R(ussell)
1894-1967(?) ... CAP-1
Earlier sketch in CA 13-16
Jackman, Jarrell C(lark) 1943- ... 120
Jackman, Leslie (Arthur James)
1919- ... CANR-29
Earlier sketch in CA 29-32R
Jackman, Michael R. 1952- ... 120
Jackman, Robert W(illiam) 1946- ... CANR-51
Earlier sketch in CA 124
Jackman, Stuart 1922- ... CANR-18
Earlier sketch in CA 101
Jackman, Sydney W(ayne) 1925- ... CANR-19
Earlier sketches in CA 1-4R, CANR-1
Jackont, Amnon 1948- ... 130
Jackowska, Nicki 1942- ... 119
Jackowski, Edward J. ... 218
Jackowski, Karol (A.) 1946(?)- ... 229
Jacks, L(awrence) P(earsall) 1860-1955 ... 190
Brief entry ... 113
See also DLB 135
Jacks, Oliver
See Gandley, Kenneth Royce
Jacks, Philip (J.) 1954- ... 223
Jackson, A(lexander) B(rooks) 1925- ... 104
Jackson, Alan 1938- ... 101
See also CP 1, 2
Jackson, Albert 1943- ... 93-96
Jackson, Albina
See Geis, Richard E(rwin)
Jackson, Alison 1953- ... 178
See also SATA 73, 108, 160
Jackson, Allan 1905(?)-1976
Obituary ... 65-68
Jackson, Allen W. 1951- ... 197
Jackson, Angela 1951- ... 216
Earlier sketch in CA 176
Autobiographical Essay in ... 216
See also BW 3
See also DLB 41
Jackson, Anna J. 1926- ... 103
Jackson, Anne
See Jackson, Anna J.
Jackson, Anne 1896(?)-1984 ... SATA-Obit 37
Jackson, Anthony 1926- ... CANR-11
Earlier sketch in CA 69-72
Jackson, Archibald Stewart 1922-2003 ... 61-64
Obituary ... 213
Jackson, Arlene M(arjorie) 1938- ... 118
Jackson, Arthur 1921-
Brief entry ... 104
Jackson, Ashley 1971- ... 197
Jackson, B(erkley) R. 1937- ... 25-28R
Jackson, Barbara (Ward) 1914-1981 ... CANR-6
Obituary ... 103
Earlier sketch in CA 45-48
Jackson, Barbara Garvey Seagrave
1929- ... 21-24R
Jackson, Basil 1920- ... CANR-8
Earlier sketch in CA 57-60
Jackson, Blair ... 190
Jackson, Blyden 1910-2000 ... 57-60
Jackson, Bo
See Jackson, Vincent Edward
Jackson, Brenda Streater 195(?)- ... 218
Jackson, Brian 1933(?)-1983
Obituary ... 110
Jackson, Brooks 1941- ... 97-100
Jackson, Bruce 1936- ... 89-92
Jackson, C(hester) O(scar) 1901-1980 ... CAP-1
Earlier sketch in CA 13-16
Jackson, C(aary) Paul 1902-1991 ... CANR-6
Earlier sketch in CA 5-8R
See also SATA 6
Jackson, Caary
See Jackson, C(aary) Paul
Jackson, Carlton (Luther) 1933- ... 21-24R
Jackson, Carole ... 104
Jackson, Charles (Reginald) 1903-1968 ... 101
Obituary ... 25-28R
See also DLB 234
Jackson, Charles O. 1935- ... 126
Brief entry ... 112
Jackson, Charlotte E. (Cobden) 1903(?)-1989
Obituary ... 128
See also SATA-Obit 62
Jackson, Christine E(lisabeth) 1936- ... CANR-47
Earlier sketch in CA 121
Jackson, Clarence J.-L.
See Bulliet, Richard W(illiams)
Jackson, Daniel
See Wingrove, David (John)
Jackson, Dave
See Jackson, J. David
Jackson, David Cooper 1931- ... 109
Jackson, (Marvin) Dennis 1945- ... 228
Jackson, Dennis Barry 1929- ... 174
Jackson, Derrick 1939- ... 77-80
Jackson, Diane 1938- ... 115
Jackson, Don(ald) D(e Avila)
1920-1968 ... CAP-1
Earlier sketch in CA 11-12
Jackson, Donald (Dean) 1919-1987 ... 17-20R
Obituary ... 124
Jackson, Donald Dale 1935- ... CANR-19
Earlier sketches in CA 49-52, CANR-1
Jackson, Dorothy Virginia Steinhauer
1924- ... 13-16R
Jackson, Douglas N. 1929- ... 37-40R
Jackson, E. F.
See Tubb, E(dwin) C(harles)
Jackson, Edgar (Newman)
1910-1994 ... CANR-29
Earlier sketches in CA 77-80, CANR-13
Jackson, Edwardo 1975- ... 203
Jackson, Elaine
See Freeman, Gillian
Jackson, Ellen B. 1943- ... 110
See also SATA 75, 115
Jackson, Elmore 1910-1989 ... 112
Jackson, Esther Merle 1922- ... 13-16R
Jackson, Eve 1943- ... 163
Jackson, Everatt
See Muggeson, Margaret Elizabeth
Jackson, Frank 1951- ... 120
Jackson, Franklin Jefferson
See Watkins, Mel
Jackson, G. Mark 1952- ... 132
Jackson, Gabriel 1921- ... 21-24R
Jackson, Gabriele Bernhard 1934- ... 29-32R
Jackson, Garnet Nelson 1944- ... SATA 87
Jackson, Geoffrey (Holt Seymour)
1915-1987 ... 61-64
Obituary ... 123
See also SATA-Obit 53
Jackson, George (Lester) 1941-1971 ... 120
Obituary ... 111
See also BW 1
Jackson, George D. 1929- ... 81-84
Jackson, George S(tuyvesant)
1906-1976 ... CAP-1
Obituary ... 61-64
Earlier sketch in CA 17-18
Jackson, Gina
See Fluke, Joanne
Jackson, Gordon 1934- ... 104
Jackson, Graham 1949- ... 112
Jackson, Guida M. 1930- ... CANR-122
Earlier sketches in CA 93-96, CANR-16, 37
See also SATA 71
Jackson, H(eather) J. ... 210
Jackson, Harvey H(ardaway III) 1943- ... 119
Jackson, Helen Hunt 1830-1885 ... DLB 42, 47, 186, 189
See also RGAL 4
Jackson, Henry 1912-1988
Obituary ... 126
Jackson, Henry F. 1939-1991 ... 129
Obituary ... 135
Jackson, Henry Martin 1912-1983
Obituary ... 110
Jackson, Herbert C(ross) 1917- ... 9-12R
Jackson, Herbert G., Jr. 1928- ... 37-40R
Jackson, Hialeah
See Whitney, Polly (Louise)
Jackson, Holbrook 1874-1948 ... 185
See also DLB 98
Jackson, Innes
See Herdan, Innes
Jackson, J. David 1944- ... CANR-136
Earlier sketches in CA 81-84, CANR-18, 57
See also SATA 91
Jackson, J. P.
See Atkins, (Arthur) Harold (Foweraker)
Jackson, J(ames) R(obert) de J(ager)
1935- ... CANR-93
Earlier sketch in CA 146
Jackson, Jack 1941- ... 224
Jackson, Jacqueline 1928- ... 45-48
See also SATA 65
Jackson, Jacquelyne Johnson 1932- ... 37-40R
Jackson, James Charles 1936-1979 ... 163
Obituary ... 117
Jackson, James P(ierre) 1925- ... CANR-14
Earlier sketch in CA 77-80
Jackson, Jay W. 1961- ... 139
Jackson, Jeremy 1973- ... 230
Jackson, Jesse, Jr. 1965- ... 204
Jackson, Jesse 1908-1983 ... CANR-27
Obituary ... 109
Earlier sketch in CA 25-28R
See also BW 1
See also CLC 12
See also CLR 28
See also CWRI 5
See also MAICYA 1, 2
See also SATA 2, 29
See also SATA-Obit 48
Jackson, Joe 1954- ... 195
Jackson, John A. 1943- ... CANR-90
Earlier sketch in CA 138
Jackson, John Archer 1929- ... 13-16R
Jackson, John E(dgar) 1942- ... 101
Jackson, John Howard 1932- ... 41-44R
Jackson, John N(icholas) 1925- ... CANR-57
Earlier sketches in CA 37-40R, CANR-14, 31
Jackson, John W. ... 181
Jackson, John Wyse ... 182
Jackson, Jon A(nthony) 1938- ... CANR-71
Earlier sketch in CA 81-84
Jackson, Jonathan (Charles) 1966- ... 116
Jackson, Joseph 1924-1987 ... CANR-11
Obituary ... 122
Earlier sketches in CAP-1, CA 9-10
Jackson, Joseph Hollister 1912-1987 ... 120
Jackson, Joy J(uanita) 1928- ... 29-32R
Jackson, Julia A(ndreasen) 1939- ... 119
Jackson, Julian 1954- ... 210
Jackson, Karl (Dion) 1942- ... 102
Jackson, Katherine Gauss 1904-1975
Obituary ... 57-60
Jackson, Kathy Merlock 1955- ... 145
Jackson, (William) Keith 1928- ... CANR-8
Earlier sketch in CA 61-64
Jackson, Kenneth T. 1939- ... CANR-141
Earlier sketch in CA 21-24R
Jackson, Kevin 1955- ... 147
Jackson, Kevin Goldstein
See Goldstein-Jackson, Kevin
Jackson, Laura (Riding) 1901-1991 ... CANR-89
Obituary ... 135
Earlier sketches in CA 65-68, CANR-28
See also Riding, Laura
See also DLB 48
See also PC 44
Jackson, Leslie C. 1945- ... 190
Jackson, Livia Bitton
See Bitton Jackson, Livia E(lvira)
Jackson, Louise A(llen) 1937- ... 93-96
Jackson, Lowell G(eorge) 1934- ... 118
Jackson, Lucille
See Strauss, (Mary) Lucille Jackson
Jackson, Lydia 1900(?)-1983
Obituary ... 110
Jackson, MacDonald P. 1938- ... CANR-110
Earlier sketch in CA 125
Jackson, Mae 1946- ... 81-84
Jackson, Maggie ... 204
Jackson, Mahalia 1911-1972
Obituary ... 33-36R
Jackson, Margaret Weymouth 1895-1974
Obituary ... 115
See also AITN 1
Jackson, Marian J. A.
See Rogers, Marian H.
Jackson, Marjorie 1928- ... SATA 127
Jackson, Mark
See Kurz, Ron
Jackson, Marni 1946- ... CANR-126
Earlier sketch in CA 149
Jackson, Martin A(lan) 1941- ... 89-92
Jackson, Mary 1924- ... 61-64
Jackson, Melanie 1956- ... 212
See also SATA 141
Jackson, Melvin H. 1914(?)-1983
Obituary ... 111
Jackson, Michael (Derek) 1940- ... 232
See also CP 7
Jackson, Michael P. 1947- ... 125
Jackson, Mick 1960- ... 215
See also CN 7
Jackson, Mike 1946- ... 155
See also SATA 91
Jackson, Miles M(errill) 1929- ... 41-44R
Jackson, Monica ... 232
Jackson, Neta J. 1944- ... CANR-136
Earlier sketches in CA 89-92, CANR-18, 57
See also SATA 91
Jackson, Neville
See Glaskin, G(erald) M(arcus)
Jackson, Nora
See Tennant, Nora Jackson
Jackson, Norman 1932- ... CANR-17
Earlier sketch in CA 25-28R
See also CP 1
Jackson, O. B.
See Jackson, C(aary) Paul
Jackson, Paul R. 1905-1999 ... CAP-1
Earlier sketch in CA 13-16
Jackson, Percival Ephrates
1891-1970 ... CANR-3
Earlier sketch in CA 1-4R
Jackson, Peter 1961- ... 171
See also AAYA 49
Jackson, Phil 1945- ... 202
Jackson, Philip W(esley) 1928- ... 21-24R
Jackson, R. E.
See Innes, Rosemary E(lizabeth Jackson)
Jackson, R(ichard) Eugene 1941- ... CANR-51
Earlier sketches in CA 109, CANR-28
Jackson, R(ichard) W(illiam) 1939- ... 119
Jackson, Reggie
See Jackson, Reginald Martinez
Jackson, Reginald Martinez 1946-
Brief entry ... 112
Jackson, Richard 1946- ... CANR-112
Earlier sketch in CA 110
Jackson, Richard A(rlen) 1937- ... 125
Jackson, Richard D(ean) W(ells) 1967- ... 170
Jackson, Richard L. 1937- ... 218
Jackson, Robert 1911- ... 9-12R
Jackson, Robert B(lake) 1926- ... CANR-6
Earlier sketch in CA 5-8R
See also SATA 8
Jackson, Robert H. 1955- ... 148
Jackson, Robert J. 1936- ... 25-28R
Jackson, Robert L(owell) 1935- ... 73-76
Jackson, Robert Louis 1923- ... 109
Jackson, Robert S(umner) 1926- ... 29-32R
Jackson, Ronald L. II 1970- ... 187
Jackson, Ruth A. ... 45-48
Jackson, Sally
See Kellogg, Jean (Defrees)
Jackson, Sam
See Trumbo, Dalton
Jackson, Sandra ... 224
Jackson, Sara
See Thomas, Sara (Sally) and Wingrove, David (John)
Jackson, Scoop
See Jackson, Henry Martin
Jackson, Shelley 1963- ... 215
Jackson, Sheneska 1970- ... 163
See also BW 3
Jackson, Sherri L. 1962- ... 233
Jackson, Shirley 1919-1965 ... CANR-52
Obituary ... 25-28R
Earlier sketches in CA 1-4R, CANR-4
See also AAYA 9
See also AMWS 9
See also BPFB 2
See also CDALB 1941-1968
See also CLC 11, 60, 87
See also DA
See also DA3
See also DAC
See also DAM MST
See also DLB 6, 234
See also EXPS
See also HGG
See also LAIT 4
See also MAL 5
See also MTCW 2
See also MTFW 2005
See also RGAL 4
See also RGSF 2
See also SATA 2
See also SSC 9, 39
See also SSFS 1
See also SUFW 1, 2
See also WLC
Jackson, Sid J. 1937- ... 231
Jackson, Stanley W(ebber) 1920-2000 ... 124
Jackson, Stephanie
See Werner, Vivian
Jackson, Teague 1938- ... 93-96
Jackson, Vincent Edward 1962- ... 141
Jackson, W. A. Douglas
See Jackson, William Arthur Douglas
Jackson, W(illiam) G(odfrey) F(othergill)
1917-1999 ... 25-28R
Obituary ... 177
See also Jackson, Sir William
Jackson, W(illiam) T(homas) H(obdell)
1915-1983 ... CANR-1
Obituary ... 117
Earlier sketch in CA 1-4R
Jackson, W(illiam) Turrentine
1915-2000 ... 13-16R
Obituary ... 188
Jackson, Wallace 1930- ... 114
Jackson, Wes 1936- ... CANR-22
Earlier sketches in CA 49-52, CANR-3
Jackson, William 1958- ... 218
Jackson, Sir William
See Jackson, W(illiam) G(odfrey) F(othergill)
Jackson, William Arthur Douglas
1923- ... CANR-28
Earlier sketch in CA 45-48
Jackson, William J(oseph) 1943- ... 139
Jackson, William M. 1936- ... CANR-87
Earlier sketch in CA 151
Jackson, William Vernon 1926- ... CANR-13
Earlier sketch in CA 21-24R
Jackson, Wilma 1929- ... CANR-12
Earlier sketch in CA 73-76
Jackson, Woody 1948- ... SATA 92
Jackson-Haight, Mabel V. 1912- ... 25-28R
Jackson-Opoku, Sandra 1953- ... 181
Jaco, E(gbert) Gartly 1923- ... CANR-1
Earlier sketch in CA 1-4R
Jacob, Alaric 1909- ... 5-8R
Jacob, Charles E. 1931- ... CANR-5
Earlier sketch in CA 13-16R
Jacob, Ernest Fraser 1894-1971 ... CANR-3
Earlier sketch in CA 1-4R
Jacob, Francois 1920- ... 102
Jacob, Fred E. 1899-1995 ... 105
Jacob, Gordon (Percival Septimus) 1895-1984
Obituary ... 113
Jacob, Helen Pierce 1927- ... 69-72
See also SATA 21
Jacob, Herbert 1933- ... 77-80
Jacob, J. R.
See Jacob, James R.
Jacob, James R. 1940- ... 132
Jacob, John 1950- ... CANR-53
Earlier sketch in CA 126
Jacob, Joseph M. 1943- ... 166
Jacob, Margaret C(andee) 1943- ... CANR-37
Earlier sketches in CA 65-68, CANR-16
Jacob, (Cyprien-)Max 1876-1944 ... 193
Brief entry ... 104
See also DLB 258
See also EWL 3
See also GFL 1789 to the Present
See also GLL 2
See also RGWL 2, 3
See also TCLC 6
Jacob, Merle (Lynn) 1945- ... 152
Jacob, Nancy L. 1943- ... 29-32R

Cumulative Index 291 Jahiz, al-

Jacob, Naomi (Ellington) 1884(?)-1964 ... 181
Obituary ... 115
See also DLB 191
See also RHW
Jacob, Paul 1940- ... 103
See also CP 1, 2
Jacob, Philip E(rnest) 1914-1985 ... CANR-4
Earlier sketch in CA 53-56
Jacob, Violet (Kennedy-Erskine) 1863-1946 ... DLB 240
Jacobi, Carl (Richard) 1908-1997 ... CANR-73
Obituary ... 160
Earlier sketches in CAP-1, CA 13-14
See also HGG
Jacobi, Friedrich Heinrich 1743-1819 .. DLB 94
Jacobi, Johann Georg 1740-1814 ... DLB 97
Jacobi, Jolande (Szekacs) 1890-1973 ... 9-12R
Jacobi, Kathy 1830-1914 ... SATA-Brief 42
Jacobowitz, Ellen 1948- ... 121
Jacobs, Al(bert T.) 1903-1985
Obituary ... 115
Jacobs, Anna 1941- ... 216
Jacobs, Arthur (David) 1922-1996 ... CANR-21
Obituary ... 155
Earlier sketches in CA 5-8R, CANR-4
Jacobs, Barbara 1947- ... 148
Jacobs, Barry (Douglas) 1932- ... 101
Jacobs, Bradford (McElderry) 1920- ... 121
Jacobs, Clyde E(dward) 1925- ... 37-40R
Jacobs, Dan(iel) N(orman) 1924- ... CANR-4
Earlier sketch in CA 5-8R
Jacobs, David Michael 1942- ... 57-60
Jacobs, Diane 1948- ... 73-76
Jacobs, Donald M(artin) 1937- ... 110
Jacobs, Donald Trent 1946- ... 229
Jacobs, Flora Gill 1918- ... CANR-21
Earlier sketch in CA 1-4R
See also SATA 5
Jacobs, Francine 1935- ... CANR-18
Earlier sketches in CA 49-52, CANR-1
See also SATA 43, 150
See also SATA-Brief 42
Jacobs, Frank 1929- ... CANR-6
Earlier sketch in CA 13-16R
See also SATA 30
Jacobs, G(enevieve) Walker 1948- ... 49-52
Jacobs, Garry (Lawrence) 1946- ... 120
Jacobs, George 1927- ... 225
Jacobs, Glenn 1940- ... 29-32R
Jacobs, Gregory S. 1969- ... 177
Jacobs, Harold 1941- ... 45-48
Jacobs, Harriet A(nn) 1813(?)-1897 .. AFAW 1, 2
See also DLB 239
See also FL 1:3
See also FW
See also LAIT 2
See also RGAL 4
Jacobs, Harvey (Collins) 1915-1997 ... 21-24R
Jacobs, Harvey 1930- ... CANR-134
Earlier sketch in CA 29-32R
See also SFW 4
Jacobs, Hayes B(enjamin) 1919- ... 9-12R
Jacobs, Helen Hull 1908-1997 ... 9-12R
Obituary ... 159
See also SATA 12
Jacobs, Herbert (Austin) 1903-1987 ... 13-16R
Obituary ... 122
Jacobs, Howard 1908-1985 ... 65-68
Jacobs, Jack L. 1953- ... 142
Jacobs, James B. 1947- ... CANR-107
Earlier sketches in CA 101, CANR-18, 39
Jacobs, Jane 1916- ... CANR-15
Earlier sketch in CA 21-24R
Jacobs, Jerome L. 1931- ... 89-92
Jacobs, Jerry 1932- ... CANR-11
Earlier sketch in CA 29-32R
Jacobs, Jill
See Bharti, Ma Satya
Jacobs, Jim 1942- ... 97-100
Interview in ... CA-97-100
See also CLC 12
Jacobs, Jo Ellen 1952- ... 230
Jacobs, John (Kedzie) 1918- ... 21-24R
Jacobs, Jonnie ... CANR-93
Earlier sketch in CA 159
Jacobs, Joseph 1854-1916 ... 136
Brief entry ... 111
See also DLB 141
See also MAICYA 1, 2
See also SATA 25
See also WCH
Jacobs, Judy 1952- ... 137
See also SATA 69
Jacobs, Laurence Wile 1939- ... 53-56
Jacobs, Laurie A. 1956- ... SATA 89
Jacobs, Leah
See Gellis, Roberta (Leah Jacobs)
Jacobs, Leland Blair 1907-1992 ... 73-76
Obituary ... 137
See also SATA 20
See also SATA-Obit 71
Jacobs, Lewis 1906-1997 ... 77-80
Obituary ... 156
Jacobs, Linda
See Altman, Linda Jacobs
Jacobs, Lou(is), Jr. 1921- ... CANR-9
Earlier sketch in CA 21-24R
See also SATA 2
Jacobs, Louis 1920- ... CANR-38
Earlier sketches in CA 1-4R, CANR-1, 17
Jacobs, Margaret (D.) 1963- ... 202
Jacobs, Melville 1902-1971 ... 1-4R
Obituary ... 103
Jacobs, Michael (Stephen) 1955- ... 123
Jacobs, Michael T. 1958- ... 139
Jacobs, Milton 1920- ... 37-40R
Jacobs, Nehama 1951- ... 126
Jacobs, Norman (Gabriel) 1924- ... 77-80
Jacobs, Paul 1918-1978 ... 13-16R
Obituary ... 73-76
Jacobs, Pepita Jimenez 1932- ... 17-20R
Jacobs, Philip E. 1914(?)-1985
Obituary ... 116
Jacobs, Renee 1962- ... 125
Jacobs, Robert D(urene) 1918-1998 ... 41-44R
Jacobs, Roderick A(rnold) 1934- ... 21-24R
Jacobs, Ruth Harriet 1924- ... CANR-87
Earlier sketches in CA 89-92, CANR-15, 33
Jacobs, Shannon K. 1947- ... CANR-92
Earlier sketch in CA 145
See also SATA 77
Jacobs, Sheldon 1931- ... 106
Jacobs, Sherry-Anne
See Jacobs, Anna
Jacobs, Sophia Yarnall 1902-1993 ... 106
Obituary ... 141
Jacobs, Steve 1955- ... 171
Jacobs, Steven L(eonard) 1947- ... 234
Jacobs, Sue-Ellen 1936- ... 111
Jacobs, Susan
See Quinn, Susan
See also SATA 30
Jacobs, T. C. H.
See Pendower, Jacques
Jacobs, Travis Beal 1936- ... 187
Brief entry ... 113
Jacobs, Vernon K(enneth) 1936- ... CANR-41
Earlier sketch in CA 117
Jacobs, Vivian 1916(?)-1981
Obituary ... 103
Jacobs, W(illiam) W(ymark) 1863-1943 ... 167
Brief entry ... 121
See also DLB 135
See also EXPS
See also HGG
See also RGEL 2
See also RGSF 2
See also SSC 73
See also SSFS 2
See also SUFW 1
See also TCLC 22
Jacobs, Walter Darnell 1922- ... 17-20R
Jacobs, Wilbur R(ipley) 1918-1998 ... 13-16R
Jacobs, William Jay 1933- ... CANR-57
Earlier sketches in CA 57-60, CANR-7
See also SATA 28, 89
Jacobsen, Douglas G. 1951- ... 141
Jacobsen, Hans Jacob 1901-1987
Obituary ... 122
Jacobsen, J. P. 1847-1885 ... DLB 300
Jacobsen, Joergen-Frantz
See Jacobsen, Jorgen-Frantz
Jacobsen, Jorgen-Frantz 1900-1938 ... DLB 214
Jacobsen, Josephine (Winder) 1908-2003 ... CANR-48
Obituary ... 218
Earlier sketches in CA 33-36R, CANR-23
See also CAAS 18
See also CCA 1
See also CLC 48, 102
See also CP 2, 3, 4, 5, 6, 7
See also DLB 244
See also PC 62
See also PFS 23
See also TCLE 1:1
Jacobsen, K(enneth) C. 1939- ... 133
Jacobsen, Lydik S. 1897(?)-1976
Obituary ... 69-72
Jacobsen, Lyle E. 1929- ... 13-16R
Jacobsen, Marion Leach 1908-1997 ... 61-64
Jacobsen, O(le) Irving 1896-1990 ... CAP-2
Earlier sketch in CA 25-28
Jacobsen, Phebe R(obinson) 1922-2000 .. 73-76
Obituary ... 189
Jacobsen, Rolf 1907-1994 ... 194
See also CWW 2
See also DLB 297
See also EWL 3
Jacobsen, Thorkild 1904-
Brief entry ... 105
Jacobsohn, Gary J. 1946- ... 89-92
Jacobson, Alan 1961- ... 196
Jacobson, Bernard Isaac 1936- ... 109
Jacobson, Beverly 1927- ... 113
Jacobson, Boyd 1942- ... 118
Jacobson, Cliff 1940- ... 85-88
Jacobson, Dan 1929- ... CANR-66
Earlier sketches in CA 1-4R, CANR-2, 25
See also AFW
See also CLC 4, 14
See also CN 1, 2, 3, 4, 5, 6, 7
See also DLB 14, 207, 225, 319
See also EWL 3
See also MTCW 1
See also RGSF 2
Jacobson, Daniel 1923- ... 53-56
See also SATA 12
Jacobson, David B(ernard) 1928- ... 53-56
Jacobson, Edith 1897(?)-1978
Obituary ... 85-88
Jacobson, Edmund 1888-1983 ... 9-12R
Jacobson, Ethel ... 37-40R
Jacobson, Frederick L(awrence) 1938- ... 49-52
Jacobson, Gary Charles 1944- ... 109
Jacobson, Gerald F. 1922-1987
Obituary ... 123
Jacobson, Harold Karan 1929- ... CANR-19
Earlier sketches in CA 9-12R, CANR-3
Jacobson, Helen S(altz) 1921- ... CANR-6
Earlier sketch in CA 57-60
Jacobson, Howard 1942- ... 205
See also CN 5, 6
See also DLB 207
Jacobson, Howard Boone 1925- ... 1-4R
Jacobson, Joanne 1952- ... 144
Jacobson, Jon 1938- ... 61-64
Jacobson, Judy 1947- ... 225
Jacobson, Julius 1922- ... 45-48
Jacobson, Marcia 1941- ... 115
Jacobson, Mark 1948- ... 136
Jacobson, Matthew Frye 1958- ... CANR-96
Earlier sketch in CA 156
Jacobson, Michael F. 1943- ... CANR-127
Earlier sketches in CA 77-80, CANR-13
Jacobson, Morris K(arl) 1906- ... CANR-3
Earlier sketch in CA 45-48
See also SATA 21
Jacobson, Nils Olof 1937-
Brief entry ... 110
Jacobson, Nolan Pliny 1909- ... CANR-23
Earlier sketches in CA 21-24R, CANR-8
Jacobson, Robert (Marshall) 1940-1987 .. 89-92
Obituary ... 122
Jacobson, Rodolfo 1915- ... 41-44R
Jacobson, Sheldon A(lbert) 1903-1992 .. 37-40R
Jacobson, Sibyl C(hafer) 1942- ... 65-68
Jacobson, Stephen A. 1934- ... 97-100
Jacobson, Steve
See Jacobson, Stephen A.
Jacobstein, J(oseph) Myron 1920-2005 ... 53-56
Obituary ... 237
Jacobus, Donald L(ines) 1887-1970 ... CANR-4
Earlier sketch in CA 5-8R
Jacobus, Elaine Wegener 1908-1986 ... 33-36R
Jacobus, Lee A. 1935- ... CANR-57
Earlier sketches in CA 33-36R, CANR-13, 30
Jacobus, Mary 1944- ... 105
See also FW
Jacoby, Henry 1905-1996 ... 77-80
Jacoby, Jeff ... 228
Jacoby, Joseph E. 1944- ... 97-100
Jacoby, Neil H(erman) 1909-1979 ... CANR-10
Obituary ... 89-92
Earlier sketch in CA 21-24R
Jacoby, Oswald 1902-1984 ... 107
Obituary ... 113
Jacoby, Russell 1945- ... CANR-95
Earlier sketches in CA 77-80, CANR-15, 42
Jacoby, Sidney B(ernard) 1908-1990
Obituary ... 130
Jacoby, Stephen M(ichael) 1940- ... 57-60
Jacoby, Susan ... CANR-95
Earlier sketch in CA 108
Jacoby, Tamar 1954- ... 172
Jacopetti, Alexandra
See Hart, Alexandra
See also SATA 14
Jacot, B. L.
See Jacot de Boinod, Bernard Louis
Jacot, Michael 1924- ... 104
Jacot de Boinod, Bernard Louis 1898-1977 ... 9-12R
Obituary ... 77-80
Jacoway, Elizabeth 1944- ... 110
Jacq, Christian 1947- ... 200
Jacquard, Roland ... 238
Jacqueline
See Carpentier (y Valmont), Alejo
Jacqueney, Mona G(raubart) ... 41-44R
Jacqueney, Theodore 1943(?)-1979
Obituary ... 89-92
Jacques, Beau
See House, R(ichard) C(alvin)
Jacques, Brian 1939- ... CANR-117
Earlier sketches in CA 127, CANR-68
See also AAYA 20
See also BYA 16
See also CLR 21
See also FANT
See also JRDA
See also MAICYA 2
See also MAICYAS 1
See also SATA 62, 95, 138
See also YAW
Jacques, David (Lawson) 1948- ... 123
Jacques, Edwin E. 1908-1996 ... 151
Jacques, Robin 1920-1995 ... MAICYA 1, 2
See also MAICYAS 1
See also SAAS 5
See also SATA 32
See also SATA-Brief 30
See also SATA-Obit 86
Jacques de Vitry c. 1160-1240 ... DLB 208
Jacquet, Constant Herbert, Jr. 1925- ... 106
Jacquette, Dale 1953- ... 207
Jade, Jacqueline
See Hyman, Jackie (Diamond)
Jaded Observer
See Zolf, Larry
Jados, Stanley S. 1912-1977 ... 33-36R
Jaeck, Lois Marie 1946- ... 137
Jaediker, Kermit 1912(?)-1986
Obituary ... 118
Jaeger, Cyril Karel Stuart 1912- ... 1-4R
Jaeger, Edmund C(arroll) 1887-1983 ... CAP-2
Obituary ... 110
Earlier sketch in CA 23-24
Jaeger, Frank
See Jaeger, Frank
Jaeger, Frank 1926-1977 ... DLB 214
See also EWL 3
Jaeger, Harry J., Jr. 1919(?)-1979
Obituary ... 85-88
Jaeger, Lorenz Cardinal 1892-1975
Obituary ... 57-60
Jaeger, Walter H(enry) E(dward) 1902(?)-1982
Obituary ... 108
Jaeggi, Urs 1931- ... 191
Jaeggy, Fleur ... 166
Jaegher, Raymond-Joseph
See De Jaegher, Raymond-Joseph
Jaekel, Susan M. 1948- ... SATA 89
Jaen, Didier Tisdel 1933- ... 29-32R
Jaenen, Cornelius John 1927- ... CANR-15
Earlier sketch in CA 85-88
Jaenzon, Julius 1885-1961 ... IDFW 3, 4
Jaernefelt, Arvid
See Jarnefelt, Arvid
Ja'far al-Sadiq c. 702-765 ... DLB 311
Jaffa, George
See Wallace-Clarke, George
Jaffa, Harry V(ictor) 1918- ... 33-36R
Jaffe, A(bram) J. 1912-1997 ... 5-8R
Obituary ... 163
Jaffe, Adam B. 1955- ... 209
Jaffe, Aniela 1903-1991 ... 125
Jaffe, Bernard 1896-1986 ... 5-8R
Obituary ... 121
Jaffe, Betsy
See Jaffe, Elizabeth Latimer
Jaffe, Dan 1933- ... CANR-17
Earlier sketch in CA 25-28R
See also CP 1
Jaffe, David 1911-1990
Obituary ... 131
Jaffe, Dennis T(heodore) 1946- ... CANR-32
Earlier sketches in CA 89-92, CANR-15
Jaffe, Elizabeth Latimer 1935- ... 135
Jaffe, Elsa
See Bartlett, Elsa Jaffe
Jaffe, Eugene D. 1937- ... 37-40R
Jaffe, Frederick S. 1925-1978 ... CANR-5
Earlier sketch in CA 9-12R
Jaffe, Gabriel Vivian 1923- ... 13-16R
Jaffe, H. L. C.
See Jaffe, Hans L(udwig) C.
Jaffe, Hans L(udwig) C. 1915-1984 ... 144
Jaffe, Harold 1940- ... CANR-30
Earlier sketch in CA 29-32R
Jaffe, Hilde 1927- ... 105
Jaffe, Irma B(lumenthal) ... CANR-1
Earlier sketch in CA 45-48
Jaffe, Joseph 1924- ... 184
Brief entry ... 113
Jaffe, Lorna S. 1941- ... 128
Jaffe, Louis Leventhal 1905-1996 ... 21-24R
Obituary ... 155
Jaffe, (Andrew) Michael 1923-1997 ... 21-24R
Obituary ... 159
Jaffe, Michele (Sharon) ... 215
Jaffe, Nina ... MAICYA 2
Jaffe, Nora Crow 1944- ... 106
Jaffe, Rona 1932- ... CANR-57
Earlier sketches in CA 73-76, CANR-24
Interview in ... CANR-24
See also AITN 1
See also BEST 90:3
See also MTCW 1
Jaffe, Sam(uel Adason) 1893(?)-1984
Obituary ... 115
Jaffe, Sandra Sohn 1943- ... 101
Jaffe, Sherril 1945- ... CANR-19
Earlier sketch in CA 103
Jaffe, William 1898-1980 ... 57-60
Obituary ... 122
Jaffee, Al(lan) 1921- ... 135
Brief entry ... 116
See also SATA 37, 66
Jaffee, Annette Williams 1945- ... 131
Jaffee, Dwight M. 1943- ... 57-60
Jaffee, Mary L.
See Lindsley, Mary F(rances)
Jaffin, David 1937- ... CANR-34
Earlier sketches in CA 65-68, CANR-15
See also CP 2, 3, 4, 5, 6, 7
Jaffrey, Saeed 1929- ... 192
Jaffrey, Zia ... 159
Jafree, Mohammed Jawaid Iqbal 1939- ... CANR-121
Earlier sketch in CA 164
Jafri, Ali Sardar 1913-2000 ... 203
Jagasich, Paul Anthony 1934- ... 203
Jagel, Beatrice Hawley 1944(?)-1985
Obituary ... 116
Jagendorf, Moritz (Adolf) 1888-1981 ... 5-8R
Obituary ... 102
See also SATA 2
See also SATA-Obit 24
Jagendorf, Zvi 1936- ... 207
Jager, Okke 1928- ... CANR-23
Earlier sketches in CA 61-64, CANR-8
Jager, Ronald (Albert) 1932- ... 41-44R
Jaggar, Alison M(ary) ... 185
Jaggard, Geoffrey (William) 1902-1970 . CAP-2
Earlier sketch in CA 21-22
Jaggard, William fl. 1591-1623 ... DLB 170
Jagger, Brenda 1936-1986 ... 167
See also RHW
Jagger, John Hubert 1880- ... CAP-1
Earlier sketch in CA 9-10
Jagger, Michael Philip
See Jagger, Mick
Jagger, Mick 1943- ... 239
See also CLC 17
Jagger, Peter (John) 1938- ... CANR-21
Earlier sketch in CA 103
Jaglom, Henry 1941- ... CANR-112
Earlier sketches in CA 127, CANR-55
Jagninski, Tom 1935- ... 137
Jago, Lucy 1968(?)- ... 215
Jagoda, Robert 1923- ... 73-76
Jagose, Annamarie 1965- ... 233
Jahan, Rounaq 1944- ... CANR-29
Earlier sketch in CA 49-52
Jaher, Frederic Cople 1934- ... 9-12R
Jahiel, Jessica ... 230
Jahier, Piero 1884-1966 ... DLB 114
Jahiz, al- c. 780-c. 869 ... DLB 311

Jahn, Ernst A(dalbert) 1929- 69-72
Jahn, Janheinz 1918-1973
Obituary 111
Jahn, Joseph C. 1914(?)-1984
Obituary 113
Jahn, Melvin E(dward) 1938- 9-12R
Jahn, Michael
See Jahn, (Joseph) Michael
Jahn, (Joseph) Michael 1943- CANR-125
Earlier sketches in CA 49-52, CANR-5
See also SATA 28
Jahn, Mike
See Jahn, (Joseph) Michael
Jahn-Clough, Lisa 1967- .... SATA 88, 152
Jahnn, Hans Henny 1894-1959 186
See also DLB 56, 124
See also EWL 3
Jahoda, Gloria (Adelaide Love)
1926-1980 .... CANR-4
Obituary 104
Earlier sketch in CA 1-4R
See also AITN 1
Jahoda, Gustav 1920- 135
Brief entry 114
Jahsmann, Allan Hart 1916- 106
See also SATA 28
Jaimes, M. Annette 1946- 137
Jaimes Freyre, Ricardo 1868-1933 ...... DLB 283
See also EWL 3
See also HW 1
See also LAW
Jain, Girilal 1923-1993 .... 9-12R
Obituary 142
Jain, Rajendra K. 1951- 134
Jain, Ravindra Kumar 1937- 29-32R
Jain, Sagar C. 1930- CANR-10
Earlier sketch in CA 25-28R
Jain, Sharad Chandra 1933- CANR-21
Earlier sketch in CA 25-28R
Jaini, Padmanabh S. 1923- 103
Jaivin, Linda 1955- CANR-115
Earlier sketch in CA 139
Jakeman, Jane 228
Jakes, John (William) 1932- 214
Earlier sketches in CA 57-60, CANR-10, 43, 66, 111, 142
Interview in CANR-10
Autobiographical Essay in 214
See also AAYA 32
See also BEST 89:4
See also BPFB 2
See also CLC 29
See also CPW
See also CSW
See also DA3
See also DAM NOV, POP
See also DLB 278
See also DLBY 1983
See also FANT
See also MTCW 1, 2
See also MTFW 2005
See also RHW
See also SATA 62
See also SFW 4
See also TCWW 1, 2
Jakes, T(homas) D(exter) 1957- 197
Jakle, John A(llais) 1939- CANR-91
Earlier sketch in CA 107
Jakober, Marie 1941- 181
Jakobina Sigurbjarnardottir
See Sigurbjarnardottir, Jakobina
Jakobovits, Immanuel 1921-1999 108
Jakobovits, Leon Alex 1938- 25-28R
Jakobsdottir, Svava 1930-2004 .... CWW 2
See also DLB 293
Jakobsen, Janet R. 222
Jakobson, Michael 1939- 146
Jakobson, Roman 1896-1982 .... CANR-31
Obituary 107
Earlier sketch in CA 77-80
See also DLB 242
Jakobsson, Jokull 1933-1978 .... DLB 293
Jakosky, Bruce M. 1955- 190
Jaksch, Wenzel 1896-1966 .... CAP-1
Earlier sketch in CA 13-14
Jaksic, Ivan (Andrades) 1954- CANR-120
Earlier sketch in CA 141
Jaksic, Ivan (Andrades) 1954-
See Jaksic, Ivan (Andrades)
Jakubauskas, Edward B(enedict) 1930- 57-60
Jakubowski, Maxim 1944- 209
Jakubowski, Patricia (Ann) 1941- 65-68
Jalan, Edi Lee
See Stivender, Ed
Jalata, Asafa 1954- CANR-92
Earlier sketch in CA 149
Jalland, Pat(ricia) 1941- CANR-82
Earlier sketch in CA 133
Jalongo, Mary Renck 1950- CANR-121
Earlier sketch in CA 166
Jamail, Milton H. 191
Jamalzadah, Muhammad Ali
1892-1997 .... WLIT 6
Jamalzadeh, Muhammad Ali
See Jamalzadah, Muhammad Ali
Jamba, Sousa 1966- 134
James I 1394-1437 .... RGEL 2
James, Alan Geoffrey 1943- 104
James, Alice 1848-1892 .... DLB 221
James, Allen
See Allen, James L(ovic), Jr.
James, Amalia
See Neggers, Carla A(malia)
James, Andrew
See Kirkup, James
James, Ann 1952- .... SATA 82, 117
James, Anne Eleanor Scott
See Scott-James, Anne Eleanor
James, Anthony
See Hanna, David
James, (Eliot) Antony Brett
See Brett-James, (Eliot) Antony
James, Bernard (Joseph) 1922-
Brief entry 110
James, Bessie (Williams) Rowland
1895-1974 107
James, Bill 1949- CANR-35
Earlier sketch in CA 173
James, Brian 1976- 211
See also SATA 140
James, Bronte
See Nash, Renea Denise
James, Bruno S(cott) 1906- 5-8R
James, (David) Burnett (Stephen)
1919-1987 .... 5-8R
Obituary 122
James, C. B.
See Coover, James B(urrell)
James, C(yril) L(ionel) R(obert)
1901-1989 .... CANR-62
Obituary 128
Brief entry 117
Earlier sketch in CA 125
See also BLCS
See also BW 2
See also CLC 33
See also CN 1, 2, 3, 4
See also DLB 125
See also MTCW 1
James, C. W.
See Cumes, J(ames) W(illiam) C(rawford)
James, Captain Lew
See Stratemeyer, Edward L.
James, Cary
See Richardson, Gladwell
James, Cary A(mory) 1935- 29-32R
James, Caryn 170
James, Charles J(oseph) 1944- CANR-5
Earlier sketch in CA 53-56
James, Charles L(yman) 1934- 29-32R
James, Clive (Vivian Leopold)
1939- CANR-117
Brief entry 105
Earlier sketch in CA 128
See also CPW
See also DAM POP
See also MTCW 1
James, Cooper
See Flint, James (Bragg)
James, Coy Hilton 1915- 103
James, Cy
See Watts, Peter Christopher
James, D(orris) Clayton 1931- 29-32R
James, D(avid) G(wilym) 1905-1968 .. CANR-4
Earlier sketch in CA 1-4R
James, Dan
See Sayers, James Denson
James, Daniel (Lewis) 1911-1988 174
Obituary 125
See also Santiago, Danny
James, David
See Hagberg, David J(ames)
James, David 1955- CANR-99
Earlier sketch in CA 119
James, David N. 1952-1996 140
James, David W(illiam) 1910- 128
James, (Darryl) Dean 226
James, Deana
See Sizer, Mona Young
James, Denise 29-32R
James, Diana
See Gunn, Diana Maureen
James, Don(ald H.) 1905-1993 .... CANR-2
Earlier sketch in CA 1-4R
James, Dorothy Buckton 1937- 185
Brief entry 109
James, Dynely
See Mayne, William (James Carter)
James, Edgar C. 1933- CANR-5
Earlier sketch in CA 13-16R
James, Edward
See Masur, Harold Q.
James, Edward (Frank Willis) 1907-1984
Obituary 115
James, Edward T(opping) 1917- 33-36R
James, Edwin
See Gunn, James E(dwin)
James, Edwin Oliver 1889-1972 .... CAP-1
Earlier sketch in CA 13-16
James, Eleanor 1912- 41-44R
James, Elizabeth 1942- 121
See also SATA 39, 45, 52, 97
James, Eloisa 1962- 221
James, Emily
See Standiford, Natalie
James, Eric Arthur 1925- CAP-1
Earlier sketch in CA 9-10
James, Erica 1960- 186
James, Estelle 1935- 37-40R
James, F(rank) Cyril 1903-1973
Obituary 114
James, Fleming, Jr. 1904-1981 .... CAP-1
Earlier sketch in CA 17-18
James, Frank
See Lala, Frank James John, Jr.
James, Frederick
See Martin, William (Flynn)
James, G(eorge) P(ayne) R(ainsford)
1799-1860 .... HGG
James, Gene Gray 1934- 114
James, George P. R. 1801-1828 .... DLB 116
James, George W(illiam)
See James, Bill
James, H(enry) Thomas 1915- 25-28R
James, Harold 1956- CANR-108
Earlier sketch in CA 127
James, Harry Clebourne 1896-1978 ... CANR-4
Earlier sketch in CA 5-8R
See also SATA 11
James, Heather 1914- CANR-31
Earlier sketch in CA 45-48
James, Henry 1843-1916 132
Brief entry 104
See also AMW
See also AMWC 1
See also AMWR 1
See also BPFB 2
See also BRW 6
See also CDALB 1865-1917
See also DA
See also DA3
See also DAB
See also DAC
See also DAM MST, NOV
See also DLB 12, 71, 74, 189
See also DLBD 13
See also EWL 3
See also EXPS
See also GL 2
See also HGG
See also LAIT 2
See also MAL 5
See also MTCW 1, 2
See also MTFW 2005
See also NFS 12, 16, 19
See also RGAL 4
See also RGEL 2
See also RGSF 2
See also SSC 8, 32, 47
See also SSFS 9
See also SUFW 1
See also TCLC 2, 11, 24, 40, 47, 64
See also TUS
See also WLC
James, Howard (Anthony, Jr.) 1935-
Brief entry 111
James, Hunter 1932- 114
James, J. Alison 1962- 220
See also SATA 83, 146
James, Jamie 163
James, Jean Rosemary Haughton
See Haughton-James, Jean Rosemary
James, John 1633(?)-1729 .... DLB 24
See also FANT
James, (David) John 1924(?)-1993 .... CANR-43
Obituary 171
Earlier sketch in CA 45-48
James, Josef C. 1916(?)-1973
Obituary 45-48
James, Joseph B. 1912-1986 .... 17-20R
James, Josephine
See Sterne, Emma Gelders
James, Judith
See Jennings, Leslie Nelson
James, Kelvin Christopher 138
See also CN 6
James, Kristin
See Camp, Candace (Pauline)
James, Laurence 1942-2000 .... TCWW 2
James, Laurie 1930- 163
James, Leigh Franklin 176
See also Little, Paul H(ugo)
James, Leonard F(rank) 1904- 49-52
James, Livia
See Reasoner, James M(orris) and Washburn, L(ivia) J(ane)
James, Lloyd E.
See Laughlin, Tom
James, (William) Louis (Gabriel) CANR-6
Earlier sketch in CA 13-16R
James, Luther 1928- CANR-87
Earlier sketch in CA 153
See also BW 2
James, M. R.
See James, Montague (Rhodes)
See also DLB 156, 201
James, M. R.
See Reasoner, James M(orris)
James, M. R. 1940- 57-60
James, Margaret
See Bennetts, Pamela
James, Marlise Ann 1945- 57-60
James, Marquis 1891-1955 144
James, Martin
See Kisner, James (Martin, Jr.)
James, Mary
See Meaker, Marijane (Agnes)
See also GLL 2
James, Matthew
See Lucey, James D(ennis)
James, Michael 1922(?)-1981
Obituary 104
James, Monica
See Nonhebel, Clare
James, Montague (Rhodes) 1862-1936 203
Brief entry 104
See also James, M. R.
See also HGG
See also RGEL 2
See also RGSF 2
See also SSC 16
See also SUFW 1
See also TCLC 6
James, Muriel 85-88
James, Naomi 1949- 102
See also DLB 204
James, Noel David Glaves 1911-1993 107
James, Norah C(ordner) (?)-1979 ...... CANR-59
Earlier sketch in CA 29-32R
James, P. D.
See White, Phyllis Dorothy James
See also BEST 90:2
See also BPFB 2
See also BRWS 4
See also CDBLB 1960 to Present
See also CLC 18, 46, 122
See also CN 4, 5, 6
See also DLB 87, 276
See also DLBD 17
See also MSW
James, Patrick 1957- 179
James, Paul
See Warburg, James Paul
James, Paul 1921- 125
James, Peter 1948- 163
See also HGG
James, Peter N. 1940- 57-60
James, Philip
See del Rey, Lester and Moorcock, Michael (John)
James, Philip S(eaforth) 1914-2001 .... CAP-1
Earlier sketch in CA 9-10
James, Preston
See Fearn, John Russell
James, Preston E(verett) 1899-1986 .. CANR-29
Earlier sketch in CA 45-48
James, Rebecca
See Elward, James (Joseph)
James, Robert A. 1946-1983
Obituary 109
James, Robert C(larke) 1918- 5-8R
James, Robert Leigh 1918- 161
James, Robert (Vidal) Rhodes
See Rhodes James, Robert (Vidal)
James, Robin
See Curtis, Sharon
James, Robin (Irene) 1953- 126
See also SATA 50
James, Ronald
See Preston, James
James, Russell 1942- CANR-95
Earlier sketch in CA 137
James, Samantha
See Kleinschmit, Sandra
James, Samuel
See Stephens, James
James, Sandra
See Kleinschmit, Sandra
James, Seumas
See Stephens, James
James, Sian 1932- 195
James, Sibyl 1946- 142
James, Simon
See Kunen, James Simon
James, Stanlie M(yrise) 231
James, Stanton
See Flemming, Nicholas Coit
James, Stephanie
See Krentz, Jayne Ann
James, Stephen
See Stephens, James
James, Susan
See Schiffer, James (M.)
James, Susan
See Griffin, Arthur J.
James, Susan E. 1945- 187
James, Susannah
See Moody, Susan (Elizabeth Howard)
James, Sydney C. 1928- 199
James, Sydney V(incent, Jr.)
1929-1993 .... CANR-21
Earlier sketch in CA 1-4R
James, Tegan
See Odgers, Sally Farrell
James, Thelma Gray 1899-1988 .... 5-8R
Obituary 124
James, Theodore, Jr. 1934- 33-36R
James, Theodore E(arle) 1913-1998 57-60
James, Thomas 1572(?)-1629 .... DLB 213
James, Thomas N.
See Neal, James T(homas)
James, Thurston 1933- 142
James, Trevor
See Constable, Trevor James
James, Vanessa
See Beauman, Sally
James, W(illiam) Martin (III) 1952- 143
James, (Arthur) Walter 1912- 5-8R
James, Walter S.
See Sheldon, Walter J(ames)
James, Warren A. 1960- 133
James, Warren E(dward) 1922- 45-48
James, Weldon (Bernard) 1912-1985 .... 1-4R
James, Will(iam Roderick) 1892-1942 137
See also BYA 4
See also CWRI 5
See also DLBD 16
See also MAICYA 1, 2
See also SATA 19
See also TCWW 1, 2
James, William
See Craddock, William J(ames)
James, William 1842-1910 193
Brief entry 109
See also AMW
See also DLB 270, 284
See also MAL 5
See also NCFS 5
See also RGAL 4
See also TCLC 15, 32
James, William C(losson) 1943- 126
James, William M.
See Harknett, Terry (Williams) and Harvey, John (Barton) and James, Laurence

Cumulative Index 293 Jasner

James, William Milbourne 1881-1973 ... CAP-1
Earlier sketch in CA 11-12
James, Wilma Roberts 1905-1996 105
James, Wilmot G. 1953- 138
James Alexander, Simone A. 221
Jameson, Anna 1794-1860 .... DLB 99, 166
Jameson, Eric
See Trimmer, Eric J.
Jameson, Fredric (R.) 1934- 196
See also CLC 142
See also DLB 67
See also LMFS 2
Jameson, J(ohn) Franklin 1859-1937 182
See also DLB 17
Jameson, Judith
See Neyland, James (Elwyn)
Jameson, Kenneth (Ambrose)
1913-1996 77-80
Jameson, Kenneth P(eter) 1942- 112
Jameson, Sam 1936- 136
Jameson, Samuel H(aig) 1896-1991 45-48
Jameson, (Margaret) Storm
1891-1986 .... CANR-47
Obituary 120
Earlier sketch in CA 81-84
See also CN 1, 2, 3, 4
See also DLB 36
See also RHW
Jameson, Vic(tor Loyd) 1924- 17-20R
Jameson, W. C. 1942- 158
See also SATA 93
James VI of Scotland 1566-1625 .... DLB 151, 172
Jamie, Kathleen 1962- CANR-91
Earlier sketch in CA 128
See also CP 7
See also CWP
Jamieson, Bill 181
Jamieson, Bob
See Jamieson, Robert John
Jamieson, Dale Walter 1947- 186
Jamieson, Ian R.
See Goulart, Ron(ald Joseph)
Jamieson, Kathleen Hall 1946- CANR-97
Earlier sketch in CA 155
Jamieson, Paul F(letcher) 1903- CAP-1
Earlier sketch in CA 9-10
Jamieson, Peter .... CP 1
Jamieson, Robert John 1943- 116
Brief entry 110
Interview in CA-116
Jamiolkowski, Raymond M. 1953- 149
See also SATA 81
Jamison, A(lbert) Leland 1911-1986 89-92
Jamison, Andrew 1948- 29-32R
Jamison, Bill 1942- 153
Jamison, Cheryl Alters 1953- 153
Jamison, Janelle
See Peterson, Tracie
Jamison, Judith 1943(?)- 206
Jamison, Kay Redfield CANR-137
Earlier sketch in CA 153
Jamme, Albert (Joseph) 1916- 5-8R
Jammer, Max 188
Jammes, Francis 1868-1938 198
See also EWL 3
See also GFL 1789 to the Present
See also TCLC 75
Jampolsky, Gerald G(ershan) 1925- 111
Jan
See Noble, John (Appelbe)
Jan, Emerson
See Bixby, Jerome Lewis
Jan, George P(okung) 1925- 21-24R
Janas, Frankie-Lee 1908- CANR-24
Earlier sketch in CA 106
Jancar, Barbara Wolfe 1935-
Brief entry 111
Jancar, Drago 1948- .... DLB 181
Jance, J. A.
See Jance, J(udith) A(nn)
Jance, J(udith) A(nn) 1944- CANR-105
Earlier sketches in CA 118, CANR-61
See also CMW 4
See also SATA-Brief 50
Jancovich, Mark 1960- 169
Janda, Kenneth (Frank) 1935- 13-16R
Jandl, Ernst 1925-2000 200
See also CLC 34
See also EWL 3
Jandl, H(enry) Ward 1946- 121
Jandt, Fred E(dmund) 1944- 53-56
Jandy, Edward Clarence 1899-1980
Obituary 97-100
Jane, Mary Childs 1909- CANR-4
Earlier sketch in CA 1-4R
See also SATA 6
Jane, Nancy 1946- 89-92
Jane, Pamela .... SATA 158
Janeczko, Paul B(ryan) 1945- CANR-155
Earlier sketches in CA 104, CANR-22, 49, 105
See also AAYA 9, 28
See also CLR 47
See also MAICYA 2
See also MAICYAS 1
See also SAAS 18
See also SATA 53, 98, 155
See also YAW
Janello, Amy (Elizabeth) 1962- 136
Janes, Clara 1940- .... DLB 134
Janes, Edward C. 1908- 93-96
See also SATA 25
Janes, J(oseph) Robert 1935- CANR-131
Earlier sketches in CA 123, CANR-49, 88, 102
See also SATA 101, 148
See also SATA-Brief 50
Janes, Percy 1922- 113
Janes, Regina (Mary) 1946- 120
Janeshutz, Patricia M(arie) 1947- CANR-73
Earlier sketch in CA 121
Janeshutz, Trish
See Janeshutz, Patricia M(arie)
Janesick, Valerie J. 210
Janevski, Slavko 1920- .... CDWLB 4
See also DLB 181
Janeway, Eliot 1913-1993 130
Obituary 140
Brief entry 112
Interview in CA-130
Janeway, Elizabeth (Hall) 1913-2005 .. CANR-2
Obituary 235
Earlier sketch in CA 45-48
See also AITN 1
See also SATA 19
Janeway, Michael 1940- 189
Janger, Allen R(obert) 1932- CANR-48
Earlier sketches in CA 29-32R, CANR-12
Janger, Kathleen N. 1940- 125
See also SATA 66
Janice
See Brustlein, Janice Tworkov
Janifer, Laurence M(ark) 1933-2002 ... CANR-5
Earlier sketch in CA 9-12R
See also SFW 4
Janik, Allan (Stanley Peter) 1941- 53-56
Janik, Carolyn 1940- CANR-33
Earlier sketches in CA 89-92, CANR-15
Janik, Del Ivan 1945- 117
Janik, Phyllis 1944- 111
Janis, Irving L(ester) 1918- CANR-23
Earlier sketches in CA 17-20R, CANR-8
Janis, J(ack) Harold 1910-2001 .... 13-16R
Janis, Sidney 1896-1989
Obituary 130
Janjigian, Robert 1957- 127
Jankelevitch, Vladimir 1903-1985
Obituary 117
Janken, Kenneth Robert 1956- 226
Janko, Richard 1955- CANR-30
Earlier sketch in CA 111
Janko, (Kathleen) Susan 1951- 149
Jankowski, James P. 1937- 150
Jankowski, Paul F. 1950- 210
Jankowsky, Kurt Robert 1928- 37-40R
Janner, Greville Ewan 1928- CANR-8
Earlier sketch in CA 13-16R
Jannuzzi, Luigi 1952- 232
Janos, Andrew C(saba) 1934- 106
Janos, James George
See Ventura, Jesse
Janos, Leo 1933- 127
Janosch
See Eckert, Horst
See also CLR 26
Janov, Arthur 1924- CANR-97
Earlier sketch in CA 116
Janov, Jill E. 1942- 149
Janover, Caroline (Davis) 1943- CANR-113
Earlier sketch in CA 155
See also SATA 89, 141
Janovy, John, Jr. 1937- CANR-41
Earlier sketches in CA 97-100, CANR-19
See also ANW
Janowitz, Anne F. 181
Janowitz, Henry D. 1918- 145
Janowitz, Morris 1919-1988 .... 13-16R
Obituary 127
Janowitz, Phyllis 1940- CANR-45
Earlier sketch in CA 93-96
Janowitz, Tama 1957- CANR-129
Earlier sketches in CA 106, CANR-52, 89
See also CLC 43, 145
See also CN 5, 6, 7
See also CPW
See also DAM POP
See also DLB 292
See also MTFW 2005
Janowski, Tadeus M(arian) 1923- 53-56
Janowsky, Oscar Isaiah 1900-1993 ..... CANR-5
Obituary 143
Earlier sketch in CA 5-8R
Janrup, (Ruth) Birgit 1931- 97-100
Jans, Zephyr
See Zekowski, Arlene
Jansen, Clifford J. 1935- 33-36R
Jansen, Erin 1967- 219
Jansen, G(odfrey) H(enry) 1919- 114
Jansen, Godfrey
See Jansen, G(odfrey) H(enry)
Jansen, Jared
See Cebulash, Mel
Jansen, John Frederick 1918- 21-24R
Jansen, Marius B(erthus) 1922- 130
Jansen, Michael (Elin) 1940- 130
Jansen, Robert B(ruce) 1922- 81-84
Jansen, Sharon L. 1951- 140
Jansma, Pamela E. 1958- 144
Janson, Anthony F(rederick) 1943- 121
Janson, Donald 1921- 5-8R
Janson, Dora Jane (Heineberg) 1916- 106
See also SATA 31
Janson, H(orst) W(oldemar)
1913-1982 .... CANR-4
Obituary 107
Earlier sketch in CA 1-4R
See also SATA 9
Janson, Hank
See Hobson, Harry and
Norwood, Victor G(eorge) C(harles)
Janson-Smith, Celina 1909-1985
Obituary 118
Janssen, Al(fred Guthrie) 1949- 121
Janssen, Jo Ann 1952- 213
Janssen, Lawrence H(arm) 1921- 13-16R
Janssen, Marian (L. M.) 1953- 159
Janssens, Paul Mary 53-56
Jansson, Bruce S. 200
Jansson, Tove (Marika) 1914-2001 .. CANR-118
Obituary 196
Earlier sketches in CA 17-20R, CANR-38
See also CLR 2
See also CWW 2
See also DLB 257
See also EWL 3
See also MAICYA 1, 2
See also RGSF 2
See also SATA 3, 41
Janszen, J., Jr.
See Greshoff, Jan
Janta, Alexander 1908-1974 101
Obituary 53-56
Jantsch, Erich 1929-1980 .... CANR-10
Earlier sketch in CA 65-68
Jantscher, Gerald R. 1939(?)-1987
Obituary 123
Jantzen, Grace M. 218
Jantzen, Hans 1881-1967
Obituary 111
Jantzen, Steven L(loyd) 1941- 77-80
Janus
See Clery, (Reginald) Val(entine)
Janus, Grete
See Hertz, Grete Janus
Janus, Sam (Shep) 1930- 134
Brief entry 111
Januz, Lauren Robert 1939- 108
Janvier, Thomas A(llibone) 1849-1913 181
See also DLB 202
Janzen, John M(arvin) 1937- 81-84
Janzen, Rod 1953- 187
Japin, Arthur 1956- 196
Japrisot, Sebastien 1931-
See Rossi, Jean-Baptiste
See also CLC 90
See also CMW 4
See also NFS 18
Jaques, Elliott 1917- CANR-6
Earlier sketch in CA 13-16R
Jaques, Faith 1923-1997 .... CANR-20
Obituary 159
Earlier sketch in CA 103
See also MAICYA 1, 2
See also SATA 21, 69, 97
Jaques, Florence Page 1890-1972 103
Obituary 104
Jaques, Francis Lee 1887-1969 ... SATA-Brief 28
Jaques-Dalcroze, Emile 1865-1950 208
Jaquette, Jane Stallmann 1942- 184
Brief entry 105
Jaquin, Noel 1894(?)-1974
Obituary 112
Jaquith, Priscilla 1908- 121
See also SATA 51
Jaramillo, Cleofas Martinez 1878-1956 179
See also DLB 122
Jaramillo, Mari-Luci 1928- 210
See also SATA 139
Jaramillo, Samuel 1925- 41-44R
Jaramillo, Stephan 1970(?)- 171
Jaramillo Levi, Enrique 1944- .... DLB 290
Jarausch, Konrad H(ugo) 1941- CANR-87
Earlier sketch in CA 130
Jarchovsky, Petr 1966- 229
Jarchow, Merrill E(arl) 1910-1993 ..... CANR-48
Earlier sketches in CA 41-44R, CANR-14
Jardim, Anne 1936- 107
Jardim, Vasco S. 1900(?)-1983
Obituary 111
Jardin, Andre 1912- 158
Jardine, Alice (Ann) 1951- 117
Jardine, Jack 1931- 21-24R
Jardine, Lisa A(nne) 1944- 195
Jareed
See Faridi, Shah Nasiruddin Mohammad
Jares, Joe 1937- CANR-12
Earlier sketch in CA 33-36R
Jarir 7th cent. -c. 730 .... DLB 311
Jarmain, W. Edwin 1938- 13-16R
Jarman, A(lfred) O(wen) H(ughes)
1911-1998 130
Jarman, Cosette C(otterell) 1909- CAP-2
Earlier sketch in CA 21-22
Jarman, Derek 1942-1994 144
Jarman, Douglas 1942- 133
Jarman, Geraint 1950- .... CP 1
Jarman, Julia 1946- 202
See also SATA 133
Jarman, Mark (F.) 1952- CANR-109
Earlier sketch in CA 171
See also CAAS 22
See also CP 7
See also CSW
See also DLB 282
Jarman, Mark Anthony 1955- 118
See also DLB 120
Jarman, Rosemary Hawley 1935- CANR-59
Earlier sketches in CA 49-52, CANR-2
See also RHW
See also SATA 7
Jarman, Thomas Leckie 1907- CANR-4
Earlier sketch in CA 5-8R
Jarman, Walton Maxey 1904-1980
Obituary 108
Jarmusch, Jim 1953(?)- 132
Jarmuth, Sylvia L. 1912-1997 .... 25-28R
Jarnes, Benjamin 1888-1949 .... EWL 3
Jarnot, Lisa 1967- 197
See also CWP
Jarnow, Jeannette 1909- 53-56
Jaroch, F(rancis) A(nthony) Randy 1947- . 89-92
Jaroch, Randy
See Jaroch, F(rancis) A(nthony) Randy
Jaroff, Leon Morton 1927- 135
Jarolimek, John 1921-
Brief entry 114
Jaron, Lou
See Spender, Lynne
Jarre, Maurice 1924- .... IDFW 3, 4
Jarreau, Al(wyn Lopez) 1940- 117
Brief entry 116
Jarrell, John W. 1908(?)-1978
Obituary 81-84
Jarrell, Mary Von Schrader 1914- CANR-88
Earlier sketch in CA 77-80
See also SATA 35
Jarrell, Randall 1914-1965 .... CANR-34
Obituary 25-28R
Earlier sketches in CA 5-8R, CANR-6
See also CABS 2
See also AMW
See also BYA 5
See also CDALB 1941-1968
See also CLC 1, 2, 6, 9, 13, 49
See also CLR 6
See also CWRI 5
See also DAM POET
See also DLB 48, 52
See also EWL 3
See also EXPP
See also MAICYA 1, 2
See also MAL 5
See also MTCW 1, 2
See also PAB
See also PC 41
See also PFS 2
See also RGAL 4
See also SATA 7
Jarrett, Amanda Jean
See Avallone, Michael (Angelo, Jr.)
Jarrett, (John) Derek 1928-2004 57-60
Obituary 225
Jarrett, H(arold) Reginald 1916- CANR-3
Earlier sketch in CA 9-12R
Jarrett, James Louis 1917- 53-56
Jarrett, Marjorie 1923- 105
Jarrett, Philip (Martin) 1946- 127
Jarrett, Roxanne
See Werner, Herma
Jarrick, Arne 1952- 222
Jarrico, Paul 1915-1997 .... IDFW 4
Jarriel, Thomas Edwin 1934- 120
Brief entry 109
Interview in CA-120
Jarriel, Tom
See Jarriel, Thomas Edwin
Jarrott, Mattie L. 1881(?)-1973
Obituary 41-44R
Jarrow, Gail 1952- 150
See also SATA 84
Jarry, Alfred 1873-1907 153
Brief entry 104
See also DA3
See also DAM DRAM
See also DFS 8
See also DLB 192, 258
See also EW 9
See also EWL 3
See also GFL 1789 to the Present
See also RGWL 2, 3
See also SSC 20
See also TCLC 2, 14, 147
See also TWA
Jarves, James Jackson 1818-1888 .... DLB 189
Jarvie, Clodagh Gibson
See Gibson-Jarvie, Clodagh
Jarvie, Gordon (Iain) 1941- 143
Jarvie, I(an) C(harles) 1937- 53-56
Jarvik, Laurence 1956- 169
Jarvik, Lissy F. 128
Jarvis, Ana C(ortesi) 1936- CANR-14
Earlier sketch in CA 65-68
Jarvis, Charles E(fthemios) 1921- 111
Jarvis, E. K.
See Ellison, Harlan (Jay)
Jarvis, F(rank) Washington 1939- 37-40R
Jarvis, Fred(erick) G(ordon, Jr.) 1930- 33-36R
Jarvis, Howard (Arnold) 1902(?)-1986 122
Obituary 120
Brief entry 111
Jarvis, Jennifer M(ary) 1935- 13-16R
Jarvis, Martin 1941- CANR-25
Earlier sketch in CA 105
Jarvis, Robert M. 1959- 188
Jarvis, Rupert Charles 1899- 103
Jarvis, Sharon 1943- CANR-120
Earlier sketches in CA 119, CANR-48
Jarvis, Simon 1963- 150
Jarvis, Will
See Jarvis, William E.
Jarvis, William Don(ald) 1913- CAP-1
Earlier sketch in CA 13-16
Jarvis, William E. 1945- 231
Jasen, David A(lan) 1937- CANR-126
Earlier sketches in CA 29-32R, CANR-27, 52
Jasenas, Michael 1912-
Brief entry 113
Jashemski, Wilhelmina (Mary) Feemster
1910- CAP-1
Earlier sketch in CA 13-16
Jaskol, Julie 1958- 197
See also SATA 127
Jaskunas, Paul 1971- 236
Jasmin, Claude 1930- 123
See also CCA 1
See also DLB 60
Jasner, W. K.
See Watson, Jane Werner

Jasny, Naum (Mikhailovich)
1883-1967 .... CAP-1
Obituary 174
Earlier sketch in CA 9-10
Jason
See Caballero, Manuel and
Munro, (Macfarlane) Hugh and
Stannus, (James) Gordon (Dawson)
Jason, Johnny
See Glut, Donald F(rank)
Jason, Kathrine 1953- 126
Jason, Ken
See Newton, D(wight) B(ennett)
Jason, Philip K(enneth) 1941- CANR-75
Earlier sketches in CA 114, CANR-35
Jason, Sonya 1927- 145
Jason, Stuart
See Avallone, Michael (Angelo, Jr.) and
Floren, Lee
Jaspan, Norman 103
Jasper, David 1951- 128
Jasper, James M(acdonald) 1957- CANR-100
Earlier sketch in CA 138
Jasper, Jan 219
Jasper, Kenji (Nathaniel) 1976- 235
Jasper, Ronald Claud Dudley 1917-1990
Obituary 131
Jaspers, Karl (Theodor) 1883-1969 122
Obituary 25-28R
Jaspersohn, William 1947- CANR-71
Earlier sketch in CA 102
Jassal, Harjinder (Singh) 1938- 111
Jassem, Kate
See Oppenheim, Joanne
Jassy, Marie-France Perrin
See Perrin Jassy, Marie-France
Jastak, Joseph Florian 1901-1979 .... CANR-4
Obituary 85-88
Earlier sketch in CA 5-8R
Jastrow, Robert 1925- CANR-18
Earlier sketch in CA 21-24R
Interview in CANR-18
Jastrun, Mieczyslaw 1903-1983 .... EWL 3
Jaubert, Maurice 1900-1940 .... IDFW 3, 4
Jauch, Lawrence R. 1943- 112
Jauncey, James 1949- 151
Jauncey, James H(enry) 1916- CANR-20
Earlier sketches in CA 1-4R, CANR-5
Jaunsudrabins, Janis 1877-1962 .... DLB 220
Jauss, Anne Marie 1902(?)-1991 .... CANR-4
Obituary 135
Earlier sketch in CA 1-4R
See also SATA 10
See also SATA-Obit 69
Jauss, David 1951- 121
See also CSW
Jaussi, Laureen Richardson 1934- 73-76
Javacheff, Christo
See Christo
Javacheff, Jeanne-Claude
See Jeanne-Claude
Javernick, Ellen 1938- 155
See also SATA 89
Javitch, Daniel Gilbert 1941- 103
Javits, Benjamin A(braham) 1894-1973
Obituary 41-44R
Javits, Eric Moses 1931- 1-4R
Javits, Jacob K(oppel) 1904-1986 ..... CANR-17
Obituary 118
Earlier sketches in CA 1-4R, CANR-1
Javor, Frank A. 1916- 135
Jawien, Andrzej
See John Paul II, Pope
Jaworska, Wladyslawa Jadwiga 1910- 53-56
Jaworski, Francis Anthony
See Javor, Frank A.
Jaworski, Leon 1905-1982 .... CAP-1
Obituary 108
Earlier sketch in CA 13-16
Jaworskyj, Michael 1921- 61-64
Jaxon, Milt
See Kimbro, John M.
Jay, Antony (Rupert) 1930- 25-28R
Jay, Bill 1940- 184
Brief entry 117
Jay, Charlotte
See Halls, Geraldine (Mary)
Jay, Donald
See Meyer, Charles R(obert)
Jay, Douglas (Patrick Thomas)
1907-1996 .... CANR-12
Earlier sketch in CA 65-68
Jay, Elisabeth (Joy) 1947- CANR-117
Earlier sketches in CA 124, CANR-54
Jay, Eric George 1907- 5-8R
Jay, G. M.
See Halls, Geraldine (Mary)
Jay, Gregory S. 1952- 130
Jay, Hilda L(ease) 1921- 117
Jay, James M(onroe) 1927- 53-56
Jay, Jamus
See Oppenheim, James
Jay, John 1745-1829 .... DLB 31
Jay, Karla 1947- 85-88
See also GLL 1
Jay, M(argaret) Ellen 1946- CANR-41
Earlier sketch in CA 118
Jay, Marion
See Spalding, Ruth
Jay, Martin (Evan) 1944- CANR-94
Earlier sketch in CA 53-56
Jay, Mel
See Fanthorpe, R(obert) Lionel
Jay, Peter 1937- CANR-101
Earlier sketch in CA 109
Jay, Peter (Anthony Charles) 1945- 97-100
See also CP 1, 2
Jay, Peter A. 1940- 101
Jay, Ricky 1949(?)- 216
Jay, Robert Ravenelle 1925- 186
Brief entry 106
Jay, Ruth I(ngrid) 1920- 93-96
Jay, Ruth Johnson
See Jay, Ruth I(ngrid)
Jay, Shannah
See Jacobs, Anna
Jay, Simon
See Alexander, Colin James
Jayawardena, Visakha Kumari
1931- CANR-59
Earlier sketch in CA 45-48
See also FW
Jayme, William North 1925-2001 .... 9-12R
Obituary 196
Jayne, Lieutenant R. H.
See Ellis, Edward S(ylvester)
Jayne, Sears 1920- 13-16R
Jaynes, Clare
See Mayer, Jane Rothschild
Jaynes, Julian 1923- 41-44R
Jaynes, Richard A(ndrus) 1935- 65-68
Jaynes, Roderick
See Coen, Ethan
Jaynes, Roger W. 1946- 85-88
Jaynes, Ruth 1899-1988 .... CAP-2
Earlier sketch in CA 25-28
Jazayery, M(ohammad) Ali 1924- CANR-9
Earlier sketch in CA 21-24R
Jeake, Samuel, Jr.
See Aiken, Conrad (Potter)
Jeakins, Dorothy 1914-1995 .... IDFW 3, 4
Jeal, Tim 1945- CANR-101
Earlier sketches in CA 21-24R, CANR-9
Jean, Gabrielle (Lucille) 1924- CANR-14
Earlier sketch in CA 37-40R
Jean, Marcel 1900- 25-28R
Jean-Bart, Leslie 1954- .... SATA 121
Jean de Meun
See Meung, Jean de
Jean-Louis
See Kerouac, Jean-Louis Lebris de
Jeanne-Claude 1935- .... AAYA 53
Jeannerat, Pierre Gabriel 1902- 5-8R
Jeanneret, Charles-Edouard 1887-1965 184
See also AAYA 66
Jeanneret, Marsh 1917-1990 132
Jeanniere, Abel 1921- CANR-28
Earlier sketch in CA 49-52
Jeans, Marylu Terral 1914-1997 89-92
Jeans, Michael 127
Jeans, Peter D(ouglas) 1936- 146
Jeanson, Henri 1900-1970 .... IDFW 3, 4
Jeansonne, Glen 1946- CANR-48
Earlier sketch in CA 122
Jeanty, Ninette Helene
See Raven, Ninette Helene Jeanty
Jebavy, Vaclav Ignac 1868-1929
See Brezina, Otokar
Jebb, (Hubert Miles) Gladwyn
1900-1996 .... 21-24R
Obituary 154
Jecks, Michael 1960- 200
Jedamus, Paul 1923- 37-40R
Jedlitzka, Maria
See Jeritza, Maria
Jedren, Susan 223
Jedrey, Christopher M(ichael) 1949- 101
Jedrzejewicz, Waclaw 1893-1993 .... 25-28R
Obituary 143
Jeef, Kalle
See Tshiamala, Kabasele
Jeeves, Malcolm A(lexander) 1926- .. CANR-12
Earlier sketch in CA 29-32R
Jeffares, A(lexander) Norman
1920- CANR-124
Earlier sketches in CA 85-88, CANR-16, 39
Jeffcoat, A(lbert) E(dward) 179
Jeffer, Marsha 1940- 41-44R
Jefferds, Vincent H(arris) 1916- 127
See also SATA 59
See also SATA-Brief 49
Jefferies, Henry A(lan) 1961- 221
Jefferies, Matthew (Martin) 1962- 154
Jefferies, Mike 1943- .... FANT
Jefferies, (John) Richard 1848-1887 ..... DLB 98,
141
See also RGEL 2
See also SATA 16
See also SFW 4
Jefferies, Susan Herring 1903-1980 .... CAP-1
Earlier sketch in CA 13-14
Jefferies, William
See Deaver, Jeffery (Wilds)
Jefferis, Barbara (Tarlton) 1917- 81-84
Jeffers, H(arry) Paul 1934- CANR-71
Earlier sketches in CA 93-96, CANR-63
See also TCWW 2
Jeffers, Jo
See Johnson, Joan Helen
Jeffers, Lance 1919-1985 .... CANR-25
Earlier sketch in CA 65-68
See also BW 1
See also DLB 41
Jeffers, (John) Robinson 1887-1962 .. CANR-35
Earlier sketch in CA 85-88
See also AMWS 2
See also CDALB 1917-1929
See also CLC 2, 3, 11, 15, 54
See also DA
See also DAC
See also DAM MST, POET
See also DLB 45, 212
See also EWL 3
See also MAL 5
See also MTCW 1, 2
See also MTFW 2005
See also PAB
See also PC 17
See also PFS 3, 4
See also RGAL 4
See also WLC
Jeffers, Susan 1942- CANR-44
Earlier sketch in CA 97-100
See also CLR 30
See also MAICYA 1, 2
See also SATA 17, 70, 129, 137
Jefferson, Alan 1921- CANR-53
Earlier sketches in CA 33-36R, CANR-13, 29
Jefferson, Blanche (Waugaman) 1909- 5-8R
Jefferson, Carter (Alfred) 1927- 17-20R
Jefferson, Ian
See Davies, L(eslie) P(urnell)
Jefferson, Janet
See Mencken, H(enry) L(ouis)
Jefferson, Omar Xavier
See Jefferson, Xavier T(homas)
Jefferson, Roland S. 1939- CANR-35
Earlier sketch in CA 111
See also BW 2
Jefferson, Sarah
See Farjeon, (Eve) Annabel
Jefferson, Thomas 1743-1826 .... AAYA 54
See also ANW
See also CDALB 1640-1865
See also DA3
See also DLB 31, 183
See also LAIT 1
See also RGAL 4
Jefferson, Xavier T(homas) 1952- CANR-13
Earlier sketch in CA 73-76
Jeffery, Anthea (J.) 231
Jeffery, Grant 1924- 1-4R
Jeffery, Lawrence 1953- 130
Jeffery, Ransom 1943- 21-24R
Jefferys, Allan 93-96
Jefferys, Margot 1916-1999 183
Jefford, Bat
See Bingley, David Ernest
Jeffords, James Merrill 1934- 224
Jeffress, Philip W. 1941-
Brief entry 111
Jeffrey, Adi-Kent Thomas 1916-1990 ..... 37-40R
Jeffrey, Christopher
See Leach, Michael
Jeffrey, David Lyle 1941- CANR-49
Earlier sketches in CA 57-60, CANR-7, 24
Jeffrey, Francis 1773-1850
See Francis, Lord Jeffrey
Jeffrey, Francis 1950- 135
Jeffrey, Jonathan D. 1960- 224
Jeffrey, Julie Roy 1941- 93-96
Jeffrey, L(illian) H(amilton) 1915- 1-4R
Jeffrey, Lawrence 1953- 130
Jeffrey, Lloyd Nicholas 1918- 37-40R
Jeffrey, Mildred (Mesurac) 5-8R
Jeffrey, Richard Carl 1926- 103
Jeffrey, Ruth
See Bell, Louise Price
Jeffrey, Thomas E. 1947- 136
Jeffrey, William
See Pronzini, Bill and
Wallmann, Jeffrey M(iner)
Jeffrey, William
See Wallmann, Jeffrey M(iner)
Jeffrey, William P., Jr. 1919- 57-60
Jeffreys, Harold 1891-1989 109
Obituary 128
Jeffreys, J. G.
See Healey, Ben (James)
Jeffreys, Montagu Vaughan Castelman
1900-1985 .... CANR-4
Obituary 117
Earlier sketch in CA 5-8R
Jeffreys, Stephen 1950- 230
See also CBD
See also CD 5, 6
Jeffreys-Jones, Rhodri 1942- CANR-13
Earlier sketch in CA 77-80
Jeffries, Charles Joseph 1896-1972 ..... CANR-4
Earlier sketch in CA 5-8R
Jeffries, Derwin J(ames) 1915- 57-60
Jeffries, Don 1940- 137
Jeffries, Graham Montague
1900-1982 .... CANR-60
Earlier sketches in CA 77-80, CANR-25
See also CMW 4
Jeffries, Ian 1942- 143
Jeffries, John C., Jr. 1948- 145
Jeffries, John Worthington 1942- 103
Jeffries, Judson L. 1965- 239
Jeffries, Lewis I(ngles) 1942- 103
Jeffries, Mike 178
Jeffries, Ona (Griffin) 1893(?)-1973
Obituary 41-44R
Jeffries, Roderic (Graeme) 1926- CANR-97
Earlier sketches in CA 17-20R, CANR-9, 25,
50, 65
See also CMW 4
See also SATA 4
Jeffries, Stuart 1962- 205
Jeffries, Virginia M(urrill) 1911-1995 .... 5-8R
Jeffs, Julian 1931- 37-40R
Jeffs, Rae 1921- 25-28R
Jefkins, Frank William 1920- CANR-9
Earlier sketch in CA 13-16R
Jege 1866-1940 .... DLB 215
Jehlen, Myra 1940- 101
Jekel, Pamela (L.) 1948- 135
Jelagin, Juri 1910-1987
Obituary 123
Jelakowitch, Ivan
See Heijermans, Herman
Jelavich, Barbara 1923- 53-56
Jelen, Ted G. 1950- 145
Jelenski, Constantin 1922- 101
Jelinek, Elfriede 1946- 154
See also CLC 169
See also DLB 85
See also FW
Jelinek, Estelle C. 1935- 102
Jelinek, Hena Maes
See Maes-Jelinek, Hena
Jellema, Roderick 1927- 41-44R
Jellicoe, (Patricia) Ann 1927- 85-88
See also CBD
See also CD 5, 6
See also CLC 27
See also CWD
See also CWRI 5
See also DLB 13, 233
See also FW
Jellicoe, Geoffrey Alan 1900-1996 .... 13-16R
Obituary 152
Jellicoe, Sidney 1906-1973 .... CAP-2
Earlier sketch in CA 33-36
Jellinek, George 1919- 89-92
Jellinek, J(oseph) Stephan 1930- 81-84
Jellinek, Paul 1897- 13-16R
Jellison, Charles Albert, Jr. 1924- CANR-27
Earlier sketch in CA 1-4R
Jellison, Katherine 1960- 147
Jelloun, Tahar ben 1944- CANR-100
Earlier sketch in CA 162
See also Ben Jelloun, Tahar
See also CLC 180
Jelly, George Oliver 1909- 103
Jemas, Bill 1958- 217
Jemie, Onwuchekwa 1940- 89-92
Jemison, Mary 1742-1833 .... DLB 239
Jemyma
See Holley, Marietta
Jen, Gish
See Jen, Lillian
See also AAL
See also AMWC 2
See also CLC 70, 198
See also CN 7
See also DLB 312
Jen, Lillian 1955- CANR-130
Earlier sketches in CA 135, CANR-89
See also Jen, Gish
Jena, Ruth Michaelis
See Ratcliff, Ruth
Jencks, Charles (Alexander) 1939- CANR-55
Earlier sketches in CA 49-52, CANR-2
Jencks, Christopher 1936- CANR-2
Earlier sketch in CA 49-52
Jencks, Harlan W(ardell) 1941- 111
Jenison, Don P. 1897-1988 .... CANR-7
Earlier sketch in CA 17-20R
Jenkin, A(lfred) K(enneth) Hamilton 1900-1980
Obituary 102
Jenkin, Len 1941- 229
See also CAD
See also CD 5, 6
Jenkin-Pearce, Susie 1943- .... SATA 80
Jenkins, Alan 1914-1993 .... CANR-6
Obituary 176
Earlier sketch in CA 57-60
Jenkins, Amy 1963- 199
Jenkins, Beverly 1951- CANR-99
Earlier sketch in CA 156
Jenkins, Catherine 1962- 203
Jenkins, Cecil 1927- 107
Jenkins, (David) Clive 1926-1999 .... CANR-5
Earlier sketch in CA 13-16R
Jenkins, Dafydd 1911- 146
Jenkins, Dan (Thomas B.) 1929- 126
Brief entry 111
See also BPFB 2
See also DLB 241
Jenkins, Daniel T(homas) 1914-2002 127
Obituary 206
Jenkins, David 1928- 97-100
Jenkins, David E(dward) 1925-
Brief entry 114
Jenkins, David L. 1931- 136
Jenkins, Debra Reid
See Reid Jenkins, Debra
Jenkins, Dorothy Helen 1907-1972
Obituary 37-40R
Jenkins, Edith A(rnstein) 1913- 137
Jenkins, (Margaret) Elizabeth (Heald)
1905- CANR-13
Earlier sketch in CA 73-76
See also DLB 155
See also NCFS 4
Jenkins, Elizabeth B. 181
Jenkins, Elwyn 1939- 219
Jenkins, Emily 1967- 214
See also SATA 144
Jenkins, Emyl 1941- 114
Jenkins, Everett, Jr. 1953- 180
Jenkins, Ferrell 1936- CANR-6
Earlier sketch in CA 57-60
Jenkins, Frances Briggs 1905-1993 .... CAP-2
Earlier sketch in CA 25-28

Cumulative Index 295 **Jessop**

Jenkins, Fred W(illiam) 1957- 159
Jenkins, Garry 232
Jenkins, Geoffrey 1920- CANR-16
  Earlier sketch in CA 5-8R
Jenkins, George 1908- .... IDFW 3, 4
Jenkins, (Thomas) Gilmour 1894-1981
  Obituary 108
Jenkins, Gladys Gardner 1901-1994 .. CANR-4
  Earlier sketch in CA 1-4R
Jenkins, Gordon (Hill) 1910-1984
  Obituary 112
Jenkins, Greg 1952- 168
Jenkins, Gwyn 1919- 1-4R
Jenkins, Hal
  See Jenkins, Harold L.
Jenkins, Harold 1909-2000 .... 9-12R
  Obituary 187
Jenkins, Harold L. 1909(?)-1987
  Obituary 124
Jenkins, Holt M. 1920- 17-20R
Jenkins, Hugh (Gater) 1908-2004 104
  Obituary 222
Jenkins, Iredell 1909-1988 106
Jenkins, James J(erome) 1923- 13-16R
Jenkins, Jean 166
  See also SATA 98
Jenkins, Jerry B(ruce) 1949- CANR-138
  Earlier sketches in CA 49-52, CANR-5, 20, 113
  See also AAYA 39
  See also MTFW 2005
  See also SATA 149
Jenkins, John (Robert Graham)
  1928- CANR-53
  Earlier sketches in CA 45-48, CANR-28
Jenkins, John A. 1950- 139
Jenkins, John Geraint 1929- 21-24R
Jenkins, John H(olmes III) 1940- CANR-10
  Earlier sketch in CA 65-68
Jenkins, John J. 1937-1987 .... CANR-90
  Earlier sketch in CA 132
Jenkins, Kenneth V(incent) 1930- 53-56
Jenkins, Lee 1942- 210
Jenkins, Lee Margaret 207
Jenkins, Linda Walsh 1944- 111
Jenkins, Louis 1942- CANR-142
  Earlier sketches in CA 53-56, CANR-4
Jenkins, Marcella 1954- CANR-87
  Earlier sketch in CA 151
Jenkins, Marie M(agdalen) 1909- 41-44R
  See also SATA 7
Jenkins, Mark 1958- CANR-126
  Earlier sketch in CA 137
Jenkins, McKay 1963- 187
Jenkins, Michael (Romilly Heald)
  1936- 25-28R
Jenkins, Nancy
  See Jenkins, Nancy (Harmon)
Jenkins, Patricia 1927-1982 106
Jenkins, Patrick 1955- .... SATA 72
Jenkins, Peter (George James) 1934-1992 ... 135
Jenkins, Peter 1951- CANR-113
  Earlier sketch in CA 89-92
Jenkins, Philip 1952- 199
Jenkins, Phyllis
  See Schwalberg, Carol(yn Ernestine Stein)
Jenkins, Ray(mond Leonard) 1935- 103
Jenkins, Reese V(almer) 1938- 65-68
Jenkins, (John) Robin 1912- CANR-135
  Earlier sketches in CA 1-4R, CANR-1
  See also CLC 52
  See also CN 1, 2, 3, 4, 5, 6, 7
  See also DLB 14, 271
Jenkins, Romilly James Heald
  1907-1969 .... CANR-5
  Earlier sketch in CA 5-8R
Jenkins, Roy (Harris) 1920-2003 ..... CANR-110
  Obituary 212
  Earlier sketches in CA 9-12R, CANR-13, 30
Jenkins, Sally 1960(?)- 232
Jenkins, Simon 1943- CANR-45
  Earlier sketch in CA 81-84
Jenkins, Steve 1952- .... MAICYA 2
  See also SATA 154
Jenkins, Steven 1952- 162
Jenkins, T(erence) A(ndrew) 1958- .. CANR-134
  Earlier sketch in CA 162
Jenkins, Valerie
  See Grove, Valerie
Jenkins, Victoria 1945- 210
Jenkins, Virginia Scott 1948- CANR-96
  Earlier sketch in CA 148
Jenkins, Will(iam) F(itzgerald)
  1896-1975 .... CANR-63
  Obituary 57-60
  Earlier sketches in CA 9-12R, CANR-4
  See also Leinster, Murray
  See also SFW 4
  See also TCWW 1, 2
Jenkins, William A(twell) 1922-1998 61-64
  See also SATA 9
Jenkins, William Marshall, Jr. 1918-
  Brief entry 105
Jenkinson, Edward B(ernard) 1930- 21-24R
Jenkinson, Michael 1938- 25-28R
Jenks, Almet 1892-1966 .... CAP-1
  Earlier sketch in CA 13-14
Jenks, C(larence) Wilfred 1909-1973 .. CANR-4
  Earlier sketch in CA 9-12R
Jenks, George C(harles) 1850-1929
  Brief entry 119
  See also TCWW 1, 2
Jenks, James M. 1922- 122
Jenks, Randolph 1912- 9-12R
Jenks, Tom 1950- 137
Jenkyns, Chris 1921- .... SATA 31
Jenkyns, Richard (Henry Austen) 1949- 108
Jenner, Bruce 1949- 110
Jenner, Chrystie 1950- 77-80
Jenner, Delia 1944- 21-24R
Jenner, Heather
  See James, Heather
Jenner, Philip Norman 1921- 89-92
Jenner, W(illiam) J(ohn) F(rancis)
  1940- CANR-12
  Earlier sketch in CA 29-32R
Jenness, Aylette 1934- 25-28R
Jennett, Sean 1912- .... CP 1
Jennifer, Susan
  See Hoskins, Robert (Phillip)
Jennings, Charles 162
Jennings, Christian 183
Jennings, Coleman A(lonzo) 1933- . CANR-115
  Earlier sketches in CA 124, CANR-51
  See also SATA 64
Jennings, Dana Andrew 1957- 158
  See also SATA 93
Jennings, Dana Close 1923- 53-56
Jennings, Dean
  See Frazee, Charles Stephen
Jennings, Dean Southern 1905-1969
  Obituary 89-92
Jennings, Edward M(orton III) 1936- 29-32R
Jennings, Elizabeth (Joan)
  1926-2001 .... CANR-127
  Obituary 200
  Earlier sketches in CA 61-64, CANR-8, 39, 66
  See also CAAS 5
  See also BRWS 5
  See also CLC 5, 14, 131
  See also CP 1, 2, 3, 4, 5, 6, 7
  See also CWP
  See also DLB 27
  See also EWL 3
  See also MTCW 1
  See also SATA 66
Jennings, Francis (Paul) 1918-2000 144
  Obituary 192
Jennings, Gary (Gayne) 1928-1999 .. CANR-81
  Obituary 177
  Earlier sketches in CA 5-8R, CANR-9, 29, 56, 59
  See also RHW
  See also SATA 9
  See also SATA-Obit 117
Jennings, (William) Ivor 1903-1965 .... 5-8R
Jennings, James M(urray) 1924- 37-40R
Jennings, Jason (William) 1952- 224
Jennings, Jerry (Edward) 1935- CANR-7
  Earlier sketch in CA 53-56
Jennings, Jesse David 1909-1997 ..... CANR-13
  Earlier sketch in CA 33-36R
Jennings, John (Edward, Jr.) 1906-1973 . CAP-1
  Obituary 45-48
  Earlier sketch in CA 13-14
Jennings, John M(ark) 1962- 181
Jennings, Karla (Mari) 1956- 134
Jennings, Kate 1948- CANR-126
  Earlier sketch in CA 169
Jennings, Kevin 1963- 219
Jennings, Lane (Eaton) 1944- CANR-19
  Earlier sketch in CA 102
Jennings, Leslie Nelson 1890-1972 .... CAP-1
  Earlier sketch in CA 9-10
Jennings, Luke 182
Jennings, Marianne Moody 1953- CANR-42
  Earlier sketch in CA 118
Jennings, Maureen CANR-127
  Earlier sketch in CA 169
Jennings, Michael Glenn 1931- CANR-24
  Earlier sketch in CA 69-72
Jennings, Patrick
  See Mayer, S(ydney) L(ouis)
Jennings, Patrick 1962- 161
  See also SATA 96, 160
Jennings, Paul (Francis) 1918- CANR-19
  Earlier sketches in CA 9-12R, CANR-4
Jennings, Paul 1943- CANR-93
  Earlier sketch in CA 170
  See also AAYA 28
  See also CLR 40
  See also MAICYA 2
  See also MAICYAS 1
  See also SATA 88
Jennings, Peter (Charles Archibald Ewart)
  1938-2005 .... CANR-120
  Brief entry 114
  Earlier sketches in CA 134, CANR-69
Jennings, Phillip C. 1946- 126
Jennings, Raymond P(olson) 1924- 110
Jennings, Richard (Wormington)
  1907-1999 .... 17-20R
  Obituary 183
Jennings, Richard (W.) 1945- 205
  See also SATA 136
Jennings, Robert
  See Hamilton, Charles (Harold St. John)
Jennings, Robert E(dward) 1931- CANR-11
  Earlier sketch in CA 61-64
Jennings, S. M.
  See Meyer, Jerome Sydney
Jennings, Sharon (Elizabeth) 1954- ... CANR-68
  Earlier sketch in CA 134
  See also SATA 95
Jennings, Talbot 1895(?)-1985
  Obituary 116
  See also IDFW 3, 4
Jennings, Ted C(harles) 1949- 81-84
Jennings, Vivien 61-64
Jennings, Waylon 1937-2002 .... CLC 21
Jennings, William Dale 1917-2000 .... 25-28R
  Obituary 188
Jennison, C. S.
  See Starbird, Kaye
Jennison, Christopher 1938- 53-56
Jennison, Keith Warren 1911-1995 73-76
  See also SATA 14
Jennison, Peter S(axe) 1922- CANR-4
  Earlier sketch in CA 9-12R
Jenny, Hans H(einrich) 1922-1998 103
Jenoff, Marvyne 1942- 117
Jens, Walter 1923- CANR-15
  Earlier sketch in CA 89-92
  See also DLB 69
Jensen, Ad(olph) E. 1899-1965 .... CAP-2
  Earlier sketch in CA 19-20
Jensen, Aksel
  See Jensen, Axel
Jensen, Alan F(rederick) 1938- 53-56
Jensen, Albert C(hristian) 1924- 85-88
Jensen, Andrew F(rederick), Jr. 1929- 57-60
Jensen, Ann 21-24R
Jensen, Arthur R(obert) 1923- CANR-73
  Earlier sketches in CA 1-4R, CANR-2
Jensen, Axel 1932-2003 202
  See also DLB 297
Jensen, Carsten 1952- 239
Jensen, Clayne R. 1930- CANR-8
  Earlier sketch in CA 17-20R
Jensen, De Lamar 1925- CANR-7
  Earlier sketch in CA 9-12R
Jensen, Derrick 232
Jensen, Dorothea 221
Jensen, Dwight 1934- 85-88
Jensen, Ejner J. 1937- 138
Jensen, Emma 204
Jensen, Erik Aalbaek
  See Jensen, Erik Aalbaek
Jensen, Erik Frederick 1906- 209
Jensen, Frede 1926- 57-60
Jensen, Gordon D(uff) 1926- 189
  Brief entry 106
Jensen, Gwendolyn Evans 1936- 57-60
Jensen, H. James 1933- CANR-92
  Earlier sketch in CA 25-28R
Jensen, Irene K(hin Khin Myint) 1925- 69-72
Jensen, Irving L. 1920-1996 .... CANR-7
  Earlier sketch in CA 17-20R
Jensen, J(ohannes) Hans D(aniel)
  1907-1973 155
Jensen, J(ohn) Vernon 1922- 49-52
Jensen, Jane 190
Jensen, Jo
  See Pelton, Beverly Jo
Jensen, Joan M(aria) 1934- CANR-56
  Earlier sketch in CA 127
Jensen, Johannes V(ilhelm) 1873-1950 170
  See also DLB 214
  See also EWL 3
  See also RGWL 3
  See also TCLC 41
Jensen, John H(jalmar) 1929- 21-24R
Jensen, John Martin 1893-1984 .... CAP-1
  Earlier sketch in CA 13-16
Jensen, Julie
  See McDonald, Julie
Jensen, Kathryn 1949- 149
  See also SATA 81
Jensen, Kristine Mary 1961- .... SATA 78
Jensen, Larry Cyril 1938- 106
Jensen, Laura (Linnea) 1948- 103
  See also CLC 37
Jensen, Lawrence N(eil) 1924- 17-20R
Jensen, Lloyd 1936- 61-64
Jensen, Margaret Ann 1948- 123
Jensen, Marlene 1947- 81-84
Jensen, Mary Ten Eyck Bard 1904-1970 .... 5-8R
  Obituary 29-32R
Jensen, Maxine Dowd 1919- 65-68
Jensen, Merrill (Monroe) 1905-1980 77-80
  Obituary 112
  See also DLB 17
Jensen, Michael C(harles) 1934- 127
Jensen, Michael C(ole) 1939- CANR-32
  Earlier sketch in CA 49-52
Jensen, Muriel 1945- CANR-133
  Earlier sketch in CA 164
Jensen, Niels 1927- 49-52
  See also SATA 25
Jensen, Ole Klindt
  See Klindt-Jensen, Ole
Jensen, Oliver (Ormerod) 1914- CANR-10
  Earlier sketch in CA 25-28R
Jensen, Paul K. 1916- 17-20R
Jensen, Paul M(orris) 1944- CANR-99
  Earlier sketch in CA 53-56
Jensen, Pauline Marie (Long)
  1900-1974 .... CAP-2
  Earlier sketch in CA 17-18
Jensen, Peter
  See Wallmann, Jeffrey M(iner)
Jensen, Richard C(arl) 1936- 49-52
Jensen, Richard J. 1941- 33-36R
Jensen, Robert (Earl) 1938-1990 111
  Obituary 132
Jensen, Rolf (Arthur) 1912- 21-24R
Jensen, Rosalie (Seymour) 1938- 57-60
Jensen, Ruby Jean 173
Jensen, Thit (Maria Kristine Dorothea)
  1876-1957 .... DLB 214
Jensen, Vernon H(ortin) 1907-1998 106
Jensen, Vickie (Dee) 1946- 149
  See also SATA 81
Jensen, Virginia Allen 1927- CANR-1
  Earlier sketch in CA 45-48
  See also SATA 8
Jensi, Muganwa Nsiku
  See Shorter, Aylward
Jenson, Robert W(illiam) 1930- CANR-9
  Earlier sketch in CA 5-8R
Jenson, William R(obert) 1946- 101
Jenson-Elliott, Cynthia L(ouise) 1962- 216
  See also SATA 143
Jentleson, Bruce W. 1951- 124
Jentz, Gaylord A. 1931- CANR-31
  Earlier sketches in CA 25-28R, CANR-14
Jenyns, R(oger) Soame 1904-1976 73-76
  Obituary 69-72
Jenyns, Soame
  See Jenyns, R(oger) Soame
Jeong-ho, Nam 1952- 212
Jephcott, E(dmund) F(rancis) N(eville) 1938-
  Brief entry 115
Jephson, Robert 1736-1803 .... DLB 89
Jeppson, J. O.
  See Asimov, Janet (Jeppson)
Jepsen, Stanley M(arius) 1912-1997 77-80
Jepson, Jill 1950- 141
Jepson, Selwyn 1899-1989
  Obituary 128
Jeram, Anita 1965- CANR-123
  Earlier sketch in CA 149
  See also MAICYA 2
  See also SATA 71, 102, 154
Jerdee, Thomas H(arlan) 1927- 118
Jeremias, Joachim 1900-1982 .... CANR-11
  Earlier sketch in CA 5-8R
Jeremy, David J(ohn) 1939- CANR-71
  Earlier sketch in CA 129
Jeremy, Sister Mary 5-8R
Jerina, Carol 1947- 126
Jeritza, Maria 1887-1982
  Obituary 107
Jermain, Clive 1966(?)-1988
  Obituary 124
Jerman, James (Auguste) 1920- 123
Jerman, Jerry 1949- 155
  See also SATA 89
Jerman, Sylvia Paul
  See Cooper, Sylvia
Jernick, Ruth 1948- 107
Jernigan, Brenda K. 1950- 217
Jernigan, E. Wesley 1940- .... SATA 85
Jernigan, Gisela (Evelyn) 1948- 151
  See also SATA 85
Jerome, Saint 345-420 .... RGWL 3
Jerome, Fred 1939- 210
Jerome, Jerome K(lapka) 1859-1927 177
  Brief entry 119
  See also DLB 10, 34, 135
  See also RGEL 2
  See also TCLC 23
Jerome, John 1932- CANR-99
  Earlier sketches in CA 45-48, CANR-2
Jerome, Joseph
  See Sewell, Brocard
Jerome, Judson (Blair) 1927-1991 ..... CANR-44
  Earlier sketches in CA 9-12R, CANR-4, 20
  See also CAAS 8
  See also CP 1, 2
  See also DLB 105
Jerome, Lawrence E(dmund) 1944- 77-80
Jerome, Mark
  See Appleman, Mark J(erome)
Jerome, Stuart 1918(?)-1983
  Obituary 111
Jerott, Michelle 173
Jerrold, Douglas William 1803-1857 . DLB 158, 159
  See also RGEL 2
Jerry, Mathers 1948- 177
Jerrybilt
  See Shields, Gerald R.
Jersild, Arthur T(homas) 1902-1994 .. CANR-21
  Obituary 143
  Earlier sketch in CA 1-4R
Jersild, Devon 1958- 199
Jersild, P. C.
  See Jersild, Per Christian
Jersild, Paul T(homas) 1931- 37-40R
Jersild, Per Christian 1935- 130
  See also CWW 2
  See also DLB 257
  See also EWL 3
Jervell, Jacob 1925- CANR-23
  Earlier sketches in CA 61-64, CANR-8
Jervey, Edward D(rewry) 1929- 133
Jervis, Robert 1940- 142
Jeschke, Marlin 1929- 45-48
Jeschke, Susan 1942- 77-80
  See also SATA 42
  See also SATA-Brief 27
Jeschke, Wolfgang 1936- 163
  See also SFW 4
Jeske, Richard Lee 1936- 111
Jesmer, Elaine 1939- 49-52
  See also AITN 1
Jespersen, James 1934- 103
Jesse, F(ryniwyd) Tennyson 1889-1958
  Brief entry 112
  See also DLB 77
Jesse, Michael
  See Baldwin, Michael
Jessel, Camilla (Ruth) 1937- CANR-122
  Earlier sketches in CA 104, CANR-23
  See also SATA 29, 143
Jessel, George (Albert) 1898-1981 89-92
  Obituary 103
Jessel, John
  See Weinbaum, Stanley Grauman
Jessen, Carl A. 1887(?)-1978
  Obituary 77-80
Jessey, Cornelia
  See Sussman, Cornelia Silver
Jessner, Lucie Ney 1896-1979
  Obituary 93-96
Jessop, Keith 1933- 200
Jessop, Thomas Edmund 1896-1980 .... 9-12R

Jessor 296 CONTEMPORARY AUTHORS

Jessor, Richard 1924- 41-44R
Jessup, Deborah Hitchcock 1934- 141
Jessup, Frances
See Van Briggle, Margaret F(rances) Jessup
Jessup, John K(nox) 1907-1979 101
Obituary 89-92
Jessup, Michael H(yle) 1937-
Brief entry 109
Jessup, Paul F(rederick) 1939- 111
Jessup, Philip C(aryl) 1897-1986 77-80
Obituary 118
Jessup, Richard 1925(?)-1982
Obituary 108
See also TCWW 1, 2
Jesty, P(eter) H(ugh) 1948- 121
Jeter, Jacky
See Jeter, Jacquelyn I.
Jeter, Jacquelyn I. 1935- 25-28R
Jeter, K. W. 1950- 158
See also HGG
See also SFW 4
Jett, (Orlando) Joseph 1958(?)- 186
Jett, Stephen C(linton) 1938- CANR-10
Earlier sketch in CA 25-28R
Jette, Fernand 1921- 5-8R
Jeune, Paul 1950- 101
Jeunet, Jean-Pierre 1955- .... AAYA 56
Jeury, Michel 1934- 161
See also SFW 4
Jevons, Frederic Raphae 1929- 61-64
Jevons, Marshall
See Breit, William (Leo) and
Elzinga, Kenneth G(erald)
Jewel
See Kilcher, Jewel
Jewel, John 1522-1571 .... DLB 236
Jewell, Derek 1927-1985 .... CANR-20
Earlier sketches in CA 33-36R, CANR-13
Jewell, Edmund F. 1896(?)-1978
Obituary 81-84
Jewell, Elizabeth
See Jewell, Elizabeth J.
Jewell, Lisa 1968- 210
Jewell, Malcolm E(dwin) 1928- CANR-5
Earlier sketch in CA 1-4R
Jewell, Nancy 1940- CANR-7
Earlier sketch in CA 61-64
See also SATA 109
See also SATA-Brief 41
Jewess, Kathleen
See Burk, Kathleen
Jewett, Alyce Lowrie (Williams) 1908- .. CAP-1
Earlier sketch in CA 13-14
Jewett, Ann E(lizabeth) 1921- 93-96
Jewett, Claudia L(owe) 1939- 112
Jewett, Eleanore Myers 1890-1967 .... 5-8R
See also SATA 5
Jewett, Paul King 1919-1991 53-56
Obituary 135
Jewett, Robert 1933- CANR-127
Earlier sketches in CA 45-48, CANR-2
Jewett, (Theodora) Sarah Orne
1849-1909 .... CANR-71
Brief entry 108
Earlier sketch in CA 127
See also AMW
See also AMWC 2
See also AMWR 2
See also DLB 12, 74, 221
See also EXPS
See also FL 1:3
See also FW
See also MAL 5
See also MAWW
See also NFS 15
See also RGAL 4
See also RGSF 2
See also SATA 15
See also SSC 6, 44
See also SSFS 4
See also TCLC 1, 22
Jewison, Norman (Frederick) 1926- 143
Brief entry 113
Jewitt, John Rodgers 1783-1821 .... DLB 99
Jewsbury, Geraldine (Endsor)
1812-1880 .... DLB 21
Jewsbury, Maria Jane 1800-1833 .... DLB 199
Jeyaretnam, Philip 1965- 212
Jezard, Alison 1919- 29-32R
See also SATA 57
See also SATA-Brief 34
Jezer, Marty 1940- CANR-27
Earlier sketch in CA 109
Jezewski, Bohdan O(lgierd) 1900-1980 .... 5-8R
Obituary 103
Jha, Akhileshwar 1932- 107
Jha, Lakshmi Kant 1913-1988
Obituary 125
Jha, Raj Kamal 1966- 189
Jhabvala, Ruth Prawer 1927- CANR-128
Earlier sketches in CA 1-4R, CANR-2, 29, 51,
74, 91
Interview in CANR-29
See also BRWS 5
See also CLC 4, 8, 29, 94, 138
See also CN 1, 2, 3, 4, 5, 6, 7
See also DAB
See also DAM NOV
See also DLB 139, 194
See also EWL 3
See also IDFW 3, 4
See also MTCW 1, 2
See also MTFW 2005
See also RGSF 2
See also RGWL 2
See also RHW
See also TEA
Jiang, Cheng An 1943- 180
See also SATA 109
Jiang, Jifang
See Ruan, Fang-fu
Jiang, Ji-li 1954- CANR-134
Earlier sketch in CA 168
See also AAYA 42
See also BYA 16
See also MTCW 2005
See also SATA 101
Jiang, Zheng An
See Jiang, Cheng An
Jianou, Ionel 1905- CANR-9
Earlier sketch in CA 21-24R
Jibran, Kahlil
See Gibran, Kahlil
Jibran, Khalil
See Gibran, Kahlil
Jidejian, Nina 1921- 29-32R
Jilemnicky, Peter 1901-1949 .... EWL 3
Jiler, John 1946- 114
See also SATA 42
See also SATA-Brief 35
Jiles, Paulette 1943- CANR-124
Earlier sketches in CA 101, CANR-70
See also CLC 13, 58
See also CWP
Jillson, Joyce 1946(?)-2004 111
Obituary 232
Jimenez, Francisco 1943- CANR-136
Earlier sketches in CA 131, CANR-90
See also AAYA 32
See also HW 1
See also MAICYA 2
See also MTFW 2005
See also SATA 108
Jimenez, Janey (Renee) 1953- 77-80
Jimenez (Mantecon), Juan Ramon
1881-1958 .... CANR-74
Brief entry 104
Earlier sketch in CA 131
See also DAM MULT, POET
See also DLB 134
See also EW 9
See also EWL 3
See also HLC 1
See also HW 1
See also MTCW 1, 2
See also MTFW 2005
See also PC 7
See also RGWL 2, 3
See also TCLC 4
Jimenez, Neal (Randall) 1960- 138
Jimenez, Ramon
See Jimenez (Mantecon), Juan Ramon
Jimenez de Wagenheim, Olga
See Jiminez Wagenheim, Olga
Jimenez Lozano, Jose 1930- 219
Jimenez Mantecon, Juan
See Jimenez (Mantecon), Juan Ramon
Jiminez Wagenheim, Olga 1941- 177
Jimson, Giles
See Graves, Roy Neil
Jin, Ha 152
See also Jin, Xuefei
See also CLC 109
See also DLB 244, 292
See also SSFS 17
Jin, Jian-Ming
See Jin, Jianming
Jin, Jianming 1962- 233
Jin, Xuefei 1956- CANR-130
Earlier sketch in CANR-91
See also Jin, Ha
See also MTFW 2005
See also SSFS 17
Jinks, Catherine 1963- CANR-140
Earlier sketches in CA 159, CANR-96
See also SATA 94, 155
See also YAW
Jinks, William Howard, Jr. 1938- 41-44R
Jinpa, Geshe Thupten
See Jinpa, Thupten
Jinpa, Thupten 1958- 151
Jipson, Wayne R(ay) 1931- 45-48
Jirasek, Alois 1851-1930 .... EWL 3
Jirgens, Karl (Edward) 1952- 158
Jiskogo
See Harrington, Mark Raymond
Jo, Yung-Hwan 1932- 45-48
Joachim, Leo H. 1898-1985
Obituary 117
Joan, Polly 1933- 101
Joanou, Phil(ip) 1961- 213
Joans, Barbara 205
Joans, Ted 1928-2003 .... CANR-25
Obituary 217
Earlier sketches in CA 45-48, CANR-2
See also CAAS 25
See also BW 1
See also DLB 16, 41
Joaquin, Nick 1917- .... EWL 3
Joas, Hans 1948- CANR-115
Earlier sketch in CA 159
Job, Amy G. 1942- 224
Jobb, Jamie 1945- 85-88
See also SATA 29
Jobe, Brock (William) 1948- 118
Jobes, Gertrude Blumenthal
1907-1972 .... CAP-1
Earlier sketch in CA 11-12
Jobling, Curtis 200
See also SATA 131
Jobling, David 168
Jobson, Gary Alan 1950- 93-96
Jobson, Hamilton 1914- 73-76
Jobson, Sandra
See Darroch, Sandra Jobson
Jocelyn, Ann Henning 1948- CANR-117
Earlier sketch in CA 156
See also SATA 92
Jocelyn, Marthe 1956- .... SATA 118, 163
Jocelyn, Richard
See Clutterbuck, Richard
Jochnowitz, George 1937- 49-52
Jochumsson, Matthias 1835-1920 .... DLB 293
Jodelle, Etienne 1532-1573 .. GFL Beginnings to
1789
Joe, Barbara
See Hoshizaki, Barbara Joe
Joe, Rita 1932- 153
See also CP 7
Joe, Yolanda 1962(?)- 230
Joedicke, Juergen 1925- 17-20R
Joel, Asher Alexander 1912-1998 108
Obituary 172
Joel, Billy
See Joel, William Martin
See also CLC 26
Joel, William Martin 1949- 108
See also Joel, Billy
Joels, Merrill E. 1915- 25-28R
Joelson, Annette 1903-1971
Obituary 29-32R
Joenpelto, Eeva (Elisabeth) 1921- 195
See also EWL 3
Joensen, Martin 1902-1966 238
Joensson, Reidar 1944- 140
Joerns, Consuelo 114
Brief entry 111
See also SATA 44
See also SATA-Brief 33
Joers, Lawrence E(ugene) C(laire)
1900-1999 .... 41-44R
Joesting, Edward Henry 1925- 103
Joey D
See Macaulay, Teresa (E.)
Jofen, Jean 1922- 37-40R
Joffe, Josef 1944- 126
Joffe, Joyce 1940- 77-80
Joha 1525-1602 .... DLB 203
Johanides, Jan 1934- .... EWL 3
Johannes, John R. 1943- 111
Johannes, R.
See Moss, Rose
Johannesen, Richard L(ee) 1937- 17-20R
Johannessen, Matthias (Haraldsson)
1930- .... CWW 2
See also DLB 293
Johannesson, Olof
See Alfven, Hannes O(lof) G(oesta)
Johannes Ur Kotlum 1899-1972 .... DLB 293
See also EWL 3
Johanningmeier, E(rwin) V(irgil) 1937- 104
Johannis, Theodore B(enjamin), Jr.
1914-1996 .... 33-36R
Johannsen, Hano D. 1933- CANR-29
Earlier sketch in CA 29-32R
Johannsen, Robert Walter 1925- CANR-96
Earlier sketches in CA 1-4R, CANR-45
Johansen, Bruce Elliott 1950- 110
Johansen, Dorothy O. 1904-1999 .... CAP-1
Earlier sketch in CA 13-14
Johansen, Iris 170
See also AAYA 38
Johansen, K(rista) V(ictoria) 1968- 198
See also SATA 129
Johansen, Ruthann Knechel 1942- 237
Johanson, Donald C(arl) 1943- CANR-48
Earlier sketch in CA 107
Johanson, Stanley Morris 1933- 45-48
Johansson, Philip 239
See also SATA 163
Johansson, Thomas (Hugo) B(ernard)
1943- CANR-19
Earlier sketch in CA 102
John, Alix
See Jones, Alice C.
John, Angela V. 1948- 125
John, B.
See John, Elizabeth Beaman
John, Betty
See John, Elizabeth Beaman
John, Bubba Free
See Jones, Franklin Albert
John, Colin
See Hagan, Chet
John, Da Free
See Jones, Franklin Albert
John, Dane
See Major, Alan P(ercival)
John, DeWitt 1915-1985
Obituary 117
John, Elizabeth Beaman 1907-1997 .... CANR-8
Earlier sketch in CA 5-8R
John, Errol 1924-1988
Obituary 126
See also DLB 233
John, Helen James 1930- 61-64
John, Joyce .... SATA 59
John, Juliet 1967- 199
John, Owen 1918-
Brief entry 117
John, Robert 29-32R
John, Sandra D(eanne Thompson) 1951- 114
John, Vera P.
See John-Steiner, Vera P(olgar)
Johnn, David
See Engle, John D(avid), Jr.
John of Dumbleton 1310(?)-1349(?) .... DLB 115
John of Garland c. 1195-c. 1272 .... DLB 208
John of the Cross, St. 1542-1591 .... RGWL 2, 3
John Paul I, Pope 1912-1978 .... CANR-29
Earlier sketch in CA 81-84
John Paul II, Pope 1920-2005 133
Obituary 238
Brief entry 106
See also CLC 128
Johnpoll, Bernard K(eith) 1918- CANR-24
Earlier sketches in CA 21-24R, CANR-9
Johns, Albert Cameron 1914- CANR-6
Earlier sketch in CA 49-52
Johns, Avery
See Cousins, Margaret
Johns, Claude J., Jr. 1930- 77-80
Johns, Edward Alistair 1936- 45-48
Johns, Elizabeth 1937- CANR-137
Earlier sketch in CA 121
Johns, Elizabeth 1943- .... SATA 88
Johns, Eric 1907-1975
Obituary 116
Johns, Foster
See Seldes, Gilbert (Vivian)
Johns, Geoff 1973- 222
Johns, Geoffrey
See Warner, (George) Geoffrey John
Johns, Glover S., Jr. 1911(?)-1976
Obituary 65-68
Johns, Janetta
See Quin-Harkin, Janet
Johns, Jasper 1930- .... AAYA 63
Johns, John E(dwin) 1921- 9-12R
Johns, June 1925- 57-60
Johns, Kenneth
See Bulmer, (Henry) Kenneth
Johns, Linda 1945- 142
Johns, Marston
See Fanthorpe, R(obert) Lionel
Johns, Ray E(arl) 1900-1991 .... 41-44R
Johns, Richard A(lton) 1929- 17-20R
Johns, Stephanie Bernardo 1947- CANR-30
Earlier sketch in CA 112
Johns, Veronica Parker 1907-1988 234
See also CMW 4
Johns, W(illiam) E(arle) 1893-1968 .... CANR-30
Earlier sketch in CA 73-76
See also CWRI 5
See also DLB 160
See also MAICYA 1, 2
See also SATA 55
Johns, Captain W. E.
See Johns, W(illiam) E(arle)
Johns, Warren L. 1929- 21-24R
Johns, Whitey
See White, John I(rwin)
Johnsen, Trevor Bernard Meldal
See Meldal-Johnsen, Trevor Bernard
Johnsgard, Karin L(uisa) 1964- 118
Johnsgard, Paul A(ustin) 1931- CANR-94
Earlier sketches in CA 49-52, CANR-1, 17, 39
Johnson, A.
See Johnson, Annabell (Jones)
Johnson, A. E.
See Johnson, Annabell (Jones) and
Johnson, Edgar (Raymond)
Johnson, Mrs. A. E. 1858(?)-1922 .... DLB 221
Johnson, A(lison) Findlay 1947- 132
Johnson, Alan P(ackard) 1929- 17-20R
Johnson, Albert (Franklin) 1904-1993 . CANR-6
Earlier sketch in CA 9-12R
Johnson, Alden Porter 1914-1972
Obituary 104
Johnson, Alexandra 1949- CANR-127
Earlier sketch in CA 164
Johnson, Alison
See Johnson, A(lison) Findlay
Johnson, Allan G. 1946- 171
Johnson, Allen 85-88
Johnson, Allison H(eartz) 1910- 41-44R
Johnson, Alvin 1874-1971
Obituary 29-32R
Johnson, Amandus 1877-1974
Obituary 49-52
Johnson, Amelia
See Johnson, Mrs. A. E.
Johnson, Amryl .... CWP
Johnson, Andrew 1949- 143
Johnson, Andrew N(isseu) 1887-1982 61-64
Obituary 120
Johnson, Angela 1961- CANR-134
Earlier sketches in CA 138, CANR-92
See also AAYA 32
See also CLR 33
See also CWRI 5
See also MAICYA 2
See also MAICYAS 1
See also SATA 69, 102, 150
Johnson, Ann Braden 1945- 135
Johnson, Ann Cox
See Saunders, Ann Loreille
Johnson, Annabel
See Johnson, Annabell (Jones)
See also BYA 7, 8
Johnson, Annabell (Jones) 1921- CANR-37
Earlier sketch in CA 9-12R
See also Johnson, Annabel
See also MAICYA 1, 2
See also SATA 2, 72
See also YAW 1
Johnson, Annette R. 1969- 239
Johnson, Arno Hollock 1901-1985
Obituary 116
Johnson, Arnold W(aldemar)
1900-1984 .... CAP-1
Earlier sketch in CA 13-14
Johnson, Art 1946- 194
See also SATA 123
Johnson, Arthur Menzies 1921- 21-24R

Cumulative Index 297 **Johnson**

Johnson, Arthur W(illiam) 1920- CANR-41
Earlier sketch in CA 117
Johnson, Aubrey Rodway 1901-1985
Obituary 117
Johnson, Audrey P(ike) 1915- CANR-15
Earlier sketch in CA 93-96
Johnson, B(owen) C(harleston) 1945- 107
Johnson, B(urdetta) F(aye) 1920- CANR-3
Earlier sketch in CA 1-4R
See also Beebe, B(urdetta) F(aye)
Johnson, B(asil) L(eonard) C(lyde) 1919- 120
Johnson, B(ryan) S(tanley William)
1933-1973 .... CANR-9
Obituary 53-56
Earlier sketch in CA 9-12R
See also CLC 6, 9
See also CN 1
See also CP 1, 2
See also DLB 14, 40
See also EWL 3
See also RGEL 2
Johnson, Barbara 1947- 173
Johnson, Barbara E. 173
Johnson, Barbara F(erry) 1923-1989 . CANR-44
Earlier sketch in CA 73-76
See also RHW
Johnson, Barclay G(iddings) 1909-1985
Obituary 116
Johnson, Barry L(ynn) 1934- 33-36R
Johnson, Barry L(ee) 1943- 61-64
Johnson, Bea (?)-1976
Obituary 65-68
Johnson, Ben E(ugene) 1940- CANR-8
Earlier sketch in CA 61-64
Johnson, Bengt Emil 1936- 192
Johnson, Benjamin A. 1937- CANR-9
Earlier sketch in CA 21-24R
Johnson, Benjamin F., of Boone
See Riley, James Whitcomb
Johnson, Benton 1928- 81-84
Johnson, Bernard 1933-2003 .... 33-36R
Obituary 218
Johnson, Bertha French 1906-1993 .... 41-44R
Johnson, Beth 1953- 118
Johnson, Bettye 1858-1919
See Rogers, Bettye
Johnson, Bob 1950- 130
Johnson, Bradford 1937- 57-60
Johnson, Braiden Rex
See Rex-Johnson, Braiden
Johnson, Brian (Martin) 1925- CANR-23
Earlier sketch in CA 106
Johnson, Bruce 1933- 33-36R
Johnson, Bryan 1948- 133
Johnson, Burges 1877-1963
Obituary 89-92
Johnson, Byron Lindberg 1917- 21-24R
Johnson, C. Edward
See Johnson, Carl E(dward)
Johnson, C. F.
See Goulart, Frances Sheridan
Johnson, Cait 1952- CANR-127
Earlier sketch in CA 170
Johnson, Carl E(dward) 1937- 25-28R
Johnson, Carl G(raves) 1915- 101
Johnson, Carol
See Bolt, Carol
Johnson, Carol Virginia 1928- CANR-6
Earlier sketch in CA 9-12R
Johnson, Carroll B(ernard) 1938- 73-76
Johnson, Caryn
See Goldberg, Whoopi
Johnson, Caryn E.
See Goldberg, Whoopi
Johnson, Cathy Marie 1956- 145
See also ANW
Johnson, Cecil Edward 1927- 33-36R
Johnson, Chalmers (Ashby) 1931- CANR-98
Earlier sketches in CA 5-8R, CANR-6
Johnson, Charlene
See Crawford, Char
Johnson, Charles 1679-1748 .... DLB 84
Johnson, Charles (Richard) 1948- ... CANR-129
Earlier sketches in CA 116, CANR-42, 66, 82
See also CAAS 18
See also AFAW 2
See also AMWS 6
See also BLC 2
See also BW 2, 3
See also CLC 7, 51, 65, 163
See also CN 5, 6, 7
See also DAM MULT
See also DLB 33, 278
See also MAL 5
See also MTCW 2
See also MTFW 2005
See also RGAL 4
See also SSFS 16
Johnson, Charles Benjamin
1928-1980 .... CANR-4
Earlier sketch in CA 5-8R
Johnson, Charles Ellicott 1920-1969 .... 1-4R
Obituary 103
Johnson, Charles Floyd 172
Johnson, Charles R. 1925- 65-68
See also SATA 11
Johnson, Charles S.
See Edwards, William B(ennett)
Johnson, Charles S(purgeon)
1893-1956 .... CANR-82
Earlier sketch in CA 125
See also BW 1, 3
See also DLB 51, 91
See also HR 1:3
Johnson, Charles W(illiam) 1934- 107
Johnson, Charlotte Buel
See von Wodtke, Charlotte Buel Johnson
See also SATA 46
Johnson, Chas. Floyd
See Johnson, Charles Floyd
Johnson, Cherry L(urae) F(lake) 1968- 165
Johnson, Chester L. 1951- 211
Johnson, Christine 1943- 123
Johnson, Christopher 1931- CANR-8
Earlier sketch in CA 13-16R
Johnson, Christopher Howard 1937-
Brief entry 106
Johnson, Chuck
See Johnson, Charles R.
Johnson, Clair 1915(?)-1980
Obituary 97-100
Johnson, Claire M. 1956- 219
Johnson, Clarence L(eonard) 1910-1990 159
Johnson, Claudia Alta (Taylor) 1912- 89-92
Johnson, Claudia D(urst) 1938- 114
Johnson, Clive (White, Jr.) 1930- 29-32R
Johnson, Colin
See Mudrooroo (Nyoongah)
See also CN 4, 5
See also CP 7
See also DLB 289
Johnson, Colin 1939- 130
Johnson, Crockett
See Leisk, David (Johnson)
See also CLR 98
Johnson, Curt(is Lee) 1928- 33-36R
Johnson, Curtiss Sherman
1899-1993 .... CANR-45
Earlier sketch in CA 45-48
Johnson, D(onald) B. 1944- .... SATA 146
Johnson, D(onald) Barton 1933- 33-36R
Johnson, D(avid) Bruce 1942- 61-64
Johnson, D(avid) Gale 1916-2003 .... 17-20R
Obituary 215
Johnson, D(ana) William 1945- 97-100
See also SATA 23
Johnson, Dale A(rthur) 1936- 37-40R
Johnson, Dale L(eonard) 1934- 130
Johnson, Daniel M. 1940- 154
Johnson, Daniel Shahid 1954- .... SATA 73
Johnson, Dave W(illiam) 1931- 93-96
Johnson, David 1927- CANR-8
Earlier sketch in CA 13-16R
Johnson, David E(dsel) 1927- 201
Johnson, David G(eorge) 1906- 9-12R
Johnson, David K. 235
Johnson, David Lawrence 1943- 114
Johnson, David Ralph 1942- 117
Johnson, Deidre A(nn) 1953- 116
Johnson, Denis 1949- CANR-99
Brief entry 117
Earlier sketches in CA 121, CANR-71
See also CLC 52, 160
See also CN 4, 5, 6, 7
See also DLB 120
See also SSC 56
Johnson, Diane 1934- CANR-95
Earlier sketches in CA 41-44R, CANR-17, 40, 62
Interview in CANR-17
See also BPFB 2
See also CLC 5, 13, 48
See also CN 4, 5, 6, 7
See also DLBY 1980
See also MTCW 1
Johnson, Dianne 1960- 199
See also Johnson, Dinah
Johnson, Dick
See Johnson, Richard A.
Johnson, Dinah
See Johnson, Dianne
See also SATA 130
Johnson, Dolores 1949- 137
See also SATA 69
Johnson, Don 1927- 168
Johnson, Don 1934- 116
Johnson, Donald Bruce 1921-1981 .. CANR-25
Earlier sketch in CA 1-4R
Johnson, Donald D. 1917- 137
Johnson, Donald Leslie 1930- 176
Johnson, Donald M(cEwen) 1909- 1-4R
Johnson, Donald McI(ntosh)
1903-1978 .... CANR-8
Earlier sketch in CA 5-8R
Johnson, Donald S. 1932- 225
Johnson, Donna Kay 1935- 106
Johnson, Donovan A(lbert) 1910- CANR-5
Earlier sketch in CA 5-8R
Johnson, Doris 1937- 219
Johnson, Doris McNeely 1941- 111
Johnson, Dorothy Biddle 1887(?)-1974
Obituary 53-56
Johnson, Dorothy E(thel) 1920- 53-56
Johnson, Dorothy M(arie)
1905-1984 .... CANR-63
Obituary 114
Earlier sketches in CA 5-8R, CANR-6
See also DLB 206
See also SATA 6
See also SATA-Obit 40
See also TCWW 1, 2
Johnson, Dorris 1914- 109
Johnson, Doug(las A.) 1952- 225
Johnson, Douglas W(ayne) 1934- CANR-21
Earlier sketches in CA 57-60, CANR-6
Johnson, E(dgar) A(gustus) J(erome)
1900-1972 .... CAP-1
Obituary 37-40R
Earlier sketch in CA 17-18
Johnson, E(arl) Ashby 1917- 33-36R
Johnson, E(ugene) Harper .... SATA 44
Johnson, E. Ned
See Johnson, Enid
Johnson, E(mily) Pauline 1861-1913 150
See also CCA 1
See also DAC
See also DAM MULT
See also DLB 92, 175
See also NNAL
See also TCWW 2
Johnson, E(mil) Richard 1937- CANR-60
Earlier sketch in CA 104
See also CMW 4
Johnson, E(dward) W(arren) 1941- 29-32R
Johnson, Earl, Jr. 1933- CANR-10
Earlier sketch in CA 61-64
Johnson, Earl S.
See Johnson, Earl Shepard
Johnson, Earl Shepard 1894-1986
Obituary 119
Johnson, Earvin, Jr. 1959- 141
See also AAYA 17
Johnson, Edgar 1901-1995 .... 9-12R
Obituary 148
See also DLB 103
Johnson, Edgar (Raymond)
1912-1990 .... CANR-37
Earlier sketch in CA 9-12R
See also BYA 7, 8
See also MAICYA 1, 2
See also SATA 2, 72
See also YAW
Johnson, Edward 1598-1672 .... DLB 24
Johnson, Edward A(ndrew) 1915- 37-40R
Johnson, Edwin Clark (Toby) 1945- .. CANR-99
Earlier sketches in CA 107, CANR-25
Johnson, Eleanor
See Seymour, Dorothy Jane Z(ander)
Johnson, Eleanor Murdock 1892-1987
Obituary 123
See also SATA-Obit 54
Johnson, Electa (Search) 1909-2004 .... 1-4R
Obituary 233
Johnson, Elizabeth 1911-1984 .... CANR-4
Obituary 117
Earlier sketch in CA 1-4R
See also SATA 7
See also SATA-Obit 39
Johnson, Elizabeth A. 1941- CANR-133
Earlier sketch in CA 168
Johnson, Ellen Argo 1933-1983 .... CANR-13
Obituary 110
Earlier sketch in CA 73-76
Johnson, Ellen H(ulda) 1910-1992 ... CANR-15
Obituary 137
Earlier sketch in CA 37-40R
Johnson, Elmer Douglas 1915- CANR-3
Earlier sketch in CA 9-12R
Johnson, Elmer Hubert 1917- CANR-67
Earlier sketch in CA 13-16R
Johnson, Elmer W. 1932- 210
Johnson, Enid 1892-1969 73-76
Johnson, Eola 1909- 49-52
Johnson, Eric W(arner) 1918-1994 ..... CANR-4
Obituary 146
Earlier sketch in CA 5-8R
See also SATA 8,
See also SATA-Obit 82
Johnson, Eugene J. 1937- CANR-56
Earlier sketch in CA 127
Johnson, Evelyne 1922- CANR-21
Earlier sketch in CA 69-72
See also SATA 20
Johnson, Eyvind (Olof Verner)
1900-1976 .... CANR-101
Obituary 69-72
Earlier sketches in CA 73-76, CANR-34
See also CLC 14
See also DLB 259
See also EW 12
See also EWL 3
Johnson, Falk S(immons) 1913-1994 ..... 17-20R
Johnson, Fenton 1888-1958 124
Brief entry 118
See also BLC 2
See also BW 1
See also DAM MULT
See also DLB 45, 50
Johnson, Fenton 1953- 159
Johnson, Ferd 1905-1996 69-72
Obituary 154
Johnson, Forrest B(ryant) 1935- 106
Johnson, Frank J. 1930- 200
Johnson, Franklyn A(rthur) 1921- CANR-4
Earlier sketch in CA 1-4R
Johnson, Fred 19(?)-1982 .... SATA 63
Johnson, Freddie Lee III 202
Johnson, Frederick 1932- 73-76
Johnson, Fridolf (Lester) 1905-1988 103
Obituary 126
Johnson, Frosty
See Johnson, Forrest B(ryant)
Johnson, G(eorge) Orville 1915- CANR-4
Earlier sketch in CA 1-4R
Johnson, G. Timothy 1936- 235
Johnson, Gaylord 1884-1972 .... CAP-1
Earlier sketch in CA 9-10
See also SATA 7
Johnson, Geoffrey 1893-1966 .... CAP-1
Earlier sketch in CA 13-14
Johnson, George 1917- 5-8R
Johnson, George (Laclede) 1952- 133
Johnson, George Lloyd 1955- 175
Johnson, Georgia Douglas (Camp)
1880-1966 125
See also BW 1
See also DLB 51, 249
See also HR 1:3
See also WP
Johnson, Gerald White 1890-1980 85-88
Obituary 97-100
See also DLB 29
See also SATA 19
See also SATA-Obit 28
Johnson, Gertrude F(alk) 1929- 57-60
Johnson, Greer 1920(?)-1974
Obituary 53-56
Johnson, Greg 1953- 140
See also DLB 234
Johnson, Guy 1945- 189
Johnson, H(arold) B(enjamin), Jr. 1931- . 29-32R
Johnson, H(erbert) Webster 1906- CANR-4
Earlier sketch in CA 5-8R
Johnson, Halvard 1936- 33-36R
Johnson, Harold L. 1924- 13-16R
Johnson, Harold Scholl 1929- 37-40R
Johnson, Harold V. 1897-1991 .... CANR-5
Earlier sketch in CA 1-4R
Johnson, Harper
See Johnson, E(ugene) Harper
Johnson, Harriett 1908-1987
Obituary 123
See also SATA-Obit 53
Johnson, Harry Alleyn 1921- CANR-31
Earlier sketch in CA 45-48
Johnson, Harry G(ordon)
1923-1977 .... CANR-29
Obituary 69-72
Earlier sketch in CA 5-8R
Johnson, Harry L. 1929- 29-32R
Johnson, Harry Morton 1917- 9-12R
Johnson, Harvey L.
See Johnson, Harvey Leroy
Johnson, Harvey Leroy 1904-1995 .... 37-40R
Johnson, Haynes (Bonner) 1931- CANR-112
Earlier sketches in CA 5-8R, CANR-12, 48
Johnson, Helen (Louise) Kendrick 1844(?)-1917
Brief entry 123
Johnson, Helene 1907-1995 181
See also DLB 51
See also HR 1:3
See also WP
Johnson, Henry
See Hammond, John (Henry, Jr.)
Johnson, Herbert A(lan) 1934- CANR-106
Earlier sketches in CA 5-8R, CANR-4
Johnson, Herbert J. 1933- 29-32R
Johnson, Hildegard Binder
1908-1993 .... CANR-3
Earlier sketch in CA 9-12R
Johnson, Hillary 190
Johnson, Howard Albert 1915-1974 .... 1-4R
Obituary 49-52
Johnson, Hubert C. 1930- 130
Johnson, Hugh 1939- CANR-39
Earlier sketches in CA 93-96, CANR-16
Johnson, Humphrey Wynne 1925-1976
Obituary 61-64
Johnson, Ian 229
Johnson, Irma Bolan 1903- CANR-1
Earlier sketch in CA 1-4R
Johnson, Irving McClure 1905-1991 .... 1-4R
Obituary 133
Johnson, J. R.
See James, C(yril) L(ionel) R(obert)
Johnson, J. Stewart 1925- 127
Johnson, Jack
See Johnson, John Arthur
Johnson, Jakobina
See Sigurbjarnardottir, Jakobina
Johnson, Jakobina
See Sigurbjarnardottir, Jakobina
See also DLB 293
Johnson, Jalmar Edwin 1905- 5-8R
Johnson, James A(llen) 1932-
Brief entry 110
Johnson, James Craig 1944- 53-56
Johnson, James E(dgar) 1927- 77-80
Johnson, James H(enry) 1930- CANR-11
Earlier sketch in CA 25-28R
Johnson, James J(ay) 1939- 33-36R
Johnson, James L. 1927- CANR-9
Earlier sketch in CA 21-24R
Johnson, James P(earce) 1937- 81-84
Johnson, James Ralph 1922- CANR-2
Earlier sketch in CA 1-4R
See also SATA 1
Johnson, James Rosser 1916- 9-12R
Johnson, James Turner 1938- CANR-100
Earlier sketch in CA 61-64

Johnson, James Weldon 1871-1938 . CANR-82
Brief entry ... 104
Earlier sketch in CA 125
See also AFAW 1, 2
See also BLC 2
See also BW 1, 3
See also CDALB 1917-1929
See also CLR 32
See also DA3
See also DAM MULT, POET
See also DLB 51
See also EWL 3
See also EXPP
See also HR 1:3
See also LMFS 2
See also MAL 5
See also MTCW 1, 2
See also MTFW 2005
See also NFS 22
See also PC 24
See also PFS 1
See also RGAL 4
See also SATA 31
See also TCLC 3, 19
See also TUS
Johnson, James William 1927- ... 53-56
Johnson, Jane 1951- ... CANR-28
Earlier sketch in CA 110
See also SATA 48
Johnson, Jane M(axine) 1914- ... 49-52
Johnson, Janis Tyler 1930- ... 141
Johnson, Jann
See Johnson, Paula Janice
Johnson, Jay 1951(?)-1990
Obituary ... 131
Johnson, (Hettie) Jean 1937- ... 126
Johnson, Jean Dye 1920- ... 21-24R
Johnson, Jenny Lees 1944- ... CWP
Johnson, Jerry Mack 1927- ... CANR-4
Earlier sketch in CA 53-56
Johnson, Jim
See Johnson, James A(llen)
Johnson, Jinna
See Johnson, Virginia
Johnson, Joan D. 1929-
Brief entry ... 106
Johnson, Joan Helen 1931-1986 ... 61-64
Johnson, Joan J. 1942- ... CANR-98
Earlier sketches in CA 122, CANR-48
See also SATA 59
Johnson, Joe Donald 1943- ... 57-60
Johnson, John Arthur 1878-1946
Brief entry ... 115
Johnson, John Bockover, Jr. 1908-1972
Obituary ... 106
Johnson, John E(mil) 1929- ... 110
See also SATA 34
Johnson, John H(arold) 1918- ... 135
Brief entry ... 128
See also DLB 137
Johnson, John J. 1912- ... 9-12R
Johnson, John L. 1945- ... 146
Johnson, John M(yrton) 1941- ... 93-96
Johnson, Johnni 1922- ... 13-16R
Johnson, Johnny 1901-1995
See Johnson, (Walter) Ryerson
Johnson, Jory (F.) 1950- ... 137
Johnson, Joseph A., Jr. 1914(?)-1979
Obituary ... 89-92
Johnson, Joseph E(arl) 1946- ... 37-40R
Johnson, Joseph M. 1883(?)-1973
Obituary ... 45-48
Johnson, Josephine W(inslow)
1910-1990 ... 25-28R
Obituary ... 131
See also ANW
See also CN 1, 2, 3, 4, 5
Johnson, Joy Duvall 1932- ... 110
Johnson, Joyce 1935- ... CANR-102
Brief entry ... 125
Earlier sketch in CA 129
See also BG 1:3
See also CLC 58
Johnson, Judith (Emlyn) 1936- ... CANR-34
Earlier sketch in CA 25-28R, 153
See also Sherwin, Judith Johnson
See also CLC 7, 15
See also CP 7
Johnson, Karen 1939- ... 69-72
Johnson, Kathryn 1929- ... 33-36R
Johnson, Keith B(arnard) 1933- ... 29-32R
Johnson, Kendall 1928- ... 69-72
Johnson, Kenneth G(ardner) 1922- ... 41-44R
Johnson, Kenneth M(itchell) 1903-1983 ... 5-8R
Johnson, Kevin R. 1958- ... 210
Johnson, Kij 1960- ... 215
Johnson, Kim 1955- ... CANR-89
Earlier sketch in CA 133
Johnson, Kim "Howard"
See Johnson, Kim
Johnson, Kristi Planck 1944- ... 57-60
Johnson, Kurt ... 188
Johnson, L. D. 1916-1981 ... CANR-28
Earlier sketch in CA 33-36R
Johnson, La Verne B(ravo) 1925- ... 65-68
See also SATA 13
Johnson, Lady Bird
See Johnson, Claudia Alta (Taylor)
Johnson, Lee Kaiser 1962- ... SATA 78
Johnson, Leland R(oss) 1937- ... 149
Johnson, Lemuel A. 1941- ... CANR-43
Earlier sketch in CA 53-56
See also BW 2
Johnson, LeRoy C. 1937- ... 126
Johnson, Lewis Kerr 1904-1983 ... 1-4R
Johnson, Lincoln F., Jr. 1920- ... 81-84
Johnson, Linnea 1946- ... 138
Johnson, Linton Kwesi 1952- ... 153
See also BW 3
See also CP 7
See also DLB 157
See also EWL 3
Johnson, Lionel (Pigot) 1867-1902 ... 209
Brief entry ... 117
See also DLB 19
See also RGEL 2
See also TCLC 19
Johnson, Lissa H(alls) 1955- ... 136
See also SATA 65
Johnson, Loch K. 1942- ... CANR-102
Earlier sketches in CA 121, CANR-48
Johnson, Lois Smith 1894-1993 ... CAP-1
Earlier sketch in CA 9-10
See also SATA 6
Johnson, Lois Walfrid 1936- ... CANR-110
Earlier sketches in CA 57-60, CANR-6, 57
See also SATA 22, 91, 130
Johnson, LouAnne 1953- ... 138
Johnson, Louis 1924-1988 ... CANR-18
Earlier sketch in CA 101
See also CP 1, 2
Johnson, Luke Timothy 1943- ... CANR-128
Brief entry ... 107
Earlier sketch in CA 127
Johnson, Lyndon Baines 1908-1973 . CANR-23
Obituary ... 41-44R
Earlier sketch in CA 53-56
Johnson, Lynn Eric 1932-
Brief entry ... 108
Johnson, Lynn Staley
See Staley, Lynn
Johnson, M. Glen 1936- ... 41-44R
Johnson, M. L.
See Abercrombie, M(innie) L(ouie) J(ohnson)
Johnson, Magic
See Johnson, Earvin, Jr.
Johnson, Malcolm (Malone) 1904-1976 .. 69-72
Obituary ... 65-68
Johnson, Malcolm L. 1937- ... 69-72
Johnson, Manly 1920- ... 89-92
Johnson, Margaret 1926- ... 37-40R
Johnson, Margaret S(weet) 1893-1964
Obituary ... 113
See also SATA 35
Johnson, Marguerite Annie
See Angelou, Maya
Johnson, Marilue Carolyn 1931- ... CANR-1
Earlier sketch in CA 45-48
Johnson, Marilynn S. 1957- ... 164
Johnson, Marion Georgina Wikeley
1912-1980 ... 9-12R
Obituary ... 97-100
Johnson, Mark 1949- ... 115
Johnson, Marshall D. 1935- ... CANR-136
Earlier sketch in CA 33-36R
Johnson, Mary Anne 1943- ... 53-56
Johnson, Mary Ellen 1949- ... 120
Johnson, Mary Frances K. 1929(?)-1979
Obituary ... 104
See also SATA-Obit 27
Johnson, Mary Louise
See King, Mary Louise
Johnson, Mary Ritz 1904-1985 ... CAP-1
Earlier sketch in CA 9-10
Johnson, Maryanna 1925- ... 33-36R
Johnson, Mat(thew) 1970- ... 222
Johnson, Maud Battle 1918(?)-1985
Obituary ... 117
See also SATA-Obit 46
Johnson, Maurice (O.) 1913-1978 ... CANR-20
Earlier sketch in CA 1-4R
Johnson, Mauritz (Jr.) 1922- ... 41-44R
Johnson, Mel
See Malzberg, Barry N(athaniel)
Johnson, Mendal W(illiam) 1928-1976 ... 101
Johnson, Meredith Merrell 1952- ... SATA 104
Johnson, Merle Allison 1934- ... 37-40R
Johnson, Michael Craft 1950- ... 216
Johnson, Michael L(illard) 1943- ... CANR-19
Earlier sketches in CA 53-56, CANR-4
Johnson, Michael P(aul) 1941- ... 132
Johnson, Mike
See Sharkey, John Michael
Johnson, Mildred D. ... 132
Johnson, Milton 1932- ... SATA 31
Johnson, Nancy 1948- ... 159
Johnson, Nancy E(dith) 1941- ... 125
Johnson, Neil 1954- ... 204
See also SATA 73, 135
Johnson, Neil (James) 1955- ... 123
Johnson, Nellie Stone 1905- ... 199
Johnson, Nicholas 1934- ... 29-32R
Johnson, Niel M(elvin) 1931- ... 41-44R
Johnson, Nora 1933- ... 106
Johnson, Norman L. 1917- ... CANR-123
Earlier sketch in CA 166
Johnson, Nunnally 1897-1977 ... 81-84
Obituary ... 69-72
See also DLB 26
See also IDFW 3, 4
Johnson, Olga Weydemeyer
1901-1988 ... CAP-2
Earlier sketch in CA 29-32
Johnson, Oliver A(dolph) 1923- ... CANR-12
Earlier sketch in CA 29-32R
Johnson, Owen (McMahon) 1878-1952 ... 159
See also DLBY 1987
Johnson, Pamela 1949- ... 195
See also SATA 71
Johnson, Pamela Hansford
1912-1981 ... CANR-28
Obituary ... 104
Earlier sketches in CA 1-4R, CANR-2
See also CLC 1, 7, 27
See also CN 1, 2, 3
See also DLB 15
See also MTCW 1, 2
See also MTFW 2005
See also RGEL 2
Johnson, Patricia E. 1951- ... 215
Johnson, Patricia Polin 1956- ... 150
See also SATA 84
Johnson, Patrick Spencer 1938- ... 9-12R
Johnson, Paul (Bede) 1928- ... CANR-100
Earlier sketches in CA 17-20R, CANR-34, 62
See also BEST 89:4
See also CLC 147
Johnson, Paul Brett 1947- ... SATA 83, 132
Johnson, Paul C(ornelius) 1904-1993 ... 81-84
Johnson, Paul E(manuel) 1898-1974 ... 13-16R
Obituary ... 134
Johnson, Paul Victor 1920- ... 1-4R
Johnson, Paula Janice 1946- ... 106
Johnson, Pauline B. ... 1-4R
Johnson, Penelope D(elafield) 1938- ... 124
Johnson, Pepper
See Johnson, Thomas
Johnson, Peter (Colpoys Paley)
1930-2003 ... 65-68
Obituary ... 217
Johnson, Peter 1951- ... 224
Johnson, Philip (Cortelyou) 1906-2005 ... 198
Obituary ... 235
Brief entry ... 106
Johnson, Philip A(rthur) 1915-1991 ... 13-16R
Obituary ... 133
Johnson, Phillip E. 1940- ... CANR-143
Earlier sketch in CA 136
Johnson, Phyllis (Anne) 1937-1985 ... 126
Brief entry ... 108
Johnson, Pierce 1921- ... 41-44R
Johnson, Quentin G. 1930- ... 9-12R
Johnson, R(odney) M(arcus) 1968- ... 202
Johnson, R(obbin) S(inclair) 1946- ... 29-32R
Johnson, Rachel H(arris) 1887-1983
Obituary ... 110
Johnson, Rafer (Lewis) 1935- ... 188
Johnson, Ralph W(hitney) 1923- ... 77-80
Johnson, Ray(mond Edward) 1927- ... 17-20R
Johnson, Ray DeForest 1926-1989 ... 65-68
Obituary ... 130
Johnson, Raynor C(arey) 1901-1987
Brief entry ... 115
Johnson, Rebecca L. 1956- ... CANR-128
Earlier sketch in CA 136
See also SATA 67, 147
Johnson, Richard
See Richey, David
Johnson, Richard
See Richardson, John
Johnson, Richard A(ugust) 1937- ... 37-40R
Johnson, Richard A. 1955- ... 135
Johnson, Richard B(righam)
1914-1977 ... 41-44R
Johnson, Richard C. 1919- ... 33-36R
Johnson, Richard D(avid) 1927- ... 109
Johnson, Richard N(ewhall) 1900-1971
Obituary ... 104
Johnson, Richard R(igby) 1942- ... 116
Johnson, Richard T.
See Pascale, Richard Tanner
Johnson, Richard Tanner
See Pascale, Richard Tanner
Johnson, Rick L. 1954- ... 147
See also SATA 79
Johnson, Rob ... 228
Johnson, Robert ... CLC 70
Johnson, Robert 1911(?)-1938 ... 174
See also BW 3
See also TCLC 69
Johnson, Robert A. 1921- ... 61-64
Johnson, Robert C(lyde) 1919- ... 5-8R
Johnson, Robert E. 1908(?)-1989
Obituary ... 128
Johnson, Robert Erwin 1923- ... 37-40R
Johnson, Robert I(var) 1933- ... 53-56
Johnson, Robert J. 1933- ... 21-24R
Johnson, Robert L. 1919- ... 33-36R
Johnson, Robert L(eon, Jr.) 1930- ... 33-36R
Johnson, Robert Owen 1926- ... 33-36R
Johnson, Robert Sherlaw 1932-2000 ... 61-64
Obituary ... 192
Johnson, Robert W(illard) 1921- ... 17-20R
Johnson, Roger 1942- ... 149
Johnson, Roger N(ylund) 1939- ... 53-56
Johnson, Rolf M(artin) 1940- ... 213
Johnson, Ronald 1935-1998 ... CANR-42
Obituary ... 165
Earlier sketches in CA 9-12R, CANR-4, 20
See also CAAS 30
See also CP 1, 2, 3, 4, 5, 6, 7
See also DLB 169
Johnson, Ronald C. 1927- ... 81-84
Johnson, Ronald M(aberry) 1936- ... 126
Brief entry ... 108
Johnson, Rossall J(ames) 1917- ... 21-24R
Johnson, Ruby Kelley 1928- ... 33-36R
Johnson, Ruth I.
See Jay, Ruth I(ngrid)
Johnson, (Walter) Ryerson
1901-1995 ... CANR-2
Obituary ... 171
Earlier sketch in CA 5-8R
See also Halliday, Brett
See also SATA 10
See also SATA-Obit 106
Johnson, S(amuel) Lawrence
1909-1978 ... CANR-12
Earlier sketch in CA 29-32R
Johnson, Sabina Thorne
See Thorne, Sabina
Johnson, Sam Houston 1914(?)-1978 ... 89-92
Obituary ... 81-84
Johnson, Samuel 1696-1772 ... DLB 24
Johnson, Samuel 1709-1784 ... BRW 3
See also BRWR 1
See also CDBLB 1660-1789
See also DA
See also DAB
See also DAC
See also DAM MST
See also DLB 39, 95, 104, 142, 213
See also LMFS 1
See also RGEL 2
See also TEA
See also WLC
Johnson, Samuel 1822-1882 ... DLB 1, 243
Johnson, Samuel A(ugustus)
1895-1979 ... 17-20R
Johnson, Sandra E. ... 215
Johnson, Sandy ... CANR-129
Earlier sketch in CA 172
Johnson, Scott 1952- ... CANR-97
Earlier sketch in CA 143
See also SATA 76, 119
Johnson, Sherman E(lbridge) 1908-1993 . 53-56
Obituary ... 141
Johnson, Sherman Ellsworth 1896-1978
Obituary ... 77-80
Johnson, Sherrie 1948- ... 151
See also SATA 87
Johnson, Shirley K(ing) 1927- ... 9-12R
See also SATA 10
Johnson, Siddie Joe 1905-1977
Obituary ... 106
See also SATA-Obit 20
Johnson, Sonia 1936- ... 118
Johnson, Spencer 1938- ... CANR-125
Earlier sketches in CA 110, CANR-95
See also SATA 145
See also SATA-Brief 38
Johnson, Stanley (Patrick) 1940- ... CANR-13
Earlier sketch in CA 21-24R
Johnson, Stanley J. F. 1920(?)-1978
Obituary ... 77-80
Johnson, Stanley L(ewis) 1920- ... 17-20R
Johnson, Stephanie 1961- ... CN 7
Johnson, (John) Stephen 1947- ... 107
Johnson, Stephen M. ... 141
Johnson, Stephen T. 1964- ... SATA 84, 141
Johnson, Steven 1968- ... 224
Johnson, Steven F(orrest) 1954- ... 156
Johnson, (Edward) Stowers ... 5-8R
Johnson, Sue Kaiser 1963- ... SATA 78
Johnson, Susan 1939- ... RHW
Johnson, Susan (Ruth) 1956- ... CANR-122
Earlier sketch in CA 137
Johnson, Susan E. 1940- ... 138
Johnson, Susan Lee 1956- ... 192
Johnson, Susanna 1730-1810 ... DLB 200
Johnson, Sylvia A. ... 171
See also SATA 104
See also SATA-Brief 52
Johnson, Terry 1955- ... 144
See also CBD
See also CD 5, 6
See also DLB 233
Johnson, Thomas 1964- ... 219
Johnson, Thomas Frank 1920- ... 9-12R
Johnson, Thomas Herbert 1902-1985 ... 124
Johnson, Thomas William 1946-
Brief entry ... 110
Johnson, Toby
See Johnson, Edwin Clark (Toby)
Johnson, U(ral) Alexis 1908-1997 ... 143
Johnson, Una E. 1905-1997 ... 134
Obituary ... 157
Brief entry ... 109
Johnson, Uwe 1934-1984 ... CANR-39
Obituary ... 112
Earlier sketches in CA 1-4R, CANR-1
See also CDWLB 2
See also CLC 5, 10, 15, 40
See also DLB 75
See also EWL 3
See also MTCW 1
See also RGWL 2, 3
Johnson, Van L(oran) 1908-1993 ... 37-40R
Johnson, Vernon E(dwin) 1920- ... 93-96
Johnson, Vicki Vaughn 1948- ... 144
Johnson, Victor Hugo 1912- ... 186
Brief entry ... 110
Johnson, Victoria 1958- ... 226
Johnson, Virginia 1914-1975 ... CAP-2
Earlier sketch in CA 33-36
Johnson, Virginia E. 1925- ... CANR-34
Earlier sketch in CA 21-24R
Johnson, Virginia W(eisel) 1910-1988 ... 17-20R
Johnson, W. Bolingbroke
See Bishop, Morris
Johnson, W(illiam) Branch 1893- ... CANR-5
Earlier sketch in CA 5-8R
Johnson, W(illiam) E(rnest) 1858-1931
Brief entry ... 122
Johnson, W(alter) R(alph) 1933- ... CANR-9
Earlier sketch in CA 65-68
Johnson, W(endell) Stacy
1927-1990 ... CANR-17
Obituary ... 131
Earlier sketches in CA 1-4R, CANR-2
Johnson, Walter 1915-1985 ... 89-92
Obituary ... 116
Johnson, Walter Frank, Jr. 1914- ... 5-8R

Cumulative Index 299 Jones

Johnson, Warren Arthur 1937- 33-36R
Johnson, Warren T(hurston) 1925-1994 131
Johnson, Wayne 1956- CANR-89
Earlier sketch in CA 135
Johnson, Wayne G(ustave) 1930- 113
Johnson, Wendell (Andrew Leroy) 1906-1965 CANR-1
Earlier sketch in CA 1-4R
Johnson, Whittington B. 1931- CANR-135
Earlier sketch in CA 157
See also BW 3
Johnson, Willard R(aymond) 1935- 105
Johnson, William Alexander 1932- 5-8R
Johnson, William C(lark, Jr.) 1945- CANR-8
Earlier sketch in CA 61-64
Johnson, William R. CANR-25
Earlier sketches in CA 17-20R, CANR-7
See also SATA 38
Johnson, William Stacy 1956- 156
Johnson, William Weber 1909-1992 CANR-46
Obituary 139
Earlier sketch in CA 17-20R
See also SATA 7
Johnson, Willis 1938- 162
Johnson, Winifred (MacNally) 1905-1998 5-8R
Johnson Abercrombie, M. L.
See Abercrombie, M(innie) L(ouie) J(ohnson)
Johnson-Acsadi, Gwendolyn 210
Johnson-Coleman, Lorraine 180
Johnson Cook, Suzan D(enise) 1957- 222
Johnson-Feelings, Dianne
See Johnson, Dianne
Johnson-Hodge, Margaret 230
Johnson-Marshall, Percy E(dwin) A(lan) 1915-1993 21-24R
Obituary 142
John-Steiner, Vera P(olgar) CANR-109
Earlier sketch in CA 121
Johnston, A(ndrew) J(ohn) B(ayly) 1949- 209
Johnston, A(aron) Montgomery 1915- CANR-11
Earlier sketch in CA 29-32R
Johnston, Agnes Christine
See Dazey, Agnes J(ohnston)
Johnston, Alan (William) 1942- 103
Johnston, Albert H. 1914-1992 69-72
Johnston, Andrew K(enneth) 1969- 238
Johnston, Angus James II 1916- 9-12R
Johnston, Annie Fellows 1863-1931
Brief entry 116
See also DLB 42
See also SATA 37
Johnston, (William) Arnold 1942- 77-80
Johnston, Arthur 1924- 21-24R
Johnston, Arvin Harry 1906- 1-4R
Johnston, Barbara Rose 1957- 150
Johnston, Basil H. 1929- CANR-66
Earlier sketches in CA 69-72, CANR-11, 28
See also DAC
See also DAM MULT
See also DLB 60
See also NNAL
Johnston, Bernard 1934- 17-20R
Johnston, Bernice Houle 1914-1971 CAP-2
Earlier sketch in CA 33-36
Johnston, Brenda A(rlivia) 1944- 57-60
Johnston, Bret Anthony 1971- 229
Johnston, Brian 1932- 65-68
Johnston, Bruce F(oster) 1919- CANR-14
Earlier sketch in CA 41-44R
Johnston, Carol 1951- 219
Johnston, Charles (Hepburn) 1912-1986 CANR-5
Obituary 119
Earlier sketch in CA 13-16R
Johnston, Colin 1946- 108
Johnston, Dan 1912-1997 123
Johnston, David (Cay Boyle) 1948- 131
Johnston, David Claypoole 1798(?)-1865 DLB 188
Johnston, (William) Denis 1901-1984 CAP-2
Obituary 113
Earlier sketch in CA 21-22
See also DLB 10
See also EWL 3
See also RGEL 2
Johnston, Donald J(ames) 1936- 162
Johnston, Dorothy Grunbock 1915-1979 CANR-5
Earlier sketch in CA 5-8R
See also SATA 54
Johnston, Ellen 1835-1873 DLB 199
Johnston, Ellen Turlington 1929- 65-68
Johnston, Fran(ces Jonsson) 1925- 13-16R
Johnston, Francine R. 1951- 177
Johnston, Francis E. 1931- CANR-4
Earlier sketch in CA 53-56
Johnston, George 1912-1970 DLB 260
Johnston, George (Benson) 1913- CANR-20
Earlier sketches in CA 1-4R, CANR-5
See also CLC 51
See also CP 1, 2, 3, 4, 5, 6, 7
See also DLB 88
Johnston, George 1913-1997 CANR-15
Earlier sketch in CA 89-92
Johnston, George Burke 1907-1995 CAP-1
Earlier sketch in CA 17-18
Johnston, Ginny 1946- SATA 60
Johnston, Gordon (Frederick) 1920-1983 122
Johnston, H(ugh) A(nthony) S(tephen) 1913-1967 CAP-2
Earlier sketch in CA 21-22
See also SATA 14
Johnston, H(ugh) J(ames) M(orton) 1939- 41-44R
Johnston, Hank
See Johnston, Henry
Johnston, Sir Harry Hamilton 1858-1927 190
See also DLB 174
Johnston, Henry 1922- 25-28R
Johnston, Herbert (Leo) 1912-1987 5-8R
Johnston, Hugh Buckner 1913-1990 69-72
Johnston, Janet 1944- SATA 71
Johnston, Jennifer (Prudence) 1930- CANR-92
Earlier sketch in CA 85-88
See also CLC 7, 150
See also CN 4, 5, 6, 7
See also DLB 14
Johnston, Jill 1929- CANR-44
Earlier sketch in CA 53-56
See also FW
See also GLL 1
Johnston, Joan 1948- CANR-126
Earlier sketch in CA 147
Johnston, Johanna 1914(?)-1982 CANR-7
Obituary 108
Earlier sketch in CA 57-60
See also SATA 12
See also SATA-Obit 33
Johnston, John H(ubert) 1921- 9-12R
Johnston, John M. 1898(?)-1979
Obituary 89-92
Johnston, Joni E. 1960- 148
Johnston, Judith 1947- 190
Johnston, Julie 1941- CANR-122
Earlier sketches in CA 146, CANR-69
See also AAYA 27
See also CLR 41
See also MAICYA 2
See also MAICYAS 1
See also SAAS 24
See also SATA 78, 110
See also SATA-Essay 128
See also YAW
Johnston, Kenneth R(ichard) 1938- CANR-95
Earlier sketch in CA 121
Johnston, Leonard 1920- CANR-11
Earlier sketch in CA 13-16R
Johnston, Lynn (Beverley) 1947- CANR-98
Earlier sketch in CA 110
See also AAYA 12, 63
See also SATA 118
Johnston, Marguerite 1917- 138
Johnston, Marilyn 1942- 169
Johnston, Mary 1870-1936
Brief entry 109
See also DLB 9
See also RHW
Johnston, Mary E(lizabeth) 1919-1989
Obituary 128
Johnston, Michael 1974- 217
Johnston, Minton C(oyne) 1900- 5-8R
Johnston, Mireille 1940-2000 49-52
Obituary 192
Johnston, Norma
See St. John, Nicole
See also AAYA 12
See also JRDA
See also SATA 29
See also WYA
Johnston, Norman (Bruce) 1921- CANR-18
Earlier sketch in CA 93-96
Johnston, Norman J. 1918- 120
Johnston, Paul 1957- 191
Johnston, Portia
See Takakjian, Portia
Johnston, R(onald) J(ohn) 1941- CANR-40
Earlier sketches in CA 101, CANR-18
Johnston, Randolph W(ardell) 1904-1992 CANR-15
Earlier sketch in CA 85-88
Johnston, Richard 1948- 164
Johnston, Richard Malcolm 1822-1898 DLB 74
Johnston, Richard W(yckoff) 1915-1981
Obituary 104
Johnston, Robert Kent 1945- CANR-120
Earlier sketch in CA 104
Johnston, Ronald 1926- 13-16R
Johnston, Ronald Carlyle 1907-1990
Obituary 131
Johnston, Russell G. 1933- 118
Johnston, S(amuel) Paul 1899-1985
Obituary 117
Johnston, Sarah Iles 1957- 219
Johnston, Sean 1966- 223
Johnston, Stanley H(oward), Jr. 1946- 137
Johnston, Stella 1959- 205
Johnston, Susan Taylor 1942- CANR-15
Earlier sketch in CA 41-44R
See also Johnston, Tony
See also SATA 83, 128
Johnston, Terry C(onrad) 1947-2001 CANR-112
Obituary 195
Earlier sketches in CA 113, CANR-63
See also TCWW 2
Johnston, Thomas 1945- 104
Johnston, Thomas E. 1931- 13-16R
Johnston, Tim(othy Patrick) 1962- 220
See also SATA 146
Johnston, Tony
See Johnston, Susan Taylor
See also SATA 8
Johnston, Velda CMW 4
See also RHW
Johnston, Velma B. 1912(?)-1977
Obituary 69-72
Johnston, Victor S. 210
Johnston, Wayne (Gerard) 1958- CANR-89
Earlier sketch in CA 125
Johnston, William 1924- 85-88
Johnston, William 1925- 33-36R
Johnston, William M(urray) 1936- 37-40R
Johnstone, Bob 233
Johnstone, Charles 1719(?)-1800(?) DLB 39
Johnstone, D(onald) Bruce 1909- 104
Johnstone, Henry W(ebb), Jr. 1920- 1-4R
Johnstone, Iain 1943- 108
Johnstone, Kathleen Yerger 1906- 9-12R
Johnstone, Keith 129
See also CBD
See also CD 6
Johnstone, Lammy Olcott 1949- CANR-14
Earlier sketch in CA 81-84
Johnstone, Nick 1970- 226
Johnstone, Parker Lochiel 1903-1995 69-72
Johnstone, Rex
See Chapman, Frank M(onroe)
Johnstone, Robert 1951- 118
Johnstone, Robert Morton, Jr. 1939- 81-84
Johnstone, T(homas) M(uir) 1924-1983
Obituary 114
Johnstone, Ted
See McDaniel, David (Edward)
Johnstone, William D(avid) G(ordon) 1935- 77-80
Johnston-Saint, Peter 1889-1974
Obituary 53-56
John XXIII, Pope 1881-1963 134
Obituary 113
Johst, Hanns 1890-1978 DLB 124
Joiner, Charles A(drian) 1932- 77-80
Joiner, Charles W(ycliffe) 1916- CANR-1
Earlier sketch in CA 1-4R
Joiner, Edward Earl 1924- 49-52
Joiner, Harry M(ason) 1944- 219
Joiner, Verna J(ones) 1896-1983 1-4R
Joinson, Carla 236
See also SATA 160
Jokemeisters
See Krauzer, Steven M(ark)
Joki, Virginia (Carville) 1909(?)-1986
Obituary 120
Jolas, Eugene 1894-1952 166
Brief entry 107
See also DLB 4, 45
Joliat, Eugene (A.) 1910-1999 49-52
Jolin, Stephen Towne 1941- 45-48
Jolivet, R(egis) 1891-1966 CAP-1
Earlier sketch in CA 9-10
Joll, (Dowrish) Evelyn (Louis) 1925-2001 101
Obituary 194
Joll, James (Bysse) 1918-1994 CANR-7
Earlier sketch in CA 5-8R
Jolley, (Monica) Elizabeth 1923- CANR-59
Earlier sketch in CA 127
See also CAAS 13
See also CLC 46
See also CN 4, 5, 6, 7
See also EWL 3
See also RGSF 2
See also SSC 19
Jolley, (Stephen) Nicholas 1948- 120
Jolley, Willie 1956- 188
Jolliffe, H(arold) R(ichard) 1904-1978 1-4R
Obituary 103
Jolliffe, J(ohn) E(dward) A(ustin) 1891-1964 CANR-89
Earlier sketch in CA 5-8R
Jolliffe, John (Hedworth) 1935- CANR-82
Earlier sketch in CA 133
Jolly, Alison 1937- CANR-93
Earlier sketches in CA 41-44R, CANR-15
Jolly, Clifford J. 1939-
Brief entry 108
Jolly, Cyril Arthur 1910- CAP-1
Earlier sketch in CA 9-10
Jolly, Hugh R. 1918-1986 85-88
Obituary 118
Jolly, Margaretta 1965- 210
Jolly, Roslyn 1963- CANR-116
Earlier sketch in CA 152
Jolly, W(illiam) P(ercy) 1922-2003 CANR-4
Obituary 215
Earlier sketch in CA 53-56
Jolly Cholly
See Grimm, Charles John
Jolson, Marvin A(rnold) 1922- CANR-1
Earlier sketch in CA 49-52
Joly, Cyril Bencraft 1918- CAP-1
Earlier sketch in CA 9-10
Jomo
See Raskin, Jonah (Seth)
Jonaitis, Aldona 1948- 139
Jonas, A(dolphe) David 1913- 107
Jonas, Ann 1919- 105
Jonas, Ann 1932- 136
Brief entry 118
See also CLR 12, 74
See also CWRI 5
See also MAICYA 1, 2
See also SATA 50, 135
See also SATA-Brief 42
Jonas, Arthur 1930- 13-16R
Jonas, Carl 1913-1976 9-12R
Obituary 69-72
Jonas, Doris F(rances) 1916- CANR-8
Earlier sketch in CA 61-64
Jonas, Franklin L. 1937- 200
Jonas, George 1935- CANR-32
Earlier sketch in CA 29-32R
See also CP 1, 2
Jonas, Gerald 1935- 65-68
Jonas, Hans 1903-1993 CANR-23
Obituary 140
Earlier sketches in CA 61-64, CANR-7
Jonas, Ilsedore B. 1920- 33-36R
Jonas, Klaus W(erner) 1920- CANR-2
Earlier sketch in CA 1-4R
Jonas, Manfred 1927- CANR-8
Earlier sketch in CA 21-24R
Jonas, Norman N. 1931-1988
Obituary 125
Jonas, Paul 1922- CANR-13
Earlier sketch in CA 73-76
Jonas, Steven 1936- 89-92
Jonas, Susan 1938- CANR-93
Earlier sketch in CA 146
Jonas, Wayne B(oice) 1955- 230
Jonasdottir, Anna G(udrun) 1942- 146
Jonassen, Christen T(onnes) 1912-1998 41-44R
Joncich, Geraldine
See Clifford, Geraldine Joncich
Jonell, Lynne 173
See also SATA 109
Jones, A(rnold) H(ugh) M(artin) 1904-1970
Obituary 89-92
Jones, A(rthur) Morris 1899- CAP-1
Earlier sketch in CA 13-14
Jones, Adam Mars
See Mars-Jones, Adam
Jones, Adrienne 1915-2000 CANR-28
Earlier sketch in CA 33-36R
See also SAAS 10
See also SATA 7, 82
Jones, Alan Griffith 1943- CANR-19
Earlier sketch in CA 103
Jones, Alan Moore, Jr. 1942- 53-56
Jones, Alan William 1940- CANR-136
Earlier sketch in CA 117
Jones, Alex S. 1946- CANR-124
Earlier sketch in CA 135
Jones, Alexander 1906-1970 CANR-2
Obituary 103
Earlier sketch in CA 1-4R
Jones, Alfred Winslow 1900-1989
Obituary 128
Jones, Alice C. 1853-1933 201
See also DLB 92
Jones, Allan Frewin 1954- YAW
Jones, Allan Gwynne
See Gwynne-Jones, Allan
Jones, Allen Morris 1970- 207
Jones, Amelia 1961- CANR-91
Earlier sketch in CA 146
Jones, Andrew 1921- 93-96
Jones, Andrew (Eric) 1950- 111
Jones, Ann (Maret) 1937- CANR-109
Earlier sketch in CA 156
Jones, Annabel
See Lewis, Mary (Christianna)
Jones, Anne Hudson 1944- 135
Jones, Antony Armstrong
See Armstrong-Jones, Antony (Charles Robert)
Jones, Aphrodite (Alicia) 1958- 222
Jones, Archer 1926- CANR-18
Earlier sketches in CA 1-4R, CANR-4
Jones, Archie N(eff) 1900-1979 CAP-1
Earlier sketch in CA 13-16
Jones, Arthur F(rederick) 1945- 81-84
Jones, Arthur Glyn Prys
See Prys-Jones, Arthur Glyn
Jones, (Alun) Arthur Gwynne 1919- 128
Brief entry 120
Jones, Arthur Hope
See Hope-Jones, Arthur
Jones, Arthur (Mervyn) Keppel
See Keppel-Jones, Arthur (Mervyn)
Jones, Arthur Llewellyn 1863-1947 179
Brief entry 104
See also Machen, Arthur and Machen, Arthur Llewelyn Jones
See also HGG
Jones, Aubrey 1911-2003 103
Obituary 215
Jones, Barbara (Mildred) 1917(?)-1978 CANR-4
Obituary 81-84
Earlier sketch in CA 1-4R
Jones, (Geraint Dyfed) Barri 1936-1999 188
Jones, Ben 1968- 230
Jones, Bessie 1902-1984
Obituary 114
Jones, Betty Millsaps 1940- 109
See also SATA 54
Jones, Bill
See Jones, William David Anthony
Jones, Bill
See Jones, William B(ryan), Jr.
Jones, Bill T.
See Jones, William T.
Jones, Billy M(ac) 1925- CANR-25
Earlier sketches in CA 21-24R, CANR-10
Jones, Bob
See Jones, Robert Reynolds, Jr.
Jones, Bobby
See Jones, Robert Tyre, Jr.
Jones, Bobi
See Jones, R(obert) M(aynard)
Jones, Brennon 1945- 136
Jones, Brian 1938- 153
Brief entry 119
See also CP 1, 2, 3, 4, 5, 6, 7
Jones, Bridget 1955- 141
Jones, Bruce 1944- 231
Jones, Bryan D(avidson) 1944- 139
Jones, Bryan L. 1945- 110
Jones, C(lifton) Clyde 1922- 109
Jones, C. M.
See Jones, C(larence) M(edleycott)
Jones, C(larence) M(edleycott) 1913(?)-1986 164
Obituary 118

Jones, C(harles) Robert 1932- ... CANR-66
Earlier sketch in CA 129
Jones, Calico
See Richardson, Gladwell
Jones, Candy 1925-1990 ... 107
Obituary ... 130
Jones, Capt. Wilbur
See Edwards, William B(ennett)
Jones, Carol 1942- ... SATA 79, 153
Jones, Caroly 1941- ... 171
Jones, Carolyn (Sue) 1933-1983 ... 29-32R
Obituary ... 110
Jones, (Horace) Charles 1906-1998 ... CAP-1
Earlier sketch in CA 9-10
Jones, Charles Alfred 1921-1982
Obituary ... 107
Jones, Charles C., Jr. 1831-1893 ... DLB 30
Jones, Charles Edwin 1932- ... CANR-47
Earlier sketches in CA 49-52, CANR-23
Jones, Charles M(artin) 1912-2002 . CANR-106
Obituary ... 202
Earlier sketch in CA 129
See also Jones, Chuck
See also SATA 53
See also SATA-Obit 133
Jones, Charles O(scar) 1931- ... CANR-7
Earlier sketch in CA 17-20R
Jones, Charles W(illiams) 1905-1989 ... 13-16R
Jones, Charlotte Foltz 1945- ... CANR-93
Earlier sketch in CA 145
See also SATA 77, 122
Jones, Cheslyn Peter Montague 1918-1987(?)
Obituary ... 125
Jones, Christina Hendry 1896-1984 ... 73-76
Jones, (Audrey) Christine 1937- ... 61-64
Jones, Christopher 1937- ... 21-24R
Jones, Christopher S. 1971- ... 234
Jones, Chuck
See Jones, Charles M(artin)
See also AAYA 2
See also IDFW 3, 4
Jones, Clifford M(erton) 1902- ... 17-20R
Jones, Cody L. 1949- ... 177
Jones, Constance 1961- ... 173
See also SATA 112
Jones, Craig 1945- ... CANR-34
Earlier sketch in CA 81-84
Jones, Cranston E(dward)
1918-1991 ... CANR-26
Obituary ... 134
Earlier sketch in CA 1-4R
Jones, Cyril Meredith 1904-1999 ... CAP-2
Earlier sketch in CA 23-24
Jones, D(ennis) F(eltham) 1917-1981 ... 163
Brief entry ... 111
See also SFW 4
Jones, D(ouglas) G(ordon) 1929- ... CANR-90
Earlier sketches in CA 29-32R, CANR-13
See also CLC 10
See also CP 1, 2, 3, 4, 5, 6, 7
See also DLB 53
Jones, D(avid) Gareth 1940- ... 106
Jones, D(onald) L(ewis) 1925- ... 25-28R
Jones, D(avid) Mervyn 1922- ... 21-24R
Jones, D. S. 1922- ... 141
Jones, Daisy (Marvel) 1906- ... 17-20R
Jones, Dan Burne 1908-1995 ... 65-68
Jones, Daniel 1881-1967 ... CANR-6
Earlier sketch in CA 5-8R
Jones, Daryl (Emrys) 1946- ... 134
Jones, David (Michael) 1895-1974 ... CANR-28
Obituary ... 53-56
Earlier sketch in CA 9-12R
See also BRW 6
See also BRWS 7
See also CDBLB 1945-1960
See also CLC 2, 4, 7, 13, 42
See also CP 1, 2
See also DLB 20, 100
See also EWL 3
See also MTCW 1
See also PAB
See also RGEL 2
Jones, David Arthur 1946- ... CANR-13
Earlier sketch in CA 73-76
Jones, David (Erik) Hay 1959- ... 133
Jones, David Lee 1948- ... 149
Jones, David Martin 1951- ... CANR-121
Earlier sketch in CA 170
Jones, David Pryce
See Pryce-Jones, David
Jones, David Rhodes 1932- ... 101
Jones, David Richard 1942- ... 125
Jones, David Robert 1947- ... CANR-104
Earlier sketch in CA 103
See also Bowie, David
Jones, David W(yn) 1950- ... 131
Jones, Denice 1965- ... 204
Jones, Dennis 1945- ... 209
Jones, Derek ... 219
Jones, Diana Wynne 1934- ... CANR-120
Earlier sketches in CA 49-52, CANR-4, 26, 56
See also AAYA 12
See also BYA 6, 7, 9, 11, 13, 16
See also CLC 26
See also CLR 23
See also DLB 161
See also FANT
See also JRDA
See also MAICYA 1, 2
See also MTFW 2005
See also SAAS 7
See also SATA 9, 70, 108, 160
See also SFW 4
See also SUFW 2
See also YAW
Jones, Dolores Blythe 1947- ... 120
Jones, Don 1924- ... 125
Jones, (Gene) Donald 1931- ... CANR-34
Earlier sketches in CA 85-88, CANR-15
Jones, Donald (Lawrence) 1938- ... 17-20R
Jones, Dorothy 1948- ... 146
Jones, Dorothy Holder 1925(?)-1991 ... 9-12R
Obituary ... 134
Jones, Dorothy V. 1927- ... 138
Jones, Douglas C(lyde) 1924-1998 ... CANR-48
Obituary ... 169
Earlier sketches in CA 21-24R, CANR-12
See also SATA 52
See also TCWW 1, 2
Jones, DuPre Anderson 1937- ... 21-24R
Jones, Dylan 1960- ... 142
Jones, E. Michael 1948- ... 191
Jones, E(li) Stanley 1884-1973 ... 93-96
Obituary ... 41-44R
Jones, E(ndsley) Terrence 1941- ... 33-36R
Jones, E(lbert) Winston 1911- ... 13-16R
Jones, Ebenezer 1820-1860 ... DLB 32
See also RGEL 2
Jones, (Hilary) Edgar 1953- ... 118
Jones, Edgar A(llen), Jr. 1921- ... 89-92
Jones, Edward A(llen) 1903-1981 ... 25-28R
Obituary ... 134
Jones, Edward E(llsworth) 1926-1993 ... 17-20R
Obituary ... 142
Jones, Edward H(arral), Jr. 1922- ... 13-16R
Jones, Edward P. 1950- ... CANR-134
Earlier sketches in CA 142, CANR-79
See also BW 2, 3
See also CLC 76
See also CSW
See also MTFW 2005
Jones, Eileen 1952- ... 147
Jones, Eileen 1962- ... 189
Jones, Eldred D(urosimi) 1925- ... CANR-30
Earlier sketch in CA 45-48
Jones, Elinor 1930- ... CANR-138
Earlier sketch in CA 174
Jones, Elizabeth B(rown) 1907- ... 61-64
Jones, Elizabeth McDavid ... 205
See also SATA 155
Jones, Elizabeth Orton 1910-2005 ... 77-80
Obituary ... 239
See also SATA 18
Jones, Elwyn 1923-1982 ... CANR-21
Obituary ... 106
Earlier sketch in CA 69-72
Jones, Emlyn (David) 1912-1975 ... CAP-2
Earlier sketch in CA 23-24
Jones, Emrys 1920- ... 17-20R
Jones, Eric Lionel 1936- ... 104
Jones, Ernest 1819-1868 ... DLB 32
Jones, (Alfred) Ernest 1879-1958
Brief entry ... 121
Jones, Eva (Eleonore) 1913-1996 ... 131
Obituary ... 151
Jones, Evan 1915-1996 ... CANR-6
Obituary ... 151
Earlier sketch in CA 9-12R
See also SATA 3
Jones, Evan 1927- ... CP 1
Jones, Evan (Lloyd) 1931- ... CP 1, 2
Jones, Evan David 1903-1987
Obituary ... 122
Jones, Eve (Spiro-John) 1924- ... 1-4R
Jones, Everett L(ee) 1915-1990 ... 13-16R
Obituary ... 131
Jones, Ezra Earl 1939- ... 57-60
Jones, F(rank) Lancaster 1937- ... 29-32R
Jones, Faustine Childress
See Jones-Wilson, Faustine C(hildress)
Jones, Felix Edward Aylmer 1889-1979 . CAP-1
Earlier sketch in CA 9-10
Jones, Francis P(rice) 1890-1975 ... 9-12R
Jones, Frank
See Fearn, John Russell
Jones, Frank 1937- ... CANR-43
Earlier sketch in CA 119
Jones, Frank E(dward) 1917- ... 13-16R
Jones, Frank Pierce 1905-1975
Obituary ... 110
Jones, Franklin Albert 1939- ... 221
Jones, Franklin Ross 1921- ... 53-56
Jones, Frederic J. 1925- ... 149
Jones, Frederick George Hall
See Hall-Jones, Frederick George
Jones, G. Brian 1935- ... 128
Jones, G(eorge) Curtis 1911-1999 ... CANR-3
Earlier sketch in CA 5-8R
Jones, G(wyn) O(wain) 1917- ... 25-28R
Jones, G(eorge) William 1931- ... CANR-11
Earlier sketch in CA 21-24R
Jones, Gail 1955- ... 188
Jones, Gareth (Elwyn) 1939- ... CANR-41
Earlier sketches in CA 102, CANR-19
Jones, Garth N(elson) 1925- ... 81-84
Jones, Gary M(artin) 1925- ... 17-20R
Jones, Gayl 1949- ... CANR-122
Earlier sketches in CA 77-80, CANR-27, 66
See also AFAW 1, 2
See also BLC 2
See also BW 2, 3
See also CLC 6, 9, 131
See also CN 4, 5, 6, 7
See also CSW
See also DA3
See also DAM MULT
See also DLB 33, 278
See also MAL 5
See also MTCW 1, 2
See also MTFW 2005
See also RGAL 4
Jones, Gene 1928- ... 21-24R
Jones, Geoffrey (Gareth) 1952- ... CANR-99
Earlier sketches in CA 122, CANR-48
Jones, George 1800-1870 ... DLB 183
Jones, George (Glenn) 1931- ... 159
Jones, George Chetwynd Griffith
See Griffith(-Jones), George (Chetwynd)
Jones, George Fenwick 1916- ... CANR-7
Earlier sketch in CA 13-16R
Jones, George Hilton 1924- ... 33-36R
Jones, George Thaddeus 1917- ... 53-56
Jones, Geraldine
See McCaughrean, Geraldine
Jones, Gerard ... 217
Jones, Gillingham
See Hamilton, Charles (Harold St. John)
Jones, Glenn R(obert) 1930- ... 223
Jones, (Morgan) Glyn 1905-1995 ... CANR-3
Earlier sketch in CA 9-12R
See also CN 1, 2, 3, 4, 5, 6, 7
See also CP 1, 2
See also DLB 15
See also RGSF 2
Jones, Gordon W(illis) 1915- ... 45-48
Jones, Goronwy J(ohn) 1915- ... 9-12R
Jones, Grant D(rummond) 1941- ... 129
Jones, Griff(ith) Rhys 1953- ... 223
Jones, Guy Salisbury
See Salisbury-Jones, Guy
Jones, Gwen 1951(?)-1988
Obituary ... 124
Jones, Gwendolyn ... 33-36R
Jones, Gwilym Peredur 1892-1975
Obituary ... 57-60
Jones, Gwyn 1907-1999 ... 124
Brief entry ... 117
See also CN 1, 2, 3, 4, 5, 6
See also DLB 15, 139
Jones, Gwyneth A(nn) 1952- ... CANR-123
Earlier sketches in CA 107, CANR-58
See also CN 7
See also FANT
See also SATA 159
See also SFW 4
See also YAW
Jones, H(ouston) G(wynne) 1924- ... CANR-13
Earlier sketch in CA 33-36R
Jones, H(enry) John F(ranklin) 1924- ... 9-12R
Jones, Hardin Blair 1914-1978
Obituary ... 77-80
Jones, Harold
See Page, Gerald W(ilburn)
Jones, Harold 1904-1992 ... CANR-49
Obituary ... 139
Earlier sketches in CA 85-88, CANR-15
See also SATA 14
See also SATA-Obit 72
Jones, Harriet
See Marble, Harriet Clement
Jones, Harry Austin
See Jons, Hal
Jones, Harry Lee 1921(?)-1983
Obituary ... 110
Jones, Helen 1917- ... 105
Jones, Helen Hinckley 1903-1991 ... CANR-5
Earlier sketch in CA 5-8R
See also SATA 26
Jones, Helen L(ouise) 1903-1973
Obituary ... 104
See also SATA-Obit 22
Jones, (Max Him) Henri 1921- ... 41-44R
Jones, Henry Albert 1889-1981
Obituary ... 103
Jones, Henry Arthur 1851-1929
Brief entry ... 110
See also DLB 10
See also RGEL 2
Jones, Hettie 1934- ... CANR-87
Earlier sketch in CA 81-84
See also SATA 42
See also SATA-Brief 27
Jones, Hortense P. 1918- ... 61-64
See also SATA 9
Jones, Howard 1940- ... CANR-94
Earlier sketch in CA 85-88
Jones, Howard Mumford 1892-1980 ... 85-88
Obituary ... 97-100
Jones, Howard P(alfry) 1899-1973
Obituary ... 111
Jones, Hugh 1692(?)-1760 ... DLB 24
Jones, Iris Sanderson 1932- ... 73-76
Jones, J. Barrie 1946- ... 131
Jones, J. Farragut
See Levinson, Leonard and
Streib, Dan(iel Thomas)
Jones, J. Gwynfor 1936- ... CANR-91
Earlier sketch in CA 146
Jones, J(ohn) Ithel 1911-1980 ... CAP-2
Earlier sketch in CA 25-28
Jones, J(on) Sydney 1948- ... 168
See also SATA 101
Jones, Jack
See Jones, James Larkin
Jones, Jack 1884-1970
Obituary ... 115
Jones, Jack 1913-1984
Obituary ... 113
Brief entry ... 109
Jones, Jack 1924- ... 85-88
Jones, Jack P(ayne) 1928- ... CANR-122
Earlier sketch in CA 168
Jones, Jacqueline 1948- ... 122
See also BW
Jones, James 1921-1977 ... CANR-6
Obituary ... 69-72
Earlier sketch in CA 1-4R
See also AITN 1, 2
See also AMWS 11
See also BPFB 2
See also CLC 1, 3, 10, 39
See also CN 1, 2
See also DLB 2, 143
See also DLBD 17
See also DLBY 1998
See also EWL 3
See also MAL 5
See also MTCW 1
See also RGAL 4
Jones, James C(linton) 1922- ... 69-72
Jones, James Earl 1931- ... 146
Jones, James Henry 1907(?)-1977
Obituary ... 73-76
Jones, James Larkin 1913- ... CANR-27
Earlier sketch in CA 109
Jones, James T. 1948- ... 124
Jones, Jeanie Schmit Kayser
See Kayser-Jones, Jeanie Schmit
Jones, Jeanne 1937- ... CANR-28
Earlier sketches in CA 61-64, CANR-12
Jones, Jeannette 1944- ... 110
Jones, Jenkin Lloyd 1911-2004 ... 9-12R
Obituary ... 224
See also DLB 127
Jones, Jennifer (Berry) 1947- ... SATA 90
Jones, Jennifer B. ... 238
Jones, Jenny 1954- ... 155
See also FANT
Jones, Jerry W. 1964- ... 211
Jones, Jessie Mae Orton 1887(?)-1983
Obituary ... 111
See also SATA-Obit 37
Jones, Jill 1945- ... 171
Jones, Jimmy
See Jones, C(larence) M(edleycott)
Jones, Jo ... 33-36R
Jones, Joanna
See Burke, John (Frederick)
Jones, Johanna 1909- ... 118
Jones, (Harry) John (Franklin) 1924- ... 158
Jones, John (Henry) 1942- ... 140
Jones, John Beauchamp 1810-1866 ... DLB 202
Jones, John Bush 1940- ... CANR-134
Earlier sketch in CA 33-36R
Jones, John F(inbar) 1929- ... 130
Jones, John Griffin 1955- ... 113
Jones, John J.
See Lovecraft, H(oward) P(hillips)
Jones, John Paul, Jr. 1912-2001 ... CANR-11
Obituary ... 198
Earlier sketch in CA 69-72
Jones, John Philip 1930- ... CANR-86
Earlier sketch in CA 130
Jones, John R(obert) 1926- ... 116
See also SATA 76
Jones, Joseph Jay 1908-1999 ... CANR-16
Earlier sketches in CA 1-4R, CANR-1
Jones, Joseph L. 1897-1980
Obituary ... 102
Jones, Joseph Marion, Jr. 1908-1990
Obituary ... 132
Jones, Judith Paterson 1938- ... 106
Jones, K. Westcott
See Westcott-Jones, K(enneth)
Jones, Karen Midkiff 1948- ... 104
Jones, Katharine M(acbeth) 1900-1977 ... 5-8R
Jones, Kathleen 1922- ... CANR-48
Earlier sketch in CA 81-84
Jones, Kathleen B. 1949- ... 191
Jones, Kathleen Eve 1944- ... CANR-46
Earlier sketch in CA 102
Jones, Kaylie (Ann) 1960- ... CANR-94
Earlier sketch in CA 123
Jones, Ken (H.) ... 222
Jones, Ken D(uane) 1930- ... CANR-31
Earlier sketch in CA 49-52
Jones, Kenley 1935- ... 69-72
Jones, Kenneth E(ffner) 1920- ... 57-60
Jones, Kenneth Glyn 1915-1995 ... 115
Jones, Kenneth LaMar 1931- ... 53-56
Jones, Kenneth S. 1919- ... 21-24R
Jones, Kenneth W. 1934-
Brief entry ... 113
Jones, Landon Y(oung) 1943- ... 105
Jones, Laurie Beth 1952- ... CANR-120
Earlier sketch in CA 155
Jones, Lawrence K. 1940- ... 143
Jones, Leon 1936-1992 ... 101
Obituary ... 137
Jones, Leonidas M(onroe) Sr. 1923- .. CANR-46
Earlier sketch in CA 45-48
Jones, LeRoi
See Baraka, Amiri
See also CLC 1, 2, 3, 5, 10, 14
See also CN 1, 2
See also CP 1, 2
See also MTCW 2
Jones, Leroy P. 1941- ... 118
Jones, Lewis 1897-1939 ... 177
See also DLB 15
Jones, Lewis Pinckney 1916- ... 61-64
Jones, Linda Phillips
See Phillips-Jones, Linda
Jones, Lisa 1961- ... 130
Jones, Lloyd 1955- ... 219
Jones, Lloyd S(cott) 1931- ... CANR-4
Earlier sketch in CA 1-4R
Jones, Louis B. 1953- ... CANR-73
Earlier sketch in CA 141
See also CLC 65

Cumulative Index 301 Jordan

Jones, Louis C(lark) 1908-1990 .... 5-8R
Obituary 133
Jones, Luke
See Watts, Peter Christopher
Jones, Lyndon Hamer 1927- CANR-45
Earlier sketches in CA 103, CANR-22
Jones, Lynne (Myfanwy) 236
Jones, M(arjorie) L(ilian) Glynne
See Glynne-Jones, M(arjorie) L(ilian)
Jones, Madeline Adams 1913-1993 .... 21-24R
Jones, Madison (Percy, Jr.) 1925- CANR-83
Earlier sketches in CA 13-16R, CANR-7, 54
See also CAAS 11
See also CLC 4
See also CN 1, 2, 3, 4, 5, 6, 7
See also CSW
See also DLB 152
Jones, Major J. 1919- 33-36R
Jones, Major Joseph
See Thompson, William Tappan
Jones, Malcolm V(ince) 1940- CANR-48
Earlier sketch in CA 103
Jones, Maldwyn Allen 1922- CANR-4
Earlier sketch in CA 1-4R
Jones, Marc Edmund 1888-1980 .... 33-36R
Jones, Marcia Thornton 1958- ..... SATA 73, 115
Jones, Marcus E. 1943- 219
Jones, Margaret Boone 25-28R
Jones, Margaret C. 1949- 146
Jones, Margaret E. W. 1938- 37-40R
Jones, Marie 1955- .... DLB 233
Jones, Marion 1975- .... CN 7
Jones, Marion Patrick 1934- .... CN 4, 5, 6
See also EWL 3
Jones, Martha T(annery) 1931- .... SATA 130
Jones, Marvin 1886-1976
Obituary 65-68
Jones, Mary (Elizabeth) 1942- 120
Jones, Mary Alice 1898(?)-1980 .... 17-20R
Obituary 118
See also SATA 6
Jones, Mary Brush 1925- 25-28R
Jones, Mary Voell 1933- 21-24R
Jones, Matthew F. 1956- 175
Jones, Maxwell (Shaw) 1907-1990 .... 25-28R
Jones, Maynard Benedict 1904-1972
Obituary 93-96
See also Jones, Nard
Jones, McClure 112
See also SATA 34
Jones, Merry Bloch 1948- CANR-142
Earlier sketch in CA 140
Jones, Mervyn 1922- CANR-91
Earlier sketches in CA 45-48, CANR-1
See also CAAS 5
See also CLC 10, 52
See also CN 1, 2, 3, 4, 5, 6, 7
See also MTCW 1
Jones, Michael (Christopher Emlyn)
1940- CANR-42
Earlier sketches in CA 104, CANR-20
Jones, Michael Owen 1942- 101
Jones, Mick 1956(?)- .... CLC 30
Jones, Miriam
See Schuchman, Joan
Jones, Morris Val 1914-1998 .... 5-8R
Jones, Nancy L.
See Holder, Nancy L.
Jones, Naomi Brooks 1941- 145
Jones, Nard
See Jones, Maynard Benedict
See also TCWW 1, 2
Jones, Neil R(onald) 1909-1988 160
See also SFW 4
Jones, Nettie (Pearl) 1941- CANR-88
Earlier sketch in CA 137
See also CAAS 20
See also BW 2
See also CLC 34
Jones, Noel 1939- 81-84
Jones, Norman (Leslie) 1951- 146
Jones, O(wen) R(ogers) 1922- 1-4R
Jones, Oakah L., Jr. 1930- CANR-8
Earlier sketch in CA 17-20R
Jones, Orlando
See Looker, Antonina (Hansell)
Jones, Owen Marshall
See Marshall, Owen
Jones, P(eter) M(ichael) 1949- CANR-120
Earlier sketches in CA 122, CANR-48
Jones, Pamela M. 1953- 146
Jones, Pat
See Jones, Virgil Carrington
Jones, Patrick 1961- 205
See also SATA 136
Jones, Paul Davis 1940- 49-52
Jones, Paul J. 1897(?)-1974
Obituary 53-56
Jones, Pauline Baird 1955- 223
Jones, Pearl Binder Elwyn
See Elwyn-Jones, Pearl Binder
Jones, Peggy 1947- 109
Jones, Penelope 1938- CANR-14
Earlier sketch in CA 81-84
See also SATA 31
Jones, Peter 1802-1856 .... NNAL
Jones, Peter 1920-2000 103
Obituary 189
Jones, Peter 1921- 5-8R
Jones, Peter (Austin) 1929- CANR-4
Earlier sketch in CA 53-56
Jones, Peter d'Alroy 1931- CANR-20
Earlier sketches in CA 5-8R, CANR-3
Jones, Peter Gaylord 1929- 73-76
Jones, Philip Howard 1937- 102
Jones, Philippe
See Roberts-Jones, Philippe
Jones, Phillip L. 1928(?)-1979
Obituary 89-92
Jones, Pirkle 1914- CANR-122
Earlier sketch in CA 29-32R
Jones, Preston 1936-1979 73-76
Obituary 89-92
See also CLC 10
See also DLB 7
Jones, Quincy (Delight) 1933- 210
See also IDFW 3, 4
Jones, R. A. 1953- 223
Jones, R(ichard) Ben(jamin) 1933- CANR-12
Earlier sketch in CA 25-28R
Jones, R. D.
See Jones, Dennis
Jones, R(obert) M(aynard) 1929- CANR-109
Earlier sketch in CA 152
Jones, R(oger) W(illiam) 1941- 128
Jones, Rachel
See Bain, Donald
Jones, Ray O. 1930- 89-92
Jones, Raymond F(isher) 1915-1994 156
Obituary 176
Brief entry 106
See also SFW 4
Jones, Rebecca C(astaldi) 1947- CANR-104
Earlier sketches in CA 106, CANR-22, 50
See also SATA 33, 99
Jones, Reginald L(anier) 1931- CANR-48
Earlier sketch in CA 45-48
Jones, Reginald Victor 1911-1997 103
Obituary 163
Jones, Reinette F. 1958- 212
Jones, Renee Gertrude 1929- 231
See also Renee
Jones, Richard 1926- CANR-2
Earlier sketch in CA 49-52
Jones, Richard 1953- 121
Jones, Richard Allan 1943- 103
Jones, Richard Granville 1926- 112
Jones, Richard H(utton) 1914-1998 49-52
Jones, Richard M(atthew) 1925- 93-96
Jones, Richard Wyn 1966- 195
Jones, Robert B(rinkley) 1942- 114
Jones, Robert Emmet 1928- CANR-2
Earlier sketch in CA 1-4R
Jones, Robert Epes 1908-1998 .... CAP-1
Earlier sketch in CA 13-14
Jones, Robert F(rancis) 1934-2003 .. CANR-118
Earlier sketches in CA 49-52, CANR-2, 61
See also CLC 7
Jones, Robert Godwin
See Godwin-Jones, Robert
Jones, Robert H(uhn) 1927- CANR-2
Earlier sketch in CA 5-8R
Jones, Robert O(wen) 1928- 29-32R
Jones, Robert R(ussell) 1927- 69-72
Jones, Robert Reynolds, Jr.
1911-1997 .... CANR-11
Obituary 162
Earlier sketch in CA 25-28R
Jones, Robert Tyre, Jr. 1902-1971
Obituary 113
Jones, Robin D(orothy) 1959- 147
See also SATA 80
Jones, Robin Lloyd
See Lloyd-Jones, Robin
Jones, Rod 1953- 128
See also CLC 50
Jones, Rodney 1950- CANR-123
Earlier sketches in CA 133, CANR-64
See also CP 7
See also CSW
See also DLB 120
Jones, Rodney W(illiam) 1943- CANR-33
Earlier sketch in CA 113
Jones, Roger (Winston) 1939- 101
Jones, Roger Stanley 1934- 113
Jones, Royston Oscar 1925-1974 85-88
Jones, Ruby Aileen Hiday 1908-2000 ... CAP-1
Earlier sketch in CA 11-12
Jones, Russell 1918-1979 106
Obituary 89-92
Jones, Russell Bradley 1894-1986 .... 1-4R
Jones, Russell Celyn 1955- 219
Jones, Ruth Ann 1928- 107
Jones, Ruth Dorval 93-96
Jones, Sally Roberts 1935- 102
See also Roberts, Sally
Jones, Sandra (Redmond) 1937- 132
Jones, Sandra L.
See Ireland, Sandra L(eora) Jones
Jones, Sandy 1943- CANR-15
Earlier sketch in CA 85-88
Jones, Sanford W.
See Thorn, John
Jones, Scott N. 1929- 29-32R
Jones, Seaborn (Gustavus), Jr. 1942- 104
Jones, Simmons 1920- 136
Jones, Simon (C.) 1957- 128
Jones, Solomon 1969(?)- 225
Jones, Sonia 1938- 127
Jones, Stacy V(anderhoof) 1894-1989 .... 1-4R
Obituary 127
Jones, Stan 1947- 184
Jones, Stanley 1916-1999 183
Jones, Stanley L(lewellyn) 1918- 9-12R
Jones, Star(let Marie) 1962- 173
Jones, Stephen (Phillip) 1935- CANR-2
Earlier sketch in CA 49-52
Jones, Stephen 1953- 134
Jones, Stephen D(wight) 1948- 112
Jones, Stephen Graham 1972- 213
Jones, Steve 1961- 143
Jones, Stuart 1933-1998 .... CANR-106
Earlier sketch in CA 146
Jones, Susan Mann
See Mann, Susan
Jones, Susanna 1967- 210
Jones, Suzanne W(hitmore) 1950- 230
Jones, T(homas) Anthony 1940- 110
Jones, Tad
See Jones, Thaddeus B.
Jones, Ted
See Jones, Theador Edward
Jones, Terence Graham Parry 1942- . CANR-93
Brief entry 112
Earlier sketches in CA 116, CANR-35
Interview in CA-116
See also Jones, Terry and
Monty Python
See also CLC 21
See also SATA 127
Jones, Terry
See Jones, Terence Graham Parry
See also SATA 67
See also SATA-Brief 51
Jones, Thaddeus B. 1952- 125
Jones, Theador Edward 1937- 138
Jones, Thom (Douglas) 1945(?)- CANR-88
Earlier sketch in CA 157
See also CLC 81
See also DLB 244
See also SSC 56
Jones, Thomas B. 1929- 25-28R
Jones, Thomas M(artin) 1916- 29-32R
Jones, Thomas W(arren) 1947- 53-56
Jones, Tim(othy) Wynne
See Wynne-Jones, Tim(othy)
Jones, Timothy K. 1955- 190
Jones, Tobias 1972- 226
Jones, Tom 1928- CANR-78
Earlier sketches in CA 53-56, CANR-6
Interview in CANR-6
Jones, Tony Armstrong
See Armstrong-Jones, Antony (Charles Robert)
Jones, Trevor Arthur 1936- 105
Jones, Trevor David 1908-1984
Obituary 114
Jones, Tristan 1924-1995 .... CANR-104
Obituary 148
Earlier sketch in CA 73-76
Jones, Turkel
See McKimmey, James
Jones, V(ictoria) M(ary) 1958- 221
See also SATA 147
Jones, Vane A. 1917- 21-24R
Jones, Veda Boyd 1948- 190
See also SATA 119
Jones, Vernon 1897-1980 53-56
Jones, (Charles) Victor 1919- 5-8R
Jones, Virgil Carrington 1906- CANR-2
Earlier sketch in CA 1-4R
Jones, Volcano
See Mitchell, Adrian
Jones, W(alton) Glyn 1928- CANR-56
Earlier sketches in CA 49-52, CANR-29
Jones, W(illiam) J(ohn) 1932- CANR-88
Earlier sketch in CA 129
Jones, W(alter) Paul 1891-1977 .... CAP-1
Earlier sketch in CA 11-12
Jones, W(illiam) T(homas) 1910-1998 ... 37-40R
Jones, Walter Benton 1893-1979 .... 1-4R
Jones, Webb
See Henley, Arthur
Jones, Weyman (B.) 1928- 17-20R
See also SAAS 11
See also SATA 4
Jones, Whitney R. D. 1924- 213
Jones, Wilbur Devereux 1916- CANR-2
Earlier sketch in CA 1-4R
Jones, William 1746-1794 .... DLB 109
Jones, William Alfred 1817-1900 177
See also DLB 59
Jones, William B(ryan), Jr. 1950- 217
Jones, William David Anthony 1946- 113
Jones, William Glynne
See Glynne-Jones, William
Jones, William H(ugh) 1939-1982 112
Obituary 108
Jones, William M(cKendrey) 1927- CANR-7
Earlier sketch in CA 61-64
Jones, William Monarch
See Guthrie, Thomas Anstey
Jones, William P(owell) 1901-1989 .... 1-4R
Jones, William R(onald) 1933- 104
Jones, William T. 1952- 206
Jones, Willis Knapp 1895-1982 .... 13-16R
Jones, Zelda
See Schuchman, Joan
Jones-Evans, Eric (John Llewellyn)
1898-1976 .... 21-24R
Jones-Jackson, Pat
See Jones Jackson, Patricia
Jones-Jackson, Patricia 1946-1986
Obituary 124
Jones-Ryan, Maureen 1943- 93-96
Jones-Wilson, Faustina C(hildress)
1927- CANR-27
Earlier sketch in CA 77-80
Jong, Erica 1942- CANR-132
Earlier sketches in CA 73-76, CANR-26, 52, 75
Interview in CANR-26
See also AITN 1
See also AMWS 5
See also BEST 90:2
See also BPFB 2
See also CLC 4, 6, 8, 18, 83
See also CN 3, 4, 5, 6, 7
See also CP 2, 3, 4, 5, 6, 7
See also CPW
See also DA3
See also DAM NOV, POP
See also DLB 2, 5, 28, 152
See also FW
See also MAL 5
See also MTCW 1, 2
See also MTFW 2005
Jong, Gerrit de, Jr.
See de Jong, Gerrit, Jr.
Jonge, Marinus de
See De Jonge, Marinus
Jongeward, Dorothy 1925- CANR-3
Earlier sketch in CA 49-52
Jong-Fast, Molly 1978- 237
Jonk, Clarence 1906-1987 .... 5-8R
See also SATA 10
Jonke, Gert F(riedrich) 1946- 177
See also DLB 85
Jonklaas, David 1932- .... CP 1
Jonnes, Jill 1952- CANR-106
Earlier sketch in CA 121
Jons, Hal .... TCWW 2
Jonsen, Albert R(upert) 1931- CANR-28
Earlier sketches in CA 25-28R, CANR-11
Jonson, Ben(jamin) 1572(?)-1637 .... BRW 1
See also BRWC 1
See also BRWR 1
See also CDBLB Before 1660
See also DA
See also DAB
See also DAC
See also DAM DRAM, MST, POET
See also DC 4
See also DFS 4, 10
See also DLB 62, 121
See also LMFS 1
See also PC 17
See also PFS 23
See also RGEL 2
See also TEA
See also WLC
See also WLIT 3
Jonsson, Erik 1922- 210
Jonsson, Jon 1917-2000
See ur Vor, Jon
Jonsson, Kristjan Niels 1860-1936
See Kainn
Jonsson, Lars O(ssian) 1952- 234
Jonsson, Reidar
See Joensson, Reidar
Jonsson, Snaebjorn 1888(?)-1978
Obituary 81-84
Jonsson, Thorsteinn (Elton) 1921-2001 231
Jonsson, Tony
See Jonsson, Thorsteinn (Elton)
Jonsson, Tor 1916-1951 .... DLB 297
Jonsson, Torsteinn Elton
See Jonsson, Thorsteinn (Elton)
Jonze, Spike 1969(?)- .... AAYA 47
Joos, Francoise 1956- .... SATA 78
Joos, Frederic 1953- .... SATA 78
Joos, Martin (George) 1907-1978 .... CAP-1
Earlier sketch in CA 13-16
Joosse, Barbara M(onnot) 1949- CANR-48
Earlier sketch in CA 109
See also SATA 52, 96
Joost, Nicholas (Teynac) 1916-1980 ...... 13-16R
Obituary 97-100
Jooste, Pamela 1946(?)- 204
Joplin, Scott 1868(?)-1917 189
Brief entry 123
Jopp, Hal
See Jopp, Harold Dowling, Jr.
Jopp, Harold Dowling, Jr. 1946- 57-60
Joppke, Christian 1959- CANR-91
Earlier sketch in CA 145
Joralemon, Ira B(eaman) 1884-1975
Obituary 61-64
Joravsky, David 1925- CANR-2
Earlier sketch in CA 1-4R
Jordan, A(rchibald) C(ampbell) 1906-1968 . 210
Jordan, Alexis Hill
See Glick, Ruth (Burtnick) and
Titchener, Louise
Jordan, Allie
See Chastain, Sandra
Jordan, Alma Theodora 1929- 33-36R
Jordan, Amos A(zariah) 1922- 33-36R
Jordan, Anne Devereaux 1943- 135
See also SATA 80
Jordan, B. B. 183
Jordan, Barbara (Charline) 1936-1995 123
Obituary 151
Brief entry 113
See also BW 1
Jordan, Bill
See Jordan, William
Jordan, Borimir 1933- 89-92
Jordan, Bryn
See Henderson, James Maddock
Jordan, Carrie
See Cudlipp, Edythe
Jordan, Clarence L(eonard) 1912-1969 .. CAP-2
Earlier sketch in CA 23-24
Jordan, Claudia E. 1954- 163

Jordan, Constance ... 168
Jordan, Dale R(oderick) 1931- ... CANR-46
Earlier sketch in CA 45-48
Jordan, Daniel P(orter), Jr. 1938- ... CANR-86
Earlier sketch in CA 130
Jordan, David C. 1935- ... 146
Jordan, David K. 1942- ... 61-64
Jordan, David M(alcolm) 1935- ... 33-36R
Jordan, David P(aul) 1939- ... 57-60
Jordan, David William 1940- ... 93-96
Jordan, Don
See Howard, Vernon (Linwood)
Jordan, Donald A. 1936- ... 65-68
Jordan, E(mil) L(eopold) 1900- ... SATA-Brief 31
Jordan, Emma Coleman 1946- ... 153
See also BW 3
Jordan, Franklin Everard 1904(?)-1983
Obituary ... 110
Jordan, Gail
See Dern, Erolie Pearl Gaddis
Jordan, Gerald Ray 1896-1964 ... CAP-1
Earlier sketch in CA 13-14
Jordan, Gilbert John 1902-1992 ... CANR-28
Earlier sketch in CA 49-52
Jordan, Gill
See Gilbert, George
Jordan, Grace Edgington -1985 ... CANR-2
Earlier sketch in CA 1-4R
Jordan, Hope Dahle 1905-1995 ... CANR-13
Earlier sketch in CA 77-80
See also SATA 15
Jordan, Jael (Michal) 1949- ... SATA 30
Jordan, John 1930- ... 103
Jordan, John E(mory) 1919- ... CANR-20
Earlier sketch in CA 1-4R
Jordan, Judy 1961- ... 195
Jordan, June (Meyer) 1936-2002 ... CANR-114
Obituary ... 206
Earlier sketches in CA 33-36R, CANR-25, 70
See also AAYA 2, 66
See also AFAW 1, 2
See also BLCS
See also BW 2, 3
See also CLC 5, 11, 23, 114
See also CLR 10
See also CP 7
See also CWP
See also DAM MULT, POET
See also DLB 38
See also GLL 2
See also LAIT 5
See also MAICYA 1, 2
See also MTCW 1
See also PC 38
See also SATA 4, 136
See also YAW
Jordan, Ken ... 232
Jordan, Laura
See Brown, Sandra
Jordan, Lee
See Scholefield, Alan
Jordan, Leonard
See Levinson, Leonard
Jordan, Lewis 1912-1983
Obituary ... 111
Jordan, Lois B(reedlove) 1912-1989 ... 57-60
Jordan, Martin George 1944- ... SATA 84
Jordan, Matt
See Linaker, Mike
Jordan, Michael (Jeffrey) 1963- ... CANR-93
Earlier sketch in CA 149
Jordan, Michele Anna 1949- ... 199
Jordan, Mildred
See Bausher, Mildred Jordan
Jordan, Mildred Arlene 1918-2001 ... 110
Jordan, Monica
See Caruba, Alan
Jordan, Neil (Patrick) 1950- ... CANR-54
Brief entry ... 124
Earlier sketch in CA 130
Interview in ... CA-130
See also CLC 110
See also CN 4, 5, 6, 7
See also GLL 2
Jordan, Norman 1938- ... 33-36R
Jordan, Pascual 1902-1982(?)
Obituary ... 112
Jordan, Pat(rick M.) 1941- ... CANR-121
Earlier sketch in CA 33-36R
See also CLC 37
Jordan, Penny 1946- ... 163
See also RHW
Jordan, Philip D(ean) 1940- ... 110
Jordan, Philip Dillon 1903-1980 ... 9-12R
Jordan, Richard Tyler 1960- ... 173
Jordan, Robert
See Rigney, James Oliver, Jr.
See also AAYA 26
See also FANT
See also SUFW 2
Jordan, Robert B. 1939- ... 141
Jordan, Robert Paul 1921- ... 29-32R
Jordan, Robert S(mith) 1929- ... CANR-1
Earlier sketch in CA 45-48
Jordan, Robin 1947- ... 65-68
Jordan, Ruth 1926-1994 ... CANR-7
Obituary ... 144
Earlier sketch in CA 57-60
Jordan, Sandra ... 236
Jordan, Sherryl 1949- ... 195
See also AAYA 45
See also CWRI 5
See also SAAS 23
See also SATA 71, 122
Jordan, Shirley 1930- ... 229
See also SATA 154
Jordan, Stello 1914-1979 ... 29-32R
Jordan, Tanis 1946- ... SATA 84
Jordan, Teresa 1955- ... 202
Jordan, Terry G.
See Jordan-Bychkov, Terry G(ilbert)
Jordan, Thomas E(dward) 1929- ... 120
Jordan, Thurston C., Jr. 1940- ... 25-28R
Jordan, Wayne 1903(?)-1979
Obituary ... 85-88
Jordan, Wendy A(dler) ... 204
Jordan, Weymouth T(yree) 1912-1968 ... CAP-2
Earlier sketch in CA 17-18
Jordan, Wilbur K(itchener)
1902-1980 ... CANR-5
Obituary ... 97-100
Earlier sketch in CA 5-8R
Jordan, William 1941-
Brief entry ... 118
Jordan, William A. 1928- ... 33-36R
Jordan, William Chester 1948- ... 221
Jordan, William H., Jr. 1944- ... 114
Jordan, William J(ohnston) 1924- ... CANR-39
Earlier sketch in CA 114
Jordan, William S(tone), Jr. 1917- ... 13-16R
Jordan, Winthrop D(onaldson) 1931- ... 25-28R
Jordan, Z(bigniew) A(ntoni) 1911-1977 ... 25-28R
Obituary ... 89-92
Jordan-Bychkov, Terry G(ilbert)
1938- ... CANR-108
Earlier sketches in CA 21-24R, CANR-9
Jordan Haight, Mary Ellen 1927- ... 136
Jordan-Smith, Paul 1885(?)-1971
Obituary ... 104
Jorden, Eleanor Harz ... CANR-8
Earlier sketch in CA 5-8R
Jorden, William John 1923- ... 140
Jordy, William H(enry) 1917-1997 ... CANR-25
Obituary ... 160
Earlier sketch in CA 1-4R
Jorge, Lidia 1946- ... EWL 3
Jorgens, Jack J(ohnstone) 1943- ... 65-68
Jorgensen, Christine 1926-1989
Obituary ... 128
Jorgensen, Ernst (Mikeal) 1951(?)- ... 221
Jorgensen, Ivar
See Ellison, Harlan (Jay) and
Garrett, (Gordon) Randall (Phillip)
Jorgensen, James (Aleck) 1931- ... CANR-19
Earlier sketch in CA 103
Jorgensen, James D(ale) 1932- ... 41-44R
Jorgensen, Johannes 1866-1956 ... DLB 300
Jorgensen, Joseph G(ilbert) 1934- ... CANR-7
Earlier sketch in CA 61-64
Jorgensen, Mary Venn -1995 ... CANR-1
Earlier sketch in CA 1-4R
See also SATA 36
Jorgensen, Neil 1934- ... 53-56
Jorgensen, Norman 1954- ... SATA 157
Jorgensen-Earp, Cheryl R(uth) 1952- ... 169
Jorgenson, Allen
See Stine, Henry Eugene
Jorgenson, Ivar
See Silverberg, Robert
Jorgenson, Lloyd P. 1912-2001 ... 125
Jorn, Asger 1914-1973
Obituary ... 41-44R
Jorstad, Erling (Theodore) 1930- ... CANR-30
Earlier sketches in CA 29-32R, CANR-12
Joscelyn, Archie L(ynn) 1899-1986 ... CANR-63
Earlier sketches in CA 1-4R, CANR-5
See also TCWW 1, 2
Jose, F(rancisco) Sionil
See Sionil Jose, F(rancisco)
Jose, F(rancisco) Sionil
See Sionil Jose, F(rancisco)
Jose, James R(obert) 1939- ... 29-32R
Josefowitz, Natasha 1926- ... CANR-40
Earlier sketch in CA 114
Josefsberg, Milt 1911-1987 ... CANR-29
Obituary ... 124
Earlier sketch in CA 81-84
Joselovitz, Ernest A. 1942- ... 108
Joselow, Beth Baruch 1948- ... CANR-36
Earlier sketch in CA 114
Joseph, Chief
See Chief Joseph
Joseph, Alexander 1907-1976 ... 13-16R
Obituary ... 120
Joseph, Anne
See Coates, Anna
Joseph, Bertram L(eon) 1915-1981 ... CANR-6
Obituary ... 104
Earlier sketch in CA 5-8R
Joseph, David I(glauer) 1941- ... 9-12R
Joseph, Don
See Holmes, Donald J.
Joseph, Dov 1899-1980
Obituary ... 93-96
Joseph, Franz
See Schnaubelt, Franz Joseph
Joseph, George Ghevarughese ... CLC 70
Joseph, Helen (Beatrice May) 1905-1992 ... 128
Obituary ... 140
Joseph, Henry 1948- ... 153
Joseph, James (Herz) 1924- ... CANR-2
Earlier sketch in CA 1-4R
See also SATA 53
Joseph, Jenny 1932- ... CANR-60
Earlier sketches in CA 107, CANR-25
See also CP 7
See also CWP
See also DLB 40
Joseph, Joan 1939- ... CANR-17
Earlier sketch in CA 25-28R
See also SATA 34
Joseph, John 1923- ... 1-4R
Joseph, Jonathan
See Fineman, Irving
Joseph, Joseph M(aron) 1903-1979 ... 5-8R
See also SATA 22
Joseph, Lawrence 1948- ... 165
Joseph, M(ichael) K(ennedy)
1914-1981 ... CANR-84
Earlier sketches in CA 9-12R, CANR-6
See also CN 1, 2, 3
See also CP 1, 2
See also SFW 4
Joseph, Marie ... CANR-59
Earlier sketch in CA 109
See also RHW
Joseph, Marjory L(ockwood) 1917- ... 77-80
Joseph, Mark (Chester) 1946- ... CANR-117
Earlier sketch in CA 120
Joseph, Patrick
See O'Malley, Kevin
Joseph, R. F.
See Joseph, Robert Farras
Joseph, Richard 1910-1976 ... CANR-6
Obituary ... 69-72
Earlier sketch in CA 1-4R
Joseph, Robert F.
See Joseph, Robert Farras
Joseph, Robert Farras 1935- ... 129
Joseph, Sheri 1967- ... 219
Joseph, Stephen 1921-1967 ... 9-12R
Obituary ... 103
Joseph, Stephen M. 1938- ... 25-28R
Joseph, William A(llen) 1947- ... CANR-41
Earlier sketch in CA 118
Josephs, Arthur
See Gottlieb, Arthur
Josephs, Jay Raphael 1912-2005 ... 9-12R
Obituary ... 238
Josephs, Ray
See Josephs, Jay Raphael
Josephs, Rebecca
See Talbot, Toby
Josephs, Stephen
See Dolmatch, Theodore B(ieley)
Josephson, Clifford A. 1922- ... 17-20R
Josephson, Elmer A. 1909-1996 ... CANR-49
Earlier sketch in CA 121
Josephson, Erland 1923- ... 192
Josephson, Halsey D. 1906(?)-1977
Obituary ... 69-72
Josephson, Hannah 1900-1976 ... CAP-2
Obituary ... 69-72
Earlier sketch in CA 29-32
Josephson, Harold 1942- ... 61-64
Josephson, Mary
See O'Doherty, Brian
Josephson, Matthew 1899-1978 ... 81-84
Obituary ... 77-80
See also DLB 4
Josephson, Paul R. 1954- ... 192
Joseph the Younger
See Chief Joseph
Josephus, Flavius c. 37-100 ... AW 2
See also DLB 176
Josephy, Alvin M., Jr. 1915- ... CANR-93
Earlier sketches in CA 17-20R, CANR-8, 48
Josey, E(lonnie) J(unius) 1924- ... CANR-42
Earlier sketch in CA 29-32R
See also BW 2
Josh
See Clemens, Samuel Langhorne
Joshee, O(m) K(umar) 1934- ... 117
Joshel, Sandra R(ae) 1947- ... 228
Joshi, Arun 1939- ... 160
See also CN 6, 7
Joshi, Irene M(arian) 1934- ... 110
Joshi, S(unand) T(ryambak) 1958- ... CANR-97
Earlier sketch in CA 131
Joshi, Shivkumar 1916- ... 77-80
Joshua, Peter
See Stone, Peter
Joshua, Wynfred 1930- ... 29-32R
Josiah Allen's Wife
See Holley, Marietta
Josipovici, Gabriel (David) 1940- ... 224
Earlier sketches in CA 37-40R, CANR-47, 84
Autobiographical Essay in ... 224
See also CAAS 8
See also CLC 6, 43, 153
See also CN 3, 4, 5, 6, 7
See also DLB 14, 319
Joskow, Paul L. 1947- ... 124
Joslin, Michael (E.) 1949- ... 219
Joslin, Sesyle
See Hine, Sesyle Joslin
See also SATA 2
Jospe, Alfred 1909-1994 ... 106
Obituary ... 147
Joss, John 1934- ... 101
Josselson, Ruthellen (Lefkowitz) 1946- ... 139
Josselyn, John 1638(?)-1675 ... DLB 24
Josten, Josef 1913-1985
Obituary ... 118
Jotischky, Andrew 1965- ... CANR-143
Earlier sketch in CA 133
Jotuni, Maria
See Haggren, Maria Gustava
Joubert, Andre J. 1924- ... 49-52
Joubert, Elsa 1922- ... EWL 3
Joubert, Ingrid 1942- ... 110
Joudry, Patricia 1921- ... 65-68
See also DLB 88
Jouhandeau, Marcel Henri 1888-1979 ... 217
Obituary ... 85-88
See also EWL 3
Jourard, Sidney M(arshall)
1926-1974 ... CANR-6
Obituary ... 53-56
Earlier sketch in CA 5-8R
Jourdain, Alice M. 1923- ... 53-56
Jourdain, Robert 1950- ... 163
Jourdain, Rose (Leonora) 1932- ... 89-92
Journet, Charles 1891-1975 ... 65-68
Obituary ... 57-60
Journlet, Marie de
See Little, Paul H(ugo)
Jouve, Nicole Ward ... 173
Jouve, Pierre Jean 1887-1976
Obituary ... 65-68
See also CLC 47
See also DLB 258
See also EWL 3
Jouvenel, Bertrand de
See de Jouvenel des Ursins, Edouard Bertrand
Jouvenel, Hugues Alain de
See de Jouvenel, Hugues Alain
Jouvet, Jean
See Strich, Christian
Jouvet, Michel 1925- ... 197
Jovanovic, Rob 1969- ... 235
Jovanovich, William (Iliya) 1920-2001 ... 107
Obituary ... 201
See also DLBY 01
Jovanovski, Meto 1928- ... 142
Jovine, Francesco 1902-1950 ... DLB 264
See also EWL 3
See also TCLC 79
Jovine, Giuseppe 1922-1998 ... DLB 128
Jowett, Garth Samuel 1940- ... CANR-10
Earlier sketch in CA 65-68
Jowett, Paul (Melville) 1959- ... 120
Jowitt, Deborah 1934- ... 103
Joy, Barbara Ellen 1898-1984 ... 5-8R
Joy, Camden 1963(?)- ... 226
Joy, David Anthony Welton 1942- ... CANR-20
Earlier sketch in CA 103
Joy, Donald Marvin 1928- ... 13-16R
Joy, Edward T(homas) 1909- ... 9-12R
Joy, Elissa
See Rashkin, Elissa J(oy)
Joy, Kenneth Ernest 1908-1980 ... CAP-2
Earlier sketch in CA 23-24
Joy, Rick 1958- ... 222
Joy, Thomas Alfred 1904-2003 ... 102
Obituary ... 215
Joyaux, Julia
See Kristeva, Julia
Joyaux, Philippe
See Sollers, Philippe
Joyce, Adrien
See Eastman, Carol
Joyce, Bill
See Joyce, William
Joyce, Brenda ... 216
Joyce, Brian T(homas) 1938- ... 106
Joyce, Bruce R(ogers) 1930- ... 186
Brief entry ... 114
Joyce, Carolyn
See Zonailo, Carolyn
Joyce, Christopher 1950- ... 140
Joyce, Davis D. 1940- ... 149
Joyce, Donald Franklin 1938- ... 139
See also BW 2
Joyce, Ernest 1899-1975 ... CAP-2
Earlier sketch in CA 33-36
Joyce, Graham 1954- ... CANR-81
Earlier sketch in CA 151
See also HGG
See also SUFW 2
Joyce, J(ames) Avery 1902-1987 ... CANR-10
Obituary ... 121
Earlier sketch in CA 65-68
See also SATA 11
See also SATA-Obit 50
Joyce, James (Augustine Aloysius)
1882-1941 ... 126
Brief entry ... 104
See also AAYA 42
See also BRW 7
See also BRWC 1
See also BRWR 1
See also BYA 11, 13
See also CDBLB 1914-1945
See also DA
See also DA3
See also DAB
See also DAC
See also DAM MST, NOV, POET
See also DC 16
See also DLB 10, 19, 36, 162, 247
See also EWL 3
See also EXPN
See also EXPS
See also LAIT 3
See also LMFS 1, 2
See also MTCW 1, 2
See also MTFW 2005
See also NFS 7
See also PC 22
See also RGSF 2
See also SSC 3, 26, 44, 64
See also SSFS 1, 19
See also TCLC 3, 8, 16, 35, 52, 159
See also TEA
See also WLC
See also WLIT 4
Joyce, James Daniel 1921- ... 9-12R
Joyce, Jon L(oyd) 1937- ... CANR-10
Earlier sketch in CA 65-68
Joyce, Joyce Ann 1949- ... 137
Joyce, Judith
See Schwartz, Ruth L.
Joyce, Julia
See Tetel, Julie
Joyce, Mary Rosera 1930- ... 29-32R
Joyce, Michael 1945- ... CANR-137
Earlier sketch in CA 148

Cumulative Index 303 **Kabir**

Joyce, Patrick 1945- 128
Joyce, Peter 1937- .... SATA 127
Joyce, R(oger) B(ilbrough) 1924- CANR-1
Earlier sketch in CA 45-48
Joyce, Robert E(dward) 1934- 29-32R
Joyce, Rosemary A. 1956- 141
Joyce, Steven James 1950- 191
Joyce, Thomas
See Cary, (Arthur) Joyce (Lunel)
Joyce, Trevor 1947- .... CP 1
Joyce, William 1957- CANR-96
Earlier sketch in CA 124
See also AAYA 38
See also CLR 26
See also CWRI 5
See also MAICYA 2
See also MAICYAS 1
See also SATA 72, 118
See also SATA-Brief 46
Joyce, William L(eonard) 1942- 111
Joyce, William W(alter) 1934- CANR-15
Earlier sketch in CA 85-88
Joyner, Charles W. 1935- 37-40R
Joyner, Jerry 1938- 107
See also SATA 34
Joyner, Stephen Christopher 1967- 144
Joyner, Tim(othy) 1922- 141
Joyner, William T. 1934- 21-24R
Joynson, R(obert) B(illington) 1922- 57-60
Joynt, Carey Bonthron 1924- 124
Joynt, Robert R(ichard) 1915-1993 106
Jozsef, Attila 1905-1937 230
Brief entry 116
See also CDWLB 4
See also DLB 215
See also EWL 3
See also TCLC 22
Jrade, Cathy L(ogin) 1949- 184
J.S-N
See Aho, Juhani
Juana Ines de la Cruz, Sor
1651(?)-1695 .... DLB 305
See also FW
See also HLCS 1
See also LAW
See also PC 24
See also RGWL 2, 3
See also WLIT 1
Juana Inez de La Cruz, Sor
See Juana Ines de la Cruz, Sor
Juan de la Cruz 1542-1591 .... DLB 318
Juarez, Tina 1942- 173
Juarroz, Roberto 1925-1995 131
See also DLB 283
See also HW 1
Juby, Susan 1969- 231
See also SATA 156
Jucker, Sita 1921- CANR-12
Earlier sketch in CA 29-32R
See also SATA 5
Jucovy, Milton Edward 1918- 109
Juda, L(yon) 1923- 9-12R
Judah, Aaron 1923- CANR-84
Earlier sketch in CA 103
See also CWRI 5
See also SATA 118
Judah, J(ay) Stillson 1911-2000 .... 21-24R
Judd, Alan
See Petty, Alan Edwin
Judd, Cyril
See Kornbluth, C(yril) M. and Merril, Judith and Pohl, Frederik
Judd, Deane B(rewster) 1900-1972 .... CAP-1
Earlier sketch in CA 13-14
Judd, Denis (O'Nan) 1938- CANR-102
Earlier sketches in CA 25-28R, CANR-13, 49
See also SATA 33
Judd, Dennis R. 1943- CANR-16
Earlier sketch in CA 93-96
Judd, Frances K. CANR-27
Earlier sketches in CAP-2, CA 19-20
See also Benson, Mildred (Augustine Wirt)
See also SATA 1
Judd, Frederick Charles 1914- CANR-6
Earlier sketch in CA 5-8R
Judd, Gerrit P(armele) 1915-1971 .... 5-8R
Obituary 29-32R
Judd, H(oward) Stanley 1936- CANR-21
Earlier sketch in CA 69-72
Judd, Harrison
See Daniels, Norman
Judd, Larry R. 1937- 45-48
Judd, Margaret Haddican 1906-1995 .... 5-8R
Judd, Naomi 1946- 146
Judd, Robert 1939- CANR-38
Earlier sketch in CA 85-88
Judd, Sara (Hutton) Bowen
See Bowen-Judd, Sara (Hutton)
Judd, Sylvester 1813-1853 .... DLB 1, 243
Jude, Conny .... SATA 81
Judelle, Beatrice 1908- 33-36R
Judge, Edward H. 1945- CANR-93
Earlier sketch in CA 145
Judge, Harry George 1928- 124
Judge, Mike 1963(?)- 156
See also AAYA 20
Judis, John B. 1941- CANR-94
Earlier sketch in CA 140
Judkins, Phil(lip Edward) 1947- 142
Judovitz, Dalia 1951- 130
Judson, Clara Ingram 1879-1960 137
See also MAICYA 1, 2
See also SATA 38
See also SATA-Brief 27
Judson, David (Malcolm) 1941- 93-96
Judson, Don 1950- 155
Judson, Edward Zane Carroll
1823-1886 .... DLB 186
Judson, Horace Freeland 1931- 89-92
Judson, John 1930- CANR-12
Earlier sketch in CA 13-16R
Judson, Lewis Van Hagen 1893-1973
Obituary 41-44R
Judson, Margaret Atwood 1899-1991 102
Obituary 134
Judson, Sylvia Shaw 1897-1978 .... 41-44R
Obituary 133
Judson, William
See Corley, Edwin (Raymond)
Judt, Tony (Robert) 1948- 187
Judy, Marvin T(hornton) 1911-1996 .... 33-36R
Judy, Stephen
See Tchudi, Stephen N.
Judy, Stephen N.
See Tchudi, Stephen N.
Judy, Susan J(ane) 1944- 107
Judy, Will(iam Lewis) 1891-1973 .... 5-8R
Juel, Donald H. 1942- CANR-35
Earlier sketch in CA 114
Juel-Hansen, Erna 1845-1922 .... DLB 300
Juel-Nielsen, Niels 1920- 106
Juengel, Eberhard 1934-
Brief entry 118
Juenger, Ernst 1895-1998 .... CANR-106
Obituary 167
Earlier sketches in CA 101, CANR-21, 47
See also Junger, Ernst
See also CLC 125
See also DLB 56
Juenger, Friedrich Georg
See Junger, Friedrich Georg
Juergens, George Ivar 1932- 109
Juergensen, Hans 1919- CANR-48
Earlier sketches in CA 21-24R, CANR-8
Juergensmeyer, Jane Stuart
See Stuart, (Jessica) Jane
Juergensmeyer, John Eli 1934- 41-44R
Juergensmeyer, Mark (Karl) 1940- CANR-95
Earlier sketch in CA 129
Jugenheimer, Donald W(ayne)
1943- CANR-52
Earlier sketch in CA 125
Juhasz, Anne McCreary 1922- 53-56
Juhasz, Ferenc 1928- .... CWW 2
Juhasz, Gyula 1883-1937 .... EWL 3
Juhasz, Leslie A.
See Shepard, Leslie Albert
Juhasz, Suzanne 1942- 85-88
Juin, Hubert
See Loescher, Hubert
Jukes, (James Thomas) Geoffrey 1928- 29-32R
Jukes, Mavis 1947- CANR-78
Brief entry 121
Earlier sketch in CA 127
Interview in CA-127
See also CWRI 5
See also MAICYA 1, 2
See also SAAS 12
See also SATA 72, 111
See also SATA-Brief 43
Jukic, Ilija 1901-1977 49-52
Obituary 103
Jukucho
See Setouchi Harumi
Julavits, Heidi 219
Jules, Jacqueline 1956- 222
See also SATA 148
Julesberg, Elizabeth Rider Montgomery
1902-1985 .... CANR-42
Obituary 115
See also Montgomery, Elizabeth Rider
Jules-Rosette, Bennetta (Washington)
1948- 112
Julia, Edgardo Rodriguez
See Rodriguez Julia, Edgardo
Julia, Edgardo Rodriguez
See Rodriguez Julia, Edgardo
Julian, Jane
See Wiseman, David
Julian of Norwich 1342(?)-1416(?) .... DLB 146
See also LMFS 1
Juliard, Pierre 1939- 41-44R
Julie
See Robbins, June
Julien, Charles-Andre 1891- 103
Julie of Colorado Springs
See Robbins, June
Julier, Virginia Cheatham 1918- 5-8R
Julin, Joseph R(ichard) 1926-1993 .... 37-40R
Juline, Ruth Bishop
See Ritchie, Ruth
Julitte, Pierre (Gaston Louis) 1910- 37-40R
Julius
See Curling, Bryan William Richard
Julius, Anthony (Robert) 1956- 226
Julius, J.
See Jaenzon, Julius
Julius, Kristjan Niels
See Jonsson, Kristjan Niels
Julius Caesar 100B.C.-44B.C.
See Caesar, Julius
See also CDWLB 1
See also DLB 211
Jullian, Philippe 1919-1977 73-76
Julqunbay
See Qadiriy, Abdullah
Julty, Sam 1927-1992 61-64
July, Robert W(illiam) 1918- 41-44R
July, William II 191
Jump, Shirley 222
Jumper, Andrew Albert 1927- 17-20R
Jumpp, Hugo
See MacPeek, Walter G.
Jumsai, Sumet 1939- 129
Jun, Jong S(up) 1936- 53-56
June, Jennie
See Croly, Jane Cunningham
Jung, C(arl) G(ustav) 1875-1961 117
See also DA3
See also DLB 296
See also EWL 3
See also MTCW 1, 2
Jung, Franz 1888-1963 .... DLB 118
Jung, Hwa Yol 1932- 37-40R
Jung, John A. 1937- 17-20R
Jung, Leo 1892-1987
Obituary 124
Jung, Patricia B. 1949- 197
Junge, Alfred 1886-1964 .... IDFW 3, 4
Junge, Mark G(ene) 1943- CANR-48
Earlier sketch in CA 122
Jungel, Eberhard
See Juengel, Eberhard
Junger, Ernst
See Juenger, Ernst
See also CDWLB 2
See also EWL 3
See also RGWL 2, 3
Junger, Sebastian 1962- CANR-130
Earlier sketch in CA 165
See also AAYA 28
See also CLC 109
See also MTFW 2005
Jungk, Peter Stephan 1952- 236
Jungk, Robert 1913-1994 85-88
Jungle Doctor
See White, Paul Hamilton Hume
Jungmann, Joseph Andreas 1889-1975 165
Jungreis, Esther 1936- CANR-127
Earlier sketch in CA 110
Jung-Stilling, Johann Heinrich
1740-1817 .... DLB 94
Juniper, Alex
See Hospital, Janette Turner
Juniper, D(ean) F(rancis) 1929- CANR-18
Earlier sketch in CA 97-100
Junius
See Luxemburg, Rosa
Junker, Karin Stensland 1916- CANR-3
Earlier sketch in CA 9-12R
Junker, Patricia 1952- CANR-127
Earlier sketch in CA 170
Junkin, Tim 1951- 196
Junkins, B(illy) E(ugene) 1925-2000 234
Junkins, Donald 1931- 33-36R
Junkyard Moondog
See Dwyer, Jim
Junkyard Moondog, Reverend
See Dwyer, Jim
Juno, Andrea 1955- 171
Junor, John 1919-1997 108
Obituary 158
Junqueiro, Abilio Manuel Guerra
1850-1923 .... DLB 287
Junzaburo, Nishiwaki
See Nishiwaki, Junzaburo
See also EWL 3
Jupo, Frank J. 1904-1981 .... CANR-2
Earlier sketch in CA 5-8R
See also SATA 7
Jupp, James 1932- CANR-11
Earlier sketch in CA 21-24R
Jupp, Kenneth 1939- 65-68
Juptner, Joseph Paul 1913-2000 .... 5-8R
Jur, Jerzy
See Lerski, George Jan
Jura
See Soyfer, Jura
Jurafsky, Daniel 1962- 206
Juraga, Dubravka 1956- 175
Jurasik, Peter 1950- 229
Jurek, Martin 1942- 77-80
Jurgela, Constantine R. 1904-1988
Obituary 124
Jurgens, Curt 1912-1982
Obituary 107
Jurgens, W(illiam) A(nthony) 1928- 41-44R
Jurgensen, Barbara (Bitting) 1928- 17-20R
Jurinski, James John 1949- 191
Juris, Hervey A(sher) 1938- CANR-5
Earlier sketch in CA 53-56
Jurjevich, Ratibor-Ray (Momchila)
1915- 37-40R
Jurji, Edward J. 1907-1990 .... 13-16R
Obituary 132
Jurkevich, Gayana 1953- 139
Jurmain, Suzanne 1945- CANR-86
Earlier sketch in CA 133
See also SATA 72
Jurnak, Sheila
See Raeschild, Sheila
Jurnaville, Clarisse
See Magritte, Renw (Francois Ghislain)
Juska, Elise 1973- 224
Juska, Jane 1933(?)- 225
Jussawalla, Adil (Jehangir) 1940- CANR-83
Earlier sketch in CA 153
See also CP 1, 7
Jussawalla, Feroza 1953- 165
Jussawalla, Meheroo 1923- 233
Jusscrand, Jean Adrien Antoine Jules
See Jusserand, Jean Jules
Jusserand, Jean Jules 1855-1932 227
Jussi
See Aho, Juhani
Jussim, Estelle 1927- CANR-29
Earlier sketch in CA 81-84
Just, Ward (Swift) 1935- CANR-87
Earlier sketches in CA 25-28R, CANR-32
Interview in CANR-32
See also CLC 4, 27
See also CN 6, 7
Juster, F. Thomas 1926- CANR-2
Earlier sketch in CA 45-48
Juster, Norton 1929- CANR-83
Earlier sketches in CA 13-16R, CANR-13, 44
See also BYA 5
See also FANT
See also JRDA
See also MAICYA 1, 2
See also SATA 3, 132
See also YAW
Justesen, Benjamin R(ay) 1949- 198
Justice, Blair 1927- CANR-1
Earlier sketch in CA 45-48
Justice, Donald (Rodney)
1925-2004 .... CANR-122
Obituary 230
Earlier sketches in CA 5-8R, CANR-26, 54, 74, 121
Interview in CANR-26
See also AMWS 7
See also CLC 6, 19, 102
See also CP 1, 2, 3, 4, 5, 6, 7
See also CSW
See also DAM POET
See also DLBY 1983
See also EWL 3
See also MAL 5
See also MTCW 2
See also PC 64
See also PFS 14
See also TCLE 1:1
Justice, Keith L(eroy) 1949-2004 169
Justice, William G(ross), Jr. 1930- CANR-20
Earlier sketches in CA 53-56, CANR-5
Justiciar
See Powell-Smith, Vincent (Walter Francis)
Justin, George 1916- .... IDFW 4
Justiss, Julia 204
Justman, Robert H. 1926- 155
Justman, Stewart 1948- 234
Justus, May 1898-1989 .... 9-12R
Obituary 171
See also SATA 1
See also SATA-Obit 106
Juta, Jan 1895-1930 49-52
Obituary 174
Juta, Rene
See Juta, Jan
Jute, Andre 1945- 131
Jutikkala, Eino Kaarlo Ilmari 1907- CAP-1
Earlier sketch in CA 9-10
Jutson, Mary Carolyn Hollers
See George, Mary Carolyn Hollers Jutson
Juvenal c. 60-c. 130 .... AW 2
See also CDWLB 1
See also DLB 211
See also RGWL 2, 3
Juvenilia
See Taylor, Ann
Juvenis
See Bourne, Randolph S(illiman)
Juviler, Peter H(enry) 1926- 77-80
Jwaideh, Nizar 1933(?)-1988
Obituary 124
Jweid, Rosann 1933- 203
Jylhae, Yrjoe
See Jylha, Yrjo
Jylland, Jorgen
See Bonnelycke, Emil (Christian Theodor)

K

K., Alice
See Knapp, Caroline
Kaaberbol, Lene
See Kaaberbol, Lene
Kaaberbol, Lene 1960- 238
See also SATA 159
Kaapu, Myrtle King 1898-1985
Obituary 119
Kaaveri
See Kannan, Lakshmi
Kaba, Lansine 1941- 61-64
Kabadi, Sunder 1898(?)-1983
Obituary 111
Kabaker, Ray 1934(?)-1990
Obituary 132
Kabakov, Sasha .... CLC 59
Kabal, A. M.
See Bhabra, H(argurchet) S(ingh)
Kabaphe, Konstantinos Petrou
See Kavafis, Konstantinos Petrou
Kabaphes, Konstantinos Petrou
See Kavafis, Konstantinos Petrou
Kabasele, Joseph
See Tshiamala, Kabasele
Kabaservice, Geoffrey (M.) 1966- 233
Kabat-Zinn, Jon 153
Kabbani, Rana 1958- 125
Kabdebo, Tamas
See Kabdebo, Thomas
Kabdebo, Thomas 1934- CANR-23
Earlier sketches in CA 53-56, CANR-7
See also SATA 10
Kabibble, Ish
See Bogue, Merwyn (Alton)
Kabibble, Osh
See Jobb, Jamie
Kabir 1398(?)-1448(?) .... PC 56
See also RGWL 2, 3

Kabira, Wanjiku Mukabi ... 168
Kabotie, Fred 1900-1986 ... 118
Kabotie, Michael 1942- ... 210
Kabraji, Fredoon 1897- ... CAP-1
Earlier sketch in CA 13-14
Kac, Arthur W(ayne) 1904-1996 ... 117
Kac, Mark 1914-1984
Obituary ... 114
Kacapyr, Elia 1956- ... 158
Kacer, Kathy 1954- ... 213
See also SATA 142
Kacew, Romain 1914-1980 ... 108
Obituary ... 102
See also Gary, Romain
Kacew, Roman
See Kacew, Romain
Kachru, Braj B(ehari) 1932- ... CANR-49
Earlier sketches in CA 61-64, CANR-8, 23
Kachtick, Keith ... 225
Kachur, Lewis ... 142
Kachur, Shirley (Bridget) 1955- ... 180
Kack-Brice, Valerie 1950- ... CANR-102
Earlier sketch in CA 150
Kaczer, Illes 1887- ... CAP-1
Earlier sketch in CA 9-10
Kaczman, James ... SATA 156
Kadai, Heino Olavi 1931- ... 21-24R
Kadans, Joseph M(ichael) 1912-1993 ... 118
Kadare, Ismail 1936- ... 161
See also CLC 52, 190
See also EWL 3
See also RGWL 3
Kadel, Andrew 1954- ... 154
Kaden-Bandrowski, Juliusz 1885-1944 ... EWL 3
Kader, Soha Abdel ... 220
Kadesch, Robert R(udstone) 1922- ... 57-60
See also SATA 31
Kadic, Ante 1910-1998 ... 185
Brief entry ... 107
Kadir, Djelal 1946- ... 147
Kadish, Alon 1950- ... CANR-90
Earlier sketch in CA 131
Kadish, Ferne 1940- ... 61-64
Kadish, Mortimer Raymond 1916- ... 186
Brief entry ... 106
Kadish, Rachel Susan 1969- ... 181
Kadler, Eric H(enry) 1922- ... 29-32R
Kadohata, Cynthia (Lynn) 1956(?)- ... CANR-124
Earlier sketch in CA 140
See also CLC 59, 122
See also SATA 155
Kadushin, Alfred 1916- ... 25-28R
Kadushin, Charles 1932- ... 25-28R
Kaegi, Walter Emil, Jr. 1937- ... CANR-10
Earlier sketch in CA 25-28R
Kael, Pauline 1919-2001 ... CANR-70
Obituary ... 198
Earlier sketches in CA 45-48, CANR-6, 44
Interview in ... CANR-6
See also DA3
See also MTCW 2
Kaelbling, Rudolf 1928-1976 ... 17-20R
Kaelin, Eugene F(rancis) 1926-1991 ... 45-48
Kaellberg, Sture 1928- ... CANR-50
Earlier sketches in CA 107, CANR-25
Kaemmer, John E. 1928- ... 145
Kaempfer, William H. 1951- ... 144
Kaempfert, Wade
See del Rey, Lester
Kaempffert, Waldemar (Bernhard) 1877-1956
Brief entry ... 113
Kaeppler, Adrienne Lois 1935- ... 186
Brief entry ... 107
Kaerkkaeinen, Veli-Matti
See Karkkainen, Veli-Matti
Kaes, Anton 1945- ... 222
Kaese, Harold 1909(?)-1975
Obituary ... 57-60
Kaestle, Carl F(rederick) 1940- ... CANR-109
Earlier sketch in CA 85-88
Kaestner, Dorothy 1920- ... 61-64
Kaestner, Erich 1899-1974 ... CANR-40
Obituary ... 49-52
Earlier sketch in CA 73-76
See also Kastner, Erich
See also CLR 4
See also DLB 56
See also MAICYA 1, 2
See also SATA 14
Kaeuper, Richard W(illiam) 1941-
Brief entry ... 115
Kafatos, Menas ... 197
Kafatos, Minas C.
See Kafatos, Menas
Kafe, Joseph Kofi Thompson 1933- ... 49-52
Kaffka, Margit 1880-1918 ... EWL 3
Kafka, Barbara 1933- ... 136
Kafka, F(rancis) L. 1926- ... 139
Kafka, Franz 1883-1924 ... 126
Brief entry ... 105
See also AAYA 31
See also BPFB 2
See also CDWLB 2
See also DA
See also DA3
See also DAB
See also DAC
See also DAM MST, NOV
See also DLB 81
See also EW 9
See also EWL 3
See also EXPS
See also LATS 1:1
See also LMFS 2
See also MTCW 1, 2
See also MTFW 2005
See also NFS 7
See also RGSF 2
See also RGWL 2, 3
See also SFW 4
See also SSC 5, 29, 35, 60
See also SSFS 3, 7, 12
See also TCLC 2, 6, 13, 29, 47, 53, 112
See also TWA
See also WLC
Kafka, Kimberly ... 199
Kafka, Paul
See Kafka-Gibbons, Paul
Kafka, Phillipa 1933- ... 229
Kafka, Sherry 1937- ... 21-24R
Kafka, Vincent W(infield) 1924- ... 61-64
Kafka-Gibbons, Paul ... 235
Kafker, Frank A. 1931- ... 37-40R
Kafu
See Nagai, Sokichi
See also MJW
Kaga, Otohiko 1929- ... 194
Kagan, Abram S. 1889(?)-1983
Obituary ... 111
Kagan, Andrew 1947- ... 123
Kagan, Benjamin 1914- ... 21-24R
Kagan, Donald 1932- ... CANR-97
Earlier sketches in CA 21-24R, CANR-9
Kagan, Elaine ... CANR-108
Earlier sketch in CA 147
Kagan, Janet 1945- ... 162
See also SFW 4
Kagan, Jerome 1929- ... CANR-88
Earlier sketches in CA 5-8R, CANR-2, 24, 49
Kagan, Norman 1931- ... 153
Kagan, Richard (Lauren) 1943- ... 57-60
Kagan, Richard C(lark) 1938- ... 53-56
Kagan, Robert A. 1938- ... 126
Kagan, Shelly 1954- ... 204
Kagan-Kans, Eva 1928- ... 49-52
Kaganoff, Nathan M. 1926-1992 ... 126
Brief entry ... 108
Kagarlitsky, Boris 1958- ... CANR-127
Earlier sketch in CA 134
Kagel, John H(enry) 1942- ... 227
Kagerer, Rudy 1931- ... 196
Kagy, Frederick D(avid) 1917-1989 ... 13-16R
Kahan, Alan S. 1959- ... 139
Kahan, Arcadius 1920-1982 ... 135
Kahan, Gerald 1923-1993 ... 33-36R
Kahan, Stanley 1931- ... 5-8R
Kahan, Stuart 1936- ... 93-96
Kahana-Carmon, Amalia 1930- ... CWW 2
See also EWL 3
Kahane, Claire 1935- ... CANR-53
Earlier sketch in CA 126
Kahane, Howard 1928-2001 ... CANR-1
Obituary ... 197
Earlier sketch in CA 49-52
Kahane, Meir (David) 1932-1990 ... 133
Brief entry ... 112
Kahanovitsch, Pinkhes
See Der Nister
Kaharl, Victoria A(nn) 1952- ... 137
Kahf, Mohja 1967- ... 210
Kahila, Hilja
See Jarnefelt, Arvid
Kahin, Audrey R. 1934- ... CANR-98
Earlier sketch in CA 121
Kahin, George McTurnan 1918-2000 ... 144
Obituary ... 187
Kahl, Ann Hammel 1929- ... 17-20R
Kahl, Jonathan (D.) 1959- ... 145
See also SATA 77
Kahl, Joseph A(lan) 1923-
Brief entry ... 109
Kahl, M(arvin) P(hilip) 1934- ... 107
See also SATA 37
Kahl, Virginia (Caroline) 1919-2004 ... CANR-83
Obituary ... 233
Earlier sketches in CA 49-52, CANR-2
See also CWRI 5
See also SATA 48
See also SATA-Brief 38
See also SATA-Obit 158
Kahle, Roger (Raymond) 1943- ... 33-36R
Kahlenberg, Mary Hunt 1940- ... CANR-2
Earlier sketch in CA 45-48
Kahlenberg, Richard D(awson)
1963- ... CANR-97
Earlier sketch in CA 138
Kahler, Erich Gabriel 1885-1970 ... CANR-7
Obituary ... 29-32R
Earlier sketch in CA 5-8R
Interview in ... CANR-7
Kahler, Hugh (Torbert) MacNair
1883-1969 ... 102
Kahler, Woodland 1895-1981 ... 1-4R
Kahlo, Frida 1907-1954 ... 153
See also AAYA 47
See also HW 2
Kahm, H(arold) S. ... 101
Kahn, Albert E(ugene) 1912-1979 ... 118
Obituary ... 89-92
Kahn, Alfred E(dward) 1917- ... 41-44R
Kahn, Alfred J. 1919- ... CANR-66
Earlier sketches in CA 5-8R, CANR-15, 32
Kahn, Alfred Reginald
See Bretnor, (Alfred) Reginald
Kahn, Alfred Reginald
See Bretnor, (Alfred) Reginald
Kahn, Alice 1943- ... 119
Kahn, Arnold Dexter 1939- ... 101
Kahn, Balthazar
See Carlisle, Thomas (Fiske)
Kahn, Charles H(enry) 1928- ... CANR-75
Earlier sketch in CA 132
Kahn, Coppelia 1939- ... 129
Kahn, Dan 1933(?)-1989
Obituary ... 129
Kahn, David 1930- ... CANR-12
Earlier sketch in CA 25-28R
Kahn, Douglas 1951- ... 191
Kahn, E(ly) J(acques), Jr. 1916-1994 ... 65-68
Obituary ... 145
Kahn, Ely Jacques 1884-1972 ... 189
Obituary ... 37-40R
Kahn, Frank J(ules) 1938- ... 33-36R
Kahn, Gilbert 1912-1971 ... CANR-6
Earlier sketch in CA 1-4R
Kahn, Grace Leboy 1891-1983
Obituary ... 109
Kahn, Gus 1886-1941 ... DLB 265
See also IDFW 3, 4
Kahn, Hannah 1911-1988 ... CANR-14
Earlier sketch in CA 77-80
See also AITN 2
Kahn, Herman 1922-1983 ... CANR-83
Obituary ... 110
Earlier sketches in CA 65-68, CANR-44
Kahn, Herta Hess 1919- ... 25-28R
Kahn, James 1947- ... CANR-83
Earlier sketches in CA 109, CANR-27
See also SFW 4
Kahn, James M. 1903(?)-1978
Obituary ... 77-80
Kahn, Joan 1914-1994 ... 77-80
Obituary ... 146
See also SATA 48
See also SATA-Obit 82
Kahn, John (Ellison) 1950- ... 135
Kahn, Judd 1940- ... 101
Kahn, Katherine Janus 1942- ... SATA 90
Kahn, Kathy 1945- ... 41-44R
Kahn, Lawrence E(dwin) 1937- ... 103
Kahn, Lothar 1922-1990 ... 25-28R
Kahn, Louis I. 1901-1974
Obituary ... 49-52
Kahn, Ludwig W(erner) 1910- ... 41-44R
Kahn, Madeleine (H.) 1955- ... 137
Kahn, Margaret 1949- ... 101
Kahn, Michael A. 1952- ... CANR-71
Earlier sketch in CA 138
Kahn, Michael D. 1936- ... CANR-27
Earlier sketch in CA 109
Kahn, Michele 1940- ... 130
Kahn, Peggy
See Katz, Bobbi
Kahn, Peter H., Jr. 1955- ... 187
Kahn, Richard (Ferdinand Karn)
1905-1989 ... 97-100
Obituary ... 128
Kahn, Robert I(rving) 1910- ... 5-8R
Kahn, Robert L(ouis) 1918-1991 ... CANR-10
Earlier sketch in CA 17-20R
Kahn, Roger 1927- ... CANR-69
Earlier sketches in CA 25-28R, CANR-44
See also CLC 30
See also DLB 171
See also SATA 37
Kahn, Samuel 1897-1981
Obituary ... 106
Kahn, Sanders A(rthur) 1919-1987 ... 89-92
Obituary ... 121
Kahn, Sandra S(utker) 1942- ... 106
Kahn, Sharon 1934- ... 200
Kahn, Sholom J(acob) 1918- ... 102
Kahn, Si(mon) 1944- ... 33-36R
Kahn, Stephen 1940-1988 ... 5-8R
Obituary ... 127
Kahn, Steve
See Kahn, Stephen
Kahn, Sy M. 1924- ... CANR-10
Earlier sketch in CA 25-28R
Kahn, Theodore C(harles) 1912- ... 33-36R
Kahne, Joseph 1964- ... 162
Kahneman, Daniel 1934- ... 222
Kahn-Fogel, Daniel (Mark) 1948- ... 97-100
Kahn-Freund, Otto 1900-1979
Obituary ... 108
Kahnweiler, Daniel-Henry 1884-1979 ... 29-32R
Obituary ... 85-88
Kahrl, George M(orrow) 1904-1994 ... 105
Kahrl, Stanley J. 1931- ... 9-12R
Kahrl, William L. 1946- ... 109
Kahukiwa, Robyn 1940- ... SATA 134
Kai, Tara ... 219
Kaid, Lynda Lee 1948- ... CANR-16
Earlier sketch in CA 89-92
Kaikini, P(rabhakar) R(amrao) 1912- ... 61-64
Kaikkonen, Gus 1951- ... 129
Kaiko, Takeshi 1930- ... 104
See also Kaiko Takeshi
Kaiko Takeshi
See Kaiko, Takeshi
See also DLB 182
Kailbourn, Thomas R. ... 218
Kaimann, Diane S. 1939- ... 239
Kaim-Caudle, Peter Robert 1916- ... 21-24R
Kain, John F(orrest) 1935-2003 ... 29-32R
Obituary ... 219
Kain, Malcolm
See Oglesby, Joseph
Kain, Philip J(oseph) 1943- ... CANR-75
Earlier sketch in CA 132
Kain, Richard M(organ) 1908-1990 ... CANR-2
Obituary ... 131
Earlier sketch in CA 5-8R
Kain, Richard Y(erkes) 1936- ... 37-40R
Kain, Saul
See Sassoon, Siegfried (Lorraine)
Kainn
See Jonsson, Kristjan Niels
See also DLB 293
Kains, Josephine
See Goulart, Ron(ald Joseph)
Kainsdatter, Marianne
See Madsen, Svend Aage
Kainz, Howard Paul 1933- ... CANR-96
Earlier sketches in CA 114, CANR-35
Kairys, Anatolijus 1914- ... CANR-74
Earlier sketches in CA 102, CANR-32
Kairys, David 1943- ... 142
Kaisari, Uri 1899(?)-1979
Obituary ... 85-88
Kaiser, Artur 1943- ... 97-100
Kaiser, Bill
See Sumner, David (W. K.)
Kaiser, Charles 1950- ... 163
Kaiser, Christopher B(arina) 1941- ... CANR-47
Earlier sketch in CA 114
Kaiser, Daniel H. 1945- ... CANR-53
Earlier sketch in CA 126
Kaiser, David E. 1947- ... CANR-95
Earlier sketch in CA 144
Kaiser, Edward J(ohn) 1935- ... 93-96
Kaiser, Edwin George 1893-1984 ... 45-48
Obituary ... 114
Kaiser, Ernest 1915- ... CANR-16
Earlier sketches in CA 49-52, CANR-1
Kaiser, Frances E(lkan) 1922- ... 57-60
Kaiser, Georg 1878-1945 ... 190
Brief entry ... 106
See also CDWLB 2
See also DLB 124
See also EWL 3
See also LMFS 2
See also RGWL 2, 3
See also TCLC 9
Kaiser, Harvey H. 1936- ... CANR-14
Earlier sketch in CA 81-84
Kaiser, Ken 1945- ... 226
Kaiser, Leo M(ax) 1918-2001 ... 116
Obituary ... 193
Kaiser, Otto 1924- ... 85-88
Kaiser, Philip M. 1913- ... 141
Kaiser, Robert Blair 1930- ... CANR-123
Earlier sketch in CA 9-12R
Kaiser, Robert G(reeley) 1943- ... CANR-119
Earlier sketches in CA 65-68, CANR-31
Kaiser, Walter (Jacob) 1931- ... CANR-36
Earlier sketches in CA 37-40R, CANR-15
Kaiser, Walter Christian, Jr. 1933- ... CANR-43
Earlier sketch in CA 114
Kaiser, Ward L(ouis) 1923- ... 53-56
Kaiser Wilhelm II
See Hohenzollern, Friedrich Wilhelm (Victor Albert)
Kaitz, Edward M. 1928- ... CANR-13
Earlier sketch in CA 29-32R
Kaizuki, Kiyonori 1950- ... SATA 72
Kajencki, Francis C(asimir) 1918- ... CANR-38
Earlier sketch in CA 115
Kakar, Sudhir 1938- ... CANR-90
Earlier sketch in CA 33-36R
Kaki
See Heinemann, Katherine
Kakimoto, Kozo 1915- ... SATA 11
Kakonen, Ulla
See Anobile, Ulla (Kakonen)
Kakonis, Thomas E. 1930- ... CANR-48
Earlier sketch in CA 57-60
Kakonis, Tom E.
See Kakonis, Thomas E.
Kaku, Michio 1947- ... 228
Kakugawa, Frances H(ideko) 1936- ... 77-80
Kaland, William J. 1915(?)-1983
Obituary ... 111
Kalashnikoff, Nicholas 1888-1961 ... 73-76
See also SATA 16
Kalb, Bernard 1932-
Brief entry ... 109
Kalb, Jonah 1926- ... CANR-4
Earlier sketch in CA 53-56
See also SATA 23
Kalb, Jonathan 1959- ... CANR-90
Earlier sketch in CA 135
Kalb, Marvin L(eonard) 1930- ... CANR-109
Earlier sketches in CA 5-8R, CANR-45
Kalb, S(am) William 1897-1992 ... 33-36R
Kalbacken, Joan 1925- ... 161
See also SATA 96
Kalberer, Augustine 1917- ... 61-64
Kalberg, Stephen ... 154
Kalcheim, Lee 1938- ... 85-88
See also CAD
See also CD 5, 6
Kaldor, Mary 1946- ... 93-96
Kaldor, Nicholas 1908-1986 ... 134

Cumulative Index 305 Kang

Kale, Arvind and
Shanta
See Gantzer, Hugh
Kale, Steven D(avid) 1957- 144
Kaleb, Vjekoslav 1905-1996 203
Kaleb, Vjekoslav 1905-1997 .... DLB 181
Kalechofsky, Roberta 1931- CANR-57
Earlier sketches in CA 49-52, CANR-2
See also DLB 28
See also SATA 92
Kaledin, Eugenia 1929- 109
Kaledin, Sergei .... CLC 59
Kalem, T(heodore) E(ustace) 1919-1985
Obituary 116
Kalemkerian, Zarouhi 1874(?)-1971
Obituary 104
Kalenik, Sandra 1945-1993 73-76
Obituary 140
Kaler, Anne K(atherine) 1935- 138
Kaler, James Otis 1848-1912 196
Brief entry 120
See also DLB 42
See also SATA 15
Kales, Emily Fox 1944- 21-24R
Kalesniko, Mark G(aston) 1958- 203
Kaleta, Kenneth C. 1948- CANR-98
Earlier sketch in CA 146
Kaletski, Alexander 1946- 143
Brief entry 118
See also CLC 39
Kalfatovic, Martin R. 1961- 141
Kalfus, Ken 1954- CANR-134
Earlier sketch in CA 174
Kalfus, Melvin 1931- 134
Kalia, Narendra Nath 1942- CANR-30
Earlier sketch in CA 112
Kalia, Ravi 1947- 161
Kalich, Jacob 1891-1975
Obituary 89-92
Kalich, Richard 1947- CANR-55
Earlier sketch in CA 127
Kalich, Robert 1947- 106
Kalicki, Jan H(enryk) 1948- 65-68
Kalidasa fl. c. 400-455 .... PC 22
See also RGWL 2, 3
Kalijarvi, Thorsten V(alentine)
1897-1980 .... CAP-1
Obituary 97-100
Earlier sketch in CA 19-20
Kalin, Jim 1959- 172
Kalin, Martin (Gregory) 1943- 53-56
Kalin, Robert 1921- CANR-8
Earlier sketch in CA 61-64
Kalin, Rudolf 1938- 45-48
Kalina, Sigmund 1911-1977 .... CANR-3
Earlier sketch in CA 49-52
Kalins, Dorothy (G.) 1942- CANR-17
Earlier sketch in CA 25-28R
Kalinsky, George 1936- CANR-143
Earlier sketches in CA 49-52, CANR-2
Kalish, Betty McKelvey 1913-1997 45-48
Obituary 157
Kalish, Claire M. 1947- .... SATA 92
Kalish, Donald 1919-2000 .... 9-12R
Obituary 188
Kalish, Richard A(llan) 1930- CANR-25
Earlier sketches in CA 5-8R, CANR-10
Kalisher, Simpson 1926- 17-20R
Kallas, Aino (Julia Maria) 1878-1956 192
See also EWL 3
Kallas, James (Gus) 1928- CANR-10
Earlier sketch in CA 17-20R
Kallaus, Norman F. 1924- 33-36R
Kallberg, Sture
See Kaellberg, Sture
Kalleen, Jake
See Wilcox, Robert K(alleen)
Kallen, (Marc) Christian 1950- 120
Kallen, Horace M(eyer) 1882-1974 93-96
Obituary 49-52
Kallen, Laurence 1944- 41-44R
Kallen, Lucille 1922-1999 97-100
Obituary 173
Kallen, Stuart A(rnold) 1955- CANR-106
Earlier sketch in CA 151
See also SATA 86, 126
Kallenbach, Joseph E(rnest) 1903-1991 77-80
Kallenbach, W(illiam) Warren 1926- 9-12R
Kallesser, Michael 1886(?)-1975
Obituary 61-64
Kallet, Arthur 1902-1972
Obituary 33-36R
Kallet, Marilyn 1946- 104
Kalley, Jacqueline A(udrey) 1945- 200
Kallgren, Beverly Hayes 1925- 146
Kallich, Martin 1918- CANR-2
Earlier sketch in CA 5-8R
Kallifatides, Theodor 1938- CANR-43
Earlier sketches in CA 85-88, CANR-15
Kallir, Jane K(atherine) 1954- CANR-119
Earlier sketches in CA 109, CANR-25, 52
Kallir, Otto 1894-1978 49-52
Obituary 81-84
Kallman, Chester (Simon) 1921-1975 .... CANR-3
Obituary 53-56
Earlier sketch in CA 45-48
See also CLC 2
See also CP 1, 2
Kallmann, Helmut Max 1922- 108
Kallsen, T(heodore) J(ohn) 1915-1997 .... 5-8R
Kalman, Bobbie 1947- .... SATA 63
Kalman, Harold David 1910- 103
Kalman, Laura 1955- 140
Kalman, Maira 1949- CANR-116
Earlier sketch in CA 161
See also CLR 32
See also MAICYA 2
See also MAICYAS 1
See also SATA 96, 137
Kalmar, Bert 1884-1947 .... DLB 265
Kalme, Egils 1909-1983 81-84
Kalmijn, Jo 1905-1991 .... CAP-2
Earlier sketch in CA 21-22
Kalmus, Ain
See Mand, Ewald
Kalmus, Hans 1906(?)-1988
Obituary 128
Kalnay, Francis 1899-1992 49-52
See also SATA 7
Kalnoky, Ingeborg L(ouise) 1909-1997 61-64
Kaloustian, Rosanne 1955- .... SATA 93
Kalow, Gert 1921- 29-32R
Kalow, Gisela 1946- 107
See also SATA 32
Kalpakian, Laura Anne 1945- CANR-15
Earlier sketch in CA 81-84
Kals, W(illiam) S(teven) 1910-1994 .... CANR-24
Earlier sketch in CA 45-48
Kalson, Albert E(ugene) 1932- 132
Kalstone, David (Michael) 1932-1986 166
Obituary 119
Kalstone, Shirlee A(nn) 1932- CANR-8
Earlier sketch in CA 61-64
Kalt, Bryson R. 1934- 33-36R
Kalt, Jeannette Chappell 1898(?)-1976
Obituary 69-72
Kaltenborn, Hans Von 1878-1965
Obituary 93-96
Kalter, Joanmarie 1951- 102
Kalu, Ogbu Uke 1944- 93-96
Kaluger, George 1921- 29-32R
Kaluger, Meriem Fair 1921- 81-84
Kalven, Harry, Jr. 1914-1974 162
Obituary 53-56
Kalyanaraman, Aiyaswamy 1903- CAP-2
Earlier sketch in CA 33-36
Kalyn, Wayne (Stephen) 1951- 239
Kamakahi, Jeffrey J(on) 1960- 139
Kamakaris, Athena 1946- 172
Kamakaris, Tina
See Kamakaris, Athena
Kamal, Aleph 1950- 134
Kamal, Sufia 1911-1999 186
Kamali, Masoud 1956- 195
Kamalipour, Yahya R. 1947- 184
Kamarck, Andrew M(artin) 1914- CANR-10
Earlier sketch in CA 21-24R
Kamarck, Lawrence 1927- CANR-32
Earlier sketch in CA 73-76
Kamath, M(adhav) V(ithal) 1921- CANR-21
Earlier sketch in CA 69-72
Kamau, Kwadwo Agymah CANR-143
Earlier sketch in CA 164
Kambanellis, Iakovos 1922- .... EWL 3
Kamber, Victor S. 181
Kambil, Ajit 231
Kamboureli, Smaro 1955- CANR-56
Earlier sketch in CA 127
Kambu, Joseph
See Amamoo, Joseph Godson
Kamen, Betty 1925- CANR-43
Earlier sketch in CA 114
Kamen, Gloria 1923- CANR-35
Earlier sketch in CA 114
See also SATA 9, 98
Kamen, Henry (Arthur Francis)
1936- CANR-122
Earlier sketches in CA 5-8R, 163, CANR-7
Kamen, Isai
See Stein, Jess
Kamen, Martin D(avid) 1913-2002 118
Obituary 206
Kamen, Paula 1967- CANR-109
Earlier sketch in CA 137
Kamen, Si 1920- 114
Kamenetsky, Ihor 1927- CANR-4
Earlier sketch in CA 1-4R
Kamenetz, Rodger 1950- CANR-47
Earlier sketches in CA 112, CANR-30
Kamenka, Eugene 1928-1994 .... CANR-2
Earlier sketch in CA 5-8R
Kamensky, Jane 1963- 173
Kamensky, Vasilii Vasil'evich
1884-1961 .... DLB 295
Kamerlingh Onnes, Heike 1853-1926 155
Kamerman, Jack B. 1940- 115
Kamerman, Sheila B(rody) 1928- CANR-10
Earlier sketch in CA 65-68
Kamerman, Sylvia E.
See Burack, Sylvia K.
Kamerschen, David R(oy) 1937- 53-56
Kamien, Marcia 1940- CANR-45
Earlier sketches in CA 105, CANR-22
Kamieniecki, Sheldon 156
Kamil, Alan C(urtis) 1941- 134
Brief entry 109
Kamil, Jill 1930- CANR-7
Earlier sketch in CA 57-60
Kamin, Blair 1957- 206
Kamin, Leon J. 1927- 103
Kamin, Nick
See Antonick, Robert J.
Kaminer, Wendy 1950(?)- CANR-139
Earlier sketch in CA 162
Kamins, Jeanette -1972 .... 5-8R
Kamins, Robert Martin 1918-
Brief entry 105
Kaminska, Ida 1899-1980
Obituary 97-100
Kaminskaya, Dina 1920- 115
Kaminski, Janusz 1959- .... IDFW 4
Kaminski, Margaret (Joan) 1944- CANR-8
Earlier sketch in CA 61-64
Kaminsky, Alice R. 33-36R
Kaminsky, Howard 1940- CANR-113
Earlier sketch in CA 105
Interview in CA-105
Kaminsky, Ilya 1977- 238
Kaminsky, Jack 1922- 21-24R
Kaminsky, Marc 1943- CANR-24
Earlier sketches in CA 53-56, CANR-5
Kaminsky, Melvin 1926- CANR-16
Earlier sketch in CA 65-68
See also Brooks, Mel
See also DFS 21
Kaminsky, Peretz 1916-2000 .... 33-36R
Kaminsky, Peter 1947(?)- 207
Kaminsky, Stuart M(elvin) 1934- CANR-89
Earlier sketches in CA 73-76, CANR-29, 53
See also CLC 59
See also CMW 4
Kaminsky, Susan Stanwood 1937- 115
Brief entry 110
Kamisar, Yale 1929- CANR-13
Earlier sketch in CA 69-72
Kamitses, Zoe 1941- 111
Kamleshwar
See Kamlesvar
Kamlesvar 1932- .... CWW 2
Kamm, Antony 1931- CANR-41
Earlier sketch in CA 117
Kamm, (Jan) Dorinda 1952- CANR-14
Earlier sketch in CA 37-40R
Kamm, Henry 1925- 151
Kamm, Herbert 1917-2002 69-72
Obituary 209
Kamm, Jacob Oswald 1918-1995 .... 5-8R
Kamm, Josephine (Hart) 1905-1989 .... CANR-83
Earlier sketches in CA 9-12R, CANR-5
See also SATA 24
See also YAW
Kamm, Phyllis S. 1918- 112
Kamman, Madeleine M(arguerite Pin)
1930- 85-88
Kamman, William 1930- 25-28R
Kammen, Michael G(edaliah)
1936- CANR-89
Earlier sketches in CA 25-28R, CANR-22, 34, 63
See also CAAS 23
See also MTCW 1
Kammerer, Gladys M. 1909-1970 .... CANR-16
Obituary 103
Earlier sketch in CA 1-4R
Kammerman, Sylvia K.
See Burack, Sylvia K.
Kammeyer, Kenneth C(arl) W(illiam)
1931- 29-32R
Kamo no Chomei 1153(?)-1216 .... DLB 203
Kamo no Nagaakira
See Kamo no Chomei
Kamp, Irene Kittle 1910-1985
Obituary 116
Kampelman, Max M. 1920- 41-44R
Kampen, Irene Trepel 1922-1998 .... CANR-1
Obituary 166
Earlier sketch in CA 1-4R
Kampen, Michael Edwin 1939- 186
Brief entry 110
Kampf, Abraham 1920- 21-24R
Kampf, Avram
See Kampf, Abraham
Kampf, Louis 1929- 33-36R
Kamphoefner, Walter D. 1948- 137
Kampmann, Christian 1939-1988 191
See also DLB 214
See also EWL 3
Kampov, Boris Nikolayevich 1908-1981 108
Obituary 104
Kampurt, Remko
See Campert, Remco Wouter
Kamrany, Nake M. 1934- CANR-14
Earlier sketch in CA 37-40R
Kamstra, Leslie D. 1920-1997 69-72
Kan, Sergei 1953- CANR-122
Earlier sketch in CA 137
Kanafani, Ghassan 1936-1972 .... EWL 3
See also WLIT 6
Kanahele, George Sanford 1930- 102
Kanaly, Michael 171
Kanan, Nabiel 182
Kanan, Sean 1966- 215
Kanar, Stephen (Patrick) 1944- 201
Kanarfogel, Ephraim 1955- 224
Kanaris, Jim 1964- 237
Kanazawa, Masakata 1934- 25-28R
Kanazawa, Roger
See Kanazawa, Masakata
Kanbar, Maurice 1950- 201
Kanchier, Carole 132
Kandall, Stephen R. 1940- 163
Kandaouroff, Berice 1912- 33-36R
Kandel, Denise Bystryn 1933- 13-16R
Kandel, I(saac) L(eon) 1881-1965 .... CANR-3
Earlier sketch in CA 1-4R
Kandel, Lenore 1932- 178
See also CP 1, 2
See also DLB 16
Kandel, Michael 1941- 159
See also SATA 93
Kandel, Robert S(amuel) 1937- 223
Kandel, Susan 1961- 235
Kandel, Thelma E. 1932- 111
Kandell, Alice S. 1938- CANR-13
Earlier sketch in CA 33-36R
See also SATA 35
Kandinsky, Nina 1896(?)-1980 101
Kandinsky, Wassily 1866-1944 155
Brief entry 118
See also AAYA 64
See also TCLC 92
Kando, Thomas M. 1941- CANR-2
Earlier sketch in CA 49-52
Kane, Aarno
See Kagan, Andrew
Kane, Alex
See Lazuta, Gene
Kane, Andrea 219
Kane, Basil G(odfrey) 1931- CANR-24
Earlier sketch in CA 69-72
Kane, Bob 1916-1998 163
Obituary 172
See also AAYA 8
See also SATA 120
Kane, Dennis Cornelius 1918-1997 .... 41-44R
Kane, E. B. 1944- 57-60
Kane, Edward J(ames) 1935- 41-44R
Kane, Elizabeth 1942- 136
Kane, Francis
See Robbins, Harold
Kane, Frank 1912-1968 .... CANR-58
Obituary 25-28R
Earlier sketch in CA 5-8R
See also CMW 4
Kane, Frank R. 1925- 77-80
Kane, George 1916- 103
Kane, Gerard Thomas Matthew
1946-1999 133
Obituary 186
Kane, Gil 1926-2000 228
Kane, Gordon L. 1937- CANR-95
Earlier sketch in CA 149
Kane, H. Victor 1906-1983 .... 29-32R
Kane, Harnett T(homas) 1910-1984
Obituary 113
Kane, Henry 1918- 156
See also McKay, Kenneth R. and
Queen, Ellery
See also CMW 4
Kane, Henry Bugbee 1902-1971 .... CANR-83
Earlier sketch in CA 73-76
See also SATA 14
Kane, J. Herbert 1910-1988 97-100
Kane, Jack
See Baker, A(lbert) A(llen)
Kane, James
See Germano, Peter B.
Kane, Jim
See Germano, Peter B.
Kane, John 1946- 167
Kane, John Joseph 1909- CAP-2
Earlier sketch in CA 13-14
Kane, Joseph Nathan 1899-2002 220
Kane, Julia
See Robins, Denise (Naomi)
Kane, Kathleen
See Child, Maureen
Kane, L. A.
See Mannetti, Lisa
Kane, Leslie 1945- 140
Kane, Mallory
See Mallory, Rickey R.
Kane, Pablo
See Zachary, Hugh
Kane, Paul
See Simon, Paul (Frederick)
Kane, Paul 1950- 207
Kane, Penelope Susan 1945- CANR-86
Earlier sketch in CA 131
Kane, Penny
See Kane, Penelope Susan
Kane, Peter E(vans) 1932- CANR-31
Earlier sketch in CA 112
Kane, Robert S. 1925-1997 .... CANR-48
Obituary 162
Earlier sketches in CA 9-12R, CANR-7, 23
Kane, Robert W. 1910- .... SATA 18
Kane, Rod
See Kane, Gerard Thomas Matthew
Kane, Sarah 1971-1999 190
See also BRWS 8
See also CD 5, 6
See also DLB 310
Kane, Thomas S. 1925- 114
Kane, William Everett 1943- 49-52
Kane, Wilson
See Bloch, Robert (Albert)
Kanefield, Teri 1960- .... SATA 135
Kaneko, Lonny 1939- .... DLB 312
Kanellos, Nicolas 1945- CANR-108
Earlier sketch in CA 131
See also HW 1
Kanengoni, Alexander 182
Kaner, Etta 1947- .... SATA 126
Kaner, Sam 171
Kanerova, Mita Castle
See Castle-Kanerova, Mita
Kanes, Eveline L. 1929- 141
Kanet, Roger E(dward) 1936- CANR-100
Earlier sketches in CA 33-36R, CANR-14, 49
Kanetzke, Howard W(illiam) 1932- 112
See also SATA 38
Kanfer, Allen 1905(?)-1983
Obituary 110
Kanfer, Frederick H. 1925-2002 .... CANR-32
Obituary 210
Earlier sketches in CA 41-44R, CANR-15
Kanfer, Stefan 1933- CANR-98
Earlier sketch in CA 103
Interview in CA-103
Kang, Chol-Hwan 1968(?)- 209
Kang, K. Connie 1942- 152
Kang, Shin T. 1935- 33-36R

Kang, Younghill 1903-1972
Obituary 37-40R
See also DLB 312
Kanigel, Robert 1946- CANR-122
Earlier sketches in CA 132, CANR-69
Kanin, Garson 1912-1999 .... CANR-78
Obituary 177
Earlier sketches in CA 5-8R, CANR-7
See also AITN 1
See also CAD
See also CLC 22
See also DLB 7
See also IDFW 3, 4
Kanin, Michael 1910-1993 .... CANR-46
Obituary 140
Earlier sketch in CA 61-64
Kanin, Ruth 1920- 107
Kanitz, Walter 1910-1986 97-100
Kaniuk, Yoram 1930- 134
See also CLC 19
See also DLB 299
Kaniut, Larry (LeRoy) 1942- CANR-129
Earlier sketch in CA 114
Kann, Mark E. 1947- 130
Kann, Robert A(dolf) 1906-1981 129
Obituary 105
Kannan, Lakshmi 1947(?)- 198
Kannappan, Subbiah 1927- 93-96
Kanner, Catherine 1954- 123
Kanner, Leo 1894-1981 .... 17-20R
Obituary 103
Kannus, (Veli) Pekka 1959- 171
Kanof, Abram 1903-1999 .... 29-32R
Kanon, Joseph A. 1946- CANR-109
Earlier sketch in CA 163
Kanovsky, Eliyahu 1922- 33-36R
Kanoza, Muriel Canfield
See Canfield, Muriel
Kansil, Joli 1943- 81-84
Kant, Hermann 1926- 159
See also DLB 75
See also EWL 3
Kant, Immanuel 1724-1804 .... DLB 94
Kantar, Edwin B(ruce) 1932- 41-44R
Kantaris, Sylvia 1936- CANR-84
Earlier sketch in CA 139
See also CP 7
See also CWP
Kantarizis, Sylvia
See Kantaris, Sylvia
Kantemir, Antiokh Dmitrievich
1708-1744 .... DLB 150
Kanter, Arnold 1945- 89-92
Kanter, Hal 1918- 81-84
Kanter, Lynn 1954- 164
Kanter, Rosabeth Moss 1943- CANR-106
Earlier sketches in CA 77-80, CANR-14
Kantha, Sachi Sri 1953- 184
Kantner, Seth 1965- 232
Kanto, Peter
See Zachary, Hugh
Kantonen, T(aito) A(lmar) 1900-1993 .... 33-36R
Kantor, Hal 1924- 77-80
Kantor, Harry 1911-1985 .... CANR-2
Earlier sketch in CA 1-4R
Kantor, Herman I. 1909- 57-60
Kantor, James 1927-1974 .... CAP-2
Earlier sketch in CA 21-22
Kantor, Leonard 1924(?)-1984
Obituary 112
Kantor, MacKinlay 1904-1977 .... CANR-63
Obituary 73-76
Earlier sketches in CA 61-64, CANR-60
See also CLC 7
See also CN 1, 2
See also DLB 9, 102
See also MAL 5
See also MTCW 2
See also RHW
See also TCWW 1, 2
Kantor, Martin 1933- 181
Kantor, Marvin 1934- CANR-2
Earlier sketch in CA 49-52
Kantor, Seth 1926-1993 81-84
Obituary 142
Kantor, Tim 1932- 128
Kantor-Berg, Friedrich 1908-1979 133
Obituary 89-92
See also Torberg, Friedrich
Kantorovich, Leonid V(italevich)
1912-1986 164
Obituary 119
Kantowicz, Edward Robert 1943- 114
Kantrowitz, Arnie 1940- 77-80
Kantrowitz, Joanne Spencer 1931- 81-84
Kantrowitz, Stephen D(avid) 1965- 197
Kantzer, Kenneth S(ealer) 1917- 106
Kanungo, R(abindra) N. 1935- 135
Kanwar, Mahfooz A. 1939- 37-40R
Kany, Charles E(mil) 1895-1968 .... CANR-3
Earlier sketch in CA 1-4R
Kanya, Maria
See Green, Maria A.
Kanyadi, Sandor 1929- 219
Kanya-Forstner, A(lexander) S(ydney)
1940- CANR-17
Earlier sketch in CA 25-28R
Kanza, Thomas R. (Nsenga) 1933- CANR-5
Earlier sketch in CA 53-56
Kanzawa, Toshiko
See Furukawa, Toshi
Kanze, Edward (J. III) 1956- 139
Kanze Kojiro Nobumitsu 1435-1516 .. DLB 203
Kanze Motokiyo
See Zeami
Kanzer, Mark 1908-1998 .... 37-40R
Kao, Charles C. L. 1932- 85-88
Kao, George 1912- 132
Kao Hsiao-sheng
See Gao, Xiaosheng
See also EWL 3
Kapel, Andrew
See Burgess, Michael (Roy)
Kapel, David E(dward) 1932- 125
Kapel, Saul M.D.
See Schanche, Don(ald) A(rthur)
Kapelner, Alan 5-8R
Kapelrud, Arvid Schou 1912-1994 102
Kaper, Bronislau 1902-1983 .... IDFW 3, 4
Kapfer, Miriam B(ierbaum) 1935- 33-36R
Kapfer, Philip G(ordon) 1936- 33-36R
Kapferer, Jean-Noel 1948- 147
Kapitsa, Pyotr L(eonidovich) 1894-1984
Obituary 112
Kaplan, Abraham 1918-1993 .... CANR-48
Obituary 141
Earlier sketch in CA 13-16R
Kaplan, Alice (Yaeger) 1954- CANR-93
Earlier sketch in CA 153
Kaplan, Alice Y.
See Kaplan, Alice (Yaeger)
Kaplan, Allan 1932- 33-36R
Kaplan, Andrew (Gary) 1941- 125
Kaplan, Andrew 1960- 146
See also SATA 78
Kaplan, Anne Bernays 1930- CANR-72
Earlier sketches in CA 1-4R, CANR-5
See also SATA 32
Kaplan, Arthur 1925- 5-8R
Kaplan, Barbara Beigun 1943- 146
Kaplan, Benjamin 1911- CANR-47
Earlier sketch in CA 1-4R
Kaplan, Bernard 1944- CANR-2
Earlier sketch in CA 49-52
Kaplan, Berton H(arris) 1930- 61-64
Kaplan, Bess 1927- 85-88
See also SATA 22
Kaplan, Boche 1926- CANR-10
Earlier sketch in CA 21-24R
See also SATA 24
Kaplan, Carter 1960- 225
Kaplan, Chaim A(ron) 1880-1942(?)
Kaplan, Charles 1919- 9-12R
Kaplan, Dana Evan 1960- 226
Kaplan, David Gordon 1908-1977 61-64
Kaplan, David Michael 1946- 187
See also CLC 50
Kaplan, Doris
See Willens, Doris
Kaplan, E(lizabeth) Ann 1936- 127
Kaplan, Edward 1946- CANR-11
Earlier sketch in CA 69-72
Kaplan, Edward S. 1942- 175
Kaplan, Elizabeth (A.) 1956- 150
See also SATA 83
Kaplan, Eugene H(erbert) 1932- 81-84
Kaplan, Flora S(tewart) 109
Kaplan, Fred
See Kaplan, Fred Michael
Kaplan, Fred 1937- CANR-91
Earlier sketches in CA 41-44R, CANR-14, 48
See also DLB 111
Kaplan, Fred M.
See Kaplan, Fred Michael
Kaplan, Fred Michael 1954- 127
Brief entry 121
Kaplan, Frederick I(srael) 1920- 21-24R
Kaplan, Gabrielle Suzanne
See Kaplan-Mayer, Gabrielle
Kaplan, H. Roy 1944- 89-92
Kaplan, Harold 1916- 17-20R
Kaplan, Helen Singer 1929-1995 102
Obituary 149
See also AITN 1
Kaplan, Hester 1959- 230
Kaplan, Howard 1950- CANR-123
Earlier sketch in CA 69-72
Kaplan, Howard B(ernard) 1932- CANR-22
Earlier sketches in CA 61-64, CANR-8
Kaplan, Hymen R. 1910- 102
Kaplan, Irma 1900- 29-32R
See also SATA 10
Kaplan, Jack A(rnold) 1947- 57-60
Kaplan, Jacob J. 1920- CANR-10
Earlier sketch in CA 21-24R
Kaplan, James 1951- CANR-121
Earlier sketch in CA 135
See also CLC 59
Kaplan, Janet A(nn) 1945- 130
Kaplan, Janice Ellen 1955- CANR-67
Earlier sketch in CA 117
Kaplan, Jean Caryl Korn 1926- 5-8R
See also SATA 10
Kaplan, Jeffrey 1954- 165
Kaplan, Jerry 1952- 152
Kaplan, Jim 1944- 126
Kaplan, Joel 1956- 134
Kaplan, Johanna 1942- CANR-83
Earlier sketch in CA 77-80
See also CN 4, 5, 6, 7
See also DLB 28
Kaplan, John 1929-1989
Obituary 130
Kaplan, Jonathan 1954- 204
Kaplan, Joseph 1916(?)-1980
Obituary 97-100
Kaplan, Justin 1925- CANR-123
Earlier sketches in CA 17-20R, CANR-8
See also DLB 111
Kaplan, Kalman J. 1941- 193
Kaplan, Lawrence Jay 1915- 21-24R
Kaplan, Lawrence S(amuel) 1924- CANR-92
Earlier sketch in CA 33-36R
Kaplan, Leonard 1918(?)-1977
Obituary 69-72
Kaplan, Louise J. 1929- 141
Kaplan, Marion A. 1946- 142
Kaplan, Martin (Harold) 1950- 65-68
Kaplan, Martin F(rancis) 1940- 93-96
Kaplan, Max 1911-1998 .... CANR-20
Obituary 169
Earlier sketches in CA 1-4R, CANR-5
Kaplan, Milton (Allen) 1910-1997 65-68
Kaplan, Milton 1918-1988
Obituary 127
Kaplan, Mordecai M(enahem) 1881-1983
Obituary 111
Kaplan, Morton A. 1921- CANR-7
Earlier sketch in CA 5-8R
Kaplan, Nelly 1936- CANR-139
Earlier sketch in CA 144
Kaplan, Norman Mayer 1931- 110
Kaplan, Philip 1916- 13-16R
Kaplan, Rachel 166
Kaplan, Richard 1929- 73-76
Kaplan, Robert B. 1928- CANR-122
Earlier sketches in CA 13-16R, CANR-7, 22
Kaplan, Robert D. 1952- CANR-96
Earlier sketch in CA 142
Kaplan, Robert S. 1940- 170
Kaplan, S(aul) Howard 1938- 25-28R
Kaplan, Samuel 1935- 21-24R
Kaplan, Sidney 1913-1993 .... CANR-47
Obituary 141
Earlier sketch in CA 85-88
Kaplan, Stephen 1940-1995 142
Kaplan, Steven B. 1953- 135
Kaplan, Steven M. 1960- 166
Kaplan, Stuart R(onald) 1932- CANR-21
Earlier sketches in CA 49-52, CANR-2
Kaplan, Sydney Janet 1939- 110
Kaplan, Vivan Jeanette 1946- 238
Kaplan, William 1957- CANR-53
Earlier sketch in CA 126
Kaplan-Mayer, Gabrielle 228
Kaplar, Richard T. 1951- 154
Kapleau, Philip 1912-2004 233
Kapler, Aleksei (Yaklovlevich) 1904(?)-1979
Obituary 89-92
Kaplinski, Jaan 1941- .... DLB 232
See also RGWL 3
Kaplon, Morton F(ischel) 1921- 21-24R
Kaplow, Herb(ert Elias) 1927- 119
Brief entry 110
Interview in CA-119
Kaplow, Jeffry 1937- 17-20R
Kaplow, Louis 1956- 233
Kaplow, Robert 1954- CANR-137
Earlier sketch in CA 138
See also SATA 70
Kapnist, Vasilii Vasil'evich
1758(?)-1823 .... DLB 150
Kapoor, Ashok 1940- 85-88
Kapoor, L(achman) D(as) 1916- 154
Kapoor, Sukhbir Singh 1937- CANR-56
Earlier sketches in CA 109, CANR-29
Kapp, Colin 1928(?)- 132
See also SFW 4
Kapp, K(arl) William 1910-1976 .... CANR-8
Obituary 65-68
Earlier sketch in CA 5-8R
Kapp, Reginald Otto 1885-1966 .... 5-8R
Kapp, Yvonne (Mayer) 1903-1999 103
Obituary 181
Kappauf, William Emil (Jr.) 1913-1983 106
Kappel, Philip 1901-1981 .... CAP-1
Earlier sketch in CA 13-16
Kappelman, Murray M(artin) 1931- 73-76
Kappel-Smith, Diana 1951- 121
See also ANW
Kappen, Charles Vaughan 1910-1999 ..... 9-12R
Kappes, Marcia Ann 1947- 151
Kappes, Sister Marcianne
See Kappes, Marcia Ann
Kapralov, Yuri 223
Kaprow, Allan 1927- 105
Kapsis, Robert E. 1943- 141
Kapsner, Oliver L(eonard) 1902-1991 116
Kapstein, I(srael) J(ames) 1904-1983
Obituary 110
Kaptchuk, Ted J(ack) 1947- CANR-27
Earlier sketch in CA 110
Kapur, Harish 1929- CANR-34
Earlier sketches in CA 85-88, CANR-15
Kapur, L. D.
See Kapoor, L(achman) D(as)
Kapur, Manju 173
Kapur, Rajiv A. 1951- 136
Kapur, Sudarshan 1940- 142
Kapuscinski, Ryszard 1932- 114
Kapusta, Paul
See Bickers, Richard (Leslie) Townshend
Kara, Juro 1940(?)- 191
Karaban, Roslyn A. 1953- 195
Karabell, Zachary 236
Karadzic, Vuk Stefanovic
1787-1864 .... CDWLB 4
See also DLB 147
Karafilly, Irena F. 1944- 171
Karageorge, Michael
See Anderson, Poul (William)
Karageorghis, Vassos 1929- CANR-86
Earlier sketches in CA 81-84, CANR-15, 33
Karam, Jana Abrams 219
Karamanski, Theodore J. 1953- 126
Karamitroglou, Fotios 1971- 202
Karamzin, Nikolai Mikhailovich
1766-1826 .... DLB 150
See also RGSF 2
Karan, Pradyumna P(rasad) 1930- CANR-93
Earlier sketches in CA 114, CANR-35
Karanen, Terry Drew 1955- 178
Karanikas, Alexander 1916- 33-36R
Karanth, Kota Shivaram 1902- .... EWL 3
Karaosmanoglu, Yakup Kadri
1889-1974 .... EWL 3
Karapanou, Margarita 1946- 101
See also CLC 13
Karas, Jim 1949-1981 126
Obituary 108
Karas, Joza 1926- 124
Karas, Phyllis 1944- 105
Karasik, Paul 1956- 232
Karason, Einar 1955- .... DLB 293
Karasu, Toksoz B(yram) 1935- 105
Karasyov, Carrie (Doyle) 1972- 229
Karasz, Ilonka 1896-1981 .... SATA-Obit 29
Karbo, Joe 1925(?)-1980
Obituary 115
Karbo, Karen (Lee) 1956(?)- CANR-99
Earlier sketch in CA 141
Kardiner, Abram 1891-1981 107
Obituary 104
Kardish, Laurence 1945- CANR-30
Earlier sketch in CA 49-52
Kardouche, G(eorge) Khalil 1935- 17-20R
Kardulias, P(aul) Nick 1952- 194
Karel, Leonard 1912-1993 49-52
Karen
See Aldrich, Sandra Picklesimer
Karen, Robert L(e Roy) 1925- 73-76
Karen, Ruth 1922-1987 .... CANR-11
Obituary 123
Earlier sketch in CA 17-20R
See also SATA 9
See also SATA-Obit 54
Karesh, William B. 193
Karetzky, Patricia E(ichenbaum) 1947- 199
Karetzky, Stephen 1946- 211
Karg, Elissa Jane 1951- 21-24R
Karger, Delmar William 1913-2001 .... CANR-8
Earlier sketch in CA 17-20R
Kargon, Robert Hugh 1938- CANR-28
Earlier sketch in CA 45-48
Kari, Daven M(ichael) 1953- 156
Kariel, Henry S. 1924- 13-16R
Karier, Thomas 1956- 148
Karin, Sidney 1943- 126
Karina
See Goud, Anne
Karinthy, Frigyes 1887-1938 170
See also DLB 215
See also EWL 3
See also TCLC 47
Kariuki, Elijah 1956- .... CWRI 5
Kariuki, Josiah Mwangi 1929- 107
See also CP 1
Kark, Nina Mary 1925-
See Bawden, Nina (Mary Mabey)
See also SATA 4, 132
Karkala, John A.
See Alphonso-Karkala, John B.
Karkala, John B. A.
See Alphonso-Karkala, John B.
Karkhanis, Sharad 1935- 110
Karkkainen, Veli-Matti
See Karkkainen, Veli-Matti
Karkkainen, Veli-Matti 212
Karkoschka, Erhard 1923- 45-48
Karl, Barry D(ean) 1927- 102
Karl, Dennis (R.) 1954-1992 134
Obituary 139
Karl, Frederick R(obert)
1927-2004 .... CANR-143
Obituary 226
Earlier sketches in CA 5-8R, CANR-3, 44
See also CLC 34
Karl, Herb 1938- .... SATA 73
Karl, Jean E(dna) 1927-2000 .... CANR-12
Obituary 189
Earlier sketch in CA 29-32R
See also SAAS 10
See also SATA 34, 122
Karl, Roger
See Trouve, Roger
Karlan, Richard 1919- 17-20R
Karle, Hellmut (William Arthur) 1932- 142
Karlen, Arno 1937- CANR-81
Earlier sketches in CA 1-4R, CANR-5
Karlen, Delmar 1912-1988 .... CANR-2
Obituary 127
Earlier sketch in CA 5-8R
Karlen, Neal (Stuart) 1959- 154
Karlfeldt, Erik Axel 1864-1931 185
Karlgren, (Klas) Bernhard (Johannes)
1889-1978 .... CAP-1
Earlier sketch in CA 9-10
Karlin, Bernie 1927- 136
See also SATA 68
Karlin, Daniel 1953- 139
Karlin, Eugene 1918- .... SATA 10
Karlin, Jules 1899-1972 .... CAP-2
Earlier sketch in CA 25-28
Karlin, Muriel S.
See Trachman, Muriel Karlin
Karlin, Nurit .... SATA 63, 103
Karlin, Robert 1918-1998 .... 9-12R
Karlin, Samuel 1924- 148
Karlin, Wayne (Stephen) 1945- 133
Karlins, Marvin 1941-1996 .... CANR-17
Earlier sketch in CA 25-28R
Karlinsky, Simon 1924- .... GLL 2
Karlowich, Robert A. 1927- 125
Karlsberg, Michele 1965- 178
Karlsson, Elis (Viktor) 1905- CAP-1
Earlier sketch in CA 13-16

Cumulative Index 307 Katz

Karlsson, T. Edward 1915(?)-1984
Obituary ... 113
Karma Karen
See Kent, Karen
Karman, James W. 1947- ... 126
Karman, Mal 1944- ... 103
Karmel, Alex 1931- ... 21-24R
Karmel, Annabel 1962(?)- ... 198
Karmel, Ilona 1925-2000 ... DLB 299
Karmel, Roberta S(arah) 1937- ... 108
Karmel-Wolfe, Henia 1923- ... 49-52
Karmen, Roman Lazarevich 1906-1978
Obituary ... 77-80
Karmi, Abdul Karim 1907(?)-1980
Obituary ... 102
Karmi, Ghada 1939- ... 224
Karmi, Hasan Said 1908- ... 45-48
Karmiloff-Smith, Annette Dionne 1938- ... 143
Karmin, Monroe William 1929-1999 ... 101
Obituary ... 173
Karnad, Girish 1938- ... 65-68
See also CD 5, 6
Karnes, Frances A. 1937- ... 180
See also SATA 110
Karnes, Merle B(riggs) 1916- ... 85-88
Karnes, Thomas L(indas) 1914- ... 21-24R
Karney, Beulah Mullen ... 13-16R
Karniewski, Janusz
See Wittlin, Thaddeus (Andrew)
Karno, Bung
See Sukarno, (Ahmed)
Karnos, David D. 1947- ... 141
Karnow, Stanley 1925- ... CANR-64
Earlier sketches in CA 57-60, CANR-31
See also MTCW 1
Karo, Aaron 1979- ... 214
Karodia, Farida 1942- ... CANR-138
Earlier sketch in CA 168
Karol, Alexander
See Kent, Arthur William Charles
Karol, K. S.
See Kewes, Karol
Karolevitz, Bob
See Karolevitz, Robert F.
Karolevitz, Robert F. 1922- ... CANR-22
Earlier sketches in CA 17-20R, CANR-7
Karolides, Nicholas J(ames) 1928- ... 21-24R
Karolyi, Catherine (Andrassy) 1898-1985
Obituary ... 116
Karon, Bertram Paul 1930- ... CANR-7
Earlier sketch in CA 61-64
Karon, Jan ... 204
Karp, Abraham J. 1921- ... CANR-40
Earlier sketches in CA 5-8R, CANR-3, 18
Karp, Alan 1947- ... 107
Karp, Carl 1954- ... 139
Karp, David 1922-1999 ... CANR-1
Obituary ... 185
Earlier sketch in CA 1-4R
See also CN 1, 2, 3
Karp, David A(llen) 1944- ... 235
Karp, Ivan C. 1926- ... 17-20R
Karp, Larry 1939- ... 200
Karp, Laurence E(dward) 1939- ... 77-80
Karp, Lila 1933- ... 25-28R
Karp, Mark 1922-1979 ... 1-4R
Karp, Naomi J. 1926- ... 81-84
See also SATA 16
Karp, Robert J. 1941- ... 151
Karp, Stephen A(rnold) 1928- ... CANR-6
Earlier sketch in CA 1-4R
Karp, Walter 1934(?)-1989
Obituary ... 129
Karpat, Kemal H(asim) 1925- ... CANR-11
Earlier sketch in CA 69-72
Karpatkin, Marvin M. 1926-1975
Obituary ... 53-56
Karpau, Uladzimir
See Karpov, Vladimir
Karpel, Bernard 1911-1986 ... 106
Obituary ... 118
Karpel, Craig S. 1944- ... 65-68
Karpeles, Maud 1885-1976 ... 25-28R
Karpf, Holly W. 1946- ... 37-40R
Karpin, Fred L(eon) 1913-1986 ... CANR-9
Obituary ... 119
Earlier sketch in CA 13-16R
Karpin, Michael ... 237
Karpinski, J. Rick
See Karpinski, John Eric
Karpinski, John Eric 1952- ... SATA 81
Karpinski, Rick
See Karpinski, John Eric
Karplus, Walter J. 1927-2001 ... 21-24R
Obituary ... 200
Karpman, Harold L(ew) 1927- ... 77-80
Karpov, Vladimir 1912(?)-1977
Obituary ... 73-76
Karr, E(arl) R(alph) 1918- ... 1-4R
Karr, Kathleen 1946- ... CANR-106
Earlier sketch in CA 149
See also AAYA 44
See also SATA 82, 127
Karr, Mary 1955- ... CANR-100
Earlier sketch in CA 151
See also AMWS 11
See also CLC 188
See also MTFW 2005
See also NCFS 5
Karr, Phyllis Ann 1944- ... CANR-84
Earlier sketches in CA 101, CANR-18, 40
See also FANT
See also SATA 119
Karras, Alex(ander G.) 1935- ... 107
Karrass, Chester L. 1923- ... 101
Karren, Keith J(ohn) 1943- ... CANR-40
Earlier sketch in CA 116
Karrer, Paul 1889-1971
Obituary ... 113
Karris, Robert J(oseph) 1938- ... CANR-5
Earlier sketch in CA 53-56
Karsavina, Jean (Faterson) 1908-1987 ... 101
Karsavina, Tamara 1885-1978
Obituary ... 77-80
Karsch, Anna Louisa 1722-1791 ... DLB 97
Karsch, Robert F(rederick) 1909-1992 ... 77-80
Karsen, Sonja (Petra) 1919- ... 41-44R
Karsh, Bernard 1921- ... 103
Karsh, Yosuf
See Karsh, Yousuf
Karsh, Yousef
See Karsh, Yousuf
Karsh, Yousuf 1908-2002 ... 33-36R
Obituary ... 207
Karshner, Roger 1928- ... 33-36R
Karst, Kenneth L(eslie) 1929- ... CANR-86
Earlier sketch in CA 132
Karsten, Peter 1938- ... CANR-123
Earlier sketches in CA 37-40R, CANR-13
Karta, Nat
See Fearn, John Russell and
Norwood, Victor G(eorge) C(harles)
Kartiganer, Donald M. 1937- ... 97-100
Karttunen, Frances 1942- ... 138
Karu, Baruch 1899-1972
Obituary ... 104
Karvas, Peter 1920- ... EWL 3
Karve, Dinakar Dhondo 1899-1980 ... 5-8R
Obituary ... 103
Karve, Irawati (Karmarkar) 1905-1970 ... CAP-1
Earlier sketch in CA 19-20
Karwoski, Gail Langer 1949- ... 197
See also SATA 127
Kary, Elizabeth N. 1947- ... 122
See also Witmer-Gow, Karen
Karyotakis, Kostas 1896-1928 ... EWL 3
Kasabov, Nikola K(irilov) 1948- ... CANR-125
Earlier sketch in CA 168
Kasack, Hermann 1896-1966 ... 182
See also DLB 69
Kasai Zenzo 1887-1927 ... DLB 180
Kasarda, John Dale 1945- ... 103
Kaschak, Ellyn 1943- ... 139
Kaschnitz, Marie Luise
See von Kaschnitz-Weinberg, Marie Luise
See also DLB 69
See also EWL 3
Kasdan, Lawrence 1949- ... 109
Interview in ... CA-109
Kasdan, Sara (Moskovitz) 1911-1999 ... 1-4R
Kasdorf, Hans 1928- ... 116
Kasdorf, Julia 1962- ... CANR-128
Earlier sketch in CA 139
Kase, Francis J(oseph) 1910-1995 ... 21-24R
Kaselow, Joseph 1912-1986
Obituary ... 119
Kaser, David 1924- ... 17-20R
Kaser, Michael (Charles) 1926- ... CANR-10
Earlier sketch in CA 17-20R
Kaser, Paul 1944- ... 104
Kasey, Michelle
See Seidick, Kathryn A(melia)
Kash, Don E(ldon) 1934- ... CANR-9
Earlier sketch in CA 21-24R
Kasha, Lawrence N(athan) 1934(?)-1990
Obituary ... 132
Kashdan, Isaac 1905-1985
Obituary ... 115
Kashima, Tetsuden 1940- ... 81-84
Kashiwagi, Isami 1925- ... SATA 10
Kashner, Rita 1942- ... CANR-27
Earlier sketch in CA 105
Kashu, Sayid
See Kashua, Sayed
Kashua, Sayed 1975- ... 232
Kasich, John R. 1952- ... 179
Kasinitz, Philip 1957- ... 137
Kasischke, Laura 1961- ... 154
Kaske, Robert Earl 1921-1989
Obituary ... 129
Kaslow, Florence (Whiteman) 1930- ... CANR-41
Earlier sketches in CA 45-48, CANR-1, 18
Kasparov, G. K.
See Kasparov, Gary (Kimovich)
Kasparov, Gari
See Kasparov, Gary (Kimovich)
Kasparov, Garry
See Kasparov, Gary (Kimovich)
Kasparov, Gary (Kimovich) 1963- ... 139
Kasper, Shirl(ey Elaine) 1948- ... 137
Kasper, Sydney H. 1911- ... 1-4R
Kasper, Walter 1933- ... CANR-83
Earlier sketch in CA 130
Kasper, Wolfgang E. 1939- ... 187
Kasperson, Roger E. 1938- ... 29-32R
Kasrils, Ronald 1938- ... 29-32R
Kass, Edward H(arold) 1917-1990 ... 129
Kass, Jerome 1923(?)-1973
Obituary ... 104
Kass, Jerome 1937- ... 57-60
Kass, Leon R(ichard) 1939- ... 185
Kass, Linda Stern 1953- ... 138
Kass, Norman 1934- ... 29-32R
Kass, Ray 1944- ... 118
Kassak, Lajos 1887-1967 ... DLB 215
See also EWL 3
Kassalow, Everett M(alcolm)
1918-1995 ... CANR-25
Obituary ... 149
Earlier sketch in CA 45-48
Kassam, Yusuf O. 1940- ... CP 1
Kassebaum, Gene G(irard) 1929- ... 17-20R
Kassem, Lou 1931- ... CANR-62
Earlier sketch in CA 128
See also AAYA 58
See also SATA 62
See also SATA-Brief 51
See also WYAS 1
Kasser, Timothy 1966- ... 214
Kassewitz, Jack 1914(?)-1984
Obituary ... 112
Kassim, Husain 1939- ... 189
Kassindja, Fauziya 1977- ... 229
Kassis, Hanna (Emmanuel) 1932- ... 125
Kassler, J. C.
See Kassler, Jamie C(roy)
Kassler, Jamie C(roy) 1938- ... 135
Kassof, Allen 1930- ... 21-24R
Kasson, John F(ranklin) 1944- ... CANR-116
Earlier sketch in CA 81-84
Kassorla, Irene Chamie 1931- ... 110
Kassy, Karen Grace 1964- ... 195
Kast, Fremont E. 1926- ... 21-24R
Kastan, David Scott 1946- ... 109
Kastein, Shulamith 1903-1983 ... 105
Obituary ... 110
Kastel, Warren
See Silverberg, Robert
Kastelan, Jure 1919-1990 ... DLB 147
Kastely, James L. 1947- ... 166
Kastenbaum, Robert (Jay) 1932- ... CANR-9
Earlier sketch in CA 13-16R
Kaster, Joseph 1912-1968(?) ... CAP-1
Earlier sketch in CA 19-20
Kastl, Albert J(oseph) 1939- ... 57-60
Kastl, Lena 1942- ... 61-64
Kastle, Herbert D(avid) 1924-1987 ... CANR-1
Obituary ... 123
Earlier sketch in CA 1-4R
Kastner, Erich
See Kaestner, Erich
See also EWL 3
See also IDFW 4
See also WCH
Kastner, Jill (Marie) 1964- ... SATA 70, 117
Kastner, Jonathan 1937- ... 25-28R
Kastner, Joseph 1907-1997 ... CANR-71
Obituary ... 156
Earlier sketch in CA 85-88
Kastner, Laura 1953- ... 218
Kastner, Marianna 1940- ... 25-28R
Kastner, Patricia Wilson
See Wilson-Kastner, Patricia
Kasulis, T(homas) P(atrick) 1948- ... 124
Kasuya, Masahiro 1937- ... CANR-29
Earlier sketch in CA 110
See also SATA 51
Kasza, Keiko 1951- ... SATA 124
Kaszner, Kurt
See Serwicher, Kurt
Kaszubski, Marek 1951- ... 105
Kaszynski, William 1953- ... 203
Kataev, Evgenii Petrovich
See Kataev, Evgeny Petrovich
Kataev, Evgeny Petrovich 1903-1942
Brief entry ... 120
See also Petrov, Evgenii and
Petrov, Evgeny
Kataev, Valentin Petrovich
1897-1986 ... DLB 272
See also EWL 3
Katagiri, Yasuhiro 1960- ... 227
Katahn, Martin 1928- ... CANR-128
Earlier sketch in CA 114
Katai, Tayama
See Rokuya, Tayama
Katan, Norma-Jean 1936- ... 113
Kataphusin
See Ruskin, John
Katayev, Valentin (Petrovich) 1897-1986 ... 131
Obituary ... 119
Brief entry ... 117
Katcha, Vahe
See Katchadourian, Vahe
Katchadourian, Herant A(ram)
1933- ... CANR-42
Earlier sketches in CA 103, CANR-20
Katchadourian, Vahe 1928- ... CANR-25
Earlier sketch in CA 29-32R
Katchen, Carole 1944- ... 61-64
See also SATA 9
Katchmer, George Andrew 1916-1997 ... 1-4R
Katchor, Ben 1951- ... 182
See also AAYA 54
Kateb, George (Anthony) 1931- ... 123
Brief entry ... 118
Kateb Yacine
See Yacine, Kateb
See also AFW
See also EWL 3
Katen, Thomas Ellis 1931- ... 53-56
Katenin, Pavel Aleksandrovich
1792-1853 ... DLB 205
Kater, Michael H(ans) 1937- ... CANR-123
Earlier sketches in CA 114, CANR-69
Kates, Brian 1946- ... 119
Kates, Carol A. 1943- ... 115
Kates, Gary (Richard) 1952- ... 125
Kates, J(ames George) 1945- ... 200
Kates, Robert W. 1929- ... CANR-24
Earlier sketches in CA 17-20R, CANR-8
Kathman, Michael D(ennis) 1943- ... 109
Kathryn
See Searle, Kathryn Adrienne
Kati
See Rekai, Kati
Katicic, Radoslav 1930- ... 37-40R
Katkov, George 1903-1985
Obituary ... 115
Katkov, Norman 1918- ... 13-16R
Kato, Hidetoshi 1930- ... 115
Kato, Shidzue 1897-2001 ... 211
Kato, Shuichi 1919- ... 37-40R
Kato, Tosio 1917-1999 ... 161
Kato, Tsuyoski 1943- ... CANR-56
Earlier sketch in CA 126
Katona, Edita 1913- ... 69-72
Katona, George 1901-1981 ... 128
Obituary ... 104
Katona, Jozsef 1791-1830
Katona, Robert 1949- ... SATA 21
Katope, Christopher G. 1918- ... 21-24R
Katoppo, (Henriette) Marianne 1943- ... 123
Katouzian, Homa 1942- ... 200
Katrak, Kersy Dady 1936- ... CP 1
Katrovas, Richard 1953- ... CANR-55
Earlier sketch in CA 126
Katsarakis, Joan Harries
See Harries, Joan
Katsaros, Thomas 1926- ... 57-60
Katsh, Abraham I(saac) 1908(?)-1998 ... CANR-8
Obituary ... 169
Earlier sketch in CA 5-8R
Katsh, M. Ethan 1945- ... 133
Katsh, Salem M(ichael) 1948- ... 110
Kattan, Naim 1928- ... CANR-44
Earlier sketches in CA 69-72, CANR-11
See also DLB 53
Katterjohn, Arthur D. 1930(?)-1980
Obituary ... 93-96
Katz, Abraham 1926- ... 49-52
Katz, Albert M(ichael) 1938- ... 93-96
Katz, Alfred
See Allan, Alfred K.
Katz, Alfred 1938- ... 77-80
Katz, Arthur M. 1942- ... 124
Katz, Avner 1939- ... 170
See also SATA 103
Katz, Barbara 1956- ... 142
Katz, Basho
See Gatti, Arthur Gerard
Katz, Benjamin 1904-1985
Obituary ... 115
Katz, Bernard S. 1932- ... 175
Katz, Bobbi 1933- ... CANR-123
Earlier sketches in CA 37-40R, CANR-16, 37
See also SATA 12
Katz, Carol 1939- ... 115
Katz, Daniel 1903-1998 ... 41-44R
Obituary ... 166
Katz, David 1953- ... 203
Katz, Elia (Jacob) 1948- ... 151
Katz, Elias 1912- ... 29-32R
Katz, Ellis 1938- ... 29-32R
Katz, Eve 1938- ... CANR-1
Earlier sketch in CA 45-48
Katz, Fred(eric Phillip) 1938- ... 49-52
See also SATA 6
Katz, Fred E(mil) 1927- ... 77-80
Katz, Friedrich 1927- ... CANR-90
Brief entry ... 113
Earlier sketch in CA 134
Katz, Gloria 1945(?)- ... 107
Katz, Herbert Melvin 1930- ... 103
Katz, Irving I. 1907-1979 ... 1-4R
Katz, Jack 1944- ... CANR-127
Earlier sketch in CA 111
Katz, Jacob 1904-1998 ... CANR-4
Obituary ... 169
Earlier sketch in CA 1-4R
Katz, James Everett 1948- ... 204
Katz, Jane B(resler) 1934- ... 85-88
See also SATA 33
Katz, Jay 1922- ... 118
Katz, Jerrold J. 1932-2002 ... 212
Katz, John Stuart 1938- ... CANR-14
Earlier sketch in CA 37-40R
Katz, Jon ... CANR-135
Earlier sketch in CA 165
See also AAYA 43
Katz, Jonathan Ned 1938- ... CANR-112
Earlier sketch in CA 85-88
Katz, Josef 1918- ... 53-56
Katz, Joseph 1910- ... CANR-2
Earlier sketch in CA 1-4R
Katz, Judith 1951- ... 139
Katz, Judith Milstein 1943- ... 106
Katz, Karen 1947- ... SATA 158
Katz, Lawrence S(anford) 1947- ... 154
Katz, Leon 1919- ... CANR-20
Earlier sketches in CA 49-52, CANR-4
Katz, Leonard 1926- ... 21-24R
Katz, Lewis R(obert) 1938- ... CANR-96
Earlier sketches in CA 116, CANR-46
Katz, Lilian G(onshaw) 1932- ... 111
Katz, Marjorie P.
See Weiser, Marjorie P(hillis) K(atz)
Katz, Marshall P. 1939- ... 153
Katz, Martin 1929- ... 21-24R
Katz, Marvin C(harles) 1930- ... 25-28R
Katz, Menke 1906-1991 ... CANR-11
Obituary ... 134
Earlier sketch in CA 13-16R
Interview in ... CANR-11
See also CAAS 9
Katz, Michael B(arry) 1939- ... CANR-48
Earlier sketches in CA 33-36R, CANR-13
Katz, Michael J(ay) 1950- ... 205
Katz, Michael M. 1956(?)-1988
Obituary ... 126
Katz, Michael Ray 1944- ... CANR-39
Earlier sketches in CA 102, CANR-18
Katz, Mickey
See Katz, Myron Meyer

Katz, Milton 1907-1995 .... CAP-1
Obituary 149
Earlier sketch in CA 11-12
Katz, Molly 170
Katz, Mort 1925- CANR-11
Earlier sketch in CA 61-64
Katz, Myron Meyer 1909-1985 81-84
Obituary 116
Katz, Ralph 1944- CANR-139
Earlier sketch in CA 173
Katz, Richard Stephen 1947- 175
Katz, Robert 1933- CANR-11
Earlier sketch in CA 25-28R
Katz, Robert L. 1917- 9-12R
Katz, Samuel 1914- CANR-12
Earlier sketch in CA 25-28R
Katz, Samuel M. 1963- 239
Katz, Sanford N. 1933-2005 .... CANR-13
Earlier sketch in CA 33-36R
Katz, Shmuel
See Katz, Samuel
Katz, Stan
See Chapman, Frank M(onroe)
Katz, Stanley Nider 1934- 9-12R
Katz, Steve 1935- CANR-12
Earlier sketch in CA 25-28R
See also CAAS 14, 64
See also CLC 47
See also CN 4, 5, 6, 7
See also DLBY 1983
Katz, Steven T(heodore) 1944- CANR-95
Earlier sketch in CA 132
Katz, Susan 1944(?)-1982
Obituary 107
Katz, Susan 1945- 231
See also SATA 156
Katz, Vincent 1960- 179
Katz, Welwyn Wilton 1948- CANR-127
Earlier sketch in CA 154
See also AAYA 19
See also CLR 45
See also JRDA
See also MAICYA 2
See also MAICYAS 1
See also SATA 62, 96
See also SATA-Essay 118
See also YAW
Katz, William 1940- 85-88
See also SATA 98
Katz, William A(rmstrong)
1924-2004 .... CANR-10
Obituary 232
Earlier sketch in CA 25-28R
Katz, William Loren 1927- CANR-130
Earlier sketches in CA 21-24R, CANR-9
See also SATA 13
Katzander, Howard L. 1911(?)-1983
Obituary 110
Katzen, Halbert 206
Katzen, Mollie 1950- 165
Katzenbach, John 1950- CANR-127
Earlier sketch in CA 119
Katzenbach, Jon R. 1932- 211
Katzenbach, Maria 1953- 77-80
Katzenbach, William E. 1904-1975
Obituary 61-64
Katzenelson, Yitzhak 1886-1944
Katzenstein, Mary Fainsod 1945- 93-96
Katzenstein, Peter J(oachim) 1945- ... CANR-17
Earlier sketch in CA 93-96
Ka-Tzetnik 135633 1917-2001 .... CANR-27
Obituary 198
Earlier sketch in CA 29-32R
See also DLB 299
Katzman, Allen 1937- CANR-43
Earlier sketch in CA 29-32R
Katzman, Anita 1920- 57-60
Katzman, David Manners 1941- CANR-5
Earlier sketch in CA 53-56
Katzman, Martin T(heodore) 1941- 111
Katzman, Melanie A. 1958- 151
Katznelson-Shazar, Rachel 1888-1975
Obituary 61-64
Katzner, Kenneth 1930-2003 .... 5-8R
Obituary 217
Kau, Michael Y. M.
See Kau, Ying-Mao
Kau, Ying-Mao 1934- 185
Brief entry 114
Kauder, Emil 1901-1982 .... 17-20R
Kaufelt, David Allan 1939- CANR-71
Earlier sketches in CA 45-48, CANR-1, 16, 38
Kauffeld, Carl F. 1911-1974
Obituary 49-52
Kauffman, Bill 1959- CANR-141
Earlier sketch in CA 156
Kauffman, Christmas Carol 1902-1969 ..... 1-4R
Kauffman, Christopher J. 1936- 107
Kauffman, Donald T(homas) 1920- ... CANR-11
Earlier sketch in CA 25-28R
Kauffman, Donna 1960(?)- 226
Kauffman, Dorotha S(trayer)
1925-1991 .... 17-20R
Kauffman, Draper L. 1946- 108
Kauffman, George B(ernard) 1930- 17-20R
Kauffman, Henry J. 1908-2001 .... 13-16R
Kauffman, J. Howard 1919- 145
Kauffman, James M(ilton) 1940- CANR-7
Earlier sketch in CA 57-60
Kauffman, Janet 1945- CANR-84
Earlier sketches in CA 117, CANR-43
See also CLC 42
See also DLB 218
See also DLBY 1986
Kauffman, Janet King 1935- 185
See also King, Janet Kauffman
Kauffman, Joseph F(rank) 1921- CANR-1
Earlier sketch in CA 45-48
Kauffman, Milo (Franklin) 1898-1988 89-92
Kauffman, Stanley L.
See Kaufman, Lloyd
Kauffman, Stuart Alan 1939- CANR-100
Earlier sketch in CA 153
Kauffmann, C. Michael 1931- 125
Kauffmann, Georg (Friedrich) 1925- 49-52
Kauffmann, Jean-Paul 1944- 238
Kauffmann, Lane 1921-1988 .... 17-20R
Obituary 125
Kauffmann, Samuel Hay 1898-1971 178
Obituary 89-92
See also DLB 127
Kauffmann, Stanley 1916- CANR-107
Earlier sketches in CA 5-8R, CANR-6
Interview in CANR-6
Kaufman, Alan 1952- CANR-96
Earlier sketch in CA 128
Kaufman, Arnold S. 1927- 25-28R
Kaufman, Arthur 1934- CANR-25
Earlier sketch in CA 107
Kaufman, Barry Neil 1942- CANR-17
Earlier sketch in CA 97-100
Kaufman, Bel CANR-13
Earlier sketch in CA 13-16R
See also AAYA 4, 65
See also SATA 57
Kaufman, Bob (Garnell) 1925-1986 . CANR-22
Obituary 118
Earlier sketch in CA 41-44R
See also BG 1:3
See also BW 1
See also CLC 49
See also CP 1
See also DLB 16, 41
Kaufman, Boris 1906-1980 .... IDFW 3, 4
Kaufman, Burton I. 1940- 33-36R
Kaufman, Charlie 1958- 206
Kaufman, Daniel 1949- 85-88
Kaufman, David 222
Kaufman, Debra Renee 1941- 109
Kaufman, Donald D(avid) 1933- 29-32R
Kaufman, Edmund George 1891-1980 73-76
Kaufman, George S. 1889-1961 108
Obituary 93-96
Interview in CA-108
See also CLC 38
See also DAM DRAM
See also DC 17
See also DFS 1, 10
See also DLB 7
See also MTCW 2
See also MTFW 2005
See also RGAL 4
See also TUS
Kaufman, Gerald (Bernard) 1930- 21-24R
Kaufman, Gershen 1943- 117
Kaufman, Gloria Joan Frances (Shapiro)
1929- CANR-103
Earlier sketches in CA 122, CANR-47
Kaufman, Gordon Dester 1925- CANR-7
Earlier sketch in CA 13-16R
Kaufman, H(arold) G(erson) 1939- 69-72
Kaufman, Herbert 1922- 137
Brief entry 115
Kaufman, I(sadore) 1892-1978
Obituary 77-80
Kaufman, Irving 1920- 21-24R
Kaufman, J. B. 171
Kaufman, Jacob J(oseph) 1914- 41-44R
Kaufman, Jason Andrew 1970- 220
Kaufman, Jeff 1955- .... SATA 84
Kaufman, Joe 1911-2001 107
See also SATA 33
Kaufman, Joseph
See Kaufman, Joe
Kaufman, Kenn 1956(?)- 170
Kaufman, Lloyd 1927- 93-96
Kaufman, Lloyd 1945- 207
Kaufman, Lynne 225
Kaufman, Martin 1940- CANR-54
Earlier sketches in CA 109, CANR-28
Kaufman, Menahem 1921- 138
Kaufman, Mervyn D. 1932- 5-8R
See also SATA 4
Kaufman, Miriam 1954- 222
Kaufman, Moises 1964- 211
See also DC 26
See also DFS 22
See also MTFW 2005
Kaufman, Pamela 237
Kaufman, Paul 1886-1979
Obituary 89-92
Kaufman, Paula T. 1946- 126
Kaufman, Philip 1936- 121
Brief entry 112
Kaufman, Polly W(elts) 1929- 114
Kaufman, Robert 1931- CANR-25
Earlier sketch in CA 17-20R
Kaufman, Roger (Alexander) 1932- CANR-9
Earlier sketch in CA 53-56
Kaufman, Rosamond (Arleen) V(an) P(oznak)
1923- CANR-7
Earlier sketch in CA 9-12R
Kaufman, Sherwin A. 1920- CANR-10
Earlier sketch in CA 25-28R
Kaufman, Shirley 1923- CANR-143
Earlier sketches in CA 49-52, CANR-73
See also CWP
Kaufman, Sidney 1910-1983
Obituary 110
Kaufman, Stuart Bruce 1942-1997 ... CANR-50
Obituary 156
Earlier sketch in CA 123
Kaufman, Sue
See Barondess, Sue K(aufman)
See also CLC 3, 8
Kaufman, Victor S(cott) 1969- 226
Kaufman, Wallace 1939- CANR-100
Earlier sketches in CA 25-28R, CANR-10, 46
Kaufman, Will 1958- 172
Kaufman, William I(rving)
1922-1995 .... CANR-24
Obituary 149
Earlier sketches in CA 13-16R, CANR-7
Kaufman, Wolfe 1905(?)-1970
Obituary 29-32R
Kaufmann, Angelika 1935- .... SATA 15
Kaufmann, David
See Kaufmann, Dovid Yisroel Ber
Kaufmann, Dovid Y. B.
See Kaufmann, Dovid Yisroel Ber
Kaufmann, Dovid Yisroel Ber 1951- 175
Kaufmann, Edgar, Jr. 1910-1989
Obituary 129
Kaufmann, Harry 1927- 45-48
Kaufmann, Helen L(oeb) 1887-1978 .. CANR-7
Earlier sketch in CA 5-8R
Kaufmann, Henry William 1913-1982 .. 41-44R
Kaufmann, John 1931- 81-84
See also SATA 18
Kaufmann, Myron S. 1921- 25-28R
Kaufmann, R(alph) James 1924- 13-16R
Kaufmann, Thomas DaCosta 1948- 129
Kaufmann, U(rlin) Milo 1934- 41-44R
Kaufmann, Ulrich George 1920- 21-24R
Kaufmann, Walter 1921-1980 .... CANR-1
Obituary 101
Earlier sketch in CA 1-4R
See also DLB 279
Kaufmann, Walter 1933- 61-64
Kaufmann, William J(ohn) III 1942- 93-96
Kaufmann, William W. 1918- 13-16R
Kaufman-Osborn, Timothy V. 1953- 233
Kaul, Donald 1934- 65-68
Kaul, Suvir 1955- 190
Kaula, Edna Mason 1906-1987 .... 5-8R
See also SATA 13
Kaumeyer, Dorothy
See Lamour, Dorothy
Kaumeyer, Mary Leta Dorothy
See Lamour, Dorothy
Kaunda, K. D.
See Kaunda, Kenneth David
Kaunda, Kenneth
See Kaunda, Kenneth David
Kaunda, Kenneth D.
See Kaunda, Kenneth David
Kaunda, Kenneth David 1924- 133
Kauper, Paul Gerhardt 1907-1974 ...... CANR-6
Obituary 49-52
Earlier sketch in CA 1-4R
Kaur, Sardarni Premka 1943- 77-80
Kaurismaki, Aki 1957- 140
Kaur Khalsa, Dayal
Obituary 129
See also Khalsa, Dayal Kaur
Kaus, Mickey 1951- 142
Kausler, Donald H(arvey) 1927- 17-20R
Kauth, Benjamin 1914- 5-8R
Kautsky, Karl (Johann) 1854-1938
Brief entry 123
Kauvar, Gerald B(luestone) 1938- 45-48
Kava, Alex 214
Kava, Sharon
See Kava, Alex
Kavafis, Konstantinos Petrou 1863-1933
Brief entry 104
See also Cavafy, C(onstantine) P(eter)
Kavaler, Lucy 1930- CANR-48
Earlier sketches in CA 57-60, CANR-7, 22
See also SATA 23
Kavaler, Rebecca 1932- CANR-16
Earlier sketch in CA 89-92
Kavan, Anna 1901-1968 .... CANR-57
Earlier sketches in CA 5-8R, CANR-6
See also BRWS 7
See also CLC 5, 13, 82
See also DLB 255
See also MTCW 1
See also RGEL 2
See also SFW 4
Kavanagh, Aidan 1929- 112
Kavanagh, Dan
See Barnes, Julian (Patrick)
Kavanagh, Dan(iel) 1946- 125
Kavanagh, Ed 1954- 210
Kavanagh, Jack 1920- 151
See also SATA 85
Kavanagh, James H. 1948- 126
Kavanagh, Jennifer 1947- 119
Kavanagh, Julie 1952- 163
See also CLC 119
Kavanagh, Michael 1945- 118
Kavanagh, P(atrick) J(oseph Gregory)
1931- CANR-45
Earlier sketch in CA 81-84
See also CP 1, 2, 3, 4, 5, 6, 7
See also DLB 40
See also SATA 122
Kavanagh, Patrick (Joseph) 1904-1967 123
Obituary 25-28R
See also BRWS 7
See also CLC 22
See also DLB 15, 20
See also EWL 3
See also MTCW 1
See also PC 33
See also RGEL 2
Kavanagh, Paul
See Block, Lawrence
Kavanagh, Peter 1916- CANR-93
Earlier sketch in CA 132
Kavanaugh, Andrea L(ee) 1951- 165
Kavanaugh, Cynthia
See Daniels, Dorothy
Kavanaugh, Ian
See Webb, Jean Francis (III)
Kavanaugh, James J(oseph) 1934- ... CANR-142
Earlier sketches in CA 13-16R, CANR-17, 38
Kavanaugh, John F(rancis) 1941- 115
Kavanaugh, Kieran 1928- 25-28R
Kavanaugh, Robert E. 1926- 29-32R
Kavasch, E(lizabeth) Barrie 1942- ... CANR-130
Earlier sketch in CA 110
Kavenagh, W(illiam) Keith 1926- 37-40R
Kaverin, Veniamin Aleksandrovich
1902-1989 .... DLB 272
See also EWL 3
Kavesh, Robert A(llyn) 1927- 17-20R
Kavet, Robert 1924- 37-40R
Kavieff, Paul R. 1947- 207
Kavifis, Konstantinos Petrou
See Kavafis, Konstantinos Petrou
Kavli, Guthorm 1917- CAP-1
Earlier sketch in CA 9-10
Kavner, Richard S. 1936- 93-96
Kavolis, Vytautas 1930- 25-28R
Kawabata, Yasunari 1899-1972 .... CANR-88
Obituary 33-36R
Earlier sketch in CA 93-96
See also Kawabata Yasunari
See also CLC 2, 5, 9, 18, 107
See also DAM MULT
See also MJW
See also MTCW 2
See also MTFW 2005
See also RGSF 2
See also RGWL 2, 3
See also SSC 17
Kawabata Yasunari
See Kawabata, Yasunari
See also DLB 180
See also EWL 3
Kawahito, Kiyoshi 1939- 37-40R
Kawai, Kazuo 1904-1963 .... 1-4R
Kawa-Jump, Shirley
See Jump, Shirley
Kawakami, Barbara Fusako 1921- CANR-95
Earlier sketch in CA 146
Kawakami, Tovo S(uvemoto)
1916-2003 .... 33-36R
Obituary 223
Kawamura, Susumu 1929- 203
Kawatski, Deanna 1951- CANR-92
Earlier sketch in CA 146
Kawin, Bruce F. 1945- CANR-13
Earlier sketch in CA 37-40R
Kawin, Ethel (?)-1969 .... CAP-1
Earlier sketch in CA 11-12
Kay, Alan N. 1965- 217
See also SATA 144
Kay, Barbara Ann 1929- 13-16R
Kay, Brian Ross 1924- 1-4R
Kay, David A(llen) 1940- 154
Brief entry 114
Kay, Donald 1939- 57-60
Kay, E(lizabeth) Alison 1928- 65-68
Kay, Ellen
See DeMille, Nelson (Richard)
Kay, Ernest 1915-1994 .... CANR-24
Earlier sketches in CA 13-16R, CANR-6
Kay, George
See Lambert, Eric
Kay, George 1924- .... CP 1
Kay, George 1936- 21-24R
Kay, Guy Gavriel 1954- CANR-85
Earlier sketch in CA 134
See also AAYA 36
See also DLB 251
See also FANT
See also SATA 121
See also SUFW 2
Kay, Harry 1919- 25-28R
Kay, Helen
See Goldfrank, Helen Colodny
Kay, J(ohn) A(nderson) 1948- 119
Kay, Jackie
See Kay, Jacqueline Margaret
See also CN 7
See also WLIT 4
Kay, Jacqueline Margaret 1961- CANR-83
Earlier sketch in CA 153
See also Kay, Jackie
See also CP 7
See also CWP
See also SATA 97
Kay, Jane Holtz 1938- CANR-73
Earlier sketches in CA 106, CANR-22
Kay, Jeremy 1942- 156
Kay, Kenneth (Edmond) 1915- CANR-6
Earlier sketch in CA 9-12R
Kay, Mara CANR-2
Earlier sketch in CA 5-8R
See also SATA 13
Kay, Mary
See Ash, Mary Kay (Wagner)
Kay, Norman (Forber) 1929-2001 45-48
Obituary 197
Kay, (Sydney Francis) Patrick (Chippendall) Healey
See Healey-Kay, (Sydney Francis) Patrick (Chippendall)
Kay, Paul 1934- 41-44R
Kay, Reed 1925- 77-80
Kay, Ronald
See Knox-Mawer, Ronald

Cumulative Index 309 **Keen**

Kay, Susan 1952- ... CANR-98
Earlier sketch in CA 144
See also HGG
Kay, Terence 1918-1999 ... 17-20R
Kay, Teresa
See de Kerpely, Theresa
Kay, Terry
See Kay, Terence
Kay, Terry (Winter) 1938- ... 110
See also CSW
Kay, Thomas O(bed) 1932- ... 1-4R
Kay, Verla 1946- ... 191
See also SATA 120
Kay, (Albert) William 1930-1976 ... CAP-2
Earlier sketch in CA 29-32
Kay, Zell
See Kemp, Roy Z(ell)
Kayal, Joseph M(itchell) 1942- ... 57-60
Kayal, Philip M(itchell) 1943- ... 57-60
Kayden, Xandra 1939- ... 127
Kaye, Alan
See Horowitz, Shel Alan
Kaye, Barbara
See Muir, Marie
Kaye, Bruce (Norman) 1939- ... 93-96
Kaye, Buddy 1918-2002 ... 81-84
Obituary ... 210
Kaye, Danny 1913-1987
Obituary ... 121
See also SATA-Obit 50
Kaye, Elizabeth 1945- ... 152
Kaye, Evelyn 1937- ... CANR-98
Earlier sketch in CA 57-60
Kaye, Geraldine (Hughesdon)
1925- ... CANR-84
Earlier sketches in CA 13-16R, CANR-7, 22, 46
See also CWRI 5
See also SATA 10, 85
Kaye, H. R.
See Knox, Hugh (Randolph)
Kaye, Harvey E(arle) 1927- ... 101
Kaye, Harvey J(ordan) 1949- ... CANR-98
Earlier sketches in CA 121, CANR-47
Kaye, Hilary 1950- ... 116
Kaye, Howard L. 1951- ... 126
Kaye, Joanne
See Payes, Rachel (Ruth) C(osgrove)
Kaye, Judy
See Baer, Judy
Kaye, Julian B(ertram) 1925-1982 ... 1-4R
Kaye, Kenneth Peter 1946- ... 111
Kaye, Lenny 1946- ... 188
Brief entry ... 121
Kaye, M(ary) M(argaret)
1908-2004 ... CANR-142
Obituary ... 223
Earlier sketches in CA 89-92, CANR-24, 60, 102
See also CLC 28
See also MTCW 1, 2
See also MTFW 2005
See also RHW
See also SATA 62
See also SATA-Obit 152
Kaye, Marie
See Garner, Sharon K.
Kaye, Marilyn 1949- ... CANR-104
Earlier sketches in CA 107, CANR-24, 49
See also SATA 56, 110
Kaye, Marvin (Nathan) 1938- ... CANR-99
Earlier sketches in CA 53-56, CANR-5, 19, 41
See also HGG
Kaye, Melanie
See Kaye-Kantrowitz, Melanie
Kaye, Mollie
See Kaye, M(ary) M(argaret)
Kaye, Myrna 1930- ... 57-60
Kaye, Peggy 1948- ... 216
Earlier sketch in CA 116
See also SATA 143
Kaye, Philip A. 1920- ... 37-40R
Kaye, Phyllis Johnson ... 102
Kaye-Kantrowitz, Melanie 1945- ... 141
Kaye-Smith, Sheila 1887-1956 ... 203
Brief entry ... 118
See also DLB 36
See also TCLC 20
Kayira, Legson Didimu 1942- ... 17-20R
See also BW 1
Kaymor, Patrice Maguilene
See Senghor, Leopold Sedar
Kaynak, Erdener 1947- ... CANR-103
Earlier sketch in CA 149
Kays, Scott A. 1960- ... 204
Kaysen, Carl 1920- ... CANR-11
Earlier sketch in CA 17-20R
Kaysen, Susanna 1948- ... CANR-99
Earlier sketch in CA 144
See also AAYA 42
Kayser, Elmer Louis 1896-1985 ... 37-40R
Obituary ... 116
Kayser, Hugh F. 1926- ... 107
Kayser-Jones, Jeanie Schmit 1935- ... 105
Kaysing, Bill
See Kaysing, William C.
Kaysing, William C. 1922-2005 ... 33-36R
Obituary ... 239
Kayyali, Abdul-Wahhab (Said) 1939-1981
Obituary ... 108
Kaza, Stephanie 1947- ... 201
Kazakov, Iurii Pavlovich
See Kazakov, Yuri Pavlovich
See also DLB 302
Kazakov, Yuri Pavlovich 1927-1982 ... CANR-36
Earlier sketch in CA 5-8R
See also Kazakov, Iurii Pavlovich and Kazakov, Yury
See also MTCW 1
See also RGSF 2
See also SSC 43
Kazakov, Yury
See Kazakov, Yuri Pavlovich
See also EWL 3
Kazamias, Andreas M. 1927- ... 17-20R
Kazan, Elia 1909-2003 ... CANR-78
Obituary ... 220
Earlier sketches in CA 21-24R, CANR-32
See also CLC 6, 16, 63
Kazan, Frances 1946- ... 125
Kazantzakis, Nikos 1883(?)-1957 ... 132
Brief entry ... 105
See also BPFB 2
See also DA3
See also EW 9
See also EWL 3
See also MTCW 1, 2
See also MTFW 2005
See also RGWL 2, 3
See also TCLC 2, 5, 33
Kazantzis, Judith 1940- ... CANR-140
Earlier sketch in CA 144
See also CP 7
See also CWP
Kazarian, Edward A(rshak) 1931- ... 53-56
Kazdin, Alan E(dward) 1945- ... 104
Kazee, Buell H(ilton) 1900-1976
Obituary ... 111
Kazemzadeh, Firuz 1924- ... 21-24R
Kazhdan, Alexander P(etrovich)
1922-1997 ... 138
Obituary ... 158
Kazickas, Jurate C(atherine) 1943- ... 102
Kazimiroff, Theodore L. 1941- ... 109
See also BYA 7
Kazin, Alfred 1915-1998 ... CANR-79
Earlier sketches in CA 1-4R, CANR-1, 45
See also CAAS 7
See also AMWS 8
See also CLC 34, 38, 119
See also DLB 67
See also EWL 3
Kazin, Michael 1948- ... CANR-98
Earlier sketch in CA 127
Kazis, Richard 1952- ... 112
Kazmer, Daniel (Raphael) 1947- ... 102
Kazmier, Leonard J(ohn) 1930- ... 107
Kazziha, Walid W. 1941- ... 65-68
Keach, James 1948- ... 206
Keach, James P. 1950- ... SATA 125
Keach, Richard L(eroy) 1919- ... 89-92
Keady, Walter 1934- ... 172
Keahey, John ... 216
Kealey, Edward J(oseph) 1936- ... CANR-14
Earlier sketch in CA 37-40R
Kealy, Sean P(atrick) 1937- ... CANR-94
Earlier sketch in CA 114
Keams, Geri 1951- ... 189
See also SATA 117
Kean, Benjamin Harrison 1912-1993 ... 103
Obituary ... 142
Kean, Charles Duell 1910-1963 ... 5-8R
Kean, Edmund (Stanley) 1915- ... 102
Kean, Jack
See Keenan, Gerald
Kean, Rob ... 230
Keane, Betty Winkler 1914-2002 ... 93-96
Keane, Bil 1922- ... CANR-13
Earlier sketch in CA 33-36R
See also SATA 4
Keane, Ellsworth McGranahan 1927- ... CP 1
Keane, John 1949- ... CANR-94
Earlier sketch in CA 148
Keane, John B(rendan) 1928-2002 ... CANR-84
Obituary ... 205
Earlier sketches in CA 29-32R, CANR-42
See also CBD
See also CD 5, 6
See also DLB 13
Keane, Marc P(eter) 1958- ... 221
Keane, Mary Nesta (Skrine) 1904-1996 ... 114
Obituary ... 151
Brief entry ... 108
See also Keane, Molly
See also RHW
Keane, Molly
Interview in ... CA-114
See also Keane, Mary Nesta (Skrine)
See also CLC 31
See also CN 5, 6
See also TCLE 1:1
Keane, Noel 1938-1997 ... 133
Keane, Patrick J(oseph) 1939- ... CANR-1
Earlier sketch in CA 45-48
Keane, Robert N. 1933- ... 236
Keaney, Brian 1954- ... 176
See also SATA 106
Keaney, Marian 1944- ... 103
Kearey, Charles 1916- ... 45-48
Kearley, F(loyd) Furman 1932- ... 57-60
Kearney, Hugh Francis 1924- ... 5-8R
Kearney, James R(obert III) 1929- ... 25-28R
Kearney, Jean Nylander 1923- ... 65-68
Kearney, Lawrence 1948- ... 210
Kearney, Milo 1938- ... 195
Kearney, Paul 1967- ... FANT
Kearney, Robert N(orman) 1930- ... 81-84
Kearney, Robert P. ... 171
Kearney, Ruth Elizabeth
See Carlson, Ruth (Elizabeth) Kearney
Kearns, Doris Helen
See Goodwin, Doris (Helen) Kearns
Kearns, Francis E(dward) 1931- ... 29-32R
Kearns, Frank 1917(?)-1986
Obituary ... 119
Kearns, Frank T. 1903-1984
Obituary ... 111
Kearns, James A(loysius) III 1949- ... 29-32R
Kearns, Josie 1954- ... 208
Kearns, Lionel 1937- ... CANR-11
Earlier sketch in CA 17-20R
See also CP 1, 2
Kearns, Martha 1945- ... 57-60
Kearns, Michael S. 1947- ... 126
Kearns, Sheila M. 1955- ... 156
Kearny, Edward N. III 1936- ... 29-32R
Kearny, Jillian
See Goulart, Ron(ald Joseph)
Kearse, Amalya (Lyle) 1937- ... 155
See also BW 3
Kearsley, Edward
See Mitchell, S(ilas) Weir
Keary, Annie 1825-1879 ... DLB 163
Keary, Eliza (Harriet) 1827-1918 ... 201
See also DLB 240
Keasey, Carol Tomlinson
See Tomlinson-Keasey, Carol
Keast, James D. 1930- ... 25-28R
Keast, William R(ea) 1914-1998 ... 13-16R
Keates, Jonathan 1946(?)- ... CANR-126
Earlier sketch in CA 163
See also CLC 34
Keating, AnaLouise 1961- ... 162
Keating, Ann Durkin 1957- ... 238
Keating, AnnLouise
See Keating, AnaLouise
Keating, Bern
See Keating, Leo Bernard
Keating, Charlotte Matthews 1927- ... 33-36R
Keating, Diane (Margaret) 1940- ... CANR-137
Earlier sketches in CA 101, CANR-18
Keating, Edward M. 1925-2003 ... 13-16R
Obituary ... 215
Keating, Frank 1944- ... 216
See also SATA 143
Keating, H(enry) R(eymond) F(itzwalter)
1926- ... CANR-117
Earlier sketches in CA 33-36R, CANR-18, 34, 64
Interview in ... CANR-18
See also CAAS 8
See also CMW 4
See also DLB 87
See also MSW
See also MTCW 1
Keating, John J. 1918(?)-1975
Obituary ... 61-64
Keating, L(ouis) Clark 1907-1991 ... 21-24R
Keating, Lawrence A. 1903-1966 ... 5-8R
See also SATA 23
Keating, Leo Bernard 1915- ... 29-32R
See also SATA 10
Keating, Michael (F.) 1932- ... 49-52
Keating, Michael (Irvine) 1943- ... CANR-64
Earlier sketch in CA 129
Keating, Micheline 1904(?)-1989
Obituary ... 127
Keating, Tom 1917-1984
Obituary ... 112
Keatley, Charlotte 1960- ... CBD
See also CD 5, 6
See also CWD
See also DLB 245
Keaton, Buster 1895-1966 ... 194
See also CLC 20
Keats, Charles B. 1905-1978 ... CAP-1
Earlier sketch in CA 13-16
Keats, Emma 1899(?)-1979(?) ... 135
See also SATA 68
Keats, Ezra Jack 1916-1983 ... CANR-85
Obituary ... 109
Earlier sketch in CA 77-80
See also AITN 1
See also CLR 1, 35
See also CWRI 5
See also DLB 61
See also MAICYA 1, 2
See also SATA 14, 57
See also SATA-Obit 34
Keats, John 1795-1821 ... AAYA 58
See also BRW 4
See also BRWR 1
See also CDBLB 1789-1832
See also DA
See also DA3
See also DAB
See also DAC
See also DAM MST, POET
See also DLB 96, 110
See also EXPP
See also LMFS 1
See also PAB
See also PC 1
See also PFS 1, 2, 3, 9, 17
See also RGEL 2
See also TEA
See also WLC
See also WLIT 3
See also WP
Keats, John C(hesswell) 1920-2000 ... 73-76
Obituary ... 192
Keats, Mark 1905-1980 ... 77-80
Keaveney, Arthur 1951- ... 124
Keaveney, Sydney Starr 1939- ... 53-56
Keay, Frederick 1915- ... 33-36R
Keay, John (Stanley Melville) 1941- ... CANR-93
Earlier sketch in CA 65-68
Kebbe, Charles Maynard 1913-2000 ... 114
Kebin, Jodi
See Lawrence, Jodi
Keble, John 1792-1866 ... DLB 32, 55
See also RGEL 2
Kebschull, Harvey G(ustav) 1932- ... 41-44R
Keck, Leander Earl 1928- ... 104
Keckley, Elizabeth 1818(?)-1907 ... 216
See also DLB 239
Keddell, Georgina (Murray) 1913- ... 25-28R
Keddie, Nikki R(agozin) 1930- ... CANR-56
Earlier sketches in CA 25-28R, CANR-13
Kedgley, Susan (Jane) 1948- ... 61-64
Kedourie, Elie 1926-1992 ... CANR-31
Obituary ... 139
Earlier sketches in CA 21-24R, CANR-10
Kedzie, Daniel Peter 1930- ... 17-20R
Kee, (Alexander) Alistair 1937- ... 89-92
Kee, Howard Clark 1920- ... CANR-10
Earlier sketch in CA 21-24R
Kee, Robert 1919- ... CANR-96
Brief entry ... 113
Earlier sketch in CA 130
Kee, Thuan Chye 1954- ... 230
See also CD 5, 6
Keeble, John 1944- ... CANR-14
Earlier sketch in CA 29-32R
See also CCA 1
See also DLBY 1983
Keeble, Neil H(oward) 1944- ... 135
Keech, Thomas (Walton) 1946- ... 149
Keech, William J(ohn) 1904-1976 ... CAP-1
Earlier sketch in CA 9-10
Keech, William R(obertson) 1939- ... 25-28R
Keedy, Mervin L(averne) 1920- ... CANR-5
Earlier sketch in CA 53-56
Keefauver, Larry ... 204
Keefe, Carolyn 1928- ... 57-60
Keefe, Donald Joseph 1924- ... 37-40R
Keefe, John Edwin 1942- ... 107
Keefe, Michael 1946- ... 93-96
Keefe, Richard S(tanley) E(dwards) 1958- ... 148
Keefe, Robert 1938- ... 89-92
Keefe, Susan E. 1947- ... 126
Keefe, Terry 1940- ... 125
Keefer, Catherine
See Ogan, George F. and Ogan, Margaret E. (Nettles)
Keefer, Janice Kulyk
See Kulyk Keefer, Janice
See also SATA 132
Keefer, T(ruman) Frederick 1930- ... 21-24R
Keeffe, Barrie (Colin) 1945- ... 144
Brief entry ... 116
See also CBD
See also CD 5, 6
See also DLB 13, 245
Keegan, Christopher
See Gorman, Edward
Keegan, Frank L. 1925- ... 45-48
Keegan, John (Desmond Patrick)
1934- ... CANR-121
Brief entry ... 130
Earlier sketch in CA 136
Interview in ... CA-136
See also BEST 90:3
Keegan, John E. 1943- ... CANR-109
Earlier sketch in CA 146
Keegan, Marcia 1943- ... CANR-32
Earlier sketch in CA 49-52
See also SATA 9, 104
Keegan, Mary Heathcott 1914- ... CANR-3
Earlier sketch in CA 5-8R
Keegan, Susanne ... 194
Keegan, Terence J(ames) 1939- ... 117
Keegan, Warren J(oseph) 1936- ... 57-60
Keegan, William (James Gregory) 1938- ... 161
Keehn, Sally M. 1947- ... 137
See also SATA 87
Keel, Frank
See Keeler, Ronald F(ranklin)
Keel, John A.
See Kiehle, John Alva
Keelan, Claudia A. 1959- ... 192
Keele, Alan (Frank) 1942- ... 152
Keele, Kenneth D(avid) 1909- ... 5-8R
Keele, Reba Lou 1941- ... 186
Brief entry ... 106
Keeler, Harry Stephen 1890-1967 ... 235
See also CMW 4
Keeler, Mary Frear 1904-1999 ... 77-80
Keeler, Robert F. 1944- ... 176
Keeler, Ronald F(ranklin) 1913-1983 ... 107
See also SATA 47
Keeley, Edmund (Leroy) 1928- ... CANR-89
Earlier sketches in CA 1-4R, CANR-1, 22
Keeley, James 1867-1934 ... 177
See also DLB 25
Keeley, Joseph C(harles) 1907-1994 ... 25-28R
Keeley, Steve 1949- ... 93-96
Keeling, Clinton Harry 1932- ... CANR-7
Earlier sketch in CA 9-12R
Keeling, E. B.
See Curl, James Stevens
Keeling, Jill Annette (Shaw) 1923- ... CANR-12
Earlier sketches in CAP-1, CA 9-10
Keely, Charles C(larke), Jr. 1934-1985
Obituary ... 116
Keely, Harry Harris 1904- ... 65-68
Keely, Jack 1951- ... SATA 119
Keely, Jane 1922- ... 107
Keelyn, Patricia
See Lewin, Patricia
Keen, Benjamin 1913-2002 ... 136
Brief entry ... 114
Keen, (John) Ernest 1937- ... 33-36R

Keen, Geraldine
See Norman, Geraldine (Lucia)
Keen, Lisa 236
Keen, M. H.
See Keen, Maurice Hugh
Keen, Martin L. 1913-1992 .... 33-36R
See also SATA 4
Keen, Maurice
See Keen, Maurice Hugh
Keen, Maurice Hugh 1933- 122
Keen, Sam 137
Keen, Suzanne 1963- 220
Keen, Tommy 1923- 108
Keenan, Angela Elizabeth 1890-1983 61-64
Obituary 111
Keenan, Boyd R(aymond) 1928- 17-20R
Keenan, Brian 1950- CANR-122
Earlier sketch in CA 145
Keenan, Deborah (Anne) 1950- CANR-56
Earlier sketches in CA 69-72, CANR-11, 30
Keenan, Desmond (Joseph) 1933- 125
Keenan, Gerald 1932- 169
Keenan, James F. 1953- 222
Keenan, Jerry
See Keenan, Gerald
Keenan, Joe 1958- .... GLL 2
Keenan, Joseph H(enry) 1900-1977
Obituary 73-76
Keenan, Martha 1927- 77-80
Keenan, Sheila 1953- CANR-115
Earlier sketch in CA 160
See also SATA 95
Keene, Ann T(odd) 1940- 151
See also SATA 86
Keene, Burt
See Bickers, Richard (Leslie) Townshend
Keene, Carolyn CANR-56
Earlier sketches in CA 17-20R, CANR-27
See also Benson, Mildred (Augustine Wirt) and
Goulart, Ron(ald Joseph) and
McFarlane, Leslie (Charles) and
Stanley, George Edward and
Stratemeyer, Edward L.
See also BYA 4
See also CCA 1
See also JRDA
See also MAICYA 1, 2
See also SATA 65, 100
Keene, Daniel 1955- 229
See also CD 5, 6
Keene, Day 1903-1969 .... CMW 4
Keene, Dennis 1934- CANR-144
Earlier sketch in CA 144
Keene, Donald 1922- CANR-119
Earlier sketches in CA 1-4R, CANR-5
See also CLC 34
Keene, J(ames) Calvin 1908- CAP-1
Earlier sketch in CA 17-18
Keene, James
See Cook, Will(iam Everett)
Keene, James A(llen) 1932- CANR-43
Earlier sketch in CA 109
Keene, John (R.), (Jr.) 1965- 151
Keene, Lt.
See Rathborne, St. George (Henry)
Keene, R. D.
See Keene, Raymond D(ennis)
Keene, Ray
See Keene, Raymond D(ennis)
Keene, Raymond D(ennis) 1948- 158
Brief entry 112
Keener, Craig S. 1960- 224
Keener, Frederick M(ichael) 1937- CANR-43
Earlier sketches in CA 53-56, CANR-15
Keeney, Charles James 1912-1996 .... 5-8R
Keeney, Chuck
See Keeney, Charles James
Keeney, Ralph L(yons) 1944- CANR-16
Earlier sketch in CA 97-100
Keeney, William (Echard) 1922- CANR-15
Earlier sketch in CA 41-44R
Keenleyside, Hugh Llewellyn
1898-1992 .... CAP-1
Earlier sketch in CA 17-18
Keenleyside, T(erence) A(shley) 1940- 77-80
Keens-Douglas, Richardo 1953- CANR-139
Earlier sketch in CA 160
See also SATA 95, 154
Keeny, S. M.
See Keeny, Spurgeon Milton
Keeny, Spurgeon Milton 1893-1988
Obituary 126
Keep, Carolyn 1940- 65-68
Keep, David (John) 1936- 61-64
Keep, John (Leslie Howard) 1926- 9-12R
Keep, Linda Lowery
See Lowery, Linda
Keeping, Charles (William James)
1924-1988 .... CANR-43
Obituary 125
Earlier sketches in CA 21-24R, CANR-11
See also AAYA 26
See also CLR 34
See also CWRI 5
See also MAICYA 1, 2
See also SATA 9, 69
See also SATA-Obit 56
Keery, James 1958- CANR-121
Earlier sketch in CA 170
Keery, Sam 1929- 124
Kees, Beverly (Ann) 1941-2004 81-84
Obituary 234
Kees, Weldon 1914-1955 .... AMWS 15
Keese, Parton 1926- 109
Keesecker, William Francis 1918-1992 . 33-36R
Keeshan, Robert J. 1927-2004 .... CANR-5
Obituary 223
Earlier sketch in CA 5-8R
See also SATA 32
See also SATA-Obit 151
Keesing, Nancy (Florence)
1923-1995 .... CANR-27
Obituary 149
Earlier sketches in CA 9-12R, CANR-6
See also CP 1
Keeslar, Oreon 1907-1995 .... CAP-1
Earlier sketch in CA 13-14
Keeter, (Charles) Scott 1951- 160
Keeton, Elizabeth B(aker) 1919- 29-32R
Keeton, George Williams 1902-1989 .... 13-16R
Keeton, Kathy 1939-1997 125
Obituary 161
See also AITN 2
Keeton, Morris Teuton 1917- CANR-4
Earlier sketch in CA 1-4R
Keeton, Robert E(rnest) 1919- CANR-2
Earlier sketch in CA 5-8R
Keeton, William T(insley) 1933-1980 124
Obituary 105
Keevak, Michael 1962- 231
Keever, Jack 1938- 53-56
Keevill, Henry J(ohn) 1914-1978 ...... CANR-63
Earlier sketches in CAP-1, CA 9-10
See also Allison, Clay and
Alvord, Burt
Keezer, Dexter Merriam 1895-1991 .... 1-4R
Kefala, Antigone 1935- CANR-83
Earlier sketch in CA 153
See also CP 7
See also CWP
See also DLB 289
Kefferstan, Jean
See Pedrick, Jean
Kegan, Adrienne Koch 1912-1971
Obituary 33-36R
Kegan, Robert G. 1946- 199
Kegel, Charles H(erbert) 1924- CANR-45
Earlier sketch in CA 1-4R
Kegg, Maude (Ellen Mitchell) 1904-1996 ... 221
Kegley, Charles W(illiam), Jr. 1944- .. CANR-82
Earlier sketches in CA 114, CANR-36
Kegley, Charles William 1912-1986 ... CANR-2
Earlier sketch in CA 5-8R
Kehayan, V. Alex 1944- 110
Kehde, Ned 1940- 143
Kehl, D(elmar) G(eorge) 1936- 33-36R
Kehl, James Arthur 1922- 112
Kehle, Roberta L(unsford) 1936- 116
Kehler, Dorothea 1936- CANR-121
Earlier sketch in CA 171
Kehm, Freda (Irma) S(amuels) CAP-2
Earlier sketch in CA 29-32
Kehoe, Alice Beck 1934- 223
Kehoe, Constance (DeMuzio) 1933- 13-16R
Kehoe, Monika 1909- 21-24R
Kehoe, Patricia D. 1951- 132
Kehoe, Patrick E(mmett) 1941- 57-60
Kehoe, William F. 1933- 13-16R
Kehrer, Daniel M(ark) 1953- 120
Kehrer, James P(aul) 1951- 117
Kehret, Peg 1936- 178
See also AAYA 40
See also BYA 12
See also SATA 73, 108, 149
See also SATA-Essay 149
Keidel, Eudene 1921- 109
Keidel, Levi (Jr.) 1927- 115
Keifetz, Norman 1932- 89-92
Keiger, John F(rederick) V(ictor) 1952- 125
Keightley, David N(oel) 1932- 97-100
Keil, (Harold) Bill 1926- 81-84
Keil, Charles 1939- 140
Keil, Sally Van Wagenen 1946- 89-92
Keiler, Allan Ronald 1938- 199
Keillor, Garrison
See Keillor, Gary (Edward)
See also AAYA 2, 62
See also BEST 89:3
See also BPFB 2
See also CLC 40, 115
See also DLBY 1987
See also EWL 3
See also SATA 58
See also TUS
Keillor, Gary (Edward) 1942- CANR-124
Brief entry 111
Earlier sketches in CA 117, CANR-36, 59
See also Keillor, Garrison
See also CPW
See also DA3
See also DAM POP
See also MTCW 1, 2
See also MTFW 2005
Keillor, Steven J(ames) 1948- 151
Keilstrup, Margaret 1945- CANR-114
Earlier sketch in CA 138
Keim, Charles J. 1921-1999 .... CANR-13
Earlier sketch in CA 33-36R
Keimberg, Allyn
See Kimbro, John M.
Kein, Sybil 1939- 163
Keinzley, Frances 1922- 85-88
Keir, Christine
See Popescu, Christine
Keir, David E(dwin) 1906-1969 .... CAP-1
Earlier sketch in CA 9-10
Keir, David Lindsay 1895-1973 .... CAP-2
Earlier sketch in CA 21-22
Keirstead, Burton Seely 1907-1973 .... 5-8R
Keiser, Bea(trice) 1931- 97-100
Keiser, Norman F(red) 1930- 13-16R
Keislar, Evan R(ollo) 1913-2003 .... 21-24R
Keisling, Bill
See Keisling, William
Keisling, William 1958- 113
Keisman, Michael E(dward) 1932- 25-28R
Keister, Douglas 1948- .... SATA 88
Keister, Elinore
See Dobson, Elinore (Lucille)
Keitges, Julie 1940- 110
Keith, Agnes Newton 1901-1982 .... 17-20R
Keith, Andrew 1952- 238
Keith, Bill
See Keith, William H(enry), Jr., Jr.
Keith, Carlos
See Lewton, Val
Keith, Caroline H(elen) 1940- 139
Keith, David
See Steegmuller, Francis
Keith, Don 1947- 224
Keith, Donald
See Monroe, Keith
Keith, Doug 1952- .... SATA 81
Keith, Elmer (Merrifield) 1899-1984 101
Keith, Eros 1942- 114
See also SATA 52
Keith, Hal 1934- .... SATA 36
Keith, Hamish
See Chapman, James (Keith)
Keith, Harold (Verne) 1903-1998 ..... CANR-83
Earlier sketches in CA 5-8R, CANR-2, 48
See also BYA 3
See also JRDA
See also MAICYA 1, 2
See also SATA 2, 74
See also YAW
Keith, Herbert F. 1895-1978 .... 37-40R
Keith, J. Kilmeny
See Malleson, Lucy Beatrice
Keith, Jean E. 1921-1979
Obituary 85-88
Keith, Jennie 1942- 116
Keith, Judith 1923- 49-52
Keith, Julie (Houghton) 1940- CANR-110
Earlier sketch in CA 151
Keith, K. Wymand 1924- 33-36R
Keith, Larry Ficquette 1947- 97-100
Keith, Lee
See Sunners, William
Keith, Leigh
See Gold, H(orace) L(eonard)
Keith, Marian 1876(?)-1961
See MacGregor, Mary Esther
See also CCA 1
See also CWRI 5
See also DLB 92
See also RHW
Keith, Michael
See Hubbard, L(afayette) Ron(ald)
Keith, Michael C(urtis) 1945- CANR-98
Earlier sketch in CA 132
Keith, Nancy 1916-1990 138
Keith, Noel L(eonard) 1903-1981 57-60
Obituary 133
Keith, Robert
See Applebaum, Stan
Keith, Ronald (A.) 1914(?)-1985
Obituary 117
Keith, Sam 1921- 65-68
Keith, Slim
See Keith, Nancy
Keith, (G.) Stuart 1931-2003 126
Obituary 215
Keith, W(illiam) J(ohn) 1934- CANR-11
Earlier sketch in CA 17-20R
Keith, William H(enry), Jr., Jr. 1950- 172
Keithley, Erwin M. 1905-1991 73-76
Keithley, George 1935- 37-40R
Keith-Lucas, Alan 1910-1995 .... CANR-42
Earlier sketches in CA 5-8R, CANR-2, 20
Keith-Lucas, Bryan 1912-1996 107
Keith-Spiegel, Patricia 1939- 41-44R
Keith X
See Armstrong, Keith F(rancis) W(hitfield)
Kekes, John 1936- CANR-135
Earlier sketch in CA 65-68
Kekkonen, Sylvi 1900(?)-1974
Obituary 53-56
Kekst, Joan 1933- 205
Kelber, Magda 1908- 5-8R
Kelby, N(icole) M. 222
Kelch, Ray Alden 1923- 85-88
Kelder, Diane 1934- CANR-40
Earlier sketches in CA 25-28R, CANR-18
Keldysh, Mstislav V(sevolodovich) 1911-1978
Obituary 77-80
Kele, Max H(erschel) 1936- 185
Brief entry 114
Keleher, Will(iam Aloysius) 1886-1972
Obituary 37-40R
Keleinikov, Andrei 1924- .... SATA 65
Keleman, Stanley 1931- CANR-49
Earlier sketches in CA 81-84, CANR-14
Kelemen, Julie 1959- 146
See also SATA 78
Kelemen, Pal 1894-1993 104
Kelen, Andras 1951- 224
Kelen, Emery 1896-1978 .... 9-12R
Obituary 103
See also SATA 13
See also SATA-Obit 26
Kelen, Stephen 1912- 107
Kelf-Cohen, Reuben 1895-1981 49-52
Kelikian, Hampar 1899(?)-1983
Obituary 110
Kell, Carl L. 1938- 213
Kell, Joseph
See Wilson, John (Anthony) Burgess
Kell, Richard (Alexander) 1927- CANR-8
Earlier sketch in CA 5-8R
See also CP 1, 2, 3, 4, 5, 6, 7
Kellam, Sheppard (Gordon) 1931- 73-76
Kelland, Clarence Budington 1881-1964
Obituary 89-92
Kellar, Kenneth C(hambers) 1906-1981 ... 45-48
Kellar, William Henry 1952- 188
Kellaway, Frank (Gerald) 1922- 9-12R
Kellaway, George P(ercival) 1909- CAP-2
Earlier sketch in CA 23-24
Kelleam, Joseph E(veridge) 1913-1975 107
See also SATA 31
Kelleher, Annette 1950- 194
See also SATA 122
Kelleher, Catherine McArdle 1939- .. CANR-53
Brief entry 115
Earlier sketch in CA 125
Kelleher, Daria Valerian 1955- 147
See also SATA 79
Kelleher, Patrick J(oseph) 1917-1985
Obituary 116
Kelleher, Stephen J(oseph) 1915-1999 69-72
Obituary 188
Kelleher, Victor (Michael Kitchener)
1939- CANR-109
Earlier sketches in CA 126, CANR-56
See also AAYA 31
See also CLR 36
See also CN 5, 6, 7
See also HGG
See also SATA 75, 129
See also SATA-Brief 52
See also YAW
Kellenberger, James 1938- 155
Keller, Allan 1904-1981 .... CANR-29
Earlier sketch in CA 29-32R
Keller, Betty 1930- 121
Keller, Beverly L(ou) CANR-57
Earlier sketches in CA 49-52, CANR-1, 17, 38
See also SATA 13, 91
Keller, Charles 1942- CANR-43
Earlier sketches in CA 49-52, CANR-2
See also SATA 8, 82
Keller, Clair W(ayne) 1932- 53-56
Keller, David H(enry) 1880-1966 161
See also HGG
See also SCFW 1, 2
See also SFW 4
Keller, Dean H(oward) 1933- 53-56
Keller, Debra 1958- 159
See also SATA 94
Keller, Dick 1923- .... SATA 36
Keller, Dolores Elaine 1926- 104
Keller, Edward A(nthony) 1942- 73-76
Keller, Edward B. 1955- 225
Keller, Emily 161
See also SATA 96
Keller, Evelyn Fox 1936- CANR-99
Earlier sketches in CA 125, CANR-51
Keller, Frances Richardson 1914- 81-84
Keller, Franklin J. 1887(?)-1976
Obituary 65-68
Keller, Fred S(immons) 1899-1996 .... CANR-11
Obituary 151
Earlier sketch in CA 69-72
Keller, Gail Faithfull
See Faithfull, Gail
Keller, Gary D. 1943- CANR-82
Earlier sketch in CA 131
See also DLB 82
See also HW 1
Keller, George 1928- 123
Keller, Gottfried 1819-1890 .... CDWLB 2
See also DLB 129
See also EW
See also RGSF 2
See also RGWL 2, 3
See also SSC 26
Keller, Helen (Adams) 1880-1968 101
Obituary 89-92
See also BYA 3
See also DLB 303
See also MTCW 1
See also MTFW 2005
See also NCFS 2
Keller, Holly 1942- 235
Brief entry 118
See also CLR 45
See also MAICYA 2
See also SATA 76, 108, 157
See also SATA-Brief 42
Keller, Howard H(ughes) 1941- 45-48
Keller, Irene (Barron) 1927-2002 116
Obituary 208
See also SATA 36
See also SATA-Obit 139
Keller, James Gregory 1900-1977
Obituary 69-72
Keller, Joe 1963- 216
Keller, John E(sten) 1917- 45-48
Keller, Karl 1933- CANR-12
Earlier sketch in CA 57-60
Keller, Laurent 1961- 148
Keller, Laurie
See Keller, Laurie Smith
Keller, Laurie 184
Keller, Laurie S.
See Keller, Laurie Smith
Keller, Laurie Smith 1945(?)- 184
Keller, Lynn 1952- 195
Keller, Marian Jean 1953- 193
Keller, Marti 1948- 97-100
Keller, Mary (L.) 1964- 224
Keller, Mitzie Stuart 111
Keller, Mollie .... SATA-Brief 50
Keller, Morton 1929- 5-8R

Cumulative Index 311 Kemble

Keller, Nora Okja 1965- 187
See also CLC 109
Keller, Pierre 1956- 185
Keller, Sharon R. 142
Keller, Suzanne 1930- CANR-140
Earlier sketch in CA 65-68
Keller, Thomas F(ranklin) 1931- CANR-3
Earlier sketch in CA 9-12R
Keller, W(alter) D(avid) 1900- 41-44R
Keller, Werner (Rudolf August Wolfgang)
1909-(?) CANR-13
Earlier sketch in CA 21-24R
Keller, William W(alton) 1950- 208
Kellerman, Barbara 1939- 110
Kellerman, Faye 1952- CANR-136
Earlier sketches in CA 120, CANR-60
See also CMW 4
Kellerman, Jonathan 1949- CANR-51
Earlier sketches in CA 106, CANR-29
Interview in CANR-29
See also AAYA 35
See also BEST 90:1
See also CLC 44
See also CMW 4
See also CPW
See also DA3
See also DAM POP
Kellermann, Bernhard 1879-1951 165
See also SFW 4
Kellert, Stephen R. 1944- CANR-120
Earlier sketch in CA 147
Kellett, Arnold 1926- CANR-41
Earlier sketches in CA 103, CANR-19
Kelley, Alden D(rew) 1903-1980 .... 1-4R
Kelley, Alec E(rvin) 1923- 143
Kelley, Alice van Buren 1944- 81-84
Kelley, (Kathleen) Alita 1932- 143
Kelley, Allen C(harles) 1937- 104
Kelley, Arleon L(eigh) 1935- 115
Kelley, (Albert) Ben 1936- 45-48
Kelley, Beverly Merrill 185
Kelley, Brooks Mather 1929- 111
Kelley, Cecil B. Sr. 1911(?)-1987
Obituary 123
Kelley, Clarence M(arion) 1911-1997 127
Obituary 160
Kelley, David E. 1956- 194
See also AAYA 41
Kelley, Dean M(aurice) 1926-1997 81-84
Obituary 158
Kelley, Donald R(eed) 1931- CANR-12
Earlier sketch in CA 29-32R
Kelley, Douglas 1957- 202
Kelley, Earl Clarence 1895-1970 .... 5-8R
Kelley, Edith Summers 1884-1956
Brief entry 109
See also DLB 9
Kelley, Emma Dunham 1863-1938 .... DLB 221
Kelley, Eugene J(ohn) 1922- 13-16R
Kelley, Florence 1859-1932 .... DLB 303
Kelley, Hubert (Williams), Jr. 1926- 5-8R
Kelley, Hugh N(aoman) 1911-1991 45-48
Kelley, J(ohn) Charles 1913-1997 97-100
Kelley, Jane Holden 1928- 45-48
Kelley, Joanna (Elizabeth) 1910-2003 .... CAP-2
Obituary 215
Earlier sketch in CA 23-24
Kelley, Jonathan 107
Kelley, Joseph J(ohn), Jr. 1914-1990 .... CANR-8
Earlier sketch in CA 61-64
Kelley, Kevin J. 1948- 120
Kelley, Kitty 1942- CANR-82
Earlier sketches in CA 81-84, CANR-27
Interview in CANR-27
Kelley, Larry D. 1955- 238
Kelley, Leo P(atrick) 1928- CANR-83
Earlier sketches in CA 107, CANR-24
See also SATA 32
See also SATA-Brief 31
See also SFW 4
See also TCWW 2
Kelley, Mary 1943- CANR-52
Earlier sketch in CA 124
Kelley, Maurice (Willyle) 1903-1996 119
Kelley, Page H(utto) 1924- 25-28R
Kelley, Patrick (G.) 1963- .... SATA 129
Kelley, Patte 1947- .... SATA 93
Kelley, Ray
See Paine, Lauran (Bosworth)
Kelley, Robert 1925- 25-28R
Kelley, Robert E(mmett) 1938- 53-56
Kelley, Robin D. G. 1962(?)- 215
Kelley, Ruby M.
See Johnson, Ruby Kelley
Kelley, Stanley, Jr. 1926- 13-16R
Kelley, True (Adelaide) 1946- CANR-47
Earlier sketches in CA 105, CANR-23
See also SATA 41, 92, 130
See also SATA-Brief 39
Kelley, William 1929-2002 .... CANR-6
Obituary 213
Earlier sketch in CA 5-8R
Kelley, William Melvin 1937- CANR-83
Earlier sketches in CA 77-80, CANR-27
See also BW 1
See also CLC 22
See also CN 1, 2, 3, 4, 5, 6, 7
See also DLB 33
See also EWL 3
Kelley, William T(homas) 1917- 37-40R
Kelley, Win 1923- 89-92
Kellin, Sally Moffet 1932- 61-64
See also SATA 9
Kelling, Furn L. 1914-2000 .... 17-20R
See also SATA 37
Kelling, George W(alton) 1944- CANR-9
Earlier sketch in CA 57-60
Kelling, Hans-Wilhelm 1932- 37-40R
Kellison, Stephen G. 1942- 53-56
Kellman, Anthony 1955- 224
Kellman, Barnet (Kramer) 1947- 174
Kellman, Steven G. 1947- CANR-97
Earlier sketches in CA 112, CANR-29, 53
Kellner, Bruce 1930- CANR-136
Earlier sketches in CA 29-32R, CANR-11, 27
Kellner, Douglas (Mackay) 1943- CANR-100
Earlier sketches in CA 116, CANR-90
Kellner, Esther 13-16R
Kellner, L. 1904- 5-8R
Kellock, Archibald P.
See Mavor, Osborne Henry
Kellogg, Alfred Latimer 1915- 41-44R
Kellogg, Ansel Nash 1832-1886 .... DLB 23
Kellogg, Charles Edwin 1902-1980
Obituary 97-100
Kellogg, Charles Flint 1909- CAP-2
Earlier sketch in CA 23-24
Kellogg, Frederick 1929- CANR-134
Earlier sketch in CA 150
Kellogg, Gene
See Kellogg, Jean (Defrees)
Kellogg, James C. III 1915-1980
Obituary 103
Kellogg, Jean (Defrees) 1916-1978 .... CANR-7
Earlier sketch in CA 9-12R
See also SATA 10
Kellogg, M. Bradley
See Kellogg, Marjorie Bradley
Kellogg, Marion S(chuyler) 1920- 120
Kellogg, Marjorie 1922- 81-84
See also CLC 2
Kellogg, Marjorie B.
See Kellogg, Marjorie Bradley
Kellogg, Marjorie Bradley 1946- CANR-128
Earlier sketch in CA 164
Kellogg, Marne Davis 1946- CANR-92
Earlier sketch in CA 152
Kellogg, Mary Alice 1948- 81-84
Kellogg, Steven (Castle) 1941- CANR-110
Earlier sketches in CA 49-52, CANR-1
See also CLR 6
See also CWRI 5
See also DLB 61
See also MAICYA 1, 2
See also SATA 8, 57, 130
Kellogg, Virginia 1907-1981
Obituary 108
Kellogg, Winthrop N(iles) 1898-1971 .... 1-4R
Kellough, Richard Dean 1935- 53-56
Kellow, Kathleen
See Hibbert, Eleanor Alice Burford
Kellow, Norman B. 1914-2000 .... 21-24R
Kells, Susannah
See Cornwell, Bernard
Kellum, D(avid) F(ranklin) 1936- 61-64
Kelly, A(ngeline) A(gnes) 1924- 128
Kelly, Alfred H. 1907-1976 .... 5-8R
Obituary 65-68
Kelly, Alison 1913- 105
Kelly, Balmer H(ancock) 1914-2000 .... 17-20R
Kelly, Brian 1954- 158
Kelly, Brigit Pegeen 1951- 219
See also PFS 22
Kelly, C(harles) Brian 1935- 89-92
Kelly, C. M. O.
See Gibbs, (Cecilia) May
Kelly, Caitlin 230
Kelly, Carla 1947- 118
Kelly, Cathy 1966- 185
Kelly, Catriona (Helen Moncrieff)
1959- CANR-94
Earlier sketch in CA 147
Kelly, Charles E. 1920(?)-1985
Obituary 114
Kelly, Charles M. 1932- 128
Kelly, Charles Patrick Bernard 1891(?)-1971
Obituary 29-32R
Kelly, Chris 1940- 154
Kelly, Clarence 1941- 61-64
Kelly, Clint 1950- 211
See also SATA 140
Kelly, Commando
See Kelly, Charles E.
Kelly, Daniel 1938- 213
Kelly, Dave
See Kelly, David M(ichael)
Kelly, David M(ichael) 1938- CANR-12
Earlier sketch in CA 29-32R
Kelly, Deirdre M. 1959- 146
Kelly, Eamonn 219
Kelly, Edward H(anford) 1930- 37-40R
Kelly, Emmett (Leo) 1898-1979
Obituary 85-88
Kelly, Eric P(hilbrook) 1884-1960
Obituary 93-96
See also BYA 3
See also CWRI 5
See also MAICYA 1, 2
See also YABC 1
Kelly, Erin E. 1972- 149
Kelly, Faye L(ucius) 1914- 21-24R
Kelly, Fiona
See Coleman, Michael (Lee) and
Oldfield, Jenny and
Welford, Sue
Kelly, Frank K. 1914- CANR-39
Earlier sketches in CA 1-4R, CANR-1, 16
Kelly, Franklin (Wood) 1953- 139
Kelly, Frederic Joseph 1922- 53-56
Kelly, Gail P(aradise) 1940-1991 81-84
Obituary 133
Kelly, Gary F(rank) 1943- 89-92
Kelly, Gene 1912-1996 159
Kelly, George (Edward) 1887-1974 177
Obituary 49-52
See also AITN 1
See also DLB 7, 249
See also MAL 5
See also RGAL 4
Kelly, George A(nthony) 1916- CANR-43
Earlier sketches in CA 17-20R, CANR-11
Kelly, George Armstrong 1932-1987
Obituary 125
Kelly, George V(incent) 1919- 93-96
Kelly, George W. 1894-1991 .... CANR-9
Earlier sketch in CA 65-68
Kelly, Gerald R(ay) 1930- 29-32R
Kelly, Grace (Patricia) 1929-1982
Obituary 107
Kelly, Guy
See Moore, Nicholas
Kelly, H(enry) A(nsgar) 1934- CANR-57
Earlier sketches in CA 25-28R, CANR-30
Kelly, Hugh 1739-1777 .... DLB 89
See also RGEL 2
Kelly, Ian
See Kelly, John Spence
Kelly, Irene 1957- .... SATA 147
Kelly, J(ohn) M(aurice) 1931-1991 109
Obituary 133
Kelly, Jack 197
Kelly, James B(urton) 1905-1983 49-52
Kelly, James Patrick 1951- CANR-85
Earlier sketch in CA 135
See also SFW 4
Kelly, James Plunkett 1920-2003 .... CANR-83
Obituary 216
Earlier sketch in CA 53-56
See also Plunkett, James
Kelly, Jeff
See Kelly, Jeffrey
Kelly, Jeffrey 1946- 136
See also SATA 65
Kelly, Jeffrey A(llen) 1948- 114
Kelly, Jerry 1933- 239
Kelly, Joan 1928(?)-1982
Obituary 107
Kelly, Joan Berlin 1939- 107
Kelly, Joanne (W.) 1934- 151
See also SATA 87
Kelly, John 1921- 73-76
Kelly, John 1943- 127
Kelly, John M., Jr. 1919- 13-16R
Kelly, John N(orman) D(avidson)
1909- CANR-5
Earlier sketch in CA 5-8R
Kelly, John Rivard 1939- 103
Kelly, John Spence 1934- 125
Kelly, Joseph F(rancis) 1945- 222
Kelly, Joyce 1933- 106
Kelly, Karen 1935- 101
Kelly, Kate 1958- 155
See also SATA 91
Kelly, Kathleen M. 1964- .... SATA 71
Kelly, Kathleen Sheridan White
1945-2000 49-52
Obituary 193
Kelly, Kevin 1934- 130
Kelly, Kevin (J.) 1952- 149
Kelly, L(ouis) G(erard) 1935- 107
Kelly, Lauren
See Oates, Joyce Carol
Kelly, Laurence 1933- CANR-119
Earlier sketches in CA 81-84, CANR-15
Kelly, Laurene 1954- 194
See also SATA 123
Kelly, Lawrence C(harles) 1932- CANR-8
Earlier sketch in CA 21-24R
Kelly, Lelia 199
Kelly, Leo J. 1925- 41-44R
Kelly, (Alison) Linda 1936- 103
Kelly, M(ilton) T(errence) 1947- CANR-84
Earlier sketches in CA 97-100, CANR-19, 43
See also CAAS 22
See also CLC 55
See also CN 6
Kelly, Maeve 1930- 144
See also CN 7
Kelly, Mahlon (George) 1939- 53-56
Kelly, Marguerite (Lelong) 1932- 65-68
Kelly, Martha Rose 1914-1983 69-72
See also SATA 37
Kelly, Marty
See Kelly, Martha Rose
Kelly, Mary (Theresa Coolican)
1927- CANR-66
Earlier sketches in CA 1-4R, CANR-2
See also CMW 4
Kelly, Mary Anne 229
Kelly, Mary J(osephine) 1944- 117
Kelly, Maurice Anthony 1931- 53-56
Kelly, Maurice N. 1919- 21-24R
Kelly, Michael 1957-2003 210
Kelly, Nora (Hickson) 1910- 101
Kelly, Nora 1945- 207
Kelly, Patrick
See Allbeury, Theodore Edward le Bouthillier
Kelly, Paula 1949- 114
Kelly, Pauline Agnes 1936- 45-48
Kelly, Philip John 1896-1972 .... 5-8R
Obituary 37-40R
Kelly, R. M.
See Kelly, Ronald
Kelly, Ralph
See Geis, Darlene Stern
Kelly, Ralph
See Geis, Darlene Stern
Kelly, Ray
See Paine, Lauran (Bosworth)
Kelly, Regina Z(immerman)
1898-1986 .... CANR-2
Earlier sketch in CA 1-4R
See also SATA 5
Kelly, Richard
See Laymon, Richard (Carl)
Kelly, Richard (Michael) 1937- CANR-72
Earlier sketches in CA 107, CANR-34
Kelly, Richard J(ohn) 1938- 41-44R
Kelly, Rita Mae 1939- 81-84
Kelly, Robert 1935- CANR-47
Earlier sketch in CA 17-20R
See also CAAS 19
See also CP 1, 2, 3, 4, 5, 6, 7
See also DLB 5, 130, 165
See also SSC 50
Kelly, Robert Glynn 1920- 1-4R
Kelly, Robert J. 1938- CANR-121
Earlier sketch in CA 164
Kelly, Ronald 1959- 154
Kelly, Rosalie (Ruth) CANR-11
Earlier sketch in CA 61-64
See also SATA 43
Kelly, Russell 1949- 123
Kelly, Saul 1957- 226
Kelly, Sean C. 1940- 145
Kelly, Stan
See Kelly-Bootle, Stan
Kelly, Stephen E(ugene) 1919-1978 110
Obituary 104
Kelly, Susan Croce 1947- 129
Kelly, Susan S. 1954- 223
Kelly, Thomas 1909-1992 .... CAP-1
Earlier sketch in CA 9-10
Kelly, Thomas 1929- 109
Kelly, Thomas 1961- 238
Kelly, Tim 1935-1998 .... CANR-47
Obituary 172
Earlier sketch in CA 13-16R
Kelly, Timothy Michael 1947- 133
Kelly, Veronica 1945- 190
Kelly, Walt(er Crawford) 1913-1973 73-76
Obituary 45-48
See also AAYA 56
See also SATA 18
Kelly, William Leo 1924- 13-16R
Kelly, William W(atkins) 1928- 9-12R
Kelly-Benjamin, Kathleen 140
Kelly-Bootle, Stan 1929- 110
Kelly-Gadol, Joan 61-64
Kelm, Karlton 1908(?)-1987
Obituary 121
Kelman, Charles D. 1930-2004 110
Obituary 228
Kelman, Herbert C(hanoch) 1927- 13-16R
Kelman, James 1946- CANR-130
Earlier sketches in CA 148, CANR-85
See also BRWS 5
See also CLC 58, 86
See also CN 5, 6, 7
See also DLB 194, 319
See also RGSF 2
See also WLIT 4
Kelman, Judith (Ann) 1945- CANR-112
Earlier sketch in CA 166
Kelman, Mark 1951- 93-96
Kelman, Steven 1948- CANR-12
Earlier sketch in CA 29-32R
Kelner, Toni L. P. CANR-117
Earlier sketch in CA 166
Kelsay, Isabel Thompson 1905-1998 121
Kelsay, Michael 1957- 226
Kelsen, Hans 1881-1973
Obituary 115
Kelsey, Alice Geer 1896-1982 .... 5-8R
See also SATA 1
Kelsey, Elin .... SATA 159
Kelsey, Elin 235
Kelsey, Joan Marshall 1907-1989 .... CANR-58
Earlier sketch in CA 5-8R
See also FANT
Kelsey, Morton T(rippe) 1917- CANR-26
Earlier sketches in CA 21-24R, CANR-10
Kelsey, Robert J(ohn) 1927- 103
Kelso, Chuck
See Gribble, Leonard (Reginald)
Kelso, Louis O(rth) 1913-1991 .... 25-28R
Obituary 133
Kelso, Ruth 1885-1986
Obituary 119
Kelson, Allen H(oward) 1940- CANR-13
Earlier sketch in CA 77-80
Keltner, John W(illiam) 1918- 29-32R
Keltner, Kim Wong 1969(?)- 230
Kelton, Elmer 1926- CANR-85
Earlier sketches in CA 21-24R, CANR-12, 36
See also AITN 1
See also BYA 9
See also DLB 256
See also TCWW 1, 2
Keltz, Martha 177
Kelvin, Norman 1924- 164
Brief entry 118
Kemal, Salim 1948- 125
Kemal, Yasar
See Kemal, Yashar
See also CWW 2
See also EWL 3
See also WLIT 6
Kemal, Yashar 1923(?)- CANR-44
Earlier sketch in CA 89-92
See also CLC 14, 29
Kemble, E(dward) W(indsor) 1861-1933 218
See also DLB 188
Kemble, Fanny 1809-1893 .... DLB 32
Kemble, James CAP-2
Earlier sketch in CA 29-32

Kemelman, Harry 1908-1996 .... CANR-71
Obituary 155
Earlier sketches in CA 9-12R, CANR-6
See also AITN 1
See also BPFB 2
See also CLC 2
See also CMW 4
See also DLB 28
Kemeny, Jean A(lexander) 1930- 117
Kemeny, John G(eorge) 1926-1992 .. CANR-46
Obituary 140
Earlier sketch in CA 33-36R
Kemeny, Peter 1938-1975 53-56
Obituary 89-92
Kemerer, Frank R(obert) 1940- CANR-115
Earlier sketches in CA 65-68, CANR-10, 26, 54
Kemery, Mary Alice
See Goodman, Linda
Kemmer, Suzanne 1959- 194
Kemmerer, Donald L(orenzo) 1905-1993 .. 1-4R
Kemmerer, Kathleen Nulton 1952- 196
Kemmis, Daniel (Orra) 1945- 161
Kemnitz, Thomas Milton, Jr. 1984- 227
See also SATA 152
Kemnitz, Tom, Jr.
See Kemnitz, Thomas Milton, Jr.
Kemp, Anthony 1939- CANR-51
Earlier sketches in CA 105, CANR-25
Kemp, Arnold 1938-
Brief entry 110
Kemp, Bernard Peter 1942- 107
Kemp, Betty 1916- 9-12R
Kemp, Charles F. 1912-1994 .... CANR-5
Earlier sketch in CA 9-12R
Kemp, Diana Moyle 1919- CAP-1
Earlier sketch in CA 9-10
Kemp, Edward C. 1929- 81-84
Kemp, Gene 1926- CANR-85
Earlier sketches in CA 69-72, CANR-12
See also CLR 29
See also CWRI 5
See also MAICYA 1, 2
See also SATA 25, 75
Kemp, Jack (French) 1935- 109
Kemp, Jan 1949- .... CWP
Kemp, Jerrold E(dwin) 1921- 77-80
Kemp, John C(rocker) 1942- 93-96
Kemp, Kenny 1955- CANR-130
Earlier sketch in CA 168
Kemp, Lysander (Schaffer, Jr.)
1920-1992 .... CANR-1
Earlier sketch in CA 45-48
Kemp, Martin (John) 1942- CANR-97
Earlier sketch in CA 108
Kemp, Patrick S(amuel) 1932- 53-56
Kemp, Penn 1944- CANR-94
Earlier sketch in CA 130
Kemp, Penny
See Kemp, Penn
Kemp, Peter (Mant Macintyre)
1915-1993 .... 25-28R
Obituary 143
Kemp, Robert 1908-1967 .... CAP-1
Earlier sketch in CA 13-16
Kemp, Roger L. 1946- 154
Kemp, Roy Z(ell) 1910- 9-12R
Kemp, Sarah
See Butterworth, Michael
Kemp, Simon 1952- 237
Kemp, Tom 1921-1993 .... 25-28R
Obituary 143
Kempadoo, Oonya 186
Kempe, C(harles) Henry 1922-1984 122
Kempe, Frederick 1954- CANR-89
Earlier sketch in CA 138
Kempe, Margery 1373(?)-1440(?) .... DLB 146
See also FL 1:1
See also RGEL 2
Kemper, Donald J. 1929- 21-24R
Kemper, Inez 1906-1980 .... CAP-1
Earlier sketch in CA 13-14
Kemper, Kathi J. 1957- 156
Kemper, R. Crosby (III) 1951- 153
Kemper, Rachel H. 1931- 102
Kemper, Robert V(an) 1945- 104
Kemper, Steve 1951- 227
Kemper, Troxey 1915- 136
Kemperman, Steve (Richard) 1955- 108
Kempfer, Lester Leroy 1932- 49-52
Kempher, Ruth Moon 1934- CANR-17
Earlier sketch in CA 25-28R
Kempinski, Tom 1938- 230
See also CBD
See also CD 5, 6
See also DLB 310
Kempner, Friederike 1836-1904 .... DLB 129
Kempner, Mary Jean 1913-1969 .... CAP-2
Earlier sketch in CA 29-32
See also SATA 10
Kempner, S. Marshall 1898-1987 85-88
Kempowski, Walter 1929- CANR-137
Brief entry 122
Earlier sketch in CA 158
See also DLB 75
Kemprecos, Paul CANR-119
Earlier sketch in CA 166
Kempson, Rachel 1910-2003 130
Obituary 216
Kempster, Mary Yates 1911- CAP-1
Earlier sketch in CA 9-10
Kempster, Norman 1936- 77-80
Kempton, Arthur 222
Kempton, James Murray, Jr. 1945(?)-1971
Obituary 33-36R
Kempton, Jean Goldschmidt 1946(?)-1971
Obituary 33-36R
Kempton, Jean Welch 1914- 49-52
See also SATA 10
Kempton, (James) Murray
1918-1997 .... CANR-51
Obituary 158
Earlier sketch in CA 97-100
Kempton, Richard 1935- 106
Kemske, Floyd 1947- CANR-101
Earlier sketch in CA 151
Kemsley, Viscount
See Berry, James Gomer
Kemsley, William George, Jr. 1928- 85-88
Kenan, Randall (G.) 1963- CANR-86
Earlier sketch in CA 142
See also BW 2, 3
See also CN 7
See also CSW
See also DLB 292
See also GLL 1
Kenaston, Denny G. 1949- 238
Kenaz, Yehoshua 1937- 200
See also EWL 3
Kenda, Margaret 1942- .... SATA 71
Kendal, Felicity 1946- 188
Kendal, Geoffrey
See Bragg, Richard Geoffrey
Kendal, Wallis 1937- 107
Kendall, Alan 1939- 131
Kendall, Aubyn 1919-1995 107
Kendall, Carol (Seeger) 1917- CANR-84
Earlier sketches in CA 5-8R, CANR-7, 25
See also MAICYA 1, 2
See also SAAS 7
See also SATA 11, 74
See also YAW
Kendall, David Evan 1944- 29-32R
Kendall, Diana (E.) 231
Kendall, Dorothy Steinbomer
1912-2002 57-60
Kendall, E(dith) Lorna 1921- 5-8R
Kendall, Edward C(alvin) 1886-1972
Obituary 111
Kendall, Elaine (Becker) 1929- 17-20R
Kendall, Elizabeth B(emis) 1947- CANR-99
Earlier sketch in CA 81-84
Kendall, Gordon
See Lewitt, Shariann (N.)
Kendall, Henry 1839-1882 .... DLB 230
Kendall, Henry Madison 1901-1966 .... 5-8R
Kendall, Jane (F.) 1952- 137
Kendall, Jerry T. 1932- 222
Kendall, Katherine
See Applegate, Katherine (Alice)
Kendall, Kenneth E(verett) 1913-1995 45-48
Kendall, Lace
See Stoutenburg, Adrien (Pearl)
Kendall, Laurel 1947- 121
Kendall, Lisa See 1955- CANR-73
Earlier sketches in CA 111, CANR-25
Kendall, Lyle H(arris), Jr. 1919- 17-20R
Kendall, Marjorie 1930- 121
Kendall, Martha E. .... SATA 87
Kendall, Maurice (George) 1907-1983
Obituary 109
Kendall, May 1861-1943 200
See also DLB 240
Kendall, Patricia Louise 1921-1990
Obituary 131
Kendall, Paul Murray 1911-1973 .... CAP-1
Earlier sketch in CA 13-16
Kendall, R(obert) T(illman) 1935- 93-96
Kendall, Richard 1946- 189
Kendall, Robert 1934- CANR-6
Earlier sketch in CA 13-16R
Kendall, Russ 1957- .... SATA 83
Kendall, T(homas) Robert 1935- 69-72
Kendall, Tim 1970- 221
Kendall, Willmoore 1909-1967 .... CANR-6
Earlier sketch in CA 5-8R
Kendle, John Edward 1937- 61-64
Kendler, Howard H(arvard) 1919- 17-20R
Kendrake, Carleton
See Gardner, Erle Stanley
Kendrick, Alexander 1911(?)-1991 143
Kendrick, Baynard H(ardwick)
1894-1977 .... CANR-60
Obituary 69-72
Earlier sketches in CA 1-4R, CANR-4
See also CMW 4
Kendrick, David Andrew 1937- CANR-9
Earlier sketch in CA 21-24R
Kendrick, Frank J(enness) 1928- 41-44R
Kendrick, John (Stafford) 1917- 121
Kendrick, John W(hitefield) 1917- 127
Brief entry 110
Kendrick, Stephen 1954- 204
Kendrick, Thomas Downing 1895-1979 .. 81-84
Kendrick, Walter M(ay Forth) 1947-1998 112
Kendricks, James
See Fox, G(ardner) F(rancis)
Kendris, Christopher 1923- CANR-24
Earlier sketches in CA 5-8R, CANR-7
Kendyl, Sharice
See Michels, Sharry C.
Keneally, Thomas (Michael) 1935- . CANR-130
Earlier sketches in CA 85-88, CANR-10, 50, 74
See also BRWS 4
See also CLC 5, 8, 10, 14, 19, 27, 43, 117
See also CN 1, 2, 3, 4, 5, 6, 7
See also CPW
See also DA3
See also DAM NOV
See also DLB 289, 299
See also EWL 3
See also MTCW 1, 2
See also MTFW 2005
See also NFS 17
See also RGEL 2
See also RHW
Kenealy, James P. 1927- 93-96
See also SATA 52
See also SATA-Brief 29
Kenealy, Jim
See Kenealy, James P.
Keneas, Alexander 1938(?)-1984
Obituary 113
Kenedi, Aaron 213
Kenelly, John W(illis, Jr.) 1935- 25-28R
Kenen, Isaiah Leo 1905-1988 107
Kenen, Peter B(ain) 1932- CANR-22
Earlier sketches in CA 5-8R, CANR-7
Kenesson, Frank G. 1913(?)-1985
Obituary 119
Kenez, Peter 1937- CANR-88
Earlier sketch in CA 29-32R
Kenian, Paul Roger
See Clifford, Martin
Kenin, Richard (Metz) 1947-1983
Obituary 111
Kenison, Katrina 1958- CANR-127
Earlier sketches in CA 138, CANR-106
Keniston, Kenneth 1930- CANR-101
Earlier sketch in CA 25-28R
Kenjo, Takashi 1940- 137
Kenkel, William F(rancis) 1925- 61-64
Kenko 1283(?)-1352(?) .... DLB 203
See also RGWL 3
Kenna, Peter (Joseph) 1930-1987 61-64
See also DLB 289
Kennamer, Lorrin, Jr. 1924-1999 .... CANR-6
Earlier sketch in CA 5-8R
Kennan, George 1845-1924 183
See also DLB 189
Kennan, George F(rost) 1904-2005 . CANR-106
Obituary 237
Earlier sketches in CA 1-4R, CANR-2, 39
Kennan, Kent (Wheeler) 1913-2003 .... 1-4R
Obituary 221
Kennard, George (Arnold Ford)
1915-1999 134
Kennaway, Adrienne 1945- .... SATA 60
Kennaway, James (Peebles Ewing)
1928-1968 103
Obituary 89-92
Kenneally, Michael 1945- CANR-100
Earlier sketch in CA 133
Kennealy, Jerry 1938- 142
Kennealy (Morrison), Patricia 1946- 120
See also FANT
Kennebeck, Edwin 1924-1996 .... 41-44R
Obituary 152
Kennebeck, Paul 1943- 53-56
Kennecott, G. J.
See Viksnins, George J(uris)
Kennedy, A(lison) L(ouise) 1965- 213
Earlier sketches in CA 168, CANR-108
Autobiographical Essay in 213
See also CD 5, 6
See also CLC 188
See also CN 6, 7
See also DLB 271
See also RGSF 2
Kennedy, Adam 1920(?)-1997 .... CANR-24
Obituary 162
Earlier sketch in CA 107
See also AITN 1
Kennedy, Adrienne (Lita) 1931- CANR-82
Earlier sketches in CA 103, CANR-26, 53
See also CAAS 20
See also AFAW 2
See also BLC 2
See also BW 2, 3
See also CABS 3
See also CAD
See also CD 5, 6
See also CLC 66
See also DAM MULT
See also DC 5
See also DFS 9
See also DLB 38
See also FW
See also MAL 5
Kennedy, Andrew (Karpati) 1931- 61-64
Kennedy, Betty 1926- 121
Kennedy, Brendan 1970- 123
See also SATA 57
Kennedy, Bruce M. 1929- 57-60
Kennedy, Carol CANR-107
Earlier sketches in CA 105, CANR-21
Kennedy, Caroline 1944- 125
Kennedy, Caroline (Bouvier) 1957- . CANR-119
Earlier sketch in CA 140
Kennedy, Charles J(oseph) 1935-1984
Obituary 114
Kennedy, Chuck
See Kennedy, Charles J(oseph)
Kennedy, Cody
See Reese, John (Henry)
Kennedy, D. James 1930- 61-64
Kennedy, Dana Forrest 1917- .... SATA 74
Kennedy, Dane K(eith) 1951- CANR-117
Earlier sketches in CA 126, CANR-56
Kennedy, David M(ichael) 1941- CANR-92
Earlier sketches in CA 29-32R, CANR-13
Kennedy, Dennis (Edward) 1940- CANR-46
Earlier sketch in CA 120
Kennedy, Don(ald) H(enry) 1911-1990 61-64
Kennedy, Dorothy M(intzlaff) 1931- . CANR-40
Earlier sketch in CA 116
See also SATA 53
Kennedy, Doug(las) 1963- .... SATA 122
Kennedy, Douglas 1955- CANR-144
Earlier sketch in CA 158
Kennedy, Eddie C(lifton) 1910- 89-92
Kennedy, Edward Moore 1932- 110
Kennedy, Edward R(idgway) 1923(?)-1975
Obituary 104
Kennedy, Elliot
See Godfrey, Lionel (Robert Holcombe)
Kennedy, (Robert) Emmet (Jr.) 1941- . CANR-93
Earlier sketch in CA 132
Kennedy, Erica 1970(?)- 236
Kennedy, Eugene C(ullen) 1928- CANR-114
Earlier sketches in CA 25-28R, CANR-44
Kennedy, Florynce (Rae) 1916-2000 155
Obituary 191
See also BW 3
Kennedy, Gail 1900-1972
Obituary 33-36R
Kennedy, Gary J. 1948- 194
Kennedy, Gavin 1940- CANR-9
Earlier sketch in CA 61-64
Kennedy, George 1899(?)-1977
Obituary 73-76
Kennedy, George (Alexander) 1928- ... CANR-2
Earlier sketch in CA 5-8R
Kennedy, Gerald (Hamilton)
1907-1980 .... CANR-6
Earlier sketch in CA 5-8R
Kennedy, Gerald Studdert
See Studdert-Kennedy, (William) Gerald
Kennedy, Gwynne 1955- 200
Kennedy, Harold J. 1915(?)-1988
Obituary 124
Kennedy, Hubert (Collings) 1931- 93-96
Kennedy, Hugh 1947- CANR-143
Earlier sketch in CA 127
Kennedy, J. Gerald 1947- 127
Kennedy, J(ames) Hardee 1915- 13-16R
Kennedy, James
See Monahan, James (Henry Francis)
Kennedy, James
See Lusby, Jim
Kennedy, James G(ettier) 1932- 81-84
Kennedy, James William 1905-1999 .. CANR-1
Obituary 177
Earlier sketch in CA 1-4R
Kennedy, James Y(oung) 1916- 77-80
Kennedy, Jimmy 1903(?)-1984
Obituary 112
Kennedy, John C. 1943- 152
Kennedy, John Fitzgerald 1917-1963 .. CANR-1
Earlier sketch in CA 1-4R
See also LAIT 5
See also MTCW 1
See also NCFS 2
See also SATA 11
Kennedy, John J(oseph) 1914-2001 57-60
Kennedy, John Pendleton 1795-1870 .... DLB 3, 248, 254
See also RGAL 4
Kennedy, Joseph Charles 1929- 201
Earlier sketches in CA 1-4R, CANR-4, 30, 40
Autobiographical Essay in 201
See also Kennedy, X. J.
See also CWRI 5
See also MAICYA 2
See also MAICYAS 1
See also SATA 14, 86, 130
See also SATA-Essay 130
Kennedy, Judith M(ary) 1935- 41-44R
Kennedy, Kathleen 1947(?)-1975
Obituary 57-60
Kennedy, Kenneth A(drian) R(aine)
1930- CANR-1
Earlier sketch in CA 45-48
Kennedy, Kieran A. 1935- 37-40R
Kennedy, Kim 171
Kennedy, L. D. 1924- 45-48
Kennedy, Lawrence W. 1952- 141
Kennedy, Leigh 1951- CANR-84
Earlier sketch in CA 122
See also SFW 4
Kennedy, Lena
See Smith, Lena (Kennedy)
Kennedy, Leo 1907-2000 178
See also DLB 88
Kennedy, Leonard Anthony 1922- 37-40R
Kennedy, Leonard M(ilton) 1925- 73-76
Kennedy, Liv 1934- 140
Kennedy, Ludovic (Henry Coverley)
1919- CANR-97
Earlier sketches in CA 65-68, CANR-46
Kennedy, Malcolm D(uncan)
1895-1984 .... 9-12R
Kennedy, Margaret 1896-1967
Obituary 25-28R
See also DLB 36
See also RHW
Kennedy, Marilyn Moats 1943- CANR-32
Earlier sketch in CA 109
Kennedy, Mary 102
Kennedy, (Matthew) Maxwell Taylor
1965- 194
Kennedy, Michael 1926- CANR-47
Earlier sketches in CA 13-16R, CANR-5, 23
Kennedy, Mimi 1948(?)- 174

Cumulative Index 313 Kerby

Kennedy, Moorhead 1930- ... 123
Kennedy, Nigel (Paul) 1956- ... 140
Kennedy, P(eter) J(ohn) 1925- ... 123
Kennedy, Pagan
See Kennedy, Pamela
Kennedy, Pamela (J.) 1946- ... 151
See also SATA 87
Kennedy, Pamela 1962- ... CANR-119
Earlier sketch in CA 146
Kennedy, Patrick 1801-1873 ... DLB 159
Kennedy, Paul (Michael) 1945- ... CANR-30
Earlier sketches in CA 65-68, CANR-9
See also BEST 89:1
Kennedy, Paul E(dward) 1929- ... 185
See also SATA 33, 113
Kennedy, Paul M.
See Kennedy, Paul (Michael)
Kennedy, Philip F. ... 173
Kennedy, Ralph Dale 1897-1965 ... 1-4R
Kennedy, Randall 1954- ... CANR-119
Earlier sketch in CA 162
Kennedy, Randy ... 230
Kennedy, Raymond A. 1934- ... 5-8R
Kennedy, Richard (Pitt) 1910-1989 ... 102
Obituary ... 127
See also SATA-Obit 60
Kennedy, (Jerome) Richard 1932- ... CANR-80
Earlier sketches in CA 57-60, CANR-7, 26
See also CWRI 5
See also SATA 22
Kennedy, Richard S(ylvester)
1920-2002 ... CANR-56
Earlier sketches in CA 5-8R, CANR-3, 29
See also DLB 111
See also DLBY 2002
Kennedy, Rick 1935- ... 175
Kennedy, Robert 1938- ... SATA 63
Kennedy, Robert E(mmet), Jr. 1937- ... 37-40R
Kennedy, Robert F(rancis), Jr. 1954- ... 110
Kennedy, Robert F(rancis) 1925-1968 . CANR-1
Earlier sketch in CA 1-4R
Kennedy, Robert L(ee) 1930- ... 57-60
Kennedy, Robert Woods 1911-1985 ... 49-52
Kennedy, Roger G(eorge) 1926- ... CANR-107
Earlier sketch in CA 115
Kennedy, Rose (Elizabeth Fitzgerald)
1890-1995 ... 53-56
Obituary ... 147
Kennedy, Sighle Aileen 1919-1996 ... 53-56
Kennedy, Stetson 1916- ... CANR-45
Earlier sketch in CA 5-8R
Kennedy, Susan Estabrook 1942- ... CANR-43
Earlier sketch in CA 45-48
Kennedy, T(eresa) A. 1953- ... 114
See also SATA 42
See also SATA-Brief 35
Kennedy, T(homas) F(illans) 1921- ... 53-56
Kennedy, Ted
See Kennedy, Edward Moore
Kennedy, Teresa
See Kennedy, T(eresa) A.
Kennedy, Theodore Reginald 1936- ... 105
Kennedy, Thomas 1920- ... 116
Kennedy, Thomas C. 1937- ... 125
Kennedy, William (Joseph) 1928- ... CANR-134
Earlier sketches in CA 85-88, CANR-14, 31, 76
Interview in ... CANR-31
See also AAYA 1
See also AMWS 7
See also BPFB 2
See also CLC 6, 28, 34, 53
See also CN 4, 5, 6, 7
See also DA3
See also DAM NOV
See also DLB 143
See also DLBY 1985
See also EWL 3
See also MAL 5
See also MTCW 1, 2
See also MTFW 2005
See also SATA 57
Kennedy, William B(ean) 1926- ... 116
Kennedy, William J(ohn) 1942- ... 117
Kennedy, X. J.
See Kennedy, Joseph Charles
See also CAAS 9
See also AMWS 15
See also CLC 8, 42
See also CLR 27
See also CP 1, 2, 3, 4, 5, 6, 7
See also DLB 5
See also SAAS 22
Kennedy-Martin, Ian 1936- ... 101
Kenneggy, Richard
See Nettell, Richard (Geoffrey)
Kennel, LeRoy E(ldon) 1930- ... 77-80
Kennell, Nigel M. 1955- ... 155
Kennell, Ruth Epperson 1893-1977 ... CAP-2
Earlier sketch in CA 29-32
See also SATA 6
See also SATA-Obit 25
Kennelly, (Timothy) Brendan 1936- .. CANR-97
Earlier sketches in CA 9-12R, CANR-5
See also CP 1, 2, 3, 4, 5, 6, 7
See also DLB 40
Kennemore, Tim 1957- ... 202
See also CWRI 5
See also SATA 133
Kenner, Charles Leroy 1933- ... 25-28R
Kenner, (William) Hugh
1923-2003 ... CANR-139
Obituary ... 221
Earlier sketches in CA 21-24R, CANR-28
See also DLB 67
Kennerly, David Hume 1947- ... 101
See also AITN 2
Kennerly, Karen 1940- ... 33-36R
Kennett, (Elizabeth) Audrey 1905-2001 ... 147
Obituary ... 201
Kennett, David 1959- ... SATA 121
Kennett, (Houn) Jiyu 1924- ... 93-96
Kennett, Lee 1931- ... CANR-109
Earlier sketch in CA 21-24R
Kennett, Peggy Teresa Nancy
See Kennett, (Houn) Jiyu
Kennett, Rick 1956- ... HGG
Kennett, Shirley 1951- ... 223
Kenney, Alice P(atricia) 1937-1985 .. CANR-10
Obituary ... 115
Earlier sketch in CA 25-28R
Kenney, Catherine (McGehee) 1948- ... 135
Kenney, Charles 1950- ... CANR-109
Earlier sketch in CA 135
Kenney, Douglas C. 1947(?)-1980 ... 107
Obituary ... 101
Kenney, Edwin James, Jr. 1942- ... 53-56
Kenney, George Churchill 1889-1977 ... CAP-1
Earlier sketch in CA 11-12
Kenney, John Paul 1920- ... 17-20R
Kenney, Lona B(ronberg) 1921- ... 115
Kenney, Padraic (Jeremiah) 1963- ... 226
Kenney, Richard (L.) 1948- ... 134
Kenney, Susan (McIlvaine) 1941- ... CANR-37
Earlier sketch in CA 115
Kenney, Sylvia W. 1922-(?) ... CAP-1
Earlier sketch in CA 19-20
Kenney, William Howland III 1940- ... 201
Kennick, W(illiam) E(lmer) 1923- ... 13-16R
Kennington, (Gilbert) Alan 1906-1986
Obituary ... 121
Kennington, Alice Eve 1935- ... 119
Kennon, Donald R. 1948- ... 122
Kennon, Patrick E. ... 236
Kenny, Anthony
See Kenny, Anthony John Patrick
Kenny, Anthony John Patrick 1931- .. CANR-23
Earlier sketch in CA 101
Kenny, Charles J.
See Gardner, Erle Stanley
Kenny, Ellsworth Newcomb 1909-1971 ... 5-8R
Obituary ... 103
See also SATA-Obit 26
Kenny, Herbert Andrew 1912-2002 ... 41-44R
See also SATA 13
Kenny, James Andrew 1933- ... CANR-51
Earlier sketches in CA 107, CANR-26
Kenny, Jean
See Freeman, Jean Kenny
Kenny, John P. 1915-1987 ... 17-20R
Kenny, John Peter 1916- ... CANR-1
Earlier sketch in CA 45-48
Kenny, Kathryn
See Bowden, Joan Chase and
Krull, Kathleen and Sanderlin, Owenita (Harrah) and
Stack, Nicolete Meredith
Kenny, Kevin
See Krull, Kathleen
Kenny, Kevin 1960- ... 191
Kenny, Lorraine Delia 1961- ... 226
Kenny, Mary 1936- ... 108
Kenny, Maurice (Francis) 1929- ... CANR-143
Earlier sketch in CA 144
See also CAAS 22
See also CLC 87
See also DAM MULT
See also DLB 175
See also NNAL
Kenny, Michael 1923-1986 ... CANR-5
Earlier sketch in CA 1-4R
Kenny, Nicholas Napoleon 1895-1975
Obituary ... 89-92
Kenny, Nick
See Kenny, Nicholas Napoleon
Kenny, Shirley (Elise) Strum 1934- ... CANR-31
Earlier sketch in CA 45-48
Kenny, Vincent 1919- ... 45-48
Kenny, W. Henry 1918- ... 37-40R
Keno, Leigh 1957(?)- ... 197
Keno, Leslie 1957(?)- ... 197
Kenofer, C(harles) Louis 1923- ... 69-72
Kenoyer, Natlee Peoples 1907- ... CANR-5
Earlier sketch in CA 5-8R
Kenrick, Donald Simon 1929- ... 81-84
Kenrick, Tony 1935- ... CANR-84
Earlier sketch in CA 104
See also CMW 4
Kenshalo, Daniel R(alph) 1922- ... 41-44R
Kensinger, George
See Fichter, George S.
Kensington, Kathryn Wesley
See Rusch, Kristine Kathryn
Kent, Alexander
See Reeman, Douglas Edward
Kent, Allegra 1938(?)- ... CANR-72
Brief entry ... 105
Earlier sketch in CA 126
Kent, Allen 1921- ... CANR-39
Earlier sketches in CA 9-12R, CANR-3, 18
Kent, Arden
See Marion, Frieda
Kent, Arthur William Charles 1925-1998 ... 102
Kent, Bill
See Kent, Carleton Volney, Jr.
Kent, Bill 1954- ... 224
Kent, Carleton Volney, Jr. 1909-1985
Obituary ... 114
Kent, Carol 1947- ... 233
Kent, Christopher 1940- ... 129
Kent, Cromwell
See Sparshott, Francis (Edward)
Kent, David
See Lambert, David (Compton)
Kent, David
See Birney, (Herman) Hoffman
Kent, Deborah Ann 1948- ... CANR-139
Earlier sketch in CA 103
See also SATA 47, 104, 155
See also SATA-Brief 41
Kent, Debra 1952- ... 208
Kent, Donald P(eterson) 1916-1972 ... 17-20R
Obituary ... 120
Kent, Edward Allen 1933- ... 45-48
Kent, Ernest W(illiam) 1940- ... 104
Kent, Fortune
See Toombs, John
Kent, Frank (Richardson, Jr.) 1907(?)-1978
Obituary ... 81-84
Kent, Frank R(ichardson) 1877-1958
Brief entry ... 121
See also DLB 29
Kent, George O(tto) 1919- ... 37-40R
Kent, George W. 1928- ... 25-28R
Kent, Gordon
See Tubb, E(dwin) C(harles)
Kent, Gordon
See Cameron, Christian
Kent, Harold W(infield) 1900-1990 ... 65-68
Kent, Helen
See Polley, Judith (Anne)
Kent, Homer A(ustin), Jr. 1926- ... CANR-3
Earlier sketch in CA 9-12R
Kent, Jack
See Kent, John Wellington
Kent, James M. 1956- ... 139
Kent, John Henry Somerset 1923- ... 9-12R
Kent, John Wellington 1920-1985 ... CANR-16
Obituary ... 117
Earlier sketch in CA 85-88
Interview in ... CANR-16
See also SATA 24
See also SATA-Obit 45
Kent, Joseph (P.) 1940- ... CANR-143
Earlier sketch in CA 172
Kent, Karen 1941- ... 159
Kent, Katherine
See Dial, Joan
Kent, Katie
See Green, Kay
Kent, Kelvin
See Kuttner, Henry
Kent, Leonard J. 1927- ... 77-80
Kent, Lisa 1942- ... 155
See also SATA 90
Kent, Louise Andrews 1886-1969 ... CANR-4
Obituary ... 25-28R
Earlier sketch in CA 1-4R
Kent, Malcolm 1932- ... 45-48
Kent, Mallory
See Lowndes, Robert A(ugustine) W(ard)
Kent, Margaret 1894- ... CAP-2
Earlier sketch in CA 25-28
See also SATA 2
Kent, Neil (Lowell) 1951- ... CANR-82
Earlier sketch in CA 129
Kent, Noel J(ay) 1944- ... 111
Kent, Nora 1899- ... CAP-1
Earlier sketch in CA 9-10
Kent, Pete
See Richardson, Gladwell
Kent, Peter C. 1938- ... 234
Kent, Philip
See Bulmer, (Henry) Kenneth
Kent, Richard G. 1951- ... 216
Kent, Rockwell 1882-1971 ... CANR-4
Obituary ... 29-32R
Earlier sketch in CA 5-8R
See also SATA 6
Kent, Sherman 1903-1986 ... 53-56
Obituary ... 118
See also SATA 20
See also SATA-Obit 47
Kent, Sherry 1955- ... 128
Kent, Simon
See Catto, Max(well Jeffrey)
Kent, Stella
See Phillips, Stella
Kent, Timothy J. 1949- ... 216
Kent, Tony
See Crechales, Anthony George
Kent, Valerie 1947- ... 114
Kente, Gibson 1932- ... 233
See also CD 5, 6
Kentfield, Calvin 1924-1975 ... 5-8R
Kentfield, J(ohn) A(lan) C. 1930- ... 165
Kenton, Leslie 1941- ... 113
Kenton, Maxwell
See Hoffenberg, Mason and
Southern, Terry
Kenton, Warren 1933- ... CANR-29
Earlier sketch in CA 29-32R
Kenvin, Roger Lee 1926- ... 180
Kenward, James (Macara) 1908- ... 5-8R
Kenward, Jean 1920- ... 108
See also SATA 42
Kenward, Michael 1945- ... 103
Kenworthy, Brian J(ohn) 1920- ... 103
Kenworthy, Eldon (G.) 1935-1998 ... 154
Kenworthy, Leonard S. 1912-1991 ... CANR-1
Earlier sketch in CA 1-4R
See also SATA 6
Kenyatta, Jomo 1891(?)-1978 ... CANR-82
Obituary ... 113
Earlier sketch in CA 124
See also BW 1, 3
See also MTCW 1
Kenyon, Bernice
See Gilkyson, Bernice Kenyon
Kenyon, Ernest M(onroe) 1920- ... 85-88
Kenyon, F(rank) W(ilson) 1912- ... CANR-1
Earlier sketch in CA 1-4R
Kenyon, J(ohn) P(hilipps)
1927-1996 ... CANR-45
Obituary ... 151
Earlier sketches in CA 9-12R, CANR-3
Kenyon, James William 1910- ... CAP-1
Earlier sketch in CA 9-10
Kenyon, Jane 1947-1995 ... CANR-69
Obituary ... 148
Earlier sketches in CA 118, CANR-44
See also AAYA 63
See also AMWS 7
See also CP 7
See also CWP
See also DLB 120
See also PC 57
See also PFS 9, 17
See also RGAL 4
Kenyon, John R(obert) 1948- ... CANR-55
Earlier sketch in CA 127
Kenyon, Karen (Smith) 1938- ... CANR-126
Earlier sketches in CA 106, CANR-92
See also SATA 145
Kenyon, Kate
See Adorjan, Carol (Madden) and
Ransom, Candice F.
Kenyon, Kathleen Mary 1906-1978 .. CANR-13
Earlier sketch in CA 21-24R
Kenyon, Kay ... 223
Kenyon, Ley 1913-1990 ... 13-16R
See also SATA 6
Kenyon, Michael 1931- ... CANR-84
Earlier sketches in CA 13-16R, CANR-12
See also CMW 4
Kenyon, Mildred Adams 1894-1980 ... 108
Obituary ... 105
Kenyon, Paul
See Freedland, Nat(haniel)
Kenyon, Robert O.
See Kuttner, Henry
Kenyon, W. A.
See Kenyon, Walter Andrew
Kenyon, Walter
See Kenyon, Walter Andrew
Kenyon, Walter A.
See Kenyon, Walter Andrew
Kenyon, Walter Andrew 1917-1986
Obituary ... 121
Kenzer, Robert C. 1955- ... 126
Kenzheev, Bakhyt Shkurullaevich
1950- ... DLB 285
Keogh, Dermot (Francis) 1945- ... 126
Keogh, James 1916- ... 45-48
Keogh, Lilian Gilmore 1927- ... 9-12R
Keogh, Pamela Clarke ... 239
Keohane, Dan 1941- ... CANR-104
Earlier sketch in CA 146
Keohane, Nannerl O(verholser) 1940- ... 106
Keohane, Robert O(wen) 1941- ... CANR-33
Earlier sketch in CA 45-48
Keough, Hugh Edmund 1864-1912 ... 203
See also DLB 171
Keown, Elizabeth ... SATA 78
Keown, Tim ... 239
Kepel, Gilles 1955- ... CANR-126
Earlier sketch in CA 149
Kepes, Gyorgy 1906-2001 ... 101
Obituary ... 202
Kepes, Juliet A(ppleby) 1919-1999 ... 69-72
See also SATA 13
Kephart, Beth 1960- ... 198
Kephart, Horace 1862-1931
Brief entry ... 119
Kephart, Newell C. 1911-1973 ... CAP-2
Earlier sketch in CA 17-18
Kephart, William M. 1921- ... 41-44R
Kepler, Thomas Samuel 1897-1963 ... 1-4R
Keppel, Charlotte
See Torday, Ursula
Keppel, Sonia 1900-1986 ... 107
Obituary ... 120
Keppel-Jones, Arthur (Mervyn) 1909- ... 118
Kepple, Ella Huff 1902-1981 ... CAP-2
Earlier sketch in CA 17-18
Keppler, Ann B(lystad) 1946- ... 117
Keppler, C(arl) F(rancis) 1909- ... 17-20R
Keppler, Herbert 1925- ... 85-88
Keppler, Victor 1904-1987
Obituary ... 124
Ker, Ian (Turnbull) ... 233
Ker, Jill
See Conway, Jill K(er)
Ker, John, third Duke of Roxburghe
1740-1804 ... DLB 213
Ker, Madeline
See Gabriel, Marius
Ker, N(eil) R(ipley) 1908-1982 ... 183
Obituary ... 107
See also DLB 201
Ker, W(illiam) P(aton) 1855-1923 ... 185
Brief entry ... 121
Ker, William Paton
See Ker, W(illiam) P(aton)
Keralio-Robert, Louise-Felicite de
1758-1822 ... DLB 313
Kerbel, Matthew Robert 1958- ... CANR-101
Earlier sketch in CA 148
Kerber, August Frank 1917- ... 21-24R
Kerber, Linda K(aufman) 1940- ... 160
Brief entry ... 115
Kerby, Anthony Paul 1953- ... 141
Kerby, Bill 1937- ... 104
Kerby, Joe Kent 1933- ... 53-56
Kerby, Mona 1951- ... 142
See also SATA 75

Kerby, Philip Pearce 1911-1993 ... 180
Brief entry ... 116
Kerby, Robert L(ee) 1934- ... 41-44R
Kerby, Susan Alice
See Burton, (Alice) Elizabeth
Kercheval, Jesse Lee 1956- ... CANR-101
Earlier sketches in CA 126, CANR-53
Kerckhoff, Alan C(hester) 1924- ... CANR-67
Earlier sketches in CA 113, CANR-32
Kerek, Andrew 1936- ... 102
Kerekes, Tibor 1893-1969 ... CAP-2
Earlier sketch in CA 17-18
Kerensky, Alexandr Fedorovich 1881-1970
Obituary ... 113
Kerensky, Oleg 1930-1993 ... CANR-12
Obituary ... 141
Earlier sketch in CA 29-32R
Kerensky, V(asil) M(ichael) 1930- ... 53-56
Keres, Paul (Petrovich) 1916-1975
Obituary ... 57-60
Kerestesi, Michael 1929- ... 109
Kereszty, Roch A(ndrew) 1933- ... 29-32R
Keret, Etgar 1967- ... 202
Kerewsky-Halpern, Barbara 1931- ... 102
Kerferd, G(eorge) B(riscoe) 1915-1998 ... 132
Obituary ... 170
Kerigan, Florence 1896-1984 ... 29-32R
See also SATA 12
Kerik, Bernard B. 1955- ... 237
Kerin, Roger A(nthony) 1947- ... CANR-26
Earlier sketch in CA 109
Kerina, Mburumba 1932- ... CANR-71
Earlier sketch in CA 129
Kerkhoff, Blair 1959- ... 201
Kerkow, H. C.
See Lewton, Val
Kerkvliet, Benedict J(ohn) 1943- ... 93-96
Kerlan, Irvin 1912-1963 ... 5-8R
See also DLB 187
Kerley, Barbara 1960- ... 209
See also SATA 138
Kerley, Jack ... 232
Kerlinger, Fred N(ichols) 1910-1991 ... CANR-2
Earlier sketch in CA 49-52
Kerman, Cynthia Earl 1923- ... 57-60
Kerman, Gertrude
See Furman, Gertrude Lerner Kerman
Kerman, Joseph (Wilfred) 1924- ... CANR-91
Earlier sketches in CA 65-68, CANR-15
Kerman, Judith (Berna) 1945- ... 77-80
Kerman, Sheppard 1928-1991 ... CANR-26
Earlier sketch in CA 85-88
Kermani, Taghi Thomas 1929- ... 25-28R
Kermode, (John) Frank 1919- ... CANR-95
Earlier sketches in CA 1-4R, CANR-1, 47
See also DLB 242
Kern, Alfred 1924- ... 33-36R
Kern, Canyon
See Raborg, Frederick A(shton), Jr.
Kern, E. R.
See Kerner, Fred
Kern, Edith 1912- ... 113
Kern, Gary 1938- ... 65-68
Kern, Gregory
See Tubb, E(dwin) C(harles)
Kern, Janet (Rosalie) 1924-1998 ... 5-8R
Obituary ... 166
Kern, Jean B(ordner) 1913-2003 ... 85-88
Kern, Jerome 1885-1945 ... 198
See also DLB 187
Kern, Mary Margaret 1906- ... 101
Kern, Robert W(illiam) 1934- ... CANR-7
Earlier sketch in CA 61-64
Kern, Seymour 1913-1987 ... 93-96
Kern, Stephen 1943- ... 69-72
Kern, Walter O(tto) 1930- ... 117
Kernaghan, Eileen 1939- ... 221
Earlier sketches in CA 111, CANR-28, 54
Autobiographical Essay in ... 221
See also BYA 13
See also DLB 251
Kernan, Alvin B(ernard) 1923- ... CANR-95
Earlier sketches in CA 49-52, CANR-33
Kernan, Jerome B(ernard) 1932- ... 25-28R
Kernan, Julia K. 1901(?)-1988
Obituary ... 125
Kernan, Michae (Jenkins), (Jr.)
1927-2005 ... 81-84
Obituary ... 239
Kerner, Elizabeth ... 201
Kerner, Fred 1921- ... CANR-47
Earlier sketches in CA 9-12R, CANR-6, 22
See also Fredericks, Frohm and
Kerr, Frederick
See also CCA 1
Kerner, Justinus 1786-1862 ... DLB 90
Kernfeld, Barry (Dean) 1950- ... CANR-135
Earlier sketch in CA 161
Kernick, Simon 1966- ... 222
Kernochan, Sarah 1947- ... 73-76
Kernodle, George R(iley) 1907-1988 ... 65-68
Kerns, Daniel R.
See Lichtenberg, Jacqueline
Kerns, Frances Casey 1937- ... 81-84
Kerns, J(ames) Alexander 1894-1975
Obituary ... 104
Kerns, Joanna 1953- ... 174
Kerns, Robert Louis 1929- ... 77-80
Kerns, Thelma 1929- ... 188
See also SATA 116
Kerns, Thomas A. 1942- ... 227
Kerouac, Jack 1922-1969
See Kerouac, Jean-Louis Lebris de
See also AAYA 25
See also AMWC 1
See also AMWS 3
See also BG 3
See also BPFB 2
See also CDALB 1941-1968
See also CLC 1, 2, 3, 5, 14, 29, 61
See also CP 1
See also CPW
See also DLB 2, 16, 237
See also DLBD 3
See also DLBY 1995
See also EWL 3
See also GLL 1
See also LATS 1:2
See also LMFS 2
See also MAL 5
See also NFS 8
See also RGAL 4
See also TCLC 117
See also TUS
See also WLC
See also WP
Kerouac, Jan
See Hackett, Jan Michele
See also DLB 16
Kerouac, Jean-Louis Lebris de
1922-1969 ... CANR-95
Obituary ... 25-28R
Earlier sketches in CA 5-8R, CANR-26, 54
See also Kerouac, Jack and
Kerouac, John
See also AITN 1
See also DA
See also DA3
See also DAB
See also DAC
See also DAM MST, NOV, POET, POP
See also MTCW 1, 2
See also MTFW 2005
Kerouac, Joan Haverty 1931-1990 ... 197
Kerouac, John
See Kerouac, Jean-Louis Lebris de
See also GLL 1
Kerpelman, Larry C(yril) 1939- ... 37-40R
Kerr, Alex(ander McBride) 1921- ... 61-64
Kerr, Alex 1952- ... 233
Kerr, Alex A. 1922- ... 125
Kerr, Andrea Moore 1940- ... 141
Kerr, Andy
See Kerr, Alex A.
Kerr, Ann Zwicker 1934- ... 148
Kerr, Barbara 1913- ... 89-92
Kerr, Ben
See Ard, William (Thomas)
Kerr, Bob 1951- ... 191
See also SATA 120
Kerr, Carole
See Carr, Margaret
Kerr, Catherine 1945- ... 102
Kerr, Clark 1911-2003 ... CANR-22
Obituary ... 222
Earlier sketches in CA 45-48, CANR-1
Kerr, D(onald) G(ordon) G(rady)
1913-1976 ... CANR-6
Earlier sketch in CA 1-4R
Kerr, Donna H(anneman) 1944- ... 112
Kerr, E. Bartlett 1924- ... 139
Kerr, E(laine) Katherine 1942- ... 215
Kerr, Elizabeth M(argaret) 1905-1991 ... 37-40R
Kerr, Frederick
See Kerner, Fred
See also CCA 1
Kerr, Graham 1934- ... 108
Kerr, Harry P(rice) 1928- ... 5-8R
Kerr, Homer L(ee) 1921- ... 120
Kerr, Howard Hastings 1931- ... 103
Kerr, Hugh Thomson 1909-1992 ... 103
Obituary ... 137
Kerr, James Lennox 1899-1963 ... CANR-83
Earlier sketch in CA 102
See also CWRI 5
Kerr, James Stolee 1928- ... 17-20R
Kerr, (Bridget) Jean (Collins)
1923(?)-2003 ... CANR-7
Obituary ... 212
Earlier sketch in CA 5-8R
Interview in ... CANR-7
See also CLC 22
Kerr, (Bridget) Jean (Collins) 1923(?)-2003
Obituary ... 212
Kerr, Jessica 1901-1991 ... CAP-2
Earlier sketch in CA 29-32
See also SATA 13
Kerr, Joan P(aterson) 1921-1996 ... 81-84
Obituary ... 154
Kerr, John 1950- ... 149
Kerr, (Anne-)Judith 1923-1970 ... CANR-83
Earlier sketch in CA 93-96
See also CWRI 5
See also SATA 24
Kerr, K(athel) Austin 1938- ... 25-28R
Kerr, Katharine 1944- ... CANR-123
Earlier sketch in CA 155
See also BYA 11
See also FANT
Kerr, LaRae Free 1944- ... 195
Kerr, M. E.
See Meaker, Marijane (Agnes)
See also AAYA 2, 23
See also BYA 1, 7, 8
See also CLC 12, 35
See also CLR 29
See also SAAS 1
See also WYA
Kerr, Malcolm (Hooper) 1931-1984 ... 97-100
Obituary ... 111
Kerr, Margaret (H.) 1954- ... 217
Kerr, Michael
See Hoskins, Robert (Phillip)
Kerr, Norman D.
See Sieber, Sam Dixon
Kerr, Orpheus C.
See Newell, Robert Henry
Kerr, Philip 1956- ... CANR-92
Earlier sketch in CA 159
See also CMW 4
Kerr, Phyllis Forbes 1942- ... 120
See also SATA 72
Kerr, Robert ... CLC 55
Kerr, Robert (a pseudonym) 1899- ... 69-72
Kerr, Rose Netzorg 1892-1974 ... CAP-2
Earlier sketch in CA 23-24
Kerr, Stanley E. 1894(?)-1976
Obituary ... 69-72
Kerr, Steven 1941- ... 171
Kerr, Tom 1950- ... SATA 77
Kerr, Walter (Francis) 1913-1996 ... CANR-77
Obituary ... 154
Earlier sketches in CA 5-8R, CANR-7
Kerrey, Bob
See Kerrey, J(oseph) Robert
Kerrey, J(oseph) Robert 1943- ... 213
Kerridge, George H. ... 238
Kerrigan, (Thomas) Anthony 1918- ... CANR-4
Earlier sketch in CA 49-52
See also CAAS 11
See also CLC 4, 6
Kerrigan, Catherine 1939- ... 117
Kerrigan, John
See Whiting, Charles (Henry)
Kerrigan, Kate Lowe
See Rickett, Frances
Kerrigan, William J(oseph) ... CANR-2
Earlier sketch in CA 49-52
Kerruish, Jessie Douglas 1884-1949 ... 188
See also HGG
Kerry, Frances
See Kerigan, Florence
Kerry, John (Forbes) 1943- ... 227
Kerry, Lois
See Duncan, Lois
Kersaudy, Francois 1948- ... 144
Kersell, John E(dgar) 1930- ... 45-48
Kersenboom, Saskia 1953- ... 152
Kersey, (Patrick) Colin 1947- ... 225
Kersey, Katharine C(lark) 1935- ... CANR-38
Earlier sketch in CA 116
Kersey, Tanya-Monique 1961- ... 138
See also BW 2
Kersh, Cyril 1925-1993 ... CANR-47
Obituary ... 141
Earlier sketch in CA 104
Kersh, Gerald 1911-1968 ... 188
Obituary ... 25-28R
See also CMW 4
See also DLB 255
See also HGG
Kershaw, Alex ... 173
Kershaw, Alister (Nasmyth) 1921- ... CANR-41
Earlier sketches in CA 5-8R, CANR-3, 19
Kershaw, Gordon Ernest 1928- ... 85-88
Kershaw, Ian 1943- ... CANR-101
Earlier sketch in CA 137
Kershaw, John (Hugh D'Allenger) ... 73-76
Kershen, (L.) Michael 1982- ... 149
See also SATA 82
Kershner, Howard E(ldred) 1891-1990 ... 73-76
Kershner, Richard B(randon) 1913-1982
Obituary ... 110
Kerslake, Susan 1943- ... CANR-17
Earlier sketch in CA 93-96
Kersnowski, Frank L. 1934- ... 41-44R
Kerstan, Lynn ... 223
Kertes, Joseph ... 166
Kertess, Klaus 1940- ... 162
Kertesz, Andre 1894-1985 ... 85-88
Obituary ... 117
Kertesz, Imre 1929- ... 205
See also DLB 299
See also DLBY 2002
Kertesz, Louise 1939- ... 102
Kertesz, Stephen D(enis) 1904-1986 ... CAP-2
Earlier sketch in CA 21-22
Kertscher, Kevin M. 1964- ... 173
Kertzer, David I(srael) 1948- ... CANR-114
Earlier sketches in CA 106, CANR-44
Kertzer, Morris Norman 1910-1983 ... CANR-1
Obituary ... 111
Earlier sketch in CA 1-4R
Kerven, Rosalind 1954- ... CANR-105
Earlier sketch in CA 150
See also SATA 83
Ker Wilson, Barbara 1929- ... CANR-99
Earlier sketches in CA 5-8R, CANR-7
See also CWRI 5
See also SAAS 18
See also SATA 20, 70, 121
Kerwood, John R. 1942- ... 53-56
Kesel, Barbara 1960- ... 224
See also AAYA 63
Keselman, Gabriela 1953- ... SATA 128
Kesey, Ken (Elton) 1935-2001 ... CANR-124
Obituary ... 204
Earlier sketches in CA 1-4R, CANR-22, 38, 66
See also AAYA 25
See also BG 1:3
See also BPFB 2
See also CDALB 1968-1988
See also CLC 1, 3, 6, 11, 46, 64, 184
See also CN 1, 2, 3, 4, 5, 6, 7
See also CPW
See also DA
See also DA3
See also DAB
See also DAC
See also DAM MST, NOV, POP
See also DLB 2, 16, 206
See also EWL 3
See also EXPN
See also LAIT 4
See also MAL 5
See also MTCW 1, 2
See also MTFW 2005
See also NFS 2
See also RGAL 4
See also SATA 66
See also SATA-Obit 131
See also TUS
See also WLC
See also YAW
Keshet, Harry F(inkelstein) 1940- ... 109
Keshishian, John M. 1923- ... 25-28R
Kesich, Veselin 1921-
Brief entry ... 111
Kesler, (William) Jackson (II) 1938- ... 102
Kesler, Jay 1935- ... CANR-51
Earlier sketches in CA 61-64, CANR-8, 26
See also SATA 65
Kesler, Robert Shaw 1968- ... 177
Kess, Joseph Francis 1942- ... 65-68
Kessel, Dmitri 1902-1995 ... 120
Kessel, John (Joseph Vincent) 1950- ... 235
Earlier sketches in CA 120, CANR-80
Autobiographical Essay in ... 235
See also SFW 4
Kessel, John H(oward) 1928- ... CANR-46
Earlier sketches in CA 21-24R, CANR-21
Kessel, Joseph (Elie) 1898-1979 ... 105
Obituary ... 89-92
See also DLB 72
Kessel, Joyce Karen 1937- ... 105
See also SATA 41
Kessel, Lipmann 1914-1986 ... 13-16R
Kessel, Martin 1901- ... 182
See also DLB 56
Kessell, John L(ottridge) 1936- ... CANR-122
Earlier sketch in CA 93-96
Kesselman, Judi R.
See Kesselman-Turkel, Judi
Kesselman, Louis Coleridge 1919-1974
Obituary ... 110
Kesselman, Mark J. ... CANR-14
Earlier sketch in CA 37-40R
Kesselman, Wendy (Ann) 1940- ... 233
See also CAD
See also CD 5, 6
See also CWD
Kesselman-Turkel, Judi 1934- ... CANR-37
Kesselring, Joseph (Otto) 1902-1967 ... 150
See also CLC 45
See also DAM DRAM, MST
See also DFS 20
Kessen, William 1925-1999 ... CANR-1
Obituary ... 177
Earlier sketch in CA 1-4R
Kessler, Carol Farley 1936- ... 188
Kessler, Daniel B. 1949- ... 231
Kessler, David 1959- ... 205
Kessler, Diane Cooksey 1947- ... 57-60
Kessler, Edward 1927- ... 61-64
Kessler, Ethel 1922- ... CANR-48
Brief entry ... 115
Earlier sketch in CA 121
See also SATA 44
See also SATA-Brief 37
Kessler, Francis P(aschal) 1944- ... 109
Kessler, Frank
See Kessler, Francis P(aschal)
Kessler, Gail 1937- ... 65-68
Kessler, Henry H(oward) 1896-1978
Obituary ... 73-76
Kessler, Herbert L(eon) 1941- ... CANR-112
Earlier sketches in CA 125, CANR-51
Kessler, Jascha (Frederick) 1929- ... CANR-111
Earlier sketches in CA 17-20R, CANR-8, 48
See also CLC 4
See also CP 1
Kessler, Judy 1947- ... 146
Kessler, Julia Braun 1926- ... CANR-70
Earlier sketch in CA 144
Kessler, Kaye (Warren) 1923- ... 112
Kessler, Lauren J. 1950- ... CANR-97
Earlier sketches in CA 127, CANR-54
Kessler, Leo
See Whiting, Charles (Henry)
Kessler, Leonard P. 1921- ... 77-80
See also SATA 14
Kessler, Merle (Bruce) 1949- ... 128
Kessler, Milton 1930-2000 ... CANR-2
Earlier sketch in CA 1-4R
See also CP 1, 2
Kessler, Rod 1949- ... 117
Kessler, Ronald (Borek) 1943- ... CANR-91
Earlier sketches in CA 69-72, CANR-13, 28, 55
Kessler, Sheila ... 57-60
Kessler, Stephen James 1947- ... 198
Kessler, Suzanne J. 1946- ... 167

Cumulative Index 315 Kiarostami

Kessler, Walter R. 1913-1978
Obituary 81-84
Kessler-Harris, Alice 1941- CANR-120
Earlier sketch in CANR-32, 65
Kessner, Lawrence 1957- 109
Kessner, Thomas 1946- CANR-11
Earlier sketch in CA 69-72
Kest, Kristin 1967- .... SATA 118
Kesteloot, Lilyan 1931- CANR-41
Earlier sketches in CA 73-76, CANR-19
Kesten, Hermann 1900-1996 178
See also DLB 56
Kestenberg, Judith S(ilberpfennig)
1910-1999 185
Kester, Dana R(ay) 1943- 116
Kesterson, David B(ert) 1938- 41-44R
Kesterton, Wilfred (Harold) 1914-1997 . 41-44R
Kesteven, G. R.
See Crosher, G. R.
Kestler, Frances Roe 1929- 135
Kestner, Joseph A(loysius) 1943- 89-92
Ketch, Jack
See Tibbetts, John C(arter)
Ketcham, Carl H(untington)
1923-1991 .... 29-32R
Ketcham, Charles B(rown) 1926- 29-32R
Ketcham, Hank
See Ketcham, Henry King
Ketcham, Henry King 1920-2001 105
Obituary 197
See also SATA 28
See also SATA-Brief 27
See also SATA-Obit 128
Ketcham, Howard 1902-1982
Obituary 106
Ketcham, Katherine 1949- CANR-97
Earlier sketch in CA 118
Ketcham, Orman W(eston)
1918-2004 .... CANR-9
Obituary 234
Earlier sketch in CA 21-24R
Ketcham, Ralph (Louis) 1927- CANR-4
Earlier sketch in CA 9-12R
Ketcham, Rodney K(enneth) 1909- CANR-4
Earlier sketch in CA 1-4R
Ketcham, Sallie 1963- .... SATA 124
Ketchin, Susan 1948- 180
Ketchum, Carlton Griswold 1892-1984 ... 85-88
Ketchum, Cliff
See Paine, Lauran (Bosworth)
Ketchum, Creston Donald 1922- 9-12R
Ketchum, Frank
See Paine, Lauran (Bosworth)
Ketchum, J.
See Frentzen, Jeffrey
Ketchum, Jack
See Paine, Lauran (Bosworth)
Ketchum, Jack
See Mayr, Dallas William
See also AAYA 61
See also HGG
See also SUFW 2
Ketchum, Liza 1946-
See Murrow, Liza Ketchum
See also SATA 132
Ketchum, Marshall D(ana) 1905-1989 .. CAP-1
Earlier sketch in CA 17-18
Ketchum, Philip (L.) 1902-1969 ..... TCWW 1, 2
Ketchum, Richard M(alcolm)
1922- CANR-123
Earlier sketch in CA 25-28R
Ketchum, Robert Glenn 1947- CANR-23
Earlier sketch in CA 107
Ketchum, William C(larence), Jr.
1931- CANR-55
Earlier sketches in CA 33-36R, CANR-12, 28
Keteyian, Armen 1953- 122
Ketner, Kenneth Laine (Sr.) 1939- 139
Ketner, Mary Grace 1946- .... SATA 75
Ketron, Larry 1947- 141
Kets de Vries, Manfred F. R. 1942- 111
Kett, Joseph F. 1938-1989 .... 25-28R
Kettani, M. Ali 1941- 133
Kettelhack, Guy 1951- 134
Kettelkamp, Larry (Dale) 1933- CANR-16
Earlier sketch in CA 29-32R
See also CLC 12
See also SAAS 3
See also SATA 2
Ketteman, Helen 1945- 186
See also SATA 73, 115
Ketterer, David (Anthony Theodor)
1942- CANR-46
Earlier sketches in CA 53-56, CANR-4, 21
Ketterman, Grace H(orst) 1926- CANR-22
Earlier sketch in CA 106
Kettl, Donald F. 1952- CANR-34
Earlier sketch in CA 111
Kettle, Arnold (Charles) 1916-1986 .... CANR-6
Obituary 121
Earlier sketch in CA 9-12R
Kettle, Jocelyn Pamela 1934- 25-28R
Kettle, Pamela
See Kettle, Jocelyn Pamela
Kettle, Peter
See Glover, Denis (James Matthews)
Kettlewell, Caroline 228
Kettner, Elmer Arthur 1906-1964 .... 1-4R
Kettner, James H(arold) 1944- 89-92
Ketton-Cremer, Robert Wyndham 1906-1969
Obituary 106
Keucher, William F. 1918- 49-52
Keuls, Eva C(lara) 1928- 123
Keuls, Hans 1910-1985
Obituary 117
Keuls, Yvonne 1931- 196
Keun, Irmgard 1905-1982 178
See also DLB 69
Kevan, Martin 1949- CANR-27
Earlier sketch in CA 110
Kevane, Bridget 231
Keve, Paul W(illard) 1913-1999 .... CANR-6
Earlier sketch in CA 9-12R
Kevelson, Roberta 1931-1998 226
Kevern, Barbara
See Shepherd, Donald (Lee)
Keveson, Peter 1919-1986
Obituary 118
Kevill-Davies, Sally 1945- 138
Kevin, Jodi
See Lawrence, Jodi
Kevles, Barbara (Lynne) 1940- 128
Kevles, Bettyann Holtzmann 1938- .. CANR-72
Earlier sketches in CA 69-72, CANR-11, 27
See also SATA 23
Kevles, Daniel J(erome) 1939- CANR-135
Earlier sketches in CA 85-88, CANR-27
Kevorkian, Jack 1928- 161
Kew, Stephen 1947- 103
Kewes, Karol 1924- 9-12R
Key, Alexander (Hill) 1904-1979 ...... CANR-85
Obituary 89-92
Earlier sketches in CA 5-8R, CANR-6
See also SATA 8
See also SATA-Obit 23
See also SFW 4
Key, Ellen (Karolina Sofia)
1849-1926 .... DLB 259
See also TCLC 65
Key, Jack D(ayton) 1934- CANR-30
Earlier sketch in CA 112
Key, Mary Ritchie 1924-2003 .... CANR-38
Obituary 221
Earlier sketches in CA 45-48, CANR-1, 16
Key, Samuel M.
See de Lint, Charles (Henri Diederick Hofsmit)
Key, Ted
See Key, Theodore
Key, Theodore 1912- 13-16R
Key, V(aldimer) O(rlando), Jr. 1908-1963 .. 1-4R
Key, William H(enry) 1919- 45-48
Key, Wilson Bryan 1925- CANR-2
Earlier sketch in CA 49-52
Keyber, Conny
See Fielding, Henry
Keyes, Alan L(ee) 1950- 155
Keyes, Claire J. 1938- 126
Keyes, Daniel 1927- 181
Earlier sketches in CA 17-20R, CANR-10, 26, 54, 74
Autobiographical Essay in 181
See also AAYA 23
See also BYA 11
See also CLC 80
See also DA
See also DA3
See also DAC
See also DAM MST, NOV
See also EXPN
See also LAIT 4
See also MTCW 2
See also MTFW 2005
See also NFS 2
See also SATA 37
See also SFW 4
Keyes, Edward 1927- 103
Keyes, Evelyn 1919(?)- 85-88
Keyes, Fenton 1915-1999 107
See also SATA 34
Keyes, Frances Parkinson
1885-1970 .... CANR-59
Obituary 25-28R
Earlier sketches in CA 5-8R, CANR-7
See also RHW
Keyes, Greg
See Keyes, J. Gregory
Keyes, J. Gregory 1963- 181
See also SATA 116
Keyes, Jessica 1950- 145
Keyes, Kenneth S(cofield), Jr.
1921-1995 .... CANR-24
Obituary 150
Earlier sketches in CA 17-20R, CANR-8
Keyes, Langley Carleton, Jr. 1938- 25-28R
Keyes, Margaret Frings 1929- 57-60
Keyes, Marian 1963- 187
Keyes, Noel
See Keightley, David N(oel)
Keyes, Ralph 1945- CANR-134
Earlier sketches in CA 49-52, CANR-3, 47
Keyes, Sidney (Arthur Kilworth)
1922-1943 .... BRW 7
See also RGEL 2
Keyfitz, Nathan 1913- CANR-10
Earlier sketch in CA 25-28R
Keyhoe, Donald E(dward) 1897-1988
Obituary 127
Keyishian, Harry 1932- 61-64
Keylock, Leslie R(obert) 1933- 117
Keylor, Arthur (W.) 1920(?)-1981
Obituary 104
Keylor, William R(obert) 1944- 89-92
Keyne, Gordon
See Bedford-Jones, H(enry James O'Brien)
Keynes, Edward 1940- 120
Keynes, Sir Geoffrey Langdon 1887-1982 .. 103
Obituary 107
See also DLB 201
Keynes, John Maynard 1883-1946 163
Brief entry 114
Earlier sketch in CA 162
See also DLBD 10
See also MTCW 2
See also MTFW 2005
See also TCLC 64
Keynes, Randal 234
Keynes, Richard Darwin 1919- 114
Keynes, Simon 1952- 175
Keys, Ancel (Benjamin) 1904-2004 61-64
Obituary 233
Keys, Donald (Fraser) 1924- 115
Keys, Ivor Christopher Banfield
1919-1995 103
Keys, John D. 1938- 9-12R
Keys, Kerry Shawn 1946- 145
Keys, Thomas Edward 1908-1995 .... CAP-1
Earlier sketch in CA 11-12
Keyser, Daniel J. 1935- 121
Keyser, (George) Gustave 1910- 77-80
Keyser, James D. 1950- 216
Keyser, Lester Joseph 1943- 105
Keyser, Marcia 1933- 116
See also SATA 42
Keyser, Samuel Jay 1935- 106
Keyser, Sarah
See McGuire, Leslie (Sarah)
Keyser, William R(ussell) 1916- 69-72
Keyserling, Eduard von 1855-1918 182
See also DLB 66
Keyserling, Leon H. 1908-1987 61-64
Obituary 123
Keyserlingk, Robert H. 1933- 131
Keyssar, Alexander 1947- CANR-100
Earlier sketch in CA 121
Keyt, David (Alan) 1930- 1-4R
Keyt, George 1901- .... CP 1
Kezdi, Paul 1914-1999 77-80
Kezys, Algimantas 1928- CANR-31
Earlier sketches in CA 81-84, CANR-14
Kgositsile, Aneb
See House, Gloria
Kgositsile, Keorapetse (William)
1938- CANR-25
Earlier sketch in CA 77-80
See also BW 2
See also CP 2
Khadduri, Majid 1909- CANR-2
Earlier sketch in CA 1-4R
Khadin, Sa'd al-
See Elkhadem, Saad (Eldin Amin)
Khadra, Yasmina
See Moulessehoul, Mohammed
Khafajah, Ibn Ibrahim ibn Abi al-Fath Abu Ishaq
See Ibn Khafajah, Ibrahim ibn Abi al-Fath Abu Ishaq
Khai-Hu'ng 1896-1947 .... EWL 3
Khair, Tabish 1966- 210
Khaketla, B. M.
See Khaketla, B(ennett) Makalo
Khaketla, B(ennett) Makalo 1913-2000
Brief entry 113
Khal, Yusuf al- 1917-1987 .... EWL 3
Khalatbari, Adel-Sultan 1901(?)-1977
Obituary 69-72
Khalid, Farooq 1950- 159
Khalid, Mansour 1931- 160
Khalidi, Rashid I(smail) 1948- 236
Khalil ibn Ahmad, al- c. 718-8th cent.
.... DLB 311
Khalsa, Dayal Kaur 1943-1989 .... CANR-85
Earlier sketch in CA 137
See also Kaur Khalsa, Dayal
See also CLR 30
See also CWRI 5
See also MAICYA 1, 2
See also SATA 62
Khalvati, Mimi 1944- CANR-120
Earlier sketch in CA 142
Khan, Adib 1949- 168
Khan, Badrul H(uda) 1958- 168
Khan, Hasan-Uddin 1947- CANR-121
Earlier sketch in CA 157
Khan, Hassina
See Ali Khan, Shirley
Khan, Ismith Mohamed 1925-2002 191
Obituary 205
See also CN 3, 4
See also DLB 125
See also EWL 3
Khan, Lurey 1927- 97-100
Khan, Mahmood H(asan) 1937- 143
Khan, Mohammed Masud R.
1927(?)-1989 129
Khan, Muhammad 1931- 185
See also Hussein, Abdullah
See also CWW 2
Khan, (Chaudhri) Muhammad Zafrulla
1893-1985
Obituary 117
Khan, Pir Vilayat Inayat
See Inayat-Khan, Vilayat
Khan, Riaz M. 1945- 142
Khan, Rukhsana 1962- .... SATA 118
Khan, Sharif N. 1970- 221
Khan, Shirley Ali
See Ali Khan, Shirley
Khan, Taidje 1920(?)-1985
Obituary 117
Khan, Zillur Rahman 1938- CANR-14
Earlier sketch in CA 41-44R
Khandekar, Vishnu Sakharam
1898-1976 .... EWL 3
Khanna, J(aswant) L(al) 1925- 21-24R
Khansa', Al-
See Al-Khansa'
Khanshendel, Chiron
See Rose, Wendy
Kharasch, Robert Nelson 1926- 103
Khare, Narayan Bhaskar 1882-1970 ...... CAP-1
Earlier sketch in CA 11-12
Kharitonov, Evgenii Vladimirovich
See Kharitonov, Yevgeny
See also DLB 285
Kharitonov, Mark Sergeevich 1937- .... DLB 285
Kharitonov, Yevgeny 1941(?)-1981
Obituary 104
See also Kharitonov, Evgenii Vladimirovich
Kharrat, Edwar al-
See al-Kharrat, Edwar
See also EWL 3
Khatchadourian, Haig 1925- 53-56
Khatena, Joe
See Khatena, Joseph
Khatena, Joseph 1925- CANR-39
Earlier sketch in CA 116
Khatibi, Abdelkebir 1938- .... EWL 3
See also RGWL 3
Khaytov, Nikolay 1919- .... DLB 181
Khayyam, Omar 1048-1131
See Omar Khayyam
See also DA3
See also DAM POET
See also PC 8
See also WLIT 6
Khazanov, Anatoly M. 1937- 154
Khazzoom, J. Daniel 1932- 17-20R
Khedouri, Franklin 1944- 101
Kheirabadi, Masoud 1951- CANR-143
Earlier sketch in CA 142
See also SATA 158
Khemir, Sabiha .... SATA 87
Khemnitser, Ivan Ivanovich
1745-1784 .... DLB 150
Kher, Inder Nath 1933- 93-96
Khera, S(ucha) S(ingh) 1903- 13-16R
Kheraskov, Mikhail Matveevich
1733-1807 .... DLB 150
Kherdian, David 1931- 192
Earlier sketches in CA 21-24R, CANR-39, 78
Autobiographical Essay in 192
See also CAAS 2
See also AAYA 42
See also CLC 6, 9
See also CLR 24
See also JRDA
See also LAIT 3
See also MAICYA 1, 2
See also SATA 16, 74
See also SATA-Essay 125
Khilnani, Sunil 1960- 149
Khlebnikov, Velimir
See Khlebnikov, Viktor Vladimirovich
See also DLB 295
See also EW 10
See also EWL 3
See also RGWL 2, 3
See also TCLC 20
Khlebnikov, Viktor Vladimirovich
1885-1922 217
Brief entry 117
See also Khlebnikov, Velimir
Khodasevich, Vladislav (Felitsianovich)
1886-1939
Brief entry 115
See also DLB 317
See also EWL 3
See also TCLC 15
Khomaini, Ayatollah Sayyed Ruholla Mousavi
See Khomeini, Ruhollah (Mussavi)
Khomeini, Ayatollah
See Khomeini, Ruhollah (Mussavi)
Khomeini, Ayatollah Ruhollah
See Khomeini, Ruhollah (Mussavi)
Khomeini, Imam
See Khomeini, Ruhollah (Mussavi)
Khomeini, Ruhollah (Mussavi)
1900(?)-1989 .... CANR-43
Obituary 128
Earlier sketch in CA 117
Khomiakov, Aleksei Stepanovich
1804-1860 .... DLB 205
Khoo Thwe, Pascal 1967- 227
Khornak, Lucille 1953- 110
Khoroche, Peter (Andrew) 1947- 136
Khosla, G(opal) D(as) 1901-1996 113
Khouri, Callie (Ann) 1957- CANR-124
Earlier sketch in CA 172
Khouri, Fred J(ohn) 1916- 25-28R
Khouri, Mounah A(bdallah) 1918- 114
Khouri, Norma 1970- 224
Khristov, Boris 1945- 192
See also DLB 181
Khrushchev, Nikita Sergeyevich
1894-1971 112
Khrushchev, Sergei (Nikitich) 1935- 136
Khubchandani, Lachman M(ulchand)
1932- 128
Khumeini, Ruhollah
See Khomeini, Ruhollah (Mussavi)
Khush, Gurdev S. 1935- 155
Khvoshchinskaia, Nadezhda Dmitrievna
1824-1889 .... DLB 238
Khvostov, Dmitrii Ivanovich
1757-1835 .... DLB 150
Khwaja, Waqas Ahmad 1952- 160
Kiam, Victor K(ermit) (II) 1926-2001 158
Obituary 197
Kiang, Ying-cheng 17-20R
Kianto, Ilmari 1874-1970
Obituary 29-32R
Kiarostami, Abbas 1940- 204

Kibbe, Pat (Hosley) ... 125
See also SATA 60
Kibbee, Roland 1914-1984
Obituary ... 113
Kibera, Leonard 1940(?)- ... 153
See also BW 2
Kiberd, Declan 1951- ... CANR-107
Earlier sketch in CA 157
Kibirov, Timur Iur'evich 1955- ... DLB 285
Kibler, James Everett, Jr. 1944- ... CANR-46
Earlier sketches in CA 105, CANR-22
Kibler, M. Alison ... 204
Kibler, Robert J(oseph) 1934- ... 29-32R
Kibler, William W. 1942- ... 37-40R
Kibre, Pearl 1902(?)-1985 ... 165
Obituary ... 116
Kicknosway, Faye 1936- ... CANR-7
Earlier sketch in CA 57-60
See also CWP
Kicza, John E(dward) 1947- ... 120
Kidd, Adam 1802(?)-1831 ... DLB 99
Kidd, Aline H(alstead) 1922-1999 ... 17-20R
Kidd, Charles (William) 1952- ... 134
Kidd, Chip 1964- ... 211
See also AAYA 62
Kidd, David Lundy 1926- ... CANR-1
Earlier sketch in CA 1-4R
Kidd, Diana 1933-2000 ... 225
See also SATA 150
Kidd, Elisabeth
See Triegel, Linda (Jeanette)
Kidd, Flora ... RHW
Kidd, Harry 1917- ... 29-32R
Kidd, I(an) G(ray) 1922- ... CANR-93
Earlier sketch in CA 132
Kidd, J(ames) R(obbins) 1915- ... CANR-3
Earlier sketch in CA 5-8R
Kidd, J. Roby
See Kidd, J(ames) R(obbins)
Kidd, Janet (Gladys) Aitken 1908(?)-1988
Obituary ... 127
Kidd, Michael 1919- ... IDFW 3, 4
Kidd, Paul 1963- ... 150
Kidd, Richard 1952- ... 227
See also SATA 152
Kidd, Ronald 1948- ... CANR-39
Earlier sketch in CA 116
See also SATA 42, 92
Kidd, Russ(ell)
See Donson, Cyril
Kidd, Sue Monk ... 202
See also MTFW 2005
Kidd, Virginia 1921-2003 ... CANR-10
Earlier sketch in CA 65-68
Kidd, Walter E. 1917- ... 21-24R
Kidde, Harald 1878-1918 ... DLB 300
Kiddell, John 1922- ... 29-32R
See also SATA 3
Kiddell-Monroe, Joan 1908-1972 ... CAP-1
Earlier sketch in CA 13-14
See also SATA 55
Kidder, Barbara (Ann) 1933- ... 41-44R
Kidder, J(onathan) Edward, (Jr.) 1922- ... 107
Kidder, Rushworth M(oulton) 1944- ... 77-80
Kidder, Tracy 1945- ... CANR-61
Earlier sketches in CA 109, CANR-40
Interview in ... CA-109
See also AAYA 35
See also BEST 90:1
See also DLB 185
See also MTCW 1
Kiddle, Lawrence B(ayard) 1907-1991 .. 33-36R
Kidger, Mark (Richard) 1960- ... 192
Kidman, Fiona (Judith) 1940- ... 159
See also CN 6, 7
Kidner, (Frank) Derek 1913- ... 41-44R
Kidney, Dorothy Boone 1919- ... CANR-3
Earlier sketch in CA 9-12R
Kidney, Walter C(urtis) 1932- ... CANR-19
Earlier sketches in CA 53-56, CANR-4
Kido, Koichi 1890(?)-1977
Obituary ... 69-72
Kidwell, Carl 1910- ... SATA 43
Kidwell, Catherine (Arthelia) 1921- ... 109
Kidwell, Clara Sue 1941- ... 150
Kieckhefer, Richard 1946- ... 93-96
Kiefer, Bill
See Kiefer, Tillman W.
Kiefer, Christie Weber 1937- ... 103
Kiefer, Frederick (Paul) 1945- ... 114
Kiefer, Irene 1926- ... CANR-11
Earlier sketch in CA 69-72
See also SATA 21
Kiefer, Kathleen Balmes 1957- ... 213
See also SATA 142
Kiefer, Louis Sr. 1936- ... 131
Kiefer, Tillman W. 1898-1973 ... CAP-2
Earlier sketch in CA 29-32
Kiefer, Warren 1929- ... 77-80
Kiefer, William Joseph 1925- ... 1-4R
Kiehle, John Alva 1930-
Brief entry ... 115
Kiehtreiber, Albert Conrad
See Guetersloh, Albert Paris
Kiel, R. Andrew 1956- ... 198
Kiell, Norman 1916- ... CANR-5
Earlier sketch in CA 13-16R
Kiell, Paul J(acob) 1930- ... 124
Brief entry ... 118
Kielland, Alexander Lange 1849-1906
Brief entry ... 104
See also TCLC 5
Kiely, Benedict 1919- ... CANR-84
Earlier sketches in CA 1-4R, CANR-2
See also CLC 23, 43
See also CN 1, 2, 3, 4, 5, 6, 7
See also DLB 15, 319
See also SSC 58
See also TCLE 1:1
Kiely, Jerome 1925- ... CP 1
Kiely, Robert (James) 1931- ... 131
Kiemel, Ann
See Anderson, Ann Kiemel
Kieniewicz, Stefan 1907-1992 ... 29-32R
Kienzle, William X(avier)
1928-2001 ... CANR-111
Obituary ... 203
Earlier sketches in CA 93-96, CANR-9, 31, 59
Interview in ... CANR-31
See also CAAS 1
See also CLC 25
See also CMW 4
See also DA3
See also DAM POP
See also MSW
See also MTCW 1, 2
See also MTFW 2005
Kiepper, Shirley Morgan 1933- ... 37-40R
See also Morgan, Shirley
Kieran, John Francis 1892-1981 ... CANR-62
Obituary ... 105
Earlier sketch in CA 101
See also DLB 171
Kieran, Sheila 1930- ... 97-100
Kierans, Eric (William) 1914-2004 ... 210
Obituary ... 227
Kierkegaard, Soren 1813-1855 ... DLB 300
See also EW 6
See also LMFS 2
See also RGWL 3
See also TWA
Kierland, Joseph Scott 1937- ... 61-64
Kierman, Frank Algerton, Jr. 1914-1992 ... 125
Kiernan, Ben 1953- ... CANR-119
Earlier sketch in CA 147
Kiernan, Brian 1937- ... 107
Kiernan, Caitlin R(ebekah) 1964- ... CANR-112
Earlier sketch in CA 173
See also AAYA 58
Kiernan, Pauline ... 204
Kiernan, Robert F(rancis) 1940- ... 115
Kiernan, Sean
See Quick, W(illiam) T(homas)
Kiernan, Thomas ... 113
Kiernan, (E.) V(ictor) G(ordon)
1913- ... CANR-11
Earlier sketch in CA 25-28R
Kiernan, Walter 1902-1978
Obituary ... 73-76
Kierstead, Vera M. 1913- ... 192
See also SATA 121
Kies, Cosette (Nell) 1936- ... 124
Kies, Marietta 1853-1899 ... DLB 270
Kieschnick, Michael Hall 1953- ... 139
Kiesel, Stanley 1925- ... 104
See also SATA 35
Kieser, Rolf 1936- ... 77-80
Kiesler, Charles A(dolphus)
1934-2002 ... CANR-10
Obituary ... 211
Earlier sketch in CA 25-28R
Kiesler, Kate (A.) 1971- ... SATA 90, 152
Kiesler, Sara B(eth) 1940- ... CANR-16
Earlier sketch in CA 25-28R
Kiesling, Christopher (Gerald)
1925-1986 ... CANR-12
Obituary ... 120
Earlier sketch in CA 29-32R
Kiesling, Herbert J. 1934- ... 45-48
Kieslowski, Krzysztof 1941-1996 ... 147
Obituary ... 151
See also CLC 120
Kiessling, Nicolas K. 1936- ... 151
Kiester, Edwin, Jr. 1927- ... 110
Kieszak, Kenneth 1939- ... 89-92
Kieth, Sam 1963- ... 219
Kiev, Ari 1933- ... CANR-3
Earlier sketch in CA 9-12R
Kiev, I. Edward 1905-1975
Obituary ... 104
Kiewiet, Cornelis W(illem) de
See de Kiewiet, Cornelis W(illem)
Kifner, John William 1941- ... 234
Kiger, Joseph Charles 1920- ... 125
Kightlinger, Laura 1964- ... 234
Kihl, Armand
See Ald, Roy A(llison)
Kihl, Young Whan 1932- ... 127
Kihlman, Christer Alfred 1930- ... 159
See also EWL 3
Kihn, Greg 1952- ... 171
See also SATA 110
Kihss, Peter (Frederick) 1912(?)-1984
Obituary ... 114
Kijewski, Karen 1943- ... 161
See also CMW 4
Kijima Hajime
See Kojima Shozo
Kikel, Rudy (John) 1942- ... 117
Kiker, B(ill) F(razier) 1937- ... 61-64
Kiker, Douglas 1930-1991 ... 65-68
Obituary ... 135
Kikuchi, Hiroshi
See Kikuchi, Kan
Kikukawa, Cecily H(arder) 1919- ... 113
See also SATA 44
See also SATA-Brief 35
Kilander, H(olger) Frederick
1900-1969 ... CAP-2
Earlier sketch in CA 17-18
Kilborne, Virginia Wylie 1912-1998 ... 21-24R
Kilbourn, Jonathan 1916(?)-1976
Obituary ... 65-68
Kilbourn, Matt
See Barrett, Geoffrey John
Kilbourn, William (Morley)
1926-1995 ... CANR-11
Earlier sketch in CA 21-24R
Kilbourne, Jean 1943- ... 189
Kilbracken, John (Raymond Godley)
1920- ... 5-8R
Kilburn, Henry
See Rigg, H(enry Hemmingway) K(ilburn)
Kilburn, Robert E(dward) 1931- ... 17-20R
Kilby, Clyde Samuel 1902-1986 ... CANR-9
Obituary ... 120
Earlier sketch in CA 13-16R
Kilby, Peter 1935- ... CANR-17
Earlier sketch in CA 25-28R
Kilcher, Jewel 1974- ... 171
See also SATA 109
Kildahl, John P. 1927- ... 89-92
Kildahl, Phillip A. 1912-1995 ... 21-24R
Kildare, Maurice
See Richardson, Gladwell
Kilduff, (Mary) Dorrell 1901-1998 ... 5-8R
Kile, Joan 1940- ... SATA 78
Kiley, Dan (Edward) 1942-1996 ... 132
Obituary ... 151
Brief entry ... 125
Interview in ... CA-132
Kiley, David 1963- ... 202
Kiley, Frederick 1932- ... CANR-15
Earlier sketch in CA 37-40R
Kiley, Jed
See Kiley, John Gerald
See also DLB 4
Kiley, John Gerald 1889-1962
Obituary ... 112
See also Kiley, Jed
Kiley, Margaret A(nn) ... 53-56
Kilgallen, Dorothy (Mae) 1913-1965
Obituary ... 89-92
Kilgallen, James L. 1888(?)-1982
Obituary ... 108
Kilgo, James 1941-2002 ... 127
Obituary ... 213
See also CSW
Kilgore, (Leslie) Bernard 1908-1967 ... 183
See also DLB 127
Kilgore, James C(olumbus) 1928-1988 .. 33-36R
Obituary ... 127
Kilgore, John
See Paine, Lauran (Bosworth)
Kilgore, Kathleen 1946- ... CANR-27
Earlier sketch in CA 109
See also BYA 6
See also SATA 42
Kilgore, William J(ackson) 1917- ... 45-48
Kilgour, John Graham 1937- ... 105
Kilgour, Raymond L(incoln) 1903- ... CAP-1
Earlier sketch in CA 13-16
Kilham, Benjamin 1953- ... 216
Kilian, Crawford 1941- ... 211
Earlier sketches in CA 105, CANR-22, 56
Autobiographical Essay in ... 211
See also DLB 251
See also SATA 35
See also SFW 4
Kilian, Michael D. 1939-2005 ... 172
Kilina, Patricia
See Warren, Patricia Nell
See also GLL 1
Kiljunen, Kimmo (Roobert) 1951- ... CANR-90
Earlier sketch in CA 132
Killam, (Gordon) Douglas 1930- ... CANR-3
Earlier sketch in CA 49-52
Killan, Gerald 1945- ... 147
Killanin, Lord
See Morris, Michael
Killdeer, John
See Mayhar, Ardath
Kille, Mary F. 1948- ... 33-36R
Killebrew, Harmon (Clayton, Jr.) 1936- ... 159
Killeen, Jacqueline 1931- ... 61-64
Killen, Linda 1945- ... 118
Killenberg, George A(ndrew) 1917- ... 77-80
Killens, John Oliver 1916-1987 ... CANR-26
Obituary ... 123
Earlier sketch in CA 77-80
See also CAAS 2
See also BW 2
See also CLC 10
See also CN 1, 2, 3, 4
See also DLB 33
See also EWL 3
Killham, Edward L(eo) 1926- ... 147
Killham, Nina ... 219
Killian, Ida F(aith) 1910- ... 65-68
Killian, James R(hyne), Jr. 1904-1988 ... 97-100
Obituary ... 124
Killian, Kevin 1952- ... CANR-138
Earlier sketch in CA 174
Killian, Larry
See Wellen, Edward (Paul)
Killian, Lewis M(artin) 1919- ... 9-12R
Killian, Ray A. 1922- ... 21-24R
Killien, Christi 1956- ... SATA 73
Killigrew, Anne 1660-1685 ... DLB 131
Killigrew, Thomas 1612-1683 ... DLB 58
See also RGEL 2
Killilea, Marie (Lyons) 1913-1991 ... 5-8R
See also SATA 2
Killingback, Julia 1944- ... SATA 63
Killinger, George G(lenn) 1908-1993 ... 102
Killinger, John 1933- ... CANR-140
Earlier sketch in CA 81-84
Killingley, Carl A(rthur) 1918- ... 118
Killingley, Siew-Yue 1940- ... CWP
Killingsworth, Frank R. 1873(?)-1976
Obituary ... 65-68
Killion, Katheryn L. 1936- ... 17-20R
Killion, Ronald G(ene) 1931- ... 61-64
Killorin, Joseph I(gnatius) 1926- ... 111
Killough, (Karen) Lee 1942- ... CANR-111
Earlier sketches in CA 89-92, CANR-15, 32, 66
See also SATA 64
See also SFW 4
Killy, Jean-Claude 1943-
Brief entry ... 115
Kilmann, Peter R(ichard) 1945- ... 118
Kilmartin, Edward J(ohn) 1923- ... 17-20R
Kilmer, (Alfred) Joyce 1886-1918
Brief entry ... 120
See also DLB 45
Kilmer, Kenton 1909-1995 ... 1-4R
Obituary ... 148
Kilmer, Nicholas (John) 1941- ... CANR-114
Earlier sketches in CA 129, CANR-56
Kilmer, Val 1959- ... 160
Kilmister, C(live) W(illiam) 1924- ... 119
Kilodney, Crad 1948- ... CANR-37
Earlier sketch in CA 115
Kilpack, Josi S. ... 236
Kilpatrick, Alan Edwin ... 170
Kilpatrick, Andrew 1943- ... 140
Kilpatrick, Carroll 1913-1984 ... 69-72
Kilpatrick, F(ranklin) P(eirce) 1920- ... 21-24R
Kilpatrick, James Jackson 1920- ... CANR-1
Earlier sketch in CA 1-4R
See also AITN 1, 2
Kilpatrick, Nancy 1946- ... CANR-140
Earlier sketches in CA 150, CANR-75
See also HGG
Kilpatrick, Sarah
See Underwood, Mavis Eileen
Kilpatrick, Terrence 1920- ... 81-84
Kilpi, Eeva Karin 1928- ... 192
See also EWL 3
Kilpi, Volter Adalbert 1874-1939 ... EWL 3
Kilreon, Beth
See Walker, Barbara (Jeanne) K(erlin)
Kilroy, James F(rancis) 1935- ... 133
Kilroy, Thomas 1934- ... 53-56
See also CBD
See also CD 5, 6
See also DLB 233
Kilson, Marion 1936- ... 37-40R
Kilson, Martin Luther, Jr. 1931- ... 103
Kilvert, B. Cory, Jr. 1930- ... 45-48
Kilvert, (Robert) Francis 1840-1879 ... RGEL 2
Kilwardby, Robert 1215(?)-1279 ... DLB 115
Kilwein Guevara, Maurice 1961- ... 204
Kilworth, Garry (D.) 1941- ... CANR-67
Earlier sketch in CA 128
See also DLB 261
See also FANT
See also SATA 94
See also SFW 4
Kim
See Simenon, Georges (Jacques Christian)
Kim, Anatolii Andreevich 1939- ... DLB 285
Kim, Ayoung M. ... 223
Kim, Byong-lo Philo 1960- ... 143
Kim, C(hong-) I(k) Eugene 1930- ... 37-40R
Kim, Chin W. 1936- ... 37-40R
Kim, Chong Lim 1937- ... 114
Kim, Choong Soon 1938- ... 116
Kim, David U(ngchon) 1932- ... 109
Kim, Derek (D.) ... 220
Kim, Elaine H(aikyung) 1942- ... CANR-100
Earlier sketch in CA 130
Kim, Hakjoon 1943- ... 147
Kim, Hee-Jin 1927- ... 106
Kim, Helen 1899-1970 ... CAP-1
Earlier sketch in CA 13-16
See also SATA 98
Kim, (Robert) Hyung-chan 1938- ... CANR-103
Earlier sketch in CA 57-60
Kim, Hyun-Hee 1962- ... 164
Kim, Il Sung 1912-1994 ... 174
Kim, Ilpyong J(ohn) 1931- ... 53-56
Kim, In S(oo) 1943- ... CANR-122
Earlier sketch in CA 164
Kim, Johnny
See Kim, Derek (D.)
Kim, Jung-Gun 1933- ... 53-56
Kim, K(wan) H(o) 1936- ... 29-32R
Kim, Kwan-Bong 1936- ... 37-40R
Kim, Kyung-Won 1936- ... 29-32R
Kim, Myung Mi 1957- ... 211
Kim, Nancy (S.) 1966- ... 191
Kim, Richard C(hong) C(hin) 1923- ... 29-32R
Kim, Richard E. 1932- ... 5-8R
See also CN 1, 2, 3, 4
See also RGAL 4
Kim, Samuel S(oonki) 1935- ... 104
Kim, Se-Jin 1933- ... 53-56
Kim, Seung Hee 1936- ... 29-32R
Kim, Sue Kwock 1968- ... 220
Kim, Suji Kwock
See Kim, Sue Kwock
Kim, Suki 1970- ... 219
Kim, Sung Bok 1932-
Brief entry ... 113
Kim, Willyce 1946- ... GLL 2
Kim, Yong Choon 1935- ... 57-60
Kim, Yong-ik 1920- ... 17-20R
Kim, Yoon Hough 1934-1976 ... 33-36R
Kim, Young Hum 1920- ... 21-24R

Cumulative Index 317 King

Kimball, Arthur G(ustaf) 1927- 41-44R
Kimball, Cheryl 1957- 216
Kimball, Dean 1912-1998 69-72
Kimball, Frank
See Paine, Lauran (Bosworth)
Kimball, Gayle 1943- CANR-116
Earlier sketches in CA 107, CANR-58
See also SATA 90
Kimball, George 1943- 53-56
Kimball, Jeffrey (P.) 1941- 194
Kimball, John P. 1941- CANR-2
Earlier sketch in CA 45-48
Kimball, John W(ard) 1931- CANR-15
Earlier sketch in CA 93-96
Kimball, Meredith M. 1944- 154
Kimball, Michael 1949- CANR-98
Earlier sketch in CA 120
Kimball, Nancy
See Upson, Norma
Kimball, Penn T(ownsend) 1915- CANR-18
Earlier sketch in CA 102
Kimball, Philip 1941- 117
Kimball, Ralph
See Paine, Lauran (Bosworth)
Kimball, Richard B(urleigh)
1816-1892 .... DLB 202
Kimball, Richard Laurance 1939- CANR-7
Earlier sketch in CA 53-56
Kimball, Robert (Eric) 1939- CANR-101
Brief entry 106
Earlier sketch in CA 159
Kimball, Roger 1953- CANR-103
Earlier sketches in CA 136, CANR-64
Kimball, Solon T(oothaker) 1909- 21-24R
Kimball, Spencer L(evan) 1918- CANR-1
Earlier sketch in CA 1-4R
Kimball, Spencer W(oolley)
1895-1985 .... CANR-39
Obituary 117
Earlier sketch in CA 45-48
Kimball, Stanley B(uchholz) 1926- ... CANR-26
Earlier sketches in CA 17-20R, CANR-10
Kimball, Violet T(ew) 1932- 196
See also SATA 126
Kimball, Warren F. 1935- 25-28R
Kimball, Yeffe 1914-1978 .... SATA 37
Kimber, Lee
See King, Albert
Kimber, Stephen 1949- 223
Kimberley, Hugh
See Morland, Nigel
Kimberly, Gail CANR-129
Earlier sketch in CA 81-84
Kimble, Daniel Porter 1934- 41-44R
Kimble, David 1921- 13-16R
Kimble, George H(erbert) T(inley) 1908- 108
Kimble, Gregory A(dams) 1917- 21-24R
Kimbrell, Grady 1933- 33-36R
Kimbrell, James 182
Kimbriel, Katherine Eliska 1956- 172
Kimbro, Harriet
See Kofalk, Harriet
Kimbro, Jean
See Kimbro, John M.
Kimbro, John M. 1929- CANR-85
Earlier sketches in CA 45-48, CANR-2
Kimbrough, Emily 1899-1989 .... 17-20R
Obituary 127
See also SATA 2
See also SATA-Obit 59
Kimbrough, Katheryn
See Kimbro, John M.
Kimbrough, Ralph B(radley) 1922-1998 .. 73-76
Kimbrough, Richard B(enito) 1931- 41-44R
Kimbrough, Robert (Alexander III)
1929- CANR-6
Earlier sketch in CA 9-12R
Kimbrough, S. T., Jr. 1936- 200
Kimbrough, Sara Dodge 1901-1990 93-96
Kimche, David 103
Kimeldorf, Martin (R.) 1948- 192
See also SATA 121
Kimenye, Barbara 1940(?)- CANR-85
Earlier sketch in CA 101
See also CWRI 5
See also SATA 121
Kimes, Beverly Rae 1939- CANR-47
Brief entry 107
Earlier sketch in CA 122
Kimmel, Allan J. 234
Kimmel, Arthur S(andor) 1930-1999 ..... 41-44R
Kimmel, Daniel M. 1955- 234
Kimmel, Douglas C(harles) 1943- 53-56
Kimmel, Eric A. 1946- CANR-104
Earlier sketches in CA 49-52, CANR-3
See also MAICYA 2
See also MAICYAS 1
See also SATA 13, 80, 125
Kimmel, Jo 1931- CANR-4
Earlier sketch in CA 53-56
Kimmel, Jordan L. 1958- 176
Kimmel, Margaret Mary 1938- 124
See also SATA 43
See also SATA-Brief 33
Kimmel, Melvin 1930- 25-28R
Kimmel, Michael S(cott) 1951- CANR-99
Earlier sketch in CA 153
Kimmel, Stanley (Preston) 1894(?)-1982
Obituary 109
Kimmel, William (Breyfogel) 1908-1982
Obituary 109
Kimmelman, Burt 1947- 187
Kimmelman, Elaine 1925- 111
Kimmelman, Leslie (Grodinsky)
1958- CANR-140
Earlier sketch in CA 132
See also SATA 85, 150
Kimmelman, Michael Simon 1958- 173
Kimmelman, Sidney
See Omarr, Sydney
Kimmens, Andrew C(harles) 1942- 124
Kimmerling, Baruch 1939- 141
Kimmey, John Lansing 1922-
Brief entry 108
Kimmich, Christoph M(artin) 1939- 69-72
Kimmich, Flora (Graham Horne) 1939- 106
Kimpel, Ben D(rew) 1915-1983 57-60
Kimpel, Ben F(ranklin) 1905-1997 .... 1-4R
Kimrey, Grace (Evelyn) Saunders
1910-2001 .... CANR-24
Earlier sketch in CA 45-48
Kim Ronyoung
See Hahn, Gloria
Kimura, Doreen 1933- 194
Kimura, Jiro 1949- 85-88
Kincaid, Alan
See Rikhoff, James C.
Kincaid, J. D.
See Dalgleish, James Corteen
See also TCWW 2
Kincaid, Jamaica 1949- CANR-133
Earlier sketches in CA 125, CANR-47, 59, 95
See also AAYA 13, 56
See also AFAW 2
See also AMWS 7
See also BLC 2
See also BRWS 7
See also BW 2, 3
See also CDALBS
See also CDWLB 3
See also CLC 43, 68, 137
See also CLR 63
See also CN 4, 5, 6, 7
See also DA3
See also DAM MULT, NOV
See also DLB 157, 227
See also DNFS 1
See also EWL 3
See also EXPS
See also FW
See also LATS 1:2
See also LMFS 2
See also MAL 5
See also MTCW 2
See also MTFW 2005
See also NCFS 1
See also NFS 3
See also SSC 72
See also SSFS 5, 7
See also TUS
See also WWE 1
See also YAW
Kincaid, James R(ussell) 1937- CANR-15
Earlier sketch in CA 65-68
Kincaid, Nanci 1950- CANR-120
Earlier sketch in CA 174
See also CSW
Kincaid, Suzanne (Moss) 1936- 9-12R
Kinch, Sam E., Jr. 1940- 45-48
Kincheloe, Raymond McFarland 1909- ... 61-64
Kincher, Jonni 1949- 147
See also SATA 79
Kinck, Hans E(rnst) 1865-1926 205
See also DLB 297
Kincl, (Gladys) Kay Owens 1955- 106
Kindall, Alva Frederick 1906-1996 .... 1-4R
Kindem, Gorham A(nders) 1948- CANR-51
Earlier sketch in CA 125
Kinder, Charles Alfonso II 1946- 210
Kinder, Chuck
See Kinder, Charles Alfonso II
Kinder, Faye 1902-1993 .... 5-8R
Kinder, Gary 1946- 109
Kinder, James S. 1895-1992 .... 13-16R
Kinder, Kathleen
See Potter, Kathleen Jill
Kinder, Marsha 1940- CANR-88
Earlier sketches in CA 41-44R, CANR-15
Kinderlehrer, Jane 1913-2001 106
Kindl, Patrice 1951- CANR-115
Earlier sketch in CA 149
See also AAYA 55
See also SATA 82, 128
Kindleberger, Charles P(oor) II
1910-2003 .... CANR-82
Obituary 218
Earlier sketches in CA 73-76, CANR-12, 36
Kindley, Jeffrey (Bowman) 1945- 130
Brief entry 125
Interview in CA-130
Kindred, Alton R(ichard) 1922-1995 109
Kindred, Leslie W(ithrow) 1905-1985 ... 41-44R
Kindred, Wendy (Good) 1937- 37-40R
See also SATA 7
Kindregan, Charles P(eter) 1935- CANR-10
Earlier sketch in CA 21-24R
Kindsvatter, Peter S. 1949- 229
Kinealy, Christine 1956- 149
Kineji, Maborushi
See Gibson, Walter B(rown)
Kiner, Ralph (McPherran) 1922- 161
Kinert, Reed (Charles) 1911(?)-1976 107
Kines, Pat Decker 1937- 65-68
See also SATA 12
Kines, Thomas Alvin 1922- 13-16R
Kines, Tom
See Kines, Thomas Alvin
King, Adam
See Hoare, Robert J(ohn)
King, Adele Cockshoot 1932- CANR-92
Earlier sketches in CA 13-16R, CANR-8
King, Alan 1927-2004 89-92
Obituary 228
King, Albert 1924-
See Wetzel, Lewis
See also TCWW 2
King, Alec Hyatt
See King, Alexander Hyatt
King, Alexander 1909- 110
King, Alexander Hyatt 1911-1995 124
Obituary 148
King, Alfred M. 1933- 25-28R
King, Algin B(raddy) 1927- CANR-15
Earlier sketch in CA 41-44R
King, Alison
See Martini, Teri
King, Alvy L(eon) 1932- 33-36R
King, Ames
See King, Albert
King, Anita 1931- 175
King, (Maria) Anna 1964- .... SATA 72
King, Annette 1941- 33-36R
King, Anthony (Stephen) 1934- 17-20R
King, Archdale Arthur 1890-1972 .... CAP-1
Earlier sketch in CA 17-18
King, Ben F(rank) 1937- 57-60
King, Bernard 1946- 156
See also FANT
King, Bert T(homas) 1927- 45-48
King, Betty (Alice) 1919- 103
King, Betty Patterson 1925- 9-12R
King, Billi
See Caulder, Colline
King, Billie Jean 1943- CANR-10
Earlier sketch in CA 53-56
See also SATA 12
King, Bob 184
King, Bob 1952- 184
King, Bruce (?)-1976
Obituary 61-64
King, Bruce (Alvin) 1933- CANR-92
Earlier sketches in CA 53-56, CANR-4, 19, 41
King, C(lyde) Richard 1924- CANR-11
Earlier sketch in CA 69-72
King, Captain Charles
See King, Charles
King, Carol Soucek 1943- CANR-96
Earlier sketch in CA 145
King, Cassandra 1944- 216
King, Cecil
See King, Cecil H(armsworth)
King, Cecil H(armsworth) 1901-1987 110
Obituary 122
King, Charles 1844-1933
Brief entry 122
See also King, General Charles
See also DLB 186
King, Charles (Lester) 1922- 57-60
King, Charles R. 1947- 148
King, Christopher (L.) 1945- .... SATA 84
King, Clarence (Rivers) 1842-1901
Brief entry 110
See also ANW
See also DLB 12
King, Clarence 1884(?)-1974
Obituary 53-56
King, (David) Clive 1924- CANR-124
Earlier sketches in CA 104, CANR-86
See also SATA 28, 144
King, Clyde S(tuart) 1919- 17-20R
King, Colbert I. 1939- 227
King, Colin 1943- .... SATA 76
King, Coretta Scott 1927- CANR-27
Earlier sketch in CA 29-32R
See also BW 1
King, Cynthia 1925- CANR-36
Earlier sketch in CA 29-32R
See also SATA 7
King, Daniel (John) 1963- 199
See also SATA 130
King, Daniel P(atrick) 1942- CANR-4
Earlier sketch in CA 53-56
King, David 1943- 168
King, Dean 230
King, Deborah 1950- CANR-31
Earlier sketch in CA 112
King, (William) Dennis 1941- 130
King, Donald B. 1913-1997 .... 13-16R
King, Edith W(eiss) 1930- CANR-14
Earlier sketch in CA 33-36R
King, Edmund J(ames) 1914-2002 ...... CANR-2
Obituary 205
Earlier sketch in CA 5-8R
King, Edmund L(udwig) 1914- CANR-49
Earlier sketches in CA 33-36R, CANR-13
King, Edward L. 1928- 81-84
King, Eleanor (Campbell) 1906-1991 209
King, Elizabeth 1953- .... SATA 83
King, Elizabeth A.
See Abravanel, Elizabeth
King, Florence 1936- CANR-41
Earlier sketches in CA 57-60, CANR-7
See also AITN 1
See also CSW
See also DLBY 1985
King, Francis (Henry) 1923- CANR-86
Earlier sketches in CA 1-4R, CANR-1, 33
See also CLC 8, 53, 145
See also CN 1, 2, 3, 4, 5, 6, 7
See also DAM NOV
See also DLB 15, 139
See also MTCW 1
King, Francis Edward 1931- 61-64
King, Francis P(aul) 1922- 13-16R
King, Frank A.
See King, Franklin Alexander
King, Frank H(enry) H(aviland)
1926- CANR-44
Earlier sketch in CA 119
King, Frank O. 1883-1969
Obituary 89-92
See also SATA-Obit 22
King, Frank P. 1939- 182
King, Frank R. 1904-1999 .... SATA 127
King, Franklin Alexander 1923- 45-48
King, Frederick Murl 1916- CANR-2
Earlier sketch in CA 5-8R
King, Gabriel
See Harrison, M(ichael) John
King, Gary C. 225
King, General Charles
See King, Charles
See also TCWW 1, 2
King, Geoff 1960- 200
King, Gilbert
See Harrison, Susan Frances (Riley)
King, Glen D. 1925- 9-12R
King, Godfre Ray
See Ballard, Guy W(arren)
King, Grace (Elizabeth) 1852(?)-1932
Brief entry 116
See also DLB 12, 78
King, Graham (Peter) 1930-1999
Obituary 179
King, Graham (Peter) 1930-1999
Obituary 179
King, Harold 1898-1990
Obituary 132
King, Harold 1945- CANR-7
Earlier sketch in CA 57-60
King, Harriet (Eleanor Baillie) Hamilton
1840-1920 183
See also DLB 199
King, Hedley 1949- 141
King, Helen H(ayes) 1937- 33-36R
King, Henry 1592-1669 .... BRWS 6
See also DLB 126
See also RGEL 2
King, Homer W. 1907-1987 .... CAP-1
Earlier sketch in CA 13-16
King, Horace Maybray
See Maybray-King, Horace
King, Irving H(enry) 1935- 89-92
King, Ivan R(obert) 1927- 89-92
King, J. L. 236
King, J. Robert 210
King, Jack
See Dowling, Allen
King, James 1942- CANR-104
Earlier sketches in CA 121, CANR-49
King, James Cecil 1924- CANR-14
Earlier sketch in CA 41-44R
King, James G. 1898(?)-1979
Obituary 89-92
King, James T(errell) 1933- 37-40R
King, James W. 1920- 9-12R
King, Jane
See Currie, Stephen
King, Janet Kauffman
Brief entry 110
See also Kauffman, Janet King
King, Jeanette (Margaret) 1959- 173
See also SATA 105
King, Jere Clemens 1910-1999 .... 5-8R
King, Jerome Babcock 1927- 103
King, (Frederick) Jerry 1941- 97-100
King, Jerry P. 1935- 139
King, Joan (M.) 1930- 123
King, Joe 1909(?)-1979
Obituary 85-88
King, John
See McKeag, Ernest L(ionel)
King, John 1944- 235
King, John 1960- 222
King, John Edward 1947- 102
King, John L(afayette) 1917- 41-44R
King, John N. 1945- CANR-109
Earlier sketches in CA 113, CANR-32
King, John O(zias) 1923-2001 237
Brief entry 108
King, John Q. Taylor 1921- 25-28R
King, Jonathon 217
King, Jonny 1965- 162
King, Josie
See Germany, (Vera) Jo(sephine)
King, Joyce
See Ching, Julia (Chia-yi)
King, K. DeWayne (Dewey) 1925- 13-16R
King, Katherine Callen 1942- CANR-56
Earlier sketch in CA 127
King, Kathleen (Marie) 1948- 114
King, Kathryn R. 217
King, Kennedy
See Brown, George Douglas
King, Kimball 1934- CANR-57
Earlier sketches in CA 110, CANR-31
King, Larry 1933- CANR-102
Brief entry 111
Earlier sketch in CA 139
King, Larry L. 1929- CANR-24
Earlier sketch in CA 13-16R
See also MTCW 1
See also SATA 66
King, Laurie R. 1952- 207
Earlier sketches in CA 140, CANR-63, 105
Autobiographical Essay in 207
See also AAYA 29
See also CMW 4
See also SATA 88
King, Leila Pier 1882-1981
Obituary 105
King, Leslie J(ohn) 1934- 186
Brief entry 106
King, Lester S(now) 1908-2002 .... 33-36R
Obituary 211
King, Lily 190

King, Louise W(ooster) ... CANR-7
Earlier sketch in CA 13-16R
King, Marcet (Alice Hines) 1922-1995 .. 25-28R
King, Margaret L(eah) 1947- ... CANR-92
Earlier sketches in CA 123, CANR-50
King, Marian 1900(?)-1986 ... CANR-2
Obituary ... 118
Earlier sketch in CA 5-8R
See also SATA 23
See also SATA-Obit 47
King, Marjorie Cameron 1909- ... 33-36R
King, Mark 1945- ... 61-64
King, Martha 1937- ... 216
King, Martha L. 1918- ... 127
Brief entry ... 109
King, Martin Luther Sr. 1899-1984 ... 125
Obituary ... 117
See also BW 1
King, Martin Luther, Jr. 1929-1968 ... CANR-44
Earlier sketches in CAP-2, CA 25-28, CANR-27
See also BLC 2
See also BW 2, 3
See also CLC 83
See also DA
See also DA3
See also DAB
See also DAC
See also DAM MST, MULT
See also LAIT 5
See also LATS 1:2
See also MTCW 1, 2
See also MTFW 2005
See also SATA 14
See also WLCS
King, Mary (Elizabeth) 1940- ... CANR-126
Earlier sketch in CA 160
King, Mary Ellen 1958- ... 158
See also SATA 93
King, Mary Louise 1911-1996 ... 21-24R
King, Michael
See Buse, Renee and
Kahane, Meir (David)
King, Michael 1945-2004 ... 194
Obituary ... 225
King, Michael J(ulius) 1941- ... 119
King, Morton Brandon 1913- ... 102
King, Nicholas 1947- ... 203
King, Noel Q(uixote) 1922- ... CANR-19
Earlier sketches in CA 1-4R, CANR-4
King, Norman A.
See Tralins, S(andor) Robert
King, O. H. P. 1902-1996 ... 1-4R
King, Patricia 1930- ... 5-8R
King, Paul
See Drackett, Phil(ip Arthur)
King, Paula
See Downing, Paula E.
King, Pauline 1917- ... 119
King, Peggy Cameron
See King, Marjorie Cameron
King, Peter 1925- ... 125
King, Peter (John) 1940-1989
Obituary ... 127
King, Philip 1904-1979 ... 103
King, Philip B(urke) 1903-1987 ... 125
Obituary ... 122
King, Philip J. 1925- ... 149
King, Preston (Theodore) 1936- ... CANR-109
Earlier sketches in CA 21-24R, CANR-10, 26
King, Rachel 1963- ... 231
King, Ray A(iken) 1933- ... 21-24R
King, Richard A(ustin) 1929- ... 21-24R
King, Richard G. 1922- ... 37-40R
King, Richard H. 1942- ... CANR-40
Earlier sketch in CA 77-80
King, Richard L(ouis) 1937- ... CANR-1
Earlier sketch in CA 45-48
King, Robert B. 1949- ... 125
King, Robert Charles 1928- ... 17-20R
King, Robert G. 1929- ... 21-24R
King, Robert H(arlen) 1935- ... 45-48
King, Robert L. 1950- ... 77-80
King, Robert R(ay) 1942- ... CANR-8
Earlier sketch in CA 61-64
King, Robin 1919- ... 5-8R
King, Roger (Frank Graham) 1947- . CANR-139
Earlier sketch in CA 139
King, Roma Alvah, Jr. 1914- ... CANR-1
Earlier sketch in CA 1-4R
King, Ronald (Wilfred) 1914-1988 ... 107
King, Ross 1962- ... 221
King, Ruchama ... 225
King, Rufus 1917-1999 ... CANR-86
Obituary ... 188
Earlier sketch in CA 25-28R
King, Ruth Rodney
See Manley, Ruth Rodney King
King, Sarah Belk ... 234
King, Spencer B(idwell), Jr. 1904-1977 .. CAP-1
Earlier sketch in CA 17-18
King, Stanley H(all) 1921-
Brief entry ... 110
King, Stella (Lennox) 1919-2002 ... 69-72
Obituary ... 211
King, Stephen (Edwin) 1947- ... CANR-134
Earlier sketches in CA 61-64, CANR-1, 30, 52, 76, 119
See also AAYA 1, 17
See also AMWS 5
See also BEST 90:1
See also BPFB 2
See also CLC 12, 26, 37, 61, 113
See also CN 7
See also CPW
See also DA3
See also DAM NOV, POP
See also DLB 143
See also DLBY 1980
See also HGG
See also JRDA
See also LAIT 5
See also MTCW 1, 2
See also MTFW 2005
See also RGAL 4
See also SATA 9, 55, 161
See also SSC 17, 55
See also SUFW 1, 2
See also WYAS 1
See also YAW
King, Stephen Michael ... SATA 157
King, Stephen W(illiam) 1947- ... 61-64
See also GL 2
King, Steve
See King, Stephen (Edwin)
King, Susan Petigru 1824-1875 ... DLB 239
King, T(homas) J(ames) 1925- ... 37-40R
King, Tabitha (Jane) 1949- ... CANR-30
Earlier sketch in CA 105
King, Teri 1940- ... 89-92
King, Terry Johnson 1929-1978 ... 17-20R
Obituary ... 77-80
King, Thomas 1943- ... CANR-95
Earlier sketch in CA 144
See also CCA 1
See also CLC 89, 171
See also CN 6, 7
See also DAC
See also DAM MULT
See also DLB 175
See also NNAL
See also SATA 96
King, Thomas F. 1942- ... 198
King, Thomas M(ulvihill) 1929- ... 57-60
King, Tom
See King, Thomas F.
King, Tony 1947- ... 109
See also SATA 39
King, Valerie
See Bosna, Valerie
King, Veronica
See King, Florence
King, Victor T(erence) 1949- ... 185
King, Vincent
See Vinson, Rex Thomas
King, Willard L. 1893-1981 ... 1-4R
Obituary ... 103
King, William 1662-1712 ... RGEL 2
King, William Donald Aelian 1910- ... 89-92
King, William R(ichard) 1938- ... CANR-8
Earlier sketch in CA 21-24R
King, Wilma 1942- ... 141
King, Winston L(ee) 1907-2000 ... 41-44R
King, Woodie, Jr. 1937- ... CANR-25
Earlier sketch in CA 103
See also BW 2
See also DLB 38
King, Zalman 1941- ... 213
Kingdom, Will
See Rickman, Philip
Kingdon, Frank 1894-1972
Obituary ... 33-36R
Kingdon, John W(ells) 1940- ... 25-28R
Kingdon, Jonathan ... 237
Kingdon, Robert M(cCune) 1927- ... 21-24R
Kingdon, Roger 1891-1984
Obituary ... 113
Kingery, Robert E(rnest) 1913-1978 ... 9-12R
Obituary ... 103
King-Farlow, John 1932- ... 111
King-Hall, Magdalen 1904-1971 ... CAP-1
Obituary ... 29-32R
Earlier sketch in CA 9-10
King-Hall, (William) Stephen (Richard)
1893-1966 ... 5-8R
King-Hamilton, Alan 1904- ... 130
King-Hele, Desmond (George)
1927- ... CANR-66
Earlier sketches in CA 29-32R, CANR-14, 32
Kinghorn, A(lexander) M(anson) 1926- ... 93-96
Kinghorn, Kenneth Cain 1930- ... CANR-57
Earlier sketches in CA 41-44R, CANR-14, 31
Kinglake, Alexander William
1809-1891 ... DLB 55, 166
Kingma, Daphne Rose 1942- ... 208
Kingman, Dong (Moy Shu) 1911-2000 ... 112
Obituary ... 188
See also SATA 44
Kingman, Kent ... 190
Kingman, Lee
See Natti, (Mary) Lee
See also CLC 17
See also CWRI 5
See also SAAS 3
See also SATA 1, 67
Kingman, Russ 1917- ... CANR-17
Earlier sketch in CA 101
Kingo, Thomas 1634-1703 ... DLB 300
Kingry, Philip L. 1942- ... 53-56
Kingsbury, Arthur 1939- ... 29-32R
Kingsbury, Donald (MacDonald)
1929- ... CANR-85
Earlier sketch in CA 124
See also DLB 251
See also SFW 4
Kingsbury, Jack Dean 1934- ... 37-40R
Kingsbury, John M(erriam) 1928- ... CANR-6
Earlier sketch in CA 13-16R
Kingsbury, Karen ... 224
Kingsbury, Noel ... 238
Kingsbury, Robert C(arrick) 1924- ... CANR-2
Earlier sketch in CA 1-4R
Kingsbury-Smith, Joseph 1908-1999 ... 133
Obituary ... 177
Kingsland, Leslie William 1912- ... 69-72
See also SATA 13
Kingsland, Rosemary 1941- ... 226
Kingsland, Sharon E. 1951- ... 124
Kingsley, April 1941- ... 140
Kingsley, Charles 1819-1875 ... CLR 77
See also DLB 21, 32, 163, 178, 190
See also FANT
See also MAICYA 2
See also MAICYAS 1
See also RGEL 2
See also WCH
See also YABC 2
Kingsley, Charlotte Mary
See Cooke, H. O. and
Dashing Charley and
Emmett, R. T. and
Hanshew, Thomas W. and
Old Cap Collier and
Old Cap Darrell
Kingsley, Daniel T(hain) 1932- ... 117
Kingsley, Emily Perl 1940- ... 107
See also SATA 33
Kingsley, G. Thomas 1936- ... 149
Kingsley, Henry 1830-1876 ... DLB 21, 230
See also RGEL 2
Kingsley, Johanna
See Perutz, Kathrin
Kingsley, Mary Henrietta 1862-1900 .. DLB 174
Kingsley, Michael J. 1918(?)-1972
Obituary ... 37-40R
Kingsley, Sidney 1906-1995 ... 85-88
Obituary ... 147
See also CAD
See also CLC 44
See also DFS 14, 19
See also DLB 7
See also MAL 5
See also RGAL 4
Kingsley-Smith, Terence 1940- ... 57-60
Kingsmill, Hugh
See Lunn, Hugh (Kingsmill)
See also DLB 149
King-Smith, Dick 1922- ... CANR-85
Earlier sketch in CA 105
See also CLR 40
See also CWRI 5
See also MAICYA 1, 2
See also SATA 47, 80, 135
See also SATA-Brief 38
Kingsnorth, George W(illiam) 1924- ... 5-8R
Kingsolver, Barbara 1955- ... CANR-133
Brief entry ... 129
Earlier sketches in CA 134, CANR-60, 96
Interview in ... CA-134
See also AAYA 15
See also AMWS 7
See also CDALBS
See also CLC 55, 81, 130
See also CN 7
See also CPW
See also CSW
See also DA3
See also DAM POP
See also DLB 206
See also INT
See also LAIT 5
See also MTCW 2
See also MTFW 2005
See also NFS 5, 10, 12
See also RGAL 4
See also TCLE 1:1
Kingston, Albert J(ames) 1917- ... 21-24R
Kingston, Christina ... 217
Kingston, Jeremy
See Betancourt, John (Gregory)
Kingston, Jeremy Henry Spencer 1931- ... 103
Kingston, Maxine (Ting Ting) Hong
1940- ... CANR-128
Earlier sketches in CA 69-72, CANR-13, 38, 74, 87
Interview in ... CANR-13
See also AAL
See also AAYA 8, 55
See also AMWS 5
See also BPFB 2
See also CDALBS
See also CLC 12, 19, 58, 121
See also CN 6, 7
See also DA3
See also DAM MULT, NOV
See also DLB 173, 212, 312
See also DLBY 1980
See also EWL 3
See also FL 1:6
See also FW
See also LAIT 5
See also MAL 5
See also MAWW
See also MTCW 1, 2
See also MTFW 2005
See also NFS 6
See also RGAL 4
See also SATA 53
See also SSFS 3
See also TCWW 2
See also WLCS
Kingston, Paul W. 1951- ... 198
Kingston, Syd
See Bingley, David Ernest
Kingston, (Frederick) Temple 1925- .. CANR-12
Earlier sketch in CA 33-36R
Kingston, Victoria 1956- ... 189
Kingston, William Henry Giles
1814-1880 ... DLB 163
Kingston-Mann, Esther ... 112
King-Stoops, Joyce 1923- ... 81-84
Kington, Miles (Beresford) 1941- ... 130
Kingwell, Mark (Gerald) 1963- ... 231
Kininmonth, Christopher 1917- ... 53-56
Kinkade, Richard P(aisley) 1939- ... CANR-31
Earlier sketches in CA 37-40R, CANR-14
Kinkade, Thomas 1958- ... 202
See also AAYA 64
Kinkaid, Matt
See Adams, Clifton
Kinkaid, Wyatt E.
See Jennings, Michael Glenn
Kinkead, Eugene (Francis)
1906-1992 ... CANR-1
Earlier sketch in CA 1-4R
Kinkead, Gwen 1951- ... 144
Kinkead-Weekes, Mark 1931- ... CANR-56
Earlier sketch in CA 124
Kinkley, Jeffrey C(arroll) 1948- ... CANR-92
Earlier sketches in CA 125, CANR-57
Kinley, Phyllis (Elaine Gillespie) 1930- ... 1-4R
Kinloch, A. Murray 1923- ... 103
Kinmonth, Earl H. 1946- ... 107
Kinnaird, Clark 1901-1983 ... CANR-1
Obituary ... 111
Earlier sketch in CA 45-48
Kinnaird, John (William) 1924-1980 ... 124
Obituary ... 97-100
Kinnaird, William M(cKee) 1928- ... 101
Kinnamon, Keneth 1932- ... 37-40R
Kinnan, Mary Lewis 1763-1848 ... DLB 200
Kinnane, John F. 1921-1987
Obituary ... 123
Kinnard, Douglas 1921- ... CANR-14
Earlier sketch in CA 77-80
Kinnear, Elizabeth K. 1902-1994 ... CAP-2
Earlier sketch in CA 33-36
Kinnear, Michael 1937- ... 37-40R
Kinneavy, James Louis 1920-1999 ... 69-72
Kinneir, (Richard) Jock 1917-1994 ... 121
Kinnell, Galway 1927- ... CANR-138
Earlier sketches in CA 9-12R, CANR-10, 34, 66, 116
Interview in ... CANR-34
See also AMWS 3
See also CLC 1, 2, 3, 5, 13, 29, 129
See also CP 1, 2, 3, 4, 5, 6, 7
See also DLB 5
See also DLBY 1987
See also EWL 3
See also MAL 5
See also MTCW 1, 2
See also MTFW 2005
See also PAB
See also PC 26
See also PFS 9
See also RGAL 4
See also TCLE 1:1
See also WP
Kinney, Arthur F(rederick) 1933- ... CANR-142
Earlier sketches in CA 37-40R, CANR-14
Kinney, C. Cle(land) 1915- ... 9-12R
See also SATA 6
Kinney, Francis S(herwood) 1915-1993 ... 106
Obituary ... 140
Kinney, Harrison 1921- ... CANR-52
Earlier sketch in CA 1-4R
See also SATA 13
Kinney, James (Joseph) 1942- ... 120
Kinney, James R(oser) 1902(?)-1978
Obituary ... 81-84
Kinney, Jean Stout 1912- ... 9-12R
See also SATA 12
Kinney, John F. 1914- ... 150
Kinney, Lucien Blair 1895-1971 ... CAP-2
Earlier sketch in CA 23-24
Kinney, Peter 1943- ... 73-76
Kinney, Richard 1924(?)-1979
Obituary ... 85-88
Kinnicutt, Susan Sibley 1926-1979 ... 77-80
Kinnison, William A(ndrew) 1932- ... 21-24R
Kinor, Jehuda
See Rothmuller, Aron Marko
Kinoshita Junji 1914- ... 124
See also EWL 3
Kinoy, Arthur 1920-2003 ... 143
Obituary ... 221
Kinross, Lord
See Balfour, (John) Patrick Douglas
Kinsale, Laura ... 230
Kinsbruner, Jay 1939- ... 25-28R
Kinsel, Paschal 1895(?)-1976
Obituary ... 69-72
Kinsella, James 1959- ... CANR-140
Earlier sketch in CA 134
Kinsella, John 1963- ... 189
See also WWE 1
Kinsella, Paul L. 1923- ... 21-24R
Kinsella, Sophie ... 211
Kinsella, Thomas 1928- ... CANR-122
Earlier sketches in CA 17-20R, CANR-15
See also BRWS 5
See also CLC 4, 19, 138
See also CP 1, 2, 3, 4, 5, 6, 7
See also DLB 27
See also EWL 3
See also MTCW 1, 2
See also MTFW 2005
See also RGEL 2
See also TEA
Kinsella, W(illiam) P(atrick) 1935- ... 222
Earlier sketches in CA 97-100, CANR-21, 35, 66, 75, 129
Interview in ... CANR-21
Autobiographical Essay in ... 222
See also CAAS 7
See also AAYA 7, 60
See also BPFB 2
See also CLC 27, 43, 166

See also CN 4, 5, 6, 7
See also CPW
See also DAC
See also DAM NOV, POP
See also FANT
See also LAIT 5
See also MTCW 1, 2
See also MTFW 2005
See also NFS 15
See also RGSF 2
Kinsey, Alfred C(harles) 1894-1956 ... 170
Brief entry ... 115
See also MTCW 2
See also TCLC 91
Kinsey, Barry Allan 1931- ... 17-20R
Kinsey, Elizabeth
See Clymer, Eleanor
Kinsey, Helen 1948- ... SATA 82
Kinsey-Jones, Brian
See Ball, Brian N(eville)
Kinsey-Warnock, Natalie 1956- ... 188
See also SATA 71, 116
Kinsley, D(aniel) A(llan) 1939- ... 45-48
Kinsley, James 1922-1984 ... CANR-2
Obituary ... 114
Earlier sketch in CA 1-4R
Kinsolving, Charles McIlvaine 1893-1984
Obituary ... 114
Kinsolving, Susan Baumann ... 194
Kinstler, Clysta (Joyce) 1931- ... 154
Kinstler, Everett Raymond 1926- ... 33-36R
Kinter, Judith 1928- ... 109
Kintgen, Eugene R(obert), Jr. 1942- ... 116
Kintner, Earl W(ilson) 1912-1991 ... CANR-1
Earlier sketch in CA 45-48
Kintner, Robert Edmonds 1909-1980
Obituary ... 103
Kintner, William R(oscoe) 1915-1997 . CANR-6
Obituary ... 156
Earlier sketch in CA 5-8R
Kinton, Jack F(ranklin) 1939- ... CANR-7
Earlier sketch in CA 57-60
Kintsch, Walter 1932- ... 29-32R
Kinyatti, Maina wa
See wa Kinyatti, Maina
Kinzel, Dorothy 1950- ... SATA 57
Kinzel, Dottie
See Kinzel, Dorothy
Kinzer, Betty 1922- ... 21-24R
Kinzer, Donald Louis 1914-2001 ... 53-56
Kinzer, H(arless) M(ahlon) 1923(?)-1975
Obituary ... 57-60
Kinzer, Nora Scott 1936- ... 126
Brief entry ... 106
Kinzer, Stephen 1951- ... CANR-118
Earlier sketch in CA 142
Kinzie, Mary 1944- ... CANR-111
Earlier sketch in CA 133
Kiparsky, Valentin (Julius Alexander)
1904-1993 ... 17-20R
Kipfer, Barbara Ann 1954- ... CANR-137
Earlier sketch in CA 134
Kiple, Kenneth F(ranklin) 1939- ... CANR-96
Earlier sketches in CA 120, CANR-46
Kipling, (Joseph) Rudyard
1865-1936 ... CANR-33
Brief entry ... 105
Earlier sketch in CA 120
See also AAYA 32
See also BRW 6
See also BRWC 1, 2
See also BYA 4
See also CDBLB 1890-1914
See also CLR 39, 65
See also CWRI 5
See also DA
See also DA3
See also DAB
See also DAC
See also DAM MST, POET
See also DLB 19, 34, 141, 156
See also EWL 3
See also EXPS
See also FANT
See also LAIT 3
See also LMFS 1
See also MAICYA 1, 2
See also MTCW 1, 2
See also MTFW 2005
See also NFS 21
See also PC 3
See also PFS 22
See also RGEL 2
See also RGSF 2
See also SATA 100
See also SFW 4
See also SSC 5, 54
See also SSFS 8, 21
See also SUFW 1
See also TCLC 8, 17, 167
See also TEA
See also WCH
See also WLC
See also WLIT 4
See also YABC 2
Kiplinger, Austin H(untington) 1918- ... 57-60
Kiplinger, Willard Monroe 1891-1967
Obituary ... 89-92
Kipnis, Aaron R. 1948- ... CANR-111
Earlier sketch in CA 137
Kipnis, Claude 1938-1981 ... 107
Obituary ... 103
Kipnis, Kenneth 1943- ... 129
Kipp, Rita Smith 1948- ... CANR-98
Earlier sketch in CA 147
Kippax, Frank
See Needle, Jan
Kippax, Janet 1926- ... 97-100
Kippax, John
See Hynam, John Charles
Kippenhahn, Rudolf 1926- ... CANR-99
Earlier sketch in CA 130
Kipphardt, Heinar 1922-1982 ... 89-92
Obituary ... 108
See also DLB 124
See also EWL 3
Kippley, John F(rancis) 1930- ... 29-32R
Kippley, Sheila K. 1939- ... 61-64
Kipps, Harriet C(lyde) 1926- ... 124
Kipury, Naomi ... 183
Kiraly, Bela (Kalman) 1912- ... CANR-8
Earlier sketch in CA 61-64
Kiraly, Marie
See Bergstrom, Elaine
Kiraly, Sherwood 1949- ... 158
Kiratli, Cemile
See Schimmel, Annemarie (Brigitte)
Kirby, (George) Blaik 1928- ... 77-80
Kirby, D(avid) P(eter) 1936- ... 25-28R
Kirby, David G. 1942- ... 101
Kirby, David K(irk) 1944- ... 53-56
See also SATA 78
Kirby, Douglas J. 1929- ... 25-28R
Kirby, E(dward) Stuart 1909- ... CANR-22
Earlier sketches in CA 13-16R, CANR-7
Kirby, Emily B(aruch) 1929- ... 117
Kirby, F(rank) E(ugene) 1928- ... 65-68
Kirby, Gilbert W(alter) 1914- ... 103
Kirby, Jack 1917-1994 ... 234
See also AAYA 49
Kirby, Jack Temple 1938- ... 25-28R
Kirby, James
See Kirby, James C(ordell), Jr.
Kirby, James C(ordell), Jr. 1928-1989
Obituary ... 130
Kirby, Jean
See McDonnell, Virginia B(leecker)
Kirby, Jean
See Robinson, Chaille Howard (Payne)
Kirby, John B(yron) 1938- ... 105
Kirby, John R. 1951- ... 146
Kirby, M(ary) Sheelah Flanagan 1916- ... 5-8R
Kirby, Margaret
See Bingley, Margaret (Jane Kirby)
Kirby, Margaret
See Bingley, Margaret (Jane Kirby)
Kirby, Mark
See Floren, Lee
Kirby, Rollin 1875-1952
Brief entry ... 118
Kirby, Susan E. 1949- ... SATA 62
Kirby, Thomas Austin 1904-1993 ... 5-8R
Kirby, William 1817-1906 ... 177
See also DLB 99
Kirch, Patrick V(inton) 1950- ... 143
Kircher, Athanasius 1602-1680 ... DLB 164
Kirchheimer, Gloria (De Vidas) ... 196
Kirchhofer, Alfred H. 1892(?)-1985
Obituary ... 117
Kirchhoff, Frederick (Thomas) 1942- ... 111
Kirchner, Audrey Burie 1937- ... CANR-12
Earlier sketch in CA 73-76
Kirchner, Bharti 1940- ... CANR-123
Earlier sketch in CA 169
Kirchner, Bill 1953- ... 199
Kirchner, Emil J(oseph) 1942- ... CANR-86
Earlier sketch in CA 130
Kirchner, Glenn 1930- ... 29-32R
Kirchner, Walther 1905-2004 ... CANR-1
Obituary ... 228
Earlier sketch in CA 1-4R
Kirchwey, Freda 1893-1976 ... 93-96
Obituary ... 61-64
Kirchwey, Karl 1956- ... 218
Kirdar, Uner 1933- ... 21-24R
Kireevsky, Ivan Vasil'evich
1806-1856 ... DLB 198
Kireevsky, Petr Vasil'evich
1808-1856 ... DLB 205
Kirgis, Frederic L(ee), Jr. 1934- ... 125
Kiriakopoulos, George C. 1925- ... 161
Kirk, Alexandra
See Woods, Sherryl
Kirk, Clara M(arburg) 1898-1976 ... CAP-1
Obituary ... 69-72
Earlier sketch in CA 17-18
Kirk, Cooper 1920- ... 116
Kirk, Daniel 1952- ... SATA 107, 153
Kirk, David 1935- ... 29-32R
Kirk, David 1955- ... SATA 117, 161
Kirk, Donald 1938- ... 37-40R
Kirk, Donald R. 1935- ... CANR-47
Earlier sketch in CA 57-60
Kirk, Elizabeth D(oan) 1937- ... 53-56
Kirk, G(eoffrey) S(tephen) 1921-2003 . CANR-2
Obituary ... 215
Earlier sketch in CA 5-8R
Kirk, George (Eden) 1911-1993 ... 1-4R
Kirk, H(enry) David 1918- ... CANR-11
Earlier sketch in CA 17-20R
Kirk, Hans 1898-1962 ... DLB 214
See also EWL 3
Kirk, Irene 1926- ... CANR-6
Earlier sketch in CA 5-8R
Kirk, Irina
See Kirk, Irene
Kirk, James A(lbert) 1929- ... 37-40R
Kirk, Janice E(mily) 1935- ... 146
Kirk, Jeremy
See Powell, Richard (Pitts)
Kirk, Jerome (Richard) 1937- ... 49-52
Kirk, John Esben 1905-1975
Obituary ... 57-60
Kirk, John Foster 1824-1904 ... 182
See also DLB 79
Kirk, John T(homas) 1933- ... 49-52
Kirk, John W. 1932- ... 129
Kirk, Lydia (Chapin) 1896-1984
Obituary ... 114
Kirk, Marshall (Kenneth) 1957- ... 135
Kirk, Mary Wallace 1889-1978 ... 57-60
Kirk, Matthew
See Wells, Angus
Kirk, Michael
See Knox, William
Kirk, Paul 1941- ... 232
Kirk, Pauline (M.) 1942- ... 157
Kirk, Philip
See Levinson, Leonard
Kirk, R.
See Dietrich, Richard V(incent)
Kirk, Richard (Edmund) 1931- ... 13-16R
Kirk, Robert Warner (?)-1980 ... 9-12R
Obituary ... 103
Kirk, Roger E(dward) 1930- ... 41-44R
Kirk, Rudolf 1898-1989
Obituary ... 130
Kirk, Russell (Amos) 1918-1994 ... CANR-60
Obituary ... 145
Earlier sketches in CA 1-4R, CANR-1, 20
Interview in ... CANR-20
See also CAAS 9
See also AITN 1
See also HGG
See also MTCW 1, 2
See also TCLC 119
Kirk, Ruth (Kratz) 1925- ... CANR-9
Earlier sketch in CA 13-16R
See also SATA 5
Kirk, Samuel A(lexander) 1904-1996 .. CANR-1
Obituary ... 152
Earlier sketch in CA 45-48
Kirk, Stuart A. 1945- ... 194
Kirk, T(homas) H(obson) 1899-2004 ... CAP-2
Obituary ... 233
Earlier sketch in CA 23-24
Kirk, Ted
See Bank, Theodore P(aul) II
Kirk, Wayne
See Kock, Winston E(dward)
Kirkaldy, John F(rancis) 1908-1990
Obituary ... 132
Kirkbride, Norma Jean 1924(?)-1983
Obituary ... 111
Kirkbride, Ronald (de Levington)
1912-1973 ... CANR-2
Earlier sketch in CA 1-4R
Kirkby, Bruce 1968- ... 195
Kirkconnell, Watson 1895-1977 ... 125
Obituary ... 108
See also CP 1
See also DLB 68
Kirkendall, Don(ald M.) 1923-1987 ... 49-52
Kirkendall, Lester A(llen) 1903-1983 .. CANR-5
Earlier sketch in CA 1-4R
Kirkendall, Richard Stewart 1928- ... 77-80
Kirker, Harold (Clark) 1921- ... 172
Kirk-Greene, Anthony (Hamilton Millard)
1925- ... CANR-54
Earlier sketches in CA 61-64, CANR-11, 27
Kirk-Greene, Anthony H. M.
See Kirk-Greene, Anthony (Hamilton Millard)
Kirk-Greene, Christopher Walter Edward
1926- ... 13-16R
Kirkham, Dinah
See Card, Orson Scott
Kirkham, E. Bruce 1938- ... 37-40R
Kirkham, George L. 1941- ... 77-80
Kirkham, Michael 1934- ... CANR-90
Earlier sketch in CA 25-28R
Kirkland, Bryant M(ays) 1914-2000 ... 21-24R
Obituary ... 189
Kirkland, Caroline M. 1801-1864 .... DLB 3, 73, 74, 250, 254
See also DLBD 13
Kirkland, Edward Chase 1894-1975 ... CANR-6
Obituary ... 104
Earlier sketch in CA 1-4R
Kirkland, Joseph 1830-1893 ... DLB 12
See also RGAL 4
Kirkland, Martha ... 166
Kirkland, Sally 1912-1989
Obituary ... 129
Kirkland, Wallace W. 1891(?)-1979
Obituary ... 89-92
Kirkland, Will
See Hale, Arlene
Kirkley, Evelyn A(nne) 1961- ... 216
Kirklighter, Cristina (C.) 1959- ... 229
Kirkman, Francis 1632-c. 1680 ... DLB 170
Kirkman, James S(pedding) 1906-1989 93-96
Obituary ... 128
Kirkpatrick, Clayton 1915-2004 ... 182
Obituary ... 228
See also DLB 127
Kirkpatrick, Diane 1933- ... 53-56
Kirkpatrick, Donald L(ee) 1924- ... 41-44R
Kirkpatrick, Doris (Upton) 1902-1984 ... 93-96
Kirkpatrick, Dow (Napier) 1917- ... 21-24R
Kirkpatrick, Evron M(aurice) 1911-1995 .. 57-60
Kirkpatrick, Frank 1924- ... 108
Kirkpatrick, Ivone Augustine
1897-1964 ... CAP-1
Earlier sketch in CA 9-10
Kirkpatrick, Jane 1946- ... 235
Kirkpatrick, Jean 1923-2000 ... 81-84
Obituary ... 188
Kirkpatrick, Jeane D(uane) J(ordan)
1926- ... CANR-7
Earlier sketch in CA 53-56
Kirkpatrick, John 1905-1991 ... 45-48
Obituary ... 136
Kirkpatrick, Katherine (Anne) 1964- ... 174
See also SATA 113
Kirkpatrick, Lyman B(ickford), Jr.
1916-1995 ... 33-36R
Kirkpatrick, Oliver (Austin) 1911-1988 49-52
Kirkpatrick, Ralph 1911-1984 ... 49-52
Obituary ... 112
Kirkpatrick, Robert J. 1953- ... 228
Kirkpatrick, Samuel A(lexander) III
1943- ... 41-44R
Kirkpatrick, Sidney D(ale) 1955- ... CANR-98
Earlier sketch in CA 136
Kirkpatrick, Smith 1922- ... 49-52
Kirkup, James 1918- ... CANR-2
Earlier sketch in CA 1-4R
See also CAAS 4
See also CLC 1
See also CP 1, 2, 3, 4, 5, 6, 7
See also DLB 27
See also SATA 12
Kirkus, Virginia
See Glick, Virginia Kirkus
Kirkwood, Annie 1937- ... CANR-112
Earlier sketch in CA 154
Kirkwood, Byron (Ray) 1946- ... 141
Kirkwood, Dianna 1946(?)- ... 216
Kirkwood, Ellen Swan 1904-1993 ... 25-28R
Kirkwood, G(ordon) M(acdonald) 1916- . 93-96
Kirkwood, James 1930(?)-1989 ... CANR-40
Obituary ... 128
Earlier sketches in CA 1-4R, CANR-6
See also AITN 2
See also CLC 9
See also GLL 2
Kirkwood, Kathryn
See Fluke, Joanne
Kirkwood, Kenneth P. 1899-1968 ... 37-40R
Kirkwood, Neville A. 1927- ... 229
Kirn, Ann Minette 1910-1997 ... 93-96
Kirn, Walter 1962- ... CANR-89
Earlier sketch in CA 142
Kirner, Joan (Elizabeth) 1938- ... 194
Kirp, David L(eslie) 1944- ... CANR-100
Earlier sketch in CA 109
Kirsch, Abigail 1930- ... 222
Kirsch, Anthony Thomas 1930- ... 103
Kirsch, Arthur C(lifford) 1932- ... 13-16R
Kirsch, Charlotte 1942- ... 109
Kirsch, George B(enson) 1945- ... CANR-111
Earlier sketch in CA 151
Kirsch, Herbert 1924(?)-1978
Obituary ... 104
Kirsch, Irving 1943- ... 136
Kirsch, James Isaac 1901-1989
Obituary ... 128
Kirsch, Jonathan 1949- ... CANR-100
Earlier sketch in CA 164
Kirsch, Leonard Joel 1934-1977 ... 37-40R
Kirsch, Paul John 1914-1993 ... 108
Kirsch, Robert R. 1922-1980 ... CANR-13
Obituary ... 102
Earlier sketch in CA 33-36R
Kirsch, Sarah 1935- ... 178
See also CLC 176
See also CWW 2
See also DLB 75
See also EWL 3
Kirschen, Leonard 1908-1983
Obituary ... 109
Kirschenbaum, Aaron 1926- ... 33-36R
Kirschenbaum, Howard 1944- ... 89-92
Kirschke, James J. 1941- ... 191
Kirschner, Allen 1930- ... 29-32R
Kirschner, David 1955- ... 214
Kirschner, Don S(tuart) 1928- ... 148
Kirschner, Fritz
See Bickers, Richard (Leslie) Townshend
Kirschner, Joseph 1930- ... 121
Kirschner, Linda Rae 1939- ... 33-36R
Kirschten, Ernest 1902-1974 ... CAP-1
Obituary ... 49-52
Earlier sketch in CA 11-12
Kirshenbaum, Binnie ... 192
See also SATA 79
Kirshenbaum, Jerry 1938- ... 107
Kirshenblatt-Gimblett, Barbara
1942- ... CANR-15
Earlier sketch in CA 81-84
Kirshner, David S. 1958- ... SATA 123
Kirshner, Gloria Ifland ... 41-44R
Kirshner, Sidney
See Kingsley, Sidney
Kirsner, Douglas 1947- ... 77-80
Kirsner, Kim 1941- ... 171
Kirsner, Robert 1921- ... 21-24R
Kirst, Hans Hellmut 1914-1989 ... CANR-83
Obituary ... 128
Earlier sketch in CA 104
See also DLB 69
Kirst, Michael W(eile) 1939- ... CANR-49
Earlier sketches in CA 45-48, CANR-24
Kirstein, George G(arland) 1909-1986
Obituary ... 118
Kirstein, Lincoln (Edward) 1907-1996 ... 128
Obituary ... 151
Brief entry ... 117
Kirsten, Grace 1900-1998 ... 104
Kirsten, Wulf 1934- ... 237
Kirtland, G. B.
See Hine, Al(fred Blakelee) and Hine, Sesyle Joslin
Kirtland, Helen Johns 1890(?)-1979
Obituary ... 89-92
Kirtland, Kathleen 1945- ... 65-68
Kirtzman, Andrew 1961- ... 189

Kirvan, John J. 1932- CANR-10
Earlier sketch in CA 21-24R
Kirwan, Albert D(ennis) 1904-1971 .... CANR-4
Earlier sketch in CA 1-4R
Kirwan, Anna 238
Kirwan, Laurence Patrick
1907-1999 .... CANR-70
Obituary 177
Earlier sketch in CA 1-4R
Kirwan, Molly (Morrow) 1906- CAP-1
Earlier sketch in CA 13-14
Kirwan-Vogel, Anna
See Kirwan, Anna
Kirwin, Harry Wynne 1911-1963 .... 1-4R
Kirzner, Israel M(ayer) 1930- CANR-142
Earlier sketches in CA 1-4R, CANR-3
Kis, Danilo 1935-1989 .... CANR-61
Obituary 129
Brief entry 109
Earlier sketch in CA 118
See also CDWLB 4
See also CLC 57
See also DLB 181
See also EWL 3
See also MTCW 1
See also RGSF 2
See also RGWL 2, 3
Kisamore, Norman D(ale) 1928- 5-8R
Kiser, Clyde V(ernon) 1904-2000 .... 25-28R
Kiser, Lisa J. 1949- 114
Kish, Eleanor M(ary) 1924- .... SATA 73
Kish, Ely
See Kish, Eleanor M(ary)
Kish, G. Hobab
See Kennedy, Gerald (Hamilton)
Kish, George 1914-1989 .... CANR-1
Earlier sketch in CA 1-4R
Kish, Kathleen Vera 1942- CANR-12
Earlier sketch in CA 69-72
Kish, Leslie 1910-2000 .... CAP-1
Obituary 191
Earlier sketch in CA 19-20
Kishel, Patricia G(unter) 1948- 117
Kishida, Eriko 1929- CANR-7
Earlier sketch in CA 53-56
See also SATA 12
Kishida, Kunio 1890-1954 194
See also Kishida Kunio
Kishida Kunio
See Kishida, Kunio
See also EWL 3
Kishkan, Theresa 1955- 209
Kishon, Ephraim 1924-2005 .... CANR-2
Obituary 235
Earlier sketch in CA 49-52
Kishore, Prem 1940- 236
Kishtainy, Khalid 1929- 115
Kisiel, Marie 1929- 112
Kisiel, Theodore J(oseph) 1930- 224
Kisinger, Grace Gelvin (Maze)
1913-1965 .... CAP-1
Earlier sketch in CA 13-14
See also SATA 10
Kisker, George W. 1912- 21-24R
Kisly, Lorraine 233
Kismaric, Carole 1942-2002 .... CANR-23
Obituary 211
Earlier sketches in CA 33-36R, CANR-8
Kisner, James (Martin, Jr.) 1947- CANR-35
Earlier sketch in CA 113
Kisor, Henry (Du Bois) 1940- 73-76
Kissam, Edward 1943- 61-64
Kissane, John M(ichael) 1928- 53-56
Kissane, Leedice McAnelly 1905-2000 . CAP-2
Earlier sketch in CA 25-28
Kissel, Susan S. 1943- 162
Kissen, Fan(ny) 1904-1978 .... CAP-1
Earlier sketch in CA 13-16
Kissick, Gary 1946- 118
Kissin, Eva H. 1923- 29-32R
See also SATA 10
Kissing, Steve 1963- 226
Kissinger, Henry A(lfred) 1923- CANR-109
Earlier sketches in CA 1-4R, CANR-2, 33, 66
See also CLC 137
See also MTCW 1
Kissinger, Rosemary K.
See Updyke, Rosemary K.
Kissinger, Warren S(tauffer) 1922- 116
Kissling, Dorothy (Hight) 1904-1969
Obituary 105
Kissling, Fred R., Jr. 1930- 21-24R
Kiste, Robert Carl 1936- 61-64
Kister, Kenneth F. 1935- 25-28R
Kistiakowsky, George B(ogdan) 1900-1982
Obituary 108
Kistiakowsky, Vera 1928- 21-24R
Kistler, John M. 1967- 236
See also SATA 160
Kistler, Mark O(liver) 1918-1995 77-80
Kistler, William 182
Kistner, Robert William 1917-1990 .. CANR-13
Earlier sketch in CA 61-64
Kisubi, Alfred T(aligoola) 1949- 175
Kita, Joe 211
Kita, Morio 1927- 205
Kitagawa, Daisuke 1910-1970 .... CAP-2
Earlier sketch in CA 17-18
Kitagawa, Joseph M. 1915-1992 .... CANR-2
Earlier sketch in CA 1-4R
Kitaj, Karma 1943- 217
Kita Morio 1927- .... DLB 182
Kitamura, Satoshi 1956- CANR-122
Earlier sketch in CA 165
See also CLR 60
See also SATA 62, 98, 143
Kitano, Harry H(aruo) L. 1926-2002 ..... 29-32R
Obituary 211
Kitao, T(imothy) Kaori 1933- 106
Kitcat, Mabel Greenhow 1859-1922 .. DLB 135
Kitch, Carolyn L. 213
Kitch, Sally L. 1946- 140
Kitchel, Denison 1908-2002 105
Obituary 213
Kitchell, Webster (Lardner) 1931- 165
Kitchen, Bert
See Kitchen, Herbert Thomas
Kitchen, Helen (Angell) CANR-47
Earlier sketches in CA 9-12R, CANR-8, 23
Kitchen, Herbert Thomas 1940- 138
See also SATA 70
Kitchen, Herminie B(roedel)
1901-1973 .... CAP-1
Earlier sketch in CA 17-18
Kitchen, Judith 1941- CANR-115
Earlier sketch in CA 147
Kitchen, Martin 1936- CANR-51
Earlier sketches in CA 61-64, CANR-10, 26
Kitchen, Paddy 1934- CANR-21
Earlier sketch in CA 25-28R
Kitchener, Richard Frank 1941- 124
Kitcher, Philip 1947- CANR-143
Earlier sketch in CA 113
Kitchin, C(lifford) H(enry) B(enn)
1895-1967 237
See also CMW 4
See also DLB 77
Kitchin, Laurence 1913-1997 104
Kite, Larry
See Schneck, Stephen
Kite, Pat 1940- 119
See also Kite, (L.) Patricia
Kite, (L.) Patricia
See Kite, Pat
See also SATA 78
Kiteley, Brian 1956- CANR-104
Earlier sketch in CA 132
Kitfield, James C. 1956- 147
Kitman, Marvin 1929- 101
Kitson, Jack William 1940- 25-28R
Kitson, Peter J. 208
Kitson Clark, George Sydney Roberts
1900-1975 .... CANR-14
Earlier sketch in CA 21-24R
Kitt, Eartha (Mae) 1928- CANR-126
Earlier sketch in CA 77-80
Kitt, Sandra (E.) 1947- CANR-91
Earlier sketch in CA 146
Kitt, Tamara
See de Regniers, Beatrice Schenk (Freedman)
Kittell, Ellen E. 191
Kittelson, David James 1931-1989 119
Obituary 142
Kittinger, Jo S(usenbach) 1955- CANR-128
Earlier sketch in CA 161
See also SATA 96, 148
Kittler, Glenn D. 1920(?)-1986
Obituary 119
Kitto, Crispin 1951- 119
Kitto, H(umphrey) D(avy) F(indley)
1897-1982 .... CAP-1
Obituary 105
Earlier sketch in CA 11-12
Kittredge, William 1932- CANR-84
Earlier sketches in CA 111, CANR-44
See also DLB 212, 244
See also TCWW 2
Kittrie, Nicholas N(orbert Nehemiah)
1928- CANR-100
Earlier sketch in CA 81-84
Kitts, Thomas M(ichael) 1955- CANR-111
Earlier sketch in CA 155
Kituomba
See Odaga, Asenath (Bole)
Kitzinger, Ernst 1912-2003 108
Obituary 214
Kitzinger, Sheila 1929- CANR-134
Earlier sketch in CA 37-40R
See also SATA 57
Kitzinger, U(we) W(ebster) 1928- CANR-1
Earlier sketch in CA 1-4R
Kiufejian, Hagop
See Oshagan, Hagop
Kiukhel'beker, Vil'gel'm Karlovich
1797-1846 .... DLB 205
Kivenson, Gilbert 1920- 112
Kivy, Peter Nathan 1934- CANR-137
Earlier sketch in CA 103
Kiwak, Barbara 1966- .... SATA 103
Kiyama, Henry Yoshitaka 1885-1951 225
See also AAYA 66
Kiyooka, Roy (Kenzie) 1926-1994 171
Kiyota, Minoru 1923- CANR-61
Earlier sketches in CA 113, CANR-32
Kizaki, Satoko
See Harada, Masako
Kizer, Carolyn (Ashley) 1925- CANR-134
Earlier sketches in CA 65-68, CANR-24, 70
See also CAAS 5
See also CLC 15, 39, 80
See also CP 1, 2, 3, 4, 5, 6, 7
See also CWP
See also DAM POET
See also DLB 5, 169
See also EWL 3
See also MAL 5
See also MTCW 2
See also MTFW 2005
See also PC 66
See also PFS 18
See also TCLE 1:1
Kjaeaerstad, Jan 1953- .... DLB 297
Kjaer, Nils
See Kjaer, Nils
Kjelgaard, James Arthur 1910-1959 .. CANR-84
Brief entry 109
Earlier sketch in CA 137
See also Kjelgaard, Jim
See also CLR 81
See also MAICYA 1, 2
See also SATA 17
Kjelgaard, Jim
See Kjelgaard, James Arthur
See also CWRI 5
See also JRDA
Kjelle, Marylou Morano 1954- 220
See also SATA 146
Kjome, June C(reola) 1920- 5-8R
Klaas, Joe 1920- CANR-12
Earlier sketch in CA 29-32R
Klaassen, Leo(nardus) H(endrik)
1920- CANR-26
Earlier sketches in CA 21-24R, CANR-11
Klaassen, Walter 1926- 115
Klabund 1890-1928 162
See also DLB 66
See also TCLC 44
Klabunde, Kenneth J. 1943- 222
Kladstrup, Don(ald) 1943- 77-80
Klafs, Carl E. 1911-1999 .... 13-16R
Klagsbrun, Francine (Lifton) CANR-138
Earlier sketch in CA 21-24R
See also SATA 36
Klaiber, Jeffrey L. 1943- 85-88
Klaich, Dolores 1936- 49-52
Klaidman, Stephen 1938- CANR-94
Earlier sketch in CA 125
Klainikite, Anne
See Gehman, Betsy Holland
Klaits, Barrie 1944- 73-76
See also SATA 52
Klaits, Joseph (Aaron) 1942- 126
Klaj, Johann 1616-1656 .... DLB 164
Klajman, Jack 1931- 213
Klam, Matthew 1964- 226
Klamer, Arjo 1953- 116
Klamkin, Charles 1923- 61-64
Klamkin, Lynn 1950- 45-48
Klamkin, Marian 1926- CANR-1
Earlier sketch in CA 49-52
Klammer, Martin (P.) 1957- 151
Klaniczay, Tibor 1923- 132
Klann, Margaret L(ydia) 1911-2000 77-80
Klaperman, Gilbert 1921- 49-52
See also SATA 33
Klaperman, Libby Mindlin 1921-1982 .... 9-12R
Obituary 107
See also SATA 33
See also SATA-Obit 31
Klapp, Orrin E. 1915-1997 .... 9-12R
Klapper, Charles F(rederick) 1905- CAP-1
Earlier sketch in CA 9-10
Klapper, Joseph T(homas) 1917-1984
Obituary 112
Klapper, M(olly) Roxana 1937- 53-56
Klapper, Marvin 1922- 17-20R
Klappert, Peter 1942- 33-36R
See also CLC 57
See also CSW
See also DLB 5
Klappholz, Kurt 1913-1975
Obituary 61-64
Klapthor, Margaret B(rown) 1922-1994 119
Klare, George R(oger) 1922- 5-8R
Klare, Hugh J(ohn) 1916- 103
Klare, Michael T(homas) 1942- 130
Klaren, Peter F(lindell) 1938- 57-60
Klarsfeld, Beate 1939- 65-68
Klarsfeld, Serge 1935- 115
Klass, Allan Arnold 1907-2000 65-68
Klass, David 1960- CANR-112
Earlier sketch in CA 152
See also AAYA 26
See also SATA 88, 142
See also WYAS 1
See also YAW
Klass, Morton 1927-2001 .... CANR-5
Obituary 194
Earlier sketch in CA 1-4R
See also SATA 11
Klass, Perri 1958- 126
Interview in CA-126
Klass, Philip J. 1919-2005 .... 25-28R
Klass, Sheila Solomon 1927- CANR-37
Earlier sketches in CA 37-40R, CANR-13
See also AAYA 34
See also SAAS 26
See also SATA 45, 99
See also SATA-Essay 126
See also YAW
Klass, Sholom 1916- 21-24R
Klassen, Albert D(ale, Jr.) 1931- 133
Klassen, Frank Roy 1910-1989 113
Klassen, Peter J(ames) 1930- CANR-1
Earlier sketch in CA 45-48
Klassen, Randolph Jacob 1933- 61-64
Klassen, Walter
See Klaassen, Walter
Klassen, William 1930- CANR-10
Earlier sketch in CA 25-28R
Klauber, John 1917-1981
Obituary 104
Klauber, Laurence M(onroe) 1883-1968
Obituary 105
Klauck, Daniel L. 1947- 69-72
Klauck, Hans-Josef 1946- 203
Klauder, Francis John 1918- 53-56
Klaue, Lola Shelton 1903- 5-8R
Klaus, Carl H. 1932- 185
Klaus, Marshall H. 1927- 181
Klaus, Phyllis H. 182
Klause, Annette Curtis 1953- CANR-83
Earlier sketch in CA 147
See also AAYA 27
See also BPFA 14
See also BYA 12
See also SATA 79
See also WYAS 1
See also YAW
Klause, John L(ouis) 1943- 118
Klausen, Jytte 1954- 239
Klausler, Alfred P(aul) 1910-1991 .... 21-24R
Klausmeier, Herbert J. 1915- CANR-20
Earlier sketches in CA 1-4R, CANR-5
Klausner, Abraham J. 1915- 108
Klausner, David N. 1941- 177
Klausner, Lawrence D(avid) 1939- 110
Klausner, Margot 1905-1976(?)
Obituary 61-64
Klausner, Samuel Z(undel) 1923- 17-20R
Klavan, Andrew 169
Klavans, J(odie) K(ay) 1956- 118
Klaveness, Jan O'Donnell 1939- 151
See also SATA 86
Klaw, Spencer 1920-2004 .... 25-28R
Obituary 228
Klawans, Harold L(eo) 1937-1998 106
Obituary 166
Klayman, Maxwell Irving 1917-1999 .... 29-32R
Klebanoff, Arthur 1951- 204
Klebe, Charles Eugene 1907-1985 .... CAP-2
Earlier sketch in CA 23-24
Klebe, Gene
See Klebe, Charles Eugene
Kleberger, Ilse 1921- CANR-39
Earlier sketches in CA 41-44R, CANR-15
See also SATA 5
Kleck, Gary 1951- 140
Klee, James B(utt) 1916-1996 109
Klee, Paul 1879-1940 155
See also AAYA 31
Kleeberg, Irene (Flitner) Cumming
1932- CANR-35
Earlier sketches in CA 61-64, CANR-12
See also SATA 65
Kleeblatt, Norman L(eslie) 1948- CANR-138
Earlier sketch in CA 128
Kleene, Stephen Cole 1909-1994 .... 41-44R
Obituary 143
Klees, Fredric (Spang) 1901-1985 .... CAP-2
Earlier sketch in CA 19-20
Kleh, Cindy (L.) 1959- 226
Klehr, Harvey 1945- CANR-69
Earlier sketches in CA 111, CANR-48
Kleier, Glenn 171
Kleiler, Frank Munro 1914-1999 89-92
Obituary 183
Kleiman, Ed 1932- 135
Kleiman, Mark A. R. 1951- 138
Kleiman, Robert 1918-2004 .... 13-16R
Obituary 225
Klein, A(braham) M(oses) 1909-1972 101
Obituary 37-40R
See also CLC 19
See also CP 1
See also DAB
See also DAC
See also DAM MST
See also DLB 68
See also EWL 3
See also RGEL 2
Klein, Aaron E. 1930-1998 .... CANR-19
Earlier sketch in CA 25-28R
See also SATA 45
See also SATA-Brief 28
Klein, Adam 225
Klein, Alan F(redric) 1911- 57-60
Klein, Alan M. 1946- 199
Klein, Alexander 1918-2002 .... CANR-14
Obituary 208
Earlier sketch in CA 5-8R
Klein, Allen 1938- 131
Klein, Anne Carolyn 1923-1974 148
Klein, Arnold William 1945- 37-40R
Klein, Bernard 1921- 17-20R
Klein, Bill 1945- .... SATA 89
Klein, Bonnie Sherr 1941- 191
Klein, Carole (Doreen Honig)
1934-2001 .... CANR-101
Obituary 200
Brief entry 118
Earlier sketch in CA 168
Klein, Charlotte 1925- 101
Klein, Christian Felix 1849-1925 170
Klein, Cornelis 1937- 145
Klein, Daniel M(artin) 1939- CANR-141
Earlier sketches in CA 61-64, CANR-11, 28
Klein, Dave 1940- 89-92
Klein, David 1919-2001 .... CANR-40
Obituary 196
Earlier sketches in CA 1-4R, CANR-1, 18
See also SATA 59
Klein, David Ballin 1897-1983 .... 41-44R
Klein, Donald C(harles) 1923- 25-28R
Klein, Donald F. 1928- 146
Klein, Donald W(alker) 1929-
Brief entry 114
Klein, Doris F.
See Jonas, Doris F(rances)
Klein, Edward 1936- 69-72
Klein, Elizabeth 1939- 110
Klein, Erica Levy 1966- 151
Klein, Ernest 1899-1983 .... CAP-2
Earlier sketch in CA 21-22
Klein, Ethel 1952- 221
Klein, Etienne 1958- 218

Klein, Fannie J. 1903-1984
Obituary ... 113
Klein, Fred 1932-
Brief entry ... 115
Klein, Frederic Shriver 1904-1987 ... 13-16R
Klein, Frederick C. 1938- ... 229
See also SATA 154
Klein, Gary (A.) 1944- ... 224
Klein, Gene 1921- ... 126
Klein, George 1925- ... CANR-144
Earlier sketch in CA 140
Klein, Gerard 1937- ... CANR-85
Earlier sketches in CA 49-52, CANR-48
See also SFW 4
Klein, Gerda Weissmann 1924- ... CANR-98
Earlier sketch in CA 116
See also SATA 44
Klein, H(erbert) Arthur ... 13-16R
See also SATA 8
Klein, Herbert G(eorge) 1918- ... 165
Klein, Herbert Sanford 1936- ... CANR-37
Earlier sketches in CA 93-96, CANR-17
Klein, Heywood 1954(?)-1984
Obituary ... 111
Klein, Holger Michael 1938- ... 65-68
Klein, Isaac 1905-1979 ... 57-60
Klein, James 1932- ... 186
See also SATA 115
Klein, Jeffrey B. 1948- ... 77-80
Klein, Joe
See Klein, Joseph
Klein, John J(acob) 1929- ... 17-20R
Klein, Jonas 1932- ... 195
Klein, Joseph 1946- ... CANR-55
Earlier sketch in CA 85-88
See also CLC 154
Klein, Josephine (F. H.) 1926- ... 1-4R
Klein, Julius 1901-1984
Obituary ... 112
Klein, K. K.
See Turner, Robert (Harry)
Klein, Karl
See Sala, Charles
Klein, Kathleen Gregory 1946- ... 130
Klein, Kurt 1920-2002 ... 217
Klein, Lawrence R(obert) 1920- ... 152
Brief entry ... 116
Klein, Leonore (Glotzer) 1916- ... CANR-1
Earlier sketch in CA 1-4R
See also SATA 6
Klein, Marcus 1928- ... 9-12R
Klein, Marjorie H(anson) 1933- ... 190
Klein, Martin A. 1934- ... 21-24R
Klein, Marymae E. 1917- ... CANR-40
Earlier sketch in CA 97-100
Klein, Maury 1939- ... CANR-95
Earlier sketch in CA 33-36R
Klein, Maxine 1934- ... CANR-10
Earlier sketch in CA 61-64
Klein, Melanie 1882-1960
Obituary ... 111
Klein, Michael 1954- ... 174
Klein, Milton M(artin) 1917- ... 93-96
Klein, Mina C(ooper) 1906-1979 ... 37-40R
Obituary ... 133
See also SATA 8
Klein, Muriel Walzer 1920- ... 29-32R
Klein, Norma 1938-1989 ... CANR-37
Obituary ... 128
Earlier sketches in CA 41-44R, CANR-15
Interview in ... CANR-15
See also AAYA 2, 35
See also BPFB 2
See also BYA 6, 7, 8
See also CLC 30
See also CLR 2, 19
See also JRDA
See also MAICYA 1, 2
See also SAAS 1
See also SATA 7, 57
See also WYA
See also YAW
Klein, Norman M. 1945- ... 171
Klein, Philip A(lexander) 1927- ... 17-20R
Klein, Philip Shriver 1909-1993 ... CANR-1
Obituary ... 140
Earlier sketch in CA 1-4R
Klein, Rachel S. 1953- ... CANR-142
Earlier sketch in CA 165
See also SATA 105
Klein, Randolph Shipley 1942- ... 73-76
Klein, Richard 1941- ... CANR-112
Earlier sketch in CA 158
Klein, Richard C. 1916(?)-1983
Obituary ... 111
Klein, Richard G. 1941- ... 120
Klein, Richard M. 1923- ... CANR-25
Earlier sketch in CA 108
Klein, Robin 1936- ... CANR-40
Earlier sketch in CA 116
See also AAYA 21
See also CLR 21
See also JRDA
See also MAICYA 1, 2
See also SATA 55, 80
See also SATA-Brief 45
See also YAW
Klein, Rose (Shweitzer) 1918- ... 21-24R
Klein, Sherwin 1932- ... 147
Klein, Stanley 1930- ... 57-60
Klein, Stanley D. 1936- ... 77-80
Klein, Stuart M(arc) 1932- ... 134
Brief entry ... 111
Klein, Suzanne Marie 1940- ... 57-60
Klein, T(heodore) E(ibon) D(onald)
1947- ... CANR-75
Earlier sketches in CA 119, CANR-44
See also CLC 34
See also HGG
Klein, Ted U. 1926- ... 25-28R
Klein, Thomas D(icker) 1941- ... 61-64
Klein, Walter J(ulian) 1923- ... 69-72
Klein, Woody 1929- ... 13-16R
Klein, Zachary 1948- ... 135
Kleinbauer, W(alter) Eugene 1937- ... 37-40R
Kleinbaum, Abby Wettan 1943- ... 113
Kleinberg, Aviad M. 1957- ... 141
Kleinberg, Seymour 1933- ... 105
Kleindienst, Kris 1953- ... 226
Kleine, Glen 1936- ... 73-76
Kleine-Ahlbrandt, W(illiam) Laird
1932- ... CANR-92
Earlier sketch in CA 29-32R
Kleiner, Art 1954- ... 124
Kleiner, Diana E(lizabeth) E(delman)
1947- ... CANR-139
Earlier sketch in CA 144
Kleiner, Dick
See Kleiner, Richard Arthur
Kleiner, Fred S. 1948- ... 163
Kleiner, Richard Arthur 1921-2002 ... 129
Obituary ... 204
Kleinfeld, Gerald R. 1936- ... 103
Kleinfeld, Judith S. 1944- ... CANR-15
Earlier sketch in CA 77-80
Kleinfeld, Vincent A. 1907-1993 ... CANR-10
Obituary ... 143
Earlier sketch in CA 17-20R
Kleinfield, N(athan) R(ichard) 1950- ... CANR-18
Earlier sketch in CA 97-100
Kleinfield, Sonny
See Kleinfield, N(athan) R(ichard)
Kleinhans, Theodore John 1924- ... 5-8R
Kleinke, Chris (Lynn) 1944- ... CANR-15
Earlier sketch in CA 89-92
Kleinman, Arthur (Michael) 1941- ... CANR-22
Earlier sketch in CA 105
Kleinman, Philip (Julian) 1932- ... 131
Kleinman, Ruth 1929- ... 125
Kleinmann, Jack H(enry) 1932- ... 21-24R
Kleinmuntz, Benjamin 1930- ... 33-36R
Kleinpell, Ruth M. 1960- ... 229
Kleinpell-Nowell, Ruth
See Kleinpell, Ruth M.
Kleinsasser, Lois ... CANR-107
Earlier sketch in CA 168
Kleinschmit, Sandra ... 230
Kleinsmith, Bruce John 1942- ... 132
Kleinzahler, August 1949- ... CANR-101
Earlier sketches in CA 125, CANR-51
Kleiser, Randal 1946- ... 166
Kleist, Ewald von 1715-1759 ... DLB 97
Kleist, Heinrich von 1777-1811 ... CDWLB 2
See also DAM DRAM
See also DLB 90
See also EW 5
See also RGSF 2
See also RGWL 2, 3
See also SSC 22
Klejment, Anne M. 1950- ... CANR-17
Earlier sketch in CA 101
Klem, Kaye Wilson 1941- ... 89-92
Klement, Frank L(udwig)
1908-1994 ... CANR-91
Earlier sketch in CA 9-12R
Klemer, Richard Hudson 1918-1972 ... CANR-4
Obituary ... 37-40R
Earlier sketch in CA 5-8R
Klemesrud, Judy 1939(?)-1985 ... 89-92
Obituary ... 117
Klemin, Diana ... 49-52
See also SATA 65
Klemke, E(lmer) D. 1926- ... CANR-10
Earlier sketch in CA 25-28R
Klemm, Barry 1945- ... 171
See also SATA 104
Klemm, Edward G., Jr. 1910-2001 ... 57-60
See also SATA 30
Klemm, Roberta K(ohnhorst) 1884-1975 ... 61-64
See also SATA 30
Klemm, W(illiam) R(obert) 1934- ... 93-96
Klemperer, Otto 1885-1973
Obituary ... 116
Klemperer, Paul (David) 1956- ... 218
Klemperer, Victor 1881-1960 ... 169
See also NCFS 3
Klempner, Irving M(ax) 1924- ... 53-56
Klempner, John 1898(?)-1972
Obituary ... 37-40R
Klempner, Joseph T(eller) 1940- ... CANR-111
Earlier sketch in CA 151
Klenbort, Charlotte
See Sempell, Charlotte
Klenicki, Leon 1930- ... 106
Klenk, Robert W(illiam) 1934- ... 29-32R
Klenz, William 1915-1988 ... 5-8R
Klepfisz, Irena 1941- ... CWP
See also GLL 2
Klerer, Melvin 1926-1992 ... 21-24R
Klerkx, Greg 1963- ... 232
Klerman, Lorraine V(ogel) 1929- ... CANR-15
Earlier sketch in CA 81-84
Klett, Guy S(oulliard) 1897-1990 ... CAP-1
Earlier sketch in CA 13-14
Kleuser, Louise C(aroline) 1889(?)-1976
Obituary ... 65-68
Kleven, Elisa 1958- ... 143
See also CLR 85
See also SATA 76
Klevin, Jill Ross 1935- ... 111
See also SATA 39
See also SATA-Brief 38
Klewin, W(illiam) Thomas 1921- ... 29-32R
Kleyman, Paul (Fred) 1945- ... 57-60
Kleypas, Lisa 1964- ... CANR-115
Earlier sketch in CA 127
Kliban, B(ernard) 1935-1990 ... 106
Obituary ... 132
See also SATA 35
See also SATA-Obit 66
Klibansky, Raymond 1905-
Brief entry ... 117
Klieman, Charles 1940- ... 140
Klier, John Doyle 1944- ... 141
Kliever, Lonnie D(ean) 1931- ... CANR-47
Earlier sketch in CA 29-32R
Kliewer, Evelyn 1933- ... 101
Kliewer, Warren 1931- ... CANR-2
Earlier sketch in CA 45-48
Kliger, Hannah 1953- ... 149
Kligerman, Jack 1938- ... 85-88
Kligman, Ruth 1930- ... 101
Klima, Ivan 1931- ... CANR-91
Earlier sketches in CA 25-28R, CANR-17, 50
See also CDWLB 4
See also CLC 56, 172
See also CWW 2
See also DAM NOV
See also DLB 232
See also EWL 3
See also RGWL 3
Kliman, Bernice W. 1933- ... 162
Kliman, Gilbert W(allace) 1929- ... 117
Klimas, Antanas 1924- ... 41-44R
Klimas, John E(dward) 1927-1975
Obituary ... 111
Klimek, David E(rnest) 1941- ... 89-92
Klimenko, Michael 1924- ... 73-76
Klimentev, Andrei Platonovich
See Klimentov, Andrei Platonovich
Klimentov, Andrei Platonovich 1899-1951 ... 232
Brief entry ... 108
See also Platonov, Andrei Platonovich and Platonov, Andrey Platonovich
See also SSC 42
See also TCLC 14
Klimisch, Sister Mary Jane 1920- ... 17-20R
Klimo, Jake
See Klimo, Vernon
Klimo, Vernon 1914-1984 ... 101
Klimowicz, Barbara 1927- ... 21-24R
See also SATA 10
Klimt, Gustav 1862-1918 ... AAYA 61
Klin, George 1931- ... 53-56
Klinck, Carl Frederick 1908-1990 ... 17-20R
Klinck, George Alfred 1903-1973 ... 9-12R
Obituary ... 103
Klindt-Jensen, Ole 1918-1980 ... CANR-10
Obituary ... 101
Earlier sketch in CA 21-24R
Kline, Christina Baker 1964- ... 161
See also SATA 101
Kline, George L(ouis) 1921- ... CANR-9
Earlier sketch in CA 17-20R
Kline, Herbert 1909-1999 ... 184
Kline, James
See Klein, James
Kline, Jim
See Kline, Jim
Kline, Linda 1940- ... 126
Kline, Lisa Williams 1954- ... 216
See also SATA 143
Kline, Lloyd W. 1931- ... 33-36R
Kline, Morris 1908-1992 ... CANR-84
Obituary ... 139
Earlier sketches in CA 5-8R, CANR-2, 46
Kline, Nancy Meadors 1946- ... 57-60
Kline, Nathan S(chellenberg)
1916-1983 ... CANR-36
Obituary ... 109
Earlier sketch in CA 81-84
Kline, Otis Adelbert 1891-1946 ... 162
See also SFW 4
Kline, Peter 1936- ... CANR-137
Earlier sketch in CA 25-28R
Kline, Ronald R. 1947- ... 148
Kline, Stephen Edward 1945- ... 132
Kline, Steve
See Kline, Stephen Edward
Kline, Suzy 1943- ... 120
See also SATA 67, 99, 152
See also SATA-Brief 48
Kline, Thomas J(efferson) 1942- ... 85-88
Klineberg, Stephen L(ouis) 1940- ... 77-80
Klinefelter, Walter 1899-1987 ... CANR-3
Earlier sketch in CA 9-12R
Klineman, George A(lfred) 1947- ... 107
Kling, Christine ... 216
Kling, Robert E(dward), Jr. 1920-2002 ... 29-32R
Obituary ... 203
Kling, Simcha 1922-1991 ... 13-16R
Kling, Woody 1926(?)-1988
Obituary ... 125
Klingelhofer, E(dwin) L(ewis) 1920- ... CANR-51
Earlier sketch in CA 124
Klingenstein, Susanne (Schloetelburg)
1959- ... 140
Klinger, Eric 1933- ... CANR-29
Earlier sketches in CA 33-36R, CANR-13
Klinger, Friedrich Maximilian von
1752-1831 ... DLB 94
Klinger, Kurt 1914- ... 17-20R
Klinghoffer, Arthur Jay 1941- ... CANR-90
Earlier sketch in CA 65-68
Klinghoffer, David 1965- ... 181
Klingman, Lawrence (Lewis) 1918-1986
Obituary ... 120
Klingsor the Magician
See Hartmann, Sadakichi
Klingstedt, Joe Lars 1938- ... 53-56
Klink, Joanna 1969- ... 220
Klink, Johanna L. 1918- ... CANR-8
Earlier sketch in CA 61-64
Klinkenberg, Jeff 1949- ... 229
Klinkenborg, Verlyn 1953(?)- ... CANR-144
Earlier sketch in CA 139
Klinkowitz, Jerome 1943- ... CANR-96
Earlier sketches in CA 45-48, CANR-1
See also CAAS 9
Klipper, Miriam Z(eldner) ... 108
Kliros, Thea 1935- ... SATA 106
Klise, Eugene Storm 1908-1973 ... 5-8R
Klise, Kate ... 237
Klise, M. Sarah 1961- ... SATA 128
Klise, Thomas S. 1928-1978 ... 57-60
Obituary ... 134
Klitzman, Robert (L.) 1958- ... CANR-96
Earlier sketch in CA 135
Kliuev, Nikolai Alekseevich
1884-1937 ... DLB 295
Kliushnikov, Viktor Petrovich
1841-1892 ... DLB 238
Klobuchar, James John 1928- ... 73-76
Klobuchar, Jim
See Klobuchar, James John
Kloepfer, Marguerite (Fonnesbeck)
1916- ... 97-100
Kloesel, Christian Johannes Wilhelm
1942- ... 113
Kloetzli, Walter, (Jr.) 1921- ... 1-4R
Klonglan, Gerald E(dward) 1936- ... 41-44R
Klonis, N. I.
See Clones, N(icholas) J.
Klonsky, Milton 1921(?)-1981
Obituary ... 105
Kloos, Peter 1936- ... 93-96
Klooster, Fred H. 1922- ... 1-4R
Klopf, Donald W(illiam) 1923- ... CANR-34
Earlier sketches in CA 89-92, CANR-15
Klopfer, Donald S(imon) 1902-1986
Obituary ... 119
See also DLBY 1997
Klopfer, Peter H(ubert) 1930- ... 85-88
Klopfer, Walter G(eorge) 1923- ... 89-92
Kloppenburg, Boaventura 1919- ... CANR-15
Earlier sketch in CA 65-68
Klopstock, Friedrich Gottlieb
1724-1803 ... DLB 97
See also EW 4
See also RGWL 2, 3
Klopstock, Meta 1728-1758 ... DLB 97
Klos, Frank W(illiam), Jr. 1924- ... 13-16R
Klose, Kevin 1940- ... 53-56
Klose, Norma Cline 1936- ... 17-20R
Klose, Robert ... 184
Klosinski, Emil 1922- ... 65-68
Kloss, Phillips 1902-1995 ... CAP-1
Earlier sketch in CA 13-16
Kloss, Robert J(ames) 1935- ... 45-48
Kloss, Robert Marsh 1938- ... 65-68
Klosterman, Chuck 1972- ... 222
Klosty, James (Michael) 1943-
Brief entry ... 112
Klotman, Phyllis Rauch ... 93-96
Klotman, Robert Howard 1918- ... 53-56
Klots, Alexander Barrett 1903-1989 ... 107
Obituary ... 128
See also SATA-Obit 62
Klotter, James C(hristopher) 1947- ... 77-80
Klotter, John C(harles) 1918- ... 93-96
Klotz, Irving M(yron) 1916-2005 ... 201
Obituary ... 238
Klotz, Lynn C(harles) 1940- ... 116
Klubertanz, George Peter 1912-1972 ... 5-8R
Kluckhohn, Frank L. 1907-1970 ... 5-8R
Obituary ... 29-32R
Klueger, Ruth
See Kluger, Ruth
Klug, Eugene F(rederick Adolf) 1917- ... CANR-1
Earlier sketch in CA 45-48
Klug, Ron(ald) 1939- ... CANR-24
Earlier sketch in CA 107
See also SATA 31
Kluge, Alexander 1932- ... 81-84
See also DLB 75
See also SSC 61
Kluge, Eike-Henner W. 1942- ... 61-64
Kluge, P(aul) F(rederick) 1942- ... CANR-96
Earlier sketches in CA 73-76, CANR-16, 37
See also DLBY 2002
Kluger, Garry Michael 1955- ... 169
Kluger, James R. 1939- ... 29-32R
Kluger, Jeffrey ... 236
Kluger, Richard 1934- ... CANR-54
Earlier sketches in CA 9-12R, CANR-6, 28
Kluger, Ruth 1914(?)-1980 ... 116
Obituary ... 108
Kluger, Ruth 1931- ... 216
Kluger, Steve 1952- ... 138
Kluger-Bell, Kim 1951- ... 173
Klugh, Henry E(licker III) 1927- ... 53-56
Klugman, Edgar 1925- ... 132
Klungel
See Campert, Remco Wouter
Kluver, Billy
See Kluver, J(ohan) Wilhelm
Kluver, J(ohan) Wilhelm
1927-2004 ... CANR-144
Obituary ... 224
Earlier sketch in CA 133
Kluwe, Mary Jean 1905-1975 ... CAP-2
Earlier sketch in CA 23-24

Klymshyn, John 1959- 228
Klyuev, Nikolay Alexeevich
1887-1937(?) .... EWL 3
Klyza, Christopher McGrory 1959- . CANR-104
Earlier sketch in CA 150
Kmoch, Hans 1897(?)-1973
Obituary 41-44R
Knaack, Twila 1944- 119
Knaak, Richard A(llen) 1961- CANR-128
Earlier sketches in CA 128, CANR-58
See also FANT
See also SATA 86
Knachel, Philip A(therton) 1926- 21-24R
Knack, Martha C(arol) 1948- 118
Knaplund, Paul (Alexander)
1885-1964 .... CAP-1
Earlier sketch in CA 11-12
Knapp, Bettina (Liebowitz) CANR-136
Earlier sketches in CA 13-16R, CANR-6, 21, 44
Knapp, Caroline 1959-2002 154
Obituary 207
See also CLC 99
Knapp, David A(llan) 1938- 41-44R
Knapp, Edward
See Kunhardt, Edith
Knapp, Herbert W. 1931- 105
Knapp, J(ohn) Merrill 1914-1993 53-56
Obituary 140
Knapp, James F(ranklin) 1940- 107
Knapp, John (Allen) II 1940- 116
Knapp, Joseph G(rant) 1900-1983 .... 37-40R
Obituary 110
Knapp, Joseph G(eorge) 1924- 41-44R
Knapp, Joseph Palmer 1864-1951 183
See also DLB 91
Knapp, Lewis M(ansfield) 1894-1976 .... 21-24R
Knapp, Mark L(ane) 1938- 81-84
Knapp, Mary L. 1931- 105
Knapp, Peggy A(nn) 1937- 119
Knapp, Robert Hampden 1915-1974 .... CAP-2
Obituary 53-56
Earlier sketch in CA 13-14
Knapp, Ron 1952- 103
See also SATA 34
Knapp, Ronald Gary 1940- CANR-116
Earlier sketches in CA 112, CANR-30, 56
Knapp, Ronald J(ames) 1935- 119
Knapp, Samuel Lorenzo 1783-1838 ..... DLB 59
Knapp, Sara D. 1936- 143
Knapp, William R. 1920(?)-1990
Obituary 132
Knapper, Christopher (Kay) 1940- CANR-12
Earlier sketch in CA 29-32R
Knappert, Jan 1927- 172
Knapton, Ernest John 1902-1989 .... CANR-1
Earlier sketch in CA 1-4R
Knaub, Richard K. 1928-1996 .... 41-44R
Knauft, Bruce M. 1954- CANR-96
Earlier sketch in CA 146
Knaus, John Kenneth 1923- 187
Knaus, William A. 1946- 105
Knauss, Peter R(ichard) 1937-1990
Obituary 131
Knauss, Sibylle 1944- 218
Knauth, Percival Roediger
See Knauth, Percy
Knauth, Percy 1914-1995 57-60
Obituary 147
Knauth, Victor W. 1895(?)-1977
Obituary 73-76
Kneale, Matthew (Nicholas Kerr)
1960- CANR-96
Earlier sketches in CA 125, CANR-52
Kneale, (Thomas) Nigel 1922- CANR-75
Earlier sketch in CA 132
See also HGG
See also SFW 4
Knebel, Fletcher 1911-1993 .... CANR-36
Obituary 140
Earlier sketches in CA 1-4R, CANR-1
See also CAAS 3
See also AITN 1
See also CLC 14
See also CN 1, 2, 3, 4, 5
See also SATA 36
See also SATA-Obit 75
Knecht, G. Bruce 213
Knecht, Heidi 1961- 170
Knecht, Robert (Jean) 1926- CANR-46
Earlier sketches in CA 33-36R, CANR-13
Knechtges, David R(ichard) 1942- 65-68
Kneebone, Geoffrey (Thomas) 1918-2003 . 5-8R
Obituary 226
Kneeland, Linda Clarke 1947- 159
See also SATA 94
Kneeland, Timothy (W.) 1962- 201
Kneese, Allen V(ictor) 1930-2001 .... CANR-8
Obituary 195
Earlier sketch in CA 13-16R
Knef, Hildegard (Frieda Albertina)
1925-2002 .... CANR-4
Obituary 201
Earlier sketch in CA 45-48
Knell, Simon J. 1955- 209
Kneller, John W(illiam) 1916- 17-20R
Kneller, Marianna 1942- 153
Knelman, Fred H. 1919- 102
Knelman, Martin 1943- CANR-130
Earlier sketch in CA 73-76
Knepler, Henry (William) 1922-1999 .... 21-24R
Knevitt, Charles (Philip Paul) 1952- 132
Knezevich, Stephen J(oseph) 1920- .. CANR-10
Earlier sketch in CA 5-8R
Kniazhnin, Iakov Borisovich
1740-1791 .... DLB 150
Knibbs, H(enry) H(erbert)
1874-1945 .... TCWW 1, 2
Knickerbocker, Charles H(errick) 1922- . 13-16R
Knickerbocker, Cholly
See Cassini, Igor (Loiewski)
Knickerbocker, Diedrich
See Irving, Washington
Knickerbocker, Kenneth L(eslie)
1905-1990 .... 5-8R
Knickerbocker, Wendy 1948- 213
Knickmeyer, Steve 1944- 85-88
Knies, Elizabeth 1941- 109
Knifesmith
See Cutler, Ivor
Kniffen, Fred B(owerman)
1900-1993 .... CANR-47
Obituary 171
Earlier sketch in CA 1-4R
Knigge, Adolph Franz Friedrich Ludwig Freiherr von 1752-1796 .... DLB 94
Knigge, Robert (R.) 1921(?)-1987
Obituary 121
See also SATA 50
Knight, Adam
See Lariar, Lawrence
Knight, Alan 1946- 125
Knight, Alanna CANR-86
Earlier sketches in CA 81-84, CANR-15, 33
Knight, Alice Valle 1922- 81-84
Knight, Amarantha
See Kilpatrick, Nancy
Knight, Amy 1946- CANR-60
Earlier sketch in CA 128
Knight, Ann Scott 190
Knight, Anne (Katherine) 1946- .... SATA 34
Knight, Arthur 1916-1991 .... 41-44R
Obituary 135
Knight, Arthur Winfield 1937- 177
Earlier sketches in CA 53-56, CANR-4, 19, 41
Autobiographical Essay in 177
See also CAAS 27
Knight, B(etty) Carolyn 1944- 118
Knight, Bernard 1931- CANR-2
Earlier sketch in CA 49-52
Knight, Bertram 1904- 103
Knight, Bob
See Knight, Robert Montgomery
Knight, Bobby
See Knight, Robert Montgomery
Knight, Brenda 185
Earlier sketch in CA 173
See also SATA 112
Knight, Charles 1910- 109
Knight, Charles Landon .... AITN 2
Knight, Charles W. 1891-1973 .... CAP-1
Earlier sketch in CA 9-10
Knight, Christopher G. 1943- 163
See also SATA 96
Knight, Clayton 1891-1969 .... CAP-1
Earlier sketch in CA 9-10
Knight, Damon (Francis)
1922-2002 .... CANR-88
Obituary 208
Earlier sketches in CA 49-52, CANR-3, 17, 36, 80
See also CAAS 10
See also DLB 8
See also SATA 9
See also SATA-Obit 139
See also SCFW 1, 2
See also SFW 4
Knight, David
See Prather, Richard S(cott)
Knight, David C(arpenter) 1925-1984 73-76
See also CLR 38
See also SATA 14
Knight, David Marcus 1936- CANR-7
Earlier sketch in CA 57-60
Knight, Denis 1921- 137
Knight, Doug(las E.) 1925- 85-88
Knight, Douglas M(aitland)
1921-2005 .... CANR-2
Obituary 235
Earlier sketch in CA 49-52
Knight, Eric (Mowbray) 1897-1943 137
See also BYA 15
See also CWRI 5
See also JRDA
See also MAICYA 1, 2
See also SATA 18
Knight, Etheridge 1931-1991 .... CANR-82
Obituary 133
Earlier sketches in CA 21-24R, CANR-23
See also BLC 2
See also BW 1, 3
See also CLC 40
See also CP 1, 2
See also DAM POET
See also DLB 41
See also MTCW 2
See also MTFW 2005
See also PC 14
See also RGAL 4
See also TCLE 1:1
Knight, Everett 1919- 33-36R
Knight, Francis Edgar 1905- CANR-84
Earlier sketch in CA 73-76
See also SATA 14
Knight, Frank
See Knight, Francis Edgar
Knight, Frank H(yneman) 1885-1972
Obituary 33-36R
Knight, Franklin W(illis) 1942- CANR-94
Earlier sketch in CA 101
Knight, Frida 1910-1996 .... CANR-2
Obituary 154
Earlier sketch in CA 49-52
Knight, G(ilfred) Norman
1891-1978 .... CANR-17
Earlier sketch in CA 25-28R
Knight, G(eorge) Wilson 1897-1985 . CANR-10
Obituary 115
Earlier sketch in CA 13-16R
Knight, Gareth
See Wilby, Basil Leslie
Knight, Geoffrey Egerton 1921-1997 122
Knight, George A(ngus) F(ulton)
1909- CANR-42
Earlier sketch in CA 1-4R
Knight, Gladys (Maria) 1944- 169
Knight, Glee 1947-1975 57-60
Obituary 120
Knight, H(erbert) Ralph 1895-1972 .... CAP-2
Earlier sketch in CA 25-28
Knight, Harold V(incent) 1907-1991 ..... 21-24R
Knight, Harry Adam
See Brosnan, John
See also HGG
Knight, Hattie M. 1908-1976 .... CAP-2
Earlier sketch in CA 29-32
Knight, Hilary 1926- 73-76
See also MAICYA 1, 2
See also SATA 15, 69, 132
Knight, Hugh McCown 1905-1983 .... 5-8R
Knight, Ian 1956- 205
Knight, Ione Kemp 1922- 37-40R
Knight, Isabel F(rances) 1930- 25-28R
Knight, James
See Schneck, Stephen
Knight, James A(llen) 1918- CANR-6
Earlier sketch in CA 13-16R
Knight, Janet M(argaret) 1940- 93-96
Knight, Jesse F. 1946- 129
Knight, Joan (MacPhail) CANR-144
Earlier sketch in CA 149
See also SATA 82, 159
Knight, Joan
See Knight, Joan (MacPhail)
Knight, John S. III .... AITN 2
Knight, John Shively 1894-1981 .... CANR-79
Obituary 103
Earlier sketch in CA 93-96
Interview in CA-93-96
See also AITN 2
See also DLB 29
Knight, Julia 1957- 143
Knight, K(enneth) G(raham) 1921- 25-28R
Knight, Karl F. 1930- 17-20R
Knight, Kathleen Moore .... CMW 4
Knight, Kathryn Lasky
See Lasky, Kathryn
Knight, Lynne 1943- 216
Knight, Mallory T.
See Hurwood, Bernhardt J.
Knight, Margaret K(ennedy) Horsey
1903- CAP-1
Earlier sketch in CA 9-10
Knight, Max 1909-1993 .... CANR-40
Obituary 142
Earlier sketch in CA 93-96
Knight, Maxwell 1900- CAP-1
Earlier sketch in CA 13-14
Knight, Michael E(mery) 1935- 105
Knight, Norman L(ouis) 1895-1972 .. CANR-84
Earlier sketches in CAP-2, CA 23-24
See also SFW 4
Knight, Oliver (Holmes) 1919- 21-24R
Knight, Paul Emerson 1925- 13-16R
Knight, R(oy) C(lement) 1907-1999 .... 13-16R
Knight, Richard S. 1936- 115
Knight, Robert Montgomery 1940- 219
Knight, Robin 1943- 73-76
Knight, Roderic C(opley) 1942- 61-64
Knight, Ruth Adams 1898-1974 .... 5-8R
Obituary 49-52
See also SATA-Obit 20
Knight, Sarah Kemble 1666-1727 . DLB 24, 200
Knight, Stephen 1951-1985 .... CANR-34
Obituary 117
Earlier sketch in CA 69-72
Knight, Theodore O. 1946- CANR-91
Earlier sketch in CA 145
See also SATA 77
Knight, Thomas J(oseph) 1937- 102
Knight, Thomas S(tanley, Jr.) 1921- 17-20R
Knight, Vick (Ralph) Sr. 1908-1984
Obituary 112
Knight, Vick R(alph), Jr. 1928- CANR-37
Earlier sketches in CA 45-48, CANR-1, 16
Knight, W(illiam) Nicholas 1939- 37-40R
Knight, Walker L(eigh) 1924- CANR-13
Earlier sketch in CA 37-40R
Knight, Wallace E(dward) 1926- CANR-11
Earlier sketch in CA 65-68
Knight, William E. 1922- CANR-136
Earlier sketches in CA 128, CANR-66
Knight-Bruce, G. W. H. 1852-1896 .... DLB 174
Knightley, Phillip 1929- CANR-141
Earlier sketches in CA 25-28R, CANR-107
Knighton, C(harles) S(tephen Richard)
1950- 224
Knight-Patterson, W. M.
See Kulski, Wladyslaw W(szebor)
Knights, John Keell 1930(?)-1981
Obituary 102
Knights, L(ionel) C(harles)
1906-1997 .... CANR-43
Earlier sketches in CA 5-8R, CANR-3
Knights, Peter R(oger) 1938- 37-40R
Knights, Ward A(rthur), Jr. 1927- 97-100
Knigin, Michael Jay 1942- 85-88
Kniker, Charles Robert 1936- 77-80
Knipe, Humphry 1941- 37-40R
Knipe, Wayne Bishop III 1946- 53-56
Knipfel, Jim 1968- 221
Knippenberg, Joseph M. 1948- 170
Knippling, Alpana Sharma 1937- 177
Knipschield, Don(ald Harold) 1940- 5-8R
Knish, Anne
See Ficke, Arthur Davison
Kniskern, David Paul 1948- 112
Knister, Raymond 1899-1932 186
See also DLB 68
See also RGEL 2
See also TCLC 56
Knittel, John (Herman Emanuel) 1891-1970
Obituary 104
Knitter, Paul F(rancis) 1939- 129
Knobel, Lance 1956- 121
Knoblauch, C(yril) H. 1945- CANR-53
Earlier sketch in CA 124
Knobler, Nathan 1926- 33-36R
Knobler, Peter (Stephen) 1946- CANR-110
Earlier sketches in CA 97-100, CANR-44
Knobloch, Dorothea 1951- CANR-111
Earlier sketch in CA 152
See also SATA 88
Knoblock, Edward 1874-1945
Brief entry 108
See also DLB 10
Knoblock, Glenn A. 1962- 237
Knock, Thomas J. 1950- 141
Knock, Warren 1932- 65-68
Knode, Helen 1957- 218
Knoebl, Kuno 1936- 25-28R
Knoedelseder, William 1947- 190
Knoepfel, Heinz E. 1931- 231
Knoepfle, John (Ignatius) 1923- CANR-84
Earlier sketches in CA 13-16R, CANR-12, 29, 53
See also CP 1, 2, 3, 4, 5, 6, 7
See also SATA 66
Knoepflmacher, U(lrich) C(amillus)
1931- CANR-115
Earlier sketches in CA 13-16R, CANR-10
Knoerle, Jeanne 1928- 45-48
Knoke, David (Harmon) 1947- CANR-51
Earlier sketches in CA 65-68, CANR-10, 26
Knoles, George Harmon 1907- 5-8R
Knoll, Erwin 1931-1994 89-92
Knoll, Gerald M. 1942- 29-32R
Knoll, Paul W(endell) 1937- 107
Knoll, Robert Edwin 1922- CANR-5
Earlier sketch in CA 1-4R
Knollenberg, Bernhard 1892-1973 .... CAP-2
Obituary 41-44R
Earlier sketch in CA 21-22
Knoop, Faith Yingling 1896-1984 97-100
Knop, Werner 1912(?)-1970
Obituary 29-32R
Knopf, Alfred A. 1892-1984 106
Obituary 113
See also DLBY 1984
Knopf, Edwin H. 1899-1982(?)
Obituary 105
Knopf, Irwin J(ay) 1924- 119
Knopf, Kenyon A(lfred) 1921- 77-80
Knopf, Marcy 1969- 142
Knopf, Robert 1961- 187
Knopf, Terry Ann 1940- CANR-17
Earlier sketch in CA 25-28R
Knopfler, Mark (Freuder) 1949- 234
Knopp, Josephine Zadovsky 1941- 103
Knopp, Lisa 1956- 158
Knorr, Albert Scofield 1929-1998 .... 25-28R
Knorr, Dandi 1949- 112
Knorr, K. E.
See Knorr, Klaus E(ugene)
Knorr, Klaus
See Knorr, Klaus E(ugene)
Knorr, Klaus E(ugene) 1911-1990 134
Obituary 131
Brief entry 113
Knorr, Marian L(ockwood) 1910-1995 102
Knorr von Rosenroth, Christian
1636-1689 .... DLB 168
Knott, Bill
See Knott, William C(ecil, Jr.)
See also CP 2, 3, 4, 5, 6, 7
Knott, John R(ay), Jr. 1937- 57-60
Knott, Kim 1955- 124
Knott, Leonard L(ewis) 1905-1992 107
Knott, William C(ecil, Jr.) 1927- CANR-63
Earlier sketches in CA 5-8R, CANR-7, 22
See also Knott, Bill and
Mitchum, Hank and
Sharpe, Jon
See also DAM POP
See also SATA 3
See also TCWW 2
Knotts, Howard (Clayton, Jr.) 1922- .. CANR-11
Earlier sketch in CA 69-72
See also SATA 25
Knowland, A(nthony) S(tephen) 1919- 116
Knowland, William Fife 1908-1974
Obituary 89-92
Knowler, John 1933(?)-1979
Obituary 85-88
Knowles, A(lbert) Sidney, Jr. 1926- 101
Knowles, Alison 1933- CANR-29
Earlier sketches in CA 17-20R, CANR-8
Knowles, Anne 1933- 102
See also SATA 37
Knowles, Asa S(mallidge) 1909-1990 .... 29-32R
Obituary 132
Knowles, Clayton 1908-1978 81-84
Obituary 73-76
Knowles, (Michael Clive) David
1896-1974 .... CANR-4
Obituary 53-56

Cumulative Index 323 Koester

Knowles, David 1966- CANR-94
Earlier sketch in CA 152
Knowles, Dorothy 1906- 25-28R
Knowles, Elizabeth 1947- 170
Knowles, Harry (Jay) 1971- 216
Knowles, Henry P(aine) 1912-1991 61-64
Knowles, James Sheridan 1784-1862 RGEL 2
Knowles, John 1926-2001 CANR-132
Obituary 203
Earlier sketches in CA 17-20R, CANR-40, 74, 76
See also AAYA 10
See also AMWS 12
See also BPFB 2
See also BYA 3
See also CDALB 1968-1988
See also CLC 1, 4, 10, 26
See also CLR 98
See also CN 1, 2, 3, 4, 5, 6, 7
See also DA
See also DAC
See also DAM MST, NOV
See also DLB 6
See also EXPN
See also MTCW 1, 2
See also MTFW 2005
See also NFS 2
See also RGAL 4
See also SATA 8, 89
See also SATA-Obit 134
See also YAW
Knowles, John H(ilton) 1926-1979 101
Obituary 85-88
See also LAIT 4
Knowles, Joseph W(illiam) 1922- 21-24R
Knowles, Louis L(eonard) 1947- 29-32R
Knowles, Mabel Winifred 1875-1949
Brief entry 122
See also May, Wynne
See also CWRI 5
Knowles, Malcolm Shepherd 1913-1997 CANR-5
Obituary 162
Earlier sketch in CA 5-8R
Knowles, Valerie (J.) 1934- CANR-59
Earlier sketch in CA 128
Knowles, Yereth K(ahn) 1920- 93-96
Knowlton, Derrick 1921- CANR-6
Earlier sketch in CA 57-60
Knowlton, Edgar C(olby), Jr. 1921- 41-44R
Knowlton, James 1943- 120
Knowlton, Robert A(lmy) 1914-1968 1-4R
Obituary 103
Knowlton, William H. 1927- 17-20R
Knox, Alan B. 1931- 147
Knox, Alexander 1907-1995 81-84
Obituary 148
Knox, Bernard M(acGregor) W(alker) 1914- 128
Brief entry 117
Knox, Bill
See Knox, William
Knox, Buddy
See Knox, Wayne
Knox, Calvin M.
See Silverberg, Robert
Knox, Caroline 1938- 120
Knox, Cleone
See King-Hall, Magdalen
Knox, Collie T. 1897-1977 77-80
Obituary 73-76
Knox, David H., Jr. 1943- 41-44R
Knox, Donald E(dward) 1936-1986 CANR-39
Obituary 119
Earlier sketch in CA 45-48
Knox, Edmund George Valpy 1881-1971 112
Obituary 29-32R
Knox, (Mary) Eleanor Jessie 1909-2000
Obituary 189
See also MAICYA 1, 2
See also SATA 30, 59
Knox, Elizabeth (Fiona) 1959- CANR-109
Earlier sketch in CA 159
See also CN 5, 6, 7
Knox, (William) Frank(lin) 1874-1944 178
See also DLB 29
Knox, George 1922- 138
Knox, George A(lbert) 1918- 121
Knox, Gilbert
See Macbeth, Madge (Hamilton)
Knox, Henry M(acdonald) 1916- 13-16R
Knox, Hugh (Randolph) 1942- 103
Knox, Israel 1906-1986
Obituary 119
Knox, James
See Brittain, William (E.)
Knox, John c. 1505-1572 DLB 132
Knox, John 1900-1990 13-16R
Obituary 132
Knox, John Armoy 1850-1906 178
See also DLB 23
Knox, John Ballenger 1909- CAP-1
Earlier sketch in CA 9-10
Knox, Jolyne 1937- SATA 76
Knox, Katharine McCook 1890(?)-1983
Obituary 110
Knox, Lucy 1845-1884 201
See also DLB 240
Knox, (Thomas) Malcolm 1900-1980 103
Obituary 97-100
Knox, Melissa 1957- 149
Knox, Oliver 1923-2002 216
Knox, Robert Buick 1918-2004 25-28R
Knox, Ronald A(rbuthnott) 1888-1957 173
Brief entry 111
See also CMW 4
See also DLB 77
See also MSW
Knox, Sanka (Lutins) 1906-1984
Obituary 112
Knox, Sara L(ouise) 1962- 174
Knox, Thomas Wallace 1835-1896 DLB 189
Knox, Vera Huntingdon 9-12R
Knox, Warren Barr 1925- 49-52
Knox, Wayne 1933-1999 181
Knox, William 1928-1999 CANR-85
Earlier sketches in CA 1-4R, CANR-1, 47
See also CMW 4
Knox-Johnston, Robin 1939- CANR-15
Earlier sketch in CA 29-32R
Knox-Mawer, June 1930- CANR-111
Earlier sketch in CA 151
Knox-Mawer, Ronald 1925- 123
Knox-Mawer, Ronnie
See Knox-Mawer, Ronald
Knuckey, Deborah 224
Knudbucker, Homer T., Jr.
See Garfinkle, Adam M.
Knudsen, Hans August Heinrich 1886-1971
Obituary 29-32R
Knudsen, Jakob 1858-1917 DLB 300
Knudsen, James 1950- CANR-47
Earlier sketch in CA 111
See also SATA 42
Knudson, Danny (Alan) 1940- CANR-11
Earlier sketch in CA 61-64
Knudson, R. R.
See Knudson, Rozanne
See also AAYA 20
See also SAAS 18
Knudson, Richard L(ewis) 1930- CANR-20
Earlier sketch in CA 104
See also SATA 34
Knudson, Rozanne 1932- CANR-85
Earlier sketches in CA 33-36R, CANR-15, 35
See also Knudson, R. R.
See also SATA 7, 79
See also YAW
Knudtson, Peter M(ichael) 1947- CANR-68
Earlier sketch in CA 129
Knuemann, Carl H(einz) 1922-1994 77-80
Knusel, Jack L(eonard) 1923-1993 25-28R
Knut, Dovid
See Fiksman, David Mironovich
See also DLB 317
Knuth, Donald E. 1938- CANR-114
Earlier sketch in CA 163
Knuth, Helen 1912- 53-56
Knutson, Donald C. 1931(?)-1990
Obituary 131
Knutson, Harold Christian 1928- 112
Knutson, Jeanne N(ickell) 1934- 41-44R
Knutson, Kent S(iguart) 1924-1973 CAP-2
Obituary 41-44R
Earlier sketch in CA 33-36
Knutson, Kimberley 182
See also SATA 115
Knutson, Roger M. 1933- 126
Knutson, Susan 1952- 224
Knye, Cassandra
See Disch, Thomas M(ichael)
Ko, Kanzein
See Isogai, Hiroshi
Ko, Tanya Hyonhye 1964- 232
Ko, Won 1925- 61-64
Kobak, Annette 230
Kobal, John 1943(?)-1991 CANR-11
Obituary 135
Earlier sketch in CA 61-64
Kobayashi, Hideo 1902-1983 193
See also Kobayashi Hideo
Kobayashi, Koji 1907-1996 133
Kobayashi, Masako Matsuno 1935- CANR-31
Earlier sketches in CA 5-8R, CANR-13
See also Matsuno, Masako
Kobayashi, Noritake 1932- 53-56
Kobayashi, Takiji 1903-1933
See Kobayashi Takiji
Kobayashi, Tetsuya 1926- 69-72
Kobayashi Hideo
See Kobayashi, Hideo
See also EWL 3
Kobayashi Takiji
See Kobayashi, Takiji
See also DLB 180
Kober, Arthur 1900-1975 CAP-1
Obituary 57-60
Earlier sketch in CA 13-14
See also DLB 11
Kobiakova, Aleksandra Petrovna 1823-1892 DLB 238
Kobler, Albert John, Jr. 1910-2000 65-68
Obituary 191
Kobler, Arthur L(eon) 1920-1999 13-16R
Kobler, (Mary) Turner S. 1930- 37-40R
Kobrak, Peter 1936- 104
Kobre, Sidney 1907-1995 65-68
Kobrin, David 1941- 41-44R
Kobrin, Janet 1942- 57-60
Kobryn, A(llen) P(aul) 1949- 93-96
Kocbek, Edvard 1904-1981 CDWLB 4
See also DLB 147
Koch, C(hristopher) J(ohn) 1932- CANR-84
Earlier sketch in CA 127
See also CLC 42
See also CN 3, 4, 5, 6, 7
See also DLB 289
Koch, Charlotte (Moskowitz) 1908-2002 85-88
Obituary 200
See also Koch, Raymond
Koch, Christopher
See Koch, C(hristopher) J(ohn)
Koch, Claude (F.) 1918- 9-12R
Koch, Dorothy Clarke 1924- 5-8R
See also SATA 6
Koch, Edward I(rving) 1924- CANR-92
Earlier sketch in CA 113
Koch, Eric 1919- CANR-98
Earlier sketch in CA 69-72
Koch, H(annsjoachim) W(olfgang) 1933- CANR-15
Earlier sketch in CA 93-96
Koch, Hans-Gerhard 1913- 17-20R
Koch, Helen L(ois) 1895-1977 CAP-2
Earlier sketch in CA 21-22
Koch, Howard 1902-1995 73-76
Obituary 149
See also DLB 26
See also IDFW 3, 4
Koch, James Harold 1926- 106
Koch, Joanne 1940- CANR-32
Earlier sketches in CA 69-72, CANR-15
Koch, Kenneth (Jay) 1925-2002 CANR-131
Obituary 207
Earlier sketches in CA 1-4R, CANR-6, 36, 57, 97
Interview in CANR-36
See also AMWS 15
See also CAD
See also CD 5, 6
See also CLC 5, 8, 44
See also CP 1, 2, 3, 4, 5, 6, 7
See also DAM POET
See also DLB 5
See also MAL 5
See also MTCW 2
See also MTFW 2005
See also PFS 20
See also SATA 65
See also WP
Koch, Kurt E(mil) 1913-1987 107
Obituary 122
Koch, Lew(is) Z. 1935- 69-72
Koch, Michael 1916(?)-1981
Obituary 103
Koch, Phyllis (Mae) McCallum 1911- CANR-4
Earlier sketch in CA 53-56
See also SATA 10
Koch, Raymond -1994 85-88
Obituary 145
Koch, Richard 1921- 29-32R
Koch, Robert 1918-2003 9-12R
Obituary 219
Koch, Stephen 1941- CANR-131
Earlier sketch in CA 77-80
Koch, Thilo 1920- CANR-11
Earlier sketch in CA 25-28R
Koch, Thomas J(ohn) 1947- 61-64
Koch, Thomas Walter 1933- 17-20R
Koch, Tom 1949- 191
Koch, William H., Jr. 1923- 17-20R
Kochalka, James 1968- 227
Kochan, Lionel 1922- 105
Kochan, Miriam (Louise) 1929- 103
Kochan, Nicholas 175
Kochan, Nick
See Kochan, Nicholas
Kochan, Paul C(ranston) 1906-1994 45-48
Kochan, Thomas A(nton) 1947- 123
Kochanek, Stanley A(nthony) 1934- CANR-38
Earlier sketch in CA 116
Kochanowski, Jan 1530-1584 RGWL 2, 3
Kochen, Manfred 1928- 21-24R
Kochenburger, Ralph J. 1919-1980 53-56
Kochendoerfer, Violet A. 1912-2001 159
Kocher, Eric 1912-1999 57-60
Kocher, Paul H(arold) 1907-1998 65-68
Kocher, Ruth Ellen 1965- 184
Kochetov, Vsevolod A(nisimovich) 1912-1973
Obituary 45-48
Kochhar-Lindgren, Gray 1955- 195
Kochina, Pelageya (Yakovlevna) Polubarinova 1899- 169
Kochiss, John (Matthew) 1926- 97-100
Kochka, Mary Murray 1894(?)-1984
Obituary 112
Kochman, Thomas 1936- 37-40R
Kocieniewski, David 230
Kocis, Robert A. 1950- 185
Kock, Winston E(dward) 1909-1982 110
Kocka, Juergen 1941- 133
Kocka, Jurgen
See Kocka, Juergen
Kockelmans, Joseph J(ohn) 1923- CANR-41
Brief entry 113
Earlier sketch in CA 117
Kocot, Noelle 1969- 214
Kocour, Ruth Anne 1947- 181
Kocsis, J. C.
See Paul, James
Kocsis, Robert
See Kossez, Robes
Koda-Callan, Elizabeth 1944- CANR-119
Earlier sketch in CA 136
See also SATA 67, 140
Kodaira, Kunihiko 1915-1997 164
Kodaly, Zoltan 1882-1967
Obituary 112
Kodama, Sanehide 1932- 120
Kodanda Rao, Pandurangi 1889- 13-16R
Koda Rohan
See Koda Shigeyuki
Koda Rohan
See Koda Shigeyuki
See also DLB 180
Koda Shigeyuki 1867-1947 183
Brief entry 121
See also Koda Rohan
See also TCLC 22
Kodera, Takashi James 1945- 111
Kodis, Michelle R. 1968- 172
Koegler, Hans-Herbert 1960- 165
Koehler, Alan (Robert) 1928- 13-16R
Koehler, Frank
See Paine, Lauran (Bosworth)
Koehler, G(eorge) Stanley 1915- 37-40R
Koehler, George E. 1930- 25-28R
Koehler, John O. 1930- 198
Koehler, Ludmila 1917- 53-56
Koehler, Lyle P(eter) 1944- 109
Koehler, Margaret (Hudson) CANR-30
Earlier sketch in CA 85-88
Koehler, Nikki 1951- 25-28R
Koehler, Phoebe 1955- 132
See also SATA 85
Koehler, Ted 1894-1973 DLB 265
Koehler, W(illiam) R. 1914-1993 9-12R
Koehler, Wolfgang 1887-1967
Obituary 111
Koehler-Pentacoff, Elizabeth 1957- 161
See also SATA 96, 160
Koehn, Ilse
See Van Zwienen, Ilse Charlotte Koehn
Koehn, Lala
See Koehn-Heine, Lala
Koehn-Heine, Lala 1936- 112
Koelb, Clayton T. 1942- 132
Koelsch, William Alvin 1933- 104
Koen, Ross Y. 1918- 1-4R
Koenig, Allen Edward 1939- 21-24R
Koenig, C(lyde) Eldo 1919- 21-24R
Koenig, Duane (Walter) 1918-1995 37-40R
Koenig, Franz 1905-2004 101
Obituary 225
Koenig, Fritz H(ans) 1940- 53-56
Koenig, Harold G. 1951- CANR-141
Earlier sketch in CA 176
Koenig, John (Thomas) 1938- 102
Koenig, Karl P. 1938- 148
Koenig, Laird CANR-32
Earlier sketch in CA 29-32R
Koenig, Linda Lee 1948- 113
Koenig, Louis William 1916- CANR-48
Earlier sketch in CA 1-4R
Koenig, Rene 1906- CANR-15
Earlier sketch in CA 81-84
Koenig, Samuel 1899-1972 CAP-2
Obituary 37-40R
Earlier sketch in CA 17-18
Koenig, Viviane 1950- 147
See also SATA 80
Koenig, Walter 1936- 104
Koenigsberg, Moses 1879-1945 178
See also DLB 25
Koenigsberger, H(elmut) G(eorg) 1918- 33-36R
Koenigswald, (Gustav Heinrich) Ralph von
See von Koenigswald, (Gustav Heinrich) Ralph
Koenker, Diane 1947- 112
Koenker, Ernest Benjamin 1920-
Brief entry 106
Koenner, Alfred 1921- CANR-40
Earlier sketches in CA 101, CANR-18
Koepf, Gerhard
See Kopf, Gerhard
Koepf, Michael 1940- 81-84
Koepke, Paul 1918- 114
Koepke, Wulf 1928- CANR-39
Earlier sketches in CA 93-96, CANR-16
Koepp, David 1964(?)- 156
Koeppel, Gary 1938- 49-52
Koeppel, Gerard T. 1957- 188
Koeppen, Wolfgang 1906-1996 183
See also DLB 69
See also EWL 3
Koering, Ursula 1921-1976 SATA 64
Koerner, David (W.) 200
Koerner, James D. 1923- 9-12R
Koerner, Joseph Leo 1958- 146
Koerner, Lisbet 204
Koerner, Stephan 1913-2000 1-4R
Koerner, Theodor 1791-1813 DLB 90
Koerner, W(illiam) H(enry) D(avid) 1878-1938 SATA 21
Koerte, Mary Norbert 1934- 103
See also Korte, Mary Norbert
Koertge, Noretta 1935- CANR-22
Earlier sketch in CA 106
Koertge, Ron(ald) 1940- CANR-58
Earlier sketches in CA 65-68, CANR-9, 25
See also AAYA 12, 43
See also BYA 6
See also DLB 105
See also MAICYA 2
See also MAICYAS 1
See also SATA 53, 92, 131
See also WYAS 1
See also YAW
Koestenbaum, Peter 1928- CANR-13
Earlier sketch in CA 29-32R
Koestenbaum, Phyllis 1930- CANR-25
Earlier sketch in CA 107
Koestenbaum, Wayne 1958- CANR-96
Earlier sketch in CA 134
Koester, Helmut 1926- 110

Koestler, Arthur 1905-1983 .... CANR-33
Obituary 109
Earlier sketches in CA 1-4R, CANR-1
See also BRWS 1
See also CDBLB 1945-1960
See also CLC 1, 3, 6, 8, 15, 33
See also CN 1, 2, 3
See also DLBY 1983
See also EWL 3
See also MTCW 1, 2
See also MTFW 2005
See also NFS 19
See also RGEL 2
Koestler, Cynthia 1928(?)-1983
Obituary 114
Koestler-Grack, Rachel A. 1973- 231
See also SATA 156
Koethe, John (Louis) 1945- CANR-126
Earlier sketch in CA 49-52
Koetzsch, Ronald E. 1944- 164
Kofalk, Harriet 1937- CANR-30
Earlier sketch in CA 112
Kofas, Jon V. 1953- 195
Koff, Richard Myram 1926- CANR-15
Earlier sketch in CA 89-92
See also SATA 62
Koffinke, Carol 1949- 149
See also SATA 82
Kofman, Sarah 1934-1994 198
Kofoed, Jack
See Kofoed, John C.
Kofoed, John C. 1894-1979 .... 5-8R
Obituary 93-96
Koford, Kenneth J. 1948-2004 140
Obituary 232
Kofsky, Frank (Joseph) 1935-1997 57-60
Obituary 162
Kogan, Bernard Robert 1920-2001 .... 9-12R
Obituary 194
Kogan, Deborah
See Kogan Ray, Deborah
See also SATA 50
Kogan, Herman 1914-1989 .... CANR-20
Obituary 128
Earlier sketches in CA 9-12R, CANR-5
Kogan, Judith 1956- 126
Kogan, Leonard S(aul) 1919-1976
Obituary 65-68
Kogan, Maurice 1930- 107
Kogan, Norman 1919- 1-4R
Kogan Ray, Deborah 1940- CANR-22
Earlier sketches in CA 57-60, CANR-7
See also Kogan, Deborah and Ray, Deborah
See also SATA 161
Kogawa, Joy Nozomi 1935- CANR-126
Earlier sketches in CA 101, CANR-19, 62
See also AAYA 47
See also CLC 78, 129
See also CN 6, 7
See also CP 1
See also CWP
See also DAC
See also DAM MST, MULT
See also FW
See also MTCW 2
See also MTFW 2005
See also NFS 3
See also SATA 99
Koger, Lisa (Jan) 1953- 133
Kogiku, K(iichiro) C(hris) 1927- 33-36R
Koginos, Manny T. 1933- 21-24R
Kogon, Eugen 1903-1897
Kogos, Frederick 1907-1974 .... CAP-2
Obituary 53-56
Earlier sketch in CA 29-32
Koh, Byung Chul 1936- 17-20R
Koh, Sung Jae 1917- 17-20R
Kohak, Erazim V. 1933- CANR-31
Earlier sketches in CA 37-40R, CANR-14
Kohake, Rosanne 1951- 114
Kohan, Rhea 89-92
Kohanov, Linda 210
Kohanski, Alexander S(iskind) 1902-1987 .. 108
Obituary 123
Kohavi, Y.
See Stern, Jay B(enjamin)
Kohen, Aharon
See Cohen, Aharon
Kohen, Hayim H.
See Cohn, Haim H(erman)
Kohen-Raz, Reuven 1921- 37-40R
Kohfeldt, Mary Lou (Stevenson) 1939- CANR-44
Earlier sketch in CA 119
Kohl, Benjamin G. 1938- CANR-56
Earlier sketch in CA 126
Kohl, Herbert 1937- CANR-79
Earlier sketches in CA 65-68, CANR-14
See also SATA 47
Kohl, Irene C(aistor) 1927- 119
Kohl, James (Virgil) 1942- 57-60
Kohl, James Vaughn 1951- 157
Kohl, Judith 219
Kohl, Marvin 1932- 85-88
Kohl, MaryAnn F(aubion) 1947- 217
See also SATA 74, 144
Kohlberg, Lawrence 1927-1987 125
Obituary 122
Kohlenberg, Robert J(oseph) 1937- 111
Kohler, Foy D(avid) 1908-1990 .... 29-32R
Obituary 133
Kohler, Heinz 1934- 21-24R
Kohler, Joachim 221
Kohler, Julilly H(ouse) 1908-1976 77-80
Obituary 69-72
See also SATA-Obit 20
Kohler, Lotte (E.) 1919- 216
Kohler, Mary Conway 1903-1986 135
Obituary 119
Kohler, Sandra 1940- 176
Kohler, Saul 1928-1999 69-72
Kohler, Sheila (May) 1941- CANR-89
Earlier sketch in CA 137
See also SSFS 18
Kohler, Sister Mary Hortense 1892-1991 ... 5-8R
Kohler, Wolfgang
See Koehler, Wolfgang
Kohlmeier, Louis M(artin), Jr. 1926- 49-52
Kohls, R. L.
See Kohls, Richard L(ouis)
Kohls, Richard L(ouis) 1921- 126
Brief entry 106
Kohlstedt, Sally Gregory 1943- 69-72
Kohmescher, Matthew Franklin 1921- 113
Kohn, Alan J(acobs) 1931- CANR-91
Earlier sketch in CA 146
Kohn, Alexander 1919- 123
Kohn, Alfie 1957- 122
Kohn, Bernice
See Hunt, Bernice (Kohn)
See also SATA 4
Kohn, Clyde Frederick 1911-1989
Obituary 130
Brief entry 109
Kohn, Eugene 1887-1977
Obituary 69-72
Kohn, George C(hilds) 1940- CANR-42
Earlier sketches in CA 103, CANR-19
Kohn, Hans 1891-1971 .... CANR-4
Obituary 29-32R
Earlier sketch in CA 1-4R
Kohn, Howard 1947- 124
Kohn, Jacob 1881-1968 .... 5-8R
Obituary 103
Kohn, John S.
See Kohn, John S(icher) Van E(isen)
Kohn, John S(icher) Van E(isen) 1906-1976 177
Obituary 104
See also DLB 187
Kohn, Livia 1956- 139
Kohn, Marek (Czeslaw Patrick) 1958- 128
Kohn, Melvin L(ester) 1928- 41-44R
Kohn, Richard H(enry) 1940- CANR-37
Earlier sketch in CA 115
Kohn, Rita (T.) 1933- .... SATA 89
Kohn, Walter S(amuel) G(erst) 1923- 107
Kohn, Wendy 183
Kohner, Frederick 1905-1986 .... CANR-1
Obituary 119
Earlier sketch in CA 1-4R
See also SATA 10
See also SATA-Obit 48
Kohno, Masaru 1962- 180
Kohon, Gregorio 1943- 159
Kohout, Pavel 1928- CANR-3
Earlier sketch in CA 45-48
See also CLC 13
Kohr, Louise Hannah 1903-2000 .... 41-44R
Kohs, Samuel C(almin) 1890-1984
Obituary 111
Koht, Halvdan 1873-1965 85-88
Kohut, Heinz 1913-1981 .... CANR-1
Obituary 105
Earlier sketch in CA 45-48
Kohut, Les
See Kohut, Nester C(larence)
Kohut, Nester C(larence) 1925- 45-48
Kohut, Thomas A. 1950- 142
Koidahl, Ilona 1924-1996 97-100
Koide, Tan 1938-1986 132
See also SATA 50
Koi Hai
See Palmer, (Nathaniel) Humphrey
Koike, Kay 1940- .... SATA 72
Koilpillai, (Jesudas) Charles 41-44R
Koilpillai, Das
See Koilpillai, (Jesudas) Charles
Koinange, Mbiyu (Peter) 1907-1981
Obituary 108
Koiner, Richard B. 1929- 17-20R
Koistinen, Paul A. C. 1933- 174
Koizumi, Yakumo
See Hearn, (Patricio) Lafcadio (Tessima Carlos)
Koja, Kathe 1960- CANR-99
Earlier sketch in CA 147
See also AAYA 59
See also HGG
See also SATA 155
See also SUFW 2
Kojecky, Roger 1943- 85-88
Kojima, Naomi 1950- 109
Kojima, Takashi 1902- CAP-1
Earlier sketch in CA 9-10
Kojima Shozo 1928- 69-72
Kokhanovskaia
See Sokhanskaia, Nadezhda Stepanovna
Kokoris, Jim 1958- 208
Kokoschka, Oskar 1886-1980 109
Obituary 93-96
See also DLB 124
Kokyshev, Lazor 1933(?)-1975
Obituary 104
Kolaja, Jiri Thomas 1919- 9-12R
Kolakowski, Leszek 1927- 49-52
Kolars, Frank 1899-1973 .... 5-8R
Obituary 37-40R
Kolasky, John 1915- 25-28R
Kolata, Gina
See Kolata, Gina Bari
Kolata, Gina Bari 1948- CANR-128
Earlier sketch in CA 171
Kolatch, Alfred Jacob 1916- 107
Kolatch, Jonathan 1943- 41-44R
Kolatkar, Arun (Balkrishna) 1932- CANR-84
Earlier sketch in CA 153
See also CP 7
Kolb, Annette 1870-1967 178
See also DLB 66
See also EWL 3
Kolb, Carolyn 1942- 89-92
Kolb, David A(llen) 1939- CANR-15
Earlier sketch in CA 65-68
Kolb, Erwin J(ohn) 1924- 37-40R
Kolb, Gwin Jackson 1919- 1-4R
Kolb, Harold H(utchinson), Jr. 1933- CANR-12
Earlier sketch in CA 29-32R
Kolb, (Gwin) Jack (II) 1946- 125
Kolb, John F. 1916(?)-1974
Obituary 53-56
Kolb, Ken(neth) 1926- 21-24R
Kolb, Lawrence 1911-1972
Obituary 37-40R
Kolb, Philip 1907-1992 .... CANR-4
Obituary 139
Earlier sketch in CA 53-56
Kolb, Robert 1941- 198
Kolba, St. Tamara 97-100
See also SATA 22
Kolbas, Grace Holden 1914-1987 93-96
Kolbe, Henry E(ugene) 1907-1985 .... 5-8R
Kolbenheyer, Erwin Guido 1878-1962 178
See also DLB 66, 124
Kolbenschlag, Madonna (Claire) 1935-2000
Brief entry 115
Kolbert, Elizabeth 1961(?)- 235
Kolbrek, Loyal 1914- 29-32R
Kolchin, Peter 1943- 41-44R
Kolde, Endel Jakob 1917- CANR-1
Earlier sketch in CA 45-48
Kolenda, Konstantin 1923-1991 .... 13-16R
Kolers, Paul A. 1926-1986 97-100
Kolesar, Paul 1927- 105
Kolesnik, Walter B(ernard) 1923- CANR-2
Earlier sketch in CA 5-8R
Kolesnikow, Tassia 1966- 223
Kolevzon, Edward R. 1913(?)-1976
Obituary 69-72
Kolibalova, Marketa
See Kolibalova, Marketa
Kolibalova, Marketa 1953- .... SATA 126
Kolin, Philip C(harles) 1945- CANR-43
Earlier sketch in CA 119
Kolins, William 1926(?)-1973
Obituary 104
Kolinski, Charles J(ames) 1916-1978 ..... 17-20R
Kolinsky, Martin 1936- CANR-8
Earlier sketch in CA 61-64
Kolitz, Zvi 1913(?)-2002 227
Koljevic, Svetozar 1930- CANR-7
Earlier sketch in CA 17-20R
Kolker, Robert Phillip 1940- CANR-101
Earlier sketch in CA 112
Kolko, Gabriel 1932- CANR-123
Earlier sketches in CA 5-8R, CANR-4
Kolko, Joyce 1933- 130
Kolkowicz, Roman 1929- 154
Brief entry 116
Kollat, David T(ruman) 1938- 41-44R
Kollek, Teddy
See Kollek, Theodore
Kollek, Theodore 1911- CAP-2
Earlier sketch in CA 29-32
Koller, Ann Marie 128
Koller, Charles W. 1896(?)-1983 61-64
Obituary 109
Koller, Jackie French 1948- CANR-141
Earlier sketch in CA 170
See also AAYA 28
See also CLR 68
See also SATA 72, 109, 157
Koller, James 1936- CANR-85
Earlier sketches in CA 49-52, CANR-2, 18, 39
See also CAAS 5
See also CP 1, 2, 3, 4, 5, 6, 7
Koller, John M. 1938- 33-36R
Koller, Larry
See Koller, Lawrence Robert
Koller, Lawrence Robert 1912-1967 ... CANR-6
Earlier sketch in CA 1-4R
Koller, Marvin Robert 1919-1997 .... 13-16R
Kolleritsch, Alfred 1931- 183
See also DLB 85
Kollmar, Dick
See Kollmar, Richard Tompkins
Kollmar, Richard Tompkins 1910-1971
Obituary 89-92
Kollock, Will(iam Raymond) 1940- 33-36R
Kollontai, Alexandra (Mikhailovna Domantovich) 1872-1952 154
Brief entry 112
See also FW
Kollstedt, Paula Lubke 1946- 113
Kollwitz, Kathe 1867-1945 .... AAYA 62
Kolmar, Gertrud 1894-1943 167
See also EWL 3
See also TCLC 40
Kolmerten, Carol A. 1946- 135
Kolmogorov, Andrei Nikolayevich 1903-1987
Obituary 123
Kolnai, Aurel (Thomas) 1900-1973 103
Kolodin, Irving 1908-1988 93-96
Obituary 125
Kolodny, Annette 1941- CANR-8
Earlier sketch in CA 61-64
See also DLB 67
Kolodny, Nancy J. 1946- 143
See also SATA 76
Kolodny, Ralph (Leonard) 1923- 116
Kolodziej, Edward Albert 1935- CANR-45
Earlier sketch in CA 97-100
Kolon, Nita
See Onadipe, (Nathaniel) Kola(wole)
Kolonitskii, Boris (Ivanovich) 236
Kolosimo, Peter 1922-1984 .... CANR-7
Earlier sketch in CA 53-56
Kolowrat-Krakowsky, Alexander 1886-1927 .... IDFW 4
Kolp, John Gilman 1943- 233
Kolpan, Steven 204
Kolpas, Norman 216
Kolpen, Jana (Fayne) 1958- 156
Kolsky, Thomas A. 1942- 135
Kolson, Clifford J(ohn) 1920-1984 .... 9-12R
Kolstoe, Oliver P(aul) 1920- 17-20R
Koltes, Bernard-Marie 1948-1989
Obituary 128
See also DLB 321
Kol'tsov, Aleksei Vasil'evich 1809-1842 .... DLB 205
Koltun, Frances Lang 69-72
Koltzow, Liv
See Koltzow, Liv
Kolumban, Nicholas 1937- CANR-116
Earlier sketches in CA 111, CANR-56
Kolve, Carolee Nance 1946- 122
Kolyer, John (McNaughton) 1933- CANR-39
Earlier sketches in CA 69-72, CANR-11
Komai, Akira 1908(?)-1983
Obituary 111
Komaiko, Jean R. 1922(?)-1984
Obituary 114
Komaiko, Leah 1954- 164
See also SATA 97
Koman, Aleta 1954(?)- 234
Komar, Kathleen L(enore) 1949- 128
Komarnicki, Tytus 1896-1967 .... CAP-1
Earlier sketch in CA 9-10
Komarov, Matvei c. 1730-1812 .... DLB 150
Komarovsky, Mirra 1907-1999 .... CAP-1
Obituary 173
Earlier sketch in CA 17-18
Komatsu, Shoei 1931- .... SFW 4
Komatsu Sakyo 1931- 162
Brief entry 113
Kome, Penney 1948- 116
Komenich, Kim 1956- 160
Komer, Robert W(illiam) 1922-2000 108
Obituary 189
Kometani, Foumiko 1930- 135
Komey, Ellis Ayitey 1927- .... CP 1
Komisar, Lucy 1942- 33-36R
See also SATA 9
Komiss, Virginia
See Guttenberg, Virginia
Kommers, Donald P. 1932- 116
Komoda, Beverly 1939- 85-88
See also SATA 25
Komoda, Kiyo 1937- .... SATA 9
Komp, Diane M. 1940- 200
Komroff, Manuel 1890-1974 .... CANR-4
Obituary 53-56
Earlier sketch in CA 1-4R
See also DLB 4
See also SATA 2
See also SATA-Obit 20
Komunyakaa, Yusef 1947- CANR-83
Earlier sketch in CA 147
See also AFAW 2
See also AMWS 13
See also BLCS
See also CLC 86, 94, 207
See also CP 7
See also CSW
See also DLB 120
See also EWL 3
See also PC 51
See also PFS 5, 20
See also RGAL 4
Konadu, Asare
See Konadu, S(amuel) A(sare)
Konadu, S(amuel) A(sare) 1932- CANR-26
Earlier sketch in CA 21-24R
See also BW 2
Konchalovsky, Andrei
See Mikhalkov-Konchalovsky, Andrei (Sergeyevich)
Konczacki, Zbigniew Andrzej 1917- CANR-10
Earlier sketch in CA 21-24R
Kondazian, Karen 1950- 214
Kondoleon, Harry 1955-1994 .... CANR-137
Obituary 144
Earlier sketch in CA 112
See also CAD
See also DLB 266
Kondracke, Morton 1939- CANR-115
Brief entry 119
Earlier sketch in CA 127
Interview in CA-127
Kondrashin, Kiril (Petrovich) 1914-1981
Obituary 108
Kondrashov, Stanislav (Nikolaevich) 1928- CANR-40
Earlier sketch in CA 69-72
Konecky, Edith 1922- 69-72
Konefsky, Samuel J. 1915-1970
Obituary 29-32R
Konek, Carol (Wolfe) 1934- 228
Brief entry 114
Koner, Marvin 1921(?)-1983
Obituary 109
Koner, Pauline 1912-2001 132
Obituary 193

Koneski, Blaze 1921-1993 .... CDWLB 4
  See also CWW 2
  See also DLB 181
Kong, Shiu Loon 1934- 108
Konick, Marcus 1914-1993 .... 37-40R
Konieczny, Vladimir 1946- 237
Konig, David Thomas 1947- 97-100
Konig, Franz
  See Koenig, Franz
Konig, Fritz H(ans)
  See Koenig, Fritz H(ans)
Konig, Rene
  See Koenig, Rene
Konigsberg, Conrad Isidore 1916-1976 . 21-24R
  Obituary 134
Konigsburg, E(laine) L(obl) 1930- CANR-106
  Earlier sketches in CA 21-24R, CANR-17, 39, 59
  Interview in CANR-17
  See also AAYA 3, 41
  See also BYA 1, 2, 3, 9
  See also CLR 1, 47, 81
  See also CWRI 5
  See also DLB 52
  See also JRDA
  See also MAICYA 1, 2
  See also MAICYAS 1
  See also MTCW 1
  See also SATA 4, 48, 94, 126
  See also TUS
  See also YAW
Koning, (Angela) Christina 1954- ... CANR-134
  Earlier sketch in CA 170
Koning, Hans 1924- CANR-102
  Earlier sketch in CANR-48
  See also Koningsberger, Hans
Koningsberger, Hans
  See Koning, Hans
  See also SATA 5
Konkel, Wilbur Stanton 1912-1992 111
Konkle, Janet Everest 1917- 1-4R
  See also SATA 12
Konner, Alfred
  See Koenner, Alfred
Konner, Linda 1951- 102
Konner, Melvin Joel 1946-
  Brief entry 116
Konnyu, Leslie 1914-1992 .... CANR-7
  Earlier sketch in CA 13-16R
Kono, Taeko 1926- 202
  See also MJW
Konopka, Gisela 1910-2003 .... 9-12R
  Obituary 222
Konovalov, Sergey 1899-1982
  Obituary 106
Konparu Zenchiku 1405-1468(?) .... DLB 203
Konrad, Evelyn 1931- CANR-45
  Earlier sketch in CA 33-36R
Konrad, George
  See Konrad, Gyorgy
Konrad, Gyorgy 1933- CANR-97
  Earlier sketch in CA 85-88
  See also CDWLB 4
  See also CLC 4, 10, 73
  See also CWW 2
  See also DLB 232
  See also EWL 3
Konrad, James
  See Maclean, Charles
Konrad, Klaus
  See Whiting, Charles (Henry)
Konrad, Thomas Edmund 1928- 220
Konrad von Wuerzburg c. 1230-1287 .... DLB 138
Konrath, J(oseph) A(ndrew) 1970- 229
Konstan, David 1940- CANR-136
  Earlier sketches in CA 113, CANR-32, 68
Konstantinov, Aleko 1863-1897 .... DLB 147
Kontos, Cecille
  See Haddix-Kontos, Cecille P.
Kontos, Peter G(eorge) 1935-1977 ... CANR-17
  Obituary 115
  Earlier sketch in CA 25-28R
Konvitz, Jeffrey 1944- CANR-75
  Earlier sketches in CA 53-56, CANR-7
  See also HGG
Konvitz, Milton Ridvas 1908-2003 ... CANR-99
  Obituary 221
  Earlier sketches in CA 1-4R, CANR-4
Konwicki, Tadeusz 1926- CANR-59
  Earlier sketches in CA 101, CANR-39
  See also CAAS 9
  See also CLC 8, 28, 54, 117
  See also CWW 2
  See also DLB 232
  See also EWL 3
  See also IDFW 3
  See also MTCW 1
Konyn, Kees
  See Greshoff, Jan
Konz, Helen S. 1922- 145
Konzak, Burt 1946- 226
  See also SATA 151
Koo, Anthony Y(ing) C(hang) 1918- 57-60
Koo, Samuel 1941- 77-80
Koo, V(i) K(yuin) Wellington 1888-1985 . 81-84
  Obituary 117
Koob, C(harles) Albert 1920- 41-44R
Koob, Derry D(elos) 1933- 37-40R
Koob, Joseph E. II 1948- 121
Koob, Theodora (J. Foth) 1918- 5-8R
  See also SATA 23
Kooiker, Leonie
  See Kooyker-Romijn, Johanna Maria
Kooiman, Gladys 1927- 89-92
Kooiman, Helen W.
  See Hosier, Helen Kooiman
Kooistra, Paul G. 1952- 141
Koolhaas, Rem(ment) CANR-106
  Earlier sketch in CA 172
Koolmatrie, Wanda
  See Carmen, Leon
Koon, George William 1942- 116
Koon, Helene Wickham 1924-1996 120
  Obituary 161
Koonce, Ray F. 1913-2002 .... 9-12R
Koons, Carolyn 136
Koons, James
  See Pernu, Dennis
Koonts, Jones Calvin 1924- 49-52
Koontz, Dean R(ay) 1945- CANR-138
  Earlier sketches in CA 108, CANR-19, 36, 52, 95
  See also AAYA 9, 31
  See also BEST 89:3, 90:2
  See also CLC 78, 206
  See also CMW 4
  See also CPW
  See also DA3
  See also DAM NOV, POP
  See also DLB 292
  See also HGG
  See also MTCW 1
  See also MTFW 2005
  See also SATA 92
  See also SFW 4
  See also SUFW 2
  See also YAW
Koontz, Harold 1908-1984 .... 41-44R
  Obituary 112
Koontz, Robin Michal 1954- 138
  See also SATA 70, 136
Koontz, Tomas M. 1967- 231
Koonz, Claudia
  See Koonz, Claudia Ann
Koonz, Claudia Ann 131
  Brief entry 126
  Interview in CA-131
Koop, Katherine C. 1923-1973 .... 17-20R
Koop, Theodore Frederick 1907(?)-1988
  Obituary 126
Kooperman, Evelyn L. 1945- 208
Koopman, LeRoy George 1935- 101
Koopmans, Tjalling (Charles) 1910-1985
  Obituary 115
Koopowitz, Harold 1940- CANR-136
  Earlier sketch in CA 114
Kooser, Ted
  See Kooser, Theodore
  See also DLB 105
  See also PFS 8
Kooser, Theodore 1939- CANR-136
  Earlier sketches in CA 33-36R, CANR-15
  See also Kooser, Ted
  See also CP 7
Kootz, Samuel Melvin 1898-1982
  Obituary 107
Kooyker, Leonie CANR-86
  See also Kooyker-Romijn, Johanna Maria
Kooyker-Romijn, Johanna Maria 1927- CANR-34
  Earlier sketch in CA 107
  See also Kooyker, Leonie
  See also SATA 48
Kooyker-Romyn, Johanna Maria
  See Kooyker-Romijn, Johanna Maria
Kopacsi, Sandor 1922-2001 218
Kopal, Zdenek 1914-1993 93-96
  Obituary 141
Kopelev, Lev (Zinovievich) 1912-1997 123
  Obituary 159
Kopelev, Raissa (Davydovna) Orlova
  See Orlova-Kopelev, Raissa (Davydovna)
Kopelke, Lisa 1963- .... SATA 154
Kopelman, Arie 1937- 113
Kopelnitsky, Raimonda 1977- 151
Kopernik, Mikolaj
  See Copernicus, Nicolaus
Koperwas, Sam 1948- CANR-22
  Earlier sketch in CA 105
Kopf, David 1930- 89-92
Kopf, Gerhard 1948- 196
Kopff, E(dward) Christian 1946- CANR-143
  Earlier sketch in CA 117
Kopinak, Kathryn 166
Kopit, Arthur (Lee) 1937- 81-84
  See also CABS 3
  See also AITN 1
  See also CAD
  See also CD 5, 6
  See also CLC 1, 18, 33
  See also DAM DRAM
  See also DFS 7, 14
  See also DLB 7
  See also MAL 5
  See also MTCW 1
  See also RGAL 4
Kopkind, Andrew D(avid) 1935-1994 ... 29-32R
  Obituary 147
Koplewicz, Harold S. 1953- CANR-143
  Earlier sketch in CA 156
Koplin, H(arry) T(homas) 1923- 33-36R
Koplinka, Charlotte
  See Lukas, Charlotte Koplinka
Koplitz, Eugene D(e Vere) 1928- 37-40R
Koplow, David A. 1951- 225
Kopman, H(enri Marshall) 1918- 89-92
Kopp, Anatole 1915-1990 .... CANR-45
  Earlier sketches in CA 29-32R, CANR-12
Kopp, Harriet Green 41-44R
Kopp, O(swald) W. 1918- 33-36R
Kopp, Richard L. 1934- CANR-13
  Earlier sketch in CA 33-36R
Kopp, Sheldon B(ernard) 1929-1999 ..... 37-40R
  Obituary 177
Kopp, William LaMarr 1930- 65-68
Koppel, Lillian 1926- 108
Koppel, Shelley R(uth) 1951- 108
Koppel, Ted 1940(?)- CANR-99
  Earlier sketch in CA 103
Koppelman, Amy 1969- 224
Koppelman, Kent L. 1948- 196
Kopper, Edward A(nthony), Jr. 1937- CANR-86
  Earlier sketches in CA 69-72, CANR-15, 33
Kopper, Lisa (Esther) 1950- 173
  See also SATA 105
  See also SATA-Brief 51
Kopper, Philip (Dana) 1937- CANR-47
  Earlier sketch in CA 97-100
Kopperman, Paul Edward 1945- 69-72
Koppeschaar, Carl (Egon) 1953- 154
Koppett, Leonard 1923-2003 .... CANR-11
  Obituary 217
  Earlier sketch in CA 25-28R
Koppitz, Elizabeth M(unsterberg) 1919-1983 .... CANR-14
  Obituary 111
  Earlier sketch in CA 13-16R
Koppman, Lionel 1920- CANR-6
  Earlier sketch in CA 9-12R
Kops, Bernard 1926- CANR-84
  Earlier sketch in CA 5-8R
  See also CBD
  See also CLC 4
  See also CN 1, 2, 3, 4, 5, 6, 7
  See also CP 1, 2, 3, 4, 5, 6, 7
  See also DLB 13
Kopulos, Stella 1906-1992 49-52
Kopycinski, Joseph V(alentine) 1923- 33-36R
Korach, Mimi 1922- .... SATA 9
Koralek, Jenny 1934- 196
  See also SATA 71, 140
Koran, Dennis 1947- 120
Korb, Lawrence J(oseph) 1939- 77-80
Korbel, John 1918- 9-12R
Korbel, Josef 1909-1977 .... 37-40R
  Obituary 73-76
Korbel, Kathleen
  See Dreyer, Eileen
Korbonski, Andrzej 1927- 9-12R
Korbonski, Stefan 1903-1989 .... CANR-5
  Obituary 128
  Earlier sketch in CA 5-8R
Korchilov, Igor 1941- 159
Korczak, Janusz
  See Goldszmit, Henryk
  See also SATA 65
Korda, Alexander 1893-1956 .... IDFW 3, 4
Korda, Michael (Vincent) 1933- CANR-85
  Earlier sketches in CA 107, CANR-39
  See also BEST 89:3
  See also CPW
Korda, Vincent 1897-1979 .... IDFW 3, 4
Kordel, Lelord 1904- 106
Korder, Howard 1958(?)- CANR-139
  Earlier sketch in CA 153
Korelitz, Jean Hanff 1961- 132
Koren, Edward (Benjamin) 1935- CANR-11
  Earlier sketch in CA 25-28R
  See also SATA 5, 148
Koren, Henry J(oseph) 1912-2002 ...... CANR-35
  Earlier sketch in CA 9-12R
Koren, Yehuda 232
Korenbaum, Myrtle 1915- 57-60
Korenblit, Joan B(ravo) 1952- 113
Korey, William 1922- 184
  Brief entry 112
Korfker, Dena 1908-1997 .... CANR-17
  Earlier sketch in CA 1-4R
Korg, Jacob 1922- CANR-2
  Earlier sketch in CA 5-8R
Korges, James 1930-1975 .... CAP-2
  Earlier sketch in CA 25-28
Korine, Harmony 173
Korinets, Iurii Iosifovich
  See Korinetz, Yuri (Iosifovich)
Korinetz, Yuri (Iosifovich) 1923- CANR-11
  Earlier sketch in CA 61-64
  See also CLR 4
  See also SATA 9
Koriyama, Naoshi 1926- .... CP 1
Korman, A. Gerd 1928- CANR-35
  Earlier sketch in CA 53-56
Korman, Bernice 1937- CANR-93
  Earlier sketch in CA 146
  See also SATA 78
Korman, Gordon (Richard) 1963- CANR-90
  Earlier sketches in CA 112, CANR-34, 56
  See also AAYA 10, 44
  See also CCA 1
  See also CLR 25
  See also CWRI 5
  See also JRDA
  See also MAICYA 1, 2
  See also SATA 49, 81, 119
  See also SATA-Brief 41
  See also WYA
Korman, Justine 1958- 138
  See also SATA 70
Korman, Keith 1956- 102
Kormendi, Ferenc 1900-1972
  Obituary 37-40R
Kormondy, Edward J(ohn) 1926- CANR-13
  Earlier sketch in CA 33-36R
Korn, Alfons L(udwig) 1906-1986 ..... CANR-34
  Obituary 119
  Earlier sketch in CA 93-96
Korn, Bertram Wallace 1918-1979 ..... CANR-1
  Earlier sketch in CA 1-4R
Korn, David A(dolph) 1930- 139
Korn, Frank J(ames) 1935- 115
Korn, Henry (James) 1945- CANR-47
  Earlier sketch in CA 69-72
Korn, Noel 1923-2000 73-76
  Obituary 188
Korn, Peggy
  See Liss, Peggy K(orn)
Korn, Peter 182
Korn, Walter 1908-1997 73-76
Kornai, J(anos) 1928- CANR-82
  Earlier sketches in CA 13-16R, CANR-35, 56
Kornblatt, Joyce Reiser 1944- CANR-27
  Earlier sketch in CA 106
Kornblatt, Judith Deutsch 1955- 141
Kornblatt, Marc 1954- CANR-128
  Earlier sketches in CA 150, CANR-100
  See also SATA 84, 147
Kornblith, Hilary (Stuart) 1954- CANR-141
  Earlier sketch in CA 144
Kornbluh, Marvin 1927-1987
  Obituary 124
Kornbluh, Peter 171
Kornblum, Allan 1949- CANR-54
  Earlier sketch in CA 69-72
Kornblum, Cinda 1950- 69-72
Kornblum, Sylvan 1927- 41-44R
Kornblum, William 219
Kornbluth, C(yril) M. 1923-1958 160
  Brief entry 105
  See also DLB 8
  See also SCFW 1, 2
  See also SFW 4
  See also TCLC 8
Kornbluth, Jesse 1946- CANR-128
  Earlier sketches in CA 25-28R, CANR-17
Korneichuk, Aleksandr Y. 1905-1972
  Obituary 33-36R
Korner, Stephan
  See Koerner, Stephan
Kornfeld, Anita Clay 1928- 97-100
Kornfeld, Paul 1889-1942 .... DLB 118
Kornfeld, Robert J(onathan) 1919- 104
Kornfield, Jack 1945- 199
Korngold, Erich Wolfgang 1897-1957 . IDFW 3, 4
Kornhauser, David H(enry) 1918-1993 .... CANR-14
  Earlier sketch in CA 41-44R
Kornhauser, Jincy
  See Willett, Jincy
Kornhauser, William 1925- 1-4R
Kornheiser, Anthony (I.) 1948- CANR-123 1
  Earlier sketch in CA 138
Kornheiser, Tony
  See Kornheiser, Anthony (I.)
Kornrich, Milton 1933- 17-20R
Kornwolf, James D. 217
Korobkin, Laura Hanft 204
Korol, Alexander G. 1900-1967 .... 5-8R
Korolenko, V. G.
  See Korolenko, Vladimir Galaktionovich
Korolenko, Vladimir
  See Korolenko, Vladimir Galaktionovich
Korolenko, Vladimir G.
  See Korolenko, Vladimir Galaktionovich
Korolenko, Vladimir Galaktionovich 1853-1921
  Brief entry 121
  See also DLB 277
  See also TCLC 22
Korotkin, Judith 1931- 53-56
Korr, Charles
  See Korr, Charles P(aul)
Korr, Charles P(aul) 1939- CANR-141
  Earlier sketch in CA 112
Kors, Alan Charles 1943- CANR-135
  Earlier sketch in CA 77-80
Korschunow, Irina .... BYA 7
Kort, Carol 1945- CANR-137
  Earlier sketch in CA 106
Kort, Wesley A(lbert) 1935- CANR-86
  Earlier sketches in CA 37-40R, CANR-34
Korte, Gene J. 1950- .... SATA 74
Korte, Mary Norbert
  See Koerte, Mary Norbert
  See also CP 2
Korten, David C(raig) 1937- CANR-34
  Earlier sketches in CA 41-44R, CANR-15
Kortepeter, C(arl) Max 1928- CANR-26
  Earlier sketch in CA 41-44R
Korth, Francis N(icholas) 1912-1995 ..... 25-28R
Korth, Philip A. 1936- 137
Kortner, Peter 1924-1991 .... 33-36R
  Obituary 133
Korty, Carol 1937- 77-80
  See also SATA 15
Korty, John Van Cleave 1936- 106
Kory, Robert B(ruce) 1950- 65-68
Korzenik, Diana 1941- CANR-82
  Earlier sketch in CA 133
Korzenny, Felipe 1947- 116
Korzybski, Alfred (Habdank Skarbek) 1879-1950 160
  Brief entry 123
  See also TCLC 61
Kos, Erih 1913-
  Brief entry 106
Kosa, John 1914-1972 .... CANR-34
  Earlier sketch in CA 5-8R
Kosch, Erich
  See Kos, Erih
Koschade, Alfred 1928- 21-24R
Koscielniak, Bruce 1947- 134
  See also SATA 67, 99, 153
Kosel, Janice E. 1940- 116
Koshetz, Herbert 1907(?)-1977
  Obituary 73-76

Koshi, George M. 1911- CAP-2
Earlier sketch in CA 29-32
Koshin, Alexander (A.) 1952- ..... SATA 86
Koshiro, Yukiko 211
Koshland, Ellen 1947- CANR-13
Earlier sketch in CA 33-36R
Kosinski, Dorothy M. 1953- 145
Kosinski, Jerzy (Nikodem)
1933-1991 ..... CANR-46
Obituary 134
Earlier sketches in CA 17-20R, CANR-9
See also AMWS 7
See also BPFB 2
See also CLC 1, 2, 3, 6, 10, 15, 53, 70
See also CN 1, 2, 3, 4
See also DA3
See also DAM NOV
See also DLB 2, 299
See also DLBY 1982
See also EWL 3
See also HGG
See also MAL 5
See also MTCW 1, 2
See also MTFW 2005
See also NFS 12
See also RGAL 4
See also TUS
Kosinski, Leonard V. 1923-1997 ..... 25-28R
Kositsky, Lynne 1947- 234
See also SATA 158
Koskenmaki, Rosalie
See Maggio, Rosalie
Koski, Mary B(ernadette) 1951- 167
Koskoff, David E(lihu) 1939- 49-52
Koslow, Connie H. 224
Koslow, Jules 1916- CANR-6
Earlier sketch in CA 1-4R
Kosma, Joseph 1905-1969 ..... IDFW 3, 4
Kosmac, Ciril 1910-1980 200
See also DLB 181
Kosmala, Hans 1904(?)-1981
Obituary 104
Kosof, Anna 1945- CANR-35
Earlier sketch in CA 85-88
Kosovel, Srecko 1904-1926 230
See also DLB 147
Koss, Amy Goldman 1954- CANR-143
Earlier sketch in CA 186
See also AAYA 45
See also SATA 115, 158
Koss, Joan
See Koss-Chioino, Joan D.
Koss, Stephen E(dward) 1940-1984 .. CANR-48
Obituary 114
Earlier sketch in CA 25-28R
Kossak, Zofia 1890-1968 ..... EWL 3
Koss-Chioino, Joan D. 1935- CANR-144
Earlier sketch in CA 144
Kosser, Mike 1941- 145
Kossez, Robes 1935- CANR-12
Earlier sketch in CA 29-32R
Kossin, Sandy (Sanford) 1926- ..... SATA 10
Kosslyn, Stephen Michael 1948- CANR-40
Earlier sketch in CA 117
Kossman, Nina 1959- CANR-112
Earlier sketch in CA 150
See also SATA 84
Kossmann, Rudolf R(ichard) 1934- 37-40R
Kossoff, David 1919-2005 ..... CANR-35
Obituary 237
Earlier sketch in CA 61-64
Kossy, Donna J. 1957- 219
Kost, Bruce 1950- 170
Kost, Mary Lu 1924- 45-48
Kost, Robert John 1913- 1-4R
Kostash, Myrna 1944- 65-68
Koste, Robert Francis 1933- 81-84
Koste, V. Glasgow
See Koste, Virginia Glasgow
Koste, Virginia Glasgow 1924- 229
Kostelanetz, Andre 1901-1980 165
Obituary 107
Kostelanetz, Richard (Cory) 1940- CANR-77
Earlier sketches in CA 13-16R, CANR-38
See also CAAS 8
See also CLC 28
See also CN 4, 5, 6
See also CP 2, 3, 4, 5, 6, 7
Kostelniuk, James 1946- 227
Kosten, Andrew 1921- 1-4R
Kostenko, Lina 1930- ..... EWL 3
Koster, Donald N(elson) 1910-2000 53-56
Koster, John (Peter, Jr.) 1945- CANR-5
Earlier sketch in CA 53-56
Koster, R(ichard) M(orton) 1934- CANR-116
Earlier sketch in CA 37-40R
Kosters, Marvin H(oward) 1933- 143
Kostich, Dragos D. 1921- CANR-10
Earlier sketch in CA 5-8R
Kostis, Nicholas 103
Kostiuk, Hryhory 1902- 77-80
Kostka, Edmund Karl 1915- 17-20R
Kostoff, Lynn 1954(?)- 227
Kostov, K. N.
See Whiting, Charles (Henry)
Kostov, L.
See Whiting, Charles (Henry)
Kostrov, Ermil Ivanovich 1755-1796 ... DLB 150
Kostrowitzki, Wilhelm Apollinaris de
1880-1918
Brief entry 104
See also Apollinaire, Guillaume
Kostrubala, Thaddeus 1930- 101
Kostyu, Frank A(lexander) 1919- CANR-1
Earlier sketch in CA 49-52
Kosygin, Alexei Nikolayevich 1904-1980
Obituary 102
Kosztolanyi, Dezso 1885-1936 ..... EW 10
See also EWL 3
Kot, Greg 238
Kot, Stanislaw 1886(?)-1976
Obituary 65-68
Kotarba, Joseph A(nthony) 1947- 111
Kotarbinski, Tadeusz (Marian) 1886-1981
Obituary 105
Kotcheff, Ted
See Kotcheff, William Theodore
Kotcheff, William Theodore 1931- 115
Kothari, Rajni 1928- CANR-35
Earlier sketch in CA 33-36R
Kotin, Armine Avakian
See Mortimer, Armine Kotin
Kotker, Norman (Richard)
1931-1999 ..... CANR-35
Obituary 177
Earlier sketches in CA 25-28R, CANR-10
Kotker, Zane 1934- CANR-109
Earlier sketches in CA 49-52, CANR-3
Kotler, Milton 1935- CANR-25
Earlier sketch in CA 29-32R
Kotler, Neil G. 1941- CANR-91
Earlier sketch in CA 146
Kotler, Philip 1931- CANR-13
Earlier sketch in CA 33-36R
Kotler, Steven 1967- 181
Kotlowitz, Alex 1955(?)- 138
See also MTFW 2005
Kotlowitz, Robert 1924- CANR-36
Earlier sketch in CA 33-36R
See also CLC 4
Kotowska, Monika 1942- 93-96
Kotowski, Joanne 1930- 57-60
Kotre, John N(icholas) 1940- 81-84
Kotrozo, Carol Donnell
See Donnell-Kotrozo, Carol
Kotschevar, Lendal H(enry) 1908- CANR-10
Earlier sketch in CA 17-20R
Kotschnig, Walter M(aria) 1901-1985
Obituary 117
Kotsilibas-Davis, James 1940- 106
Kotsuji, Abraham S(etsuzau)
1899-1973 ..... CAP-1
Obituary 45-48
Earlier sketch in CA 13-16
Kotsyubynsky, Mykhaylo 1864-1913 ..... EWL 3
Kott, Jan 1914-2001 ..... 13-16R
Obituary 203
Kotter, John P(aul) 1947- 216
Kottler, Dorothy 1918- 97-100
Kottler, Jeffrey (A.) 1951- 136
Kottman, Richard N(orman) 1932- 25-28R
Kotto, Yaphet (Fredrick) 1944(?)- 166
Kotz, Cappy 1955- ..... GLL 2
Kotz, David M(ichael) 1943- 81-84
Kotz, Mary Lynn 1936- 104
Kotz, Nick 1932- CANR-32
Earlier sketch in CA 29-32R
Kotz, Samuel 1930- CANR-82
Earlier sketches in CA 13-16R, CANR-7, 34
Kotzebue, August (Friedrich Ferdinand) von
1761-1819 ..... DLB 94
Kotzin, Michael C(harles) 1941- 37-40R
Kotzwinkle, William 1938- CANR-129
Earlier sketches in CA 45-48, CANR-3, 44, 84
See also BPFB 2
See also CLC 5, 14, 35
See also CLR 6
See also CN 7
See also DLB 173
See also FANT
See also MAICYA 1, 2
See also SATA 24, 70, 146
See also SFW 4
See also SUFW 2
See also YAW
Koubourlis, Demetrius J(ohn) 1938- 57-60
Kouf, Jim
See Kouf, M(arvin) James, Jr.
Kouf, M(arvin) James, Jr. 1951- 141
Koufax, Sandy
See Koufax, Sanford
Koufax, Sanford 1935- 89-92
Kouhi, Elizabeth 1917- 126
See also SATA 54
See also SATA-Brief 49
Kouka, Hone 1968- 230
See also CD 5, 6
Koulack, David 1938- 102
Koumoulides, John (Thomas Anastassios)
1938- CANR-34
Earlier sketch in CA 41-44R
Koupal, Nancy Tystad 1947- CANR-116
Earlier sketch in CA 158
Koupernik, Cyrille 1917- CANR-35
Earlier sketch in CA 57-60
Kourdakov, Sergei 1951-1973
Obituary 115
Kourilsky, Francoise 1933- 148
Kourouma, Ahmadou 1927-2003 ... CANR-128
Obituary 224
Earlier sketch in CA 143
See also BW 2
See also EWL 3
See also RGWL 3
Kourvetaris, George A.
See Kourvetaris, Yorgos A.
Kourvetaris, Yorgos A. 1933- 127
Kousoulas, D(imitrios) George 1923- 17-20R
Kousser, J(oseph) Morgan 1943- CANR-32
Earlier sketch in CA 57-60
Koutoukas, H. M. 1947- CANR-83
Earlier sketches in CA 69-72, CANR-47
See also CAD
See also CD 5, 6
Kouts, Anne 1945- 29-32R
See also SATA 8
Kouts, Hertha Pretorius 1922-1973 ..... 1-4R
Obituary 103
Koutsky, Jan Dale 1955- ..... SATA 146
Kouwenhoven, John A(tlee) 1909-1990 ..... 1-4R
Obituary 132
Kouyate, Djeli Mamoudou ..... EFS 1
Kouyoumdjian, Dikran
See Arlen, Michael
Kovach, Barbara (Ellen) L(usk) 1941-2003 .. 107
Obituary 219
Kovach, Barbara L(usk) Forisha
See Kovach, Barbara (Ellen) L(usk)
Kovach, Bill 1932- CANR-11
Earlier sketch in CA 69-72
Kovach, Francis J(oseph) 1918- CANR-35
Earlier sketch in CA 61-64
Kovach, Gay H(aff) 1956- 149
Kovach, Kenneth A. 1946- CANR-142
Earlier sketch in CA 144
Kovach, Thomas A(llen) 1949- 129
Kovacic, Ante 1854-1889 ..... DLB 147
Kovacs, Alexander 1930(?)-1977
Obituary 73-76
Kovacs, Deborah 1954- 148
See also SATA 79, 132
Kovacs, Diane K. 1962- 223
Kovacs, Imre 1913-1980 ..... CANR-34
Obituary 102
Earlier sketch in CA 21-24R
Kovacs, Laszlo 1933- ..... IDFW 3, 4
Kovacs, Steven 1946- 130
Kovaleff, Theodore Philip 1943- 116
Kovalev, Mikhail A(leksandrovich) 1893-1981
Obituary 108
Kovalevskaia, Sof'ia Vasil'evna
1850-1891 ..... DLB 277
Kovalic, John 1962- 220
Kovalik, Nada 1926- 25-28R
Kovalik, Vladimir 1928- 25-28R
Kovalski, Maryann 1951- 163
See also CLR 34
See also SAAS 21
See also SATA 58, 97
Kovarik, Bill
See Kovarik, William
Kovarik, William 1951- 113
Kovarsky, Irving 1918-1982 ..... 29-32R
Kovel, Joel S. 1936- CANR-137
Earlier sketches in CA 29-32R, CANR-14, 32, 66
Kovel, Ralph CANR-48
Earlier sketches in CA 17-20R, CANR-8, 23
Kovel, Terry 1928- CANR-48
Earlier sketches in CA 17-20R, CANR-8, 23
Koves, Andras 1938- 145
Kovic, Kajetan 1931- ..... DLB 181
Kovic, Ron 1946- CANR-135
Earlier sketch in CA 138
Kovner, Aba
See Kovner, Abba
Kovner, Abba 1918-1987 ..... CANR-111
Obituary 123
Kovner, B.
See Adler, Jacob (P.)
Kovrig, Bennett 1940- CANR-12
Earlier sketch in CA 29-32R
Kowaleski, Maryanne 1952- 150
Kowalewski, David 1943- 112
Kowalewski, Michael (John) 1956- 140
Kowalke, Kim H. 1948- 132
Kowalski, Frank 1907-1974 ..... 37-40R
Kowalski, Gary A. 173
Kowalski, Kathiann M. 1955- CANR-121
Earlier sketch in CA 161
See also SATA 96, 151
Kowalski, William J. 1970- 222
Kowet, Don 1937- CANR-35
Earlier sketches in CA 57-60, CANR-10
Kowit, Steve 1938- 118
Kowitt, Sylvia
See Crosbie, Sylvia Kowitt
Kowitz, Gerald T(homas) 1928-1994 ..... 33-36R
Kowna, Stancy
See Szymborska, Wislawa
Kownslar, Allan O(wen) 1935- CANR-35
Earlier sketch in CA 61-64
Koya, Tatsuhito 1964- 144
Koyama, Kosuke 1929- CANR-35
Earlier sketches in CA 57-60, CANR-7
Koykka, Arthur S(idney) 1937- 116
Koyo, Ozaki
See Ozaki, Tokutaro
Koyre, Alexandre 1892-1964
Obituary 111
Kozak, Harley Jane
See Kozak, Susan Jane
Kozak, Jan B(lahoslav) 1889(?)-1974
Obituary 45-48
Kozak, Roman 1948(?)-1988
Obituary 126
Kozak, Susan Jane 1957- 230
Kozak, Warren 1951- 237
Kozar, Andrew Joseph 1930- 103
Kozelka, Paul 1909- CAP-2
Earlier sketch in CA 25-28
Kozer, Jose 1940- CANR-82
Earlier sketches in CA 49-52, CANR-2, 34
See also CAAS 29
Kozicki, Henry 1924- 103
Kozicki, Richard J(oseph) 1929- 125
Brief entry 118
Koziebrodzki, Leopold B(olesta)
1906-1999 ..... 41-44R
Kozintsev, Grigori (Mikhailovich)
1905-1973 53-56
Kozlenko, William 1917- 57-60
Kozloff, Max 1933- CANR-136
Brief entry 114
Earlier sketch in CA 127
Kozloski, Lillian D. 1934- 150
Kozlov, Ivan Ivanovich 1779-1840 ..... DLB 205
Kozlow, Mark J.
See Newton, Michael
Kozlowski, Theodore T(homas)
1917- CANR-124
Earlier sketches in CA 9-12R, CANR-4, 19
Kozol, Jonathan 1936- CANR-96
Earlier sketches in CA 61-64, CANR-16, 45
See also AAYA 46
See also CLC 17
See also MTFW 2005
Kozoll, Michael 1940(?)- ..... CLC 35
Kozulin, Alex 1949- 122
Kpomassie, Tete-Michel 1941- 123
Kra, Siegfried J. 1930- CANR-128
Earlier sketches in CA 129, CANR-67
Kraay, Colin M(ackennal) 1918-1982
Obituary 116
Kracauer, Siegfried 1889-1966 ..... DLB 296
Kracmar, John Z. 1916- 37-40R
Krader, Lawrence 1919-1998 ..... 21-24R
Kraditor, Aileen S. 1928- CANR-35
Earlier sketch in CA 13-16R
Kraehe, Enno E(dward) 1921- CANR-82
Earlier sketches in CA 9-12R, CANR-35
Kraemer, Kenneth L(eo) 1936- CANR-35
Earlier sketch in CA 111
Kraemer, Richard H(oward) 1920- CANR-82
Earlier sketches in CA 53-56, CANR-4, 35
Kraenzel, Carl F(rederick) 1906-1980 73-76
Kraenzel, Margaret (Powell) 1899-1988 ..... 1-4R
Kraeuter, David W. 1941- 143
Kraf, Elaine 1946- CANR-11
Earlier sketch in CA 65-68
See also DLBY 1981
Krafft, C(onrad) James 1923- 119
Krafft, Jim
See Krafft, C(onrad) James
Krafft, Maurice 1946-1991 ..... CANR-10
Obituary 134
Earlier sketch in CA 65-68
Krafsur, Richard Paul 1940- 103
Kraft, Barbara 1939- 97-100
Kraft, Betsy Harvey 1937- CANR-141
Earlier sketch in CA 89-92
See also SATA 157
Kraft, Charles H(oward) 1932- CANR-16
Earlier sketches in CA 45-48, CANR-1
Kraft, Charlotte 1922-1985 103
Kraft, Chris(topher Columbus, Jr.) 204
Kraft, Dean 1950- 114
Kraft, Eric (Lance) 1944- CANR-123
Earlier sketch in CA 108
Kraft, Hy(man Solomon) 1899-1975 . CANR-36
Obituary 57-60
Earlier sketch in CA 41-44R
Kraft, Joseph 1924-1986 ..... CANR-34
Obituary 118
Earlier sketch in CA 9-12R
Kraft, Ken(neth) 1907- CANR-1
Earlier sketch in CA 1-4R
Kraft, Kenneth 1949- 207
Kraft, Kenneth H. Sr. 1896-1983
Obituary 111
Kraft, Leo 1922- 41-44R
Kraft, Leonard E(dward) 1923- 29-32R
Kraft, Robert Alan 1934- 37-40R
Kraft, Stephanie (Barlett) 1944- 105
Kraft, Virginia 1932- 21-24R
Kraft, Walter Andreas
See Friedlander, Walter A(ndreas)
Kraft, William F. 1938- 33-36R
Kragen, Jinx
See Morgan, Judith A(dams)
Kragh, Helge S(terjnholm) 1944- 194
Krahn, Betina 199
Krahn, Fernando 1935- CANR-11
Earlier sketch in CA 65-68
See also CLR 3
See also SATA 49
See also SATA-Brief 31
Kraig, Bruce 1939- CANR-18
Earlier sketch in CA 102
Krailsheimer, Alban John 1921-2001 .. CANR-2
Obituary 196
Earlier sketch in CA 5-8R
Kraines, Oscar 1916- 97-100
Kraines, Samuel H(enry) 1906-1989 77-80
Kraizer, Sherryll Kerns 1948- 164
Krajenke, Robert William 1939- 29-32R
Krajewski, Frank R. 1938- CANR-10
Earlier sketch in CA 65-68
Krajewski, Robert J(oseph) 1940- 97-100
Krakauer, Hoong Yee Lee 1955- ..... SATA 86
Krakauer, Jon 1954- CANR-131
Earlier sketch in CA 153
See also AAYA 24
See also BYA 9
See also MTFW 2005
See also SATA 108
Krakel, Dean (Fenton) 1923-1998 ..... CANR-47
Earlier sketch in CA 45-48
Krakowski, Lili 1930- 85-88
Krall, Hanna 1937-
Kralovec, Etta 224
Kraly, Hanns 1885-1950 ..... IDFW 3, 4
Kram, Mark 1932-2002 233
Kramarae, Cheris 1938- 221
Kramarz, Joachim 1931- 25-28R
Kramer, A(lfred) T(heodore) 1892- CAP-1
Earlier sketch in CA 11-12

Cumulative Index 327 **Kreskin**

Kramer, Aaron 1921-1997 .... CANR-12
Obituary 157
Earlier sketch in CA 21-24R
Kramer, Anthony .... SATA-Brief 42
Kramer, Bernard M(ordecai) 1923- 77-80
Kramer, Charles 1915-1988
Obituary 125
Kramer, Dale 1936- CANR-5
Earlier sketch in CA 53-56
Kramer, Daniel C(aleb) 1934- 53-56
Kramer, Douglas 1950- 138
Kramer, Edith 1916- 33-36R
Kramer, Edna E.
See Kramer-Lassar, Edna Ernestine
Kramer, Edward (E.) 1961- 146
Kramer, Eugene F(rancis) 1921-1992 ..... 37-40R
Kramer, Frank Raymond 1908-2001 ...... CAP-1
Earlier sketch in CA 11-12
Kramer, Fritz W. 1941- 147
Kramer, Gene 1927- 69-72
Kramer, George
See Heuman, William
Kramer, Helen 1946- 146
Kramer, Hilton 1928- CANR-102
Brief entry 109
Earlier sketch in CA 113
Kramer, Jack N. 1923-1983 .... CANR-47
Earlier sketch in CA 41-44R
Kramer, Jacqueline 1951- 236
Kramer, Jane 1938- CANR-140
Earlier sketches in CA 102, CANR-68
Interview in CA-102
See also DLB 185
Kramer, Joel (Herbert) 1937- 97-100
Kramer, Joel P. 1976(?)- 235
Kramer, John Eichholtz, Jr. 1935- 108
Kramer, Jonathan D. 1942-2004 130
Obituary 228
Kramer, Jonathan M. 1946- 121
Kramer, Judith Rita 1933-1970 .... 1-4R
Obituary 103
Kramer, Kathryn 19(?)- .... CLC 34
Kramer, Larry 1935- CANR-132
Brief entry 124
Earlier sketches in CA 126, CANR-60
See also CLC 42
See also DAM POP
See also DC 8
See also DLB 249
See also GLL 1
Kramer, Lawrence (Eliot) 1946- CANR-94
Earlier sketches in CA 120, CANR-45
Kramer, Leonie Judith 1924- CANR-39
Earlier sketches in CA 81-84, CANR-17
Kramer, Linda Konheim 1939- CANR-94
Earlier sketch in CA 146
Kramer, Lloyd S. 1949- CANR-128
Earlier sketch in CA 165
Kramer, Lotte (Karoline) 1923- CANR-84
Earlier sketch in CA 153
See also CP 7
See also CWP
Kramer, Mark (William) 1944- CANR-68
Earlier sketches in CA 97-100, CANR-17
See also DLB 185
Kramer, Martin 1954- CANR-114
Earlier sketch in CA 160
Kramer, Milton D. 1915-1973
Obituary 37-40R
Kramer, Nancy 1942- 101
Kramer, Nora 1896(?)-1984 107
Obituary 113
See also SATA 26
See also SATA-Obit 39
Kramer, (Simon) Paul 1914- 21-24R
Kramer, Paul J(ackson) 1904-1995 ...... CANR-1
Obituary 149
Earlier sketch in CA 45-48
Kramer, Peter (D.) 1948- CANR-109
Earlier sketch in CA 145
Kramer, Remi (Thomas) 1935- .... SATA 90
Kramer, Rita 1929- CANR-57
Earlier sketches in CA 69-72, CANR-31
Kramer, Roberta 1935- 103
Kramer, Roland Laird 1898-1976 .... 5-8R
Kramer, Samuel Noah 1897-1990 .... 9-12R
Obituary 133
Kramer, Ted
See Steward, Samuel M(orris)
See also GLL 1
Kramer, Theodor 1897-1958 .... EWL 3
Kramer, Victor A. 1939- CANR-16
Earlier sketch in CA 85-88
Kramer-Lassar, Edna Ernestine 1902-1984 .. 107
Obituary 113
Kramish, Arnold 1923- CANR-7
Earlier sketch in CA 5-8R
Kramm, Joseph 1907-1991 210
See also DFS 15
Krammer, Arnold Paul 1941- CANR-27
Earlier sketches in CA 61-64, CANR-11
Kramnick, Isaac 1938- 139
Kramon, Florence 1920- 25-28R
Kramrisch, Stella 1896(?)-1993 .... CAP-2
Obituary 142
Earlier sketch in CA 21-22
Krancher, Jan A. 1939- 237
Kranendonk, Anke 1959- 231
Kranidas, Kathleen
See Collins, Kathleen
Kranish, Michael 232
Kranjcevic, Silvije Strahimir
1865-1908 .... DLB 147
Krannich, Caryl Rae 1943- 191
Krannich, Ronald Louis 191
Krantz, Grover S. 1931-2002 146
Obituary 201
Krantz, Hazel (Newman) CANR-40
Earlier sketches in CA 1-4R, CANR-1, 16
See also SATA 12
Krantz, Judith 1927- CANR-110
Earlier sketches in CA 81-84, CANR-11, 33, 66
See also BEST 89:1
See also BPFB 2
See also CPW
See also DA3
See also DAM NOV, POP
See also MTCW 1
Krantz, Les(lie Jay) 1945- 120
Krantz, Steven G. 1951- CANR-122
Earlier sketch in CA 165
Kranz, E(dwin) Kirker 1949- 33-36R
Kranz, Stewart D(uane) 1924- 101
Kranzberg, Melvin 1917-1995 .... CANR-11
Obituary 150
Earlier sketch in CA 21-24R
Kranzler, David 1930- 93-96
Kranzler, George G(ershon) 1916- CANR-12
Earlier sketch in CA 57-60
See also SATA 28
Kranzler, Gershon
See Kranzler, George G(ershon)
Krapf, Norbert 1943- 117
Krapp, R. M.
See Adams, Robert Martin
Krar, Stephen Frank 1924- CANR-42
Earlier sketches in CA 53-56, CANR-4, 20
Kraselchik, R.
See Dyer, Charles (Raymond)
Krashen, Stephen D. 1941- 132
Krasilovsky, Alexis 1950- 214
Krasilovsky, M(arvin) William 1926- 61-64
Krasilovsky, Phyllis 1926- CANR-85
Earlier sketches in CA 29-32R, CANR-11, 45
See also CLR 83
See also CWRI 5
See also MAICYA 1, 2
See also SAAS 5
See also SATA 1, 38
Krasinski, Zygmunt 1812-1859 .... RGWL 2, 3
Kraske, Robert 226
Brief entry 116
See also SATA-Brief 36
Krasker, Robert 1913-1981 .... IDFW 3, 4
Krasko, Ivan 1876-1958 .... DLB 215
See also EWL 3
Kraslow, David 1926- 29-32R
Krasna, Norman 1909-1984 164
Obituary 114
See also DLB 26
See also IDFW 3, 4
Krasne, Betty
See Levine, Betty K(rasne)
Krasner, Jack Daniel 1921-1978 .... CANR-3
Earlier sketch in CA 49-52
Krasner, Leonard 1924- 33-36R
Krasner, Milton 1901-1988 .... IDFW 3, 4
Krasner, Stephen D(avid) 1942- CANR-15
Earlier sketch in CA 85-88
Krasner, Steven 1953- 229
See also SATA 154
Krasner, William 1917- CANR-86
Earlier sketches in CA 37-40R, CANR-15, 35
Krasney, Samuel A. 1922- 1-4R
Krasno, Rena 1923- CANR-132
Earlier sketch in CA 171
See also SATA 104
Krasnov, Vladislav Georgievich 1937- 132
Krasnow, Erwin G(ilbert) 1936- 103
Krasnow, Iris 1954(?)- 163
Krasovskaya, Vera (Mikhailovna)
1915-1999 130
Obituary 183
Brief entry 106
Krass, Alfred C(harles) 1936- 116
Krasser, Wilhelm 1925(?)-1979
Obituary 89-92
Krassner, Paul 1932- CANR-11
Earlier sketch in CA 21-24R
Krasso, Miklos 1929(?)-1986
Obituary 118
Krasznahorkai, Laszlo 1954- 197
Kratcoski, Peter C(harles) 1936- 111
Kratochvil, Paul 1932- 25-28R
Kratos
See Power, Norman S(andiford)
Kratovil, Robert 1910-1989 .... CANR-5
Earlier sketch in CA 5-8R
Kratz, Martin P. J. 1955- 143
Kratzenstein, Jossef J. 1904-1990 .... CAP-2
Earlier sketch in CA 17-18
Krauch, Velma 1916- 37-40R
Kraues, Judith E. 101
Kraus, Albert L(awson) 1920-1996 .... 41-44R
Obituary 151
Kraus, Barbara 1929-1977 102
Kraus, Bruce R. 1954- 97-100
Kraus, C(lyde) Norman 1924- CANR-86
Earlier sketches in CA 41-44R, CANR-15, 33
Kraus, Caroline (M. H.) 231
Kraus, Charles E. 1946- 111
Kraus, Constantine Raymond 1900-1990 129
Kraus, George 1930- 25-28R
Kraus, H. P.
See Kraus, Hans P(eter)
Kraus, Hans P(eter) 1907-1988 .... CAP-2
Obituary 127
Earlier sketch in CA 29-32
See also DLB 187
Kraus, Joanna Halpert 1937- CANR-85
Earlier sketches in CA 104, CANR-21, 44
See also CWRI 5
See also SATA 87
Kraus, Joe 1939- CANR-15
Earlier sketch in CA 89-92
Kraus, Joseph 1925- CANR-4
Earlier sketch in CA 53-56
Kraus, Karl 1874-1936 216
Brief entry 104
See also DLB 118
See also EWL 3
See also TCLC 5
Kraus, Krandall 1944- 188
Kraus, Michael 1901-1990 .... 5-8R
Obituary 132
Kraus, Nicola 1974(?)- 212
Kraus, Richard G(ordon) 1923-2002 . CANR-11
Obituary 207
Earlier sketch in CA 13-16R
Kraus, (Herman) Robert 1925-2001 .. CANR-54
Obituary 199
Earlier sketch in CA 33-36R
See also CWRI 5
See also MAICYA 1, 2
See also SAAS 11
See also SATA 4, 65, 93
See also SATA-Obit 130
Kraus, Sidney 1927- CANR-10
Earlier sketch in CA 5-8R
Kraus, W. Keith 1934- 21-24R
Krause, Bernie 1938- 186
Krause, Chester L. 1923- 199
Krause, David 1917- 168
Krause, Frank H(arold) 1942- 104
Krause, Harry D(ieter) 1932- 33-36R
Krause, Herbert (Arthur)
1905-1976 .... CANR-120
Obituary 103
Earlier sketches in CA 49-52, CANR-63
See also DLB 256
See also TCWW 1, 2
Krause, Jill A.
See Steans, Jill A.
Krause, Lawrence Berle 1929- 113
Krause, Pat 1930- CANR-37
Earlier sketch in CA 114
Krause, Paul 1951- 139
Krause, Shari Stamford
See Stamford Krause, Shari
Krause, Sydney J(oseph) 1925- 21-24R
Krause, Walter 1917- CANR-1
Earlier sketch in CA 1-4R
Kraushaar, John L. 1917-1974 45-48
Kraushaar, Otto F(rederick) 1901-1989 . 37-40R
Krauskopf, Konrad B(ates) 1910- 77-80
Krauss, Bob
See Krauss, Robert G.
Krauss, Bruno
See Bulmer, (Henry) Kenneth
Krauss, Clifford 1953- 136
Krauss, Ellis S(aunders) 1944- CANR-8
Earlier sketch in CA 61-64
Krauss, Herbert Harris 1940- 85-88
Krauss, Lawrence M. 1954- CANR-98
Earlier sketch in CA 147
Krauss, Nicole 216
Krauss, Paul Gerhardt 1905-1995 .... 1-4R
Krauss, Robert G. 1924- CANR-2
Earlier sketch in CA 1-4R
Krauss, Robert M. 1931- 17-20R
Krauss, Rosalind E(pstein) 1940- CANR-89
Earlier sketch in CA 81-84
Krauss, Ruth (Ida) 1911-1993 .... CANR-83
Obituary 141
Earlier sketches in CA 1-4R, CANR-1, 13, 47
See also CAD
See also CLR 42
See also CWD
See also CWRI 5
See also DLB 52
See also MAICYA 1, 2
See also SATA 1, 30
See also SATA-Obit 75
Krausz, Ernest 1931- 104
Krausz, Michael 1942- CANR-4
Earlier sketch in CA 53-56
Krausz, Norman G(eorge) P(hilip)
1920- 41-44R
Kraut, Benny 1947- 113
Kraut, Richard 1944- 130
Krauthammer, Charles 1950- 127
Brief entry 121
Interview in CA-127
Krautheimer, Richard 1897-1994 103
Obituary 147
Krautter, Elisa (Bialk) 1912(?)-1990 ..... CANR-1
Obituary 131
Earlier sketch in CA 1-4R
See also SATA 1
See also SATA-Obit 65
Krautwurst, Terry 1946- .... SATA 79
Krauze, Andrzej 1947- 197
See also SATA-Brief 46
Krauzer, Steven M(ark) 1948- CANR-83
Earlier sketches in CA 109, CANR-25, 51
See also TCWW 2
Kravetz, Nathan 1921- 9-12R
Kravis, Irving B(ernard) 1916-1992 ..... CANR-7
Earlier sketch in CA 17-20R
Kravitz, Nathan
See Kravitz, Nathaniel
Kravitz, Nathaniel 1905-1979 49-52
Krawiec, Richard 1952- CANR-96
Earlier sketch in CA 122
Krawiec, T(heophile) S(tanley)
1913-1995 .... CANR-10
Earlier sketch in CA 25-28R
Krawitz, Henry 1947- 45-48
Krawitz, Herman E(verett) 1925- 61-64
Krawitz, Ruth (Lifshitz) 1929- 9-12R
Kray, Robert Clement 1930- .... SATA 82
Kraybill, Donald B(rubaker) 1945- 69-72
Kraynak, Robert P. 1949- 236
Kraynay, Anton
See Gippius, Zinaida (Nikolaevna)
Krebs, Alfred H. 1920- 21-24R
Krebs, Hans (Adolf) 1900-1981 129
Obituary 108
Krebs, Nina Boyd 1938- 193
Krech, David 1909-1977
Obituary 73-76
Krech, Shepard III 1944- CANR-97
Earlier sketch in CA 119
Kredel, Fritz 1900-1973
Obituary 41-44R
See also SATA 17
Kredenser, Gail 1936- 21-24R
Kreeft, Peter 1937- CANR-57
Earlier sketches in CA 81-84, CANR-14, 31
Krefetz, Gerald 1932- CANR-15
Earlier sketch in CA 33-36R
Krefetz, Ruth 1931-1972 .... CAP-2
Obituary 37-40R
Earlier sketch in CA 33-36
Kregel, J(an) A(llen) 1944- 41-44R
Kreh, Bernard 1925- 57-60
Kreider, Barbara 1942- 41-44R
Kreider, Carl 1914-2002 .... 37-40R
Kreider, Jan F(rederick) 1942- 111
Kreidl, John Francis 1939- 81-84
Kreig, Margaret B. (Baltzell)
1922-1998 .... 13-16R
Obituary 164
Kreighbaum, Mark 183
Kreikemeier, Gregory Scott 1965- .... SATA 85
Krein, David F(rederick) 1942- 85-88
Kreindler, Lee (Stanley) 1924-2003 .... 17-20R
Obituary 213
Kreingold, Shana 1889(?)-1972
Obituary 37-40R
Kreinin, Mordechai 1930- 9-12R
Kreisel, Henry 1922-1991 .... CANR-42
Earlier sketch in CA 61-64
See also CCA 1
See also DAC
See also DAM MST
See also DLB 88
Kreiser, B(ernard) Robert 1943- 116
Kreisler, Fritz 1875-1962
Obituary 115
Kreisman, Leonard T(heodore) 1925- 13-16R
Kreisman, Marvin 1933(?)-1979(?)
Obituary 102
Kreit, Carol 1936- 203
Kreitler, Hans 1916- 45-48
Kreitler, Shulamith 1938- 45-48
Kreitzman, Leon 236
Krejci, Jaroslav 1916- CANR-57
Earlier sketches in CA 41-44R, CANR-14, 31
Kremen, Bennett 1936- 57-60
Kremenliev, Boris A(ngeloff) 1911-1988 .. 45-48
Obituary 125
Krementz, Jill 1940- CANR-112
Earlier sketches in CA 41-44R, CANR-23, 46
Interview in CANR-23
See also AITN 1, 2
See also CLR 5
See also MAICYA 1, 2
See also SAAS 8
See also SATA 17, 71, 134
Kremenyuk, Victor (A.) 1940- 200
Kremer, Laura Evelyn 1921- 103
Kremer, Marcie
See Sorenson, Margo
Kremer, Rudiger
See Kremer, Ruediger
Kremer, Ruediger 1942- 139
Kremer, S. Lillian 1939- 187
Kremer, William F. 1919- 69-72
Kreml, Anne Lee 1930- 21-24R
Kreml, William P. 1941- CANR-121
Earlier sketch in CA 165
Kremmer, Christopher 1958- 216
Krempel, Daniel S(partakus) 1926- 33-36R
Kren, George M. 1926- 102
Krenek, Ernst 1900-1991 57-60
Obituary 136
Krenina, Katya 1968- .... SATA 101
Krenkel, John H(enry) 1906-1985 .... CAP-2
Earlier sketch in CA 33-36
Krensky, Stephen (Alan) 1953- CANR-135
Earlier sketches in CA 73-76, CANR-13, 46, 67
See also BYA 1
See also SATA 47, 93, 136
See also SATA-Brief 41
Krentel, Mildred White 1921- 5-8R
Krents, Harold Eliot 1944-1987 .... 37-40R
Obituary 121
Krentz, Edgar (Martin) 1928- 21-24R
Krentz, Jayne Ann 1948- CANR-108
Earlier sketches in CA 139, CANR-63
See also RHW
Krepon, Michael 1946- 128
Krepps, Robert W(ilson) 1919-1980 ... CANR-1
Earlier sketch in CA 1-4R
Kreps, Juanita M(orris) 1921- 130
Kresge, George Joseph, Jr.
See Kreskin
Kresh, Paul 1919-1997 .... CANR-13
Obituary 156
Earlier sketch in CA 13-16R
See also SATA 61
See also SATA-Obit 94
Kreskin 1935- 101

Kress, Nancy 1948- CANR-109
Earlier sketches in CA 126, CANR-60
See also AAYA 28
See also SATA 85, 147
See also SATA-Essay 147
See also SFW 4
See also SUFW 2
Kress, Paul F(rederick) 1935- 29-32R
Kress, Robert (Lee) 1932- CANR-8
Earlier sketch in CA 61-64
Kress, Roy A(lfred) 1916- 107
Kress, Stephen W. 1945- 122
Kressel, Kenneth 1942- 119
Kressel, Neil J. 1957- CANR-109
Earlier sketch in CA 152
Kressley, Carson 1969- 233
Kressy, Michael 1936- CANR-8
Earlier sketch in CA 61-64
Krestovsky, V.
See Khvoshchinskaia, Nadezhda Dmitrievna
Krestovsky, Vsevolod Vladimirovich
1839-1895 .... DLB 238
Kretsch, Robert W. 1913(?)-1979
Obituary 89-92
Kretzmann, Adalbert Raphael
1903-1989 .... CAP-1
Earlier sketch in CA 13-16
Kretzmann, Norman 1928-1998 49-52
Kretzmer, Herbert 1925- CANR-130
Earlier sketch in CA 105
Kreuder, Ernst 1903-1972 182
See also DLB 69
Kreuger, Miles 1934- 81-84
Kreusler, Abraham A(rthur) 1897-1983 65-68
Kreuter, Kent 1932- 29-32R
Kreuz, Roger J(ames) 1961- 180
Kreuzer, James R. 1913-1971 .... CAP-1
Earlier sketch in CA 11-12
Kreve (Mickevicius), Vincas 1882-1954 170
See also DLB 220
See also EWL 3
See also TCLC 27
Krevitsky, Nathan I. 1914-1991 .... 9-12R
Krevitsky, Nik
See Krevitsky, Nathan I.
Krevolin, Nathan 1927-1995 .... CANR-14
Earlier sketch in CA 41-44R
Krewer, Semyon E(fimovich) 1915-1985 105
Kreyche, Gerald F. 1927- 37-40R
Kreyche, Robert J(oseph) 1920-1974 ..... 13-16R
Obituary 133
Kreymborg, Alfred 1883-1966 178
Obituary 25-28R
See also DLB 4, 54
See also MAL 5
Krich, A. M.
See Krich, Aron
Krich, Aron 1916-1995 120
Krich, Aron M.
See Krich, Aron
Krich, John 1951- 108
Krich, Rochelle
See Krich, Rochelle Majer
Krich, Rochelle Majer CANR-110
Earlier sketch in CA 166
Kricher, John C. 1944- 175
See also SATA 113
Kricorian, Nancy 1960- CANR-139
Earlier sketch in CA 169
Krieg, Joann P(eck) 1932- 143
Krieg, Joyce 1950- 221
Krieg, Robert Anthony 1946- CANR-91
Earlier sketch in CA 145
Krieg, Saul 1917- 81-84
Kriegel, Gail 1942- 108
Kriegel, Harriet 104
Kriegel, Leonard 1933- CANR-12
Earlier sketch in CA 33-36R
Kriegel, Mark 238
Krieger, Frieda Frome 1925-1993 128
Krieger, Leonard 1918-1990 .... CANR-7
Obituary 132
Earlier sketch in CA 17-20R
Krieger, Martin H. 1944- 138
Krieger, Melanie 161
See also SATA 96
Krieger, Michael J. 1940- CANR-139
Earlier sketch in CA 146
Krieger, Murray 1923-2000 .... CANR-50
Earlier sketches in CA 1-4R, CANR-2
See also DLB 67
Krieghbaum, Hillier (Hiram)
1902-1993 .... CANR-2
Earlier sketch in CA 5-8R
Kriegman, Oscar M(arvin) 1930- 9-12R
Kriendler, H(arold) Peter 1905-2001 239
Kriendler, Peter
See Kriendler, H(arold) Peter
Kriensky, Morris (Edward) 1917-1998 57-60
Obituary 166
Krier, James E(dward) 1939- 81-84
Krier, Leon 1946- 173
Krier, Rob 1938- 190
Kriesberg, Louis 1926- CANR-12
Earlier sketch in CA 29-32R
Krige, Uys 1910- .... CN 1, 2, 3, 4
Krikorian, Yervant H(ovhannes)
1892-1977 .... CANR-2
Obituary 73-76
Earlier sketch in CA 45-48
Krim, Seymour 1922-1989 .... CANR-4
Obituary 129
Earlier sketch in CA 5-8R
See also DLB 16
Krimerman, Leonard Isaiah 1934- 17-20R
Krims, Milton Robert 1904(?)-1988
Obituary 126
Krimsky, George A. 1942- 156
Krimsky, Joseph (Hayylm) 1883(?)-1971
Obituary 104
Krimsky, Sheldon 1941- CANR-86
Earlier sketches in CA 113, CANR-33
Krin, Sylvie
See Fantoni, Barry (Ernest)
Krinard, Susan 199
Kring, Hilda Adam 1921- 77-80
Kring, Walter Donald 1916-1999 116
Obituary 173
Kringle, Karen 1947- 140
Krinsky, Carol Herselle 1937- 37-40R
Kripalani, J(iwatram) B(hagwandas) 1888-1982
Obituary 110
Kripke, Dorothy Karp 17-20R
See also SATA 30
Kripke, Saul A(aron) 1940- 130
See also DLB 279
Krippendorff, Klaus 1932- 77-80
Krippner, Stanley (Curtis) 1932- CANR-68
Earlier sketches in CA 81-84, CANR-15, 32
Krisch, Henry 1931- 134
Brief entry 111
Krise, Raymond (Owens, Jr.) 1949- 109
Krise, Thomas W(arren) 1961- 193
Krisher, Bernard 1931- CANR-18
Earlier sketch in CA 77-80
Krisher, Trudy (B.) 1946- 151
See also AAYA 32
See also SATA 86, 160
See also WYAS 1
See also YAW
Krishna, Gopi
See Shivpuri, Gopi Krishna
Krishna, K(owligi) R. 1954- 239
Krishnamurti, Jiddu 1895-1986 .... CANR-69
Obituary 118
Earlier sketches in CA 61-64, CANR-11, 39
Krishnaswami, Uma 1956- 217
See also SATA 144
Kriska, Laura 173
Krislov, Alexander
See Lee Howard, Leon Alexander
Krislov, Joseph 1927- 41-44R
Krislov, Samuel 1929- CANR-18
Earlier sketches in CA 9-12R, CANR-3
Krispyn, Egbert 1930- 13-16R
Kriss, Ronald P(aul) 1934- 69-72
Krist, Gary (Michael) 1957- CANR-123
Earlier sketch in CA 132
Kristal, Efrain 1959- 204
Kristein, Marvin M(ichael) 1926- 29-32R
Kristeller, Paul Oskar 1905-1999 .... CANR-6
Obituary 181
Earlier sketch in CA 9-12R
Kristensen, Thorkil 1899-1989 130
Kristensen, (Aage) Tom 1893-1974 192
Kristensen, Tom 1893-1974 .... DLB 214
See also EWL 3
Kristeva, Julia 1941- CANR-99
Earlier sketch in CA 154
See also CLC 77, 140
See also DLB 242
See also EWL 3
See also FW
See also LMFS 2
Kristian, Hans
See Neerskov, Hans Kristian
Kristmundsson, Adalsteinn
See Kristmundsson, Aoalsteinn
Kristmundsson, Aoalsteinn 1908-1958
See Steinarr, Steinn
Kristof, Agota 1935- 168
Kristof, Jane 1932- 29-32R
See also SATA 8
Kristof, Ladis K(ris) D(onabed) 1918- 61-64
Kristof, Nicholas D(onabet) 1959- .. CANR-100
Earlier sketches in CA 126, CANR-53
Kristofferson, Kris 1936- 104
See also CLC 26
Kristol, Irving 1920- CANR-28
Earlier sketch in CA 25-28R
Kristol, William 1952- 228
Kritsick, Stephen M(ark) 1951-1994 112
Obituary 143
Kritz, Mary M. 138
Kritzeck, James 1930- 5-8R
Kritzer, Amelia Howe 1947- 146
Kritzer, Hyman W. 1918-2002 .... DLBY 2002
Krivich, Mikhail 173
Krivulin, Viktor Borisovich
1944-2001 .... DLB 285
Kriwaczek, Paul 1937- 224
Kriyananda
See Walters, J. Donald
Kriyananda, S.
See Walters, J. Donald
Kriyananda, Sri
See Walters, J. Donald
Kriyananda, Swami
See Walters, J. Donald
Krizanc, John 1956- 187
See also CLC 57
Krizay, John 1926-1992 61-64
Krleza, Miroslav 1893-1981 .... CANR-50
Obituary 105
Earlier sketch in CA 97-100
See also CDWLB 4
See also CLC 8, 114
See also DLB 147
See also EW 11
See also RGWL 2, 3
Krmpotic, Vesna 1932- CANR-44
Earlier sketches in CA 102, CANR-20
Kroc, Ray(mond Albert) 1902-1984 118
Obituary 111
Kroch, Adolph A. 1882-1978
Obituary 81-84
Krochmal, Arnold 1919-1993 .... CANR-14
Earlier sketch in CA 69-72
Krochmal, Connie 1949- 41-44R
Krock, Arthur 1887-1974 .... CAP-2
Obituary 49-52
Earlier sketch in CA 33-36
See also AITN 1
See also DLB 29
Krodel, Gerhard 1926- 61-64
Kroeber, A(lfred) L(ouis) 1876-1960 129
Obituary 110
Kroeber, Clifton B(rown) 1921- CANR-32
Earlier sketch in CA 110
Kroeber, Donald W(alter) 1934- 115
Kroeber, Karl 1926- CANR-66
Earlier sketches in CA 57-60, CANR-32
Kroeber, Theodora (Kracaw)
1897-1979 .... CANR-32
Obituary 89-92
Earlier sketches in CA 5-8R, CANR-5
See also BYA 2
See also LAIT 2
See also SATA 1
Kroeger, Arthur 1908-1998 .... 13-16R
Kroeger, Brooke 1949- 146
Kroeger, Frederick P(aul) 1921- 33-36R
Kroeger, Mary Kay 1950- .... SATA 92
Kroepcke, Karol
See Krolow, Karl (Gustav Heinrich)
Kroes, Rob 1940- 214
Kroetsch, Robert (Paul) 1927- CANR-38
Earlier sketches in CA 17-20R, CANR-8
See also CCA 1
See also CLC 5, 23, 57, 132
See also CN 2, 3, 4, 5, 6, 7
See also CP 7
See also DAC
See also DAM POET
See also DLB 53
See also MTCW 1
Kroetz, Franz
See Kroetz, Franz Xaver
Kroetz, Franz Xaver 1946- CANR-142
Earlier sketch in CA 130
See also CLC 41
See also CWW 2
See also EWL 3
Krog, Antjie 1952- 194
Kroger, William S. 1906-1995 .... CAP-1
Earlier sketch in CA 13-14
Krohn, Aino
See Kallas, Aino (Julia Maria)
Krohn, Claus-Dieter 1941- 146
Krohn, Ernst C(hristopher) 1888-1975 ... 37-40R
See also AITN 1
Krohn, Katherine E(lizabeth) 1961- . CANR-105
Earlier sketch in CA 150
See also SATA 84, 125
Krohn, Norman Odya 1920- 116
Krohn, Robert 1937- 45-48
Kroker, Arthur (W.) 1945- 161
See also CLC 77
Krok-Paszkowski, Jan 1925- 130
Kroll, Burt
See Rowland, D(onald) S(ydney)
Kroll, Ernest 1914-1993 97-100
Kroll, Francis Lynde 1904-1973 .... CAP-1
Earlier sketch in CA 13-16
See also SATA 10
Kroll, John (Leon) 1925-1986
Obituary 119
Kroll, Judith 1943- 65-68
Kroll, Morton 1923-2004 49-52
Obituary 223
Kroll, Steven 1941- CANR-94
Earlier sketches in CA 65-68, CANR-9, 25, 35, 50
See also SAAS 7
See also SATA 19, 66, 125, 135
See also SATA-Essay 135
Kroll, Virginia L(ouise) 1948- 186
Earlier sketch in CA 143
See also SATA 76, 114
Kroll, Woodrow (M.) 1944- 191
Kroller, Eva-Marie 1949- 128
Krolow, Karl (Gustav Heinrich) 1915- 81-84
See also CWW 2
See also EWL 3
Kromer, Helen CANR-34
Earlier sketch in CA 93-96
Kromm, David E. 1938- 144
Krommes, Beth 1956- .... SATA 128
Kromminga, John H(enry) 1918-1995 77-80
Krondorfer, Bjorn 1959-
See Krondorfer, Bjorn
Krondorfer, Bjorn 1959- CANR-111
Earlier sketch in CA 151
Kronegger, Maria Elisabeth 1932- 25-28R
Kronen, Steve 1953- 140
Kronenberg, Henry Harold 1902-1980 ...... 1-4R
Kronenberg, Maria Elizabeth 1881(?)-1970
Obituary 104
Kronenberger, Louis 1904-1980 .... CANR-2
Obituary 97-100
Earlier sketch in CA 1-4R
Kronenfeld, Jennie J(acobs) 1949- CANR-93
Earlier sketch in CA 146
Kronenwetter, Michael 1943- .... SATA 62
Kroner, Richard 1884-1974 .... 9-12R
Kronhausen, Eberhard W(ilhelm)
1915- CANR-6
Earlier sketch in CA 9-12R
Kronhausen, Phyllis C(armen) 1929- .. CANR-6
Earlier sketch in CA 9-12R
Kronick, David A(braham) 1917- 9-12R
Kronick, Joseph G. 1953- 122
Kroninger, Robert H(enry) 1923- 13-16R
Kroninger, Stephen 227
Kroniuk, Lisa
See Berton, Pierre (Francis de Marigny)
Kronk, Gary (Wayne) 1956- 115
Kronman, Anthony T(ownsend) 1945- 113
Kronstadt, Henry L(ippin) 1915- 73-76
Kronus, Sidney J., Jr. 1937-
Brief entry 107
Krook, Dorothea 1920- 123
Krooss, Herman E. 1912-1975 .... CAP-2
Obituary 57-60
Earlier sketch in CA 17-18
Krooth, Dick
See Krooth, Richard
Krooth, Richard 1935- CANR-96
Earlier sketch in CA 146
Kropf, Linda S(toddart) 1947- 49-52
Kropf, Richard W(illiam Bartlett)
1932- CANR-10
Earlier sketch in CA 65-68
Kropotkin, Peter (Aleksieevich) 1842-1921 . 219
Brief entry 119
See also Kropotkin, Petr Alekseevich
See also TCLC 36
Kropotkin, Petr Alekseevich
See Kropotkin, Peter (Aleksieevich)
See also DLB 277
Kropp, (Lars Olaf) Goran 1966-2002 194
Obituary 209
Kropp, Lloyd 25-28R
Kropp, Paul (Stephan) 1948- CANR-96
Earlier sketch in CA 112
See also CLR 96
See also SATA 38
See also SATA-Brief 34
See also YAW
Krosby, H(ans) Peter 1929- 89-92
Krosney, Mary Stewart 1939- 17-20R
Krosoczka, Jarrett J. 1977- .... SATA 155
Kross, Jaan 1920- .... DLB 232
See also RGWL 3
Krotki, Karol J(ozef) 1922- 41-44R
Krotkov, Yuri 1917-1981 102
See also CLC 19
Krouse, Erika Dawn 1969- 202
Krout, John Allen 1896-1979 97-100
Obituary 85-88
Krstic, Radivoj V(ase) 1935- 142
Kruchenykh, Aleksei Eliseevich
1886-1968 .... DLB 295
Kruchkow, Diane 1947- 69-72
Kruck, William E(vert) 1942- 114
Kruckeberg, Arthur R(ice) 1920- 137
Kruczkowski, Leon 1900-1962 .... EWL 3
Krudy, Gyula 1878-1933 .... DLB 215
See also EWL 3
Krueger, Anne O. 1934- CANR-32
Earlier sketches in CA 37-40R, CANR-15
Krueger, Arnd
See Kruger, Arnd
Krueger, Caryl Waller 1929- 175
Krueger, Christoph 1937- 33-36R
Krueger, Hardy 1928- 77-80
Krueger, Henrik S. 1938- 130
Krueger, John R(ichard) 1927- CANR-33
Earlier sketches in CA 21-24R, CANR-10
Krueger, Lesley 225
Krueger, Lorenz 1932- 136
Krueger, Marj 158
Krueger, Ralph R. 1927-1999 .... CANR-2
Earlier sketch in CA 49-52
Krueger, Robert B(lair) 1928-1994 57-60
Krueger, Thomas A. 1936- 21-24R
Krueger, William Kent 194
Kruell, Marianne 1936- 132
Kruess, James
See Kruss, James
See also CLR 9
Krug, Achim
See Krug, Hans-Joachim
Krug, Edward August 1911-1980 .... CANR-4
Earlier sketch in CA 5-8R
Krug, Hans-Joachim 1919- 222
Krug, Mark M. 1915-2004 185
Obituary 234
Brief entry 109
Krug, Samuel E(dward) 1943- 121
Kruger, Arnd 1944-
See Kruger, Arnd
Kruger, Arnd 1944- CANR-122
Earlier sketch in CA 163
Kruger, Arthur N(ewman) 1916- CANR-1
Earlier sketch in CA 1-4R
Kruger, Daniel H(erschel) 1922- 25-28R
Kruger, Ehren 1972- 226
Kruger, Hardy
See Krueger, Hardy
Kruger, Lorenz
See Krueger, Lorenz
Kruger, Michael 1943- 231
Kruger, Mollee (Coppel) 1929- CANR-45
Earlier sketches in CA 69-72, CANR-21
Kruger, Paul
See Sebenthall, R(oberta) E(lizabeth)
Kruger, (Charles) Rayne -2002 .... 5-8R
Obituary 213
Kruger, Wolf
See Hutson, Shaun
Kruglak, Haym 1909- 53-56
Krugman, Paul R. 1953- 174
Kruh, David (S.) 1956- 138
Kruh, Louis 1923- 138
Kruise, Carol Sue 1939- 125
Kruk, Herman (Hersh) 1897-1944
Krukowski, Lucian 1929- 125

Cumulative Index 329 **Kunanbaev**

Krulewitch, Melvin Levin 1895-1978 ... 103
Krulik, Stephen 1933- ... CANR-8
Earlier sketch in CA 17-20R
Krull, Felix
See White, Stanley
Krull, Kathleen 1952- ... CANR-132
Earlier sketch in CA 106
See also CLR 44
See also MAICYA 2
See also MAICYAS 1
See also SATA 52, 80, 149
See also SATA-Brief 39
See also SATA-Essay 106
Krull, Marianne
See Kruell, Marianne
Kruman, Marc W. 1949- ... 166
Krumb
See Crumb, R(obert)
Krumboltz, John D(wight) 1928-
Brief entry ... 110
Krumgold, Joseph (Quincy)
1908-1980 ... CANR-7
Obituary ... 101
Earlier sketch in CA 9-12R
See also BYA 1, 2
See also CLC 12
See also MAICYA 1, 2
See also SATA 1, 48
See also SATA-Obit 23
See also YAW
Krumm, John McGill 1913-1995 ... 109
Obituary ... 150
Krummel, Donald William 1929- ... 106
Krump, John M. 1929(?)-1990
Obituary ... 132
Krumpelmann, John T(heodore)
1892-1986 ... 41-44R
Krumwitz
See Crumb, R(obert)
Krupat, Arnold 1941- ... 126
Krupat, Edward 1945- ... 77-80
Krupinski, Loretta 1940- ... SATA 67, 102, 161
Krupnick, Karen 1947- ... CANR-113
Earlier sketch in CA 155
See also SATA 89
Krupnick, Mark L. 1939- ... 130
Krupnik, Baruch
See Karu, Baruch
Krupp, E(dwin) C(harles) 1944- ... CANR-101
Earlier sketches in CA 105, CANR-21
See also SATA 53, 123
Krupp, Nate 1935- ... CANR-10
Earlier sketch in CA 21-24R
Krupp, Robin Rector 1946- ... 135
See also SATA 53
Krupp, Sherman Roy 1926-1988 ... 1-4R
Obituary ... 125
Krusch, Werner E. 1927- ... 5-8R
Kruschke, Earl R(oger) 1934- ... 41-44R
Kruse, Alexander Z. 1888(?)-1972
Obituary ... 33-36R
Kruse, Harry D(ayton) 1900-1977
Obituary ... 73-76
Kruse, John 1919- ... CANR-35
Earlier sketch in CA 114
Krusenstjerna, Agnes von
See von Krusenstjerna, Agnes (Julie Frederika)
Krush, Beth 1918- ... MAICYA 1, 2
See also SATA 18
Krush, Joe 1918-
See Krush, Joseph P.
See also MAICYA 1
See also SATA 18
Krush, Joseph P. 1918-
See Krush, Joe
See also MAICYA 2
Krusich, Walter S(teve) 1922- ... 49-52
Kruskal, William H(enry) 1919-2005 ... 33-36R
Obituary ... 238
Kruss, James 1926-1997 ... CANR-5
Earlier sketch in CA 53-56
See also Kruess, James
See also MAICYA 1, 2
See also SATA 8
Kruszewski, Z. Anthony 1928- ... 134
Brief entry ... 113
Krutch, Joseph Wood 1893-1970 ... CANR-4
Obituary ... 25-28R
Earlier sketch in CA 1-4R
See also ANW
See also CLC 24
See also DLB 63, 206, 275
Krutilla, John Vasil 1922-2003 ... CANR-9
Obituary ... 217
Earlier sketch in CA 21-24R
Krutzch, Gus
See Eliot, T(homas) S(tearns)
Kruuk, Hans 1937- ... 61-64
Kruzas, Anthony T(homas)
1914-1999 ... CANR-17
Earlier sketches in CA 1-4R, CANR-2
Krych, Margaret A. 1942- ... 194
Kryder, Daniel (Thomas) ... 230
Krygier, Leora ... 238
Krygsman, Nancy (Patricia Rice) 1943- ... 190
See also Tudor, Nancy (Patricia Rice)
Krykorka, Vladyana 1945- ... SATA 96
Krylov, Ivan Andreevich
1768(?)-1844 ... DLB 150
Krymov, Iurii Solomonovich
1908-1941 ... DLB 272
Krymow, Virginia P(auline) 1930- ... 69-72
Krynicki, Ryszard 1943- ... EWL 3
Krypton
See Graham, Lloyd M.
Krysl, Marilyn 1943- ... CANR-86
Earlier sketch in CA 105
Krystal, Henry 1925- ... 214
Krythe, Maymie Richardson -1969 ... 17-20R
Krzywan, Jozef
See Krotki, Karol J(ozef)
Krzyzaniak, Marian 1911-1993 ... 9-12R
Krzyzanowski, Jerzy R(oman) 1922- ... 37-40R
Krzyzanowski, Ludwik 1907(?)-1986
Obituary ... 118
Kselman, Thomas A. 1948- ... 110
K-Turkel, Judi
See Kesselman-Turkel, Judi
Kubal, David L(awrence) 1936- ... 45-48
Kubat, Daniel 1928-
Brief entry ... 114
Kubeck, James (Ernest) 1920- ... 17-20R
Kubek, Anthony 1920- ... 104
Kubelka, Susanna 1942- ... 113
Kube-McDowell, Michael P(aul)
1954- ... CANR-83
Earlier sketch in CA 119
See also SFW 4
Kuberski, Philip 1952- ... 145
Kubert, Joe ... AAYA 58
Kubert, Joe 1926- ... 225
Kubey, Robert W(illiam) 1952- ... 165
Kubiak, Greg D. 1960- ... 147
Kubiak, T(imothy) J(ames) 1942- ... 61-64
Kubiak, William J. 1929- ... 33-36R
Kubicek, Robert V(incent) 1935- ... CANR-47
Earlier sketch in CA 29-32R
Kubie, Eleanor Gottheil
See Kubie, Nora Gottheil Benjamin
Kubie, Lawrence S. 1896(?)-1973
Obituary ... 45-48
Kubie, Nora Benjamin
See Kubie, Nora Gottheil Benjamin
Kubie, Nora Gottheil Benjamin
1899-1988 ... 5-8R
Obituary ... 126
See also SATA 39
See also SATA-Obit 59
Kubik, Gerhard 1934- ... 189
Kubin, Alfred (Leopold Isidor)
1877-1959 ... CANR-104
Brief entry ... 112
Earlier sketch in CA 149
See also DLB 81
See also TCLC 23
Kubinyi, Laszlo 1937- ... CANR-68
Earlier sketch in CA 85-88
See also SATA 17, 94
Kubis, Pat 1928- ... 25-28R
Kubler, George (Alexander) 1912-1996 ... 9-12R
Obituary ... 154
Kubler-Ross, Elisabeth
See Kubler-Ross, Elisabeth
Kubler-Ross, Elisabeth 1926-2004 ... CANR-106
Obituary ... 230
Earlier sketch in CA 25-28R
Kublicki, Nicolas M. ... 216
Kublin, Hyman 1919-1982 ... 9-12R
Kubly, Herbert (Oswald Nicholas)
1915-1996 ... CANR-44
Obituary ... 153
Earlier sketches in CA 5-8R, CANR-4
Kubo, Sakae 1926- ... CANR-7
Earlier sketch in CA 57-60
Kubose, Gyomay M(asao) 1905-2000 ... 49-52
Kubota, Akira 1932- ... 37-40R
Kubrick, Stanley 1928-1999 ... CANR-33
Obituary ... 177
Earlier sketch in CA 81-84
See also AAYA 30
See also CLC 16
See also DLB 26
See also TCLC 112
Kucera, Henry 1925- ... 21-24R
Kucera, Jaroslav 1929-1991 ... IDFW 3
Kuch, K(athy) D(iane) ... 176
Kucharek, Casimir (Anthony) 1928- ... 57-60
Kucharski, Kasimir
See Koch, Kurt E(mil)
Kucharsky, David (Eugene) 1931- ... 65-68
Kucherov, Alexander 1927-1985
Obituary ... 117
Kucich, John (Richard) 1952- ... 112
Kuczkir, Mary 1933- ... CANR-90
Brief entry ... 111
Earlier sketches in CA 115, CANR-42
Interview in ... CA-115
See also RHW
Kuczmarski, Susan Smith 1951- ... CANR-105
Earlier sketch in CA 150
Kuczmarski, Thopmas D(ale) 1951- ... 150
Kuczynski, Pedro-Pablo 1938- ... 77-80
Kudian, Mischa ... 107
Kudlinski, Kathleen V. 1950- ... 225
See also SATA 150
Kudrle, Robert Thomas 1942- ... 112
Kudrova, I(rma) V. ... 230
Kuebrich, David 1943- ... 134
Kuehl, John 1928-1998 ... 21-24R
Kuehl, Linda 1939(?)-1978
Obituary ... 104
Kuehl, Stefan 1966- ... 146
Kuehl, Warren F(rederick)
1924-1987 ... CANR-7
Earlier sketch in CA 17-20R
Kuehn, Dieter
See Kuhn, Dieter
Kuehn, Dorothy Dalton
See Dalton, Dorothy
Kuehn, Heinz R(ichard) 1919- ... 130
Kuehn, Paul
See Grant, Roto
Kuehn, Thomas James 1950- ... 116
Kuehnelt-Leddihn, Erik (Maria) Ritter von
1909- ... CANR-44
Earlier sketches in CA 9-12R, CANR-3, 20
Kuemmerly, Walter 1903- ... 49-52
Kuen, Alfred (F.) 1921- ... CANR-53
Earlier sketches in CA 107, CANR-25
Kuenàn, Philip Henry 1902-1976
Obituary ... 116
Kueng, Hans
See Kung, Hans
Kuenne, Robert E(ugene) 1924- ... 5-8R
Kuenster, Kenneth 1931- ... 187
Kuenstler, Morton 1927- ... SATA 10
Kuenzli, Alfred E(ugene) 1923-1989 ... 17-20R
Kuernberger, Ferdinand 1821-1879 ... DLB 129
Kuesel, Harry N. 1892(?)-1977
Obituary ... 73-76
Kuester, David 1938- ... 53-56
Kuether, Edith Lyman 1915- ... 49-52
Kufeldt, George 1923- ... 37-40R
Kuffler, Stephen 1913-1980
Obituary ... 105
Kufner, Herbert L(eopold) 1927- ... 5-8R
Kugel, James 1945- ... CANR-79
Earlier sketch in CA 29-32R
Kugelman, Richard 1908-1981 ... 41-44R
Kugelmass, J. Alvin 1910-1972 ... CANR-4
Obituary ... 33-36R
Earlier sketch in CA 5-8R
Kugi, Constance Todd 1939- ... 127
Kuh, Charlotte 1892(?)-1985
Obituary ... 115
See also SATA-Obit 43
Kuh, Edwin 1925-1986 ... CANR-36
Obituary ... 119
Earlier sketch in CA 21-24R
Kuh, Frederick Robert 1895-1978
Obituary ... 89-92
Kuh, Katharine (W.) 1904-1994 ... 13-16R
Obituary ... 143
Kuh, Patric 1964- ... 233
Kuh, Richard H. 1921- ... 21-24R
Kuharski, Janice 1947- ... 198
See also SATA 128
Kuhatschek, Jack 1949- ... 122
Kuhfeld, Mary Pulver 1943- ... 128
Kuhl, Ernest Peter 1881-1981 ... CANR-39
Obituary ... 133
Earlier sketch in CA 41-44R
Kuhl, Stefan
See Kuehl, Stefan
Kuhlken, Ken(neth Wayne) 1945- ... CANR-99
Earlier sketch in CA 102
Kuhlman, Erika A. 1961- ... 181
Kuhlman, James A(llen) 1941- ... 85-88
Kuhlman, John M(elville) 1923- ... 17-20R
Kuhlman, Kathryn 1910(?)-1976 ... CANR-12
Obituary ... 65-68
Earlier sketch in CA 57-60
Kuhlmann, Quirinus 1651-1689 ... DLB 168
Kuhlmann, Susan
See Lohafer, Susan
Kuhn, Alfred 1914-1981 ... CANR-37
Earlier sketches in CA 9-12R, CANR-3
Kuhn, Annette 1945- ... CANR-53
Earlier sketches in CA 111, CANR-29
Kuhn, Bowie (Kent) 1926- ... 126
Kuhn, Delia (Wolf) 1903-1989 ... 130
Kuhn, Edward, Jr. 1924(?)-1979 ... 102
Obituary ... 93-96
Kuhn, Ferdinand 1905-1978 ... CANR-36
Obituary ... 81-84
Earlier sketch in CA 5-8R
Kuhn, Harold B(arnes) 1911-1994 ... 49-52
Kuhn, Heinz R(ichard)
See Kuehn, Heinz R(ichard)
Kuhn, Irene Corbally -1995 ... CAP-1
Earlier sketch in CA 9-10
Kuhn, Karl F(rancis) 1939- ... CANR-37
Earlier sketch in CA 65-68
Kuhn, Maggie
See Kuhn, Margaret E.
Kuhn, Margaret E. 1905-1995
Obituary ... 148
Brief entry ... 109
Kuhn, Martin A(rno) 1924- ... 9-12R
Kuhn, Reinhard (Clifford)
1930-1980 ... CANR-34
Earlier sketch in CA 45-48
Kuhn, Thomas S(amuel) 1922-1996 ... CANR-83
Obituary ... 152
Earlier sketches in CA 21-24R, CANR-11
See also DLB 279
Kuhn, Tillo E. 1919- ... 5-8R
Kuhn, W. E.
See Kuhn, William Ernst
Kuhn, William Ernst 1922-1998 ... CANR-142
Earlier sketch in CA 37-40R
Kuhn, Wolfgang Erasmus 1914-2003 ... 5-8R
Obituary ... 215
Kuhnau, Johann 1660-1722 ... DLB 168
Kuhne, Cecil 1952- ... 93-96
Kuhne, Marie (Ahnighito Peary) 1893-1978
Obituary ... 77-80
Kuhner, Herbert 1935- ... 25-28R
Kuhns, Dennis R(ay) 1947- ... 113
Kuhns, Dorothy
See Heyward, Dorothy (Hartzell Kuhns)
Kuhns, Elizabeth ... 235
Kuhns, Faith
See Eidse, Faith
Kuhns, Grant (Wilson) 1929- ... 9-12R
Kuhns, Richard F(rancis, Jr.) 1924- ... CANR-36
Earlier sketch in CA 37-40R
Kuhns, William 1943- ... 21-24R
Kuhre, W. Lee 1947- ... 154
Kuhse, Helga 1940- ... CANR-101
Earlier sketches in CA 122, CANR-47
Kuic, Vukan 1923- ... 37-40R
Kuiper, Gerard Peter 1905-1973 ... CAP-2
Obituary ... 45-48
Earlier sketch in CA 17-18
Kuipers, Joel C(orneal) 1954- ... 184
Kuisel, Richard F(rancis) 1935- ... 21-24R
Kuist, J(ames) M(arquis) 1935- ... 124
Kuitenbrouwer, Kathryn (Ann Frances)
1965- ... 233
Kuitert, H(arminus) Martinus 1924- ... CANR-37
Earlier sketch in CA 25-28R
Kujawa, Duane 1938- ... 33-36R
Kujoory, Parvin 1936- ... 204
Kujoth, Jean Spealman 1935-1975 ... CAP-2
Earlier sketch in CA 25-28
See also SATA-Obit 30
Kukla, Jon 1948- ... 223
Kukla, Robert J(ohn) 1932- ... 49-52
Kuklick, Bruce 1941- ... CANR-136
Earlier sketch in CA 41-44R
Kuklin, Susan 1941- ... CANR-67
Earlier sketch in CA 130
See also AAYA 27
See also CLR 51
See also MAICYA 2
See also SATA 63, 95, 163
Kukol'nik, Nestor Vasil'evich
1809-1868 ... DLB 205
Kukreja, Veena 1960- ... 143
Kukrit Pramoj
See Pramoj, M(on) R(ajawong) Kukrit
See also EWL 3
Kukrit Pramoj, M. R.
See Pramoj, M(on) R(ajawong) Kukrit
Kukucin, Martin 1860-1928 ... CDWLB 4
See also DLB 215
See also EWL 3
Kula, Witold 1916-1988 ... 159
Kuleshov, Arkady A. 1914-1978
Obituary ... 77-80
Kuletz, Valerie L. ... 222
Kulick, John
See Pinchot, Ann (Kramer)
Kulka, Richard A. 1945- ... 130
Kulkarni, Hemant B(alvantrao)
1916-1994 ... CANR-1
Earlier sketch in CA 45-48
Kulkarni, R(amchandra) G(anesh)
1931- ... 29-32R
Kulkarni, Venkatesh S(rinivas) 1945-1998 ... 113
Kulkin, Mary-Ellen
See Siegel, Mary-Ellen (Kulkin)
Kull, A. Stoddard
See Kull, Andrew
Kull, Andrew 1947- ... 138
Kull, Steven 1951- ... 128
Kulling, Monica 1952- ... CANR-111
Earlier sketch in CA 155
See also SATA 89
Kullman, Colby H(aight) 1945- ... 165
Kullman, Harry 1919-1982 ... CANR-39
Earlier sketch in CA 93-96
See also SATA 35
Kulshrestha, Chirantan 1946- ... 107
Kulski, Julian (Eugeniusz) 1929- ... CANR-14
Earlier sketch in CA 21-24R
Kulski, Wladyslaw W(szebor)
1903-1989 ... CANR-37
Earlier sketch in CA 5-8R
Kulstein, David J. 1916-1974 ... CAP-2
Earlier sketch in CA 25-28
Kultermann, Udo 1927- ... 85-88
Kulukundis, Elias 1937- ... 21-24R
Kulyk Keefer, Janice 1952- ... 127
See also Keefer, Janice Kulyk
Kumar, Alok 1954- ... 142
Kumar, Dharma 1928-2001 ... 221
Kumar, (Jagdish) Krishan 1942- ... 130
Kumar, Krishna 1942- ... CANR-45
Earlier sketch in CA 109
Kumar, Satish 1933- ... 112
Kumar, Shiv K(umar) 1921- ... CANR-94
Earlier sketches in CA 9-12R, CANR-7
See also CP 7
Kumar, Udaya 1960- ... 142
Kumayama, Akihisa 1942- ... 189
Kumbel
See Hein, Piet
Kumigai, Fumie 1943- ... 175
Kumin, Maxine (Winokur) 1925- ... CANR-140
Earlier sketches in CA 1-4R, CANR-1, 21, 69, 115
See also CAAS 8
See also AITN 2
See also AMWS 4
See also ANW
See also CLC 5, 13, 28, 164
See also CP 2, 3, 4, 5, 6, 7
See also CWP
See also DA3
See also DAM POET
See also DLB 5
See also EWL 3
See also EXPP
See also MTCW 1, 2
See also MTFW 2005
See also PAB
See also PC 15
See also PFS 18
See also SATA 12
Kummel, Bernhard 1919-1980 ... 33-36R
Kummerly, Walter
See Kuemmerly, Walter
Kun, Michael (Stuart) 1962- ... 132
Kunanbaev, Abai 1845-1904 ... EWL 3

Kunce, Joseph T(yree) 1928- 41-44R
Kuncewicz, Maria (Szczepanska) 1899-1989 .... CAP-1
Earlier sketch in CA 9-10
See also DLB 215
See also RGWL 3
Kuncewiczowa, Maria
See Kuncewicz, Maria (Szczepanska)
Kunda, Gideon 1952- 141
Kundahl, George G. 1940- 214
Kundera, Milan 1929- CANR-144
Earlier sketches in CA 85-88, CANR-19, 52, 74
See also AAYA 2, 62
See also BPFB 2
See also CDWLB 4
See also CLC 4, 9, 19, 32, 68, 115, 135
See also CWW 2
See also DA3
See also DAM NOV
See also DLB 232
See also EW 13
See also EWL 3
See also MTCW 1, 2
See also MTFW 2005
See also NFS 18
See also RGSF 2
See also RGWL 3
See also SSC 24
See also SSFS 10
Kundsin, Ruth Blumfeld 1916- 106
Kunen, James Simon 1948- 25-28R
Kunene, Mazisi (Raymond) 1930- CANR-81
Earlier sketch in CA 125
See also BW 1, 3
See also CLC 85
See also CP 1, 7
See also DLB 117
Kuner, M(ildred) C(hristophe) 1922- 41-44R
Kunert, Guenter 1929- 178
See also Kunert, Gunter
See also DLB 75
Kunert, Gunter
See Kunert, Guenter
See also CWW 2
See also EWL 3
Kung, Hans
See Kung, Hans
See also CLC 130
Kung, Hans 1928- CANR-134
Earlier sketches in CA 53-56, CANR-66
See also Kung, Hans
See also MTCW 1, 2
See also MTFW 2005
Kung, Shien Woo 1905- 1-4R
Kunhappa, Murkot 1905- 69-72
Kunhardt, Dorothy (Meserve) 1901-1979 ... 107
Obituary 93-96
See also MAICYA 2
See also SATA 53
See also SATA-Obit 22
Kunhardt, Edith 1937- 134
See also SATA 67
Kunhardt, Philip B(radish) Jr. 1928- .. CANR-37
Earlier sketch in CA 85-88
Kunhi Krishnan, T(aramal) V(anmeri) 1919- 61-64
Kuni, Ibrahim al- 1948- .... EWL 3
Kuniczak, W(ieslaw) S(tanislaw) 1930- CANR-42
Earlier sketch in CA 85-88
Kuniholm, Bruce Robellet 1942- CANR-27
Earlier sketch in CA 93-96
Kuniholm, Whitney 1954- 112
Kunikida, Tetsuo
See Kunikida Doppo
Kunikida Doppo 1869(?)-1908
See Doppo, Kunikida
See also DLB 180
See also EWL 3
Kunikida Tetsuo
See Kunikida Doppo
Kunin, Madeleine May 1933- 93-96
Kunin, Richard A(llen) 1932- 107
Kunin, Seth Daniel 194
Kunitz, Joshua 1896(?)-1980
Obituary 97-100
Kunitz, Stanley (Jasspon) 1905- CANR-98
Earlier sketches in CA 41-44R, CANR-26, 57
Interview in CANR-26
See also AMWS 3
See also CLC 6, 11, 14, 148
See also CP 1, 2, 3, 4, 5, 6, 7
See also DA3
See also DLB 48
See also MAL 5
See also MTCW 1, 2
See also MTFW 2005
See also PC 19
See also PFS 11
See also RGAL 4
Kunjufu, Jawanza 1953- .... SATA 73
Kunjufu, Johari M. Amini 1935- 41-44R
See also Amini, Johari M.
See also BW 1
Kunkel, Francis L(eo) 1921- 45-48
Kunkel, H(arriott) O. 1922- 202
Kunnes, Richard 1941- 33-36R
Kuno, Susumu 1933- 41-44R
Kunreuther, Howard Charles 1938- .. CANR-37
Earlier sketch in CA 25-28R
Kunst, David W(illiam) 1939- 85-88
Kunstel, Marcia 182
Kunstler, James Howard 1948- CANR-114
Earlier sketches in CA 101, CANR-18
Kunstler, Morton
See Kuenstler, Morton
Kunstler, William M(oses) 1919-1995 . CANR-5
Obituary 149
Earlier sketch in CA 9-12R
Interview in CANR-5
Kuntz, J(ohn) Kenneth 1934- CANR-9
Earlier sketch in CA 21-24R
Kuntz, J(ohn) L. 1947- 155
See also SATA 91
Kuntz, Jerry 1956- 202
See also SATA 133
Kuntz, Kenneth A. 1916-1984 .... 1-4R
Kuntz, Paul G. 1915- 5-8R
Kuntzleman, Charles T(homas) 1940- CANR-22
Earlier sketches in CA 57-60, CANR-7
Kunz, Kathleen 1935- 143
Kunz, Marji 1939(?)-1979
Obituary 89-92
Kunz, Phillip Ray 1936- CANR-41
Earlier sketches in CA 37-40R, CANR-19
Kunz, Roxane (Brown) 1932- 121
See also SATA-Brief 53
Kunz, Virginia B(rainard) 1921- CANR-37
Earlier sketch in CA 21-24R
Kunze, Michael 1943- 169
Kunze, Reiner 1933- 93-96
See also CLC 10
See also CWW 2
See also DLB 75
See also EWL 3
Kunzle, David Mark 1936- CANR-36
Earlier sketches in CA 53-56, CANR-5
Kunzru, Hari 1971(?)- 204
Kunzur, Sheela
See Geis, Richard E(rwin)
Kuo, Helena 1911-1999 .... DLB 312
Kuo, J. David 1968- 217
Kuo, Mo-Jo 1892-1978
Obituary 77-80
See also EWL 3
Kuo, Pao Kun 1939-2002 218
See also CD 5, 6
Kuo, Ping-chia 1908- 5-8R
Kuo, Shirley W. Y. 1930- 115
Kuo, Ting-yee 1904(?)-1975
Obituary 61-64
Kup, Alexander Peter 1924- CANR-9
Earlier sketch in CA 13-16R
Kup, Karl 1903-1981
Obituary 104
Kupchan, Charles A. 227
Kupcinet, Irv(ing) 1912-2003 166
Kuper, Adam (Jonathan) 1941- CANR-94
Earlier sketches in CA 103, CANR-20, 42
Kuper, Hilda Beemer 1911-1992 .... CANR-2
Earlier sketch in CA 1-4R
Kuper, Jack 1932- 21-24R
Kuper, Jenny Riva 1948- 175
Kuper, Leo 1908-1994 .... CANR-35
Obituary 145
Earlier sketches in CA 21-24R, CANR-11
Kuper, Peter 1958- 227
See also AAYA 67
Kuper, Yuri
See Kuperman, Yuri
Kuperman, Yuri 1940- 102
Kupfer, Allen C(onrad) 231
Kupfer, Fern 1946- CANR-36
Earlier sketch in CA 106
Kupferberg, Audrey E. 1949- 218
Kupferberg, Feiwel 1946- 235
Kupferberg, Herbert 1918-2001 .... 29-32R
Obituary 193
See also SATA 19
Kupferberg, Naphtali 1923- CANR-13
Earlier sketch in CA 21-24R
See also Kupferberg, Tuli
Kupferberg, Tuli
See Kupferberg, Naphtali
See also DLB 16
Kupperman, Joel J. 1936- CANR-36
Earlier sketch in CA 33-36R
Kupperman, Karen Ordahl 1939- ... CANR-106
Earlier sketch in CA 111
Kuppner, Frank 1951- CANR-83
Earlier sketch in CA 153
See also CP 7
Kuprin, Aleksander Ivanovich 1870-1938 ... 182
Brief entry 104
See also Kuprin, Aleksandr Ivanovich and Kuprin, Alexandr Ivanovich
See also TCLC 5
Kuprin, Aleksandr Ivanovich
See Kuprin, Aleksander Ivanovich
See also DLB 295
Kuprin, Alexandr Ivanovich
See Kuprin, Aleksander Ivanovich
See also EWL 3
Kuraev, Mikhail Nikolaevich 1939- .... DLB 285
Kurahashi, Yumiko 1935- 184
See also Kurahashi Yumiko
See also MJW
Kurahashi Yumiko
See Kurahashi, Yumiko
See also DLB 182
Kuralt, Charles (Bishop) 1934-1997 .... CANR-138
Obituary 159
Earlier sketches in CA 89-92, CANR-43
See also CSW
Kurath, Gertrude Prokosch 1903-1992 .. 13-16R
Kurath, Hans 1891-1992 .... 9-12R
Kuratomi, Chizuko 1939- CANR-10
Earlier sketch in CA 21-24R
See also CLR 32
See also SATA 12
Kurczok, Belinda 1978- .... SATA 121
Kurdi, Abdulrahman Abdulkadir 1941- CANR-86
Earlier sketch in CA 133
Kurdsen, Stephen
See Noon, Brian
Kureishi, Hanif 1954- CANR-113
Earlier sketch in CA 139
See also BRWS 11
See also CBD
See also CD 5, 6
See also CLC 64, 135
See also CN 6, 7
See also DC 26
See also DLB 194, 245
See also GLL 2
See also IDFW 4
See also WLIT 4
See also WWE 1
Kurelek, William 1927-1977 .... CANR-85
Earlier sketches in CA 49-52, CANR-3
See also CCA 1
See also CLR 2
See also CWRI 5
See also JRDA
See also MAICYA 1, 2
See also SATA 8
See also SATA-Obit 27
Kuri, Yoji 1928- .... IDFW 3, 4
Kurian, George 1928- 107
See also SATA 65
Kurian, George Thomas 1931- 175
Kuriansky, Judith (Anne Brodsky) 1947- 132
Kurien, C(hristopher) T(homas) 1931- CANR-13
Earlier sketch in CA 33-36R
Kurihara, Kenneth Kenkichi 1910-1972 .... CANR-6
Obituary 37-40R
Earlier sketch in CA 1-4R
Kurihara, Sadako 1913- .... MJW
Kurjian, Judi(th M.) 1944- .... SATA 127
Kurkjian, Stephen A(noosh) 1943- 129
Brief entry 116
Kurkov, Andrei 1961- 215
Kurkul, Edward 1916-1997 .... 25-28R
Kurland, Geoffrey 1947- 216
Kurland, Gerald 1942- CANR-14
Earlier sketch in CA 41-44R
See also SATA 13
Kurland, Michael (Joseph) 1938- CANR-83
Earlier sketches in CA 61-64, CANR-11
See also SATA 48, 118
See also SFW 4
Kurland, Philip B. 1921-1996 .... CANR-7
Obituary 151
Earlier sketch in CA 9-12R
Kurlansky, Mark 1948- CANR-108
Earlier sketch in CA 163
Kurman, George 1942- 53-56
Kurnitz, Harry 1909-1968
Obituary 25-28R
Kuroda, Yasumasa 1931- CANR-93
Earlier sketches in CA 45-48, CANR-35
Kuroi, Ken 1947- .... SATA 120
Kurokawa, Mitsuhiro 1954- 152
See also SATA 88
Kuropas, Myron B(ohdon) 1932- 45-48
Kurosawa, Akira 1910-1998 .... CANR-46
Obituary 170
Earlier sketch in CA 101
See also AAYA 11, 64
See also CLC 16, 119
See also DAM MULT
Kurosawa, Susan 188
Kurowski, Eugeniusz
See Dobraczynski, Jan
Kurrik, Maire Jaanus 1940- 101
Kursh, Charlotte Olmsted 1912- 9-12R
Kursh, Harry 1919- 9-12R
Kurson, Ken 1969- 216
Kurson, Robert 1963(?)- 229
Kurten, Bjorn (Olof) 1924-1988 .... CANR-56
Earlier sketches in CA 25-28R, CANR-20
See also SATA 64
Kurth, Peter 1953- CANR-114
Earlier sketch in CA 139
Kurth-Voigt, Lieselotte E. 1923-
Brief entry 110
Kurtis, Arlene Harris 1927- 25-28R
Kurtis, Bill
See Kurtis, William Horton
Kurtis, William Horton 1940- 133
Brief entry 124
Interview in CA-133
Kurtz, C(larence) Gordon 1902-1987 65-68
Kurtz, David L(ee) 1941- 41-44R
Kurtz, Don 1951- 152
Kurtz, Donn M. II 168
Kurtz, Donna Carol 1943- 93-96
Kurtz, Ernest 1935- 112
Kurtz, Harold 1913- 17-20R
Kurtz, Howard 1953- 141
Kurtz, Irma 1935- 118
Kurtz, Jane 1952- 155
See also SATA 91, 139
Kurtz, Katherine (Irene) 1944- CANR-106
Earlier sketches in CA 29-32R, CANR-25, 50, 85
See also AAYA 21
See also BPFB 2
See also FANT
See also SATA 76, 126
See also SFW 4
See also SUFW 2
Kurtz, Kenneth H(assett) 1928- 33-36R
Kurtz, Lester R. 1949- 126
Kurtz, Maurice 1913- 214
Kurtz, Michael L(ouis) 1941- CANR-82
Earlier sketches in CA 107, CANR-36
Kurtz, Paul 1925- CANR-25
Earlier sketches in CA 13-16R, CANR-5
Kurtz, Stephen G(uild) 1926- 9-12R
Kurtz, Sylvie 232
Kurtzman, Harvey 1924-1993 216
Kurtzman, Jeffrey G(ordon) 1940- 110
Kurtzman, Joel 1947- CANR-30
Earlier sketch in CA 29-32R
Kurtz-Phelan, James L(anham) 1946- 49-52
Kuryluk, Ewa 1946- 135
Kurys, Diane 1949- CANR-59
Earlier sketch in CA 125
Kurz, Artur R.
See Scortia, Thomas N(icholas)
Kurz, Isolde 1853-1944 183
See also DLB 66
Kurz, Mordecai 1934- CANR-12
Earlier sketch in CA 29-32R
Kurz, Otto 1908-1975 107
Obituary 104
Kurz, Paul Konrad 1927- CANR-48
Earlier sketch in CA 29-32R
Kurz, Ron 1940- CANR-14
Earlier sketch in CA 81-84
Kurz, Rudolf 1952- .... SATA 95
Kurzer, Siegmund F. 1907(?)-1973
Obituary 104
Kurzke, Hermann 1943- 194
Kurzman, Dan 1927- CANR-116
Earlier sketches in CA 69-72, CANR-14, 32
Kurzman, Paul A(lfred) 1938- CANR-13
Earlier sketch in CA 33-36R
Kurzweg, Bernhard F. 1926- 17-20R
Kurzweil, Allen 1960- CANR-109
Earlier sketch in CA 168
Kurzweil, Arthur 1951- 97-100
Kurzweil, Edith 110
Kurzweil, Raymond (C.) 1948- 134
Kurzweil, Zvi Erich 1911-1992 .... CANR-36
Earlier sketches in CAP-1, CA 11-12
Kurzydlowski, Krzysztof Jan 1954- 155
Kusan, Ivan 1933- CANR-6
Earlier sketch in CA 9-12R
Ku Sang 1919- .... CWW 2
Kusano Shimpei 1903-1988 167
Kusch, Robert 1934- 206
Kusche, Larry
See Kusche, Lawrence David
Kusche, Lawrence David 1940- CANR-5
Earlier sketch in CA 53-56
Kusenberg, Kurt 1904-1983 183
See also DLB 69
Kushchevsky, Ivan Afanas'evich 1847-1876 .... DLB 238
Kushel, Gerald 1930- CANR-11
Earlier sketch in CA 25-28R
Kushigian, Julia A. 1950- 143
Kushlan, James A. 1947- 142
Kushner, Aleksandr (Semenovich) 1936- .... CWW 2
Kushner, Carol 1950- 133
Kushner, David 1968- 224
Kushner, David Z(arkeri) 1935- 53-56
Kushner, Donn (J.) 1927- CANR-35
Earlier sketch in CA 113
See also CLR 55
See also CWRI 5
See also SATA 52
Kushner, Ellen (Ruth) 1955- CANR-141
Earlier sketch in CA 155
See also FANT
See also SATA 98
Kushner, Eve 1968- CANR-141
Earlier sketch in CA 174
Kushner, Harold S(amuel) 1935- CANR-84
Earlier sketches in CA 107, CANR-36
See also BEST 90:2
Kushner, Harvey W(olf) 1941- CANR-142
Earlier sketch in CA 110
Kushner, Howard I(rvin) 1943- CANR-91
Earlier sketch in CA 81-84
Kushner, Irving 1929- 119
Kushner, James A(lan) 1945- CANR-75
Earlier sketch in CA 132
Kushner, Jill Menkes 1951- .... SATA 62
Kushner, Lawrence 1943- CANR-109
Earlier sketch in CA 150
See also SATA 83
Kushner, Malcolm 1952- 134
Kushner, Rose 1929-1990 61-64
Obituary 130
Kushner, Sam 1915(?)-1987
Obituary 123
Kushner, Tony 1956- CANR-130
Earlier sketches in CA 144, CANR-74
See also AAYA 61
See also AMWS 9
See also CAD
See also CD 5, 6
See also CLC 81, 203
See also DA3
See also DAM DRAM
See also DC 10
See also DFS 5
See also DLB 228
See also EWL 3
See also GLL 1
See also LAIT 5
See also MAL 5
See also MTCW 2
See also MTFW 2005
See also RGAL 4
See also SATA 160
Kushnick, Louis 1938- 216

Kusin, Vladimir V(ictor) 1929- CANR-13
  Earlier sketch in CA 33-36R
Kuske, Martin 1940- 97-100
Kuskin, Karla (Seidman) 1932- CANR-136
  Earlier sketches in CA 1-4R, CANR-4, 22, 41
  See also CLR 4
  See also CWRI 5
  See also MAICYA 1, 2
  See also SAAS 3
  See also SATA 2, 68, 111
Kuslan, Louis I(saac) 1922- CANR-1
  Earlier sketch in CA 45-48
Kusmer, Kenneth L(eslie) 1945- CANR-114
  Earlier sketch in CA 102
Kusnet, David 1951- 160
Kusnick, Barry A. 1910- CANR-37
  Earlier sketch in CA 53-56
Kusniewicz, Andrzej 1904-1993 107
Kuspit, Donald B(urton) 1935- CANR-137
  Earlier sketches in CA 97-100, CANR-37
Kussmaul, Ann (Sturm) 1945- 110
Kusterer, Ken(neth) C. 1945- 190
Kustermeir, Rudolf 1893(?)-1977
  Obituary 73-76
Kustow, Michael (David) 1939-
  Brief entry 106
Kusturica, Emir 1955- 156
Kusugak, Michael (Arvaarluk) 1948- 215
  See also CWRI 5
  See also SATA 143
Kusz, Natalie 1962- 141
Kutash, Samuel Benjamin
  1912-1979 .... CANR-2
  Earlier sketch in CA 1-4R
Kutchins, Herb 218
Kuten, Jay 1935-
  Brief entry 108
Kuter, Laurence S(herman) 1905-1979
  Obituary 113
Kutler, Laurence 1953- 142
Kutler, Stanley I. 1934- CANR-128
  Earlier sketches in CA 21-24R, CANR-36
Kutner, Luis 1908-1993 109
  Obituary 140
Kutner, Nanette 1906(?)-1962 .... 1-4R
Kutsche, Paul 1927- 114
Kutscher, Charles L(awrence) 1936- 77-80
Kutsky, Roman Joseph 1922-
  Brief entry 110
Kuttna, Mari 1934-1983
  Obituary 109
Kuttner, Henry 1915-1958 157
  Brief entry 107
  See also DLB 8
  See also FANT
  See also SCFW 1, 2
  See also SFW 4
  See also TCLC 10
Kuttner, Paul 1922- CANR-56
  Earlier sketches in CA 77-80, CANR-13, 30
  See also SATA 18
Kuttner, Robert (Louis) 1943- CANR-134
  Earlier sketch in CA 168
Kuttner, Sharland Trotter
  See Trotter, Sharland
Kutty, Madhavi
  See Das, Kamala
Kutz, LeRoy M. 1922- 13-16R
Kutza, Elizabeth Ann 111
Kuusisto, Stephen 1955- 234
Kuvshinoff, Boris W. 1922- 146
Kuwayama, George 1925- CANR-39
  Earlier sketch in CA 116
Kuyck, A. L. van
  See Greshoff, Jan
Kuyk, Dirk (A., Jr.) 1934- 135
Kuykendall, Eleanor 1938-
  Brief entry 109
Kuykendall, Jack L(awrence) 1940- 57-60
Kuykendall, Ralph S(impson) 1885-1963 .. 1-4R
Kuyper, Sjoerd 1952- 202
Kuyten, Anton
  See Quintana, Anton
Kuzio, Taras 205
Kuzma, Greg 1944- CANR-70
  Earlier sketch in CA 33-36R
  See also CLC 7
Kuzma, Kay 1941- CANR-23
  Earlier sketch in CA 106
  See also SATA 39
Kuzmich, Natalie 1932- 127
Kuzmin, Mikhail (Alekseevich)
  1872(?)-1936 170
  See also DLB 295
  See also EWL 3
  See also TCLC 40
Kuzneski, Chris 1969- 217
Kuznets, Simon (Smith) 1901-1985 158
  Obituary 116
  Brief entry 108
Kuznetsov, (Edward) 1939- CANR-39
  Earlier sketch in CA 57-60
Kuznetsov, Anatoli(i) 1929-1979
  Obituary 89-92
  See also DLB 299, 302
Kuznetsov, Nickolaj 1955- 158
Kuzniewski, Anthony J(oseph) 1945- 107
Kuzwayo, Ellen (Kate) 1914- 134
Kvale, Velma R(uth) 1898-1979 .... CAP-2
  Earlier sketch in CA 25-28
  See also SATA 8
Kvam, Wayne (Eugene) 1938- 45-48
Kvasnicka, Robert M(ichael) 1935- 97-100
Kvasnosky, Laura McGee 1951- CANR-121
  Earlier sketch in CA 159
  See also SATA 93, 142
Kvistad, Gregg O(wen) 205
Kvitka, Laryssa Kosach 1871-1913
  See Ukrayinka, Lesya
Kwa, Lydia 1959- 220
Kwabena Nketia, J. H.
  See Nketia, J(oseph) H(anson) Kwabena
Kwakye, Benjamin 1967- CANR-140
  Earlier sketch in CA 174
Kwamena-Poh, M(ichael Albert) 1932- 132
Kwan, Kian M(oon) 1929- 17-20R
Kwan, Michael David 1934-2001 201
Kwan, Michelle (Wing) 1980- 238
Kwant, R. C.
  See Kwant, Remigius C(ornelis)
Kwant, Remigius C(ornelis) 1918- CANR-18
  Earlier sketches in CA 9-12R, CANR-3
Kwant, Remy C.
  See Kwant, Remigius C(ornelis)
Kwanten, Luc 1944- 93-96
Kwasney, Michelle D. 1960- 238
  See also SATA 162
Kwavnick, David 1940- 45-48
Kweder, Adele 1910-1979 .... 5-8R
Kweder, David James 1905-1991 .... 5-8R
Kweit, Robert W(illiam) 1946- CANR-37
  Earlier sketch in CA 112
Kwiatkowska, Hanna Yaxa 1907(?)-1980
  Obituary 97-100
Kwitny, Jonathan 1941-1998 .... CANR-92
  Obituary 172
  Earlier sketches in CA 49-52, CANR-1, 23
Kwolek, Constance
  See Porcari, Constance Kwolek
Kwon, O. Yul 1936- 234
Kwong, Julia C. 1946- 171
Kwong, Peter 173
Kyburg, Henry (Guy) E(ly), Jr. 1928- . CANR-36
  Earlier sketches in CA 5-8R, CANR-8
Kyd, Thomas
  See Harbage, Alfred (Bennett)
Kyd, Thomas 1558-1594 .... BRW 1
  See also DAM DRAM
  See also DC 3
  See also DFS 21
  See also DLB 62
  See also IDTP
  See also LMFS 1
  See also RGEL 2
  See also TEA
  See also WLIT 3
Kydd, Sam(uel) 1917-1982 109
  Obituary 106
Kyemba, Henry 1939- 81-84
Kyes, Robert L(ange) 1933- CANR-37
  Earlier sketch in CA 49-52
Kyffin, Maurice 1560(?)-1598 .... DLB 136
Kyger, Joanne (Elizabeth) 1934- CANR-140
  Earlier sketches in CA 101, CANR-17, 40
  See also CAAS 16
  See also BG 1:3
  See also CP 1, 2, 3, 4, 5, 6, 7
  See also CWP
  See also DLB 16
  See also PFS 23
Kyle, Barbara J. 223
Kyle, Benjamin
  See Gottfried, Theodore Mark
Kyle, Duncan
  See Broxholme, John Franklin
Kyle, Elisabeth
  See Dunlop, Agnes M. R.
  See also BYA 1
Kyle, Keith 1925- CANR-99
  Earlier sketch in CA 137
Kyle, Marlaine
  See Hager, Jean
Kyle, Molly M. 1959- 146
Kyle, Richard (G.) 1938- 177
Kyle, Robert
  See Terrall, Robert
Kyle, Sefton
  See Vickers, Roy C.
Kyle, Stephen
  See Kyle, Barbara J.
Kyle, Susan (Spaeth) 1946- CANR-140
  Earlier sketch in CA 141
  See also RHW
Kyle, Susan S.
  See Kyle, Susan (Spaeth)
Kyme, Ernest Hector 1906- 103
Kynaston, David 173
Kyndrup, Morten 1952- 140
Kyne, Peter B(ernard) 1880-1957 182
  See also DLB 78
  See also TCWW 1, 2
Kynett, Harold Havelock 1889-1973
  Obituary 106
Kyogoku Tamekane 1254-1332 .... DLB 203
Kyoka
  See Izumi, Kyoka
  See also MJW
Kyper, Frank 1940- 85-88
Kyprianos, Iossif
  See Samarakis, Antonis
Kyre, Joan Randolph 1935- 25-28R
Kyre, Martin (Theodore, Jr.) 1928- 25-28R
Kyrklund, Paul Wilhelm 1921-
  See Kyrklund, Willy
Kyrklund, Willy 1921-
  See Kyrklund, Paul Wilhelm
  See also DLB 257
Kyrle, Roger (Ernie) Money
  See Money-Kyrle, Roger (Ernie)
Kysar, Robert (Dean) 1934- CANR-22
  Earlier sketch in CA 69-72
Kyselka, Will 1921- 106
Kyte, Kathy S. 1946- .... SATA 50
  See also SATA-Brief 44
Kytle, Elizabeth 112
Kytle, Ray(mond) 1941- 29-32R
Kyvig, David E(dward) 1944- CANR-82
  Earlier sketches in CA 101, CANR-36

L

L., Barry
  See Longyear, Barry B(rookes)
L., Jimmy Boy
  See Ferrara, Abel
L. S.
  See Stephen, Sir Leslie
L., Tommy
  See Lorkowski, Thomas V(incent)
Laake, Deborah 1954(?)-2000 167
Layamon
  See Layamon
  See also DLB 146
La-Anyane, Seth 1922- 9-12R
Laas, Virginia J(eans) 1943- 139
Laas, William M. 1910(?)-1975
  Obituary 61-64
Laban, Rudolf von 1879-1958 209
Laband, John (Paul Clow) 1947- 145
Labanyi, Jo 1946- CANR-87
  Earlier sketch in CA 154
LaBar, Tom 1937- 25-28R
Labaree, Benjamin Woods 1927- CANR-6
  Earlier sketch in CA 9-12R
Labaree, Leonard W(oods) 1897-1980 73-76
  Obituary 97-100
Labarge, Margaret Wade 1916- CANR-11
  Earlier sketch in CA 25-28R
LaBarge, William Howard 1948- 116
La Barr, Creighton
  See von Block, Bela W(illiam)
La Barre, Weston 1911-1996 .... CANR-22
  Obituary 171
  Earlier sketch in CA 1-4R
LaBastille, Anne 1938- CANR-8
  Earlier sketch in CA 57-60
  See also AMWS 10
  See also ANW
L'Abate, Luciano 1928- 111
Labatut, Jean 1899-1986
  Obituary 121
Labbe, Armand J(oseph) 1944-2005 185
  Obituary 238
Labbe, John T. CANR-17
  Earlier sketch in CA 97-100
La Beau, Dennis (George) 1941- 97-100
LaBelle, Maurice Marc 1939- 113
Laber, Jeri (Lidsky) 1931- CANR-122
  Earlier sketches in CA 65-68, CANR-9
Laberge, Albert 1871-1960 189
  See also CCA 1
  See also DLB 68
La Berge, Ann F. 1944- 143
Laberge, Marie 1950- 177
  See also DLB 60
Labiche, Eugene 1815-1888 .... DLB 192
  See also GFL 1789 to the Present
LaBier, Douglas 1944- 124
Labin, Suzanne (Devoyon)
  1913-2001 .... CANR-32
  Earlier sketches in CA 29-32R, CANR-14
Labiner, Norah 182
Labinger, Jay A(lan) 1947- 219
Laboda, Lawrence R. 1952- 150
La Boetie, Etienne de
  1530-1563 .... GFL Beginnings to 1789
Labor, Earle G. 1928- 21-24R
LaBorde, Rene
  See Neuffer, Irene LaBorde
Laborteaux, Patrick
  See Labyorteaux, Patrick
Labounsky, Ann 1939- 205
Labovitz, I(srael) M(ilton) 1907-1992 .... 5-8R
  Obituary 174
Labovitz, Trudy A. 1954- 207
Labowitz, Shoni 181
Labrador, James
  See Hamel Peifer, Kathleen
Labrador, Judy
  See Hamel Peifer, Kathleen
LaBrecque, Claude X. 85-88
La Bree, Clifton 1933- 207
La Brie, Henry George III 1946- 57-60
Labrie, Roger P(aul) 1952- 113
Labrie, Ross (E.) 1936- CANR-130
  Earlier sketch in CA 171
Labriola, Jerry 218
Labro, Philippe (Christian) 1936- 167
  See also EWL 3
Labroca, Mario 1897(?)-1973
  Obituary 41-44R
LaBrot, Matthew 1988(?)- 229
Labrunie, Gerard
  See Nerval, Gerard de
La Bruyere, Jean de 1645-1696 .... DLB 268
  See also EW 3
  See also GFL Beginnings to 1789
Labus, Marta Haake 1943- 109
Labuta, Joseph A(nthony) 1931- 57-60
Labuz, Ronald M. 1953- 123
Labyorteaux, Patrick 1965- 232
Labys, Walter C(arl) 1937- CANR-86
  Earlier sketches in CA 73-76, CANR-34
La Calprenede, Gautier de Costes
  1610(?)-1663 .... DLB 268
  See also GFL Beginnings to 1789
La Camera, Anthony 1914(?)-1984
  Obituary 114
Lacan, Jacques (Marie Emile) 1901-1981 ... 121
  Obituary 104
  See also CLC 75
  See also DLB 296
  See also EWL 3
  See also TWA
LaCapra, Dominick 1939- CANR-52
  Earlier sketches in CA 109, CANR-28
La Capria, Raffaele 1922- CANR-117
  Earlier sketches in CA 9-12R, CANR-4
  See also DLB 196
Lacarriere, Jacques 1925-
  Brief entry 125
La Casce, Steward 1935- 37-40R
Laccetti, (Silvio) Richard 1941- CANR-13
  Earlier sketch in CA 37-40R
Lace, O(live) Jessie 1906- 17-20R
Lace, William W. 1942- 196
  See also SATA 126
Lacerda, Carlos 1914-1977
  Obituary 69-72
Lacey, A(lan) R(obert) 1926- 112
Lacey, Archie L(ouis) 1923- 9-12R
Lacey, Douglas R(aymond) 1913-1973 .. 29-32R
  Obituary 134
Lacey, Earnest Edward 1939- 163
Lacey, Elizabeth A. 1954- 132
Lacey, Jeannette F. 77-80
Lacey, John
  See Alexander, Boyd
Lacey, Louise 1940- 81-84
Lacey, Nicola 1958- CANR-86
  Earlier sketch in CA 130
Lacey, Paul A. 1934- 41-44R
Lacey, Peter 1929-1995 .... 21-24R
Lacey, Robert 1944- CANR-127
  Earlier sketches in CA 33-36R, CANR-16, 43
  Interview in CANR-16
Lacey, W(alter) K(irkpatrick) 1921- ... CANR-11
  Earlier sketch in CA 25-28R
Lach, Donald F(rederick) 1917-2000 102
  Obituary 192
La Chapelle, Mary 1955- 132
La Charite, Virginia Anding 1937- 29-32R
La Chaussee, Pierre-Claude Nivelle de
  See Nivelle de la Chaussee, Pierre-Claude
  See also DLB 313
Lachenbruch, David 1921-1996 89-92
  Obituary 154
Lachenmeyer, Charles W(illiam) 1943- 105
Lachman, Barbara 1938- CANR-121
  Earlier sketch in CA 163
Lachman, Marvin 166
Lachman, Seymour P. 1933- 154
Lachmann, Frank M(ichael) 1929- 103
Lachner, Dorothea
  See Knobloch, Dorothea
Lachnit, Carrolll 176
Lachs, John 1934- 21-24R
Lack, David Lambert 1910-1973 .... CANR-4
  Obituary 89-92
  Earlier sketch in CA 5-8R
Lack, Paul D. 1944- 140
Lack, Simon
  See Strunge, Michael
Lackey, Douglas Paul 1945- 103
Lackey, Kris 1953- 162
Lackey, Mercedes R(itchie) 1950- CANR-97
  Earlier sketches in CA 126, CANR-51
  See also AAYA 13
  See also BPFB 2
  See also FANT
  See also SATA 81, 127
  See also SUFW 2
  See also YAW
Lacki, Al Francis 1930- 196
Lackmann, Ron(ald) 1934- CANR-130
  Earlier sketches in CA 29-32R, CANR-13
Lackner, Stephan Ernest 1910-2000 .. CANR-15
  Earlier sketch in CA 29-32R
Lacks, Cecilia 1945- 69-72
Lacks, Cissy
  See Lacks, Cecilia
Lacks, Roslyn 1933- 102
La Clair, Earl E(dward) 1916-1975 ...... 21-24R
  Obituary 176
La Claustra, Vera Berneicia (Derrick)
  1903-1995 53-56
  Obituary 198
Laclos, Pierre-Ambroise Francois
  1741-1803 .... DLB 313
  See also EW 4
  See also GFL Beginnings to 1789
  See also RGWL 2, 3
LaCocque, Andre (Marie) 1927- CANR-31
  Earlier sketch in CA 112
Lacocque, Pierre-Emmanuel 1952- 112
Lacoe, Addie .... SATA 78
La Colere, Francois
  See Aragon, Louis
Lacolere, Francois
  See Aragon, Louis
Lacombe, Gabriel 1905(?)-1973
  Obituary 37-40R
Lacome, Julie 1961- .... SATA 80
LaCoste, Lilly
  See Harris, Yvonne L.
Lacoste, Paul 1923- CANR-1
  Earlier sketch in CA 45-48
La Coste, Warren 1941- 141
Lacouture, Jean Marie Gerard
  1921- CANR-92
  Earlier sketches in CA 101, CANR-43
Lacretelle, Jacques de
  See Lacretelle, Jacques
Lacretelle, Jacques de 1888-1985 .... DLB 65
  See also GFL 1789 to the Present

La Croix, I(sobyl) F. 1933- ... 142
Lacroix, Louise
See Swift, Helen C(ecilia)
LaCroix, Mary 1937- ... CANR-22
Earlier sketch in CA 106
Lacroix, Ramon
See McKeag, Ernest L(ionel)
LaCrosse, E. Robert 1937- ... 33-36R
Lacy, A(lexander) D(acre) 1894-1969 ... CAP-2
Earlier sketch in CA 25-28
Lacy, Allen 1935- ... CANR-97
Earlier sketch in CA 159
Lacy, Charles
See Hippisley Coxe, Antony D(acres)
Lacy, Creighton (Boutelle) 1919- ... 13-16R
Lacy, Dan (Mabry) 1914-2001 ... 37-40R
Obituary ... 195
Lacy, Donald Charles 1933- ... CANR-59
Earlier sketch in CA 105
Lacy, Ed 1911-1968 ... AMWS 15
See also CMW 4
See also DLB 226
Lacy, Eric Russell 1933- ... 17-20R
Lacy, Gene M(elvin) 1934- ... 53-56
Lacy, Gerald M(orris) 1940- ... 77-80
Lacy, Leslie Alexander 1937- ... 33-36R
See also SATA 6
Lacy, Mary Lou (Pannill) 1914-1984 ... 17-20R
Lacy, Norris J(oiner) 1940- ... CANR-23
Earlier sketches in CA 61-64, CANR-8
Lacy, Sam(uel Harold) 1903-2003 ... 192
Obituary ... 216
See also DLB 171
Lacy, Tira
See Estrada, Rita Clay
Ladany, L.
See Ladany, Laszlo
Ladany, Laszlo 1914-1990
Obituary ... 132
Ladas, Alice Kahn ... 129
Ladas, Gerasimos 1937- ... 53-56
Ladas, Stephen P(ericles) 1898-1976 ... 102
Ladd, Brian 1957- ... 137
Ladd, Bruce 1936- ... 25-28R
Ladd, Cheryl (Jean) 1951- ... 174
See also SATA 113
Ladd, Edward T(aylor) 1918-1973 ... CANR-4
Earlier sketch in CA 5-8R
Ladd, Everett Carll, (Jr.) 1937-1999 ... CANR-88
Obituary ... 188
Earlier sketches in CA 25-28R, CANR-11
Ladd, George E(ldon) 1911-1982 ... CANR-5
Earlier sketch in CA 5-8R
Ladd, Helen F. 1945- ... 111
Ladd, Jerrold J. 1970- ... 145
Ladd, John 1917- ... 81-84
Ladd, Joseph Brown 1764-1786 ... DLB 37
Ladd, Justin
See Reasoner, James M(orris)
Ladd, Linda ... 211
Ladd, Louise 1943- ... 154
See also SATA 97
Ladd, Tony 1942- ... 187
Ladd, Veronica
See Miner, Jane Claypool
Ladd-Taylor, Molly ... 171
Ladell, John L. 1924- ... 147
Laden, Nina 1962- ... SATA 85, 148
Ladenson, Alex 1907- ... 17-20R
Ladenson, Robert Franklin 1943- ... 113
Lader, Lawrence 1919- ... CANR-2
Earlier sketch in CA 1-4R
See also SATA 6
Laderman, Carol (C.) ... CANR-47
Earlier sketch in CA 121
La Deshabilleuse
See Simenon, Georges (Jacques Christian)
Ladman, Jerry R. 1935- ... 128
Ladner, Joyce A(nn) 1943- ... 124
Brief entry ... 122
See also BW 2
Ladner, Kurt
See DeMille, Nelson (Richard)
Ladner, Mildred D. 1918- ... 97-100
Lado, Robert 1915- ... CANR-7
Earlier sketch in CA 9-12R
LaDoux, Rita C. 1951- ... SATA 74
Ladow, Beth ... 203
La Due, William J. 1928- ... 206
LaDuke, Betty 1933- ... 143
LaDuke, Winona 1959- ... CANR-100
Earlier sketch in CA 168
Ladurie, Emmanuel Le Roy
See Le Roy Ladurie, Emmanuel (Bernard)
Lady, A
See Taylor, Ann
Lady Barker
See Stewart, Mary Anne
Lady Broome
See Stewart, Mary Anne
Lady Culross
See Melville, Elizabeth
Lady Gregory
See Gregory, Lady Isabella Augusta (Persse)
Ladyman, Phyllis ... 103
Lady Masham, Dumaris Cudworth
1659-1708 ... DLB 252
Lady Mears
See Tempest, Margaret Mary
Lady of Quality, A
See Bagnold, Enid
Lady Strange
See Evans, (Jean) Cherry (Drummond)
Ladyzhensky, Oleg S. 1963- ... 230
Lael, Richard L(ee) 1946- ... 111
Laemmar, Jack W. 1909- ... 1-4R
Laemmle, Carl Sr. 1867-1939 ... IDFW 3, 4
Laemmle, Carl, Jr. 1908-1979 ... IDFW 3, 4
Laermer, Richard 1960- ... 213
Laertes, Joseph
See Saltzman, Joseph
Laestadius, Lars-Levi 1909-1982
Obituary ... 107
Laeuchli, Samuel 1924- ... CANR-4
Earlier sketch in CA 5-8R
Laevastu, Taivo 1923- ... CANR-15
Earlier sketch in CA 41-44R
LaFantasie, Glenn W(arren) 1949- ... 125
Lafarge, Albert (R.) 1963- ... 189
La Farge, Oliver (Hazard Perry)
1901-1963 ... CANR-84
Earlier sketches in CA 81-84, CANR-30
See also BYA 2
See also DLB 9
See also RGAL 4
See also SATA 19
See also TCWW 1, 2
Lafarge, Paul 1970- ... 212
La Farge, Phyllis ... 73-76
See also SATA 14
Lafarge, Rene 1902- ... CAP-2
Earlier sketch in CA 29-32
LaFargue, Michael ... 179
LaFargue, Michael ... 179
La Fargue, Michael ... 179
LaFauci, Horatio M(ichael) 1917-2000 . 33-36R
LaFavor, Carole S. ... 170
LaFaye, A(lexandria R. T.) 1970- ... CANR-141
Earlier sketches in CA 162, CANR-95
See also AAYA 44
See also BYA 16
See also SATA 105, 156
Lafayette, Carlos
See Boiles, Charles Lafayette (Jr.)
La Fayette, Marie-(Madelaine Pioche de la
Vergne) 1634-1693
See Lafayette, Marie-Madeleine
See also GFL Beginnings to 1789
See also RGWL 2, 3
Lafayette, Marie-Madeleine
See La Fayette, Marie-(Madelaine Pioche de
la Vergne)
See also DLB 268
Lafayette, Rene
See Hubbard, L(afayette) Ron(ald)
LaFeber, Walter (Fredrick) 1933- ... CANR-84
Earlier sketches in CA 9-12R, CANR-5, 48
LaFemina, Gerry 1968- ... 193
Laferriere, Daniel
See Rancour-Laferriere, Daniel
Laferriere, Dany 1953- ... 142
Laffal, Julius 1920- ... 49-52
Laffan, Kevin (Barry) 1922-2003 ... 37-40R
Obituary ... 215
See also CBD
See also CD 5, 6
Laffan, Mrs. R. S. de Courcy
See Adams, Bertha Leith
Laffeaty, Christina ... RHW
Lafferty, Perry (Francis) 1917- ... CANR-6
Earlier sketch in CA 9-12R
Lafferty, R(aphael) A(loysius)
1914-2002 ... CANR-116
Obituary ... 205
Earlier sketches in CA 57-60, CANR-12, 32
See also DLB 8
See also SFW 4
See also SUFW 1, 2
Laffin, John (Alfred Charles) 1922- ... CANR-23
Earlier sketches in CA 53-56, CANR-7
See also SATA 31
Laffont, Jean-Pierre 1935- ... 115
Laffrado, Laura 1959- ... 138
LaFitte, Pat Chew 1950- ... 107
La Flesche, Francis 1857(?)-1932 ... CANR-83
Earlier sketch in CA 144
See also DLB 175
See also NNAL
LaFleur, William R. 1936- ... 115
La Follette, Marcel (Evelyn) Chotkowski
1944- ... 114
La Follette, Melvin Walker 1930- ... CP 1
La Follette, Suzanne 1894(?)-1983
Obituary ... 109
LaFond, Carolyn Street 1951- ... 196
LaFontaine, Blanche
See Schwalberg, Carol(yn Ernestine Stein)
LaFontaine, Bruce 1948- ... 186
See also SATA 114
LaFontaine, Charles Vivian 1936- ... 57-60
LaFontaine, Gary 1945-2002 ... 214
La Fontaine, Jean de 1621-1695 ... DLB 268
See also EW 3
See also GFL Beginnings to 1789
See also MAICYA 1, 2
See also RGWL 2, 3
See also SATA 18
Lafore, Laurence Davis 1917-1985 ... 13-16R
Obituary ... 118
Laforest, Guy 1955- ... 149
LaForet (Diaz), Carmen 1921- ... CWW 2
See also DLB 322
See also EWL 3
Laforgue, Jules 1860-1887 ... DLB 217
See also EW 7
See also GFL 1789 to the Present
See also PC 14
See also RGWL 2, 3
See also SSC 20
La Forte, Robert S(herman) 1933- ... CANR-141
Earlier sketch in CA 57-60
La Fountaine, George 1934- ... CANR-41
Earlier sketches in CA 57-60, CANR-7
Lafourcade, Bernard 1934-1986 ... 115
Obituary ... 118
LaFourcade, Enrique 1927- ... EWL 3
LaFoy, Leslie ... 235
LaFrance, David G(erald) 1948- ... 221
LaFraniere, Sharon 1955- ... 136
La Freniere, (B. Marie) Celine 1950- ... 132
Lafreniere, Gyslaine F. 1948- ... 116
la Fuente, Patricia de
See de la Fuente, Patricia
Lagace, Louise Lambert
See Lambert-Lagace, Louise
la Garza, Rodolfo O(ropea) de
See de la Garza, Rodolfo O(ropea)
Lagatree, Kirsten 1948- ... 170
LaGattuta, Margo 1942- ... CANR-38
Earlier sketch in CA 115
Lagemann, Ellen Condliffe 1945- ... 128
Lager, Claude
See Lapp, Christiane (Germain)
Lager, Fred "Chico" 1955(?)- ... 168
Lager, Marilyn 1939- ... 121
See also SATA 52
Lagercrantz, Olof 1911- ... 184
Lagercrantz, Rose (Elsa) 1947- ... 108
See also SATA 39
Lagerkvist, Paer (Fabian) 1891-1974 ... 85-88
Obituary ... 49-52
See also Lagerkvist, Par
See also CLC 7, 10, 13, 54
See also DA3
See also DAM DRAM, NOV
See also MTCW 1, 2
See also MTFW 2005
See also TCLC 144
See also TWA
Lagerkvist, Par
See Lagerkvist, Paer (Fabian)
See also DLB 259
See also EW 10
See also EWL 3
See also RGSF 2
See also RGWL 2, 3
See also SSC 12
Lagerloef, Selma (Ottiliana Lovisa)
Brief entry ... 108
See also Lagerlof, Selma (Ottiliana Lovisa)
See also MTCW 2
See also TCLC 4, 36
Lagerlof, Selma (Ottiliana Lovisa)
1858-1940 ... 188
See also Lagerloef, Selma (Ottiliana Lovisa)
See also CLR 7
See also DLB 259
See also RGWL 2, 3
See also SATA 15
See also SSFS 18
Lagerwall, Edna ... 45-48
Lagerwerff, Ellen Best 1919- ... 85-88
Lagevi, Bo
See Blom, Karl Arne
Lago, Mary M(cClelland) 1919- ... CANR-15
Earlier sketch in CA 85-88
Lagorio, Gina 1922- ... DLB 196
LaGrand, James B. 1968- ... 238
LaGrand, Louis E. 1935- ... 33-36R
La Grange, Henry Louis De
See La Grange, Henry-Louis de
La Grange, Henry-Louis de 1924- ... CANR-92
Earlier sketch in CA 69-72
LaGravenese, Richard 1960- ... 173
La Greca, Annette M(arie) 1950- ... 142
LaGuardia, Cheryl M. ... 221
LaGuardia, David M(ichael) 1943- ... 118
La Guardia, Fiorello (Henry) 1882-1947 ... 168
Brief entry ... 120
Laguerre, Andre 1915(?)-1979 ... 97-100
Obituary ... 85-88
Laguerre, Enrique A(rturo) 1906- ... 131
See also EWL 3
See also HW 1
See also LAW
Laguerre, Michel S(aturnin) 1945- ... 115
La Guma, (Justin) Alex(ander)
1925-1985 ... CANR-81
Obituary ... 118
Earlier sketches in CA 49-52, CANR-25
See also AFW
See also BLCS
See also BW 1, 3
See also CDWLB 3
See also CLC 19
See also CN 1, 2, 3
See also CP 1
See also DAM NOV
See also DLB 117, 225
See also EWL 3
See also MTCW 1, 2
See also MTFW 2005
See also TCLC 140
See also WLIT 2
See also WWE 1
La Gumina, Salvatore John 1928- ... 77-80
Laguna, Sofie 1968- ... 234
See also SATA 158
Lahaise, Francoise-Guillaume 1888-1969 .. 178
See also Delahaye, Guy
Laham, Nicholas 1954- ... 175
La Harpe, Jean-Francois de
1739-1803 ... DLB 313
LaHaye, Tim(othy) F. 1926- ... CANR-113
Earlier sketches in CA 65-68, CANR-9
See also AAYA 39
See also SATA 149
Lahee, Frederic Henry 1884-1968 ... CAP-2
Earlier sketch in CA 19-20
Lahey, Edwin A(loysius) 1902-1969
Obituary ... 115
Lahiri, Jhumpa 1967- ... CANR-134
Earlier sketch in CA 193
See also AAYA 56
See also MTFW 2005
See also SSFS 19
Lahontan, Louis-Armand de Lom d'Arce Baron
1666-1715(?) ... DLB 99
LaHood, Marvin J(ohn) 1933- ... CANR-10
Earlier sketch in CA 25-28R
Lahr, John (Henry) 1941- ... CANR-96
Earlier sketches in CA 25-28R, CANR-21
Lahr, Raymond M(errill) 1914-1973
Obituary ... 41-44R
Lahue, Kalton C. 1934- ... CANR-7
Earlier sketch in CA 13-16R
Lahuti, Abulqasim 1887-1957 ... EWL 3
Lai, David Chuenyan 1937- ... 138
Lai, Francis 1932- ... IDFW 3, 4
Lai, Him Mark 1925- ... 195
Lai, Larissa 1967- ... 157
Lai, T'ien-Ch'ang 1921- ... CANR-11
Earlier sketch in CA 69-72
Lai, Violet Lau 1916- ... 119
Laidlaw, A. K.
See Grieve, C(hristopher) M(urray)
Laidlaw, Harry Hyde, Jr. 1907- ... 5-8R
Laidlaw, James 1963- ... 239
Laidlaw, Marc 1960- ... CANR-45
Earlier sketch in CA 119
Laidlaw, Ross 1931- ... CANR-44
Earlier sketch in CA 118
Laidlaw, W(illiam) A(llison) 1898-1983
Obituary ... 109
Laidler, Harry W(ellington)
1884-1970 ... CANR-5
Obituary ... 29-32R
Earlier sketch in CA 5-8R
La Iglesia, Maria Elena De
See De La Iglesia, Maria Elena
Laiken, Deirdre S(usan) 1948- ... 104
See also SATA 48
See also SATA-Brief 40
Laikin, Paul 1927- ... 5-8R
Laimgruber, Monika 1946- ... SATA 11
Laimo, Michael 1966- ... 227
Lain, Anna
See Lamb, Nancy
Laine, Barry 1951-1987
Obituary ... 123
Laine, Daniel
See Laine, Daniel
Laine, Daniel 1949- ... 229
Laine, Gloria
See Hanna, David
Laine, Jimmy
See Ferrara, Abel
Laine, Pascal 1942- ... 192
Lain Entralgo, Pedro 1908-2001 ... 211
Lainez, Manuel Mujica
See Mujica Lainez, Manuel
See also HW 1
Laing, Alastair 1944- ... 127
Laing, Alexander (Kinnan)
1903-1976 ... CANR-79
Obituary ... 65-68
Earlier sketches in CA 5-8R, CANR-4
See also HGG
See also SATA 117
Laing, Anne C.
See Schachterle, Nancy (Lange)
Laing, Frederick ... 105
Laing, Jennifer 1948- ... 106
Laing, Kojo 1946- ... 185
See also DLB 157
See also EWL 3
Laing, Lloyd (Robert) 1944- ... CANR-5
Earlier sketch in CA 53-56
Laing, Martha
See Celestino, Martha Laing
Laing, R(onald) D(avid) 1927-1989 .. CANR-34
Obituary ... 129
Earlier sketch in CA 107
See also CLC 95
See also MTCW 1
Laingen, L(owell) Bruce 1922- ... 139
Laino, E. J. Miller 1948- ... 208
Laiou, Angeliki Evangelos 1941- ... 193
Lair, Clara
See Munoz, Mercedes Negron
Lair, Jacqueline Carey 1930- ... 119
Lair, Jess K. 1926-2000 ... CANR-14
Obituary ... 188
Earlier sketch in CA 41-44R
Lair, Robert L(eland) 1932- ... 53-56
Laird, Betty A(nn) 1925- ... CANR-33
Earlier sketches in CA 33-36R, CANR-15
Laird, Brian Andrew 1964- ... 151
Laird, Carobeth 1895-1983 ... CANR-8
Obituary ... 110
Earlier sketch in CA 61-64
See also DLBY 1982
Laird, Charlton G(rant) 1901-1984 ... 13-16R
Laird, Christa 1944- ... 178
See also AAYA 30
See also SAAS 26
See also SATA 108
See also SATA-Essay 120
Laird, David
See Laird, W(ilbur) David, Jr.
Laird, Donald A(nderson) 1897-1969 ... 5-8R
Obituary ... 25-28R
Laird, Dorothy
See Carr, Dorothy Stevenson Laird
Laird, Dugan 1920- ... CANR-12
Earlier sketch in CA 73-76

Cumulative Index 333 Lamparski

Laird, Eleanor Childs 1908- 73-76
Laird, Elizabeth (Mary Risk) 1943- .. CANR-127
Earlier sketches in CA 128, CANR-65
See also AAYA 63
See also CLR 65
See also SATA 77, 114, 159
Laird, Gordon 182
Laird, Helen 1933- 122
Laird, Holly A. 1953- 239
Laird, J(ohn) T(udor) 1921- 69-72
Laird, Jean E(louise) 1930- CANR-6
Earlier sketch in CA 9-12R
See also SATA 38
Laird, Marc 194
Laird, Melvin R(obert) 1922- 65-68
Laird, Robbin F. 1946- 113
Laird, Ross 1947- 175
Laird, Roy D(ean) 1925- CANR-33
Earlier sketches in CA 33-36R, CANR-15
Laird, Sally 233
Laird, Thomas (Calvin) 1953(?)- 235
Laird, W(ilbur) David, Jr. 1937- 113
Laishley, Alex
See Booth, Martin
Lait, Robert 1921- CANR-2
Earlier sketch in CA 1-4R
Laite, Gordon 1925- .... SATA 31
Laite, William Edward, Jr. 1932- 37-40R
Laithwaite, Eric Roberts 1921-1997 103
Laitin, Joseph 1914-2002 136
Obituary 204
Laitin, Ken 1963- 102
Laitin, Lindy 1968- 108
Laitin, Steve 1965- 102
Laje, Zilia L. 1941- 227
Lajer-Burcharth, Ewa 215
Lajoie, Antoine Gerin 1824-1882 .... DLB 99
Lajolo, Davide 1913(?)-1984
Obituary 113
Lakatos, Imre 1922-1974
Obituary 116
Lake, Alice (Dannenberg) 1916-1990
Obituary 131
Lake, Carolyn 1932- 25-28R
Lake, David J(ohn) 1929- CANR-83
Earlier sketches in CA 65-68, CANR-10, 41
See also SFW 4
Lake, Deryn
See Lampitt, Dinah
Lake, Don(ald) 1953- 206
Lake, Frank 1914-1982 .... CANR-10
Earlier sketch in CA 21-24R
Lake, Harriet
See Taylor, Paula (Wright)
Lake, Inez Hollander 1965- 195
Lake, Jo-Anne 1941- 225
Lake, Kenneth R(obert) 1931- CANR-5
Earlier sketch in CA 53-56
Lake, M. D.
See Simpson, Allen
Lake, Paul 1951- .... DLB 282
Lake, Simon
See Grant, Charles L(ewis)
Lake, Timothy
See Bates, Tom
Lakeland, Paul 1946- 137
Lakeman, Enid 1903-1995 107
Laken, Bob
See Holman, Robert
Laker, Rosalind
See Ovstedal, Barbara
Lakey, George (Russell) 1937- CANR-7
Earlier sketch in CA 17-20R
Lakhu
See Khubchandani, Lachman M(ulchand)
Lakin, Martin 1925- 73-76
Lakin, Patricia 1944- 219
Laklan, Carli 1907-1988 .... CANR-1
Earlier sketch in CA 1-4R
See also SATA 5
Lakoff, George 1941- CANR-27
Earlier sketch in CA 29-32R
Lakoff, Robin Tolmach 1942- CANR-27
Earlier sketch in CA 103
Lakoff, Sanford A(llan) 1931- CANR-1
Earlier sketch in CA 1-4R
Lakos, Amos 1946- 143
Lakritz, Esther Himmelman 1928- 1-4R
Lal, Brij V. 1952- 139
Lal, Deepak (Kumar) 1940- 189
Lal, Gobind Behari 1890(?)-1982
Obituary 106
Lal, Kishori Saran 1920- 21-24R
Lal, P. 1929- CANR-9
Earlier sketch in CA 13-16R
See also CP 1, 2
Lala, Frank James John, Jr. 181
Laliberte, Norman 1925- 104
Lalic, Ivan V. 1931-1996 210
See also CWW 2
See also DLB 181
Lalic, Mihailo 1914-1992 .... DLB 181
See also EWL 3
Lalicki, Barbara 119
See also SATA 61
Lalita, K. 1953- 144
Lalley, Joseph M. 1897(?)-1980
Obituary 102
Lalli, Judy 1949- 110
Lally, Michael (David) 1942- CANR-32
Earlier sketches in CA 77-80, CANR-14
Lally, Richard 238
Lally, Soinbhe 1945- 186
See also SATA 119
La Londe, Bernard J. 1933- 33-36R
Lalonde, Marc P(hilippe) 1961- 197
Lalonde, Michele 1937- 178
See also DLB 60
Lalonde, Robert 1947- 109
Laluah, Aquah
See Casely-Hayford, Gladys May
Lalumia, Joseph 1916- 21-24R
Lam, Charlotte (Dawson) 1924- 37-40R
Lam, Quang Thi
See Lam Quang Thi
Lam, Truong Buu 1933- 25-28R
Laman, Russell 1907-1987 .... CAP-1
Earlier sketch in CA 9-10
LaMancusa, Katherine C.
See Koop, Katherine C.
Lamanna, Dolores B. 1930-1980 .... 9-12R
Obituary 97-100
Lamantia, Philip 1927-2005 117
Obituary 237
Brief entry 111
See also CP 1, 2
See also DLB 16
Lamar, Howard R(oberts) 1923- 17-20R
Lamar, Jake 1961- CANR-108
Earlier sketch in CA 137
Lamar, Lavoisier 1907- 5-8R
Lamar, Nedra Newkirk -1997 69-72
LaMarche, Jim .... SATA 162
Lamarque, Peter 1948- 120
LaMarre, Virgil E. 1910(?)-1985
Obituary 115
LaMarsh, Judy
See LaMarsh, Julia Verlyn
LaMarsh, Julia Verlyn 1924-1980 ..... CANR-13
Obituary 105
Earlier sketch in CA 29-32R
Lamartine, Alphonse (Marie Louis Prat) de
1790-1869 .... DAM POET
See also DLB 217
See also GFL 1789 to the Present
See also PC 16
See also RGWL 2, 3
LaMay, Craig L. 173
Lamazares, Ivonne 1962- 189
Lamb, Andrew (Martin) 1942- 137
Lamb, Antonia 1943- 21-24R
Lamb, Arnette 169
Lamb, Beatrice Pitney 1904-1997 .... 5-8R
See also SATA 21
Lamb, Brian 1941- 169
Lamb, Charles 1775-1834 .... BRW 4
See also CDBLB 1789-1832
See also DA
See also DAB
See also DAC
See also DAM MST
See also DLB 93, 107, 163
See also RGEL 2
See also SATA 17
See also TEA
See also WLC
Lamb, Charles Bentall 1914-1981 102
Obituary 105
Lamb, Charles M(oody) 1945- 124
Lamb, Charlotte
See Holland, Sheila
See also RHW
Lamb, Christina 1965- CANR-89
Earlier sketch in CA 140
Lamb, Connie 1947- 139
Lamb, Dana S(torrs) 1900-1986 134
Obituary 120
Lamb, David 1940- CANR-122
Earlier sketch in CA 110
Lamb, Edward 1902-1987 108
Obituary 122
Lamb, Eleanor 1917- 69-72
Lamb, Elizabeth Searle 1917- 33-36R
See also SATA 31
Lamb, F(rank) Bruce 1913-1992 .... 33-36R
Lamb, G(eoffrey) F(rederick) CANR-41
Earlier sketches in CA 53-56, CANR-4, 19
See also SATA 10
Lamb, H(ubert) H(orace) 1913-1997 ..... 21-24R
Lamb, Harold (Albert) 1892-1962 101
Obituary 89-92
See also SATA 53
Lamb, Helen B.
See Lamont, Helen Lamb
Lamb, Hugh 1946- CANR-1
Earlier sketch in CA 49-52
Lamb, James B(arrett) 1919- 133
Lamb, Joyce (L.) 1965- 221
Lamb, Karl A(llen) 1933- CANR-18
Earlier sketches in CA 5-8R, CANR-3
Lamb, Lady Caroline 1785-1828 .... DLB 116
Lamb, Lawrence E(dward) 1926- 97-100
Lamb, Lynton (Harold) 1907-1977 ..... CANR-4
Earlier sketch in CA 1-4R
See also SATA 10
Lamb, Marion M(inerva) 1905-2000 .... 5-8R
Lamb, Mary Ann 1764-1847 .... DLB 163
See also SATA 17
Lamb, Milton T.
See Powell, (Oval) Talmage
Lamb, Nancy 1939- 148
See also SATA 80
Lamb, (Margaret) Pansy Felicia (Pakenham)
1904-1999 183
Lamb, Patricia Clare 1935- 211
Lamb, Patricia Frazer 1931- 126
Lamb, Ramdas 1945- 232
Lamb, Richard 1911- 197
Lamb, Robert (Boyden) 1941- CANR-35
Earlier sketch in CA 29-32R
See also SATA 13
Lamb, Ruth S(tanton) CANR-21
Earlier sketch in CA 45-48
Lamb, Sharon 1955- 217
Lamb, Simon 215
Lamb, Sydney M(acDonald) 1929- 33-36R
Lamb, Wally 140
See also Lamb, Walter
See also MTFW 2005
Lamb, Walter 1950- CANR-104
See also Lamb, Wally
Lamb, William
See Jameson, (Margaret) Storm
Lamb, William Kaye 1904-1999 81-84
Lambasa, Frank Slavko 1921-1987
Obituary 123
Lambdin, Dewey (W.) 1945- CANR-103
Earlier sketch in CA 140
Lambdin, Laura Cooner 1961- 177
Lambdin, Robert Thomas 1958- 177
Lambdin, William 1936- 102
Lambec, Zoltan
See Kimbro, John M.
Lamberg, Robert F(elix) 1929- 65-68
Lamberg-Karlovsky, Clifford Charles
1937- 85-88
Lambersy, Werner 1941- 192
Lambert, Angela
See Lambert, Angela Maria
See also DLB 271
Lambert, Angela Maria 1940- 138
See also Lambert, Angela
Lambert, Anne-Therese de
1647-1733 .... DLB 313
Lambert, B. Geraldine 1922- 41-44R
Lambert, Barbara 196
Lambert, Betty
See Lambert, Elizabeth (Minnie)
See also DLB 60
Lambert, Byron Cecil 1923- 97-100
Lambert, Darwin (Seymour) 1916- CANR-2
Earlier sketch in CA 5-8R
Lambert, David (Compton) 1932- 122
See also SATA 84
See also SATA-Brief 49
Lambert, Derek 1929-2001 .... CANR-101
Earlier sketches in CA 25-28R, CANR-17, 69
See also CMW 4
Lambert, Eleanor 1903-2003 102
Obituary 220
Lambert, Elisabeth
See Ortiz, Elisabeth Lambert
Lambert, Elizabeth (Minnie) 1933-1983 102
See also Lambert, Betty
Lambert, Eric 1918-1966 .... CAP-1
Earlier sketch in CA 13-14
Lambert, Gavin 1924-2005 .... CANR-96
Earlier sketches in CA 1-4R, CANR-1
Lambert, Hazel Margaret (?)-1968 .... 1-4R
Lambert, Herbert H. 1929- 69-72
Lambert, J(ack) W(alter) 1917-1986 108
Obituary 120
Lambert, Jacques Edward 1901- CAP-2
Earlier sketch in CA 23-24
Lambert, Janet 1895(?)-1973
Obituary 41-44R
See also SATA 25
Lambert, John (Robin) 1936- CANR-8
Earlier sketch in CA 5-8R
Lambert, Katherine 234
Lambert, Mark 1942- 73-76
Lambert, Martha L. 185
See also SATA 113
Lambert, Mercedes
See Munson, Douglas Anne
Lambert, Page 1952- 154
Lambert, Philip 1958- 174
Lambert, Ronald Dick 1936- 108
Lambert, Roy Eugene 1918- 37-40R
Lambert, Royston James 1932-1982
Obituary 108
Lambert, Saul 1928- 106
See also SATA 23
Lambert, Sheila 1926- 85-88
Lambert, William Wilson 1919- 9-12R
Lamberti, Marjorie 1937- 103
Lambert-Lagace, Louise 1941- CANR-29
Earlier sketch in CA 111
Lamberton, Donald McLean 1927- 103
Lamberton, Ken 1958- 197
Lamberts, J(acob) J. 1910- 37-40R
Lambeth, Edmund Barry 1932- 123
Lamb-Faffelberger, Margarete 1954- 236
Lambi, Ivo Nikolai 1931- 132
Lambley, Peter 1946- 109
Lambo, Thomas Adeoye 1923- 29-32R
Lamborn, LeRoy L(eslie) 1937- 21-24R
Lambot, Isobel 1926- 73-76
Lambourne, John
See Lamburn, John Battersby Crompton
Lambrecht, Bill 208
Lambrecht, Frank L. 1915- 164
Lambrecht, P(atricia) J. 230
Lambrecht, Traci 230
Lambrick, Hugh Trevor 1904-1982 .... CANR-6
Earlier sketch in CA 9-12R
Lambright, Evelyn 238
Lambright, Slim
See Lambright, Evelyn
Lambright, William Henry 1939- 103
Lambro, Donald (Joseph) 1940- CANR-25
Earlier sketches in CA 57-60, CANR-7
Lambton, Anne (Patricia St. Clair) 1918- . 85-88
Lamburn, John Battersby Crompton
1893- CAP-1
Earlier sketch in CA 9-10
Lamburn, Richmal Crompton
1890-1969 .... CANR-83
Obituary 25-28R
Earlier sketches in CAP-1, CA 9-10
See also Crompton, Richmal
See also CWRI 5
See also SATA 5
Lame Deer 1903(?)-1976
Obituary 69-72
See also NNAL
Lamennais, Hugues-Felicite Robert de
1782-1854 .... GFL 1789 to the Present
Lamensdorf, Len
See Lamensdorf, Leonard
Lamensdorf, Leonard 1930- CANR-95
Earlier sketch in CA 29-32R
See also SATA 120
La Meri
See Hughes, Russell Meriwether
La Mettrie, Julien Offroy de
1709-1751 .... DLB 313
L'Ami, Charles Ernest 1896-1981 102
Laminack, Lester L. 1956- 191
See also SATA 120, 163
Lamirande, Emilien 1926- CANR-8
Earlier sketch in CA 17-20R
Lamis, Alexander P. 1946- CANR-52
Earlier sketch in CA 125
Lamm, Joyce 1933- 57-60
Lamm, Leonard Jonathan 1945 146
Lamm, Maurice 1930- 17-20R
Lamm, Norman 1927- CANR-28
Earlier sketch in CA 49-52
Lamme, Linda Leonard 1942- 102
Lammers, Stephen E. 1938- 170
Lammers, Wayne P. 1951- 140
Lamming, George (William) 1927- ... CANR-76
Earlier sketches in CA 85-88, CANR-26
See also BLC 2
See also BW 2, 3
See also CDWLB 3
See also CLC 2, 4, 66, 144
See also CN 1, 2, 3, 4, 5, 6, 7
See also CP 1
See also DAM MULT
See also DLB 125
See also EWL 3
See also MTCW 1, 2
See also MTFW 2005
See also NFS 15
See also RGEL 2
Lamming, R. M. 1949- 125
Brief entry 119
Interview in CA-125
Lammon, Martin 1958- CANR-93
Earlier sketch in CA 162
LaMon, Jacqueline Jones 213
Lamon, Lester C(rawford) 1942- 89-92
Lamond, Henry George 1885-1969
Obituary 25-28R
Lamonde, Yvan 171
Lamont, Corliss 1902-1995 .... CANR-11
Obituary 148
Earlier sketch in CA 13-16R
Lamont, Douglas Felix 1937- 41-44R
Lamont, Helen Lamb 1906(?)-1975
Obituary 61-64
Lamont, Lansing 1930- CANR-11
Earlier sketch in CA 17-20R
Lamont, Marianne
See Rundle, Anne
Lamont, Michele 1957- 143
Lamont, N. B.
See Barnitt, Nedda Lemmon
Lamont, Nedda
See Barnitt, Nedda Lemmon
Lamont, Norman Stewart Hughson 1942- .. 194
Lamont, Rosette C(lementine) 33-36R
Lamont, William D(awson) 1901-1982 . CAP-1
Obituary 108
Earlier sketch in CA 11-12
Lamont-Brown, Raymond 1939- CANR-66
Earlier sketches in CA 73-76, CANR-14, 32
Lamorisse, Albert (Emmanuel) 1922-1970 .. 101
See also SATA 23
La Mothe Le Vayer, Francois de
1588-1672 .... DLB 268
Lamott, Anne 1954- CANR-135
Earlier sketches in CA 144, CANR-74
See also NCFS 3
Lamott, Kenneth (Church) 1923-1979 ... 25-28R
Obituary 89-92
la Motte, Antoine-Charles de Houdar de
See Houdar de la Motte, Antoine-Charles de
Lamotte, Etienne 1904(?)-1983
Obituary 109
Lamour, Dorothy 1914-1996 134
Brief entry 105
L'Amour, Louis (Dearborn)
1908-1988 .... CANR-40
Obituary 125
Earlier sketches in CA 1-4R, CANR-3, 25
See also AAYA 16
See also AITN 2
See also BEST 89:2
See also BPFB 2
See also CLC 25, 55
See also CPW
See also DA3
See also DAM NOV, POP
See also DLB 206
See also DLBY 1980
See also MTCW 1, 2
See also MTFW 2005
See also RGAL 4
See also TCWW 1, 2
Lamparski, Richard 21-24R

Lampe, David 1923- ... CANR-1
Earlier sketch in CA 1-4R
Lampe, Gregory P. 1954- ... 212
Lampedusa, Giuseppe (Tomasi) di ... 164
See also Tomasi di Lampedusa, Giuseppe
See also EW 11
See also MTCW 2
See also MTFW 2005
See also RGWL 2, 3
See also TCLC 13
Lampell, Millard 1919-1997 ... 9-12R
Obituary ... 162
Lampert, Ada 1942- ... 175
Lampert, Catherine 1946- ... 229
Lampert, Emily 1951- ... 121
See also SATA 52
See also SATA-Brief 49
Lampert, Hope 1960- ... 143
Lamphear, John 1941- ... 147
Lamphere, Louise (Anne) 1940- ... 89-92
Lamphere, Robert J. 1918-2002 ... 214
Lampitt, Dinah 1937- ... CANR-101
Earlier sketches in CA 132, CANR-83
See also RHW
Lampkin, William R(obert) 1932- ... 106
Lampl, Paul 1915-
Brief entry ... 104
Lamplugh, Lois 1921- ... CANR-83
Earlier sketches in CA 13-16R, CANR-9, 24
See also CWRI 5
See also SATA 17
Lampman, Archibald 1861-1899 ... DLB 92
See also RGEL 2
See also TWA
Lampman, Ben Hur 1886-1954
Brief entry ... 111
Lampman, Evelyn Sibley
1907-1980 ... CANR-84
Obituary ... 101
Earlier sketches in CA 13-16R, CANR-11
See also BYA 5
See also CWRI 5
See also SATA 4, 87
See also SATA-Obit 23
Lampman, Robert James 1920-1997 ... 103
Obituary ... 157
Lampo, Hubert 1920-
Brief entry ... 105
Lamport, Felicia 1916-1999 ... 1-4R
Lamppa, William R(ussell) 1928- ... 53-56
Lamprecht, Sterling P(ower)
1890-1973 ... CAP-1
Earlier sketch in CA 17-18
Lamprey, Louise 1869-1951 ... 184
Brief entry ... 117
See also YABC 2
Lampson, Robin 1900-1978
Obituary ... 77-80
Lampton, Chris
See Lampton, Christopher F.
Lampton, Christopher
See Lampton, Christopher F.
Lampton, Christopher F. ... CANR-37
Earlier sketch in CA 125
See also SATA 67
See also SATA-Brief 47
Lams, Victor J. 1935- ... 232
Lamsa, George M(amishisho)
1890-1975 ... CANR-9
Earlier sketches in CAP-2, CA 23-24
Lamsley, Terry 1941- ... HGG
Lamson, Peggy 1912-1996 ... 25-28R
Lamstein, Sarah Marwil 1943- ... SATA 126
La Mure, Pierre 1909-1976
Obituary ... 104
Lan, David 1952- ... CANR-84
Earlier sketches in CA 97-100, CANR-24
See also CD 5, 6
Lana, Robert E(dward) 1932- ... 33-36R
Lanagan, Margo 1960- ... 239
See also SATA 163
Lancaster, Bob 1943- ... 111
Lancaster, Bruce 1896-1963 ... CANR-70
Earlier sketches in CAP-1, CA 9-10
See also CLC 36
See also SATA 9
Lancaster, Burt(on Stephen) 1913-1994 ... 122
Obituary ... 147
Brief entry ... 116
Lancaster, Clay 1917-2000 ... CANR-8
Obituary ... 193
Earlier sketch in CA 5-8R
Lancaster, David
See Heald, Tim(othy Villiers)
Lancaster, Evelyn
See Sizemore, Chris(tine) Costner
Lancaster, F. Donald
See Fredriksson, Don
Lancaster, F(rederick) Wilfrid 1933- .. CANR-42
Earlier sketches in CA 53-56, CANR-4, 19
Lancaster, Jane F(airchild) 1940- ... CANR-102
Earlier sketch in CA 150
Lancaster, Kelvin (John) 1924-1999 ... 33-36R
Obituary ... 185
Lancaster, Kurt 1967- ... 198
Lancaster, Lydia
See Meaker, Eloise
Lancaster, Lynne C. ... 210
Lancaster, Marie-Jaqueline 1922- ... 25-28R
Lancaster, Matthew 1973(?)-1983
Obituary ... 117
See also SATA-Obit 45
Lancaster, Michael (L.) 1928- ... 154
Lancaster, Osbert 1908-1986 ... 105
Obituary ... 119
Lancaster, Otis Ewing 1909-1992 ... 103
Lancaster, Richard ... 21-24R
Lancaster, Roger N(elson) 1959- ... 143
Lancaster, Roy ... 185
Lancaster, Sheila
See Holland, Sheila
Lancaster-Brown, Peter 1927- ... CANR-19
Earlier sketches in CA 53-56, CANR-4
Lance, Derek (Paul) 1932- ... CANR-9
Earlier sketch in CA 13-16R
Lance, H(ubert) Darrell 1935- ... 115
Lance, James Waldo 1926- ... 65-68
Lance, Jamie Westin
See Cayson, Joyce A.
Lance, Kathryn 1943- ... 122
See also SATA 76
Lance, LaBelle D(avid) 1931- ... 81-84
Lance, Leslie
See Swatridge, Charles (John)
Lance, Peter ... 172
Lancer, Jack ... CANR-27
Earlier sketch in CAP-2
Lanchester, Elsa 1902-1986 ... 134
Obituary ... 121
Lanchester, John 1962- ... 194
See also CLC 99
See also DLB 267
Lanchner, Carolyn ... 182
Lanci, Giuseppe 1942- ... IDFW 3, 4
Lanciano, Claude O(lwen), Jr. 1922- .. CANR-1
Earlier sketch in CA 45-48
Lancour, Gene
See Fisher, Gene L(ouis)
Lancour, (Adlore) Harold 1908-1981 .... 21-24R
Obituary ... 105
Lancy, David F(alcon) 1945- ... 110
Land
See Landry, Robert John
Land, Aubrey C(hristian) 1912-1993 ..... 41-44R
Land, Barbara (Neblett) 1923- ... 81-84
See also SATA 16
Land, Ben
See Rosenberg, Robert
Land, (Reginald) Brian 1927- ... 101
Land, Edwin H(erbert) 1909-1991 ... 155
Land, George T(homas) Lock 1933- ... 53-56
Land, Jane
See Borland, Kathryn Kilby and
Speicher, Helen Ross S(mith)
Land, Jon 1960- ... 191
Land, Milton 1920-2000
See Powell, (Oval) Talmage
Land, Myrick (Ebben) 1922-1998 ..... CANR-11
Earlier sketch in CA 13-16R
See also SATA 15
Land, Ross
See Borland, Kathryn Kilby and
Speicher, Helen Ross S(mith)
Landar, Herbert (Jay) 1927- ... 33-36R
Landau, Edmund Georg Hermann
1877-1938 ... 170
Landau, Elaine 1948- ... CANR-120
Earlier sketches in CA 53-56, CANR-5
See also SATA 10, 94, 141
Landau, Genevieve Millet 1927-1993 ... 107
Obituary ... 141
Landau, Jacob 1917- ... SATA 38
Landau, Jacob M. 1924- ... CANR-24
Earlier sketches in CA 17-20R, CANR-8
Landau, Lev Davidovich 1908-1968 ... 158
Obituary ... 113
Landau, Mark Alexandrovich
See Aldanov, Mark (Alexandrovich)
Landau, Martin 1921-2004 ... 45-48
Obituary ... 234
Landau, Paul Stuart 1962- ... 153
Landau, Rom 1899-1974 ... CANR-4
Obituary ... 49-52
Earlier sketch in CA 1-4R
Landau, Saul (I.) 1936- ... 130
Landau, Sidney I(van) 1933- ... CANR-7
Earlier sketch in CA 57-60
Landau, Sol 1920- ... CANR-31
Earlier sketch in CA 49-52
Landau, Susan 1954- ... CANR-101
Earlier sketch in CA 166
Landau, Tina ... 206
Landau, Zbigniew Wladyslaw 1931- ... 196
Landau-Aldanov, Mark Alexandrovich
See Aldanov, Mark (Alexandrovich)
Landauer, Carl 1891-1983 ... CANR-21
Earlier sketch in CA 1-4R
Landauer, Jerry Gerd 1932-1981 ... 109
Obituary ... 103
Lande, Henry F(rank) 1920-1999 ... 29-32R
Lande, Lawrence (Montague) 1906- ... 105
Lande, Nathaniel 1939- ... 104
Landeck, Beatrice 1904-1978 ... 73-76
See also SATA 15
Landecker, Manfred 1929- ... 29-32R
Landeen, William M. 1891-1982
Obituary ... 109
Landeira, Ricardo L(opez) 1917- ... 81-84
Landen, Robert Geran 1930- ... 21-24R
Lander, Ernest McPherson, Jr. 1915- ... CANR-4
Earlier sketch in CA 1-4R
Lander, Jack Robert 1921- ... 101
Lander, Jeannette 1931- ... 33-36R
Lander, Kim
See Schirmbeck, Heinrich Wilhelm
Lander, Louise 1938- ... 85-88
Lander, Mamie Stubbs 1891(?)-1975
Obituary ... 53-56
Landers, Ann
See Lederer, Esther Pauline (Friedman)
Landers, Gunnard W(illiam) 1944- ... 93-96
Landers, John 1952- ... 231
Landers, Scott 1952- ... 231
Landes, David S(aul) 1924- ... CANR-129
Earlier sketches in CA 103, CANR-22
Landes, Marie Gisele
See Landes-Fuss, Marie-Gisele
Landes, Richard 1949-1998 ... 154
Landes, Ruth 1908-1991 ... CAP-2
Obituary ... 133
Earlier sketch in CA 29-32
Landes, Sonia 1925- ... CANR-22
Earlier sketch in CA 104
Landes-Fuss, Marie-Gisele 1936- ... 129
Landesman, Charles 1932- ... 85-88
Landesman, Fran(ces) 1927- ... CANR-55
Brief entry ... 120
Earlier sketch in CA 127
See also DLB 16
Landesman, Jay (Irving) 1919- ... 127
Brief entry ... 118
See also DLB 16
Landesman, Peter 1965- ... 154
Landeta, Matilde Soto 1910-1999 ... 219
Landgrebe, Ludwig 1902-1991 ... 142
Landgren, Marchal E. 1907(?)-1983
Obituary ... 109
Landi, Ferruccio Rossi
See Rossi-Landi, Ferruccio
Landin, Les 1923- ... 5-8R
See also SATA 2
Landis, Benson Y. 1897-1966 ... CAP-1
Earlier sketch in CA 13-14
Landis, Bill 1959- ... 219
Landis, Dennis Channing 1947- ... 110
Landis, Fred S(imon) 1943- ... 107
Landis, Geoffrey A(lan) 1955- ... CANR-102
Earlier sketch in CA 159
See also SFW 4
Landis, J(ames) D(avid) 1942- ... CANR-101
Earlier sketch in CA 126
See also SATA 60
See also SATA-Brief 52
Landis, James D.
See Landis, J(ames) D(avid)
Landis, Jerry
See Simon, Paul (Frederick)
Landis, Jessie Royce 1904-1972
Obituary ... 33-36R
Landis, Jill Marie 1948- ... CANR-109
Earlier sketch in CA 161
See also SATA 101
Landis, John 1950- ... CANR-128
Brief entry ... 112
Earlier sketch in CA 122
See also CLC 26
Landis, Judson R(ichard) 1935- ... 33-36R
Landis, Lincoln 1922- ... 45-48
Landis, Marie A. ... 161
Landis, Paul H(enry) 1901-1985 ... CANR-5
Earlier sketch in CA 5-8R
Landman, David 1917- ... CANR-11
Earlier sketch in CA 69-72
Landman, Jessica C. 1955- ... 149
Lando, Barry Mitchell 1939- ... 77-80
Landolfi, Tommaso 1908-1979 ... 127
Obituary ... 117
See also CLC 11, 49
See also DLB 177
See also EWL 3
Landon, Carolyn 1945- ... 194
Landon, Donald D. 1930- ... 25-28R
Landon, H(oward) C(handler) Robbins
1926- ... CANR-94
Earlier sketches in CA 77-80, CANR-13, 34
Landon, Letitia Elizabeth 1802-1838 .... DLB 96
Landon, Lucinda 1950- ... 123
See also SATA 56
See also SATA-Brief 51
Landon, Margaret (Dorothea Mortenson)
1903-1993 ... CAP-1
Obituary ... 143
Earlier sketch in CA 13-14
See also SATA 50
Landon, Michael de L(aval) 1935- CANR-57
Earlier sketches in CA 29-32R, CANR-30
Landor, Walter Savage 1775-1864 ... BRW 4
See also DLB 93, 107
See also RGEL 2
Landorf, Joyce 1932- ... 124
See also AITN 1
Landow, George P(aul) 1940- ... CANR-41
Earlier sketches in CA 53-56, CANR-4, 19
Landowska, Wanda (Aleksandra) 1879-1959
Brief entry ... 122
Landreth, Bill 1964- ... 138
Landreth, Catherine 1899-1995 ... 77-80
Landreth, Marsha Ann 1947- ... 140
Landrith, Harold Fochone 1919-1984 ... 103
Landro, Laura 1954- ... 193
Landrum, Gene N. 1935- ... CANR-98
Earlier sketch in CA 147
Landrum, Graham (Gordon) 1922-1995 148
Landrum, Larry N. ... 219
Landrum, Phil 1939- ... 81-84
Landry, Hilton (James) 1924- ... 13-16R
Landry, Napoleon-Philippe 1884-1956 ... 182
See also DLB 92
Landry, Robert John 1903-1991 ... 69-72
Obituary ... 134
Landry, Thomas Wade 1924-2000 ... 141
Obituary ... 188
Landry, Tom
See Landry, Thomas Wade
Landsberg, Brian K. 1937- ... 165
Landsberg, Hans H(ermann)
1913-2001 ... CANR-10
Obituary ... 202
Earlier sketch in CA 17-20R
Landsberg, Helmut Erich 1906-1985 ... 107
Obituary ... 118
Landsberg, Melvin 1926- ... 142
Landsberg, Michele 1939- ... 123
Landsbergis, Algirdas J. 1924- ... CANR-45
Earlier sketches in CA 33-36R, CANR-13
Landsburg, Alan William 1933- ... 103
Landsburg, Sally (Breit) 1933- ... 57-60
Landsburg, Steven E(lliot) 1954- ... 168
Landshoff, Fritz Helmut 1901-1988
Obituary ... 125
Landshoff, Ursula 1908-1989 ... 29-32R
See also SATA 13
Landskroner, Ronald A. 1946- ... 165
Landsman, Ned C. 1951- ... 126
Landsteiner, Karl (Otto) 1868-1943 ... 158
Landstrom, Bjorn O(lof) 1917- ... 13-16R
Landstrom, Lena 1943- ... SATA 146
Landstrom, Olof 1943- ... SATA 146
Landsverk, O(le) G(odfred) 1901-1987 61-64
Landvater, Dorothy 1927- ... 103
Landvik, Lorna 1954- ... 192
See also DLB 292
Landwehr, Arthur J. II 1934- ... 37-40R
Landwirth, Heinz 1927- ... CANR-7
Earlier sketch in CA 9-12R
See also Lind, Jakov
Landy, David 1917- ... 77-80
Landy, Eugene E(llsworth) 1934- ... 41-44R
Landy, John (Michael) 1930- ... 128
Landy, Marcia 1931- ... CANR-129
Earlier sketch in CA 168
Landynski, Jacob W. 1930- ... 21-24R
Lane, Abbe 1935- ... 140
Lane, Allen 1902-1970
Obituary ... 29-32R
Lane, Ann J(udith) 1931- ... 126
Brief entry ... 110
Lane, Anthony 1916- ... 13-16R
Lane, Anthony 1962- ... 219
Lane, Arthur (Ernest) 1937- ... 41-44R
Lane, Carl D(aniel) 1899-1995 ... 105
Lane, Carolyn 1926-1993 ... CANR-12
Earlier sketch in CA 29-32R
See also SATA 10
Lane, Charles
See Gatti, Arthur Gerard
Lane, Charles 1800-1870 ... DLB 1, 223
Lane, Christopher 1966- ... 194
Lane, Dakota 1959- ... 162
See also SATA 105
Lane, David (Stuart) ... CANR-39
Earlier sketches in CA 29-32R, CANR-17
Lane, Dixie
See Salazar, Dixie
Lane, E(ugene Numa) 1936- ... 37-40R
Lane, Edward
See Dick, Kay
Lane, F. C. 1885-1984 ... 203
See also Lane, Ferdinand Cole
See also DLB 241
Lane, Ferdinand Cole 1885-1984 ... 203
See also Lane, F. C.
Lane, Frank Walter 1908-1988 ... 9-12R
Lane, Frederic C(hapin) 1900-1984 ... 105
Obituary ... 114
Lane, Gary 1943- ... 37-40R
Lane, Grant
See Fisher, Stephen (Gould)
Lane, Hana Umlauf 1946- ... 118
Lane, Harlan (Lawson) 1936- ... 126
Brief entry ... 111
Lane, Helen 1920- ... 123
Lane, Helen R(uth) 1921(?)-2004 ... CANR-2
Obituary ... 230
Earlier sketch in CA 45-48
Lane, Irving M(ark) 1944- ... 53-56
Lane, Jack C(onstant) 1932- ... CANR-4
Earlier sketch in CA 53-56
Lane, James B(uchanan) 1942- ... 93-96
Lane, Jane
See Dakers, Elaine Kidner
Lane, Jan-Erik 1946- ... 138
Lane, Jerry
See Martin, Patricia Miles
Lane, Jim R. 1944- ... 188
Lane, Joel 1963- ... 194
See also HGG
Lane, John (Richard) 1932- ... 106
See also SATA 15
Lane, Laura Gordon 1913-2001 ... 102
Lane, Laurence W. 1890-1967 ... 178
See also DLB 91
Lane, M(illicent) Travis 1934- ... CANR-44
Earlier sketch in CA 112
See also DLB 60
Lane, Marc J(ay) 1946- ... CANR-46
Earlier sketches in CA 105, CANR-21
Lane, Margaret 1907-1994 ... CANR-29
Obituary ... 144
Earlier sketches in CA 25-28R, CANR-13
See also BYA 3
See also SATA 65
See also SATA-Brief 38
See also SATA-Obit 79
Lane, Mark 1927- ... CANR-21
Earlier sketch in CA 61-64
Lane, Mary (Lois) B(eauchamp)
1911- ... CANR-9
Earlier sketch in CA 13-16R
Lane, Mary D.
See Delaney, Mary Murray
Lane, Michael (John) 1941- ... 85-88
Lane, Nancy 1947- ... 147
Lane, Nick ... 226

Cumulative Index 335 Lansbury

Lane, Patrick 1939- CANR-54
Earlier sketch in CA 97-100
Interview in CA-97-100
See also CLC 25
See also CP 7
See also DAM POET
See also DLB 53
Lane, Pinkie Gordon 1923- CANR-25
Earlier sketch in CA 41-44R
See also BW 2
See also DLB 41
Lane, Raymond A. 1894(?)-1974
Obituary 53-56
Lane, Richard 1926- CANR-10
Earlier sketch in CA 21-24R
Lane, Robert E(dwards) 1917- CANR-6
Earlier sketch in CA 1-4R
Lane, Roger 1934- 105
Lane, Ronnie M(ack) 1949- 41-44R
Lane, Rose Wilder 1887-1968 .... CANR-63
Earlier sketch in CA 102
See also SATA 29
See also SATA-Brief 28
See also TCWW 2
Lane, Roumelia
See Green, Kay
Lane, Sherry
See Smith, Richard Rein
Lane, Simon 1957- 171
Lane, Sylvia 1916- CANR-8
Earlier sketch in CA 5-8R
Lane, Terry 1939- 165
Lane, Thomas A(lphonsus) 1906-1975 .. 13-16R
Obituary 125
Lane, Wheaton J. 1902-1983
Obituary 111
Lane, William G(uerrant) 1919- 25-28R
Lane, William L(ister) 1931- CANR-27
Earlier sketch in CA 29-32R
Lane, Yoti 1-4R
Lanegran, David A(ndrew) 1941- CANR-37
Earlier sketches in CA 89-92, CANR-16
Lanes, Selma Gordon 1929- 25-28R
See also SATA 3
Laneuville, Eric (Gerard) 1952- 213
Laney, Al 1896-1988 .... CANR-62
Earlier sketch in CA 108
See also DLB 4, 171
Laney, J(ohn) Carl 1948- CANR-82
Earlier sketches in CA 114, CANR-35
Laney, James Thomas 1927- 103
Lanford, H(orace) W(haley) 1919- 41-44R
Lanfredi, Judy 1964- .... SATA 83
Lang, Allen Kim 1928- 17-20R
Lang, Andrew 1844-1912 .... CANR-85
Brief entry 114
Earlier sketch in CA 137
See also CLR 101
See also DLB 98, 141, 184
See also FANT
See also MAICYA 1, 2
See also RGEL 2
See also SATA 16
See also TCLC 16
See also WCH
Lang, Anthony E. 1951- 204
Lang, Barbara 1935-.............................. 9-12R
Lang, Berel 1933- CANR-73
Earlier sketches in CA 41-44R, CANR-15, 34
Lang, Charles B. 1902-1998 .... IDFW 3, 4
Lang, Daniel 1915-1981 .... CANR-4
Obituary 105
Earlier sketch in CA 5-8R
Lang, David 1913- 106
Lang, David Marshall 1924-1991 ..... CANR-17
Obituary 134
Earlier sketches in CA 5-8R, CANR-2
Lang, Derek (Boileau) 1913-2001 102
Obituary 194
Lang, Frances
See Mantle, Winifred (Langford)
Lang, Fritz 1890-1976 .... CANR-30
Obituary 69-72
Earlier sketch in CA 77-80
See also AAYA 65
See also CLC 20, 103
Lang, George 1924- 101
Lang, Gottfried O(tto) 1919- 45-48
Lang, Grace
See Floren, Lee
Lang, Gregor
See Birren, Faber
Lang, H. Jack 1904-1996 115
Lang, Isaac
See Goll, Yvan
Lang, Jack (Frederick) 1921- 5-8R
Lang, Jeannie
See Brewer, Jeannie A.
Lang, Jenifer Harvey 1951- 138
Lang, Jovian Peter 1919- CANR-15
Earlier sketch in CA 41-44R
Lang, Judith 1939- 165
Lang, Kenneth R(obert) 1941- 237
Lang, King
See Tubb, E(dwin) C(harles)
Lang, Kurt 1924- 33-36R
Lang, Mabel L(ouise) 1917- CANR-95
Brief entry 106
Earlier sketch in CA 126
Lang, Martin
See Birren, Faber
Lang, Martin A(ndrew) 1930- 115
Lang, Maud
See Williams, Claerwen
Lang, Michel (Jules Jean Marcel) 1939- 129
Lang, Miriam (Milman) 1915- 5-8R
Lang, Nancy M.
See Mace, Nancy L(awson)
Lang, Ned
See Sheckley, Robert
Lang, Paul 1948- 150
See also SATA 83
Lang, Paul Henry 1901-1991 103
Obituary 135
Lang, Robert (Peregrine) 1912-2001 ...... 41-44R
Obituary 195
Lang, Ronald William 1933- 103
Lang, Rupert
See Turner, E(rnest) S(ackville)
Lang, Susan S. 1950- 136
See also SATA 68
Lang, T. T.
See Taylor, Theodore
Lang, William L. 1942- 165
Lang, William Rawson 1909- CANR-21
Earlier sketch in CA 103
Langa, Mandla 1950- CANR-112
Earlier sketch in CA 168
Langacker, Ronald W(ayne) 1942- 21-24R
Langan, Ruth Ryan 1937- CANR-24
Earlier sketch in CA 107
Langan, Thomas 1929- CANR-17
Earlier sketch in CA 1-4R
Langart, Darrell T.
See Garrett, (Gordon) Randall (Phillip)
Langbaum, Robert (Woodrow) 1924- . CANR-1
Earlier sketch in CA 45-48
Langbein, John H(arriss) 1941- CANR-53
Earlier sketch in CA 124
Langdale, Cecily 1939- CANR-53
Earlier sketch in CA 126
Langdale, Eve
See Craig, E(velyn) Quita
Langdo, Bryan 1973- 209
See also SATA 138
Langdon, Charles 1934- 77-80
Langdon, Danny G. 1938- 215
Langdon, E(sther) Jean Matteson 1944- 146
Langdon, Frank C(orriston) 1919- 21-24R
Langdon, George D(orland), Jr. 1933- ... 21-24R
Langdon, Grace 1889-1970 .... 1-4R
Langdon, John 1913-1980 .... 5-8R
Langdon, Margaret Hoffmann (Storms) 1926-
Brief entry 107
Langdon, Philip 1947- CANR-66
Earlier sketch in CA 129
Langdon, Robert Adrian 1924- CANR-42
Earlier sketches in CA 104, CANR-20
Lange, Arthur D. 1952- 145
Lange, Dorothea 1895-1965 148
Obituary 107
See also AAYA 14
Lange, Frederick Douglas
See Lange, Tom
Lange, Gerald 1946- 69-72
Lange, James E(dward) T(homas) 142
Lange, John
See Crichton, (John) Michael
Lange, John Frederick, Jr. 1931- CANR-85
Earlier sketches in CA 97-100, CANR-8, 25, 54
See also Norman, John
See also FANT
See also SFW 4
Lange, (Leo) Joseph (Jr.) 1932- CANR-8
Earlier sketch in CA 17-20R
Lange, Kelly CANR-120
Earlier sketch in CA 89-92
Lange, Martin 1955- 130
Lange, Oliver (a pseudonym) 1927- . CANR-23
Earlier sketch in CA 103
Lange, Oskar (Richard) 1904-1965
Obituary 116
Lange, Suzanne 1945- 29-32R
See also SATA 5
Lange, Tom 1945- 158
Lange, (Hermann Walter) Victor
1908-1996 .... 9-12R
Obituary 152
Langendoen, D(onald) Terence 1939- ... 33-36R
Langer, Adam 228
Langer, Elinor 1939- 121
See also CLC 34
Langer, Ellen J(ane) 1947- CANR-72
Earlier sketches in CA 49-52, CANR-30
Langer, Erick D. 1955- 137
Langer, Frantisek 1888-1965
Langer, Howard 1929- 175
Langer, Jonas 1936- 33-36R
Langer, Lawrence L(ee) 1929- CANR-41
Earlier sketches in CA 65-68, CANR-11
Langer, Marshall J. 1928- 105
Langer, Susanne (Katherina) K(nauth)
1895-1985 .... CANR-34
Obituary 116
Earlier sketch in CA 41-44R
See also DLB 270
See also MTCW 1
Langer, Sydney 1914- 109
Langer, Thomas Edward 1929- 5-8R
Langer, Walter Charles 1899-1981 102
Obituary 104
Langer, William L(eonard)
1896-1977 .... CANR-14
Obituary 73-76
Earlier sketch in CA 29-32R
Langevin, Andre 1927- 178
See also CWW 2
See also DLB 60
See also EWL 3
Langevin, Sister Jean Marie 1917- 53-56
Langewiesche, William 102
Langford, Alec J. 1926- 97-100
Langford, David 1953- CANR-85
Earlier sketch in CA 135
See also DLB 261
See also SFW 4
Langford, Gary R(aymond) 1947- CANR-45
Earlier sketches in CA 103, CANR-20
Langford, George 1939- 53-56
Langford, Gerald 1911-2003 .... CANR-32
Earlier sketch in CA 1-4R
Langford, James R(ouleau) 1937- 53-56
Langford, Jane
See Mantle, Winifred (Langford)
Langford, Jeremy 205
Langford, Jerome J.
See Langford, James R(ouleau)
Langford, Thomas Anderson 1929-2000 . 9-12R
Obituary 187
Langford, Walter McCarty 1908-2001 ... 33-36R
Langgaesser, Elisabeth (Maria) 1899-1950 .. 179
Brief entry 121
See also Langgasser, Elisabeth
Langgasser, Elisabeth (Maria)
See Langgaesser, Elisabeth (Maria)
Langgasser, Elisabeth
See Langgaesser, Elisabeth (Maria)
See also DLB 69
Langguth, A(rthur) J(ohn) 1933- CANR-100
Earlier sketches in CA 61-64, CANR-30
Langhart, Janet
See Cohen, Janet Langhart
Langhoff, Severin Peter, Jr. 1910-1987
Obituary 122
Langholm, Neil
See Bulmer, (Henry) Kenneth and
James, Laurence
Langhorne, Elizabeth (Coles) 1909- .. CANR-40
Earlier sketch in CA 49-52
Langhorne, John 1735-1779 .... DLB 109
See also RGEL 2
Langhorne, Richard (Tristan Bailey) 1940- .. 122
Langiade de la Renta, Francoise de
See de la Renta, Francoise de Langiade
Langiulli, Nino 1932- 53-56
Langlais, Jacques 1921- 141
Langland, Elizabeth 1948- 112
Langland, Joseph (Thomas) 1917- CANR-8
Earlier sketch in CA 5-8R
See also CP 1, 2
Langland, William 1332(?)-1400(?) .... BRW 1
See also DA
See also DAB
See also DAC
See also DAM MST, POET
See also DLB 146
See also RGEL 2
See also TEA
See also WLIT 3
Langley, Adria (Locke) 1899(?)-1983
Obituary 110
Langley, Andrew 1949- 171
See also SATA 104
Langley, Bob 1936- 85-88
Langley, Charles P(itman) III 1949- . CANR-122
Earlier sketch in CA 170
See also SATA 103
Langley, Dorothy
See Kissling, Dorothy (Hight)
Langley, Gill(ian Rose) 1952- 133
Langley, Harold D. 1925- 21-24R
Langley, Helen
See Rowland, D(onald) S(ydney)
Langley, James Maydon 1916-1983 102
Obituary 109
Langley, John .... TCWW 1, 2
Langley, Jonathan 1952- 195
See also SATA 122
Langley, Lee 1932- CANR-114
Earlier sketch in CA 159
Langley, Lester D(anny) 1940- CANR-41
Earlier sketches in CA 102, CANR-19
Langley, Liz 226
Langley, Michael (John) 1933- 97-100
Langley, Noel 1911-1980 .... CANR-83
Obituary 102
Earlier sketches in CA 13-16R, CANR-30
See also FANT
See also SATA-Obit 25
Langley, Raymond J. 1935-
Brief entry 108
Langley, Roger 1930- 73-76
Langley, Stephen G(ould) 1938-1997 .... 41-44R
Obituary 159
Langley, Tania
See Armstrong, Tilly
Langley, Wright 1935- 57-60
Langlois, Walter G(ordon) 1925- CANR-9
Earlier sketch in CA 21-24R
Langman, Ida Kaplan 1904-1991 .... CAP-1
Earlier sketch in CA 13-16
Langman, Larry 1930- 109
Langmead, Donald 1939- 175
Langner, Lawrence 1890-1962
Obituary 116
Langner, Nola
See Malone, Nola Langner
See also SATA 8
Langone, John (Michael) 1929- CANR-1
Earlier sketch in CA 49-52
See also SATA 46
See also SATA-Brief 38
Langreuter, Jutta 1944- 194
See also SATA 122
Langsam, Walter Consuelo
1906-1985 .... CANR-2
Obituary 117
Earlier sketch in CA 1-4R
Langsen, Richard C. 1953- 160
See also SATA 95
Lang-Sims, Lois Dorothy 1917- 106
Langsley, Donald G(ene) 1925- CANR-4
Earlier sketch in CA 53-56
Langstaff, J(ohn) Brett 1889-1985 ..... CANR-29
Obituary 115
Earlier sketch in CA 1-4R
Langstaff, John (Meredith) 1920- CANR-49
Earlier sketches in CA 1-4R, CANR-4
See also CLR 3
See also MAICYA 1, 2
See also SATA 6, 68
Langstaff, Josephine
See Herschberger, Ruth (Margaret)
Langstaff, Launcelot
See Irving, Washington
Langstaff, Nancy 1925- CANR-12
Earlier sketch in CA 73-76
Langston, Douglas C. 1950- 208
Langton, Anne 1804-1893 .... DLB 99
Langton, Clair V(an Norman) 1895-1973 .. 5-8R
Langton, Daniel J(oseph) 1927- 93-96
Langton, Jane (Gillson) 1922- CANR-109
Earlier sketches in CA 1-4R, CANR-1, 18, 40, 83
See also BYA 5
See also CLR 33
See also CMW 4
See also MAICYA 1, 2
See also SAAS 5
See also SATA 3, 68, 129, 140
See also SATA-Essay 140
See also YAW
Langton, Kenneth P(atrick) 1933- 25-28R
Langton, Rae 1961- 185
Languirand, Jacques 1931- 166
Langum, David J. 1940- 141
Langwill, Lyndesay Graham
1897-1983 .... 13-16R
Langworth, Richard M(ichael) 1941- 73-76
Langworthy, Harry W(ells III) 1939- 57-60
Lanham, Charles Trueman 1902-1978
Obituary 81-84
Lanham, Edwin (Moultrie) 1904-1979 ..... 9-12R
Obituary 89-92
See also DLB 4
Lanham, Frank W(esley) 1914-2002 ... CANR-6
Earlier sketch in CA 1-4R
Lanham, Richard Alan 1936- CANR-10
Earlier sketch in CA 25-28R
Lanham, Url(ess Norton) 1918-1999 ..... 25-28R
Lanier, Alison Raymond 1917-1993 . CANR-12
Obituary 142
Earlier sketch in CA 17-20R
Lanier, Drew Noble 1962- 233
Lanier, Sidney (Clopton) 1842-1881 . MAICYA 2
Lanier, Sidney 1842-1881 .... AMWS 1
See also DAM POET
See also DLB 64
See also DLBD 13
See also EXPP
See also MAICYA 1
See also PC 50
See also PFS 14
See also RGAL 4
See also SATA 18
Lanier, Sterling E(dmund) 1927- 162
Brief entry 118
See also SATA 109
See also SFW 4
Lanier, Virginia 1930-2003 .... CANR-144
Earlier sketch in CA 169
Lanigan, Catherine 1947- 108
Laning, Edward 1906-1981 53-56
Lanino, Deborah 1964- .... SATA 123
Lank, Edith H(andleman) 1926- 109
Lanker, Brian T(imothy) 1947- 134
Lankevich, George J(ohn) 1939- CANR-13
Earlier sketch in CA 77-80
Lankford, John (Errett) 1934- 17-20R
Lankford, Mary D. 1932- 145
See also SATA 77, 112
Lankford, Mike 1951- 163
Lankford, Nelson D. 1948- CANR-123
Earlier sketch in CA 138
Lankford, Philip Marlin 1945- CANR-7
Earlier sketch in CA 57-60
Lankford, T(homas) Randall 1942- 65-68
Lankford, Terrill Lee 234
Lankov, Andrei N(ikolaevich) 1963- 232
Lanks, Herbert C(harles) 1899-1987
Obituary 122
Lanne, William F.
See Leopold, Nathan F.
Lanner, Ronald Martin 1930- 107
Lannin, Joanne (A.) 1951- 192
See also SATA 121
Lanning, Edward P(utnam) 1930-1985 .. 17-20R
Lanning, George (William), Jr.
1925-1995 .... 9-12R
Obituary 198
Lanning, John Tate 1902-1976
Obituary 108
Lannoy, Richard 1928- 194
Lannoy, Violet Dias 1925-1973 168
Lanoil, Georgia Hope Witkin
See Witkin-Lanoil, Georgia Hope
Lanoue, Fred Richard 1908-1965 .... CAP-1
Earlier sketch in CA 13-14
La Noue, George R(ichard) 1937- 73-76
Lanouette, William (John) 1940- 136
Lanoux, Armand 1913-1983
Obituary 109
Lansbury, Angela 1946- 81-84
Lansbury, Coral 1933-1991 143

Lansdale, Edward Geary 1908-1987
Obituary ... 121
Lansdale, Joe R(ichard) 1951- ... CANR-95
Earlier sketches in CA 113, CANR-32, 50, 83
See also AAYA 50
See also CMW 4
See also HGG
See also SATA 116
See also SFW 4
See also SUFW 2
See also TCWW 2
Lansdale, Robert Tucker 1900-1980
Obituary ... 103
Lansdowne, J(ames) F(enwick)
1937- ... CANR-30
Earlier sketch in CA 49-52
Lanser, Susan Sniader ... 107
Lansing, Alfred 1921-1975 ... 13-16R
Obituary ... 61-64
See also SATA 35
Lansing, Elisabeth Carleton Hubbard
1911- ... 5-8R
Lansing, Gerrit (Yates) 1928- ... 73-76
See also CP 1
Lansing, Henry
See Rowland, D(onald) S(ydney)
Lansing, John
See Andrews, Patrick E.
Lansing, John B(elcher) 1919-1970
Obituary ... 108
Lansing, Karen E. 1954- ... SATA 71
Lansing, Sherry 1944- ... IDFW 4
Lansky, Bruce 1941- ... CANR-29
Earlier sketch in CA 109
Lansky, Vicki 1942- ... CANR-53
Earlier sketches in CA 81-84, CANR-26
Lanson, Lucienne (Therese) 1930-
Brief entry ... 108
Lant, Harvey
See Rowland, D(onald) S(ydney)
Lant, Jeffrey Ladd 1947- ... CANR-30
Earlier sketch in CA 109
Lantange, Cecile de
See Cloutier-Wojciechowska, Cecile
Lanterman, Ray(mond E.) 1916-1994 ... 106
Lantier-Sampon, Patricia 1952- ... 156
See also SATA 92
Lantis, David W(illiam) 1917- ... 13-16R
Lantis, Margaret (Lydia) 1906- ... CAP-2
Earlier sketch in CA 29-32
Lantry, Mike
See Tubb, E(dwin) C(harles)
Lantz, Fran
See Lantz, Francess L(in)
Lantz, Francess L(in) 1952-2004 ... CANR-39
Obituary ... 233
Earlier sketch in CA 115
See also Dixon, Franklin W.
See also AAYA 37
See also SATA 63, 109, 153
See also SATA-Essay 153
See also SATA-Obit 159
Lantz, Herman R. 1919-1987 ... 37-40R
Obituary ... 122
Lantz, Louise K. 1930- ... 45-48
Lantz, Paul 1908- ... SATA 45
Lantz, Walter 1900-1994
Obituary ... 144
Brief entry ... 108
See also IDFW 3, 4
See also SATA 37
See also SATA-Obit 79
Lanyer, Aemilia 1569-1645 ... DLB 121
See also PC 60
Lanyon, Anna ... 234
Lanyon, Carla 1906-1971 ... CAP-1
Earlier sketch in CA 13-14
Lanza, Alejandro
See Bahr, Hermann
Lanza, Barbara 1945- ... SATA 101
Lanza, Joseph 1955- ... 154
Lanzillotti, Robert F(ranklin) 1921- ... 77-80
Lanzmann, Claude 1925- ... 139
Lao, Kan 1907- ... 41-44R
Lao Khamhom
See Srinawk, Khamsing
See also EWL 3
Laor, Yitzhak 1948- ... 214
Lao She
See Shu, Ch' ing-ch'un
See also EWL 3
See also RGWL 3
Lao-Tzu
See Lao Tzu
Lapage, Geoffrey 1888-1971 ... CAP-1
Earlier sketch in CA 9-10
La Pallo, A. Elise ... 128
LaPalma, Marina deBellagente 1949- ... 207
La Palombara, Joseph 1925- ... CANR-57
Earlier sketches in CA 1-4R, CANR-6, 31
Lapaquellerie, Yvon
See Bizardel, Yvon
Lapati, Americo D. 1924-1992 ... CANR-1
Earlier sketch in CA 1-4R
Lapatin, Kenneth D. S. 1961- ... 222
La Patra, Jack W(illiam) 1927- ... 93-96
Lape, Esther Everett 1881-1981
Obituary ... 108
Lape, Fred 1900-1985 ... 102
Lapedes, Daniel N. 1913(?)-1979
Obituary ... 93-96
Lapena, Frank Raymond
See Lapena, Frank Raymond
Lapena, Frank Raymond 1937- ... 219
Lapena-Bonifacio, Amelia 1930- ... 130
LaPenta, Anthony V(incent), Jr. 1943- ... 69-72
Lapeza, David (Henry) 1950- ... 73-76
Lapham, Arthur L(owell) 1922- ... 49-52
Lapham, David ... 194
Lapham, Lewis H(enry) 1935- ... CANR-88
Earlier sketches in CA 77-80, CANR-33
Interview in ... CANR-33
Lapham, Maxwell E(dward) 1900(?)-1983
Obituary ... 110
Lapham, Samuel, Jr. 1892-1972
Obituary ... 106
Lapid, Haim 1948- ... 219
Lapide, Phinn E.
See Lapide, Pinchas E.
Lapide, Pinchas E. 1922- ... CANR-13
Earlier sketch in CA 21-24R
Lapides, Robert 1940- ... 145
Lapidge, Michael 1942- ... 219
Lapidus, Elaine 1939- ... 21-24R
Lapidus, Jacqueline (Anita) 1941- ... 97-100
Lapidus, Morris 1902-2001 ... 77-80
Obituary ... 193
Lapierre, Dominique 1931- ... CANR-125
Earlier sketches in CA 69-72, CANR-19, 42
LaPierre, Janet 1933- ... 190
LaPierre, Laurier L. 1929- ... CANR-129
Brief entry ... 107
Earlier sketch in CA 164
LaPierre, Wayne R. ... 173
La Pietra, Mary 1929- ... 61-64
Lapin, Howard S(idney) 1922-1993 ... 17-20R
Lapin, Jackie 1951- ... 85-88
Lapine, James (Elliot) 1949- ... CANR-128
Brief entry ... 123
Earlier sketches in CA 130, CANR-54
Interview in ... CA-130
See also CLC 39
Lapinski, Susan 1948- ... 115
La Place, John 1922- ... 103
LaPlante, Eve ... 234
La Plante, Lynda 1943(?)- ... 232
LaPlante, Royal 1929- ... 195
LaPointe, Frank 1936- ... 93-96
Lapointe, (Joseph-)Gatien(-Fernand)
1931-1983 ... 148
See also DLB 88
Lapointe, Paul-Marie 1929- ... 196
Brief entry ... 109
See also DLB 88
Laponce, Jean Antoine 1925- ... 53-56
Laporte, Jean 1924- ... 41-44R
Laporte, Maurice 1901(?)-1987
Obituary ... 123
LaPorte, Robert, Jr. 1940- ... 41-44R
Lapotaire, Jane (Elizabeth Marie) 1944- ... 214
Lapp, Charles (Leon) 1914-1991 ... CANR-1
Earlier sketch in CA 45-48
Lapp, Christiane (Germain) 1948- ... SATA 74
Lapp, Chuck
See Lapp, Charles (Leon)
Lapp, Eleanor J. 1936- ... 69-72
Lapp, Eunice Willis Bodine 1905-1991 ... 123
Lapp, John Allen 1933- ... 41-44R
Lapp, John Clarke 1917-1977 ... 85-88
Lapp, Ralph Eugene 1917-2004 ... 81-84
Obituary ... 231
Lapp, Rudolph M(athew) 1915- ... 113
Lappe, Frances Moore 1944- ... CANR-115
Earlier sketch in CA 37-40R
Lappe, Frances Moore 1944-
See Lappe, Frances Moore
Lappe, Marc
See Lappe, Marc (Alan)
Lappe, Marc (Alan) 1943-2005 ... CANR-128
Obituary ... 239
Earlier sketches in CA 126, CANR-56
Lappin, Ben
See Lappin, Bernard William
Lappin, Bernard William 1916- ... 9-12R
Lappin, Elena ... 184
Lappin, Peter 1911-1999 ... CANR-50
Earlier sketches in CA 57-60, CANR-7, 25
See also SATA 32
Lapping, Brian 1937- ... 25-28R
Laprade, William Thomas 1883-1975
Obituary ... 89-92
LaPray, (Margaret) Helen 1916- ... CANR-7
Earlier sketch in CA 53-56
Lapsley, Hilary 1949- ... 197
Lapsley, James N(orvell) 1930- ... 25-28R
La Puma, Salvatore 1929- ... 136
Laqueur, Thomas Walter 1945- ... 172
Laqueur, Walter (Ze'ev) 1921- ... CANR-94
Earlier sketches in CA 5-8R, CANR-23
See also CAAS 19
Laquian, Aprodicio A(rcilla) 1935- ... CANR-26
Earlier sketch in CA 29-32R
Lara
See Griffith(-Jones), George (Chetwynd)
Lara, Adair 1952- ... 203
Lara, Agustin 1900-1970
Obituary ... 104
Lara, Jan
See Hinkemeyer, Michael T(homas)
Laramore, Darryl 1928- ... 101
Larangeira, Crispin 1940- ... 129
Laraque, Paul 1920- ... 215
Larbalestier, Justine ... 223
Larbaud, Valery (Nicolas) 1881-1957 ... 152
Brief entry ... 106
See also EWL 3
See also GFL 1789 to the Present
See also TCLC 9
Larco, Isabel Granda 1911(?)-1983
Obituary ... 109
Larcom, Lucy 1824-1893 ... AMWS 13
See also DLB 221, 243
Lardas, Konstantinos 1927-1996 ... 13-16R
Lardner, George, Jr. 1934- ... 73-76
Lardner, James 1948- ... CANR-98
Earlier sketch in CA 118
Lardner, John (Abbot) 1912-1960 ... 182
Obituary ... 93-96
See also DLB 171
Lardner, Kate ... 232
Lardner, Ring
See Lardner, Ring(gold) W(ilmer)
See also BPFB 2
See also CDALB 1917-1929
See also DLB 11, 25, 86, 171
See also DLBD 16
See also RGAL 4
See also RGSF 2
Lardner, Ring(gold Wilmer), Jr.
1915-2000 ... CANR-109
Obituary ... 191
Earlier sketches in CA 25-28R, CANR-13
Interview in ... CANR-13
See also DLB 26
See also IDFW 3, 4
Lardner, Ring W., Jr.
See Lardner, Ring(gold) W(ilmer)
Lardner, Ring(gold) W(ilmer) 1885-1933 ... 131
Brief entry ... 104
See also Lardner, Ring
See also AMW
See also MAL 5
See also MTCW 1, 2
See also MTFW 2005
See also SSC 32
See also TCLC 2, 14
See also TUS
Lardner-Burke, Desmond William 1909-1984
Obituary ... 114
Lardy, Nicholas R. 1946- ... 140
Laredo, Betty
See Codrescu, Andrei
Laredo, Johnny
See Caesar, (Eu)Gene (Lee)
la Renta, Francoise de Langiade de
See de la Renta, Francoise de Langiade
La Reyniere
See Courtine, Robert
Large, David C(lay) 1945- ... CANR-102
Earlier sketch in CA 140
Large, E(rnest) C(harles) (?)-1976 ... 160
Large, Peter Somerville
See Somerville-Large, Peter
Large, R(ichard) Geddes 1901-1988 ... 102
Large, Stephen S(toker) 1942- ... 120
Largo, Michael 1950- ... CANR-88
Earlier sketch in CA 73-76
Lariar, Lawrence 1908-1981 ... CAP-1
Earlier sketch in CA 9-10
Larimore, Bertha B(urnham) 1915-1999 .. 61-64
La Rivers, Ira II 1915-1977 ... 41-44R
Larkey, Patrick Darrel 1943- ... 85-88
Larkin, Amy
See Burns, Olive Ann
Larkin, Emmet 1927- ... CANR-9
Earlier sketch in CA 13-16R
Larkin, Joan 1939- ... 193
Larkin, John A(lan) 1936- ... 41-44R
Larkin, John Day 1897-1986
Obituary ... 118
Larkin, Maia
See Wojciechowska, Maia (Teresa)
Larkin, Maurice (John Milner) 1932-2004 .. 102
Obituary ... 223
Larkin, Miriam Therese 1930-
Brief entry ... 108
Larkin, Oliver Waterman 1896-1970 ... 1-4R
Obituary ... 29-32R
Larkin, Philip (Arthur) 1922-1985 ... CANR-62
Obituary ... 117
Earlier sketches in CA 5-8R, CANR-24
See also BRWS 1
See also CDBLB 1960 to Present
See also CLC 3, 5, 8, 9, 13, 18, 33, 39, 64
See also CP 1, 2
See also DA3
See also DAB
See also DAM MST, POET
See also DLB 27
See also EWL 3
See also MTCW 1, 2
See also MTFW 2005
See also PC 21
See also PFS 3, 4, 12
See also RGEL 2
Larkin, R. T.
See Larkin, Rochelle
Larkin, Rochelle 1935- ... CANR-13
Earlier sketch in CA 33-36R
Larkin, Sarah
See Loening, Sarah (Elizabeth) Larkin
Larlham, Hattie 1914-1996 ... 113
Larminie, Margaret Beda 1924- ... CANR-89
Earlier sketches in CA 5-8R, CANR-2, 18, 59
See also CMW 4
Larmore, Lewis 1915-1995 ... 45-48
Larn, Richard (James Vincent)
1930- ... CANR-20
Earlier sketch in CA 103
Larnach, Rupert
See Nevill, Barry St-John
Larner, Christina (Ross) (?)-1983
Obituary ... 115
Larner, Jeremy 1937- ... 9-12R
See also CN 1, 2
Larner, John (Patrick) 1930- ... CANR-81
Earlier sketch in CA 81-84
Larneuil, Michel
See Batbedat, Jean
Laroche, Giles 1956- ... SATA 71, 126
Laroche, Loretta 1939- ... 204
Laroche, Rene
See McKeag, Ernest L(ionel)
La Roche, Sophie von 1730-1807 ... DLB 94
La Rochefoucauld, Francois VI
1613-1680 ... DLB 268
See also EW 3
See also GFL Beginnings to 1789
See also RGWL 2, 3
LaRochelle, David 1960- ... 186
See also SATA 115
Larock, Bruce Edward 1940- ... 53-56
La Rocque, Gilbert 1943-1984 ... 148
See also DLB 60
Larom, Henry V. 1903(?)-1975
Obituary ... 61-64
See also SATA-Obit 30
Laroque, Francois G. 1948- ... 140
Laroque de Roquebrune, Robert
See Roquebrune, Robert (Laroque) de
La Rosa, Pablo 1944- ... 161
La Rosa, Paul (Frank) 1953- ... 113
LaRose, Lawrence 1964(?)- ... 235
LaRose, Linda ... SATA 125
Larose, Paul 1947- ... 114
LaRouche, Lyndon H(ermyle), Jr. 1922- ... 138
Brief entry ... 124
Larrabee, Carroll Burton 1896-1983
Obituary ... 110
Larrabee, Eric 1922-1990 ... CANR-1
Obituary ... 133
Earlier sketch in CA 1-4R
Larrabee, Harold A(tkins) 1894-1979 ... CAP-1
Obituary ... 85-88
Earlier sketch in CA 11-12
Larrabee, Lisa 1947- ... 150
See also SATA 84
Larranaga, Robert O. 1940- ... 49-52
Larrea, Jean-Jacques 1960- ... 45-48
Larrecq, John M(aurice) 1926-1980 ... SATA 44
See also SATA-Obit 25
Larreta, Enrique 1875-1961 ... LAW
Larrick (Crosby), Nancy 1910-2004 ... CANR-1
Obituary ... 233
Earlier sketch in CA 1-4R
See also DLB 61
See also SATA 4
Larrie, Reginald R. 1928-1997 ... 123
Brief entry ... 118
Larrison, Earl J(unior) 1919-1987 ... CANR-9
Earlier sketch in CA 57-60
Larrowe, Charles P(atrick) 1916- ... 41-44R
Larry
See Parkes, Terence
Lars, Claudia 1899-1974 ... DLB 283
Larsen, Anita 1942- ... SATA 78
Larsen, Beverly (Namen) 1929- ... 17-20R
Larsen, Carl 1934- ... CANR-27
Earlier sketch in CA 77-80
Larsen, Charles E(dward) 1923- ... 33-36R
Larsen, David C(harles) 1944- ... 73-76
Larsen, E(gner) John 1926- ... CANR-16
Earlier sketch in CA 25-28R
Larsen, Egon 1904- ... CANR-3
Earlier sketch in CA 9-12R
See also SATA 14
Larsen, Elyse 1957- ... 41-44R
Larsen, Eric 1941- ... 132
See also CLC 55
Larsen, Erik 1911- ... 41-44R
Larsen, Erling 1909-1976 ... 13-16R
Larsen, Ernest 1946- ... 106
Larsen, Gaylord 1932- ... CANR-30
Earlier sketch in CA 112
Larsen, J(akob) A(ll) O(tteson) 1888-1974
Obituary ... 111
Larsen, Jack Lenor 1927- ... 126
Larsen, Jeanne (Louise) 1950- ... CANR-112
Earlier sketch in CA 134
Larsen, Jens Peter 1902-1988
Obituary ... 126
Larsen, Kalee 1952- ... 41-44R
Larsen, Knud S(onderhede) 1938- ... 53-56
Larsen, Lawrence H(arold) 1931- ... 21-24R
Larsen, Marianne 1951- ... 189
See also EWL 3
Larsen, Nella 1893(?)-1963 ... CANR-83
Earlier sketch in CA 125
See also AFAW 1, 2
See also BLC 2
See also BW 1
See also CLC 37
See also DAM MULT
See also DLB 51
See also FW
See also HR 1:3
See also LATS 1:1
See also LMFS 2
Larsen, Otto N. 1922- ... CANR-2
Earlier sketch in CA 1-4R
Larsen, Paul E(manuel) 1933- ... 93-96
Larsen, Peter 1933- ... CANR-22
Earlier sketch in CA 29-32R
Larsen, Rebecca 1944- ... 122
See also SATA 54
Larsen, Ronald J(ames) 1948- ... 41-44R
Larsen, Roy E(dward) 1899-1979
Obituary ... 89-92
Larsen, Scott ... 224
Larsen, Stephen 1941- ... 69-72
Larsen, Susan C(arol) 1946- ... 125
Larsen, Thoger 1875-1928 ... DLB 300
Larsen, Tony 1949- ... 107
Larsen, Torben B. 1944- ... 143
Larsen, Wendy Wilder 1940- ... 120
Larsen, William E(dward) 1936- ... 17-20R
Larsgaard, Chris 1967- ... 225
Larsgaard, Mary L(ynette) 1946- ... 122

Cumulative Index 337 **Lattany**

Larson, Albert J. 1934- 112
Larson, Andrew Karl 1899-1983 .... CAP-2
Earlier sketch in CA 33-36
Larson, (Lewis) Arthur 1910-1993 ...... CANR-1
Obituary 141
Earlier sketch in CA 1-4R
Larson, Bob 1944- CANR-5
Earlier sketch in CA 53-56
Larson, Bruce 1925-1998 .... CANR-56
Earlier sketches in CA 57-60, CANR-13, 30
Larson, Bruce L(lewellyn) 1936- 85-88
Larson, Calvin J(ames) 1933- CANR-31
Earlier sketch in CA 49-52
Larson, Carl M. 1916- 41-44R
Larson, Carole 1940- 147
Larson, Cedric Arthur 1908-1996 65-68
Larson, Charles 1922- 25-28R
Larson, Charles R(aymond) 1938- .. CANR-121
Earlier sketches in CA 53-56, CANR-4
See also CLC 31
Larson, Charles U(rban) 1940- 97-100
Larson, Clem
See Fearn, John Russell
Larson, Clinton F(oster) 1919-1994 . CANR-118
Earlier sketch in CA 57-60
See also DLB 256
Larson, Donald (Norman) 1925- 57-60
Larson, Doran 1957- 124
Larson, E. Richard 1944- 105
Larson, Edward J(ohn) 1953- CANR-88
Earlier sketch in CA 158
Larson, Ellen 1953- 221
Larson, Erik 1954- 192
See also AAYA 65
Larson, Esther Elisabeth 1908-1978 .... 17-20R
Obituary 134
Larson, Eve
See St. John, Wylly Folk
Larson, Gary 1950- CANR-60
Earlier sketches in CA 118, CANR-41
See also AAYA 1, 62
See also BYA 12
See also DAM POP
See also SATA 57
Larson, Gary O(tto) 1949- 115
Larson, George C(harles) 1942- CANR-9
Earlier sketch in CA 65-68
Larson, Gerald James 1938- 93-96
Larson, Glen A. 1937(?)-
Brief entry 115
Larson, Gustive O(lof) 1897-1978 .... 29-32R
Obituary 125
Larson, Harold J. 1934- 53-56
Larson, Henrietta M(elia) 1894-1983 ..... CAP-2
Obituary 110
Earlier sketch in CA 23-24
Larson, Ingrid D(ana) 1965- 156
See also SATA 92
Larson, James F(rederick) 1947- 115
Larson, Janet Karsten 1945- CANR-99
Earlier sketch in CA 104
Larson, Jean Russell 1930- CANR-99
Earlier sketch in CA 21-24R
See also SATA 121
Larson, Jeanne 1920- 57-60
Larson, Jennifer 1965- 152
Larson, Jonathan 1960-1996 156
See also AAYA 28
See also CLC 99
See also MTFW 2005
Larson, Kate Clifford 232
Larson, Kirby 1954- 161
See also SATA 96
Larson, Knute (G.) 1919-1976 .... 9-12R
Larson, Kris 1953- 77-80
Larson, Magali Sarfatti 1936- 97-100
Larson, Martin Alfred 1897-1994 .... CANR-2
Earlier sketch in CA 5-8R
Larson, Mel(vin Gunnard) 1916-1972 .... 5-8R
Larson, Muriel 1924- CANR-49
Earlier sketches in CA 21-24R, CANR-9, 24
Larson, Norita D(ittberner) 1944- 105
See also SATA 29
Larson, Orvin Prentiss 1910-1985 77-80
Larson, P(aul) Merville 1903-1986 .... 41-44R
Larson, Peggy (Ann Pickering) 1931- 81-84
Larson, Rebecca 1959- 200
Larson, Reed (W.) 1950- 128
Larson, Richard Francis 1931- CANR-15
Earlier sketch in CA 41-44R
Larson, Robert H(erbert) 1942- 113
Larson, Robert W. 1927- 85-88
Larson, Rodger .... BYA 12
Larson, Sidner J. 1949- 149
Larson, Simeon 1925- 61-64
Larson, Stephanie Greco 1960- 144
Larson, T(aft) A(lfred) 1910-2001 .... 33-36R
Larson, Thomas B(ryan) 1914- 25-28R
Larson, Victor E. 1898-1981 .... 25-28R
Obituary 134
Larson, Wendy 200
Larson, William H. 1938- 21-24R
See also SATA 10
Larsson, Carl (Olof) 1853-1919
Brief entry 115
See also SATA 35
Larsson, Flora (Benwell) 1904-2000 93-96
Lartigue, Jacques-Henri 1894-1986 .... 33-36R
Obituary 120
La Rue, Daniel Wolford, Jr. 1878-1969
Obituary 116
Larue, Gerald A(lexander) 1916- 21-24R
LaRue, L. H. 1938- 135
LaRusso, Dominic A(nthony) 1924- 33-36R
Lary, N(ikita) M(ichael) 1940- 61-64
Larzelere, Alex 1936- 166
Lasagna, Louis (Cesare) 1923-2003
Obituary 219
Brief entry 106
La Sale, Antoine de c. 1386-1460(?) ... DLB 208
LaSalle, Barbara 219
LaSalle, Charles A.
See Ellis, Edward S(ylvester)
LaSalle, Charles E.
See Ellis, Edward S(ylvester)
La Salle, Donald (Philip) 1933- 29-32R
La Salle, Dorothy (Marguerite)
1895-1980 .... 5-8R
Obituary 126
LaSalle, Mick 219
LaSalle, Peter 1947- 103
La Salle, Victor
See Fanthorpe, R(obert) Lionel and
Glasby, John S.
Lasar, Matthew 1954- 184
Lasater, Alice E(lizabeth) 1936- 57-60
Lasby, Clarence G(eorge) 1933- 105
Las Casas, Bartolome de 1474-1566
See Casas, Bartolome de las
See also DLB 318
See also HLCS
See also LAW
Lascelles, Mary (Madge) 1900-1995 201
Lasch, Christopher 1932-1994 .... CANR-118
Obituary 144
Earlier sketches in CA 73-76, CANR-25
See also CLC 102
See also DLB 246
See also MTCW 1, 2
See also MTFW 2005
Lasch, Robert 1907-1998 102
Obituary 167
Laschever, Barnett D. 1924- CANR-6
Earlier sketch in CA 1-4R
Lasch-Quinn, Elisabeth 1959- 207
LaScola, Ray(mond) L. 1915- 1-4R
Lasdun, James 1958- CANR-111
Earlier sketch in CA 137
See also DLB 319
Lasdun, Susan 1929- 111
Lasell, Elinor H. 1929- CANR-7
Earlier sketch in CA 5-8R
See also SATA 19
Lasell, Fen H.
See Lasell, Elinor H.
Lasenby, Jack 1931- CANR-83
Earlier sketch in CA 130
See also CWRI 5
See also SATA 65, 103
Laser, Marvin 1914-1985 .... 9-12R
Laser, Michael 1954- 189
See also SATA 117
Lash, Jeffrey N. 1949- 136
Lash, Jennifer 1938-1993 168
Lash, Joseph P. 1909-1987 .... CANR-16
Obituary 123
Earlier sketch in CA 17-20R
See also SATA 43
Lash, Nicholas (Langrishe Alleyne) 1934- ... 144
La Shelle, Joseph 1905-1989 .... IDFW 3, 4
Lasher, Albert C. 1928- 25-28R
Lasher, Faith B. 1921- 37-40R
See also SATA 12
Lashley, Cliff 1935- .... CP 1
Lashmar, Paul (Christopher) 1954- 189
Lashner, William 1956(?)- CANR-71
Earlier sketch in CA 152
Laska
See Laska, P(eter) J(erome)
Laska, P(eter) J(erome) 1938- CANR-15
Earlier sketch in CA 65-68
Laska, Vera
See Laska, Vera O(ravec)
Laska, Vera O(ravec) 1923- 119
Laskas, Gretchen Moran 223
Lasker, David 1950- 112
See also SATA 38
Lasker, Edward 1885-1981 .... 5-8R
Obituary 103
Lasker, Gabriel Ward 1912- 1-4R
Lasker, Joe
See Lasker, Joseph Leon
See also SAAS 17
See also SATA 83
Lasker, Joseph Leon 1919- CANR-38
Earlier sketches in CA 49-52, CANR-1
See also Lasker, Joe
See also SATA 9
Lasker, Judith N. 1947- 130
Lasker, Lawrence 1949- 166
Lasker, Michael
See Elman, Richard (Martin)
Lasker-Schueler, Else 1869-1945 183
See also Lasker-Schuler, Else
See also DLB 66, 124
See also TCLC 57
Lasker-Schuler, Else
See Lasker-Schueler, Else
See also EWL 3
Laski, Audrey Louise 1931-2003 224
Laski, Harold J(oseph) 1893-1950 188
See also TCLC 79
Laski, Marghanita 1915-1988 .... CANR-75
Obituary 124
Earlier sketch in CA 105
See also HGG
See also SATA 55
Laskier, Michael M. 1949- 142
Laskin, Bora 1912-1984
Obituary 112
Laskin, David 1953- CANR-100
Earlier sketch in CA 146
Laskin, Pamela L. 1954- 142
See also SATA 75
Lasko, Peter (Erik) 1924-2003 150
Obituary 216
Laskowski, Jerzy 1919- 77-80
Lasky, Betty 1927- 119
Lasky, Jesse L. 1880-1958 .... IDFW 3, 4
Lasky, Jesse Louis, Jr. 1910-1988 ...... CANR-20
Earlier sketches in CA 1-4R, CANR-4
See also AITN 1
Lasky, Kathryn 1944- CANR-141
Earlier sketches in CA 69-72, CANR-11, 84
See also AAYA 19
See also BYA 6
See also CLR 11
See also JRDA
See also MAICYA 1, 2
See also SATA 13, 69, 112, 157
See also WYA
See also YAW
Lasky, Melvin J(onah) 1920-2004 53-56
Obituary 228
Lasky, Pat
See Carleton, Barbara
Lasky, Victor 1918-1990 .... CANR-10
Obituary 131
Earlier sketch in CA 5-8R
Interview in CANR-10
See also AITN 1
Lasky, William R(aymond) 1921- 97-100
Lasky Knight, Kathryn
See Lasky, Kathryn
Laslett, John H(enry) M(artin) 1933- . CANR-12
Earlier sketch in CA 29-32R
Laslett, Peter 1915-2001 .... CANR-12
Obituary 200
Earlier sketch in CA 73-76
Lasley, Jack
See Lasley, John Wayne III
Lasley, John Wayne III 1925- 17-20R
Lasnier, Rina 1915- .... DLB 88
LaSor, William Sanford 1911-1991 ... CANR-21
Obituary 133
Earlier sketches in CA 1-4R, CANR-2
La Sorte, A(ntonio) Michael 1931- 13-16R
La Spina, (Fanny) Greye 1880-1969 ...... CAP-1
Obituary 199
Earlier sketch in CA 13-14
Lass, Abraham H(arold) 1907-2001 .... 9-12R
Lass, Betty (Lipschitz) 1908(?)-1976
Obituary 69-72
Lass, Bonnie .... SATA 131
Lass, Roger 1937- 132
Lass, William E(dward) 1928- CANR-2
Earlier sketch in CA 1-4R
Lass, William M. 1910(?)-1975
Obituary 104
Lassaigne, Jacques 1910(?)-1982 129
Lassalle, C. E.
See Ellis, Edward S(ylvester)
Lassalle, Ferdinand 1825-1864 .... DLB 129
Lassally, Walter 1926- .... IDFW 3, 4
Lassam, Robert (Errington) 1914- 112
Lassang, Iwan
See Goll, Yvan
Lassen-Willems, James
See Willems, J. Rutherford
Lasser, Scott 212
Lasserre, Philippe 1939- 159
Lassers, Willard J. 1919-1997 .... 17-20R
Lasseter, John 1957- .... AAYA 65
Lassimonne, Denise 25-28R
Lassiter, Adam
See Krauzer, Steven M(ark)
Lassiter, Isaac Steele 1941- 33-36R
Lassiter, Mary
See Hoffman, Mary (Margaret)
See also SATA 59
Lassiter, (Albin) Perry (Jr.) 1935- 97-100
Lassiter, Rhiannon 1977- 233
See also SATA 157
Lassiter, Roy L(eland), Jr. 1927- 21-24R
Lassiter, Sybil M. 1928- 175
Lassner, Jacob 1935- CANR-42
Earlier sketches in CA 29-32R, CANR-20
Lasson, Kenneth (Lee) 1943- CANR-94
Earlier sketches in CA 33-36R, CANR-13
Lasswell, Harold D. 1902-1978
Obituary 104
Lasswell, Marcia 1927- 97-100
Lasswell, Thomas Ely 1919- 17-20R
Lasswitz, Kurd 1848-1910 168
See also SFW 4
Last, Jef
See Last, Josephus Carel Franciscus
Last, Joan 1908- 107
Last, Josephus Carel Franciscus
1898-1972 .... CAP-2
Earlier sketch in CA 33-36
Laster, Ann A(ppleton) 1936- 29-32R
Laster, James H. 1934- 209
Laszlo, Ernest 1896-1984 .... IDFW 3, 4
Laszlo, Ervin 1932- 41-44R
Laszlo, Miklos 1904(?)-1973
Obituary 41-44R
La Taille, Jean de 1533(?)-c.
1607 .... GFL Beginnings to 1789
Latane, Bibb 1937- 37-40R
Latch, William 1950(?)-1985
Obituary 117
Latchaw, Marjorie Elizabeth 1914- 5-8R
Lateef, Tolen S.
See Sanders, Clinton R.
Lateiner, Donald 1944- 135
Latell, Brian 1941- 175
Lateur, Frank
See Streuvels, Stijn
Latham, Aaron 1943- CANR-107
Earlier sketch in CA 33-36R
Latham, Agnes (Mary Christabel)
1905-1996 221
Latham, Alison 226
Latham, Angela J(oy) 1961- 190
Latham, Barbara 1896- .... SATA 16
Latham, Caroline S. 1940- 125
Latham, Donald Crawford 1932- 9-12R
Latham, Earl Ganson 1907-1977 103
Latham, Frank B(rown) 1910-2000 49-52
See also SATA 6
Latham, Harold Strong 1887-1969 .... CAP-1
Earlier sketch in CA 9-10
Latham, Ian 1956- 109
Latham, Jean Lee 1902-1995 .... CANR-84
Earlier sketches in CA 5-8R, CANR-7
See also AITN 1
See also BYA 1
See also CLC 12
See also CLR 50
See also MAICYA 1, 2
See also SATA 2, 68
See also YAW
Latham, John H. 1917- 5-8R
Latham, Joyce 1943- 73-76
Latham, Lenn Learner 1901-1970(?) 1-4R
Obituary 135
Latham, Lorraine 1948- 65-68
Latham, Marte Hooper 1924-1988 .... 9-12R
Latham, Mavis
See Clark, Mavis Thorpe
Latham, Peter 1910- CAP-1
Earlier sketch in CA 11-12
Latham, Philip
See Richardson, Robert S(hirley)
Latham, Robert C(lifford)
1912-1995 .... CANR-89
Earlier sketch in CA 158
See also DLB 201
Latham, Roger M. 1914(?)-1979
Obituary 85-88
Latham, Sean (Patrick) 1971- 224
Lathen, Emma
See Hennissart, Martha and
Latsis, Mary J(ane)
See also BPFB 2
See also CLC 2
See also CMW 4
See also DLB 306
Lather, Patti 1948- 163
Lathey, Gillian 1949- 216
Lathrop, Dorothy P(ulis) 1891-1980 73-76
Obituary 102
See also DLB 22
See also MAICYA 1, 2
See also SATA 14
See also SATA-Obit 24
Lathrop, Francis
See Leiber, Fritz (Reuter, Jr.)
Lathrop, George Parsons 1851-1898 .... DLB 71
Lathrop, Irvin T(unis) 1927- CANR-22
Earlier sketch in CA 45-48
Lathrop, JoAnna 1931- 61-64
Lathrop, John, Jr. 1772-1820 .... DLB 37
Lathrop, Philip H. 1916-1995 .... IDFW 4
Latimer, Dean 1945- 129
See also AAYA 2
Latimer, H(enry) C. 1893-1982 .... 29-32R
Latimer, Hugh 1492(?)-1555 .... DLB 136
Latimer, Jim 1943- .... SATA 80
Latimer, Jonathan (Wyatt) 1906-1983
Obituary 110
See also CMW 4
Latimer, Rebecca H. 1905- 194
Latman, Alan 1930-1984
Obituary 113
Latner, Helen (Stambler) 1918- 106
Latner, Pat Wallace
See Strother, Pat Wallace
Latorre, Dolores L(aguarta Blasco)
1903-1999 65-68
Latorre, Felipe A(ugusto) 1907-1997 65-68
Latour, Frank
See Streuvels, Stijn
Latour, Jose 1940- 197
La Tour du Pin, Patrice de 1911-1975
Obituary 115
See also DLB 258
See also EWL 3
Latourelle, Rene 1918- CANR-85
Earlier sketch in CA 130
La Tourette, Aileen 1946- 119
Latourette, Kenneth Scott 1884-1967 .... CAP-2
Earlier sketch in CA 23-24
La Tourrette, Jacqueline 1926- CANR-86
Earlier sketches in CA 49-52, CANR-34
Latow, (Muriel) Roberta 1931-2003 .. CANR-40
Obituary 218
Earlier sketch in CA 116
Latreille, Stanley 234
Latsis, Mary J(ane) 1927-1997 85-88
Obituary 162
See also Lathen, Emma
See also CMW 4
Latta, Rich
See Latta, Richard
Latta, Richard 1946- CANR-41
Earlier sketches in CA 53-56, CANR-4, 19
See also SATA 113
Latta, William (Charlton, Jr.) 1929- 115
Lattany, Kristin
See Lattany, Kristin (Elaine Eggleston) Hunter
Lattany, Kristin (Eggleston) Hunter
1931- .... SATA 132, 154
See also SATA-Essay 154

Lattany, Kristin (Elaine Eggleston) Hunter
1931- CANR-108
Earlier sketches in CA 13-16R, CANR-13
Interview in CANR-13
See also Hunter, Kristin
See also AITN 1
See also BW 1
See also BYA 3
See also CLC 35
See also CLR 3
See also CN 7
See also DLB 33
See also MAICYA 1, 2
See also SAAS 10
See also SATA 12, 132
See also YAW
Latterman, Terry A. 219
Lattes, Jean-Claude J. 1941- 201
Lattimer, John Kingsley 1914- 106
Lattimore, Deborah Nourse .... CWRI 5
Lattimore, Eleanor Frances
1904-1986 .... CANR-85
Obituary 119
Earlier sketches in CA 9-12R, CANR-6
See also CWRI 5
See also SATA 7
See also SATA-Obit 48
Lattimore, Jessie
See Dresser, Norine and
Fontes, Montserrat
Lattimore, Owen 1900-1989 97-100
Obituary 128
Lattimore, Richmond (Alexander)
1906-1984 .... CANR-1
Obituary 112
Earlier sketch in CA 1-4R
See also CLC 3
See also CP 1, 2
See also MAL 5
Lattin, Ann
See Cole, Lois Dwight
Lattin, Harriet Pratt 1898- 33-36R
Lattis, James M. 1954- 150
Latuchie, Karen 1954- 232
Latukefu, Sione 1927- 73-76
Latymer, William 1498-1583 .... DLB 132
Latynin, Leonid (Aleksandrovich) 1938- 226
Latzer, Barry 1945- 170
Latzer, Beth Good 1911- 65-68
Lau, Charles Richard 1933-1984
Obituary 112
Lau, Charley
See Lau, Charles Richard
Lau, Evelyn 1970- 155
Lau, Joseph S(hui) M(ing) 1934- CANR-87
Earlier sketch in CA 77-80
Laub, (Martin) Julian 1929- 37-40R
Laubach, David C. 1939- 216
Laubach, Frank Charles 1884-1970 .... CAP-1
Earlier sketch in CA 9-10
Laube, Clifford J(ames) 1891-1974
Obituary 53-56
Laube, Heinrich 1806-1884 .... DLB 133
Laubenbacher, Reinhard C. 1954- 148
Laubenthal, Sanders Anne 1943- 61-64
Lauber, Lynn 1952- 133
Lauber, Patricia (Grace) 1924- CANR-117
Earlier sketches in CA 9-12R, CANR-6, 24, 38
See also CLR 16
See also JRDA
See also MAICYA 1, 2
See also SATA 1, 33, 75, 138
Lauber, Volkmar 1944- 132
Laubin, Gladys (Winifred) 111
Laubin, Reginald K(arl) -2000 111
Laucanno, Christopher Sawyer
See Sawyer-Laucanno, Christopher
Lauck, Carol 1934- 93-96
Lauck, Jennifer 1964- 204
Lauck, Jon K. 201
Laud, William 1573-1645 .... DLB 213
Laudan, Larry L. 1941- 129
Lauder, George
See Dick-Lauder, George (Andrew)
Lauder, George (Andrew) Dick
See Dick-Lauder, George (Andrew)
Lauder, Peter
See Cunningham, Peter
Lauder, Phyllis (Anna Lynn) 1898- 93-96
Lauder, Robert E(dward) 1934- 134
Lauderdale, Pat 1944- 101
Laudicina, Paul A(ndrew) 1949- 93-96
Laudin, Harvey 1922- 77-80
Laue, Max Theodor Felix von 1879-1960
Obituary 113
Lauer, Evelyn G(erda) 1938- 29-32R
Lauer, Jeanette C(arol) 1935- CANR-43
Earlier sketches in CA 104, CANR-19
Lauer, Jean-Philippe 1902- 85-88
Lauer, (Joseph) Quentin 1917- 152
Lauer, Robert H(arold) 1933- CANR-43
Earlier sketches in CA 53-56, CANR-4, 19
Lauer, Rosemary Zita 1919-1988 .... 5-8R
Lauer, Theodore E. 1931- 37-40R
Lauerman, David A(nthony) 1931- 17-20R
Lauersen, Niels H(elth) 1939- CANR-33
Earlier sketches in CA 85-88, CANR-15
Lauf, Detlef I. Charles 1936- 103
Laufe, Abe 1906- 17-20R
Laufenberg, Cindy 1965- 147
Laufer, Leopold 1925- 21-24R
Laufer, Robert S. 1942(?)-1989
Obituary 129
Lauffer, Armand A(lbert) 1933- CANR-19
Earlier sketches in CA 53-56, CANR-5
Laugesen, Mary E(akin) 1906-1995 .... CAP-2
Earlier sketch in CA 29-32
See also SATA 5
Laugesen, Peter 1942- .... EWL 3
Laughbaum, Steve 1945- .... SATA 12
Laughlin, Clarence John 1905-1985
Obituary 114
Laughlin, Florence Young 1910-2001 .... 9-12R
See also SATA 3
Laughlin, Henry Prather 1916- CANR-8
Earlier sketch in CA 61-64
Laughlin, James 1914-1997 .... CANR-47
Obituary 162
Earlier sketches in CA 21-24R, CANR-9
See also CAAS 22
See also CLC 49
See also CP 1, 2
See also DLB 48
See also DLBY 1996, 1997
Laughlin, Ledlie Irwin 1890-1977 .... 37-40R
Laughlin, P. S.
See Shea, Patrick
Laughlin, Rosemary 1941- 194
See also SATA 123
Laughlin, Tom 1938(?)- 138
Brief entry 116
Laughton, Bruce (Kyle Blake) 1928- 133
Laughton, Tom 1904(?)-1984
Obituary 112
Laugier, Odile 1956- 108
Laugier, R.
See Cumberland, Marten
Lauinger, Joseph L. 1947- 187
Laumann, Edward O(tto) 1938- CANR-128
Earlier sketch in CA 33-36R
Laumer, (John) Keith 1925-1993 .... CANR-51
Earlier sketches in CA 9-12R, CANR-7
See also DLB 8
See also SFW 4
Launay, Andre (Joseph) 1930- 25-28R
Launay, Droo
See Launay, Andre (Joseph)
Launay, Jacques F(orment) de
See de Launay, Jacques F(orment)
Laune, Paul Sidney 1899- 17-20R
Launer, Donald 1926- 162
Launitz-Schurer, Leopold (Sidney), Jr.
1942- 103
Launius, Roger D. 1954- CANR-118
Earlier sketch in CA 154
Launko, Okinba
See Osofisan, Femi
Lauper, Cyndi 1953- 213
Laurance, Alfred D.
See Tralins, S(andor) Robert
Laurance, Alice (a pseudonym) 1938- 101
Laurance, William F. 1957- 197
Laure, Ettagale
See Blauer, Ettagale
Laure, Jason 1940- 104
See also SATA 50
See also SATA-Brief 44
Laurel, Alicia Bay 1949- 41-44R
Lauremberg, Johann 1590-1658 .... DLB 164
Lauren, Linda
See Bunce, Linda Susan (Staines)
Laurence, Dan H. 1920- CANR-66
Earlier sketches in CA 17-20R, CANR-13, 32
Laurence, Ester Hauser 1935- 29-32R
See also SATA 7
Laurence, Gerald (Robert) 1948- 131
Laurence, Helen
See Kennedy, Leo
Laurence, Janet 1937- 140
Laurence, John 1939- CANR-116
Earlier sketch in CA 69-72
Laurence, (Jean) Margaret (Wemyss)
1926-1987 .... CANR-33
Obituary 121
Earlier sketch in CA 5-8R
See also BYA 13
See also CLC 3, 6, 13, 50, 62
See also CN 1, 2, 3, 4
See also DAC
See also DAM MST
See also DLB 53
See also EWL 3
See also FW
See also MTCW 1, 2
See also MTFW 2005
See also NFS 11
See also RGEL 2
See also RGSF 2
See also SATA-Obit 50
See also SSC 7
See also TCWW 2
Laurence, Michael M(arshall) 1940- 33-36R
Laurence, Will
See Smith, Willard L(aurence)
Laurence, William Leonard 1888-1977 77-80
Obituary 69-72
Laurens, Camille
See Ruel-Mezieres, Laurence
Laurens, Jeannine 1950- 151
Laurens, Stephanie 212
Laurent, Antoine 1952- .... CLC 50
Laurent, John (Angus) 1947- 231
Laurent, Lawrence (Bell) 1925- 69-72
Laurent, Pauline 1945- 178
Laurent, Pierre-Henri 1933- 174
Laurenti, Joseph L(ucian) 1931- CANR-57
Earlier sketches in CA 49-52, CANR-31
Laurentin, Rene 1917- CANR-48
Earlier sketch in CA 106
Laurentius von Schnuffis 1633-1702 .... DLB 168
Laurents, Arthur 1917- CANR-113
Earlier sketches in CA 13-16R, CANR-8, 73
Interview in CANR-8
See also CAD
See also CD 5, 6
See also DLB 26
See also LAIT 4
See also RGAL 4
Lauri, Olavi
See Paavolainen, Olavi (Lauri)
Lauria, Frank (Jonathan) 1935- 103
Laurie, Annie
See Black, Winifred
Laurie, Annie
See Scarberry, Alma Sioux
Laurie, Bruce 1943- 115
Laurie, Clayton D. 1954- 153
Laurie, Edward J(ames) 1925- CANR-8
Earlier sketch in CA 17-20R
Laurie, Harry C.
See Cahn, Zvi
Laurie, Hugh 1959- 164
Laurie, James 1947- 69-72
Laurie, Michael M. 1932- 126
Laurie, Peter 1937- 158
Laurie, Rona 1916- CANR-33
Earlier sketches in CA 85-88, CANR-15
See also SATA 55
Laurimore, Jill Frances 1947- 203
Laurin, Anne
See McLaurin, Anne
Lauritsen, John (Phillip) 1939- 57-60
Lauritzen, Elizabeth Moyes 1909- CAP-1
Earlier sketch in CA 13-16
Lauritzen, Jonreed 1902-1979 .... 5-8R
See also SATA 13
Lauri-Volpi, Giacomo 1893(?)-1979
Obituary 85-88
Lauro, Shirley (Shapiro) Mezvinsky 1933- .. 126
Interview in CA-126
Laursen, John Christian 1952- CANR-91
Earlier sketch in CA 145
Laursen, Keld 1967- 198
Laury, Jean Ray 1928- 77-80
Lauscher, Hermann
See Hesse, Hermann
Laut, Agnes Christina 1871-1936 193
See also DLB 92
Lautenbach, Renee 1932- 110
Lautens, Gary 1928-1993(?) 144
Lauter
See Chamson, Andre J(ules) L(ouis)
Lauter, Geza Peter 1932-2002 .... 41-44R
Obituary 206
Lauter, Paul 1932- 13-16R
Lauterbach, Albert 1904- CANR-1
Earlier sketch in CA 1-4R
Lauterbach, Ann 1942- CANR-103
Earlier sketch in CA 175
See also CWP
See also DLB 193
Lauterborn, Robert F. 1936- 146
Lauterstein, Ingeborg 1935- 130
Lautreamont 1846-1870
See Lautreamont, Isidore Lucien Ducasse
See also GFL 1789 to the Present
See also RGWL 2, 3
See also SSC 14
Lautreamont, Isidore Lucien Ducasse
See Lautreamont
See also DLB 217
Lauture, Denize 1946- 152
See also SATA 86
Lauwerys, Joseph (Albert) 1902-1981 .... 13-16R
Obituary 104
Laux, Connie
See Laux, Constance
Laux, Constance 1952- 151
See also SATA 97
Laux, Dorianne (Louise) 1952- 195
Laux, Dorothy 1920- 61-64
See also SATA 49
Laux, James M(ichael) 1927- 33-36R
Laux, P(eter) J(ohn) 1922- 25-28R
Lavaca, Pere
See Torrent, Ferran
Lavagnino, Allessandra 1927- CANR-2
Earlier sketch in CA 45-48
LaValle, Irving H(oward) 1939- 33-36R
LaValle, Victor D. 1972- 194
Lavallee, Barbara 1941- .... SATA 74
Lavan, Spencer 1937- CANR-8
Earlier sketch in CA 57-60
Lavater, Johann Kaspar 1741-1801 .... DLB 97
Lave, Lester B(ernard) 1939- CANR-33
Earlier sketches in CA 41-44R, CANR-15
Lavelle, Mike 1933- 65-68
Lavelle, Sheila 1939- 109
Lavender, Abraham D(onald)
1940- CANR-112
Earlier sketch in CA 151
Lavender, David (Sievert)
1910-2003 .... CANR-40
Obituary 217
Earlier sketches in CA 1-4R, CANR-2, 18
See also SATA 64, 97
See also SATA-Obit 145
Lavender, William D. 1921- CANR-122
Earlier sketches in CA 65-68, CANR-10
See also SATA 143
Lavenson, James H. 1919-1998 103
Obituary 170
Lavenson, Jim
See Lavenson, James H.
Laver, James 1899-1975 .... CANR-3
Obituary 57-60
Earlier sketch in CA 1-4R
Laver, Michael (John) 1949- CANR-46
Earlier sketches in CA 107, CANR-23
Laver, Rod(ney George) 1938-
Brief entry 112
La Verdiere, Eugene Armand 1936- .. CANR-19
Earlier sketch in CA 102
Lavers, Annette 1932- 130
Lavers, Chris(topher) P. 1965- 206
Lavers, Norman 1935- CANR-93
Earlier sketch in CA 104
Lavert, Gwendolyn Battle 1951-
See Battle-Lavert, Gwendolyn
See also SATA 131
Laverty, Carroll D(ee) 1906- 77-80
Laverty, Donald
See Blish, James (Benjamin) and
Knight, Damon (Francis)
Lavery, Bryony 1947- 229
See also CBD
See also CD 5, 6
See also CWD
Lavery, David 1949- CANR-134
Earlier sketch in CA 163
Lavery, Emmet (Godfrey) 1902-1986
Obituary 118
Laves, Walter H(erman) C(arl) 1902-1983
Obituary 111
La Vey, (Howard) Anton Szandor
1930-1997 158
Obituary 162
Brief entry 109
Laviera, Tato 1951- .... LLW
Lavigne, Louis-Dominique 165
See also SATA 107
Lavin, David E(dwin) 1931- CANR-2
Earlier sketch in CA 1-4R
Lavin, Henry St. C. 1921-1985
Obituary 114
Lavin, Irving 1927- 158
Lavin, J(oseph) A(nthony) 1932- 33-36R
Lavin, Marilyn Aronberg 1925- 106
Lavin, Mary 1912-1996 .... CANR-33
Obituary 151
Earlier sketch in CA 9-12R
See also CLC 4, 18, 99
See also CN 1, 2, 3, 4, 5, 6
See also DLB 15, 319
See also FW
See also MTCW 1
See also RGEL 2
See also RGSF 2
See also SSC 4, 67
Lavin, Maud 1954- CANR-109
Earlier sketch in CA 142
Lavin, S(tuart) R. 1945- 219
Lavin, Sylvia 1960- 142
Lavine, David 1928- .... SATA 31
Lavine, Harold 1915-1984 .... 41-44R
Obituary 113
Lavine, Richard A. 1917- 21-24R
Lavine, Sigmund Arnold 1908-1986 . CANR-41
Earlier sketches in CA 1-4R, CANR-4, 19
See also CLR 35
See also SATA 3, 82
Lavine, Steven D(avid) 1947- 139
Lavington, H(arold) Dude 1907- 117
Lavinson, Joseph
See Kaye, Marvin (Nathan)
Laviolette, Emily A.
1923(?)-1975 .... SATA-Brief 49
Lavitt, Wendy (Adler) 1939- 127
Lavond, Paul Dennis
See Kornbluth, C(yril) M. and
Lowndes, Robert A(ugustine) W(ard) and
Pohl, Frederik
Lavori, Nora 1950- 93-96
Lavrentiev, Alexander (Nikolaevich) 1954- . 135
Lavrin, Janko Matthew 1887-1986 .... 9-12R
Obituary 120
Law, Alexander 1904-1995 128
Law, Carol Russell 106
Law, Cheukyiu
See Law, Clara
Law, Clara 1957- 208
Law, Elizabeth
See Peters, Maureen
Law, Graham 1953- 214
Law, Howard W(illiam) 1919- 21-24R
Law, Janice
See Trecker, Janice Law
Law, John
See Harkness, Margaret (Elise)
Law, John 1946- 145
Law, Jonathan 1961- CANR-124
Earlier sketch in CA 154
Law, Marie Hamilton 1884-1981
Obituary 106
Law, Richard 1901-1980
Obituary 105
Law, Virginia W.
See Shell, Virginia Law
Lawder, Douglas W(ard) 1934- CANR-1
Earlier sketch in CA 45-48
Lawes, Henry 1596-1662 .... DLB 126
Lawford, J(ames) P(hilip)
1915-1977 .... CANR-28
Earlier sketch in CA 33-36R
Lawford, Paula Jane 1960- 125
See also Martyr, Paula (Jane)
See also SATA-Brief 53
Lawhead, Stephen R. 1950- CANR-89
Earlier sketch in CA 155
See also AAYA 29
See also FANT
See also SATA 109
Lawhead, Steve
See Lawhead, Stephen R.

Cumulative Index 339 Layden

Lawhead, Victor B(ernard) 1919- 41-44R
Lawhorne, Clifton O. 1927-1983 104
Obituary 110
Lawler, Donald L(ester) 1935- 105
Lawler, Edmund 1953- 229
Lawler, James R. 1929- 57-60
Lawler, Lillian B. 1898-1990 .... 13-16R
Lawler, Nancy Ellen 227
Lawler, Patrick 1948- 136
Lawler, Peter Augustine 1951- CANR-119
Earlier sketch in CA 169
Lawler, Philip F(rederick) 1950- 110
Lawler, Ray
See Lawler, Raymond Evenor
See also DLB 289
Lawler, Raymond Evenor 1922- 103
See also Lawler, Ray
See also CD 5, 6
See also CLC 58
See also RGEL 2
Lawler, Ronald (David) 1926- 126
Brief entry 110
Lawless, Anthony
See MacDonald, Philip
Lawless, Bettyclare Hamilton 1915- 61-64
Lawless, Dorothy (Mae) Kennedy 1906- ... 5-8R
Lawless, Edward W(illiam) 1931- 114
Lawless, Elaine J. 1947- CANR-53
Earlier sketch in CA 126
Lawless, Emily 1845-1913 201
See also DLB 240
Lawless, Gary 1951- CANR-13
Earlier sketch in CA 73-76
Lawless, John
See Best, Don(ald M.)
Lawless, The Hon. Emily
See Lawless, Emily
Lawlor, Eric 184
Lawlor, Florine 1925- 65-68
Lawlor, John (James) 1918-1999 .... 5-8R
Obituary 178
Lawlor, Laurie 1953- 207
See also SATA 80, 137
Lawlor, Mary 214
Lawlor, Monica (Mary) 1926- 9-12R
Lawlor, Pat
See Lawlor, Patrick Anthony
Lawlor, Patrick Anthony 1893-1979 ...... CAP-1
Earlier sketch in CA 9-10
Lawlor, Rob(ert Thomas) 1936- 127
Lawlor, William 1951- 176
Lawn, Judy 1953- 238
Lawner, Lynne 1935- 9-12R
Lawrence, A. R.
See Foff, Arthur R(aymond)
Lawrence, Alexander Atkinson 1906-1979 . 102
Lawrence, Ann (Margaret)
1942-1987 .... CANR-85
Earlier sketch in CA 104
See also CWRI 5
See also SATA 41
See also SATA-Obit 54
Lawrence, Ariadne
See Ling, Amy
Lawrence, Barbara Kent 194
Lawrence, Berta 73-76
Lawrence, Bill 1930- 25-28R
Lawrence, Bruce B. 173
Lawrence, C(lifford) H(ugh) 1921- CANR-90
Earlier sketch in CA 132
Lawrence, Carole 212
Lawrence, Cynthia Miller 218
Lawrence, D. Baloti 1950- CANR-32
Earlier sketch in CA 113
Lawrence, D(avid) H(erbert Richards)
1885-1930 .... CANR-131
Brief entry 104
Earlier sketch in CA 121
See also Chambers, Jessie
See also BPFB 2
See also BRW 7
See also BRWR 2
See also CDBLB 1914-1945
See also DA
See also DA3
See also DAB
See also DAC
See also DAM MST, NOV, POET
See also DLB 10, 19, 36, 98, 162, 195
See also EWL 3
See also EXPP
See also EXPS
See also LAIT 2, 3
See also MTCW 1, 2
See also MTFW 2005
See also NFS 18
See also PC 54
See also PFS 6
See also RGEL 2
See also RGSF 2
See also SSC 4, 19, 73
See also SSFS 2, 6
See also TCLC 2, 9, 16, 33, 48, 61, 93
See also TEA
See also WLC
See also WLIT 4
See also WP
Lawrence, Daniel 1940- 57-60
Lawrence, David, Jr. 1942- 73-76
Lawrence, David 1888-1973 .... CANR-70
Obituary 41-44R
Earlier sketch in CA 102
See also DLB 29
Lawrence, David 1942- 234
Lawrence, David M(eade) 1961- 219
Lawrence, E. S.
See Bradburne, E(lizabeth) S.
Lawrence, Eddie
See Eisler, Lawrence
Lawrence, Edward
See Eisler, Lawrence
Lawrence, Elizabeth Atwood 1929-2003 214
Obituary 221
Lawrence, Elizabeth L. 1904-1985 124
Lawrence, Emeric Anthony 1908- CANR-5
Earlier sketch in CA 1-4R
Lawrence, Francis L(eo) 1937- 49-52
Lawrence, Frederick M. 197
Lawrence, Gale 1941- 126
Lawrence, George H(ill Mathewson) 1910-1978
Obituary 81-84
Lawrence, Greg 236
Lawrence, H(enry) L(ionel) 1908- CAP-1
Earlier sketch in CA 9-10
Lawrence, Iain 1955- 198
See also AAYA 51
See also SATA 135
Lawrence, Irene
See Marsh, John
Lawrence, Isabelle (Wentworth) .. SATA-Brief 29
Lawrence, J. D.
See Lawrence, James Duncan
Lawrence, J. T.
See Rowland-Entwistle, (Arthur) Theodore (Henry)
Lawrence, Jack
See Fitzgerald, Lawrence P(ennybaker)
Lawrence, Jacob 1917-2000 196
See also AAYA 30
Lawrence, James Duncan 1918- CANR-27
Earlier sketch in CA 17-20R
Lawrence, Jerome 1915-2004 .... CANR-44
Obituary 224
Earlier sketch in CA 41-44R
See also CAD
See also CD 5, 6
See also DFS 2, 16
See also DLB 228
See also SATA 65
Lawrence, Jim
See Lawrence, James Duncan
Lawrence, Jock
See Lawrence, Justus Baldwin
Lawrence, Jodi 1938- CANR-3
Earlier sketch in CA 45-48
Lawrence, John
See Lawrence, Jodi
Lawrence, John (Waldemar) 1907-1999 .. 81-84
Obituary 187
Lawrence, John 1933- CANR-24
Earlier sketch in CA 107
See also SATA 30
Lawrence, John A. 1908-1976
Obituary 65-68
Lawrence, John S(helton) 1938- 123
Brief entry 107
Lawrence, Joseph D(ouglas) 1895-1990 126
Lawrence, Josephine 1890(?)-1978 77-80
See also SATA-Obit 24
Lawrence, Justus Baldwin 1903-1987
Obituary 122
Lawrence, Karen 1949- 126
Lawrence, Karen 1951- 126
Lawrence, Karl
See Foff, Arthur R(aymond)
Lawrence, Kathleen Rockwell 1945- 136
Lawrence, Kathy
See Martin, Kat
Lawrence, Kenneth G.
See Ringgold, Gene
Lawrence, Lesley
See Lewis, Lesley
Lawrence, Louise 1943- 97-100
See also BYA 6, 7
See also SATA 38, 78, 119
See also YAW
Lawrence, Louise de Kiriline
1894-1992 .... 25-28R
See also SATA 13
Lawrence, Lynn
See Garland, Sherry
Lawrence, Margaret K.
See Keilstrup, Margaret
Lawrence, Margaret Morgan 1914- 33-36R
Lawrence, Margery H. 1889-1969 202
See also HGG
See also SATA 120
Lawrence, Margot
See Thompson, Margot
Lawrence, Marjorie 1909-1979
Obituary 85-88
Lawrence, Martha C. 1956- CANR-109
Earlier sketch in CA 165
See also AAYA 61
Lawrence, Martin
See Greif, Martin and
Grow, Lawrence
Lawrence, Mary
See Young, Mary Lou Daves
Lawrence, Mary Margaret 1920- 93-96
Lawrence, Melinda
See Weinhouse, Beth (R)
Lawrence, Merle 1915- 21-24R
Lawrence, Michael
See Lariar, Lawrence
Lawrence, Michael 1943- 201
See also SATA 132
Lawrence, Mildred Elwood
1907-1997 .... CANR-5
Earlier sketch in CA 1-4R
See also SATA 3
Lawrence, Nathaniel (Morris)
1917-1986 .... CANR-22
Earlier sketch in CA 45-48
Lawrence, P.
See Tubb, E(dwin) C(harles)
Lawrence, Paul Frederic 1912-1999 . CANR-87
Earlier sketch in CA 153
See also BW 2
Lawrence, Paul Roger 1922- CANR-136
Earlier sketch in CA 158
Lawrence, Peter 1921-1988
Obituary 124
Lawrence, R(onald) D(ouglas)
1921- CANR-51
Earlier sketches in CA 65-68, CANR-11
See also SATA 55
Lawrence, Rae
See Liebman, Ruth
Lawrence, Richard A.
See Leopold, Nathan F.
Lawrence, Robert
See Beum, Robert (Lawrence)
Lawrence, Robert 1912(?)-1981
Obituary 105
Lawrence, Robert A(llen) 1948- 118
Lawrence, Roy 1930- 45-48
Lawrence, Samuel A. 1928- 21-24R
Lawrence, Seymour 1926-1994 ...... DLBY 1994
Lawrence, Sharon 1945- 65-68
Lawrence, Starling 165
Lawrence, Steven C.
See Murphy, Lawrence A(gustus)
See also TCWW 1, 2
Lawrence, T(homas) E(dward) 1888-1935 .. 167
Brief entry 115
See also Dale, Colin
See also BRWS 2
See also DLB 195
See also TCLC 18
Lawrence, Thomas
See Roberts, Thom(as Sacra)
Lawrence, Vera Brodsky
1909-1996 .... CANR-100
Brief entry 109
Lawrence, William Howard 1916-1972
Obituary 33-36R
Lawrence, William J(ohn) C(ooper)
1899(?)-1985
Obituary 118
Lawrence of Arabia
See Lawrence, T(homas) E(dward)
Lawrenny, H.
See Simcox, Edith Jemima
Lawrenson, Helen 1907-1982 117
Obituary 106
Lawrenson, Thomas Edward 1918-1982
Obituary 106
Lawrinson, Julia 1969- 212
See also SATA 141
Lawry, Jon Sherman 1924- 5-8R
Laws, G(eorge) Malcolm, Jr.
1919-1994 .... 37-40R
Laws, Priscilla W(atson) 1940- 73-76
Laws, Sophie 1957- 238
Laws, Stephen 1952- 168
See also HGG
Lawshe, C(harles) H(ubert) 1908-2000 .. CAP-2
Earlier sketch in CA 23-24
Lawson, (Richard) Alan 1934- 53-56
Lawson, Amy
See Gordon, Amy
Lawson, Annetta 1939- 116
Lawson, Annette 1936- 129
Lawson, Carol (Antell) 1946- .... SATA 42
Lawson, Chet
See Tubb, E(dwin) C(harles)
Lawson, David 1927- 57-60
Lawson, Don(ald Elmer) 1917-1990 . CANR-26
Earlier sketches in CA 1-4R, 130, CANR-2
See also SATA 9
Lawson, Donna Roberta 1937- 41-44R
Lawson, Doug 212
Lawson, E(verett) LeRoy 1938- CANR-19
Earlier sketches in CA 53-56, CANR-4
Lawson, Evelyn 1917- 57-60
Lawson, F(loyd) Melvyn 1907-1997 53-56
Lawson, Frederick Henry 1897-1983
Obituary 109
Lawson, George 1598-1678 .... DLB 213
Lawson, Greg 1944- 164
Lawson, H(orace) L(owe) 1900-1981 .... 5-8R
Lawson, H. Lowe
See Lawson, H(orace) L(owe)
Lawson, Henry (Archibald Hertzberg)
1867-1922 181
Brief entry 120
See also DLB 230
See also RGEL 2
See also RGSF 2
See also SSC 18
See also TCLC 27
Lawson, Jacob
See Burgess, Michael (Roy)
Lawson, James 1938- 65-68
Lawson, Joan 1906- 103
See also SATA 55
Lawson, John (?)-1711 .... DLB 24
Lawson, John 1909- CANR-3
Earlier sketch in CA 1-4R
Lawson, John Howard 1894-1977 .... CANR-84
Obituary 73-76
Earlier sketches in CAP-1, CA 13-16
See also CAD
See also DLB 228
See also MAL 5
See also RGAL 4
Lawson, Johnny
See Newton, D(wight) B(ennett)
Lawson, JonArno Burhans 1968- 171
Lawson, Julie 1947- 196
See also CLR 89
See also SATA 79, 126
Lawson, Kay 1933- 104
Lawson, L. (M.) 1949- 193
Lawson, Lewis A. 1931- 21-24R
Lawson, Linda 1952- 148
Lawson, Louisa Albury 1848-1920 ..... DLB 230
Lawson, M. C.
See Lawson, H(orace) L(owe)
Lawson, M(ichael) K(enneth) 1950- 238
Lawson, Marion Tubbs 1896-1994 .... CAP-1
Earlier sketch in CA 9-10
See also SATA 22
Lawson, Mark 1962- 139
Lawson, Mary 1946- 215
Lawson, Michael
See Ryder, M(ichael) L(awson)
Lawson, Nigella 1960- 210
Lawson, Philip 1949-1995 146
Lawson, Philip J. 1908(?)-1978
Obituary 77-80
Lawson, (Phillippe) Reed 1929- 5-8R
Lawson, Richard H(enry) 1919- CANR-8
Earlier sketch in CA 17-20R
Lawson, Robert 1892-1957 137
Brief entry 118
See also BYA 5
See also CLR 2, 73
See also CWRI 5
See also DLB 22
See also MAICYA 1, 2
See also SATA 100
See also WCH
See also YABC 2
Lawson, Robert G. 1938- 118
Lawson, Ronald (Lynton) 1940- 126
Lawson, Ruth C(atherine) 1911-1990 ...... 9-12R
Lawson, S. Alexander 1912- 57-60
Lawson, Sarah (Anne) 1943- CANR-96
Earlier sketches in CA 120, CANR-45
Lawson, Steve
See Turner, Robert (Harry)
Lawson, Steven F(red) 1945- CANR-48
Earlier sketch in CA 122
Lawson, Victor F. 1850-1925 184
See also DLB 25
Lawson, W. B.
See Jenks, George C(harles)
Lawton, Barbara (Perry) 1930- CANR-122
Earlier sketch in CA 144
Lawton, Charles
See Heckelmann, Charles N(ewman)
Lawton, Clive A. 1951- 218
See also SATA 145
Lawton, David 1943- 156
Lawton, Dennis
See Faust, Frederick (Schiller)
Lawton, Harry Wilson 1927- 33-36R
Lawton, John 1949- CANR-143
Earlier sketch in CA 168
Lawton, Manny
See Lawton, Marion R(ussell)
Lawton, Marion R(ussell) 1918-1986 118
Lawton, Paul 1924- 148
Lawton, Sherman P(axton) 1908- CAP-2
Earlier sketch in CA 19-20
Lawyer, Annabel Glenn 1906(?)-1974
Obituary 53-56
Law Yone, Edward Michael 1911(?)-1980
Obituary 101
Law-Yone, Wendy 1947- 210
Lax, Eric 1944- 138
Lax, Robert 1915-2000 .... CANR-115
Obituary 189
Earlier sketches in CA 25-28R, CANR-11, 27
Lax, Scott 1952- 187
Laxalt, Robert P(eter) 1923-2001 .... CANR-103
Obituary 194
Earlier sketches in CA 13-16R, CANR-38
Laxdal, Vivienne 1962- 173
See also SATA 112
Laxness, Halldor (Kiljan)
See Gudjonsson, Halldor Kiljan
See also CWW 2
Lay, Bennett 1910-1993 .... CAP-1
Earlier sketch in CA 11-12
Lay, Bierne, Jr. 1909-1982
Obituary 107
Lay, Daniel W(ayne) 1914-2002 118
Lay, K. Edward 1932- 190
Lay, Nancy Duke S. 1938- CANR-21
Earlier sketch in CA 105
Lay, Norvie L(ee) 1940- 49-52
Lay, S(amuel) Houston 1912-1987 .... 33-36R
Lay, Shawn 1953- CANR-89
Earlier sketch in CA 124
Layamon fl. c. 1200-
See Layamon
See also DLB 146
See also RGEL 2
Layard, Sir Austen Henry 1817-1894 .. DLB 166
Layard, (Peter) Richard (Grenville) 1934- ... 128
Laybourne, Lawrence E. 1914(?)-1976
Obituary 65-68
Laycock, Ellen (Mae) 1921- 112
Laycock, George (Edwin) 1921- CANR-41
Earlier sketches in CA 5-8R, CANR-4, 19
See also SATA 5
Laycock, Harold R. (I. O.) 1916- 5-8R
Layden, Joe 1959- 223

Laye, Camara 1928-1980 ... CANR-25
Obituary ... 97-100
Earlier sketch in CA 85-88
See also Camara Laye
See also AFW
See also BLC 2
See also BW 1
See also CLC 4, 38
See also DAM MULT
See also MTCW 1, 2
See also WLIT 2
Layman, Carol Spurlock 1937- ... 140
Layman, Constance 1943- ... 111
Layman, Emma McCloy 1910- ... 81-84
Layman, Richard 1947- ... CANR-35
Earlier sketch in CA 65-68
Laymon, Carl
See Laymon, Richard (Carl)
Laymon, Carla
See Laymon, Richard (Carl)
Laymon, Charles Martin 1904-1991 ... CANR-7
Earlier sketch in CA 9-12R
Laymon, Richard (Carl)
1947-2001 ... CANR-121
See also HGG
Layne, Bobby
See Layne, Robert Lawrence
Layne, Laura
See Knott, William C(ecil, Jr.)
Layne, Robert Lawrence 1927-1986
Obituary ... 121
Layton, Andrea
See Bancroft, Iris (May Nelson)
Layton, Aviva 1933- ... 116
Layton, Clare
See Wright, (Idonea) Daphne
Layton, Deborah 1953- ... 192
Layton, Edwin T(homas), Jr. 1928- ... 29-32R
Layton, Felix 1910-1991 ... CAP-2
Earlier sketch in CA 23-24
Layton, Irving (Peter) 1912- ... CANR-129
Earlier sketches in CA 1-4R, CANR-2, 33, 43, 66
See also CLC 2, 15, 164
See also CP 1, 2, 3, 4, 5, 6, 7
See also DAC
See also DAM MST, POET
See also DLB 88
See also EWL 3
See also MTCW 1, 2
See also PFS 12
See also RGEL 2
Layton, Marilyn Smith 1941- ... 114
Layton, Max 1946- ... 128
Layton, Neal (Andrew) 1971- ... 195
See also SATA 152
Layton, Robert 1930- ... 21-24R
Layton, Thomas Arthur 1910-1988 ... 9-12R
Layton, Wilbur L. 1922-
Brief entry ... 106
Layton, William (Isaac) 1913-1996 ... 17-20R
Lazang, Iwan
See Goll, Yvan
Lazar, Irving (Paul) 1907-1993 ... 149
Lazar, Swifty
See Lazar, Irving (Paul)
Lazar, Wendy 1939- ... 104
Lazar, Zachary 1968- ... 174
Lazard, Naomi ... CP 1
Lazare, Daniel (Henry) 1950- ... CANR-115
Earlier sketch in CA 154
Lazare, Gerald John 1927- ... SATA 44
Lazare, Jerry
See Lazare, Gerald John
Lazareff, Pierre 1907-1972
Obituary ... 33-36R
Lazareth, William Henry 1928- ... CANR-16
Earlier sketches in CA 1-4R, CANR-1
Lazarevic, Laza K. 1851-1890 ... DLB 147
Lazarevich, Mila 1942- ... SATA 17
Lazaron, Hilda R(othschild) 1895-1982 ... 49-52
Lazarre, Jane D(eitz) 1943- ... 101
Lazarsfeld, Paul F(elix) 1901-1976 ... CANR-29
Obituary ... 69-72
Earlier sketch in CA 73-76
Lazarus, A(rnold) L(eslie)
1914-1992 ... CANR-11
Earlier sketch in CA 25-28R
Lazarus, Arnold A(llan) 1932- ... CANR-14
Earlier sketch in CA 41-44R
Lazarus, Arthur 1892(?)-1978
Obituary ... 77-80
Lazarus, Edward H. 1959- ... 122
Lazarus, Felix
See Cable, George Washington
Lazarus, George 1904-1997 ... DLB 201
Lazarus, Harold 1927- ... 21-24R
Lazarus, Henry
See Slavitt, David R(ytman)
Lazarus, John 1947- ... 132
Lazarus, Keo Felker 1913-1993 ... 41-44R
Obituary ... 198
See also SATA 21
See also SATA-Obit 129
Lazarus, Marguerite 1916- ... CANR-85
Earlier sketch in CA 106
See also RHW
Lazarus, Mell 1927- ... CANR-11
Earlier sketch in CA 17-20R
Lazarus, Pat 1935- ... 130
Lazarus, Paul N. 1913-1997 ... 126
Lazarus, Richard S(tanley)
1922-2002 ... CANR-5
Obituary ... 210
Earlier sketch in CA 1-4R
Lazarus, Simon 1941- ... 57-60
Lazarus-Black, Mindie ... 151
Lazear, Edward P. 1948- ... CANR-65
Earlier sketch in CA 129
LaZebnik, Claire Scovell ... 227
LaZebnik, Edith 1897-1988 ... 85-88
Lazell, James Draper, Jr. 1939- ... 65-68
Lazenby, Edith P. 1945- ... 161
Lazenby, J(ohn) F(rancis) 1934- ... 147
Lazenby, Nat ... TCWW 2
Lazenby, Norman 1914- ... TCWW 2
Lazenby, Walter S(ylvester), Jr. 1930- ... 65-68
Lazer, Hank
See Lazer, Henry Alan
Lazer, Henry Alan 1950- ... 173
Autobiographical Essay in ... 173
See also CAAS 27
Lazer, William 1924- ... CANR-19
Earlier sketches in CA 1-4R, CANR-4
Lazere, Donald 1935- ... 105
Lazerowitz, Alice Ambrose 1906- ... CANR-17
Earlier sketches in CA 49-52, CANR-1
Lazerowitz, Morris 1907-1987 ... CANR-17
Earlier sketches in CA 9-12R, CANR-3
Lazerson, Joshua N(athaniel) 1959- ... 148
Lazhechnikov, Ivan Ivanovich
1790(?)-1869 ... DLB 198
Lazic, Radmila 1949- ... PFS 22
Lazlo, Kate
See Angus, Sylvia
Lazo, Hector 1899-1965 ... CANR-3
Earlier sketch in CA 1-4R
Lazreg, Marnia 1941- ... 69-72
Lazuta, Gene 1959- ... CANR-71
Earlier sketch in CA 148
Le, Duan 1908(?)-1986
Obituary ... 119
Le, Thi Diem Thuy 1972-
See Le Thi Diem Thuy
Lea, Alec 1907- ... 73-76
See also SATA 19
Lea, David A(lexander) M(aclure)
1934- ... CANR-10
Earlier sketch in CA 21-24R
Lea, F(rank) A(lfred) 1915-1977 ... CANR-3
Earlier sketch in CA 1-4R
Lea, Frederick (Measham) 1900-1984
Obituary ... 113
Lea, Henry Charles 1825-1909
Brief entry ... 122
See also DLB 47
Lea, James F(ranklin) 1945- ... 130
Lea, Joan
See Neufeld, John (Arthur)
Lea, John Sedgwick 1910(?)-1987
Obituary ... 124
Lea, Kathleen M(arguerite) 1903-1995 ... 119
Lea, Sydney (L. Wright, Jr.) 1942- ... CANR-70
Earlier sketches in CA 106, CANR-22
See also DLB 120, 282
Lea, Timothy
See Wood, Christopher (Hovelle)
Lea, Tom 1907-2001
Obituary ... 192
Brief entry ... 115
See also DLB 6
See also TCWW 1, 2
Leab, Daniel Josef 1936- ... CANR-11
Earlier sketch in CA 29-32R
Leabo, Dick A. 1921- ... 9-12R
Leacacos, John P. 1908-1986 ... 25-28R
Obituary ... 121
Leach, Aroline (Arnett) Beecher
1899-1981 ... 61-64
Leach, Barry Arthur 1930- ... 102
Leach, Bernard Howell 1887-1979 ... 97-100
Obituary ... 85-88
Leach, Douglas Edward 1920- ... 17-20R
Leach, E. R.
See Leach, Edmund Ronald
Leach, Edmund
See Leach, Edmund Ronald
Leach, Edmund R.
See Leach, Edmund Ronald
Leach, Edmund Ronald 1910-1989
Obituary ... 127
Leach, Eleanor Winsor 1937- ... 103
Leach, Gerald (Adrian) 1933-2004 ... CANR-21
Obituary ... 234
Earlier sketch in CA 5-8R
Leach, Graham (John) 1948- ... 122
Leach, John Robert 1922- ... 21-24R
Leach, Joseph (Lee) 1921- ... 29-32R
Leach, Maria 1892-1977 ... 53-56
Obituary ... 69-72
See also SATA 39
See also SATA-Brief 28
Leach, Marjorie S. 1911-1998 ... 142
Leach, (Richard) Max(well) 1909- ... 41-44R
Leach, Michael 1940- ... 73-76
Leach, Paul Roscoe 1890-1977
Obituary ... 73-76
Leach, Penelope (Jane) 1937- ... CANR-44
Earlier sketches in CA 97-100, CANR-21
Leach, Richard H(eald) 1922-2004 ... 127
Obituary ... 227
Brief entry ... 113
Leach, Robert J. 1916- ... 29-32R
Leach, (Carson) Wilford
1934(?)-1988 ... CANR-2
Obituary ... 125
Earlier sketch in CA 45-48
Leach, William (R.) 1944- ... CANR-93
Earlier sketch in CA 146
Leachman, Robert Briggs 1921- ... 104
Leacock, Eleanor Burke 1922-1987 ... CANR-15
Obituary ... 122
Earlier sketch in CA 37-40R
Leacock, Elspeth 1946- ... 200
See also SATA 131
Leacock, John 1729-1802 ... DLB 31
Leacock, Ruth 1926- ... 37-40R
Leacock, Stephen (Butler)
1869-1944 ... CANR-80
Brief entry ... 104
Earlier sketch in CA 141
See also DAC
See also DAM MST
See also DLB 92
See also EWL 3
See also MTCW 2
See also MTFW 2005
See also RGEL 2
See also RGSF 2
See also SSC 39
See also TCLC 2
Leacroft, Helen (Mabel Beal) 1919- ... CANR-2
Earlier sketch in CA 5-8R
See also SATA 6
Leacroft, Richard (Vallance Becher)
1914- ... CANR-2
Earlier sketch in CA 5-8R
See also SATA 6
Lead, Jane Ward 1623-1704 ... DLB 131
Leadbetter, Eric 1892(?)-1971
Obituary ... 104
Leadbitter, Mike 1942- ... 41-44R
Leader, (Evelyn) Barbara (Blackburn)
1898- ... 61-64
Leader, Charles
See Smith, Robert Charles
Leader, Darian ... 161
Leader, Mary 1948- ... CANR-107
Earlier sketch in CA 159
Leader, Mary (Bartelt) 1948- ... 85-88
Leader, Ninon 1933- ... 21-24R
Leader, Shelah Gilbert 1943- ... CANR-27
Earlier sketch in CA 110
Leader, Zachary 1946- ... CANR-135
Earlier sketch in CA 138
Leaf, David 1952- ... 117
Leaf, Margaret P. 1909(?)-1988
Obituary ... 124
See also SATA-Obit 55
Leaf, (Wilbur) Munro 1905-1976 ... CANR-85
Obituary ... 69-72
Earlier sketches in CA 73-76, CANR-29
See also CLR 25
See also CWRI 5
See also MAICYA 1, 2
See also SATA 20
Leaf, Murray J(ohn) 1939- ... CANR-1
Earlier sketch in CA 45-48
Leaf, Paul 1929- ... 132
Leaf, Russell C(harles) 1935- ... 21-24R
Leaf, VaDonna Jean 1929- ... 57-60
See also SATA 26
Leagans, John Paul 1911-2001 ... 103
Leah, Devorah
See Devorah-Leah
Leahey, Michael I. 1956- ... 207
Leahy, Donna 1961- ... 210
Leahy, James E. 1919- ... 138
Leahy, Syrell Rogovin 1935- ... CANR-56
Earlier sketches in CA 57-60, CANR-12, 29
Leake, Chauncey D(epew)
1896-1978 ... CANR-3
Obituary ... 73-76
Earlier sketch in CA 49-52
Leake, Jane Acomb 1928- ... 21-24R
Leakey, Caroline Woolmer
1827-1881 ... DLB 230
Leakey, Louis S(eymour) B(azett)
1903-1972 ... 97-100
Obituary ... 37-40R
See also MTCW 1
Leakey, Mary (Douglas Nicol)
1913-1996 ... CANR-60
Obituary ... 155
Earlier sketches in CA 97-100, CANR-18
Leakey, Richard E(rskine Frere)
1944- ... CANR-114
Earlier sketches in CA 93-96, CANR-18
See also SATA 42
Leal, Luis 1907- ... 131
See also HW 1
Leale, B(arry) C(avendish) 1930- ... 132
Leal Massey, Cynthia 1956- ... 218
Leaman, David R(ay) 1947- ... 115
Leamer, Edward E(mery) 1944- ... 29-32R
Leamer, Laurence Allen 1941- ... CANR-35
Earlier sketches in CA 65-68, CANR-13
Leaming, Barbara ... CANR-88
Earlier sketches in CA 107, CANR-25, 50
Leamon, Warren (Coleman) 1938- ... 181
Lean, Arthur E(dward) 1909-1992 ... 73-76
Lean, David 1908-1991 ... 134
Brief entry ... 111
See also AAYA 65
Lean, E(dward) Tangye 1911-1974
Obituary ... 53-56
Lean, Garth Dickinson 1912-1993 ... CANR-86
Obituary ... 143
Earlier sketches in CA 29-32R, CANR-17
Leander, Ed
See Richelson, Geraldine
Leaney, Alfred Robert Clare
1909-1995 ... CANR-2
Obituary ... 148
Earlier sketch in CA 5-8R
Leaning, Jennifer 1945- ... 132
Leanne, Shelly 1968(?)- ... 224
Leap, Harry P(atrick) 1908-1976 ... 1-4R
Obituary ... 103
Leapman, Michael (Henry) 1938- ... CANR-41
Earlier sketch in CA 109
Leapor, Mary 1722-1746 ... DLB 109
Lear, Edward 1812-1888 ... AAYA 48
See also BRW 5
See also CLR 1, 75
See also DLB 32, 163, 166
See also MAICYA 1, 2
See also PC 65
See also RGEL 2
See also SATA 18, 100
See also WCH
See also WP
Lear, Floyd Seyward 1895-1975 ... CAP-1
Earlier sketch in CA 17-18
Lear, John 1909- ... 37-40R
Lear, Linda J(ane) 1940- ... 166
Lear, Martha Weinman 1930- ... CANR-9
Earlier sketch in CA 9-12R
Lear, Melva Gwendoline Bartlett 1917- ... 5-8R
Lear, Norman (Milton) 1922- ... 73-76
See also CLC 12
Lear, Patricia 1944- ... 150
See also CSW
Lear, Peter
See Lovesey, Peter (Harmer)
Leard, G(eorge) Earl 1918- ... 9-12R
Leard, John E(arnshaw) 1916-2003 ... 73-76
Obituary ... 213
Learmonth, Andrew Thomas Amos
1916- ... 13-16R
Learned, Edmund Philip 1900-1991 ... 104
Learning, Walter J. 1938- ... 130
Lears, Laurie 1955- ... SATA 127
Lears, T. J. Jackson 1947- ... 221
Leary, Ann (Lembeck) 1963(?)- ... 231
Leary, David E. 1945- ... CANR-51
Earlier sketch in CA 124
Leary, Denis 1958- ... 154
Leary, Edward A(ndrew) 1913-1997 ... CANR-12
Earlier sketch in CA 29-32R
Leary, James F. 1942- ... 126
Leary, John P(atrick) 1919- ... 9-12R
Leary, Lewis (Gaston) 1906-1990 ... CANR-4
Obituary ... 131
Earlier sketch in CA 1-4R
Leary, Paris 1931- ... 17-20R
See also CP 1
Leary, Timothy (Francis) 1920-1996 ... CANR-92
Obituary ... 152
Earlier sketch in CA 107
Interview in ... CA-107
See also DA3
See also DLB 16
See also MTCW 1
See also NCFS 2
Leary, William G(ordon) 1915- ... CANR-31
Earlier sketch in CA 49-52
Leary, William M., Jr. 1934- ... 93-96
Leas, Speed 1937- ... CANR-30
Earlier sketch in CA 49-52
Lease, Benjamin 1917-
Brief entry ... 114
Lease, Gary 1940- ... CANR-38
Earlier sketch in CA 45-48
Lease, Joseph 1960- ... 174
Leasher, Evelyn M(arie) 1941- ... 115
Leask, Ian Graham 1951- ... 138
Leask, Nigel 1958- ... CANR-143
Earlier sketch in CA 145
Leaska, Mitchell A(lexander) 1934- ... CANR-91
Earlier sketches in CA 77-80, CANR-13, 39
Leasor, (Thomas) James 1923- ... CANR-2
Earlier sketch in CA 1-4R
See also CMW 4
See also SATA 54
Least Heat-Moon, William
See Trogdon, William (Lewis)
See also ANW
Leasure, Robert E. 1921- ... 112
Leather, Edwin (Hartley Cameron)
1919-2005 ... 97-100
Obituary ... 238
Leather, George
See Swallow, Norman
Leatherbarrow, W(illiam) J(ohn) 1947- ... 145
Leatherman, LeRoy 1922-1984 ... 21-24R
Obituary ... 112
Leatherwood, (James) Stephen 1943-1997 ... 146
Leaton, Anne 1932- ... 130
Leautaud, Paul 1872-1956 ... 203
See also DLB 65
See also GFL 1789 to the Present
See also TCLC 83
Leavell, Landrum P(inson) II 1926- ... 89-92
Leavell, Linda 1954- ... 154
Leavengood, Betty 1939- ... 187
Leavenworth, Carol 1940- ... CANR-14
Earlier sketch in CA 81-84
Leavenworth, Geoffrey (M.) 1953- ... 238
Leavenworth, James Lynn 1915-1988 ... 21-24R
Leaver, Robin Alan 1939- ... CANR-9
Earlier sketch in CA 61-64
Leavey, James 1947- ... 213
Leavey, John P(eter), Jr. 1951- ... 127
Leavis, F(rank) R(aymond)
1895-1978 ... CANR-44
Obituary ... 77-80
Earlier sketch in CA 21-24R
See also BRW 7
See also CLC 24
See also DLB 242
See also EWL 3
See also MTCW 1, 2
See also RGEL 2

Cumulative Index 341 Lee

Leavis, Q(ueenie) D(orothy)
1906-1981 97-100
Obituary 108
Leavitt, Caroline 1952- CANR-115
Earlier sketch in CA 150
Leavitt, David 1961- CANR-134
Brief entry 116
Earlier sketches in CA 122, CANR-50, 62, 101
Interview in CA-122
See also CLC 34
See also CPW
See also DA3
See also DAM POP
See also DLB 130
See also GLL 1
See also MAL 5
See also MTCW 2
See also MTFW 2005
Leavitt, Harold J(ack) 1922- 125
Brief entry 117
Leavitt, Hart Day 1909- 13-16R
Leavitt, Harvey R(obert) 1934- 65-68
Leavitt, Jack 1931- 97-100
Leavitt, Jerome E(dward) 1916- CANR-17
Earlier sketches in CA 1-4R, CANR-1
See also SATA 23
Leavitt, Judith A(nn) 1947- CANR-27
Earlier sketch in CA 110
Leavitt, Judith Walzer 1940- CANR-115
Earlier sketch in CA 158
Leavitt, Martine 1953- 237
Leavitt, Richard Freeman 1929- 89-92
Leavitt, Ruby R.
See Rohrlich, Ruby
Leavitt, William J. 1928-1984
Obituary 112
Leavy, Barbara Fass 1936- 145
Leavy, Stanley A(rnold) 1915- 120
LeBar, Lois E(mogene) 1907-1997 .... 21-24R
LeBar, Mary E(velyn) 1910-1982 ...... CANR-25
Earlier sketch in CA 107
See also SATA 35
LeBaron, Charles W. 1943- CANR-9
Earlier sketch in CA 61-64
Lebbon, Tim 1969- 221
LeBeau, Roy
See Smith, Mitchell
Lebeaux, Richard 1946- CANR-12
Earlier sketch in CA 73-76
Lebed, Alexander (Ivanovich) 1950-2002 ... 172
Obituary 204
Lebedoff, David (Michael) 1938- 126
Leber, George L. 1917(?)-1976
Obituary 61-64
Lebergott, Stanley 1918- 103
Lebert, Benjamin 1982- 207
Lebert, Norbert 1929-1993 205
Lebert, Randy
See Brannon, William T.
Lebert, Stephan 1961- 210
Lebesgue, Henri (Leon) 1875-1941 155
Lebeson, Anita Libman 1896-1987 .... 29-32R
Obituary 121
LeBey, Barbara Sydell 1939- 205
LeBlanc, Adrian Nicole 219
LeBlanc, Annette M. 1965- .... SATA 68
LeBlanc, L(ee) 1913- .... SATA 54
Leblanc, Maurice (Marie Emile) 1864-1941
Brief entry 110
See also CMW 4
See also TCLC 49
LeBlanc, Rena Dictor 1938- 104
Lebling, Dave .... AAYA 64
Leblon, Jean (Marcel Jules) 1928- 41-44R
Le Blond, (Elizabeth) Aubrey
1861-1934 .... DLB 174
Lebo, Dell 1922-1978 57-60
LeBoeuf, Michael 1942- CANR-128
Earlier sketches in CA 93-96, CANR-15
Lebon, Rachel L. 1951- 194
LeBor, Adam 232
Le Boutillier, Cornelia Geer 1894(?)-1973
Obituary 45-48
Lebovich, William Louis 1948- CANR-37
Earlier sketch in CA 115
Lebovics, Herman 1935- 193
Lebovitz, Harold Paul 1916- 77-80
Lebow, Barbara 1936-
Lebow, Eileen F. 1925- CANR-123
Earlier sketch in CA 132
Lebow, Jeanne 1951- 135
Lebow, Richard Ned 1942- 129
Lebow, Victor 1902-1980 .... 37-40R
Obituary 133
Lebowitz, Alan 1934- 25-28R
Lebowitz, Albert 1922- 73-76
See also CN 1, 2
Lebowitz, Fran(ces Ann) 1951(?)- CANR-70
Earlier sketches in CA 81-84, CANR-14, 60
Interview in CANR-14
See also CLC 11, 36
See also MTCW 1
Lebowitz, Naomi 1932- 37-40R
LeBox, Annette 1943- 218
See also SATA 145
Leboyer, Frederick 1918- 106
Lebra, Joyce C(hapman) CANR-1
Earlier sketch in CA 45-48
Lebra, Takie Sugiyama 1930- 77-80
Lebra, William P(hilip) 1922-1986 .... 33-36R
Lebrecht, Norman 1948- 117
Lebrecht, Peter
See Tieck, (Johann) Ludwig
Lebreo, Steward
See Weiner, Stewart
Lebreo, Stewart
See Weiner, Stewart
Le Breton, Auguste
See Montfort, Auguste
Le Breton, Binka 1942- 142
Lebreton, J(ean) D(ominique) 1950- 146
Le Bris, Michel 1944- 131
Le Brown, Andreas
See Brown, Andreas Le
Lebrun, Claude 1929- 136
See also SATA 66
LeBrun, Gautier
See Gibson, Walter B(rown)
LeBrun, George P. 1862-1966 .... 5-8R
Lebrun, Richard Allen 1931- 41-44R
Lebsock, Suzanne (Dee) 1949- 153
le Cagat, Benat
See Whitaker, Rod(ney)
Le Cain, Errol (John) 1941-1989 .... CANR-42
Obituary 127
Earlier sketches in CA 33-36R, CANR-13
See also MAICYA 1, 2
See also SATA 6, 68
See also SATA-Obit 60
Lecale, Errol
See McNeilly, Wilfred (Glassford)
Lecar, Helene Lerner 1938- 25-28R
le Carre, John
See Cornwell, David (John Moore)
See also AAYA 42
See also BEST 89:4
See also BPFB 2
See also BRWS 2
See also CDBLB 1960 to Present
See also CLC 3, 5, 9, 15, 28
See also CMW 4
See also CN 1, 2, 3, 4, 5, 6, 7
See also CPW
See also DLB 87
See also EWL 3
See also MSW
See also MTCW 2
See also RGEL 2
See also TEA
Lecavele, Roland -1973 204
Le Chanois, Jean-Paul
See Drefus, Jean-Paul Etienne
Lechleidner, Mary L. 1947- CANR-126
Earlier sketch in CA 149
Lechlitner, Ruth N. 1901-1989 105
See also DLB 48
Lechner, Robert F(irman) 1918- 33-36R
Lechon, Jan
See Serafinowicz, Leszek
See also EWL 3
Lecht, Charles Philip 1933- 21-24R
Lecht, Leonard A. 1920- CANR-28
Earlier sketches in CA 25-28R, CANR-11
Lechtenberg, Richard 1947- 125
Lecker, Robert 1951- CANR-28
Earlier sketch in CA 111
Leckey, Andrew A. 1949- 199
Leckey, Dolores (Conklin) 1933- 109
Leckie, Keith (Ross) 1952- 130
Leckie, Robert (Hugh) 1920- 13-16R
Leckie, Ross 1957- 157
Leckie, Shirley A(nne) 1937- CANR-95
Earlier sketch in CA 146
Leckie, William H. 1915- 21-24R
Lecky-Thompson, Guy W. 1974- 217
LeClair, Mark S. 1958- 197
LeClair, Thomas 1944- CANR-43
Earlier sketch in CA 113
LeClair, Tom
See LeClair, Thomas
LeClaire, Anne D(ickinson) 1942- 150
LeClaire, Gordon (M.) 1905-1989 69-72
Leclant, Jean 1920- 132
Leclerc, Felix 1914-1988 181
See also DLB 60
Leclerc, Ivor 1915-1999 .... 33-36R
Leclerc, Victor
See Parry, Albert
Le Clercq, Jacques Georges Clemenceau
1898-1972
Obituary 37-40R
Leclercq, Jean 1911-1993 149
Le Clezio, J(ean) M(arie) G(ustave) 1940- ... 128
Brief entry 116
See also CLC 31, 155
See also CWW 2
See also DLB 83
See also EWL 3
See also GFL 1789 to the Present
See also RGSF 2
Le Cocq, Rhoda P(riscilla) 1921-1988 73-76
Lecoin, Louis 1888(?)-1971
Obituary 33-36R
Lecomber, Brian 1945- CANR-13
Earlier sketch in CA 73-76
LeCompte, (Nancy) Jane 1948- 133
Lecompte, Janet 1923- 122
LeCompte, Mary Lou 1935- 146
Le Comte, Edward (Semple) 1916- CANR-5
Earlier sketch in CA 1-4R
Lecomte du Nouey
See Lecomte du Nouey, Pierre(-Andre-Leon)
Lecomte du Nouey, P.
See Lecomte du Nouey, Pierre(-Andre-Leon)
Lecomte du Nouey, Pierre(-Andre-Leon)
1883-1947
Brief entry 119
Lecomte du Nouy, Pierre (-Andre-Leon)
See Lecomte du Nouey, Pierre(-Andre-Leon)
Leconte de Lisle, Charles-Marie-Rene
1818-1894 .... DLB 217
See also EW 6
See also GFL 1789 to the Present
Le Coq, Monsieur
See Simenon, Georges (Jacques Christian)
Le Corbusier
See Jeanneret, Charles-Edouard
Lecourt, Nancy (Hoyt) 1951- .... SATA 73
Le Couteur, Penny 1942- 228
LeCroy, Anne K(ingsbury) 1930- CANR-16
Earlier sketch in CA 41-44R
LeCroy, Ruth Brooks 45-48
Ledbetter, J(ack) T(racy) 1934- 73-76
Ledbetter, Jack Wallace 1930- 5-8R
Ledbetter, Joe O(verton) 1927- 45-48
Ledbetter, Ken(neth Lee) 1931- CANR-40
Earlier sketch in CA 117
Ledbetter, Les 1941(?)-1985
Obituary 116
Ledbetter, Suzann 1953- CANR-117
Earlier sketch in CA 144
See also SATA 119
Ledbetter, Virgil C. 1918-1967(?) CAP-1
Earlier sketch in CA 13-16
Ledderose, Lothar 1942- 85-88
Leddy, Mary Jo 1946- 164
Le Debonnaire, Sixte
See Dugas, Marcel
Ledeen, Michael A(rthur) 1941- CANR-103
Earlier sketch in CA 144
Leder, Jane Mersky 1945- 117
See also SATA 61
See also SATA-Brief 51
Leder, Lawrence H. 1927- 25-28R
Leder, Mary M(ackler) 1916(?)- 206
Leder, Rudolf
See Hermlin, Stephan
Lederberg, Joshua 1925- 156
Lederer, Charles 1910-1976
Obituary 65-68
See also DLB 26
See also IDFW 3, 4
Lederer, Chloe 1915- 77-80
Lederer, Edith Madelon 1943- 97-100
Lederer, Eppie
See Lederer, Esther Pauline (Friedman)
Lederer, Esther Pauline (Friedman)
1918-2002 89-92
Obituary 206
Lederer, Ivo J(ohn) 1929-1998 .... 9-12R
Obituary 181
Lederer, Jiri 1922-1983
Obituary 111
Lederer, Joseph 1927- 73-76
Lederer, Lajos 1904-1985
Obituary 118
Lederer, Laura 1951- 121
Lederer, Muriel 1929- 77-80
See also SATA 48
Lederer, Paul Joseph 1944- CANR-79
Earlier sketch in CA 111
See also Winters, Logan
Lederer, Rhoda Catharine (Kitto)
1910-1990 .... CANR-22
Earlier sketches in CA 9-12R, CANR-6
Lederer, Richard 1938- CANR-135
Earlier sketch in CA 132
Lederer, William J(ulius) 1912- CANR-5
Earlier sketch in CA 1-4R
See also SATA 62
Lederman, Leonard L(awrence) 1931- 61-64
Ledermann, Erich Kurt 1908- 107
Ledermann, Walter 1911- CANR-30
Earlier sketch in CA 49-52
Ledesert, (Dorothy) Margaret 1916- .. CANR-28
Earlier sketch in CA 45-48
Ledesert, R(ene) P(ierre) L(ouis)
1913-1984 .... CANR-28
Obituary 114
Earlier sketch in CA 45-48
Le Doeuff, Michele 1948- 143
LeDoux, Joseph E. 176
Ledoux, Paul (Martin) 1949- 131
Le Duc, Don R(aymond) 1933- CANR-31
Earlier sketch in CA 49-52
Leduc, Violette 1907-1972 .... CANR-69
Obituary 33-36R
Earlier sketches in CAP-1, CA 13-14
See also CLC 22
See also EWL 3
See also GFL 1789 to the Present
See also GLL 1
Ledwidge, Francis 1887(?)-1917 203
Brief entry 123
See also DLB 20
See also TCLC 23
Ledwidge, Michael 1971- 208
Ledwidge, William (Bernard) John
1915-1998 103
Ledwith, Frank 1907- 103
Ledyard, Gleason H(ines) 1919- 5-8R
Lee, A. R.
See Ash, Rene Lee
Lee, A(rthur) Robert 1941- 130
Lee, Addison E(arl) 1914-1992 .... 9-12R
Lee, Adrian Iselin, Jr. 1920- 89-92
Lee, Al(fred Matthew) 1938- 45-48
See also CP 1
Lee, Alfred McClung 1906-1992 ...... CANR-19
Obituary 137
Earlier sketches in CA 1-4R, CANR-3
Lee, Alvin A. 1930- 33-36R
Lee, Amanda
See Baggett, Nancy and
Buckholtz, Eileen (Garber) and
Glick, Ruth (Burtnick)
Lee, Amber
See Baldwin, Faith
Lee, Andrea
See Toona, Elin(-Kai)
Lee, Andrea 1953- CANR-82
Earlier sketch in CA 125
See also BLC 2
See also BW 1, 3
See also CLC 36
See also DAM MULT
Lee, Andrew
See Auchincloss, Louis (Stanton)
Lee, Andrew H. 235
Lee, Ang 1954- CANR-116
Earlier sketch in CA 157
See also AAYA 44
Lee, Anthony W. 1960- 235
Lee, Arthur M(atthias) 1918- 41-44R
Lee, Asher 1909- 73-76
Lee, Audrey 25-28R
Lee, Austin 1904-(?) CANR-84
Earlier sketches in CAP-1, CA 13-16
Lee, Barbara 1932- 109
Lee, Barbara (Moore) 1934- CANR-9
Earlier sketch in CA 53-56
Lee, Barbara A(nne) 1949- 128
Lee, Benjamin 1921- 104
See also SATA 27
Lee, Bernie 1926- 144
Lee, Betsy 1949- 106
See also SATA 37
Lee, Betty
See Lambert, Elizabeth (Minnie)
Lee, Betty 1921- 103
Lee, Bill
See Lee, William Saul
Lee, Bob
See McGrath, Robert L(ee)
Lee, Brother Basil Leo 1909-1974
Obituary 53-56
Lee, C(live) H(oward) 1942- 126
Lee, C(larence) P(endleton) 1913- 49-52
Lee, Calvin B. T. 1934- 33-36R
Lee, Carol
See Fletcher, Helen Jill
Lee, Carolina
See Dern, Erolie Pearl Gaddis
Lee (Hammond), Carvel (Anita Gail Bigham)
1910- CAP-1
Earlier sketch in CA 13-14
Lee, Chana Kai 1962- 207
Lee, Chang-rae 1965- CANR-89
Earlier sketch in CA 148
See also CLC 91
See also CN 7
See also DLB 312
See also LATS 1:2
Lee, Charles 1913-2002 .... 33-36R
Lee, Charles Robert, Jr. 1929- 5-8R
Lee, Charlotte I(rene) 1909- 21-24R
Lee, Cherylene 1953- .... DLB 312
Lee, Chin-Chuan 1946- 150
Lee, Chong-Sik 1931- CANR-15
Earlier sketch in CA 41-44R
Lee, Christine Eckstrom 1952- 110
Lee, Christopher 1913- .... CP 1
Lee, Christopher 1941- CANR-110
Earlier sketch in CA 149
Lee, Christopher Frank Carandini 1922- .. 73-76
Lee, Cora
See Anderson, Catherine Corley
Lee, C(hin)-Y(ana) 1917- 9-12R
Lee, (William) David 1944- CANR-99
Earlier sketches in CA 111, CANR-29
Lee, David Dale 1948- 117
Lee, Debra (a pseudonym) 227
Lee, Deemer 1905-1979 111
Lee, Dennis (Beynon) 1939- CANR-119
Earlier sketches in CA 25-28R, CANR-11, 31, 57, 61
See also CLR 3
See also CP 1, 2, 3, 4, 5, 6, 7
See also CWRI 5
See also DAC
See also DLB 53
See also MAICYA 1, 2
See also SATA 14, 102
Lee, Derek 1937- 107
Lee, (Henry) Desmond (Pritchard)
1908-1993 102
Lee, Devon
See Pohle, Robert W(arren), Jr.
Lee, Dom 1959- .... SAAS 26
See also SATA 83, 146
See also SATA-Essay 121
Lee, Don 1959- 231
Lee, Don L.
See Madhubuti, Haki R.
See also CLC 2
See also CP 2
Lee, Doris Emrick 1905-1983
Obituary 110
See also SATA 44
See also SATA-Obit 35
Lee, Dorris M(ay Potter) 1905-1985 ...... 13-16R
Lee, Douglas A(llen) 1932- 53-56
Lee, Dwight E(rwin) 1898-1986 .... 5-8R
Lee, Eddie H. 1917- 69-72
Lee, Edward Edson 1884-1944 128
See also AITN 1
Lee, Edward N(icholls) 1935- 29-32R
Lee, Elizabeth Briant 1908- 37-40R
Lee, Elizabeth Rogers 1940- .... SATA 90
Lee, Elsie 1912-1987 .... CANR-84
Earlier sketch in CA 85-88
Lee, Eric
See Lee, Fleming and
Page, Gerald W(ilburn)
Lee, Essie E. 1920- CANR-4
Earlier sketch in CA 49-52
Lee, Eugene (Huey) 1941- 49-52

Lee, Fleming 1933- CANR-7
Earlier sketch in CA 9-12R
Lee, Florence Henry 1910-1998 CAP-1
Earlier sketch in CA 17-18
Lee, Frances E. 1968- 199
Lee, Francis Nigel 1934- CANR-8
Earlier sketch in CA 57-60
Lee, Frank F(reeman) 1920- 1-4R
Lee, Fred 1927- 109
Lee, G. Avery 1916- 104
Lee, Gentry 1942- 140
Lee, George J. 1920(?)-1976
Obituary 65-68
Lee, George Leslie
See Lee, Brother Basil Leo
Lee, George W(ashington)
1894-1976 CANR-83
Earlier sketch in CA 125
See also BLC 2
See also BW 1
See also CLC 52
See also DAM MULT
See also DLB 51
Lee, Georgia 1926- 194
Lee, Gerard (Majella) 1951- 93-96
Lee, Ginffa 1900(?)-1976
Obituary 69-72
Lee, Gordon C(anfield) 1916-1972 13-16R
Obituary 135
Lee, Gus 1946- CANR-126
Earlier sketch in CA 142
See also DLB 312
Lee, Gwen 222
Lee, Gypsy Rose
See Hovick, Rose Louise
Lee, H. Alton 1942- 81-84
Lee, Hahn-Been 1921- CANR-11
Earlier sketch in CA 25-28R
Lee, Harold N(ewton) 1899-1990 37-40R
Lee, (Nelle) Harper 1926- CANR-128
Earlier sketches in CA 13-16R, CANR-51
See also AAYA 13
See also AMWS 8
See also BPFB 2
See also BYA 3
See also CDALB 1941-1968
See also CLC 12, 60, 194
See also CSW
See also DA
See also DA3
See also DAB
See also DAC
See also DAM MST, NOV
See also DLB 6
See also EXPN
See also LAIT 3
See also MAL 5
See also MTCW 1, 2
See also MTFW 2005
See also NFS 2
See also SATA 11
See also WLC
See also WYA
See also YAW
Lee, Harriet 1757-1851 DLB 39
Lee, Harry J., Jr. 1914-1985
Obituary 118
Lee, Hector (Haight) 1908-1992 97-100
Lee, Hector Viveros 1962- 186
See also SATA 115
Lee, Helen Clara 1919- 49-52
Lee, Helen Elaine 1959(?)- 148
See also CLC 86
Lee, Helen Jackson 1908-1997 81-84
Lee, Helene 1947(?)- 226
Lee, Helie 1964- 210
Lee, Henry (Walsh) 1911-1993 5-8R
Obituary 142
Lee, Henry C(hang-Yuh) 1938- 161
Lee, Henry F(oster) 1913-1994 89-92
Lee, Herbert d'H.
See Kastle, Herbert D(avid)
Lee, Hermione 1948- CANR-119
Earlier sketches in CA 73-76, CANR-15
Lee, Howard N.
See Goulart, Ron(ald Joseph)
Lee, Howard N.
See Goulart, Ron(ald Joseph)
Lee, Huy Voun 1969- SATA 129
Lee, Irvin H. 1932-1980 21-24R
Obituary 133
Lee, J. Cleo
See Johnson, Leland R(oss)
Lee, J(oseph) Edward 1953- 199
See also SATA 130
Lee, J(erry) W(allace) 1932- 93-96
Lee, Jae 1972- 225
Lee, James A(lvin) 1922- CANR-113
Earlier sketches in CA 126, CANR-53
Lee, James F. 1905(?)-1975
Obituary 61-64
Lee, James Michael 1931- CANR-30
Earlier sketches in CA 17-20R, CANR-13
Lee, James W. 1931- 25-28R
Lee, Janet 1904-1988
Obituary 127
Lee, Janet 1954- 222
Lee, Janice (Jeanne) 1944- 33-36R
Lee, Jarena 1783-(?) AFAW 2
Lee, Jeanne M. 1943- 199
See also SATA 138
Lee, Jennie
See Lee, Janet
Lee, Jennifer 1968- 225
Lee, Joann Faung Jean 203
Lee, Joe Won 1921- 41-44R
Lee, John CLC 70
Lee, John FANT
Lee, John (Darrell) 1931- CANR-83
Earlier sketches in CA 25-28R, CANR-9
Lee, John A(lexander) 1891-1982 CANR-7
Earlier sketch in CA 53-56
See also CN 3
See also RGEL 2
Lee, John Eric 1919- 33-36R
Lee, John Michael 1932- CANR-6
Earlier sketch in CA 13-16R
Lee, John R(obert) 1923-1976 57-60
Obituary 120
See also SATA 27
Lee, Joie Susannah 1962(?)- 216
Lee, Jordan
See Scholefield, Alan
Lee, Josephine (D.) 169
Lee, Judith Yaross 1949- 137
Lee, Judy
See Carlson, Judith Lee
Lee, Julian
See Latham, Jean Lee
Lee, Jung Young 1935- 33-36R
Lee, Kathryn Louise 1919- 188
Lee, Katie
See Lee, Kathryn Louise
Lee, Kay
See Kelly, Karen
Lee, Kelley 1962- 177
Lee, L(awrence) L(ynn) 1924- 73-76
Lee, Lamar, Jr. 1911-1988 17-20R
Lee, Lance 1942- CANR-13
Earlier sketch in CA 77-80
Lee, Larry
See Lee, Lawrence
Lee, Laura 1969- 191
Lee, Laurel 1945-2004 138
Brief entry 113
Lee, Laurie 1914-1997 CANR-73
Obituary 158
Earlier sketches in CA 77-80, CANR-33
See also CLC 90
See also CP 1, 2
See also CPW
See also DAB
See also DAM POP
See also DLB 27
See also MTCW 1
See also RGEL 2
Lee, Lawrence 1903-1978 CANR-44
Earlier sketch in CA 25-28R
Lee, (Enoch) Lawrence 1912-1996 13-16R
Lee, Lawrence 1941-1990 CANR-43
Obituary 131
See also CLC 34
Lee, Leo Ou-fan 1939- 102
Lee, Leslie (E.) 1935- 233
See also DLB 266
Lee, Lilian NFS 19
Lee, Lily Xiao Hong 1939- 203
Lee, Lincoln 1922- 9-12R
Lee, Linda 1947- CANR-13
Earlier sketch in CA 77-80
Lee, Linda Francis 218
Lee, Li-Young 1957- CANR-118
Earlier sketch in CA 153
See also AMWS 15
See also CLC 164
See also CP 7
See also DLB 165, 312
See also LMFS 2
See also PC 24
See also PFS 11, 15, 17
Lee, Liz
See Lee, Elizabeth Rogers
Lee, Loyd Ervin 1939- 102
Lee, Lucy
See Talbot, Charlene Joy
Lee, Lyn 1953- SATA 128
Lee, M(ark) Owen 1930- CANR-94
Earlier sketch in CA 33-36R
Lee, Mabel 1886-1985 134
Lee, Mabel Barbee 1886(?)-1978
Obituary 85-88
Lee, Malka 1905(?)-1976
Obituary 65-68
Lee, Manfred B(ennington)
1905-1971 CANR-2
Obituary 29-32R
Earlier sketch in CA 1-4R
See also Queen, Ellery
See also CLC 11
See also CMW 4
See also DLB 137
Lee, Manning de Villeneuve 1894-1980
Obituary 104
See also SATA 37
See also SATA-Obit 22
Lee, Maria Berl 1924- CANR-9
Earlier sketch in CA 61-64
Lee, Marian
See Clish, (Lee) Marian
Lee, Marie G. 1964- CANR-110
Earlier sketches in CA 149, CANR-71
See also AAYA 27
See also BYA 12
See also SATA 81, 130
Lee, Marjorie 1921-1999 CANR-4
Obituary 179
Earlier sketch in CA 1-4R
Lee, Mark 1950- 226
Lee, Mark W. 1923- CANR-18
Earlier sketches in CA 9-12R, CANR-3
Lee, Martha F(rances) 1962- 160
Lee, Martin A. 1954- CANR-47
Earlier sketch in CA 121
Lee, Mary 1949- 29-32R
Lee, Mary Effie
See Newsome, (Mary) Effie Lee
Lee, Mary Price 1934- CANR-24
Earlier sketches in CA 57-60, CANR-9
See also SATA 8, 82
Lee, Maryat 1923-1989 25-28R
Obituary 129
Lee, Matt
See Merwin, (W.) Sam(uel Kimball), Jr.
Lee, Maurice (duPont), Jr. 1925- CANR-21
Earlier sketch in CA 45-48
Lee, Meredith 1945- 93-96
Lee, Michael 1946- 215
Lee, Mildred
See Scudder, Mildred Lee
See also SAAS 12
See also SATA 6
Lee, Molly K(yung) S(ook) C(hang)
1934- 53-56
Lee, Mona 1939- 203
Lee, Muna 1895-1965
Obituary 25-28R
Lee, Nata
See Frackman, Nathaline
Lee, Nathaniel 1645(?)-1692 DLB 80
See also RGEL 2
Lee, Norma E. 1924- 65-68
Lee, Oliver M(inseem) 1927- 41-44R
Lee, Pali Jae 1929- CANR-31
Earlier sketches in CA 29-32R, CANR-13
Lee, Parker
See Turner, Robert (Harry)
Lee, Patricia 1941- 115
Lee, Patrick
See Andrews, Patrick E.
Lee, Patrick C(ornelius) 1936- 65-68
Lee, Peter 1947- 127
Lee, Peter H(acksoo) 1929- CANR-97
Earlier sketches in CA 9-12R, CANR-3
Lee, Philip J. 1932- 124
Lee, Philip Randolph 1924- 149
Lee, Polly Jae
See Lee, Pali Jae
Lee, R(oy) Alton 1931- CANR-140
Earlier sketch in CA 21-24R
Lee, Rachel 217
Lee, Ranger
See Snow, Charles H(orace)
Lee, Raymond 1910(?)-1974
Obituary 49-52
Lee, Raymond L(awrence) 1911-1999 41-44R
Lee, Rebecca Smith 1894-1990 5-8R
Lee, Rensselaer W(right) 1898-1984
Obituary 114
Lee, Richard
See Lee, Richard B(orshay)
Lee, Richard B(orshay) 1937- CANR-20
Earlier sketch in CA 45-48
Lee, Richard S. 1927- SATA 82
Lee, Robert
See Fairman, Paul W.
Lee, Robert 1929- CANR-3
Earlier sketch in CA 5-8R
Lee, Robert 1947- 169
Lee, Robert C. 1931- CANR-10
Earlier sketch in CA 25-28R
See also SATA 20
Lee, Robert E(arl) 1906- 53-56
See also AITN 1
Lee, Robert E(dwin) 1918-1994 CANR-2
Obituary 146
Earlier sketch in CA 45-48
See also CAD
See also DFS 2, 16
See also DLB 228
See also SATA 65
See also SATA-Obit 82
Lee, Robert E. A. 1921- 9-12R
Lee, Robert Edson 1921- 25-28R
Lee, Robert Edward 1912-1993 111
Lee, Robert Greene 1886-1978(?) CANR-3
Earlier sketch in CA 1-4R
Lee, Robert J. 1921- SATA 10
Lee, Roberta
See McGrath, Robert L(ee)
Lee, Ronald 1934- 37-40R
Lee, Rowena
See Bartlett, Marie (Swan)
Lee, Roy
See Hopkins, Clark
Lee, Roy Stuart 1899- CAP-1
Earlier sketch in CA 9-10
Lee, Russel V(an Arsdale) 1895-1982
Obituary 110
Lee, Ruth (Wile) 1892-1983 CAP-2
Earlier sketch in CA 23-24
Lee, S(amuel) E(dgar) 1894-1988 73-76
Lee, S(idney) G(illmore) M(cKenzie)
1920-1973 CAP-2
Earlier sketch in CA 33-36
Lee, Sally 1943- 134
See also SATA 67
Lee, Samuel J(ames) 1906- CAP-2
Earlier sketch in CA 29-32
Lee, Sander H. 1951- 219
Lee, Sandra
See Cusick, Heidi Haughy
Lee, Sharon 1952- CANR-127
Earlier sketch in CA 166
Lee, Shelton Jackson 1957(?)- CANR-42
Earlier sketch in CA 125
See also Lee, Spike
See also BLCS
See also BW 2, 3
See also CLC 105
See also DAM MULT
Lee, Sherman Emery 1918- CANR-1
Earlier sketch in CA 1-4R
Lee, Sir Sidney
See Lee, Solomon (Lazarus)
See also DLB 149, 184
Lee, Simon Francis 1957- 194
Lee, Sky 1952- 161
See also CN 6, 7
Lee, Solomon (Lazarus) 1859-1926
See Lee, Sir Sidney
Lee, Sophia 1750-1824 DLB 39
Lee, Spike
See Lee, Shelton Jackson
See also AAYA 4, 29
Lee, Stan 1922- CANR-129
Brief entry 108
Earlier sketch in CA 111
Interview in CA-111
See also AAYA 5, 49
See also CLC 17
See also MTFW 2005
Lee, Stewart M(unro) 1925- 57-60
Lee, Susan 135
Lee, Susan 1944- 110
Lee, Susan Dye 1939- 85-88
Lee, Tammie
See Townsend, Thomas L.
Lee, Tanith 1947- CANR-102
Earlier sketches in CA 37-40R, CANR-53
See also AAYA 15
See also CLC 46
See also DLB 261
See also FANT
See also SATA 8, 88, 134
See also SFW 4
See also SUFW 1, 2
See also YAW
Lee, Terence R(ichard) 1938- 29-32R
Lee, Tom(my L.) 1950- 65-68
Lee, Tonya Lewis 234
Lee, Vernon
See Paget, Violet
See also DLB 57, 153, 156, 174, 178
See also GLL 1
See also SSC 33
See also SUFW 1
See also TCLC 5
Lee, Virginia 1905(?)-1981
Obituary 105
Lee, Virginia (Yew) 1927- 9-12R
Lee, W. Storrs
See Lee, William Storrs
Lee, Walt(er William, Jr.) 1931- 61-64
Lee, Warner
See Battin, B(rinton) W(arner)
Lee, Warren M. 1908-1978 77-80
Lee, Wayne C(yril) 1917- CANR-141
Earlier sketches in CA 1-4R, CANR-2, 17, 41
See also TCWW 1, 2
Lee, Wen Ho 1940- 215
Lee, William
See Burroughs, William S(eward)
See also GLL 1
Lee, William R(owland) 1911-1996 CANR-42
Earlier sketches in CA 9-12R, CANR-4, 19
Lee, William Saul 1938- 104
Lee, William Storrs 1906- CANR-1
Earlier sketch in CA 1-4R
Lee, Willy
See Burroughs, William S(eward)
See also GLL 1
Lee, Yur Bok 1934- 29-32R
Leeb, Donna 1948- 231
Leeb, Stephen 1946- 231
Leech, Alfred B. 1918(?)-1974
Obituary 49-52
Leech, Ben
See Bowkett, Stephen
Leech, Bryan Jeffery 1931- 93-96
Leech, Clifford 1909-1977 CANR-4
Earlier sketch in CA 1-4R
Leech, Geoffrey N(eil) 1936- CANR-53
Earlier sketches in CA 29-32R, CANR-12, 29
Leech, John 1925- 139
Leech, Kenneth 1939- 103
Leech, Margaret (Kernochan)
1893-1974 93-96
Obituary 49-52
Leecing, Walden A. 1932- 33-36R
Leed, Eric J. 1942- 89-92
Leed, Jacob R. 1924- CANR-7
Earlier sketch in CA 17-20R
Leed, Richard L. 1929- 13-16R
Leed, Theodore W(illiam) 1927- 126
Brief entry 106
Leeder, Elaine J. 1944- CANR-98
Earlier sketch in CA 147
Leedham, Charles 1926- 13-16R
Leedham, John 1912- CANR-13
Earlier sketch in CA 21-24R
Leeds, Anthony 1925- 17-20R
Leeds, Barry H. 1940- CANR-94
Earlier sketch in CA 29-32R
Leeds, Morton (Harold) 1921-1998 13-16R
Leeds, Patricia (Miriam) 1920(?)-1985
Obituary 114
Leedy, Jack J. 1921- 21-24R
Leedy, Loreen (Janelle) 1959- CANR-99
Earlier sketches in CA 122, CANR-48
See also SATA 54, 84, 128
See also SATA-Brief 50
Leedy, Paul D. 1908-2003 CANR-1
Earlier sketch in CA 1-4R
Leefeldt, Christine 1941- 93-96
Leefeldt, Ed 1946- 219
Leegant, Joan 1951(?)- 239
Lee Geok Lan 1939- CP 1

Cumulative Index 343 Lehring

Lee-Hamilton, Eugene (Jacob) 1845-1907 .. 234
Brief entry ... 117
See also TCLC 22
Lee-Hostetler, Jeri 1940- ... SATA 63
Lee Howard, Leon Alexander 1914-1979(?)
Obituary ... 104
Leek, Margaret
See Bowen-Judd, Sara (Hutton)
Leek, Sybil 1917-1982 ... 102
Obituary ... 108
Leekley, Richard N. 1912-1976
Obituary ... 69-72
Leekley, Thomas B(riggs) 1910-2001 ... 5-8R
See also SATA 23
Leeman, Wayne A(lvin) 1924- ... 13-16R
Leeming, David Adams 1937- ... CANR-119
Earlier sketch in CA 49-52
Leeming, Donald 1944- ... 114
Leeming, Glenda 1943- ... CANR-4
Earlier sketch in CA 53-56
Leeming, Jo Ann
See Leeming, Joseph
Leeming, John F(ishwick) 1900- ... CAP-1
Earlier sketch in CA 9-10
Leeming, Joseph 1897-1968 ... 73-76
See also SATA 26
Leeming, Owen (Alfred) 1930- ... CANR-15
Earlier sketch in CA 65-68
See also CP 1, 2
Leemis, Ralph B. 1954- ... SATA 72
Leenhouts, Keith J(ames) 1925- ... 61-64
Leepa, Allen 1919- ... 45-48
Leeper, Sarah (Lou) H(ammond)
1912-1992 ... 57-60
Obituary ... 139
Leepson, Marc 1945- ... CANR-89
Earlier sketch in CA 111
Leer, Norman Robert 1937- ... 17-20R
Leerburger, Benedict A., Jr. 1932- ... 9-12R
Lees, Andrew 1940- ... 122
Lees, Carlton Brown 1924-1989 ... 103
Lees, Charles J. 1919- ... 25-28R
Lees, Dan 1927- ... CANR-13
Earlier sketch in CA 33-36R
Lees, Francis A(nthony) 1931- ... CANR-9
Earlier sketch in CA 65-68
Lees, Gene 1928- ... CANR-106
Earlier sketches in CA 21-24R, CANR-9, 24, 49
Lees, Hannah
See Fetter, Elizabeth Head
Lees, Hilda Frances 1900-1983
Obituary ... 111
Lees, John D(avid) 1936- ... 53-56
Lees, John G(arfield) 1931- ... 57-60
Lees, Lynn Hollen 1941- ... 113
Lees, Ray 1931- ... CANR-8
Earlier sketch in CA 61-64
Lees, Richard 1948- ... CANR-26
Earlier sketch in CA 108
Lees, Stella 1931- ... 150
Leese, Elizabeth 1937- ... 85-88
Leese, Jennifer L.B. 1970- ... 239
See also SATA 163
Leese, Peter (Jeremy) ... 226
Lee Six, Abigail (Etta) 1960- ... CANR-86
Earlier sketch in CA 132
Lees-Milne, James 1908-1997 ... CANR-31
Obituary ... 163
Earlier sketches in CA 9-12R, CANR-13
Leeson, C(harles) Roland 1926- ... 93-96
Leeson, Howard A(lfred) 1942- ... 118
Leeson, Muriel 1920- ... SATA 54
Leeson, R. A.
See Leeson, Robert (Arthur)
Leeson, Robert (Arthur) 1928- ... CANR-46
Earlier sketches in CA 105, CANR-22
See also MAICYA 1, 2
See also SATA 42, 76
See also YAW
Leeson, Ted 1954- ... CANR-120
Earlier sketch in CA 145
Leet, Judith 1935- ... 187
See also CLC 11
Lee Tzu Pheng 1946- ... CP 1
Leeuw, Hendrik de
See de Leeuw, Hendrik
Leevy, Carroll (Moton) 1920- ... 158
Le Fanu, Joseph Sheridan 1814-1873 ... CMW 4
See also DA3
See also DAM POP
See also DLB 21, 70, 159, 178
See also GL 3
See also HGG
See also RGEL 2
See also RGSF 2
See also SSC 14, 84
See also SUFW 1
LeFanu, Sarah 1953- ... 149
Lefco, Helene 1922- ... 53-56
Lefcoe, George 1938- ... 21-24R
Lefcourt, Peter 1941- ... CANR-103
Earlier sketch in CA 140
Lefcowitz, Barbara F(reedgood)
1935- ... CANR-116
Earlier sketch in CA 104
Lefebure, Leo D. 1952- ... 150
Lefebure, Marcus 1933- ... 113
Lefebure, Molly ... 57-60
Lefebvre, Henri 1901-1991 ... CANR-11
Earlier sketch in CA 25-28R
Lefebvre d'Argence, Rene-Yvon
1928- ... CANR-11
Earlier sketch in CA 21-24R
Lefens, Tim 1953- ... 216
Lefer, Diane ... 197
Le Feuvre, Amy (?)-1929
Brief entry ... 111
Lefever, D(avid) Welty 1901-1992 ... 49-52
Lefever, Ernest W(arren) 1919- ... CANR-1
Earlier sketch in CA 1-4R
Lefevere, Andre A. 1945- ... 151
LeFevre, Adam 1950- ... 81-84
Lefevre, Carl A(nthony) 1913-2002 ... CANR-7
Earlier sketch in CA 9-12R
Lefevre, Gui
See Bickers, Richard (Leslie) Townshend
Lefevre, Helen (Elveback) ... 17-20R
LeFevre, Perry D(eyo) 1921- ... CANR-25
Earlier sketches in CA 21-24R, CANR-10
LeFevre, Robert (Thomas) 1911-1986 . CANR-9
Obituary ... 119
Earlier sketch in CA 57-60
Lefevre d'Etaples, Jacques c.
1460-1536 ... GFL Beginnings to 1789
Leff, Arthur A(llen) 1935-1981
Obituary ... 105
Leff, Gordon 1926- ... CANR-3
Earlier sketch in CA 9-12R
Leff, Julian P(aul) 1938- ... 219
Leff, Leonard J. 1942- ... 128
Leff, Nathaniel H. 1938- ... 25-28R
Leffelaar, Hendrik Louis 1929-1980 ... 5-8R
Obituary ... 145
Lefferts, George 1921- ... CANR-14
Earlier sketch in CA 69-72
Leffland, Ella 1931- ... CANR-82
Earlier sketches in CA 29-32R, CANR-35, 78
Interview in ... CANR-35
See also CLC 19
See also DLBY 1984
See also SATA 65
Leffler, Melvyn Paul 1945- ... 89-92
Leffler, William J. 1929- ... 197
Lefkoe, Morty R. 1937- ... CANR-103
Earlier sketch in CA 29-32R
Lefkovitz, Lori Hope 1956- ... 210
Lefkowitz, Annette S(ara) 1922- ... 17-20R
Lefkowitz, Bernard 1937-2004 ... CANR-81
Obituary ... 227
Earlier sketches in CA 29-32R, CANR-30
Lefkowitz, Joel M. 1940- ... 45-48
Lefkowitz, Mary Rosenthal 1935- ... CANR-41
Earlier sketches in CA 103, CANR-19
Lefkowitz, R(obert) J. 1942- ... 45-48
Leflar, Robert A(llen) 1901-1997 ... 29-32R
Le Fleming, Christopher (Kaye) 1908-1985
Obituary ... 117
Lefler, Hugh Talmage 1901-1981 ... 5-8R
Lefler, Irene (Whitney) 1917- ... CANR-1
Earlier sketch in CA 45-48
See also SATA 12
Leflore, Ron(ald) 1948(?)- ... 182
Brief entry ... 115
Le Fontaine, Joseph (Raymond) 1927- ... 106
le Fort, Gertrud (Petrea) von
1876-1971 ... CANR-31
Obituary ... 33-36R
Earlier sketch in CA 69-72
See also DLB 66
Lefranc, Pierre 1927- ... 41-44R
Lefrancois, Guy R(enald) 1940- ... CANR-18
Earlier sketches in CA 45-48, CANR-2
Lefton, Robert Eugene 1931- ... CANR-31
Earlier sketch in CA 49-52
Leftwich, James (Adolf) 1902-1987 .. CANR-15
Earlier sketch in CA 41-44R
Leftwich, Jim 1956- ... CAAS 25
Leftwich, Joseph 1892-1983 ... 5-8R
Obituary ... 109
Leftwich, Richard Henry 1920- ... CANR-5
Earlier sketch in CA 13-16R
LeGalley, Donald P(aul) 1901-1985 ... CAP-2
Earlier sketch in CA 17-18
Le Gallienne, Eva 1899-1991 ... 45-48
Obituary ... 134
See also SATA 9
See also SATA-Obit 68
Le Gallienne, Richard 1866-1947
Brief entry ... 107
See also DLB 4
Legany, Dezso 1916- ... 157
Legare, Hugh Swinton 1797-1843 ... DLB 3, 59, 73, 248
Legare, James Mathewes 1823-1859 ... DLB 3, 248
Legaret, Jean 1913-1976 ... CAP-2
Earlier sketch in CA 29-32
Legarreta, Dorothy 1926- ... 118
Legat, Michael (Ronald) 1923- ... 122
Legato, Marianne J. 1935- ... 171
Legault, Albert 1938- ... 53-56
Leger, Alexis
See Leger, (Marie-Rene Auguste) Alexis Saint-Leger
Leger, (Marie-Rene Auguste) Alexis Saint-Leger
1887-1975 ... CANR-43
Obituary ... 61-64
Earlier sketch in CA 13-16R
See also Perse, Saint-John and Saint-John Perse
See also CLC 4, 11, 46
See also DAM POET
See also MTCW 1
See also PC 23
Leger, Antoine-J 1880-1950 ... DLB 88
Leger, Antoine-J(oseph) 1880-1950 ... 186
Leger, Fernand 1881-1955 ... 165
Brief entry ... 123
Leger, Saintleger
See Leger, (Marie-Rene Auguste) Alexis Saint-Leger
Legeros, Michael J. 1965- ... 229
Legeza, (Ireneus) Laszlo 1934- ... CANR-32
Earlier sketch in CA 65-68
Legg, Gerald 1947- ... 216
See also SATA 143
Legg, Sarah Martha Ross Bruggeman
(?)-1982 ... SATA-Obit 40
Legg, (Francis) Stuart 1910-1988
Obituary ... 126
Leggatt, Alexander (Maxwell) 1940- . CANR-93
Earlier sketch in CA 97-100
Legge, Elisabeth Schwarzkopf
See Schwarzkopf-Legge, Elisabeth
Legge, Gordon 1961- ... 174
Legge, J(ohn) D(avid) 1921- ... CANR-2
Earlier sketch in CA 1-4R
Legge, M(ary) Dominica 1905-1986
Obituary ... 121
Legge-Bourke, (Edward Alexander) Henry
1914-1973 ... CAP-1
Earlier sketch in CA 9-10
Leggett, B(obby) J(oe) 1938- ... 53-56
Leggett, Eric
See Rimel, Duane (Weldon)
Leggett, Glenn 1918-2003 ... CANR-5
Obituary ... 217
Earlier sketch in CA 13-16R
Leggett, John (Ward) 1917- ... CANR-143
Earlier sketches in CA 1-4R, CANR-2
Leggett, John C. 1930- ... 25-28R
Leggett, Linda 1941- ... 108
Leggett, Paul 1946- ... 219
Leggett, Richard G. 1953- ... 226
Leggett, Stephen 1949- ... 77-80
Leggett, William 1801-1839 ... DLB 250
Leggitt, (Samuel) Hunter (Jr.) 1935- ... 65-68
Leggott, Michele 1956- ... CWP
Legh, Kathleen Louise Wood
See Wood-Legh, Kathleen Louise
Legler, Gretchen 1960- ... 166
Legler, Henry M. 1897-1979 ... 97-100
Legler, Philip 1928-1992 ... 9-12R
Legman, G(ershon) 1917-1999 ... CANR-15
Obituary ... 177
Earlier sketch in CA 21-24R
Legrain, Philippe ... 227
LeGrand
See Henderson, LeGrand
Legrand, Catherine Carlisle 1947- ... 126
Legrand, Lucien 1926- ... 5-8R
Legrand, Michel (Jean) 1932- ... 186
Brief entry ... 114
See also IDFW 3, 4
Legters, Lyman H(oward) 1928- ... CANR-15
Earlier sketch in CA 33-36R
Le Guin, Ursula K(roeber) 1929- ... CANR-132
Earlier sketches in CA 21-24R, CANR-9, 32, 52, 74
Interview in ... CANR-32
See also AAYA 9, 27
See also AITN 1
See also BPFB 2
See also BYA 5, 8, 11, 14
See also CDALB 1968-1988
See also CLC 8, 13, 22, 45, 71, 136
See also CLR 3, 28, 91
See also CN 2, 3, 4, 5, 6, 7
See also CPW
See also DA3
See also DAB
See also DAC
See also DAM MST, POP
See also DLB 8, 52, 256, 275
See also EXPS
See also FANT
See also FW
See also JRDA
See also LAIT 5
See also MAICYA 1, 2
See also MAL 5
See also MTCW 1, 2
See also MTFW 2005
See also NFS 6, 9
See also SATA 4, 52, 99, 149
See also SCFW 1, 2
See also SFW 4
See also SSC 12, 69
See also SSFS 2
See also SUFW 1, 2
See also WYA
See also YAW
Leguizamo, John 1965(?)- ... 169
See also AAYA 64
See also HW 2
Legum, Colin 1919-2003 ... CANR-4
Obituary ... 217
Earlier sketch in CA 1-4R
See also SATA 10
Legvold, Robert 1940- ... 85-88
Lehan, Richard (D'Aubin Daniel)
1930- ... 21-24R
Lehane, Brendan 1936- ... CANR-117
Earlier sketches in CA 21-24R, CANR-10, 26
Lehane, Cornelius ... 216
Lehane, Dennis 1965- ... CANR-136
Earlier sketches in CA 154, CANR-72, 112
See also AAYA 56
See also MTFW 2005
Lehiste, Ilse 1922- ... 37-40R
Lehman, Anita Jacobs 1920-1997 ... 21-24R
Lehman, Barbara 1963- ... SATA 115
Lehman, Bob ... SATA 91
Lehman, Celia 1928- ... CANR-1
Earlier sketch in CA 49-52
Lehman, Chester K. 1895-1980 ... CANR-1
Earlier sketch in CA 1-4R
Lehman, Dale 1920- ... 9-12R
Lehman, David 1948- ... CANR-24
Earlier sketches in CA 57-60, CANR-8
See also CP 7
Lehman, Donna (Jean) 1940- ... 143
Lehman, Elaine ... SATA 91
Lehman, Ernest 1920- ... IDFW 3, 4
Lehman, Ernest Paul 1915-2005 ... CANR-129
Earlier sketches in CA 85-88, CANR-69
See also DLB 44
Lehman, F(rederick) K. 1924- ... 9-12R
Lehman, Godfrey ... 25-28R
Lehman, Harold D(aniel) 1921- ... 81-84
Lehman, John 1941- ... 206
Lehman, John F(rancis), Jr. 1942- ... 13-16R
Lehman, John H. 1932- ... 141
Lehman, Milton 1917-1966 ... CAP-1
Earlier sketch in CA 13-14
Lehman, Paul Evan ... TCWW 1, 2
Lehman, Peter 1944- ... CANR-134
Earlier sketch in CA 115
Lehman, Sam 1899-1974 ... 49-52
Lehman, Warren (Winfred, Jr.) 1930- ... 21-24R
Lehman, Yvonne 1936- ... CANR-12
Earlier sketch in CA 29-32R
Lehmann, A(ndrew) George 1922- ... CANR-4
Earlier sketch in CA 1-4R
Lehmann, Arno 1901-1984 ... CAP-2
Earlier sketch in CA 29-32
Lehmann, Geoffrey (John) 1940-
Brief entry ... 107
See also CP 1, 2, 3, 4, 5, 6, 7
Lehmann, Irving J(ack) 1927- ... 53-56
Lehmann, Johannes 1929- ... CANR-14
Earlier sketch in CA 37-40R
Lehmann, (Rudolph) John (Frederick)
1907-1987 ... CANR-74
Obituary ... 122
Earlier sketches in CA 9-12R, CANR-8
Interview in ... CANR-8
See also CP 1, 2
See also DLB 27, 100
Lehmann, Linda 1906- ... 85-88
Lehmann, Lotte 1888-1976 ... 73-76
Obituary ... 69-72
Lehmann, Martin Ernest 1915- ... 5-8R
Lehmann, Michael Boas 1941- ... 119
Lehmann, Paul Louis 1906-1994 ... 85-88
Obituary ... 144
Lehmann, Peter 1938- ... 57-60
Lehmann, Robert A(rthur) 1932- ... 57-60
Lehmann, Rosamond (Nina)
1901-1990 ... CANR-73
Obituary ... 131
Earlier sketches in CA 77-80, CANR-8
See also CLC 5
See also CN 1, 2, 3, 4
See also DLB 15
See also MTCW 2
See also RGEL 2
See also RHW
Lehmann, Theo 1934- ... 41-44R
Lehmann, Traugott
See zur Muhlen, Hermynia
Lehmann, Wilhelm 1882-1968 ... 182
See also DLB 56
Lehmann, Winfred P(hilipp)
1916-2000 ... 33-36R
Lehmann-Haupt, Christopher (Charles Herbert)
1934- ... 109
Interview in ... CA-109
Lehmann-Haupt, Hellmut (Emile)
1903-1992 ... 9-12R
Obituary ... 137
Lehmberg, Paul 1946- ... 102
Lehmberg, Stanford Eugene 1931- ... CANR-2
Earlier sketch in CA 1-4R
Lehn, Cornelia 1920- ... CANR-12
Earlier sketch in CA 29-32R
See also SATA 46
Lehne, Judith Logan 1947- ... CANR-116
Earlier sketch in CA 158
See also SATA 93
Lehner, Christine (Reine) 1952- ... 109
Lehner, David 1955- ... 187
Lehnert, Herbert (Hermann) 1925- ... 41-44R
Lehning, James R(obert) 1947- ... CANR-117
Earlier sketch in CA 105
Lehninger, Albert L(ester) 1917-1986 ... 153
Obituary ... 119
Lehnus, Donald James 1934- ... CANR-9
Earlier sketch in CA 57-60
Lehnus, Opal (Hull) 1920- ... 9-12R
Lehovich, Eugenie Ouroussow
See Ouroussow, Eugenie
Lehr, Delores 1920- ... 17-20R
See also SATA 10
Lehr, Dick 1944(?)- ... 237
Lehr, Norma 1930- ... SATA 71
Lehr, Paul E(dwin) 1918- ... 65-68
Lehr, Robert 1919- ... 153
Lehr, Valerie D. 1961- ... 184
Lehrack, Otto J(ohn III) 1938- ... 139
Lehrer, Adrienne (Joyce) 1937- ... 29-32R
Lehrer, James (Charles) 1934- ... CANR-90
Brief entry ... 109
Earlier sketches in CA 114, CANR-43
Lehrer, Jim
See Lehrer, James (Charles)
Lehrer, Kate 1939- ... 138
Lehrer, Keith 1936- ... 17-20R
Lehrer, Robert N(athaniel) 1922- ... 61-64
Lehrer, Stanley 1929- ... CANR-2
Earlier sketch in CA 5-8R
Lehrer, Thomas Andrew 1928- ... 123
Lehrer, Tom
See Lehrer, Thomas Andrew
Lehring, Gary L. 1966- ... 235

Lehrman, Harold Arthur 1911-1988
  Obituary ... 127
Lehrman, Liza
  See Williams, Liza
Lehrman, Nat 1929- ... 93-96
Lehrman, Robert L(awrence) 1921- ... CANR-7
  Earlier sketch in CA 5-8R
Lehrman, Simon Maurice 1900- ... CAP-1
  Earlier sketch in CA 9-10
Lehrmann, Chanan
  See Lehrmann, Charles C(uno)
Lehrmann, Charles C(uno) 1905-1977 .. 33-36R
Lehrmann, Cuno Chanan
  See Lehrmann, Charles C(uno)
Lehtinen, Hilja Onerva
  See Onerva, L.
Lehtinen-Madetoja, Hilja Onerva
  See Onerva, L.
Lehtonen, Joel 1881-1934 ... EWL 3
Le Hunte, Bem 1964- ... 221
Leib, Amos Patten 1917-1977 ... 45-48
  Obituary ... 133
Leib, Franklin A(llen) 1944- ... CANR-98
  Earlier sketch in CA 138
Leibbrand, Kurt 1914- ... 45-48
Leibel, Charlotte P(ollack) 1899- ... 33-36R
Leibenguth, Charla Ann
  See Banner, Charla Ann Leibenguth
Leibenstein, Harvey 1922-1994 ... 103
  Obituary ... 144
Leiber, Fritz (Reuter, Jr.) 1910-1992 .. CANR-86
  Obituary ... 139
  Earlier sketches in CA 45-48, CANR-2, 40
  See also AAYA 65
  See also BPFB 2
  See also CLC 25
  See also CN 2, 3, 4, 5
  See also DLB 8
  See also FANT
  See also HGG
  See also MTCW 1, 2
  See also MTFW 2005
  See also SATA 45
  See also SATA-Obit 73
  See also SCFW 1, 2
  See also SFW 4
  See also SUFW 1, 2
Leiber, Justin Fritz 1938- ... CANR-39
  Earlier sketches in CA 97-100, CANR-17
Leibert, Julius A(mos) 1888-1968 ... CAP-2
  Earlier sketch in CA 17-18
Leiblum, Sandra R. ... 193
Leibniz, Gottfried Wilhelm von
  1646-1716 ... DLB 168
Leibold, Jay 1957- ... 123
  See also SATA 57
  See also SATA-Brief 52
Leibold, (William) John 1926- ... 37-40R
Leibovitz, Annie 1949- ... 140
  See also AAYA 11, 61
Leibovitz, Clement 1923- ... 178
Leibowitz, Herbert A. 1935- ... 25-28R
Leibowitz, Herschel W. 1925- ... CANR-8
  Earlier sketch in CA 17-20R
Leibowitz, Irving 1922-1979 ... 9-12R
  Obituary ... 85-88
Leibowitz, Rene 1913-1972
  Obituary ... 37-40R
Leibson, Jacob J. 1883(?)-1971
  Obituary ... 33-36R
Leiby, Adrian C(oulter) 1904-1976 ... CAP-1
  Obituary ... 65-68
  Earlier sketch in CA 9-10
Leiby, James 1924- ... 33-36R
Leichman, Seymour 1933- ... 25-28R
  See also SATA 5
Leichter, Otto 1898(?)-1973
  Obituary ... 41-44R
Leick, Gwendolyn 1951- ... 237
Leiden, Carl 1922- ... 5-8R
Leider, Emily Wortis 1937- ... CANR-72
  Earlier sketch in CA 81-84
Leider, Frida 1888-1975
  Obituary ... 57-60
Leider, Richard J. ... 200
Leidner, Alan C. ... 208
Leidner, Gordon 1954- ... 202
Leier, Mark 1956- ... 164
Leigh, Amy
  See Beagley, Brenda E.
Leigh, Carolyn 1926-1983
  Obituary ... 111
  See also DLB 265
Leigh, David 1946- ... 144
Leigh, Egbert Giles, Jr. 1940- ... 57-60
Leigh, Eugene
  See Seltzer, Leon E(ugene)
Leigh, James L(eighton) 1930- ... 9-12R
Leigh, Janet ... CANR-120
  Obituary ... 232
  See also Morrison, Jeanette Helen
Leigh, Matthew Andrew
  See Chervokas, John V(incent)
Leigh, Michael 1914- ... 13-16R
Leigh, Mike 1943- ... CANR-68
  Earlier sketches in CA 109, CANR-31
  See also CBD
  See also CD 5, 6
Leigh, Nila K. 1981- ... 149
  See also SATA 81
Leigh, Palmer
  See Palmer, Pamela Lynn
Leigh, Ralph Alexander 1915-1987
  Obituary ... 124
Leigh, Richard (Harris) 1943- ... 140
Leigh, Robert
  See Randisi, Robert J(oseph)
Leigh, Robin
  See Hatcher, Robin Lee
Leigh, Spencer 1945- ... 102
Leigh, Stephen (W.) 1951- ... 135
  See also SFW 4
Leigh, Susannah 1938- ... CANR-15
  Earlier sketch in CA 81-84
Leigh, Tera 1964- ... 237
Leigh, Tom 1947- ... SATA 46
Leigh, W. R. 1866-1955 ... DLB 188
Leigh, W(illiam) R(obinson) 1866-1955 ... 199
Leigh Fermor, Patrick (Michael)
  1915- ... CANR-82
  Earlier sketches in CA 81-84, CANR-35
  See also Fermor, Patrick Leigh
  See also MTCW 1
Leigh-Pemberton, John 1911-1997 ... 108
  See also SATA 35
Leight, Robert L(ewis) 1932- ... 110
Leight, Warren 1957- ... DFS 19
Leighton, Albert C(hester) 1919- ... 37-40R
Leighton, Alexander H(amilton) 1908- .. 41-44R
Leighton, Ann
  See Smith, Isadore Leighton Luce
Leighton, Clare (Veronica Hope)
  1899-1989 ... 108
  See also SATA 37
Leighton, David S(truan) R(obertson)
  1928- ... CANR-2
  Earlier sketch in CA 5-8R
Leighton, Edward
  See Barrett, Geoffrey John
Leighton, Frances Spatz ... CANR-58
  Earlier sketches in CA 81-84, CANR-30
Leighton, Jack Richard 1918- ... 1-4R
Leighton, Lauren G(ray) 1934- ... 118
Leighton, Lee
  See Overholser, Wayne D.
Leighton, Len
  See Patten, Lewis B(yford)
Leighton, Margaret (Carver) 1896-1987 ... 9-12R
  Obituary ... 123
  See also BYA 3
  See also SATA 1
  See also SATA-Obit 52
Leiken, Robert S. 1939- ... 145
Leikind, Morris C. 1906(?)-1976
  Obituary ... 65-68
Leimbach, Martha 1963- ... 130
  See also Leimbach, Marti
Leimbach, Marti
  See Leimbach, Martha
  See also CLC 65
Leimbach, Patricia Penton 1927- ... 57-60
Leimberg, Stephan R(obert) 1943- ... 117
Leimert, Lucille 1895(?)-1983
  Obituary ... 110
Lein, Glenna R. Schroeder
  See Schroeder-Lein, Glenna R(uth)
Leinbach, Esther V(ashti) 1924- ... 61-64
Leiner, Al(an) 1938- ... SATA 83
Leiner, Katherine 1949- ... CANR-90
  Earlier sketches in CA 132, CANR-61
  See also SATA 93
Leinfellner, Werner (Hubertus) 1921- . CANR-5
  Earlier sketch in CA 53-56
Leininger, Madeleine M. 1925- ... 33-36R
Leino, Eino
  See Lonnbohm, Armas Eino Leopold
  See also EWL 3
  See also TCLC 24
Leinsdorf, Erich 1912-1993 ... 119
  Obituary ... 142
  Brief entry ... 112
Leinster, Murray
  See Jenkins, Will(iam) F(itzgerald)
  See also DLB 8
  See also SCFW 1, 2
Leinwand, Gerald 1921- ... CANR-110
  Earlier sketches in CA 5-8R, CANR-9
Leinwand, Theodore B. ... 207
Leip, Hans 1893-1983
  Obituary ... 110
Leipart, Charles 1944- ... 108
Leiper, Henry Smith 1891-1975
  Obituary ... 53-56
Leipold, L. Edmond 1902-1983 ... 69-72
  See also SATA 16
Leiris, Michel (Julien) 1901-1990 ... 128
  Obituary ... 132
  Brief entry ... 119
  See also CLC 61
  See also EWL 3
  See also GFL 1789 to the Present
Leiser, Bill
  See Leiser, William Frederick
Leiser, Burton M. 1930- ... CANR-42
  Earlier sketches in CA 29-32R, CANR-12
Leiser, Erwin (Moritz) 1923- ... CANR-14
  Earlier sketch in CA 29-32R
Leiser, Gary 1946- ... 153
Leiser, William Frederick 1898-1965 ... 216
  See also DLB 241
Leiserson, Michael 1939- ... 37-40R
Leisewitz, Johann Anton 1752-1806 ... DLB 94
Leishman, J(ames) Blair 1902-1963 ... CANR-6
  Earlier sketch in CA 5-8R
Leishman, Thomas L. 1900-1978
  Obituary ... 81-84
Leisk, David (Johnson) 1906-1975 ... 9-12R
  Obituary ... 57-60
  See also Johnson, Crockett
  See also CLR 98
  See also CWRI 5
  See also MAICYA 1, 2
  See also SATA 1, 30
  See also SATA-Obit 26
Leiss, William 1939- ... 41-44R
Leister, Mary 1917- ... CANR-11
  Earlier sketch in CA 65-68
  See also SATA 29
Leistritz, F(redrick) Larry 1945- ... 104
Leistyna, Pepi 1963- ... 234
Leisy, James (Franklin) 1927- ... CANR-20
  Earlier sketches in CA 9-12R, CANR-4
Leitch, Adelaide 1921- ... 101
Leitch, D(avid) B(ruce) 1940- ... 57-60
Leitch, Ione Skye
  See Skye, Ione
Leitch, Maurice 1933- ... CANR-40
  Earlier sketch in CA 102
  See also DLB 14
Leitch, Patricia 1933- ... CANR-9
  Earlier sketch in CA 61-64
  See also SATA 11, 98
Leitch, Thomas M. 1964- ... 224
Leitch, Vincent Barry 1944- ... CANR-119
  Earlier sketch in CA 113
Leitenberg, Milton 1933- ... CANR-19
  Earlier sketch in CA 101
Leiter, Louis (Henry) 1921- ... 37-40R
Leiter, Marcia 1942- ... 116
Leiter, Robert D(avid) 1922-1976 ... CANR-4
  Obituary ... 69-72
  Earlier sketch in CA 5-8R
Leiter, Samuel L(ouis) 1940- ... CANR-116
  Earlier sketches in CA 93-96, CANR-31, 56
Leiter, Sharon 1942- ... 57-60
Leites, Edmund 1939- ... 126
Leites, Nathan Constantin 1912-1987 ... 126
  Obituary ... 122
Leith, (James) Andrew 1931- ... CANR-20
  Earlier sketch in CA 45-48
Leith, Denise J. 1954- ... 237
Leith, J(ames) Clark 1937- ... 57-60
Leith, John H(addon) 1919-2002 ... CANR-3
  Obituary ... 206
  Earlier sketch in CA 5-8R
Leith, Linda 1949- ... 131
Leith, Prudence (Margaret) 1940- ... 218
Leith, Prue
  See Leith, Prudence (Margaret)
Leith, Valery
  See Sullivan, Tricia
Leithauser, Brad 1953- ... CANR-81
  Earlier sketches in CA 107, CANR-27
  See also CLC 27
  See also CP 7
  See also DLB 120, 282
Leithauser, Gladys Garner 1925- ... CANR-27
  Earlier sketch in CA 13-16R
Leith-Ross, Prudence 1922- ... CANR-90
  Earlier sketch in CA 132
Leitmann, George 1925- ... 53-56
Leitner, Isabella 1924- ... 152
  See also SATA 86
Leitner, Moses J. 1908- ... CAP-1
  Earlier sketch in CA 13-16
Leitz, Robert C(harles) III 1944- ... CANR-93
  Earlier sketch in CA 133
Leivick, H.
  See Halpern, Leivick
Leivick, Halper
  See Halpern, Leivick
le Jars de Gournay, Marie
  See de Gournay, Marie le Jars
Le Jumel de Barneville, Marie-Catherine
  1650(?)-1705 ... DLB 268
Lekachman, Robert 1920-1989
  Obituary ... 127
  Brief entry ... 106
Lekai, J(ulius) Louis 1916-1994 ... 33-36R
Lekis, Lisa 1917-1995 ... 9-12R
Lekson, Stephen H(enry) 1950- ... CANR-91
  Earlier sketches in CA 122, CANR-48
Leland, Bob 1956- ... SATA 92
Leland, Charles G(odfrey) 1824-1903
  Brief entry ... 118
  See also DLB 11
Leland, Christopher Towne 1951- ... CANR-99
  Earlier sketch in CA 108
Leland, David 1947- ... 172
Leland, Henry 1923- ... CANR-18
  Earlier sketch in CA 89-92
Leland, Jeremy (Francis David)
  1932- ... CANR-13
  Earlier sketch in CA 33-36R
Leland, John 1503(?)-1552 ... DLB 136
Leland, Robert E.
  See Leland, Bob
Leland, Timothy 1937- ... 102
Lelchuk, Alan 1938- ... CANR-70
  Earlier sketches in CA 45-48, CANR-1
  See also CAAS 20
  See also CLC 5
  See also CN 3, 4, 5, 6, 7
Lele, Uma 1941- ... 73-76
Leliaert, Richard Maurice 1940- ... 101
le Lievre, Audrey 1923- ... 132
Lellenberg, Jon L. 1946- ... CANR-114
  Earlier sketch in CA 165
Lelouch, Claude (Barruck Joseph) 1937-
  Brief entry ... 113
LeLoup, Lance T. 1949- ... 110
Lelwica, Michelle Mary ... 197
Lelyveld, Arthur J(oseph) 1913-1996 ... 25-28R
  Obituary ... 152
Lelyveld, Joseph (Salem) 1937- ... CANR-107
  Brief entry ... 117
  Earlier sketch in CA 126
  Interview in ... CA-126
Lem, Stanislaw 1921- ... CANR-32
  Earlier sketch in CA 105
  See also CAAS 1
  See also CLC 8, 15, 40, 149
  See also CWW 2
  See also MTCW 1
  See also SCFW 1, 2
  See also SFW 4
Lem, Winnie 1955- ... 228
Lemagny, Jean-Claude 1931- ... 136
LeMahieu, D(an) L(loyd) 1945- ... 69-72
LeMair, H(enriette) Willebeek
  1889-1966 ... SATA-Brief 29
LeMaire, Charles 1897-1985 ... IDFW 3, 4
LeMaire, H. Paul 1933- ... 113
Lemaitre, Corene 1967- ... 207
Lemaitre, Georges E(douard)
  1898-1973 ... CAP-2
  Obituary ... 37-40R
  Earlier sketch in CA 25-28
Lemann, Bernard 1905-2000 ... CANR-21
  Earlier sketch in CA 41-44R
Lemann, Nancy (Elise) 1956- ... CANR-121
  Brief entry ... 118
  Earlier sketch in CA 136
  See also CLC 39
Lemann, Nicholas 1954- ... CANR-88
  Earlier sketch in CA 138
Lemarchand, Elizabeth (Wharton)
  1906-2000 ... CANR-64
  Earlier sketches in CA 25-28R, CANR-10, 26
  See also CMW 4
Lemarchand, Rene 1932- ... 13-16R
LeMaster, Carolyn Gray ... 150
LeMaster, J(immie) R(ay) 1934- ... CANR-30
  Earlier sketches in CA 33-36R, CANR-13
LeMaster, Leslie Jean 1943- ... 125
LeMay, Alan 1899-1964
  Obituary ... 115
  See also TCWW 1, 2
Lemay, Harding 1922- ... CANR-21
  Earlier sketches in CA 45-48, CANR-1
Lemay, J(oseph) A(lberic) Leo 1935- . CANR-49
  Earlier sketches in CA 17-20R, CANR-9, 24
Lemay, Laura ... 170
Lemay, Pamphile 1837-1918 ... 181
  See also DLB 99
le May, Reginald Stuart 1885-1972 ... 5-8R
Lemay, Shawna 1966- ... 200
Lembark, Connie W. 1934- ... 144
Lembeck, Ruth (Louise) 1919- ... 105
Lember, Barbara Hirsch 1941- ... SATA 92
Lembke, Janet (Nutt) 1933- ... 45-48
Lembo, Diana L.
  See Spirt, Diana L(ouise)
Lembo, John M(ario) 1937- ... 29-32R
Lembourn, Hans Joergen 1923- ... 105
Lemco, Jonathan 1956- ... 139
Lemelin, Roger 1919-1992 ... 210
  See also DLB 88
Lemelle, Wilbert J. 1931- ... 45-48
Lemercier, Louis-Jean-Nepomucene
  1771-1840 ... DLB 192
Lemerle, Paul (Emile) 1903-1989
  Obituary ... 129
Lemert, Charles C(lay) 1937- ... 111
Lemert, Edwin M(cCarty) 1912-1996 ... 93-96
Lemert, James B(olton) 1935- ... 73-76
Lemert, Jim
  See Lemert, James B(olton)
Lemesurier, Peter
  See Britton, Peter Ewart
LeMieux, A(nne) C(onnelly) 1954- ... CANR-97
  Earlier sketch in CA 155
  See also LeMieux, Anne
  See also AAYA 40
  See also SATA 90, 125
LeMieux, Anne
  See LeMieux, A(nne) C(onnelly)
  See also WYAS 1
Lemieux, Joanne (Hero) 1946- ... 114
Lemieux, Lucien 1934- ... 41-44R
Lemieux, Marc 1948- ... 102
Lemieux, Michele 1955- ... SATA 139
Lemir, Andre
  See Rimel, Duane (Weldon)
Lemire, Beverly 1950- ... 141
Le Mire, Eugene D(ennis) 1929- ... 41-44R
Lemire, Robert A(rthur) 1933- ... 101
Lemish, John 1921-1998 ... 5-8R
Lemke, Horst 1922- ... 107
  See also SATA 38
Lemlin, Jeanne 1953- ... 150
Lemme, Janet E(llen) 1941- ... 29-32R
Lemmon, David (Hector) 1931-1998 ... 131
  Obituary ... 171
Lemmon, Kenneth 1911- ... 65-68
Lemmon, Sarah McCulloh 1914-2002 .. 21-24R
Lemmons, Thom 1955- ... CANR-114
  Earlier sketch in CA 134
Lemoine, Ernest
  See Roy, Ewell Paul
Le Moine, James MacPherson 1825-1912 .. 218
  See also DLB 99
LeMon, Cal 1945- ... 53-56
Lemon, James Thomas 1929- ... 37-40R
Lemon, Lee T(homas) 1931- ... 17-20R
LeMon, Lynn
  See Wert, Lynette L(emon)
Lemon, Mark 1809-1870 ... DLB 163
Lemon, Ralph 1952- ... 209
LeMoncheck, Linda 1954- ... 171
LeMond, Alan 1938- ... CANR-9
  Earlier sketch in CA 61-64
Lemonnier, (Antoine Louis) Camille 1844-1913
  Brief entry ... 121
  See also TCLC 22

Cumulative Index 345 **Leplin**

Lemons, J. Stanley 1938- 37-40R
Lemont, George 1927- 65-68
Lemos, Ramon M(arcelino) 1927- 37-40R
Le Moyne, Jean 1913-1996 163
  See also DLB 88
Lemperly, Paul 1858-1939 183
  See also DLB 187
Lena, Dan 1955- 134
Lena, Marie
  See Lena, Marie H(oward)
Lena, Marie H(oward) 1956- 134
Lenanton, Carola Mary Anima Oman
  See Oman, Carola (Mary Anima)
Lenarcic, R(aymond) J(ames) 1942- 49-52
Lenard, Alexander 1910-1972 .... CANR-4
  Obituary 89-92
  Earlier sketch in CA 5-8R
  See also SATA-Obit 21
Lenard, Yvone 1921- CANR-101
  Earlier sketches in CA 53-56, CANR-7
Lenardon, Robert J(oseph) 1928- 33-36R
Lenburg, Greg 1956- 105
Lenburg, Jeff 1956- CANR-20
  Earlier sketch in CA 104
Lencioni, Patrick 1965- 235
Lenczowski, George 1915-2000 .... CANR-4
  Obituary 187
  Earlier sketch in CA 1-4R
Lendon, Kenneth Harry 1928- 9-12R
Lendvai, Paul 1929- CANR-33
  Earlier sketches in CA 85-88, CANR-15
Lenehan, William T. 1930-1993 .... 21-24R
Lenero, Vicente 1933- 180
  See also DLB 305
  See also EWL 3
L'Enfant, Julie 1944- 109
Lenfestey, (William Frederick) Thompson
  1925- 153
Leng, Russell J. 1938- CANR-142
  Earlier sketch in CA 144
Lengel, Frances
  See Trocchi, Alexander
Lengle, James I(rvin) 1949- 106
L'Engle, Madeleine (Camp Franklin)
  1918- CANR-107
  Earlier sketches in CA 1-4R, CANR-3, 21, 39, 66
  See also AAYA 28
  See also AITN 2
  See also BPFB 2
  See also BYA 2, 4, 5, 7
  See also CLC 12
  See also CLR 1, 14, 57
  See also CPW
  See also CWRI 5
  See also DA3
  See also DAM POP
  See also DLB 52
  See also JRDA
  See also MAICYA 1, 2
  See also MTCW 1, 2
  See also MTFW 2005
  See also SAAS 15
  See also SATA 1, 27, 75, 128
  See also SFW 4
  See also WYA
  See also YAW
Lengyel, Alfonz 1921- CANR-87
  Earlier sketch in CA 116
Lengyel, Cornel Adam 1915- CANR-24
  Earlier sketches in CA 1-4R, CANR-1
  See also SATA 27
Lengyel, Emil 1895-1985 .... CANR-3
  Obituary 115
  Earlier sketch in CA 9-12R
  See also SATA 3
  See also SATA-Obit 42
Lengyel, Jozsef 1896-1975 .... CANR-71
  Obituary 57-60
  Earlier sketch in CA 85-88
  See also CLC 7
  See also RGSF 2
Lengyel, Melchior 1879(?)-1974
  Obituary 53-56
Lengyel, Olga
Lenhoff, Alan (Stuart) 1951- 73-76
Lenica, Jan 1928- .... IDFW 3, 4
Lenier, Sue 1957- 120
Lenihan, Eddie 1950- 228
Lenihan, John (Howard) 1941- 105
Lenihan, Kenneth J. 1928-1998 97-100
  Obituary 167
Lenin 1870-1924 168
  Brief entry 121
  See also Lenin, V. I.
Lenin, N.
  See Lenin
Lenin, Nikolai
  See Lenin
Lenin, V. I.
  See Lenin
  See also TCLC 67
Lenin, Vladimir I.
  See Lenin
Lenin, Vladimir Ilyich
  See Lenin
Lenn, Theodore I. 1914- 45-48
Lennard, John (Chevening) 1964- 137
Lennart, Isobel 1915-1971 182
  Obituary 29-32R
  See also DLB 44
  See also IDFW 3
Lenneberg, Eric H. 1921-1975 .... CANR-7
  Obituary 57-60
  Earlier sketch in CA 53-56
Lennig, Arthur 1933- CANR-101
  Earlier sketch in CA 57-60
Lennon, Donald R. 1938- 139
Lennon, Florence Becker (Tanenbaum)
  1895-1984 .... 13-16R
Lennon, Helen M.
  See Goulart, Frances Sheridan
Lennon, J. Robert 1970- CANR-114
  Earlier sketch in CA 173
Lennon, John (Ono) 1940-1980 102
  See also CLC 12, 35
  See also SATA 114
Lennon, Joseph Luke 1919- 33-36R
Lennon, Nigey 1954- 109
Lennon, Sister M. Isidore 1901- 41-44R
Lennon, Thomas M. 1942- CANR-56
  Earlier sketch in CA 125
Lennox, Charlotte Ramsay
  1729(?)-1804 .... DLB 39
  See also RGEL 2
Lennox, John 1945- 169
Lennox, Terry
  See Harvey, John (Barton)
Lennox-Short, Alan 1913- 102
Lennox-Smith, Judith (Elizabeth) 1953- 134
Leno, Jay 1950- CANR-124
  Earlier sketch in CA 159
  See also SATA 154
Lenoir, Jacques
  See Laraque, Paul
LeNoir, Janice 1941- 155
  See also SATA 89
Lenormand, Henri-Rene 1882-1951 219
Lenox, James 1800-1880 .... DLB 140, 254
Lens, Sidney 1912-1986 .... CANR-17
  Obituary 119
  Earlier sketches in CA 1-4R, CANR-1
  See also SATA 13
  See also SATA-Obit 48
Lensen, George Alexander
  1923-1980 .... CANR-2
  Earlier sketch in CA 1-4R
Lensink, Judy Nolte 1948- 127
Lenski, Gerhard Emmanuel, Jr.
  1924- CANR-128
  Earlier sketch in CA 1-4R
Lenski, Lois 1893-1974 .... CANR-80
  Obituary 53-56
  Earlier sketches in CAP-1, CA 13-14, CANR-41
  See also BYA 3
  See also CLR 26
  See also CWRI 5
  See also DLB 22
  See also MAICYA 1, 2
  See also SATA 1, 26, 100
Lenson, David (Rollar) 1945- 73-76
Lent, Blair CANR-111
  Earlier sketches in CA 21-24R, CANR-11
  See also MAICYA 1, 2
  See also SATA 2, 133
Lent, D(ora) Geneva 1904-1965 .... 5-8R
Lent, Henry Bolles 1901-1973 73-76
  See also SATA 17
Lent, Jeffrey 238
Lent, John 1948- 169
  See also SATA 108
Lent, John A(nthony) 1936- CANR-57
  Earlier sketches in CA 29-32R, CANR-12, 30
Lentfoehr, Therese 1902-1981 97-100
Lentilhon, Robert Ward 1925- 9-12R
Lentin, Antony 1941- 103
Lentin, Ronit 1944- 203
Lentner, Howard H(enry) 1931- 106
Lenton, Henry Trevor 1924- 103
Lentricchia, Frank, (Jr.) 1940- CANR-106
  Earlier sketches in CA 25-28R, CANR-19
  See also CLC 34
  See also DLB 246
Lentz, Donald A. 1910- 17-20R
Lentz, Harold H(erbert) 1910-2004 57-60
  Obituary 225
Lentz, Harris M(onroe) III 1955- 172
Lentz, John C(layton), Jr. 1957- 146
Lentz, Perry 1943- 21-24R
Lenz, Carolyn Ruth Swift
  See Swift, Carolyn Ruth
Lenz, Elinor 1928- 145
Lenz, Frederick (P.), (Jr.) 1950-1998 .. CANR-52
  Obituary 167
  Earlier sketch in CA 97-100
Lenz, Gunter .... CLC 65
Lenz, Hermann 1913-1998 185
  See also DLB 69
Lenz, Jakob Michael Reinhold
  1751-1792 .... DLB 94
  See also RGWL 2, 3
Lenz, Siegfried 1926- CANR-80
  Earlier sketch in CA 89-92
  See also CLC 27
  See also CWW 2
  See also DLB 75
  See also EWL 3
  See also RGSF 2
  See also RGWL 2, 3
  See also SSC 33
Lenz, William E(rnest) 1950- 118
Lenzner, Robert 1935- 145
Leo, John P. 1935- 207
Leo, Mabel Maglone
  See Leo, Mabel R.
Leo, Mabel R. 1937- CANR-123
  Earlier sketch in CA 166
Leo, Richard C. 1952- 139
Leodhas, Sorche Nic
  See Alger, Leclaire (Gowans)
LeoGrande, William M(ark) 1949- 122
Leokum, Arkady 1916(?)- 116
  See also SATA 45
Leon, David
  See Jacob, (Cyprien-)Max
Leon, Donna 1942- 183
Leon, Frances
  See Swadesh, Frances Leon
Leon, Henry Cecil 1902-1976
  Obituary 115
  See also CMW 4
Leon, Luis de 1527-1591 .... DLB 318
Leon, Nick
  See Grant, Graeme
Leon, Pierre R. 1926- CANR-43
  Earlier sketches in CA 45-48, CANR-1, 17
Leon, Sharon 1959- 148
  See also SATA 79
Leon, Vicki 1942- 132
Leonard, Alison 1944- 138
  See also SATA 70
Leonard, Calista V(erne) 1919- 21-24R
Leonard, Charlene M(arie) 1928- 33-36R
Leonard, Constance (Brink) 1923- CANR-28
  Earlier sketch in CA 49-52
  See also SATA 42
  See also SATA-Brief 40
Leonard, Diana 1941- 137
Leonard, Edith Marian CAP-1
  Earlier sketch in CA 13-16
Leonard, Elizabeth D. 229
Leonard, Elmore (John, Jr.) 1925- CANR-133
  Earlier sketches in CA 81-84, CANR-12, 28, 53, 76, 96
  Interview in CANR-28
  See also AAYA 22, 59
  See also AITN 1
  See also BEST 89:1, 90:4
  See also BPFB 2
  See also CLC 28, 34, 71, 120
  See also CMW 4
  See also CN 5, 6, 7
  See also CPW
  See also DA3
  See also DAM POP
  See also DLB 173, 226
  See also MSW
  See also MTCW 1, 2
  See also MTFW 2005
  See also RGAL 4
  See also SATA 163
  See also TCWW 1, 2
Leonard, Eugenie Andruss 1888-1980 ... CAP-2
  Obituary 97-100
  Earlier sketch in CA 17-18
Leonard, Frances 1939- 141
Leonard, Frank G. 1935(?)-1974
  Obituary 49-52
Leonard, George (Jay) 1946- 112
Leonard, George B(urr) 1923- CANR-20
  Earlier sketches in CA 9-12R, CANR-3
Leonard, George E(dward) 1931- 21-24R
Leonard, George H. 1921- 65-68
Leonard, George K., Jr. 1915- 17-20R
Leonard, Gerald 1960- 227
Leonard, Gladys Osborne 1882-1968
  Obituary 112
Leonard, Graham Douglas 1921- 103
Leonard, Hugh
  See Byrne, John Keyes
  See also CBD
  See also CD 5, 6
  See also CLC 19
  See also DFS 13
  See also DLB 13
Leonard, Irving A(lbert) 1896-1996 .... CANR-5
  Earlier sketch in CA 5-8R
Leonard, J. S.
  See Leonard, James S.
Leonard, James S. 1947- 142
Leonard, Jason
  See Escott, Jonathan
Leonard, John 1939- CANR-88
  Earlier sketches in CA 13-16R, CANR-12
Leonard, Jonathan N(orton) 1903-1975 ... 61-64
  Obituary 57-60
  See also SATA 36
Leonard, Joseph T. 1916- 9-12R
Leonard, Justin W(ilkinson) 1909-1975 . CAP-1
  Earlier sketch in CA 19-20
Leonard, Karen Isaksen 1939- CANR-135
  Earlier sketch in CA 144
Leonard, Kathy S. 1952- CANR-140
  Earlier sketch in CA 174
Leonard, Laura 1923- 142
  See also SATA 75
Leonard, Lawrence 1928- CANR-47
  Earlier sketch in CA 121
Leonard, Leo D(onald) 1938- CANR-5
  Earlier sketch in CA 53-56
Leonard, Maurice 1939- 107
Leonard, Neil 1927- 1-4R
Leonard, Phyllis B. 1929- 117
Leonard, Phyllis G(rubbs) 1924- CANR-12
  Earlier sketch in CA 69-72
Leonard, Richard 1954- 141
Leonard, Richard Anthony 1900(?)-1979
  Obituary 85-88
Leonard, Robert 1928-1984
  Obituary 112
Leonard, Robert C(arl) 1928- 45-48
Leonard, Roger Ashley 1940- 25-28R
Leonard, Ruth S(haw) 1906- CAP-2
  Earlier sketch in CA 23-24
Leonard, Stephen J. 1941- 147
Leonard, Thomas C(harles) 1944- CANR-53
  Earlier sketch in CA 77-80
Leonard, Thomas M. 1937- CANR-102
  Earlier sketches in CA 122, CANR-48
Leonard, Tom 1944- CANR-31
  Earlier sketches in CA 77-80, CANR-13
  See also CP 2, 3, 4, 5, 6, 7
Leonard, V(ivian) A(nderson)
  1898-1984 .... CANR-15
  Earlier sketch in CA 37-40R
Leonard, William Ellery 1876-1944 182
  See also DLB 54
Leonard, William N. 1912- 37-40R
Leonard, William Torbert 1918- 107
Leonard-Barton, Dorothy 1942- 155
Leonardi, Susan J. 1946- 131
Leondes, Cornelius Thomas 1927- 17-20R
Leone, Bruno 1939- 110
Leone, Daniel 1969- 165
Leone, Leonard 1914- 115
Leone, Mark P(aul) 1940- 93-96
Leone, Robert A. 1945-1999 122
Leone, Sergio 1929(?)-1989 123
  Obituary 128
Leong, Albert 1935-2002 218
Leong, Charles L. 1911(?)-1984
  Obituary 112
Leong, Gor Yun
  See Ellison, Virginia H(owell)
Leong, Russell (C.) 1950- CANR-99
  Earlier sketch in CA 142
  See also DLB 312
Leonhard, Charles 1915- 5-8R
Leonhard, Wolfgang 1921- 144
Leonhardt, Alice 1950- 227
  See also SATA 152
Leonhardt, David W. J. 1962- 213
Leonhardt, Fritz 1909-1999 .... CANR-49
  Earlier sketch in CA 123
Leonhardt, Rudolf Walter 1921- CANR-3
  Earlier sketch in CA 9-12R
Leoni, Edgar (Hugh) 1925- CANR-38
  Earlier sketch in CA 125
Leonov, Leonid (Maximovich)
  1899-1994 .... CANR-76
  Earlier sketch in CA 129
  See also Leonov, Leonid Maksimovich
  See also CLC 92
  See also DAM NOV
  See also EWL 3
  See also MTCW 1, 2
  See also MTFW 2005
Leonov, Leonid Maksimovich
  See Leonov, Leonid (Maximovich)
  See also DLB 272
Leonowens, Anna (Harriet Crawford)
  1834-1914 183
  See also DLB 99, 166
Leon-Portilla, Miguel 1926- CANR-32
  Earlier sketches in CA 21-24R, CANR-11
  See also HW 1
Leont'ev, Konstantin Nikolaevich
  1831-1891 .... DLB 277
Leontiades, Milton 1932- 110
Leontief, Wassily 1906(?)-1999 .... CAP-1
  Obituary 177
  Earlier sketch in CA 17-18
Leontyev, Lev Abramovich 1901-1974
  Obituary 49-52
Leopardi, (Conte) Giacomo 1798-1837 ... EW 5
  See also PC 37
  See also RGWL 2, 3
  See also WLIT 7
  See also WP
Leopold, A(ldo) Starker 1913-1983
  Obituary 110
Leopold, Aldo 1886-1948 141
  See also AMWS 14
  See also ANW
  See also DLB 275
Leopold, Allison Kyle 1955- 112
Leopold, Carolyn Clugston 1923- 73-76
Leopold, Christopher
  See Synge, Allen
Leopold, Ellen 1944- 223
Leopold, Jan Hendrik 1865-1925 197
  See also EWL 3
Leopold, Luna B(ergere) 1915- CANR-31
  Earlier sketch in CA 49-52
Leopold, Nathan F. 1904-1971 .... CAP-1
  Obituary 29-32R
  Earlier sketch in CA 13-16
Leopold, Richard William 1912- CANR-2
  Earlier sketch in CA 1-4R
Leopold, Werner F. 1896-1984 45-48
Leopold III 1901-1983
  Obituary 110
Le Page, Rand
  See Glasby, John S.
Lepage, Robert 1957- CANR-109
  Earlier sketch in CA 162
Le Pan, Douglas (Valentine) 1914-1998 129
  Brief entry 117
  See also CP 1, 2, 3, 4, 5, 6, 7
  See also DLB 88
Le Patourel, John Herbert 1909-1981 .... CAP-1
  Obituary 104
  Earlier sketch in CA 9-10
Lepawsky, Albert 1908-1992 45-48
Le Pelley, Guernsey 1910-1990 81-84
Lepetit, Charles
  See Sala, Charles
Lepidus, Henry 1916(?)-1983
  Obituary 110
Lepik, Kalju 1920-1999 .... DLB 232
Lepko, E.
  See Kopelev, Lev (Zinovievich)
Lepley, Jean Elizabeth 1931- 69-72
Lepley, Paul M(ichael) 1933- 53-56
Leplin, Jarrett 1944- 170

Le Poer Trench, (William Francis) Brinsley 1911-1995
Brief entry ... 116
Le Poidevin, Robin (David) 1962- ... 185
Lepore, D(ominick) J(ames) 1911-1992 ... 45-48
Lepore, Jill 1966- ... CANR-144
Earlier sketch in CA 170
Le Poulain, Jean 1924-1988
Obituary ... 125
Lepovitz, Helena Waddy 1945- ... 135
Lepp, Henry 1922-1990 ... 53-56
Leppek, Christopher 1954- ... CANR-139
Earlier sketch in CA 173
Leppmann, Peter K. 1931- ... 25-28R
Leppmann, Wolfgang Arthur 1922- ... CANR-37
Earlier sketch in CA 1-4R
Leppzer, Robert 1958- ... 105
Leprohon, Pierre 1903- ... CANR-1
Earlier sketch in CA 45-48
Leprohon, Rosanna Eleanor 1829-1879 ... DLB 99
Le Quesne, A(lfred) L(aurence) 1928- ... 116
Le Quesne, Laurence
See Le Quesne, A(lfred) L(aurence)
Le Queux, William (Tufnell) 1864-1927 ... 185
Brief entry ... 109
See also DLB 70
Lerangis, Peter 1955- ... SATA 72
Lerbinger, Otto 1925- ... 21-24R
Lerche, Charles O(lsen), Jr. 1918-1966 ... 5-8R
Le Reveler
See Artaud, Antonin (Marie Joseph)
le Riche, William Harding 1916- ... 107
Lerman, Eleanor 1952- ... CANR-124
Earlier sketches in CA 85-88, CANR-69
See also CLC 9
Lerman, Leo 1914-1994 ... 45-48
Obituary ... 146
Lerman, Liz (A.) 1947- ... 213
Lerman, Paul 1926- ... 97-100
Lerman, Rhoda 1936- ... CANR-70
Earlier sketch in CA 49-52
See also CLC 56
Lermontov, Mikhail Iur'evich
See Lermontov, Mikhail Yuryevich
See also DLB 205
Lermontov, Mikhail Yuryevich 1814-1841
See Lermontov, Mikhail Iur'evich
See also EW 6
See also PC 18
See also RGWL 2, 3
See also TWA
Lernat-Holenia, Alexander 1898(?)-1976 ... DLB 85
Lerner, Aaron Bunsen 1920- ... 108
See also SATA 35
Lerner, Abba P(tachya) 1903-1982 ... CANR-2
Obituary ... 108
Earlier sketch in CA 1-4R
Lerner, Alan Jay 1918-1986 ... CANR-31
Obituary ... 119
Earlier sketch in CA 77-80
See also DLB 265
Lerner, Andrea 1954- ... 134
Lerner, Arthur 1915-1998 ... 102
Obituary ... 167
Lerner, Barron H. 1960- ... 208
Lerner, Carol 1927- ... CANR-70
Earlier sketch in CA 102
See also CLR 34
See also MAICYA 2
See also MAICYAS 1
See also SAAS 12
See also SATA 33, 86
Lerner, Daniel 1917-1980 ... CANR-6
Obituary ... 97-100
Earlier sketch in CA 1-4R
Lerner, Eugene Max 1928- ... 17-20R
Lerner, Gerda 1920- ... CANR-130
Earlier sketches in CA 25-28R, CANR-26, 45, 70
See also FW
See also SATA 65
Lerner, Harriet 1944- ... CANR-143
Earlier sketch in CA 168
See also SATA 101
Lerner, Henry M. ... 226
Lerner, Herbert J. 1933- ... 53-56
Lerner, I. Michael 1910-1977 ... 41-44R
Lerner, Janet W(eiss) 1926- ... CANR-7
Earlier sketch in CA 57-60
Lerner, Jimmy ... 210
Lerner, Joel J. 1936- ... 53-56
Lerner, Laurence (David) 1925- ... CANR-101
Earlier sketches in CA 5-8R, CANR-3, 20
See also CN 1, 2
See also CP 1, 2, 3, 4, 5, 6, 7
Lerner, Lily Gluck 1928- ... 117
Lerner, Linda ... 73-76
Lerner, Lisa 1960- ... 218
Lerner, Louis A. 1935-1984
Obituary ... 114
Lerner, Marguerite Rush 1924-1987 ... 13-16R
Obituary ... 122
See also SATA 11
See also SATA-Obit 51
Lerner, Martin 1936- ... 141
Lerner, Maura 1953- ... 97-100
Lerner, Max(well Alan) 1902-1992 ... CANR-25
Obituary ... 137
Earlier sketch in CA 13-16R
See also AITN 1
See also DLB 29
Lerner, Michael G(ordon) 1943- ... 49-52
Lerner, Michael P(hillip) 1943- ... 45-48
Lerner, Motti 1949- ... 215
Lerner, Richard E(dward) 1941- ... 73-76
Lerner, Richard M(artin) 1946- ... 93-96
Lerner, Robert E. 1940- ... CANR-8
Earlier sketch in CA 21-24R
Lerner, Sharon (Ruth) 1938-1982 ... CANR-3
Obituary ... 106
Earlier sketch in CA 5-8R
See also SATA 11
See also SATA-Obit 29
Lerner, Steve 1946- ... CANR-123
Earlier sketch in CA 167
Lerner, Warren 1929- ... 29-32R
Lernet-Holenia, Alexander 1898(?)-1976 ... 183
Obituary ... 65-68
Lernoux, Penny (Mary) 1940-1989 ... 77-80
Obituary ... 129
Leroe, Ellen W(hitney) 1949- ... CANR-40
Earlier sketch in CA 116
See also SATA 61, 99
See also SATA-Brief 51
Leroi, Armand Marie 1964- ... 235
Le Roi, David (de Roche) 1905- ... CANR-3
Earlier sketch in CA 9-12R
Leroi-Gourhan, Andre (Georges Leandre) 1911-1986
Obituary ... 118
Le Rossignol, James 1866-1969 ... 148
See also DLB 92
Leroux, Etienne
See Leroux, S(tephanus) P(etrus) D(aniel)
Leroux, Gaston 1868-1927 ... CANR-69
Brief entry ... 108
Earlier sketch in CA 136
See also CMW 4
See also MTFW 2005
See also NFS 20
See also SATA 65
See also TCLC 25
Leroux, S(tephanus) P(etrus) D(aniel) 1922- ... CANR-2
Earlier sketch in CA 49-52
Leroux-Hugon, Helene 1955- ... 201
See also SATA 132
Le Roy, Bruce Murdock 1920-1999 ... 185
Brief entry ... 106
LeRoy, Dave
See LeRoy, (Lemuel) David
LeRoy, (Lemuel) David 1920-1998 ... 81-84
Obituary ... 181
LeRoy, Douglas 1943- ... CANR-18
Earlier sketches in CA 49-52, CANR-3
LeRoy, Gaylord C(larke) 1910-1995 ... 37-40R
LeRoy, Gen ... 134
Brief entry ... 115
See also SATA 52
See also SATA-Brief 36
Leroy, Gilles 1958- ... CANR-134
Earlier sketch in CA 157
LeRoy, J. T. 1980- ... 200
Leroy, Maurice (A. L.) 1909- ... 25-28R
LeRoy, Mervyn 1900-1987 ... 166
Obituary ... 123
Brief entry ... 108
Le Roy Ladurie, Emmanuel (Bernard) 1929- ... CANR-102
Earlier sketches in CA 113, CANR-49
Lerrigo, Marion Olive 1898-1968
Obituary ... 109
See also SATA-Obit 29
Lerro, Anthony Joseph 1932- ... 33-36R
Lerski, George Jan 1917-1992 ... 73-76
Lerteth, Oban
See Fanthorpe, R(obert) Lionel
Lerude, Warren (Leslie) 1937- ... 146
Brief entry ... 122
Lesage, Alain-Rene 1668-1747 ... DLB 313
See also EW 3
See also GFL Beginnings to 1789
See also RGWL 2, 3
Le Sage, Laurent 1913- ... CANR-25
Earlier sketch in CA 1-4R
Lescarbot, Marc c. 1570-1642 ... DLB 99
Lesch, David W. 1960- ... 167
Lesch, John E(mmett) 1945- ... 132
Leschak, Peter M. 1951- ... CANR-134
Earlier sketches in CA 126, CANR-52
Lescoe, Francis J(oseph) 1916- ... 61-64
Lescroart, John T. 1948- ... CANR-106
Earlier sketches in CA 122, CANR-61
See also CMW 4
Lesesne, J(oab) Mauldin 1899-1993 ... CAP-2
Earlier sketch in CA 33-36
LeSeur, Geta ... 193
LeShan, Eda J(oan) 1922-2002 ... CANR-21
Obituary ... 205
Earlier sketch in CA 13-16R
See also CLR 6
See also SATA 21
LeShan, Lawrence L(ee) 1920- ... CANR-21
Earlier sketch in CA 17-20R
Le Shana, David C(harles) 1932- ... 29-32R
Lesher, Phyllis A(senath Bayers) 1912-1982 ... CANR-17
Earlier sketch in CA 25-28R
Lesher, Stephan 1935- ... 103
Leshoai, Benjamin Letholoa 1920- ... 153
See also BW 2
LeSieg, Theo.
See Dr. Seuss and
Geisel, Theodor Seuss and
Seuss, Dr. and
Stone, Rosetta
Lesieur, Henry R(ichard) 1946- ... 77-80
Lesikar, Raymond Vincent 1922- ... CANR-2
Earlier sketch in CA 1-4R
Lesikin, Joan 1947- ... 93-96
Lesins, Knuts 1909- ... 73-76
Lesinski, Jeanne M. 1960- ... 191
See also SATA 120
Lesko, George 1932- ... 17-20R
Lesko, Leonard Henry 1938- ... CANR-8
Earlier sketch in CA 61-64
Lesko, Wendy
See Schaetzel, Wendy
Leskov, N(ikolai) S(emenovich) 1831-1895
See Leskov, Nikolai (Semyonovich)
Leskov, Nikolai (Semyonovich) 1831-1895
See Leskov, Nikolai Semenovich
See also SSC 34
Leskov, Nikolai Semenovich
See Leskov, Nikolai (Semyonovich)
See also DLB 238
Lesky, Albin (Hans) 1896-1981 ... 85-88
Leslau, Wolf 1906- ... 104
Lesley, Blake
See Duckworth, Leslie Blakey
Lesley, Cole
See Cole, Leonard Leslie
Lesley, Craig ... 190
Leslie, A. L.
See Lazarus, A(rnold) L(eslie)
Leslie, Aleen ... 5-8R
Leslie, Anita 1914-1985 ... CANR-32
Obituary ... 117
Earlier sketch in CA 49-52
Leslie, Anne
See Leslie, Anita
Leslie, Cecilie 1914- ... 17-20R
Leslie, Charles M. 1923- ... 5-8R
Leslie, Clare Walker 1947- ... 108
Leslie, Conrad 1923- ... 29-32R
Leslie, Desmond 1921-2001 ... 9-12R
Leslie, Donald Daniel 1922- ... 102
Leslie, Doris
See Fergusson Hannay, Doris
Leslie, Eliza 1787-1858 ... DLB 202
Leslie, F(rederic) Andrew 1927- ... CANR-7
Earlier sketch in CA 17-20R
Leslie, Frank 1821-1880 ... DLB 43, 79
Leslie, Gerald R(onnell) 1925- ... 17-20R
Leslie, Jacques (Robert), (Jr.) 1947- ... 213
Leslie, Jane
See Coade, Jessie
Leslie, John 1944- ... CANR-71
Earlier sketch in CA 148
Leslie, John Andrew 1940- ... CANR-118
Earlier sketches in CA 112, CANR-30, 56
Leslie, Josephine Aimee Campbell 1898-1979 ... 85-88
Leslie, Kenneth 1892-1974 ... 93-96
Obituary ... 53-56
See also CP 1, 2
Leslie, (Virginia) Kent A(nderson) 1942- ... 149
Leslie, Michael 1952- ... 118
Leslie, Miriam
See Ketchum, Philip (L.)
Leslie, O. H.
See Slesar, Henry
Leslie, Phil 1909(?)-1988
Obituary ... 126
Leslie, Richard
See Bickers, Richard (Leslie) Townshend
Leslie, Robert B.
See Wooley, John (Steven)
Leslie, Robert C(ampbell) 1917- ... 33-36R
Leslie, Robert Franklin 1911-1990 ... CANR-28
Earlier sketch in CA 49-52
See also SATA 7
Leslie, Rochelle
See Diamond, Graham
Leslie, Roger (James) 1961- ... 233
Leslie, Roy F. 1922- ... 41-44R
Leslie, S(amuel) Clement 1898-1980 ... 85-88
Leslie, San
See Crook, Bette (Jean)
Leslie, Sarah
See McGuire, Leslie (Sarah)
Leslie, Seymour 1890(?)-1979
Obituary ... 89-92
Leslie, (John Randolph) Shane 1885-1971
Obituary ... 33-36R
Leslie, Sir Shane
See Leslie, (John Randolph) Shane
Leslie, Ward S.
See Ward, Elizabeth Honor (Shedden)
Leslie, Warren III 1927- ... 9-12R
Leslie-Melville, Betty 1929-2005 ... 81-84
Leslie-Melville, Jock
See Leslie-Melville, John D.
Leslie-Melville, John D. 1933-1984 ... 81-84
Obituary ... 112
Lesly, Philip 1918-1997 ... CANR-44
Earlier sketches in CA 81-84, CANR-14
Lesmian, Boleslaw 1878-1937 ... DLB 215
See also EWL 3
Lesniak, Rose 1955- ... 147
Lesnoff-Caravaglia, Gari ... 41-44R
LeSourd, Catherine
See Marshall, (Sarah) Catherine (Wood)
LeSourd, Leonard (Earle) 1919-1996 ... 135
Obituary ... 151
Lesourne, Jacques 1928- ... 142
Lesowitz, Robert I(rwin) 1939- ... 57-60
Lesperance, John 1835(?)-1891 ... DLB 99
L'Esperance, Wilford L(ouis) III 1930-1982 ... CANR-27
Earlier sketch in CA 33-36R
Lespinasse, Julie de 1732-1776 ... DLB 313
Lessa, William A(rmand) 1908-1995 ... 61-64
Lessac, Arthur 1910-
Brief entry ... 110
Lessac, Frane
See Lessac, Frane
Lessac, Frane 1954- ... CANR-131
Earlier sketch in CA 127
See also SATA 61, 148
Lessard, Bill 1966(?)- ... 208
Lessard, Michel 1942- ... 104
Lessard, Suzannah ... 166
Lessel, William M. 1906-1995 ... CAP-2
Earlier sketch in CA 33-36
Lessem, Dino Don
See Lessem, Don
Lessem, Don 1951- ... CANR-134
Earlier sketch in CA 164
See also SATA 97, 155
Lesser, Alexander 1902-1982 ... CANR-28
Obituary ... 107
Earlier sketch in CA 49-52
Lesser, Charles H(uber) 1944- ... 73-76
Lesser, Eugene (Bernard) 1936- ... 49-52
Lesser, Gerald S(amuel) 1926- ... 97-100
Lesser, Margaret 1899(?)-1979
Obituary ... 93-96
See also SATA-Obit 22
Lesser, Michael 1939- ... CANR-120
Earlier sketch in CA 102
Lesser, Milton
See Marlowe, Stephen
Lesser, R(oger) H(arold) 1928- ... CANR-14
Earlier sketch in CA 73-76
Lesser, Rika 1953- ... CANR-96
Earlier sketch in CA 118
See also SATA 53
Lesser, Robert C. 1933- ... 104
Lesser, Wendy 1952- ... CANR-105
Earlier sketch in CA 140
Lessere, Samuel E. 1892-1975 ... CAP-2
Earlier sketch in CA 21-22
Lessig, Lawrence 1961- ... 230
Lessing, Bruno 1870-1940 ... DLB 28
Lessing, Doris (May) 1919- ... CANR-122
Earlier sketches in CA 9-12R, CANR-33, 54, 76
See also CAAS 14
See also AAYA 57
See also AFW
See also BRWS 1
See also CBD
See also CD 5, 6
See also CDBLB 1960 to Present
See also CLC 1, 2, 3, 6, 10, 15, 22, 40, 94, 170
See also CN 1, 2, 3, 4, 5, 6, 7
See also CWD
See also DA
See also DA3
See also DAB
See also DAC
See also DAM MST, NOV
See also DFS 20
See also DLB 15, 139
See also DLBY 1985
See also EWL 3
See also EXPS
See also FL 1:6
See also FW
See also LAIT 4
See also MTCW 1, 2
See also MTFW 2005
See also RGEL 2
See also RGSF 2
See also SFW 4
See also SSC 6, 61
See also SSFS 1, 12, 20
See also TEA
See also WLCS
See also WLIT 2, 4
Lessing, Gotthold Ephraim 1729-1781 ... CDWLB 2
See also DC 26
See also DLB 97
See also EW 4
See also RGWL 2, 3
Lessiter, Mike (J.) 1969- ... 135
Lessler, Richard Sigmund 1924- ... 1-4R
Lessmann, Paul G. 1919-1992 ... 17-20R
Lessnoff, Michael 1940- ... CANR-125
Earlier sketch in CA 169
LesStrang, Jacques 1926- ... CANR-17
Earlier sketch in CA 65-68
Lester, Alison 1952- ... CANR-109
Earlier sketches in CA 125, CANR-52
See also MAICYA 2
See also MAICYAS 1
See also SATA 50, 90, 129
Lester, Andrew D(ouglas) 1939- ... CANR-54
Earlier sketches in CA 109, CANR-26
Lester, Anthony 1936- ... 37-40R
Lester, David 1942- ... CANR-57
Earlier sketches in CA 33-36R, CANR-12, 31
Lester, Frank
See Usher, Frank (Hugh)
Lester, Gene
See Mercer, Jean
Lester, Godfrey Allen 1943- ... CANR-28
Earlier sketch in CA 111
Lester, Helen 1936- ... CANR-126
Earlier sketches in CA 115, CANR-38, 58
See also SATA 46, 92, 145
Lester, James
See Blake, L(eslie) J(ames)
Lester, James D. 1935- ... CANR-15
Earlier sketch in CA 89-92
Lester, James P(inkney) 1944- ... CANR-82
Earlier sketches in CA 114, CANR-35
Lester, Joan Steinau 1940- ... 238
Lester, John
See Werner, Vivian

Cumulative Index 347 Levine

Lester, Julius (Bernard) 1939- CANR-129
Earlier sketches in CA 17-20R, CANR-8, 23, 43
See also AAYA 12, 51
See also BW 2
See also BYA 3, 9, 11, 12
See also CLR 2, 41
See also JRDA
See also MAICYA 1, 2
See also MAICYAS 1
See also MTFW 2005
See also SATA 12, 74, 112, 157
See also YAW
Lester, Margot Carmichael 1962- 164
Lester, Mark
See Russell, Martin
Lester, Mike 1955- .... SATA 131
Lester, Reginald Mounstephens 1896- ... CAP-1
Earlier sketch in CA 9-10
Lester, Richard 1932- .... CLC 20
Lester, Richard A(llen) 1908-1997 102
Obituary 163
Lester, Richard K. 173
Lester, Robert C(arlton) 1933- 73-76
Lester, Robin 1939- 213
Lester, Tanya 1956- 138
Lester, William 57-60
Lester-Rands, A.
See Judd, Frederick Charles
LeStourgeon, Diana E. 1927- 13-16R
L'Estrange, Anna
See Ellerbeck, Rosemary (Anne L'Estrange)
Le Sueur, Lucille 1908(?)-1977
Obituary 111
Le Sueur, Meridel 1900-1996 .... CANR-121
Obituary 154
Earlier sketches in CA 49-52, CANR-2, 30, 83
See also DLB 303
See also SATA 6
See also TCWW 2
LeSueur, Stephen C. 1952- 133
LeSueur, William Dawson 1840-1917 210
See also DLB 92
Lesure, Francois 1923-
Brief entry 108
Lesure, Thomas B(arbour) 1923- 102
Leszlei, Marta
See Dosa, Marta Leszlei
L'Etang, Hugh J(oseph) C(harles) J(ames) 1917- 45-48
LeTarte, Clyde E(dward) 1938- 53-56
Letellier, Robert Ignatius 1953- CANR-118
Earlier sketch in CA 151
Leterman, Elmer G(oldsmith) 1897-1982 .... 25-28R
Letessier, Dorothee 1953- 158
Lethbridge, Rex
See Meyers, Roy (Lethbridge)
Lethbridge, Robert (David) 1947- 135
Lethbridge, T(homas) C(harles) 1901-1971 .... CAP-2
Earlier sketch in CA 29-32
Lethem, Jonathan (Allen) 1964- CANR-138
Earlier sketches in CA 150, CANR-80
See also AAYA 43
See also CN 7
See also MTFW 2005
See also SFW 4
Le Thi Diem Thuy
See Le, Thi Diem Thuy
Letiche, John M(arion) 1918- 49-52
Letley, Emma 1949- 131
Letnanova, Elena 1942- 140
Le Tord, Bijou 1945- CANR-68
Earlier sketches in CA 65-68, CANR-31
See also SATA 49, 95
LeTourneau, Richard H(oward) 1925-2004 .... CANR-23
Obituary 229
Earlier sketches in CA 53-56, CANR-7
Letrusco
See Martini, Virgilio
Lettau, Reinhard 1929-1996 .... CANR-70
Earlier sketches in CA 17-20R, CANR-9
See also DLB 75
Lette, Kathy 1958- CANR-101
Earlier sketch in CA 136
Letterman, David (Michael) 1947- 139
See also AAYA 10, 61
Letterman, Edward John 1926- 29-32R
Lettis, Richard 1928- 5-8R
Letts, Billie 1938- CANR-99
Earlier sketch in CA 151
See also SATA 121
Letts, Tracy 1965- 223
Lettvin, Maggie 1927- 73-76
Letwin, Shirley Robin 1924-1993 .... 17-20R
Obituary 141
Letwin, William L(ouis) 1922- 9-12R
Leuba, Clarence J(ames) 1899-1985 ...... 37-40R
Leubsdorf, Carl P(hilipp) 1938- 73-76
Leuchtenburg, William E(dward) 1922- CANR-105
Earlier sketches in CA 5-8R, CANR-12
Leuci, Bob
See Leuci, Robert
Leuci, Robert 1940- CANR-50
Earlier sketch in CA 125
Leuck, Laura 1962- .... SATA 85, 146
Leukel, Francis 1922- 53-56
Leung, Brian (J.) 229
Leung, John K(ong-cheong) 1949- 127
Leupp, Gary P. 1956- CANR-142
Earlier sketch in CA 144
Leutenegger, Gertrud 1948- .... EWL 3
Leuthner, Stuart 1939- 125
Leuthold, David Allen 1932- 21-24R
Leutscher, Alfred (George) 1913- 73-76
See also SATA 23
Lev, Daniel S(aul) 1933- 41-44R
Lev, Peter 1948- CANR-95
Earlier sketch in CA 146
Levack, Brian P(aul) 1943- 53-56
Levai, Blaise 1919- 108
See also SATA 39
Levandoski, Rob 1949- 193
Levant, Howard 1929- 89-92
Levant, Oscar 1906-1972
Obituary 37-40R
Levant, Victor 1947- CANR-52
Earlier sketch in CA 126
Levantrosser, William F(rederick) 1925- 21-24R
Levanway, Russell W(ilford) 1919-
Brief entry 107
Levarie, Siegmund 1914- 13-16R
Le Vay, David 1915-2001 89-92
Obituary 199
LeVay, Simon 1943- CANR-98
Earlier sketch in CA 142
Levell, Byrd 1911(?)-1979
Obituary 89-92
Levelt, Willem J(ohannes) M(aria) 1938- 133
Leven, Boris 1912-1986 .... IDFW 3, 4
Leven, Charles L(ouis) 1928- CANR-14
Earlier sketch in CA 41-44R
Leven, Jeremy 1941- 102
See also HGG
Levenback, Karen L. 1951- 220
Levendosky, Charles (Leonard) 1936-2004 .... CANR-12
Obituary 225
Earlier sketch in CA 29-32R
Levene, Malcolm 1937- 45-48
Levene, Mark 1953- CANR-144
Earlier sketch in CA 142
Levenkron, Steven 1941- CANR-79
Earlier sketches in CA 109, CANR-52
See also SATA 86
See also YAW
Levenson, Alan Ira 1935- 45-48
Levenson, Alec R. 1966- 150
Levenson, Christopher 1934- 29-32R
See also CP 1, 2, 3, 4, 5, 6, 7
Levenson, Dorothy (Perkins) 1927- 9-12R
Levenson, Edgar A. 1924- 128
Brief entry 108
Levenson, J(acob) C(lavner) 1922- 25-28R
Levenson, Jay .... CLC 70
Levenson, Jordan 1936- CANR-23
Earlier sketches in CA 57-60, CANR-7
Levenson, Joseph Richmond 1920-1969 .... CANR-6
Earlier sketch in CA 1-4R
Levenson, Myron H(erbert) 1926-1974 ... 53-56
Levenson, Sam(uel) 1911-1980 .... CANR-26
Obituary 101
Earlier sketch in CA 65-68
See also AITN 1
Levenson, William B. 1907-1982 .... CAP-2
Earlier sketch in CA 25-28
Levenstein, Aaron 1910-1986 .... CAP-1
Obituary 119
Earlier sketch in CA 19-20
Levenstein, Harvey A(llan) 1938- 106
Levenstein, Sidney 1917-1974 .... 9-12R
Leventhal, Albert Rice 1907-1976 65-68
Obituary 61-64
Leventhal, Bennett (L.) 1949- 135
Leventhal, Donald B(ecker) 1930-1984 ... 45-48
Leventhal, Fred Marc 1938-
Brief entry 109
Leventhal, Herbert 1941- 69-72
Leventhal, Lance A. 1945- CANR-27
Earlier sketch in CA 110
Leventhal, Lionel 1937- 213
Leventman, Seymour 1930- CANR-1
Earlier sketch in CA 1-4R
Lever, Charles (James) 1806-1872 .... DLB 21
See also RGEL 2
Lever, (Tresham) Christopher (Arthur Lindsay) 1932- 136
Lever, J(ulius) W(alter) 1913-1975 .... CAP-2
Obituary 61-64
Earlier sketch in CA 23-24
Lever, Janet 1946- 85-88
Lever, Judy 1947- 107
Lever, Katherine 1916-1999 .... 17-20R
Lever, Ralph 1527-1585 .... DLB 236
Lever, Tresham (Joseph Philip) 1900-1975 .... 13-16R
Obituary 57-60
Lever, Walter
See Lever, J(ulius) W(alter)
Levere, Trevor H(arvey) 1944- CANR-120
Earlier sketches in CA 147, CANR-102
Leverence, William John 1946- 102
Leverich, Kathleen 1948- 137
See also SATA 103
Levering, Frank (Graham) 1952- CANR-43
Earlier sketch in CA 119
Levering, Ralph (Brooks) 1947- 85-88
Levering, Robert 1944- 160
Leveritt, Mara 215
Leverson, Ada Esther 1862(?)-1933(?) 202
Brief entry 117
See also Elaine
See also DLB 153
See also RGEL 2
See also TCLC 18
LeVert, (William) John 1946- 122
See also SATA 55
Levert, Liberte E
See Bleiler, Everett F(ranklin)
Levertov, Denise 1923-1997 178
Obituary 163
Earlier sketches in CA 1-4R, CANR-3, 29, 50, 108
Interview in CANR-29
Autobiographical Essay in 178
See also CAAS 19
See also AMWS 3
See also CDALBS
See also CLC 1, 2, 3, 5, 8, 15, 28, 66
See also CP 1, 2, 3, 4, 5, 6
See also CWP
See also DAM POET
See also DLB 5, 165
See also EWL 3
See also EXPP
See also FW
See also MAL 5
See also MTCW 1, 2
See also PAB
See also PC 11
See also PFS 7, 17
See also RGAL 4
See also TUS
See also WP
Levesque, John 1953- 165
Levesque, Rene 1922-1987
Obituary 125
Levete, Sarah 1961- 228
See also SATA 153
Levey, Martin 1913-1970 .... CANR-10
Earlier sketch in CA 13-16R
Levey, Michael (Vincent) 1927- CANR-137
Earlier sketches in CA 5-8R, CANR-4, 25
Levey, Samuel 1932- CANR-2
Earlier sketch in CA 45-48
Levi, Albert William 1911-1988
Brief entry 107
Levi, Anthony H(erbert) T(igar) 1929-2004 .... CANR-105
Obituary 234
Earlier sketches in CA 13-16R, CANR-9, 24
Levi, Barbara Goss 1943- 144
Levi, Carlo 1902-1975 .... CANR-10
Obituary 53-56
Earlier sketch in CA 65-68
See also EWL 3
See also RGWL 2, 3
See also TCLC 125
Levi, Darrell E(rville) 1940- 131
Levi, Edward H(irsch) 1911-2000 .... CANR-2
Obituary 189
Earlier sketch in CA 49-52
Levi, Gershon
See Levi, S(amuel) Gershon
Levi, Hans 1935- 41-44R
Levi, Helen I(sabel) 1929- 117
Levi, Isaac 1930- 97-100
Levi, Jan Heller 1954- 199
Levi, Jonathan 197
See also CLC 76
Levi, Julian (Edwin) 1900-1982
Obituary 106
Levi, Lennart 1930- CANR-8
Earlier sketch in CA 17-20R
Levi, Louise Landes 1944- 213
Levi, Maurice (David) 1945- CANR-43
Earlier sketch in CA 111
Levi, Peter (Chad Tigar) 1931-2000 .. CANR-80
Obituary 187
Earlier sketches in CA 5-8R, CANR-34
See also CLC 41
See also CP 1, 2, 3, 4, 5, 6, 7
See also DLB 40
Levi, Primo 1919-1987 .... CANR-132
Obituary 122
Earlier sketches in CA 13-16R, CANR-12, 33, 61, 70
See also CLC 37, 50
See also DLB 177, 299
See also EWL 3
See also MTCW 1, 2
See also MTFW 2005
See also RGWL 2, 3
See also SSC 12
See also TCLC 109
See also WLIT 7
Levi, S(amuel) Gershon 1908-1990
Obituary 131
Levi, Vicki Gold 1941- 101
Levi, Werner 1912-2005 .... CANR-37
Obituary 236
Earlier sketches in CA 25-28R, CANR-16
Levi, Y(ehudah) Leo 1926- CANR-94
Earlier sketches in CA 114, CANR-36
Leviant, Curt 217
Leviatin, David 1961- 130
Levi-Civita, Tullio 1873-1941 163
Levi D'Ancona, Mirella
See D'Ancona, Mirella Levi
LeVie, Donn, Jr. 1951- 134
Levien, Sonya -1960
See Hovey, Sonya
See also DLB 44
See also IDFW 3, 4
Levieux, Eleanor 1937- 199
Levieux, Michel 222
Levi-Montalcini, Rita 1909- 149
Levin, Alexandra Lee 1912-1997 .... 9-12R
Levin, Alfred 1908-1984 .... 13-16R
Levin, Alvin Irving 1921- CANR-1
Earlier sketch in CA 45-48
Levin, Amy K. 1957- 145
Levin, Beatrice Schwartz 1920- CANR-18
Earlier sketches in CA 9-12R, CANR-3
Levin, Benjamin H. 49-52
Levin, Betty 1927- CANR-116
Earlier sketches in CA 65-68, CANR-9, 25, 50, 53, 79
See also AAYA 23
See also CWRI 5
See also MAICYA 2
See also MAICYAS 1
See also SAAS 11
See also SATA 19, 84, 137
Levin, Bob
See Levin, Robert A.
Levin, Dan 1914-
Brief entry 108
Levin, Dana 1965- 188
Levin, David 1924-1998 .... CANR-8
Earlier sketch in CA 5-8R
Levin, Donna 1954- 134
Levin, Doron P. 1950- 130
Levin, Gail 1948- CANR-53
Earlier sketch in CA 102
Levin, Gerald H(enry) 1929- CANR-33
Earlier sketches in CA 33-36R, CANR-15
Levin, Hanoch 1943-1999 217
Levin, Harold L(eonard) 1929- 93-96
Levin, Harry (Tuchman) 1912-1994 .... CANR-2
Obituary 145
Earlier sketch in CA 1-4R
Levin, Harry 1925-1993 109
Levin, Harvey J(oshua) 1924-1992 .... 9-12R
Obituary 137
Levin, Henry M(ordecai) 1938- 122
Levin, Hillel 1954- 222
Levin, Igor 1931- 144
Levin, Ira 1929- CANR-139
Earlier sketches in CA 21-24R, CANR-17, 44, 74
See also CLC 3, 6
See also CMW 4
See also CN 1, 2, 3, 4, 5, 6, 7
See also CPW
See also DA3
See also DAM POP
See also HGG
See also MTCW 1, 2
See also MTFW 2005
See also SATA 66
See also SFW 4
Levin, Irina 1937- CANR-142
Earlier sketch in CA 144
Levin, Jack 1941- CANR-41
Earlier sketches in CA 53-56, CANR-4, 19
Levin, James (Benesch) 1940- 111
Levin, Jane Whitbread 1914- 184
Brief entry 106
Levin, Janna 221
Levin, Jeff 1959- 230
Levin, Jenifer 1955- CANR-26
Earlier sketch in CA 108
Levin, John 1944- 107
Levin, Jonathan 1960- 190
Levin, Jonathan V(ictor) 1927- 9-12R
Levin, Kenneth 1944-
Brief entry 115
Levin, Kim 73-76
Levin, Kristine Cox 1944- 65-68
Levin, Marcia Obrasky 1918- 13-16R
See also SATA 13
Levin, Marlin 1921- CANR-9
Earlier sketch in CA 65-68
Levin, Meyer 1905-1981 .... CANR-15
Obituary 104
Earlier sketch in CA 9-12R
See also AITN 1
See also CLC 7
See also CN 1, 2, 3
See also DAM POP
See also DLB 9, 28
See also DLBY 1981
See also MAL 5
See also SATA 21
See also SATA-Obit 27
Levin, Michael (Graubart) 1958- 135
Levin, Michael Eric 1943- CANR-79
Earlier sketch in CA 131
Levin, Milton 1925- 25-28R
Levin, Miriam (Ramsfelder) 1962- 164
See also SATA 97
Levin, Molly Apple 61-64
Levin, N. Gordon, Jr. 1935- 25-28R
Levin, Nora 1916-1989 .... 25-28R
Obituary 130
Levin, Phillis 1954- .... DLB 282
Levin, Richard Louis 1922- 1-4R
Levin, Robert A. 1942- 81-84
Levin, Robert E. 1955- 160
Levin, Robert J. 1921(?)-1976
Obituary 65-68
Levin, Saul 1921- 13-16R
Levin, Ted 1948- CANR-144
Earlier sketch in CA 172
Levin, William C. 1946- 105
Levinas, Emmanuel 1906-1995 .... DLB 296
Levine, A(aron) L(awrence) 1925- 21-24R
Levine, Abby 1943- 126
See also SATA 54
See also SATA-Brief 52
Levine, Adeline 1925- 49-52
Levine, Alan J. 1950- 176
Levine, Albert Norman 1924- .... CN 7
Levine, Allan 1956- CANR-137
Earlier sketch in CA 135
Levine, Andrew 1944- 65-68
Levine, Arthur E(lliott) 1948- 73-76
Levine, Barbara Hoberman 1937- 139
Levine, Barry B(ernard) 1941- 101
Levine, Bernard 1934- 29-32R

Levine, Betty K(rasne) 1933- ... 93-96
See also SATA 66
Levine, Bob
See Levine, Robert
Levine, Caroline Anne 1942- ... 89-92
Levine, Charles H(oward)
1939-1988 ... CANR-35
Obituary ... 126
Earlier sketches in CA 89-92, CANR-15
Levine, Daniel 1934- ... 13-16R
Levine, Daniel H(arris) 1942- ... 73-76
Levine, Daniel Urey 1935- ... 57-60
Levine, David 1926- ... 116
Brief entry ... 113
See also SATA 43
See also SATA-Brief 35
Levine, David 1928- ... 17-20R
Levine, David O(scar) 1955- ... 124
Levine, Donald N(athan) 1931- ... 53-56
Levine, Edna S(imon) ... 85-88
See also SATA 35
Levine, Edward M(onroe) 1924- ... 21-24R
Levine, Edwin Burton 1920- ... 25-28R
Levine, Eliot 1967- ... 237
Levine, Ellen 1939- ... CANR-22
Earlier sketch in CA 69-72
Levine, Erwin L(eon) 1926- ... 9-12R
Levine, Evan 1962- ... 145
See also SATA 74, 77
Levine, Faye (Iris) 1944- ... CANR-3
Earlier sketch in CA 49-52
Levine, Frederick S(pencer) 1945- ... 120
Levine, Gail Carson 1947- ... CANR-118
Earlier sketch in CA 166
See also AAYA 37
See also BYA 11
See also CLR 85
See also MAICYA 2
See also SATA 98, 161
Levine, Gary 1938- ... 61-64
Levine, Gene N(orman) 1930- ... 5-8R
Levine, George 1931- ... CANR-42
Earlier sketches in CA 25-28R, CANR-20
Levine, George R. 1929- ... 21-24R
Levine, Gustav 1926- ... 149
Levine, Herbert S(amuel) 1928- ... 128
Brief entry ... 107
Levine, I(srael) E. 1923-2003 ... CANR-1
Obituary ... 217
Earlier sketch in CA 1-4R
See also SATA 12
See also SATA-Obit 146
Levine, Irving R(askin) 1922- ... 13-16R
Levine, Isaac Don 1892-1981 ... CANR-11
Obituary ... 103
Earlier sketch in CA 13-16R
Levine, Isidore N. 1909-1972 ... 41-44R
Levine, Israel 1893(?)-1988(?)
Obituary ... 125
Levine, Jeffrey P. 1957- ... 168
Levine, Joan Goldman ... 61-64
See also SATA 11
Levine, Joel S. 1942- ... 165
Levine, John R. 1954- ... 150
Levine, Joseph 1910- ... 108
See also SATA 33
Levine, Joseph E. 1905-1987 ... IDFW 3, 4
Levine, Judith 1952- ... CANR-122
Earlier sketch in CA 139
Levine, Laura (Sue) 1943- ... 211
Levine, Laurence William 1931- ... 103
Levine, Lawrence 1916- ... 9-12R
Levine, Lawrence W(illiam) 1933- . CANR-122
Brief entry ... 115
Earlier sketch in CA 145
Levine, Lois (Elaine) L. 1931- ... 106
Levine, Louis 1921-
Brief entry ... 116
Levine, Marge 1934- ... SATA 81
Levine, Mark 1965- ... 183
Earlier sketch in CA 182
Levine, Mark Lee 1943- ... CANR-2
Earlier sketch in CA 49-52
Levine, Marvin J. 1930- ... CANR-21
Earlier sketch in CA 45-48
Levine, Maurice 1902-1971 ... 85-88
Levine, Mel
See Levine, Melvin D.
Levine, Michael 1939- ... 133
Levine, Michael 1954- ... 89-92
Levine, Milton I(sra) 1902-1993 ... 109
Obituary ... 143
Levine, Miriam 1939- ... 116
Levine, Mortimer 1922- ... 17-20R
Levine, Murray 1928- ... CANR-29
Earlier sketch in CA 49-52
Levine, Nancy D. 1955- ... 146
Levine, Noah 1971(?)- ... 226
Levine, Norman 1924- ... CANR-70
Earlier sketches in CA 73-76, CANR-14
See also CAAS 23
See also CLC 54
See also CN 1, 2, 3, 4, 5, 6
See also CP 1
See also DLB 88
Levine, Norman D(ion) 1912-1999 ... 85-88
Levine, Paul (J.) 1948- ... CANR-72
Earlier sketch in CA 137
Levine, Peter D. 1944- ... CANR-118
Earlier sketches in CA 126, CANR-52
Levine, Philip 1928- ... CANR-116
Earlier sketches in CA 9-12R, CANR-9, 37, 52
See also AMWS 5
See also CLC 2, 4, 5, 9, 14, 33, 118
See also CP 1, 2, 3, 4, 5, 6, 7
See also DAM POET
See also DLB 5
See also EWL 3
See also MAL 5
See also PC 22
See also PFS 8
Levine, Rhoda ... 73-76
See also SATA 14
Levine, Rick ... 215
Levine, Robert 1944- ... 121
LeVine, Robert A(lan) 1932- ... CANR-13
Earlier sketch in CA 21-24R
Levine, Robert M. 1910(?)-1981
Obituary ... 108
Levine, Robert M. 1941- ... CANR-11
Earlier sketch in CA 21-24R
Levine, Sarah 1970- ... 125
See also SATA 57
Levine, Saul V. 1938- ... 123
Levine, Shar 1953- ... 200
See also SATA 131
Levine, Sol 1914-1987 ... 9-12R
Obituary ... 124
Levine, Solomon B. 1920- ... 104
Levine, Stacey 1960- ... 145
Levine, Stephen 1937- ... CANR-120
Earlier sketches in CA 45-48, CANR-35
Levine, Stuart (George) 1932- ... 17-20R
Levine, Suzanne Jill 1946- ... CANR-99
Earlier sketches in CA 49-52, CANR-13, 31
Levine, Terri 1957- ... 195
LeVine, Victor T(heodore) 1928- ... 13-16R
Levine-Freidus, Gail
See Provost, Gail Levine
Levine-Shneidman, Conalee 1930- ... 119
Levinger, Elma Ehrlich 1887-1958 ... BYA 1
Levinger, George 1927- ... CANR-2
Earlier sketch in CA 49-52
Levins, Richard 1930- ... 119
Levinsohn, Florence H(amlish) 1926-1998 . 132
Obituary ... 171
Levinson, Alan 1943- ... 150
Levinson, Barry 1942- ... CANR-140
Earlier sketch in CA 149
See also AAYA 25
Levinson, Boris M(ayer) 1907-1984 .. CANR-13
Obituary ... 112
Earlier sketch in CA 33-36R
Levinson, Bradley A. U. 1963- ... 228
Levinson, Charles 1920- ... CANR-21
Earlier sketch in CA 45-48
Levinson, Daniel Jacob 1920-1994 ... 102
Obituary ... 145
Levinson, David L. 1947- ... 223
Levinson, Deirdre 1931- ... CANR-70
Earlier sketch in CA 73-76
See also CLC 49
Levinson, Harold M(yer) 1919- ... 21-24R
Levinson, Harry 1922- ... CANR-29
Earlier sketches in CA 1-4R, CANR-1
Levinson, Henry Samuel 1948- ... CANR-26
Earlier sketch in CA 109
Levinson, Horace C(lifford)
1895-1968(?) ... CAP-1
Earlier sketch in CA 19-20
Levinson, Irene
See Zahava, Irene
Levinson, Jay Conrad ... CANR-137
Earlier sketch in CA 169
Levinson, Jerrold 1948- ... CANR-116
Earlier sketch in CA 156
Levinson, Leonard 1935- ... CANR-31
Earlier sketches in CA 77-80, CANR-14
Levinson, Leonard L. 1905(?)-1974
Obituary ... 45-48
Levinson, Marjorie 1951- ... 127
Levinson, Nancy Smiler 1938- ... CANR-119
Earlier sketches in CA 107, CANR-23, 47
See also SATA 33, 80, 140
Levinson, Olga May ... 103
Levinson, Paul 1947- ... CANR-141
Earlier sketch in CA 174
Levinson, Peter J. ... 230
Levinson, Richard (Leighton)
1934-1987 ... CANR-41
Obituary ... 121
Earlier sketches in CA 73-76, CANR-13
Levinson, Riki ... CANR-37
Earlier sketch in CA 121
See also MAICYA 1, 2
See also SATA 52, 99
See also SATA-Brief 49
Levinson, Robert E. 1925- ... 132
Levinson, Robert S. ... 214
Levinson, Sanford Victor 1941- ... 190
Levinthal, Charles F(rederick) 1945- . CANR-54
Earlier sketch in CA 127
Levinthal, Israel Herbert 1888-1982 ... 13-16R
Levis, Donald J(ames) 1936- ... 41-44R
Levis, Larry (Patrick) 1946-1996 ... CANR-80
Obituary ... 152
Earlier sketches in CA 77-80, CANR-71
See also CAAS 23
See also AMWS 11
See also CP 7
See also DLB 120
Levison, Andrew 1948- ... 93-96
Levison, Iain 1963- ... 217
Levi-Strauss, Claude 1908- ... CANR-57
Earlier sketches in CA 1-4R, CANR-6, 32
See also CLC 38
See also DLB 242
See also EWL 3
See also GFL 1789 to the Present
See also MTCW 1, 2
See also TWA
Levit, Herschel 1912-1986 ... 111
Levit, Martin 1918-1999 ... 45-48
Levit, Rose 1922- ... 73-76
Levitan, Donald 1928- ... 104
Levitan, Max 1921- ... 53-56
Levitan, Sar A. 1914-1994 ... CANR-3
Obituary ... 145
Earlier sketch in CA 9-12R
Levitan, Tina (Nellie) 1928- ... 9-12R
Levitas, Gloria B(arach) 1931- ... CANR-21
Earlier sketch in CA 45-48
Levitas, Irving M(ilton) 1908-1999 ... 185
Levitas, Louise
See Henriksen, Louise Levitas
Levitas, Maurice 1917- ... 77-80
Levitch, Joel A. 1942- ... 37-40R
Levith, Murray J(ay) 1939- ... 81-84
Levitin, Daniel J. 1957- ... 234
Levitin, Sonia (Wolff) 1934- ... CANR-79
Earlier sketches in CA 29-32R, CANR-14, 32
See also AAYA 13, 48
See also CLC 17
See also CLR 53
See also JRDA
See also MAICYA 1, 2
See also SAAS 2
See also SATA 4, 68, 119, 131
See also SATA-Essay 131
See also YAW
Levitine, George 1916-1989 ... 41-44R
Levitov, Aleksandr Ivanovich
1835(?)-1877 ... DLB 277
Levitsky, David A(aron) 1942- ... 116
Levitt, Arthur, Jr. 1931- ... 222
Levitt, B. Blake 1948- ... 139
Levitt, Gene 1920-1999 ... 189
Levitt, I(srael) M(onroe) 1908-2004 ... 45-48
Levitt, Jesse 1919- ... 45-48
Levitt, Leonard 1941- ... 104
Levitt, Morris J(acob) 1938- ... CANR-15
Earlier sketch in CA 41-44R
Levitt, Mortimer 1907-2005 ... 118
Levitt, Morton 1920-1980 ... 61-64
Levitt, Morton P(aul) 1936- ... CANR-43
Earlier sketch in CA 111
Levitt, Norman 1943- ... 192
Levitt, Saul 1911-1977 ... 81-84
Obituary ... 73-76
Levitt, Sidney (Mark) 1947- ... SATA 68
Levitzky, Sergei A. 1909-1983
Obituary ... 110
Levon, Fred
See Ayvazian, L. Fred
Levon, O. U.
See Kesey, Ken (Elton)
Le Vot, Andre 1921- ... 130
Levoy, Myron ... CANR-81
Earlier sketches in CA 93-96, CANR-18, 40
See also AAYA 19
See also SATA 49
See also SATA-Brief 37
See also YAW
Levtzion, Nehemia 1935- ... CANR-4
Earlier sketch in CA 53-56
Levy, Adrian 1965- ... 216
Levy, Alan 1932-2004 ... CANR-46
Obituary ... 226
Earlier sketches in CA 9-12R, CANR-6, 21
Levy, Amy 1861-1889 ... DLB 156, 240
Levy, Andrea 1956- ... 236
Levy, Andrew (Gordon) 1962- ... 172
Levy, Babette May 1907-1977 ... 81-84
Obituary ... 73-76
Levy, Barbara ... 177
Levy, Barrie ... 173
See also SATA 112
Levy, Benn W(olfe) 1900-1973 ... 101
Obituary ... 45-48
See also DLB 13
See also DLBY 1981
Levy, Bernard 1907- ... 61-64
Levy, Bernard Henri
See Levy, Bernard Henri
Levy, Bernard Henri 1949- ... CANR-99
Earlier sketch in CA 122
Levy, Bernard-Henri
See Levy, Bernard Henri
Levy, Bill
See Levy, William V.
Levy, Burt S. ... 190
Levy, Charles K(ingsley) 1924- ... 120
Levy, Claude 1924-1995 ... 129
Levy, Clifford J. 1967- ... 227
Levy, Constance 1931- ... 211
See also SAAS 22
See also SATA 73, 140
Levy, D(arryl) A(llen) 1942-1968 ... CAP-2
Earlier sketch in CA 19-20
Levy, Daniel S. 1959- ... 167
Levy, Darline Gay Shapiro 1939- ... 102
Levy, David 1913-2000 ... 13-16R
Obituary ... 187
Levy, David A(rthur) 1955- ... 108
Levy, David H. 1948- ... 204
Levy, David M(ordecai) 1892-1977 ... 73-76
Obituary ... 69-72
Levy, David N(eil) L(aurence) 1945- ... 119
Levy, David W(illiam) 1937- ... CANR-139
Earlier sketch in CA 41-44R
Levy, Deborah 1959- ... CANR-80
Earlier sketch in CA 147
See also CBD
See also CD 5, 6
See also CWD
See also DLB 310
Levy, Donald 1936- ... 164
Levy, Elinor 1942- ... 223
Levy, Elizabeth 1942- ... CANR-87
Earlier sketches in CA 77-80, CANR-15, 34
See also CWRI 5
See also MAICYA 1, 2
See also SAAS 18
See also SATA 31, 69, 107
Levy, Emanuel 1947- ... CANR-107
Earlier sketches in CA 108, CANR-26
Levy, Eugene Donald 1933- ... 102
Levy, Faye 1951- ... CANR-51
Earlier sketch in CA 125
Levy, Frank 1941- ... 181
Levy, Fred D(avid), Jr. 1937- ... CANR-14
Earlier sketch in CA 37-40R
Levy, G(ertrude) Rachel 1883-1966 ... 5-8R
Levy, Harold B(ernard) 1918- ... 73-76
Levy, Harry 1944- ... 171
Levy, Harry L(ouis) 1906-1981 ... 33-36R
Obituary ... 103
Levy, Helen Fiddyment 1937- ... 142
Levy, Herta Hess
See Kahn, Herta Hess
Levy, Howard S(eymour) 1923- ... CANR-25
Earlier sketches in CA 17-20R, CANR-10
Levy, Hyman 1889-1975
Obituary ... 57-60
Levy, Ian Hideo 1950- ... 217
Levy, Isaac Jack 1928- ... 41-44R
Levy, Jack Steven 1948- ... 115
Levy, Jefery 1958- ... 216
Levy, Jill Meryl ... CANR-123
Earlier sketch in CA 169
Levy, JoAnn 1941- ... 134
Levy, John 1954- ... 128
Levy, Jonathan 1935- ... CANR-10
Earlier sketch in CA 61-64
Levy, Joseph V(ictor) 1928- ... 106
Levy, Julien 1906-1981
Obituary ... 103
Levy, Leonard W(illiams) 1923- ... CANR-69
Earlier sketches in CA 1-4R, CANR-1, 20
Levy, Lester S(tern) 1896-1989 ... 61-64
Levy, Lillian (Rae Berliner) 1918-1986 .. 17-20R
Obituary ... 120
Levy, Lorelei
See Schwalberg, Carol(yn Ernestine Stein)
Levy, Marc 1961- ... 208
Levy, Marilyn 1937- ... 135
See also SATA 67
Levy, Marion Joseph, Jr. 1918-2002 ... 73-76
Obituary ... 205
Levy, Matthys 1929- ... 139
Levy, Michael E(rnst) 1929- ... CANR-2
Earlier sketch in CA 5-8R
Levy, Michael R(ichard) 1946- ... 77-80
Levy, Morton 1930- ... 77-80
Levy, Naomi ... 194
Levy, Nathan 1945- ... SATA 63
Levy, Neil 1967- ... 220
Levy, Owen 1948- ... 118
Levy, Peter B. 1956- ... CANR-143
Earlier sketch in CA 168
Levy, Raphael 1900-1969 ... CAP-1
Earlier sketch in CA 13-16
Levy, Reynold 1945- ... 97-100
Levy, Richard C. 1947- ... 73-76
Levy, Robert 1926- ... 77-80
Levy, Robert 1945- ... CANR-120
Earlier sketch in CA 149
See also SATA 82
Levy, Robert Calmann
See Calmann-Levy, Robert
Levy, Robert J(oseph) 1931- ... 37-40R
Levy, Roger (P.) 1950- ... 134
Levy, Rosalie Marie 1889-1980 ... CAP-1
Earlier sketch in CA 9-10
Levy, S. Jay 1922- ... 108
Levy, Shawn 1961- ... 219
Levy, Sidney Jay 1921- ... 184
Brief entry ... 106
Levy, Stephen 1947- ... 105
Levy, Steven 1951- ... CANR-108
Earlier sketch in CA 149
Levy, Sue 1936- ... CANR-8
Earlier sketch in CA 57-60
Levy, Wilbert J. 1917-1986 ... CANR-6
Earlier sketch in CA 57-60
Levy, William Turner 1922- ... CANR-88
Earlier sketch in CA 25-28R
Levy, William V. 1930- ... 9-12R
Levytskjy, Borys 1915- ... 65-68
Lew, Alan 1943- ... 206
Lewald, Fanny 1811-1889 ... DLB 129
Lewald, H(erald) Ernest 1922-1982 ... 21-24R
Obituary ... 114
Lewald, (Theo) Roon 1942- ... 93-96
Lewallen, John 1942- ... 69-72
Lewalski, Barbara Kiefer 1931- ... CANR-142
Earlier sketch in CA 104
Lewandowski, Dan 1947- ... 77-80
Lewandowski, Stephen 1947- ... 93-96
Lewanski, Richard C(asimir)
1918-1996 ... 17-20R
LeWarne, Charles P(ierce) 1930- ... 57-60
Lewbin, Hyman J(oseph) 1894-1980 ... 61-64
Lewcock, Ronald (B.) 1929- ... CANR-96
Earlier sketches in CA 121, CANR-46
Lewees, John
See Stockton, Francis Richard

Lewellen, T(ed) C(harles) 1940- CANR-6
Earlier sketch in CA 13-16R
Lewellyn, Les
See Paine, Lauran (Bosworth)
Lewels, Francisco J(ose), Jr. 1944- 104
Lewenstein, Morris R. 1923- 13-16R
Lewes, Darby 1946- 153
Lewes, George Henry 1817-1878 . DLB 55, 144
Lewes, Lettie
See Cleveland, Philip Jerome
Lewesdon, John
See Daniell, Albert Scott
Lewicki, Roy J. 1942- 235
Lewiecki-Wilson, Cynthia 1948- 147
Lewin, Abraham 1893-1942(?)
Lewin, Bertram D(avid) 1896-1971 65-68
Lewin, Betsy 1937- CANR-116
Earlier sketches in CA 104, CANR-58
See also SATA 32, 90
See also SATA-Essay 115
Lewin, C. L.
See Brister, Richard
Lewin, Ellen 1946- 156
Lewin, Elsa 118
Lewin, Esther 1922- 61-64
Lewin, Hugh 1939- CANR-38
Earlier sketch in CA 113
See also CLR 9
See also MAICYA 1, 2
See also SATA 72
See also SATA-Brief 40
Lewin, L.
See Lewin, Leonard
Lewin, Leonard 1919- CANR-28
Earlier sketch in CA 49-52
Lewin, Leonard C(ase) 1916-1999 .... 17-20R
Obituary 174
Lewin, Michael Z(inn) 1942- CANR-88
Earlier sketches in CA 73-76, CANR-59
See also CMW 4
Lewin, Moshe 1921- 152
Lewin, Nathan 1936- 101
Lewin, Patricia 224
Lewin, Rhoda G. 1929- 135
Lewin, Roger A. 1946- CANR-111
Earlier sketch in CA 161
Lewin, (George) Ronald 1914-1984 . CANR-13
Obituary 111
Earlier sketch in CA 25-28R
Lewin, Ted 1935- CANR-50
Earlier sketches in CA 69-72, CANR-25
See also MAICYA 2
See also MAICYAS 1
See also SATA 21, 76, 119
See also SATA-Essay 115
Lewine, Richard 1910-2005 81-84
Obituary 239
Lewing, Anthony Charles 1933- 81-84
Lewinson, Paul 1900-1988
Obituary 127
LeWinter, Oswald 1931- 1-4R
Lewis, A(rthur) J(ames) 1914- 5-8R
Lewis, A(drian) S(teven) 1945- 116
Lewis, Adele
See Corwin, Adele Beatrice Lewis
Lewis, Adrian R. 1952- 201
Lewis, Agnes Smith 1843-1926 .... DLB 174
Lewis, Albert 1885(?)-1978
Obituary 77-80
Lewis, Alfred Allan 1929- CANR-100
Earlier sketches in CA 73-76, CANR-15
Lewis, Alfred E. 1912-1968
Obituary 111
See also SATA-Brief 32
Lewis, Alfred Henry 1857-1914
Brief entry 120
See also DLB 25, 186
See also TCWW 1, 2
Lewis, Alice C. 1936- .... SATA 46
Lewis, Alice Hudson 1895(?)-1971
Obituary 109
See also SATA-Obit 29
Lewis, Allan 1905-1991 .... 13-16R
Lewis, Alun 1915-1944 188
Brief entry 104
See also BRW 7
See also DLB 20, 162
See also PAB
See also RGEL 2
See also SSC 40
See also TCLC 3
Lewis, Amanda 1955- .... SATA 80
Lewis, (Joseph) Anthony 1927- 9-12R
See also SATA 27
Lewis, Anthony 1966- .... SATA 120
Lewis, Anthony Carey 1915-1983
Obituary 110
Lewis, Archibald Ross 1914-1990 81-84
Obituary 130
Lewis, Arnold 1930- 166
Lewis, Arthur H. 1906-1995 .... CANR-1
Earlier sketch in CA 1-4R
Lewis, Arthur O(rcutt), Jr. 1920- 9-12R
Lewis, Arthur William 1905-1970 .... CAP-1
Earlier sketch in CA 9-10
Lewis, Barbara 1928-1984
Obituary 113
Lewis, Barbara A. 1943- .... SATA 73
Lewis, Benjamin F. 1918- 45-48
Lewis, Bernard 1916- CANR-130
Brief entry 113
Earlier sketches in CA 118, CANR-44, 78
Interview in CA-118
Lewis, Beth Irwin 1934- 33-36R
Lewis, Beverly 1949- 148
Obituary 179
See also SATA 80
Lewis, Bill
See Lewis, William
Lewis, Bill H. 1927- 1-4R
Lewis, Brad (Alan) 1954- 127
Lewis, Brenda Ralph 1932- .... SATA 72
Lewis, Brian 1963- 198
See also SATA 128
Lewis, C. Day
See Day Lewis, C(ecil)
See also CN 1
Lewis, C(larence) I(rving) 1883-1964 .... 5-8R
See also DLB 270
Lewis, C(live) S(taples) 1898-1963 . CANR-132
Earlier sketches in CA 81-84, CANR-33, 71
See also AAYA 3, 39
See also BPFB 2
See also BRWS 3
See also BYA 15, 16
See also CDBLB 1945-1960
See also CLC 1, 3, 6, 14, 27, 124
See also CLR 3, 27
See also CWRI 5
See also DA
See also DA3
See also DAB
See also DAC
See also DAM MST, NOV, POP
See also DLB 15, 100, 160, 255
See also EWL 3
See also FANT
See also JRDA
See also LMFS 2
See also MAICYA 1, 2
See also MTCW 1, 2
See also MTFW 2005
See also RGEL 2
See also SATA 13, 100
See also SCFW 1, 2
See also SFW 4
See also SUFW 1
See also TEA
See also WCH
See also WLC
See also WYA
See also YAW
Lewis, Cecil Day
See Day Lewis, C(ecil)
Lewis, Charles
See Dixon, Roger
Lewis, Charles Bertrand 1842-1924
Brief entry 114
See also DLB 11
Lewis, Charles R. III 1953- 222
Lewis, Claude A. 1934- 9-12R
Lewis, Claudia (Louise) 1907-2001 .... CANR-6
Earlier sketch in CA 5-8R
See also SATA 5
Lewis, Clay(ton Wilson) 1936- 101
Lewis, Craig A. 1955- 132
Lewis, Cynthia Copeland 1960- 182
See also SATA 111
Lewis, D. B.
See Bixby, Jerome Lewis
Lewis, D(ominic) B(evan) Wyndham 1894-1969
Obituary 25-28R
Lewis, D(es) F. 1948- 152
See also HGG
Lewis, Daniel 1944- 189
Lewis, Daniel K(eith) 1953- 182
Lewis, Dave
See Lewis, David V.
Lewis, David
See Lewis, David Kellogg
See also DLB 279
Lewis, David 1909-1981 104
Lewis, David 1922- 41-44R
Lewis, David 1942- CANR-12
Earlier sketch in CA 69-72
Lewis, David B(enjamin) 1965- 111
Lewis, David Kellogg 1941-2001 ..... CANR-86
Obituary 202
Earlier sketches in CA 81-84, CANR-15, 33
See also Lewis, David
Lewis, David L(anier) 1927- 69-72
Lewis, David Levering 1936- CANR-105
Earlier sketches in CA 45-48, CANR-2, 50
Lewis, David Marshall
See Cook, Michael Lewis
Lewis, David T(revor) 1920- 45-48
Lewis, David V. 1923- 5-8R
Lewis, Deborah
See Grant, Charles L(ewis)
Lewis, Derek 1946- 164
Lewis, Diane 1936- 129
Lewis, Donald Earle 1925- 5-8R
Lewis, Dorothy Otnow 1937- 181
Lewis, Dorothy Roe 1904-1985
Obituary 115
Lewis, E(arl) B(radley) 1956- .... SATA 93, 124
Lewis, E. M. CANR-101
Earlier sketches in CA 69-72, CANR-77
See also SATA 20, 123
Lewis, Earl 200
Lewis, Edith 1882(?)-1972
Obituary 111
Lewis, Edward W(illiams) 1899-1986
Obituary 118
Lewis, Edwin C(lark) 1933- 25-28R
Lewis, Eils Moorhouse 1919- 106
Lewis, Elizabeth Foreman
1892-1958 .... CANR-77
Earlier sketch in CA 137
See also BYA 3
See also MAICYA 1, 2
See also SATA 121
See also YABC 2
See also YAW
Lewis, Elliott (Bruce) 1917-1990 ...... CANR-22
Obituary 131
Earlier sketch in CA 104
Lewis, Eugene 1940- CANR-4
Earlier sketch in CA 53-56
Lewis, (E.) Faye (Cashatt) 1896-1982 .... 25-28R
Obituary 135
Lewis, Felice (Elizabeth) Flanery 1920- ... 73-76
Lewis, Finlay 1938- 101
Lewis, Flora 1922-2002 127
Obituary 206
Brief entry 119
Lewis, Francine
See Wells, Helen
Lewis, Francis Ames
See Ames-Lewis, Francis
Lewis, Freeman 1908-1976
Obituary 69-72
Lewis, Fulton, Jr. 1903-1966
Obituary 89-92
Lewis, G(ranville) Douglass 1934- 106
Lewis, Gene D. 1931- 45-48
Lewis, Geoffrey (Lewis) 1920- 13-16R
Lewis, George 1941- 29-32R
Lewis, George 1943- 77-80
Lewis, George H(allam) 1943- 53-56
Lewis, George L. 1916- CANR-3
Earlier sketch in CA 45-48
Lewis, George Q. 1916-1979 .... 21-24R
Obituary 135
Lewis, Gilbert Newton 1875-1946 160
Lewis, Gordon R(ussell) 1926- CANR-50
Earlier sketches in CA 21-24R, CANR-10, 25
Lewis, Gregg (Allan) 1951- 141
Lewis, Grover Virgil 1934-1995 106
Obituary 148
Lewis, Gwyneth 1959- .... CWP
Lewis, H(ywel) D(avid) 1910-1992 ..... CANR-3
Earlier sketch in CA 9-12R
Lewis, H(enry) H(arrison) Walker
1904-1999 .... CAP-2
Earlier sketch in CA 19-20
Lewis, H. W. 1923- 167
Lewis, H. Warren 1924- 29-32R
Lewis, Harold M. 1891(?)-1973
Obituary 45-48
Lewis, Harry 1917- 109
Lewis, Harry 1942- CANR-3
Earlier sketch in CA 49-52
Lewis, Heather 182
Lewis, Helen (Lillian) Block 1913-1987 110
Obituary 121
Lewis, Henry Clay 1825-1850 .... DLB 3, 248
Lewis, Henry T(rickey) 1928- 73-76
Lewis, Herbert S(amuel) 1934- 17-20R
Lewis, Hilda (Winifred) 1896-1974 .. CANR-78
Obituary 49-52
Earlier sketch in CA 93-96
See also CWRI 5
See also SATA-Obit 20
Lewis, Horacio D(elano) 1944- 57-60
Lewis, Howard R(obert) 1934- CANR-10
Earlier sketch in CA 25-28R
Lewis, Hunter 1947- 109
Lewis, I(oan) M(yrddin) 1930- CANR-21
Earlier sketches in CA 9-12R, CANR-5
Lewis, Ian
See Bensman, Joseph
Lewis, J(ohn) P(aul) Sinclair 232
See also MAL 5
Lewis, J. Patrick 1942- CANR-128
Earlier sketch in CA 138
See also SATA 69, 104, 162
Lewis, J. R.
See Lewis, (John) Roy(ston)
Lewis, Jack P(earl) 1919- CANR-82
Earlier sketches in CA 37-40R, CANR-34
See also SATA 65
Lewis, James, Jr. 1930- CANR-12
Earlier sketch in CA 29-32R
Lewis, James 1935- 65-68
Lewis, James E(ldon), Jr. 1964- 178
Lewis, James R. 1949- 202
Lewis, Jan (Ellen) 1949- 115
Lewis, Janet 1899-1998 .... CANR-63
Obituary 172
Earlier sketches in CAP-1, CA 9-12R, CANR-29
See also Winters, Janet Lewis
See also CLC 41
See also CN 1, 2, 3, 4, 5, 6
See also DLBY 1987
See also RHW
See also TCWW 2
Lewis, Jayne Elizabeth 185
Lewis, Jean 1924- CANR-28
Earlier sketches in CA 21-24R, CANR-11
See also SATA 61
Lewis, Jeffrey M. 200
Lewis, Jeremy 1942- 173
Lewis, Jerry 1926- 121
Brief entry 113
Lewis, Jim 183
Lewis, Johanna Miller 1961- 151
Lewis, John 1889- CANR-5
Earlier sketch in CA 5-8R
Lewis, John (Noel Claude)
1912-1996 .... CANR-19
Earlier sketch in CA 102
Lewis, (F.) John 1916- 133
Lewis, John D(onald) 1905-1988 65-68
Obituary 124
Lewis, John E(arl) 1931- CANR-44
Earlier sketches in CA 57-60, CANR-6, 21
Lewis, John P(rior) 1921- 9-12R
Lewis, John Parry 1927- 107
Lewis, John S(impson), (Jr.) 1941- 239
Lewis, John W(ilson) 1930- 9-12R
Lewis, Joseph 1889-1968 .... CAP-1
Earlier sketch in CA 13-14
Lewis, Judith Mary 1921- 97-100
Lewis, Judy 1935- 152
Lewis, Julian Herman 1891-1989 161
Lewis, Julinda
See Lewis-Ferguson, Julinda
Lewis, June E(thelyn) 1905-1987 .... CAP-2
Earlier sketch in CA 29-32
Lewis, Kim 1951- .... SATA 84, 136
Lewis, Lange
See Brandt, Jane Lewis
Lewis, Larry L(ynn) 1935- 115
Lewis, Lawrence E(dwin) 1928- 69-72
Lewis, Leon 1904-1977 .... CAP-1
Earlier sketch in CA 13-16
Lewis, Leon Ray 1883-1966 .... CAP-1
Earlier sketch in CA 9-10
Lewis, Lesley 1909- 102
Lewis, Linda 1927- 93-96
Lewis, Linda (Joy) 1946- 135
See also SATA 67
Lewis, Lionel Stanley 1933- CANR-5
Earlier sketch in CA 53-56
Lewis, Lucia Z.
See Anderson, Lucia (Lewis)
Lewis, Margaret (B.) 1942- 135
Lewis, Margie M. 1923- 101
Lewis, Marianna Olmstead 1923- 9-12R
Lewis, Marilyn Jaye 1960- 217
Lewis, Marjorie 1929- 108
See also SATA 40
See also SATA-Brief 35
Lewis, Martha E(llen) 1941- CANR-10
Earlier sketch in CA 25-28R
Lewis, Martin W. 1956- 139
Lewis, Martyn (John Dudley) 1945- 141
Lewis, Marvin 1923-1971 .... CAP-2
Earlier sketch in CA 21-22
Lewis, Mary (Christianna)
1907(?)-1988 .... CANR-79
Obituary 125
Earlier sketches in CA 77-80, CANR-13, 43
See also Brand, Christianna
See also CMW 4
See also CWRI 5
See also SATA 64
See also SATA-Obit 56
Lewis, Mary F. W.
See Bond, Mary Fanning Wickham
Lewis, Matthew Gregory 1775-1818 ... DLB 39, 158, 178
See also GL 3
See also HGG
See also LMFS 1
See also RGEL 2
See also SUFW
Lewis, Maynah 1919-1988 .... CANR-77
Earlier sketches in CA 25-28R, CANR-16
See also RHW
Lewis, Meriwether 1774-1809 .... DLB 183, 186
Lewis, Mervyn
See Frewer, Glyn (M.)
Lewis, Mervyn K(eith) 1941- CANR-51
Earlier sketch in CA 125
Lewis, Michael
See Untermeyer, Louis
Lewis, Michael 1937- CANR-1
Earlier sketch in CA 45-48
Lewis, Michael 1960- 140
See also BEST 90:2
Lewis, Michael Arthur 1890-1970 ...... CANR-5
Obituary 29-32R
Earlier sketch in CA 5-8R
Lewis, Mildred D. 1912- 13-16R
Lewis, Mindy 1952- 221
Lewis, Mort(imer) R(eis) 1908-1991 105
Obituary 134
Lewis, Naomi CANR-124
Earlier sketch in CA 143
See also SATA 76, 144
Lewis, Naphtali 1911- 110
Lewis, Nigel (Stephen) 1948- 116
Lewis, Nolan D(on) C(arpenter)
1889-1979 .... 5-8R
Lewis, Norman 1908-2003 129
Obituary 218
Brief entry 112
See also DLB 204
See also MTCW 1
Lewis, Norman 1912- CANR-3
Earlier sketch in CA 9-12R
Lewis, Norman 1940- 136
Lewis, Oren Ritter 1902-1983
Obituary 110
Lewis, Oscar 1893-1992 .... CANR-46
Obituary 139
Earlier sketch in CA 5-8R
Lewis, Oscar 1914-1970 .... CAP-1
Obituary 29-32R
Earlier sketch in CA 19-20
Lewis, Padmore
See Lewis, Sandra Padmore
Lewis, Patricia Ann 1933- 112
Lewis, Paul
See Gerson, Noel Bertram
Lewis, Paul H. 1937- 73-76
Lewis, Peirce F(ee) 1927- 41-44R
Lewis, Peter
See Lewis, Peter Elvet (Elfed)
Lewis, Peter 1922- 9-12R
Lewis, Peter 1938- CANR-21
Earlier sketch in CA 45-48
Lewis, Peter Elvet (Elfed) 1937- 133
Lewis, Philip 1913- 1-4R

Lewis, R. Duffy 1908-1975 ... CAP-1
Earlier sketch in CA 11-12
Lewis, R(ichard) W(arrington) B(aldwin) 1917-2002 ... CANR-119
Obituary ... 206
Earlier sketches in CA 102, CANR-71
See also DLB 111
Lewis, Ralph F(erguson) 1918-1979 ... 29-32R
Obituary ... 89-92
Lewis, Ralph L(oren) 1919- ... 117
Lewis, Randolph R. 1966- ... 222
Lewis, Richard 1700(?)-1734 ... DLB 24
Lewis, Richard 1935- ... CANR-135
Earlier sketches in CA 9-12R, CANR-5, 45
See also SATA 3
Lewis, Richard S. 1916- ... CANR-9
Earlier sketch in CA 57-60
Lewis, Rob 1962- ... SATA 72
Lewis, Robert 1932- ... 97-100
Lewis, Robert T(urner) 1923- ... 85-88
Lewis, Robert W. 1930- ... 143
Lewis, Roger
See Zarchy, Harry
Lewis, Ronello B. 1909-1986 ... CAP-1
Earlier sketch in CA 17-18
Lewis, (Ernest Michael) Roy 1913-1996 ... CANR-3
Earlier sketch in CA 5-8R
Lewis, (John) Roy(ston) 1933- ... CANR-117
Earlier sketches in CA 105, CANR-64
See also CMW 4
Lewis, Rupert 1947- ... 142
Lewis, Samella S(anders) 1924-
Brief entry ... 112
Lewis, Sandra Padmore 1957- ... 153
See also BW 3
Lewis, Sara 1954- ... 183
Lewis, Sasha Gregory 1947- ... CANR-15
Earlier sketch in CA 85-88
Lewis, Saunders 1893-1985 ... 190
Obituary ... 117
See also DLB 310
See also EWL 3
Lewis, Sean Day
See Day-Lewis, Sean (Francis)
Lewis, Selma S. 1921- ... 123
Lewis, Shannon
See Llywelyn, Morgan
Lewis, Shari 1934-1998 ... CANR-19
Obituary ... 169
Earlier sketch in CA 89-92
See also SATA 35
See also SATA-Brief 30
See also SATA-Obit 104
Lewis, Sherry ... 166
Lewis, (Harry) Sinclair 1885-1951 .. CANR-132
Brief entry ... 104
Earlier sketch in CA 133
See also AMW
See also AMWC 1
See also BPFB 2
See also CDALB 1917-1929
See also DA
See also DA3
See also DAB
See also DAC
See also DAM MST, NOV
See also DLB 9, 102, 284
See also DLBD 1
See also EWL 3
See also LAIT 3
See also MTCW 1, 2
See also MTFW 2005
See also NFS 15, 19, 22
See also RGAL 4
See also TCLC 4, 13, 23, 39
See also TUS
See also WLC
Lewis, Stephen (C.) 1942- ... 201
Lewis, Stephen 1947(?)-1981
Obituary ... 103
See also AITN 1
Lewis, Stephen Richmond, Jr. 1939- ... 41-44R
Lewis, Sydney 1952- ... 200
Lewis, Sylvan R.
See Aronson, Virginia
Lewis, T(heodore) G(yle) 1941- ... 111
Lewis, Ted
See Lewis, Edward W(illiams)
Lewis, Theophilus 1891-1974 ... 125
See also BW 1
Lewis, Therese 1912(?)-1984
Obituary ... 113
Lewis, Thomas A. 1942- ... 128
Lewis, Thomas H. 1919- ... 141
Lewis, Thomas P(arker) 1936- ... CANR-45
Earlier sketch in CA 29-32R
See also SATA 27
Lewis, Thomas S(pottswood) W(ellford) 1942- ... CANR-31
Earlier sketch in CA 49-52
Lewis, Tom 1940- ... 105
Lewis, Tony 1938- ... 122
Lewis, Trudy 1961- ... 147
Lewis, Voltaire
See Ritchie, Edwin
Lewis, W(illiam) Arthur 1915-1991 .. CANR-13
Obituary ... 134
Brief entry ... 111
Earlier sketch in CA 17-20R
Lewis, W(alter) David 1931- ... CANR-9
Earlier sketch in CA 13-16R
Lewis, Ward B., (Jr.) 1938- ... 168
Lewis, Warren 1940- ... 115
Lewis, Wendy A. 1966- ... 225
See also BYA 15
See also SATA 150
Lewis, William 1946- ... 120
Lewis, William Hubert 1928- ... 13-16R
Lewis, Willie Newbury 1891-1985 ... 93-96
Obituary ... 116
Lewis, Wilmarth Sheldon 1895-1979 ... CANR-76
Obituary ... 89-92
Earlier sketches in CA 65-68, CANR-15, 74
See also DLB 140
Lewis, (Percy) Wyndham 1884(?)-1957 ... 157
Brief entry ... 104
See also BRW 7
See also DLB 15
See also EWL 3
See also FANT
See also MTCW 2
See also MTFW 2005
See also RGEL 2
See also SSC 34
See also TCLC 2, 9, 104
Lewis-Ferguson, Julinda 1955- ... 152
See also SATA 85
Lewisohn, Ludwig 1883-1955 ... 203
Brief entry ... 107
See also DLB 4, 9, 28, 102
See also MAL 5
See also TCLC 19
Lewisohn, Mark 1958- ... CANR-86
Earlier sketch in CA 130
Lewison, Jeremy 1955- ... 198
Lewiston, Robert R(ueben) 1909-1979 .. CAP-2
Earlier sketch in CA 23-24
Lewis-Williams, J(ames) David 1934- ... CANR-137
Earlier sketches in CA 117, CANR-41
See also SFW 4
Lewiton, Mina 1904-1970 ... CAP-2
Obituary ... 29-32R
Earlier sketch in CA 23-24
See also SATA 2
Lewitt, Maria 1924-
Lewitt, S. N.
See Lewitt, Shariann (N.)
Lewitt, Shariann (N.) 1954- ... CANR-101
Earlier sketch in CA 119
Lewittes, Mordecai Henry
See Lewittes, Morton H(enry)
Lewittes, Morton H(enry) 1911-1990 ... 25-28R
Obituary ... 133
Lewontin, Richard Charles 1929- ... CANR-98
Earlier sketch in CA 104
Lewontin, Timothy (Andrew) 1955- ... 130
Lewsen, Phyllis 1916-2001 ... 109
Obituary ... 193
Lewton, Val 1904-1951 ... 199
See also IDFW 3, 4
See also TCLC 76
Lewton-Brain, James 1923- ... 97-100
Lewty, Marjorie 1906-2002 ... CANR-77
Obituary ... 204
Earlier sketches in CAP-1, CA 9-10
See also RHW
Lewy, Guenter 1923- ... CANR-21
Earlier sketches in CA 9-12R, CANR-3
Lexau, Joan M. ... CANR-110
Earlier sketches in CA 17-20R, CANR-11, 78
See also SATA 1, 36, 130
Ley, Alice Chetwynd 1913- ... CANR-77
Earlier sketches in CA 13-16R, CANR-6, 21, 44
See also RHW
Ley, Arthur Gordon 1911-1968
Obituary ... 102
See also Sellings, Arthur
See also SFW 4
Ley, Charles David 1913- ... 9-12R
Ley, Ralph 1929- ... 41-44R
Ley, Robert Arthur
See Ley, Arthur Gordon
Ley, Sandra 1944- ... 57-60
Ley, Willy 1906-1969 ... 9-12R
Obituary ... 25-28R
See also SATA 2
Leyburn, Ellen Douglass 1907-1966 ... CAP-2
Earlier sketch in CA 25-28
Leyburn, James G(raham) 1902-1993 ... 5-8R
Leyda, Jay 1910-1988 ... 108
Obituary ... 124
Leydet, Francois G(uillaume) 1927-1997 ... 9-12R
Leydon, Rita (Floden) 1949- ... SATA 21
Leyendecker, J(oseph) C(hristian) 1874-1951 ... 188
See also DLB 188
Leygraf, Christofer 1946- ... 214
Leyhart, Edward
See Edwards, Elwyn Hartley
Leyland, Eric (Arthur) 1911- ... SATA 37
Leyland, Mal(colm Rex) 1944- ... 108
Leyland, Winston 1940- ... CANR-71
Earlier sketch in CA 107
See also GLL 2
Leymarie, Isabelle ... 223
Leynard, Martin
See Berger, Ivan (Bennett)
Leyner, Mark 1956- ... CANR-53
Earlier sketches in CA 110, CANR-28
See also CLC 92
See also DA3
See also DLB 292
See also MTCW 2
See also MTFW 2005
Leypoldt, Martha M. 1918-1975 ... CAP-2
Earlier sketch in CA 23-24
Leys, Mary Dorothy Rose 1890- ... 5-8R
Leys, Simon
See Ryckmans, Pierre
Leys, Wayne A(lbert) R(isser) 1905-1973 ... CAP-1
Earlier sketch in CA 17-18
Leyser, Karl Joseph 1920-1992 ... 112
Obituary ... 137
Leyton, Elliott (Hastings) 1939- ... 120
Leyton, Sophie
See Walsh, Sheila
Leyva, Ricardo
See Valdes, Nelson P.
Lezama Lima, Jose 1910-1976 ... CANR-71
Earlier sketch in CA 77-80
See also CLC 4, 10, 101
See also DAM MULT
See also DLB 113, 283
See also EWL 3
See also HLCS 2
See also HW 1, 2
See also LAW
See also RGWL 2, 3
Lezardiere, Marie-Charlotte-Pauline Robert de 1754-1835 ... DLB 313
Lezra, Grizzella Paull 1934- ... 61-64
Lhamon, W(illiam) T(aylor), Jr. 1945- ... CANR-137
Earlier sketch in CA 65-68
L'Hermite, Tristan
See Tristan L'Hermite
Lhermitte, Thierry 1952- ... 208
L'Heureux, Bill
See L'Heureux, W(illard) J(oseph)
L'Heureux, John (Clarke) 1934- ... CANR-88
Earlier sketches in CA 13-16R, CANR-23, 45
See also CLC 52
See also CP 1, 2
See also DLB 244
L'Heureux, W(illard) J(oseph) 1918- ... 5-8R
L'Homme, Pierre 1930- ... IDFW 4
L'Hommedieu, Dorothy Keasley 1885-1961
Obituary ... 109
See also SATA-Obit 29
Li, Ang 1952-
See Li Ang
See also RGWL 3
Li, C(hing) C(hun) 1912-2003 ... 17-20R
Obituary ... 220
Li, Chenyang 1956- ... 194
Li, Chiang-Kwang 1915- ... 73-76
Li, Choh Hao 1913-1987 ... 164
Li, Choh-Ming 1912-1991 ... 1-4R
Li, David H(siang-fu) 1928- ... 13-16R
Li, Fang Kuei 1902-1987 ... 112
Li, Guofang 1972- ... 233
Li, Hui-Lin 1911- ... CANR-15
Earlier sketch in CA 85-88
Li, Leslie 1945- ... 148
Li, Qiao 1934- ... 221
Li, Shu Hua 1890(?)-1979
Obituary ... 89-92
Li, Tien-yi 1915- ... 37-40R
Li, Tze-chung 1927- ... CANR-14
Earlier sketch in CA 41-44R
Li, Xiao Jun 1952- ... SATA 86
Li, Xiaobing 1954- ... 210
Li, Xueqin 1933- ... 136
Li, Yao-wen 1924- ... 106
Li, Zhisui 1919-1995 ... 152
Li Ang
See Li, Ang
See also EWL 3
Liang, Chin-tung 1893-1987 ... 81-84
Liang, Heng 1954- ... 142
Liang, Ssu-ch'eng 1901-1972 ... 162
Liang, Yen 1908-2000 ... 5-8R
Liang Jinguang 1932-
See Hao Ran
Liao, David C. E. 1925- ... 41-44R
Liao, Kang 1955- ... 177
Lias, Edward J(ohn) 1934- ... 120
Lias, Godfrey ... 5-8R
Liatsos, Sandra Olson 1942- ... 170
See also SATA 103
Li Bai 701(?)-762 ... RGWL 2, 3
Libaire, Jardine ... 236
Libaw, William H. 1923- ... 206
Libbey, Elizabeth 1947- ... 110
Libbey, James K(eith) 1942- ... 81-84
Libbey, Laura Jean 1862-1924 ... DLB 221
See also RHW
Libby, Anthony 1942- ... 118
Libby, Barbara M. ... SATA 153
Libby, Bill
See Libby, William M.
Libby, Leona Marshall 1919-1986 ... 101
Obituary ... 121
Libby, Ronald T(heodore) 1941- ... 135
Libby, Violet K(elway) 1892(?)-1981
Obituary ... 105
Libby, Willard F(rank) 1908-1980 ... 160
Obituary ... 113
Libby, William C(harles) ... 104
Libby, William M. 1927-1984 ... CANR-10
Obituary ... 113
Earlier sketch in CA 25-28R
See also SATA 5
See also SATA-Obit 39
Libedinsky, Iurii Nikolaevich 1898-1959 ... DLB 272
Libera, Antoni 1949- ... 200
Liberace
See Liberace, Wladziu Valentino
Liberace, Wladziu Valentino 1919-1987 ... CANR-22
Obituary ... 121
Earlier sketch in CA 89-92
Liberman, Alexander 1912-1999
Obituary ... 186
Brief entry ... 113
Liberman, Anatoly 1937- ... CANR-40
Earlier sketch in CA 116
Liberman, Evsei Grigorevich 1897-1983
Obituary ... 109
Liberman, Judith 1929- ... 73-76
Liberman, M(yron) M(andell) 1921-1995 ... 57-60
Liberman, Robert Paul 1937- ... CANR-49
Earlier sketches in CA 61-64, CANR-7, 22
Liberman, Rosette B. ... 200
Liberman, Yevsei Grigorievich
See Liberman, Evsei Grigorevich
Libersat, Henry 1934- ... 53-56
Libertson, Joseph 1946- ... 199
Liberty, Gene 1924- ... CANR-8
Earlier sketch in CA 5-8R
See also SATA 3
Libin, Laurence (Elliot) 1944- ... 119
Liblit, Jerome ... 13-16R
Libman, Carol 1928- ... 113
Libo, Kenneth (Harold) 1937- ... 133
Brief entry ... 109
Libo, Lester M(artin) 1923- ... 77-80
Libov, Charlotte 1950- ... CANR-93
Earlier sketch in CA 145
Librach, Jan 1904(?)-1973
Obituary ... 41-44R
LiBretto, Ellen V. 1947- ... 110
Lich, G(len) E(rnst) 1948- ... 139
Lichbach, Mark Irving 1951- ... 152
Lichello, Robert 1926- ... 13-16R
Lichfield, Leonard II fl. 1671-1685 ... DLB 170
Lichine, Alexis 1913-1989 ... 9-12R
Obituary ... 128
Licht, Fred (Stephen) 1928- ... 101
Licht, H. William 1915- ... 145
Licht, Sidney Herman 1907-1979
Obituary ... 108
Lichtblau, Myron (Ivor) 1925-2002 ... 17-20R
Obituary ... 207
Lichten, Joseph L. 1906(?)-1987
Obituary ... 125
Lichtenberg, Elisabeth Jacoba 1913- ... 13-16R
Lichtenberg, Georg Christoph 1742-1799 ... DLB 94
Lichtenberg, Jacqueline 1942- ... CANR-59
Earlier sketch in CA 73-76
See also SFW 4
Lichtenberg, Peter A. 1959- ... 149
Lichtenberg, Philip 1926- ... CANR-13
Earlier sketch in CA 37-40R
Lichtenberg, Ronna ... 238
Lichtenheld, Tom ... SATA 152
Lichtenstadter, Ilse 1907-1991 ... CANR-13
Obituary ... 134
Earlier sketch in CA 33-36R
Lichtenstein, Aharon 1933- ... 17-20R
Lichtenstein, Alice 1958- ... 199
Lichtenstein, Grace 1941- ... CANR-22
Earlier sketches in CA 49-52, CANR-2
Lichtenstein, Nelson 1944- ... CANR-120
Earlier sketch in CA 155
Lichter, S. Robert 1948- ... 236
Lichtheim, George 1912-1973
Obituary ... 41-44R
Lichtman, Allan J. 1947- ... 124
Lichtman, Celia S(chmukler) 1932- ... 41-44R
Lichtman, Wendy 1946- ... 114
Lichty, George M(aurice) 1905-1983 ... 104
Obituary ... 110
Lichty, Lawrence W(ilson) 1937- ... 53-56
Lichty, Ron 1950- ... CANR-18
Earlier sketch in CA 101
Licklider, Roy E(ilers) 1941- ... 33-36R
Lickona, Thomas Edward 1943- ... 113
Lico, Laurie E.
See Albanese, Laurie Lico
Lida, Denah (Levy) 1923- ... 21-24R
Lidchi, Maggi
See Lidchi Grassi, Maggi
Lidchi Grassi, Maggi 1930- ... 132
Liddell, Brendan E(dwin) A(lexander) 1927- ... 29-32R
Liddell, C. H.
See Kuttner, Henry
Liddell, Kenneth 1912-1975 ... SATA 63
Liddell, (John) Robert 1908-1992 ... CANR-46
Obituary ... 139
Earlier sketch in CA 13-16R
See also CN 1, 2
Liddell Hart, Basil Henry 1895-1970 ... 103
Obituary ... 89-92
Lidderdale, Halliday Adair 1917- ... 21-24R
Liddicoat, Richard T(homas), Jr. 1918-2002 ... 45-48
Obituary ... 208
Liddington, Jill 1946- ... 187
Liddle, Peter H(ammond) 1934- ... CANR-107
Earlier sketches in CA 102, CANR-18
See also DLBY 1997
Liddle, William 1925- ... 77-80
Liddy, G(eorge) Gordon (Battle) 1930- ... CANR-66
Earlier sketch in CA 114
Interview in ... CA-114
Liddy, James (Daniel Reeves) 1934- . CANR-99
Earlier sketches in CA 13-16R, CANR-5, 20, 43
See also AITN 2
See also CP 1
Lide, David R. 1928- ... CANR-93
Earlier sketch in CA 146

Lide, Mary CANR-79
  Brief entry 127
  Earlier sketch in CA 132
  Interview in CA-132
Lidman, David 1905-1982 69-72
Lidman, Sara (Adela) 1923-2004 193
  Obituary 228
  See also CWW 2
  See also DLB 257
  See also EWL 3
Lidoff, Joan (Ilene) 1944-1989 115
  Obituary 130
Lidtke, Vernon L. 1930- 21-24R
Lidz, Jane .... SATA 120
Lidz, Theodore 1910-2001 .... 29-32R
  Obituary 195
Lie, John 1959- CANR-113
  Earlier sketch in CA 152
Lie, Jonas (Lauritz Idemil) 1833-1908(?)
  Brief entry 115
  See also TCLC 5
Lie, Trygve (Halvdan) 1896-1968
  Obituary 113
Lieb, Fred(erick George) 1888-1980 . CANR-62
  Obituary 97-100
  Earlier sketch in CA 69-72
  See also DLB 171
Lieb, Irwin Chester 1925-1992 232
  Brief entry 105
Lieb, Michael 1940- CANR-93
  Earlier sketch in CA 65-68
Lieb, Robert C. 1944- 37-40R
Lieb, Sandra 112
Liebe, German
  See Seyppel, Joachim (Hans)
Liebenow, J. Gus 1925-1993 45-48
  Obituary 141
Lieber, Arnold L(ou) 1937-
  Brief entry 113
Lieber, Joel 1937-1971 73-76
  Obituary 29-32R
  See also CLC 6
Lieber, Robert J(ames) 1941- CANR-57
  Earlier sketches in CA 29-32R, CANR-12, 30
Lieber, Stanley Martin
  See Lee, Stan
Lieber, Todd M(ichael) 1944- 45-48
Lieberg, Owen S. 1896-1973 .... CAP-2
  Earlier sketch in CA 25-28
Lieberman, Arnold (Leo) 1903-1993 .... CAP-1
  Earlier sketch in CA 19-20
Lieberman, David J. 212
Lieberman, Donald 1927- 111
Lieberman, E(dwin) James 1934- CANR-22
  Earlier sketch in CA 45-48
  See also SATA 62
Lieberman, Elias 1883-1969 .... 5-8R
Lieberman, Fredric 1940- CANR-7
  Earlier sketch in CA 53-56
Lieberman, Gerald F. 1923-1986 85-88
  Obituary 119
Lieberman, Herbert (Henry) 1933- CANR-19
  Earlier sketches in CA 9-12R, CANR-5
  Interview in CANR-19
Lieberman, J. Ben 1914-1984
  Obituary 113
Lieberman, Jethro K(oller) 1943- CANR-10
  Earlier sketch in CA 21-24R
Lieberman, Joseph I. 1942- CANR-96
  Earlier sketch in CA 17-20R
Lieberman, Laurence (James) 1935- .. CANR-89
  Earlier sketches in CA 17-20R, CANR-8, 36
  See also CLC 4, 36
  See also CP 1, 2, 3, 4, 5, 6, 7
Lieberman, Mark 1942- 29-32R
Lieberman, Mendel Halliday 1913-1988 106
Lieberman, Morton A(lexander) 1931- .. 41-44R
Lieberman, Myron 1919- CANR-8
  Earlier sketch in CA 5-8R
Lieberman, Phil 1940- 194
Lieberman, Philip 1934- 93-96
Lieberman, Richard 1946- 207
Lieberman, Richard K. 233
Lieberman, Robert (Howard)
  1941- CANR-141
  Earlier sketches in CA 57-60, CANR-10
  See also AITN 1
Lieberman, Rosalie -1979 .... 9-12R
Lieberman, Samuel 1911-1981 .... 17-20R
  Obituary 134
Lieberman, Saul 1898-1983
  Obituary 109
Lieberman, Susan (Abel) 1942- 170
Liebers, Arthur 1913-1984 .... CANR-3
  Earlier sketch in CA 5-8R
  See also SATA 12
Liebers, Ruth 1910-1983 .... CAP-1
  Earlier sketch in CA 9-10
Lieberson, Goddard 1911-1977 .... CAP-2
  Earlier sketch in CA 25-28
Lieberson, Jonathan 1949(?)-1989
  Obituary 128
Lieberson, Stanley 1933- CANR-38
  Earlier sketches in CA 1-4R, CANR-1, 17
Lieberstein, Stanley H. 1934- 105
Liebert, Burt 1925- 33-36R
Liebert, Doris 1934- 105
Liebert, Robert M. 1942- 41-44R
Liebert, Robert S. 1930-1988
  Obituary 125
Lieberthal, Kenneth G. 1943- CANR-86
  Earlier sketch in CA 130
Lieberthal, Milton M(orton) 1911-1989 117
Liebeschuetz, Hans 1893(?)-1978(?)
  Obituary 85-88
Liebeschuetz, John Hugo W(olfgang) G(ideon)
  1927- 141
Liebhafsky, Herbert Hugo 1919-1993 .... 5-8R
Liebhafsky, Herman A(lfred) 1905-1982 .. 53-56
Liebich, Andre 1948- 166
Lieblich, Amia 1939- 93-96
Lieblich, Irene 1923- .... SATA 22
Liebling, A(bbott) J(oseph)
  1904-1963 .... CANR-63
  Obituary 89-92
  Earlier sketch in CA 104
  See also DLB 4, 171
  See also MTCW 2
  See also MTFW 2005
Liebman, Arthur 1926- CANR-6
  Earlier sketch in CA 57-60
Liebman, Charles S(eymour) 1934- 61-64
Liebman, Herbert 1935- 175
Liebman, Marcel 1930(?)-1986
  Obituary 118
Liebman, Ron(ald S.) 1943- CANR-99
  Earlier sketch in CA 120
Liebman, Roy 1936- 170
Liebman, Ruth 210
Liebman, Seymour B(ertrand)
  1907-1986 .... CANR-7
  Obituary 120
  Earlier sketch in CA 17-20R
Liebmann, George W. 1939- 175
Liebow, Averill A(braham) 1911-1978
  Obituary 111
Liebowitz, Daniel 1921- 164
Liebowitz, Jay 1981- 217
Liebrecht, Savyon 1948- 177
Liebreich, Karen 239
Liederbach, Clarence Andrew
  1910-1991 93-96
Liederman, Judith 1927- 85-88
Liedholm, Carl (Edward) 1940- 41-44R
Liedloff, Jean 81-84
Liedtke, Kurt E(rnst) H(einrich) 1919- 17-20R
Lief, Judith L. 1946- 162
Lief, N. H.
  See Bayes, Ronald H(omer)
Lief, Nina R. 1907-2000 118
Lief, Philip 1947- 107
Liehm, Antonin J. 1924- 102
Lieknis, Edvarts 1883-1940
  See Virza, Edvarts
Lieksman, Anders
  See Haavikko, Paavo Juhani
Liel, Alon 1948- 210
Liem, Nguyen Dang 1936- 57-60
Lien, Arnold J. 1920-1979 .... 21-24R
  Obituary 122
Lien, Pei-te 1957- 230
Lienhard, John H(enry IV) 1930- CANR-4
  Earlier sketch in CA 53-56
Lienhard, Joseph T(homas) 1940- 191
Lientz, Bennet Price 1942- CANR-8
  Earlier sketch in CA 61-64
Liepmann, Hans Wolfgang (Leopold Edmund
  Eugen Victor) 1914- 155
Liepolt, Werner 1944- 25-28R
Liers, Emil E(rnest) 1890-1975 107
  See also SATA 37
Lies, Brian 1963- .... SATA 131
Liesner, Hans Hubertus (Karl Kurt Otto)
  1929- 104
Liestman, Vicki 1961- .... SATA 72
Lietaer, Bernard A(rthur) 1942- 33-36R
Lietaert Peerbolte, Maarten 1905- 25-28R
Lietz, Gerald S. 1918- .... SATA 11
Lieuwen, Edwin 1923- CANR-5
  Earlier sketch in CA 1-4R
Lieven, Anatol 1960- CANR-101
  Earlier sketch in CA 145
Lieven, Dominic 202
Liew, Kit Siong 1932- 77-80
Lifar, Serge 1905-1986
  Obituary 121
Lifchitz, Boris 1895-1984
  Obituary 114
Life, Kay (Guinn) 1930- .... SATA 83
Li Fei-kan 1904- 105
  See also Ba Jin and
  Pa Chin
  See also TWA
Liffring, Joan Louise 1929- 17-20R
Lifshin, Lyn (Diane) 1944- 210
  Earlier sketches in CA 33-36R, CANR-8, 25, 50, 78, 102
  Autobiographical Essay in 210
  See also CAAS 10
  See also CP 2, 3, 4, 5, 6, 7
  See also CWP
Lifshitz, Felice 1959- 198
Lifson, David S. 1908-1996 .... CANR-32
  Obituary 154
  Earlier sketch in CA 33-36R
Liftin, Hilary (L.) 1969- 222
Lifton, Betty Jean CANR-78
  Earlier sketches in CA 5-8R, CANR-12, 27
  See also SATA 6, 118
Lifton, Robert Jay 1926- CANR-78
  Earlier sketches in CA 17-20R, CANR-27
  Interview in CANR-27
  See also CLC 67
  See also SATA 66
Lifton, Walter M. 1918- CANR-16
  Earlier sketch in CA 33-36R
Liggero, John 1921- 25-28R
Liggett, Clayton E(ugene) 1930-1995 .... 29-32R
Liggett, Hunter
  See Paine, Lauran (Bosworth)
Liggett, John 1923- 57-60
Liggett, Thomas 1918- 5-8R
Light, Albert 1927- 93-96
Light, Ivan 1941- 73-76
Light, James F. 1921- CANR-1
  Earlier sketch in CA 1-4R
Light, Martin 1927-1999 53-56
Light, P(aul) H. 1947- 128
Light, Patricia Kahn 1939- 61-64
Lightbody, Charles Wayland 1904- 5-8R
Lightbody, Donna Mae 1920-1976
  Obituary 110
Lightbown, Ronald William 1932- 104
Lightburn, Ron 1954- .... SATA 91
Lightburn, Sandra 1955- 155
  See also SATA 91
Lighter, J(onathan) E. 1949(?)- 147
Lightfoot, Alfred 1936- CANR-4
  Earlier sketch in CA 53-56
Lightfoot, Claude M. 1910-1991 123
  See also BW 1
Lightfoot, D. J.
  See Sizemore, Deborah Lightfoot
Lightfoot, David (William) 1945- 116
Lightfoot, Gordon 1938-
  Brief entry 109
  See also CLC 26
Lightfoot, Neil R(oland) 1929- 81-84
Lightfoot, Paul 1946- 110
Lightfoot, Sara Lawrence 142
  See also BW 2
Lighthall, William Douw 1857-1954 181
  See also DLB 92
Lightman, Alan P(aige) 1948- CANR-138
  Earlier sketches in CA 141, CANR-63, 105
  See also CLC 81
  See also MTFW 2005
Lightman, Bernard 1950- 116
Lightner, A. M.
  See Hopf, Alice (Martha) L(ightner)
Lightner, Alice
  See Hopf, Alice (Martha) L(ightner)
Lightner, David L(ee) 1942- 188
Lightner, Robert P(aul) 1931- CANR-37
  Earlier sketches in CA 49-52, CANR-1, 16
Lightner, Theodore 1893(?)-1981
  Obituary 113
Lightwood, Martha B. 1923-1991 .... 33-36R
Lignell, Lois 1911- .... SATA 37
Ligocka, Roma 1938- 224
Ligomenides, Panos A. 1928- 29-32R
Ligon, Ernest M(ayfield) 1897-1984 .... CAP-1
  Earlier sketch in CA 9-10
Ligon, Samuel 225
Ligotti, Thomas (Robert) 1953- CANR-135
  Earlier sketches in CA 123, CANR-49
  See also CLC 44
  See also HGG
  See also SSC 16
  See also SUFW 2
Liguori, Frank E. 1917-1980 .... 21-24R
  Obituary 134
Lihani, John 1927- CANR-14
  Earlier sketch in CA 37-40R
Lihn, Enrique 1929-1988 .... CANR-94
  Earlier sketches in CA 104, CANR-32
  See also DLB 283
  See also EWL 3
  See also HW 1
Li Ho 791-817 .... PC 13
Liiv, Juhan 1864-1913 .... EWL 3
Lijphart, Arend 1936- CANR-100
  Earlier sketches in CA 21-24R, CANR-10, 25, 50
Li Jui 1950- .... EWL 3
Likeness, George C(lark) 1927-1999 .... 17-20R
Likert, Rensis 1903-1981 93-96
Likhachev, Dmitriy Sergeyevich
  1906-1999 186
Likhovski, Eliahou 1927- 45-48
Lila, Kim 1966- 165
Lilar, Francoise
  See Mallet-Joris, Francoise
Lilar, Suzanne 1901-1992 194
Lilburn, Tim 1950- 215
Liles, Bruce (Lynn) 1934- 53-56
Liles, Maurine Walpole 1935- CANR-102
  Earlier sketch in CA 149
  See also SATA 81
Liley, Helen Margaret Irwin 1928- 25-28R
Liliencron, (Friedrich Adolf Axel) Detlev von
  1844-1909
  Brief entry 117
  See also TCLC 18
Lilienfeld, Abraham M(orris) 1920-1984
  Obituary 113
Lilienfeld, Jane 203
Lilienfeld, Robert Henry 1927- CANR-1
  Earlier sketch in CA 1-4R
Lilienheim, Henry 1908-2002 150
  Obituary 211
Lilienthal, Alfred M(orton) 1913- 37-40R
Lilienthal, David E(li) 1899-1981 .... CANR-3
  Obituary 102
  Earlier sketch in CA 5-8R
Li Ling-Ai 77-80
Lili'uokalani, Queen 1838-1917 .... DLB 221
Lilje, Hanns 1899-1977
  Obituary 69-72
Lill, Wendy (Elizabeth) 1950- 190
  See also CD 5, 6
Lillard, Charles (Marion) 1944- CANR-8
  Earlier sketch in CA 61-64
Lillard, Paula Polk 1931- 73-76
Lillard, Richard G(ordon) 1909-1990 .... 21-24R
  Obituary 131
Lille, Alain de
  See Alain de Lille
Liller, William 1927- CANR-93
  Earlier sketch in CA 145
L'Illettre
  See Bernard, Harry
Lilley, Dorothy B(race) 1914-1998 113
Lilley, Peter 1943- 77-80
Lilley, Stephen R(ay) 1950- 164
  See also SATA 97
Lillibridge, G(eorge) D(onald) 1921- 13-16R
Lillich, Meredith Parsons 1932-
  Brief entry 105
Lillich, Richard B(onnot) 1933-1996 119
  Obituary 153
Lillie, Beatrice (Gladys) 1898(?)-1989
  Obituary 127
Lillie, Helen
  See Marwick, Helen Lillie
Lillie, John Adam 1884-1983
  Obituary 110
Lillie, Ralph D(ougall) 1896-1979
  Obituary 89-92
Lillie, William 1899- 5-8R
Lillington, Kenneth (James)
  1916-1998 .... CANR-77
  Earlier sketches in CA 5-8R, CANR-3
  See also SATA 39
  See also YAW
Lillo, George 1691-1739 .... DLB 84
  See also RGEL 2
Lilloy, Raul A. 1953- 217
Lilly, Charles .... SATA-Brief 33
Lilly, Doris 1926-1991 .... CANR-11
  Obituary 135
  Earlier sketch in CA 29-32R
Lilly, Eli 1885-1977
  Obituary 69-72
Lilly, J(osiah) K(irby), Jr. 1893-1966 184
  See also DLB 140
Lilly, John C(unningham) 1915-2001 .. CANR-1
  Obituary 198
  Earlier sketch in CA 1-4R
Lilly, John F. 1954- 210
Lilly, Mark 1950- 136
Lilly, Ray
  See Curtis, Richard (Alan)
Lilly, Ray
  See Fisher, David
Lily, William c. 1468-1522 .... DLB 132
Lim, Catherine 1942- CANR-127
  Earlier sketch in CA 160
  See also CN 6, 7
Lim, Genevieve 1946- CANR-77
  Earlier sketches in CA 116, CANR-39
  See also Lim, Genny
Lim, Genny
  See Lim, Genevieve
  See also RGAL 4
Lim, John 1932- 116
  See also SATA 43
Lim, Johnson T. K. 1952- 226
Lim, Paul Stephen 1944- CANR-25
  Earlier sketch in CA 108
Lim, Shirley Geok-lin 1944- CANR-100
  Earlier sketch in CA 140
  See also CWP
  See also DLB 312
Lima, Carolyn W(omack) 1938- 118
Lima, Frank 1939- CANR-108
  Earlier sketch in CA 73-76
Lima, Jorge de 1893-1953 .... DLB 307
  See also LAW
Lima, Jose Lezama
  See Lezama Lima, Jose
Lima, Patrick 234
Lima, Robert 1935- CANR-94
  Earlier sketch in CA 9-12R
Lima Barreto, Afonso Henrique de
  1881-1922 181
  Brief entry 117
  See also Lima Barreto, Afonso Henriques de
  See also LAW
  See also TCLC 23
Lima Barreto, Afonso Henriques de
  See Lima Barreto, Afonso Henrique de
  See also DLB 307
Liman, Arthur L(awrence) 1932-1997 185
Liman, Claude Gilbert 1943- 57-60
Liman, Ellen (Fogelson) 1936- CANR-13
  Earlier sketch in CA 61-64
  See also SATA 22
Limb, Sue 1946- CANR-143
  Earlier sketches in CA 115, CANR-37
  See also SATA 158
Limbacher, James L. 1926- CANR-17
  Earlier sketches in CA 5-8R, CANR-2
Limbaugh, Rush H. III 1951(?)- 142
  See also CPW 1
Limburg, James 1935- CANR-95
  Earlier sketches in CA 112, CANR-46
Limburg, Peter R(ichard) 1929- 33-36R
  See also SATA 13
Limentani, Uberto 1913-1989(?) 17-20R
  Obituary 129
Limerick, Jeffrey W. 1948- 102
Limerick, Patricia Nelson 1951- 228
Limmer, Ruth 1927-2001 .... CANR-1
  Obituary 200
  Earlier sketch in CA 45-48
Limon, Graciela 1938- 195
  See also DLB 209
  See also LLW
Limon, Jerzy 1950- CANR-110
  Earlier sketch in CA 153
Limon, Jose (Arcadio) 1908-1972 209
Limon, Jose Eduardo 1944- 191
Limon, Martin 1948- 163
Limonov, Eduard
  See Limonov, Edward
  See also DLB 317

Limonov, Edward 1944- 137
See also Limonov, Eduard
See also CLC 67
Limpert, John A. 1934- 77-80
Lin, Adet J(usu) 1923- 5-8R
Lin, Chia-Chiao 1916- 170
Lin, Florence (Shen) CANR-12
Earlier sketch in CA 61-64
Lin, Frank
See Atherton, Gertrude (Franklin Horn)
Lin, Gang 1953- 238
Lin, Grace 1974- .... SATA 111, 162
Lin, Henry B. 210
Lin, Hwai-Min 1947- 217
Lin, Jami 1956- CANR-123
Earlier sketch in CA 164
Lin, Julia C(hang) 1928- 73-76
Lin, Maya 1959- .... AAYA 20
Lin, Nan 1938- 73-76
Lin, Robert K(wan-Hwan) 1937- CANR-10
Earlier sketch in CA 65-68
Lin, San-su C(hen) 1916- 17-20R
Lin, Tai-yi 1926- 9-12R
See also RGAL 4
Lin, Tan (Anthony) 1957- 161
Lin, Wallace
See Leong, Russell (C.)
Lin, Yu-sheng 1934- 89-92
Lin, Yutang 1895-1976 .... CANR-2
Obituary 65-68
Earlier sketch in CA 45-48
See also RGAL 4
See also TCLC 149
Linaker, Mike 1940- .... TCWW 2
Linamen, Harold Frederick 1921- 17-20R
Linaweaver, Brad 1952- 156
See also SFW 4
Lincecum, Jerry Bryan 1942- CANR-126
Earlier sketch in CA 168
Lincicome, Bernard Wesley
See Lincicome, Bernie
Lincicome, Bernie 1941- 136
Linck, Orville F. 1906- 5-8R
Lincke, Jack 1909- CAP-2
Earlier sketch in CA 29-32
Lincoff, Gary Henry 1942- 112
Lincoln, Abraham 1809-1865 .... LAIT 2
Lincoln, Alan Jay 1945- 123
Lincoln, Bruce 1948- CANR-138
Earlier sketches in CA 105, CANR-22, 45
Lincoln, C(harles) Eric 1924-2000 .... CANR-27
Obituary 189
Earlier sketches in CA 1-4R, CANR-1
See also BW 2
See also SATA 5
Lincoln, Edith Maas 1891-1977
Obituary 73-76
Lincoln, G(eorge) Gould 1880-1974
Obituary 113
See also AITN 1
Lincoln, George Arthur 1907-1975 .... 1-4R
Obituary 57-60
Lincoln, Harry B. 1922- 25-28R
Lincoln, Henry 110
Lincoln, James
See Bates, Katharine Lee
See also GLL 2
Lincoln, James Finney 1883-1965 .... 1-4R
Lincoln, James H. 1916- 25-28R
Lincoln, Kenneth Robert 1943- CANR-82
Earlier sketches in CA 114, CANR-36
Lincoln, Les
See Swatridge, Charles (John)
Lincoln, Murray D. 1892-1966 .... CAP-2
Earlier sketch in CA 19-20
Lincoln, Roger J(ohn) 1942- 117
Lincoln, Victoria 1904-1981 .... CAP-1
Obituary 104
Earlier sketch in CA 17-18
Lincoln, W(illiam) Bruce
1938-2000 .... CANR-29
Obituary 189
Earlier sketch in CA 85-88
Lind, Alan R(obert) 1940- CANR-12
Earlier sketch in CA 61-64
Lind, Andrew W(illiam) 1901-1988 .. CANR-21
Earlier sketch in CA 45-48
Lind, Jakov
See Landwirth, Heinz
See also CAAS 4
See also CLC 1, 2, 4, 27, 82
See also DLB 299
See also EWL 3
Lind, L(evi) R(obert) 1906- CANR-4
Earlier sketch in CA 5-8R
Lind, Michael 1962- CANR-130
Earlier sketch in CA 152
Lind, Millard C. 1918- 115
Lind, Sidney Edmund 1914-2002 .... 37-40R
Lind, William S(turgiss) 1947- CANR-49
Earlier sketch in CA 123
Linda Bloodworth
See Bloodworth-Thomason, Linda (Joyce)
Lindal, Amalia 1926-1989 181
Lindal, Tryggvi V(altyr) 1951- 181
Lindaman, Edward B. 1920-1982 77-80
Obituary 107
Lindars, Barnabas 1923-1991 .... CANR-27
Obituary 135
Earlier sketches in CA 25-28R, CANR-11
Lindau, Joan
See Alden, Joan
Lindauer, John Howard 1937- 21-24R
Lindauer, Lois Lyons 1933- CANR-35
Earlier sketch in CA 49-52
Lindauer, Martin 1918- 5-8R
Linday, Ryllis Elizabeth Paine 1919- 13-16R
Lindbeck, (K.) Assar (E.) 1930- 37-40R
Lindberg, Carter (Harry) 1937- CANR-98
Earlier sketches in CA 112, CANR-47
Lindberg, David C. 1935- CANR-11
Earlier sketch in CA 69-72
Lindberg, Gary H(ans) 1941- 65-68
Lindberg, Gladys 1905(?)-1990
Obituary 131
Lindberg, Leon N. 1932- 33-36R
Lindberg, Lucile 1913-1992 .... 37-40R
Lindberg, Paul M(artin) 1905-1992 .... 5-8R
Lindberg, Rich
See Lindberg, Richard C.
Lindberg, Richard C. 1953- CANR-94
Earlier sketches in CA 110, CANR-27, 52
Lindberg, Stanley W(illiam) 1939-2000 112
Lindbergh, Anne
See Sapieyevski, Anne Lindbergh
See also SATA 81
Lindbergh, Anne (Spencer) Morrow
1906-2001 .... CANR-73
Obituary 193
Earlier sketches in CA 17-20R, CANR-16
See also BPFB 2
See also CLC 82
See also DAM NOV
See also MTCW 1, 2
See also MTFW 2005
See also SATA 33
See also SATA-Obit 125
See also TUS
Lindbergh, Charles A(ugustus, Jr.)
1902-1974 .... CANR-80
Obituary 53-56
Earlier sketches in CA 93-96, CANR-16
See also SATA 33
Lindbergh, Reeve 1945- 181
See also SATA 116, 163
Lindberg-Seyersted, Brita 1923- 111
Lindblom, Charles E(dward) 1917- . CANR-105
Earlier sketches in CA 1-4R, CANR-1
Lindblom, (Christian) Johannes 1882-1974
Obituary 53-56
Lindblom, Steven (Winther) 1946- CANR-47
Earlier sketches in CA 106, CANR-23
See also SATA 42, 94
See also SATA-Brief 39
Linde, Gunnel 1924- CANR-27
Earlier sketches in CA 21-24R, CANR-11
See also SATA 5
Linde, Nancy 1949- 160
Linde, Shirley Motter 1929- CANR-18
Earlier sketches in CA 45-48, CANR-1
Lindeburg, Franklin Alfred 1918- 5-8R
Lindegren, Erik 1910-1968 .... EWL 3
Lindell, Colleen 1963- 169
Lindeman, Jack 1924- 21-24R
Lindemann, Albert S(hirk) 1938- 49-52
Lindemann, Constance 1923- 61-64
Lindemann, Herbert Fred 1909-1995 .... 29-32R
Linden, Catherine 1939- 110
Linden, Eugene 1947(?)- 192
Linden, George William 1938- 65-68
Linden, Kathryn (Wolaver) 1925- 37-40R
Linden, Oliver
See Abrahams, Doris Caroline
Linden, Patricia
See Nutting, Patricia Fink
Linden, Sara
See Bartlett, Marie (Swan)
Lindenau, Judith Wood 1941- 77-80
Lindenbaum, Pija 1955- CANR-124
Earlier sketches in CA 145, CANR-95
See also SATA 77, 144
Lindenberger, Herbert (Samuel)
1929- CANR-93
Earlier sketches in CA 5-8R, CANR-3
Lindenfeld, David Frank 1944- 106
Lindenfeld, Frank 1934- 33-36R
Lindenmeyer, Otto J. 1936- 77-80
Lindenmuth, Kevin J. 1965- 211
Linder, Bertram L. 1931- CANR-2
Earlier sketch in CA 49-52
Linder, Bill R(oyce) 1937-2000 112
Obituary 188
Linder, Darwyn E(llsworth) 1939- 57-60
Linder, Erich 1925(?)-1983
Obituary 109
Linder, Ivan H. 1894-1977 .... CAP-1
Earlier sketch in CA 9-10
Linder, Laura R. 1954- 212
Linder, Leslie (?)-1973
Obituary 41-44R
Linder, Marc 1946- CANR-93
Earlier sketch in CA 142
Linder, Mark 1944- 120
Linder, Norma West 1928- 97-100
Linder, Robert D(ean) 1933- 41-44R
Linder, Staffan B.
See Linder, Staffan Burenstam
Linder, Staffan Burenstam 1931-2000 152
Brief entry 105
Linder, Steven 1953- 112
Linderman, Earl W. 1931- 33-36R
Linderman, Gerald F(loyd) 1934- 85-88
Linderman, Lawrence 1940- 128
Linderman, Winifred B. -1993 .... CAP-2
Earlier sketch in CA 25-28
Lindesmith, Alfred Ray 1905-1991 .... CAP-1
Earlier sketch in CA 9-10
Lindey, Christine 1947- CANR-53
Earlier sketch in CA 126
Lindfors, Judith Wells 1937- CANR-90
Earlier sketch in CA 117
Lindfors, Viveca 1920-1995 128
Lindgren, Alvin J. 1917- CANR-8
Earlier sketch in CA 17-20R
Lindgren, Astrid (Anna Emilia Ericsson)
1907-2002 .... CANR-117
Obituary 204
Earlier sketches in CA 13-16R, CANR-39, 80
See also BYA 5
See also CLR 1, 39
See also CWW 2
See also DLB 257
See also MAICYA 1, 2
See also SATA 2, 38
See also SATA-Obit 128
See also TWA
Lindgren, Barbro 1937- CANR-119
Earlier sketch in CA 149
See also CLR 20, 86
See also SATA 63, 120
See also SATA-Brief 46
Lindgren, David T(readwell) 1939- 225
Lindgren, Ernest H. 1910-1973 .... CAP-1
Earlier sketch in CA 13-14
Lindgren, Ethel John
See Lindgren-Utsi, E(thel) J(ohn)
Lindgren, Henry Clay 1914- CANR-1
Earlier sketch in CA 1-4R
Lindgren, James M. 1950- 146
Lindgren, Torgny 1938- CANR-101
Earlier sketch in CA 136
See also DLB 257
See also EWL 3
Lindgren-Utsi, E(thel) J(ohn) 1905-1988
Obituary 125
Lindheim, Irma Levy 1886-1978 .... 5-8R
Obituary 77-80
Lindholdt, Paul J. 1954- 137
Lindholm, Anna Margaret
See Haycraft, Anna (Margaret)
Lindholm, Charles T. 1946- 134
Lindholm, Megan 155
See also Ogden, Margaret (Astrid) Lindholm
See also FANT
Lindholm, Richard W(adsworth)
1914- CANR-5
Earlier sketch in CA 1-4R
Lindisfarne, Nancy 1944- 143
Lindisfarne-Tapper, Nancy
See Lindisfarne, Nancy
Lindley, Betty G(rimes) 1900(?)-1976
Obituary 65-68
Lindley, David 1956- 230
Lindley, Denver 1904-1982
Obituary 106
Lindley, Erica
See Quigley, Aileen
Lindley, Ernest K(idder) 1899-1979
Obituary 89-92
Lindley, Hilda 1919(?)-1980
Obituary 102
Lindley, Kenneth (Arthur) 1928- CANR-10
Earlier sketch in CA 5-8R
Lindman, Maj (Jan) 1886-1972 .... SATA 43
Lindner, D. Berry
See Du Breuil, (Elizabeth) L(or)inda
Lindner, Edgar T(heodore) 1910-1985 57-60
Lindner, Koenraad J(an) 1941- 165
Lindop, Audrey (Beatrice Noel) Erskine
See Erskine-Lindop, Audrey (Beatrice Noel)
Lindop, Christine (Robin) 1949- 128
Lindop, Edmund 1925- CANR-38
Earlier sketches in CA 5-8R, CANR-2, 17
See also SATA 5
Lindop, Grevel 1948- CANR-29
Earlier sketches in CA 61-64, CANR-13
Lindow, John Frederick 1946- 113
Lindow, Wesley 1910-1995 45-48
Lindquist, Donald 1930-1981 65-68
Lindquist, E(veret) F(ranklin) 1901-1978
Obituary 77-80
Lindquist, Emory Kempton
1908-1992 .... CANR-31
Obituary 136
Earlier sketch in CA 49-52
Lindquist, Jennie Dorothea 1899-1977 73-76
Obituary 69-72
See also SATA 13
Lindquist, John H(enry) 1931- 41-44R
Lindquist, Mark 1959- CANR-101
Earlier sketch in CA 136
Lindquist, N(ancy) J(ane) 1948- 193
Lindquist, Ray (Irving) 1941- 45-48
Lindquist, Rowena Cory 1958- 165
See also SATA 98
Lindquist, Willis 1908-1988 73-76
See also SATA 20
Lindqvist, Sven (Oskar) 1932- 227
Lindsay, Alexander William
1812-1880 .... DLB 184
Lindsay, Caroline Blanche Elizabeth Fitzroy
Lindsay
See Lindsay, Lady
Lindsay, Catherine Brown 1928- 21-24R
Lindsay, Cressida 1934- 21-24R
Lindsay, Dave
See Lindsay, David (Bruce)
Lindsay, David 1878(?)-1945 187
Brief entry 113
See also DLB 255
See also FANT
See also SFW 4
See also SUFW 1
See also TCLC 15
Lindsay, David (Bruce) 1984- 200
Lindsay, Sir David c. 1485-1555 .... DLB 132
See also RGEL 2
Lindsay, Dorothy 1902(?)-1983
Obituary 110
Lindsay, Frank Whiteman 1909- 104
Lindsay, Frederic 1933- 143
Lindsay, Geoff 173
Lindsay, Harold Arthur 1900-1969 .... 5-8R
Lindsay, Howard 1889-1968
Obituary 25-28R
See also DFS 19
Lindsay, Ian G(ordon) 1906-1966 .... CAP-1
Earlier sketch in CA 9-10
Lindsay, Inabel (Frances) B(urns) 1900-1983
Obituary 110
Lindsay, J(ohn) Robert 1925- 13-16R
Lindsay, Jack 1900-1990 .... CANR-81
Obituary 131
Earlier sketches in CA 9-12R, CANR-11
See also Preston, Richard
See also CN 1, 2, 3, 4
See also DLBY 1984
See also RGEL 2
See also RHW
Lindsay, James Martin 1924- 29-32R
Lindsay, Jean 1926- CANR-11
Earlier sketch in CA 25-28R
Lindsay, Jeanne Warren 1929- CANR-22
Earlier sketch in CA 106
Lindsay, Jeff
See Lindsay, Jeffry P.
Lindsay, Jeffry P. 230
Lindsay, John
See Ladell, John L.
Lindsay, John (Joseph) 1921-1988
Obituary 127
Lindsay, John Vliet 1921-2000 101
Obituary 191
Lindsay, Kenneth C(lement) 1919- 112
Lindsay, Lady 1844-1912 .... DLB 199
Lindsay, Loelia (Mary) 1902-1993 133
Obituary 143
Lindsay, Martin Alexander 1905-1981
Obituary 103
Lindsay, Mary
See Nonhebel, Clare
Lindsay, (John) Maurice 1918- CANR-47
Earlier sketches in CA 9-12R, CANR-6, 22
See also CP 1, 2, 3, 4, 5, 6, 7
Lindsay, Merrill K(irk) 1915-1985 73-76
Obituary 115
Lindsay, Michael (Francis Morris)
1909-1994 .... CANR-1
Obituary 144
Earlier sketch in CA 45-48
Lindsay, Norman Alfred William
1879-1969 .... CANR-79
Earlier sketch in CA 102
See also CLR 8
See also CWRI 5
See also DLB 260
See also SATA 67
Lindsay, Paul 1943- 221
Lindsay, Perry
See Dern, Erolie Pearl Gaddis
Lindsay, R(obert) Bruce 1900-1975 .... CANR-8
Earlier sketch in CA 13-16R
Lindsay, Rachel .... RHW
Lindsay, Rae 109
Lindsay, Robert 1924- 77-80
Lindsay, Thomas Fanshawe 1910-1977 . 21-24R
Lindsay, (Nicholas) Vachel
1879-1931 .... CANR-79
Brief entry 114
Earlier sketch in CA 135
See also AMWS 1
See also CDALB 1865-1917
See also DA
See also DA3
See also DAC
See also DAM MST, POET
See also DLB 54
See also EWL 3
See also EXPP
See also MAL 5
See also PC 23
See also RGAL 4
See also SATA 40
See also TCLC 17
See also WLC
See also WP
Lindsay, William 1956- 231
Lindsay, Zaidee 1923- 29-32R
Lindsay-Poland, John 1960- 226
Lindsell, Harold 1913-1998 .... CANR-5
Obituary 164
Earlier sketch in CA 13-16R
Lindsey, Alfred J. 1931- 41-44R
Lindsey, Almont 1906-1993 .... 1-4R
Lindsey, Alton A(nthony) 1907-1999 131
Obituary 188
Lindsey, David 1914-1989 .... 9-12R
See also TCWW 2
Lindsey, David L. 1944- 162
See also HGG
Lindsey, George R(oy) 1920- 65-68
Lindsey, Hal CANR-22
Earlier sketch in CA 104
Lindsey, Jim 1957- 65-68
Lindsey, (Helen) Johanna 1952- CANR-102
Earlier sketches in CA 73-76, CANR-18, 40, 66
Interview in CANR-18
See also CPW
See also RHW
Lindsey, Karen 1944- 73-76
Lindsey, Kathleen D(orothy) 1949- 228
See also SATA 153
Lindsey, Robert (Hughes) 1935- CANR-50
Earlier sketches in CA 97-100, CANR-22
Interview in CANR-22
Lindsey-Stevens, Jennifer
See Crowell, Jenn(ifer Lindsey)

Cumulative Index 353 Lisboa

Lindskold, Jane M. 1962- ... 147
See also AAYA 55
Lindskoog, Kathryn (Ann) 1934-2003 ... CANR-50
Earlier sketches in CA 65-68, CANR-10, 25
Lindsley, Mary F(rances) ... CANR-30
Earlier sketches in CA 61-64, CANR-9
Lindstrom, Carl E(inar) 1896-1969 ... 1-4R
Obituary ... 103
Lindstrom, Lamont (Carl) 1953- ... 143
Lindstrom, Matthew J. 1969- ... 219
Lindstrom, Naomi (Eva) 1950- ... CANR-95
Earlier sketches in CA 112, CANR-30
Lindstrom, Thais (Stakhy) 1917- ... 21-24R
Lindt, Gillian 1932- ... 107
Lindvall, Michael L(loyd) 1947- ... CANR-143
Earlier sketch in CA 146
Line, David
See Davidson, Lionel
Line, Les 1935- ... 73-76
See also SATA 27
Line, Maurice Bernard 1928- ... 107
Lineaweaver, Thomas H(astings) III 1926- ... 73-76
Lineback, Richard H(arold) 1936- ... CANR-31
Earlier sketch in CA 29-32R
Linebarger, J(ames) M(orris) 1934- ... CANR-2
Earlier sketch in CA 49-52
Linebarger, Paul M(yron) A(nthony) 1913-1966 ... CANR-79
Earlier sketches in CA 5-8R, CANR-6
See also Smith, Cordwainer
See also SFW 4
Lineberry, John H(arvey) 1926- ... 1-4R
Lineberry, Robert L(eon) 1942- ... CANR-18
Earlier sketch in CA 73-76
Linecar, Howard (Walter Arthur) 1912- ... 110
Linedecker, Clifford L. 1931- ... 73-76
Linen, James A. III 1912-1988
Obituary ... 124
Linenger, Jerry M. 1955- ... 196
Linenthal, Edward Tabor 1947- ... CANR-30
Earlier sketch in CA 112
Lines, Kathleen Mary 1902-1988
Obituary ... 127
See also SATA-Obit 61
Lines, William J. 1952- ... 187
Linet, Beverly 1929- ... CANR-22
Earlier sketch in CA 89-92
Linett, Deena 1938- ... 113
Linfield, Esther ... 112
See also SATA 40
Linford, Dee -1971 ... TCWW 2
Ling, Amy 1939- ... 137
Ling, Arthur (William) 1901- ... 5-8R
Ling, Cyril Curtis 1936- ... 17-20R
Ling, Dwight L(eroy) 1923- ... CANR-11
Earlier sketch in CA 21-24R
Ling, H(sien) C(hang) 1910-1991 ... 57-60
Ling, Hung-hsun 1894(?)-1981
Obituary ... 105
Ling, Jack (Chieh Sheng) 1930- ... 25-28R
Ling, Mona ... 9-12R
Ling, Peter J(ohn) 1956- ... 135
Ling, Roger (John) 1942- ... CANR-41
Earlier sketches in CA 103, CANR-19
Ling, Trevor 1920- ... CANR-11
Earlier sketch in CA 21-24R
Lingard, Jeanette ... 173
Lingard, Joan (Amelia) 1932- ... CANR-79
Earlier sketches in CA 41-44R, CANR-18, 40
See also AAYA 38
See also BYA 12
See also CLR 89
See also JRDA
See also MAICYA 1, 2
See also SAAS 5
See also SATA 8, 74, 114, 130
See also SATA-Essay 130
See also YAW
Lingeman, Richard R(oberts) 1931- ... CANR-127
Earlier sketches in CA 17-20R, CANR-11
Lingenfelter, Richard Emery 1934- ... CANR-5
Earlier sketch in CA 13-16R
Lingenfelter, Sherwood Galen 1941- ... 53-56
Lingis, Alphonso Frank 1933- ... CANR-15
Earlier sketch in CA 37-40R
Lingren, Art(hur James) 1943- ... 212
Lings, Martin 1909-2005 ... 57-60
Obituary ... 239
Linhart, Robert 1944- ... 130
Linington, (Barbara) Elizabeth 1921-1988 ... CANR-65
Obituary ... 125
Earlier sketches in CA 1-4R, CANR-20
See also CMW 4
Link, Al 1945- ... 222
Link, Arthur S(tanley) 1920-1998 ... CANR-3
Obituary ... 165
Earlier sketch in CA 1-4R
See also DLB 17
Link, Edwin A(lbert) 1904-1981
Obituary ... 108
Link, Eugene P(erry) 1907- ... 37-40R
Link, Frederick M(artin) 1930- ... CANR-4
Earlier sketch in CA 53-56
Link, (S.) Gordden 1907-1986 ... 120
Link, Howard Anthony 1934- ... 127
Link, John R(einhardt) 1907- ... 17-20R
Link, Kelly 1969- ... 211
See also AAYA 53
Link, Mark J(oseph) 1924- ... CANR-42
Earlier sketches in CA 13-16R, CANR-5, 20
Link, Martin 1934- ... 106
See also SATA 28
Link, Matthew 1969- ... 167
Link, (Eugene) Perry, (Jr.) 1944- ... CANR-122
Earlier sketch in CA 105
Link, Robert G(rant) 1918-1984
Obituary ... 113
Link, Ruth 1923- ... 29-32R
Link, Theodore Carl 1905(?)-1974
Obituary ... 104
Link, William 1933- ... CANR-41
Earlier sketches in CA 73-76, CANR-13
Linke, Maria (Zeitner) 1908-1978 ... 65-68
Linke-Poot
See Doeblin, Alfred
Linker, Robert White 1905-1976 ... 104
Linkin, Harriet 1956- ... 170
Linklater, Andro ... CANR-107
Earlier sketch in CA 168
Linklater, Eric (Robert Russell) 1899-1974 ... CANR-79
Obituary ... 53-56
Earlier sketches in CAP-2, CA 13-14
See also CN 1, 2
See also CWRI 5
See also RGEL 2
See also RGSF 2
Linklater, Magnus (Duncan) 1942- ... 131
Linklater, Richard 1962(?)- ... 152
See also AAYA 28
Linkletter, Art(hur Gordan) 1912- ... CANR-4
Earlier sketch in CA 9-12R
Interview in ... CANR-4
Linkletter, John A(ustin) 1923-1985 ... 69-72
Obituary ... 115
Links, Bo 1949- ... 150
Links, J(oseph) G(luckenstein) 1904-1997 ... 81-84
Obituary ... 162
Linkugel, Wil(mer) A(lbert) 1929- ... CANR-13
Earlier sketch in CA 17-20R
Linley, John (William) 1916- ... 41-44R
Lin Mao
See Shen, Congwen
Linn, Bill
See Linn, William J(oseph)
Linn, Charles F. 1930- ... 85-88
Linn, Ed(ward Allen) 1922-2000 ... CANR-117
Obituary ... 187
Earlier sketch in CA 97-100
See also DLB 241
Linn, John Blair 1777-1804 ... DLB 37
Linn, John Gaywood 1917- ... 25-28R
Linn, Karen 1957- ... 139
Linn, Margot
See Ziefert, Harriet
Linn, Susan ... 236
Linn, William J(oseph) 1943- ... 117
Linna, Vaino (Valtteri) 1920-1992 ... 189
See also EWL 3
See also RGWL 2, 3
Linnea, Ann 1949- ... 151
Linnea, Sharon 1956- ... 149
See also SATA 82
Linnell, Charles Lawrence Scruton 1915- ... 5-8R
Linnell, David 1928- ... 146
Linnell, Robert H(artley) 1922- ... 53-56
Linneman, Robert E. 1928- ... 29-32R
Linneman, William R(ichard) 1926- ... 125
Brief entry ... 118
Linner, Birgitta 1920- ... CANR-10
Earlier sketch in CA 21-24R
Linney, Peter 1931- ... 145
Linney, Romulus 1930- ... CANR-79
Earlier sketches in CA 1-4R, CANR-40, 44
See also CAD
See also CD 5, 6
See also CLC 51
See also CSW
See also RGAL 4
Linowes, David F(rancis) 1917- ... 49-52
Linowitz, Sol M(yron) 1913-2005 ... 221
Obituary ... 237
Lins, Osman 1924-1978 ... 182
Brief entry ... 105
See also DLB 145, 307
Linscomb, Shadrach 1971- ... 164
Linscott, Gillian 1944- ... CANR-107
Earlier sketch in CA 128
Lins do Rego, Jose
See do Rego, Jose Lins
See also LAW
Linsenmeyer, Helen Walker 1906- ... CANR-1
Earlier sketch in CA 45-48
Linsky, Leonard 1922- ... 134
Brief entry ... 112
Linsley, Leslie ... 237
Linsley, William A(llan) 1933- ... 25-28R
Linson, Art 1942(?)- ... 232
Linstone, Harold A(drian) 1924- ... 112
Linstrum, Derek 1925- ... 107
Linthicum, Robert Charles 1936- ... 65-68
Lintner, John (Virgil) 1916-1983 ... 104
Obituary ... 110
Linton, Barbara Leslie 1945- ... 33-36R
Linton, Calvin D(arlington) 1914-2002 ... CANR-5
Obituary ... 210
Earlier sketch in CA 13-16R
Linton, David (Hector) 1923- ... 9-12R
Linton, Eliza Lynn 1822-1898 ... DLB 18
Linton, Harold 1947- ... 204
Linton, James M(ichael) 1946- ... 123
Linton, Robert R. 1909(?)-1979
Obituary ... 89-92
Linton, Ron(ald) M. 1929- ... 41-44R
Linton, William James 1812-1897 ... DLB 32
Lintot, Barnaby Bernard 1675-1736 ... DLB 170
Lintott, Andrew (William) 1936- ... CANR-88
Earlier sketch in CA 116
Lintrey, Alan R.
See Gordon, W. Terrence
Lintz, Harry McCormick ... 1-4R
Linz, Cathie ... 237
Linzee, David (Augustine Anthony) 1952- ... 73-76
Linzer, Anna 1950- ... 203
Linzey, Andrew 1952- ... 149
Linzey, Donald Wayne 1939- ... CANR-13
Earlier sketch in CA 61-64
Lionberger, Herbert F(rederick) 1912-2000 ... 73-76
Lionel, Robert
See Fanthorpe, R(obert) Lionel
Lionni, Leo(nard) 1910-1999 ... CANR-38
Obituary ... 187
Earlier sketch in CA 53-56
See also CLR 7, 71
See also CWRI 5
See also DLB 61
See also MAICYA 1, 2
See also SATA 8, 72
See also SATA-Obit 118
Liotta, P. H. 1956- ... 136
Liou, K(uo-) N(an) 1943- ... 145
Lipe, Dewey 1933- ... 85-88
Lipetz, Ben-Ami 1927- ... 33-36R
Lipez, Richard 1938- ... CANR-134
Earlier sketches in CA 101, CANR-18
Lipham, James Maurice 1927-1986 ... 81-84
Li Pi-Hua
See Lee, Lilian
Li Pik-Wah
See Lee, Lilian
Lipinski, Tomas A. ... 219
Lipinsky de Orlov, Lino S. 1908- ... SATA 22
Lipkin, Gladys B(albus) 1925- ... CANR-2
Earlier sketch in CA 49-52
Lipkin, Mack, Jr. 1943- ... CANR-18
Earlier sketch in CA 101
Lipkin, Randie 1953- ... 173
Lipkin, Semyon Izrailevich 1911- ... EWL 3
Lipkin, Steven N. 1951- ... 220
Lipkina, Lawrence (Irwin) 1934- ... 41-44R
Lipkind, William 1904-1974 ... CANR-79
Obituary ... 53-56
Earlier sketch in CA 101
See also CWRI 5
See also SATA 15
Lipking, Lawrence 1934- ... CANR-73
Earlier sketch in CA 130
Lipkowitz, Myron A. 1938- ... 149
Lipman, Aaron 1925-1992 ... 21-24R
Lipman, Burton E(llis) 1931- ... 109
Lipman, David 1931- ... 21-24R
See also SATA 21
Lipman, Elinor 1950- ... CANR-81
Earlier sketch in CA 136
Lipman, Eugene Jay 1919-1994 ... 9-12R
Obituary ... 143
Lipman, Ira A 1940- ... 65-68
Lipman, Jean (H.) 1909-1998 ... CANR-28
Obituary ... 169
Earlier sketches in CA 21-24R, CANR-10
Lipman, Marilyn 1938- ... 69-72
Lipman, Matthew 1923- ... CANR-32
Earlier sketches in CA 33-36R, CANR-13
See also SATA 14
Lipman, Maureen (Diane) 1946- ... 141
Lipman, Samuel 1934-1994 ... 77-80
Obituary ... 147
Lipman, Victoria M. 1949- ... 176
Lipman, Vivian David 1921-1990 ... 9-12R
Obituary ... 131
Lipman-Blumen, Jean 1933- ... 201
Lipmann, Fritz Albert 1899-1986 ... 159
Obituary ... 119
Li Po 701-763 ... PC 29
See also PFS 20
See also WP
Lipp, Frederick (John) 1916-1995 ... 106
Lipp, Martin R(obert) 1940- ... 106
Lipp, Solomon 1913-
Brief entry ... 111
Lippard, George 1822-1854 ... DLB 202
Lippard, Lucy R. 1937- ... CANR-88
Earlier sketches in CA 25-28R, CANR-20
Lippe, Toinette 1939- ... 212
Lippens, Ronnie L. G. 1962- ... 215
Lipper, Arthur III 1931- ... 127
Lipper, Joanna ... 234
Lippert, Clarissa Start 1917- ... 77-80
Lipphard, William B(enjamin) 1886-1971 ... CAP-2
Earlier sketch in CA 29-32
Lippi, Rosina 1956- ... 170
Lippi-Green, Rosina
See Lippi, Rosina
Lippincott, Bertram 1898(?)-1985
Obituary ... 115
See also SATA-Obit 42
Lippincott, David (McCord) 1925-1984 ... CANR-9
Obituary ... 196
Earlier sketch in CA 61-64
Lippincott, Gary A. 1953- ... SATA 73, 119
Lippincott, Gertrude (Lawton) 1913-1996 ... 215
Lippincott, Joseph W(harton) 1887-1976 ... CANR-79
Obituary ... 69-72
Earlier sketch in CA 73-76
See also SATA 17
Lippincott, Kristen (Clarke) 1954- ... 185
Lippincott, Robin ... 221
Lippincott, Sara Jane Clarke 1823-1904
Brief entry ... 120
See also DLB 43
Lippincott, Sarah Lee 1920- ... 17-20R
See also SATA 22
Lippitt, Gordon L(eslie) 1920-1985 ... CANR-12
Earlier sketch in CA 29-32R
Lippitt, Ronald O. 1914-1986 ... 37-40R
Lippman, Edward A. 1920- ... CANR-94
Earlier sketch in CA 122
Lippman, Laura ... 207
Lippman, Leopold 1919-1985 ... 49-52
Lippman, Peter J. 1936- ... CANR-26
Earlier sketch in CA 108
See also SATA 31
Lippman, Theo, Jr. 1929- ... 33-36R
Lippman, Thomas W. 1940- ... 202
Lippmann, Walter 1889-1974 ... CANR-61
Obituary ... 53-56
Earlier sketches in CA 9-12R, CANR-6
See also AITN 1
See also DLB 29
See also MTCW 1, 2
See also NCFS 1
Lippy, Charles H(oward) 1943- ... CANR-99
Earlier sketch in CA 138
Lipschutz, Ilse Hempel 1923- ... 41-44R
Lipscomb, Commander F. W.
See Lipscomb, F(rank) W(oodgate)
Lipscomb, David M(ilton) 1935- ... CANR-1
Earlier sketch in CA 49-52
Lipscomb, Elizabeth J(ohnston) 1938- ... 115
Lipscomb, F(rank) W(oodgate) 1903-1983 ... 29-32R
Obituary ... 126
Lipscomb, James 1926- ... 85-88
Lipsen, Charles B. 1925- ... 73-76
Lipset, David 1951- ... 129
Lipset, Seymour Martin 1922- ... CANR-106
Earlier sketches in CA 1-4R, CANR-1, 69
Lipsett, Laurence Cline 1915-1996 ... 9-12R
Lipsett, Suzanne 1943- ... 132
Lipsey, David (Lawrence) 1948- ... CANR-101
Earlier sketch in CA 130
Lipsey, Richard A(llan) 1930- ... CANR-23
Earlier sketch in CA 107
Lipsey, Richard G(eorge) 1928- ... CANR-17
Earlier sketch in CA 97-100
Lipsey, Robert E(dward) 1926- ... CANR-40
Earlier sketches in CA 5-8R, CANR-2, 18
Lipsitz, George R(aymond) 1947- ... CANR-32
Earlier sketch in CA 113
Lipsitz, Lou 1938- ... CANR-18
Earlier sketch in CA 101
See also CP 1, 2
Lipska, Ewa (Aleksandra) 1945- ... 132
See also CWW 2
Lipski, Alexander 1919- ... CANR-28
Earlier sketch in CA 49-52
Lipsky, David Bruce 1939- ... 103
Lipsky, Eleazar 1911-1993
Brief entry ... 115
Lipsky, Michael 1940- ... 61-64
Lipsky, Mortimer 1915- ... 73-76
Lipson, Charles 1948- ... CANR-104
Earlier sketches in CA 123, CANR-49
Lipson, Goldie 1905-1992 ... 33-36R
Lipson, Harry A(aron, Jr.) 1919- ... 61-64
Lipson, Leon Samuel 1921-1996 ... 104
Obituary ... 153
Lipson, Leslie (Michel) 1912-2000 ... 106
Obituary ... 189
Lipson, Milton 1913-2003 ... 65-68
Obituary ... 214
Lipson, Shelley 1948- ... 119
Lipstadt, Deborah E(sther) 1947- ... 111
Lipstein, Kurt 1909- ... 117
Lipstreu, Otis 1919-1970 ... CAP-1
Earlier sketch in CA 13-16
Lipsyte, Marjorie (Rubin) 1932- ... 105
Lipsyte, Robert (Michael) 1938- ... CANR-57
Earlier sketches in CA 17-20R, CANR-8
See also AAYA 7, 45
See also CLC 21
See also CLR 23, 76
See also DA
See also DAC
See also DAM MST, NOV
See also JRDA
See also LAIT 5
See also MAICYA 1, 2
See also SATA 5, 68, 113, 161
See also WYA
See also YAW
Lipsyte, Sam 1968- ... 209
Lipton, David R(obert) 1947- ... 97-100
Lipton, Dean 1919-1992 ... CANR-31
Earlier sketch in CA 29-32R
Lipton, Eunice ... 140
Lipton, Lawrence 1898-1975 ... 93-96
Obituary ... 57-60
See also DLB 16
Lipton, Lenny 1940- ... 101
Lipton, Peter 1954- ... 138
Liptzin, Sol(omon) 1901-1995 ... 9-12R
Obituary ... 150
Li-Qun, David Su ... 194
Liquori, Martin William, Jr. 1949- ... 130
Liquori, Marty
See Liquori, Martin William, Jr.
Lirio
See Brunclair, Victor
Liroff, Richard A(lan) 1948- ... CANR-11
Earlier sketch in CA 69-72
Lisagor, Peter 1915-1976
Obituary ... 69-72
Lisandrelli, Elaine Slivinski 1951- ... 159
See also SATA 94
Lisanti, Thomas 1961- ... 230
Lisboa, Irene 1892-1958 ... DLB 287

Lisboa, Maria Manuel 1963- CANR-81
Earlier sketch in CA 157
See also HW 2
Lisca, Peter 1925- 37-40R
Lischer, Richard 1943- 101
Lisci, Leonardo Ginori
See Ginori Lisci, Leonardo
Liscomb, Kathlyn Maurean 1950- 145
Liscombe, R. M.
See Windsor-Liscombe, Rhodri
Liscombe, R. W.
See Windsor-Liscombe, Rhodri
Liscow, Christian Ludwig 1701-1760 .... DLB 97
Lisee, Jean-Francois 184
Lish, Gordon (Jay) 1934- CANR-79
Brief entry 113
Earlier sketch in CA 117
Interview in CA-117
See also CLC 45
See also DLB 130
See also SSC 18
Lishka, Gerald R 1949- 89-92
Lisi, Albert 1929- 25-28R
Lisicky, Paul (Alexander) 1959- 194
Lisio, Donald J(ohn) 1934- 124
Lisk, Jill 1938- 25-28R
Liska, Edward G. 1914(?)-1984
Obituary 113
Liska, George 1922- 104
Lisker, Sonia O. 1933- CANR-2
Earlier sketch in CA 49-52
See also SATA 44
Lisle, Holly 1960- CANR-103
Earlier sketch in CA 157
See also FANT
See also SATA 98
Lisle, Janet Taylor 1947- CANR-134
Earlier sketches in CA 153, CANR-79
See also AAYA 60
See also CWRI 5
See also MAICYA 2
See also MAICYAS 1
See also SAAS 14
See also SATA 59, 96, 150
See also SATA-Brief 47
Lisle, Laurie 1942- 133
Lisle, Rebecca 232
See also SATA 162
Lisle, Seward D.
See Ellis, Edward S(ylvester)
Lison-Tolosana, Carmelo 1929- CANR-13
Earlier sketch in CA 21-24R
Lisowski, Gabriel 1946- 97-100
See also SATA 47
See also SATA-Brief 31
Lispector, Clarice 1925(?)-1977 .... CANR-71
Obituary 116
Earlier sketch in CA 139
See also CDWLB 3
See also CLC 43
See also DLB 113, 307
See also DNFS 1
See also EWL 3
See also FW
See also HLCS 2
See also HW 2
See also LAW
See also RGSF 2
See also RGWL 2, 3
See also SSC 34
See also WLIT 1
Liss, David 1966- 199
Liss, Howard 1922-1995 .... CANR-16
Obituary 147
Earlier sketch in CA 25-28R
See also SATA 4
See also SATA-Obit 84
Liss, Jerome 1938- 53-56
Liss, Peggy K(orn) 1927- 41-44R
Liss, Robert E. 1945(?)-1979
Obituary 115
Liss, Sheldon B. 1936-1994 .... 21-24R
Obituary 147
Lissak, Moshe (Avraham) 1928- 97-100
Lissakers, Karin 1944- 141
Lissim, Simon 1900-1981
Obituary 109
See also SATA-Brief 28
Lissitzyn, Oliver J(ames) 1912-1994 45-48
Lissner, Will 1908-2000 101
Obituary 189
Lisson, Deborah 1941- 180
See also SATA 71, 110
List, Ilka Katherine 1935- 37-40R
See also SATA 6
List, Jacob Samuel 1896-1967 .... CAP-1
Earlier sketch in CA 19-20
List, Robert Stuart 1903-1983
Obituary 109
List, Shelley Steinmann 1930-1996 144
Obituary 152
Lister, Eric 1926(?)-1988(?)
Obituary 125
Lister, Hal
See Lister, Harold
Lister, Harold 1922-1987 73-76
Lister, Laurier L. 1907-1986
Obituary 120
Lister, R(ichard) P(ercival) 1914- CANR-5
Earlier sketch in CA 9-12R
Lister, Raymond (George)
1919-2001 .... CANR-49
Obituary 204
Earlier sketches in CA 13-16R, CANR-8, 24
Listfield, Emily 1957- 127
Liston, Jack
See Maloney, Ralph Liston
Liston, Mary Dawn 1936- 53-56
Liston, Robert A. 1927- CANR-30
Earlier sketches in CA 17-20R, CANR-12
See also SATA 5
Listowel, Judith (de Marffy-Mantuano)
1904-2003 .... 13-16R
Obituary 218
Litan, Robert E(li) 1950- 131
Litchfield, Ada B(assett) 1916-1999 .. CANR-10
Earlier sketch in CA 25-28R
See also SATA 5
Litchfield, Harry R(obert) 1898-1973
Obituary 41-44R
Litchfield, Jo 1973- .... SATA 116
Litchfield, Robert O(rbin) (?)-1977
Obituary 73-76
Lite, Jams
See Schneck, Stephen
Lithgow, John (Arthur) 1945- 217
See also SATA 145
Lithman, Yngve Georg 1943- 132
Lithwick, Norman Harvey 1938- 61-64
Litoff, Judy Barrett 1944- 85-88
Litowinsky, Olga (Jean) 1936- 81-84
See also SATA 26
Litsey, Sarah -1996 .... 5-8R
Litt, Jacquelyn S. 1958- 215
Litt, Toby 1968- 223
See also DLB 267, 319
Littauer, Florence 1928- 115
Littauer, Raphael (Max) 1925-
Brief entry 109
Littauer, Vladimir S. 1893-1989
Obituary 129
Littell, Eliakim 1797-1870 .... DLB 79
Littell, Franklin H(amlin) 1917- 134
Brief entry 112
Littell, Robert 1896-1963
Obituary 93-96
Littell, Robert 1935(?)- CANR-115
Brief entry 109
Earlier sketches in CA 112, CANR-64
See also CLC 42
See also CMW 4
Littell, Robert S. 1831-1896 .... DLB 79
Litten, Julian (William Sebastian) 1947- 136
Litterer, Joseph A(ugust) 1926-1995 .. CANR-35
Earlier sketches in CA 9-12R, CANR-3
Littke, Lael J. 1929- CANR-119
Earlier sketches in CA 85-88, CANR-15, 33
See also SATA 51, 83, 140
Little, A. Edward
See Klein, Aaron E.
Little, Alan M(acNaughton) G(ordon)
1901-1987
Obituary 124
Little, Anne C(olclogh) 1944- 173
Little, Bentley 1960- CANR-106
Earlier sketch in CA 164
See also HGG
See also SUFW 2
Little, Bryan (Desmond Greenway)
1913- CANR-22
Earlier sketch in CA 104
Little, Carl (von Kienbusch) 1954- 238
Little, Charles E. 1931- 128
Little, Cynthia M. 239
Little, David 1933- CANR-48
Earlier sketch in CA 29-32R
Little, Denise 1957- 179
Little, Dennis 1957- 179
Little, Douglas 1942- 161
See also SATA 96
Little, Eddie 1956(?)-2003 176
Obituary 216
Little, Elbert L(uther), Jr. 1907- 57-60
Little, Elbert Payson 1912(?)-1983
Obituary 110
Little, Geraldine C(linton) 109
Little, Ian M(alcolm) D(avid) 1918- .. CANR-34
Earlier sketches in CA 21-24R, CANR-15
Little, Jack
See Little, John D(utton)
Little, Jane Sneddon 1942-
Brief entry 113
Little, Jason 1970- 224
Little, (Flora) Jean 1932- CANR-121
Earlier sketches in CA 21-24R, CANR-42, 66
See also AAYA 43
See also CLR 4
See also CWRI 5
See also DAC
See also DAM MST
See also JRDA
See also MAICYA 1, 2
See also SAAS 17
See also SATA 2, 68, 106, 149
See also YAW
Little, John D(utton) 1894-1988 65-68
Little, Kenneth
See Scotland, James
Little, Kenneth L(indsay) 1908-1991 ...... 17-20R
Little, Lawrence Calvin 1897-1976 .... CANR-3
Earlier sketch in CA 1-4R
Little, Lessie Jones 1906-1986 .... CANR-79
Obituary 121
Earlier sketch in CA 101
See also CWRI 5
See also SATA 60
See also SATA-Obit 50
Little, Lester Knox 1935- 103
Little, Linda 1959- 215
Little, Loyd (Harry), Jr. 1940- 81-84
Little, Malcolm 1925-1965 .... CANR-82
Obituary 111
Earlier sketch in CA 125
See also Malcolm X
See also BW 1, 3
See also DA
See also DA3
See also DAB
See also DAC
See also DAM MST, MULT
See also MTCW 1, 2
See also MTFW 2005
Little, Mary E. 1912-1999 105
See also SATA 28
Little, Nina Fletcher 1903-1993 127
Brief entry 106
Little, Paul E. 1928-1975 .... CAP-2
Earlier sketch in CA 21-22
Little, Paul H(ugo) 1915-1987 .... CANR-13
Obituary 122
Earlier sketch in CA 17-20R
See also James, Leigh Franklin
Little, Paula
See Little, Paul H(ugo)
Little, Pippa 1958- 123
Little, Ray 1918(?)-1980
Obituary 102
Little, Richard 1944- 114
Little, Roger W(illiam) 1922- 29-32R
Little, Royal (D.) 1896-1989 106
Obituary 127
Little, S. George 1903-1974
Obituary 49-52
Little, Sara (Pamela) 1919- 116
Little, Stuart W. 1921- CANR-1
Earlier sketch in CA 45-48
Little, Thomas Russell 1911- 13-16R
Little, Tom
See Little, Thomas Russell
Little, William Alfred
See Little, Wm. A.
Little, Wm. A. 1929- 57-60
Littleboy, Sheila M.
See Ary, Sheila M(ary Littleboy)
Littlechild, George 1958- .... SATA 85
Littledale, Freya (Lota) 1929-1992 .... CANR-25
Earlier sketches in CA 21-24R, CANR-10
See also SATA 2, 74
Littledale, Harold (Aylmer) 1927- 5-8R
Littlefair, Duncan (Elliot) 1912- 45-48
Littlefield, Bill 1948- CANR-102
Earlier sketch in CA 150
See also SATA 83
Littlefield, David Joseph 1928- 41-44R
Littlefield, Holly 1963- CANR-138
Earlier sketch in CA 164
See also SATA 97
Littlefield, James Edward 1932- 53-56
Littlehawk, Jay
See Goingback, Owl
Littlejohn, (Cameron) Bruce 1913- 61-64
Littlejohn, David 1937- CANR-88
Earlier sketches in CA 41-44R, CANR-14
Littlejohn, Duffy 1953- 146
Littlesugar, Amy 1953- 195
See also SATA 122
Littleton, C(ovington) Scott 1933- ... CANR-123
Earlier sketch in CA 21-24R
Littleton, Carol 1948- .... IDFW 3, 4
Littleton, Harvey K(line) 1922- 53-56
Littleton, Mark R. 1950- CANR-121
Earlier sketch in CA 155
See also SATA 89, 142
Little Turtle, Carm(elita) 1952- 217
Littlewit, Humphrey Gent.
See Lovecraft, H(oward) P(hillips)
Littlewood, Joan (Maud) 1914-2002 149
Obituary 209
Brief entry 116
See also DLB 13
Littlewood, Robert Percy 1910- 5-8R
Littlewood, Thomas B. 1928- 29-32R
Littman, Jonathan (Russell) 1958- 153
Littman, Robert J. 1943- 81-84
Littmann, Mark Evan 1939- 188
Litto, Fredric M. 1939- 25-28R
Litto, Gertrude 1929- 69-72
Litvag, Irving 1928- 57-60
Litvak, Isaiah A(llan) 1936- 13-16R
Litvinoff, Barnet 1917- 17-20R
Litvinoff, Emanuel 1915- CANR-79
Brief entry 117
Earlier sketch in CA 129
See also CN 1, 2, 3, 4, 5, 6
See also CP 1
Litvinoff, Saul 1925- 41-44R
Litvinov, Ivy 1890(?)-1977
Obituary 69-72
Litvinov, Pavel 1940- 89-92
Litwack, Leon F(rank) 1929- CANR-101
Earlier sketches in CA 1-4R, CANR-1
Litwak, Eugene 1925- 237
Brief entry 114
Litwak, Leo (E.) 1924- CANR-22
Earlier sketch in CA 5-8R
See also CN 1, 2
Litweiler, John (Berkey) 1940- 142
Litwos
See Sienkiewicz, Henryk (Adam Alexander Pius)
Litz, A(rthur) Walton (Jr.) 1929- 33-36R
Litzel, Otto 1901-1981 57-60
Litzinger, Boyd (A., Jr.) 1929- CANR-20
Earlier sketches in CA 13-16R, CANR-5
Liu, Aimee E. 1953- CANR-143
Earlier sketches in CA 89-92, CANR-49
See also DLB 312
Liu, Alan P(ing-) L(in) 1937- 61-64
Liu, Catherine 1964- 212
Liu, Da 1910-2000 85-88
Liu, David
See Liu, Da
Liu, E. 1857-1909 190
Brief entry 115
See also TCLC 15
Liu, Eric 1968- CANR-91
Earlier sketch in CA 146
Liu, James J(o) Y(u) 1926- CANR-7
Earlier sketch in CA 5-8R
Liu, James T(zu) C(hien) 1919-1993 ...... 21-24R
Liu, Jung-Chao 1929- 29-32R
Liu, Leo Yueh-yun 1940- 41-44R
Liu, Sarah 1943- CANR-38
Earlier sketch in CA 115
Liu, Shaozhong 1963- 195
Liu, Sola 1955- 217
Liu, Sydney (Chieh) 1920- 103
Liu, Timothy 1965- CANR-97
Earlier sketch in CA 169
Liu, Tzu-chien
See Liu, James T(zu) C(hien)
Liu, William T(homas) 1930- CANR-13
Earlier sketch in CA 21-24R
Liu, Wu-chi 1907-2002 .... CANR-50
Obituary 210
Earlier sketches in CA 13-16R, CANR-10, 25
Liu, Yong
See Liu, William T(homas)
Liu Binyan 1925- 136
See also CWW 2
Liu Hsin-Wu
See Liu Xinwu
Liu Pin-Yen
See Liu Binyan
Liu Xinwu 1942- .... CWW 2
Liu Ya-Tzu 1887-1958 .... EWL 3
Liu Zongren 1940- 116
Livant, Rose Adleman 1899(?)-1986
Obituary 120
Lively, Adam 1961- CANR-135
Earlier sketch in CA 147
Lively, Penelope (Margaret) 1933- .. CANR-131
Earlier sketches in CA 41-44R, CANR-29, 67, 79
See also BPFB 2
See also CLC 32, 50
See also CLR 7
See also CN 5, 6, 7
See also CWRI 5
See also DAM NOV
See also DLB 14, 161, 207
See also FANT
See also JRDA
See also MAICYA 1, 2
See also MTCW 1, 2
See also MTFW 2005
See also SATA 7, 60, 101
See also TEA
Lively, Walter
See Elliott, Bruce (Walter Gardner Lively Stacy)
Liverani, Giuseppe 1903- CANR-6
Earlier sketch in CA 5-8R
Liverani, Mary Rose 1939- 104
Livergood, Norman D(avid) 1933- 37-40R
Livermore, Jean
See Sanville, Jean
Livermore, Seward W. 1901(?)-1984
Obituary 112
Livermore, Shaw 1902-1986 .... CAP-2
Earlier sketch in CA 19-20
Liversidge, (Henry) Douglas 1913- CAP-1
Earlier sketch in CA 9-10
See also SATA 8
Liversidge, Joan (Eileen Annie)
1915(?)-1984 103
Obituary 112
Liverton, Joan 1913- CAP-1
Earlier sketch in CA 9-10
Livesay, Dorothy (Kathleen)
1909-1996 .... CANR-67
Earlier sketches in CA 25-28R, CANR-36
See also CAAS 8
See also AITN 2
See also CLC 4, 15, 79
See also CP 1, 2
See also DAC
See also DAM MST, POET
See also DLB 68
See also FW
See also MTCW 1
See also RGEL 2
See also TWA
Livesay, Florence Randal 1874-1953 183
See also DLB 92
Livesey, Claire (Warner) 1927- 29-32R
See also SATA 127
Livesey, James 1963- 220
Livesey, Margot 1953- 190
Livgren, Kerry 1949- 114
Livia, Anna 1955- CANR-71
Earlier sketch in CA 119
See also GLL 2
Livie-Noble, Frederick Stanley
1899-1970 .... CAP-1
Earlier sketch in CA 9-10
Livingood, James W(eston) 1910- CANR-32
Earlier sketches in CA 17-20R, CANR-8
Livings, Henry 1929-1998 .... CANR-71
Earlier sketch in CA 13-16R
See also CBD
See also DLB 13
Livingston, A(lfred) D(elano) 1932- ... CANR-13
Earlier sketch in CA 17-20R

Cumulative Index 355 Locke

Livingston, Anne Home 1763-1841 ..... DLB 37, 200
Livingston, Bernard 1911-2000 81-84
Livingston, Carole 1941- 105
See also SATA 42
Livingston, Dorothy Michelson 1906- 49-52
Livingston, Elizabeth J(ane) 1952- 113
Livingston, George Herbert 1916- 53-56
Livingston, Gordon (S.) 1938- 149
Livingston, Harold 1924- 1-4R
Livingston, (M.) Irene 1932- .... SATA 150
Livingston, J(oseph) A(rnold) 1905-1989 ... 1-4R
Obituary 130
Livingston, James C(raig) 1930- CANR-21
Earlier sketch in CA 45-48
Livingston, Jane S(helton) 1944- CANR-129
Earlier sketch in CA 107
Livingston, Jay 1915-2001 .... DLB 265
Livingston, Jayson 1965- 136
Livingston, John A. 1937- 166
Livingston, Jon 1944- 49-52
Livingston, M. Jay
See Livingston, Myran Jabez, Jr.
Livingston, Martha 1945- 115
Livingston, Myra Cohn 1926-1996 ... CANR-58
Obituary 153
Earlier sketches in CA 1-4R, CANR-1, 33
Interview in CANR-33
See also CLR 7
See also CWRI 5
See also DLB 61
See also MAICYA 1, 2
See also MAICYAS 1
See also SAAS 1
See also SATA 5, 68
See also SATA-Obit 92
Livingston, Myran Jabez, Jr. 1934- CANR-22
Earlier sketch in CA 105
Livingston, Nancy 1935-1994 .... CANR-62
Earlier sketch in CA 134
See also CMW 4
Livingston, Paisley 1951- 136
Livingston, Peter Van Rensselaer
See Townsend, James B(arclay) J(ermain)
Livingston, Richard R(oland) 1922- 45-48
See also SATA 8
Livingston, Robert Burr 1918-2002 97-100
Obituary 205
Livingston, Robert Henry 1934- 134
Livingston, William 1723-1790 .... DLB 31
Livingston, William S. 1920- CANR-3
Earlier sketch in CA 9-12R
Livingstone, Angela 1934- 119
Livingstone, Bernard L. 1907(?)-1984
Obituary 112
Livingstone, David 1813-1873 .... DLB 166
Livingstone, Douglas (James)
1932-1996 .... CANR-20
Earlier sketches in CA 13-16R, CANR-5
See also CP 1, 2, 3, 4, 5, 6, 7
See also DLB 225
Livingstone, Harrison Edward
1937- CANR-52
Earlier sketch in CA 33-36R
Livingstone, J. B.
See Jacq, Christian
Livingstone, J(ohn) Leslie 1932- 73-76
Livingstone, Leon 1912- 33-36R
Livingstone, Marco (Eduardo)
1952- CANR-103
Earlier sketches in CA 107, CANR-24, 49
Livio, Mario 1945- 219
Livo, Norma J. 1929- CANR-49
Earlier sketch in CA 123
See also SATA 76
Livoni, Cathy 1956- 113
Livsey, Clara G(rabois) 1924- 107
Livshits, Benedikt Konstantinovich
1886-1938(?) .... DLB 295
Livson, Norman 1924- 49-52
Livy c. 59B.C.-c. 12 .... AW 2
See also CDWLB 1
See also DLB 211
See also RGWL 2, 3
Li Yaotang
See Li Fei-kan
Li Yikai 1932- 141
Liyong, Taban lo 1938(?)- CANR-79
Earlier sketch in CA 105
See also Taban, Liyong and
Taban lo Liyong
See also BW 2
See also CP 2
Lizardi, Jose Joaquin Fernandez de
1776-1827 .... LAW
Lizardi, Joseph 1941- CANR-81
Earlier sketch in CA 129
See also HW 1, 2
Lizarraga, Sylvia S. 1925- 185
See also DLB 82
Lizotte, Ken 1948- 126
Ljoka, Daniel J. 1935- 49-52
Ljubomir, Simovic 1935- .... DLB 181
Llamazares, Julio 1955- .... DLB 322
Llano, George A(lbert) 1911-2003 125
Obituary 213
Lleo, Manuel Urrutia
See Urrutia Lleo, Manuel
Llerena, Mario 1913- 81-84
Llerena Aguirre, Carlos (Antonio) 1952- .. 77-80
See also SATA 19
Llewellyn, Claire 1954- 215
See also SATA 77, 143
Llewellyn, D(avid) W(illiam) Alun
1903-1987 57-60
See also SFW 4
Llewellyn, Edward
See Llewellyn-Thomas, Edward
Llewellyn, Grace (Katherine) 1964- 180
See also SATA 110
Llewellyn, Kate 1940- CANR-79
Earlier sketch in CA 153
See also CP 7
Llewellyn, Richard
See Llewellyn Lloyd, Richard Dafydd Vivian
See also DLB 15
Llewellyn, Sam 1948- CANR-97
Earlier sketch in CA 140
See also SATA 95
Llewellyn-Jones, Derek 1923-1997 .. CANR-90
Earlier sketches in CA 37-40R, CANR-15, 34
Llewellyn Lloyd, Richard Dafydd Vivian
1906-1983 .... CANR-71
Obituary 111
Earlier sketches in CA 53-56, CANR-7
See also Llewellyn, Richard
See also CLC 7, 80
See also DLB 15
See also SATA 11
See also SATA-Obit 37
Llewellyn-Thomas, Edward 1917-1984 104
Llewellyn-Williams, Hilary (Maria) 1951- ... 127
Llewelyn, T. Harcourt
See Hamilton, Charles (Harold St. John)
Llewelyn-Davies, Richard 1912-1981 ... 13-16R
Obituary 105
Llewelyn-Owens, Joan (Margaret)
1919- CANR-36
Lliteras, D.S. 1949- 172
Llorens, Vicente 1906-1979
Obituary 89-92
Llorens, Washington 1900-1989 153
See also HW 1
Llorens Torres, Luis 1876-1944 .... DLB 290
Lloret, Antoni 1935- 29-32R
Llosa, (Jorge) Mario (Pedro) Vargas
See Vargas Llosa, (Jorge) Mario (Pedro)
See also RGWL 3
Llosa, Mario Vargas
See Vargas Llosa, (Jorge) Mario (Pedro)
Llosa, Ricardo Pau
See Pau-Llosa, Ricardo
Lloyd, A(lan) R(ichard) 1927- CANR-110
Earlier sketch in CA 155
See also FANT
See also SATA 97
Lloyd, Adrien
See Gelb, Alan Lloyd
Lloyd, Alan
See Lloyd, A(lan) R(ichard)
Lloyd, Alan C(hester) 1915- CANR-1
Earlier sketch in CA 1-4R
Lloyd, Albert Lancaster 1908-1982
Obituary 107
Lloyd, Charles
See Birkin, Charles (Lloyd)
Lloyd, (Charles) Christopher 1906-1986
Obituary 119
Lloyd, Christopher 1921- CANR-46
Earlier sketch in CA 120
Lloyd, Craig 1940- CANR-99
Earlier sketch in CA 61-64
Lloyd, Cynthia B(rown) 1943- CANR-8
Earlier sketch in CA 61-64
Lloyd, Dan (Edward) 1953- 228
Lloyd, David 1946- 89-92
Lloyd, David Demarest 1911-1962 .... CAP-1
Earlier sketch in CA 11-12
Lloyd, Dennis 1915-1992 .... 13-16R
Lloyd, E. James
See James, Elizabeth
Lloyd, Elisabeth A. 1956- 139
Lloyd, Errol 1943- 101
See also SATA 22
Lloyd, Fran 222
Lloyd, Francis V(ernon), Jr. 1908-1993 .. CAP-2
Earlier sketch in CA 21-22
Lloyd, G(eoffrey) E(rnest) R(ichard)
1933- 57-60
Lloyd, Grant
See Wordsworth, Elizabeth
Lloyd, Howell Arnold 1937- 103
Lloyd, Hugh
See Fitzhugh, Percy Keese
Lloyd, Hugh (Pughe) 1894-1981
Obituary 108
Lloyd, J. Ivester 1905- 13-16R
Lloyd, Jack Ivester
See Lloyd, J. Ivester
Lloyd, James
See James, Elizabeth
Lloyd, James Barlow 1945- 112
Lloyd, John Ivester
See Lloyd, J. Ivester
Lloyd, John S. B. Selwyn
See Selwyn-Lloyd, John S. B.
Lloyd, Levanah
See Peters, Maureen
Lloyd, Linda Marie 1941- 173
Lloyd, Lisa
See Lloyd, Elisabeth A.
Lloyd, Manda
See Mander, (Mary) Jane
Lloyd, Margaret Glynne 1946- 130
Lloyd, Marjorie 1909- CANR-8
Earlier sketch in CA 5-8R
Lloyd, Megan 1958- .... SATA 77, 117
Lloyd, Nigel
See Tubb, E(dwin) C(harles)
Lloyd, Norman 1909-1980 .... CANR-28
Obituary 101
Earlier sketch in CA 37-40R
See also SATA-Obit 23
Lloyd, (Mary) Norris 1908-1993 .... CANR-85
Obituary 140
Earlier sketches in CA 1-4R, CANR-1
See also SATA 10
See also SATA-Obit 75
Lloyd, P(eter) J(ohn) 1937- 208
Lloyd, Peter C(utt) 1927- CANR-11
Earlier sketch in CA 25-28R
Lloyd, Peter Edward 1938- 107
Lloyd, Robert
See Tubb, E(dwin) C(harles)
Lloyd, Robin 1925- 73-76
Lloyd, Ronald
See Friedland, Ronald Lloyd
Lloyd, Roseann 1944- 209
Lloyd, Rosemary (Helen) 1949- CANR-107
Earlier sketch in CA 116
Lloyd, Sarah
See Cox, Jennifer Lloyd
Lloyd, Seton (Howard Frederick)
1902-1996 132
Obituary 151
Lloyd, Stephanie
See Golding, Morton J(ay)
Lloyd, Trevor (Owen) 1934- 25-28R
Lloyd Evans, Barbara 1924- CANR-37
Earlier sketch in CA 93-96
Lloyd Evans, Gareth 1923-1984
Obituary 117
Lloyd George (of Dwyor), Frances (Louise
Stevenson) 1888(?)-1972
Obituary 37-40R
Lloyd-Jones, Esther McDonald
1901-1991 .... 13-16R
Lloyd-Jones, (Peter) Hugh (Jefferd)
1922- CANR-21
Earlier sketches in CA 5-8R, CANR-4
Lloyd-Jones, Robin 1934- 111
Lloyd Owen, David Lanyon 1917-2001 117
Obituary 195
Lloyd-Thomas, Catherine 1917- 65-68
Lloyd Webber, Andrew 1948- 149
Brief entry 116
See also Webber, Andrew Lloyd
See also AAYA 1, 38
See also DAM DRAM
See also SATA 56
Llywelyn, Morgan 1937- CANR-100
Earlier sketches in CA 81-84, CANR-16
Interview in CANR-16
See also AAYA 29
See also SATA 109
Llywelyn-Williams, Alun 1913- CAP-1
Earlier sketch in CA 9-10
Lo, Irving Yucheng 1922- 57-60
Lo, Ruth Earnshaw 1910- 106
Lo, Samuel E. 1931- 29-32R
Lo, Steven C. 1949- 132
Lo, Winston W. 1938- 133
Loader, William Reginald 1916- 1-4R
Loades, David Michael 1934- 17-20R
Loane, Marcus L(awrence) 1911- CANR-2
Earlier sketch in CA 1-4R
Loasby, Brian John 1930- 93-96
Loase, John F. 1947- 229
Lobato, Jose Bento Monteiro 1882-1948 179
See also DLB 307
See also EWL 3
See also SATA 114
Lobb, Charlotte 1935- CANR-15
Earlier sketch in CA 65-68
Lobb, Ebenezer
See Upward, Allen
Lobban, Carolyn Fluehr
See Fluehr-Lobban, Carolyn
Lobban, Richard A., Jr. 1943- 144
Lobdell, Helen 1919- 9-12R
Lobdell, Jared C(harles) 1937- CANR-28
Earlier sketch in CA 49-52
Lobel, Anita (Kempler) 1934- CANR-68
Earlier sketches in CA 53-56, CANR-9, 33
See also CWRI 5
See also MAICYA 1, 2
See also SATA 6, 55, 96, 162
Lobel, Arnold (Stark) 1933-1987 ...... CANR-79
Obituary 124
Earlier sketches in CA 1-4R, CANR-2, 33
See also AITN 1
See also CLR 5
See also CWRI 5
See also DLB 61
See also MAICYA 1, 2
See also SATA 6, 55
See also SATA-Obit 54
Lobel, Brana 1942- 97-100
Lobel, Edgar 1889-1982
Obituary 107
Lobel, Stanley 1937- 111
Lo Bello, Nino 1921- CANR-53
Earlier sketches in CA 29-32R, CANR-12, 28
Loberg, Mary Alice 1943- 29-32R
Lobinger, Fritz 1929- 225
Lobkowicz, Nicholas 1931- CANR-32
Earlier sketches in CA 21-24R, CANR-10
Lobley, Robert (John) 1934- CANR-29
Earlier sketch in CA 29-32R
Lobo, Anthony S(avio) 1937- 49-52
Lobo Antunes, Antonio 1942- 193
Lobsenz, Amelia 13-16R
See also SATA 12
Lobsenz, Norman M(itchell) 1919- CANR-4
Earlier sketch in CA 9-12R
See also SATA 6
Loch, Joice N.
See Loch, Joice N(anKivell)
Loch, Joice N(anKivell) 1893-1982 .. CANR-85
Obituary 108
Earlier sketch in CA 25-28R
Lochak, Michele 1936- 106
See also SATA 39
Lochard, Metz T(ullus) P(aul) 1896-1984
Obituary 112
Lochbiler, Don 1908-1987 49-52
Locher, Dick
See Locher, Richard (Earl)
Locher, Frances C(arol) CANR-17
Earlier sketch in CA 97-100
Locher, Richard (Earl) 1929- CANR-16
Earlier sketch in CA 85-88
Lochhead, Douglas (Grant) 1922- .. CANR-142
Earlier sketches in CA 45-48, CANR-1, 16, 39
See also CP 1
Lochhead, Liz 1947- CANR-79
Earlier sketch in CA 81-84
See also CBD
See also CD 5, 6
See also CP 2, 3, 4, 5, 6, 7
See also CWD
See also CWP
See also DLB 310
Lochhead, Marion Cleland
1902-1985 .... CANR-85
Obituary 115
Earlier sketch in CA 101
Lochlons, Colin
See Jackson, C(aary) Paul
Lochman, Jan Milic 1922- CANR-28
Earlier sketches in CA 29-32R, CANR-12
Lochnan, Katharine A. 1946- 127
Lochner, Louis P(aul) 1887-1975 65-68
Obituary 53-56
Lochridge, Betsy Hopkins
See Fancher, Betsy
Lochrie, Karma 195
Lochte, Dick
See Lochte, Richard S(amuel)
Lochte, Richard S(amuel) 1944- CANR-144
Earlier sketches in CA 105, CANR-23, 47, 66
See also CMW 4
LoCicero, Donald 1937- CANR-134
Earlier sketch in CA 25-28R
Lock, C(lara) B(eatrice) Muriel 1914- 49-52
Lock, C. J. S.
See Lock, Charles (John Somerset)
Lock, Charles (John Somerset) 1955- 146
Lock, Dennis (Laurence) 1929- .... CANR 32
Earlier sketches in CA 41-44R, CANR-14
Lock, F(rederick) P(eter) 1948- CANR-119
Earlier sketch in CA 118
Lock, Fred
See Lock, F(rederick) P(eter)
Lock, Joan 1933- CANR-97
Earlier sketch in CA 132
Lock, Margaret M. 1936- 126
Lock, Samuel 1926- 188
Lockard, Craig Alan 1942- 122
Lockard, (Walter) Duane 1921- 17-20R
Lockard, Isabel 1915- 141
Lockard, Leonard
See Thomas, Theodore L.
Locke, Alain (Le Roy) 1886-1954 ..... CANR-79
Brief entry 106
Earlier sketch in CA 124
See also AMWS 14
See also BLCS
See also BW 1, 3
See also DLB 51
See also HR 1:3
See also LMFS 2
See also MAL 5
See also RGAL 4
See also TCLC 43
Locke, Charles O. 1896(?)-1977
Obituary 69-72
See also TCWW 2
Locke, Christopher 1947- 199
Locke, Clinton W. CANR-26
Earlier sketches in CAP-2, CA 19-20
See also SATA 1
Locke, David M(illard) 1929- 41-44R
Locke, David Ross 1833-1888
See Nasby, Petroleum Vesuvius
See also DLB 11, 23
Locke, Duane CANR-1
Earlier sketch in CA 49-52
Locke, Edwin A. III 1938- 13-16R
Locke, Elsie (Violet) 1912-2001 .... CANR-88
Earlier sketches in CA 25-28R, CANR-11, 26, 53
See also CWRI 5
See also SATA 87
Locke, Frederick W. 1918- 13-16R
Locke, Hubert G. 1934- 29-32R
Locke, John 1632-1704 .... DLB 31, 101, 213, 252
See also RGEL 2
See also WLIT 3
Locke, Joseph
See Garton, Ray
Locke, Louis G(lenn) 1912-1991 .... 33-36R
Locke, Lucie 1904-1989 53-56
See also SATA 10
Locke, Martin
See Duncan, W(illiam) Murdoch
Locke, Maryel 144
Locke, Michael (Stephen) 1943- 73-76
Locke, Peter
See McCutchan, J(ohn) Wilson
Locke, R. E.
See Raffelock, David
Locke, Ralph P(aul) 1949- CANR-110
Earlier sketches in CA 124, CANR-53

Locke 356 CONTEMPORARY AUTHORS

Locke, Richard Adams 1800-1871 .... DLB 43
Locke, Robert 1944- 129
See also Bess, Clayton
See also SATA 63
Locke, Robert R. 1932- 163
Locke, Steven E(lliot) 1945- 127
Locke, Wende 1945- 33-36R
Locke-Elliott, Sumner
See Elliott, Sumner Locke
Locker, Thomas 1937- CANR-91
Earlier sketches in CA 128, CANR-66
See also CLR 14
See also MAICYA 1, 2
See also SATA 59, 109
Lockerbie, D(onald) Bruce 1935- CANR-14
Earlier sketch in CA 37-40R
Lockerbie, Jeanette W. Honeyman CANR-5
Earlier sketch in CA 9-12R
Lockerbie, Jeannie 1938- CANR-13
Earlier sketch in CA 73-76
Locker-Lampson, Frederick
1821-1895 .... DLB 35, 184
See also RGEL 2
Lockert, (Charles) Lacy (Jr.) 1888-1974 .. CAP-2
Earlier sketch in CA 25-28
Lockert, Lucia (Alicia Ungaro Fox)
1928- CANR-14
Earlier sketch in CA 73-76
Lockett, Reginald (Franklin) 1947- 153
See also BW 2, 3
Lockhard, Leonard
See Harness, Charles L(eonard)
Lockhart, (Jeanne) Aileene Simpson
1911- 13-16R
Lockhart, Caroline 1875-1962 .... TCWW 2
Lockhart, Freda Bruce 1909-1987
Obituary 124
Lockhart, George
See Lokert, George
Lockhart, Jack Herbert 1909-1985
Obituary 117
Lockhart, John Gibson 1794-1854 ..... DLB 110, 116, 144
Lockhart, Robert (Hamilton) Bruce 1886-1970
Obituary 89-92
Lockhart, Russell A(rthur) 1938- CANR-21
Earlier sketch in CA 45-48
Locklair, Wriston 1924(?)-1984
Obituary 112
Lockley, Lawrence Campbell
1899-1969 .... CAP-1
Earlier sketch in CA 11-12
Lockley, Martin Gaudin 1950- 190
Lockley, Ronald M(athias)
1903-2000 .... CANR-22
Obituary 189
Earlier sketches in CA 9-12R, CANR-5
Locklin, Gerald (Ivan) 1941- CANR-96
Earlier sketches in CA 37-40R, CANR-14, 32
Locklin, (David) Philip 1897-1989 .... 1-4R
Lockmann, Ronald F(rederick) 1942- 117
Lockmiller, David A(lexander) 1906- 77-80
Lockridge, Ernest (Hugh) 1938- 25-28R
See also AITN 1
Lockridge, Frances Louise 1896-1963
Obituary 93-96
See also CMW 4
See also DLB 306
Lockridge, Hildegarde (Dolson)
1908-1981 .... CANR-87
Obituary 102
Earlier sketches in CA 5-8R, CANR-3
See also Dolson, Hildegarde
See also SATA 121
Lockridge, Kenneth A(lan) 1940- 134
Brief entry 107
Lockridge, Laurence S(hockley)
1942- CANR-90
Earlier sketch in CA 130
Lockridge, Norman
See Roth, Samuel
Lockridge, Richard 1898-1982 .... CANR-62
Obituary 107
Earlier sketch in CA 85-88
See also DLB 306
Lockridge, Ross (Franklin), Jr.
1914-1948 .... CANR-79
Brief entry 108
Earlier sketch in CA 145
See also DLB 143
See also DLBY 1980
See also MAL 5
See also RGAL 4
See also RHW
See also TCLC 111
Lockspeiser, Edward 1905-1973 .... CANR-6
Earlier sketch in CA 5-8R
Lockwood, Allison 1920- 115
Lockwood, C. C. 1949- CANR-136
Earlier sketches in CA 117, CANR-41
Lockwood, Charles Andrews 1890-1967 ... 1-4R
Lockwood, Douglas (Wright)
1918-1980 .... 21-24R
Lockwood, Guy C. 1943- 65-68
Lockwood, Jeffrey A(lan) 1960- 234
Lockwood, Lee 1932- 37-40R
Lockwood, Lewis 1930- 215
Lockwood, M(ichael) J(ohn) 1950- 128
Lockwood, Margo 1939- CANR-41
Earlier sketch in CA 117
Lockwood, Mary
See Spelman, Mary
Lockwood, Michael 1944- 122
Lockwood, Robert
See Johnson, Robert
Lockwood, Theodore Davidge 1924- . CANR-1
Earlier sketch in CA 1-4R
Lockwood, W(illiam) B(urley) 1917- 29-32R
Lockwood, William W(irt) 1906- CAP-2
Earlier sketch in CA 23-24
Lockyer, Herbert 1888(?)-1984
Obituary 115
Lockyer, Judith 1949- 138
Lockyer, Roger 1927- CANR-12
Earlier sketch in CA 17-20R
Locre, Peter E.
See Cole, E(ugene) R(oger)
Lodder, Christina (Anne) 1948- 125
Lode, Rex
See Goldstein, William Isaac
Lodeizen, Hans
See Lodeizen, Johannes August Frederick
Loden, Barbara (Ann) 1937-1980
Obituary 101
Loden, Rachel 1948- 223
Loder, John 1898-1988
Obituary 128
Lodge, Bernard 1933- 107
See also SATA 33, 107
Lodge, David (John) 1935- CANR-139
Earlier sketches in CA 17-20R, CANR-19, 53, 92
Interview in CANR-19
See also BEST 90:1
See also BRWS 4
See also CLC 36, 141
See also CN 1, 2, 3, 4, 5, 6, 7
See also CPW
See also DAM POP
See also DLB 14, 194
See also EWL 3
See also MTCW 1, 2
See also MTFW 2005
Lodge, George Cabot 1873-1909
Brief entry 123
See also DLB 54
Lodge, George Cabot 1927- 17-20R
Lodge, Henry Cabot 1850-1924 180
See also DLB 47
Lodge, Henry Cabot, (Jr.)
1902-1985 .... CANR-85
Obituary 115
Earlier sketch in CA 53-56
Lodge, Jeff 1952- 164
Lodge, Jo 1966- 184
See also SATA 112
Lodge, Oliver (Joseph) 1851-1940
Brief entry 117
Lodge, Orlan Robert 1917-1975
Obituary 57-60
Lodge, Thomas 1558-1625 .... DLB 172
See also RGEL 2
Lodrick, Deryck O(scar) 1942- 106
Loeb, Arthur L. 1923- 145
Loeb, Benjamin S. 1914- 128
Loeb, Catherine (Roberta) 1949- 89-92
Loeb, Gerald M(artin) 1899-1974 .... CAP-1
Obituary 49-52
Earlier sketch in CA 13-16
Loeb, Harold A(lbert) 1891-1974 106
Obituary 45-48
See also DLB 4
Loeb, Jacques 1859-1924 161
Loeb, Jeffrey 1946- 123
See also SATA 57
Loeb, Jeph 1958- 225
Loeb, Karen 1946- 144
Loeb, Madeleine H. 1905(?)-1974
Obituary 45-48
Loeb, Marshall Robert 1929- 21-24R
Loeb, Paul Rogat 1952- CANR-128
Earlier sketch in CA 109
Loeb, Robert F(rederick) 1895-1973
Obituary 45-48
Loeb, Robert H., Jr. 1917- CANR-12
Earlier sketch in CA 29-32R
See also SATA 21
Loeb, Sara(h) 1928- 221
Loeb, William 1905-1981 .... CANR-71
Obituary 104
Earlier sketch in CA 93-96
Interview in CA-93-96
See also DLB 127
Loebl, Eugen 1907-1987
Obituary 123
Loebl, Suzanne CANR-112
Earlier sketch in CA 69-72
Loeffelholz, Mary 1958- 141
Loeffler, Jack 1936- 213
Loefgren, Ulf 1931- CANR-16
Earlier sketch in CA 25-28R
See also SATA 3
Loefstedt, Bengt 1931- CANR-1
Earlier sketch in CA 45-48
Loehfelm, Bill 1969- 228
See also SATA 153
Loehlin, John C(linton) 1926- 21-24R
Loemker, Leroy E(arl) 1900-1985 .... 41-44R
Loen, Raymond O(rdell) 1924- 146
Loengard, John 1934- CANR-97
Earlier sketch in CA 133
Loening, Grover C. 1889(?)-1976
Obituary 65-68
Loening, Sarah (Elizabeth) Larkin
1896-1988 .... CANR-85
Obituary 124
Earlier sketches in CA 45-48, CANR-21
Loeoef, Jan 1940- 81-84
Loeper, John J(oseph) 1929- CANR-96
Earlier sketches in CA 29-32R, CANR-12
See also SATA 10, 118
Loertscher, David V. 1940- 126
Loesch, Juli(anne) 1951- 89-92
Loescher, Ann Dull 1942- CANR-9
Earlier sketch in CA 61-64
See also SATA 20
Loescher, Gil(burt Damian) 1945- CANR-9
Earlier sketch in CA 61-64
See also SATA 20
Loeschke, Maravene Sheppard 1947- 115
Loeser, Herta 1921- 57-60
Loeser, Katinka 1913-1991 .... CANR-85
Obituary 133
Earlier sketch in CA 17-20R
Loesser, Francis Henry 1910-1969
Obituary 112
See also Loesser, Frank
Loesser, Frank
See Loesser, Francis Henry
See also DLB 265
Loest, Erich 1926- 192
Loether, Herman J(ohn) 1930- 21-24R
Loetscher, Lefferts A(ugustine) 1904-1981 . 5-8R
Loevinger, Jane 1918- 41-44R
Loevinger, Lee 1913-2004 .... CANR-15
Obituary 226
Earlier sketch in CA 81-84
Loevy, Robert D(ickinson) 1935- 175
Loew, Marcus 1870-1927 .... IDFW 4
Loew, Ralph William 1907-1996 .... CAP-1
Earlier sketch in CA 19-20
Loew, Sebastian 1939- CANR-19
Earlier sketch in CA 103
Loewald, Hans W. 1906-1993 .... CANR-46
Obituary 140
Earlier sketch in CA 101
Loewe, Michael 1922- CANR-86
Earlier sketch in CA 133
Loewe, Ralph E. 1923-1997 .... 21-24R
Loewe, Raphael J(ames) 1919- CANR-42
Earlier sketch in CA 118
Loewen, James W. 1942- CANR-92
Earlier sketches in CA 37-40R, CANR-14, 50
Loewenberg, Bert James 1905-1974 ... CANR-5
Earlier sketch in CA 9-12R
Loewenberg, Frank M(eyer) 1925- CANR-2
Earlier sketch in CA 45-48
Loewenberg, Gerhard 1928- CANR-9
Earlier sketch in CA 21-24R
Loewenberg, J(orn) Joseph 1933- 33-36R
Loewenberg, Peter J(acob) 1933- 109
Loewenberg, Robert J(ames) 1938-
Brief entry 114
Loewenfeld, Claire 1899-1974 .... CAP-2
Earlier sketch in CA 23-24
Loewenstein, Bernice .... SATA-Brief 40
Loewenstein(-Wertheim-Freudenberg), Hubertus (Friedrich Maria Johannes Leopold Ludwig)
1906-1984 .... CANR-29
Obituary 114
Earlier sketches in CA 5-8R, CANR-4
Loewenstein, Joseph (F.) 1952- CANR-143
Earlier sketch in CA 124
Loewenstein, Karl 1891-1973
Obituary 41-44R
Loewenstein, Louis Klee 1927- 37-40R
Loewenstein, Prince Hubertus (F. zu)
See Loewenstein(-Wertheim-Freudenberg), Hubertus (Friedrich Maria Johannes Leopold Ludwig)
Loewenstein, Rudolph M(aurice)
1898-1976 .... CAP-2
Obituary 65-68
Earlier sketch in CA 21-22
Loewenstein, Werner R(andolph) 1926- 185
Loewenthal, L(eonard) J(oseph) A(lfonso) . 61-64
Loewer, Jean Jenkins
See Jenkins, Jean
Loewer, (Henry) Peter 1934- CANR-120
Earlier sketch in CA 138
See also SATA 98
Loewinsohn, Ron(ald William)
1937- CANR-71
Earlier sketch in CA 25-28R
See also CLC 52
See also CP 1, 2
Loewith, Karl 1897-1973
Obituary 116
Loewy, Ariel G(ideon) 1925-2001 89-92
Obituary 194
Loewy, Erich H. 1927- 139
Loewy, Raymond Fernand
1893-1986 .... CANR-85
Obituary 119
Earlier sketch in CA 104
LoFaro, Jerry 1959- .... SATA 77
Lofaro, Michael Anthony 1948- 89-92
Lofas, Jeannette 1940- 157
Loffelholz, Franz
See Mon, Franz
Lofficier, Jean-Marc 1954- 224
Lofland, John (Franklin) 1936- CANR-12
Earlier sketch in CA 33-36R
Lofland, Lyn (Hebert) 1937- 61-64
Loflin, Christine 1959- 183
Lofo
See Heimann, Rolf
Lofstedt, Bengt
See Loefstedt, Bengt
Loftas, Tony 1940- 21-24R
Lofthouse, Jessica 1916-1988 .... CANR-85
Obituary 125
Earlier sketch in CA 29-32R
Lofthus, Myrna 1935- 115
Loftin, T(helma) L(ois) 1922-2003
Obituary 232
See also Snell, Tee Loftin
Lofting, Hugh (John) 1886-1947 .... CANR-73
Brief entry 109
Earlier sketch in CA 137
See also BYA 5
See also CLR 19
See also CWRI 5
See also DLB 160
See also FANT
See also MAICYA 1, 2
See also SATA 15, 100
See also TEA
See also WCH
Loftis, Anne 1922- 45-48
Loftis, John (Clyde, Jr.) 1919- CANR-3
Earlier sketch in CA 1-4R
Lofton, John (Marion) 1919- CANR-6
Earlier sketch in CA 9-12R
Lofts, Norah (Robinson) 1904-1983 . CANR-80
Obituary 110
Earlier sketches in CA 5-8R, CANR-6
Interview in CANR-6
See also AITN 2
See also RHW
See also SATA 8
See also SATA-Obit 36
Loftus, Elizabeth F. 1944- 105
Loftus, Ernest Achey 1884-1987
Obituary 123
Loftus, John (Joseph) 1950- 117
Loftus, Richard J. 1929- 13-16R
Lo Gaiter Del Besos
See Solsona, Ramon
Logan, Albert Boyd 1909- 53-56
Logan, Anne
See Colley, Barbara
Logan, Cait
See Kleinsasser, Lois
Logan, Chuck 1942- 226
Logan, Daniel 1936- 25-28R
Logan, Deborah Norris 1761-1839 ..... DLB 200
Logan, Don
See Crawford, William (Elbert)
Logan, Elizabeth D(ulaney) 1914- 61-64
Logan, F(rancis) Donald 1930- 45-48
Logan, Ford
See Newton, D(wight) B(ennett)
Logan, Frank A(nderson) 1924- 41-44R
Logan, Gene A(dams) 1922- CANR-7
Earlier sketch in CA 9-12R
Logan, George M(eredith) 1941- 131
Logan, Gerald E(lton) 1924- 73-76
Logan, Jake
See Knott, William C(ecil, Jr.) and
Krepps, Robert W(ilson) and
Pearl, Jacques Bain and
Riefe, Alan and
Rifkin, Shepard and
Smith, Martin Cruz
Logan, Jake
See Edmondson, G(arry) C(otton)
Logan, James 1674-1751 .... DLB 24, 140
Logan, James Phillips 1921- 37-40R
Logan, Jane
See Gardner, Virginia (Marberry)
Logan, John (Burton) 1923-1987 ...... CANR-45
Obituary 124
Earlier sketch in CA 77-80
See also CLC 5
See also CP 1, 2
See also DLB 5
Logan, John A(rthur), Jr. 1923- 1-4R
Logan, Joshua (Lockwood)
1908-1988 .... CANR-85
Obituary 126
Earlier sketch in CA 89-92
Interview in CA-89-92
See also AITN 1
Logan, Lillian M(ay) 1909- CANR-1
Earlier sketch in CA 1-4R
Logan, Mark
See Nicole, Christopher (Robin)
Logan, Martha Daniell 1704(?)-1779 .. DLB 200
Logan, Matt
See Whitehead, David
Logan, Michael F. 1950- 157
Logan, Onnie Lee 1910(?)-1995 144
Obituary 149
Logan, Rayford W(hittingham)
1897-1982 .... CANR-25
Obituary 108
Earlier sketches in CA 1-4R, CANR-1
See also BW 1
Logan, Sara
See Haydon, June and
Simpson, Judith H(olroyd)
Logan, Shirley Wilson 1943- CANR-93
Earlier sketch in CA 151
See also BW 3
Logan, Sister Mary Francis Louise 1928- ... 5-8R
Logan, Spencer 1912(?)-1980
Obituary 93-96
Logan, Terence P(atrick) 1936- 57-60
Logan, Virgil G(lenn) 1904-1987 .... 21-24R
Logan, William 1950- CANR-88
Earlier sketch in CA 136
See also DLB 120
Loganbill, G. Bruce 1938- 37-40R
Logelin, Warren E. 1940(?)-1985
Obituary 117
Logghe, Joan 1947- 188
Loggins, Vernon 1893-1968 .... 5-8R
Loggins, William Kirk 1946- 77-80
Logie Robertson, James
See Robertson, James Logie
Logsdon, John M(ortimer III) 1937-
Brief entry 115
Logsdon, Joseph 1938- 25-28R

Cumulative Index 357 Longman

Logsdon, Richard Henry 1912-1997 .. CANR-2
Earlier sketch in CA 5-8R
Logsdon, Thomas S(tanley) 1937- CANR-46
Earlier sketches in CA 57-60, CANR-6, 21
Logsdon, Tom
See Logsdon, Thomas S(tanley)
Logston, Anne 1962- 173
See also SATA 112
Logue, Antonia 236
Logue, Cal(vin McLeod) 1935- 127
Brief entry 105
Logue, Christopher 1926- CANR-79
Earlier sketches in CA 9-12R, CANR-3, 42
See also CP 1, 2, 3, 4, 5, 6, 7
See also DLB 27
See also SATA 23
Logue, Jeanne 1921- 89-92
Logue, John 1933- 126
Logue, John A(lan) 1947- 141
Logue, Mary 1952- CANR-114
Earlier sketch in CA 173
See also SATA 112, 161
Logue, Robert 1971- 184
Logue, William (Herbert) 1934- 45-48
Loh, Jules 1931- 33-36R
Loh, Morag 1935- .... SATA 73
Loh, Pichon P(ei) Y(ung) 1928- 17-20R
Loh, Robert 1924- 17-20R
Loh, Sandra Tsing 1962- CANR-115
Earlier sketch in CA 166
Loh, Vyvyane 229
Lohafer, Susan 1942- CANR-37
Lohans, Alison 1949- 160
See also SATA 101
See also YAW
Lohenstein, Daniel Casper von
1635-1683 .... DLB 168
Lohf, Kenneth A. 1925-2002 .... CANR-3
Obituary 208
Earlier sketch in CA 9-12R
Lohman, Joseph D(ean) 1910-1968 .... CAP-2
Earlier sketch in CA 23-24
Lohnes, Walter F. W. 1925- CANR-29
Earlier sketch in CA 49-52
Lohr, Steve 213
Lohr, Thomas F. 1926- 77-80
Lohrer, M(ary) Alice 1907-2002 .... 17-20R
Obituary 211
Lohrey, David T. 1955- 225
Lohrli, Anne 1906- 111
Lohrman, Paul
See Fairman, Paul W.
Lohse, Eduard 1924- CANR-46
Earlier sketch in CA 107
Lois, George 1931- 127
Loisy, Alfred (Firmin) 1857-1940 182
Brief entry 120
Loizeaux, Elizabeth Bergmann 1950- 219
Lo-Johansson, (Karl) Ivar
1901-1990 .... CANR-137
Obituary 131
Earlier sketches in CA 102, CANR-20, 79
See also DLB 259
See also EWL 3
See also RGWL 2, 3
Loken, Newton Clayton 1919- 1-4R
See also SATA 26
Lokert, George c. 1485-1547 .... DLB 281
Loki
See Pearson, Karl
Lokken, Roy N(orman) 1917-1984 53-56
Lokos, Lionel 1928- 25-28R
Loll, Leo M(arius), Jr. 1923-1968 .... CAP-2
Earlier sketch in CA 25-28
Lollar, Coleman Aubrey (Jr.) 1946-1993 .. 49-52
Obituary 141
Lolli, Giorgio 1905-1979 .... CANR-2
Obituary 85-88
Earlier sketch in CA 1-4R
Lollis, Lorraine 1911- CAP-2
Earlier sketch in CA 29-32
Lolos, Kimon 1917- 1-4R
Lom, Herbert 1917- 166
Lomas, Charles W(yatt) 1907-1999 .... CAP-1
Earlier sketch in CA 13-14
Lomas, Derek 1933- 29-32R
Lomas, Frank T.
See Tubb, E(dwin) C(harles)
Lomas, Geoffrey (Robert) 1950- 93-96
Lomas, Herbert 1924- CANR-81
Earlier sketch in CA 144
See also CP 7
Lomas, Peter 1923- 21-24R
Lomas, Steve
See Brennan, Joseph Lomas
Lomask, Milton (Nachman)
1909-1991 .... CANR-44
Obituary 135
Earlier sketches in CA 1-4R, CANR-1
See also SATA 20
Lomax, Alan 1915-2002 .... CANR-1
Obituary 207
Earlier sketch in CA 1-4R
Lomax, Bliss
See Drago, Harry Sinclair
Lomax, Derek W(illiam) 1933-1992 . CANR-85
Obituary 137
Earlier sketch in CA 130
Lomax, John A(lbert) 1930- 61-64
Lomax, Louis E(manuel) 1922-1970 ...... CAP-2
Earlier sketch in CA 25-28
See also BW 1
Lomax, Marion 1953- CANR-82
Earlier sketch in CA 133
Lomax, Pearl
See Cleage, Pearl (Michelle)
Lomax, Richard G. 1954- 177
Lomax, Yve 1952- 196
Lombard, C(harles) M(orris) 1920- CANR-1
Earlier sketch in CA 49-52
Lombard, Helen
See Vischer, Helen (Cassin Lombard) Carusi
Lombard, Lawrence Brian 1944- 124
Lombard, Nap
See Johnson, Pamela Hansford
Lombardi, John V(incent) 1942- CANR-20
Earlier sketches in CA 53-56, CANR-5
Lombardi, Mary 1940- 61-64
Lombardo, Josef Vincent 1908-1992 .... 5-8R
Lombardo, Mary A. 1938- 235
Lombreglia, Ralph 181
LoMedico, Brian T.
See Monteleone, Thomas F(rancis)
Lomer, Mary
See Lide, Mary
Lommasson, Robert C(urtis)
1917-1996 .... 41-44R
Lomnitz, Cinna 1925- 150
Lomnitz, Larissa Adler
See Adler, Larissa
LoMonaco, Palmyra 1932- 169
See also HW 2
See also SATA 102
Lomonosov, Mikhail Vasil'evich
1711-1765 .... DLB 150
Lomosia, Andrew
See Stern, Jay B(enjamin)
Lomperis, Timothy J. 1947- CANR-52
Earlier sketch in CA 126
Lomupo, Brother Robert 1939- 13-16R
London, Artur 1915-1986 .... CANR-85
Obituary 120
Earlier sketches in CA 65-68, CANR-12
London, Asher
See Stone, Kurt F(ranklin)
London, Cait
See Kleinsasser, Lois
London, Carolyn 1918- 57-60
London, Ephraim 1911-1990
Obituary 131
London, Fritz Wolfgang 1900-1954 161
London, H(oyt) H(obson) 1900-1990 49-52
London, Hannah R. 1894-1988 .... 29-32R
London, Herbert I(ra) 1939- CANR-12
Earlier sketch in CA 33-36R
London, Jack 1876-1916
See London, John Griffith
See also AAYA 13
See also AITN 2
See also AMW
See also BPFB 2
See also BYA 4, 13
See also CDALB 1865-1917
See also DLB 8, 12, 78, 212
See also EWL 3
See also EXPS
See also LAIT 3
See also MAL 5
See also NFS 8
See also RGAL 4
See also RGSF 2
See also SATA 18
See also SFW 4
See also SSC 4, 49
See also SSFS 7
See also TCLC 9, 15, 39
See also TCWW 1, 2
See also TUS
See also WLC
See also WYA
See also YAW
London, Jack 1915-1988 .... CANR-85
Obituary 126
Earlier sketches in CA 89-92, CANR-25
London, Jane
See Geis, Darlene Stern
London, Jane
See Geis, Darlene Stern
London, Joan 1901-1971 .... CAP-2
Earlier sketch in CA 25-28
London, Joan 1948- 227
London, John Griffith 1876-1916 ..... CANR-73
Brief entry 110
Earlier sketch in CA 119
See also London, Jack
See also DA
See also DA3
See also DAB
See also DAC
See also DAM MST, NOV
See also JRDA
See also MAICYA 1, 2
See also MTCW 1, 2
See also MTFW 2005
See also NFS 19
London, Jonathan (Paul) 1947- CANR-141
Earlier sketch in CA 185
See also SATA 74, 113, 157
London, Julius 1917- 118
London, Kurt L(udwig) 1900-1985 ..... CANR-6
Earlier sketch in CA 1-4R
London, Laura
See Curtis, Sharon and
Curtis, Thomas Dale
See also RHW
London, Lawrence Steven 1950- 146
London, Mel 1923- CANR-49
Earlier sketches in CA 107, CANR-24
London, Perry 1931-1992 .... CANR-49
Obituary 139
Earlier sketch in CA 45-48
London, Roy (Laird) 1943-1993 .... CANR-85
Obituary 141
Earlier sketch in CA 108
Londre, Felicia Hardison 1941- CANR-21
Earlier sketch in CA 105
Lonergan, Bernard J(oseph) F(rancis)
1904-1984 .... CANR-85
Obituary 114
Earlier sketches in CA 53-56, CANR-11
Lonergan, (Pauline) Joy (MacLean) 1909- .. 1-4R
See also SATA 10
Lonergan, Kenneth 1963(?)- 215
Lonesome Cowboy
See White, John I(rwin)
Lone Star Ranger
See White, John I(rwin)
Lonette, Reisie (Dominee) 1924- .... SATA 43
Lone Wolf, Terry
See Karanen, Terry Drew
Loney, Glenn (Meredith) 1928- CANR-14
Earlier sketch in CA 33-36R
Loney, Martin 1944- CANR-18
Earlier sketch in CA 102
Long, A(nthony) A(rthur) 1937- CANR-29
Earlier sketches in CA 33-36R, CANR-13
Long, Ann Marie
See Jensen, Pauline Marie (Long)
Long, Benjamin 1967- 217
Long, Carolyn Morrow 1940- 204
Long, Cathryn J. 1946- CANR-137
Earlier sketch in CA 155
See also SATA 89
Long, Charles 1938- 65-68
Long, Charles R(ussell) 1904-1978 .... CAP-1
Earlier sketch in CA 11-12
Long, Chester Clayton 1932- 25-28R
Long, Clayton
See Long, Chester Clayton
Long, Cynthia 1956- 126
Long, D. Stephen 1960- 151
Long, David 1948- CANR-56
Earlier sketch in CA 127
See also DLB 244
See also MTFW 2005
Long, David E(dwin) 1937- 89-92
Long, David F(oster) 1917- CANR-8
Earlier sketch in CA 61-64
Long, E(verette) B(each) 1919-1981 .. CANR-85
Obituary 103
Earlier sketches in CA 1-4R, CANR-1
Long, Earlene (Roberta) 1938- 126
See also SATA 50
Long, Edward LeRoy, Jr. 1924- CANR-22
Earlier sketches in CA 5-8R, CANR-7
Long, Elgen M. 1927- 208
Long, Elliot
See Bennett, Reginald George Stephen
See also TCWW 2
Long, Emmett
See Leonard, Elmore (John, Jr.)
Long, Esmond R(ay) 1890-1979
Obituary 89-92
Long, Eugene Thomas (III) 1935- 25-28R
Long, Father Valentine W. 1902-1998 ... 17-20R
Long, Fern CAP-2
Earlier sketch in CA 23-24
Long, Frank Belknap 1903-1994 ...... CANR-75
Obituary 143
Earlier sketches in CA 81-84, CANR-16
See also HGG
See also SFW 4
See also SUFW 1
Long, Franklin A(sbury) 1910-1999 127
Obituary 177
Long, Frederick Lawrence 1917- 9-12R
Long, Goldberry 1967(?)- 219
Long, Haniel (Clark) 1888-1956
Brief entry 122
See also DLB 45
Long, Helen Beecher CANR-26
Earlier sketches in CAP-2, CA 19-20
See also SATA 1
Long, Howard Rusk 1906- CANR-3
Earlier sketch in CA 5-8R
Long, Huey P(ierce) 1893-1935 166
Brief entry 115
Long, J(ohn) C(uthbert) 1892-1980 .... CAP-1
Earlier sketch in CA 9-10
Long, James M. 1907-1979
Obituary 85-88
Long, Jeff 208
Long, John D(ouglas) 1920- 17-20R
Long, John H(enderson) 1916- 13-16R
Long, John L(atham) 1932- 111
Long, Judith Elaine 1953- 65-68
See also SATA 20
Long, Judy
See Long, Judith Elaine
Long, Kim 1949- 129
See also SATA 69
Long, Laura Mooney 1892-1967
Obituary 109
See also SATA-Obit 29
Long, Lois 1901-1974
Obituary 104
Long, Loren 1966(?)- .... SATA 151
Long, Louise 37-40R
Long, Lucile
See Brandt, Lucile (Long Strayer)
Long, Luman H(arrison) 1907-1971 108
Obituary 104
Long, Lyda Belknap
See Long, Frank Belknap
Long, M(olly) 1916- 21-24R
Long, Marie K. 207
Long, Melinda 1960- .... SATA 152
Long, Naomi Cornelia
See Madgett, Naomi Long
Long, Norton E. 1910-1993 45-48
Long, Pamela O. 235
Long, Priscilla 1943- 29-32R
Long, Quincy 1945- 230
See also CD 5, 6
Long, Ralph B(ernard) 1906- 5-8R
Long, Ray 1878-1935 183
See also DLB 137
Long, Richard A(lexander)
1927-1974 .... CANR-42
Earlier sketches in CA 37-40R, CANR-24
See also BW 2
Long, Robert 1954- CANR-117
Earlier sketches in CA 110, CANR-30
Long, Robert Emmet 1934- CANR-116
Earlier sketches in CA 122, CANR-48
Long, Steven 1944- 125
Long, Sylvia 1948- .... SATA 120
Long, T(heodore) Dixon 1933- 121
Brief entry 118
Long, Theodore E(dward) 1944- 126
Long, Thomas (Joseph) 1938- 119
Long, Wesley
See Smith, George O(liver)
Long, William Stuart
See Stuart, (Violet) Vivian (Finlay)
Longaberger, Dave
See Longaberger, David
Longaberger, David 1935(?)-1999 203
Longacre, Edward G(eorge) 1946- CANR-99
Earlier sketches in CA 53-56, CANR-5, 22
Longacre, Robert E(dmondson)
1922- CANR-19
Earlier sketches in CA 53-56, CANR-4
Longacre, William A(tlas) II 1937- CANR-12
Earlier sketch in CA 29-32R
Longaker, Richard P(ancoast) 1924- ... CANR-1
Earlier sketch in CA 1-4R
Longbaugh, Harry
See Goldman, William (W.)
Longbeard, Frederick
See Longyear, Barry B(rookes)
Longden, Deric 173
Longeaux y Vasquex, Enriqueta 1930- 57-60
Longenbach, James 1959- 127
Longenecker, Dwight 195
Longenecker, Justin G. 1917- CANR-1
Earlier sketch in CA 1-4R
Longenecker, Richard N(orman) 1930- .. 13-16R
Longest, George C(alvin) 1938- 107
Longeville, Jean
See Goll, Yvan
Longfellow, Henry Wadsworth
1807-1882 .... AMW
See also AMWR 2
See also CDALB 1640-1865
See also CLR 99
See also DA
See also DA3
See also DAB
See also DAC
See also DAM MST, POET
See also DLB 1, 59, 235
See also EXPP
See also PAB
See also PC 30
See also PFS 2, 7, 17
See also RGAL 4
See also SATA 19
See also TUS
See also WLCS
See also WP
Longfellow, Layne (A.) 1937- 169
See also SATA 102
Longfellow, Samuel 1819-1892 .... DLB 1
Longfield, Bradley J(ames) 1955- 139
Longfish, George (C.) 1942- 213
Longford, Lord
See Pakenham, Francis Aungier
Longford, Elizabeth (Harmon Pakenham)
1906-2002 .... CANR-46
Obituary 213
Earlier sketch in CA 5-8R
See also DLB 155
Longford, Frank
See Pakenham, Francis Aungier
Longgood, William (Frank) 1917- CANR-17
Earlier sketch in CA 1-4R
Longhurst, Henry Carpenter 1909-1978 .. 85-88
Obituary 81-84
Longino, Charles F(reeman), Jr.
1938- CANR-24
Earlier sketches in CA 53-56, CANR-7
Longinus c. 1st cent. - .... AW 2
See also DLB 176
Longland, Jean R(ogers) 1913- CANR-10
Earlier sketch in CA 21-24R
Longleigh, Peter J., Jr.
See Korges, James
Longley, John Lewis, Jr. 1920- 5-8R
Longley, Lawrence D(ouglas)
1939-2002 .... 41-44R
Obituary 207
Longley, Michael 1939- 102
See also BRWS 8
See also CLC 29
See also CP 1, 2, 3, 4, 5, 6, 7
See also DLB 40
Longley, Richmond W(ilberforce) 1907- .. 73-76
Longley, W. B.
See Randisi, Robert J(oseph)
Longman, Harold S. 1919- 25-28R
See also SATA 5
Longman, Jere 199
Longman, Lester Duncan 1905-1987
Obituary 121
Longman, Mark Frederic Kerr 1916-1972
Obituary 37-40R
Longman, Tremper III 1952- 184

Longmate, Norman Richard 1925- ... CANR-28
Earlier sketches in CA 9-12R, CANR-6
Longmore, George 1793(?)-1867 .... DLB 99
Longmore, Laura 5-8R
Long-Neck Woman
See Cheatham, Karyn Follis
Longo, Lucas 1919-1992 .... 25-28R
Longrigg, Clare 221
Longrigg, Jane Chichester 1929- 9-12R
Longrigg, Roger (Erskine) 1929-2000 .. CANR-3
Obituary 187
Earlier sketch in CA 1-4R
See also CMW 4
Longrigg, Stephen Hemsley 1893-1979
Obituary 89-92
Longstreet, Augustus Baldwin
1790-1870 .... DLB 3, 11, 74, 248
See also RGAL 4
Longstreet, Chauncey
See Longstreet, Stephen
Longstreet, Stephen 1907-2002 .... CANR-7
Obituary 201
Earlier sketch in CA 9-12R
Longstreet, Wilma S. 1935- 93-96
Longstreth, Edward 1894-1971(?) CAP-1
Earlier sketch in CA 13-16
Longstreth, Richard 1946- 132
Longstreth, T(homas) Morris 1886-1975 .... 5-8R
Longstreth, W(illiam) Thacher 1920-2003 .. 134
Obituary 215
Longsworth, Polly 1933- CANR-96
Earlier sketch in CA 106
See also SATA 28
Longsworth, Robert M. 1937- 21-24R
Longtemps, Kenneth 1933- .... SATA 17
Longway, A. Hugh
See Lang, Andrew
Longworth, Alice Lee (Roosevelt) 1884-1980
Obituary 93-96
Longworth, I(an) H(eaps) 1935- 120
Longworth, James J., Jr. 1954- 217
Longworth, Norman 1936- 187
Longworth, Philip 1933- CANR-28
Earlier sketches in CA 21-24R, CANR-10
Longworth, Richard C(ole) 1935- 85-88
Longyard, William H(enry) 1958- 152
Longyear, Barry B(rookes) 1942- CANR-78
Earlier sketch in CA 102
See also SATA 117
See also SFW 4
Longyear, Christopher R(udston) 1929- 105
Longyear, Marie Marcia Bernstein 1928- 115
Longyear, Rey M(organ) 1930- CANR-22
Earlier sketch in CA 45-48
Lonn, Oystein
See Lonn, Oystein
Lonn, Oystein 1936- .... DLB 297
Lonnbohm, Armas Eino Leopold
See Lonnbohm, Armas Eino Leopold
Lonnbohm, Armas Eino Leopold 1878-1926
Brief entry 123
See also Leino, Eino
Lonnrot, Elias 1802-1884 .... EFS 1
Lonsdale, Adrian L. 1927- 13-16R
Lonsdale, Frederick 1881-1954
Brief entry 109
See also DLB 10
See also RGEL 2
Lonsdale, Gordon Arnold 1923(?)-1970
Obituary 104
Lonsdale, Kathleen (Yardley) 1903-1971 ... 5-8R
Obituary 33-36R
Lonsdale, Richard E. 1926- CANR-13
Earlier sketch in CA 21-24R
Lonsdale, Roger ed. .... CLC 65
Lonsdale, Steven (Hancock) 1952- ... CANR-36
Earlier sketch in CA 114
Looby, Christopher 193
Look, Al 1893-1992 57-60
Look, Dennis 1949- 73-76
Looker, Antonina (Hansell) -1987 .... 29-32R
Looker, (Reginald) Earle 1895-1976 ...... CAP-2
Obituary 65-68
Earlier sketch in CA 29-32
Lookout
See Noble, John (Appelbe)
Lookstein, Haskel 1932- 119
Loomans, Diane 1955- 155
See also SATA 90
Loomba, N(arendra) Paul 1927- 57-60
Loomes, Brian 1938- CANR-116
Earlier sketches in CA 69-72, CANR-12, 30, 56
Loomie, Albert Joseph 1922- 5-8R
Loomis, Albertine (G.) 1895-1985 .... CANR-85
Obituary 117
Earlier sketch in CA 93-96
Loomis, Burdett A. 1945- CANR-65
Earlier sketch in CA 129
Loomis, Charles P(rice) 1905-1995 .. CANR-13
Earlier sketch in CA 21-24R
Loomis, Chauncey C(hester), Jr. 1930- .. 33-36R
Loomis, Christine 173
See also SATA 113, 160
Loomis, Edward 1924- CANR-2
Earlier sketch in CA 1-4R
Loomis, Jennifer A. 1942- 168
See also SATA 101
Loomis, Noel M(iller) 1905-1969 ..... CANR-68
Obituary 25-28R
Earlier sketch in CA 1-4R
See also TCWW 1, 2
Loomis, Rae
See Steger, Shelby
Loomis, Robert D. 17-20R
See also SATA 5
Loomis, Roger Sherman 1887-1966 ... CANR-8
Earlier sketch in CA 5-8R
Loomis, Stanley 1922-1972 .... CAP-1
Obituary 37-40R
Earlier sketch in CA 11-12
Loomis, Susan Herrmann 1955- CANR-107
Earlier sketch in CA 140
Loomis, Zona Kemp 1911-1996 45-48
Looney, Dennis (Oscar III) 1955- 217
Looney, Douglas S. 1942- 144
Looney, Robert E(dward) 1941- 104
Loori, John Daido 1931- CANR-101
Earlier sketch in CA 154
Loory, Stuart H. 1932- 25-28R
Loos, Anita 1893(?)-1981 .... CANR-77
Obituary 104
Earlier sketches in CA 21-24R, CANR-26
See also AITN 1
See also CN 2, 3
See also DLB 11, 26, 228
See also DLBY 1981
See also IDFW 3, 4
See also MTCW 2
See also MTFW 2005
Loos, Mary .... AITN 1
Loose, Gerhard 1907-2000 45-48
Loose, H.
See Lourie, Dick
Looser, Devoney 1967- 217
Loosley, William Robert
See Langford, David
Loots, Barbara Kunz 1946- 57-60
Loovis, David (Mactavish) 1926- CANR-1
Earlier sketch in CA 1-4R
Lopach, James J. 1942- 135
Lopata, Helena Znaniecka 1925-2003 104
Obituary 213
Lopate, Carol
See Ascher, Carol
Lopate, Phillip 1943- CANR-88
Earlier sketch in CA 97-100
Interview in CA-97-100
See also CLC 29
See also DLBY 1980
Lopatin, Judy 1954- 124
Lope de Rueda 1510(?)-1565(?) .... DLB 318
Loper, William C. 1927- 13-16R
Lopes, Dominic (M. McIver) 1964- 157
See also HW 2
Lopes, Fernao 1380(?)-1460(?) .... DLB 287
Lopes, Henri (Marie-Joseph) 1937- ... CANR-90
Earlier sketch in CA 132
See also BW 2
See also EWL 3
Lopes, Michael 1943- 57-60
Lopez, Adalberto 1943- 103
Lopez, Andrew 1910-1986
Obituary 120
Lopez, Angelo (Cayas) 1967- .... SATA 83
Lopez, Barry (Holstun) 1945- CANR-92
Earlier sketches in CA 65-68, CANR-7, 23, 47, 68
Interview in .... CANR-7, -23
See also AAYA 9, 63
See also ANW
See also CLC 70
See also DLB 256, 275
See also MTCW 1
See also RGAL 4
See also SATA 67
Lopez, Cecilia L(uisa) 1941- 53-56
Lopez, Claude-Anne 1920- 104
Lopez, Diana 1948- 153
See also Rios, Isabella
See also HW 1, 2
Lopez, Ella B. 1900(?)-1978
Obituary 81-84
Lopez, Enrique 1921(?)-1985
Obituary 117
Lopez, Felix Manuel, Jr. 1917- 13-16R
Lopez, Jack 1950- 225
Lopez, Josefina 1969- .... DLB 209
Lopez, Laura 1957- 136
Lopez, Manuel Dennis 1934- CANR-22
Earlier sketch in CA 105
Lopez, Nancy (Marie) 1957-
Brief entry 113
Lopez, Ralph I. 1942- 238
Lopez, Robert S(abatino) 1910-1986
Obituary 119
Brief entry 112
Lopez, Steve 1953- CANR-136
Earlier sketch in CA 171
Lopez, Vincent (Joseph) 1895-1975
Obituary 61-64
Lopez, Willebaldo
See Lopez, Willebaldo
Lopez de Mendoza, Inigo
See Santillana, Inigo Lopez de Mendoza, Marques de
Lopez-Morillas, Frances M. 1918- 149
Lopez-Morillas, Juan 1913-1997 .... CANR-1
Earlier sketch in CA 1-4R
Lopez Portillo (y Pacheco), Jose
1920-2004 129
Obituary 224
See also CLC 46
See also HW 1
Lopez-Rey, Jose 1905-1991 .... 37-40R
Lopez-Rey (y Arrojo), Manuel
1902-1987 .... CANR-85
Obituary 124
Earlier sketch in CA 29-32R
Lopez Suria, Violeta 1926- .... HW 1
Lopez Velarde, Ramon 1888-1921 ..... DLB 290
See also LAW
Lopez y Fuentes, Gregorio 1897(?)-1966 131
See also CLC 32
See also EWL 3
See also HW 1
Lopez Y Rivas, Gilberto 1943- 97-100
LoPiccolo, Joseph 1943- CANR-15
Earlier sketch in CA 81-84
Lo Pinto, Maria 1900(?)-1970
Obituary 104
Lopreato, Joseph 1928- 33-36R
Lopresti, Lucia (Longhi) 1895-1985 202
See also Banti, Anna
Lopresti, Robert 1954- 137
Lopshire, Robert M(artin) 1927- CANR-30
Earlier sketches in CA 5-8R, CANR-8
See also MAICYA 2
See also SATA 6
Loptson, Peter 1945- 223
Lopukhov, Fyodor V(asilevich) 1886-1973
Obituary 41-44R
Loquasto, Santo 1944- .... IDFW 3, 4
Lora, Josephine
See Alexander, Josephine
Lora, Ronald 1938- 41-44R
Lorac, E. C. R.
See Rivett, Edith Caroline
Loraine, Connie
See Reece, Colleen L.
Loraine, Philip
See Estridge, Robin
Loram, Ian Craig 1917- 5-8R
Loran, Martin
See Baxter, John
Lorand, (Alexander) Sandor
1893(?)-1987 .... CANR-85
Obituary 123
Earlier sketches in CAP-1, CA 9-10
Lorang, Ruth Mary
See Lorang, Sister Mary Corde
Lorang, Sister Mary Corde 1904-1978 49-52
Loranger, Jean-Aubert 1896-1942 181
See also DLB 92
Lorant, Stefan 1901-1997 .... CANR-9
Obituary 162
Earlier sketch in CA 5-8R
See also AITN 1
Lorayne, Harry 1926- 41-44R
Lorber, Judith 1931- 150
Lorberg, Aileen Dorothy 1910-1998 ... CANR-2
Earlier sketch in CA 5-8R
Lorbiecki, Marybeth 1959- 192
See also MAICYA 2
See also SATA 121
Lorca, Federico Garcia
See Garcia Lorca, Federico
See also DFS 4
See also EW 11
See also PFS 20
See also RGWL 2, 3
See also WP
Lorca de Tagle, Lillian 1914- CANR-91
Earlier sketch in CA 145
Lorch, Edgar R(aymond) 1907-1990
Obituary 131
Lorch, Robert Stuart 1925- 73-76
Lord, Albert Bates 1912-1991 .... CANR-85
Obituary 135
Earlier sketch in CA 103
Lord, Alison
See Ellis, Julie
Lord, Athena V. 1932- CANR-46
Earlier sketch in CA 109
See also SATA 39
Lord, Audre
See Lorde, Audre (Geraldine)
See also EWL 3
Lord, Beman 1924-1991 .... CANR-85
Obituary 135
Earlier sketch in CA 33-36R
See also SATA 5
See also SATA-Obit 69
Lord, Bette Bao 1938- CANR-79
Earlier sketches in CA 107, CANR-41
Interview in CA-107
See also AAL
See also BEST 90:3
See also BPFB 2
See also CLC 23
See also SATA 58
Lord, Chalfont
See Jones, (Alun) Arthur Gwynne
Lord, Charles R. 1950- 196
Lord, Clifford L(ee) 1912-1980 .... CANR-8
Obituary 102
Earlier sketch in CA 13-16R
Lord, David Thomas 200
Lord, Donald Charles 1930- 37-40R
Lord, Douglas
See Cooper, Douglas
Lord, (Doreen Mildred) Douglas 1904- . CAP-1
Earlier sketch in CA 13-14
See also SATA 12
Lord, Eda 1907-1976
Obituary 104
Lord, Edith Elizabeth 1907-1989 .... 41-44R
Lord, Eugene Hodgdon 1894-1981 .... 1-4R
Lord, Francis A(lfred) 1911- 17-20R
Lord, Frederic Mather 1912-2000 .... 37-40R
Obituary 187
Lord, Gabrielle 1946- 106
Lord, George deF(orest) 1919- CANR-25
Earlier sketches in CA 65-68, CANR-10
Lord, Graham 1943- CANR-92
Earlier sketches in CA 53-56, CANR-4
Lord, James 1922- 226
Lord, Jeffrey
See Ellis, Julie and
Green, Roland (James) and
Nelson, R(adell) Faraday
Lord, Jeremy
See Redman, Ben Ray
Lord, Jess Rollin 1911- 65-68
Lord, John Keast 1818-1872 .... DLB 99
Lord, John Vernon 1939- 53-56
See also SATA 21
Lord, M(ary) G(race) 1955- 127
Lord, Mary Stinson Pillsbury 1904-1978 . 85-88
Obituary 81-84
Lord, Nancy
See Titus, Eve
Lord, Nancy J. 1952- 204
Lord, Patricia C. 1927-1988 .... SATA-Obit 58
Lord, Peter 1953(?)- 201
Lord, Phillips H.
See Yolen, Will(iam Hyatt)
Lord, Priscilla Sawyer 1908-1991 .... 9-12R
Lord, Robert (Needham) 1945-1992 61-64
Lord, Shirley
See Rosenthal, Shirley Lord
Lord, Tom
See Braun, Matt
Lord, Tony 1949- 225
Lord, Vivian
See Strother, Pat Wallace
Lord, Walter 1917-2002 .... CANR-22
Obituary 205
Earlier sketches in CA 1-4R, CANR-5
See also SATA 3
Lord, William Jackson, Jr. 1926- 5-8R
Lord Altrincham
See Grigg, John (Edward Poynder)
Lordan, (Ellenora) Beth 1948- CANR-93
Earlier sketch in CA 130
Lord Astor of Hever
See Astor, Gavin
Lord Auch
See Bataille, Georges
Lord Beloff
See Beloff, Max
Lord Beveridge
See Beveridge, William (Henry)
Lord Blake
See Blake, Robert (Norman William)
Lord Boyle of Handsworth
See Boyle, Edward Charles Gurney
Lord Brooke
See Greville, Fulke
Lord Butler of Saffron Walden
See Butler, Richard Austen
Lord Byron
See Byron, George Gordon (Noel)
Lord Chalfont
See Jones, (Alun) Arthur Gwynne
Lord Crowther-Hunt
See Crowther-Hunt, Norman Crowther
Lord Denning
See Denning, Alfred Thompson
Lord Denning
See Denning, Alfred Thompson
Lord Dunsany
See Dunsany, Edward John Moreton Drax Plunkett
Lorde, Audre (Geraldine)
1934-1992 .... CANR-82
Obituary 142
Earlier sketches in CA 25-28R, CANR-16, 26, 46
See also Domini, Rey and
Lord, Audre
See also AFAW 1, 2
See also BLC 2
See also BW 1, 3
See also CLC 18, 71
See also CP 2
See also DA3
See also DAM MULT, POET
See also DLB 41
See also FW
See also MAL 5
See also MTCW 1, 2
See also MTFW 2005
See also PC 12
See also PFS 16
See also RGAL 4
Lorde, Diana
See Reno, Dawn E(laine)
Lord Eccles
See Eccles, David (McAdam)
Lord Energlyn
See Evans, William David
Lord Evans of Hungershall
See Evans, Benjamin Ifor
Lord Francis Williams
See Williams, Edward Francis
Lord George-Brown
See George-Brown, George Alfred
Lord Gillmore of Thamesfield
See Gillmore, David (Howe)
Lord Hailsham of St. Marylebone
See Hogg, Quintin McGarel
Lord Home
See Home, Alexander Frederick (Douglas-)
Lord Houghton
See Milnes, Richard Monckton
Lord Howe of Aberavon
See Howe, (Richard Edward) Geoffrey
Lordi, Robert J(oseph) 1923- 89-92
Lord Jeffrey
See Jeffrey, Francis
Lord Kames
See Home, Henry

Cumulative Index 359 Lovelace

Lord Killanin
See Morris, Michael
Lord Longford
See Pakenham, Francis Aungier
Lord Mancroft
See Mancroft, Stormont Mancroft Samuel
Lord Moran
See Wilson, (Richard) John (McMoran)
Lord Mountbatten
See Mountbatten, Louis (Francis Albert Victor Nicholas)
Lord Nolan
See Nolan, Michael Patrick
Lord Pakenham
See Pakenham, Francis Aungier
Lord Rhyl
See Birch, (Evelyn) Nigel (Chetwode)
Lord Roll of Ipsden
See Roll, Eric
Lord Rothschild
See Rothschild, Nathaniel Mayer Victor
Lords, Traci (Elizabeth) 1968- 222
Lord Snowdon
See Armstrong-Jones, Antony (Charles Robert)
Lord Strange
See Drummond, John
Lord Thomas
See Thomas, (William) Miles (Webster)
Lord Windlesham
See Hennessy, David James George
Lord Young of Darlington
See Lord Young of Darlington
Loreaux, Nichol .... CLC 65
Loree, Kate (Lambie) 1920- 21-24R
Lorek, Daniel N. 1958(?)-1983
Obituary 110
Loren, Sophia 1936- 142
Brief entry 111
Lorence, James J(ohn) 1937- CANR-119
Earlier sketch in CA 148
Lorens, M. K.
See Keilstrup, Margaret
Lorenz, Albert 1941- 186
See also SATA 115
Lorenz, Alfred Lawrence 1937- 45-48
Lorenz, Edward N(orton) 1917- 162
Lorenz, J(ames) D(ouglas) 1938- 102
Lorenz, Konrad Zacharias
1903-1989 .... CANR-61
Obituary 128
Earlier sketches in CA 61-64, CANR-35
See also MTCW 1, 2
Lorenz, Lee (Sharp) 1932- 150
Brief entry 124
See also SATA-Brief 39
Lorenz, Sarah E.
See Winston, Sarah
Lorenzen, Coral Elsie 1925-1988 113
Lorenzen, David N(eal) 1940- 33-36R
Lorenzini, Carlo 1826-1890
See Collodi, Carlo
See also MAICYA 1, 2
See also SATA 29, 100
Lorenzo, Carol Lee 1939- CANR-50
Earlier sketch in CA 53-56
Lorenzo, Heberto Padilla
See Padilla (Lorenzo), Heberto
Lorenzo, Orestes 148
Loreto, Charles A. 1903(?)-1990
Obituary 132
Loria, Jeffrey H. 1940- 17-20R
Lorie, James Hirsch 1922- 103
Lorig, Kate R. 1942- 117
Loriga, Ray 1967- 233
Lorimer, Frank 1894-1985
Obituary 116
Lorimer, George Horace 1867-1937 183
See also DLB 91
Lorimer, James 1942- 123
Lorimer, Janet 1941- .... SATA 60
Lorimer, Lawrence T(heodore) 1941- .. CANR-6
Earlier sketch in CA 57-60
Lorimer, Sara 1970- 230
Lorimer, Scat
See Fuentes, Martha Ayers
Loring, Ann 1915- 97-100
Loring, Emilie (Baker) 1864(?)-1951 .... RHW
See also SATA 51
Loring, J. M.
See Warner-Crozetti, R(uth G.)
Loring, Murray 1917-1992 .... CANR-22
Earlier sketch in CA 45-48
Loring, Peter
See Shellabarger, Samuel
Lorini, Alessandra 1949- 188
Lorion, R(aymond) P(aul) 1946- 85-88
Loris
See Hofmannsthal, Hugo von
Loris, Joseph James 1943-1987
Obituary 125
Lorkowski, Thomas V(incent) 1950- .... SATA 92
Lorkowski, Tom
See Lorkowski, Thomas V(incent)
Lorme, Anna
See Markowa, Nina Alexandrovna
Lornquest, Olaf
See Rips, Ervine M(ilton)
Lorrah, Jean CANR-41
Earlier sketches in CA 103, CANR-19
Lorraine, Paul
See Fearn, John Russell and Glasby, John S.
Lorraine, Walter (Henry) 1929- .... SATA 16
Lorrance, Arleen 1939- 85-88
Lorrimer, Claire CANR-42
See also Clark, Patricia Denise
See also RHW
Lorsch, Jay William 1932- 97-100
Lorsch, Susan E. 1950- 116
Lortie, Alain 1955- CANR-141
See also Sernine, Daniel
Lortie, Dan C(lement) 1926- 115
Lortz, Richard 1917-1980 .... CANR-11
Obituary 102
Earlier sketch in CA 57-60
Lorusso, Edward N. S. 1949- 133
Lorwin, Val Rogin 1907-1982
Obituary 111
Lory, Robert (Edward) 1936- CANR-75
Earlier sketches in CA 53-56, CANR-10
See also HGG
Los, George
See Amabile, George
Losada (Goya), Jose Manuel 1962- 168
Losang, Rato Khyongla Ngawang 1923- .. 81-84
Los Bros Hernandez
See Hernandez, Jaime
Losch, Richard R. 1933- 208
Lose, M(argaret) Phyllis 1925- CANR-18
Earlier sketch in CA 101
Loseff, Lev 1937- 202
Losev, S(ergei) A(ndreevich) 1927-1988
Obituary 126
Losey, Joseph (Walton) 1909-1984
Obituary 113
Losey, Patricia 1930- 144
Loshak, David (Leslie Ivor) 1933- 41-44R
Loshitzky, Yosefa 158
Losoncy, Lawrence J. 1941- CANR-32
Earlier sketches in CA 37-40R, CANR-14
Losoncy, Mary Jan 1942- 37-40R
los Reyes, Gabriel de
See de los Reyes, Gabriel
los Rios, Francisco Giner de
See Giner de los Rios, Francisco
Loss, Joan 1933- .... SATA 11
Loss, Louis 1914-1997 .... CANR-2
Obituary 163
Earlier sketch in CA 5-8R
Loss, Richard (Archibald John) 1938- 65-68
Losse, Deborah N(ichols) 1944- 147
Lossing, Benson J. 1813-1891 .... DLB 30
Lossky, Andrew 1917-1997 93-96
Lossy, Rella 1934- 81-84
Lotarev, Igor' Vasil'evich 1887-1941
See Severianin, Igor'
Lotchin, Roger W. 1935- 139
Loth, Calder 1943- 73-76
Loth, David 1899-1988 .... CANR-85
Obituary 125
Earlier sketches in CA 1-4R, CANR-1
Lothar, Ernst 1890-1974 185
See also DLB 81
Lothian, John Maule 1896-1970 .... CAP-1
Earlier sketch in CA 9-10
Lothringen, Geza Louis Eusebius Gebhard Ralphael Albert Maria
See von Habsburg(-Lothringen), Geza Louis Eusebius Gebhard Ralphael Albert Maria
Lothrop, Harriet Mulford Stone
1844-1924 204
See also DLB 42
See also MAICYA 2
See also MAICYAS 1
See also SATA 20
Lothstein, Leslie Martin 1942- 126
Loti, Pierre
See Viaud, (Louis Marie) Julien
See also DLB 123
See also GFL 1789 to the Present
See also TCLC 11
Lott, Arnold S(amuel) 1912-1992 ..... CANR-46
Obituary 139
Earlier sketch in CA 13-16R
Lott, Bret 1958- 126
See also CSW
Lott, Clarinda Harriss
See Harriss, Clarinda
Lott, Davis Newton 1913- CANR-10
Earlier sketch in CA 21-24R
Lott, Emmeline .... DLB 166
Lott, Eric 1959- 149
Lott, Milton 1919-1996 .... CANR-64
Earlier sketch in CA 17-20R
See also TCWW 1, 2
Lott, Monroe
See Howard, Edwin
Lott, Robert F(ugene) 1926- CANR-4
Earlier sketch in CA 5-8R
Lott, Tim 1956- 195
Lottich, Kenneth V(erne) 1904- 17-20R
Lottie
See Grimke, Charlotte L(ottie) Forten
Lottinville, Savoie 1906-1997 105
Lottman, Eileen 1927- CANR-56
Earlier sketches in CA 57-60, CANR-12, 30
Lottman, Herbert R. 1927- CANR-128
Earlier sketches in CA 105, CANR-71, 121
Interview in CA-105
See also CAAS 12
Lottor, Elisa (Sandra) 1942- 230
Lottridge, Celia Barker 1936- CANR-141
Earlier sketch in CA 184
See also SATA 112, 157
LoTurco, Laura 1963- .... SATA 84
Lotz, Anne Graham 1948- CANR-141
Earlier sketch in CA 165
Lotz, David W(alter) 1937-
Brief entry 115
Lotz, James Robert 1929- CANR-14
Earlier sketches in CA 37-40R, CANR-31
Lotz, Jim
See Lotz, James Robert
Lotz, John 1913-1973
Obituary 45-48
Lotz, Wolfgang 1912-1981 .... CANR-34
Earlier sketch in CA 81-84
See also SATA 65
Lotze, Dieter P(aul) 1933- 132
Lou, Henri
See Andreas-Salome, Lou
Loubere, Leo A(lbert) 1923- 130
Louca, Francisco 1956- 218
Louch, A(lfred) R(ichard) 1927- 17-20R
Louchheim, Kathleen 1903-1991 ..... CANR-85
Obituary 133
Earlier sketch in CA 21-24R
Louchheim, Katie
See Louchheim, Kathleen
Loucks, William Negele 1899-1983 .... 1-4R
Loud, G(raham) A(nthony) 1953- 136
Loud, Pat(ricia Russell) 1926- 184
Brief entry 114
Loud, Patricia C(ummings) 135
Louden, Bruce 1954- 191
Louden, J(ames) Keith 1905-1994 132
Louden, Robert B. 1953- CANR-91
Earlier sketch in CA 139
Louden, Robert Stuart 1912- 5-8R
Loudon, David L. 1944- 142
Loudon, Irvine 1924- CANR-116
Earlier sketches in CA 126, CANR-53
Louganis, Greg(ory Efthimios) 1960- 189
Lougee, Robert Wayne 1919- 5-8R
Loughary, John W(illiam) 1930- 41-44R
Loughery, John 1953- 138
Loughhead, LaRue A(lvin) 1927- 61-64
Loughlin, Caroline 1940- 126
Loughlin, James 1948- 153
Loughlin, Richard L(awrence)
1907-1997 .... CANR-21
Obituary 171
Earlier sketch in CA 45-48
Loughmiller, Campbell 1906-1993 ... CANR-13
Earlier sketch in CA 77-80
Loughran, Bernice B(ingham) 1919- 5-8R
Loughran, Peter 1938- 25-28R
Lougy, Robert E. 1940- 118
Louie, Ai-Ling 1949- 112
See also SATA 40
See also SATA-Brief 34
Louie, Andrea 1966- 152
Louie, David Wong 1954- CANR-120
Earlier sketch in CA 139
See also CLC 70
Louis, Adrian C. 223
See also NNAL
Louis, Arthur M(urray) 1938- 106
Louis, Cindi 1962- 208
Louis, David
See Carroll, David L.
Louis, Debbie 1945- 29-32R
Louis, Father M.
See Merton, Thomas (James)
Louis, J(ack) C(harles), Jr. 1949- 105
Louis, Jean 1907- .... IDFW 3, 4
Louis, Joe
See Barrow, Joseph Louis
Louis, Murray 1926- 126
Louis, Pat
See Francis, Dorothy Brenner
Louis, Paul P(anickavede) 1918- CANR-12
Earlier sketch in CA 61-64
Louis, Pierre(-Felix) 1870-1925
Brief entry 105
See also Louys, Pierre
Louis, Ray Baldwin 1949- 65-68
Louis, Tobi 1940- 57-60
Louis, Valerie
See Salvatore, Diane
Louisburgh, Sheila Burnford
See Burnford, Sheila (Philip Cochrane Every)
Louise, Anita
See Riggio, Anita
Louise, Heidi
See Erdrich, (Karen) Louise
Louise, Regina 224
Louisell, David William 1913-1977 ... CANR-4
Obituary 73-76
Earlier sketch in CA 1-4R
Louiso, Todd 1970- 213
Loukes, Harold 1912- 17-20R
Loulan, JoAnn 1948- .... GLL 2
Lounsberry, Barbara 1946- 138
Lounsbury, Carl (Reavis) 1952- 189
Lounsbury, Myron O. 1940- 37-40R
Lounsbury, Ruth Ozeki
See Ozeki, Ruth L.
Lounsbury, Thomas R(aynesford)
1838-1915 182
See also DLB 71
Loup, Jacques 1942- 120
Lourdeaux, Lee 1951- 136
Louria, Donald B(ruce) 1928- 107
Lourie, Dick 1937- 33-36R
Lourie, Eugene 1905-1991 .... IDFW 3, 4
Lourie, Helen
See Storr, Catherine (Cole)
Lourie, Peter (King) 1952- CANR-121
Earlier sketch in CA 137
See also SATA 82, 142
Lourie, Richard 1940- CANR-89
Brief entry 125
Earlier sketch in CA 131
Interview in CA-131
Loury, Glenn C(artman) 1948- CANR-109
Earlier sketch in CA 152
Lousley, J(ob) E(dward) 1907-1976
Obituary 104
Louthan, Robert 1951- 109
Louv, Richard 1949- 154
Louviere, Vernon Ray 1920-1986 108
Louvish, Misha 1909- CANR-1
Earlier sketch in CA 45-48
Louvish, Simon 1947- CANR-98
Earlier sketch in CA 121
Louw, Nicholaas Petrus Van Wyk 1906-1970
Obituary 89-92
Loux, Ann Kimble 1943- 168
Loux, Michael Joseph 1942- 103
Louys, Pierre
See Louis, Pierre(-Felix)
See also DLB 123
See also GFL 1789 to the Present
Lovaas, O(le) Ivar 1927- CANR-22
Earlier sketch in CA 45-48
Lovasik, Lawrence George
1913-1986 .... CANR-20
Earlier sketches in CA 1-4R, CANR-1
Lovato, Charles F(rederick) 1937-1987 225
Lovatt, Edwin A(lbert) 1944- 119
Love, Alan C(arson) 1937- 53-56
Love, (Kathleen) Ann 1947- 148
See also SATA 79
Love, Barbara J. 1937- 37-40R
Love, Charles (Ross) 1932- 25-28R
Love, Charles K.
See Swicegood, Thomas L. P.
Love, D. Anne 1949- CANR-127
Earlier sketches in CA 149, CANR-103
See also SATA 96, 145
Love, Douglas 1967- 156
See also SATA 92
Love, Edmund G(eorge) 1912-1990 .. CANR-85
Obituary 132
Earlier sketches in CA 1-4R, CANR-4
Love, Glen A. 1932- 29-32R
Love, Harold (Halford Russell) 1937- 190
Love, Iris Cornelia 1933- 29-32R
Love, Janet
See Ferrier, Janet Mackay
Love, Jean O. 1920- 29-32R
Love, Joseph L., (Jr.) 1938- 29-32R
Love, Katherine (Isabel) 1907- .... SATA 3
Love, Kathy 236
Love, Kennett 1924- 77-80
Love, Philip H(ampton) 1905-1977 77-80
Obituary 73-76
Love, Richard S. 1923- 81-84
Love, Ronald S(cott) 1955- 217
Love, Sandra (Weller) 1940- CANR-11
Earlier sketch in CA 69-72
See also SATA 26
Love, Susan M. 168
Love, Sydney F(rancis) 1923- 81-84
Love, Thomas Teel 1931- 13-16R
Love, William F. 1932- 132
Love-Ananda, Da
See Jones, Franklin Albert
Lovecraft, H(oward) P(hillips)
1890-1937 .... CANR-106
Brief entry 104
Earlier sketch in CA 133
See also AAYA 14
See also BPFB 2
See also DA3
See also DAM POP
See also HGG
See also MTCW 1, 2
See also MTFW 2005
See also RGAL 4
See also SCFW 1, 2
See also SFW 4
See also SSC 3, 52
See also SUFW
See also TCLC 4, 22
Love Doctor, The
See Tessina, Tina B.
Lovegrove, J. M. H.
See Lovegrove, James (Matthew Henry)
Lovegrove, James (Matthew Henry) 1965- .. 193
See also HGG
Lovegrove, Philip
See Ray, John (Philip)
Lovehill, C. B.
See Beaumont, Charles
Loveid, Cecilie (Meyer) 1951- 194
See also CWW 2
See also DLB 297
Loveid, Cecilie 1951-
See Loveid, Cecilie (Meyer)
Lovejoy, Arthur O. 1873-1962 .... DLB 270
Lovejoy, Bahija Fattuhi 1914-1999 .... 5-8R
Lovejoy, Clarence Earle 1894-1974 .... 5-8R
Obituary 45-48
Lovejoy, David Sherman 1919-1999 103
Lovejoy, Elijah P(arish) 1940- 45-48
Lovejoy, Jack 1937- CANR-82
Earlier sketches in CA 114, CANR-35
See also SATA 116
Lovejoy, L(awrence) C(lark) 1893-1971 ..... 1-4R
Obituary 176
Lovejoy, Paul E(llsworth) 1943- 115
Lovejoy, Thomas E. 1941- 143
Lovelace, Delos Wheeler 1894-1967 .... 5-8R
Obituary 25-28R
See also SATA 7
Lovelace, Earl 1935- CANR-114
Earlier sketches in CA 77-80, CANR-41, 72
See also BW 2
See also CD 5, 6
See also CDWLB 3
See also CLC 51
See also CN 1, 2, 3, 4, 5, 6, 7
See also DLB 125
See also EWL 3
See also MTCW 1

Lovelace, Linda
See Marchiano, Linda Boreman
Lovelace, Marc Hoyle 1920- ... 37-40R
Lovelace, Maud Hart 1892-1980 ... CANR-79
Obituary ... 104
Earlier sketches in CA 5-8R, CANR-39
See also CWRI 5
See also FW
See also MAICYA 1, 2
See also SATA 2
See also SATA-Obit 23
Lovelace, Merline (A.) 1946- ... CANR-106
Earlier sketch in CA 158
Lovelace, Richard 1618-1657 ... BRW 2
See also DLB 131
See also EXPP
See also PAB
See also RGEL 2
Lovelace, Richard Franz 1930- ... 101
Loveland, Anne C(arol) 1938- ... CANR-56
Brief entry ... 114
Earlier sketch in CA 126
Loveless, E(dward) E. 1919- ... 57-60
Lovell, Ann 1933- ... CANR-41
Earlier sketches in CA 97-100, CANR-19
Lovell, (Alfred Charles) Bernard
1913- ... CANR-6
Earlier sketch in CA 13-16R
Lovell, Colin Rhys 1917-1969 ... 5-8R
Lovell, Ernest J(ames), Jr.
1918-1975 ... CANR-85
Obituary ... 103
Earlier sketch in CA 1-4R
Lovell, Glenville 1955- ... 166
See also BW 3
Lovell, Ingraham
See Bacon, Josephine Dodge (Daskam)
Lovell, John, Jr. 1907-1974 ... CAP-2
Obituary ... 49-52
Earlier sketch in CA 33-36
Lovell, John P(hilip) 1932- ... CANR-15
Earlier sketch in CA 29-32R
Lovell, Marc
See McShane, Mark
Lovell, Mark 1934- ... CANR-8
Earlier sketch in CA 61-64
Lovell, Mary S(ybilla) 1941- ... CANR-119
Earlier sketch in CA 140
Lovell, Michael Christopher 1930- ... 33-36R
Lovell, Ronald P. 1937- ... CANR-13
Earlier sketch in CA 73-76
Lovell, Stanley P(latt) 1890-1976 ... 5-8R
Lovell, Stephen ... 223
Lovelock, J. E.
See Lovelock, James (Ephraim)
Lovelock, James (Ephraim) 1919- ... 123
Loveman, Brian E(lliot) 1944- ... CANR-99
Earlier sketches in CA 89-92, CANR-17
Loveman, Samuel 1885(?)-1976
Obituary ... 65-68
Lovenstein, Meno 1909-1993 ... CANR-3
Earlier sketch in CA 5-8R
Lovequist, Gwendlelynn
See Stafford, Linda (Crying Wind)
Lover, Samuel 1797-1868 ... DLB 159, 190
See also RGEL 2
Loverde, Lorin (James Bell) 1943- ... 45-48
LoVerde, Mary ... 229
Loveridge, Ronald O. 1938- ... 33-36R
Lovering, Joseph Paul 1921- ... 104
Loverseed, Amanda (Jane) 1965- ... 142
See also SATA 75
Lovesey, Peter (Harmer) 1936- ... CANR-99
Earlier sketches in CA 41-44R, CANR-28, 59
See also CMW 4
See also DLB 87
See also MTCW 1
Lovestrand, Harold 1925- ... 21-24R
Lovett, A(lbert) W(inston) 1944- ... 124
Lovett, Clara Maria 1939- ... CANR-16
Earlier sketch in CA 93-96
Lovett, Gabriel H(arry) 1921- ... 65-68
Lovett, Margaret (Rose) 1915- ... 61-64
See also SATA 22
Lovett, Robert W. 1913-1996 ... 33-36R
Lovett, Sarah 1953- ... 200
Loveyouth, Willis
See Homer, Winslow
Lovin, Clifford R(amsey) 1937- ... 37-40R
Lovin, Roger Robert 1941- ... CANR-6
Earlier sketch in CA 57-60
Lovinescu, Eugen 1881-1943 ... CDWLB 4
See also DLB 220
See also EWL 3
Loving, Jerome MacNeill 1941- ... CANR-56
Earlier sketches in CA 112, CANR-30
Lovins, Amory B(loch) 1947- ... CANR-32
Earlier sketch in CA 69-72
Lovins, L. Hunter 1950- ... 191
Lovisi, Gary 1952- ... 195
Lovoll, Odd Sverre 1934- ... CANR-7
Earlier sketch in CA 61-64
Lovoos, Janice
See Garbutt, Janice (D.) Lovoos
Low, Alfred D(avid) 1913- ... 33-36R
Low, Alice 1926- ... CANR-141
Earlier sketches in CA 61-64, CANR-8
See also SATA 11, 76, 156
Low, Ann Marie 1912-1998 ... 118
Low, Anthony 1935- ... CANR-13
Earlier sketch in CA 37-40R
Low, D(onald) A(nthony) 1927- ... 73-76
Low, David (Alexander Cecil) 1891-1963
Obituary ... 89-92
Low, Dorothy Mackie
See Low, Lois Dorothea
Low, Elizabeth Hammond 1898-1991 ... CAP-2
Earlier sketch in CA 19-20
See also SATA 5
Low, Francis 1893-1972
Obituary ... 115
Low, Gardner
See Rodda, Charles
Low, George M(ichael) 1926-1984
Obituary ... 113
Low, Ivy
See Litvinov, Ivy
Low, Joseph 1911- ... CANR-49
Earlier sketches in CA 85-88, CANR-15
See also MAICYA 1, 2
See also SATA 14
Low, Kathleen ... 153
Low, Lisa 1952- ... 204
Low, Lois Dorothea 1916- ... CANR-15
Earlier sketch in CA 37-40R
Low, Rachael 1923- ... 125
Low, Samuel 1765-(?) ... DLB 37
Low, Setha M. 1948- ... CANR-138
Earlier sketch in CA 156
Low, Victor N. 1931- ... CANR-1
Earlier sketch in CA 49-52
Lowachee, Karin 1973- ... 223
Lowam, Ron
See Tubb, E(dwin) C(harles)
Lowance, Mason I(ra), Jr. 1938- ... 57-60
Lowbury, Edward (Joseph Lister)
1913-2001(?) ... CANR-81
Earlier sketches in CA 29-32R, CANR-12, 29, 54
See also CP 1, 2, 3, 4, 5, 6, 7
Lowden, Desmond 1937- ... 53-56
Lowder, Jerry 1932- ... 65-68
Lowder, Paul D(aniel) 1929- ... 93-96
Lowdermilk, W(alter) C(lay) 1888-1974
Obituary ... 49-52
Lowe, A(lfred) Mifflin 1948- ... 128
Lowe, Alfonso
See Loewenthal, L(eonard) J(oseph) A(lfonso)
Lowe, Ben(no P.) 1956- ... 163
Lowe, C(arrington) Marshall 1930- ... 29-32R
Lowe, Carl 1949- ... 125
Lowe; Corke
See Pepper, Choral
Lowe, David A(llan) 1948- ... CANR-29
Earlier sketch in CA 111
Lowe, David Garrard 1933- ... CANR-113
Earlier sketches in CA 104, CANR-22, 47
Lowe, Donald M. 1928- ... 21-24R
Lowe, E. J. 1950- ... 189
Lowe, Gordon R(obb) 1928- ... 49-52
Lowe, Gustav E. 1901-1977 ... CAP-2
Earlier sketch in CA 23-24
Lowe, James 1941- ... 151
Lowe, Jay, Jr.
See Loeper, John J(oseph)
Lowe, Jeanne R. 1924(?)-1972
Obituary ... 33-36R
Lowe, John (Evelyn) 1928- ... CANR-103
Earlier sketches in CA 123, CANR-49
Lowe, John W(esley) G(uinn) 1946- ... 121
Lowe, Judah
See Lyon, Christopher (Leslie)
Lowe, Marjorie G(riffiths) Lowe 1909- ... 1-4R
Lowe, Michael Ellenwood
See Lowe, Mick
Lowe, Mick 1947- ... 165
Lowe, Pardee 1904- ... AAL
Lowe, Richard Barrett 1902-1972
Obituary ... 33-36R
Lowe, Richard G. 1942- ... CANR-49
Earlier sketch in CA 123
Lowe, Robert W. 1910- ... CAP-1
Earlier sketch in CA 13-14
Lowe, Roberta (Justine) 1940- ... CANR-24
Earlier sketches in CA 61-64, CANR-8
Lowe, Rodney 1946- ... CANR-95
Earlier sketch in CA 146
Lowe, Sam Jack
See Rummel, (Louis) Jack(son)
Lowe, Sarah M. 1956- ... 153
Lowe, Stephen 1947- ... 231
See also CBD
See also CD 5, 6
Lowe, Stephen R(obert) 1966- ... 190
Lowe, Sue Davidson 1922- ... 118
Lowe, Victor (Augustus) 1907-1988 ... CANR-85
Obituary ... 127
Earlier sketch in CA 17-20R
Lowe, Victoria Lincoln
See Lincoln, Victoria
Lowe, Wendy
See Besmann, Wendy Lowe
Lowe, William T(ebbs) 1929- ... 73-76
Lowe-Evans, Mary 1941- ... 145
Lowell, Amy 1874-1925 ... 151
Brief entry ... 104
See also AAYA 57
See also AMW
See also DAM POET
See also DLB 54, 140
See also EWL 3
See also EXPP
See also LMFS 2
See also MAL 5
See also MAWW
See also MTCW 2
See also MTFW 2005
See also PC 13
See also RGAL 4
See also TCLC 1, 8
See also TUS
Lowell, C. Stanley 1909- ... CANR-6
Earlier sketch in CA 5-8R
Lowell, Elizabeth
See Maxwell, Ann (Elizabeth)
Lowell, James Russell 1819-1891 ... AMWS 1
See also CDALB 1640-1865
See also DLB 1, 11, 64, 79, 189, 235
See also RGAL 4
Lowell, Jon 1938- ... 97-100
Interview in ... CA-97-100
Lowell, Juliet 1901-1998 ... CANR-1
Earlier sketch in CA 1-4R
Lowell, Mildred Hawksworth
1905-1974 ... CAP-2
Earlier sketch in CA 33-36
Lowell, Robert (Traill Spence, Jr.)
1917-1977 ... CANR-60
Obituary ... 73-76
Earlier sketches in CA 9-12R, CANR-26
See also CABS 2
See also AMW
See also AMWC 2
See also AMWR 2
See also CAD
See also CDALBS
See also CLC 1, 2, 3, 4, 5, 8, 9, 11, 15, 37, 124
See also CP 1, 2
See also DA
See also DA3
See also DAB
See also DAC
See also DAM MST, NOV
See also DLB 5, 169
See also EWL 3
See also MAL 5
See also MTCW 1, 2
See also MTFW 2005
See also PAB
See also PC 3
See also PFS 6, 7
See also RGAL 4
See also WLC
See also WP
Lowell, Susan 1950- ... CANR-106
Earlier sketch in CA 126
See also SATA 81, 127
Lowell, Tex
See Turner, George E(ugene)
Lowen, Alexander 1910- ... 17-20R
Lowenberg, Anton D(avid) 1957- ... CANR-135
Earlier sketch in CA 144
Lowenberg, Carlton 1919-1996 ... 146
Lowenberg, Susan 1957- ... 146
Lowenfeld, Andreas F(rank) 1930- ... CANR-8
Earlier sketch in CA 61-64
Lowenfeld, Berthold 1901-1994 ... 17-20R
Lowenfels, Walter 1897-1976 ... CANR-3
Obituary ... 65-68
Earlier sketch in CA 1-4R
See also CP 1, 2
See also DLB 4
Lowenfish, Lee (Elihu) 1942- ... 106
Lowenherz, David H. 1951- ... 213
Lowenkopf, Shelly A(lan) 1931- ... CANR-4
Earlier sketch in CA 49-52
Lowenrosen, Richard
See Krooth, Richard
Lowens, Irving 1916-1983 ... CANR-85
Obituary ... 111
Earlier sketches in CA 17-20R, CANR-11
Lowenstein, Dyno 1914-1996 ... 9-12R
See also SATA 6
Lowenstein, Michael W. 1942- ... 154
Lowenstein, Ralph Lynn 1930- ... 17-20R
Lowenstein, Sallie 1949- ... 188
See also SATA 116
Lowenstein, Sharon R. 1937- ... 122
Lowenstein, Tom 1941- ... 93-96
Lowenthal, Abraham F(rederic) 1941- ... 127
Lowenthal, Cynthia J. 1952- ... CANR-127
Earlier sketch in CA 145
Lowenthal, David 1923- ... CANR-69
Earlier sketches in CA 115, CANR-41
Lowenthal, Gary T(obias) ... 231
Lowenthal, Leo 1900-1993 ... CANR-46
Obituary ... 140
Earlier sketches in CA 1-4R, CANR-5, 20
Lowenthal, Marjorie Fiske
See Fiske, Marjorie
Lowenthal, Michael (Francis)
1969- ... CANR-115
Earlier sketch in CA 150
See also CLC 119
Lower, Arthur R(eginald) M(arsden)
1889-1988 ... CANR-85
Obituary ... 124
Earlier sketches in CA 9-12R, CANR-4
Lower, J(oseph) Arthur 1907- ... 21-24R
Lowerre, Susan (K.) 1962- ... 134
Lowery, Bruce Arlie 1931- ... CANR-1
Earlier sketch in CA 1-4R
Lowery, Daniel L(orne) 1929- ... 113
Lowery, James L(incoln), Jr. 1932- ... 45-48
Lowery, Linda 1949- ... CANR-135
Earlier sketch in CA 141
See also SATA 74, 151
Lowery, Lynn 1949- ... 93-96
Lowery, Robert G. 1941- ... 130
Lowery, Thomas V(incent) 1919- ... 37-40R
Lowi, Theodore J(ay) 1931- ... 37-40R
Lowidski, Witt
See Clinton, (Lloyd) D(eWitt)
Lowing, Anne
See Geach, Christine
Lowinsky, Edward E(lias)
1908-1985 ... CANR-85
Obituary ... 117
Earlier sketches in CAP-1, CA 13-14
Lowith, Karl
See Loewith, Karl
Lowitz, Anson C. 1901(?)-1978 ... 81-84
Obituary ... 73-76
See also SATA 18
Lowitz, Leza 1962- ... CAAS 26
Lowitz, Sadyebeth Heath 1901-1969 ... 85-88
See also SATA 17
Lowman, Charles LeRoy 1880(?)-1977
Obituary ... 69-72
Lowman, Eleanor B(arry) 1906-1983
Obituary ... 110
Lowman, Josephine (Cherry) 1899(?)-1983
Obituary ... 110
Lowman, Margaret D(alzell) 1953- ... 179
Lowman, Meg
See Lowman, Margaret D(alzell)
Lowndes, Betty 1929- ... 61-64
Lowndes, George Alfred Norman 1897- ... 5-8R
Lowndes, Marie Adelaide (Belloc) 1868-1947
Brief entry ... 107
See also CMW 4
See also DLB 70
See also RHW
See also TCLC 12
Lowndes, Natalya
See Symmons, Sarah
Lowndes, Robert A(ugustine) W(ard)
1916-1998 ... CANR-78
Obituary ... 174
Brief entry ... 113
Earlier sketch in CA 128
See also SATA 117
See also SFW 4
Lowndes, William 1914- ... 13-16R
Lowndes, William Thomas
1798-1843 ... DLB 184
Lownes, Humphrey fl. 1590-1630 ... DLB 170
Lowney, Paul Benjamin 1922- ... CANR-93
Earlier sketches in CA 93-96, CANR-17
Lowrey, Janette Sebring 1892-1986 ... 13-16R
See also MAICYA 2
See also SATA 43
Lowrey, Kathleen 1943- ... 57-60
Lowrey, P(errin) H(olmes) 1923-1965 ... CAP-1
Earlier sketch in CA 11-12
Lowrey, Sara 1897-1991 ... 17-20R
Lowrie, Donald A(lexander) 1889-1974 ... 5-8R
Obituary ... 53-56
Lowrie, Jean E(lizabeth) 1918- ... 45-48
Lowry, Albert J(ames) 1927- ... 129
Brief entry ... 118
Lowry, Bates 1923-2004 ... CANR-1
Obituary ... 225
Earlier sketch in CA 1-4R
Lowry, Betty (T.) 1927- ... 217
Lowry, Beverly (Fey) 1938- ... 101
See also CSW
Lowry, Bullitt 1936- ... 165
Lowry, Charles W(esley) 1905-1998 ... 37-40R
Lowry, Fern 1896(?)-1983
Obituary ... 111
Lowry, Joan (Catlow) 1911- ... 13-16R
Lowry, Lois (Hammersburg) 1937- ... 200
Earlier sketches in CA 69-72, CANR-13, 43, 70, 131
Interview in ... CANR-13
Autobiographical Essay in ... 200
See also AAYA 5, 32
See also BYA 4, 6, 14
See also CLR 6, 46, 72
See also DLB 52
See also JRDA
See also MAICYA 1, 2
See also MAICYAS 1
See also MTCW 2
See also MTFW 2005
See also NFS 3
See also SAAS 3
See also SATA 23, 70, 111
See also SATA-Essay 127
See also WYA
See also YAW
Lowry, (Clarence) Malcolm
1909-1957 ... CANR-105
Brief entry ... 105
Earlier sketches in CA 131, CANR-62
See also BPFB 2
See also BRWS 3
See also CDBLB 1945-1960
See also DLB 15
See also EWL 3
See also MTCW 1, 2
See also MTFW 2005
See also RGEL 2
See also SSC 31
See also TCLC 6, 40
Lowry, Martin John Clement 1940- ... 107
Lowry, Mina Gertrude 1882-1966 ... 113
See also Loy, Mina
Lowry, Nan
See MacLeod, Ruth
Lowry, Peter 1953- ... 49-52
See also SATA 7
Lowry, Ritchie P(eter) 1926- ... 17-20R
Lowry, Robert (James Collas) 1919-1994 ... 61-64
See also CN 1, 2, 3
Lowry, S(tanley) Todd 1927- ... 126
Lowry, Shirley Park 1933- ... 109
Lowry, Thomas P(ower) 1932- ... CANR-100
Earlier sketch in CA 21-24R
Lowry, William R. 1953- ... 142
Lowther, Christine 1967- ... 223
Lowther, George F. 1913-1975
Obituary ... 57-60
See also SATA-Obit 30
Lowther, Kevin G(eorge) 1941- ... 81-84

Cumulative Index 361 **Lufkin**

Lowther, Pat 1935-1975 ... 153
See also DLB 53
Lowther, William (Anthony) 1942- ... 136
Lowy, George 1924- ... 17-20R
Lowy, Jonathan ... 239
Loxley, James 1968- ... 173
Loxsmith, John
See Brunner, John (Kilian Houston)
Loxterkamp, David ... 166
Loxton, (Charles) Howard 1934- ... CANR-27
Earlier sketches in CA 25-28R, CANR-11
Loy, J(ohn) Robert 1918-1985 ... 201
Brief entry ... 108
Loy, Jane M.
See Rausch, Jane M(eyer)
Loy, Mina
See Lowry, Mina Gertrude
See also CLC 28
See also DAM POET
See also DLB 4, 54
See also PC 16
See also PFS 20
Loy, Rosetta 1931- ... CANR-99
Earlier sketch in CA 138
Loyd, Marianne 1955- ... 115
Loye, David (Elliot) 1925- ... 33-36R
Loyie, Larry 1933- ... SATA 150
Loyn, H(enry) R(oyston) 1922-2000 . CANR-41
Obituary ... 191
Earlier sketch in CA 117
Loyn, Henry
See Loyn, H(enry) R(oyston)
Loyn, Henry R.
See Loyn, H(enry) R(oyston)
Loynaz, Dulce Maria 1902-1997 ... DLB 283
Loyson-Bridet
See Schwob, Marcel (Mayer Andre)
Loza, Steven (Joseph) ... 208
Lozano, Wendy 1941- ... 102
Lozansky, Edward D. 1941- ... SATA 62
Lozeau, Albert 1878-1924 ... 182
See also DLB 92
Lozier, Herbert 1915- ... 49-52
See also SATA 26
Lozoff, Bo 1947- ... 222
Lozowick, Lee 1943- ... 160
Lozowick, Louis 1892-1973
Obituary ... 107
Lu, David J(ohn) 1928- ... CANR-5
Earlier sketch in CA 9-12R
Lu, K'uan-yu
See Luk, Charles
Lu, Ning 1955- ... 172
Lu, Paul Hsien 1926- ... 41-44R
Luard, (David) Evan (Trant)
1926-1991 ... CANR-1
Earlier sketch in CA 1-4R
Luard, Nicholas 1937-2004 ... CANR-70
Obituary ... 229
Earlier sketch in CA 85-88
See also FANT
Lubalin, Herb(ert Frederick) 1918-1981
Obituary ... 104
Lubans, John, Jr. 1941- ... 57-60
Lubar, David 1954- ... 202
See also AAYA 52
See also SATA 133
Lubar, Joel F. 1938- ... 37-40R
Lubar, Robert 1920-1995 ... 73-76
Obituary ... 148
Lubar, Steven D. 1954- ... 205
Lubbe, Catherine Case ... AITN 1
Lubbock, (Mary Katherine) Adelaide
1906- ... 29-32R
Lubbock, Mark Hugh 1898-1986
Obituary ... 121
Lubbock, Percy 1879-1965 ... CANR-72
Earlier sketch in CA 85-88
See also DLB 149
Lubbren, Nina 1962- ... 227
Lubchenco, Jane 1947- ... 161
Lubeck, Steven G. 1944- ... 29-32R
Lubell, Cecil 1912-2000 ... CANR-4
Earlier sketch in CA 9-12R
See also SATA 6
Lubell, Harold 1925- ... 9-12R
Lubell, Samuel 1911-1987 ... CANR-86
Obituary ... 123
Earlier sketch in CA 13-16R
Lubell, Winifred (A. Milius) 1914- ... CANR-4
Earlier sketch in CA 49-52
See also SATA 6
Lubenow, William (Cornelius) 1939-
Brief entry ... 107
Luber, Philip 1948- ... 124
Lubertozzi, Alex ... 222
Lubetski, Edith 1940- ... 112
Lubetski, Meir 1938- ... 112
Lubin, Bernard 1923- ... CANR-9
Earlier sketch in CA 21-24R
Lubin, David M. 1950- ... 120
Lubin, Ernest 1916-1977 ... 41-44R
Lubin, Isador 1896-1978
Obituary ... 77-80
Lubin, Leonard
See Lubin, Leonard B.
Lubin, Leonard B. 1943-1994 ... CANR-38
Brief entry ... 115
Earlier sketch in CA 125
See also MAICYA 1, 2
See also SATA 45
See also SATA-Brief 37
Lubis, Mochtar 1922- ... 29-32R
Lubitz, Raymond 1937-1984
Obituary ... 113
Lubka, S. Ruth 1948- ... SATA 154
Lubove, Roy 1934- ... 21-24R
Lubow, Arthur 1952- ... 140
Lubow, Robert E. 1932- ... 77-80
Lubowe, Irwin I(rville) 1905-1989 ... 53-56
Lubrano, Linda L. 1943- ... 126
Brief entry ... 108
Luby, Thia 1954- ... SATA 124
Lucado, Max (Lee) 1955- ... 163
See also SATA 104
Lucan 39-65 ... AW 2
See also DLB 211
See also EFS 2
See also RGWL 2, 3
Lucanio, Patrick 1949- ... 228
Lucas, Alec 1913- ... 101
Lucas, Barbara
See Wall, Barbara
Lucas, Bryan Keith
See Keith-Lucas, Bryan
Lucas, C. Payne 1933- ... 85-88
Lucas, Carol 1929-1999 ... 17-20R
Lucas, Cedric 1962- ... SATA 101
Lucas, Celia 1938- ... CANR-24
Earlier sketch in CA 107
Lucas, Christopher J(ohn) 1940- ... 25-28R
Lucas, Craig 1951- ... CANR-142
Earlier sketches in CA 137, CANR-71, 109
See also CAD
See also CD 5, 6
See also CLC 64
See also GLL 2
See also MTFW 2005
Lucas, D(onald) W(illiam)
1905-1985 ... CANR-86
Obituary ... 116
Earlier sketches in CAP-1, CA 13-14
Lucas, Darrel B(laine) 1902-1995 ... CAP-1
Earlier sketch in CA 9-10
Lucas, Dione (Narnona Margaris Wilson)
1909-1971
Obituary ... 104
Lucas, E(dna) Louise 1899-1970 ... CAP-2
Earlier sketch in CA 25-28
Lucas, E(dward) V(errall) 1868-1938 ... 176
See also DLB 98, 149, 153
See also SATA 20
See also TCLC 73
Lucas, Eileen 1956- ... 143
See also SATA 76, 113
Lucas, F(rank) L(aurence) 1894-1967 . CANR-4
Obituary ... 25-28R
Earlier sketch in CA 1-4R
Lucas, George 1944- ... CANR-30
Earlier sketch in CA 77-80
See also AAYA 1, 23
See also CLC 16
See also SATA 56
Lucas, Hans
See Godard, Jean-Luc
Lucas, Henry C(ameron), Jr. 1944- . CANR-133
Earlier sketches in CA 109, CANR-28, 52
Lucas, J. K.
See Paine, Lauran (Bosworth)
Lucas, J(ohn) R(andolph) 1929- ... CANR-86
Earlier sketches in CA 21-24R, CANR-11, 35
Lucas, J(ames) R(aymond) 1950- ... CANR-42
Earlier sketch in CA 118
Lucas, James (Sidney) 1923-2002 ... 219
Lucas, Jason 1904-1975 ... CAP-1
Earlier sketch in CA 9-10
Lucas, Jeremy 1953- ... 108
Lucas, Jerry 1940- ... 108
See also SATA 33
Lucas, Jim Griffing 1914-1970
Obituary ... 104
Lucas, John 1937- ... CANR-69
Earlier sketches in CA 37-40R, CANR-14, 32
Lucas, John A. 1927- ... 143
Lucas, Joseph 1928- ... 69-72
Lucas, Joyce 1927- ... 57-60
Lucas, Lawrence E(dward) 1933- ... 65-68
Lucas, Marion B(runson) 1935- ... 81-84
Lucas, Martin 1944- ... 111
Lucas, Michele Claire 1937- ... 239
Lucas, N. B. C. 1901- ... 81-84
Lucas, Noah 1927- ... 57-60
Lucas, Phil 1942- ... 181
Lucas, Robert 1904-1984 ... CANR-85
Obituary ... 111
Earlier sketch in CA 101
Lucas, Robert Emerson, Jr. 1937- ... CANR-138
Earlier sketch in CA 107
Lucas, Robert Harold 1933- ... 37-40R
Lucas, Russell 1930-2002 ... 137
Obituary ... 211
Lucas, Ruth (Baxendale) 1909- ... CAP-2
Earlier sketch in CA 19-20
Lucas, Scott 1937- ... 93-96
Lucas, Stephen E. 1946- ... 125
Lucas, T(homas) E(dward) 1919- ... 77-80
Lucas, Tim(othy) 1956- ... 188
See also HGG
Lucas, Victoria
See Plath, Sylvia
Lucas, W(ilmer) F(rancis, Jr.) 1927- ... 77-80
See also BW 1
Lucash, Frank S. 1938- ... 120
Lucashenko, Melissa 1967- ... 171
See also SATA 104
Lucas Phillips, C(ecil) E(rnest)
1897-1984 ... CANR-86
Obituary ... 112
Earlier sketches in CA 1-4R, CANR-3
Luccarelli, Vincent 1923- ... 155
See also SATA 90
Lucchesi, Aldo
See von Block, Bela W(illiam)
Luce, Celia (Geneva Larsen) 1914- ... 61-64
See also SATA 38
Luce, Clare Boothe 1903-1987 ... CANR-85
Obituary ... 123
Earlier sketch in CA 45-48
See also DFS 19
See also DLB 228
Luce, Don 1934- ... CANR-12
Earlier sketch in CA 29-32R
Luce, Gay Gaer 1930- ... 103
Luce, Henry R(obinson) 1898-1967 ... 104
Obituary ... 89-92
See also DLB 91
See also MTCW 1
Luce, J(ohn) V(ictor) 1920- ... 61-64
Luce, T(orry) James, (Jr.) 1932- ... 129
Luce, Willard (Ray) 1914-1990 ... 61-64
See also SATA 38
Luce, William (Aubert) 1931- ... CANR-25
Earlier sketches in CA 65-68, CANR-11
See also LAIT 2
Lucebert
See Swaanswijk, Lubertus Jacobus
See also CWW 2
See also EWL 3
Lucena, Juan de c. 1430-1501 ... DLB 286
Lucente, Gregory L. 1948- ... 120
Lucentini, Mauro 1924- ... 69-72
Lucero, Roberto
See Meredith, Robert C(hidester)
Lucey, James D(ennis) 1923- ... 25-28R
Luchetti, Cathy 1945- ... CANR-114
Earlier sketch in CA 162
Lu-ch'iao
See Wu, Nelson I(kon)
Luchins, Abraham S(amuel) 1914- ... CANR-11
Earlier sketch in CA 69-72
Luchins, Edith H(irsch) 1921- ... CANR-11
Earlier sketch in CA 17-20R
Luchsinger, Elaine King 1902-1976 ... CAP-2
Earlier sketch in CA 17-18
Lucht, Irmgard 1937- ... SATA 82
Lucia, Ellis (Joel) 1922- ... CANR-22
Earlier sketches in CA 1-4R, CANR-4
Lucia, Salvatore Pablo 1901-1984 ... CANR-86
Obituary ... 112
Earlier sketch in CA 13-16R
Luciak, Ilja A. 1956- ... 231
Lucian c. 125-c. 180 ... AW 2
See also DLB 176
See also RGWL 2, 3
Luciani, Vincent 1906-1980 ... 61-64
Lucid, Robert F(rancis) 1930- ... 25-28R
Lucie, Doug 1953- ... 231
See also CBD
See also CD 5, 6
Lucier, Charles B(rooks) 1956- ... 195
Lucie-Smith, (John) Edward (McKenzie)
1933- ... CANR-7
Earlier sketch in CA 13-16R
See also CP 1, 2, 3, 4, 5, 6, 7
See also DLB 40
Lucilius c. 180B.C.-102B.C. ... DLB 211
Lucini, Gian Pietro 1867-1914 ... DLB 114
Lucire, Yolande ... 231
Luciuk, Lubomyr Y(aroslav) 1953- ... 132
Luck, David Johnston 1912- ... CANR-4
Earlier sketch in CA 53-56
Luck, G(eorge) Coleman 1913-1976 ... 13-16R
Luck, George Hans 1926- ... 5-8R
Luck, Thomas Jefferson 1922- ... 5-8R
Lucker, Andrew M. 1965- ... 197
Luckert, Karl W(ilhelm) 1934- ... 81-84
Luckett, Dave 1951- ... 176
See also SATA 106
Luckett, Hubert Pearson 1916-1988 ... 77-80
Luckett, Karen Beth 1944- ... 77-80
Luckey, Eleanore Braun 1915-1994 ... 33-36R
Luckhardt, C(harles) Grant 1943- ... 93-96
Luckhardt, Mildred Corell 1898-1990 ... 13-16R
See also SATA 5
Luckless, John
See Burkholz, Herbert and
Irving, Clifford Michael
Luckmann, Thomas 1927- ... CANR-81
Earlier sketches in CA 101, CANR-19, 44
Luckmann, William H. 1926- ... 153
Luckock, Elizabeth 1914- ... 21-24R
Luckovich, Mike 1960(?)- ... 144
Luckyj, George S(tephen) N(estor)
1919- ... CANR-46
Earlier sketches in CA 45-48, CANR-21
Luco Cruchaga, German 1894-1936 .. DLB 305
Lucretius c. 94B.C.-c. 49B.C. ... AW 2
See also CDWLB 1
See also DLB 211
See also EFS 2
See also RGWL 2, 3
Ludden, Allen (Ellsworth) 1918(?)-1981
Obituary ... 104
See also SATA-Obit 27
Ludden, David 1948- ... 127
Ludel, Jacqueline 1945- ... 111
See also SATA 64
Ludemann, Gerd 1946- ... 238
Luder, Peter c. 1415-1472 ... DLB 179
Luder, William Fay 1910-1998 ... 29-32R
Ludington, (Charles) Townsend
1936- ... CANR-25
Earlier sketches in CA 45-48, CANR-9
Ludlam, Charles 1943-1987 ... CANR-86
Obituary ... 122
Earlier sketches in CA 85-88, CANR-72
See also CAD
See also CLC 46, 50
See also DLB 266
Ludlow, Geoffrey
See Meynell, Laurence Walter
Ludlow, George
See Kay, Ernest
Ludlow, Howard T(homas) 1921- ... 21-24R
Ludlow, Ian
See Perdue, Lewis
Ludlow, James Minor 1917-1974
Obituary ... 53-56
Ludlum, Mabel Cleland
See Widdemer, Mabel Cleland
Ludlum, Robert 1927-2001 ... CANR-131
Obituary ... 195
Earlier sketches in CA 33-36R, CANR-25, 41, 68, 105
See also AAYA 10, 59
See also BEST 89:1, 90:3
See also BPFB 2
See also CLC 22, 43
See also CMW 4
See also CPW
See also DA3
See also DAM NOV, POP
See also DLBY 1982
See also MSW
See also MTCW 1, 2
See also MTFW 2005
Ludlum, Robert P(hillips)
1909-1987 ... CANR-86
Obituary ... 122
Earlier sketches in CAP-1, CA 13-16
Ludmerer, Kenneth M. 1947- ... CANR-89
Earlier sketches in CA 45-48, CANR-27
Ludovici, Anthony M(ario)
1882-1971(?) ... CAP-1
Earlier sketch in CA 11-12
Ludovici, L. J.
See Ludovici, Lorenz James
Ludovici, Laurence James
See Ludovici, Lorenz James
Ludovici, Lorenz James 1910- ... CANR-10
Earlier sketch in CA 21-24R
Ludowyk, E(velyn) F(rederick) C(harles)
1906-1985 ... CANR-86
Obituary ... 117
Earlier sketches in CAP-1, CA 11-12
Ludtke, James Buren 1924- ... 1-4R
Ludvigsen, Karl (Eric) 1934- ... 73-76
Ludvigson, Susan 1942- ... CANR-71
Earlier sketches in CA 57-60, CANR-7
See also DLB 120
Ludwickson, John 1948- ... 144
Ludwig, Charles Shelton 1918- ... CANR-42
Earlier sketches in CA 9-12R, CANR-5, 20
Ludwig, Coy (L.) 1939- ... 236
Ludwig, Ed(ward William) 1920-1990 ... 97-100
Obituary ... 171
Ludwig, Edward W.
See Ludwig, Ed(ward William)
Ludwig, Eric
See Grunwald, Stefan
Ludwig, Frederic
See Grunwald, Stefan
Ludwig, Helen ... SATA 33
Ludwig, Jack 1922- ... CANR-81
Earlier sketches in CA 1-4R, CANR-1, 72
See also CN 1, 2, 3, 4, 5, 6
See also DLB 60
Ludwig, Jerry 1934- ... 81-84
Ludwig, Ken 1950- ... 195
See also CAD
See also CD 6
See also CLC 60
Ludwig, Lyndell 1923- ... CANR-38
Earlier sketch in CA 115
See also SATA 63
Ludwig, Myles Eric 1942- ... 25-28R
Ludwig, Otto 1813-1865 ... DLB 129
Ludwig, Richard M(ilton) 1920-2003 ... 17-20R
Obituary ... 216
Ludwig, William 1912-1999 ... 181
Ludwigson, Kathryn Romaine 1921- .. CANR-6
Earlier sketch in CA 53-56
Ludwikowski, Rett R. 1943- ... 139
Luebbermann, Mimi 1945- ... 150
Luebke, Frederick Carl 1927- ... CANR-12
Earlier sketch in CA 33-36R
Luecke, Janemarie 1924-1987 ... CANR-21
Earlier sketch in CA 104
Lueders, Edward (George) 1923- ... CANR-5
Earlier sketch in CA 13-16R
See also SATA 14
Luedtke, Kurt (Mamre) 1939- ... 111
Brief entry ... 109
Interview in ... CA-111
Lueker, Erwin L(ouis) 1914- ... CANR-23
Earlier sketches in CA 17-20R, CANR-8
Luellen, Valentina
See Polley, Judith (Anne)
Luening, Otto 1900-1996 ... 102
Obituary ... 153
Luenn, Nancy 1954- ... CANR-39
Earlier sketch in CA 116
See also SATA 51, 79
Luera, Yolanda 1953- ... 181
See also DLB 122
Lueschen, Guenther R(udolf) 1930- ... CANR-4
Earlier sketch in CA 53-56
Luescher, Max 1923- ... 101
Luetgen, Kurt (Bodo Heinrich) 1911- ... 108
Luethi, Max 1909- ... 29-32R
Luetzelschwab, John (William) 1940- ... 121
Brief entry ... 118
Lufburrow, William 1931(?)-1986
Obituary ... 118
Luff, S(tanley) G(eorge) A(nthony) 1921- . 9-12R
Lufkin, Raymond H. 1897- ... SATA 38

Luft, David Sheers 1944- ... 106
Luft, Lorna 1952- ... 173
Luft, Lya Fett 1938- ... 175
See also DLB 145
See also HW 2
Lugansky, Kazak Vladimir
See Dal', Vladimir Ivanovich
Lugard, Flora Louisa Shaw
1852-1929 ... SATA 21
Luger, Harriett Mandelay 1914- ... CANR-1
Earlier sketch in CA 45-48
See also SATA 23
Lugg, George Wilson 1902-1988 ... 105
Lugger, Phyllis M. 1954- ... 142
Lugn, Kristina 1948- ... DLB 257
Lugo, Ariel E(milio) 1943- ... 41-44R
Lugo, James O. 1928- ... 29-32R
Lugones, Leopoldo 1874-1938 ... CANR-104
Brief entry ... 116
Earlier sketch in CA 131
See also DLB 283
See also EWL 3
See also HLCS 2
See also HW 1
See also LAW
See also TCLC 15
Lugt, Herbert Vander
See Vander Lugt, Herbert
Luhan, Mabel Dodge 1879-1962 ... DLB 303
Luhr, William 1946- ... 106
Luhrmann, Baz 1963(?)- ... 201
Luhrmann, T(anya) M(arie) 1959- ... CANR-100
Earlier sketch in CA 130
Luhrmann, Winifred B(ruce) 1934- ... 61-64
See also SATA 11
Lu Hsun
See Shu-Jen, Chou
See also EWL 3
See also SSC 20
See also TCLC 3
Luick, John F(rancis) 1920- ... 25-28R
Luis, Earlene W. 1929- ... 61-64
See also SATA 11
Luis, William 1948- ... CANR-144
Earlier sketch in CA 172
See also HW 2
Luisada, Aldo A(ugusto) 1901-1987
Obituary ... 124
Luiselli, James K. 1949- ... 233
Luisi, Billie M(eisner) 1940- ... 73-76
Lujan, Leonardo Lopez 1964- ... 148
Luk, Charles 1898-1978 ... 9-12R
Luka, Ronald 1937- ... 61-64
Lukach, Joan M(ickelson) 1935- ... 118
Lukacher, Ned 1950- ... CANR-46
Earlier sketch in CA 120
Lukacs, George
See Lukacs, Gyorgy (Szegeny von)
See also CLC 24
Lukacs, Gyorgy (Szegeny von)
1885-1971 ... CANR-62
Obituary ... 29-32R
Earlier sketch in CA 101
See also Lukacs, George
See also CDWLB 4
See also DLB 215, 242
See also EW 10
See also EWL 3
See also MTCW 1, 2
Lukacs, John (Adalbert) 1924- ... CANR-88
Earlier sketches in CA 1-4R, CANR-1, 17
Lukaczer, Moses 1911-1984
Obituary ... 112
Lukas, Charlotte Koplinka 1954- ... 93-96
Lukas, Ellen ... 97-100
Lukas, J(ay) Anthony 1933-1997 ... CANR-73
Obituary ... 159
Earlier sketches in CA 49-52, CANR-2, 19
See also MTCW 1
Lukas, Mary ... 101
Lukas, Richard C. 1937- ... 33-36R
Lukas, Susan 1940- ... 53-56
Lukashevich, Stephen 1931- ... 33-36R
Luke, Helen M. 1924-1995 ... 206
Luke, Hugh J(ay) 1932-1988 ... 89-92
Luke, Mary M(unger) 1919-1993 ... CANR-86
Obituary ... 143
Earlier sketches in CA 21-24R, CANR-14
Luke, Pearl 1958- ... 207
Luke, Peter (Ambrose Cyprian)
1919-1995 ... CANR-72
Obituary ... 147
Earlier sketch in CA 81-84
See also CBD
See also CD 5, 6
See also CLC 38
See also DLB 13
Luke, Thomas
See Masterton, Graham
Lukeman, Noah ... 219
Lukenbill, Willis B(ernard) 1939- ... 103
Luker, Kristin Carol 1946- ... 61-64
Luker, Nicholas (John Lydgate)
1945- ... CANR-92
Earlier sketch in CA 130
Luker, Ralph E(dlin) 1940- ... 139
Lukes, Steven (Michael) 1941- ... CANR-53
Earlier sketches in CA 93-96, CANR-16
Lukins, Sheila 1942- ... 139
Lukken, Miriam 1960- ... 226
Lukodianov, Isai (Borisovich) 1913-1984 ... 101
Lukonin, Mikhail K. 1920(?)-1977
Obituary ... 69-72
Lule, Jack 1954- ... 197
Lum, Peter
See Crowe, (Bettina) Peter Lum
Lumby, Catharine 1963(?)- ... 224
Lumet, Sidney 1924- ... 169
Lumian, Norman C. 1928- ... 29-32R
Lumiansky, R(obert) M(ayer) 1913-1987
Obituary ... 122
Lumley, Brian 1937- ... CANR-104
Brief entry ... 120
Earlier sketches in CA 132, CANR-54
See also DAM POP
See also HGG
Lummis, Charles F. 1859-1928 ... DLB 186
Lummis, Charles Fletcher 1859-1928 ... 197
Lummis, Keith 1904- ... 104
Lummis, Trevor 1930- ... 174
Lumpkin, Aaron 1951- ... 203
Lumpkin, Angela 1950- ... CANR-32
Earlier sketch in CA 112
Lumpkin, Beatrice 1918- ... 193
Lumpkin, Betty S(tewart) 1934- ... 146
Lumpkin, Grace ... 69-72
Lumpkin, Henry H(ope) 1913-1988 ... 122
Lumpkin, Susan 1954(?)- ... 238
Lumpkin, William Latane 1916- ... CANR-4
Earlier sketch in CA 1-4R
Lumry, Amanda (R.) ... 235
See also SATA 159
Lumsden, Charles J(ohn) 1949- ... CANR-29
Earlier sketch in CA 111
Lumsden, D(an) Barry 1939- ... CANR-21
Earlier sketch in CA 45-48
Lumsden, Linda J. 1953- ... 169
Lunan, Duncan (Alasdair) 1945- ... 107
Lunar, Dennis
See Mungo, Raymond
Lunch, Lydia 1959- ... CANR-38
Earlier sketch in CA 115
Lund, A. Morten 1926- ... 13-16R
Lund, Deb ... SATA 157
Lund, Doris Herold 1919- ... 17-20R
See also SATA 12
Lund, Gerald N. 1939- ... CANR-13
Earlier sketch in CA 33-36R
Lund, Gilda E. 1909- ... 5-8R
Lund, Herb(ert Frederick) 1926- ... 45-48
Lund, James
See Stonehouse, John (Thomson)
Lund, JoAnna M. 1944- ... 180
Lund, Michael 1945- ... 145
Lund, Orval 1940- ... 191
Lund, Philip R(eginald) 1938- ... 57-60
Lund, Robert P. 1915- ... 1-4R
Lund, Robert T. 1924- ... 126
Lund, Thomas A. 1922- ... 33-36R
Lundahl, Gene 1933- ... 21-24R
Lundberg, Dan
See Lundberg, Daniel
Lundberg, Daniel 1912-1986 ... CANR-86
Obituary ... 119
Earlier sketch in CA 114
Lundberg, Donald E(mil) 1916- ... CANR-12
Earlier sketch in CA 33-36R
Lundberg, Erik F(ilip) 1907-1987 ... CANR-38
Earlier sketches in CA 25-28R, CANR-17
Lundberg, (Edgar) Ferdinand
1905-1995 ... CAP-1
Obituary ... 148
Earlier sketch in CA 9-10
Lundberg, George D. 1933- ... 199
Lundberg, Margaret (Jessie) 1919- ... 61-64
Lundborg, Louis B(illings) 1906-1981 ... 81-84
Lundbye, Vagn 1933- ... 190
Lunde, David (Eric) 1941- ... 158
Lunde, Donald T(heodore) 1937- ... 101
Lunde, Karl (Roy) 1931- ... 122
Lunde, Paul 1943- ... 234
Lunden, Joan 1950- ... CANR-124
Earlier sketch in CA 145
Lunden, Walter A(lbin) 1899-1990 ... 21-24R
Lundestad, Geir 1945- ... 200
Lundgren, P. A. 1911- ... IDFW 3, 4
Lundgren, Paul Arthur 1925-1981
Obituary ... 103
Lundgren, Regina (E.) 1959- ... 221
Lundgren, William R. 1918- ... 13-16R
Lundin, Robert W(illiam) 1920- ... 1-4R
Lundin, Steve (Rune) 1959- ... 232
Lundkvist, (Nils) Artur
1906-1991(?) ... CANR-125
Brief entry ... 117
Earlier sketch in CA 147
See also DAM POET
See also DLB 259
See also EWL 3
Lundman, Richard J. 1944- ... 138
Lundquist, James (Carl) 1941- ... 65-68
Lundquist, Leslie (Dwynn Heeler) ... 154
Lundqvist, Lennart J. 1939- ... 129
Lundsgaarde, Henry P(eder) 1938- ... CANR-14
Earlier sketch in CA 73-76
Lundsteen, Sara W. ... 109
Lundstrom, David E. 1929- ... 126
Lundstrom, John B(ernard) 1948- ... CANR-119
Earlier sketch in CA 148
Lundvall, Bengt-Ake 1941- ... 233
Lundwall, Sam J(errie) 1941- ... CANR-81
Earlier sketches in CA 49-52, CANR-1, 17, 37
See also SFW 4
Lundy, Derek 1946- ... 187
Lundy, Mike
See Bain, Donald
Lundy, Robert F(ranklin) 1937- ... 5-8R
Lundyall, Bengt-Ake
See Lundvall, Bengt-Ake
Lunenfeld, Marvin C. 1934- ... 61-64
Lunenfeld, Peter 1962- ... 189
Lung, Chang
See Rigney, James Oliver, Jr.
Lunge-Larsen, Lise 1955- ... 208
See also SATA 138
Lunin, Lois F(ranklin) ... 102
Lunn, Arnold 1888-1974 ... 81-84
Obituary ... 49-52
Lunn, Carolyn (Kowalczyk) 1960- ... 136
See also SATA 67
Lunn, Eugene 1941- ... 45-48
Lunn, Hugh (Kingsmill) 1889-1949 ... 191
See also Kingsmill, Hugh
Lunn, Janet (Louise Swoboda)
1928- ... CANR-80
Earlier sketches in CA 33-36R, CANR-22
See also AAYA 38
See also CLR 18
See also CWRI 5
See also JRDA
See also MAICYA 1, 2
See also SAAS 12
See also SATA 4, 68, 110
Lunn, John Edward 1930- ... 41-44R
Lunneborg, Patricia W(ells) 1933- ... 216
Lunsford, Cin Forshay
See Forshay-Lunsford, Cin
Lunt, Elizabeth Graves 1922- ... 33-36R
Lunt, Horace G(ray) 1918- ... 134
Brief entry ... 107
Lunt, James D(oiran) 1917-2001 ... CANR-3
Obituary ... 202
Earlier sketch in CA 1-4R
Lunt, Lois
See Metz, Lois Lunt
Lunt, Richard D(eForest) 1933- ... 13-16R
Lunts, Lev Natanovich 1901-1924 ... DLB 272
Luoma, Jon R. 1951- ... CANR-101
Earlier sketch in CA 127
Luomala, Katharine 1907-1992 ... 37-40R
Luongo, C. Paul 1930- ... 105
Luongo, Edward Parker 1912(?)-1989
Obituary ... 128
Luongo-Orlando, Katherine 1969- ... 231
Lupack, Alan ... 200
Lupack, Barbara Tepa 1951- ... 219
Luper, Harold L(ee) 1924-1996 ... 17-20R
Luper, Steven 1956- ... CANR-134
Earlier sketch in CA 162
Lupica, Michael (Thomas) 1952- ... CANR-97
Earlier sketch in CA 142
Lupica, Mike
See Lupica, Michael (Thomas)
Lupo, Alan 1938- ... CANR-111
Earlier sketch in CA 41-44R
Lupoff, Dick
See Lupoff, Richard A(llen)
Lupoff, Richard A(llen) 1935- ... CANR-80
Earlier sketches in CA 21-24R, CANR-9, 25, 50
See also SATA 60
See also SFW 4
Lupold, Harry F. 1936- ... 139
Lupul, Manoly R(obert) 1927- ... 127
Brief entry ... 106
Lupus of Ferrieres c. 805-c. 862 ... DLB 148
Luraghi, Raimondo 1921- ... 164
Lurgan, Lester
See Knowles, Mabel Winifred
Luria, Alexander R(omanovich)
1902-1977 ... CANR-33
Obituary ... 73-76
Earlier sketch in CA 25-28R
See also MTCW 1
Luria, Maxwell Sidney 1932- ... 37-40R
Luria, S(alvador) E(dward)
1912-1991 ... CANR-86
Obituary ... 133
Earlier sketch in CA 61-64
Lurie, Alison 1926- ... CANR-88
Earlier sketches in CA 1-4R, CANR-2, 17, 50
See also BPFB 2
See also CLC 4, 5, 18, 39, 175
See also CN 1, 2, 3, 4, 5, 6, 7
See also DLB 2
See also MAL 5
See also MTCW 1
See also SATA 46, 112
See also TCLE 1:1
Lurie, Edward 1927- ... CANR-7
Earlier sketch in CA 9-12R
Lurie, Harry L. 1892(?)-1973
Obituary ... 41-44R
Lurie, Jonathan 1939- ... 132
Lurie, Morris 1938- ... CANR-92
Earlier sketch in CA 133
See also CN 4, 5, 6, 7
See also SATA 72
Lurie, Nancy Oestreich 1924- ... CANR-16
Earlier sketch in CA 1-4R
Lurie, Ranan R(aymond) 1932- ... 57-60
Lurie, Richard G. 1919-1981 ... 21-24R
Lurie, Toby 1925- ... 45-48
Luriya, Aleksander Romanovich
See Luria, Alexander R(omanovich)
Lusby, Jim ... 233
Luschei, Eugene C(harles) 1928- ... 37-40R
Luscher, Max
See Luescher, Max
Luscombe, David Edward 1938- ... 41-44R
Luscombe, William 1912- ... 5-8R
Lusinchi, Victor 1912-1985
Obituary ... 115
Lusk, John ... 233
Luskin, Bernard J(ay) 1937- ... 33-36R
Luskin, Fred 1954- ... 222
Luskin, John 1908-1988 ... 45-48
Lussert, Anneliese 1929- ... 168
See also SATA 101
Lussier, (Joseph) Ernest 1911-1979 ... CANR-9
Earlier sketch in CA 57-60
Lussu, Emilio 1890-1975 ... DLB 264
Lussu, Joyce (Salvadori) 1912-1998 ... CANR-14
Earlier sketch in CA 29-32R
Lust, John (Benedict) 1920- ... 116
Lust, Peter 1911- ... 103
Lustbader, Eric Van 1946- ... CANR-106
Earlier sketches in CA 85-88, CANR-14, 42, 66
Interview in ... CANR-14
See also BEST 90:2
See also CPW
See also DAM POP
See also FANT
See also MTCW 2
Lusted, Marcia Amidon 1962- ... 216
See also SATA 143
Lustgarten, Edgar (Marcus)
1907-1978 ... CANR-60
Earlier sketches in CA 25-28R, CANR-22
See also CMW 4
Lustgarten, Karen 1944- ... 85-88
Lustick, Ian Steven 1949- ... CANR-40
Earlier sketch in CA 117
Lustig, Arnost 1926- ... CANR-102
Earlier sketches in CA 69-72, CANR-47
See also AAYA 3
See also CLC 56
See also CWW 2
See also DLB 232, 299
See also EWL 3
See also SATA 56
Lustig, Loretta 1944- ... SATA 46
Lustig, Nora (Claudia) 1951- ... CANR-95
Earlier sketch in CA 145
Lustig, R(ichard) Jeffrey 1943- ... 112
Lustig, T(imothy) J(ohn) 1961- ... 150
Lustig-Arecco, Vera 1942- ... 101
Lutes, Catherine Urell 1900(?)-1983
Obituary ... 110
Lutes, Jason (Haynes) 1967- ... 212
See also AAYA 54
Lutetius
See Stearns, Harold Edmund
Lutgen, Kurt
See Luetgen, Kurt (Bodo Heinrich)
Luthans, Fred 1939- ... 29-32R
Luther, Edward T(urner) 1928- ... 77-80
Luther, Frank 1905-1980
Obituary ... 102
See also SATA-Obit 25
Luther, James W(allace) 1940- ... 69-72
Luther, Jim
See Luther, James W(allace)
Luther, Martin 1483-1546 ... CDWLB 2
See also DLB 179
See also EW 2
See also RGWL 2, 3
Luther, Ray
See Ley, Arthur Gordon
Luther, Rebekah (Lyn) S(tiles) 1960- ... 155
See also SATA 90
Luthi, Max
See Luethi, Max
Luthuli, A. J.
See Luthuli, Albert John
Luthuli, Albert John 1898(?)-1967 ... 153
Obituary ... 113
See also BW 2
Lutin, Michael 1940- ... 89-92
Luttbeg, Norman R. 1938- ... CANR-10
Earlier sketch in CA 25-28R
Luttmann, Gail
See Damerow, Gail (Jane)
Luttrell, Guy L. 1938- ... 97-100
See also SATA 22
Luttrell, Ida (Alleene) 1934- ... CANR-52
Earlier sketches in CA 110, CANR-27
See also SATA 40, 91
See also SATA-Brief 35
Luttrell, Mark H. 1914-1994 ... 97-100
Luttrell, William (J. III) 1954- ... SATA 149
Luttwak, Edward N(icholae) 1942- ... CANR-88
Earlier sketches in CA 25-28R, CANR-11, 48
Lutwack, Leonard 1917- ... 41-44R
Lutyens, (Agnes) Elisabeth 1906-1983
Obituary ... 109
Lutyens, Mary 1908-1999 ... CANR-90
Earlier sketch in CA 25-28R
See also RHW
Lutz, Alma 1890-1973 ... CAP-1
Obituary ... 45-48
Earlier sketch in CA 9-10
Lutz, Catherine A. 1952- ... CANR-116
Earlier sketches in CA 145, CANR-66
Lutz, Charles P(aul) 1931- ... 115
Lutz, Cora Elizabeth 1906-1985 ... CANR-86
Obituary ... 115
Earlier sketch in CA 102
Lutz, Frank W. 1928- ... 33-36R
Lutz, Gertrude May 1899-1988 ... 33-36R
Lutz, Giles A(lfred) 1910-1982 ... TCWW 1, 2
Lutz, Harley L. 1882-1975
Obituary ... 53-56
Lutz, Jerry 1939- ... 89-92
Lutz, Jessie Gregory 1925- ... 13-16R
Lutz, John (Thomas) 1939- ... CANR-100
Earlier sketches in CA 65-68, CANR-9, 24, 49
See also CMW 4
Lutz, Lorry 1928- ... 184
Lutz, Norma Jean 1943- ... 195
See also SATA 122
Lutz, Paul E(ugene) 1934- ... 61-64
Lutz, Thomas M. ... 199
Lutz, William D. 1940- ... 33-36R
Lutz, William W(alter) 1919- ... 49-52

Cumulative Index 363 Lyons

Lutze, Karl E(rnst) 1920- ... 89-92
Lutzeier, Elizabeth 1952- ... SATA 72
Lutzer, Erwin W(esley) 1941- ... CANR-2
Earlier sketch in CA 45-48
Lutzker, Edythe 1904-1991 ... CANR-85
Obituary ... 135
Earlier sketch in CA 37-40R
See also SATA 5
Luvaas, Jay 1927- ... 13-16R
Luvaas, William 1945- ... 121
Lux, Jimmy
See Obrecht, Jas
Lux, Maureen K. 1956- ... 226
Lux, Thomas 1946- ... CANR-90
Earlier sketches in CA 41-44R, CANR-53
See also CP 7
Luxbacher, Irene M. 1970- ... SATA 153
Luxemburg, Rosa 1870(?)-1919
Brief entry ... 118
See also TCLC 63
Luxenburg, Norman 1927- ... 41-44R
Luxmoore, Jonathan ... 221
Luxon, Thomas H. 1954- ... 155
Luxton, Leonora Kathrine 1895-1985 ... 85-88
Luxton, Richard (Neil) 1950- ... 110
Lu Xun 1881-1936 ... RGSF 2
See also RGWL 2, 3
Luyben, Helen L. 1932- ... 17-20R
Luytens, David (Edwin) Bulwer 1929- ... 13-16R
Luza, Radomir 1922- ... CANR-24
Earlier sketches in CA 9-12R, CANR-9
Luzadder, Patrick 1954- ... SATA 89
Luzbetak, Louis J(oseph) 1918- ... 33-36R
Luzi, Mario (Egidio Vincenzo) 1914-2005 ... CANR-70
Obituary ... 236
Earlier sketches in CA 61-64, CANR-9
See also CLC 13
See also CWW 2
See also DLB 128
See also EWL 3
Luzkow, Jack Lawrence 1941- ... 194
Luzma
See Umpierre (Herrera), Luz Maria
Luzwick, Dierdre 1945- ... 65-68
Luzzati, Emanuele 1921- ... 29-32R
See also SATA 7
Luzzatto, Paola Caboara 1938- ... 112
See also SATA 38
L'vov, Arkady ... CLC 59
L'vov, Nikolai Aleksandrovich 1751-1803 ... DLB 150
Lwoff, Andre Michel 1902-1994 ... 160
Lyall, Gavin (Tudor) 1932-2003 ... CANR-59
Obituary ... 213
Earlier sketches in CA 9-12R, CANR-4, 26
See also CMW 4
See also DLB 87
Lyall, Katharine Elizabeth 1928- ... CANR-7
Earlier sketch in CA 5-8R
Lyall, Leslie T(heodore) 1905-1996 ... 13-16R
Lyandres, Yulian Semenovich 1931-1993 ... CANR-86
Obituary ... 142
Earlier sketch in CANR-35
Lybbert, Tyler 1970- ... SATA 88
Lycan, Gilbert L(ester) 1909-1998 ... CAP-2
Earlier sketch in CA 33-36
Lycett, Andrew 1948- ... 188
Lycett Green, Candida 1942- ... 217
Lychack, William 1966(?)- ... 236
Lyday, Leon F(aidherbee) III 1939- ... 33-36R
Lydecker, Beatrice 1938- ... 106
Lyden, Fremont J(ames) 1926-1994 ... 25-28R
Lyden, Jacki 1954- ... 162
Lydenberg, John 1913-1987 ... 37-40R
Lydgate, John c. 1370-1450(?) ... BRW 1
See also DLB 146
See also RGEL 2
Lydolph, Paul E. 1924- ... 13-16R
Lydon, James G(avin) 1927- ... 126
Brief entry ... 105
Lydon, John (Joseph) 1956- ... 158
Lydon, Michael 1942- ... 85-88
See also SATA 11
Lydon, Susan Gordon 1943-2005 ... 152
Lye, Len 1901-1980 ... IDFW 3, 4
Lyfick, Warren
See Reeves, Lawrence F.
Lyford, Joseph Philip 1918-1992 ... CANR-86
Obituary ... 140
Earlier sketch in CA 37-40R
Lyford-Pike, Margaret (Prudence) 1911- ... 109
Lyftogt, Kenneth L. 1951- ... 150
Lygre, David G(erald) 1942- ... 93-96
Lykiard, Alexis (Constantine) 1940- ... 81-84
Lykins, Jenny ... 168
Lykke, Ivar
See James, Caryn
Lykken, David Thoreson 1928- ... 105
Lyle, Albert Walter 1944- ... 124
Brief entry ... 117
Lyle, David 1927- ... 118
Lyle, Guy R(edvers) 1907-1994 ... 61-64
Lyle, Jack 1929- ... 13-16R
Lyle, Jerolyn R(oss) 1937- ... 89-92
Lyle, Katie Letcher 1938- ... CANR-90
Earlier sketches in CA 49-52, CANR-29, 53
See also BYA 6
See also SATA 8
See also YAW
Lyle, Rob(ert Francis Xavier) 1920- ... CP 1
Lyle, Sparky
See Lyle, Albert Walter
Lyles, Vina Honish 1935- ... 9-12R
Lyles, William H(using) 1946- ... 111
Lyle-Smythe, Alan 1914- ... CANR-86
Earlier sketch in CA 103
Lyly, John 1554(?)-1606 ... BRW 1
See also DAM DRAM
See also DC 7
See also DLB 62, 167
See also RGEL 2
L'Ymagier
See Gourmont, Remy(-Marie-Charles) de
Lyman, Albert Robison 1880-1973 ... CAP-1
Earlier sketch in CA 13-16
Lyman, Darryl (Dean) 1944- ... 151
Lyman, Francesca 1951- ... 133
Lyman, Helen (Lucille) Huguenor 1910-2002 ... 65-68
Obituary ... 213
Lyman, Howard B(urbeck) 1920- ... 41-44R
Lyman, Howard F. 1939- ... 219
Lyman, Irene (Vera) Ponting ... 5-8R
Lyman, Lauren D(wight) 1891-1972
Obituary ... 89-92
Lyman, Marilyn F(lorence) 1925- ... 93-96
Lyman, Mary Ely 1887-1975
Obituary ... 53-56
Lyman, Stanford M(orris) 1933- ... CANR-32
Earlier sketches in CA 29-32R, CANR-12
Lyman, Susan Elizabeth 1906-1976
Obituary ... 69-72
Lymington, John
See Chance, John Newton
Lynas, Mark 1973- ... 236
Lynch, Allen C. 1955- ... 145
Lynch, B. Suarez
See Borges, Jorge Luis
Lynch, Benito 1885-1951 ... HW 1
See also LAW
Lynch, Beverly ... GLL 2
Lynch, Charles B. 1919-1994 ... 137
Lynch, Chris 1962- ... 154
See also AAYA 19, 44
See also BYA 10, 12, 15
See also CLR 58
See also MAICYA 2
See also MAICYAS 1
See also SATA 95, 131
See also WYA
See also YAW
Lynch, Daniel 1946- ... CANR-117
Earlier sketch in CA 139
Lynch, David (Keith) 1946- ... CANR-111
Brief entry ... 124
Earlier sketch in CA 129
See also AAYA 55
See also CLC 66, 162
Lynch, Edith M. (Carstensen) 1912-1986 ... CANR-85
Obituary ... 119
Earlier sketch in CA 105
Lynch, Eric
See Bingley, David Ernest
Lynch, Etta Lee 1924- ... 69-72
Lynch, Frances
See Compton, D(avid) G(uy)
Lynch, Hayden Wood 1927(?)-1979
Obituary ... 89-92
Lynch, Henry T(homson) 1928- ... 89-92
Lynch, Hollis Ralph 1935- ... CANR-1
Earlier sketch in CA 45-48
Lynch, J(ohn) Joseph 1894-1987
Obituary ... 123
Lynch, James
See Andreyev, Leonid (Nikolaevich)
Lynch, James 1936- ... CANR-40
Earlier sketches in CA 101, CANR-18
Lynch, James F. 1919(?)-1985
Obituary ... 117
Lynch, James J(oseph) 1938- ... 73-76
Lynch, Jennifer 1968- ... 142
Lynch, John 1927- ... 85-88
Lynch, Kathleen M(artha) 1898-1984 ... 73-76
Lynch, Kevin (Andrew) 1918-1984 ... CANR-85
Obituary ... 112
Earlier sketches in CA 5-8R, CANR-3
Lynch, Lee 1945- ... GLL 2
Lynch, Lorenzo 1932- ... 29-32R
See also SATA 7
Lynch, Malcolm 1922- ... 119
Lynch, Marietta 1947- ... 106
See also SATA 29
Lynch, Marilyn 1938- ... 89-92
Lynch, Marta 1925-1985 ... EWL 3
Lynch, Martin 1950- ... DLB 310
Lynch, Michael 1946- ... 203
Lynch, Michael P(atrick) 1966- ... 203
Lynch, Owen M(artin) 1931- ... CANR-11
Earlier sketch in CA 29-32R
Lynch, P(atrick) J(ames) 1962- ... MAICYA 2
See also SATA 79, 122
Lynch, Patricia (Nora) 1898-1972 ... CANR-70
Earlier sketches in CAP-1, CA 11-12
See also CWRI 5
See also DLB 160
See also SATA 9
Lynch, Patrick
See Geary, Joseph and Sington, Philip
Lynch, Patrick B(eavis) 1927- ... 9-12R
Lynch, Peter S. 1944- ... 154
Lynch, Richard Chigley 1932- ... 172
Lynch, Sarah-Kate ... 222
Lynch, Thomas 1948- ... CANR-129
Earlier sketch in CA 164
Lynch, Thomas Francis 1938- ... 45-48
Lynch, W(illiam) E(dward) 1930- ... CANR-10
Earlier sketch in CA 17-20R
Lynch, W. Ware 1914(?)-1989
Obituary ... 128
Lynch, William F. 1908-1987 ... CANR-85
Obituary ... 121
Earlier sketches in CA 1-4R, CANR-3
Lynche, Richard fl. 1596-1601 ... DLB 172
Lynch-Fraser, Diane 1953- ... 111
Lynch-Watson, Janet 1936- ... 93-96
Lynd, Barry
See Cannell, Charles (Henry)
Lynd, Helen Merrell 1896-1982
Obituary ... 105
Lynd, Robert 1879-1949 ... 181
See also DLB 98
Lynd, Robert S. 1892-1970
Obituary ... 29-32R
Lynd, Staughton (Craig) 1929- ... 133
Brief entry ... 112
Lynde, Stan 1931- ... 65-68
Lynden, Patricia 1937- ... 73-76
Lyndon, Amy
See Radford, Richard F(rancis), Jr.
Lyndon, Diana
See Anthony, Diana
Lynds, Dennis 1924-2005 ... CANR-22
Earlier sketches in CA 1-4R, CANR-6
See also CMW 4
See also DLB 306
See also SATA 47
See also SATA-Brief 37
Lynds, Gayle (Hallenbeck) ... 160
Lyndsay, Sir David 1485-1555 ... RGEL 2
Lyne, John Alexander 1909- ... 97-100
Lyneis, Richard George 1935- ... 81-84
Lynen, John Fairbanks 1924- ... CANR-2
Earlier sketch in CA 1-4R
Lynes, (Joseph) Russell (Jr.) 1910-1991 ... CANR-85
Obituary ... 135
Earlier sketches in CA 1-4R, CANR-3
Lyngseth, Joan
See Davies, Joan
Lyngstad, Alexandra Halina 1925-1998 ... 37-40R
Lyngstad, Sverre 1922- ... CANR-37
Earlier sketches in CA 37-40R, CANR-16
Lynk, Carol ... GLL 2
Lynk, Miles V(andahurst) 1871-1956 ... 155
See also BW 3
Lynn
See Brown, Velma Darbo
Lynn, Adele B. 1953- ... 167
Lynn, Allison ... 238
Lynn, Andrea E. 1944- ... 214
Lynn, Arthur D(ellert), Jr. 1921- ... CANR-10
Earlier sketch in CA 25-28R
Lynn, Conrad J. 1908-1995 ... CAP-2
Obituary ... 150
Earlier sketch in CA 23-24
Lynn, David B(randon) 1925- ... 57-60
Lynn, Edward S(hird) 1919- ... 57-60
Lynn, Edwin Charles 1935- ... 45-48
Lynn, Elizabeth A(nne) 1946- ... CANR-58
Earlier sketch in CA 81-84
See also FANT
See also SATA 99
See also SFW 4
Lynn, Frank
See Leisy, James (Franklin)
Lynn, Irene
See Rowland, D(onald) S(ydney)
Lynn, Janet
See Salomon, Janet Lynn (Nowicki)
Lynn, Jeannette Murphy 1905-1984 ... CAP-2
Earlier sketch in CA 21-22
Lynn, (Dorcas) Joanne (Harley) 1951- ... CANR-53
Earlier sketch in CA 125
Lynn, John A(lbert) 1943- ... CANR-93
Earlier sketch in CA 146
Lynn, Jonathan 1943- ... 104
Lynn (Ruiz), Kathryn 1953- ... 175
Lynn, Kenneth S(chuyler) 1923-2001 ... CANR-65
Obituary ... 196
Earlier sketches in CA 1-4R, CANR-3, 27
See also CLC 50
Lynn, Laurence Edwin, Jr. 1937- ... 105
Lynn, Loretta (Webb) 1932(?)- ... CANR-106
Earlier sketch in CA 81-84
Lynn, Margaret
See Battye, Gladys Starkey
Lynn, Mary
See Brokamp, Marilyn
Lynn, Naomi B. 1933- ... 61-64
Lynn, Patricia
See Watts, Mabel Pizzey
Lynn, Richard 1930- ... CANR-64
Earlier sketch in CA 37-40R
Lynn, Roa 1937- ... 101
Lynn, Robert A(than) 1930- ... 17-20R
Lynn, Robert Wood 1925- ... 21-24R
Lynn, Ruth Nadelman 1948- ... 103
Lynne, Becky
See Zawadsky, Patience
Lynne, Gloria 1931- ... 194
Lynne, James Broom 1920-1988 ... 77-80
Lynskey, Winifred 1904-1986 ... CAP-2
Earlier sketch in CA 23-24
Lynson, Jane
See Michaels, Lynn
Lynton, Ann
See Rayner, Claire (Berenice)
Lynton, Harriet Ronken 1920- ... 73-76
Lynton, Mark (Oliver Lawrence) 1920-1997 ... 150
Lynx
See West, Rebecca
Lyon, Annabel 1971- ... 202
Lyon, Bentley 1929- ... 140
Lyon, Bryce Dale 1920- ... CANR-52
Brief entry ... 106
Earlier sketch in CA 126
Lyon, Buck
See Paine, Lauran (Bosworth)
Lyon, Christopher (Leslie) 1949- ... 132
Brief entry ... 118
Lyon, David 1948- ... CANR-98
Earlier sketch in CA 148
Lyon, E(lijah) Wilson 1904-1989 ... CANR-85
Obituary ... 128
Earlier sketch in CA 97-100
Lyon, Elinor 1921- ... CANR-90
Earlier sketch in CA 25-28R
See also SATA 6
Lyon, Elizabeth Redditt 1950- ... 239
Lyon, Eugene 1929- ... 106
Lyon, George Ella 1949- ... CANR-46
Earlier sketch in CA 120
See also CSW
See also MAICYA 2
See also SATA 68, 119, 148
See also SATA-Essay 148
Lyon, Harold C(lifford), Jr. 1935- ... 41-44R
Lyon, James K(arl) 1934- ... CANR-1
Earlier sketch in CA 45-48
Lyon, Janet ... 208
Lyon, Jeff(rey R.) 1943- ... 130
Interview in ... CA-130
Lyon, Jessica
See DeLeeuw, Cateau
Lyon, John 1932- ... CANR-15
Earlier sketch in CA 41-44R
Lyon, Katherine
See Mix, Katherine Lyon
Lyon, Linda Gale
See Van Voorhis, Linda Lyon
Lyon, Lyman R.
See de Camp, L(yon) Sprague
Lyon, Matthew 1749-1822 ... DLB 43
Lyon, Matthew (McTee) 1956-2002 ... 228
Lyon, Melvin (Ernest) 1927- ... 33-36R
Lyon, Peter 1915-1996 ... CANR-5
Obituary ... 154
Earlier sketch in CA 5-8R
Lyon, Peyton V(aughan) 1921- ... CANR-3
Earlier sketch in CA 9-12R
Lyon, Phyllis Ann 1924- ... 224
Lyon, Quinter M(arcellus) 1898-1981 ... CAP-1
Earlier sketch in CA 19-20
Lyon, Thomas Edgar, Jr. 1939- ... 37-40R
Lyon, William Henry 1926- ... 13-16R
Lyon, Winston
See Woolfolk, William
Lyons, Albert S. 1912- ... 126
Lyons, Arthur (Jr.) 1946- ... CANR-112
Earlier sketches in CA 29-32R, CANR-12, 35, 61
See also CMW 4
Lyons, Augusta Wallace ... 85-88
Lyons, Barbara (Baldwin) 1912-2001 ... 93-96
Lyons, Catherine 1944- ... 85-88
Lyons, Christine 1943- ... 136
Lyons, Daniel 1920- ... 41-44R
Lyons, David (Barry) 1935- ... 33-36R
Lyons, Delphine C.
See Smith, Evelyn E.
Lyons, Dorothy M(arawee) 1907-1997 ... CANR-24
Earlier sketch in CA 1-4R
See also SATA 3
Lyons, Elena
See Fairburn, Eleanor
Lyons, Enid (Muriel) 1897-1981 ... CANR-86
Obituary ... 108
Earlier sketch in CA 21-24R
Lyons, Eugene 1898-1985 ... CANR-86
Obituary ... 114
Earlier sketch in CA 9-12R
Lyons, F(rancis) S(tewart) L(eland) 1923-1983 ... CANR-86
Obituary ... 110
Earlier sketch in CA 29-32R
Lyons, Gene 1943- ... 126
Lyons, Grant 1941- ... CANR-15
Earlier sketch in CA 41-44R
See also SATA 30
Lyons, Ivan 1934- ... CANR-45
Earlier sketches in CA 101, CANR-19
Lyons, J. B. 1922- ... CANR-17
Earlier sketch in CA 97-100
Lyons, James
See Loewen, James W.
Lyons, John 1932- ... 132
Lyons, John O(rmsby) 1927- ... 1-4R
Lyons, John T. 1926- ... 29-32R
Lyons, Joseph 1918- ... 13-16R
Lyons, Len 1942- ... 93-96
Lyons, Leonard 1906-1976
Obituary ... 69-72
Lyons, Louis 1937-1998 ... 143
Lyons, Louis M. 1897-1982
Obituary ... 106
Lyons, Marcus
See Blish, James (Benjamin)
Lyons, Mark Joseph 1910-2001 ... 5-8R
Lyons, Mary E(velyn) 1947- ... CANR-124
Earlier sketch in CA 159
See also AAYA 26
See also CWRI 5
See also MAICYA 2
See also MAICYAS 1
See also SATA 93, 142
Lyons, Nan 1935- ... CANR-45
Earlier sketches in CA 101, CANR-19

Lyons, Nick 1932- CANR-99
Earlier sketches in CA 53-56, CANR-4
Lyons, Paul 1942- 162
Lyons, Paul 1958- 238
Lyons, Phyllis I. 1942- 126
Lyons, Richard D(aniel) 1928- 69-72
Lyons, Richard E(ugene) 1920- CANR-21
Earlier sketch in CA 45-48
Lyons, Richard K. 1961- 237
Lyons, Sister Jeanne Marie 1904- CAP-1
Earlier sketch in CA 11-12
Lyons, Thomas Tolman 1934- CANR-3
Earlier sketch in CA 9-12R
Lyons, Timothy J(ames) 1944- 73-76
Lyons, Tom W(allace) 1943- 116
Lyons, William (Edward) 1939- 216
Lyotard, Jean-Francois 1924-1998 ...... DLB 242
See also EWL 3
See also TCLC 103
Ly-Qui, Chung 1940- 29-32R
Lyre, Pinchbeck
See Sassoon, Siegfried (Lorraine)
Lys, Daniel 1924- 21-24R
Lysaght, Averil M(argaret) 85-88
Lysaught, Jerome Paul 1930- CANR-6
Earlier sketch in CA 5-8R
Lysenko, T(rofim) D(enisovich) 1898-1976
Obituary 69-72
Lysias c. 459B.C.-c. 380B.C. .... DLB 176
Lysne, Robin
See Lysne, Robin Heerens
Lysne, Robin Heerens 1953- 198
Lysne, Robin Lopez
See Lysne, Robin Heerens
Lysons, Kenneth 1923- CANR-33
Earlier sketches in CA 85-88, CANR-15
Lyssiotis, Tes 231
See also CD 5, 6
See also CWD
Lystad, Mary (Hanemann) 1928- CANR-26
Earlier sketches in CA 65-68, CANR-10
See also SATA 11
Lystad, Robert A(rthur Lunde)
1920-2004 .... 13-16R
Obituary 228
Lystra, Karen 234
Lyte, Charles 1935- 104
Lyte, Richard
See Whelpton, (George) Eric
Lytle, Andrew (Nelson) 1902-1995 ... CANR-70
Obituary 150
Earlier sketch in CA 9-12R
See also CLC 22
See also CN 1, 2, 3, 4, 5, 6
See also CSW
See also DLB 6
See also DLBY 1995
See also RGAL 4
See also RHW
Lytle, Clifford M(erle) 1932- 93-96
Lytle, Elizabeth Stewart 1949- 148
See also SATA 79
Lytle, Guy Fitch (III) 1944- 118
Lytle, Robert A. 1944- 190
See also SATA 119
Lytle, Ruby (Coker) 1917-1970(?) CAP-1
Earlier sketch in CA 13-16
Lyttelton, George 1709-1773 .... RGEL 2
Lyttelton, George (William) 1883-1962 134
Lyttelton, Humphrey (Richard Adeane)
1921- 129
Brief entry 118
Lyttle, Charles Harold 1885(?)-1980 109
Obituary 97-100
Lyttle, G(erald) R(oland) 1908- CAP-1
Earlier sketch in CA 9-10
Lyttle, Jean
See Garrett, Eileen J(eanette)
Lyttle, Richard B(ard) 1927- CANR-13
Earlier sketch in CA 33-36R
See also SATA 23
Lytton, David 1927- .... CN 1, 2, 3
Lytton, Edward G(eorge) E(arle) L(ytton)
Bulwer-Lytton Baron 1803-1873 ...... SATA 23
Lytton, Edward Robert Bulwer
1831-1891 .... DLB 32
Lytton, Hugh 1921- 45-48
Lytton, Noel (Anthony Scawen)
1900-1985 .... CANR-86
Obituary 115
Earlier sketches in CAP-1, CA 9-10
Lytton of Knebworth, Baron
See Bulwer-Lytton, Edward (George Earle Lytton)
Lytton-Sells, Iris (Esther) 1903- 29-32R
Lyudvinskaya, Tatyana 1885(?)-1976
Obituary 65-68

M

M., S.
See Morison, Stanley (Arthur)
Ma, Jian 1953- 215
Ma, John T(a-jen) 1920- CANR-31
Earlier sketch in CA 49-52
Ma, Liping 1951- 199
Ma, Nancy Chih 1919- CANR-10
Earlier sketch in CA 65-68
Ma, Pearl (Pik Chun) 1928(?)-1989
Obituary 130
Ma, Wenhai 1954- .... SATA 84
Ma, Yinchu 1882-1982
Obituary 110
Maakestad, William J(ohn) 1951- 126
Maalouf, Amin 1949- 212
Maar, Leonard (Frank, Jr.) 1927- 106
See also SATA 30
Maartens, Maretha 1945- .... SATA 73
Maas, Audrey Gellen 1936-1975 .... CAP-2
Obituary 57-60
Earlier sketch in CA 23-24
Maas, Frederica Sagor 1900- 201
Maas, Henry 1929- 25-28R
Maas, Jeremy (Stephen) 1928- CANR-32
Earlier sketch in CA 29-32R
Maas, Peter 1929-2001 93-96
Obituary 201
Interview in CA-93-96
See also CLC 29
See also MTCW 2
See also MTFW 2005
Maas, Selve -1997 69-72
See also SATA 14
Maas, Sharon 1951- 217
Maas, Virginia H(argrave) 1913- 105
Maas, Willard 1911-1971 .... CAP-1
Obituary 29-32R
Earlier sketch in CA 13-14
Maasarani, Aly Mohamed 1927- 49-52
Maass, Arthur 1917- 193
Brief entry 105
Maass, Joachim 1901-1972 182
Obituary 37-40R
See also DLB 69
Maass, John 1918-
Brief entry 108
Maass, Vera Sonja 1931- 231
Maathai, Wangari (Muta) 1940- CANR-80
Earlier sketch in CA 155
See also BW 3
Mabberley, D(avid) J(ohn) 1948- 122
Mabbett, I(an) W(illiam) 1939- 29-32R
Mabbott, John David 1898-1988 ...... CANR-86
Obituary 124
Earlier sketch in CA 13-16R
Mabee, Carleton 1914- CANR-21
Earlier sketch in CA 1-4R
Maberly, Allan 1922-1977 103
Maberly, Norman C(harles) 1926- 33-36R
Mabery, D. L. 1953- 121
See also SATA-Brief 53
Mabey, Richard (Thomas) 1941- CANR-92
Earlier sketches in CA 21-24R, CANR-9, 26
Mabie, Grace
See Mattern, Joanne
Mabie, Hamilton Wright 1845-1916 195
See also DLB 71
Mabie, Margot C(auldwell) J(ones) 1944- ... 125
Mabley, Edward (Howe) 1906-1984 . CANR-86
Obituary 114
Earlier sketch in CA 29-32R
Mabley, Jack 1915- 105
Mabogunje, Akin(lawon) L(adipo)
1931- CANR-16
Earlier sketch in CA 77-80
Mabon, John Scott 1910(?)-1980
Obituary 104
Mabry, Bevars Dupre 1928- 45-48
Mabry, Donald J(oseph) 1941- CANR-37
Earlier sketch in CA 49-52
Mabry, Marcus 1967- 152
See also BW 3
Mac
See Maccari, Ruggero and MacManus, Seumas
Mac, Bernie 1957- 209
Mac, Carm
See Armstrong, Keith F(rancis) W(hitfield)
MacAdam, Eve
See Leslie, Cecilie
MacAdam, Preston
See Preston, John
See also GLL 1
MacAdams, Lewis (Perry, Jr.) 1944- 97-100
See also CP 1, 2
MacAdams, William 1944- 150
MacAfee, Norman 1943- 122
Mac A'Ghobhainn, Iain
See Smith, Iain Crichton
MacAgy, Douglas G(uernsey) 1913-1973 ... 102
Macainsh, Noel Leslie 1926- 103
See also CP 1
MacAlan, Peter
See Ellis, Peter Berresford
Macalaster, Elizabeth G. 1951- 186
See also SATA 115
MacAlister, Ian
See Albert, Marvin H(ubert)
MacAlister, Katie 217
See also SATA 159
MacAlpin, Rory
See Mackinnon, Charles Roy
MacAlpine, Margaret H(esketh Murray)
1907- CAP-1
Earlier sketch in CA 11-12
Macan, T(homas) T(ownley) 1910- 107
MacAndrew, Elizabeth 1924-1983(?) 126
Macao, Marshall
See Tuleja, Thaddeus F(rancis)
MacAodhagain, Eamon
See Egan, E(dward) W(elstead)
MacApp, C. C.
See Capps, Carroll M.
Macardle, Dorothy 1889-1958 189
See also HGG
Macari, Anne Marie 1955- 196
Macarov, David 1918- CANR-53
Earlier sketches in CA 29-32R, CANR-12, 28
MacArthur, Bessie J.B. 1889- .... CP 1
MacArthur, Brian 1940- 190
MacArthur, Burke
See Burks, Arthur J.
MacArthur, Charles 1895-1956
Brief entry 108
See also DFS 9
See also DLB 7, 25, 44
See also IDFW 3, 4
See also RGAL 4
MacArthur, D(avid) Wilson
1903-1981 .... CANR-5
Earlier sketch in CA 9-12R
MacArthur, Douglas 1880-1964
Obituary 113
MacArthur, John F., Jr. 1939- 81-84
MacArthur, John R. 1956- CANR-95
Earlier sketch in CA 140
MacArthur, Robert H(elmer) 1930-1972 167
Obituary 37-40R
MacArthur-Onslow, Annette Rosemary
1933- 102
See also SATA 26
Macartney, (Carlile) Aylmer
1895-1978 .... CANR-86
Obituary 125
Earlier sketch in CA 17-20R
Macartney, Frederick Thomas Bennett
1887- .... CP 1
Macaulay, Catherine 1731-1791 .... DLB 104
Macaulay, David (Alexander) 1946- . CANR-34
Earlier sketches in CA 53-56, CANR-5
Interview in CANR-34
See also AAYA 21
See also BEST 89:2
See also BYA 1
See also CLR 3, 14
See also CWRI 5
See also DLB 61
See also MAICYA 2
See also SATA 46, 72, 137
See also SATA-Brief 27
Macaulay, John (Ure) 1925- 107
Macaulay, Neill (Webster, Jr.) 1935- 21-24R
Macaulay, Ronald K. S. 1927- 146
Macaulay, (Emilie) Rose 1881(?)-1958
Brief entry 104
See also DLB 36
See also EWL 3
See also RGEL 2
See also RHW
See also TCLC 7, 44
Macaulay, Stewart 1931- 77-80
Macaulay, Susan Schaeffer 1941- 120
Macaulay, Teresa (E.) 1947- 160
See also SATA 95
Macaulay, Thomas Babington
1800-1859 .... BRW 4
See also CDBLB 1832-1890
See also DLB 32, 55
See also RGEL 2
Macauley, Robie Mayhew
1919-1995 .... CANR-92
Obituary 150
Earlier sketches in CA 1-4R, CANR-3
See also CN 1, 2, 3, 4, 5, 6
MacAusland, Earle R(utherford) 1893-1980
Obituary 101
MacAvoy, Paul W(ebster) 1934- 126
Brief entry 105
MacAvoy, Roberta Ann 1949- CANR-59
Earlier sketch in CA 113
See also FANT
See also SFW 4
See also YAW
MacBean, Dilla Whittemore 1895-1973 ... 5-8R
MacBeth, George (Mann)
1932-1992 .... CANR-66
Obituary 136
Earlier sketches in CA 25-28R, CANR-61
See also CLC 2, 5, 9
See also CP 1, 2
See also DLB 40
See also MTCW 1
See also PFS 8
See also SATA 4
See also SATA-Obit 70
Macbeth, Madge (Hamilton)
1880(?)-1965 .... CANR-90
Earlier sketch in CA 148
See also DLB 92
See also RHW
Macbeth, Norman 1910-1989 .... CAP-2
Earlier sketch in CA 33-36
MacBride, Robert O(liver) 1926- 17-20R
MacBride, Roger Lea 1929-1995 ...... CANR-86
Obituary 147
Earlier sketch in CA 81-84
See also SATA 85
MacBride, Sean 1904-1988
Obituary 124
MacCabe, Colin (Myles Joseph) 1949- 187
Maccabee, Bruce S. 1942- 195
MacCaffrey, Isabel Gamble 1924-1978 ... 81-84
Obituary 77-80
MacCaffrey, Wallace T(revethic) 1920- 134
Brief entry 112
MacCaig, Norman (Alexander)
1910-1996 .... CANR-34
Earlier sketches in CA 9-12R, CANR-3
See also BRWS 6
See also CLC 36
See also CP 1, 2
See also DAB
See also DAM POET
See also DLB 27
See also EWL 3
See also RGEL 2
MacCall, Libby
See Machol, Libby
MacCallum, Hugh R. 1928- 127
MacCallum Scott, John Hutchison
1911- 25-28R
MacCampbell, James C(urtis)
1916-1990 .... 9-12R
MacCann, Donnarae 1931- CANR-1
Earlier sketch in CA 45-48
MacCann, Richard Dyer 1920- CANR-5
Earlier sketch in CA 9-12R
MacCannell, Juliet Flower 1943- CANR-56
Earlier sketch in CA 127
Maccari, Ruggero 1919(?)-1989
Obituary 128
MacCarter, Don 1944- .... SATA 91
MacCarthy, Sir (Charles Otto) Desmond
1877-1952 167
See also TCLC 36
MacCarthy, Fiona 1940- CANR-102
Earlier sketches in CA 105, CANR-48
MacCarthy, J(oseph) A(idan) 1913- 107
MacCauley, Sister Rose Agnes 1911- 37-40R
Macchiarola, Frank Joseph 1941- 145
Macciocchi, Maria Antonietta 1922- 73-76
MacClancy, Jeremy 1953- CANR-138
Earlier sketch in CA 144
MacClintock, Dorcas 1932- CANR-6
Earlier sketch in CA 57-60
See also SATA 8
MacCloskey, Monro 1902-1983 .... CANR-5
Earlier sketch in CA 9-12R
Maccoby, Eleanor E(mmons) 1917- 188
Brief entry 113
Maccoby, Hyam 1924-2004 143
Obituary 228
Maccoby, Michael 1933- CANR-144
Earlier sketches in CA 33-36R, CANR-14
MacCollam, Joel A(llan) 1946- 105
MacCombie, John 1932- 37-40R
MacCorkle, Stuart A(lexander)
1903-1982 .... 17-20R
MacCormac, Earl Ronald 1935- 85-88
MacCormack, Sabine G(abriele) 1941- 106
MacCormick, Austin H(arbutt) 1893-1979
Obituary 93-96
MacCormick, (Donald) Neil 1941- 129
MacCorquodale, Patricia (Lee) 1950- 101
MacCoun, Catherine 1953- 131
MacCracken, Calvin D(odd) 1919-1999 116
Obituary 186
MacCracken, Henry Noble 1880-1970 . CAP-1
Obituary 29-32R
Earlier sketch in CA 19-20
MacCracken, Mary 1926- CANR-30
Earlier sketch in CA 49-52
MacCraig, Hugh
See Ward, Craig
MacCreagh, Gordon 1886-1953 216
MacCulloch, Diarmaid 1951- CANR-95
Earlier sketch in CA 125
MacCullum, Hugh R. 1928- 127
MacCurdy, Marian (Mesrobian) 195
MacCurdy, Raymond R(alph, Jr.) 1916- . 41-44R
MacDermot, Thomas Henry 1870-1933 167
MacDermott, Mercia 1927- 106
MacDiarmid, Hugh
See Grieve, C(hristopher) M(urray)
See also CDBLB 1945-1960
See also CLC 2, 4, 11, 19, 63
See also CP 1, 2
See also DLB 20
See also EWL 3
See also PC 9
See also RGEL 2
MacDonagh, Donagh 1912-1968
Obituary 93-96
MacDonald, Aeneas
See Thomson, George Malcolm
Macdonald, Alastair (A.) 1920- 136
MacDonald, Amy 1951- CANR-115
Earlier sketch in CA 135
See also SATA 76, 136, 156
See also SATA-Essay 156
MacDonald, Andrew
See Pierce, William L(uther)
MacDonald, Anne Elizabeth Campbell Bard -1958
See MacDonald, Betty
See also MAICYA 1, 2
Macdonald, Anne L. 1920- 136
MacDonald, Ann-Marie 1958- 192
See also CN 7
MacDonald, Anson
See Heinlein, Robert A(nson)
MacDonald, Bernell 1948- 113
MacDonald, Betty 1908-1958 136
See also MacDonald, Anne Elizabeth Campbell Bard
See also YABC 1
Macdonald, Blackie
See Emrich, Duncan (Black Macdonald)
MacDonald, Bonnie 1941- 117
MacDonald, Callum A. 1947- 144
Macdonald, Caroline 1948- CANR-90
Obituary 171
Earlier sketch in CA 152
See also CLR 60
See also CWRI 5
See also SATA 86
See also SATA-Obit 111
MacDonald, Cecilia
See MacDonald, Sharman
MacDonald, Cese
See MacDonald, Sharman
MacDonald, Charles B(rown)
1922-1990 .... CANR-87
Obituary 133
Earlier sketches in CA 9-12R, CANR-6, 23
Macdonald, Coll 1924- 17-20R

Cumulative Index 365 Machlin

Macdonald, Copthorne 1936- ... CANR-93
Earlier sketch in CA 145
MacDonald, Craig 1949- ... CANR-9
Earlier sketch in CA 57-60
Macdonald, Cynthia 1928- ... CANR-44
Earlier sketches in CA 49-52, CANR-4
See also CLC 13, 19
See also DLB 105
Macdonald, David W(hyte) 1951- ... 106
MacDonald, Dennis Ronald 1946- ... CANR-47
Earlier sketch in CA 111
Macdonald, Douglas J. 1947- ... 138
Macdonald, Dwight 1906-1982 ... CANR-85
Obituary ... 108
Earlier sketch in CA 29-32R
See also MAL 5
See also SATA 29
See also SATA-Obit 33
MacDonald, Edgar E(dgeworth) 1919- ... 115
MacDonald, Edwin A(nderson)
1907-1988 ... 41-44R
Macdonald, Eleanor 1910-2004 ... CAP-1
Obituary ... 223
Earlier sketch in CA 9-10
Macdonald, Elisabeth 1926- ... 65-68
MacDonald, Elizabeth P.
See McIntosh, Elizabeth P.
Macdonald, Finlay J. 1925- ... 132
MacDonald, George 1824-1905 ... CANR-80
Brief entry ... 106
Earlier sketch in CA 137
See also AAYA 57
See also BYA 5
See also CLR 67
See also DLB 18, 163, 178
See also FANT
See also MAICYA 1, 2
See also RGEL 2
See also SATA 33, 100
See also SFW 4
See also SUFW
See also TCLC 9, 113
See also WCH
Macdonald, Gerard 1940- ... 119
Macdonald, Gina L. 1942- ... 236
MacDonald, Golden
See Brown, Margaret Wise
MacDonald, Gordon (James Fraser) 1929- ... 155
Macdonald, Gordon A(ndrew)
1911-1978 ... CANR-15
Earlier sketch in CA 65-68
Macdonald, H(enry) Malcolm 1914- ... 17-20R
Mac Donald, Heather 1956- ... 198
Macdonald, Hector (R.) 1973- ... 215
Macdonald, Hope 1928- ... 135
MacDonald, Ian 1948- ... 182
MacDonald, J. Fred(erick) 1941- ... 130
Brief entry ... 117
MacDonald, Jake (M.) 1949- ... CANR-136
Earlier sketch in CA 126
Macdonald, James D. 1954- ... CANR-137
Earlier sketch in CA 170
See also Appleton, Victor
See also SATA 81, 114
MacDonald, Jerry (Paul) 1953- ... 150
Macdonald, John
See Millar, Kenneth
Macdonald, John (Barfoot) 1918- ... CANR-1
Earlier sketch in CA 49-52
Macdonald, John (Edward) 1929- ... 186
MacDonald, John D(ann)
1916-1986 ... CANR-60
Obituary ... 121
Earlier sketches in CA 1-4R, CANR-1, 19
See also BPFB 2
See also CLC 3, 27, 44
See also CMW 4
See also CPW
See also DAM NOV, POP
See also DLB 8, 306
See also DLBY 1986
See also MSW
See also MTCW 1, 2
See also MTFW 2005
See also SFW 4
Macdonald, John M(arshall) ... CANR-2
Earlier sketch in CA 1-4R
Macdonald, John Ross
See Millar, Kenneth
Macdonald, Julie 1926- ... 17-20R
MacDonald, Kenneth 1905-2004 ... 73-76
Obituary ... 229
Macdonald, Lyn ... 235
Macdonald, Malcolm
See Ross-Macdonald, Malcolm J(ohn)
MacDonald, Malcolm John
1901-1981 ... CANR-85
Obituary ... 102
Earlier sketch in CA 9-12R
MacDonald, Malcolm M(urdoch)
1935- ... 41-44R
Macdonald, Marcia
See Hill, Grace Livingston
MacDonald, Margaret Read 1940- ... CANR-126
Earlier sketches in CA 110, CANR-27, 56
See also SATA 94
Macdonald, Marianne 1934- ... CANR-97
Earlier sketch in CA 176
See also SATA 113
Macdonald, Mary
See Gifford, Griselda
MacDonald, Maryann 1947- ... SATA 72
MacDonald, Marylee 1945- ... 144
MacDonald, Michael Patrick 1966- ... 234
Macdonald, Nancy (Gardiner Rodman)
1910-1996 ... 126
Obituary ... 155
Macdonald, Neil (William) 1936- ... 89-92
Macdonald, Nina Hansell
See Looker, Antonina (Hansell)
Macdonald, Norman Malcolm
1927-1998 ... CANR-86
Earlier sketch in CA 130
MacDonald, Philip 1896-1980 ... CANR-58
Earlier sketch in CA 81-84
See also CMW 4
See also DLB 77
Macdonald, R. Ross 1923(?)-1983
Obituary ... 110
See also MAL 5
Macdonald, Robert M(unro) 1923- ... 9-12R
Macdonald, Robert S. 1925- ... 13-16R
Macdonald, Robert W. 1922- ... 17-20R
MacDonald, Ron(ald) 1932- ... 149
MacDonald, Ronald St. John 1928- ... 103
Macdonald, Ross
See Millar, Kenneth
See also AMWS 4
See also BPFB 2
See also CLC 1, 2, 3, 14, 34, 41
See also CN 1, 2, 3
See also DLBD 6
See also MSW
See also RGAL 4
MacDonald, Ruby (DeAngelo Norton)
1930- ... 115
MacDonald, Sandy 1949- ... 103
Macdonald, Sarah ... 235
MacDonald, Scott 1942- ... 215
MacDonald, Shari ... 182
MacDonald, Sharman 1951- ... 231
See also CBD
See also CD 5, 6
See also CWD
See also DLB 245
Macdonald, Shelagh 1937- ... 97-100
See also SATA 25
MacDonald, Simon G(avin) G(eorge)
1923- ... 53-56
MacDonald, Suse 1940- ... CANR-127
Earlier sketches in CA 125, CANR-70
See also SATA 54, 109
See also SATA-Brief 52
MacDonald, Timothy I(gnatius) 1941- ... 121
MacDonald, (Allan) William Colt 1891-c.
1935 ... TCWW 1, 2
MacDonald, William L. 1921- ... 21-24R
MacDonald, Wilson (Pugsley) 1880-1967 ... 148
See also DLB 92
Macdonald, Zillah K(atherine)
1885-1979 ... CAP-1
Earlier sketch in CA 9-10
See also SATA 11
Macdonnell, James Edmond 1917- ... CANR-8
Earlier sketch in CA 5-8R
MacDonnell, Kevin 1919- ... CANR-31
Earlier sketch in CA 45-48
MacDonnell, Lawrence J. 1944- ... 206
MacDonnell, Megan
See Stevens, Serita (Deborah)
MacDonogh, Giles 1955- ... CANR-98
Earlier sketch in CA 132
MacDonogh, Katharine ... 237
MacDonogh, Steve 1949- ... CANR-91
Earlier sketch in CA 145
MacDouall, Robertson
See Mair, George Brown
MacDougal, Bonnie 1953- ... CANR-139
Earlier sketch in CA 164
MacDougal, Gary E. 1936- ... 200
MacDougal, John
See Blish, James (Benjamin) and
Lowndes, Robert A(ugustine) W(ard)
MacDougal, John
See Blish, James (Benjamin)
MacDougal, Sheila X.
See Manly, Peter L.
MacDougall, A(llan) Kent 1931- ... CANR-29
Earlier sketch in CA 45-48
Macdougall, Bruce 1960- ... 196
MacDougall, Curtis D(aniel)
1903-1985 ... CANR-29
Obituary ... 117
Earlier sketch in CA 53-56
MacDougall, David 1939- ... 202
MacDougall, (George) Donald (Alastair)
1912-2004 ... 106
Obituary ... 225
MacDougall, Fiona
See MacLeod, Robert F(redric)
MacDougall, Malcolm D(ouglas) 1928-
Brief entry ... 110
MacDougall, Mary Katherine ... CANR-12
Earlier sketch in CA 29-32R
MacDougall, Ruth Doan 1939- ... CANR-93
Earlier sketches in CA 17-20R, CANR-8
MacDowell, Douglas M(aurice)
1931- ... CANR-6
Earlier sketch in CA 5-8R
MacDowell, John
See Parks, Tim(othy Harold)
Mace, Betty Webb
See Webb, Betty
Mace, C(ecil) Alec 1894-1971 ... CAP-1
Earlier sketch in CA 13-14
Mace, Carroll Edward 1926- ... 41-44R
Mace, David Robert 1907-1990 ... CANR-87
Obituary ... 133
Earlier sketches in CA 57-60, CANR-7, 23
Mace, Don 1899(?)-1983
Obituary ... 109
Mace, Elisabeth 1933- ... CANR-23
Earlier sketch in CA 77-80
See also SATA 27
Mace, Elizabeth Rhoda 1943- ... CANR-38
Mace, Gordon 1947- ... 202
Mace, Myles L(a Grange) 1911-2000 ... 185
Obituary ... 189
Brief entry ... 110
Mace, Nancy L(awson) 1941- ... CANR-137
Earlier sketch in CA 119
Mace, Varian 1938- ... SATA 49
Mace, Vera C(hapman) 1902- ... 113
MacEachern, Diane 1952- ... 133
Macedo, Stephen 1957- ... 138
MacEoin, Denis 1949- ... 141
See also HGG
MacEoin, Gary 1909-2003 ... CANR-2
Obituary ... 218
Earlier sketch in CA 1-4R
Macer-Story, E(ugenia) 1945- ... CANR-23
Earlier sketch in CA 107
Macesich, George 1927- ... 13-16R
MacEwan, Arthur 1942- ... 222
MacEwan, J(ohn) W(alter) Grant
1902-2000 ... 41-44R
MacEwan, Paul W. 1943- ... CANR-7
Earlier sketch in CA 61-64
MacEwen, Gwendolyn (Margaret)
1941-1987 ... CANR-22
Obituary ... 124
Earlier sketches in CA 9-12R, CANR-7
See also CLC 13, 55
See also CP 1, 2
See also DLB 53, 251
See also SATA 50
See also SATA-Obit 55
MacEwen, Malcolm 1911-1996 ... 110
Obituary ... 152
Macey, Carn
See Barrett, Geoffrey John
Macey, Samuel L(awson) 1922- ... 102
Macfadden, Bernarr 1868-1955 ... DLB 25, 91
MacFadden, Bruce J. 1949- ... 146
MacFadyen, David 1964- ... 204
MacFall, Russell P(atterson)
1903-1983 ... CANR-86
Obituary ... 110
Earlier sketches in CAP-1, CA 11-12
Macfarlan, Allan A. 1892-1982 ... 107
See also SATA 35
MacFarlane, Alan (Donald James)
1941- ... CANR-143
Earlier sketch in CA 170
Macfarlane, (Robert) Gwyn 1907-1987 ... 131
Obituary ... 122
MacFarlane, Iris 1922- ... 89-92
See also SATA 11
MacFarlane, James Douglas 1916- ... 132
MacFarlane, Kenneth
See Walker, Kenneth Macfarlane
Macfarlane, Leslie John 1924- ... 21-24R
MacFarlane, Louise 1917(?)-1979
Obituary ... 89-92
MacFarlane, Malcolm M. 1958- ... 214
Macfarlane, Malcolm R. 1942- ... 226
MacFarlane, Neil 1936- ... 127
Macfarlane, Robert 1976- ... 226
MacFarlane, Stephen
See Cross, John Keir
MacFarquhar, Roderick 1930- ... CANR-89
Earlier sketches in CA 21-24R, CANR-13
MacFee, Maxwell
See Rennie, James Alan
MacGaffey, Wyatt 1932- ... 73-76
MacGhill-Eain, Somhairle
See MacLean, Sorley
MacGibbon, Jean 1913-2002 ... CANR-90
Earlier sketch in CA 97-100
MacGill, Patrick 1890(?)-1963 ... 116
MacGill, Mrs. Patrick 1881-1958 ... RHW
MacGill-Callahan, Sheila 1926-2000 ... 146
See also SATA 78
MacGillivray, John H(enry) 1899-1984 ... CAP-2
Earlier sketch in CA 25-28
MacGorman, J(ohn) W(illiam) 1920- ... 102
MacGowan, Christopher (John)
1948- ... CANR-86
Earlier sketch in CA 133
Macgowan, Jonathan
See Thurlow, David (Michael)
MacGowan, Kenneth 1888-1963
Obituary ... 93-96
See also IDFW 3, 4
MacGowan, Shane 1957- ... 201
MacGoye, Marjorie (King) Oludhe
1928- ... CANR-129
Earlier sketch in CA 168
See also EWL 3
MacGraw, Ali 1939- ... 139
MacGregor, Alasdair Alpin (Douglas)
1899-1970 ... CAP-1
Obituary ... 29-32R
Earlier sketch in CA 11-12
MacGregor, Bruce (Alan) 1945- ... 77-80
MacGregor, Carol Lynn ... 228
See also SATA 153
MacGregor, David Roy 1925- ... 93-96
MacGregor, Ellen 1906-1954 ... CANR-90
Brief entry ... 111
Earlier sketch in CA 137
See also MAICYA 1, 2
See also SATA 39
See also SATA-Brief 27
MacGregor, Frances (M.) Cooke
1906-2001 ... CANR-1
Obituary ... 204
Earlier sketch in CA 1-4R
MacGregor, (John) Geddes
1909-1998 ... CANR-45
Obituary ... 174
Earlier sketches in CA 1-4R, CANR-2, 21
MacGregor, Gregory Michael ... 183
Macgregor, James (Murdoch) 1925- ... CANR-90
Earlier sketches in CA 13-16R, CANR-5
See also SFW 4
MacGregor, James G(rierson)
1905-1989 ... CANR-10
Earlier sketch in CA 25-28R
MacGregor, John 1825-1892 ... DLB 166
MacGregor, John M. 1941- ... CANR-129
Earlier sketch in CA 133
MacGregor, Loren J. 1950- ... 126
MacGregor, Malcolm D(ouglas) 1945- ... 102
MacGregor, Mary Esther 1876-1961 ... 158
See also Keith, Marian
MacGregor, Morris J. 1931- ... 198
MacGregor, Neil 1946- ... CANR-107
Earlier sketch in CA 145
MacGregor, Rob ... 194
MacGregor, Robert Mercer 1911-1974
Obituary ... 104
MacGregor, T. J.
See Janeshutz, Patricia M(arie)
MacGregor-Hastie, Roy (Alasdhair Niall)
1929- ... CANR-20
Earlier sketches in CA 1-4R, CANR-2
See also SATA 3
Macgregor-Morris, Pamela 1925- ... CANR-25
Earlier sketch in CA 29-32R
MacGrory, Yvonne 1948- ... 213
See also SATA 142
MacGuigan, Mark R(udolph) 1931- ... 21-24R
MacGuire, James 1952- ... 142
Mach, Elyse (Janet) 1941- ... 131
Machado, Ana Maria 1941- ... CANR-135
Earlier sketch in CA 194
See also MAICYA 2
See also SATA 150
Machado (y Ruiz), Antonio 1875-1939 ... 174
Brief entry ... 104
See also DLB 108
See also EW 9
See also EWL 3
See also HW 2
See also PFS 23
See also RGWL 2, 3
See also TCLC 3
Machado, Eduardo 1953- ... 131
See also CAD
See also CD 5, 6
See also HW 1
Machado (y Ruiz), Manuel 1874-1947 ... 211
See also DLB 108
Machado, Manuel Anthony, Jr. 1939- ... 29-32R
Machado de Assis, Joaquim Maria
1839-1908 ... CANR-91
Brief entry ... 107
Earlier sketch in CA 153
See also BLC 2
See also DLB 307
See also HLCS 2
See also LAW
See also RGSF 2
See also RGWL 2, 3
See also SSC 24
See also TCLC 10
See also TWA
See also WLIT 1
Machan, Tibor R(ichard) 1939- ... CANR-1
Earlier sketch in CA 45-48
Machann, Clinton (John) 1947- ... CANR-90
Earlier sketch in CA 131
Machar, Agnes Maule 1837-1927 ... 181
See also DLB 92
Machar, Josef Svatopluk 1864-1942 ... EWL 3
MacHardy, Charles 1926- ... 104
Machaut, Guillaume de c.
1300-1377 ... DLB 208
Machedon, Luminita 1952- ... 199
Machen, Arthur ... 179
See also Jones, Arthur Llewellyn
See also DLB 156, 178
See also RGEL 2
See also SSC 20
See also SUFW 1
See also TCLC 4
Machen, Arthur Llewelyn Jones
See Jones, Arthur Llewellyn
See also DLB 36
Macherey, Pierre 1938- ... DLB 296
Machetanz, Frederick 1908- ... SATA 34
Machetanz, Sara Burleson 1918- ... 1-4R
Machiavelli
See McCready, Warren T(homas)
Machiavelli, Niccolo 1469-1527 ... AAYA 58
See also DA
See also DAB
See also DAC
See also DAM MST
See also DC 16
See also EW 2
See also LAIT 1
See also LMFS 1
See also NFS 9
See also RGWL 2, 3
See also TWA
See also WLCS
See also WLIT 7
Machin, G(eorge) Ian T(hom) 1937- ... 13-16R
Machin Goodall, Daphne (Edith) ... CANR-7
Earlier sketch in CA 5-8R
See also SATA 37
Machlin, Milton Robert 1924- ... CANR-2
Earlier sketch in CA 1-4R

Machlis, Joseph 1906-1998 .... CANR-90
Obituary 171
Earlier sketches in CA 1-4R, CANR-2, 22
Interview in CANR-22
Machlowitz, Marilyn M(arcia) 1952- 101
Machlup, Fritz 1902-1983 .... CANR-86
Obituary 109
Earlier sketches in CA 1-4R, CANR-6
Machol, Libby 1916-1998 .... 21-24R
Machol, Robert E(ngel) 1917-1998 .... 37-40R
Macholtz, James Donald 1926-1985 53-56
Machor, James L(awrence) 1950- 140
MacHorton, Ian
See Machorton, Ian (Duncan)
Machorton, Ian (Duncan) 1923- CANR-8
Earlier sketch in CA 17-20R
Machotka, Otakar (Richard) 1899-1970 .... CAP-1
Obituary 29-32R
Earlier sketch in CA 13-16
Machotka, Pavel 1936- CANR-131
Earlier sketch in CA 161
Machowicz, Richard J. 233
Macht, Joel 1938- 57-60
Macht, Norman L(ee) 1929- 194
See also SATA 122
Machtan, Lothar 1949- 215
Machung, Anne 1947- 133
Macia, Rafael 1946- 97-100
Mac Iain Deorsa, Deorsa
See Hay, George Campbell
Maciel, Judi(th Anne) 1942- 33-36R
MacIlmaine, Roland fl. 1574- .... DLB 281
MacInnes, Colin 1914-1976 .... CANR-21
Obituary 65-68
Earlier sketch in CA 69-72
See also CLC 4, 23
See also CN 1, 2
See also DLB 14
See also MTCW 1, 2
See also RGEL 2
See also RHW
MacInnes, Helen (Clark) 1907-1985 .... CANR-58
Obituary 117
Earlier sketches in CA 1-4R, CANR-1, 28
See also BPFB 2
See also CLC 27, 39
See also CMW 4
See also CN 1, 2
See also CPW
See also DAM POP
See also DLB 87
See also MSW
See also MTCW 1, 2
See also MTFW 2005
See also SATA 22
See also SATA-Obit 44
MacInnes, Mairi 1925- 141
MacInnes, Patricia 1954- 148
MacInnis, Donald E(arl) 1920- 41-44R
Macintosh, Brownie 1950- 166
See also SATA 98
MacIntosh, J(ohn) J(ames) 1934- 37-40R
MacIntosh, Joan 1924- 107
MacIntosh, Keitha 1954- 112
MacIntosh, Robert 1923- 137
MacIntyre, Alasdair (Chalmers) 1929- 128
Brief entry 118
Macintyre, Angus (Donald) 1935-1994 118
Macintyre, Ben 1963- CANR-70
Earlier sketch in CA 143
MacIntyre, Christine Melba 1939-1987
Obituary 123
Macintyre, Donald George (Frederick Wyville) 1904-1981 .... 5-8R
MacIntyre, Elisabeth 1916- CANR-93
Earlier sketches in CA 9-12R, CANR-5
See also CWRI 5
See also SATA 17
MacIntyre, Michael 1939- 131
MacIntyre, Rod(erick Peter) 1947- 132
MacIntyre, Sheila Scott 1910-1960 170
Macintyre, Stuart (Forbes) 1947- CANR-107
Earlier sketch in CA 131
Mac Intyre, Tom 1931- .... DLB 245
Maclre, Esor B.
See Ambrose, Eric (Samuel)
MacIsaac, David 1935- CANR-31
Earlier sketches in CA 77-80, CANR-14
MacIsaac, Robert 175
MacIsaac, Sharon 57-60
Maciulis, Jonas
See Maironis, Jonas
Maciuszko, Jerzy J. 1913- 25-28R
Maciuszko, Kathleen L(ynn) 1947- 113
MacIver, Robert M(orrison) 1882-1970 .. CAP-1
Obituary 25-28R
Earlier sketch in CA 11-12
Mack, Arien 1931- 141
Mack, Beverly (B.) 1952- 143
Mack, Carol K. 130
Mack, Charles R. 1940- 126
Mack, Dana 1954- CANR-141
Earlier sketch in CA 165
Mack, David (A.) 232
Mack, David (W.) 228
Mack, Edward C. 1905(?)-1973
Obituary 45-48
Mack, Evalina
See McNamara, Lena Brooke
Mack, Gerstle 1894-1983 129
Obituary 109
Mack, J. A. 1906- 65-68
Mack, James D(ecker) 1916- 21-24R
Mack, Jerry
See Johnson, Jerry Mack
Mack, John E(dward) 1929-2004 106
Obituary 231
Mack, Karin E(ileen) 1946- 97-100
Mack, Kibibi Voloria C.
See Mack-Shelton, Kibibi Voloria C.
Mack, Kirby
See McEvoy, Harry K(irby)
Mack, L. V.
See Kimmelman, Burt
Mack, Marjorie
See Dixon, Marjorie (Mack)
Mack, Mary Peter 1927-1973 .... CANR-85
Obituary 103
Earlier sketch in CA 1-4R
Mack, Max Noble 1916- 61-64
Mack, Maynard 1909-2001 .... CANR-50
Obituary 194
Earlier sketches in CA 9-12R, CANR-25
See also DLB 111
Mack, Raneta Lawson 1963- 234
Mack, Raymond (Wright) 1927- 13-16R
Mack, Stan(ley) 85-88
See also SATA 17
Mack, Tracy 1968- 198
See also SATA 128
Mack, Walter Staunton 1895-1990 109
Mack, William P(aden) 1915-2003 127
Obituary 212
Mackal, Roy P(aul) 1925- 73-76
Mackall, Dandi D(aley) 1949- 190
See also SATA 118
MacKall, Leonard L. 1879-1937 213
Mackall, Leonard L. 1879-1937 .... DLB 140
Mackaman, Douglas P(eter) 184
Mackaman, Frank H(indes) II 1950- 111
Mackarness, Richard 1916- 103
MacKay, Mrs.
See MacKay, Isabel Ecclestone (Macpherson)
Mackay, Alan L(indsay) 1926- 137
MacKay, Alfred F(arnum) 1938- 104
MacKay, Alistair McColl 1931- 81-84
MacKay, Barbara E. 1944- 77-80
Mackay, Claire 1930- CANR-92
Earlier sketches in CA 105, CANR-22, 50
See also CLR 43
See also CWRI 5
See also SATA 40, 97
See also SATA-Essay 124
Mackay, Constance D'Arcy (?)-1966 . CANR-92
Earlier sketch in CA 102
See also SATA 125
MacKay, D(onald) I(ain) 1937- CANR-24
Earlier sketch in CA 29-32R
Mackay, Donald (Alexander) 1914- .. CANR-55
Earlier sketch in CA 136
See also SATA 81
MacKay, Donald 1925- 144
MacKay, Donald M(acCrimmon) 1922-1987 .... CANR-86
Obituary 121
Earlier sketches in CA 29-32R, CANR-13
Mackay, Florence Ruth
See Gilbert, (Florence) Ruth
See also CP 1
Mackay, Harvey (B.) 1933(?)- 130
See also BEST 89:3
MacKay, Isabel Ecclestone (Macpherson) 1875-1928 194
See also DLB 92
Mackay, James (Alexander) 1936- CANR-89
Earlier sketches in CA 53-56, CANR-7, 23
Mackay, Jane 1920-1986 .... CANR-45
Mackay, John Alexander 1889-1983
Obituary 110
MacKay, Joy 1918-1997 65-68
MacKay, Louis Alexander 1901- .... CP 1
Mackay, Malcolm George 1919- 108
Mackay, Mary 1855-1924 177
Brief entry 118
See also Corelli, Marie
See also FANT
See also RHW
Mackay, Mercedes (Isabelle) 1906- CAP-1
Earlier sketch in CA 11-12
MacKay, Robert A(lexander) 1894- 9-12R
Mackay, Ruddock F(inlay) 1922- 102
Mackay, Shena 1944- CANR-139
Earlier sketches in CA 104, CANR-88
See also CLC 195
See also DLB 231, 319
See also MTFW 2005
MacKay, William 1943(?)-
Brief entry 110
MacKaye, Benton 1879-1975
Obituary 61-64
MacKaye, Milton 1901-1979 93-96
Obituary 85-88
MacKaye, Percy (Wallace) 1875-1956
Brief entry 113
See also DLB 54
See also MAL 5
See also RGAL 4
See also SATA 32
MacKaye, William Ross 1934-
Brief entry 109
Mack Bride, Johnny
See McGeough, John
See also TCWW 2
MacKeever, Maggie
See Clark, Gail
MacKeith, Ronald Charles 1908-1977
Obituary 77-80
Mackel, Kathryn 1950- 236
See also SATA 162
Mackel, Kathy
See Mackel, Kathryn
MacKellar, William 1914- CANR-13
Earlier sketch in CA 33-36R
See also SATA 4
Mackelprang, Romel W. 1955- 206
Mackelworth, R(onald) W(alter) 1930-2000 .... CANR-90
Earlier sketch in CA 29-32R
See also SFW 4
Macken, Walter 1915-1967 .... CANR-89
Obituary 25-28R
Earlier sketches in CAP-1, CA 13-14
See also CWRI 5
See also DLB 13
See also SATA 36
Mackendrick, John 1946- 81-84
MacKendrick, Paul Lachlan 1914-1998 .... CANR-1
Earlier sketch in CA 1-4R
MacKenna, John 1952- 149
See also DLB 319
MacKenney, Richard 1953- 157
Mackensen, Heinz Friedrich 1921-1997 187
Brief entry 107
Mackenzie, Alastair (Ian Folliott) 1933- 118
Mackenzie, Alexander 1755-1820 .... DLB 99
Mackenzie, Alexander Slidell 1803-1848 .... DLB 183
MacKenzie, Andrew (Carr) 1911-2001 .... CANR-29
Earlier sketch in CA 49-52
Mackenzie, Basil William Sholto 1900-1983
Obituary 111
MacKenzie, Christine Butchart 1917- 13-16R
Mackenzie, Compton (Edward Montague) 1883-1972 .... CAP-2
Obituary 37-40R
Earlier sketch in CA 21-22
See also CLC 18
See also CN 1
See also DLB 34, 100
See also RGEL 2
See also TCLC 116
MacKenzie, Craig 1960- 234
MacKenzie, David 1927- 21-24R
Mackenzie, Donald (Fraser) 1913-1999 186
MacKenzie, Donald 1918-1993 .... CANR-60
Obituary 142
Earlier sketches in CA 25-28R, CANR-21
See also CMW 4
MacKenzie, Donald (Angus) 1950- 166
MacKenzie, Fred 1905-1982 .... CAP-2
Earlier sketch in CA 25-28
MacKenzie, Garry 1921- .... SATA-Brief 31
Mackenzie, Henry 1745-1831 .... DLB 39
See also RGEL 2
MacKenzie, Jean 1928- 93-96
MacKenzie, (Daisy) Jeanne 1922-1986 130
Obituary 120
MacKenzie, Jill (Kelly) 1947- 142
See also SATA 75
MacKenzie, John P(ettibone) 1930- 65-68
Mackenzie, Kathleen Guy 1907- 5-8R
Mackenzie, Kenneth (Ivo Brownley) 1913-1955
Brief entry 122
See also DLB 260
See also RGEL 2
Mackenzie, Kenneth Donald 1937- 37-40R
Mackenzie, Lee
See Bowden, Jean
MacKenzie, Lewis (Wharton) 1940- 155
Mackenzie, Locke L. 1900(?)-1977
Obituary 69-72
MacKenzie, Louise (Wilks) 1920- 29-32R
Mackenzie, Manfred 1934- 65-68
MacKenzie, Norman (Ian) 1921- 130
MacKenzie, Norman H(ugh) 1915- 21-24R
MacKenzie, Ossian 1907-1980 .... CANR-86
Obituary 120
Earlier sketch in CA 25-28R
MacKenzie, R(oderick) A(ndrew) F(rancis) 1911-1994 .... 5-8R
Mackenzie, R. Alec
See Mackenzie, Richard Alexander
MacKenzie, Rachel 1909-1980 102
Obituary 97-100
Mackenzie, Richard Alexander 1923- 109
Mackenzie, Seaforth
See Mackenzie, Kenneth (Ivo Brownley)
Mackenzie, Suzanne 1950- 136
Mackenzie, W(illiam) J(ames) M(illar) 1909- 104
Mackenzie, William 1758-1828 .... DLB 187
Mackenzie-Grieve, Averil (Salmond) 1903- 9-12R
Mackerras, Colin Patrick 1939- CANR-86
Earlier sketches in CA 85-88, CANR-15, 33
Mackesy, Piers G(erald) 1924- CANR-3
Earlier sketch in CA 9-12R
MacKethan, Lucinda Hardwick 1945- 102
Mackey, Ernan
See McInerny, Ralph (Matthew)
Mackey, Frank 1947- 222
Mackey, Helen T. 1918- 5-8R
Mackey, J(ames) P(atrick) 1934- CANR-9
Earlier sketch in CA 65-68
Mackey, Louis H(enry) 1926- 33-36R
Mackey, Mary 1945- 177
Earlier sketches in CA 77-80, CANR-15, 50, 97
Autobiographical Essay in 177
See also CAAS 27
Mackey, Nathaniel (Ernest) 1947- ... CANR-114
Earlier sketch in CA 153
See also CP 7
See also DLB 169
See also PC 49
Mackey, Richard A. 176
Mackey, Sandra 1937- CANR-123
Earlier sketches in CA 127, CANR-54
Mackey, Thomas C. 1956- 231
Mackey, William Francis 1918- 37-40R
Mackey, William J., Jr. 1902(?)-1972
Obituary 37-40R
Mackey, William Wellington 1937- 124
Brief entry 120
See also BW 1
See also DLB 38
Mackie, Alastair 1925- 17-20R
See also CP 2
Mackie, Albert D(avid) 1904-1985 .... CAP-1
Earlier sketch in CA 9-10
See also CP 1
Mackie, Carole 1967- 185
Mackie, J(ohn) L(eslie) 1917- CANR-7
Earlier sketch in CA 57-60
Mackie, (Benjamin) James 1932- 41-44R
Mackie, John
See Levinson, Leonard
Mackie, Margaret Davidson 1914- 102
Mackie, Maron
See McNeely, Jeannette
Mackie, Philip 1918-1985 .... CANR-85
Obituary 118
Earlier sketch in CA 103
Mackie, Richard Somerset 1957- 190
Mackiewicz, Jozef 1902-1985
Obituary 116
MacKillop, Ian D(uncan) 1939-2004 166
Obituary 229
MacKillop, James (John) 1939- 113
Mackin, Anita
See Donson, Cyril
Mackin, Catherine (Patricia) 1939-1982 109
Obituary 108
Mackin, Cooper R(icherson) 1933- 41-44R
Mackin, Dorothy (May Mabee) 1917-1996 107
Mackin, Edward
See McInerny, Ralph (Matthew)
Mackin, Jeanne 1951- CANR-110
Earlier sketch in CA 134
Mackin, John H(oward) 1921- 33-36R
Mackin, Theodore 1922- 116
Mackinlay, Leila Antoinette Sterling 1910- CANR-90
Earlier sketches in CAP-1, CA 11-12, CANR-24
See also RHW
Mackinlock, Duncan
See Watts, Peter Christopher
Mackinnon, A(lexander) J(ames) 1963- 224
MacKinnon, Bernie 1957- 137
See also SATA 69
MacKinnon, Catharine A. 1946- CANR-140
Brief entry 128
Earlier sketches in CA 132, CANR-73
See also CLC 181
See also FW
See also MTCW 2
See also MTFW 2005
Mackinnon, Charles Roy 1924- CANR-7
Earlier sketch in CA 9-12R
MacKinnon, Edward M(ichael) 1928- CANR-12
Earlier sketch in CA 61-64
MacKinnon, Frank 1919- 49-52
MacKinnon, John Ramsay 1947- 103
MacKinnon, Kenneth 1942- 238
Mackinnon, Marianne 1925- 128
MacKinnon, Stephen Robert 1940- .. CANR-36
Earlier sketch in CA 107
MacKinnon Groomer, Vera 1915- .... SATA 57
MacKinstry, Elizabeth 1879-1956 .... SATA 42
Mackintosh, Athole S(palding) 1926-1977 .... CANR-85
Obituary 134
Earlier sketch in CA 5-8R
Mackintosh, Elizabeth 1896(?)-1952
Brief entry 110
See also Daviot, Gordon and Tey, Josephine
See also CMW 4
MacKintosh, Graham (D.) 1951- 132
MacKintosh, Ian 1940- 73-76
Mackintosh, Sir James 1765-1832 ...... DLB 158
Mackintosh, John (Pitcairn) 1929-1978 103
Mackintosh, (John) Malcolm 1921- 5-8R
Mackintosh, N(icholas) J(ohn) 1935- 124
Mackintosh, Prudence 1944- 124
Mackintosh-Smith, Tim 1961- 201
Mackle, Jeff
See McLeod, John F(reeland)
Mackler, Bernard 1934- 21-24R
Mackler, Carolyn 1973- 239
See also AAYA 56
See also SATA 156
Mackley, George 1900-1983
Obituary 109
Macklin, Barbara J(une) 1925- 185
Brief entry 118
Macklin, Charles 1699-1797 .... DLB 89
See also RGEL 2
Macklin, Elizabeth (Jean) 1952- CANR-97
Earlier sketch in CA 141
Macklin, F. Anthony 1937- 194
Macklin, June
See Macklin, Barbara J(une)
Macklin, Tony
See Macklin, F. Anthony
MacKnight, Nancy (Margaret) 1940- 118
Mackowski, Richard M(artin) 1929- 106
Macksey, (Catherine Angela) Joan 1925- . 65-68
Macksey, Kenneth J. 1923- CANR-56
Earlier sketches in CA 25-28R, CANR-11, 30

Cumulative Index 367 MacPherson

Macksey, Major K. J.
  See Macksey, Kenneth J.
Macksey, Richard (Alan) 1930- 101
Mack-Shelton, Kibibi Voloria C. 229
Mack Smith, Denis 1920- CANR-39
  Earlier sketches in CA 21-24R, CANR-17
Mackworth, Cecily 57-60
Mackworth, Jane F. 1917-1986 .... 37-40R
Macky, Peter W(allace) 1937- 53-56
MacLachlan, Ian (Robertson) 1952- 230
MacLachlan, James Angell 1891-1967 .. CAP-2
  Earlier sketch in CA 19-20
Maclachlan, Lewis 1894-1980 .... CANR-6
  Earlier sketch in CA 5-8R
MacLachlan, Patricia 1938- CANR-130
  Brief entry 118
  Earlier sketch in CA 136
  See also AAYA 18
  See also BYA 3
  See also CLR 14
  See also CWRI 5
  See also JRDA
  See also MAICYA 1, 2
  See also SATA 62, 107
  See also SATA-Brief 42
Maclagan, Bridget
  See Borden, Mary
Maclagan, Michael 1914-2003 .... 5-8R
  Obituary 219
MacLaine, Allan H(ugh) 1924- 13-16R
MacLaine, Shirley 1934- CANR-99
  Earlier sketches in CA 103, CANR-32
MacLane, Jack
  See Crider, (Allen) Bill(y)
MacLane, Mary 1881-1929 156
Mac Lane, Saunders 1909-2005 158
  Obituary 238
MacLaren, A. Allan 1938- 106
Maclaren, Colin Shaw 1898-1985
  Obituary 116
Maclaren, Hamish 1901- .... CP 1
Maclaren, Ian
  See Watson, John
MacLaren, James
  See Grieve, C(hristopher) M(urray)
MacLaren, Roy 1934- 206
MacLaren, Sherrill M. 1939- 124
MacLaren-Ross, Julian 1912-1964 ...... DLB 319
MacLaverty, Bernard 1942- CANR-88
  Brief entry 116
  Earlier sketches in CA 118, CANR-43
  Interview in CA-118
  See also CLC 31
  See also CN 5, 6, 7
  See also DLB 267
  See also RGSF 2
Maclay, George 1943- 45-48
Maclay, Joanna Hawkins 1938- 112
Maclean, Alasdair 1926-
  Brief entry 113
  See also CP 7
MacLean, Alistair (Stuart)
  1922(?)-1987 .... CANR-61
  Obituary 121
  Earlier sketches in CA 57-60, CANR-28
  See also CLC 3, 13, 50, 63
  See also CMW 4
  See also CP 2, 3, 4, 5, 6, 7
  See also CPW
  See also DAM POP
  See also DLB 276
  See also MTCW 1
  See also SATA 23
  See also SATA-Obit 50
  See also TCWW 2
Maclean, Art
  See Shirreffs, Gordon D(onald)
Maclean, Arthur
  See Tubb, E(dwin) C(harles)
MacLean, Barbara Anne Hutmacher
  See Hutmacher (MacLean), Barbara Anne
Maclean, Charles 1946- 109
Maclean, Donald Duart 1913-1983
  Obituary 109
Maclean, Fitzroy (Hew) 1911-1996 .. CANR-31
  Obituary 152
  Earlier sketches in CA 29-32R, CANR-14
MacLean, Frederick
  See MacDonald, Wilson (Pugsley)
MacLean, Glynne 1964- 225
  See also SATA 150
MacLean, Harry N(orman) 1942- 130
  See also BEST 90:3
Maclean, Iain S(tewart) 1956- 187
MacLean, Jane 1935- 101
MacLean, Janet Rockwood 1917- 33-36R
Maclean, John N. 223
MacLean, Katherine 1925- CANR-88
  Earlier sketch in CA 33-36R
  See also DLB 8
  See also SCFW 2
  See also SFW 4
Maclean, Lady
  See Maclean, Lady Veronica
Maclean, Norman (Fitzroy)
  1902-1990 .... CANR-49
  Obituary 132
  Earlier sketch in CA 102
  See also AMWS 14
  See also CLC 78
  See also CPW
  See also DAM POP
  See also DLB 206
  See also SSC 13
  See also TCWW 2
Maclean, Rory Howe 1954- 168
MacLean, Sorley 1911-1996 .... CANR-96
  Earlier sketches in CA 154, CANR-91
  See also CP 7
Maclean, Una 1925- 69-72
Maclean, Lady Veronica
  1920-2005 .... CANR-141
  Obituary 235
  Earlier sketch in CA 144
MacLear, Kyo 1970- 203
MacLeish, Andrew 1923- 17-20R
MacLeish, Archibald 1892-1982 ...... CANR-63
  Obituary 106
  Earlier sketches in CA 9-12R, CANR-33
  See also AMW
  See also CAD
  See also CDALBS
  See also CLC 3, 8, 14, 68
  See also CP 1, 2
  See also DAM POET
  See also DFS 15
  See also DLB 4, 7, 45
  See also DLBY 1982
  See also EWL 3
  See also EXPP
  See also MAL 5
  See also MTCW 1, 2
  See also MTFW 2005
  See also PAB
  See also PC 47
  See also PFS 5
  See also RGAL 4
  See also TUS
MacLeish, Kenneth 1917-1977 81-84
  Obituary 73-76
MacLeish, Rod(erick) 1926- 41-44R
MacLeish, William H(itchcock)
  1928- CANR-110
  Earlier sketches in CA 120, CANR-46
MacLennan, David Alexander
  1903-1978 .... CANR-2
  Earlier sketch in CA 1-4R
MacLennan, (John) Hugh
  1907-1990 .... CANR-33
  Obituary 142
  Earlier sketch in CA 5-8R
  See also CLC 2, 14, 92
  See also CN 1, 2, 3, 4
  See also DAC
  See also DAM MST
  See also DLB 68
  See also EWL 3
  See also MTCW 1, 2
  See also MTFW 2005
  See also RGEL 2
  See also TWA
MacLennan, Toby 1939- 115
Macleod, Alison 1920- 53-56
MacLeod, Alistair 1936- 123
  See also CCA 1
  See also CLC 56, 165
  See also DAC
  See also DAM MST
  See also DLB 60
  See also MTCW 2
  See also MTFW 2005
  See also RGSF 2
  See also TCLE 1:2
MacLeod, Ann 1940- 138
MacLeod, Beatrice (Beach) 1910- CAP-1
  Earlier sketch in CA 19-20
  See also SATA 10, 162
MacLeod, Catriona 1963- 207
MacLeod, Celeste (Lipow) 1931- 105
MacLeod, Charlotte (Matilda)
  1922-2005 .... CANR-141
  Obituary 235
  Earlier sketches in CA 21-24R, CANR-18, 40, 66
  See also BYA 6
  See also CMW 4
  See also SATA 28
  See also SATA-Obit 160
Macleod, David I(rving, Jr.) 1943- 123
Macleod, Donald 1914- 17-20R
MacLeod, Doug 1959- 112
  See also SATA 60
MacLeod, Duncan J(ohn) 1939- 61-64
MacLeod, Earle Henry 1907- CAP-1
  Earlier sketch in CA 9-10
MacLeod, Elizabeth 234
  See also SATA 158
MacLeod, Ellen Jane (Anderson)
  1916- CANR-3
  Earlier sketch in CA 5-8R
  See also SATA 14
Macleod, Fiona
  See Sharp, William
  See also RGEL 2
  See also SUFW
MacLeod, Ian R. 1959- 158
MacLeod, Jay 1961- 126
MacLeod, Jean Sutherland 1908- CANR-90
  Earlier sketches in CA 9-12R, CANR-3
  See also RHW
Macleod, Jennifer Selfridge 1929- 102
MacLeod, Joan 1954- 165
Macleod, John 1966- 201
Macleod, Joseph (Todd Gordon)
  1903-1984(?) CANR-85
  Obituary 112
  Earlier sketch in CA 65-68
  See also Drinan, Adam
  See also CP 2
Macleod, Norman (Wicklund)
  1906-1985 .... CANR-86
  Obituary 116
  Earlier sketch in CA 73-76
  See also DLB 4
MacLeod, Robert
  See Knox, William
MacLeod, Robert 1906- .... TCWW 1, 2
MacLeod, Robert F(redric) 1917-2003 77-80
  Obituary 212
MacLeod, Roderick 1892(?)-1984
  Obituary 113
MacLeod, Ruth 1903-1990 93-96
MacLeod, Sheila 1939- 162
  See also SFW 4
MacLeod, Wendy 233
Mac Liaimmhoir, Micheal
  See Mac Liammoir, Micheal
Mac Liammhoir, Micheal
  See Mac Liammoir, Micheal
Mac Liammoir, Micheal 1899-1978 ... CANR-3
  Obituary 77-80
  Earlier sketch in CA 45-48
Mac Low, Jackson 1922-2004 .... CANR-90
  Obituary 234
  Earlier sketch in CA 81-84
  See also CAD
  See also CD 5, 6
  See also CP 1, 2, 3, 4, 5, 6, 7
  See also DLB 193
Maclure, (John) Stuart 1926- 61-64
MacLysaght, Edward Anthony
  1887-1986 .... CANR-86
  Obituary 118
  Earlier sketches in CA 1-4R, CANR-1
Macmahon, Arthur W(hittier)
  1890-1980 .... CANR-85
  Obituary 135
  Earlier sketch in CA 17-20R
MacMahon, Bryan (Michael)
  1909-1998 .... CANR-47
  Earlier sketches in CA 41-44R, CANR-23
  See also DLB 319
MacMahon, Candace W(addell) 1950- 112
Macmann, Elaine
  See Willoughby, Elaine Macmann
MacManus, James
  See MacManus, Seumas
MacManus, Seumas 1869-1960 102
  Obituary 93-96
  See also SATA 25
Macmanus, Sheila 1946- 111
MacManus, Susan A(nn) 1947- CANR-40
  Earlier sketch in CA 116
MacManus, Yvonne 1931- CANR-45
  Earlier sketches in CA 25-28R, CANR-11
MacMaster, Eve (Ruth) B(owers) 1942- 112
  See also SATA 46
MacMaster, Richard Kerwin 1935- 115
Mac Master, Robert E(llsworth) 1919- ... 33-36R
MacMillan, Annabelle
  See Quick, Annabelle
Macmillan, C(harles) J(ames) B(arr)
  1935- 21-24R
MacMillan, Cecile 1898(?)-1986
  Obituary 120
Macmillan, David S(tirling) 1925- 113
MacMillan, Dianne M(arie) 1943- .. CANR-105
  Earlier sketch in CA 150
  See also SATA 84, 125
MacMillan, Donald L(ee) 1940- 57-60
Macmillan, (John) Duncan 1939- 142
MacMillan, Gail 1944- 97-100
Macmillan, (Maurice) Harold 1894-1986 ... 128
  Obituary 121
  Brief entry 113
MacMillan, Ian T. 1941- 191
Macmillan, James
  See Brown, Hamish M.
Macmillan, Malcolm (Bruce) 1929- 225
Macmillan, Margaret (Owen) 1943- 205
Macmillan, Maurice Victor 1921-1984
  Obituary 112
Macmillan, Mona 1908- 33-36R
MacMillan, Norma 1947- 149
Macmillan, Norman 1892-1976 .... CAP-1
  Obituary 69-72
  Earlier sketch in CA 11-12
Macmillan, William Miller
  1885-1974 .... CANR-9
  Obituary 53-56
  Earlier sketches in CAP-1, CA 11-12
MacMullan, Charles Walden Kirkpatrick
  1889-1973
  Obituary 89-92
MacMullen, Ramsay 1928- CANR-116
  Earlier sketches in CA 21-24R, CANR-13
Macnab, Francis Auchline 1931- 25-28R
MacNab, P(eter) A(ngus) 1903- 33-36R
Macnab, Roy 1923- 65-68
  See also CP 1, 2, 3, 4, 5, 6, 7
MacNalty, Arthur (Salusbury)
  1880-1969 .... CANR-5
  Earlier sketch in CA 5-8R
MacNamara, Brinsley
  See Weldon, John
  See also DLB 10
  See also RGEL 2
Mac Namara, Desmond 1918- 146
Mac Namara, Donal E(oin) J(oseph)
  1916- CANR-14
  Earlier sketch in CA 33-36R
Macnamara, Ellen 1924- 103
Macnamara, John (Theodore) 1929- . CANR-13
  Earlier sketch in CA 21-24R
Macnamara, Michael Raymond Harley
  1925- .... CP 1
Macnaughton, William R(obert) 1939- 119
MacNeice, Jill 1956- 115
MacNeice, (Frederick) Louis
  1907-1963 .... CANR-61
  Earlier sketch in CA 85-88
  See also BRW 7
  See also CLC 1, 4, 10, 53
  See also DAB
  See also DAM POET
  See also DLB 10, 20
  See also EWL 3
  See also MTCW 1, 2
  See also MTFW 2005
  See also PC 61
  See also RGEL 2
MacNeil, Beatrice (Theresa) 1945- 238
MacNeil, Duncan
  See McCutchan, Philip (Donald)
Macneil, Ian R(oderick) 1929- 33-36R
MacNeil, Neil
  See Ballard, (Willis) Todhunter
MacNeil, Neil 1891-1969 .... CAP-1
  Obituary 29-32R
  Earlier sketch in CA 19-20
MacNeil, Robert (Breckenridge Ware)
  1931- CANR-80
  Brief entry 108
  Earlier sketches in CA 114, CANR-53
  Interview in CA-114
  See also BEST 89:3
MacNeill, Alastair (John) 1960- 130
MacNeill, Dand
  See Fraser, George MacDonald
MacNeill, Earl S(chwom) 1893-1972
  Obituary 37-40R
MacNeill, Ian 1919- 193
Macneill, Janet
  See McNeely, Jeannette
Macneill, Norma 1922- 117
MacNeish, Richard S(tockton)
  1918-2001 .... 37-40R
  Obituary 193
Macnell, James
  See Macdonnell, James Edmond
MacNelly, C(larence) L(amont) 1920(?)-1986
  Obituary 118
MacNelly, Jeff(rey Kenneth) 1947-2000 102
  Obituary 188
MacNib
  See Mackie, Albert D(avid)
MacNicholas, John (Malcolm) 1943- 123
  Brief entry 118
Macnicol, Eona K(athleen) Fraser 1910- .. 9-12R
MacNiven, Ian S. 76
MacNutt, Francis S. 1925- CANR-12
  Earlier sketch in CA 73-76
Macomber, Daria
  See Robinson, Patricia Colbert
Macomber, Debbie 170
Macomber, William (Butts, Jr.)
  1921-2003 61-64
  Obituary 221
Mac Orlan, Pierre
  See Dumarchais, Pierre
Macourek, Milos 1926- 140
MacPatterson, Fred
  See Ernsting, Walter
MacPeek, Walter G. 1902-1973 .... CAP-2
  Obituary 41-44R
  Earlier sketch in CA 29-32
  See also SATA 4
  See also SATA-Obit 25
Macphail, Andrew 1864-1938 224
  See also DLB 92
MacPhail, Catherine 1946- 199
  See also SATA 130
MacPhearson, James
  See Wright, John L.
MacPhee, Ross D(ouglas) E(arle) 1949- 149
Macpherson, C(rawford) Brough
  1911-1987 .... CANR-86
  Obituary 123
  Earlier sketches in CA 5-8R, CANR-2
Macpherson, Isabel
  See MacKay, Isabel Ecclestone (Macpherson)
Macpherson, James 1736-1796
  See Ossian
  See also BRWS 8
  See also DLB 109
  See also RGEL 2
Macpherson, James (Campbell) 1942- 136
Macpherson, (Jean) Jay 1931- CANR-90
  Earlier sketch in CA 5-8R
  See also CLC 14
  See also CP 1, 2, 3, 4, 5, 6, 7
  See also CWP
  See also DLB 53
Macpherson, Jeanie 1884-1946
  Brief entry 123
  See also DLB 44
  See also IDFW 3, 4
Macpherson, Kenneth 1903(?)-1971
  Obituary 29-32R
MacPherson, Malcolm C(ook)
  1943- CANR-24
  Earlier sketch in CA 102
MacPherson, Margaret 1908- CANR-86
  Earlier sketch in CA 49-52
  See also SAAS 4
  See also SATA 9
MacPherson, Myra 237
MacPherson, Rett 213
MacPherson, Thomas George
  1915-1976 .... CANR-4
  Earlier sketch in CA 1-4R
  See also SATA-Obit 30
MacPherson, William 1926- 233

MacPherson, Winnie 1930- ... SATA 107
Macquarrie, Alan (Denis) 1954- ... 122
Macquarrie, Heath Nelson 1919- ... CANR-20
Earlier sketch in CA 41-44R
Macquarrie, John 1919- ... CANR-29
Earlier sketches in CA 1-4R, CANR-1
Macqueen, James G(alloway) 1932- ... 17-20R
MacQueen, John 1929- ... CANR-86
Earlier sketch in CA 133
MacQueen, Winifred (Wallace)
1928- ... CANR-82
Earlier sketch in CA 133
Macquet, Dominique 1966- ... 202
MacQuitty, William 1905-2004 ... CANR-7
Obituary ... 223
Earlier sketch in CA 17-20R
MacRae, C(hristopher) Fred(erick) 1909- ... 45-48
MacRae, Donald E. 1907-1981 ... 93-96
MacRae, Donald G. 1921-1997 ... 13-16R
Obituary ... 167
MacRae, Duncan (Jr.) 1921- ... 21-24R
MacRae, George W(insor) 1928-1985
Obituary ... 117
Macrae, John, Jr. 1898(?)-1983
Obituary ... 111
Macrae, Marjorie Knight (?)-1973
Obituary ... 41-44R
Macrae, Mason
See Rubel, James Lyon
See also TCWW 1, 2
Macrae, Norman 1923- ... CANR-22
Earlier sketch in CA 106
Macrae, Travis
See Feagles, Anita M(acRae)
MacRaild, Donald M. 1965- ... 189
MacRaois, Cormac 1944- ... SATA 72
MacRaye, Lucy Betty
See Webling, Lucy
Macridis, Roy C(onstantine)
1918-1991 ... CANR-85
Obituary ... 136
Earlier sketch in CA 115
Macro, Eric 1920- ... CANR-32
Earlier sketch in CA 29-32R
Macrorie, Ken(neth) 1918- ... 65-68
Macrow, Brenda G(race Joan) Barton
1916- ... 9-12R
Macsai, Gwen ... 201
MacShane, Denis 1948- ... 109
MacShane, Frank 1927-1999 ... CANR-33
Obituary ... 186
Earlier sketches in CA 9-12R, CANR-3
See also CLC 39
See also DLB 111
MacStiofain, Sean
See Stephenson, John Edward Drayton
MacSweeney, Barry 1948-2000 ... CANR-20
Earlier sketch in CA 25-28R
See also CP 1, 2, 3, 4, 5, 6, 7
MacTaggart, Morna Doris
See Brown, Morna Doris
MacThomais, Ruaraidh
See Thomson, Derick S(mith)
Macu, Pavel
See Magocsi, Paul Robert
Macumber, Mari
See Sandoz, Mari(e Susette)
Macura, Paul 1924- ... CANR-8
Earlier sketch in CA 17-20R
MacVane, John (Franklin)
1912-1984 ... CANR-16
Obituary ... 111
Earlier sketch in CA 65-68
Macvaugh, Gilbert S(tillman) 1902-1990
Obituary ... 131
MacVeagh, Lincoln 1890-1972
Obituary ... 33-36R
MacVean, Jean ... 131
Macvey, John W(ishart) 1923- ... CANR-7
Earlier sketch in CA 17-20R
MacVicar, Angus 1908- ... CANR-103
Earlier sketches in CA 13-16R, CANR-10, 30, 89
See also CWRI 5
Macy, Helen 1904(?)-1978
Obituary ... 81-84
Macy, Joanna Rogers 1929- ... CANR-52
Earlier sketch in CA 125
Macy, John W(illiams), Jr.
1917-1986 ... CANR-86
Obituary ... 121
Earlier sketch in CA 33-36R
Macy, Mike 1951- ... 122
Macy, Sue 1954- ... CANR-112
Earlier sketch in CA 152
See also SATA 88, 134
Madachy, Joseph S(teven) 1927- ... 5-8R
Madame Simone
See Porche, Simone (Benda)
Madan, T(riloki) N(ath) 1931- ... CANR-7
Earlier sketch in CA 17-20R
Madar, Wendy ... 183
Madaras, Area 1969- ... 116
Madaras, Lynda 1947- ... CANR-135
Earlier sketch in CA 107
See also SATA 151
Madariaga, Isabel de
See de Madariaga, Isabel
Madariaga (Y Rojo), Salvador de
1886-1978 ... CANR-32
Obituary ... 81-84
Earlier sketches in CA 9-12R, CANR-6
See also HW 1
Maday, Bela C(harles) 1912-1997 ... 41-44R
Madden, Arthur Gerard 1911- ... 1-4R
Madden, Betty I(senbarger) 1915- ... 57-60
Madden, Bill 1945- ... 133
Madden, Carl H(alford) 1920-1978 ... 41-44R
Obituary ... 81-84
Madden, Cecil (Charles) 1902-1987
Obituary ... 122
Madden, Charles F(rank) 1921- ... 25-28R
Madden, Chris (Casson) 1948- ... 233
Madden, Daniel Michael 1916- ... 65-68
Madden, (Jerry) David 1933- ... CANR-45
Earlier sketches in CA 1-4R, CANR-4
See also CAAS 3
See also CLC 5, 15
See also CN 3, 4, 5, 6, 7
See also CSW
See also DLB 6
See also MTCW 1
Madden, David W(illiam) 1950- ... 188
Madden, Deirdre 1960- ... CANR-141
Earlier sketches in CA 133, CANR-59
See also CN 7
Madden, Don 1927- ... 25-28R
See also SATA 3
Madden, Donald L(eo) 1937- ... CANR-4
Earlier sketch in CA 53-56
Madden, E(dward) S(tanislaus) 1919- ... 9-12R
Madden, Edward H. 1925- ... CANR-1
Earlier sketch in CA 1-4R
Madden, Sir Frederick 1801-1873 ... DLB 184
Madden, Henry Miller 1912-1982
Obituary ... 108
Madden, Myron C(rowson) 1918- ... 115
Madden, Peter 1939- ... 115
Madden, Richard Raymond 1924- ... 5-8R
Madden, Susan
See Johnson, Susan E.
Madden, Tara Roth 1942- ... 126
Madden, Thomas F. 1960- ... 191
Madden, W. C. 1947- ... 166
Madden, Warren
See Cameron, Kenneth Neill
Madden, William A. 1923- ... 21-24R
Maddern, Al(an)
See Ellison, Harlan (Jay)
Madderom, Gary 1937- ... 45-48
Maddex, Jack P(endleton), Jr. 1941-
Brief entry ... 111
Maddi, Salvatore R(ichard) 1933- ... 13-16R
Maddison, Ada Isabel 1869-1950 ... 169
Maddison, Angela Mary 1923- ... CANR-89
Earlier sketch in CA 53-56
See also Banner, Angela
See also CWRI 5
See also SATA 10
Maddison, Angus 1926- ... CANR-10
Earlier sketch in CA 13-16R
Maddison, Carol Hopkins 1923- ... 17-20R
Maddock, Brent 1950- ... 81-84
Maddock, Kenneth (?)-1971
Obituary ... 104
Maddock, Larry
See Jardine, Jack
Maddock, Mary (Denise Catharine Majdak)
1951- ... 116
Maddock, Reginald (Bertram)
1912-1994 ... 81-84
See also SATA 15
Maddocks, Margaret (Kathleen Avern)
1906- ... CANR-90
Earlier sketch in CA 116
See also RHW
Maddocks, Morris Henry St. John 1928- ... 116
Maddow, Ben 1909-1992 ... 180
See also Wolff, David
See also DLB 44
See also IDFW 3, 4
Maddox, Brenda 1932- ... CANR-88
Earlier sketches in CA 97-100, CANR-22
Maddox, Bruno 1969- ... 207
Maddox, Carl
See Tubb, E(dwin) C(harles)
Maddox, Conroy (Ronald) 1912-2005 ... 101
Obituary ... 235
Maddox, Gaynor -1985 ... 9-12R
Maddox, George L(amar), Jr. 1925- ... 17-20R
Maddox, James G(ray) 1907-1973 ... CAP-2
Obituary ... 45-48
Earlier sketch in CA 21-22
Maddox, Jerrold (Warren) 1932- ... 17-20R
Maddox, John (Royden) 1925- ... 209
Maddox, Lester (Garfield) 1915-2003
Obituary ... 217
Brief entry ... 112
Maddox, Marion Errol 1910-1977 ... 21-24R
Maddox, Marjorie Lee 1959- ... 172
Maddox, Rebecca 1953- ... 152
Maddox, Robert James 1931- ... 33-36R
Maddox, Russell W(ebber), Jr. 1921- ... 1-4R
Maddox, Sara Higgins Sturm
See Sturm-Maddox, Sara Higgins
Maddox-Hafer, Marjorie Lee
See Maddox, Marjorie Lee
Maddux, (Juanita) Rachel 1912-1983 ... CANR-5
Obituary ... 176
Earlier sketch in CA 1-4R
See also DLB 234
See also DLBY 1993
Maddy, Monique (Adesemi) 1962- ... 236
Maddy, Pat Amadu
See Maddy, Yulisa Amadu
Maddy, Yulisa Amadu 1936- ... 231
See also CD 5, 6
Madeleva, Sister Mary
See Wolff, Mary Evaline
Madelin, Alain 1946- ... 184
Madelung, A. Margaret (Arent) 1926- ... 13-16R
Madenski, Melissa (Ann) 1949- ... 146
See also SATA 77
Mader, (Stanley) Chris(topher, Jr.) 1943(?)-1980
Obituary ... 103
Mader, Katherine 1948- ... 126
Madetoja, Hilja Onerva
See Onerva, L.
Madge, Charles Henry 1912-1996 ... 97-100
See also CP 1, 2
Madge, John (Hylton) 1914-1968 ... CAP-1
Earlier sketch in CA 9-10
Madge, Nicola 1949- ... 130
Madge, Violet 1916-(?) ... CAP-2
Earlier sketch in CA 21-22
Madgett, Naomi Long 1923- ... CANR-73
Earlier sketches in CA 33-36R, CANR-13, 29
See also CAAS 23
See also BW 2
See also CWP
See also DLB 76
See also EXPP
See also PFS 10
Madgwick, P(eter) J(ames) 1925- ... CANR-24
Earlier sketch in CA 29-32R
Madhavan, A. 1933- ... CP 1
Madhubuti, Haki R. 1942- ... CANR-139
Earlier sketches in CA 73-76, CANR-24, 51, 73
See also Lee, Don L.
See also BLC 2
See also BW 2, 3
See also CLC 6, 73
See also CP 3, 4, 5, 6, 7
See also CSW
See also DAM MULT, POET
See also DLB 5, 41
See also DLBD 8
See also EWL 3
See also MAL 5
See also MTCW 2
See also MTFW 2005
See also PC 5
See also RGAL 4
Madian, Jon 1941- ... 61-64
See also SATA 9
Madigan, Brian 1949- ... 165
Madigan, Marian East 1898-1988 ... CAP-2
Earlier sketch in CA 19-20
Madigan, Mark J. 1961- ... 147
Madigan, Mary Jean Smith 1941- ... CANR-134
Earlier sketch in CA 110
Madigan, Patrick 1945- ... CANR-142
Earlier sketch in CA 144
Madigan, Tim(othy S.) 1957- ... 210
Madison, Alfreda Louise 1911-1989
Obituary ... 129
Madison, Arnold 1937- ... CANR-9
Earlier sketch in CA 21-24R
See also SATA 6
Madison, Charles A(llan) 1895-1970 ... CANR-1
Earlier sketch in CA 1-4R
Madison, Frank
See Hutchins, Francis Gilman
Madison, Gary (Brent) 1940- ... 131
Madison, Hank
See Rowland, D(onald) S(ydney)
Madison, Holt ... TCWW 2
Madison, James 1751-1836 ... DLB 37
Madison, James H. 1944- ... CANR-109
Earlier sketch in CA 138
Madison, Jane
See Horne, Hugh Robert
Madison, Joyce
See Mintz, Joyce Lois
Madison, Peter 1918- ... 9-12R
Madison, Russ 1929- ... 25-28R
Madison, Susan
See Moody, Susan (Elizabeth Howard)
Madison, Thomas A(lvin) 1926- ... 57-60
Madison, Tom
See Madison, Thomas A(lvin)
Madison, Winifred ... 37-40R
See also SATA 5
Madle, Dorothy
See Madlee, Dorothy (Haynes)
Madlee, Dorothy (Haynes)
1917-1980 ... CANR-10
Earlier sketch in CA 17-20R
Mado, Michio 1909- ... 236
Madonna 1958- ... 143
See also SATA 149
Madott, Darlene (Patrice) 1952- ... 123
Madow, Leo 1915- ... CANR-13
Earlier sketch in CA 33-36R
Madow, Pauline (Reichberg) ... 9-12R
Madrick, Jeffrey G. 1947- ... 222
Madrigal, Alfonso Fernandez de c.
1405-1455 ... DLB 286
Madrigal, Margarita 1912(?)-1983
Obituary ... 110
Madruga, Lenor 1942- ... 102
Madsen, Axel 1930- ... CANR-86
Earlier sketches in CA 25-28R, CANR-33
Madsen, Borge Gedso 1920- ... 1-4R
Madsen, Brigham Dwaine 1914- ... 103
Madsen, David Lawrence 1929- ... 21-24R
Madsen, (Mark) Hunter 1955- ... 133
Madsen, Richard (Paul) 1941- ... CANR-114
Earlier sketches in CA 123, CANR-50
Madsen, Ross Martin 1946- ... 149
See also SATA 82
Madsen, Roy Paul 1928- ... 89-92
Madsen, Susan A(rrington) 1954- ... 155
See also SATA 90
Madsen, Svend Aage 1939- ... CANR-114
Earlier sketch in CA 150
See also DLB 214
See also EWL 3
Madsen, Truman Grant 1926-
Brief entry ... 106
Madubuike, Ihechukwu (Chiedozie) 1943- ... 134
Maduell, Charles Rene, Jr. 1918- ... 73-76
Mae, Eydie
See Hunsberger, Edith Mae
Maechler, Stefan 1957- ... 226
Maeda, John 1966- ... 196
Maeder, Thomas 1951- ... 132
Maedke, Wilmer O(tto) 1922-1986 ... 57-60
Maehl, William H(arvey) 1915- ... 89-92
Maehl, William Henry, Jr. 1930- ... 21-24R
Maehlqvist, (Karl) Stefan 1943- ... CANR-50
Earlier sketches in CA 107, CANR-24
See also Mahlqvist, (Karl) Stefan
Maenchen, Otto John 1894-1969
Obituary ... 109
Maenchen-Helfen, Otto J.
See Maenchen, Otto John
Maend, Evald
See Mand, Ewald
Maepenn, Hugh
See Kuttner, Henry
Maepenn, K. H.
See Kuttner, Henry
Maeroff, Gene I(rving) 1939- ... 61-64
Maertz, Richard Charles 1935- ... 73-76
Maes, Yvonne (M.) 1940(?)- ... 235
Maes-Jelinek, Hena 1929- ... 107
Maestro, Betsy (Crippen) 1944- ... CANR-37
Earlier sketches in CA 61-64, CANR-8, 23
See also CLR 45
See also MAICYA 1, 2
See also SATA 59, 106
See also SATA-Brief 30
Maestro, Giulio 1942- ... CANR-37
Earlier sketches in CA 57-60, CANR-8, 23
See also CLR 45
See also MAICYA 1, 2
See also SATA 8, 59, 106
Maestro and
Maestro
Maestro
See Maestro, Betsy (Crippen) and
Maestro, Giulio
Maeterlinck, Maurice 1862-1949 ... CANR-80
Brief entry ... 104
Earlier sketch in CA 136
See also DAM DRAM
See also DLB 192
See also EW 8
See also EWL 3
See also GFL 1789 to the Present
See also LMFS 2
See also RGWL 2, 3
See also SATA 66
See also TCLC 3
See also TWA
Maffei, Paolo 1926- ... CANR-25
Earlier sketch in CA 108
Maffi, Mario 1947- ... CANR-109
Earlier sketch in CA 153
Mafham, Rod Preston
See Preston-Mafham, Rod(ney Arthur)
Magalaner, Marvin 1920- ... CANR-1
Earlier sketch in CA 1-4R
Magaret, Helene 1906- ... 1-4R
Magarshack, David 1899-1977 ... CANR-29
Earlier sketch in CA 5-8R
Magary, Alan 1944- ... CANR-8
Earlier sketch in CA 61-64
Magary, James F(rederick) 1933- ... 25-28R
Magary, Kerstin Fraser 1947- ... CANR-12
Earlier sketch in CA 61-64
Magas, Branka ... 233
Magdalany, Philip 1936(?)-1985
Obituary ... 117
Magdaleno, Mauricio 1906-1986 ... 194
See also EWL 3
Magdol, Edward 1918- ... CANR-9
Earlier sketch in CA 21-24R
Magee, Bryan 1930- ... CANR-106
Earlier sketches in CA 5-8R, CANR-2
Magee, David (Bickersteth) 1905-1977 ... 81-84
Obituary ... 73-76
See also DLB 187
Magee, Doug 1947- ... 146
See also SATA 78
Magee, John
See Edward, John
Magee, John 1901-1987
Obituary ... 122
Magee, Wes 1939- ... CANR-90
Earlier sketches in CA 107, CANR-23
See also CP 7
See also SATA 64
Mager, George C(lyde) 1937- ... 49-52
Mager, Hugo 1967- ... 176
Mager, Nathan H. 1912-1986 ... CANR-18
Earlier sketches in CA 45-48, CANR-2
Maggal, Moshe M(orris) 1908-1994 ... CAP-2
Earlier sketch in CA 23-24
Maggi, Maria E. 1951- ... 223
Maggin, Elliot S. 1950- ... 102
Maggio, Joe 1938- ... CANR-1
Earlier sketch in CA 45-48
Maggio, Mike 1952- ... 208
Maggio, Rosalie 1943- ... 130
See also SATA 69
Maggio, Theresa (Marion) 1952- ... 234
Maggiolo, Marcio E. Veloz
See Veloz Maggiolo, Marcio E.
Maggiolo, Walter A(ndrew) 1908-2000 ... 85-88
Obituary ... 189
Maggs, Peter B(lount) 1936- ... CANR-95
Earlier sketches in CA 17-20R, CANR-8, 23, 46

Cumulative Index 369 Mains

Maggs, Will(iam) Colston 1912- 13-16R
Maghut, al- Muhammad 1934- .... CWW 2
See also EWL 3
Magid, Barry 1949- 220
Magid, Ken(neth Marshall) 128
See also SATA 65
Magida, Arthur J. 1945- 163
Magidoff, Robert 1905-1970 .... CAP-1
Earlier sketch in CA 19-20
Magidson, Herbert (Adolph) 1906-1986
Obituary 118
Magill, Frank N(orthen) 1907-1997 .... CANR-6
Obituary 158
Earlier sketch in CA 5-8R
Magill, Kathleen 1948- 116
Magill, Marcus
See Hill, Brian (Merrikin)
Magill, Robert S(amuel) 1941- 89-92
Maginn, Simon 1961- CANR-91
Earlier sketch in CA 150
See also HGG
Maginn, William 1794-1842 ...... DLB 110, 159
Maginnis, Andrew Francis 1923- 45-48
Magister, Joseph
See Grant, Louis T(heodore)
Magistrale, Tony 1952- 144
Magloire-Saint-Aude, Clement
1912-1971 .... 13-16R
Magnan, Pierre 1922- 224
Magnarella, Paul J(oseph) 93-96
Magnarelli, Sharon 1946- 147
Magner, James A. 1901-1994 .... CAP-1
Earlier sketch in CA 13-14
Magner, James Edmund, Jr. 1928- CANR-7
Earlier sketch in CA 17-20R
Magner, Lois N. 1943- CANR-93
Earlier sketch in CA 143
Magner, Thomas F(reeman) 1918- 17-20R
Magnin, Cyril I(saac) 1899-1988 ...... CANR-86
Obituary 125
Earlier sketch in CA 107
Magnus, Erica 1946- 145
See also SATA 77
Magnus, Philip
See Magnus-Allcroft, Philip (Montefiore)
Magnus, Samuel Woolf 1910-1992 .... CAP-1
Earlier sketch in CA 9-10
Magnus-Allcroft, Philip (Montefiore)
1906-1988 .... CANR-85
Obituary 127
Earlier sketches in CAP-1, CA 11-12
Magnuson, Don(ald Hammer) 1911-1979
Obituary 89-92
Magnuson, Edward F. 1926- 102
Magnuson, Keith (Arlen) 1947- 93-96
Magnuson, Mike 1964(?)- 182
Magnuson, Paul 1939- 69-72
Magnuson, Paul Budd 1884-1968
Obituary 106
Magnuson, Warren G(rant) 1905-1989 85-88
Magnussen, Daniel Osar 1919- 65-68
Magnusson, A(ugusta) L(ynne)
See Magnusson, Lynne
Magnusson, Charles 1878-1948 .... IDFW 3, 4
Magnusson, Gudmundur 1873-1918
See Trausti, Jon
Magnusson, Lynne 1953- 237
Magnusson, Magnus 1929- CANR-23
Earlier sketch in CA 105
Magocsi, Paul Robert 1945- CANR-102
Earlier sketch in CA 148
Magoffin, Susan Shelby 1827-1855 .... DLB 239
Magog, Paul Dowsey
See Dowsey-Magog, Paul
Magona, Sindiwe 1943- 170
See also BW 3
Magoon, Robert A(rnold) 1922- CANR-24
Earlier sketch in CA 107
Magorian, Christopher 1959- 111
Magorian, James 1942- CANR-58
Earlier sketches in CA 102, CANR-18, 40
See also SATA 32, 92
Magorian, Michelle 1947- CANR-90
Earlier sketch in CA 135
See also AAYA 49
See also BYA 1
See also JRDA
See also MAICYA 1, 2
See also SATA 67, 128
See also YAW
Magoun, F(rederick) Alexander
1896-1968 .... CAP-2
Earlier sketch in CA 17-18
Magoun, Francis P(eabody), Jr.
1895-1979(?) 107
Magovern, Peg .... SATA 103
Magowan, Robin 1936- CANR-20
Earlier sketches in CA 9-12R, CANR-4
Magrath, Allan J. 1949- 142
Magrath, C(laude) Peter 1933- 17-20R
Magrelli, Valerio 1957- 196
Magrid, Henry M. 1918(?)-1979
Obituary 89-92
Magriel, Paul (David) 1906(?)-1990
Obituary 132
Magris, Claudio 1939- CANR-114
Earlier sketch in CA 133
Magritte, Rene (Francois Ghislain) 1898-1967
See Magritte, Renw (Francois Ghislain)
Magritte, Renw (Francois Ghislain)
1898-1967 191
See also AAYA 41
Magruder, Jeb Stuart 1934- 101
Magsam, Charles Michael 1907-1990 ... CAP-1
Earlier sketch in CA 13-16
Magubane, Bernard (Makhosezwe)
1930- 93-96
Maguen, David
See Markish, David
Maguinness, W(illiam) Stuart
1903-1982 .... CANR-85
Obituary 108
Earlier sketches in CAP-1, CA 13-16
Maguire, Anne
See Nearing, Penny
Maguire, Daniel Charles 1931- CANR-32
Earlier sketch in CA 49-52
Maguire, Francis T(homas) 1911-1976
Obituary 69-72
Maguire, Gregory (Peter) 1954- 226
Earlier sketches in CA 81-84, CANR-53, 89, 109
Autobiographical Essay in 226
See also AAYA 22
See also BYA 14
See also CWRI 5
See also SAAS 22
See also SATA 28, 84, 129
Maguire, Henry Pownall 1943- 111
Maguire, Jack 1920-2000 81-84
See also SATA 74
Maguire, Jesse
See Smith, Sherwood
Maguire, Jessie
See Smith, Sherwood
Maguire, John David 1932- CANR-9
Earlier sketch in CA 21-24R
Maguire, John T(homas) 1917- 1-4R
Maguire, Michael 1945- 104
Maguire, R(obert) A(ugustine) J(oseph)
1898- 5-8R
Maguire, Robert A(lan) 1930-2005 73-76
Maguire, Sarah 1957- .... CP 7
See also CWP
Magun, Carol 1949- 147
Magwood, John McLean 1912- 106
Mah, Adeline Yen 1937- CANR-139
Earlier sketch in CA 169
Mahaffey, Vicki 1952- 133
Mahajan, Vidya Dhar 1913-1990 ..... CANR-29
Earlier sketches in CA 25-28R, CANR-11
Mahajani, Usha 1933- 53-56
Mahan, Alfred Thayer 1840-1914 180
See also DLB 47
Mahan, Bill
See Mahan, William Allen
Mahan, Pat
See Wheat, Patte
Mahan, Patte Wheat
See Wheat, Patte
Mahan, William Allen 1930- CANR-15
Earlier sketch in CA 85-88
Mahapatra, Jayanta 1928- CANR-87
Earlier sketches in CA 73-76, CANR-15, 33, 66
See also CAAS 9
See also CLC 33
See also CP 7
See also DAM MULT
Mahar, J. Michael 1929- 13-16R
Mahar, William J(ohn) 1938- 189
Maharaj, Mac (Sathyandranath R.) 1935- ... 210
Maharaj, Rabindranath 173
Maharani of Jaipur
See Devi, Gayatri
Maharidge, Dale (Dimitro) 1956- ... CANR-102
Earlier sketch in CA 148
Mahdi, Muhsin S(ayyid) 1926- CANR-3
Earlier sketch in CA 1-4R
Maher, Bill 1956- CANR-101
Earlier sketch in CA 154
See also AAYA 56
Maher, Brendan A(rnold) 1924- 25-28R
Maher, Eamon 233
Maher, James T(homas) 1917- 65-68
Maher, John E. 1925- 17-20R
Maher, Mary 1940- 140
Maher, Mary Z. 1941- 163
Maher, Peter Kevin 1960- 166
Maher, Ramona 1934- CANR-9
Earlier sketch in CA 21-24R
See also SATA 13
Maher, Robert F. 1922- 17-20R
Maher, Trafford P(atrick) 1914- 21-24R
Maheshwari, Shriram 1931- CANR-30
Earlier sketches in CA 21-24R, CANR-11
Maheu, Marlene M. 1954- 222
Maheux-Forcier, Louise 1929- 162
See also DLB 60
Mahfouz, Naguib (Abdel Aziz Al-Sabilgi)
1911(?)- CANR-101
Earlier sketches in CA 128, CANR-55
See also Mahfuz, Najib (Abdel Aziz al-Sabilgi)
See also AAYA 49
See also BEST 89:2
See also CLC 153
See also DA3
See also DAM NOV
See also MTCW 1, 2
See also MTFW 2005
See also RGWL 2, 3
See also SSC 66
See also SSFS 9
Mahfuz, Najib (Abdel Aziz al-Sabilgi)
See Mahfouz, Naguib (Abdel Aziz Al-Sabilgi)
See also AFW
See also CLC 52, 55
See also CWW 2
See also DLBY 1988
See also EWL 3
See also RGSF 2
See also WLIT 6
Mahin, John Lee 1902(?)-1984 184
Obituary 112
See also DLB 44
Mahindra, Indira 1926- 136
Mahjoub, Jamal .... CN 7
Mahl, George F(ranklin) 1917- 93-96
Mahl, Mary R. 1914- 25-28R
Mahl, Thomas E. 1943- 236
Mahlendorf, Ursula R. 1929- 49-52
Mahler, Gregory S. 1950- CANR-50
Earlier sketch in CA 123
Mahler, Gustav 1860-1911 170
Mahler, Jane Gaston 1906- 37-40R
Mahler, Margaret S(choenberger)
1897-1985 .... CANR-85
Obituary 117
Earlier sketch in CA 103
Mahler-Werfel, Alma 1879-1964 204
Mahlqvist, (Karl) Stefan
See Maehlqvist, (Karl) Stefan
See also SATA 30
Mahmood, Iftekhar 223
Mahmood, Mamdani 1946- 105
Mahmoody, Betty 1945(?)- 142
Mahmud, Shabana 144
Maholick, Leonard T(homas) 1921- CANR-1
Earlier sketch in CA 1-4R
Mahon, Basil 1937- 234
Mahon, Derek 1941- CANR-88
Brief entry 113
Earlier sketch in CA 128
See also BRWS 6
See also CLC 27
See also CP 1, 2, 3, 4, 5, 6, 7
See also DLB 40
See also EWL 3
See also PC 60
Mahon, John K(eith) 1912- 17-20R
Mahon, Julia C(unha) 1916- 61-64
See also SATA 11
Mahon, Thomas (Cavan) 1944- 119
Mahone, Colt
See Lazenby, Norman
Mahoney, Dan 1947- 141
Mahoney, Irene 1921- 61-64
Mahoney, J. Daniel 1931- 61-64
Mahoney, John (Francis) 1929- 41-44R
Mahoney, John Leo 1928- CANR-14
Earlier sketch in CA 33-36R
Mahoney, John Thomas 1905-1981 .. CANR-85
Obituary 104
Earlier sketches in CAP-1, CA 11-12
Mahoney, Michael J(ohn) 1946- CANR-8
Earlier sketch in CA 53-56
Mahoney, Olivia 1952- 133
Mahoney, Patrick 1927- 81-84
Mahoney, Paul F. 1938- 155
Mahoney, Richard D. 1952- 235
Mahoney, Robert F. 1914- 13-16R
Mahoney, Rosemary 1961- 135
Mahoney, Thomas (Arthur) 1928-2004 ...... 1-4R
Obituary 230
Mahoney, Thomas H(enry) D(onald)
1913-1997 .... 13-16R
Obituary 157
Mahoney, Tim 1947- 123
Mahoney, Tom
See Mahoney, John Thomas
Mahony, Devin (Adair) 1963- 130
Mahony, Elizabeth Winthrop 1948- 41-44R
See also Winthrop, Elizabeth
See also SATA 8
Mahony, Patrick
See O'Mahony, Patrick (Frederick)
Mahony, Patrick J(oseph) 1932- 162
Mahony, Peter (Bernard) 1931- 118
Mahony, Phillip 1955- 207
Mahood, Kenneth 1930- 103
See also SATA 24
Mahood, Ruth I. 1908-1981 .... CAP-1
Earlier sketch in CA 19-20
Mahowald, Mary Briody 1935- CANR-86
Earlier sketch in CA 146
Mahrer, Alvin R(aymond) 1927- 21-24R
Mahy, Margaret (May) 1936- CANR-77
Earlier sketches in CA 69-72, CANR-13, 30, 38
See also AAYA 8, 46
See also BYA 6, 7, 8
See also CLR 7, 78
See also CWRI 5
See also FANT
See also JRDA
See also MAICYA 1, 2
See also MAICYAS 1
See also SATA 14, 69, 119
See also WYA
See also YAW
Mai, Ludwig H(ubert) 1898-1982 73-76
Maiakovskii, Vladimir
See Mayakovski, Vladimir (Vladimirovich)
See also IDTP
See also RGWL 2, 3
Maiakovsky, Vladimir Vladimirovich
1893-1930 .... DLB 295
Maibaum, Richard 1909-1991 .... CANR-85
Obituary 133
Earlier sketch in CA 102
Interview in CA-102
Maiden, Cecil (Edward) 1902-1981 73-76
See also SATA 52
Maiden, Jennifer 1949- CANR-91
Earlier sketch in CA 154
See also CP 7
See also CWP
Maidoff, Illia
See List, Ilka Katherine
Maier, Anne McDonald 1954- 142
Maier, Charles S(teven) 1939- CANR-66
Earlier sketch in CA 69-72
Maier, Ernest L(ouis) 1938- 105
Maier, Howard 1906(?)-1983
Obituary 109
Maier, Joseph (Ben) 1911- 21-24R
Maier, Karl George 1957- 216
Maier, Norman R(aymond) F(rederick)
1900-1977 .... CANR-4
Obituary 73-76
Earlier sketch in CA 1-4R
Maier, Paul L(uther) 1930- CANR-2
Earlier sketch in CA 5-8R
Maier, Pauline (Rubbelke) 1938- CANR-143
Earlier sketch in CA 37-40R
Maier, Philipp 1971- 237
Maier, Thomas 1956- 148
Maier, (Henry) William (Jr.) 1901-1981 ..... 1-4R
Maifair, Linda Lee 1947- 150
See also SATA 83
Maik, Henri
See Hecht, Henri Joseph
Maikov, Apollon Nikolaevich
1821-1897 .... DLB 277
Maikov, Vasilii Ivanovich 1728-1778 . DLB 150
Mailer, Adele 166
Mailer, Norman (Kingsley) 1923- CANR-130
Earlier sketches in CA 9-12R, CANR-28, 74, 77
See also CABS 1
See also AAYA 31
See also AITN 2
See also AMW
See also AMWC 2
See also AMWR 2
See also BPFB 2
See also CDALB 1968-1988
See also CLC 1, 2, 3, 4, 5, 8, 11, 14, 28, 39, 74, 111
See also CN 1, 2, 3, 4, 5, 6, 7
See also CPW
See also DA
See also DA3
See also DAB
See also DAC
See also DAM MST, NOV, POP
See also DLB 2, 16, 28, 185, 278
See also DLBD 3
See also DLBY 1980, 1983
See also EWL 3
See also MAL 5
See also MTCW 1, 2
See also MTFW 2005
See also NFS 10
See also RGAL 4
See also TUS
Maillard, Keith 1942- CANR-98
Earlier sketch in CA 93-96
Maillart, Ella 1903-1997 158
See also DLB 195
Maillet, Adrienne 1885-1963 .... DLB 68
Maillet, Antonine 1929- CANR-134
Brief entry 115
Earlier sketches in CA 120, CANR-46, 74, 77
Interview in CA-120
See also CCA 1
See also CLC 54, 118
See also CWW 2
See also DAC
See also DLB 60
See also MTCW 2
See also MTFW 2005
Mailloux, Steven 1950- CANR-53
Earlier sketches in CA 107, CANR-25
Maillu, David G(ian) 1939- 172
See also BW 3
See also DLB 157
See also MAICYA 2
See also SATA 111
Mails, Thomas E. 1920(?)- 134
Brief entry 111
Maiman, Jaye 1957- CANR-72
Earlier sketch in CA 145
Maimane, Arthur 1932- 219
Maimon, Morton A. 1931- 33-36R
Maimonides, Moses 1135-1204 .... DLB 115
Main, Elizabeth
See Le Blond, (Elizabeth) Aubrey
Main, Gloria (Jean) L(und) 1933- 112
Main, Jackson Turner 1917- CANR-1
Earlier sketch in CA 1-4R
Main, Jeremy 1929- 175
Main, Mildred Miles 1898-1980 .... CAP-1
Earlier sketch in CA 13-16
Main, Mrs.
See Le Blond, (Elizabeth) Aubrey
Maina wa kinyatti
See wa Kinyatti, Maina
Maine, Charles Eric
See McIlwain, David
Maine, David
See Avice, Claude (Pierre Marie)
Maine, Trevor
See Catherall, Arthur
Maines, Leah 1962- 200
Maines, Rachel P(earl) 1950- 185
Maingot, Anthony P. 1937- 151
Maingot, Rodney 1893-1982
Obituary 105
Mainland, William Faulkner 1905-1988(?)
Obituary 125
Mainprize, Don 1930- CANR-7
Earlier sketch in CA 17-20R
Mains, David R(andall) 1936- 93-96
Mains, Randolph P. 1946- 148
See also SATA 80

Mainstone, Rowland J(ohnson)
1923- CANR-23
Earlier sketch in CA 107
Mainwaring, Daniel 1902-1977 204
See also CMW 4
See also DLB 44
See also IDFW 4
Mainwaring, Marion 1922- CANR-102
Earlier sketches in CA 1-4R, CANR-3
Mainwaring, Scott 1954- CANR-93
Earlier sketch in CA 145
Maio, Samuel (Joseph) 1955- 171
Maiolo, Joseph 1938- 49-52
Maiorano, Robert 1946- 116
See also SATA 43
Mair, Alistair 1924- 9-12R
Mair, Charles 1838-1927 182
See also DLB 99
See also RGEL 2
Mair, (Alexander) Craig 1948- 102
Mair, George Brown 1914- CANR-12
Earlier sketch in CA 13-16R
Mair, George F(isk) 1922-1978
Obituary 111
Mair, George L. 1929- 129
Mair, John c. 1467-1550 .... DLB 281
Mair, Lucy Philip 1901-1986
Obituary 119
Mair, Margaret
See Crompton, Margaret (Norah Mair)
Mair, Victor H(enry) 1943- CANR-90
Earlier sketches in CA 113, CANR-32
Maira, Sunaina 1969- 197
Maire
See O'Grianna, Seamus
Mairet, Jean de 1604-1686 .. GFL Beginnings to 1789
Maironis, Jonas 1862-1932 .... CDWLB 4
See also DLB 220
Mairowitz, David Zane 1943- CANR-48
Earlier sketch in CA 122
Mairs, Nancy (Pedrick) 1943- CANR-114
Earlier sketch in CA 136
Mais, Roger 1905-1955 .... CANR-82
Brief entry 105
Earlier sketch in CA 124
See also BW 1, 3
See also CDWLB 3
See also DLB 125
See also EWL 3
See also MTCW 1
See also RGEL 2
See also TCLC 8
Mais, S(tuart) P(etre) B(rodie) 1885-1975 . 69-72
Obituary 57-60
Maisel, Herbert 1930- 53-56
Maisel, Louis Sandy 1945- 117
Maisel, Sherman J(oseph) 1918- CANR-19
Earlier sketches in CA 5-8R, CANR-4
Maisels, Maxine S. 1939- 49-52
Maisky, Ivan (Mikhailovich) 1884-1975 .. 65-68
Obituary 61-64
Maisner, Heather 1947- .... SATA 89
Maison, Della
See Katz, Bobbi
Maison, Margaret M(ary Bowles)
1920- 17-20R
Maissi, Elie 1911(?)-1983
Obituary 110
Maister, David H. 1947- 221
Maistre, Joseph 1753-1821 ..... GFL 1789 to the Present
Maital, Sharone L(evow) 1947- 131
Maital, Shlomo 1942- CANR-52
Earlier sketches in CA 108, CANR-25
Maitland, Antony Jasper 1935- 101
See also SATA 25
Maitland, Barbara 169
See also SATA 102
Maitland, Barry 217
Maitland, David J(ohnston) 1922- CANR-38
Earlier sketch in CA 116
Maitland, Derek 1943- CANR-23
Earlier sketch in CA 29-32R
Maitland, Frederic William
1850-1906 .... TCLC 65
Maitland, Margaret
See Du Breuil, (Elizabeth) L(or)inda and Wallmann, Jeffrey M(iner)
Maitland, Sara (Louise) 1950- CANR-59
Earlier sketches in CA 69-72, CANR-13
See also BRWS 11
See also CLC 49
See also DLB 271
See also FW
Maitra, Priyatosh 1930- 107
Maizel, C. L.
See Maizel, Clarice Matthews
Maizel, Clarice Matthews 1919- 9-12R
Maizel, Leah
See Maizel, Clarice Matthews
Maizels, John 1945- CANR-115
Earlier sketch in CA 157
Maja-Pearce, Adewale 1953- 126
Majault, Joseph 1916- 101
Majd, Kam 227
Majerova, Marie 1882-1967 .... EWL 3
Majerus, Janet 1936- 65-68
Majeski, Bill
See Majeski, William
Majeski, William 1927- CANR-18
Earlier sketch in CA 25-28R
Majka, Linda C. 1947- 124
Majonica, Ernst 1920- 29-32R
Major, Alan P(ercival) 1929- CANR-7
Earlier sketch in CA 57-60
Major, Andre 1942- 166
See also DLB 60
Major, Charles 1856-1913 186
See also DLB 202
Major, Clarence 1936- CANR-82
Earlier sketches in CA 21-24R, CANR-13, 25, 53
See also CAAS 6
See also AFAW 2
See also BLC 2
See also BW 2, 3
See also CLC 3, 19, 48
See also CN 3, 4, 5, 6, 7
See also CP 2, 3, 4, 5, 6, 7
See also CSW
See also DAM MULT
See also DLB 33
See also EWL 3
See also MAL 5
See also MSW
major, devorah 1952- CANR-124
Earlier sketch in CA 158
See also BW 3
Major, Geraldyn Hodges
1894-1984 .... CANR-85
Obituary 113
Earlier sketch in CA 85-88
Major, Gerri
See Major, Geraldyn Hodges
Major, H. M.
See Jarvis, Sharon
Major, Henriette 1933- 109
Major, J(ames) Russell 1921- CANR-2
Earlier sketch in CA 5-8R
Major, Jean-Louis 1937- CANR-40
Earlier sketches in CA 49-52, CANR-2, 18
Major, John 1936- 233
Major, John (Roy) 1943- 187
Major, John M(cClellan) 1918- 13-16R
Major, Kevin (Gerald) 1949- CANR-112
Earlier sketches in CA 97-100, CANR-21, 38
Interview in CANR-21
See also AAYA 16
See also CLC 26
See also CLR 11
See also DAC
See also DLB 60
See also JRDA
See also MAICYA 1, 2
See also MAICYAS 1
See also SATA 32, 82, 134
See also WYA
See also YAW
Major, Mabel (I.) 1893-1974 45-48
Major, Mark Imre 1923- 65-68
Major, Ralph Hermon 1884-1970 .... CAP-1
Earlier sketch in CA 9-10
Major, Reginald W. 1926- 29-32R
Major-Ball, Terry 1932- 153
Major-General of Marsland
See Duncan, Ronald
Major-Poetzl, Pamela 1943- 116
Majors, Richard G. III 148
Majors, Simon
See Fox, G(ardner) F(rancis)
Majumdar, R(amesh) C(handra) 1888- ... 33-36R
Majumder, Sanat K(umer) 1929- 33-36R
Majure, Janet 1954- CANR-121
Earlier sketch in CA 161
See also SATA 96
Mak, Geert 1946- 196
Makalani, Jabulani K.
See Semmes, Clovis E.
Makanin, Vladimir Semenovich
1937- .... DLB 285
Makanowitzky, Barbara
See Norman, Barbara
Makarenko, Anton Semenovich
1888-1939 .... DLB 272
Makarova, Marina 1942- 120
Makarova, Natalia 1940- 113
Makary
See Iranek-Osmecki, Kazimierz
Makavejev, Dusan 1946- 157
Makaveli
See Shakur, Tupac (Amaru)
Makdisi, Jean Said 155
Makeba, (Zensi) Miriam 1932- 104
See also BW 1
Makely, William O(rson) 1932- 53-56
Makemie, Francis 1658(?)-1708 .... DLB 24
Makepeace, Anne 1947- 208
Makepeace, Joanna
See York, Margaret Elizabeth
Makepeace, R(oyston) W(illiam) 1950- 116
Makerney, Edna Smith 1921- 61-64
Maki, Fumihiko 1928- 190
Maki, James
See Ozu, Yasujiro
Maki, John M(cGilvrey) 1909- 109
Makie, Pam 1943- .... SATA 37
Makin, Peter (Julian) 1946- 93-96
Makine, Andrei 1957- CANR-103
Earlier sketch in CA 176
See also CLC 198
See also MTFW 2005
Makinen, Merja 1953- 156
Makino, Seiichi 1935- 113
Makins, Clifford 1924-1990
Obituary 132
Makins, Roger Mellor 1904-1996 111
Makkai, Adam 1935- CANR-10
Earlier sketch in CA 57-60
Makkreel, Rudolf A. 1939- CANR-48
Earlier sketch in CA 122
Makovsky, Sergei 1877-1962 .... DLB 317
Makow, Henry 1949- 5-8R
Makower, Addie (Gertrude Leonaura)
1906- 65-68
Makower, Joel 1952- 124
Makowski, Elizabeth 206
Makowski, Silk
See Makowski, Silvia Ann
Makowski, Silvia Ann 1940- 168
See also SATA 101
Makowsky, Veronica A(nn) 1954- CANR-38
Earlier sketch in CA 116
Maksimov, Vladimir (Yemelyanovich)
See Maximov, Vladimir (Yemelyanovich)
Maksimov, Vladimir Emel'ianovich
See Maximov, Vladimir (Yemelyanovich)
See also DLB 302
Maksimovic, Desanka 1898-1993 193
See also CDWLB 4
See also DLB 147
See also EWL 3
Maktari, Abdulla M. A. 1936- 37-40R
Maktos, John 1902-1977
Obituary 69-72
Makuck, Peter 1940- 222
Makumi, Joel 1945(?)- .... BW 2
Mal
See Hancock, Malcolm Cyril
Malabaila, Damiano
See Levi, Primo
Malabre, Alfred L(eopold), Jr. 1931- . CANR-28
Earlier sketches in CA 65-68, CANR-12
Malahide, Patrick
See Duggan, P(atrick) G.
Mala'ika, al- Nazik 1922- .... EWL 3
Malam, John 1957- 227
See also SATA 89, 152
Malamud, Bernard 1914-1986 .... CANR-114
Obituary 118
Earlier sketches in CA 5-8R, CANR-28, 62
See also CABS 1
See also AAYA 16
See also AMWS 1
See also BPFB 2
See also BYA 15
See also CDALB 1941-1968
See also CLC 1, 2, 3, 5, 8, 9, 11, 18, 27, 44, 78, 85
See also CN 1, 2, 3, 4
See also CPW
See also DA
See also DA3
See also DAB
See also DAC
See also DAM MST, NOV, POP
See also DLB 2, 28, 152
See also DLBY 1980, 1986
See also EWL 3
See also EXPS
See also LAIT 4
See also LATS 1:1
See also MAL 5
See also MTCW 1, 2
See also MTFW 2005
See also NFS 4, 9
See also RGAL 4
See also RGSF 2
See also SSC 15
See also SSFS 8, 13, 16
See also TCLC 129
See also TUS
See also WLC
Malamud, Phyllis Carole 1938- 125
Malamud, Randy 1962- 142
Malamud-Goti, Jaime 1943- 147
Malan, Herman
See Bosman, Herman Charles and Bosman, Herman Charles
Malan, Rian 1954- 133
See also BEST 90:3
Malan, Roy Mark 1911- 41-44R
Malancioiu, Ileana 1940- .... DLB 232
Maland, David 1929- 103
Malanga, Gerard (Joseph) 1943- 128
Brief entry 112
See also CAAS 17
See also CP 1
Malanos, George J(ohn) 1919-1962 .. CANR-85
Obituary 103
Earlier sketch in CA 1-4R
Malanowski, Jamie 1953- 140
Malaparte, Curzio 1898-1957 .... DLB 264
See also TCLC 52
Malarek, Victor 1948- 123
Malatesta, Peter J. 1932-1990
Obituary 130
Malaurie, Jean Leonard 1922- 212
Malavie, M. J. 1920- 29-32R
Malbin, Michael J(acob) 1943- CANR-17
Earlier sketch in CA 73-76
Malcolm, Andrew (Ian) 1927- 97-100
Malcolm, Andrew H(ogarth) 1943- 53-56
Malcolm, Dan
See Silverberg, Robert
Malcolm, Donald 1932(?)-1975
Obituary 104
Malcolm, Ian
See Malcolm, Andrew (Ian)
Malcolm, Jahnna N.
See Beecham, Jahnna
Malcolm, Janet 1934- CANR-89
Earlier sketch in CA 123
See also CLC 201
See also NCFS 1
Malcolm, John
See Andrews, John (Malcolm)
Malcolm, Joyce Lee 1942- CANR-114
Earlier sketch in CA 152
Malcolm, Margaret
See Kuether, Edith Lyman
Malcolm, Noel 159
Malcolm, Norman (Adrian)
1911-1990 .... CANR-86
Obituary 132
Earlier sketch in CA 37-40R
Malcolmson, Anne
See von Storch, Anne B.
Malcolmson, David 1899-1978 .... 5-8R
See also SATA 6
Malcolmson, Patrick N. 1953- 172
Malcolmson, Robert W(illiam)
1943- CANR-19
Earlier sketch in CA 103
Malcolm X
See Little, Malcolm
See also BLC 2
See also CLC 82, 117
See also LAIT 5
See also NCFS 3
See also WLCS
Malcom, Robert E. 1933- 17-20R
Malcomson, R(osalie) M(ary) 1925- 119
Malcomson, Scott L. 1961- 137
Malcomson, William L. 1932- 25-28R
Malcoskey, Edna Walker 17-20R
Malden, Karl 1914- 169
Maldonado-Denis, Manuel 1933- 131
Brief entry 113
See also HW 1
Male, Belkis Cuza
See Cuza Male, Belkis
Male, David Arthur 1928- 57-60
Male, Roy R(aymond) 1919- 104
Malebranche, Nicolas
1638-1715 .... GFL Beginnings to 1789
Malecki, Edward S(tanley) 1938- 41-44R
Malefakis, Edward E(manuel) 1932- 29-32R
Malefijt, Annemarie de Waal
See de Waal Malefijt, Annemarie
Malek, Frederic Vincent 1937- 81-84
Malek, James S(tanley) 1941- 57-60
Malenbaum, Wilfred 1913-1996 .... CANR-1
Earlier sketch in CA 1-4R
Malerba, Luigi 1927- 142
See also DLB 196
See also EWL 3
Malerich, Edward P. 1940- 33-36R
Maleska, Eugene Thomas
1916-1993 .... CANR-86
Obituary 142
Earlier sketches in CA 1-4R, CANR-1
Malet, (Baldwyn) Hugh (Grenville)
1928-2005 .... 17-20R
Obituary 237
Malet, Lucas 1852-1931
See Harrison, Mary St. Leger Kingsley
See also DLB 153
Maletta, Dr. Arlene
See Feltenstein, Arlene (H.)
Maley, William 1957- 224
Malgonkar, Manohar (Dattatray)
1913- CANR-40
Earlier sketches in CA 1-4R, CANR-1, 18
See also CN 1, 2, 3, 4, 5, 6
See also EWL 3
Malherbe, Abraham J(ohannes)
1930- CANR-1
Earlier sketch in CA 49-52
Malherbe, Ernst Gideon 1895-1982 ...... CAP-1
Earlier sketch in CA 13-14
Malherbe, Francois de
1555-1628 .... GFL Beginnings to 1789
Malherbe, Janie Antonia (Nel) 1897- CAP-1
Earlier sketch in CA 13-16
Malhotra, Ashok Kumar 1940- 110
Malhotra, Inder 1930- 135
Mali, Jane Lawrence 1937-1995 ...... CANR-36
Obituary 149
Earlier sketch in CA 114
See also SATA 51
See also SATA-Brief 44
See also SATA-Obit 86
Mali, Paul 1926- CANR-8
Earlier sketch in CA 57-60
Malia, Martin (Edward)
1924-2004 .... CANR-101
Obituary 233
Earlier sketch in CA 148
Malick, Terrence 1943- 101
Malick, Terry
See Malick, Terrence
Malickson, David L. 1928- 110
Malik, Charles Habib 1906-1987 ..... CANR-86
Obituary 124
Earlier sketches in CA 45-48, CANR-7
Malik, Habib C. 1954- 175
Malik, Hafeez 1930- CANR-21
Earlier sketch in CA 77-80
Malik, Iftikhar H(aider) 1949- 195
Malik, Yogendra K(umar) 1929- 81-84
Malikin, David 1913-1980 77-80
Malimoto
See Puri, Shamlal
Malin, David (Frederick) 1941- CANR-91
Earlier sketch in CA 118
Malin, Edward 1923- 187
Malin, Irving 1934- CANR-6
Earlier sketch in CA 13-16R
Malin, James Claude 1893-1979
Obituary 113
Malin, Jo (Ellen) 1942- 206
Malin, Peter
See Conner, Patrick Reardon
Malina, Bruce J(ohn) 1933- 112

Cumulative Index 371 Mancini

Malina, Frank J(oseph) 1912-1981 ... CANR-86
Obituary ... 108
Earlier sketch in CA 93-96
Malina, Judith 1926- ... CANR-18
Earlier sketch in CA 102
Maling, Arthur (Gordon) 1923- ... CANR-22
Earlier sketches in CA 49-52, CANR-3
Malinin, Theodore I 1933- ... 93-96
Malino, Frances 1940- ... 115
Malinovsky, Aleksandr Aleksandrovich (Bogdanov) 1873-1928
See Bogdanov, Aleksandr Aleksandrovich
Malinowitz, Harriet ... 160
Malinowski, Bronislaw (Kasper) 1884-1942 ... 216
Brief entry ... 114
Malinowski, Ivan 1926-1989 ... 192
See also EWL 3
Malins, Edward (Greenway) 1910- ... 103
Malins, Penelope 1929- ... 126
Malipiero, Gian Francesco 1882-1973
Obituary ... 45-48
Malkiel, Burton G(ordon) 1932- ... CANR-143
Earlier sketches in CA 49-52, CANR-31, 57
Malkiel, Yakov 1914- ... 25-28R
Malkiewicz, J(an) Kris 1931- ... 57-60
Malkin, Irad ... 207
Malkin, Lawrence 1930- ... 126
Malkin, Maurice L. 1900-1977 ... 49-52
Malkin, Michael R(obert) 1943- ... 129
Malkin, Michelle 1970- ... 235
Malkin, Sol(omon) M. 1910-1986
Obituary ... 118
Malkmus, Lizbeth 1937- ... 139
Malkoff, Karl 1938- ... 17-20R
Malkus, Alida Wright 1899-1976 ... 5-8R
Mall, E. Jane 1920- ... CANR-13
Earlier sketch in CA 21-24R
Mall, Viktor
See Beskow, Bo
Mallaby, (Howard) George 1902-1978
Obituary ... 108
Mallaby, Sebastian 1964- ... 138
Malladi, Amulya 1974- ... 221
Mallalieu, Herbert B. 1914- ... CP 1
Mallalieu, John Percival William 1908-1980 ... 129
Obituary ... 97-100
Mallan, Lloyd 1914-1983(?) ... 5-8R
Mallarme, Stephane 1842-1898 ... DAM POET
See also DLB 217
See also EW 7
See also GFL 1789 to the Present
See also LMFS 2
See also PC 4
See also RGWL 2, 3
See also TWA
Malle, Louis 1932-1995 ... 101
Obituary ... 150
Mallea, Eduardo 1903-1982(?) ... 153
Obituary ... 114
See also EWL 3
See also HW 1
See also LAW
Mallen, Bruce E. 1937- ... CANR-14
Earlier sketch in CA 21-24R
Mallery, David 1923- ... 5-8R
Malleson, Andrew (Graeme) 1931- ... 185
Brief entry ... 112
Malleson, Lucy Beatrice 1899-1973 . CANR-59
Obituary ... 49-52
Earlier sketch in CA 97-100
See also Gilbert, Anthony
Mallet, David c. 1705-1765 ... RGEL 2
Mallet-Joris, Francoise 1930- ... CANR-17
Earlier sketch in CA 65-68
See also CLC 11
See also CWW 2
See also DLB 83
See also EWL 3
See also GFL 1789 to the Present
Mallett, Anne 1913-2001 ... 49-52
Mallett, Daryl F(urumi) 1969- ... 149
Mallett, Jerry J. 1939- ... SATA 76
Malley, Ern
See McAuley, James Phillip and Stewart, Harold Frederick
Mallick, Ross ... 153
Mallie, Eamonn 1950- ... 219
Mallin, Jay 1927- ... 17-20R
Mallin, Tom 1927(?)-1978
Obituary ... 89-92
Mallinson, Allan ... 238
Mallinson, George Greisen 1918- ... CANR-1
Earlier sketch in CA 1-4R
Mallinson, Jeremy (John Crosby) 1937- ... CANR-6
Earlier sketch in CA 57-60
Mallinson, Vernon 1910- ... 5-8R
Malliol, William
See McInenly, William T(homas)
Mallis, Jackie
See Mallis, Jacqueline
Mallis, Jacqueline 1922- ... 113
Malloch, Peter
See Duncan, W(illiam) Murdoch
Mallock, W(illiam) H(urrell) 1849-1923 ... 185
See also DLB 18, 57
See also RGEL 2
Mallon, Bill 1952- ... 119
Mallon, Thomas 1951- ... CANR-92
Earlier sketches in CA 110, CANR-29, 57
See also CLC 172
Mallone, George 1944- ... 115
Mallone, Ronald Stephen 1916- ... CAP-1
Earlier sketch in CA 9-10
Mallonee, Richard C(arvel) II 1923- ... 100
Mallory, Bob F(ranklin) 1932- ... 89-92
Mallory, Drew
See Garfield, Brian (Francis Wynne)
Mallory, Enid Lorraine 1938- ... 105
Mallory, J(ames) P(atrick) 1945- ... CANR-88
Earlier sketch in CA 136
Mallory, Kenneth 1945- ... CANR-107
Earlier sketch in CA 124
See also SATA 128
Mallory, Mark
See Reynolds, Dallas McCord
Mallory, Rickey R. 1947- ... 230
Mallory, Tess ... 218
Mallory, Walter Hampton 1892-1980 ... CANR-86
Obituary ... 101
Earlier sketch in CA 9-12R
Mallough, Don 1914- ... 21-24R
Mallow, Judy M(ofield) 1949- ... 163
Mallowan, Agatha Christie
See Christie, Agatha (Mary Clarissa)
Mallowan, Max (Edgar Lucien) 1904-1978 ... CANR-21
Obituary ... 81-84
Earlier sketch in CA 69-72
Mallows, (Edward) Wilfrid (Nassau) 1905- .. 119
Malloy, Brian 1960- ... 221
Malloy, Jerry 1946- ... 152
Malloy, Lester
See Meares, Leonard Frank
Malloy, Ruth Lor 1932- ... CANR-22
Earlier sketch in CA 69-72
Malloy, Terry 1950- ... 69-72
Mally, E(mma) Louise 1908-1977 ... 33-36R
Malm, F(inn) T(heodore) 1919- ... 17-20R
Malm, William P(aul) 1928- ... 9-12R
Malmberg, Carl 1904-1979 ... 33-36R
See also SATA 9
Malmgren, Dallin 1949- ... 133
See also SATA 65
Malmgren, Harald B(ernard) 1935- ... CANR-27
Earlier sketch in CA 45-48
Malmo, Robert Beverley 1912- ... 61-64
Malmont, Valerie S(kuse) 1937- ... 150
Malmqvist, N(ils) G(oran) D(avid) 1924- ... 208
Malmstad, John E. 1941- ... 219
Malmstroem, Vincent H(erschel)
See Malmstrom, Vincent H(erschel)
Malmstrom, Jean 1908-1996 ... 53-56
Malmstrom, Vincent H(erschel) 1926- ... 112
Malo, John W. 1911-2000 ... CANR-12
Earlier sketch in CA 33-36R
See also SATA 4
Malocsay, Zoltan 1946- ... 81-84
Malof, Joseph F(etler) 1934- ... 29-32R
Maloff, Chalda (Irene) 1946- ... 129
Maloff, Saul 1922- ... 33-36R
See also CLC 5
Malone, Bill C(harles) 1934- ... CANR-137
Earlier sketch in CA 65-68
Malone, Colonel Dick
See Malone, Richard S(ankey)
Malone, Dave 1968- ... 171
Malone, Dick
See Malone, Richard S(ankey)
Malone, Dumas 1892-1986 ... CANR-2
Obituary ... 121
Earlier sketch in CA 1-4R
See also DLB 17
Malone, Edmond 1741-1812 ... DLB 142
Malone, Elmer Taylor, Jr. 1943- ... CANR-17
Earlier sketches in CA 49-52, CANR-1
Malone, Hank 1940- ... CANR-102
Earlier sketch in CA 158
Malone, James Hiram 1930- ... 157
See also SATA 84
Malone, Joseph James 1924-1983
Obituary ... 111
Malone, Kemp 1889-1971
Obituary ... 89-92
Malone, Louis
See MacNeice, (Frederick) Louis
Malone, Margaret Gay 1939- ... 112
Malone, Mary ... CANR-2
Earlier sketch in CA 1-4R
Malone, Mary T. 1938- ... 227
Malone, Michael (Christopher) 1942- ... CANR-114
Earlier sketches in CA 77-80, CANR-14, 32, 57
See also CLC 43
Malone, Michael P. 1940-1999 ... CANR-96
Earlier sketches in CA 29-32R, CANR-12
Malone, Michael S(hawn) 1954- ... 197
Malone, Nola Langner 1930-2003 ... CANR-41
Obituary ... 224
Earlier sketches in CA 37-40R, CANR-15
See also Langner, Nola
See also SATA-Obit 151
Malone, Patricia 1932- ... 230
See also SATA 155
Malone, Paul
See Newton, Michael
Malone, Paul B. III 1929- ... 166
Malone, Paul Scott 1952- ... 150
Malone, R. S.
See Malone, Richard S(ankey)
Malone, Richard S(ankey) 1909-1985 ... 129
Obituary ... 116
Brief entry ... 107
Malone, Ruth 1918- ... 93-96
Malone, Susan (Mary) 1957- ... 150
Malone, Ted
See Malone, Elmer Taylor, Jr.
Malone, Wex S(mathers) 1906-1988 ... 9-12R
Maloney, Arnold Hamilton 1888-1955 ... 162
Maloney, Frank E(dward) 1918-1980 ... 73-76
Obituary ... 97-100
Maloney, George A(nthony) 1924- ... CANR-8
Earlier sketch in CA 21-24R
Maloney, J(oseph) J(ohn) 1940-1999 ... 109
Maloney, Joan M(arie) 1931- ... 37-40R
Maloney, Pat
See Markun, Patricia Maloney
Maloney, Ralph Liston 1927-1973 ... CANR-3
Obituary ... 45-48
Earlier sketch in CA 1-4R
Maloney, Ray 1951- ... 133
Malony, H(enry) Newton 1931- ... 104
Malory, Sir Thomas 1410(?)-1471(?) ... BRW 1
See also BRWR 2
See also CDBLB Before 1660
See also DA
See also DAB
See also DAC
See also DAM MST
See also DLB 146
See also EFS 2
See also RGEL 2
See also SATA 59
See also SATA-Brief 33
See also TEA
See also WLCS
See also WLIT 3
Malossi, Giannino ... 182
Malouf, (George Joseph) David 1934- ... CANR-76
Earlier sketches in CA 124, CANR-50
See also CLC 28, 86
See also CN 3, 4, 5, 6, 7
See also CP 1, 7
See also DLB 289
See also EWL 3
See also MTCW 2
See also MTFW 2005
Malouf, Pyrrha 1929- ... 117
Maloy, Kate 1944- ... 214
Malpas, J(effery) E(dward) 1958- ... CANR-94
Earlier sketch in CA 144
Malpass, E(ric) L(awson) 1910-1996 . CANR-18
Obituary ... 154
Earlier sketches in CA 9-12R, CANR-3
See also RHW
Malpass, Leslie F(rederick) 1922- ... CANR-8
Earlier sketch in CA 17-20R
Malpede, Karen (Sophia) 1945- ... CANR-26
Earlier sketch in CA 45-48
See also CD 5, 6
See also DLB 249
See also FW
Malpott, Virgule
See Ghnassia, Maurice (Jean-Henri)
Malquiades
See Hayes, (Robert) Dennis
Malraux, (Georges-)Andre 1901-1976 ... CANR-58
Obituary ... 69-72
Earlier sketches in CAP-2, CA 21-22, CANR-34
See also BPFB 2
See also CLC 1, 4, 9, 13, 15, 57
See also DA3
See also DAM NOV
See also DLB 72
See also EW 12
See also EWL 3
See also GFL 1789 to the Present
See also MTCW 1, 2
See also MTFW 2005
See also RGWL 2, 3
See also TWA
Malraux, Clara (Goldschmidt) 1897(?)-1982
Obituary ... 108
Malraux-Goldschmidt, Clara
See Malraux, Clara (Goldschmidt)
Malroux, Claire ... 215
See also PFS 21
Malta, Demetrio Aguilera
See Aguilera Malta, Demetrio
Maltby, Arthur 1935- ... CANR-10
Earlier sketch in CA 25-28R
Maltby, William S(aunders) 1940- ... CANR-110
Brief entry ... 113
Earlier sketch in CA 152
Malten, William 1902-1993 ... CAP-2
Earlier sketch in CA 23-24
Maltese, John Anthony 1960- ... 143
Maltese, Michael 1909(?)-1981
Obituary ... 103
See also SATA-Obit 24
Malthus, Thomas Robert 1766-1834 . DLB 107, 158
See also RGEL 2
Malti-Douglas, Fedwa 1946- ... 193
Maltin, Leonard 1950- ... CANR-95
Earlier sketches in CA 29-32R, CANR-12, 28
Maltman, Kim 1950- ... 112
Maltz, Albert 1904-1985 ... CANR-85
Obituary ... 115
Earlier sketch in CA 41-44R
See also CN 2, 3
See also DLB 102
See also MAL 5
Maltz, Maxwell 1899-1975 ... 65-68
Obituary ... 57-60
Maltz, Stephen 1932- ... 57-60
Maluf, Chafic 1905(?)-1976
Obituary ... 69-72
Malvasi, Mark G. 1957- ... 170
Malvasi, Meg Greene ... 216
See also SATA 143
Malveaux, Julianne M(arie) 1953- ... CANR-23
Earlier sketch in CA 105
Malvern, Corinne 1905-1956 ... 183
Brief entry ... 115
See also SATA 34
Malvern, Gladys (?)-1962 ... 73-76
See also SATA 23
Malville, J. McKim
See Malville, John McKim
Malville, John McKim 1934- ... 120
Malville, Kim
See Malville, John McKim
Maly, Eugene H. 1920-1981 ... CANR-14
Earlier sketch in CA 21-24R
Malz, Betty 1929- ... CANR-32
Earlier sketch in CA 113
Malzahn, Manfred 1955- ... 146
Malzberg, Barry N(athaniel) 1939- ... CANR-16
Earlier sketch in CA 61-64
See also CAAS 4
See also CLC 7
See also CMW 4
See also DLB 8
See also SFW 4
Malzberg, Benjamin 1893-1975 ... CAP-1
Obituary ... 57-60
Earlier sketch in CA 13-16
Mama G.
See Davis, Grania
Mama G.
See Davis, Grania
Mamalakis, Markos J(ohn) 1932- ... CANR-52
Earlier sketches in CA 45-48, CANR-27
Maman, Andre 1927- ... 73-76
Mamatey, Victor S(amuel) 1917- ... 9-12R
Mamedkulizade, Djalil 1866-1932 ... EWL 3
Mamedov, Seville 1964- ... 150
Mamet, David (Alan) 1947- ... CANR-129
Earlier sketches in CA 81-84, CANR-15, 41, 67, 72
See also CABS 3
See also AAYA 3, 60
See also AMWS 14
See also CAD
See also CD 5, 6
See also CLC 9, 15, 34, 46, 91, 166
See also DA3
See also DAM DRAM
See also DC 4, 24
See also DFS 2, 3, 6, 12, 15
See also DLB 7
See also EWL 3
See also IDFW 4
See also MAL 5
See also MTCW 1, 2
See also MTFW 2005
See also RGAL 4
Mamin, Dmitrii Narkisovich 1852-1912 ... DLB 238
Mamina
See Costa, Nino
Mamin-Sibiriak, D.
See Mamin, Dmitrii Narkisovich
Mamis, Justin E. 1929- ... 9-12R
Mamleev, Yury
See Mamleyev, Yuri
Mamleyev, Yuri 1931- ... 85-88
Mammano, Julie (Lynn) 1962- ... SATA 107
Mammeri, Mouloud 1917-1989 ... EWL 3
Mamonova, Tatyana 1943- ... 114
See also SATA 93
Mamoulian, Rouben (Zachary) 1897-1987 ... CANR-85
Obituary ... 124
Earlier sketch in CA 25-28R
See also CLC 16
Man, Felix H.
See Baumann, Hans Felix S(iegismund)
Man, John 1941- ... CANR-91
Earlier sketches in CA 93-96, CANR-16
Manach (Robato), Jorge 1898(?)-1961
Obituary ... 111
See also LAW
Manaka, Matsemela 1956- ... 140
See also BW 2
See also CD 5, 6
See also DLB 157
Manard, Barbara Bolling 1945- ... 121
Manarin, Louis H(enry) 1932- ... 21-24R
Manas, Jose Angel 1971- ... DLB 322
Manaster, Benjamin 1938- ... 149
Manaster, Kenneth A. 1942- ... 207
Mana-Zucca
See Cassel, Mana-Zucca
Mancewicz, Bernice Winslow 1917- ... 37-40R
Manch, Joseph (Rodman) 1910-1988 ... 53-56
Manchee, Fred B. 1903(?)-1981
Obituary ... 105
Manchee, William L. 1947- ... 229
Manchel, Frank 1935- ... CANR-14
Earlier sketch in CA 37-40R
See also SATA 10
Manchester, Harland 1898-1977 ... 1-4R
Obituary ... 73-76
Manchester, Paul T(homas) 1893-1995 ... 61-64
Manchester, William (Raymond) 1922-2004 ... CANR-59
Obituary ... 228
Earlier sketches in CA 1-4R, CANR-3, 31
See also AITN 1
See also BEST 89:2
See also CPW
See also DAM POP
See also MTCW 1, 2
See also SATA 65
Mancini, Anthony 1939- ... CANR-98
Earlier sketch in CA 73-76
Mancini, Henry 1924-1994 ... IDFW 3, 4

Mancini, Pat McNees
See McNees, Pat
Mancke, Richard B(ell) 1943- 81-84
Mancroft, Stormont Mancroft Samuel
1914- CANR-28
Earlier sketch in CA 49-52
Mancusi-Ungaro, Harold R(aymond), Jr.
1947- 97-100
Mancuso, Joe
See Mancuso, Joseph R.
Mancuso, Joseph R. 1941- 93-96
Mand, Ewald 1906- 17-20R
Mandel, Adrienne Schizzano 1934- 37-40R
Mandel, (Mark) Babaloo 1949(?)- 154
Mandel, Benjamin 1891(?)-1973
Obituary 45-48
Mandel, Bernard 1920- 1-4R
Mandel, Brett H. 1969- CANR-129
Earlier sketch in CA 161
See also SATA 108
Mandel, Charlotte 1925- CANR-108
Earlier sketch in CA 140
Mandel, Eli(as Wolf) 1922-1992 .... CANR-43
Earlier sketches in CA 73-76, CANR-15
See also CP 1, 2
See also DLB 53
Mandel, Ernest 1923-1995 .... CANR-15
Earlier sketch in CA 37-40R
Mandel, George 1920- 1-4R
Mandel, Jerome 1937- 37-40R
Mandel, Johnny 1925- .... IDFW 4
Mandel, Leon III 1928-2002 .... CANR-13
Obituary 205
Earlier sketch in CA 77-80
Mandel, Loring 1928- 73-76
Mandel, Miriam B. 1942- 225
Mandel, Morris 1911- CANR-6
Earlier sketch in CA 5-8R
Mandel, Oscar 1926- CANR-48
Earlier sketches in CA 1-4R, CANR-2, 21
Mandel, Peter (Bevan) 1957-1998 152
See also SATA 87
Mandel, Ruth Blumenstock 1938- 105
Mandel, Sally (Elizabeth) 1944- CANR-119
Earlier sketch in CA 102
See also SATA 64
Mandel, Sheila 1930(?)-1987
Obituary 124
Mandel, Sidney Albert 1923- 93-96
Mandel, Siegfried 1922- CANR-20
Earlier sketches in CA 1-4R, CANR-5
Mandel, William M(arx) 1917- 9-12R
Mandela, Nelson R(olihlahla) 1918- . CANR-82
Earlier sketches in CA 125, CANR-43, 59
See also BW 2, 3
See also DAM MULT
See also WLIT 2
Mandela, (Nomzamo) Winnie (Madikileza)
1936- 125
See also BW 1
Mandelbaum, Allen 111
Mandelbaum, Bernard 1922-2001 130
Obituary 199
Mandelbaum, David G(oodman)
1911-1987 .... CANR-85
Obituary 122
Earlier sketch in CA 41-44R
Mandelbaum, Maurice (H.) 1908-1987 131
Obituary 121
Brief entry 113
Mandelbaum, Michael 1946- CANR-136
Earlier sketch in CA 101
Mandelbaum, Paul 1959- 238
Mandelbaum, Seymour J. 1936- 17-20R
Mandelbaum, W. Adam 235
Mandelbrot, Benoit B. 1924- CANR-130
Earlier sketch in CA 161
Mandelker, Amy 1953- 149
Mandelker, Daniel Robert 1926- CANR-43
Earlier sketches in CA 1-4R, CANR-5, 20
Mandelkorn, Eugenia Miller 1916- 9-12R
Mandell, Arnold Joseph 1934- 101
Mandell, Betty Reid 1924- CANR-8
Earlier sketch in CA 61-64
Mandell, Daniel 1895-1987 .... IDFW 3, 4
Mandell, Fran Gare 1939- 115
Mandell, Gail Porter 1940- 123
Mandell, Maurice I(ra) 1925- CANR-11
Earlier sketch in CA 25-28R
Mandell, Mel 1926- 41-44R
Mandell, Muriel (Hortense Levin) 1921- . 9-12R
See also SATA 63
Mandell, Richard Donald 1929- CANR-10
Earlier sketch in CA 25-28R
Mandelman, Avner 1947- 193
Mandelshtam, Nadezhda
See Mandelstam, Nadezhda (Yakovlevna)
Mandel'shtam, Nadezhda Iakovlevna
See Mandelstam, Nadezhda (Yakovlevna)
See also DLB 302
Mandelshtam, Osip
See Mandel'shtam, Osip Emil'evich and
Mandelstam, Osip (Emilievich)
See also EW 10
See also EWL 3
See also RGWL 2, 3
Mandel'shtam, Osip Emil'evich
See Mandelshtam, Osip
See also DLB 295
Mandelstam, Nadezhda (Yakovlevna)
1899-1980 110
Obituary 102
See also Mandel'shtam, Nadezhda Iakovlevna
Mandelstam, Osip (Emilievich)
1891(?)-1943(?) 150
Brief entry 104
See also Mandelshtam, Osip
See also MTCW 2
See also PC 14
See also TCLC 2, 6
See also TWA
Mandelstamm, Allan B(eryle) 1928- 41-44R
Mander, A(lfred) E(rnest) 1894- CAP-1
Earlier sketch in CA 11-12
Mander, Anica Vesel 1934-2002 .... CANR-8
Obituary 208
Earlier sketch in CA 61-64
Mander, Christine 1927- 136
Mander, Gertrud 1927- 93-96
Mander, (Mary) Jane 1877-1949 162
See also RGEL 2
See also TCLC 31
Mander, Jerry 1936- 81-84
Mander, Raymond (Josiah Gale)
1911(?)-1983 .... CANR-85
Obituary 111
Earlier sketch in CA 101
Mander, Rosalie Grylls 5-8R
Manderino, John 1949- 175
Mandery, Evan J. 236
Mandeville, Bernard 1670-1733 .... DLB 101
Mandeville, Sir John fl. 1350- .... DLB 146
Mandiargues, Andre Pieyre de
See Pieyre de Mandiargues, Andre
See also CLC 41
See also DLB 83
Mandino, Augustine A.
See Mandino, Og
Mandino, Og 1923-1996 103
Obituary 153
Mandler, George 1924- CANR-19
Earlier sketches in CA 1-4R, CANR-4
Mandler, Jean Matter 1929- CANR-19
Earlier sketch in CA 13-16R
Mandler, Peter 1958- 165
Mandrake, Ethel Belle
See Thurman, Wallace (Henry)
Mandrell, Barbara (Ann) 1948- 139
Mandrepelias, Loizos
See Hartocollis, Peter
Mane, Robert 1926- 37-40R
Manea, Norman 1936- CANR-97
Earlier sketch in CA 142
See also DLB 232
Manegold, Catherine S. 1955- 190
Manella, Raymond L(awrence)
1917-2004 .... 17-20R
Obituary 233
Manent, Maria 1898-1988 211
Manent, Pierre 1949- 171
Maner, Martin 1946- CANR-95
Earlier sketch in CA 135
Manes, Christopher 1957- 133
Manes, Stephen 1949- CANR-100
Earlier sketch in CA 97-100
See also SATA 42, 99
See also SATA-Brief 40
Maness, Lonnie (E.) 1929- 206
Manet, Edouard 1832-1883 .... AAYA 58
Manet, Eduardo 1930(?)- .... CWW 2
Manetti, Larry 1947- 235
Manfred, Frederick (Feikema)
1912-1994 .... CANR-85
Obituary 146
Earlier sketch in CA 9-12R
See also CAAS 18
See also CN 1, 2, 3, 4, 5
See also DLB 6, 212, 227
See also SATA 30
See also TCWW 1, 2
Manfred, Freya 1944- 69-72
Manfred, Robert
See Marx, Erica Elizabeth
Manfredi, Gianfranco 1948- .... DLB 196
Manfredi, John Francis 1920- 109
Manfredi, Nino 1921-2004 226
Manfredi, Renee 1962- 144
Manfredi, V.
See Musciano, Walter A.
Manfredi, Valerio Massimo 1943- 215
Mang, Karl 1922- 101
Mangalam, J(oseph) J(oseph) 1924- 37-40R
Mangan, James Clarence 1803-1849 .... RGEL 2
Mangan, James J. 1907- 139
Mangan, James Thomas 1896-1970 ...... CAP-2
Earlier sketch in CA 19-20
Mangan, (John Joseph) Sherry 1904-1961 ... 211
Obituary 112
See also DLB 4
Manganelli, Giorgio 1922-1990 .... DLB 196
Manganiello, Dominic 1951- 124
Mangat, J(agjit) S(ingh) 1937- 73-76
Manger, Itsik 1901-1969 .... EWL 3
Mangin, Marie France 1940- .... SATA 59
Mangini (Gonzalez), Shirley 1946- 149
Mangione, Gerlando 1909-1998 ...... CANR-42
Obituary 169
See also Mangione, Jerre
See also CN 7
Mangione, Jerre
See Mangione, Gerlando
See also CN 1, 2, 3, 4, 5, 6
See also SATA 6
See also SATA-Obit 104
Mango, Andrew 1926(?)- 221
Mango, Cyril (Alexander) 1928- CANR-143
Earlier sketch in CA 109
Mango, Karin N. 1936- CANR-50
Earlier sketch in CA 123
See also SATA 52
Mangold, James 1964(?)- 171
Mangold, Tom 1934- 69-72
Mangua, Charles 168
Manguel, Alberto (Adrian) 1948- CANR-87
Earlier sketches in CA 131, CANR-44
See also HW 1
Mangum, Garth L(eroy) 1926- 81-84
Mangurian, David 1938- CANR-10
Earlier sketch in CA 57-60
See also SATA 14
Manhattan, Avro 1914- CANR-30
Earlier sketches in CA 9-12R, CANR-5
Manheim, Camryn 1961- 192
Manheim, Debra Francis
See Manheim, Debra Francis
Manheim, Emanuel 1897-1988
Obituary 125
Manheim, Jarol B(ruce) 1946- CANR-21
Earlier sketches in CA 57-60, CANR-6
Manheim, Leonard (Falk) 1902-1983 .... CAP-2
Earlier sketch in CA 21-22
Manheim, Michael 1928- CANR-93
Earlier sketch in CA 81-84
Manheim, Ralph 1907(?)-1992 159
Brief entry 115
Manheim, Sylvan D. 1897-1977
Obituary 73-76
Manheim, Theodore 1921-
Brief entry 108
Manheim, Werner 1915- 53-56
Manhein, Mary H(uffman) 203
Manhire, Bill 1946- CANR-20
Earlier sketch in CA 103
See also CP 2, 3, 4, 5, 6, 7
See also EWL 3
Manhoff, Bill
See Manhoff, Wilton
Manhoff, Wilton 1919-1974
Obituary 49-52
Mania, Cathy 1950- 169
See also SATA 102
Mania, Robert (C.) 1952- 169
See also SATA 102
Maniam, K. S. 1942- .... CD 6
Maniates, Maria Rika 1937- 113
Maniatty, Taramesha 1978- .... SATA 92
Maniaty, Anthony 1949- 119
Maniaty, Tony
See Maniaty, Anthony
Manicas, Peter T(heodore) 1934- 53-56
Manicka, Rani 225
Manicom, Jacqueline 1935-1976 .... EWL 3
Maniere, J.-E.
See Giraudoux, Jean(-Hippolyte)
Manifold, J(ohn) S(treeter) 1915- CANR-24
Earlier sketch in CA 69-72
See also CP 1, 2
Manigault, Edward 1897(?)-1983
Obituary 109
Manigault, Sandra L. 1945- 180
Manilius fl. 1st cent. - .... DLB 211
Manilla, James 97-100
Manis, Jerome G. 1917- 25-28R
Manis, Melvin 1931- 21-24R
Maniscalco, Joseph 1926- CANR-8
Earlier sketch in CA 5-8R
See also SATA 10
Maniu, Adrian 1891-1968 .... EWL 3
Manji, Irshad 1971(?)- 230
Manjon, Maite
See Manjon De Read, Maria Teresa
Manjon De Read, Maria Teresa
1931- CANR-38
Mank, Gregory William 1950- 89-92
Mankekar, D. R. 1910- CANR-13
Earlier sketch in CA 21-24R
Mankell, Henning 1948- 187
Mankiewicz, Don M(artin) 1922- 13-16R
See also CN 1, 2
Mankiewicz, Frank (Fabian) 1924- 89-92
Mankiewicz, Herman (Jacob) 1897-1953 ... 169
Brief entry 120
See also DLB 26
See also IDFW 3, 4
See also TCLC 85
Mankiewicz, Joseph L(eo)
1909-1993 .... CANR-87
Obituary 140
Earlier sketch in CA 73-76
See also DLB 44
Mankiewicz, Thomas F. 1942- 128
Brief entry 124
Mankiewicz, Tom
See Mankiewicz, Thomas F.
Mankiller, Wilma (Pearl) 1945- 146
Mankin, Paul A. 1924- 37-40R
Mankoff, Allan H. 1935- 45-48
Mankowitz, (Cyril) Wolf 1924-1998 ... CANR-5
Obituary 169
Earlier sketch in CA 5-8R
See also CBD
See also CD 5, 6
See also CN 1, 2, 3, 4, 5, 6
See also DLB 15
See also IDFW 3
Mankowska, Joyce Kells Batten 1919- ... CAP-1
Earlier sketch in CA 9-10
Manley, Deborah 1932- CANR-22
Earlier sketch in CA 105
See also SATA 28
Manley, (Mary) Delariviere
1672(?)-1724 .... DLB 39, 80
See also RGEL 2
Manley, Frank 1930- CANR-125
Earlier sketch in CA 5-8R
Manley, Joey 1965- 138
Manley, John F(rederick) 1939- 77-80
Manley, Lawrence (Gordon) 1949- 109
Manley, Michael Norman
1924-1997 .... CANR-27
Obituary 157
Earlier sketch in CA 85-88
Manley, Rachel 1947- 209
Manley, Ruth Rodney King 1907(?)-1973
Obituary 41-44R
Manley, Seon 1921- 85-88
See also CLR 3
See also SAAS 2
See also SATA 15
Manley-Tucker, Audrie 1924(?)-1983(?)
Obituary 108
See also RHW
Manlove, Colin Nicholas 1942- CANR-86
Earlier sketches in CA 113, CANR-32
Manly, Marline
See Rathborne, St. George (Henry)
Manly, Peter L. 1945- 144
Mann, A. Philo
See Ald, Roy A(llison)
Mann, Abby 1927- 109
Interview in CA-109
See also DLB 44
Mann, Abel
See Creasey, John
Mann, (Francis) Anthony 1914- CAP-1
Earlier sketch in CA 9-10
Mann, Arthur 1922-1993 109
Obituary 140
Mann, Avery
See Breetveld, Jim Patrick
Mann, Barbara Alice 1947- 192
Mann, Bob 1948- 61-64
Mann, Catherine 1943- 139
Mann, Charles
See Heckelmann, Charles N(ewman)
Mann, Charles F. 1946- 149
Mann, Charles W(illiam), Jr.
1929-1998 .... 41-44R
Obituary 169
Mann, Chris(topher Michael Zithulele)
1948- 126
See also CP 7
Mann, (Robert Francis) Christopher Stephen
1917- 89-92
Mann, Chuck
See Heckelmann, Charles N(ewman)
Mann, D. J.
See Freeman, James Dillet
Mann, Dale 1938- 61-64
Mann, David Douglas 1934- CANR-52
Earlier sketches in CA 49-52, CANR-28
Mann, Dean Edson 1927- CANR-5
Earlier sketch in CA 9-12R
Mann, Deborah
See Bloom, Ursula (Harvey)
Mann, Donald Nathaniel 1920-1985
Obituary 114
Mann, Douglas 236
Mann, E(dward) B(everly) 1902- .... TCWW 1, 2
Mann, Edward
See Fried, Emanuel
Mann, Edward Andrew 1932- 103
Mann, Elizabeth 1948- .... MAICYA 2
See also SATA 153
Mann, Emily 1952- CANR-55
Earlier sketch in CA 130
See also CAD
See also CD 5, 6
See also CWD
See also DC 7
See also DLB 266
Mann, Erika 1905-1969
Obituary 25-28R
Mann, Esther Kingston
See Kingston-Mann, Esther
Mann, Floyd C(hristopher) 1917- 1-4R
Mann, Georg K(arl) F(riedrich)
1913-1980 .... 1-4R
Mann, Golo 1909-1994 97-100
Obituary 145
Mann, Harold W(ilson) 1925- 17-20R
Mann, (Luiz) Heinrich 1871-1950 181
Brief entry 106
Earlier sketch in CA 164
See also DLB 66, 118
See also EW 8
See also EWL 3
See also RGWL 2, 3
See also TCLC 9
Mann, Horace 1796-1859 .... DLB 1, 235
Mann, Jack
See Cannell, Charles (Henry)
Mann, Jack 1917(?)-1995 143
Mann, Jackie
See Mann, Jack
Mann, James
See Harvey, John (Barton)
Mann, James 1946- 229
Mann, Janet 1960- 208
Mann, Jeff(rey A.) 1959- 204
Mann, Jessica 1937- CANR-111
Earlier sketches in CA 49-52, CANR-2, 24, 60
See also CMW 4
Mann, John H. 1928- CANR-88
Earlier sketch in CA 85-88
Mann, Josephine
See Pullein-Thompson, Josephine (Mary Wedderburn)
Mann, Judith (W.) 1950- 208
Mann, Judy 1943-2005 146
Mann, Julia de Lacy 1891-1985
Obituary 116
Mann, Katharina 1883(?)-1980
Obituary 97-100

Cumulative Index 373 Mara

Mann, Kenneth Walker 1914- 29-32R
Mann, Kenny 1946- 155
See also SATA 91
Mann, Klaus (Heinrich) 1906-1949 204
See also DLB 56
Mann, Leonard 1895- .... CN 1, 2, 3
See also CP 1
Mann, Lucile Q.
See Mann, Lucile Quarry
Mann, Lucile Quarry 1897(?)-1986
Obituary 121
Mann, Marty 1904-1980 103
Obituary 101
Mann, Mary Peabody 1806-1887 .... DLB 239
Mann, Michael 1919-1977 .... CANR-3
Obituary 69-72
Earlier sketch in CA 49-52
Mann, Michael K. 1943- 134
Brief entry 120
Mann, Milton B(ernard) 1937- 45-48
Mann, Pamela 1946- 155
See also SATA 91
Mann, Patrick
See Waller, Leslie
Mann, Paul (James) 1947- CANR-73
Earlier sketch in CA 143
Mann, Peggy
See Houlton, Peggy Mann
See also SATA 6
Mann, Peter (Clifford) 1948- 93-96
Mann, Peter H. 1926- CANR-12
Earlier sketch in CA 25-28R
Mann, Philip A(lan) 1934- 73-76
Mann, (Anthony) Phillip 1942- .... SFW 4
Mann, Ralph 1943- 112
Mann, Richard G(eorge) 1949- 124
Mann, Robert 1958- CANR-115
Earlier sketch in CA 140
Mann, Steve 1962- 212
Mann, Sunnie 1914(?)-1992 143
Mann, Susan 1943- 128
Mann, (Paul) Thomas 1875-1955 ... CANR-133
Brief entry 104
Earlier sketch in CA 128
See also BPFB 2
See also CDWLB 2
See also DA
See also DA3
See also DAB
See also DAC
See also DAM MST, NOV
See also DLB 66
See also EW 9
See also EWL 3
See also GLL 1
See also LATS 1:1
See also LMFS 1
See also MTCW 1, 2
See also MTFW 2005
See also NFS 17
See also RGSF 2
See also RGWL 2, 3
See also SSC 5, 80, 82
See also SSFS 4, 9
See also TCLC 2, 8, 14, 21, 35, 44, 60, 168
See also TWA
See also WLC
Mann, W(illiam) Edward 1918- CANR-121
Earlier sketches in CA 49-52, CANR-28
Mann, William D'Alton 1839-1920 236
See also DLB 137
Mann, William J. 1963- CANR-109
Earlier sketch in CA 162
Mann, William S(omervell) 1924-1989 109
Obituary 129
Mann, Zane B. 1924- 101
Mann-Borgese, Elisabeth
See Borgese, Elisabeth Mann
Manne, Henry G. 1928- 33-36R
Mannello, George Jr. 1913-1990 .... 33-36R
Manner, Eeva-Liisa 1921-1995 202
See also EWL 3
Mannering, Julia
See Bingham, Madeleine (Mary Ebel)
Manners, Alexandra
See Rundle, Anne
Manners, Ande Miller 1923(?)-1975
Obituary 57-60
Manners, David X. 1912- CANR-46
Earlier sketch in CA 106
Manners, Elizabeth (Maude) 1917- 49-52
Manners, Gerald 1932- 37-40R
Manners, John (Errol) 1914- 106
Manners, Julia
See Greenaway, Gladys
Manners, Robert A(lan) 1913-1996 .... 33-36R
Obituary 152
Manners, William 1907-1994 65-68
Mannes, Marya 1904-1990 .... CANR-3
Obituary 132
Earlier sketch in CA 1-4R
Mannetti, Lisa 1953- 125
See also SATA 57
See also SATA-Brief 51
Manngian, Peter
See Monger, (Ifor) David
Mannheim, Grete (Salomon) 1909-1986 . 9-12R
See also SATA 10
Mannheim, Karl 1893-1947 204
See also TCLC 65
Manniche, Lise 1943- CANR-101
Earlier sketches in CA 107, CANR-25
See also SATA 31
Mannin, Ethel (Edith) 1900-1984 .... CANR-8
Obituary 114
Earlier sketch in CA 53-56
See also CN 2, 3
See also DLB 191, 195
Manning, Adelaide Frances Oke .... CMW 4
Manning, Ambrose N(uel) 1922- 114
Manning, Bayless Andrew 1923- CANR-9
Earlier sketch in CA 13-16R
Manning, Beverley J(ane) 1942- 109
Manning, Brennan 195
Manning, Brian 1927-2004 239
Manning, Christel (J.) 1961- 234
Manning, Clarence A(ugustus) 1893-1972
Obituary 37-40R
Manning, David
See Faust, Frederick (Schiller)
Manning, David John 1938- 103
Manning, Emily 1845-1890 .... DLB 230
Manning, Frank E(dward) 1944- CANR-7
Earlier sketch in CA 53-56
Manning, Frederic 1882-1935 216
Brief entry 124
See also DLB 260
See also TCLC 25
Manning, Harvey (Hawthorne)
1925- CANR-115
Earlier sketches in CA 112, CANR-30, 56
Manning, Helen Taft 1891(?)-1987
Obituary 121
Manning, Jack 1920-2001 69-72
Obituary 204
See also Mendelsohn, Jack
Manning, Jo 1940- 222
Manning, Joe 1941- 202
Manning, Kate 205
Manning, Laurence (Edward)
1899-1972 .... CANR-117
Earlier sketch in CA 160
See also DLB 251
See also SFW 4
Manning, Margaret Raymond 1921-1984
Obituary 114
Manning, Marie 1873(?)-1945 202
See also DLB 29
Manning, Marsha
See Grimstead, Hettie
Manning, Martha M. 1952- CANR-119
Earlier sketch in CA 149
Manning, Martin
See Smith, R(eginald) D(onald)
Manning, Mary Louise
See Cameron, Lou
Manning, Matthew 1955- 183
Brief entry 111
Manning, Maurice 1966- 215
Manning, Michael 1940- 65-68
Manning, Mick 1959- 190
Manning, Olivia 1915-1980 .... CANR-29
Obituary 101
Earlier sketch in CA 5-8R
See also CLC 5, 19
See also CN 1, 2
See also EWL 3
See also FW
See also MTCW 1
See also RGEL 2
Manning, Paul 1912-1995 107
Manning, Peter J. 1942- CANR-56
Earlier sketch in CA 125
Manning, Peter K(irby) 1940- CANR-86
Earlier sketches in CA 37-40R, CANR-14, 34
Manning, Philip 1930(?)-1983
Obituary 110
Manning, Phyllis A(nne) Sergeant
1903-1999 .... 5-8R
Manning, Preston 1942- 141
Manning, Reg(inald West) 1905-1986
Obituary 118
Manning, Richard Dale 1951- 200
Manning, Robert (Joseph) 1919- 69-72
Manning, Robert D. 1957- 201
Manning, Roberta Thompson 1940- 130
Manning, Rosemary
See Cole, Margaret Alice
Manning, Rosemary (Joy)
1911-1988 .... CANR-70
Earlier sketches in CA 1-4R, CANR-1, 25
See also Davys, Sarah and
Voyle, Mary
See also CWRI 5
See also SATA 10
Manning, Roy
See West, Tom
Manning, Sarra 238
See also SATA 162
Manning, Stanley Arthur 1921- 110
Manning, Sylvia 1943- 81-84
Manning, Thomas Davys 1898-1972 ..... CAP-1
Earlier sketch in CA 19-20
Manning-Sanders, Ruth (Vernon)
1895(?)-1988 .... CANR-41
Obituary 126
Earlier sketch in CA 73-76
See also CWRI 5
See also MAICYA 1, 2
See also SATA 15, 73
See also SATA-Obit 57
Mannino, Mary Ann Vigilante 1943- 209
Mannion, John J(oseph) 1941- 73-76
Mannix, Edward 1928- 13-16R
Mannon, James M(onroe) 1942- 110
Mannon, Warwick
See Hopkins, (Hector) Kenneth
Mannoni, Octave 1899-1989 102
Mannyng, Robert fl. 1303-1338 .... DLB 146
Mano, D. Keith 1942- CANR-57
Earlier sketches in CA 25-28R, CANR-26
See also CAAS 6
See also CLC 2, 10
See also DLB 6
Mano, M(oshe) Morris 1927- 103
Manocchia, Benito 1934- 69-72
Manoff, Robert Karl 1944- 126
Manogaran, Chelvadurai 1935- 124
Manolson, Frank 1925- 17-20R
Manoni, Mary H(allahan) 1924- CANR-4
Earlier sketch in CA 49-52
Manoogian, Haig P. 1916(?)-1980
Obituary 97-100
Manor, Jason
See Hall, Oakley (Maxwell)
Manos, Charley 1923-1985 .... 29-32R
Obituary 116
Manosevitz, Martin 1938- 29-32R
Manrique, Gomez 1412(?)-1490 .... DLB 286
Manrique (Ardila), Jaime 1949- CANR-89
Earlier sketch in CA 139
Manrique, Jorge 1440-1479 .... DLB 286
Manross, William Wilson 1905- 57-60
Manry, Robert 1918-1971 .... CAP-2
Obituary 29-32R
Earlier sketch in CA 21-22
Mansbach, Richard W(allace) 1943- 53-56
Mansberg, Ruth 1924- 130
Mansbridge, Francis 1943- 133
Mansbridge, John 1901(?)-1981
Obituary 105
Manschreck, Clyde Leonard 1917- CANR-5
Earlier sketch in CA 9-12R
Mansel, Philip 1943- 209
Mansell, Darrel (Lee, Jr.) 1934- 57-60
Mansell, Gerard (Evelyn Herbert) 1921- 130
Manser, Martin H(ugh) 1952- CANR-123
Earlier sketches in CA 118, CANR-42
Mansergh, (Philip) Nicholas (Seton)
1910-1991 .... CANR-86
Obituary 133
Earlier sketch in CA 105
Mansfield, Bruce Edgar 1926- 103
Mansfield, Comins 1896-1984
Obituary 112
Mansfield, Edwin 1930-1997 .... CANR-18
Obituary 162
Earlier sketches in CA 9-12R, CANR-3
Mansfield, Elizabeth
See Schwartz, Paula
Mansfield, Harold H. 1912-1989 .... 17-20R
Mansfield, Harvey C(laflin)
1905-1988 .... CANR-86
Obituary 125
Earlier sketch in CA 1-4R
Mansfield, Howard 1957- CANR-92
Earlier sketch in CA 146
Mansfield, Irving 1908(?)-1988
Obituary 126
Mansfield, John M(aurice) 1936- 29-32R
Mansfield, Katherine
See Beauchamp, Kathleen Mansfield
See also BPFB 2
See also BRW 7
See also DAB
See also DLB 162
See also EWL 3
See also EXPS
See also FW
See also GLL 1
See also RGEL 2
See also RGSF 2
See also SSC 9, 23, 38, 81
See also SSFS 2, 8, 10, 11
See also TCLC 2, 8, 39, 164
See also WLC
See also WWE 1
Mansfield, Libby
See Schwartz, Paula
Mansfield, Nick 1959- 176
Mansfield, Norman
See Gladden, E(dgar) Norman
Mansfield, Peter 1928-1996 65-68
Obituary 151
Mansfield, Roger (Ernest) 1939- CANR-11
Earlier sketch in CA 25-28R
Manship, David 1927- 25-28R
Manski, Charles F. 1948- 138
Manso, Peter 1940- CANR-44
Earlier sketch in CA 29-32R
See also CLC 39
Manson, Ainslie Kertland 1938- 180
See also SATA 115
Manson, Beverlie 1945- 113
See also SATA 57
See also SATA-Brief 44
Manson, Cynthia 171
Manson, JoAnn E. 1953- 221
Manson, Marilyn
See Warner, Brian
Manson, Richard 1939- 29-32R
Mansoor, Menahem 1911-2001 .... CANR-15
Obituary 202
Earlier sketch in CA 41-44R
Mansur, Ina 1910-1988 .... CANR-38
Earlier sketch in CA 116
Mantecon, Juan Jimenez
See Jimenez (Mantecon), Juan Ramon
Mantel, Hilary (Mary) 1952- CANR-101
Earlier sketches in CA 125, CANR-54
See also CLC 144
See also CN 5, 6, 7
See also DLB 271
See also RHW
Mantel, Samuel J(oseph), Jr. 1921- 13-16R
Mantell, Leroy H. 1919- 37-40R
Mantell, Martin E(den) 1936- 45-48
Manternach, Janaan 1927- 116
Mantey, Julius Robert 1890-1981 .... CAP-1
Earlier sketch in CA 11-12
Manthorpe, Helen 1958- 195
See also SATA 122
Mantinband, Gerda (B.) 1917- .... SATA 74
Mantle, Jonathan 1954- CANR-88
Earlier sketch in CA 129
Mantle, Mickey (Charles) 1931-1995 89-92
Obituary 149
Mantle, Winifred (Langford) CANR-6
Earlier sketch in CA 13-16R
Manto, Saadat Hasan 1912-1955 .... RGSF 2
See also SSFS 15
Manton, Jo
See Gittings, Jo (Grenville) Manton
Manton, Kenneth G. 1947- 143
Manton, Peter
See Creasey, John
Manton, Sidnie Milana 1902-1979 167
Mantovano
See Spagnola, Giovanni Battista
Mantsios, Gregory 1950- 171
Mantyla, Martti 1955- 161
Manuel, E(spiridion) Arsenio 1909- 118
See also CAAS 9
Manuel, Frank Edward 1910-2003 ... CANR-92
Obituary 215
Earlier sketches in CA 9-12R, CANR-6, 29, 53
Manuel, Fritzie Prigohzy 1910- 219
Manuel, George 1921-1989 107
Manuel, Lynn 1948- .... SATA 99
Manuel, Niklaus c. 1484-1530 .... DLB 179
Manus, Mavis 1929- 116
Manus, Willard 1930- CANR-53
Earlier sketches in CA 108, CANR-28
Manushkin, Fran(ces) 1942- CANR-61
Earlier sketches in CA 49-52, CANR-1
See also SATA 7, 54, 93
Manvell, (Arnold) Roger 1909-1987 . CANR-86
Obituary 124
Earlier sketches in CA 1-4R, CANR-6, 23
Manville, W(illiam) H(enry) 1930- 93-96
Interview in CA-93-96
Manwell, Reginald D(ickinson)
1897-1987 .... 37-40R
Man Without a Spleen, A
See Chekhov, Anton (Pavlovich)
Man Xibo
See Porkert, Manfred (Bruno)
Many, Paul 1947- 191
Many, Seth E(dward) 1939- 97-100
Manyan, Gladys 1911- 57-60
Manz, Charles C. 203
Manzalaoui, Mahmoud (Ali) 1924- .. CANR-12
Earlier sketch in CA 29-32R
Manzarek, Ray(mond Daniel) 1939- 212
Manzella, David (Bernard) 1924- 5-8R
Manzini, Gianna 1896-1974
Obituary 53-56
See also DLB 177
Manzoni, Alessandro 1785-1873 .... EW 5
See also RGWL 2, 3
See also TWA
See also WLIT 7
Manzoni, Jean-Francois 226
Manzoni, Pablo Michelangelo 1939-
Brief entry 106
Mao, James C. T. 1925- 37-40R
Mao, Tse-tung 1907-1976 .... CANR-46
Obituary 69-72
Earlier sketch in CA 73-76
See also MTCW 1, 2
Maor, Eli 1937- 226
Mao Tun
See Yen-Ping, Shen
See also EWL 3
Mapanje, (John Alfred Clement) Jack
1944(?)- 166
See also BW 3
See also CP 7
See also DLB 157
See also WWE 1
Mapel, William 1902-1984
Obituary 112
Mapes, Arthur Franklin 1913-1986
Obituary 118
Mapes, Mary A.
See Ellison, Virginia H(owell)
Maple, Eric William 1915- CANR-6
Earlier sketch in CA 53-56
Maple, Jack
See Maple, John Edward
Maple, John Edward 1952-2001 194
Maple, Marilyn 1931- 148
See also SATA 80
Maple, Terry 1946- CANR-1
Earlier sketch in CA 49-52
Maples, Evelyn Palmer 1919- CANR-17
Earlier sketches in CA 5-8R, CANR-2
Maponya, Maishe 1951- 229
See also CD 5, 6
Mapp, Alf J(ohnson), Jr. 1925- CANR-1
Earlier sketch in CA 1-4R
Mapp, Edward C(harles) 33-36R
Mappin, Strephyn 1956- 180
See also SATA 109
Mapson, Jo-Ann CANR-143
Earlier sketch in CA 174
Maquet, Jacques Jerome Pierre
1919- CANR-29
Earlier sketches in CA 61-64, CANR-8
Maquet, Paul G. J. 1928- 211
Mar, M. Elaine 1966- 221
Mara, Barney
See Roth, Arthur J(oseph)

Mara 374 CONTEMPORARY AUTHORS

Mara, Jeanette
See Cebulash, Mel
Mara, Rachna
See Gilmore, Rachna
Mara, Sally
See Queneau, Raymond
Mara, Thalia 1911-2003 ... 9-12R
Obituary ... 220
Marable, Manning 1950- ... CANR-144
Earlier sketch in CA 110
Maracle, Lee 1950- ... 149
See also NNAL
Marahiman, Ismail 1934- ... 136
Marai, Sandor 1900-1989
Obituary ... 128
Maraini, Dacia 1936- ... CANR-91
Earlier sketches in CA 5-8R, CANR-11
See also CWW 2
See also DLB 196
See also EWL 3
See also WLIT 7
Maraini, Fosco 1912-2004
Obituary ... 228
Brief entry ... 116
Maraire, J. Nozipo 1966- ... 179
Marais, Eugene Nielen 1871-1936 ... 216
Marais, Josef 1905-1978
Obituary ... 77-80
See also SATA-Obit 24
Maraise, Marie-Catherine-Renee Darcel de
1737-1822 ... DLB 314
Maramorosch, Karl 1915- ... 212
Maramzin, Vladimir Rafailovich
1934- ... DLB 302
Maran, Rene 1887-1960 ... 125
Obituary ... 107
See also BW 1
See also EWL 3
Maran, Stephen P(aul) 1938- ... 57-60
Maranda, Elli Kongas 1932-
Brief entry ... 107
Maranda, Pierre 1930- ... 37-40R
Maranell, Gary M. 1932- ... 37-40R
Marangell, Virginia J(ohnson) 1924- ... 93-96
Maraniss, David 1949- ... 147
Maraniss, James E(lliott) 1945- ... CANR-101
Earlier sketch in CA 139
Marano, Michael 1964- ... 196
Maranto, Gina (Lisa) 1955- ... 154
Marantz, Kenneth A. 1927- ... 142
Marantz, Sylvia S. 1929- ... 142
Maras, Karl
See Bulmer, (Henry) Kenneth
Marasmus, Seymour
See Rivoli, Mario
Marath, Laurie
See Roberts, Suzanne
Marath, Sparrow
See Roberts, Suzanne
Maravich, Pete(r Press) 1947(?)-1988
Obituary ... 124
Marazzi, Rich(ard Thomas) 1943- ... 102
Marbach, Ethel
See Pochocki, Ethel (Frances)
Marback, Richard (C.) ... 197
Marber, Patrick 1964- ... 203
See also CD 5, 6
Marberry, M. M(arion) 1905-1968 ... CAP-2
Earlier sketch in CA 21-22
Marble, Allan Everett 1939- ... 147
Marble, Harriet Clement 1903-1975 ... 73-76
Marble, Samuel D(avey) 1915- ... 106
Marbrook, Del
See Marbrook, Djelloul
Marbrook, Djelloul 1934- ... 73-76
Marbut, F(rederick) B(rowning)
1905-1989 ... 33-36R
Marc
See Boxer, (Charles) Mark (Edward)
Marc, David 1951- ... 138
Marcal, Annette B.
See Callaway, Bernice (Anne)
Marcal, Maria Merce 1952-1998 ... 216
Marcantel, Pamela 1949- ... 162
Marcatante, John 1930- ... CANR-10
Earlier sketch in CA 25-28R
Marceau, Felicien
See Carette, Louis
Marceau, LeRoy 1907- ... CAP-1
Earlier sketch in CA 19-20
Marceau, Marcel 1923- ... 85-88
Marcel, Gabriel Honore 1889-1973 ... 102
Obituary ... 45-48
See also CLC 15
See also EWL 3
See also MTCW 1, 2
Marcelin, Pierre 1908- ... 106
See also EWL 3
Marcelino
See Agnew, Edith J(osephine)
Marcell, David Wyburn 1937- ... 41-44R
Marcell, Jacqueline 1950- ... 199
Marcellino, Fred 1939-2001 ... SATA 68, 118
See also SATA-Obit 127
Marcello, Leo Luke 1945- ... 219
Marcello, Ronald E. 1939- ... 144
March, Andrew Lee 1932- ... 110
March, Anthony 1912-1973
Obituary ... 45-48
March, Bill
See March, William Joseph
March, Carl
See Fleischman, (Albert) Sid(ney)
March, Hilary
See Adcock, Almey St. John
March, James Gardner 1928- ... 13-16R
March, Jessica
See Africano, Lillian
March, Joseph Moncure 1899-1977 ... 149
Obituary ... 69-72
March, Josie
See Titchener, Louise
March, Robert H(erbert) 1934- ... 61-64
March, Valerie
See Beecher, Maureen Ursenbach
March, William ... 216
See also Campbell, William Edward March
See also DLB 9, 86, 316
See also MAL 5
See also TCLC 96
March, William J. 1915- ... 13-16R
March, William Joseph 1941-1990
Obituary ... 132
Marchaj, C(zeslaw) A(ntony) 1918- ... CANR-5
Earlier sketch in CA 9-12R
Marchak, M(aureen) Patricia
1936- ... CANR-144
Earlier sketches in CA 111, CANR-29, 54
Marchak, Maureen
See Marchak, M(aureen) Patricia
Marcham, Frederick George
1898-1992 ... CANR-86
Obituary ... 140
Earlier sketch in CA 13-16R
Marchand, C(harles) Roland 1933-1997
Brief entry ... 110
Marchand, Leslie A(lexis)
1900-1999 ... CANR-12
Obituary ... 185
Earlier sketch in CA 65-68
See also DLB 103
Marchand, Philip (Edward) 1946- ... 130
Marchant, Anyda 1911- ... CANR-53
Earlier sketches in CA 13-16R, CANR-29
Marchant, Bessie 1862-1941 ... 184
See also CWRI 5
See also DLB 160
See also YABC 2
Marchant, Catherine
See Cookson, Catherine (McMullen)
Marchant, Fred 1946- ... 207
Marchant, Herbert S(tanley) ... 106
Marchant, Ian 1958- ... 235
Marchant, John H. 1951- ... 125
Marchant, Leslie R(onald) 1924-
Brief entry ... 110
Marchant, Maurice P(eterson) 1927- ... 110
Marchant, R(ex) A(lan) 1933- ... 13-16R
Marchant, Tony 1959- ... 230
See also CBD
See also CD 5, 6
See also DLB 245
Marchant, William 1923-1995 ... 69-72
Obituary ... 150
Marchbanks, Samuel
See Davies, (William) Robertson
See also CCA 1
Marchenko, Anastasiia Iakovlevna
1830-1880 ... DLB 238
Marchenko, Anatoly (Timofeevich)
1938-1986 ... 25-28R
Obituary ... 121
Marcher, Marion Walden 1890-1987 ... 1-4R
See also SATA 10
Marchese, John 1961- ... 208
Marchesi, Stephen 1951- ... SATA 114
Marchesi, Steve
See Marchesi, Stephen and
Older, Effin and
Older, Jules
Marchessault, Jovette 1938- ... 161
See also DLB 60
Marchetta, Camille ... 217
Marchetta, Melina 1965- ... 238
Marchetti, Albert 1947- ... 89-92
Marchetti, Victor
Brief entry ... 108
Marchi, Giacomo
See Bassani, Giorgio
Marchiano, Linda Boreman 1949(?)-2002 ... 129
Obituary ... 207
Brief entry ... 114
Marchione, Margherita (Frances)
1922- ... CANR-15
Earlier sketch in CA 37-40R
Marciano, Francesca ... CANR-114
Earlier sketch in CA 173
Marciano, John Bemelmans 1971- ... CLR 93
See also SATA 118
Marciniak, Ed(ward) A. 1917-2004 ... 29-32R
Obituary ... 229
Marcinkevicius, Justinas 1930- ... DLB 232
Marcinko, Richard 1940- ... CANR-108
Earlier sketch in CA 143
Marckwardt, Albert H(enry)
1903-1975 ... CANR-4
Obituary ... 61-64
Earlier sketch in CA 1-4R
Marco
See Mountbatten, Louis (Francis Albert Victor Nicholas)
Marco
See Charlier, Roger H(enri)
Marco, Anton N(icholas) 1943- ... 110
Marco, Barbara (Starkey) 1934- ... 9-12R
Marco, Guy A(nthony) 1927- ... 118
Marco, Lou
See Gottfried, Theodore Mark
Marcom, Micheline Aharonian 1968- ... 201
Marcombe, Edith Marion
See Shiffert, Edith (Marcombe)
Marconi, Catherine Lewallen ... 183
Marconi, Guglielmo 1874-1937 ... 160
Marconi, Joe 1945- ... 169
Marcos, Ferdinand E(dralin) 1917-1989 ... 130
Marcos (de Barros), Plinio 1935-1999 ... 188
See also DLB 307
Marcosson, Isaac Frederick 1877-1961
Obituary ... 89-92
Marcosson, Samuel A. 1961- ... 222
Marcot, Bruce G. 1953- ... 145
Marcotte, Gilles 1925- ... 166
Marcovich, Miroslav 1919- ... 115
Marcson, Simon 1910-1984 ... 49-52
Marcum, John A(rthur) 1927- ... CANR-14
Earlier sketch in CA 25-28R
Marcus, Aaron 1943- ... 53-56
Marcus, Adrianne 1935- ... CANR-108
Earlier sketches in CA 45-48, CANR-1
Marcus, Alan I. 1949- ... 163
Marcus, Alfred A(llen) 1950- ... CANR-43
Earlier sketch in CA 118
Marcus, Amy Dockser 1965- ... 189
Marcus, Anne M(ulkeen) 1927- ... 73-76
Marcus, Ben 1967- ... CANR-119
Earlier sketch in CA 165
Marcus, Betty Blum 1923-1984
Obituary ... 113
Marcus, David 1926- ... 134
Brief entry ... 110
Marcus, Donald (Edwin) 1946- ... 134
Marcus, Edward 1918- ... CANR-14
Earlier sketch in CA 21-24R
Marcus, Ellis 1918(?)-1990
Obituary ... 132
Marcus, Eric 1958- ... GLL 2
Marcus, Frank 1928-1996 ... CANR-2
Obituary ... 153
Earlier sketch in CA 45-48
See also CBD
See also DLB 13
Marcus, Fred H(arold) 1921- ... 104
Marcus, Genevieve Grafe 1932- ... 111
Marcus, George E. 1946- ... CANR-112
Earlier sketches in CA 124, CANR-52
Marcus, George H. 1939- ... 120
Marcus, Greil (Gerstley) 1945- ... CANR-102
Earlier sketch in CA 122
See also AAYA 58
Marcus, Harold G. 1936- ... 37-40R
Marcus, Irwin M. 1919- ... 45-48
Marcus, Jacob Rader 1896-1995 ... CANR-28
Obituary ... 152
Earlier sketch in CA 21-24R
Marcus, James ... 233
Marcus, Jana 1962- ... 165
Marcus, Jerry 1924- ... 97-100
Marcus, Joanna
See Andrews, Lucilla (Mathew)
Marcus, Joe 1933- ... 65-68
Marcus, K(aren) Melissa 1956- ... 153
Marcus, Larry
See Marcus, Lawrence B.
Marcus, Laurence R. 1947-1999 ... 135
Marcus, Lawrence B. 1925-2001 ... 133
Obituary ... 201
Marcus, Leonard S. 1950- ... CANR-111
Earlier sketch in CA 134
See also SATA 133
Marcus, Lyn
See LaRouche, Lyndon H(ermyle), Jr.
Marcus, Maeva 1941-
Brief entry ... 108
Marcus, Martin 1933- ... 25-28R
Marcus, Mildred Rendl 1928- ... CANR-2
Earlier sketch in CA 1-4R
Marcus, Millicent 1946- ... 146
Marcus, Mordecai 1925- ... CANR-38
Earlier sketches in CA 77-80, CANR-17
Marcus, Morton 1936- ... 218
Earlier sketch in CA 105
Autobiographical Essay in ... 218
Marcus, Paul 1953- ... 149
See also SATA 82
Marcus, Phillip L. 1941- ... 134
Brief entry ... 111
Marcus, Rebecca B(rian) 1907- ... CANR-1
Earlier sketch in CA 5-8R
See also SATA 9
Marcus, Robert D. 1936-2000 ... 184
Brief entry ... 110
Marcus, Ruth Barcan 1921- ... 41-44R
Marcus, Sheldon 1937-
Brief entry ... 106
Marcus, Stanley 1905-2002 ... 53-56
Obituary ... 204
Marcus, Steven 1928- ... CANR-117
Earlier sketch in CA 41-44R
Marcus Aurelius
See Aurelius, Marcus
See also AW 2
Marcuse, Aida E. 1934- ... 155
See also SATA 89
Marcuse, F(rederick) L(awrence)
1916-1997 ... 9-12R
Marcuse, Gary 1949- ... CANR-112
Earlier sketch in CA 154
Marcuse, Herbert 1898-1979 ... 188
Obituary ... 89-92
See also DLB 242
Marcuse, Ludwig 1894-1971
Obituary ... 33-36R
Marden, Charles F(rederick)
1902-1988 ... 37-40R
Marden, Orison Swett 1850-1924 ... 216
See also DLB 137
Marden, William (Edward) 1947- ... 61-64
Marder, Arthur (Jacob) 1910-1980 ... 105
Obituary ... 102
Marder, Daniel 1923- ... 21-24R
Marder, Herbert 1934- ... CANR-97
Earlier sketch in CA 69-72
Marder, Louis 1915- ... 5-8R
Marder, Norma 1934- ... 144
Mardock, Robert W(inston) 1921- ... 17-20R
Mardon, Austin Albert 1962- ... CANR-129
Earlier sketch in CA 164
Mardon, Ernest George 1928- ... 168
Mardon, Michael (Claude) 1919- ... 13-16R
Mardor, Munya Meir 1913- ... 17-20R
Mardus, Elaine Bassler 1914- ... 9-12R
Mare, W(illiam) Harold 1918- ... 105
Marechal, Leopoldo 1900-1970 ... 153
See also EWL 3
See also HW 1
See also LAW
See also RGWL 2, 3
Marechera, Dambudzo 1952-1987 ... 166
See also BW 3
See also CN 4
See also DLB 157
See also EWL 3
Marei, Sayed (Ahmed) 1913- ... 73-76
Marein, Shirley 1926- ... CANR-1
Earlier sketch in CA 45-48
Marek, George R(ichard) 1902-1987 ... CANR-1
Obituary ... 121
Earlier sketch in CA 49-52
Marek, Hannelore M(arie) C(harlotte)
1926- ... 13-16R
Marek, Kurt W(illi) 1915-1972 ... CAP-2
Obituary ... 33-36R
Earlier sketch in CA 17-18
Marek, Margot L. 1934(?)-1987
Obituary ... 123
See also SATA-Obit 54
Marek, Richard (William) 1933- ... 126
Marelli, Leonard R(ussell) 1933-1973 ... CAP-1
Earlier sketch in CA 13-16
Maremaa, Thomas 1945- ... 85-88
Marenbon, John (Alexander) 1955- ... CANR-90
Earlier sketch in CA 131
Marenco, Ethne (Elsie) K(aplan) 1925- ... 103
Marer, Paul 1936- ... 105
Mares, E. A. 1938- ... 179
See also DLB 122
Mares, F(rancis) H(ugh) 1925- ... 25-28R
Mares, Michael A(llen) 1945- ... CANR-122
Earlier sketch in CA 138
Mares, Theun 1952- ... 169
Maresca, Thomas Edward 1938- ... 85-88
Mareth, Glenville
See Gilbert, Willie
Marett, Robert Hugh Kirk 1907- ... 25-28R
Marevna
See Vorobeva, Maria
Margadant, Ted W(inston) 1941- ... 93-96
Margalit, Avishai 1939- ... CANR-138
Earlier sketch in CA 184
Margalith, Pinhas Z(alman) 1926- ... 110
Margaret, Karla
See Andersdatter, Karla M(argaret)
Margenau, Henry 1901-1997 ... CANR-14
Obituary ... 156
Earlier sketch in CA 37-40R
Marger, Mary Ann 1934- ... 93-96
Margerson, David
See Davies, David Margerison
Margetson, Stella 1912-1992 ... CANR-40
Earlier sketches in CA 33-36R, CANR-13
Marghieri, Clotilde 1901(?)-1981
Obituary ... 105
Margold, Stella ... 81-84
Margolian, Howard T. 1957- ... 193
Margolick, David ... 208
Margolies, Alan 1933- ... 125
Margolies, Edward 1925- ... CANR-92
Earlier sketches in CA 65-68, CANR-11
Margolies, Joseph A(aron) 1889-1982
Obituary ... 108
Margolies, Luise 1945- ... 102
Margolies, Marjorie 1942- ... CANR-13
Earlier sketch in CA 65-68
Margolin, Edythe ... 69-72
Margolin, Harriet
See Ziefert, Harriet
Margolin, Judith B(elle) 1946- ... 117
Margolin, Malcolm 1940- ... 57-60
Margolin, Phillip (Michael) 1944- ... CANR-97
Earlier sketch in CA 145
Margolin, Victor 1941- ... 65-68
Margolis, Anne T(hrone) 1949- ... 128
Margolis, Diane Rothbard 1933- ... 97-100
Margolis, Ellen (Edelman) 1934- ... 1-4R
Margolis, Gary 1945- ... 73-76
Margolis, Howard 1932- ... CANR-89
Earlier sketch in CA 130
Margolis, Jack S 1934- ... 69-72
Margolis, Jeffrey A. 1948- ... 168
See also SATA 108
Margolis, John D(avid) 1941- ... 134
Brief entry ... 113
Margolis, Jonathan 1955- ... CANR-102
Earlier sketch in CA 139
Margolis, Joseph (Zalman) 1924- ... CANR-100
Earlier sketch in CA 37-40R
Margolis, Julius 1920- ... 195
Brief entry ... 109
Margolis, Maxine L(uanna) 1942- ... 53-56
Margolis, Michael (Stephen) 1940- ... 93-96
Margolis, Nadia 1949- ... 140
Margolis, Richard J(ules) 1929-1991 ... CANR-25
Obituary ... 134
Earlier sketch in CA 29-32R
See also SATA 4, 86
See also SATA-Obit 67
Margolis, Seth J(acob) ... 166

Margolis, Sue 194
Margolis, Susan Spector 1941- 81-84
Margolis, Susanna 1944- 107
Margolis, Vivienne 1922- .... SATA 46
Margolius, Sidney (Senier) 1911-1980 .... CANR-11
 Obituary 93-96
 Earlier sketch in CA 21-24R
Margon, Lester 1892-1980 .... CAP-1
 Earlier sketch in CA 13-16
Margoshes, Dave 1941- CANR-117
 Earlier sketches in CA 111, CANR-29, 54
Margroff, Robert E. 1930- 134
Mar Gudmundsson, Einar
 See Gudmundsson, Einar Mar
Marguenat de Courcelles, Anne-Therese de
 See Lambert, Anne-Therese de
Marguerite
 See de Navarre, Marguerite
Marguerite d'Angouleme
 See de Navarre, Marguerite
 See also GFL Beginnings to 1789
Marguerite de Navarre
 See de Navarre, Marguerite
 See also RGWL 2, 3
Margulies, Donald 1954- 200
 See also AAYA 57
 See also CD 6
 See also CLC 76
 See also DFS 13
 See also DLB 228
Margulies, Harry D. 1907(?)-1980
 Obituary 97-100
Margulies, Herbert F(elix) 1928- 77-80
Margulies, Jimmy 1951- CANR-86
 Earlier sketch in CA 133
Margulies, Leo 1900-1975
 Obituary 61-64
Margulies, Newton 1932- 61-64
Margulis, Lynn 1938- CANR-126
 Earlier sketches in CA 53-56, CANR-4
Margull, Hans J(ochen) 1925- 9-12R
Marhoefer, Barbara (McGeary) 1936- 61-64
Maria Del Rey, Sister 1908-2000 .... 5-8R
Mariah, Paul 1937-1996 .... CANR-4
 Earlier sketch in CA 53-56
Mariana
 See Foster, Marian Curtis
Mariana, Juan de 1535(?)-1624 .... DLB 318
Mariani, John Francis 1945- CANR-41
 Earlier sketch in CA 117
Mariani, Paul L(ouis) 1940- CANR-104
 Earlier sketches in CA 29-32R, CANR-12
 See also DLB 111
Mariano, Frank 1931(?)-1976
 Obituary 69-72
Marias, Javier 1951- CANR-139
 Earlier sketches in CA 167, CANR-109
 See also DLB 322
 See also HW 2
 See also MTFW 2005
Marias (Aguilera), Julian 1914- CANR-48
 Earlier sketches in CA 9-12R, CANR-5, 22
Mariategui, Jose Carlos 1894-1930 .... LAW
Marie, Beverly Sainte
 See Sainte-Marie, Beverly
Marie, Buffy Sainte
 See Sainte-Marie, Beverly
Marie, Geraldine 1949- 108
 See also SATA 61
Marie, Jeanne
 See Wilson, Marie B(eatrice)
Marie, Rose 1923- 218
Marie-Andre du Sacre-Coeur, Sister 1899- 5-8R
Marie de France c. 12th cent. - .... DLB 208
 See also FW
 See also PC 22
 See also RGWL 2, 3
Marien, Mary Warner 218
Marien, Michael 1938- CANR-16
 Earlier sketches in CA 49-52, CANR-1
Mariengof, Anatoly Borisovich 1897-1962 . 218
Marier, Captain Victor
 See Griffith, D(avid Lewelyn) W(ark)
Marie Therese, Mother 1891- CAP-1
 Earlier sketch in CA 13-14
Marie-Victorin, Frere 1885-1944 218
 See also DLB 92
Maril, Nadja 1954- CANR-17
 Earlier sketch in CA 85-88, 186
Maril, Robert Lee 1947- 222
Marill, Alvin H(erbert) 1934- CANR-12
 Earlier sketch in CA 73-76
Marilla, E(smond) L(inworth) 1900-1970 .... CAP-2
 Earlier sketch in CA 23-24
Marillier, Juliet 207
 See also AAYA 50
Marilue
 See Johnson, Marilue Carolyn
Marimow, William K. 1947- 93-96
Marin, A. C.
 See Coppel, Alfred
Marin, Biagio 1891-1985 .... DLB 128
Marin, Cheech
 See Marin, Richard Anthony
Marin, Diego 1914- 17-20R
Marin, Luis Munoz
 See Munoz Marin, (Jose) Luis (Alberto)
Marin, Mindy 1960- 163
Marin, Richard Anthony 1946- 148
 Brief entry 112
Marin, Rick 1962- 223
Marinacci, Barbara 1933- CANR-9
 Earlier sketch in CA 21-24R
Marinaccio, Anthony 1912- 53-56
Marin Canas, Jose 1904- .... EWL 3
 See also LAW
Marine, David 1880(?)-1976
 Obituary 69-72
Marine, Gene 1926- 65-68
Marine, Nick
 See Oursler, Will(iam Charles)
Marineau, Michele 1955- 166
Marinelli, Peter V(incent) 1933- 41-44R
Mariner, David
 See Smith, David MacLeod
Mariner, Scott
 See Pohl, Frederik
Marinetti, Filippo Tommaso 1876-1944
 Brief entry 107
 See also DLB 114, 264
 See also EW 9
 See also EWL 3
 See also TCLC 10
 See also WLIT 7
Maring, Joel M(arvin) 1935- 49-52
Maring, Norman H(ill) 1914- 17-20R
Marini, Frank N(ick) 1935- 45-48
Marinina, Aleksandra 1957- .... DLB 285
Marinkovic, Ranko 1913-2001 182
 See also CDWLB 4
 See also DLB 147
 See also EWL 3
Marino, Anne (N.) 199
Marino, Carolyn Fitch 1942- 110
Marino, Dorothy Bronson 1912- 73-76
 See also SATA 14
Marino, Giambattista 1569-1625 .... WLIT 7
Marino, Jan 1936- 186
 See also AAYA 39
 See also SATA 114
Marino, John J. 1948- 106
Marino, Joseph D. 1912(?)-1983
 Obituary 109
Marino, Nick
 See Deming, Richard
Marino, Susan
 See Ellis, Julie
Marino, Trentino J(oseph) 1917- 65-68
Marinoff, Lou 1951- 223
Marinoni, Rosa Zagnoni 1888-1970 .... CAP-1
 Earlier sketch in CA 13-14
Mario, Anna
 See Odgers, Sally Farrell
Marion, Frances 1886-1973 177
 Obituary 41-44R
 See also DLB 44
 See also IDFW 3, 4
Marion, Frieda 1912- CANR-8
 Earlier sketch in CA 61-64
Marion, Henry
 See del Rey, Lester
Marion, John Francis 1922- CANR-3
 Earlier sketch in CA 5-8R
Marion, Robert W. 1952- 130
Mariotti, (Raffaello) Marcello 1938- 29-32R
Marique, Joseph M(arie-) F(elix) 1899-1979 .... 33-36R
Maris, Roger (Eugene) 1934-1985
 Obituary 118
Maris, Ron .... SATA 71
 See also SATA-Brief 45
Marisa
 See Nucera, Marisa Lonette
Mariscal, Richard N(orth) 1935- 53-56
Maristed, Kai 239
Maritain, Jacques 1882-1973 85-88
 Obituary 41-44R
Maritano, Nino 1919- 13-16R
Marius, Richard (Curry) 1933-1999 .. CANR-91
 Obituary 186
 Earlier sketches in CA 25-28R, CANR-29, 56
 See also DLBY 1985
Marivaux, Pierre Carlet de Chamblain de 1688-1763 .... DC 7
 See also DLB 314
 See also GFL Beginnings to 1789
 See also RGWL 2, 3
 See also TWA
Marix Evans, Martin 1939- 196
Mariz, Linda 1948- 139
Marjolin, Robert (Ernest) 1911-1986 154
 Obituary 119
Marjoram, J.
 See Mottram, R(alph) H(ale)
Mark, Charles Christopher 1927-1998 .... CANR-1
 Obituary 165
 Earlier sketch in CA 1-4R
Mark, David 1922- 1-4R
Mark, Edwina
 See Fadiman, Edwin, Jr.
Mark, Irving 1908-1987 .... CAP-1
 Obituary 121
 Earlier sketch in CA 19-20
Mark, Jan(et Marjorie) 1943- CANR-77
 Earlier sketches in CA 93-96, CANR-17, 42
 See also CLR 11
 See also MAICYA 1, 2
 See also SATA 22, 69, 114
 See also YAW
Mark, Joan T. 1937- CANR-89
 Earlier sketch in CA 130
 See also SATA 122
Mark, Jon
 See Du Breuil, (Elizabeth) L(or)inda
Mark, Julius 1898-1977 81-84
 Obituary 73-76
Mark, Mary Ellen 1940- .... AAYA 52
Mark, Matthew
 See Babcock, Frederic
Mark, Max 1910-1982 73-76
Mark, Michael L(aurence) 1936- 93-96
Mark, Norman (Barry) 1939- 113
Mark, Pauline (Dahlin) 1913-1997 .... CANR-7
 Earlier sketch in CA 17-20R
 See also SATA 14
Mark, Polly
 See Mark, Pauline (Dahlin)
Mark, Rebecca 1955- 150
Mark, Robert 1930- 110
Mark, Samuel Eugene 1953- 170
Mark, Shelley M(uin) 1922- CANR-1
 Earlier sketch in CA 1-4R
Mark, Steven Joseph 1913-2003 .... 17-20R
Mark, Ted
 See Gottfried, Theodore Mark
Mark, Theonie Diakidis 1938- 69-72
Mark, Yudel 1897-1975
 Obituary 61-64
Markandaya, Kamala
 See Taylor, Kamala (Purnaiya)
 See also BYA 13
 See also CLC 8, 38
 See also CN 1, 2, 3, 4, 5, 6, 7
 See also EWL 3
Markbreit, Jerry 1935- 49-52
Marke, Julius J(ay) 1913- 17-20R
Markel, Geraldine (Ponte) 1939- 108
Markel, Helen 1919(?)-1990
 Obituary 130
Markel, Howard 1960- 154
Markel, Lester 1894-1977 .... 37-40R
 Obituary 73-76
Markels, Julian 1925- 25-28R
Marken, Bill
 See Marken, William Riley
Marken, Jack W(alter) 1922- CANR-31
 Earlier sketch in CA 49-52
Marken, William Riley 1942- 226
Marker, Frederick (Joseph, Jr.) 1936- CANR-39
 Earlier sketches in CA 41-44R, CANR-16
Marker, Gary 1948- 125
Marker, Lise-Lone (Christensen) 1934- CANR-39
 Earlier sketches in CA 61-64, CANR-8
Marker, Rita 1940- 148
Marker, Sherry 1941- 143
 See also SATA 76
Markert, Jennifer 1965- 150
 See also SATA 83
Markert, Jenny
 See Markert, Jennifer
Market Man
 See Lake, Kenneth R(obert)
Markevich, Boleslav Mikhailovich 1822-1884 .... DLB 238
Markevitch, Igor 1912-1983
 Obituary 109
Markey, Dorothy
 See Page, Myra
Markey, Gene 1895-1980 .... CANR-85
 Obituary 97-100
 Earlier sketches in CAP-1, CA 11-12
Markey, Kevin 1965- 143
Markfield, Wallace (Arthur) 1926-2002 .. 69-72
 Obituary 208
 See also CAAS 3
 See also CLC 8
 See also CN 1, 2, 3, 4, 5, 6, 7
 See also DLB 2, 28
 See also DLBY 2002
Markgraf, Carl 1928- CANR-57
 Earlier sketches in CA 49-52, CANR-31
Markham, Beryl 1902-1986
 Obituary 119
 See also LATS 1:2
Markham, Clarence M(atthew), Jr. 1911-1995 69-72
Markham, Dewey 1904-1981
 Obituary 108
Markham, E(dward) A(rchibald) 1939- CANR-144
 Earlier sketch in CA 154
 See also CP 7
 See also DLB 319
Markham, Edwin 1852-1940 160
 See also DLB 54, 186
 See also MAL 5
 See also RGAL 4
 See also TCLC 47
Markham, Felix (Maurice Hippisley) 1908-1992 .... CAP-1
 Obituary 139
 Earlier sketch in CA 11-12
Markham, Ian Stephen 1962- CANR-113
 Earlier sketch in CA 154
Markham, James M(orris IV) 1943-1989 .. 93-96
 Obituary 129
Markham, James W(alter) 1910-1972 .... CAP-2
 Earlier sketch in CA 21-22
Markham, Jesse William 1916- 9-12R
Markham, Lynne 1947- 169
 See also SATA 102
Markham, Marion M. 1929- 129
 See also SATA 60
Markham, Meeler 1914- CANR-12
 Earlier sketch in CA 25-28R
Markham, Pigmeat
 See Markham, Dewey
Markham, Reed 1957- CANR-104
 Earlier sketch in CA 110
Markham, Robert
 See Amis, Kingsley (William)
Marki, Ivan 1934- 97-100
Markides, Constantinos C. 1960- ... CANR-135
 Earlier sketch in CA 162
Markides, Kyriacos (Costa) 1942- 81-84
Markie, Peter J(oseph) 1950- CANR-50
 Earlier sketch in CA 123
Markins, W. S.
 See Jenkins, Marie M(agdalen)
Markish, David 1938- 69-72
 See also DLB 317
Markish, Peretz 1895-1952 .... EWL 3
Markle, (William) Fletcher 1921-1991 177
 See also DLB 68
 See also DLBY 1991
Markle, Joyce B(onners) 1942- 69-72
Markle, Sandra L(ee) 1946- CANR-131
 Earlier sketches in CA 111, CANR-58
 See also SATA 57, 92, 148
 See also SATA-Brief 41
Markley, Kenneth A(lan) 1933- 61-64
Markley, R(ayner) W(are) 1934- 111
Marklin, Megan
 See Harrington, William
Marklund, Liza 1962- 221
Markman, Howard (Joel) 1950- 69-72
Markman, Ronald A. 1936- 145
Markman, Sherwin J. 1929- 104
Markman, Sidney David 1911- CAP-2
 Earlier sketch in CA 33-36
Markmann, Charles Lam 1913-1976 .... 13-16R
Marko, Katherine D(olores) CANR-15
 Earlier sketch in CA 29-32R
 See also SATA 28
Markoe, Glenn E. 1951- 162
Markoe, Karen 1942- 81-84
Markoe, Merrill 211
Markoff, John 1949- 160
Markoosie
 See Patsauq, Markoosie
 See also CLR 23
 See also DAM MULT
 See also NNAL
Markov, Andrei Andreevich 1856-1922 161
Markov, Georgi 1929(?)-1978
 Obituary 104
Markov, Vladimir 1920- 17-20R
Markova, Alicia 1910-2004 .... CAP-2
 Obituary 234
 Earlier sketch in CA 19-20
Markovic, Mihailo (M.) 1923- 131
Markovic, Miroslav
 See Marcovich, Miroslav
Markovic, Vida E. 1916- 33-36R
Markovich, Mariia Aleksandrovna 1833-1907 228
 See also Vovchok, Marko
Markovitz, Irving Leonard 1934- 33-36R
Markowa, Nina Alexandrovna 1925- 142
Markowitz, Norman Daniel 1943- 45-48
Marks, Alan 1957- 145
 See also SATA 77, 151
Marks, Alfred H(arding) 1920- CANR-47
 Earlier sketches in CA 45-48, CANR-23
Marks, Barry A(lan) 1926- 17-20R
Marks, Bayly Ellen 1943- 115
Marks, Burton 1930- 107
 See also SATA 47
 See also SATA-Brief 43
Marks, Charles 1922- CANR-5
 Earlier sketch in CA 53-56
Marks, Claude (Mordecai) 1915-1991 61-64
 Obituary 134
Marks, Copeland H. 1921-1999 167
 Obituary 188
Marks, Corey 1970- 204
Marks, David (Francis) 1945- 132
Marks, Edith Bobroff 1924- 17-20R
Marks, Edward S(tanford) 1936- 45-48
Marks, Elaine 1930- CANR-23
 Earlier sketches in CA 17-20R, CANR-7
Marks, Eli S(amplin) 1911-1991 85-88
 Obituary 133
Marks, Frederick (William III) 1940- 97-100
Marks, Geoffrey 1906-1985 .... 33-36R
Marks, Gil(bert S.) 1952- 175
 Earlier sketch in CA 168
Marks, Graham 234
 See also SATA 158
Marks, Hannah K.
 See Trivelpiece, Laurel
Marks, Henry S(eymour) 1933- 73-76
Marks, J.
 See Highwater, Jamake (Mamake)
Marks, J
 See Highwater, Jamake (Mamake)
Marks, J(ames) M(acdonald) 1921- 61-64
 See also SATA 13
Marks, James R(obert) 1932- 17-20R
Marks, Jane (A. Steinberg) 1943- 113
Marks, Jeffrey 1960- 215
Marks, John 1943- 110
Marks, John 1963- 229
Marks, John David 1909-1985
 Obituary 117
Marks, John H(enry) 1923- 17-20R
Marks, Johnny
 See Marks, John David
Marks, Kathy (L.) 1953- 153
Marks, Lara Vivienne 1963- 203
Marks, Laurie J. 1957- CANR-141
 Earlier sketch in CA 135
 See also FANT
 See also SATA 68
Marks, (Amelia) Lee 1948- 137
Marks, Leo 1921-2001 184
 Obituary 193
Marks, Margaret L. 1911(?)-1980
 Obituary 101
 See also SATA-Obit 23
Marks, Marjorie
 See Bitker, Marjorie M(arks)

Marks, Mickey Klar -1986 ... CANR-6
Earlier sketch in CA 1-4R
See also SATA 12
Marks, Mitchell Lee 1955- ... 165
Marks, Norton E(lliott) 1932- ... 21-24R
Marks, Pat R.
See Feinman, Jeffrey
Marks, Paula Mitchell 1951- ... 135
Marks, Peter
See Smith, Robert Kimmel
Marks, Richard Lee 1923(?)-2003 ... 140
Obituary ... 213
Marks, Rita 1938- ... 106
See also SATA 47
Marks, Robert B. 1949- ... 188
Marks, Sally (Jean) 1931- ... 102
Marks, Sema 1942- ... 29-32R
Marks, Stan(ley) ... CANR-57
Earlier sketches in CA 29-32R, CANR-12, 31
See also SATA 14
Marks, Stuart A. 1939- ... 69-72
Marks, Thomas A. 1950- ... 164
Marks, Vic(tor James) 1955- ... 118
Marks, Walter 1934- ... 218
Marksberry, Mary Lee ... 13-16R
Marks-Highwater, J
See Highwater, Jamake (Mamake)
Marks-Highwater, J.
See Highwater, Jamake (Mamake)
Markson, David M(errill) 1927- ... CANR-91
Earlier sketches in CA 49-52, CANR-1
See also CLC 67
See also CN 5, 6
Markstein, David L. 1920- ... 29-32R
Markstein, George 1929-1987
Obituary ... 121
Markun, Alan Fletcher 1925- ... 45-48
Markun, Patricia Maloney 1924- ... CANR-4
Earlier sketch in CA 5-8R
See also SATA 15
Markus, Julia 1939- ... CANR-101
Earlier sketch in CA 105
Interview in ... CA-105
Markus, R(obert) A(ustin) 1924- ... CANR-16
Earlier sketch in CA 65-68
Markusen, Ann Roell 1946- ... 142
Markusen, Bruce (Stanley Rodriguez)
1965- ... 212
See also SATA 141
Markusen, Eric 1946- ... 156
Marl, David J. ... FANT
Marland, Christina
See Pemberton, Margaret
Marland, Edward Allen 1912- ... 17-20R
Marland, Michael 1934- ... 103
Marland, Sidney P(ercy, Jr.) 1914-1992 ... 53-56
Obituary ... 137
Marlatt, Daphne (Buckle) 1942- ... CANR-39
Earlier sketches in CA 25-28R, CANR-17
See also CLC 168
See also CN 6, 7
See also CP 7
See also CWP
See also DLB 60
See also FW
Marlborough
See Oaksey, John
Marles, Robin J(ames) 1955- ... 226
Marlette
See Marlette, Doug(las Nigel)
Marlette, Doug(las Nigel) 1949- ... CANR-110
Earlier sketch in CA 145
Marley, Augusta Anne (?)-1973
Obituary ... 41-44R
Marley, Bob
See Marley, Robert Nesta
See also CLC 17
Marley, Louise 1952- ... 191
See also SATA 120
Marley, Rita 1947- ... 234
Marley, Robert Nesta 1945-1981 ... 107
Obituary ... 103
See also Marley, Bob
Marley, Stephen 1946- ... 155
See also FANT
Marlin, Alice Tepper 1944- ... 123
Marlin, Henry
See Giggal, Kenneth
Marlin, Hilda
See Van Stockum, Hilda
Marlin, Jeannie
See Woods, Jeannie Marlin
Marlin, Jeffrey 1940- ... 45-48
Marlin, John Tepper 1942- ... 124
Marling, Karal Ann 1943- ... CANR-98
Earlier sketch in CA 148
Marling, William 1951- ... 123
Marling, Yvonne Rodd
See Rodd-Marling, Yvonne
Marlis, Stefanie 1951- ... 169
Marlitt, E. 1825-1887 ... DLB 129
Marlo, John A. 1934- ... 29-32R
Marlor, Clark Strang 1922- ... 37-40R
Marlot, Raymond
See Angremy, Jean-Pierre
Marlow, Cecilia Ann 1952- ... 121
Marlow, David 1943- ... 107
Marlow, Edwina
See Huff, T(om) E.
Marlow, John Robert ... 229
Marlow, Joyce
See Connor, Joyce Mary
Marlow, Louis
See Wilkinson, Louis (Umfreville)
Marlow, Max
See Nicole, Christopher (Robin)
Marlowe, Alan Stephen 1937- ... 21-24R
Marlowe, Amy Bell ... CANR-26
Earlier sketches in CAP-2, CA 19-20
See also SATA 1, 67
Marlowe, Ann 1958- ... 196
Marlowe, Christopher 1564-1593 ... BRW 1
See also BRWR 1
See also CDBLB Before 1660
See also DA
See also DA3
See also DAB
See also DAC
See also DAM DRAM, MST
See also DC 1
See also DFS 1, 5, 13, 21
See also DLB 62
See also EXPP
See also LMFS 1
See also PC 57
See also PFS 22
See also RGEL 2
See also TEA
See also WLC
See also WLIT 3
Marlowe, Dan J(ames) 1914-1987 ... CANR-60
Earlier sketches in CA 1-4R, CANR-1
See also CMW 4
Marlowe, Derek 1938-1996 ... CANR-59
Earlier sketches in CA 17-20R, CANR-11
See also CMW 4
Marlowe, Don ... 61-64
Marlowe, Hugh
See Patterson, Harry
Marlowe, Katherine
See Allen, Charlotte Vale
Marlowe, Katherine
See Allen, Charlotte Vale
Marlowe, Kenneth 1926- ... 13-16R
Marlowe, Stephen 1928- ... CANR-55
Earlier sketches in CA 13-16R, CANR-6
See also Queen, Ellery
See also CLC 70
See also CMW 4
See also SFW 4
Marlowe, Webb
See McComas, J(esse) Francis
Marlyn, John 1912- ... 9-12R
See also DLB 88
Marmariadis, Yiannis 1902-
See Haris, Petros
Marmerrode, Ludovicus van
See Greshoff, Jan
Marmion, Harry A. 1931- ... 25-28R
Marmion, Shakerley 1603-1639 ... DLB 58
See also RGEL 2
Marmol, Jose 1817-1871 ... LAW
Marmon, William F., Jr. 1942- ... 77-80
Marmontel, Jean-Francois 1723-1799 . DLB 314
Marmor, Judd 1910-2003 ... CANR-12
Obituary ... 222
Earlier sketch in CA 25-28R
Marmor, T(heodore) R(ichard)
1939- ... CANR-52
Earlier sketches in CA 29-32R, CANR-27
Marmot, Michael (Gideon) 1945- ... 232
Marmur, Dow 1935- ... CANR-47
Earlier sketch in CA 121
Marmur, Jacland 1901-1970 ... 9-12R
Marmur, Mildred 1930- ... 5-8R
Marnell, William H. 1907- ... 21-24R
Marner, Der c. 1230-c. 1287 ... DLB 138
Marney, (Leonard) Carlyle 1916-1978 ... 57-60
Obituary ... 135
Marney, Dean 1952- ... CANR-52
Earlier sketches in CA 110, CANR-28
See also SATA 90
Marney, John 1933- ... 69-72
Marnham, Patrick 1943- ... CANR-90
Earlier sketches in CA 102, CANR-46
See also DLB 204
Marokvia, Artur 1909- ... SATA 31
Marokvia, Mireille (Journet) 1918- ... 29-32R
See also SATA 5
Marol, Jean-Claude 1946- ... CANR-89
Earlier sketch in CA 130
See also SATA 125
Maron, Margaret ... CANR-66
Earlier sketches in CA 122, CANR-44, 50
See also CMW 4
Maron, Monika 1941- ... 201
See also CLC 165
Maroon, Fred J. 1924-2001 ... 132
Obituary ... 200
Marossi, Ruth
See Krefetz, Ruth
Marosy, John Paul 1951- ... 212
Marot, Clement 1496-1544 .. GFL Beginnings to 1789
Marot, Marc
See Koch, Kurt E(mil)
Marotti, Arthur F(rancis) 1940- ... 199
Marouane, Leila 1960- ... 216
Marple, Allen Clark 1901(?)-1968
Obituary ... 106
Marple, Hugo D(ixon) 1920- ... 53-56
Marples, William F(rank) 1907- ... CAP-1
Earlier sketch in CA 13-16
Marquand, John P(hillips)
1893-1960 ... CANR-73
Earlier sketch in CA 85-88
See also AMW
See also BPFB 2
See also CLC 2, 10
See also CMW 4
See also DLB 9, 102
See also EWL 3
See also MAL 5
See also MTCW 2
See also RGAL 4
Marquand, Josephine
See Gladstone, Josephine
Marquand, Robert 1957- ... 136
Marquard, Leo(pold) 1897-1974 ... 5-8R
Marquardt, Dorothy Ann 1921- ... 13-16R
Marquardt, Virginia C. Hagelstein 1945- ... 168
Marquart, Debra 1956- ... 201
Marques, Helena 1935- ... DLB 287
Marques, Rene 1919-1979 ... CANR-78
Obituary ... 85-88
Earlier sketch in CA 97-100
See also CLC 96
See also DAM MULT
See also DLB 305
See also EWL 3
See also HLC 2
See also HW 1, 2
See also LAW
See also RGSF 2
Marquess, Harlan E(arl) 1931- ... 49-52
Marquess, William Henry 1954- ... 126
Marquess of Anglesey
See Paget, George Charles Henry Victor
Marquez, Gabriel (Jose) Garcia
See Garcia Marquez, Gabriel (Jose)
Marquez, Robert 1942- ... 53-56
Marquina, Eduardo 1879-1946 ... 211
Marquis, Alice Goldfarb 1930- ... CANR-119
Earlier sketch in CA 156
Marquis, Arnold ... 57-60
Marquis, Dave 1951- ... 113
Marquis, Don(ald Robert Perry)
1878-1937 ... 166
Brief entry ... 104
See also DLB 11, 25
See also MAL 5
See also RGAL 4
See also TCLC 7
Marquis, Donald G(eorge) 1908-1973
Obituary ... 45-48
Marquis, G(eorge) Welton 1916- ... 17-20R
Marquis, Max ... CANR-69
Earlier sketch in CA 136
Marquis de Sade
See Sade, Donatien Alphonse Francois
Marquit, Amanda 1986(?)- ... 239
Marqusee, Mike 1953- ... 148
Marr, Andrew William Stevenson 1959- ... 199
Marr, David G(eorge) 1937- ... CANR-28
Earlier sketch in CA 33-36R
Marr, James Pratt 1898-1986
Obituary ... 121
Marr, John S(tuart) 1940- ... 81-84
See also SATA 48
Marranca, Bonnie 1947- ... CANR-9
Earlier sketch in CA 65-68
Marreco, Anne
See Wignall, Anne
Marric, J. J.
See Butler, William (Arthur) Vivian and Creasey, John
See also MSW
Marrin, Albert 1936- ... CANR-106
Earlier sketches in CA 49-52, CANR-30, 58
See also AAYA 35
See also CLR 53
See also MAICYA 2
See also MAICYAS 1
See also SATA 53, 90, 126
See also SATA-Brief 43
Marriner, Brian 1937- ... 141
Marriner, Ernest (Cummings)
1891-1983 ... CANR-28
Obituary ... 109
Earlier sketch in CA 37-40R
Marriner Tomey, Ann 1943- ... 168
Marrington, Pauline 1921- ... CANR-10
Earlier sketch in CA 65-68
Marriott, Alice Lee 1910-1992 ... CANR-86
Obituary ... 137
Earlier sketch in CA 57-60
See also SATA 31
See also SATA-Obit 71
Marriott, (Joyce) Anne 1913-1997 ... CANR-18
Earlier sketch in CA 102
See also CP 1
See also DLB 68
Marriott, Edward 1966- ... 199
Marriott, Janice 1946- ... 203
See also SATA 134
Marriott, Kim 1961- ... 171
Marriott, Pat(ricia) 1920- ... SATA 35
Marriott, William H. 1909(?)-1986
Obituary ... 118
Marriott-Watson, Nan 1899-1982
Obituary ... 107
Marris, Peter (Horsey) 1927- ... CANR-29
Earlier sketch in CA 111
Marris, Robin Lapthorn 1924- ... CANR-8
Earlier sketch in CA 5-8R
Marris, Ruth 1948- ... 106
Marrison, L(eslie) W(illiam) 1901- ... 29-32R
Marr-Johnson, Diana (Maugham)
1908- ... 13-16R
Marrocco, W(illiam) Thomas
1909-1999 ... 9-12R
Marron, Kevin (Christopher Gerard) 1947- . 127
Marrone, Robert 1941- ... 77-80
Marrone, Steven P(hillip) 1947- ... 130
Marroquin, Patricio
See Markun, Patricia Maloney
Marrow, Alfred J. 1905-1978 ... 81-84
Obituary ... 77-80
Marrow, Bernard ... CCA 1
Marrow, Stanley B. 1931- ... CANR-26
Earlier sketches in CA 25-28R, CANR-10
Marrs, Edwin W(ilson), Jr. 1928- ... 25-28R
Marrs, Jim 1943- ... CANR-98
Earlier sketch in CA 139
Marrus, Michael R(obert) 1941- ... CANR-12
Earlier sketch in CA 33-36R
Marryat, Frederick 1792-1848 ... DLB 21, 163
See also RGEL 2
See also WCH
Mars, Alastair 1915-1985
Obituary ... 116
Mars, Florence L. 1923- ... 101
Mars, Gerald 1933- ... 132
Mars, Jean Price
See Price-Mars, Jean
Mars, Kasey
See Martin, Kat
Mars, Perry 1941- ... 193
Mars, W. T.
See Mars, Witold Tadeusz J.
Mars, Witold Tadeusz J. 1912-1985 ... 25-28R
See also SATA 3
Marsa, Linda J. 1948- ... 161
Marsack, Robyn (Louise) 1953- ... CANR-54
Earlier sketch in CA 127
Marsano, Ramon
See Dinges, John (Charles)
Marsden, Alexander
See Waddington, Patrick (Haynes)
Marsden, Carolyn 1950- ... 211
See also SATA 140
Marsden, George (Mish) 1939- ... CANR-142
Earlier sketches in CA 73-76, CANR-12
Marsden, James
See Creasey, John
Marsden, John 1950- ... CANR-129
Earlier sketch in CA 135
See also AAYA 20
See also CLR 34
See also MAICYA 2
See also MAICYAS 1
See also SAAS 22
See also SATA 66, 97, 146
See also YAW
Marsden, Lorna R(uth) 1942- ... 85-88
Marsden, Malcolm Morse 1922- ... 5-8R
Marsden, Peter (Richard Valentine)
1940- ... CANR-47
Earlier sketches in CA 77-80, CANR-14
Marsden, Philip Kitson 1916-1984
Obituary ... 113
Marsden-Smedley, Hester 1901-1982
Obituary ... 107
Marsden-Smedley, Philip 1961- ... 135
Marse, Juan 1933- ... DLB 322
Marsella, Anne (Francesca) 1964- ... 146
Marsh, Analyticus
See Morrison, Marsh
Marsh, Andrew
See O'Donovan, John
Marsh, Carole 1946- ... 197
See also SATA 127
Marsh, Charles R. 1958- ... 200
Marsh, Clifton E. 1946- ... 77-80
Marsh, Corinna (Reiman) 1891-1990
Obituary ... 132
Marsh, Dave 1950- ... CANR-41
Earlier sketches in CA 97-100, CANR-17
See also AAYA 52
See also SATA 66
Marsh, David Charles 1917- ... 103
Marsh, Edward 1872-1953 ... TCLC 99
Marsh, Edwin
See Schorb, E(dwin) M(arsh)
Marsh, Fabienne 1957- ... 211
Marsh, Geoffrey
See Grant, Charles L(ewis)
Marsh, George Perkins 1801-1882 .. DLB 1, 64, 243
Marsh, Henry
See Saklatvala, Beram
Marsh, Irving T. 1907-1982 ... CANR-85
Obituary ... 107
Earlier sketch in CA 9-12R
Marsh, J. E.
See Marshall, Evelyn
Marsh, James 1794-1842 ... DLB 1, 59
Marsh, James 1946- ... SATA 73
Marsh, Jan 1942- ... CANR-98
Earlier sketch in CA 145
Marsh, Jean
See Marshall, Evelyn
Marsh, Jeanne C(ay) 1948- ... 111
Marsh, Jeri 1940- ... 85-88
Marsh, Joan
See Marsh, John
Marsh, Joan F. 1923- ... CANR-102
Earlier sketch in CA 150
See also SATA 83
Marsh, John 1904-1994
Obituary ... 144
Marsh, John 1907-1997 ... CANR-60
Earlier sketches in CAP-1, CA 13-16
See also Woodward, Lilian
Marsh, John L(eslie) 1927- ... CANR-1
Earlier sketch in CA 45-48

Cumulative Index 377 Martin

Marsh, Leonard (Charles) 1906-1982 .... 37-40R
Marsh, Leonard (George) 1930- CANR-13
Earlier sketch in CA 73-76
Marsh, Lucy Allen 1941- 189
Marsh, Margaret Sammartino 1945- 106
Marsh, Mary Val 1925- CANR-52
Earlier sketches in CA 69-72, CANR-11, 26
Marsh, Meredith 1946- 77-80
Marsh, Narcissus 1638-1713 .... DLB 213
Marsh, (Edith) Ngaio 1895-1982 ...... CANR-58
Earlier sketches in CA 9-12R, CANR-6
See also CLC 7, 53
See also CMW 4
See also CN 1, 2, 3
See also CPW
See also DAM POP
See also DLB 77
See also MSW
See also MTCW 1, 2
See also RGEL 2
See also TEA
Marsh, Norman Stayner 1913- 117
Marsh, Patrick O(tis) 1928- 25-28R
Marsh, Paul
See Hopkins, (Hector) Kenneth
Marsh, Peter T(imothy) 1935- 33-36R
Marsh, Philip M(errill) 1893-1975 .... 9-12R
Marsh, Rebecca
See Neubauer, William Arthur
Marsh, Richard
See Heldmann, Richard Bernard
See also HGG
Marsh, Robert (Harrison) 1926-1979 ..... 17-20R
Obituary 134
Marsh, Robert C(harles) 1924- 13-16R
Marsh, Robert M(ortimer) 1931- CANR-2
Earlier sketch in CA 1-4R
Marsh, Ronald (James) 1914- 13-16R
Marsh, Rosalind
See Marsh, Rosalind J(udith)
Marsh, Rosalind J(udith) 1950- 132
Marsh, Spencer 1931- 61-64
Marsh, Susan (Sherry Raymond) 1914- 9-12R
Marsh, Susan H. 1926- 148
Marsh, U(lysses) Grant 1911- 57-60
Marsh, Valerie 1954- .... SATA 89
Marsh, Willa
See Marsh, Willa
Marsh, Willard 1922-1970 .... CAP-2
Earlier sketch in CA 25-28
Marshak, Robert Eugene
1916-1992 .... CANR-85
Obituary 140
Earlier sketch in CA 107
Marshak, Ronni T. 222
Marshak, Samuil Yakovlevich 1887-1964
Obituary 111
Marshal, Nell 1933- 171
Marshall, Adre 1942- 170
Marshall, Alan 1902-1984 85-88
See also DLB 260
Marshall, Alfred 1884-1965 .... 5-8R
Marshall, Allen
See Westlake, Donald E(dwin)
Marshall, Andrew 1967- 215
Marshall, Annie Jessie 1922- CAP-1
Earlier sketch in CA 9-10
Marshall, Anthony 196
Marshall, Anthony D(ryden) 1924- 29-32R
See also SATA 18
Marshall, (Charles) Arthur (Bertram) 1910-1989
Obituary 127
Marshall, Bev 1945- 230
Marshall, Bill 1937- CANR-17
Earlier sketch in CA 65-68
Marshall, Bonnie C. 1941- 212
See also SATA 18, 141
Marshall, Bridget M(ary) 1974- 170
See also SATA 103
Marshall, Bruce 1899-1987 .... CANR-86
Obituary 123
Earlier sketch in CA 5-8R
See also CN 1, 2, 3, 4
Marshall, Burke 1922-2003 .... 13-16R
Obituary 217
Marshall, Byron K. 1936- 33-36R
Marshall, (Sarah) Catherine (Wood)
1914-1983 .... CANR-79
Obituary 109
Earlier sketches in CA 17-20R, CANR-8, 57
See also BPFB 2
See also SATA 2
See also SATA-Obit 34
Marshall, Charles Burton 1908-1999 .... 37-40R
Obituary 188
Marshall, Charles F(rancis) 1915- 146
Marshall, Charles Wheeler 1906-1997 110
Marshall, Christopher D(avid) 1953- 226
Marshall, Cynthia L. 1956- 187
Marshall, D(onald) Bruce 1931- 65-68
Marshall, David F(ranklin) 1938- 25-28R
Marshall, Don
See Marshall, Donovan
Marshall, Donald G. 1943- 145
Marshall, Donald R. 1934- 93-96
Marshall, Donald S(tanley) 1919- 29-32R
Marshall, Donovan 1908- 117
Marshall, Dorothy 1900-1994 .... CAP-1
Obituary 144
Earlier sketch in CA 13-14
Marshall, Douglas
See McClintock, Marshall
Marshall, E(dmund) Jesse 1888-1974 .... CAP-1
Earlier sketch in CA 11-12
Marshall, Edison 1894-1967 .... CAP-1
Obituary 29-32R
Earlier sketch in CA 9-10
See also DLB 102
See also RHW
Marshall, Edmund
See Hopkins, (Hector) Kenneth
Marshall, Edward
See Marshall, James (Edward)
Marshall, Edward 1932- .... DLB 16
Marshall, Emily
See Hall, Bennie Caroline (Humble)
Marshall, Emma 1828-1899 .... DLB 163
Marshall, Evan 1956- 223
Marshall, Evelyn 1897-1991 .... CANR-18
Earlier sketches in CA 5-8R, CANR-2
See also RHW
See also SATA 11
Marshall, F(reddie) Ray 1928- CANR-8
Earlier sketch in CA 17-20R
Marshall, Felicity 1950- 188
See also SATA 116
Marshall, Frank 1946- .... IDFW 3, 4
Marshall, Garry 1934- 111
See also AAYA 3
See also CLC 17
See also SATA 60
Marshall, Gary
See Snow, Charles H(orace)
Marshall, George C(atlett), Jr. 1880-1959
Brief entry 115
Marshall, George N(ichols)
1920(?)-1993 .... CANR-46
Obituary 140
Earlier sketch in CA 77-80
Marshall, George O(ctavius), Jr. 1922- .. 17-20R
Marshall, H. H.
See Jahn, (Joseph) Michael
Marshall, Helen E(dith) 1899-1989 .... 37-40R
Marshall, Helen Lowrie 1904-1975 103
Marshall, Herbert (Percival James)
1906-1991 .... CANR-29
Earlier sketch in CA 25-28R
Marshall, Herbert Hedley 1909(?)-1982
Obituary 112
Marshall, Hermine H(alprin) 1935- .. CANR-14
Earlier sketch in CA 41-44R
Marshall, Howard D(rake) 1924-1972 ... CAP-2
Obituary 37-40R
Earlier sketch in CA 23-24
Marshall, Howard Wight 1944- 107
Marshall, Hubert (Ray) 1920- 21-24R
Marshall, I(an) Howard 1934- CANR-50
Earlier sketch in CA 122
Marshall, I. N. 1931- 134
Marshall, Ian 1954- 175
Marshall, J(ohn) D(uncan) 1919- CANR-31
Earlier sketch in CA 73-76
Marshall, Jack 1937- 97-100
See also CP 1, 2, 3, 4, 5, 6, 7
Marshall, James 1896-1986 .... 41-44R
Obituary 120
Marshall, James (Edward)
1942-1992 .... CANR-77
Obituary 139
Earlier sketches in CA 41-44R, CANR-38
See also CLR 21
See also CWRI 5
See also DLB 61
See also MAICYA 1, 2
See also MAICYAS 1
See also SATA 6, 51, 75
Marshall, James M(orse) 1924- 120
Marshall, James Vance
See Payne, Donald Gordon
Marshall, James Vance 1887-1964 .... CAP-1
Earlier sketch in CA 11-12
Marshall, Janet (Perry) 1938- 164
See also SATA 97
Marshall, Jeff
See Laycock, George (Edwin)
Marshall, Joanne
See Rundle, Anne
Marshall, John 1905(?)-1985(?)
Obituary 116
Marshall, John 1922- CANR-43
Earlier sketches in CA 89-92, CANR-15
Marshall, John David 1928- CANR-41
Earlier sketches in CA 9-12R, CANR-3, 19
Marshall, John Douglas 1947- CANR-93
Earlier sketch in CA 145
Marshall, John Ross 1912-1988 109
Marshall, John S(edberry) 1898-1979 .... CAP-1
Earlier sketch in CA 19-20
Marshall, Joyce 1913- 102
See also DLB 88
Marshall, June 1947- 215
Marshall, Kathryn 1951- 57-60
See also AITN 1
Marshall, Kim
See Marshall, Michael (Kimbrough)
Marshall, Lenore Guinzburg
1899-1971 .... CAP-2
Obituary 33-36R
Earlier sketch in CA 25-28
See also CP 1
Marshall, Lorna 1898-2002 230
Marshall, Lovat
See Duncan, W(illiam) Murdoch
Marshall, Margaret 1901(?)-1974
Obituary 104
Marshall, Margaret Wiley 1908-1995 .... CAP-1
Earlier sketch in CA 9-10
Marshall, Martin V(ivan) 1922- 1-4R
Marshall, Max Lawrence 1922- 17-20R
Marshall, Max S(kidmore) 1897-1985 ... CAP-1
Earlier sketch in CA 13-14
Marshall, Megan 1954- 124
Marshall, Mel(vin D.) 1911- CANR-12
Earlier sketch in CA 29-32R
Marshall, Michael
See Smith, Michael Marshall
Marshall, Michael (Kimbrough)
1948- CANR-3
Earlier sketch in CA 49-52
See also SATA 37
Marshall, Muriel 106
Marshall, Nancy Rose 203
Marshall, Natalie J(unemann) 1929- 41-44R
Marshall, Norman 1901-1980
Obituary 108
Marshall, Owen 1941- CANR-137
Earlier sketch in CA 160
See also CN 5, 6, 7
See also RGSF 2
Marshall, Paul A. 1948- CANR-143
Earlier sketch in CA 165
Marshall, Paule 1929- CANR-129
Earlier sketches in CA 77-80, CANR-25, 73
See also AFAW 1, 2
See also AMWS 11
See also BLC 3
See also BPFB 2
See also BW 2, 3
See also CLC 27, 72
See also CN 1, 2, 3, 4, 5, 6, 7
See also DA3
See also DAM MULT
See also DLB 33, 157, 227
See also EWL 3
See also LATS 1:2
See also MAL 5
See also MTCW 1, 2
See also MTFW 2005
See also RGAL 4
See also SSC 3
See also SSFS 15
Marshall, Penny 1943- .... AAYA 10, 62
Marshall, Percy
See Young, Percy M(arshall)
Marshall, Peter 1902-1949
Brief entry 112
Marshall, Peter (H.) 1946- 140
Marshall, Ray
See Marshall, F(reddie) Ray
Marshall, Raymond
See Raymond, Rene (Brabazon)
Marshall, Richard (D.) 1947- 125
Marshall, Robert G. 1919- 37-40R
Marshall, Robert L(ewis) 1939- 104
Marshall, Robert O. 1939- 206
Marshall, Roderick 1903-1975
Obituary 53-56
Marshall, Ronald 1905- CAP-2
Earlier sketch in CA 33-36
Marshall, Rosalind Kay CANR-41
Earlier sketches in CA 53-56, CANR-4, 19
Marshall, Rosamond (Van der Zee)
1902-1957 .... RHW
Marshall, S(amuel) L(yman) A(twood)
1900-1977 81-84
Obituary 73-76
See also SATA 21
Marshall, Shirley E(velyn) 1925- 21-24R
Marshall, Sybil Mary (Edwards)
1913- CANR-1
Earlier sketch in CA 1-4R
Marshall, T(homas) H(umphrey)
1893-1981 109
Obituary 105
Marshall, Teresa 1962- 210
Marshall, Thomas Archibald 1938- .. CANR-38
Earlier sketches in CA 49-52, CANR-1, 17
See also Marshall, Tom
Marshall, Thomas F(rederic)
1908-1991 .... CAP-2
Earlier sketch in CA 23-24
Marshall, Thomas R. 1949- 115
Marshall, Tom
See Marshall, Thomas Archibald
See also CP 1
See also DLB 60
Marshall, Tyler 1941- 136
Marshall, W. Gerald 1948- 145
Marshall, William
See Marshall, William Leonard
Marshall, William H(arvey) 1925-1968 . CAP-1
Earlier sketch in CA 11-12
Marshall, William Leonard 1944- CANR-62
Brief entry 127
Earlier sketch in CA 133
Interview in CA-133
See also CMW 4
Marshall-Cornwall, James (Handyside)
1887-1985 107
Obituary 118
Marshallik
See Zangwill, Israel
Marshburn, Joseph Hancock 1890-1975 109
Obituary 106
Marshner, Connaught Coyne 1951- .. CANR-16
Earlier sketch in CA 93-96
Marsilius of Padua 1275(?)-1342(?) ..... DLB 115
Mars-Jones, Adam 1954- CANR-134
Earlier sketches in CA 109, CANR-27
See also CN 5, 6, 7
See also DLB 207, 319
Marsland, Amy 1924- CANR-19
Earlier sketch in CA 103
Marsman, Hendrik 1899-1940 .... EWL 3
Marsman, Hendrik Jan 1937- 192
Marsoli, Lisa Ann 1958- 120
See also SATA 101
See also SATA-Brief 53
Marson, Bonnie 230
Marson, Philip 1892-1971 .... 9-12R
Marson, Una (Maude) 1905-1965 176
See also BW 3
See also DLB 157
Marsteller, Bill
See Marsteller, William A.
Marsteller, William A. 1914-1987
Obituary 123
Marsten, Richard
See Hunter, Evan
Marston, David W(eese) 1942- 125
Marston, Edward
See Miles, Keith
Marston, Elsa 1933- CANR-87
Earlier sketches in CA 113, CANR-32
See also SATA 156
Marston, Hope Irvin 1935- CANR-106
Earlier sketch in CA 101
See also SATA 31, 127
Marston, John 1576-1634 .... BRW 2
See also DAM DRAM
See also DLB 58, 172
See also RGEL 2
Marston, John E(merson) 1911-2000 .... 5-8R
Marston, John Westland 1819-1890 ...... RGEL 2
Marston, Philip Bourke 1850-1887 .... DLB 35
Marston, Thomas Ewart 1904-1984
Obituary 112
Marszalek, John F(rancis, Jr.) 1939- .. CANR-45
Earlier sketches in CA 37-40R, CANR-14
Marta, Suzy Yehl 1945- 238
Martchenko, Michael 1942- 160
See also SATA 50, 95, 154
Marte, Fred
See Marte, Leonard Ferdinand
Marte, Leonard Ferdinand 1942- 156
Marteka, Vincent (James) 1936- 13-16R
Martel, Gordon 208
Martel, Jane G. 1926- 57-60
Martel, Leon C. 1933- CANR-113
Earlier sketch in CA 125
Martel, Suzanne 1924- 160
See also SATA 99
Martel, Yann 1963- CANR-114
Earlier sketch in CA 146
See also AAYA 67
See also CLC 192
See also MTFW 2005
Martell, Aimee
See Thurlo, Aimee and
Thurlo, David
Martell, Christopher R. 1956- 226
Martell, Dominic
See Reaves, Sam
Martell, James
See Bingley, David Ernest
Martell, Joanne 1926- 187
Martell, Mike
See Sasser, Charles W(ayne)
Martell, Paul 1921(?)-1985
Obituary 116
Martellaro, Joseph A. 1924-1995 .... 17-20R
Martelli, Leonard J. 1938(?)-1988
Obituary 125
Marten, Jacqueline (Lee) 1923- 141
Marten, James 1956- 187
Marten, Michael 1947- 132
Martens, Adolphe-Adhemar
See Ghelderode, Michel de
Martens, E. A.
See Martens, Elmer A(rthur)
Martens, Elmer A(rthur) 1930- CANR-113
Earlier sketches in CA 127, CANR-54
Martens, Kurt 1870-1945 237
See also DLB 66
Martens, Lorna 1946- 157
Martens, Margaret Hosmer 1942- 151
Marter, Joan M. 1946- CANR-113
Earlier sketches in CA 124, CANR-52
Marth, Del 1925- 61-64
Martha, Henry
See Harris, Mark
Marti, Fritz 1894-1991 107
Marti, Jose
See Marti (y Perez), Jose (Julian)
See also DLB 290
Marti (y Perez), Jose (Julian) 1853-1895
See Marti, Jose
See also DAM MULT
See also HLC 2
See also HW 2
See also LAW
See also RGWL 2, 3
See also WLIT 1
Martial c. 40-c. 104 .... AW 2
See also CDWLB 1
See also DLB 211
See also PC 10
See also RGWL 2, 3
Martianoff, Nicholas 1893-1984
Obituary 112
Martien, Jerry 1939- CANR-115
Earlier sketch in CA 154
Martignoni, Margaret E. 1908(?)-1974
Obituary 104
See also SATA-Obit 27
Marti-Ibanez, Felix 1912(?)-1972
Obituary 33-36R
Martin, Albert
See Mehan, Joseph Albert and
Nussbaum, Al(bert F.)
Martin, Albro 1921- 77-80
Martin, Alex 1953- 137
Martin, Alexander M(ichael) 1964- 229
Martin, Alfred 1916- 117

Martin, Alfred Manuel 1928-1989 ... CANR-79
Obituary ... 130
Earlier sketch in CA 108
Martin, Allana ... 171
Martin, Allie Beth 1914-1976
Obituary ... 65-68
Martin, Anamae 1919- ... 9-12R
Martin, Andre
See Jacoby, Henry
Martin, Andrew 1906-1985 ... 137
Obituary ... 115
Martin, Andrew 1952- ... CANR-116
Earlier sketch in CA 137
Martin, Andy
See Martin, Andrew
Martin, Ann Bodenhamer 1927- ... CANR-11
Earlier sketch in CA 69-72
Martin, Ann M(atthews) 1955- ... CANR-106
Earlier sketches in CA 111, CANR-32
Interview in ... CANR-32
See also AAYA 6, 42
See also BYA 8, 14
See also CLR 32
See also JRDA
See also MAICYA 1, 2
See also SATA 44, 70, 126
See also SATA-Brief 41
Martin, April
See Sherrill, Dorothy
Martin, Arlan Stone 1932- ... 69-72
Martin, Augustine 1935-1995 ... 93-96
Martin, Barclay (Cluck) 1923- ... 73-76
Martin, Ben(jamin S.) 1921-2004 ... 1-4R
Obituary ... 230
Martin, Benjamin F(ranklin, Jr.)
1947- ... CANR-93
Earlier sketch in CA 89-92
Martin, Bernard (Davis) 1897- ... CAP-1
Earlier sketch in CA 9-10
Martin, Bernard 1905- ... CAP-1
Earlier sketch in CA 11-12
Martin, Bernard 1928- ... CANR-4
Earlier sketch in CA 53-56
Martin, Betty
See Martin, Elizabeth DuVernet
Martin, Bill, Jr.
See Martin, William Ivan, Jr.
See also CLR 97
See also SATA 67
See also SATA-Brief 40
Martin, Billy
See Martin, Alfred Manuel
Martin, Boyd A(rcher) 1911-1998 ... 37-40R
Martin, Brian P(hilip) 1947- ... CANR-38
Earlier sketch in CA 116
Martin, Bruce
See Paine, Lauran (Bosworth)
Martin, Bruce 1922- ... 168
Martin, C(arol) Dianne 1943- ... 113
Martin, C(harles) Leslie 1897-1974 ... 5-8R
Martin, C. Lewis 1915- ... 25-28R
Martin, Calvin (Luther) 1948- ... 195
Brief entry ... 113
Martin, Carol A. 1941- ... 149
Martin, Carter W(illiams) 1933- ... 25-28R
Martin, Catherine 1847-1937 ... DLB 230
Martin, Charles 1906-1997 ... 1-4R
Martin, Charles 1942- ... 187
See also DLB 120, 282
Martin, Charles B(asil) 1930- ... 93-96
Martin, Charles Burton 1924- ... 25-28R
Martin, Charles E(lmer)
See Mastrangelo, Charles E(lmer)
See also SATA 69, 70
Martin, Charles-Noel 1923- ... 29-32R
Martin, Chip
See Martin, Stoddard (Hammond), Jr.
Martin, Christopher
See Hoyt, Edwin P(almer), Jr.
Martin, Chryssee MacCasler Perry
1940- ... CANR-56
Earlier sketch in CA 126
Martin, Chuck 1891-1954 ... TCWW 2
Martin, Claire 1914- ... 164
See also DLB 60
Martin, Claire 1933- ... 143
See also SATA 76
Martin, Constance R. 1923- ... 158
Martin, Cort
See Sherman, Jory (Tecumseh)
Martin, Curtis 1915- ... 53-56
Martin, Dannie M. 1939- ... 145
Martin, David 1915-1997 ... CANR-49
Earlier sketches in CA 103, CANR-24
See also CP 1
See also CWRI 5
See also DLB 260
Martin, David (Lozell) 1946- ... CANR-101
Earlier sketches in CA 89-92, CANR-27
See also HGG
Martin, David Alfred 1929- ... 107
Martin, David C(lark) 1943- ... 102
Martin, David Grant 1939- ... 65-68
Martin, David L(incoln) 1947- ... 119
Martin, David S. 1937- ... 142
Martin, David Stone 1913-1992 ... SATA 39
Martin, Del
See Martin, Dorothy L.
See also GLL 1
Martin, Don 1931-2000 ... 101
Obituary ... 187
Martin, Don W. 1934- ... CANR-52
Earlier sketch in CA 126
Martin, Donald
See Honig, Donald
Martin, Donald Franklin 1944- ... 65-68
Martin, Donald L(loyd) 1939- ... 111
Martin, Dorothy 1921- ... CANR-6
Earlier sketch in CA 57-60
See also SATA 47
Martin, Dorothy L. 1921- ... 138
See also Martin, Del
See also FW
Martin, Douglas (Ivor) 1939- ... CANR-82
Earlier sketch in CA 133
Martin, Dwight 1921-1978
Obituary ... 77-80
Martin, E(rnest) W(alter) 1914-2005 . CANR-20
Obituary ... 238
Earlier sketches in CA 9-12R, CANR-5
Martin, Earl S(auder) 1944- ... 102
Martin, Edward A(lexander) 1927- ... 120
Martin, Elizabeth A(nn) 1945- ... CANR-90
Earlier sketch in CA 132
Martin, Elizabeth DuVernet 1910-1996 ... 103
Martin, Ellis
See Ryan, Marah Ellis
Martin, Emily 1944- ... CANR-27
Earlier sketch in CA 49-52
Martin, Esmond Bradley 1941- ... CANR-16
Earlier sketch in CA 93-96
Martin, Eugene ... CANR-26
Earlier sketches in CAP-2, CA 19-20
See also SATA 1
Martin, Eva M. 1939- ... 126
See also SATA 65
Martin, F(rancis) David 1920- ... 33-36R
Martin, F(rancis) X(avier)
1922-2000 ... CANR-30
Obituary ... 187
Earlier sketches in CA 21-24R, CANR-13
Martin, Fenton S(trickland) 1943- ... 157
Martin, Frances M(cEntee) 1906-1998 ... 61-64
See also SATA 36
Martin, Francesca 1947- ... 168
See also SATA 101
Martin, Francis
See Reid, Charles (Stuart)
Martin, Fred 1948- ... 190
See also SATA 119
Martin, Frederick M(orris) 1923-1985
Obituary ... 115
Martin, Fredric
See Christopher, Matt(hew Frederick)
Martin, G(eoffrey) H(oward) 1928- ... 5-8R
Martin, Gail Gaymer ... 224
Martin, Gary M. 1936- ... 89-92
Martin, Ged
See Martin, Gerald Warren
Martin, Geoffrey John 1934- ... CANR-14
Earlier sketch in CA 37-40R
Martin, George (Whitney) 1926- ... CANR-44
Earlier sketches in CA 9-12R, CANR-3, 21
Martin, George E. 1932- ... 143
Martin, George R(aymond) R(ichard)
1948- ... CANR-79
Earlier sketch in CA 81-84
See also AAYA 35
See also HGG
See also SATA 118
See also SFW 4
See also SUFW 2
Martin, Gerald Warren 1945- ... CANR-38
Earlier sketches in CA 45-48, CANR-1, 17
Martin, Graham Dunstan 1932- ... CANR-47
Earlier sketches in CA 106, CANR-23
See also FANT
Martin, Greg
See Miller, George Louquet
Martin, Harold Clark 1917- ... 9-12R
Martin, Harold Harber 1910-1994 ... CANR-7
Obituary ... 146
Earlier sketch in CA 61-64
Martin, Harold S(heaffer) 1930- ... 57-60
Martin, Herbert 1913- ... 29-32R
Martin, Herbert Woodward 1933- ... CANR-52
Earlier sketches in CA 73-76, CANR-27
See also BW 1
Martin, Hubert M., Jr. 1932- ... 103
Martin, Ian Kennedy
See Kennedy-Martin, Ian
Martin, Ira Jay III 1911-1983 ... 53-56
Martin, J(ohn) P(ercival) 1880(?)-1966 ... 81-84
See also SATA 15
Martin, J(ulia) Wallis ... 208
Martin, Jack
See Etchison, Dennis (William)
Martin, Jack 1950- ... 199
Martin, Jacqueline Briggs 1945- ... CANR-132
Earlier sketch in CA 165
See also SATA 98, 149
Martin, James 1921- ... 119
Martin, James (Thomas) 1933- ... 134
Brief entry ... 112
Martin, James Alfred, Jr. 1917- ... 73-76
Martin, James Gilbert 1926- ... 9-12R
Martin, James J(oseph) 1916- ... CANR-8
Earlier sketch in CA 5-8R
Martin, James Kirby 1943- ... CANR-53
Earlier sketch in CA 125
Martin, James L. 1948- ... 81-84
Martin, James Perry 1923- ... 5-8R
Martin, Jane ... CD 5, 6
Martin, Jane Read 1957- ... 150
See also SATA 84
Martin, Jane Roland 1929- ... CANR-97
Earlier sketches in CA 119, CANR-43
Martin, Janet
See Garfinkel, Bernard Max
Martin, Jay
See Golding, Morton J(ay)
Martin, Jay (Herbert) 1935- ... CANR-96
Earlier sketches in CA 5-8R, CANR-21
See also DLB 111
Martin, Jeremy
See Levin, Marcia Obrasky
Martin, Jesse 1981- ... 215
Martin, Joanna 1951- ... 173
Martin, John 1893-1985
Obituary ... 116
Martin, John B.
See Martin, Bruce
Martin, John Bartlow 1915-1987 ... CANR-8
Obituary ... 121
Earlier sketch in CA 13-16R
Martin, John Hanbury 1892-1983
Obituary ... 109
Martin, John Henry 1915- ... 102
Martin, John Rupert 1916-2000 ... 17-20R
Martin, John Sayre 1921- ... 103
Martin, John Stuart 1900-1977 ... 9-12R
Obituary ... 69-72
Martin (Montes), Jose L(uis) 1921- ... CANR-12
Earlier sketch in CA 61-64
See also HW 1
Martin, Josef
See Bauer, Henry H.
Martin, Joseph George 1915-1981 ... 108
Obituary ... 102
Martin, Joy 1922- ... 57-60
Martin, Judith (Sylvia) 1938- ... CANR-103
Earlier sketches in CA 97-100, CANR-12
Interview in ... CANR-12
Martin, Julie (Breyer) 1938- ... 133
Martin, June Hall
See McCash, June Hall
Martin, Justin 1964- ... 232
Martin, Kat 1947- ... CANR-119
Earlier sketch in CA 150
Martin, Kathryn 1908-1990 ... 108
Martin, Ken
See Hubbard, L(afayette) Ron(ald)
Martin, Kenneth R(obert) 1938- ... CANR-38
Earlier sketches in CA 45-48, CANR-1, 17
Martin, Kevin
See Pelton, Robert W(ayne)
Martin, (Basil) Kingsley 1897-1969 ... CANR-11
Obituary ... 25-28R
Earlier sketch in CA 5-8R
Martin, L(eslie) John 1921- ... CANR-46
Earlier sketches in CA 57-60, CANR-6, 22
Martin, Larry Jay ... 203
Martin, Laura C(oogle) 1952- ... 117
Martin, Laurence W(oodward) 1928- . CANR-7
Earlier sketch in CA 5-8R
Martin(-Berg), Laurey K(ramer) 1950- ... 143
Martin, Lawrence 1895-1980 ... CAP-1
Earlier sketch in CA 9-10
Martin, Lee
See Wingate, (Martha) Anne (Guice)
Martin, Lee Nicholson 1916(?)-1987
Obituary ... 124
Martin, Les
See Schulman, L(ester) M(artin)
Martin, Linda 1961- ... SATA 82
Martin, Linda G. 1947- ... 128
Martin, Lisa L. ... 232
Martin, Lucien
See Gabel, Joseph
Martin, Luis 1927- ... 131
See also HW 1
Martin, Luther H(oward), Jr. 1937- ... 124
Martin, Lynne 1923- ... 65-68
See also SATA 21
Martin, M(arilynn) Kay 1942- ... 65-68
Martin, Malachi 1921-1999 ... CANR-70
Obituary ... 185
Earlier sketch in CA 81-84
See also AITN 1
Martin, Marcia
See Levin, Marcia Obrasky
Martin, Margaret Joan 1928- ... 69-72
Martin, Marianne K. 1945- ... 175
Martin, Marie-Louise 1912-1990 ... 69-72
Martin, Mario, Jr.
See Monteleone, Thomas F(rancis)
Martin, Marjorie 1942-1997 ... 53-56
Martin, Marta San
See San Martin, Marta
Martin, Marvin 1926- ... 196
See also SATA 126
Martin, Mary 1913(?)-1990 ... CANR-79
Obituary ... 132
Brief entry ... 111
Earlier sketch in CA 113
Martin, Mary Steichen
See Calderone, Mary S(teichen)
Martin, Maurice 1946- ... 115
Martin, Melanie
See Pellowski, Michael (Joseph)
Martin, Michael L. 1932- ... 17-20R
Martin, Michael T. 1947- ... 226
Martin, Michael William 1946- ... CANR-98
Earlier sketches in CA 121, CANR-47
Martin, Michelle 1957- ... 119
Martin, Mike W.
See Martin, Michael William
Martin, Milward Wyatt 1895-1974 ... CAP-1
Earlier sketch in CA 19-20
Martin, Morgan 1921- ... 17-20R
Martin, Murray S(impson) 1928-1998 ... 112
Martin, Nancy
See Salmon, Annie Elizabeth
Martin, Noah S(ensenig) 1940- ... 69-72
Martin, Norma F(rances) 1936- ... 113
Martin, Oliver
See Smith, R(eginald) D(onald)
Martin, Ovid A. 1904-1979
Obituary ... 89-92
Martin, Patricia Miles 1899-1986 ... CANR-37
Obituary ... 119
Earlier sketches in CA 1-4R, CANR-2
See also MAICYA 1, 2
See also SATA 1, 43
See also SATA-Obit 48
Martin, Patricia Preciado 1939- ... 199
See also Preciado Martin, Patricia
Martin, Paul
See Deale, Kenneth Edwin Lee
Martin, Paul Sidney 1899-1974 ... CANR-8
Earlier sketch in CA 5-8R
Martin, Pete
See Martin, William Thorton
Martin, Peter
See Chaundler, Christine
Martin, (Roy) Peter 1931- ... CANR-63
Brief entry ... 120
Earlier sketch in CA 125
Interview in ... CA-125
See also Melville, James
See also CMW 4
Martin, Peter W(illiam) 1939- ... 89-92
Martin, Philip (John Talbot) 1931- ... CANR-24
Earlier sketches in CA 61-64, CANR-9
Martin, Philip R. 1943- ... 202
Martin, Phyllis Cook 1908-1994 ... 5-8R
Martin, Phyllis R(odgers) ... 130
Martin, Quinn 1922-1987
Obituary ... 123
Martin, R. Johnson
See Mehta, Rustam Jehangir
Martin, R(ichard) M(ilton) 1916- ... CANR-15
Earlier sketch in CA 41-44R
Martin, Ralph 1942- ... CANR-9
Earlier sketch in CA 57-60
Martin, Ralph C. 1924- ... 9-12R
Martin, Ralph G(uy) 1920-1997 ... CANR-104
Earlier sketches in CA 5-8R, CANR-50
Martin, Ralph P(hilip) ... CANR-9
Earlier sketch in CA 65-68
Martin, Randy (L.) 1957- ... 229
Martin, Reginald 1956- ... 126
See also BW 2
Martin, Rene 1891-1977 ... SATA 42
See also SATA-Obit 20
Martin, Renee C(ohen) 1928- ... 49-52
Martin, Rhona 1922- ... 121
Brief entry ... 116
See also RHW
Martin, Richard
See Creasey, John
Martin, Richard 1946-1999 ... 124
Obituary ... 186
Martin, Robert (Lee) 1908-1976 ... 1-4R
Obituary ... 103
Martin, Robert A(llen) 1930- ... 110
Martin, Robert Bernard 1918- ... CANR-25
Earlier sketches in CA 1-4R, CANR-2
Martin, Robert F. 1946- ... 218
Martin, Robert K(essler) 1941- ... 102
Martin, Robert M. 1942- ... 143
Martin, Robert Sidney 1949- ... 122
Martin, Robert W.
See Pelton, Robert W(ayne)
Martin, Roderick 1940- ... CANR-12
Earlier sketch in CA 29-32R
Martin, Roger H(arry) 1943- ... CANR-90
Earlier sketch in CA 132
Martin, Ron 1941- ... 122
Martin, Ronald E(dward) 1933- ... 17-20R
Martin, Roscoe C(oleman) 1903-1972 ... CAP-1
Obituary ... 33-36R
Earlier sketch in CA 19-20
Martin, Ross M(urdoch) 1929- ... 222
Martin, Rupert (Claude) 1905- ... SATA 31
Martin, Russell 1952- ... CANR-103
Earlier sketch in CA 143
Martin, Ruth
See Rayner, Claire (Berenice)
Martin, S. R.
See Mappin, Strephyn
Martin, Sam
See Moskowitz, Sam
Martin, Samuel Elmo 1924-
Brief entry ... 105
Martin, Sandy Dwayne ... 205
Martin, Shannon E. (Rossi) 1952- ... 237
Martin, Stefan 1936- ... SATA 32
Martin, Stella
See Heyer, Georgette
Martin, Stephen-Paul 1949- ... 145
Martin, Steve 1945- ... CANR-140
Earlier sketches in CA 97-100, CANR-30, 100
See also AAYA 53
See also CLC 30
See also DFS 19
See also MTCW 1
See also MTFW 2005
Martin, Stoddard (Hammond), Jr. 1948- ... 117
Martin, Susan B(oyles) 1959- ... 128
Martin, Susan Ehrlich 1940- ... 124
Martin, Sylvia (Pass) 1913-1981 ... 17-20R
Obituary ... 135
Martin, Taffy 1945- ... 125
Martin, Thom(as) Francis 1934- ... 5-8R
Martin, Thomas 1696-1771 ... DLB 213
Martin, Thomas Lyle, Jr. 1921- ... 9-12R
Martin, Thomas R. ... 183
Martin, Timothy (Peter) 1950- ... 138
Martin, Tom
See Paine, Lauran (Bosworth)
Martin, Tony 1942- ... CANR-52
Earlier sketches in CA 57-60, CANR-6, 26
See also BW 2

Cumulative Index 379 Masetti

Martin, Valerie 1948- CANR-89
Earlier sketches in CA 85-88, CANR-49
See also BEST 90:2
See also CLC 89
Martin, Vance G(regory) 1949- 114
Martin, Vernon N(orthfleet) 1930- 45-48
Martin, Vicky
See Storey, Victoria Carolyn
Martin, Violet Florence 1862-1915 .... SSC 56
See also TCLC 51
Martin, Wallace 1933- 122
Martin, Walter Ralston 1928-1989
Obituary 129
Martin, Walter T(ilford) 1917- 9-12R
Martin, Warren Bryan 1925- CANR-20
Earlier sketch in CA 41-44R
Martin, Webber
See Silverberg, Robert
Martin, Wendy
See Martini, Teri
Martin, Wendy 1940- 37-40R
Martin, Wilfred B(enjamin) W(eldon)
1940- 116
Martin, William (Flynn) 1950- CANR-108
Earlier sketch in CA 140
Martin, William C. 1937- CANR-41
Earlier sketches in CA 77-80, CANR-14
Martin, William Ivan, Jr. 1916-2004 130
Obituary 229
Brief entry 117
See also Martin, Bill, Jr.
See also MAICYA 1, 2
See also SATA 40, 145
Martin, William Keble 1877-1969
Obituary 104
Martin, William Thorton 1901(?)-1980
Obituary 102
Martina, Daniella
See Klein, Daniel M(artin)
Martinac, Paula 1954- 164
See also GLL 1
Martinco, John P. 1917(?)-1986
Obituary 118
Martindale, Charles (Anthony) 1949- 124
Martindale, Colin (Eugene) 1943- 61-64
Martindale, Don (Albert) 1915- CANR-6
Earlier sketch in CA 13-16R
Martindale, Patrick Victor
See White, Patrick (Victor Martindale)
Martin du Gard, Roger 1881-1958 ... CANR-94
Brief entry 118
See also DLB 65
See also EWL 3
See also GFL 1789 to the Present
See also RGWL 2, 3
See also TCLC 24
Martine
See Woolfolk, Joanna Martine
Martine, James J(ohn) 1937- 57-60
Martineau, Gilbert CANR-17
Earlier sketch in CA 29-32R
Martineau, Harriet 1802-1876 .... DLB 21, 55, 159, 163, 166, 190
See also FW
See also RGEL 2
See also YABC 2
Martineau, James 1805-1900
Brief entry 122
Martineau, Robert Arnold Schurhoff
1913-1999 106
Martine-Barnes, Adrienne 1942- 110
Martinelli, Marco 1956- .... WLIT 7
Martinelli, Ricardo
See Brandon, Johnny
Martines, Julia
See O'Faolain, Julia
Martines, Lauro 1927- CANR-12
Earlier sketch in CA 25-28R
Martinet, Andre 1908-1999 .... CAP-1
Earlier sketch in CA 11-12
Martinet, Jeanne 1958- CANR-101
Earlier sketch in CA 148
See also SATA 80
Martinetti, Ronald 1945- 57-60
Martinetz, V(ivian) L. 1927- 61-64
Martinez, Al 1929- CANR-104
Earlier sketch in CA 57-60
Martinez, Andres 1966- 239
Martinez, Demetria 1960- 179
See also DLB 209
See also LLW
Martinez, Dionisio D. 1956- 201
See also LLW
Martinez, Ed(ward) 1954- .... SATA 98
Martinez, Eliud 1935- 179
See also DLB 122
Martinez, Elizabeth Coonrod 1954- . CANR-80
Earlier sketch in CA 152
See also HW 2
See also SATA 85
Martinez, Elizabeth Sutherland 1925- 121
Martinez, Enrique Gonzalez
See Gonzalez Martinez, Enrique
Martinez, Jacinto Benavente y
See Benavente (y Martinez), Jacinto
Martinez, Joseph G. R. 145
Martinez, Julio A(ntonio) 1931- CANR-18
Earlier sketch in CA 101
See also HW 1
Martinez, Manuel Luis 1966- 200
Martinez, Max(imiano) 1943- 131
See also DLB 82
See also HW 1
Martinez, Nancy C. CANR-93
Earlier sketch in CA 145
Martinez, Nina Marie 228
Martinez, Orlando 1924- 138
Martinez, Oscar J(aquez) 1943- 120
Martinez, Rafael Arevalo
See Arevalo Martinez, Rafael
Martinez, Rafael V. 1923- 9-12R
Martinez, Raymond J(oseph) 1889-1982 . 61-64
Martinez, Ruben 1962- .... DLB 209
Martinez, S(ally) A. 1938- 81-84
Martinez, Tomas Eloy 1934- CANR-144
Earlier sketches in CA 131, CANR-62
See also HW 1, 2
See also LAWS 1
See also WLIT 1
Martinez, Victor 1954- 159
See also LATS 1:2
See also SATA 95
See also YAW
Martinez-Alier, Joan 1939- 238
Martinez de la Rosa, Francisco de Paula
1787-1862 .... TWA
Martinez de Toledo, Alfonso
1398(?)-1468 .... DLB 286
Martinez Estrada, Ezequiel 1895-1964 ... EWL 3
See also LAW
Martinez-Fernandez, Luis
See Martinez-Fernandez, Luis
Martinez-Fernandez, Luis 1960- CANR-134
Earlier sketch in CA 174
See also HW 2
Martinez Moreno, Carlos 1917-1986 131
See also HW 1
Martinez Ruiz, Jose 1873-1967 93-96
See also Azorin and
Ruiz, Jose Martinez
See also HW 1
Martinez Sierra, Gregorio 1881-1947
Brief entry 115
See also EWL 3
See also TCLC 6
Martinez Sierra, Maria (de la O'LeJarraga)
1874-1974
Obituary 115
See also EWL 3
See also TCLC 6
Marting, Diane E. 1952- 138
Martin Gaite, Carmen 1925- .... CWW 2
See also EWL 3
Martini, Steve(n Paul) 1946- CANR-108
Earlier sketches in CA 140, CANR-62
See also CMW 4
Martini, Teri 1930- CANR-2
Earlier sketch in CA 5-8R
See also SATA 3
Martini, Therese
See Martini, Teri
Martini, Virgilio 1903-1986 .... 37-40R
Martinich, A. P. 1946- 191
Martino, Bill 1933- 57-60
Martino, Joseph P(aul) 1931- 61-64
Martino, Rick 1947- 226
Martino, Rocco L(eonard) 1929- 13-16R
Martino, Teresa Tsimmu 1965(?)- 223
Martin-Perdue, Nancy J(ean) 1934- 164
Martins, Maria 1898(?)-1973
Obituary 41-44R
Martins, Maria Isabel Barreno de Faria
1939- 105
See also Barreno, Maria Isabel
Martins, Peter 1946- 113
Martins, Wilson 1921- 17-20R
Martin-Santos, Luis 1924-1964 .... DLB 322
Martin-Santos, Luis 1925-1964 .... EWL 3
Martinsen, Ella Barbara Lung 1901-1977 ... 103
Martinsen, Martin
See Follett, Ken(neth Martin)
Martinson, David (Keith) 1946- CANR-1
Earlier sketch in CA 45-48
Martinson, Floyd M(ansfield) 1916-2000 . 93-96
Obituary 189
Martinson, Harry (Edmund)
1904-1978 .... CANR-130
Earlier sketches in CA 77-80, CANR-34
See also CLC 14
See also DLB 259
See also EWL 3
Martinson, Ida M(arie) 1936- 157
Martinson, Janis
See Herbert, Janis
Martinson, (Helga Maria) Moa
1890-1964 .... DLB 259
Martinson, Robert M. 1927- 41-44R
Martinson, Ruth A(lice) 1915- CANR-17
Earlier sketch in CA 25-28R
Martinson, Tom L. 1941- 77-80
Martinson, William D. 1924-1979 .... 21-24R
Obituary 135
Martland, Thomas R(odolphe) 1926- 5-8R
Marton, Beryl M(itchell) 1922- CANR-11
Earlier sketch in CA 69-72
Marton, Endre 1910-2005 .... 37-40R
Marton, George 1900-1979 .... 29-32R
Marton, Jirina 1946- 160
See also SATA 95, 144
Marton, Kati (Ilona) 1949- CANR-111
Earlier sketch in CA 140
Marton, Pierre
See Stone, Peter
Martone, John 1952- .... CAAS 30
Martone, Michael 1955- CANR-96
Brief entry 118
Earlier sketches in CA 124, CANR-56
Interview in CA-124
See also DLB 218
Martos, Borys 1879-1977
Obituary 73-76
Martos, Joseph (John) 1943- CANR-100
Earlier sketch in CA 103
Martson, Del
See Lupoff, Richard A(llen)
Marty, Martin E(mil) 1928- 194
Earlier sketches in CA 5-8R, CANR-21, 49, 77
Interview in CANR-21
Autobiographical Essay in 194
Marty, Myron A. 1932- CANR-99
Earlier sketches in CA 25-28R, CANR-11
Marty, Sid 1944- 108
Martyn, Edward 1859-1923 179
See also DLB 10
See also RGEL 2
See also TCLC 131
Martyn, Howe 1906-1989 .... 9-12R
Obituary 129
Martyn, J(ames) Louis 1925- 126
Brief entry 105
Martyn, Kenneth A(lfred) 1926- 21-24R
Martyn, Philip
See Tubb, E(dwin) C(harles)
Martynov, Leonid (Nikolaevich) 1905-1980
Brief entry 116
Martyr, Paula (Jane)
See Lawford, Paula Jane
See also SATA 57
Martz, John D(anhouse) 1934-1998 ... CANR-1
Earlier sketch in CA 45-48
Martz, Lawrence J. 1933- 69-72
Martz, Linda 1939- 135
Martz, Louis L(ohr) 1913-2001 .... CANR-5
Obituary 204
Earlier sketch in CA 13-16R
Martz, Sandra (Haldeman) 1944- 149
Martz, William J. 1928- CANR-9
Earlier sketch in CA 21-24R
Maruki, Toshi 1912-2000 .... CLR 19
See also SATA 112
Marut, Ret
See Traven, B.
Marut, Robert
See Traven, B.
Maruya, Saiichi 1925- 135
Maruyama, Masao 1914-1996 107
Obituary 153
Earlier sketch in CA 13-16R
Marvel, Thomas S. 1935- 145
Marvel, Tom 1901-1970
Obituary 104
Marvel, William 1949- CANR-100
Earlier sketch in CA 139
Marvell, Andrew 1621-1678 .... BRW 2
See also BRWR 2
See also CDBLB 1660-1789
See also DA
See also DAB
See also DAC
See also DAM MST, POET
See also DLB 131
See also EXPP
See also PC 10
See also PFS 5
See also RGEL 2
See also TEA
See also WLC
See also WP
Marvick, Elizabeth Wirth 1925- CANR-41
Earlier sketch in CA 117
Marvin, Burton Wright 1913-1979
Obituary 85-88
Marvin, David Keith 1921- 13-16R
Marvin, Dorothy Betts 1894(?)-1975
Obituary 57-60
Marvin, Garry 1952- 127
Marvin, Harold Myers 1893-1977 .... 5-8R
Obituary 73-76
Marvin, Isabel R(idout) 1924- 150
See also SATA 84
Marvin, James W.
See James, Laurence
Marvin, Jay 1953(?)- 232
Marvin, John R(obert) 1923- 117
Marvin, John T. 1906-1988 .... 17-20R
Marvin, Julie
See Ellis, Julie
Marvin, Philip (Roger) 1916-1993 .... CANR-13
Earlier sketch in CA 37-40R
Marvin, Richard
See Ellis, Julie
Marvin, Susan
See Ellis, Julie
Marvin, W. R.
See Cameron, Lou and
James, Laurence
Marvin X
See El Muhajir
See also DLB 38
Marwell, Gerald 1937- 41-44R
Marwick, Arthur 1936- CANR-57
Earlier sketches in CA 29-32R, CANR-13, 30
Marwick, Helen Lillie 1915-2003 65-68
Obituary 212
Marwick, Lawrence 1909-1981
Obituary 106
Marwick, M(axwell) G(ay) 1916- 37-40R
Marwil, Jonathan L(evy) 1940- CANR-35
Earlier sketch in CA 114
Marwood, William
See Morton, James (Severs)
Marx, Anne CANR-56
Earlier sketches in CA 29-32R, CANR-12, 30
Marx, Anthony W. 1959- 143
Marx, Arthur 1893-1964
Obituary 113
See also Marx, Harpo
Marx, Arthur 1921- CANR-24
Earlier sketch in CA 81-84
Marx, Elisabeth 235
Marx, Erica Elizabeth 1909-1967 .... CAP-1
Earlier sketch in CA 13-14
Marx, Eva 176
Marx, Gary T. 1938- CANR-32
Earlier sketches in CA 37-40R, CANR-14
Marx, Groucho
See Marx, Julius Henry
Marx, Harpo 175
See also Marx, Arthur
Marx, Herbert L(ewis), Jr. 1922- CANR-6
Earlier sketch in CA 9-12R
Marx, Jenifer (Grant) 1940- 101
Marx, Jerry
See Bernstein, Jerry Marx
Marx, Julius Henry 1890-1977 81-84
Obituary 73-76
Marx, Karl (Heinrich) 1818-1883 .... DLB 129
See also LATS 1:1
See also TWA
Marx, Kenneth S(amuel) 1939- 69-72
Marx, Leo 1919- CANR-98
Earlier sketch in CA 126
Marx, Melvin H(erman) 1919- CANR-6
Earlier sketch in CA 5-8R
Marx, Patricia Windschill 1948- 184
See also SATA 112, 160
Marx, Paul 1920- 37-40R
Marx, Robert F(rank) 1936- CANR-6
Earlier sketch in CA 9-12R
See also SATA 24
Marx, Samuel 1902-1992 103
Obituary 137
Marx, Steven 1942- 193
Marx, Trish
See Marx, Patricia Windschill
Marx, Werner 1910-1994 81-84
Marx, Wesley 1934- CANR-12
Earlier sketch in CA 21-24R
Marxhausen, Joanne G. 1935- 37-40R
Mary Agnes Therese, Sister 1910-1992 ..... 1-4R
Mary Francis, Mother
See Aschmann, Alberta
Mary Kay
See Ash, Mary Kay (Wagner)
Mary Madeleine, Sister 1916-1974 .... CAP-1
Earlier sketch in CA 13-16
Marzan, Julio 1946- CANR-81
Brief entry 113
Earlier sketch in CA 131
See also HW 1, 2
Marzani, Carl (Aldo) 1912-1994 61-64
See also SATA 12
Marzials, Theo(phile-Jules-Henri)
1850-1920 184
See also DLB 35
Marzolf, Marion Tuttle 1930- CANR-52
Brief entry 114
Earlier sketch in CA 124
Marzollo, Jean 1942- CANR-90
Earlier sketches in CA 81-84, CANR-15
See also MAICYA 2
See also SAAS 15
See also SATA 29, 77, 130
Mas, Joan 1926- .... CP 1
Mas'adi, Mahmud 1911- .... EWL 3
Masalha, Nur 1957- 143
Masani, Shakuntala 112
Masani, Zareer 1947- 97-100
Masannat, George S. 1933- 25-28R
Masao, Maruyama
See Maruyama, Masao
Masaoka, Shiki -1902
See Masaoka, Tsunenori
See also RGWL 3
See also TCLC 18
Masaoka, Tsunenori 1867-1902 191
Brief entry 117
See also Masaoka, Shiki and
Masaoka Shiki
See also TWA
Masaoka Shiki
See Masaoka, Tsunenori
See also EWL 3
Masatsugu, Mitsuyuki 1924- 129
Mascall, Eric L(ionel) 1905-1993 .... 5-8R
Mascall, Jennifer (Wootton) 1952- 212
Mascarenhas, Margaret 206
Masciangelo, Bill
See Masciangelo, William R., Jr.
Masciangelo, William R., Jr. 1944- 139
Mascott, Trina 81-84
Masefield, Geoffrey Bussell 1911-2001 ..... 5-8R
Obituary 201
Masefield, John (Edward)
1878-1967 .... CANR-33
Obituary 25-28R
Earlier sketches in CAP-2, CA 19-20
See also CDBLB 1890-1914
See also CLC 11, 47
See also DAM POET
See also DLB 10, 19, 153, 160
See also EWL 3
See also EXPP
See also FANT
See also MTCW 1, 2
See also PFS 5
See also RGEL 2
See also SATA 19
Masefield, (John) Richard (William) 1943- .. 119
Masekela, Hugh (Ramapolo) 1939- 231
Maser, Chris 1938- 132
Maser, Edward A(ndrew)
1923-1988 .... CANR-28
Obituary 126
Earlier sketch in CA 15-16
Maser, Jack D(avid) 1937- 57-60
Masetti, Jorge 1955- 224

Masey, Mary Lou(ise) 1932-1991 ... 21-24R
Obituary ... 134
Masha
See Stern, Marie
Masheck, Joseph (Daniel) 1942- ... 105
Masia, Seth 1948- ... CANR-28
Earlier sketch in CA 110
Masing, Uku 1909- ... EWL 3
Masini, Donna 1954- ... 193
Masini, Eleonora Barbieri 1928- ... 130
Masino, Paola 1908-1989 ... DLB 264
Masinton, Charles G(erald) 1938- ... 77-80
Maskarinec, Gregory G(abriel) 1951- ... CANR-115
Earlier sketch in CA 150
Maskin, Eric S. 1950- ... 195
Maskinen, Oskari
See Hamalainen, Pertti (Olavi)
Maslach, Christina 1946- ... 111
Maslen, Elizabeth 1935- ... CP 1
Maslenikov, Oleg A(lexander) 1907-1972
Obituary ... 111
Maslin, Alice 1914(?)-1981
Obituary ... 104
Maslin, Bonnie L(ynn) 1947- ... 107
Maslow, Abraham H. 1908-1970 ... CANR-4
Obituary ... 29-32R
Earlier sketch in CA 1-4R
See also MTCW 1, 2
Maslow, Jonathan Evan 1948- ... CANR-63
Earlier sketch in CA 126
Maslowski, Peter 1944- ... 97-100
Maslowski, Raymond M(arion) 1931- ... 93-96
Maslowski, Stanley 1937- ... 21-24R
Masnata, Albert 1900- ... 93-96
Maso, Carole (?)- ... 170
See also CLC 44
See also CN 7
See also GLL 2
See also RGAL 4
Masoff, Joy 1951- ... SATA 118
Mason, A(lfred) E(dward) W(oodley) 1865-1948 ... 177
See also CMW 4
See also DLB 70
See also RGEL 2
See also RHW
Mason, Adrienne 1962- ... 239
See also SATA 163
Mason, Alpheus Thomas 1899-1989 ... CANR-32
Obituary ... 130
Earlier sketch in CA 1-4R
Mason, Anita (Frances) 1942- ... CANR-144
Earlier sketch in CA 139
Mason, Betty (Oxford) 1930- ... 37-40R
Mason, Bill 1940- ... 236
Mason, Bobbie Ann 1940- ... CANR-125
Earlier sketches in CA 53-56, CANR-11, 31, 58, 83
Interview in ... CANR-31
See also AAYA 5, 42
See also AMWS 8
See also BPFB 2
See also CDALBS
See also CLC 28, 43, 82, 154
See also CN 5, 6, 7
See also CSW
See also DA3
See also DLB 173
See also DLBY 1987
See also EWL 3
See also EXPS
See also MAL 5
See also MTCW 1, 2
See also MTFW 2005
See also NFS 4
See also RGAL 4
See also RGSF 2
See also SSC 4
See also SSFS 3, 8, 20
See also TCLE 1:2
See also YAW
Mason, Bruce B(onner) 1923- ... 9-12R
Mason, Bruce Edward George 1921-1982 .. 129
Obituary ... 110
See also RGEL 2
Mason, Carl
See King, Albert
Mason, Carola
See Zentner, Carola
Mason, Christopher ... 231
Mason, Chuck
See Rowland, D(onald) S(ydney)
Mason, Clarence (Eugene), Jr. 1904-1985 ... 57-60
Mason, Connie 1930- ... CANR-117
Earlier sketch in CA 164
Mason, Daniel
See Mason, Jeffrey D(aniel)
Mason, Daniel 1976- ... 217
Mason, David 1951- ... 147
Mason, David 1954- ... CANR-144
Earlier sketch in CA 166
See also DLB 282
Mason, David E(rnest) 1928- ... 21-24R
Mason, Douglas R(ankine) 1918- ... CANR-17
Earlier sketches in CA 49-52, CANR-1
See also SFW 4
Mason, Edmund (John) 1911-1993 ... 103
Mason, Edward S(agendorph) 1899-1992 ... 73-76
Obituary ... 137
Mason, Edwin A. 1905-1979 ... CAP-2
Obituary ... 89-92
Earlier sketch in CA 25-28
See also SATA-Obit 32
Mason, Ellsworth (Goodwin) 1917- ... 126
Mason, Ernst
See Pohl, Frederik
Mason, Eudo C(olecestra) 1901-1969 ... CAP-1
Earlier sketch in CA 9-10
Mason, F(rancis) van Wyck 1901-1978 ... CANR-58
Obituary ... 81-84
Earlier sketches in CA 5-8R, CANR-8
See also CMW 4
See also DLB 306
See also RHW
See also SATA 3
See also SATA-Obit 26
Mason, Francis K(enneth) 1928- ... 103
Mason, Frank Earl 1893-1979
Obituary ... 89-92
Mason, Frank W.
See Mason, F(rancis) van Wyck
Mason, Gabriel Richard 1884-1979
Obituary ... 85-88
Mason, Gene (William) 1928- ... 89-92
Mason, George E(van) 1932- ... CANR-30
Earlier sketches in CA 29-32R, CANR-12
Mason, George Frederick 1904-2000 ... 73-76
See also SATA 14
Mason, Harry M. 1908-2000 ... 139
Mason, Haydn T(revor) 1929- ... CANR-3
Earlier sketch in CA 9-12R
Mason, Herbert Molloy, Jr. 1927- ... CANR-6
Earlier sketch in CA 13-16R
Mason, Herbert Warren, Jr. 1932- ... CANR-38
Earlier sketches in CA 85-88, CANR-16
Mason, Hunni B.
See Sternheim, (William Adolf) Carl
Mason, Jackie 1934- ... 188
Mason, James (Neville) 1909-1984 ... 146
Mason, Jeffrey D(aniel) 1952- ... 201
Mason, Jim 1940- ... 145
Mason, John
See Tubb, E(dwin) C(harles)
Mason, John Brown 1904-1992 ... 49-52
Mason, Joseph B(igsbee) 1903-1989 ... 125
Mason, Julian D(ewey) Jr. 1931- ... 37-40R
Mason, Laura 1957- ... 219
Mason, Lee W.
See Malzberg, Barry N(athaniel)
Mason, Linda 1954- ... 226
Mason, Lowell Blake 1893-1983
Obituary ... 110
Mason, Madeline 1913-1990 ... 9-12R
Mason, Marilyn (J.) 1933- ... CANR-115
Earlier sketch in CA 159
Mason, Mark 1953- ... 163
Mason, Mark 1955- ... 138
Mason, Marsha 1942- ... 203
Mason, Michael 1939- ... 120
Mason, Michael A. 1954- ... 187
Mason, Michael Henry 1900-1982
Obituary ... 108
Mason, Mike 1952- ... 126
Mason, Miriam E(vangeline) 1900-1973 ... CANR-15
Obituary ... 103
Earlier sketch in CA 1-4R
See also SATA 2
See also SATA-Obit 26
Mason, Nicholas (Charles Sheppard) 1938- ... CANR-24
Earlier sketch in CA 104
Mason, Nick 1945- ... CLC 35
Mason, Pamela 1918(?)-1996
Obituary ... 152
Brief entry ... 105
Mason, Paul T(aylor) 1937- ... 33-36R
Mason, Peter (Geoffrey) 1914- ... CANR-82
Earlier sketches in CA 114, CANR-35
Mason, Philip 1906-1999 ... CANR-3
Obituary ... 174
Earlier sketch in CA 9-12R
Mason, Philip (Parker) 1927- ... CANR-38
Earlier sketch in CA 17-20R
Mason, R.
See Reasoner, James M(orris)
Mason, R(ichard) A(nthony) 1932- ... 119
Mason, R(onald) A(lison) K(ells) 1905-1971
Obituary ... 89-92
See also CP 1
See also RGEL 2
Mason, Raymond 1926- ... 9-12R
Mason, Richard (Lakin) 1919-1997 ... 9-12R
Obituary ... 162
Mason, Richard 1978- ... 187
Mason, Robert C(averly) 1942- ... 134
Brief entry ... 128
Interview in ... CA-134
Mason, Robert E(mmett) 1914-1998 . CANR-17
Earlier sketch in CA 1-4R
Mason, Ronald (Charles) 1912-2001 ... CANR-24
Earlier sketch in CA 13-16R
Mason, Ronald M. 1949- ... 111
Mason, Ruth Fitch 1890-1974
Obituary ... 53-56
Mason, Sarah J. 1949- ... CANR-144
Earlier sketch in CA 167
Mason, Stephen F(inney) 1923- ... 141
Mason, Tally
See Derleth, August (William)
Mason, Ted
See Mason, Theodore C(harles)
Mason, Theodore C(harles) 1921- ... 109
Mason, Thomas A(lexander) 1944- ... 120
Mason, Todd ... 231
Mason, Tyler
See Mason, Madeline
Mason, Van Wyck
See Mason, F(rancis) van Wyck
Mason, Will Edwin 1912-1993 ... 5-8R
Mason, William 1725-1797 ... DLB 142
See also RGEL 2
Masotti, Louis H(enry) 1934- ... 41-44R
Mass, Anna ... CLC 59
Mass, Jeffrey P(aul) 1940-2001 ... 183
Obituary ... 195
Brief entry ... 111
Mass, Wendy 1967- ... 234
See also SATA 158
Mass, William
See Gibson, William
Massa, Ann 1940- ... 29-32R
Massa, Mark S(tephen) ... 235
Massa, Richard W(ayne) 1932- ... 57-60
Massad, (Leslie) Stewart (Jr.) 1958- ... 144
Massanari, Jared (Dean) 1943- ... 65-68
Massaquoi, Hans J(urgen) 1926- ... 69-72
Massarik, Fred 1926- ... CANR-35
Earlier sketch in CA 1-4R
Massel, Mark S. 1910-1989 ... CAP-1
Earlier sketch in CA 11-12
Masselink, Ben 1919-2000 ... 17-20R
Obituary ... 187
Masselman, George 1897-1971 ... 9-12R
See also SATA 19
Massengale, John (Edward) Montague 1951- ... 125
Masserman, Jules H(oman) 1905-1994 ... 69-72
Massey, Calvin R(andolph) 1949- ... CANR-115
Earlier sketch in CA 152
Massey, Don 1948- ... 186
Massey, Ellen Gray 1921- ... CANR-42
Earlier sketch in CA 118
Massey, Erika 1900-1978 ... 61-64
Massey, Floyd, Jr. 1915-2003 ... 65-68
Obituary ... 220
Massey, Gerald 1828-1907 ... 177
See also DLB 32
Massey, Gerald J. 1934- ... 89-92
Massey, Harrie Stewart Wilson 1908-1983
Obituary ... 111
Massey, Irving (Joseph) 1924- ... 77-80
Massey, James A(ldege) 1939- ... 121
Massey, James Earl 1930- ... CANR-12
Earlier sketch in CA 29-32R
Massey, Joseph Earl 1897-1986 ... 29-32R
Massey, Linton R. 1900-1974 ... DLB 187
Massey, Linton R(eynolds) 1900-1974 ... 202
Massey, Mary Elizabeth 1915-1970(?) ... CAP-2
Earlier sketch in CA 23-24
Massey, Raymond (Hart) 1896-1983 ... 104
Obituary ... 110
Interview in ... CA-104
Massey, Reginald 1932- ... 21-24R
See also CP 1
Massey, Sujata 1964- ... 215
Massey, Victoria ... 199
Massialas, Byron G. 1929- ... CANR-8
Earlier sketch in CA 21-24R
Massie, Allan (Johnstone) 1938- ... CANR-91
Earlier sketch in CA 145
See also CN 4, 5, 6, 7
See also DLB 271
Massie, Dianne Redfield 1938- ... CANR-105
Earlier sketch in CA 81-84
See also SATA 16, 125
Massie, Elizabeth ... CANR-144
Earlier sketch in CA 169
See also SATA 108
Massie, Joseph Logan 1921- ... CANR-2
Earlier sketch in CA 1-4R
Massie, Robert K(inloch) 1929- ... CANR-138
Earlier sketches in CA 77-80, CANR-14, 40
Interview in ... CANR-14
See also MTFW 2005
Massie, Robert K(inloch) 1956- ... 219
Massie, Sonja ... 233
Massie, Suzanne 1931- ... 142
Massine, Leonide
See Myassin, Leonid Fedorovich
Massing, Hede 1899-1981
Obituary ... 108
Massinger, Philip 1583-1640 ... BRWS 11
See also DLB 58
See also RGEL 2
Massingham, Harold William 1932- ... 65-68
See also CP 1, 2
Massis, Henri 1886-1970
Obituary ... 29-32R
Massman, Patti 1945- ... CANR-41
Earlier sketch in CA 117
Massman, Virgil Frank 1929- ... 37-40R
Masson, Andre (Aime Rene) 1896-1987
Obituary ... 124
Masson, David 1822-1907 ... DLB 144
Masson, David I(rvine) 1915- ... CANR-59
Earlier sketch in CA 25-28R
See also SFW 4
Masson, Georgina
See Johnson, Marion Georgina Wikeley
Masson, J. Moussaieff
See Masson, Jeffrey Moussaieff
Masson, Jeffrey M.
See Masson, Jeffrey Moussaieff
Masson, Jeffrey Moussaieff 1941- ... CANR-89
Earlier sketch in CA 122
Masson, Loyes 1915-1969 ... CAP-1
Earlier sketch in CA 13-14
Masson, Marilyn 1958- ... 228
Masson, Paul R(obert) 1946- ... 142
Masson, Sophie 1959- ... 202
See also AAYA 43
See also SATA 133
Massow, Rosalind ... 89-92
Massy, William F(rancis) 1934- ... 41-44R
Mast, Gerald 1940-1988 ... CANR-76
Obituary ... 126
Earlier sketches in CA 69-72, CANR-12
Mast, Russell L. 1915- ... 13-16R
Master Lao
See Lao Tzu
Masterman, John Cecil 1891-1977 ... CANR-64
Obituary ... 69-72
Earlier sketches in CA 9-12R, CANR-6
See also CMW 4
Masterman-Smith, Virginia 1937- ... 110
Master of Life, The
See Olisah, Sunday Okenwa
Masters, Alexis 1949- ... 202
Masters, Anthony (Richard) 1940-2003 ... CANR-45
Obituary ... 217
Earlier sketch in CA 25-28R
See also SATA 112
See also SATA-Obit 145
Masters, Anthony 1948(?)-1985
Obituary ... 115
Masters, Brian 1939- ... CANR-43
Earlier sketch in CA 118
Masters, Dexter (Wright) 1908-1989
Obituary ... 127
Masters, Edgar Lee 1868-1950 ... 133
Brief entry ... 104
See also AMWS 1
See also CDALB 1865-1917
See also DA
See also DAC
See also DAM MST, POET
See also DLB 54
See also EWL 3
See also EXPP
See also MAL 5
See also MTCW 1, 2
See also MTFW 2005
See also PC 1, 36
See also RGAL 4
See also TCLC 2, 25
See also TUS
See also WLCS
See also WP
Masters, Elaine 1932- ... 57-60
Masters, G(eorge) Mallary 1936- ... 25-28R
Masters, Hardin (Wallace) 1899(?)-1979
Obituary ... 89-92
Masters, Hilary 1928- ... 217
Earlier sketches in CA 25-28R, CANR-13, 47, 97
Autobiographical Essay in ... 217
See also CLC 48
See also CN 6, 7
See also DLB 244
Masters, Joan
See Murphey, Cecil B(laine)
Masters, John 1914-1983 ... 110
Brief entry ... 108
Interview in ... CA-110
See also CN 1, 2, 3
See also RHW
Masters, Kelly R(ay) 1897-1987 ... 1-4R
See also SATA 3
Masters, Mildred 1932- ... 110
See also SATA 42
Masters, Nicholas A. 1929- ... 13-16R
Masters, Olga 1919-1986 ... CANR-76
Obituary ... 135
Earlier sketch in CA 121
See also RGSF 2
Masters, Roger D(avis) 1933- ... 21-24R
Masters, Susan Rowan 1943- ... 156
Masters, William
See Cousins, Margaret
Masters, William H(owell) 1915-2001 ... CANR-34
Obituary ... 195
Earlier sketch in CA 21-24R
See also AITN 1
Masters, Zeke
See Bensen, Donald R. and Goulart, Ron(ald Joseph)
Masterson, B. L. H.
See Sternau, Cynthia
Masterson, Dan 1934- ... 81-84
Masterson, Daniel M. 1945- ... 140
Masterson, Dave 1951- ... 118
Masterson, J. B.
See Edmondson, G(arry) C(otton)
Masterson, James F(rancis) 1925- ... 69-72
Masterson, Patrick 1936- ... 73-76
Masterson, Peter 1934- ... 153
Masterson, Thomas R(obert) 1915- ... 25-28R
Masterson, Whit
See Miller, (H.) Bill(y) and Wade, Robert (Allison)
Masterson, William Henry 1914-1983 ... 123
Masterton, Elsie (Lipstein) 1914-1966 ... 5-8R
Masterton, Graham 1946- ... CANR-79
Earlier sketches in CA 105, CANR-22, 45
See also HGG
Masthay, Carl (David) 1941- ... 142
Mastnak, Lynne
See Jones, Lynne (Myfanwy)
Mastny, Vojtech 1936- ... CANR-29
Earlier sketches in CA 33-36R, CANR-13
Maston, T(homas) B(uford) 1897-1988 ... CANR-76
Obituary ... 128
Earlier sketches in CA 5-8R, CANR-2, 18
Mastoon, Adam 1962- ... 176
Mastrangelo, Charles E(lmer) 1910-1995 ... 113
See also Martin, Charles E(lmer)
Mastro, Susan (Duff) 1945- ... 69-72

Mastronardi, Lucio 1930-1979 .... DLB 177
See also EWL 3
Mastrosimone, William 1947- 186
See also CAD
See also CD 5, 6
See also CLC 36
Masud
See Choudhury, Masudul Alam
Masuda, Sayo 1925- 232
Masuda, Takeshi 1944- CANR-50
Earlier sketch in CA 123
See also Aska, Warabe
Masuda, Yoneji 1909- 109
Masumoto, David Mas 1954- CANR-143
Earlier sketch in CA 150
Masur, Gerhard Strassman
1901-1975 .... CANR-4
Earlier sketch in CA 1-4R
Masur, Harold Q. 1909-1995 .... CANR-65
Earlier sketches in CA 77-80, CANR-13
See also CMW 4
Masur, Jenny 1948- 65-68
Mata, Daya 1914- 77-80
Matacena, Orestes 230
Matalin, Mary 1953(?)- 147
Matalon, Ronit 1959- 211
Matanzo, Jane Brady 1940- 103
Matarazzo, James M. 1941- CANR-49
Earlier sketches in CA 37-40R, CANR-14
Matarazzo, Joseph D(ominic) 1925- 57-60
Matarese, Susan M. 203
Matas, Carol 1949- CANR-144
Earlier sketch in CA 158
See also AAYA 22
See also BYA 15
See also CLR 52
See also MAICYA 2
See also MAICYAS 1
See also SATA 93
See also SATA-Essay 112
See also YAW
Matas, David 1943- 156
Matatu, Michael
See Puri, Shamlal
Matcha, Jack 1919- CANR-2
Earlier sketch in CA 1-4R
Matchett, William H(enry) 1923- 13-16R
See also CP 1, 2
Matchette, Katharine E. 1941- 53-56
See also SATA 38
Matczak, Sebastian A(lexander) 1914- 9-12R
Mate, Rudolph 1898-1964 .... IDFW 3, 4
Matejic, Mateja 1924- CANR-56
Earlier sketches in CA 112, CANR-30
Matejka, Ladislav 1919- 73-76
Matejko, Alexander J. 1924- CANR-49
Earlier sketches in CA 57-60, CANR-6, 22
Matek, Ord 1922- 89-92
Matelski, Marilyn J. 1950- 175
Matenko, Percy 1901-1987 .... CANR-1
Earlier sketch in CA 45-48
Mateosian, S. Richard 1941- 111
Matera, D. M.
See Matera, Dary
Matera, Dary 1955- 232
Matera, Lia 1952- CANR-136
Earlier sketch in CA 170
See also CMW 4
Materer, Timothy (John) 1940- 89-92
Materson, Ray 1954- 227
Mates, Julian 1927- CANR-31
Earlier sketch in CA 1-4R
Mates, Susan Onthank 1950- 148
Matesky, Ralph 1913-1979 .... 5-8R
Matevossian, Hrant 1935- .... EWL 3
Matevski, Mateja 1929- .... CDWLB 4
See also DLB 181
Math, Irwin 1940- 112
See also SATA 42
Mathabane, Mark 1960- 183
Earlier sketches in CA 125, CANR-51, 73, 115
Autobiographical Essay in 183
See also AAYA 4, 39
See also BW 2, 3
See also DA3
See also DAM MULT
See also MAICYA 2
See also MTCW 2
See also MTFW 2005
See also NCFS 4
See also SATA 123
See also YAW
Mathai, M. O. 1909-1981
Obituary 108
Mathay, Francis 1925- 57-60
Mathe, Albert
See Camus, Albert
Matheny, Albert R(alston III) 1950- 152
Mather, Anne .... RHW
Mather, Berkely
See Davies, John Evan Weston
Mather, Bertrand 1914- CAP-1
Earlier sketch in CA 9-10
Mather, Bob
See Mather, Robert E(dward)
Mather, Cotton 1663-1728 .... AMWS 2
See also CDALB 1640-1865
See also DLB 24, 30, 140
See also RGAL 4
See also TUS
Mather, Eleanore Price 1910-1985 116
Mather, Increase 1639-1723 .... DLB 24
Mather, Jean 1946- 115
Mather, June 1924- 107
Mather, Kenneth 1911-1990
Obituary 131
Mather, Kirtley F(letcher)
1888-1978 .... CANR-35
Earlier sketch in CA 17-20R
See also SATA 65
Mather, Melissa
See Brown, Melissa Mather
Mather, Richard 1596-1669 .... DLB 24
Mather, Richard B(urroughs) 1913- 73-76
Mather, Robert E(dward) 1945- 115
Mathers, Michael 1945- 65-68
Mathers, Peter 1931- 130
Brief entry 116
See also CN 3, 4, 5, 6, 7
Mathers, Petra 1945- 194
See also CLR 76
See also CWRI 5
See also SATA 119
Mathes, Charles (Elliott) 1949- 141
Mathes, J(ohn) C(harles) 1931- CANR-139
Earlier sketch in CA 49-52
Mathes, Valerie Sherer 1941- 195
Mathes, W(illiam) Michael 1936- CANR-52
Earlier sketches in CA 61-64, CANR-8, 26
Matheson, Ann 1940- CANR-86
Earlier sketch in CA 133
Matheson, Annie 1853-1924 201
See also DLB 240
Matheson, Don(ald S.) 1948- 126
Matheson, Joan (Transue) 1924-1995 97-100
Obituary 198
Matheson, John Ross 1917- CANR-23
Earlier sketch in CA 106
Matheson, Richard (Burton) 1926- ... CANR-99
Earlier sketches in CA 97-100, CANR-88
Interview in CA-97-100
See also AAYA 31
See also CLC 37
See also DLB 8, 44
See also HGG
See also SCFW 1, 2
See also SFW 4
See also SUFW 2
Matheson, Richard (Christian) 1953- 190
See also HGG
See also SATA 119
See also SUFW 1
Matheson, Shirlee Smith 1942- 230
See also SATA 155
Matheson, Sylvia A.
See Schofield, Sylvia Anne
Matheson, T. J.
See Matheson, Terry
Matheson, Terry 1944- 184
Matheson, William H(oward) 1929- 21-24R
Matheus, John F(rederick) 1887-1983 124
See also BW 1
See also DLB 51
Mathew, David 1902-1975 .... CAP-2
Earlier sketch in CA 25-28
Mathew, (Anthony) Gervase 1905-1976 .. 9-12R
Mathew, Ray(mond Frank) 1929- 17-20R
See also CP 1
Mathewes-Green, Frederica 172
Mathews, Adrian 1957- 196
Mathews, Aidan (Carl) 1956(?)- 152
See also DLB 319
Mathews, Anthony Stuart 1930- 93-96
Mathews, Arthur 1903(?)-1980
Obituary 102
Mathews, Cornelius 1817(?)-1889 ... DLB 3, 64, 250
Mathews, Denise
See Mathews, Patricia J.
Mathews, Donald G. 1932- 17-20R
Mathews, Donald K(enneth) 1923- 57-60
Mathews, Eleanor Muth 1923- 13-16R
Mathews, Evelyn Craw 1906- CAP-2
Earlier sketch in CA 19-20
Mathews, F(rancis) X. 1935- 25-28R
Mathews, H(arry) Lee 1939- 37-40R
Mathews, Harry (Burchell) 1930- CANR-98
Earlier sketches in CA 21-24R, CANR-18, 40
See also CAAS 6
See also CLC 6, 52
See also CN 5, 6, 7
Mathews, J(oseph) Howard
1881-1970 .... CANR-75
Obituary 103
Earlier sketch in CA 9-12R
Mathews, Jackson 1907(?)-1978
Obituary 104
Mathews, Jane DeHart 1936- 21-24R
Mathews, Janet 1914-1992 115
See also SATA 41
Mathews, (Thomas) Jay (II) 1945- ... CANR-101
Earlier sketch in CA 147
Mathews, John Joseph 1894-1979 .... CANR-45
Obituary 142
Earlier sketches in CAP-2, CA 19-20
See also CLC 84
See also DAM MULT
See also DLB 175
See also NNAL
See also TCWW 1, 2
Mathews, Judith
See Goldberger, Judith M.
See also SATA 80
Mathews, Louise
See Tooke, Louise Mathews
Mathews, Marcia Mayfield 9-12R
Mathews, Mitford M(cLeod) 1891-1985
Obituary 115
Mathews, Nancy Mowll 212
Mathews, Nieves 1917- 156
Mathews, Patricia J. 1929(?)-1983
Obituary 100
Mathews, Richard (Barrett) 1944- CANR-1
Earlier sketch in CA 45-48
Mathews, Russell Lloyd 1921- 109
Mathews, Thomas G(eorge) 1925- 49-52
Mathews, Virginia H(opper) 1925- 121
Mathews, Walter M(ichael) 1942- 110
Mathewson, Rufus Wellington, Jr. 1919(?)-1978
Obituary 81-84
Mathewson, William (Glen, Jr.) 1940- 106
Mathez, Edmond A. 234
Mathias, Frank Furlong 1925- CANR-97
Earlier sketches in CA 61-64, CANR-12
Mathias, Peter 1928- 17-20R
Mathias, Roland (Glyn) 1915- CANR-41
Earlier sketches in CA 97-100, CANR-19
See also CLC 45
See also CP 1, 2, 3, 4, 5, 6, 7
See also DLB 27
Mathias, Sean (Gerard) 1956- 158
Mathiesen, Egon 1907-1976
Obituary 109
See also SATA-Obit 28
Mathiesen, Thomas J(ames) 1947- CANR-94
Earlier sketches in CA 113, CANR-34
Mathieson, John A(ndrew) 1949- 111
Mathieson, Muir 1911-1975 .... IDFW 3, 4
Mathieson, Theodore 1913- 9-12R
Mathieu, Beatrice 1904-1976
Obituary 65-68
Mathieu, Bertrand 1936- 73-76
Mathieu, Joe
See Mathieu, Joseph P.
Mathieu, Joseph P. 1949- CANR-68
Brief entry 117
Earlier sketch in CA 125
See also SATA 43, 94
See also SATA-Brief 36
Mathieu, Noel Jean 1916-1984 130
Obituary 113
See also Emmanuel, Pierre
Mathis, (Byron) Claude 1927- 45-48
Mathis, Cleopatra 1947- 104
Mathis, Deborah 1953- 228
Mathis, (Luster) Doyle 1936- 45-48
Mathis, Edward 1927- 119
Mathis, F(erdinand) John 1941- 37-40R
Mathis, James L. 1925- 105
Mathis, June 1892-1927 180
See also DLB 44
See also IDFW 3, 4
Mathis, (Gerald) Ray 1937-1981 ...... CANR-31
Obituary 113
Earlier sketch in CA 37-40R
Mathis, Sharon Bell 1937- 41-44R
See also AAYA 12
See also BW 2
See also CLR 3
See also DLB 33
See also JRDA
See also MAICYA 1, 2
See also SAAS 3
See also SATA 7, 58
See also YAW
Mathison, Melissa 1950- 165
Mathison, Richard Randolph
1919-1980 .... CANR-3
Earlier sketch in CA 1-4R
Mathison, Stuart L. 1942- 29-32R
Mathur, Anurag 212
Mathur, Dinesh C(handra) 1918- 41-44R
Mathur, Y. B. 1930- 49-52
Matias, David 1961-1996 183
Matias, Waldemar 1934- 5-8R
Matilal, Bimal Krishna 1935-1991 .... CANR-30
Obituary 134
Earlier sketches in CA 21-24R, CANR-13
Matilsky, Sarah
See Ruthchild, Rochelle Goldberg
Matisoff, James A(lan) 1937- 103
Matisoff, Susan 1940- 104
Matisse, Henri (Emile Benoit) 1869-1954
Brief entry 122
See also AAYA 34
Matkovic, Marijan 1915-1985 .... DLB 181
Matlaw, Myron 1924-1990 .... 33-36R
Matlaw, Ralph E. 1927-1990
Obituary 131
Matless, David 186
Matlin, David 1944- CANR-114
Earlier sketch in CA 141
Matlin, Margaret White 1944- CANR-44
Earlier sketch in CA 119
Matlin, Marlee (Beth) 1965- 228
Matlins, Stuart M. 1940- 212
Matlock, Jack F., Jr. 1929- 153
Matloff, Gregory 1945- .... SATA 73
Matloff, Maurice 1915-1993 .... CANR-6
Obituary 141
Earlier sketch in CA 13-16R
Mat' Mariia
See Skobtsova, Elizaveta Kuz'mina-Karavaeva
See also DLB 317
Matney, Bill
See Matney, William C., Jr.
Matney, William C., Jr. 1924-2001 69-72
Obituary 198
Matos, Antun Gustav 1873-1914 .... DLB 147
Matos, Luis Pales
See Pales Matos, Luis
Matos Paoli, Francisco
See Matos Paoli, Francisco
See also HW 1
Matos Paoli, Francisco 1915-2000 131
See also Matos Paoli, Francisco
See also DLB 290
See also HW 1
Matossian, Mary Kilbourne 1930- 125
Matossian, Nouritza 1945- 124
Matott, Justin 1961- CANR-133
Earlier sketch in CA 171
See also SATA 109
Matranga, Frances Carfi 1922- 146
See also SATA 78
Matras, Christian 1903-1977 .... IDFW 3, 4
Matrat, Jean 1915- 61-64
Matray, James I(rving) 1948- 135
See also SATA 161
Matschat, Cecile H. 1895(?)-1976
Obituary 65-68
Matsen, Brad
See Matsen, Bradford (Conway)
Matsen, Bradford (Conway) 1944- .. CANR-142
Earlier sketch in CA 144
Matsen, Herbert Stanley 1926- 57-60
Matshoba, Mtutuzeli 1950- 221
Matsier, Nicolaas
See Reinsma, Tjit
Matson, Albert Thomas 1915(?)-1987
Obituary 124
Matson, Cathy 170
Matson, Clive 1941- 129
Matson, Emerson N(els) 1926- 45-48
See also SATA 12
Matson, Floyd W(illiam) 1921- 13-16R
Matson, Molly 1921- 139
Matson, Norman H(aghejm) 1893-1965 .. FANT
Matson, Suzanne 1959- CANR-101
Earlier sketch in CA 144
Matson, Theodore E. 1906-1987 .... 1-4R
Matson, Virginia (Mae) Freeberg 1914- . 33-36R
Matson, Wallace I(rving) 1921- 13-16R
Matsuba, Moshe 1917- 37-40R
Matsuda, Mari J. 140
Matsui, Tadashi 1926- 41-44R
See also SATA 8
Matsui, Yayori 1934-2002 225
Matsumoto, Seicho 1909-1992
See Matsumoto Seicho
See also CMW 4
Matsumoto, Toru 1914(?)-1979
Obituary 89-92
Matsumoto Seicho
See Matsumoto, Seicho
See also DLB 182
Matsumura, Takao 1942- 132
Matsunaga, Alicia 1936- 29-32R
Matsunaga, Daigan Lee 1941- 41-44R
Matsunaga, Spark M(asayuki) 1916-1990 ... 128
Obituary 131
Matsuno, Masako
See Kobayashi, Masako Matsuno
See also SATA 6
Matsuo Basho 1644(?)-1694
See Basho, Matsuo
See also DAM POET
See also PC 3
See also PFS 2, 7, 18
Matsuoka, Takashi 217
Matsushita, Konosuke 1894-1989
Obituary 128
Matsutani, Miyoko 1925- 69-72
Matsuura, Kumiko 1955- 140
Matt, Daniel C(hanan) 1950- 116
Matt, Joe 1963- 224
Matt, Paul R(obert) 1926- 33-36R
Mattam, Donald 1909- 45-48
Matte, (Encarnacion) L'Enc 1936- .... SATA 22
Matte, Robert G., Jr. 1948- CANR-16
Earlier sketch in CA 65-68
Matteo, P. B., Jr.
See Ringgold, Gene
Matteo, Sherri 1951- 141
Matter, Joseph Allen 1901-1990 .... 29-32R
Mattera, John 1953- CANR-82
Earlier sketch in CA 131
Mattera, Philip 1953- 133
Mattern, Joanne 1963- 195
See also SATA 122
Mattersdorf, Leo 1903-1985
Obituary 117
Mattes, Merrill J(ohn) 1910-1996 .... 41-44R
Obituary 152
Matteson, Michael T(ownsend)
1943- CANR-16
Earlier sketch in CA 89-92
Matteson, Stefanie (Newton) 1946- 160
Mattessich, Richard V(ictor) 1922- CANR-9
Earlier sketch in CA 13-16R
Matthaei, Julie Ann 1951- 110
Matthau, Carol (Grace Marcus)
1932-2003 139
Obituary 218
Matthee, Dalene 1938- 141
Matthee, Rodney
See Creasey, John
Matthew, Christopher C(harles) F(orrest)
1939- CANR-134
Brief entry 116
Earlier sketches in CA 129, CANR-69
Matthew, Colin
See Matthew, Henry Colin Gray
Matthew, Donald J(ames) A(lexander)
1930- CANR-15
Earlier sketch in CA 5-8R
Matthew, H. C. G.
See Matthew, Henry Colin Gray
Matthew, Henry Colin Gray 1941-1999 .. 53-56
Obituary 187
Matthew, Kathryn I. 1950- 215
Matthew of Vendome c. 1130-c.
1200 .... DLB 208
Matthews, Alex CANR-137
Earlier sketch in CA 168

Matthews, Andrew 1948- 209
See also SATA 138
Matthews, Anne 1957- 141
Matthews, Anthony
See Barker, Dudley
Matthews, Bonnye L. 1943- 145
Matthews, Brad
See DeMille, Nelson (Richard)
Matthews, (James) Brander 1852-1929 181
See also DLB 71, 78
See also DLBD 13
See also TCLC 95
Matthews, C(onstance) M(ary) 1908- 25-28R
Matthews, Caitlin 1952- 180
See also SATA 122
Matthews, Carola 1937- 25-28R
Matthews, Carole 234
Matthews, Carole Smith 1943- 111
Matthews, Clayton (Hartley) 1918- ... CANR-25
Earlier sketches in CA 53-56, CANR-9
Matthews, Clyde 1917- 103
Matthews, (Robert) Curt(is, Jr.) 1934- 73-76
Matthews, Dakin 230
Matthews, Denis (James)
1919-1988 .... CANR-75
Obituary 127
Earlier sketch in CA 103
Matthews, Desmond S. 1922- 21-24R
Matthews, Donald Henry 1952- 186
Matthews, Donald Rowe 1925- CANR-2
Earlier sketch in CA 1-4R
Matthews, Downs 1925- .... SATA 71
Matthews, Elizabeth W(oodfin) 1927- 161
Matthews, Ellen
See Bache, Ellyn
Matthews, Ellen 1950- 89-92
See also SATA 28
Matthews, Elmora Messer 1925- 21-24R
Matthews, Gareth B(lanc) 1929- 135
Matthews, Geoffrey M. 1920-1984
Obituary 115
Matthews, Glenna C. 1938- 126
Matthews, Greg 1949- 135
See also CLC 45
Matthews, Harry G(len) 1939- 73-76
Matthews, Herbert Lionel 1900-1977 . CANR-2
Obituary 73-76
Earlier sketch in CA 1-4R
Matthews, Honor 1901- CAP-2
Earlier sketch in CA 23-24
Matthews, J(ohn) H(erbert) 1930- CANR-20
Earlier sketches in CA 13-16R, CANR-5
Matthews, Jack
See Matthews, John H(arold)
See also CAAS 15
See also CN 3, 4, 5, 6, 7
See also DLB 6
Matthews, Jack 1917- 9-12R
Matthews, Jacklyn Meek
See Meek, Jacklyn O'Hanlon
Matthews, Jessie 1907-1981
Obituary 108
Matthews, Jill Julius 1949- 222
Matthews, Joan E(thel) 1914- 21-24R
Matthews, John (Pengwerne) 1927- .. CANR-41
Earlier sketch in CA 118
Matthews, John (Kentigern) 1948- 182
See also SATA 116
Matthews, John H(arold) 1925- 228
Earlier sketches in CA 33-36R, CANR-15
Autobiographical Essay in 228
See also Matthews, Jack
Matthews, Joseph R(onald) 1942- 235
Matthews, Kathy 1949- CANR-119
Earlier sketches in CA 110, CANR-27
Matthews, Kevin
See Fox, G(ardner) F(rancis)
Matthews, L(eonard) Harrison
1901-1986 .... CANR-76
Obituary 121
Earlier sketches in CA 53-56, CANR-4
Matthews, L(aura) S. 239
Matthews, Lewis J. 1943- 230
Matthews, Liz
See Pellowski, Michael (Joseph)
Matthews, Lloyd J. 1929- 141
Matthews, Morgan
See Pellowski, Michael (Joseph)
Matthews, Patricia (Anne) 1927- CANR-25
Earlier sketches in CA 29-32R, CANR-9
Interview in CANR-25
See also DAM POP
See also MTCW 1
See also RHW
See also SATA 28
Matthews, Patrick 1953- 223
Matthews, Ralph 1904(?)-1978 85-88
Obituary 81-84
Matthews, Richard K(evin) 1952- 117
Matthews, Robert J(ames) 1926- 65-68
Matthews, Roy A(nthony) 1927- CANR-13
Earlier sketch in CA 33-36R
Matthews, Roy T(homas) 1932- 109
Matthews, Rupert O(liver) 1961- 118
Matthews, Stanley 1915-2000 134
Obituary 187
Brief entry 115
Matthews, Stanley G(oodwin) 1924- 21-24R
Matthews, Steven 1961- 217
Matthews, Susan R. 220
Matthews, T(homas) S(tanley)
1901-1991 .... CANR-76
Obituary 133
Earlier sketches in CAP-1, CA 11-12, CANR-18
Matthews, Tom
See Klewin, W(illiam) Thomas
Matthews, Victor Monroe 1921- 93-96
Matthews, Victoria (Ann) 1941- 163
Matthews, Victoria Earle 1861-1907 ... DLB 221
Matthews, Walter Robert 1881-1973 ..... CAP-1
Earlier sketch in CA 13-14
Matthews, William (Richard) 1905-1975 . 61-64
Obituary 57-60
Matthews, William (Procter III)
1942-1997 .... CANR-57
Obituary 162
Earlier sketches in CA 29-32R, CANR-12
See also CAAS 18
See also AMWS 9
See also CLC 40
See also CP 2
See also DLB 5
Matthews, William Henry III 1919- 9-12R
See also SATA 45
See also SATA-Brief 28
Matthews-Simonton, Stephanie 1947- 132
Matthias, Catherine 1945- 110
See also SATA-Brief 41
Matthias, John (Edward) 1941- CANR-56
Earlier sketch in CA 33-36R
See also CLC 9
See also CP 7
Matthiessen, F(rancis) O(tto) 1902-1950 185
See also DLB 63
See also MAL 5
See also TCLC 100
Matthiessen, Peter 1927- CANR-138
Earlier sketches in CA 9-12R, CANR-21, 50, 73, 100
See also AAYA 6, 40
See also AMWS 5
See also ANW
See also BEST 90:4
See also BPFB 2
See also CLC 5, 7, 11, 32, 64
See also CN 1, 2, 3, 4, 5, 6, 7
See also DA3
See also DAM NOV
See also DLB 6, 173, 275
See also MAL 5
See also MTCW 1, 2
See also MTFW 2005
See also SATA 27
Matthieu, Martial
See Gegauff, Paul
Matthis, Raimund Eugen 1928- 37-40R
Mattick, Paul 1904-1981
Obituary 115
Mattil, Edward La Marr 1918- 127
Brief entry 106
Mattill, A(ndrew) J(acob), Jr. 1924- ... CANR-58
Earlier sketches in CA 37-40R, CANR-14, 31
Mattingley, Christobel (Rosemary)
1931- CANR-47
Earlier sketches in CA 97-100, CANR-20
See also CLR 24
See also CWRI 5
See also MAICYA 1, 2
See also SAAS 18
See also SATA 37, 85
Mattingly, Carol 1945- 186
Mattingly, Garrett 1900-1962
Obituary 111
Mattingly, George E. 1950- 105
Mattingly, Paul H(avey) 1941- 129
Mattioli, Raffaele 1895-1973
Obituary 45-48
Mattis, George 1905-1982 .... CAP-2
Earlier sketch in CA 29-32
Mattison, Alice 1942- CANR-89
Earlier sketch in CA 110
Mattison, Chris
See Mattison, Christopher
Mattison, Christopher 1949- CANR-100
Earlier sketch in CA 125
Mattison, Judith 1939- CANR-24
Earlier sketches in CA 61-64, CANR-8
Mattlin, Paula Plotnick 1934(?)-1981
Obituary 104
Matto de Turner, Clorinda 1852-1909 .... LAW
Mattos, Gregorio de 1636-1695 .... LAW
Mattson, George E(dward) 1937- 5-8R
Mattson, Kevin 1966- CANR-139
Earlier sketch in CA 162
Mattson, Lloyd 1923- CANR-17
Earlier sketch in CA 93-96
Mattusch, Carol C. 1947- 163
Matulay, Laszlo 1912- .... SATA 43
Matulka, Jan 1890-1972 .... SATA-Brief 28
Matura, Mustapha 1939- CANR-63
Earlier sketches in CA 65-68, CANR-12
See also CD 5, 6
Matura, Thaddee 1922- 132
Maturin, Charles Robert 1780(?)-1824 . BRWS 8
See also DLB 178
See also GL 3
See also HGG
See also LMFS 1
See also RGEL 2
See also SUFW
Matus, Greta 1938- 93-96
See also SATA 12
Matus, Irvin Leigh 1941- 129
Matusow, Allen J(oseph) 1937- 142
Matusow, Barbara 1938- 143
Matuszak, John (Daniel) 1950-1989
Obituary 130
Matute (Ausejo), Ana Maria 1925- . CANR-129
Earlier sketch in CA 89-92
See also CLC 11
See also CWW 2
See also DLB 322
See also EWL 3
See also MTCW 1
See also RGSF 2
Matz, Marc 206
Mau, Bruce Douglas 1959- 172
Mau, Ernest E(ugene) 1945- 112
Mau, James A. 1935- 25-28R
Mauceri, Philip 1961- 163
Mauch, Christof 1960- CANR-126
Earlier sketch in CA 163
Mauchline, Mary 1915- 53-56
Maud, John P. R.
See Redcliffe-Maud, John Primatt
Maud, John Primatt Redcliffe
See Redcliffe-Maud, John Primatt
Maud, Ralph (Noel) 1928- 129
Maude, George 1931- CANR-33
Earlier sketch in CA 113
Maude, H(enry) E(vans) 1906- 103
Maududi, Maulana Abdul Ala 1903(?)-1979
Obituary 89-92
Maue, Kenneth 1947- 97-100
Mauer, Marc 233
Mauermann, Mary Anne 1927- 33-36R
Maugham, Diana
See Marr-Johnson, Diana (Maugham)
Maugham, Robert Cecil Romer
1916-1981 .... CANR-40
Obituary 103
Earlier sketch in CA 9-12R
See also Maugham, Robin
Maugham, Robin
See Maugham, Robert Cecil Romer
See also CN 1, 2
See also GLL 1
Maugham, W. S.
See Maugham, W(illiam) Somerset
Maugham, W(illiam) Somerset
1874-1965 .... CANR-127
Obituary 25-28R
Earlier sketches in CA 5-8R, CANR-40
See also AAYA 55
See also BPFB 2
See also BRW 6
See also CDBLB 1914-1945
See also CLC 1, 11, 15, 67, 93
See also CMW 4
See also DA
See also DA3
See also DAB
See also DAC
See also DAM DRAM, MST, NOV
See also DFS 22
See also DLB 10, 36, 77, 100, 162, 195
See also EWL 3
See also LAIT 3
See also MTCW 1, 2
See also MTFW 2005
See also RGEL 2
See also RGSF 2
See also SATA 54
See also SSC 8
See also SSFS 17
See also WLC
Maugham, William Somerset
See Maugham, W(illiam) Somerset
Maughan, A(nne) M(argery) 53-56
Maughan, Jackie Johnson 1948- CANR-116
Earlier sketch in CA 153
Mauk, David C. 1945- 171
Mauldin, Bill
See Mauldin, William Henry
Mauldin, William Henry 1921-2003
Obituary 214
Brief entry 111
Maule, Christopher J(ohn) 1934- 37-40R
Maule, Hamilton Bee 1915- CANR-3
Earlier sketch in CA 1-4R
Maule, Harry E(dward) 1886-1971
Obituary 104
Maule, Henry (Ramsay) 1915-1981 133
Maule, Tex
See Maule, Hamilton Bee
Maultash Warsh, Sylvia E. 202
Maultsby, Maxie C(larence), Jr. 1932- 81-84
Maund, Alfred (Thomas, Jr.) 1923- 1-4R
Maunder, Elwood R(ondeau) 1917- 85-88
Maunder, W(illiam) J(ohn) 1932- 33-36R
Maung, Mya 1933-1998 .... 37-40R
Maung Lun
See U Lun
Maupassant, (Henri Rene Albert) Guy de
1850-1893 .... BYA 14
See also DA
See also DA3
See also DAB
See also DAC
See also DAM MST
See also DLB 123
See also EW 7
See also EXPS
See also GFL 1789 to the Present
See also LAIT 2
See also LMFS 1
See also RGSF 2
See also RGWL 2, 3
See also SSC 1, 64
See also SSFS 4, 21
See also SUFW
See also TWA
See also WLC
Maupertuis, Pierre-Louis Moreau de
1698-1759 .... DLB 314
Maupin, Armistead (Jones, Jr.)
1944- CANR-101
Brief entry 125
Earlier sketches in CA 130, CANR-58
Interview in CA-130
See also CLC 95
See also CPW
See also DA3
See also DAM POP
See also DLB 278
See also GLL 1
See also MTCW 2
See also MTFW 2005
Maura, Sister
See Eichner, Maura
Maureen, Sister Mary 1924- 21-24R
Maurensig, Paolo 1943- 168
Maurer, Armand A(ugustine) 1915- 21-24R
Maurer, Charles Benes 1933- 33-36R
Maurer, Daphne (Jean) 1946- 128
Maurer, David J(oseph) 1935- 102
Maurer, David W(arren) 1906-1981 . CANR-75
Obituary 104
Earlier sketch in CA 17-20R
Maurer, Diane Philippoff
See Maurer-Mathison, Diane V(ogel)
Maurer, Diane Vogel
See Maurer-Mathison, Diane V(ogel)
Maurer, Joan Howard 1927- 119
Maurer, John G. 1937- 37-40R
Maurer, Otto
See Mason, Eudo C(olecestra)
Maurer, Rose
See Somerville, Rose M(aurer)
Maurer, Warren R(ichard) 1929- 146
Maurer-Mathison, Diane V(ogel)
1944- CANR-111
Earlier sketch in CA 155
See also SATA 89
Maurhut, Richard
See Traven, B.
Mauriac, Claude 1914-1996 89-92
Obituary 152
See also CLC 9
See also CWW 2
See also DLB 83
See also EWL 3
See also GFL 1789 to the Present
Mauriac, Francois (Charles) 1885-1970 . CAP-2
Earlier sketch in CA 25-28
See also CLC 4, 9, 56
See also DLB 65
See also EW 10
See also EWL 3
See also GFL 1789 to the Present
See also MTCW 1, 2
See also MTFW 2005
See also RGWL 2, 3
See also SSC 24
See also TWA
Maurice, David (John Kerr) 1899- CAP-1
Earlier sketch in CA 11-12
Maurice, Frederick Denison
1805-1872 .... DLB 55
Maurice, Roger
See Asselineau, Roger (Maurice)
Mauricio, Victoria Courtney 1928- 106
Maurina, Zenta 1897-1978
Obituary 85-88
Maurois, Andre 1885-1967 .... CAP-2
Obituary 25-28R
Earlier sketch in CA 21-22
See also DLB 65
See also EWL 3
See also MTCW 1, 2
See also MTFW 2005
See also SFW 4
Mauron, Charles (Paul) 1899-1966 .... CAP-1
Earlier sketch in CA 9-10
Maurras, Charles(-Marie-Photius)
1868-1952 .... GFL 1789 to the Present
Maury, Inez 1909-1984 61-64
Maury, James 1718-1769 .... DLB 31
Maury, Reuben 1899-1981
Obituary 103
Mauser, Ferdinand F. 1914-1994 .... CANR-2
Earlier sketch in CA 1-4R
Mauser, Patricia Rhoads CANR-22
Earlier sketch in CA 106
See also McCord, Patricia
See also SATA 37
Maushart, Susan 1958- 206
Mauskopf, Seymour Harold 1938- 104
Mauss, Armand L(ind) 1928- 111
Mausser, Wayne 206
Mauterer, Erin Marie 229
Mautner, Franz H(einrich)
1902-1995 .... CANR-12
Earlier sketch in CA 61-64
Mautner, Thomas 1935- CANR-111
Earlier sketch in CA 151
Mauzey, Merritt 1897-1975 102
Mauzy, Peter
See Burgess, Michael (Roy)
Maverick, Liz 237
Maves, Carl (Edwin) 1940- 69-72
Maves, Karl
See Maves, Carl (Edwin)
Maves, Mary Carolyn 1916- 49-52
See also SATA 10
Maves, Paul B(enjamin) 1913-1994 . CANR-17
Earlier sketches in CA 45-48, CANR-1
See also SATA 10
Mavin, John
See Rickword, (John) Edgell

Cumulative Index 383 Mayfield

Mavis, Walter Curry 1905-1998 ... 5-8R
Mavity, Hubert
See Bond, Nelson S(lade)
Mavor, Carol ... 196
Mavor, Elizabeth (Osborne) 1927- ... 107
See also CN 2, 3, 4, 5, 6, 7
See also DLB 14
Mavor, Osborne Henry 1888-1951
Brief entry ... 104
See also Bridie, James
Mavor, Salley 1955- ... SATA 125
Mavrodes, George I(on) 1926- ... 21-24R
Mavrogordato, J(ohn) G(eorge) 1905-1987
Obituary ... 122
Mavrogordato, Jack G.
See Mavrogordato, J(ohn) G(eorge)
Mavrogordatos, George T(hemistocles) 1945- ... 115
Mawby, Janet
See Garton, Janet
Mawdsley, James 1973- ... 217
Mawdsley, Norman
See Hargreaves-Mawdsley, W(illiam) Norman
Mawer, June
See Knox-Mawer, June
Mawer, Ronald Knox
See Knox-Mawer, Ronald
Mawer, Ronnie Knox
See Knox-Mawer, Ronald
Mawer, Simon 1948- ... CANR-140
Earlier sketch in CA 182
Mawhiney, Anne-Marie 1953- ... 227
Mawicke, Tran 1911- ... SATA 15
Mawsilili, Ahmad
See Moussalli, Ahmad S.
Mawson, Robert 1956(?)- ... 172
Max 1906-1989
See Diop, Birago (Ismael)
Max, Nicholas
See Asbell, Bernard
Max, Peter 1939- ... 116
See also SATA 45
Maxa, Rudolph Joseph, Jr. 1949- ... 65-68
Maxa, Rudy
See Maxa, Rudolph Joseph, Jr.
Maxcy, Spencer J. 1939- ... 110
Maxey, Chester Collins 1890-1984 ... CAP-1
Earlier sketch in CA 13-16
Maxey, David R(oy) 1936-1984 ... CANR-75
Obituary ... 112
Earlier sketch in CA 73-76
Maxfield, Doris Morris 1953- ... 129
Maxfield, Elizabeth
See Miller, Elizabeth Maxfield
Maxford, Howard 1964- ... 165
Maxhim, Tristan
See Jones, (Max Him) Henri
Maxidiwiac
See Buffalo Bird Woman
Maxim, John R. 1937- ... CANR-128
Earlier sketches in CA 118, CANR-70
Maximin, Daniel 1947- ... EWL 3
Maximov, Vladimir (Yemelyanovich) 1930-1995 ... 104
Obituary ... 148
See also Maksimov, Vladimir Emel'ianovich
Maximovich, Stanley P. 1957- ... 217
Maxmen, Jerrold S(amuel) 1942- ... CANR-27
Earlier sketch in CA 106
Maxner, Joyce (Karen Leopold) 1929- ... 133
Maxon, Anne
See Best, (Evangel) Allena Champlin
Maxon, John 1916-1977
Obituary ... 69-72
Maxon, Lou R(ussell) 1900-1971
Obituary ... 116
Maxted, Anna 1969- ... 205
Maxton, Hugh
See McCormack, W(illiam) J(ohn)
Maxtone Graham, James Anstruther 1924- ... 69-72
Maxtone-Graham, John 1929- ... CANR-96
Earlier sketch in CA 69-72
Maxtone Graham, Ysenda (May) 1962- ... 217
Maxwell, A. E.
See Maxwell, Ann (Elizabeth)
Maxwell, A(lbert) E(rnest) 1916- ... 5-8R
Maxwell, Ann (Elizabeth) 1944- ... CANR-103
Earlier sketches in CA 105, CANR-58
See also RHW
Maxwell, Arthur S. 1896-1970 ... CAP-1
Earlier sketch in CA 9-10
See also SATA 11
Maxwell, Cassandre 1942- ... 117
Maxwell, Catherine (Fern) 1953- ... CANR-111
Earlier sketch in CA 160
Maxwell, Cathy
See Maxwell, Catherine (Fern)
Maxwell, Colin 1956- ... 132
Maxwell, D(esmond) E(rnest) S(tewart) 1925- ... 33-36R
Maxwell, Donald R. 1929- ... 193
Maxwell, Edith 1923- ... 49-52
See also SATA 7
Maxwell, Edward
See Allan, Ted
Maxwell, Elisabeth (Meynard) 1921- ... 151
Maxwell, Elsa 1883-1963
Obituary ... 89-92
Maxwell, Gavin 1914-1969 ... CANR-114
Obituary ... 25-28R
Earlier sketches in CA 5-8R, CANR-61
See also DLB 204
See also MTCW 1
See also SATA 65
Maxwell, Gilbert 1910-1979 ... CANR-76
Obituary ... 93-96
Earlier sketches in CAP-1, CA 9-10
Maxwell, Glyn 1962- ... CANR-88
Earlier sketch in CA 154
See also CP 7
See also PFS 23
Maxwell, Grant
See Richardson, Gladwell
Maxwell, Grover (Edward) 1918-1981 ... CANR-9
Earlier sketch in CA 5-8R
Maxwell, Jack
See McKeag, Ernest L(ionel)
Maxwell, James A. 1912-1984 ... 13-16R
Maxwell, John
See Freemantle, Brian (Harry)
Maxwell, John C. 1947- ... 208
Maxwell, Katie
See MacAlister, Katie
Maxwell, Kenneth (Robert) 1941- ... CANR-33
Earlier sketches in CA 85-88, CANR-15
Maxwell, Kenneth E(ugene) 1908- ... 73-76
Maxwell, Margaret F(inlayson) 1927- ... 109
Maxwell, Maurice 1910-1982
Obituary ... 107
Maxwell, Neville (George Anthony) 1926- ... CANR-4
Earlier sketch in CA 49-52
Maxwell, Nicholas 1937- ... 132
Maxwell, Nicole (Hughes) 1905(?)-1998 ... 1-4R
Obituary ... 167
Maxwell, Patricia 1942- ... CANR-106
Earlier sketches in CA 29-32R, CANR-12, 28, 52
See also RHW
Maxwell, Rhonda 1950- ... 112
Maxwell, Richard 1948- ... 152
Maxwell, Richard C(allender) 1919- ... 41-44R
Maxwell, (Ian) Robert 1923-1991 ... 9-12R
Obituary ... 135
Maxwell, Robert S(idney) 1911-1990 ... 57-60
Maxwell, Robin 1948- ... CANR-119
Earlier sketch in CA 162
Maxwell, Ronald
See Smith, Ronald Gregor
Maxwell, Sister Mary 1913-1996 ... 37-40R
Maxwell, Vicky
See Worboys, Anne(tte Isobel) Eyre
Maxwell, W(illiam) David 1926- ... 61-64
Maxwell, William
See Allan, Ted
See also MAL 5
Maxwell, William (Keepers, Jr.) 1908-2000 ... CANR-95
Obituary ... 189
Earlier sketches in CA 93-96, CANR-54
Interview in ... CA-93-96
See also AMWS 8
See also CLC 19
See also CN 1, 2, 3, 4, 5, 6, 7
See also DLB 218, 278
See also DLBY 1980
See also SATA-Obit 128
Maxwell-Hudson, (Rachel) Clare 1946- ... 69-72
Maxwell-Hyslop, Miranda 1968- ... SATA 154
Maxwell-Lefroy, Cecil Anthony 1907- ... CAP-1
Earlier sketch in CA 13-16
Maxymuk, John M. 1957- ... 205
May, Allan 1923- ... 85-88
May, Arthur James 1899-1968 ... CAP-1
Earlier sketch in CA 11-12
May, Brian 1959- ... 165
May, Charles E(dward) 1941- ... CANR-41
Earlier sketch in CA 117
May, Charles Paul 1920- ... CANR-5
Earlier sketch in CA 1-4R
See also SATA 4
May, Clifford D. 1951- ... 136
May, Daryl (Alden) 1936- ... 139
May, Dean E(dward) 1944- ... 57-60
May, Derwent (James) 1930- ... CANR-141
Earlier sketches in CA 25-28R, CANR-11, 28
May, Edgar 1929- ... 9-12R
May, Elaine 1932- ... 142
Brief entry ... 124
See also CAD
See also CLC 16
See also CWD
See also DLB 44
May, Elaine Tyler 1947- ... CANR-57
Earlier sketches in CA 111, CANR-30
See also SATA 120
May, Elizabeth 1907- ... CAP-2
Earlier sketch in CA 19-20
May, Ernest R(ichard) 1928- ... CANR-108
Earlier sketches in CA 1-4R, CANR-6, 22
May, Eugene 1906-1994 ... 1-4R
May, Florissa
See Green, Kay
May, Francis Barns 1915- ... 9-12R
May, George S(mith) 1924- ... 65-68
May, Georges (Claude) 1920-2003 ... CANR-6
Obituary ... 213
Earlier sketch in CA 13-16R
May, Gerald G(ordon) 1940-2005 ... 206
Obituary ... 238
Brief entry ... 112
May, Gita 1929- ... CANR-13
Earlier sketch in CA 29-32R
May, H(enry) J(ohn) 1903- ... 13-16R
May, Henry F(arnham) 1915- ... 9-12R
May, Herbert Gordon 1904-1977 ... CANR-6
Obituary ... 89-92
Earlier sketch in CA 5-8R
May, Irvin M(arion), Jr. 1939- ... 123
May, J. C.
See May, Julian
May, Jacques M. 1896-1975
Obituary ... 57-60
May, James Boyer 1904-1981 ... CAP-1
Earlier sketch in CA 11-12
May, Jesse 1970(?)- ... 235
May, John 1942- ... 239
May, John D(ickinson) 1932- ... 45-48
May, John R(ichard) 1931- ... CANR-18
Earlier sketches in CA 45-48, CANR-2
May, Jonathan
See James, Laurence
May, Judy Gail 1943- ... 57-60
May, Julian 1931- ... CANR-127
Earlier sketches in CA 1-4R, CANR-6, 54
See also AAYA 17
See also FANT
See also SATA 11
See also SFW 4
May, Karl 1842-1912 ... DLB 129
May, Kenneth Ownsworth 1915-1977
Obituary ... 73-76
May, Lary L. 1944- ... CANR-119
Earlier sketch in CA 130
May, Lawrence Alan 1948- ... 106
May, Philip Radford 1928- ... 45-48
May, Robert E(van) 1943- ... 57-60
May, Robert Lewis 1905-1976
Obituary ... 104
See also SATA-Obit 27
May, Robert M(cCredie) 1936- ... 69-72
May, Robert Stephen 1929-1996 ... CANR-30
Earlier sketches in CA 29-32R, CANR-13
See also SATA 46
May, Robin
See May, Robert Stephen
May, Rollo (Reece) 1909-1994 ... 111
Obituary ... 147
Interview in ... CA-111
May, Sophie
See Clarke, Rebecca Sophia
May, Stephen 1946- ... CANR-97
Earlier sketch in CA 124
May, Steven W. 1941- ... 141
May, Thomas 1595(?)-1650 ... DLB 58
See also RGEL 2
May, Thomas 1964- ... 223
May, Timothy C(laude) 1940- ... 73-76
May, Todd Gifford 1955- ... 145
May, William E(ugene) 1928- ... CANR-14
Earlier sketch in CA 41-44R
May, Wynne
See Knowles, Mabel Winifred
See also RHW
Mayakovski, Vladimir (Vladimirovich) 1893-1930 ... 158
Brief entry ... 104
See also Maiakovskii, Vladimir and Mayakovsky, Vladimir
See also EWL 3
See also MTCW 2
See also MTFW 2005
See also SFW 4
See also TCLC 4, 18
See also TWA
Mayakovsky, Vladimir
See Mayakovski, Vladimir (Vladimirovich)
See also EW 11
See also WP
Mayall, David 1953- ... 119
Mayall, R(obert) Newton 1904-1989 ... CAP-1
Earlier sketch in CA 11-12
Maybarduk, Linda ... 185
Maybaum, Ignaz 1897-1976 ... CAP-1
Earlier sketch in CA 9-10
Mayberry, Florence V(irginia) Wilson ... 9-12R
See also SATA 10
Mayberry, Genevieve 1900-1991 ... CAP-1
Earlier sketch in CA 19-20
Maybray-King, Horace 1901-1986 ... 29-32R
Obituary ... 120
Maybury, Anne
See Buxton, Anne (Arundel)
Maybury, Richard J. 1946- ... SATA 72
Maybury-Lewis, David H(enry) P(eter) 1929- ... 17-20R
Maye, Patricia 1940- ... 53-56
Mayer, Adrian C(urtius) 1922- ... 1-4R
Mayer, Agatha
See Maher, Ramona
Mayer, Albert 1897-1981 ... 73-76
Obituary ... 105
Mayer, Albert Ignatius, Jr. 1906-1994
Obituary ... 200
Obituary ... 109
See also SATA-Obit 29
Mayer, Alfred 1903(?)-1984
Obituary ... 114
Mayer, (Henri) Andre (Van Huysen) 1946- ... 110
Mayer, Ann M(argaret) 1938- ... 57-60
See also SATA 14
Mayer, Arno J. 1926- ... CANR-111
Earlier sketch in CA 85-88
Mayer, Arthur L(oeb) 1886-1981
Obituary ... 108
Mayer, Barbara 1939- ... 145
Mayer, Bernadette 1945- ... CANR-132
Earlier sketches in CA 33-36R, CANR-70
See also CWP
See also DLB 165
Mayer, Bob 1959- ... 137
Mayer, Carl 1894-1944 ... IDFW 3, 4
Mayer, Carl J. 1959- ... 122
Mayer, Charles Leopold 1881-1971 ... CANR-6
Earlier sketch in CA 1-4R
Mayer, Christa Charlotte
See Thurman, Christa C(harlotte) Mayer
Mayer, Clara Woollie 1895-1988 ... CAP-2
Earlier sketch in CA 19-20
Mayer, Danuta 1958- ... SATA 117
Mayer, Debby
See Mayer, Deborah Anne
Mayer, Deborah Anne 1946- ... 109
Mayer, Ellen Moers
See Moers, Ellen
Mayer, Fanny (Alice) Hagin 1899-1990 ... 118
Mayer, Gary (Richard) 1945- ... 53-56
Mayer, Gerda (Kamilla) 1927- ... 106
See also CP 7
See also CWP
Mayer, Hannelore Valencak 1929- ... 116
See also Valencak, Hannelore
Mayer, Hans (Heinrich) 1907- ... 133
Brief entry ... 113
Mayer, Hans 1912-1978
See Amery, Jean
Mayer, Harold M(elvin) 1916- ... 41-44R
Mayer, Harry F(rederick) 1912-1993 ... 101
Mayer, Henry 1941-2000 ... CANR-96
Obituary ... 189
Earlier sketch in CA 122
Mayer, Herbert Carleton 1893-1978 ... 41-44R
Mayer, Herbert T. 1922- ... 33-36R
Mayer, Jane ... 158
Mayer, Jane Rothschild 1903-2001 ... 9-12R
Obituary ... 202
See also SATA 38
Mayer, Jean 1920-1993 ... 129
Obituary ... 140
Brief entry ... 117
Mayer, Jeremy D. 1968- ... 221
Mayer, Lawrence C(lark) 1936- ... 97-100
Mayer, Leo V. 1936- ... 73-76
Mayer, Louis B. 1885-1957 ... IDFW 3, 4
Mayer, Lynne Rhodes 1926- ... 73-76
Mayer, Marianna 1945- ... 93-96
See also SATA 32, 83, 132
Mayer, Martin (Prager) 1928- ... 5-8R
Mayer, Mercer 1943- ... CANR-109
Earlier sketches in CA 85-88, CANR-38, 77
See also CLR 11
See also CWRI 5
See also DLB 61
See also MAICYA 1, 2
See also SATA 16, 32, 73, 129, 137
Mayer, Michael F. 1917- ... 13-16R
Mayer, Milton (Sanford) 1908-1986 ... 37-40R
Obituary ... 119
Mayer, Musa 1943- ... 135
Mayer, Orlando Benedict 1818-1891 ... DLB 3, 248
Mayer, Parm 1915- ... CP 1
Mayer, (Ulrich) Philip 1910-1995 ... 49-52
Mayer, Ralph 1895-1979 ... CANR-28
Obituary ... 89-92
Earlier sketch in CA 29-32R
Mayer, Raymond Richard 1924- ... 1-4R
Mayer, Robert 1879-1985
Obituary ... 115
Mayer, Robert 1939- ... 136
Mayer, S(ydney) L(ouis) 1937- ... 103
Mayer, Sigrid 1933- ... CANR-123
Earlier sketch in CA 121
Mayer, Thomas 1927- ... CANR-9
Earlier sketch in CA 21-24R
Mayer, Tom 1943- ... 9-12R
Mayers, Daniel E. 1933(?)-1988
Obituary ... 129
Mayers, David (Allan) 1951- ... 131
Mayers, Lewis 1890-1975
Obituary ... 61-64
Mayers, Marvin K(eene) 1927- ... CANR-43
Earlier sketch in CA 41-44R
Mayerson, Charlotte Leon ... 13-16R
See also SATA 36
Mayerson, Evelyn Wilde 1935- ... 101
See also SATA 55
Mayerson, Keith 1966- ... 230
Mayerson, Philip 1918- ... 41-44R
Mayer-Thurman, Christa C.
See Thurman, Christa C(harlotte) Mayer
Mayes, (Anthony) Bernard Duncan 1929- ... 197
Mayes, Edythe Beam 1902-1990 ... CANR-7
Earlier sketch in CA 53-56
Mayes, Frances ... CANR-137
Earlier sketches in CA 81-84, CANR-74
Mayes, Herbert R(aymond) 1900-1987 ... 105
Obituary ... 124
See also DLB 137
Mayes, Linda C(arol) 1951- ... 225
Mayes, Stanley (Herbert) 1911- ... 1-4R
Mayes, Wendell 1919(?)-1992 ... CANR-80
Obituary ... 137
Earlier sketch in CA 103
Interview in ... CA-103
See also DLB 26
Mayeux, Peter E(dmond) 1942- ... 119
Mayfair, Bertha
See Raborg, Frederick A(shton), Jr.
Mayfair, Franklin
See Mendelsohn, Felix, Jr.
Mayfield, Chris 1951- ... 107
Mayfield, Guy 1905-1976 ... 5-8R
Obituary ... 122
Mayfield, Jack
See Cooper, Parley J(oseph)
Mayfield, James Bruce 1934- ... 69-72
Mayfield, John S. 1904-1983
Obituary ... 109
Mayfield, Julia
See Hastings, Phyllis (Dora Hodge)

Mayfield, Julian (Hudson)
1928-1984 ... CANR-26
Obituary ... 114
Earlier sketch in CA 13-16R
See also BW 1
See also CN 1, 2, 3
See also DLB 33
See also DLBY 1984
Mayfield, Katherine 1958- ... 190
See also SATA 118
Mayfield, L(afayette) H(enry) II 1910- ... CAP-2
Earlier sketch in CA 19-20
Mayfield, Marlys 1931- ... CANR-27
Earlier sketches in CA 25-28R, CANR-10
Mayfield, Robert C(harles) 1928- ... 37-40R
Mayfield, Sara (Martin) 1905-1979 ... CANR-76
Obituary ... 85-88
Earlier sketch in CA 25-28R
Mayfield, Sue 1963- ... SATA 72, 146
Mayfield, Terry L. 1953- ... 217
Mayhall, Jane (Francis) 1921- ... CANR-8
Earlier sketch in CA 17-20R
Mayhall, Mildred P(ickle) 1902-1987 . CANR-1
Earlier sketch in CA 1-4R
Mayhar, Ardath 1930- ... CANR-42
Earlier sketches in CA 103, CANR-19
See also BYA 7
See also SATA 38
See also SFW 4
Mayhew, Christopher Paget 1915-1997
Brief entry ... 106
Mayhew, David R(aymond) 1937- ... 17-20R
Mayhew, Edgar deNoailles 1913-1991 .. 37-40R
Mayhew, Elizabeth
See Bear, Joan
Mayhew, Henry 1812-1887 ... DLB 18, 55, 190
Mayhew, James (John) 1964- ... SATA 85, 149
Mayhew, Jonathan 1720-1766 ... DLB 31
Mayhew, Lenore 1924- ... 49-52
Mayhew, Lewis B. 1917- ... CANR-4
Earlier sketch in CA 1-4R
Mayhew, Margaret 1936- ... 235
Mayhew, Nicholas ... 196
Mayhue, Richard L(ee) 1944- ... 116
Mayle, Peter 1939(?)- ... CANR-109
Earlier sketches in CA 139, CANR-64
See also CLC 89
Mayleas, William 1927- ... 120
Mayman, Martin 1924- ... 9-12R
Maynard, Alan (Keith) 1944- ... CANR-7
Earlier sketch in CA 57-60
Maynard, Bill ... 195
Maynard, Chris
See Maynard, Christopher
Maynard, Christopher 1949- ... 203
Brief entry ... 118
See also SATA-Brief 43
Maynard, Donald Pemberton 1937- ... CP 1
Maynard, Fredelle (Bruser) 1922- ... 85-88
Maynard, Geoffrey W(alter) 1921- ... 5-8R
Maynard, Harold Bright 1902-1975 . CANR-75
Obituary ... 103
Earlier sketch in CA 9-12R
Maynard, Isabelle 1929- ... 162
Maynard, John (Rogers) 1941- ... CANR-40
Earlier sketch in CA 65-68
Maynard, Joyce 1953- ... CANR-64
Brief entry ... 111
Earlier sketch in CA 129
See also CLC 23
Maynard, (Daphne) Joyce 1953- ... CANR-114
Maynard, Olga 1920- ... 114
See also SATA 40
Maynard, Richard Allen 1942- ... 33-36R
Maynard, Robert C(lyve)
1937-1993 ... CANR-76
Obituary ... 142
Brief entry ... 110
Earlier sketch in CA 115
Interview in ... CA-115
Mayne, Ethel(ind Frances) Colburn
1865-1941 ... DLB 197
Mayne, Jasper 1604-1672 ... DLB 126
See also RGEL 2
Mayne, Richard (John) 1926- ... CANR-6
Earlier sketch in CA 13-16R
Mayne, Seymour 1944- ... CANR-47
Earlier sketches in CA 101, CANR-18
See also CCA 1
See also CP 2, 3, 4, 5, 6, 7
See also DLB 60
Mayne, William (James Carter)
1928- ... CANR-100
Earlier sketches in CA 9-12R, CANR-37, 80
See also AAYA 20
See also CLC 12
See also CLR 25
See also FANT
See also JRDA
See also MAICYA 1, 2
See also MAICYAS 1
See also SAAS 11
See also SATA 6, 68, 122
See also SUFW 2
See also YAW
Maynert, Helga
See Henningsen, Agnes (Kathinka Malling)
Maynes, E(dwin) Scott 1922- ... CANR-30
Earlier sketch in CA 45-48
Maynes, J. O. Rocky, Jr.
See Maynes, J. Oscar, Jr.
Maynes, J. Oscar, Jr. 1929- ... 115
See also SATA 38
Mayo, Bernard 1902-1979
Obituary ... 89-92
Mayo, C(atherine) M(ansell) 1961- ... 154
Mayo, Charles G(eorge) 1931-1985
Obituary ... 116
Mayo, E(dward) L(eslie) 1904-1979 ... 97-100
See also CP 1, 2
Mayo, Gretchen Will 1936- ... 239
See also SATA 84, 163
Mayo, James
See Coulter, Stephen
Mayo, Janet 1949- ... 121
Mayo, Jim
See L'Amour, Louis (Dearborn)
Mayo, Lida (Smith) 1904-1978
Obituary ... 112
Mayo, Lucy Graves 1909-1963 ... 5-8R
Mayo, Margaret (Mary) 1935- ... CANR-68
Earlier sketch in CA 107
See also SATA 38, 96
Mayo, Margot (Booth) 1910-1974 ... CAP-1
Earlier sketch in CA 13-16
Mayo, Mark
See Lane, Yoti
Mayo, Nick 1922-1983 ... CANR-76
Obituary ... 110
Earlier sketch in CA 103
Mayo, Patricia Elton 1915- ... 103
Mayo, Wendell 1953- ... CANR-88
Earlier sketch in CA 161
Mayo, William L. 1931- ... 17-20R
Mayor, A(lpheus) Hyatt 1901-1980 ... CANR-1
Obituary ... 97-100
Earlier sketch in CA 45-48
Mayor, Adrienne 1946- ... 199
Mayor, Alfred Hyatt 1934- ... 65-68
Mayor, Archer
See Mayor, Archer H(untington)
Mayor, Archer H(untington) 1950- .. CANR-118
Earlier sketches in CA 134, CANR-65
See also CMW 4
Mayor, Beatrice (?)-1971 ... CAP-1
Earlier sketch in CA 9-10
Mayor, Federico 1934- ... 154
See also HW 2
Mayor, Flora MacDonald 1872-1932 ... 179
See also DLB 36
Mayor, Stephen (Harold) 1927- ... 21-24R
Mayotte, Judy A. 1937- ... 144
Mayoux, Jean-Jacques 1901(?)-1987(?)
Obituary ... 125
Mayr, Dallas William 1946-
See Ketchum, Jack
Mayr, Ernst (Walter) 1904-2005 ... CANR-118
Obituary ... 236
Earlier sketches in CA 5-8R, CANR-2
Mayrant, Drayton
See Simons, Katherine Drayton Mayrant
Mayrocker, Friedericke ... CANR-125
See also Mayroecker, Friederike
See also EWL 3
Mayroecker, Friederike 1924- ... CANR-125
Earlier sketch in CA 179
See also Mayrocker, Friedericke
See also DLB 85
Mays, Benjamin E(lijah) 1894-1984 . CANR-25
Obituary ... 112
Earlier sketch in CA 45-48
See also BW 1
Mays, Buddy (Gene) 1943- ... CANR-30
Earlier sketches in CA 73-76, CANR-12
Mays, Cedric Wesley 1907- ... 29-32R
Mays, David John 1896-1971 ... 218
Mays, James A(rthur) 1939- ... CANR-25
Earlier sketch in CA 57-60
See also BW 1
Mays, John Barron 1914-1987
Obituary ... 123
Mays, John Bentley 1941- ... CANR-138
Earlier sketch in CA 164
Mays, Lucinda L(a Bella) 1924- ... 101
See also SATA 49
Mays, Spike
See Mays, Cedric Wesley
Mays, (Lewis) Victor (Jr.) 1927- ... 25-28R
See also SATA 5
Mays, Willie (Howard, Jr.) 1931- ... 105
Mayshark, Cyrus 1926-1976 ... CANR-76
Obituary ... 134
Earlier sketch in CA 17-20R
Maysi, Kadra
See Simons, Katherine Drayton Mayrant
Maysles, Albert 1926- ... 29-32R
See also CLC 16
Maysles, David 1932-1987 ... 191
See also CLC 16
Maytham, Thomas N(orthrup) 1931- ... 103
Maza, Regino Sainz de la
See Sainz de la Maza, Regino
Maza, Sarah C. 1953- ... 234
Mazani, Eric C.F. Nhando 1948- ... CP 1
Maze, Edward 1925- ... 5-8R
Mazer, Anne 1953- ... 135
See also SATA 67, 105
Mazer, Harry 1925- ... CANR-129
Earlier sketches in CA 97-100, CANR-32
Interview in ... CA-97-100
See also AAYA 5, 36
See also BYA 6
See also CLR 16
See also JRDA
See also MAICYA 1, 2
See also SAAS 11
See also SATA 31, 67, 105
See also WYA
See also YAW
Mazer, Milton 1911- ... 85-88
Mazer, Norma Fox 1931- ... CANR-129
Earlier sketches in CA 69-72, CANR-12, 32, 66
See also AAYA 5, 36
See also BYA 1, 8
See also CLC 26
See also CLR 23
See also JRDA
See also MAICYA 1, 2
See also SAAS 1
See also SATA 24, 67, 105
See also WYA
See also YAW
Mazia, Marjorie
See Guthrie, Marjorie (Greenblatt Mazia)
Maziarz, Edward A(nthony) 1915- ... 37-40R
Mazille, Capucine 1953- ... SATA 96
Mazis, Glen A. 1951- ... 237
Mazlish, Bruce 1923- ... CANR-88
Earlier sketches in CA 5-8R, CANR-2
Mazmanian, Arthur B(arkev) 1931- ... 77-80
Mazmanian, Daniel (Aram) 1945- ... CANR-5
Earlier sketch in CA 53-56
Mazo, Earl 1919- ... 37-40R
Mazo, Joseph H(enry) 1938- ... 69-72
Mazonowicz, Douglas (Howcroft)
1920-2001 ... 57-60
Obituary ... 193
Mazor, Julian 1929- ... 238
Mazour, Anatole G. 1900-1982 ... 13-16R
Mazow, Julia Wolf 1937- ... 103
Mazower, Mark ... 175
Mazrui, Ali A(l'Amin) 1933- ... CANR-13
Earlier sketch in CA 21-24R
See also BW 2
See also DLB 125
Mazumdar, Maxim 1952(?)-1988
Obituary ... 125
Mazur, Allan Carl 1939- ... 105
Mazur, Gail 1937- ... 77-80
Mazur, Grace Dane ... 188
Mazur, Laurie Ann 1961- ... 150
Mazur, Paul M(yer) 1892-1979 ... 102
Obituary ... 89-92
Mazur, Ronald Michael 1934- ... 25-28R
Mazuranic, Ivan 1814-1890 ... DLB 147
Mazurkiewicz, Albert J. 1926- ... CANR-3
Earlier sketch in CA 9-12R
Mazursky, Paul 1930- ... CANR-24
Earlier sketch in CA 77-80
See also DLB 44
Mazza, Adriana 1928- ... CANR-4
Earlier sketch in CA 1-4R
See also SATA 19
Mazza, Cris 1956- ... CANR-108
Earlier sketch in CA 132
Mazza, Joan 1948- ... 189
Mazzarins, Laimdota 1945- ... 159
Mazzaro, Jerome 1934- ... CANR-45
Earlier sketches in CA 33-36R, CANR-13
Mazze, Edward M(ark) 1941- ... CANR-5
Earlier sketch in CA 13-16R
Mazzei, George 1941- ... 117
Mazzeo, Guido E(ttore) 1914-1984 .. CANR-28
Obituary ... 113
Earlier sketch in CA 45-48
Mazzeo, Joseph Anthony 1923-1998 ... 17-20R
Obituary ... 169
Mazzetti, Lorenza 1933- ... 9-12R
Mazzio, Joann 1926- ... SATA 74
Mazzotta, Giuseppe 1942- ... CANR-37
Earlier sketches in CA 93-96, CANR-16
Mazzuca Toops, Laura 1955- ... 202
Mazzulla, Fred 1903- ... CAP-2
Earlier sketch in CA 29-32
Mbaku, John Mukum 1950- ... 194
Mbaye, Marietou (Bileoma) 1948- ... 139
See also Bugul, Ken
Mbeki, Govan 1910-2001 ... 204
Mberi, Antar Sudan Katara 1949- ... 81-84
Mbiti, John S(amuel) 1931- ... CANR-11
Earlier sketch in CA 21-24R
See also BW 1
See also CP 1
Mbuende, Kaire (Munionganda) 1953- ... 155
See also BW 3
Mbugua, Kioi Wa 1962- ... SATA 83
McAdam, Charles Vincent 1892-1985
Obituary ... 116
McAdam, Colin 1971- ... 231
McAdam, Doug 1951- ... CANR-55
Earlier sketch in CA 126
McAdam, Ian 1960- ... 200
Mc Adam, Robert E(verett) 1920- ... 81-84
McAdams, Charles
See Richardson, Gladwell
McAdams, Dan P. 1954- ... 141
McAdams, Janet 1957- ... 203
McAdoo, Henry Robert 1916-1998 ... 107
Obituary ... 172
McAfee, Carol 1955- ... CANR-121
Earlier sketch in CA 149
See also SATA 81
McAfee, John P. 1947- ... 141
McAfee, Paul ... TCWW 2
McAfee, (James) Thomas 1928-1982 .. CANR-1
Earlier sketch in CA 45-48
McAfee, Ward M(erner) 1939- ... 57-60
McAlary, Mike 1957-1998 ... 210
McAleavey, David 1946- ... 65-68
McAleavy, Henry 1912-1968 ... CAP-2
Earlier sketch in CA 21-22
McAleer, John J(oseph) 1923-2003 ... CANR-13
Obituary ... 221
Earlier sketch in CA 21-24R
McAleer, Neil 1942- ... 119
McAlester, A(rcie) Lee 1933- ... 118
McAlester, Lee
See McAlester, A(rcie) Lee
McAlester, Virginia 1943- ... 120
McAlindon, Thomas 1932- ... 97-100
McAlister, Elizabeth (A.) 1963- ... 236
McAlister, Luther Durwood 1927- ... 134
McAlister, Neil Harding 1952- ... 110
McAlister, W(alter) Robert 1930- ... 69-72
McAll, Christopher 1948- ... 137
McAllaster, Elva 1922- ... 33-36R
McAllen, Jack 1929- ... 145
McAllen, John Banks
See McAllen, Jack
McAllester, Matthew 1969- ... 212
McAllister, Alister 1877-1943
Brief entry ... 121
McAllister, Amanda
See Dowdell, Dorothy (Florence) Karns and
Hager, Jean and
Meaker, Eloise
McAllister, Annie Laurie
See Cassiday, Bruce (Bingham)
McAllister, Bruce (Hugh) 1946- ... 33-36R
See also SFW 4
McAllister, Casey
See Battin, B(rinton) W(arner)
McAllister, Harry E(dward) ... 5-8R
McAllister, Ian 1950- ... 128
McAllister, Lester G(rover) 1919- ... 41-44R
McAllister, Margaret 1956- ... 189
See also SATA 117
McAllister, Troon
See Gruenfeld, Lee
McAlmon, Robert (Menzies) 1895-1956 ... 168
Brief entry ... 107
See also DLB 4, 45
See also DLBD 15
See also GLL 1
See also TCLC 97
McAlpin, Heller 1955- ... 109
McAlpine, Alistair 1942- ... 167
McAlpine, Donald 1934- ... IDFW 4
McAlpine, Ken 1959- ... 230
McAlpine, Rachel (Taylor) 1940- ... CWP
McAnally, Mary E(llen) 1939- ... CANR-46
Earlier sketches in CA 105, CANR-21
McAndrew, John 1904-1978
Obituary ... 77-80
McAndrews, John
See Steward, Samuel M(orris)
See also GLL 1
McAnelly, James R. 1932- ... 57-60
McAnuff, Des 1952- ... 203
McArdle, Catherine
See Kelleher, Catherine McArdle
McArdle, Hugh M(c Lure) 1905- ... 107
McArdle, John 1949- ... 213
McArdle, Karen 1936- ... 129
McArdle, Phil 1939- ... 129
McArdle, William D(aniel) 1939- ... 110
McArthur, Benjamin 1951- ... 167
McArthur, Charles C(ampbell) 1920- ... 41-44R
McArthur, Edwin Douglas 1907-1987 ... 17-20R
Obituary ... 121
McArthur, Harvey K(ing) 1912- ... 25-28R
McArthur, John
See Wise, Arthur
McArthur, Maxine 1962- ... 186
McArthur, Nancy ... CANR-124
Earlier sketch in CA 161
See also SATA 96
McArthur, Peter 1866-1924 ... 179
See also DLB 92
McAtee, Robert E(mmet) 1948- ... 201
McAulay, John D(avid) 1912-2000 ... 13-16R
McAuley, James J(ohn) 1936- ... 77-80
See also CP 1, 2, 3, 4, 5, 6, 7
McAuley, James Phillip 1917-1976 ... 97-100
See also CLC 45
See also CP 1, 2
See also DLB 260
See also RGEL 2
McAuley, Patricia Ann Calistro
See Calistro McAuley, Patricia Ann
McAuley, Paul J. 1955- ... CANR-97
Earlier sketch in CA 157
See also SFW 4
McAuliffe, Clarence 1903-1990 ... CAP-2
Earlier sketch in CA 19-20
McAuliffe, Jody 1954- ... 230
McAuliffe, Johanna
See McAuliffe, Jody
McAuliffe, Kevin Michael 1949-2000 ... 81-84
Obituary ... 189
McAuliffe, Mary Sperling 1943- ... 81-84
McAvoy, Jim 1972- ... 213
See also SATA 142
McAvoy, Thomas T(imothy)
1903-1969 ... CANR-15
Earlier sketch in CA 1-4R
McBain, Donald J(ames) 1945- ... 45-48
McBain, Ed
See Hunter, Evan
See also MSW
McBain, Gordon D(uncan) III 1946-1992 ... 106
McBain, John M(aurice) 1921- ... 41-44R
McBain, Laurie 1949- ... 97-100
See also RHW
McBath, James Harvey 1922- ... 17-20R
McBeath, Gerald A. 1942- ... 203
McBee, Mary Louise 1924- ... 103

Cumulative Index 385 McCarthy

McBratney, Sam 1943- ... CANR-115
Earlier sketch in CA 155
See also CLR 44
See also CWRI 5
See also MAICYA 2
See also MAICYAS 1
See also SATA 89
McBrearty, James C(onnell) 1941-
Brief entry ... 113
McBrearty, Robert (Garner) 1954- ... 185
McBreen, Joan 1947- ... CANR-101
Earlier sketch in CA 151
McBriar, Alan M(arne) 1918- ... 5-8R
McBride, Alfred 1928- ... CANR-6
Earlier sketch in CA 13-16R
McBride, (Mary) Angela Barron
1941- ... CANR-1
Earlier sketch in CA 49-52
McBride, Bunny 1950- ... 190
McBride, Chris(topher James) 1941- ... 81-84
McBride, David P(aul) 1947- ... 116
McBride, Donald O(pie) 1903-1978
Obituary ... 77-80
McBride, Dwight A. ... 238
McBride, Earl Duwain 1891-1975 ... CAP-1
Earlier sketch in CA 13-14
McBride, Genevieve G. 1949- ... 149
McBride, James C. 1957- ... CANR-113
Earlier sketch in CA 153
See also BW 3
See also MTFW 2005
McBride, James H(ubert) 1924- ... 25-28R
McBride, Jim 1941- ... 157
McBride, John Cosgrove 1911-1983
Obituary ... 110
McBride, John G. 1919- ... 9-12R
McBride, Joseph (Pierce) 1947- ... CANR-114
Earlier sketch in CA 41-44R
McBride, Jule 1959- ... 166
McBride, Katharine 1904-1976
Obituary ... 65-68
Mcbride, Mary ... 217
McBride, Mary Margaret 1899-1976 ... 69-72
Obituary ... 65-68
McBride, Patricia
See Bartz, Patricia McBride
McBride, Regina 1956- ... 209
McBride, Richard William 1928- ... 17-20R
McBride, Robert 1941-
Brief entry ... 116
McBride, Robert H(enry) 1918-1983 ... 107
Obituary ... 111
McBride, Stephen 1947- ... CANR-101
Earlier sketch in CA 148
McBride, Susan ... 204
McBride, Theresa Marie 1947- ... 112
McBride, William Leon 1938- ... CANR-6
Earlier sketch in CA 57-60
McBrien, Richard P(eter) 1936- ... CANR-118
Earlier sketches in CA 17-20R, CANR-10
McBrien, William (Augustine)
1930- ... CANR-90
Earlier sketch in CA 107
See also CLC 44
McBrier, Michael
See Older, Effin and
Older, Jules
McBroom, R. Curtis 1910-1999 ... CAP-2
Earlier sketch in CA 21-22
McBurney, James H(oward) 1905-1986 . 17-20R
McBurney, Simon ... 223
McCabe, Bernard P(atrick), Jr. 1933- ... 53-56
McCabe, Cameron
See Borneman, Ernest
McCabe, Charles B. 1899-1970
Obituary ... 89-92
McCabe, Charles Raymond 1915-1983
Obituary ... 109
McCabe, Cynthia Jaffee 1943-1986 ... 117
Obituary ... 120
McCabe, David Aloysius 1884(?)-1974
Obituary ... 45-48
McCabe, Eugene 1930- ... CANR-120
Earlier sketch in CA 158
See also CBD
See also CD 5, 6
McCabe, Herbert 1926-2001 ... 13-16R
Obituary ... 198
McCabe, James P(atrick) 1937- ... 101
McCabe, John (Charles III) III
1920- ... CANR-106
Earlier sketches in CA 1-4R, CANR-1
McCabe, Joseph E. 1912-2001 ... 17-20R
McCabe, Patrick 1955- ... CANR-90
Earlier sketches in CA 130, CANR-50
See also BRWS 9
See also CLC 133
See also CN 6, 7
See also DLB 194
McCabe, Peter 1945- ... 140
McCabe, Sybil Anderson 1902-1996 ... CAP-1
Earlier sketch in CA 13-16
McCabe, Victoria 1948- ... 29-32R
McCafferty, Jane 1960- ... 141
McCafferty, Jim 1954- ... 150
See also SATA 84
McCafferty, Lawrence ... 25-28R
McCafferty, Maureen 1954- ... 175
McCafferty, Megan ... 205
See also AAYA 59
McCafferty, Owen 1961- ... DLB 310
McCafferty, (Barbara) Taylor 1946- . CANR-130
Earlier sketches in CA 134, CANR-74
McCaffery, Dan 1952- ... 129
McCaffery, Edward J. 1958- ... 215
McCaffery, Janet 1936- ... SATA 38
McCaffery, John K(erwin) M(ichael)
1914(?)-1983
Obituary ... 111
McCaffery, Larry 1946- ... 115
McCaffery, Margo (Smith) 1938- ... 37-40R
McCaffery, Steve 1947- ... CANR-109
Earlier sketch in CA 154
See also CP 7
McCaffrey, Anne (Inez) 1926- ... 227
Earlier sketches in CA 25-28R, CANR-15, 35, 55, 96
Autobiographical Essay in ... 227
See also AAYA 6, 34
See also AITN 2
See also BEST 89:2
See also BPFB 2
See also BYA 5
See also CLC 17
See also CLR 49
See also CPW
See also DA3
See also DAM NOV, POP
See also DLB 8
See also JRDA
See also MAICYA 1, 2
See also MTCW 1, 2
See also MTFW 2005
See also SAAS 11
See also SATA 8, 70, 116, 152
See also SATA-Essay 152
See also SFW 4
See also SUFW 2
See also WYA
See also YAW
McCaffrey, Donald W. 1926-
Brief entry ... 114
McCaffrey, James M. 1946- ... 143
McCaffrey, Joseph A. 1940- ... 37-40R
McCaffrey, K(en) T. 1947- ... 235
McCaffrey, Lawrence John 1925- ... 25-28R
McCaffrey, Mary
See Szudek, Agnes S(usan) P(hilomena)
McCaffrey, Phillip 1945- ... CANR-15
Earlier sketch in CA 77-80
McCagg, William O., Jr. 1930- ... 93-96
McCaghy, Charles H(enry) 1934- ... 25-28R
McCague, James (P.) 1909-1977 ... CANR-2
Earlier sketch in CA 1-4R
McCahery, James R. 1934-1995 ... 204
McCahill, Thomas 1907(?)-1975
Obituary ... 104
McCaig, Donald 1940- ... CANR-47
Earlier sketches in CA 104, CANR-14
McCaig, Robert Jesse 1907-1982 ... CANR-64
Earlier sketches in CA 1-4R, CANR-1
See also TCWW 1, 2
McCaig, Snee
See McCaig, Donald
McCain, Becky Ray 1954- ... 209
See also SATA 138
McCain, Gillian 1966- ... 204
McCain, John (Sidney III) 1936- ... 185
McCain, Murray (David, Jr.)
1926-1981 ... CANR-15
Obituary ... 105
Earlier sketch in CA 1-4R
See also SATA 7
See also SATA-Obit 29
McCairen, Patricia 1940- ... 169
McCaleb, Robert Bruce 1950- ... 111
McCaleb, Walter Flavius 1873-1967 ... CAP-1
Earlier sketch in CA 9-10
McCall, Anthony
See Kane, Henry
McCall, Bruce 1935(?)- ... 174
McCall, Christina 1935-2005 ... 162
Obituary ... 239
See also Newman, Christina McCall
McCall, Dan (Elliott) 1940- ... 135
Brief entry ... 113
McCall, Daniel F(rancis) 1918- ... 17-20R
McCall, Dorothy Lawson 1889(?)-1982 ... 109
Obituary ... 106
McCall, Edith (Sansom) 1911- ... CANR-43
Earlier sketches in CA 1-4R, CANR-4, 19
See also SATA 6
McCall, George J(ohn) 1939- ... CANR-9
Earlier sketch in CA 21-24R
McCall, Grant 1943- ... 107
McCall, John Corey
See Morland, Nigel
McCall, John R(obert) 1920- ... CANR-1
Earlier sketch in CA 45-48
McCall, Marsh H(oward), Jr. 1939- ... 29-32R
McCall, Mary C(aldwell), Jr. 1904-1986
Obituary ... 118
McCall, Nathan 1955(?)- ... CANR-88
Earlier sketch in CA 146
See also AAYA 59
See also BW 3
See also CLC 86
McCall, Robert B(ooth) 1940- ... CANR-14
Earlier sketch in CA 33-36R
McCall, Storrs 1930- ... 147
McCall, Thomas (Lawson) 1913-1983
Obituary ... 108
McCall, Thomas S(creven) 1936- ... CANR-1
Earlier sketch in CA 49-52
McCall, Tom
See McCall, Thomas (Lawson)
McCall, Vincent
See Morland, Nigel
McCall, Virginia Nielsen
1909-2000 ... CANR-39
Earlier sketches in CA 1-4R, CANR-1, 17
See also SATA 13
McCall, Wendell
See Pearson, Ridley
McCall, William A(nderson)
1891-1982 ... CAP-1
Earlier sketch in CA 19-20
McCalley, John W(allace) 1916-1983 ... 110
McCall-Newman, Christina
See McCall, Christina
McCall Smith, Alexander 1948- ... SATA 73
McCallum, George E(dward) 1931- ... 37-40R
McCallum, Ian R(obert) M(ore)
1919-1987 ... 13-16R
Obituary ... 124
McCallum, James Dow 1893-1971
Obituary ... 104
McCallum, John D(ennis) 1924-1988 . CANR-4
Obituary ... 127
Earlier sketch in CA 53-56
McCallum, Neil 1916- ... 13-16R
McCallum, Phyllis
See Koch, Phyllis (Mae) McCallum
McCallum, Ronald Buchanan 1898-1973 . 5-8R
Obituary ... 89-92
McCallum, Shara 1972- ... 199
McCallum, Stephen 1960- ... SATA 91
McCallum, Taffy Gould 1942- ... 141
McCally, David 1949- ... 211
McCamant, James D. 1933- ... 211
McCamant, Jim
See McCamant, James D.
McCamant, John F. 1933- ... 25-28R
McCammon, Robert R(ick) 1952- ... CANR-88
Earlier sketches in CA 81-84, CANR-40
See also AAYA 17
See also DAM POP
See also HGG
See also SUFW 2
McCampbell, Darlene Z. 1942- ... SATA 83
McCampbell, James M. 1924- ... 49-52
McCamy, James L(ucian) 1906-1995 ... 5-8R
McCandless, Anthony
See McConville, Michael (Anthony)
McCandless, George T., Jr. 1947- ... 139
McCandless, Hugh (Douglas) 1907- ... 5-8R
McCandless, Perry 1917- ... CANR-1
Earlier sketch in CA 49-52
McCandless, Ruth Strout 1909-1994 ... 128
McCandlish, George E(dward)
1914-1975 ... 65-68
Obituary ... 61-64
McCanles, Michael (Frederick) 1936- ... 69-72
McCanless, Christel Ludewig 1939- ... 215
McCann, Arthur
See Campbell, John W(ood, Jr.)
McCann, Colum 1965- ... CANR-99
Earlier sketch in CA 152
See also DLB 267
McCann, Coolidge
See Fawcett, F(rank) Dubrez
McCann, Dennis P(atrick) 1945- ... 115
McCann, Eamonn 1943-
Brief entry ... 117
McCann, Edson
See del Rey, Lester and
Pohl, Frederik
McCann, Francis Daniel, Jr. 1938- ... CANR-43
Earlier sketch in CA 117
McCann, Frank D., Jr.
See McCann, Francis Daniel, Jr.
McCann, Gerald 1916- ... SATA 41
McCann, Graham 1961- ... 134
McCann, Helen 1948- ... 142
See also SATA 75
McCann, Jim 1951- ... 168
McCann, Kevin 1904-1981
Obituary ... 103
McCann, Maria 1956- ... 226
McCann, Richard (J.) 1940- ... 204
McCann, Sean 1929- ... 134
Brief entry ... 115
McCann, Thomas 1934- ... 73-76
McCann, Timmothy B. 1963- ... 200
McCannon, Dindga ... 114
See also SATA 41
McCannon, John 1967- ... 158
McCants, Olga 1901- ... CANR-14
Earlier sketch in CA 73-76
McCants, Sister Dorothea Olga
See McCants, Olga
McCants, William D. 1961- ... 149
See also SATA 82
McCardell, John (Malcolm, Jr.) 1949- ... 101
McCardle, Carl W(esley) 1904(?)-1972 . 37-40R
McCardle, Dorothy Bartlett 1904-1978 ... 85-88
Obituary ... 81-84
McCarey, Peter 1956- ... 138
McCargar, James (Goodrich) 1920- ... 137
McCarr, Ken(neth George) 1903-1977 ... 109
Obituary ... 106
McCarrick, Chris Shea
See Gorman, Edward
McCarrick, Earlean M. 1930- ... 103
McCarriston, Linda 1943- ... 206
See also CAAS 28
See also AMWS 14
McCarroll, Marion C(lyde) 1893(?)-1977
Obituary ... 73-76
McCarroll, Tolbert (Henry) 1931- ... CANR-116
Earlier sketch in CA 110
McCarry, Charles 1930- ... CANR-41
Earlier sketch in CA 103
McCart, Joyce 1936- ... 215
McCarten, Anthony (Peter Chanel Thomas
Aquinas) 1961- ... 206
See also CD 5, 6
McCarten, John (Bernard Francis James)
1916(?)-1974
Obituary ... 115
McCarter, Alan 1943- ... 107
McCarter, Neely Dixon 1929- ... 109
See also SATA 47
McCarter, P(ete) Kyle, (Jr.) 1945- ... 105
McCarthy, Agnes 1933- ... 17-20R
See also SATA 4
McCarthy, Barry (Wayne) 1943- ... CANR-61
Earlier sketches in CA 113, CANR-32
McCarthy, Bryan Eugene 1930- ... CP 1
McCarthy, Cavan 1943- ... 61-64
See also CP 1
McCarthy, Charlene B(arbara) 1929- ... 41-44R
McCarthy, Charles, Jr. 1933- ... CANR-101
Earlier sketch in CANR-42, 69
See also McCarthy, Cormac
See also CPW
See also CSW
See also DA3
See also DAM POP
See also MTCW 2
See also MTFW 2005
McCarthy, Clarence F. 1909-1982 ... 29-32R
McCarthy, Colin (John) 1951- ... 145
See also SATA 77
McCarthy, Cormac ... CANR-10
Earlier sketch in CA 13-16R
See also McCarthy, Charles, Jr.
See also AAYA 41
See also AMWS 8
See also BPFB 2
See also CLC 4, 57, 101, 204
See also CN 6, 7
See also DLB 6, 143, 256
See also EWL 3
See also LATS 1:2
See also MAL 5
See also TCLE 1:2
See also TCWW 2
McCarthy, Darry 1930- ... CANR-82
Earlier sketches in CA 5-8R, CANR-35
McCarthy, David (Edgar) 1925- ... 1-4R
McCarthy, David Seymour 1935- ... 115
McCarthy, Dennis John 1924- ... 21-24R
McCarthy, E(dmund) Jerome 1928-
Brief entry ... 112
McCarthy, Edward V., Jr. 1924- ... 93-96
McCarthy, Emily J(eannette) 1945- ... CANR-32
Earlier sketch in CA 113
McCarthy, Eugene J(oseph) 1916- ... CANR-2
Earlier sketch in CA 1-4R
McCarthy, Gary 1943- ... CANR-64
Earlier sketches in CA 69-72, CANR-22
See also TCWW 1, 2
McCarthy, Harold T. 1920- ... 127
McCarthy, James J(erome) 1927- ... 41-44R
McCarthy, Jenny 1972- ... 167
McCarthy, Joe
See McCarthy, Joseph Weston
McCarthy, John 1898-1994 ... 45-48
McCarthy, John J(oseph) 1909- ... 130
McCarthy, John P(atrick) 1938- ... 97-100
McCarthy, Joseph M(ichael) 1940- . CANR-104
Earlier sketch in CA 97-100
McCarthy, Joseph Raymond 1908-1957
Brief entry ... 111
McCarthy, Joseph Weston
1915-1980 ... CANR-1
Obituary ... 97-100
Earlier sketch in CA 1-4R
McCarthy, Justin 1945- ... 163
McCarthy, Kevin 1914- ... 214
McCarthy, Kevin M. 1940- ... CANR-134
Earlier sketches in CA 120, CANR-45
McCarthy, Kyle 1954- ... CANR-54
Earlier sketch in CA 127
McCarthy, Martha M(ay) 1945- ... CANR-31
Earlier sketch in CA 111
McCarthy, Marvin 1902-1983
Obituary ... 110
McCarthy, Mary (Therese)
1912-1989 ... CANR-64
Obituary ... 129
Earlier sketches in CA 5-8R, CANR-16, 50
Interview in ... CANR-16
See also AMW
See also BPFB 2
See also CLC 1, 3, 5, 14, 24, 39, 59
See also CN 1, 2, 3, 4
See also DA3
See also DLB 2
See also DLBY 1981
See also EWL 3
See also FW
See also MAL 5
See also MAWW
See also MTCW 1, 2
See also MTFW 2005
See also RGAL 4
See also SSC 24
See also TUS
McCarthy, Michael 1939- ... 127
McCarthy, Mignon ... 138
McCarthy, Nan(cy J.) 1961- ... 160
McCarthy, Patrick A. 1945- ... CANR-93
Earlier sketch in CA 145
McCarthy, Patrick Joseph 1922- ... 9-12R
McCarthy, Paul Eugene 1921- ... 103
McCarthy, Pete 1951-2004 ... 234
McCarthy, R(uby) Delphina (Polley)
1894-1977 ... CAP-1
Earlier sketch in CA 13-16
McCarthy, Ralph F. 1950- ... CANR-118
Earlier sketch in CA 145
See also SATA 139

McCarthy, Ray 1920(?)-1984
Obituary ... 112
McCarthy, Richard D(ean Max) 1927- ... 41-44R
McCarthy, Shaun (Lloyd) 1928- ... CANR-65
Earlier sketches in CA 9-12R, CANR-6
See also Cory, Desmond
See also CMW 4
McCarthy, Susan ... 235
McCarthy, Teresa
See Anderson, Teresa
McCarthy, Thomas 1954- ... 133
See also CP 7
McCarthy, Thomas N. 1927- ... 37-40R
McCarthy, Thomas P. 1920- ... 13-16R
McCarthy, Timothy G. 1929- ... 158
McCarthy, (Daniel) Todd 1950- ... 105
McCarthy, Wil 1966- ... CANR-104
Earlier sketch in CA 166
McCarthy, William E(dward) J(ohn)
1925- ... CANR-6
Earlier sketch in CA 9-12R
McCarthy-Tucker, Sherri N. 1958- ... 151
See also SATA 83
McCartney, Christine Maye 1949- ... 116
McCartney, James H(arold) 1925- ... 73-76
McCartney, Mike
See McCartney, Peter Michael
McCartney, (James) Paul 1942- ... CANR-111
Earlier sketch in CA 146
See also CLC 12, 35
McCartney, Peter Michael 1944- ... 109
McCartney, Scott 1960- ... 138
McCarty, Cheryl R. 1963- ... 222
McCarty, Clifford 1929- ... 17-20R
McCarty, Doran Chester 1931- ... CANR-31
Earlier sketches in CA 65-68, CANR-10
McCarty, Frederick H.
See McCarty, Hanoch
McCarty, Hanoch 1940- ... 161
McCarty, John 1944- ... 234
McCarty, Maclyn 1911-2005 ... 120
Obituary ... 235
McCarty, Norma
See Crandall, Norma
McCarty, Rega Kramer 1904-1986 ... 5-8R
See also SATA 10
McCary, James Leslie 1919-1978 ... 85-88
McCash, June Hall 1938- ... CANR-111
Earlier sketch in CA 37-40R
McCasland, S(elby) Vernon 1896-1970 ... 5-8R
McCaslin, Nellie 1914-2005 ... 33-36R
Obituary ... 236
See also SATA 12
McCaslin, Richard B(ryan) 1961- ... CANR-93
Earlier sketch in CA 144
McCaughey, Ellen
See Koshland, Ellen
McCaughey, Robert A(nthony) 1939- ... 77-80
McCaughrean, Geraldine 1951- ... CANR-111
Earlier sketches in CA 117, CANR-52
See also AAYA 23
See also CLR 38
See also MAICYA 2
See also MAICYAS 1
See also SATA 87, 139
See also YAW
McCaughren, Tom 1936- ... 142
See also CWRI 5
See also SATA 75
McCauley, Adam 1965- ... SATA 128
McCauley, Barbara 1939- ... 185
McCauley, Carole Spearin 1939- ... CANR-50
Earlier sketches in CA 57-60, CANR-8, 25
McCauley, Elfrieda B(abnick) 1915- ... 9-12R
McCauley, Leon 1908(?)-1984
Obituary ... 112
McCauley, Martin 1934- ... CANR-46
Earlier sketches in CA 107, CANR-23
McCauley, Michael F(rederick) 1947- . CANR-9
Earlier sketch in CA 61-64
McCauley, Michael J. 1961- ... 138
McCauley, Stephen (D.) 1955- ... 141
See also CLC 50
McCauley, Sue (Montgomery) 1941- ... 140
See also CN 5, 6, 7
McCaull, M. E.
See Bohlman, (Mary) Edna McCaull
McCaw, Kenneth Malcolm 1907-1989 ... 109
McCaw, Mabel Niedermeyer
1899-1995 ... CAP-2
Earlier sketch in CA 19-20
McCay, Bill ... BYA 10
McCay, (Zenas) Winsor 1869-1934 ... 169
See also AAYA 44
See also DLB 22
See also IDFW 3, 4
See also SATA 41, 134
McChesney, Kathryn 1936- ... 115
McClafferty, Carla Killough 1958- ... 207
See also SATA 137
McClain, Alva J. 1888-1968 ... 65-68
McClain, Carl S. 1899-1986 ... 37-40R
McClain, John O. 1942- ... CANR-30
Earlier sketch in CA 110
McClain, Leanita 1952(?)-1984
Obituary ... 112
McClain, Molly L. 1966- ... 213
McClain, Russell H(arding) 1910- ... CAP-2
Earlier sketch in CA 21-22
McClanahan, Ed 1932- ... 232
See also CSW
McClanahan, Rebecca ... 223
McClanan, Anne L. 1966- ... 227
McClane, A(lbert) J(ules) 1922-1991 ... 126
Obituary ... 136
Brief entry ... 106
See also DLB 171
McClane, Kenneth Anderson, Jr.
1951- ... CANR-21
Earlier sketches in CA 57-60, CANR-6
McClaren, Peter ... CLC 70
McClary, Andrew 1927- ... 61-64
McClary, Ben Harris 1931- ... CANR-3
Earlier sketch in CA 9-12R
McClary, Jane Stevenson 1919-1990 .. CANR-1
Obituary ... 130
Earlier sketch in CA 1-4R
See also SATA-Obit 64
McClary, Susan 1946- ... 154
McClatchy, C(harles) K(enny) 1858-1936 ... 179
See also DLB 25
McClatchy, Eleanor Grace 1895(?)-1980
Obituary ... 102
McClatchy, J(oseph) D(onald, Jr.)
1945- ... CANR-101
Earlier sketches in CA 105, CANR-44
See also AMWS 12
McClaurin, Irma Pearl 1952- ... 57-60
McClay, Wilfred M(ark) 1951- ... 149
McClean, Joseph Lucius 1919- ... CAP-1
Earlier sketch in CA 9-10
McCleary, Elliott H(arold) 1927- ... 57-60
McCleary, Robert A(ltwig) 1923-1973 ... 17-20R
Obituary ... 134
McCleary, William J(ames) 1938- ... 119
McCleery, Patsy R. 1925- ... CANR-111
Earlier sketch in CA 160
See also SATA 88, 133
McCleery, William (Thomas)
1911-2000 ... CANR-5
Obituary ... 188
Earlier sketch in CA 1-4R
McClellan, A(rchibald) W(illiam) 1908- ... 77-80
McClellan, Albert (Alfred) 1922- ... 122
McClellan, B(ernard) Edward 1939- ... 199
McClellan, Edwin 1925-
Brief entry ... 115
McClellan, George Marion 1860-1934 ... 125
See also BW 1
See also DLB 50
McClellan, Grant S(amuel) 1914-1989
Brief entry ... 114
McClellan, James (Paul) 1937- ... CANR-113
Earlier sketch in CA 21-24R
McClellan, James Edward, Jr. 1922- ... 25-28R
McClellan, Norris 1905-1984
Obituary ... 116
McClellan, Robert F., Jr. 1934- ... 33-36R
McClellan, Stephen T. 1942- ... 133
McClellan, Tierney
See McCafferty, (Barbara) Taylor
McClellan, William B.
See Strong, Charles S(tanley)
McClelland, Charles A. 1917- ... 85-88
McClelland, Charles E(dgar III) 1940- ... 33-36R
McClelland, David C(larence)
1917-1998 ... 25-28R
Obituary ... 165
McClelland, Diane Margaret 1931- .. CANR-59
Earlier sketch in CA 105
See also RHW
McClelland, Doug 1934- ... CANR-57
Earlier sketches in CA 41-44R, CANR-14, 31
McClelland, Ivy Lilian 1908- ... 29-32R
McClelland, Lucille Hudlin 1920- ... 21-24R
McClelland, Michael 1958- ... 219
McClelland, V(incent) Alan 1933- ... CANR-96
Earlier sketch in CA 103
McClendon, James William, Jr.
1924-2000 ... CANR-98
Obituary ... 192
Earlier sketches in CA 9-12R, CANR-5, 49
McClendon, Lise (Webb) 1952- ... CANR-73
Earlier sketch in CA 146
McClendon, Sarah (Newcomb)
1910-2003 ... 73-76
Obituary ... 214
McClennen, Sandra Elaine 1942- ... 103
McClintick, David 1940- ... 146
McClintock, Barbara 1902-1992 ... 161
McClintock, Barbara 1955- ... 160
See also SATA 57, 95, 146
McClintock, Marshall 1906-1967 ... CAP-1
Earlier sketch in CA 9-10
See also SATA 3
McClintock, May Garelick
See Garelick, May
McClintock, Mike
See McClintock, Marshall
McClintock, Robert (Mills) 1909-1976 .. CAP-2
Earlier sketch in CA 21-22
McClintock, Theodore 1902-1971 ... 73-76
Obituary ... 33-36R
See also SATA 14
McClinton, Katharine Morrison
1899-1993 ... CANR-5
Obituary ... 140
Earlier sketch in CA 1-4R
McClinton, Leon 1933- ... 65-68
See also SATA 11
McClory, Robert J(oseph) 1932- ... CANR-13
Earlier sketch in CA 77-80
McCloskey, Deirdre N(ansen)
1942- ... CANR-126
Earlier sketches in CA 57-60, CANR-8, 31
McCloskey, Donald N.
See McCloskey, Deirdre N(ansen)
McCloskey, Eunice (Loncoske)
1906-1983 ... 9-12R
McCloskey, H(enry) J(ohn) 1925- ... 110
McCloskey, Kevin 1951- ... SATA 79
McCloskey, Mark 1938- ... CANR-1
Earlier sketch in CA 45-48
See also CP 1
McCloskey, Maxine E(laine) 1927- ... 33-36R
McCloskey, Patrick 1948- ... CANR-38
Earlier sketch in CA 115
McCloskey, Paul N., Jr. 1927- ... 37-40R
McCloskey, (John) Robert
1914-2003 ... CANR-47
Obituary ... 217
Earlier sketch in CA 9-12R
See also CLR 7
See also CWRI 5
See also DLB 22
See also MAICYA 1, 2
See also SATA 2, 39, 100
See also SATA-Obit 146
McCloskey, William B(ertine), Jr. 1928- ... 101
McCloud, Jed
See Fearn, John Russell
McCloud, Scott
See McLeod, Scott Willard
McCloy, Helen (Worrell Clarkson)
1904-1994(?) ... CANR-44
Earlier sketch in CA 25-28R
See also CMW 4
See also DLB 306
See also MSW
McCloy, James F(loyd) 1941- ... 103
See also SATA 59
McCloy, Shelby Thomas 1898-1973(?) .. CAP-2
Earlier sketch in CA 23-24
McClung, Floyd, Jr. 1945- ... 61-64
McClung, Nellie Letitia 1873-1951 ... 181
See also DLB 92
See also FW
McClung, Patricia A. 1950- ... 119
McClung, Robert M(arshall) 1916- .. CANR-113
Earlier sketches in CA 13-16R, CANR-6, 21, 46, 77
See also AITN 2
See also CLR 11
See also MAICYA 1, 2
See also SAAS 15
See also SATA 2, 68, 135
McClung, William Alexander 1944- ... 113
McClure, Arthur F(rederick) II
1936- ... CANR-10
Earlier sketch in CA 65-68
McClure, Charles R(obert) 1949- ... CANR-53
Earlier sketches in CA 111, CANR-29
McClure, Gillian Mary 1948- ... 103
See also SATA 31
McClure, Grace 1918- ... 123
McClure, Hal 1921- ... 81-84
McClure, James (Howe) 1939- ... CANR-66
Earlier sketches in CA 69-72, CANR-44
See also CMW 4
See also DLB 276
See also MSW
McClure, Joanna 1930-
Brief entry ... 116
See also DLB 16
McClure, John A. 1945- ... 132
McClure, Larry 1941- ... CANR-26
Earlier sketch in CA 69-72
McClure, Laura (Kathleen) 1959- ... 208
McClure, Michael (Thomas) 1932- . CANR-131
Earlier sketches in CA 21-24R, CANR-17, 46, 77
See also BG 1:3
See also CAD
See also CD 5, 6
See also CLC 6, 10
See also CP 1, 2, 3, 4, 5, 6, 7
See also DLB 16
See also WP
McClure, Ron 1941- ... 37-40R
McClure, Ruth Koonz ... 107
McClure, S(amuel) S(idney) 1857-1949 ... 183
See also DLB 91
McClure, Sandy 1948- ... 154
McCluskey, John (A.), Jr. 1944- ... CANR-24
Earlier sketches in CA 57-60, CANR-7
See also BW 1
See also DLB 33
McCluskey, Neil Gerard 1921- ... CANR-12
Earlier sketch in CA 25-28R
McCole, John 1954- ... 148
McColgan, John (Joseph) 1946- ... 132
McCollam, James Graham
1913-1997 ... CANR-4
Earlier sketch in CA 45-48
McCollam, Jim
See McCollam, James Graham
McColley, Diane Kelsey 1934- ... 130
McColley, Kevin 1961- ... 148
See also SAAS 23
See also SATA 80
McColley, Robert (McNair) 1933- ... 13-16R
McCollough, Albert W. 1917- ... 102
McCollough, Celeste 1926- ... 13-16R
McCollough, Charles R(andolph)
1934- ... CANR-42
Earlier sketch in CA 118
McCollum, Audrey T(almage) 1924- ... 107
McCollum, Elmer Verner 1879-1967 ... CAP-1
Earlier sketch in CA 13-14
McCollum, Michael (Allen) 1946- ... 147
McComas, Annette Peltz 1911-1994 ... 109
Obituary ... 198
McComas, J(esse) Francis 1911-1978
Obituary ... 104
McComb, David G(lendinning)
1934- ... CANR-28
Earlier sketches in CA 29-32R, CANR-12
McComb, K(atherine Woods)
1895-1990 ... 13-16R
McCombs, Davis 1969- ... 195
McCombs, Don 1948- ... 115
McCombs, Judith 1939- ... 102
McCombs, Maxwell E(lbert) 1938- ... CANR-58
Earlier sketches in CA 73-76, CANR-12, 31
McCombs, Philip A(lgie) 1944- ... 49-52
McConagha, Alan 1932- ... 77-80
McConahay, John B. 1938- ... 110
McCondach, J. P. 1912-1996 ... 117
McConduit, Denise Walter 1950- ... 155
See also SATA 89
McCone, R(obert) Clyde 1915- ... 77-80
McConica, James Kelsey 1930- ... CANR-44
Earlier sketches in CA 33-36R, CANR-13
McConkey, Clarence 1925- ... 29-32R
McConkey, Dale Durant 1928- ... 93-96
McConkey, James (Rodney) 1921- ... CANR-41
Earlier sketch in CA 17-20R
McConkey, Kevin M(alcolm) 1952- ... 182
McConkie, Bruce R(edd) 1915-1985
Obituary ... 115
McConnel, Ian ... 237
McConnel, Patricia 1931- ... CANR-111
Earlier sketch in CA 133
McConnell, Allen 1923- ... 77-80
McConnell, Campbell R(obertson) 1928- .. 5-8R
McConnell, Dorothy 1900(?)-1989
Obituary ... 129
McConnell, Frank D(eMay)
1942-1999 ... CANR-70
Earlier sketch in CA 104
McConnell, Grant 1915-1993 ... 65-68
McConnell, James Douglas Rutherford
1915-1988 ... CANR-22
Obituary ... 125
Earlier sketches in CA 9-12R, CANR-6
See also SATA 40
See also SATA-Obit 56
McConnell, James V(ernon) 1925-1990 ... 5-8R
Obituary ... 131
McConnell, Jane ... 206
McConnell, Jean 1928- ... CANR-39
Earlier sketches in CA 85-88, CANR-16
McConnell, John Lithgow Chandos
1918- ... 53-56
McConnell, John W(ilkinson) 1907-1997 ... 107
McConnell, Jon Patrick 1928- ... 21-24R
McConnell, Malcolm 1939- ... 106
McConnell, Marie-Antoinette
1939- ... CANR-128
Earlier sketch in CA 163
McConnell, Raymond A(rnott) 1915-1979
Obituary ... 89-92
McConnell, Roland C(alhoun) 1910- ... 73-76
McConnell, T. R.
See McConnell, Thomas Raymond
McConnell, Terrance C(allihan)
1948- ... CANR-99
Earlier sketch in CA 110
McConnell, Thomas Raymond 1901-1989 . 118
McConnell, Virginia (McCorison)
1928- ... 13-16R
McConnell, William C 1917- ... 180
See also DLB 88
McConnell, William T(ate) 1941- ... 115
McConnochie, Mardi 1971- ... 208
McConnor, Vincent 1907-1997 ... CANR-23
Earlier sketch in CA 106
McConville, Michael (Anthony) 1925- ... 144
McConville, Sean 1943- ... 137
McCool, Charles 1964- ... 215
McCoole, Sinead ... 235
McCord, Anne 1942- ... 109
See also SATA 41
McCord, Arline F(ujii) 1934- ... CANR-1
Earlier sketch in CA 45-48
McCord, David (Thompson Watson)
1897-1997 ... CANR-38
Obituary ... 157
Earlier sketch in CA 73-76
See also CLR 9
See also CWRI 5
See also DLB 61
See also MAICYA 1, 2
See also MAICYAS 1
See also SATA 18
See also SATA-Obit 96
McCord, Guy
See Reynolds, Dallas McCord
McCord, Howard 1932- ... CANR-40
Earlier sketches in CA 9-12R, CANR-4, 18
See also CAAS 9
McCord, James I(ley) 1919- ... 21-24R
McCord, James W(alter), Jr. 1918(?)- ... AITN 1
McCord, Jean 1924- ... 49-52
See also SATA 34
McCord, John H(arrison) 1934- ... CANR-17
Earlier sketch in CA 25-28R
McCord, Louisa S. 1810-1879 ... DLB 248
McCord, Margaret 1916-2004 ... 161
Obituary ... 225
McCord, Pat Mauser
See McCord, Patricia
McCord, Patricia 1943-
See Mauser, Patricia Rhoads
See also SATA 159
McCord, Ted 1898-1976 ... IDFW 3, 4
McCord, Whip
See Norwood, Victor G(eorge) C(harles)
McCord, William Maxwell
1930-1992 ... CANR-46
Earlier sketches in CA 1-4R, 139, CANR-1
McCorduck, Pamela (Ann) 1940- ... CANR-36
Earlier sketches in CA 81-84, CANR-15
McCorison, Marcus Allen 1926- ... 33-36R
McCorkle, Chester O(liver), Jr. 1925- ... 110

Cumulative Index 387 McCutcheon

McCorkle, Jill (Collins) 1958- CANR-113
Earlier sketch in CA 121
See also CLC 51
See also CSW
See also DLB 234
See also DLBY 1987
McCorkle, Samuel Eusebius
1746-1811 .... DLB 37
McCormac, John W. 1926- 41-44R
McCormack, Arthur Gerard
1911-1992 .... CANR-47
Obituary 140
Earlier sketch in CA 5-8R
McCormack, Derek 231
McCormack, Eric 1938- 229
McCormack, Gavan Patrick 1937- ... CANR-22
Earlier sketch in CA 105
McCormack, Jerusha (Hall) 185
McCormack, John (E.) 187
McCormack, Mark H(ume)
1930-2003 .... CANR-97
Obituary 216
Earlier sketches in CA 49-52, CANR-17
Mccormack, Mike 1965- 171
McCormack, S(usan) Allison 1943- 111
McCormack, W(illiam) J(ohn)
1947- CANR-109
Earlier sketch in CA 145
McCormack, William A. 1932- 25-28R
McCormick, Anita Louise 1957- 146
McCormick, Anne (Elizabeth) O'Hare
1882(?)-1954
Brief entry 118
See also DLB 29
McCormick, Blaine 239
McCormick, Brooks
See Adams, William Taylor
McCormick, Charles H(oward) 1932- 170
McCormick, Claire
See Labus, Marta Haake
McCormick, David H. 1965- 174
McCormick, Dell J. 1892-1949 .... SATA 19
McCormick, Diana Festa
See Festa-McCormick, Diana
McCormick, (George) Donald (King)
1911-1998 .... CANR-65
Earlier sketches in CA 73-76, CANR-14, 32
See also SATA 14
McCormick, E(dward) Allen 1925- 107
McCormick, E(ric) H(all) 1906-1995 103
McCormick, Edgar L(indsley) 1914- 5-8R
McCormick, Edith (Joan) 1934- .... SATA 30
McCormick, Ernest J(ames) 1911-1990 93-96
McCormick, Jack (Sovern)
1929-1979 .... CANR-5
Obituary 85-88
Earlier sketch in CA 9-12R
McCormick, James (Phillip) 1920-2000 . 25-28R
Obituary 191
McCormick, James P(atton) 1911-1988
Obituary 125
McCormick, John O(wen) 1918- 17-20R
McCormick, Kenneth Dale
1906-1997 .... DLBY 1997
McCormick, Kimberly A. 1960- 228
See also SATA 153
McCormick, Mary
See McCormick, Sister Rose M(atthew)
McCormick, Merla Jean 1938- 97-100
McCormick, Mona 77-80
McCormick, Patricia 1956- 198
See also SATA 128
McCormick, Peter J(oseph) 1940- 112
McCormick, Richard Arthur
1922-2000 .... CANR-22
Obituary 188
Earlier sketch in CA 105
McCormick, Richard P(atrick) 1916- 9-12R
McCormick, Robert (K.) 1911-1985 115
Obituary 117
McCormick, Robert Rutherford
1880-1955 180
See also DLB 29
McCormick, Scott, Jr. 1929- 17-20R
McCormick, Sister Rose M(atthew)
1914- 21-24R
McCormick, Theresa E. 1939- 150
McCormick, Theresa Mickey
See McCormick, Theresa E.
McCormick, Virginia E(vans) 1934- 239
McCormick, Wilfred 1903-1983 .... CANR-1
Earlier sketch in CA 1-4R
McCormmach, Russell (Keith) 1933- 118
Brief entry 112
McCorquodale, Barbara
See Cartland, Barbara (Hamilton)
McCorquodale, Robin (Hunt) 121
McCorry, Vincent P(atrick) 1909-1990
Obituary 131
McCorvey, Norma (Leah) 1947- 147
McCourt, Edward (Alexander)
1907-1972 .... 9-12R
Obituary 103
See also CN 1, 2
See also DLB 88
See also SATA-Obit 28
McCourt, Frank 1930- CANR-138
Earlier sketches in CA 157, CANR-97
See also AAYA 61
See also AMWS 12
See also CLC 109
See also MTFW 2005
See also NCFS 1
McCourt, James 1941- CANR-98
Earlier sketch in CA 57-60
See also CLC 5
McCourt, Lisa 1964- 235
See also SATA 117, 159
McCourt, Malachy 1931- .... CLC 119
See also SATA 126
McCowen, Alec
See McCowen, Alexander Duncan
McCowen, Alexander Duncan 1925- 129
McCowen, George S(mith), Jr. 1935- 89-92
McCown, Clint 1952- 209
McCown, Edna 1947- 140
McCown, James Hart 1911-1991 89-92
McCown, Wayne (Gordon) 1942- 111
McCoy, Alfred W. 1945- CANR-17
Earlier sketch in CA 29-32R
McCoy, Andrew 117
McCoy, Arch
See Miller, Victor (Brooke)
McCoy, Charles A(llan) 1920- CANR-16
Earlier sketch in CA 65-68
McCoy, Charles W., Jr. 1946- 213
McCoy, D(onald) E(dward) 1923- 37-40R
McCoy, Donald R(ichard) 1928-1996 . CANR-2
Obituary 154
Earlier sketch in CA 5-8R
McCoy, Edain
See Taylor, Carol MacKenzie
McCoy, Elaine 1945- 119
McCoy, Esther 1904-1989
Obituary 130
McCoy, F(lorence) N(ina) 1925- 65-68
McCoy, Horace (Stanley) 1897-1955 155
Brief entry 108
See also AMWS 13
See also CMW 4
See also DLB 9
See also TCLC 28
McCoy, Iola Fuller 13-16R
See also SATA 3
McCoy, J(oseph) J(erome) 1917- CANR-6
Earlier sketch in CA 13-16R
See also SATA 8
McCoy, John P(leasant) 1906(?)-1974
Obituary 49-52
McCoy, Joseph A(loysius) 1911-1981 .... 1-4R
McCoy, Karen Kawamoto 1953- .... SATA 82
McCoy, Kathleen 1945- CANR-47
Earlier sketches in CA 81-84, CANR-22
McCoy, Kathy
See McCoy, Kathleen
McCoy, Lois (Rich) 1941- CANR-22
Earlier sketch in CA 101
See also SATA 38
McCoy, Malachy
See Caulfield, Malachy Francis
McCoy, Marjorie Casebier 1934-1985
Obituary 114
McCoy, Marshall
See Meares, Leonard Frank
McCoy, Maureen 1949- 119
McCoy, Max 1958- 153
McCoy, Mick
See Fearn, John Russell
McCoy, Ralph E(dward) 1915- 37-40R
McCoy, Ronald 1947- 81-84
McCoy, Roy 1935- 29-32R
McCoy, Samuel (Duff) 1882-1964
Obituary 93-96
McCoy, Tim(othy John Fitzgerald)
1891-1978 81-84
Obituary 77-80
McCoy, William C. 1945- 231
McCracken, (James) David 1939- 119
McCracken, Elizabeth 1966- CANR-109
Earlier sketch in CA 167
McCracken, Esther 1902-1971
Obituary 33-36R
McCracken, George E(nglert)
1904-1986 .... 17-20R
McCracken, Glenn 1908- 5-8R
McCracken, Harold 1894-1983 107
McCracken, J(ohn) L(eslie) 1914- 25-28R
McCracken, James (Eugene) 1926-1988
Obituary 126
McCracken, Karen Harden 1905-1992 122
McCracken, Kay
See McCracken, Karen Harden
McCracken, Kenneth David 1901-1983
Obituary 109
McCracken, Linda D. 1950- 215
McCracken, Mary Lou 1943- 61-64
McCracken, Paul Winston 1915- CANR-6
Earlier sketch in CA 5-8R
McCracken, Samuel 111
McCrackin, Mark (Owens) 1949- 107
McCrady, Lady 1951- 93-96
See also SATA 16
McCrae, Hugh 1876-1958 .... DLB 260
McCrae, John 1872-1918
Brief entry 109
See also DLB 92
See also PFS 5
See also TCLC 12
McCrank, Lawrence J(oseph) 1945- .. CANR-29
Earlier sketch in CA 110
McCrary, Crystal
See Anthony, Crystal McCrary
McCrary, (James) Peyton 1943- 85-88
McCraw, James Edward 1943- 101
McCraw, Louise Harrison 1893-1975 .... 1-4R
Obituary 103
McCraw, Thomas K(incaid) 1940- .. CANR-126
Earlier sketches in CA 33-36R, CANR-17
McCray, Mike
See Preston, John
See also GLL 1
McCrea, James (Craig, Jr.) 1920- CANR-8
Earlier sketch in CA 5-8R
See also SATA 3
McCrea, Joan Marie Ryan 1922- 57-60
McCrea, Ruth (Pirman) 1921- CANR-8
Earlier sketch in CA 5-8R
See also SATA 3
McCrea, William Hunter 1904-1999 107
McCreadie, Marsha A. 1943- 111
McCready, Jack
See Powell, (Oval) Talmage
McCready, Warren T(homas) 1915- 21-24R
McCreary, Alf(red) 1940- CANR-31
Earlier sketch in CA 69-72
McCreary, W(illiam) Burgess
1894-1981 .... CAP-1
Earlier sketch in CA 19-20
McCreery, Charles (Anthony Selby)
1942- 25-28R
McCreigh, James
See Pohl, Frederik
McCrimmon, Barbara (Smith) 1918- 108
McCrimmon, James M(cNab) 1908- 9-12R
McCrindle, Joseph F(eder) 1923- 29-32R
McCrohan, Donna 1947- 111
McCrone, John (Robert) 1957- 139
McCrone, Kathleen E. 1941- 130
McCrorey, Sanders
See Counselman, Mary Elizabeth
McCrorie, Edward (P.) 1936- 153
McCrory, Donald P(eter) 1943- 225
McCrory, Moy (Ellen) 1953- 130
McCroskey, James C(layborne)
1936- CANR-13
Earlier sketch in CA 77-80
McCrossen, V(incent) A(loysius) 1918- 53-56
McCrosson, Doris Ross 1923- 17-20R
McCrum, Mark 1958- 198
McCrum, Robert 1953- 101
McCrumb, Sharyn 1948- CANR-143
Earlier sketch in CA 168
See also AAYA 27
See also CMW 4
See also CSW
See also DLB 306
See also SATA 109
McCuaig, Ronald 1908- 114
See also CP 1, 2
McCue, Frances 1962- 139
McCue, George R(obert) 1910- 110
McCue, Lillian Bueno 1902-1993 .... CANR-63
Obituary 142
Earlier sketches in CA 1-4R, CANR-2
See also CMW 4
McCue, Lisa (Emiline) 1959- 136
See also SATA 65
McCuen, Jo Ray 1929- 85-88
McCuen, John J(oachim) 1926- 21-24R
McCullagh, Joseph B. 1842-1896 .... DLB 23
McCullagh, Sheila K(athleen) 1920- 110
McCullagh, Suzanne Folds 1951- 127
McCullar, Michael 1951- 122
McCullen, Andrew
See Arthur, Robert, (Jr.)
McCullers, (Lula) Carson (Smith)
1917-1967 .... CANR-132
Obituary 25-28R
Earlier sketches in CA 5-8R, CANR-18
See also CABS 1, 3
See also AAYA 21
See also AMW
See also AMWC 2
See also BPFB 2
See also CDALB 1941-1968
See also CLC 1, 4, 10, 12, 48, 100
See also DA
See also DA3
See also DAB
See also DAC
See also DAM MST, NOV
See also DFS 5, 18
See also DLB 2, 7, 173, 228
See also EWL 3
See also EXPS
See also FW
See also GLL 1
See also LAIT 3, 4
See also MAL 5
See also MAWW
See also MTCW 1, 2
See also MTFW 2005
See also NFS 6, 13
See also RGAL 4
See also RGSF 2
See also SATA 27
See also SSC 9, 24
See also SSFS 5
See also TCLC 155
See also TUS
See also WLC
See also YAW
McCulley, Johnston 1883-1958
Brief entry 115
See also TCWW 1, 2
McCullin, Don(ald) 1935- 141
Brief entry 106
McCulloch, Alan McLeod 1907- 104
McCulloch, Derek (Ivor Breashur) 1897-1967
Obituary 109
See also SATA-Obit 29
McCulloch, Frank E(liot) 1898-1984 112
McCulloch, John I(rvin) B(eggs) 1909(?)-1983
Obituary 110
McCulloch, John Tyler
See Burroughs, Edgar Rice
McCulloch, Joseph 1900-1990
Obituary 131
McCulloch, Sarah
See Ure, Jean
McCulloch, Thomas 1776-1843 .... DLB 99
McCulloch, Warren S(turgis)
1898-1969 .... CAP-2
Earlier sketch in CA 21-22
McCulloh, William Ezra 1931- 49-52
McCullough, Bob 1956- 235
McCullough, Bonnie Runyan 1944- . CANR-18
Earlier sketch in CA 102
McCullough, Colleen 1937- CANR-139
Earlier sketches in CA 81-84, CANR-17, 46, 67, 98
See also AAYA 36
See also BPFB 2
See also CLC 27, 107
See also CPW
See also DA3
See also DAM NOV, POP
See also MTCW 1, 2
See also MTFW 2005
See also RHW
McCullough, Constance Mary
1912-1988 .... CANR-5
Earlier sketch in CA 1-4R
McCullough, Dale Richard 1933- 125
McCullough, David (Gaub) 1933- .. CANR-107
Earlier sketches in CA 49-52, CANR-2, 31, 53
See also MTFW 2005
See also SATA 62
McCullough, David Willis 1937- CANR-104
Earlier sketch in CA 143
McCullough, Donald W. 1949- CANR-142
Earlier sketch in CA 130
McCullough, Edo
See McCullough, Edward Joseph Tilyou
McCullough, Edward Joseph Tilyou
1901(?)-1987
Obituary 123
McCullough, Frances Monson 1938- 41-44R
See also SATA 8
McCullough, Helen Craig 1918- 151
McCullough, James P., Jr. 1936- 225
McCullough, John Gerard 1917-1984
Obituary 111
McCullough, Kate 1961- 226
McCullough, Ken(neth Douglas)
1943- CANR-22
Earlier sketch in CA 45-48
McCullough, Sharon Pierce 1943- 200
See also SATA 131
McCullough, W. S.
See McCullough, W(illiam) Stewart
McCullough, W(illiam) Stewart
1902-1982 .... 21-24R
Obituary 135
McCully, Emily Arnold 180
See also Arnold, Emily
See also CLR 46
See also SAAS 7
See also SATA 5, 110, 134
See also SATA-Essay 134
McCully, Ethel Walbridge 1896-1980
Obituary 103
McCully, Helen 1902(?)-1977 81-84
Obituary 73-76
McCully, Marilyn 234
McCully, Robert (Stephen) 1921- 53-56
McCune, Dan
See Haas, Dorothy F.
McCune, Shannon (Boyd-Bailey)
1913-1993 .... CANR-46
Obituary 140
Earlier sketches in CA 77-80, CANR-13
McCunn, Ruthanne Lum 1946- CANR-96
Earlier sketches in CA 119, CANR-43
See also AAL
See also DLB 312
See also LAIT 2
See also SATA 63
McCurdy, Charles Robert 1926- 5-8R
McCurdy, Frances Lea 1906-1981 .... 41-44R
McCurdy, Harold Grier 1909-1999 .... CANR-7
Earlier sketch in CA 17-20R
McCurdy, Howard E(arl) 1941- CANR-120
Earlier sketch in CA 81-84
McCurdy, Jack 1933- 69-72
McCurdy, Michael (Charles) 1942- ... CANR-50
Earlier sketches in CA 69-72, CANR-25
See also MAICYA 2
See also MAICYAS 1
See also SATA 13, 82, 147
McCurley, Foster R., Jr. 1937- 134
Brief entry 107
McCurtin, Peter .... TCWW 1, 2
McCusker, John J(ames) 1939- 102
McCutchan, Ann 196
McCutchan, J(ohn) Wilson 1909- 5-8R
McCutchan, Philip (Donald)
1920-1996 .... CANR-66
Earlier sketches in CA 9-12R, CANR-5, 22, 46
See also CMW 4
See also RHW
McCutchen, Samuel Proctor
1909-1966 .... CAP-1
Earlier sketch in CA 9-10
McCutcheon, Elsie (Mary Jackson) 1937- ... 133
See also SATA 60
McCutcheon, George Barr 1866-1928 ..... RHW
McCutcheon, Hugh Davie-Martin
1909-1999 .... CANR-5
Earlier sketch in CA 9-12R
McCutcheon, James
See Lundgren, Paul Arthur
McCutcheon, James M(iller) 1932- 45-48
McCutcheon, John 1952- 164
See also SATA 97

McCutcheon 388 CONTEMPORARY AUTHORS

McCutcheon, John Tinney, Jr. 1917- 69-72
McCutcheon, Lynn E(llis) 1944- 57-60
McCutcheon, W(illiam) A(lan) 1934- 53-56
McCutcheon, W(illiam) J(ohn) 1928- 41-44R
McDade, Thomas M. 1907- CAP-1
Earlier sketch in CA 13-16
McDaniel, Becky Bring 1953- 117
See also SATA 61
McDaniel, Bruce A. 1946- 227
McDaniel, C. Yates 1907(?)-1983
Obituary 109
McDaniel, David (Edward)
1939-1977 .... CANR-10
Earlier sketch in CA 21-24R
McDaniel, Elsiebeth 65-68
McDaniel, Eugene B(arker) 1931- 65-68
McDaniel, George William 1944- 116
McDaniel, Gerald 1936- 213
McDaniel, Gerald G(reen)
1945-2001 .... CANR-99
Earlier sketch in CA 122
McDaniel, Herman 1938- 111
McDaniel, John N(oble) 1941- 57-60
McDaniel, Joseph Milton, Jr. 1902-1980
Obituary 97-100
McDaniel, Lurlene 1944- CANR-118
Earlier sketch in CA 148
See also AAYA 15, 38
See also SATA 71, 146
McDaniel, Roderick D. 1927- 37-40R
McDaniel, Ruel R(obly) 1896-1971 .... CAP-1
Earlier sketch in CA 13-14
McDaniel, Sylvia (J.) 1956- 217
McDaniel, Walton Brooks 1871-1978 77-80
Obituary 81-84
McDaniels, Carl 1930- 93-96
McDaniels, Darryl 1964- 224
McDaniels, Pellom III 1968- 192
See also SATA 121
McDarrah, Fred W(illiam) 1926- CANR-114
Earlier sketches in CA 81-84, CANR-24, 49
McDavid, John E., Jr. 1934- 37-40R
McDavid, John W(alter, Jr.) 1933- 41-44R
McDavid, Raven I(oor), Jr. 1911-1984 ... 41-44R
Obituary 114
McDavid, Virginia (Glenn) 1926- 37-40R
McDearmon, Kay CANR-11
Earlier sketch in CA 69-72
See also SATA 20
McDermid, Val 1955- 228
McDermott, A(gnes) Charlene Senape
1937- 77-80
McDermott, Alice 1953- CANR-126
Earlier sketches in CA 109, CANR-40, 90
See also CLC 90
See also CN 7
See also DLB 292
See also MTFW 2005
McDermott, Beatrice Schmulling 17-20R
McDermott, Beverly Brodsky 1941- . CANR-16
Earlier sketch in CA 65-68
See also SATA 11
McDermott, Catherine 1952- 125
McDermott, Charles J(ames)
1905-1985 .... CAP-1
Earlier sketch in CA 13-16
McDermott, Eleni .... SATA 156
McDermott, Geoffrey (Lyster) 1912- 73-76
McDermott, Gerald (Edward) 1941- 85-88
See also AITN 2
See also CLR 9
See also CWRI 5
See also MAICYA 1, 2
See also SATA 16, 74, 163
McDermott, Jeanne 1955- 199
McDermott, John F(rancis), Jr. 1929-
Brief entry 114
McDermott, John Francis (III)
1902-1981 .... CANR-6
Earlier sketch in CA 5-8R
McDermott, John J(oseph) 1932- CANR-101
Earlier sketch in CA 73-76
McDermott, John R(alph) 1921-1977
Obituary 69-72
McDermott, Michael 1962- .... SATA 76
McDermott, Richard A. 1948- 204
McDermott, Robert
See Hawley, Donald Thomas
McDermott, Robert A(nthony) 1939- 57-60
McDermott, Sister Maria Concepta
1913-1989 .... 17-20R
McDermott, Thomas J. 1915- 9-12R
McDermott, Walsh 1909-1981
Obituary 105
McDevitt, Jack 1935- CANR-100
Earlier sketches in CA 149, CANR-88
See also SFW 4
McDevitt, John Charles
See McDevitt, Jack
See also SATA 94, 155
McDill, Edward L. 1930- 77-80
McDole, Carol
See Farley, Carol (J.)
McDollu, Michael A. 1946- .... DLBY 1987
McDonagh, Don(ald Francis) 1932- ... CANR-1
Earlier sketch in CA 49-52
McDonagh, Enda 1930- 101
McDonagh, John Michael 1944- 109
McDonagh, Martin 1970(?)- CANR-141
Earlier sketch in CA 171
See also CD 6
McDonald, Alan (Patrick) 1949- 124
McDonald, Angus Henry 1904(?)-1990
Obituary 130
McDonald, Angus W(illiam), Jr. 1941- 105
McDonald, Archie P(hilip) 1935- CANR-15
Earlier sketch in CA 81-84
McDonald, Brix 1952- 175
McDonald, Christie (V.) 1942- 144
McDonald, Claude C(omstock), Jr.
1925- 29-32R
McDonald, Collin 1943- 148
See also SATA 79
McDonald, David J(ohn) 1902-1979 45-48
Obituary 125
McDonald, Dianna
See Shomaker, Dianna
McDonald, Elvin 1937- CANR-34
Earlier sketches in CA 5-8R, CANR-8
McDonald, Erwin L(awrence) 1907- 73-76
McDonald, Eva (Rose) 1909-1998 ...... CANR-6
Earlier sketch in CA 13-16R
McDonald, Forrest 1927- CANR-103
Earlier sketches in CA 9-12R, CANR-5
See also DLB 17
McDonald, Frank J(ames) 1941- 97-100
McDonald, Gerald D(oan) 1905-1970 .. CAP-1
Earlier sketch in CA 11-12
See also SATA 3
Mcdonald, Gregory (Christopher)
1937- CANR-77
Earlier sketches in CA 5-8R, CANR-3, 42
See also CMW 4
McDonald, Hugh C(hisholm)
1913-1984 65-68
McDonald, Hugh Dermot 1910- CANR-3
Earlier sketch in CA 9-12R
McDonald, Ian .... SFW 4
McDonald, Ian A(rchie) 1933- CANR-52
Earlier sketches in CA 29-32R, CANR-26
See also CP 1, 7
McDonald, Iverach 1908- 138
McDonald, J. I(an) H. 1933- CANR-119
Earlier sketch in CA 148
McDonald, James Robert 1934- 41-44R
McDonald, Jamie
See Heide, Florence Parry
McDonald, Janet 1953- 184
See also SATA 148
McDonald, Jeanne Gray 1917-1996 180
McDonald, Jerry N(ealon) 1944- CANR-31
Earlier sketch in CA 105
McDonald, Jill (Masefield)
1927-1982 .... CANR-12
Obituary 105
Earlier sketch in CA 65-68
See also SATA 13
See also SATA-Obit 29
McDonald, John D(ennis) 1906-1998 ... CAP-2
Obituary 172
Earlier sketch in CA 19-20
McDonald, Joyce 1946- 168
See also AAYA 47
See also SATA 101
McDonald, Julie 1929- CANR-43
Earlier sketches in CA 29-32R, CANR-12
McDonald, Julie Jensen
See McDonald, Julie
McDonald, Kay L(aureen) 1934- 57-60
McDonald, Lee Cameron 1925- 5-8R
McDonald, Linda 1939- CANR-4
Earlier sketch in CA 49-52
McDonald, Lucile Saunders
1898-1992 .... CANR-18
Earlier sketches in CA 1-4R, CANR-4
See also SATA 10
McDonald, (Mary) Lynn 1940- 101
McDonald, Mary Ann 1956- .... SATA 84
McDonald, Mary Reynolds 1888- CAP-1
Earlier sketch in CA 13-16
McDonald, Megan 1959- CANR-131
Earlier sketch in CA 135
See also CLR 94
See also SATA 67, 99, 148, 151
See also SATA-Essay 151
McDonald, Meme 1954- 184
See also MAICYA 2
See also SATA 112
McDonald, Mercedes 1956- 164
See also SATA 97
McDonald, Nan(cy May) 1921- .... CP 1, 2
McDonald, Nicholas 1923- 13-16R
McDonald, Paula 1939(?)- .... AITN 1
McDonald, Pauline 1907- 33-36R
McDonald, (Duncan) Peter 1962- 124
McDonald, Richard C. 1935(?)- .... AITN 1
McDonald, Robert 1943- 115
McDonald, Roger 1941- 101
See also CN 2
McDonald, Stephen L(ee) 1924- 89-92
McDonald, Walter (Robert) 1934- CANR-58
Earlier sketches in CA 73-76, CANR-12, 31
See also DLB 105
See also DLBD 9
McDonald, William Andrew
1913-2000 .... 41-44R
McDonald, William Francis
1898-1976 .... 37-40R
McDonald, William U(lma), Jr. 1927- ... 17-20R
McDonell, Chris 1960- 208
See also SATA 138
McDonell, J(oan) M. CANR-130
Earlier sketch in CA 149
McDonell, Nick 1984- 205
McDonnell, Christine 1949- CANR-23
Earlier sketch in CA 107
See also SATA 34, 115
McDonnell, Evelyn 236
McDonnell, Flora (Mary) 1963- ... SATA 90, 146
McDonnell, Helen M(argaret)
1923- CANR-13
Earlier sketch in CA 33-36R
McDonnell, Jinny
See McDonnell, Virginia B(leecker)
McDonnell, Kilian (Perry) 1921- CANR-89
Earlier sketches in CA 33-36R, CANR-34
McDonnell, Lois Eddy 1914-2001 .... 5-8R
See also SATA 10
McDonnell, Patrick 1956- 225
McDonnell, Rea 1942- 127
McDonnell, Robert F. 1928- 17-20R
McDonnell, Virginia B(leecker)
1917- CANR-8
Earlier sketch in CA 21-24R
McDonogh, Gary Wray 1952- 127
McDonough, George Edward 1924- 41-44R
McDonough, Jack 1944- 125
McDonough, James Lee 1934- 73-76
McDonough, James R(ichard) 1946- 146
McDonough, Jerome 1946- CANR-27
Earlier sketch in CA 109
McDonough, Jerry
See McDonough, Jerome
McDonough, Jimmy 1960(?)- 208
McDonough, Kathryn Susan
1943- CANR-127
See also McDonough, Kaye
McDonough, Kaye
See McDonough, Kathryn Susan
See also CAAS 29
McDonough, Nancy 1935- 57-60
McDonough, Peter 1939- CANR-117
Earlier sketch in CA 138
McDonough, Sheila 1928- 77-80
McDonough, Thomas E(dmund) 1929- . 21-24R
McDonough, Tom 1969- 231
McDonough, William K. 1900-1982 ..... CAP-1
Earlier sketch in CA 9-10
McDonough, Yona Zeldis 1957- 191
See also SATA 73
McDormand, Thomas Bruce
1904-1988 .... CAP-1
Earlier sketch in CA 19-20
McDougal, Dennis 1947- CANR-136
Earlier sketch in CA 169
McDougal, James B. 1941-1998 174
McDougal, Jim
See McDougal, James B.
McDougal, Myres Smith 1906-1998 .. CANR-6
Obituary 169
Earlier sketch in CA 5-8R
McDougal, Stan
See Diamant, Lincoln
McDougal, Stuart Y(eatman) 1942- .. CANR-13
Earlier sketch in CA 73-76
McDougal, Susan 1954- 218
McDougall, Anne 1926- 104
McDougall, Bonnie S. 1941- 127
McDougall, Colin (Malcolm) 1917-1984 153
See also DLB 68
Mcdougall, Derek 1945- 191
McDougall, Donald 1907- 81-84
McDougall, Gay J. 1947- 155
See also BW 3
McDougall, John Lorne 1900- 37-40R
McDougall, Joyce 1920- CANR-82
McDougall, Joyce 1926- CANR-36
Earlier sketches in CA 25-28R, CANR-11
McDougall, Marina 1945- 97-100
McDougall, Walter A(llan) 1946- CANR-77
Brief entry 121
Earlier sketch in CA 126
Interview in CA-126
McDow, Gerald
See Scortia, Thomas N(icholas)
McDowall, Robert William 1914-1987
Obituary 123
McDowall, Roddy 1928-1998 167
McDowell, (Ho)Bart (Kelliston, Jr.)
1923- 25-28R
McDowell, Charles (Rice), Jr. 1926- 1-4R
McDowell, Crosby
See Freeman, John Crosby
McDowell, David 1918(?)-1985
Obituary 115
McDowell, Dimmes 1925(?)-1976
Obituary 69-72
McDowell, Edward Allison, Jr.
1898-1975 .... CAP-2
Earlier sketch in CA 21-22
McDowell, Edwin (Stewart) 1935- 9-12R
McDowell, Elizabeth Tibbals 1912-1981 .. 5-8R
McDowell, Frank 1911-1981 53-56
McDowell, Frederick P(eter) W(oll)
1915- CANR-5
Earlier sketch in CA 1-4R
McDowell, Gary L. 1949- 145
McDowell, John (Henry) 1942- 103
McDowell, John Holmes 1946- 97-100
McDowell, Katharine Sherwood Bonner
1849-1883
See Bonner, Sherwood
See also DLB 239
McDowell, L(ee) R(ussell) 1941- 218
McDowell, Margaret B(laine) 1923- 69-72
McDowell, Michael (McEachern)
1950-1999 .... CANR-75
Obituary 188
Earlier sketches in CA 93-96, CANR-29
See also HGG
McDowell, Michael P(aul) Kube
See Kube-McDowell, Michael P(aul)
McDowell, R(obert) B(rendan) 1913- 227
McDowell, Robert 1953- CANR-120
Earlier sketch in CA 127
See also DLB 282
McDowell, Robert Emmett 1914-1975 ...... 1-4R
Obituary 103
McDowell, Virginia (Duncan) H(ecker)
1933- 85-88
McDuff, Margaret Dusa 1945- 169
McEachern, Theodore 1928- 21-24R
McEachin, James 1930- CANR-99
Earlier sketch in CA 160
McElaney, (Joseph) Paul 1922- 9-12R
McElderry, Bruce R., Jr. 1900-1970 .... CAP-1
Earlier sketch in CA 13-14
McEldowney, (Richard) Dennis 1926- 103
McEldowney, Eugene 1943- 158
McEleney, Neil Joseph 1927-2004 115
Obituary 229
McElfresh, (Elizabeth) Adeline 1918- 1-4R
See also RHW
McElhaney, James W(illson) 1937- 85-88
McElhanon, K(enneth) A(ndrew)
1939- CANR-5
Earlier sketch in CA 53-56
McElheny, Victor K(ing) 1935- 195
McEllhenney, John Galen 1934- 53-56
McElligott, Matt(hew) 1968- .... SATA 135
McElmeel, Sharron L. 1942- CANR-92
Earlier sketch in CA 145
See also SATA 128
McElmurray, Karen Salyer 1956- 203
McElmurry, Jill .... SATA 159
McElrath, Damian (Edmund) 1928-
Brief entry 111
McElrath, Dennis Cornealius 1929- 45-48
McElrath, Frances .... TCWW 2
McElrath, Joseph R(ichard), Jr. 1945- 65-68
McElrath, William N. 1932- CANR-93
Earlier sketches in CA 77-80, CANR-35
See also SATA 65
McElrath-Eslick, Lori 1960- .... SATA 96
McElroy, Bernard (Patrick, Jr.)
1938-1991 61-64
Obituary 136
McElroy, Colleen J(ohnson) 1935- CANR-38
Earlier sketches in CA 49-52, CANR-2, 17
See also CAAS 21
See also BW 2
See also EXPP
See also PFS 3
McElroy, Davis Dunbar 1917- 37-40R
McElroy, Elam E. 1922- 57-60
McElroy, John Alexander 1913- 17-20R
McElroy, John Harmon 1934- 201
McElroy, Joseph (Prince) 1930- 17-20R
See also CLC 5, 47
See also CN 3, 4, 5, 6, 7
McElroy, Lee
See Kelton, Elmer
McElroy, Paul Simpson 1902-1989 .... 5-8R
McElroy, Susan Chernak 1952- 176
McElroy, Thomas P(arker), Jr.
1914-1994 73-76
McElroy, Wendy CANR-102
Earlier sketch in CA 152
McElvaine, Robert S(tuart) 1947- CANR-104
Earlier sketch in CA 114
McElwee, William (Lloyd) 1907-1979 57-60
Obituary 104
McEnery, John H. 1925- 134
McEnroe, Colin (Welles) 1954- 127
McEnroe, John 1959- 217
McEntee, Dorothy (Layng) 1902- .... SATA 37
McEntire, Reba (Nell) 1954(?)- 147
McEuen, Melissa A(nn) 1961- 188
McEvedy, Colin (Peter) 1930- 97-100
McEvilley, Thomas 1939- 140
McEvoy, Dennis 1918- 73-76
McEvoy, Harry K(irby) 1910-1993 .... 17-20R
McEvoy, Hubert 1899- 5-8R
McEvoy, James III 1940-1976 .... CAP-2
Earlier sketch in CA 33-36
McEvoy, Marjorie Harte 1909-1989 . CANR-40
Earlier sketches in CA 5-8R, CANR-2, 18
McEwan, Barbara 1926- 139
McEwan, Ian (Russell) 1948- CANR-132
Earlier sketches in CA 61-64, CANR-14, 41, 69, 87
See also BEST 90:4
See also BRWS 4
See also CLC 13, 66, 169
See also CN 3, 4, 5, 6, 7
See also DAM NOV
See also DLB 14, 194, 319
See also HGG
See also MTCW 1, 2
See also MTFW 2005
See also RGSF 2
See also SUFW 2
See also TEA
McEwan, Jenny 1951- 124
McEwan, Keith 1926- 21-24R
McEwan, (John) Neil 1946- 130
McEwan, Peter J(ames) M(ichael)
1924- CANR-17
Earlier sketch in CA 25-28R
McEwen, Bruce S. 1938- 224
McEwen, Christian 1956- CANR-121
Earlier sketch in CA 162
McEwen, Helena 1961- 199
McEwen, Robert (Lindley) 1926-1980
Obituary 101
See also SATA-Obit 23
Mcfadden, Bernard Adolphus 1868-1955 ... 184
Mcfadden, Bernarr
See Mcfadden, Bernard Adolphus
Mcfadden, Bernice L. 1965- 224
McFadden, Charles Joseph 1909-1990 77-80
McFadden, Cyra 1937- 77-80
McFadden, David 1940- 104
Interview in CA-104
See also CLC 48
See also CP 1, 2, 3, 4, 5, 6, 7
See also DLB 60
McFadden, Dorothy Loa 1902-1997 ..... 17-20R

Cumulative Index 389 McGrath

McFadden, George 1916- 111
McFadden, James A., Jr. 1913-2000 ...... 17-20R
McFadden, Johnjoe 1956- 231
McFadden, Kevin Christopher
1961(?)- CANR-141
Earlier sketches in CA 136, CANR-66
See also Pike, Christopher
See also AAYA 13
See also CLR 29
See also HGG
See also JRDA
See also MAICYA 2
See also SATA 68, 156
See also YAW
McFadden, Maggie
See McFadden, Margaret (H.)
McFadden, Margaret (H.) 1941- CANR-92
Earlier sketch in CA 115
McFadden, Robert D(ennis) 1937- ... CANR-15
Earlier sketch in CA 85-88
McFadden, Roy 1921-1999 144
Obituary 185
Brief entry 111
See also CP 1, 2
McFadden, Steven (S. H.) 1948- 138
McFadden, Thomas M(ore) 1935- 89-92
McFadyean, Melanie 1950- 127
McFague, Sallie 1933- CANR-11
Earlier sketch in CA 21-24R
McFall, Christie 1918- 5-8R
See also SATA 12
McFall, Frances Elizabeth Clarke
See Grand, Sarah
McFall, Kathleen 1960- 182
McFall, Lynne 1948- 206
McFarlan, Donald M(aitland) 1915- . CANR-10
Earlier sketch in CA 65-68
See also SATA 59
McFarlan, F. Warren 1937- 17-20R
McFarland, Andrew S(tuart) 1940- CANR-13
Earlier sketch in CA 25-28R
McFarland, C(harles) K(eith) 1934- 29-32R
McFarland, Carl 1904-1979
Obituary 85-88
McFarland, Dalton E(dward) 1919- CANR-2
Earlier sketch in CA 5-8R
McFarland, Dennis 1950- CANR-110
Earlier sketch in CA 165
See also CLC 65
McFarland, Dorothy Tuck 1938- 9-12R
McFarland, Ernest W(illiam) 1894-1984
Obituary 114
McFarland, Gerald Ward 1938- 85-88
McFarland, Henry Hammer
See McFarland, Henry O.
McFarland, Henry O. 1934- 216
See also SATA 143
McFarland, John 1943- 116
McFarland, Keith D(onavon) 1940- 57-60
McFarland, Kenton D(ean) 1920- 61-64
See also SATA 11
McFarland, M(alcolm) Carter 1912- 85-88
McFarland, Martha
See Smith-Ankrom, M. E.
McFarland, Marvin W(ilks) 1919-1985
Obituary 115
McFarland, Philip (James) 1930- CANR-12
Earlier sketch in CA 73-76
McFarland, Ron(ald Earl) 1942- 213
Earlier sketches in CA 113, CANR-32, 69
Autobiographical Essay in 213
See also DLB 256
McFarland, Ross A(rmstrong)
1901-1976 .... CAP-2
Earlier sketch in CA 21-22
McFarland, Stephen L. 1950- 139
McFarland, Thomas (Alfred, Jr.)
1926- CANR-101
Earlier sketch in CA 41-44R
McFarlane, Alexander C. 1952- CANR-115
Earlier sketch in CA 157
McFarlane, Basil Clare 1922- .... CP 1
McFarlane, Brian 1931- 122
McFarlane, Bruce John 1936- CANR-16
Earlier sketch in CA 81-84
McFarlane, I(an) D(alrymple) 1915- 107
McFarlane, James Walter 1920-1999 . CANR-5
Earlier sketch in CA 1-4R
McFarlane, K. B. 1903-1966
Obituary 114
McFarlane, Leslie (Charles)
1902-1977 .... CANR-37
Earlier sketch in CA 112
See also Dixon, Franklin W. and
Ferris, James Cody and
Keene, Carolyn and
Rockwood, Roy
See also DLB 88
See also MAICYA 1, 2
See also SATA 31
McFarlane, Peter (William) 1940- 160
See also SATA 95
McFarlane, Sheryl P. 1954- .... CWRI 5
See also SATA 86
McFarlane, Todd 1961- .... AAYA 34
See also SATA 117
McFate, Patricia Ann 1932- 103
McFather, Nelle 1936- CANR-4
Earlier sketch in CA 49-52
McFeat, Tom Farrar Scott 1919- 103
McFee, J. Scott
See Johnson, Don
McFee, June King 1917- CANR-16
Earlier sketch in CA 81-84
McFee, Michael 1954- CANR-57
Earlier sketches in CA 112, CANR-30
McFee, Oonah 1922- 116
McFee, William (Morley Punshon)
1881-1966 185
Obituary 116
See also DLB 153
McFeely, Eliza 1956- 200
McFeely, Mary Drake 1932- CANR-97
Earlier sketches in CA 110, CANR-27
McFeely, William S(hield) 1930- CANR-90
Earlier sketches in CA 33-36R, CANR-15, 50
McFerran, Ann
See Townsend, Doris McFerran
McFerran, Doris
See Townsend, Doris McFerran
McFerran, Douglass David 1934- 65-68
McFerrin, Linda Watanabe 1953- 188
McGaa, Ed 1936- 97-100
McGaffin, William 1910-1975 .... CAP-2
Earlier sketch in CA 25-28
McGahan, Andrew 1967- 168
McGahern, John 1934- CANR-113
Earlier sketches in CA 17-20R, CANR-29, 68
See also CLC 5, 9, 48, 156
See also CN 1, 2, 3, 4, 5, 6, 7
See also DLB 14, 231, 319
See also MTCW 1
See also SSC 17
McGahey, Michael J(oseph) 1948- 116
McGann, George T(homas) 1913- 93-96
McGann, Jerome J(ohn) 1937- CANR-102
Earlier sketches in CA 45-48, CANR-1, 14
McGann, Michael
See Naha, Ed
McGann, Thomas F. 1920- 13-16R
McGannon, J(ohn) Barry 1924- 13-16R
McGarey, Gladys T(aylor) 1920- 57-60
McGarey, William A. 1919- 57-60
McGarrigle, Francis Joseph 1888-1971 ..... 5-8R
McGarrity, Mark 1943-2002 .... CANR-110
Obituary 207
Earlier sketches in CA 45-48, CANR-1, 17, 37, 63
See also CMW 4
McGarrity, Michael 202
McGarry, Daniel D(oyle) 1907- CAP-1
Earlier sketch in CA 11-12
McGarry, Jean 1952- CANR-129
Earlier sketch in CA 126
McGarry, Kevin J(ohn) 1935- 102
McGarry, Michael B(rett) 1948- 102
McGarvey, Robert 1948- 113
McGaugh, James L(afayette) 1931- CANR-7
Earlier sketch in CA 57-60
McGaughey, (Florence) Helen
1904-1997 .... 37-40R
McGaughey, Neil 1951-1999 .... CANR-70
Obituary 185
Earlier sketch in CA 152
McGavin, E(lmer) Cecil 1900-1975 .... CAP-1
Earlier sketch in CA 11-12
McGavran, Donald (Anderson)
1897-1990(?) 13-16R
Obituary 132
McGaw, Charles James 1910-1978
Obituary 106
McGaw, Jessie Brewer 1913-1997 .... 1-4R
See also SATA 10
McGaw, Naomi Blanche Thoburn
1920- 9-12R
McGaw, William C(ochran) 1914- 101
McGeachy, D(aniel) P(atrick) III
1929- CANR-8
Earlier sketch in CA 61-64
McGear, Mike
See McCartney, Peter Michael
McGee, Barbara 1943- 25-28R
See also SATA 6
McGee, (Doctor) Frank 1921-1974 105
Obituary 89-92
Mcgee, Garry 1966- 227
McGee, Glenn 1967- 203
McGee, Greg(ory William) 1950- 231
See also CD 5, 6
McGee, Harold 1951- 118
McGee, Mark
See McGee, Mark T(homas)
McGee, Mark T(homas) 1947- 134
McGee, Marni 239
See also SATA 163
McGee, Reece (Jerome) 1929- CANR-17
Earlier sketches in CA 5-8R, CANR-2
McGee, Robert W(illiam) 1947- 112
McGee, Spike
See Moody, Fred
McGee, T. D.
See Savage, Teresa
McGee, T(erence) G(ary) 1936- CANR-10
Earlier sketch in CA 21-24R
McGee, Teresa Rhodes 1957- 222
McGee, Thomas D'Arcy 1825-1868 ..... DLB 99
McGee, Victor (Errol) 1935- 41-44R
McGee, William L. 1925- 217
McGeehan, Robert 1933- 33-36R
McGeehan, William O'Connell
1879-1933 184
See also DLB 25, 171
McGeeney, Patrick John 1918- 5-8R
McGeezer, Mark
See McGee, Mark T(homas)
McGehee, Helen 1921- 217
McGehee, Nicole 1956- 141
McGehee, Ralph W(alter) 1928- 112
McGeough, John 1926-
See Mack Bride, Johnny
McGeough, Paul 1954- 229
McGeown, Patrick 1897- CAP-2
Earlier sketch in CA 23-24
McGerr, Patricia 1917-1985 .... CANR-61
Obituary 116
Earlier sketches in CA 1-4R, CANR-1
See also AITN 1
See also CMW 4
McGhan, Barry (Robert) 1939- 69-72
McGhee, Alison 1960- 238
McGhee, George (Crews) 152
McGhie, Andrew 1926- 97-100
McGiffert, Michael 1928- 13-16R
McGiffert, Robert C(arnahan) 1922- 49-52
McGiffin, (Lewis) Lee (Shaffer)
1908-1978 .... CAP-1
Earlier sketch in CA 13-16
See also SATA 1
McGilchrist, Iain 1953- 132
McGill, Alice 235
See also SATA 159
McGill, Dan M(ays) 1919- 134
Brief entry 107
McGill, Ian
See Allegro, John Marco
McGill, Leonard J(ames) 1956- 115
McGill, Ormond 1913- CANR-58
Earlier sketches in CA 49-52, CANR-2
See also SATA 92
McGill, Ralph (Emerson) 1898-1969 .... 5-8R
Obituary 25-28R
See also DLB 29
McGill, Thomas E(merson) 1930- 17-20R
McGill, William J(ames) 1922-1997 190
McGilligan, Patrick (Michael)
1951- CANR-79
Earlier sketches in CA 65-68, CANR-10
McGilvery, Laurence 1932- 33-36R
McGimpsey, David 1962- CANR-129
Earlier sketch in CA 174
McGimsey, Charles Robert III 1925- 37-40R
McGinley, Jerry 1948- 188
See also SATA 116
McGinley, Patrick (Anthony) 1937- .. CANR-56
Brief entry 120
Earlier sketch in CA 127
Interview in CA-127
See also CLC 41
McGinley, Phyllis 1905-1978 .... CANR-19
Obituary 77-80
Earlier sketch in CA 9-12R
See also CLC 14
See also CP 1, 2
See also CWRI 5
See also DLB 11, 48
See also MAL 5
See also PFS 9, 13
See also SATA 2, 44
See also SATA-Obit 24
McGinn, Bernard John 1937- 113
McGinn, Colin 1950- 197
McGinn, Donald Joseph 1905-1994 ..... CAP-2
Earlier sketch in CA 23-24
McGinn, Elinor Myers 1923- 149
McGinn, John T. 1900(?)-1972
Obituary 33-36R
McGinn, Matt 1928-1977 106
McGinn, Maureen Ann
See Sautel, Maureen Ann
McGinn, Noel F(rancis) 1934- 73-76
McGinn, Richard 1939- 126
McGinnies, Elliott M(orse) 1921- 77-80
McGinnies, W(illiam) G(rovenor)
1899-1990 .... CANR-7
Earlier sketch in CA 57-60
McGinnis, Bruce 1941- 97-100
McGinnis, Dorothy Jean 1920- 29-32R
McGinnis, Duane
See Niatum, Duane
McGinnis, K. K.
See Page, Grover, Jr.
McGinnis, Lila S(prague) 1924- 93-96
See also SATA 44
McGinnis, Marilyn 1939- 57-60
McGinnis, Robert 1927-2001 45-48
Obituary 194
McGinnis, Thomas C(harles) 1925-1987 . 65-68
Obituary 123
McGinniss, Joe 1942- CANR-70
Earlier sketches in CA 25-28R, CANR-26
Interview in CANR-26
See also AITN 2
See also BEST 89:2
See also CLC 32
See also CPW
See also DLB 185
McGinty, Alice B. 1963- 203
See also SATA 134
McGirk, Tim(othy Stephen) 1952- 136
McGirr, Michael 212
McGirt, Dan(iel) 1967- 155
See also FANT
McGirt, James E(phraim)
1874-1930 .... CANR-87
Earlier sketch in CA 153
See also BW 2
See also DLB 50
McGivering, John H. 1923- 25-28R
McGivern, Justin 1985- .... SATA 129
McGivern, Maureen Daly
See Daly, Maureen
McGivern, William P(eter)
1922-1982 .... CANR-62
Obituary 108
Earlier sketches in CA 49-52, CANR-7
See also CMW 4
McGlade, Francis S(tanley) 1930- 41-44R
McGlamry, Beverly 1932- CANR-43
Earlier sketch in CA 119
McGlashan, Alan (Fleming) 1898-1997 . 41-44R
Obituary 158
McGlathery, James M(elville) 1936- 178
McGlennon, John J(oseph) 1949- 119
McGlinchee, Claire CAP-2
Earlier sketch in CA 23-24
McGlinchey, Charles 1861-1954 218
McGlinn, Dwight
See Brannon, William T.
McGloin, John Bernard 1912-1988 .... 33-36R
McGloin, Joseph T(haddeus)
1917-1993 .... CANR-39
Earlier sketches in CA 1-4R, CANR-1, 18
McGlone, Edward Leon 1941-
Brief entry 108
McGlothlen, Ronald L(ee) 1947- 143
McGlothlin, William J(oseph)
1908-1978 .... CAP-2
Earlier sketch in CA 19-20
McGlynn, Christopher
See Ginder, Richard
McGlynn, James V(incent) 1919-1973 ...... 1-4R
Obituary 103
McGoey, John Heck 1915- CANR-21
Earlier sketches in CA 9-12R, CANR-6
McGoldrick, Desmond Francis 1919- ... 17-20R
McGoldrick, Edward J., Jr. 1909-1967 ... CAP-1
Earlier sketch in CA 19-20
McGoldrick, James A. 237
McGoldrick, Joseph D. 1901-1978
Obituary 97-100
McGoldrick, May
See McGoldrick, James A. and
McGoldrick, Nikoo
McGoldrick, Nikoo 237
McGoldstein, Paddy
See Page, William
McGonigle, Thomas 1944- 137
McGoogan, Ken 1947- CANR-122
Earlier sketch in CA 144
McGoon, Clifford D. 1939- 113
McGough, Elizabeth (Hemmes) 1934- 107
See also SATA 33
McGough, Roger 1937- CANR-128
Earlier sketches in CA 105, CANR-44
See also CP 1, 2, 3, 4, 5, 6, 7
See also CWRI 5
See also DLB 40
McGovern, Ann 1930- CANR-44
Earlier sketches in CA 49-52, CANR-2
See also CLR 50
See also MAICYA 1, 2
See also SAAS 17
See also SATA 8, 69, 70, 132
McGovern, Arthur F(rancis)
1929-2000 .... CANR-40
Earlier sketch in CA 116
McGovern, Constance M(adeline) 1938- 120
McGovern, George S(tanley)
1922- CANR-103
Earlier sketches in CA 45-48, CANR-8, 63
McGovern, James (Walter)
1923-1989 .... CANR-7
Obituary 129
Earlier sketch in CA 17-20R
McGovern, James R(ichard) 1928- 108
McGovern, John P(hillip) 1921- CANR-44
Earlier sketches in CA 21-24R, CANR-13
McGovern, Robert 1927- CANR-28
Earlier sketch in CA 49-52
McGowan, Christopher 1942- 208
McGowan, Jack 1896(?)-1977
Obituary 69-72
McGowan, James A(lfred) 1932- 97-100
McGowan, Joe A., Jr.
See McGowan, Joseph A., Jr.
McGowan, John J. 1936(?)-1982
Obituary 106
McGowan, John P. 1953- 135
McGowan, Joseph A., Jr. 1931- 133
McGowan, Margaret M(ary) 69-72
McGowen, Charles H(ammond) 1936- ... 69-72
McGowen, Randall 1948- 213
McGowen, Thomas E. 1927- CANR-101
Earlier sketches in CA 21-24R, CANR-8, 25, 50
See also SATA 2, 109
McGowen, Tom
See McGowen, Thomas E.
McGown, Jill 1947- 221
See also CMW 4
McGrade, Arthur Stephen 1934- 25-28R
McGrady, Donald Lee 1935- 25-28R
McGrady, Mike 1933- CANR-2
Earlier sketch in CA 49-52
See also SATA 6
McGrady, Patrick M(ichael), Jr.
1932-2003 .... CANR-12
Earlier sketch in CA 29-32R
McGrady, Patrick Michael Sr. 1908-1980 ... 103
Obituary 97-100
McGrail, Anna 1957- 174
McGrail, Joie 1922(?)-1977
Obituary 69-72
McGrail, Sean Francis 1928- 217
McGrane, Bernard 1947- 133
McGrath, Alice (Greenfield) 1917- 112
McGrath, Alister E(dgar) 1953- CANR-98
Earlier sketch in CA 134
McGrath, Barbara Barbieri 1953- 169
See also SATA 108
McGrath, Campbell 1962- CANR-120
Earlier sketch in CA 164
McGrath, Camellia 1960- 203
McGrath, Charles 1947- 232
McGrath, Dennis 1946- 139

McGrath, Doyle
See Schorb, E(dwin) M(arsh)
McGrath, Eamonn 1929- ... 139
McGrath, Earl James 1902-1993 ... CAP-1
Obituary ... 140
Earlier sketch in CA 19-20
McGrath, Edward G(orham) 1917- ... 25-28R
McGrath, Francis E. 1903(?)-1976
Obituary ... 61-64
McGrath, J. H. 1923- ... 29-32R
McGrath, James Bernard, Jr. 1917- ... 5-8R
McGrath, Joan Rosita (Torr) 1895(?)-1967
Obituary ... 116
See also Forbes, Rosita
McGrath, John (Peter) 1935-2002 ... CANR-95
Obituary ... 204
Brief entry ... 112
Earlier sketch in CA 145
See also CBD
See also CD 5, 6
See also DLB 233
McGrath, Kristina 1950- ... CANR-99
Earlier sketch in CA 148
McGrath, Lee Parr 1933- ... 29-32R
McGrath, Malcolm (Frederick) 1963- ... 236
McGrath, Melanie ... 217
McGrath, Patrick 1950- ... CANR-65
Earlier sketch in CA 136
See also CLC 55
See also CN 5, 6, 7
See also DLB 231
See also HGG
See also SUFW 2
McGrath, Renee J. Vaillancourt 1969- ... 221
McGrath, Robert L(ee) 1920- ... 97-100
McGrath, Roberta (Wilson) 1956- ... 229
McGrath, Robin 1949- ... 192
See also SATA 121
McGrath, Roger D. 1947- ... 118
McGrath, Sean
See Douglas, John (Frederick James)
McGrath, Susan 1955- ... 121
McGrath, Sylvia Wallace 1937- ... 61-64
McGrath, Thomas (Matthew)
1916-1990 ... CANR-95
Obituary ... 132
Earlier sketches in CA 9-12R, CANR-6, 33
See also AMWS 10
See also CLC 28, 59
See also CP 1, 2
See also DAM POET
See also MAL 5
See also MTCW 1
See also SATA 41
See also SATA-Obit 66
McGrath, Tom 1940- ... 130
See also CBD
See also CD 5, 6
McGrath, William J(ames) 1937- ... 85-88
McGrath, William Thomas 1917- ... 103
McGratty, Arthur R. 1909-1975
Obituary ... 53-56
McGraw, Eloise Jarvis 1915-2000 ... CANR-82
Obituary ... 191
Earlier sketches in CA 5-8R, CANR-4, 19, 36
See also AAYA 41
See also BYA 16
See also MAICYA 1, 2
See also SAAS 6
See also SATA 1, 67
See also SATA-Obit 123
See also YAW
McGraw, Erin 1957- ... CANR-116
Earlier sketch in CA 158
McGraw, Harold Whittlesey Sr. 1890(?)-1970
Obituary ... 29-32R
McGraw, James (Paul) 1913-1977 ... 1-4R
McGraw, James R. 1935- ... 93-96
McGraw, Milena 1944- ... 171
McGraw, Phillip C. 1950- ... 201
McGraw, Walter John, Jr. 1919(?)-1978
Obituary ... 81-84
McGraw, William Corbin
1916-1999 ... CANR-36
Earlier sketch in CA 29-32R
See also SATA 3
McGreal, Elizabeth
See Yates, Elizabeth
McGreal, Ian Philip 1919- ... 77-80
McGreevey, William Paul 1938- ... CANR-11
Earlier sketch in CA 69-72
McGreevy, John T. ... 225
McGreevy, Susan Brown 1934- ... 126
McGregor
See Hurley, Doran
McGregor, Barbara 1959- ... SATA 82
McGregor, Craig 1933- ... CANR-13
Earlier sketch in CA 21-24R
See also SATA 8
McGregor, Elizabeth ... 222
McGregor, Iona 1929- ... 105
See also CWRI 5
See also SATA 25
McGregor, James H. 1946- ... CANR-119
Earlier sketch in CA 138
McGregor, John C(harles) 1905-1992 ... CAP-1
Earlier sketch in CA 19-20
McGregor, Jon 1976- ... 211
McGregor, Malcolm Francis 1910-1989 .. 45-48
McGregor, Rob Roy, Jr. 1929- ... 108
McGregor, Tom
See Grant, Graeme
McGrew, William W. 1933- ... 122
McGrory, Brian 1962(?)- ... 232
McGrory, Mary 1918-2004 ... 106
Obituary ... 227
Interview in ... CA-106
See also AITN 2
McGuane, Thomas (Francis III)
1939- ... CANR-94
Earlier sketches in CA 49-52, CANR-5, 24, 49
Interview in ... CANR-24
See also AITN 2
See also BPFB 2
See also CLC 3, 7, 18, 45, 127
See also CN 2, 3, 4, 5, 6, 7
See also DLB 2, 212
See also DLBY 1980
See also EWL 3
See also MAL 5
See also MTCW 1
See also MTFW 2005
See also TCWW 1, 2
McGuckian, Medbh 1950- ... 143
See also BRWS 5
See also CLC 48, 174
See also CP 7
See also CWP
See also DAM POET
See also DLB 40
See also PC 27
McGuckin, John Anthony 1952- ... 187
McGuffey, Alexander Hamilton
1816-1896 ... SATA 60
McGuffey, William Holmes
1800-1873 ... DLB 42
McGuffie, Tom H(enderson) 1902- ... CAP-2
Earlier sketch in CA 19-20
McGuffin, Mark
See McGee, Mark T(homas)
McGuigan, Dorothy Gies
1914-1982 ... CANR-11
Earlier sketch in CA 21-24R
McGuigan, F(rank) J(oseph)
1924-1998 ... CANR-8
Earlier sketch in CA 5-8R
McGuigan, Mary Ann 1949- ... 176
See also SATA 106
McGuinness, Arthur E(dward) 1936- ... 25-28R
McGuinness, Diane 1933- ... 186
McGuinness, Frank 1953- ... 188
See also CBD
See also CD 5, 6
See also DLB 245
McGuire, Christine ... 194
McGuire, Don 1919-1979 ... 167
McGuire, E(dward) Patrick 1932- ... 25-28R
McGuire, Edna 1899- ... CANR-2
Earlier sketch in CA 5-8R
See also SATA 13
McGuire, Frances Margaret (Cheadle) ... CAP-1
Earlier sketch in CA 9-10
McGuire, James Dean 1936- ... 21-24R
McGuire, Jerry 1934- ... 93-96
McGuire, Joseph William 1925- ... 9-12R
McGuire, Leslie (Sarah) 1945- ... CANR-69
Earlier sketch in CA 107
See also SATA 52, 94
See also SATA-Brief 45
McGuire, Martin C. 1933- ... 37-40R
McGuire, Martin Rawson Patrick 1897-1969
Obituary ... 111
McGuire, Meredith Anne (Black) 1944- ... 118
McGuire, Michael Terrance 1929- ... 41-44R
McGuire, (Dominic) Paul 1903-1978 ... CMW 4
McGuire, Richard L(en) 1940- ... 57-60
McGuire, Robert G. (III) 1938(?)-1975
Obituary ... 61-64
McGuire, Thomas (Vertin) 1945- ... 73-76
McGuire, Thomas G. 1950- ... 111
McGuire, William 1917- ... 143
McGuirk, Bernard 1949- ... 129
McGuirk, Carol ... 193
McGuirk, Leslie (A.) 1960- ... SATA 152
McGurk, Patrick (Maurice) 1928- ... 118
McGurk, Slater
See Roth, Arthur J(oseph)
McGurn, Barrett 1914- ... CANR-1
Earlier sketch in CA 1-4R
McGurn, James (Edward) 1953- ... 136
McGurn, William 1958- ... 126
McGwire, Michael 1924- ... 128
McHale, John 1922-1978 ... CANR-17
Earlier sketch in CA 61-64
McHale, Philip John 1928- ... 103
McHale, Tom 1942(?)-1982 ... 77-80
Obituary ... 106
See also AITN 1
See also CLC 3, 5
See also CN 1, 2, 3
McHale, Vincent E(dward) 1939- ... 112
McHam, David 1933- ... 73-76
McHaney, Thomas L(afayette)
1936- ... CANR-24
Earlier sketches in CA 65-68, CANR-9
McHarg, Ian L(ennox) 1920-2001 ... CANR-66
Obituary ... 195
Earlier sketch in CA 29-32R
McHargue, Georgess 1941- ... CANR-24
Earlier sketch in CA 25-28R
See also CLR 2
See also JRDA
See also SAAS 5
See also SATA 4, 77
McHenry, Dean E(ugene) 1910-1998 ... 109
Obituary ... 167
McHenry, James 1785-1845 ... DLB 202
McHenry, Leemon B. 1956- ... 140
McHenry, Paul G(raham), Jr. 1924-2002 . 61-64
Obituary ... 208
McHugh, Arona (Lipman) 1924-1996 ... 5-8R
Obituary ... 152
McHugh, Edna ... 69-72
McHugh, (Berit) Elisabet 1941- ... CANR-32
Earlier sketch in CA 113
See also SATA 55
See also SATA-Brief 44
McHugh, Heather 1948- ... CANR-92
Earlier sketches in CA 69-72, CANR-11, 28, 55
See also CP 7
See also CWP
See also PC 61
McHugh, John (Francis) 1927- ... 103
McHugh, Leroy 1891(?)-1975
Obituary ... 104
McHugh, Mary 1928- ... 85-88
McHugh, Maureen F. 1959- ... CANR-115
Earlier sketch in CA 139
See also AAYA 56
See also SFW 4
McHugh, Maxine Davis 1899(?)-1978
Obituary ... 77-80
McHugh, P(atrick) J(oseph) 1922- ... 21-24R
McHugh, Roger Joseph 1908-1987 ... 5-8R
McHugh, Roland 1945- ... CANR-10
Earlier sketch in CA 65-68
McHugh, Ruth Nelson
See Nelson, Ruth
McHugh, Stuart
See Rowland, D(onald) S(ydney)
McHugh, Thomas Cannell 1926- ... 103
McHugh, Tom
See McHugh, Thomas Cannell
McHugh, Vincent 1904-1983
Obituary ... 109
McHughen, Alan 1954- ... 189
McIlhany, William H(erbert) II 1951- . CANR-6
Earlier sketch in CA 57-60
McIlroy, Brian 1959- ... 199
McIlroy, Thad 1956- ... 122
McIlvaine, Betsy 1945- ... 123
McIlvaine, Jane
See McClary, Jane Stevenson
McIlvanney, William 1936- ... CANR-61
Earlier sketch in CA 25-28R
See also CLC 42
See also CMW 4
See also DLB 14, 207
McIlvoy, Kevin 1953- ... 175
McIlwain, Charles Howard 1871-1968 ... 102
McIlwain, David 1921-1981 ... 109
See also SFW 4
McIlwain, William (Franklin, Jr.)
1925- ... CANR-1
Earlier sketch in CA 1-4R
McIlwraith, Jean Newton 1859-1938 ... 189
See also DLB 92
McIlwraith, Maureen Mollie Hunter
See Hunter, Mollie
See also SATA 2
McInenly, William T(homas) 1932- ... 124
McInerney, Jay 1955- ... CANR-116
Brief entry ... 116
Earlier sketches in CA 123, CANR-45, 68
Interview in ... CA-123
See also AAYA 18
See also BPFB 2
See also CLC 34, 112
See also CN 5, 6, 7
See also CPW
See also DA3
See also DAM POP
See also DLB 292
See also MAL 5
See also MTCW 2
See also MTFW 2005
McInerney, Judith W(hitelock) 1945- ... 118
See also SATA 49
See also SATA-Brief 46
McInerney-Whiteford, Merry
See Whiteford, Merry
McInerny, Dennis Q(uentin) 1936- ... 97-100
McInerny, Ralph (Matthew) 1929- .. CANR-105
Earlier sketches in CA 21-24R, CANR-12, 34, 63
See also CMW 4
See also DLB 306
See also MSW
See also SATA 93
McInnes, Edward 1935- ... 109
McInnes, Graham (Campbell)
1912-1970 ... CAP-2
Earlier sketch in CA 25-28
McInnes, Ian (Andrew Stuart Fraser)
1925- ... 25-28R
McInnes, Neil 1924- ... 77-80
McInnis, Edgar Wardwell 1899-1973 ... 5-8R
McInnis, Judy B. 1943- ... 193
McInnis, Noel F. 1936- ... CANR-14
Earlier sketch in CA 33-36R
McInnis, Raymond G(eorge) 1936- ... 110
McIntire, C(arl) T(homas) 1939- ... CANR-101
Earlier sketch in CA 130
McIntire, Roger W(arren) 1935- ... 53-56
McIntosh, Alexander 1947- ... CANR-2
Earlier sketch in CA 45-48
McIntosh, Carey 1934- ... 77-80
McIntosh, Christopher 1943- ... 33-36R
McIntosh, Dave
See McIntosh, David Norman
McIntosh, David Norman 1921- ... 142
McIntosh, Donal W. 1919- ... 69-72
McIntosh, Douglas M. 1909-1998 ... CAP-1
Earlier sketch in CA 13-14
McIntosh, E. 1894(?)-1970
Obituary ... 104
McIntosh, Elizabeth P. 1915- ... 171
McIntosh, J. T.
See Macgregor, James (Murdoch)
McIntosh, James (Henry) 1934- ... 104
McIntosh, John 1930-1970 ... CAP-2
Earlier sketch in CA 21-22
McIntosh, Kinn Hamilton 1930- ... CANR-58
Earlier sketches in CA 25-28R, CANR-27
See also CMW 4
McIntosh, Louis
See Johnson, Christopher
McIntosh, Maria Jane 1803-1878 ... DLB 239, 248
McIntosh, Marjorie Keniston 1940- ... 144
McIntosh, Michael (Scott) 1945- ... 107
McIntosh, Peter Chisholm 1915- ... 102
McIntosh, Sandy
See McIntosh, Alexander
McInturff, Roy A(rthur) 1905-1979 ... 53-56
McIntyre, Carly
See Upcher, Caroline
McIntyre, Clare ... 229
See also CBD
See also CD 5, 6
See also CWD
McIntyre, Dennis 1943(?)-1990
Obituary ... 130
McIntyre, Hope
See Upcher, Caroline
McIntyre, Ian (James) 1931- ... 157
McIntyre, James 1827-1906 ... 177
See also DLB 99
McIntyre, John A(rmin) 1920- ... 57-60
McIntyre, Kenneth E. 1918- ... CANR-9
Earlier sketch in CA 21-24R
McIntyre, Lee C(ameron) 1962- ... 163
McIntyre, Michael P(erry) 1921- ... 41-44R
McIntyre, O(scar) O(dd) 1884-1938 ... 184
See also DLB 25
McIntyre, Thomas (Alfred) 1952- ... 120
McIntyre, Thomas J(ames) 1915-
Brief entry ... 114
McIntyre, Vonda N(eel) 1948- ... CANR-69
Earlier sketches in CA 81-84, CANR-17, 34
See also CLC 18
See also MTCW 1
See also SFW 4
See also YAW
McIntyre, W(illiam) David 1932- ... CANR-51
Earlier sketches in CA 21-24R, CANR-10, 26
McIntyre, William (Alexander) 1916- ... 37-40R
McIver, J(ohn) R(abie) 1931- ... 25-28R
McIver, Ray 1913-1985 ... 25-28R
McIver, Stuart B(etts) 1921- ... 69-72
McJimsey, George T(ilden) 1936- ... CANR-101
Earlier sketch in CA 93-96
McJimsey, Harriet Tilden 1902-1988 ... 5-8R
Obituary ... 199
McKain, David W. 1937- ... CANR-5
Earlier sketch in CA 9-12R
See also CAAS 14
McKale, Donald M(arshall) 1943- ... CANR-70
Earlier sketches in CA 53-56, CANR-5
McKane, William 1921-2004 ... 117
Obituary ... 231
McKaughan, Larry (Scott) 1941- ... 142
See also SATA 75
McKay, Alexander G(ordon) 1924- ... 37-40R
McKay, (Herbert) Alwyn (Cochrane)
1913-1997 ... 119
McKay, Arthur R(aymond) 1918- ... 5-8R
McKay, Claude
See McKay, Festus Claudius
See also AFAW 1, 2
See also AMWS 10
See also BLC 3
See also DAB
See also DLB 4, 45, 51, 117
See also EWL 3
See also EXPP
See also GLL 2
See also HR 1:3
See also LAIT 3
See also LMFS 2
See also MAL 5
See also PAB
See also PC 2
See also PFS 4
See also RGAL 4
See also TCLC 7, 41
See also WLC
See also WP
McKay, Claudia 1934- ... 171
McKay, Derek 1942- ... 81-84
McKay, Don(ald) 1932- ... 33-36R
McKay, Don 1942- ... CANR-114
Earlier sketch in CA 163
McKay, Donald 1895- ... SATA 45
McKay, Douglas R(ich) 1936- ... CANR-7
Earlier sketch in CA 57-60
McKay, Elizabeth Norman 1931- ... 172
McKay, Ernest A. 1918- ... 21-24R
McKay, Festus Claudius 1889-1948 .. CANR-73
Brief entry ... 104
Earlier sketch in CA 124
See also McKay, Claude
See also BW 1, 3
See also DA
See also DAC
See also DAM MST, MULT, NOV, POET
See also MTCW 1, 2
See also MTFW 2005
See also TUS
McKay, Gardner 1932-2001 ... 206
McKay, George Frederick 1899-1970
Obituary ... 106

Cumulative Index **391** **McLaughlin**

McKay, Hilary (Jane) 1959- CANR-119
  Earlier sketch in CA 156
  See also CWRI 5
  See also SAAS 23
  See also SATA 92, 145
McKay, Jim
  See McManus, James Kenneth
McKay, John H(arvey) 1923-2001
  Obituary 198
  Brief entry 115
McKay, John P(atrick) 1938- 29-32R
McKay, Kenneth R.
  See Kane, Henry
McKay, Lawrence, Jr. 1948- 186
  See also SATA 114
McKay, Quinn G(unn) 1926- 57-60
McKay, Robert B(udge) 1919-1990 57-60
  Obituary 132
McKay, Robert W. 1921- CANR-10
  Earlier sketch in CA 13-16R
  See also SATA 15
McKay, Ron 1949- 156
McKay, Simon
  See Nicole, Christopher (Robin)
McKay, Vernon 1912-1985 .... 5-8R
McKay, William Paul 1951- 116
McKeachie, Wilbert J(ames) 1921- 21-24R
McKeag, Ernest L(ionel) 1896-1976 .... CAP-1
  Earlier sketch in CA 13-16
McKean, Charles (Alexander) 1946- 137
McKean, Dave
  See McKean, David (Jeff)
McKean, David (Jeff) 1963- 217
McKean, Dayton D(avid) 1904-1977 .... CAP-1
  Earlier sketch in CA 19-20
McKean, Erin 1971- 205
McKean, Gil(bert S.) 1918- 5-8R
McKean, Hugh Ferguson 1908-1995 102
  Obituary 148
McKean, John (Maule) 1943- 107
McKean, John Richard 1939- 33-36R
McKean, Keith F. 1915- 37-40R
McKean, Margaret A(nne) 1946- 108
McKean, Robert B. 1943- 135
McKean, Robert C(laud) 1920- 13-16R
McKean, Roland N(eely) 1917- 33-36R
McKean, William V. 1820-1903 .... DLB 23
McKeating, Eileen 1957- .... SATA 81
McKeating, Henry 1932- 37-40R
McKeay, Eileen
  See McKeag, Ernest L(ionel)
McKechnie, Paul (Richard) 1957- 137
McKee, Alasdair 1963- 132
McKee, Alexander (Paul Charrier)
  1918- CANR-11
  Earlier sketch in CA 9-12R
McKee, Barbara H(astings) 1902-1998 57-60
McKee, Christopher (Fulton) 1935- 77-80
McKee, David (John) 1935- CANR-143
  Earlier sketch in CA 137
  See also CLR 38
  See also CWRI 5
  See also MAICYA 1, 2
  See also SATA 70, 107, 158
McKee, Edwin D(inwiddie) 1906-1984 ... 57-60
McKee, Eric
  See McKee, J. E. G.
McKee, J. E. G. (?)-1983
  Obituary 111
McKee, Jeffrey Kevin 1958- 189
McKee, John DeWitt 1919- 41-44R
McKee, LaVonne L. 1932- 145
McKee, Louis 1951- CANR-96
  Earlier sketches in CA 110, CANR-46
McKee, Paul Gordon 1897-1974 .... CAP-1
  Earlier sketch in CA 11-12
McKee, Robert 1941- 184
McKee, Tim 1970- 182
  See also SATA 111
McKeefery, William James 1918-1987
  Obituary 123
McKeen, William 1954- CANR-104
  Earlier sketch in CA 145
McKeever, James Ross 1909(?)-1986
  Obituary 120
McKeever, Marcia
  See Laird, Jean E(louise)
McKellar, Don 1963- 200
McKelvey, Blake F. 1903-2000 .... 17-20R
McKelvey, Carole A. 1942- 135
  See also SATA 78
McKelvey, James Lee 1934- 45-48
McKelvey, John J(ay), Jr. 1917- CANR-8
  Earlier sketch in CA 61-64
McKelvy, Charles 1950- .... SATA 124
McKelvy, Natalie 1950- 138
McKelway, Alexander J(effery) 1932- 13-16R
McKelway, Benjamin M. 1895-1976
  Obituary 69-72
McKelway, St. Clair 1905-1980 .... 5-8R
  Obituary 93-96
McKemy, Kay 1924- 29-32R
McKendrick, (Hector) Fergus 1933- 115
McKendrick, James (Stewart) 1955- 235
McKendrick, Jamie
  See McKendrick, James (Stewart)
McKendrick, Melveena (Christine)
  1941- CANR-111
  Earlier sketches in CA 93-96, CANR-17, 37
  See also SATA 55
McKendry, John (Joseph) 1933-1975
  Obituary 61-64
McKenna, A. Daniel
  See Corson-Finnerty, Adam Daniel
McKenna, Christine A.
  See Adams, (Butch) Christine A(nn)
McKenna, Colleen O'Shaughnessy
  1948- CANR-115
  Earlier sketch in CA 143
  See also SATA 76, 136
McKenna, Evelyn
  See Joscelyn, Archie L(ynn)
McKenna, F(rancis) E(ugene) 1921-1978
  Obituary 85-88
McKenna, George 1937- CANR-14
  Earlier sketch in CA 81-84
McKenna, J(ane) J(essica) 1945- 93-96
McKenna, J(ohn) W(illiam) 1938- 37-40R
McKenna, Kevin (E.) 1950- 218
McKenna, Lindsay 1946- .... RHW
McKenna, Marian Cecilia 1926- CANR-22
  Earlier sketch in CA 1-4R
McKenna, Michael C(layton) 1947- 116
McKenna, Patrick J. 1951- 204
McKenna, Richard (Milton)
  1913-1964 .... CANR-13
  Earlier sketch in CA 5-8R
  See also SFW 4
McKenna, Sister Margaret Mary 1930- .. 21-24R
McKenna, Sister Mary Lawrence
  See McKenna, Sister Margaret Mary
McKenna, Stephen 1888-1967 .... CAP-1
  Earlier sketch in CA 9-10
  See also DLB 197
McKenna, Terry 1949- 109
McKenney, Kenneth 1929- CANR-75
  Earlier sketch in CA 69-72
  See also HGG
McKenney, Mary 1946- 61-64
McKenney, Ruth 1911-1972 93-96
  Obituary 37-40R
McKennon, Joe
  See McKennon, Joseph W(esley)
McKennon, Joseph W(esley) 1907- CANR-2
  Earlier sketch in CA 49-52
Mc Kenny, Margaret 73-76
McKenzie, Barbara 1934- 21-24R
McKenzie, Donald Francis 1931-1999 186
McKenzie, Dorothy Clayton
  1910-1981 .... SATA-Obit 28
McKenzie, Doug
  See Thomas, Dave
McKenzie, Ellen Kindt 1928- .... SATA 80
McKenzie, Evan 1951- 148
McKenzie, Garry D(onald) 1941- 41-44R
McKenzie, George W(ashington) 1939- ... 69-72
McKenzie, John D. 1924- CANR-99
  Earlier sketch in CA 156
McKenzie, John L(awrence) 1910-1991 .. 9-12R
  Obituary 133
McKenzie, Judith (Sheila) 1957- 235
McKenzie, Leon R(oy) 1932- 29-32R
McKenzie, Michael 1954- 127
McKenzie, Nancy Affleck 1948- 225
McKenzie, Paige
  See Blood, Marje
McKenzie, Robert T(relford)
  1917-1981 .... 17-20R
  Obituary 105
McKenzie, Steven L. 1953- 197
McKenzie, William P. 1954- 130
McKeon, Doug(las Jude) 1966- 215
McKeon, Richard P(eter) 1900-1985
  Obituary 115
McKeon, Zahava Karl 1927- 126
McKeown, Charles 165
McKeown, James E(dward) 1919- 13-16R
McKeown, Thomas 1912-1988
  Obituary 125
McKeown, Tom 1937- CANR-20
  Earlier sketches in CA 45-48, CANR-2
  See also CP 1, 2, 3, 4, 5, 6, 7
McKercher, Berneth N(oble) 1915- 53-56
McKercher, Brian J. C. 196
McKern, Leo
  See McKern, Reginald
McKern, Reginald 1920-2002 134
  Obituary 210
McKern, Sharon S(mith) 1941- 37-40R
McKernan, John J(oseph) 1942- 110
McKernan, John R(ettie), Jr. 1948- 151
McKernan, Michael 1945- 230
McKernan, Victoria 1957- 140
McKerrow, Mary 1915- 132
McKerrow, R(onald) B(runlees) 1872-1940 . 184
  See also DLB 201
McKersie, R. B.
  See McKersie, Robert Bruce
McKersie, Robert Bruce 1929-
  Brief entry 116
McKevett, G. A.
  See Massie, Sonja
McKhann, Charles Fremont 1930- 112
McKibben, Bill
  See McKibben, William (Ernest)
  See also ANW
McKibben, William (Ernest) 1960- CANR-66
  Earlier sketch in CA 130
  See also McKibben, Bill
McKibbin, Alma E(stelle Baker)
  1871-1974 .... CAP-1
  Earlier sketch in CA 19-20
McKibbin, Frank L(owell) 1917- 65-68
McKibbin, Jean 1919- 65-68
McKibbin, Ross 181
McKie, Robin 173
  See also MTFW 2005
  See also SATA 112
McKie, Ronald (Cecil Hamlyn)
  1909-1994 .... CANR-6
  Earlier sketch in CA 9-12R
McKiernan, Dennis L. 1932- 230
McKillen, Elizabeth 1957-1998 156
McKillip, Patricia A(nne) 1948- CANR-106
  Earlier sketches in CA 49-52, CANR-4, 18, 63
  Interview in CANR-18
  See also AAYA 14
  See also BPFB 2
  See also BYA 7, 11
  See also FANT
  See also JRDA
  See also MAICYA 2
  See also MAICYAS 1
  See also MTCW 1
  See also SATA 30, 80, 126
  See also SFW 4
  See also SUFW 1, 2
  See also YAW
McKillop, A. B(rian) 1946- 222
McKillop, Alan D(ugald) 1892-1974 ..... CAP-1
  Obituary 53-56
  Earlier sketch in CA 19-20
McKillop, Menzies 1929- 77-80
McKillop, Norman 1892-1974 .... 5-8R
McKillop, Susan Regan 1929- CANR-8
  Earlier sketch in CA 61-64
McKim, Audrey Margaret 1909-1999 . CANR-4
  Earlier sketch in CA 1-4R
  See also SATA 47
McKim, Donald K(eith) 1950- CANR-17
  Earlier sketch in CA 93-96
McKimmey, James 1923- CANR-22
  Earlier sketch in CA 85-88
McKimson, Robert 1910-1976 .... IDFW 3, 4
McKinlay, Brian John 1933- CANR-19
  Earlier sketch in CA 103
McKinley, Catherine E(lizabeth) 1967- 218
McKinley, Daniel (Lawson) 1924- 25-28R
McKinley, David Hopwood 1906-1986 . CAP-2
  Earlier sketch in CA 33-36
McKinley, James (Courtright) 1935- 69-72
McKinley, (Jennifer Carolyn) Robin
  1952- CANR-110
  Earlier sketches in CA 107, CANR-31, 64
  See also AAYA 4, 33
  See also BYA 4, 5, 6, 12, 16
  See also CLR 10, 81
  See also DLB 52
  See also FANT
  See also JRDA
  See also LAIT 1
  See also MAICYA 1, 2
  See also MTFW 2005
  See also SATA 50, 89, 130
  See also SATA-Brief 32
  See also YAW
McKinley, Tamara 220
McKinnell, James 1933- CANR-12
  Earlier sketch in CA 61-64
McKinnell, Robert Gilmore 1926- 102
McKinney, Anne
  See Sleem, Patricia Anne
McKinney, Barbara Shaw 1951- 188
  See also SATA 116
McKinney, Blanaid 1961- 212
McKinney, D. J.
  See Cooper, Parley J(oseph)
McKinney, David Walter, Jr. 1920- 37-40R
McKinney, Don(ald Lee) 1923- 73-76
McKinney, Donald 1909- CANR-7
  Earlier sketch in CA 57-60
McKinney, Eleanor Ruth 1918- 33-36R
McKinney, Eugene 1922- CANR-15
  Earlier sketch in CA 73-76
McKinney, Fred 1908-1981 .... 17-20R
  Obituary 135
McKinney, Gene
  See McKinney, Eugene
McKinney, George Dallas, Jr. 1932- 5-8R
McKinney, George W(esley), Jr. 1922- 57-60
McKinney, Gordon B(artlett) 1943- 85-88
McKinney, H(enry) Lewis 1935- 41-44R
McKinney, Jack
  See Daley, Brian
McKinney, John William 1908-1989 .... 1-4R
McKinney, Joseph A. 1943- 218
McKinney, Kathleen 1954- 139
McKinney, Meagan 1961- CANR-103
  Earlier sketch in CA 139
McKinney, Mel 186
McKinney, Nadine 1938- 155
  See also SATA 91
McKinney, Sally (Brown) 1933- 149
McKinney, Virginia (Marie) 1940- 57-60
McKinney, William 1946- 121
McKinney-Whetstone, Diane 197
McKinnon, Alastair Thomson 1925- 102
McKinnon, James 1932- 128
Mckinnon, Karen 218
McKinnon, K.C.
  See Pelletier, Cathie
McKinnon, Ray 1961(?)- 215
McKinnon, Robert Scott 1937- 37-40R
McKinnon, Ronald I(an) 1935- 131
McKinsey, Elizabeth 1947- 139
McKinzie, Clinton 1969- 218
McKinzie, Richard D. 1936- 77-80
McKisack, May 1900-1981 107
  Obituary 103
McKissack, Fredrick L(emuel) 1939- . CANR-96
  Earlier sketches in CA 120, CANR-49
  See also BYA 15
  See also CLR 55
  See also CWRI 5
  See also SATA 73, 117, 162
  See also SATA-Brief 53
McKissack, Patricia (L'Ann) C(arwell)
  1944- CANR-96
  Earlier sketches in CA 118, CANR-38
  See also AAYA 38
  See also BW 2
  See also BYA 15
  See also CLR 23, 55
  See also CWRI 5
  See also JRDA
  See also MAICYA 1, 2
  See also MAICYAS 1
  See also SATA 51, 73, 117, 162
McKissack and
  McKissack
  McKissack
  See McKissack, Fredrick L(emuel) and
  McKissack, Patricia (L'Ann) C(arwell)
McKissick, Floyd Bixler 1922-1991 49-52
  Obituary 134
McKitrick, Eric Louis 1919-2002 .... 21-24R
  Obituary 208
McKitterick, David John 1948- 176
McKittrick, David 1938- 61-64
McKivigan, John R(aymond) 1949- 119
McKnight, Allan Douglas 1918- 104
McKnight, Brian Emerson 1938- 106
McKnight, C. A.
  See Russell, Rosalind
McKnight, C(olbert) A(ugustus) 1916-1986
  Obituary 120
McKnight, Edgar V(ernon) 1931- 21-24R
McKnight, Gerald 1919- 13-16R
McKnight, John P(roctor) 1908(?)-1987
  Obituary 123
McKnight, Linton W. 1942- 159
McKnight, Reginald CANR-111
  Earlier sketch in CA 129
  See also DLB 234
McKnight, Scot 229
McKnight, Stephen A. 1944- 143
McKnight, Thomas Lee
  See McKnight, Tom Lee
McKnight, Tom Lee 1928-2004 .... CANR-5
  Earlier sketch in CA 9-12R
McKowen, Clark 1929- 41-44R
McKown, Dave Ross 1895-1992 97-100
McKown, Delos B. 1930- 141
McKown, Robert 1908-1973
  Obituary 104
McKown, Robin (?)-1976 .... CANR-1
  Earlier sketch in CA 1-4R
  See also SATA 6
McKuen, Rod 1933- CANR-40
  Earlier sketch in CA 41-44R
  See also AITN 1
  See also CLC 1, 3
  See also CP 1
McKusick, Marshall Bassford 1930- CANR-9
  Earlier sketch in CA 13-16R
McLachlan, Alexander 1818-1896 .... DLB 99
McLachlan, Ian 1938- 69-72
McLaglen, John J.
  See Harvey, John (Barton) and
  James, Laurence
McLanathan, Richard 1916- 81-84
McLandress, Herschel
  See Galbraith, John Kenneth
  See also CCA 1
McLane, Charles B(ancroft) 1919- 25-28R
McLane, Helen J. CANR-4
  Earlier sketch in CA 9-12R
McLane, John R. 1935- 97-100
McLane, Paul Elliott 1907- CAP-1
  Earlier sketch in CA 9-10
McLaren, Angus 1942- 221
McLaren, Brian D. 1956- 229
McLaren, Clemence 1938- CANR-130
  Earlier sketch in CA 164
  See also BYA 10
  See also SATA 105, 158
McLaren, Colin Andrew 1940- CANR-27
  Earlier sketch in CA 106
McLaren, Floris (Marion) Clark 1904-1978 . 148
  See also DLB 68
McLaren, Homer D. 1887-1980 .... CAP-2
  Earlier sketch in CA 29-32
McLaren, Ian A. 1928- 103
McLaren, Ian Francis 1912-2000 ...... CANR-24
  Earlier sketch in CA 106
McLaren, John (David) 1932- 29-32R
McLaren, Joseph 1948- 226
McLaren, (R.) Keith 1949- 236
McLaren, Moray (David Shaw) 1901-1971 . 103
McLaren, N(orman) Loyall 1892(?)-1977
  Obituary 73-76
McLaren, Norman 1914-1987 .... IDFW 3, 4
McLaren, Philip 1943- 168
McLaren, Robert Bruce 1923- 29-32R
McLarey, Myra 1942- 150
McLarin, Kim CANR-128
  Earlier sketch in CA 175
McLarry, Newman R(ay) 1923- 13-16R
McLaughlin, Andree N.
  See McLaughlin, Andree Nicola
McLaughlin, Andree Nicola 1948- 133
McLaughlin, Andrew 203
McLaughlin, Ann L. 1928- 135
McLaughlin, Arthur Leo 1921- 17-20R
McLaughlin, Bill
  See Phillips, James W.
McLaughlin, Brian P. 1949- 141
McLaughlin, Charles Bernard 1937- 61-64
McLaughlin, Corinne 1947- 147
McLaughlin, Curtis P. 1932- CANR-5
  Earlier sketch in CA 53-56
McLaughlin, David J(ohn) 1936- 73-76

McLaughlin, Dean (Jr.) 1931- ... 9-12R
See also SFW 4
McLaughlin, Elizabeth Taylor 1923- ... 93-96
McLaughlin, Ellen 1957- ... 220
McLaughlin, Emma 1964(?)- ... 212
McLaughlin, Emma Maude 1901-1991 ... 65-68
McLaughlin, Frank 1934- ... SATA 73
McLaughlin, Jack
See McLaughlin, John Joseph
McLaughlin, John Joseph 1926- ... CANR-65
Earlier sketch in CA 129
McLaughlin, Joseph (D.) 1940- ... CANR-100
Earlier sketches in CA 45-48, CANR-4, 20
McLaughlin, Joseph F., Jr. 1919-1978
Obituary ... 77-80
McLaughlin, Kathleen 1898-1990
Obituary ... 132
McLaughlin, Lorrie (Bell) 1924-1971 .. CANR-5
Earlier sketch in CA 5-8R
McLaughlin, Martin L. ... 233
McLaughlin, Michael 1949-2002 ... 141
Obituary ... 207
McLaughlin, Mignon -1983 ... 9-12R
McLaughlin, Ritta ... 227
McLaughlin, Robert (Emmet) 1908-1973 ... 1-4R
Obituary ... 45-48
McLaughlin, Robert William 1900-1989 ... 1-4R
McLaughlin, Samuel Clarke 1924- ... 89-92
McLaughlin, Sister Raymond
1897-1985 ... 25-28R
McLaughlin, Ted J(ohn) 1921- ... 13-16R
McLaughlin, Terence (Patrick) 1928- ... 33-36R
McLaughlin, Virginia Yans
See Yans-McLaughlin, Virginia
McLaughlin, William (DeWitt) 1918- ... 107
McLaughlin, William Raffian Davidson
1908- ... CAP-1
Earlier sketch in CA 11-12
McLaurin, Anne 1953- ... 106
See also SATA 27
McLaurin, Melton A(lonza) 1941- ... CANR-28
Earlier sketch in CA 81-84
McLaurin, R(onald) D(e) 1944- ... CANR-17
Earlier sketch in CA 65-68
McLaurin, Tim 1953-2002 ... 232
See also CSW
McLaverty, James 1947- ... 219
McLaverty, Michael 1904-1992 ... CAP-1
Earlier sketch in CA 13-14
See also DLB 15
McLean, Alan A(ngus) 1925-1999 ... 157
Obituary ... 181
McLean, Albert F(orbes), Jr. 1928- ... 17-20R
McLean, Allan Campbell 1922- ... CANR-4
Earlier sketch in CA 1-4R
See also CWRI 5
McLean, Andrew 1946- ... 185
See also SATA 113
McLean, Anne (Julia) 1951- ... 120
McLean, Antonio (Maxwell) 1919- ... 130
McLean, Beth Bailey 1892-1976 ... CAP-2
Earlier sketch in CA 19-20
McLean, Don(ald George) 1932- ... 122
McLean, Donald 1905-1975 ... CANR-4
Earlier sketch in CA 1-4R
McLean, Duncan 1964- ... CANR-109
Earlier sketch in CA 149
See also DLB 267
McLean, George 1905(?)-1983
Obituary ... 109
McLean, George F(rancis) 1929- ... CANR-6
Earlier sketch in CA 13-16R
McLean, Gordon R(onald) 1934- ... CANR-2
Earlier sketch in CA 49-52
McLean, Helen 1927- ... 224
McLean, Hugh 1925- ... 65-68
McLean, Iain (S.) 1946- ... 135
McLean, J. Sloan
See Gillette, Virginia M(ary) and
Wunsch, Josephine (McLean)
McLean, J. W. 1922- ... 143
McLean, Janet 1946- ... 185
See also SATA 113
McLean, Janice W(alker) 1944- ... 119
McLean, John R. 1848-1916 ... DLB 23
McLean, Joseph E(rigina) 1915-1985
Obituary ... 118
McLean, Kathryn (Anderson)
1909-1966 ... CAP-2
Obituary ... 25-28R
Earlier sketch in CA 21-22
See also SATA 9
McLean, Malcolm Dallas 1913- ... CANR-39
Earlier sketches in CA 93-96, CANR-16
McLean, Maria Coletta 1946- ... 218
McLean, Robert 1891-1980
Obituary ... 103
McLean, Robert Colin 1927- ... 17-20R
McLean, (John David) Ruari 1917- . CANR-115
Earlier sketch in CA 21-24R
McLean, Sammy Kay 1929- ... 37-40R
McLean, Scott A. 1963- ... 232
McLean, Susan 1937- ... 106
McLean, Teresa 1951- ... 143
McLean, Virginia Overton 1946- ... 155
See also SATA 90
McLean, William L. 1852-1931 ... 183
See also DLB 25
McLean-Carr, Carol 1948- ... SATA 122
McLeave, Hugh George 1923- ... CANR-86
Earlier sketches in CA 5-8R, CANR-6, 27
McLeavy, Gus 1951- ... 105
McLees, Ainslie Armstrong 1947- ... 135
McLeish, Garen
See Stine, Whitney Ward
McLeish, John 1917- ... CANR-7
Earlier sketch in CA 57-60
McLeish, Kenneth 1940-1997 ... CANR-45
Earlier sketches in CA 29-32R, CANR-13
See also SATA 35
McLellan, David 1940- ... CANR-33
Earlier sketches in CA 33-36R, CANR-15
McLellan, David S(tanley) 1924- ... 103
McLellan, Diana 1937- ... CANR-101
Earlier sketch in CA 114
Interview in ... CA-114
McLellan, Robert 1907-1985 ... CANR-95
Obituary ... 115
Earlier sketch in CA 41-44R
See also CP 1
McLemore, S(amuel) Dale 1928- ... 9-12R
McLendon, Gloria H(ouston) 1940- ... 112
McLendon, Gordon (Barton) 1921-1986 ... 133
Obituary ... 120
McLendon, Jacquelyn Y. 1943- ... 167
McLendon, James (Nelson) 1942-1982 . 41-44R
Obituary ... 106
McLendon, Jonathon C(ollins)
1919-1977 ... 17-20R
Obituary ... 134
McLendon, Will L(oving) 1925- ... 9-12R
McLendon, Winzola Poole ... 93-96
McLenighan, Valjean 1947- ... 108
See also SATA 46
See also SATA-Brief 40
McLennan, Barbara N(ancy) 1940- ... 85-88
McLennan, Scotty
See McLennan, William L., Jr.
McLennan, Will
See Wisler, G(ary) Clifton
McLennan, William 1856-1904 ... 184
See also DLB 92
McLennan, William L., Jr. 1948- ... 187
See also McNab, David T.
McLeod, Alan L(indsey) 1928- ... 9-12R
McLeod, Carolyn 1969- ... 239
McLeod, Chum 1955- ... SATA 95
McLeod, Emilie Warren 1926-1982 ... 33-36R
Obituary ... 108
See also SATA 23
See also SATA-Obit 31
McLeod, Enid (Devoge) 1896-1985 ... 134
Obituary ... 116
McLeod, Grover S(tephen) 1923- ... 143
McLeod, Jack (T.) 1932- ... 129
McLeod, James R(ichard) 1942- ... CANR-99
Earlier sketch in CA 41-44R
McLeod, John F(reeland) 1917-1989 ... 69-72
Obituary ... 128
McLeod, Joseph (Bertram) 1929- ... 156
McLeod, Kembrew 1970- ... 237
McLeod, Ken 1948- ... 220
McLeod, Kirsty
See Hudson, (Margaret) Kirsty
McLeod, Malcolm Donald 1941- ... 110
McLeod, Margaret Vail
See Holloway, Teresa (Bragunier)
McLeod, Mary Alice 1937- ... 112
McLeod, Raymond, Jr. 1932- ... CANR-19
Earlier sketches in CA 49-52, CANR-3
McLeod, Ross
See Feldman, Herbert (H. S.)
McLeod, Scott Willard 1960- ... 148
See also MTFW 2005
McLeod, Wallace (Edmond) 1931- ... CANR-57
Earlier sketches in CA 37-40R, CANR-14, 31
McLerran, Alice 1933- ... CANR-116
Earlier sketch in CA 136
See also SATA 68, 137
McLin, Jon (Blythe) 1938- ... 102
McLin, Ruth (Arlene) 1924- ... 61-64
McLoughlin, John C. 1949- ... 108
See also SATA 47
McLoughlin, Leslie J. 1935- ... 146
McLoughlin, R. B.
See Mencken, H(enry) L(ouis)
McLoughlin, Tim 1959- ... 220
McLoughlin, William G. 1922-1993 .. CANR-6
Obituary ... 140
Earlier sketch in CA 13-16R
McLouth, Gary (Michael) 1944- ... 119
McLowery, Frank
See Keevill, Henry J(ohn)
McLuhan, (Thomas) Eric (Marshall)
1942- ... CANR-100
Earlier sketch in CA 130
McLuhan, (Herbert) Marshall
1911-1980 ... CANR-61
Obituary ... 102
Earlier sketches in CA 9-12R, CANR-12, 34
Interview in ... CANR-12
See also CLC 37, 83
See also DLB 88
See also MTCW 1, 2
See also MTFW 2005
McLure, Charles E., Jr. 1940- ... CANR-58
Earlier sketches in CA 57-60, CANR-8, 28
McLure, James ... 232
See also CAD
See also CD 5, 6
McLynn, Frank ... 197
McMahan, Ian (D.) ... 232
See also SATA-Brief 45
McMahan, Jeff(erson Allen) 1954- ... 220
McMahon, Bob 1944-2000 ... 111
McMahon, Bryan T(homas) 1950- ... CANR-35
Earlier sketch in CA 45-48
McMahon, Charles P. 1916(?)-1983
Obituary ... 109
McMahon, Darrin ... 208
McMahon, Donna 1959- ... 228
McMahon, Dorothy 1912-1984
Obituary ... 112
McMahon, Ed(ward Leo Peter, Jr.) 1923- . 89-92
McMahon, Edwin Mansfield 1930- ... 126
McMahon, Eileen M. 1957- ... 151
McMahon, Francis E(lmer) 1906-1987
Obituary ... 123
McMahon, Jeremiah 1919- ... 109
McMahon, Joseph H(enry) 1930-1987 ... 9-12R
Obituary ... 124
McMahon, Maureen M. 1952- ... 217
McMahon, Michael 1943- ... 69-72
McMahon, Pat
See Hoch, Edward D(entinger)
McMahon, Robert
See Weverka, Robert
McMahon, Robert J. 1949- ... 109
McMahon, Sean 1931- ... 196
McMahon, Thomas 1923(?)-1972
Obituary ... 37-40R
McMahon, Thomas (Arthur)
1943-1999 ... CANR-45
Earlier sketches in CA 33-36R, CANR-15
McMane, Fred 1940- ... 192
McManis, Douglas R. ... 69-72
McManners, (Joseph) Hugh 1952- ... 132
McManners, John 1916- ... CANR-14
Earlier sketch in CA 37-40R
McManus, Antonia 1952- ... 225
McManus, Declan Patrick Aloysius
See Costello, Elvis
McManus, Edgar J. 1924- ... 97-100
McManus, Frederick R(ichard) 1923- ... 1-4R
McManus, James 1951- ... CANR-67
Earlier sketch in CA 117
McManus, James Kenneth 1921- ... 85-88
McManus, Jason 1934- ... 125
McManus, John C. 1965- ... 176
McManus, Marjorie 1950- ... 73-76
McManus, Michael 1967- ... 239
McManus, Michael J. 1941- ... 231
McManus, Patrick F(rancis) 1933- ... CANR-87
Earlier sketch in CA 105
See also SATA 46
McManus, Ruth 1971- ... 232
McMartin, Barbara 1931- ... 234
McMaster, Beth 1935- ... CANR-30
Earlier sketch in CA 112
McMaster, Gerald 1953- ... 211
McMaster, H. R. 1962- ... 170
McMaster, John Bach 1852-1932 ... 203
See also DLB 47
McMaster, Juliet 1937- ... 37-40R
McMaster, Rhyll 1947- ... CANR-111
Earlier sketch in CA 154
See also CP 7
See also CWP
McMaster, Susan 1950- ... 208
McMath, Robert C(arroll), Jr. 1944- ... 129
McMeekin, Clark
See McMeekin, Isabel McLennan
McMeekin, Dorothy 1932- ... 125
McMeekin, Isabel McLennan 1895-1973 .. 5-8R
See also SATA 3
McMenemey, William Henry
1905-1977 ... CAP-1
Earlier sketch in CA 11-12
McMenemy, Nickie 1925- ... 97-100
McMenemy, Sarah 1965- ... SATA 156
McMichael, George 1927- ... 103
McMichael, James 1939- ... 69-72
McMichael, Joan K(atharine) 1906-1989 ... 107
McMillan, Alan D. 1945- ... 130
McMillan, Ann 1952- ... 192
McMillan, Bruce 1947- ... CANR-110
Earlier sketches in CA 73-76, CANR-13, 35, 89
See also CLR 47
See also MAICYA 1, 2
See also SATA 22, 70, 129
McMillan, Colin 1923- ... 29-32R
McMillan, Constance (VanBrunt Johnson)
1949- ... 85-88
McMillan, Douglas J. 1931- ... 192
McMillan, George 1913-1987 ... 102
Obituary ... 123
McMillan, Ian 1956- ... CANR-143
Earlier sketch in CA 132
McMillan, James B. 1907- ... 85-88
McMillan, James F(rancis) 1948- ... 122
McMillan, John 1951- ... CANR-120
Earlier sketch in CA 138
McMillan, Naomi
See Grimes, Nikki
McMillan, Polly Miller 1920- ... 1-4R
McMillan, Priscilla Johnson 1928- ... 41-44R
McMillan, Roddy 1923-1979
Obituary ... 109
McMillan, Sally 1929- ... 145
McMillan, Terry (L.) 1951- ... CANR-131
Earlier sketches in CA 140, CANR-60, 104
See also AAYA 21
See also AMWS 13
See also BLCS
See also BPFB 2
See also BW 2, 3
See also CLC 50, 61, 112
See also CN 7
See also CPW
See also DA3
See also DAM MULT, NOV, POP
See also MAL 5
See also MTCW 2
See also MTFW 2005
See also RGAL 4
See also YAW
McMillen, Howard 1938- ... 57-60
McMillen, Neil R(aymond) 1939- ... 33-36R
McMillen, S(im) I. (Socrates) 1898-1990 ... 5-8R
McMillen, Sally G(regory) 1944- ... CANR-93
Earlier sketch in CA 133
McMillen, Wheeler 1893-1992 ... 33-36R
McMillin, (Joseph) Laurence, (Jr.)
1923- ... 33-36R
McMillin, (Harvey) Scott 1934- ... 126
McMillion, Bonner 1921- ... 13-16R
McMorey, James L.
See Moyer, Terry J.
McMorran, Susan
See Beattie, Susan
McMorris, Jenny 1946-2002 ... 218
McMorrow, Annalisa 1969- ... 171
See also SATA 104
McMorrow, Fred 1925-2000 ... 57-60
Obituary ... 189
McMullan, Frank (Alonzo) 1907- ... 5-8R
McMullan, Gordon 1962- ... 149
McMullan, Jim 1934- ... SATA 87, 150
McMullan, Kate
See McMullan, Kate (Hall)
McMullan, Kate (Hall) 1947- ... CANR-114
Earlier sketch in CA 123
See also SATA 52, 87, 132
See also SATA-Brief 48
McMullan, Margaret 1960- ... CANR-99
Earlier sketch in CA 145
McMullen, Jay L. 1921-1992 ... 118
Obituary ... 137
Brief entry ... 114
Interview in ... CA-118
McMullen, Jeremy (John) 1948- ... 103
McMullen, Lorraine 1926- ... CANR-41
Earlier sketch in CA 117
McMullen, Mary
See Reilly, Mary
McMullen, Michael 1965- ... 221
McMullen, Roy 1911-1984 ... 25-28R
Obituary ... 113
McMullen, Sean (Christopher)
1948- ... CANR-99
Earlier sketch in CA 161
See also SFW 4
McMullen, William Wallace 1952- ... 151
McMullin, Ernan 1924- ... CANR-49
Earlier sketches in CA 13-16R, CANR-6, 22
McMullin, Ruth R(oney) 1942- ... 61-64
McMurdie, Annie Laurie
See Cassiday, Bruce (Bingham)
McMurray, George R(ay) 1925- ... 103
McMurray, Nancy A(rmistead) 1936- ... 41-44R
McMurrin, Sterling M(oss) 1914-1996 ... 29-32R
Obituary ... 152
McMurry, James Burton 1941- ... 69-72
McMurry, Linda O. 1945- ... CANR-88
Earlier sketch in CA 106
McMurry, Richard M. 1939- ... 132
McMurry, Robert N(oleman)
1901-1985 ... 17-20R
McMurry, Sarah L. 1944- ... 123
McMurtrey, Martin A(loysias) 1921- ... 69-72
See also SATA 21
McMurtry, Jo 1937- ... 89-92
McMurtry, Larry (Jeff) 1936- ... CANR-103
Earlier sketches in CA 5-8R, CANR-19, 43, 64
See also AAYA 15
See also AITN 2
See also AMWS 5
See also BEST 89:2
See also BPFB 2
See also CDALB 1968-1988
See also CLC 2, 3, 7, 11, 27, 44, 127
See also CN 2, 3, 4, 5, 6, 7
See also CPW
See also CSW
See also DA3
See also DAM NOV, POP
See also DLB 2, 143, 256
See also DLBY 1980, 1987
See also EWL 3
See also MAL 5
See also MTCW 1, 2
See also MTFW 2005
See also RGAL 4
See also TCWW 1, 2
McMurtry, R(obert) Gerald 1906-1988 .. CAP-1
Obituary ... 127
Earlier sketch in CA 11-12
McNab, Andy ... 185
McNab, Claire 1940- ... 193
McNab, David T. 1947- ... 187
McNab, Jeb
See Fearn, John Russell
McNab, Oliver
See Frede, Richard
McNab, Thomas 1933- ... 108
McNab, Tom
See McNab, Thomas
McNabb, Linda 1963- ... 221
See also SATA 147
McNail, Eddie Gathings 1905-1994 ... CANR-6
Earlier sketch in CA 57-60
McNair, Clement John 1915-1989
Obituary ... 129
McNair, Harold M. 1933- ... 169
McNair, Kate ... 17-20R
See also SATA 3
McNair, Malcolm P(errine) 1894-1985 .. CAP-1
Obituary ... 117
Earlier sketch in CA 11-12
McNair, Marie 1900(?)-1989
Obituary ... 130
McNair, Philip Murray Jourdan 1924- ... 21-24R
McNair, Sylvia 1924-2002 ... 121
Obituary ... 210
See also SATA 74
McNair, Wesley C. 1941- ... 175

McNairn, Jeffrey L. 1967- 218
McNair Scott, Ronald (Guthrie)
1906-1995 111
Obituary 148
McNairy, Philip F(rederick) 1911-1989 . 17-20R
McNall, Bruce 1950- 233
McNall, P(reston) E(ssex) 1888-1981 ..... 29-32R
Obituary 135
McNall, Scott G(rant) 1941- CANR-11
Earlier sketch in CA 25-28R
McNally, Clare 230
See also HGG
McNally, Curtis
See Birchall, Ian H(arry)
McNally, Dennis 1949- CANR-119
Earlier sketch in CA 103
McNally, Gertrude Bancroft 1908(?)-1985
Obituary 115
McNally, John 1914- 17-20R
McNally, John (Raymond) 1965- 215
McNally, Raymond T(homas)
1931-2002 .... CANR-14
Obituary 211
Earlier sketch in CA 37-40R
McNally, Robert 1946- 107
McNally, Robert E(dward)
1917-1978 .... CANR-11
Earlier sketch in CA 21-24R
McNally, T. M. 1961- .... CLC 82
McNally, Terrence 1939- CANR-116
Earlier sketches in CA 45-48, CANR-2, 56
See also AAYA 62
See also AMWS 13
See also CAD
See also CD 5, 6
See also CLC 4, 7, 41, 91
See also DA3
See also DAM DRAM
See also DFS 16, 19
See also DLB 7, 249
See also EWL 3
See also GLL 1
See also MTCW 2
See also MTFW 2005
McNally, Tom 1923-2002 85-88
Obituary 207
McNally, Vincent J. 1943- 192
McNamara, Brooks 1937- 25-28R
McNamara, Dennis L. 1945- 136
McNamara, Eugene (Joseph) 1930- .. CANR-53
Earlier sketches in CA 21-24R, CANR-10, 26
See also CP 1
McNamara, Jo Ann 1931- CANR-15
Earlier sketch in CA 85-88
McNamara, John J(oseph), Jr.
1932-1986 .... 41-44R
Obituary 120
McNamara, John S. 1908(?)-1977
Obituary 69-72
McNamara, Kathleen R. 1962- 176
McNamara, Kevin (John) 1926-1987 ..... 25-28R
Obituary 122
McNamara, Lena Brooke 1891-1983 .... CAP-1
Earlier sketch in CA 11-12
McNamara, Margaret C(raig)
1915-1981 .... SATA-Obit 24
McNamara, Michael M. 1940-1979
Obituary 89-92
McNamara, Peter 1959- 186
McNamara, Robert (James) 1950- 218
McNamara, Robert S(trange)
1916- CANR-109
Brief entry 112
Earlier sketches in CA 129, CANR-63
McNamara, Sister Marie Aquinas
See Schaub, Marilyn McNamara
McNamara, William E. 1926- CANR-4
Earlier sketch in CA 1-4R
McNamee, Eoin 1961- CANR-116
Earlier sketch in CA 152
McNamee, James 1904- 5-8R
McNamee, Lawrence F. 1917- 25-28R
McNamee, Maurice B(asil) 1909- 5-8R
McNamee, Thomas 1947- 125
McNamer, Deirdre 1950- 188
McNamer, Deirdre 1950- .... CLC 70
McNarie, Alan Decker 1954- 143
McNaron, Toni (A. H.) 1937- 139
McNaspy, Clement James 1915- CANR-2
Earlier sketch in CA 5-8R
McNaught, Brian Robert 1948- 105
McNaught, Harry 106
See also SATA 32
McNaught, Judith 1944- CANR-135
Earlier sketch in CA 138
See also RHW
McNaught, Kenneth (William Kirkpatrick)
1918- 29-32R
McNaughton, Arnold 1930- 57-60
McNaughton, Brian 1935-2004 229
McNaughton, Colin 1951- CANR-112
Earlier sketches in CA 112, CANR-47
See also CLR 54
See also SATA 39, 92, 134
McNaughton, Deborah (L.) 1950- 233
McNaughton, Frank 1906(?)-1978
Obituary 81-84
McNaughton, Howard (Douglas) 1945- .. 57-60
McNaughton, Janet 1953- 172
See also SATA 110, 162
McNaughton, Wayne L. 1902-1982 .... 1-4R
McNaughton, William (Frank) 1933- 41-44R
McNeal, Patricia 1942- 144
McNeal, Robert H(atch) 1930- 9-12R
Mcneal, Shay 1946- 219
McNeal, Tom .... CLC 119
McNear, Robert 1930(?)-1985
Obituary 117
McNeely, Jeannette 1918- 41-44R
See also SATA 25
McNeely, Jerry Clark 1928- 193
Brief entry 115
McNeer, May (Yonge) 1902-1994 ...... CANR-2
Obituary 146
Earlier sketch in CA 5-8R
See also SATA 1, 81
McNees, Pat 1940- CANR-128
Earlier sketches in CA 57-60, CANR-7
McNeese, Tim 1953- 210
See also SATA 139
McNeil, Art 1944- 124
McNeil, Barbara L(aurie) 1951- 97-100
McNeil, Bill
See McNeil, William Russell
McNeil, Elton B(urbank) 1924-1974 ...... CAP-2
Earlier sketch in CA 25-28
McNeil, Florence 1940- 116
See also CCA 1
See also CP 7
See also CWP
See also DLB 60
McNeil, Jean 1968- 220
McNeil, John 1939- 131
McNeil, Larry 1955- 212
McNeil, Legs
See McNeil, Roderick Edward
McNeil, Linda L. 1946- 170
McNeil, Mary 134
McNeil, Maureen (Christena) 1948- 128
McNeil, Roderick Edward 1956- 168
McNeil, W. K. 1940- 154
McNeil, William F. 1932- CANR-121
Earlier sketch in CA 166
McNeil, William Russell 1924- 133
McNeile, Herman Cyril 1888-1937 184
See also Sapper
See also CMW 4
See also DLB 77
McNeill, Anthony 1941- 97-100
See also BW 2
See also CP 2, 3, 4, 5, 6, 7
McNeill, Christine 1953- 153
McNeill, Daniel 1947- 141
McNeill, Donald P(aul) 1936- 107
McNeill, Elisabeth
See Taylor, Elisabeth (D.)
McNeill, J(ohn) R(obert) CANR-98
Earlier sketch in CA 144
McNeill, Janet
See Alexander, Janet
See also SATA 1, 97
McNeill, John J. 1925- 65-68
McNeill, John Thomas 1885-1975 ... CANR-10
Obituary 57-60
Earlier sketches in CAP-1, CA 11-12
McNeill, Louise 1911-1993 139
McNeill, Robert B(lakely) 1915- 17-20R
McNeill, Stuart 1942- 65-68
McNeill, William H(ardy) 1917- CANR-2
Earlier sketch in CA 5-8R
McNeilly, Wilfred (Glassford)
1921-1983 .... CANR-28
Earlier sketch in CA 29-32R
See also HGG
McNeir, Waldo F(orest) 1908-1991 .... 17-20R
McNeish, James 1931- CANR-29
Earlier sketches in CA 69-72, CANR-12
See also CN 3, 7
McNelly, Theodore (Hart) 1919- 5-8R
McNelly, Willis E(verett) 1920-2003 107
Obituary 216
McNew, Ben(nie) B(anks) 1931- CANR-3
Earlier sketch in CA 9-12R
McNicholl, Damian 236
McNichols, Charles L(ongstreth)
1887- .... TCWW 1, 2
McNickle, (William) D'Arcy
1904-1977 .... CANR-45
Obituary 85-88
Earlier sketches in CA 9-12R, CANR-5
See also CLC 89
See also DAM MULT
See also DLB 175, 212
See also NNAL
See also RGAL 4
See also SATA-Obit 22
See also TCWW 1, 2
McNicoll, Alan (Wedel Ramsay) 1908-1987
Obituary 124
McNicoll, Robert E. 1907- 37-40R
McNicoll, Sylvia (Marilyn) 1954- ... CANR-139
Earlier sketch in CA 163
See also CLR 99
See also SATA 113
McNiece, Harold Francis 1923-1972
Obituary 37-40R
McNierney, Mary Alice 9-12R
McNiff, William John 1899-1987
Obituary 122
McNitt, Gale 1921- 57-60
McNiven, Malcolm A(lbert) 1929- 29-32R
McNown, John S(tephenson) 1916- 57-60
McNulty, Edward N. 1936- CANR-25
Earlier sketches in CA 65-68, CANR-10
McNulty, Faith 1918-2005 .... CANR-118
Obituary 238
Earlier sketches in CA 49-52, CANR-1, 25
See also ANW
See also SATA 12, 84, 139
McNulty, James Edmund, Jr. 1924-1965 .... 1-4R
Obituary 103
McNulty, James Francis 1934-1979
Obituary 113
McNulty, John K. 1934- 195
McNutt, Dan James 1938- 61-64
McNutt, James (Allen) 1944- 49-52
McNutt, Patrick A. 1957- 165
McNutt, Randy 1948- 193
McOwan, Rennie 1933- CANR-37
Earlier sketch in CA 115
McPhail, David M(ichael) 1940- CANR-119
Earlier sketches in CA 85-88, CANR-22, 38, 56
See also MAICYA 1, 2
See also SATA 47, 81, 140
See also SATA-Brief 32
McPhail, Helen 1939- 197
McPhail, Kate
See Lynn (Ruiz), Kathryn
McPharlin, Paul 1903-1948
Brief entry 110
See also SATA-Brief 31
McPhaul, Jack
See McPhaul, John J.
McPhaul, John J. 1904-1983 .... 9-12R
Obituary 110
McPhee, Arthur G(ene) 1945- 185
Brief entry 116
Mcphee, James
See James, Laurence
McPhee, Jenny 208
McPhee, John (Angus) 1931- CANR-121
Earlier sketches in CA 65-68, CANR-20, 46, 64, 69
See also AAYA 61
See also AMWS 3
See also ANW
See also BEST 90:1
See also CLC 36
See also CPW
See also DLB 185, 275
See also MTCW 1, 2
See also MTFW 2005
See also TUS
McPhee, Martha (A.) 1964- CANR-123
Earlier sketch in CA 165
McPhee, Norma H. 1928- 160
See also SATA 95
McPhee, Richard B(yron) 1934- 111
See also SATA 41
McPhee, Sarah (Collyer) 1960- 225
McPhee, William N(orvell) 1921- 17-20R
McPherson, Anna Talbott 1904- CANR-19
Earlier sketches in CA 1-4R, CANR-4
McPherson, Conor 1971- 229
See also CD 5, 6
McPherson, Gertrude H(untington)
1923- 45-48
McPherson, Harry Cummings, Jr. 1929- 104
McPherson, Holt 1907(?)-1979
Obituary 89-92
McPherson, Hugo (Archibald) 1921- 29-32R
McPherson, James Alan 1943- CANR-140
Earlier sketches in CA 25-28R, CANR-24, 74
See also CAAS 17
See also BLCS
See also BW 1, 3
See also CLC 19, 77
See also CN 3, 4, 5, 6
See also CSW
See also DLB 38, 244
See also EWL 3
See also MTCW 1, 2
See also MTFW 2005
See also RGAL 4
See also RGSF 2
McPherson, James Lowell 1921- 13-16R
McPherson, James M(unro) 1936- .. CANR-120
Earlier sketches in CA 9-12R, CANR-31, 95
Interview in CANR-31
See also AAYA 57
See also MTCW 1
See also SATA 16, 141
McPherson, John 1925- 119
McPherson, Sandra 1943- CANR-70
Earlier sketches in CA 29-32R, CANR-12
See also CAAS 23
See also CP 7
See also CWP
See also DLBY 1986
McPherson, Thomas Herdman 1925- 17-20R
McPherson, William (Alexander)
1933- CANR-28
Earlier sketch in CA 69-72
Interview in CANR-28
See also CLC 34
McPherson, William 1939- 57-60
McPhie, Walter E(van) 1926- 29-32R
McQuade, Ann Aikman 1928- CANR-34
Earlier sketch in CA 1-4R
McQuade, De Rosset Morrissey 1934(?)-1978
Obituary 81-84
McQuade, Donald A(nthony) 1941- . CANR-16
Earlier sketch in CA 65-68
McQuade, Walter 1922- 103
McQuaid, Kim 1947- CANR-49
Earlier sketches in CA 107, CANR-24
McQuaig, Jack Hunter 9-12R
McQuaig, Linda 1951- 127
McQuain, Jeffrey Hunter 1955- 203
McQuarrie, Christopher 1968- 198
McQuay, Mike
See Goulart, Ron(ald Joseph)
McQuay, Peri Phillips 1945- 202
McQueen, Cilla 1949- 154
See also CP 7
See also CWP
McQueen, Cyrus B. 1951-1999 135
McQueen, Ian 1930- 104
McQueen, Lucinda 1950- .... SATA 58
See also SATA-Brief 48
McQueen, Mildred Hark 1908-1978 ..... CAP-1
Earlier sketch in CA 9-10
See also SATA 12
McQueen, Rod 231
McQueen, William A. 1926- 21-24R
McQuigg, R. Bruce 1927- 17-20R
McQuilkin, Frank 1936- CANR-13
Earlier sketch in CA 33-36R
McQuillan, Karin 1950- 133
McQuillan, Kevin 1951- 192
McQuin, Susan Coultrap
See Coultrap-McQuin, Susan (M.)
McQuiston, Joanne W(orth) 1922(?)-1985
Obituary 117
McQuiston, Liz 1952- 238
McQuown, F(rederic) R(ichard) 1907- 9-12R
McQuown, Judith H(ershkowitz) 1941- 107
McQuown, Norman A(nthony) 1914- 126
Brief entry 106
McRae, Barry (Donald) 1935- 136
McRae, Donald 228
McRae, Edward (Actun) 1932- 178
McRae, Hamish (Malcolm Donald)
1943- 57-60
McRae, Kenneth D(ouglas)
1925-1997 .... CANR-17
Earlier sketch in CA 1-4R
McRae, Lindsay
See Sowerby, A(rthur) L(indsay) M(cRae)
McRae, Robert (Forbes) 1914- 77-80
McRae, Russell (William) 1934- 129
See also SATA 63
McRae, William John 1933- 106
McReynolds, David 1929- 29-32R
McReynolds, Edwin C(larence)
1890-1967 .... CAP-1
Earlier sketch in CA 19-20
McReynolds, Patricia Justiniani 1926- 177
McReynolds, Ronald W(eldon) 1934- 49-52
McRobbie, Kenneth A(lan) 1929- 203
See also CP 1
McRoberts, Agnesann
See Meek, Pauline Palmer
McRoberts, Omar Maurice 229
McRoberts, R(obert) Lewis 1944- 33-36R
McShan, James 1937- 69-72
McShane, Fred
See Elman, Richard (Martin)
McShane, Joseph M(ichael) 1949- 127
McShane, Mark 1930- CANR-61
Earlier sketches in CA 17-20R, CANR-7, 22
See also CMW 4
McShane, Philip 1932- 69-72
McShean, Gordon 1936- 108
See also SATA 41
McSherry, Frank D(avid), Jr.
1927-1997 .... CANR-47
Obituary 198
Earlier sketches in CA 107, CANR-23
McSherry, James E(dward) 1920- CANR-28
Earlier sketch in CA 49-52
McShine, Kynaston
See McShine, Kynaston L(eigh)
McShine, Kynaston L(eigh) 1935- 134
Brief entry 115
McSorley, Jean Sarah 1958- 133
McSorley, Joseph 1874-1963 .... CAP-1
Earlier sketch in CA 13-16
McSweeney, Kerry 1941- 220
McSweeny, Maxine 1905- 61-64
Mc Swigan, Marie 1907-1962 73-76
See also SATA 24
McTaggart, Fred 1939- 65-68
McTaggart, J. McT. Ellis
See McTaggart, John McTaggart Ellis
McTaggart, John McTaggart Ellis 1866-1925
Brief entry 120
See also DLB 262
See also TCLC 105
McTaggart, Lynne (Ann) 1951- CANR-140
Brief entry 113
Earlier sketch in CA 145
McTeer, Wilson 1905-1987 .... 41-44R
McVaugh, Michael R(ogers) 1938- ... CANR-99
Earlier sketch in CA 147
McVay, Gordon 1941- 73-76
McVean, James
See Luard, Nicholas
McVeigh, Malcolm J(ames) 1931- 61-64
McVeity, Jen 222
See also SATA 148
McVey, Ruth T(homas) 1930- 109
McVey, Vicki 1946- 148
See also SATA 80
McVickar, Elinor Guthrie 1902(?)-1982
Obituary 106
McVicker, Charles (Taggart) 1930- .... SATA 39
McVicker, Chuck
See McVicker, Charles (Taggart)
McVicker, Daphne Alloway 1895-1979
Obituary 85-88
McVicker, Steve 223
McWaters, Barry 1937- 108
McWhiney, Grady 1928- CANR-6
Earlier sketch in CA 5-8R
McWhinney, Edward Watson 1926- . CANR-52
Earlier sketches in CA 29-32R, CANR-12, 28
McWhinnie, Donald 1920-1987
Obituary 123
McWhirter, A(lan) Ross 1925-1975 .. CANR-46
Obituary 61-64
Earlier sketch in CA 17-20R
See also SATA 37
See also SATA-Obit 31

McWhirter 394 CONTEMPORARY AUTHORS

McWhirter, George 1939- CANR-13
Earlier sketch in CA 77-80
See also CP 2, 3, 4, 5, 6, 7
See also DLB 60
McWhirter, Glenna S. 1929- 89-92
McWhirter, Nickie
See McWhirter, Glenna S.
McWhirter, Norris (Dewar)
1925-2004 .... CANR-50
Obituary 227
Earlier sketch in CA 13-16R
See also SATA 37
McWhirter, Teresa A. 1971- 223
McWhorter, Diane 200
McWhorter, John H. 193
McWhorter, Kathleen T. 1944- 190
McWilliam, Candia 1955- CANR-144
Earlier sketch in CA 136
See also CN 6, 7
See also DLB 267
McWilliams, Carey 1905-1980 .... CANR-2
Obituary 101
Earlier sketch in CA 45-48
See also DLB 137
McWilliams, John P(robasco), Jr.
1940- CANR-101
Earlier sketches in CA 49-52, CANR-28
McWilliams, Karen 1943- 133
See also SATA 65
McWilliams, Kelly 1987- 238
McWilliams, Margaret (Ann Edgar)
1929- CANR-26
Earlier sketches in CA 17-20R, CANR-8
McWilliams, Peter 1949-2000 .... CANR-72
Obituary 188
Earlier sketch in CA 41-44R
McWilliams, Wilson Carey
1933-2005 .... CANR-40
Obituary 237
Earlier sketches in CA 103, CANR-19
Mda, Zakes
See Mda, Zanemvula (Kizito Gatyeni)
See also CD 6
Mda, Zanemvula (Kizito Gatyeni) 1948- 205
See also Mda, Zakes
See also CD 5
See also DLB 225
Mdurvwa, Hajara E. 1962- 156
See also SATA 92
Meacham, Beth 1951- 166
Meacham, Ellis K. 1913-1998 .... 25-28R
Meacham, Harry M(onroe) 1901-1975 .. CAP-2
Earlier sketch in CA 25-28
Meacham, Jon 1969- 230
Meacham, Margaret 1952- CANR-42
Earlier sketch in CA 118
See also SATA 95
Meacham, Standish (Jr.) 1932- CANR-100
Brief entry 110
Earlier sketch in CA 135
Meacher, Michael Hugh 1939- 109
Meachum, Virginia 1918- CANR-111
Earlier sketch in CA 151
See also SATA 87, 133
Meacock, Heather 1949- 211
Mead, Alice 1952- CANR-127
Earlier sketch in CA 159
See also AAYA 59
See also SATA 94, 146
Mead, Chris(topher John) 1940-2003 228
Mead, Chris 1959- 142
Mead, Christopher Curtis 1953- 140
Mead, D(onald) Eugene 1934- 65-68
Mead, Edgar T(horn), Jr. 1922- 113
Mead, Frank Spencer 1898-1982 .... CANR-9
Obituary 107
Earlier sketches in CAP-1, CA 19-20
Mead, G(eorge) R(obert) S(tow) 1863-1933
Brief entry 122
Mead, George Herbert 1863-1931 212
See also DLB 270
See also TCLC 89
Mead, Harold C(harles) H(ugh) 1910- ... CAP-1
Earlier sketch in CA 13-14
Mead, Jane 1958- 199
Mead, Jude 1919- 25-28R
Mead, Margaret 1901-1978 .... CANR-4
Obituary 81-84
Earlier sketch in CA 1-4R
See also AITN 1
See also CLC 37
See also DA3
See also FW
See also MTCW 1, 2
See also SATA-Obit 20
Mead, Matthew 1924- 101
See also CAAS 13
See also CP 1, 2, 3, 4, 5, 6, 7
See also DLB 40
Mead, Peter (Willan) 1911- 116
Mead, Philip (Stirling) 1953- 154
See also CP 7
Mead, Robert Douglas 1928-1983 .... 41-44R
Obituary 110
Mead, Russell
See Koehler, Margaret (Hudson)
Mead, Russell (M., Jr.) 1935- 9-12R
See also SATA 10
Mead, (Edward) Shepherd 1914-1994 ..... 9-12R
Obituary 198
Mead, Sidney E(arl) 1904-1999 .... CAP-1
Earlier sketch in CA 9-10
Mead, Sidney (Hirini) Moko 1927- . CANR-105
Earlier sketches in CA 106, CANR-23, 49
Mead, Stella (?)-1981
Obituary 103
See also SATA-Obit 27
Mead, Taylor 1931(?)- 126
Brief entry 116
See also DLB 16
Mead, Walter B(ruce) 1934- 37-40R
Mead, Walter Russell 1952- 233
Mead, William B(owmar) 1934- CANR-32
Earlier sketches in CA 85-88, CANR-15
Mead, William Richard 1915- 103
Meade, Bill C.
See Rogers, Paul T(aylor)
Meade, Dorothy (Joan Sampson) 1923- .. 9-12R
Meade, Elizabeth Thomasina 1854(?)-1914(?)
Brief entry 112
See also Meade, L. T.
Meade, Ellen
See Roddick, Ellen
See also SATA 5
Meade, Everard 1914-2000 .... 25-28R
Meade, Glenn 170
Meade, Holly 237
Meade, James Edward 1907-1995 ...... CANR-2
Obituary 150
Earlier sketch in CA 1-4R
Meade, L. T.
See Meade, Elizabeth Thomasina
See also DLB 141
Meade, Marion 1934- 236
Earlier sketches in CA 49-52, CANR-1, 53, 98
Autobiographical Essay in 236
See also SATA 23, 127
Meade, Mary
See Church, Ruth Ellen (Lovrien)
Meade, Richard
See Haas, Ben(jamin) L(eopold)
Meade, Richard A(ndrew) 1911-1983 45-48
Meade, Robert Douthat 1903-1970(?) CAP-2
Earlier sketch in CA 25-28
Meader, Jonathan 1943- 173
Meader, Stephen W(arren) 1892-1977 ...... 5-8R
See also CWRI 5
See also SATA 1
Meades, Jonathan (Turner) 1947- CANR-140
Earlier sketch in CA 130
Meadmore, Susan
See Sallis, Susan (Diana)
Meador, Roy 1929- CANR-11
Earlier sketch in CA 69-72
Meadow, Barry 1947- CANR-94
Earlier sketch in CA 125
Meadow, Charles T(roub) 1929- CANR-15
Earlier sketch in CA 29-32R
See also SATA 23
Meadow, Kathryn Pendleton 1929- CANR-7
Earlier sketch in CA 57-60
Meadowcroft, Enid LaMonte
See Wright, Enid Meadowcroft (LaMonte)
Meadowes, Alicia
See Burak, Linda (Gallina) and
Zieg, Joan (Gallina)
Meadows, A(rthur) J(ack) 1934- 137
Meadows, Audrey 1924(?)-1996 160
Meadows, Eddie S(pencer) 1939- 109
Meadows, Edward 1944- 101
Meadows, Graham (W.) 1934- 237
See also SATA 161
Meadows, Jack
See Meadows, A(rthur) J(ack)
Meadows, Lee E. 1951- 214
Meadows, Paul 1913-1984 .... 41-44R
Meadows, Peter
See Lindsay, Jack
Meagher, John C(arney)
1935-2003 .... CANR-136
Earlier sketches in CA 17-20R, CANR-11
Meagher, Paul Kevin 1907-1976
Obituary 69-72
Meagher, Robert E(mmett) 1943- CANR-10
Earlier sketch in CA 25-28R
Meagher, Robert F. 1927- 41-44R
Meaker, Eloise 1915- CANR-28
Earlier sketch in CA 105
Meaker, M. J.
See Meaker, Marijane (Agnes)
Meaker, Marijane (Agnes) 1927- CANR-63
Earlier sketches in CA 107, CANR-37
Interview in CA-107
See also Aldrich, Ann and
James, Mary and
Kerr, M. E. and
Packer, Vin
See also JRDA
See also MAICYA 1, 2
See also MAICYAS 1
See also MTCW 1
See also SATA 20, 61, 99, 160
See also SATA-Essay 111
See also YAW
Meakin, David 1943- 69-72
Meallet, Sandro 1965- 209
Meaney, John 1957- 239
Means, David 205
Means, Florence Crannell
1891-1980 .... CANR-37
Obituary 103
Earlier sketch in CA 1-4R
See also CLR 56
See also MAICYA 1, 2
See also SATA 1
See also SATA-Obit 25
See also YAW
Means, Gardiner C(oit) 1896-1988
Obituary 124
Means, Gordon P(aul) 1927- 33-36R
Means, Howard 1944- 141
Means, John Barkley 1939- 33-36R
Means, Louis Edgar 1902-1983 .... CANR-2
Earlier sketch in CA 5-8R
Means, Marianne Hansen 1934- 9-12R
Means, Richard K(eith) 1929- CANR-17
Earlier sketches in CA 5-8R, CANR-2
Means, Russell (Charles) 1939- 158
Meany, George 1894-1980
Obituary 97-100
Meany, Tom 1903-1964 193
See also DLB 171
Meara, (Mary) Jane (Frances) Cavolina
1954- 120
Meara, Mary Jane Frances Cavolina
See Meara, (Mary) Jane (Frances) Cavolina
Meares, Ainslie Dixon 1910-1986 .... CANR-11
Earlier sketch in CA 25-28R
Meares, Leonard Frank 1921-
See Grover, Marshall
Mearian, Judy Frank 1936- 101
See also SATA 49
Mearns, Barbara (Crawford) 1955- ... CANR-82
Earlier sketch in CA 132
Mearns, David Chambers 1899-1981 .... 1-4R
Obituary 104
Mearns, Richard (James) 1950- CANR-90
Earlier sketch in CA 132
Mears, Brainerd, Jr. 1921- 53-56
Mears, Gillian 1964- 168
Mears, Richard Chase 1935- 101
Mears, Walter R(obert) 1935- CANR-138
Brief entry 111
Earlier sketch in CA 113
Interview in CA-113
Mearsheimer, John J(oseph) 1947- .. CANR-109
Earlier sketch in CA 117
Measday, George
See Soderberg, Percy Measday
Measham, D(onald) C. 1932- 21-24R
Measures, (William) Howard 1894- CAP-1
Earlier sketch in CA 13-14
Meath, Michael
See Marquis, Max
Mebane, John (Harrison) 1909-1987 ..... 13-16R
Mebane, Mary E(lizabeth) 1933- CANR-30
Earlier sketch in CA 73-76
Mebus, Scott 1974- 233
Mecca, Judy Truesdell 1955- 197
See also SATA 127
Mech, Dave
See Mech, L(ucyan) David
Mech, L(ucyan) David 1937- CANR-14
Earlier sketch in CA 33-36R
Mecham, John Lloyd 1893-1992 .... 1-4R
Mechanic, David 1936- CANR-19
Earlier sketches in CA 5-8R, CANR-3
Mechanic, Sylvia (Gertrude) 1920- 69-72
Mechik, Sergei
See Dovlatov, Sergei
Mechin, Jacques Benoist
See Benoist-Mechin, Jacques
Mechthild von Magdeburg c. 1207-c.
1282 .... DLB 138
Meckel, Christoph 1935- 192
See also EWL 3
Meckel, Richard A(lan) 1948- 135
Meckier, Jerome (Thomas) 1941- 33-36R
Meckler, Alan Marshall 1945- 57-60
Meckley, Richard F(rederick) 1928- 37-40R
Mecklin, John Martin 1918-1971
Obituary 33-36R
Meckstroth, Jacob A. 1887(?)-1985
Obituary 115
Meckstroth, Jake
See Meckstroth, Jacob A.
Medalia, Leon S. 1881-1980 85-88
Medary, Marjorie 1890-1980 73-76
See also SATA 14
Medavoy, Mike 1941- 206
Medawar, Jean (Shinglewood Taylor)
1913-2005 .... CANR-100
Obituary 239
Earlier sketch in CA 134
Medawar, Peter Brian 1915-1987 97-100
Obituary 123
Medd, Charles Leighton 1928-1989
Obituary 130
Medd, Patrick 1919-1995 150
Meddaugh, Susan 1944- CANR-105
Earlier sketch in CA 106
See also MAICYA 2
See also MAICYAS 1
See also SATA 29, 84, 125
Meddeb, Abdelwahab 1946- 233
Meddis, Ray 1944- 77-80
Medea, Andra 1953- 57-60
Medearis, Angela Shelf 1956- 194
See also MAICYA 2
See also SATA 72, 123
Medearis, John 1963- 226
Medearis, Mary 1915- 69-72
See also SATA 5
Medeiros, Earl Caton 1933- 89-92
Medeiros, Teresa 1962- CANR-97
Earlier sketch in CA 142
Medford, Margaret
See Graves, Roy Neil
Medhin, Tsegaye (Kawessa) Gabre
See Gabre-Medhin, Tsegaye (Kawessa)
Medhurst, Joan
See Liverton, Joan
Medhurst, Martin J. 1952- CANR-124
Earlier sketch in CA 161
Medici, Lorenza de
See de Medici, Lorenza
Medici, Marino de
See de Medici, Marino
Medicine-Eagle, Brooke 1943- CANR-116
Earlier sketch in CA 140
Medicus II
See Philipp, Elliot Elias
Medill, Joseph 1823-1899 .... DLB 43
Medina, Jane 1953- 195
See also SATA 122
Medina, Jeremy T(yler) 1942- CANR-11
Earlier sketch in CA 69-72
Medina, Pablo 1948- CANR-127
Earlier sketch in CA 177
See also HW 2
Medina, Robert C. 1924- 153
See also HW 1
Medina, William A.
See Medina, William Antonio
Medina, William Antonio 1935-1985
Obituary 117
Medley, Anne
See Borchard, Ruth (Berendsohn)
Medley, (Rachel) Margaret 1918-2000 .. 13-16R
Obituary 188
Medley, Morris L(ee) 1942- 57-60
Medlicott, Alexander G(uild), Jr. 1927- . 37-40R
Medlicott, Joan 1932(?)- 214
Medlicott, Margaret P(aget) 1913- 29-32R
Medlicott, Mary 1946- 152
See also SATA 88
Medlicott, William Norton 1900-1987 .... 9-12R
Obituary 123
Medlin, Virgil D(ewain) 1943- 57-60
Mednick, Murray 1939- 21-24R
See also CAD
See also CD 5, 6
Medoff, Jeslyn 1951- 128
Medoff, Jillian 1963- 166
Medoff, Mark (Howard) 1940- CANR-5
Earlier sketch in CA 53-56
Interview in CANR-5
See also AITN 1
See also CAD
See also CD 5, 6
See also CLC 6, 23
See also DAM DRAM
See also DFS 4
See also DLB 7
Medsger, Betty (Louise) 1942- 113
Medsker, Leland L. 1905-1978 .... CANR-2
Earlier sketch in CA 1-4R
Medusa
See Harrison, Susan Frances (Riley)
Medved, Diane 1951- 132
Medved, Harry 1961(?)- 93-96
Medved, Michael 1948- CANR-45
Earlier sketches in CA 65-68, CANR-11
Medvedev, Grigori 1933- 141
Medvedev, P. N.
See Bakhtin, Mikhail Mikhailovich
Medvedev, Roy (Alexandrovich)
1925- CANR-110
Earlier sketch in CA 81-84
Medvedev, Zhores A(leksandrovich)
1925- 69-72
Medwall, Henry 1461- .... RGEL 2
Medway, Gareth J. 227
Medwed, Mameve CANR-140
Earlier sketch in CA 160
Medwick, Cathleen 1948- 188
Mee, Bob 225
Mee, Charles L., Jr. 1938- CANR-50
Earlier sketches in CA 45-48, CANR-3
See also CD 5, 6
See also SATA 8, 72
Mee, Fiona 1946(?)-1978
Obituary 104
Mee, John F(ranklin) 1908-1985 .... CAP-1
Earlier sketch in CA 9-10
Mee, Susie (B.) 1938- 154
Meechan, Hugh L(awrence) 1933- 17-20R
Meed, Vladka 1923-
Meehan, Brenda 1942- 229
Meehan, Daniel Joseph 1930-1978
Obituary 77-80
Meehan, Danny
See Meehan, Daniel Joseph
Meehan, Eugene J(ohn) 1923- CANR-14
Earlier sketch in CA 37-40R
Meehan, Francis X(avier) 1937- 116
Meehan, Michael 196
Meehan, Paula 1955- CANR-116
Earlier sketch in CA 154
See also CP 7
See also CWP
Meehan, Richard Lawrence 1939- 107
Meehan, Thomas Edward 1932- CANR-28
Earlier sketch in CA 29-32R
Meehan-Waters, Brenda
See Meehan, Brenda
Meehl, Paul E(verett) 1920-2003 93-96
Obituary 213
Meek, Alexander Beaufort 1814-1865 ... DLB 3,
248
Meek, Edwin 1951- 196
Meek, Forrest B(urns) 1928- 110
Meek, H(arold) A(lan) 1922- CANR-71
Earlier sketch in CA 129
Meek, Jacklyn O'Hanlon 1933- 77-80
See also SATA 51
See also SATA-Brief 34
Meek, Jay 1937- CANR-25
Earlier sketch in CA 107
Meek, Joseph
See Randisi, Robert J(oseph)
Meek, Lois Hayden
See Stolz, Lois (Hayden) Meek
Meek, Loyal George 1918- 73-76

Meek, M(argaret) R(eid) D(uncan) 1918- ... CANR-114
Earlier sketches in CA 142, CANR-66
See also CMW 4
Meek, Margaret
See Meek Spencer, Margaret (Diston)
Meek, Pauline Palmer 1917- ... 106
Meek, Ronald L(indley) 1917-1978 ... CANR-6
Earlier sketch in CA 9-12R
Meek, S(terner St.) P(aul) 1894-1972 ... CANR-88
Obituary ... 103
Earlier sketch in CA 1-4R
See also SATA-Obit 28
See also SFW 4
Meeke, Mary (?)-1816(?) ... DLB 116
Meeker, Alice (MacCutcheon) 1904-1987 ... CAP-2
Earlier sketch in CA 25-28
Meeker, Clare Hodgson 1952- ... 161
See also SATA 96
Meeker, Joseph W(arren) 1932- ... CANR-28
Earlier sketch in CA 49-52
Meeker, Mary Nacol 1928- ... 53-56
Meeker, Oden 1919(?)-1976 ... 73-76
Obituary ... 65-68
See also SATA 14
Meeker, Richard
See Brown, Fornan
Meeker, Richard Kilburn 1925-(?) ... CAP-2
Earlier sketch in CA 19-20
Meeks, Christopher (Nelson) 1953- ... 193
Meeks, Esther MacBain ... 1-4R
See also SATA 1
Meeks, John E. ... 33-36R
Meeks, Kenneth 1963- ... 195
Meeks, Linda A.
See Brower, Linda A.
Meeks, M(errill) Douglas 1941- ... 93-96
Meeks, Wayne A. 1932- ... CANR-54
Earlier sketches in CA 13-16R, CANR-5, 28
Meek Spencer, Margaret (Diston) 1925- ... CANR-21
Earlier sketch in CA 105
Meen, Victor Ben 1910-1971
Obituary ... 106
Meenan, James F(rancis) 1910-1987 ... 124
Meer, Fatima 1929- ... 73-76
Meerhaeghe, M(arcel) A(lfons) G(ilbert) Van
See Van Meerhaeghe, M(arcel) A(lfons) G(ilbert)
Meerloo, Joost A(braham) M(aurits) 1903-1976 ... CANR-4
Obituary ... 69-72
Earlier sketch in CA 1-4R
Meeropol, Abel 1903(?)-1986
Obituary ... 121
Meeropol, Robert 1947(?)- ... 224
Meerson, Lazare 1900-1938 ... IDFW 3, 4
Meese, Elizabeth Ann 1943- ... 122
Meeter, Glenn 1934- ... CANR-12
Earlier sketch in CA 33-36R
Meeth, Louis Richard 1934- ... 17-20R
Meeuse, Bastiaan (Jacob Dirk) 1916-1999 .. 119
Obituary ... 185
Meezan, William 1947- ... 117
Megargee, Edwin I(nglee) 1937- ... CANR-7
Earlier sketch in CA 17-20R
Megarry, Tim 1941- ... CANR-137
Earlier sketch in CA 162
Meged, Aharon
See Megged, Aharon
Meged, Aron
See Megged, Aharon
Megged, Aharon 1920- ... CANR-140
Earlier sketches in CA 49-52, CANR-1
See also CAAS 13
See also CLC 9
See also EWL 3
Meggendorfer, Lothar 1847-1925
Brief entry ... 115
See also SATA-Brief 36
Meggers, Betty J(ane) 1921- ... 17-20R
Meggitt, M(ervyn) J(ohn) 1924- ... 13-16R
Meggs, Brown (Moore) 1930-1997 ... CANR-7
Obituary ... 162
Earlier sketch in CA 61-64
Meggs, Libby Phillips 1943- ... SATA 130
Meggs, Philip B(axter) 1942-2002 ... 116
Obituary ... 211
Meggyesy, Dave
See Meggyesy, David M.
Meggyesy, David M. 1941- ... 33-36R
Megill, Kenneth Alden 1939-
Brief entry ... 106
Megivern, James J(oseph) 1931- ... 167
Meglin, Nick 1935- ... CANR-124
Earlier sketches in CA 69-72, CANR-21, 45
Meglitsch, Paul A(llen) 1914-1982 ... 53-56
Mego, Al
See Roberts, Arthur O.
Megrah, Maurice Henry 1896-1985
Obituary ... 116
Megson, Barbara 1930- ... 29-32R
Mehaffey, Karen Rae 1959- ... 140
Mehaffy, Robert E(ugene) 1935- ... 113
Mehan, Joseph Albert 1929- ... 101
Mehdevi, Alexander (Sinclair) 1947- ... 49-52
See also SATA 7
Mehdevi, Anne (Marie) Sinclair 1947- ... 5-8R
See also SATA 8
Mehdi, M(ohammed) T(aki) 1928-1998 ... CANR-8
Obituary ... 167
Earlier sketch in CA 17-20R
Mehegan, John (Francis) 1920(?)-1984 ... 5-8R
Obituary ... 112
Meher Baba
See Baba, Meher
Mehl, Roger 1912-1997 ... CANR-21
Earlier sketches in CA 9-12R, CANR-6
Mehlinger, Howard D(ean) 1931- ... CANR-6
Earlier sketch in CA 9-12R
Mehlmann, Marilyn 1939- ... 119
Mehnert, Klaus 1906-1984 ... CANR-2
Obituary ... 111
Earlier sketch in CA 1-4R
Meho, Lokman I. 1968- ... 175
Mehr, Joseph (John) 1941-
Brief entry ... 113
Mehrabian, Albert 1939- ... 33-36R
Mehren, Stein 1935- ... EWL 3
Mehrens, William A(rthur) 1937- ... 37-40R
Mehring, Walter 1896-1981 ... 202
Obituary ... 105
See also EWL 3
Mehrotra, Arvind Krishna 1947- ... CANR-116
Earlier sketch in CA 154
See also CP 7
Mehrotra, S(ri) Ram 1931- ... CANR-8
Earlier sketch in CA 13-16R
Mehrtens, Susan E(mily) 1945- ... 53-56
Mehta, Deepa 1950- ... CLC 208
Mehta, Gaganvihari L(allubhai) 1900-1974
Obituary ... 49-52
Mehta, Gita 1943- ... 225
See also CLC 179
See also CN 7
See also DNFS 2
Mehta, J. L. 1912(?)-1988
Obituary ... 126
Mehta, Rustam Jehangir 1912- ... 9-12R
Mehta, Shahnaz ... 106
Mehta, Ved (Parkash) 1934- ... 212
Earlier sketches in CA 1-4R, CANR-2, 23, 69
Autobiographical Essay in ... 212
See also CLC 37
See also MTCW 1
See also MTFW 2005
Mei, Ko-Wang 1918- ... CANR-2
Earlier sketch in CA 45-48
Mei, Lev Aleksandrovich 1822-1862 .. DLB 277
Meidell, Sherry 1951- ... SATA 73
Meiden, Walter 1907- ... CANR-8
Earlier sketch in CA 13-16R
Meier, August 1923-2003 ... CANR-3
Obituary ... 215
Earlier sketch in CA 9-12R
Meier, Barry ... 230
Meier, C(arl) A(lfred) 1905-1995 ... 130
Meier, Christian 1929- ... 174
Meier, Gerald M(arvin) 1923- ... CANR-56
Earlier sketches in CA 112, CANR-30
Meier, Heinz K(arl) 1929- ... 61-64
Meier, Joel F(rancis) 1940- ... 109
Meier, Leslie
See Ruhmkorf, Peter
Meier, Leslie 1948- ... 190
Meier, Mary Jane ... 228
Meier, Matt S(ebastian) 1917-2003 ... CANR-43
Obituary ... 219
Earlier sketches in CA 41-44R, CANR-14
Meier, Minta 1906- ... SATA 55
Meier, Paul D. ... 136
Meier, Richard (Alan) 1934- ... 143
Meier, Richard L(ouis) 1920- ... 17-20R
Meierhenry, Wesley Carl 1915- ... 41-44R
Meiggs, Russell 1902-1989 ... 103
Obituary ... 129
Meighan, Donald Charles 1929- ... CANR-49
Earlier sketches in CA 107, CANR-24
See also SATA 30
Meigs, Alexander James 1921- ... 104
Meigs, Cornelia Lynde 1884-1973 ... 9-12R
Obituary ... 45-48
See also BYA 2
See also CLR 55
See also JRDA
See also MAICYA 1, 2
See also SATA 6
See also WCH
See also YAW
Meigs, Mary 1917- ... 132
Meigs, Peveril 1903-1979 ... 37-40R
Obituary ... 133
Meigs, Walter B(erkeley) 1912-1997 ... 21-24R
Meij, Jacob L(ouis) 1900-1996 ... 5-8R
Meijer, M(arinus) J(ohan) 1912- ... 69-72
Meikle, Clive
See Brooks, Jeremy
Meikle, Jeffrey L(ee) 1949- ... CANR-64
Earlier sketch in CA 101
Meikle, William 1958- ... 217
Meiklejohn, Alexander 1872-1964
Obituary ... 111
Meilach, Dona Z(weigoron) 1926- ... CANR-22
Earlier sketches in CA 9-12R, CANR-5
See also SATA 34
Meilach, Michael D(avid) 1932- ... CANR-2
Earlier sketch in CA 5-8R
Meilaender, Gilbert 1946- ... CANR-116
Earlier sketch in CA 109
Meilen, Bill 1932- ... 69-72
Meillassoux, Claude 1925- ... 25-28R
Meilman, Philip W(arren) 1951- ... 148
See also SATA 79
Mein, Margaret ... 61-64
Meine, Curt 1958- ... 126
Meiners, R(oger) K(eith) 1932- ... CANR-3
Earlier sketch in CA 5-8R
Meiners, Roger Evert 1948- ... 110
Meinesz, Alexandre ... 203
Meinhold, (Johann) Wilhelm 1797-1851 ... SUFW
Meinig, Donald William 1924- ... 112
Meinke, Peter 1932- ... CANR-109
Earlier sketches in CA 25-28R, CANR-29, 53
See also CP 7
See also DLB 5
Meinkoth, Norman A(ugust) 1913-1987 ... 113
Meinstereifel, Ronald L. 1960- ... 203
See also SATA 134
Meintjes, Johannes 1923-1980 ... CANR-8
Earlier sketch in CA 17-20R
Meintjes, Louise 1960- ... 227
Meir, Avinoam 1946- ... CANR-121
Earlier sketch in CA 168
Meir, Golda 1898-1978 ... 89-92
Obituary ... 81-84
Meireles, Cecilia 1901-1964 ... 184
See also DLB 307
See also EWL 3
See also LAW
Meiring, Desmond
See Rice, Desmond Charles
Meiring, Jane (Muriel) 1920- ... CANR-20
Earlier sketch in CA 103
Meisch, Lynn A. 1945- ... 105
Meisch, Richard A(lden) 1943- ... 33-36R
Meisel, Anthony C(lark) 1943- ... 105
Meisel, Gerald Stanley 1937- ... 9-12R
Meisel, John 1923- ... 17-20R
Meisel, Martin 1931- ... CANR-15
Earlier sketch in CA 5-8R
Meisel, Perry 1949- ... CANR-86
Earlier sketch in CA 102
Meisel, Tony
See Meisel, Anthony C(lark)
Meiselas, Susan 1948- ... 106
Meiselman, David I(srael) 1924- ... 13-16R
Meisenhelder, Susan Edwards 1951- ... 221
Meisenholder, Robert 1915- ... 37-40R
Meisler, Richard 1940- ... 124
Meisler, Stanley 1931- ... CANR-51
Earlier sketch in CA 73-76
Meisner, Maurice 1931- ... 21-24R
Meiss, Millard (Lazare) 1904-1975 ... 61-64
Obituary ... 57-60
Meissner, Collin ... 219
Meissner, Hans-Otto 1909- ... CANR-2
Earlier sketch in CA 49-52
Meissner, Kurt 1885-1976 ... CAP-2
Earlier sketch in CA 29-32
Meissner, W(illiam) W. 1931- ... CANR-29
Earlier sketches in CA 33-36R, CANR-13
Meister, Anton D(iderik) 1944- ... 118
Meister, Barbara 1932- ... 102
Meister, Maureen 1953- ... 195
Meister, Peter 1948- ... 192
Meister, Richard J(ulius) 1938- ... 57-60
Meister, Robert 1926- ... CANR-9
Earlier sketch in CA 5-8R
Meixner, John A(lbert) 1925- ... 5-8R
Mejia, Arthur, Jr. 1934- ... 81-84
Mejia, Pedro 1497-1551 ... DLB 318
Mejia Vallejo, Manuel 1923-1998 ... 178
See also DLB 113
See also EWL 3
See also HW 2
Mekas, Jonas 1922-
Brief entry ... 113
Meketa, Jacqueline
See Meketa, Jacqueline Dorgan
Meketa, Jacqueline Dorgan 1926- ... 125
Mekler, Eva 1945- ... CANR-116
Earlier sketch in CA 158
Melady, John 1938- ... CANR-128
Earlier sketches in CA 122, CANR-49
See also SATA-Brief 49
Melady, Thomas Patrick 1927- ... CANR-5
Earlier sketch in CA 9-12R
Melahn, Martha 1924- ... 107
Melamed, Leo 1932- ... 162
Melamid, Alexander 1914-2001 ... 45-48
Melanchthon, Philipp 1497-1560 ... DLB 179
Melancon, Robert 1947- ... 202
See also DLB 60
Meland, Bernard Eugene 1899-1993 ... 17-20R
Melanson, Richard A(llen) 1944- ... 113
Melanter
See Blackmore, R(ichard) D(oddridge)
Melantzon, Ricardo Aguilar
See Aguilar Melantzon, Ricardo
Melaragno, Michele G. 1928- ... 163
Melaro, Constance L(oraine) 1929- ... 17-20R
Melas, Evi 1930- ... 65-68
Melber, Jehuda 1916- ... 29-32R
Melbin, Murray 1927- ... 45-48
Melbo, Irving Robert 1908-1995 ... 49-52
Obituary ... 148
Melby, Ernest O(scar) 1891-1987
Obituary ... 121
Melby, John Fremont 1913-1992
Brief entry ... 106
Melcher, Daniel 1912-1985 ... CANR-49
Obituary ... 116
Earlier sketch in CA 33-36R
See also SATA-Obit 43
Melcher, Frederic Gershom 1879-1963
Obituary ... 89-92
See also SATA-Obit 22
Melcher, Marguerite Fellows 1879-1969 ... 5-8R
See also SATA 10
Melcher, Robert Augustus 1910-1983 ... 17-20R
Melchert, Norman Paul 1933- ... 25-28R
Melchett, Sonia
See Sinclair, Sonia
Melchinger, Siegfried 1906-1988 ... 81-84
Melchior, Ib (Jorgen) 1917- ... CANR-22
Earlier sketches in CA 45-48, CANR-2
Melchiori, Barbara Arnett 1926- ... 142
Meldal-Johnsen, Trevor Bernard 1944- ... CANR-19
Earlier sketch in CA 101
Melden, A(braham) I(rving) 1910-1991 . 17-20R
Melder, Keith E(ugene) 1932- ... 81-84
Meldrum, James
See Broxholme, John Franklin
Mele, Alfred R. 1951- ... 138
Mele, Christopher ... 208
Mele, Frank Michael 1935- ... 53-56
Mele, Jim 1950- ... 113
Melendez (Ramirez), Concha 1895-1983 ... HW 1
Melendez, Conchita
See Melendez (Ramirez), Concha
Melendez, Edwin 1951- ... 142
Melendez, Francisco 1964- ... SATA 72
Melendez, Miguel 1948(?)- ... 223
Melendy, H(oward) Brett 1924- ... CANR-23
Earlier sketches in CA 17-20R, CANR-8
Meleski, Patricia F(erguson) 1935- ... 61-64
Melezh, Ivan 1921(?)-1976
Obituary ... 69-72
Melfi, Leonard 1935- ... 73-76
See also CAD
Melfi, Mary 1951- ... CANR-71
Earlier sketches in CA 113, CANR-32
Melford, Austin (Alfred) 1884-1971
Obituary ... 115
Melford, Michael (Austin) 1916-1999 ... 183
Melges, Buddy
See Melges, Harry C., Jr.
Melges, Harry C., Jr. 1930- ... 130
Melhem, D(iana) H(elen) ... CANR-42
Earlier sketches in CA 49-52, CANR-2
Melhorn, Charles M(ason) 1918-1983 ... 57-60
Obituary ... 111
Melhuish, George (William Seymour) 1916-1985
Obituary ... 117
Melich, Tanya 1936- ... 154
Melick, Arden Davis 1940- ... 106
Melies, Georges 1861-1938 ... TCLC 81
Melikow, Loris
See Hofmannsthal, Hugo von
Melin, Charlotte Ann 1952- ... 196
Melin, Grace Hathaway 1892-1973 ... CAP-2
Obituary ... 45-48
Earlier sketch in CA 21-22
See also SATA 10
Melion, Walter S. 1952- ... 144
Mell
See Lazarus, Mell
Mell, Donald C(harles), Jr. 1931- ... 115
Mell, Max 1882-1971 ... 183
See also DLB 81, 124
Mellaart, James 1925- ... 161
Brief entry ... 118
Mellan, Eleanor 1905-1984 ... 5-8R
Mellan, Ibert 1901-1975 ... 5-8R
Mellan, Olivia 1946- ... CANR-93
Earlier sketch in CA 146
Mellanby, Kenneth 1908-1993 ... 85-88
Obituary ... 143
Mellander, Gustavo Adolfo 1935- ... 33-36R
Mellard, James Milton 1938- ... 105
Mellen, Ida M(ay) 1877-1970 ... 5-8R
Mellen, Joan 1941- ... CANR-11
Earlier sketch in CA 65-68
Mellencamp, Virginia Lynn 1917- ... 9-12R
Meller, Norman 1913-2000 ... 25-28R
Mellers, Wilfrid (Howard) 1914- ... CANR-118
Earlier sketches in CA 5-8R, CANR-4
Mellersh, H(arold) E(dward) L(eslie) 1897- ... CANR-9
Earlier sketch in CA 53-56
See also SATA 10
Mellert, Robert B(oros) 1937- ... 61-64
Mellichamp, Josephine 1923- ... 93-96
Mellin, Jeanne 1929- ... CANR-24
Earlier sketch in CA 49-52
Mellin, Robert 1950- ... 227
Melling, O. R.
See Whelan, G(eraldine) V(alerie)
Melling, Orla
See Whelan, G(eraldine) V(alerie)
Mellinger, Philip J. 1940- ... 156
Mellini, Peter 1935- ... 93-96
Mellinkoff, David 1914-1999 ... 13-16R
Obituary ... 188
Mellinkoff, Ruth 1924- ... CANR-14
Earlier sketch in CA 37-40R
Mellins, Thomas 1957- ... CANR-95
Earlier sketches in CA 122, CANR-49
Mellizo (Cuadrado), Carlos 1942- ... CANR-88
Earlier sketch in CA 130
See also HW 1
Mello, Michael A. 1957- ... 197
Melloan, George 1927- ... 180
Mellon, Constance A. 1938- ... 123
Mellon, James R(oss) 1942- ... 69-72
Mellon, John C(raig) 1933-
Brief entry ... 107
Mellon, Knox
See Mellon, William Knox, Jr.
Mellon, Matthew T(aylor) 1897-1992 ... 29-32R
Mellon, Stanley 1927-
Brief entry ... 108
Mellon, William Knox, Jr. 1925- ... 37-40R
Mellor, Anne Kostelanetz 1941- ... 45-48
Mellor, D. H. 1938- ... 203
Mellor, J(ohn) Leigh 1928- ... 17-20R
Mellor, John W(illiams) 1928- ... 33-36R
Mellor, William Bancroft 1906-1980 ... 61-64
Mellors, John (Parkin) 1920- ... 65-68
Mellors, Samantha
See Lottman, Eileen

Mellos, Elias 1904-1973
See Venezis, Elias
Mellow, James R(obert) 1926-1997 .. CANR-89
Obituary ... 162
Earlier sketches in CA 105, CANR-29
See also DLB 111
Mellown, Elgin W(endell, Jr.) 1931- ... 17-20R
Mellows, Joan ... 77-80
Melly, Diana 1937- ... 130
Melly, George 1926- ... 81-84
Melman, Seymour 1917-2004 ... CANR-114
Obituary ... 234
Earlier sketches in CA 1-4R, CANR-4
Melman, Yossi (Bili) 1950- ... 140
Melmoth, Sebastian
See Wilde, Oscar (Fingal O'Flahertie Wills)
Melnick, Donald 1926-1977
Obituary ... 69-72
Melnick, Jack 1929- ... 89-92
Melnick, Jeffrey Paul ... 202
Melnick, Ralph 1946- ... CANR-125
Earlier sketch in CA 167
Melnikoff, Pamela (Rita) ... 164
See also SATA 97
Mel'nikov, Pavel Ivanovich
1818-1883 ... DLB 238
Melnitz, William W(olf) 1900-1989
Obituary ... 127
Melnyczuk, Askold 1954- ... CANR-107
Earlier sketch in CA 146
Melnyk, Eugenie (?)-1999 ... 236
Melnyk, Steven A. 1953- ... 142
Melnyk, Z(inowii) Lew 1928- ... 41-44R
Meloan, Taylor W(ells) 1919-2002 ... CANR-29
Obituary ... 213
Earlier sketch in CA 45-48
Meloen, Josien
See van Keulen, Mensje
Melone, Albert P(hilip) 1942- ... CANR-52
Earlier sketches in CA 109, CANR-27
Melone, Joseph J(ames) 1931- ... 13-16R
Melo Neto, Joao Cabral de
See Cabral de Melo Neto, Joao
See also CWW 2
See also EWL 3
Meloney, Franken (?)-
See Franken, Rose D(orothy Lewin)
Meloney, William Brown 1905-1971
Obituary ... 104
Melonio, Francoise 1951- ... CANR-121
Earlier sketch in CA 169
Meloon, Marion 1921- ... 65-68
Melosh, Barbara 1950- ... CANR-89
Earlier sketch in CA 130
Melosi, Martin Victor 1947- ... CANR-13
Earlier sketch in CA 77-80
Melot, Michel 1943- ... 132
Meloy, Ellen (Ditzler) 1946-2004 ... 226
Obituary ... 233
Meloy, Maile ... 214
Melrose, Andrea La Sonde
See Anastos, Andrea La Sonde (Melrose)
Melsa, James L(ouis) 1938- ... 104
Melson, Robert 1937- ... 85-88
Melton, David 1934- ... CANR-22
Earlier sketch in CA 69-72
Melton, J(ohn) Gordon 1942- ... 110
Melton, John L. 1920- ... 9-12R
Melton, Judith 1941- ... 199
Melton, Julius W(emyss), Jr. 1933- ... 21-24R
Melton, William 1920- ... 37-40R
Meltsner, Arnold J(erry) 1931- ... 57-60
Meltsner, Michael (Charles) 1937-
Brief entry ... 108
Meltzer, Allan H. 1928- ... CANR-39
Earlier sketches in CA 5-8R, CANR-3, 18
Meltzer, Bernard N(athan) 1916- ... 21-24R
Meltzer, Brad 1970- ... CANR-104
Earlier sketch in CA 167
Meltzer, David 1937- ... 178
Earlier sketches in CA 9-12R, CANR-6, 35
Autobiographical Essay in ... 178
See also CAAS 26
See also CP 1, 2, 3, 4, 5, 6, 7
See also DLB 16
See also SFW 4
Meltzer, Jack 1921- ... 119
Meltzer, Milton 1915- ... CANR-107
Earlier sketches in CA 13-16R, CANR-38, 92
See also AAYA 8, 45
See also BYA 2, 6
See also CLC 26
See also CLR 13
See also DLB 61
See also JRDA
See also MAICYA 1, 2
See also SAAS 1
See also SATA 1, 50, 80, 128
See also SATA-Essay 124
See also WYA
See also YAW
Meltzer, Morton F. 1930- ... 21-24R
Meltzer, Peter D. 1951- ... 120
Meltzoff, Julian 1921- ... 21-24R
Meltzoff, Nancy 1952- ... 93-96
Meluch, R(ebecca) M. 1956- ... CANR-116
Earlier sketches in CA 109, CANR-56
See also SFW 4
Melvill, Harald 1895- ... 5-8R
Melville, A(lan) D(avid) 1912-1994 ... 137
Melville, Alan
See Caverhill, William Melville
Melville, Annabelle McConnell
1910-1991 ... 5-8R
Melville, Anne
See Potter, Margaret (Newman)
Melville, Arabella 1948- ... 130
Melville, Charles (Peter) 1951- ... 138
Melville, Elizabeth c. 1585-1640 ... DLB 172
Melville, Herman 1819-1891 ... AAYA 25
See also AMW
See also AMWR 1
See also CDALB 1640-1865
See also DA
See also DA3
See also DAB
See also DAC
See also DAM MST, NOV
See also DLB 3, 74, 250, 254
See also EXPN
See also EXPS
See also GL 3
See also LAIT 1, 2
See also NFS 7, 9
See also RGAL 4
See also RGSF 2
See also SATA 59
See also SSC 1, 17, 46
See also SSFS 3
See also TUS
See also WLC
Melville, J. Keith 1921- ... 53-56
Melville, James
See Martin, (Roy) Peter
See also DLB 276
Melville, Jennie
See Butler, Gwendoline Williams
Melville, Jock Leslie
See Leslie-Melville, John D.
Melville, John D. Leslie
See Leslie-Melville, John D.
Melville, Joy 1932- ... 85-88
Melville, Keith 1945- ... 41-44R
Melville, Pauline 1948- ... 173
See also CN 7
Melvin, A(rthur) Gordon 1894-1990 ... 9-12R
Melvin, Ann (Patricia) Skene
See Skene-Melvin, Ann (Patricia)
Melvin, (Lewis) David (St. Columb) Skene
See Skene-Melvin, (Lewis) David (St. Columb)
Melwani, Murli Das 1939- ... 61-64
Melwood, Mary
See Lewis, E. M.
Melzack, Ronald 1929- ... CANR-15
Earlier sketch in CA 41-44R
See also SATA 5
Melzer, John Henry 1908-1967 ... CAP-1
Earlier sketch in CA 13-14
Melzi, Robert C. 1915- ... 37-40R
Members, Mark
See Powell, Anthony (Dymoke)
Membreno, Alejandro ... CLC 59
Memling, Carl 1918-1969 ... CANR-4
Earlier sketch in CA 1-4R
See also SATA 6
Memmi, Albert 1920- ... CANR-32
Earlier sketches in CA 81-84, CANR-14
See also AFW
See also CWW 2
See also EWL 3
See also RGWL 3
See also WLIT 2
Memmott, David R. 1948- ... 159
Memmott, Roger Ladd 1944- ... 218
Mena, Janet Gonzalez
See Gonzalez-Mena, Janet
Mena, Juan de 1411-1456 ... DLB 286
Mena, Maria Cristina 1893-1965 ... DLB 209, 221
Menache, Sophia ... 202
Menacker, Julius 1933- ... 41-44R
Menaker, Daniel 1941- ... 65-68
See also DLBY 1997
Menand, Louis 1952- ... 200
See also CLC 208
Menander c. 342B.C.-c. 293B.C. ... AW 1
See also CDWLB 1
See also DAM DRAM
See also DC 3
See also DLB 176
See also LMFS 1
See also RGWL 2, 3
Menard, H(enry) William 1920-1986 ... 37-40R
Obituary ... 118
Menard, Jean 1930(?)-1977
Obituary ... 69-72
Menard, Orville D. 1933- ... 21-24R
Menard, Russell 1942- ... 126
Menasco, Norman
See Guin, Wyman (Woods)
Menashe, Louis 1935- ... 21-24R
Menashe, Samuel 1925- ... 115
Brief entry ... 111
Interview in ... CA-115
See also CAAS 11
Menasse, Robert 1954-
Mencher, Melvin 1927- ... 73-76
Menchin, Robert S(tanley) 1923- ... CANR-13
Earlier sketch in CA 21-24R
Menchu, Rigoberta 1959- ... CANR-135
Earlier sketch in CA 175
See also CLC 160
See also DNFS 1
See also HLCS 2
See also WLIT 1
Mencke, Johann Burckhard
1674-1732 ... DLB 168
Mencken, H(enry) L(ouis) 1880-1956 ... 125
Brief entry ... 105
See also AMW
See also CDALB 1917-1929
See also DLB 11, 29, 63, 137, 222
See also EWL 3
See also MAL 5
See also MTCW 1, 2
See also MTFW 2005
See also NCFS 4
See also RGAL 4
See also TCLC 13
See also TUS
Menczer, Bela 1902-1983
Obituary ... 110
Mendel, Arthur 1905-1979 ... CANR-29
Obituary ... 89-92
Earlier sketch in CA 41-44R
Mendel, Arthur P(aul) 1927-1988 ... 13-16R
Obituary ... 124
Mendel, Douglas H(eusted), Jr. 1921- ... 17-20R
Mendel, Jo
See Bond, Gladys Baker and
Gilbertson, Mildred Geiger
Mendel, Sydney 1925-
Brief entry ... 109
Mendel, Werner M(ax) 1927- ... CANR-11
Earlier sketch in CA 21-24R
Mendele mocher seforim
See Abramowitz, Shalom Jacob
Mendele Mocher Seforim
See Abramowitz, Shalom Jacob
Mendell, Clarence W(hittlesey)
1883-1970 ... CAP-1
Earlier sketch in CA 19-20
Mendeloff, Henry 1917-1984
Obituary ... 113
Mendelowitz, Daniel M(arcus)
1905-1980 ... 9-12R
Obituary ... 135
Mendels, Joseph 1937- ... 29-32R
Mendels, Ora 1936- ... 124
Mendelsohn, Allan R(obert) 1928- ... 45-48
Mendelsohn, Daniel (Adam) 1960- ... 190
Mendelsohn, Erich 1887-1953 ... 185
Mendelsohn, Everett (Irwin) 1931- ... CANR-28
Earlier sketches in CA 17-20R, CANR-11
Mendelsohn, Ezra 1940- ... 130
Mendelsohn, Felix, Jr. 1906-1990 ... 29-32R
Obituary ... 182
Mendelsohn, Harold 1923- ... 49-52
Mendelsohn, Jack
See Manning, Jack
Mendelsohn, Jack 1920- ... CANR-1
Earlier sketch in CA 1-4R
See also Manning, Jack
Mendelsohn, Jane 1965- ... CANR-94
Earlier sketch in CA 154
See also CLC 99
Mendelsohn, Martin 1935- ... CANR-13
Earlier sketch in CA 33-36R
Mendelsohn, Michael John 1931- ... 85-88
Mendelsohn, Oscar (Adolf)
1896-1978 ... CANR-22
Earlier sketch in CA 9-12R
Mendelsohn, Pamela 1944- ... 101
Mendelsohn, Robert S(aul) 1926-1988
Obituary ... 125
Mendelsohn, Stefan 1930(?)-1987(?)
Obituary ... 122
Mendelson, Cheryl 1946- ... 201
Mendelson, Edward (James) 1946- ... CANR-87
Earlier sketches in CA 65-68, CANR-11
Mendelson, Lee 1933- ... 33-36R
Mendelson, Mary Adelaide (Jones)
1917- ... 85-88
Mendelson, Morris 1922- ... CANR-2
Earlier sketch in CA 5-8R
Mendelson, Sara Heller 1947- ... CANR-89
Earlier sketch in CA 126
Mendelson, Steven T. 1958-1995 ... SATA 86
Mendelson, Wallace 1911- ... 1-4R
Mendelssohn, Kurt (Alfred Georg)
1906-1980 ... CANR-7
Obituary ... 105
Earlier sketch in CA 53-56
Mendelssohn, Moses 1729-1786 ... DLB 97
Mendenhall, Corwin (Guy, Jr.) 1916- ... 134
Mendenhall, George E(mery) 1916- ... 33-36R
Mendenhall, James Edgar 1903-1971
Obituary ... 33-36R
Mendenhall, John D(ale) 1911(?)-1983
Obituary ... 110
Mendenhall, Ruth Dyar 1912-1989 ... 65-68
Obituary ... 128
Mendenhall, Thomas C(orwin II)
1910-1998 ... 115
Obituary ... 169
Mender, Mona (Siegler) 1926- ... 141
Mendes, Catulle 1841-1909 ... DLB 217
Mendes, Irene Vilar 1969- ... 203
Mendes, Pedro Rosa
See Rosa Mendes, Pedro
Mendes, Sam 1965- ... AAYA 63
Mendes, Valerie 1939- ... SATA 157
Mendes-Flohr, Paul R(obert) 1941- ... 196
Mendes France, Pierre 1907-1982 ... CANR-43
Obituary ... 108
Earlier sketch in CA 81-84
Mendez, Antonio J. 1940- ... 214
Mendez, Charlotte (Walker) 1935- ... 120
Mendez, Eugenio Fernandez
See Fernandez Mendez, Eugenio
Mendez, Jonna Hiestand 1945- ... 214
Mendez, Miguel 1930- ... CANR-138
Earlier sketches in CA 131, CANR-66
See also DAM MULT
See also DLB 82
See also HW 1, 2
See also MTCW 2
See also MTFW 2005
See also NFS 12
See also RGAL 4
Mendez, Raymond A. 1947- ... SATA 66
Mendl, Robert William Sigismund 1892-1983
Obituary ... 111
Mendlovitz, Saul H. 1925- ... 21-24R
Mendonca, Susan
See Smith, Susan Vernon
See also SATA-Brief 45
Mendonsa, Eugene L(ouis) 1942- ... 109
Mendoza, Diego Hurtado de
1504-1575 ... DLB 318
Mendoza, Eduardo 1943- ... DLB 322
Mendoza, George 1934- ... 73-76
See also SAAS 7
See also SATA 41
See also SATA-Brief 39
Mendoza, Inigo Lopez de
See Santillana, Inigo Lopez de Mendoza, Marques de
Mendoza, Lisa 1958- ... 202
Mendoza, Manuel G. 1936- ... 53-56
Mendoza, Tony 1941- ... 128
Mendoza, Vincent L. 1947- ... 162
Mendras, Henri 1927- ... CANR-13
Earlier sketch in CA 73-76
Mendus, Susan 1951- ... 123
Mendyk, Stan A. E. 1953- ... 135
Menefee, Sarah 1946- ... CAAS 26
Meneghello, Luigi 1927(?)- ... 237
Menen, (Salvator) Aubrey (Clarence)
1912-1989 ... CANR-76
Obituary ... 127
Earlier sketches in CA 1-4R, CANR-2
See also CN 1, 2, 3
Menendez, Albert J(ohn) 1942- ... CANR-46
Earlier sketches in CA 53-56, CANR-7, 22
Menendez, Ana (Maria) 1970- ... 204
Menendez, Shirley (C.) 1937- ... 220
See also SATA 146
Menendez Pidal, Ramon 1869-1968 ... 153
Obituary ... 116
See also HW 1
Meneses, Enrique 1929- ... CANR-27
Earlier sketches in CA 25-28R, CANR-11
Meng, Heinz (Karl) 1924- ... 69-72
See also SATA 13
Meng, John J(oseph) 1906-1988
Obituary ... 124
Menges, Chris 1940- ... IDFW 3, 4
Menges, Karl (Heinrich) 1908-1999 ... 37-40R
Obituary ... 185
Menhennet, Alan 1933- ... 97-100
Menikoff, Barry 1939- ... 37-40R
Menken, Alan 1949- ... IDFW 3, 4
Menkiti, Ifeanyi 1940- ... 65-68
Menkus, Belden 1931- ... CANR-58
Earlier sketches in CA 17-20R, CANR-31
Mennel, Robert McKisson 1938-
Brief entry ... 109
Mennell, Stephen (John) 1944- ... CANR-94
Earlier sketch in CA 107
Mennen, Ingrid 1954- ... SATA 85
Menning, J(ack) H(arwood)
1915-1973 ... CANR-77
Obituary ... 134
Earlier sketch in CA 21-24R
Menninger, Edwin A(rnold)
1896-1995 ... CANR-29
Earlier sketch in CA 9-12R
Menninger, Karl A(ugustus)
1893-1990 ... CANR-61
Obituary ... 132
Earlier sketches in CA 17-20R, CANR-29
See also MTCW 1, 2
Menninger, W(illiam) Walter 1931- ... 111
Menninger, Walt
See Menninger, W(illiam) Walter
Menninger, William C(laire) 1899-1966
Obituary ... 25-28R
Menninghaus, Winfried 1952- ... 234
Mennis, Bernard 1938- ... 41-44R
Meno, Joe 1975- ... 208
Menocal, Narciso G(arcia) 1936- ... 199
Menolascino, Frank J(oseph) 1930- ... 73-76
Menon, Dilip M(adhav) 1962- ... 147
Menon, K(umara) P(admanabha) S(ivasankara)
1898-1982 ... CANR-76
Obituary ... 108
Earlier sketches in CA 5-8R, CANR-5
Menon, R(amakrishna) Rabindranath
1927- ... CANR-11
Earlier sketch in CA 65-68
Menon, Ritu 1948- ... 167
Menon, Vallathol Narayana 1878-1958 . EWL 3
Menotti, Gian Carlo 1911- ... 104
See also SATA 29
Menshikov, Marina 1928(?)-1979
Obituary ... 93-96
Mensoian, Michael G(eorge), Jr. 1927- ... 85-88
Mente, Boye de
See De Mente, Boye
Menton, Francisco de
See Chin, Frank (Chew, Jr.)
Menton, Seymour 1927- ... CANR-31
Earlier sketch in CA 45-48
Mentor
See Lake, Kenneth R(obert)
Mentschikoff, Soia 1915-1984
Obituary ... 113

Mentzer, Michael J(ohn) 1949- 118
Mentzer, Raymond A. 1945- 148
Menuhin, Hephzibah 1920-1981
Obituary 108
Menuhin, Sir Yehudi 1916-1999 .... CANR-2
Earlier sketch in CA 45-48
See also SATA 40
See also SATA-Obit 113
Menut, Albert D(ouglas Bartlett)
1894-1981 .... CANR-75
Obituary 135
Earlier sketch in CA 25-28R
Menville, Douglas 1935- 57-60
See also SATA 64
Menyuk, Paula 1929- 37-40R
Menz, Deb 1954- 169
Menzel, Barbara Jean 1946- 114
See also SATA 63
Menzel, Donald H(oward) 1901-1976 .. CAP-2
Obituary 69-72
Earlier sketch in CA 21-22
Menzel, Johanna
See Meskill, Johanna Menzel
Menzel, Otto J. 178
Menzel, Paul T(heodore) 1942- 53-56
Menzel, Roderich 1907- 93-96
Menzies, Edna O(live) 1921- 116
Menzies, Elizabeth G(rant) C(ranbrook)
1915- 17-20R
Menzies, Ian Stuart 1920- 180
Menzies, Robert Gordon 1894-1978 81-84
Obituary 77-80
Menzies, William Cameron
1896-1957 .... IDFW 3, 4
Menzies, William W(atson) 1931-
Brief entry 110
Meo, Lucy Dorothy 1920- 25-28R
Mera, Koichi 1933- 197
Merak, A.J.
See Glasby, John S.
Meras, Phyllis 1931- CANR-37
Earlier sketches in CA 41-44R, CANR-16
Merback, Mitchell B. 224
Merbaum, Michael 1933- 65-68
Mercado, Tununa 1939- 206
Mercatante, Anthony Stephen 1940- 41-44R
Mercati, Maria (B.) 1951- 175
Mercer, Blaine (Eugene) 1921- CANR-2
Earlier sketch in CA 1-4R
Mercer, Cecil William 1885-1960
Obituary 114
See also Yates, Dornford
Mercer, Charles (Edward)
1917-1988 .... CANR-75
Obituary 127
Earlier sketches in CA 1-4R, CANR-2
See also BYA 1
See also SATA 16
See also SATA-Obit 61
Mercer, Colin 1952- 117
Mercer, David 1928-1980 .... CANR-23
Obituary 102
Earlier sketch in CA 9-12R
See also CBD
See also CLC 5
See also DAM DRAM
See also DLB 13, 310
See also MTCW 1
See also RGEL 2
Mercer, Derrik 1944- 130
Mercer, Diana 1964- 228
Mercer, James L(ee) 1936- CANR-125
Earlier sketches in CA 112, CANR-30, 56
Mercer, Jane R. 45-48
Mercer, Jean 1941- CANR-13
Earlier sketch in CA 33-36R
Mercer, Jessie CANR-2
Earlier sketch in CA 1-4R
See also Shannon, Terry
Mercer, Joan Bodger 1923-2002 101
Obituary 208
Mercer, John
See Morris, Eric C(ecil)
Mercer, John 1704-1768 .... DLB 31
Mercer, Johnny 1906-1976
Obituary 65-68
See also DLB 265
See also IDFW 3, 4
Mercer, Judy CANR-100
Earlier sketch in CA 166
Mercer, Marilyn 1923-
Brief entry 107
Mercer, Paul 1950- 111
Mercer, Virginia Fletcher 1916- 5-8R
Mercey, Arch Andrew 1906-1980
Obituary 102
Merchant, Carolyn 1936- CANR-144
Earlier sketch in CA 113
Merchant, Ismail 1936- .... IDFW 3, 4
Merchant, Jane (Hess) 1919-1972 ...... CANR-4
Obituary 33-36R
Earlier sketch in CA 1-4R
Merchant, Larry 1931- 102
Merchant, Paul
See Ellison, Harlan (Jay)
Mercie, Jean-Luc Henri 1939- 49-52
Mercier, Jean Doyle 1916- 1-4R
Mercier, Louis-Sebastien 1740-1814 ... DLB 314
Mercier, Richard 1949- 177
Mercier, Vivian (Herbert Samuel)
1919-1989 .... CANR-76
Obituary 130
Earlier sketch in CA 81-84
Mercouri, Melina 1925-1994
Obituary 144
Brief entry 106
Mercury
See Allen, Cecil J(ohn)
Meredith, Anne
See Malleson, Lucy Beatrice
Meredith, Arnold
See Hopkins, (Hector) Kenneth
Meredith, Burgess 1909(?)-1997 147
Obituary 162
Meredith, Char(lotte) 1921- 106
Meredith, Christopher (Laurence) 1954- 126
Meredith, D(oris) R. 1944- CANR-143
Earlier sketch in CA 128
Meredith, David William
See Miers, Earl Schenck
Meredith, Dean
See Dean, Edith M(ae)
Meredith, Don 1938- 102
Meredith, George 1828-1909 ....: CANR-80
Brief entry 117
Earlier sketch in CA 153
See also CDBLB 1832-1890
See also DAM POET
See also DLB 18, 35, 57, 159
See also PC 60
See also RGEL 2
See also TCLC 17, 43
See also TEA
Meredith, George (Marlor)
1923-1998 .... CANR-4
Earlier sketch in CA 9-12R
Meredith, George Patrick 1904-1978
Obituary 108
Meredith, James Howard 1933- 77-80
Meredith, Joel L(yman) 1935- 116
Meredith, Joseph C(harlton) 1914-2002 .. 53-56
Meredith, Louisa Anne 1812-1895 .... DLB 166, 230
Meredith, Marilyn 1933- 221
Meredith, Martin 233
Meredith, Nicolete
See Stack, Nicolete Meredith
Meredith, Owen
See Lytton, Edward Robert Bulwer
Meredith, Richard A. 1948- 216
Meredith, Richard C(arlton) 1937-1979 ... 85-88
See also SFW 4
Meredith, Robert (King) 1923- 5-8R
Meredith, Robert C(hidester) 1921- 5-8R
Meredith, Roy 1914(?)-1984
Obituary 111
Meredith, Scott 1923-1993 .... CANR-75
Obituary 140
Earlier sketches in CA 9-12R, CANR-3
Meredith, Ted Jordan 1950- 216
Meredith, William (Morris) 1919- ... CANR-129
Earlier sketches in CA 9-12R, CANR-6, 40
See also CAAS 14
See also CLC 4, 13, 22, 55
See also CP 1, 2, 3, 4, 5, 6, 7
See also DAM POET
See also DLB 5
See also MAL 5
See also PC 28
Meredyth, Bess 1890(?)-1969 .... IDFW 3
Merendino, James 1967- 210
Meretzky, Steve 1957- .... AAYA 65
Merewitz, Leonard (Alan) 1943- 69-72
Merezhkovsky, Dmitrii Sergeevich
See Merezhkovsky, Dmitry Sergeyevich
See also DLB 295
Merezhkovsky, Dmitry Sergeevich
See Merezhkovsky, Dmitry Sergeyevich
See also EWL 3
Merezhkovsky, Dmitry Sergeyevich
1865-1941 169
See also Merezhkovsky, Dmitrii Sergeevich and Merezhkovsky, Dmitry Sergeevich
See also TCLC 29
Merezhkovsky, Zinaida
See Gippius, Zinaida (Nikolaevna)
Mergen, Bernard 1937- CANR-93
Earlier sketch in CA 112
Meri, Veijo 1928- 184
See also EWL 3
Merians, Linda E. 1955- 168
Merick, Wendell S. 1928(?)-1988
Obituary 124
Merideth, Robert 1935- 49-52
Merillat, Herbert C(hristian) L(aing)
1915- 29-32R
Merimee, Prosper 1803-1870 ..... DLB 119, 192
See also EW 6
See also EXPS
See also GFL 1789 to the Present
See also RGSF 2
See also RGWL 2, 3
See also SSC 7, 77
See also SSFS 8
See also SUFW
Merin, Peter
See Bihalji-Merin, Oto
Meringoff, Laurene Krasny
See Brown, Laurene Krasny
Merino, Gustavo Gutierrez
See Gutierrez Merino, Gustavo
Merino, Jose Maria 1941- .... DLB 322
Meritt, Lucy Shoe 1906-2003 .... 37-40R
Merivale, John Herman 1779-1844 ...... DLB 96
Merivale, Patricia 1934- 29-32R
Meriwether, James B. 1928- 13-16R
Meriwether, James H. 1963- 236
Meriwether, Lee 1862-1966
Obituary 116
Meriwether, Louise 1923- 77-80
See also BW 1
See also DLB 33
See also SATA 52
See also SATA-Brief 31
Merk, Frederick 1887-1977 .... 41-44R
Obituary 73-76
Merkel, Miles Adair 1929- 53-56
Merkhofer, Miley W(esson Lee) 1947- 147
Merkin, Daphne 1954- 123
See also CLC 44
Merkin, Donald H. 1945- 69-72
Merkin, Robert (Bruce) 1947- 109
Merkl, Peter H(ans) 1932- CANR-49
Earlier sketches in CA 5-8R, CANR-7, 24
Merkle, Edgar A. 1900(?)-1984
Obituary 113
Merkle, Judith A. 105
See also Riley, Judith (Astria) Merkle
Merklinghaus, Michele 1965- 116
Merle, Robert (Jean Georges)
1908-2004 93-96
Obituary 226
Merleau-Ponty, Maurice 1908-1961 114
Obituary 89-92
See also DLB 296
See also GFL 1789 to the Present
See also TCLC 156
Merli, Frank J(ohn) 1929-
Brief entry 113
Merlin, Arthur
See Blish, James (Benjamin)
Merlin, Christina
See Heaven, Constance (Christina)
Merlin, David
See Moreau, David Merlin
Merlin, Jan 1925- 108
Merlin, Mark D(avid) 118
Merlin, Samuel 1910- 115
Merlis, George 1940- 33-36R
Merlis, Mark 1950- 223
Merliss, Reuben 1915- 17-20R
Merman, Ethel
See Zimmermann, Ethel Agnes
Mermin, Samuel 1912- 53-56
Merne, Oscar James 1943- 102
Mernissi, Fatima 1940- 152
See also CLC 171
See also FW
Mernit, Susan 1953- 69-72
Meroff, Deborah 1948- 89-92
Meron, Theodor 1930- 138
Merquior, J(ose) G(uilherme) 1941- 143
Merrell, James H. 1953- 127
Merrell, James L(ee) 1930- 17-20R
Merrell, Jo Ann 1945- 113
Merrell, Karen Dixon 1936- CANR-6
Earlier sketch in CA 13-16R
Merrell, V(ictor) Dallas 1936- 9-12R
Merrens, H(arry) Roy 1931- 9-12R
Merrett, Christopher 1951- CANR-111
Earlier sketch in CA 151
Merrett, Robert James 1944- 111
Merriam, Alan P(arkhurst)
1923-1980 .... CANR-1
Earlier sketch in CA 1-4R
Merriam, Eve 1916-1992 .... CANR-80
Obituary 137
Earlier sketches in CA 5-8R, CANR-29
See also CLR 14
See also DLB 61
See also EXPP
See also MAICYA 1, 2
See also PFS 6
See also SATA 3, 40, 73
See also YAW
Merriam, Harold G(uy) 1883-1981 .. CANR-10
Earlier sketch in CA 61-64
Merriam, Robert E(dward) 1918- 5-8R
Merriam, Sharan B. 1943- 135
Merrick, Gordon 1916-1988 .... CANR-76
Obituary 125
Earlier sketches in CA 13-16R, CANR-11
See also GLL 2
Merrick, Hugh
See Meyer, H(arold) A(lbert)
Merrick, Mark
See Rathborne, St. George (Henry)
Merrick, William 1916-1969 .... CAP-1
Earlier sketch in CA 11-12
Merridale, Catherine 1959- 200
Merril, Judith 1923-1997 .... CANR-15
Obituary 161
Earlier sketch in CA 13-16R
Interview in CANR-15
See also DLB 251
See also MTCW 1
See also SCFW 1, 2
See also SFW 4
Merrill, Antoinette June 1912- 45-48
Merrill, Arch 1895(?)-1974
Obituary 49-52
Merrill, Bob
See Merrill, Robert Alexander
Merrill, Boynton, Jr. 1925- 69-72
Merrill, Christopher (Lyall) 1957- CANR-96
Earlier sketch in CA 130
Merrill, David W. 1928- 108
Merrill, Dean 1943- CANR-142
Earlier sketches in CA 61-64, CANR-8, 27
Merrill, Dick
See Merrill, Henry Tindall
Merrill, (Edwin) Durwood 1938- 172
Merrill, Edward C(lifton), Jr. 1920- 21-24R
Merrill, Edward H. 1903-1993 .... CAP-1
Earlier sketch in CA 13-16
Merrill, Francis E(llsworth) 1904-1969 .. CAP-1
Earlier sketch in CA 19-20
Merrill, Frederick Thayer 1905-1974
Obituary 53-56
Merrill, Gary (Franklin) 1915(?)-1990
Obituary 131
Merrill, Harwood F(erry) 1904-1984
Obituary 114
Merrill, Helen Abbot 1864-1949 170
Merrill, Henry Tindall 1897-1982
Obituary 108
Merrill, Hugh (Davis) (III) 1942- 151
Merrill, James (Ingram) 1926-1995 . CANR-108
Obituary 147
Earlier sketches in CA 13-16R, CANR-10, 49, 63
Interview in CANR-10
See also AMWS 3
See also CLC 2, 3, 6, 8, 13, 18, 34, 91
See also CP 1, 2
See also DA3
See also DAM POET
See also DLB 5, 165
See also DLBY 1985
See also EWL 3
See also MAL 5
See also MTCW 1, 2
See also MTFW 2005
See also PAB
See also PC 28
See also PFS 23
See also RGAL 4
Merrill, James M(ercer) 1920- 9-12R
Merrill, Jane 1946- .... SATA 42
Merrill, Jean (Fairbanks) 1923- CANR-38
Earlier sketches in CA 1-4R, CANR-4
See also BYA 5
See also CLR 52
See also CWRI 5
See also MAICYA 1, 2
See also SATA 1, 82
Merrill, John Calhoun 1924- CANR-13
Earlier sketch in CA 73-76
Merrill, John N(igel) 1943- CANR-22
Earlier sketch in CA 103
Merrill, Lisa 206
Merrill, M. David 1937- CANR-16
Earlier sketch in CA 41-44R
Merrill, P. J.
See Roth, Holly
Merrill, Phil
See Filstrup, Jane (Merrill)
Merrill, Robert 1919-2004 81-84
Obituary 232
Merrill, Robert 1944- 89-92
Merrill, Robert Alexander 1958- 136
Merrill, Thomas F. 1932- 29-32R
Merrill, Toni
See Merrill, Antoinette June
Merrill, Walter M. 1915- CANR-13
Earlier sketch in CA 21-24R
Merrill, Wilfred K. 1903-1990 .... 9-12R
Merrill, William C. 1934- 29-32R
Merrim, Stephanie 198
Merriman, Alex
See Silverberg, Robert
Merriman, Ann Lloyd 1934- 77-80
Merriman, Beth
See Taylor, Demetria
Merriman, Catherine 1949- 140
Merriman, Chad
See Cheshire, Giff(ord Paul)
Merriman, Jerry Johnson 1939- 25-28R
Merriman, John 1924-1974
Obituary 104
Merriman, Marion 1909-1991 133
Merriman, Pat
See Atkey, Philip
Merriman, Rachel 1971- .... SATA 98, 149
Merrin, Jeredith 1944- CANR-117
Earlier sketch in CA 160
Merriner, James L. 1947- 214
Merrit, Elizabeth
See Goudge, Eileen
Merrit, Elizabeth
See Goudge, Eileen
Merritt, A.
See Merritt, A(braham P.)
Merritt, A(braham P.) 1884-1943 167
Brief entry 120
See also FANT
See also SCFW 1, 2
See also SFW 4
See also SUFW 1
Merritt, Constance 1966- 203
Merritt, Dixon Lanier 1879-1972
Obituary 33-36R
Merritt, Don 1945- CANR-22
Earlier sketch in CA 106
Merritt, E. B.
See Waddington, Miriam
Merritt, Helen Henry 1920- 17-20R
Merritt, James D. 1934- 33-36R
Merritt, LeRoy Charles 1912-1970 .... CAP-2
Earlier sketch in CA 33-36
Merritt, Miriam 1925- 17-20R
Merritt, Muriel 1905-1997 69-72
Merritt, Ray E(merson), Jr. 1948- 73-76
Merritt, Raymond H(arland) 1936- 85-88
Merritt, Richard L(awrence) 1933- 41-44R
Merritt, William E. 1945- 132
Merry, Henry J(ohn) 1908-2000 .... 37-40R
Merry, Robert William 1946- 153
Mersand, Joseph 1907- CANR-1
Earlier sketch in CA 1-4R
Merser, Cheryl 1951- 141

Mersereau, John, Jr. 1925- CANR-2
Earlier sketch in CA 1-4R
Mersky, Roy M. 1925- 37-40R
Mersmann, James Frederick 1938- 61-64
Mertens, Lawrence E(dwin) 1929- 85-88
Mertens, Thomas R(obert) 1930- CANR-6
Earlier sketch in CA 57-60
Mertes, Kate 1955- 129
Mertins, Herman, Jr. 1931- 41-44R
Mertins, (Marshall) Louis 1885-1973 ..... 41-44R
Merton, Andrew H(arris) 1944- 107
Merton, Giles
See Curran, Mona (Elisa)
Merton, Robert K(ing) 1910-2003 ..... CANR-31
Obituary 214
Earlier sketch in CA 41-44R
Merton, Stephen 1912-1998 .... 21-24R
Merton, Thomas (James)
1915-1968 .... CANR-131
Obituary 25-28R
Earlier sketches in CA 5-8R, CANR-22, 53, 111
See also AAYA 61
See also AMWS 8
See also CLC 1, 3, 11, 34, 83
See also DA3
See also DLB 48
See also DLBY 1981
See also MAL 5
See also MTCW 1, 2
See also MTFW 2005
See also PC 10
Mertus, Julie A. 1963- 232
Mertvago, Peter 1946- 154
Mertz, Annelise 227
Mertz, Barbara (Gross) 1927- CANR-135
Earlier sketches in CA 21-24R, CANR-11, 36, 63, 82
Interview in CANR-36
See also AAYA 24
See also BEST 90:4
See also CMW 4
See also CN 6, 7
See also CPW
See also RHW
See also SATA 49
Mertz, Richard R(olland) 1927- 21-24R
Merullo, Roland 1953- CANR-104
Earlier sketch in CA 136
Mervosh, Edward M. 1941(?)-1998 181
Merwe, A. v. d.
See Geyl, Pieter (Catharinus Arie)
Merwin, Decie 1894-1961
Obituary 111
See also SATA-Brief 32
Merwin, (W.) Sam(uel Kimball), Jr.
1910-1996 131
Obituary 196
See also SFW 4
Merwin, W(illiam) S(tanley) 1927- . CANR-140
Earlier sketches in CA 13-16R, CANR-15, 51, 112
Interview in CANR-15
See also AMWS 3
See also CLC 1, 2, 3, 5, 8, 13, 18, 45, 88
See also CP 1, 2, 3, 4, 5, 6, 7
See also DA3
See also DAM POET
See also DLB 5, 169
See also EWL 3
See also MAL 5
See also MTCW 1, 2
See also MTFW 2005
See also PAB
See also PC 45
See also PFS 5, 15
See also RGAL 4
Mery, Fernand 1897-1984 .... CANR-29
Earlier sketch in CA 105
Merz, Charles 1893-1977
Obituary 73-76
Merzer, Meridee 1947- 102
Mesa-Lago, Carmelo 1934- CANR-53
Earlier sketches in CA 25-28R, CANR-10, 26
Meschel, Susan V. 1936- .... SATA 83
Meserve, Walter Joseph, Jr. 1923- ... CANR-100
Earlier sketches in CA 1-4R, CANR-1
Meshack, B(illie) A(ugusta) 1922- 93-96
Meshenberg, Michael J(ay) 1942- CANR-16
Earlier sketch in CA 93-96
Mesibov, Gary B. 1945- 170
Meske, Eunice Boardman 1926- CANR-4
Earlier sketch in CA 9-12R
Meskill, Johanna Menzel 1930- 17-20R
Meskill, Robert 1918(?)-1970
Obituary 104
Mesle, C. Robert 1949- CANR-98
Earlier sketch in CA 147
Mesne, Eugene (Frederick Peter Cheshire) de
See de Mesne, Eugene (Frederick Peter Cheshire)
Mesquita, Bruce James Bueno de
See Bueno de Mesquita, Bruce James
Messager, Charles 1882-1971
Obituary 93-96
Messaoudi, Khalida 1958- 192
Messdeck Annie
See Coade, Jessie
Messegue, Maurice 1921- 103
Messel, Harry 1922- CANR-21
Earlier sketch in CA 103
Messenger, Charles (Rynd Milles)
1942- CANR-31
Earlier sketches in CA 73-76, CANR-13
See also SATA 59
Messenger, Christian K(arl) 1943- CANR-56
Earlier sketch in CA 132
Messenger, Elizabeth Margery (Esson)
1908-1965 .... CAP-1
Earlier sketch in CA 11-12
Messenger, Phyllis (E.) Mauch 1950- 132
Messent, Peter Ronald 1949- 106
Messer, Alfred A(mes) 1922- 29-32R
Messer, Donald E(dward) 1941- 138
Messer, Richard 1965- 147
Messer, Ronald Keith 1942- 57-60
Messer, Sarah 235
Messer, Sarah Carlin 1924(?)-1984
Obituary 112
Messer, Thomas M. 1920- 111
Brief entry 106
Messer-Davidow, Ellen 1941- 228
Messerer, Asaf Mikhailovich
1903-1992 .... CANR-76
Obituary 137
Earlier sketch in CA 104
Messerli, Douglas 1947- CANR-39
Earlier sketch in CA 116
Messerli, Jonathan C(arl) 1926-2004 ..... 41-44R
Obituary 233
Messerly, John G. 1955- 165
Messick, Dale 1906-2005 .... SATA 64
See also SATA-Brief 48
Messick, Hank
See Messick, Henry H(icks)
Messick, Henry H(icks) 1922-1999 .... CANR-2
Obituary 186
Earlier sketch in CA 45-48
Messier, Claire 1956- 170
See also SATA 103
Messieres, Nicole de
See de Messieres, Nicole
Messimer, Dwight R. 1937- 214
Messina, Lynn 222
Messing, Shep 1949-
Brief entry 111
Messing, Simon D(avid) 1922- 57-60
Messinger, C. F. 1913- 21-24R
Messinger, Sheldon L(eopold)
1925-2003 .... 25-28R
Obituary 215
Messman, Jon
See Sharpe, Jon
Messmer, Otto 1892(?)-1983
Obituary 111
See also IDFW 3, 4
See also SATA 37
Messner, Fred(rick) R(ichard) 1926- 13-16R
Messner, Gerald 1935- 29-32R
Messner, Johannes 1891-1984
Obituary 112
Messner, Michael A. 1952- CANR-100
Earlier sketch in CA 138
Messner, Reinhold 1944- CANR-82
Earlier sketches in CA 81-84, CANR-15, 35
Messner, Stephen Dale 1936- 21-24R
Messori, Vittorio 1941- 204
Messter, Oskar 1866-1943 .... IDFW 3, 4
Messud, Claire 1966- 202
Mesta, Perle 1891(?)-1975
Obituary 57-60
Mester, Terri A. 1948- 165
Mesthene, Emmanuel George 1920- 77-80
Meston, John 1915(?)-1979
Obituary 85-88
Mestre, Ernesto 184
Mestrovic, Stjepan G. 1955- 168
Meszaros, Istvan 1930- CANR-9
Earlier sketch in CA 57-60
Meszaros, Marta 1931- 127
Meszoly, Miklos
See Molnar, Miklos
See also DLB 232
See also EWL 3
Meta
See Tomkiewicz, Mina
Metalious, Grace (de Repentigny)
1924-1964 .... CAP-2
Earlier sketch in CA 21-22
See also BPFB 2
See also MTCW 2
See also RHW
Metastasio, Pietro 1698-1782 .... RGWL 2, 3
Metaxas, B(asil) N(icolas) 1925- 37-40R
Metcalf, Alida C. 1954- 143
Metcalf, Allan (Albert) 1940- 233
Metcalf, Doris H(unter) .... SATA 91
Metcalf, E(ugene) W(esley) 1945- 65-68
Metcalf, George R. 1914-2002 .... 25-28R
Metcalf, John 1938- 113
See also CLC 37
See also CN 4, 5, 6, 7
See also DLB 60
See also RGSF 2
See also SSC 43
See also TWA
Metcalf, Kenneth N(olan) 1923-1965 .... 5-8R
Metcalf, Keyes DeWitt 1889-1983 ... CANR-76
Obituary 111
Earlier sketch in CA 17-20R
Metcalf, Lawrence E(ugene) 1915- 21-24R
Metcalf, Paul 1917-1999 .... CANR-39
Obituary 174
Earlier sketches in CA 45-48, CANR-1, 17
Metcalf, Peter 116
Metcalf, Suzanne
See Baum, L(yman) Frank
Metcalf, Thomas R. 1934- 13-16R
Metcalf, Vicky 1901- 89-92
Metcalfe, John 1891-1965 221
See also HGG
See also SUFW
Metcalfe, John Wallace 1901-1982
Obituary 107
Metcalfe, Philip (Earle) 1946- 149
Metcalfe, Steve 1953- 108
Metchnikoff, Elie 1845-1916 160
Metellus, Jean 1937- .... EWL 3
Metereau, Rebecca Bell
See Bell-Metereau, Rebecca
Metesky, George
See Hoffman, Abbie
Methold, Kenneth (Walter) 1931- CANR-32
Earlier sketch in CA 13-16R
Methvin, Eugene H. 1934- 29-32R
Metos, Thomas H(arry) 1932- 93-96
See also SATA 37
Metoyer, Cynthia Chavez 1965- 214
Metraux, Guy S(erge) 1917- 9-12R
Metraux, Rhoda 1914- 57-60
Metress, James F.
See Metress, Seamus P.
Metress, Seamus P. 1933- CANR-44
Earlier sketches in CA 57-60, CANR-6, 21
Metropolis, N.
See Metropolis, Nicholas Constantine
Metropolis, Nicholas Constantine
1915-1999 110
Obituary 187
Mets, David Raymond 1928- 118
Mettee, Stephen Blake 1947- 228
Metter, Bert(ram Milton) 1927- .... SATA 56
Mettler, Barbara 1907- 217
Mettler, George B(arry) 1934- 93-96
Metty, Russell 1906-1978 .... IDFW 3, 4
Metwally, M(okhtar) M(ohamed)
1939- CANR-15
Earlier sketch in CA 65-68
Metz, Allan (Sheldon) 1950- 175
Metz, Don 1940- 135
Metz, Donald L(ehman) 1935- 21-24R
Metz, Donald S(hink) 1916- 45-48
Metz, Jerred 1943- CANR-22
Earlier sketch in CA 104
Metz, Leon C(laire) 1930- CANR-36
Earlier sketches in CA 45-48, CANR-1, 16
Metz, Lois Lunt 1906-1998 .... CAP-1
Earlier sketch in CA 9-10
Metz, Mary (Seawell) 1937- 53-56
Metz, Mary Haywood 1939- CANR-15
Earlier sketch in CA 85-88
Metz, Robert (Henry) 1928- CANR-13
Earlier sketch in CA 61-64
Metz, William 1918- 77-80
Metzdorf, Robert F(rederic) 1912-1975
Obituary 57-60
Metzenthen, David 1958- 176
See also SATA 106
Metzger, Barbara 1944- CANR-119
Earlier sketch in CA 110
Metzger, Bruce Manning 1914- CANR-118
Earlier sketches in CA 9-12R, CANR-4
Metzger, Charles R(eid) 1921- 25-28R
Metzger, Deena P. 1936- CANR-89
Earlier sketch in CA 130
Metzger, Erika A(lma) 1933- 33-36R
Metzger, H(owell) Peter 1931-
Brief entry 107
Metzger, Lois 1955- 206
Metzger, Michael M(oses) 1935- 21-24R
Metzger, Norman 1924- CANR-9
Earlier sketch in CA 53-56
Metzger, Philip W. 1931- 45-48
Metzger, Robert 1950- 117
Metzger, Robert A(lan) 1956- 225
Metzger, Stanley D. 1916- 9-12R
Metzger, Thomas A(lbert) 1933- 97-100
Metzger, Walter P. 1922- CANR-17
Earlier sketch in CA 61-64
Metzker, Isaac 1901-1984 45-48
Metzl, Jamie (Frederic) 230
Metzler, Ken(neth Theodore) 1929- CANR-4
Earlier sketch in CA 53-56
Metzler, Lloyd A(ppleton) 1913-1980 104
Metzler, Paul 1914- CANR-6
Earlier sketch in CA 57-60
Metzner, Erno 1892-1953 .... IDFW 3, 4
Metzner, Ralph 1936- 69-72
Metzner, Seymour 1924- 21-24R
Meudt, Edna Kritz 1906-1989 .... CANR-9
Earlier sketch in CA 13-16R
Meung, Jean de c. 1240-c. 1305 .... RGWL 2
See also TWA
Meurant, Georges 1948- 135
Meurice, Blanca
See von Block, Bela W(illiam)
Meux, Milton O(tto) 1930- 45-48
Meves, Christa 1925- CANR-102
Earlier sketches in CA 93-96, CANR-24, 49
Mew, Charlotte (Mary) 1870-1928 189
Brief entry 105
See also DLB 19, 135
See also RGEL 2
See also TCLC 8
Mewburn, Martin
See Hitchin, Martin Mewburn
Mewhinney, Bruce 1949- 118
Mews, Constant J(an) 1954- 221
Mews, Hazel 1909-1975 .... CAP-2
Earlier sketch in CA 29-32
Mews, Siegfried 1933- CANR-99
Earlier sketches in CA 57-60, CANR-7, 22, 45
Mewshaw, Michael 1943- CANR-47
Earlier sketches in CA 53-56, CANR-7
See also CLC 9
See also DLBY 1980
Mey, Jacob Lovis
See Meij, Jacob L(ouis)
Meyen, Edward L. 1937- 33-36R
Meyendorff, John 1926-1992 .... CANR-47
Obituary 138
Earlier sketches in CA 21-24R, CANR-9
Meyer, Adam 1961- 213
Meyer, Agnes E(lizabeth Ernst) 1887-1970
Obituary 29-32R
Meyer, Albert Julius 1919-1983
Obituary 111
Meyer, Alfred (Herman Ludwig)
1893-1988 .... CAP-1
Earlier sketch in CA 13-14
Meyer, Alfred George 1920- 17-20R
Meyer, Anthony 1920-2004 134
Obituary 234
Meyer, Armin Henry 1914- 85-88
Meyer, Barbara 1939- .... SATA 77
Meyer, Ben F(ranklin) 1927- CANR-43
Earlier sketches in CA 37-40R, CANR-14
Meyer, Bernard C. 1910-1988 73-76
Meyer, Bernard F. 1891(?)-1975
Obituary 57-60
Meyer, Bruce 1957- 234
Earlier sketch in CA 228
Autobiographical Essay in 234
See also DLB 282
Meyer, Carl S(tamm) 1907-1972 .... CAP-1
Earlier sketch in CA 13-16
Meyer, Carol H. 1924-1996 .... CANR-13
Obituary 155
Earlier sketch in CA 73-76
Meyer, Carolyn (Mae) 1935- CANR-121
Earlier sketches in CA 49-52, CANR-2, 57
See also AAYA 16, 48
See also BYA 7, 8
See also JRDA
See also MAICYA 1, 2
See also SAAS 9
See also SATA 9, 70, 118, 142
See also SATA-Essay 142
See also WYAS 1
See also YAW
Meyer, Charles R. 1920- 33-36R
Meyer, Charles R(obert) 1926- 69-72
Meyer, Clarence 1903-1997 97-100
Meyer, Conrad Ferdinand 1825-1898 . DLB 129
See also EW
See also RGWL 2, 3
See also SSC 30
Meyer, Cord, Jr. 1920-2001 144
Obituary 194
Meyer, D. Swing 1938- 17-20R
Meyer, David R. 1943- 65-68
Meyer, Donald (Burton) 1923- 21-24R
Meyer, Donald H(arvey) 1935-
Brief entry 113
Meyer, Doris (L.) 1942- CANR-33
Earlier sketch in CA 89-92, 179
See also HW 1, 2
Meyer, Douglas K. 219
Meyer, Duane Gilbert 1926- 5-8R
Meyer, E. Y.
See Meyer, Peter
See also EWL 3
Meyer, Edith Patterson 1895-1993 ...... CANR-1
Earlier sketch in CA 1-4R
See also SATA 5
Meyer, Elizabeth C(ooper) 1958- 69-72
Meyer, Ellen Hope 1928- 119
Meyer, Erika 1904-1994 73-76
Meyer, Ernst Hermann 1905-1988(?)
Obituary 127
Meyer, Eugene 1875-1959 192
See also DLB 29
Meyer, Eugene L. 1942- 135
Meyer, F(ranklyn) E(dward) 1932- 1-4R
See also SATA 9
Meyer, Frank S(traus) 1909-1972 .... CAP-1
Obituary 33-36R
Earlier sketch in CA 9-10
Meyer, Fred(erick Robert) 1922-1985 57-60
Obituary 117
Meyer, George H(erbert) 1928- 116
Meyer, Gladys (Eleanor) 1908-1986 166
Obituary 118
Meyer, Gustav 1868-1932 190
Brief entry 117
See also Meyrink, Gustav
Meyer, H(arold) A(lbert) 1898-1980 ... CANR-4
Obituary 102
Earlier sketch in CA 5-8R
Meyer, H. K. Houston
See Meyer, Heinrich
Meyer, Harding 1928- 130
Meyer, Harold D(iedrich) 1892-1974(?) . CAP-2
Earlier sketch in CA 19-20
Meyer, Harold G. 1909(?)-1986
Obituary 118
Meyer, Heinrich 1904-1977 49-52
Obituary 85-88
Meyer, Henry Cord 1913-2001 206
Meyer, Herbert W(alter) 1892-1981 ...... CAP-2
Earlier sketch in CA 33-36
Meyer, Herman 1911- 21-24R
Meyer, Howard N(icholas) 1914- CANR-99
Earlier sketch in CA 13-16R
Meyer, Jean Shepherd .... SATA 11
Meyer, Jerome Sydney 1895-1975 ...... CANR-4
Obituary 57-60
Earlier sketch in CA 1-4R
See also SATA 3
See also SATA-Obit 25
Meyer, Joachim-Ernst 1917- 57-60
Meyer, Joanne 231
Meyer, John Robert 1927- CANR-9
Earlier sketch in CA 13-16R
Meyer, June
See Jordan, June (Meyer)

Cumulative Index 399 Mickolus

Meyer, Karl E(rnest) 1928- CANR-91
Earlier sketches in CA 1-4R, CANR-1
Meyer, L. A.
See Meyer, Louis A(lbert), Jr.
Meyer, Laurence H. 1944- 236
Meyer, Lawrence (Robert) 1941- CANR-34
Earlier sketch in CA 73-76
Meyer, Leisa D. 159
Meyer, Leonard B. 1918- 13-16R
Meyer, Lillian Nicholson 1917(?)-1983
Obituary 109
Meyer, Linda D(oreen) 1948- CANR-37
Earlier sketches in CA 93-96, CANR-16
Meyer, Louis A(lbert), Jr. 1942- CANR-124
Earlier sketch in CA 37-40R
See also SATA 12, 144
Meyer, Lynn
See Slavitt, David R(ytman)
Meyer, Lysle E(dward) 1932- 144
Meyer, Mabel H. 1890(?)-1976
Obituary 61-64
Meyer, Marie-Louise 1936- 97-100
Meyer, Marvin W(ayne) 1948- 212
Meyer, Mary Keysor 1919- 102
Meyer, Michael (Leverson)
1921-2000 .... CANR-64
Obituary 189
Earlier sketches in CA 25-28R, CANR-13
See also DLB 155
Meyer, Michael A. 1937- CANR-96
Earlier sketch in CA 21-24R
Meyer, Michael C. 1935- CANR-10
Earlier sketch in CA 21-24R
Meyer, Michael J. 1956- 139
Meyer, Nicholas 1945- CANR-87
Earlier sketches in CA 49-52, CANR-7
Meyer, Peter 1946- .... DLB 75
Meyer, Peter (Barrett) 1950- 141
Meyer, Philip (Edward) 1930- CANR-10
Earlier sketch in CA 65-68
Meyer, Renate 1930- 53-56
See also SATA 6
Meyer, Richard E. 1939- 150
Meyer, Robert H. 1934- 37-40R
Meyer, Ronald 1952- 135
Meyer, Roy W(illard) 1925- 17-20R
Meyer, Ruth F(ritz) 1910- CAP-2
Earlier sketch in CA 23-24
Meyer, Sam 1917(?)-2003 225
Meyer, Stewart (Martin) 1947- 118
Meyer, Susan E. 1940- CANR-19
Earlier sketches in CA 45-48, CANR-2
See also SATA 64
Meyer, Thomas 1947- CANR-1
Earlier sketch in CA 49-52
Meyer, William Eugene 1923- 45-48
Meyer, William R(obert) 1949- 77-80
Meyer de Schauensee, Rodolphe
See De Schauensee, Rodolphe Meyer
Meyerhof, Otto Fritz 1884-1951 162
Meyerhoff, Arthur E(dward) 1895-1986
Obituary 120
Meyerhoff, Howard A(ugustus)
1899-1982 .... CAP-2
Earlier sketch in CA 19-20
Meyering, Ralph A. 1930- 29-32R
Meyering, Sheryl L. 1948- 148
Meyer-Meyrink, Gustav
See Meyer, Gustav
Meyerowitz, Eva (Leonie) L(ewin-)
R(ichter) 9-12R
Meyerowitz, Joanne 1954- CANR-123
Earlier sketch in CA 146
Meyerowitz, Patricia 1933- 21-24R
Meyers, Albert L. 1904(?)-1981
Obituary 102
Meyers, Annette (Brafman) 1934- CANR-90
Earlier sketches in CA 132, CANR-74
Meyers, Bert(ram) 1928-1979 101
See also CP 2
Meyers, Carlton R(oy) 1922- 57-60
Meyers, Carol L(yons) 1942- CANR-32
Earlier sketch in CA 113
Meyers, Carole Terwilliger 1945- CANR-137
Earlier sketch in CA 69-72
Meyers, Cecil H(arold) 1920- 29-32R
Meyers, David W. 1942- 29-32R
Meyers, Edward 1934- 101
Meyers, Eric M(ark) 1940- 110
Meyers, Gertrude Barlow 1902- 1-4R
Meyers, Harold Burton 1924- .... BYA 6
Meyers, Jeffrey 1939- 186
Earlier sketches in CA 73-76, CANR-54, 102
Autobiographical Essay in 186
See also CLC 39
See also DLB 111
Meyers, Joan Simpson 1927- CANR-14
Earlier sketch in CA 17-20R
Meyers, Kent 1956(?)- 203
Meyers, Lawrence Stanley 1943- 57-60
Meyers, Maan
See Meyers, Annette (Brafman) and
Meyers, Martin
Meyers, Martin 1934- CANR-138
Earlier sketches in CA 146, CANR-73
Meyers, Marvin 1921-
Brief entry 108
Meyers, Mary Ann 1937- 116
Meyers, Michael Jay 1946- 65-68
Meyers, Nancy 1950- 138
See also AAYA 44
Meyers, Odette 1934- 164
Meyers, Richard
See Hell, Richard
Meyers, Robert Rex 1923- 17-20R
Meyers, Roy (Lethbridge) 1910-1974 ...... CAP-2
Earlier sketch in CA 25-28
Meyers, Ruth S(chlaff) 1923- 117
Meyers, Susan
See Falk, Susan Meyers
Meyers, Susan 1942- CANR-13
Earlier sketch in CA 21-24R
See also SATA 19, 108
Meyers, Walter E(arl) 1939- CANR-6
Earlier sketch in CA 53-56
Meyerson, Adam 1953- 128
Meyerson, Debra E. 1957- 227
Meyerson, Edward L(eon)
1904-1980 .... CANR-12
Earlier sketch in CA 61-64
Meyerson, Harvey 1937- 212
Meyerson, Martin 1922-
Brief entry 115
Meyerson, Michael I. 204
Meynell, Alice (Christina Gertrude Thompson)
1847-1922 177
Brief entry 104
See also DLB 19, 98
See also RGEL 2
See also TCLC 6
Meynell, Alix (Hester M.) 1903-1999 128
Obituary 183
Meynell, Francis Meredith Wilfrid
1891-1975 .... CAP-2
Obituary 57-60
Earlier sketch in CA 19-20
Meynell, Hugo A. 1936- 130
Meynell, Laurence Walter
1899-1989 .... CANR-73
Obituary 128
Earlier sketches in CA 81-84, CANR-15
See also CWRI 5
See also SATA-Obit 61
Meynell, Viola (Mary Gertrude)
1885-1956 .... DLB 153
Meyners, J. Robert 1922- 104
Meynier, Yvonne (Pollet) 1908- 73-76
See also SATA 14
Meyrink, Gustav
See Meyer, Gustav
See also DLB 81
See also EWL 3
See also TCLC 21
Meza, Pedro Thomas 1941- 37-40R
Mezerick, Avrahm G. 1901-1986
Obituary 119
Mezey, Michael L(loyd) 1943- 118
Mezey, Robert 1935- CANR-7
Earlier sketch in CA 57-60
See also CP 1, 2, 3, 4, 5, 6, 7
See also SATA 33
Mezieres, Philippe de c. 1327-1405 ... DLB 208
Mezieres Riccoboni, Marie-Jeanne de Heurles
Laboras de
See Riccoboni, Marie-Jeanne
Mezlekia, Nega 1958- 201
Mezrich, Ben 1969- 214
Mezvinsky, Edward M. 1937- 103
Mezvinsky, Shirley
See Lauro, Shirley (Shapiro) Mezvinsky
Mezzrow, Mezz
See Mezzrow, Milton
Mezzrow, Milton 1899-1972 .... 37-40R
Miall, Robert
See Burke, John (Frederick)
Mian, Mary (Lawrence Shipman)
1902- .... SATA-Brief 47
Micale, Albert 1913- .... SATA 22
Micallef, Benjamin A(nthony)
1925-1980 53-56
Obituary 103
Micallef, John 1923- 25-28R
Micaud, Charles Antoine 1910-1974 .... 5-8R
Miceli, Frank 1932- 57-60
Miceli, Vincent P(eter) 1915-1991 229
Brief entry 114
Michael, Aloysius 1938- 189
Michael, Colette V(erger) 1937- 139
Michael, David J. 1944- 29-32R
Michael, Franz H(enry) 1907- CANR-4
Earlier sketch in CA 5-8R
Michael, George 1919- 41-44R
Michael, Henry N(athaniel) 1913- 33-36R
Michael, Ian (Lockie) 1915- 104
See also CMW 4
Michael, Ib 1945- 196
See also DLB 214
Michael, James
See Scagnetti, Jack
Michael, John A(rthur) 1921- 133
Michael, Judith
See Barnard, Judith
Michael, Livi 1960- .... DLB 267
Michael, Manfred
See Winterfeld, Henry
Michael, Paul Martin 1934- CANR-10
Earlier sketch in CA 17-20R
Michael, Phyllis C(allender) 1908- CANR-2
Earlier sketch in CA 5-8R
Michael, S(tanley) T(heodore)
1912-1986 .... 13-16R
Michael, Sami 1926- 211
Michael, Thomas A. 1933- 33-36R
Michael, Tom
See Michael, Thomas A.
Michael, William B(urton) 1922- 45-48
Michael, Wolfgang F(riedrich)
1909-1994 .... CANR-14
Earlier sketch in CA 41-44R
Michaeles, M. M.
See Golding, Morton J(ay)
Michaelides, Constantine E. 1930- 25-28R
Michaelis, David (Todd) 1957- CANR-80
Earlier sketch in CA 114
Michaelis, John U(dell) 1912-1996 69-72
Michaelis, Karin 1872-1950 .... DLB 214
Michaelis-Jena, Ruth
See Ratcliff, Ruth
Michaelowa, Axel 1968- 204
Michaels, Anne 1958- CANR-96
Earlier sketch in CA 157
See also CN 7
See also DLB 299
Michaels, Barbara
See Mertz, Barbara (Gross)
Michaels, Carolyn Leopold
See Leopold, Carolyn Clugston
Michaels, Dale
See Rifkin, Shepard
Michaels, Fern
See Anderson, Roberta and
Kuczkir, Mary
Michaels, J. Ramsey 1931- CANR-38
Earlier sketch in CA 116
Michaels, Joanne 1950- CANR-23
Earlier sketch in CA 107
Michaels, Joanne Louise
See Teitelbaum, Michael
Michaels, Joe
See Saltzman, Joseph
Michaels, Kasey
See Seidick, Kathryn A(melia)
Michaels, Kristin
See Williams, Jeanne
Michaels, Leonard 1933-2003 .... CANR-119
Obituary 216
Earlier sketches in CA 61-64, CANR-21, 62
See also CLC 6, 25
See also CN 3, 45, 6, 7
See also DLB 130
See also MTCW 1
See also SSC 16
See also TCLE 1:2
Michaels, Lisa 1966- 171
Michaels, Lorne 1944- CANR-78
Earlier sketch in CA 142
See also AAYA 12, 62
See also CCA 1
Michaels, Lynn 238
Michaels, Lynn
See Strongin, Lynn
Michaels, Molly
See Untermeyer, Louis
Michaels, Neal
See Teitelbaum, Michael
Michaels, Norman 97-100
Michaels, Philip
See Magocsi, Paul Robert and
van Rjndt, Philippe
Michaels, Ralph
See Filicchia, Ralph
Michaels, Sidney R(amon) 1927- 17-20R
Michaels, Ski
See Pellowski, Michael (Joseph)
Michaels, Steve
See Avallone, Michael (Angelo, Jr.)
Michaels, Steve 1955- .... SATA 71
Michaels, Walter Benn 239
Michaels, William M. 1917- .... SATA 77
Michaelson, L(ouis) W. 1917- CANR-14
Earlier sketch in CA 77-80
Michaely, Michael 1928- 103
Michalak, Stanley (J., Jr.) 1938- 232
Michalak, Virginia
See Koste, Virginia Glasgow
Michalczyk, John Joseph 1941- 104
Michalopoulos, Andre 1897-1982 .... CAP-2
Earlier sketch in CA 23-24
Michalos, Alex C. 1935- 37-40R
Michalowski, Kazimierz 1901-1981
Obituary 108
Michalski, John 1934- 25-28R
Michalski, Sergiusz 1951- 198
Michalson, Carl (Donald, Jr.) 1915-1965 ... 1-4R
Michalson, Karen 1960- 219
Michas, Takis 1948- 222
Michaud, Charles Regis 1910- CAP-2
Earlier sketch in CA 19-20
Michaud, Stephen G(age) 1948- CANR-100
Earlier sketch in CA 109
Michaud, W. W.
See Dunbar, Wylene (Wisby)
Michaux, Henri 1899-1984 85-88
Obituary 114
See also CLC 8, 19
See also DLB 258
See also EWL 3
See also GFL 1789 to the Present
See also RGWL 2, 3
Michaux, William W(hitehead) 1919- ... 41-44R
Miche, Giuseppe
See Bochenski, Joseph M.
Micheaux, Oscar (Devereaux) 1884-1951 .. 174
See also BW 3
See also DLB 50
See also TCLC 76
See also TCWW 2
Micheels, Peter A. 1945- 132
Michel, Anna 1943- 85-88
See also SATA 49
See also SATA-Brief 40
Michel, Beth
See Dubus, Elizabeth Nell
Michel, Francois 1948- .... SATA 82
Michel, Georges 1926- CANR-31
Earlier sketch in CA 25-28R
Michel, Henri (Jules) 1907-1986 ...... CANR-19
Earlier sketches in CA 53-56, CANR-4
Michel, Joseph 1922- CANR-13
Earlier sketch in CA 25-28R
Michel, Michel Georges
See Georges-Michel, Michel
Michel, Pierre 1934- 57-60
Michel, Sandra (Seaton) 1935- 77-80
Michel, Sandy
See Michel, Sandra (Seaton)
Michel, (Milton) Scott 1916-1992 .... 1-4R
Obituary 196
Michel, Walter 1922- 81-84
Michelangelo 1475-1564 .... AAYA 43
Michelet, Jules 1798-1874 .... EW 5
See also GFL 1789 to the Present
Micheli, Lyle Joseph 1940- CANR-20
Earlier sketch in CA 97-100
Micheline, Jack 1929-1998 122
Obituary 165
Brief entry 114
Interview in CA-122
See also DLB 16
Michell, John (F.) 1933- CANR-88
Earlier sketches in CA 107, CANR-23
Michelman, Herbert 1913-1980
Obituary 102
Michelman, Irving S(imon) 1917- 69-72
Michelmore, Peter 1930- CANR-7
Earlier sketch in CA 5-8R
Michel of Northgate, Dan c. 1265-c.
1340 .... DLB 146
Michelon, L. C. 1918- CANR-1
Earlier sketch in CA 45-48
Michels, Caroll Chesy 1943- 117
Michels, Christine
See Michels, Sharry C.
Michels, Robert 1876-1936 212
See also TCLC 88
Michels, Sharry C. 1957- 232
Michelsen, G. F. 234
Michelson, Albert (Abraham) 1852-1931 163
Michelson, Bruce (N.) 1948- CANR-101
Earlier sketch in CA 139
Michelson, Edward J(ulias) 1915- 77-80
Michelson, Florence B. CAP-2
Earlier sketch in CA 21-22
Michelson, Karin 1953- 225
Michelson, Peter 1937- CANR-1
Earlier sketch in CA 45-48
Michelson, Stephan 1938- 93-96
Michelson, William M. 1940- 33-36R
Michelucci, Stefania 1963- 222
Michener, Anna J. 1977- 176
Michener, Charles D(uncan) 1918- 117
Michener, Charles Thomson 1940- 104
Michener, James A(lbert)
1907(?)-1997 .... CANR-68
Obituary 161
Earlier sketches in CA 5-8R, CANR-21, 45
See also AAYA 27
See also AITN 1
See also BEST 90:1
See also BPFB 2
See also CLC 1, 5, 11, 29, 60, 109
See also CN 1, 2, 3, 4, 5, 6
See also CPW
See also DA3
See also DAM NOV, POP
See also DLB 6
See also MAL 5
See also MTCW 1, 2
See also MTFW 2005
See also RHW
See also TCWW 1, 2
Michener, Marian 219
Michie, Allan (Andrew) 1915-1973
Obituary 45-48
Michie, Donald 1923- 121
Michie, James 1927- 164
Brief entry 116
See also CP 1, 2, 3, 4, 5, 6, 7
Michie, Jonathan 1957- 132
Michihiko Hachiya MD .... LAIT 4
Michman, Dan 1947- 229
Michman, Ronald D(avid) 1931- CANR-7
Earlier sketch in CA 57-60
Michod, Richard E. 1951- CANR-98
Earlier sketch in CA 147
Michel, Paul .... SATA 74
Mickel, Emanuel J(ohn), Jr. 1937- CANR-99
Earlier sketch in CA 37-40R
Mickelbury, Penny 1948- 146
Mickelsen, A(nton) Berkeley 1920- 9-12R
Mickelsen, Olaf 1912-1999 .... 17-20R
Mickelson, Monty (Phillip) 1956- 141
Mickelson, Sig 1913-2000 111
Obituary 189
Micken, Charles M. 1918- 13-16R
Mickey, Paul A(lbert) 1937- CANR-1
Earlier sketch in CA 49-52
Mickiewicz, Adam 1798-1855 .... EW 5
See also PC 38
See also RGWL 2, 3
Mickiewicz, Ellen Propper 1938- CANR-49
Earlier sketches in CA 21-24R, CANR-9, 24
Mickle, Shelley Fraser 1944- CANR-110
Earlier sketch in CA 132
Micklejohn, George 1717(?)-1818 .... DLB 31
Micklem, Nathaniel 1888-1976 103
Micklem, Sarah 1955- 233
Mickler, Ernest M(atthew) 1940(?)-1988
Obituary 127
Micklethwait, (Richard) John 1962- 237
Micklish, Rita 1931- 49-52
See also SATA 12
Micklos, John J., Jr. 1956- 198
See also SATA 129
Mickolus, Edward F(rancis) 1950- 106

Micks, Marianne H(offman) 1923-1997 ... CANR-12
Earlier sketch in CA 17-20R
Micou, Paul 1959- ... 140
Micucci, Charles (Patrick), Jr. 1959- ... CANR-124
Micucci, Charles (Patrick, Jr.) 1959- ... 137
See also SATA 82, 144
Micunovic, Veljko 1916-1982 ... 109
Obituary ... 107
Midda, Sara 1951- ... 135
Middeldorf, Ulrich Alexander 1901-1983
Obituary ... 109
Middendorf, John Harlan 1922- ... 104
Middlebrook, Christina 1941- ... 156
Middlebrook, David
See Rosenus, Alan (Harvey)
Middlebrook, Diane Wood 1939- ... CANR-97
Earlier sketches in CA 81-84, CANR-15
Middlebrook, Jonathan 1940- ... 65-68
Middlebrook, (Norman) Martin 1932- ... CANR-57
Earlier sketches in CA 37-40R, CANR-14, 31
Middlekauff, Robert (Lawrence) 1929- ... 130
Brief entry ... 112
Middleman, Ruth J. Rosenbloom 1923- ... 104
Middlemas, Keith
See Middlemas, Robert Keith
Middlemas, Robert Keith 1935- ... CANR-12
Earlier sketch in CA 29-32R
Middlemiss, Robert (William) 1938- . CANR-12
Earlier sketch in CA 73-76
Middleton, Bernard C(hester) 1924- ... CANR-116
Earlier sketch in CA 41-44R
Middleton, (John) Christopher 1926- ... CANR-117
Earlier sketches in CA 13-16R, CANR-29, 54
See also CLC 13
See also CP 1, 2, 3, 4, 5, 6, 7
See also DLB 40
Middleton, Darren J. N. 1966- ... 157
Middleton, David L. 1940- ... 37-40R
Middleton, Dorothy 1909-1999 ... 184
Middleton, Drew 1914(?)-1990
Obituary ... 130
Brief entry ... 110
Middleton, George 1880-1967
Obituary ... 25-28R
Middleton, Haydn 1955- ... CANR-90
Earlier sketch in CA 132
See also SATA 85, 152
Middleton, Michael (Humfrey) 1917- ... CANR-51
Earlier sketch in CA 124
Middleton, Michael L. 1945- ... 145
Middleton, Nicholas J. ... 236
Middleton, Nick
See Middleton, Nicholas J.
Middleton, Nigel (Gordon) 1918- ... CANR-25
Earlier sketch in CA 45-48
Middleton, O(sman) E(dward Gordon) 1925- ... CANR-81
Earlier sketch in CA 81-84
See also CN 1, 2, 3, 4, 5, 6
See also RGSF 2
Middleton, Richard (Barham) 1882-1911 ... 187
See also DLB 156
See also HGG
See also TCLC 56
Middleton, Richard 1945- ... 109
Middleton, Roger 1955- ... 126
Middleton, Stanley 1919- ... CANR-81
Earlier sketches in CA 25-28R, CANR-21, 46
See also CAAS 23
See also CLC 7, 38
See also CN 1, 2, 3, 4, 5, 6, 7
See also DLB 14
Middleton, Stephen 1954- ... CANR-141
Earlier sketch in CA 144
Middleton, Thomas 1580-1627 ... BRW 2
See also DAM DRAM, MST
See also DC 5
See also DFS 18, 22
See also DLB 58
See also RGEL 2
Middleton-Murry, Colin
See Middleton-Murry, John, (Jr.)
Middleton-Murry, John, (Jr.) 1926-2002 ... CANR-81
Obituary ... 206
Earlier sketches in CA 5-8R, CANR-3
See also Cowper, Richard
See also SFW 4
Middleton Murry, Mary
See Murry, Mary Middleton
Midelfort, H(ans) C(hristian) Erik 1942- ... CANR-26
Earlier sketch in CA 45-48
Midgett, Elwin W(ilburn) 1911-1993 ... CAP-2
Earlier sketch in CA 29-32
Midgett, Wink
See Midgett, Elwin W(ilburn)
Midgette, Anne ... 236
Midgley, David A(lan) 1898-1987 ... 17-20R
Midgley, E(rnest) B(rian) F(rancis) 1927- .. 93-96
Midgley, Graham 1923-1999 ... 73-76
Obituary ... 178
Midgley, Louis C(asper) 1931- ... 41-44R
Midgley, Mary 1919- ... CANR-43
Earlier sketches in CA 89-92, CANR-20
Midkiff, Mary D. 1955- ... 202
Midlarsky, Manus I(ssacher) 1937- ... 57-60
Midler, Bette 1945- ... 106
Midtlyng, Joanna 1927- ... 61-64
Midwinter, E(ric) C(lare) 1932-1998 . CANR-26
Earlier sketch in CA 29-32R
Midwood, Bart(on A.) 1938- ... 172
Mieczkowski, Bogdan 1924- ... 111
Miegel, Agnes 1879-1964 ... DLB 56
Miel, Alice Marie 1906-1998 ... CANR-20
Obituary ... 164
Earlier sketches in CA 1-4R, CANR-5
Mielczarek, Eugenie Vorburger ... 213
Mielke, Arthur W(illard) 1912-1978 ... CANR-4
Earlier sketch in CA 1-4R
Mielziner, Jo 1901-1976 ... 45-48
Obituary ... 65-68
Miernyk, William Henry 1918- ... 17-20R
Miers, Earl Schenck 1910-1972 ... CANR-2
Obituary ... 37-40R
Earlier sketch in CA 1-4R
See also SATA 1
See also SATA-Obit 26
Miers, Suzanne (Doyle) 1922- ... 61-64
Mierzejewski, Alfred C. 1953- ... 196
Mierzenski, Stanislaw 1903-1964 ... 1-4R
Miesel, Sandra (Louise) 1941- ... 128
Mies van der Rohe, Ludwig 1886-1969 ... 185
See also AAYA 54
Mieth, Dietmar 1940- ... 176
Miethe, Terry Lee 1948- ... 105
Mieville, China 1973(?)- ... CANR-138
Earlier sketch in CA 196
See also AAYA 52
See also MTFW 2005
Miewald, Robert D(ale) 1938- ... 117
Miezelaitis, Eduardas 1919-1997 ... DLB 220
Mifflin, Margot ... 181
Migdal, Joel S(amuel) 1945- ... CANR-142
Earlier sketches in CA 57-60, CANR-6
Migdale, Lawrence 1951- ... SATA 89
Migdalski, Edward C(harles) 1918- ... CANR-4
Earlier sketch in CA 9-12R
Migel, Parmenia
See Ekstrom, Parmenia Migel
Mighetto, Lisa 1955- ... 141
Mighton, John 1957- ... 166
Mighty Sparrow, The 1935- ... CP 7
Migliore, R. Henry 1940- ... 110
Migliorini, Bruno 1896-1975
Obituary ... 116
Miglis, John 1950- ... CANR-20
Earlier sketch in CA 81-84
Mignani, Rigo 1921- ... 37-40R
Mignola, Mike 1962- ... 224
See also AAYA 54
Mignon, Charles W. 1933- ... CANR-139
Earlier sketch in CA 172
Mignot, Claude 1943- ... 197
Migueis, Jose Rodrigues 1901-1980 ... CLC 10
See also DLB 287
Miguez-Bonino, Jose 1924- ... 49-52
Mihailovic, Dragoslav 1930- ... 202
See also DLB 181
Mihailovich, Vasa D. 1926- ... CANR-14
Earlier sketch in CA 41-44R
Mihajlov, Mihajlo 1934- ... CANR-89
Brief entry ... 105
Earlier sketch in CA 130
Mihalas, Dimitri M(anuel) 1939- ... CANR-4
Earlier sketch in CA 53-56
Mihalic, Slavko 1928- ... CWW 2
See also DLB 181
Mihaly, Mary E(llen) 1950- ... 97-100
Mihanovich, Clement Simon 1913-1998 .. 5-8R
Mihesuah, Devon ... 201
Mihura, Miguel 1905-1977 ... 214
Mijuskovic, Ben Lazare 1937- ... 132
Mikaelsen, Ben(jamin John) 1952- ... 139
See also AAYA 37
See also SATA 73, 107
Mikalson, Jon D. 1943- ... 140
Mikan, Baron
See Barba, Harry
Mikdashi, Zuhayr 1933- ... CANR-39
Earlier sketches in CA 89-92, CANR-17
Mikes, George 1912-1987 ... CANR-83
Obituary ... 123
Earlier sketches in CA 9-12R, CANR-6
Mikesell, Arthur M. 1932- ... 13-16R
Mikesell, John L(ee) 1942- ... 102
Mikesell, Marvin Wray 1930- ... CANR-4
Earlier sketch in CA 1-4R
Mikesell, Raymond F(rech) 1913- ... CANR-41
Earlier sketches in CA 1-4R, CANR-4, 19
Mikesell, Rufus Merrill 1893-1972 ... CAP-2
Earlier sketch in CA 25-28
Mikesell, William H(enry) 1887-1969 ... CAP-2
Earlier sketch in CA 19-20
Mikhail, E(dward) H(alim) 1926- ... CANR-58
Earlier sketches in CA 37-40R, CANR-14, 31
Mikhailov, A.
See Sheller, Aleksandr Konstantinovich
Mikhailov, M.
See Mihajlov, Mihajlo
Mikhailov, Mikhail Larionovich 1829-1865 ... DLB 238
Mikhailovsky, Nikolai Konstantinovich 1842-1904 ... DLB 277
Mikhalkov, Sergei Vladimirovich 1913-
Brief entry ... 116
Mikhalkov-Konchalovsky, Andrei (Sergeyevich) 1937- ... 127
Miki, Chihan
See Naruse, Mikio
Mikkelsen, Ejnar 1881(?)-1971
Obituary ... 29-32R
Miklowitz, Gloria D. 1927- ... CANR-109
Earlier sketches in CA 25-28R, CANR-10, 26, 51, 81
See also AAYA 6, 64
See also BYA 13
See also JRDA
See also MAICYA 1, 2
See also SAAS 17
See also SATA 4, 68, 129
See also WYA
See also YAW
Miklowitz, Paul S(tephen) 1956- ... 185
Mikolaycak, Charles 1937-1993 ... CANR-38
Obituary ... 141
Earlier sketches in CA 61-64, CANR-8, 23
See also MAICYA 1, 2
See also MAICYAS 1
See also SAAS 4
See also SATA 9, 78
See also SATA-Obit 75
Mikolyzk, Thomas A. 1953- ... 138
Mikszath, Kalman 1847-1910 ... 170
See also TCLC 31
Mikulas, William Lee 1942- ... 53-56
Mikus, Joseph A(ugust) 1909-2005 ... 61-64
Obituary ... 239
Milano, Paolo 1904-1988
Obituary ... 125
Milbank, Dana ... 200
Milbank, (Alasdair) John ... 202
Milberg, Warren H(oward) 1941- ... 109
Milbrath, Lester W(alter) 1925- ... CANR-4
Earlier sketch in CA 9-12R
Milburn, George 1906-1966
Obituary ... 109
See also TCWW 1, 2
Milburn, Josephine F(ishel) 1928- ... CANR-13
Earlier sketch in CA 21-24R
Milburn, Joyce 1953- ... 114
Milburn, Michael A. 1950- ... 191
Milburn, Robert (Leslie Pollington) 1907- ... 130
Milch, Robert J(effrey) 1938- ... 25-28R
Milcsik, Margie 1950- ... 110
Mild, Warren (Paul) 1922- ... CANR-8
Earlier sketch in CA 21-24R
See also SATA 41
Mildner, Gerard C. S. 1959- ... 138
Mileck, Joseph 1922- ... 107
Milelli, Pascal 1965- ... SATA 135
Milenkovitch, Michael M. 1932- ... 37-40R
Milenski, Paul Edward 1942- ... 128
Miles, Lady -1969 ... RHW
Miles, Angela R(ose) 1946- ... 122
Miles, Barry 1943- ... CANR-102
Earlier sketch in CA 134
Miles, (Louise) Bebe 1924-1980 ... CANR-9
Earlier sketch in CA 61-64
Miles, Bernard 1907-1991 ... 133
Miles, Betty 1928- ... CANR-79
Earlier sketches in CA 1-4R, CANR-5, 20, 48
See also BYA 2
See also JRDA
See also SAAS 9
See also SATA 8, 78
See also YAW
Miles, Beverly Parkhurst 1940- ... 107
Miles, Charles 1894- ... 5-8R
Miles, Christopher (John) 1939- ... 176
Miles, David H(olmes) 1940- ... 57-60
Miles, Dione 1921- ... 220
Miles, Dorien K(lein) 1915- ... CANR-8
Earlier sketch in CA 61-64
Miles, Dudley (Robert Alexander) 1947- ... 131
Miles, Edwin A(rthur) 1926- ... 1-4R
Miles, Elliot
See Ludvigsen, Karl (Eric)
Miles, Elton (Roger) 1917- ... 37-40R
Miles, Gary Britten 1940- ... 102
Miles, George C(arpenter) 1904-1975
Obituary ... 61-64
Miles, Herbert J(ackson) 1907- ... 21-24R
Miles, Ian (Douglas) 1948- ... 115
Miles, Jack ... 200
See also CLC 100
Miles, John
See Bickham, Jack M(iles)
Miles, John Russiano
See Miles, Jack
Miles, Josephine (Louise) 1911-1985 ... CANR-55
Obituary ... 116
Earlier sketches in CA 1-4R, CANR-2
See also CLC 1, 2, 14, 34, 39
See also CP 1, 2
See also DAM POET
See also DLB 48
See also MAL 5
See also TCLE 1:2
Miles, Joyce C(rudgington) 1927- ... 105
Miles, Judith Mary (Huhta) 1937- ... 65-68
Miles, Keith 1940- ... CANR-144
Earlier sketches in CA 139, CANR-103
See also CMW 4
Miles, Leland (Weber, Jr.) 1924- ... 13-16R
Miles, Margaret R(uth) 1937- ... 117
Miles, Mary Lillian (Brown) 1908-1986 ... 13-16R
Miles, Matthew B(ailey) 1926- ... CANR-36
Earlier sketches in CA 81-84, CANR-15
Miles, Michael W. 1945- ... 33-36R
Miles, Miska
See Martin, Patricia Miles
Miles, O. Thomas 1923- ... 21-24R
Miles, (Mary) Patricia 1930- ... CANR-27
Earlier sketches in CA 69-72, CANR-11
See also SATA 29
Miles, Patricia A.
See Martin, Patricia Miles
Miles, Peter
See Miles, Richard
Miles, Richard 1938- ... 105
Miles, Robert H. 1944- ... 118
Miles, Robert L(ee) 1939- ... 107
Miles, Russell Hancock 1895-1983 ... CAP-1
Earlier sketch in CA 9-10
Miles, Sara 1952- ... 198
Miles, Stanley 1911-1987
Obituary ... 123
Miles, Susan
See Roberts, Ursula (Wyllie)
See also DLB 240
Miles, Sylva
See Miles, Dorien K(lein) and Mularchyk, Sylva
Miles, T(homas) R(ichard) 1923- ... CANR-38
Earlier sketches in CA 49-52, CANR-1, 17
Miles, William F. S. 1955- ... 151
Milestone, Lewis 1895-1980
Obituary ... 101
Miletich, Leo N(ick) 1946- ... 148
Miletus, Rex
See Burgess, Michael (Roy)
Milford, D(avid) S(umner) 1905-1984
Obituary ... 113
Milford, Nancy (Winston) 1938- ... CANR-117
Earlier sketch in CA 29-32R
Milgate, Rodney Armour 1934- ... 107
Milgram, Gail Gleason 1942- ... 29-32R
Milgram, Morris 1916-1997 ... 73-76
Obituary ... 159
Milgram, Stanley 1933-1984 ... CANR-29
Obituary ... 114
Earlier sketch in CA 105
Milgrim, David ... 219
See also SATA 158
Milgrom, Harry 1912-1978 ... CANR-3
Earlier sketch in CA 1-4R
See also SATA 25
Milgrom, Jacob 1923- ... 53-56
Milhaud, Darius 1892-1974
Obituary ... 49-52
See also IDFW 3, 4
Milhaven, John Giles 1927- ... 29-32R
Milhorn, H(oward) Thomas, Jr. 1936- ... 146
Milhous, Judith 1946- ... 129
Milhous, Katherine 1894-1977
Obituary ... 104
See also SATA 15
Milhouse, Paul W(illiam) 1910- ... CANR-27
Earlier sketches in CA 25-28R, CANR-11
Mili, Gjon 1904-1984
Obituary ... 112
Milic, Louis T(onko) 1922- ... 21-24R
Milio, Nancy 1938- ... CANR-13
Earlier sketch in CA 29-32R
Milios, Rita 1949- ... 148
See also SATA 79
Milis, Ludo(vicus) J. R. 1940- ... 145
Militant
See Sandburg, Carl (August)
Militello, Pietro
See Natali, Alfred Maxim
Milius, John 1945- ... 101
Interview in ... CA-101
See also DLB 44
Miljkovic, Branko 1934-1962 ... DLB 181
Milkomane, George Alexis Milkomanovich 1903-1996 ... CANR-20
Earlier sketch in CA 104
Milks, Harold Keith 1908-1979 ... 108
Obituary ... 93-96
Mill, C. R.
See Crnjanski, Milos
Mill, Harriet (Hardy) Taylor 1807-1858 ... FW
Mill, James 1773-1836 ... DLB 107, 158, 262
Mill, John Stuart 1806-1873 ... CDBLB 1832-1890
See also DLB 55, 190, 262
See also FW 1
See also RGEL 2
See also TEA
Millais, Raoul 1901- ... SATA 77
Milland, Jack
See Milland, Ray
Milland, Ray 1908(?)-1986
Obituary ... 118
Brief entry ... 113
Millar, Barbara F. 1924- ... 25-28R
See also SATA 12
Millar, Fergus (G. B.) 1935- ... CANR-88
Earlier sketches in CA 13-16R, CANR-5, 20
Millar, George (Reid) 1910-2005 ... 73-76
Obituary ... 236
Millar, Gilbert John 1939- ... 104
Millar, J(ohn) Halket 1899-1978 ... 9-12R
Millar, James Primrose Malcolm 1893-1989 ... CAP-1
Earlier sketch in CA 9-10
Millar, James R(obert) 1936- ... 29-32R
Millar, Jeff(ery Lynn) 1942- ... CANR-11
Earlier sketch in CA 69-72
Millar, (Minna Henrietta) Joy 1914- ... 93-96

Cumulative Index 401 **Miller**

Millar, Kenneth 1915-1983 .... CANR-107
Obituary 110
Earlier sketches in CA 9-12R, CANR-16, 63
See also Macdonald, Ross
See also CLC 14
See also CMW 4
See also CPW
See also DA3
See also DAM POP
See also DLB 2, 226
See also DLBD 6
See also DLBY 1983
See also MTCW 1, 2
See also MTFW 2005
Millar, Margaret (Ellis Sturm)
1915-1994 .... CANR-81
Obituary 144
Earlier sketches in CA 13-16R, CANR-16, 44
See also CMW 4
See also CN 2, 3, 4, 5
See also MSW
See also SATA 61
See also SATA-Obit 79
Millar, Oliver (Nicholas) 1923- 142
Millar, Ronald (Graeme) 1919-1998 73-76
Obituary 167
See also CBD
See also CD 5, 6
Millar, T(homas) B(ruce) CANR-26
Earlier sketch in CA 29-32R
Millard, A(lan) R(alph) 1937- CANR-11
Earlier sketch in CA 25-28R
Millard, Andre 1947- 136
Millard, Charles W(arren III) 1932- 153
Brief entry 115
Millard, Gregory B. 1947(?)-1984
Obituary 114
Millard, Joe
See Millard, Joseph (John)
Millard, Joseph (John) 1908-1989 ..... CANR-71
Obituary 171
Earlier sketch in CA 13-16R
See also TCWW 1, 2
Millas, Juan Jose 1946- .... DLB 322
Millay, E. Vincent
See Millay, Edna St. Vincent
Millay, Edna St. Vincent 1892-1950 130
Brief entry 104
See also Boyd, Nancy
See also AMW
See also CDALB 1917-1929
See also DA
See also DA3
See also DAB
See also DAC
See also DAM MST, POET
See also DLB 45, 249
See also EWL 3
See also EXPP
See also FL 1:6
See also MAL 5
See also MAWW
See also MTCW 1, 2
See also MTFW 2005
See also PAB
See also PC 6, 61
See also PFS 3, 17
See also RGAL 4
See also TCLC 4, 49, 169
See also TUS
See also WLCS
See also WP
Millbank, Captain H. R.
See Ellis, Edward S(ylvester)
Millburn, Cynthia
See Brooks, Anne Tedlock
Milldyke, (John) William 1937-1983 77-80
Obituary 111
Mille, Agnes de
See Prude, Agnes George de Mille
Millen, C(ynthia) M. 1955- 186
See also SATA 114
Millen, Clifford H. 1901(?)-1972
Obituary 104
Millender, Dharathula H(ood) 1920- 17-20R
Miller, Abraham H(irsh) 1940- 104
Miller, Al 1936- 65-68
Miller, Alan 1954- 226
Miller, Alan Robert 1929- 73-76
Miller, Alan S. 1949- 147
Miller, Alan W. 1926- 29-32R
Miller, Albert G(riffith) 1905-1982 ...... CANR-1
Obituary 107
Earlier sketch in CA 1-4R
See also SATA 12
See also SATA-Obit 31
Miller, Albert Jay 1928- CANR-1
Earlier sketch in CA 45-48
Miller, Alden D(ykstra) 1940(?)-1984
Obituary 113
Miller, Alden Holmes 1906-1965
Obituary 109
Miller, Alex 1936- 196
See also CN 6, 7
Miller, Alfred W. 1893(?)-1983
Obituary 111
Miller, Alice 142
Miller, Alice Ann 1958- .... SATA 150
Miller, Alice P(atricia McCarthy) CANR-44
Earlier sketch in CA 29-32R
See also SATA 22
Miller, Alicia (Metcalf) 1939- 127
Miller, Andrew M. 1960- CANR-116
Earlier sketch in CA 159
See also DLB 267
Miller, Anesa 1934- 156
Miller, Anistatia R. 1952- 182
Miller, Anita 1926- CANR-91
Earlier sketches in CA 111, CANR-29, 53
Miller, Ann
See Collier, Lucille Ann
Miller, Arthur 1915-2005 .... CANR-132
Obituary 236
Earlier sketches in CA 1-4R, CANR-2, 30, 54, 76
See also CABS 3
See also AAYA 15
See also AITN 1
See also AMW
See also AMWC 1
See also CAD
See also CD 5, 6
See also CDALB 1941-1968
See also CLC 1, 2, 6, 10, 15, 26, 47, 78, 179
See also DA
See also DA3
See also DAB
See also DAC
See also DAM DRAM, MST
See also DC 1
See also DFS 1, 3, 8
See also DLB 7, 266
See also EWL 3
See also LAIT 1, 4
See also LATS 1:2
See also MAL 5
See also MTCW 1, 2
See also MTFW 2005
See also RGAL 4
See also TUS
See also WLC
See also WYAS 1
Miller, Arthur B(urton) 1922- 37-40R
Miller, Arthur C. 1895-1970 .... IDFW 3, 4
Miller, Arthur R(aphael) 1934- 150
Brief entry 114
Miller, Arthur S(elwyn) 1917-1988 ... CANR-11
Obituary 125
Earlier sketch in CA 69-72
Miller, Barbara D(iane) 1948- CANR-23
Earlier sketch in CA 106
Miller, Barbara S(toler) 1940-1993 ... CANR-47
Obituary 141
Earlier sketches in CA 25-28R, CANR-11, 27
Miller, Barry 1946- 33-36R
Miller, Benj.
See Loomis, Noel M(iller)
Miller, Benjamin F(rank) 1907-1971 ... CANR-4
Obituary 29-32R
Earlier sketch in CA 1-4R
Miller, Bernard S. 1920- 106
Miller, Beth 1941- 136
Miller, Beulah Montgomery 1917- 61-64
Miller, (H.) Bill(y) 1920-1961 .... CANR-62
Earlier sketch in CA 108
See also Miller, Wade
Miller, Bill D. 1936- 102
Miller, Blair 1955- 153
Miller, Brent C(arlton) 1947- 112
Miller, (Harvey) Brown 1943- 101
Miller, Byron Strongman 1912(?)-1978
Obituary 77-80
Miller, C(larence) William 1914- 53-56
Miller, Calvin 1936- CANR-104
Earlier sketches in CA 21-24R, CANR-13
Miller, Carlene 1935- 187
Miller, Caroline (Pafford) 1903-1992 179
See also DLB 9
Miller, Carroll H(iram) 1907-1970(?) CAP-1
Earlier sketch in CA 19-20
Miller, Casey (Geddes) 1919-1997 69-72
Obituary 156
Miller, Cathleen (A.) 1956- 173
Miller, Cecilia Parsons 1909-1994 .... CANR-12
Earlier sketch in CA 21-24R
Miller, Cecille (Boyd) 1908- 9-12R
Miller, Char
See Miller, Frank L(ubbock) IV
Miller, Charles 1918- 77-80
Miller, Charles A. 1937- 29-32R
Miller, Charles D(avid) 1942- CANR-32
Earlier sketch in CA 69-72
Miller, Charles E. 1929- 33-36R
Miller, Charles Henderson 1905-1996 ... CAP-2
Earlier sketch in CA 19-20
Miller, Charles Leslie 1908-1999 49-52
Miller, Christian 1920- 108
Miller, Christopher L. 1950(?)- 219
Miller, Cincinnatus Hiner 1839(?)-1913 202
Miller, Clarence H(arvey) 1930- 102
Miller, Clarence J(ohn) 1916- CANR-13
Earlier sketch in CA 21-24R
Miller, Clement (Albin) 1915-2005 .... 41-44R
Obituary 235
Miller, Conrad
See Strung, Norman
Miller, D(ean) A(rthur) 1931- 21-24R
Miller, D. Quentin 1967- 213
Miller, Daniel Adlai II 1918- 37-40R
Miller, Danny 1947- CANR-53
Earlier sketch in CA 126
Miller, Danny L(ester) 1949- 166
Miller, Darlis A(nn) 1939- 125
Miller, David (Leslie) 1946- 130
Miller, David 1950- 172
Autobiographical Essay in 172
See also CAAS 30
Miller, David C. 1951- 147
Miller, David E(ugene) 1909-1978 45-48
Obituary 103
Miller, David Harry 1938- 57-60
Miller, David L(eroy) 1936- 49-52
Miller, David Lee 1951- 122
Miller, David Louis 1903-1986 .... 21-24R
Obituary 118
Miller, David Merlin 1934- 93-96
Miller, David W. 1940- 49-52
Miller, Debbie (S.) 1951- 133
See also SATA 103, 160
Miller, Deborah 1957- 201
Miller, Deborah Uchill 1944- 116
See also SATA 61
Miller, Delbert C(harles) 1913-1998 ...... 25-28R
Miller, Don 1923- .... SATA 15
Miller, Donald 1893-1986
Obituary 119
Miller, Donald 1934- 97-100
Miller, Donald C(urtis) 1933- CANR-6
Earlier sketch in CA 57-60
Miller, Donald Eugene 1929- CANR-24
Earlier sketch in CA 106
Miller, Donald George 1909-1997 ..... CANR-4
Earlier sketch in CA 5-8R
Miller, Donald L. 216
Miller, Donald L(ane) 1918- 17-20R
Miller, Doris R.
See Mosesson, Gloria R(ubin)
Miller, Dorothy (Ryan)
See Ryan, Dorothy (Barger)
Miller, Douglas T(aylor) 1937- 21-24R
Miller, E(ugene) Ethelbert 1950- CANR-115
Earlier sketch in CA 143
See also BW 2
See also CP 7
See also DLB 41
Miller, E. F.
See Pohle, Robert W(arren), Jr.
Miller, E(dwin) S(hepard) 1904-2000 45-48
Miller, E(ugene) Willard 1915- CANR-40
Earlier sketches in CA 5-8R, CANR-2, 17
Miller, Ed(die) L(eRoy) 1937- 37-40R
Miller, Eddie
See Miller, Edward
Miller, Edmund 1943- 188
Miller, Edna Anita 1920- 112
See also SATA 29
Miller, Edward 1905-1974 .... CAP-2
Earlier sketch in CA 25-28
See also SATA 8
Miller, Edward A., Jr. 1927- 171
Miller, Edward A. Jr 1927- 171
Miller, Edward G. 1958- 150
Miller, Edwin Haviland 1918- 110
Miller, Elizabeth 1933- 117
See also SATA 41
Miller, Elizabeth Kubota 1932- 13-16R
Miller, Elizabeth Maxfield 1910- 45-48
Miller, Ella May 1915- CANR-11
Earlier sketch in CA 21-24R
Miller, Ellanita 1957- .... SATA 87
Miller, Ellen 1967(?)- 234
Miller, Elmer S(chaffner) 1931- 152
Miller, Elwood E. 1925- 122
Miller, Errol Louis 1939- 198
Miller, Ethel Prince 1893-1981 .... CAP-1
Earlier sketch in CA 13-14
Miller, Eugene 1925- 101
See also SATA 33
Miller, Eugene E. 1930- 135
Miller, Eugenia
See Mandelkorn, Eugenia Miller
Miller, F(rederick) W(alter) G(ascoyne)
1904-1996 .... CANR-11
Earlier sketch in CA 25-28R
Miller, Faren (Carol) 1950- .... FANT
Miller, Florence B. 1895(?)-1976
Obituary 69-72
Miller, Floyd C. 1912-1988 .... CANR-2
Earlier sketch in CA 1-4R
Miller, Forrestt A. 1931- 25-28R
Miller, Frances A. 1937- 123
See also SATA 52
See also SATA-Brief 46
See also YAW
Miller, Francis Pickens 1895-1978 69-72
Obituary 135
Miller, Frank
See Loomis, Noel M(iller)
Miller, Frank 1925-1983
Obituary 109
Miller, Frank 1957- 224
See also AAYA 45
Miller, Frank L(ubbock) IV 1951- CANR-105
Earlier sketches in CA 113, CANR-34
Miller, Fred D., Jr. 1944- 129
Miller, G. R.
See Judd, Frederick Charles
Miller, G(eorge) Wayne 1954- 198
Miller, Gabriel 1948- 115
Miller, Gary M(ichael) 1941- 113
Miller, Gene Edward 1928- 97-100
Miller, Genevieve 1914- 17-20R
Miller, Geoffrey 1921-1984
Obituary 112
Miller, Geoffrey F. 1965- 208
Miller, Geoffrey Samuel 1945- 104
Miller, George (Eric) 1943- CANR-14
Earlier sketch in CA 73-76
Miller, George 1945- 157
Miller, George A(rmitage) 1920- CANR-1
Earlier sketch in CA 1-4R
Miller, George H(all) 1919- 33-36R
Miller, George Louquet 1934- 89-92
Miller, Gerald 1928(?)-1970
Obituary 104
Miller, Gerald R(aymond) 1931- CANR-16
Earlier sketch in CA 93-96
Miller, Glenn T(homas) 194?- 171
Brief entry 110
Miller, Glenn W. 1956- 217
Miller, Gordon W(esley) 1918- 89-92
Miller, Gus
See Miller, Gustavus Hindman
Miller, Gustavus Hindman 1857-1929
Brief entry 120
Miller, H. Orlo
See Miller, Hanson Orlo
Miller, Hanson Orlo 1911-1993 138
Miller, Harvey 1935-1999 181
Miller, Haskell M(orris) 1910- CAP-2
Earlier sketch in CA 23-24
Miller, Heather Ross 1939- CANR-91
Earlier sketches in CA 13-16R, CANR-5
See also DLB 120
Miller, Helen Hill 1899-1995 .... 9-12R
Obituary 150
Miller, Helen M(arkley) -1984 .... CANR-2
Earlier sketch in CA 1-4R
See also SATA 5
Miller, Helen Topping 1884-1960
Obituary 109
See also SATA-Obit 29
Miller, Henry (Valentine)
1891-1980 .... CANR-64
Obituary 97-100
Earlier sketches in CA 9-12R, CANR-33
See also AMW
See also BPFB 2
See also CDALB 1929-1941
See also CLC 1, 2, 4, 9, 14, 43, 84
See also CN 1, 2
See also DA
See also DA3
See also DAB
See also DAC
See also DAM MST, NOV
See also DLB 4, 9
See also DLBY 1980
See also EWL 3
See also MAL 5
See also MTCW 1, 2
See also MTFW 2005
See also RGAL 4
See also TUS
See also WLC
Miller, Henry Knight 1920- CANR-2
Earlier sketch in CA 1-4R
Miller, Herbert E(lmer) 1914- CANR-11
Earlier sketch in CA 17-20R
Miller, Hope (Deupree) Ridings
1906(?)-2005 .... 25-28R
Obituary 239
Miller, Howard S(mith) 1936- 29-32R
Miller, Hubert John 1927- 37-40R
Miller, Hugh 1802-1856 .... DLB 190
Miller, Hugh 1897(?)-1979
Obituary 89-92
Miller, Hugh 1937- CANR-12
Earlier sketch in CA 61-64
Miller, Hugh Milton 1908-1986 .... 33-36R
Miller, Ian
See Milne, John
Miller, Isabel
See Routsong, Alma
See also GLL 1
Miller, Ivor L. 1960- 222
Miller, J(ohn) D(onald) B(ruce)
1922- CANR-13
Earlier sketch in CA 73-76
Miller, J. Dale 1923- 105
Miller, J(oseph) Hillis 1928- 85-88
See also DLB 67
Miller, J. Innes 1892-1976 .... CAP-2
Earlier sketch in CA 29-32
Miller, J(ames) Maxwell 1937- 110
Miller, J(ames) P(inckney)
1919-2001 .... CANR-49
Obituary 204
Earlier sketch in CA 25-28R
See also AITN 1, 2
Miller, J(ohn) Robert 1913- 45-48
Miller, Jake C. 1929- 126
Miller, James 1947- 137
Miller, James A. 1957- 126
Miller, James C(lifford) III 1942- CANR-10
Earlier sketch in CA 25-28R
Miller, James Edward 1945- 135
Miller, James Edwin (Jr.) 1920- CANR-1
Earlier sketch in CA 1-4R
Miller, James G(rier) 1916-2002 .... 21-24R
Obituary 219
Miller, James M. 1933- CANR-121
Earlier sketch in CA 170
Miller, Jane (Judith) 1925-1989 .... CANR-34
Earlier sketches in CA 77-80, CANR-13
See also SATA 15
Miller, Jane 1949- 146
Miller, Jason 1939(?)-2001 .... CANR-130
Obituary 197
Earlier sketch in CA 73-76
See also AITN 1
See also CAD
See also CLC 2
See also DFS 12
See also DLB 7
Miller, Jay W(ilson) 1893-1975 .... CAP-1
Earlier sketch in CA 13-14
Miller, Jean Baker 1927- 154
Brief entry 108
See also FW
Miller, Jeffrey G. 1941- 144
Miller, Jerome G. 1931- 139
Miller, Jerome K. 1931- CANR-44
Earlier sketch in CA 105
Miller, Jewel 1956- .... SATA 73
Miller, Jim .... TCWW 2

Miller, Jim Wayne 1936-1996 ... CANR-92
Earlier sketches in CA 49-52, CANR-1, 20, 45
See also CAAS 15
See also YAW
Miller, Joan I(rene) 1944- ... CANR-41
Earlier sketch in CA 117
Miller, Joan M(ary) 1941- ... 108
Miller, Joaquin 1837-1913 ... DLB 186
See also RGAL 4
Miller, John
See Samachson, Joseph
Miller, John 1937- ... 231
Miller, John (Laurence) 1947- ... 93-96
Miller, John C. 1916(?)-1979
Obituary ... 89-92
Miller, John Chester 1907-1991 ... 73-76
Obituary ... 136
Miller, John Grider 1935- ... 133
Miller, John Harold 1925- ... 5-8R
Miller, John N. 1933- ... 33-36R
Miller, John P(earse, Jr.) 1943- ... CANR-27
Earlier sketch in CA 69-72
Miller, John Ramsey 1949- ... 188
Miller, Johnny
See Miller, John (Laurence)
Miller, Jolonda 1945- ... 108
Miller, Jon (Gordon) 1921- ... 53-56
Miller, Jonathan (Wolfe) 1934- ... 115
Brief entry ... 110
Miller, Jordan Y(ale) 1919- ... CANR-2
Earlier sketch in CA 1-4R
Miller, Joseph C(alder) 1939- ... 93-96
Miller, Judi ... CANR-95
Earlier sketch in CA 106
See also SATA 117
Miller, Judith 1948- ... CANR-112
Earlier sketches in CA 140, CANR-61
Miller, Judith von Daler 1940- ... 69-72
Miller, Julian M. 1922-1976
Obituary ... 69-72
Miller, June 1923- ... 89-92
Miller, K(eith) Bruce 1927- ... 33-36R
See also AITN 1
Miller, Karl (Fergus Connor) 1931- ... CANR-92
Brief entry ... 107
Earlier sketch in CA 145
Miller, Katherine C. Hill
See Hill-Miller, Katherine C(ecelia)
Miller, Keith G.
See Graber Miller, Keith Allen
Miller, Kenneth Dexter 1887-1968 ... CAP-1
Earlier sketch in CA 13-14
Miller, Kenneth E(ugene) 1926- ... 21-24R
Miller, Kenneth R(aymond) 1948- ... 195
Miller, Kent S(amuel) 1927-
Brief entry ... 109
Miller, Kerby A. 1944- ... CANR-90
Earlier sketch in CA 132
Miller, Kit 1956(?)- ... 208
Miller, Kristie 1944- ... 142
Miller, Lanora 1932- ... 61-64
Miller, Lee 1907-1977 ... 149
Miller, Lenore 1924- ... 107
Miller, Leon Gordon 1917- ... 104
Miller, Leslie Adrienne 1956- ... 225
Miller, Levi 1944- ... 113
Miller, Lewis (Ames) 1928- ... 93-96
Miller, Liam 1924(?)-1987
Obituary ... 122
Miller, Libuse (Lukas) 1915-1973 ... 1-4R
Obituary ... 103
Miller, Lillian B(eresnack)
1923-1997 ... CANR-52
Obituary ... 162
Earlier sketches in CA 21-24R, CANR-9, 25
Miller, Lily Poritz 1938- ... 126
Miller, Linda B. 1937- ... 21-24R
Miller, Linda Lael 1949- ... CANR-91
Earlier sketches in CA 110, CANR-30
See also RHW
Miller, Linda Patterson 1946- ... 135
Miller, Louise (Rolfe) 1940- ... 143
See also SATA 76
Miller, Luree 1926-1996 ... 93-96
Obituary ... 152
Miller, Lyle L. 1919- ... CANR-6
Earlier sketch in CA 13-16R
Miller, Lynn F(ieldman) 1938- ... 109
Miller, Lynn H(ellwarth) 1937- ... 37-40R
Miller, Lynne (Ellen) 1945- ... 89-92
Miller, M. Hughes 1913-1989
Obituary ... 130
Miller, M. L. ... SATA 85
Miller, Madelaine Hemingway 1904-1995 . 103
See also AITN 2
Miller, Madge 1918- ... CANR-92
Brief entry ... 117
Earlier sketch in CA 123
See also SATA 63
Miller, Mara (Jayne) 1944- ... 97-100
Miller, Marc S(cott) 1947- ... CANR-31
Earlier sketch in CA 105
Miller, Margaret
See Bambola, Sylvia
Miller, Margaret J.
See Dale, Margaret J(essy) Miller
Miller, Margery
See Welles, Margery Miller
Miller, Marilyn (Jean) 1925- ... SATA 33
Miller, Marilyn McMeen
See Brown, Marilyn McMeen Miller
Miller, Marjorie M. 1922- ... 101
Miller, Mark 1951- ... 224
Miller, Mark Crispin 1949(?)- ... 237
Miller, Marshall Lee 1942- ... CANR-9
Earlier sketch in CA 57-60
Miller, Martha
See Ivan, Martha Miller Pfaff
Miller, Martha Porter 1897(?)-1983
Obituary ... 109
Miller, Martin A. 1938- ... 65-68
Miller, Marvin ... 133
See also SATA 65
Miller, Mary
See Northcott, (William) Cecil
Miller, Mary Agnes 1888(?)-1973
Obituary ... 45-48
Miller, Mary Beth 1942- ... 61-64
See also SATA 9
Miller, Mary Britton 1883-1975 ... CANR-16
Obituary ... 57-60
Earlier sketch in CA 1-4R
Miller, Maryann 1943- ... SATA 73
Miller (Riis), Maurine 1910- ... 118
Miller, Max (Carlton) 1899-1967 ... CANR-16
Obituary ... 25-28R
Earlier sketch in CA 1-4R
Miller, May 1899-1995 ... 142
See also BW 2
See also DLB 41
Miller, Melvin H(ull) 1920- ... 13-16R
Miller, Merl Kem 1942- ... 111
Miller, Merle 1919-1986 ... CANR-80
Obituary ... 119
Earlier sketches in CA 9-12R, CANR-4
See also AITN 1
Miller, Merton Howard 1923-2000 ... 134
Obituary ... 188
Brief entry ... 109
Miller, Michael M. 1910(?)-1977
Obituary ... 73-76
Miller, Milt 1916- ... 117
Miller, Minnie M. 1899-1983 ... CAP-2
Obituary ... 110
Earlier sketch in CA 21-22
Miller, Miranda 1950- ... 132
Miller, Morris 1914- ... 17-20R
Miller, Muriel
See Minor, Muriel Miller
Miller, N(ewton) Edd 1920-2004 ... 25-28R
Obituary ... 233
Miller, Naomi 1928- ... 111
Miller, Natalie 1917-1976 ... SATA 35
Miller, Nathan 1927-2004 ... CANR-97
Obituary ... 232
Earlier sketches in CA 53-56, CANR-4
Miller, Neal E(lgar) 1909-2002 ... 81-84
Obituary ... 205
Miller, Neil 1945- ... 204
See also GLL 1
Miller, Nicole Puleo 1944- ... 49-52
Miller, Nina 1958- ... 239
Miller, Nina Hull 1894-1974 ... CAP-1
Earlier sketch in CA 9-10
Miller, Nolan 1912- ... 9-12R
Miller, Norman 1933- ... 37-40R
Miller, Norman C(harles) 1934- ... 37-40R
Miller, Nyle H. 1907- ... CAP-2
Earlier sketch in CA 23-24
Miller, Olga K(omarkova) 1908-1990 ... 107
Miller, Orlo
See Miller, Hanson Orlo
Miller, Orson K., Jr. 1930- ... 126
Brief entry ... 110
Miller, Osborn (Maitland) 1896(?)-1979
Obituary ... 89-92
Miller, Oscar J. 1913-2002 ... 37-40R
Miller, P(eter) Schuyler 1912-1974 ... SFW 4
Miller, Patrick Dwight, Jr. 1935- ... 112
Miller, Paul 1906-1991 ... 215
See also DLB 127
Miller, Paul D. 1970- ... 234
Miller, Paul Martin 1914-1998 ... CANR-10
Earlier sketch in CA 17-20R
Miller, Paul R(ichard) 1929- ... 21-24R
Miller, Paul William 1926- ... 41-44R
Miller, Perry 1905-1963 ... 182
Obituary ... 93-96
See also DLB 17, 63
Miller, Peter 1920- ... CP 1
Miller, (Mitchell) Peter 1934- ... 37-40R
Miller, Peter G. 1945- ... 129
Miller, Peter M(ichael) 1942- ... CANR-25
Earlier sketch in CA 69-72
Miller, Philip L(ieson) 1906-1996 ... CAP-1
Earlier sketch in CA 11-12
Miller, Phyllis (Steinfurth) 1920- ... 131
Miller, R(onald) Baxter 1948- ... 115
Miller, R. Craig 1946- ... 135
Miller, R. S. 1936- ... 45-48
Miller, Ralph J. Sr. 1925- ... 187
Miller, Randall Martin 1945- ... CANR-75
Earlier sketches in CA 81-84, CANR-15, 34
Miller, Randolph Crump 1910-2002 ... CANR-1
Obituary ... 208
Earlier sketch in CA 1-4R
Miller, Raymond W(iley) 1895-1988
Obituary ... 124
Miller, Rene Fueloep
See Fueloep-Miller, Rene
Miller, Rene Fulop
See Fueloep-Miller, Rene
Miller, Rex 1929- ... CANR-30
Earlier sketch in CA 110
Miller (Spangberg), Rex 1939-2004 ... HGG
Miller, Richard
See Pietschmann, Richard John III
Miller, Richard (Connelly) 1925- ... CANR-90
Earlier sketches in CA 17-20R, CANR-26
Miller, Richard B. 1927- ... 146
Miller, Richard I(rwin) 1924- ... 41-44R
Miller, Richard Lawrence 1949- ... 134
Miller, Richard S(herwin) 1930- ... 21-24R
Miller, Richard Ulric 1932- ... CANR-17
Earlier sketch in CA 41-44R
Miller, Risa 1954(?)- ... 221
Miller, Rob(ert) Hollis 1944- ... CANR-87
Earlier sketch in CA 37-40R
Miller, Robert A(llen) 1932- ... 33-36R
Miller, Robert H(enry) 1889-1979 ... 33-36R
Miller, Robert H. 1944- ... 155
See also SATA 91
Miller, Robert Henry 1938- ... CANR-93
Earlier sketch in CA 110
Miller, Robert Keith 1949- ... CANR-35
Earlier sketch in CA 114
Miller, Robert L. 1928- ... 25-28R
Miller, Robert Moats 1924- ... 184
Brief entry ... 105
Miller, Robert Ryal 1923- ... 41-44R
Miller, Robin Feuer 1947- ... 130
Miller, Roger LeRoy 1943-
Brief entry ... 107
Miller, Ron 1947- ... 117
Miller, Ronald E(ugene) 1933- ... CANR-107
Earlier sketch in CA 5-8R
Miller, Roy Andrew 1924- ... CANR-40
Earlier sketches in CA 5-8R, CANR-2, 18
Miller, Ruby 1890(?)-1976
Obituary ... 65-68
Miller, Ruby M. 1911- ... 141
Miller, Russell 1938- ... CANR-129
Earlier sketch in CA 133
Miller, Russell E(lliott) 1916-
Brief entry ... 117
Miller, Ruth -1969
See Jacobs, Ruth Harriet
Miller, Ruth 1919-1969 ... 213
Miller, Ruth 1921-
Brief entry ... 106
Miller, Ruth White
See White, Ruth (C.)
Miller, S(eymour) M(ichael) 1922- ... 17-20R
Miller, Sally M. 1937- ... CANR-51
Earlier sketches in CA 45-48, CANR-26
Miller, Samuel Jefferson 1919- ... 53-56
Miller, Sandra (Peden) 1948- ... CANR-38
Earlier sketch in CA 115
See also Miller, Sandy (Peden)
Miller, Sandy (Peden)
See Miller, Sandra (Peden)
See also SATA 41
See also SATA-Brief 35
Miller, Sasha ... 181
Miller, Seton I. 1902-1974 ... IDFW 3, 4
Miller, Seumas 1953- ... 141
Miller, Shane 1907- ... CAP-2
Earlier sketch in CA 21-22
Miller, Shirley 1920- ... 93-96
Miller, Sigmund Stephen 1917-1998 .. CANR-4
Obituary ... 171
Earlier sketch in CA 1-4R
Miller, Stanley 1916(?)-1977
Obituary ... 69-72
Miller, Stanley L(loyd) 1930- ... 45-48
Miller, Stanley S. 1924- ... 13-16R
Miller, Stephen J(ohn) 1936- ... 33-36R
Miller, Stephen M. 1964- ... 236
Miller, Steve(n R.) 1950- ... CANR-113
Earlier sketch in CA 165
Miller, Stuart 1937- ... 41-44R
Miller, Stuart Creighton 1927- ... 33-36R
Miller, Sue 1943- ... CANR-128
Earlier sketches in CA 139, CANR-59, 91
See also AMWS 12
See also BEST 90:3
See also CLC 44
See also DA3
See also DAM POP
See also DLB 143
Miller, Susan 1944- ... CANR-139
Earlier sketch in CA 107
See also CAD
See also CD 5, 6
See also CWD
Miller, Teresa 1952- ... 105
Miller, Thomas Lloyd 1913-1995 ... 25-28R
Miller, Thomas W. 1943- ... 167
Miller, Tice L. 1938- ... 143
Miller, Timothy (Alan) 1944- ... CANR-94
Earlier sketches in CA 126, CANR-56
Miller, Tom
See Miller, William Thomas
Miller, Tom 1947- ... CANR-115
Earlier sketches in CA 73-76, CANR-14
Miller, Tony
See Penrose, Antony
Miller, Vassar 1924-1998 ... CANR-4
Obituary ... 171
Earlier sketch in CA 9-12R
See also CP 1, 2
See also CSW
See also DLB 105
Miller, Victor (Brooke) 1940- ... 107
Miller, Virgil 1887-1974 ... IDFW 3, 4
Miller, Virginia
See Austin, Virginia
Miller, Wade
See Miller, (H.) Bill(y) and
Wade, Robert (Allison)
See also CMW 4
Miller, Walter James 1918- ... 81-84
Miller, Walter M(ichael, Jr.)
1923-1996 ... CANR-108
Earlier sketch in CA 85-88
See also BPFB 2
See also CLC 4, 30
See also DLB 8
See also SCFW 1, 2
See also SFW 4
Miller, Warne
See Rathborne, St. George (Henry)
Miller, Warren 1921-1966 ... 143
Obituary ... 25-28R
See also BW 2
Miller, Warren E(dward) 1924-1999 . CANR-11
Obituary ... 174
Earlier sketch in CA 13-16R
Miller, Wayne Charles 1939- ... CANR-1
Earlier sketch in CA 45-48
Miller, Webb 1892-1940
See Miller, Webster
See also DLB 29
Miller, Webster 1892-1940 ... 191
See also Miller, Webb
Miller, William (Moseley) 1909-1989 ... 81-84
Obituary ... 129
Miller, William Alvin 1931- ... CANR-17
Earlier sketches in CA 49-52, CANR-1
Miller, William D. 1916- ... 13-16R
Miller, William Hugh 1905-1975 ... 1-4R
Miller, William Ian 1946- ... CANR-105
Earlier sketch in CA 163
Miller, William J. 1913(?)-1989
Obituary ... 128
Miller, William L(ockley) 1943- ... CANR-93
Earlier sketch in CA 130
Miller, William Lee 1926- ... CANR-117
Earlier sketches in CA 127, CANR-65
Miller, William McElwee 1892-1993 .. CANR-6
Earlier sketch in CA 57-60
Miller, William R. 1959- ... 181
See also SATA 116
Miller, William Robert 1927-1970 ... CAP-1
Obituary ... 29-32R
Earlier sketch in CA 11-12
Miller, William Thomas 1945- ... 192
Miller, Wilma H(ildruth) 1936- ... CANR-58
Earlier sketches in CA 33-36R, CANR-12, 30
Miller, Wright (Watts) 1903-1974 ... 17-20R
Obituary ... 120
Miller, Zane L. 1934- ... CANR-27
Earlier sketches in CA 25-28R, CANR-12
Miller-Pogacar, Anesa
See Miller, Anesa
Millerson, Geoffrey L. 1931- ... 17-20R
Millet, Catherine 1948- ... 201
Millet, Lydia 1968- ... CANR-100
Earlier sketch in CA 152
Millet, Stanton 1931- ... 25-28R
Millett, Allan R(eed) 1937- ... CANR-104
Earlier sketch in CA 21-24R
Millett, Fred B(enjamin) 1890-1976
Obituary ... 61-64
Millett, John (Antill) 1922- ... CANR-94
Earlier sketches in CA 103, CANR-20, 43
Millett, John D(avid) 1912-1993 ... CANR-82
Obituary ... 143
Earlier sketch in CA 104
Millett, Kate 1934- ... CANR-110
Earlier sketches in CA 73-76, CANR-32, 53, 76
See also AITN 1
See also CLC 67
See also DA3
See also DLB 246
See also FW
See also GLL 1
See also MTCW 1, 2
See also MTFW 2005
Millett, Larry 1947- ... 219
Millett, Martin 1955- ... CANR-82
Earlier sketch in CA 133
Millett, Paul ... 203
Millett, Richard L(eroy) 1938- ... 117
Millezr, William Lee 1926- ... 127
Millgate, Jane 1937- ... 57-60
Millgate, Michael (Henry) 1929- ... CANR-137
Earlier sketches in CA 29-32R, CANR-28, 48
Millgram, Abraham E(zra) 1901-1998 ... 33-36R
Millham, C(harles) B(lanchard) 1936- ... 37-40R
Millhauser, Milton 1910-1985 ... CAP-1
Earlier sketch in CA 13-16
Millhauser, Steven (Lewis) 1943- ... CANR-133
Brief entry ... 110
Earlier sketches in CA 111, CANR-63, 114
Interview in ... CA-111
See also CLC 21, 54, 109
See also CN 6, 7
See also DA3
See also DLB 2
See also FANT
See also MAL 5
See also MTCW 2
See also MTFW 2005
See also SSC 57
Millhiser, Marlys (Joy) 1938- ... CANR-143
Earlier sketches in CA 53-56, CANR-73
See also HGG
Millican, Arthenia Jackson Bates 1920- ... 105
See also BW 2
See also DLB 38
Millicent
See Jordan, Mildred Arlene
Millichap, Joseph R(obert) 1940- ... 116
Millidge, Gary Spencer 1961- ... 235
Millies, Suzanne 1943- ... 49-52
Milligan, Alice 1866-1953 ... 201
See also DLB 240
Milligan, Edward Archibald
1903-1977 ... 41-44R
Milligan, Jeffrey Ayala 1959- ... 238
Milligan, Martin 1923-1993 ... 236
Milligan, Peter ... 221
Milligan, Spike
See Milligan, Terence Alan
See also CLR 92

Cumulative Index 403 Miner

Milligan, Terence Alan 1918-2002 ... CANR-64
  Obituary ... 207
  Earlier sketches in CA 9-12R, CANR-4, 33
  See also Milligan, Spike
  See also MTCW 1
  See also SATA 29
  See also SATA-Obit 134
Millikan, Ruth Garrett 1933- ... 128
Milliken, Ernest Kenneth 1899- ... 5-8R
Milliken, Stephen F(rederick) 1928- ... 93-96
Milliken, William Mathewson
  1889-1978 ... CAP-2
  Earlier sketch in CA 23-24
Millimaki, Robert H. 1931- ... 57-60
Millin, Sarah Gertrude 1889-1968 ... 102
  Obituary ... 93-96
  See also CLC 49
  See also DLB 225
  See also EWL 3
Milling, Michael C. Crowley
  See Crowley-Milling, Michael C.
Millington, Ada
  See Deyneka, Anita
Millington, Barry 1951- ... CANR-43
  Earlier sketch in CA 119
Millington, Frances Ryan 1899-1977
  Obituary ... 69-72
Millington, Mil 1963(?)- ... 235
Millington, Patrick 1910-1982
  Obituary ... 107
Millington, Roger 1939- ... 65-68
Millinship, William 1929- ... 145
Million, Elmer M(ayse) 1912-1990 ... 41-44R
Million, Joelle 1946(?)- ... 234
Millis, Walter 1899-1968 ... CAP-1
  Obituary ... 37-40R
  Earlier sketch in CA 9-10
Millman, Brock 1963- ... 211
Millman, Gregory J. ... 239
Millman, Isaac 1933- ... 211
  See also SATA 140
Millman, Joan (M.) 1931- ... 135
Millman, Lawrence 1946- ... CANR-144
  Earlier sketches in CA 93-96, CANR-17, 38
Millman, Marcia (Honey) 1946- ... 207
Millner, Cork 1931- ... 134
Millner, Denene ... 201
Millon, Henry (Armand) 1927- ... 97-100
Millon, Rene 1921- ... 116
  Brief entry ... 113
Millon, Robert Paul 1932- ... 21-24R
Millon, Theodore 1929- ... 57-60
Milloy, John S(heridan) ... 196
Mills, A(nthony) D(avid) 1935- ... 145
Mills, Adam
  See Stanley, George Edward
Mills, Alison 1951- ... 53-56
Mills, Barriss 1912-1984 ... CANR-12
  Earlier sketch in CA 25-28R
Mills, Belen Collantes 1930- ... 37-40R
Mills, Betty (Lidstrom) 1926- ... 9-12R
Mills, Brenda J. 1940- ... 120
Mills, C(harles) Wright 1916-1962 ... 212
  Obituary ... 107
Mills, Carley 1897-1962 ... 1-4R
  Obituary ... 103
Mills, Clarence A(lonzo) 1891-1974 ... CAP-1
  Obituary ... 53-56
  Earlier sketch in CA 13-16
Mills, Claudia 1954- ... CANR-125
  Earlier sketches in CA 109, CANR-27, 58
  See also SATA 44, 89, 145
  See also SATA-Brief 41
Mills, Constance (Quinby) 1898-1987
  Obituary ... 122
Mills, Craig (Allan) 1955-2002 ... 174
Mills, Daniel Quinn 1941- ... CANR-57
  Earlier sketches in CA 112, CANR-30
Mills, David Harlow 1932- ... 104
Mills, Dorothy
  See Howard, Dorothy Gray
Mills, Edward D(avid) 1915-1998 ... CANR-19
  Obituary ... 164
  Earlier sketches in CA 5-8R, CANR-4
Mills, Elaine (Rosemary) 1941- ... SATA 72
Mills, Enos (Abijah) 1870-1922 ... ANW
Mills, G(len) E(arl) 1908-1988 ... CAP-1
  Earlier sketch in CA 13-14
Mills, Gary B(ernard) 1944- ... 81-84
Mills, George S(torginne) 1906- ... 97-100
Mills, Gordon H(arrison) 1914-1978
  Obituary ... 117
Mills, Helen 1923- ... CANR-16
  Earlier sketch in CA 97-100
Mills, Hilary (Paterson) 1950- ... 115
Mills, Irving 1894-1985
  Obituary ... 115
Mills, J(anet) M(elanie) A(ilsa)
  1894-1987 ... 69-72
Mills, Jack
  See Molina, Jacinto
Mills, James R(obert) 1927- ... 85-88
Mills, Jane (Kathryn) 1948- ... 139
Mills, Jeannie 1939- ... 93-96
Mills, John 1908-2005 ... 108
  Obituary ... 238
Mills, John 1930- ... 81-84
Mills, John FitzMaurice 1917- ... 103
Mills, John W(illiam) 1933- ... 69-72
Mills, Joyce C. 1944- ... 169
  See also SATA 102
Mills, Judith Christine 1956- ... 199
  See also SATA 130
Mills, Kathi
  See Mills, Kathleen Lorraine
Mills, Kathleen Lorraine 1948- ... 121
Mills, Kay ... 181
Mills, Kyle 1966- ... 221
Mills, Leonard Russell 1917- ... 45-48
Mills, Liston O. 1928- ... 107
Mills, Magnus 1954- ... 196
  See also DLB 267
Mills, Margaret A(nn) 1946- ... 141
Mills, (William) Mervyn 1906-2000 ... CAP-1
  Earlier sketch in CA 11-12
Mills, Nicolaus 1938- ... 214
Mills, Patricia J(agentowicz) 1944- ... 151
Mills, Peter R. 1962- ... 227
Mills, Ralph J(oseph), Jr. 1931- ... CANR-39
  Earlier sketches in CA 9-12R, CANR-3, 18
Mills, Richard W. 1945- ... 203
  Brief entry ... 112
Mills, Robert P(ark) 1920-1986 ... 97-100
  Obituary ... 118
Mills, Stephanie (Ellen) 1948- ... CANR-122
  Earlier sketch in CA 149
Mills, Stephen (Paul) 1952- ... 130
Mills, Terry Kenneth 1949- ... 107
Mills, Theodore M(ason) 1920- ... 21-24R
Mills, Watson Early 1939- ... CANR-48
  Earlier sketch in CA 57-60
Mills, Wendy H. 1973- ... 229
Mills, William 1935-
  Brief entry ... 118
Mills, William Donald 1925- ... 33-36R
Mills, Wilmer 1969- ... 239
Mills, Yaroslava Surmach 1925- ... SATA 35
Millspaugh, Ben P. 1936- ... 145
  See also SATA 77
Millstead, Thomas E. ... 106
  See also SATA 30
Millstein, Rose Silverman 1903(?)-1975
  Obituary ... 61-64
Millu, Liana 1915(?)- ... 141
Millum, Trevor 1945- ... CANR-44
  Earlier sketches in CA 104, CANR-21
Millus, Donald (J.) 1939- ... 219
Millward, Celia M(cCullough) 1935- ... 53-56
Millward, Eric (Geoffrey William) 1935- . 65-68
  See also CP 2
Millward, John S(candrett) 1924- ... 13-16R
Millward, Pamela 1937- ... CP 1
Milman, Donald S. 1924- ... 134
  Brief entry ... 111
Milman, Henry Hart 1796-1868 ... DLB 96
Milman, Miriam 1928- ... 112
Milne, A(lan) A(lexander) 1882-1956 ... 133
  Brief entry ... 104
  See also BRWS 5
  See also CLR 1, 26
  See also CMW 4
  See also CWRI 5
  See also DA3
  See also DAB
  See also DAC
  See also DAM MST
  See also DLB 10, 77, 100, 160
  See also FANT
  See also MAICYA 1, 2
  See also MTCW 1, 2
  See also MTFW 2005
  See also RGEL 2
  See also SATA 100
  See also TCLC 6, 88
  See also WCH
  See also YABC 1
Milne, Antony 1942- ... 101
Milne, Christopher (Robin)
  1920-1996 ... CANR-27
  Obituary ... 152
  Earlier sketches in CA 61-64, CANR-11
  See also AITN 2
Milne, Edward Arthur 1896-1950 ... 158
Milne, Edward James 1915-1983
  Obituary ... 109
Milne, Evander Mackay 1920- ... 5-8R
Milne, (Charles) Ewart 1903-1987 ... CANR-16
  Obituary ... 121
  Earlier sketch in CA 97-100
  See also CP 1, 2
Milne, G(eorge) W. A. 1937- ... 154
Milne, (William) Gordon 1921- ... 21-24R
Milne, Jean (Killgrove) 1920- ... 17-20R
Milne, John 1952- ... CANR-66
  Earlier sketch in CA 143
  See also CMW 4
Milne, Lorna 1959- ... 169
Milne, Lorus J. ... CANR-14
  Earlier sketch in CA 33-36R
  See also CLR 22
  See also SAAS 18
  See also SATA 5
Milne, Margery ... CANR-14
  Earlier sketch in CA 33-36R
  See also CLR 22
  See also SAAS 18
  See also SATA 5
Milne, Roseleen 1945- ... CANR-13
  Earlier sketch in CA 73-76
Milne, Seumas 1958- ... 135
Milne, Terry
  See Milne, Theresa Ann
Milne, Theresa Ann 1964- ... SATA 84
Milner, Christina 1942- ... 49-52
Milner, Clyde A. II 1948- ... CANR-26
  Earlier sketch in CA 108
Milner, Esther 1918- ... 21-24R
Milner, Ian Frank George 1911-1991 ... 104
Milner, Jay
  See Morton, James (Severs)
Milner, Jay (Dunston) 1926- ... 1-4R
Milner, Lucille Bernheimer 1888(?)-1975
  Obituary ... 61-64
Milner, Marion (Blackett) 1900-1998 ... 9-12R
  Obituary ... 169
Milner, Michael
  See Cooper, Saul
Milner, Murray, Jr. 1935- ... 41-44R
Milner, Neal A(lan) 1941-
  Brief entry ... 112
Milner, Richard B(ruce) 1941- ... 49-52
Milner, Ron(ald) 1938-2004 ... CANR-81
  Obituary ... 230
  Earlier sketches in CA 73-76, CANR-24
  See also AITN 1
  See also BLC 3
  See also BW 1
  See also CAD
  See also CD 5, 6
  See also CLC 56
  See also DAM MULT
  See also DLB 38
  See also MAL 5
  See also MTCW 1
Milnes, Eric Charles 1912-1984
  Obituary ... 112
Milnes, Gerald ... 236
Milnes, Irma McDonough 1924- ... 168
  See also SATA 101
Milnes, Richard Monckton
  1809-1885 ... DLB 32, 184
Milnor, John (Willard) 1931- ... 161
Milns, R(obert) D(avid) 1938- ... 33-36R
Milo, Ronald D(mitri) 1935- ... 25-28R
Milofsky, Carl 1948- ... 139
Milofsky, David 1946- ... CANR-136
  Earlier sketch in CA 175
Milonas, Rolf
  See Myller, Rolf
Miloradovich, Milo 1901(?)-1972
  Obituary ... 37-40R
Milord, Susan 1954- ... 221
  See also SATA 74, 147
Milosh, Joseph E(dmund) 1936- ... 21-24R
Miloslavsky, Nikolai Dimitrievich Tolstoy
  See Tolstoy(-Miloslavsky), Nikolai (Dimitrievich)
Milosz, Czeslaw 1911-2004 ... CANR-126
  Obituary ... 230
  Earlier sketches in CA 81-84, CANR-23, 51, 91
  See also AAYA 62
  See also CDWLB 4
  See also CLC 5, 11, 22, 31, 56, 82
  See also CWW 2
  See also DA3
  See also DAM MST, POET
  See also DLB 215
  See also EW 13
  See also EWL 3
  See also MTCW 1, 2
  See also MTFW 2005
  See also PC 8
  See also PFS 16
  See also RGWL 2, 3
  See also WLCS
Milotte, Alfred G(eorge) 1904-1989 ... CAP-1
  Obituary ... 128
  Earlier sketch in CA 19-20
  See also SATA 11
  See also SATA-Obit 62
Milotte, Elma (Moore) 1908(?)-1989
  Obituary ... 128
Milsen, Oscar
  See Mendelsohn, Oscar (Adolf)
Milson, Fred(erick William) 1912-1983 ... 73-76
Milstead, Jessica L(ee) 1939- ... CANR-14
  Earlier sketch in CA 33-36R
Milstead, John 1924- ... 49-52
Milsted, David 1954- ... 132
Milstein, Linda 1954- ... SATA 80
Milstein, Mike M(yron) 1937- ... 81-84
Miltner, Robert F. 1949- ... CANR-133
  Earlier sketch in CA 168
Milton, Ann ... SATA 134
Milton, Arthur 1922- ... CANR-27
  Earlier sketch in CA 109
Milton, Charles R(udolph) 1925- ... 53-56
Milton, David Scott 1934- ... CANR-13
  Earlier sketch in CA 73-76
Milton, Hilary (Herbert) 1920- ... CANR-21
  Earlier sketches in CA 57-60, CANR-6
  See also SATA 23
Milton, Jack
  See Kimbro, John M.
Milton, John 1608-1674 ... AAYA 65
  See also BRW 2
  See also BRWR 2
  See also CDBLB 1660-1789
  See also DA
  See also DA3
  See also DAB
  See also DAC
  See also DAM MST, POET
  See also DLB 131, 151, 281
  See also EFS 1
  See also EXPP
  See also LAIT 1
  See also PAB
  See also PC 19, 29
  See also PFS 3, 17
  See also RGEL 2
  See also TEA
  See also WLC
  See also WLIT 3
  See also WP
Milton, John R(onald) 1924- ... 33-36R
  See also SATA 24
Milton, Joyce 1946- ... CANR-89
  Earlier sketch in CA 106
  See also MAICYA 2
  See also SATA 52, 101
  See also SATA-Brief 41
Milton, Mark
  See Pelton, Robert W(ayne)
Milton, Oliver
  See Hewitt, Cecil Rolph
Milton, Pat ... 235
Milunsky, Aubrey 1936- ... 103
Milverton, Charles A.
  See Penzler, Otto
Milvy, Paul 1931-1989
  Obituary ... 129
Milward, Alan S. 1935- ... CANR-45
  Earlier sketch in CA 45-48
Milward, Peter 1925- ... 101
Mimouni, Rachid 1945-1995 ... EWL 3
Mims, Forrest M(arion) III 1944- ... CANR-39
  Earlier sketches in CA 97-100, CANR-16
Mims, George L. 1934- ... 129
Mims, Lambert C. 1930- ... 29-32R
Mims, Roddey Earl 1936(?)-1982
  Obituary ... 108
Min, Anchee 1957- ... CANR-137
  Earlier sketches in CA 146, CANR-94
  See also CLC 86
  See also MTFW 2005
Min, Pyong Gap 1942- ... 219
Min, Tu-ki 1932- ... 138
Mina, Denise 1966- ... 228
Mina, Hanna 1924- ... EWL 3
Mina, V. K. 1979(?)- ... 236
Minadeo, Richard (William) 1929- ... 25-28R
Minahan, John 1933- ... CANR-2
  Earlier sketch in CA 45-48
Minahan, John A. 1956- ... 142
  See also SATA 92
Minakami Tsutomu 1919- ... DLB 182
Minale, Marcello 1938-2000 ... 108
  Obituary ... 191
Minamoto no Sanetomo 1192-1219 ... DLB 203
Minar, Barbra (Goodyear) 1940- ... 148
  See also SATA 79
Minar, David W(illiam) 1925-1973
  Obituary ... 111
Minard, Rosemary 1939- ... SATA 63
Minarik, Else Holmelund 1920- ... CANR-91
  Earlier sketches in CA 73-76, CANR-48
  See also CLR 33
  See also CWRI 5
  See also MAICYA 1, 2
  See also SATA 15, 127
Minarik, John Paul 1947- ... CANR-103
  Earlier sketches in CA 73-76, CANR-13
Minatoya, Lydia (Yuriko) 1950- ... 238
Minatoya, Lydia Yuri
  See Minatoya, Lydia (Yuriko)
Minc, Alain J. R. 1949- ... 146
Mincer, Jacob 1922-
  Brief entry ... 114
Minchin, Timothy J. 1969- ... CANR-135
  Earlier sketch in CA 166
Minchinton, W(alter) E(dward)
  1921-1996 ... CANR-29
  Earlier sketches in CA 29-32R, CANR-12
Mincieli, Rose Laura 1912- ... CANR-4
  Earlier sketch in CA 5-8R
Minckler, (Sherwood) Leon 1906- ... 57-60
Minco, Marga 1920- ... 196
  See also DLB 299
Minco, Sara
  See Minco, Marga
Minczeski, John 1947- ... 137
Mindadze, Aleksandr 1949- ... IDFW 4
Mindel, Eugene D. 1934- ... 41-44R
Mindell, Amy (Kaplan) 1958- ... 217
Mindell, Arnold 1940- ... 219
Mindell, Earl L(awrence) 1940- ... 105
Mindlin, Michael 1923-2004 ... 133
  Obituary ... 225
Mindlin, Murray 1924(?)-1987
  Obituary ... 122
Mindszenty, Jozsef 1892-1975 ... 65-68
  Obituary ... 57-60
Mindt, Heinz R. 1940- ... 193
  Brief entry ... 115
Minear, Paul Sevier 1906- ... CANR-3
  Earlier sketch in CA 1-4R
Minear, Richard H(offman) 1938- ... CANR-93
  Earlier sketch in CA 33-36R
Minehaha, Cornelius
  See Wedekind, (Benjamin) Frank(lin)
Mineka, Francis Edward 1907-
  Brief entry ... 106
Miner, Caroline Eyring 1907- ... CANR-27
  Earlier sketches in CA 25-28R, CANR-11
Miner, Charles S(ydney) 1906-1996 ... CAP-1
  Earlier sketch in CA 19-20
Miner, Dwight Carroll 1904-1978
  Obituary ... 81-84
Miner, Earl (Roy) 1927- ... CANR-1
  Earlier sketch in CA 1-4R
Miner, Ellis D(evere, Jr.) 1937- ... CANR-141
  Earlier sketch in CA 144
Miner, H. Craig 1944- ... CANR-16
  Earlier sketches in CA 45-48, CANR-1
Miner, (Opal) Irene Sevrey (Frazine)
  1906- ... 5-8R
Miner, Jane Claypool 1933- ... CANR-27
  Earlier sketch in CA 106
  See also Claypool, Jane
  See also SATA 38
  See also SATA-Brief 37
Miner, John B(urnham) 1926- ... CANR-20
  Earlier sketches in CA 9-12R, CANR-5

Miner 404 CONTEMPORARY AUTHORS

Miner, Joshua L. 1920-2002 106
 Obituary 204
Miner, Lewis S. 1909-1971 .... CAP-1
 Earlier sketch in CA 11-12
 See also SATA 11
Miner, Mary Green 1928- 69-72
Miner, Matthew
 See Wallmann, Jeffrey M(iner)
Miner, Robert C. 1970- 237
Miner, Valerie 1947- CANR-59
 Earlier sketch in CA 97-100
 See also CLC 40
 See also FW
 See also GLL 2
Miner, Ward L(ester) 1916- 9-12R
Minerbrook, Scott 1951- 156
Mines, Jeanette (Marie) 1948- 119
 See also SATA 61
Mines, Samuel 1909-1998 .... CANR-1
 Earlier sketch in CA 45-48
Mines, Stephanie 1944- 77-80
Minetor, Randi (S.) 1958- 225
Minetree, Harry 1935- 93-96
Minford, John (Michael) 1946- 130
Mingay, G(ordon) E(dmund) 1923- ... CANR-45
 Earlier sketches in CA 17-20R, CANR-11
Minge, Ward Alan 1924- 97-100
Minghella, Anthony 1954- 165
 See also CBD
 See also CD 5, 6
Minghi, Julian V(incent) 1933- 29-32R
Mingi, Akili
 See Puri, Shamlal
Mingione, Enzo 1947- 141
Mingus, Charles 1922-1979 93-96
 Obituary 85-88
Minhinnick, Robert 1952- 126
 See also CP 7
Minichiello, Sharon 126
Minick, Michael 1945- 65-68
Minier, Nelson
 See Stoutenburg, Adrien (Pearl)
Minifie, James MacDonald 1900-1974 49-52
Minihan, Janet
 See Oppenheim, Janet
Minimo, Duca
 See D'Annunzio, Gabriele
Minio-Paluello, Lorenzo 1907-1986
 Obituary 119
Minirth, Frank B. 136
Minium, Edward W(headon) 1917- 29-32R
Mink, Joanna Stephens 1947- CANR-119
 Earlier sketch in CA 138
Mink, Louis Otto, Jr. 1921-1983 104
 Obituary 109
Mink, Nelson G. 1907- 123
Minkema, Kenneth (Pieter) 1958- 212
Minkler, Meredith 1946- 162
Minkoff, Randy 1949- 141
Minkovitz, Moshe
 See Shokeid, Moshe
Minkow, Rosalie 1927- 135
Minkowitz, Donna 1964- 228
Minne, Richard 1891-1965 239
Minnelli, Vincente 1910(?)-1986 153
 Obituary 119
 Brief entry 117
Minnery, Tom 220
Minney, R(ubeigh) J(ames)
 1895-1979 .... CANR-5
 Earlier sketch in CA 5-8R
Minnich, Elizabeth (Anne)
 Kamarck CANR-118
 Earlier sketch in CA 158
Minnich, Helen Benton 1892-1975 .... CAP-1
 Earlier sketch in CA 9-10
Minnick, Wayne C. 1915- 25-28R
Minnick, Wendell L. 1962- 144
Minnigerode, Meade 1887-1967
 Obituary 116
Minnion, John (Lawrence) 1939- 130
Minnitt, Ronda Jacqueline
 See Armitage, David
Minns, Susan 1839-1938 215
 See also DLB 140
Minock, Daniel 1944- 165
Minogue, Kenneth R(obert) 1930- 5-8R
Minogue, Valerie Pearson 1931- CANR-89
 Earlier sketch in CA 132
Minor, Andrew Collier 1918- 13-16R
Minor, Anthropopagus
 See Conniff, James C(lifford) G(regory)
Minor, Audax
 See Ryall, George (Francis Trafford)
Minor, Edward Orville 1920- 9-12R
Minor, Marz 1928- 103
Minor, Muriel Miller 1908-1987
 Obituary 122
Minor, Nono 1932- 103
Minor, Wendell G. 1944- 180
 See also CWRI 5
 See also DLBY 2002
 See also SATA 78, 109
Minot, Eliza 1970- 188
Minot, George 1959- 229
Minot, Stephen 1927- CANR-17
 Earlier sketch in CA 13-16R
Minot, Susan (Anderson) 1956- CANR-118
 Earlier sketch in CA 134
 See also AMWS 6
 See also CLC 44, 159
 See also CN 6, 7
Minott, Rodney G(lisan) 1928- 9-12R
Minow, Martha 1954- 137
Minow, Newton N(orman) 1926- CANR-55
 Earlier sketch in CA 13-16R

Minrath, William R(ichard) 1900-1971 .. CAP-1
 Obituary 89-92
 Earlier sketch in CA 9-10
Minshall, Merlin (Theodore) 1906-1987
 Obituary 123
Minshall, Vera (Wild) 1924- 13-16R
Minshull, Evelyn 1929- 37-40R
Minshull, Roger (Michael) 1935- 21-24R
Minsky, Betty Jane (Toebe) 1932- 5-8R
Minsky, Hyman P(hilip) 1919-1996 85-88
 Obituary 154
Minsky, Marvin (Lee) 1927- 21-24R
Minsky, Morton 1902-1987 135
 Obituary 122
Minsky, Nikolai 1855-1937 .... DLB 317
Minta, Stephen 1947- 132
Minter, David L. 1935- CANR-12
 Earlier sketch in CA 25-28R
Minter, J(onathan)
 See Schrank, Ben
Minter, William 1942- 124
Minters, Arthur Herman 1932- 102
Minthorn, P. Y. 1960- 228
Minto-Cowen, Frances
 See Munthe, Frances
Minton, Henry L. 1934- 138
Minton, Lynn 107
Minton, Madge Rutherford 1920- 45-48
Minton, Paula
 See Little, Paul H(ugo)
Minton, Robert 1918-2000 57-60
Minton, Sandra Cerny 1943- 184
Minton, Sherman A(nthony), Jr.
 1890-1965 45-48
Mintonye, Grace 25-28R
 See also SATA 4
Minturn, Leigh 1928- 21-24R
Minty, Judith 1937- CANR-21
 Earlier sketches in CA 49-52, CANR-2
 See also CWP
Mintz, Alan L. 139
Mintz, Barbara 1931- 110
Mintz, Donald E(dward) 1932- 17-20R
Mintz, Elizabeth E(mmons) 1913-1997 73-76
 Obituary 159
Mintz, Joel A(lan) 1949- CANR-103
 Earlier sketch in CA 167
Mintz, Joyce Lois 1933- 65-68
Mintz, Lannon W. 1938-1988 126
Mintz, Leigh W(ayne) 1939- 57-60
Mintz, Max M. 1919- 33-36R
Mintz, Morton A. 1922- 13-16R
Mintz, Norman N(elson) 1934- 41-44R
Mintz, Ruth Finer 1919- 13-16R
Mintz, Samuel I(saiah) 1923- 5-8R
Mintz, Sidney W(ilfred) 1922- CANR-21
 Earlier sketches in CA 1-4R, CANR-5
Mintz, Steven (Harry) 1953- 118
Mintz, Thomas 1931- 108
Mintzberg, Henry 1939- CANR-1
 Earlier sketch in CA 45-48
Mintzer, Yvette 1947- 77-80
Minuchin, Salvador 1921- CANR-144
 Earlier sketch in CA 144
Minus, Ed 1938- 185
 See also CLC 39
Minus, Paul M(urray, Jr.) 1935- 118
Minutaglio, Bill 197
Minyana, Philippe 1946- .... DLB 321
Minyard, John Douglas 1943-1990 120
 Obituary 145
Miola, Robert S(teven) 1951- 129
Mira Bai 1498-1546(?) .... RGWL 2, 3
Mirabai 1498(?)-1550(?) .... PC 48
Mirabehn
 See Slade, Madeleine
Mirabelli, Eugene (Jr.) 1931- 25-28R
Miracle, Andrew W., (Jr.) 1945- 146
Miracle, Gordon E. 1930- 33-36R
Miracle, Marvin P(reston) 1933- 17-20R
Miranda, Anne 1954- 180
 See also SATA 71, 109
Miranda, Javier
 See Bioy Casares, Adolfo
 See also CWW 2
Miranda, Javier .... CWW 2
Mirande, Alfredo M(anuel) 1940- 115
Mirbeau, Octave 1848-1917 216
 See also DLB 123, 192
 See also GFL 1789 to the Present
 See also TCLC 55
Mireaux, Emile 1885(?)-1969
 Obituary 104
Mirecki, Paul (A.) 214
Mireles, Marina 1927(?)-1986
 Obituary 119
Mirelman, Victor A. 1943- 136
Mirenburg, Barry (Leonard Steffan) 1952- ... 101
Mirepoix, Camille 1926- 105
Mirikitani, Janice 1942- 211
 See also AAL
 See also DLB 312
 See also RGAL 4
Mirisch, Walter 1921- .... IDFW 3, 4
Mirk, John (?)-c. 1414 .... DLB 146
Mirkin, Gabe 1935- 129
Miro (Ferrer), Gabriel (Francisco Victor)
 1879-1930 185
 Brief entry 104
 See also DLB 322
 See also EWL 3
 See also TCLC 5
Miro, Joan 1893-1983 121
 Obituary 111
 See also AAYA 30
Miro, Ricardo 1883-1940 .... DLB 290
Mirochnik, Elijah 1952- 227

Miron, Dan 1934- 77-80
Miron, Gaston 1928-1996 180
 See also DLB 60
Miron, Murray S(amuel) 1932- 81-84
Miron, Salvador Diaz
 See Diaz Miron, Salvador
Mironov, Boris N(ikolaevich) 1942- 220
Mirow, Kurt Rudolf 1936- 130
Mirrlees, Hope 1887-1978 .... CANR-117
 Earlier sketch in CA 155
 See also FANT
 See also SUFW
Mirsky, Jeannette 1903-1987 .... CAP-2
 Obituary 122
 Earlier sketch in CA 19-20
 See also SATA 8
 See also SATA-Obit 51
Mirsky, Mark Jay 1939- 176
 Earlier sketches in CA 25-28R, CANR-44
 Autobiographical Essay in 176
 See also CAAS 30
 See also CN 3, 4, 5, 6, 7
Mirsky, Prince D. S.
 See Sviatopolk-Mirsky, Prince Dimitrii Petrovich
 See also DLB 317
Mirsky, Reba Paeff 1902-1966 .... 1-4R
 See also SATA 1
Mirsky, Stanley 1929- 110
Miruka, Okumba 170
Mirvis, Tova 1972- 222
Mirvish, Robert Franklin 1921- 1-4R
Misbin, Robert I. 1947- 146
Miscall, Peter D(arwin) 1943- 111
Misch, Robert J(ay) 1905-1990 .... 21-24R
Mische, Gerald F(rederick) 1926- 97-100
Mische, Patricia M(ary) 1939- CANR-16
 Earlier sketch in CA 93-96
Mischke, Bernard Cyril 1926- 13-16R
Mischke, Fridolin 1916- 117
Mischke, Fritz
 See Mischke, Fridolin
Miscione, Lisa 1970- 218
Mises, Ludwig (Edler) von
 1881-1973 .... CANR-19
 Obituary 45-48
 Earlier sketch in CA 5-8R
Mises, Margit von 1896-1993 .... CANR-19
 Earlier sketch in CA 89-92
Mish, Charles C(arroll) 1913-1992 .... 33-36R
 Obituary 140
Mishael, Bert
 See Mishael, Herbert Stanley
Mishael, Herbert Stanley 1900(?)-1985
 Obituary 117
Mishan, E(zra) J(oshua) 1917- CANR-30
 Earlier sketches in CA 73-76, CANR-13
Misharin, Alexandr .... CLC 59
Misheiker, Betty Fairly 1919- 9-12R
Mishica, Clare 1960- 155
 See also SATA 91
Mishima, Yukio
 See Hiraoka, Kimitake
 See also AAYA 50
 See also BPFB 2
 See also CLC 2, 4, 6, 9, 27
 See also DC 1
 See also GLL 1
 See also MJW
 See also RGSF 2
 See also RGWL 2, 3
 See also SSC 4
 See also SSFS 5, 12
 See also TCLC 161
Mishima Yukio
 See Hiraoka, Kimitake
 See also DLB 182
 See also EWL 3
Mishkin, Paul J. 1927- 17-20R
Mishkin, Tracy 234
Mishler, Clayton (R.) 1908-1992 146
Mishler, William (Thomas Earle II)
 1947- CANR-52
 Earlier sketch in CA 125
Mishne, Judith 1932- CANR-121
 Earlier sketch in CA 162
Mishra, Pankaj 1969- 201
Mishra, Sudesh (Raj) 1962- CANR-86
 Earlier sketch in CA 154
 See also CP 7
Mishra, Vishwa Mohan 1937- 61-64
Misiak, Henryk 1911-1992 .... CANR-5
 Earlier sketch in CA 1-4R
Misiunas, Romuald John 1945- 109
Miskimin, Harry A(lvin, Jr.) 1932-
 Brief entry 109
Miskimon, Robert 1943- 194
Miskovits, Christine 1939- 53-56
 See also SATA 10
Misner, Arthur J(ack) 1921- 21-24R
Misner, Paul 1936- 138
Misra, Bankey Bihari 1909- 104
Misra, Vaidyanath
 See Nagarjun
Miss C. L. F.
 See Grimke, Charlotte L(ottie) Forten
Miss Elbee
 See Baker, Lillian (L.)
Missen, Leslie R(obert) 1897-1983
 Obituary 110
Miss Frances
 See Horwich, Frances R(appaport)
Missildine, (Whitney) Hugh 1915- 77-80
Missinne, Leo E(miel) 1927- CANR-39
 Earlier sketch in CA 116
Missiroli, Mario 1886-1974
 Obituary 53-56

Miss Lou
 See Bennett-Coverley, Louise
Miss Manners
 See Martin, Judith (Sylvia)
Miss Read
 See Saint, Dora Jessie
Mister Rogers
 See Rogers, Fred McFeely
Mister X
 See Hoch, Edward D(entinger)
Mistral, Frederic 1830-1914 213
 Brief entry 122
 See also GFL 1789 to the Present
 See also TCLC 51
Mistral, Gabriela
 See Godoy Alcayaga, Lucila
 See also DLB 283
 See also DNFS 1
 See also EWL 3
 See also LAW
 See also RGWL 2, 3
 See also WP
Mistry, Rohinton 1952- CANR-114
 Earlier sketches in CA 141, CANR-86
 See also BRWS 10
 See also CCA 1
 See also CLC 71, 196
 See also CN 6, 7
 See also DAC
 See also SSC 73
 See also SSFS 6
Misurella, Fred 1940-1997 143
Mitcalfe, Barry 1930-1986 110
Mitcham, Carl 1941- CANR-37
 Earlier sketches in CA 85-88, CANR-16
Mitcham, Gilroy
 See Newton, William Simpson
Mitcham, Judson 1948- 235
Mitcham, Samuel W(ayne), Jr. 1949- 106
Mitchard, Jacquelyn 1953- CANR-119
 Earlier sketch in CA 157
 See also AAYA 34
 See also SATA 98
Mitchel, Jonathan 1624-1668 .... DLB 24
Mitchell, Adam
 See Pyle, Hilary
Mitchell, Adrian 1932- CANR-87
 Earlier sketch in CA 33-36R
 See also CBD
 See also CD 5, 6
 See also CN 1, 2, 3
 See also CP 1, 2, 3, 4, 5, 6, 7
 See also DLB 40
 See also SATA 104
Mitchell, Alan 1922- CANR-27
 Earlier sketches in CA 57-60, CANR-8
Mitchell, Alexander Ross Kerr 1934- 73-76
Mitchell, Allan 1933- 102
Mitchell, Allison
 See Butterworth, W(illiam) E(dmund III)
Mitchell, Andrew W. 1953- 124
Mitchell, Arnold 1918- 131
Mitchell, Arthur A(ustin) 1926- 9-12R
Mitchell, Austin (Vernon) 1934- CANR-12
 Earlier sketch in CA 25-28R
Mitchell, B(etty) J(o) 1931- 187
 See also SATA 120
Mitchell, B(rian) R(edman) 1929- 49-52
Mitchell, Barbara 1941- 117
Mitchell, Barbara A. 1939- 25-28R
Mitchell, Basil George 1917- 104
Mitchell, Bennett 220
Mitchell, Betty L(ou) 1947- 107
Mitchell, Bonner 1929- 25-28R
Mitchell, Breon 1942- 112
Mitchell, Broadus 1892-1988 .... CANR-5
 Obituary 125
 Earlier sketch in CA 1-4R
Mitchell, Bruce M. 1929- 175
Mitchell, Burroughs 1914(?)-1979 129
 Obituary 89-92
Mitchell, Carlton
 See Marshall, Mel(vin D.)
Mitchell, Charles 1912-1995 .... 9-12R
 Obituary 150
Mitchell, Chris 1964- 235
Mitchell, Clyde
 See Ellison, Harlan (Jay)
Mitchell, Colin W(are) 1927-1996 73-76
 Obituary 152
Mitchell, Curtis Cornelius, Jr. 1927- 105
Mitchell, Cynthia 1922- 106
 See also SATA 29
Mitchell, Daniel J(esse) B(rody)
 1942- CANR-50
 Earlier sketch in CA 123
Mitchell, David (John) 1924- CANR-12
 Earlier sketch in CA 53-56
Mitchell, David (John) 1940- .... CP 2
Mitchell, David 1969- 210
Mitchell, Don(ald Earl) 1947- CANR-31
 Earlier sketches in CA 33-36R, CANR-14
Mitchell, Donald (Charles Peter)
 1925- CANR-100
 Earlier sketch in CA 103
Mitchell, Donald Grant 1822-1908 184
 See also DLB 1, 243
 See also DLBD 13
 See also RGAL 4
Mitchell, Edgar D(ean) 1930- 53-56
Mitchell, Edward B. 1937- 21-24R
Mitchell, Elizabeth P(ryse) 1946- 101
Mitchell, Ellinor R. 1930- 159
Mitchell, Elma 1919- .... CWP

Cumulative Index 405 Moberg

Mitchell, (Sibyl) Elyne (Keith) 1913- . CANR-86
Earlier sketches in CA 53-56, CANR-5, 21, 44
See also CWRI 5
See also SATA 10
Mitchell, Emerson Blackhorse Barney
1945- 45-48
See also NNAL
Mitchell, Erica
See Posner, Richard
Mitchell, Ewan
See Janner, Greville Ewan
Mitchell, Fay Langellier 1884-1964 .... 5-8R
Mitchell, Felicia 1956- 238
Mitchell, Frank
See Mitchell, George Francis
Mitchell, Frank Vincent 1919-(?) 9-12R
Mitchell, Franklin D. 1932-
Brief entry 118
Mitchell, G(eoffrey) Duncan
1921-1999 .... CANR-11
Earlier sketch in CA 29-32R, 183
Mitchell, George Francis 1912-1997 77-80
Mitchell, George J(ohn) 1933- CANR-89
Earlier sketch in CA 141
Mitchell, Giles 1928- 93-96
Mitchell, Gladys (Maude Winifred)
1901-1983 .... CANR-63
Obituary 110
Earlier sketches in CA 9-12R, CANR-9
See also CMW 4
See also DLB 77
See also SATA 46
See also SATA-Obit 35
Mitchell, Greg 1947- CANR-70
Earlier sketch in CA 73-76
Mitchell, Harold P(aton) 1900-1983 .... 9-12R
Obituary 109
Mitchell, (Arthur) Harris 1916- 119
Mitchell, Helen Buss 1941- 193
Mitchell, Helen S(wift) 1895-1984 .... 25-28R
Obituary 114
Mitchell, Henry (Clay II) 1923-1993 130
Obituary 143
Mitchell, Henry H(eywood) 1919- ... CANR-10
Earlier sketch in CA 57-60
Mitchell, (William) Hobart 1908- 119
Mitchell, Howard E(still) 1921- 108
Mitchell, J(ames) Clyde 1918- CANR-9
Earlier sketch in CA 13-16R
Mitchell, Jack 1925- 9-12R
Mitchell, Jackson
See Matcha, Jack
Mitchell, James 1926-2002 .... CANR-66
Obituary 209
Earlier sketches in CA 13-16R, CANR-12
See also CMW 4
Mitchell, James (Alexander Hugh) 1939-1985
Obituary 115
Mitchell, James Leslie 1901-1935 188
Brief entry 104
See also Gibbon, Lewis Grassic
See also DLB 15
Mitchell, Jay
See Roberson, Jennifer
Mitchell, Jay P. 1940- 145
Mitchell, Jeremy 1929- 41-44R
Mitchell, Jerome 1935- 25-28R
Mitchell, Jerry 1905(?)-1972
Obituary 33-36R
Mitchell, Joan Cattermole 1920- CAP-1
Earlier sketch in CA 9-10
Mitchell, John 1930- 143
Mitchell, John Ames 1845-1918 184
See also DLB 79
Mitchell, John C. 1955- 170
Mitchell, John D(ietrich) 1917- 49-52
Mitchell, John D(avid) B(awden) 1917-1980
Obituary 105
Mitchell, John Hanson 1940- CANR-116
Earlier sketch in CA 142
See also ANW
Mitchell, John Howard 1921-1995 .... 9-12R
Mitchell, John J(oseph) 1941- CANR-1
Earlier sketch in CA 45-48
Mitchell, Joni 1943- 112
See also CCA 1
See also CLC 12
Mitchell, Joseph (Quincy)
1908-1996 .... CANR-69
Obituary 152
Earlier sketch in CA 77-80
See also CLC 98
See also CN 1, 2, 3, 4, 5, 6
See also CSW
See also DLB 185
See also DLBY 1996
Mitchell, Joseph B(rady) 1915-1993 .... 9-12R
Obituary 140
Mitchell, Joyce Slayton 1933- CANR-121
Earlier sketches in CA 65-68, CANR-15
See also SATA 46, 142
See also SATA-Brief 43
Mitchell, Judith Paige CANR-40
Earlier sketches in CA 85-88, CANR-18
Interview in CANR-18
Mitchell, (Charles) Julian (Humphrey)
1935- CANR-87
Earlier sketches in CA 5-8R, CANR-5, 39
See also CBD
See also CD 5, 6
See also CN 1, 2, 3, 4, 5, 6, 7
See also DLB 14
Mitchell, Julie 1959- 128
Mitchell, Juliet (Constance Wyatt)
1940- CANR-29
Earlier sketch in CA 45-48
See also FW
Mitchell, K. L.
See Lamb, Elizabeth Searle
Mitchell, Kathy 1948- .... SATA 59
Mitchell, Keith
See Coogan, Keith
Mitchell, Ken(neth Ronald) 1940- .. CANR-103
Earlier sketches in CA 93-96, CANR-16, 37
See also CD 5, 6
See also DLB 60
Mitchell, Kenneth R. 1930- 17-20R
Mitchell, Kerry
See Wilkes-Hunter, R(ichard)
Mitchell, Kirk (John) 1950- CANR-107
Earlier sketch in CA 128
Mitchell, Lane 1907- CAP-1
Earlier sketch in CA 19-20
Mitchell, Langdon (Elwyn) 1862-1935
Brief entry 120
See also DLB 7
See also RGAL 4
Mitchell, Larry 1938- 152
Mitchell, Lee M(ark) 1943- CANR-1
Earlier sketch in CA 49-52
Mitchell, Leeds 1912-1998 89-92
Mitchell, Leonel Lake 1930- 89-92
Mitchell, Leslie (Scott Falconer)
1905-1985 156
Obituary 118
Mitchell, Lionel H. 1942- 106
Mitchell, Loften 1919-2001 .... CANR-26
Obituary 197
Earlier sketch in CA 81-84
See also BW 1
See also CAD
See also CD 5, 6
See also DLB 38
Mitchell, Lori 1961- .... SATA 128
Mitchell, Marcia L(ouise) 1942- 113
Mitchell, Margaree King 1953- 150
See also SATA 84
Mitchell, Margaret (Munnerlyn)
1900-1949 .... CANR-94
Brief entry 109
Earlier sketches in CA 125, CANR-55
See also AAYA 23
See also BPFB 2
See also BYA 1
See also CDALBS
See also DA3
See also DAM NOV, POP
See also DLB 9
See also LAIT 2
See also MAL 5
See also MTCW 1, 2
See also MTFW 2005
See also NFS 9
See also RGAL 4
See also RHW
See also TCLC 11
See also TUS
See also WYAS 1
See also YAW
Mitchell, Margaretta K. 1935- CANR-14
Earlier sketch in CA 29-32R
Mitchell, Marianne 1947- 218
See also SATA 145
Mitchell, Marianne Helen 1937- 85-88
Mitchell, Mark 1961- CANR-115
Earlier sketch in CA 156
Mitchell, Memory F(armer) 1924- 37-40R
Mitchell, Michele 1961(?)- 223
Mitchell, Mozella G. 1934- 189
Mitchell, Nancy 208
Mitchell, Otis C. 1935- CANR-13
Earlier sketch in CA 37-40R
Mitchell, P(hilip) M(arshall) 1916- CANR-43
Earlier sketches in CA 104, CANR-20
Mitchell, Paige
See Mitchell, Judith Paige
Mitchell, Pamela Holsclaw 1940- CANR-6
Earlier sketch in CA 57-60
Mitchell, Peggy
See Mitchell, Margaret (Munnerlyn)
Mitchell, Peter M(cQuilkin) 1934- 85-88
Mitchell, Reid 1955- 140
Mitchell, Rhonda .... SATA 89
Mitchell, Richard G., Jr. 1942- 212
Mitchell, Richard H(anks) 1931- 21-24R
Mitchell, Robert H(ughes) 1921- 117
Mitchell, Roger (Sherman) 1935- 25-28R
Mitchell, Ruth K. 33-36R
Mitchell, S. Valentine
See Gammell, Susanna Valentine Mitchell
Mitchell, S(ilas) Weir 1829-1914 165
See also DLB 202
See also RGAL 4
See also TCLC 36
Mitchell, Sally 1937- 110
Mitchell, Scott
See Godfrey, Lionel (Robert Holcombe)
Mitchell, Sharon 1962- 172
Mitchell, Sidney Alexander 1895-1966 ..... 5-8R
Obituary 134
Mitchell, Stephen 1948- CANR-144
Earlier sketch in CA 146
Mitchell, Stephen A. 1946-2000 133
Obituary 191
Mitchell, Stephen Arnold 1903-1974
Obituary 49-52
Mitchell, Stephen O. 1930- 13-16R
Mitchell, Susan 1944- CANR-86
Earlier sketch in CA 154
See also CP 7
See also CWP
Mitchell, Susanna (Ryland) 1941- 161
Mitchell, Syne 1970- 218
Mitchell, Thomas N(oel) 1939- 103
Mitchell, Thomas R. 1950- 202
Mitchell, Tony William 1949- 218
Mitchell, Verner D. 1957- 196
Mitchell, W. J. T. 1942- CANR-89
Earlier sketches in CA 81-84, CANR-14
See also DLB 246
Mitchell, W(illiam) O(rmond)
1914-1998 .... CANR-43
Obituary 165
Earlier sketches in CA 77-80, CANR-15
See also CLC 25
See also CN 1, 2, 3, 4, 5, 6
See also DAC
See also DAM MST
See also DLB 88
See also TCLE 1:2
Mitchell, Wayne 219
Mitchell, William (Lendrum) 1879-1936 213
See also TCLC 81
Mitchell, William E(dward) 1927- 81-84
Mitchell, William E. 1936- 93-96
Mitchell, William Hamilton 1907(?)-1982
Obituary 107
Mitchell, William J. 1944- 146
Mitchell, William P. 1937- 141
Mitchell, Yvonne 1925-1979 .... CANR-10
Obituary 85-88
Earlier sketch in CA 17-20R
See also SATA-Obit 24
Mitchelson, Marvin M. 1928-2004 104
Obituary 231
Mitchelson, Mitch
See Mitchelson, Peter Richard
Mitchelson, Peter Richard 1950- 171
See also SATA 104
Mitcheltree, Thomas James 1946- 171
Mitcheltree, Tom
See Mitcheltree, Thomas James
Mitchenson, Francis Joseph Blackett
1911-1992 101
Obituary 139
Mitchenson, Joe
See Mitchenson, Francis Joseph Blackett
Mitchinson, Wendy 1947- 237
Mitchison, (Sonja) Lois 1-4R
Mitchison, Naomi (Margaret Haldane)
1897-1999 .... CANR-144
Obituary 174
Earlier sketches in CA 77-80, CANR-15, 83
See also CN 1, 2, 3, 4, 5, 6
See also CWRI 5
See also DLB 160, 191, 255, 319
See also RGSF 2
See also RHW
See also SATA 24
See also SATA-Obit 112
Mitchison, Rosalind (Mary) 1919-2002 . 33-36R
Obituary 209
Mitchll, John
See Slater, Patrick
Mitchner, Stuart 1938- 61-64
Mitchnik, Helen 1901-1982 117
See also SATA 41
See also SATA-Brief 35
Mitchum, Hank
See Knott, William C(ecil, Jr.) and
Murray, Stuart A. P. and
Newton, D(wight) B(ennett) and
Sherman, Jory (Tecumseh)
See also TCWW 2
Mitelman, Bonnie Cossman 1941- 111
Mitford, Jessica 1917-1996 .... CANR-60
Obituary 152
Earlier sketches in CA 1-4R, CANR-1
See also CAAS 17
See also MTFW 2005
Mitford, Mary Russell 1787-1855 ...... DLB 110, 116
See also RGEL 2
Mitford, Nancy 1904-1973 .... 9-12R
See also BRWS 10
See also CLC 44
See also CN 1
See also DLB 191
See also RGEL 2
Mitgang, Herbert 1920- CANR-93
Earlier sketches in CA 9-12R, CANR-4
Mitgang, Lee D. 1949- 77-80
Mitgutsch, Ali 1935- 143
See also SATA 76
Mitra, Subrata 1930- .... IDFW 3, 4
Mitrany, David 1888-1975 65-68
Obituary 61-64
Mitroff, Ian I. 1938- 201
Mitrokhin, Vasili (Nikitich) 1922-2004 237
Mitrokhina, Yelena
See Costa, (Elena) Alexandra
Mitry, Jean 1907-1988 173
Mit-sata Maung Hmaing
See U Lun
Mitscherlich, Alexander Joseph 1908-1982
Obituary 107
Mitson, Eileen N(ora) 1930- 25-28R
Mitsuhashi, Yoko .... SATA 45
See also SATA-Brief 33
Mitsui, James Masao 1940- 213
Mittelholzer, Edgar Austin 1909-1965 ... CAP-1
Earlier sketch in CA 13-14
See also BW 1
See also CDWLB 3
See also DLB 117
See also EWL 3
See also RGEL 2
Mittelman, James H(oward) 1944- CANR-13
Earlier sketch in CA 73-76
Mittelpunkt, Hillel 1949- 213
Mitter, Rana 1969- 236
Mitterer, Erika 1906(?)- 180
See also DLB 85
Mitterer, Felix 1948- .... DLB 124
Mitterling, Philip Ira 1926- 102
Mittermeier, Russell (Alan) 1949- 161
Mittermeyer, Helen (Hayton Monteith)
1930- 124
Mitternacht, Johann Sebastian
1613-1679 .... DLB 168
Mittlebeeler, Emmet V(aughn) 1915- 57-60
Mittman, Stephanie 1950- 167
Mitton, Bruce H(arold) 1950- 108
Mitton, Charles Leslie 1907-1998 ...... CANR-4
Earlier sketch in CA 1-4R
Mitton, Jacqueline 1948- 97-100
See also SATA 66, 115, 162
Mitton, Simon 1946- 97-100
See also SATA 66
Mitton, Tony 1951- CANR-131
Earlier sketch in CA 171
See also SATA 104, 149
Mittra, S(id) 1930- 41-44R
Mitzman, Arthur Benjamin 1931- ... CANR-122
Earlier sketch in CA 104
Mitzman, Max E. 1908- 97-100
Miura, Akira 1927- 117
Miura, Ayako 1922- 73-76
Miura, Chizuko 1931- 133
See also Sono, Ayako
Miura, Hiroshi 1944- 164
Mix, C(larence) Rex 1935- 29-32R
Mix, Katherine Lyon 53-56
Mix, Paul E(merson) 1934- 45-48
Mix, Susan Shank 1943- 29-32R
Mixon, Laura J. CANR-143
Earlier sketch in CA 165
Mixter, Elisabeth W.
See Morss, Elisabeth W.
Mixter, Keith Eugene 1922- 41-44R
Mixter, Russell Lowell 1906- CAP-1
Earlier sketch in CA 13-16
Miyagawa, Kazuo 1908- .... IDFW 3, 4
Miyakawa, T(etsuo) Scott 1906-1981 .... 17-20R
Miyamoto, Kazuo 1900-1988 .... CAP-1
Earlier sketch in CA 11-12
Miyamoto, Kenji 1908- 192
Miyamoto, Shigeru 1952- .... AAYA 58
Miyamoto, (Chujo) Yuriko 1899-1951 174
Earlier sketch in CA 170
See also Miyamoto Yuriko
See also TCLC 37
Miyamoto Yuriko
See Miyamoto, (Chujo) Yuriko
See also DLB 180
Miyazaki, Hayao 1941- 213
See also AAYA 37
Miyazawa, Kenji 1896-1933 157
See also Miyazawa Kenji
See also RGWL 3
See also TCLC 76
Miyazawa Kenji
See Miyazawa, Kenji
See also EWL 3
Miyoshi, Masao 1928- 29-32R
Mize, B. Ray 1946- 218
Mizejewski, Linda 1952- CANR-89
Earlier sketch in CA 144
Mizener, Arthur (Moore) 1907-1988 ... CANR-5
Obituary 124
Earlier sketch in CA 5-8R
See also DLB 103
Mizner, Elizabeth Howard 1907- 13-16R
See also SATA 27
Mizoguchi, Kenji 1898-1956 167
See also TCLC 72
Mizrahi, Isaac 1961- 169
Mizruchi, Ephraim H(arold) 1926- 41-44R
Mizruchi, Mark S(heldon) 1953- CANR-30
Earlier sketch in CA 110
Mizruchi, Susan L. 1959- 177
Mizumura, Kazue 85-88
See also SATA 18
Mizumura, Minae 1951- 227
Mjelde, Michael Jay 1938- 69-72
Mlodinow, Leonard 1954- 225
Mlynar, Zdenek 1930-1997 213
Mlynowski, Sarah 1977(?)- 218
Mnacko, Ladislav 1919-1994 .... CANR-31
Earlier sketch in CA 29-32R
See also CWW 2
See also EWL 3
Mnookin, Robert H(arris) 1942- CANR-104
Earlier sketch in CA 140
Mnookin, Wendy M. 1946- 207
Mnouchkine, Alexandre 1908-1993 . IDFW 3, 4
Mo, Timothy (Peter) 1950- CANR-128
Earlier sketch in CA 117
See also CLC 46, 134
See also CN 5, 6, 7
See also DLB 194
See also MTCW 1
See also WLIT 4
See also WWE 1
Moak, Lennox L. 1912-1982 .... 21-24R
Moak, Samuel K(uhn) 1929- 37-40R
Moan, Terrence 1947- 97-100
Moat, John 1936- CANR-29
Earlier sketches in CA 33-36R, CANR-13
See also CP 1, 2
Moats, Alice-Leone 1908(?)-1989 .... CAP-1
Obituary 128
Earlier sketch in CA 13-16
Moats, David 1947- 232
Moats, Lillian 1946- 180
Moberg, David O(scar) 1922- CANR-18
Earlier sketches in CA 1-4R, CANR-2

Moberg, (Carl Arthur) Vilhelm
1898-1973 ... CANR-135
Obituary ... 45-48
Earlier sketch in CA 97-100
See also DLB 259
See also EW 11
See also EWL 3
Moberly, R(obert) B(asil) 1920- ... 29-32R
Moberly, Walter (Hamilton) 1881-1974 . CAP-2
Earlier sketch in CA 29-32
Moberly-Bell, E(nid Hester Chataway)
1881- ... 5-8R
Mobius, Martin
See Bierbaum, Otto Julius
Mobley, Charles M(urray) 1954- ... 139
Mobley, Harris W(itsel) 1929- ... 37-40R
Mobley, James Bryce 1934- ... CANR-48
Mobley, Joe A. 1945- ... 155
See also SATA 91
Mobley, Tony Allen 1938- ... 102
Mobley, Walt
See Burgess, Michael (Roy)
Moche, Dinah (Rachel) L(evine)
1936- ... CANR-57
Earlier sketch in CA 89-92
See also SATA 44
See also SATA-Brief 40
Mochi, Ugo (A.) 1889-1977 ... SATA 38
Mochizuki, Ken 1954- ... CANR-127
Earlier sketch in CA 149
See also SAAS 22
See also SATA 81, 146
Mock, Edward J(oseph) 1934- ... 21-24R
Mock, Michele L. 1962- ... 187
Mocker, Donald W(ilbur) 1935- ... 102
Mockler, Anthony 1937- ... 69-72
Mockler, Mike 1945- ... 109
Mockler, Robert J. 1932- ... 33-36R
Mockridge, Norton 1915-2004
Obituary ... 226
Brief entry ... 110
Mocsy, Andras 1929- ... 65-68
Moczarski, Kazimierz 1907-1975
Modahl, Mary 1962- ... 199
Modak, Manorama Ramkrishna
1895-1986 ... 97-100
Modarressi, Mitra 1967- ... SATA 126
Modarressi, Taghi (M.) 1931-1997 ... 134
Brief entry ... 121
Interview in ... CA-134
See also CLC 44
Mode, Heinz (Adolf) 1913-1992 ... 185
Brief entry ... 111
Model, Lisette 1906-1983
Obituary ... 109
Modell, Frank B. 1917- ... CANR-39
Earlier sketch in CA 116
See also SATA 39
See also SATA-Brief 36
Modell, John 1941- ... 93-96
Modell, Judith Schachter 1941- ... 111
Modelski, George 1926- ... CANR-2
Earlier sketch in CA 49-52
Modert, (Betty) Jo 1921- ... 132
Modesitt, Jeanne 1953- ... SATA 92, 143
Modesitt, L(eland) E(xton), Jr.
1943- ... CANR-110
Earlier sketches in CA 109, CANR-27, 58, 101
See also AAYA 33
See also FANT
See also SATA 91
Modgil, Celia 1937- ... 124
Modgil, Sohan (Lal) 1938- ... 124
Modiano, Patrick (Jean) 1945- ... CANR-115
Earlier sketches in CA 85-88, CANR-17, 40
See also CLC 18
See also CWW 2
See also DLB 83, 299
See also EWL 3
Modigliani, Andre 1940- ... 53-56
Modigliani, Jeanne 1918(?)-1984
Obituary ... 113
Modinos, Antonis 1938- ... 160
Modisane, Bloke
See Modisane, William
Modisane, William 1923-1986
Obituary ... 118
See also CP 1
Modjeska, Drusilla 1946- ... 189
Modleski, Tania 1949- ... 191
Modley, Rudolph 1906-1976
Obituary ... 69-72
Modotti, Tina 1896-1942 ... AAYA 53
Modras, Ronald E(dward) 1937- ... CANR-9
Earlier sketch in CA 21-24R
Modrell, Dolores 1933- ... SATA 72
Moe, Barbara 1937- ... 69-72
See also SATA 20
Moe, Christian (Hollis) 1929- ... 41-44R
Moe, Doug ... 207
Moe, Edith Monroe 1896(?)-1987
Obituary ... 122
Moe, Jorgen (Ingebretsen) 1813-1882 ... WCH
Moe, Nelson 1961- ... 230
Moe, Richard 1936- ... 145
Moebius, Martin
See Bierbaum, Otto Julius
Moehlman, Arthur H(enry) 1907- ... 9-12R
Moehlmann, F. Herbert 1893-1991 ... 93-96
Moelleken, Wolfgang W. 1934- ... 33-36R
Moeller, Charles 1912-1986 ... 73-76
Moeller, Dade W. 1927- ... 138
Moeller, Dorothy W(ilson) 1902-1995 ... 45-48
Moeller, Helen (Elaine) 1921- ... CANR-13
Earlier sketch in CA 21-24R
Moeller, Susan D. ... 181
Moellering, Ralph L(uther) 1923- ... 13-16R
Moellhausen, Balduin 1825-1905 ... DLB 129
Moen, Matthew C. 1958- ... 143
Moenkemeyer, Heinz 1914-1985 ... 102
Moenssens, Andre A. 1930- ... 29-32R
Moeran, Brian 1944- ... 127
Moerbeek, Kees 1955- ... 166
See also SATA 98
Moerck, Paal
See Roelvaag, O(le) E(dvart)
Moeri, Louise 1924- ... CANR-61
Earlier sketches in CA 65-68, CANR-9
See also AAYA 33
See also SAAS 10
See also SATA 24, 93
See also YAW
Moerk, Ernst L(orenz) 1937- ... 126
Moerman, Daniel E(llis) 1941- ... 105
Moerman, Michael (Harris) 1934- ... 25-28R
Moerne, Arvid
See Morne, Arvid
Moerner, Magnus 1924- ... 132
Moers, Ellen 1928-1979 ... CANR-59
Obituary ... 89-92
Earlier sketch in CA 9-12R
See also FW
Moers, Walter 1957- ... 219
Moes, Joh(a)n E(rnst) 1926- ... 1-4R
Moeser, John V(ictor) 1942- ... 116
Moffat, Abbot Low 1901- ... 1-4R
Moffat, Alexander W(hite) 1891- ... 69-72
Moffat, Anne Simon 1947- ... 107
Moffat, Frances 1912- ... 97-100
Moffat, Gwen 1924- ... CANR-66
Earlier sketches in CA 13-16R, CANR-10, 27, 52
See also CMW 4
Moffat, Ivan 1918-2002 ... 239
Moffat, John Lawrence 1916- ... 103
Moffat, Mary Jane 1933- ... CANR-17
Earlier sketch in CA 97-100
Moffat, Riley M(oore) 1947- ... 220
Moffatt, Doris 1919- ... 105
Moffatt, (Marston) Michael 1944- ... CANR-20
Earlier sketch in CA 85-88
Moffeit, Tony A. 1942- ... 211
Moffet, Thomas 1553-1604 ... DLB 136
Moffett, Eileen Flower 1928- ... 123
Moffett, George D(inwiddie) III 1943- ... 118
Moffett, Hugh (Oliver) 1910-1985 ... 73-76
Obituary ... 115
Moffett, Jami 1952- ... SATA 84
Moffett, Judith 1942- ... CANR-83
Earlier sketches in CA 69-72, CANR-14, 48
See also CP 7
See also SFW 4
Moffett, Kenworth W(illiam) 1934- ... 167
Brief entry ... 118
Moffett, Marian (Scott) 1949-2004 ... 149
Obituary ... 231
Moffett, Martha (Leatherwood) 1934- ... 37-40R
See also SATA 8
Moffett, Samuel Hugh 1916- ... CANR-5
Earlier sketch in CA 9-12R
Moffett, (Anthony) Toby 1944- ... 85-88
Moffitt, Donald (Anthony) 1936-
Brief entry ... 111
Moffitt, John 1908-1987 ... CANR-10
Earlier sketch in CA 25-28R
Moffitt, Peggy 1937- ... 138
Moffitt, Phillip 1946- ... 114
Brief entry ... 110
Interview in ... CA-114
Moffitt, Sharon McMahon 1947- ... 227
Moffitt, William J. 1930- ... 57-60
Mofolo, Thomas (Mokopu)
1875(?)-1948 ... CANR-83
Brief entry ... 121
Earlier sketch in CA 153
See also AFW
See also BLC 3
See also DAM MULT
See also DLB 225
See also EWL 3
See also MTCW 2
See also MTFW 2005
See also TCLC 22
See also WLIT 2
Mofsie, Louis B. 1936- ... SATA-Brief 33
Mogal, Doris P(ick) 1918- ... 69-72
Mogan, Joseph J(ohn), Jr. 1924- ... 49-52
Mogel, Leonard Henry 1922- ... 104
Mogelon, Ronna 1960- ... 211
Mogensen, Suzanne A(ncher) 1946- .. SATA 129
Moger, Allen W(esley) 1905- ... CAP-2
Earlier sketch in CA 25-28
Moger, Art 1911- ... 120
Moggach, Deborah 1948- ... CANR-99
Earlier sketches in CA 89-92, CANR-18
Moggridge, D(onald) E(dward) 1943- ... 29-32R
Moghadam, Valentine M. 1952- ... 146
Mogil, Christopher ... 197
Mogil, Cindy R. 1954- ... 232
Moglen, Helene 1936- ... 65-68
Mogulof, Melvin B(ernard) 1926- ... 105
Mohamad Haji Salleh 1942- ... CP 1
Mohamed
See Muhammad
Mohammed Riza Pahlevi
See Pahlevi, Mohammed Riza
Mohan, Beverly Moffett 1918- ... 5-8R
Mohan, Brij 1939- ... CANR-57
Earlier sketches in CA 110, CANR-29
Mohan, Peter John 1930- ... CANR-10
Earlier sketch in CA 61-64
Mohan, Rakesh 1948- ... 151
Mohan, Robert Paul 1920- ... 41-44R
Mohanraj, Mary Anne 1971- ... 199
Mohanti, Prafulla 1936- ... 134
Mohanty, Gopinath 1914- ... EWL 3
Mohanty, Jitendra N(ath) 1928- ... 117
Mohar, Bojan 1956- ... 208
Moher, Francis Anthony Peter 1955- ... 133
Moher, Frank
See Moher, Francis Anthony Peter
Mohin, Ann ... 170
Mohl, Raymond A(llen) 1939- ... CANR-30
Earlier sketches in CA 33-36R, CANR-13
Mohl, Ruth 1891- ... CAP-1
Earlier sketch in CA 13-16
Mohle, Robert L. 1949- ... 167
Mohlenbrock, Robert H. 1931- ... CANR-5
Earlier sketch in CA 53-56
Mohler, Charles 1913- ... 29-32R
Mohler, James A(ylward) 1923- ... CANR-47
Earlier sketches in CA 21-24R, CANR-8, 23
Mohn, Peter B(urnet) 1934- ... 106
See also SATA 28
Mohn, Viola Kohl 1914- ... SATA 8
Mohr, Charles (Henry) 1929-1989
Obituary ... 128
Mohr, Clarence L(ee) 1946- ... 137
Mohr, Gordon 1916- ... CANR-12
Earlier sketch in CA 25-28R
Mohr, Hal 1894-1974 ... IDFW 3, 4
Mohr, Jack
See Mohr, Gordon
Mohr, James C(rail) 1943- ... 73-76
Mohr, Jay 1970- ... 234
Mohr, Merilyn
See Simonds, Merilyn
Mohr, Nicholasa 1938- ... CANR-64
Earlier sketches in CA 49-52, CANR-1, 32
See also AAYA 8, 46
See also CLC 12
See also CLR 22
See also DAM MULT
See also DLB 145
See also HLC 2
See also HW 1, 2
See also JRDA
See also LAIT 5
See also LLW
See also MAICYA 2
See also MAICYAS 1
See also RGAL 4
See also SAAS 8
See also SATA 8, 97
See also SATA-Essay 113
See also WYA
See also YAW
Mohr, Richard D(rake) 1950- ... 140
Mohrenschildt, Dimitri Sergius Von
See Von Mohrenschildt, Dimitri Sergius
Mohrhardt, Foster E(dward) 1907- ... CAP-1
Earlier sketch in CA 13-16
Mohrmann, Christine A(ndrina) E(lisabeth)
M(aria) 1903-1988 ... CAP-1
Earlier sketch in CA 9-10
Mohrt, Michel 1914- ... 13-16R
Mohun, Arwen Palmer ... 231
Mohundro, Lynn
See Lynn (Ruiz), Kathryn
Moi, Toril 1953- ... CANR-102
Earlier sketch in CA 154
See also CLC 172
See also FW
Moinot, Pierre 1920- ... 207
Moir, Alfred 1924- ... CANR-49
Earlier sketches in CA 21-24R, CANR-9, 24
Moir, Duncan Wilson 1930-1983
Obituary ... 110
Moir, John S(argent) 1926- ... 41-44R
Moir, May A(rstad) 1907- ... 111
Moir, Ronald Eugene 1928- ... 29-32R
Moise, Edwin E(variste) 1946-1998 ... 130
Moise, Lotte E(lla) 1917- ... 103
Moissan, (Ferdinand Frederic) Henri
1852-1907 ... 168
Moix (Meseguer), Ana Maria 1947- ... DLB 134
Mojica, Jose 1896-1974
Obituary ... 53-56
Mojtabai, A(nn) G(race) 1938- ... CANR-88
Earlier sketch in CA 85-88
See also CLC 5, 9, 15, 29
Mok, Esther 1953- ... 159
See also SATA 93
Mok, Paul P. 1934- ... 9-12R
Mokashi-Punekar, Shankar 1925- ... 97-100
See also CP 1, 2
Mokgatle, (Monyadio Moreleba) Naboth
1911-1985 ... CAP-2
Obituary ... 115
Earlier sketch in CA 33-36
Mokgatle, Naboth Nyadioe
See Mokgatle, (Monyadio Moreleba) Naboth
Mokgatle, Nyadioe Naboth
See Mokgatle, (Monyadio Moreleba) Naboth
Mokres, James A(llen) 1945- ... 49-52
Mokyr, Joel 1946- ... 136
Mol, Hans
See Mol, J(ohannis) J(acob)
Mol, J(ohannis) J(acob) 1922- ... CANR-43
Earlier sketches in CA 49-52, CANR-2, 18
Molan, Christine 1943- ... SATA 84
Molan, Dorothy L(ennon) 1911- ... 9-12R
Molan, Pat Carlson 1941- ... 112
Molarsky, Osmond 1909- ... CANR-48
Earlier sketch in CA 25-28R
See also SATA 16
Molavi, Afshin ... 214
Molchanov, Mikhail A(leksandrovich)
1961- ... 236
Moldafsky, Annie 1930- ... 61-64
Moldea, Dan E. 1950- ... 122
Moldenhauer, Hans 1906-1987 ... CANR-3
Earlier sketch in CA 1-4R
Moldenhauer, Joseph J(ohn) 1934- ... 33-36R
Moldenhauer, Rosaleen 1926- ... 97-100
Moldon, Peter L(eonard) 1937- ... 121
See also SATA 49
Moldovsky, Joel S(amuel) 1939- ... 97-100
Mole, Gary D(avid) 1964- ... 237
Mole, John 1941- ... CANR-83
Earlier sketches in CA 101, CANR-18, 41
See also CLR 61
See also CP 2, 3, 4, 5, 6, 7
See also SATA 36, 103
Mole, Robert L. 1923- ... 29-32R
Molen, Ronald Lowry 1929- ... 65-68
Molenaar, Dee 1918- ... 37-40R
Moler, Kenneth Lloyd 1938- ... 89-92
Moleski, Martin X. 1952- ... 215
Molesworth, Carl 1947- ... 147
Molesworth, Charles 1941- ... CANR-18
Earlier sketch in CA 77-80
Molesworth, Mary Louisa 1839-1921 ... 165
See also DLB 135
See also HGG
See also SATA 98
See also WCH
Molette, Barbara Jean 1940- ... CANR-56
Earlier sketches in CA 45-48, CANR-26
See also BW 1
Molette, Carlton W(oodard) II
1939- ... CANR-25
Earlier sketches in CA 45-48, CANR-1
See also BW 1
Moley, Raymond (Charles) 1886-1975 ... 61-64
Molho, Anthony 1939-
Brief entry ... 106
Moliere 1622-1673 ... DA
See also DA3
See also DAB
See also DAC
See also DAM DRAM, MST
See also DC 13
See also DFS 13, 18, 20
See also DLB 268
See also EW 3
See also GFL Beginnings to 1789
See also LATS 1:1
See also RGWL 2, 3
See also TWA
See also WLC
Molin, Charles
See Mayne, William (James Carter)
Molin, James
See Molina, Jacinto
Molin, Sven Eric 1929- ... 17-20R
Molina, Antonio Munoz 1956- ... DLB 322
Molina, Enrique 1910- ... HW 1
Molina, Jacinto 1934- ... 216
Molina, Juan Ramon 1875-1908 ... LAW
Molina, Silvia 1946- ... CANR-87
Earlier sketch in CA 151
See also SATA 97
Molinari, Ricardo E. 1898- ... LAW
Molinaro, Edouard 1928- ... 202
Molinaro, Julius A(rthur) 1918- ... 41-44R
Molinaro, Matie A. 1922- ... 128
Molinaro, Ursule (?)-2000 ... CANR-91
Obituary ... 189
Earlier sketches in CA 69-72, CANR-48
Molinaro Herndon, Ursule
See Molinaro, Ursule
Moline, Jon Nelson 1937- ... 111
Moline, Karen ... 169
Moline, Mary 1932- ... CANR-7
Earlier sketch in CA 57-60
Molinsky, Joan Sandra 1933- ... 123
Brief entry ... 116
Molk, Laurel 1957- ... SATA 92, 162
Moll, Elick 1907- ... CANR-2
Earlier sketch in CA 1-4R
Moll, Ernest George 1900- ... CP 1
Molland, Einar 1908-1987 ... 53-56
Mollegen, Albert Theodore 1906-1984
Obituary ... 111
Mollegen, Anne Rush
See Smith, Anne Mollegen
Mollel, Tololwa M. 1952- ... 137
See also CWRI 5
See also SATA 88
Mollenhoff, Clark R(aymond)
1921-1991 ... CANR-83
Obituary ... 133
Earlier sketches in CA 17-20R, CANR-13
Mollenkamp, Carrick 1969- ... 175
Mollenkott, Virginia R(amey) 1932- .. CANR-12
Earlier sketch in CA 33-36R
Moller, Poul Martin 1794-1838 ... DLB 300
Moller, Richard Jay 1952- ... 106
Molleur, (Michael B.) Joseph 1962- ... 215
Mollier, Jean-Yves ... 175
Mollinger, Robert N. 1945- ... 106
Mollo, Andrew 1940- ... CANR-15
Earlier sketch in CA 65-68
Mollo, Terry (Madeline) 1949- ... 102
Mollo, Victor 1909-1987 ... CANR-20
Obituary ... 123
Earlier sketches in CA 9-12R, CANR-5
Molloy, Anne Baker 1907-1999 ... 13-16R
See also SATA 32
Molloy, Frances
See Brady, Ann
Molloy, John T. 1937(?)- ... 81-84
Molloy, Johnny 1961- ... 168
Molloy, Julia Sale 1905-1983 ... CANR-1
Obituary ... 110
Earlier sketch in CA 1-4R

Cumulative Index 407 Montapert

Molloy, M(ichael) J(oseph) 1917-1994 103
See also CBD
Molloy, Michael (John) 1940- 238
See also SATA 162
Molloy, Paul (George) 1924- CANR-17
Earlier sketch in CA 1-4R
See also SATA 5
Molloy, Robert (William) 1906-1977 ..... CAP-2
Obituary 69-72
Earlier sketch in CA 29-32
Molloy, Sylvia 1938- .... GLL 2
Molloy, Tom 1948- 107
Molnar, Ferenc 1878-1952 .... CANR-83
Brief entry 109
Earlier sketch in CA 153
See also CDWLB 4
See also DAM DRAM
See also DLB 215
See also EWL 3
See also RGWL 2, 3
See also TCLC 20
Molnar, Imre
See Lakatos, Imre
Molnar, Maria 1910(?)-1985
Obituary 117
Molnar, Michael 1946- 147
Molnar, Miklos 1921-
See Meszoly, Miklos
Molnar, Thomas 1921- CANR-42
Earlier sketches in CA 1-4R, CANR-3, 19
Molodowsky, Kadia 1894-1975 219
Molodowsky, Kadya
See Molodowsky, Kadia
Molody, Konan Trofimovich
See Lonsdale, Gordon Arnold
Moloi, Godfrey 1934-1998 175
Moloney, Ed 1948- 221
Moloney, James 1954- 159
See also SATA 94, 144
See also SATA-Essay 144
See also YAW
Moloney, Susie 170
Molotch, Harvey L(uskin) 1940- CANR-15
Earlier sketch in CA 41-44R
Molotov, V.
See Molotov, Viacheslav Mikhailovich
Molotov, V. M.
See Molotov, Viacheslav Mikhailovich
Molotov, Viacheslav Mikhailovich 1890-1986
Obituary 121
Molt, Cynthia Marylee 1957- 138
Moltmann, Juergen 1926- 93-96
Molton, Stephen 1951- 127
Molumby, Lawrence E. 1932- 21-24R
Molz, (Redmond) Kathleen 1928- 49-52
Momaday, N(avarre) Scott 1934- CANR-134
Earlier sketches in CA 25-28R, CANR-14, 34, 68
Interview in CANR-14
See also AAYA 11, 64
See also AMWS 4
See also ANW
See also BPFB 2
See also BYA 12
See also CDALBS
See also CLC 2, 19, 85, 95, 160
See also CN 2, 3, 4, 5, 6, 7
See also CPW
See also DA
See also DA3
See also DAB
See also DAC
See also DAM MST, MULT, NOV, POP
See also DLB 143, 175, 256
See also EWL 3
See also EXPP
See also LAIT 4
See also LATS 1:2
See also MAL 5
See also MTCW 1, 2
See also MTFW 2005
See also NFS 10
See also NNAL
See also PC 25
See also PFS 2, 11
See also RGAL 4
See also SATA 48
See also SATA-Brief 30
See also TCWW 1, 2
See also WLCS
See also WP
See also YAW
Momboisse, Raymond M. 1927- 29-32R
Momen, Moojan 1950- CANR-102
Earlier sketches in CA 122, CANR-48
Moment, David 1925- 9-12R
Momigliano, Arnaldo (Dante) 1908-1987
Obituary 123
Mommsen, Hans 1930- 164
Mommsen, Katharina 1925- 69-72
Mommsen, (Christian Matthias) Theodor
1817-1903 202
Mommsen, Wolfgang J(ustin) 1930-2004 101
Obituary 229
Mon, Franz 1926- 202
See also EWL 3
Monaco, James 1942- CANR-33
Earlier sketches in CA 69-72, CANR-15
Monaco, Paul 1942- 191
Monaco, Richard 1950- CANR-86
Earlier sketches in CA 65-68, CANR-15, 33
See also FANT
Monagan, Charles A(ndrew) 1950- 109
Monagan, John S(tephen) 1911-2005 126
Monaghan, David (Mark) 1941- 133
Monaghan, E(dith) Jennifer 1933- 115
Monaghan, (James) Jay (IV) 1891-1981 . 41-44R
Obituary 103
Monaghan, (Mary) Patricia 1946- ... CANR-143
Earlier sketches in CA 107, CANR-23
Monaghan, Patrick C. 1903(?)-1972
Obituary 37-40R
Monagle, Bernie 1957- 192
See also SATA 121
Monahan, Arthur P(atrick) 1928- 57-60
Monahan, Brent J(effrey) 1948- 93-96
See also HGG
Monahan, James (Henry Francis) 1912-1985
Obituary 118
See also CP 1
Monahan, Jean 1959- 218
Monahan, John
See Burnett, W(illiam) R(iley)
Monahan, John 1946- 149
Monahan, Kaspar .... AITN 1
Monahan, Patrick J. 1954- 148
Monahan, William G(regory) 1927(?)- 132
Monas, Sidney 1924- 13-16R
Monash, Paul 1914-2003 201
Obituary 214
Monaster, Nathan 1916(?)-1990
Obituary 131
Monath, Elizabeth 1907- 5-8R
Monbeck, Michael E(ugene) 1942- CANR-2
Earlier sketch in CA 49-52
Monbiot, George (Joshua) 1963- 132
Monclova, Lidio Cruz
See Cruz Monclova, Lidio
Moncreiffe, (Rupert) Iain (Kay) 1919-1985
Obituary 115
Moncrieff, David (William Hardy) Scott
See Scott-Moncrieff, David (William Hardy)
Moncrieff, Earnest
See Chi, Richard Hu See-Yee
Moncrieff, Elspeth 1959- 160
Moncrieff, Martha Christian Scott
See Scott Moncrieff, Martha Christian
Moncrieff, William Thomas
1794-1857 .... RGEL 2
Moncure, Jane Belk 1926- CANR-6
Earlier sketch in CA 9-12R
See also SATA 23
Mondadori, Alberto 1914(?)-1976
Obituary 65-68
Mondadori, Arnoldo 1889-1971
Obituary 29-32R
Mondale, Joan Adams 1930- 41-44R
Mondale, Walter F(rederick) 1928- 65-68
Monday, James 1951- 61-64
Monday, Michael
See Ginder, Richard
Mondey, David (Charles) 1917- 93-96
Mondor, Henri 1885(?)-1962
Obituary 111
Mondrian, Piet 1872-1944 .... AAYA 63
Mone, Gregory 231
Monegal, Emir Rodriquez
See Rodriguez Monegal, Emir
Monelle, Raymond 1937- 207
Monelli, Paolo 1894(?)-1984
Obituary 114
Monenembo, Tierno
See Diallo, Tierno Saidou
See also EWL 3
Mones, Nicole 1951(?)- CANR-136
Earlier sketch in CA 174
Mones, Paul 138
Monesson, Harry S. 1935- CANR-93
Earlier sketch in CA 133
Monet, Claude 1840-1926 .... AAYA 25
Monet, Dorothy 1927- 81-84
Monet, Jacques 1930- CANR-11
Earlier sketch in CA 65-68
Monet, Jean 1932- 167
Monette, Paul 1945-1995 139
Obituary 147
See also AMWS 10
See also CLC 82
See also CN 6
See also GLL 1
Money, A. E. 1920- 188
Money, David Charles 1918- 107
Money, James (Henry) 1918- 133
Money, John (William) 1921- CANR-41
Earlier sketches in CA 45-48, CANR-1, 18
Money, Keith 1935- 107
Money, Tony
See Money, A. E.
Moneyhon, Carl H. 1944- CANR-96
Earlier sketches in CA 120, CANR-46
Money-Kyrle, Roger (Ernie) 1898-1980
Obituary 101
Monfalcone, Wesley R. 1942- 109
Monfolo, Rodolpho 1899(?)-1976
Obituary 69-72
Monfredo, Miriam Grace 166
Monfried, Henri De
See De Monfried, Henri
Monger, Christopher 1950- 158
Monger, (Ifor) David 1908-1972 .... 5-8R
Mongerson, Paul 1922- 175
Mong-Lan 1970- 203
Mongre, Dr. Paul
See Hausdorff, Felix
Monguio, Luis 1908- 5-8R
Monheim, Leonard M. 1911-1971
Obituary 33-36R
Monhoff, June Hildegarde Flanner 1899-1987
Obituary 122
See also Flanner, Hildegarde
Monhollon, Michael L. 1959- 168
Monie, Willis J. 1945- 112
Moniere, Denis 1947- 167
Monier-Williams, Randall Herbert 1892(?)-1984
Obituary 113
Monig, Christopher
See Crossen, Kendell Foster
Monin, Lydia 218
Monjo, F(erdinand) N(icholas III)
1924-1978 .... CANR-83
Earlier sketches in CA 81-84, CANR-37
See also CLR 2
See also CWRI 5
See also MAICYA 1, 2
See also SATA 16
Monk, Alan
See Kendall, Willmoore
Monk, Galdo
See Riseley, Jerry B(urr, Jr.)
Monk, Isabell 1952- 199
See also SATA 136
Monk, Janice J(ones) 1937- 93-96
Monk, Katherine 213
Monk, Lorraine (Althea Constance) 101
Monk, Meredith (Jane) 1942- 172
Monk, Ray(mond) 1925- CANR-109
Earlier sketch in CA 136
Monk, Robert C(larence) 1930- 21-24R
Monka, Paul 1935- 29-32R
Monkhouse, Allan 1858-1936 184
See also DLB 10
Monkhouse, Francis John
1914-1975 .... CANR-10
Obituary 57-60
Earlier sketch in CA 13-16R
Monkkonen, Eric H(enry) 1942-2005 61-64
Obituary 239
Monkman, Leslie
See Monkman, Leslie G.
Monkman, Leslie G. 1946- CANR-52
Earlier sketch in CA 125
Monmonier, Mark Stephen 1943- CANR-27
Earlier sketch in CA 109
Monnet, Jean (Omer Marie) 1888-1979 102
Monnett, John 198
Monnier, Genevieve 1939- 156
Monninger, Joseph 1953- 121
Monnow, Peter
See Croudace, Glynn
Monod, Jacques 1910-1976 69-72
Obituary 65-68
Monod, Rene
See Koch, Kurt E(mil)
Monod, Sylvere 1921- 21-24R
Monod, (Andre) Theodore 1902-2000 65-68
Obituary 192
Monongo
See Clytus, John
Monopoli, Paula A. 1958- 224
Monoson, S. Sara 1960- 225
Monro, Gavin
See Monro-Higgs, Gertrude
Monro, Harold (Edward) 1879-1932 189
See also DLB 19
See also RGEL 2
Monro, Isabel S(tevenson) 1884-1977 ... CAP-2
Earlier sketch in CA 19-20
Monro, Kate M(argaret) 1883-1971(?) CAP-2
Earlier sketch in CA 19-20
Monroe, Alan D(ouglas) 1944- 57-60
Monroe, Alan Houston 1903-1975 .... 5-8R
Monroe, Bill
See Monroe, William Blanc, Jr.
Monroe, Carole 1944- 105
Monroe, Charles R(exford) 1905-1996 73-76
Monroe, Debra 1958- 134
Monroe, Elizabeth 1905-1986 .... 13-16R
Obituary 118
Monroe, Frank
See Chapman, Frank M(onroe)
Monroe, Harriet 1860-1936 204
Brief entry 109
See also DLB 54, 91
See also TCLC 12
Monroe, Jonathan B(eck) 1954- 126
Monroe, Keith 1917- CANR-2
Earlier sketch in CA 5-8R
Monroe, Kristen Renwick 1946- 187
Monroe, Lyle
See Heinlein, Robert A(nson)
Monroe, (Marilyn) Lynn Lee 1935- 53-56
Monroe, Margaret E(llen) 1914-2004 .... 5-8R
Obituary 234
Monroe, Marilyn
See Baker, Norma Jean
Monroe, Marion
See Cox, Marion Monroe
See also SATA-Obit 34
Monroe, Mary 1951- 216
Monroe, Steve 1961- 208
Monroe, William Blanc, Jr. 1920-1996 108
Interview in CA-108
Monro-Higgs, Gertrude 1905- 105
Monsaingeon, Bruno 1943- CANR-110
Earlier sketch in CA 142
Monsarrat, Ann Whitelaw 1937- 73-76
Monsarrat, Nicholas (John Turney)
1910-1979 .... CANR-3
Earlier sketch in CA 1-4R
See also BPFB 2
See also CN 1, 2
See also DLB 15
Monsell, Helen Albee 1895-1971 .... CAP-1
Earlier sketch in CA 9-10
See also SATA 24
Monsen, R(aymond) Joseph, Jr. 1931- 9-12R
Monsey, Derek 1921-1979 .... CANR-2
Obituary 85-88
Earlier sketch in CA 1-4R
Monshipouri, Mahmood 1952- 151
Monsivais, Carlos 1938- 161
Monsky, Mark 1941- 65-68
Monsma, James E. 1929- 29-32R
Monsma, Stephen V(os) 1936- 33-36R
Monsman, Gerald Cornelius 1940- CANR-8
Earlier sketch in CA 21-24R
Monson, Charles H., Jr. 1924- 5-8R
Monson, Ingrid (T.) 1955- 165
Monson, Karen Ann 1945-1988 .... CANR-20
Obituary 124
Earlier sketch in CA 97-100
Monson-Burton, Marianne 1975- 210
See also SATA 139
Monsour, Sally A. 1929- 21-24R
Monsour, Theresa 233
Montag, Thomas 1947- 103
Montag, Tom
See Montag, Thomas
Montagnes, Ian 1932- 45-48
Montagnier, Luc (Antoine) 1932- CANR-104
Earlier sketch in CA 160
Montagu, Ashley 1905-1999 .... CANR-78
Obituary 186
Earlier sketches in CA 5-8R, CANR-5
Interview in CANR-5
Montagu, Elizabeth 1720-1800 .... FW
Montagu, Elizabeth 1917- 9-12R
Montagu, Ewen (Edward Samuel)
1901-1985 77-80
Obituary 116
Montagu, Ivor (Goldsmid Samuel)
1904-1984 .... 13-16R
Obituary 114
Montagu, Jeremy (Peter Samuel) 1927- ... 93-96
Montagu, John Drogo 1923- 232
Montagu, Mary (Pierrepont) Wortley
1689-1762 .... DLB 95, 101
See also FL 1:1
See also PC 16
See also RGEL 2
Montagu, Robert 1949- 128
Montagu, W. H.
See Coleridge, Samuel Taylor
Montague, C(harles) E(dward) 1867-1928 .. 184
See also DLB 197
Montague, Gene Bryan 1928- 93-96
Montague, George T(homas) 1929- 133
Montague, Jeanne
See Yarde, Jeanne Betty Frances
Montague, Joel B(enjamin), Jr. 1912- 5-8R
Montague, John (Patrick) 1929- CANR-121
Earlier sketches in CA 9-12R, CANR-9, 69
See also CLC 13, 46
See also CP 1, 2, 3, 4, 5, 6, 7
See also DLB 40
See also EWL 3
See also MTCW 1
See also PFS 12
See also RGEL 2
See also TCLE 1:2
Montague, Lisa
See Shulman, Sandra (Dawn)
Montague, Peter Gunn 1938- 85-88
Montague-Smith, Patrick Wykeham 1920- . 107
Montagu of Beaulieu, Edward John Barrington
1926- CANR-6
Earlier sketch in CA 9-12R
Montaigne, Fen 1952- 171
Montaigne, Michel (Eyquem) de
1533-1592 .... DA
See also DAB
See also DAC
See also DAM MST
See also EW 2
See also GFL Beginnings to 1789
See also LMFS 1
See also RGWL 2, 3
See also TWA
See also WLC
Montaigne, Sanford H(oward) 1935- 65-68
Montal, Lionel .... CCA 1
Montalbano, William D(aniel)
1940-1998 .... CANR-142
Obituary 167
Earlier sketches in CA 105, CANR-22
Montalcini, Rita Levi
See Levi-Montalcini, Rita
Montale, Eugenio 1896-1981 .... CANR-30
Obituary 104
Earlier sketch in CA 17-20R
See also CLC 7, 9, 18
See also DLB 114
See also EW 11
See also EWL 3
See also MTCW 1
See also PC 13
See also PFS 22
See also RGWL 2, 3
See also TWA
See also WLIT 7
Montalvo, Garci Rodriguez de c. 1450-c. 1505 .... DLB 286
Montalvo, Jose 1946-1994 .... DLB 209
Montalvo, Juan 1832-1889 .... LAW
Montalvo, Luis Galvez de
See Avalle-Arce, Juan Bautista de
Montana, Bob 1920-1975
Obituary 89-92
See also SATA-Obit 21
Montana, Joe 1956- 169
Montana, Patrick J(oseph) 1937- CANR-10
Earlier sketch in CA 25-28R
Montanari, A(delio) J(oseph) 1917- 104
Montanari, Richard 1955(?)- 236
Montandon, Pat 57-60
Montapert, Alfred Armand 1906- 108
Montapert, William D(avid) 1930- 107

Montauredes 408 CONTEMPORARY AUTHORS

Montauredes, Rita 165
Montchrestien, Antoine de
1575(?)-1621 .... GFL Beginnings to 1789
Montclair, Dennis
See Sladen, Norman St. Barbe
Montebello, Guy -Philippe Lannes de
See de Montebello, Guy-Philippe Lannes
Montecino, Marcel 1945- 137
Brief entry 131
Montee, Kelly 196
Montee, Kristy 196
Montefiore, Hugh (William)
1920-2005 .... CANR-86
Obituary 239
Earlier sketch in CA 133
Montefiore, Simon Sebag
See Sebag-Montefiore, Simon
Monteilh, Marissa 205
Monteilhet, Hubert 1928-
Brief entry 117
See also CMW 4
Monteiro, George 1932- CANR-7
Earlier sketch in CA 17-20R
Monteiro, Longteine de
See de Monteiro, Longteine
Monteiro, Luis (Infante de la Cerda) de Sttau
1926-1993 .... CANR-10
Obituary 142
Earlier sketch in CA 13-16R
Monteith, Hayton
See Mittermeyer, Helen (Hayton Monteith)
Montejo, Victor (D.) 1951- 139
Monteleone, Elizabeth E. 237
Monteleone, Thomas F(rancis)
1946- CANR-79
Brief entry 109
Earlier sketches in CA 113, CANR-50
Interview in CA-113
See also HGG
See also SFW 4
Montell, William Lynwood 1931- CANR-11
Earlier sketch in CA 29-32R
Montemayor, Carlos 1947- 152
Montemayor, Jorge de
1521(?)-1561(?) .... DLB 318
Montenegro, Laura Nyman 1953- .. CANR-135
Earlier sketch in CA 160
See also SATA 95
Monter, E. William 1936- 21-24R
Montero, Darrel Martin 1946- 101
Montero, Gloria 1933- 171
See also SATA 109
Montero, Mayra 1952- 192
Montero, Rosa 1951- .... DLB 322
Monterosso, Carlo 1921- 29-32R
Monterroso, Augusto 1921-2003 .... CANR-79
Obituary 214
Earlier sketch in CA 153
See also DLB 145
See also HW 1
See also LAWS 1
See also RGSF 2
Montes, Antonio Llano 1924- CANR-14
Earlier sketch in CA 69-72
Montes, Marisa 1951- 217
See also SATA 144
Montes de Oca, Marco Antonio 1932- 114
See also HW 1
Montes-Huidobro, Matias 1931- .... EWL 3
Montesi, Albert Joseph 1921- 37-40R
Montesquieu, Charles-Louis de Secondat
1689-1755 .... DLB 314
See also EW 3
See also GFL Beginnings to 1789
See also TWA
Montesquiou, Robert de 1855-1921 ... DLB 217
Montessori, Maria 1870-1952 147
Brief entry 115
See also TCLC 103
Monteux, Doris (Hodgkins) 1894-1984 . CAP-2
Obituary 112
Earlier sketch in CA 19-20
Montey, Vivian M(arie) 1956- 105
Montfort, Auguste 1913-1999 .... CANR-41
Earlier sketches in CA 101, CANR-18
Montfort, Guy de
See Johnson, Donald McI(ntosh)
Montgomerie, Alexander
1550(?)-1598 .... DLB 167
See also RGEL 2
Montgomerie, Norah (Mary) 1913- 105
See also SATA 26
Montgomerie, William 1904- .... CP 1
Montgomery, Albert A. 1929- 13-16R
Montgomery, Bernard Law 1887-1976 69-72
Obituary 65-68
Montgomery, Brian (Frederick)
1903-1989 53-56
Obituary 128
Montgomery, (Robert) Bruce 1921(?)-1978 . 179
Obituary 104
See also Crispin, Edmund
See also CMW 4
Montgomery, Charles F(ranklin)
1910-1978 81-84
Obituary 77-80
Montgomery, Constance
See Cappel, Constance
Montgomery, David 1927- 81-84
Montgomery, David 1928- 148
Montgomery, David Bruce 1938- 29-32R
Montgomery, Diane 1940- 162
Montgomery, Edward F(inley) 1918- 9-12R
Montgomery, Elizabeth
See Julesberg, Elizabeth Rider Montgomery
Montgomery, Elizabeth Rider
See Julesberg, Elizabeth Rider Montgomery
See also SATA 3, 34
See also SATA-Obit 41
Montgomery, Elizabeth Wakefield
1891- 41-44R
Montgomery, Helen
See Gunn, Helen Montgomery
Montgomery, Herbert J. 1933- CANR-40
Earlier sketches in CA 49-52, CANR-3, 18
Montgomery, Horace 1906-2001 .... 9-12R
Obituary 193
Montgomery, Hugh (Edward) 1962- 220
See also SATA 146
Montgomery, James 1771-1854 .... DLB 93, 158
Montgomery, John (McVey) 1919- 25-28R
See also DLB 16
Montgomery, John D(ickey) 1920- CANR-18
Earlier sketches in CA 5-8R, CANR-3
Montgomery, John Warwick 1931- ... CANR-89
Earlier sketches in CA 21-24R, CANR-10, 25
Montgomery, L(ucy) M(aud) 1874-1942 137
Brief entry 108
See also AAYA 12
See also BYA 1
See also CLR 8, 91
See also DA3
See also DAC
See also DAM MST
See also DLB 92
See also DLBD 14
See also JRDA
See also MAICYA 1, 2
See also MTCW 2
See also MTFW 2005
See also RGEL 2
See also SATA 100
See also TCLC 51, 140
See also TWA
See also WCH
See also WYA
See also YABC 1
Montgomery, M(aurice) R(ichard) 1938- 143
Montgomery, Marion H., Jr. 1925- ... CANR-48
Earlier sketches in CA 1-4R, CANR-3
See also AITN 1
See also CLC 7
See also CSW
See also DLB 6
Montgomery, Maureen E. 175
Montgomery, Max
See Davenport, Guy (Mattison, Jr.)
Montgomery, Michael B. 1950- 122
Montgomery, Nancy S(chwinn) 93-96
Montgomery, Raymond A. (Jr.)
1936- CANR-16
Earlier sketch in CA 97-100
See also SATA 39
Montgomery, Robert 1904-1981
Obituary 108
Montgomery, Robert L(angford), Jr. 1927- . 5-8R
Montgomery, Ruth Shick -2001 .... CANR-17
Obituary 198
Earlier sketches in CA 1-4R, CANR-2
See also AITN 1
Montgomery, Rutherford George
1894-1985 .... CANR-70
Earlier sketch in CA 9-12R
See also SATA 3
See also TCWW 1, 2
Montgomery, Scott L. 231
Montgomery, Stuart 1940- .... CP 1
Montgomery, Sy 1958- 202
Earlier sketches in CA 186, CANR-100
Autobiographical Essay in 202
See also MAICYA 2
See also SATA 114, 132
See also SATA-Essay 132
See also TCLE 1:2
Montgomery, Thomas (Andrew) 1925- 49-52
Montgomery, Tommie Sue 1942- 112
Montgomery, Vivian 102
See also SATA 36
Monthan, Doris Born 1924- CANR-37
Earlier sketch in CA 115
Montherlant, Henry (Milon) de
1896-1972 85-88
Obituary 37-40R
See also CLC 8, 19
See also DAM DRAM
See also DLB 72, 321
See also EW 11
See also EWL 3
See also GFL 1789 to the Present
See also MTCW 1
Monti, Dean 1957- 207
Monti, Laura V(irginia) 1930- 111
Monti, Nicolas 1956- 128
Monti, Ricardo 1944- .... DLB 305
Montias, John Michael 1928-2005 ..... CANR-2
Earlier sketch in CA 1-4R
Monticello, Roberto 1954- 142
Monticone, Ronald Charles 1937- 73-76
Montiel, Dito 1970(?)- 223
Montier, Jean-Pierre 1956- 165
Montigny, Edgar-Andre 1965- 212
Montigny, Louvigny de 1876-1955 205
See also DLB 92
Montini, Giovanni Battista (Enrico Antonio
Maria) 1897-1978 .... CANR-30
Obituary 77-80
Earlier sketch in CA 81-84
Montoya, Jose 1932- 131
See also DLB 122
See also HW 1
See also RGAL 4
Montoya, Peter 233
Montparker, Carol 234
Montpetit, Charles 1958- 160
See also SATA 101
Montresor, Beni 1926-2001 .... CANR-28
Earlier sketch in CA 29-32R
See also MAICYA 1, 2
See also SAAS 4
See also SATA 3, 38
Montreuil, Claire
See Martin, Claire
Montrose, Graham
See Mackinnon, Charles Roy
Montrose, James St. David
See Appleman, John Alan
Montrose, Sarah
See Bosna, Valerie
Montross, David
See Backus, Jean L(ouise)
Montville, Leigh 206
Monty, Jeanne R(uth) 1935- 49-52
Monty Python
See Chapman, Graham and
Cleese, John (Marwood) and
Gilliam, Terry (Vance) and
Idle, Eric and
Jones, Terence Graham Parry and Palin, Michael (Edward)
See also AAYA 7
Monzo, Joaquim 1952- 211
Monzo, Quim
See Monzo, Joaquim
Mood, Alexander M(cFarlane) 1913- 53-56
Mood, John J(ordan) L(indemann) 1932- . 57-60
Mood, Terry Ann 1945- 154
Moodie, Fiona 1952- .... SATA 133
Moodie, Graeme C(ochrane) 1924- CANR-2
Earlier sketch in CA 1-4R
Moodie, John Wedderburn Dunbar
1797-1869 .... DLB 99
Moodie, Susanna (Strickland)
1803-1885 .... DLB 99
Moodie, T(homas) Dunbar 1940- 77-80
Moody, Anne 1940- 65-68
See also BW 1
See also MTFW 2005
See also NCFS 3
Moody, Bill 1941- CANR-129
Earlier sketches in CA 154, CANR-73
Moody, Dale 1915- 17-20R
Moody, Eric N(elson) 1946- 116
Moody, Ernest A(ddison) 1903-1975 ..... 13-16R
Obituary 61-64
Moody, Fred 1949- 153
Moody, G. F.
See Hamel Peifer, Kathleen
Moody, Hiram (F. III) 1961- CANR-112
Earlier sketches in CA 138, CANR-64
See also Moody, Rick
See also MTFW 2005
Moody, J. Carroll 1934- 33-36R
Moody, Jess C. 1925- 21-24R
Moody, John (Henry) 1953- 138
Moody, Joseph Nestor 1904-1994 .... CANR-1
Obituary 145
Earlier sketch in CA 49-52
Moody, Joshua 1633(?)-1697 .... DLB 24
Moody, Mary 1950- 144
Moody, Minerva
See Alcott, Louisa May
Moody, Paul Amos 1903-1986 53-56
Moody, Paul E(lliot) 1936- 118
Moody, Peter R(ichard, Jr.) 1943- 130
Brief entry 107
Moody, R. Bruce 1933- 17-20R
Moody, Ralph Owen 1898-1982 .... CAP-1
Earlier sketch in CA 9-10
See also SATA 1
Moody, Raymond Avery, Jr. 1944- 93-96
Moody, Richard 1911-1996 .... 33-36R
Obituary 151
Moody, Rick
See Moody, Hiram (F. III)
See also CLC 147
Moody, Ron 1924- 108
Moody, Skye Kathleen 180
Moody, Susan (Elizabeth Howard) 238
See also CMW 4
Moody, T(heodore) W(illiam) 1907- 13-16R
Moody, William Vaughan 1869-1910 178
Brief entry 110
See also DLB 7, 54
See also MAL 5
See also RGAL 4
See also TCLC 105
Mooers, Vernon 197
Mookerjee, Ajit 1915- 157
Mookerjee, Ajitcoomar
See Mookerjee, Ajit
Mookini, Esther T. 1928- 135
Moolb, Leinad
See Bloom, Daniel Halevi
Moolson, Melusa
See Solomon, Samuel
Moomaw, I(ra) W(ilbur) 1894-1990 .... CAP-1
Earlier sketch in CA 13-14
Moon, Carl 1879(?)-1948 184
Brief entry 111
See also SATA 25
Moon, Douglas Mark 1937- 17-20R
Moon, Elaine Latzman 1939- 147
Moon, (Susan) Elizabeth (Norris)
1945- CANR-107
Earlier sketches in CA 134, CANR-83
See also FANT
Moon, G(eoff) J. H. 1915- 105
Moon, Grace (Purdie) 1877(?)-1947 190
Brief entry 113
See also SATA 25
Moon, Harold K(ay) 1932- 53-56
Moon, Henry Lee 1901-1985
Obituary 116
Moon, Jeremy 1955- 149
Moon, Lily
See Warnes, Tim(othy)
Moon, Michael E(lliott) 1948- 85-88
Moon, Nicola 1952- CANR-128
Earlier sketch in CA 148
See also SATA 96, 147
Moon, Pat 1946- 185
See also SATA 113
Moon, (Edward) Penderel 1905-1987 145
Obituary 122
Moon, Rexford G(eorge), Jr. 1922- 41-44R
Moon, Robert 1925- 73-76
Moon, Sheila (Elizabeth) 1910-1991 ..... 25-28R
Obituary 182
See also SATA 5
See also SATA-Obit 114
Moon, Susan (Ichi Su) 1942- 173
Moon, Warren G. 1946- 125
Moonblood, Q.
See Stallone, Sylvester (Enzio)
Mooney, Bel 1946- CANR-69
Earlier sketch in CA 138
See also SATA 95
Mooney, Bill 195
See also Mooney, William F.
See also SATA 122
Mooney, Booth 1912-1977 .... CANR-3
Obituary 69-72
Earlier sketch in CA 49-52
Mooney, Brian C. 235
Mooney, Canice (Albert James)
1911-1963 .... 5-8R
Mooney, Chase C(urran) 1913-1972 .... CAP-2
Earlier sketch in CA 19-20
Mooney, Chris 230
Mooney, Christopher F(rancis)
1925-1993 .... CANR-14
Obituary 142
Earlier sketch in CA 37-40R
Mooney, Edward 1951- 130
See also Mooney, Ted
Mooney, Elizabeth C(omstock)
1918-1986 .... CANR-9
Obituary 119
Earlier sketch in CA 61-64
See also SATA-Obit 48
Mooney, Eugene F. 1930- 17-20R
Mooney, George A(ustin) 1911-1979
Obituary 89-92
Mooney, Harry J(ohn), Jr. 1927- 5-8R
Mooney, Mark P. 1956- 228
Mooney, Michael M.
See Mooney, Michael Macdonald
Mooney, Michael Macdonald
1930-1985 .... CANR-21
Obituary 117
Earlier sketch in CA 65-68
Mooney, Nan 1970- 214
Mooney, Patrick 1937- 115
Mooney, Robert 226
Mooney, Ted
See Mooney, Edward
See also CLC 25
Mooney, William F. 1919(?)-1985
Obituary 116
See also Mooney, Bill
Mooneyham, W(alter) Stanley
1926-1991 .... CANR-6
Obituary 134
Earlier sketch in CA 13-16R
Moonitz, Maurice 1910- CANR-2
Earlier sketch in CA 5-8R
Moonman, Eric 1929- 103
Moor, Emily
See Deming, Richard
Mooradian, Karlen 1935- 97-100
Moorcock, Michael (John) 1939- CANR-122
Earlier sketches in CA 45-48, CANR-2, 17, 38, 64
See also Bradbury, Edward P.
See also CAAS 5
See also AAYA 26
See also CLC 5, 27, 58
See also CN 5, 6, 7
See also DLB 14, 231, 261, 319
See also FANT
See also MTCW 1, 2
See also MTFW 2005
See also SATA 93
See also SCFW 1, 2
See also SFW 4
See also SUFW 1, 2
Moorcraft, Paul L. 1948- 222
Moore, Acel 1940- 69-72
Moore, Alan 1953- CANR-138
Earlier sketch in CA 204
See also AAYA 51
See also DLB 261
See also MTFW 2005
See also SFW 4
Moore, Alan 1960- 123
Moore, Alexis 1951- 162
Moore, Alice Ruth
See Nelson, Alice Ruth Moore Dunbar
Moore, Alison 1951- 153
Moore, Allan F. 1954- CANR-93
Earlier sketch in CA 146
Moore, Alma Chesnut 1901- CAP-1
Earlier sketch in CA 13-14

Cumulative Index **409** **Moore**

Moore, Amos
See Hubbard, George (Barron)
See also TCWW 1, 2
Moore, Andrew
See Binder, Frederick Moore
Moore, Ann (Schweinler) 1959- ... 221
Moore, Anne Carroll 1871-1961 ... 73-76
See also SATA 13
Moore, Archie Lee 1916-1998 ... 33-36R
Obituary ... 172
Moore, Arden 1957(?)- ... 223
Moore, Arthur 1906(?)-1977
Obituary ... 69-72
Moore, Arthur James 1888-1974 ... 5-8R
Obituary ... 49-52
Moore, Austin
See Muir, (Charles) Augustus (Carlow)
Moore, Barbara
See Lee, Barbara (Moore)
Moore, Barrington, Jr. 1913- ... 117
Moore, Basil John 1933- ... 21-24R
Moore, Bernard 1904-1988 ... CANR-13
Earlier sketch in CA 69-72
Moore, Bidwell 1917- ... 33-36R
Moore, Bob 1948- ... 61-64
Moore, Brenda L(ee) 1950- ... 159
Moore, Brian 1921-1999 ... CANR-63
Obituary ... 174
Earlier sketches in CA 1-4R, CANR-1, 25, 42
See also Bryan, Michael
See also BRWS 9
See also CCA 1
See also CLC 1, 3, 5, 7, 8, 19, 32, 90
See also CN 1, 2, 3, 4, 5, 6
See also DAB
See also DAC
See also DAM MST
See also DLB 251
See also EWL 3
See also FANT
See also MTCW 1, 2
See also MTFW 2005
See also RGEL 2
Moore, C(atherine) L(ucile)
1911-1987 ... CANR-83
Earlier sketch in CA 104
Interview in ... CA-104
See also DLB 8
See also FANT
See also SCFW 1, 2
See also SFW 4
See also SUFW
Moore, Carey Armstrong 1930- ... 37-40R
Moore, Carl L(eland) 1921- ... CANR-15
Earlier sketch in CA 5-8R
Moore, Carman L(eroy) 1936- ... 61-64
Moore, Cassandra Chrones ... 166
Moore, Charles
See Moore, Reg(inald Charles Arthur)
Moore, Charles A(lexander)
1901-1967 ... CANR-3
Earlier sketch in CA 1-4R
Moore, Charles Garrett Ponsonby
1910-1989 ... 108
Moore, Charlotte E(mma) 1898-1990 ... 160
Moore, Chauncey O. 1895-1965 ... CAP-1
Earlier sketch in CA 11-12
Moore, Cheri
See Ladd, Cheryl (Jean)
Moore, Christine Palamidessi 1951- ... 151
Moore, Christopher (Hugh) 1950- .. CANR-143
Earlier sketch in CA 119
Moore, Clayton
See Brandner, Gary (Phil) and
Henderson, M(arilyn) R(uth)
Moore, Clement Clarke 1779-1863 ... DLB 42
See also MAICYA 1, 2
See also SATA 18
Moore, Clyde B. 1886-1973 ... CANR-4
Earlier sketch in CA 1-4R
Moore, Colleen 1902(?)-1988
Obituary ... 124
Moore, Cora R. 1902-1987 ... CAP-2
Earlier sketch in CA 25-28
Moore, Cory
See Sturgeon, Wina
Moore, Cyd 1957- ... SATA 83, 133
Moore, Dan Tyler 1908-1998 ... 5-8R
Moore, Daniel G(eorge) 1899-1977 ... 57-60
Obituary ... 126
Moore, David G. 1918- ... CANR-2
Earlier sketch in CA 1-4R
Moore, David Moresby 1933- ... 112
Moore, Deborah Dash 1946- ... CANR-120
Earlier sketch in CA 108
Moore, Dick
See Moore, John Richard, Jr.
Moore, Dinty W. 1955- ... 150
Moore, Don W. 1905(?)-1986
Obituary ... 119
See also SATA-Obit 48
Moore, Donald Joseph 1929- ... 57-60
Moore, Dora Mavor 1888-1979 ... 148
See also DLB 92
Moore, Doris Langley 1903(?)-1989 . CANR-83
Obituary ... 128
Earlier sketches in CA 1-4R, CANR-1
See also RHW
Moore, Dorothea (Mary) 1881-1933
Brief entry ... 121
See also CWRI 5
Moore, Dorothy N(elson) 1915- ... CANR-44
Earlier sketches in CA 89-92, CANR-21
Moore, Douglas Stuart 1893-1969 ... CAP-1
Earlier sketch in CA 13-16
Moore, Dudley (Stuart John) 1935-2002 ... 167
Obituary ... 205
Moore, E(velyn) Garth 1906-1990 ... CAP-1
Earlier sketch in CA 11-12
Moore, Edmund A(rthur) 1903-1996 ... 5-8R
Moore, Edward
See Muir, Edwin
See also RGEL 2
Moore, Edward C(arter) 1917- ... CANR-5
Earlier sketch in CA 1-4R
Moore, Edward J(ames) 1935- ... 65-68
Moore, Edward M(umford) 1940- ... 57-60
Moore, Elaine 1944- ... 151
See also SATA 86
Moore, Elizabeth
See Atkins, Meg Elizabeth
Moore, Ethel Pauline Perry 1902- ... CAP-1
Earlier sketch in CA 11-12
Moore, Eva 1942- ... 45-48
See also SATA 20, 103
Moore, Everett T(homson) 1909-1988 ... CAP-1
Earlier sketch in CA 11-12
Moore, Fenworth ... CANR-26
Earlier sketches in CAP-2, CA 19-20
Moore, Francis D(aniels) 1913-2001
Obituary ... 200
Brief entry ... 113
Moore, Francis Edward 1898-1978 ... CAP-1
Earlier sketch in CA 9-10
Moore, Frank Harper 1920- ... 5-8R
Moore, Frank Ledlie 1923-1999 ... 5-8R
Obituary ... 185
Moore, Franklin G. 1905- ... 1-4R
Moore, G(ranville) Alexander Jr. 1937- . 21-24R
Moore, G. E. 1873-1958 ... DLB 262
See also TCLC 89
Moore, Gary T(homas) 1945- ... CANR-15
Earlier sketch in CA 85-88
Moore, Gene D. 1919- ... 21-24R
Moore, Geoffrey H(oyt) 1914-2000 .. CANR-41
Obituary ... 189
Earlier sketches in CA 81-84, CANR-19
Moore, Geoffrey Herbert 1920-1999 ... 109
Moore, George Augustus 1852-1933 ... 177
Brief entry ... 104
See also BRW 6
See also DLB 10, 18, 57, 135
See also EWL 3
See also RGEL 2
See also RGSF 2
See also SSC 19
See also TCLC 7
Moore, George Ellis 1916- ... 5-8R
Moore, Gerald 1899-1987 ... CANR-5
Obituary ... 122
Earlier sketch in CA 1-4R
Moore, Glover 1911-2004 ... 107
Obituary ... 233
Moore, Greg 1946- ... 170
Moore, Gwyneth
See Bannister, Patricia Valeria
Moore, (David) Harmon 1911-1982 ... 13-16R
Moore, Harold A. 1913-1981 ... 33-36R
Moore, Harold G(regory, Jr.) 1922- ... 144
Moore, Harris
See Harris, Alf(red)
Moore, Harry Estill 1897-1966 ... CAP-1
Earlier sketch in CA 13-14
Moore, Harry T(hornton) 1908-1981 .. CANR-3
Obituary ... 103
Earlier sketch in CA 5-8R
Moore, Henry (Spencer) 1898-1986 ... 126
Obituary ... 121
Moore, Honor 1945- ... CANR-118
Earlier sketch in CA 85-88
See also CWP
Moore, Ishbel (Lindsay) 1954- ... 211
See also SATA 140
Moore, J(ohn) Preston 1906-1995 ... 65-68
Moore, J. Stuart 1953- ... 147
Moore, J(ohn) William 1928- ... 5-8R
Moore, Jack (William) 1941- ... 112
See also SATA 46
See also SATA-Brief 32
Moore, Jack B(ailey) 1933- ... 33-36R
Moore, Jack L(ynne) 1920- ... 89-92
Moore, James 1928- ... 97-100
Moore, James A. ... 235
Moore, James R(ichard) 1947- ... CANR-22
Earlier sketch in CA 105
Moore, James T. III 1939- ... CANR-31
Earlier sketch in CA 29-32R
Moore, James T(almadge) 1936- ... 139
Moore, James Tice 1945- ... 73-76
Moore, Jane Ann 1931- ... 37-40R
Moore, Janet Gaylord 1905-1992 ... 77-80
See also SATA 18
Moore, Jean S. ... 130
Moore, Jeffrey ... 196
Moore, Jenny 1923-1973
Obituary ... 45-48
Moore, Jerome (Aaron) 1903-1986 ... 81-84
Moore, Jerrold Northrup 1934- ... 104
Moore, Jessie Eleanor 1886-1969(?) ... CAP-1
Earlier sketch in CA 19-20
Moore, Jim 1946- ... SATA 42
Moore, Jimmy
See Moore, James T. III
Moore, John 1729-1802 ... RGEL 2
Moore, John (Cecil) 1907- ... 5-8R
Moore, John A.
See Moore, John Allen
Moore, John A(lexander) 1915- ... CANR-55
Earlier sketches in CA 45-48, CANR-26
Moore, John A(ndrew) 1918-1972
Obituary ... 37-40R
Moore, John Allen 1912-1996 ... 110
Moore, John C(lare) 1933- ... 49-52
Moore, John H. 1935- ... 118
Moore, John Hammond 1924- ... 57-60
Moore, John Hebron 1920- ... 21-24R
Moore, John L. ... 181
Moore, John Michael 1935- ... 104
Moore, John Norton 1937- ... CANR-14
Earlier sketch in CA 37-40R
Moore, John R(obert) 1928- ... CANR-3
Earlier sketch in CA 1-4R
Moore, John Rees 1918- ... 33-36R
Moore, John Richard, Jr. 1925- ... 17-20R
Moore, John Robert 1890-1973 ... CAP-1
Earlier sketch in CA 9-10
Moore, John Travers 1908- ... CANR-3
Earlier sketch in CA 5-8R
See also SATA 12
Moore, Judith 1940- ... 159
Moore, Judith K. 1939- ... 158
Moore, Julia A. (Davis) 1847-1920
Brief entry ... 116
Moore, (Una) Katharine 1898-2001 . CANR-20
Obituary ... 203
Earlier sketch in CA 89-92
Moore, Katherine Davis 1915- ... 13-16R
Moore, Kathryn ... 237
Moore, Kay 1948- ... 130
Moore, Keith L(eon) 1925- ... 69-72
Moore, Kenneth Clark 1943- ... 102
Moore, Kenneth E(ugene) 1930- ... 73-76
Moore, Kenny
See Moore, Kenneth Clark
Moore, L(ittleton) Hugh 1935- ... 49-52
Moore, L. Silas (Jr.) 1936- ... 41-44R
Moore, Lamont 1909- ... SATA-Brief 29
Moore, Lander
See Fensch, Thomas
Moore, Laurie ... 232
Moore, Lenard D(uane) 1958- ... 210
Moore, Lester L(ee) 1924- ... 33-36R
Moore, Lilian 1909-2004 ... CANR-116
Obituary ... 229
Earlier sketches in CA 103, CANR-38
See also CLR 15
See also MAICYA 1, 2
See also SATA 52, 137
See also SATA-Obit 155
Moore, Lillian 1917-1967 ... CANR-2
Earlier sketch in CA 1-4R
Moore, Linda Perigo 1946- ... CANR-28
Earlier sketch in CA 107
Moore, Lisa
See Chater, Elizabeth (Eileen Moore)
Moore, Liz
See Moore, M. Elizabeth
Moore, Lorrie
See Moore, Marie Lorena
See also AMWS 10
See also CLC 39, 45, 68
See also CN 5, 6, 7
See also DLB 234
See also SSFS 19
Moore, Louis 1946- ... CANR-134
Earlier sketch in CA 130
Moore, M. Elizabeth 1959- ... SATA 156
Moore, Madeline (Roberta) 1934- ... 124
Moore, Marcia 1928-1979 ... CANR-13
Earlier sketch in CA 61-64
Moore, Margaret A.
See Moore-Hart, Margaret A.
Moore, Margaret R(umberger) 1903- ... 9-12R
See also SATA 12
Moore, Marianne (Craig)
1887-1972 ... CANR-61
Obituary ... 33-36R
Earlier sketches in CA 1-4R, CANR-3
See also AMW
See also CDALB 1929-1941
See also CLC 1, 2, 4, 8, 10, 13, 19, 47
See also CP 1
See also DA
See also DA3
See also DAB
See also DAC
See also DAM MST, POET
See also DLB 45
See also DLBD 7
See also EWL 3
See also EXPP
See also FL 1:6
See also MAL 5
See also MAWW
See also MTCW 1, 2
See also MTFW 2005
See also PAB
See also PC 4, 49
See also PFS 14, 17
See also RGAL 4
See also SATA 20
See also TUS
See also WLCS
See also WP
Moore, Marie Drury 1926- ... 33-36R
Moore, Marie Lorena 1957- ... CANR-139
Earlier sketches in CA 116, CANR-39, 83
See also Moore, Lorrie
See also CLC 165
See also DLB 234
See also MTFW 2005
Moore, Marna
See Reynolds, (Marjorie) Moira Davison
Moore, Martha 1950- ... 152
Moore, (Georgina) Mary (Galbraith) 1930-
Brief entry ... 112
Moore, Mary Tyler 1936- ... 165
Moore, Maureen (Audrey) 1943- ... 135
Moore, (James) Mavor 1919- ... CANR-83
Earlier sketch in CA 132
See also CD 5, 6
See also DLB 88
Moore, Maxine 1927- ... 73-76
Moore, Michael
See Harris, Herbert
Moore, Michael 1954- ... 166
See also AAYA 53
Moore, Monica
See Wilson, Mona
Moore, Nicholas 1918- ... 69-72
See also CP 1, 2
Moore, P(eter) G(erald) 1928- ... CANR-26
Earlier sketch in CA 45-48
Moore, Pamela 1937-1964 ... 1-4R
Moore, Pat(ricia A.) 1952- ... 144
Moore, Patrick (Alfred Caldwell)
1923- ... CANR-57
Earlier sketches in CA 13-16R, CANR-8
See also SAAS 8
See also SATA 49
See also SATA-Brief 39
See also SFW 4
Moore, Paul, Jr. 1919-2003 ... 89-92
Obituary ... 216
Moore, Paul L. 1917-1976 ... 1-4R
Obituary ... 103
Moore, Peter D(ale) 1942- ... CANR-58
Earlier sketch in CA 127
Moore, Philip N(icholas) 1957- ... 170
Moore, R(obert) Laurence 1940- ... 29-32R
Moore, Ray (S.) 1905(?)-1984
Obituary ... 111
See also SATA-Obit 37
Moore, Ray 1941(?)-1989
Obituary ... 127
Moore, Rayburn Sabatzky 1920- ... CANR-37
Earlier sketches in CA 1-4R, CANR-2, 17
Moore, Raylyn 1928-2005 ... 29-32R
Moore, Raymond Arthur, Jr. 1925- ... 5-8R
Moore, Raymond Cecil 1892-1974 ... 156
Moore, Raymond S. 1915- ... CANR-49
Earlier sketches in CA 29-32R, CANR-21
Moore, Reg(inald Charles Arthur) 1930- ... 104
Moore, Regina
See Dunne, Mary Collins
Moore, Richard (Thomas) 1927- ... CANR-65
Earlier sketches in CA 33-36R, CANR-20
See also DLB 105
Moore, Richard B. 1893(?)-1978
Obituary ... 81-84
Moore, Richard H(arlan) 1945- ... 121
Moore, Richard R. 1934- ... 105
Moore, Robert
See Williams, Robert Moore
Moore, Robert (Samuel) 1936- ... CANR-11
Earlier sketch in CA 25-28R
Moore, Robert E(verett) 1914- ... 57-60
Moore, Robert Etheridge 1919- ... 61-64
Moore, Robert Hamilton 1913-1984
Obituary ... 114
Moore, Robert L(owell), Jr. 1925- ... 13-16R
See also AITN 1
Moore, Robin
See Moore, Robert L(owell), Jr.
Moore, Robin 1950- ... 134
Moore, Rogan H. 1955- ... 203
Moore, Roger George 1927- ... 109
Moore, Rosalie (Gertrude)
1910-2001 ... CANR-3
Earlier sketch in CA 5-8R
See also Brown, Rosalie
Moore, Roy L. 1947- ... CANR-119
Earlier sketch in CA 147
Moore, Russell Franklin 1920- ... CANR-6
Earlier sketch in CA 9-12R
Moore, Ruth (Ellen) 1908-1989 ... CANR-6
Obituary ... 127
Earlier sketch in CA 1-4R
See also SATA 23
Moore, Ruth Nulton 1923- ... CANR-15
Earlier sketch in CA 81-84
See also SATA 38
Moore, S(arah) E. ... CANR-2
Earlier sketch in CA 49-52
See also SATA 23
Moore, Sally Falk 1924- ... CANR-6
Earlier sketch in CA 57-60
Moore, Sam 1931(?)- ... 171
Moore, Samuel Taylor 1893-1974
Obituary ... 53-56
Moore, Sandra Crockett 1945- ... 139
Moore, Sebastian 1917- ... 21-24R
Moore, Sonia 1902-1995 ... CANR-2
Earlier sketch in CA 45-48
Moore, Steven 1951- ... 123
Moore, Susanna 1948- ... CANR-52
Earlier sketch in CA 109
Moore, T. Inglis
See Moore, Tom Inglis
Moore, T. M. 1949- ... 208
Moore, T(homas) Sturge 1870-1944
Brief entry ... 118
See also DLB 19
See also RGEL 2
Moore, Tara 1950- ... CANR-38
Earlier sketch in CA 116
See also SATA 61
Moore, Terry 1929- ... 231
Moore, Thomas 1779-1852 ... DLB 96, 144
See also RGEL 2
Moore, Thomas (William) 1940- ... CANR-123
Earlier sketches in CA 132, CANR-57
Moore, Thomas Gale 1930- ... CANR-12
Earlier sketch in CA 29-32R
Moore, Thomas S(cott) 1945- ... 160

Moore, Tim 1964- 233
Moore, Timothy J. 1959- 207
Moore, Tom 1950- CANR-18
Earlier sketch in CA 101
Moore, Tom Inglis 1901-1978(?) 21-24R
Obituary 135
See also CP 1
Moore, Trevor Wyatt 1924- CANR-12
Earlier sketch in CA 29-32R
Moore, Tui De Roy 1953- 107
Moore, Vardine (Russell) 1906-1993 ..... 41-44R
Obituary 198
Moore, Virginia Dryden 1911- 17-20R
Moore, W(illiam) Glenn 1925- 49-52
Moore, Walter (John) 1918-2001 ...... CANR-86
Obituary 203
Earlier sketch in CA 131
Moore, Walter Lane 1905-1978 .... CAP-1
Earlier sketch in CA 19-20
Moore, Ward 1903-1978 .... CAP-2
Obituary 113
Earlier sketch in CA 29-32
See also DLB 8
See also SFW 4
Moore, Warner O(land),, Jr. 1942-1992(?) .. 167
Moore, Warren (M., Jr.) 1923- 25-28R
Moore, Wilbert E(llis) 1914-1987 .... CANR-5
Earlier sketch in CA 1-4R
Moore, Wilfred George 1907- CANR-4
Earlier sketch in CA 9-12R
Moore, William Howard 1942- 73-76
Moore, William L(eonard, Jr.) 1943- 93-96
Moore, Yvette 1958- 135
See also JRDA
See also SATA 69, 70, 154
Moore-Colyer, Richard 1945- 141
Moore-Gilbert, Bart 1952- 158
Moore-Hart, Margaret A. 1946- 151
Moorehead, Agnes 1906-1974
Obituary 49-52
Moorehead, Alan (McCrae)
1910-1983 .... CANR-6
Obituary 110
Earlier sketch in CA 5-8R
See also DLB 204
Moorehead, Caroline 1944- CANR-122
Earlier sketches in CA 101, CANR-18, 39
Moore-Rinvolucri, Mina Josephine 1902- ... 107
Moores, Dick
See Moores, Richard (Arnold)
Moores, Richard (Arnold) 1909-1986 69-72
Obituary 119
See also SATA-Obit 48
Moore-Sitterly, Charlotte Emma
See Moore, Charlotte E(mma)
Moorey, P(eter) R(oger) S(tuart) 1937-2004 . 132
Obituary 234
Moorey, Roger
See Moorey, P(eter) R(oger) S(tuart)
Moorhead, Diana 1940- 105
Moorhead, Hugh S. 1922- 130
Moorhead, James H(owell) 1947- 124
Moorhead, John (Anthony) 1948- 142
Moorhead, Max L(eon) 1914-1981 .... 21-24R
Obituary 135
Moorhouse, Charles Edmund 1911- 108
Moorhouse, Frank 1938- CANR-92
Earlier sketch in CA 118
See also CN 3, 4, 5, 6, 7
See also DLB 289
See also RGSF 2
See also SSC 40
Moorhouse, Geoffrey 1931- CANR-99
Earlier sketches in CA 25-28R, CANR-49
See also DLB 204
Moorhouse, Hilda Vansittart CAP-1
Earlier sketch in CA 11-12
Moorman, Charles (Wickliffe) 1925-
Brief entry 114
Moorman, John Richard Humpidge
1905-1989 .... CANR-2
Earlier sketch in CA 1-4R
Moorman, Mary C(aroline Trevelyan)
1905-1994 .... DLB 155
Moorshead, Henry
See Pine, Leslie Gilbert
Moorsom, Sasha 1931- CANR-14
Earlier sketch in CA 69-72
Moorsteen, Richard H. 1926(?)-1975
Obituary 57-60
Moorti, Sujata 213
Moos, Malcolm C(harles) 1916-1982 .... 37-40R
Obituary 105
Moos, Rudolf H. 1934- CANR-1
Earlier sketch in CA 49-52
Moosa, Matti 1924- CANR-55
Earlier sketch in CA 127
Moose, Ruth 1938- CANR-118
Earlier sketch in CA 101
Mooser, Stephen 1941- CANR-15
Earlier sketch in CA 89-92
See also SATA 28, 75
Moote, A(lanson) Lloyd 1931- 33-36R
Mootoo, Shani 1957(?)- 174
Moquin, Wayne(-Francis) 1930- 33-36R
Mora, Carl J(ose) 1936- 109
Mora, Francisco X(avier) 1952- .... SATA 90
Mora, George 1923- CANR-1
Earlier sketch in CA 45-48
Mora, Pat(ricia) 1942- CANR-112
Earlier sketches in CA 129, CANR-57, 81
See also AMWS 13
See also CLR 58
See also DAM MULT
See also DLB 209
See also HLC 2
See also HW 1, 2
See also LLW
See also MAICYA 2
See also MTFW 2005
See also SATA 92, 134
Morabito, Rocco 1920- 134
Morace, Robert A(nthony) 1947- 113
Morad, Gowhar
See Sa'edi, Gholam-Hossein
Moraes, Dom(inic Frank) 1938-2004 .... 25-28R
Obituary 228
See also CP 1, 2, 3, 4, 5, 6, 7
See also RGEL 2
Moraes, Frank Robert 1907-1974 .... CAP-1
Obituary 49-52
Earlier sketch in CA 13-14
Moraes, (Marcus) Vinicius (Cruz) de (Mello)
1913-1980
Obituary 101
See also DLB 307
Moraga, Cherrie 1952- CANR-66
Earlier sketch in CA 131
See also CLC 126
See also DAM MULT
See also DC 22
See also DLB 82, 249
See also FW
See also GLL 1
See also HW 1, 2
See also LLW
Morain, Lloyd L. 1917- 69-72
Morais, Vamberto 1921- 69-72
Moral, Tony Lee 1971- 236
Morales, Alejandro 1944- CANR-90
Earlier sketch in CA 131
See also DLB 82
See also HW 1
See also LLW
See also RGAL 4
See also SSFS 19
Morales, Angel Luis 1919- 49-52
See also HW 1
Morales, Edmundo 1943- CANR-87
Earlier sketch in CA 153
Morales, Gregorio 1952- 217
Morales, Jorge Luis 1930(?)- 153
See also HW 1
Morales, Mario Roberto 1947- 178
See also DLB 145
Morales, Rafael 1919- 176
See also DLB 108
See also HW 2
Morales, Rebecca (Hope) 147
Morales, Waltraud Queiser 1947- 144
Morales, Yuyi .... SATA 154
Morales Carrion, Arturo 1914(?)-1989 131
Obituary 129
See also HW 1
Moramarco, Fred Stephen 1938- 57-60
Moran, Barbara B. 1944- 124
Moran, Charles 1936- 144
Moran, Charles McMoran Wilson
See Wilson, Charles McMoran
Moran, Daniel
See Vardeman, Robert E(dward)
Moran, Daniel Keys 1962- 206
Moran, Emilio F(ederico) 1946- 117
Moran, Gabriel 1935- CANR-107
Earlier sketches in CA 53-56, CANR-4
Moran, George 1942- 115
Moran, Hugh Anderson 1881-1977
Obituary 73-76
Moran, J. L.
See Whitaker, Rod(ney)
Moran, James P. 1958- 146
Moran, James S(terling) 1909-1999 .. CANR-12
Obituary 187
Earlier sketch in CA 9-12R
Moran, Jeffrey P. 1966- 214
Moran, Jim
See Moran, James S(terling)
Moran, John 1930- 45-48
Moran, John C(harles) 1942- CANR-27
Earlier sketch in CA 110
Moran (Kegley), Lindsay 239
Moran, Mary Hurley 1947- CANR-119
Earlier sketch in CA 148
Moran, Maya 1934- 175
Moran, Michael 1946- 195
Moran, Michael G. 1947- 138
Moran, Mike
See Ard, William (Thomas)
Moran, Patrick Alfred Pierce 1917- 9-12R
Moran, Richard (Jerome) 1942- 121
Moran, Ronald (Wesson, Jr.) 1936- 37-40R
Moran, Thomas 224
Moran, Tom 1943- CANR-29
Earlier sketch in CA 111
See also SATA 60
Moran, Victoria 1950- 160
Moran, William 1934- 224
Moran, William E(dward), Jr. 1916- 13-16R
Morand, Paul 1888-1976 184
Obituary 69-72
See also CLC 41
See also DLB 65
See also EWL 3
See also SSC 22
Morano, Donald V(ictor) 1934- 45-48
Morante, Elsa 1918-1985 .... CANR-35
Obituary 117
Earlier sketch in CA 85-88
See also CLC 8, 47
See also DLB 177
See also EWL 3
See also MTCW 1, 2
See also MTFW 2005
See also RGWL 2, 3
See also WLIT 7
Morantz, Regina Markell
See Morantz-Sanchez, Regina (Ann) Markell
Morantz-Sanchez, Regina (Ann) Markell
1943- 124
Moranville, Sharelle Byars 227
See also SATA 152
Morash, Christopher 1963- 151
Morasky, Robert Louis 1940- 105
Morata, Olympia Fulvia 1526-1555 ... DLB 179
Moraud, Marcel I(an) 1917- 53-56
Moravec, Hans P(eter) 1948- 142
Moravec, Ivo 1948- 168
Moravia, Alberto
See Pincherle, Alberto
See also CLC 2, 7, 11, 27, 46
See also DLB 177
See also EW 12
See also EWL 3
See also MTCW 2
See also RGSF 2
See also RGWL 2, 3
See also SSC 26
See also WLIT 7
Morawetz, Thomas H(ubert) 1942- 101
Morawski, Stefan T(adeusz) 1921- 81-84
Moray, Helga 89-92
Moray, Neville (Peter) 1935- 29-32R
Moray Williams, Ursula 1911- CANR-121
Earlier sketches in CA 111, CANR-26, 88
See also Williams, Ursula Moray
See also CWRI 5
See also MAICYA 1, 2
See also SAAS 9
See also SATA 73, 142
Morch, Dea Trier 1941-2001 202
See also Trier Morch, Dea
Morck, Irene 181
Morck, Paul
See Roelvaag, O(le) E(dvart)
Morcom, John Brian 1925- 5-8R
Mordaunt, Elinor
See Wiehe, Evelyn May Clowes
Mordaunt, Walter J(ulius) de
See De Mordaunt, Walter J(ulius)
Mordden, Ethan (Christopher)
1947- CANR-114
Earlier sketches in CA 73-76, CANR-65
Mordecai, Carolyn 1936- 176
Mordecai, Pamela (Claire) 1942- 134
Mordechai, Ben
See Gerber, Israel J(oshua)
Mordell, Louis (Joel) 1888-1972 170
Mordock, John B. 1938- 61-64
Mordovtsev, Daniil Lukich
1830-1905 .... DLB 238
Mordvinoff, Nicolas 1911-1973 73-76
Obituary 41-44R
See also SATA 17
More, Caroline
See Cone, Molly (Lamken) and
Strachan, Margaret Pitcairn
More, Daphne 1929- 65-68
More, Hannah 1745-1833 . DLB 107, 109, 116,
158
See also RGEL 2
More, Harry W(illiam) 1929- CANR-44
Earlier sketches in CA 53-56, CANR-4, 20
More, Henry 1614-1687 .... DLB 126, 252
More, Jasper 1907-1987 .... CAP-1
Obituary 124
Earlier sketch in CA 9-10
More, Julian 1928- CANR-137
Earlier sketch in CA 144
More, Kenneth 1914-1982
Obituary 107
More, Sir Thomas 1478(?)-1535 .... BRWC 1
See also BRWS 7
See also DLB 136, 281
See also LMFS 1
See also RGEL 2
See also TEA
Moreas, Jean
See Papadiamantopoulos, Johannes
See also GFL 1789 to the Present
See also TCLC 18
Moreau, Daniel 1949- 125
Moreau, David Merlin 1927- 93-96
Moreau, Emil
See Wood, Edward D(avis), Jr.
Moreau, John Adam 1938- 37-40R
Moreau, Jules Laurence 1917-1971 .... 1-4R
Obituary 103
Moreau, Marcel 1933- 190
Moreau, Reginald E(rnest) 1897-1970
Obituary 104
Morecambe, Eric 1926-1984
Obituary 112
Moreh, Shmuel 1932- 141
Morehead, Albert H(odges) 1909-1966 . CAP-1
Earlier sketch in CA 13-14
Morehead, James B. 1916- 166
Morehead, Joe
See Morehead, Joseph H(yde), Jr.
Morehead, Joseph H(yde), Jr. 1931- .. CANR-27
Earlier sketches in CA 57-60, CANR-6
Morehouse, Clifford P(helps) 1904-1977 . 9-12R
Obituary 134
Morehouse, Laurence E(nglemohr)
1913-1995 .... CANR-4
Earlier sketch in CA 9-12R
Morehouse, Thomas A(lvin) 1937- 124
Morehouse, Ward 1899(?)-1966
Obituary 25-28R
Morejon, Nancy
See Morejon, Nancy
See also DLB 283
Morejon, Nancy 1944- 179
Morel, Dighton
See Warner, Kenneth (Lewis)
Morel, Nina
See Markowa, Nina Alexandrovna
Moreland, Lois B. 45-48
Moreland, Richard C. 1953- 135
Morell, David 1939- 110
Morell, James B. 1956- 144
Morell, Virginia 1949- CANR-109
Earlier sketch in CA 156
Morella, Joe
See Morella, Joseph (James)
Morella, Joseph (James) 1949- CANR-48
Earlier sketch in CA 104
Morellet, Andre 1727-1819 .... DLB 314
Morello, Karen Berger 1949- 126
Moremen, Grace E(llen Partin) 1930- . CANR-1
Earlier sketch in CA 45-48
Moren, Halldis
See Vesaas, Halldis Moren
Moren, Sally M(oore) 1947- 97-100
Morency, Pierre 1942- 204
See also DLB 60
Moreno, Antonio Elosequi 1918- 33-36R
Moreno, Baldomero Fernandez
See Fernandez Moreno, Baldomero
Moreno, Carlos Martinez
See Martinez Moreno, Carlos
Moreno, Cesar Fernandez
See Fernandez Moreno, Cesar
Moreno, Dorinda 1939- 176
See also DLB 122
See also HW 2
Moreno, Francisco Jose 1934- 29-32R
Moreno, Jacob L. 1892-1974 .... CAP-2
Obituary 49-52
Earlier sketch in CA 19-20
Moreno, Jonathan D. 1952- 201
Moreno, Jose A. 1928- 25-28R
Moreno, Martin
See Swartz, Harry (Felix)
Moreno, Pedro R. 1947- 69-72
Moreno, Vincent
See Campert, Remco Wouter
Moreno, Virginia 1935- .... CP 1
Moreno-Duran, Rafael Humberto
1946- .... EWL 3
Morentz, Ethel Irene 29-32R
Morentz, Pat
See Morentz, Ethel Irene
Morenus, Constance Gay 1895(?)-1985
Obituary 117
Moreton, Andrew Esq.
See Defoe, Daniel
Moreton, John
See Cohen, Morton N(orton)
Moreton, N. Edwina 1950- 135
Moretti, Marino 1885(?)-1979
Obituary 89-92
See also DLB 114, 264
Morewedge, Parviz 1934- 93-96
Morey, Ann-Janine 1951- 144
Morey, Charles
See Fletcher, Helen Jill
Morey, James H. 1961- 215
Morey, Robert A(lbert) 1946- CANR-32
Earlier sketch in CA 113
Morey, Roy D. 1937- 17-20R
Morey, Walt(er Nelson) 1907-1992 .. CANR-31
Obituary 136
Earlier sketch in CA 29-32R
See also CWRI 5
See also JRDA
See also MAICYA 1, 2
See also SAAS 9
See also SATA 3, 51
See also SATA-Obit 70
Morey-Gaines, Ann-Janine
See Morey, Ann-Janine
Morford, Mark P(ercy) O(wen) 1929-
Brief entry 111
Morgan, Al(bert Edward) 1920- CANR-1
Earlier sketch in CA 45-48
Morgan, Alfred P(owell) 1889-1972 107
See also SATA 33
Morgan, Alison (Mary) 1930- CANR-92
Earlier sketches in CA 49-52, CANR-1, 18, 51
See also CWRI 5
See also SATA 30, 85
Morgan, Alison 1959- 137
Morgan, Alyssa
See Delatush, Edith G.
Morgan, Angela
See Paine, Lauran (Bosworth)
Morgan, Ann Lee 1941- 125
Morgan, Anne 1954- 192
See also SATA 121
Morgan, Anne Hodges 1940- 117
Morgan, Arlene
See Paine, Lauran (Bosworth)
Morgan, Arthur Ernest 1878-1975 ...... CANR-3
Obituary 61-64
Earlier sketch in CA 5-8R
Morgan, Austen 1949- 130
Morgan, B(ayard) Q(uincy) 1883-1967 .. CAP-1
Earlier sketch in CA 11-12

Cumulative Index 411 **Morlan**

Morgan, Bailey
See Brewer, Gil
Morgan, Barton 1889- CAP-1
Earlier sketch in CA 9-10
Morgan, Bernice B. 170
Morgan, Berry 1919-2002 49-52
Obituary 208
See also CLC 6
See also DLB 6
Morgan, Bill 1949- CANR-30
Earlier sketch in CA 110
Morgan, Brian 1919- 5-8R
Morgan, Bryan S(tanford) 1923-1976 . CANR-9
Earlier sketch in CA 5-8R
Morgan, By
See Morgan, Byron
Morgan, Byron 1921- 165
Morgan, Cary
See Cutler, Roland
Morgan, Charles, Jr. 1930- CANR-13
Earlier sketch in CA 17-20R
Morgan, Charles (Landridge) 1894-1958 185
See also DLB 34, 100
See also RGEL 2
Morgan, Charles H(ill) 1902-1984 .... 37-40R
Obituary 112
Morgan, Charlotte (G.) 1946- 177
Morgan, Chester A(lan) 1914-1980 .... 17-20R
Morgan, Christine 1904-1996 166
Morgan, Christopher 1952- CANR-48
Earlier sketch in CA 105
Morgan, Claire
See Highsmith, (Mary) Patricia
See also GLL 1
Morgan, Clifford T(homas)
1915-1976 .... CANR-4
Obituary 65-68
Earlier sketch in CA 1-4R
Morgan, Dale L. 1914-1971
Obituary 104
Morgan, Dan 1925- CANR-14
Earlier sketch in CA 37-40R
Morgan, Dan 1937- 143
Morgan, Daniel C(roxton), Jr. 1931- 17-20R
Morgan, Dareion
See Walz, Marjorie A.
Morgan, Darold H. 1924- 21-24R
Morgan, David (Rhys) 1937- CANR-92
Earlier sketches in CA 45-48, CANR-45
Morgan, David 1957- 198
Morgan, David 1960- 203
Morgan, David P(age) 1927- 123
Brief entry 118
Morgan, David T(aft, Jr.) 1937- 69-72
Morgan, Dewi (Lewis) 1916-1993 ...... CANR-1
Earlier sketch in CA 1-4R
Morgan, Donald G(rant) 1911-1985 ...... 17-20R
Morgan, Donn F(arley) 1943- 113
Morgan, Douglas
See Macdonald, James D.
Morgan, Edmund S(ears) 1916- CANR-134
Earlier sketches in CA 9-12R, CANR-4, 49
See also DLB 17
Morgan, Edward James Ranembe 1900-1978
Obituary 108
Morgan, Edward P(addock) 1910-1993 . CAP-1
Obituary 140
Earlier sketch in CA 19-20
Morgan, Edwin (George) 1920- CANR-90
Earlier sketches in CA 5-8R, CANR-3, 43
See also BRWS 9
See also CLC 31
See also CP 1, 2, 3, 4, 5, 6, 7
See also DLB 27
Morgan, Elaine (Neville) 1920- CANR-73
Earlier sketch in CA 41-44R
Morgan, Elizabeth 1947- 108
Interview in CA-108
Morgan, Elizabeth Anne 1940- .... CSW
Morgan, Elizabeth Seydel 1939- 233
Morgan, Ellen
See Bumstead, Kathleen Mary
Morgan, Emanuel
See Bynner, Witter
Morgan, Fidelis 1952- CANR-105
Earlier sketches in CA 127, CANR-57
Morgan, Frank
See Paine, Lauran (Bosworth)
Morgan, Fred Bruce, Jr. 1919-1975 65-68
Obituary 61-64
Morgan, Fred Troy 1926- 89-92
Morgan, (George) Frederick
1922-2004 .... CANR-144
Obituary 224
Earlier sketches in CA 17-20R, CANR-21
See also CLC 23
See also CP 2, 3, 4, 5, 6, 7
Morgan, G. J.
See Rowland, D(onald) S(ydney)
Morgan, Geoffrey 1916- 21-24R
See also SATA 46
Morgan, Gerald 1925- 41-44R
Morgan, Glebe
See Rowland, D(onald) S(ydney)
Morgan, Glenn G(uy) 1926- 9-12R
Morgan, Gordon D. 1931- 180
Morgan, Gwen 101
Morgan, Gwyneth
See Beal, Gwyneth
Morgan, H(oward) Wayne 1934- CANR-40
Earlier sketches in CA 5-8R, CANR-2, 18
Morgan, Hal
See Morgan, Henry A.
Morgan, Harriet
See Mencken, H(enry) L(ouis)
Morgan, Harry 1926- 175
Morgan, Helen (Gertrude Louise)
1921-1990 57-60
See also CWRI 5
See also SATA 29
Morgan, Henry
See von Ost, Henry Lerner
Morgan, Henry A. 1954- 112
Morgan, Hilda Campbell 1892-1985
Obituary 118
Morgan, Irvonwy 1907-1982
Obituary 107
Morgan, J(ill) M(eredith) 1946- 137
Morgan, James 1944- 189
Morgan, James N(ewton) 1918- 21-24R
Morgan, Jane
See Cooper, James Fenimore and
Franklin, Jane (Morgan) and
Moren, Sally M(oore)
Morgan, Janet 1945- 65-68
See also CLC 39
Morgan, Jean (Werner) 1922- 102
Morgan, Jeanne
See Zarucchi, Jeanne Morgan
Morgan, (Walter) Jefferson 1940- CANR-29
Earlier sketches in CA 73-76, CANR-12
Morgan, Jim 1950- 45-48
Morgan(-Murray), Joan 221
Morgan, Joan 1905-2004 .... 5-8R
Obituary 229
Morgan, Joe 1943- 186
Morgan, Joe Warner 1912- 9-12R
Morgan, John
See Paine, Lauran (Bosworth)
Morgan, John A(ndrew), Jr. 1935- 49-52
Morgan, John Medford
See Fox, G(ardner) F(rancis)
Morgan, John Pierpont, Jr.
1867-1943 .... DLB 140
Morgan, John Pierpont 1837-1913 193
See also DLB 140
Morgan, John S. 1921- 13-16R
Morgan, Joseph G. 1953- 167
Morgan, Joy Elmer 1889-1986
Obituary 119
Morgan, Judith A(dams) 1939- 49-52
Morgan, Kathryn L. 117
Morgan, Kay Summersby 1909-1975
Obituary 53-56
Morgan, Kenneth Owen 1934- CANR-23
Earlier sketches in CA 13-16R, CANR-7
Morgan, Kenneth R(emsen) 1916- 13-16R
Morgan, Lady 1776(?)-1859 .... DLB 116, 158
See also RGEL 2
Morgan, Lael 1936- CANR-5
Earlier sketch in CA 53-56
Morgan, Lenore H. 1908-1976 .... CAP-2
Earlier sketch in CA 33-36
See also SATA 8
Morgan, Lorrie (Loretta Lynn) 1959- 170
Morgan, Louise 9-12R
Morgan, Lucy 1940- 108
Morgan, M(argaret) Ruth 1942(?)-1983
Obituary 109
Morgan, Marabel 1937- CANR-2
Earlier sketch in CA 49-52
See also AITN 1
Morgan, Marion (Nora Eluned)
1942- CANR-46
Earlier sketch in CA 120
Morgan, Marjorie
See Chibnall, Marjorie (McCallum)
Morgan, Mark
See Overholser, Wayne D.
Morgan, Marlo 1936- 173
Morgan, Mary 1943- 132
Morgan, Mary 1957- 186
See also SATA 81, 114
Morgan, McKayla
See Basile, Gloria Vitanza
Morgan, Memo
See Avallone, Michael (Angelo, Jr.)
Morgan, Meredith
See Morgan, J(ill) M(eredith)
Morgan, Michael Croke 1911- 93-96
Morgan, Michaela
See Basile, Gloria Vitanza
Morgan, Murray 1916-2000 107
Morgan, Neil 1924- CANR-2
Earlier sketch in CA 5-8R
Morgan, Nicholas
See Morgan, Thomas Bruce
Morgan, Nicholas H. 1953- 144
Morgan, Nicola 1961- 237
See also SATA 161
Morgan, Nina 1953- 180
See also SATA 110
Morgan, Patricia 1944- 89-92
Morgan, Patrick M. 1940- 37-40R
Morgan, Paul 1928- 61-64
Morgan, (Colin) Pete(r) 1939- CANR-92
Earlier sketch in CA 133
See also CP 2, 3, 4, 5, 6, 7
Morgan, Peter F(rederick) 1930- 113
Morgan, Philip D. 1949- 176
Morgan, Philippa
See Gooden, Philip
Morgan, Pierr 1952- 145
See also SATA 77, 122
Morgan, Raleigh, Jr. 1916-1998 .... 41-44R
Morgan, Rebecca
See Forrest, Richard (Stockton)
Morgan, Rhodri 1939- 162
Morgan, Richard E(rnest) 1937- CANR-15
Earlier sketch in CA 41-44R
Morgan, Richard K. 1965- 224
Morgan, Robert
See Turner, Robert (Harry)
Morgan, Robert 1921-1994 .... CANR-42
Earlier sketches in CA 103, CANR-20
See also CP 1, 2
Morgan, Robert (R.) 1944- 201
Earlier sketches in CA 33-36R, CANR-21, 89, 144
Autobiographical Essay in 201
See also CAAS 20
See also CP 7
See also CSW
See also DLB 120, 292
Morgan, Robert C. 1943- 148
Morgan, Roberta 1953- CANR-15
Earlier sketch in CA 93-96
Morgan, Robin (Evonne) 1941- CANR-68
Earlier sketches in CA 69-72, CANR-29
See also CLC 2
See also FW
See also GLL 2
See also MTCW 1
See also SATA 80
Morgan, Roger P(earce) 1932- CANR-12
Earlier sketch in CA 17-20R
Morgan, Rosemarie (Anne Louise) CANR-86
Earlier sketch in CA 131
Morgan, Roxanne
See Gentle, Mary
Morgan, Roy A(mos) 1916- 41-44R
Morgan, Ruth P. 1934- 37-40R
Morgan, Sally (Jane) 1951- 134
Morgan, Sarah (Williams) 1901- CAP-1
Earlier sketch in CA 9-10
Morgan, Sarah (Nicola) 1959- 136
See also SATA 68
Morgan, Scott
See Kuttner, Henry
Morgan, Seth 1949(?)-1990 185
Obituary 132
See also CLC 65
Morgan, Sharon A(ntonia) 1951- 61-64
Morgan, Shirley
See Kiepper, Shirley Morgan
See also SATA 10
Morgan, Speer 1946- CANR-112
Earlier sketch in CA 97-100
Morgan, Stacy T(owle) 1959- 171
See also SATA 104
Morgan, Stanley 1929- 69-72
Morgan, Steven Michael 1942- 115
Morgan, Stevie
See Davies, Nicola
Morgan, Susan 1943- 137
Morgan, Ted 1932- CANR-3
See also CAAS 4
Morgan, (Joseph) Theodore 1910- 17-20R
See also CAAS 3
Morgan, Thomas (Bruce) 1885(?)-1972
Obituary 37-40R
Morgan, Thomas Bruce 1926- 13-16R
Morgan, Thomas Hunt 1866-1945 156
Morgan, Tom 1942- 108
See also SATA 42
Morgan, Valerie
See Paine, Lauran (Bosworth)
Morgan, Virginia
See Mundis, Hester
Morgan, Wendy
See Staub, Wendy Corsi
Morgan, Wesley
See Bennett, Isadora
Morgan, William 1944- 109
Morgan, William (Frend) de
See De Morgan, William (Frend)
Morgan-Grenville, Gerard (Wyndham)
1931- 57-60
Morganstern, Anne McGee 1936- 195
Morgan-Vanroyen, Mary
See Morgan, Mary
Morgan-Witts, Max 1931- CANR-40
Earlier sketch in CA 29-32R
Morgello, Clemente Frank 1923- 103
Morgenroth, Barbara
Brief entry 117
See also SATA-Brief 36
Morgenroth, Kate 1972- 194
Morgenstein, Gary 1952- 116
Morgenstern, Christian (Otto Josef Wolfgang)
1871-1914 191
Brief entry 105
See also EWL 3
See also TCLC 8
Morgenstern, Dan (Michael) 1929- 127
Brief entry 111
Morgenstern, Julian 1881-1976 .... CAP-1
Obituary 89-92
Earlier sketch in CA 19-20
Morgenstern, Oskar 1902-1977 .... CANR-5
Obituary 73-76
Earlier sketch in CA 9-12R
Morgenstern, S.
See Goldman, William (W.)
Morgenstern, Soma 1891(?)-1976
Obituary 65-68
Morgenstern, Susie Hoch 1945- 202
See also SATA 133
Morgenthau, Hans Joachim
1904-1980 .... CANR-82
Obituary 101
Earlier sketch in CA 9-12R
Morgenthau, Henry, Jr. 1904-1967
Obituary 116
Morghen, Raffaello 1896-1983
Obituary 109
Morgner, Irmtraud 1933-1990 184
See also DLB 75
Morgulas, Jerrold 1934- CANR-13
Earlier sketch in CA 21-24R
Morhaim, Victoria Kelrich 1937- 1-4R
Morhof, Daniel Georg 1639-1691 .... DLB 164
Mori, Hana 1909-1990(?) .... SATA 88
Mori, Kyoko 1957- CANR-102
Earlier sketch in CA 153
See also AAYA 25
See also BYA 13
See also CLR 64
See also DLB 312
See also LATS 1:2
See also MAICYA 2
See also MAICYAS 1
See also MTFW 2005
See also NFS 15
See also SAAS 26
See also SATA 122
See also SATA-Essay 126
See also WYAS 1
See also YAW
Mori, Kyozo 1907(?)-1984
Obituary 112
Mori, Rintaro
Brief entry 110
See also Mori Ogai
Mori, Toshio 1910-1980
Brief entry 116
See also DLB 312
See also RGSF 2
See also SSC 83
Moriarty, Alice Marie Ewell 1917- 21-24R
Moriarty, Christopher 1936- 81-84
Moriarty, Florence Jarman 104
Moriarty, Frederick Leo 1913- CANR-2
Earlier sketch in CA 5-8R
Moriarty, Jaclyn 238
See also SATA 162
Moriarty, Liane 238
Moriarty, Marilyn F(rances) 1953- 168
Moriarty, Michael 1941- 163
Moriarty, Tim 1923- 61-64
Moriarty, William J. 1930- .... SATA 127
Morice, Anne
See Shaw, Felicity
Morice, Dave 1946- CANR-61
Earlier sketch in CA 109
See also SATA 93
Morich, Stanton
See Griffith(-Jones), George (Chetwynd)
Morick, Harold 1933- 25-28R
Moricz, Zsigmond 1879-1942 165
See also DLB 215
See also EWL 3
See also TCLC 33
Morier, James Justinian 1782(?)-1849 .. DLB 116
Morike, Eduard (Friedrich)
1804-1875 .... DLB 133
See also RGWL 2, 3
Morillas, Frances M. Lopez
See Lopez-Morillas, Frances M.
Morillo, Stephen (Reeder) 1958- 156
Morimoto, Anri 1956- 154
Morimoto, Junko 1932- .... MAICYA 2
Morin, Claire
See Dore, Claire (Morin)
Morin, Edgar 1921- 107
Morin, Isobel V. 1928- 180
See also SATA 110
Morin, Paul 1889-1963 184
See also DLB 92
Morin, Relman George 1907-1973 ..... CANR-4
Obituary 41-44R
Earlier sketch in CA 1-4R
Morin, William J(ames) 1939- CANR-105
Earlier sketch in CA 111
Morine, Hoder
See Conroy, John Wesley
Moring, John (R.) 1946-2002 233
Moring, Marcel 1957- 191
Morini, Simona 1932- 110
Morinis, Alan 1949- 143
Mori Ogai 1862-1922 164
See also Ogai
See also DLB 180
See also EWL 3
See also RGWL 3
See also TCLC 14
See also TWA
Morisey, A. Alexander 1913-1979
Obituary 89-92
Morison, David Lindsay 1920- 13-16R
Morison, Richard 1514(?)-1556 .... DLB 136
Morison, Samuel Eliot 1887-1976 ...... CANR-4
Obituary 65-68
Earlier sketch in CA 1-4R
See also AMWS 1
See also DLB 17
Morison, Stanley (Arthur) 1889-1967 . DLB 201
Morisseau, James J(oseph) 1929- 41-44R
Morita, James R. 1931- 103
Morita, Yuzo 1940- CANR-1
Earlier sketch in CA 45-48
Moritz, A(lbert) F(rank) 1947- 110
Moritz, Charles Fredric 1917- 118
Moritz, Karl Philipp 1756-1793 .... DLB 94
Moritz, Theresa
See Moritz, Theresa Anne
Moritz, Theresa Anne 1948- 127
Morken, Lucinda Oakland 1906-1997 61-64
Morkovin, Bela V.
See Morkovin, Boris V(ladimir)
Morkovin, Boris V(ladimir) 1882-1968 .. CAP-1
Earlier sketch in CA 19-20
Morlan, A(rlette) R(enee)
See Morlan, A(rlette) R(enee)
See also HGG
Morlan, A(rlette) R(enee) 1958- 187
See also Morlan, A(rlette) R(enee)

Morlan, George K(olmer) 1904-1993 ... 29-32R
Morlan, John E(dmund) 1930- ... 9-12R
Morlan, Robert L(oren) 1920-1985 ... 17-20R
Obituary ... 118
Morland, Dick
See Hill, Reginald (Charles)
Morland, Howard 1942- ... 107
Morland, (John) Kenneth 1916- ... 41-44R
Morland, Nigel 1905-1986 ... CANR-63
Obituary ... 119
Earlier sketch in CA 53-56
See also CMW 4
Morland, Peter Henry
See Faust, Frederick (Schiller)
Morle, Albert Henry George 1919- ... 5-8R
Morley, Christopher (Darlington)
1890-1957 ... 213
Brief entry ... 112
See also DLB 9
See also MAL 5
See also RGAL 4
See also TCLC 87
Morley, David 1923- ... 108
Morley, Don 1937- ... 108
Morley, Felix M(uskett) 1894-1982 ... 166
Obituary ... 106
Morley, Frank V(igor) 1899-1980 ... 105
Obituary ... 102
Morley, (John) Geoffrey (Nicholson) 1905-1983
Obituary ... 109
Morley (Wolpe), Hilda 1919(?)-1998 ... 147
Obituary ... 167
Morley, Hugh 1908(?)-1978
Obituary ... 77-80
Morley, James William 1921- ... CANR-100
Earlier sketch in CA 13-16R
Morley, John 1838-1923 ... 185
See also DLB 57, 144, 190
Morley, John(athan) David 1948- ... 126
Morley, John F(rancis) 1936- ... 132
Morley, Margaret 1941- ... 140
Morley, Neville (G. D.) ... 207
Morley, Patricia (Ann) 1929- ... CANR-89
Earlier sketch in CA 73-76
Morley, R.
See Morley, Robert (Adolph Wilton)
Morley, Robert (Adolph Wilton)
1908-1992 ... CANR-80
Obituary ... 137
Brief entry ... 113
Earlier sketch in CA 130
Morley, S(ylvanus) Griswold 1878-1970 ... 5-8R
Morley, Samuel A. 1934- ... 37-40R
Morley, Sheridan 1941- ... 29-32R
Morley, Steve 1953- ... 132
Morley, Susan
See Cross, John Keir
Morley, Wilfred Owen
See Lowndes, Robert A(ugustine) W(ard)
Morman, Jean Mary 1925- ... 61-64
Morn, Frank T(homas) 1937- ... 107
Morneau, Robert F(ealey) 1938- ... CANR-109
Earlier sketch in CA 113
Mornell, Pierre 1935- ... 131
Morner, Magnus
See Moerner, Magnus
Mornin, Daniel 1956- ... 230
See also CBD
See also CD 5, 6
Morninghouse, Sundaira
See Wilson, Carletta
Morningstar, Connie 1927- ... 69-72
Morningstar, Mildred (Whaley) 1912-1997 . 127
Obituary ... 182
See also SATA 61
See also SATA-Obit 114
Moro, Cesar 1903-1956 ... 131
See also DLB 290
See also HW 1
Moro, Javier 1955- ... 227
Morone, James A. 1951- ... CANR-141
Earlier sketch in CA 142
Moroney, John R. 1939- ... CANR-17
Earlier sketch in CA 41-44R
Morowitz, Harold Joseph 1927- ... 104
Morozumi, Atsuko ... 172
See also SATA 110
Morpurgo, J(ack) E(ric) 1918-2000 ... CANR-4
Earlier sketch in CA 9-12R
Morpurgo, Michael 1943- ... CANR-122
Earlier sketch in CA 158
See also AAYA 37
See also BYA 15
See also CLR 51
See also MAICYA 2
See also MAICYAS 1
See also SATA 93, 143
See also YAW
Morr, Kenyon
See Sumner, Mark (C.)
Morra, Marion Eleanor ... 104
Morra, Umberto (?)-1981
Obituary ... 105
Morrah, Dave
See Morrah, David Wardlaw, Jr.
Morrah, David Wardlaw, Jr. 1914-1991 ... 1-4R
Obituary ... 134
See also SATA 10
Morrah, Dermot (Michael Macgregor)
1896-1974 ... CAP-2
Obituary ... 53-56
Earlier sketch in CA 29-32
Morrall, John B. 1923- ... 25-28R
Morray, Joseph Parker 1916- ... 5-8R
Morreale, Ben 1924- ... 57-60
Morreim, E. Haavi 1950- ... 156
Morrell, David 1943- ... CANR-89
Earlier sketches in CA 57-60, CANR-7, 43
See also HGG
Morrell, David C. 1929- ... 81-84
Morrell, Robert E(llis) 1930- ... 121
Morrell, William Parker 1899-1986 ... CANR-1
Earlier sketch in CA 1-4R
Morren, Lee Fishman
See Fishman, Lisa
Morren, Theophil
See Hofmannsthal, Hugo von
Morressy, John 1930- ... CANR-92
Earlier sketches in CA 21-24R, CANR-8, 28, 52
See also FANT
See also SATA 23
See also SFW 4
Morrice, J(ames) K(enneth) W(att)
1924-2002 ... CANR-41
Obituary ... 207
Earlier sketch in CA 118
Morrice, Ken
See Morrice, J(ames) K(enneth) W(att)
Morricone, Ennio 1928- ... IDFW 3, 4
Morrie
See Turner, Morris
Morrill, Allen C(onrad) 1904-1989 ... 101
Morrill, Claire 1900(?)-1981
Obituary ... 103
Morrill, Eleanor D(unlap) 1907- ... 101
Morrill, George Percival 1920- ... 33-36R
Morrill, John S. 1946- ... 130
Morrill, Leslie H(olt) 1934-2003 .. MAICYA 1, 2
See also SAAS 22
See also SATA 48
See also SATA-Brief 33
See also SATA-Obit 148
Morrill, Richard
See Schreck, Everett M.
Morrill, Richard L(eland) 1934- ... CANR-82
Earlier sketches in CA 29-32R, CANR-35
Morris, A(ndrew) J(ames) A(nthony)
1936- ... CANR-12
Earlier sketch in CA 73-76
Morris, Adalaide K(irby) 1942- ... 57-60
Morris, Alan 1955- ... 156
Morris, Aldyth V(ernon) 1901-1997 ... 29-32R
Obituary ... 176
Morris, Alton C(hester) 1903-1979 ... 13-16R
Morris, Ben(jamin Stephen) 1910-1990 ... 113
Obituary ... 132
Morris, Benny 1948- ... 194
Morris, Berenice Robinson 1909(?)-1990
Obituary ... 132
Morris, Bernadine (Taub) 1925- ... 102
Morris, Bertram 1908-1981 ... CANR-18
Earlier sketch in CA 1-4R
Morris, Bill 1952- ... 225
See also CLC 76
Morris, Brian (Robert) 1930-2001 ... CANR-18
Obituary ... 195
Earlier sketch in CA 29-32R
Morris, Bruce R(obert) 1909-2000 ... 5-8R
Morris, C(harles) R(ichard) 1898-1990
Obituary ... 131
Morris, Celia 1935- ... CANR-110
Earlier sketch in CA 138
Morris, Charles (William) 1901-1979 ... 13-16R
Obituary ... 135
Morris, Charles Lee 1943(?)-1986
Obituary ... 118
Morris, Chris(topher Crosby) 1946- ... 133
See also SATA 66
Morris, Christopher 1938- ... 21-24R
Morris, Christopher W. 1949- ... CANR-98
Earlier sketch in CA 147
Morris, Clyde M(cMahon) 1921- ... 93-96
Morris, (Edward) Craig 1939- ... 123
Morris, Cynthia Taft 1928- ... 25-28R
Morris, Dan (H.) 1912- ... 21-24R
Morris, David 1945- ... 85-88
Morris, David Brown 1942- ... CANR-48
Earlier sketches in CA 105, CANR-22
Morris, Deborah 1956- ... 155
See also SATA 91
Morris, Desmond (John) 1928- ... CANR-107
Earlier sketches in CA 45-48, CANR-2, 18, 38, 62
See also MTCW 1
See also SATA 14
Morris, Dick 1948- ... CANR-116
Earlier sketch in CA 160
Morris, Don 1954- ... SATA 83
Morris, Donald R. 1924- ... 17-20R
Morris, Edgar Poe
See Kinnaird, Clark
Morris, Edita (deToll) -1988 ... CANR-1
Earlier sketch in CA 1-4R
Morris, Edmund 1940- ... CANR-120
Earlier sketch in CA 89-92
Morris, (Murrell) Edward 1935- ... CANR-31
Earlier sketches in CA 69-72, CANR-14
Morris, Edwin Bateman 1881-1971
Obituary ... 112
Morris, Eric 1940- ... 81-84
Morris, Eric C(ecil) 1917- ... 185
Morris, Everett B. 1899-1967 ... CAP-1
Earlier sketch in CA 9-10
Morris, Frances 1959- ... 144
Morris, Freda 1933- ... CANR-4
Earlier sketch in CA 53-56
Morris, G. Scott 1954- ... 216
Morris, Gareth (Charles Walter) 1920- ... 144
Morris, George Pope 1802-1864 ... DLB 73
Morris, Gerald (Paul) 1963- ... CANR-134
Earlier sketch in CA 196
See also AAYA 44
See also SATA 107, 150
Morris, Gilbert (Leslie) 1929- ... CANR-121
Earlier sketch in CA 117
See also SATA 104
Morris, Grant Harold 1940- ... CANR-107
Earlier sketch in CA 29-32R
Morris, Gregory L(ynn) 1950- ... 119
Morris, Harry (Caesar) 1924- ... 9-12R
Morris, Harvey 1946- ... 134
Morris, Helen 1909-1995 ... CANR-18
Earlier sketch in CA 101
Morris, Henriette Hampton 1924- ... 238
Morris, Henry M(adison, Jr.) 1918- ... CANR-29
Earlier sketches in CA 37-40R, CANR-13
Morris, Herbert 1928- ... CANR-1
Earlier sketch in CA 1-4R
Morris, Ira (Victor) 1903- ... 9-12R
Morris, Ivan (Ira Esme) 1925-1976 ... CANR-11
Obituary ... 65-68
Earlier sketch in CA 9-12R
Morris, J(ohn) H(umphrey) C(arlile) 1910- . 5-8R
Morris, J(ames) Kenneth 1896-1987 ... 5-8R
Morris, J. R. 1914(?)-1977
Obituary ... 73-76
Morris, Jackie ... SATA 151
Morris, Jackson E(dgar) 1918- ... 17-20R
Morris, James (Humphrey)
See Morris, Jan
Morris, James A(lvin) 1938- ... CANR-46
Earlier sketch in CA 120
Morris, James E(lliot) 1942- ... 112
Morris, James M(atthew) 1935- ... 89-92
Morris, Jan 1926- ... CANR-97
Earlier sketches in CA 1-4R, CANR-1, 61
See also BRWS 10
See also DLB 204
See also MTCW 1
Morris, Jane
See Ardmore, Jane Kesner
Morris, Janet (Ellen) 1946- ... CANR-90
Earlier sketches in CA 73-76, CANR-13, 35
See also FANT
See also SATA 66
See also SFW 4
Morris, Jay
See Tatham, Julie Campbell
Morris, (Margaret) Jean 1924- ... CANR-92
Brief entry ... 116
Earlier sketch in CA 153
See also CWRI 5
See also FANT
See also SATA 98
Morris, Jeffrey B(randon) 1941- ... 156
See also SATA 92
Morris, Jerrold (A.) 1911- ... CANR-11
Earlier sketch in CA 21-24R
Morris, Jill 1936- ... 190
See also SATA 119
Morris, Jim 1964- ... 201
Morris, Joan 1901- ... 45-48
Morris, Joe A(lex) 1904-1990 ... 65-68
Obituary ... 130
Morris, Joe Alex, Jr. 1927- ... 73-76
Morris, John
See Hearne, John (Edgar Caulwell)
Morris, John ... CCA 1
Morris, John 1895-1980
Obituary ... 102
Morris, John D(avid) 1946- ... 111
Morris, John G. ... 194
Morris, John N(elson) 1931- ... 33-36R
See also CAAS 13
Morris, John O(sgood) 1918- ... 41-44R
Morris, John W(esley) 1907- ... CANR-6
Earlier sketch in CA 13-16R
Morris, Jonas 1933- ... 117
Morris, Juddi ... 152
See also SATA 85
Morris, Judy K. 1936- ... 116
See also SATA 61
Morris, Julian
See West, Morris L(anglo)
Morris, Katharine ... CAP-1
Earlier sketch in CA 13-16
Morris, Ken 1953(?)- ... 222
Morris, Kenneth (Vennor) 1879-1937 ... FANT
Morris, Kenneth Earl 1955- ... 127
Morris, Kenneth M. 1945- ... 171
Morris, Kenneth T(hompson) 1941- ... 57-60
Morris, Kevin L. 1954- ... 129
Morris, Leon (Lamb) 1914- ... CANR-43
Earlier sketches in CA 9-12R, CANR-4, 20
Morris, Lewis 1833-1907 ... 185
See also DLB 35
Morris, Loverne Lawton 1896-1994 ... 5-8R
Morris, Lynn ... 167
Morris, M.
See Thibaudeau, Colleen
Morris, Margaret 1737-1816 ... DLB 200
Morris, Margaret 1891-1980
Obituary ... 97-100
Morris, Margaret Francine 1938- ... 57-60
Morris, Marilyn (A.) 1957- ... 167
Morris, Mark 1963- ... CANR-75
Earlier sketch in CA 150
See also HGG
Morris, Mary (Elizabeth Davis)
1913-1986 ... 53-56
Obituary ... 121
Morris, Mary 1947- ... CANR-136
Earlier sketches in CA 132, CANR-71
Morris, Mary Lee ... 120
Morris, Mary (Joan) McGarry
1943- ... CANR-140
Earlier sketches in CA 139, CANR-97
See also DLB 292
See also MTFW 2005
Morris, Max 1913- ... 109
Morris, Mel (Merrill) 1930- ... 69-72
Morris, Mervyn 1937- ... CANR-92
Earlier sketch in CA 154
See also CP 1, 7
See also EWL 3
Morris, Michael 1914-1999 ... CANR-5
Earlier sketch in CA 5-8R
Morris, Michael (Spence Lowdell)
1940- ... CANR-23
Earlier sketch in CA 107
Morris, Michelle 1941- ... 108
Morris, Miggs Wynne 1938- ... 220
Morris, Milton D(onald) 1939- ... 57-60
Morris, Monica B. 1928- ... 195
Brief entry ... 113
Morris, Nobuko
See Albery, Nobuko
Morris, Norman S. 1931- ... 33-36R
Morris, Norval 1923-2004 ... 37-40R
Obituary ... 223
Morris, Oradel Nolen ... 198
See also SATA 128
Morris, Oswald 1915- ... IDFW 3, 4
Morris, Phyllis 1894-1982
Obituary ... 106
Morris, Phyllis Sutton 1931- ... 104
Morris, R(oger) J(ohn) B(owring) 1946- ... 93-96
Morris, Rachel ... 173
Morris, Raymond N. 1936- ... 25-28R
Morris, Raymond Philip 1904-1990 ... 45-48
Morris, Richard (Ward) 1939- ... CANR-39
Earlier sketches in CA 45-48, CANR-1, 18
Morris, Richard B(randon)
1904-1989 ... CANR-80
Obituary ... 128
Earlier sketches in CA 49-52, CANR-2
See also DLB 17
Morris, Richard J(ules) 1942- ... CANR-16
Earlier sketch in CA 89-92
Morris, Richard K(nowles) 1915- ... 21-24R
Morris, Robert 1910- ... CANR-16
Earlier sketch in CA 89-92
Morris, Robert (Lyle) 1942-2004
Obituary ... 229
Brief entry ... 116
Morris, Robert A(da) 1933- ... 49-52
See also SATA 7
Morris, Robert C. 1942- ... 135
Morris, Robert Kerwin 1933- ... 33-36R
Morris, Roger 1938- ... CANR-108
Earlier sketch in CA 140
Morris, Ronald 1930- ... 221
Morris, Roy, Jr. ... 221
Morris, Ruby Turner 1908- ... CANR-1
Earlier sketch in CA 1-4R
Morris, Ruth
See Webb, Ruth Enid Borlase Morris
Morris, S(tephen) Brent 1950- ... 175
Morris, Sally ... 177
Morris, Sara
See Burke, John (Frederick)
Morris, Sarah M(iller) 1906-1985 ... 81-84
Morris, Scot 1942- ... 101
Morris, Stephen 1935- ... CANR-20
Earlier sketch in CA 103
Morris, Steveland Judkins 1950(?)-
Brief entry ... 111
See also Wonder, Stevie
Morris, Suzanne 1944- ... CANR-17
Earlier sketch in CA 89-92
Morris, Sylvia Jukes ... 170
Morris, T(homas) B(aden) 1900- ... CANR-2
Earlier sketch in CA 5-8R
Morris, Taylor 1923- ... 103
Morris, Terry Lesser 1914-1993 ... 9-12R
Obituary ... 142
Morris, Thomas D(ean) 1938-
Brief entry ... 112
Morris, Thomas Victor 1952- ... CANR-46
Earlier sketch in CA 120
Morris, Timothy 1959- ... 150
Morris, Tina 1941- ... CANR-12
Earlier sketch in CA 29-32R
Morris, W. R. 1936- ... 77-80
Morris, William 1834-1896 ... BRW 5
See also CDBLB 1832-1890
See also DLB 18, 35, 57, 156, 178, 184
See also FANT
See also PC 55
See also RGEL 2
See also SFW 4
See also SUFW
Morris, William 1913-1994 ... CANR-12
Obituary ... 143
Earlier sketch in CA 17-20R
See also SATA 29
Morris, William E(dgar) 1926- ... 9-12R
Morris, William O. 1922- ... 37-40R
Morris, William Sparkes 1916-1983 ... 141
Morris, William T(homas) 1928- ... 17-20R
Morris, Willie 1934-1999 ... CANR-13
Obituary ... 183
Earlier sketch in CA 17-20R
See also AITN 2
See also CSW
See also DLBY 1980

Cumulative Index 413 Morton

Morris, Wright (Marion) 1910-1998 . CANR-81
Obituary ... 167
Earlier sketches in CA 9-12R, CANR-21
See also AMW
See also CLC 1, 3, 7, 18, 37
See also CN 1, 2, 3, 4, 5, 6
See also DLB 2, 206, 218
See also DLBY 1981
See also EWL 3
See also MAL 5
See also MTCW 1, 2
See also MTFW 2005
See also RGAL 4
See also TCLC 107
See also TCWW 1, 2
Morrisey, George L(ewis) 1926- ... CANR-14
Earlier sketch in CA 73-76
Morris-Goodall, Vanne 1909-2000 ... 29-32R
Morrish, (Ernest) Ivor (James) 1914- ... 33-36R
Morris-Jones, W(yndraeth) H(umphreys)
1918- ... CANR-11
Earlier sketch in CA 21-24R
Morrison, Arnold Telford 1928- ... 110
Morrison, Arthur 1863-1945 ... 157
Brief entry ... 120
See also CMW 4
See also DLB 70, 135, 197
See also RGEL 2
See also SSC 40
See also TCLC 72
Morrison, Bill 1935- ... CANR-90
Brief entry ... 115
Earlier sketch in CA 135
See also CBD
See also CD 5
See also SATA 66
See also SATA-Brief 37
Morrison, Bill 1940- ... CD 6
Morrison, (Philip) Blake 1950- ... CANR-120
Earlier sketches in CA 138, CANR-92
See also CP 7
See also EWL 3
Morrison, Bruce 1904(?)-1983
Obituary ... 109
Morrison, Carl V(incent) 1908-1980 ... 93-96
Morrison, Charles Clayton 1874-1966 ... 189
Obituary ... 89-92
See also DLB 91
Morrison, Cheryl 1947- ... 107
Morrison, Chloe Anthony Wofford
See Morrison, Toni
Morrison, Claudia C(hristopherson)
1936- ... 29-32R
Morrison, Clinton (Dawson, Jr.) 1924- ... 13-16R
Morrison, Craig S. 1946- ... 171
Morrison, Danny 1953- ... 206
Morrison, David (Douglas) 1940- ... CANR-30
Earlier sketch in CA 112
Morrison, Dennis L(ewis) 1949- ... 219
Morrison, Denton E(dward) 1932- ... CANR-6
Earlier sketch in CA 57-60
Morrison, Donald George 1938- ... 85-88
Morrison, Dorothy Nafus ... CANR-49
Earlier sketches in CA 61-64, CANR-8, 24
See also SATA 29
Morrison, Edward
See Humphrey, Paul
Morrison, Eleanor S(helton) 1921- ... CANR-1
Earlier sketch in CA 49-52
Morrison, Eula Atwood 1911- ... 25-28R
Morrison, Frank G. 1894(?)-1983
Obituary ... 111
Morrison, Frank M. 1914-1981 ... 37-40R
Morrison, Fred L. 1939-
Brief entry ... 112
Morrison, G. F.
See Bernstein, Gerry
Morrison, Gertrude W. ... CANR-26
Earlier sketches in CAP-2, CA 19-20
Morrison, Gordon 1944- ... SATA 87, 128
Morrison, Grant 1960- ... 227
Morrison, Helen 1942- ... 235
Morrison, Hobe 1904-2000 ... 77-80
Obituary ... 188
Morrison, Howard A(lexander) 1955- ... 118
Morrison, Ida Edith -1989 ... 1-4R
Morrison, J.
See Moore, James A.
Morrison, J. S.
See Morrison, J(ohn) S(inclair)
Morrison, J(ohn) S(inclair)
1913-2000 ... CANR-48
Obituary ... 191
Earlier sketch in CA 122
Morrison, Jack 1912-1997 ... 105
Morrison, James (Harris) 1918- ... 73-76
Morrison, James (Ryan) 1924- ... 105
Morrison, James Douglas
1943-1971 ... CANR-40
Earlier sketch in CA 73-76
See also Morrison, Jim
Morrison, James F(rederic) 1937- ... 25-28R
Morrison, James L(unsford), Jr. 1923- ... 57-60
Morrison, James R(oy) 1940- ... 123
Brief entry ... 118
Morrison, Jeanette Helen 1927-2004 ... 134
See also Leigh, Janet
Morrison, Jim
See Morrison, James Douglas
See also CLC 17
Morrison, Joan 1922- ... 133
See also SATA 65
Morrison, John 1949- ... 137
See also RGSF 2
Morrison, John Gordon 1904-1998 .. CANR-92
Earlier sketch in CA 103
See also DLB 260
Morrison, Joseph L(ederman) 1918-1970 .. 5-8R
Obituary ... 122
Morrison, Keith 1942- ... 155
See also BW 3
Morrison, Kristin (Diane) 1934- ... CANR-14
Earlier sketch in CA 37-40R
Morrison, Lester M(arvin) 1907-1991 ... CAP-1
Obituary ... 134
Earlier sketch in CA 13-16
Morrison, Lillian 1917- ... CANR-121
Earlier sketches in CA 9-12R, CANR-7, 22
See also SATA 3, 108
Morrison, Lucile Phillips 1896- ... SATA 17
Morrison, Margaret Mackie 19(?)-1973
Obituary ... 41-44R
Morrison, Marsh 1902-1985 ... CANR-10
Earlier sketch in CA 61-64
Morrison, Martha A. 1948- ... 145
See also SATA 77
Morrison, Meighan 1966- ... SATA 90
Morrison, N(ancy Agnes) Brysson (Inglis)
(?)-1986 ... 13-16R
Obituary ... 118
Morrison, Paul Fix 1902-1983
Obituary ... 111
Morrison, Peggy
See Morrison, Margaret Mackie
Morrison, Perry 1959- ... 134
Morrison, Philip 1915-2005
Obituary ... 238
Brief entry ... 106
Morrison, Phylis 1927- ... 117
Morrison, R(obert) H(ay) 1915- ... 135
Morrison, Richard
See Lowndes, Robert A(ugustine) W(ard)
Morrison, Robert
See Lowndes, Robert A(ugustine) W(ard)
Morrison, Robert H(aywood) 1927- ... 5-8R
Morrison, Robert S(tanley) 1909- ... 65-68
Morrison, Roberta
See Webb, Jean Francis (III)
Morrison, Susan Dudley
See Gold, Susan Dudley
Morrison, Taylor 1971- ... CANR-144
Earlier sketch in CA 160
See also SATA 95, 159
Morrison, Theodore 1901-1988 ... CANR-1
Obituary ... 127
Earlier sketch in CA 1-4R
Morrison, Toni 1931- ... CANR-124
Earlier sketches in CA 29-32R, CANR-27, 42, 67, 113
See also AAYA 1, 22, 61
See also AFAW 1, 2
See also AMWC 1
See also AMWS 3
See also BLC 3
See also BPFB 2
See also BW 2, 3
See also CDALB 1968-1988
See also CLC 4, 10, 22, 55, 81, 87, 173, 194
See also CLR 99
See also CN 3, 4, 5, 6, 7
See also CPW
See also DA
See also DA3
See also DAB
See also DAC
See also DAM MST, MULT, NOV, POP
See also DLB 6, 33, 143
See also DLBY 1981
See also EWL 3
See also EXPN
See also FL 1:6
See also FW
See also GL 3
See also LAIT 2, 4
See also LATS 1:2
See also LMFS 2
See also MAL 5
See also MAWW
See also MTCW 1, 2
See also MTFW 2005
See also NFS 1, 6, 8, 14
See also RGAL 4
See also RHW
See also SATA 57, 144
See also SSFS 5
See also TCLE 1:2
See also TUS
See also YAW
Morrison, Tony 1936- ... 81-84
Morrison, Van 1945- ... 168
Brief entry ... 116
See also CLC 21
Morrison, Velma Ford 1909- ... 9-12R
See also SATA 21
Morrison, Victor
See Glut, Donald F(rank)
Morrison, Wilbur Howard 1915- ... CANR-1
Earlier sketch in CA 1-4R
See also SATA 64
Morrison, William
See Samachson, Joseph
Morrison, William R(obert) 1942- ... 124
Morrison-Reed, Mark D(ouglas) 1949- ... 116
Morrisroe, Patricia 1951- ... 154
Morriss, Frank 1923- ... CANR-3
Earlier sketch in CA 5-8R
Morriss, James E(dward) 1932- ... 57-60
See also SATA 8
Morriss, J.-H.
See Ghnassia, Maurice (Jean-Henri)
Morriss, Mack 1920(?)-1976
Obituary ... 65-68
Morrisseau, Norval 1932- ... 211
Morrissette, Bruce A(rcher) 1911-2000 .. 17-20R
Morrissey, Charles Thomas 1933- ... 108
Morrissey, Donna 1956- ... 212
Morrissey, Kevin L. 1952- ... 154
Morrissey, L(eroy) J(ohn) 1935- ... CANR-1
Earlier sketch in CA 49-52
Morrissey, Leonard E., Jr. 1925- ... 9-12R
Morrissey, Mary Manin ... 207
Morrissey, Stephen 1950- ... 115
Morrissey, Thomas J(oseph) 1929- ... 216
Morris-Suzuki, Tessa 1951- ... 123
Morrissy, Mary 1957- ... 205
See also CLC 99
See also DLB 267
Morritt, Hope 1930- ... CANR-16
Earlier sketch in CA 97-100
Morrow, Ann Patricia 1934- ... 130
Morrow, Baker H(arrison) 1946- ... 127
Morrow, Barry (Nelson) 1948- ... 166
Morrow, Betty
See Bacon, Elizabeth
Morrow, Bradford 1951- ... CANR-119
Earlier sketches in CA 113, CANR-32
Morrow, Charlotte
See Kirwan, Molly (Morrow)
Morrow, Dennis 1952- ... CANR-82
Earlier sketch in CA 132
Morrow, E(verett) Frederic
1909-1994 ... CANR-2
Obituary ... 146
Earlier sketch in CA 5-8R
See also BW 1
Morrow, Felix 1906-1988 ... 107
Morrow, Glenn R(aymond)
1895-1970(?) ... CAP-1
Earlier sketch in CA 19-20
Morrow, Honore Willsie 1880-1940 .. TCWW 2
Morrow, James (Kenneth) 1947- ... 180
Earlier sketches in CA 108, CANR-55, 138
Autobiographical Essay in ... 180
See also FANT
See also MTCW 2
See also MTFW 2005
See also SFW 4
See also SUFW 2
Morrow, John Howard, Jr. 1944- ... 113
Morrow, John Howard 1910-2000 ... 25-28R
Obituary ... 188
Morrow, Lance 1939- ... 153
Brief entry ... 119
Morrow, Mable 1892-1977
Obituary ... 106
Morrow, Mark 1952- ... 167
Morrow, Mary Lou 1926- ... 61-64
Morrow, Patrick David 1940- ... CANR-102
Earlier sketches in CA 61-64, CANR-8
Morrow, Skip
See Morrow, Dennis
Morrow, Stephen 1939- ... 73-76
Morrow, Susan Brind ... 174
Morrow, W(illiam) C(hambers) 1853-1923 . 219
See also HGG
Morrow, William L(ockhart) 1935- ... 33-36R
Mors, Victor
See Roeseler, W(olfgang) G(uenter)
Mors, Wallace Peter 1911-2001 ... 17-20R
Morsberger, Katharine M. 1931- ... 105
Morsberger, Robert Eustis 1929- ... CANR-3
Earlier sketch in CA 5-8R
Morscher, Betsy 1939- ... 115
Morse, A. Reynolds 1914-2000 ... CANR-7
Obituary ... 189
Earlier sketch in CA 17-20R
Morse, Anne Christensen 1915- ... 1-4R
See also YAW
Morse, Arthur David 1920-1971
Obituary ... 29-32R
Morse, B. J. (?)-1977
Obituary ... 73-76
Morse, Carol
See Yeakley, Marjory Hall
Morse, Chandler 1906-1988 ... 5-8R
Morse, Charles A. 1898-1990 ... CAP-1
Earlier sketch in CA 19-20
Morse, David E. 1940- ... CANR-94
Earlier sketch in CA 37-40R
Morse, Donald E. 1936- ... 37-40R
Morse, Donald R(oy) 1931- ... CANR-21
Earlier sketch in CA 105
Morse, Dorothy B(ayley)
1906-1979 ... SATA-Obit 24
Morse, Edward Lewis 1942- ... CANR-7
Earlier sketch in CA 57-60
Morse, Flo 1921- ... 106
See also SATA 30
Morse, Grant W(esley) 1926- ... 17-20R
Morse, H(enry) Clifton IV 1924- ... 9-12R
Morse, Harold Marston 1892-1977
Obituary ... 69-72
Morse, Hermann Nelson 1887-1977
Obituary ... 73-76
Morse, J(osiah) Mitchell 1912- ... 65-68
Morse, James Herbert 1841-1923 ... 184
See also DLB 71
Morse, Jedidiah 1761-1826 ... DLB 37
Morse, John D. 1906-1985 ... 104
Morse, John T., Jr. 1840-1937 ... 192
See also DLB 47
Morse, Kitty 1947- ... 214
Morse, L(arry) A(lan) 1945- ... CANR-86
Earlier sketch in CA 107
See also BPFB 2
Morse, Melvin (L.) 1953- ... CANR-97
Earlier sketch in CA 111
Morse, Peter 1935- ... CANR-14
Earlier sketch in CA 73-76
Morse, Philip M(cCord) 1903-1985 .. CANR-83
Obituary ... 117
Earlier sketch in CA 108
Morse, Richard M(cGee)
1922-2001 ... CANR-10
Obituary ... 194
Earlier sketch in CA 13-16R
Morse, Roger A(lfred) 1927-2000 ... CANR-47
Obituary ... 189
Earlier sketches in CA 57-60, CANR-8, 23
Morse, Samuel French 1916- ... CANR-4
Earlier sketch in CA 9-12R
Morse, Theresa Adler 1901-1980 ... 89-92
Obituary ... 97-100
Morse, Thomas S(purr) 1925- ... 109
Morse, Tony 1953- ... SATA 129
Morse, Wayne (Lyman) 1900-1974
Obituary ... 49-52
Morse-Boycott, Desmond (Lionel)
1892-1979 ... 107
Obituary ... 104
Morselli, Guido 1912-1973 ... 211
See also DLB 177
Morsey, Royal J(oseph) 1910-1994 ... 73-76
Morshead, Ian 1922- ... 111
Morshiel, George
See Shiels, George
Morsi, Pamela 1951- ... CANR-70
Earlier sketch in CA 145
Morson, Gary S(aul) 1948- ... CANR-70
Earlier sketch in CA 121
Morson, Ian (Nairne) ... 165
Morss, Elisabeth W. 1918- ... 41-44R
Morsy, Magali 1933- ... CANR-100
Earlier sketch in CA 132
Mort, John 1947- ... 236
Mort, Vivian
See Cromie, Alice Hamilton
Mortensen, Ben(jamin) F. 1928- ... 104
Mortensen, C. David 1939- ... 37-40R
Morthland, John 1947- ... 129
Mortimer, Anne 1958- ... SATA 116
Mortimer, Anthony 1936- ... 116
Mortimer, Armine Kotin 1943- ... CANR-41
Earlier sketch in CA 117
Mortimer, Carole 1960- ... RHW
Mortimer, Chapman
See Chapman-Mortimer, William Charles
Mortimer, Edward (James) 1943- ... 234
Mortimer, Favell Lee 1802-1878 ... DLB 163
Mortimer, John (Clifford) 1923- ... CANR-109
Earlier sketches in CA 13-16R, CANR-21, 69
Interview in ... CANR-21
See also CBD
See also CD 5, 6
See also CDBLB 1960 to Present
See also CLC 28, 43
See also CMW 4
See also CN 5, 6, 7
See also CPW
See also DA3
See also DAM DRAM, POP
See also DLB 13, 245, 271
See also MSW
See also MTCW 1, 2
See also MTFW 2005
See also RGEL 2
Mortimer, John L(ynn) 1908-1977 ... 69-72
Obituary ... 135
Mortimer, Mary H.
See Coury, Louise Andree
Mortimer, Penelope (Ruth)
1918-1999 ... CANR-88
Obituary ... 187
Earlier sketches in CA 57-60, CANR-45
See also CLC 5
See also CN 1, 2, 3, 4, 5, 6
Mortimer, Peter
See Roberts, Dorothy James
Mortimer, Richard ... 237
Mortimer, Sir John
See Mortimer, John (Clifford)
Mortimore, Olive 1890-1986 ... 49-52
Mortimore, Roger ... 197
Mortlake, G. N.
See Stonov, Natasha
Mortman, Doris c. 1945-
Brief entry ... 129
See also BEST 89:4
Mortmane, J. D.
See Kiefer, Louis Sr.
Mortola, Jacopo P(rospero A.) 1949- ... 213
Morton, A(rthur) L(eslie) 1903-1987 ... 9-12R
Obituary ... 124
Morton, A(ndrew) Q(ueen) 1919- ... 105
Morton, Adam 1945- ... 128
Morton, Alexander C(lark) 1936- ... CANR-12
Earlier sketch in CA 25-28R
Morton, Alexandra (Hubbard) 1957- ... 217
See also SATA 144
Morton, Andrew 1953- ... 141
Morton, Anthony
See Arthur, Robert, (Jr.)
Morton, Anthony
See Creasey, John
Morton, Brian 1942- ... 167
Morton, Brian 1954- ... 176
Morton, Brian 1955- ... 169
Morton, C(lement) Manly 1884-1976 ... CAP-2
Earlier sketch in CA 29-32
Morton, Carlos 1947- ... CANR-87
Earlier sketches in CA 73-76, CANR-32
See also DLB 122
See also HW 1
Morton, Desmond 1937- ... CANR-32
Earlier sketches in CA 29-32R, CANR-15
Morton, Donald E(dward) 1938- ... 57-60

Morton, Frederic 1924- CANR-43
Earlier sketches in CA 1-4R, CANR-3, 20
See also MAL 5
Morton, Glen
See Lazenby, Norman
Morton, Gregory 1911-1986 102
Obituary 118
Morton, H(enry Canova) V(ollam)
1892-1979 103
Obituary 89-92
See also DLB 195
Morton, Harry 1925- CANR-15
Earlier sketch in CA 81-84
Morton, Henry W(alter) 1929- 13-16R
Morton, James (Severs) 1938- 133
Morton, Jane 1931- 93-96
See also SATA 50
Morton, Jocelyn 1912- 73-76
Morton, John (Cameron Andrieu) Bingham
(Michael) 1893-1979 93-96
Obituary 85-88
Morton, Joseph
See Richmond, Al
Morton, Joseph C. 1932- 231
See also SATA 156
Morton, Laura 182
Morton, Lee Jack, Jr. 1928- .... SATA 32
Morton, Lena Beatrice 1901-1981 .... 17-20R
Morton, Lisa R. 1958- 229
Morton, Louis 1913-1976 .... CANR-21
Obituary 65-68
Earlier sketch in CA 69-72
Morton, Lucie T. 1950- 118
Morton, Lynne 1952- 106
Morton, Marcia Colman 1927- 73-76
Morton, Marian J(ohnson) 1937- 77-80
Morton, Miriam 1918(?)-1985 .... CANR-2
Obituary 117
Earlier sketch in CA 49-52
See also SATA 9
See also SATA-Obit 46
Morton, Nathaniel 1613-1685 .... DLB 24
Morton, Newton 1901-1967 .... CAP-1
Earlier sketch in CA 19-20
Morton, Oliver 217
Morton, Patricia
See Golding, Morton J(ay)
Morton, Patricia 1945- 176
Morton, Patricia A. 1955- 221
Morton, Phyllis Digby (?)-1984
Obituary 113
Morton, R(obert) S(teel) 1917- 49-52
Morton, Richard (Everett) 1930- 37-40R
Morton, Richard Lee 1889-1974 ...... CANR-16
Obituary 53-56
Earlier sketch in CA 1-4R
Morton, Robert 1934- 69-72
Morton, Robert L(ee) 1889-1976 45-48
Obituary 134
Morton, Sarah Wentworth 1759-1846 .. DLB 37
Morton, Stanley
See Freedgood, Morton
Morton, T(homas) Ralph 1900-1977 ..... 29-32R
Morton, Thomas 1579(?)-1647(?) .... DLB 24
See also RGEL 2
Morton, W(illiam) L(ewis) 1908-1981 ... CAP-1
Earlier sketch in CA 19-20
Morton, W(illiam) Scott 1908- 81-84
Morton, Ward McKinnon 1907- 1-4R
Morton, William C(uthbert) 1875-1971 . CAP-2
Earlier sketch in CA 25-28
Morwood, James 1943- 124
Morwood, Peter 1956- .... FANT
Mosatche, Harriet (S.) 1949- 195
See also SATA 122
Mosby, Aline 1922-1998 130
Obituary 169
Mosby, Katherine 1957- 238
Mosby, Rebekah Presson 1952- 203
Mosca, Gaetano 1858-1941 .... TCLC 75
Moscati, Sabatino 1922-1997 77-80
Obituary 161
Moschella, David C. 1954- CANR-121
Earlier sketch in CA 165
Moscherosch, Johann Michael
1601-1669 .... DLB 164
Moschonas, Andreas 1941- 176
Mosco, Vincent 1948- CANR-35
Earlier sketch in CA 114
Moscoe, Mike 166
Moscotti, Albert D(ennis) 1920- 65-68
Moscovitch, Allan 1946- 111
Moscovitz, Judy 1942- CANR-50
Earlier sketch in CA 123
Moscow, Alvin 1925- CANR-45
Earlier sketches in CA 1-4R, CANR-4
See also SATA 3
Moscow, Henry (I.) 1904(?)-1983
Obituary 108
Moscow, Warren 1908-1992 .... 21-24R
Obituary 174
Moscowitz, Raymond 1938- 111
Mosel, Arlene (Tichy) 1921-1996 49-52
See also SATA 7
Mosel, Tad 1922- 73-76
See also CAD
See also CD 5, 6
Moseley, David (Victor) 1939- 97-100
Moseley, Edward H(olt) 1931- 132
Moseley, Edwin M(aurice)
1916-1978 .... CANR-8
Earlier sketch in CA 5-8R
Moseley, George (V. H. III) 1931- 49-52
Moseley, Humphrey fl. 1627-1661 ..... DLB 170
Moseley, J(oseph) Edward 1910-1973 ... 37-40R
Moseley, James G(wyn) 1946- CANR-38
Earlier sketch in CA 116
Moseley, James W(illett) 1931- 210
See also SATA 139
Moseley, Michael E(dward) 1941- 139
Moseley, Ray 1932- 85-88
Moseley, Roy 198
Moseley, Spencer A(ltemont) 1925- 93-96
Moseley, Virginia D(ouglas) 1917- 21-24R
Mosely, Philip Edward 1905-1972
Obituary 33-36R
Moseng, Elisabeth 1967- .... SATA 90
Moser, Barry (A.) 1940- 196
See also CLR 49
See also MAICYA 1, 2
See also SAAS 15
See also SATA 56, 79, 138
Moser, Charles A. 1935- 29-32R
Moser, Don(ald Bruce) 1932- 106
See also SATA 31
Moser, Edward P. 1958- 152
Moser, Justus 1720-1794 .... DLB 97
Moser, Lawrence E. 1939- 33-36R
Moser, Mary Beck 1924- 122
Moser, Nancy 1955(?)- 205
Moser, Norman Calvin 1931- CANR-10
Earlier sketch in CA 57-60
See also CP 1
Moser, Paul K. 1957- CANR-92
Earlier sketch in CA 145
Moser, Reta C(arol) 1936- 13-16R
Moser, Shia 1906- CAP-2
Earlier sketch in CA 25-28
Moser, Stephanie 214
Moser, Thomas (Colborn) 1923- 5-8R
Moses, Anna Mary Robertson 1860-1961
Obituary 93-96
Moses, Claire Goldberg 1941- CANR-43
Earlier sketch in CA 113
Moses, Daniel David 1952- 186
See also NNAL
Moses, Elbert R(aymond), Jr.
1908-1999 .... CAP-1
Earlier sketch in CA 13-16
Moses, Gerald Robert 1938- 57-60
Moses, Grandma
See Moses, Anna Mary Robertson
Moses, (Russell) Greg(ory) 1954- 168
Moses, Joel C(harles) 1944- CANR-10
Earlier sketch in CA 65-68
Moses, Kate 1962- 224
Moses, Michael Valdez 1957- 176
Moses, Norton H(olmes) 1935- 175
Moses, Robert 1888-1981 45-48
Obituary 104
Moses, Robert P(arris) 1935- 199
Moses, Sheila P. 1961- 237
Moses, W(illiam) R(obert) 1911-2001 ...... 9-12R
Moses, Will 1956- 191
See also SATA 120
Moses, Wilson Jeremiah 1942- CANR-93
Earlier sketch in CA 85-88
Mosesson, Gloria R(ubin) 41-44R
See also SATA 24
Mosettig, Michael David 1942- 233
Mosey, Anne Cronin 1938- 49-52
Mosey, Don(ald) 1924-1999 186
Moshe, David
See Winkelman, Donald M.
Mosher, Arthur Theodore 1910-1992 85-88
Mosher, Frederick C(amp) 1913-1990 ... 37-40R
Obituary 131
Mosher, Howard Frank 1943- CANR-115
Earlier sketches in CA 139, CANR-65
See also CLC 62
Mosher, Ralph Lamont 1928-1998 ...... CANR-7
Earlier sketch in CA 17-20R
Mosher, Richard 1949- 165
See also SATA 120
Mosher, Steven W(estley) 1948- 116
Mosher, (Christopher) Terry 1942- 93-96
Moshier, W(illiam) Franklyn 1929- 97-100
Moshiri, Farnoosh 1951- 193
Moshiri, Farrokh 1961- 142
Mosier, John F. 1944- 201
Mosiman, Billie Sue (Stahl) 1947- .. CANR-127
Earlier sketch in CA 119
Mosimann, Anton 1947- 141
Mosk
See Moskowitz, Gene
Moskin, J(ohn) Robert 1923- 17-20R
Moskin, Julia 233
Moskin, Marietta D(unston) 1928- CANR-13
Earlier sketch in CA 73-76
See also SATA 23
Moskof, Martin Stephen 1930- 29-32R
See also SATA 27
Moskos, Charles C. 1934- CANR-118
Earlier sketches in CA 25-28R, CANR-10, 26, 56
Moskow, Michael H. 1938- CANR-14
Earlier sketch in CA 37-40R
Moskow, Shirley Blotnick 1935- CANR-55
Earlier sketch in CA 127
Moskowitz, Anita F(iderer) 1937- 150
Moskowitz, Eva S. 200
Moskowitz, Faye (Stollman) 1930- 146
Moskowitz, Gene 1921(?)-1982
Obituary 108
Moskowitz, Ira 1912-2001 102
Moskowitz, Moses 1911(?)-1990
Obituary 131
Brief entry 114
Moskowitz, Robert (A.) 1946- CANR-57
Earlier sketch in CA 109
Moskowitz, Sam 1920-1997 .... CANR-4
Obituary 157
Earlier sketch in CA 5-8R
Interview in CANR-4
Moskvin, Andrei 1901-1961 .... IDFW 3, 4
Moskvitin, Jurij 1938- 93-96
Mosley, Charlotte 1952- 145
Mosley, Diana 1910-2003 106
Obituary 219
Mosley, Francis 1957- .... SATA 57
Mosley, J(ohn) Brooke (Jr.) 1915-1988
Obituary 125
Mosley, Jean Bell 1913- 9-12R
Mosley, Leonard O(swald)
1913-1992 .... CANR-75
Obituary 139
Brief entry 108
Earlier sketch in CA 109
Interview in CA-109
Mosley, Melissa M. 1961- 213
Mosley, Nicholas 1923- CANR-108
Earlier sketches in CA 69-72, CANR-41, 60
See also CLC 43, 70
See also CN 1, 2, 3, 4, 5, 6, 7
See also DLB 14, 207
Mosley, Oswald (Ernald)
1896-1980 .... CANR-76
Obituary 102
Earlier sketches in CAP-2, CA 25-28
Mosley, Philip 1947- CANR-89
Earlier sketch in CA 130
Mosley, Steven 1952- 133
Mosley, Walter 1952- CANR-136
Earlier sketches in CA 142, CANR-57, 92
See also AAYA 57
See also AMWS 13
See also BLCS
See also BPFB 2
See also BW 2
See also CLC 97, 184
See also CMW 4
See also CN 7
See also CPW
See also DA3
See also DAM MULT, POP
See also DLB 306
See also MSW
See also MTCW 2
See also MTFW 2005
Moss, Arthur 1889-1969 181
Obituary 112
See also DLB 4
Moss, Barbara 1946- 116
Moss, Bernard H(aym) 1943- 183
Brief entry 115
Moss, Bobby Gilmer 1932- 49-52
Moss, C(laude) Scott 1924- CANR-8
Earlier sketch in CA 17-20R
Moss, Carolyn (J.) 1932- CANR-121
Earlier sketch in CA 163
Moss, Cynthia F. 1957- 163
Moss, Cynthia J(ane) 1940- CANR-12
Earlier sketch in CA 65-68
Moss, Don(ald) 1920- .... SATA 11
Moss, Elaine (Dora) 1924- 191
Brief entry 110
See also SATA 57
See also SATA-Brief 31
Moss, Eric Owen 1943- 225
Moss, Frank Edward 1911-2003 .... CANR-13
Obituary 214
Earlier sketch in CA 61-64
Moss, Gordon E(rvin) 1937- 57-60
Moss, Howard 1922-1987 .... CANR-44
Obituary 123
Earlier sketches in CA 1-4R, CANR-1
See also CLC 7, 14, 45, 50
See also CP 1, 2
See also DAM POET
See also DLB 5
Moss, J. Joel 1922- 45-48
Moss, James A(llen) 1920- 33-36R
Moss, Jeff(rey) 1942-1998 140
Obituary 171
See also SATA 73
See also SATA-Obit 106
Moss, John 1940- CANR-17
Earlier sketch in CA 97-100
Moss, Kay K. 197
Moss, Leonard (Jerome) 1931- 25-28R
Moss, Marissa 1959- CANR-130
Earlier sketch in CA 171
See also SATA 71, 104, 163
Moss, Michael (Stanley) 1947- 108
Moss, Miriam 1955- CANR-119
Earlier sketch in CA 143
See also SATA 76, 140
Moss, Nancy
See Moss, Robert (Alfred)
Moss, Norman 1928- CANR-138
Earlier sketch in CA 49-52
Moss, (Victor) Peter (Cannings)
1921- CANR-2
Earlier sketch in CA 49-52
Moss, Ralph W(alter) 1943- 101
Moss, Robert (Alfred) 1903- CAP-1
Earlier sketch in CA 11-12
Moss, Robert (John) 1946- 146
Brief entry 118
Moss, Robert F. 1942- CANR-20
Earlier sketch in CA 81-84
Moss, Roberta
See Moss, Robert (Alfred)
Moss, Roger 1951- 124
Moss, Rosalind (Louisa Beaufort) 1890-1990
Obituary 131
Moss, Rose 1937- 49-52
Moss, Sanford Alexander III 1939- 118
Moss, Sidney P(hil) 1917- 5-8R
Moss, Stanley 1925- 97-100
See also CP 1, 2
Moss, Stephen Joseph 1935- 103
Moss, Stirling 1929- 5-8R
Moss, Thylias (Rebecca Brasier) 1954- 169
See also AAYA 37
See also BW 3
See also CP 7
See also CWP
See also DLB 120
See also SATA 108
Moss, Walter (Gerald) 1938- 65-68
Mossberger, Karen 1954- 213
Mosse, George L(achmann)
1918-1999 .... CANR-52
Obituary 174
Earlier sketches in CA 5-8R, CANR-12, 28
Mosse, Werner E(ugen Emil) 1918- 9-12R
Mossgiel, Rab
See Burns, Robert
Mossiker, Frances (Sanger)
1906-1985 .... CANR-75
Obituary 116
Earlier sketch in CA 9-12R
Mossing, Doug(las) 1952- 213
Mossman, Burt
See Keevill, Henry J(ohn)
Mossman, Dow 1943- 45-48
Mossman, Frank H(omer) 1915- CANR-5
Earlier sketch in CA 1-4R
Mossman, Jennifer 1944- CANR-38
Earlier sketches in CA 97-100, CANR-17
Mossner, Ernest C(ampbell) 1907-1986 123
Obituary 120
Mossop, D(eryk) J(oseph) 1919- 1-4R
Mossop, Irene
See Swatridge, Irene Maude (Mossop)
Most, Bernard 1937- CANR-52
Earlier sketches in CA 104, CANR-27
See also SATA 48, 91, 134
See also SATA-Brief 40
Most, Glenn W(arren) 1952- 112
Most, Kenneth S. 1924- 144
Most, William G(eorge) 1914-1999 49-52
Mostel, Kate
See Mostel, Kathryn Harkin
Mostel, Katherine Harkin
See Mostel, Kathryn Harkin
Mostel, Kathryn Harkin 1918-1986 .. CANR-75
Obituary 118
Earlier sketch in CA 81-84
Mostel, Samuel Joel 1915-1977 89-92
Mostel, Zero
See Mostel, Samuel Joel
Mosteller, (Charles) Frederick 1916- . CANR-23
Earlier sketches in CA 17-20R, CANR-7
Mostert, Noel 1929- 105
Mostofsky, David I(saac) 1931- 17-20R
Mostyn, Trevor 1946- CANR-66
Earlier sketch in CA 129
Mota, Avelino Teixeira da
See Teixeira da Mota, Avelino
Motavalli, Jim 1952- 195
Motchenbacher, C(urt) D. 1931- 146
Mother Love 198
Mother Mary Anthony
See Weinig, Jean Maria
Mothershead, Harmon Ross 1931- 33-36R
Mother Teresa 1910-1997 164
Motherwell, Cathryn 1957- 132
Mothner, Ira S(anders) 1932- CANR-13
Earlier sketch in CA 21-24R
Motion, Andrew (Peter) 1952- CANR-142
Earlier sketches in CA 146, CANR-90
See also BRWS 7
See also CLC 47
See also CP 7
See also DLB 40
See also MTFW 2005
Motley, Annette 1888-1962 .... RHW
Motley, Arthur H(arrison) 1900-1984
Obituary 112
See also AITN 2
Motley, John Lothrop 1814-1877 ..... DLB 1, 30, 59, 235
Motley, Mary
See De Reneville, Mary Margaret Motley Sheridan
Motley, Mary Penick 1920- 73-76
Motley, Red
See Motley, Arthur H(arrison)
Motley, Willard (Francis)
1909-1965 .... CANR-88
Obituary 106
Earlier sketch in CA 117
See also BW 1
See also CLC 18
See also DLB 76, 143
Motley, Wilma E(lizabeth) 1912- 41-44R
Motmot, Snik P.
See Tompkins, Everett Thomas
Motoyama, Hiroshi 1925- 110
Mott, Evelyn Clarke 1962- .... SATA 75, 133
Mott, Frank Luther 1886-1964 .... 1-4R
Mott, George Fox 1907-1987 .... CANR-76
Obituary 123
Earlier sketch in CA 13-16R
Mott, Lucretia Coffin 1793-1880 .... DLB 239
See also FW
Mott, Michael (Charles Alston)
1930- CANR-29
Earlier sketches in CA 5-8R, CANR-7
See also CAAS 7
See also CLC 15, 34
Mott, N(evill) F(rancis) 1905-1996 129
Obituary 153
Mott, Paul E. 103
Mott, Robert L. 144

Cumulative Index 415 Mueller

Mott, Sir Nevill
See Mott, N(evill) F(rancis)
Mott, Stephen Charles 1940- ... CANR-38
Earlier sketch in CA 116
Mott, Vincent Valmon 1916- ... 41-44R
Mott, Wesley T. 1946- ... 175
Motta, Dick 1931- ... 134
Brief entry ... 111
Mottahedeh, Roy Parviz 1940- ... CANR-21
Earlier sketch in CA 104
Mottaz, Carole A. 1953- ... 221
Mottelson, Ben R. 1926- ... 168
Motter, Alton M(yers) 1907- ... CAP-1
Earlier sketch in CA 11-12
Motteux, Peter Anthony 1663-1718 ... DLB 80
Motto, Anna Lydia ... 41-44R
Motto, Carmine J. 1914-2002 ... 33-36R
Motton, Gregory 1961- ... 230
See also CBD
See also CD 5, 6
Mottram, Anthony John 1920- ... 5-8R
Mottram, (Vernon) Henry 1882-1976(?) . CAP-1
Earlier sketch in CA 11-12
Mottram, R(alph) H(ale) 1883-1971 ... 108
Obituary ... 29-32R
See also DLB 36
Mottram, Tony
See Mottram, Anthony John
Motyl, Alexander J(ohn) 1953- ... 144
Motz, Lloyd 1909- ... CANR-4
Earlier sketch in CA 9-12R
See also SATA 20
Mouat, Kit
See Mackay, Jane
Moulakis, Athanasios 1945- ... CANR-101
Earlier sketch in CA 147
Mould, Daphne D(esiree) C(harlotte) Pochin
1920- ... CANR-4
Earlier sketch in CA 9-12R
Mould, Edwin
See Whitlock, Ralph
Mould, George 1894- ... 57-60
Moule, C(harles) F(rancis) D(igby)
1908- ... CANR-5
Earlier sketch in CA 1-4R
Moulessehoul, Mohammed 1956- ... 227
Moulier, (Antoine) Fernand 1913-1985 ... 81-84
Moulin, Annie 1946- ... 140
Moulin, Marie-Annie
See Moulin, Annie
Moult, Edward (Walker) 1926-1986
Obituary ... 120
Moult, Ted
See Moult, Edward (Walker)
Moult, Thomas 1895-1974
Obituary ... 89-92
Moulton, Candy (L.) 1955- ... 223
Moulton, Candy Vyvey
See Moulton, Candy (L.)
Moulton, Carl
See Tubb, E(dwin) C(harles)
Moulton, Edward C. 1936- ... 77-80
Moulton, Eugene R(ussell)
1916-1981 ... CANR-11
Earlier sketch in CA 21-24R
Moulton, Forest Ray 1872-1952 ... 159
Moulton, Gary E(van) 1942- ... 115
Moulton, Harland B. 1925- ... 37-40R
Moulton, J(ames) L(ouis) 1906-1993 ... 21-24R
Moulton, Nancy 1946- ... 116
Moulton, Phillips P(rentice) 1909- ... 37-40R
Moulton, William G(amwell)
1914-2000 ... 9-12R
Mouly, Francoise ... 224
See also SATA 155
Mouly, George J(oseph) 1915- ... CANR-17
Earlier sketch in CA 1-4R
Mounce, R(obert H.) 1921- ... CANR-110
Earlier sketch in CA 1-4R
See also Mounce, Robert H.
Mounce, Robert H. 1921- ... CANR-110
See also Mounce, R(obert H.)
Mount, Charles Merrill 1928- ... 13-16R
Mount, Elisabeth
See Dougherty, Betty
Mount, Ellis 1921- ... CANR-39
Earlier sketch in CA 116
Mount, (William Robert) Ferdinand
1939- ... CANR-88
Earlier sketches in CA 21-24R, CANR-11
See also DLB 231
Mount, Marshall Ward 1927- ... 73-76
Mountain, Fiona 1974(?)- ... 237
Mountain, Julian
See Cowie, Donald
Mountain, Marian
See Wisberg, Marian Aline
Mountain, Robert
See Montgomery, Raymond A. (Jr.)
Mountain Wolf Woman 1884-1960 . CANR-90
Earlier sketch in CA 144
See also CLC 92
See also NNAL
Mountbatten, Louis (Francis Albert Victor
Nicholas) 1900-1979 ... 133
Obituary ... 113
Mountbatten, Richard
See Wallmann, Jeffrey M(iner)
Mountfield, David
See Grant, Neil
Mountfield, Stuart 1903(?)-1984
Obituary ... 115
Mountfort, Guy 1905-2003 ... 17-20R
Obituary ... 216
Mountjoy, Christopher
See Miles, Keith
Mountjoy, Craig
See Cox, Howard A.
Mountjoy, Roberta Jean
See Sohl, Jerry
Mountrose, Phillip 1950- ... CANR-112
Earlier sketch in CA 163
Mountsier, Robert 1888(?)-1972
Obituary ... 37-40R
Mouque, Georges
See Kosma, Joseph
Mouradian, George 1927- ... 222
Mourant, John A(rthur) 1903-1994 ... CAP-1
Earlier sketch in CA 9-10
Moure, Erin 1955- ... 113
See also CLC 88
See also CP 7
See also CWP
See also DLB 60
Moure, Kenneth ... 175
Moure, Nancy D(ustin) W(all) 1943- ... 187
Mourelatos, Alexander P(hoebus) D(ionysiou)
1936- ... 29-32R
Mourgues, Odette (Marie Helene Louise) de
See de Mourgues, Odette (Marie Helene Louise)
Mourier, Marguerite
See Boulton, Marjorie
Mourning Dove 1885(?)-1936 ... CANR-90
Earlier sketch in CA 144
See also DAM MULT
See also DLB 175, 221
See also NNAL
Moursund, David G. 1936- ... CANR-30
Earlier sketches in CA 25-28R, CANR-12
Moursund, Janet (Peck) 1936- ... CANR-30
Earlier sketch in CA 45-48
Moussa, Pierre L(ouis) 1922- ... 13-16R
Moussalli, Ahmad S. 1956- ... 201
Moussard, Jacqueline 1924- ... CANR-8
Earlier sketch in CA 61-64
See also SATA 24
Moustache, Vieux
See Homer, Winslow
Mouton, Jane Srygley 1930- ... 123
Moutoux, John T. 1901(?)-1979
Obituary ... 89-92
Mouzelis, Nicos P. 1939- ... 33-36R
Mouzon, Olin T(errell) 1912-1983 ... 5-8R
Mow, Anna Beahm 1893-1985 ... CANR-3
Earlier sketch in CA 9-12R
Mowat, C(harles) L(och) 1911-1970 ... CAP-1
Earlier sketch in CA 13-16
Mowat, Claire (Angel Wheeler)
1933- ... CANR-93
Earlier sketch in CA 131
See also SATA 123
Mowat, David 1943- ... 77-80
See also CBD
See also CD 5, 6
Mowat, Farley (McGill) 1921- ... CANR-108
Earlier sketches in CA 1-4R, CANR-4, 24, 42, 68
Interview in ... CANR-24
See also AAYA 1, 50
See also BYA 2
See also CLC 26
See also CLR 20
See also CPW
See also DAC
See also DAM MST
See also DLB 68
See also JRDA
See also MAICYA 1, 2
See also MTCW 1, 2
See also MTFW 2005
See also SATA 3, 55
See also YAW
Mowat, R(obert) C(ase) 1913- ... 29-32R
Mowatt, Anna Cora 1819-1870 ... RGAL 4
Mowatt, Ian 1948- ... 41-44R
Mowery, William Byron 1899-1957 . TCWW 1, 2
Mowitt, John 1952- ... 140
Mowitz, Robert J(ames) 1920- ... CANR-3
Earlier sketch in CA 5-8R
Mowl, Timothy 1951- ... 180
Mowrer, Edgar Ansel 1892-1977 ... CAP-1
Obituary ... 69-72
Earlier sketch in CA 13-16
See also DLB 29
Mowrer, Lilian Thomson 1889(?)-1990 ... 65-68
Obituary ... 132
Mowrer, O(rval) Hobart 1907- ... CANR-1
Earlier sketch in CA 1-4R
Mowrer, Paul Scott 1887-1971 ... CANR-4
Obituary ... 29-32R
Earlier sketch in CA 5-8R
See also DLB 29
Mowry, George E(dwin) 1909-1984 . CANR-17
Earlier sketch in CA 1-4R
Mowry, Jess 1960- ... 133
See also AAYA 29
See also BYA 10
See also CLR 65
See also MAICYA 2
See also SATA 109, 131
See also SATA-Essay 131
See also YAW
Mowshowitz, Abbe 1939- ... 109
Moxham, Robert Morgan 1919-1978
Obituary ... 77-80
Moxham, Roy 1939- ... 201
Moxley, Gina ... 216
Moxley, Sheila 1966- ... 163
See also SATA 96
Moxon, Joseph fl. 1647-1684 ... DLB 170
Moy, James S. 1948- ... 146
Moya, Jose C. 1952- ... 176
Moyano, Daniel 1930- ... 131
See also HW 1
Moye, Catherine 1960- ... 136
Moye, Guan 1956(?)- ... 201
See also Mo Yen and
Yan, Mo
Mo Yen
See Moye, Guan
See also EWL 3
Moyer, Albert E. 1945- ... 172
Moyer, Carolyn
See Swayze, Carolyn (Norma)
Moyer, Claire B. (Inch) 1905-1995 ... CAP-2
Earlier sketch in CA 19-20
Moyer, Elgin Sylvester 1890-1985 ... 5-8R
Moyer, Kenneth E(van) 1919- ... CANR-13
Earlier sketch in CA 33-36R
Moyer, Kermit 1943- ... 136
Moyer, Marsha ... 214
Moyer, Terry J. 1937- ... 159
See also SATA 94
Moyers, Bill 1934- ... CANR-52
Earlier sketches in CA 61-64, CANR-31
See also AITN 2
See also CLC 74
Moyes, John Stoward 1884-1972 ... CAP-1
Earlier sketch in CA 13-14
Moyes, Norman Barr 1931- ... 37-40R
Moyes, Patricia
See Haszard, Patricia Moyes
See also DLB 276
See also SATA 63
Moyler, Alan (Frank Powell) 1926- ... SATA 36
Moyles, R(obert) Gordon 1939- ... CANR-17
Earlier sketch in CA 65-68
Moynahan, Brian 1941- ... CANR-139
Earlier sketch in CA 173
Moynahan, John F. 1912-1985
Obituary ... 115
Moynahan, Julian (Lane) 1925- ... CANR-1
Earlier sketch in CA 1-4R
Moynahan, Molly 1957- ... 133
Moyne, Ernest J(ohn) 1916-1976 ... CAP-2
Earlier sketch in CA 25-28
Moynihan, Daniel P(atrick)
1927-2003 ... CANR-43
Obituary ... 215
Earlier sketch in CA 5-8R
Moynihan, Danny ... 229
Moynihan, John Dominic 1932- ... 103
Moynihan, Maurice (Gerard) 1902-1999 ... 107
Moynihan, Michael 1969- ... 169
Moynihan, Ruth B(arnes) 1933- ... CANR-41
Earlier sketch in CA 117
Moynihan, William T. 1927- ... 21-24R
Moyse-Bartlett, Hubert 1902(?)-1973(?)
Obituary ... 104
Moyser, George H. 1945- ... 134
Mozley, Charles 1915- ... SATA 43
See also SATA-Brief 32
Mphahlele, Es'kia
See Mphahlele, Ezekiel
See also AFW
See also CDWLB 3
See also CN 4, 5, 6
See also DLB 125, 225
See also RGSF 2
See also SSFS 11
Mphahlele, Ezekiel 1919- ... CANR-76
Earlier sketches in CA 81-84, CANR-26
See also Mphahlele, Es'kia
See also BLC 3
See also BW 2, 3
See also CLC 25, 133
See also CN 1, 2, 3
See also DA3
See also DAM MULT
See also EWL 3
See also MTCW 2
See also MTFW 2005
See also SATA 119
Mqhayi, S(amuel) E(dward) K(rune Loliwe)
1875-1945 ... CANR-87
Earlier sketch in CA 153
See also BLC 3
See also DAM MULT
See also TCLC 25
Mr. Cleveland
See Seltzer, Louis B(enson)
Mr. Kenneth
See Marlowe, Kenneth
Mr. Magic Realism
See Taylor, Bruce
Mr. McGillicuddy
See Abisch, Roslyn Kroop
Mr. Metropolitan Opera
See Robinson, Francis (Arthur)
Mr. Pete.
See Kriendler, H(arold) Peter
Mr. Sniff
See Abisch, Roslyn Kroop
Mr. Tivil
See Lorkowski, Thomas V(incent)
Mr. Trend
See Torekull, Bertil
Mr. Wizard
See Herbert, Don(ald Jeffrey)
Mrabet, Mohammed
See el Hajjam, Mohammed ben Chaib
Mraz, John 1943- ... 235
Mrazek, James E(dward) 1914- ... 33-36R
Mrazek, Robert J. 1945- ... 226
Mrkvicka, Edward Francis, Jr. 1944- ... 203
Mrosovsky, Kitty ... 128
Mrozek, Donald J(ohn) 1945- ... 107
Mrozek, Slawomir 1930- ... CANR-29
Earlier sketch in CA 13-16R
See also CAAS 10
See also CDWLB 4
See also CLC 3, 13
See also CWW 2
See also DLB 232
See also EWL 3
See also MTCW 1
Mrs. Belloc-Lowndes
See Lowndes, Marie Adelaide (Belloc)
Mrs. Bishop
See Bishop, Isabella Lucy (Bird)
Mrs. Elliot Handler
See Handler, Ruth
Mrs. Fairstar
See Horne, Richard Henry Hengist
Mrs. G.
See Griffiths, Kitty Anna
Mrs. Miggy
See Krentel, Mildred White
Mrs. R. F. D.
See Peden, Rachel (Mason)
M'Taggart, John M'Taggart Ellis
See McTaggart, John McTaggart Ellis
M'Timkulu, Donald (Guy Sidney)
1910-2000 ... 97-100
Mtshali, Oswald Mbuyiseni 1940- ... CANR-87
Earlier sketch in CA 142
See also BW 2
See also CP 1, 2, 3, 4, 5, 6, 7
See also DLB 125, 225
Mtwa, Percy (?)- ... CD 6
See also CLC 47
Mu, Yang
See Wang, C(hing) H(sien)
Mubarrad, al- 826-898(?) ... DLB 311
Mucha, Jiri 1915-1991 ... CANR-82
Obituary ... 134
Earlier sketches in CA 21-24R, CANR-11, 26
Mucha, Zak ... 204
Muchmore, Jo Ann 1937- ... 170
See also SATA 103
Muchnic, Helen (Lenore) 1903-2000 . CANR-5
Earlier sketch in CA 1-4R
Muckenhoupt, Margaret ... 202
Mudd, Emily Hartshorne 1898-1998 ... 13-16R
Obituary ... 169
Mudd, Harvey (Seeley II) 1940- ... 130
Mudd, Roger H(arrison) 1928- ... 105
Mudd, Stuart 1893-1975 ... 9-12R
Obituary ... 57-60
Muddiman, John 1947- ... CANR-135
Earlier sketch in CA 136
Mude, O.
See Gorey, Edward (St. John)
Mudford, William 1782-1848 ... DLB 159
Mudge, Jean McClure 1933- ... CANR-6
Earlier sketch in CA 5-8R
Mudge, Lewis Seymour 1929- ... 89-92
Mudgeon, Apeman
See Mitchell, Adrian
Mudgett, Herman W.
See White, William A(nthony) P(arker)
Mudie, Ian (Mayelston) 1911-1976 ... 25-28R
Obituary ... 135
See also CP 1, 2
Mudimbe, V. Y. 1941- ... 141
See also BW 2
See also EWL 3
Mudrick, Marvin 1921- ... CANR-20
Earlier sketch in CA 25-28R
Mudrooroo (Nyoongah) 1938- ... 154
See also Johnson, Colin
See also CN 6, 7
Muecke, D(ouglas) C(olin) 1919- ... 53-56
Mueggler, Erik 1962- ... 206
Muehl, Lois Baker 1920- ... CANR-18
Earlier sketch in CA 1-4R
Muehl, (Ernest) William 1919- ... 45-48
Muehlbach, Luise 1814-1873 ... DLB 133
Muehlen, Maria
See von Finckenstein, Maria
Muehlen, Norbert 1909-1981 ... 69-72
Obituary ... 104
Muehsam, Gerd 1913(?)-1979
Obituary ... 93-96
Muelder, Walter George 1907- ... CAP-1
Earlier sketch in CA 13-14
Mueller, Amelia 1911- ... 57-60
Mueller, Barbara R(uth) 1925- ... 9-12R
Mueller, Charles S(teinkamp) 1929- .. CANR-20
Earlier sketches in CA 13-16R, CANR-5
Mueller, Claus 1941- ... CANR-60
Earlier sketches in CA 65-68, CANR-31
Mueller, Daniel ... 234
Mueller, David L. 1929- ... 29-32R
Mueller, Dennis C(ary) 1940- ... CANR-39
Earlier sketch in CA 116
Mueller, Dorothy 1901-1989 ... 102
Mueller, Dorothy 1949(?)-1989
Obituary ... 130
Mueller, Erwin W. 1911-1977
Obituary ... 69-72
Mueller, Gerald F(rancis) 1927- ... 13-16R
Mueller, Gerhard G(ottlob) 1930- ... CANR-36
Earlier sketches in CA 25-28R, CANR-12
Mueller, Gerhard O. W. 1926- ... CANR-44
Earlier sketches in CA 1-4R, CANR-5, 20
Mueller, Gerhardt
See Bickers, Richard (Leslie) Townshend
Mueller, Gustav Emil 1898-1987 ... CANR-7
Earlier sketch in CA 17-20R
Mueller, Heiner 1929- ... DLB 124
Mueller, Ingo 1942- ... 142
Mueller, James R. 1951- ... 138
Mueller, James W(illiam) 1941- ... 57-60

Mueller, Janel M(ulder) 1938- CANR-107
Earlier sketch in CA 132
Mueller, Joachim W(ilhelm) 1953- 139
Mueller, John E(rnest) 1937- CANR-56
Earlier sketches in CA 37-40R, CANR-14
Mueller, Jorg 1942- 136
See also CLR 43
See also MAICYA 2
See also SATA 67
Mueller, Kate Hevner 1898-1984 .... 41-44R
Mueller, Klaus Andrew 1921- CANR-4
Earlier sketch in CA 49-52
Mueller, Lisel 1924- 93-96
See also CLC 13, 51
See also CP 7
See also DLB 105
See also PC 33
See also PFS 9, 13
Mueller, M(ax) G(erhard) 1925- 17-20R
Mueller, Maler 1749-1825 .... DLB 94
Mueller, Marlies K(uhfuss) 1937- 114
Mueller, Marnie (Grace Elberson) 1942- 198
Mueller, Melissa 1967- 209
Mueller, Merrill 1916-1980
Obituary 103
Mueller, Red
See Mueller, Merrill
Mueller, Reuben Herbert 1897-1982
Obituary 107
Mueller, Robert E(mmett) 1925- 1-4R
Mueller, Robert Kirk 1913-1999 .... CANR-12
Obituary 183
Earlier sketch in CA 73-76
Mueller, Virginia 1924- CANR-57
Earlier sketches in CA 65-68, CANR-10, 27
See also SATA 28
Mueller, Wilhelm 1794-1827 .... DLB 90
Mueller, Willard Fritz 1925- 17-20R
Mueller, William R(andolph) 1916- CANR-2
Earlier sketch in CA 1-4R
Mueller-Vollmer, Kurt 1928- 126
Muenchausen, Boerries von
See Munchhausen, Borries von
Muenchen, Al(fred) 1917- 49-52
Muesing, Edith E(lizabeth)
See Muesing-Ellwood, Edith E(lizabeth)
Muesing-Ellwood, Edith E(lizabeth) 1947- ... 114
Muffett, D(avid) J(oseph) M(ead) 1919- ... 45-48
Muggeridge, Malcolm (Thomas)
1903-1990 .... CANR-63
Earlier sketches in CA 101, CANR-33
See also AITN 1
See also MTCW 1, 2
See also TCLC 120
Muggeson, Margaret Elizabeth 1942- 103
Muggs
See Watkins, Lois
Mugny, Gabriel 1949- 140
Mugo, Micere Githae 1942- 164
Muhajir, Nazzam Al Fitnah
See El Muhajir
Muhammad 570-632 .... DA
See also DAB
See also DAC
See also DAM MST
See also DLB 311
See also WLCS
Muhammadiev, Fazluddin Aminovich
1928-1986 .... EWL 3
Muhanji, Cherry 1939- .... GLL 2
Muheim, Harry Miles 1920-2003 85-88
Obituary 214
Muhlen, Norbert
See Muehlen, Norbert
Muhlenfeld, Elisabeth 1944- CANR-24
Earlier sketch in CA 108
Muhlhausen, John Prague 1940- 61-64
Muhlstein, Anka 1935- CANR-100
Earlier sketch in CA 114
Mui, Hoh-cheung 1916- 45-48
Mui, Lorna H(olbrook) 1915- 133
Muileman, Kathryn Saltzman 1946- 85-88
Muilenburg, Grace (Evelyn) 1913- 61-64
Muir, (Charles) Augustus (Carlow)
1893(?)-1989 .... 13-16R
Obituary 128
Muir, Barbara K(enrick Gowing) 1908- ... 9-12R
Muir, Bernard J(ames) 1951- 236
Muir, Dexter
See Gribble, Leonard (Reginald)
Muir, Diana
See Appelbaum, Diana Muir Karter
Muir, Edwin 1887-1959 193
Brief entry 104
See also Moore, Edward
See also BRWS 6
See also DLB 20, 100, 191
See also EWL 3
See also PC 49
See also RGEL 2
See also TCLC 2, 87
Muir, Frank (Herbert) 1920-1998 ...... CANR-29
Obituary 164
Earlier sketch in CA 81-84
See also SATA 30
Muir, Helen 1911(?)- .... AITN 2
Muir, Helen 1937- 130
See also DLB 14
See also SATA 65
Muir, James A.
See Wells, Angus
Muir, Jane
See Petrone, Jane Muir
Muir, Jean 1906-1973 .... CAP-2
Obituary 41-44R
Earlier sketch in CA 29-32
Muir, John 1838-1914 165
See also AMWS 9
See also ANW
See also DLB 186, 275
See also TCLC 28
Muir, John Kenneth 1969- 183
Muir, Kenneth (Arthur) 1907-1996 ... CANR-44
Obituary 153
Earlier sketches in CA 1-4R, CANR-4
Muir, Lynette R(oss) 1930- CANR-48
Earlier sketch in CA 122
Muir, Malcolm, Jr. 1914-1984
Obituary 113
Muir, Malcolm 1885-1979 93-96
Obituary 85-88
Muir, Marie 1904-1998 .... CANR-5
Earlier sketch in CA 1-4R
Muir, Percival H(orace) 1894-1979 .... CANR-5
Obituary 97-100
Earlier sketch in CA 9-12R
See also Muir, Percy
Muir, Percy
See Muir, Percival H(orace)
See also DLB 201
Muir, Percy H.
See Muir, Percival H(orace)
Muir, Richard 1943- CANR-23
Earlier sketch in CA 106
Muir, Rory 1962- CANR-123
Earlier sketch in CA 156
Muir, Star A. 1958- 175
Muir, Willa 1890-1970 192
Muir, William Ker, Jr. 1931- 53-56
Muirhead, Bruce 1954- 192
Muirhead, Ian A(dair) 1913-1983 .... 13-16R
Muirhead, John G. 1918- 236
Muirhead, Thorburn 1899- 5-8R
Mujica, Barbara 1943- CANR-105
Earlier sketch in CA 138
Mujica, Elisa 1918-1984 .... EWL 3
Mujica Lainez, Manuel 1910-1984 .. CANR-32
Obituary 112
Earlier sketch in CA 81-84
See also Lainez, Manuel Mujica
See also CLC 31
See also EWL 3
See also HW 1
Muju Ichien 1226-1312 .... DLB 203
Mukasa, Ham 1868(?)-1956 171
Mukerjee, Madhusree 1961(?)- 228
Mukerji, Chandra 1945- 113
Mukerji, Dhan Gopal 1890-1936 ..... CANR-90
Brief entry 119
Earlier sketch in CA 136
See also BYA 5
See also CLR 10
See also CWRI 5
See also MAICYA 1, 2
See also SATA 40
Mukerji, Kshitimohon 1920- 17-20R
Mukherjee, Bharati 1940- 232
Earlier sketches in CA 107, CANR-45, 72, 128
Autobiographical Essay in 232
See also AAL
See also AAYA 46
See also BEST 89:2
See also CLC 53, 115
See also CN 5, 6, 7
See also DAM NOV
See also DLB 60, 218
See also DNFS 1, 2
See also EWL 3
See also FW
See also MAL 5
See also MTCW 1, 2
See also MTFW 2005
See also RGAL 4
See also RGSF 2
See also SSC 38
See also SSFS 7
See also TUS
See also WWE 1
Mukherjee, Meenakshi 1937- 65-68
Mukherjee, Rabin 1932- 204
Mukherjee, Ramkrishna 1919- CANR-7
Earlier sketch in CA 57-60
Mula, Frank (Charles) 158
Mulac, Margaret E(lizabeth) 1912- CANR-2
Earlier sketch in CA 5-8R
Mulaisho, Dominic (Chola) 1933- 97-100
Mulan, Don 1956- 176
Mularchyk, Sylva 93-96
Mulari, Mary 1947- 222
Mulay, Larry L. 1904(?)-1987
Obituary 122
Mulcahy, Greg CANR-93
Earlier sketch in CA 145
Mulcahy, Lisa 239
Mulcahy, Lucille Burnett 5-8R
See also SATA 12
Mulcaster, Richard c. 1531-1611 .... DLB 167
Mulchrone, Vincent 1919(?)-1977
Obituary 73-76
Mulder, John M(ark) 1946-
Brief entry 112
Muldoon, Paul 1951- CANR-91
Brief entry 113
Earlier sketches in CA 129, CANR-52
Interview in CA-129
See also BRWS 4
See also CLC 32, 72, 166
See also CP 2, 3, 4, 5, 6, 7
See also DAM POET
See also DLB 40
See also PFS 7, 22
See also TCLE 1:2
Muldoon, Roland W. 1941- 105
Muldowny, John 1931- 127
Mule, Marty 1944- 108
Mulesko, Angelo
See Oglesby, Joseph
Mulfinger, Dale 1943- 221
Mulford, Charles W. 1951- 229
Mulford, Clarence E(dward)
1883-1956 .... TCWW 1, 2
Mulford, David Campbell 1937- 9-12R
Mulford, Philippa G(reene) 1948- 116
See also SATA 43, 112
Mulford, Wendy 1941- .... CWP
Mulgan, Catherine 1931- CANR-11
Earlier sketch in CA 25-28R
See also Gough, Catherine
Mulgan, John (Alan Edward)
1911-1945 .... RGEL 2
Mulgrew, Ian 1957- 211
Mulgrew, Peter David 1927- 13-16R
Mulhauser, Ruth (Elizabeth)
1913-1980 .... CANR-7
Earlier sketch in CA 5-8R
Mulhearn, John 1932- 65-68
Mulholland, James 1960- 236
Mulholland, Jim 1949- CANR-48
Earlier sketch in CA 61-64
Mulholland, John 1898-1970 .... 5-8R
Obituary 89-92
Mulholland, John F(ield) 1903-1989 ..... 41-44R
Mulila, Vigad G.
See Maillu, David G(ian)
Mulisch, Harry (Kurt Victor) 1927- . CANR-110
Earlier sketches in CA 9-12R, CANR-6, 26, 56
See also CLC 42
See also CWW 2
See also DLB 299
See also EWL 3
Mulkeen, Anne
See Marcus, Anne M(ulkeen)
Mulkeen, Thomas P(atrick) 1923- 85-88
Mulkerne, Donald James Dennis 1921- .. 9-12R
Mulkerns, Val 1925- .... CN 7
See also DLB 319
Mull, Martin 1943- 105
See also CLC 17
Mullally, Frederic 1920- CANR-1
Earlier sketch in CA 1-4R
Mullaly, Edward (Joseph) 1941- 41-44R
Mullan, Bob 1950- 123
Mullan, David George 1951- CANR-86
Earlier sketch in CA 130
Mullan, Don 1956- 176
Mullan, Fitzhugh 1942- CANR-143
Earlier sketch in CA 69-72
Mullan, Harry
See Mullan, (Patrick) Henry (Pearse)
Mullan, (Patrick) Henry (Pearse)
1946-1999 185
Mullan, Pat 1939- 210
Mullan, Phil 221
Mullan, Robert 1950- CANR-50
Mullane, (R.) Mike 1945- 143
Mullaney, Marie Marmo 1953- 112
Mullaney, Thomas E. 1922(?)-1978 93-96
Obituary 81-84
Mullard, Chris(topher Paul) 1944-
Brief entry 112
Mullay, Alexander John 1947- 168
Mullay, Sandy
See Mullay, Alexander John
Mullen, Barbara 1914-1979
Obituary 85-88
Mullen, Bill V. 1959- 202
Mullen, C. J. J.
See Mullen, Cyril J.
Mullen, Cyril J. 1908-1989 61-64
Mullen, Dore
See Mullen, Dorothy
Mullen, Dorothy 1933- 104
Mullen, Edward John, Jr. 1942- CANR-17
Earlier sketches in CA 49-52, CANR-2
Mullen, Harris H. 1924- 69-72
Mullen, Harryette (Romell) 1953- 218
Mullen, James H. 1924- 1-4R
Mullen, Jane 1948- 194
Mullen, Laura 194
Mullen, Michael 1937- CANR-87
Earlier sketches in CA 116, CANR-39
See also CWRI 5
See also SATA 122
Mullen, Patrick B. 1941- 143
Mullen, Robert R(odolph) 1908-1986 .... CAP-1
Earlier sketch in CA 19-20
Mullen, Thomas J(ames) 1934- CANR-5
Earlier sketch in CA 9-12R
Mullen, William Charles 1944- 73-76
Mullenbach, Philip 1912-1989
Obituary 128
Mullendore, William Clinton 1892-1983
Obituary 111
Muller, Alexander V(ilhelm) 1932- 45-48
Muller, Billex
See Ellis, Edward S(ylvester)
Muller, Charles G(eorge Geoffrey)
1897-1987 .... CANR-2
Earlier sketch in CA 1-4R
Muller, Charles Geoffrey
See Muller, Charles G(eorge Geoffrey)
Muller, Dorothy
See Mueller, Dorothy
Muller, Eddie 1959- 203
Muller, Edward John 1916- 57-60
Muller, Filip
Muller, Gilbert H(enry) 1941- CANR-14
Earlier sketch in CA 41-44R
Muller, Heiner
See Muller, Heiner
Muller, Heiner 1929-1995 193
See also CWW 2
See also EWL 3
Muller, Herbert J(oseph) 1905-1998 ... CANR-1
Earlier sketch in CA 1-4R
Muller, Herman J(oseph) 1909- 73-76
Muller, Hermann Joseph 1890-1967 161
Obituary 106
Muller, Herta 1953- 175
Muller, Hilgard 1914-1985
Obituary 117
Muller, Ingo
See Mueller, Ingo
Muller, James W(aldemar) 1953- 132
Muller, Jan-Werner 1970- 235
Muller, Jerry Z(ucker) 1954- CANR-137
Earlier sketch in CA 144
Muller, Joachim W.
See Mueller, Joachim W(ilhelm)
Muller, John E.
See Fanthorpe, R(obert) Lionel
Muller, John P(aul) 1940- 103
Muller, Jorg
See Mueller, Jorg
Muller, Karin 1965- 172
Muller, Leo C., Jr. 1924- 5-8R
Muller, Marcia 1944- CANR-97
Earlier sketches in CA 81-84, CANR-41, 62
See also AAYA 25
See also CMW 4
See also DLB 226
Muller, Peter O. 1942- CANR-93
Earlier sketches in CA 110, CANR-45
Muller, Priscilla E(lkow) 1930- 61-64
Muller, Robby 1940- .... IDFW 3, 4
Muller, Robert George 1923- 103
Muller, (Lester) Robin 1953- CANR-87
Earlier sketches in CA 127, CANR-52
See also CWRI 5
See also SATA 86
Muller, Ronald E(rnst) 1939- 107
Muller, Siegfried H(ermann)
1902-1965 .... CAP-1
Earlier sketch in CA 11-12
Mulligan, Hugh A. 1925- CANR-11
Earlier sketch in CA 21-24R
Mulligan, James J. 1936- 45-48
Mulligan, John Joseph 1918- 33-36R
Mulligan, Raymond A(lexander) 1914- .. 37-40R
Mulligan, Robert S(mith) 1941- 65-68
Mulliken, Robert Sanderson 1896-1986 109
Obituary 120
Mullin, Caryl Cude 1969- 199
See also SATA 130
Mullin, Chris(topher John) 1947- 132
Mullin, Glenn H. 1949- 179
Mullin, Michael (Albert) 1944-2003 103
Obituary 217
Mullin, Robert Bruce 1953- 217
Mullin, Robert N(orville) 1893-1982 89-92
Mullin, Willard 1902-1978
Obituary 89-92
Mullings, Leith (Patricia) 1945- 223
Mullings, Llewellyn M. 1932- 37-40R
Mullins, (George) Aloysius 1910- CAP-1
Earlier sketch in CA 13-14
Mullins, Ann
See Dally, Ann
Mullins, Carolyn J(ohns) 1940- CANR-10
Earlier sketch in CA 65-68
Mullins, Claud 1887-1968 .... CAP-1
Earlier sketch in CA 13-14
Mullins, Edward S(wift) 1922- 17-20R
See also SATA 10
Mullins, Edwin (Brandt) 1933- CANR-92
Earlier sketches in CA 53-56, CANR-4, 22, 46
See also RHW
Mullins, Helene 1899-1991 77-80
Mullins, Hilary 1962- 150
See also SATA 84
Mullins, June B(onner) 1927- 126
Mullins, Larry E(dward) 1935- 117
Mullins, Nicholas C(reed) 1939- 33-36R
Mullins, Pat(rick Joseph) 1923- CANR-66
Earlier sketch in CA 128
Mullins, Vera (Annie) Cooper
1903-1987 61-64
Mullis, Kary B(anks) 1944- 185
Mulloy, Elizabeth D(ibert) 1945- 93-96
Mulock, Dinah Maria
See Craik, Dinah Maria (Mulock)
See also RGEL 2
Multatuli 1820-1881 .... RGWL 2, 3
Multhauf, Robert P(hilip) 1919-2004 93-96
Obituary 228
Mulvaney, (Derek) John 1925- 189
Mulvaney, Robert J(oseph) 1937- 126
Mulvanity, George 1903(?)-1976
Obituary 69-72
Mulvey, Ruth Watt
See Harmer, Ruth Mulvey
Mulvihill, Edward Robert 1917- 9-12R
Mulvihill, Maureen E. 1944- 135
Mulvihill, William Patrick 1923- 1-4R
See also SATA 8
Mulville, Frank 1924- 107
Mumaw, Barton 1912- 211
Mumey, Glen A(llen) 1933- 73-76
Mumford, Bob 1930- 103
Mumford, Emily (Hamilton)
1920(?)-1987 57-60
Obituary 123
Mumford, Erika 1935(?)-1988
Obituary 126

Mumford, Lewis 1895-1990 .... CANR-5
Obituary 130
Earlier sketch in CA 1-4R
See also AMWS 2
See also DLB 63
See also MAL 5
Mumford, Ruth 1919- CANR-87
Earlier sketch in CANR-51
See also Dallas, Ruth
See also CWRI 5
See also SATA 86
Mumford, Tex
See Heckelmann, Charles N(ewman)
Mumma, Howard E. 1909- 218
Mumms, Hardee
See McLellan, Diana
Mumy, Bill 1954- 173
See also SATA 112
Mun
See Leaf, (Wilbur) Munro
Munari, Bruno 1907-1998 .... CANR-38
Earlier sketch in CA 73-76
See also CLR 9
See also MAICYA 1, 2
See also SATA 15
Munby, A(lan) N(oel) L(atimer) 1913-1974 . 182
Obituary 53-56
See also DLB 201
See also HGG
Munby, Arthur Joseph 1828-1910 184
See also DLB 35
Munby, D(enys) L(awrence)
1919-1976 .... CANR-2
Earlier sketch in CA 1-4R
Munby, Jonathan 201
Munce, Ruth Hill 1898- CAP-1
Earlier sketch in CA 9-10
See also SATA 12
Munch, Edvard 1863-1944 .... AAYA 29
Munch, Peter A(ndreas) 1908-1984 .... 29-32R
Obituary 111
Munch, Theodore W(illiam) 1919- 57-60
Munck, Victor C. de
See de Munck, Victor C.
Muncy, Raymond Lee 1928- 49-52
Mund, Vernon A(rthur) 1906-1993 ... CANR-20
Earlier sketch in CA 1-4R
Munday, Anthony 1560-1633 .... DLB 62, 172
See also RGEL 2
Mundel, Marvin E(verett) 1916- 21-24R
Mundell, Robert A(lexander) 1932- CANR-2
Earlier sketch in CA 45-48
Mundell, William Daniel 1913-1997 73-76
Obituary 163
Mundis, Hester 1938- CANR-82
Earlier sketches in CA 69-72, CANR-15, 34
Mundis, Jerrold 1941- CANR-11
Earlier sketch in CA 69-72
Mundlak, Max 1899- CAP-1
Earlier sketch in CA 9-10
Mundt, Clara
See Muehlbach, Luise
Mundt, Theodor 1808-1861 .... DLB 133
Mundy, John Hine 1917- CANR-45
Earlier sketch in CA 45-48
Mundy, Max
See Schofield, Sylvia Anne
Mundy, Simon (Andrew James Hainault)
1954- CANR-65
Earlier sketch in CA 128
See also SATA 64
Mundy, Talbot 1879-1940 155
See also FANT
See also SUFW
Mune, Ian 1941- 233
Munevar, Gonzalo 1945- 225
Munford, Robert 1737(?)-1783 .... DLB 31
Munford, W(illiam) A(rthur) 1911-2002 116
Obituary 214
Mungai, Anne M. 1952- 220
Mungazi, Dickson A(dlai) 1934- 191
Mungello, David Emil 1943- 110
Munger, Al
See Unger, Maurice Albert
Munger, Frank James 1929-1981 .... CANR-1
Obituary 116
Earlier sketch in CA 1-4R
Munger, Hortense Roberta
See Roberts, Hortense Roberta
Munger, Robert Boyd 1910-2001 77-80
Obituary 195
Mungo, Raymond 1946- CANR-2
Earlier sketch in CA 49-52
See also CLC 72
Mungoshi, Charles L. 1947- 168
See also BW 3
See also DLB 157
See also EWL 3
Munhall, Edgar 1933- 150
Munholland, John K(im) 1934- CANR-25
Earlier sketch in CA 29-32R
Munif, 'Abd al-Rahman
See Munif, Abdelrahman
See also CWW 2
See also EWL 3
See also WLIT 6
Munif, Abdelrahman 1933-2004 144
Obituary 224
See also Strydom, (Barend) Piet(er)
See also EWL 3
Munir, Muhammad 1895-1981
Obituary 108
Munitz, Milton K(arl) 1913-1995 ...... CANR-36
Obituary 149
Earlier sketches in CA 93-96, CANR-16
Muniz, Angelina 1936- 131
See also HW 1
Muniz, Olga M. 217
Munk, Arthur W. 1909-1992 .... CANR-7
Earlier sketch in CA 13-16R
Munk, Christian
See Weisenborn, Guenther
Munk, Erika 1939- 17-20R
Munk, Kaj 1898-1944 .... DLB 214
See also EWL 3
Munk, Nina 1968- 230
Munker, Dona 1945- 138
Munn, Geoffrey C(harles) 1953- CANR-47
Earlier sketch in CA 118
Munn, Glenn (Gaywaine) 1890(?)-1977
Obituary 73-76
Munn, H(arold) Warner 1903-1981 .. CANR-75
Earlier sketches in CA 21-24R, CANR-11
See also FANT
See also HGG
Munnecke, Wilbur C(heney) 1906-1984
Obituary 112
Munnell, Alicia H(aydock) 1942- CANR-30
Earlier sketches in CA 73-76, CANR-13
Munonye, John (Okechukwu)
1929- CANR-101
Earlier sketches in CA 103, CANR-87
See also CN 3, 4, 5, 6, 7
See also DLB 117
See also WLIT 2
Munowitz, Ken 1935-1977 .... SATA 14
Munoz, Braulio 1946- 110
Munoz, Elias Miguel .... LLW
Munoz, Heraldo 1948- 111
Munoz, Jose Esteban 185
Munoz, Mercedes Negron 1895(?)-1973 189
Munoz, William 1949- .... SATA 42, 92
Munoz Marin, (Jose) Luis (Alberto)
1898-1980 153
Obituary 97-100
See also HW 1
Munro, Alice (Anne) 1931- CANR-114
Earlier sketches in CA 33-36R, CANR-33, 53, 75
See also AITN 2
See also BPFB 2
See also CCA 1
See also CLC 6, 10, 19, 50, 95
See also CN 1, 2, 3, 4, 5, 6, 7
See also DA3
See also DAC
See also DAM MST, NOV
See also DLB 53
See also EWL 3
See also MTCW 1, 2
See also MTFW 2005
See also RGEL 2
See also RGSF 2
See also SATA 29
See also SSC 3
See also SSFS 5, 13, 19
See also TCLE 1:2
See also WLCS
See also WWE 1
Munro, Bertha 1887-1983 45-48
Munro, C. K.
See MacMullan, Charles Walden Kirkpatrick
Munro, Dana Gardner 1892-1990 .... 1-4R
Obituary 131
Munro, David
See Devine, D(avid) M(cDonald)
Munro, Donald J(acques) 1931- 133
Munro, Duncan H.
See Russell, Eric Frank
Munro, Eleanor 1928- 1-4R
See also SATA 37
Munro, H(ector) H(ugh)
1870-1916 .... CANR-104
Brief entry 104
Earlier sketch in CA 130
See also Saki
See also AAYA 56
See also CDBLB 1890-1914
See also DA
See also DA3
See also DAB
See also DAC
See also DAM MST, NOV
See also DLB 34, 162
See also EXPS
See also MTCW 1, 2
See also MTFW 2005
See also RGEL 2
See also SSFS 15
See also WLC
Munro, Hector H.
See Munro, H(ector) H(ugh)
Munro, (Macfarlane) Hugh 9-12R
Munro, Ian S. 29-32R
Munro, James
See Cave, Roderick (George James Munro) and Mitchell, James
Munro, Jane 1943- 112
Munro, John (Henry Alexander) 1938- .. 41-44R
Munro, John M(urchinson) 1932- CANR-11
Earlier sketch in CA 69-72
Munro, Leslie Knox 1901-1974
Obituary 49-52
Munro, Mary
See Howe, Doris Kathleen
Munro, Neil 1864-1930 188
See also DLB 156
See also RHW
Munro, Rona 1959- 230
See also CBD
See also CD 5, 6
See also CWD
Munro, Roxie 1945- 238
See also SATA 58, 136
Munro, Sheila 1953- 214
Munro, Thomas 1897-1974 .... CANR-3
Earlier sketch in CA 5-8R
Munroe, Elizabeth L(ee) 1900-1993 ... CANR-2
Earlier sketch in CA 17-20R
Munroe, Jim 1972- 218
Munroe, John A(ndrew) 1914- 49-52
Munroe, Kirk 1850-1930
Brief entry 123
See also DLB 42
Munrow, David John 1942-1976 103
Obituary 106
Munsch, Bob
See Munsch, Robert (Norman)
Munsch, Robert (Norman) 1945- CANR-87
Earlier sketches in CA 121, CANR-37
See also CLR 19
See also CWRI 5
See also MAICYA 1, 2
See also SATA 50, 83, 120
See also SATA-Brief 48
Munsell, F(loyd) Darrell 1934- 129
Munsey, Cecil (Richard, Jr.) 1935- CANR-17
Earlier sketch in CA 41-44R
Munsey, Frank A(ndrew) 1854-1925
Brief entry 116
See also DLB 25, 91
Munshi, Kiki Skagen 1943- CANR-15
Earlier sketch in CA 37-40R
Munshi, Shehnaaz
See Munshi, Kiki Skagen
Munshower, Suzanne 1945- 97-100
Munsinger, Harry 1935- 45-48
Munsinger, Lynn 1951- .... SATA 33, 94
Munslow, Barry 1950- CANR-41
Earlier sketch in CA 117
Munson, Amelia H. (?)-1972
Obituary 33-36R
Munson, Byron Edwin 1921- 41-44R
Munson, Carol (Barr) Swayze 1944- 231
Munson, Charlie E(llis) 1877-1975 57-60
Obituary 134
Munson, Derek 1970- 200
See also SATA 139
Munson, Don 1908-1978 73-76
Obituary 133
Munson, Douglas Anne 1949(?)-2003 169
Obituary 222
Munson, Fred C(aleb) 1928- 33-36R
Munson, Gorham B(ert) 1896-1969 ...... CAP-1
Earlier sketch in CA 11-12
Munson, Harold L(ewis) 1923- 29-32R
Munson, Henry (Lee), Jr. 1946- CANR-40
Earlier sketch in CA 115
Munson, James (Edward Bradbury)
1944- CANR-113
Earlier sketch in CA 124
Munson, Kenneth (George) 1929- 127
Brief entry 111
Munson, Lou
See Munson, Mary Lou (Easley)
Munson, Lynne A(nn) 1968- 198
Munson, Mary Lou (Easley) 1935- 9-12R
Munson, Noel J. 1938- 231
Munson, R. W.
See Karl, Jean E(dna)
Munson, Thomas N(olan) 1924- CANR-20
Earlier sketch in CA 1-4R
Munson, Thurman (Lee) 1947-1979 108
Obituary 89-92
Munson-Benson, Tunie 1946- 77-80
See also SATA 15
Munsterberg, Hugo 1916- CANR-2
Earlier sketch in CA 5-8R
Munsterberg, Peggy 1921- 169
See also SATA 102
Munsterhjelm, Erik 1905- 49-52
Munter, Robert (L.) 1926- 21-24R
Munthe, Adam John 1946- 107
Munthe, Frances 1915- 9-12R
See also RHW
Munthe, Malcolm Grane 1920- 5-8R
Munthe, Nelly 1947- 117
See also SATA 53
Munting, Roger 1945- 127
Munton, Alan (Guy) 1945- CANR-24
Earlier sketch in CA 107
Muntyan, Miodrag 1914-1985
Obituary 117
Muntz, (Isabelle) Hope 1907- 13-16R
Muntz, James
See Crowcroft, Peter
Munves, James (Albert) 1922- CANR-3
Earlier sketch in CA 5-8R
See also SATA 30
Munz, Peter 1921- 13-16R
Munz, Philip Alexander 1892-1974 .... 5-8R
Munzer, Martha E. 1899-1999 .... CANR-4
Earlier sketch in CA 1-4R
See also SATA 4
Mura, David (Alan) 1952- 209
Earlier sketches in CA 138, CANR-110
Autobiographical Essay in 209
See also DLB 312
Mura, Toshio 1925- 144
Murabito, Stephen J. 1956- 198
Murad, Anatol 1904- 73-76
Murad, Gauhar-i
See Sa'Idi, Ghulam Husayn
Murakami, Haruki 1949- CANR-102
Earlier sketch in CA 165
See also Murakami Haruki
See also CLC 150
See also MJW
See also RGWL 3
See also SFW 4
Murakami, Ryu(nosuke) 1952- 162
Murakami Haruki
See Murakami, Haruki
See also CWW 2
See also DLB 182
See also EWL 3
Muraki, Yoshiro 1924- .... IDFW 3, 4
Murari, Timeri N(rupendra) 1941- 102
Murarka, Shyam P. 1940- 144
Murasaki, Lady
See Murasaki Shikibu
Murasaki Shikibu 978(?)-1026(?) .... EFS 2
See also LATS 1:1
See also RGWL 2, 3
Murat, Ines 1939- 130
Murata, Kiyoaki 1922- 130
Muratov, Pavel 1881-1950 .... DLB 317
Muravchik, Joshua 1947- CANR-122
Earlier sketch in CA 136
Murav'ev, Mikhail Nikitich
1757-1807 .... DLB 150
Murav'eva, Irina
See Muravyova, Irina
Muravin, Victor 1929- 85-88
Muravyova, Irina 1952- 218
Murawski, Benjamin J(oseph) 1926- 45-48
Murayama, Milton (A.) 1923- CANR-142
Earlier sketch in CA 173
See also DLB 312
Murbarger, Nell Lounsberry
1909-1991 .... CAP-1
Earlier sketch in CA 13-16
Murch, Edward (William Lionel) 1920- ... 61-64
Murch, James DeForest 1892-1973 .... CANR-4
Earlier sketch in CA 5-8R
Murch, Mel
See Manes, Stephen
Murch, Walter (Scott) 1943- 222
See also IDFW 3, 4
Murchie, Guy 1907-1997 .... CANR-27
Obituary 159
Earlier sketch in CA 1-4R
See also CAAS 19
Murchie, Noel 1935- 199
Murchison, Thomas Moffat 1907-1984
Obituary 111
Murchison, William 1942- 147
Murchland, Bernard 1929- 112
Murcott, Anne 147
Murden, Forrest D(ozier), Jr. 1921-1977
Obituary 73-76
Murdick, Robert Gordon 1920- CANR-6
Earlier sketch in CA 5-8R
Murdin, Paul 1942- CANR-23
Earlier sketch in CA 106
Murdoch, Brian (Oliver) 1944- 141
Murdoch, David H(amilton) 1937- 161
See also SATA 96
Murdoch, (Henry) Derrick 1909-1985 89-92
Obituary 116
Murdoch, (Jean) Iris 1919-1999 ...... CANR-142
Obituary 179
Earlier sketches in CA 13-16R, CANR-8, 43, 68, 103
Interview in CANR-8
See also BRWS 1
See also CBD
See also CDBLB 1960 to Present
See also CLC 1, 2, 3, 4, 6, 8, 11, 15, 22, 31, 51
See also CN 1, 2, 3, 4, 5, 6
See also CWD
See also DA3
See also DAB
See also DAC
See also DAM MST, NOV
See also DLB 14, 194, 233
See also EWL 3
See also MTCW 1, 2
See also MTFW 2005
See also NFS 18
See also RGEL 2
See also TCLE 1:2
See also TEA
See also WLIT 4
Murdoch, J. Campbell
See Wells, John Campbell
Murdoch, Joseph S(impson) F(erguson)
1919- 102
Murdoch, Norman H. 1939- CANR-107
Earlier sketch in CA 154
Murdoch, (Keith) Rupert 1931- 239
Brief entry 111
See also DLB 127
Murdock, Eugene C(onverse) 1921- . CANR-48
Earlier sketches in CA 33-36R, CANR-13
Murdock, George Peter 1897-1985 .... CAP-1
Earlier sketch in CA 13-14
Murdock, Kenneth Ballard 1895-1975 65-68
Obituary 61-64
Murdock, Laurette P. 1900-1994 101
Murdock, M(elinda) S(eabrooke)
1947- CANR-32
Earlier sketch in CA 113
Murdock, Maureen 224
Murdock, Myrtle Cheney 1886(?)-1980
Obituary 97-100
Murdy, Louise Baughan 1935- 33-36R
Mure, David (William Alexander)
1912-1986 134
Obituary 120
Mure, G(eoffrey) R(eginald) G(ilchrist)
1893-1979 107
Muren, Dennis 1946- .... IDFW 3, 4
Murena, H. A.
See Alvarez Murena, Hector Alberto
Murena, Hector Alberto Alvarez
See Alvarez Murena, Hector Alberto

Murfin 418 CONTEMPORARY AUTHORS

Murfin, James Vernon 1930(?)-1987
Obituary 122
Murfin, Ross C. 1948- 125
Murfree, Mary Noailles 1850-1922 176
Brief entry 122
See also DLB 12, 74
See also RGAL 4
See also SSC 22
See also TCLC 135
Murger, Henry 1822-1861 ..... DLB 119
See also GFL 1789 to the Present
Murger, Louis-Henri
See Murger, Henry
Murguia, Alejandro 1949- 177
See also HW 2
Murhall, J(acqueline) J(ane) 1964- 215
See also SATA 143
Murie, Margaret (Elizabeth) 1902-2003 110
Obituary 220
Murkoff, Bruce 1953- 235
Murnaghan, Sheila Herron 1951- 185
Murnane, Gerald 1939- 164
See also CN 5, 6, 7
See also DLB 289
See also SFW 4
Murnau, Friedrich Wilhelm
See Plumpe, Friedrich Wilhelm
Murner, Thomas 1475-1537 ..... DLB 179
Murnion, Philip (Joseph) 1938-2003 116
Obituary 219
Muro, Amado (Jesus)
See Seltzer, Chester E.
See also DLB 82
Muro, Diane Patricia 1940- 65-68
Muro, James J(oseph) 1934- 33-36R
Murph, Roxane C. 1928- 175
Murphet, Howard 1906-1994(?) 61-64
Murphey, Cecil B(laine) 1933- CANR-110
Earlier sketch in CA 176
Murphey, Murray Griffin 1928- CANR-6
Earlier sketch in CA 5-8R
Murphey, Rhoads 1919- 33-36R
Murphey, Robert W(entworth) 1916- 13-16R
Murphey, Sallyann J. 1954- 190
Murphy, Agnes Louise Keating
1912-1995 ..... 1-4R
Murphy, Andrew 194
Murphy, Ann Pleshette 236
Murphy, Annie 1948(?)- 145
Murphy, Arthur 1727-1805 ..... DLB 89, 142
See also RGEL 2
Murphy, Arthur Lister 1906-1985 77-80
Murphy, Arthur Richard, Jr. 1915-1987
Obituary 123
Murphy, Austin 1961(?)- 235
Murphy, Barbara Beasley 1933- CANR-110
Earlier sketches in CA 41-44R, CANR-20
See also BYA 12, 13
See also SATA 5, 130
Murphy, Beatrice M. 1908-1992 ..... CANR-9
Obituary 137
Earlier sketch in CA 53-56
See also BW 2
See also DLB 76
Murphy, Brenda C(arol) 1950- 120
Murphy, Brian (Michael) 1931- CANR-13
Earlier sketch in CA 21-24R
Murphy, Brian 1939- 108
Murphy, Buck
See Whitcomb, Ian
Murphy, C. L.
See Murphy, Charlotte A(lice) and
Murphy, Lawrence A(gustus)
Murphy, Caroline P. 1969- 230
Murphy, Caryle 1946- 214
Murphy, Charles J(ohn) V(incent) 1904-1987
Obituary 124
Murphy, Charlotte A(lice) 1924- 105
Murphy, Claire Rudolf 1951- CANR-116
Earlier sketch in CA 143
See also SATA 76, 137
Murphy, Cornelius Francis, Jr. 1933- 89-92
Murphy, Cullen 1952- CANR-144
Earlier sketch in CA 143
Murphy, David E. 1921- 237
Murphy, Dervla (Mary) 1931- CANR-88
Earlier sketches in CA 103, CANR-21
See also DLB 204
Murphy, Dorothy Dey 1911(?)-1983
Obituary 110
Murphy, E(mmett) Jefferson 1926- 25-28R
See also SATA 4
Murphy, Earl Finbar 1928- 13-16R
Murphy, Ed
See Murphy, Edward Francis
Murphy, Edward Francis 1914-1985 102
Murphy, Edward J. 1927- 37-40R
Murphy, Emily (Gowan Ferguson)
1868-1933 180
See also DLB 99
Murphy, Emmy Lou Osborne 1910-1985 .. 5-8R
Murphy, Francis 1932- CANR-7
Earlier sketch in CA 13-16R
Murphy, Francis Xavier 1914-2002 154
Obituary 207
Murphy, Frank Hughes 1940- 61-64
Murphy, Fred P. 1889-1979
Obituary 89-92
Murphy, Gardner 1895-1979 93-96
Obituary 85-88
Murphy, Garth 235
Murphy, George E(dward), Jr. 1948- . CANR-13
Earlier sketch in CA 77-80
Murphy, George G(regory) S(tanislaus)
1924- 21-24R
Murphy, George Lloyd 1902-1992 45-48
Murphy, Geraldine (Joanne) 1920-1990
Obituary 131
Murphy, Grace E. Barstow 1888-1975
Obituary 57-60
Murphy, Gregory L(eo) 226
Murphy, Haughton
See Duffy, James H(enry)
Murphy, Hazel
See Thurston, Hazel (Patricia)
Murphy, Herta A(lbrecht) 1908-1998 49-52
Murphy, Irene L(yons) 1920- 53-56
Murphy, J(ohn) Carter 1921- 13-16R
Murphy, Jack 1923-1980
See Murphy, John Patrick
See also DLB 241
Murphy, James Bernard 1958- 146
Murphy, James F(redrick) 1943- CANR-8
Earlier sketch in CA 61-64
Murphy, James H(enry) 1959- 176
Murphy, James J(erome) 1923- CANR-27
Earlier sketches in CA 33-36R, CANR-12
Murphy, James M(artin) 1917- 29-32R
Murphy, James M(aurice) 1932-1966(?) . CAP-1
Earlier sketch in CA 11-12
Murphy, James S. 1934- 134
Murphy, Jane Brevoort Walden 1902(?)-1980
Obituary 97-100
Murphy, Jeffrie G(uy) 1940-
Brief entry 118
Murphy, Jill (Frances) 1949- CANR-121
Earlier sketches in CA 105, CANR-44, 50, 84
See also CLR 39
See also CWRI 5
See also MAICYA 1, 2
See also SATA 37, 70, 142
Murphy, Jim 1947- 111
See also AAYA 20
See also BYA 10, 11, 16
See also CLR 53
See also CWRI 5
See also MAICYA 2
See also MAICYAS 1
See also SATA 37, 77, 124
See also SATA-Brief 32
Murphy, John
See Grady, Ronan Calistus, Jr.
Murphy, John C. 1947- 165
Murphy, John H. III 1916- 182
See also DLB 127
Murphy, John L(awrence) 1924- CANR-20
Earlier sketch in CA 1-4R
Murphy, John Patrick 1923-1980 201
See also Murphy, Jack
Murphy, John W(illiam) 1948- CANR-30
Earlier sketch in CA 112
Murphy, Joseph E., Jr. 1930- 156
Earlier sketch in CA 133
See also SATA 65
Murphy, Karen A(lee) 1945- 115
Murphy, Kelly 1977- ..... SATA 143
Murphy, Larry
See Murphy, Lawrence R(ichard)
Murphy, Lawrence A(gustus) 1924- .. CANR-64
Earlier sketch in CA 104
See also Lawrence, Steven C.
Murphy, Lawrence R(ichard) 1942- 105
Murphy, Lois Barclay 1902-2003 ..... CANR-41
Obituary 224
Earlier sketches in CA 1-4R, CANR-4, 19
Murphy, Louis J.
See Hicks, Tyler Gregory
Murphy, Louise 1943- 230
See also SATA 155
Murphy, Margaret 1959- 186
Murphy, Marilyn Anne 1955- ..... FANT
Murphy, Mario
See Edmondson, G(arry) C(otton)
Murphy, Marion Fisher 1902-1998 53-56
Murphy, Mark A. 235
Murphy, Martha W(atson) 1951- 136
Murphy, (Gavin) Martin (Hedd) 1934- 132
Murphy, Michael 1930- 73-76
Murphy, N(orman) T. P. 1933- 125
Murphy, Nonie Carol
See Caroll, Nonie
Murphy, Orville T. 1926- 174
Murphy, P(eter) J(ohn) 1946- 136
Murphy, Pat
See Murphy, E(mmett) Jefferson
Murphy, Pat(rice Ann) 1955- CANR-84
Earlier sketch in CA 137
See also SCFW 2
See also SFW 4
Murphy, Patricia J. 1963- 201
See also SATA 132
Murphy, Patrick J. 1946- 208
Earlier sketch in CA 207
Murphy, Patrick T(homas) 1939- 108
Murphy, Patrick V(incent) 1920- 105
Murphy, Paul 1917(?)-1983
Obituary 111
Murphy, Paul J(ames) 1943- 112
Murphy, Paul L(loyd) 1923- CANR-7
Earlier sketch in CA 17-20R
Murphy, Peter 1956- CANR-124
Earlier sketch in CA 163
Murphy, Rae Allan 1935- 142
Murphy, Raymond E(dward)
1898-1986 ..... 41-44R
Murphy, Redmond D. 1910- ..... CP 1
Murphy, Reg 1934- 33-36R
Murphy, Richard 1927- 29-32R
See also BRWS 5
See also CLC 41
See also CP 1, 2, 3, 4, 5, 6, 7
See also DLB 40
See also EWL 3
Murphy, Richard T. A. 1908-1998 ..... CANR-1
Earlier sketch in CA 1-4R
Murphy, Robert (William) 1902-1971 ..... CAP-1
Obituary 29-32R
Earlier sketch in CA 9-10
See also SATA 10
Murphy, Robert 1947- 144
Murphy, Robert Cushman 1887-1973 ... CAP-2
Obituary 41-44R
Earlier sketch in CA 23-24
Murphy, Robert D(aniel) 1894-1978 ..... CAP-1
Obituary 73-76
Earlier sketch in CA 9-10
Murphy, Robert F(rancis) 1924- 118
Murphy, Roland E(dmund)
1917-2002 ..... CANR-6
Obituary 214
Earlier sketch in CA 5-8R
Murphy, Romaine 1941- 77-80
Murphy, Shane M. 1957- 150
Murphy, Sharon M. 1940- 77-80
Murphy, Sheila E. 1951- 185
Autobiographical Essay in 185
See also CAAS 26
Murphy, Shirley Rousseau 1928- CANR-95
Earlier sketches in CA 21-24R, CANR-13, 29, 56
See also AAYA 45
See also BYA 7
See also FANT
See also JRDA
See also MAICYA 1, 2
See also SAAS 18
See also SATA 36, 71, 126
See also YAW
Murphy, Stuart J. 1942- CANR-141
Earlier sketch in CA 186
See also SATA 115, 157
Murphy, Sylvia 1937- 121
See also CLC 34
Murphy, Terrence J(ohn) 1920-2004 ..... 5-8R
Obituary 223
Murphy, Thomas (Bernard) 1935- 101
See also Murphy, Tom
See also CLC 51
Murphy, Thomas Basil, Jr. 1935- CANR-11
Earlier sketch in CA 69-72
See also Murphy, Tom
See also CD 5
Murphy, Thomas P(atrick) 1931- CANR-16
Earlier sketch in CA 41-44R
Murphy, Tim
See Murphy, Jim
Murphy, Timothy 1951- 221
Murphy, Tom
See Murphy, Thomas (Bernard)
See also DLB 310
Murphy, Tom
See Murphy, Thomas Basil, Jr.
See also CBD
See also CD 6
Murphy, Vi 1924(?)-1987
Obituary 124
Murphy, Walter F(rancis) 1929- CANR-2
Earlier sketch in CA 1-4R
Murphy, Warren B. 1933- CANR-84
Earlier sketches in CA 33-36R, CANR-13, 31
See also CMW 4
Murphy, William Francis 1906-1996 ..... 17-20R
Murphy, William M(ichael) 1916- 85-88
Murphy, Yannick 183
Murphy-Gibb, Dwina ..... FANT
Murphy-O'Connor, Jerome James
1935- CANR-5
Earlier sketch in CA 13-16R
Murr, Naeem CANR-137
Earlier sketch in CA 172
Murra, John V(ictor) 1916- CANR-1
Earlier sketch in CA 45-48
Murrah, David Joe 1941- 106
Murray, Adrian
See Curran, Mona (Elisa)
Murray, Albert L. 1916- CANR-78
Earlier sketches in CA 49-52, CANR-26, 52
See also BW 2
See also CLC 73
See also CN 7
See also CSW
See also DLB 38
See also MTFW 2005
Murray, Alexander 1934- 186
Murray, Andrew Evans 1917- 25-28R
Murray, Beatrice
See Posner, Richard
Murray, Bruce C(hurchill) 1931- 103
Murray, Charles (Alan) 1943- CANR-63
Earlier sketch in CA 147
Murray, Charles Shaar 1950(?)- 237
Murray, Chris
See Murray, Christopher John
Murray, Christopher 1940- 117
Murray, Christopher John 235
Murray, Clara Elizabeth 1894- CAP-1
Earlier sketch in CA 9-10
Murray, Cromwell
See Morgan, Murray
Murray, D(avid) L(eslie) 1888-1962 ..... RHW
Murray, D. Stark
See Murray, David Stark
Murray, Daniel E(dward) 1925- 45-48
Murray, David (J.) 1945- CANR-101
Earlier sketch in CA 133
Murray, David Stark 1900-1977
Obituary 111
Murray, Dick 1924- 106
Murray, Don(ald Patrick) 1929- 156
Murray, Donald M(orison) 1924- CANR-84
Earlier sketches in CA 1-4R, CANR-17
Murray, Dorothy Garst 1915- 21-24R
Murray, Eden-Lee 230
Murray, Edmund P(atrick) 1930- 81-84
Murray, Edna
See Rowland, D(onald) S(ydney)
Murray, Edward (James, Jr.) 1928- CANR-1
Earlier sketch in CA 49-52
Murray, Edward J(ames) 1928- 13-16R
Murray, Elaine 1941- 144
Murray, Elwood 1897-1988 73-76
Murray, Eugene Bernard 1927- 104
Murray, Fiona
See Bevan, Gloria (Isabel)
Murray, Frances
See Booth, Rosemary Frances
Murray, Frederic W(illiam) 1933- 176
See also HW 2
Murray, G(erald) E(dward, Jr.) 1945- ... CANR-5
Earlier sketch in CA 53-56
Murray, G. T. 1927- 145
Murray, Gale Barbara 1945- 140
Murray, Geoffrey 1942- 188
Murray, George (McIntosh) 1900-1970 . CAP-1
Earlier sketch in CA 13-14
Murray, (Jesse) George 1909-1996 ..... 17-20R
Murray, George 1971- 223
Murray, (George) Gilbert (Aime) 1866-1957
Brief entry 110
See also DLB 10
Murray, Glen 1955- 168
Murray, Hallard T(homas), Jr. 1937- 17-20R
Murray, Henry A(lexander) 1893-1988
Obituary 125
Brief entry 116
Murray, Irene
See Witherspoon, Irene Murray
Murray, J(ohn) Alex 41-44R
Murray, J. Harley 1910(?)-1977
Obituary 73-76
Murray, J(ohn) Joseph 1915-1993 ..... CANR-4
Earlier sketch in CA 5-8R
Murray, James 1946- CANR-1
Earlier sketch in CA 49-52
Murray, James Augustus Henry
1837-1915 ..... TCLC 117
Murray, James Patrick 1919-1998 ... CANR-117
Obituary 169
Earlier sketches in CA 65-68, CANR-15, 34, 82
See also DLB 241
Murray, Janet Horowitz 1946- 144
Murray, Jean Shaw 1927(?)-1985
Obituary 116
Murray, Jerome T(homas) 1928- 33-36R
Murray, Jim
See Murray, James Patrick
Murray, Joan 1943- 124
Murray, Joan 1945- CANR-123
Earlier sketch in CA 77-80
Murray, Joan E. 1941- 81-84
Murray, Jocelyn (Margaret) 1929- 113
Murray, John 1923- CANR-19
Earlier sketches in CA 5-8R, CANR-4
See also SATA 39
Murray, John A. 1954- 138
Murray, John Bernard 1915- 41-44R
Murray, John Courtney 1904-1967
Obituary 106
Murray, John E(dward), Jr. 1932- CANR-31
Earlier sketch in CA 45-48
Murray, John F(rancis) 1923-1977 ..... CAP-2
Obituary 69-72
Earlier sketch in CA 29-32
Murray, John L(arry) 1937- 108
Murray, John MacDougall 1910-1997 ... 33-36R
Murray, Judith Sargent 1751-1820 ..... DLB 37, 200
Murray, K. F.
See Carlisle, Fred
Murray, K(atherine) M(aud) Elisabeth
1909-1998 ..... CANR-70
Earlier sketch in CA 77-80
Murray, Keith A. 1910-2000 ..... CAP-2
Earlier sketch in CA 33-36
Murray, Ken
See Turner, Robert (Harry)
Murray, Ken 1903-1988
Obituary 126
Murray, Kirsty 1960- 178
See also SATA 108
Murray, Les(lie Allan) 1938- CANR-103
Earlier sketches in CA 21-24R, CANR-11, 27, 56
See also BRWS 7
See also CLC 40
See also CP 1, 2, 3, 4, 5, 6, 7
See also DAM POET
See also DLB 289
See also DLBY 2001
See also EWL 3
See also RGEL 2
Murray, Lieutenant
See Ballou, Maturin Murray
Murray, Linda Charlton 1936(?)-1986
Obituary 118
Murray, Lois Smith 1906- 37-40R
Murray, Margaret Alice 1863-1963 ..... 5-8R
Murray, Marguerite 1917- ..... SATA 63
Murray, Marian 41-44R
See also SATA 5
Murray, Martin J(ulius) 1945- 132
Murray, Martine 1965- ..... SATA 125
Murray, Mary (Morrison) 1925- 25-28R
Murray, Matt 194

Cumulative Index 419 **Myers**

Murray, Maynard 1911(?)-1983
Obituary 110
Murray, Merrill G. 1900(?)-1976
Obituary 69-72
Murray, Michael
See McLaren, Moray (David Shaw)
Murray, Michael 1943- 228
Murray, Michael V(ivian) 1906- 5-8R
Murray, (Judith) Michele (Freedman)
1933-1974 49-52
See also SATA 7
Murray, Nicholas 197
Murray, Ossie 1938- .... SATA 43
Murray, Paul 1975- 238
Murray, Paul T(hom, Jr.) 1944- 146
Murray, (Anna) Pauli(ne)
1910-1985 .... CANR-87
Obituary 116
Earlier sketch in CA 125
See also BW 2
See also DLB 41
Murray, Peter
See Hautman, Pete(r Murray)
Murray, Peter (John) 1920-1992 ...... CANR-10
Obituary 137
Earlier sketch in CA 13-16R
Murray, Philip 1924- 65-68
Murray, Ralph L(a Verne) 1921- 13-16R
Murray, Raymond C. 1929- 142
Murray, Rebecca (Jean) 1936- 57-60
Murray, Robert A. 1929- 29-32R
Murray, Robert Keith 1922- 53-56
Murray, Robin 1940- CANR-55
Earlier sketch in CA 126
Murray, Roger N(icholas) 1932- 21-24R
Murray, Rona 1924- 154
See also CP 7
See also CWP
Murray, Ruth Lovell 1900-1991 103
Murray, Sabina 210
Murray, Sinclair
See Sullivan, (Edward) Alan
Murray, Sister Mary Verona 1909- 17-20R
Murray, Sonia Bennett 1936- 65-68
Murray, Stuart A. P. 1948- 192
See also Mitchum, Hank
Murray, Thomas J(oseph) 1943- 77-80
Murray, Venetia 1932- 189
Murray, Victoria Christopher 234
Murray, W(illiam) H(utchison)
1913-1996 .... CANR-4
Obituary 151
Earlier sketch in CA 9-12R
Murray, Walter I(saiah) 1910-1978 85-88
Obituary 73-76
Murray, William 1926-2005 173
Obituary 237
Murray, William Cotter 1929- 53-56
Murray, William J(oseph) III 1946- ... CANR-46
Earlier sketch in CA 110
Murray, William J(ames) 1937- 202
Murray, Yxta Maya 225
Murray-Brown, Jeremy 1932- 77-80
Murray-Smith, Joanna 1964- 230
See also CD 5, 6
Murray-Smith, Stephen 1922- 103
Murrell, Elsie Kathleen Seth-Smith
1883- CAP-1
Earlier sketch in CA 9-10
Murrell, Glenn
See Meares, Leonard Frank
Murrell, Jim
See Murrell, Vernon James
Murrell, John 1945- 230
See also CD 5, 6
Murrell, K(eith) F(rank) H(ywel) 1908(?)-1984
Obituary 112
Murrell, Nathaniel S(amuel) 1945- 169
Murrell, Sam
See Murrell, Nathaniel S(amuel)
Murrell, Vernon James 1934-1994 132
Murren, Doug(las) 1951- 136
Murrett, John Charles 1892-1971 .... 1-4R
Murrik, Ella
See Wuolijoki, Hella
Murrin, John Matthew 1935- 224
Murrow, Casey 1945- 97-100
Murrow, Edward R(oscoe) 1908-1965 103
Obituary 89-92
Murrow, Liza Ketchum 1946- CANR-142
Earlier sketch in CA 146
See also Ketchum, Liza
See also SATA 78
Murry, Colin
See Middleton-Murry, John, (Jr.)
Murry, J. Middleton
See Murry, John Middleton
Murry, John Middleton, Jr.
See Middleton-Murry, John, (Jr.)
Murry, John Middleton 1889-1957 217
Brief entry 118
See also DLB 149
See also TCLC 16
Murry, Katherine Middleton 1925- 133
Murry, Mary Middleton 1897-1983
Obituary 110
Murstein, Bernard I(rving) 1929- CANR-140
Earlier sketches in CA 9-12R, CANR-3
Murtagh, John M(artin) 1911-1976 .... 17-20R
Obituary 61-64
Murtagh, William J. 1923- 25-28R
Murton, Jessie Wilmore 5-8R
Murton, Mary 1933- 117
Murton, Thomas O'Rhelius 1929-1990
Obituary 132
Murton, Tom
See Murton, Thomas O'Rhelius
Musa, Mark 1934- 13-16R
Musacchio, George 1938- 143
Musaeus, Johann Karl August
1735-1787 .... DLB 97
See also SUFW
Musafir
See Tagore, Amitendranath
Musah, Havagah
See Smilansky, Moshe
Musaphia, Joseph 1935- CANR-17
Earlier sketch in CA 97-100
See also CD 5, 6
Musarurwa, Willie 1928(?)-1990
Obituary 131
Muscat, Robert J. 1931- 17-20R
Muscatine, Charles 1920- 21-24R
Muscatine, Doris (Corn) 1926- 9-12R
Muschamp, Thomas
See Lloyd-Thomas, Catherine
Muschenheim, Carl 1905-1977
Obituary 69-72
Muschenheim, William (Emil)
1902-1990 .... CAP-1
Obituary 130
Earlier sketch in CA 13-16
Muschg, Adolf 1934- 185
See also DLB 75
See also EWL 3
Musciano, Walt
See Musciano, Walter A.
Musciano, Walter A. 1922- 121
Muse, Beatriz de Regil 1901(?)-1983
Obituary 109
Muse, Benjamin 1898-1986 .... CANR-1
Earlier sketch in CA 1-4R
Muse, Clarence 1889-1979
Obituary 104
Muse, Daphne P. 1944- 112
Muse, Ken 1925- 111
Muse, Patricia (Alice) 1923- 69-72
Muses, C. A.
See Muses, Charles Arthur
Muses, Charles Arthur 1919- 135
Brief entry 115
Musetto, Andrew P(aul) 1945- 111
Musgrave, Barbara S(tewart) 1913-1993 ... 5-8R
Musgrave, Clifford 1904-1982
Obituary 107
Musgrave, Florence 1902-1999 .... CAP-1
Earlier sketch in CA 13-14
See also SATA 3
Musgrave, Gerald L. 1942- 143
Musgrave, Michael 1942- 191
Musgrave, Richard Abel 1910- 113
Musgrave, Susan 1951- CANR-84
Earlier sketches in CA 69-72, CANR-45
See also CCA 1
See also CLC 13, 54
See also CP 2, 3, 4, 5, 6, 7
See also CWP
Musgrave, Toby 1967- 186
Musgraves, Don 1935- 65-68
Musgrove, Frank 1922- CANR-6
Earlier sketch in CA 13-16R
Musgrove, Margaret W(ynkoop) 1943- 65-68
See also SATA 26, 124
Musgrove, Philip 1940- CANR-11
Earlier sketch in CA 29-32R
Musgrove, Stanley (E.) 1924-1986 108
Obituary 118
Mushabac, Jane 1944- 108
Mushkat, Jerome 1931- CANR-94
Earlier sketch in CA 81-84
Mushkat, Mari'on 1919- 120
Mushkin, Selma J. 1913-1979
Obituary 93-96
Musial, Joe 1905(?)-1977
Obituary 69-72
Musial, Stan(ley Frank) 1920- 93-96
Musicant, Elke (Alice) 1919- 107
Musicant, Ivan 1943-1999 168
Musicant, Tobias (Ted) 1921- 108
Musiker, Reuben 1931- 57-60
Musil, Robert (Edler von)
1880-1942 .... CANR-84
Brief entry 109
Earlier sketch in CANR-55
See also CDWLB 2
See also DLB 81, 124
See also EW 9
See also EWL 3
See also MTCW 2
See also RGSF 2
See also RGWL 2, 3
See also SSC 18
See also TCLC 12, 68
Muske, Carol
See Muske-Dukes, Carol (Anne)
See also CLC 90
Muske, Irmgard (Gertrud) 1912- CANR-18
Earlier sketch in CA 25-28R
Muske-Dukes, Carol (Anne) 1945- 203
Earlier sketches in CA 65-68, CANR-32, 70
Autobiographical Essay in 203
See also Muske, Carol
See also CWP
Muskett, Netta (Rachel) 1887- .... RHW
Muskie, Edmund S(ixtus) 1914-1996 .. CANR-2
Obituary 151
Earlier sketch in CA 49-52
Musmanno, Michael A(ngelo)
1898(?)-1968 .... CAP-1
Earlier sketch in CA 9-10
Musolf, Lloyd D(aryl) 1919- CANR-9
Earlier sketch in CA 17-20R
Musselman, George Paul 1855-1907
Obituary 123
Musselman, Vernon A(rmor) 1912- 37-40R
Mussen, Paul Henry 1922-2000 159
Obituary 189
Brief entry 114
Musser, Elizabeth 1960- 220
Musser, Joe
See Musser, Joseph L.
Musser, Joseph L. 1936- CANR-100
Earlier sketches in CA 29-32R, CANR-12
Musset, (Louis Charles) Alfred de
1810-1857 .... DLB 192, 217
See also EW 6
See also GFL 1789 to the Present
See also RGWL 2, 3
See also TWA
Musset, Paul de 1804-1880 .... GFL 1789 to the Present
Mussey, Virginia Howell
See Ellison, Virginia H(owell)
Mussey, Virginia T.H.
See Ellison, Virginia H(owell)
Mussi, Mary 1907-1991 .... CANR-84
Earlier sketches in CA 53-56, CANR-6
See also RHW
Mussio, Laurence B. 1964- 209
Mussoff, Lenore 1927- 21-24R
Mussolini, Benito (Amilcare Andrea) 1883-1945
Brief entry 116
See also TCLC 96
Mussolini, Rachele Guidi 1890-1979
Obituary 111
Mussulman Joseph A(gee) 1928- 37-40R
Must, Dennis (Patrick) 1934- 191
Mustafa, Zaki 1934- 41-44R
Mustaghanmi, Ahlam 1953- .... EWL 3
Mustazza, Leonard 1952- 175
Muste, A(braham) J(ohannes)
1885-1967 .... DLB 303
Muste, John M(artin) 1927- 21-24R
Musteikis, Antanas 1914- 45-48
Musto, Barry 1930- 106
Musto, David Franklin 1936- 104
Musto, Michael 1955- 132
Musto, Ronald G. 1948- 127
Mustoe, Anne 1933- 211
Musuraca, Nicholas 1892-1975 .... IDFW 3, 4
Musurillo, Herbert (Anthony Peter)
1917-1974 .... CAP-1
Obituary 49-52
Earlier sketch in CA 13-14
Mutafchieva, Vera 1929- .... DLB 181
Mutanabbi, Al-
See al-Mutanabbi, Ahmad ibn al-Husayn Abu al-Tayyib al-Jufi al-Kindi
See also WLIT 6
Mutchler, David E(dward) 1941- 33-36R
Mutel, Cornelia F. 1947- .... SATA 74
Muth, John F(raser) 1930- 13-16R
Muth, Richard F(erris) 1927- 13-16R
Mutharika, B(rightson) W(ebster) T(hom)
1934- CANR-46
Earlier sketch in CA 41-44R
Muthesius, Stefan 1939- CANR-50
Earlier sketch in CA 61-64
Mutiga, Josiah G. 1940- .... CP 1
Mutis, Alvaro 1923- CANR-118
Earlier sketch in CA 149
See also DLB 283
See also EWL 3
See also HW 1
See also LAWS 1
Mutke, Peter H(ans) C(hristoph) 1927- 93-96
Muto, Susan Annette 1942- CANR-53
Earlier sketches in CA 110, CANR-29
Mutton, Alice F. A. 1908-1979 .... 5-8R
Mutz
See Kuenstler, Morton
Muus, Bent J(oergen) 1926- 103
Muus, Flemming B(ruun) 1907-1982
Obituary 110
Muuss, Rolf E(duard Helmut) 1924- 9-12R
Muzumdar, Ammu Menon 1919- 21-24R
Mwangi, Meja 1948- CANR-78
Earlier sketch in CA 143
See also AFW
See also BW 2, 3
See also DLB 125
Myassin, Leonid Fedorovich
1895-1979 97-100
Obituary 85-88
My Brother's Brother
See Chekhov, Anton (Pavlovich)
Mycue, Edward 1937- CANR-45
Earlier sketches in CA 53-56, CANR-4
Mydans, Carl 1907-2004 97-100
Obituary 230
Mydans, Shelley Smith 1915-2002 145
Obituary 205
Brief entry 105
Myddleton, Robert
See Hebblethwaite, Peter
Myer, Dillon S(eymour) 1891-1982 .... CAP-2
Obituary 116
Earlier sketch in CA 29-32
Myer, John Colby 1912-1987 45-48
Myer, John Randolph 1927- 5-8R
Myerhoff, Barbara G. 1936(?)-1985
Obituary 114
Myers, A(lexander) J(ohn) William
1877-1975 .... CAP-1
Earlier sketch in CA 11-12
Myers, Albert M(orris) 1917- 118
Myers, Alec Reginald
See Myers, Alexander Reginald
Myers, Alexander Reginald
1912-1980 .... CANR-10
Earlier sketch in CA 13-16R
Myers, Alonzo F(ranklin) 1895-1970
Obituary 104
Myers, Amy 1938- 209
Myers, Andrew Breen 1920-1998 61-64
Obituary 171
Myers, Anna 236
See also SATA 160
Myers, Arthur 1917- CANR-58
Earlier sketches in CA 17-20R, CANR-7
See also SATA 35, 91
Myers, Arthur Sim 1928-1984
Obituary 113
Myers, Bernard S(amuel)
1908-1993 .... CANR-48
Obituary 140
Earlier sketch in CA 65-68
Myers, Bernice CANR-55
Earlier sketches in CA 61-64, CANR-8
See also SATA 9, 81
Myers, Bettye (Blanche) 1926-
Brief entry 107
Myers, Bill 1953- CANR-123
Earlier sketch in CA 163
Myers, C. F.
See Fairbanks, Carol
Myers, C(hauncie) Kilmer 1916-1981
Obituary 108
Myers, Carol Fairbanks
See Fairbanks, Carol
Myers, Caroline Elizabeth Clark
1887-1980 .... 29-32R
Obituary 134
See also SATA 28
Myers, Charles A(ndrew) 1913-2000 85-88
Myers, Charles B(ennett) 1939- 57-60
Myers, Christopher 1975- .... CLR 97
Myers, D. E.
See Myers, Doris T(hompson)
Myers, David G. 1942- CANR-95
Earlier sketches in CA 106, CANR-22, 46
Myers, (Eugene Victor) Debs 1911-1971
Obituary 104
Myers, Desaix B. III 1945- 104
Myers, Doris T(hompson) 1934- 178
Myers, Drew(fus Young, Jr.) 1946-1997 145
Myers, Edward 1950- CANR-50
Earlier sketch in CA 116
See also SATA 96
Myers, Elisabeth P(erkins) 1918- CANR-3
Earlier sketch in CA 5-8R
See also SATA 36
Myers, Eric 233
Myers, Eugene A(braham) 1910-1996 45-48
Myers, Francis Milton 1917- 5-8R
Myers, Frederic W(illiam) H(enry)
1843-1901 .... DLB 190
Myers, Gail E(ldridge) 1923- CANR-1
Earlier sketch in CA 49-52
Myers, Garry Cleveland 1884-1971 ...... CAP-2
Earlier sketch in CA 29-32
Myers, Gay Nagle 1943- 102
Myers, George (Francis), Jr. 1953- 119
Myers, Gerald E(ugene) 1923- 29-32R
Myers, Gustavus 1872-1942
Brief entry 123
See also DLB 47
Myers, Harriet Kathryn
See Whittington, Harry (Benjamin)
Myers, Helen CANR-88
Earlier sketch in CA 145
Myers, (Mary) Hortense (Powner)
1913-1987 .... CANR-2
Obituary 123
Earlier sketch in CA 1-4R
See also SATA 10
Myers, Irma A(shley) 1924- 112
Myers, J(ohn) William 1919- CANR-57
Earlier sketches in CA 33-36R, CANR-12, 30
Myers, Jack 1913- 150
See also SATA 83
Myers, (Elliott) Jack 1941- 73-76
Myers, Jacob M(artin) 1904-1991 .... 17-20R
Myers, Jane E. 1948- 177
Myers, John Bernard 1920(?)-1987
Obituary 123
Myers, John H(olmes) 1915-1993 .... 9-12R
Obituary 143
Myers, John L. 1958- 141
Myers, John Myers 1906-1988 .... CANR-65
Obituary 171
Earlier sketches in CA 1-4R, CANR-1
See also FANT
See also TCWW 1, 2
Myers, Katherine 1952- CANR-28
Earlier sketch in CA 110
Myers, L(eopold) H(amilton) 1881-1944 157
See also DLB 15
See also EWL 3
See also RGEL 2
See also TCLC 59
Myers, L(ouis) M(cCorry) 1901-1988 ..... 21-24R
Myers, Lois E. 1946- 139
Myers, Lonny 1922- 65-68
Myers, Lou(is) 1915- CANR-55
Earlier sketch in CA 136
See also SATA 81
Myers, M(arvin) Scott 1922- 69-72
Myers, Marshall 1943- 198
Myers, Martha A. 1948- 189
Myers, Martin 1927- CANR-20
Earlier sketch in CA 29-32R
Myers, Mary Ruth 1947- CANR-16
Earlier sketch in CA 85-88
Myers, Mike 1963- 165
See also AAYA 34
Myers, Minor, Jr. 1942-2003 133
Obituary 218

Myers, Neil 1930- ... 105
Myers, Norma 1929- ... 61-64
Myers, Norman 1934- ... CANR-20
Earlier sketches in CA 49-52, CANR-1
Myers, Patricia 1929- ... 37-40R
Myers, Paul 1932- ... 123
Myers, R(obert) E(ugene) 1924- ... CANR-94
Earlier sketches in CA 77-80, CANR-23, 47, 89
See also SATA 119
Myers, Ramon H. 1929- ... 113
Myers, Raymond E(dward) 1902-1988 .. CAP-1
Earlier sketch in CA 13-16
Myers, Robert J(ulius) 1912- ... CANR-6
Earlier sketch in CA 13-16R
Myers, Robert J(ohn) 1924- ... CANR-27
Earlier sketch in CA 107
Myers, Robert Manson 1921- ... 37-40R
Myers, Rollo Hugh 1892-1984(?) ... 17-20R
Obituary ... 115
Myers, Samuel 1897(?)-1983
Obituary ... 109
Myers, Tamar 1948- ... CANR-73
Earlier sketch in CA 154
Myers, Thomas G. 1961- ... 220
Myers, Tim (Brian) 1953- ... 221
See also SATA 147
Myers, Vernon C. 1911-1990
Obituary ... 130
Myers, W. David 1956- ... 159
Myers, Walter Dean 1937- ... CANR-108
Earlier sketches in CA 33-36R, CANR-20, 42, 67
Interview in ... CANR-20
See also AAYA 4, 23
See also BLC 3
See also BW 2
See also BYA 6, 8, 11
See also CLC 35
See also CLR 4, 16, 35
See also DAM MULT, NOV
See also DLB 33
See also JRDA
See also LAIT 5
See also MAICYA 1, 2
See also MAICYAS 1
See also MTCW 2
See also MTFW 2005
See also SAAS 2
See also SATA 41, 71, 109, 157
See also SATA-Brief 27
See also WYA
See also YAW
Myers, Walter M.
See Myers, Walter Dean
Myers, Wayne A(lan) 1931- ... 138
Myers, William 1939- ... 132
Myerscough-Walker, Raymond 1912-1984
Obituary ... 113
Myerson, Allen R(euben) 1955-2002 ... 213
Myerson, Bess 1924- ... 108
Myerson, Joel 1945- ... CANR-97
Earlier sketches in CA 102, CANR-19, 41
Myerson, Julie 1960- ... 183
See also DLB 267
Myerson, Michael 1940- ... 73-76
Myhers, John 1921-1992 ... 105
Obituary ... 137
Myhill, Henry (James) 1925-1977 ... 103
Mykle, Agnar 1915-1994 ... 13-16R
See also DLB 297
Mykolaitis, Vincas
See Mykolaitis-Putinas, Vincas
See also EWL 3
Mykolaitis-Putinas, Vincas 1893-1967
See Mykolaitis, Vincas
See also DLB 220
Mylander, Maureen 1937- ... CANR-5
Earlier sketch in CA 53-56
Myler, Joseph L. 1905(?)-1973
Obituary ... 41-44R
Myles, Eileen 1949- ... CANR-106
Earlier sketch in CA 148
See also DLB 193
Myles, Eugenie Louise (Butler) 1905- CAP-1
Earlier sketch in CA 11-12
Myles, Symon
See Follett, Ken(neth Martin)
Myller, Rolf 1926- ... CANR-8
Earlier sketch in CA 5-8R
See also SATA 27
Mylonas, George Emmanuel 1898-1988
Obituary ... 125
Mylroie, Laurie 1953- ... 139
Mynors, Roger A(ubrey) B(askerville) 1903-1989 ... 5-8R
Obituary ... 129
Mynton, Henry ... 231
Myomu, Zentatsu
See Baker Roshi, Richard
Myra, Harold L(awrence) 1939- ... CANR-74
Earlier sketches in CA 61-64, CANR-8
See also SATA 46
See also SATA-Brief 42
Myracle, Lauren 1969- ... 236
Myracle, Lauren 1969- ... SATA 162
Myrdal, Alva Reimer 1902-1986 ... CANR-83
Obituary ... 118
Earlier sketch in CA 69-72
See also FW
Myrdal, (Karl) Gunnar 1898-1987 ... CANR-4
Obituary ... 122
Earlier sketch in CA 9-12R
Myrdal, Jan 1927- ... CANR-117
Brief entry ... 117
Earlier sketch in CA 132
See also CWW 2
See also DLB 257
Myrer, Anton (Olmstead) 1922-1996 .. CANR-3
Obituary ... 151
Earlier sketch in CA 1-4R
Myres, J(ohn) N(owell) L(inton) 1902-1989 ... 123
Obituary ... 129
Myres, Sandra Lynn 1933- ... CANR-14
Earlier sketch in CA 33-36R
Myrick, David F. ... CANR-6
Earlier sketch in CA 13-16R
Myrick, Robert D(eWayne) 1935- ... CANR-17
Earlier sketch in CA 41-44R
Myrick, William J(ennings, Jr.) 1932- ... 73-76
Myrivilis, Stratis 1892-1969 ... EWL 3
Myrland, Doug 1952- ... 117
Myron, Robert 1926- ... 13-16R
Myrsiades, Kostas J. 1940- ... CANR-94
Earlier sketches in CA 109, CANR-27, 52
Myrsiades, Linda (Suny) 1941- ... 207
Myrus, Donald (Richard) 1927- ... CANR-4
Earlier sketch in CA 1-4R
See also SATA 23
Mysak, Edward D(amien) 1930-1989
Obituary ... 130
Myss, Caroline 1953(?)- ... 168
Mysterious Traveler, The
See Arthur, Robert, (Jr.)

N

Na, An ... 203
See also AAYA 53
See also SATA 149
Na'allah, Abdul-Rasheed 1962- ... 189
Naamani, Israel (Levi) T(arkow) 1913(?)-1979 ... 124
Obituary ... 171
Brief entry ... 106
Naar, Jon 1920- ... 102
Naas, Michael ... 223
Nabb, Magdalen 1947- ... CMW 4
Nabbes, Thomas 1605(?)-1641 ... DLB 58
See also RGEL 2
Nabhan, Gary Paul 1952- ... CANR-109
Earlier sketch in CA 143
See also ANW
Nabholtz, John R(obert) 1931- ... 65-68
Nabl, Franz 1883-1974 ... 204
See also DLB 81
Nabokov, Dmitri 1934- ... CANR-99
Earlier sketch in CA 132
Nabokov, Nicolas 1903-1978 ... 85-88
Obituary ... 77-80
Nabokov, Peter (Francis) 1940- ... CANR-120
Earlier sketches in CA 21-24R, CANR-9, 27
Nabokov, Vladimir (Vladimirovich) 1899-1977 ... CANR-102
Obituary ... 69-72
Earlier sketches in CA 5-8R, CANR-20
See also AAYA 45
See also AMW
See also AMWC 1
See also AMWR 1
See also BPFB 2
See also CDALB 1941-1968
See also CLC 1, 2, 3, 6, 8, 11, 15, 23, 44, 46, 64
See also CN 1, 2
See also CP 2
See also DA
See also DA3
See also DAB
See also DAC
See also DAM MST, NOV
See also DLB 2, 244, 278, 317
See also DLBD 3
See also DLBY 1980, 1991
See also EWL 3
See also EXPS
See also LATS 1:2
See also MAL 5
See also MTCW 1, 2
See also MTFW 2005
See also NCFS 4
See also NFS 9
See also RGAL 4
See also RGSF 2
See also SSC 11
See also SSFS 6, 15
See also TCLC 108
See also TUS
See also WLC
Nacci, Chris (Natale) 1909-2000 ... 41-44R
Nachbar, Herbert 1930(?)-1980
Obituary ... 97-100
Nachbar, Jack 1941- ... 53-56
Nachman, Elana ... GLL 2
Nachman, Gerald 1938- ... CANR-37
Earlier sketches in CA 65-68, CANR-16
Nachtigal, Paul M. 1930- ... 112
Nachtigall, Lila Ehrenstein 1934-
Brief entry ... 105
Nachtmann, Francis Weldon 1913-1982 ... 37-40R
Obituary ... 133
Nacos, Brigitte L(ebens) ... 231
Nadan, Paul 1933(?)-1978
Obituary ... 104
Nadar 1820-1910 ... GFL 1789 to the Present
Nadas, Peter
See Nadas, Peter
Nadas, Peter 1942- ... CANR-103
Earlier sketch in CA 166
See also EWL 3
Nadasi, Ladislav
See Jege
Naddor, Eliezer 1920-1987 ... 21-24R
Nadeau, Adel 1940- ... 168
Nadeau, Maurice 1911- ... 49-52
Nadeau, R(aymond) E(rnest) 1913-2001
Brief entry ... 107
Nadeau, Ray E.
See Nadeau, R(aymond) E(rnest)
Nadeau, Remi A(llen) 1920- ... CANR-2
Earlier sketch in CA 1-4R
Nadeau, Robert (L.) 1944- ... 195
Nadeau, Roland 1928- ... CANR-4
Earlier sketch in CA 53-56
Nadel, Frances 1905(?)-1977
Obituary ... 69-72
Nadel, Gerald H. 1944-1977 ... 81-84
Obituary ... 73-76
Nadel, Ira Bruce 1943- ... CANR-122
Earlier sketches in CA 102, CANR-18, 39
Nadel, Jennifer 1962- ... 144
Nadel, Laurie 1948- ... SATA 74
Nadel, Mark V(ictor) 1943- ... 33-36R
Nadel, Norman (Sanford) 1915- ... 106
Nadelhoffer, Hans (L.) 1940-1988 ... 137
Nadelmann, Ethan A. 1957- ... 150
Nadelson, Reggie ... 184
Naden, Constance 1858-1889 ... DLB 199
Naden, Corinne J. 1930- ... 148
See also SATA 79
Nader, George, (Jr.) 1921-2002 ... 187
Obituary ... 204
Brief entry ... 109
Nader, George Albert 1940- ... 111
Nader, Laura 1930- ... CANR-7
Earlier sketch in CA 17-20R
Nader, Ralph 1934- ... CANR-105
Earlier sketch in CA 77-80
Nadezhdin, Nikolai Ivanovich 1804-1856 ... DLB 198
Nadich, Judah 1912- ... CANR-55
Earlier sketch in CA 127
Nadler, David A. 1948- ... 177
Earlier sketch in CA 169
Nadler, Harvey 1933- ... 13-16R
Nadler, Leonard 1922- ... CANR-20
Earlier sketches in CA 53-56, CANR-5
Nadler, Paul S(tephen) 1930- ... 25-28R
Nadler, Steven M. 1958- ... 223
Nadler, Susan
See Gantry, Susan Nadler
Nadler, Zeace 1925- ... 121
Nadolny, Sten 1942- ... 228
Nadson, Semen Iakovlevich 1862-1887 ... DLB 277
Naef, Weston J(ohn) 1942-
Brief entry ... 111
Naeslund, Erik 1948- ... 103
Naess, Harald Sigurd 1925- ... 41-44R
Naether, Carl (Albert) 1892-1990 ... 25-28R
Naevius c. 265B.C.-201B.C. ... DLB 211
Naff, Clayton 1956- ... 146
Nafisi, Azar 1950(?)- ... 222
Naftali, Timothy ... 166
Nafziger, E(stel) Wayne 1938- ... 85-88
Nafziger, George F(rancis) 1949- ... 132
Nag
See Grauer, Neil A(lbert)
Nag, Moni 1925- ... 41-44R
Nagahiro, Toshio 1905- ... 158
Nagai, Kafu
See Nagai, Sokichi
See also DLB 180
See also TCLC 51
Nagai, Sokichi 1879-1959
Brief entry ... 117
See also Kafu and
Nagai, Kafu and
Nagai Kafu
Nagai Berthrong, Evelyn 1946- ... 115
Nagai Kafu
See Nagai, Sokichi
See also EWL 3
Nagara, Susumu 1932- ... CANR-3
Earlier sketch in CA 45-48
Nagarjun 1911- ... CWW 2
Nagata, Linda 1960- ... CANR-141
Earlier sketch in CA 172
Nagatsu, Toshiharu 1930- ... 107
Nagatsuka, Ryuji 1924-
Brief entry ... 125
na gCopaleen, Myles
See O Nuallain, Brian
Nagel, Andreas Fischer
See Fischer-Nagel, Andreas
Nagel, Ernest 1901-1985 ... 93-96
Obituary ... 117
See also DLB 279
Nagel, Heiderose Fischer
See Fischer-Nagel, Heiderose
Nagel, James (Edward) 1940- ... CANR-27
Earlier sketch in CA 29-32R
Nagel, Otto 1894-1967
Obituary ... 106
Nagel, Paul C(hester) 1926- ... CANR-81
Earlier sketches in CA 9-12R, CANR-5, 22
Nagel, Shirley 1922- ... 93-96
Nagel, Stuart S(amuel) 1934- ... CANR-86
Earlier sketches in CA 33-36R, CANR-14, 33
Nagel, Thomas 1937- ... CANR-122
Earlier sketches in CA 53-56, CANR-4
Nagel, William G(eorge) 1916- ... 49-52
Nagele, Rainer
See Nagele, Rainer
Nagele, Rainer 1943- ... 207
Nagem, Monique F. 1941- ... 140
Nagenda, John 1938- ... 142
See also BW 2
Nagenda, Musa
See Howard, Moses L(eon)
Nagera, Humberto 1927- ... 57-60
Nagi, Mostafa H. 1934- ... 33-36R
Nagi, Saad Z. 1925- ... 29-32R
Nagibin, Iurii Markovich
See Nagibin, Yury Markovich
See also DLB 302
Nagibin, Yury Markovich 1920-1994
See Nagibin, Iurii Markovich
See also EWL 3
Nagl, John A. 1966- ... 228
Nagl-Docekal, Herta 1944- ... 215
Nagle, James J. 1909-1978 ... 85-88
Obituary ... 81-84
Nagle, P. G. ... 197
Naglee, David Ingersoll 1930-1998 ... 53-56
Nagler, Alois Maria 1907-1993 ... CANR-19
Obituary ... 141
Earlier sketch in CA 103
Nagler, Barney 1912-1990 ... 17-20R
Obituary ... 132
Nagler, Michael N(icholas) 1937- ... CANR-13
Earlier sketch in CA 73-76
na Gopaleen, Myles
See O Nuallain, Brian
Nagorski, Andrew 1947- ... CANR-135
Earlier sketch in CA 93-96
Nagorski, Zygmunt, Jr. 1912- ... 73-76
Nagorski, Zygmunt 1885(?)-1973
Obituary ... 41-44R
Nagourney, Adam 1954- ... 207
Nagourney, Peter (Jon) 1940- ... 37-40R
Nagrin, Daniel 1917- ... CANR-120
Earlier sketch in CA 148
Nagrodskaia, Evdokiia Apollonovna 1866-1930 ... DLB 295
Naguib, Mohammed 1902(?)-1984
Obituary ... 113
Nagurney, Anna ... 193
Nagy, Ferenc 1903-1979
Obituary ... 89-92
Nagy, Gil D. 1933- ... 25-28R
Nagy, Gloria ... CANR-109
Earlier sketch in CA 148
Nagy, Gregory 1942- ... CANR-112
Earlier sketch in CA 102
Nagy, Imre 1895(?)-1958
Brief entry ... 118
Nagy, Lajos 1883-1954 ... EWL 3
Nagy, Laszlo 1925-1978 ... 129
Obituary ... 112
See also CLC 7
Nagy, Phyllis 1962- ... 230
See also CD 5, 6
Nagy-Talavera, Nicholas M(anuel) 1929- ... 33-36R
Naha, Ed 1950- ... CANR-57
Earlier sketch in CA 109
See also SFW 4
Nahai, Gina Barkhordar 1961(?)- ... 207
Nahal, Chaman (Lal) 1927- ... CANR-84
Earlier sketches in CA 37-40R, CANR-17
See also CN 4, 5, 6, 7
Nahas, Gabriel G(eorges) 1920- ... CANR-17
Earlier sketches in CA 49-52, CANR-1
Nahas, Rebecca 1946- ... 69-72
Nahaylo, Bohdan ... 217
Nahem, Joseph 1917-1992 ... 113
Nahem, Rachel
See Loden, Rachel
Nahm, Milton C(harles) 1903-1991 ... 13-16R
Obituary ... 133
Nahshon, Edna ... 203
Nahum, Lucien 1930(?)-1983
Obituary ... 111
Naidis, Mark 1918-1990 ... 33-36R
Naidoo, Beverley 1943- ... CANR-113
Earlier sketch in CA 160
See also AAYA 23
See also CLR 29
See also MAICYA 2
See also MAICYAS 1
See also SATA 63, 135
See also YAW
Naidu, Prabhakar S. 1937- ... CANR-121
Earlier sketch in CA 163
Naidu, Sarojini 1879-1949 ... EWL 3
See also RGEL 2
See also TCLC 80
Naifeh, Steven Woodward 1952- ... CANR-126
Earlier sketches in CA 102, CANR-40
Naik, Madhukar Krishna 1926- ... CANR-25
Earlier sketches in CA 21-24R, CANR-10
Naim, Asher 1929- ... 226
Naim, C(houdhri) M(ohammed) 1936-
Brief entry ... 112
Naiman, Arthur 1941- ... CANR-29
Earlier sketch in CA 108
Naimy, Mikhail 1889-1988
Obituary ... 124
See also Nu'ayma, Mikhail

Naipaul, Shiva(dhar Srinivasa)
1945-1985 .... CANR-33
Obituary 116
Brief entry 110
Earlier sketch in CA 112
See also CLC 32, 39
See also CN 2, 3
See also DA3
See also DAM NOV
See also DLB 157
See also DLBY 1985
See also EWL 3
See also MTCW 1, 2
See also MTFW 2005
See also TCLC 153
Naipaul, V(idiadhar) S(urajprasad)
1932- CANR-126
Earlier sketches in CA 1-4R, CANR-1, 33, 51, 91
See also BPFB 2
See also BRWS 1
See also CDBLB 1960 to Present
See also CDWLB 3
See also CLC 4, 7, 9, 13, 18, 37, 105, 199
See also CN 1, 2, 3, 4, 5, 6, 7
See also DA3
See also DAB
See also DAC
See also DAM MST, NOV
See also DLB 125, 204, 207
See also DLBY 1985, 2001
See also EWL 3
See also LATS 1:2
See also MTCW 1, 2
See also MTFW 2005
See also RGEL 2
See also RGSF 2
See also SSC 38
See also TWA
See also WLIT 4
See also WWE 1
Nair, Anita 206
Nair, Meera 1963- 210
Nair, Raj (G.) 1967- 228
Nairn, Ian (Douglas) 1930-1983
Obituary 110
Nairn, Ronald C(harles) 1922- 21-24R
Nairn, Tom (Cunningham) 1932- 176
Nairne, Katharine Davina 1949- 128
Nairne, Kathy
See Nairne, Katharine Davina
Naisawald, L. Van Loan 1920- CANR-6
Earlier sketch in CA 5-8R
Naisbitt, John 1929- CANR-89
Brief entry 113
Earlier sketch in CA 128
See also BEST 90:3
Naismith, Grace (Akin) 1904-1983 .. CANR-20
Obituary 111
Earlier sketch in CA 65-68
Naismith, Helen 1929- 69-72
Naismith, Horace
See Helmer, William J(oseph)
Naismith, James 1861-1939
Brief entry 118
Naismith, Marion (Overend) 1922- 29-32R
Naismith, Robert J. 1916- CANR-47
Earlier sketch in CA 121
Naj, Amal K. 1951-1998 140
Najafi, Najmeh 25-28R
Najarian, Nevart 1901(?)-1985
Obituary 117
Najder, Zdzislaw 1930- 17-20R
Najemy, John Michael 1943- 118
Najera, Rick 181
Naka, Yuji .... AAYA 59
Nakadate, Neil Edward 1943- 115
Nakae, Noriko 1940- 49-52
See also SATA 59
Nakagami, Kenji 1946-1992 195
See also Nakagami Kenji
See also MJW
Nakagami Kenji
See Nakagami, Kenji
See also DLB 182
Nakamura, Hajime 1912-1999 .... CANR-10
Earlier sketch in CA 53-56
Nakamura, James I. 1919- 21-24R
Nakamura, Yasuo 1919- 45-48
Nakanishi, Don T(oshiaki) 1949- 114
Nakanishi, Marsha
See Hirano-Nakanishi, Marsha J(oyce)
Nakanishi, Marsha J(oyce) Hirano
See Hirano-Nakanishi, Marsha J(oyce)
Nakano, Desmond 134
Nakano, Hirotaka 1942- 33-36R
Nakano'in Masatada no Musume
See Nijo, Lady
Nakarai, Toyozo W(ada) 1898-1984 ..... 41-44R
Obituary 174
Nakashima, George Katsutoshi 1905-1990 . 106
Nakatani, Chiyoko 1930-1981 77-80
See also CLR 30
See also SATA 55
See also SATA-Brief 40
Nakayama, Shigeru 1928- 29-32R
Nakdimon, Shlomo 1936- CANR-60
Earlier sketch in CA 128
Nakell, Martin 1945- 194
Nakhimovsky, Alice Stone 1950- 139
Nakhleh, Emile A. 1938- 77-80
Nakhnikian, George 1920- CANR-2
Earlier sketch in CA 1-4R
Nakkim, Lynn Kalama
See Nakkim, Lynn L.
Nakkim, Lynn L. 1937- 178
Nakos, Lilika 1903-1989 217
Nakos, Lilika 1903(?)-1989 .... CLC 29
Nalder, Eric C(hristopher) 1946- 89-92
Nale, Sharon Anne 1944- 108
Nale Roxlo, Conrado 1898-1971 178
See also HW 2
Nalkowska, Zofia 1884-1954 .... DLB 215
See also EWL 3
Nall, Barry T(homas) 1948- 141
Nall, Hiram Abiff 1950- 57-60
Nall, T(orney) Otto 1900-1989 .... 17-20R
Nallin, Walter E. 1917(?)-1978
Obituary 77-80
Nally, Susan W. 1947- 155
See also SATA 90
Nalty, Bernard Charles 1931- CANR-18
Earlier sketch in CA 102
Nam, Charles B(enjamin) 1926- CANR-10
Earlier sketch in CA 65-68
Nam, Koon Woo 1928- 61-64
Namath, Joe
See Namath, Joseph William
Namath, Joseph William 1943- 89-92
Namba, Toshio 1910-1987
Obituary 124
Nambiar, O. K. 1910- 13-16R
Nameroff, Rochelle 1943- 41-44R
Namias, June 1941- 81-84
Namier, Julia 1893-1977 61-64
Obituary 120
Namier, Lewis Bernstein 1888-1960
Obituary 113
Namikawa, Banri 1931- CANR-8
Earlier sketch in CA 53-56
Namikawa, Ryo 1905- 93-96
Namioka, Lensey 1929- CANR-141
Earlier sketches in CA 69-72, CANR-11, 27, 52, 84
See also AAYA 27
See also CLR 48
See also MAICYA 2
See also SAAS 24
See also SATA 27, 89, 157
See also SATA-Essay 116
See also YAW
Namir, Mordecai 1897-1975
Obituary 57-60
Namjoshi, Suniti 1941- CANR-115
Earlier sketches in CA 113, CANR-59
See also CP 1
See also CWP
See also FW
Namora, Fernando (Goncalves) 1919-1989
Obituary 127
See also DLB 287
See also EWL 3
Namovicz, Gene Inyart 1927- 17-20R
See also Inyart, Gene
Nana Diane
See Kaimann, Diane S.
Nanassy, Louis C(harles) 1913- CANR-41
Earlier sketches in CA 53-56, CANR-4, 19
Nance, Guinevera Ann 1939- 106
Nance, James Clark 1893(?)-1984
Obituary 113
Nance, John J. 1946- CANR-91
Earlier sketch in CA 137
Nance, Joseph Milton 1913-1997 ...... CANR-1
Earlier sketch in CA 1-4R
Nanda, B(al) R(am) 1917- CANR-47
Earlier sketches in CA 13-16R, CANR-7, 23
Nandakumar, Prema 1939- 9-12R
Nandy, Pritish 1947- CANR-12
Earlier sketch in CA 65-68
See also CP 1, 2, 3, 4, 5, 6, 7
Nangia, Sudesh 1942- CANR-22
Earlier sketches in CA 53-56, CANR-4
Nanji, Shenaaz 1954- .... SATA 131
NanKivell, Joice M.
See Loch, Joice N(anKivell)
Nannes, Caspar Harold 1906-1978 .. CANR-76
Obituary 81-84
Earlier sketch in CA 9-12R
Nanogak Agnes 1925- .... SATA 61
Nanry, Charles (Anthony) 1938- 73-76
Nanus, Burt 1936- 115
Napier, B(unyan) Davie 1915- CANR-4
Earlier sketch in CA 1-4R
Napier, Bill 1940- 130
Napier, Geraldine
See Glemser, Bernard
Napier, Mark
See Laffin, John (Alfred Charles)
Napier, Mary
See Wright, (Mary) Patricia
Napier, Nancy J. 1945- 144
Napier, Priscilla 1908-1998 .... 21-24R
Obituary 171
Napier, Susan 1954- .... RHW
Napier, William
See Seymour, William Napier
Napjus, Alice James 1913-2000 .... 21-24R
Napjus, James
See Napjus, Alice James
Naples, Nancy A. 1950(?)- 228
Napley, David 1915-1994 .... CANR-76
Obituary 146
Earlier sketch in CA 129
Napley, Sir David
See Napley, David
Napoleon
See Yamamoto, Hisaye
Napoleon, Art
See Sudhalter, Richard M(errill)
Napoli, Donna Jo 1948- CANR-96
Earlier sketch in CA 156
See also AAYA 25
See also BYA 10, 11
See also CLR 51
See also MAICYA 2
See also SAAS 23
See also SATA 92, 137
See also WYAS 1
See also YAW
Napolitan, Joseph 1929- 37-40R
Napolitane, Catherine A(nn) Durrum
1936- 85-88
Napolitano, Ann 230
Napora, Joseph S. 1944- 200
Nappa, Mike 1963- 199
Na Prous Boneta c. 1296-1328 .... DLB 208
Naqvi, Maniza 1960- 190
Naraghi, Ehsan 1926- 147
Narahashi, Keiko 1959- 186
See also SATA 79, 115
Narain, Jai Prakash
See Narayan, Jayaprakash
Narang, Gopi Chand 1931-1997 ...... CANR-31
Earlier sketches in CA 29-32R, CANR-14
Naranjo, Carmen 1930- 175
See also DLB 145
See also EWL 3
See also HW 2
Naranjo, Claudio 1932- 147
Narasimhachar, K. T.
See Narasimha Char, K. T.
Narasimha Char, K. T. 1903- CANR-5
Earlier sketch in CA 53-56
Narasimhan, Chakravarthi V. 1915- 17-20R
Narayan, Jayaprakash 1902-1979 97-100
Obituary 89-92
Narayan, Ongkar 1926- 103
Narayan, R(asipuram) K(rishnaswami)
1906-2001 .... CANR-112
Obituary 196
Earlier sketches in CA 81-84, CANR-33, 61
See also BPFB 2
See also CLC 7, 28, 47, 121, 211
See also CN 1, 2, 3, 4, 5, 6, 7
See also DA3
See also DAM NOV
See also DNFS 1
See also EWL 3
See also MTCW 1, 2
See also MTFW 2005
See also RGEL 2
See also RGSF 2
See also SATA 62
See also SSC 25
See also SSFS 5
See also WWE 1
Narayn, Deane 1929- 1-4R
Narbikova, Valeria 1958- 187
See also Narbikova, Valeriia Spartakovna
See also EWL 3
Narbikova, Valeriia Spartakovna
See Narbikova, Valeria
See also DLB 285
Nardi, James B. 1948- 127
Nardi, Peter M. 1947- CANR-93
Earlier sketch in CA 144
Nardin, Terry 1942- 41-44R
Nardini, Gloria 1942- 192
Nardo, Don 1947- 236
Narell, Irena 1923- CANR-1
Earlier sketch in CA 1-4R
Naremore, James 1941- CANR-11
Earlier sketch in CA 69-72
Narezhny, Vasilii Trofimovich
1780-1825 .... DLB 198
Naroll, Raoul 1920-1985 .... CANR-75
Obituary 116
Earlier sketch in CA 33-36R
Narrache, Jean
See Coderre, Emile
See also CCA 1
See also DLB 92
Narramore, Stanley Bruce 1941- 57-60
Naruse, Mikio 1905-1969 118
Narveson, Jan F(redric) 1936- CANR-24
Earlier sketches in CA 21-24R, CANR-9
Nasar, Jack L. 1947- CANR-122
Earlier sketch in CA 164
Nasar, Sylvia 173
Nasatir, A(braham) P(hineas)
1904-1991 .... CANR-5
Earlier sketch in CA 9-12R
Nasatir, David 1934- 41-44R
Nasaw, David 1945- CANR-96
Earlier sketch in CA 116
Nasaw, Jonathan Lewis 1947- CANR-103
Earlier sketches in CA 61-64, CANR-63
Nasby, A(sher Gordon) 1909-1983
Obituary 109
Nasby, Judith (Mary) 1945- 238
Nasby, Petroleum Vesuvius
See Locke, David Ross
See also RGAL 4
Naschy, Paul
See Molina, Jacinto
Nascimbene, Yan 1949- .... SATA 133
Nasdijj 1950- 226
Nash, Alanna 1950- 129
Nash, Allan N(ylin) 1932- 41-44R
Nash, Bruce M(itchell) 1947- CANR-15
Earlier sketch in CA 85-88
See also SATA 34
Nash, Daniel
See Loader, William Reginald
Nash, David T(heodore) 1929- 93-96
Nash, Elizabeth (Hamilton) 1934- CANR-93
Earlier sketch in CA 142
Nash, Eno
See Stevens, Austin N(eil)
Nash, Eric P(eter) 1956- 191
Nash, Ethel Miller 1909-1973 .... CAP-1
Earlier sketch in CA 13-16
Nash, Father Stephen
See Kavanaugh, James J(oseph)
Nash, Gary B. 1933- CANR-140
Earlier sketch in CA 37-40R
Nash, George (E.) 1948- 138
Nash, Gerald D(avid) 1928-2000 ..... CANR-93
Obituary 192
Earlier sketches in CA 21-24R, CANR-8
Nash, Howard P(ervear), Jr.
1900-1981 .... CANR-75
Obituary 133
Earlier sketch in CA 73-76
Nash, Isabel
See Eberstadt, Isabel
Nash, J(essie) Madeleine 1943- CANR-119
Earlier sketch in CA 69-72
Nash, James E(dward) 1933- 29-32R
Nash, Jay Robert 1937- 21-24R
Nash, Joyce D. 1940- 203
Nash, June (Caprice) 1927- CANR-143
Earlier sketch in CA 29-32R
Nash, (Cyril) Knowlton 1927- 135
Nash, Lee (Marten) 1927- 41-44R
Nash, Linell
See Smith, Linell Nash
Nash, Manning 1924-2000 .... 17-20R
Nash, Mary (Hughes) 1925- 5-8R
See also SATA 41
Nash, Mary 1947- 163
Nash, Michael R. 1951- 148
Nash, N. Richard 1913-2000 .... CANR-14
Obituary 191
Earlier sketch in CA 85-88
Interview in CANR-14
See also CD 5, 6
Nash, Nancy 1943- 21-24R
Nash, Newlyn
See Howe, Doris Kathleen
Nash, (Frediric) Ogden 1902-1971 ... CANR-61
Obituary 29-32R
Earlier sketches in CAP-1, CA 13-14, CANR-34
See also CLC 23
See also CP 1
See also DAM POET
See also DLB 11
See also MAICYA 1, 2
See also MAL 5
See also MTCW 1, 2
See also PC 21
See also RGAL 4
See also SATA 2, 46
See also TCLC 109
See also WP
Nash, Padder
See Sewart, Alan
Nash, Paul 1924-1993 .... 17-20R
Nash, Ralph (Lee) 1925- CANR-129
Earlier sketch in CA 17-20R
Nash, Ray 1905-1982
Obituary 106
Nash, Renea Denise 1963- 149
See also SATA 81
Nash, Robert 1902- CAP-1
Earlier sketch in CA 9-10
Nash, Roderick 1939- 17-20R
Nash, Roger 1942- 199
Nash, Ronald H. 1936- CANR-93
Earlier sketches in CA 5-8R, CANR-8, 23, 49
Nash, Simon
See Chapman, Raymond
Nash, Stan
See Nash, Stanley D.
Nash, Stanley D. 1946- 147
Nash, Susan Smith 1958- 185
Autobiographical Essay in 185
See also CAAS 25
Nash, William (Wray), Jr. 1928- 85-88
Nashe, Thomas 1567-1601(?) .... DLB 167
See also RGEL 2
Naske, Claus-M(ichael) 1935- CANR-57
Earlier sketches in CA 77-80, CANR-13, 31
Naslund, Erik
See Naeslund, Erik
Naslund, Sena Jeter 198
Nasmyth, Peter 188
Nason, Alvin 1919-1978
Obituary 77-80
Nason, Donna 1944- 97-100
Nason, Jerry 1910-1986 200
See also Nason, Paul Edward
See also DLB 241
Nason, Leonard H(astings) 1895-1970
Obituary 114
Nason, Leslie J. 5-8R
Nason, Paul Edward 1910-1986 200
See also Nason, Jerry
Nason, Tema 138
Nason, Thelma
See Nason, Tema
Nasr, Kameel 1949- 141
Nasr, Seyyed Hossein 1933- CANR-129
Earlier sketches in CA 21-24R, CANR-10
See also DLB 279
Nasrin, Taslima 1962- CANR-128
Earlier sketch in CA 171
Nass, Elyse (Linda) 1947- 111
Nass, Cheryl J(eanne) 1966- 200
Nass, Stanley 1940- 115
Nassaar, Christopher S(uhayl) 1944- 97-100

Nassar, Eugene Paul 1935- 33-36R
Nassau, Wilhelmina Helena Pauline Maria 1880-1962
Obituary 113
Nassauer, Rudolf 1924- 105
Nasser, Gamal Abdel 1918-1970
Obituary 113
Nassivera, John 1950- 109
Nasson, Bill 1952- 139
Nassour, Ellis (Michael) 1941- CANR-43
Earlier sketch in CA 119
Nast, Conde (Montrose) 1873-1942 184
See also DLB 91
Nast, Elsa Ruth
See Watson, Jane Werner
Nast, Thomas 1840-1902 185
Brief entry 112
See also AAYA 56
See also DLB 188
See also SATA 51
See also SATA-Brief 33
Nastasijevic, Momcilo 1894-1938 ...... DLB 147
See also EWL 3
Nastick, Sharon 1954- 114
See also SATA 41
Natale, Samuel M(ichael) 1943- 116
Natali, Alfred Maxim 1915-1999 57-60
Natanson, George 1928- 73-76
Natanson, Maurice (Alexander) 1924-1996 .... CANR-12
Obituary 153
Earlier sketch in CA 17-20R
Natarajan, Nalini 1956- 176
Natchez, Gladys W. 1915-1994 .... CANR-76
Obituary 145
Earlier sketches in CA 9-12R, CANR-4
Natella, Arthur A(ristides), Jr. 1941- .. CANR-43
Earlier sketches in CA 89-92, CANR-15
Nathan, Adele (Gutman) 1900(?)-1986 73-76
Obituary 119
See also SATA-Obit 48
Nathan, Amy CANR-139
Earlier sketch in CA 171
See also SATA 155
Nathan, Amy .... SATA 104
Nathan, Andrew J(ames) 1943- CANR-121
Earlier sketch in CA 65-68
Nathan, Daniel
See Dannay, Frederic
Nathan, David 1926- CANR-12
Earlier sketch in CA 29-32R
Nathan, Debbie 160
Nathan, Dorothy (Goldeen) (?)-1966 81-84
See also SATA 15
Nathan, George Jean 1882-1958 169
Brief entry 114
See also Hatteras, Owen
See also DLB 137
See also MAL 5
See also TCLC 18
Nathan, Hans 1910-1989 .... CANR-1
Obituary 176
Earlier sketch in CA 1-4R
Nathan, James A. 1942- CANR-16
Earlier sketch in CA 85-88
Nathan, Jean
See Levinsohn, Florence H(amlish)
Nathan, Joan 1943- 61-64
Nathan, Joe 1948- 115
Nathan, Leonard E(dward) 1924- CANR-69
Earlier sketches in CA 5-8R, CANR-7
See also CP 1, 2, 3, 4, 5, 6, 7
Nathan, Melissa 238
Nathan, Norman 1915- CANR-1
Earlier sketch in CA 1-4R
Nathan, Otto 1893-1987
Obituary 121
Nathan, Paul S. 1913- 148
Brief entry 116
Nathan, Peter E. 1935- CANR-93
Earlier sketch in CA 73-76
Nathan, Richard P(erle) 1935- CANR-7
Earlier sketch in CA 57-60
Nathan, Robert (Gruntal) 1894-1985 .... CANR-55
Obituary 116
Earlier sketches in CA 13-16R, CANR-6
See also CN 1, 2, 3
See also DLB 9
See also FANT
See also SATA 6
See also SATA-Obit 43
See also SUFW
Nathan, Robert Stuart 1948- 81-84
Nathanson, Carol (Edna) 1922- 132
Nathanson, Jerome 1908-1975
Obituary 57-60
Nathanson, Laura Walther 1941- 123
See also SATA 57
Nathanson, Leonard 1933- 21-24R
Nathanson, Nathaniel L(ouis) 1908-1983 89-92
Obituary 111
Nathanson, Paul 1947- CANR-114
Earlier sketch in CA 140
Nathanson, Stephen (Lewis) 1943- 176
Nathanson, Yale S(amuel) 1895-1989 77-80
Obituary 199
Nathiri, N. Y. 1948- 141
Nation, Carry A(melia Moore) 1846-1911 .. 218
See also DLB 303
Nations, Opal (Louis) 1941- 112
Natkin, Rick 1952- 129
Natoli, Joseph
See Natoli, Joseph P.
Natoli, Joseph P. 1943- CANR-141
Earlier sketch in CA 132
Natow, Annette 1933- 114
Natsis, James J. 1958- 223
Natsuki, Shizuko 1938- .... CMW 4
Natsume, Kinnosuke
See Natsume, Soseki
Natsume, Soseki 1867-1916 195
Brief entry 104
See also Natsume Soseki and Soseki
See also RGWL 2, 3
See also TCLC 2, 10
See also TWA
Natsume Soseki
See Natsume, Soseki
See also DLB 180
See also EWL 3
Natta, Giulio 1903-1979
Obituary 113
Nattel, Lilian 1956- 180
Natti, (Mary) Lee 1919- CANR-2
Earlier sketch in CA 5-8R
See also Kingman, Lee
Natti, Susanna 1948- .... SATA 32, 125
Nattiez, Jean-Jacques 1945- 146
Natusch, Sheila (Ellen) 1926- CANR-44
Earlier sketches in CA 103, CANR-20
Natwar-Singh, K. 1931- 13-16R
Nau, Erika S(chwager) 1918-2000 65-68
Nau, Henry R(ichard) 1941- 135
Naude, (Aletta) Adele da Fonseca-Wollheim 1910-1981 .... 9-12R
See also CP 1, 2
Nauer, Barbara Joan 1932- 191
Brief entry 105
Naughton, Bill
See Naughton, William John (Francis)
See also CN 1, 2, 3, 4, 5
Naughton, James Franklin 1957- 132
See also SATA 85
Naughton, Jim
See Naughton, James Franklin
Naughton, John P. 1933- CANR-120
Earlier sketch in CA 57-60
Naughton, William John (Francis) 1910-1992 .... CANR-61
Obituary 136
Earlier sketches in CA 105, CANR-36
See also Naughton, Bill
See also CWRI 5
See also DLB 13
See also MTCW 1
See also SATA 86
Naugle, Helen Harrold 1920- 53-56
Naugle, John E(arl) 1923- 65-68
Nauheim, Ferd(inand Alan) 1909-1986 .... CANR-16
Earlier sketches in CA 49-52, CANR-1
Naum, Gellu 1915-2001 206
Nauman, St. Elmo, Jr. 1935- 53-56
Naumann, Anthony Frank 1921-1971 ... 21-24R
Obituary 89-92
Naumann, Marina 1938- 93-96
Naumann, Oscar E(dward) 1912-1994 77-80
Obituary 196
Naumann, Rose 1919- 65-68
Naumburg, Margaret 1890-1983
Obituary 109
Naumoff, Lawrence 1946- CANR-66
Earlier sketch in CA 128
Naureckas, Jim 1964- 154
Nauticus
See Waltari, Mika (Toimi)
Nava, Gregory 1949- 131
See also HW 1
Nava, Julian 1927- 61-64
See also HW 1
Nava, Michael 1954- CANR-125
Earlier sketch in CA 124
See also DLB 306
Nava, Roberto 1906(?)-1983
Obituary 111
Navarra, Fernand Jean 1915- 108
Navarra, John Gabriel 1927- 41-44R
See also SATA 8
Navarra, Tova 1948- CANR-104
Earlier sketch in CA 149
Navarre, Marguerite de
See de Navarre, Marguerite
Navarre, Yves (Henri Michel) 1940-1994 .... CANR-83
Obituary 143
Earlier sketch in CA 133
Navarro, Antonio 1922- 107
Navarro, Joe 1953- .... DLB 209
Navarro (Gerassi), Marysa 1934- 106
Navarro, Peter 1949- 118
Navarro, Yvonne 1957- 168
See also HGG
Navas, Deborah 1943- CANR-94
Earlier sketch in CA 112
Navasky, Victor S(aul) 1932- CANR-120
Earlier sketches in CA 21-24R, CANR-10
Interview in CANR-10
Navas-Ruiz, Ricardo 1932-
Brief entry 107
Navone, John J(oseph) 1930- CANR-52
Earlier sketches in CA 21-24R, CANR-10, 28
Navrozov, Andrei 1956- 144
Navrozov, Lev 1928- 61-64
Nawrocki, Sarah 1966- 181
Naydler, Merton 1920- 45-48
Nayfeh, Ali Hasan 1933- 201
Naylor, Chris(topher Michael) 1947- 118
Naylor, Clare 1971- 228
Naylor, Eric W(oodfin) 1936- CANR-99
Earlier sketch in CA 45-48
Naylor, Gloria 1950- CANR-130
Earlier sketches in CA 107, CANR-27, 51, 74
See also AAYA 6, 39
See also AFAW 1, 2
See also AMWS 8
See also BLC 3
See also BW 2, 3
See also CLC 28, 52, 156
See also CN 4, 5, 6, 7
See also CPW
See also DA
See also DA3
See also DAC
See also DAM MST, MULT, NOV, POP
See also DLB 173
See also EWL 3
See also FW
See also MAL 5
See also MTCW 1, 2
See also MTFW 2005
See also NFS 4, 7
See also RGAL 4
See also TCLE 1:2
See also TUS
See also WLCS
Naylor, Harriet H. 1915-1985 .... CANR-9
Earlier sketch in CA 21-24R
Naylor, James C(harles) 1932- CANR-1
Earlier sketch in CA 45-48
Naylor, John 1920- 93-96
Naylor, Margot Ailsa (Lodge) 1907-1972 .... 9-12R
Obituary 134
Naylor, Penelope 1941- 37-40R
See also SATA 10
Naylor, Phyllis 1933-
See Naylor, Phyllis Reynolds
See also MAICYA 2
Naylor, Phyllis Reynolds 1933- CANR-121
Earlier sketches in CA 21-24R, CANR-8, 24, 59
See also Naylor, Phyllis
See also AAYA 4, 29
See also BYA 7, 8
See also CLR 17
See also CWRI 5
See also JRDA
See also MAICYA 1, 2
See also MAICYAS 1
See also SAAS 10
See also SATA 12, 66, 102, 152
See also SATA-Essay 152
See also WYA
See also YAW
Naylor, R. T(homas) 1945- 237
Nayman, Michele 147
Nazareth, Peter 1940- 101
See also EWL 3
Nazarian, Nikki
See Nichols, Cecilia Fawn
Nazario, Sonia 1960- 224
Nazaroff, Alexander I(vanovich) 1898-1981 .... 33-36R
See also SATA 4
Nazer, Mende 1981(?)- 229
Nazor, Vladimir 1876-1949 .... DLB 147
Nazrul Islam
See Islam, Kazi Nazrul
See also EWL 3
Nazzaro, Anthony M. 1927- 187
Brief entry 106
Ndao, Cheikh Aliou 1933- .... EWL 3
Ndebele, Njabulo (Simakahle) 1948- 184
See also DLB 157, 225
See also EWL 3
Ndebele, (Nimrod) Njabulo S(imakahle) 1913- .... CN 6, 7
Ndiaye, Marie 1967- 193
Ndu, Pol Nnamezie 1940- .... CP 1
Neagle, Anna 1904-1986
Obituary 119
Neagley, Ross Linn 1907-1999 106
Neagoe, Anna (Frankel) 1885(?)-1986
Obituary 120
Neagoe, Peter 1881-1960 105
See also DLB 4
Neal, Alfred C. 1912-2000 121
Obituary 189
Neal, Ann Parker 1934- 158
Brief entry 114
Neal, Arminta Pearl 1921- 85-88
Neal, Bruce W(alter) 1931- 21-24R
Neal, Charles Dempsey 1908-2001 ... CANR-5
Earlier sketch in CA 5-8R
Neal, Emily Gardiner CANR-3
Earlier sketch in CA 5-8R
Neal, Ernest G(ordon) 1911-1998 .... 13-16R
Obituary 165
Neal, Fred Warner 1915-1996 .... CANR-2
Earlier sketch in CA 5-8R
Neal, Harry
See Bixby, Jerome Lewis
Neal, Harry Edward 1906-1993 .... CANR-83
Obituary 141
Earlier sketches in CA 5-8R, CANR-2
See also SATA 5
See also SATA-Obit 76
Neal, Helen Keating 1907-1987 124
Obituary 122
Neal, Hilary
See Norton, Olive (Claydon)
Neal, James M(adison) 1925- 73-76
Neal, James T(homas) 1936- 57-60
Neal, John 1793-1876 .... DLB 1, 59, 243
See also FW
See also RGAL 4
Neal, Joseph C. 1807-1847 .... DLB 11
Neal, Julia 1905-1995 69-72
Neal, Larry
See Neal, Lawrence (P.)
See also DLB 38
Neal, Lawrence (P.) 1937-1981 81-84
Obituary 102
See also Neal, Larry
See also BW 1
See also CP 2
Neal, Marie Augusta 1921- CANR-35
Earlier sketches in CA 114, CANR-32
Neal, Mark Anthony 188
Neal, Michael
See Teitelbaum, Michael
Neal, Nelson 1921(?)-1983
Obituary 109
Neal, Patsy 1938- 61-64
Neal, W(illiam) Keith 1905-1990
Obituary 131
Neale, Gay Weeks 1935- 113
Neale, John E(rnest) 1890-1975 65-68
Obituary 61-64
Neale, R(onald) S(tanley) 1927-1985 157
Neale, Robert George 1919-
Brief entry 108
Neale, Walter Castle 1925- CANR-7
Earlier sketch in CA 5-8R
Neale-Silva, Eduardo 1905-
Brief entry 106
Nealon, Eleanor (O'Donoghue) 1940(?)-1999 103
Obituary 187
Nealon, Thomas E. 1933- 33-36R
Neaman, Judith S(ilverman) 1936- 61-64
Neame, Alan John 1924- CANR-2
Earlier sketch in CA 1-4R
See also CP 1
Neame, Ronald 1911- .... IDFW 4
Near, Holly 1949- 143
Nearing, Guy 1890-1986
Obituary 118
Nearing, Helen K(nothe) 1904-1995 . CANR-11
Obituary 149
Earlier sketch in CA 29-32R
Nearing, Penny 1916- 81-84
See also SATA 47
See also SATA-Brief 42
Nearing, Scott 1883-1983 .... CANR-11
Obituary 110
Earlier sketch in CA 41-44R
See also DLB 303
Neary, John (Anthony, Jr.) 1937-
Brief entry 107
Neary, John M. 1952- 187
Neatby, H(erbert) Blair 1924-
Brief entry 111
Neatby, Leslie Hamilton 1902-1997 ... CANR-3
Earlier sketch in CA 5-8R
Neate, Frank Anthony 1928- 105
Neate, Patrick 1970- 197
Neave, Airey (Middleton Sheffield) 1916-1979 85-88
Neaverson, Bob 1967- 225
Neavles, Janet (Morrison) Talmadge 1919-1988 .... 5-8R
Obituary 202
Nebel, Frederick 1903-1967 .... CMW 4
See also DLB 226
Nebel, Gustave E. .... SATA 45
See also SATA-Brief 33
Nebel, Mimouca
See Nebel, Gustave E.
Nebenzahl, Kenneth 1927- 111
Brief entry 109
Nebrensky, Alex
See Cooper, Parley J(oseph)
Nebrija, Antonio de 1442(?)-1522 ...... DLB 286
Nebylitsyn, Vladimir Dmitrievich 1930(?)-1972
Obituary 37-40R
Necati -1509 .... WLIT 6
Necatigil, Behcet 1916-1979 .... EWL 3
Nechas, Eileen (T.) 1944- 146
Necheles, Ruth F. 1936- 41-44R
Neck, Christopher P. 203
Necker, Claire (Kral) 1917- 33-36R
Neder, Dennis W. 1959- 234
Nederhood, Joel H(oman) 1930- 29-32R
Nedreaas, Torborg 1906-1987 .... DLB 297
Nee, Brett de Bary 1943- 101
Nee, Kay Bonner CANR-31
Earlier sketches in CA 49-52, CANR-2
See also SATA 10
Needham, David C. 1929- 118
Needham, Hal 1937- .... IDFW 3
Needham, (Noel) Joseph (Terence Montgomery) 1900-1995 .... CANR-34
Obituary 148
Earlier sketches in CA 9-12R, CANR-5
Needham, Kate 1962- 160
See also SATA 95
Needham, Richard (John) 1912-1996 101
Needham, Rodney 1923- CANR-15
Earlier sketch in CA 81-84
Needham, (Amy) Violet 1876-1967
Obituary 116
See also CWRI 5
Needle, Jan 1943- CANR-84
Earlier sketches in CA 106, CANR-28
See also AAYA 23
See also CLR 43
See also SAAS 23
See also SATA 30, 98
See also YAW
Needleman, Jacob 1934- CANR-115
Earlier sketches in CA 29-32R, CANR-12
See also SATA 6

Cumulative Index 423 Nelson

Needleman, Morriss H(amilton)
1907-1980 ... 25-28R
Obituary ... 199
Needler, Howard I(an) 1937- ... 111
Needler, Martin C(yril) 1933- ... CANR-18
Earlier sketches in CA 5-8R, CANR-2
Needles, Robert Johnson 1903-1979 ... CAP-1
Obituary ... 202
Earlier sketch in CA 11-12
Neef, Elton T.
See Fanthorpe, R(obert) Lionel
Neel, (Louis) Boyd 1905-1981
Obituary ... 108
Neel, David 1960- ... 212
See also SATA 82
Neel, Janet
See Cohen, Janet
Neel, Jasper 1946- ... 151
Neel, Joanne Loewe 1920- ... 25-28R
Neel, Louis (Eugene Felix) 1904-2000 ... 167
Obituary ... 192
Neel, Preston 1959- ... SATA 93
Neeld, Elizabeth Harper 1940- ... 141
Neels, Betty 1909- ... RHW
Neely, Barbara 1941- ... CANR-120
Earlier sketch in CA 170
Neely, Bill 1930- ... CANR-28
Earlier sketches in CA 33-36R, CANR-13
Neely, Carol Thomas 1939- ... 128
Brief entry ... 107
Neely, James C. 1926- ... 109
Neely, Mark E(dward), Jr. 1944- ... CANR-25
Earlier sketch in CA 106
Neely, Martina 1939- ... 61-64
Neely, Richard (Forlani) 1941- ... CANR-28
Earlier sketch in CA 107, 175
See also CMW 4
Neenan, Benedict 1949- ... 218
Neenan, Colin 1958- ... 151
Neenan, William B(raunger) 1929- ... 41-44R
Neeper, Carolyn 1937- ... 57-60
Neeper, Cary
See Neeper, Carolyn
Neera
See Zuccari, Anna
See also WLIT 7
Neerskov, Hans Kristian 1932- ... 65-68
Nees, Lawrence 1949- ... 139
Nef, Evelyn Stefansson 1913- ... CANR-20
Earlier sketch in CA 49-52
Nef, John Ulric 1899-1988 ... CANR-82
Obituary ... 127
Earlier sketches in CA 1-4R, CANR-20
Nefedova, Tatyana 1949- ... 166
Neff, Alan (Henry) 1949- ... 117
Neff, Debra ... CLC 59
Neff, Donald (Lloyd) 1930- ... CANR-28
Earlier sketch in CA 77-80
Neff, Emery E. 1892-1983 ... 5-8R
Obituary ... 109
Neff, H(arry) Richard 1933- ... 33-36R
Neff, Hildegard
See Knef, Hildegard (Frieda Albertina)
Neff, James ... 205
Neff, John B. 1931- ... 234
Neff, John C. 1913-1987 ... 17-20R
Neff, Kirk Powis 1950- ... 163
Neff, Lyle ... 217
Neff, Miriam 1945- ... 115
Neff, Renfreu (de St. Laurence) 1938- ... 29-32R
Neff, Robert W(ilbur) 1936- ... 106
Neff, Walter S(cott) 1910-1997 ... CAP-2
Earlier sketch in CA 25-28
Neff, William Lee 1906-1973 ... 1-4R
Obituary ... 103
Neft, David S(amuel) 1937- ... 41-44R
Negandhi, A(nant) R(anchoddas) 1933- . 33-36R
Negash, Tekeste ... 206
Negev, Eilat ... 232
Neggers, Carla A(malia) 1955- ... CANR-102
Earlier sketches in CA 112, CANR-30
Negley, Glenn (Robert) 1907-1988 ... 17-20R
Obituary ... 125
Negnevitsky, Michael 1956- ... 231
Negoitescu, Ion 1921-1993 ... DLB 220
See also EWL 3
Negri, Ada 1870-1945 ... DLB 114
Negri, Antonio 1933- ... 235
Negri, Rocco 1932- ... SATA 12
Negrino, Tom ... 222
Negroponte, Nicholas Peter 1943- ... 29-32R
Negus, Arthur George 1903-1985
Obituary ... 116
Negus, Kenneth George 1927- ... 17-20R
Nehamas, Alexander 1946- ... CANR-120
Earlier sketch in CA 126
Neher, Andre 1914-1988 ... CANR-26
Earlier sketch in CA 109
Neher, Clark D(umont) 1938- ... 118
Neher, Erwin 1944- ... 156
Neher, Jack 1918- ... 118
Nehr, Ellen -1995 ... 204
Nehring, James 1958- ... 140
Nehrling, Arno H. 1886-1974 ... 9-12R
Obituary ... 53-56
Nehrling, Irene (Thelma) Dahlberg
1900-1996 ... 9-12R
Obituary ... 198
Nehrt, Lee Charles 1926- ... CANR-13
Earlier sketch in CA 21-24R
Nehru, Jawaharlal 1889-1964 ... CANR-34
Earlier sketch in CA 85-88
See also MTCW 1
Neiberg, Michael (S.) 1969- ... 189
Neiburg, Gladys Eudas 1898-1983 ... 61-64
Obituary ... 203
Neider, Charles 1915-2001 ... CANR-115
Obituary ... 201
Earlier sketches in CA 17-20R, CANR-24
Interview in ... CANR-24
Neiderman, Andrew 1940- ... CANR-127
Earlier sketches in CA 33-36R, CANR-13, 75
See also HGG
Neidermyer, Dan 1947- ... CANR-24
Earlier sketch in CA 45-48
Neidhardt, W(ilfried) S(teffen) 1941- ... 65-68
Neidhart von Reuental c. 1185-c.
1240 ... DLB 138
Neidpath, James
See Charteris, James Donald
Neier, Aryeh 1937- ... CANR-128
Earlier sketch in CA 57-60
See also SATA 59
Neighbour, Ralph W(ebster)
1906-2000 ... CANR-1
Earlier sketch in CA 1-4R
Neighbour, Rhona M.
See Martin, Rhona
Neighbours, Kenneth Franklin 1915- ... 61-64
Neigoff, Anne ... 41-44R
See also SATA 13
Neigoff, Mike 1920- ... CANR-2
Earlier sketch in CA 5-8R
See also SATA 13
Neihardt, John Gneisenau
1881-1973 ... CANR-65
Earlier sketches in CAP-1, CA 13-14
See also CLC 32
See also DLB 9, 54, 256
See also LAIT 2
See also TCWW 1, 2
Neihart, Ben 1965- ... 198
Neikirk, William (Robert) 1938- ... 117
Neil, Barbara ... 214
Neil, Hugh Michael 1930-
Brief entry ... 109
Neil, J. Meredith 1937- ... 33-36R
Neil, Randolph L. 1941- ... 93-96
Neil, Randy
See Neil, Randolph L.
Neil, William 1909-1979 ... CANR-6
Obituary ... 93-96
Earlier sketch in CA 9-12R
Neilan, Sarah ... CANR-84
Earlier sketch in CA 69-72
Neilands, J(ohn) B(rian) 1921- ... 97-100
Neill, A(lexander) S(utherland) 1883-1973 . 101
Obituary ... 45-48
Neill, Christopher Harry Douglas 1955- ... 117
Neill, Michael ... 181
Neill, Stephen Charles 1900-1984 ... CANR-82
Obituary ... 113
Earlier sketches in CA 9-12R, CANR-7
Neill, Thomas Patrick 1915-1970 ... CANR-3
Earlier sketch in CA 5-8R
Neill, William 1922- ... 206
Neillands, Robin ... 212
Neils, Jenifer 1950- ... 212
Neilson, Andrew 1946- ... CANR-27
Earlier sketch in CA 110
Neilson, Eric
See Cockrell, Amanda
Neilson, Frances Fullerton (Jones)
1910-2001 ... 73-76
See also SATA 14
Neilson, James Warren 1933- ... 1-4R
Neilson, John Shaw 1872-1942 ... 202
See also DLB 230
See also RGEL 2
Neilson, Marguerite
See Tompkins, Julia (Marguerite Hunter Manchee)
Neilson, Melany 1958- ... CANR-104
Earlier sketch in CA 132
Neilson, N(eils) P. 1895-1988 ... CANR-2
Earlier sketch in CA 5-8R
Neiman, David 1921-2004 ... 69-72
Obituary ... 224
Neiman, Fraser 1911-1993 ... 25-28R
Neiman, Morris 1910(?)-1989
Obituary ... 130
Neiman, Susan 1955- ... 226
Neimanis, George J(uris) 1932- ... 175
Neimark, Anne E. 1935- ... CANR-36
Earlier sketches in CA 29-32R, CANR-16
See also SATA 4, 145
Neimark, Edith D(eborah) 1928- ... 41-44R
Neimark, Paul G. 1934- ... 135
Brief entry ... 115
See also SATA 80
See also SATA-Brief 37
Nein, Jo
See Anker, Nini Magdalene Roll
Neipris, Janet
See Wille, Janet Neipris
Neisser, Eric (Robert) 1947-1999 ... 188
Neisser, Hans P(hilip) 1895-1975 ... CAP-1
Obituary ... 53-56
Earlier sketch in CA 13-16
Neisser, Ulric 1928- ... CANR-84
Earlier sketches in CA 108, CANR-26, 55
Neitzel, Shirley 1941- ... SATA 77, 134
Neiwert, David A. 1956- ... 234
Ne Jame, Adele 1945- ... 194
Nekrasov, Nikolai Alekseevich
1821-1878 ... DLB 277
Nekrasov, Viktor (Platonovich) 1911-1987
Obituary ... 123
See also DLB 302
Nekrich, Aleksandr M(oisei) 1920-1993 .. 81-84
Nel, Philip (W.) 1969- ... 220
Neledinsky-Meletsky, Iurii Aleksandrovich
1752-1828 ... DLB 150
Neligan, David 1899-1983 ... CAP-2
Earlier sketch in CA 29-32
Nelkin, Dorothy (Wolfers)
1933-2003 ... CANR-105
Obituary ... 216
Earlier sketches in CA 41-44R, CANR-14, 31
Nell
See Hanna, Nell(ie L.)
Nell, Edward John 1935- ... 65-68
Nell, Victor 1935- ... 136
Nelles, Henry Vivian 1942- ... CANR-104
Earlier sketch in CA 103
Nelli, Humbert S(teven) 1930- ... CANR-14
Earlier sketch in CA 41-44R
Nelligan, Emile 1879-1941 ... 204
Brief entry ... 114
See also DLB 92
See also EWL 3
See also TCLC 14
Nellis, Muriel ... 102
Nellist, John B(owman) 1923- ... 25-28R
Nellist, John G. 1927- ... 192
Nelms, C(larice) E. 1919- ... 25-28R
Nelms, Henning C(unningham) 1900-1986
Obituary ... 119
Nelsen, Anne Kusener 1942- ... 97-100
Nelsen, Hart M(ichael) 1938- ... CANR-8
Earlier sketch in CA 53-56
Nelson, A(ndrew) Thomas 1933- ... 5-8R
Nelson, Alan H(olm) 1938- ... 104
Nelson, Alice Fray 1911(?)-1983
Obituary ... 110
Nelson, Alice Ruth Moore Dunbar
1875-1935 ... CANR-82
Brief entry ... 122
Earlier sketch in CA 124
See also Dunbar-Nelson, Alice
See also BW 1, 3
See also DLB 50
See also FW
See also MTCW 1
Nelson, Alvin F(redolph) 1917-1973 ... CAP-2
Earlier sketch in CA 25-28
Nelson, Amirtharaj 1934- ... 57-60
Nelson, Andrew N(athaniel)
1893-1975 ... CANR-3
Earlier sketch in CA 5-8R
Nelson, Anne 1954- ... CANR-137
Earlier sketch in CA 123
Nelson, Antonya 1961- ... CANR-97
Earlier sketch in CA 138
See also DLB 244
Nelson, Barbara 1947- ... 191
Nelson, Barney
See Nelson, Barbara
Nelson, Benjamin N. 1911-1977 ... CANR-28
Obituary ... 73-76
Earlier sketch in CA 81-84
Nelson, Benjamin N(athaniel) 1935- .. CANR-1
Earlier sketch in CA 1-4R
Nelson, Beth
See Nelson, Mary Elizabeth
Nelson, Betty (Joan) Palmer
1938-1998 ... CANR-112
Earlier sketch in CA 134
Nelson, Bobby Jack 1938- ... 172
Nelson, C(arl) Ellis 1916- ... 108
Nelson, Carl Leroy 1910- ... 104
Nelson, Carnot E(dward) 1941- ... 37-40R
Nelson, Carolyn W(illiamson) 1942- ... 150
Nelson, Cary (Robert) 1946- ... CANR-96
Earlier sketch in CA 49-52
Nelson, Catherine Chadwick 1926- ... SATA 87
Nelson, Charles Lamar 1917- ... 69-72
Nelson, Charles R(owe) 1942- ... 37-40R
Nelson, Cholmondeley M. 1903-1991 ... 5-8R
Nelson, Claudia (Baxter) 1960- ... 150
Nelson, Clifford Ansgar 1906-1994 ... CAP-1
Earlier sketch in CA 11-12
Nelson, Conny E(dwin) 1933-
Brief entry ... 108
Nelson, Cordner (Bruce) 1918- ... 29-32R
See also SATA 54
See also SATA-Brief 29
Nelson, Dalmas H(ildor) 1925- ... 119
Nelson, Daniel 1941- ... CANR-99
Earlier sketch in CA 25-28R
Nelson, David Moir 1920- ... CANR-38
Earlier sketches in CA 1-4R, CANR-17
Nelson, Donald F. 1929- ... 37-40R
Nelson, Dorothy ... 239
Nelson, Drew 1952- ... 145
See also SATA 77
Nelson, E(ugene) Clifford 1911- ... 13-16R
Nelson, Edna Deu Pree ... 5-8R
Nelson, Elof G. 1924-1998 ... CANR-35
Earlier sketch in CA 21-24R
Nelson, Emmanuel S(ampath) 1954- ... 142
Nelson, Eric 1952- ... 195
Nelson, Eric Hilliard 1940-1985
Obituary ... 118
Nelson, Esther L. 1928- ... CANR-53
Earlier sketches in CA 69-72, CANR-11, 28
See also SATA 13
Nelson, Ethel Florence 1913- ... CANR-6
Earlier sketch in CA 53-56
Nelson, Eugene 1929- ... 61-64
Nelson, F(rancis) William 1922- ... 13-16R
Nelson, Geoffrey K(enneth) 1923- ... CANR-49
Earlier sketches in CA 29-32R, CANR-24
Nelson, George (H.) 1908-1986 ... 81-84
Obituary ... 118
Nelson, George (Carl) E(dward)
1900-1982 ... CANR-24
Earlier sketch in CA 45-48
Nelson, Gideon E(dmund, Jr.) 1924- ... 53-56
Nelson, Harold A(lfred) 1932- ... 114
Nelson, Harold L(ewis) 1917- ... 93-96
Nelson, Herbert B(enjamin)
1903-1987 ... CAP-2
Earlier sketch in CA 19-20
Nelson, Howard 1947- ... 136
Nelson, Indiana 1940- ... 97-100
Nelson, J. Bryan 1932- ... CANR-10
Earlier sketch in CA 25-28R
Nelson, J(oseph) Raleigh 1873-1961
Obituary ... 110
Nelson, J(ohn) Robert 1920-2004 ... CANR-19
Obituary ... 230
Earlier sketches in CA 9-12R, CANR-3
Nelson, Jack
See Nelson, John Howard
Nelson, Jack L. 1932- ... CANR-10
Earlier sketch in CA 25-28R
Nelson, Jacquelyn S. 1950- ... 137
Nelson, James B(ruce) 1930- ... CANR-17
Earlier sketches in CA 49-52, CANR-1
Nelson, James C(ecil) 1908-2000 ... CANR-13
Earlier sketch in CA 77-80
Nelson, James G(raham) 1929- ... 9-12R
Nelson, James L. 1962- ... CANR-93
Earlier sketch in CA 159
Nelson, Jan Alan 1935- ... 41-44R
Nelson, Jane Armstrong 1927-
Brief entry ... 105
Nelson, Janet 1930- ... 115
Nelson, Jean Erichsen
See Erichsen-Nelson, Jean
Nelson, Jill 1952- ... 163
Nelson, Jim A.
See Stotter, Mike
Nelson, Jim A.
See Stotter, Mike
Nelson, John Charles 1925- ... 49-52
Nelson, John Howard 1929- ... 29-32R
Nelson, John Oliver 1909-1990 ... 37-40R
Obituary ... 131
Nelson, Johnny
See Meares, Leonard Frank
Nelson, Joseph Schieser 1937- ... 73-76
Nelson, Julie L. 1970- ... 189
See also SATA 117
Nelson, June Kompass 1920- ... 73-76
Nelson, Kadir ... SATA 154
Nelson, Katherine Shaw 1926- ... 110
Nelson, Kay Shaw
See Nelson, Katherine Shaw
Nelson, Keith L(ebahn) 1932- ... 203
Brief entry ... 113
Nelson, Kent 1943- ... CANR-89
Earlier sketch in CA 77-80
See also DLB 234
Nelson, Kris
See Rusch, Kristine Kathryn
Nelson, L(ester) Ivar 1941- ... 119
Nelson, Lawrence E(rnest) 1928-1977 ... 53-56
Obituary ... 103
See also SATA-Obit 28
Nelson, Lawrence Emerson 1893-1978 . 17-20R
Obituary ... 134
Nelson, Lee J. 1954- ... 223
Nelson, Liza 1950- ... 190
Nelson, Lois (Ney) 1930- ... 61-64
Nelson, Lowry, Jr. 1926-1994 ... CANR-39
Earlier sketch in CA 5-8R
Nelson, Maggie
See Nelson, Margaret
Nelson, Malcolm A. 1934- ... 45-48
Nelson, Marcia Z. ... 206
Nelson, Marg (Raibley) 1899-1986 ... CANR-2
Earlier sketch in CA 1-4R
Nelson, Margaret 1973- ... 210
Nelson, Margaret K. ... 198
Nelson, Marguerite
See Floren, Lee
Nelson, Mariah Burton 1956- ... CANR-93
Earlier sketch in CA 146
Nelson, Marilyn 1946- ... CANR-114
Earlier sketch in CANR-51
See also Waniek, Marilyn Nelson
See also CAAS 23
See also DLB 282
See also MAICYA 2
See also SATA 151
Nelson, Marion Harvey 1925- ... 9-12R
Nelson, Martha 1923- ... 29-32R
Nelson, Mary Carroll 1929- ... CANR-16
Earlier sketches in CA 49-52, CANR-1
See also SATA 23
Nelson, Mary Elizabeth 1926- ... 93-96
Nelson, Michael Harrington 1921- ... CANR-2
Earlier sketch in CA 170
Nelson, Miriam E. ... 213
Nelson, Nina
See Nelson, Ethel Florence
Nelson, O. Terry 1941- ... SATA 62
Nelson, Oliver W(endell) 1904-1991 ... 29-32R
Nelson, Oswald George 1907-1975 ... 93-96
Obituary ... 57-60
Nelson, Ozzie
See Nelson, Oswald George
Nelson, P.
See Scott, Whitney
Nelson, Paul David 1941- ... CANR-45
Earlier sketch in CA 120
Nelson, Peter
See Solow, Martin
Nelson, Peter 1940- ... CANR-12
Earlier sketch in CA 61-64
Nelson, Peter N. 1953- ... 140
See also SATA 73
Nelson, Philip Bradford 1951- ... 113

Nelson 424 CONTEMPORARY AUTHORS

Nelson, R(adell) Faraday 1931- CANR-84
Earlier sketches in CA 69-72, CANR-26
See also SFW 4
Nelson, Rachel W(est) 1955- 117
Nelson, Ralph 1916-1987 49-52
Obituary 124
Nelson, Ralph C(arl) 1927- 53-56
Nelson, Randy F(ranklin) 1948- 125
Brief entry 110
Nelson, Ray
See Nelson, R(adell) Faraday
Nelson, Raymond S(tanley) 1921- CANR-36
Earlier sketches in CA 45-48, CANR-1, 16
Nelson, Richard 1950- CANR-134
Brief entry 123
Earlier sketch in CA 129
Interview in CA-129
See also CAD
See also CD 5, 6
See also RGAL 4
Nelson, Richard K(ing) 1941- CANR-30
Earlier sketches in CA 29-32R, CANR-12
See also ANW
See also DLB 275
See also SATA 65
Nelson, Richard R(obinson) 1930- ... CANR-16
Earlier sketch in CA 97-100
Nelson, Rick
See Nelson, Eric Hilliard
Nelson, Ricky
See Nelson, Eric Hilliard
Nelson, Robert James 1925- CANR-8
Earlier sketch in CA 5-8R
Nelson, Robert M(cDowell, Jr.) 1945- 146
Nelson, Robert S. 1947- 222
Nelson, Robin Laura 1971- 212
See also SATA 141
Nelson, Rosanne E(ierdanz) 1939- 49-52
Nelson, Rowland Whiteway 1902-1979
Obituary 105
Nelson, Roy Paul 1923- CANR-45
Earlier sketches in CA 17-20R, CANR-7, 22
See also SATA 59
Nelson, Ruben F(rederick) W(erthenbach)
1939- CANR-58
Earlier sketches in CA 112, CANR-31
Nelson, Ruth 1914- 41-44R
Nelson, Ruth Youngdahl 1904(?)-1984
Obituary 112
Nelson, Samuel H. 1946- 227
Nelson, Sarah Milledge 184
Nelson, Severina E(laine) 1896-1978 .... 5-8R
Nelson, Sharlene (P.) 1933- CANR-130
Earlier sketch in CA 161
See also SATA 96
Nelson, Sharon H. 1948- 113
Nelson, Shirley 181
Nelson, Sioban 1943- 218
Nelson, Stanley 1933- CANR-39
Earlier sketches in CA 49-52, CANR-1, 18
Nelson, T. G. A. 1940- 154
Nelson, Ted (W.) 1931- CANR-134
Earlier sketch in CA 161
See also SATA 96
Nelson, Theresa 1948- 148
See also AAYA 25
See also SATA 79, 143
See also SATA-Essay 143
See also YAW
Nelson, Thomas P. 1925(?)-1983
Obituary 110
Nelson, Tim Blake 1964(?)- 231
Nelson, Truman (John Seymour)
1911-1987 .... CANR-1
Obituary 123
Earlier sketch in CA 1-4R
Nelson, Victoria 1945- 205
Nelson, W(esley) Dale 1927- 77-80
Nelson, Walter Henry 1928- CANR-7
Earlier sketch in CA 13-16R
Nelson, Warren L. 1940- 89-92
Nelson, William 1908-1978 49-52
Obituary 103
See also DLB 103
Nelson, William R(ichard) 1924- 25-28R
Nelson, William Rockhill 1841-1915 179
See also DLB 23
Nelson, Willie 1933- CANR-114
Earlier sketch in CA 107
See also CLC 17
Nelson-Pallmeyer, Jack 223
Nelton, Sharon (Lee) 1937- 123
Nemanic, Gerald Carl 1941- 107
Nemec, David 1938- CANR-2
Earlier sketch in CA 49-52
Nemerov, Howard (Stanley)
1920-1991 .... CANR-53
Obituary 134
Earlier sketches in CA 1-4R, CANR-1, 27
Interview in CANR-27
See also CABS 2
See also AMW
See also CLC 2, 6, 9, 36
See also CN 1, 2, 3
See also CP 1, 2
See also DAM POET
See also DLB 5, 6
See also DLBY 1983
See also EWL 3
See also MAL 5
See also MTCW 1, 2
See also MTFW 2005
See also PC 24
See also PFS 10, 14
See also RGAL 4
See also TCLC 124
Nemeshegyi, Peter 1923- 130
Nemeth, Laszlo 1901-1975 93-96
Obituary 57-60
See also DLB 215
See also EWL 3
Nemir, Alma 1902-1971 .... CAP-2
Earlier sketch in CA 29-32
Nemiro, Beverly Anderson 1925- CANR-5
Earlier sketch in CA 53-56
Nemiroff, Robert
Brief entry 116
See also AITN 2
Nemirow, Steven 1949- 110
Nemmers, Erwin Esser 1916-1988 .... 9-12R
Obituary 201
Nemoianu, Virgil (Petre) 1940- 130
Nemow, A.
See Neznansky, Friedrich
Nemser, Cindy 1937- 61-64
Nemunelis, Vyte
See Brazdzionis, Bernardas
Nena
See Saarikoski, Pentti (Ilmari)
Nenae
See Saarikoski, Pentti (Ilmari)
Nenni, Pietro 1891-1980
Obituary 105
Nepaulsingh, Colbert I(vor) 1943- 155
Nepos c. 100B.C.-c. 27B.C. .... DLB 211
Nerbovig, Marcella H. 1919- 89-92
Nerburn, Kent Michael 1946- CANR-109
Earlier sketch in CA 166
Nere, Jacques 1917- 57-60
Nerhood, Harry W(arren) 1910- 29-32R
Neri, Kris 1948- 198
Nerin, William F. 1926- 142
Neris, Salomeja 1904-1945 .... CDWLB 4
See also DLB 220
Nerlich, Graham 73-76
Nerlove, Marc L(eon) 1933- 104
Nerlove, Miriam 1959- 121
See also SATA 53
See also SATA-Brief 49
Nernst, (Hermann) Walther 1864-1941 157
Nersessian, Edward 1944- 162
Nersessian, V(rej) N. 1948- 170
Neruda, Pablo 1904-1973 .... CANR-131
Obituary 45-48
Earlier sketches in CAP-2, CA 19-20
See also CLC 1, 2, 5, 7, 9, 28, 62
See also DA
See also DA3
See also DAB
See also DAC
See also DAM MST, MULT, POET
See also DLB 283
See also DNFS 2
See also EWL 3
See also HLC 2
See also HW 1
See also LAW
See also MTCW 1, 2
See also MTFW 2005
See also PC 4, 64
See also PFS 11
See also RGWL 2, 3
See also TWA
See also WLC
See also WLIT 1
See also WP
Nerval, Gaston
See Diez de Medina, Raul
Nerval, Gerard de 1808-1855 .... DLB 217
See also EW 6
See also GFL 1789 to the Present
See also PC 13
See also RGSF 2
See also RGWL 2, 3
See also SSC 18
Nervi, Pier Luigi 1891-1979 184
Obituary 113
Nervo, (Jose) Amado (Ruiz de) 1870-1919 . 131
Brief entry 109
See also DLB 290
See also EWL 3
See also HLCS 2
See also HW 1
See also LAW
See also TCLC 11
Nesaule, Agate 1938- 159
Nesbin, Esther W(inter) 1910- 41-44R
Nesbit, Andrew
See Kelly, Ronald
Nesbit, E(dith) 1858-1924 137
Brief entry 118
See also BYA 5
See also CLR 3, 70
See also CWRI 5
See also DLB 141, 153, 178
See also FANT
See also HGG
See also MAICYA 1, 2
See also MTCW 2
See also RGEL 2
See also SATA 100
See also WCH
See also YABC 1
Nesbit, Malcolm
See Chester, Alfred
Nesbit, Molly 1952- 142
Nesbit, Robert C(arrington) 1917-1999 ... 45-48
Nesbit, Troy
See Folsom, Franklin (Brewster)
Nesbitt, Cathleen 1888-1982
Obituary 107
Nesbitt, Elizabeth 1897(?)-1977
Obituary 73-76
Nesbitt, George L(yman) 1903-1985 ..... 41-44R
Nesbitt, John D. 1948- CANR-98
Earlier sketch in CA 153
Nesbitt, Marc 226
Nesbitt, Paul H(omer) 1904-1985 77-80
Nesbitt, Ralph Beryl 1891(?)-1975
Obituary 61-64
Nesbitt, Rosemary (Sinnett) 1924- 81-84
Neshamith, Sara
See Dushnitzky-Shner, Sara
Nesin, Aziz
See Nesin, Mehmet Nusret
See also EWL 3
Nesin, Mehmet Nusret 1915-1995
See Nesin, Aziz
Nesmith, Robert I. 1891-1972 .... CANR-15
Obituary 103
Earlier sketch in CA 1-4R
Nesovich, Peter
See Naumoff, Lawrence
Nespojohn, Katherine V(eronica)
1912-1975 .... 37-40R
See also SATA 7
Ness, Evaline (Michelow)
1911-1986 .... CANR-37
Obituary 120
Earlier sketches in CA 5-8R, CANR-5
See also CLR 6
See also CWRI 5
See also DLB 61
See also MAICYA 1, 2
See also SAAS 1
See also SATA 1, 26
See also SATA-Obit 49
Ness, Gayl D(eForrest) 1929- 29-32R
Ness, Immanuel 1958- 200
Ness, John H., Jr. 1919- 21-24R
Nesse, Randolph M. 1948- 150
Nessen, (Lewis) Robert 1932- 107
Nessen, Ron(ald Harold) 1934-
Brief entry 106
Nesset, Kirk 1957- 150
Nessi, Pio Baroja y
See Baroja (y Nessi), Pio
Nester, William R. 1956- CANR-92
Earlier sketch in CA 146
Nestle, Joan 1940- 181
See also GLL 1
Nestle, John Francis 1912- 89-92
Nestle, Marion 1936- 222
Nestler, Eric J. 1954- CANR-92
Earlier sketch in CA 145
Nestor, Larry 1940- 223
See also SATA 149
Nestor, William P(rodromos) 1947- .. CANR-26
Earlier sketch in CA 109
See also SATA 49
Nestroy, Johann 1801-1862 .... DLB 133
See also RGWL 2, 3
Nesvadba, Josef 1926-2005 97-100
See also SFW 4
Netanyahu, B(enzion) 1910- CANR-52
Earlier sketch in CA 61-64
Netanyahu, Benjamin 1949- 152
Netanyahu, Binyamin
See Netanyahu, Benjamin
Netanyahu, Jonathan 1946(?)-1976
Obituary 114
Netanyahu, Yonatan
See Netanyahu, Jonathan
Netboy, Anthony 1906-1993 .... CANR-7
Earlier sketch in CA 17-20R
Neter, John 1923- 53-56
Netherclift, Beryl (Constance) 1911- 93-96
Nethercot, Arthur H(obart)
1895-1981 .... CANR-28
Obituary 182
Earlier sketch in CA 1-4R
Nethery, Mary 159
See also SATA 93
Netifnet, Dadisi Mwende 1959- 145
Netland, Dwayne 1932- 110
Neto, Antonio Agostinho 1922-1979 101
Obituary 89-92
See also AFW
Nettel, Reginald 1899- 13-16R
Nettelbeck, F(red) A(rthur) 1950- 184
Earlier sketch in CA 118
Autobiographical Essay in 184
Nettell, Richard (Geoffrey) 1907- CAP-2
Earlier sketch in CA 25-28
Nettels, Curtis Putnam 1898-1981 ..... CANR-1
Obituary 201
Earlier sketch in CA 1-4R
Nettels, Elsa 1931- 77-80
Netter, (Jean) Patrick 1952- 119
Netterville, Luke
See O'Grady, Standish (James)
Netting, Robert M(cCorkle) 1934- 61-64
Nettis, Joseph 1928- 9-12R
Nettl, Bruno 1930- 17-20R
Nettl, J(ohn) P(eter) 1926-1968 .... CAP-2
Earlier sketch in CA 23-24
Nettl, Paul 1889-1972 .... CAP-1
Obituary 33-36R
Earlier sketch in CA 9-10
Nettle, Daniel 1970- 218
Nettleford, Rex M. 37-40R
Nettler, Gwynn 1913- 33-36R
Nettles, Thomas Julian 1946- 117
Nettles, Tom
See Nettles, Thomas Julian
Nettleship, R. L. 1846-1892 .... DLB 262
Netzen, Klaus
See James, Laurence
Netzer, Dick 1928-
Brief entry 112
Netzer, Lanore A. 1916-1998 .... 17-20R
Neu, Charles E(ric) 1936- CANR-121
Earlier sketch in CA 21-24R
Neu, Jerome 1947- 138
Neubauer, Alex(ander) 1959- 135
Neubauer, David William 1944- 65-68
Neubauer, John 1933- 101
Neubauer, William Arthur 1916-1982 ..... 9-12R
Neubeck, Gerhard 1918- 41-44R
Neubeck, Kenneth J. 216
Neuberger, Egon 1925- CANR-30
Earlier sketch in CA 25-28R
Neuberger, Julia (Babette Sarah)
1950- CANR-121
Earlier sketch in CA 135
See also SATA 78, 142
Neuberger, Richard Lewis 1912-1960
Obituary 89-92
Neuberger, Roy S(alant) 1942- 192
Neubert, Christopher J. 1948- 106
Neuburg, Paul 1939- 45-48
Neuburg, Victor E. 1924- 33-36R
Neuenschwander, John A. 1941-
Brief entry 113
Neufeld, Andrew 1961- 224
Neufeld, Elizabeth F(ondal) 1928- 161
Neufeld, James (E.) 1944- 164
Neufeld, John (Arthur) 1938- CANR-56
Earlier sketches in CA 25-28R, CANR-11, 37
See also AAYA 11
See also CLC 17
See also CLR 52
See also MAICYA 1, 2
See also SAAS 3
See also SATA 6, 81, 131
See also SATA-Essay 131
See also YAW
Neufeld, Maurice Frank 1910- 1-4R
Neufeld, Michael J. 1951- CANR-100
Earlier sketch in CA 148
Neufeld, Peter Lorenz 1931- 25-28R
Neufeld, Rose 1924- 29-32R
Neufelder, Jerome M(ichael) 1929- 115
Neufeldt, Leonard N(ick) 1937- 108
Neufer Emswiler, Sharon
See Emswiler, Sharon Neufer
Neuffer, Claude Henry 1911-1984 .... 41-44R
Neuffer, Irene LaBorde 1919- 61-64
Neugeboren, Jay (Michael) 1938- CANR-96
Earlier sketches in CA 17-20R, CANR-21
Interview in CANR-21
See also CN 1, 2, 3, 4, 5, 6, 7
See also DLB 28
Neuharth, Allen .... AITN 2
Neuhaus, David 1958- .... SATA 83
Neuhaus, Denise 152
Neuhaus, Richard John 1936- CANR-120
Earlier sketch in CA 33-36R
Neuhaus, Ruby (Hart) 1932- 103
Neuhouser, Frederick 1957- 204
Neukirch, Benjamin 1665-1729 .... DLB 168
Neulinger, John 1924-1991 .... CANR-75
Obituary 134
Earlier sketches in CA 41-44R, CANR-16
Neuls-Bates, Carol 1939- 114
Neuman, Abraham A(aron) 1890-1970
Obituary 104
Neuman, Betty Mavine 1924- 33-36R
Neuman, E(rnst) Jack 1921-1998 185
Brief entry 127
Neuman, Fredric (Jay) 1934- CANR-20
Earlier sketch in CA 97-100
Neuman, Ladd A. 1942- 97-100
Neuman, Shirley Carol 1946- CANR-48
Earlier sketch in CA 121
Neuman, William Frederick 1919-1981
Obituary 103
Neumann, Alfred 1895-1952 183
See also DLB 56
See also TCLC 100
Neumann, Dietrich 1956- 223
Neumann, Emanuel 1893-1980
Obituary 105
Neumann, Ferenc
See Molnar, Ferenc
Neumann, Gareth William 1930- 61-64
Neumann, Gerhard 1917-1997 132
Neumann, John von
See von Neumann, John
Neumann, Jonathan 1950- 85-88
Neumann, Robert 1897-1975 103
Obituary 89-92
Neumann, Robert G(erhard) 1916-1999 ... 5-8R
Obituary 181
Neumann, William Louis 1915-1971 .... CAP-1
Obituary 33-36R
Earlier sketch in CA 11-12
Neumark, Georg 1621-1681 .... DLB 164
Neumeister, Erdmann 1671-1756 .... DLB 168
Neumeyer, Alfred 1900(?)-1973
Obituary 41-44R
Neumeyer, Ken(neth Walter) 1953- 107
Neumeyer, M(artin) Henry 1892-1983 .. CAP-2
Earlier sketch in CA 19-20
Neumeyer, Peter F(lorian) 1929- CANR-30
Earlier sketch in CA 33-36R
See also SATA 13
Neurath, Marie (Reidemeister)
1898-1986 .... 13-16R
See also SATA 1
Neurath, Otto 1882-1945
Brief entry 117
Neuschel, Richard F(rederick)
1915-1995 .... 13-16R
Neuschuetz, Karin 1946- 116
Neuschutz, Karin
See Neuschuetz, Karin
Neuschwander, Cindy 1953- ..... SATA 107, 157

Cumulative Index 425 Newman

Neuse, Erna Kritsch 1923- 105
Neusner, Jacob 1932- CANR-144
Earlier sketches in CA 13-16R, CANR-7, 22
See also SATA 38
Neustadt, Bertha C(ummings) 1921(?)-1984
Obituary 112
Neustadt, Egon 1898(?)-1984
Obituary 112
Neustadt, Richard E(lliott)
1919-2003 .... CANR-85
Obituary 220
Earlier sketches in CA 9-12R, CANR-27
Neustadt, Richard M(itchells) 1948- . CANR-27
Earlier sketch in CA 45-48
Neutra, Richard Joseph 1892-1970 .... CANR-5
Obituary 29-32R
Earlier sketch in CA 5-8R
Neutrelle, Dale 1937- 61-64
Neuville, H(enry) Richmond, Jr. 1937- .. 21-24R
Nevai, Lucia 1945- 166
Neve, Herbert T(heodore) 1931- 25-28R
Neve, Lloyd 1923- 53-56
Nevell, Dick
See Nevell, Richard (William Babcock)
Nevell, Richard (William Babcock) 1947- .. 102
Nevelson, Louise 1899(?)-1988 .... CANR-76
Obituary 125
Earlier sketch in CA 108
Neveux, Georges 1900-1982
Obituary 108
Nevill, Barry St-John 1941- 119
Neville, Anna
See Fairburn, Eleanor
Neville, B(arbara) Alison (Boodson)
1925-1993 .... CANR-83
Earlier sketches in CA 5-8R, CANR-11
Neville, Charles
See Bodsworth, (Charles) Fred(erick)
Neville, Emily Cheney 1919- CANR-85
Earlier sketches in CA 5-8R, CANR-3, 37
See also BYA 2
See also CLC 12
See also JRDA
See also MAICYA 1, 2
See also SAAS 2
See also SATA 1
See also YAW
Neville, Graham 1922- 196
Neville, Gwen Kennedy 1938- CANR-93
Earlier sketches in CA 114, CANR-35
Neville, Heather Buckley
See Buckley Neville, Doris Heather
Neville, Helen F(rances Fowler) 1943- 169
Neville, James Edmund Henderson 1897-1982
Obituary 107
Neville, Jill 1932-1997 .... 21-24R
Neville, John F(rancis) 1952- 176
Neville, Joyce 115
Neville, Katherine 1945- 204
Neville, Kris (Ottman) 1925-1980 .... CANR-83
Obituary 117
Earlier sketch in CA 132
See also SFW 4
Neville, Mary
See Woodrich, Mary Neville
Neville, Pauline 1924- 29-32R
Neville, Richard F. 1931-2004 85-88
Obituary 225
Neville, Robert
See Hutson, Shaun
Neville, Robert 1905-1970
Obituary 104
Neville, Robert C(ummings) 1939- ... CANR-29
Earlier sketches in CA 25-28R, CANR-11
Neville, Susan 1951- 119
Nevin, David 1927- CANR-103
Earlier sketch in CA 121
See also TCWW 2
Nevin, Evelyn C. 1910-1995 .... 17-20R
Nevins, Albert (Francis) J(erome)
1915-1997 .... CANR-41
Obituary 163
Earlier sketches in CA 5-8R, CANR-5, 19
See also SATA 20
Nevins, (Joseph) Allan 1890-1971 .... CANR-30
Obituary 29-32R
Earlier sketch in CA 5-8R
See also DLB 17
See also DLBD 17
Nevins, Deborah 1947- 105
Nevins, Edward M(ichael) 1938- 29-32R
Nevins, Francis M(ichael), Jr. 1943- .. CANR-83
Earlier sketches in CA 41-44R, CANR-16, 43
See also CMW 4
Nevinson, C(hristopher) R(ichard) W(ynne)
1889-1946
Brief entry 120
Nevinson, Henry Woodd 1856-1941 . DLB 135
Nevitt, H(enry) J(ohn) Barrington
1908-1995 .... CANR-14
Earlier sketch in CA 37-40R
Nevius, Blake (Reynolds) 1916-1994 .... 17-20R
Nevo, Ruth 1924- 61-64
New, Anthony (Sherwood Brooks)
1924- CANR-23
Earlier sketch in CA 107
New, Christopher 116
New, Elisa 191
New, Lloyd Kiva 1916-2002 213
New, Melvyn 1938- 142
New, William H(erbert) 1938- CANR-90
Brief entry 114
Earlier sketch in CA 148
Newall, Christopher 1951- 128
Newall, Martin 1935- 37-40R
Newberg, Andrew B. 185
Newberger, Devra
See Speregen, Devra Newberger
Newberger, Eli H(erbert) 1940- 205
Newberry
See Vellacott, Jo
Newberry, Clare Turlay 1903-1970 .... CAP-2
Earlier sketch in CA 19-20
See also SATA 1
See also SATA-Obit 26
Newberry, Lida 1909-1980 97-100
Obituary 171
Newberry, Vellacott
See Vellacott, Jo
Newberry, Wilma (Jean) 1927- 73-76
Newbery, John 1713-1767 .... MAICYA 1, 2
See also SATA 20
Newbery, Linda 1952- 213
See also SATA 142
Newbigin, (James Edward) Lesslie
1909-1998 .... CANR-26
Earlier sketches in CA 13-16R, CANR-10
Newbill, James Guy 1931- 61-64
Newbold, H(erbert) L(eon, Jr.)
1921-1994 .... CANR-5
Earlier sketch in CA 1-4R
Newbold, Robert T(homas, Jr.)
1920-1976 89-92
Newbold, Stokes
See Adams, Richard N(ewbold)
Newbolt, Henry (John) 1862-1938 173
Brief entry 118
See also DLB 19
Newborn, Jud 1952- 125
Newbound, Bernard Slade 1930- CANR-49
Earlier sketch in CA 81-84
See also Slade, Bernard
See also CD 5
See also DAM DRAM
Newbury, Colin (Walter) 1929- CANR-8
Earlier sketch in CA 5-8R
Newbury, Will 1912- 45-48
Newby, Eric 1919- CANR-44
Earlier sketch in CA 5-8R
See also DLB 204
Newby, Gordon D(arnell) 1939- 222
Newby, I(dus) A. 1931- 17-20R
Newby, James R(ichard) 1949- 112
Newby, Leroy Winfred 1921- 114
Newby, P(ercy) H(oward)
1918-1997 .... CANR-67
Obituary 161
Earlier sketches in CA 5-8R, CANR-32
See also CLC 2, 13
See also CN 1, 2, 3, 4, 5, 6
See also DAM NOV
See also DLB 15
See also MTCW 1
See also RGEL 2
Newby-Alexander, Cassandra L. 1957- 239
Newcastle
See Cavendish, Margaret Lucas
Newcomb, Benjamin H. 1938- 45-48
Newcomb, Charles King 1820-1894 ..... DLB 1, 223
Newcomb, Covelle 1908-2001 .... CAP-2
Earlier sketch in CA 19-20
Newcomb, Duane G(raham) 1929- CANR-5
Earlier sketch in CA 53-56
Newcomb, Ellsworth
See Kenny, Ellsworth Newcomb
Newcomb, Franc(es Lynette) J(ohnson)
1887-1970 .... 17-20R
Newcomb, John (Robert) 1937- 123
Newcomb, Kerry 1946- CANR-99
Earlier sketches in CA 65-68, CANR-10
Newcomb, Lori Humphrey 228
Newcomb, Norma
See Neubauer, William Arthur
Newcomb, Richard F(airchild) 1913- 1-4R
Newcomb, Robert N(orman)
1925-1970 .... 21-24R
Newcomb, Simon 1835-1909
Brief entry 108
Newcomb, Theodore Mead
1903-1984 .... CANR-76
Obituary 114
Earlier sketch in CA 33-36R
Newcomb, Wilburn Wendell 1935- 17-20R
Newcomb, William W(ilmon), Jr. 1921- 102
Newcombe, Eugene A. 1923-1990 ... CANR-42
Obituary 130
See also Newcombe, Jack
Newcombe, Jack
See Newcombe, Eugene A.
See also SATA 45
See also SATA-Brief 33
Newcombe, John (David) 1944- CANR-25
Earlier sketch in CA 69-72
Newcombe, Park Judson 1930- 106
Newcome, Robert 1955- 155
See also SATA 91
Newcome, Zita 1959- .... SATA 88
Newcomer, James (William) 1912- ... CANR-15
Earlier sketch in CA 41-44R
Newcomer, Robert (J.) 1943- 168
Newell, Allen 1927-1992 104
Newell, Arlo F(rederic) 1926- 114
Newell, Barbara Warne 1929- 1-4R
Newell, Charles J. 1956- 149
Newell, Clayton R. 1942- 232
Newell, Crosby
See Bonsall, Crosby Barbara (Newell)
Newell, D. A.
See Musciano, Walter A.
Newell, David McCheyne 1898(?)-1986
Obituary 120
Newell, Dianne 1943- 203
Newell, Edythe W(eatherford)
1910-1989 65-68
See also SATA 11
Newell, Fred D(elmer) 1912-1980 97-100
Newell, Gordon 1913-1991 .... CANR-20
Earlier sketches in CA 9-12R, CANR-4
Newell, Helen M(arie) 1909-1981 93-96
Newell, Homer E(dward)
1915-1983 .... CANR-75
Obituary 110
Earlier sketch in CA 97-100
Newell, Hope Hockenberry 1896-1965 .. 73-76
See also SATA 24
Newell, J. Philip 1953- 192
Newell, Kenneth B(ernard) 1930- 41-44R
Newell, Linda King 1941- 156
Newell, Margaret Ellen 1962- 228
Newell, Norman D(ennis)
1909-2005 .... CANR-21
Obituary 238
Earlier sketch in CA 104
Newell, Peter (Sheaf Hersey) 1862-1924
Brief entry 122
See also DLB 42
Newell, Peter F(rancis) 1915- 13-16R
Newell, Richard S. 1933- 134
Brief entry 112
Newell, Robert Henry 1836-1901
Brief entry 111
See also DLB 11
Newell, Rosemary 1922- 49-52
Newell, William H(are) 1922- 103
Newell, William T(hrift) 1929- 37-40R
Newey, Glen 1961- 224
Newey, Vincent 1943- 132
Newfeld, Frank 1928- 105
See also SATA 26
Newfield, Jack (Abraham)
1939-2004 .... CANR-121
Obituary 234
Earlier sketches in CA 21-24R, CANR-13
Newhafer, Richard L. 1922-1974 .... 13-16R
Newhall, Beaumont 1908-1993 .... CANR-47
Obituary 140
Earlier sketch in CA 9-12R
Newhall, David S(owle) 1929- 140
Newhall, Nancy 1908-1974
Obituary 49-52
Newhall, Richard A. 1888-1973
Obituary 41-44R
Newhouse, Edward 1911- 97-100
See also CN 1, 2, 3
Newhouse, John 181
Newhouse, Joseph P. 1942- 111
Newhouse, Neville H. 1919- 21-24R
Newhouse, Norman N(athan) 1906-1988
Obituary 127
Newhouse, Samuel I(rving) 1895-1979
Obituary 89-92
See also DLB 127
Newhouse, Thomas 1950- 192
Newhouse, Victoria 184
Newick, John 1919- CAP-1
Earlier sketch in CA 11-12
Newkirk, Glen A. 1931- 37-40R
Newland, Kathleen 1951- 97-100
Newland, T. Ernest 1903-1992 105
Newlands, George (McLeod) 1941- 129
Newley, Anthony (George) 1931-1999 105
Obituary 177
Newlin, Dika 1923- 107
Newlin, Margaret Rudd 1925- CANR-1
Earlier sketch in CA 49-52
Newlon, (Frank) Clarke
1905(?)-1982 .... CANR-10
Obituary 108
Earlier sketch in CA 49-52
See also SATA 6
See also SATA-Obit 33
Newlove, Donald 1928- CANR-25
Earlier sketch in CA 29-32R
See also CLC 6
Newlove, John (Herbert) 1938- CANR-25
Earlier sketches in CA 21-24R, CANR-9
See also CLC 14
See also CP 1, 2, 3, 4, 5, 6, 7
Newlyn, Lucy 1956- 150
Newlyn, Walter T(essier) 1915-2002 ..... 21-24R
Obituary 210
Newman, Adrien Ann 1941- 102
Newman, Albert H. 1913(?)-1987
Obituary 122
Newman, Alfred 1901-1970 .... IDFW 3, 4
Newman, Alyse 1953- 107
Newman, Amy 1949- 197
Newman, Andrea 1938- 73-76
Newman, Andrew 1948- 144
Newman, Arnold 1941- 137
Newman, Arthur J. 1939- 117
Newman, Aubrey N(orris) 1927- CANR-25
Earlier sketch in CA 29-32R
Newman, Barbara
See Newman, Mona Alice Jean
Newman, Barbara (Pollock) 1939- 132
Newman, Barclay M., Jr. 1931- CANR-9
Earlier sketch in CA 17-20R
Newman, Bernard (Charles)
1897-1968 .... CANR-84
Obituary 25-28R
Earlier sketch in CA 97-100
Newman, (Jerry) C(oleman) J(oseph) 1938- . 172
See also CN 3, 4, 5, 6
Newman, Cecil Earl 1903-1976 .... DLB 127
Newman, Charles 1900-1989
Obituary 129
Newman, Charles (Hamilton) 1938- . CANR-84
Earlier sketch in CA 21-24R
See also CLC 2, 8
See also CN 3, 4, 5, 6
Newman, Charles L. 1923- CANR-6
Earlier sketch in CA 13-16R
Newman, Christina McCall 1935- 112
See also McCall, Christina
Newman, Coleman J. 1935- 77-80
Newman, Daisy 1904-1994 .... CANR-75
Obituary 143
Earlier sketch in CA 37-40R
See also SATA 27
See also SATA-Obit 78
Newman, Dan 1969- 176
Newman, David 1937-2003 102
Obituary 217
Interview in CA-102
See also DLB 44
Newman, Debra Lynn
See Ham, Debra Newman
Newman, E. J. 1943- 61-64
Newman, Edwin (Harold) 1919- CANR-5
Earlier sketch in CA 69-72
See also AITN 1
See also CLC 14
Newman, Elmer S(imon) 1919-2003 106
Obituary 222
Newman, Eric P(feiffer) 1911- 5-8R
Newman, Ernest
See Roberts, William
Newman, Frances 1883(?)-1928 190
Brief entry 110
See also DLBY 1980
Newman, Francis William
1805-1897 .... DLB 190
Newman, Frank
See Abrams, Sam(uel)
Newman, G(ordon) F. 1942- CANR-61
Earlier sketch in CA 104
See also CBD
See also CD 5, 6
See also CMW 4
See also DLB 310
Newman, George 1936- 106
Newman, Gerald 1939- 101
See also SATA 46
See also SATA-Brief 42
Newman, Greatrex 1892-1984(?)
Obituary 112
Newman, Harold 1899-1993 .... CANR-10
Earlier sketch in CA 65-68
Newman, Harold 1927- 53-56
Newman, Herbert Ellis 1914-1998 .... 25-28R
Newman, Howard 1911-1977 57-60
Obituary 73-76
Newman, Isadore 1942- CANR-121
Earlier sketch in CA 163
Newman, Jacob 1914- 9-12R
Newman, James L. 1939- 151
Newman, Jay 1948- CANR-121
Earlier sketch in CA 168
Newman, Jay Hartley 1951- CANR-9
Earlier sketch in CA 65-68
Newman, Jeremiah Joseph 1926- CANR-8
Earlier sketch in CA 5-8R
Newman, Jerry 1935- 149
See also SATA 82
Newman, John Henry 1801-1890 .... BRWS 7
See also DLB 18, 32, 55
See also RGEL 2
Newman, John Kevin 1928- CANR-50
Earlier sketch in CA 123
Newman, Jon O(rmond) 1932- 21-24R
Newman, Joseph 1912-1995 .... CANR-17
Obituary 148
Earlier sketch in CA 89-92
Newman, Joseph W(illiam) 1918- 37-40R
Newman, Judie 1950- CANR-40
Earlier sketch in CA 117
Newman, Judith 1961(?)- 228
Newman, Katharine D(ealy)
1911-2001 .... 37-40R
Newman, Katherine S. 1953- CANR-143
Earlier sketch in CA 152
Newman, Kim (James) 1959- CANR-61
Earlier sketch in CA 119
See also FANT
See also HGG
See also SUFW 2
Newman, L(eonard) Hugh 1909-1993 .... 9-12R
Newman, Lea Bertani Vozar
1926- CANR-103
Earlier sketch in CA 120
Newman, Lee Scott 1953- CANR-15
Earlier sketch in CA 65-68
Newman, Leslea 1955- CANR-107
Earlier sketches in CA 126, CANR-94
See also GLL 1
See also SATA 71, 128, 134
Newman, Loretta Marie 1911-1993 45-48
Newman, Louis Israel 1893-1972 .... CAP-1
Obituary 33-36R
Earlier sketch in CA 19-20
Newman, Margaret
See Potter, Margaret (Newman)
Newman, Marjorie 220
See also SATA 146
Newman, Matthew (Harrison) 1955- ... SATA 56
Newman, Michael 1946- CANR-40
Earlier sketch in CA 116
Newman, Mildred (Rubenstein)
1920-2001 206
Newman, Mona Alice Jean CANR-31
Earlier sketch in CA 102
Newman, Nanette 1934- 238
See also SATA 162

Newman, Nell 1960(?)- 224
Newman, Oscar 1935- 102
Newman, P(aul) B(aker) 1919-(?) 33-36R
Newman, Parley Wright 1923-
Brief entry 106
Newman, Paul S. 1924-1999 186
Newman, Peter (Kenneth) 1928-2001 ... 17-20R
Obituary 200
Newman, Peter C(harles) 1929- CANR-29
Earlier sketches in CA 9-12R, CANR-3
Newman, Philip L(ee) 1931- 17-20R
Newman, Phyllis 1933- 206
Newman, Ralph Abraham
1892-1986 .... CANR-6
Earlier sketch in CA 1-4R
Newman, Ralph G(eoffrey)
1911-1998 .... CANR-25
Obituary 169
Earlier sketch in CA 45-48
Newman, Randolph H. 1904-1975
Obituary 61-64
Newman, Richard (Alan) 1930-2003 110
Obituary 218
Newman, Robert (Howard)
1909-1988 .... CANR-84
Obituary 127
Earlier sketches in CA 1-4R, CANR-4, 19, 51
See also CWRI 5
See also SATA 4, 87
See also SATA-Obit 60
Newman, Robert Chapman 1941- 115
Newman, Robert D(ouglas) 1951- 120
Newman, Robert P(reston) 1922- 1-4R
Newman, Robert S. 1935- 65-68
Newman, Ruth (May) G(allert) 1914- 105
Newman, Sandra 1965- 223
Newman, Sharan 1949- CANR-73
Earlier sketches in CA 106, CANR-25
See also AAYA 40
Newman, Shirlee P(etkin) CANR-117
Earlier sketches in CA 5-8R, CANR-59
See also SATA 10, 90, 144
Newman, Shirley S. 1924- 123
Newman, Stephen A(aron) 1946- 97-100
Newman, Stephen L. 1952- 132
Newman, Stewart A(lbert) 1907- CAP-2
Earlier sketch in CA 23-24
Newman, Terence 1927- 5-8R
Newman, Terry
See Newman, Terence
Newman, Thelma R(ita) 1925-1978 ... CANR-7
Obituary 81-84
Earlier sketch in CA 13-16R
Newman, Thomas 1955- .... IDFW 4
Newman, Walter (Brown) 1916(?)-1993
Obituary 143
Brief entry 110
Newman, William H(erman) 1909- .. CANR-19
Earlier sketches in CA 5-8R, CANR-3
Newman, William Mark 1943- 57-60
Newman, William S(tein) 1912-2000 . CANR-3
Earlier sketch in CA 1-4R
Newmar, Rima
See Wagman, Naomi
Newmarch, Rosa Harriet 1857-1940 201
See also DLB 240
Newmark, Joseph 1943- 53-56
Newmark, Leonard 1929- 17-20R
Newmyer, R(obert) Kent 1930- CANR-114
Earlier sketch in CA 77-80
Newport, Cris 1960- 168
Newport, John P(aul) 1917- CANR-29
Earlier sketches in CA 33-36R, CANR-13
Newport, John Paul, Jr. 1954- 135
Newquist, Jerreld L. 1919-1976 .... CANR-77
Obituary 134
Earlier sketch in CA 17-20R
Newquist, Roy 1925- 13-16R
Newsham, Ian (Alan) 1953- 115
Newsham, Wendy (Elizabeth) 1952- 117
Newsholme, Christopher (Mansford)
1920- 146
Newsinger, John 1948- 189
Newsom, Carol 1948- .... SATA 40, 92
Newsom, Carroll V(incent)
1904-1990 .... CANR-75
Obituary 130
Earlier sketches in CAP-2, CA 17-18
Newsom, Doug(las Ann) 1934- 73-76
Newsom, Tom 1944- .... SATA 80
Newsome, Arden J(eanne) 1932- 29-32R
Newsome, David Hay 1929-2004 .... CANR-17
Obituary 226
Earlier sketch in CA 89-92
Newsome, (Mary) Effie Lee 1885-1979 181
See also DLB 76
Newsome, George L(ane), Jr. 1923- 29-32R
Newsome, Walter L(ee) 1941- 105
Newson, Elizabeth (Palmer) 1929- CANR-5
Earlier sketch in CA 9-12R
Newson, John 1925- 9-12R
Newson, Tony 1953- 124
Newth, Mette 1942- 204
See also AAYA 48
See also SATA 140
Newth, Rebecca 1940- CANR-108
Earlier sketch in CA 33-36R
Newton, A. Edward 1864-1940 199
See also DLB 140
Newton, Brian 1928- 49-52
Newton, Byron Louis 1913-1995 53-56
Newton, Candelas 1948- CANR-87
Earlier sketch in CA 153
Newton, Corky 1947- 198
Newton, D(wight) B(ennett) 1916- ... CANR-17
Earlier sketches in CA 5-8R, CANR-2
See also Mitchum, Hank
See also TCWW 1, 2
Newton, David C.
See Chance, John Newton
Newton, David E(dward) 1933- 135
See also SATA 67
Newton, Derek A(rnold) 1930- 120
Newton, (Bryan Leslie) Douglas
1920-2001 104
Obituary 201
Newton, Earle Williams 1917- 41-44R
Newton, Eric 1893-1965 .... CAP-1
Earlier sketch in CA 13-16
Newton, Esther 1940- CANR-105
Earlier sketch in CA 149
Newton, Francis
See Hobsbawm, Eric J(ohn Ernest)
Newton, Helmut 1920-2004 203
Obituary 222
Newton, Huey P(ercy) 1942-1989
Obituary 129
Brief entry 114
Newton, Ian 1940- CANR-101
Earlier sketch in CA 123
Newton, (Sir) Isaac 1642-1727 .... DLB 252
Newton, Ivor 1892-1981
Obituary 108
Newton, James R(obert) 1935- 101
See also SATA 23
Newton, June 198
Newton, Kenneth 1940- CANR-16
Earlier sketch in CA 29-32R
Newton, Lionel 1961(?)- 152
Newton, Macdonald
See Newton, William Simpson
Newton, Maxwell 1929- 126
Newton, Merlin Owen 1935- 150
Newton, Michael 1951- CANR-97
Earlier sketch in CA 108
See also Newton, Mike
Newton, Michael Duff 1931- 201
Newton, Mike
See Newton, Michael
See also TCWW 2
Newton, Norman (Lewis) 1929- 9-12R
Newton, Norman Thomas 1898-1992 104
Newton, Peter 1906-1984 .... CAP-1
Earlier sketch in CA 9-10
Newton, Peter A(nthony) 1935-1987
Obituary 124
Newton, Ray C(lyde) 1935- 77-80
Newton, Robert (Henry) G(erald)
1903- CAP-1
Earlier sketch in CA 9
Newton, Robert P(arr) 1929- 113
Newton, Roger G(erhard) 1924- CANR-95
Earlier sketch in CA 146
Newton, Roy 1904(?)-1974
Obituary 104
Newton, Stu
See Whitcomb, Ian
Newton, Suzanne 1936- CANR-14
Earlier sketch in CA 41-44R
See also BYA 7
See also CLC 35
See also JRDA
See also SATA 5, 77
Newton, Verne W. 1944- 141
Newton, Virgil Miller, Jr.
1904-1977 .... CANR-76
Obituary 103
Earlier sketch in CA 1-4R
Newton, William Simpson 1923- CANR-7
Earlier sketch in CA 53-56
New York Dept. of Ed. .... CLC 70
Nexo, Martin Andersen 1869-1954 202
See also DLB 214
See also EWL 3
See also TCLC 43
Ney, James W(alter) 1932- CANR-15
Earlier sketch in CA 41-44R
Ney, John 1923- 115
See also SATA 43
See also SATA-Brief 33
Ney, Patrick
See Bolitho, (Henry) Hector
Ney, Richard 1917(?)-2004 .... AITN 1
Ney, Ronald E., (Jr.) 1936- 151
Ney, Virgil 1905-1979
Obituary 85-88
Neyland, James (Elwyn) 1939- 103
Neyman, Jerzy 1899-1981
Obituary 108
Neyrey, Jerome H(enry) 1940- 126
Nez, John .... SATA 155
Neznansky, Friedrich 1932- 128
Nezval, Vitezslav 1900-1958
Brief entry 123
See also CDWLB 4
See also DLB 215
See also EWL 3
See also TCLC 44
Nfah-Abbenyi, Juliana Makuchi 1958- 190
Ng, David 1934- 115
Ng, Fae Myenne 1957(?)- 146
See also BYA 11
See also CLC 81
Ng, Franklin CANR-103
Earlier sketch in CA 149
See also SATA 82
Ng, Larry K. Y. 1940- CANR-9
Earlier sketch in CA 17-20R
Ng, Man-lun 1946- 168
Ng, Mei 1966- 169
Nga, Tran Thi
See Tran Thi Nga
Ngagoyeanes, Nicholas 1939- 49-52
Ngai, Sianne 191
Ngara, Emmanuel 1947- 109
Ngcobo, Lauretta 1931- 165
Ngema, Mbongeni 1955- CANR-84
Earlier sketch in CA 143
See also BW 2
See also CD 5, 6
See also CLC 57
Ngoc, Nguyen Huy
See Nguyen, Ngoc Huy
Ngor, Haing S. 1947(?)-1996 159
Ngubane, Jordan K(hush) 1917- 121
Ngugi, James T(hiong'o)
See Ngugi wa Thiong'o
See also CLC 3, 7, 13, 182
See also CN 1, 2
Ngugi wa Thiong'o
See Ngugi wa Thiong'o
See also CD 3, 4, 5, 6, 7
See also DLB 125
See also EWL 3
Ngugi wa Thiong'o 1938- CANR-58
Earlier sketches in CA 81-84, CANR-27
See also Ngugi, James T(hiong'o) and
Ngugi wa Thiong'o
See also AFW
See also BLC 3
See also BRWS 8
See also BW 2
See also CDWLB 3
See also CLC 36, 182
See also DAM MULT, NOV
See also DNFS 2
See also MTCW 1, 2
See also MTFW 2005
See also RGEL 2
See also WWE 1
Nguyen, Dinh Hoa 1924- CANR-10
Earlier sketch in CA 21-24R
Nguyen, Kien 1967- 200
Nguyen, Ngoc Huy 1924- 126
Nguyen, Vuong Hung 1922(?)-1985
Obituary 118
Nguyen Cong Hoan 1903-1977 .... EWL 3
Nguyen huong
See Nguyen-Vo, Thu-huong
Nguyen Ngoc Bich 1937- CANR-15
Earlier sketch in CA 81-84
Nguyen Tuan 1910-1990 .... EWL 3
Nguyen Tuong-Tam 1906-1963
See Nhat-Linh
Nguyen-Vo, Thu-huong 1962- 146
Nhat Lang
See Nguyen Tuan
Nhat-Linh
See Nguyen Tuong-Tam
See also EWL 3
Ni, Hua-Ching 1925- 164
Niall, Sean
See Mangan, (John Joseph) Sherry
Nias, D(avid) K(enneth) B(oydell) 1940- 105
Niatum, Duane 1938- CANR-83
Earlier sketches in CA 41-44R, CANR-21, 45
See also DLB 175
See also NNAL
Niblett, W(illiam) R(oy) 1906-2005 .... CANR-3
Obituary 239
Earlier sketch in CA 1-4R
Niccolini, Dianora 1936- 113
Nice, David C. 1952- 148
Nice, Jill 1940- 138
Nice, Margaret Morse 1883-1974 156
Nicely, Thomas S(hryock), Jr. 1939- 93-96
Nicely, Tom
See Nicely, Thomas S(hryock), Jr.
Nichelson, F(loyd) Patrick 1942- 33-36R
Nichol, B(arrie) P(hillip) 1944-1988 53-56
See also CLC 18
See also CP 1, 2
See also DLB 53
See also SATA 66
Nichol, John Thomas 1928- 17-20R
Nicholas, Anna Katherine 1917- 93-96
Nicholas, (John Keiran) Barry (Moylan)
1919-2002 .... 5-8R
Obituary 204
Nicholas, David M(ansfield) 1939- 49-52
Nicholas, Denise 1944- 208
Nicholas, Donald 1909- 5-8R
Nicholas, Elizabeth 1915-1985
Obituary 117
Nicholas, Herbert George
1911-1998 .... CANR-26
Obituary 169
Earlier sketch in CA 1-4R
Nicholas, John (Morton) 1944- 118
Nicholas, Laura F(arnsworth) 1960- 158
Nicholas, Leslie 1913-1994 81-84
Nicholas, Louise D.
See Watkins, Dawn L.
Nicholas, Louise D.
See Watkins, Dawn L.
Nicholas, Robert L(eon) 1937- 53-56
Nicholas, Sian (Helen) 1964- 168
Nicholas, Ted
See Peterson, Ted Nicholas
Nicholas, Tracy (Christine) 1952- 121
Nicholas, William
See Thimmesch, Nicholas Palen
Nicholas-Hill, Denise
See Nicholas, Denise
Nicholas of Cusa 1401-1464 .... DLB 115
Nicholds, Elizabeth (Beckwith) -1999 ... CAP-1
Earlier sketch in CA 11-12
Nicholl, Charles 1950- 174
Nicholl, Louise Townsend
1890(?)-1981 .... CANR-75
Obituary 105
Earlier sketch in CA 97-100
See also CP 1, 2
Nicholls, C(hristine) S(tephanie)
1943- CANR-127
Earlier sketch in CA 133
Nicholls, David 1948- 97-100
Nicholls, Elizabeth L. 1946- 168
Nicholls, F(rederick) F(rancis) 1926- 5-8R
Nicholls, Judith (Ann) 1941- CANR-47
Earlier sketch in CA 121
See also SATA 61
Nicholls, Mark
See Frewin, Leslie Ronald
Nicholls, Peter (Douglas) 1939- 105
Nicholls, (C. G.) William 1921- 17-20R
Nichols, Adelaide
See Baker, Adelaide N(ichols)
Nichols, Albert L. 1951- 122
Nichols, Anne 1891(?)-1966 .... DLB 249
Nichols, Ashton 1953- 194
Nichols, (John) Beverley 1898-1983 . CANR-62
Obituary 110
Earlier sketches in CA 93-96, CANR-17
See also CMW 4
See also DLB 191
Nichols, Bill
See Nichols, William James
Nichols, Cecilia Fawn 1906-1987 .... CAP-1
Earlier sketch in CA 13-16
See also SATA 12
Nichols, Charles H(arold) 1919- CANR-6
Earlier sketch in CA 53-56
See also BW 1
Nichols, Dale (William) 1904-1995 ...... CAP-2
Earlier sketch in CA 17-18
Nichols, Dave
See Frost, Helen
Nichols, David 1956- 133
Nichols, David A(llen) 1939- 104
Nichols, Deborah L. 1952- 173
Nichols, Dudley 1895-1960
Obituary 89-92
See also DLB 26
See also IDFW 3, 4
Nichols, Edward J(ay) 1900- 5-8R
Nichols, Eve K(aufman) 1952- 128
Nicholls, Fred Joseph 1939- 114
Nichols, Frederick Adams 1907-1983
Obituary 111
Nichols, Grace 1950- CANR-84
Earlier sketch in CA 154
See also CP 7
See also CWP
See also DLB 157
See also EWL 3
See also SATA 98
Nichols, Harold 1903- CAP-1
Earlier sketch in CA 13-16
Nichols, Irby C(oghill), Jr. 1926- 41-44R
Nichols, J(ohn) G(ordon) 1930- 33-36R
See also CAAS 2
Nichols, Jack
See Nichols, John
Nichols, James Hastings 1915-
Brief entry 114
Nichols, James R(ichard) 1938- 105
Nichols, Janet (Louise) 1952- 135
See also SATA 67
Nichols, Jeannette 1931- 77-80
Nichols, Jeannette Paddock
1890-1982 .... CANR-76
Obituary 107
Earlier sketch in CA 9-12R
Nichols, Joan Kane 1938- 182
Nichols, John 1938-2005 .... 41-44R
Obituary 239
Nichols, John (Treadwell) 1940- 190
Earlier sketches in CA 9-12R, CANR-6, 70, 121
Autobiographical Essay in 190
See also CAAS 2
See also AMWS 13
See also CLC 38
See also DLBY 1982
See also LATS 1:2
See also MTFW 2005
See also TCWW 1, 2
Nichols, Joseph C. 1905(?)-1984
Obituary 114
Nichols, Judy 1947- .... SATA 124
Nichols, K(enneth) D(avid) 1907-2000 126
Obituary 188
Nichols, Leigh
See Koontz, Dean R(ay)
Nichols, Lewis 1903-1982
Obituary 106
Nichols, Maggie
See Nichols, Margaret
Nichols, Margaret 1931- 81-84
Nichols, Marie Hochmuth 1908-1978 103
Nichols, Marion 1921- 102
Nichols, Mary Sargeant (Neal) Gove
1810-1884 .... DLB 1, 243
Nichols, Mike 1931- 207
Nichols, Nadia
See Gray, Penny
Nichols, Nichelle 1933(?)- 155
Nichols, Nina (Marianna) da Vinci
1932- CANR-14
Earlier sketch in CA 73-76
Nichols, Paul
See Hawks, Robert
Nichols, Paul D(yer) 1938- 109

Nichols, Peter
See Youd, (Christopher) Samuel
Nichols, Peter (Richard) 1927- ... CANR-86
Earlier sketches in CA 104, CANR-33
See also CBD
See also CD 5, 6
See also CLC 5, 36, 65
See also DLB 13, 245
See also MTCW 1
Nichols, Peter 1928-1989
Obituary ... 127
Nichols, R(oy) Eugene 1914-2002 ... 29-32R
Nichols, Robert (Molise Bowyer) 1919- .. 93-96
Nichols, Roger 1939- ... 108
Nichols, Roger L(ouis) 1933- ... CANR-5
Earlier sketch in CA 13-16R
Nichols, Roy F(ranklin) 1896-1973 ... CANR-3
Obituary ... 37-40R
Earlier sketch in CA 5-8R
See also DLB 17
Nichols, (Joanna) Ruth 1948- ... CANR-84
Earlier sketches in CA 25-28R, CANR-16, 37
See also CWRI 5
See also DLB 60
See also FANT
See also JRDA
See also SATA 15
Nichols, Scott
See Scortia, Thomas N(icholas)
Nichols, Stephen G(eorge, Jr.)
1936- ... CANR-31
Earlier sketch in CA 45-48
Nichols, Sue ... 9-12R
Nichols, Victoria (Sorensen) 1944- ... 132
Nichols, William James 1942- ... 93-96
Nichols, William Thomas 1927- ... 41-44R
Nicholsen, Margaret E(sther)
1904-1999 ... 29-32R
Nicholson, Arnold 1902-2001 ... CAP-2
Earlier sketch in CA 19-20
Nicholson, Ben 1894-1982
Obituary ... 110
Nicholson, C(harles) A. III 1922- ... 41-44R
Nicholson, C. R.
See Nicole, Christopher (Robin)
Nicholson, Charles (Edward) 1946- ... 136
Nicholson, Christina
See Nicole, Christopher (Robin)
Nicholson, Colin 1944- ... 150
Nicholson, Dorothy Nelis 1923-
Brief entry ... 109
Nicholson, Edward Williams Byron
1849-1912 ... DLB 184
Nicholson, Geoff 1953- ... 206
Earlier sketches in CA 130, CANR-89
Autobiographical Essay in ... 206
See also DLB 271
Nicholson, Geoffrey (George)
1929-1999 ... CANR-8
Obituary ... 183
Earlier sketch in CA 5-8R
Nicholson, Gerald W(illiam) L(ingen)
1902-1980 ... 101
Nicholson, Hubert 1908-1996 ... 13-16R
Obituary ... 151
Nicholson, Jack 1937- ... 143
Brief entry ... 116
Nicholson, Jane
See Steen, Marguerite
Nicholson, Joe
See Nicholson, Joseph Hugh, Jr.
Nicholson, John Greer 1929-1995 ... 45-48
Obituary ... 148
Nicholson, Joseph Hugh, Jr. 1943- ... 81-84
Nicholson, Joyce Thorpe 1919- ... CANR-5
Earlier sketch in CA 9-12R
See also SATA 35
Nicholson, Linda ed. ... CLC 65
Nicholson, Lois P. 1949- ... 152
See also SATA 88
Nicholson, Mavis 1930- ... 150
Nicholson, (Edward) Max 1904-2003
Obituary ... 219
Brief entry ... 106
Nicholson, Nicholas B. A. ... 230
Nicholson, Norman (Cornthwaite)
1914-1987 ... CANR-24
Obituary ... 122
Earlier sketches in CA 9-12R, CANR-3
See also BRWS 6
See also CP 1, 2
See also DLB 27
See also RGEL 2
Nicholson, Norman L(eon) 1919- ... CANR-3
Earlier sketch in CA 9-12R
Nicholson, Patrick J(ames) 1920- ... CANR-45
Earlier sketch in CA 120
Nicholson, Paul (Joseph), Jr. 1937- ... 73-76
Nicholson, Peggy ... 229
Nicholson, Peter 1950- ... 217
Nicholson, Philip Y(ale) 1940- ... 198
Nicholson, Ranald (George) 1931- ... 37-40R
Nicholson, Robert Lawrence 1908-1985 . 53-56
Obituary ... 117
Nicholson, Robin
See Nicole, Christopher (Robin)
Nicholson, Scott 1962- ... 214
Nicholson, Shirley J. 1925- ... CANR-55
Earlier sketches in CA 29-32R, CANR-26
Nicholson, Simon 1934- ... 114
Nicholson, Virginia ... 230
Nicholson, W(illiam) G(eorge) 1935- ... 93-96
Nicholson, William ... 238
See also AAYA 47
See also DFS 11
Nicholson, William 1872-1949 ... CLR 76
See also CWRI 5
See also DLB 141
Nichter, Mark (Andrew) 1949- ... 144
Nichter, Rhoda 1926- ... 81-84
Nichtern, Sol 1920-1988 ... 17-20R
Obituary ... 126
Ni Chuilleanain, Eilean 1942- ... CANR-83
Earlier sketches in CA 126, CANR-53
See also CP 7
See also CWP
See also DLB 40
See also PC 34
Nicieza, Fabian 1961- ... 226
Nickel, Herman 1928- ... 73-76
Nickel, Mildred L(ucille) 1912-1993 ... 108
Nickell, Joe 1944- ... CANR-46
Earlier sketch in CA 110
See also SATA 73
Nickell, Lesley J(acqueline) 1944- ... 103
Nickels, William G(eorge) 1939- ... 108
Nickelsburg, George W(illiam) E(lmer), Jr.
1934- ... CANR-19
Earlier sketches in CA 53-56, CANR-5
Nickelsburg, Janet 1893-1983 ... 65-68
See also SATA 11
Nickerson, Betty 1922- ... 77-80
See also Nickerson, Elizabeth
Nickerson, Catherine Ross ... 191
Nickerson, Clarence B(entley) 1906-1991 . 5-8R
Nickerson, Elizabeth
See Nickerson, Betty
See also SATA 14
Nickerson, Jan -1975 ... 1-4R
Nickerson, Jane Soames (Bon)
1900-1988 ... CANR-28
Obituary ... 124
Earlier sketch in CA 77-80
Nickerson, John Mitchell 1937- ... 53-56
Nickerson, Joseph 1914-1990
Obituary ... 131
Nickerson, Roy 1927- ... CANR-35
Earlier sketch in CA 114
Nickerson, Sheila B(unker) 1942- ... CANR-120
Earlier sketches in CA 118, CANR-43
Nickerson, William (Ernest) 1908-1999 ... 1-4R
Obituary ... 186
Nickl, Barbara (Elisabeth) 1939- ... SATA 56
Nicklanovich, Michael David 1941- ... 107
Nicklaus, Carol ... SATA 62
See also SATA-Brief 33
Nicklaus, (Charles) Frederick 1936- ... 37-40R
Nicklaus, Jack (William) 1940- ... CANR-144
Earlier sketches in CA 89-92, CANR-16, 39
Nickle, Keith Fullerton 1933- ... 115
Nickless, Will 1902-1979(?) ... 81-84
See also SATA 66
Nickson, Arthur 1902(?)-1974
See Winstan, Matt
See also TCWW 2
Nickson, J. Richard 1917- ... 129
Niclas, Yolla 1900-1977 ... 25-28R
Nic Leodhas, Sorche
See Alger, Leclaire (Gowans)
Nicol, Abioseh
See Nicol, Davidson (Sylvester Hector Willoughby)
See also CN 1, 2, 3, 4
See also CP 1
Nicol, Ann
See Turnbull, Ann (Christine)
Nicol, Charles (David) 1940- ... 115
Nicol, D(onald) M(acGillivray)
1923-2003 ... CANR-4
Obituary ... 220
Earlier sketch in CA 53-56
Nicol, Davidson (Sylvester Hector Willoughby)
1924-1994 ... CANR-82
Obituary ... 147
Earlier sketches in CA 61-64, CANR-26
See also Nicol, Abioseh
See also BW 1
Nicol, Eric (Patrick) 1919- ... CANR-36
Earlier sketches in CA 49-52, CANR-1, 16
See also DLB 68
Nicol, Jean 1919- ... 21-24R
Nicola, Andree
See McLaughlin, Andree Nicola
Nicolaeff, Ariadne 1915- ... 57-60
Nicolai, Friedrich 1733-1811 ... DLB 97
Nicolaisen, (Agnes) Ida (Benedicte) 1940- .. 148
Nicolas
See Mordvinoff, Nicolas
Nicolas, Claire
See White, Claire Nicolas
Nicolas, F. R. E.
See Freeling, Nicolas
Nicolas de Clamanges c. 1363-1437 .. DLB 208
Nicolay, Helen 1866-1954 ... 192
Brief entry ... 121
See also YABC 1
Nicolay, John G(eorge) 1832-1901
Brief entry ... 122
See also DLB 47
Nicolaysen, Bruce 1934- ... 105
Nicole, Christopher (Robin) 1930- ... CANR-68
Earlier sketches in CA 13-16R, CANR-45
See also CMW 4
See also CN 1, 2, 3
See also RHW
See also SATA 5
Nicole, Pierre 1625-1695 ... DLB 268
See also GFL Beginnings to 1789
Nicoll, (John Ramsay) Allardyce
1894-1976 ... CANR-5
Obituary ... 65-68
Earlier sketch in CA 9-12R
Nicoll, Bruce H. 1913(?)-1983
Obituary ... 111
Nicoll, Helen 1937- ... CANR-83
Earlier sketches in CA 122, CANR-51
See also CWRI 5
See also SATA 87
Nicoll, Ruaridh 1969- ... 218
Nicolle, Jacques Maurice Raoul 1901- ... 9-12R
Nicoloff, Philip Loveless 1926- ... 1-4R
Nicolson, Adela Florence Cory
1865-1904 ... 201
See also Hope, Laurence
Nicolson, (Lionel) Benedict
1914-1978 ... CANR-6
Earlier sketch in CA 13-16R
Nicolson, Catherine ... 121
Nicolson, Cynthia Pratt 1949- ... 212
See also SATA 141
Nicolson, Harold George 1886-1968 ... CAP-1
Earlier sketch in CA 13-16
See also DLB 100, 149
Nicolson, I(an) F(erguson) 1921- ... 29-32R
Nicolson, James R(obert) 1934- ... CANR-9
Earlier sketch in CA 65-68
Nicolson, Marjorie Hope
1894-1981 ... CANR-78
Obituary ... 103
Earlier sketch in CA 9-12R
Nicolson, Nigel 1917-2004 ... CANR-102
Obituary ... 231
Earlier sketch in CA 101
See also DLB 155
Nicosia, Francesco M(ichael) 1933- ... 81-84
Nicosia, Franco M.
See Nicosia, Francesco M(ichael)
Nicosia, Gerald (Martin) 1949- ... 176
Earlier sketch in CA 115
Autobiographical Essay in ... 176
See also CAAS 28
Nida, Eugene A(lbert) 1914- ... CANR-17
Earlier sketches in CA 1-4R, CANR-1
Nidditch, Peter (Harold) 1928-1983
Obituary ... 109
Niddrie, David Lawrence 1917-1997 ... 25-28R
Nideffer, Robert M(orse) 1942- ... CANR-9
Earlier sketch in CA 65-68
Nidetch, Jean 1923- ... 89-92
Ni Dhomhnaill, Nuala 1952- ... 190
See also CWP
Ni Dhuibhne, Eilis 1954- ... CANR-92
Earlier sketch in CA 155
See also CN 7
See also CWRI 5
See also DLB 319
See also SATA 91
Niditch, Susan 1950- ... 143
Nie, Martin A. ... 224
Nie, Norman H. 1943- ... CANR-15
Earlier sketch in CA 65-68
Niebuhr, Gary Warren 1954- ... 146
Niebuhr, H(elmut) Richard 1894-1962
Obituary ... 116
Niebuhr, Reinhold 1892-1971 ... 41-44R
Obituary ... 29-32R
See also AMW
See also DLB 17
See also DLBD 17
See also MAL 5
Niebuhr, Richard R. 1926- ... 77-80
Niebuhr, Ursula 1907-1997 ... 89-92
Obituary ... 156
Nieburg, H(arold) L. 1927- ... 9-12R
Niedecker, Lorine 1903-1970 ... CAP-2
Earlier sketch in CA 25-28
See also CLC 10, 42
See also DAM POET
See also DLB 48
See also PC 42
Niederauer, David J(ohn) 1924- ... 45-48
Niederhoffer, Arthur 1917-1981
Obituary ... 103
Niederland, William G(ugliemo)
1904-1993 ... CANR-78
Obituary ... 142
Earlier sketch in CA 81-84
Niederman, Derrick ... 201
Niedzielski, Henri 1931- ... 49-52
Nieh, Hualing 1925- ... 81-84
Niehans, Juerg 1919- ... 133
Niehans, Jurg
See Niehans, Juerg
Niehaus, Paddy Bouma
See Bouma, Paddy
Niehoff, Arthur H. 1921- ... CANR-87
Earlier sketches in CA 21-24R, CANR-67
Niekerk, Marlene van
See van Niekerk, Marlene
Nielander, William Ahlers 1901-1976 ... 5-8R
Nield, Howard (Kingsley) 1949- ... 135
Nielsen, Aage Rosendal 1921- ... 25-28R
Nielsen, Aldon Lynn 1950- ... 136
Nielsen, Dulcimer 1943- ... 93-96
Nielsen, Eduard 1923- ... 29-32R
Nielsen, Gary (Elton) 1939- ... 97-100
Nielsen, Helen Berniece
1918-2002 ... CANR-61
Obituary ... 208
Earlier sketches in CA 1-4R, CANR-1
See also CMW 4
Nielsen, Jean Sarver 1922- ... 5-8R
Nielsen, Jerri 1951- ... 208
See also Nielsen, Leslie
Nielsen, Kay (Rasmus) 1886-1957 ... 177
See also CLR 16
See also MAICYA 1, 2
See also SATA 16
Nielsen, Knut Schmidt
See Schmidt-Nielsen, Knut
Nielsen, Laura F(arnsworth) 1960- ... 158
See also SATA 93
Nielsen, Leslie 1926- ... 208
See also Nielsen, Jerri
Nielsen, Margaret A(nne) ... 105
Nielsen, Nancy J. 1951- ... 145
See also SATA 77
Nielsen, Niels Christian, Jr. 1921- ... CANR-3
Earlier sketch in CA 9-12R
Nielsen, Niels Juel
See Juel-Nielsen, Niels
Nielsen, Oswald 1904-1981 ... CAP-2
Earlier sketch in CA 19-20
Nielsen, Robert F. 1937- ... 122
Nielsen, Sven Sigurd 1901-1976
Obituary ... 104
Nielsen, Torben 1918-
Brief entry ... 114
Nielsen, Veneta Leatham 1909-1998 ... 89-92
Nielsen, Virginia
See McCall, Virginia Nielsen
Nielsen, Waldemar August 1917- ... 103
Nielsen Hayden, Patrick (James)
1959- ... CANR-106
Earlier sketch in CA 163
Nielson, James 1958- ... 154
Nielssen, Eric
See Ludvigsen, Karl (Eric)
Nieman, Egbert William 1909- ... CAP-1
Earlier sketch in CA 11-12
Nieman, Lucius W(illiam) 1857-1935 ... 180
See also DLB 25
Nieman, Valerie Gail 1955- ... 197
Niemann, Linda (Grant) 1946- ... CANR-86
Earlier sketch in CA 133
Niemeier, Jean (Gilbreath) 1912-2000 ... 25-28R
Niemela, Pirkko 1939- ... 146
Niemeyer, Eberhardt Victor, Jr. 1919- ... 102
Niemeyer, Gerhart 1907-1997 ... CANR-30
Obituary ... 159
Earlier sketch in CA 1-4R
Niemeyer, Roy K(urt) 1922- ... 1-4R
Niemi, Albert (William), Jr. 1942- ... 73-76
Niemi, John A(rvo) 1932-2004 ... 77-80
Obituary ... 230
Niemi, Richard G(ene) 1941- ... 41-44R
Nieminen, Raija 1939- ... BYA 8
Nieminen, Risto Matti 1948- ... 176
Niemoeller, (Friedrich Gustav Emil) Martin
1892-1984
Obituary ... 112
See also Niemoller, (Friedrich Gustav Emil) Martin
Niemoller, Ara
See Llerena, Mario
Niemoller, (Friedrich Gustav Emil) Martin
See Niemoeller, (Friedrich Gustav Emil) Martin
Niemonen, Jack (Edwin) 1952- ... 222
Nienhauser, William H., Jr. 1943- ... 125
Nierenberg, Gerard I. 1923- ... 25-28R
Nierman, M. Murray 1918- ... 1-4R
Nies, Judith 1941- ... 77-80
Niesewand, Peter 1944-1983 ... CANR-76
Obituary ... 109
Earlier sketch in CA 101
Niess, Robert Judson 1911-1981 ... CAP-2
Earlier sketch in CA 29-32
Niethammer, Carolyn 1944- ... 85-88
Nieto, Sonia 1943- ... 186
Nietz, John Alfred 1888-1970 ... 1-4R
Nietzke, Ann 1945- ... 105
Nietzsche, Friedrich (Wilhelm) 1844-1900 . 121
Brief entry ... 107
See also CDWLB 2
See also DLB 129
See also EW 7
See also RGWL 2, 3
See also TCLC 10, 18, 55
See also TWA
Nieuwsma, Milton J(ohn) 1941- ... 213
See also SATA 142
Nieva, Francisco 1927- ... CWW 2
Nievergelt, Jurg 1938- ... CANR-26
Earlier sketch in CA 29-32R
Nievo, Stanislao 1928- ... DLB 196
Niewyk, Donald L. 1940- ... 33-36R
Nigam, Sanjay (Kumar) 1959- ... 170
Nigg, Joe
See Nigg, Joseph E(ugene)
Nigg, Joseph E(ugene) 1938- ... CANR-93
Earlier sketches in CA 114, CANR-35
Niggli, Josefina (Maria) 1910-1983 ... CANR-32
Earlier sketches in CAP-2, CA 21-24R
See also DLBY 1980
See also HW 1
Nighbert, David F(ranklin) 1948- ... CANR-70
Earlier sketch in CA 141
Nightingale, Anne Redmon 1943- ... 103
See also Redmon, Anne
Nightingale, Barbra 1949- ... 187
Nightingale, Benedict 1939- ... 132
Nightingale, Earl (Clifford) 1921-1989
Obituary ... 128
Nightingale, Elena O(ttolenghi) 1932- ... 123
Nightingale, Florence 1820-1910 ... 188
See also DLB 166
See also TCLC 85
Nightingale, Pamela 1938- ... 158
Nightingale, Sandy 1953- ... SATA 76
Nightingale, Sir Geoffrey (Slingsby)
1904-1972 ... CAP-1
Earlier sketch in CA 13-14
Nightmare, M. Macha 1943- ... 231

Nightrate, Emil
See Spielmann, Peter James
Nigro, August John 1934- 199
Nigro, Felix A(nthony) 1914- CANR-14
Earlier sketch in CA 37-40R
Nihalani, Govind 1940- .... IDFW 3, 4
Nihal Singh, Surendra 1929- 93-96
Niizaka, Kazuo 1943- 77-80
Nijhoff, Martinus 1894-1953 195
See also EWL 3
See also RGWL 2, 3
Nijinska, Bronislava 1891-1972 117
Nijinsky, Romola Flavia 1891-1978
Obituary 81-84
Nijinsky, Vaslav (Fomitch) 1890-1950 168
Brief entry 115
Nijo, Lady 1258-1306(?) .... DLB 203
Nijo Yoshimoto 1320-1388 .... DLB 203
Nik. T. O.
See Annensky, Innokenty (Fyodorovich)
Nikelly, Arthur G(eorge) 1927- 17-20R
Nikitenko, Aleksandr Vasilievich
See Nikitenko, Aleksandr Vasilievich
Nikitenko, Aleksandr Vasilievich
1804-1877 231
Nikitin, Ivan Savvich 1824-1861 .... DLB 277
Nikitin, Nikolai Nikolaevich
1895-1963 .... DLB 272
Nikkel, David H. 1952- 165
Niklas, Gerald R. 1933- 118
Niklas, Karl J(oseph) 1948- 145
Niklaus, Robert 1910-2001 .... 9-12R
Niklaus, Thelma (Jones) 1912-1970 . CANR-76
Obituary 134
Earlier sketch in CA 9-12R
Nikolaev, Vsevolod A(postolov)
1909-1987 130
Nikolajeva, Maria 1952- 197
See also SATA 127
Nikola-Lisa, W. 1951- .... SATA 71
Nikolay, Michael 1941- 97-100
Nikolev, Nikolai Petrovich
1758-1815 .... DLB 150
Nikolic, Mile
See Djilas, Milovan
Niland, D'Arcy Francis 1920-1967 ..... CANR-3
Earlier sketch in CA 1-4R
Niland, Deborah 1951- 106
See also SATA 27
Niland, Kilmeny .... SATA 75
Niland, Powell 1919- 21-24R
Nile, Dorothea
See Avallone, Michael (Angelo, Jr.)
Niles, D(aniel) T(hambyrajah) 1908-1970
Obituary 29-32R
Niles, Douglas CANR-120
Earlier sketch in CA 160
See also FANT
Niles, Gwendolyn 1914-1994 .... 9-12R
Niles, Hezekiah 1777-1839 .... DLB 43
Niles, John D(eWitt) 1945- 125
Niles, John Jacob 1892-1980 .... CANR-33
Obituary 97-100
Earlier sketch in CA 41-44R
Nill, Michael 1942- 124
Nilles, Jack M(athias) 1932- 108
Nilsen, Alleen Pace 1936- 112
Nilsen, Anna
See Bassil, Andrea
Nilsen, Don L(ee) F(red) 1934- CANR-15
Earlier sketch in CA 41-44R
Nilsson, Birgit (Marta) 1918- 129
Nilsson, Eleanor 1939- CANR-94
Earlier sketch in CA 149
See also SAAS 23
See also SATA 81, 117
Nilsson, Jenny Lind 165
Nilsson, Per 1954- 235
See also SATA 159
Nilsson, Usha Saksena 1930- 41-44R
Niman, Michael I. 1957- 164
Nimble, Jack B.
See Burgess, Michael (Roy)
Nimeth, Albert J. 1918-1984 .... CANR-77
Obituary 114
Earlier sketch in CA 25-28R
Nimitz, Chester W(illiam) 1885-1966
Obituary 113
Nimmanhemin, M. L. Buppha Kunjara
1905-1963
See Dokmai Sot
Nimmer, Melville B(ernard)
1923-1985 .... CANR-76
Obituary 117
Earlier sketch in CA 49-52
Nimmo, Dan D(ean) 1933- CANR-7
Earlier sketch in CA 13-16R
Nimmo, Derek Robert
1933(?)-1999 .... CANR-28
Obituary 177
Earlier sketch in CA 109
Nimmo, Jenny 1944- CANR-124
Earlier sketches in CA 108, CANR-52, 83
See also CLR 44
See also CWRI 5
See also FANT
See also MAICYA 2
See also SATA 87, 144
Nimnicht, Nona 1930- 73-76
Nimocks, Walter 1930- 41-44R
Nimoy, Leonard 1931- CANR-126
Earlier sketches in CA 57-60, CANR-25
Nims, Charles F(rancis) 1906-1988 .. CANR-76
Obituary 127
Earlier sketch in CA 17-20R
Nims, John Frederick 1913-1999 ... CANR-135
Obituary 174
Earlier sketches in CA 13-16R, CANR-6, 35
See also CAAS 17
See also CP 1, 2
See also DLB 5
Nin, Anais 1903-1977 .... CANR-53
Obituary 69-72
Earlier sketches in CA 13-16R, CANR-22
See also AITN 2
See also AMWS 10
See also BPFB 2
See also CLC 1, 4, 8, 11, 14, 60, 127
See also CN 1, 2
See also DAM NOV, POP
See also DLB 2, 4, 152
See also EWL 3
See also GLL 2
See also MAL 5
See also MAWW
See also MTCW 1, 2
See also MTFW 2005
See also RGAL 4
See also RGSF 2
See also SSC 10
Nineham, Dennis (Eric) 1921- 85-88
Ning, Pu 1917- 181
Ningkun, Wu 1921- 140
Ninh, Bao 1952(?)- 152
Ninh, Kim N(goc) B(ao) 1965- 229
Nininger, H(arvey) H(arlow)
1887-1986 .... CANR-76
Obituary 118
Earlier sketch in CA 21-24R
Ninkovich, Thomas 1943- 137
Ninkovich, Tom
See Ninkovich, Thomas
Nino, Carlos Santiago 1943- 141
Nino, Jairo Anibal 1941- .... EWL 3
Nino, Raul 1961- .... DLB 209
Nioche, Brigitte 109
Niosi, Jorge 1945- CANR-126
Earlier sketches in CA 129, CANR-65
See also HW 1, 2
Nir, Yehuda 1930- 107
Nirenberg, David 1964- 187
Nirenberg, Jesse S(tanley) 1921- 69-72
Nirgad, Lia 222
Nirgad, Liyah
See Nirgad, Lia
Nirmala-Kumara, V
See Bose, N(irmal) K(umar)
Niro, Shelly 1954- 212
Nirodi, Hira 1930- 5-8R
Nisan, Mordechai 1947- 229
Nisbet, Ada Blanche 1907-1994 .... 41-44R
Nisbet, Hume 1849(?)-1921 191
See also HGG
Nisbet, Jack 1949- 234
Nisbet, Robert A(lexander)
1913-1996 .... CANR-17
Obituary 153
Earlier sketch in CA 25-28R
Interview in CANR-17
See also TCLC 117
Nisbet, Stanley (Donald) 1912-2004 ..... CAP-1
Earlier sketch in CA 13-14
Nisbett, (Thomas) Alec 1930- CANR-22
Earlier sketch in CA 81-84
Nisbett, Richard E. 1941- 37-40R
Nisenson, Eric 1946-2003 221
Nisetich, Frank Joseph 1942- 97-100
Nish, Ian Hill 1926- CANR-17
Earlier sketch in CA 21-24R
Nishida, Kitaro 1870-1945 .... TCLC 83
Nishihara, Masashi 1937- CANR-93
Earlier sketches in CA 69-72, CANR-12
Nishimura, Kae 232
Nishio, Suehiro 1891-1981
Obituary 108
Nishiwaki, Junzaburo 1894-1982 194
Obituary 107
See also Junzaburo, Nishiwaki
See also MJW
See also PC 15
See also RGWL 3
Nishiyama, Chiaki 1924-
Brief entry 110
Niskala, Brenda 1955- 199
Niskanen, William Arthur, Jr.
1933- CANR-106
Earlier sketches in CA 41-44R, CANR-54
Nisker, Wes 1942- 177
Nisker, Wes "Scoop"
See Nisker, Wes
Nissel, Angela 1974- 201
Nissel, Muriel 1921- 198
Nissen, Axel 223
Nissen, Bruce 1948- 173
Nissen, Lowell A(llen) 1932- CANR-103
Earlier sketch in CA 33-36R
Nissen, Thisbe 1972- 198
Nissenbaum, Stephen 1941- 77-80
Nissenson, Hugh 1933- CANR-108
Earlier sketches in CA 17-20R, CANR-27
See also CLC 4, 9
See also CN 5, 6
See also DLB 28
Nissenson, Marilyn 1939- 146
Nissman, Albert 1930-1998 .... 37-40R
Nissman, Barbara 1944- 228
Nissman, Blossom S. 1928- CANR-19
Earlier sketch in CA 37-40R
Nist, John (Albert) 1925-1981 .... CANR-11
Earlier sketch in CA 21-24R
Nister, Der
See Der Nister
See also EWL 3
Nitchie, George W(ilson) 1921- 9-12R
Nitske, W(illiam) Robert 1909-(?) CANR-5
Earlier sketch in CA 13-16R
Nittler, Alan H(opkins) 1918-1981 ... CANR-13
Earlier sketch in CA 61-64
Nityanandan, P(erumpilavil) M(adhava Menon)
1926- 9-12R
Nitze, Paul H(enry) 1907-2004 140
Obituary 232
Nitzsche, Jack 1937-2000 .... IDFW 3, 4
Nitzsche, Jane Chance 1945- CANR-108
See also Chance, Jane
Nivelle de la Chaussee, Pierre-Claude
1692(?)-1754
See La Chaussee, Pierre-Claude Nivelle de
See also GFL Beginnings to 1789
Niven, Alastair 1944- CANR-16
Earlier sketch in CA 81-84
Niven, Alexander Curt 1920-1993 ..... CANR-2
Earlier sketch in CA 5-8R
Niven, (James) David (Graham)
1910-1983 .... CANR-31
Obituary 110
Earlier sketch in CA 77-80
Niven, Frederick John 1878-1944 182
See also DLB 92
See also RHW
See also TCWW 1, 2
Niven, John 1921- 65-68
Niven, Larry
See Niven, Laurence Van Cott
See also AAYA 27
See also BPFB 2
See also BYA 10
See also CLC 8
See also DLB 8
See also SCFW 1, 2
Niven, Laurence Van Cott 1938- 207
Earlier sketches in CA 21-24R, CANR-14, 44, 66, 113
Autobiographical Essay in 207
See also Niven, Larry
See also CAAS 12
See also CPW
See also DAM POP
See also MTCW 1, 2
See also SATA 95
See also SFW 4
Niven, Marian
See Alston, Mary Niven
Niven, (Cecil) Rex 1898-1993 120
Niven, Vern
See Grier, Barbara G(ene Damon)
See also GLL 1
Nivens, Beatryce 1948- 114
Niver, Garry 1938- 138
Nivison, David Shepherd 1923- 103
Nivola, Claire A. 1947- .... SATA 84, 140
Niwa, Tamako 1922- 184
Brief entry 106
Niwano, Nikkyo 1906-1999 130
Nix, Garth 1963- CANR-122
Earlier sketch in CA 164
See also AAYA 27
See also BYA 14, 16
See also CLR 68
See also SATA 97, 143
See also YAW
Nixon, Agnes Eckhardt 1927- 110
See also CLC 21
Nixon, Allan 1918-1995 .... 17-20R
Obituary 148
Nixon, Clarence H., Jr. 1908(?)-1990
Obituary 130
Nixon, Cornelia 193
Nixon, Edna (Mary) 5-8R
Nixon, George 1924- 49-52
Nixon, Hershell Howard 1923- 89-92
See also SATA 42
Nixon, Howard Millar 1909-1983 183
Obituary 109
See also DLB 201
Nixon, Ivor Gray 1905- CAP-2
Earlier sketch in CA 29-32
Nixon, Joan Lowery 1927-2003 ..... CANR-135
Obituary 217
Earlier sketches in CA 9-12R, CANR-7, 24, 38
See also AAYA 12, 54
See also BYA 16
See also CLR 24
See also JRDA
See also MAICYA 1, 2
See also MAICYAS 1
See also SAAS 9
See also SATA 8, 44, 78, 115
See also SATA-Obit 146
See also WYA
See also YAW
Nixon, John Erskine 1917- 101
Nixon, K.
See Nixon, Kathleen Irene (Blundell)
Nixon, Kathleen Irene (Blundell)
1894-1988(?) CANR-76
Obituary 126
Earlier sketch in CA 73-76
See also SATA 14
See also SATA-Obit 59
Nixon, Lucille M. 1908-1963 .... 5-8R
Nixon, Marion 1930- 49-52
Nixon, Richard M(ilhous)
1929-1994 .... CANR-61
Obituary 147
Earlier sketches in CA 73-76, CANR-33
See also BEST 90:3
See also MTCW 1
Nixon, Rob 1954- 199
Nixon, Robert E(arl, Jr.) 1918- 5-8R
Nixon, St. John Cousins 1885- 5-8R
Nixon, William R(ussell) 1918- 29-32R
Nixson, Frederick Ian 1943- CANR-44
Earlier sketches in CA 104, CANR-20
Nizami of Ganja .... WLIT 6
Nizan, Paul 1905-1940 161
See also DLB 72
See also EWL 3
See also GFL 1789 to the Present
See also TCLC 40
Nizer, Louis 1902-1994 .... CANR-76
Obituary 147
Earlier sketch in CA 53-56
Njau, Rebecca
See Njau, Rebeka
Njau, Rebeka 1932- 142
See also BW 2
Njegos, Petar II Petrovic 1813-1851 . CDWLB 4
See also DLB 147
Njeri, Itabari (Lord) CANR-71
Earlier sketch in CA 139
See also BW 2, 3
Njoroge, J(ames) K(ingangi) 1933- 153
See also BW 2
Njururi, Ngumbu 1930- 17-20R
Nkala, Nathan 1941- 170
See also BW 3
Nketia, J(oseph) H(anson) Kwabena
1921- CANR-7
Earlier sketch in CA 9-12R
Nkosi, Lewis 1936- CANR-81
Earlier sketches in CA 65-68, CANR-27
See also BLC 3
See also BW 1, 3
See also CBD
See also CD 5, 6
See also CLC 45
See also DAM MULT
See also DLB 157, 225
See also WWE 1
Nkrumah, Kwame 1909-1972 132
Obituary 113
See also BW 2
Nnadozie, Emmanuel 1956- 164
Noad, Frederick (McNeill) 1929- CANR-4
Earlier sketch in CA 9-12R
Noah, Harold J(ulius) 1925- CANR-30
Earlier sketches in CA 33-36R, CANR-13
Noah, Joseph W(atson) 1928- 81-84
Noah, Mordecai M. 1785-1851 .... DLB 250
Noah, Robert 1926- 168
Noailles, Anna de 1876-1933 .... DLB 258
Noakes, Jeremy 1941- 101
Noakes, Vivien 1937- 65-68
Noall, Roger 1935- 9-12R
Noam, Eli Michael 1946- 145
Nobbs, David 1935- 138
Nobile, Philip 1941- 152
Nobile, Umberto 1885-1978
Obituary 81-84
Nobisso, Josephine 1953- CANR-89
Earlier sketch in CA 146
See also SATA 78, 121
Noble, Allen G(eorge) 1930- 116
Noble, Charles
See Pawley, Martin Edward
Noble, David Watson 1925- CANR-1
Earlier sketch in CA 49-52
Noble, Dennis L. 1939- CANR-135
Earlier sketch in CA 171
Noble, Dudley (Henry) 1893(?)-1970
Obituary 104
Noble, Elizabeth 1969(?)- 236
Noble, Elizabeth Marian 1945- CANR-9
Earlier sketch in CA 65-68
Noble, G(eorge) Bernard 1892-1972 ..... CAP-2
Obituary 37-40R
Earlier sketch in CA 33-36
Noble, Iain (Andrew) 1949- 128
Noble, Iris (Davis) 1922-1986 .... CANR-76
Obituary 120
Earlier sketches in CA 1-4R, CANR-2
See also SATA 5
See also SATA-Obit 49
Noble, J(ames) Kendrick, Jr.
1928-2000 .... 17-20R
Noble, J(ames) Kendrick 1896(?)-1978
Obituary 104
Noble, Jeanne L(aveta) 1926-2002
Obituary 210
Brief entry 112
Noble, John (Appelbe) 1914- CANR-1
Earlier sketch in CA 45-48
Noble, John (Darcy) 1923-2003 45-48
Obituary 220
Noble, John Wesley 1913-1975 .... 9-12R
Noble, Joseph Veach 1920- 61-64
Noble, June (Solveig) 1924-1984 ..... CANR-18
Earlier sketch in CA 97-100
Noble, Kathleen D(iane) 1950- CANR-95
Earlier sketch in CA 146
Noble, Marguerite (Buchanan) 1910- 105
Noble, Marianne 196
Noble, Marty 1947- CANR-105
See also SATA 97, 125
Noble, Stanley R(odman) 1904(?)-1977
Obituary 104

Cumulative Index 429 **Norman**

Noble, Trinka Hakes CANR-101
Brief entry 116
Earlier sketch in CA 171
See also SATA 123
See also SATA-Brief 37
Noble, William Charles 1935- 107
Noble, William P(arker) 1932- CANR-39
Earlier sketches in CA 101, CANR-18
Nobles, Edward 1954- 191
Nobre, Antonio 1867-1900 .... DLB 287
Nocera, Joseph 238
Nochlin, Linda Weinberg 1931- CANR-88
Earlier sketches in CA 9-12R, CANR-6
Nock, Albert Jay 1870(?)-1945 166
Brief entry 122
Nock, Francis J. 1905-1969 .... CAP-1
Earlier sketch in CA 13-14
Nock, O(swald) S(tevens)
1905-1994 .... CANR-16
Earlier sketch in CA 85-88
Nockolds, Harold 1907-1982
Obituary 108
Noddings, Nel 1929- CANR-115
Earlier sketches in CA 115, CANR-48
Noddings, Thomas C. 1933- CANR-2
Earlier sketch in CA 49-52
Nodel, Sol 1912-1976
Obituary 107
Nodelman, Perry 1942- 160
See also AAYA 30
See also SATA 101
Nodier, (Jean) Charles (Emmanuel)
1780-1844 .... DLB 119
See also GFL 1789 to the Present
Nodset, Joan L.
See Lexau, Joan M.
Noe, Kenneth W. 1957- 150
Noe, Randolph 1939- 206
Noe, Thomas R. 1947- 112
Noe, Tom
See Noe, Thomas R.
Noegel, Scott B. 1962- 193
Noel, Christopher 1960- 127
Noel, Daniel C(alhoun) 1936- 101
Noel, Hilda Bloxton, Jr.
See Schroetter, Hilda Noel
Noel, John
See Bird, Dennis L(eslie)
Noel, John V(avasour), Jr.
1912-1991 .... CANR-15
Earlier sketch in CA 21-24R
Noel, Marie 1883-1967 .... DLB 258
Noel, Roden 1834-1894 .... DLB 35
Noel, Roger Arthur 1942- 144
Noel, Ruth (Swycaffer) 1947- 69-72
Noel, Sterling 1903-1984
Obituary 114
Noel, Thomas Jacob 1945- CANR-93
Earlier sketches in CA 107, CANR-24, 49
Noel-Baker, Philip John 1889-1982
Obituary 108
Noel Hume, Ivor 1927- CANR-12
Earlier sketch in CA 13-16R
See also SATA 65
Noer, David M. 1939-1997 145
Noer, Thomas John 1944- 102
Noestlinger, Christine
See Nostlinger, Christine
Noether, Emiliana P. 101
Noever, Peter 1941- 221
Nof, Shimon Y. 1946- 135
Nofi, Albert A(urelio) 1944- 112
Nofziger, (Frank)Lyn (C.) 1924- CANR-93
Earlier sketch in CA 145
Nofziger, Margaret 1946- CANR-30
Earlier sketch in CA 110
Nogales, Patti D(iane) 1961- 198
Nogami, Yaeko 1885-1985
See Nogami Yaeko
Nogami Yaeko
See Nogami, Yaeko
See also DLB 180
Nogee, Joseph Lippman 1929- 17-20R
Noggle, Burl L. 1924- 134
Brief entry 107
Nogo, Rajko Petrov 1945- .... DLB 181
Noguchi, Hideyo Seisaku 1876-1928 162
Noguchi, Isamu 1904-1988 217
See also AAYA 52
Noguchi, Rick 1967- 162
Noguchi, Yone 1875-1947 .... TCLC 80
Noguera, Magdalena
See Conde (Abellan), Carmen
Noguere, Suzanne 1947- 107
See also SATA 34
Nohl, Frederick 1927- CANR-3
Earlier sketch in CA 5-8R
Nohria, Nitin 1962- 190
Nohrnberg, James (Carson) 1941- 69-72
Nojiri, Kiyohiko 1897-1973 93-96
Obituary 41-44R
Nojumi, Neamatollah 217
Nokes, David 1948- CANR-73
Earlier sketch in CA 141
Nokes, Gerald Dacre 1899-1971
Obituary 104
Nolan, Alan T. 1923- 1-4R
Nolan, Albert 1934- 117
Nolan, Bob 1908(?)-1980
Obituary 101
Nolan, Brian
See O Nuallain, Brian
Nolan, Carroll A(nthony) 1906-1976 .... 17-20R
Nolan, Cathal J. 1956- 180
Nolan, Christopher 1965- CANR-88
Earlier sketch in CA 111
See also CLC 58
Nolan, Chuck
See Edson, J(ohn) T(homas)
Nolan, David (Joseph) 1946- 132
Nolan, Dennis 1945- CANR-59
Earlier sketches in CA 112, CANR-32
See also SATA 42, 92
See also SATA-Brief 34
Nolan, Edward Francis 1915-
Brief entry 108
Nolan, Frederick William 1931- CANR-83
Earlier sketch in CA 147
See also Christian, Frederick H.
See also RHW
Nolan, Han 1956- CANR-141
Earlier sketch in CA 170
See also AAYA 28
See also BYA 16
See also MAICYA 2
See also SATA 109, 157
See also YAW
Nolan, James 1947- CANR-5
Earlier sketch in CA 53-56
Nolan, James L., Jr. 1962- 175
Nolan, Janet 1956- 218
See also SATA 145
Nolan, Janne E. 140
Nolan, Jeannette Covert 1897-1974 .... CANR-4
Obituary 53-56
Earlier sketch in CA 5-8R
See also SATA 2
See also SATA-Obit 27
Nolan, Keith W(illiam) 1964- CANR-36
Earlier sketch in CA 114
Nolan, Madeena Spray 1943- 89-92
Nolan, Michael 1940- 126
Nolan, Michael Patrick 1921- 177
Nolan, Paul T(homas) 1919- CANR-2
Earlier sketch in CA 5-8R
See also SATA 48
Nolan, Richard Thomas 1937- CANR-10
Earlier sketch in CA 25-28R
Nolan, Simon 1961- 218
Nolan, Tom 1948- CANR-89
Earlier sketch in CA 77-80
Nolan, William F(rancis) 1928- CANR-103
Earlier sketches in CA 1-4R, CANR-1, 63
See also CAAS 16
See also CMW 4
See also DLB 8
See also SATA 88
See also SATA-Brief 28
See also SFW 4
Nolan, Winefride (Bell) 1913- 13-16R
Noland, C. F. M. 1810(?)-1858 .... DLB 11
Noland, Ronald G(ene) 1936- 41-44R
Nolde, O(tto) Frederick 1899-1972 .... CAP-2
Obituary 37-40R
Earlier sketch in CA 29-32
Nolen, Barbara 1902- 104
Nolen, Claude H. 1921- 21-24R
Nolen, Jerdine 1953- 173
See also MAICYA 2
See also SATA 105, 157
Nolen, Stephanie 1971- 223
Nolen, William A(nthony)
1928-1986 .... CANR-76
Obituary 121
Earlier sketches in CA 77-80, CANR-15
Nolin, Bertil 1926- CANR-52
Earlier sketch in CA 65-68
Noling, A(lfred) W(ells) 1899-1982 .... CAP-2
Earlier sketch in CA 29-32
Noll, Bink
See Noll, Lou Barker
Noll, Ingrid 1935- 172
Noll, Lou Barker 1927- 5-8R
Noll, Mark A(llan) 1946- CANR-113
Earlier sketches in CA 115, CANR-38
Noll, Martin
See Buxbaum, Martin (David)
Noll, Norbert
See Soyfer, Jura
Noll, Peter 1926-1982 142
Noll, Richard 1959- 134
Noll, Roger G(ordon) 1940- CANR-113
Earlier sketches in CA 53-56, CANR-8, 27, 55
Noll, Sally 1946- .... SATA 82
Nollau, Gunther 1911- 5-8R
Nollen, Scott Allen 1963- 211
Nollen, Stanley D(ale) 1940- 110
Nolletti, Arthur (Ernest, Jr.) 1941- CANR-94
Earlier sketch in CA 145
Nollman, Jim 1947- 212
Nolte, Carl William 1933- 77-80
Nolte, David 1959- 218
Nolte, Elleta 1919- 61-64
Nolte, M(ervin) Chester 1911- 9-12R
Nolte, William H(enry) 1928-1999 .... 33-36R
Nolting, Frederick (Ernest, Jr.) 1911-1989
Obituary 130
Nolting, Orin F(rederyc) 1903-1997 .... 29-32R
Noltingk, B(ernard) E(dward) 1918- 17-20R
Noma, Koremichi 1938(?)-1987
Obituary 122
Noma, Shoichi 1911-1984
Obituary 113
Nomad, Max 1880(?)-1973
Obituary 41-44R
Noma Hiroshi 1915-1991 .... DLB 182
Nomberg-Przytyk, Sara 1915-1996
Nomura, Masayasu 1927- 164
Noname
See Senarens, Luis P(hilip)
Nonis, Elisabeth 1919- 119
Nonet, Philippe 1939- 57-60
Nonhebel, Clare 1953- 119
Nonni
See Sveinsson, Jon Stefan
Noon, Brian 1919- 49-52
Noon, Jeff 1957- CANR-83
Earlier sketch in CA 148
See also CLC 91
See also DLB 267
See also SFW 4
Noon, William T(homas) 1912-1975 65-68
Obituary 53-56
Noonan, Diana 1960- 220
See also CWRI 5
See also SATA 146
Noonan, John Ford 1943- 85-88
See also CAD
See also CD 5, 6
Noonan, John T(homas), Jr. 1926- CANR-73
Earlier sketches in CA 13-16R, CANR-13
Noonan, Julia 1946- CANR-65
Earlier sketch in CA 33-36R
See also SATA 4, 95, 148
Noonan, Lowell G(erald) 1922- 29-32R
Noonan, Michael John 1921-2000 .... 21-24R
Noonan, Miles
See McConville, Michael (Anthony)
Noonan, Peggy 1950- CANR-95
Earlier sketch in CA 132
See also BEST 90:3
Noonan, Robert
See Tressell, Robert
Noonan, Robert Phillipe
See Tressell, Robert
Noonan, Tom 1951- CANR-130
Earlier sketch in CA 158
Noone, Edwina
See Avallone, Michael (Angelo, Jr.)
Noone, John 1936- 226
Brief entry 109
See also DLB 14
Noone, Richard 1918(?)-1973
Obituary 104
Noonuccal, Oodgeroo
See Walker, Kath
See also EWL 3
Noorbergen, Rene 1928-1995 77-80
Noordervliet, Nelleke 1945- 194
Nooteboom, Cees 1933- CANR-120
Brief entry 124
Earlier sketch in CA 130
See also EWL 3
See also RGWL 3
Nora, Eugenio de 1923- .... DLB 134
Nora, James Jackson 1928- CANR-42
Earlier sketches in CA 104, CANR-20
Norall, Frank 1918- 133
Norback, Craig T(homas) 1943- 113
Norbeck, Edward 1915-1991 .... CANR-1
Obituary 196
Earlier sketch in CA 1-4R
Norberg-Schulz, Christian 1926- 81-84
Norbrook, David (G. E.) 1950- 231
Norbu, Jamyang 196
Norbu, Thubten Jigme
See Thubten, Jigme Norbu
Norcliffe, Glen (B.) 1943- 229
Norcross, John
See Conroy, John Wesley
Norcross, Lisabet
See Gladstone, Arthur M.
Norcutt, Bill
See Norcutt, William E.
Norcutt, William E. 1946-
Brief entry 118
Nord, Ole C. 1935- 13-16R
Nord, Paul 1900(?)-1981
Obituary 103
Nord, Walter R(obert) 1939- 37-40R
Nordan, Lewis (Alonzo) 1939- CANR-121
Earlier sketches in CA 117, CANR-40, 72
See also CSW
See also DLB 234
Nordan, Robert W(arren) 1934-2004 202
Obituary 233
See also SATA 133
Nordberg, H(arold) Orville 1916- 1-4R
Nordberg, Robert B. 1921- 13-16R
Nordbrandt, Henrik 1945- 192
See also CWW 2
See also DLB 214
See also EWL 3
Nordby, Vernon James 1945- 57-60
Nordell, (Hans) Roderick 1925- 104
Norden, Albert 1904-1982
Obituary 107
Norden, Astor E.
See Herbert, (Alfred Francis) Xavier
Norden, Charles
See Durrell, Lawrence (George)
Norden, Denis 1922- CANR-29
Earlier sketch in CA 104
Norden, Heinz 1905-1978 53-56
Norden, Helen Brown
See Lawrenson, Helen
Nordham, George Washington
1929- CANR-87
Earlier sketches in CA 106, CANR-23, 47
Nordhaug, Odd 1953- 140
Nordhaus, Jean 1939- 211
Nordhaus, William D(awbney) 1941- 97-100
Nordhoff, Charles Bernard 1887-1947 211
Brief entry 108
See also DLB 9
See also LAIT 1
See also RHW 1
See also SATA 23
See also TCLC 23
Nordholm, Harriet 1912- 29-32R
Nordicus
See Snyder, Louis L(eo)
Nordin, D(ennis) Sven 1942- 61-64
Nordland, Gerald John 1927- 104
Nordland, Rod(ney Lee) 1949- 118
Nordlicht, Lillian 105
See also SATA 29
Nordlinger, Eric A. 1939- 77-80
Nordloh, David J(oseph) 1942- 137
Nordlund, Willis J. 1942- 175
Nordmann, Joseph (Behrens) 1922- 25-28R
Nordness, Lee 1924- 9-12R
Nordoff, Paul 1909-1977 102
Nordquist, Barbara K(ay) 1940- 77-80
Nordskog, John Eric 1893-1974 .... CANR-77
Obituary 120
Earlier sketch in CA 1-4R
Nordstroem, Ludvig Anshelm
See Nordstrom, Ludvig Anshelm
Nordstrom, Byron J. 1943- 206
Nordstrom, Ursula 1910-1988 .... CANR-75
Obituary 126
Earlier sketch in CA 13-16R
See also SATA 3
See also SATA-Obit 57
Nordtvedt, Matilda 1926- 124
See also SATA 67
Nordyke, Eleanor C(ole) 1927- 107
Nordyke, James W(alter) 1930- 49-52
Noreen, Robert Gerald 1938- 77-80
Norelli, Martina R(oudabush) 1942- 73-76
Noren, Catherine (Hanf) 1938- CANR-16
Earlier sketch in CA 65-68
Noren, Lars 1944- 193
See also CWW 2
See also DLB 257
See also EWL 3
Noren, Paul Harold Andreas
1910-1999 .... CAP-1
Earlier sketch in CA 11-12
Norfleet, Barbara P. 1926-
Brief entry 107
Norfleet, Celeste O. 1959- 217
Norfleet, Mary Crockett 1919-1999 .... 1-4R
Norfolk, Lawrence 1963- CANR-85
Earlier sketch in CA 144
See also CLC 76
See also CN 6, 7
See also DLB 267
Norfolk, Sherry 1952- 187
Norgate, Matthew 1901- 103
Norgay, Tenzing 1914-1986
Obituary 119
Nori, Claude 1949- CANR-18
Earlier sketch in CA 101
Noriega, Chon A. 1961- 141
Norinsky, Marvin 1927-1994 130
Norland, Howard Bennett 1932- 49-52
Norling, Bernard 1924- 29-32R
Norling, Beth 1969- .... SATA 149
Norling, Jo(sephine Stearns) -1972 .... 1-4R
Norling, Rita 61-64
Norman, A. V. B.
See Norman, Alexander Vesey Bethune
Norman, Adrian R(oger) D(udley)
1938- CANR-26
Earlier sketch in CA 29-32R
Norman, Alexander Vesey Bethune
1930-1998 .... CANR-9
Obituary 169
Earlier sketch in CA 21-24R
Norman, Barbara 33-36R
Norman, Barry 151
Norman, Bruce 1936- 61-64
Norman, C. J.
See Barrett, Norman (S.)
Norman, Cecilia 1927- CANR-23
Earlier sketches in CA 57-60, CANR-7
Norman, Charles 1904-1996 107
Obituary 153
See also DLB 111
See also SATA 38
See also SATA-Obit 92
Norman, Diana 1935- 135
Norman, Don(ald) Cleveland 1909(?)-1979
Obituary 89-92
Norman, Donald A(rthur) 1935- CANR-1
Earlier sketch in CA 49-52
Norman, Dorothy 1905-1997 .... 25-28R
Obituary 157
Norman, E. D.
See Goodwin, Bennie Eugene II
Norman, Edward (Robert)
1938-1997 .... CANR-27
Earlier sketches in CA 17-20R, CANR-10
Norman, Elizabeth M. 1951- 198
Norman, Frank 1930-1980 .... CANR-6
Obituary 102
Earlier sketch in CA 1-4R
Norman, Geraldine (Lucia) 1940- 93-96
Norman, Greg(ory John) 1955- 133
Norman, Hilary 126
Norman, Howard
See Norman, Howard A.
Norman, Howard A. 1949- CANR-78
Brief entry 129
Earlier sketch in CA 137
Interview in CA-137
See also CN 7
See also SATA 81
Norman, James
See Schmidt, James Norman
Norman, Jay
See Arthur, Robert, (Jr.)
Norman, Jillian 1940- 25-28R
Norman, Joe
See Heard, J(oseph) Norman

Norman, John
See Lange, John Frederick, Jr.
See also BPFB 2
Norman, John 1912-2002 ... 17-20R
Norman, Joyce Ann 1937- ... 65-68
Norman, Kerry
See Le Pelley, Guernsey
Norman, Lilith 1927- ... CANR-52
Earlier sketches in CA 45-48, CANR-1
See also CWRI 5
See also SATA 86, 120
Norman, Lisanne ... 181
Norman, Lloyd (Henry) 1913-1987 .. CANR-76
Obituary ... 124
Earlier sketch in CA 102
Norman, Louis
See Whittemore, Don
Norman, Marc 1941- ... CANR-130
Earlier sketch in CA 49-52
Norman, Marsha (Williams) 1947- . CANR-131
Earlier sketches in CA 105, CANR-41
See also CABS 3
See also CAD
See also CD 5, 6
See also CLC 28, 186
See also CSW
See also CWD
See also DAM DRAM
See also DC 8
See also DFS 2
See also DLB 266
See also DLBY 1984
See also FW
See also MAL 5
Norman, Mary 1931- ... SATA 36
Norman, Maxwell H(erbert)
1917-1984 ... 29-32R
Norman, Michael 1947- ... 129
Norman, Mick
See James, Laurence
Norman, Nick
See Norman, Alexander Vesey Bethune
Norman, Nicole
See Cudlipp, Edythe
Norman, Philip 1943- ... 156
Norman, Richard (J.) ... 228
Norman, Rick (J.) 1954- ... 137
Norman, Ruth 1903(?)-1977
Obituary ... 73-76
Norman, Steve
See Pashko, Stanley
Norman, Sylva 1901- ... CAP-1
Earlier sketch in CA 13-14
Norman, Theodore 1910-1987 ... 124
Obituary ... 122
Norman, Vesey
See Norman, Alexander Vesey Bethune
Norman, W. S.
See Wilson, N(orman) Scarlyn
Norman, Yvonne
See Seely, Norma
Normanton, John 1918- ... CP 1
Norment, Lisa 1966- ... 155
See also SATA 91
Normyx
See Douglas, (George) Norman
Norodom Sihanouk (Varman), Samdech Preah
1922- ... 129
Brief entry ... 106
Norquest, Carrol 1901-1981 ... CANR-75
Obituary ... 133
Earlier sketch in CA 41-44R
Norquist, Richard F(ranklin) 1933- ... 113
Norrander, Barbara 1954- ... 141
Norrell, Gregory T. 1960- ... 160
Norrell, Robert J(efferson) 1952- ... 139
Norretranders, Tor ... 173
Norrie, Ian 1927- ... CANR-49
Earlier sketches in CA 106, CANR-23
Norrington, Ruth 1922- ... 214
Norris, Charles G(ilman Smith)
1881-1945 ... 155
Brief entry ... 118
See also DLB 9
Norris, Christopher (Charles) 1947- .. CANR-53
Earlier sketches in CA 111, CANR-29
Norris, Christopher Neil Foxley
See Foxley-Norris, Christopher Neil
Norris, Clarence 1912-1989
Obituary ... 127
Norris, David A. 1931- ... 220
Norris, Donald F(ranklin) 1942- ... CANR-2
Earlier sketch in CA 49-52
Norris, Dorothy E. Koch 1907- ... CAP-2
Earlier sketch in CA 21-22
Norris, Edgar Poe
See Kinnaird, Clark
Norris, Frances ... 239
Norris, Francis Hubert 1909- ... 5-8R
Norris, (Benjamin) Frank(lin, Jr.)
1870-1902 ... 160
Brief entry ... 110
See also AAYA 57
See also AMW
See also AMWC 2
See also BPFB 2
See also CDALB 1865-1917
See also DLB 12, 71, 186
See also LMFS 2
See also NFS 12
See also RGAL 4
See also SSC 28
See also TCLC 24, 155
See also TCWW 1, 2
See also TUS
Norris, Frank C(allan) 1907-1967
Obituary ... 25-28R
See also MAL 5
Norris, Frederick W(alter) 1941- ... 222
Norris, Gunilla Brodde 1939- ... 93-96
See also SATA 20
Norris, H. T. ... 160
Norris, Harold 1918- ... 108
Norris, Helen 1916- ... CSW
Norris, Hoke 1913-1977 ... 9-12R
Obituary ... 73-76
See also CN 1, 2
Norris, J(ames) A(lfred) 1929- ... 25-28R
Norris, James Donald 1930- ... 17-20R
Norris, Joan 1943- ... 73-76
Norris, John 1657-1712 ... DLB 252
Norris, John 1925- ... 9-12R
Norris, Kathleen (Thompson) 1880-1966
Obituary ... 25-28R
See also RHW
Norris, Kathleen 1947- ... CANR-113
Earlier sketch in CA 160
Norris, Katrin
See FitzHerbert, Katrin
Norris, Ken 1951- ... 113
Norris, Kenneth S(tafford) 1924-1998 ... 77-80
Obituary ... 169
Norris, Leslie 1921- ... CANR-117
Earlier sketches in CAP-1, CA 11-12, CANR-14
See also CLC 14
See also CP 1, 2, 3, 4, 5, 6, 7
See also DLB 27, 256
Norris, Louanne 1930- ... CANR-20
Earlier sketch in CA 53-56
Norris, Louis William 1906-1986 ... CAP-1
Earlier sketch in CA 9-10
Norris, Margot 1944- ... 189
Norris, Maureen
See Cudlipp, Edythe
Norris, Nigel (Harold) 1943- ... 65-68
Norris, Pamela ... 208
Norris, Pippa 1953- ... 134
Norris, Richard A(lfred), Jr. 1930- ... 17-20R
Norris, Robert S(tandish) 1943- ... 215
Norris, Ronald V. 1940- ... 116
Norris, Ruby Turner
See Morris, Ruby Turner
Norris, Russell Bradner (Jr.) 1942- ... 53-56
Norris, Theo L. 1926- ... 21-24R
Norris, William R. 1973- ... 202
Norse, Harold (George) 1916- ... CANR-4
Earlier sketch in CA 53-56
See also CAAS 18
See also CP 1, 2, 3, 4, 5, 6, 7
See also DLB 16
Norst, Joel
See Mitchell, Kirk (John)
Norstein, Yuri 1942- ... IDFW 3, 4
Norte, Marisela 1955- ... DLB 209
North, Alex 1910-1991 ... IDFW 3, 4
North, Alvin J(ohn) 1917- ... 49-52
North, Andrew
See Norton, Andre
North, Anthony
See Koontz, Dean R(ay)
North, Captain George
See Stevenson, Robert Louis (Balfour)
North, Carol S. 1954- ... 128
North, Charles 1941- ... 175
North, Charles W.
See Bauer, Erwin A(dam)
North, Chris
See Gorman, Edward
North, Christopher
See Wilson, John
North, Christopher R(ichard) 1888-1975
Obituary ... 61-64
North, Colin
See Bingley, David Ernest
North, Darian ... 166
North, Edmund H(all) 1911-1990 ... CANR-76
Obituary ... 132
Earlier sketch in CA 121
North, Eleanor B(eryl) 1898-1982 ... 49-52
North, Elizabeth 1932- ... 81-84
North, Gary 1942- ... CANR-38
Earlier sketches in CA 65-68, CANR-16
North, Captain George
See Stevenson, Robert Louis (Balfour)
North, Gil
See Horne, Geoffrey
North, Helen Florence 1921- ... 104
North, Howard
See Trevor, Elleston
North, Iris
See Morgan, Joan
North, (Wheeler) James 1922-2002 ... 101
Obituary ... 213
North, Joan 1920- ... 13-16R
See also SATA 16
North, John (Francis Allen) 1894-1973 ... 107
Obituary ... 104
North, John (David) 1934- ... CANR-79
Earlier sketch in CA 148
North, Jonathan 1969- ... 214
North, Joseph 1904-1976 ... CANR-4
Obituary ... 69-72
Earlier sketch in CA 1-4R
North, Marianne 1830-1890 ... DLB 174
North, Mark
See Miller, Wright (Watts)
North, Milou
See Erdrich, (Karen) Louise
North, Morgan 1915(?)-1978
Obituary ... 104
North, Oliver L(aurence) 1943- ... CANR-142
Earlier sketch in CA 142
North, Rebecca
See Ferguson, Jo Ann
North, Rick
See Brenner, Mayer Alan
North, Robert
See Withers, Carl A.
North, Robert Carver 1914-2002 ... CANR-4
Obituary ... 207
Earlier sketch in CA 5-8R
North, Robert Grady 1916- ... 17-20R
North, Sara
See Bonham, Barbara Thomas and
Hager, Jean
North, Sterling 1906-1974 ... CANR-84
Obituary ... 53-56
Earlier sketches in CA 5-8R, CANR-40
See also BYA 3
See also CWRI 5
See also JRDA
See also MAICYA 1, 2
See also SATA 1, 45
See also SATA-Obit 26
See also YAW
Northam, Ray M(ervyn) 1929- ... 73-76
Northart, Leo J(oseph) 1929- ... 69-72
Northcote, Peter
See Cotes, Peter
Northcott, (William) Cecil
1902-1987 ... CANR-75
Obituary ... 124
Earlier sketch in CA 9-12R
See also SATA-Obit 55
Northcott, Kenneth J(ames) 1922- ... CANR-29
Earlier sketch in CA 45-48
Northcutt, Wayne 1944- ... 138
Northeast, Brenda V(ictoria) 1948- ... 176
See also SATA 106
Northedge, Frederick Samuel
1918-1985 ... CANR-76
Obituary ... 115
Earlier sketch in CA 104
Northen, Helen 1914- ... CANR-13
Earlier sketch in CA 33-36R
Northen, Henry T(heodore) 1908-1979 . 97-100
Northen, Rebecca Tyson 1910- ... 105
Northgrave, Anne
See Tibble, Anne
Northmore, Elizabeth Florence
1906-1974 ... CANR-85
Earlier sketches in CAP-2, CA 19-20
See also SATA 122
Northouse, Cameron (George) 1948- ... 81-84
Northrop, Filmer S(tuart) C(uckow)
1893-1992 ... CANR-76
Obituary ... 139
Earlier sketches in CA 1-4R, CANR-17
Northrop, J. H.
See Northrop, John H(oward)
Northrop, John H(oward) 1891-1987
Obituary ... 123
Northrup, B. A.
See Hubbard, L(afayette) Ron(ald)
Northrup, Herbert Roof 1918- ... 9-12R
Northrup, Mary (Wirtz) 1952- ... 199
North Staffs
See Hulme, T(homas) E(rnest)
Northumbrian Gentleman, The
See Tegner, Henry (Stuart)
Northway, Mary L(ouise) 1909-1987 ... 45-48
Northwood, Lawrence K(ing)
1917-1985 ... 13-16R
Nortje, Arthur (Kenneth) 1942-1970 . CANR-93
Earlier sketch in CA 141
See also BW 2
See also DLB 125, 225
See also WWE 1
Norton, Alan (Lewis) 1926- ... CANR-15
Earlier sketch in CA 81-84
Norton, Alden H(olmes) 1903-1987 ... 101
Obituary ... 200
Norton, Alice 1926- ... 33-36R
Norton, Alice Mary
See Norton, Andre
See also MAICYA 1
See also SATA 1, 43
Norton, Andre 1912-2005 ... CANR-68
Obituary ... 237
Earlier sketch in CA 1-4R
See also Norton, Alice Mary
See also AAYA 14
See also BPFB 2
See also BYA 4, 10, 12
See also CLC 12
See also CLR 50
See also DLB 8, 52
See also JRDA
See also MAICYA 2
See also MTCW 1
See also SATA 91
See also SUFW 1, 2
See also YAW
Norton, Andrews 1786-1853 ... DLB 1, 235
Norton, Augustus Richard 1946- ... CANR-48
Earlier sketch in CA 113
Norton, Bess
See Norton, Olive (Claydon)
Norton, Bettina A(ntonia) 1936- ... 93-96
Norton, Boyd 1936- ... 37-40R
Norton, Bram
See Bramesco, Norton J.
Norton, Browning
See Norton, Frank R. B(rowning)
Norton, Bryan G(eorge) 1944- ... 143
Norton, Caroline 1808-1877 ... DLB 21, 159, 199
Norton, Charles A(lbert) 1920- ... 109
Norton, Charles Eliot 1827-1908 ... 183
See also DLB 1, 64, 235
Norton, David Fate 1937- ... 107
Norton, David L. 1930- ... 37-40R
Norton, Eleanor Holmes
See Holmes Norton, Eleanor
Norton, (William) Elliot 1903-2003 ... 226
Brief entry ... 109
Norton, Eric ... GLL 2
Norton, Frank R. B(rowning) 1909-1989 . 61-64
See also SATA 10
Norton, Frederick H(arwood)
1896-1986 ... 61-64
Obituary ... 199
Norton, Glyn P(eter) 1941- ... 122
Norton, Harry N(eugebauer) 1922- ... 142
Norton, Herman A. 1921-1992 ... CANR-7
Earlier sketch in CA 5-8R
Norton, Howard Melvin 1911-1994 . CANR-76
Obituary ... 144
Earlier sketches in CA 1-4R, CANR-3
Norton, Hugh S(tanton) 1921-1999 ... 9-12R
Norton, John 1606-1663 ... DLB 24
Norton, Joseph L(ouis) 1918- ... 29-32R
Norton, Lucy 1902-1989
Obituary ... 129
Norton, M. D. Herter
See Crena de Iongh, Mary (Dows Herter Norton)
Norton, Mary 1903-1992 ... 139
Earlier sketch in CA 97-100
See also CLR 6
See also CWRI 5
See also DLB 160
See also FANT
See also MAICYA 1, 2
See also MAICYAS 1
See also SATA 18, 60
See also SATA-Obit 72
See also TEA
Norton, Mary Beth 1943- ... CANR-125
Earlier sketches in CA 49-52, CANR-5
Norton, Mary E(lizabeth) 1913- ... 41-44R
Norton, Olive (Claydon) 1913-1973 ... 9-12R
See also RHW
Norton, Paul Foote 1917- ... 41-44R
Norton, Perry L. 1920- ... 13-16R
Norton, Peter (John) 1913-1995 ... 13-16R
Obituary ... 148
Norton, Philip 1951- ... 143
Norton, Rictor 1945- ... 165
Norton, Robert L. 1939- ... 143
Norton, Roger C(ecil) 1921- ... 114
Norton, Thomas 1532-1584 ... DLB 62
See also RGEL 2
Norton, Thomas Elliot 1942- ... 61-64
Norton, Victor 1906-1983
Obituary ... 109
Norton, Wesley 1923-1994 ... 114
Norton-Smith, John 1931-1988 ... CANR-76
Obituary ... 127
Earlier sketch in CA 107
Norton-Taylor, Duncan 1904-1982 .. CANR-76
Obituary ... 107
Earlier sketch in CA 102
Norvil, Manning
See Bulmer, (Henry) Kenneth
Norville, Warren 1923- ... 73-76
Norwak, Mary 1929- ... 109
Norway, Kate
See Norton, Olive (Claydon)
Norway, Nevil Shute 1899-1960 ... CANR-85
Obituary ... 93-96
Earlier sketch in CA 102
See also Shute, Nevil
See also MTCW 2
Norwich, (Lord) John Julius (Cooper)
1929- ... CANR-95
Earlier sketches in CA 49-52, CANR-5, 29, 60
Norwich, Viscount
See Norwich, (Lord) John Julius (Cooper)
Norwich, William 1954- ... 157
Norwid, Cyprian Kamil 1821-1883 ... RGWL 3
Norwood, Fred W(ayland) 1920-
Brief entry ... 112
Norwood, Frederick Abbott
1914-1995 ... CANR-42
Earlier sketches in CA 1-4R, CANR-5, 20
Norwood, Gilbert 1880-1954
Brief entry ... 116
Norwood, John
See Stark, Raymond
Norwood, Mandi 1963- ... 225
Norwood, Paul
See Nettl, J(ohn) P(eter)
Norwood, Robert (Winkworth) 1874-1932 . 155
See also DLB 92
Norwood, Robin ... 128
Norwood, Stephen (Harlan) 1951- ... 194
Norwood, Victor G(eorge) C(harles)
1920-1983 ... CANR-64
Earlier sketches in CA 21-24R, CANR-10
See also TCWW 2
Norwood, Warren C. 1945-2005 ... CANR-83
Earlier sketch in CA 112
See also SFW 4
Nosaka, Claude
See Nosaka Akiyuki
Nosaka Akiyuki 1930- ... 184
See also DLB 182
Nosanow, Barbara Shissler 1931- ... CANR-28
Earlier sketch in CA 29-32R
Nosco, Peter 1950- ... 93-96
Nosille, Nabrah
See Ellison, Harlan (Jay)
Nosredna, Trebor
See Anderson, Bob

Cumulative Index 431 Nuttgens

Noss, John Boyer 1896- 85-88
Noss, Luther (Melancthon) 1907-1995 ...... 5-8R
Nossack, Hans Erich 1901-1978 93-96
Obituary 85-88
See also CLC 6
See also DLB 69
See also EWL 3
Nossal, Frederick (Christian)
1927-1979 .... CANR-76
Obituary 89-92
Earlier sketch in CA 5-8R
Nossal, Gustav Joseph Victor 1931- 109
Nossiter, Adam 1961- 208
Nossiter, Bernard D(aniel)
1926-1992 .... CANR-47
Obituary 138
Earlier sketch in CA 41-44R
Nostlinger, Christine 1936- CANR-38
Brief entry 115
Earlier sketch in CA 123
See also CLR 12
See also MAICYA 1, 2
See also SATA 64, 162
See also SATA-Brief 37
See also YAW
Nostradamus, Merlin
See Cobbe, Frances Power
Nostrand, Howard Lee 1910- 9-12R
Nostrand, Richard L(ee) 1939- 239
Nostwich, T(heodore) D. 127
Nosu, Chuji
See Ozu, Yasujiro
Notar, Stephen 1926- 119
Notarius
See Martin, Andrew
Notehelfer, F(red) G(eorge) 1939- 81-84
Notenburg, Eleanora (Genrikhovna) von
See Guro, Elena (Genrikhovna)
Notestein, Frank Wallace 1902-1983
Obituary 109
Notestein, Wallace 1878-1969 .... CAP-1
Earlier sketch in CA 9-10
Noth, Martin D. 1902-1968 .... CAP-2
Earlier sketch in CA 21-22
Nothing Venture
See Finney, Humphrey S.
Nothof, Anne (F.) 1944- 194
Nothomb, Amelie 1967- 205
Notker Balbulus c. 840-912 .... DLB 148
Notker III of Saint Gall c. 950-1022 ... DLB 148
Notker von Zwiefalten (?)-1095 .... DLB 148
Notlep, Robert
See Pelton, Robert W(ayne)
Notley, Alice 1945- CANR-85
Brief entry 124
Earlier sketch in CA 154
See also CAAS 27
See also CP 7
See also CWP
Noto, Lore(nzo) 1923-2002 134
Obituary 207
Nott, David 1928- 45-48
Nott, Kathleen Cecilia 1905-1999 ...... CANR-3
Obituary 177
Earlier sketch in CA 1-4R
See also CN 1, 2
See also CP 1, 2
Notterman, Joseph M(elvin) 1923- 17-20R
Nottingham, Elizabeth K(ristine)
1900-1994 93-96
Obituary 198
Nottingham, William Jesse 1927- 25-28R
Notz, Rebecca Love 1888-1974
Obituary 104
Nourbese Philip, M(arlene)
See Philip, M(arlene) Nourbese
Nourie, Alan (Raymond) 1942- 138
Nourie, Barbara (Livingston) 1947- 138
Nourissier, Francois 1927- 81-84
Nourse, Alan E(dward) 1928-1992 ... CANR-84
Obituary 145
Earlier sketches in CA 1-4R, CANR-3, 21, 45
See also CLR 33
See also DLB 8
See also SATA 48
See also SFW 4
Nourse, Edwin G(riswold) 1883-1974
Obituary 49-52
Nourse, Hugh O(liver) 1933-
Brief entry 107
Nourse, James G(regory) 1947- 105
Nourse, Joan Thellusson 1921- 9-12R
Nourse, Mary Augusta 1880(?)-1971
Obituary 33-36R
Nourse, Robert Eric Martin 1938- 21-24R
Nouveau, Arthur
See Whitcomb, Ian
Nouwen, Henri J(osef Machiel)
1932-1996 73-76
Obituary 153
Nova, Craig 1945- CANR-127
Earlier sketches in CA 45-48, CANR-2, 53
See also CLC 7, 31
Novacek, Michael 1948- 216
Novack, Cynthia (Jean) 1947-1996 235
Novack, Evelyn Reed 1906(?)-1979
Obituary 85-88
Novack, George (Edward)
1905-1992 .... CANR-47
Obituary 139
Earlier sketch in CA 49-52
Novak, Barbara 97-100
Novak, Bogdan C(yril) 1919- 33-36R
Novak, Brenda S. 1964- 221
Novak, Dagmar 1937- 214
Novak, David 1941- 93-96
Novak, Jane Dailey 1917- 105
Novak, Joe
See Novak, Joseph
Novak, Joseph
See Kosinski, Jerzy (Nikodem)
Novak, Joseph 1898-1982 .... CAP-1
Earlier sketch in CA 11-12
Novak, Karen 1958- 216
Novak, Lorna 1927- 17-20R
Novak, Matt 1962- CANR-134
Earlier sketch in CA 125
See also SATA 60, 104
See also SATA-Brief 52
Novak, Maximillian E(rwin) 1930- ... CANR-12
Earlier sketch in CA 33-36R
Novak, Michael 1933- CANR-119
Earlier sketches in CA 1-4R, CANR-1, 30
Novak, Michael Paul 1935- 49-52
Novak, Robert
See Levinson, Leonard
Novak, Robert D(avid) 1931- CANR-97
Earlier sketches in CA 13-16R, CANR-12
Novak, Rose 1940- CANR-22
Earlier sketch in CA 105
Novak, Slobodan 1924- 198
See also DLB 181
Novak, Stephen R(obert) 1922- 85-88
Novak, Vjenceslav 1859-1905 .... DLB 147
Novak, William (Arnold) 1948- CANR-26
Earlier sketch in CA 93-96
Novakovich, Josip 1956- 149
See also DLB 244
Novalis 1772-1801 .... CDWLB 2
See also DLB 90
See also EW 5
See also RGWL 2, 3
Novaro, Mario 1868-1944 .... DLB 114
Novarr, David 1917-1987 .... 17-20R
Obituary 197
Novas, Himilce 1944- 156
Novas Calvo, Lino 1905-1983 .... DLB 145
See also EWL 3
See also HW 1
Nove, Alec 1915-1994 .... CANR-76
Obituary 145
Earlier sketches in CA 1-4R, CANR-3
Novelli, Florence 1931- 112
Novelli, Luca 1947- .... SATA 61
Novello, Don 1943- CANR-44
Earlier sketch in CA 107
Noventa, Giacomo 1898-1960
See Ca'Zorci, Giacomo
See also DLB 114
Nover, Barnet 1899-1973
Obituary 41-44R
Noverr, Douglas A(rthur) 1942- 102
Novick, David 1906-1991 .... 33-36R
Obituary 196
Novick, Julius Lerner 1939- 103
Novick, Marian 1951- 123
Novick, Paul 1891-1989
Obituary 130
Novick, Peter 1934- 188
See also CLC 164
Novick, Sheldon M. 1941- 144
Novik, Mary 1945- 61-64
Novikov, Nikolai Ivanovich
1744-1818 .... DLB 150
Novins, Stuart 1914(?)-1989
Obituary 130
Novis, Emile
See Weil, Simone (Adolphine)
Novitski, Joseph (W. D.) 1940- 124
Novitz, Charles R. 1934- 69-72
Novitz, David 1945- 139
Novo, Salvador 1904-1974 131
Obituary 110
See also EWL 3
See also HW 1
Novoa, John David Bruce
See Bruce-Novoa, Juan D.
Novoa, Juan Bruce
See Bruce-Novoa, Juan D.
Novogrod, R(eevan) Joseph 1916- 29-32R
Novomesky, Laco
See Novomesky, Ladislav
See also DLB 215
See also EWL 3
Novomesky, Ladislav 1904-1976
Obituary 69-72
See also Novomesky, Laco
Novotny, Ann M. 1936-1982 .... CANR-77
Obituary 108
Earlier sketch in CA 25-28R
Novotny, Fritz 1903-1983(?) CANR-18
Earlier sketch in CA 65-68
Novotny, Louise Miller 1889-1987 .... CAP-2
Obituary 196
Earlier sketch in CA 23-24
Novy, Marianne (Lucille) 1945- 118
Nowacki, Walenty 1906-2000 .... 37-40R
Nowak, Jan 1913- 143
Nowak, Mariette 1941- 102
Nowak, Mark 1964- 191
Nowakowski, Marek 1935- 119
Nowell, Elizabeth Cameron CANR-1
Earlier sketch in CA 1-4R
See also SATA 12
Nowlan, Alden (Albert) 1933-1983 .... CANR-5
Earlier sketch in CA 9-12R
See also CLC 15
See also CP 1, 2
See also DAC
See also DAM MST
See also DLB 53
See also PFS 12
Nowlan, James Dunlap 1941-
Brief entry 105
Nowlan, Philip Francis 1888-1940 164
Brief entry 108
See also SFW 4
Nowlan, Robert Anthony, Jr. 1934- .. CANR-32
Earlier sketch in CA 113
Nowlis, Helen H(oward) 1913-1986
Obituary 197
Brief entry 111
Nowra, Louis 1950- 195
See also CD 5, 6
See also IDTP
Noxon, James Herbert 1924- 85-88
Noyce, Gaylord B. 1926- CANR-53
Earlier sketches in CA 37-40R, CANR-13, 29
Noyes, Alfred 1880-1958 188
Brief entry 104
See also DLB 20
See also EXPP
See also FANT
See also PC 27
See also PFS 4
See also RGEL 2
See also TCLC 7
Noyes, Charles Edmund 1904-1972 ...... 37-40R
Noyes, Crosby S. 1825-1908 .... DLB 23
Noyes, Crosby S(tuart) 1921-1988
Obituary 125
Noyes, Crosby Stuart 1825-1908 204
Noyes, David 1898(?)-1981
Obituary 104
Noyes, Deborah
See Wayshak, Deborah Noyes
Noyes, Gary 1943- 219
Noyes, Henry (Halsey) 1910- 133
Noyes, James H(oyt) 1927- 118
Noyes, Jeanice W. 1914-1999 .... 25-28R
Noyes, Joan 1935- 115
Noyes, Kathryn Johnston 1930- 17-20R
Noyes, Martha H. 1949- 192
Noyes, Morgan Phelps 1891-1972 .... CAP-1
Obituary 37-40R
Earlier sketch in CA 11-12
Noyes, Nell Braly 1921- 37-40R
Noyes, Nicholas 1647-1717 .... DLB 24
Noyes, Peter R. 1930- 49-52
Noyes, Russell 1901-1980 .... 25-28R
Obituary 197
Noyes, Stanley 1924- CANR-35
Earlier sketches in CA 45-48, CANR-1
Noyes, Theodore W(illiams) 1858-1946 187
See also DLB 29
Noyes-Kane, Dorothy 1906-2000 .... CAP-1
Earlier sketch in CA 13-14
Noyle, Ken(neth Alfred Edward) 1922- 85-88
Nozick, Martin 1917- 37-40R
Nozick, Robert 1938-2002 .... CANR-120
Obituary 203
Earlier sketch in CA 61-64
See also DLB 279
Nriagu, Jerome O. 1942- 135
Nsarkoh, J. K(wasi) 1931- 13-16R
Ntsoni, Marcel 1947-1995
See Tansi, Sony Labou
Nu'ayma, Mikhail
See Naimy, Mikhail
See also EWL 3
Nuccetelli, Susana 1954- 220
Nucera, Marisa Lonette 1959- 17-20R
Nuchtern, Jean 1939- 25-28R
Nuckolls, James L(awton) 1938-1987
Obituary 123
Nudel, Adele Rice 1927-1998 124
Nudel, Ida 1931- 134
Nudelman, Jerrold 1942- 33-36R
Nuechterlein, Donald Edwin 1925- CANR-1
Earlier sketch in CA 1-4R
Nuelle, Helen S(hearman)
1923-1994 .... CANR-12
Earlier sketch in CA 61-64
Nuernberger, Phil 1942- CANR-35
Earlier sketch in CA 114
Nuessel, Frank H(enry) 1943- CANR-117
Earlier sketches in CA 111, CANR-31, 56
Nuetzel, Charles (Alexander) 1934- 105
Nugent, Bruce
See Nugent, Richard Bruce
Nugent, (Donald) Christopher 1930- 139
Nugent, Donald G(ene) 1930- 45-48
Nugent, Elliott (John) 1899-1980 .... 5-8R
Obituary 101
Nugent, Frances Roberts 1904-1964(?) 5-8R
Nugent, Frank S(tanley) 1908-1965 179
See also DLB 44
See also IDFW 3, 4
Nugent, Jeffrey B(ishop) 1936- 93-96
Nugent, John Peer 1930- 13-16R
Nugent, Nancy 1938- CANR-16
Earlier sketch in CA 65-68
Nugent, Neill 1947- 133
Nugent, Nicholas 1949- .... SATA 73
Nugent, Richard Bruce 1906(?)-1987 125
See also BW 1
See also DLB 51
See also GLL 2
See also HR 1:3
Nugent, Robert 1920- 61-64
Nugent, Rory 183
Nugent, Tom 1943- 49-52
Nugent, Vincent Joseph 1913-2002 ...... 41-44R
Nugent, Walter T(erry) K(ing) 1935- . CANR-90
Earlier sketches in CA 5-8R, CANR-5
Nuland, Sherwin B. 1930- CANR-136
Earlier sketch in CA 173
Null, Gary CANR-122
Earlier sketches in CA 65-68, CANR-17
Nulman, Macy 1923- 57-60
Nulty, William H(arry) 1932- 136
Numbers, Ronald L(eslie) 1942- CANR-18
Earlier sketch in CA 101
Numeroff, Laura Joffe 1953- CANR-118
Earlier sketches in CA 106, CANR-58
See also CLR 85
See also MAICYA 2
See also SATA 28, 90, 142
Nummi, Seppo (Antero Yrjoepoika) 1932-1981
Obituary 108
Nunan, Desmond J. 1927- 17-20R
Nunes, Claude 1924- 134
Brief entry 112
Nunes, Lygia Bojunga 1932- CANR-138
Earlier sketch in CA 142
See also Bojunga, Lygia
See also SATA 75, 154
Nunes, Rhoda (Gwylleth) 1938- 189
Brief entry 113
Nunez, Ana Rosa 1926- CANR-14
Earlier sketch in CA 69-72
Nunez, Elizabeth 1944- 223
Nunez, Sigrid 1951- .... DLB 312
Nunez-Harrell, Elizabeth
See Nunez, Elizabeth
Nunis, Doyce B(lackman), Jr. 1924- . CANR-42
Earlier sketches in CA 5-8R, CANR-3, 19
Nunley, Maggie Rennert
See Rennert, Maggie
Nunn, Frederick M. 1937- 33-36R
Nunn, G(odfrey) Raymond 1918- CANR-55
Earlier sketches in CA 33-36R, CANR-13
Nunn, Henry L(ightfoot) 1878-1972
Obituary 37-40R
Nunn, John 1955- 115
Nunn, Kem 159
See also CLC 34
Nunn, Laura (Donna) Silverstein
1968- .... SATA 124
Nunn, Marshall E(arl) 1928- 112
Nunn, Pamela Gerrish 1953- 202
Nunn, Walter (Harris) 1942- CANR-23
Earlier sketch in CA 45-48
Nunn, William Curtis 1908-2001 .... CANR-1
Earlier sketch in CA 1-4R
Nunnally, Tiina 1952- CANR-144
Earlier sketches in CA 158, CANR-73
Nunnerley, (Gould) David 1947- 45-48
Nuquist, Andrew E(dgerton) 1905-1975
Obituary 61-64
Nuraini
See Sim, Katharine (Thomasset)
Nurcombe, Barry 1933- 65-68
Nurenberg, Thelma
See Greenhaus, Thelma Nurenberg
Nurge, Ethel 1920- 33-36R
Nurkse, D(ennis) 1949- 217
Nurmi, Martin Karl 1920- CANR-17
Earlier sketch in CA 1-4R
Nurnberg, Maxwell 1897-1984 .... CANR-76
Obituary 114
Earlier sketches in CA 5-8R, CANR-2
See also SATA 27
See also SATA-Obit 41
Nurnberg, Walter 1907-1991 .... 13-16R
Nurse, Malcolm Ivan Meredith 1902-1959
Brief entry 119
Nurse, Peter H(arold) 1926- 9-12R
Nusbaum, N. Richard
See Nash, N. Richard
Nusbaum, Rosemary 1907-1990 113
Obituary 197
Nusic, Branislav 1864-1938 .... CDWLB 4
See also DLB 147
See also EWL 3
Nussbaum, Aaron 1910-1981 .... CANR-76
Obituary 104
Earlier sketch in CA 49-52
Nussbaum, Al(bert F.) 1934- 85-88
Nussbaum, Martha Craven 1947- ... CANR-102
Earlier sketch in CA 134
See also CLC 203
Nussbaum, Paul David 1963- 169
Nussbaumer, Paul (Edmund) 1934- 93-96
See also SATA 16
Nusser, J(ames) L(ivingston) 1925- 1-4R
Nute, Grace Lee 1895-1990
Obituary 131
Nute, Kevin 1958- 145
Nutini, Hugo G(ino) 1928- CANR-88
Brief entry 109
Earlier sketch in CA 155
Nutt, Grady 1934- 97-100
Nutt, Ken 1951- .... MAICYA 2
See also MAICYAS 1
See also SATA 97, 163
Nutt, Paul C. 1939- CANR-127
Earlier sketch in CA 142
Nuttall, A(nthony) D(avid) 1937- CANR-11
Earlier sketch in CA 21-24R
Nuttall, Geoffrey Fillingham 1911- ... CANR-25
Earlier sketches in CA 13-16R, CANR-10
Nuttall, Jeff 1933-2004 .... CANR-14
Obituary 223
Earlier sketch in CA 29-32R
See also CP 1, 2
Nuttall, Kenneth 1907- 17-20R
Nuttall-Smith, Margaret Emily Noel
1919- CANR-45
Earlier sketch in CA 104
See also Fortnum, Peggy
Nutter, G(ilbert) Warren 1923-1979 ... CANR-2
Obituary 85-88
Earlier sketch in CA 1-4R
Nuttgens, Patrick 1930-2004 128
Obituary 226

Nutting, (Harold) Anthony 1920-1999 .... CANR-7
Obituary 177
Earlier sketch in CA 5-8R
Nutting, Patricia Fink 1926- 129
Nutting, Willis D(wight) 1900-1975 .... CAP-2
Earlier sketch in CA 25-28
Nutzle, Futzie
See Kleinsmith, Bruce John
Nuwer, Hank
See Nuwer, Henry Joseph
Nuwer, Henry Joseph 1946- CANR-102
Earlier sketches in CA 128, CANR-57
Nuwere, Ejovi 1981(?)- 216
Nuygen, Mathieu 1967- .... SATA 80
Nuytten, Bruno 1945- 153
See also IDFW 3, 4
Nwagboso, Maxwell Nkem 171
Nwanko, Agwuncha A.
See Nwankwo, Arthur Agwuncha
Nwankwo, Arthur Agwuncha 1942- 181
Nwankwo, Nkem 1936- 65-68
See also BW 2
Nwankwo, Victor 1944-2002 226
Nwapa, Flora (Nwanzuruaha) 1931-1993 .... CANR-83
Earlier sketch in CA 143
See also BLCS
See also BW 2
See also CDWLB 3
See also CLC 133
See also CWRI 5
See also DLB 125
See also EWL 3
See also WLIT 2
Nwoauau, Edwin Ifeanyichukwu 1933- 17-20R
Nyabongo, Akiki K. 1905-1975
Obituary 61-64
Nyad, Diana 1949- 136
Brief entry 111
Nyagumbo, Maurice (Tapfumaneyi) 1924-1989
Obituary 128
Nyamfukudza, S(tanley) 1951- 169
See also BW 3
Nyanaponika 1901-1994 .... CAP-1
Earlier sketch in CA 9-10
Nybakken, Elizabeth I. 1940- 114
Nybakken, Oscar Edward 1904-1997 93-96
Obituary 197
Nyberg, David (Alan) 1943- 107
Nyberg, Kathleen Neill 1919- 21-24R
Nyberg, (Everett Wayne) Morgan 1944- 127
See also SATA 87
Nyce, (Nellie) Helene von Strecker 1885-1969 .... SATA 19
Nyce, Vera 1862-1925 .... SATA 19
Nye, Andrea 1939- 189
Nye, Bill
See Nye, Edgar Wilson
Nye, Doug(las Charles) 1945-
Brief entry 114
Nye, Edgar Wilson 1850-1896 .... DLB 11, 23, 186
Nye, F(rancis) Ivan 1918- CANR-21
Earlier sketches in CA 9-12R, CANR-6
Nye, Hermes 1908-1981 .... CAP-2
Obituary 182
Earlier sketch in CA 19-20
Nye, Joseph S(amuel), Jr. 1937- CANR-93
Earlier sketches in CA 25-28R, CANR-12, 35
Nye, Loyal 1921- 106
Nye, Miriam (Maurine Hawthorn) Baker 1918-1999 85-88
Nye, Naomi Shihab 1952- CANR-126
Earlier sketches in CA 146, CANR-70
See also AAYA 27
See also AMWS 13
See also CLR 59
See also CP 7
See also CSW
See also CWP
See also DLB 120
See also MAICYA 2
See also MTFW 2005
See also SATA 86, 147
Nye, Nelson C(oral) 1907-1997 .... CANR-77
Obituary 176
Earlier sketches in CA 5-8R, CANR-4
See also TCWW 1, 2
Nye, Robert 1939- CANR-107
Earlier sketches in CA 33-36R, CANR-29, 67
See also BRWS 10
See also CLC 13, 42
See also CN 1, 2, 3, 4, 5, 6, 7
See also CP 1, 2, 3, 4, 5, 6, 7
See also CWRI 5
See also DAM NOV
See also DLB 14, 271
See also FANT
See also HGG
See also MTCW 1
See also RHW
See also SATA 6
Nye, Robert D(onald) 1934- 73-76
Nye, Robert Evans 1911- CANR-1
Earlier sketch in CA 1-4R
Nye, Russel B(laine) 1913-1993 .... CANR-76
Obituary 142
Earlier sketches in CA 1-4R, CANR-4
Nye, Simon (Beresford) 1958- CANR-75
Earlier sketch in CA 131
Nye, Vernice Trousdale 1913-1996 .... CANR-1
Obituary 174
Earlier sketch in CA 1-4R
Nye, Wilbur S. 1898-1970 .... CANR-15
Obituary 103
Earlier sketch in CA 1-4R
Nyembezi, C(yril) L(incoln) S(ibusiso) 1919-2000 218
Nyenhuis, Jacob E(ugene) 1935- CANR-137
Brief entry 117
Nyerere, Julius K(ambarage) 1922-1999 125
Obituary 187
Brief entry 105
See also BW 2
Nygaard, Anita 1934- 65-68
Nygaard, Norman E. 1897-1971 .... CANR-2
Earlier sketch in CA 1-4R
Nygard, Roald 1935- 103
Nygren, Anders T(heodor) S(amuel) 1890-1978 .... 9-12R
Nyhart, Nina 1934- 135
Nyiszli, Miklos 1901-1956
Nyka-Niliunas, Alfonsas 1919- .... DLB 220
Nykoruk, Barbara (Christine) 1949-
Brief entry 115
Nykvist, Sven 1922- .... IDFW 3, 4
Nylander, Carl 1932- 33-36R
Nylander, Jane C. 1938- CANR-134
Earlier sketch in CA 143
Nylund, Eric S. 1964- 169
Nynych, Stephanie J.
See Caulder, Colline
Nyquist, Ewald B(erger) 1914-1987
Obituary 171
Brief entry 113
Nyquist, Richard Allen 1928- 232
Nyquist, Thomas E. 1931- 41-44R
Nyren, Dorothy Elizabeth 1927- CANR-5
Earlier sketch in CA 1-4R
Nyren, Karl 1921-1988
Obituary 126
Nyro, Laura 1947-1997 194
See also CLC 17
Nystrom, Carolyn 1940- CANR-97
Earlier sketches in CA 114, CANR-37
See also SAAS 67, 130
Nystrom, David P. 1959- 209
Nystrom, Debra 1954- 194
Nzekwu, Onuora 1928- .... BW 2
Nzimiro, Ikenna 1927- CANR-2
Earlier sketch in CA 45-48

O

O(rdonez), Jaime E(dmundo) Rodriguez
See Rodriguez O(rdonez), Jaime E(dmundo)
Oak, Liston M. 1895-1970
Obituary 104
Oakes, Andy 1952- 233
Oakes, Elizabeth H. 1964- 201
See also SATA 132
Oakes, James 1953- 107
Oakes, John Bertram 1913-2001 .... 13-16R
Obituary 195
Oakes, Meredith 1946- 234
See also CD 5, 6
Oakes, Philip (Barlow) 1928- 178
Earlier sketches in CA 53-56, CANR-4, 29
Autobiographical Essay in 178
See also CAAS 25
See also CP 1, 2, 3, 4, 5, 6, 7
Oakes, Urian 1631(?)-1681 .... DLB 24
Oakes, Vanya 1909-1983 .... CANR-76
Obituary 111
Earlier sketch in CA 33-36R
See also SATA 6
See also SATA-Obit 37
Oakeshott, Michael (Joseph) 1901-1990 .... CANR-64
Obituary 133
Earlier sketches in CA 1-4R, CANR-27
Oakeshott, Walter (Fraser) 1903-1987 .... CANR-76
Obituary 123
Earlier sketch in CA 13-16R
Oakes Smith, Elizabeth
See Smith, Elizabeth Oakes (Prince)
See also DLB 239, 243
Oakie, Jack
See Offield, Lewis Delaney
Oakland, Thomas David 1939- 53-56
Oakley, Allen 1943- CANR-53
Earlier sketch in CA 126
Oakley, Ann (Rosamund) 1944- CANR-106
Earlier sketches in CA 57-60, CANR-6, 25, 50
See also FW
Oakley, Barry K(ingham) 1931- 104
See also CN 2, 3
Oakley, Charles Allen 1900-1993 108
Oakley, Don(ald G.) 1927- 29-32R
See also SATA 8
Oakley, Eric Gilbert 1916- 9-12R
Oakley, Francis (Christopher) 1931- 13-16R
Oakley, Giles (Francis) 1946- 103
Oakley, Graham 1929- CANR-85
Earlier sketches in CA 106, CANR-38, 54
See also CLR 7
See also CWRI 5
See also MAICYA 1, 2
See also SATA 30, 84
Oakley, Helen (McKelvey) 1906- 17-20R
See also SATA 10
Oakley, J. Ronald 1941- 121
Oakley, John H(enry) 1949- CANR-122
Earlier sketch in CA 165
Oakley, Josephine 1903(?)-1978
Obituary 81-84
Oakley, K. P.
See Oakley, Kenneth Page
Oakley, Kenneth P.
See Oakley, Kenneth Page
Oakley, Kenneth Page 1911-1981 122
Obituary 108
Oakley, Mary Ann B. 1940- 45-48
Oakley, Stewart P(hilip) 1931- CANR-87
Earlier sketch in CA 21-24R
Oakley, Violet 1874-1961 219
See also DLB 188
Oakman, Barbara F(rances) 1931- 57-60
Oaks, Dallin H(arris) 1932- 25-28R
Oaksey, John 1929- 105
Oana, Katherine 1929- 108
See also SATA 53
See also SATA-Brief 37
Oates, Eddie H. 1943- .... SATA 88
Oates, Jeannette 1912(?)-1984
Obituary 112
Oates, John (Frederick) 1944- 69-72
Oates, John F. 1934- 17-20R
Oates, Joyce Carol 1938- CANR-129
Earlier sketches in CA 5-8R, CANR-25, 45, 74, 113
Interview in CANR-25
See also AAYA 15, 52
See also AITN 1
See also AMWS 2
See also BEST 89:2
See also BPFB 2
See also BYA 11
See also CDALB 1968-1988
See also CLC 1, 2, 3, 6, 9, 11, 15, 19, 33, 52, 108, 134
See also CN 1, 2, 3, 4, 5, 6, 7
See also CP 7
See also CPW
See also CWP
See also DA
See also DA3
See also DAB
See also DAC
See also DAM MST, NOV, POP
See also DLB 2, 5, 130
See also DLBY 1981
See also EWL 3
See also EXPS
See also FL 1:6
See also FW
See also GL 3
See also HGG
See also LAIT 4
See also MAL 5
See also MAWW
See also MTCW 1, 2
See also MTFW 2005
See also NFS 8
See also RGAL 4
See also RGSF 2
See also SATA 159
See also SSC 6, 70
See also SSFS 1, 8, 17
See also SUFW 2
See also TUS
See also WLC
Oates, Stephen B(aery) 1936- CANR-74
Earlier sketches in CA 9-12R, CANR-4, 26, 50
Interview in CANR-26
See also MTCW 2
See also MTFW 2005
See also SATA 59
Oates, Wallace Eugene 1937- CANR-14
Earlier sketch in CA 37-40R
Oates, Wayne Edward 1917-1999 .... CANR-88
Obituary 187
Earlier sketch in CA 85-88
Oates, Whitney J(ennings) 1904-1973 .... CANR-3
Obituary 45-48
Earlier sketch in CA 5-8R
Oathout, John D(avid) 1913-1997 111
Obituary 171
Oatley, Keith 1939- 45-48
Oatman, Eric F(urber) 1939- CANR-19
Earlier sketch in CA 103
Oatts, Balfour
See Oatts, Lewis Balfour
Oatts, Henry Augustus 1898-1980 .... CANR-76
Obituary 103
Earlier sketch in CA 5-8R
Oatts, Lewis Balfour 1902-1992 110
Oba, Minako 1930- 196
See also Oba Minako
Obach, Robert 1939- 106
Obafemi, Olu 1950- .... CD 5, 6
Obaldia, Rene de 1918- 133
Brief entry 116
O'Ballance, Edgar 1918- CANR-7
Earlier sketch in CA 5-8R
Obama, Barack (A.) 1961- 236
Oba Minako
See Oba, Minako
See also DLB 182
See also EWL 3
O'Banion, Terry 1936- 33-36R
O'Bannon, Dan(iel Thomas) 1946- 138
O'Barr, Jean (Fox) 1942- 163
O'Barr, William M(cAlston) 1942- 49-52
Obed, Ellen Bryan 1944- .... SATA 74
O'Beirne, T(homas) H(ay) 1915-1982 .... CANR-76
Obituary 120
Earlier sketch in CA 17-20R
Obejas, Achy 1956- 171
See also HW 2
See also LLW
Obele, Norma Taylor 1933- 104
Obenchain, Anne DeCroes 1914(?)-1984
Obituary 112
Obenhaus, Victor 1903-1994 .... CANR-76
Obituary 145
Earlier sketches in CAP-1, CA 13-14
Ober, Frederick Albion 1849-1913 201
See also DLB 189
Ober, Richard 1960- 150
Ober, Stuart Alan 1946- 103
Ober, Warren U(pton) 1925- 13-16R
Ober, William 1920-1993 .... DLBY 1993
Oberdeck, Kathryn J. 228
Oberdorf, Charles (Donnell) 1941- 126
Oberdorfer, Don 1931- CANR-81
Earlier sketch in CA 129
Oberg, Alcestis R. 1949- 128
Oberg, Arthur K. 1938-1977
Obituary 112
Oberg, James E(dward) 1944- CANR-117
Earlier sketches in CA 108, CANR-26, 56
Oberg, Michael Leroy 224
Oberhansli, Trudi
See Schlapbach-Oberhansli, Trudi
Oberhelman, Harley D(ean) 1928- 53-56
Oberholtzer, Ellis Paxson 1868-1936 183
See also DLB 47
Oberholtzer, Peter
See Brannon, William T.
Oberholtzer, W(alter) Dwight 1939- 101
Oberholzer, Emil, Jr. 1926(?)-1981
Obituary 102
Oberle, Joseph 1958- 136
See also SATA 69
Oberman, Heiko Augustinus 1930-2001 .... CANR-25
Obituary 194
Earlier sketches in CA 5-8R, CANR-7
Oberman, Sheldon 1949-2004 .... CANR-120
Obituary 226
Earlier sketch in CA 152
See also CLR 54
See also SAAS 26
See also SATA 85
See also SATA-Essay 114
See also SATA-Obit 153
Obermann, C. Esco 1904-1999 53-56
Obermayer, Herman J. 1924- 65-68
Obermeyer, Barrett John 1937- 5-8R
Obermeyer, Henry 1899-1990 .... CAP-2
Earlier sketch in CA 29-32
Obermeyer, Marion Barrett 5-8R
Oberndorf, Charles G. 1959- 165
See also SFW 4
Oberschall, Antony R. 1936- 97-100
Obert, Genevieve 1959- 195
Obert, John C. 1924-1987
Obituary 122
Oberth, Hermann Julius 1894-1989
Obituary 113
Obets, Bob .... TCWW 1, 2
Obey, Andre 1892-1975 97-100
Obituary 57-60
Obeyesekere, Ranjini D. 1933- 207
Obichere, Boniface Ihewunwa 1932- 41-44R
Obiechina, Emmanuel Nwanonye 1933- CANR-15
Earlier sketch in CA 41-44R
Obika, Akili Addae 1969- CANR-87
Earlier sketch in CA 150
O'Biso, Carol (Anne) 1953- 133
Obligado, Lilian (Isabel) 1931- 134
See also SATA 61
See also SATA-Brief 45
Oboe, Peter
See Jacobs, Walter Darnell
Obojski, Robert 1929- CANR-103
Earlier sketches in CA 108, CANR-24, 49
Obolensky, Dimitri 1918-2001 .... CANR-25
Obituary 200
Earlier sketch in CA 45-48
Oboler, Arch 1909(?)-1987 .... CANR-88
Obituary 122
Brief entry 105
Oboler, Eli M(artin) 1915-1983 .... CANR-76
Obituary 110
Earlier sketches in CA 57-60, CANR-6
Oboro, Harunoya
See Yuzo, Tsubouchi
Obourn, Ellsworth Scott 1897-1972 .... CAP-2
Obituary 174
Earlier sketch in CA 17-18
O'Boyle, Thomas F(rancis) 1955- 187
Obradovic, Dositej 1740(?)-1811 .... DLB 147
Obradovic, Nadezda 1936- 171
O'Brady, Frederic Michel Maurice 1903- CANR-3
Earlier sketch in CA 9-12R
Obrant, Susan 1946- .... SATA 11
O'Brawes, Tarnel
See La Barre, Weston
Obrecht, James Carlton
See Obrecht, Jas
Obrecht, Jas 1952- 135
Obregon, Mauricio 1921-1998 .... CANR-110
Earlier sketches in CA 45-48, CANR-1
Obrestad, Tor 1938- 190
O'Brian, E. G.
See Clarke, Arthur C(harles)
O'Brian, Frank
See Garfield, Brian (Francis Wynne)
O'Brian, Jack 1914-2000 103
Obituary 192
O'Brian, John Lord 1874-1973
Obituary 41-44R

Cumulative Index 433 O'Connor

O'Brian, Patrick 1914-2000 .... CANR-74
Obituary 187
Earlier sketch in CA 144
See also AAYA 55
See also CLC 152
See also CPW
See also MTCW 2
See also MTFW 2005
See also RHW
O'Briant, Walter H(erbert) 1937- 25-28R
O'Brien, Andrew William 1910- CANR-17
Earlier sketch in CA 25-28R
O'Brien, Andy
See O'Brien, Andrew William
O'Brien, Anne Sibley 1952- 122
See also SATA 53, 80
See also SATA-Brief 48
O'Brien, Charlotte Grace 1845-1909 201
See also DLB 240
O'Brien, Conor Cruise 1917- CANR-120
Earlier sketches in CA 65-68, CANR-47
O'Brien, Cyril C(ornelius) 1906-1994 53-56
Obituary 176
O'Brien, D(enis) P(atrick) 1939- 158
O'Brien, Dan(iel) 1947- CANR-109
Earlier sketch in CA 160
O'Brien, Darcy 1939-1998 .... CANR-59
Obituary 167
Earlier sketches in CA 21-24R, CANR-8
See also CLC 11
O'Brien, David J(oseph) 1938- CANR-87
Earlier sketch in CA 25-28R
O'Brien, David M(ichael) 1951- 143
O'Brien, Dean D.
See Binder, Otto O(scar)
O'Brien, Des(mond John) 1930- 114
O'Brien, Edna 1932- CANR-102
Earlier sketches in CA 1-4R, CANR-6, 41, 65
See also BRWS 5
See also CDBLB 1960 to Present
See also CLC 3, 5, 8, 13, 36, 65, 116
See also CN 1, 2, 3, 4, 5, 6, 7
See also DA3
See also DAM NOV
See also DLB 14, 231, 319
See also EWL 3
See also FW
See also MTCW 1, 2
See also MTFW 2005
See also RGSF 2
See also SSC 10, 77
See also WLIT 4
O'Brien, Edward C.
See Schrodt, Philip A(ndrew)
O'Brien, Elmer 1911- 17-20R
O'Brien, Esse Forrester 1895(?)-1975
Obituary 61-64
See also SATA-Obit 30
O'Brien, Fitz-James 1828-1862 .... DLB 74
See also RGAL 4
See also SUFW
O'Brien, Flann
See O Nuallain, Brian
See also BRWS 2
See also CLC 1, 4, 5, 7, 10, 47
See also DLB 231
See also EWL 3
See also RGEL 2
O'Brien, Frances (Kelly) 1906-1981 ...... CAP-2
Earlier sketch in CA 17-18
O'Brien, Francis J(oseph) 1903- 81-84
O'Brien, Geoffrey 1948- 106
O'Brien, George 1945- CANR-74
Earlier sketch in CA 131
O'Brien, George Dennis 1931- 103
O'Brien, (Warren) Greg(ory) 1966- 235
O'Brien, Gregory (C., Jr.) 1945- 117
O'Brien, Gregory 1961- 191
O'Brien, J(ohn) W(ilfrid) 1931- 13-16R
O'Brien, Jacqueline Robin 1949- 105
O'Brien, James A(loysius) 1936-
Brief entry 110
O'Brien, James J. 1929- CANR-9
Earlier sketch in CA 17-20R
O'Brien, John 1943- 222
O'Brien, John 1953- 132
O'Brien, John Anthony 1893-1980 ..... CANR-1
Obituary 97-100
Earlier sketch in CA 1-4R
O'Brien, John J(oseph) 1937- 111
O'Brien, Justin (McCortney)
1906-1968 .... CANR-87
Earlier sketches in CA 5-8R, CANR-5
O'Brien, K.
See O'Brien, Katherine
O'Brien, Kate 1897-1974 .... CANR-85
Obituary 53-56
Earlier sketch in CA 93-96
See also DLB 15
See also FW
See also RGEL 2
See also RHW
See also TCLE 1:2
O'Brien, Katherine 1915-1982
Obituary 118
O'Brien, Kevin P. 1922- 53-56
O'Brien, Lawrence Francis 1917-1990 57-60
O'Brien, Lee 1948- 61-64
O'Brien, Lucy 1961- CANR-112
Earlier sketch in CA 152
O'Brien, Margaret 204
O'Brien, Marian P(lowman) 1915- 53-56
O'Brien, Maureen 1943- 216
O'Brien, Michael 1943- 126
O'Brien, Michael 1948- 121
O'Brien, Michael J. 1920- 25-28R
O'Brien, (William Joseph) Pat(rick) 1899-1983
Obituary 111
O'Brien, Pat 1948- 231
O'Brien, Patrick 1932- 21-24R
O'Brien, Peggy
See O'Brien, Margaret
O'Brien, Richard 1934- 73-76
O'Brien, Richard 1942- 124
See also CLC 17
O'Brien, Robert C.
See Conly, Robert Leslie
See also AAYA 6
See also CLR 2
O'Brien, Robert W(illiam) 1907- CANR-25
Earlier sketch in CA 45-48
O'Brien, Saliee
See Janas, Frankie-Lee
O'Brien, Sean 1952- CANR-83
Earlier sketch in CA 154
See also CP 7
O'Brien, Sister Mary Celine 1922- 21-24R
O'Brien, Thomas C(lement) 1938- 106
See also SATA 29
O'Brien, (William) Tim(othy)
1946- CANR-133
Earlier sketches in CA 85-88, CANR-40, 58
See also AAYA 16
See also AMWS 5
See also CDALBS
See also CLC 7, 19, 40, 103, 211
See also CN 5, 6, 7
See also CPW
See also DA3
See also DAM POP
See also DLB 152
See also DLBD 9
See also DLBY 1980
See also LATS 1:2
See also MAL 5
See also MTCW 2
See also MTFW 2005
See also RGAL 4
See also SSC 74
See also SSFS 5, 15
See also TCLE 1:2
O'Brien, Timothy (Brian) 1929- CANR-140
Earlier sketch in CA 172
O'Brien, Vincent 1916- 9-12R
O'Brien, William V(incent) 1923-2003 . 13-16R
Obituary 218
O'Brien, Willis H. 1886-1962 .... IDFW 3, 4
O'Broin, Leon 1902-1990 .... CANR-87
Earlier sketches in CA 61-64, CANR-8
O'Brynt, Jon
See Barnum, W(illiam) Paul
Observer
See Velikovsky, Immanuel
Obst, Frances Melanie 17-20R
Obst, Lynda (Rosen) 1950- 232
Obstfeld, Raymond 1952- CANR-127
Earlier sketch in CA 116
Obstfelder, Sigbjoern 1866-1900
Brief entry 123
See also TCLC 23
Oca, Marco Antonio Montes de
See Montes de Oca, Marco Antonio
O Cadhain, Mairtin 1905-1970 .... DLB 319
O'Callaghan, Denis F(rancis) 1931- 17-20R
O'Callaghan, Joseph F(rancis) 1928- 81-84
O'Callaghan, Julie 1954- 117
See also SATA 113
O'Callaghan, Sean 1954- 172
O'Callahan, Jay 1938- 152
See also SATA 88
Ocampo, Jose Antonio 1952- 235
Ocampo, Silvina 1906-1993 .... CANR-87
Earlier sketch in CA 131
See also CWW 2
See also HW 1
See also RGSF 2
Ocampo, Victoria 1891-1979 105
Obituary 85-88
See also HW 1
See also LAW
O'Carroll, Brendan 1955- 239
O'Carroll, Ryan
See Markun, Patricia Maloney
O'Casey, Brenda
See Haycraft, Anna (Margaret)
O'Casey, Eileen (Kathleen Reynolds)
1903-1995 133
Obituary 148
Brief entry 112
O'Casey, Sean 1880-1964 .... CANR-62
Earlier sketch in CA 89-92
See also BRW 7
See also CBD
See also CDBLB 1914-1945
See also CLC 1, 5, 9, 11, 15, 88
See also DA3
See also DAB
See also DAC
See also DAM DRAM, MST
See also DC 12
See also DFS 19
See also DLB 10
See also EWL 3
See also MTCW 1, 2
See also MTFW 2005
See also RGEL 2
See also TEA
See also WLCS
See also WLIT 4
O'Cathasaigh, Donal
See Casey, Daniel J(oseph)
O'Cathasaigh, Sean
See O'Casey, Sean
Occom, Samson 1723-1792 .... DLB 175
See also NNAL
Occomy, Marita (Odette) Bonner
1899(?)-1971 142
See also Bonner, Marita
See also BW 2
See also DFS 13
See also DLB 51, 228
Ocean, Julian
See de Mesne, Eugene (Frederick Peter Cheshire)
O Ceithearnaigh, Seumas
See Carney, James (Patrick)
Ochart (Torres), (Luz) Yvonne 1949- 193
Ochester, Ed(win Frank) 1939- CANR-51
Earlier sketches in CA 45-48, CANR-25
Ochiltree, Dianne 1953- .... SATA 117
Ochiltree, Paul
See Ochiltree, Thomas H.
Ochiltree, Thomas H. 1912-1993 77-80
Obituary 182
Ochoa, Enrique C(orrado) 1964- 200
Ochoa, Holly Byers 1951- 149
Ochojski, Paul M(aximilian)
1916-1983 .... CANR-20
Earlier sketch in CA 25-28R
Ochorowicz, Julian 1850-1917
Brief entry 114
Ochs, Adolph S(imon) 1858-1935 181
Brief entry 118
See also DLB 25
Ochs, Carol (Rebecca) 1939- CANR-107
Earlier sketches in CA 114, CANR-36
Ochs, Donovan J(oseph) 1938- 45-48
Ochs, Michael 1943- CANR-43
Earlier sketch in CA 119
Ochs, Phil(ip David) 1940-1976 185
Obituary 65-68
See also CLC 17
Ochs, Robert J. 1930- 29-32R
Ochs, Vanessa (L.) 1953- CANR-113
Earlier sketch in CA 134
Ochse, Orpha Caroline 1925- 93-96
Ochsenschalger, Edward L(loyd) 1932- . 17-20R
Ochsner, (Edward William) Alton
1896-1981 .... CANR-76
Obituary 105
Earlier sketch in CA 17-20R
Ochsner, Jeffrey Karl 1950- 111
Ochs-Oakes, George Washington
1861-1931 210
See also DLB 137
Ockenga, Harold John 1905-1985 ... CANR-76
Obituary 115
Earlier sketches in CA 1-4R, CANR-1
Ockenga, Starr 1938- 134
Ocker, Christopher (Michael) 1958- 227
Ockham, Joan Price
See Price, Joan
Ockham, William of 1285(?)-1347 ..... DLB 115
O'Clair, Robert M. 1923- 77-80
O'Clery, Helen (Gallagher) 1910- 9-12R
O'Collins, Gerald Glynn 1931- CANR-34
Earlier sketches in CA 85-88, CANR-15
O'Connell, Brian (Vincent) J(ohn) 1923-
Brief entry 113
O'Connell, Carol 1947- CANR-121
Earlier sketch in CA 152
See also CMW 4
O'Connell, Caroline 1953- 139
O'Connell, Daniel Patrick
1924-1979 .... CANR-25
Obituary 89-92
Earlier sketch in CA 29-32R
O'Connell, David 1940- 102
O'Connell, David F. 1953- 234
O'Connell, Frank 1892-1971 .... 5-8R
O'Connell, Jack 1959- CANR-129
Earlier sketch in CA 137
O'Connell, Jeffrey 1928- CANR-11
Earlier sketch in CA 25-28R
O'Connell, Jeremiah Joseph 1932- CANR-7
Earlier sketch in CA 13-16R
O'Connell, John James III 1921-1982
Obituary 107
O'Connell, Laurence J. 1945- 157
O'Connell, Margaret F(orster)
1935-1977 73-76
See also SATA 30
See also SATA-Obit 30
O'Connell, Marvin R(ichard) 1930- 134
Brief entry 111
O'Connell, Mary 206
O'Connell, Maurice R. 1922- 17-20R
O'Connell, Michael (William) 1943- 101
O'Connell, Nicholas 1957- 187
O'Connell, P. J. 1935- 144
O'Connell, Peg
See Ahern, Margaret McCrohan
O'Connell, Rebecca 1968- 199
See also SATA 130
O'Connell, Richard L(eo), Jr.
1912-1975 .... 41-44R
O'Connell, Sean 1944- 187
O'Connell, Timothy E(dward) 1943- . CANR-12
Earlier sketch in CA 73-76
O'Connell, Walter E(dward) 1925- 41-44R
O'Conner, Bert
See Paine, Lauran (Bosworth)
O'Conner, Clint
See Paine, Lauran (Bosworth)
O'Conner, Patricia T. 206
O'Conner, R(ay) L. 1928- 17-20R
O'Connor, A(nthony) M(ichael)
1939- CANR-11
Earlier sketch in CA 21-24R
O'Connor, Alan 1955- 133
O'Connor, Anthony (?)-1983(?)
Obituary 109
O'Connor, Barbara 1950- 229
See also SATA 154
O'Connor, Colin 1928- 150
O'Connor, Daniel William 1925- 33-36R
O'Connor, David 1949- 110
O'Connor, Dick 1930- 97-100
O'Connor, Edward Dennis 1922- 41-44R
O'Connor, Edwin (Greene) 1918-1968 93-96
Obituary 25-28R
See also CLC 14
See also MAL 5
O'Connor, Egan 1937- 119
O'Connor, Elizabeth (Anita) 1921- ... CANR-30
Earlier sketch in CA 25-28R
O'Connor, (Mary) Flannery
1925-1964 .... CANR-41
Earlier sketches in CA 1-4R, CANR-3
See also AAYA 7
See also AMW
See also AMWR 2
See also BPFB 3
See also BYA 16
See also CDALB 1941-1968
See also CLC 1, 2, 3, 6, 10, 13, 15, 21, 66, 104
See also DA
See also DA3
See also DAB
See also DAC
See also DAM MST, NOV
See also DLB 2, 152
See also DLBD 12
See also DLBY 1980
See also EWL 3
See also EXPS
See also LAIT 5
See also MAL 5
See also MAWW
See also MTCW 1, 2
See also MTFW 2005
See also NFS 3, 21
See also RGAL 4
See also RGSF 2
See also SSC 1, 23, 61, 82
See also SSFS 2, 7, 10, 19
See also TCLC 132
See also TUS
See also WLC
O'Connor, Fleann Patrick 1944- .... CP 1
O'Connor, Francine M(arie) 1930- ... CANR-59
Earlier sketch in CA 111
See also SATA 90
O'Connor, Francis V(alentine)
1937- CANR-13
Earlier sketch in CA 21-24R
O'Connor, Frank
See O'Donovan, Michael Francis
See also CLC 23
See also DLB 162
See also EWL 3
See also RGSF 2
See also SSC 5
See also SSFS 5
O'Connor, Garry 1938- CANR-97
Earlier sketches in CA 89-92, CANR-20, 45
O'Connor, Genevieve A. 1914- .... SATA 75
Oconnor, Geoffrey 181
O'Connor, Harvey 1897-1987 .... CANR-76
Obituary 123
Earlier sketch in CA 5-8R
O'Connor, Jack
See O'Connor, John Woolf
See also TCWW 1, 2
O'Connor, James I(gnatius) 1910-1988 .. CAP-1
Obituary 126
Earlier sketch in CA 13-16
O'Connor, Jane 1947- CANR-143
Earlier sketch in CA 124
See also SATA 59, 103, 150
See also SATA-Brief 47
O'Connor, John (Morris) 1937- 29-32R
O'Connor, John E. 1943- 127
Brief entry 109
O'Connor, John J(oseph) 1918- 73-76
O'Connor, John Joseph 1904-1978
Obituary 77-80
O'Connor, John P. 1892-1986
Obituary 119
O'Connor, John Woolf 1902-1978 ... CANR-64
Obituary 77-80
Earlier sketches in CA 5-8R, CANR-3
See also O'Connor, Jack
O'Connor, Joseph 1963- .... CN 7
See also DLB 267
O'Connor, June (Elizabeth) 1941- 114
O'Connor, Karen 1938- CANR-59
Earlier sketches in CA 89-92, CANR-28
See also SATA 34, 89
O'Connor, Leo F. 1936- 141
O'Connor, Lillian M. 1894(?)-1987
Obituary 122
O'Connor, M.
See O'Connor, Michael Patrick
O'Connor, Mallory McCane 1943- 151
O'Connor, Mark 1945- CANR-31
Earlier sketches in CA 65-68, CANR-11
O'Connor, Marty 1924(?)-1990
Obituary 131
O'Connor, Mary 1947- 133
O'Connor, Michael Patrick 1950- CANR-45
Earlier sketch in CA 113
O'Connor, Pat 1950- 143
O'Connor, Patricia Walker 1931- CANR-38
Earlier sketches in CA 37-40R, CANR-17

O'Connor, Patrick
See Wibberley, Leonard (Patrick O'Connor)
O'Connor, Patrick ... 77-80
O'Connor, Patrick 1949- ... 130
O'Connor, Patrick J(oseph) 1947- ... 113
O'Connor, Patrick Joseph 1924- ... 53-56
O'Connor, Philip F(rancis) 1932- ... CANR-28
Earlier sketch in CA 33-36R
O'Connor, Philip Marie Constant Bancroft
1916-1998 ... 9-12R
Obituary ... 169
See also CP 1
O'Connor, Raymond G(ish) 1915- ... CANR-4
Earlier sketch in CA 5-8R
O'Connor, Rebecca K. 1971- ... 226
O'Connor, Richard ... 203
O'Connor, Richard 1915-1975 ... CANR-85
Obituary ... 57-60
Earlier sketch in CA 61-64
See also SATA-Obit 21
O'Connor, Robert 1959- ... 140
O'Connor, Robert F. 1943- ... 128
O'Connor, Rory 1951- ... 109
O'Connor, Rosalie 1970- ... 236
O'Connor, Sandra Day 1930- ... 203
O'Connor, Sister Mary Catharine ... CAP-2
Earlier sketch in CA 17-18
O'Connor, Stephen 1952- ... 200
O'Connor, Thomas H(enry) 1922- ... CANR-107
Earlier sketch in CA 33-36R
O'Connor, Timothy Edward 1951- ... 145
O'Connor, Ulick 1928- ... CANR-120
Earlier sketches in CA 9-12R, CANR-4
O'Connor, William E(dmund) 1922- ... 37-40R
O'Connor, William P., Jr. 1916- ... 9-12R
O'Connor, William Van 1915-1966 ... CANR-87
Obituary ... 25-28R
Earlier sketches in CA 1-4R, CANR-1
O'Connor Howe, Josephine (Mary) 1924- ... 119
O'Conor, Jane 1958- ... SATA 78
O'Conor, John F(rancis) 1918- ... 33-36R
O'Conor, Joseph 1916- ... 201
October, John
See Portway, Christopher (John)
Octopus
See Drachman, Julian M(oses)
O Cuilleanain, Cormac 1950- ... 146
Oculi, Okello 1942- ... 143
See also BW 2
Ocvirk, Otto G(eorge) 1922- ... 61-64
Oda, Makoto 1932- ... 139
Odaga, Asenath (Bole) 1937- ... CANR-110
Earlier sketches in CA 124, CANR-43, 84
See also BW 2
See also CWRI 5
See also MAICYA 1, 2
See also SAAS 19
See also SATA 67, 130
Odahl, Charles Matson 1944- ... 37-40R
O'Dair, Barbara ... 180
Odajnyk, Walter 1938- ... 13-16R
O'Daly, William 1951- ... 137
O Danachair, Caoimhin
See Danaher, Kevin
Odanaka, Barbara ... SATA 159
O'Daniel, Janet 1921- ... 29-32R
See also SATA 24
O'Daniel, Therman B(enjamin)
1908-1986 ... CANR-76
Obituary ... 133
Earlier sketch in CA 45-48
See also BW 1
Oda Sakunosuke 1913-1947 ... DLB 182
O'Day, Alan (Earl) ... 143
O'Day, Cathy
See Crane, Barbara (Joyce)
O'Day, Edward Francis 1925- ... 29-32R
O'Day, Rey 1947- ... 105
Odber (de Baubeta), Patricia (Anne)
1953- ... CANR-122
Earlier sketch in CA 168
Odd, Gilbert E(dward) 1902- ... 110
Oddner, Georg 1923- ... 129
Oddo, Gilbert L. 1922- ... CANR-1
Earlier sketch in CA 1-4R
Oddo, Sandra (Schmidt) 1937- ... 65-68
O'Dea, Agnes C(ecelia) 1911-1993 ... 124
O'Dea, Thomas F(rancis) 1915-1974 ... CAP-2
Obituary ... 53-56
Earlier sketch in CA 23-24
Odean, Kathleen 1953- ... CANR-143
Earlier sketch in CA 128
Odegaard, Charles Edwin 1911-1999
Obituary ... 186
Brief entry ... 106
Odegard, Douglas Andrew 1935- ... 108
Odegard, Holtan P(eter) 1923-1983 ... CANR-88
Earlier sketch in CA 61-64
Odeku, Emmanuel Latunde 1927- ... 153
See also BW 2
O'Dell, Andrew C(harles) 1909-1966 ... CAP-1
Earlier sketch in CA 13-16
Odell, George H. 1942- ... CANR-117
Earlier sketch in CA 160
Odell, Gill
See Gill, Traviss
Odell, Jonathan 1737-1818 ... DLB 31, 99
Odell, Jonathan 1951- ... 232
Odell, Ling Chung 1945- ... 45-48
O'Dell, M(ary) E(lise) ... 9-12R
Odell, Peter R(andon) 1930- ... 97-100
Odell, Rice 1928- ... 77-80
Odell, Robin 1935- ... CANR-12
Earlier sketch in CA 73-76
O'Dell, Scott 1898-1989 ... CANR-112
Obituary ... 129
Earlier sketches in CA 61-64, CANR-12, 30
See also AAYA 3, 44
See also BPFB 3
See also BYA 1, 2, 3, 5
See also CLC 30
See also CLR 1, 16
See also DLB 52
See also JRDA
See also MAICYA 1, 2
See also SATA 12, 60, 134
See also WYA
See also YAW
O'Dell, Tawni ... 203
O'Dell, William F(rancis) 1909- ... CANR-12
Earlier sketch in CA 25-28R
Odem, J.
See Rubin, Jacob A.
Oden, Clifford 1916-1996 ... 65-68
Oden, Gloria (Catherine) 1923- ... CANR-25
Earlier sketch in CA 108
Oden, Marilyn Brown 1937- ... 33-36R
Oden, Thomas C(lark) 1931- ... CANR-43
Earlier sketches in CA 9-12R, CANR-5, 19
Oden, William E(ugene) 1923- ... 37-40R
Odenwald, Neil G. 1935- ... 141
Odenwald, Robert P(aul) 1899-1965 ... 1-4R
See also SATA 11
Odenwald, Sten F. ... 199
Oderman, Kevin ... 196
Oderman, Stuart (Douglas) 1940- ... CANR-120
Earlier sketch in CA 148
Odescalchi, Esther Kando 1938- ... 69-72
Odets, Clifford 1906-1963 ... CANR-62
Earlier sketch in CA 85-88
See also AMWS 2
See also CAD
See also CLC 2, 28, 98
See also DAM DRAM
See also DC 6
See also DFS 3, 17, 20
See also DLB 7, 26
See also EWL 3
See also MAL 5
See also MTCW 1, 2
See also MTFW 2005
See also RGAL 4
See also TUS
Odets, Walt (Whitman) 1947- ... 151
Odgers, Merle Middleton 1900-1983
Obituary ... 110
Odgers, Sally
See Odgers, Sally Farrell
Odgers, Sally Farrell 1957- ... 205
See also SATA 72, 139
Odhiambo, David Nandi 1965- ... 234
Odier, Daniel 1945- ... CANR-29
Earlier sketch in CA 29-32R
Odio, Eunice 1922-1974 ... DLB 283
See also EWL 3
Odiorne, George Stanley
1920-1992 ... CANR-76
Obituary ... 136
Earlier sketches in CA 1-4R, CANR-1
Odishaw, Hugh 1916-1984
Obituary ... 112
Odjig, Daphne 1919- ... 212
Odle, Joe T(aft) 1908-1980 ... CANR-76
Obituary ... 97-100
Earlier sketch in CA 33-36R
Odling-Smee, John (Charles) 1943- ... 112
Odlum, Doris Maude 1890-1985 ... CANR-76
Obituary ... 118
Earlier sketches in CAP-1, CA 13-14
Odoevsky, Aleksandr Ivanovich
1802-1839 ... DLB 205
Odoevsky, Vladimir Fedorovich
1804(?)-1869 ... DLB 198
See also RGSF 2
Odoevtseva, Irina 1895(?)-1990 ... DLB 317
O'Doherty, Brian 1928- ... CANR-108
O'Doherty, Brian 1928- ... CANR-108
Earlier sketch in CA 105
See also CLC 76
O'Doherty, E(amonn) F(elchin) 1918- ... 37-40R
O'doherty, Malachi 1951- ... 175
O'Doire, Annraoi
See Beechhold, Henry F(rank)
Odom, Anne Curtis 1935- ... 180
Odom, Mel 1950- ... 237
Odom, William E(ldridge) 1932- ... CANR-88
Earlier sketch in CA 73-76
O'Donnell, Bernard 1929-1983 ... CANR-76
Obituary ... 133
Earlier sketch in CA 41-44R
O'Donnell, Brennan (Patrick) 1958- ... 156
O'Donnell, Clifford R. ... 196
O'Donnell, Cyril 1900-1976 ... CAP-1
Obituary ... 196
Earlier sketch in CA 11-12
O'Donnell, Dick
See Lupoff, Richard A(llen) and
Thompson, Don(ald Arthur)
O'Donnell, Donat
See O'Brien, Conor Cruise
O'Donnell, Edward T. 1963- ... 225
O'Donnell, Elliott 1872-1965 ... CANR-75
Earlier sketches in CAP-1, CA 13-16
See also HGG
O'Donnell, Francis (?)-1984
Obituary ... 114
O'Donnell, Guillermo A. ... 200
O'Donnell, Harry J(ames) 1914-1985
Obituary ... 117
O'Donnell, James H(owlett) III
1937- ... CANR-27
Earlier sketch in CA 45-48
O'Donnell, James J(oseph, Jr.)
1950- ... CANR-16
Earlier sketch in CA 89-92
O'Donnell, James Kevin 1951- ... CANR-6
Earlier sketch in CA 57-60
O'Donnell, James P(reston) 1917-1990
Obituary ... 131
O'Donnell, Jim
See O'Donnell, James Kevin
O'Donnell, John A. 1916- ... 17-20R
O'Donnell, John P. 1923- ... 17-20R
O'Donnell, K. M.
See Malzberg, Barry N(athaniel)
O'Donnell, (Philip) Kenneth 1924-1977 ... 81-84
Obituary ... 73-76
O'Donnell, Kenneth P.
See O'Donnell, (Philip) Kenneth
O'Donnell, Kevin, Jr. 1950- ... CANR-23
Earlier sketch in CA 106
See also SFW 4
O'Donnell, L. A. 1925- ... 175
O'Donnell, Lawrence
See Kuttner, Henry and
Moore, C(atherine) L(ucile)
O'Donnell, Lawrence F(rancis), Jr. 1951- ... 117
O'Donnell, Lillian Udvardy 1926- ... CANR-60
Earlier sketches in CA 5-8R, CANR-3, 18
See also CMW 4
O'Donnell, Margaret Jane 1899- ... 5-8R
O'Donnell, Mark (Patrick) 1954- ... CANR-86
Earlier sketches in CA 104, CANR-21, 45
O'Donnell, Patrick (James) 1948- ... 114
O'Donnell, Patrick K. 1969- ... 217
O'Donnell, Peadar 1893-1986 ... 135
Obituary ... 119
O'Donnell, Peter 1920- ... CANR-71
Brief entry ... 114
Earlier sketch in CA 117
Interview in ... CA-117
See also Brent, Madeleine
See also CMW 4
See also DLB 87
O'Donnell, Red
See O'Donnell, Francis
O'Donnell, Roseann 1962- ... 218
O'Donnell, Rosie
See O'Donnell, Roseann
O'Donnell, Ruan ... 206
O'Donnell, Thomas Francis 1915- ... CANR-1
Earlier sketch in CA 1-4R
O'Donnell, Thomas J(oseph) 1918- ... 65-68
O'Donnell, William H. 1940- ... 128
O'Donnevan, Finn
See Sheckley, Robert
O'Donoghue, Bernard 1945- ... CANR-88
Earlier sketch in CA 137
O'Donoghue, Bryan 1921- ... 77-80
O'Donoghue, David 1952- ... 195
O'Donoghue, Gregory 1951- ... 114
Brief entry ... 109
O'Donoghue, Joseph 1931- ... 21-24R
O'Donoghue, Michael 1940-1994 ... CANR-76
Obituary ... 147
Earlier sketch in CA 128
O'Donohoe, Nicholas Benjamin
See O'Donohoe, Nick
O'Donohoe, Nick 1952- ... 167
O'Donohue, William T. 1957- ... 197
O'Donovan, John 1921- ... CANR-11
Earlier sketch in CA 25-28R
O'Donovan, Katherine 1942- ... 123
O'Donovan, Michael Francis
1903-1966 ... CANR-84
Earlier sketch in CA 93-96
See also O'Connor, Frank
See also CLC 14
O'Dor, Ronald Keith 1944- ... 163
Odor, Ruth Shannon 1926- ... 120
See also SATA-Brief 44
O'Dowd, Bernard Patrick 1866-1953 ... DLB 230
O'Dowd, Liam 1947- ... 116
O'Driscoll, Dennis 1954- ... CANR-83
Earlier sketches in CA 127, CANR-54
See also CP 7
O'Driscoll, Gerald P(atrick), Jr. 1947- ... 133
O'Driscoll, Robert 1938- ... CANR-35
Earlier sketch in CA 53-56
Odunke
See Nkala, Nathan
O'Dwyer, James F. 1939- ... 33-36R
O'Dwyer, (Peter) Paul 1907-1998 ... 97-100
Obituary ... 181
O'Dwyer, Tess 1966- ... CANR-120
Earlier sketch in CA 147
Odysseus
See Johnson, Donald McI(ntosh)
Oe, Kenzaburo 1935- ... CANR-126
Earlier sketches in CA 97-100, CANR-36, 50, 74
See also Oe Kenzaburo
See also CLC 10, 36, 86, 187
See also DA3
See also DAM NOV
See also DLB 182
See also DLBY 1994
See also LATS 1:2
See also MJW
See also MTCW 1, 2
See also MTFW 2005
See also RGSF 2
See also RGWL 2, 3
See also SSC 20
Oechsli, Kelly 1918-1999 ... CANR-16
Earlier sketch in CA 97-100
See also SATA 5
Oeffinger, John C. 1952- ... 206
Oehlenschlager, Adam 1779-1850 ... DLB 300
Oehmke, T(homas) H(arold) 1947- ... CANR-11
Earlier sketch in CA 65-68
Oehser, Paul H(enry) 1904-1996 ... CANR-12
Obituary ... 155
Earlier sketch in CA 29-32R
Oe Kenzaburo
See Oe, Kenzaburo
See also CWW 2
See also EWL 3
Oeksenholt, Svein 1925-1991
Brief entry ... 106
Oelschlaeger, Max 1943- ... 141
Oenslager, Donald (Mitchell)
1902-1975 ... 61-64
Obituary ... 57-60
Oepik, Ernst Julius 1893-1985
Obituary ... 118
Oeppen, J. E.
See Oeppen, Jim (E.)
Oeppen, Jim (E.) ... 236
Oerkeny, Istvan
See Orkeny, Istvan
Oernsbo, Jess
See Ornsbo, Jess
Oerum, Poul (Erik) 1919- ... CANR-32
Earlier sketches in CA 65-68, CANR-13
Oesterle, John A(rthur) 1912-1977 ... 5-8R
Obituary ... 196
Oesterle, Virginia Rorby
See Rorby, Ginny
Oesterling, Anders
See Osterling, Anders (Johan)
Oesterreicher, John M(aria)
1904-1993 ... CANR-76
Obituary ... 141
Earlier sketches in CA 29-32R, CANR-26
Oettinger, Anthony Gervin 1929- ... CANR-31
Earlier sketch in CA 1-4R
Oettinger, Elmer R(osenthal, Jr.) 1913- ... 29-32R
o Fagain, Padraig
See Fagan, Patrick
O'Faolain, Eileen 1902-1988 ... CWRI 5
O'Faolain, Julia 1932- ... CANR-61
Earlier sketches in CA 81-84, CANR-12
See also CAAS 2
See also CLC 6, 19, 47, 108
See also CN 2, 3, 4, 5, 6, 7
See also DLB 14, 231, 319
See also FW
See also MTCW 1
See also RHW
O'Faolain, Nuala 1940- ... CANR-135
Earlier sketch in CA 171
O'Faolain, Sean 1900-1991 ... CANR-66
Obituary ... 134
Earlier sketches in CA 61-64, CANR-12
See also CLC 1, 7, 14, 32, 70
See also CN 1, 2, 3, 4
See also DLB 15, 162
See also MTCW 1, 2
See also MTFW 2005
See also RGEL 2
See also RGSF 2
See also SSC 13
See also TCLC 143
Ofari, Earl 1945- ... 41-44R
O'Farrell, John ... 230
O'Farrell, Maggie 1972- ... 219
O'Farrell, Patrick (James) 1933- ... CANR-42
Earlier sketches in CA 103, CANR-20
Ofek, Uriel 1926- ... CANR-18
Earlier sketch in CA 101
See also CLR 28
See also SATA 36
Offen, Karen (Marie Stedtfeld)
1939- ... CANR-34
Earlier sketch in CA 113
Offen, Neil 1946- ... 49-52
Offen, Ron 1930- ... 45-48
Offenbacher, Ami 1958- ... 155
See also SATA 91
Offer, Daniel 1930- ... CANR-11
Earlier sketch in CA 21-24R
Offerle, Mildred (Gladys Goodnell)
1912-1996 ... 77-80
Obituary ... 171
Officer, Charles B. ... 205
Offield, Lewis Delaney 1903-1978
Obituary ... 111
Offiong, Daniel A(sukwo) 1942- ... 118
Offit, Avodah K(omito) 1931- ... CANR-13
Earlier sketch in CA 77-80
Offit, Sidney 1928- ... CANR-1
Earlier sketch in CA 1-4R
See also SATA 10
Offner, Arnold A. 1937- ... CANR-120
Earlier sketch in CA 25-28R
Offner, Eric D(elmonte) 1928- ... CANR-9
Earlier sketch in CA 17-20R
Offner, Richard 1889-1965 ... 191
Offord, Carl Ruthven 1910-1990 ... 142
See also BW 2
See also DLB 76
Offord, Lenore Glen 1905-1991 ... CANR-86
Obituary ... 182
Earlier sketch in CA 77-80
Offutt, Andrew J(efferson V)
1934(?)- ... CANR-85
Earlier sketch in CA 41-44R
See also FANT
See also SFW 4

Cumulative Index 435 Oken

Offutt, Chris 1958- ... CANR-90
Earlier sketch in CA 154
See also CSW
O Fiaich, Tomas (Seamus)
1923-1990 ... CANR-78
Obituary ... 131
Earlier sketch in CA 103
O'Finn, Thaddeus
See McGloin, Joseph T(haddeus)
O'Flaherty, James C(arneal) 1914-2002 . 21-24R
O'Flaherty, Liam 1896-1984 ... CANR-35
Obituary ... 113
Earlier sketch in CA 101
See also CLC 5, 34
See also CN 1, 2, 3
See also DLB 36, 162
See also DLBY 1984
See also MTCW 1, 2
See also MTFW 2005
See also RGEL 2
See also RGSF 2
See also SSC 6
See also SSFS 5, 20
O'Flaherty, Louise 1920- ... CANR-6
Earlier sketch in CA 57-60
O'Flaherty, Terrence 1917- ... 73-76
O'Flaherty, Wendy Doniger 1940- ... CANR-23
Earlier sketch in CA 65-68
O'Flynn, Criostoir 1927- ... 181
O'Flynn, Peter
See Fanthorpe, R(obert) Lionel
Ofomata, G(odfrey) E(zediaso) K(ingsley)
1936- ... 93-96
Oforiwaa, Yaa 1949- ... 152
Ofosu-Appiah, L(awrence) H(enry)
1920- ... 33-36R
See also SATA 13
Ofrat, Gideon 1945- ... 175
Ofri, Danielle ... 223
Ofshe, Richard 1941- ... 89-92
Og, Liam
See O'Neill, William
Ogai
See Mori Ogai
See also MJW
Ogali, Ogali A(gu) 1931- ... 153
See also BW 2
O'Gallagher, Liam 1917- ... 45-48
Ogan, George F. 1912-1983 ... CANR-4
Earlier sketch in CA 9-12R
See also SATA 13
Ogan, M. G.
See Ogan, George F. and
Ogan, Margaret E. (Nettles)
Ogan, Margaret E. (Nettles)
1923-1979 ... CANR-4
Earlier sketch in CA 9-12R
See also SATA 13
O'Gara, Geoffrey H. 1950- ... 207
O'Gara, James Vincent, Jr. 1918-1979 ... 69-72
Obituary ... 85-88
Ogarev, Nikolai Platonovich
1813-1877 ... DLB 277
Ogata, Sadako (Nakamura) 1927- ... CANR-9
Earlier sketch in CA 17-20R
Ogawa, Dennis Masaaki 1943- ... 37-40R
Ogawa, Tetsuro 1912-1978 ... 41-44R
Ogbaa, Kalu 1945- ... 141
See also BW 2
Ogbu, John U(zor) 1939-2003 ... 93-96
Obituary ... 219
Ogburn, Charlton (Jr.) 1911-1998 ... CANR-3
Obituary ... 171
Earlier sketch in CA 5-8R
See also SATA 3
See also SATA-Obit 109
Ogburn, Jacqueline K. ... SATA 162
Ogburn, William Fielding 1886-1959 ... 182
Brief entry ... 122
Ogden, Christol
See English, Thomas Dunn
Ogden, Christopher (Bennett) 1945- . CANR-88
Earlier sketch in CA 133
Ogden, Clint
See King, Albert
Ogden, Daniel 1963- ... 196
Ogden, Daniel M(iller), Jr. 1922- ... 9-12R
Ogden, Dunbar H. ... 53-56
Ogden, Gina 1935- ... 81-84
Ogden, Howard
See Winokur, Jon
Ogden, Margaret (Astrid) Lindholm
1952- ... CANR-97
See also Lindholm, Megan
Ogden, Margaret Sinclair 1909-1988 ... 198
Brief entry ... 107
Ogden, (John) Michael (Hubert) 1923- .. 13-16R
Ogden, Samuel R(obinson) 1896-1985 . 29-32R
Obituary ... 182
Ogden, Schubert Miles 1928- ... CANR-45
Earlier sketches in CA 104, CANR-21
Ogden, Scott 1957- ... 138
Ogede, Ode 1956- ... 202
Ogg, Alex ... 218
Ogg, Oscar (John) 1908-1971 ... CAP-1
Obituary ... 33-36R
Earlier sketch in CA 11-12
Ogilvie, Elisabeth May 1917- ... CANR-85
Earlier sketches in CA 103, CANR-19, 42
See also RHW
See also SATA 40
See also SATA-Brief 29
Ogilvie, Gordon (Bryant) 1934- ... CANR-8
Earlier sketch in CA 61-64
Ogilvie, Lloyd John 1930- ... 73-76
Ogilvie, Mardel 1910-1986 ... CANR-29
Obituary ... 176
Earlier sketch in CA 1-4R
Ogilvie, Marilyn Bailey 1936- ... 203
Ogilvie, Robert Maxwell
1932-1981 ... CANR-78
Obituary ... 105
Earlier sketches in CA 13-16R, CANR-6
Ogilvie, William G(eorge) 1899-1996 ... 130
Ogilvy, C(harles) Stanley 1913-2000 .. CANR-4
Obituary ... 188
Earlier sketch in CA 5-8R
Ogilvy, David (Mackenzie) 1911-1999 ... 186
Obituary ... 185
Brief entry ... 105
Ogilvy, Eliza (Anne Harris) 1822-1912 ... 184
See also DLB 199
Ogilvy, Gavin
See Barrie, J(ames) M(atthew)
Ogilvy, Stewart Marks 1914-1985(?)
Obituary ... 118
Oglanby, Elva
See Clairmont, Elva
Ogle, James Lawrence 1911-2005 ... 5-8R
Ogle, Jim
See Ogle, James Lawrence
Ogle, Lucille Edith 1904-1988 .... SATA-Obit 59
Ogle, Robert 1926(?)-1984
Obituary ... 112
Oglesby, Joseph 1931- ... CANR-17
Earlier sketch in CA 97-100
Oglesby, Richard E(dward) 1931- ... CANR-6
Earlier sketch in CA 9-12R
Oglesby, Virgil 1929- ... 192
Oglesby, William B(arr), Jr. 1916-1994 .. 25-28R
Ogletree, Earl Joseph 1930- ... CANR-10
Earlier sketch in CA 65-68
Ogletree, Thomas W(arren) 1933- ... CANR-87
Earlier sketch in CA 17-20R
Ognall, Leopold Horace
1908-1979 ... CANR-60
Earlier sketches in CA 9-12R, CANR-12
See also CMW 4
Ognibene, Peter J(ohn) 1941- ... 110
O'Gorman, Edward Charles 1929- ... CANR-87
Earlier sketch in CA 81-84
See also O'Gorman, Ned
O'Gorman, Frank 1940- ... CANR-87
Earlier sketch in CA 61-64
O'Gorman, Gerald 1916- ... 21-24R
O'Gorman, Hubert J(oseph) 1925-1990
Obituary ... 131
O'Gorman, James F(rancis) 1933- .. CANR-136
Earlier sketches in CA 53-56, CANR-95
See also MTFW 2005
O'Gorman, John
See MacGill, Patrick
O'Gorman, Ned
See O'Gorman, Edward Charles
See also CP 1, 2
O'Gorman, Richard F. 1928- ... 37-40R
O'Gorman, Samuel F.
See Cusack, Michael J(oseph)
Ogorzaly, Michael A. 1948- ... 188
Ogot, Grace 1930- ... CANR-87
Earlier sketch in CA 142
See also BW 2
See also DLB 125
See also EWL 3
See also SSFS 15
O'Grada, Sean
See O'Grady, John (Patrick)
O'Grady, Anne ... 53-56
O'Grady, Desmond (James Bernard)
1935- ... CANR-85
Earlier sketches in CA 25-28R, CANR-14, 38
See also CP 1, 2, 3, 4, 5, 6, 7
See also DLB 40
O'Grady, Francis Dominic 1909-1987 .. CAP-1
Earlier sketch in CA 9-10
O'Grady, Frank
See O'Grady, Francis Dominic
O'Grady, Jean (Mary) 1943- ... 222
O'Grady, John (Patrick) 1907-1981 ... 104
O'Grady, John F(rancis) 1939- ... 93-96
O'Grady, John P. 1958- ... CANR-113
Earlier sketch in CA 145
O'Grady, Joseph P(atrick) 1934- ... 41-44R
O'Grady, Paul 1964- ... 235
O'Grady, Rohan
See Skinner, June O'Grady
O'Grady, Ron 1930- ... 114
O'Grady, Standish (James) 1846-1928 ... 157
Brief entry ... 104
See also TCLC 5
O'Grady, Timothy 1951- ... 138
See also CLC 59
O'Grady, Tom 1943- ... 191
O'Grady, Tony
See Clemens, Brian (Horace)
Ogram, Ernest W(illiam), Jr. 1928- ... 57-60
O'Green, Jennifer
See Roberson, Jennifer
O'Green, Jennifer Roberson
See Roberson, Jennifer
Ogrin, Dusan 1929- ... 151
O'Griofa, Martin
See Greif, Martin
Ogrodnick, Margaret 1956- ... 198
Oguibe, Olu 1964- ... 199
Ogul, Morris S(amuel) 1931- ... 13-16R
Ogundipe-Leslie, 'Molara ... 154
See also BW 3
Ogunyemi, Chikwenye Okonjo 1939- ... 168
See also BW 3
Ogunyemi, (Ola)wale 1939(?)-2001 . CANR-81
Obituary ... 202
Earlier sketch in CA 153
See also BW 2
See also CD 5, 6
See also DLB 157
Oh, John Kie-chiang 1930- ... 29-32R
Ohaegbulam, Festus Ugboaja ... 239
O'Hagan, Andrew 1968- ... 192
See also CN 7
O'Hagan, Caroline 1946- ... 111
See also SATA 38
O'Hagan, Howard 1902-1982 ... 1-4R
See also DLB 68
O'Hagan, Joan 1926- ... CANR-84
Earlier sketch in CA 132
O'Hair, Madalyn (Mays) Murray
1919-2001 ... CANR-44
Earlier sketches in CA 61-64, CANR-12
O'Hallion, Sheila
See Allen, Sheila Rosalynd
O'Halpin, Eunan 1954- ... 128
Ohanian, Susan 1941- ... 191
O'Hanlon, Ardal 1965- ... 176
O'Hanlon, Bill
See O'Hanlon, William Hudson
O'Hanlon, Daniel John 1919-1992 .. CANR-47
Obituary ... 139
Earlier sketch in CA 61-64
O'Hanlon, Ellis ... 237
O'Hanlon, Jacklyn
See Meek, Jacklyn O'Hanlon
O'Hanlon, Michael David Peter 1950- ... 207
O'Hanlon, Michael E(dward) ... 204
O'Hanlon, Redmond (Douglas) 1947- ... 123
See also BRWS 11
O'Hanlon, Thomas J(oseph) 1933- ... 61-64
O'Hanlon, William Hudson ... 194
Ohanneson, Joan 1930- ... 130
O'Hara, Charles E. 1912-1984 ... 29-32R
Obituary ... 125
O'Hara, Dale
See Gillese, John Patrick
O'Hara, Elizabeth
See Ni Dhuibhne, Eilis
O'Hara, Frank 1926-1966 ... CANR-33
Obituary ... 25-28R
Earlier sketch in CA 9-12R
See also CLC 2, 5, 13, 78
See also DA3
See also DAM POET
See also DLB 5, 16, 193
See also EWL 3
See also MAL 5
See also MTCW 1, 2
See also MTFW 2005
See also PC 45
See also PFS 8, 12
See also RGAL 4
See also WP
O'Hara, Frederic James 1917- ... 103
O'Hara, Georgina 1956- ... 126
O'Hara, John (Henry) 1905-1970 ... CANR-60
Obituary ... 25-28R
Earlier sketches in CA 5-8R, CANR-31
See also AMW
See also BPFB 3
See also CDALB 1929-1941
See also CLC 1, 2, 3, 6, 11, 42
See also DAM NOV
See also DLB 9, 86
See also DLBD 2
See also EWL 3
See also MAL 5
See also MTCW 1, 2
See also MTFW 2005
See also NFS 11
See also RGAL 4
See also RGSF 2
See also SSC 15
O'Hara, Kenneth
See Morris, (Margaret) Jean
O'Hara, Kevin
See Cumberland, Marten
O'Hara, Marjorie (Doreen) 1928- ... 135
O'Hara, Mary
See Alsop, Mary O'Hara
See also TCWW 2
O'Hara (Alsop), Mary
See Alsop, Mary O'Hara
O'Hara, Maureen
See FitzSimons, Maureen
O'Hare, Jeff(rey A.) 1958- ... 173
See also SATA 105
O'Hare, Kate Richards 1876-1948 ... DLB 303
Ohashi, Wataru 1944- ... 73-76
O'Hayre, John 1923-1986
Obituary ... 121
O'hearn, Peter J(oseph) T(homas)
1917- ... 17-20R
O'Heffernan, Patrick 1944- ... 117
O'Hegarty, P(atrick) S(arsfield) 1879-1955 .. 183
See also DLB 201
O Hehir, Diana 1922- ... 93-96
See also CLC 41
O hEithir, Breandan 1930-1990
Obituary ... 132
O'Heithir, Ruairi
See o heithir, Ruairi
Ohi, Ruth 1964- ... SATA 95
O'Higgins, Donal Peter 1922-1984 ... 77-80
Obituary ... 112
O'Higgins, Paul 1927- ... 130
Ohira, Masayoshi 1910-1980
Obituary ... 105
Ohiyesa
See Eastman, Charles A(lexander)
Ohkawa, Kazushi 1908- ... 85-88
Ohl, John Kennedy 1942- ... 220
Ohl, (Mary) Suzanne Sickler 1923- ... 69-72
Ohles, John Ford 1920-1988 ... 57-60
Ohlig, Karl-Heinz 1938- ... CANR-13
Earlier sketch in CA 69-72
Ohlin, Bertil 1899(?)-1979
Obituary ... 89-92
Ohlin, Lloyd E(dgar) 1918- ... 104
Ohlinger, Gustavus 1877-1972
Obituary ... 37-40R
Ohlmeyer, Jane H. 1962- ... CANR-104
Earlier sketch in CA 149
Ohlsen, Merle M(arvel) 1914- ... CANR-15
Earlier sketch in CA 37-40R
Ohlsson, Ib 1935- ... SATA 7
Ohmae, Kenichi 1943- ... 152
Ohman, Jack 1960- ... 110
Brief entry ... 108
Interview in ... CA-110
Ohmann, Carol Burke 1929(?)-1989
Obituary ... 129
Ohmann, Richard (Malin) 1931- ... 13-16R
Ohmer, Merlin M(aurice) 1923- ... 57-60
Ohmi, Ayano 1959- ... 186
See also SATA 115
Ohon
See Barba, Harry
Ohrt, Wallace 1919- ... CANR-122
Earlier sketch in CA 170
Ohsberg, H(arry) Oliver 1926- ... 114
Ohtomo, Yasuo 1946- ... SATA 37
o huigin, sean 1942- ... 208
See also CLR 75
See also SATA 138
Ohye, Bonnie ... 203
Oinas, Felix J(ohannes) 1911- ... CANR-54
Earlier sketches in CA 33-36R, CANR-13, 29
Oiseau
See Moseley, James W(illett)
Oison
See O'Neill, Joseph James
Oiwa, Keibo ... 138
Oja, Carol J. 1953- ... 135
Ojaide, Tanure 1948- ... CANR-94
Earlier sketch in CA 171
See also AFW
See also BW 3
See also EWL 3
Ojany, Francis Frederick 1935- ... 77-80
Ojikutu, Bayo ... 221
Ojo, G. J. Afolabi 1930- ... 25-28R
Ojo-Ade, Femi ... 181
Oka, Takashi 1924- ... 135
Okada, John 1923-1971 ... 212
See also AAL
See also BYA 14
See also DLB 312
Okada, Sumie 1940- ... 132
Okafor, Chinyere Grace 1953- ... EWL 3
Okai, John 1967- ... CANR-85
Earlier sketch in CA 154
See also CP 1, 2, 3, 4, 5, 6, 7
Okamoto, Kanoko 1889-1939 ... 202
Okamoto, Katsunari 1949- ... 197
Okamoto, Kido 1872-1939 ... 192
Okamoto, Shumpei 1932- ... 29-32R
O'Kane, James M. 1941- ... 143
O'Kane, Leslie ... 180
O'Kane, Rosemary H(eather) T(eresa)
1947- ... 143
Okara, Gabriel Imomotimi Gbaingbain
1921- ... 105
See also AFW
See also BW 1
See also CDWLB 3
See also CP 1, 2, 3, 4, 5, 6, 7
See also DLB 125
See also EWL 3
See also RGEL 2
Okasha, Elisabeth 1942- ... 45-48
Oke, Janette 1935- ... CANR-58
Earlier sketch in CA 111
See also AAYA 30
See also SATA 97
O'Keefe, Bernard J(oseph) 1919-1989 ... 120
Obituary ... 129
O'Keefe, Daniel Lawrence 1928-
Brief entry ... 116
O'Keefe, Deborah (Janney) 1939- ... 227
O'Keefe, M(aurice) Timothy 1943- ... 77-80
O'Keefe, Patrick E.
See Grace, John Patrick
O'Keefe, Paul 1900(?)-1976
Obituary ... 65-68
O'Keefe, Richard R(obert) 1934- ... 57-60
O'Keefe, Sister Maureen 1917- ... 5-8R
O'Keefe, Susan Heyboer ... 239
See also SATA 133
O'Keeffe, Frank 1938- ... 160
See also SATA 99
O'Keeffe, Georgia 1887-1986 ... 156
Obituary ... 118
Earlier sketch in CA 110
See also AAYA 20
O'Keeffe, John 1747-1833 ... DLB 89
See also RGEL 2
O'Keeffe, (Peter) Laurence 1931-2003 ... 122
Obituary ... 217
Okeke, Uchefuna 1933- ... 97-100
O'Kelley, Mattie Lou 1908-1997 ... 116
Obituary ... 159
See also SATA 36, 97
O'Kelly, Charlotte G. 1946- ... 111
O'Kelly, Elizabeth 1915- ... CANR-20
Earlier sketch in CA 103
Oken, Alan C(harles) 1944- ... 45-48

Okenfuss, Max J. 1938- 156
Okes, Nicholas fl. 1607-1645 ..... DLB 170
O'Key
See Radwanski, Pierre A(rthur)
Okigbo, Christopher (Ifenayichukwu) 1932-1967 ..... CANR-74
Earlier sketch in CA 77-80
See also AFW
See also BLC 3
See also BW 1, 3
See also CDWLB 3
See also CLC 25, 84
See also DAM MULT, POET
See also DLB 125
See also EWL 3
See also MTCW 1, 2
See also MTFW 2005
See also PC 7
See also RGEL 2
Okigbo, P(ius) N(wabufo) C. 1924- CANR-87
Earlier sketch in CA 17-20R
Okihiro, Gary Y(ukio) 1945- CANR-94
Earlier sketches in CA 120, CANR-45
Okimoto, Jean Davies 1942- CANR-83
Earlier sketches in CA 97-100, CANR-16, 37
See also AAYA 31
See also SATA 34, 103
See also YAW
Okin, Susan Moller 1946-2004 93-96
Obituary 225
Okker, Patricia 1960- 151
Oklahoma Peddler
See Gilles, Albert S(imeon) Sr.
Okland, Einar
See Okland, Einar (Andreas)
Okland, Einar (Andreas) 1940- 190
Okner, Benjamin A. 1936- 21-24R
Okoampa-Ahoofe, Kwame, Jr. 1963- 187
Okomfo, Amasewa
See Cousins, Linda
Okonjo, Chukuka 1928- 29-32R
Okoro, Anezi 1929- ..... CWRI 5
Okpaku, Joseph (Ohiomogben) 1943- ... 29-32R
See also BW 1
Okpara, Mzee Lasana
See Hord, Frederick (Lee)
Okpewho, Isidore (Chukwudozi Oghenerhuele) 1941- CANR-89
Earlier sketches in CA 49-52, CANR-3
See also DLB 157
See also WLIT 2
Okrent, Daniel 1948- CANR-45
Earlier sketches in CA 105, CANR-22
Okri, Ben 1959- CANR-128
Brief entry 130
Earlier sketches in CA 138, CANR-65
Interview in CA-138
See also AFW
See also BRWS 5
See also BW 2, 3
See also CLC 87
See also CN 5, 6, 7
See also DLB 157, 231, 319
See also EWL 3
See also MTCW 2
See also MTFW 2005
See also RGSF 2
See also SSFS 20
See also WLIT 2
See also WWE 1
Oksenberg, Michel Charles 1938-2001 111
Obituary 193
Oksenholt, Svein
See Oeksenholt, Svein
Oktenberg, Adrian 1947- 173
Okubo, Genji 1915- 25-28R
Okudzhava, Bulat Shalvovich 1924-1997 .. 129
Obituary 159
Brief entry 116
See also EWL 3
Okuizumi, Hikaru
See Okuizumi, Yasuhiro
Okuizumi, Yasuhiro 1956- 195
Okun, Arthur M. 1928-1980 ..... CANR-11
Obituary 97-100
Earlier sketch in CA 61-64
Okun, Lawrence E(ugene) 1929- 101
Okwu, Julian C. R. 1957(?)- 171
Olafson, Frederick A(rlan) 1924- CANR-87
Earlier sketch in CA 17-20R
Olafsson, Olaf
See Olafsson, Olafur Johann
Olafsson, Olafur Johann
See Olafsson, Olafur Johann
Olafsson, Olafur Johann 1962- CANR-102
Earlier sketch in CA 146
Olaguer, Valdemar O. 1922- ..... CP 1
Olaleye, Isaac O. 1941- 145
See also SAAS 23
See also SATA 96
Olalquiaga, Celeste 180
Olan, Ben 1923- 111
Olan, Levi Arthur 1903-1984 109
O'Laoghaire, Liam
See O'Leary, Liam
Olasky, Marvin 1950- CANR-95
Earlier sketch in CA 139
Olbracht, Ivan
See Zeman, Kamil
See also EWL 3
Olbricht, Thomas H. 1929- 33-36R
Olby, Robert C(ecil) 1933- 21-24R
Olcheski, Bill 1925- CANR-8
Earlier sketch in CA 61-64
Olcott, Anthony 1950- 106
Olcott, Frances Jenkins 1872(?)-1963 .. SATA 19
Olcott, Henry Steel 1832-1907
Brief entry 118
Olcott, Jack 1932- 53-56
Old, Bruce S(cott) 1913- CANR-17
Earlier sketch in CA 1-4R
Old, Wendie C(orbin) 1943- 229
See also SATA 154
Old Boy
See Hughes, Thomas
Old Cap Collier
See Hanshew, Thomas W.
Old Cap Darrell
See Hanshew, Thomas W.
Olden, Marc 179
Oldenburg, Carl
See Oldenburg, Ray
Oldenburg, Claes (Thure) 1929- 121
Brief entry 117
Oldenburg, E(gbert) William 1936-1974 105
See also SATA 35
Oldenburg, Ray 1932- CANR-118
Earlier sketch in CA 132
Older, Effin 1942- 186
See also SATA 114
Older, Fremont 1856-1935 184
See also DLB 25
Older, Jules 1940- 186
See also SATA 114, 156
Older, Julia 1941- CANR-14
Earlier sketch in CA 73-76
Olderman, Murray 1922- CANR-1
Earlier sketch in CA 45-48
Olderman, Raymond M. 1937- 41-44R
Olderr, Steven 1943- 146
Old Fag
See Bell, Robert S(tanley) W(arren)
Oldfeld, Peter
See Bartlett, (Charles) Vernon (Oldfield)
Oldfield, A(rthur) Barney 1909-2003 105
Obituary 216
Oldfield, J(ohn) R(ichard) 1953- 151
Oldfield, James E(dmund) 1921- 89-92
Oldfield, Jenny 1949- 211
See also SATA 140
Oldfield, Margaret J(ean) 1932- ..... SATA 56
Oldfield, Michael 1950- 135
Oldfield, Mike
See Oldfield, Michael
Oldfield, Pamela 1931- ..... CWRI 5
See also RHW
See also SATA 86
Oldfield, R(ichard) C(harles) 1909-1972 ..... CAP-2
Earlier sketch in CA 25-28
Oldfield, Ruth L(atzer) 1922- 13-16R
Oldham, Frank 1903- 9-12R
Oldham, John 1653-1683 ..... DLB 131
See also RGEL 2
Oldham, John (M.) 1940- 138
Oldham, June 138
See also SATA 70
Oldham, Mary 1944- 109
See also SATA 65
Oldham, Nick 1956- 224
Oldham, Perry (Donald) 1943- 107
Oldham, W(illiam) Dale 1903-1984 ..... 9-12R
Oldie, Henry Lion
See Gromov, Dmitry E. and Ladyzhensky, Oleg S.
Old Jowett
See Fantoni, Barry (Ernest)
Oldman, C(ecil) B(ernard) 1894-1969 183
See also DLB 201
Oldman, Mark 1969(?)- 235
Oldman, Oliver 1920- 33-36R
Oldroyd, Harold 1913-1978 77-80
Olds, Bruce 1951- CANR-109
Earlier sketch in CA 152
Olds, Elizabeth 1896-1991 ..... 5-8R
Obituary 133
See also SATA 3
See also SATA-Obit 66
Olds, Elizabeth Fagg 1913-1995 123
Obituary 149
Olds, Helen Diehl 1895-1981 ..... CANR-3
Obituary 103
Earlier sketch in CA 1-4R
See also SATA 9
See also SATA-Obit 25
Olds, Sally Wendkos 1933- CANR-39
Earlier sketches in CA 45-48, CANR-1, 18
Olds, Sharon 1942- CANR-135
Earlier sketches in CA 101, CANR-18, 41, 66, 98
See also AMWS 10
See also CLC 32, 39, 85
See also CP 7
See also CPW
See also CWP
See also DAM POET
See also DLB 120
See also MAL 5
See also MTCW 2
See also MTFW 2005
See also PC 22
See also PFS 17
Old Settler, The
See Lyman, Albert Robison
Oldsey, Bernard 1923- CANR-7
Earlier sketch in CA 5-8R
Oldson, William O(rville) 1940- 53-56
Old Stager
See Gore, John Francis
Oldstyle, Jonathan
See Irving, Washington
Olea, Maria Florencia Varas 1938- 105
Olearius, Adam 1599-1671 ..... DLB 164
O'Leary, A. P. 1950- 161
O'Leary, Bradley S. 196
O'Leary, Brian (Todd) 1940- CANR-20
Earlier sketch in CA 33-36R
See also SATA 6
O'Leary, Cecilia E(lizabeth) 1949- 185
O'Leary, Chester F.
See Kuehnelt-Leddihn, Erik (Maria) Ritter von
O'Leary, Denyse 1950- 214
O'Leary, Ellen 1831-1889 ..... DLB 240
O'Leary, Frank(lin) J. 1922- 5-8R
O'Leary, Juan E. 1879-1969 ..... DLB 290
O'Leary, K. Daniel 1940- 41-44R
O'Leary, Les
See O'Leary, A. P.
O'Leary, Liam 1910-1992 109
O'Leary, Patrick 1920- 134
O'Leary, Patrick G. 1952- 211
O'Leary, Patsy B(aker) 1937- 164
See also SATA 97
O'Leary, Rosemary 1955- 149
O'Leary, Thomas V(incent) 1910-1972 ..... 5-8R
Oleck, Howard L(eoner) 1911-1995 ... CANR-4
Earlier sketch in CA 9-12R
Olegario, Rowena 232
Oleinik, Olga Arsenievna 1925- 170
Oleksiw, Susan (Prince) 1945- CANR-142
Earlier sketches in CA 141, CANR-73
Oleksy, Walter 1930- CANR-17
Earlier sketches in CA 45-48, CANR-1
Olen, Jeffrey 1946- 112
Olendorf, Bill
See Olendorf, William
Olendorf, William 1924-1996 ..... CANR-41
Earlier sketch in CA 117
Olesha, Iurii
See Olesha, Yuri (Karlovich)
See also RGWL 2
Olesha, Iurii Karlovich
See Olesha, Yuri (Karlovich)
See also DLB 272
Olesha, Yuri (Karlovich) 1899-1960 85-88
See also Olesha, Iurii and Olesha, Iurii Karlovich and Olesha, Yury Karlovich
See also CLC 8
See also EW 11
See also RGWL 3
See also SSC 69
See also TCLC 136
Olesha, Yury Karlovich
See Olesha, Yuri (Karlovich)
See also EWL 3
Oleszek, Walter J(oseph) 1941- 120
O'Levenson, Jordan
See Levenson, Jordan
Oleyar, Rita Balkey
See Balkey, Rita
Olford, Stephen F(rederick) 1918- 17-20R
Olfson, Lewy 1937- 93-96
Olgyay, Victor 1910-1970 ..... 5-8R
Obituary 103
Oliansky, Joel 1935-2002 133
Obituary 211
Olien, Diana Davids 1943- CANR-32
Earlier sketch in CA 113
Olien, Michael D(avid) 1937- CANR-3
Earlier sketch in CA 49-52
Olien, Roger M. 1938- 113
Olin, John C(harles) 1915- CANR-52
Earlier sketch in CA 126
Olin, Spencer C(arl), Jr. 1937- 93-96
Olin, William 1929- 106
Oliner, Samuel P. 1930- 129
Olins, Wally 1930- 120
Oliphant, Mrs.
See Oliphant, Margaret (Oliphant Wilson)
See also SUFW
Oliphant, B. J.
See Tepper, Sheri S.
Oliphant, Dave
See Oliphant, Edward Davis
Oliphant, Dave (Edward Davis) 1939- CANR-110
See also Oliphant, Edward Davis
Oliphant, Edward Davis 1939- CANR-110
Earlier sketch in CA 151
See also Oliphant, Dave (Edward Davis)
Oliphant, J(ames) Orin 1894-1979
Obituary 85-88
Oliphant, Laurence 1829(?)-1888 . DLB 18, 166
Oliphant, Margaret (Oliphant Wilson) 1828-1897
See Oliphant, Mrs.
See also BRWS 10
See also DLB 18, 159, 190
See also HGG
See also RGEL 2
See also RGSF 2
See also SSC 25
Oliphant, Patrick (Bruce) 1935- 101
Interview in CA-101
Oliphant, Robert (Thompson) 1924- 102
Olisah, Sunday Okenwa 1936-1964(?) 153
See also BW 2
Olitzky, Kerry M. 1954- CANR-122
Earlier sketch in CA 143
Oliva, JudyLee 1952- 224
Oliva, L(awrence) Jay 1933- 13-16R
Oliva, Leo E. 1937- CANR-49
Earlier sketches in CA 21-24R, CANR-9, 24
Oliva, Pavel 1923- 132
Olivares, Julian (Jr.) 1940- CANR-42
Earlier sketch in CA 118
Oliveira, Antonio Ramos
See Ramos-Oliveira, Antonio
Oliveira, Carlos de 1921-1981 ..... DLB 287
Oliveira, Paulo C(arlos) de
See de Oliveira, Paulo C(arlos)
Oliveira Salazar, Antonio de
See Salazar, Antonio de Oliveira
Olivella, Manuel Zapata
See Zapata Olivella, Manuel
Olivelle, Patrick 1942- 138
Oliven, John F. 1915(?)-1975
Obituary 53-56
Oliver, A. Richard 1912-1976 ..... 13-16R
Oliver, Amy Roberta
See Ruck, Amy Roberta
Oliver, Andrew 1906-1981 109
Obituary 105
Oliver, Anthony 1923-1995 ..... CANR-60
Earlier sketches in CA 103, CANR-20
See also CMW 4
Oliver, Bernard John Jr. 1918-1966 ..... 5-8R
Oliver, Bill 1949- 169
Oliver, Burton
See Burt, Olive Woolley
Oliver, Carl Russell 1941- 106
Oliver, Chad
See Oliver, Symmes C(hadwick)
See also DLB 8
See also SCFW 1, 2
Oliver, Covey T(homas) 1913- 111
Oliver, Dawn 1942- 123
Oliver, Douglas (Dunlop) 1937-2000 173
Autobiographical Essay in 173
See also CAAS 27
Oliver, Douglas L(lewellyn) 1913- CANR-87
Earlier sketch in CA 97-100
Oliver, Edward James 1911-1992 ..... CANR-87
Earlier sketch in CA 9-12R
Oliver, Egbert S(amuel) 1902-1989 103
Oliver, Eloise Dolores 1947- 204
Oliver, G(uillaume) Raymond 1909-1990 ..... CAP-2
Earlier sketch in CA 25-28
Oliver, George
See Onions, (George) Oliver
Oliver, Gloria I. 1964- 224
Oliver, H(arold) J(ames) 1916-1982
Obituary 111
Oliver, Herman 1885-1970 ..... CAP-1
Earlier sketch in CA 11-12
Oliver, James (Anthony) 1956- 232
Oliver, James A(rthur) 1914-1981
Obituary 106
Oliver, James Henry 1905-1981 ..... CANR-17
Earlier sketch in CA 1-4R
Oliver, Jamie 1975- 218
Oliver, Jane
See Rees, Helen Christina Easson (Evans)
Oliver, Jim 1940- 180
Oliver, John
See Davis, Owen (Gould)
Oliver, John Edward 1933- 33-36R
See also SATA 21
Oliver, Kelly 1959- 169
Oliver, Kenneth A(rthur) 1912- 53-56
Oliver, Kitty
See Oliver, Eloise Dolores
Oliver, Lawrence J. 1949- 159
Oliver, Maria-Antonia 1946- 217
Oliver, Marie
See Beck, K(athrine) K(ristine)
Oliver, Marilyn Tower 1935- 155
See also SATA 89
Oliver, Marina (Yvonne) 1934- ..... RHW
Oliver, Mark
See Tyler-Whittle, Michael Sidney
Oliver, Mary 1935- CANR-138
Earlier sketches in CA 21-24R, CANR-9, 43, 84, 92
See also AMWS 7
See also CLC 19, 34, 98
See also CP 7
See also CWP
See also DLB 5, 193
See also EWL 3
See also MTFW 2005
See also PFS 15
Oliver, Mary Hempstone 1885(?)-1973
Obituary 41-44R
Oliver, Narelle 1960- ..... SATA 152
Oliver, Paul (Hereford) 1927- CANR-87
Earlier sketches in CA 1-4R, CANR-1
Oliver, R(ichard) A(lexander) C(avaye) 1904-1998 ..... CAP-1
Earlier sketch in CA 11-12
Oliver, Raymond (Guillaume) 1909-1990
Obituary 132
Oliver, Raymond (Davies) 1936- CANR-26
Earlier sketch in CA 109
Oliver, Reggie
See Oliver, Reginald Rene St. John
Oliver, Reginald Rene St. John 1952- 181
Oliver, Revilo P(endleton) 1910-1994 121
Oliver, Richard (Bruce) 1942-1985 116
Oliver, Robert (Shelton) 1934- 105
Oliver, Robert T(arbell) 1909-2000 ..... CANR-41
Earlier sketches in CA 5-8R, CANR-4, 19
Oliver, Robert W. 1922-1998 135
Obituary 169
Oliver, Roland Anthony 1923- CANR-87
Earlier sketches in CA 73-76, CANR-12
Oliver, Rupert
See Matthews, Rupert O(liver)
Oliver, Shirley (Louise Dawkins) 1958- ..... SATA 74
Oliver, Smith Hempstone 1912-2001 ..... 25-28R

Cumulative Index 437 **Oneal**

Oliver, Symmes C(hadwick) 1928-1993 113
Obituary 174
See also Oliver, Chad
See also SATA 101
See also SFW 4
Oliver, (McWhorter) Thomas 1950- 127
Oliver, W. Andrew 1941- 37-40R
Oliver, W(illiam) H(osking) 1925- ...... CP 1
Oliver, William Irvin 1926- 17-20R
Olivera, Otto 1919- 49-52
Oliveri, Mario 1944- 107
Oliveri I Cabrer, Maria-Antonia 1946- ... EWL 3
Olivier, Charles P(ollard) 1884-1975
Obituary 61-64
Olivier, Fernande 1881(?)-1966 205
Olivier, Laurence (Kerr) 1907-1989 150
Obituary 129
Brief entry 111
See also CLC 20
Olivier, Robert L(ouis) 1903-1986 93-96
Oliviero, Jamie 1950- ...... SATA 84
Olivova, Vera 1926- 81-84
Olkes, Cheryl 1948- 127
Olkin, Rhoda 1953- 204
Olkowski, Helga 1931- 85-88
Olkowski, William 1941- 97-100
Olkyrn, Iris
See Milligan, Alice
Ollard, Richard (Laurence) 1923- ... CANR-100
Earlier sketches in CA 93-96, CANR-20
Oller, John W(illiam), Jr. 1943- CANR-5
Earlier sketch in CA 53-56
Ollerenshaw, Kathleen (Mary) 1912-
Brief entry 107
Olleson, Philip 206
Ollestad, Norman (Tennyson) 1935- 21-24R
Olli, John B. 1893(?)-1984
Obituary 112
Ollier, Claude 1922- 199
See also DLB 83
See also EWL 3
Ollier, Cliff(ord) David 1931- 61-64
Ollif, Lorna (Anne) 1918- 93-96
Olliff, Donathan C(arnes) 1933- 115
Ollman, Bertell 1935- CANR-16
Earlier sketch in CA 85-88
Olm, Kenneth W(illiam) 1924-1990 ...... 21-24R
Olmert, Michael 1940- 140
Olmo, Jorge
See Garcia Ponce, Juan
Olmstead, Alan H. 1907(?)-1980
Obituary 101
Olmstead, Andrea (Louise) 1948- 127
Olmstead, Clifton Earl 1926-1962 ...... 1-4R
Olmstead, Earl P. 1920- 137
Olmstead, Robert 1954- 129
Olmsted, Charlotte
See Kursh, Charlotte Olmsted
Olmsted, Frederick Law 1822-1903
Brief entry 120
See also AAYA 56
Olmsted, John Charles 1942- 93-96
Olmsted, Lorena Ann 1890-1989 ...... 29-32R
See also SATA 13
Olmsted, Robert W(alsh) 1936- 41-44R
Olmsted, Sterling P(itkin) 1915- 25-28R
Olney, James 1933- CANR-86
Earlier sketch in CA 77-80
Olney, Richard 1927-1999 189
Olney, Ross R. 1929- CANR-7
Earlier sketch in CA 13-16R
See also SATA 13
Olorunsola, Victor A. 1939- CANR-7
Earlier sketch in CA 57-60
O'Loughlin, Carleen CAP-2
Earlier sketch in CA 25-28
Olowu, (Claudius) Dele 1952- 135
O.L.S.
See Russell, George William
Olscamp, Paul James 1937- 104
Olschewski, Alfred (Erich) 1920- CANR-87
Earlier sketch in CA 41-44R
See also SATA 7
Olschki, G. Cesare 1890-1971
Obituary 104
Olsen, Alfa-Betty 1947- 103
Olsen, Alfred Johannes, Jr. 1884-1956
Brief entry 113
Olsen, Barbara ...... SATA 148
Olsen, Bob
See Olsen, Alfred Johannes, Jr.
Olsen, Brad(ford C.) 1965- 231
Olsen, Carol 1945- ...... SATA 89
Olsen, D. B. 1907-1973 ...... CMW 4
Olsen, Donald J(ames) 1929-1997 ...... 13-16R
Obituary 158
Olsen, Edward G(ustave)
1908-2000 ...... CANR-11
Earlier sketches in CAP-1, CA 9-10
Olsen, Gary 1948- 160
Olsen, Hans Christian, Jr. 1929-
Brief entry 106
Olsen, Ib Spang 1921- CANR-56
Earlier sketches in CA 49-52, CANR-3, 37
See also MAICYA 1, 2
See also SATA 6, 81
Olsen, Jack
See Olsen, John Edward
Olsen, James 1933- 49-52
Olsen, John Edward 1925-2002 ...... CANR-99
Obituary 207
Earlier sketches in CA 17-20R, CANR-9, 29, 55
Olsen, Lance (M.) 1956- 200
Olsen, Larry Dean 1939- 69-72
Olsen, Marvin E(lliott) 1936- CANR-26
Earlier sketch in CA 29-32R
Olsen, Otto H(arald) 1925- 33-36R
Olsen, R(obert) Arthur 1910-1992 ...... CAP-2
Earlier sketch in CA 23-24
Olsen, Richard E(llison) 1941- 81-84
Olsen, Stein Haugom 1946- 128
Olsen, T(heodore) V(ictor)
1932-1993 ...... CANR-84
Earlier sketches in CA 1-4R, CANR-3, 18, 39
See also TCWW 1, 2
Olsen, Tillie 1912- CANR-132
Earlier sketches in CA 1-4R, CANR-1, 43, 74
See also AAYA 51
See also AMWS 13
See also BYA 11
See also CDALBS
See also CLC 4, 13, 114
See also CN 2, 3, 4, 5, 6, 7
See also DA
See also DA3
See also DAB
See also DAC
See also DAM MST
See also DLB 28, 206
See also DLBY 1980
See also EWL 3
See also EXPS
See also FW
See also MAL 5
See also MTCW 1, 2
See also MTFW 2005
See also RGAL 4
See also RGSF 2
See also SSC 11
See also SSFS 1
See also TCLE 1:2
See also TCWW 2
See also TUS
Olsen, V(iggo) Norskov 1916-1999 53-56
Olsen, Violet (Mae) 1922-1991 113
Obituary 134
See also SATA 58
Olsen, William 1954- CANR-116
Earlier sketch in CA 128
Olshaker, Bennett 1921-
Brief entry 108
Olshaker, Mark 1951- 73-76
Olshaker, Thelma 114
Olshan, Joseph 1956- 128
Olshan, Neal H(ugh) 1947- 119
Olshansky, S. Jay 1954- 200
Olshen, Barry N(eil) 1944- 89-92
Olshewsky, Thomas M(ack) 1934- 37-40R
Olson, Alan M(elvin) 1939- CANR-8
Earlier sketch in CA 61-64
Olson, Alison Gilbert 1931- 186
Brief entry 109
Olson, (Elizabeth) Ann 1953- 126
Olson, Arielle North 1932- 134
See also SATA 67
Olson, Arnold O(rville) 1917- 45-48
Olson, Barbara (Kay) 1955-2001 199
Olson, Bernhard Emanuel
1910-1975 ...... CANR-24
Obituary 61-64
Earlier sketch in CA 45-48
Olson, Carl 1941- CANR-36
Earlier sketch in CA 114
Olson, Charles (John) 1910-1970 ..... CANR-61
Obituary 25-28R
Earlier sketches in CAP-1, CA 13-16, CANR-35
See also CABS 2
See also AMWS 2
See also CLC 1, 2, 5, 6, 9, 11, 29
See also CP 1
See also DAM POET
See also DLB 5, 16, 193
See also EWL 3
See also MAL 5
See also MTCW 1, 2
See also PC 19
See also RGAL 4
See also WP
Olson, Clair C(olby) 1901-1972 ...... 41-44R
Olson, (Carl Bernard) David 1904-1993 . 61-64
Olson, David F. 1938- 49-52
Olson, David John 1941- 53-56
Olson, David R(ichard) 1935- 33-36R
Olson, Donald 1938- 65-68
Olson, Elder (James) 1909-1992 ...... CANR-31
Obituary 139
Earlier sketches in CA 5-8R, CANR-6
See also CAAS 12
See also CP 1, 2
See also DLB 48, 63
Olson, Eric 1944- 53-56
Olson, Everett C. 1910-1993 53-56
Obituary 143
Olson, Gary A. 1954- CANR-102
Earlier sketch in CA 148
Olson, Gene 1922- 106
See also SATA 32
Olson, Harry E(dwin), Jr. 1932- 61-64
Olson, Harry F(erdinand) 1901-1982 .... 37-40R
Olson, Harvey S(tuart) 1908-1985 ...... CANR-1
Obituary 118
Earlier sketch in CA 1-4R
Olson, Helen Kronberg CANR-12
Earlier sketch in CA 29-32R
See also SATA 48
Olson, Herbert Waldo 1927- 1-4R
Olson, James C(lifton) 1917- CANR-86
Earlier sketch in CA 37-40R
Olson, James R(obert) 1938- 49-52
Olson, Jane Virginia 1916- 89-92
Olson, Keith W(aldemar) 1931- CANR-129
Earlier sketch in CA 49-52
Olson, Ken(neth John) 1930- 97-100
Olson, Kirby 1956- 208
Olson, Lawrence Alexander 1918-1992
Obituary 137
Brief entry 110
Olson, Lester C. 1955- 142
Olson, Linda Steffel 1949- 167
Olson, Lois Ellen 1941- 105
Olson, Mancur, Jr. 1932-1998 ...... CANR-94
Obituary 165
Earlier sketch in CA 13-16R
Olson, Marianne
See Mitchell, Marianne
Olson, McKinley C(lar) 1931- 110
Olson, Mildred Thompson 1922- 21-24R
Olson, Paul R(ichard) 1925- 21-24R
Olson, Philip G(ilbert) 1934- 9-12R
Olson, Richard G(eorge) 1940- CANR-17
Earlier sketch in CA 89-92
Olson, Richard Paul 1934- CANR-49
Earlier sketches in CA 61-64, CANR-8, 24
Olson, Robert G(oodwin) 1924- 29-32R
Olson, Robert W(illiam) 1940- CANR-93
Earlier sketch in CA 136
Olson, Roger E(ugene) 1952- 223
Olson, Sidney 1908-1995 ...... CAP-1
Earlier sketch in CA 11-12
Olson, Sigurd F(erdinand)
1899-1982 ...... CANR-86
Obituary 105
Earlier sketches in CA 1-4R, CANR-1
See also ANW
See also DLB 275
Olson, Stanley 1948-1989 89-92
Obituary 130
Olson, Steve E. 1956- 226
Olson, Steven 1950- 149
Olson, Ted
See Olson, Theodore B.
Olson, Theodore B. 1899-1981 ...... CANR-86
Earlier sketch in CA 49-52
Olson, Toby 1937- CANR-84
Earlier sketches in CA 65-68, CANR-9, 31
See also CLC 28
See also CP 7
Olson, Walter K. 1954- 135
Olson, Willard Clifford 1899-1978
Obituary 111
Olsson, Axel Adolf 1889-1977
Obituary 73-76
Olsson, Jennifer 1959- 157
Olsson, Karl A(rthur) 1913-1996 ...... CANR-4
Earlier sketch in CA 5-8R
Olsson, Nils 1909- 73-76
Olstad, Charles (Frederick)
1932-1976 ...... CANR-76
Obituary 134
Earlier sketch in CA 17-20R
Olszewski, Krystyn 1921-
Olthuis, James H(erman) 1938- 61-64
Oltmans, Willem L(eonard) 1925- 57-60
Olton, Charles S(haw) 1938-
Brief entry 108
Olton, Roy 1922- 103
Oltuski, Enrique 1930- 223
Oludhe-Macgoye, Marjorie 1928- CANR-82
Earlier sketch in CA 133
Olugebefola, Ademole 1941- ...... SATA 15
Oluonye, Mary N(kechi) 1955- 182
See also SATA 111
Olyan, Saul M(itchell) 1959- 223
Olyesha, Yuri
See Olesha, Yuri (Karlovich)
Olzendam, Roderic Marble 1892-1986
Obituary 121
Om
See Gorey, Edward (St. John)
O'Mahoney, Rich
See Warner-Crozetti, R(uth G.)
O'Mahony, Patrick (Frederick)
1911-1979 ...... 13-16R
O'Malley, Brian (Jack Morgan) 1918(?)-1980
Obituary 101
O'Malley, Charles Donald 1907-1970
Obituary 109
O'Malley, Frank
See O'Rourke, Frank
O'Malley, J(ohn) Steven 1942- 53-56
O'Malley, John W(illiam) 1927- 185
Brief entry 114
O'Malley, Joseph James 1930- 37-40R
O'Malley, Kevin
See Hossent, Harry
O'Malley, Kevin 1961- ...... SATA 157
O'Malley, Lady Mary Dolling (Sanders)
1889-1974 ...... CANR-59
Earlier sketch in CA 65-68
See also DLB 191
See also RHW
O'Malley, Mary 1954- 222
Brief entry 110
See also CBD
See also CWD
O'Malley, Mary Josephine 1941- 156
See also CD 5, 6
O'Malley, Michael (Anthony) 1-4R
O'Malley, Padraig 139
O'Malley, Patrick
See O'Rourke, Frank
O'Malley, Penelope Grenoble 233
O'Malley, Richard K(ilroy) 1911-1999 ... 97-100
O'Malley, Suzanne 1951- 110
O'Malley, Vincent (J.) 1945- 199
O'Malley, William J(ohn) 1931- CANR-31
Earlier sketches in CA 73-76, CANR-12
Oman, Carola (Mary Anima)
1897-1978 ...... CANR-84
Earlier sketches in CA 5-8R, CANR-4
See also RHW
See also SATA 35
Oman, Charles Chichele
1901-1982 ...... CANR-75
Obituary 105
Earlier sketch in CA 103
Oman, Julia Trevelyan 1930-2003 126
Obituary 220
Omang, Joanne (Brenda) 1943- 135
Omansky, Dorothy Linder 1905(?)-1977
Obituary 73-76
O Maolain, Ciaran 1958- 123
O'Maonaigh, Cainneach
See Mooney, Canice (Albert James)
O'Mara, Peggy (Noreen) 1947- 201
Omari, T(hompson) Peter 1930- 29-32R
O'Marie, Carol Anne 1933- CANR-142
Earlier sketches in CA 136, CANR-63
See also CMW 4
See also MSW
O'Marie, Sister Carol Anne
See O'Marie, Carol Anne
Omar Khayyam
See Khayyam, Omar
See also RGWL 2, 3
Omar Mohammad Noor 1941- ...... CP 1
Omarr, Sydney -2003
Obituary 212
Brief entry 116
O'Meally, Robert G(eorge) 1948- 130
O'Meara, John 1953- 191
O'Meara, John J. 1915- CANR-3
Earlier sketch in CA 1-4R
O'Meara, Patrick 1938- 113
O'Meara, Thomas F(ranklin) 1935- . CANR-144
Earlier sketch in CA 110
O'Meara, Walter (Andrew)
1897-1989 ...... CANR-77
Obituary 129
Earlier sketch in CA 13-16R
See also SATA 65
Omer, Garth St.
See St. Omer, Garth
Omissi, David 1960- 186
Ommanney, F(rancis) D(ownes)
1903-1980 ...... CANR-7
Obituary 101
Earlier sketch in CA 13-16R
See also SATA 23
Ommundsen, Wenche 1952- 147
O'More, Peggy
See Blocklinger, Peggy O'More
O'Morrison, Kevin CANR-9
Earlier sketch in CA 53-56
Omotoso, Kole 1943- CANR-78
Earlier sketch in CA 143
See also AFW
See also BW 2, 3
See also DLB 125
O Mude
See Gorey, Edward (St. John)
Omulevsky, Innokentii Vasil'evich
1836(?)-1883 ...... DLB 238
O'Mullane, Tess De Araugo
See De Araugo, Tess (S.)
Ona, Pedro de 1570-1643(?) ...... LAW
Onacewicz, Wlodzimierz 1893(?)-1986
Obituary 120
Onadipe, (Nathaniel) Kola(wole) 1922- 101
O'Nair, Mairi
See Evans, Constance May
O'Nan, Stewart 1961- CANR-81
Earlier sketch in CA 146
See also CN 7
Onate, Andres David 1940-
Brief entry 112
Ondaatje, Christopher 1933- 49-52
Ondaatje, (Philip) Michael 1943- ... CANR-133
Earlier sketches in CA 77-80, CANR-42, 74, 109
See also AAYA 66
See also CLC 14, 29, 51, 76, 180
See also CN 5, 6, 7
See also CP 1, 2, 3, 4, 5, 6, 7
See also DA3
See also DAB
See also DAC
See also DAM MST
See also DLB 60
See also EWL 3
See also LATS 1:2
See also LMFS 2
See also MTCW 2
See also MTFW 2005
See also PC 28
See also PFS 8, 19
See also TCLE 1:2
See also TWA
See also WWE 1
Ondego, Ogova 1968- 217
Ondricek, Miroslav 1934- ...... IDFW 3, 4
O'Neal, Bill
See O'Neal, John W(illiam)
O'Neal, Charles E. 1904-1996 ...... CAP-2
Obituary 153
Earlier sketch in CA 19-20
O'Neal, Cothburn M(adison) 1907- .. CANR-86
Earlier sketch in CA 1-4R
Oneal, Elizabeth 1934- CANR-84
Earlier sketches in CA 106, CANR-28
See also Oneal, Zibby
See also MAICYA 1, 2
See also SATA 30, 82
See also YAW

O'Neal, Forest Hodge 1917- 5-8R
O'Neal, Glenn (Franklin) 1919- 49-52
O'Neal, Hank 1940- 134
O'Neal, John W(illiam) 1942- 89-92
O'Neal, Reagan
  See Rigney, James Oliver, Jr.
O'Neal, William B(ainter) 1907- 73-76
Oneal, Zibby
  See Oneal, Elizabeth
  See also AAYA 5, 41
  See also BYA 13
  See also CLC 30
  See also CLR 13
  See also JRDA
  See also WYA
Onega, Susana
  See Onega Jaen, Susana
Onega Jaen, Susana
  See Onega Jaen, Susana
Onega Jaen, Susana 1948- 190
O'Neil, Daniel J. 1936- 89-92
O'Neil, Dennis 1939- 97-100
O'Neil, Eric
  See Barnum, W(illiam) Paul
O'Neil, Ginger
  See O'Neil, Mary Garvin
O'Neil, Isabel MacDonald 1908(?)-1981
  Obituary 105
O'Neil, Mary Garvin 1930- 213
O'Neil, Patrick H. 1966- 182
O'Neil, Paul E. 1909(?)-1988
  Obituary 125
  See also DFS 2,4,5,6
O'Neil, Robert M(archant) 1934- 106
O'Neil, Terry 1949- 61-64
O'Neil, W(illiam) M(atthew)
  1912-1991 .... CANR-32
  Earlier sketch in CA 113
O'Neil, Will(iam Daniel III) 1938- 101
O'Neill, Alexandre 1924-1986 .... EWL 3
O'Neill, Alexis 1949- 236
O'Neill, Amanda 1951- 182
  See also SATA 111
O'Neill, Anthony 1964- 218
O'Neill, Archie
  See Henaghan, Jim
O'Neill, Barbara Powell 1929- 17-20R
O'Neill, Brian Juan 1950- 153
O'Neill, Carlota 1918- 101
O'Neill, Carlotta Monterey 1888-1970
  Obituary 29-32R
O'Neill, Charles Edwards 1927- CANR-9
  Earlier sketch in CA 21-24R
O'Neill, Cherry Boone 1954- 112
O'Neill, Daniel Joseph 1905-
  Brief entry 106
O'Neill, David P(atrick) 1918- CANR-86
  Earlier sketch in CA 17-20R
O'Neill, Dennis (Bernard) 1947- 114
O'Neill, E. Bard 1941- 85-88
O'Neill, Egan
  See Linington, (Barbara) Elizabeth
O'Neill, Eugene (Gladstone)
  1888-1953 .... CANR-131
  Brief entry 110
  Earlier sketch in CA 132
  See also AAYA 54
  See also AITN 1
  See also AMW
  See also AMWC 1
  See also CAD
  See also CDALB 1929-1941
  See also DA
  See also DA3
  See also DAB
  See also DAC
  See also DAM DRAM, MST
  See also DC 20
  See also DFS 2, 4, 5, 6, 9, 11, 12, 16, 20
  See also DLB 7
  See also EWL 3
  See also LAIT 3
  See also LMFS 2
  See also MAL 5
  See also MTCW 1, 2
  See also MTFW 2005
  See also RGAL 4
  See also TCLC 1, 6, 27, 49
  See also TUS
  See also WLC
O'Neill, Eugene 1922- 77-80
O'Neill, Frank (Quale) 1943- 120
O'Neill, Frank F. 1926(?)-1983
  Obituary 109
O'Neill, George 1921(?)-1980
  Obituary 102
  See also AITN 1
O'Neill, Gerard (Michael) 1942- 69-72
O'Neill, Gerard K(itchen)
  1927-1992 .... CANR-75
  Obituary 137
  Earlier sketches in CA 93-96, CANR-21
  See also SATA 65
O'Neill, J(erry) M. 1921-1999 229
O'Neill, James E(dward) 1929-1987 . CANR-75
  Obituary 121
  Earlier sketch in CA 117
O'Neill, Jamie 1962- 216
O'Neill, John 1933- 53-56
O'Neill, John Joseph 1920- 21-24R
O'Neill, Joseph 1964- CANR-122
  Earlier sketch in CA 164
O'Neill, Joseph Harry 1915- 13-16R
O'Neill, Joseph James 1878-1952 162
  See also SFW 4
O'Neill, Judith (Beatrice) 1930- CANR-85
  Earlier sketches in CA 109, CANR-26, 51
  See also SATA 34
  See also YAW
O'Neill, Mary L(e Duc) 1908(?)-1990 . CANR-4
  Obituary 130
  Earlier sketch in CA 5-8R
  See also SATA 2
  See also SATA-Obit 64
O'Neill, Michael 1953- CANR-85
  Earlier sketch in CA 133
O'Neill, Michael J. 104
  See also CBD
  See also CD 5, 6
O'Neill, Michael J. 1913- 13-16R
O'Neill, Michael J(ames) 1922- 112
  Brief entry 108
  Interview in CA-112
O'Neill, Nena .... AITN 1
O'Neill, Olivia
  See Barstow, Phyllida
O'Neill, Patrick Geoffrey 1924- 21-24R
O'Neill, Paul 1928- 107
O'Neill, Reginald F. 1915- 1-4R
O'Neill, Richard W(inslow) 1925-
  Brief entry 107
O'Neill, Robert J(ohn) 1936- 25-28R
O'Neill, Seosamh
  See O'Neill, Joseph James
O'Neill, Shane
  See O'Neill, William
O'Neill, Susan 1947- 224
O'Neill, Terence Marne 1914-1990 108
O'Neill, Thomas Philip, Jr. 1912-1994 159
O'Neill, Tim 1918- 1-4R
O'Neill, Timothy J. 1949- 153
O'Neill, Timothy P. 1941- 85-88
O'Neill, Timothy R. 1943- 128
O'Neill, Tip
  See O'Neill, Thomas Philip, Jr.
O'Neill, William 1927- 37-40R
O'Neill, William F. 1931- 29-32R
O'Neill, William L. 1935- CANR-85
  Earlier sketches in CA 21-24R, CANR-12, 34
O'Neill of the Maine, Baron of Ahoghill
  See O'Neill, Terence Marne
O'Nell, Carl William 1925- 73-76
Oness, Elizabeth 1960- 200
Onetti, Juan Carlos 1909-1994 .... CANR-63
  Obituary 145
  Earlier sketches in CA 85-88, CANR-32
  See also CDWLB 3
  See also CLC 7, 10
  See also CWW 2
  See also DAM MULT, NOV
  See also DLB 113
  See also EWL 3
  See also HLCS 2
  See also HW 1, 2
  See also LAW
  See also MTCW 1, 2
  See also MTFW 2005
  See also RGSF 2
  See also SSC 23
  See also TCLC 131
Ong, Han 1968- 208
Ong, Walter J(ackson) 1912-2003 .... CANR-21
  Obituary 219
  Earlier sketches in CA 1-4R, CANR-4
Ongaro, Alberto 1925- 25-28R
Onians, Dick
  See Onians, Richard (Lathbury)
Onians, John 1942- 189
Onians, Richard (Lathbury) 1940-1999 216
O'Niell, C. M.
  See Wilkes-Hunter, R(ichard)
Onions, Charles Talbut 1873-1965
  Obituary 107
Onions, Oliver
  See Oliver, George
Onions, (George) Oliver 1872-1961 166
  See also DLB 153
  See also HGG
  See also SUFW
Onley, David C(harles) 1950- 112
Onlooker
  See Grange, Cyril
Onnes, Heike Kamerlingh
  See Kamerlingh Onnes, Heike
Ono, Chiyo 1941- CANR-12
  Earlier sketch in CA 29-32R
Ono, Yoko 1933- 235
Onoda, Hiroo 1922(?)-
  Brief entry 108
Onofri, Arturo 1885-1928 .... DLB 114
O'Nolan, Brian
  See O Nuallain, Brian
  See also DLB 231
Onopa, Robert 1943- 112
Onorato, Richard James 1933-
  Brief entry 108
Onslow, Annette Rosemary MacArthur
  See MacArthur-Onslow, Annette Rosemary
Onslow, John 1906-1985
  Obituary 118
  See also SATA-Obit 47
Onstott, Kyle 1887-1966 .... CANR-85
  Obituary 126
  Earlier sketch in CA 5-8R
  See also RHW 1
Ontoya, Jose 1932- 131
O Nuallain, Brian 1911-1966 .... CAP-2
  Obituary 25-28R
  Earlier sketch in CA 21-22
  See also O'Brien, Flann and
  O'Nolan, Brian
  See also DLB 231
  See also FANT
  See also TEA
Onwueme, (Osonye) Tess
  See Onwueme, Tess Akaeke
  See also EWL 3
Onwueme, Tess Akaeke 1954- 168
  See also Onwueme, (Osonye) Tess
Onwueme, Tess Osonye
  See Onwueme, Tess Akaeke
Onwumechili, Chukwuka Agodi 1960- 188
Onyeama, (Charles) Dillibe 1951- 125
  See also BW 1
Onyefulu, Ifeoma 1959- 187
  See also SATA 81, 115, 157
Oodgeroo
  See Walker, Kath
  See also DLB 289
Ooi Jin-Bee 1931- 73-76
Ooiman, Jo Ann
  See Robinson, Jo Ann Ooiman
Ooka, Makoto 1931- 191
Ooka, Shohei 1909-1988 195
Oost, Stewart Irvin 1921-1981 .... 29-32R
  Obituary 135
Oosterhuis, Harry 1958- 200
Oosterman, Gordon 1927- 49-52
Oosterwal, Gottfried 1930- 93-96
Oosthuizen, G(erhardus) C(ornelis)
  1922- CANR-52
  Earlier sketches in CA 29-32R, CANR-27
Oparin, Aleksandr (Ivanovich) 1894-1980
  Obituary 108
Opdahl, Keith Michael 1934- 61-64
Opdahl, Richard D(ean) 1924- 21-24R
Opdyke, Irene Gut 1918-2003 192
  Obituary 216
Opgenoorth, Winfried 1939- .... SATA-Brief 50
Ophuls, Max 1902-1957
  Brief entry 113
  See also TCLC 79
Ophuls, Patrick 1934- CANR-118
  Earlier sketch in CA 135
Ophuls, William
  See Ophuls, Patrick
Opie, Amelia 1769-1853 .... DLB 116, 159
  See also RGEL 2
Opie, Anne 1946- 145
Opie, Iona (Margaret Balfour)
  1923- CANR-101
  Earlier sketches in CA 61-64, CANR-84
  See also CWRI 5
  See also MAICYA 2
  See also MAICYAS 1
  See also SAAS 6
  See also SATA 3, 63, 118
Opie, John 1934- 29-32R
Opie, Peter (Mason) 1918-1982 .... CANR-84
  Obituary 106
  Earlier sketches in CA 5-8R, CANR-2
  See also CWRI 5
  See also MAICYA 2
  See also MAICYAS 1
  See also SATA 3, 63, 118
  See also SATA-Obit 28
Opie, Redvers 1900-1984
  Obituary 112
Opik, E.
  See Oepik, Ernst Julius
Opik, Ernst
  See Oepik, Ernst Julius
Opik, Ernst J.
  See Oepik, Ernst Julius
Opik, Ernst Julius
  See Oepik, Ernst Julius
Opitz, Edmund A. 1914- CANR-86
  Earlier sketch in CA 29-32R
Opitz, Martin 1597-1639 .... DLB 164
Opitz, May
  See Ayim, May
Opland, Jeff 1943- 106
Opler, Marvin K(aufmann) 1914-1981 .. 21-24R
  Obituary 133
Opler, Morris E(dward) 1907-1996 ... CANR-29
  Earlier sketch in CA 45-48
Opotowsky, Stan(ford L.) 1923-1997 .. CANR-1
  Obituary 161
  Earlier sketch in CA 1-4R
Oppedisano, Jeannette M. 1943- 237
Oppel, Kenneth 1967- 160
  See also AAYA 53
  See also MAICYA 2
  See also SATA 99, 153
Oppelt, Norman T. 1930- 139
Oppen, George 1908-1984 .... CANR-82
  Obituary 113
  Earlier sketches in CA 13-16R, CANR-8
  See also CLC 7, 13, 34
  See also CP 1, 2
  See also DLB 5, 165
  See also PC 35
  See also TCLC 107
Oppen, Mary 1908-1990 119
  Obituary 131
Oppenheim, A(dolph) Leo 1904-1974
  Obituary 49-52
Oppenheim, E(dward) Phillips 1866-1946 .. 202
  Brief entry 111
  See also CMW 4
  See also DLB 70
  See also TCLC 45
Oppenheim, Felix E(rrera) 1913- 1-4R
Oppenheim, Frank Mathias 1925- CANR-93
  Earlier sketch in CA 116
Oppenheim, Irene 1928- 77-80
Oppenheim, James 1882-1932 184
  See also DLB 28
Oppenheim, Janet 1948- 117
Oppenheim, Joanne 1934- CANR-115
  Earlier sketches in CA 21-24R, CANR-9, 25, 50
  See also SATA 5, 82, 136
Oppenheim, Lois Hecht 1948- CANR-103
  Earlier sketch in CA 149
Oppenheim, Lois Susan
  See Oppenheim, Lois Hecht
Oppenheim, Micha Falk 1937- 147
Oppenheim, Michael 1940- 138
Oppenheim, Paul 1885(?)-1977
  Obituary 69-72
Oppenheim, Philip 1956- 138
Oppenheim, S(aul) Chesterfield 1897-1988
  Obituary 124
Oppenheim, Shulamith (Levey) 1930- 73-76
Oppenheimer, Andres 1951- 145
Oppenheimer, Evelyn 1907-1998 .... CANR-3
  Earlier sketch in CA 1-4R
Oppenheimer, George 1900-1977 .... CANR-93
  Obituary 73-76
  Earlier sketch in CA 13-16R
Oppenheimer, Gregg 1951- 160
Oppenheimer, Harold L. 1919- 17-20R
Oppenheimer, J(ulius) Robert
  1904-1967 .... CANR-34
  Earlier sketch in CA 103
  See also MTCW 1
Oppenheimer, Jess 1913(?)-1988
  Obituary 127
Oppenheimer, Joan L(etson) 1925- ... CANR-37
  Earlier sketches in CA 37-40R, CANR-17
  See also SATA 28
Oppenheimer, Joe A(llan) 1941- 111
Oppenheimer, Joel (Lester)
  1930-1988 .... CANR-21
  Obituary 126
  Earlier sketches in CA 9-12R, CANR-4
  See also CP 1, 2
  See also DLB 5, 193
Oppenheimer, Mark 1974- 238
Oppenheimer, Martin 1930- CANR-88
  Earlier sketch in CA 29-32R
Oppenheimer, Max, Jr. 1917- 17-20R
Oppenheimer, Michael 1924- 226
Oppenheimer, Paul 1939- CANR-100
  Earlier sketch in CA 21-24R
Oppenheimer, Samuel P(hilip)
  1903-1982 .... 33-36R
Oppenheimer, Todd 233
Opper, F.
  See Opper, Frederick (Burr)
Opper, Frederick (Burr) 1857-1937
  Brief entry 118
  See also AITN 1
Opper, Jacob 1935- 49-52
Opperby, Preben 1924- 110
Opperman, D(iederik) J(ohannes)
  1914-1985 216
Oppersdorff, Mathias T. 1935- 233
Oppersdorff, Tony 1945- 137
Oppitz, Rene 1905(?)-1976
  Obituary 65-68
Oppong, Christine 1940- CANR-7
  Earlier sketch in CA 57-60
Oppong, Joseph Ransford 1953- 236
  See also SATA 160
Optic, Oliver
  See Adams, William Taylor and
  Stratemeyer, Edward L.
Opton, Edward M., Jr. 1936- CANR-11
  Earlier sketch in CA 21-24R
Opuls, Max
  See Ophuls, Max
O'Quill, Scarlett
  See Mossman, Dow
O'Quinn, Garland 1935- 21-24R
O'Quinn, Hazel Hedick 37-40R
O'R., P.
  See Dark, Eleanor
Orage, A(lfred) R(ichard) 1873-1934
  Brief entry 122
  See also TCLC 157
Oraison, Marc 1914-1979 85-88
Oram, Hiawyn 1946- 106
  See also CWRI 5
  See also SATA 56, 101
Oram, Malcolm 1944(?)-1976
  Obituary 104
O'Ramus, Seamus
  See O'Neill, William
O'Rand, Angela M(etropulos) 1945- 104
O'Rane, Patricia
  See Dark, Eleanor
Oras, Ants 1900-1982 .... CAP-1
  Earlier sketch in CA 13-16
Orbaan, Albert F. -1983 .... CANR-88
  Earlier sketches in CA 5-8R, CANR-8
Orbach, Ruth Gary 1941- 65-68
  See also SATA 21
Orbach, Susie 1946- CANR-96
  Earlier sketches in CA 85-88, CANR-19, 42
Orbach, William W(olf) 1946- 73-76
Orban, Christine 234
Orban, Clara (Elizabeth) 1960- 198
Orbanes, Philip E. 1947- 233
Orbell, Margaret 1934- 158
Orben, Robert 1927- CANR-70
  Earlier sketches in CA 81-84, CANR-31
Orbis, Victor
  See Powell-Smith, Vincent (Walter Francis)

Cumulative Index 439 Ortiz

Orcutt, Georgia 1949- 112
Orcutt, Jane 238
Orczy, Emma
See Orczy, Baroness Emmuska
See also DLB 70
Orczy, Emma Magdalena Rosalia Maria Josefa
See Orczy, Baroness Emmuska
Orczy, Emmuska
See Orczy, Baroness Emmuska
Orczy, Baroness Emmuska 1865-1947 167
Brief entry 104
See also Orczy, Emma
See also CMW 4
See also SATA 40
Ord, John E. 1917-1993 81-84
Orde, A. J.
See Tepper, Sheri S.
Orde, Lewis 1943- CANR-28
Earlier sketch in CA 109
Ord-Hume, Arthur W. J. G. 101
Ordinans, Nicholas J. 1950- 217
Ordish, (Francis) George
1908(?)-1991 .... CANR-90
Obituary 133
Earlier sketches in CA 61-64, CANR-9
Ordover, Sondra T. 1929-1988
Obituary 127
Ordway, Frederick I(ra) III 1927- CANR-112
Earlier sketches in CA 5-8R, CANR-5, 20, 49
Ordway, Sally 1939- 57-60
Ore, Rebecca 1948- CANR-102
Earlier sketch in CA 164
See also SFW 4
Oreamuno, Yolanda 1916-1956 .... EWL 3
O'Regan, Richard Arthur 1919- 73-76
O'Regan, Valerie R. 1956- 204
O'Reilly, Bill 173
O'Reilly, Bill 173
O'Reilly, Don 1913-2000 111
O'Reilly, Jackson
See Rigney, James Oliver, Jr.
O'Reilly, Jane 1936- CANR-31
Earlier sketch in CA 73-76
O'Reilly, John (Thomas) 1945- 29-32R
O'Reilly, Kenneth 1951- 155
O'Reilly, Montagu
See Andrews, Wayne
O'Reilly, Robert P. 1936- 29-32R
O'Reilly, Timothy 1954- CANR-23
Earlier sketch in CA 106
O'Reilly, Victor 1944- 156
Orel, Harold 1926- CANR-43
Earlier sketches in CA 5-8R, CANR-3, 19
Orellana, Sandra L. 1941- 126
O'Relley, Z(oltan) Edward 1940- 119
Orem, R(eginald) C(alvert) 1931- 17-20R
Oren, Aras 1939- 197
Oren, Dan A. 1958- 138
Oren, Michael B(ornstein) 216
Oren, Uri 1931- 65-68
Orend, Brian (D.) 1971- 197
Orengo, Charles 1913(?)-1974
Obituary 104
Orenstein, Denise Gosliner 1950- CANR-141
Earlier sketch in CA 110
See also SATA 157
Orenstein, Frank (Everett) 1919- CANR-54
Earlier sketches in CA 111, CANR-30
Orenstein, Gloria Feman 1938- 65-68
Orenstein, Henry 1924-1980 .... 13-16R
Orenstein, Peggy 1961- CANR-96
Earlier sketch in CA 147
Orent, Norman B. 1920- 17-20R
Orent, Wendy 239
Oreshnik, A. F.
See Nussbaum, Al(bert F.)
Oresick, Peter (Michael) 1955- CANR-56
Earlier sketches in CA 73-76, CANR-13, 30
Orest
See Bedrij, Orest (John)
Oretti, Carlos
See Harsch, Rick
Orewa, George Oka 1928- 5-8R
Orey, Michael 202
Orfalea, Gregory (M.) 1949- 128
Orff, Carl 1895-1982
Obituary 106
Orfield, Olivia 1922- 103
Orga, Ates 1944- 93-96
Organ, John 1925- CANR-7
Earlier sketch in CA 5-8R
Organ, Troy Wilson 1912-1992 .... CANR-89
Earlier sketch in CA 37-40R
Organski, A(bramo) F(imo) K(enneth)
1923-1998 103
Orgel, Doris 1929- CANR-131
Earlier sketches in CA 45-48, CANR-2
See also AITN 1
See also CLR 48
See also SAAS 19
See also SATA 7, 85, 148
See also YAW
Orgel, Joseph Randolph 1902-1987 .... CAP-1
Obituary 123
Earlier sketch in CA 11-12
Orgel, Stephen (Kitay) 1933- CANR-14
Earlier sketch in CA 73-76
Orgill, Douglas 1922-1984 .... CANR-29
Earlier sketch in CA 81-84
Orgill, Michael (Thomas) 1946- 61-64
Orians, George H(arrison) 1900-1985 49-52
Orians, Gordon H(owell) 1932- CANR-30
Earlier sketch in CA 45-48
Oriard, Michael (Vincent) 1948- 110
Origo, Iris (Margaret Cutting)
1902-1988 .... CANR-89
Earlier sketches in CA 105, CANR-47
See also DLB 155
O'Riley, Warren
See Richardson, Gladwell
Oring, Elliott 1945- 111
Oriolo, Joe
See Oriolo, Joseph D.
Oriolo, Joseph D. 1913-1985
Obituary 118
See also SATA-Obit 46
Orion
See Naylor, John
O'Riordan, Kate 1960- .... DLB 267
O'Riordan, Robert (Garrett) 1943- 119
Orizio, Riccardo 1961- 226
Orjuela, Hector H(ugo) 1930- CANR-32
Earlier sketches in CA 45-48, CANR-2
See also HW 1
Orkeny, Antal 1954- 143
Orkeny, Istvan 1912-1979 .... CANR-84
Obituary 89-92
Earlier sketch in CA 103
See also RGSF 2
Orkin, Harvey 1918(?)-1975
Obituary 61-64
Orkin, Ruth 1921-1985 119
Obituary 114
Orland, Claude 1915-1997
See Roy, Claude
Orlandersmith, Dael 1960- 222
Orlando, Guido 1908(?)-1988
Obituary 126
Orlando, Tony 1944- 222
Orlans, Harold 1921- CANR-15
Earlier sketch in CA 33-36R
Orlean, Susan 1955- CANR-102
Earlier sketch in CA 134
See also AAYA 64
Orleans, Ilo 1897-1962 .... CANR-15
Earlier sketch in CA 1-4R
See also SATA 10
Orleans, Leo A(nton) 1924- CANR-32
Earlier sketches in CA 41-44R, CANR-15
Orleans, Marion (de Bourbon) d' 1941- 211
Orleans, Thibaut (Louis Denis Humbert de
Bourbon) d' 1948-1983 224
Orleck, Annelise 1959- 149
Orledge, Robert (Nicholas) 1948- 113
Orlen, Steve 1942- 101
Orlev, Uri 1931- CANR-113
Earlier sketches in CA 101, CANR-34, 84
See also AAYA 20
See also CLR 30
See also MAICYA 2
See also MAICYAS 1
See also SAAS 19
See also SATA 58, 135
See also YAW
Orlich, Donald C(harles) 1931- CANR-45
Earlier sketches in CA 13-16R, CANR-7, 22
Orlick, Terrance D(ouglas) 1945- CANR-45
Earlier sketches in CA 57-60, CANR-6, 21
Orlick, Terry
See Orlick, Terrance D(ouglas)
Orlicky, Joseph A. 1922-1986 .... 25-28R
Orlier, Blaise
See Sylvestre, (Joseph Jean) Guy
Orlinsky, Harry M(eyer) 1908-1992 .... CANR-83
Obituary 137
Earlier sketch in CA 85-88
Orlob, Helen (Seaburg) 1908-1991 .... CANR-89
Earlier sketch in CA 5-8R
Orlock, Carol (Ellen) 1947- CANR-48
Earlier sketch in CA 122
Orloff, Ed(gar Sam) 1923-1983 .... CANR-77
Obituary 110
Earlier sketch in CA 69-72
Orloff, Erica 180
Orloff, Judith 1951- CANR-92
Earlier sketch in CA 155
Orloff, Max
See Crowcroft, Peter
Orlofsky, Myron 1928(?)-1976
Obituary 69-72
Orloski, Richard J(ohn) 1947- 97-100
Orlova, Alexandra (Anatol'evna)
1911- CANR-82
Earlier sketch in CA 133
Orlova, R.
See Orlova-Kopelev, Raissa (Davydovna)
Orlova, R. D.
See Orlova-Kopelev, Raissa (Davydovna)
Orlova, Raisa
See Orlova-Kopelev, Raissa (Davydovna)
Orlova-Kopelev, Raissa (Davydovna)
1918- 123
Orlovitz, Gil 1918-1973 77-80
Obituary 45-48
See also CLC 22
See also CN 1
See also CP 1, 2
See also DLB 2, 5
Orlovsky, Peter 1933- CANR-9
Earlier sketch in CA 13-16R
See also CP 1
See also DLB 16
Orlow, Dietrich (Otto) 1937- CANR-89
Earlier sketch in CA 65-68
Ormai, Stella .... SATA 57
See also SATA-Brief 48
Orman, Suze 174
Orme, Antony R(onald) 1936- CANR-94
Earlier sketches in CA 73-76, CANR-35
Ormerod, Jan 1946- CANR-35
Earlier sketch in CA 113
See also CLR 20
See also MAICYA 1, 2
See also SATA 55, 70, 132
See also SATA-Brief 44
Ormerod, Roger 1920- CANR-63
Earlier sketches in CA 77-80, CANR-15, 35
See also CMW 4
Ormes, Jackie
See Ormes, Zelda J.
Ormes, Robert M. 1904-1994 .... CAP-1
Earlier sketch in CA 11-12
Ormes, Robert Verner 1921-1984
Obituary 112
Ormes, Zelda J. 1914-1986
Obituary 118
See also SATA-Obit 47
Ormesson, Jean (Bruno Waldemar
Francois-de-Paule Lefevre) d'
See d'Ormesson, Jean (Bruno Waldemar
Francois-de-Paule Lefevre)
Ormesson, Wladimir d' 1888-1973
Obituary 45-48
Ormiston, Roberta
See Fletcher, Adele (Whitely)
Ormond, (Willard) Clyde
1906-1985 .... CANR-36
Obituary 115
Earlier sketch in CA 9-12R
Ormond, Frederic
See Dey, Frederic (Merrill) Van Rensselaer
Ormond, John 1923- CANR-32
Earlier sketch in CA 65-68
See also CP 1, 2
See also DLB 27
Ormond, Leonee (Jasper) 1940- 85-88
Ormond, Richard (Louis) 1939- CANR-82
Earlier sketches in CA 41-44R, CANR-15, 35
Ormondroyd, Edward 1925- CANR-84
Earlier sketch in CA 73-76
See also CWRI 5
See also SATA 14
Ormont, Louis Robert 1918- CANR-35
Earlier sketch in CA 13-16R
Ormrod, Richard (James) 1946- 119
Ormsbee, David
See Longstreet, Stephen
Ormsby, Eric (Linn) 1941- CANR-140
Earlier sketch in CA 174
Ormsby, Frank 1947- CANR-143
Earlier sketches in CA 107, CANR-23
See also CP 7
Ormsby, Virginia H(aire)
1906-1990 .... CANR-89
Earlier sketch in CA 9-12R
See also SATA 11
Ormsby, William (George) 1921- 73-76
Orna, Mary Virginia 1934- 29-32R
Ornati, Oscar A(braham)
1922-1991 .... CANR-75
Obituary 136
Earlier sketches in CA 37-40R, CANR-14
Ornis
See Winchester, Clarence
Ornish, Dean 1953- CANR-70
Earlier sketch in CA 142
Ornitz, Samuel (Badisch) 1890-1957
Brief entry 117
See also DLB 28, 44
Ornstein, Allan C(harles) 1941- CANR-4
Earlier sketch in CA 53-56
Ornstein, Dolph 1947- 77-80
Ornstein, J. L.
See Ornstein-Galicia, J(acob) L(eonard)
Ornstein, Jack H(ervey) 1938- 103
Ornstein, Norman J(ay) 1948- 93-96
Ornstein, Robert 1925- 1-4R
Ornstein, Robert E. 1942- CANR-35
Earlier sketch in CA 53-56
Ornstein-Galicia, J(acob) L(eonard)
1915- 93-96
Oropeza, Renato Prada
See Prada Oropeza, Renato
Orosz, Joel J. 1957- 199
O'Rourke, Andrew P(atrick) 1933- 126
O'Rourke, Edmund N., Jr. 1923- 213
O'Rourke, Edward William 1917-1999 112
Obituary 185
O'Rourke, F.M.
See O'Rourke, Michael
O'Rourke, Francis Michael
See O'Rourke, Michael
O'Rourke, Frank 1916-1989 .... CANR-118
Obituary 128
Brief entry 114
Earlier sketches in CA 118, CANR-65
Interview in CA-118
See also TCWW 1, 2
O'Rourke, James S. IV 1946- 201
O'Rourke, John James Joseph 1926- 33-36R
O'Rourke, John T(homas) 1900-1983
Obituary 111
O'Rourke, Lawrence Michael 1938- CANR-35
Earlier sketch in CA 69-72
O'Rourke, Michael -2001 173
O'Rourke, P(atrick) J(ake) 1947- CANR-111
Earlier sketches in CA 77-80, CANR-13, 41, 67
See also CLC 209
See also CPW
See also DAM POP
See also DLB 185
O'Rourke, Terrence James
1932-1992 .... CANR-75
Obituary 136
Earlier sketch in CA 41-44R
O'Rourke, Timothy G(erald) 1949- 111
O'Rourke, William (Andrew)
1945- CANR-118
Earlier sketches in CA 45-48, CANR-1, 35
Orozco, Olga 1920-1999 .... DLB 283
See also HW 1
See also LAWS 1
Orpaz, Yitzhak 1923- 101
Orpen, Eve 1926(?)-1978
Obituary 104
Orpen, Neil (Newton D'Arcy) 1913- 120
Orpen, Neil D.
See Orpen, Neil (Newton D'Arcy)
Orr, Bobby
See Orr, Robert Gordon
Orr, Daniel 1933- 29-32R
Orr, David 1929- 33-36R
Orr, David W. 1944- 235
Orr, Elaine Neil 1954- 237
Orr, Gregory (Simpson) 1947- 217
Earlier sketches in CA 105, CANR-22, 45, 85
Autobiographical Essay in 217
See also CP 7
Orr, Helen Frances Burton 1913-1989
Obituary 129
Orr, J(ames) Edwin 1912-1987 .... CANR-4
Earlier sketch in CA 9-12R
Orr, John Boyd 1880-1971
Obituary 113
Orr, Katherine S(helley) 1950- .... SATA 72
Orr, Linda 1943- CANR-35
Earlier sketch in CA 97-100
Orr, Mary
See Denham, Mary Orr
Orr, Mary E. E. McCombe 1918-1983 .... 5-8R
Orr, Oliver H(amilton), Jr. 1921- 1-4R
Orr, Robert Gordon 1948- 112
Orr, Robert R(ichmond) 1930- 25-28R
Orr, Robert T. 1908-1994 .... CANR-76
Obituary 146
Earlier sketch in CA 33-36R
Orr, Wendy 1953- CANR-112
Earlier sketch in CA 155
See also SATA 90, 141
Orr, William F(ridell) 1907- 108
Orrell, John (Overton) 1934-2003 .... CANR-35
Obituary 220
Earlier sketches in CA 37-40R, CANR-15
Orrery
See Boyle, Roger
Orris
See Ingelow, Jean
Orrmont, Arthur 1922- CANR-35
Earlier sketches in CA 1-4R, CANR-4
Orsborn, Carol 1948- 124
Orsi, Robert A. 1936- 186
Orsini, Gian Napoleone Giordano
1903-1976(?) 5-8R
Orsini, Joseph E(mmanuel) 1937- 37-40R
Orso, Kathryn Wickey 1921-1979 .... CANR-76
Obituary 85-88
Earlier sketch in CA 57-60
Orsy, Ladislas M. 1921- 25-28R
Orszagh, Laszlo 1907-1984
Obituary 112
Ort, Ana
See Andrews, Arthur (Douglas, Jr.)
Ortberg, John 230
Ortega, Bob
See Ortega, Robert Edward
Ortega, James M. 1932- 144
Ortega, Rafael Enrique 1952- 181
Ortega, Robert Edward 1958- 182
Ortega y Gasset, Jose 1883-1955 130
Brief entry 106
See also DAM MULT
See also EW 9
See also EWL 3
See also HLC 2
See also HW 1, 2
See also MTCW 1, 2
See also MTFW 2005
See also TCLC 9
Ortego, Philip D.
See Ortego y Gasca, Philip D.
Ortego y Gasca, Philip D. 1926- 131
See also HW 1
Orten, Jiri 1919-1941 .... DLB 215
Ortenberg, Veronica 1961- 139
Ortese, Anna Maria 1914-1998 .... CLC 89
See also DLB 177
See also EWL 3
Orth, Charles D. III 1921-2000 .... 5-8R
Orth, Penelope 1938- 45-48
Orth, Ralph H(arry) 1930- 21-24R
Orth, Richard
See Gardner, Richard (M.)
Orthwine, Rudolf 1900(?)-1970
Obituary 104
Ortiz, Adalberto 1914- 131
See also HW 1
Ortiz, Alfonso A(lex) 1939-1997 .... 29-32R
Obituary 156
Ortiz, Dianna 1958- 221
Ortiz, Elisabeth Lambert 1915-2003 .... CANR-93
Obituary 224
Earlier sketches in CA 97-100, CANR-35
Ortiz, Lourdes 1943- .... DLB 322

Ortiz, Simon J(oseph) 1941- CANR-118
Earlier sketches in CA 134, CANR-69
See also AMWS 4
See also CLC 45, 208
See also CP 7
See also DAM MULT, POET
See also DLB 120, 175, 256
See also EXPP
See also MAL 5
See also NNAL
See also PC 17
See also PFS 4, 16
See also RGAL 4
See also TCWW 2
Ortiz, Victoria 1942- 107
Ortiz Cofer, Judith
See Cofer, Judith Ortiz
See also DNFS 1, 2
See also LLW
Ortiz de Montellano, Thelma 1906-1999 ... 162
Ortiz y Pino, Jose III 1932- 112
Ortlip, Carol A(ileen) 1954- 220
Ortlund, Anne 1923- 106
Ortlund, Raymond C(arl) 1923- 114
Ortman, E(lmore) Jan 1884-1969 .... CAP-2
Earlier sketch in CA 25-28
Ortman, Elmer John
See Ortman, E(lmore) Jan
Ortner, Donald John 1938- 117
Ortner, Robert 1927- 135
Ortner, Sherry B(eth) 1941- CANR-86
Earlier sketch in CA 130
Ortner, Toni 1941- CANR-42
Ortner-Zimmerman, Toni
See Ortner, Toni
Orton, Alvin E. 1906-1987
Obituary 122
Orton, Anthony 1937- CANR-123
Earlier sketch in CA 163
Orton, Barry 1949- 111
Orton, Harold 1898-1975
Obituary 57-60
Orton, Joe
See Orton, John Kingsley
See also BRWS 5
See also CBD
See also CDBLB 1960 to Present
See also CLC 4, 13, 43
See also DC 3
See also DFS 3, 6
See also DLB 13, 310
See also GLL 1
See also RGEL 2
See also TCLC 157
See also TEA
See also WLIT 4
Orton, John Kingsley 1933-1967 ...... CANR-66
Earlier sketches in CA 85-88, CANR-35
See also Orton, Joe
See also DAM DRAM
See also MTCW 1, 2
See also MTFW 2005
Orton, Lawrence D(wayne) 1941-
Brief entry 118
Orton, Vrest (Teachout) 1897-1986 .. CANR-35
Obituary 121
Earlier sketch in CA 33-36R
Orttung, Robert W. 1964- 202
Ortzen, Len
See Ortzen, Leonard Edwin
Ortzen, Leonard Edwin 1912-1979 118
Brief entry 114
Orum, Anthony M(endl) 1939- 41-44R
Orvell, Miles 1944- 181
Earlier sketch in CA 41-44R
Orvil, Ernst
See Nilsen, Ernst
Orwell, George
See Blair, Eric (Arthur)
See also BPFB 3
See also BRW 7
See also BYA 5
See also CDBLB 1945-1960
See also CLR 68
See also DAB
See also DLB 15, 98, 195, 255
See also EWL 3
See also EXPN
See also LAIT 4, 5
See also LATS 1:1
See also NFS 3, 7
See also RGEL 2
See also SCFW 1, 2
See also SFW 4
See also SSC 68
See also SSFS 4
See also TCLC 2, 6, 15, 31, 51, 128, 129
See also TEA
See also WLC
See also WLIT 4
See also YAW
Orwell, Sonia 1919(?)-1980
Obituary 102
Orwen, (Phillips) Gifford -1997 .... 37-40R
Orwin, Clifford 181
Orwin, Joanna 1944- 212
See also SATA 141
Ory, Carlos Edmundo de 1923- .... DLB 134
Ory, Edward 1886-1973
Obituary 41-44R
Ory, Kid
See Ory, Edward
Ory, Marcia G. 1950- 141
Ory, Robert L(ouis) 1925- 142
Orzeck, Arthur Z(alman) 1921-2000 .. CANR-1
Earlier sketch in CA 45-48
Osa, Osayimwense 1951- CANR-87
Earlier sketch in CA 152
Osanka, Franklin Mark 1936- 5-8R
Osaragi, Jiro
See Nojiri, Kiyohiko
Osbeck, Kenneth W. 1924- CANR-41
Earlier sketches in CA 1-4R, CANR-3, 19
Osbey, Brenda Marie 1957- 197
See also DLB 120
Osbon, B(radley) S(illick) 1827-1912 183
See also DLB 43
Osborn, Albert D. 1896(?)-1972
Obituary 104
Osborn, Alex(ander) F(aickney) 1888-1966
Obituary 106
Osborn, Arthur W(alter) 1891- 21-24R
Osborn, Barbara M(onroe)
See Henkel, Barbara Osborn
Osborn, Carolyn 1934- 93-96
Osborn, Catherine B. 1914- 29-32R
Osborn, E. Margaret 1912- 165
Osborn, Elinor 1939- 218
See also SATA 145
Osborn, Eric (Francis) 1922- 65-68
Osborn, Frederic J(ames) 1885-1978 .. CANR-5
Earlier sketch in CA 5-8R
Osborn, Frederick (Henry)
1889-1981 .... CANR-76
Obituary 102
Earlier sketch in CA 25-28R
Osborn, George C(oleman)
1904-1982 .... CANR-19
Earlier sketch in CA 25-28R
Osborn, Ian 1946- 167
Osborn, James M(arshall)
1906-1976 .... CANR-90
Obituary 69-72
Earlier sketches in CAP-2, CA 25-28
Osborn, John Jay, Jr. 1945- CANR-6
Earlier sketch in CA 57-60
Osborn, Karen 1954- CANR-138
Earlier sketch in CA 162
Osborn, Lois D(orothy) 1915- 116
See also SATA 61
Osborn, Margot
See Osborn, E. Margaret
Osborn, Mary Elizabeth 1898-1979 . CANR-89
Earlier sketch in CA 5-8R
Osborn, Merton B(idwell) 1908-1987 ... 25-28R
Osborn, Paul 1901-1988 112
Obituary 125
Brief entry 108
Interview in CA-112
Osborn, Percy George 1899(?)-1972
Obituary 104
Osborn, Robert (Chesley) 1904-1994 .... 13-16R
Osborn, Robert T(appan) 1926- 21-24R
Osborn, Ronald E(dwin) 1917-1998 ...... 13-16R
Osborn, Sarah 1714-1796 .... DLB 200
Osborn, Stella Brunt
See Osborn, Stellanova
Osborn, Stellanova 1894-1988
Obituary 125
Osborn, Susan (E.) 1954- 139
Osborn, Thomas Noel II 1940- 114
Osborne, Adam 1939-2003 109
Obituary 215
Osborne, (Reginald) Arthur
1906-1970 .... CANR-75
Obituary 125
Earlier sketch in CA 17-20R
Osborne, Ben 1974- 238
Osborne, Betsy
See Boswell, Barbara (S.)
Osborne, C(harles) H(umfrey) C(aulfeild)
1891- 5-8R
Osborne, Cecil G. 1904-1999 .... CANR-1
Earlier sketch in CA 45-48
Osborne, Charles 1927- CANR-34
Earlier sketches in CA 13-16R, CANR-13
See also CP 1
See also SATA 59
Osborne, Chester G(orham)
1915-1987 .... CANR-35
Earlier sketches in CA 21-24R, CANR-9
See also SATA 11
Osborne, Dan 1948(?)-1983
Obituary 110
Osborne, David
See Silverberg, Robert
Osborne, David (E.) 1923- 134
Brief entry 109
Osborne, Dorothy (Gladys) Yeo 1917- 9-12R
Osborne, Eliza 1946- 206
Osborne, Elsie L(etitia) 1924-1995 118
Obituary 151
Osborne, Ernest (Glenn) 1903-1963 . CANR-88
Earlier sketch in CA 5-8R
Osborne, G(erald) S(tanley) 1926- 21-24R
Osborne, Geoffrey 1930- 110
Osborne, George
See Silverberg, Robert
Osborne, George E(dward) 1893-1977 .. CAP-2
Earlier sketch in CA 23-24
Osborne, Harold 1905-1987 .... CANR-76
Obituary 122
Earlier sketches in CA 13-16R, CANR-6
Osborne, Harold W(ayne) 1930- 57-60
Osborne, Helena
See Moore, (Georgina) Mary (Galbraith)
Osborne, J(ulius) K(enneth) 1941- 33-36R
Osborne, John (Franklin)
1907-1981 .... CANR-10
Obituary 108
Earlier sketch in CA 61-64
Osborne, John (James) 1929-1994 .... CANR-56
Obituary 147
Earlier sketches in CA 13-16R, CANR-21
See also BRWS 1
See also CBD
See also CDBLB 1945-1960
See also CLC 1, 2, 5, 11, 45
See also DA
See also DAB
See also DAC
See also DAM DRAM, MST
See also DFS 4, 19
See also DLB 13
See also EWL 3
See also MTCW 1, 2
See also MTFW 2005
See also RGEL 2
See also TCLC 153
See also WLC
Osborne, John W(alter) 1927- 33-36R
Osborne, Juanita Tyree 1916-1997 ... CANR-23
Earlier sketches in CA 61-64, CANR-8
Osborne, Lawrence 1958- 189
See also CLC 50
Osborne, Leone Neal 1914-1996 .... 21-24R
See also SATA 2
Osborne, Linda Barrett 1949- 65-68
Osborne, Maggie
See Osborne, Margaret Ellen
Osborne, Margaret 1909- 13-16R
Osborne, Margaret Ellen 1941- CANR-136
Earlier sketches in CA 102, CANR-18, 40
Osborne, Martha Lee 1928- 113
Osborne, Mary Pope 1949- CANR-124
Earlier sketches in CA 111, CANR-29, 62
See also CLR 88
See also SATA 41, 55, 98, 144
Osborne, Maureen 1924- 109
Osborne, Milton Edgeworth 1936- CANR-99
Earlier sketches in CA 13-16R, CANR-9
Osborne, Richard (Ellerker) 1943- .. CANR-137
Earlier sketch in CA 123
Osborne, Richard Horsley 1925- 21-24R
Osborne, Will 1949- 132
Osborne, William (Terry, Jr.) 1934- 25-28R
Osborne, William A(udley) 1919- 61-64
Osborne, William S(tewart) 1923- 53-56
Osbourn, R(ichard) A(lton) 1930- 120
Osbourne, Ivor Livingstone 1951- 108
Osbourne, Lloyd 1868-1947 .... TCLC 93
Osburn, Charles B(enjamin) 1939- ... CANR-13
Earlier sketch in CA 33-36R
Osceola
See Blixen, Karen (Christentze Dinesen)
Osen, James L. 1934- 175
Osen, Lynn M(oses) 1920- 65-68
Osenenko, John 1918-1983
Obituary 109
Oser, Jacob 1915-1982 .... CANR-2
Earlier sketch in CA 5-8R
Oser, Marie 1946- 202
Osers, Ewald 1917- 139
Osgood, Charles
See Wood, Charles Osgood III
Osgood, Charles E(gerton) 1916-1991 .. 17-20R
Osgood, Charles Grosvenor
1871-1964 .... CANR-4
Earlier sketch in CA 5-8R
Osgood, Cornelius 1905-1985
Obituary 114
Osgood, David William 1940- 89-92
Osgood, Don(ald W.) 1930- CANR-11
Earlier sketch in CA 61-64
Osgood, Ernest S(taples) 1888-1983 ...... CAP-1
Earlier sketch in CA 11-12
Osgood, Frances Sargent 1811-1850 .. DLB 250
Osgood, Herbert L(evi) 1855-1918
Brief entry 122
See also DLB 47
Osgood, Lawrence 1929- 85-88
Osgood, Robert Endicott
1921-1986 .... CANR-75
Obituary 121
Earlier sketches in CA 1-4R, CANR-3
Osgood, Samuel M(aurice) 1920-1975 . 33-36R
Osgood, William E(dward) 1926- 33-36R
See also SATA 37
Oshagan, Hagop 1883-1948 .... EWL 3
O'Shaughnessy, Andrew Jackson 231
O'Shaughnessy, Arthur 1844-1881 .... DLB 35
O'Shaughnessy, Brian 1925- 132
O'Shaughnessy, Darren 1972- 198
See also Shan, Darren
See also SATA 129
O'Shaughnessy, Ellen Cassels 1937- . CANR-93
Earlier sketch in CA 146
See also SATA 78
O'Shaughnessy, Mary 221
O'Shaughnessy, Pamela 221
O'Shaughnessy, Perri
See O'Shaughnessy, Mary and
O'Shaughnessy, Pamela
O'Shea, Kathleen 1944- 175
O'Shea, (Martin) Lester 1938- 108
O'Shea, (Catherine) Pat(ricia Shiels)
1931- CANR-84
Earlier sketch in CA 145
See also CLR 18
See also CWRI 5
See also FANT
See also SATA 87
O'Shea, Sean
See Tralins, S(andor) Robert
O'Shea, Stephen 205
Osherow, Jacqueline 1956- CANR-74
Earlier sketch in CA 137
Osherson, Samuel 1945- 205
Oshima, Nagisa 1932- CANR-78
Brief entry 116
Earlier sketch in CA 121
See also CLC 20
Oshinsky, David M. 1944- 165
O'Siadhail, Micheal 1947- 158
Osiek, Betty Tyree 1931- 45-48
Osing, Gordon T. 1937- 136
O Siochain, P(adraig) A(ugustine)
1905-1996 .... CAP-2
Earlier sketch in CA 17-18
Osipov, Nikolai Petrovich
1751-1799 .... DLB 150
Osipow, Samuel H(erman) 1934- CANR-1
Earlier sketch in CA 49-52
Osis, Karlis 1917- 85-88
Oskam, Bob
See Oskam, Robert T(heo)
Oskam, Robert T(heo) 1945- 108
Oskamp, Stuart 1930- CANR-12
Earlier sketch in CA 29-32R
Oski, Frank A(ram) 1932-1996 119
Obituary 155
Oskison, John Milton 1874-1947 ...... CANR-84
Earlier sketch in CA 144
See also DAM MULT
See also DLB 175
See also NNAL
See also TCLC 35
Osler, Margaret Jo 1942- 126
Osler, Robert Willard 1911-1984 ...... CANR-17
Obituary 114
Earlier sketch in CA 1-4R
Osler, Sir William 1849-1919 190
See also DLB 184
Osley, A(rthur) S(idney) 1917-1987 125
Oslin, George P(oer) 1899-1996 143
Obituary 154
Osman, Betty B(arshad) 1929- CANR-35
Earlier sketch in CA 93-96
Osman, Jack D(ouglas) 1943- CANR-35
Earlier sketches in CA 61-64, CANR-11
Osman, John 1907(?)-1978
Obituary 77-80
Osmanczyk, Edmund Jan 1913-1989
Obituary 130
Osmer, Margaret 93-96
Osmond, Andrew 1938-1999 .... 25-28R
Obituary 177
Osmond, Edward 1900- CANR-89
Earlier sketches in CAP-1, CA 13-14
See also SATA 10
Osmond, Humphry (Fortescue)
1917-2004 .... CANR-28
Obituary 223
Earlier sketch in CA 21-24R
Osmond, John 1946- 154
Osmond, Jonathan 1953- 146
Osmond, Marie 1959- CANR-126
Brief entry 112
Earlier sketch in CA 134
Osmond-Smith, David 1946- CANR-45
Earlier sketch in CA 120
Osmun, Mark 1952- 93-96
Osmunson, Robert Lee 1924- 9-12R
Osofisan, Femi 1946- CANR-84
Earlier sketch in CA 142
See also AFW
See also BW 2
See also CD 5, 6
See also CDWLB 3
See also DLB 125
See also EWL 3
Osofisan, Sola 1964- 169
Osofsky, Gilbert 1935-1974 65-68
Obituary 53-56
Osokina, Elena A(leksandrovna) 1959- 208
Osorgin, M. A.
See Ilyin, Mikhail Andreyevich
See also EWL 3
Osorio Benitez, Miguel Angel
See Barba-Jacob, Porfirio
Osserman, Richard A. 1930- 29-32R
Osserman, Robert 1926- 150
Ossian c. 3rd cent. -
See Macpherson, James
Osslinger, Kurt
See Allen, Bob
Ossman, David (H.) 1936- 9-12R
Ossman, Susan 1959- 213
Ossoli, Sarah Margaret (Fuller) 1810-1850
See Fuller, Margaret and
Fuller, Sarah Margaret
See also CDALB 1640-1865
See also FW
See also LMFS 1
See also SATA 25
Ossorgin, Mikhail
See Ilyin, Mikhail Andreyevich
Ossowska, Maria 1896-1974 .... 29-32R
Ossowski, Stanislaw 1897-1963 .... CAP-1
Earlier sketch in CA 13-14
Ost, David H(arry) 1940- CANR-6
Earlier sketch in CA 53-56
Ost, John William Philip 1931- 37-40R
Ostaijen, Paul van 1896-1928 .... EWL 3
See also RGWL 2, 3
Ostaro
See Goele, Dhruv
Ostayen, Paul van
See Ostaijen, Paul van
O'Steen, Sam 1923- .... IDFW 3, 4
Osten, Gar 1923- 65-68

Cumulative Index 441 Owen

Ostendorf, (Arthur) Lloyd, (Jr.)
1921-2000 .... CANR-6
Obituary 192
Earlier sketch in CA 1-4R
See also SATA 65
See also SATA-Obit 125
Ostenso, Martha 1900-1963 .... CANR-67
Earlier sketches in CAP-1, CA 13-16
See also CCA 1
See also DLB 92
See also TCWW 1, 2
Oster, Clinton Victor, Jr. 1947- 139
Oster, Jerry 1943- CANR-35
Earlier sketch in CA 77-80
Oster, Ludwig (Friedrich) 1931- 53-56
Oster, Patrick (Ralph) 1944- 131
Osterbrock, Donald E. 1924- CANR-127
Earlier sketch in CA 165
Osterburg, James W(illiam) 1917- 45-48
Ostergaard, G(eoffrey) N(ielsen)
1926-1990 .... CANR-75
Obituary 131
Earlier sketch in CA 25-28R
Osterhaven, M(aurice) Eugene 1915- 49-52
Osterhoudt, Robert G(erald) 1942- ... CANR-35
Earlier sketch in CA 53-56
Osterlund, Steven 1943- 77-80
Osterman, Paul 208
Osterritter, John F. 1923- 45-48
Osterweis, Rollin G(ustav)
1907-1982 .... CANR-91
Obituary 106
Earlier sketch in CA 41-44R
Ostheimer, John 1938- 41-44R
Ostle, Bernard 1921- 5-8R
Ostlere, Gordon (Stanley) 1921- CANR-105
Earlier sketch in CA 107
Ostling, Joan K. 225
Ostling, Richard N(eil) 1940- CANR-82
Earlier sketches in CA 53-56, CANR-35
Ostow, Mortimer 1918- CANR-82
Earlier sketches in CA 49-52, CANR-35
Ostrander, Gilman Marston 1923- 65-68
Ostrauskas, Kostas 1926- .... DLB 232
Ostriker, Alicia (Suskin) 1937- CANR-99
Earlier sketches in CA 25-28R, CANR-10, 30, 62
See also CAAS 24
See also CLC 132
See also CWP
See also DLB 120
See also EXPP
See also PFS 19
Ostrinsky, Meir Simha 1906-1992 .... CAP-2
Earlier sketch in CA 29-32
Ostroff, Anthony J(ames) 1923-1978 .. CANR-3
Obituary 77-80
Earlier sketch in CA 5-8R
Ostrom, Alan (Baer) 1925- 21-24R
Ostrom, Hans 1954- CANR-137
Earlier sketch in CA 139
Ostrom, John Ward 1903-1993 .... 1-4R
Ostrom, Thomas M. 1936- 37-40R
Ostrom, Vincent (Alfred) 1919-
Brief entry 113
Ostrov, Eric 1941- CANR-34
Earlier sketch in CA 113
Ostrovsky, Aleksandr Nikolaevich
See Ostrovsky, Alexander
See also DLB 277
Ostrovsky, Alexander 1823-1886
See Ostrovsky, Aleksandr Nikolaevich
Ostrovsky, Eugene 1938- 147
Ostrovsky, Nikolai Alekseevich 1904-1936
See Ostrovsky, Nikolay Alexeevich
See also DLB 272
Ostrovsky, Nikolay Alexeevich
See Ostrovsky, Nikolai Alekseevich
See also EWL 3
Ostrovsky, Victor 1949- 140
Ostrow, Joanna 1938- 29-32R
Ostrow, Ronald J. 1931- 130
Ostrower, Alexander 1901-1979 .... 17-20R
Obituary 120
Ostrower, Gary B. 1939- 154
Ostrowski, Jan K. 1947- 193
Ostrowsky
See Holmquist, Anders
Ostry, Sylvia 1927- CANR-15
Earlier sketch in CA 41-44R
Ostwald, Martin 1922- CANR-35
Earlier sketch in CA 33-36R
Ostwald, Peter F(rederic) 1928-1996 .... 17-20R
O Suilleabhain, Sean 1903-1996 ..... CANR-18
Earlier sketch in CA 25-28R
O'Sullivan, Gerry 1959- 135
O'Sullivan, Joan (D'Arcy) 77-80
O'Sullivan, John 1942- 132
O'Sullivan, John J. 1939-2000
Brief entry 114
O'Sullivan, Judith 1942- 120
O'Sullivan, Maggie 1951- .... CWP
O'Sullivan, Mark 219
O'Sullivan, Maurice
See O Suileabhain, Muiris
O'Sullivan, Michael 1957- 222
O'Sullivan, P. Michael 1940-2004 93-96
Obituary 231
O'Sullivan, Sean
See O Suilleabhain, Sean
O'Sullivan, Vincent 1868-1940 .... HGG
O'Sullivan, Vincent (Gerard) 1937- .. CANR-95
Earlier sketches in CA 97-100, CANR-35
See also CD 5, 6
See also CN 6, 7
See also CP 1, 2, 3, 4, 5, 6, 7
See also EWL 3
Osundare, Niyi 1947- 176
See also AFW
See also BW 3
See also CDWLB 3
See also DLB 157
Osusky, Stefan 1889-1973
Obituary 45-48
Oswald, Alice 1966- 223
See also CWP
Oswald, Eleazer 1755-1795 .... DLB 43
Oswald, Ian 1929- CANR-13
Earlier sketch in CA 17-20R
Oswald, J(oseph) Gregory 1922- 104
Oswald, Russell G. 1908-1991 45-48
Oswald von Wolkenstein c.
1376-1445 .... DLB 179
Oswalt, John N(ewell) 1940- CANR-93
Earlier sketch in CA 117
Oswalt, Sabine
See MacCormack, Sabine G(abriele)
Oswalt, Wendell H(illman) 1927- CANR-35
Earlier sketches in CA 17-20R, CANR-12
Ota, Yoko 1903-1963 .... MJW
Ota, Yuzo 1943- 186
Otake, Sadao 1913(?)-1983
Obituary 109
Otchis, Ethel (Herberg) 1920- 13-16R
Otero, Blas de 1916-1979 89-92
See also CLC 11
See also DLB 134
See also EWL 3
Otero, Gerardo 1952- 195
Otero, Miguel Antonio (II) 1859-1944 153
See also DLB 82
See also HW 1
Otero, Nina 1881-1965 .... DLB 209
Otero Silva, Miguel 1908-1985 175
See also DLB 145
See also HW 2
Otfinoski, Steven 1949- 188
See also SATA 56, 116
Otfried von Weißenburg c. 800-c.
875(?) .... DLB 148
Otis, George
See Mellen, Ida M(ay)
Otis, Jack 1923- 1-4R
Otis, James
See Kaler, James Otis
Otis, James, Jr. 1725-1783 .... DLB 31
Otis, Johnny 1921- CANR-99
Earlier sketch in CA 147
Otomo, Katsuhiro 1954- 226
O'Toole, Fintan 1958- CANR-127
Earlier sketch in CA 172
O'Toole, G(eorge) J(oseph) A(nthony)
1936-2001 141
Obituary 197
O'Toole, James (Joseph) 1945- 126
O'Toole, James M. 1950- 206
O'Toole, Judith Hansen 1953- 142
O'Toole, Lawrence 171
O'Toole, Peter (Seamus) 1932- 160
O'Toole, Rex
See Tralins, S(andor) Robert
O'Toole, Thomas 1941- .... SATA 71
Ototake, Hirotada 1976- 198
O'Trigger, Sir Lucius
See Horne, Richard Henry Hengist
Otsup, Nikolai 1894-1958 .... DLB 317
Ott, Attiat F(arag) 1935- CANR-10
Earlier sketch in CA 21-24R
Ott, David Jackson 1934-1975 .... CANR-8
Earlier sketch in CA 5-8R
Ott, Maggie Glen
See Ott, Virginia
Ott, Peter
See von Hildebrand, Dietrich
Ott, Thomas O(liver) III 1938- 49-52
Ott, Virginia 1917- 77-80
Ott, William Griffith 1909-1998 .... CANR-1
Earlier sketch in CA 1-4R
Ottaviani, Jim 202
Ottaway, James 1911-2000 182
See also DLB 127
Ottaway, Marina (Seassaro) 1943- 142
Otte, Jean-Pierre 1949- 220
Ottemiller, John H(enry) 1916-1968 ...... CAP-2
Earlier sketch in CA 17-18
Otten, Anna 21-24R
Otten, C. Michael 1934- 33-36R
Otten, Charlotte F(ennema) 1926- CANR-96
Earlier sketch in CA 131
See also SATA 98
Otten, Charlotte M(arie) 1915- CANR-35
Earlier sketch in CA 29-32R
Otten, Terry (Ralph) 1938- CANR-75
Earlier sketches in CA 37-40R, CANR-15, 35
Ottenberg, Miriam 1914-1982 .... CANR-10
Obituary 108
Earlier sketch in CA 5-8R
Ottenberg, Simon 1923- CANR-82
Earlier sketches in CA 33-36R, CANR-35
Ottendorfer, Oswald 1826-1900
Brief entry 123
See also DLB 23
Otter, Anthony 1896-1986
Obituary 118
Otterbein, Keith Frederick 1936- CANR-82
Earlier sketches in CA 21-24R, CANR-35
Ottersen, (John) Ottar 1918- 33-36R
Ottesen, Thea Tauber 1913-1991 .... 5-8R
Otteson, Schuyler Franklin 1917-
Brief entry 106
Ottieri, Ottiero 1924-2002 204
See also DLB 177
See also EWL 3
Ottley, Matt 1962- 169
See also SATA 102
Ottley, Reginald Leslie 1909-1985 ... CANR-34
Earlier sketch in CA 93-96
See also CLR 16
See also MAICYA 1, 2
See also SATA 26
Ottley, Roi (Vincent) 1906-1960 .... CANR-87
Obituary 89-92
Earlier sketch in CA 153
See also BW 2
Ottlik, Geza 1912-1990 .... CANR-39
Obituary 132
Earlier sketch in CA 17-20R
Ottman, Robert W(illiam) 1914- CANR-3
Earlier sketch in CA 1-4R
Otto, Beatrice K. 1963- 199
Otto, Calvin P. 1930- 29-32R
Otto, Henry J. 1901-1975 .... CAP-2
Earlier sketch in CA 13-14
Otto, Herbert Arthur 1922- CANR-1
Earlier sketch in CA 45-48
Otto, Lon 1948- 130
Otto, Luther B(enedict) 1937- 133
Otto, Margaret Glover 1909-1976
Obituary 61-64
See also SATA-Obit 30
Otto, Rudolf 1869-1937 .... TCLC 85
Otto, Svend
See Soerensen, Svend Otto
Otto, Wayne (R.) 1931- CANR-11
Earlier sketch in CA 29-32R
Otto, Whitney 1955- CANR-120
Earlier sketch in CA 140
See also CLC 70
Otto-Peters, Louise 1819-1895 .... DLB 129
Ottum, Bob
See Ottum, Robert K., Jr.
Ottum, Robert K., Jr. 1925(?)-1986
Obituary 119
Otway, Thomas 1652-1685 .... DAM DRAM
See also DC 24
See also DLB 80
See also RGEL 2
Otway-Ruthven, Jocelyn 1909-1989
Obituary 128
Otway-Ward, Patricia
See Weenolsen, Patricia
Otwell, John H(erbert) 1915-1987 73-76
Ouchi, William G(eorge) 1943- CANR-127
Earlier sketch in CA 129
Oudaii, Hashmi el
See McGirk, Tim(othy Stephen)
Ouellette, Fernand 1930- CANR-17
Earlier sketches in CA 49-52, CANR-2
See also CAAS 13
See also DLB 60
Ouellette, Laurie 222
Ouellette, Pierre 1945- 166
Oufkir, Malika 1953- 192
Oughton, Frederick 1923- CANR-29
Earlier sketch in CA 1-4R
Oughton, Jerrie (Preston) 1937- 143
See also AAYA 44
See also SATA 76, 131
Oughton, John P. 202
Oughton, (William) Taylor 1925- .... SATA 104
Ouida
See De la Ramee, Marie Louise (Ouida)
See also DLB 18, 156
See also RGEL 2
See also TCLC 43
Ouimette, Victor 1944- 73-76
Oulahan, Richard 1918-1985 .... CANR-36
Obituary 117
Earlier sketch in CA 33-36R
Oulanoff, Hongor 1929- 25-28R
Ounissi, Zhor
See Wanissi, Zuhur
Ouologuem, Yambo 1940- 176
Brief entry 111
See also CLC 146
Our Man Stanley
See Hamburger, Philip (Paul)
Ouroussoff, Peter Sergeivich 1900(?)-1984
Obituary 114
Ouroussow, Eugenie 1908-1975
Obituary 53-56
Oursler, Fulton, Jr. 1932-
Brief entry 116
Oursler, (Charles) Fulton 1893-1952
Brief entry 108
Oursler, Will(iam Charles)
1913-1985 .... CANR-35
Obituary 115
Earlier sketches in CA 5-8R, CANR-2
Ousby, Ian (Vaughan Kenneth)
1947-2001 .... CANR-120
Obituary 199
Earlier sketches in CA 89-92, CANR-35
Ouseley, Gideon
See Paranjape, Makarand (Ramachandra)
Ousley, Odille 1896-1976 .... CAP-1
Earlier sketch in CA 11-12
See also SATA 10
Ousmane, Sembene 1923- CANR-81
Brief entry 117
Earlier sketch in CA 125
See also Sembene, Ousmane
See also BLC 3
See also BW 1, 3
See also CLC 66
See also CWW 2
See also MTCW 1
Ouston, Philip (Anfield) 1924(?)-1988(?)
Obituary 125
Outcalt, Todd 1960- 194
See also SATA 123
Outerbridge, David E(ugene) 1933- .. CANR-38
Earlier sketches in CA 93-96, CANR-16
Outhwaite, Leonard 1892-1978 53-56
Obituary 171
Outhwaite, (Richard) William
1949- CANR-86
Earlier sketch in CA 130
Outka, Gene 1937- 41-44R
Outland, Charles (Faulkner)
1910-1988 .... CANR-40
Earlier sketch in CA 9-12R
Outland, Orland 181
Outler, Albert C(ook) 1908-1989 .... CANR-1
Earlier sketch in CA 1-4R
Outram, Dorinda 1949- 132
Outram, Richard Daley 1930- .... CP 1, 7
Out to Lunch
See Watson, Ben
Ouverson, Marlin D(ean) 1952- 111
Ovard, Glen F. 1928- 33-36R
Ove, Robert S. 1927- 164
Oved, Iaacov
See Oved, Yaacov
Oved, Yaacov 1929- 159
Ovenden, Keith William 1943- 185
Overacker, Louise 1891-1982 .... CANR-89
Earlier sketches in CAP-2, CA 29-32
Overall, Christine (Dorothy) 1949- ... CANR-94
Earlier sketch in CA 138
Overbeck, Pauletta 1915- 97-100
Overbeek, J(ohannes) 1932- 73-76
Overberg, Kenneth R(ichard) 1944- .. CANR-75
Earlier sketches in CA 114, CANR-35
Overbury, Stephen 1954- 119
Overbury, Sir Thomas c. 1581-1613 ... DLB 151
Overbye, Dennis 1944- CANR-98
Earlier sketch in CA 142
Overgard, William (Thomas, Jr.)
1926-1990 138
Obituary 131
Overholser, Stephen 1944- CANR-16
Earlier sketch in CA 97-100
Overholser, Wayne D. 1906-1996 .... CANR-64
Earlier sketches in CA 5-8R, CANR-2, 16
See also TCWW 1, 2
Overholt, Thomas (William) 1935- 163
Overholt, William H. 1945- 117
Overland, Arnulf
See Overland, Arnulf
Overland, Arnulf 1889-1968 190
See also DLB 297
See also EWL 3
Overman, Michael 1920- 108
Overman-Edmiston, Karen 1963- 189
Overmeyer, Eric 1951(?)- CANR-85
Earlier sketch in CA 153
See also CAD
See also CD 5, 6
Overmyer, James E. 1946- 152
See also SATA 88
Overstreet, Bonaro (Wilkinson)
1902-1985 142
Obituary 117
Overstreet, Harry Allen 1875-1970 .... CAP-1
Obituary 29-32R
Earlier sketch in CA 13-16
Overton, Ariana M. 1950- 229
Overton, Jenny (Margaret Mary)
1942- CANR-85
Earlier sketch in CA 57-60
See also CWRI 5
See also SATA 52
See also SATA-Brief 36
Overton, Richard Cleghorn 1907- 108
Overton, Robert
See Knox-Mawer, Ronald
Overton, Ron 1943- 147
Overy, Paul 1940- CANR-82
Earlier sketches in CA 29-32R, CANR-35
Overy, R(ichard) J(ames) 1947- CANR-120
Earlier sketch in CA 119
Ovesen, Ellis
See Smith, Shirley M(ae)
Ovid 43B.C.-17 .... AW 2
See also CDWLB 1
See also DA3
See also DAM POET
See also DLB 211
See also PC 2
See also PFS 22
See also RGWL 2, 3
See also WP
Oviedo y Valdes, Gonzalo Fernandez de
1478-1557 .... DLB 318
See also LAW
Ovington, Mary White 1865-1951 166
Ovstedal, Barbara 1931- CANR-85
Earlier sketch in CA 130
Ovsyanikov, Nikita 1952- 162
Owen, Alan Robert George 1919- 9-12R
Owen, Alun (Davies) 1925-1994 ...... CANR-82
Obituary 147
Earlier sketches in CA 5-8R, CANR-34
See also CBD
Owen, Annie 1949- .... SATA 75
Owen, Bob
See Geis, Richard E(rwin)
Owen, Bruce M(anning) 1943- CANR-35
Earlier sketch in CA 57-60
Owen, Caroline Dale
See Snedeker, Caroline Dale (Parke)
Owen, Charles A(braham), Jr.
1914-1998 .... CANR-36
Earlier sketch in CA 53-56

Owen, Clifford
See Hamilton, Charles (Harold St. John)
Owen, D(enis) F(rank) 1931- ... CANR-35
Earlier sketches in CA 53-56, CANR-4
Owen, David (Edward) 1898-1968 .. CANR-36
Earlier sketches in CAP-1, CA 13-16
Owen, David (Anthony Llewellyn)
1938- ... CANR-121
Earlier sketches in CA 129, CANR-65
Owen, David E(lystan) 1912-1987 ... 124
Owen, David Lanyon Lloyd
See Lloyd Owen, David Lanyon
Owen, Dean
See Dean (McGaughy), Dudley
Owen, Dilys
See Gater, Dilys
Owen, Dolores B(ullock) ... CANR-86
Earlier sketches in CA 53-56, CANR-34
Owen, Douglas David Roy
1922-2003 ... CANR-35
Obituary ... 215
Earlier sketch in CA 89-92
Owen, Edmund
See Teller, Neville
Owen, (Benjamin) Evan 1918-1984 ... 109
See also SATA 38
Owen, Frank 1907(?)-1979
Obituary ... 85-88
See also FANT
Owen, G(ail) L(ee) 1937- ... 45-48
Owen, G(eorge) Vale 1869-1931
Brief entry ... 119
Owen, Gail R.
See Owen-Crocker, Gale R(edfern)
Owen, (John) Gareth 1936-2002 .... CANR-101
Earlier sketch in CA 150
See also CLR 31
See also CWRI 5
See also SAAS 14
See also SATA 83, 162
Owen, George Earle 1908-1993 ... 77-80
Owen, Guy (Jr.) 1925-1981 ... CANR-36
Obituary ... 104
Earlier sketches in CA 1-4R, CANR-3
See also CN 2, 3
See also DLB 5
Owen, Gwilym Ellis Lane 1922-1982
Obituary ... 107
Owen, (William) Harold 1897-1971 ..... 13-16R
Obituary ... 89-92
Owen, Henry D. 1920- ... 195
Brief entry ... 111
Owen, Howard (Wayne) 1949- ... CANR-98
Earlier sketch in CA 141
Owen, Hugh
See Faust, Frederick (Schiller)
Owen, Irvin 1910- ... 97-100
Owen, Jack 1929- ... CANR-37
Earlier sketch in CA 33-36R
Owen, Jan 1940- ... CANR-85
Earlier sketch in CA 154
See also CP 7
See also CWP
Owen, Jennifer 1936- ... CANR-38
Earlier sketch in CA 116
Owen, John 1564-1622 ... DLB 121
Owen, John E. 1919- ... CANR-4
Earlier sketch in CA 9-12R
Owen, John M(alloy) 1962- ... 206
Owen, Lewis 1915- ... 29-32R
Owen, Lewis J(ames) 1925-
Brief entry ... 116
Owen, Marsha
See Stanford, Sally
Owen, Norman G. 1944- ... 126
Owen, Oliver S. 1920- ... 104
Owen, Philip
See Philips, Judson (Pentecost)
Owen, Reginald 1887-1972
Obituary ... 37-40R
Owen, Richard 1947- ... 127
Owen, Robert 1771-1858 ... DLB 107, 158
Owen, Robert N.
See Geis, Richard E(rwin)
Owen, Roderic
See Fenwick-Owen, Roderic (Franklin Rawnsley)
Owen, Roderic Fenwick
See Fenwick-Owen, Roderic (Franklin Rawnsley)
Owen, Roger C(orey) 1928- ... CANR-37
Earlier sketch in CA 77-80
Owen, Thomas
See Burtot, Gerald
Owen, Thomas C. 1943- ... 188
Owen, Thomas Richard 1918- ... CANR-10
Earlier sketch in CA 21-24R
Owen, Tobias Chant 1936- ... CANR-29
Earlier sketch in CA 111
Owen, Tom
See Watts, Peter Christopher
Owen, W(arwick) J(ack) B(urgoyne)
1916-2002 ... 134
Obituary ... 211
Brief entry ... 111
Owen, Wilfred (Edward Salter) 1893-1918 . 141
Brief entry ... 104
See also BRW 6
See also CDBLB 1914-1945
See also DA
See also DAB
See also DAC
See also DAM MST, POET
See also DLB 20
See also EWL 3
See also EXPP
See also MTCW 2
See also MTFW 2005
See also PC 19
See also PFS 10
See also RGEL 2
See also TCLC 5, 27
See also WLC
See also WLIT 4
Owen, Wilfred 1912-2001 ... CANR-36
Obituary ... 201
Earlier sketch in CA 37-40R
Owen, William Vern 1894-1975 ... CAP-2
Earlier sketch in CA 17-18
Owen, Wyn F(oster) 1923-
Brief entry ... 115
Owen-Crocker, Gale R(edfern)
1947- ... CANR-109
Earlier sketch in CA 128
Owendoff, Robert S(cott) 1945- ... 17-20R
Owens, Agnes 1926- ... CANR-60
Earlier sketch in CA 128
Owens, Bill 1938- ... 73-76
Owens, Bryant 1968- ... SATA 116
Owens, Carole (Ehrlich) 1942- ... CANR-129
Earlier sketch in CA 116
Owens, Carolyn 1946- ... 109
Owens, Craig 1950-1990
Obituary ... 132
Owens, E(dwin) J(ohn) 1950- ... 139
Owens, Edgar (Leonard) 1924-1987
Obituary ... 124
Owens, Elizabeth 1948- ... 201
Owens, Gail 1939- ... SATA 54
Owens, Gary 1936- ... 97-100
Owens, Janis E(llen) 1960- ... 208
Owens, Jesse 1913-1980 ... 110
Owens, John E. 1948- ... CANR-134
Earlier sketch in CA 162
Owens, John R(obert) 1926- ... 77-80
Owens, Joseph 1908- ... CANR-20
Earlier sketches in CA 5-8R, CANR-5
Owens, Kenneth N. 1933- ... 147
Owens, Louis (Dean) 1948-2002 ... 179
Obituary ... 207
Earlier sketches in CA 137, CANR-71
Autobiographical Essay in ... 179
See also CAAS 24
See also NNAL
Owens, Pat(rick) J. 1929- ... 73-76
Owens, Richard Meredith 1944- ... CANR-37
Earlier sketch in CA 61-64
Owens, Robert Goronwy 1923- ... CANR-28
Earlier sketch in CA 29-32R
Owens, Rochelle 1936- ... CANR-39
Earlier sketch in CA 17-20R
See also CAAS 2
See also CAD
See also CD 5, 6
See also CLC 8
See also CP 1, 2, 3, 4, 5, 6, 7
See also CWD
See also CWP
Owens, Suzanne (R.) ... 209
Owens, Thelma 1905-1987 ... 69-72
Owens, Thomas S(heldon) 1960- ... 151
See also SATA 86
Owens, Tom
See Owens, Thomas S(heldon)
Owens, Virginia Stem 1941- ... CANR-14
Earlier sketch in CA 81-84
Owens, William A. 1905-1990 ... CANR-127
Obituary ... 133
Earlier sketches in CA 9-12R, CANR-36
Owensby, Brian P(hilip) 1959- ... 201
Owenson, Sydney 1775(?)-1859 ... RGEL 2
Ower, John 1942- ... 77-80
Owings, Alison 1944- ... 216
Owings, Loren C(lyde) 1928- ... 37-40R
Owings, Mark (Samuel) 1945-
Brief entry ... 114
Owings, Nathaniel Alexander
1903-1984 ... CANR-35
Obituary ... 113
Earlier sketch in CA 61-64
Ownby, Ted M. 1960- ... 187
Owomoyela, Oyekan 1938- ... 112
Owsley, Frank L(awrence) 1890-1956
Brief entry ... 116
See also DLB 17
Owsley, Harriet Chappell 1901-1999 ... 81-84
Owusu, Martin 1943- ... CD 5, 6
Oxenbury, Helen 1938- ... CANR-133
Earlier sketches in CA 25-28R, CANR-35, 79
See also CLR 22, 70
See also CWRI 5
See also MAICYA 1, 2
See also SATA 3, 68, 149
Oxendine, Bess Holland 1933- ... 155
See also SATA 90
Oxenham, Elsie J.
See Dunkerley, Elsie Jeanette
Oxenhandler, Neal 1926- ... CANR-6
Earlier sketch in CA 13-16R
Oxenhandler, Noelle 1952- ... 199
Oxenhorn, Harvey 1952(?)-1990
Obituary ... 131
Oxford, Cheryl 1955- ... 148
Oxhorn, Philip D. ... 151
Oxley, Dorothy (Anne) 1948- ... 116
Oxley, William 1939- ... 73-76
See also CP 2, 3, 4, 5, 6, 7
Oxnam, Robert B(romley) 1942- ... CANR-5
Earlier sketch in CA 53-56
Oxnard, Charles (Ernest) 1933- ... CANR-42
Earlier sketches in CA 45-48, CANR-1, 16
Oxorn, Harry 1920- ... CANR-42
Earlier sketch in CA 111
Oxtoby, Willard Gurdon 1933- ... CANR-37
Earlier sketch in CA 49-52
OyamO
See Gordon, Charles F.
See also CD 6
See also DLB 266
Oyen, Else (Sjorup) ... 165
Oyle, Irving 1925-1995 ... CANR-6
Earlier sketch in CA 57-60
Oyler, Philip (Tom) 1879- ... CAP-1
Earlier sketch in CA 9-10
Oyono, Ferdinand 1929- ... AFW
See also EWL 3
See also WLIT 2
Oyono-Mbia, Guillaume 1939- ... CWW 2
Oy-Vik
See Holmvik, Oyvind
Oz, Amos 1939- ... CANR-138
Earlier sketches in CA 53-56, CANR-27, 47, 65, 113
See also CLC 5, 8, 11, 27, 33, 54
See also CWW 2
See also DAM NOV
See also EWL 3
See also MTCW 1, 2
See also MTFW 2005
See also RGSF 2
See also RGWL 3
See also SSC 66
See also WLIT 6
Oz, Frank (Richard) 1944- ... SATA 60
Ozaki, Robert S(higeo) 1934- ... CANR-35
Earlier sketch in CA 49-52
Ozawa, Terutomo 1935- ... CANR-34
Earlier sketch in CA 85-88
Ozbudun, Ergun 1937- ... 126
Ozeki, Ruth L. ... 181
Ozer, Jerome S. 1927- ... 107
See also SATA 59
Ozer, Mark N(orman) 1932- ... CANR-30
Earlier sketch in CA 112
Ozerov, Vladislav Aleksandrovich
1769-1816 ... DLB 150
Ozick, Cynthia 1928- ... CANR-116
Earlier sketches in CA 17-20R, CANR-23, 58
Interview in ... CANR-23
See also AMWS 5
See also BEST 90:1
See also CLC 3, 7, 28, 62, 155
See also CN 3, 4, 5, 6, 7
See also CPW
See also DA3
See also DAM NOV, POP
See also DLB 28, 152, 299
See also DLBY 1982
See also EWL 3
See also EXPS
See also MAL 5
See also MTCW 1, 2
See also MTFW 2005
See also RGAL 4
See also RGSF 2
See also SSC 15, 60
See also SSFS 3, 12
Ozieblo, Barbara 1948- ... 195
Ozinga, James Richard 1932- ... CANR-37
Earlier sketch in CA 97-100
Ozment, Robert V. 1927- ... 17-20R
Ozment, Steven E(dgar) 1939- ... CANR-92
Earlier sketches in CA 108, CANR-35
Ozmon, Howard A. ... 25-28R
Ozon, Francois 1967- ... 202
Ozsvath, Zsuzsanna 1934- ... 201
Ozu, Yasujiro 1903-1963 ... 112
See also CLC 16
Ozy
See Rosset, B(enjamin) C(harles)

P

P., Kare
See Anker, Nini Magdalene Roll
P. L. K.
See Kirk-Greene, Anthony (Hamilton Millard)
P. Q.
See Quennell, Peter (Courtney)
P., Sergije
See Vojnovik, Ivo
Paak, Carl Erich 1922-1991 ... 106
Paananen, Eloise (Katherine)
1923-1993 ... CANR-18
Obituary ... 171
Earlier sketches in CA 1-4R, CANR-2
See also Engle, Eloise
Paananen, Victor Niles 1938- ... 73-76
Paarlberg, Don(ald) 1911- ... 21-24R
Paasche, Carol L(evine) 1937- ... 5-8R
Paauw, Douglas Seymour 1921- ... 103
Pab
See Blooman, Percy A.
Pabst, G. W. 1885-1967 ... TCLC 127
Paca, Lillian Grace (Baker) 1883-1978 .. CAP-1
Earlier sketch in CA 11-12
Pacaut, Marcel 1920- ... 29-32R
Pace, C(harles) Robert 1912- ... 81-84
Pace, David 1944- ... 130
Pace, Denny F. 1925- ... 49-52
Pace, DeWanna 1954- ... 162
Pace, Donald Metcalf 1906-1982
Obituary ... 108
Pace, Eric 1936- ... 45-48
Pace, J. Blair 1916- ... 69-72
Pace, Lorenzo 1943- ... SATA 131
Pace, Mildred Mastin 1907- ... CANR-5
Earlier sketch in CA 5-8R
See also SATA 46
See also SATA-Brief 29
Pace, Nathaniel 1925- ... 110
Pace, Peter
See Burnett, David (Benjamin Foley)
Pace, R(alph) Wayne 1931- ... CANR-1
Earlier sketch in CA 45-48
Pace, Richard 1482(?)-1536 ... DLB 167
Pace, Robert Lee 1924- ... 1-4R
Pacelle, Mitchell ... 208
Pacernick, Gary 1941- ... CANR-93
Earlier sketch in CA 73-76
Pacey, Arnold 1937- ... 198
Pacey, (William Cyril) Desmond
1917-1975 ... CANR-4
Earlier sketch in CA 5-8R
See also DLB 88
Pachai, Bridglal 1927- ... CANR-17
Earlier sketch in CA 93-96
Pacheco, C.
See Pessoa, Fernando (Antonio Nogueira)
Pacheco, Catherine Chapman 1927- ... 130
Pacheco, Ferdie 1927- ... 81-84
Pacheco, Henricus Luis
See Pacheco, Henry L(uis)
Pacheco, Henry L(uis) 1947- ... 49-52
See also HW 1
Pacheco, Jose Emilio 1939- ... CANR-65
Brief entry ... 111
Earlier sketch in CA 131
See also CWW 2
See also DAM MULT
See also DLB 290
See also EWL 3
See also HLC 2
See also HW 1, 2
See also RGSF 2
Pachen, Ani 1933-2002 ... 200
Pa Chin
See Li Fei-kan
See also CLC 18
See also EWL 3
Pachmuss, Temira 1927- ... CANR-44
Earlier sketches in CA 9-12R, CANR-4, 20
Pachter, Hedwig (?)-1988 ... SATA 63
Pachter, Henry M(aximillian)
1907-1980 ... CANR-91
Earlier sketch in CA 9-12R
Pachter, Josh 1951- ... 132
Pacifici, Sergio 1925- ... CANR-3
Earlier sketch in CA 1-4R
Pacifico, Carl 1921- ... 21-24R
Pack, Ellen 1963(?)- ... 197
Pack, Janet 1952- ... 145
See also SATA 77
Pack, Robert 1929- ... CANR-82
Earlier sketches in CA 1-4R, CANR-3, 44
See also CLC 13
See also CP 1, 2, 3, 4, 5, 6, 7
See also DLB 5
See also SATA 118
Pack, Roger A(mbrose) 1907-1993 ... CAP-1
Earlier sketch in CA 13-16
Pack, S(tanley) W(alter) C(roucher)
1904-1977 ... 13-16R
Obituary ... 125
Pack, Spencer J. 1953- ... 140
Packard, Andrew 1929- ... 1-4R
Packard, Cindy
See Richmond, Cindy Packard
Packard, Edward 1931- ... CANR-121
Earlier sketches in CA 114, CANR-59
See also SATA 47, 90, 148
Packard, Frederick Clifton, Jr. 1899-1985
Obituary ... 116
Packard, George R(andolph) III 1932- ... 127
Brief entry ... 112
Packard, Jerrold M(ichael) 1943- CANR-118
Earlier sketches in CA 106, CANR-23
Packard, Karl 1911(?)-1977
Obituary ... 69-72
Packard, Reynolds 1903-1976 ... 73-76
Obituary ... 69-72
Packard, Robert 1916- ... 134
Packard, Robert G(eorge) 1933- ... 57-60
Packard, Rosa Covington 1935- ... 97-100
Packard, Rosalie ... 1-4R
Packard, Russell C. 1946- ... 119
Packard, Sidney R(aymond) 1893-1980 .. 61-64
Packard, Vance (Oakley) 1914-1996 .. CANR-7
Obituary ... 155
Earlier sketch in CA 9-12R
See also AITN 1
Packard, William 1933-2002 ... CANR-7
Obituary ... 211
Earlier sketch in CA 13-16R
Packenham, Robert Allen 1937- ... 73-76
Packer, Arnold H. 1935- ... 37-40R
Packer, B(arbara) L(ee) 1947- ... 133
Packer, Bernard J(ules) 1934- ... CANR-19
Earlier sketch in CA 65-68
Packer, David W(illiam) 1937- ... 9-12R
Packer, George 1960(?)- ... CANR-110
Earlier sketch in CA 177
Packer, George c.
See Packer, George

Cumulative Index 443 Pakula

Packer, Herbert L(eslie) 1925-1972 .. CANR-91
Earlier sketch in CA 37-40R
Packer, J(ames) I(nnell) 1926- CANR-99
Earlier sketches in CA 49-52, CANR-1, 16, 37
Packer, Joan Garrett 1947- 139
Packer, Joy (Petersen) 1905-1977 ..... CANR-91
Earlier sketches in CA 1-4R, CANR-3
Packer, Kenneth L. 1946- 188
See also SATA 116
Packer, Lady
See Packer, Joy (Petersen)
Packer, Miriam 207
Packer, Nancy Huddleston 1925- 65-68
Packer, Randall (Martin) 1953- 200
Packer, Rod Earle 1931- 109
Packer, Vin
See Meaker, Marijane (Agnes)
See also GLL 2
Packer, ZZ 221
Packman, David 1949- 123
Pacosz, Christina V(ivian) 1946- 77-80
Pacult, F. Paul 1949- 175
Pacyga, Dominic A. 1949- 128
Paczkowski, Andrzej 1938- 231
Pad, Peter
See Stratemeyer, Edward L.
Padberg, Daniel I(van) 1931- 33-36R
Padberg, John W(illiam) 1926- 25-28R
Padden, R(obert) C(harles) 1922- 21-24R
Paddison, Ronan 1945- 117
Paddison, Sara 1953- 143
Paddleford, Clementine Haskin 1900-1967
Obituary 89-92
Paddock, Jennifer 239
Paddock, John 1918- 17-20R
Paddock, Lisa (Olson) 1951- CANR-143
Earlier sketch in CA 172
Paddock, Paul (Ezekiel, Jr.) 1907-1975 .. CAP-2
Obituary 61-64
Earlier sketch in CA 21-22
Paddock, William (Carson) 1921- CANR-88
Earlier sketch in CA 21-24R
Pade, Victoria 1953- 113
Padel, Ruth 1946- CANR-122
Earlier sketch in CA 134
Paden, Ross
See Paine, Lauran (Bosworth)
Paden, William D(oremus, Jr.) 1941- 124
Paden, William E. 1939- 142
Padev, Michael Alexander 1915-1989
Obituary 128
Padfield, Harland (Irvine) 1926- 186
Brief entry 112
Padfield, Peter 1932- CANR-26
Earlier sketch in CA 101
Padgett, (Mary) Abigail 1942- CANR-115
Earlier sketches in CA 141, CANR-66
See also CMW 4
Padgett, Desmond
See von Block, Bela W(illiam)
Padgett, Dora 1893(?)-1976
Obituary 61-64
Padgett, Lewis
See Kuttner, Henry and
Moore, C(atherine) L(ucile)
Padgett, Ron 1942- CANR-141
Earlier sketches in CA 25-28R, CANR-12, 30, 57
See also CP 1, 2, 3, 4, 5, 6, 7
See also DLB 5
See also WP
Padgett, Stephen 1951- 139
Padilla, Ernesto Chavez 1944- 181
See also DLB 122
Padilla, Genaro M(iguel) 1949- 128
Padilla (Lorenzo), Heberto 1932-2000 131
Obituary 189
Brief entry 123
See also AITN 1
See also CLC 38
See also CWW 2
See also EWL 3
See also HW 1
Padilla, Ignacio 1968- 235
Padilla, Raymond V. 1944- CANR-87
Earlier sketch in CA 130
See also HW 1
Padilla, Victoria 1907-1986 103
Obituary 120
Padley, Walter Ernest 1916-1984
Obituary 112
Padmore, George
See Nurse, Malcolm Ivan Meredith
Padoa-Schioppa Rostoris, Fiorella
1945- CANR-54
Earlier sketch in CA 148
Padovano, Anthony T(homas)
1934- CANR-94
Earlier sketches in CA 17-20R, CANR-7, 22, 45
Padover, Saul K(ussiel) 1905-1981 ..... CANR-2
Obituary 103
Earlier sketch in CA 49-52
Padt, Maartje 1954- 187
Padwick, E(ric) W(illiam) 1923- 119
Pae, Sung Moon 1939- 146
Paerdurabo, Frater
See Crowley, Edward Alexander
Paesler, Michael 1946- 158
Paetro, Maxine 1946- 123
Paffard, Michael Kenneth 1928-2000 103
Pafford, John Henry Pyle
1900-1996 .... CANR-21
Obituary 151
Earlier sketch in CA 104
Pagan Ferrer, Gloria M. 1921-
See Palma, Marigloria
See also HW 1
Pagden, Anthony 1945- 101
Page, Benjamin I(ngrim) 1940- CANR-98
Earlier sketch in CA 112
Page, Carl 1957- 154
Page, Carole Gift 1942- 117
Page, Charles H(unt) 1909-1992 .... CANR-4
Obituary 136
Earlier sketch in CA 5-8R
Page, Christopher H. 1952- 137
Page, Clarence 1947- 145
Page, Curtis C(arling) 1914-1981 .... 21-24R
Page, Diana (Preuthun) 1946- 126
Page, Dorothy Myra
See Page, Myra
Page, Drew 1905-1990 105
Page, Eileen
See Heal, Edith
Page, Eleanor
See Coerr, Eleanor (Beatrice)
Page, Ellis Batten 1924-2005 .... 13-16R
Obituary 239
Page, Emma
See Tirbutt, Honoria
Page, Evelyn 1902-1977 .... 5-8R
Page, G. S.
See Galbraith, Georgie Starbuck
Page, Geoff(rey Donald) 1940- CANR-94
Earlier sketches in CA 133, CANR-79, 82
See also CP 7
Page, George (H.) 222
Page, Gerald W(ilburn) 1939- 93-96
Page, Grover, Jr. 1918- 17-20R
Page, Harry Robert 1915- 9-12R
Page, Homer (Gordon) 1918-1985
Obituary 117
Page, Jake
See Page, James K(eena), Jr.
Page, James A(llen) 1918- 107
Page, James D. 1910-1984 73-76
Page, James K(eena), Jr. 1936- CANR-73
Earlier sketches in CA 97-100, CANR-35
See also SATA 81
Page, James Patrick 1944- 204
See also Page, Jimmy
Page, Jimmy 1944-
See Page, James Patrick
See also CLC 12
Page, Joseph A(nthony) 1934- CANR-65
Earlier sketches in CA 81-84, CANR-14
Page, Karen 1962- 170
Page, Katherine Hall 1947- CANR-126
Earlier sketches in CA 136, CANR-73
Page, Kathy 1958- CANR-137
Earlier sketch in CA 133
Page, Lorna
See Rowland, D(onald) S(ydney)
Page, Lou Williams 1912-1997 .... CANR-5
Earlier sketch in CA 5-8R
See also SATA 38
Page, Louise 1955- CANR-76
Earlier sketch in CA 140
See also CBD
See also CD 5, 6
See also CLC 40
See also CWD
See also DLB 233
Page, Malcolm 1935- CANR-31
Earlier sketch in CA 45-48
Page, Marian 69-72
Page, Martin 1938-2003 .... CANR-12
Obituary 220
Earlier sketch in CA 17-20R
Page, Mary
See Heal, Edith
Page, Max 224
Page, Melvin E. 1944- 198
Page, Myra 1897-1993 166
Page, N. Wooten
See Page, Norvell W(ooten)
Page, Nick 223
Page, Norman 1930- CANR-119
Earlier sketches in CA 61-64, CANR-8, 31
Page, Norvell W(ooten) 1904-1961 155
See also FANT
Page, P(atricia) K(athleen) 1916- CANR-65
Earlier sketches in CA 53-56, CANR-4, 22
See also Cape, Judith
See also CLC 7, 18
See also CP 1, 2, 3, 4, 5, 6, 7
See also DAC
See also DAM MST
See also DLB 68
See also MTCW 1
See also PC 12
See also RGEL 2
Page, Penny B(ooth) 1949- 140
Page, Philip 1942- 195
Page, Reba Neukom 1942- 139
Page, Robert Collier 1908-1977
Obituary 73-76
Page, Robert J(effress) 1922- 17-20R
Page, Robert Morris 1903-1992 .... CAP-2
Earlier sketch in CA 17-18
Page, Robin 1943- CANR-138
Earlier sketch in CA 103
See also SATA 154
Page, Roch 1939- 33-36R
Page, Russell 1906-1985
Obituary 114
Page, Ruth 1899-1991 212
Page, Stanton
See Fuller, Henry Blake
Page, Stanton
See Fuller, Henry Blake
Page, Thomas 1942- 81-84
Page, Thomas Nelson 1853-1922 177
Brief entry 118
See also DLB 12, 78
See also DLBD 13
See also RGAL 4
See also SSC 23
Page, Thornton (Leigh) 1913-1996 ..... CANR-2
Earlier sketch in CA 5-8R
Page, Tim 1944- 176
Page, Tim 1954- CANR-142
Earlier sketch in CA 176
Page, Vicki
See Avey, Ruby
Page, Walter Hines 1855-1918 183
See also DLB 71, 91
Page, Warren (Kempton) 1910-1977
Obituary 111
Page, William 1929- CANR-82
Earlier sketches in CA 114, CANR-35
Page, William 1946- 115
Page, William Roberts 1904- 21-24R
Page, Willie F. 1929- 210
Pagel, Stephen 1955- 177
Pagel, Walter T. U. 1898-1983 129
Obituary 109
Pagels, Elaine Hiesey 1943- CANR-51
Earlier sketches in CA 45-48, CANR-2, 24
See also CLC 104
See also FW
See also NCFS 4
Pagels, Heinz R(udolf) 1939-1988 .... CANR-81
Obituary 126
Earlier sketches in CA 107, CANR-23
Pages, Pedro
See Alba, Victor
Paget, Francis Edward 1806-1882 ...... DLB 163
Paget, George Charles Henry Victor
1922- 17-20R
Paget, John
See Aiken, John (Kempton)
Paget, Julian 1921- 21-24R
Paget, Margaret
See Medlicott, Margaret P(aget)
Paget, Violet 1856-1935 166
Brief entry 104
See also Lee, Vernon
See also GLL 1
See also HGG
Paget-Fredericks, Joseph E. P. Rous-Marten
1903-1963 .... SATA-Brief 30
Paget-Lowe, Henry
See Lovecraft, H(oward) P(hillips)
Pagis, Dan 1930-1986 206
Paglia, Camille (Anna) 1947- CANR-139
Earlier sketches in CA 140, CANR-72
See also CLC 68
See also CPW
See also FW
See also GLL 2
See also MTCW 2
See also MTFW 2005
Pagliarani, Elio 1927- 184
See also DLB 128
Paglin, Morton 1922- 97-100
Pagnol, Marcel (Paul) 1895-1974 128
Obituary 49-52
See also DLB 321
See also EWL 3
See also GFL 1789 to the Present
See also MTCW 1
See also RGWL 2, 3
Pagnucci, Susan 1944- .... SATA 90
Pagonis, William G. 1941- 139
Pagter, Carl R(ichard) 1934- CANR-54
Earlier sketch in CA 127
Paher, Stanley W(illiam) 1940- 29-32R
Pahl, R(aymond) E(dward) 1935- 25-28R
Pahlavi, Mohammed Riza
See Pahlevi, Mohammed Riza
Pahlen, Kurt 1907-2003 .... CANR-7
Obituary 218
Earlier sketch in CA 13-16R
See also SATA-Obit 147
Pahlevi, Mohammed Riza 1919-1980
Obituary 106
Pahor, Boris 1913- CANR-110
Earlier sketch in CA 156
Pahz, (Anne) Cheryl Suzanne 1949- ... CANR-8
Earlier sketch in CA 53-56
See also SATA 11
Pahz, James Alon 1943- CANR-8
Earlier sketch in CA 53-56
See also SATA 11
Pai, Anna C(hao) 1935- 89-92
Pai, Young 1929- 33-36R
Paice, Eric 1927(?)-1989
Obituary 129
Paice, Margaret 1920- CANR-20
Earlier sketch in CA 29-32R
See also SATA 10
Paier, Robert (David) 1943- 89-92
Paiewonsky, Michael 1939- 137
Paige, Connie 1945- 130
Paige, David
See Whittingham, Richard
Paige, Glenn D(urland) 1929- 25-28R
Paige, Harry W(orthington) 1922- CANR-32
Earlier sketch in CA 113
See also SATA 41
See also SATA-Brief 35
Paige, Leo
See Cochrane, William E.
Paige, Leroy Robert 1907(?)-1982
Obituary 107
Paige, Michele Anna 1969- 141
Paige, Richard
See Koontz, Dean R(ay)
Paige, Richard E(aton) 1904-1988 111
Obituary 126
Paige, Robin
See Albert, Susan Wittig
Paige, Satchel
See Paige, Leroy Robert
Pai Hsien-yung 1937- .... EWL 3
Paikeday, Thomas M. 1926- CANR-65
Earlier sketch in CA 128
Paikin, Steve 1960- 224
Pailin, David A. 1936- 129
Pain, Barry (Eric Odell) 1864-1928
Brief entry 109
See also DLB 135, 197
See also FANT
See also SUFW
Pain, Philip (?)-1666(?) .... DLB 24
Paine, Albert Bigelow 1861-1937
Brief entry 108
Paine, J. Lincoln
See Kramish, Arnold
Paine, Jeffery 1944- 187
Paine, Lauran (Bosworth) 1916- CANR-96
Earlier sketches in CA 45-48, CANR-7, 31
See also Bishop, Martin
See also TCWW 2
Paine, Penelope Colville 1946- .... SATA 87
Paine, Philbrook 1910- CAP-1
Earlier sketch in CA 11-12
Paine, R(ussell) Howard 1922- 5-8R
Paine, Robert Treat, Jr. 1773-1811 .... DLB 37
Paine, Roberta M. 1925- 33-36R
See also SATA 13
Paine, Roger W(arde) III 1942- 65-68
Paine, Sheila 1929- 146
Paine, Stephen William 1908-1992 .... 1-4R
Paine, Thomas 1737-1809 .... AMWS 1
See also CDALB 1640-1865
See also DLB 31, 43, 73, 158
See also LAIT 1
See also RGAL 4
See also RGEL 2
See also TUS
Paine, Tom 203
Painter, Charlotte CANR-91
Earlier sketches in CA 1-4R, CANR-3
Painter, Daniel
See Burgess, Michael (Roy)
Painter, George D(uncan) 1914- 101
See also DLB 155
Painter, Helen W(elch) 1913- 33-36R
Painter, John 1935- CANR-121
Earlier sketch in CA 166
Painter, Nell Irvin 1942- CANR-19
Earlier sketch in CA 65-68
See also BW 1
Painter, Pamela 1941- 122
Painter, William 1540(?)-1594 .... DLB 136
Pairault, Pierre 1922-2003 53-56
Pairo, Preston (A. III) 1958- CANR-70
Earlier sketch in CA 142
Pais, Abraham 1918-2000 109
Obituary 188
Paish, F(rank) W(alter) 1898-1988 .... CANR-91
Obituary 125
Earlier sketch in CA 17-20R
Paisley, Melvyn 1924-2001 139
Obituary 200
Paisley, Tom 1932- CANR-15
Earlier sketch in CA 61-64
See also Bethancourt, T. Ernesto
See also SATA 78
See also YAW
Paisley, Vicki 139
Paisner, Daniel 1960(?)- 175
Paisner, Milton 1915- 113
Pak, Gary 182
Pak, Soyung 236
Pak, Tu-Jin
See Pak Tu-jin
Pak Chong-Hui
See Park Chung Hee
Pakenham, Lord
See Pakenham, Francis Aungier
Pakenham, Antonia
See Fraser, Antonia (Pakenham)
Pakenham, Edward Arthur Henry 1902-1961
Obituary 114
Pakenham, Elizabeth
See Longford, Elizabeth (Harmon Pakenham)
Pakenham, Francis Aungier
1905-2001 .... CANR-46
Obituary 199
Earlier sketch in CA 109
Pakenham, Frank
See Pakenham, Francis Aungier
Pakenham, Simona Vere
1916-1988 .... CANR-91
Earlier sketches in CA 1-4R, CANR-3
Pakenham, Thomas (Frank Dermot)
1933- CANR-46
Earlier sketch in CA 109
Interview in CA-109
Pakenham, Valerie 1939- 206
Paker, Saliha 143
Pakkala, Teuvo
See Frosterus, Theodor Oskar
Paksoy, H(asan) B(ulent) 1948- 195
Pakstas, Algirdas 1958- 224
Pak Tu-jin 1916- .... EWL 3
Pakula, Alan J(ay) 1928-1998 .... CANR-93
Obituary 172
Brief entry 124
Earlier sketch in CA 130

Pakula, Hannah (Cohn) 1933- CANR-55
Earlier sketch in CA 139
Pakula, Marion Broome 1926- CANR-7
Earlier sketch in CA 57-60
Pal, George 1908-1980 171
See also IDFW 3, 4
Pal, Pratapaditya 1935- CANR-144
Earlier sketch in CA 37-40R
Pal, Rajinderpal S. 1967- 234
Palacio Valdes, Armando 1853-1933 ..... EWL 3
Palahniuk, Chuck 1962- CANR-140
Earlier sketch in CA 198
See also AAYA 59
See also MTFW 2005
Palais, James B. 1934- 165
Palamas, Costis
See Palamas, Kostes
Palamas, Kostes 1859-1943 190
Brief entry 105
See also Palamas, Kostis
See also RGWL 2, 3
See also TCLC 5
Palamas, Kostis
See Palamas, Kostes
See also EWL 3
Palamidessi Moore, Christine
See Moore, Christine Palamidessi
Palamountain, Joseph Cornwall, Jr.
1920-1987 45-48
Obituary 124
Palance, (Walter) Jack 1920- 229
Palance, Walter
See Palance, (Walter) Jack
Palance, Walter Jack
See Palance, (Walter) Jack
Palandri, Angela (Chin-ying) Jung
1926- 37-40R
Palandri, Enrico 1956- 211
Palange, Anthony (Jr.) 1942- 37-40R
Palast, Greg 212
Palatini, Margie 230
See also SATA 134
Palau, Luis, Jr. 1934- CANR-117
Earlier sketches in CA 116, CANR-39
Palazchenko, Pavel 1949- 168
Palazzeschi, Aldo 1885-1974 89-92
Obituary 53-56
See also CLC 11
See also DLB 114, 264
See also EWL 3
Palazzo, Anthony D.
See Palazzo, Tony
Palazzo, Tony 1905-1970 .... CANR-4
Obituary 29-32R
Earlier sketch in CA 5-8R
See also SATA 3
Palazzolo, Daniel J. 139
Palchi, Alfredo de
See de Palchi, Alfredo
Palda, Filip 1962- 148
Palder, Edward L. 1922- .... SATA 5
Paldiel, Mordecai 1937- 145
Palecek, Josef 1932- .... SATA 56
Palecek, Libuse 1937- 155
See also SATA 89
Paleckis, Justas (Ignovich) 1899-1980
Obituary 105
Palei, Marina Anatol'evna 1955- .... DLB 285
Palen, J(oseph) John 1939- CANR-15
Earlier sketch in CA 41-44R
Palen, Jennie M. 5-8R
Palencia, Alfonso de 1424-1492 .... DLB 286
Palencia, Elaine Fowler 1946- CANR-94
Earlier sketch in CA 142
Palermo, David Stuart 1929- 17-20R
Palermo, James 1937- 220
Pales Matos, Luis 1898-1959
See Pales Matos, Luis
See also DLB 290
See also HLCS 2
See also HW 1
See also LAW
Palestrant, Simon S. 1907- CAP-1
Earlier sketch in CA 9-10
Paley, Alan L(ouis) 1943- 69-72
Paley, Grace 1922- CANR-118
Earlier sketches in CA 25-28R, CANR-13, 46, 74
Interview in CANR-13
See also AMWS 6
See also CLC 4, 6, 37, 140
See also CN 2, 3, 4, 5, 6, 7
See also CPW
See also DA3
See also DAM POP
See also DLB 28, 218
See also EWL 3
See also EXPS
See also FW
See also MAL 5
See also MAWW
See also MTCW 1, 2
See also MTFW 2005
See also RGAL 4
See also RGSF 2
See also SSC 8
See also SSFS 3, 20
Paley, Maggie 1939- 121
Paley, Morton D(avid) 1935- CANR-100
Earlier sketches in CA 33-36R, CANR-13
Paley, Nicholas M(iroslav)
1911-1994 .... CANR-15
Earlier sketch in CA 41-44R
Paley, Vivian Gussin 1929- CANR-119
Earlier sketches in CA 93-96, CANR-30, 58
Paley, William 1743-1805 .... DLB 252
Paley, William S(amuel) 1901-1990 . CANR-83
Obituary 132
Earlier sketch in CA 110
Palffy-Alpar, Julius 1908-2001 .... CAP-2
Obituary 193
Earlier sketch in CA 23-24
Palfrey, Evelyn 1950- 231
Palfrey, John Gorham 1796-1881 .... DLB 1, 30, 235
Palfrey, Thomas R(ossman) 1895-1973 61-64
Palgrave, Francis Turner 1824-1897 ..... DLB 35
Palin, Michael (Edward) 1943- CANR-109
Earlier sketches in CA 107, CANR-35
See also Monty Python
See also CLC 21
See also SATA 67
Palinchak, Robert S(tephen) 1942- 49-52
Paling, Chris 1956- CANR-141
Earlier sketch in CA 156
Palinurus
See Connolly, Cyril (Vernon)
Palisca, Claude V(ictor) 1921-2001 .... 17-20R
Obituary 192
Palissot de Montenoy, Charles
1730-1814 .... GFL Beginnings to 1789
Palkovic, Mark 1954- 137
Pall, Ellen Jane 1952- CANR-115
Earlier sketches in CA 93-96, CANR-59
Palladini, David (Mario) 1946- .... MAICYA 1, 2
See also SATA 40
See also SATA-Brief 32
Pallas, Dorothy Constance 1933-1971
Obituary 33-36R
Pallas, Norvin 1918-1983 .... CANR-90
Earlier sketches in CA 1-4R, CANR-3
See also SATA 23
Pallavera, Franco
See Soldati, Mario
Palle, Albert 1916- 13-16R
Pallen, Thomas A. 1944- 194
Pallenberg, Corrado 1912- CANR-89
Earlier sketch in CA 13-16R
Pallette, Edward M. 1929- 203
Palley, Julian I(rving) 1925- 73-76
Palley, Marian Lief 1939- CANR-8
Earlier sketch in CA 61-64
Palli, Pitsa
See Hartocollis, Peter
Pallidini, Jodi
See Robbin, (Jodi) Luna
Palling, (Studley) Bruce 1949- CANR-87
Earlier sketch in CA 155
Pallis, Alexander (Anastasius) 1883-1975
Obituary 61-64
Pallis, Athanasios A. 1966- 235
Palliser, Charles 1947- CANR-76
Earlier sketch in CA 136
See also CLC 65
See also CN 5, 6, 7
Pallister, Janis L(ouise) 1926- CANR-14
Earlier sketch in CA 41-44R
Pallister, John C(lare) 1891-1980 .... 5-8R
Obituary 103
See also SATA-Obit 26
Pallone, Dave 1951- 140
Pallone, Nathaniel (John) 1935- CANR-115
Earlier sketches in CA 21-24R, CANR-10, 29
Pallotta-Chiarolli, Maria 1960- 189
See also SATA 117
Palm, Daniel C. 1957- 220
Palm, Goeran 1931- 29-32R
Palm, Goran
See Palm, Goeran
Palm, John Daniel 1924-
Brief entry 106
Palma, Marigloria
See Pagan Ferrer, Gloria M.
See also HW 1
Palma, Michael 1945- 207
Palma, Ricardo 1833-1919 168
See also LAW
See also TCLC 29
Palmatier, Robert Allen 1926- 37-40R
Palmedo, Roland 1895-1977 53-56
Obituary 69-72
Palmen, Connie 1955- 197
Palmer, Alan Warwick 1926- CANR-97
Earlier sketches in CA 13-16R, CANR-6
Palmer, Alexandra 1957- 221
Palmer, Archie M(acInnes) 1896-1985 .. 13-16R
Obituary 116
Palmer, Arnold (Daniel) 1929- 85-88
Palmer, B. C.
See Schmidt, Laura M(arie)
Palmer, Bernard (Alvin) 1914-1998 .. CANR-64
Obituary 176
Earlier sketches in CA 57-60, CANR-7, 12
See also SATA 26
See also TCWW 2
Palmer, Beverly Wilson 1936- 148
Palmer, Brooks 1900(?)-1974
Obituary 45-48
Palmer, Bruce (Hamilton)
1932-2000 .... CANR-90
Earlier sketches in CA 1-4R, CANR-3
Palmer, Bryan D(ouglas) 1951- CANR-109
Earlier sketch in CA 151
Palmer, C(yril) Everard 1930- CANR-79
Earlier sketch in CA 41-44R
See also BW 1
See also CWRI 5
See also SATA 14
Palmer, C(edric) King 1913-1999 .... 13-16R
Palmer, (Ruth) Candida 1926- 61-64
See also SATA 11
Palmer, (John) Carey (Bowden) 1943- 103
Palmer, Catherine (Leilani Cummings)
1956- 204
Palmer, Charles Earl 1919- 13-16R
Palmer, (Thomas) Cruise 1917- 69-72
Palmer, Dave Richard 1934- CANR-1
Earlier sketch in CA 45-48
Palmer, David (Walter) 1928- CANR-28
Earlier sketch in CA 21-24R
Palmer, Diana
See Kyle, Susan (Spaeth)
Palmer, Don
See Benson, Mildred (Augustine Wirt)
Palmer, Donald C. 1934- 53-56
Palmer, Dorothy Ann 1935- 57-60
Palmer, E(dgar) P(oole), Jr. 1938- 116
Palmer, Earl Frank 1931- 113
Palmer, Edgar Z(avitz) 1898-1977 .... 21-24R
Obituary 135
Palmer, Edward L. 1938- 101
Palmer, Elizabeth 1942- 142
Palmer, Elsie Pavitt 1922- 5-8R
Palmer, Eve 1916- 21-24R
Palmer, Everett W(alter) 1906-1970 .... CAP-2
Earlier sketch in CA 17-18
Palmer, Frank 1933- CANR-69
Earlier sketch in CA 139
Palmer, Frank R. 1922- 17-20R
Palmer, Gabrielle G. 1938- 128
Palmer, George 1915(?)-1986
Obituary 119
Palmer, George E. 1908-1994 .... 1-4R
Palmer, George Herbert 1842-1933
Brief entry 121
Palmer, Gerald Eustace Howell 1904-1984
Obituary 112
Palmer, (James) Gregory 1938- 121
Palmer, Hap 1942- 136
See also SATA 68
Palmer, Heidi 1948- .... SATA 15
Palmer, Helen H. 1911-1999 .... 21-24R
Palmer, Helen Marion
See Geisel, Helen
Palmer, Henry R(obinson), Jr.
1911-1993 .... 21-24R
Palmer, (Nathaniel) Humphrey
1930- CANR-31
Earlier sketches in CA 29-32R, CANR-12
Palmer, James B. 1929- 25-28R
Palmer, Jerome Robert 1904-1993 45-48
Palmer, Jessica 1953- .... HGG
See also SATA 120
Palmer, Jim
See Palmer, James B.
Palmer, Joe H. 1904-1952 212
See also DLB 171
Palmer, John (Leslie) 1885-1944 173
Brief entry 121
Palmer, John A(lfred)
See Lacey, Douglas R(aymond)
Palmer, John A(lfred) 1926-1982 .... 29-32R
Palmer, John D. 1932- CANR-118
Earlier sketch in CA 158
Palmer, John L(ogan) 1943- 73-76
Palmer, Joseph (Mansergh) 1912- 5-8R
Palmer, Joyce 205
Palmer, Judd 1972- .... SATA 153
Palmer, Juliette 1930- 81-84
See also SATA 15
Palmer, Kate Salley 1946- 163
See also SATA 97
Palmer, Kenneth T. 1937- 77-80
Palmer, L(eonard) R(obert)
1906-1984 .... CANR-88
Obituary 114
Earlier sketch in CA 25-28R
Palmer, Larry Garland 1938- 17-20R
Palmer, Larry I. 1944- 199
Palmer, Laura
See Schmidt, Laura M(arie)
Palmer, Lilli
See Peiser, Maria Lilli
Palmer, Lynn
See Palmer, Pamela Lynn
Palmer, Madelyn 1910- 103
Palmer, Maria
See Brennan, J(ames) H(erbert) and Strachan, Ian
Palmer, Marian 1930- 53-56
Palmer, Marjorie 1919- CANR-12
Earlier sketch in CA 57-60
Palmer, Martha
See Cheney, Martha
Palmer, Martin (Giles) 1953- 204
Palmer, Michael (Stephen) 1942- CANR-35
Earlier sketch in CA 114
See also CP 7
See also CPW
See also DAM POET
See also DLB 169
Palmer, Michael D. 1933- 37-40R
Palmer, Nettie 1885-1964 .... DLB 260
Palmer, Nicholas 1950- CANR-15
Earlier sketch in CA 89-92
Palmer, Noreen E. 1960- 206
Palmer, Norman D(unbar)
1909-1996 .... CANR-41
Earlier sketches in CA 1-4R, CANR-3, 19
Palmer, Pamela Lynn 1951- CANR-4
Earlier sketch in CA 53-56
Palmer, Parker J. 1939- CANR-89
Earlier sketches in CA 115, CANR-38
Palmer, Pete
See Palmer, E(dgar) P(oole), Jr.
Palmer, Peter
See Palmer, Elsie Pavitt
Palmer, Peter John 1932- CANR-42
Earlier sketches in CA 103, CANR-20
Palmer, R(obert) R(oswell) 1909-2002 ... 13-16R
Obituary 206
Palmer, Ralph Simon 1914- 73-76
Palmer, Randy 1953-2002 164
Palmer, Raymond A. 1910-1977
Obituary 111
See also SFW 4
Palmer, Raymond Edward 1927- 77-80
Palmer, Richard 1904-1993 97-100
Palmer, Richard Edward 1933- CANR-1
Earlier sketch in CA 45-48
Palmer, Richard Phillips 1921- 57-60
Palmer, Robert (Franklin, Jr.) 1945-1997 128
Obituary 162
Brief entry 121
Palmer, Robert C(harles) 1947- 113
Palmer, Robert E(verett) A(llen) 1932-
Brief entry 114
Palmer, Robin 1909-2000 109
See also SATA 43
Palmer, Roy (Ernest) 1932- CANR-23
Earlier sketches in CA 61-64, CANR-8
Palmer, Shirley 214
Palmer, Spencer J(ohn) 1927- CANR-10
Earlier sketch in CA 61-64
Palmer, Stanley H. 1944- 135
Palmer, (Charles) Stuart 1905-1968 ...... CMW 4
Palmer, Stuart 1924- CANR-3
Earlier sketch in CA 1-4R
Palmer, Susan J(ean) 236
Palmer, Susann(a Louisa) 1923- 132
Palmer, Thomas (Coryell) 1955- CANR-39
Earlier sketch in CA 109
Palmer, Tim(othy) 1948- CANR-138
Earlier sketch in CA 121
Palmer, Tobias
See Weathers, Winston
Palmer, Tony 1941- 195
Brief entry 111
Palmer, (Edward Vivian) Vance
1885-1959 .... RGEL 2
Palmer, Vance 1885-1959 .... DLB 260
Palmer, William J. 1943- CANR-72
Earlier sketch in CA 134
Palmer, Winthrop Bushnell 1899-1988 ... 65-68
Obituary 126
Palmieri, Anthony Francis 1920- 114
Palmore, Erdman B. 1930- 37-40R
Palmquist, Peter E. 1936-2003 211
Palms, Roger C(urtis) 1936- CANR-38
Earlier sketches in CA 93-96, CANR-17
Paloczi-Horvath, George
1908-1973 .... CANR-90
Obituary 37-40R
Earlier sketch in CA 5-8R
Palombo, Joseph 1928- 208
Palombo, Stanley R(obert) 1934- 122
Palomino, Rafael 1963- 173
Palomo, G(aspar) J(esus) 1952- 61-64
Palovic, Clara Lora 1918- 25-28R
Pals, Daniel L. 1946- 206
Paltenghi, Madeleine
See Anderson, Madeleine Paltenghi
Paltock, Robert 1697-1767 .... DLB 39
See also RGEL 2
Paltrowitz, Donna (Milman) 1950- 119
See also SATA 61
See also SATA-Brief 50
Paltrowitz, Stuart 1946- 118
See also SATA 61
See also SATA-Brief 50
Paludan, (Stig Henning) Jacob (Puggaard)
1896-1975 190
Obituary 115
See also DLB 214
See also EWL 3
Paludan, Phillip S(haw) 1938- 73-76
Paludan-Muller, Frederik 1809-1876 .. DLB 300
Paludi, Michele A. 1954- 140
Paluello, Lorenzo Minio
See Minio-Paluello, Lorenzo
Palumbi, Stephen R. 208
Palumbo, Dennis J(ames) 1929- CANR-55
Earlier sketches in CA 29-32R, CANR-28
Palumbo-Liu, David 199
Palusci, Larry 1916- 29-32R
Paluszny, Maria Janina 1939- 103
Palyi, Melchior 1892(?)-1970
Obituary 104
Pampel, Fred C. 1950- 141
Pamuk, Orhan 1952- CANR-127
Earlier sketches in CA 142, CANR-75
See also CLC 185
See also CWW 2
See also WLIT 6
Pan, Hermes 1910-1990 .... IDFW 3, 4
Pan, Peter
See Bartier, Pierre
Pan, Stephen C(hao) Y(ing) 1915- 45-48
Panaev, Ivan Ivanovich 1812-1862 ..... DLB 198
Panaeva, Avdot'ia Iakovlevna
1820-1893 .... DLB 238
Panagariya, Arvind 1952- 167
Panagopoulos, Epaminondas Peter
1915-1997 .... 13-16R
Panagopoulos, Janie Lynn 223
See also SATA 149
Panama, Norman 1914-2003 104
Obituary 213
See also DLB 26
Panassie, Hugues (Louis Marie Henri)
1912-1974 97-100
Obituary 53-56
Panati, Charles 1943- 81-84
See also SATA 65
Panayi, Panikos 1962- 143

Cumulative Index 445 Parish

Panayotopoulos, I(oannis) M(ichael)
1901-1982 .... EWL 3
Pancake, Ann 1963- 204
Pancake, Breece Dexter 1952-1979 123
Obituary 109
See also Pancake, Breece D'J
Pancake, Breece D'J
See Pancake, Breece Dexter
See also CLC 29
See also DLB 130
See also SSC 61
Pancake, John S(ilas) 1920-1986 53-56
Pancaldi, Giuliano 238
Panchenko, Nikolai .... CLC 59
Panchyk, Richard 1970- 208
See also SATA 138
Pancol, Katherine 1954- 211
Pandey, B(ishwa) N(ath) 1929-1982 . CANR-20
Obituary 108
Earlier sketch in CA 25-28R
Pandiri, Ananda M(ohan) 1930- 177
Pandit, Vijaya Lakshmi 1900-1990 104
Panduro, Leif (Thormod) 1923-1977 192
See also DLB 214
See also EWL 3
Panek, LeRoy Lad 1943- CANR-32
Earlier sketch in CA 113
Panek, Richard 235
Panella, Vincent 1939- CANR-99
Earlier sketch in CA 97-100
Panero, Leopoldo 1909-1962 176
See also DLB 108
See also HW 2
Panetta, George 1915-1969 .... CANR-108
Earlier sketch in CA 81-84
See also SATA 15
Panetta, Joseph N. 1953- 161
See also SATA 96
Panetta, Leon Edward 1938- 101
Panford, Kwamina 1955- 193
Pang, May 1950- 118
Pangborn, Edgar 1909-1976 .... CANR-79
Earlier sketches in CA 1-4R, CANR-4
See also DLB 8
See also SFW 4
Panger, Daniel 1926- 93-96
Panglaykim, J(usuf Pangestu) 1922- .. CANR-15
Earlier sketch in CA 21-24R
Pangle, Thomas L(ee) 1944- CANR-1
Earlier sketch in CA 49-52
Pangrazzi, Arnaldo 1947- 115
Paniagua Bermudez, Domingo 1880(?)-1973
Obituary 41-44R
Panichas, George A(ndrew) 1930- .. CANR-119
Earlier sketches in CA 25-28R, CANR-10, 25
Panik, Sharon 1952- 149
See also SATA 82
Paniker, Raimundo
See Panikkar, Raimon
Panikkar, K(avalam) Madhava
1895-1963 .... CANR-90
Earlier sketches in CAP-1, CA 13-16
Panikkar, Raimon 1918- CANR-51
Earlier sketches in CA 81-84, CANR-25
Panikkar, Raymond
See Panikkar, Raimon
Panin, Dimitri (Mikhailovich) 1911-1987
Obituary 124
Panitch, Leo (Victor) 1945- 119
Panitt, Merrill 1917-1994 106
Panitz, Esther L(eah) CANR-40
Earlier sketch in CA 116
Panizzi, Sir Anthony 1797-1879 .... DLB 184
Pankey, Eric 1959- CANR-91
Earlier sketch in CA 120
Pankhurst, Christabel (Harriette)
1880-1958 234
See also FW
Pankhurst, Emmeline (Goulden) 1858-1928
Brief entry 116
See also FW
See also TCLC 100
Pankhurst, Helen 1964- 143
Pankhurst, Richard (Keir Pethick)
1927- CANR-90
Earlier sketches in CA 9-12R, CANR-6, 21, 44
Pankhurst, (Estelle) Sylvia 1882-1960 .... FW
Pankin, Robert M. 1935- 114
Panko, Rudy
See Gogol, Nikolai (Vasilyevich)
Pannabecker, Samuel Floyd 1896-1977 .. 65-68
Pannell, Anne Gary 1910- CAP-2
Earlier sketch in CA 23-24
Pannenberg, Wolfhart (Ulrich)
1928- CANR-48
Earlier sketches in CA 25-28R, CANR-11
Panneton, Philippe 1895-1960 148
See also Ringuet
See also CCA 1
Pannick, David 1956- 130
Panning, Anne 1966- 138
Pannor, Reuben 1922- 61-64
Pannwitz, Rudolf 1881-1969
Obituary 89-92
Pano, Nicholas C(hristopher) 1934- 37-40R
Panofsky, Erwin 1892-1968 .... CANR-101
Obituary 113
Earlier sketches in CA 117, CANR-81
Panofsky, Ruth 1958- CANR-110
Earlier sketch in CA 172
Panos, Chris(tos) 1935- 65-68
Panos, Louis G. 1925- 136
Panourgia, Neni K(onstantinou) 1958- 154
Panourgia, Nenny
See Panourgia, Neni K(onstantinou)
Panov, Valery (Shulman) 1938- 102
Panova, Vera (Fedorovna) 1905-1973 102
Obituary 89-92
See also Panova, Vera Fyodorovna
See also DLB 302
See also MTCW 1
Panova, Vera Fyodorovna
See Panova, Vera (Fedorovna)
See also EWL 3
Panowski, Eileen Thompson 1920- 5-8R
See also SATA 49
Panshin, Alexei 1940- CANR-82
Earlier sketch in CA 57-60
See also DLB 8
See also SFW 4
Panshin, Cory (Seidman) 1947- 185
Brief entry 112
Pansy
See Alden, Isabella (Macdonald)
Pantaeva, Irina 1974(?)- 176
Pantell, Dora (Fuchs) 111
See also SATA 39
Panter, Carol 1936- 49-52
See also SATA 9
Panter, Gideon G. 1935- 77-80
Panter, Peter
See Tucholsky, Kurt
Panter-Downes, Mollie Patricia
1906-1997 101
Obituary 156
Panting, Phyllis
See Morton, Phyllis Digby
Pantoja, Antonia 1922-2002 212
Pantoliano, Joe 1951- 218
Panych, Morris 1952- CANR-108
Earlier sketch in CA 166
Panzarella, Andrew 1940- 25-28R
Panzarella, Joseph John, Jr. 1919-1984 85-88
Panzer, Mary (Caroline) 1955- 171
Panzer, Pauline (Richman) 1911(?)-1972
Obituary 37-40R
Pao, Ping-Nie 1922- 103
Paolazzi, Leo 1935-1989
See Porta, Antonio
Paoletti, John T(homas) 1939- 112
Paoli, Pia 1930- 25-28R
Paolini, Christopher 1983- 219
See also CLR 102
See also SATA 157
Paolini, Gilberto 1928- CANR-45
Earlier sketches in CA 45-48, CANR-22
Paolucci, Anne (Attura) CANR-102
Earlier sketches in CA 73-76, CANR-47
Paolucci, Henry 1921-1999 102
Obituary 174
Paone, Anthony J(oseph) 1913- 5-8R
Paor, Richard de
See Power, Richard
Papachristou, Judy 1930- 93-96
Papadat-Bengescu, Hortensia
1876-1955 .... DLB 220
See also EWL 3
Papadiamantis, Alexandros 1851-1911 168
See also EWL 3
See also TCLC 29
Papadiamantopoulos, Johannes 1856-1910
Brief entry 117
See also Moreas, Jean
Papadimitriou, Dimitri B. 1946- CANR-103
Earlier sketch in CA 147
Papaleo, Joseph 1925- CANR-117
Earlier sketch in CA 25-28R
Papandreou, Andreas G(eorge)
1919-1996 .... 37-40R
Obituary 152
Papandreou, Margaret C. 1923- 29-32R
Papanek, Ernst 1900-1973 .... CANR-4
Earlier sketch in CA 1-4R
Papanek, Gustav F(ritz) 1926- CANR-1
Earlier sketch in CA 45-48
Papanicolaou, George (Nicholas)
1883-1962 167
Papanikolas, Zeese 1942- 156
Papantonio, Michael 1907-1978 .... DLB 187
Papas, Bill
See Papas, William
Papas, William 1927-2000 .... CANR-12
Obituary 188
Earlier sketch in CA 25-28R
See also SATA 50
Papashvily, George 1898-1978 .... CANR-100
Obituary 77-80
Earlier sketch in CA 81-84
See also SATA 17
Papashvily, Helen (Waite)
1906-1996 .... CANR-100
Earlier sketch in CA 81-84
See also SATA 17
Papazian, Dennis R(ichard) 1931- 45-48
Papazoglou, Orania 1951- CANR-108
Earlier sketches in CA 126, CANR-65
See also CMW 4
Pape, D. L.
See Pape, Donna (Lugg)
Pape, Donna (Lugg) 1930- CANR-50
Earlier sketches in CA 21-24R, CANR-9, 25
See also SATA 2, 82
Pape, Gordon 1936- CANR-25
Earlier sketch in CA 105
Pape, Greg 1947- 113
See also CP 7
Papenfuse, Edward C(arl), Jr. 1943- CANR-8
Earlier sketch in CA 57-60
Paper, Herbert H(arry) 1925- CANR-1
Earlier sketch in CA 45-48
Paper, Jordan 1938- 177
Paper, Lewis Jay 1946- 146
Brief entry 114
Paperny, Myra (Green) 1932- 69-72
See also SATA 51
See also SATA-Brief 33
Papert, Emma N. 1926- 101
Papes, Robert 1943- 211
Papi, G(iuseppe) Ugo 1893-1989 .... 25-28R
Papich, Stephen 1925- 69-72
Papier, Judith Barnard 1932- 21-24R
Papin, Joseph 1914-1982 65-68
Papineau, David 1947- CANR-86
Earlier sketch in CA 130
Papini, Giovanni 1881-1956 180
Brief entry 121
See also DLB 264
See also TCLC 22
Papke, David (Ray) 1947- 193
Papp, Charles Steven 1917- CANR-15
Earlier sketch in CA 41-44R
Pappageotes, George C(hristos)
1926-1963 .... CANR-2
Earlier sketch in CA 1-4R
Pappano, Marilyn 204
Pappas, George 1929- 29-32R
Pappas, Lou Seibert 1930- CANR-47
Earlier sketches in CA 61-64, CANR-8, 23
Pappas, Milt 1939- 234
Pappe, Ilan 1954- 234
Pappworth, M(aurice) H(enry)
1910-1994 .... 21-24R
Paprika
See Holmvik, Oyvind
Papus
See Encausse, Gerard (Anaclet Vincent)
Paquet, Alfons (Hermann) 1881-1944 .. DLB 66
Paquet, Laura
See Paquet, Laura Byrne
Paquet, Laura Byrne 1965- 217
Paracelsus 1493-1541 .... DLB 179
Paradeise, Catherine 1946- 138
Paradis, Adrian A(lexis) 1912- CANR-40
Earlier sketches in CA 1-4R, CANR-3, 18
See also SAAS 8
See also SATA 1, 67
Paradis, James G(ardiner) 1942- 93-96
Paradis, Marjorie Bartholomew
1886(?)-1970 .... CANR-103
Obituary 29-32R
Earlier sketch in CA 73-76
See also SATA 17
Paradis, Peter 1964- 221
Paradis, Suzanne 1936- .... DLB 53
Paradise, Louis V(incent) 1946- 114
Paradise, Paul R. 1950- 137
Parakh, Jal Sohrab 1932-
Brief entry 105
Paral, Vladimir 1932- 206
See also DLB 232
See also EWL 3
Parandowski, Jan 1895-1978 .... CAP-1
Earlier sketch in CA 11-12
See also EWL 3
Paranjape, Makarand (Ramachandra)
1960- 150
Parascandola, Louis J. 1952- 193
Parasol, Peter
See Stevens, Wallace
Parasuram, T(attamangalam) V(iswanatha Iyer)
1923- 106
Paratore, Angela 1912- 13-16R
Paravisini-Gebert, Lizabeth 1953- .. CANR-127
Earlier sketch in CA 139
Parberry, Ian 1959- 150
Parchman, William E(ugene) 1936- 93-96
Pardeck, John T. 1947- 210
Pardee, Michael 1945- 113
Pardey, Larry
See Pardey, Lawrence Fred
Pardey, Lawrence Fred 1939- 93-96
Pardey, (Mary) Lin 1944- CANR-82
Earlier sketch in CA 93-96
Pardo Bazan, Emilia 1851-1921 .... EWL 3
See also FW
See also RGSF 2
See also RGWL 2, 3
See also SSC 30
Pardoe, Julia 1804-1862 .... DLB 166
Pardoe, M(argot Mary) 1902-1996 .... CWRI 5
Pardue, Diana F. 203
Paredes, Americo 1915-1999 .... 37-40R
Obituary 179
See also DLB 209
See also EXPP
See also HW 1
Pareek, Udai (Narain) 1925- CANR-53
Earlier sketches in CA 21-24R, CANR-11, 28
Pareja Diezcanseco, Alfredo 1908-1993 174
See also DLB 145
See also EWL 3
See also HW 2
Pareja y Diez Canseco, Alfredo
See Pareja Diezcanseco, Alfredo
Parelius, Ann Parker 1943- 81-84
Parelius, Robert J. 1941- 81-84
Parens, Henri 1928- 89-92
Parent, David J(oseph) 1931- CANR-9
Earlier sketch in CA 57-60
Parent, Gail 1940- 101
Interview in CA-101
Parent, Ronald 1937-1982
Obituary 107
Parent, William A. 1944- 127
Parente, Pascal P(rosper) 1890-1971 ..... CAP-1
Obituary 33-36R
Earlier sketch in CA 17-18
Parente, Stephen L. 1961- 226
Parenteau, Shirley Laurolyn 1935- ... CANR-71
Earlier sketches in CA 85-88, CANR-15, 33
See also SATA 47
See also SATA-Brief 40
Parenti, Christian 218
Parenti, Michael 1933- CANR-104
Earlier sketch in CA 73-76
Pares, Marion (Stapylton) 1914- CANR-12
Earlier sketch in CA 17-20R
Paret, Peter 1924- 198
Brief entry 114
Pareto, Vilfredo 1848-1923 175
See also TCLC 69
Paretsky, Sara 1947- CANR-95
Brief entry 125
Earlier sketches in CA 129, CANR-59
Interview in CA-129
See also AAYA 30
See also BEST 90:3
See also CLC 135
See also CMW 4
See also CPW
See also DA3
See also DAM POP
See also DLB 306
See also MSW
See also RGAL 4
Paretti, Sandra 1935(?)-1994 .... CANR-7
Obituary 144
Earlier sketch in CA 53-56
Parezo, Nancy Jean 1951- 114
Parfenie, Maria
See Codrescu, Andrei
Parfit, Derek 1942- .... DLB 262
Parfit, Michael 1947- 119
Parfitt, George (Albert Ekins) 1939- .. CANR-26
Earlier sketch in CA 109
Parfitt, Tudor (Vernon) 1944- CANR-138
Earlier sketch in CA 123
Parfitt, Will 217
Pargeter, Edith Mary 1913-1995 .... CANR-41
Obituary 149
Earlier sketches in CA 1-4R, CANR-4, 24
See also Peters, Ellis
See also AAYA 31
See also CMW 4
See also CN 6
See also MTCW 1
See also RHW
Pargeter, Margaret 1885-1961 .... RHW
Parham, Joseph Byars 1919-1980 65-68
Obituary 135
Parham, Robert Randall 1943- 57-60
Parham, William 1914- 103
Parham, William Thomas 1913- CANR-20
Earlier sketch in CA 103
Parhokh, Sofiia Iakovlevna
See Parnok, Sophia (Yakovlevna)
Pari, Susanne 1957- 171
Parillo, Mark P. 1955- 211
Parini, Jay (Lee) 1948- 229
Earlier sketches in CA 97-100, CANR-32, 87
Autobiographical Essay in 229
See also CAAS 16
See also CLC 54, 133
Parins, James William 1939- 109
Paris, Ann
See Papazoglou, Orania
Paris, Arthur E. 127
Paris, Barry CANR-107
Earlier sketch in CA 153
Paris, Bernard J. 1931- CANR-7
Earlier sketch in CA 17-20R
Paris, David C. 1949- 154
Paris, Erna 1938- CANR-118
Earlier sketch in CA 105
Paris, Ginette 1946- 123
Paris, I. Mark 1950- 141
Paris, Jeanne 1918- 1-4R
Paris, Michael 1949- 135
Paris, Mike
See Paris, Michael
Parise, Goffredo 1929-1986 132
Obituary 120
See also DLB 177
See also EWL 3
Pariseau, Earl J(oseph) 1928- 9-12R
Parish, Charles 1927- 25-28R
Parish, David 1932- CANR-14
Earlier sketch in CA 73-76
Parish, Helen Rand 1912-
Brief entry 115
Parish, James 1904-1973
Obituary 114
Parish, James Robert 1944- CANR-117
Earlier sketches in CA 33-36R, CANR-37
Parish, Margaret (Cecile)
1927-1988 .... CANR-81
Obituary 127
Earlier sketches in CA 73-76, CANR-18, 38
See also Parish, Peggy
See also CWRI 5
See also MAICYA 1, 2
See also SATA 73
Parish, Margaret Holt
See Holt, Margaret
Parish, Mitchell 1900-1993 .... DLB 265
Parish, Peggy
See Parish, Margaret (Cecile)
See also CLR 22
See also SATA 17
See also SATA-Obit 59
Parish, Peter J(oseph) 1929-2002 57-60
Obituary 207
Parish, Steven M. 1953- 157
Parish, Townsend
See Pietschmann, Richard John III

Parisi, Joseph 1944- CANR-127
Earlier sketch in CA 93-96
Parizeau, Alice (Poznanska) 1930- 157
See also DLB 60
Park, Barbara 1947- CANR-101
Earlier sketch in CA 113
See also CLR 34
See also MAICYA 2
See also SATA 40, 78, 123
See also SATA-Brief 35
Park, Bert Edward 1947- 128
Park, Bill
See Park, W(illiam) B(ryan)
Park, Charles F(rederick), Jr. 1903-1990 .. 57-60
Park, Clara Claiborne 1923- CANR-94
Earlier sketches in CA 21-24R, CANR-39
Park, D. U.
See Woods, Clee
Park, David 1919- 105
Park, Ed 1930- 73-76
Park, Edwards 1917-2005 CANR-49
Obituary 236
Earlier sketch in CA 123
Park, Elm
See Dunbar, Charles Stuart
Park, Frances 1955- 205
Park, George 1925- 77-80
Park, Ginger 205
Park, Jacqueline 1925- 179
Park, Jacquelyn Holt 180
Park, James (Robert) 1956- 120
Park, James William 1936- 121
Park, Janie Jaehyun SATA 150
Park, Joe 1913-1993 21-24R
Park, Jordan
See Kornbluth, C(yril) M. and Pohl, Frederik
Park, Joseph H. 1890(?)-1979
Obituary 89-92
Park, Jung-Dong 1960- 175
Park, Keith K. H. 1964- 143
Park, Linda Sue 1960- 197
See also AAYA 49
See also CLR 84
See also MAICYA 2
See also SATA 127
Park, Maeva
See Dobner, Maeva Park
Park, Myung-sook
See Park Myung-sook
Park, Nick 1958- 185
See also AAYA 32
See also IDFW 3, 4
See also SATA 113
Park, O'Hyun 1940- 53-56
Park, Paul (Claiborne) 1954- CANR-129
Earlier sketch in CA 128
See also SFW 4
Park, Peter 1929- 29-32R
Park, Richard L(eonard) 1920-1980 77-80
Park, Robert E(zra) 1864-1944 165
Brief entry 122
See also TCLC 73
Park, Robert L. 1932- 89-92
Park, Roberta J. 1931- 159
Park, (Rosina) Ruth (Lucia) 1923(?)- .. CANR-65
Earlier sketch in CA 105
See also CLR 51
See also DLB 260
See also MAICYA 2
See also SATA 25, 93
Park, Severna 1948- 196
Park, Sung-Bae 1933- 115
Park, Therese 1941- 181
Park, Tim(othy) (K.) 1948- 202
Park, W(illiam) B(ryan) 1936- CANR-39
Earlier sketches in CA 97-100, CANR-17
See also SATA 22
Park, William John 1930- 49-52
Park Chung Hee 1917-1979 CANR-10
Obituary 97-100
Earlier sketch in CA 61-64
Parke, Herbert William 1903-1986 105
Parke, John 1754-1789 DLB 31
Parke, Lawrence 1922- 149
Parke, Margaret Bittner 1901-1983 89-92
Parke, Marilyn 1928- 149
See also SATA 82
Parke, Richard H. 1909(?)-1989
Obituary 128
Parke, Ross D(uke) 1938- CANR-38
Earlier sketches in CA 45-48, CANR-1, 16
Parke, Simon 1957- 187
Parker, Adrian David 1947- 103
Parker, Alastair
See Parker, R(obert) A(lexander) C(larke)
Parker, Alexander A(ugustine)
1908-1989 CANR-16
Earlier sketch in CA 21-24R
Parker, Alfred Browning 1916- 17-20R
Parker, Angela
See Thirkell, Angela (Margaret)
Parker, Ann
See Neal, Ann Parker
Parker, Arthur C(aswell) 1881-1955
Brief entry 115
Parker, Barbara J. CANR-99
Earlier sketch in CA 160
Parker, Barbara Keevil 1938- 233
See also SATA 157
Parker, Barry R(ichard) 1935- CANR-119
Earlier sketches in CA 112, CANR-31, 57
Parker, Beatrice
See Huff, T(om) E.
Parker, Bert
See Ellison, Harlan (Jay)
Parker, Bertha Morris 1890-1980 CANR-5
Obituary 102
Earlier sketch in CA 5-8R
Parker, Betty June 1929- CANR-22
Earlier sketches in CA 57-60, CANR-7
Parker, Beulah 1912- 81-84
Parker, Brant Julian 1920-
Brief entry 114
Parker, Brother Michael
See Parker, Kenneth L(eroy)
Parker, Claire 1907-1980 IDFW 3, 4
Parker, Clifford S(tetson) 1891-1972 5-8R
Parker, Clyde A. 1927- 41-44R
Parker, D(avid) C. 1953- CANR-121
Earlier sketch in CA 167
Parker, D(avid) S(tuart) 1960- 179
Parker, Dan(iel Francis) 1893-1967 200
See also DLB 241
Parker, David 1941- 132
Parker, David B. 1956- 135
Parker, David L(ambert) 1935- 108
Parker, David Marshall 1929- 77-80
Parker, Dee
See Parker, David L(ambert)
Parker, (William George) Derek
1932- CANR-119
Earlier sketches in CA 29-32R, CANR-23, 49
See also CP 1
Parker, Don(ald) H(enry) 1912-2000 .. CANR-6
Obituary 188
Earlier sketch in CA 5-8R
Parker, Donald Dean 1899-1983 CANR-34
Earlier sketch in CA 37-40R
Parker, Donn B(lanchard) 1929- CANR-9
Earlier sketch in CA 65-68
Parker, Dorian Leigh 1920- 145
Parker, Dorothy (Rothschild)
1893-1967 CAP-2
Obituary 25-28R
Earlier sketch in CA 19-20
See also AMWS 9
See also CLC 15, 68
See also DA3
See also DAM POET
See also DLB 11, 45, 86
See also EXPP
See also FW
See also MAL 5
See also MAWW
See also MTCW 1, 2
See also MTFW 2005
See also PC 28
See also PFS 18
See also RGAL 4
See also RGSF 2
See also SSC 2
See also TCLC 143
See also TUS
Parker, Dorothy 1922- 93-96
Parker, Dorothy Mills -2005 CANR-11
Obituary 239
Earlier sketch in CA 21-24R
Parker, Douglas Hugh 1926- 1-4R
Parker, Edna Jean 1935- 101
Parker, Edwin B(urke) 1932- 13-16R
Parker, Elinor Milnor 1906- CANR-3
Earlier sketch in CA 1-4R
See also SATA 3
Parker, Elliott S(evern) 1939- 103
Parker, Francis H(oward) 1920- 21-24R
Parker, Frank J(oseph) 1940- 49-52
Parker, Frank R. 1940-1997 136
Obituary 159
Parker, Franklin 1921- CANR-22
Earlier sketches in CA 33-36R, CANR-7
Parker, Franklin D(allas) 1918- 13-16R
Parker, Gail Thain 1943- 104
Parker, Gary E. 1953- 225
Parker, Geoffrey 1933- 49-52
Parker, Geoffrey 1943- 214
Parker, (Horatio) Gilbert 1862(?)-1932 192
Parker, Gilbert 1862-1932 DLB 99
Parker, Glenn M. 1938- 203
Parker, Gordon 1940- 103
Parker, Gwendolyn M(cDougand) 1950- 155
Parker, H(enry) M(ichael) D(enne) 1896(?)-1971
Obituary 104
Parker, Harold T(albot) 1907- CANR-9
Earlier sketch in CA 21-24R
Parker, Hershel 1935- CANR-123
Earlier sketches in CA 33-36R, CANR-13, 30, 57
Parker, Howard J(ohn) 1948- 57-60
Parker, I(ngrid) J. 222
Parker, J(ohn) Carlyle 1931- CANR-106
Earlier sketches in CA 57-60, CANR-7, 24, 50
Parker, Jack Horace 1914- 113
Parker, James
See Newby, Eric
Parker, James 1714(?)-1770 DLB 43
Parker, James Reid 1909-1984
Obituary 111
Parker, Jean
See Chandra, G. S. Sharat and Sharat Chandra, G(ubbi) S(hankara Chetty)
Parker, Joan H. 1932- 85-88
Parker, John
See Wyatt, John
Parker, (Herbert) John (Harvey)
1906-1987 CANR-34
Obituary 124
Earlier sketch in CA 5-8R
Parker, John 1923- CANR-5
Earlier sketch in CA 5-8R
Parker, John Thomas 1950- CANR-41
Earlier sketch in CA 118
Parker, Julia (Louise) 1932- CANR-48
Earlier sketches in CA 101, CANR-23
Parker, Julie F. 1961- 156
See also SATA 92
Parker, Kenneth L(eroy) 1954- 132
Parker, Kristy 1957- 126
See also SATA 59
Parker, Laura
See Castoro, Laura (Ann)
Parker, Leslie
See Thirkell, Angela (Margaret)
Parker, Lois M(ay) 1912-1996 CANR-39
Earlier sketches in CA 69-72, CANR-11
See also SATA 30
Parker, L.P.E. 1933- 172
Parker, Margot M. 1937- 122
See also SATA 52
Parker, Marjorie Blain 1960- 218
See also SATA 145
Parker, Marsha Zurich 1952- 107
Parker, Mary Jessie 1948- SATA 71
Parker, Matthew 231
Parker, Matthew 1504-1575 DLB 213
Parker, Michael 1959- CANR-109
Earlier sketch in CA 140
Parker, Nancy Winslow 1930- CANR-106
Earlier sketches in CA 49-52, CANR-1, 22, 49
See also MAICYA 1, 2
See also SAAS 20
See also SATA 10, 69, 132
Parker, Nathan Carlyle 1960- 102
Parker, Noel
See Shreffler, Philip A.
Parker, Pat 1944-1989 CANR-90
Earlier sketches in CA 57-60, CANR-42
See also BW 2
Parker, Pauline E. 1916- 236
Parker, Percy Spurlark 1940- 53-56
See also BW 2
Parker, Peter (Robert Nevill) 1954- 136
Parker, R(obert) A(lexander) C(larke)
1927-2001 205
Parker, Richard 1915-1990 CANR-76
Earlier sketch in CA 73-76
See also CWRI 5
See also SATA 14
Parker, Robert
See Boyd, Waldo T.
Parker, Robert 1920- CANR-13
Earlier sketch in CA 77-80
Parker, Robert Allerton 1889(?)-1970
Obituary 29-32R
Parker, Robert B(rown) 1932- CANR-128
Earlier sketches in CA 49-52, CANR-1, 26, 52, 89
Interview in CANR-26
See also AAYA 28
See also BEST 89:4
See also BPFB 3
See also CLC 27
See also CMW 4
See also CPW
See also DAM NOV, POP
See also DLB 306
See also MSW
See also MTCW 1
See also MTFW 2005
Parker, Robert Miles 1939- 118
Parker, Robert Stewart 1915- 103
Parker, Rolland (Sandau) 1928- CANR-2
Earlier sketch in CA 45-48
Parker, Ron
See Parker, Ronald B(ruce)
Parker, Ronald B(ruce) 1932- 117
Parker, Ronald K(eith) 1939- 108
Parker, Rowland 1912-1989 CANR-10
Obituary 128
Earlier sketch in CA 65-68
Parker, Sanford S. 1919(?)-1980
Obituary 97-100
Parker, Scott 1950- 113
Parker, Stanley R(obert) 1927- CANR-19
Earlier sketch in CA 103
Parker, Stephen Jan 1939- 118
Parker, (James) Stewart 1941-1988 ... CANR-76
Obituary 127
Earlier sketches in CA 103, CANR-32
See also CBD
See also CP 1
See also DLB 245
Parker, T(homas) H(enry) L(ouis)
1916- CANR-6
Earlier sketch in CA 5-8R
Parker, T(homas) Jefferson 183
Parker, Theodore 1810-1860 DLB 1, 235
Parker, Thomas F(rancis) 1932- 73-76
Parker, Thomas Maynard 1906-1985 ..... CAP-2
Earlier sketch in CA 17-18
Parker, Tom
See Parker, John Thomas
Parker, Tom 1943-1997 130
Parker, Toni Trent 1947- 213
See also SATA 142
Parker, Trey 1969- 168
See also AAYA 27
Parker, Una-Mary 1930- 140
Parker, W(illiam) H(enry)
1912-1996 CANR-13
Earlier sketch in CA 33-36R
Parker, W(ilford) Oren 1911- 41-44R
Parker, Watson 1924- 106
Parker, William Riley 1906-1968 CAP-2
Earlier sketch in CA 17-18
See also DLB 103
Parker, Willie J. 1924- 77-80
Parker, Wyman W(est) 1912-1998 13-16R
Parker-Pope, Tara 197
Parkerson, Donald H. 1946- 151
Parkerson, John 1885(?)-1978
Obituary 77-80
Parkerson, Michelle (Denise) 1953- 153
See also BW 2
Parkes, Bessie Rayner 1829-1925 205
See also DLB 240
Parkes, Colin Murray 1928- 81-84
Parkes, Frank 1932- CP 1
Parkes, Graham 1949- CANR-58
Earlier sketch in CA 127
Parkes, Henry B. 1904-1972
Obituary 33-36R
Parkes, James William 1896-1981
Obituary 104
Parkes, K. Stuart 1943- 127
Parkes, Lucas
See Harris, John (Wyndham Parkes Lucas) Beynon
Parkes, M(alcolm) B(eckwith) 1930- 145
Parkes, (Grahem) Roger 1933- 53-56
Parkes, Terence 1927-2003 104
Obituary 217
Parkes, Walter F. 1951- 167
Parket, I(rwin) Robert 1931- 114
Parkhill, Forbes 1892-1974 CANR-90
Earlier sketch in CA 1-4R
Parkhill, John
See Cox, William R(obert)
Parkhill, Wilson 1901-1978 5-8R
Parkhurst, Helen 1887-1973
Obituary 41-44R
Parkhurst, Louis Gifford, Jr. 1946- 113
Parkhurst, Winthrop 1892(?)-1983
Obituary 110
Parkin, Alan 1934- 29-32R
Parkin, David 1940- CANR-30
Earlier sketches in CA 25-28R, CANR-13
Parkin, Frank 1940- 147
See also CLC 43
Parkin, G(eorge) Raleigh 1896-1977(?)
Obituary 106
Parkin, Molly 1932- 104
Parkin, Peter Hubert 1917-1984
Obituary 113
Parkin, Ray 1910- 196
Parkin, Sara (Lamb) 1946- 153
Parkinson, C(yril) Northcote
1909-1993 CANR-59
Obituary 140
Earlier sketches in CA 5-8R, CANR-5
See also RHW
Parkinson, (Frederick) Charles Douglas
1916- CAP-1
Earlier sketch in CA 11-12
Parkinson, Claire L(ucille) 1948- CANR-103
Earlier sketches in CA 120, CANR-49
Parkinson, Cornelia M. 1925- CANR-15
Earlier sketch in CA 81-84
Parkinson, Dan 1935- TCWW 2
Parkinson, David 1961- 145
Parkinson, Ethelyn M(inerva)
1906-1999 CANR-1
Earlier sketch in CA 49-52
See also SATA 11
Parkinson, J(ohn) R(ichard) 1922- 102
Parkinson, Kathryn N. 1954- CANR-49
Earlier sketch in CA 120
See also Parkinson, Kathy
Parkinson, Kathy
See Parkinson, Kathryn N.
See also SATA 71
Parkinson, Michael 1944- CANR-27
Earlier sketch in CA 29-32R
Parkinson, R(ichard) B(ruce) 1963- . CANR-139
Earlier sketch in CA 174
Parkinson, Roger 1939-1978 106
Parkinson, Siobhan 1954- CWRI 5
Parkinson, Stanley 1941- 149
Parkinson, T(erry) L(ee) 1949-1993 239
See also HGG
Parkinson, Thomas (Francis)
1920-1992 CANR-83
Obituary 136
Earlier sketches in CA 5-8R, CANR-3
See also CP 1, 2
Parkinson, Thomas P(aul) 102
Parkinson, Tom
See Parkinson, Thomas P(aul)
Parkman, Francis, Jr. 1823-1893 AMWS 2
See also DLB 1, 30, 183, 186, 235
See also RGAL 4
Park Myung-sook 1950- 231
Parks, Aileen Wells 1901-1986 5-8R
Parks, Arva Moore 1939- 103
Parks, David 1944- 25-28R
Parks, Deborah A. 1948- CANR-110
Earlier sketch in CA 155
See also SATA 91, 133
Parks, Douglas R(ichard) 1942- 111
Parks, Edd Winfield 1906-1968 CANR-92
Earlier sketch in CA 5-8R
See also SATA 10
Parks, Edmund 1911- 69-72
Parks, Edna D(orintha) 1910-2001 13-16R

Parks, Gordon (Alexander Buchanan)
1912- CANR-66
Earlier sketches in CA 41-44R, CANR-26
See also AAYA 36
See also AITN 2
See also BLC 3
See also BW 2, 3
See also CLC 1, 16
See also DA3
See also DAM MULT
See also DLB 33
See also MTCW 2
See also MTFW 2005
See also SATA 8, 108
Parks, Joseph Howard 1903-1992 .... CANR-90
Earlier sketch in CA 1-4R
Parks, Lloyd Clifford 1922- 57-60
Parks, Lydia
See Baker, Sarah H.
Parks, Michael 1943- 126
Parks, Pat 1918- 61-64
Parks, Peggy J. 1951- 216
See also SATA 143
Parks, PJ
See Parks, Peggy J.
Parks, Richard 1955- 223
Parks, Robert James 1940- 65-68
Parks, Rosa (Louise Lee)
1913-2005 .... CANR-102
Earlier sketch in CA 150
See also SATA 83
Parks, Stephen Robert 1940- 65-68
Parks, Suzan-Lori 1964(?)- 201
See also AAYA 55
See also CAD
See also CD 5, 6
See also CWD
See also DC 23
See also DFS 22
See also RGAL 4
Parks, Tim(othy Harold) 1954- CANR-144
Brief entry 126
Earlier sketches in CA 131, CANR-77
Interview in CA-131
See also CLC 147
See also CN 7
See also DLB 231
Parks, Van Dyke 1943- .... SATA 62
Parks, William 1698(?)-1750 .... DLB 43
Parksmith, George
See Bush, George S(idney)
Parlakian, Nishan 1925- 133
Parlato, Salvatore J(oseph), Jr. 1936- 73-76
Parlett, David (Sidney) 1939- CANR-20
Earlier sketch in CA 103
Parley, Peter
See Goodrich, Samuel Griswold
Parlin, Bradley W(illiam) 1938- 69-72
Parlin, John
See Graves, Charles Parlin
Parloff, Roger (Harris) 1955- 159
Parma, Clemens
See Menzel, Roderich
Parman, Donald L(ee) 1932- 65-68
Parmar, Pratibha 1960- .... GLL 2
Parmelee, Alice 1903-1994 .... CANR-90
Earlier sketches in CAP-2, CA 21-22
Parmelee, David Freeland 1924- 143
Parmenides c. 515B.C.-c. 450B.C. ..... DLB 176
Parmenter, (Charles) Ross
1912-1999 .... CANR-92
Obituary 187
Earlier sketch in CA 17-20R
Parmer, J(ess) Norman 1925- 5-8R
Parmet, Herbert S. 1929- CANR-11
Earlier sketch in CA 21-24R
Parmet, Robert D(avid) 1938- 77-80
Parmet, Simon 1897-1969 .... CAP-1
Earlier sketch in CA 13-14
Parnaby, Owen Wilfred 1921- 9-12R
Parnall, Peter 1936- 81-84
See also MAICYA 1, 2
See also SAAS 11
See also SATA 16, 69
Parnas, Raymond I. 1937- 33-36R
Parnell, Mary Davies 1936- 140
Parnell, Michael
See Elman, Richard (Martin)
Parnell, (David) Michael 1934-1991 130
Parnell, Peter 1953- 143
Parnell, Thomas 1679-1718 .... DLB 95
See also RGEL 2
Parnes, Herbert S(aul) 1919- CANR-34
Earlier sketches in CA 41-44R, CANR-15
Parnes, Sidmore 1928-1984
Obituary 113
Parnes, Sidney J. 1922- CANR-10
Earlier sketch in CA 21-24R
Parnicki, Teodor 1908-1988 .... DLB 215
See also EWL 3
Parnok, Sofiia Iakovlevna
See Parnok, Sophia (Yakovlevna)
See also DLB 295
Parnok, Sophia (Yakovlevna) 1885-1932 148
See also Parnok, Sofiia Iakovlevna and Polyanin, Andrey
Paroissien, David (Harry) 1939- 111
Parot, Joseph (John) 1940- 126
Parotti, Phillip (Elliott) 1941- 161
See also SATA 109
Parque, Richard (Anthony) 1935- 124
Parr, A. H.
See Parr, Adolf Henry
Parr, Adolf Henry 1909-1999
Obituary 132
Parr, Ann 1943- 217
See also SATA 144
Parr, Catherine c. 1513(?)-1548 .... DLB 136
Parr, Charles McKew 1884-1976 ...... CANR-90
Earlier sketches in CAP-1, CA 11-12
Parr, Danny
See Parr, Ann
Parr, Delia
See Lechleidner, Mary L.
Parr, James A(llan) 1936- 49-52
Parr, John (Lloyd) 1928- 102
Parr, Letitia (Evelyn) 1906-1985(?) 103
See also SATA 37
Parr, Lucy 1924- 29-32R
See also SATA 10
Parr, Michael 1927- 17-20R
See also CP 1
Parr, Todd .... SATA 134
Parra, Nicanor 1914- CANR-32
Earlier sketch in CA 85-88
See also CLC 2, 102
See also CWW 2
See also DAM MULT
See also DLB 283
See also EWL 3
See also HLC 2
See also HW 1
See also LAW
See also MTCW 1
See also PC 39
Parramore, Thomas C(ustis) 1932-2004 112
Obituary 222
Parra Sanojo, Ana Teresa de la 1890-1936
See de la Parra, (Ana) Teresa (Sonojo)
See also HLCS 2
See also LAW
Parrinder, E(dward) Geoffrey 1910- .. CANR-10
Earlier sketch in CA 21-24R
Parrinder, (John) Patrick 1944- 127
Parrington, Vernon L(ouis) 1817-1929
Brief entry 113
See also DLB 17, 63
See also MAL 5
Parrini, Carl P. 1933- 185
Brief entry 107
Parrino, John J(oseph) 1942- 101
Parrino, Michael 1915(?)-1976
Obituary 65-68
Parriott, Sara 1953- 107
Parris, Addison W(ilson) 1923-1975 ...... CAP-2
Earlier sketch in CA 25-28
Parris, Guichard 1903-1990 81-84
Obituary 133
Parris, Judith (Ann) H(eimlich) 1939- 57-60
Parris, Matthew (Francis) 1949- 134
Parrish, Anne 1888-1957
Brief entry 115
See also CWRI 5
See also SATA 27
Parrish, Bernard P. 1936- 103
Parrish, Bernie
See Parrish, Bernard P.
Parrish, Carl (George) 1904-1965 ..... CANR-97
Earlier sketch in CA 5-8R
Parrish, Eugene
See Harding, Donald Edward
Parrish, John A(lbert) 1939- 37-40R
Parrish, Louis E. 1927- 186
Brief entry 107
Parrish, Mary
See Cousins, Margaret
Parrish, Mary Frances
See Fisher, M(ary) F(rances) K(ennedy)
Parrish, Maxfield
See Parrish, (Frederick) Maxfield
Parrish, (Frederick) Maxfield 1870-1966 195
See also AAYA 59
See also DLB 188
See also MAICYA 2
See also MAICYAS 1
See also SATA 14
Parrish, Michael E(merson) 1942- CANR-43
Earlier sketch in CA 29-32R
Parrish, Nancy C. 1952- 179
Parrish, P. J.
See Montee, Kelly and Montee, Kristy
Parrish, Patt
See Bucheister, Patt
Parrish, Richard 168
Parrish, Robert 1916-1995 .... IDFW 3, 4
Parrish, Robert (Reese) 1916-1995 81-84
Obituary 150
Parrish, Stephen Maxfield 1921- 104
Parrish, T(homas) Michael 1953- 143
Parrish, Thomas (Douglas) 1927- 93-96
Parrish, Tim 1958- 217
Parrish, Wayland Maxfield
1887-1970(?) CAP-2
Earlier sketch in CA 23-24
Parrish, Wendy (Louise) 1950-1977 73-76
Obituary 133
Parrish, William E(arl) 1931- CANR-3
Earlier sketch in CA 1-4R
Parronchi, Alessandro 1914- .... DLB 128
Parrott, Bruce 1945- 128
Parrott, Cecil (Cuthbert) 1909-1984 103
Obituary 113
Parrott, Fred J(ames) 1913- 41-44R
Parrott, Ian 1916- CANR-2
Earlier sketch in CA 5-8R
Parrott, Les III 200
Parrott, (Alonzo) Leslie 1922- 97-100
Parrott, Leslie L. 1964- 200
Parrott, Lindesay 1901-1987
Obituary 123
Parrott, Lora Lee 1923- 25-28R
Parry, Albert 1901-1992 .... CANR-6
Earlier sketch in CA 1-4R
Parry, Caroline (Balderston) 1945- 128
Parry, Clive 1917-1982
Obituary 107
Parry, David 1908- 113
Parry, Ellwood C(omly) III 1941- 93-96
Parry, Graham 1940- CANR-131
Earlier sketch in CA 162
Parry, Hugh J(ones) 1916- 13-16R
Parry, J(ohn) H(orace) 1914-1982 .... CANR-6
Earlier sketch in CA 5-8R
Parry, John
See Whelpton, (George) Eric
Parry, Linda (Alberta) 1945- 111
Parry, Marian 1924- 41-44R
See also SATA 13
Parry, Michael Patrick 1947- 101
Parry, Owen
See Peters, Ralph
Parry, Richard (Gittings) 1942- CANR-99
Earlier sketch in CA 162
Parry, Thomas H. 1904-1985
Obituary 116
Parry-Jones, Daniel 1891-1981 .... 13-16R
Parseghian, Ara (Raoul) 1923-
Brief entry 105
Parsegian, V(ozcan) Lawrence
1908-1996 57-60
Obituary 152
Parshchikov, Aleksei 1954-
See Parshchikov, Aleksei Maksimovich
See also CLC 59
Parshchikov, Aleksei Maksimovich
See Parshchikov, Aleksei
See also DLB 285
Parsifal
See Curl, James Stevens
Parsipur, Shahrnush 1946- 187
Parsloe, Guy Charles 1900-1985 .... CAP-1
Earlier sketch in CA 13-14
Parson, Professor
See Coleridge, Samuel Taylor
Parson, Ann B(olton) 1950- CANR-104
Earlier sketch in CA 153
Parson, Mary Jean 1934- 133
Parson, Ruben L(eRoy) 1907- 13-16R
Parson Lot
See Kingsley, Charles
Parson-Nesbitt, Julie 1957- 153
Parsons, Alexander 205
Parsons, Alexandra 1947- 156
See also SATA 92
Parsons, C(hristopher) J(ames) 1941- 103
Parsons, Charles (Dacre) 1933- 45-48
Parsons, Charles H(enry III) 1940- 134
Parsons, Coleman O(scar) 1905-1991 ... CAP-1
Obituary 134
Earlier sketch in CA 13-16
Parsons, Cynthia 1926- CANR-45
Earlier sketches in CA 45-48, CANR-21
Parsons, Denys 1914- CANR-12
Earlier sketch in CA 13-16R
Parsons, Ellen
See Dragonwagon, Crescent
Parsons, Elmer E. 1919- 25-28R
Parsons, Frances M. 1923- 129
Parsons, Geoffrey 1908-1981
Obituary 105
Parsons, George W. 1927- 156
Parsons, Harriet Oettinger 1906(?)-1983(?)
Obituary 108
Parsons, Howard L(ee) 1918- CANR-17
Earlier sketches in CA 49-52, CANR-1
Parsons, Ian (Macnaghten) 1906-1980 .. 97-100
Obituary 102
Parsons, Jack 1920- 104
Parsons, James Bunyan 1921- 29-32R
Parsons, John (Anthony) 1938- CANR-45
Earlier sketch in CA 120
Parsons, Kermit Carlyle 1927- 29-32R
Parsons, Kitty (?)-1976 .... 13-16R
Obituary 120
Parsons, Louella (Oettinger) 1881-1972 .. 93-96
Obituary 37-40R
Parsons, Malcolm B(arningham)
1919-1993 195
Brief entry 108
Parsons, Martin 1907- 53-56
Parsons, Martin (Leslie) 1951- 188
See also SATA 116
Parsons, Michael L. 1940- 151
Parsons, (Quentin) Neil 1944- 170
Parsons, Paul 1952- 132
Parsons, R(ichard) A(ugustus) 101
Parsons, Sara Mitchell 1912- 219
Parsons, Stanley B., Jr. 1927- CANR-21
Earlier sketch in CA 45-48
Parsons, Talcott 1902-1979 .... CANR-35
Obituary 85-88
Earlier sketches in CA 5-8R, CANR-4
See also MTCW 1
Parsons, Thornton H(arris) 1921- 73-76
Parsons, Tom
See MacPherson, Thomas George
Parsons, Tony 197
Parsons, William Edward, Jr. 1936- 21-24R
Parsons, William T(homas) 1923- 65-68
Parssinen, Terry Mitchell 1941- 181
Partain, Floydene 1924- 114
Partch, Virgil Franklin II 1916-1984 108
Obituary 113
See also SATA 39
See also SATA-Obit 39
Parthasarathy, R(ajagopal) 1934- CANR-79
Earlier sketch in CA 154
See also CP 1, 7
Partington, F. H.
See Yoxall, Harry W(aldo)
Partington, Martin 1944- 124
Partington, Susan Trowbridge 1924- 9-12R
Partlow, Vern 1910(?)-1987
Obituary 121
Partner, Peter (David) 1924- 85-88
Partnow, Elaine T. 1941- CANR-92
Earlier sketch in CA 147
Parton, Anthony 1959- 133
Parton, Dolly (Rebecca) 1946- 150
See also SATA 94
Parton, James 1822-1891 .... DLB 30
Parton, Margaret 1915-1981 .... CANR-92
Earlier sketch in CA 97-100
Parton, Sara Payson Willis 1811-1872 . DLB 43, 74, 239
Partridge, Anthony
See Oppenheim, E(dward) Phillips
Partridge, Astley Cooper 1901- 103
Partridge, Benjamin W(aring), Jr.
1915-2005 .... 25-28R
Obituary 238
See also SATA 28
See also SATA-Obit 163
Partridge, Cora Cheney
See Cheney, Cora
Partridge, Derek 1945- 135
Partridge, Edward B(ellamy) 1916- 65-68
Partridge, Elinore Hughes 1937- 115
Partridge, Elizabeth 203
See also SATA 134
Partridge, Eric (Honeywood)
1894-1979 .... CANR-3
Obituary 85-88
Earlier sketch in CA 1-4R
Partridge, Ernest 1935- 115
Partridge, Frances (Catherine)
1900-2004 .... CANR-134
Obituary 223
Earlier sketches in CA 29-32R, CANR-30
Partridge, Jenny (Lilian) 1947- CANR-26
Earlier sketch in CA 109
See also SATA 52
See also SATA-Brief 37
Partridge, Larry (Harold) 1949- 114
Partridge, Norman 1958- CANR-119
Earlier sketch in CA 166
See also HGG
Partridge, William L(ee) 1944- CANR-1
Earlier sketch in CA 45-48
Parulski, George R(ichard), Jr.
1954- CANR-17
Earlier sketch in CA 97-100
Parun, Vesna 1922- .... CDWLB 4
See also DLB 181
Parvin, Betty 1916- CANR-17
Earlier sketch in CA 97-100
See also CP 1, 2
Parvin, Manoucher 1934- 225
Parvin, Roy 181
Parx, C. C.
See Gilmore, Christopher Cook
Parzen, Herbert 1896-1985 .... 25-28R
Pas, Julian F(rancis) 1929- 177
Pasachoff, Jay M(yron) 1943- CANR-40
Earlier sketch in CA 117
Pasachoff, Naomi 1947- CANR-128
Earlier sketch in CA 190
See also SATA 147
Pasamanik, Luisa 1930- 101
Pasarell, Emilio J(ulio) 1891-(?) .... HW 1
Pascal, Anthony H(enry) 1933- CANR-16
Earlier sketch in CA 29-32R
Pascal, Blaise 1623-1662 .... DLB 268
See also EW 3
See also GFL Beginnings to 1789
See also RGWL 2, 3
See also TWA
Pascal, David 1918- 9-12R
See also SATA 14
Pascal, Francine 1938- CANR-97
Brief entry 115
Earlier sketches in CA 123, CANR-39, 50
See also AAYA 1, 40
See also CLR 25
See also JRDA
See also MAICYA 1, 2
See also SATA 51, 80, 143
See also SATA-Brief 37
See also YAW
Pascal, Gerald Ross 1907-1984 .... 37-40R
Obituary 133
Pascal, John Robert 1932(?)-1981
Obituary 102
Pascal, Paul 1925- 21-24R
Pascal, Roy 1904-1980 .... CANR-6
Earlier sketch in CA 5-8R
Pascale, Richard Tanner 1938- CANR-104
Earlier sketches in CA 53-56, CANR-25
Pascarella, Perry (James) 1934- 93-96
Paschal, George H., Jr. 1925- 29-32R
Paschal, Nancy
See Trotter, Grace V(iolet)
Paschall, H. Franklin 1922- 25-28R
Paschen, Elise (Maria) 1959- 202
Pascoe, Bruce 1947- 199
Pascoe, Elaine 1946- 124
Pascoe, Elizabeth Jean 69-72
Pascoe, John (Dobree) 1908-1972 .. CANR-107
Earlier sketches in CAP-1, CA 13-14
Pascoe, Natalie T(aylor) 1966- 177
Pascoe, Peggy 1954- 136
Pascoli, Giovanni 1855-1912 170
See also EW 7
See also EWL 3
See also TCLC 45
Pascu, Stefan 1914- 117

Pascudniak, Pascal
See Lupoff, Richard A(llen)
Pasewark, William R(obert) 1924- ... CANR-35
Earlier sketches in CA 33-36R, CANR-15
Pashko, Stanley 1913-1982 ... 97-100
See also SATA 29
Pashkow, Fredric J. 1945- ... 199
Pashman, Susan 1942- ... 162
Pasick, Robert 1946- ... 134
Pasinetti, P(ier-) M(aria) 1913- ... 73-76
See also DLB 177
Pask, Gordon 1928-1996 ... 111
Pask, Raymond (Frank) 1944- ... CANR-22
Earlier sketch in CA 105
Paskowicz, Patricia
See Molan, Pat Carlson
Pasley, Virginia Schmitz 1905-1986
Obituary ... 119
Pasmanik, Wolf 1924- ... 101
Paso, Fernando del
See del Paso, Fernando
See also CWW 2
Pasolini, Pier Paolo 1922-1975 ... CANR-63
Obituary ... 61-64
Earlier sketch in CA 93-96
See also CLC 20, 37, 106
See also DLB 128, 177
See also EWL 3
See also MTCW 1
See also PC 17
See also RGWL 2, 3
Pasqua, Thomas M(ario), Jr. 1938-1998 ... 131
Pasqua, Tom
See Pasqua, Thomas M(ario), Jr.
Pasquier, Marie-Claire 1933- ... 29-32R
Pasquini
See Silone, Ignazio
Pass, Gail 1940- ... 65-68
Passage, Charles Edward 1913-1983 ... 33-36R
Obituary ... 110
Passailaigue, Thomas E.
See Paisley, Tom
Passante, Dom
See Fearn, John Russell
Passantino, Gretchen 1953- ... 110
Passantino, Robert Louis 1951-2003 ... 108
Obituary ... 221
Passarella, J. G.
See Gangemi, Joseph and
Passarella, John
Passarella, John ... 197
Passaro, Maria (C. Pastore) 1948- ... 165
Passel, Anne W(onders) 1918- ... CANR-11
Earlier sketch in CA 29-32R
Passell, Peter 1944- ... CANR-2
Earlier sketch in CA 45-48
Passer, Ivan 1933- ... 169
Passerin D'Entreves, Alessandro
1902-1985 ... 69-72
Passerini, Luisa 1941- ... 226
Passeron, Jean-Claude 1930- ... 151
Passeron, Rene (Jean) 1920- ... CANR-17
Earlier sketch in CA 97-100
Passes(-Pazolski), Alan 1943- ... 85-88
Passin, Herbert 1916-2003 ... CANR-20
Obituary ... 213
Earlier sketches in CA 45-48, CANR-1
Passman, Brian 1934- ... 25-28R
Passmore, John (Arthur) 1914- ... CANR-6
Earlier sketch in CA 13-16R
Passmore, Reg 1910-1999 ... 189
Passmore, Richard E. (?)-1982
Obituary ... 107
Passonneau, Joseph Russell 1921- ... 17-20R
Passow, A(aron) Harry 1920-1996 ... CANR-3
Earlier sketch in CA 1-4R
Passwater, Richard (Albert) 1937- ... CANR-19
Earlier sketch in CA 97-100
Past, Ray(mond Edgar) 1918- ... 29-32R
Pastan, Linda (Olenik) 1932- ... CANR-113
Earlier sketches in CA 61-64, CANR-18, 40, 61
See also CLC 27
See also CP 7
See also CSW
See also CWP
See also DAM POET
See also DLB 5
See also PFS 8
Pasternack, Stefan A(lan) 1939- ... 186
Brief entry ... 108
Pasternak, Boris (Leonidovich) 1890-1960 . 127
Obituary ... 116
See also BPFB 3
See also CLC 7, 10, 18, 63
See also DA
See also DA3
See also DAB
See also DAC
See also DAM MST, NOV, POET
See also DLB 302
See also EW 10
See also MTCW 1, 2
See also MTFW 2005
See also PC 6
See also RGSF 2
See also RGWL 2, 3
See also SSC 31
See also TWA
See also WLC
See also WP
Pasternak, Burton 1933- ... 127
Brief entry ... 109
Pasternak, Joe 1901-1991 ... IDFW 3, 4
Pasternak, Velvel 1933- ... 73-76
Pasti, Umberto ... 226
Pastine, Maureen (Diane) 1944- ... CANR-8
Earlier sketch in CA 57-60
Paston, George 1860-1936
See Symonds, Emily Morse
See also DLB 149, 197
Paston, Herbert S. 1928- ... 49-52
Pastor, Robert (Alan) 1947- ... 105
Pastore, Arthur R(alph), Jr. 1922- ... 17-20R
Pastore, Nicholas 1916- ... 29-32R
Pastorius, Francis Daniel 1651-1720(?) . DLB 24
Pastor X
See Johnson, Merle Allison
Pastos, Spero 1940- ... 126
Pastoureau, Michel 1947- ... 207
Pastre, Genevieve ... GLL 2
Paszkowski, Jan Krok
See Krok-Paszkowski, Jan
Pasztory, Esther 1943- ... 181
Patai, Daphne 1943- ... CANR-118
Earlier sketches in CA 113, CANR-33
Patai, Raphael 1910-1996 ... CANR-33
Obituary ... 152
Earlier sketches in CA 29-32R, CANR-20
Pataki, George (Elmer) 1945- ... 172
Pataky, Denes 1921- ... 13-16R
Patane, Joe 1970- ... 228
Patanne, Maria
See La Pietra, Mary
Patapoff, Elizabeth 1917- ... 29-32R
Patch, William L. 1953- ... 186
Patchen, Kenneth 1911-1972 ... CANR-35
Obituary ... 33-36R
Earlier sketches in CA 1-4R, CANR-3
See also BG 1:3
See also CLC 1, 2, 18
See also CN 1
See also CP 1
See also DAM POET
See also DLB 16, 48
See also EWL 3
See also MAL 5
See also MTCW 1
See also RGAL 4
Patchen, Martin 1932- ... 57-60
Patchett, Ann 1963- ... CANR-110
Earlier sketches in CA 139, CANR-64
See also AMWS 12
See also MTFW 2005
Patchett, Mary Elwyn 1897-1989 ... CANR-84
Earlier sketches in CA 5-8R, CANR-3
See also CWRI 5
Pate, Alexs D. 1950- ... 182
Pate, Billie 1932- ... 61-64
Pate, J'Nell L(aVerne) 1938- ... CANR-94
Earlier sketch in CA 139
Pate, Martha B. Lucas 1912-1983
Obituary ... 110
Patel, Essop 1943- ... 220
Patel, Gieve 1940- ... CANR-82
Earlier sketch in CA 154
See also CD 5, 6
See also CP 1, 7
Patel, Harshad C(hhotabhia) 1934- ... 53-56
Patel, I(ndraprasad) G(ordhanbhai) 1924- ... 126
Patel, Kant 1946- ... 229
Pateman, Carole 1940- ... 85-88
Pateman, Kim
See Levin, Kim
Pateman, Robert 1954- ... SATA 84
Pateman, Roy 1935- ... 215
Pateman, Trevor 1947- ... 49-52
Patent, Dorothy Hinshaw 1940- ... CANR-98
Earlier sketches in CA 61-64, CANR-9, 24
See also CLR 19
See also MAICYA 1, 2
See also SAAS 13
See also SATA 22, 69, 120, 162
See also SATA-Essay 162
Pater, Elias
See Friedman, John
See also CP 1
Pater, Walter (Horatio) 1839-1894 ... BRW 5
See also CDBLB 1832-1890
See also DLB 57, 156
See also RGEL 2
See also TEA
Paterek, Josephine 1916- ... 148
Paternostro, Silvana ... 189
Paternot, Stephan 1974- ... 208
Paterson, A(ndrew) B(arton) 1864-1941 ... 155
See also DLB 230
See also RGEL 2
See also SATA 97
See also TCLC 32
Paterson, Alistair (Ian Hughes) 1929- ... 107
See also CP 7
Paterson, Allen P(eter) 1933- ... 93-96
Paterson, Ann 1916- ... 33-36R
Paterson, Banjo
See Paterson, A(ndrew) B(arton)
Paterson, Barbara (Olive) 1933- ... 112
Paterson, Diane (R. Cole) 1946- ... 101
See also SATA 59
See also SATA-Brief 33
Paterson, Don(ald) 1963- ... CANR-82
Earlier sketch in CA 154
See also CP 7
Paterson, George W(illiam) 1931- ... 103
Paterson, Hugh
See Bower, Ursula Violet Graham
Paterson, Huntley
See Ludovici, Anthony M(ario)
Paterson, Isabel M. (Bowler) 1885-1961 .. RHW
Paterson, Janet M. 1944- ... 151
Paterson, John 1887-1967 ... CAP-1
Earlier sketch in CA 13-14
Paterson, John (Barstow) 1932- ... 186
See also SATA 114
Paterson, John Harris 1923- ... CANR-6
Earlier sketch in CA 5-8R
Paterson, Judith
See Jones, Judith Paterson
Paterson, Katherine (Womeldorf)
1932- ... CANR-111
Earlier sketches in CA 21-24R, CANR-28, 59
See also AAYA 1, 31
See also BYA 1, 2, 7
See also CLC 12, 30
See also CLR 7, 50
See also CWRI 5
See also DLB 52
See also JRDA
See also LAIT 4
See also MAICYA 1, 2
See also MAICYAS 1
See also MTCW 1
See also SATA 13, 53, 92, 133
See also WYA
See also YAW
Paterson, Kent 1956- ... 195
Paterson, (James Edmund) Neil
1916-1995 ... 13-16R
Paterson, R(onald) W(illiam) K(eith)
1933- ... CANR-90
Earlier sketch in CA 33-36R
Paterson, Richard 1947- ... 148
Paterson, Thomas G(raham) 1941- ... CANR-16
Earlier sketches in CA 45-48, CANR-1
Paterson, William E(dgar) 1941- ... CANR-13
Earlier sketch in CA 61-64
Paterson-Jones, Judith
See Jones, Judith Paterson
Patey, Douglas Lane 1952- ... 176
Pathe, Charles 1863-1957 ... IDFW 3, 4
Patience, John 1949- ... 155
See also SATA 90
Patin, Thomas A., Jr. 1948- ... 175
Patinkin, Don 1922-1995 ... CANR-10
Obituary ... 149
Earlier sketch in CA 17-20R
Patinkin, Mark 1953- ... 133
Patka, Frederick 1922- ... 9-12R
Patman, (John William) Wright 1893-1976 . 109
Obituary ... 107
Patmore, Coventry Kersey Dighton
1823-1896 ... DLB 35, 98
See also PC 59
See also RGEL 2
See also TEA
Patmore, Derek Coventry 1908-1972 ... 5-8R
Obituary ... 103
Patmore, John Allan 1931- ... 104
Patneaude, David 1944- ... CANR-144
Earlier sketch in CA 151
See also SATA 85, 159
Patner, Andrew 1959- ... 128
Paton, Alan (Stewart) 1903-1988 ... CANR-22
Obituary ... 125
Earlier sketches in CAP-1, CA 13-16
See also AAYA 26
See also AFW
See also BPFB 3
See also BRWS 2
See also BYA 1
See also CLC 4, 10, 25, 55, 106
See also CN 1, 2, 3, 4
See also DA
See also DA3
See also DAB
See also DAC
See also DAM MST, NOV
See also DLB 225
See also DLBD 17
See also EWL 3
See also EXPN
See also LAIT 4
See also MTCW 1, 2
See also MTFW 2005
See also NFS 3, 12
See also RGEL 2
See also SATA 11
See also SATA-Obit 56
See also TCLC 165
See also TWA
See also WLC
See also WLIT 2
See also WWE 1
Paton, David Macdonald
1913-1992 ... CANR-47
Obituary ... 139
Earlier sketch in CA 114
Paton, George (Whitecross) 1902-1985 . CAP-1
Earlier sketch in CA 11-12
Paton, Herbert James 1887-1969 ... CAP-1
Earlier sketch in CA 13-14
Paton, Jane (Elizabeth) 1934- ... SATA 35
Paton, Joseph Noel 1821-1901 ... DLB 35
Paton, Priscilla 1952- ... 166
See also SATA 98
Paton, Steven C. 1928(?)-1980
Obituary ... 97-100
Paton Walsh, Gillian 1937- ... CANR-83
Earlier sketch in CANR-38
See also Paton Walsh, Jill and
Walsh, Jill Paton
See also AAYA 11
See also CLC 35
See also CLR 2, 65
See also DLB 161
See also JRDA
See also MAICYA 1, 2
See also SAAS 3
See also SATA 4, 72, 109
See also YAW
Paton Walsh, Jill
See Paton Walsh, Gillian
See also AAYA 47
See also BYA 1, 8
Patoski, Joe Nick 1951- ... CANR-126
Earlier sketch in CA 141
Patoski, Margaret (Nancy Pearson)
1930- ... 69-72
Patra, Atul Chandra 1915- ... 57-60
Patras, Louis 1931- ... CANR-15
Earlier sketch in CA 85-88
Patriarca, Gianna 1951- ... 221
Patrice, Ann
See Galbraith, Georgie Starbuck
Patrick, Alison (Mary Houston) 1921- ... 49-52
Patrick, Clarence H(odges) 1907-1999 .. 33-36R
Patrick, Cuthbert Melvin 1914-1985
Obituary ... 116
Patrick, Diane ... 222
Patrick, Douglas Arthur 1905- ... 17-20R
Patrick, Edwin Hill 1901-1964 ... 212
See also DLB 137
Patrick, Hugh 1930- ... 41-44R
Patrick, J(ohn) Max 1911-1996 ... CANR-5
Obituary ... 182
Earlier sketch in CA 5-8R
Patrick, James (Arthur) 1933- ... CANR-20
Earlier sketch in CA 104
Patrick, Jennifer 1965- ... 239
Patrick, John 1905-1995 ... CANR-131
Obituary ... 150
Earlier sketch in CA 89-92
Interview in ... CA 89-92
See also CAD
See also DFS 13
See also DLB 7
Patrick, Johnstone G(illespie) 1918- ... CANR-2
Earlier sketch in CA 5-8R
Patrick, Leal
See Stone, Patti
Patrick, Lilian
See Keogh, Lilian Gilmore
Patrick, Martha 1956- ... 109
Patrick, Maxine
See Maxwell, Patricia
Patrick, Q.
See Wheeler, Hugh (Callingham)
Patrick, Rembert Wallace 1909-1967 ... 5-8R
Obituary ... 134
Patrick, Robert 1937- ... CANR-57
Earlier sketches in CA 45-48, CANR-1, 30
See also AITN 2
See also CAD
See also CD 5, 6
See also GLL 1
Patrick, Ruth 1907- ... 156
Patrick, Susan
See Clark, Patricia Denise
Patrick, Ted -1964
See Patrick, Edwin Hill
Patrick, Vincent 1935- ... CANR-22
Earlier sketch in CA 104
Interview in ... CANR-22
Patrick, Walton Richard 1909-1986 ... 37-40R
Patrick, William 1948- ... 225
Patrick, William B. ... 196
Patrick-Wexler, Diane
See Patrick, Diane
Patrides, C(onstantinos) A(postolos)
1930- ... CANR-20
Earlier sketches in CA 13-16R, CANR-5
Patrikeyev
See Healey-Kay, (Sydney Francis) Patrick (Chippendall)
Patron, Susan 1948- ... 143
See also SATA 76
Patrouch, Joseph F(rancis), Jr. 1935- ... 49-52
Patrouch, Joseph F. III 1960- ... 188
Patry, Jean-Luc (P.) 1947- ... 143
Patsauq, Markoosie 1942- ... 101
See also Markoosie
See also CWRI 5
Patschke, Steve 1955- ... SATA 125
Patsouras, Louis
See Patras, Louis
Patt, Richard B. 1954- ... 145
Pattee, Fred Lewis 1863-1950 ... 197
See also DLB 71
Pattee, Howard Hunt, Jr. 1926-
Brief entry ... 109
Pattemore, Arnel W(ilfred) 1934- ... 53-56
Patten, Alan ... 217
Patten, Bebe H(arrison) 1913-2004 ... 61-64
Obituary ... 223
Patten, Brian 1946- ... CANR-85
Earlier sketches in CA 25-28R, CANR-43
See also CP 1, 2, 3, 4, 5, 6, 7
See also CWRI 5
See also SATA 29, 152
Patten, Chris 1944- ... 176
Patten, Lewis B(yford) 1915-1981 ... CANR-84
Obituary ... 103
Earlier sketches in CA 25-28R, CANR-21
See also TCWW 1, 2

Cumulative Index 449 Pavenstedt

Patten, Marguerite 1915- 186
Patten, Nigel 1940- 25-28R
Patten, Priscilla C(arla) 1950- 117
Patten, (Bebe) Rebecca 1950- 117
Patten, Robert L(owry) 1939- 109
Patten, Thomas H., Jr. 1929- 21-24R
Patterson, A(lfred) Temple
1902-1983 .... CANR-75
Obituary 111
Earlier sketch in CA 103
Patterson, Alicia Brooks 1906-1963 221
Obituary 89-92
See also DLB 127
Patterson, Barbara 1944- 110
Patterson, Barbara McMartin
See McMartin, Barbara
Patterson, Benton Rain 1929- CANR-114
Earlier sketch in CA 122
Patterson, Bradley H., Jr. 1921- CANR-123
Earlier sketch in CA 136
Patterson, C(ecil) H(olden) 1912- CANR-16
Earlier sketch in CA 21-24R
Patterson, Carolyn Bennett 1921-2003 106
Obituary 218
Patterson, Charles 1935- CANR-41
Earlier sketch in CA 117
See also SATA 59
Patterson, Charles D(arold) 1928- 122
Patterson, Charles E(dwin), Jr. 1934- 41-44R
Patterson, Charles H(enry) 1896-1986 .. 37-40R
Patterson, Charlotte (Buist) 1942- 29-32R
Patterson, Craig E(ugene) 1945- 93-96
Patterson, David S(ands) 1937- 65-68
Patterson, E. Britt 1954- 142
Patterson, Edwin W(ilhite)
1889-1965 .... CANR-27
Earlier sketch in CA 1-4R
Patterson, Eleanor Medill 1881(?)-1948 201
Brief entry 118
See also DLB 29
Patterson, Elinor Josephine
See Patterson, Eleanor Medill
Patterson, Elizabeth C. 29-32R
Patterson, Emma L. 1904-1984 .... CANR-75
Obituary 135
Earlier sketches in CAP-2, CA 25-28
Patterson, Eric James 1891-1972 .... CAP-1
Earlier sketch in CA 11-12
Patterson, Eugene C(orbett) 1923- 182
See also DLB 127
Patterson, Evelyn Roelofs 1917- 5-8R
Patterson, Francine (G.) 1947- 147
Patterson, Frank Harmon 1912-
Brief entry 109
Patterson, Frank M(organ) 1931- CANR-25
Earlier sketch in CA 45-48
Patterson, Franklin (Kessel) 1916- 45-48
Patterson, Frederick D(ouglass)
1901-1988 155
See also BW 3
Patterson, Gardner 1916-1998
Obituary 181
Brief entry 106
Patterson, Geoffrey 1943- 103
See also SATA 54
See also SATA-Brief 44
Patterson, George N(eilson) 1920- 137
Patterson, Gerald R. 1926- 41-44R
Patterson, Glenn 1961- 154
Patterson, Harriet-Louise H(olland)
1903-1995 .... CAP-1
Earlier sketch in CA 13-16
Patterson, Harry 1929- CANR-115
Earlier sketches in CA 13-16R, CANR-33, 63
See also Higgins, Jack
See also CMW 4
See also CPW
See also DAM POP
Patterson, Henry
See Patterson, Harry
Patterson, Horace L. 1947- 145
Patterson, James (Tyler) 1935- 21-24R
Patterson, James (B.) 1947- CANR-113
Earlier sketches in CA 133, CANR-72
See also AAYA 25
Patterson, Jane
See Britton, Mattie Lula Cooper
Patterson, Janet McFadden 1915- 89-92
Patterson, Jefferson 1891-1977
Obituary 115
Patterson, Jerry E(ugene) 1931- 185
Brief entry 107
Patterson, Jerry L. 1934- 145
Patterson, John McCready 1913-1983
Obituary 109
Patterson, Joseph Medill 1879-1946
Brief entry 118
See also DLB 29
Patterson, June (Marie) 1924- 126
Patterson, K(arl) David 1941- 65-68
Patterson, Kevin 1956(?)-1988 203
Obituary 126
Patterson, L(loyd) G(eorge), Jr.
1929-1999 .... 41-44R
Patterson, L(yman) Ray 1929- 33-36R
Patterson, Lawrence Thomas II 1937- 104
Patterson, Letha L(emon) 1913-1984 .... 5-8R
Patterson, Lillie G. -1999 73-76
See also SATA 14, 88
Patterson, Lindsay 1942- 77-80
See also BW 1
Patterson, Margaret C(leveland)
1923- CANR-7
Earlier sketch in CA 57-60
Patterson, Mary H(agelin) 1910-1975
Obituary 37-40R
Patterson, Michael 1939- 111
Patterson, (James) Milton 1927- 53-56
Patterson, Nancy Ruth 1944- 222
See also SATA 72, 148
Patterson, Olive
See Rowland, D(onald) S(ydney)
Patterson, (Horace) Orlando (Lloyd)
1940- CANR-84
Earlier sketches in CA 65-68, CANR-27
See also BLCS
See also BW 1
See also CN 1, 2, 3, 4, 5, 6
Patterson, (Leighton) Paige 1942- CANR-10
Earlier sketch in CA 25-28R
Patterson, Paul 1909- 85-88
Patterson, Paul E. 1926- 197
Patterson, Peter
See Terson, Peter
Patterson, Raymond R(ichard)
1929-2001 .... 29-32R
Obituary 195
See also CP 2, 3, 4, 5, 6, 7
Patterson, Rebecca Elizabeth Coy
1911-1975 103
Patterson, Richard 1908(?)-1976
Obituary 69-72
Patterson, Richard North 1947- CANR-128
Earlier sketches in CA 85-88, CANR-41, 73
Patterson, Robert B(enjamin) 1934- 73-76
Patterson, Robert Leet 1893-1980 .... 17-20R
Patterson, Ruth P(olk) 1930- 119
Patterson, Samuel C(harles) 1931- CANR-22
Earlier sketches in CA 17-20R, CANR-7
Patterson, Samuel White 1883-1975 ..... CAP-2
Obituary 61-64
Earlier sketch in CA 17-18
Patterson, Sheila Caffyn 1918- 9-12R
Patterson, Sheron C. 1959- 198
Patterson, Sparrow L. 1974- 204
Patterson, Sylvia W.
See Iskander, Sylvia Patterson
Patterson, Sylvia W(iese) 1940- 61-64
Patterson, Ted 1944- 237
Patterson, Thomas E. 229
Patterson, Tom
See Patterson, (Harry) Tom
Patterson, (Harry) Tom 1920-2005 128
Obituary 236
Patterson, Virginia 1931- 102
Patterson, W. M(acLean) 1912(?)-1976
Obituary 69-72
Patterson, W. Morgan 1925- 65-68
Patterson, Walter C(ram) 1936- CANR-20
Earlier sketch in CA 103
Patterson, Ward L(amont) 1933- CANR-23
Earlier sketches in CA 57-60, CANR-8
Patterson, Wayne 1946- CANR-16
Earlier sketch in CA 85-88
Patterson, Webster T. 1920- 25-28R
Patterson, William Dudley 1910-1986
Obituary 119
Patterson, William L(orenzo)
1890-1980 .... CANR-76
Obituary 97-100
Earlier sketch in CA 41-44R
Patti, Archimedes L(eonida) A(ttilio)
1913-1998 106
Patti, Ercole 1904(?)-1976
Obituary 69-72
Patti, Paul 1956- 136
Pattie, Alice 1906-1991 .... CAP-2
Earlier sketch in CA 29-32
Pattie, Donald L. 1933- 215
Pattillo, Donald M. 1940- 218
Pattillo, Henry 1726-1801 .... DLB 37
Pattillo, James W(ilson) 1937- CANR-11
Earlier sketch in CA 17-20R
Pattillo, Manning M., Jr. 1919- 21-24R
Pattinson, Nancy Evelyn -1979
Brief entry 117
See also Asquith, Nan
Pattison, Darcy (S.) 1954- .... SATA 72, 126
Pattison, Eliot 1951- 197
Pattison, O(live) R(uth) B(rown) 1916- .. 29-32R
Pattison, Robert 1945- 129
Pattison, Walter Thomas 1903-1992 81-84
Patton, Alva Rae 1908-1997 .... 5-8R
Patton, Arch 1908-1996 .... CAP-1
Obituary 154
Earlier sketch in CA 13-16
Patton, Bobby R(ay) 1935- CANR-17
Earlier sketches in CA 45-48, CANR-1
Patton, Brian (Lee) 1943- 123
Patton, Frances Gray 1906-2000 101
Obituary 189
See also CN 1, 2
Patton, Frank
See Palmer, Raymond A. and
Shaver, Richard S(harpe)
Patton, George S(mith), Jr. 1885-1945 189
See also TCLC 79
Patton, Gerald W(ilson) 1947- 112
Patton, James W(elch) 1900-1973 .... CAP-1
Earlier sketch in CA 11-12
Patton, Kenneth L(eo) 1911-1994 .... CANR-7
Earlier sketch in CA 17-20R
Patton, Oliver B(eirne) 1920-2002 81-84
Obituary 213
Patton, Phil 1952- CANR-122
Earlier sketch in CA 133
Patton, Rob(ert Warren) 1943- 37-40R
Pattullo, George 1879-1967
Obituary 115
See also TCWW 1, 2
Pattullo, Polly 1946- 168
Patty, C. Robert 1925- CANR-10
Earlier sketch in CA 25-28R
Patty, Ernest N(ewton) 1894-1976 .... CAP-2
Earlier sketch in CA 25-28
Patty, James S(ingleton) 1925- 53-56
Paturi, Felix R.
See Mindt, Heinz R.
Patz (Blaustein), Nancy .... SATA 154
Patzert, Rudolph W. 1911-2000 146
Obituary 188
Pauck, Wilhelm 1901-1981 .... CANR-28
Obituary 104
Earlier sketch in CA 81-84
Pauk, Walter 1914- CANR-39
Earlier sketches in CA 5-8R, CANR-2, 18
Pauker, Guy J(ean) 1916-2002 .... CANR-1
Obituary 213
Earlier sketch in CA 45-48
Pauker, John 1920-1991 .... CANR-75
Obituary 133
Earlier sketch in CA 25-28R
Pauker, Samuel L. 1948- 127
Pauker, Ted
See Conquest, (George) Robert (Acworth)
Paul, Aileen 1917- CANR-19
Earlier sketch in CA 41-44R
See also SATA 12
Paul, Ann Whitford 1941- 143
See also SATA 76, 110
Paul, Anthony (Marcus) 1937- 77-80
Paul, (John) Anthony 1941- 77-80
Paul, Auren
See Uris, Auren
Paul, Barbara
See Ovstedal, Barbara
Paul, Barbara 1931- CANR-62
Earlier sketch in CA 132
See also CMW 4
Paul, Celeste 1952- 140
Paul, Charles B. 1931- 105
Paul, Charlotte 1916-1989 .... CANR-75
Obituary 129
Earlier sketches in CA 5-8R, CANR-7
Paul, Daniel
See Kessel, Lipmann
Paul, Danielle
See Mittermeyer, Helen (Hayton Monteith)
Paul, David (Tyler) 1934-1988
Obituary 125
See also SATA-Obit 56
Paul, David W(arren) 1944- 107
Paul, Elizabeth
See Crow, Donna Fletcher
Paul, Elliot (Harold) 1891-1958 196
Brief entry 107
See also CMW 4
See also DLB 4
Paul, Emily
See Eicher, (Ethel) Elizabeth
Paul, F. W.
See Fairman, Paul W.
Paul, Florrie 1928- 61-64
Paul, Geoffrey John 1921-1983
Obituary 110
Paul, George F(ranklin) 1954- CANR-123
Earlier sketch in CA 167
Paul, Gordon L. 1935- CANR-7
Earlier sketch in CA 17-20R
Paul, Grace 1908- 17-20R
Paul, Hamish Vigne Christie 1951- .... CLR 87
See also SATA 151
Paul, Hugo
See Little, Paul H(ugo)
Paul, I(rving) H. 1928- 103
Paul, James 1936- .... SATA 23
Paul, Jim 1950- 224
Paul, Jordan 1936- 97-100
Paul, Judith Edison 1939- CANR-16
Earlier sketch in CA 29-32R
Paul, Korky
See Paul, Hamish Vigne Christie
Paul, Leslie (Allen) 1905-1985 .... CANR-83
Obituary 117
Earlier sketches in CA 1-4R, CANR-3
Paul, Louis
See Placet, Leroi
Paul, Margaret 1939- 97-100
Paul, Norman L(eo) 1926- 61-64
Paul, Pamela 1971(?)- 221
Paul, Raymond 1940- 106
Paul, Robert
See Roberts, John G(aither)
Paul, Robert S(idney) 1918- CANR-3
Earlier sketch in CA 1-4R
Paul, Rodman Wilson 1912-1987 ...... CANR-3
Obituary 122
Earlier sketch in CA 1-4R
Paul, Roland A(rthur) 1937- 41-44R
Paul, Sheri
See Resnick, Sylvia (Safran)
Paul, Sherman 1920-1995 .... CANR-3
Obituary 148
Earlier sketch in CA 5-8R
Paul, T. V. 1956- 214
Paul, Terri 1945- 182
Paul, Tessa 1944- 170
See also SATA 103
Paul, William
See Eicher, (Ethel) Elizabeth
Paulden, Sydney (Maurice) 1932- CANR-12
Earlier sketch in CA 29-32R
Paulding, James Kirke 1778-1860 ... DLB 3, 59, 74, 250
See also RGAL 4
Pauley, Barbara Anne 1925- CANR-61
Earlier sketch in CA 89-92
See also DLIW
Pauley, Bruce F. 1937- 41-44R
Pauley, (Margaret) Jane 1950- 106
Paulhan, Jean 1884-1968
Obituary 25-28R
See also EWL 3
Pauli, Hertha (Ernestine) 1909-1973 ... CANR-2
Obituary 41-44R
Earlier sketch in CA 1-4R
See also SATA 3
See also SATA-Obit 26
Paulin, Thomas Neilson 1949- CANR-98
Brief entry 123
Earlier sketch in CA 128
See also Paulin, Tom
See also CP 7
Paulin, Tom
See Paulin, Thomas Neilson
See also CLC 37, 177
See also DLB 40
Pauling, Linus (Carl) 1901-1994 .... CANR-68
Obituary 146
Brief entry 110
Earlier sketches in CA 116, CANR-45
Interview in CA-116
See also MTCW 1, 2
Paull, Grace A. 1898- .... SATA 24
Paull, Raymond Allan 1906-1972 .... CAP-1
Earlier sketch in CA 9-10
Pau-Llosa, Ricardo 1954- CANR-87
Earlier sketch in CA 111
See also HW 1
Paulon, Flavia 1907(?)-1987
Obituary 122
Paulos, John Allen 1945- 136
Brief entry 128
Interview in CA-136
See also BEST 89:3
See also MTFW 2005
Pauls, John P. 1916- 45-48
Paulsell, William Oliver 1935- 111
Paulsen, F(rank) Robert 1922- 21-24R
Paulsen, Gary 1939- CANR-126
Earlier sketches in CA 73-76, CANR-30, 54, 83
See also AAYA 2, 17
See also BYA 6, 7, 8, 10, 11
See also CLR 19, 54, 82
See also JRDA
See also MAICYA 1, 2
See also MAICYAS 1
See also SATA 22, 50, 54, 79, 111, 158
See also TCWW 2
See also WYA
See also YAW
Paulsen, Lois (Thompson) 1905-1991 ... CAP-2
Earlier sketch in CA 19-20
Paulsen, Wolfgang 1910-1998 .... CANR-11
Earlier sketch in CA 17-20R
Paulson, Belden 1927- 21-24R
Paulson, Jack
See Jackson, C(aary) Paul
Paulson, Michael G. 1945- 139
Paulson, Morton C. 1923- 111
Paulson, Ronald (Howard) 1930- CANR-33
Earlier sketches in CA 17-20R, CANR-15
Paulson, Terry L. 1945- 136
Paulsson, Bjoern 1932- 61-64
Paulsson, Martin W. 1942- 149
Paulsson, Thomas A(lfred) 1923- 9-12R
Paulston, Christina Bratt CANR-10
Earlier sketch in CA 65-68
Paulston, Rolland G(lenn) 1929- CANR-13
Earlier sketch in CA 33-36R
Paulu, Burton 1910- 13-16R
Paulus, John Douglas 1917- 69-72
Paul VI, Pope
See Montini, Giovanni Battista (Enrico Antonio Maria)
Pauly, Louis W. 1952- CANR-130
Earlier sketch in CA 171
Pauly, Rebecca M. 1942- CANR-98
Earlier sketch in CA 147
Pauly, Thomas H(arry) 1940- 115
Paun, Maggie
See Voysey, Margaret
Pauquet, Gina Ruck
See Ruck-Pauquet, Gina
Pausacker, Jenny 1948- .... SAAS 23
See also SATA 72
Pausewang, Gudrun 1928- 171
See also SATA 104
Paustovsky, Konstantin (Georgievich)
1892-1968 93-96
Obituary 25-28R
See also CLC 40
See also DLB 272
See also EWL 3
Pautler, Albert J., Jr. 1935- 33-36R
Pautz, Peter D(ennis) 1952- 198
Pauw, Berthold Adolf 1924- 9-12R
Pauwels, Louis 1920-1997 187
Brief entry 111
Pavalko, Ronald M(ichael) 1934- 57-60
Pavarotti, Luciano 1935- 181
Brief entry 112
Pavel, Frances 1907- 21-24R
See also SATA 10
Pavelich, Matt 235
Pavenstedt, Eleanor 1903-1993 .... 21-24R

Pavese, Cesare 1908-1950 ... 169
Brief entry ... 104
See also DLB 128, 177
See also EW 12
See also EWL 3
See also PC 13
See also PFS 20
See also RGSF 2
See also RGWL 2, 3
See also SSC 19
See also TCLC 3
See also TWA
See also WLIT 7
Pavey, Don 1922- ... 107
Pavic, Milorad 1929- ... 136
See also CDWLB 4
See also CLC 60
See also CWW 2
See also DLB 181
See also EWL 3
See also RGWL 3
Pavitranda, Swami 1896(?)-1977
Obituary ... 73-76
Pavlakis, Christopher 1928- ... 73-76
Pavletich, Aida ... 101
Pavlik, Evelyn Marie 1954- ... 97-100
Pavlik, John V(ernon) ... CANR-143
Earlier sketch in CA 154
Pavlov, Ivan Petrovich 1849-1936 ... 180
Brief entry ... 118
See also TCLC 91
Pavlov, Konstantin 1933- ... DLB 181
Pavlov, Nikolai Filippovich
1803-1864 ... DLB 198
Pavlova, Karolina Karlovna
1807-1893 ... DLB 205
Pavlovic, Miodrag
See Pavlovic, Miodrag
See also CDWLB 4
See also DLB 181
Pavlovic, Miodrag 1928- ... 201
See also Pavlovic, Miodrag
See also CWW 2
See also EWL 3
See also RGWL 3
Pavlovsky, Eduardo 1933- ... DLB 305
Pavlowitch, Stevan K. 1933- ... CANR-53
Earlier sketches in CA 33-36R, CANR-13, 29
Pavord, Anna 1940- ... CANR-119
Earlier sketches in CA 115, CANR-37
Pawel, Ernst 1920-1994 ... 131
Pawel, Rebecca C. 1977- ... 222
Pawelczynska, Anna 1922- ... 101
Pawlak, Mark 1948- ... CANR-92
Earlier sketch in CA 145
Pawle, Gerald Strachan 1913-1991 ... 5-8R
Obituary ... 135
Pawley, Bernard C(linton) 1911-1981 ... 25-28R
Obituary ... 105
Pawley, Christine 1945- ... 214
Pawley, Martin Edward 1938- ... 101
Pawley, Thomas Desire III 1917- ... 29-32R
Pawlick, Thomas F(rancis) 1941- ... 119
Pawlicki, T(homas) B(ert) 1930- ... 109
Pawlikowski, John T. 1940- ... CANR-24
Earlier sketches in CA 21-24R, CANR-9
Pawlowicz, Sala Kaminska 1925- ... 5-8R
Pawlowski, Gareth L(ee) 1939-1995 ... 29-32R
Obituary ... 148
Pawson, G(eoffrey) P(hilip) H(enry) 1904- . 5-8R
Pax
See Cholmondeley, Mary
Pax, Clyde 1928- ... 49-52
Paxman, Jeremy (Dickson) 1950- ... CANR-100
Earlier sketch in CA 108
Paxson, Bud
See Paxson, Lowell (White)
Paxson, Diana L(ucile) 1943- ... CANR-115
Earlier sketch in CA 157
See also FANT
Paxson, Ethel 1885-1982 ... 25-28R
Paxson, Frederic L(ogan) 1877-1948 ... 217
Paxson, Lowell (White) 1935(?)- ... 177
Paxton, Dr. John
See Lawton, Sherman P(axton)
Paxton, Jack
See Lawton, Sherman P(axton)
Paxton, Jack 1939-1985
Obituary ... 117
Paxton, Jean
See Powers, Martha (Jean)
Paxton, John 1911-1985 ... 183
Obituary ... 114
See also DLB 44
See also IDFW 3, 4
Paxton, John 1923- ... CANR-125
Earlier sketches in CA 129, CANR-67
Paxton, Lois
See Low, Lois Dorothea
Paxton, Mary Jean Wallace 1930- ... 109
Paxton, Nancy L. 1949- ... 195
Paxton, Robert O(wen) 1932- ... CANR-82
Earlier sketches in CA 73-76, CANR-42
Paxton, Thomas R. 1937- ... CANR-44
Earlier sketch in CA 105
See also Paxton, Tom
Paxton, Tom
See Paxton, Thomas R.
See also SATA 70
Payack, Paul J. J. 1950- ... CANR-113
Earlier sketches in CA 69-72, CANR-31
Payan, Gregory ... 238
Paye, Robert
See Campbell, (Gabrielle) Margaret (Vere)
Payelle, Raymond-Gerard 1898-1971
Obituary ... 33-36R
Payer, Cheryl Ann 1940- ... 61-64
Payer, Lynn (Jeanine) 1945-2001 ... 128
Obituary ... 199
Payes, Rachel (Ruth) C(osgrove)
1922-1998 ... CANR-16
Obituary ... 196
Earlier sketches in CA 49-52, CANR-1
Payn, James 1830-1898 ... DLB 18
Payne, A. J.
See Payne, Anthony
Payne, Alan
See Jakes, John (William)
Payne, Alexander 1961- ... 223
Payne, Alma Smith
See Ralston, Alma (Smith Payne)
Payne, Anthony 1952- ... CANR-56
Earlier sketch in CA 125
Payne, B(en) Iden 1888-1976 ... 73-76
Obituary ... 65-68
Payne, Basil 1928- ... 81-84
See also CP 1, 2
Payne, Bernal C., Jr. 1941- ... SATA 60
Payne, Bruce 1911-1997 ... 9-12R
Payne, C. D. 1949- ... 195
See also AAYA 43
See also SATA 133
Payne, Charles 1909-1994 ... 103
Payne, Daniel G. 1958- ... 167
Payne, Darwin 1937- ... 143
Payne, (William) David (A.) 1955- ... CANR-99
Earlier sketch in CA 154
See also CSW
Payne, David A(llen) 1935- ... 25-28R
Payne, Deborah C. 1952- ... 150
Payne, Donald Gordon 1924- ... CANR-104
Earlier sketches in CA 13-16R, CANR-9, 24
See also SATA 37
Payne, Emmy
See West, Emily Govan
Payne, Eric Francis Jules 1895-1983 ... 57-60
Payne, Ernest A(lexander) 1902-1980 . CANR-9
Obituary ... 105
Earlier sketch in CA 9-12R
Payne, F(rances) Anne 1932- ... 73-76
Payne, F. M.
See English, Thomas Dunn
Payne, J(ohn) Barton 1922- ... CANR-3
Earlier sketch in CA 1-4R
Payne, J(ames) Gregory 1949- ... 123
Payne, Jack 1926- ... 33-36R
Payne, James L. 1939- ... 33-36R
Payne, Joan Balfour (?)-1973
Obituary ... 41-44R
Payne, John 1842-1916 ... 206
See also DLB 35
Payne, John Howard 1791-1852 ... DLB 37
See also RGAL 4
Payne, Johnny 1958- ... 189
Payne, Karen 1951- ... 111
Payne, Katharine 1937(?)- ... 224
Payne, Katy
See Payne, Katharine
Payne, Ladell 1933- ... 134
Brief entry ... 111
Payne, Larry ... 226
Payne, Laurence 1919- ... CANR-63
Earlier sketch in CA 5-8R
See also CMW 4
Payne, LaVeta Maxine 1916- ... 37-40R
Payne, Leanne 1932- ... CANR-37
Earlier sketch in CA 115
Payne, Leigh A. 1956- ... 147
Payne, Michael 1941- ... CANR-12
Earlier sketch in CA 29-32R
Payne, Mildred Y(ounger) 1906-1994 ... 41-44R
Payne, Neil F. 1939- ... CANR-106
Earlier sketch in CA 149
Payne, Nina ... 204
See also SATA 135
Payne, Oliver
See Murray, Stuart A. P.
Payne, Peggy 1949- ... CANR-104
Earlier sketch in CA 128
Payne, Rachel Ann
See Jakes, John (William)
Payne, Richard A. 1934- ... 97-100
Payne, (Pierre Stephen) Robert
1911-1983 ... CANR-31
Obituary ... 109
Earlier sketch in CA 25-28R
Payne, Robert O. 1924- ... 97-100
Payne, Ronald 1926- ... 97-100
Payne, Stanley G(eorge) 1934- ... CANR-3
Earlier sketch in CA 1-4R
Payne-Gaposchkin, Cecilia (Helena)
1900-1979 ... 167
Paynter, David H. 1921- ... 135
Paynter, Will(iam) 1903-1984
Obituary ... 115
Paynter, William Henry 1901- ... 13-16R
Paynton, Clifford T. 1929- ... 37-40R
Payro, Roberto J(orge) 1867-1928 ... EWL 3
See also HW 1
See also LAW
Payson, Dale 1943- ... CANR-3
Earlier sketch in CA 49-52
See also SATA 9
Payson, Herb(ert III) 1927- ... 115
Payton, Rodney J. 1940- ... 144
Payzant, Charles ... SATA 18
Paz, A.
See Pahz, James Alon
Paz, Carlos F(ernando) 1937- ... 109
Paz, Gil
See Lugones, Leopoldo
Paz, Octavio 1914-1998 ... CANR-104
Obituary ... 165
Earlier sketches in CA 73-76, CANR-32, 65
See also AAYA 50
See also CLC 3, 4, 6, 10, 19, 51, 65, 119
See also CWW 2
See also DA
See also DA3
See also DAB
See also DAC
See also DAM MST, MULT, POET
See also DLB 290
See also DLBY 1990, 1998
See also DNFS 1
See also EWL 3
See also HLC 2
See also HW 1, 2
See also LAW
See also LAWS 1
See also MTCW 1, 2
See also MTFW 2005
See also PC 1, 48
See also PFS 18
See also RGWL 2, 3
See also SSFS 13
See also TWA
See also WLC
See also WLIT 1
Paz, Zan
See Pahz, (Anne) Cheryl Suzanne
Pazder, Lawrence Henry 1936- ... 107
Paz Soldan, (Jose) Edmundo 1967- ... 237
Pazzi, Roberto 1946- ... 204
See also DLB 196
See also EWL 3
p'Bitek, Okot 1931-1982 ... CANR-82
Obituary ... 107
Earlier sketch in CA 124
See also AFW
See also BLC 3
See also BW 2, 3
See also CLC 96
See also CP 1, 2
See also DAM MULT
See also DLB 125
See also EWL 3
See also MTCW 1, 2
See also MTFW 2005
See also RGEL 2
See also TCLC 149
See also WLIT 2
Pea, Enrico 1881-1958 ... DLB 264
Peabody, Barbara 1933- ... 122
Peabody, Elizabeth Palmer 1804-1894 .. DLB 1, 223
Peabody, Josephine Preston
1874-1922 ... DLB 249
Peabody, Oliver William Bourn
1799-1848 ... DLB 59
Peabody, Richard (Myers, Jr.) 1951- ... 143
Peabody, Robert Lee 1931- ... 9-12R
Peabody, Velton 1936- ... 53-56
Peace, David ... 203
Peace, David (Brian) 1915-2003 ... 192
Obituary ... 213
Peace, Frank
See Cook, Will(iam Everett)
Peace, Mary
See Finley, Mary Peace
Peace, Richard (Arthur) 1933- ... CANR-75
Earlier sketch in CA 131
Peace, Richard 1938- ... CANR-14
Earlier sketch in CA 25-28R
Peace, Roger Craft 1899-1968
Obituary ... 89-92
See also DLB 127
Peach, Lawrence du Garde 1890-1974 ... 101
Peach, William Bernard 1918- ... 127
Peach, William Nelson 1912-1984 ... 21-24R
Peacham, Henry 1578-1644(?) ... DLB 151
Peacham the Elder, Henry
1547-1634 ... DLB 172, 236
Peacher, Georgiana M(elicent) 1919- ... 25-28R
Peachey, Laban 1927- ... 17-20R
Peachey, Paul 1918- ... 219
Peachment, Christopher ... 225
Peacock, Alan T(urner) 1922- ... CANR-3
Earlier sketch in CA 1-4R
Peacock, Basil 1898-1991 ... 103
Peacock, Carlos (Charles Hanbury) ... 132
Peacock, D(avid) P(hilip) S(pencer) 1939- .. 123
Peacock, Daniel J. 1919- ... 125
Peacock, Dick
See Peacock, Richard
Peacock, James Craig 1888(?)-1977
Obituary ... 73-76
Peacock, James L(owe) 1937-
Brief entry ... 113
Peacock, L(elon) J(ames) 1928- ... 21-24R
Peacock, Mary (Willa) 1942- ... 69-72
Peacock, Mary Reynolds (Bradshaw)
1916- ... 57-60
Peacock, Molly 1947- ... CANR-84
Earlier sketches in CA 103, CANR-52
See also CAAS 21
See also CLC 60
See also CP 7
See also CWP
See also DLB 120, 282
Peacock, Nancy 1954- ... 190
Peacock, Richard 1933- ... 107
Peacock, Ronald 1907-1993 ... CANR-5
Obituary ... 141
Earlier sketch in CA 53-56
Peacock, Thomas Love 1785-1866 ... BRW 4
See also DLB 96, 116
See also RGEL 2
See also RGSF 2
Peacock, Wilbur Scott 1915(?)-1979
Obituary ... 89-92
Peacocke, A(rthur) R(obert) 1924- ... 41-44R
Peacocke, Christopher 1950- ... 124
Peacocke, Isabel Maud 1881-1973
Obituary ... 116
Pead, Deuel (?)-1727 ... DLB 24
Pead, Greg
See Serious, Yahoo
Peairs, Lillian Gehrke 1925- ... 103
Peairs, Richard Hope 1929-
Brief entry ... 105
Peak, David 1953- ... 133
Peak, John A. ... CANR-136
Earlier sketch in CA 168
Peake, C(harles) H. 1920(?)-1988
Obituary ... 124
Peake, Lilian (Margaret) 1924-
Brief entry ... 115
See also RHW
Peake, Mervyn 1911-1968 ... CANR-3
Obituary ... 25-28R
Earlier sketch in CA 5-8R
See also CLC 7, 54
See also DLB 15, 160, 255
See also FANT
See also MTCW 1
See also RGEL 2
See also SATA 23
See also SFW 4
Peake, Miriam Morrison 1901-1993 ... 57-60
Peake, Thomas H(arold) 1947- ... 206
See also Perlmutter, Amos
Peake,, Tom H.
See Peake, Thomas H(arold)
Peake, Tony 1951- ... 222
Peaker, G(ilbert) F. 1903(?)-1983(?)
Obituary ... 109
Peale, Norman Vincent 1898-1993 .. CANR-55
Obituary ... 143
Earlier sketches in CA 81-84, CANR-29
See also AITN 1
See also MTCW 1
See also SATA 20
See also SATA-Obit 78
Peale, Rembrandt 1778-1860 ... DLB 183
Peale, Ruth Stafford 1906- ... CANR-29
Earlier sketch in CA 73-76
Peano, Giuseppe 1858-1932 ... 163
Pear, David (Adrian) 1957- ... 141
Pear, Lillian Myers ... 73-76
Pearce, Ann Philippa
See Pearce, Philippa
Pearce, Arthur Williams 1913(?)-1983
Obituary ... 111
Pearce, Brian Louis 1933- ... CANR-42
Earlier sketches in CA 103, CANR-19
Pearce, Charles A. 1906-1970
Obituary ... 104
Pearce, David (Robert) 1937-2001 ... 126
Obituary ... 202
Pearce, David W(illiam) 1941- ... CANR-93
Earlier sketch in CA 146
Pearce, Dick
See Pearce, Richard Elmo
Pearce, Donald R(oss) 1917- ... 119
Pearce, Donn 1928- ... 13-16R
Pearce, Ellen 1946- ... 179
See also CP 1
Pearce, Frank 1909- ... 109
Pearce, J(ohn) Kenneth 1898-1991 ... 45-48
Pearce, J. Winston 1907-1985(?) ... 130
Brief entry ... 106
Pearce, Jacqueline 1962- ... 220
See also SATA 146
Pearce, Janice 1931- ... 61-64
Pearce, John Kingston 1925- ... 118
Pearce, Joseph 1961- ... 188
Pearce, Joseph Chilton 1926- ... CANR-144
Earlier sketch in CA 173
Pearce, Kenneth 1921- ... CANR-119
Earlier sketch in CA 120
Pearce, Margaret ... CANR-121
Earlier sketch in CA 171
See also SATA 104
Pearce, Mary E(mily) 1932- ... CANR-31
Earlier sketch in CA 69-72
Pearce, Michael 1933- ... 213
Pearce, Moira ... 103
Pearce, Philippa ... CANR-109
Earlier sketches in CA 5-8R, CANR-4
See also Christie, Philippa
See also CWRI 5
See also FANT
See also MAICYA 2
Pearce, Richard 1932- ... 41-44R
Pearce, Richard Elmo 1909-1990 ... 1-4R
Pearce, Roy Harvey 1919- ... CANR-3
Earlier sketch in CA 1-4R
Pearce, Thomas Matthews
1902-1986 ... CANR-7
Earlier sketch in CA 17-20R
Pearce, William M(artin) 1913-1999 ... 9-12R
Pearcey, Nancy ... 203
Pearcy, G(eorge) Etzel 1905-1980 ... CANR-3
Earlier sketch in CA 1-4R
Peard, Julyan G. 1947- ... 214
Peardon, Thomas Preston 1899-1985
Obituary ... 116
Peare, Catherine Owens 1911- ... 5-8R
See also SATA 9
Pearl, Arthur 1922- ... 13-16R
Pearl, Chaim 1919- ... 49-52

Cumulative Index 451 Peet

Pearl, Cyril (Altson) 1906-1987(?)
Obituary ... 122
Pearl, Daniel 1963-2002 ... 204
Pearl, David 1944- ... 133
Pearl, Eric
See Elman, Richard (Martin)
Pearl, Esther Elizabeth
See Ritz, David
Pearl, Hal 1914(?)-1975
Obituary ... 61-64
Pearl, Jack
See Pearl, Jacques Bain
Pearl, Jacques Bain 1923-1992 ... CANR-60
Obituary ... 196
Earlier sketches in CA 5-8R, CANR-23
Pearl, Joseph L. 1886(?)-1974
Obituary ... 53-56
Pearl, Leon 1922- ... 5-8R
Pearl, Leonard (Brent) 1911-1993 ... CAP-2
Earlier sketch in CA 33-36
Pearl, Mariane ... 224
Pearl, Matthew 1975(?)- ... 208
Pearl, Minnie
See Cannon, Sarah Ophelia Colley
Pearl, Nancy Linn 1945- ... 236
Pearl, Ralph 1910- ... 73-76
Pearl, Richard M(axwell) 1913-1980 ... CANR-3
Earlier sketch in CA 9-12R
Pearl, Virginia L(ou) 1930- ... 61-64
Pearlman, Bill 1943- ... 195
Pearlman, Daniel (David) 1935- ... CANR-24
Earlier sketch in CA 61-64, 158
Pearlman, Jeff ... 233
Pearlman, Maurice 1911-1992 ... CANR-6
Earlier sketch in CA 5-8R
Pearlman, Michael D. 1944- ... 197
Pearlman, Mickey 1938- ... 134
Pearlman, Moshe
See Pearlman, Maurice
Pearlstein, Howard J. 1942- ... 57-60
Pearman, Jean R(ichardson) 1915- ... 49-52
Pears, Charles 1870-1958 ... 181
Brief entry ... 114
See also SATA-Brief 30
Pears, David Francis 1921- ... 65-68
Pears, Iain (George) 1955- ... CANR-129
Earlier sketches in CA 130, CANR-71
Pears, Tim 1956- ... 143
Pearsall, Derek (Albert) 1931- ... CANR-49
Earlier sketches in CA 107, CANR-24
Pearsall, (F.) Paul ... CANR-55
Earlier sketch in CA 126
Pearsall, Robert Brainard 1920- ... CANR-2
Earlier sketch in CA 45-48
Pearsall, Ronald 1927- ... CANR-73
Earlier sketches in CA 21-24R, CANR-14, 31
Pearsall, Thomas E. 1925- ... 25-28R
Pearsall, William Harold 1891-1964
Obituary ... 106
Pearse, Peter H(ector) 1932- ... 138
Pearson, Andrew Russell 1897-1969 ... CANR-6
Obituary ... 25-28R
Earlier sketch in CA 5-8R
See also MTCW 1
Pearson, B(enjamin) H(arold)
1893-1984 ... 65-68
Pearson, Bill
See Pearson, William Harrison
See also CN 1, 2, 3, 4, 5, 6
Pearson, Bruce L. 1932- ... 73-76
Pearson, Carol 1944- ... 57-60
Pearson, Carol Lynn 1939- ... 133
Pearson, David E. 1953- ... 127
Pearson, Diane
See McClelland, Diane Margaret
Pearson, Drew
See Pearson, Andrew Russell
Pearson, Frederic S(tephen) 1944- ... 113
Pearson, Gayle 1947- ... CANR-97
Earlier sketch in CA 122
See also BYA 12
See also SATA 53, 119
Pearson, (Edward) Hesketh (Gibbons)
1887-1964 ... 5-8R
See also DLB 149
Pearson, Hugh ... 231
Pearson, James Larkin 1879-1981
Obituary ... 104
Pearson, Jim Berry 1924- ... 17-20R
Pearson, Joanne (E.) ... 232
Pearson, John 1934- ... CANR-4
Earlier sketch in CA 49-52
Pearson, Karl 1857-1936 ... 211
Brief entry ... 119
Pearson, Kit 1947- ... CANR-71
Earlier sketch in CA 145
See also AAYA 19
See also CCA 1
See also CLR 26
See also JRDA
See also MAICYA 2
See also MAICYAS 1
See also SATA 77
See also SATA-Essay 117
See also YAW
Pearson, Lester B(owles) 1897-1972 ... 121
Obituary ... 37-40R
Pearson, (Edith) Linnea 1942- ... 65-68
Pearson, Lionel (Ignatius Cusack)
1908-1988 ... 1-4R
Obituary ... 126
Pearson, Lon
See Pearson, Milo Lorentz
Pearson, M(ichael) N(aylor) 1941- ... 195
Brief entry ... 118
Pearson, Mary E. 1955- ... 203
See also SATA 134
Pearson, Michael ... 102
Pearson, Milo Lorentz 1939- ... CANR-99
Earlier sketch in CA 73-76
Pearson, Neville P(ershing) 1917- ... 45-48
Pearson, Norman Holmes 1909-1975 ... CAP-1
Obituary ... 61-64
Earlier sketch in CA 13-16
Pearson, Patricia 1964- ... 232
Pearson, R(obert) A(rthur) 1945- ... 128
Pearson, Richard Joseph 1938- ... 65-68
Pearson, Ridley 1953- ... CANR-122
Earlier sketches in CA 135, CANR-71
See also AAYA 44
Pearson, Robert Paul 1938- ... 65-68
Pearson, Ronald Hooke 1915- ... 13-16R
Pearson, Roy 1914-1996 ... 1-4R
Pearson, Ryne Douglas 1965(?)- ... 219
Pearson, Scott Roberts 1938- ... CANR-11
Earlier sketch in CA 29-32R
Pearson, Susan 1946- ... CANR-58
Earlier sketches in CA 65-68, CANR-14
See also SATA 39, 91
See also SATA-Brief 27
Pearson, Sybille 1937- ... 156
Pearson, T(homas) R(eid) 1956- ... CANR-97
Brief entry ... 120
Earlier sketch in CA 130
Interview in ... CA-130
See also CLC 39
See also CSW
Pearson, Thomas S(pencer) 1949- ... 132
Pearson, Tracey Campbell 1956- . SATA 64, 155
Pearson, William Harrison 1922- ... CANR-83
Earlier sketch in CA 57-60
See also Pearson, Bill
Peart, Norman A(nthony) 1961- ... 200
Peary, Dannis 1949- ... CANR-127
Earlier sketches in CA 109, CANR-27
Peary, Danny
See Peary, Dannis
Peary, Marie Ahnighito
See Kuhne, Marie (Ahnighito Peary)
Peascod, Bill
See Peascod, William
Peascod, William 1920(?)-1985
Obituary ... 116
Pease, Dorothy Wells 1896-1984 ... 5-8R
Pease, (Clarence) Howard
1894-1974 ... CANR-41
Obituary ... 106
Earlier sketch in CA 5-8R
See also CWRI 5
See also MAICYA 1
See also SATA 2
See also SATA-Obit 25
Pease, Howard 1894-1974 ... MAICYA 2
Pease, Jane H(anna) 1929- ... CANR-4
Earlier sketch in CA 9-12R
Pease, Louise
See McNeill, Louise
Pease, Victor Philip 1938- ... 107
Pease, William H(enry) 1924- ... CANR-4
Earlier sketch in CA 9-12R
Peaston, Monroe 1914- ... 49-52
Peat, F. David 1938- ... CANR-142
Earlier sketch in CA 132
Peate, Iorwerth C.
See Peate, Iorwerth Cyfeiliog
Peate, Iorwerth Cyfeiliog 1901-1982 ... 120
Obituary ... 108
Peate, Patricia Flynn 1911(?)-1983
Obituary ... 111
Peatman, John Gray 1904-1997 ... 5-8R
Obituary ... 157
Peattie, Donald Culross 1898-1964 ... 102
See also DLB 275
Peattie, Lisa Redfield 1924- ... CANR-10
Earlier sketch in CA 25-28R
Peattie, Mark R(obert) 1930- ... CANR-8
Earlier sketch in CA 61-64
Peavler, Terry J. 1942- ... 135
Peavy, Charles D(ruery) 1931- ... 25-28R
Peavy, John W(esley) III 1944- ... 119
Peavy, Linda 1943- ... CANR-31
Earlier sketch in CA 109
See also SATA 54
Pebworth, Ted-Larry 1936- ... 121
Peccei, Aurelio 1908-1984
Obituary ... 112
Peccorini, Francisco L(etona) 1915- . CANR-25
Earlier sketch in CA 45-48
Pech, Stanley Z. 1924- ... 33-36R
Pechefsky, Rebecca ... 215
Pechel, Peter (Rudolf) 1920- ... 135
Pechersky, Andrei
See Mel'nikov, Pavel Ivanovich
Pechman, Joseph A(aron)
1918-1989 ... CANR-83
Obituary ... 129
Earlier sketch in CA 85-88
Pecht, Michael G. 1952- ... 145
Pechter, Edward 1941- ... 85-88
Peck, Abe 1945- ... 73-76
Peck, Anne Merriman 1884-1976 ... 77-80
See also SATA 18
Peck, Beth 1957- ... SATA 79
Peck, Dale 1967- ... CANR-127
Earlier sketches in CA 146, CANR-72
See also CLC 81
See also GLL 2
Peck, David R. 1938- ... 143
Peck, David W(arner) 1902-1990 ... 1-4R
Obituary ... 132
Peck, Ellen 1942-
Brief entry ... 113
Peck, Frederic Taylor 1920(?)-1983
Obituary ... 110
Peck, George (Willis) 1931-1990
Obituary ... 130
Peck, George W(ilbur) 1840-1916
Brief entry ... 115
See also DLB 23, 42
Peck, Harry Thurston 1856-1914 ... 212
See also DLB 71, 91
Peck, Helen E(stelle) 1910- ... 5-8R
Peck, Ira 1922- ... 77-80
Peck, Jan ... SATA 159
Peck, Jane Cary 1932-1990
Obituary ... 132
Peck, Jeanie J. 1967- ... 221
See also SATA 147
Peck, John (Frederick) 1941- ... CANR-100
Earlier sketches in CA 49-52, CANR-3
See also CLC 3
See also CP 7
Peck, John B. 1918(?)-1973
Obituary ... 104
Peck, Kathryn Blackburn 1904-1975 ... CAP-2
Earlier sketch in CA 25-28
Peck, M(organ) Scott 1936- ... CANR-100
Earlier sketches in CA 89-92, CANR-20, 45, 66
See also BEST 89:2
See also CPW
See also DAM POP
Peck, Marshall III 1951- ... SATA 92
Peck, Merton J(oseph) 1925- ... 13-16R
Peck, Paula 1927(?)-1972
Obituary ... 104
Peck, Ralph H(arold-Henry) 1926- ... CANR-22
Earlier sketch in CA 69-72
Peck, Richard (Wayne) 1934- ... CANR-129
Earlier sketches in CA 85-88, CANR-19, 38
Interview in ... CANR-19
See also AAYA 1, 24
See also BYA 1, 6, 8, 11
See also CLC 21
See also CLR 15
See also JRDA
See also MAICYA 1, 2
See also SAAS 2
See also SATA 18, 55, 97, 110, 158
See also SATA-Essay 110
See also WYA
See also YAW
Peck, Richard E(arl) 1936- ... CANR-31
Earlier sketch in CA 81-84
Peck, Robert F. 1919- ... 13-16R
Peck, Robert McCracken 1952- ... 112
Peck, Robert Newton 1928- ... 182
Earlier sketches in CA 81-84, CANR-31, 63, 127
Autobiographical Essay in ... 182
See also AAYA 3, 43
See also BYA 1, 6
See also CLC 17
See also CLR 45
See also DA
See also DAC
See also DAM MST
See also JRDA
See also LAIT 3
See also MAICYA 1, 2
See also SAAS 1
See also SATA 21, 62, 111, 156
See also SATA-Essay 108
See also WYA
See also YAW
Peck, Robert S(tephen) 1953- ... 141
Peck, Russell A(lbert) 1933- ... 108
Peck, Ruth L. 1915- ... 29-32R
Peck, Seymour 1917-1985
Obituary ... 114
Peck, Sidney M. 1926- ... 5-8R
Peck, Stacey 1925- ... 123
Peck, Suzy
See Carlson, Maureen
Peck, Sylvia 1953- ... CANR-111
Earlier sketch in CA 135
See also SATA 133
Peck, Theodore P(arker) 1924- ... 103
Pecka
See Heikel, Karin Alice
Peckenpaugh, Angela J(ohnson) 1942- ... 104
Peckham, Howard Henry 1910-1995 ... 9-12R
Peckham, James O. 1903(?)-1984
Obituary ... 113
Peckham, Lawton (Parker Greenman)
1904-1979
Obituary ... 89-92
Peckham, Morse 1914-1993 ... CANR-1
Earlier sketch in CA 1-4R
Peckham, Richard
See Holden, Raymond (Peckham)
Peckinpah, (David) Sam(uel)
1925-1984 ... CANR-82
Obituary ... 114
Earlier sketch in CA 109
See also CLC 20
Peck-Whiting, Jeanie J.
See Peck, Jeanie J.
Pecsok, Mary Bodell 1919- ... 5-8R
Peddicord, Jo (Anne) 1925- ... 154
Peden, Henry C(lint), Jr. 1946- ... 207
Peden, Margaret Sayers 1927- ... CANR-14
Earlier sketch in CA 37-40R
Peden, Rachel (Mason) 1901-1975 ... 110
Peden, W. Creighton 1935- ... 144
Peden, William (Harwood) 1913-1999 . 21-24R
See also DLB 234
Pedersen, Elsa Kienitz 1915- ... CANR-2
Earlier sketch in CA 1-4R
Pedersen, (Thelma) Jean J(orgenson)
1934- ... CANR-21
Earlier sketches in CA 57-60, CANR-6
Pedersen, Knut 1859-1952 ... CANR-63
Brief entry ... 104
Earlier sketch in CA 119
See also Hamsun, Knut
See also MTCW 1, 2
Pedersen, Laura 1967- ... 193
Pedersen, Paul B(odholdt) 1936- ... 41-44R
Pedersen, Vernon L. 1955- ... 225
Pederson, Jay P(orter) 1961- ... 165
Pederson, Kern O(wen) 1910-1997 ... 102
Pederson, Sharleen
See Collicott, Sharleen
Pederson, William D(avid) 1946- ... 176
Pedicord, Harry William 1912-1994 ... 33-36R
Pedler, Christopher Magnus Howard
1927-1981 ... 97-100
Obituary ... 197
Pedler, Frederick Johnson 1908-1991 ... 107
Obituary ... 134
Pedler, Kit
See Pedler, Christopher Magnus Howard
Pedler, Margaret (Bass) ... RHW
Pedley, Robin 1914-1988 ... 9-12R
Obituary ... 127
Pedoe, Daniel 1910-1998 ... 65-68
Pedolsky, Andrea 1951- ... CANR-38
Earlier sketch in CA 115
Pedrazas, Allan ... 168
Pedreira, Antonio (Salvador) 1899(?)-1939 . 188
Pedretti, Erica 1930- ... 193
Pedrick, Jean 1922- ... CANR-6
Earlier sketch in CA 57-60
Pedrolo, Manuel de 1918-1990 ... EWL 3
Pedrosa, Carmen Navarro 1941- ... 128
Pedulla, Walter 1930- ... 211
Peebles, Anne
See Galloway, Priscilla
Peebles, Dick 1918-1980 ... 77-80
Obituary ... 97-100
Peek, Bertrand Meigh 1891-1964
Obituary ... 111
Peek, Dan William 1945- ... 218
Peek, Merle 1938- ... CANR-22
Earlier sketch in CA 105
See also SATA 39
Peek, Philip M. 1943- ... 222
Peek, Walter W(illiam) 1922- ... 45-48
Peel, Bruce Braden 1916- ... 17-20R
Peel, Colin D(udley) 1936- ... 119
Peel, Edwin A(rthur) 1911-1992 ... 13-16R
Obituary ... 139
Peel, H(azel) M(ary) 1930- ... CANR-4
Earlier sketch in CA 9-12R
Peel, J(ohn) D(avid) Y(eadon)
1941- ... CANR-107
Earlier sketch in CA 33-36R
Peel, John 1954- ... SATA 79
Peel, John Donald 1908-1989 ... 33-36R
Peel, Kendal J(ohn) 1940- ... 116
Peel, Malcolm Lee 1936- ... 29-32R
Peel, Norman Lemon
See Hirsch, Phil
Peel, Robert 1909-1992 ... 77-80
Obituary ... 136
Peel, Ronald Francis (Edward Waite) 1912-1985
Obituary ... 117
Peel, Wallis
See Peel, H(azel) M(ary)
Peele, David A(rnold) 1929-1985 ... 102
Obituary ... 118
Peele, George 1556-1596 ... BRW 1
See also DLB 62, 167
See also RGEL 2
Peele, Stanton 1946- ... 57-60
Peeler, Tim 1957- ... 225
Peelor, Harry N. 1922- ... 17-20R
Peeples, Edwin A(ugustus, Jr.)
1915-1994 ... 9-12R
See also SATA 6
Peeples, Samuel Anthony ... TCWW 2
Peer, Lyndon A. 1899(?)-1977
Obituary ... 73-76
Peeradina, Saleem 1944- ... 154
See also CP 7
Peerbolte, Maarten Lietaert
See Lietaert Peerbolte, Maarten
Peerce, Jan 1904-1984 ... 101
Obituary ... 114
Peerman, Dean G(ordon) 1931- ... 13-16R
Peers, Judi(th May West) 1956- ... 190
See also SATA 119
Peers, William R(aymond) 1914-1984 ... 13-16R
Obituary ... 112
Peery, Janet 1948- ... 157
Peery, Nelson 1923- ... 149
Peery, Paul D(enver) 1906-1981 ... CAP-2
Earlier sketch in CA 29-32
Peeslake, Gaffer
See Durrell, Lawrence (George)
Peet, Bill
See Peet, William Bartlett
See also CLR 12
Peet, C(harles) Donald, Jr. 1927- ... 13-16R
Peet, Creighton B. 1899-1977 ... 106
Obituary ... 69-72
See also SATA 30
Peet, Louise Jenison 1885-1983 ... 5-8R

Peet, William Bartlett 1915-2002 ... CANR-84
Obituary ... 207
Earlier sketches in CA 17-20R, CANR-38
See also Peet, Bill
See also CWRI 5
See also MAICYA 1, 2
See also SATA 2, 41, 78
See also SATA-Obit 137
Peffer, Randall S(cott) 1948- ... 101
Pegge, C(ecil) Denis 1902- ... CAP-1
Earlier sketch in CA 13-16
Pegis, Anton Charles 1905-
Brief entry ... 106
Pegis, Jessie Corrigan 1907- ... CAP-1
Earlier sketch in CA 13-14
Pegler, (James) Westbrook
1894-1969 ... CANR-62
Obituary ... 89-92
Earlier sketch in CA 103
See also DLB 171
Pegram, Marjorie Anne (Dykes) 1925- ... 9-12R
Pegram, Thomas R. 1955- ... 143
Pegrum, Dudley F(rank) 1898-1989 ... 33-36R
Peguero, Leone ... 205
See also SATA 116
Pegues, Franklin J(ohnson) 1924- ... 5-8R
Peguy, Charles (Pierre) 1873-1914 ... 193
Brief entry ... 107
See also DLB 258
See also EWL 3
See also GFL 1789 to the Present
See also TCLC 10
Pehnt, Wolfgang 1931- ... CANR-24
Earlier sketch in CA 107
Pehrson, Justine Davis Randers
See Randers-Pehrson, Justine Davis
Pei, I(eoh) M(ing) 1917- ... AAYA 39
Pei, Lowry 1947- ... BYA 6
Pei, Mario A(ndrew) 1901-1978 ... CANR-5
Obituary ... 77-80
Earlier sketch in CA 5-8R
Peierls, Rudolf (Ernst) 1907-1995 ... 128
Obituary ... 149
Peierls, Rudolf E.
See Peierls, Rudolf (Ernst)
Peifer, Claude J(ohn) 1927- ... 17-20R
Peifer, Kathleen Hamel
See Hamel Peifer, Kathleen
Peikoff, Leonard 1933- ... 108
Peil, Margaret 1929- ... CANR-8
Earlier sketch in CA 61-64
Peirce, Charles Sanders 1839-1914 ... 194
See also DLB 270
See also TCLC 81
Peirce, J(ames) F(ranklin) 1918- ... 41-44R
Peirce, Neal R. 1932- ... CANR-21
Earlier sketch in CA 25-28R
Peirce, Penney 1949- ... 215
Peirce, Waldo 1884-1970 ... SATA-Brief 28
Peiris, Denzil 1918(?)-1985
Obituary ... 116
Peiser, Maria Lilli 1914-1986 ... CANR-82
Obituary ... 118
Brief entry ... 110
Earlier sketch in CA 116
Peissel, Michel (Francois) 1937- ... CANR-30
Earlier sketches in CA 25-28R, CANR-12
Peitchinis, Stephen G(abriel) 1925- .. CANR-49
Earlier sketches in CA 45-48, CANR-24
Pejovich, Svetozar 1931- ... CANR-12
Earlier sketch in CA 17-20R
Pejovich, Ted
See Pejovich, Theodore Peter
Pejovich, Theodore Peter 1945- ... 131
Pekar, Harvey 1939- ... 224
Pekarik, Andrew J(oseph) 1946- ... 112
Pekarkova, Iva 1963- ... 147
Pekic, Borislav 1930-1992 ... CANR-47
Obituary ... 139
Earlier sketch in CA 69-72
See also CDWLB 4
See also DLB 181
Pekkanen, John 1939- ... 153
Pela, Robrt L. 1962- ... 223
Peladeau, Marius B(eaudoin) 1935- ... 73-76
Pelaez, Jill 1924- ... 33-36R
See also SATA 12
Pelan, John ... 204
Pelavin, Cheryl 1946- ... 106
Pelecanos, George P. 1957- ... CANR-122
Earlier sketch in CA 138
See also DLB 306
Peleg, Ilan 1944- ... 161
Pelenski, Jaroslaw 1929- ... 153
Brief entry ... 111
Peletier du Mans, Jacques
1517-1582 ... GFL Beginnings to 1789
Pelevin, Victor 1962- ... CANR-88
Earlier sketch in CA 154
See also Pelevin, Viktor Olegovich
Pelevin, Viktor Olegovich
See Pelevin, Victor
See also DLB 285
Pelfrey, William 1947- ... 33-36R
Pelger, Lucy J. 1913-1971 ... CAP-2
Earlier sketch in CA 21-22
Pelham, David 1938- ... 138
See also SATA 70
Peli, Pinchas H(acohen) 1930(?)-1989
Obituary ... 128
Pelikan, Jaroslav Jan 1923- ... CANR-85
Earlier sketches in CA 1-4R, CANR-1, 41
Pelikan, Pavel 1935- ... 239
Pelin, Elin 1877-1949 ... 215
Pelissier, Anthony 1912-1988
Obituary ... 125
Pelissier, Roger 1924-1972 ... CAP-2
Obituary ... 37-40R
Earlier sketch in CA 23-24
Pelka, Fred 1954- ... CANR-138
Earlier sketch in CA 173
Pell, Arthur R. 1920- ... CANR-120
Earlier sketches in CA 29-32R, CANR-11, 26, 51
Pell, Claiborne (de Borda) 1918- ... 49-52
Pell, Derek 1947- ... 77-80
Pell, Ed(ward) 1950- ... 233
See also SATA 157
Pell, Eve 1937- ... 33-36R
Pell, John (Howland Gibbs) 1904-1987
Obituary ... 123
Pell, Olive Bigelow 1886-1980
Obituary ... 103
Pell, Robert
See Hagberg, David J(ames)
Pell, Walden II 1902-1983
Obituary ... 109
Pella, Milton O(rville) 1914- ... 17-20R
Pellegreno, Ann Holtaren ... 33-36R
Pellegrini, Angelo 1904-1991 ... CANR-40
Earlier sketch in CA 17-20R
See also CAAS 11
Pellegrini, Ann ... 222
Pellegrini, Anthony D(avid) 1949- ... 117
Pellegrino, Charles R. 1953- ... CANR-104
Earlier sketch in CA 136
Pellegrino, Edmund D. 1920- ... 175
Pellegrino, Victoria Y(urasits) 1944- ... 107
Peller, Sigismund 1890-1985
Obituary ... 116
Pellerano, Maria B. 1957- ... 133
Pelletier, Cathie 1953(?)- ... 146
Pelletier, Francine 1959- ... DLB 251
Pelletier, Ingrid 1912-1980 ... 29-32R
Pelletier, Kenneth R. 1946- ... CANR-29
Earlier sketches in CA 69-72, CANR-11
Pelletier, Nancy 1923- ... 136
Pelletreau, John 1925(?)-1983
Obituary ... 111
Pellew, Jill (Hosford) 1942- ... 109
Pelli, Moshe 1936- ... CANR-90
Earlier sketch in CA 132
Pellicer, Carlos 1897(?)-1977 ... 153
Obituary ... 69-72
See also DLB 290
See also EWL 3
See also HLCS 2
See also HW 1
Pelling, Henry Mathison 1920-1997 ... 61-64
Pellow, Deborah 1945- ... CANR-13
Earlier sketch in CA 73-76
Pellowski, Anne 1933- ... CANR-9
Earlier sketch in CA 21-24R
See also SATA 20
Pellowski, Michael (Joseph) 1949- . CANR-135
Earlier sketches in CA 110, CANR-29
See also SATA 88, 151
See also SATA-Brief 48
Pellowski, Michael Morgan
See Pellowski, Michael (Joseph)
Pells, Richard Henry 1941- ... 53-56
Pelly, David F. 1948- ... 124
Pelosi, Olimpia 1957- ... 219
Pelshe, Arvid Yanovich 1899-1983
Obituary ... 109
Pelta, Kathy 1928- ... 85-88
See also SATA 18
Peltason, J(ack) W(alter) 1923- ... CANR-4
Earlier sketch in CA 1-4R
Peltier, Leslie C(opus) 1900-1980 ... 17-20R
See also SATA 13
Pelto, Bert
See Pelto, Pertti J(uho)
Pelto, Pertti J(uho) 1927- ... 97-100
Pelton, Alan R. 1953- ... 145
Pelton, Barry C(lifton) 1935- ... 61-64
Pelton, Beverly Jo 1939- ... 49-52
Pelton, Joseph N(eal) 1943- ... 107
Pelton, Leroy H. 1940- ... 190
Pelton, Robert D(oane) 1935- ... 103
Pelton, Robert Stuart 1921- ... 170
Pelton, Robert W(ayne) 1934- ... CANR-28
Earlier sketch in CA 29-32R
Pelton, Warren J. 1923- ... 133
Peltonen, Carla ... 238
Peltz, Mary Ellis 1896-1981 ... 85-88
Obituary ... 105
Peluso, Joseph L(ouis) 1929- ... 97-100
Pelz, Lotte A(uguste) Hensl 1924- ... 9-12R
Pelz, Stephen Ernest 1942- ... 114
Brief entry ... 110
Pelz, Werner 1921- ... 9-12R
Pelzer, David J. ... 182
Peman, Jose Maria 1897-1981
Obituary ... 104
Pemberton, Cintra 1935- ... 187
Pemberton, Gayle Renee 1948- ... 143
See also BW 2
Pemberton, John E(dward) 1930- ... 33-36R
Pemberton, John Leigh
See Leigh-Pemberton, John
Pemberton, Madge 1880(?)-1970
Obituary ... 29-32R
Pemberton, Margaret 1943- ... CANR-83
Earlier sketches in CA 93-96, CANR-17, 38
See also RHW
Pemberton, Max 1863-1950 ... 204
Brief entry ... 120
See also DLB 70
Pemberton, Nan
See Pykare, Nina
Pemberton, William Baring 1897- ... 5-8R
Pemberton, William E(rwin) 1940- ... 97-100
Pemble, John ... 236
Pembrook, Linda 1942- ... 61-64
Pembrooke, Kenneth
See Page, Gerald W(ilburn)
Pembury, Bill
See Groom, Arthur William
Pempel, T. J. 1942- ... CANR-30
Earlier sketch in CA 112
Pemsteen, Hans
See Manes, Stephen
Pen, Jan 1921- ... CANR-17
Earlier sketch in CA 1-4R
Pena, Humberto J(ose) 1928- ... 73-76
Pena, Milagros 1955- ... CANR-87
Earlier sketch in CA 152
Pena, Ramon del Valle y
See Valle-Inclan, Ramon (Maria) del
Pena, Terri de la
See de la Pena, (Mary) Terri
See also DLB 209
Pencavel, John (H.) 1943- ... 140
Pence, Caprial A. 1963- ... 208
Pence, Gregory E. 1948- ... 226
Pence, Joanne ... 227
Penczak, Christopher 1973- ... 223
Pendar, Kenneth 1906-1972
Obituary ... 37-40R
Pendarvis, China Clark
See Clark-Pendarvis, China
Pendell, Elmer 1894-1982 ... CAP-1
Earlier sketch in CA 11-12
Pendennis, Arthur Esquir
See Thackeray, William Makepeace
Pender, Lex
See Pendower, Jacques
Pender, Lydia Podger 1907- ... CANR-2
Earlier sketch in CA 5-8R
See also SATA 61
Pender, Marilyn
See Pendower, Jacques
Pendergast, Charles 1950- ... 65-68
Pendergast, Chuck
See Pendergast, Charles
Pendergast, Richard J. 1927- ... 93-96
Pendergrass, Tess ... 238
Pendery, Rosemary (Schmitz) ... 53-56
See also SATA 7
Pendexter, Hugh 1875-1940 ... TCWW 2
Pendle, Alexy 1943- ... SATA 29
Pendle, George 1906-1977 ... 5-8R
Obituary ... 103
See also SATA-Obit 28
Pendle, Karin 1939- ... 141
Pendlebury, B(evis) J(ohn) 1898- ... CAP-2
Earlier sketch in CA 33-36
Pendleton, Conrad
See Kidd, Walter E.
Pendleton, Don
See Cunningham, Chet and Garside, (Clifford) Jack and Jagninski, Tom and Krauzer, Steven M(ark) and Obstfeld, Raymond
Pendleton, Don(ald Eugene)
1927-1995 ... CANR-55
Obituary ... 150
Earlier sketch in CA 33-36R
See also CMW 4
Pendleton, Ford
See Cheshire, Gifford Paul)
Pendleton, James D(udley) 1930- ... 107
Pendleton, Mary ... 65-68
Pendleton, Winston K. 1910-2000 ... CAP-1
Earlier sketch in CA 13-16
Pendo, Stephen 1947- ... 65-68
Pendower, Jacques 1899-1976 ... 9-12R
Obituary ... 89-92
See also Pendower, T(homas) C(urtis) H(icks)
Pendower, T(homas) C(urtis) H(icks)
See Pendower, Jacques
See also TCWW 2
Pendower, T(homas) C(urtis) H(icks)
1899-1976 ... TCWW 2
Pendray, Edward
See Pendray, George Edward
Pendray, G. Edward
See Pendray, George Edward
Pendray, George Edward 1901-1987
Obituary ... 123
Pendreigh, Brian 1957- ... 226
Pendse, Sripad Narayan 1913- ... CWW 2
Pene du Bois, William (Sherman)
1916-1993 ... CANR-41
Obituary ... 140
Earlier sketches in CA 5-8R, CANR-17
See also CLR 1
See also CWRI 5
See also DLB 61
See also MAICYA 1, 2
See also SATA 4, 68
See also SATA-Obit 74
Penelope
See Boyden, Sarah B.
Penelope, Julia 1941- ... 145
See also GLL 2
Penfield, Edward 1866-1925 ... DLB 188
Penfield, Thomas 1903-1973 ... 5-8R
Penfield, Wilder (Graves) 1891-1976 . CANR-3
Obituary ... 65-68
Earlier sketch in CA 5-8R
Pengelley, Eric T. 1919- ... 89-92
Penick, Harvey 1904-1995 ... 147
Penick, James (Lal), Jr. 1932- ... 33-36R
Penman, Sharon K(ay)
See Penman, Sharon Kay
See also AAYA 43
See also RHW
Penman, Sharon Kay ... 200
See also Penman, Sharon K(ay)
See also BYA 10
Penn, Anne
See Pendower, Jacques
Penn, Arthur
See Matthews, (James) Brander
Penn, Arthur (Hiller) 1922- ... 130
Brief entry ... 112
Penn, Asher 1908(?)-1979
Obituary ... 93-96
Penn, Audrey 1950- ... CANR-13
Earlier sketch in CA 77-80
See also Zellan, Audrey Penn
Penn, Christopher
See Lawlor, Patrick Anthony
Penn, David
See Balsiger, David (Wayne)
Penn, James R. 1949- ... CANR-120
Earlier sketch in CA 169
Penn, John
See Harcourt, Palma
Penn, Margaret (?)-1981
Obituary ... 105
Penn, Richard
See Sproat, Iain (MacDonald)
Penn, Ruth Bonn
See Rosenberg, Eth(el) Clifford
Penn, Sean 1960- ... 163
Penn, W(illiam) S. 1949- ... CANR-101
Earlier sketch in CA 145
Penn, William 1644-1718 ... DLB 24
Penna, Sandro 1906-1977 ... 183
See also DLB 114
See also GLL 1
Pennac, Daniel 1944- ... CANR-139
Earlier sketch in CA 168
See also SATA 155
Pennage, E. M.
See Finkel, George (Irvine)
Pennar, Jaan 1924-
Brief entry ... 115
Pennekamp, John (David) 1897-1978
Obituary ... 89-92
See also AITN 2
Pennell, Joseph 1857-1926 ... 198
See also DLB 188
Penner, Fred (Ralph Cornelius) 1946- ... 136
See also SATA 67
Penner, Jonathan 1940- ... CANR-39
Earlier sketches in CA 97-100, CANR-17
See also DLBY 1983
Penner, Peter 1925- ... 129
Penney, Annette Culler 1916- ... 45-48
Penney, Edmund F. 1926- ... 132
Penney, Grace Jackson 1904-2000 ... 5-8R
See also SATA 35
Penney, Ian 1960- ... SATA 76
Penney, J(ames) C(ash) 1875-1971
Obituary ... 29-32R
Penney, Jennifer 1946- ... 122
Penney, Sue 1957- ... CANR-136
Earlier sketch in CA 169
See also SATA 102, 152
Pennick, Nigel Campbell 1946- ... CANR-88
Earlier sketches in CA 110, CANR-28
Pennie, Hester
See Taylor, Elisabeth (D.)
Penniman, Clara 1914- ... 185
Brief entry ... 111
Penniman, Howard R(ae) 1916- ... CANR-12
Earlier sketch in CA 13-16R
Penniman, Thomas Kenneth 1896(?)-1977
Obituary ... 69-72
Penninger, F(rieda) Elaine 1927- ... 57-60
Penningroth, Paul W(illiam) 1901-1974 .. 49-52
Obituary ... 103
Penning-Rowsell, Edmund 1913-2002 ... 127
Obituary ... 208
Pennington, Albert Joe 1950- ... 57-60
Pennington, Anne (Elizabeth) 1934-1981
Obituary ... 114
Pennington, Chester Arthur 1916- ... 104
Pennington, Donald Henshaw 1919- ... 5-8R
Pennington, Eunice 1923- ... 57-60
See also SATA 27
Pennington, Howard (George) 1923- ... 49-52
Pennington, John Selman 1924(?)-1980
Obituary ... 102
Pennington, Lee 1939- ... CANR-67
Earlier sketches in CA 69-72, CANR-31
See also DLBY 1982
Pennington, Lillian Boyer 1904- ... SATA 45
Pennington, Lucinda 1945- ... 117
Pennington, M. (Robert John) Basil
1931- ... CANR-37
Earlier sketches in CA 93-96, CANR-16
Pennington, Penny
See Galbraith, Georgie Starbuck
Pennington, Reina 1956- ... 221
Pennington, Robert (Roland) 1927- ... 73-76
Pennington, Stuart
See Galbraith, Georgie Starbuck
Pennington, W(eldon) J(erry) 1919-1985
Obituary ... 115
Pennink, (John Jacob) Frank 1913- ... 5-8R
Pennock, J(ames) Roland
1906-1995 ... CANR-29
Obituary ... 148
Earlier sketches in CA 33-36R, CANR-13
Penny, J. Leith 1955- ... 127
Penny, Julie 1945- ... 117
Penny, Prudence
See Goldberg, Hyman
Penny, Ruthanna (Merrick) 1914-1983 .. 17-20R
Pennycuick, John 1943- ... 97-100
Penrod, James 1934- ... 77-80

Penrose, Antony 1947- CANR-112
Earlier sketch in CA 137
Penrose, Boies 1902-1976
Obituary 65-68
Penrose, Edith Tilton 1914-1996 .... 25-28R
Obituary 154
Penrose, Gordon 1925- 127
See also SATA 66
Penrose, Harald 1904-1996 .... CANR-44
Earlier sketches in CA 13-16R, CANR-6, 21
Penrose, Margaret CANR-27
Earlier sketches in CAP-2, CA 19-20
Penrose, Roger 1931- CANR-100
Earlier sketch in CA 139
See also BEST 90:2
Penrose, Roland (Algernon) 1900-1984 ... 85-88
Obituary 112
Pensack, Robert Jon 1951- 148
Pensky, Max 1961- 144
Penslar, Derek J(onathan) 1958- 136
Penson, Mary E. 1917- 146
See also SATA 78
Pentak, Stephen 1951- 236
Pentecost, Edward C(lyde) 1917- 57-60
Pentecost, Hugh
See Philips, Judson (Pentecost)
Pentecost, J(ohn) Dwight 1915- CANR-2
Earlier sketch in CA 5-8R
Pentecost, Martin
See Hearn, John
Penton, Brian 1904-1951 .... DLB 260
Pentony, DeVere Edwin 1924- CANR-8
Earlier sketch in CA 5-8R
Pentreath, A(rthur Godolphin) Guy C(arleton)
1902-1985 .... CAP-1
Obituary 118
Earlier sketch in CA 13-14
Pentz, Croft Miner CANR-9
Earlier sketch in CA 5-8R
Pentz, Lundy H(urd) 1951- 116
Penuel, Arnold M(cCoy) 1936- 57-60
Penuelas, Marcelino C. 1916- 25-28R
Penycate, John (Vincent George) 1943- 144
Penzel, Fred 230
Penzel, Frederick 1948- 85-88
Penzik, Irena
See Narell, Irena
Penzl, Herbert 1910-1995 .... CANR-24
Earlier sketch in CA 45-48
Penzler, Otto 1942- CANR-75
Earlier sketches in CA 81-84, CANR-35
See also DLBY 1996
See also SATA 38
Peoples, Morgan D. 1919-1998 133
Pepe, John Frank 1920- 9-12R
Pepe, Phil(ip) 1935- CANR-18
Earlier sketch in CA 25-28R
See also SATA 20
PEPECE
See Prado (Calvo), Pedro
Pepelasis, Adam(antios) A. 1923- CANR-2
Earlier sketch in CA 1-4R
Peper, George Frederick 1950- CANR-25
Earlier sketch in CA 108
Pepetela 1941- .... AFW
See also EWL 3
See also WLIT 2
Pepin, Ernest 1950- 198
Pepin, Jacques (Georges) 1935- CANR-109
Earlier sketches in CA 103, CANR-25
Pepinsky, Harold E(ugene) 1945- 119
Pepitone, Albert (Davison) 1923- 9-12R
Pepitone, Joe 1940-
Brief entry 109
Pepitone, Joseph Anthony
See Pepitone, Joe
Peploe, Clare .... IDFW 4
Peploe, Mark CANR-130
Earlier sketch in CA 164
Peppard, Murray B(isbee) 1917-1974 .... CAP-2
Obituary 53-56
Earlier sketch in CA 21-22
Peppe, Rodney (Darrell) 1934- 33-36R
See also MAICYA 1, 2
See also SAAS 10
See also SATA 4, 74
Pepper, Adeline 41-44R
Pepper, Art(hur Edward) 1925-1982
Obituary 107
Pepper, Choral 1918- 25-28R
Pepper, Claude Denson 1900-1989
Obituary 128
Pepper, Curtis Bill
See Pepper, Curtis G.
Pepper, Curtis G. 1920- CANR-10
Earlier sketch in CA 21-24R
Pepper, Frank S. 1910-1988
Obituary 127
See also SATA-Obit 61
Pepper, Joan
See Wetherell-Pepper, Joan Alexander
Pepper, John 1942- 117
Pepper, Martin
See Krich, John
Pepper, Stephen C(oburn)
1891-1972 .... CANR-32
Obituary 103
Earlier sketch in CA 1-4R
See also DLB 270
Pepper, Thomas 1939- CANR-16
Earlier sketch in CA 97-100
Pepper, William M(ullin), Jr.
1903-1975 97-100
Obituary 57-60
Pepperberg, Irene M(axine) 1949- 202
Peppercorn, David 1931- 118
Peppercorn, Lisa M(argot) 1913-2004 138
Peppiatt, Michael 1941- CANR-82
Earlier sketches in CA 118, CANR-42
Peppin, Brigid (Mary) 1941- 65-68
Peppler, Alice Stolper 1934- 53-56
Pepys, Samuel 1633-1703 .... BRW 2
See also CDBLB 1660-1789
See also DA
See also DA3
See also DAB
See also DAC
See also DAM MST
See also DLB 101, 213
See also NCFS 4
See also RGEL 2
See also TEA
See also WLC
See also WLIT 3
Pera, Pia 1956- 192
Peradotto, John Joseph 1933- 41-44R
Perani, Judith 208
Perata, David D. 1953- 198
Perazich, George (Nikolas) 1905-1999 185
Perceval-Maxwell, M(ichael) 1933- 53-56
Percival, Alicia C(onstance) 1903- 9-12R
Percival, John 1927- 33-36R
Percival, Walter 1896- CAP-1
Earlier sketch in CA 11-12
Percy
See Walton, Priscilla L.
Percy, Charles H(arting) 1919- 65-68
Percy, Charles Henry
See Smith, Dorothy Gladys
Percy, Douglas Cecil 1914-1995 .... CANR-3
Earlier sketch in CA 5-8R
Percy, Herbert R(oland) 1920- 5-8R
Percy, John R(ees) 1941- 140
Percy, Rachel 1930- .... SATA 63
Percy, Thomas 1729-1811 .... DLB 104
Percy, Walker 1916-1990 .... CANR-64
Obituary 131
Earlier sketches in CA 1-4R, CANR-1, 23
See also AMWS 3
See also BPFB 3
See also CLC 2, 3, 6, 8, 14, 18, 47, 65
See also CN 1, 2, 3, 4
See also CPW
See also CSW
See also DA3
See also DAM NOV, POP
See also DLB 2
See also DLBY 1980, 1990
See also EWL 3
See also MAL 5
See also MTCW 1, 2
See also MTFW 2005
See also RGAL 4
See also TUS
Percy, William 1575-1648 .... DLB 172
Percy, William A., Jr. 1933- 29-32R
Percy, William Alexander 1885-1942 163
See also MTCW 2
See also TCLC 84
Perdrizet, Marie-Pierre 1952- 148
See also SATA 79
Perdue, Charles L., Jr. 1930- 135
Perdue, Lewis 1949- 219
Perdue, Theda 1949- CANR-16
Earlier sketch in CA 93-96
Perdurabo, Frater
See Crowley, Edward Alexander
See also GLL 1
Perec, Georges 1936-1982 141
See also CLC 56, 116
See also DLB 83, 299
See also EWL 3
See also GFL 1789 to the Present
See also RGWL 3
Pereda (y Sanchez de Porrua), Jose Maria de
1833-1906
Brief entry 117
See also TCLC 16
Pereda y Porrua, Jose Maria de
See Pereda (y Sanchez de Porrua), Jose Maria de
Peregoy, George Weems
See Mencken, H(enry) L(ouis)
Peregrine
See Deutscher, Isaac
Peregrini, Gino
See Doty, Gene Warren
Pereira, Hal 1905-1983 .... IDFW 3, 4
Pereira, Harold Bertram 1890- 9-12R
Pereira, Jose Maria dos Reis 1901-1969
See Regio, Jose
Pereira, Sam 1949- 111
Pereira, W(ilfred) D(ennis) 1921- CANR-42
Earlier sketches in CA 104, CANR-20
Pereira Carneiro, Maurina 1899(?)-1983
Obituary 111
Perel, Solomon 1925- 182
Perel, William M. 1927- 33-36R
Pereleshin, Valery 1913-1992 .... GLL 2
Perella, Nicholas James 1927- 73-76
Perelman, Bob 1947- CANR-85
Earlier sketch in CA 154
See also CP 7
See also DLB 193
See also RGAL 4
Perelman, Chaim 1912-1984 103
Perelman, Lewis J(oel) 1946- 73-76
Perelman, Michael 1939- CANR-130
Earlier sketch in CA 111
Perelman, S(idney) J(oseph)
1904-1979 .... CANR-18
Obituary 89-92
Earlier sketch in CA 73-76
See also AITN 1, 2
See also BPFB 3
See also CLC 3, 5, 9, 15, 23, 44, 49
See also DAM DRAM
See also DLB 11, 44
See also MTCW 1, 2
See also MTFW 2005
See also RGAL 4
See also SSC 32
Perenyi, Constance (Marie) 1954- 159
See also SATA 93
Perenyi, Eleanor (Spencer Stone)
1918- CANR-120
Brief entry 113
Earlier sketch in CA 133
Perera, Gretchen G(ifford) 1940- 93-96
Perera, Hilda 1926- 173
See also SATA 105
Perera, Thomas Biddle 1938- CANR-48
Earlier sketches in CA 37-40R, CANR-21
See also SATA 13
Perera, Victor (Haim) 1934-2003 .... 29-32R
Obituary 217
Peres, Richard 1947- 93-96
Peres, Shimon 1923- 85-88
Peres Da Costa, Suneeta 194
Peret, Benjamin 1899-1959 186
Brief entry 117
See also GFL 1789 to the Present
See also PC 33
See also TCLC 20
Peretti, Burton W(illiam) 1961- 144
Peretti, Frank E. 1951- CANR-120
Earlier sketches in CA 136, CANR-65, 102
See also AAYA 48
See also MTCW 2
See also MTFW 2005
See also SATA 80, 141
Peretz, Don 1922- CANR-94
Earlier sketches in CA 9-12R, CANR-4, 19, 41
Peretz, Isaac Leib 201
See also Peretz, Isaac Loeb
Peretz, Isaac Loeb 1851(?)-1915
Brief entry 109
See also Peretz, Isaac Leib
See also SSC 26
See also TCLC 16
Peretz, Yitzkhok Leibush
See Peretz, Isaac Loeb
Pereyra, Lillian A(nita) 1920- 21-24R
Perez, George 1954- 226
Perez, Gilberto (Guillermo) 1943- 171
See also HW 2
Perez, Joseph F(rancis) 1930- CANR-36
Earlier sketches in CA 29-32R, CANR-16
Perez, Loida Maritza 1963- 223
Perez, Louis A., Jr. 1943- CANR-90
Earlier sketch in CA 121
Perez, Louis C(elestino) 1923- 77-80
Perez, Louis G. 1946- 187
Perez, Mireya 189
Perez, Raymundo
See Perez, Raymundo
See also DLB 122
Perez, Raymundo 1946- 181
See also Perez, Raymundo
Perez, Rolando 1957- CANR-117
Earlier sketch in CA 160
Perez, Sofia A(na) 1963- 168
Perez, Tigre
See Perez, Raymundo
Perez de Ayala, Ramon 1881-1962
Obituary 93-96
See also DLB 322
See also EWL 3
See also RGWL 2, 3
Perez de Guzman, Fernan c. 1377-c.
1460 .... DLB 286
Perez-Firmat, Gustavo (Francisco)
1949- CANR-100
Earlier sketches in CA 123, CANR-49
See also LLW
Perez Galdos, Benito 1843-1920 153
Brief entry 125
See also Galdos, Benito Perez
See also EWL 3
See also HLCS 2
See also HW 1
See also RGWL 2, 3
See also TCLC 27
Perez-Gomez, Alberto 1949- CANR-86
Earlier sketch in CA 130
See also HW 1
Perez Lopez, Francisco 1916- 49-52
Perez-Marchand, Monelisa L(ina) 1918- 153
See also HW 1
Perez-Petit, Manuel 1967- 226
Perez-Reverte, Arturo 1951-
See Perez-Reverte, Arturo
See also DLB 322
Perez-Reverte, Arturo 1951- CANR-120
Earlier sketch in CA 163
See also Perez-Reverte, Arturo
See also HW 2
Perez-Stable, Marifeli 1949(?)- CANR-87
Earlier sketch in CA 151
Perfetti, Charles A. 1940- 139
Pergaud, Louis 1882-1915 217
Perham, Margery (Freda)
1895-1982 .... CANR-83
Obituary 106
Earlier sketches in CA 1-4R, CANR-1
Pericoli, Ugo 1923- 97-100
Perier, Odilon-Jean
See Perier, Odilon-Jean
Perigoe, J. Rae 1910- 61-64
Perillo, Joseph M. 1933- 17-20R
Perin, Constance 29-32R
Perin, Roberto 1948- CANR-82
Earlier sketch in CA 133
Perinal, Georges 1897-1965 .... IDFW 3, 4
Perinbanayagam, Robert S(idharthan)
1934- CANR-134
Earlier sketch in CA 109
Perino, Joseph 1946- 106
Perino, Sheila C. 1948- 106
Peripatus
See Whittington-Egan, Richard
Peri Rossi, Cristina 1941- CANR-81
Earlier sketches in CA 131, CANR-59
See also CLC 156
See also CWW 2
See also DLB 145, 290
See also EWL 3
See also HLCS 2
See also HW 1, 2
Peristiany, John G(eorge) 1911-1987 ..... 17-20R
Obituary 124
Peritz, Rene 1933- 45-48
Perkel, Colin N. 1956- 216
Perkens, Duco
See du Perron, Edgar
Perkes, Dan 1931- CANR-21
Earlier sketch in CA 69-72
Perkin, Harold (James) 1926-2004 ... CANR-14
Obituary 232
Earlier sketch in CA 77-80
Perkin, J(ames) R(ussell) C(onway) 1928- 113
Perkin, Joan 1926- CANR-86
Earlier sketch in CA 131
Perkin, Robert L(yman) 1914-1978
Obituary 77-80
Perkins, Agnes (Regan) 1926- CANR-10
Earlier sketch in CA 57-60
Perkins, Al(bert Rogers) 1904-1975 107
Obituary 57-60
See also SATA 30
Perkins, Ann (Louise) 1915-
Brief entry 113
Perkins, Anthony B. 196
Perkins, Bradford 1925- 1-4R
Perkins, Carl (Lee) 1932-1998 102
Obituary 164
Perkins, David 1928- 77-80
Perkins, David (Lee) 1939- CANR-13
Earlier sketch in CA 73-76
Perkins, Dawson 238
Perkins, Dexter 1889-1984 .... 5-8R
Obituary 113
Perkins, Dwight Heald 1934- CANR-22
Earlier sketches in CA 17-20R, CANR-7
Perkins, E(rnest) Benson 1881-1964 .... 5-8R
Obituary 134
Perkins, Edward A., Jr. 1928- CANR-14
Earlier sketch in CA 21-24R
Perkins, Edwin Judson 1939- 106
Perkins, Emily 1970- 171
Perkins, (Useni) Eugene 1932- 142
See also BW 2
See also DLB 41
Perkins, Faith
See Bramer, Jennie (Perkins)
Perkins, George (Burton, Jr.) 1930- ... CANR-99
Earlier sketch in CA 13-16R
Perkins, Hugh V(ictor) 1918-1988 93-96
Obituary 124
Perkins, James Alfred 1911-1998 108
Obituary 169
Perkins, James Ashbrook 1941- 73-76
Perkins, James Oliver Newton 1924- 9-12R
Perkins, James S(cudday) 1899-1991 89-92
Perkins, John (William) 1935- CANR-13
Earlier sketch in CA 73-76
Perkins, John Allen 1919- 114
Perkins, John Bryan Ward
See Ward-Perkins, John Bryan
Perkins, John H. 1942- 176
Perkins, Kathy A(nne) 1954- 186
Perkins, Ken 1926- 137
Perkins, Lawrence A. 1917(?)-1979
Obituary 89-92
Perkins, Leeman L(loyd) 1932- 200
Perkins, Leigh H. 1927- 196
Perkins, Lucy Fitch 1865-1937 .... CANR-85
Brief entry 122
Earlier sketch in CA 137
See also MAICYA 1, 2
See also SATA 72
Perkins, Lynne Rae 200
See also SATA 131
Perkins, (Richard) Marlin 1905-1986 103
Obituary 119
See also SATA 21
See also SATA-Obit 48
Perkins, Merle Lester 1919- 45-48
Perkins, Michael 1942- CANR-8
Earlier sketch in CA 17-20R
Perkins, Mitali 1963- 152
See also SATA 88
Perkins, Newton Stephens 1925- 49-52
Perkins, Ralph 1913- 13-16R
Perkins, Robert L(ee) 1930- 25-28R
Perkins, Rollin M(orris) 1889-1993 53-56
Perkins, Steve
See Perkins, Newton Stephens
Perkins, Van L. 1930- 185
Brief entry 106
Perkins, Virginia Chase 1902-1987 .... CAP-2
Earlier sketch in CA 33-36
Perkins, Whitney Trow 1921- 106

Perkins, (Robert) Wilder 1921-1999 230
Perkins, William 1558-1602 .... DLB 281
Perkins, William H(ughes) 1923- 53-56
Perkins, Wilma Lord 1897-1976
Obituary 104
Perkinson, Henry J(oseph) 1930- CANR-12
Earlier sketch in CA 17-20R
Perkoff, Stuart Z. 1930-1974 212
Obituary 113
See also CP 1
See also DLB 16
Perkowitz, Sidney 1939- 234
Perkowski, Jan Louis 1936- CANR-2
Earlier sketch in CA 45-48
Perks, Anne-Marie 1955- .... SATA 122
Perl, Arnold 1914-1971
Obituary 33-36R
Perl, Gisella 1907-1988
Perl, Jed 1951- 203
Perl, Jeffrey M(ichael) 1952- 138
Perl, Lila CANR-134
Earlier sketch in CA 33-36R
See also JRDA
See also SATA 6, 72
Perl, Ruth June 1929- 25-28R
Perl, Susan 1922-1983 .... CANR-11
Obituary 110
Earlier sketch in CA 17-20R
See also SATA 22
See also SATA-Obit 34
Perl, Teri (Hoch) 1926- CANR-42
Earlier sketches in CA 93-96, CANR-19
Perl, William R. 1906-1998 126
Obituary 172
Perlata
See Peret, Benjamin
Perlberg, Deborah 1948- 118
Perlberg, Mark 1929- 37-40R
Perle, George 1915- CANR-3
Earlier sketch in CA 1-4R
Perles, Alfred 1897-1990(?)
Obituary 130
Perles, Benjamin Max 1922- 45-48
Perley, Michael 1946- 114
Perley, Moses Henry 1804-1862 .... DLB 99
Perlin, John 1944- 134
Perlin, Seymour 1925- 121
Perlinski, Jerome 1940- 112
Perlis, Vivian 1928- 85-88
Perlman, Bennard B(loch) 1928- 89-92
Perlman, Helen Harris 1905-2004 ..... CANR-3
Obituary 231
Earlier sketch in CA 1-4R
Perlman, Janice E(laine) 1943- 61-64
Perlman, Jess 1891-1984 89-92
Perlman, John N(iels) 1946- CANR-113
Earlier sketches in CA 33-36R, CANR-12
Perlman, Mark 1923- CANR-57
Earlier sketches in CA 1-4R, CANR-3, 19
Perlman, Samuel 1905-1975 .... CAP-2
Earlier sketch in CA 33-36
Perlmutter, Amos 1932(?)-2001 206
See also Peake, Thomas H(arold)
Perlmutter, Emanuel 1907(?)-1986
Obituary 118
Perlmutter, Jerome H. 1924- 17-20R
Perlmutter, Nathan 1923-1987 .... CANR-49
Obituary 123
Earlier sketch in CA 13-16R
Perlmutter, O(scar) William 1920-1975 ... 57-60
See also SATA 8
Perlmutter, Ruth Ann 1924- 109
Perlo, Victor 1912-1999 .... CANR-2
Obituary 188
Earlier sketch in CA 5-8R
Perloff, Harvey S(tephen) 1915-1983 129
Obituary 110
Perloff, Marjorie G(abrielle) 1931- . CANR-104
Earlier sketches in CA 57-60, CANR-7, 22, 49
See also CLC 137
Perloff, Richard M. 1951- 146
Perlongo, Bob 1933- 112
Perls, Eugenia Soderberg 1904(?)-1973
Obituary 37-40R
Perls, Frederick S(alomon) 1893-1970 101
Perls, Fritz
See Perls, Frederick S(alomon)
Perls, Hugo 1886(?)-1977
Obituary 73-76
Perlstein, Gary R(obert) 1940- 57-60
Perlstein, Rick 1969- 214
Permal, Lindy
See Palmer, Randy
Perman, Dagmar Horna 1926(?)-1978
Obituary 77-80
Perman, Michael 1942-
Brief entry 113
Pern, Stephen (Antony Nigel) 1950- 128
Pernet, A(nn) 1940- 107
Perniciaro, Tony 1917- 41-44R
Pernick, Martin S(teven) 1948- CANR-67
Earlier sketch in CA 128
Pernoud, Regine 1909- 102
Pernu, Dennis 1970- 152
See also SATA 87
Peroff, Nicholas C(arl) 1944- 113
Peron, Juan (Domingo) 1895-1974
Obituary 49-52
Perone, James E. 1958- 175
Perosa, Sergio 1933- CAP-1
Earlier sketch in CA 13-16
Perot, H(enry) Ross 1930- 142
Peroutka, Ferdinand 1895(?)-1978
Obituary 77-80
Perovsky, Aleksei Alekseevich
1787-1836 .... DLB 198
Perowne, Barry
See Atkey, Philip
Perowne, Stewart Henry 1901-1989 .. CANR-3
Obituary 128
Earlier sketch in CA 1-4R
Perrault, Charles 1628-1703 .... BYA 4
See also CLR 79
See also DLB 268
See also GFL Beginnings to 1789
See also MAICYA 1, 2
See also RGWL 2, 3
See also SATA 25
See also WCH
Perreard, Suzanne Louise Butler
1919- .... SATA-Brief 29
Perreault, John 1937- CANR-1
Earlier sketch in CA 45-48
See also CP 1
Perreault, William D(aniel), Jr. 1948- 110
Perrella, Robert 1917- 61-64
Perrenod, Virginia Marion (Lacy) 1928- 117
Perret, Gene (Richard) 1937- CANR-49
Brief entry 114
Earlier sketch in CA 117
Interview in CA-117
See also SATA 76
Perret, Geoffrey 1940- CANR-117
Earlier sketches in CA 53-56, CANR-4, 63
Perret, Patti 1955- 168
Perrett, Bryan 1934- CANR-48
Earlier sketches in CA 29-32R, CANR-20
Perri, Henri
See Perri, Henry
Perri, Henry 1561-1617 .... DLB 236
Perriam, Wendy 1940- CANR-105
Earlier sketch in CA 136
Perricone, Nicholas V. 1948(?)- 237
Perrigo, Lynn I(rwin) 1904-1992 .... 33-36R
Perrin, Alice 1867-1934 213
See also DLB 156
Perrin, Blanche Chenery 1894-1973 .... 5-8R
Obituary 41-44R
Perrin, Dennis 231
Perrin, Don 1964- 158
Perrin, Gail 1938- 136
Perrin, (Edwin) Noel 1927-2004 .... CANR-92
Obituary 233
Earlier sketches in CA 13-16R, CANR-31, 57
See also ANW
Perrin, (Horace) Norman
1920-1976 .... CANR-11
Earlier sketch in CA 13-16R
Perrin, Porter Gale 1896-1962
Obituary 113
Perrin, Robert 1939- 97-100
Perrin, Robert G(eorge) 1945- 111
Perrin, Ursula 1935- CANR-57
Earlier sketch in CA 101
Perrine, Laurence 1915- CANR-3
Earlier sketch in CA 1-4R
Perrine, Mary 1913-1976 .... 25-28R
See also SATA 2
Perrin Jassy, Marie-France 1942- 93-96
Perrins, Lesley 1953- 123
See also SATA 56
Perron, Edgar du
See du Perron, Edgar
See also EWL 3
Perrone, Charles A. 1951- 132
Perrott, John (R.) 1932- 139
Perrotta, Tom 1961- CANR-99
Earlier sketch in CA 162
Perrottet, Philippe (Louis Gaston)
1921-1982 .... 25-28R
Obituary 122
Perrottet, Tony 213
Perrow, Angeli 1954- 192
See also SATA 121
Perroy, Edouard (Marie Joseph) 1901-1974
Obituary 53-56
Perrucci, Robert 1931- CANR-34
Earlier sketches in CA 85-88, CANR-15
Perruchot, Henri 1917-1967 .... CAP-1
Earlier sketch in CA 9-10
Perry, Andrea 1956- 222
See also SATA 148
Perry, Ann 1953- 224
Perry, Anne 1938- CANR-84
Earlier sketches in CA 101, CANR-22, 50
See also CLC 126
See also CMW 4
See also CN 6, 7
See also CPW
See also DLB 276
Perry, Barbara Fisher
See Fisher, Barbara
Perry, Ben Edwin 1892-1968 .... CAP-2
Earlier sketch in CA 23-24
Perry, Bernard (Berenson) 1910-1985
Obituary 117
Perry, Bliss 1860-1954 185
See also DLB 71
Perry, Brighton
See Sherwood, Robert E(mmet)
Perry, Carmen .... AITN 2
Perry, Charles 1941- 124
Perry, Charles Edward .... AITN 2
Perry, Charner M(arquis) 1902-1985
Obituary 117
Perry, Collin 1949- 108
Perry, David L. 1931- 33-36R
Perry, David Thomas 1946- 37-40R
Perry, Dick 1922-2002 .... 13-16R
Perry, Edgar C(loud) 1900-1995 117
Perry, Elaine 1959- 184
Perry, Eleanor (Rosenfeld Bayer)
1915(?)-1981 111
Obituary 103
See also DLB 44
Perry, Elisabeth Israels 1939- 111
Perry, Elizabeth Jean 1948- CANR-100
Earlier sketch in CA 104
Perry, Erma (Jackson McNeil) 89-92
Perry, Gaylord (Jackson) 1938-
Brief entry 113
Perry, George 1935- CANR-26
Earlier sketch in CA 103
Perry, George Sessions 1910-1956 .... TCWW 1, 2
Perry, Gordon Arthur 1914- 108
Perry, Grace 1927-1987 .... CANR-20
Earlier sketch in CA 102
See also CP 1, 2
Perry, Helen Swick 1911-2001 148
Obituary 201
Perry, Henry Ten Eyck 1890-1973 .... CAP-2
Earlier sketch in CA 19-20
Perry, Huey 1936- 49-52
Perry, James M(oorhead) 1927- CANR-95
Earlier sketch in CA 13-16R
Perry, Jim (Angelo) 1942- 53-56
Perry, John 1914-1998 .... CANR-6
Obituary 171
Earlier sketch in CA 5-8R
Perry, John Curtis 1930- CANR-97
Earlier sketch in CA 104
Perry, John D(elbert), Jr. 1940- 25-28R
Perry, John Oliver 1929- 93-96
Perry, Joseph M(cGarity) 1936- 37-40R
Perry, Kenneth F(rederick) 1902-1974 ... CAP-2
Earlier sketch in CA 19-20
Perry, Kenneth I. 1929- 29-32R
Perry, Kenneth W(ilbur) 1919- 57-60
Perry, Laura 1965- 229
Perry, Lewis (Curtis) 1938- CANR-1
Earlier sketch in CA 45-48
Perry, Linette (Purbi) 108
Perry, Lloyd M(erle) 1916-1998 .... CANR-9
Obituary 165
Earlier sketch in CA 21-24R
Perry, Louis B(arnes) 1918- CAP-1
Earlier sketch in CA 13-14
Perry, Margaret 1933- 89-92
See also BW 1
Perry, Mark 1950- 181
Perry, Matthew 1794-1858 .... DLB 183
Perry, Michael (Charles) 1933- 101
Perry, Milton F(reeman) 1926- 13-16R
Perry, Nicolette E. 1949- 119
Perry, Octavia Jordan 1894-1991 .... CAP-1
Earlier sketch in CA 13-14
Perry, Patricia 1949- 106
See also SATA 30
Perry, Paul 1950- CANR-99
Earlier sketch in CA 140
Perry, Peter John 1937- 49-52
Perry, Phillip M. 1948- 29-32R
Perry, Phyllis Alesia 232
Perry, Phyllis J(ean) 1933- CANR-122
Earlier sketch in CA 168
See also SATA 60, 101, 152
Perry, Ralph Barton 1876-1957
Brief entry 123
Perry, Regenia (Alfreda) 1941- 126
Perry, Richard 41-44R
Perry, Richard 1944- 115
See also BW 1
Perry, Richard S. 1924- 13-16R
Perry, Ritchie (John Allen) 1942- CANR-61
Earlier sketches in CA 45-48, CANR-1, 21
See also CMW 4
See also SATA 105
Perry, Robin 1917- 65-68
Perry, Roger 1933- CANR-14
Earlier sketch in CA 77-80
See also SATA 27
Perry, Ronald Peter Lee 1932- .... CP 1
Perry, Rosalie Sandra 1945- 53-56
Perry, Rufus
See Gibson, Walter B(rown)
Perry, Ruth (Fuller) 1892- 131
Perry, Ruth 1943- 118
Perry, Sampson 1747-1823 .... DLB 158
Perry, Shauneille 1930- 113
Perry, Steve(n Carl) 1947- CANR-85
Earlier sketch in CA 143
See also BYA 10
See also FANT
See also SATA 76
See also SFW 4
Perry, Stewart E(dmond) 1928- 17-20R
Perry, (Charles) Stuart 1908- 107
Perry, Susan
See Perry, Susan M.
Perry, Susan (K.) 200
Perry, Susan M. 1950- 124
Perry, T. Anthony 1938- 81-84
Perry, Thomas 1947- 213
Brief entry 123
Earlier sketches in CA 130, CANR-64, 108
Autobiographical Essay in 213
Perry, Thomas Whipple 1925- 9-12R
Perry, Troy D(eroy) 1940-
Brief entry 109
Perry, Walter (Laing Macdonald) 1921- 113
Perry, Will 1933- 65-68
Perry, William E(dward) 1931- 111
Perry, William J(ames) 1927- 183
Perry, Wilma I. 1912-1992 105
Perse, St.-John
See Leger, (Marie-Rene Auguste) Alexis Saint-Leger
Perse, Saint-John
See Leger, (Marie-Rene Auguste) Alexis Saint-Leger
See also DLB 258
See also RGWL 3
Pershall, Mary K. 1951- 138
See also SATA 70
Pershing, John J(oseph) 1860-1948 227
Pershing, Marie
See Schultz, Pearle Henriksen
Persichetti, Vincent 1915-1987
Obituary 124
Persico, Joseph E(dward) 1930- CANR-117
Earlier sketches in CA 93-96, CANR-21
Persinger, Michael A. 1945- 69-72
Persis
See Haime, Agnes Irvine Constance (Adams)
Persius 34-62 .... AW 2
See also DLB 211
See also RGWL 2, 3
Perske, Robert 1927- 106
See also SATA 57
Persky, Mordecai 1931- 81-84
Persky, Mort
See Persky, Mordecai
Persky, Stan 1941- CANR-39
Earlier sketches in CA 101, CANR-18
Person, Amy L. 1896-1973 .... CAP-2
Earlier sketch in CA 23-24
Person, Bernard 1895(?)-1981
Obituary 103
Person, James E(llis), Jr. 1955- 201
Person, Peter P. 1889-1984 .... CAP-1
Earlier sketch in CA 11-12
Persons, Robert H(odge), Jr. 1922- CANR-13
Earlier sketch in CA 17-20R
Persons, Stow Spaulding 1913- 103
Persun, Morgan Reed
See Watkins, Dawn L.
Persun, Morgan Reed
See Watkins, Dawn L.
Pertinax
See Geraud, (Charles Joseph) Andre and Haws, Duncan
Pertman, Adam 1953- 191
Pertschuk, Michael 1933- CANR-117
Earlier sketches in CA 109, CANR-26
Pertwee, Michael (Henry Roland)
1916-1991 154
Brief entry 124
Pertwee, Roland 1885-1963
Obituary 93-96
Perutz, Kathrin 1939- CANR-85
Earlier sketches in CA 1-4R, CANR-3
See also CN 1, 2, 3, 4, 5, 6, 7
Perutz, Leo(pold) 1882-1957 147
See also DLB 81
See also TCLC 60
Perutz, Max (Ferdinand) 1914-2002 156
Obituary 205
Pervin, Lawrence A. 1936- CANR-8
Earlier sketch in CA 21-24R
Pescadero, Joey
See Obrecht, Jas
Pescadero, Julia
See Obrecht, Jas
Pesce, Dolores 198
Peschel, Enid Rhodes 1943- 110
Pescow, Jerome K(enneth) 1929- 45-48
Peseenz, Tulio F.
See Lopez y Fuentes, Gregorio
Pesek, Boris P(eter) 1926- 21-24R
Pesek, Ludek 1919-1999 .... 29-32R
Pesetsky, Bette 1932- 133
See also CLC 28
See also DLB 130
Peshkin, Alan 1931- 81-84
Peshkov, Alexei Maximovich
1868-1936 .... CANR-83
Brief entry 105
Earlier sketch in CA 141
See also Gor'kii, Maksim and Gorky, Maxim
See also DA
See also DAC
See also DAM DRAM, MST, NOV
See also MTCW 2
See also MTFW 2005
Pesic, Peter (Dragan) 1948- 226
Pesin, Harry 1919-1984 .... 29-32R
Obituary 197
Peskett, William 1952- CANR-85
Earlier sketch in CA 154
See also CP 7
Peskin, Allan 1933- 189
Brief entry 109
Pesnot, Patrick 1943- 101
Pessanha, Camilo 1867-1926 .... DLB 287
Pessen, Beth 1943- 97-100
Pessen, Edward 1920-1992 .... CANR-82
Obituary 140
Earlier sketches in CA 37-40R, CANR-14
Pessina, Giorgio 1902(?)-1977
Obituary 73-76
Pessino, Clara Park 1899(?)-1985
Obituary 116
Pesso, Albert 1929- 73-76

Pessoa, Fernando (Antonio Nogueira)
1888-1935 183
Brief entry 125
See also DAM MULT
See also DLB 287
See also EW 10
See also EWL 3
See also HLC 2
See also PC 20
See also RGWL 2, 3
See also TCLC 27
See also WP
Pestalozzi, Johann Heinrich
1746-1827 .... DLB 94
Pestana, Carla Gardina 1958- 141
Pestelli, Giorgio 1938- 124
Pestieau, Phyllis Smith 1946- 97-100
Petacco, Arrigo 1929- CANR-21
Earlier sketch in CA 103
Petach, Heidi .... SATA 149
Petacque, Art(hur M.) 1924-2001 136
Obituary 196
Petaja, Emil (Theodore) 1915-2000 .. CANR-85
Obituary 189
Earlier sketch in CA 25-28R
See also SFW 4
Pete, Eric E. 1968- 200
Peter
See Stratemeyer, Edward L.
Peter, Armistead (III) 1896(?)-1983
Obituary 111
Peter, Elizabeth O. 1863-1924 .... RHW
Peter, James (Fletcher) 1919- 17-20R
Peter, John (Desmond) 1921- CANR-3
Earlier sketch in CA 1-4R
Peter, Katherine 1918- 197
Peter, Laurence J(ohnston)
1919-1990 .... CANR-17
Obituary 130
Earlier sketch in CA 17-20R
See also DLB 53
Peterfreund, Sheldon P(aul) 1917- 21-24R
Peterfreund, Stuart (Samuel) 1945- ... CANR-58
Earlier sketches in CA 33-36R, CANR-13, 30
Peterkiewicz, Jerzy (Michal) 1916- ... CANR-83
Earlier sketches in CA 5-8R, CANR-5
See also CN 1, 2, 3, 4, 5, 6, 7
Peterkin, Allan David 182
Peterkin, Julia Mood 1880-1961 102
See also CLC 31
See also DLB 9
Peterman, Michael A(lan) 1942- 111
Peterman, Ruth 1924- 57-60
Peter of Spain 1205(?)-1277 .... DLB 115
Peters, Alexander
See Hollander, Zander
Peters, Andrew Fusek 1965- .... SATA 107
Peters, Arthur Anderson 1913-1979
Obituary 93-96
See also Peters, Fritz
Peters, Arthur King 1919- 104
Peters, Barney
See Bauer, Erwin A(dam)
Peters, Caroline
See Betz, Eva Kelly
Peters, Catherine 1930- 127
Peters, Charles (Given, Jr.) 1926- 122
Brief entry 116
Peters, Christina 1942- 85-88
Peters, Curtis H. 1942- 147
Peters, Daniel (James) 1948- CANR-39
Earlier sketches in CA 85-88, CANR-15
Peters, David 214
See also David, Peter (Allen)
Peters, David A(lexander) 1923- 25-28R
Peters, Donald L. 1925- 21-24R
Peters, Edward (Murray) 1936- CANR-40
Earlier sketches in CA 101, CANR-18
Peters, Elizabeth
See Mertz, Barbara (Gross)
Peters, Ellis
See Pargeter, Edith Mary
See also DLB 276
See also MSW
Peters, Emma
See Price, Karen
Peters, Eugene H(erbert) 1929- 41-44R
Peters, F(rancis) E(dward) 1927- CANR-12
Earlier sketch in CA 73-76
Peters, Flossie E.
See Thompson-Peters, Flossie E.
Peters, Frederick George 1935- 104
Peters, Fritz
See Peters, Arthur Anderson
See also GLL 2
Peters, Gabriel
See Matott, Justin
Peters, Geoffrey
See Palmer, Madelyn
Peters, George W(illiam) 1907- CANR-24
Earlier sketch in CA 45-48
Peters, H. Frederick 1910-1990 73-76
Peters, J. Ross 1936- 29-32R
Peters, Jean (Rae) 1935- 116
Peters, Joan K(aren) 1945- CANR-109
Earlier sketch in CA 158
See also CLC 39
Peters, John F(red) 1935- 185
Peters, Julie Anne 1952- CANR-103
Earlier sketch in CA 149
See also AAYA 44
See also BYA 16
See also SATA 82, 128
Peters, Ken(neth Walter) 1929- 17-20R
Peters, Lane
See Lapidus, Elaine
Peters, Lawrence
See Davies, L(eslie) P(urnell)
Peters, Lenrie (Wilfred Leopold)
1932- CANR-85
Earlier sketch in CA 108
See also BW 1
See also CP 1, 2, 3, 4, 5, 6, 7
See also DLB 117
See also EWL 3
Peters, Leslie
See Peters, Donald L.
Peters, Linda
See Catherall, Arthur
Peters, Lisa N. 1957- 189
Peters, Lisa Westberg 1951- 141
See also SATA 74, 115, 161
Peters, Ludovic
See Brent, Peter (Ludwig)
Peters, Marcia
See Gouled, Vivian G(loria)
Peters, Margaret Evelyn 1936- 53-56
Peters, Margot 1933- CANR-12
Earlier sketch in CA 73-76
Peters, Maureen 1935- CANR-141
Earlier sketches in CA 33-36R, CANR-65
See also RHW
Peters, Max S(tone) 1920- 57-60
Peters, Michael
See Hornsby-Smith, Michael P(eter)
Peters, Michael (Adrian) 1948- 163
Peters, Michael Bartley 1943- 110
Brief entry 108
Interview in CA-110
Peters, Mike
See Peters, Michael Bartley
Peters, Natasha
See Cleaver, Anastasia N.
Peters, Nell
See Pietila, Nellie
Peters, Patricia 1953- .... SATA 84
Peters, R(ichard) S(tanley) 1919- CANR-16
Earlier sketch in CA 21-24R
Peters, Ralph 1952- CANR-122
Earlier sketch in CA 140
Peters, Randolph 1959- 185
Peters, Richard Dorland 1910-1984
Obituary 114
Peters, Robert Anthony 1926- 49-52
Peters, Robert Henry 1946-1996 143
Peters, Robert L(ouis) 1924- 13-16R
See also CAAS 8
See also CLC 7
See also CP 1, 7
See also DLB 105
Peters, Ronald M., Jr. 1947- 85-88
Peters, Roy
See Nickson, Arthur
Peters, Russell M. 1929- 146
See also SATA 78
Peters, Ruth Marie 1913(?)-1978
Obituary 104
Peters, S. H.
See Porter, William Sydney and
Proffitt, Nicholas (Charles)
Peters, S. T.
See Brannon, William T.
Peters, Sally 1938- 229
Peters, Shawn Francis 1966- 225
Peters, Stephen 1907(?)-1990
Obituary 130
Peters, Steven
See Geiser, Robert L(ee)
Peters, Ted
See Peters, Theodore F(rank)
Peters, Theodore F(rank) 1941- 81-84
Peters, Thomas J. 1942- CANR-71
Brief entry 123
Earlier sketch in CA 135
See also Peters, Tom
Peters, Tom
See Peters, Thomas J.
See also BEST 89:1
Peters, Victor 1915- 17-20R
Peters, Virginia Bergman 1918- 93-96
Peters, William 1921- CANR-20
Earlier sketches in CA 9-12R, CANR-3
Petersen, Arnold 1885-1976
Obituary 65-68
Petersen, Carol Otto 1914- 57-60
Petersen, Clarence G. 1933- 77-80
Petersen, David 1946- CANR-123
Earlier sketch in CA 180
See also SATA 62, 109
Petersen, David M(uir) 1939- 41-44R
Petersen, Donald 1928- 13-16R
See also CP 1, 2
Petersen, E. Allen 1903(?)-1987
Obituary 122
Petersen, Gwenn Boardman 1924- CANR-2
Earlier sketch in CA 45-48
See also Boardman, Gwenn R.
See also SATA 61
Petersen, James R(eeve) 1948- 114
Petersen, Karen Daniels 1910- 73-76
Petersen, Mark E. 1900-1984 132
Obituary 111
Petersen, Melba F(rances) Runtz 1919- 5-8R
Petersen, Nis 1897-1943 .... EWL 3
Petersen, P(eter) J(ames) 1941- CANR-30
Earlier sketch in CA 112
See also JRDA
See also MAICYA 1, 2
See also SATA 48, 83, 118
See also SATA-Brief 43
See also YAW
Petersen, Palle 1943- .... SATA 85
Petersen, Peter (Barron) 1932- 57-60
Petersen, Sigurd Damskov 1904-1981 .... 9-12R
Petersen, Verner C. 1946- 234
Petersen, William 1912- CANR-3
Earlier sketch in CA 1-4R
Petersen, William J. 1929- CANR-9
Earlier sketch in CA 21-24R
Petersen, William John 1901-1989 .... 5-8R
Petersen, Wolfgang 1941- 181
Petersham, Maud (Sylvia Fuller)
1890-1971 .... CANR-84
Obituary 33-36R
Earlier sketches in CA 73-76, CANR-29
See also CLR 24
See also CWRI 5
See also DLB 22
See also MAICYA 1, 2
See also SATA 17
Petersham, Miska 1888-1960 .... CANR-83
Earlier sketches in CA 73-76, CANR-29
See also CLR 24
See also CWRI 5
See also DLB 22
See also MAICYA 1, 2
See also SATA 17
Peterson, A(lexander) D(uncan) C(ampbell)
1908-1988 108
Obituary 126
Peterson, Agnes F(ischer) 1923- 29-32R
Peterson, Arthur L(aVerne) 1926- 9-12R
Peterson, Audrey CANR-120
Earlier sketch in CA 131
Peterson, Benjamin
See Allen, Robert L(ee)
Peterson, Brenda 1950- 197
See also ANW
Peterson, Brent D(an) 1942- 120
Peterson, Carl 1896(?)-1983
Obituary 110
Peterson, Carol R. 1942- 176
Peterson, Carolyn Sue 1938- CANR-12
Earlier sketch in CA 73-76
Peterson, Carroll V(alleen) 1929- 45-48
Peterson, Charles 1900(?)-1976
Obituary 69-72
Peterson, Charles Jacobs 1819-1887 .... DLB 79
Peterson, Charles S. 1927- 49-52
Peterson, Chris(tine Louise) 1957- 141
Peterson, Christian A. 1953- 144
Peterson, Christmas
See Christmas, Joyce
Peterson, Cris 1952- CANR-124
Earlier sketch in CA 150
See also SATA 84, 145
Peterson, Dale 1944- CANR-127
Earlier sketch in CA 109
Peterson, Dawn 1934- .... SATA 86
Peterson, Donald 1956- 135
Peterson, Donald R(obert) 1923- 25-28R
Peterson, Douglas L(ee) 1924- 41-44R
Peterson, Edward N(orman) 1925- 29-32R
Peterson, Edwin (Lewis) 1904-1972
Obituary 37-40R
Peterson, Edwin Loose 1915- 5-8R
Peterson, Eldridge 1905(?)-1977
Obituary 73-76
Peterson, Eleanor M. 1912- 25-28R
Peterson, Elmer 1930- 37-40R
Peterson, Esther (Allen) 1934- CANR-16
Earlier sketch in CA 89-92
See also SATA 35
Peterson, Eugenie Vasilievna
See Devi, Indra
Peterson, Evan T(ye) 1925- 45-48
Peterson, F. Ross 1941- 97-100
Peterson, Forrest H(arold)
1912-1988 .... CANR-25
Earlier sketch in CA 45-48
Peterson, Franklynn 1938- CANR-37
Earlier sketch in CA 110
Peterson, Fred W. 1932- 140
Peterson, Frederick Alvin 1920- 49-52
Peterson, (P.) Geoff(rey) 1946- 196
Peterson, Gilbert Allan 1935- CANR-82
Earlier sketches in CA 114, CANR-35
Peterson, Hans 1922- CANR-1
Earlier sketch in CA 49-52
See also SATA 8
Peterson, Harold 1939- 29-32R
Peterson, Harold F(erdinand) 1900-1983 .. 5-8R
Peterson, Harold L(eslie) 1922-1978 .. CANR-4
Obituary 73-76
Earlier sketch in CA 1-4R
See also SATA 8
Peterson, Helen Stone 1910- 37-40R
See also SATA 8
Peterson, Houston 1897-1981 107
Obituary 103
Peterson, Ivars 168
Peterson, James
See Zeiger, Henry A(nthony)
Peterson, James Alfred 1913-1992 104
Obituary 137
Peterson, James Allan 1932- 29-32R
Peterson, Jean Sunde 1941- CANR-121
Earlier sketch in CA 169
See also SATA 108
Peterson, Jeanne Whitehouse
1939- CANR-144
See also Whitehouse, Jeanne
See also SATA 159
Peterson, Jim
See Crawford, William (Elbert)
Peterson, John Eric 1933- 53-56
Peterson, John J. 1918- 53-56
Peterson, John W(illard) 1921- 97-100
Peterson, Kathleen B. 1951- .... SATA 119
Peterson, Keith
See Klavan, Andrew
Peterson, Kenneth G(erard) 1927- 33-36R
Peterson, Len
See Peterson, Leonard (Byron)
Peterson, Leonard (Byron) 1917- 204
See also DLB 88
Peterson, Levi S(avage) 1933- CANR-51
Earlier sketches in CA 109, CANR-26
See also DLB 206
Peterson, Linda H(aenlein) 1948- CANR-93
Earlier sketches in CA 121, CANR-46
Peterson, Lloyd R(ichard) 1922-
Brief entry 107
Peterson, Lorraine 1940- 113
See also SATA 56
See also SATA-Brief 44
Peterson, Louis (Stamford), (Jr.) 1922-1998 . 153
Obituary 166
See also BW 2
See also DLB 76
Peterson, M(ildred) Jeanne 1937- 103
Peterson, Marilyn Ann 1933- 57-60
Peterson, Martin Severin 1897-1986 .. CANR-3
Earlier sketch in CA 1-4R
Peterson, Melvin N. A. 1929-1995 144
Obituary 149
Peterson, Mendel (Lazear) 1918-2003 73-76
Obituary 218
Peterson, Merrill D(aniel) 1921- CANR-44
Earlier sketches in CA 1-4R, CANR-3, 19
Peterson, Michael L. 1950- CANR-120
Earlier sketch in CA 148
Peterson, Nancy J. 1958- 213
Peterson, Nancy L(ee) 1939- 105
Peterson, Norma Lois 1922- 13-16R
Peterson, Ottis 1907- 21-24R
Peterson, Owen M. 1924- CANR-51
Earlier sketches in CA 108, CANR-26
Peterson, Paul E(lliott) 1940- CANR-24
Earlier sketch in CA 45-48
Peterson, Paula W. 230
Peterson, Peter G. 1926- 151
Peterson, R(odney) D(elos) 1932- 41-44R
Peterson, Reona 1941- 73-76
Peterson, Richard A(ustin) 1932- 25-28R
Peterson, Richard F(rank) 1939- 128
Peterson, Richard H(ermann) 1942- 137
Peterson, Richard S(cot) 1938- 133
Peterson, Robert 1924- CANR-17
Earlier sketch in CA 25-28R
See also CP 1
Peterson, Robert E(ugene) 1928- 13-16R
Peterson, Robert W. 1925- CANR-92
Earlier sketch in CA 33-36R
Peterson, Roger Tory 1908-1996 .... CANR-1
Obituary 152
Earlier sketch in CA 1-4R
Peterson, Russell Arthur 1922- 33-36R
Peterson, Shelley 1952- 220
See also SATA 146
Peterson, Simone
See Thomson, Daisy H(icks)
Peterson, Steven A. 1947- 138
Peterson, Susan (Annette) H(arnly)
1925- 57-60
Peterson, Ted Nicholas 1934- 121
Peterson, Theodore (Bernard)
1918-1997 .... 9-12R
Obituary 160
Peterson, Tracie 204
Peterson, Trudy H(uskamp) 1945- 116
Peterson, V. Spike 1946- 144
Peterson, Virgil W(allace) 1904-1989
Obituary 127
Peterson, Virgilia 1904-1966
Obituary 25-28R
Peterson, Wallace Carroll 1921- 5-8R
Peterson, Walter Scott 1944- 21-24R
Peterson, Wilferd Arlan 1900-1995 .... CANR-6
Earlier sketch in CA 9-12R
Peterson, Willard James 1938- 103
Peterson, William R. 1943-1990
Obituary 132
Peterson, William S(amuel) 1939- CANR-11
Earlier sketch in CA 29-32R
Peterson del Mar, David
See del Mar, David Peterson
Petersson, Robert T. 1918- 45-48
Peterzell, Jay 1952- 118
Petesch, Natalie L(evin) M(aines)
1924- CANR-21
Earlier sketches in CA 57-60, CANR-6
See also CAAS 12
Petgen, Dorothea 1903(?)-1985
Obituary 115
Petgen, Dorothy
See Petgen, Dorothea
Pethybridge, Roger 1934- 5-8R
Petie, Haris
See Petty, Roberta
See also SATA 10
Petievich, Gerald 1944- CANR-62
Earlier sketch in CA 105
See also CMW 4
Petiot, Henri Jules Charles 1901-1965
Obituary 114
Petit, Chris 1949- 224
Petit, Gaston 1930- 73-76
Petit, Susan 1945- 142
Petitclair, Pierre 1813-1860 .... DLB 99
Petitclerc, Denne Bart 1929- 93-96
Petite, Irving (Laurence) 1920-
Brief entry 113
Petitfils, Pierre (Robert) 1908- 137
Petkas, Peter (James) 1945- 37-40R
Petkovsek, Marko 1955- 165

Petley, Dexter 1955- ... 239
Petmecky, Ben (Joe) 1922- ... 1-4R
Peto
  See White, Stanley
Peto, James
  See White, Stanley
Petofi, Sandor 1823-1849 ... RGWL 2, 3
Petrakis, Harry Mark 1923- ... CANR-85
  Earlier sketches in CA 9-12R, CANR-4, 30
  See also CLC 3
  See also CN 1, 2, 3, 4, 5, 6, 7
Petranek, Stephen Lynn 1944- ... 133
Petrarch 1304-1374 ... DA3
  See also DAM POET
  See also EW 2
  See also LMFS 1
  See also PC 8
  See also RGWL 2, 3
  See also WLIT 7
Petras, James Frank 1937- ... CANR-47
  Earlier sketches in CA 61-64, CANR-7, 22
Petras, John W. 1940- ... 29-32R
Petrement, Simone 1907- ... 77-80
Petres, Robert E(van) 1939- ... 104
Petrescu, Camil 1894-1957 ... DLB 220
  See also EWL 3
Petri, Gyorgy
  See Petri, Gyorgy
Petri, Gyorgy 1943-2000 ... 210
  See also CWW 2
Petric, Vlada
  See Petric, Vladimir
Petric, Vladimir 1928- ... 129
Petrich, Patricia Barrett 1942- ... 61-64
Petrides, Avra ... 123
Petrides, George Athan 1916-
  Brief entry ... 106
Petrides, Heidrun 1944- ... SATA 19
Petrie, Alexander 1881- ... CAP-1
  Earlier sketch in CA 13-16
Petrie, Anne 1946- ... 172
Petrie, Asenath 1914-2001 ... 21-24R
Petrie, Catherine 1947- ... 109
  See also SATA 52
  See also SATA-Brief 41
Petrie, Charles (Alexander)
  1895-1977 ... CANR-8
  Obituary ... 89-92
  Earlier sketch in CA 17-20R
Petrie, Duncan 1963- ... 164
Petrie, Mildred McClary 1912-1995 ... 21-24R
Petrie, Paul J(ames) 1928- ... CANR-18
  Earlier sketches in CA 9-12R, CANR-3
  See also CP 1, 2, 3, 4, 5, 6, 7
Petrie, Rhona
  See Buchanan, Marie
Petrie, Sidney 1923- ... 21-24R
Petrik, James M. 1961- ... 213
Petrino, Elizabeth (Anne) 1962- ... 233
Petrinovich, Lewis 1930- ... 41-44R
Petro, Joseph 1944- ... 238
Petro, Nicolai N. 1958- ... 135
Petro, Pamela J. 1960- ... CANR-122
  Earlier sketch in CA 169
Petro, Peter 1946- ... 144
Petro, Sylvester 1917- ... 1-4R
Petrocelli, Orlando R(alph) 1930- ... CANR-1
  Earlier sketch in CA 45-48
Petrone, Jane Muir 1929- ... 5-8R
Petrone, Penny 1923- ... 194
Petroni, Frank A. 1936- ... 85-88
Petroni, Guglielmo 1911-1993 ... 188
Petronius c. 20-66 ... AW 2
  See also CDWLB 1
  See also DLB 211
  See also RGWL 2, 3
Petropoulos, Jonathan G. 1961- ... 153
Petropulos, John A(nthony) 1929-1999 ... 25-28R
Petroski, Catherine (Ann Groom)
  1939- ... CANR-22
  Earlier sketch in CA 106
  See also SATA 48
Petroski, Henry 1942- ... 188
  See also MTFW 2005
Petrou, David Michael 1949- ... 73-76
Petrov, Aleksander 1938- ... DLB 181
Petrov, Evgenii
  See Kataev, Evgeny Petrovich
  See also DLB 272
Petrov, Evgeny
  See Kataev, Evgeny Petrovich
  See also TCLC 21
Petrov, Fyodor 1877(?)-1973
  Obituary ... 41-44R
Petrov, Gavriil 1730-1801 ... DLB 150
Petrov, Michel
  See Visson, Lynn
Petrov, Valeri 1920- ... DLB 181
Petrov, Vasilii Petrovich 1736-1799 ... DLB 150
Petrov, Victor P. 1907-2000 ... CANR-51
  Obituary ... 189
  Earlier sketches in CA 21-24R, CANR-10, 26
Petrov, Vladimer 1915-1999 ... 21-24R
  Obituary ... 177
Petrov, Yevgeny
  See Kataev, Evgeny Petrovich
Petrova, Olga 1884(?)-1977
  Obituary ... 73-76
Petrovic, Rastko 1898-1949 ... CDWLB 4
  See also DLB 147
Petrovich, Michael B(oro) 1922- ... 108
  See also SATA 40
Petrovska, Marija 1926- ... 107
Petrovskaya, Kyra
  See Wayne, Kyra Petrovskaya
Petrovsky, Boris
  See Beauchamp, Kathleen Mansfield
  See also GLL 1
Petrovsky, N.
  See Poltoratzky, N(ikolai) P(etrovich)
Petrucci, Armando 1932- ... CANR-118
  Earlier sketch in CA 159
Petrucci, Kenneth R(occo) 1947- ... 57-60
Petruccio, Steven James 1961- ... SATA 67
Petrushevskaia, Liudmila (Stefanovna)
  See Petrushevskaya, Ludmila
  See also CWW 2
Petrushevskaya, Ludmila 1938-
  See Petrushevskaia, Liudmila (Stefanovna)
  See also DLB 285
  See also EWL 3
Petrushevskaya, Lyudmila
  See Petrushevskaya, Ludmila
Petry, Alice Hall 1951- ... CANR-120
  Earlier sketch in CA 130
Petry, Ann (Lane) 1908-1997 ... CANR-46
  Obituary ... 157
  Earlier sketches in CA 5-8R, CANR-4
  See also CAAS 6
  See also AFAW 1, 2
  See also BPFB 3
  See also BW 1, 3
  See also BYA 2
  See also CLC 1, 7, 18
  See also CLR 12
  See also CN 1, 2, 3, 4, 5, 6
  See also DLB 76
  See also EWL 3
  See also JRDA
  See also LAIT 1
  See also MAICYA 1, 2
  See also MAICYAS 1
  See also MTCW 1
  See also RGAL 4
  See also SATA 5
  See also SATA-Obit 94
  See also TCLC 112
  See also TUS
Petry, Carl Forbes 1943- ... 106
Petry, R(ay) C. 1903-1992 ... 5-8R
Petsales-Diomedes, Nikos
  See Petsalis-Diomidis, Nicholas
Petsalis-Diomidis, Nicholas 1943- ... 200
Pettas, Mary 1918- ... 25-28R
Pettee, George S(awyer) 1904(?)-1989
  Obituary ... 130
Petterson, Donald K. 1930- ... 192
Petterson, Henry William 1922- ... 9-12R
Petterson, Steve D. 1948- ... 138
Petterssen, Sverre 1898-1974
  Obituary ... 53-56
Pettersson, Karl-Henrik 1937- ... 65-68
Pettes, Dorothy E. ... CANR-12
  Earlier sketch in CA 25-28R
Pettie, George 1548(?)-1589 ... DLB 136
Pettifer, James 1949- ... CANR-93
  Earlier sketch in CA 146
Pettifer, Julian 1935- ... 136
Pettigrew, Judith Hoyt 1943- ... 170
Pettigrew, Judy
  See Pettigrew, Judith Hoyt
Pettigrew, Thomas Fraser 1931- ... CANR-30
  Earlier sketches in CA 33-36R, CANR-13
Pettinger, Peter 1945-1998 ... 184
Pettingill, Amos
  See Harris, William Bliss
Pettingill, Olin Sewall, Jr. 1907- ... CANR-1
  Earlier sketch in CA 45-48
Pettit, Arthur G. 1938-1977 ... 53-56
  Obituary ... 135
Pettit, Clyde Edwin 1932- ... 65-68
Pettit, Henry (Jewett) 1906-1994 ... 1-4R
Pettit, Jayne 1932- ... 178
  See also SATA 108
Pettit, Lawrence K. 1937- ... 33-36R
Pettit, Michael (Edwin) 1950- ... 114
Pettit, Norman 1929- ... 17-20R
Pettit, Philip 1945- ... CANR-97
  Earlier sketches in CA 97-100, CANR-17, 37
Pettit, Rhonda S(ue) 1955- ... 204
Pettitt, George A(lbert) 1901-1976 ... CAP-2
  Earlier sketch in CA 29-32
Pettoello, Decio (Egberto Saadi) 1886-1984
  Obituary ... 113
Petty, Alan Edwin 1946- ... CANR-97
  Earlier sketch in CA 139
Petty, Anne C(otton) 1945- ... 115
Petty, Bruce M. 1945- ... 228
Petty, Mary 1899-1976
  Obituary ... 65-68
Petty, Norman 1927(?)-1984
  Obituary ... 113
Petty, Roberta 1915- ... CANR-10
  Earlier sketch in CA 61-64
  See also Petie, Haris
Petty, Walter T. 1918- ... CANR-9
  Earlier sketch in CA 21-24R
Petty, William Henry 1921- ... 65-68
  See also CP 2
Petuchowski, Jakob Josef
  1925-1991 ... CANR-18
  Obituary ... 136
  Earlier sketches in CA 1-4R, CANR-3
Petulla, Joseph M. 1932- ... CANR-9
  Earlier sketch in CA 21-24R
Petzinger, Thomas, Jr. 1955- ... 136
Petzold, Charles 1953- ... 185
Petzold, Paul 1940- ... CANR-9
  Earlier sketch in CA 61-64
Petzoldt, Paul Kiesow 1908-1999 ... 57-60
  Obituary ... 187
Petzoldt, Richard 1907-1974
  Obituary ... 111
Peukert, Detlev
  See Peukert, Detlev J(ulio) K.
Peukert, Detlev J(ulio) K. 1950- ... 133
Pevar, Stephen L. 1946- ... 237
Pevsner, Nikolaus (Bernhard Leon)
  1902-1983 ... CANR-64
  Obituary ... 110
  Earlier sketches in CA 9-12R, CANR-7
  See also MTCW 1
Pevsner, Stella ... CANR-27
  Earlier sketch in CA 57-60
  See also AAYA 15
  See also JRDA
  See also MAICYA 2
  See also MAICYAS 1
  See also SAAS 14
  See also SATA 8, 77, 131
  See also WYA
Peychinovich
  See Vazov, Ivan (Minchov)
Peyer, Bernd C. 1946- ... 166
Peyo
  See Culliford, Pierre
Peyre, Henri (Maurice) 1901-1988 ... CANR-82
  Obituary ... 127
  Earlier sketches in CA 5-8R, CANR-3
Peyrefitte, Alain Antoine
  1925-1999 ... CANR-97
  Obituary ... 186
  Earlier sketch in CA 85-88
Peyrefitte, (Pierre) Roger 1907-2000 ... CANR-47
  Obituary ... 192
  Earlier sketch in CA 65-68
Peyser, Joan 1931- ... 187
  Brief entry ... 112
Peyser, Joseph (L.) 1925- ... 189
Peyser, Randy 1955- ... 224
Peyton, A(nthony) J(oseph) 1962- ... 147
Peyton, John (Wynne William) 1919- ... 234
Peyton, K. M.
  See Peyton, Kathleen Wendy (Herald)
  See also AAYA 20
  See also CLR 3
  See also DLB 161
  See also SAAS 17
  See also WYA
Peyton, Karen (Hansen) 1897-1960(?) ... CAP-1
  Earlier sketch in CA 9-10
Peyton, Kathleen Wendy (Herald)
  1929- ... CANR-142
  Earlier sketches in CA 69-72, CANR-32, 69
  See also Peyton, K. M.
  See also JRDA
  See also MAICYA 1, 2
  See also SATA 15, 62, 157
  See also YAW
Peyton, Myron A(lvin) 1909-1998 ... 185
  Brief entry ... 114
Peyton, Patrick J(oseph) 1909-1992 ... CANR-75
  Obituary ... 137
  Earlier sketches in CAP-2, CA 23-24
Pezeshki, Charles 1962- ... 203
Pezeshkzad, Iraj 1928- ... 206
Pezzullo, Ralph 1951- ... 135
Pezzulo, Ted 1936(?)-1979
  Obituary ... 89-92
Pezzuti, Thomas Alexander 1936- ... 61-64
Pfadt, Robert Edward 1915- ... 73-76
Pfaff, Daniel W. 1940- ... 136
Pfaff, Richard W(illiam) 1936- ... CANR-61
  Earlier sketch in CA 128
Pfaff, William (Wendle III) 1928- ... CANR-49
  Earlier sketches in CA 5-8R, CANR-24
Pfaffe Konrad fl. c. 1172- ... DLB 148
Pfaffe Lamprecht fl. c. 1150- ... DLB 148
Pfaffenberger, Bryan 1949- ... 118
Pfaffenberger, Clarence J. 1889-1967 ... CAP-1
  Earlier sketch in CA 13-14
Pfahl, John K(erch) 1927- ... CANR-1
  Earlier sketch in CA 1-4R
Pfaltz, Marilyn 1933- ... 103
Pfaltzgraff, Robert L., Jr. 1934- ... CANR-24
  Earlier sketches in CA 21-24R, CANR-9
Pfanner, Helmut Franz 1933- ... CANR-108
  Earlier sketch in CA 57-60
Pfanner, (Anne) Louise 1955- ... 136
  See also SATA 68
Pfanz, Harry W. 1921- ... CANR-109
  Earlier sketches in CA 128, CANR-60
Pfarrer, Donald 1934- ... 111
Pfatteicher, Philip H(enry) 1935- ... 114
Pfau, Hugo 1908-1978 ... 29-32R
Pfau, Richard Anthony 1942- ... 120
Pfeffer, J(ay) Alan 1907- ... CANR-3
  Earlier sketch in CA 1-4R
Pfeffer, Jeffrey 1946- ... 109
Pfeffer, Leo 1910-1993 ... CANR-22
  Earlier sketches in CA 13-16R, CANR-7
Pfeffer, Rose 1908-1985
  Obituary ... 115
Pfeffer, Susan Beth 1948- ... CANR-58
  Earlier sketches in CA 29-32R, CANR-31
  See also AAYA 12, 55
  See also BYA 8
  See also CLR 11
  See also JRDA
  See also MAICYA 2
  See also MAICYAS 1
  See also SAAS 17
  See also SATA 4, 83
  See also WYA
Pfeffer, Wendy 1929- ... CANR-121
  Earlier sketch in CA 146
  See also SATA 78, 142
Pfefferle, Seth 1955- ... 128
Pfeffermann, Guy 1941- ... 25-28R
Pfeifer, Carl J(ames) 1929- ... 49-52
Pfeifer, Luanne 1928- ... CANR-16
  Earlier sketch in CA 89-92
Pfeiffer, Bruce Brooks 1930- ... CANR-123
  Earlier sketches in CA 121, CANR-46
Pfeiffer, C(urtis) Boyd 1937- ... 57-60
Pfeiffer, Carl Curt 1908- ... 101
Pfeiffer, Charles F. 1919-1976 ... CANR-4
  Obituary ... 65-68
  Earlier sketch in CA 1-4R
Pfeiffer, Emily 1827-1890 ... DLB 199
Pfeiffer, Eric 1935- ... CANR-10
  Earlier sketch in CA 13-16R
Pfeiffer, Janet (B.) 1949- ... CANR-124
  Earlier sketch in CA 161
  See also SATA 96
Pfeiffer, John E(dward) 1914-1999 ... 101
Pfeiffer, Karl G(raham) -1984 ... 1-4R
Pfeiffer, Marcella
  See Syracuse, Marcella Pfeiffer
Pfeiffer, Steven I(ra) 1950- ... 213
Pfeiffer, William (Sanborn) 1947- ... 191
Pfeil, (John) Fred(erick) 1949- ... 133
Pfeilschifter, Boniface 1900-1985 ... CAP-2
  Earlier sketch in CA 19-20
Pfenninger, Leslie J. 1955- ... 170
Pferd, William (III) 1922(?)-1987
  Obituary ... 121
Pfiffner, John M(cDonald) 1893-1968 ... 5-8R
Pfingston, Roger 1940- ... CANR-20
  Earlier sketch in CA 104
Pfister, Arthur 1949- ... 45-48
Pfister, Marcus ... 185
  See also CLR 42
  See also MAICYA 2
  See also SATA 83, 150
Pfister, Patrick 1949- ... 153
Pfitsch, Patricia Curtis 1948- ... 222
  See also SATA 148
Pflanze, Otto (Paul) 1918- ... 5-8R
Pflaum, Irving Peter 1906-1985 ... CANR-75
  Obituary ... 115
  Earlier sketch in CA 13-16R
Pflaum, Melanie L(oewenthal) 1909- ... CANR-6
  Earlier sketch in CA 13-16R
Pflaum, Susanna Whitney 1937- ... 110
  Brief entry ... 106
Pflaum-Connor, Susanna
  See Pflaum, Susanna Whitney
Pflieger, Elmer F. 1908- ... 17-20R
Pflieger, Pat 1955- ... 150
  See also SATA 84
Pflock, Karl T. 1943- ... 235
Pflug, Melissa A. 1955- ... 169
Pflum, John (Edward) 1934- ... 186
  Brief entry ... 107
Pfordresher, John 1943- ... 65-68
Pforzheimer, Carl H. 1879-1957 ... DLB 140
Pfouts, Ralph W(illiam) 1920- ... 41-44R
Pfoutz, Shirley Eclov 1922- ... 1-4R
Pfriem, John E. 1923(?)-1983
  Obituary ... 110
Pfuetze, Paul E(ugene) 1904-1985 ... CANR-76
  Obituary ... 118
  Earlier sketch in CA 1-4R
Phaedrus c. 15B.C.-c. 50 ... DLB 211
Phaer, Thomas 1510(?)-1560 ... DLB 167
Phair, Judith Turner 1946- ... 61-64
Phalle, Thibaut de Saint
  See de Saint Phalle, Thibaut
Pham, Andrew X. 1967- ... 186
Phan, Peter C(ho) 1943- ... 114
Phares, Donald 1942- ... 81-84
Phares, Ross (Oscar) 1908- ... CAP-1
  Earlier sketch in CA 11-12
Phares, Timothy B. 1954- ... 97-100
Pharies, David (Arnold) 1951- ... 227
Pharr, Emory Charles 1896(?)-1981
  Obituary ... 104
Pharr, Robert Deane 1916-1992 ... CANR-75
  Obituary ... 137
  Earlier sketches in CA 49-52, CANR-27
  See also BW 1
  See also DLB 33
  See also TCLE 1:2
Pharr, Susan J(ane) 1944- ... 105
Phathanothai, Sirin 1947- ... 147
Phayer, Michael 1935- ... 193
Phelan, Anna Hamilton ... 165
Phelan, Francis (Joseph) 1925- ... CANR-36
  Earlier sketch in CA 5-8R
Phelan, James 1912-1997 ... 144
  Obituary ... 161
Phelan, James Pius X 1951- ... CANR-35
  Earlier sketch in CA 114
Phelan, Jay ... 208
Phelan, John Leddy 1924-1976 ... CANR-12
  Earlier sketch in CA 21-24R
Phelan, John Martin 1932- ... 73-76
Phelan, Josephine 1905- ... SATA-Brief 30
Phelan, Mary Kay 1914- ... CANR-4
  Earlier sketch in CA 1-4R
  See also SATA 3
Phelan, Mary Michenfelder 1936- ... 97-100
Phelan, Nancy 1913- ... 101
Phelan, Shane 1956- ... 137
Phelan, Terence
  See Mangan, (John Joseph) Sherry
Phelan, Terry Wolfe 1941- ... 97-100
  See also SATA 56
Phelan, Thomas Joseph 1940- ... CANR-135
  Earlier sketch in CA 161
Phelan, Tom
  See Phelan, Thomas Joseph
Phelge, Nanker
  See Richards, Keith

Cumulative Index 457 Phillips

Phelps, Anthony 1928- .... EWL 3
Phelps, Arthur Warren 1909-1991 49-52
Phelps, Ashton 1913-1983
Obituary 109
Phelps, Barry 1941- 140
Phelps, Christopher 1965- 171
Phelps, D(udley) Maynard 1897-1993 ... CAP-2
Earlier sketch in CA 25-28
Phelps, Daphne 232
Phelps, Digger
See Phelps, Richard
Phelps, Donald (Norman) 1929- CANR-122
Earlier sketches in CA 45-48, CANR-25
Phelps, Edmund S. 1933- 166
Phelps (Ward), Elizabeth Stuart
See Phelps, Elizabeth Stuart
See also FW
Phelps, Elizabeth Stuart 1815-1852 ... DLB 202, 221
Phelps, Elizabeth Stuart 1844-1911
See Phelps (Ward), Elizabeth Stuart
See also DLB 74
See also TCLC 113
Phelps, Ethel Johnston 1914-1984 106
See also SATA 35
Phelps, Frederic
See McCulley, Johnston
Phelps, Gilbert (Henry, Jr.)
1915-1993 .... CANR-47
Obituary 141
Earlier sketches in CA 5-8R, CANR-7, 26
See also CN 2, 3, 4, 5
Phelps, Humphrey 1927- 111
Phelps, J(oseph) Alfred 1927- 135
Phelps, Jack 1926- 29-32R
Phelps, O(rme) Wheelock 1906-2003 .... 1-4R
Obituary 218
Phelps, Peter 1960- 231
Phelps, Phelps 1897-1981
Obituary 104
Phelps, Richard 103
Phelps, Robert 1922-1989 .... CANR-75
Obituary 129
Earlier sketches in CA 17-20R, CANR-19
Phelps, Roger P(aul) 1920- 49-52
Phelps, Thomas Ross 1929- 61-64
Phenix, Philip Henry 1915-2002 .... 5-8R
Pheto, Molefe 1935- 118
Phialas, Peter George 1914-1999 .... 25-28R
Phibbs, Brendan (Pearse) 1916- 33-36R
Phifer, Kenneth G. 1915- 17-20R
Philalethes
See Butler, Josephine (Elizabeth)
Philander, S. George H. 1942- 172
Philbin, Regis (Francis Xavier) 1933(?)- 197
Philbrick, Allen Kellogg 1914- 117
Philbrick, Charles (Horace) II
1922-1971 .... CANR-4
Earlier sketch in CA 1-4R
Philbrick, Helen L. 1910- 103
Philbrick, Joseph Lawrence 1927- 45-48
Philbrick, Nathaniel 1957(?)- 221
Philbrick, Rodman
See Philbrick, (W.) Rodman
Philbrick, (W.) Rodman 1951- CANR-100
Earlier sketch in CA 171
See also Philbrick, W. R.
See also AAYA 31
See also SATA 122, 163
See also WYAS 1
Philbrick, W. R.
See Philbrick, (W.) Rodman
See also SATA 163
Philbrook, Clem(ent E.) 1917- 104
See also SATA 24
Philby, H(arry) St. John B(ridger)
1885-1960 183
See also DLB 195
Philby, Harold Adrian Russell 1912-1988
Obituary 125
Philby, Kim
See Philby, Harold Adrian Russell
Philip, Cynthia Owen 1928- 49-52
Philip, George 1951- 156
Philip, J(ames) A(llenby) 1901- CAP-2
Earlier sketch in CA 23-24
Philip, John Robert 1927-1999 108
Obituary 181
Philip, Leila 1961- CANR-116
Earlier sketch in CA 137
Philip, Lotte Brand
See Foerster, Lotte B(rand)
Philip, M(arlene) Nourbese 1947- 163
See also BW 3
See also CWP
See also DLB 157
Philipp, Elliot Elias 1915- CANR-3
Earlier sketch in CA 9-12R
Philippatos, George Crito 1938-
Brief entry 106
Philippe, Charles-Louis 1874-1909 191
See also DLB 65
Philippi, Donald L. 1930- 108
Philippide, Alexandru 1900-1979 .... EWL 3
Philips, Ambrose 1674-1749 .... RGEL 2
Philips, Cyril Henry 1912- 103
Philips, G(eorge) Edward 1926- 41-44R
Philips, J. Stanley
See Gibilisco, Stan
Philips, John 1676-1708 .... DLB 95
See also RGEL 2
Philips, Judson (Pentecost)
1903-1989 .... CANR-72
Obituary 128
Earlier sketches in CA 89-92, CANR-14
Interview in CANR-14
See also AITN 1
See also CMW 4
Philips, Katherine 1632-1664 .... DLB 131
See also PC 40
See also RGEL 2
Philips, Michael 1942- 125
Philips, Thomas
See Davies, L(eslie) P(urnell)
Philipsen, Dirk 1959- 139
Philipson, Ilene J. 1950- 219
Philipson, Morris H. 1926- CANR-4
Earlier sketch in CA 1-4R
See also CLC 53
Philipson, Susan Sacher 1934-1994 . CANR-76
Obituary 146
Earlier sketch in CA 9-12R
Philliber, William W(esley) 1943- 111
Phillifent, John Thomas 1916-1976
Obituary 102
See also SFW 4
Phillippi, Wendell Crane 1918- 136
Phillipps, Sidney
See Rehfisch, Hans Jose
Phillipps, Sir Thomas 1792-1872 .... DLB 184
Phillips, Adam CANR-127
Earlier sketch in CA 174
Phillips, Aileen Paul
See Paul, Aileen
Phillips, Alan
See Stauderman, Albert P(hilip)
Phillips, Alan Meyrick Kerr 1916- 5-8R
Phillips, Alice H(erz) 1909-1986 114
Phillips, Allen
See Allen, (Evelyn) Elizabeth
Phillips, Almarin 1925- CANR-1
Earlier sketch in CA 1-4R
Phillips, Anita 182
Phillips, Anne G(arvey) 1929- 73-76
Phillips, Arthur 1969- 205
See also AAYA 65
Phillips, (Elizabeth Margaret Ann) Barty
1933- CANR-24
Earlier sketches in CA 61-64, CANR-8
Phillips, Beeman N(oal) 1927- 122
Phillips, Bernard S. 1931- CANR-12
Earlier sketch in CA 25-28R
Phillips, Bernice Maxine 1925- 45-48
Phillips, Betty Lou
See Phillips, Elizabeth Louise
Phillips, Billie M(cKindra) 1925- 102
Phillips, Bluebell
See Phillips, Bluebell Stewart
Phillips, Bluebell S.
See Phillips, Bluebell Stewart
Phillips, Bluebell Stewart 1904- 131
Phillips, Bob 1940- CANR-124
Earlier sketches in CA 69-72, CANR-68
See also SATA 95
Phillips, C(ecil) E(rnest) Lucas
See Lucas Phillips, C(ecil) E(rnest)
Phillips, Cabell (Beverly Hatchett)
1904-1975 97-100
Obituary 61-64
Phillips, Carl 1959- CANR-104
Earlier sketch in CA 172
See also PFS 23
Phillips, Carla Rahn 1943- CANR-60
Earlier sketch in CA 128
Phillips, Carly
See Drogin, Karen
Phillips, Carole 1938- 108
Phillips, Caryl 1958- CANR-140
Earlier sketches in CA 141, CANR-63, 104
See also BLCS
See also BRWS 5
See also BW 2
See also CBD
See also CD 5, 6
See also CLC 96
See also CN 5, 6, 7
See also DA3
See also DAM MULT
See also DLB 157
See also EWL 3
See also MTCW 2
See also MTFW 2005
See also WLIT 4
See also WWE 1
Phillips, Cecil R(andolph) 1933- 13-16R
Phillips, Celeste R(ose Nagel) 1933- 110
Phillips, Charles F(ranklin), Jr. 1934- .. CANR-2
Earlier sketch in CA 5-8R
Phillips, Charles F(ranklin, Jr.)
1910-1998 85-88
Obituary 167
Phillips, Christopher 1959- 200
Phillips, Claude S., Jr. 1923- 9-12R
Phillips, Clifton J(ackson) 1919- 37-40R
Phillips, Clyde 235
Phillips, (Preswly) Craig 1922- 9-12R
Phillips, D(ennis) J(ohn Andrew)
1924- CANR-60
Earlier sketches in CA 13-16R, CANR-10
See also CMW 4
Phillips, Dale Ray 1955- 230
Phillips, Dale Wesley 1954- .... CSW
Phillips, Dave 1951- 197
Phillips, David Atlee 1922-1988 .... CANR-75
Obituary 126
Earlier sketches in CA 69-72, CANR-12
Phillips, David Graham 1867-1911 176
Brief entry 108
See also DLB 9, 12, 303
See also RGAL 4
See also TCLC 44
Phillips, Debora R(othman) 1939- 93-96
Phillips, Delores 1950- 232
Phillips, Dennis
See Phillips, D(ennis) J(ohn Andrew)
Phillips, Dennis 1951- 141
Phillips, Derek L(ee) 1934- CANR-18
Earlier sketch in CA 33-36R
Phillips, Dewi Zephaniah 1934- CANR-51
Earlier sketches in CA 17-20R, CANR-9, 25
Phillips, Dorothy
See Garlock, Dorothy
Phillips, Dorothy S(anborn) 1893-1972
Obituary 37-40R
Phillips, Dorothy W. 1906-1977
Obituary 73-76
Phillips, Douglas 1929- .... CP 1
Phillips, Douglas A. 1949- 237
See also SATA 161
Phillips, E(lmo) Bryant 1905-1975 ...... CANR-6
Earlier sketch in CA 5-8R
Phillips, E(wing) Lakin 1915-1994 .... CANR-76
Obituary 144
Earlier sketch in CA 37-40R
Phillips, E(ugene) Lee 1941- CANR-40
Earlier sketch in CA 115
Phillips, Edward O. 1931- 124
Phillips, Edwin A(llen) 1915- 53-56
Phillips, Elizabeth C(row) 1906-1980 .... 41-44R
Phillips, Elizabeth Louise .... SATA 58
See also SATA-Brief 48
Phillips, Emma Julia 1900-1991 .... CAP-1
Earlier sketch in CA 13-14
Phillips, Frances Lucas 1896-1986
Obituary 119
Phillips, Frank
See Nowlan, Philip Francis
Phillips, Gary 1955- CANR-102
Earlier sketch in CA 161
Phillips, Gene D(aniel) 1935- CANR-38
Earlier sketches in CA 45-48, CANR-1, 17
Phillips, George H(oward) 1907- 112
Phillips, Gerald M. 1928-1995 .... CANR-29
Earlier sketches in CA 33-36R, CANR-13
Phillips, Gordon Lewis 1911-1982
Obituary 108
Phillips, Hal
See Phillips, Thomas Hal
Phillips, Hal Thomas
See Phillips, Thomas Hal
Phillips, Henry 183
Phillips, Herbert P. 1929- 13-16R
Phillips, Hiram Stone 1912(?)-1979 85-88
Phillips, Hugh D. 1952- 139
Phillips, Irv(ing W.) 1905-2000 .... CANR-31
Obituary 192
Earlier sketch in CA 65-68
See also SATA 11
See also SATA-Obit 125
Phillips, J(ohn) B(ertram)
1906-1982 .... CANR-75
Obituary 108
Earlier sketch in CA 106
Phillips, Jack
See Sandburg, Carl (August)
Phillips, James E(merson, Jr.) 1912-1979 101
Obituary 89-92
Phillips, James E(merson, Jr.) 1912-1979
Obituary 89-92
Phillips, James M(cJunkin) 1929- 106
Phillips, James W. 1922- 33-36R
Phillips, Jayne Anne 1952- CANR-96
Earlier sketches in CA 101, CANR-24, 50
Interview in CANR-24
See also AAYA 57
See also BPFB 3
See also CLC 15, 33, 139
See also CN 4, 5, 6, 7
See also CSW
See also DLBY 1980
See also MTCW 1, 2
See also MTFW 2005
See also RGAL 4
See also RGSF 2
See also SSC 16
See also SSFS 4
Phillips, Jerome C.
See Cleveland, Philip Jerome
Phillips, Jewell Cass 1900-1995 .... CAP-2
Earlier sketch in CA 33-36
Phillips, Jill (Meta) 1952- CANR-39
Earlier sketches in CA 65-68, CANR-14
Phillips, Johanna
See Garlock, Dorothy
Phillips, John 1914-1996 147
Obituary 153
Phillips, John 1950- 194
Phillips, John A(llen) 1949-1998 .... CANR-86
Earlier sketch in CA 133
Phillips, John L(awrence), Jr. 1923- 33-36R
Phillips, Jonathan P. 231
Phillips, Josephine E(lvira Frye)
1896-1975 .... 5-8R
Obituary 61-64
Phillips, Julia (Miller) 1944-2002 140
Obituary 204
Phillips, Julien L(ind) 1945- 77-80
Phillips, Kate 1966- 157
Phillips, Kathleen C(oleman) 1920- .. CANR-39
Earlier sketch in CA 116
Phillips, Keith W(endall) 1946- 102
Phillips, Kenneth J. H. 1946- 143
Phillips, Kevin (Price) 1940- CANR-124
Earlier sketches in CA 65-68, CANR-40
Phillips, Klaus (Peter) 1947- 116
Phillips, L(ouis) C(hristopher) 1939- 57-60
Phillips, Laughlin 1924- 102
Phillips, Leon
See Gerson, Noel Bertram
Phillips, Leona Rasmussen 1925- CANR-14
Earlier sketch in CA 65-68
Phillips, Leroy, Jr. 1935- 232
Phillips, Lisa 1956- 139
Phillips, Lois (Elisabeth) 1926-
Brief entry 114
Phillips, Loretta (Hosey) 1893-1987 ...... CAP-1
Earlier sketch in CA 13-16
See also SATA 10
Phillips, Louis 1942- CANR-20
Earlier sketches in CA 49-52, CANR-3
See also SATA 8, 102
Phillips, Mac
See Phillips, Maurice J(ack)
Phillips, Margaret 1892(?)-1985
Obituary 116
Phillips, Margaret Mann 1906-1987 . CANR-75
Obituary 123
Earlier sketch in CA 13-16R
Phillips, Margaret McDonald 1910(?)-1978
Obituary 77-80
Phillips, Marjorie (Fell) 5-8R
Phillips, Mark
See Garrett, (Gordon) Randall (Phillip) and Janifer, Laurence M(ark)
Phillips, Mary Geisler 1881-1964 .... 5-8R
See also SATA 10
Phillips, Mary L. 1930- 116
Phillips, Maurice J(ack) 1914-1976 .... 5-8R
Obituary 103
Phillips, Max 237
Phillips, Melicia 1960- 149
Phillips, Michael
See Nolan, William F(rancis)
Phillips, Michael 1938- 108
Phillips, Michael Joseph 1937- CANR-18
Earlier sketches in CA 49-52, CANR-3
Phillips, Michael R(ay) 1946- 114
Phillips, (Holly) Michelle 1944- 137
Phillips, Mickey
See Phillips, Alan Meyrick Kerr
Phillips, Mike .... CN 7
Phillips, O(wen) Hood 1907- CANR-2
Earlier sketch in CA 5-8R
Phillips, O(wen) M(artin) 1930- 89-92
Phillips, Osborne
See Barcynski, Leon Roger
Phillips, Patricia 1935- 103
Phillips, Paul 1938- CANR-14
Earlier sketch in CA 73-76
Phillips, Paul T(homas) 1942- 138
Phillips, Pauline (Esther Friedman)
1918- CANR-19
Earlier sketch in CA 1-4R
Phillips, (Woodward) Prentice
1894-1981 .... CAP-1
Earlier sketch in CA 13-16
See also SATA 10
Phillips, R. Hart
See Phillips, Ruby Hart
Phillips, Rachel 1934- 49-52
Phillips, Ray C. 1922- CANR-10
Earlier sketch in CA 25-28R
Phillips, Richard
See Dick, Philip K(indred)
Phillips, Richard C(laybourne) 1934- 65-68
Phillips, Robert (Schaeffer) 1938- CANR-8
Earlier sketch in CA 17-20R
See also CAAS 13
See also CLC 28
See also DLB 105
Phillips, Robert H. 1948- 181
Phillips, Robert L(eRoy), Jr. 1940- 77-80
Phillips, Roderick (Goler) 1947- CANR-94
Earlier sketch in CA 131
Phillips, Rog 1909-1965 .... SFW 4
Phillips, Roger CANR-130
Earlier sketch in CA 171
Phillips, Ruby Hart 1902-1985
Obituary 117
Phillips, Samantha
See Gelles-Cole, Sandi
Phillips, Sian 1934- 214
Phillips, Sky 1921- 140
Phillips, Stella 1927- CANR-11
Earlier sketch in CA 21-24R
Phillips, Stephen 1864-1915
Brief entry 111
See also DLB 10
See also RGEL 2
Phillips, Stephen H. 1950- 160
Phillips, Steve
See Whittington, Harry (Benjamin)
Phillips, Steven 1947- 103
Phillips, Susan Elizabeth CANR-104
Earlier sketch in CA 142
Phillips, Susan S. 1954- 154
Phillips, T. J.
See Savage, Tom
Phillips, Thomas Hal 1922- 222
Phillips, Tom
See Drotning, Phillip T(homas)
Phillips, Tom 1937- CANR-73
Earlier sketch in CA 128
Phillips, Ulrich B(onnell) 1877-1934 184
See also DLB 17
Phillips, Velma 1894-1977 .... CAP-2
Earlier sketch in CA 19-20
Phillips, Vic 1941- 128

Phillips, Ward
See Lovecraft, H(oward) P(hillips)
Phillips, Warren (Henry) 1926- 107
Interview in CA-107
Phillips, Wendell 1921-1975 .... CAP-2
Obituary 61-64
Earlier sketch in CA 23-24
See also DLB 235
Phillips, Willard 1784-1873 .... DLB 59
Phillips, William 1907-2002 .... CANR-82
Obituary 211
Earlier sketches in CA 29-32R, CANR-35
See also DLB 137
Phillips, William G. 1924(?)-1990
Obituary 130
Phillips-Birt, Douglas Hextall Chedzey
1920-1977 .... CANR-1
Earlier sketch in CA 1-4R
Phillips-Jones, Linda 1943- CANR-26
Earlier sketch in CA 109
Phillipson, David 1930- 57-60
Phillipson, David W(alter) 1942- 107
Phillipson, Michael 1940- 133
Phillpotts, (Mary) Adelaide Eden
1896-1993 .... CANR-37
Earlier sketch in CA 115
See also DLB 191
Phillpotts, Eden 1862-1960 .... CANR-85
Obituary 93-96
Earlier sketch in CA 102
See also DLB 10, 70, 135, 153
See also FANT
See also SATA 24
See also SUFW
Philmus, Robert M. 1943- 33-36R
Philo c. 20B.C.-c. 50 .... DLB 176
Philomythes
See Dewart, Leslie
Philp, Howard Littleton 1902- 5-8R
Philp, Kenneth R(oy) 1941- 65-68
Philp, (Dennis Alfred) Peter 1920- 5-8R
Philp, Richard B(lain) 1934- CANR-126
Earlier sketch in CA 154
Philp, Richard Nilson 1943- CANR-11
Earlier sketch in CA 69-72
Philpott, David G(oodwin) 1927- 123
Philpott, Kent 1942- 61-64
Philpott, Tom 1951- 198
Phin
See Thayer, Ernest Lawrence
Phipps, Christine 1945- 123
Phipps, Frances (Lucille Walker) 1924(?)-1986
Obituary 119
Phipps, Grace May Palk 1901- CANR-4
Earlier sketch in CA 9-12R
Phipps, Joe (Kenneth) 1921- 139
Phipps, Joyce 1942- 49-52
Phipps, Marilene 1960- 194
Phipps, Nicholas 1913-1980
Obituary 97-100
Phipps, William E(ugene) 1930- CANR-30
Earlier sketches in CA 29-32R, CANR-12
Phipson, Joan
See Fitzhardinge, Joan Margaret
See also AAYA 14
See also CLR 5
See also SAAS 3
Phiz
See Browne, Hablot Knight
Phleger, Fred B. 1909-1993 .... CANR-21
Earlier sketch in CA 1-4R
See also SATA 34
Phleger, Marjorie Temple 1908(?)-1986 ... 9-12R
Obituary 118
See also SATA 1
See also SATA-Obit 47
Phoenix, John
See Derby, George Horatio
Phoenix, Pat
See Pilkington, Pat
Phrynichus fl. 420B.C.- .... LMFS 1
Phypers, David (John) 1939- 114
Physick, John Frederick 1923- 114
Phythian, B(rian) A(rthur)
1932-1993 .... CANR-10
Earlier sketch in CA 21-24R
Piacentino, Edward J(oseph) 1945- 191
Piaf, Edith 1915-1963
Obituary 113
Piaget, Jean 1896-1980 .... CANR-31
Obituary 101
Earlier sketch in CA 21-24R
See also MTCW 1, 2
See also SATA-Obit 23
Pian, Rulan Chao 1922- CANR-94
Earlier sketch in CA 21-24R
Piano, Celeste
See Lykiard, Alexis (Constantine)
Piasecki, Bruce 1955- CANR-12
Earlier sketch in CA 69-72
Piatigorsky, Alexander 1929- 124
Piatigorsky, Gregor 1903-1976
Obituary 69-72
Piatt, Bill
See Piatt, Robert William, Jr.
Piatt, Robert William, Jr. 1950- 146
Piatti, Celestino 1922- CANR-81
Earlier sketch in CA 73-76
See also SATA 16
Piazza, Ben 1934-1991 .... 9-12R
Piazza, Thomas (Leonard) 182
Piazza, Tom 1955- 155

Picano, Felice 1944- 225
Earlier sketches in CA 69-72, CANR-11, 27, 52, 91
Autobiographical Essay in 225
See also CAAS 13
See also DAM POP
See also GLL 1
Picard, Barbara Leonie 1917- CANR-58
Earlier sketches in CA 5-8R, CANR-2
See also CWRI 5
See also MAICYA 1, 2
See also SAAS 10
See also SATA 2, 89
Picard, Elizabeth 1944- 158
Picard, Robert G(eorge) 1951- 127
Picardie, Ruth 1964-1997 229
Picasso, Pablo (Ruiz) 1881-1973 97-100
Obituary 41-44R
See also AAYA 10
Picazo, Jose 1910- CAP-1
Earlier sketch in CA 13-14
Piccard, Auguste 1884-1962 157
Obituary 113
Piccard, Bertrand 1958- 195
Piccard, Betty
See Piccard, Elizabeth J(ane)
Piccard, Elizabeth J(ane) 1925- 65-68
Piccard, Jacques 1922- 65-68
Piccard, Joan Russell 29-32R
Picchi, Blaise 1946- 179
Picchio, Riccardo 1923- CANR-24
Earlier sketch in CA 45-48
Piccioni, Giuseppe 1953- 208
Piccirilli, Thomas Edward 1965- CANR-140
Earlier sketch in CA 171
Piccirilli, Tom
See Piccirilli, Thomas Edward
Picco, Giandomenico 1948- 195
Piccoli, (Jacques Daniel) Michel 1925- 208
Piccolo, Lucio 1901-1969 97-100
See also CLC 13
See also DLB 114
See also EWL 3
Pichaske, David R(ichard) 1943- CANR-96
Earlier sketches in CA 45-48, CANR-1
Pichette, Henri 1924-2000 .... DLB 321
Pichois, Claude 1925- 132
Pick, Hella 160
Pick, J(ohn) B(arclay) 1921- CANR-5
Earlier sketch in CA 1-4R
Pick, John 1911-1981 .... CAP-2
Earlier sketch in CA 33-36
Pick, (Frederick) Michael 1949- 123
Pick, Robert 1898-1978 .... CANR-8
Obituary 77-80
Earlier sketch in CA 17-20R
Pickard, Charles 1932- .... SATA 36
Pickard, Dorothea Wilgus 1902-1986 ... 21-24R
Pickard, John Benedict 1928- 1-4R
Pickard, John Q.
See Borg, Jack
Pickard, Nancy 1945- CANR-73
Earlier sketch in CA 153
See also CMW 4
Pickard, Tom 1946- CANR-83
Earlier sketches in CA 81-84, CANR-44
See also CP 1, 2, 3, 4, 5, 6, 7
See also DLB 40
Pickell, Charles N(orman) 1927- 17-20R
Pickell, David 225
Pickem, Peter
See Stearns, Harold Edmund
Picken, Mary Brooks 1886(?)-1981
Obituary 103
Picken, Stuart D(onald) B(lair) 1942- 106
Pickens, Cathy
See Anderson, S. Catherine
Pickens, Donald Kenneth 1934- 53-56
Pickens, Robert S. 1900(?)-1978
Obituary 81-84
Pickens, Roy 1939- 57-60
Pickens, T. Boone, Jr. 1928- 147
Picker, Fred 1927- 81-84
Picker, Ingrid 1932- 25-28R
Picker, Martin 1929- CANR-7
Earlier sketch in CA 17-20R
Pickerell, Albert G(eorge) 1912-1999 .... 25-28R
Pickerill, Don 1928- 77-80
Pickering, David (Hugh) 1958- CANR-122
Earlier sketch in CA 139
Pickering, Eileen Marion
See Falcon, Mark
Pickering, Ernest 1893(?)-1974
Obituary 53-56
Pickering, Frederick Pickering 1909-1981 .. 105
Pickering, George (White) 1904-1980 73-76
Obituary 105
Pickering, George W. 1937-2002 136
Pickering, James H(enry) 1937- CANR-53
Earlier sketches in CA 33-36R, CANR-13, 29
Pickering, James Sayre 1897-1969 ... CANR-16
Obituary 103
Earlier sketch in CA 1-4R
See also SATA 36
See also SATA-Obit 28
Pickering, Jerry V(ane) 1931- 57-60
Pickering, Paul 1952- 138
Pickering, Percival
See Stirling, Anna Maria Diana Wilhelmina (Pickering)
Pickering, R(obert) E(aston) 1934- 21-24R
Pickering, Robert B. 1950- 158
See also SATA 93
Pickering, Sam
See Pickering, Samuel F(rancis), Jr.
See also CSW

Pickering, Samuel F(rancis), Jr. 1941- 208
See also Pickering, Sam
Pickering, Stephen 1947- 57-60
Pickersgill, J(ohn) W(hitney) 1905-1997 .. 45-48
Pickett, Calder M. 1921- 53-56
Pickett, Carla 1944- 37-40R
Pickett, J(arrell) Waskom 1890-1981 ..... CAP-1
Earlier sketch in CA 13-16
Pickett, Rex 1952- 239
Pickett, Robert S. 1931- 33-36R
Pickett, William B. 1940- 198
Pickford, Cedric Edward 1926-1983 107
Obituary 109
Pickford, Mary 1893-1979
Obituary 85-88
Pickle, Hal B(rittain) 1929- CANR-21
Earlier sketches in CA 57-60, CANR-6
Pickles, (Maud) Dorothy 1903-1994 77-80
Pickles, M(abel) Elizabeth 1902- CAP-1
Earlier sketch in CA 9-10
Pickles, Wilfred 1904-1978(?) 108
Picknett, Lynn 1947- 224
Pickoff, David 1930(?)-1986
Obituary 118
Pickover, Clifford A. 1957- CANR-89
Earlier sketch in CA 141
Pickrel, Paul (Murphy) 1917- 9-12R
Pickstock, Catherine 1970- 186
Pickthall, Marjorie L(owry) C(hristie) 1883-1922
Brief entry 107
See also DLB 92
See also TCLC 21
Pickthorn, Helen 1927- 25-28R
Pickus, Keith H. 199
Pico, Rafael 1912-1998 45-48
Pico della Mirandola, Giovanni
1463-1494 .... LMFS 1
Picon, Molly 1898-1992 104
Picon Salas, Mariano 1901-1965 178
See also HW 2
See also LAW
Picot, Derek 1952- 151
Picott, J(ohn) Rupert 1916(?)-1989
Obituary 129
Picou, Alphonse
See Ghnassia, Maurice (Jean-Henri)
Picoult, Jodi 1966- CANR-138
Earlier sketches in CA 138, CANR-100
See also DLB 292
See also MTFW 2005
Picton, Bernard
See Knight, Bernard
Pidal, Ramon Menendez
See Menendez Pidal, Ramon
Piddock, Jim 1956- 172
Pidgeon, Mary E. 1890(?)-1979
Obituary 89-92
Piechocki, Joachim von Lang
See von Lang-Piechocki, Joachim
Pieczenik, Steve .... BYA 10, 11
Piediscalzi, Nicholas 1931- 122
Brief entry 112
Pied Piper
See Mallalieu, John Percival William
Piehl, Mel (Willis) 1946- 111
Piehler, Paul 1929-
Brief entry 111
Piekalkiewicz, Jaroslaw A. 1926- 81-84
Piel, Gerard 1915-2004 .... CANR-138
Obituary 231
Earlier sketch in CA 57-60
See also DLB 137
Pielichaty, Helena 1955- 213
See also SATA 142
Pielke, Roger A. Sr. 186
Pielmeier, John 1949- CANR-79
Brief entry 125
Earlier sketch in CA 132
Interview in CA-132
See also CAD
See also CD 5, 6
See also DLB 266
Pienkowski, Jan (Michal) 1936- CANR-38
Earlier sketches in CA 65-68, CANR-11
See also CLR 6
See also MAICYA 1, 2
See also SATA 6, 58, 131
Pieper, Josef 1904-1997 .... CANR-44
Earlier sketch in CA 119
Piepkorn, Arthur Carl 1907-1973 .... 41-44R
Pier, Arthur Stanhope 1874(?)-1966
Obituary 25-28R
Pierard, Richard Victor 1934- CANR-38
Earlier sketches in CA 29-32R, CANR-17
Pieratt, Asa B. 1938- 77-80
Pierce, Anne Whitney 1953- 221
Pierce, Arthur 1959- 154
Pierce, Arthur Dudley 1897-1967 .... 1-4R
Obituary 103
Pierce, Bessie Louise 1888-1974
Obituary 53-56
Pierce, Charles P. 1953- 196
Pierce, Chonda 200
Pierce, David 1947- 141
Pierce, E(ugene) 1924- 13-16R
Pierce, Edith Gray 1893-1977 61-64
See also SATA 45
Pierce, Edward T. 1917(?)-1978
Obituary 77-80
Pierce, F(ranklin) David 1947- 153
Pierce, George Gilbert 1923- 5-8R
Pierce, Gerald S(wetnam) 1933- 45-48
Pierce, Gillian Borland 183
Pierce, Glenn
See Dumke, Glenn S.
Pierce, Jack P. 1889-1968 .... IDFW 3, 4
Pierce, James Smith 1930- 21-24R

Pierce, Janis V(aughn) 1934- 45-48
Pierce, Joe E. 1924-1994 .... 33-36R
Pierce, John Leonard, Jr. 1921- 9-12R
Pierce, John Robinson 1910-2002 .... 17-20R
Obituary 205
Pierce, Katherine
See St. John, Wylly Folk
Pierce, Lawrence C(olman) 1936- 85-88
Pierce, Meredith Ann 1958- CANR-106
Earlier sketches in CA 108, CANR-26, 48, 87
See also AAYA 13, 60
See also BYA 5
See also CLR 20
See also FANT
See also JRDA
See also MAICYA 1, 2
See also SATA 67, 127
See also SATA-Brief 48
See also YAW
Pierce, Michael D(ale) 1940- 142
Pierce, Milton Plotz 1933- 106
Pierce, Ovid Williams 1910-1987 ...... CANR-4
Earlier sketch in CA 1-4R
Pierce, Patricia (May) 1943- 120
Pierce, Patricia Jobe 1943- CANR-98
Earlier sketch in CA 148
Pierce, Paul 1910-1998 69-72
Pierce, Philip E(arly) 1912-1984 110
Pierce, Richard A(ustin) 1918-2004 .... CANR-2
Obituary 231
Earlier sketch in CA 5-8R
Pierce, Robert
See Drake, Timothy A.
Pierce, Robert N(ash) 1931- 104
Pierce, Ronald K. 1944- 142
Pierce, Roy 1923-(?) 37-40R
Pierce, Ruth (Ireland) 1936- 29-32R
See also SATA 5
Pierce, Sharon
See McCullough, Sharon Pierce
Pierce, Tamora 1954- CANR-120
Earlier sketches in CA 118, CANR-69
See also AAYA 26
See also BYA 8
See also MAICYA 2
See also SATA 51, 96, 153
See also SATA-Brief 49
See also YAW
Pierce, Willard Bob 1914-1978 .... 13-16R
Pierce, William L(uther) 1933-2002 184
Obituary 209
Piercy, Josephine Ketcham 1895-1995 .. CAP-1
Earlier sketch in CA 13-16
Piercy, Marge 1936- 187
Earlier sketches in CA 21-24R, CANR-13, 43, 66, 111
Autobiographical Essay in 187
See also CAAS 1
See also BPFB 3
See also CLC 3, 6, 14, 18, 27, 62, 128
See also CN 3, 4, 5, 6, 7
See also CP 1, 2, 3, 4, 5, 6, 7
See also CWP
See also DLB 120, 227
See also EXPP
See also FW
See also MAL 5
See also MTCW 1, 2
See also MTFW 2005
See also PC 29
See also PFS 9, 22
See also SFW 4
Pierik, Robert 1921- 37-40R
See also SATA 13
Pierman, Carol J 1947- 77-80
Pierotti, John 1911-1987 133
Obituary 122
Pierpaoli, Paul G., Jr. 1962- 187
Pierpoint, Katherine 1961- 153
Pierpoint, Robert (Charles) 1925- 107
Interview in CA-107
Pierpont, Claudia Roth 196
Pierre, Andrew J. 1934- CANR-1
Earlier sketch in CA 45-48
Pierre, Clara 1939- 65-68
Pierre, D. B. C.
See Finlay, Peter (Warren)
Pierre, Jose 1927-1999 143
Pierrepont
See Church, William Conant
Pierro, Albino 1916-1995 184
See also DLB 128
Pierrot, George Francis 1898-1980 .... 5-8R
Obituary 103
See also AITN 2
Piers, Maria W(eigl) 1911-1997 .... CANR-8
Obituary 158
Earlier sketch in CA 21-24R
Piers, Robert
See Anthony, Piers
Piersanti, Claudio 1954- 234
Piersen, William D. 1942- CANR-53
Earlier sketch in CA 126
Pierson, Christopher 1956- 149
Pierson, Don 1944- 185
Pierson, Frank
See Pierson, Frank R(omer)
Pierson, Frank R(omer) 1925- 123
Brief entry 114
Interview in CA-123
Pierson, G(eorge) W(ilson)
1904-1993 .... CANR-3
Obituary 143
Earlier sketch in CA 9-12R
Pierson, Howard 1922- 49-52
Pierson, Jan 1937- 112
Pierson, John 221

Cumulative Index 459 Pinkwater

Pierson, John H(erman) G(roesbeck)
1906- CANR-4
Earlier sketch in CA 9-12R
Pierson, Melissa Holbrook 1957- 172
Pierson, Paul Everett 1927- 108
Pierson, Peter O'Malley 1932- 97-100
Pierson, Robert H. 1911-1989 .... 21-24R
Pierson, Stanley 1925- 85-88
Pierson, Stephanie 224
Pierson, William H(arvey), Jr. 1911- 122
Piet, John H(enry) 1914-1992 .... 29-32R
Pietila, Hilkka 183
Pietila, Nellie 1932- 156
Pietri, Arturo Uslar
See Uslar Pietri, Arturo
Pietri, Pedro (Juan) 1943-2004 .... CANR-87
Obituary 225
Earlier sketches in CA 97-100, CANR-32
See also HW 1
See also LLW
Pietrofesa, John J(oseph) 1940- 57-60
Pietropinto, Anthony 1938- 89-92
Pietrusza, David 1949- 135
Pietrzyk, Leslie (Jeanne) 1961- 184
Pietsch, Paul Andrew 1929- 104
Pietschmann, Richard John III 1940- 69-72
Pieyre de Mandiargues, Andre
1909-1991 .... CANR-82
Obituary 136
Earlier sketches in CA 103, CANR-22
See also Mandiargues, Andre Pieyre de
See also EWL 3
See also GFL 1789 to the Present
Pifer, Alan J(ay Parrish) 1921- 127
Pifer, Ellen 1942- CANR-103
Earlier sketches in CA 106, CANR-23
Pig, Edward
See Gorey, Edward (St. John)
Pigg, Kenneth E. 1945- 139
Piggott, C. M.
See Guido, (Cecily) Margaret
Piggott, (Alan) Derek 1923- CANR-37
Earlier sketch in CA 115
Piggott, Stuart 1910-1996 134
Piglia, Ricardo (Emilio) 1941(?)- 230
See also EWL 3
See also LAWS 1
Pigman, William Ward 1910-1977
Obituary 73-76
Pigney, Joseph Pape 1908-1987 .... 1-4R
Pignotti, Lamberto 1926- 184
See also DLB 128
Pihera, Larry 1933- CANR-1
Earlier sketch in CA 45-48
Pihl, Marshall R(alph) 1933- 49-52
Piirto, Jane 1941- 144
Pijewski, John 1952- 111
Piji
See Williams, Ann, Jr.
Pike, Albert 1809-1891 .... DLB 74
Pike, B(arry) A(ustin) 1935- 150
Pike, Bob
See Pike, Robert W(ilson)
Pike, Burton 1930- CANR-33
Earlier sketch in CA 1-4R
Pike, Charles R.
See Bulmer, (Henry) Kenneth and
Harknett, Terry (Williams)
Pike, Charles R.
See Wells, Angus
Pike, Christopher CANR-66
See also McFadden, Kevin Christopher
See also MAICYAS 1
See also WYAS 1
Pike, Dag 1933- 69-72
Pike, Deborah 1951- .... SATA 89
Pike, Diane Kennedy 1938- 37-40R
Pike, Douglas Eugene 1924-2002 153
Obituary 205
Pike, E(dgar) Royston 1896-1980 .... 9-12R
Obituary 125
See also SATA 22
See also SATA-Obit 56
Pike, Eunice V(ictoria) 1913- CANR-20
Earlier sketch in CA 97-100
Pike, James A(lbert) 1913-1969 .... CANR-4
Obituary 25-28R
Earlier sketch in CA 1-4R
Pike, Kenneth Lee 1912-2000 .... CANR-94
Earlier sketches in CA 120, CANR-46
Pike, Margaret (Prudence) Lyford
See Lyford-Pike, Margaret (Prudence)
Pike, Marion
See Marion, Frances
Pike, Nelson C. 1930- 184
Brief entry 111
Pike, Norman 1901-1982 .... CAP-2
Earlier sketch in CA 25-28
Pike, R. William 1956- 156
See also SATA 92
Pike, Rafford
See Peck, Harry Thurston
Pike, Robert E(vording) 1905-1997 .... 5-8R
Obituary 160
Pike, Robert L.
See Fish, Robert L(loyd)
Pike, Robert W(ilson) 1931- 169
See also SATA 102
Pike, Ruth 1931- 134
Brief entry 112
Pike, William H. 1943- 115
Pike, Zebulon Montgomery
1779-1813 .... DLB 183
Pikelny, Philip S. 1951- 107
Pikoulis, John 1941- 113
Pikunas, Justin 1920- 25-28R
Pilapil, Vicente R. 1941- 37-40R
Pilardi, Jo-Ann 1941- 233
Pilarski, Laura 1926- 29-32R
See also SATA 13
Pilat, O. R.
See Pilat, Oliver (Ramsay)
Pilat, Oliver (Ramsay) 1903-1987 .... 5-8R
Obituary 123
Pilbeam, Pamela M. 226
Pilbrow, Richard (Hugh) 1933- 29-32R
Pilcer, Sonia 1949- CANR-119
Earlier sketches in CA 89-92, CANR-13
Interview in CANR-13
Pilch, John J(oseph) 1936- CANR-25
Earlier sketch in CA 108
Pilch, Judah 1902-1986 .... CANR-6
Earlier sketch in CA 5-8R
Pilcher, George William 1935- 105
Pilcher, Robin 1950- 204
Pilcher, Rosamunde 1924- CANR-95
Earlier sketches in CA 57-60, CANR-27, 58
Interview in CANR-27
See also BEST 89:1, 90:4
See also CPW
See also DA3
See also DAM POP
See also MTCW 1
See also RHW
Pilcher, William W. 1930- 45-48
Pilditch, James (George Christopher)
1929-1995 .... 9-12R
Pile, John F(rederick) 1924- CANR-82
Earlier sketches in CA 93-96, CANR-16, 36
Pileggi, Nicholas 1933- CANR-52
Earlier sketch in CA 124
Pilger, John Richard 1939- 141
Pilgrim, Anne
See Allan, Mabel Esther
Pilgrim, David
See Palmer, John (Leslie) and
Saunders, Hilary Aidan St. George
Pilgrim, David 1950- 120
Pilgrim, Geneva Hanna 1914-2000 .... 25-28R
Pilgrim, Walter E(dward) 1934- 113
Piliawsky, Monte 1944- 111
Pilibosian, Helene 1933- 219
Pilinszky, Janos 1921-1981 142
Obituary 104
See also EWL 3
Pilio, Gerone
See Whitfield, John Humphreys
Pilipp, Frank 1961- 141
Pilisuk, Marc 1934- 29-32R
Pilk, Henry
See Campbell, Ken
Pilkey, Dav(id Murray, Jr.) 1966- CANR-122
Earlier sketch in CA 136
See also CLR 48
See also MAICYA 2
See also SATA 68, 115
Pilkey, Orrin H. 1934- CANR-127
Earlier sketches in CA 97-100, CANR-40
Pilkington, Betty 69-72
Pilkington, Cynthia
See Horne, Cynthia Miriam
Pilkington, E(dward) C(ecil) A(rnold)
1907- CAP-2
Earlier sketch in CA 25-28
Pilkington, Francis Meredyth 1907- CAP-2
Earlier sketch in CA 25-28
See also SATA 4
Pilkington, John, Jr. 1918- 17-20R
Pilkington, John 1948- 235
Pilkington, Pat 1923-1986 123
Obituary 120
Pilkington, Roger (Windle)
1915-2003 .... CANR-5
Obituary 216
Earlier sketch in CA 1-4R
See also SATA 10
See also SATA-Obit 144
Pilkington, Walter (?)-1983
Obituary 109
Pilkington, William T(homas, Jr.)
1939- CANR-8
Earlier sketch in CA 61-64
Pill, Erastes
See Madsen, (Mark) Hunter
Pill, Virginia 1922- 61-64
Pillai, Karnam Chengalvaroya 1901-1970 . 5-8R
Pillar, James Jerome 1928- 13-16R
Pillat, Ion 1891-1945 .... DLB 220
See also EWL 3
Pillecijn, Filip de 1891-1962 .... EWL 3
Pillemer, David B. 1950- 233
Piller, Charles 1955- 237
Pillin, William 1910-1985 .... 9-12R
Obituary 116
See also CP 1, 2
Pilling, Ann 1944- .... CWRI 5
Pilling, Arnold R(emington) 1926- CANR-3
Earlier sketch in CA 1-4R
Pilling, Christopher Robert 1936- CANR-91
Earlier sketches in CA 101, CANR-19, 44
See also CP 2, 3, 4, 5, 6, 7
Pilling, John 1946- 153
Pillinger, Douglass 1906(?)-1983
Obituary 111
Pillon, Nancy Bach 1917- 110
Pil'niak, Boris
See Vogau, Boris Andreyevich
See also RGSF 2
See also RGWL 2, 3
Pil'niak, Boris Andreevich
See Vogau, Boris Andreyevich
See also DLB 272
Pilnyak, Boris 1894-1938
See Vogau, Boris Andreyevich
See also EWL 3
See also SSC 48
See also TCLC 23
Pilo, Giuseppe Maria 1929- CANR-5
Earlier sketch in CA 9-12R
Pilon, Jean-Guy 1930- 161
See also DLB 60
Pilon, Juliana Geran 1947- 97-100
Pilou
See Bardot, Louis
Pilpel, Harriet F(leischl) CAP-2
Earlier sketch in CA 21-22
Pilpel, Robert H(arry) 1943- CANR-9
Earlier sketch in CA 65-68
Pim, Sheila 1909-1995 201
Pimentel, David 1925- 167
Pimlott, Ben(jamin John)
1945-2004 .... CANR-81
Obituary 226
Earlier sketch in CA 144
Pimm, Stuart L(eonard) 1949- CANR-109
Earlier sketch in CA 142
Pimsleur, Meira Goldwater
1905(?)-1979 .... 13-16R
Obituary 89-92
Pimsleur, Paul 1927-1976 .... CAP-2
Obituary 65-68
Earlier sketch in CA 33-36
Pina, Laura (?)-1984
Obituary 113
Pina, Leslie A. 1947- 138
Pina-Cabral, Joao de 1954- 136
Pinar, Florencia fl. 15th cent. - .... DLB 286
Pinar, William 1947- 57-60
Pinard, (J. L.-M.) Maurice 1929- 41-44R
Pinch, Richard G. E. 1954- 145
Pinch, Trevor (John) 1952- CANR-143
Earlier sketch in CA 147
Pinchback, Eugene
See Toomer, Jean
Pincher, (Henry) Chapman 1914- CANR-93
Earlier sketches in CA 13-16R, CANR-12, 34
Pincherle, Alberto 1907-1990 .... CANR-142
Obituary 132
Earlier sketches in CA 25-28R, CANR-33, 63
See also Moravia, Alberto
See also CLC 11, 18
See also DAM NOV
See also MTCW 1
See also MTFW 2005
Pincherle, Marc 1888-1974
Obituary 49-52
Pinchin, Jane Lagoudis 1942- 69-72
Pinchot, Ann (Kramer) -1998 .... CANR-4
Earlier sketch in CA 1-4R
Pinchot, David 1914(?)-1983
Obituary 109
See also SATA-Obit 34
Pinciss, Gerald M. 1936- 222
Pinckney, Catherine L(arkum) 17-20R
Pinckney, Cathey
See Pinckney, Catherine L(arkum)
Pinckney, Darryl 1953- CANR-79
Earlier sketch in CA 143
See also BW 2, 3
See also CLC 76
Pinckney, Edward R(obert) 1924- 17-20R
Pinckney, Eliza Lucas 1722-1793 .... DLB 200
Pinckney, Josephine (Lyons Scott) 1895-1957
Brief entry 107
See also DLB 6
Pincus, Edward R. 1938- CANR-12
Earlier sketch in CA 33-36R
Pincus, Fred L. 1942- 233
Pincus, Gregory Goodwin 1903-1967
Obituary 113
Pincus, Harriet 1938- 102
See also SATA 27
Pincus, Jonathan H. 1935- 213
Pincus, Joseph 1919-1997 .... 25-28R
Pincus, Lily 1898-1981 .... CANR-5
Obituary 105
Earlier sketch in CA 53-56
Pinczes, Elinor J(ane) 1940- 149
See also SATA 81
Pindar 518(?)B.C.-438(?)B.C. .... AW 1
See also CDWLB 1
See also DLB 176
See also PC 19
See also RGWL 2
Pindar, Peter
See Wolcot, John
See also RGWL 3
Pindell, Terry 1947- 133
Pinder, Chuck
See Donson, Cyril
Pinder, John H(umphrey) M(urray) CANR-39
Earlier sketches in CA 9-12R, CANR-3, 18
Pinder, Leslie Hall
See Hall, Leslie
Pindyck, Robert (Stephen) 1945- 89-92
Pine, Leslie Gilbert 1907-1987 .... 13-16R
Obituary 122
Pine, Nicholas 1951- 155
See also SATA 91
Pine, Robert 1928- 129
Pine, Theodore
See Petaja, Emil (Theodore)
Pine, Tillie S(chloss) 1896-1999 69-72
See also SATA 13
Pine, William
See Harknett, Terry (Williams)
Pineau, Gisele 1956- .... EWL 3
Pineau, Roger 1916-1993 .... 25-28R
Obituary 143
Pineda, Cecile 1942- 118
See also CLC 39
See also DLB 209
Pineiro, R. J. 1961- CANR-120
Earlier sketch in CA 152
Pinelli, Tullio 1908- .... IDFW 3, 4
Pineo, Ronn 1954- 196
Pinera, Virgilio 1912-1979 131
See also EWL 3
See also HW 1
Pinero, Arthur Wing 1855-1934 153
Brief entry 110
See also DAM DRAM
See also DLB 10
See also RGEL 2
See also TCLC 32
Pinero, Miguel (Antonio Gomez)
1946-1988 .... CANR-90
Obituary 125
Earlier sketches in CA 61-64, CANR-29
See also CAD
See also CLC 4, 55
See also DLB 266
See also HW 1
See also LLW
Pines, Ayala Malach 1945- 193
Pines, Dinora 1918-2002 218
Pines, Maya 13-16R
Pines, Paul (Andre) 1941- 112
Ping, Charles J. 1930- 17-20R
Pingeot, Mazarine 1974- 228
Pinget, Robert 1919-1997 85-88
Obituary 160
See also CLC 7, 13, 37
See also CWW 2
See also DLB 83
See also EWL 3
See also GFL 1789 to the Present
Pini, Richard (Alan) 1950- 150
See also AAYA 12
See also SATA 89
Pini, Wendy 1951- CANR-78
Earlier sketch in CA 150
See also AAYA 12
See also SATA 89
Pinion, F(rancis) B(ertram)
1908-1997 .... CANR-52
Earlier sketches in CA 25-28R, CANR-12, 28
Pinka, Patricia G(arland) 1935- 126
Pinker, Steven Arthur 1954- CANR-108
Earlier sketch in CA 150
Pinkerton, Edward C(askin) 1911-1985 108
Pinkerton, James R(onald) 1932- CANR-24
Earlier sketch in CA 45-48
Pinkerton, Jan 1934-
Brief entry 112
Pinkerton, Joan Trego 1928- 107
Pinkerton, Kathrene Sutherland (Gedney)
1887-1967 .... 1-4R
Obituary 103
See also SATA-Obit 26
Pinkerton, Marjorie Jean 1934- 45-48
Pinkerton, Robert E(ugene) 1882-1970
Obituary 29-32R
Pinkerton, Todd 1917- 69-72
Pinkerton, W. Anson
See Steele, Henry
Pinkett, Harold T(homas) 1914-2001 .... 29-32R
Pinkett, Jada
See Smith, Jada Pinkett
Pink Floyd
See Barrett, (Roger) Syd and
Gilmour, David and Mason, Nick and
Waters, Roger and
Wright, Rick
Pinkham, Mary Ellen 1946- CANR-141
Earlier sketch in CA 101
Pinkney, Alphonso 1929- 25-28R
Pinkney, Andrea Davis 1963- CANR-113
Earlier sketch in CA 185
See also CWRI 5
See also MAICYA 2
See also SATA 113, 160
Pinkney, (Jerry) Brian 1961- .... CLR 54
See also CWRI 5
See also MAICYA 2
See also MAICYAS 1
See also SATA 74, 148
Pinkney, David H(enry) 1914-1993 .... 9-12R
Obituary 146
Pinkney, Edward 1802-1828 .... DLB 248
Pinkney, Gloria Jean 1941- .... SATA 85
Pinkney, J. Brian
See Pinkney, (Jerry) Brian
Pinkney, Jerry 1939- .... CLR 43
See also MAICYA 1, 2
See also MAICYAS 1
See also SAAS 12
See also SATA 41, 71, 107, 151
See also SATA-Brief 32
Pinkney, John 164
See also SATA 97
Pinkney, Sandra L. 198
See also SATA 128
Pinkowski, Edward 1916- 9-12R
Pinkston, Joe M. 1931- 5-8R
Pinkston, Tristi 1976- 233
Pinkus, Oscar 1927- CANR-27
Earlier sketch in CA 5-8R
Pinkus, Philip 1922- 185
Brief entry 113
Pinkwater, D. Manus
See Pinkwater, Daniel Manus
Pinkwater, Daniel
See Pinkwater, Daniel Manus
Pinkwater, Daniel M.
See Pinkwater, Daniel Manus

Pinkwater, Daniel Manus 1941- CANR-143
Earlier sketches in CA 29-32R, CANR-12, 38, 89
See also AAYA 1, 46
See also BYA 9
See also CLC 35
See also CLR 4
See also CSW
See also FANT
See also JRDA
See also MAICYA 1, 2
See also SAAS 3
See also SATA 8, 46, 76, 114, 158
See also SFW 4
See also YAW
Pinkwater, Manus
See Pinkwater, Daniel Manus
Pinn, Anthony B(ernard) 1964- CANR-130
Earlier sketch in CA 162
Pinna, Giovanni 1939- CANR-4
Earlier sketch in CA 49-52
Pinner, David 1940- CANR-19
Earlier sketch in CA 25-28R
See also CBD
See also CD 5, 6
Pinner, Erna 1896- CAP-1
Earlier sketch in CA 11-12
Pinner, Joma
See Werner, Herma
Pinner, Patty 1957- 235
Pinney, Lucy (Catherine) 1952- 136
Pinney, Peter (Patrick) 1922- 25-28R
Pinney, Roy 1911- CANR-6
Earlier sketch in CA 5-8R
Pinney, Thomas 1932- CANR-101
Earlier sketches in CA 85-88, CANR-21
Pinney, Wilson G(ifford) 1929- 45-48
Pinnock, Winsome 1961- 232
See also CBD
See also CD 5, 6
See also CWD
Pino, E.
See Wittermans, Elizabeth (Pino)
Pino, Jose Ortiz y III
See Ortiz y Pino, Jose III
Pinoak, Justin Willard
See Prosser, H(arold) L(ee)
Pinon, Nelida 1937- 175
See also CWW 2
See also DLB 145, 307
See also EWL 3
See also LAWS 1
Pinsdorf, Marion K(atheryn) 1932- 124
Pinsent, Arthur 1888- CAP-2
Earlier sketch in CA 29-32
Pinsent, Gordon (Edward) 1930- 106
Pinsker, Sanford 1941- CANR-60
Earlier sketches in CA 33-36R, CANR-12, 31
Pinsky, Robert 1940- CANR-138
Earlier sketches in CA 29-32R, CANR-58, 97
See also CAAS 4
See also AMWS 6
See also CLC 9, 19, 38, 94, 121
See also CP 7
See also DA3
See also DAM POET
See also DLBY 1982, 1998
See also MAL 5
See also MTCW 2
See also MTFW 2005
See also PC 27
See also PFS 18
See also RGAL 4
See also TCLE 1:2
Pinson, Hermine (Dolorez) 1953- CANR-87
Earlier sketch in CA 153
See also BW 2
Pinson, William M(eredith), Jr. 1934- . CANR-9
Earlier sketch in CA 17-20R
Pinstrup-Andersen, Per 1939- 221
Pinta, Harold
See Pinter, Harold
Pintak, Larry 1955- 132
Pintauro, Joseph 1930- 81-84
Pintel, Gerald 1922- CANR-4
Earlier sketch in CA 49-52
Pinter, Harold 1930- CANR-112
Earlier sketches in CA 5-8R, CANR-33, 65
See also BRWR 1
See also BRWS 1
See also CBD
See also CD 5, 6
See also CDBLB 1960 to Present
See also CLC 1, 3, 6, 9, 11, 15, 27, 58, 73, 199
See also CP 1
See also DA
See also DA3
See also DAB
See also DAC
See also DAM DRAM, MST
See also DC 15
See also DFS 3, 5, 7, 14
See also DLB 13, 310
See also EWL 3
See also IDFW 3, 4
See also LMFS 2
See also MTCW 1, 2
See also MTFW 2005
See also RGEL 2
See also TEA
See also WLC
Pinter, Walter S. 1928- 102
Pinthus, Kurt 1886-1975 194
Pinti, Pietro 1927- 237
Pintner, Walter McKenzie 1931- 21-24R
Pinto, David 1937- 61-64
Pinto, Edward Henry 1901-1972 .... CAP-1
Earlier sketch in CA 13-14
Pinto, Fernao Mendes 1509(?)-1583 ... DLB 287
Pinto, John A. 1948- CANR-54
Earlier sketch in CA 127
Pinto, Peter
See Berne, Eric (Lennard)
See also CCA 1
Pinto, Ricardo 1961- 224
Pinto, Vivian de Sola 1895-1969 ...... CANR-10
Earlier sketch in CA 5-8R
Pinto-Correia, Clara 174
Pintoff, Ernest 1931-2002 .... 17-20R
Obituary 203
Pintoro, John 1947- 103
Pinxten, Hendrik
See Pinxten, Rik
Pinxten, Rik 1947- CANR-94
Earlier sketch in CA 131
Pioneer
See Yates, Raymond F(rancis)
Piontek, Heinz 1925- CANR-34
Earlier sketches in CA 25-28R, CANR-13
See also DLB 75
See also EWL 3
Piore, Michael J(oseph) 1940- 130
Piotrow, Phyllis Tilson 1933- 122
Piotrowski, Andrew 1939- 131
Piotrowski, Tadeusz
See Piotrowski, Thaddeus M.
Piotrowski, Thaddeus M. 1940- CANR-115
Earlier sketch in CA 151
Piovene, Guido 1907-1974 97-100
Obituary 53-56
See also EWL 3
Piowaty, Kim Kennelly 1957- 115
See also SATA 49
Piozzi, Hester Lynch (Thrale) 1741-1821 .... DLB 104, 142
Pipa, Arshi 1920- CANR-10
Earlier sketch in CA 25-28R
Piper, Adrian (Margaret Smith) 1948- 193
Piper, Anson C(onant) 1918-2004 .... 41-44R
Obituary 224
Piper, David (Towry) 1918-1990 147
Piper, Don Courtney 1932- CANR-15
Earlier sketch in CA 41-44R
Piper, Eileen 1906- 122
Piper, H(enry) Beam 1904-1964 .... CANR-79
Obituary 110
Earlier sketch in CA 117
See also DLB 8
See also SFW 4
Piper, H(erbert) W(alter) 1915- 5-8R
Piper, Henry Dan 1918- 17-20R
Piper, Jim 1937- 97-100
Piper, Jon Kingsbury 1957- 140
Piper, Otto A(lfred) 1891-1982 .... 5-8R
Piper, Roger
See Fisher, John (Oswald Hamilton)
Piper, Watty 137
See also DLB 22
See also MAICYA 1, 2
Piper, William Bowman 1927- CANR-12
Earlier sketch in CA 61-64
Pipes, Daniel 1949- CANR-92
Earlier sketch in CA 145
Pipes, Richard (Edgar) 1923- CANR-88
Earlier sketch in CA 158
Pipher, Mary (Bray) 1947- CANR-121
Earlier sketches in CA 145, CANR-72
See also AAYA 39
See also MTFW 2005
Pipin
See Ferreras, Francisco
Pippert, Wesley Gerald 1934- 53-56
Pippett, (Winifred) Aileen 1895-1974 .... CAP-1
Earlier sketch in CA 13-14
Pippin, Frank Johnson 1906-1968 .... CAP-2
Earlier sketch in CA 19-20
Pippin, Robert B. 1948- 130
Pipping, Ella (Geologica) 1897- 61-64
Piquefort, Jean
See Routhier, Adolphe Basil
Piquet, Howard S(amuel) 1903-1983 .... CANR-16
Obituary 111
Earlier sketches in CAP-2, CA 19-20
Piquet-Wicks, Eric 1915- 5-8R
Pirages, Dennis (Clark) 1942- 116
Pirandello, Luigi 1867-1936 .... CANR-103
Brief entry 104
Earlier sketch in CA 153
See also DA
See also DA3
See also DAB
See also DAC
See also DAM DRAM, MST
See also DC 5
See also DFS 4, 9
See also DLB 264
See also EW 8
See also EWL 3
See also MTCW 2
See also MTFW 2005
See also RGSF 2
See also RGWL 2, 3
See also SSC 22
See also TCLC 4, 29
See also WLC
See also WLIT 7
Piraro, Dan 1958- 225
Pirckheimer, Caritas 1467-1532 .... DLB 179
Pirckheimer, Willibald 1470-1530 ...... DLB 179
Pires, Joe
See Stout, Robert Joe
Pires, Jose Cardoso 1925-1998
See Cardoso Pires, Jose (Augusto Neves)
See also DLB 287
See also EWL 3
Pirie, Bruce A. 1953- 231
Pirie, David (Alan Tarbat) 1946- CANR-139
Earlier sketches in CA 97-100, CANR-21
Pirie, N(orman) W(ingate) 1907- 29-32R
Pirie-Gordon, (Charles) Harry (Clinton) 1883(?)-1969
Obituary 104
Pirkle, John Paul 1958- 178
Pirmantgen, Pat
See Pirmantgen, Patricia H.
Pirmantgen, Patricia H. 1933- 45-48
Pirner, Connie White 1955- .... SATA 72
Piro, Richard 1934- 49-52
See also SATA 7
Pirogov, Peter A. 1920-1987
Obituary 121
Pirone, Pascal P(ompey) 1907-2003 .... 9-12R
Obituary 214
Pirosh, Robert 1910-1989
Obituary 130
Pirot, Alison Lohans
See Lohans, Alison
Pirsig, Robert M(aynard) 1928- CANR-74
Earlier sketches in CA 53-56, CANR-42
See also CLC 4, 6, 73
See also CPW 1
See also DA3
See also DAM POP
See also MTCW 1, 2
See also MTFW 2005
See also SATA 39
Pirson, Sylvain J. 1905-1983 .... 5-8R
Pirtle, Caleb (Jackson) III 1941- CANR-26
Earlier sketches in CA 69-72, CANR-11
Pirtle, Carol J(une) 1938- 187
Pisan, Christine de
See de Pisan, Christine
Pisano, Ronald G(eorge) 1948- CANR-44
Earlier sketches in CA 102, CANR-20
Pisar, Samuel 1929- CANR-27
Earlier sketch in CA 29-32R
See also DLBY 1983
Pisarev, Dmitrii Ivanovich
See Pisarev, Dmitry Ivanovich
See also DLB 277
Pisarev, Dmitry Ivanovich 1840-1868
See Pisarev, Dmitrii Ivanovich
Pisemsky, Aleksei Feofilaktovich 1821-1881 .... DLB 238
Piserchia, Doris (Elaine) 1928- CANR-79
Brief entry 107
Earlier sketch in CA 125
See also SFW 4
Pishkin, Vladimir 1931- CANR-24
Earlier sketch in CA 45-48
Pisier, Marie-France 1944- 208
Pisk, Paul A(madeus) 1893-1990 .... CAP-1
Earlier sketch in CA 13-14
Pismire, Osbert
See Hivnor, Robert
Pisor, Robert (Louis) 1939- 109
Pistole, Elizabeth (Smith) 1920- CANR-8
Earlier sketch in CA 17-20R
Piston, Walter 1894-1976
Obituary 69-72
Piston, William Garrett 1953- 191
Pistone, Joseph D. 1939(?)- 171
Piszkiewicz, Dennis 1941- 186
Pita
See Rendon, Maria
Pitas, I(oannis) 1957- 213
Pitavy, Francois L(ouis) 1934- 73-76
Pitcairn, Frank
See Cockburn, (Francis) Claud
Pitcairn, Leonora 1912- 21-24R
Pitcher, Caroline (Nell) 1948- CANR-93
Earlier sketch in CA 132
See also SATA 128
Pitcher, Evelyn G(oodenough) 1915- 17-20R
Pitcher, George (Willard) 1925- 21-24R
Pitcher, Gladys 1890-1996 .... CAP-1
Earlier sketch in CA 9-10
Pitcher, Harvey (John) 1936- CANR-3
Earlier sketch in CA 45-48
Pitcher, Oliver 1923(?)- 153
See also BW 2
Pitcher, Robert W(alter) 1918- 29-32R
Pitchford, Kenneth S(amuel) 1931- 104
See also CP 1, 2
Pitino, Rick 1952- 165
Pitkin, Dorothy (Horton) 1899(?)-1972
Obituary 37-40R
Pitkin, Hanna Fenichel 1931- 122
Brief entry 111
Pitkin, Thomas M(onroe) 1901-1988 ..... 17-20R
Pitkin, Timothy 1766-1847 .... DLB 30
Pitkin, Walter, Jr. 1913- 13-16R
Pitman, (Isaac) James 1901-1985 .... CAP-2
Obituary 117
Earlier sketch in CA 29-32
See also SATA-Obit 46
Pitot, Genevieve 197
Pitre, Felix 1949- .... SATA 84
Pitrone, Jean Maddern 1920- CANR-89
Earlier sketches in CA 17-20R, CANR-8
See also SATA 4
Pitseolak, Peter 1902-1973 93-96
Pitsula, James (Michael) 1950- 137
Pitt, Barrie (William Edward) 1918- .. CANR-20
Earlier sketch in CA 5-8R
Pitt, David C(harles) 1938- CANR-37
Earlier sketches in CA 29-32R, CANR-16
Pitt, David G(eorge) 1921- 126
Pitt, Jeremy
See Wynne-Tyson, (Timothy) Jon (Lyden)
Pitt, Peter (Clive Crawford) 1933- 33-36R
Pitt, Valerie Joan 1925- 5-8R
Pitt-Aikens, Tom 1940-1999 131
Pittenger, W(illiam) Norman 1905-1997 .... CANR-20
Obituary 159
Earlier sketches in CA 1-4R, CANR-5
Pitter, Ruth 1897-1992 .... CAP-1
Obituary 137
Earlier sketch in CA 13-14
See also CP 1, 2
See also DLB 20
See also EWL 3
Pitt-Kethley, Fiona 1954- 129
See also CP 7
See also CWP
Pittman, David J(oshua) 1927- CANR-6
Earlier sketch in CA 5-8R
Pittman, Helena Clare 1945- .... SATA 71
Pittock, Joan (Hornby) 1930- CANR-26
Earlier sketch in CA 107
Pittock, Murray (G. H.) 1962- 138
Pitt-Rivers, Julian Alfred 1919-2001 101
Obituary 199
Pitts, Denis (Trewin) 1930-1994 65-68
Obituary 145
Pitts, Leonard J., Jr. 1957- 238
Pitts, Michael R. 1947- CANR-93
Earlier sketch in CA 146
Pitts, Robert F. 1908-1977
Obituary 69-72
Pittwood, James Beattie
See Ritchie, (Harry) Ward
Pitz, Henry C(larence) 1895-1976 ...... CANR-9
Obituary 69-72
Earlier sketch in CA 9-12R
See also SATA 4
See also SATA-Obit 24
Pitzer, Sara 1938- 107
Pivar, David J. 1933- 45-48
Piven, Frances Fox 1932- 49-52
Piven, Joshua L. 1971- 200
Piver, M. Steven 1934- 138
Pix, Mary (Griffith) 1666-1709 .... DLB 80
Pixerecourt, (Rene Charles) Guilbert de 1773-1844 .... DLB 192
See also GFL 1789 to the Present
Pixley, Jorge V. 1937- CANR-37
Earlier sketches in CA 45-48, CANR-1, 16
Pizarnik, Alejandra 1936-1972 .... DLB 283
Pizarro (de Rayo), Agueda 1941- CANR-87
Earlier sketch in CA 131
See also HW 1
Pizer, Donald 1929- CANR-123
Earlier sketch in CA 9-12R
Pizer, Harry F(rancis) 1947- 101
Pizer, John 1953- 152
Pizer, Vernon 1918- CANR-4
Earlier sketch in CA 1-4R
See also SATA 21
Piziks, Steven 236
Pizzat, Frank J(oseph) 1924- 49-52
Pizzey, Erin 1939- CANR-129
Earlier sketches in CA 81-84, CANR-61
See also RHW
Pizzo, Peggy 1946- 118
Pjerrou, Mary 1945- 137
Pla, Josefina 1909-1999 .... DLB 290
Pla, Josep 1897-1981
Obituary 103
Plaatje, Sol(omon) T(shekisho) 1878-1932 .... CANR-79
Earlier sketch in CA 141
See also BLCS
See also BW 2, 3
See also DLB 125, 225
See also TCLC 73
Place, Irene Magdaline (Glazik) 1912- CANR-1
Earlier sketch in CA 1-4R
Place, Janey Ann 1946- 73-76
Place, Marian T(empleton) 1910- CANR-20
Earlier sketches in CA 1-4R, CANR-5
See also SATA 3
Place, Milner 1930- 150
Place, Robin (Mary) 1926- .... SATA 71
Placere, Morris N.
See Gupta, S(ushil) (Kumar)
Placet, Leroi 1901-1970
Obituary 29-32R
Placksin, Sally 1948- 111
Placzek, Adolf Kurt 1913-2000 112
Obituary 189
Plagemann, (William) Bentz 1913-1991 .... CANR-81
Obituary 134
Earlier sketches in CA 1-4R, CANR-4
Plagens, Peter (L.) 1941- 187
Brief entry 107
Plager, Sheldon J. 1931- 25-28R
Plaidy, Jean
See Hibbert, Eleanor Alice Burford
Plain, Belva 1919- CANR-107
Earlier sketches in CA 81-84, CANR-14, 29, 53
Interview in CANR-29
See also BEST 89:4
See also CPW
See also DA3
See also DAM POP
See also RHW
See also SATA 62
Plaine, Alfred R. 1898(?)-1981
Obituary 105
See also SATA-Obit 29

Cumulative Index 461 Plympton

Plaister, Ted
See Plaister, Theodore H.
Plaister, Theodore H. 1923- 185
Brief entry 113
Plait, Philip C. 1964(?)- 211
Plaja, Guillermo Diaz
See Diaz Plaja, Guillermo
Plamenatz, John Petrov 1912-1975 .... CANR-5
Earlier sketch in CA 13-16R
Planche, James Robinson 1796-1880 .... RGEL 2
Planchon, Roger 1931- .... DLB 321
Planck, Annika 1941- 139
Planck, Carolyn H(eine) 1910-1986 73-76
Planck, Charles Evans 1896-1987 73-76
Obituary 121
Planck, Max (Karl Ernst Ludwig)
1858-1947 182
Brief entry 115
Planer, Franz 1894-1963 .... IDFW 3, 4
Plank, Emma N(uschi) 1905-1990 .... CAP-2
Obituary 171
Earlier sketch in CA 33-36
Plank, Robert 1907-1983 .... CANR-12
Earlier sketch in CA 25-28R
Plankinton, John (Clark) 1917- 196
Plano, Jack Charles 1921- CANR-39
Earlier sketches in CA 5-8R, CANR-2, 17
Plant, Marcus L(eo) 1911-1984 .... 1-4R
Plant, Raymond 1945- CANR-21
Earlier sketch in CA 29-32R
Plant, Robert 1948- .... CLC 12
Plant, Sadie 1964- 170
Plante, David (Robert) 1940- CANR-82
Earlier sketches in CA 37-40R, CANR-12, 36, 58
Interview in CANR-12
See also CLC 7, 23, 38
See also CN 2, 3, 4, 5, 6, 7
See also DAM NOV
See also DLBY 1983
See also MTCW 1
Plante, (Joseph) Jacques (Omer) 1929-1986
Obituary 118
Brief entry 108
Plante, Julian G(erard) 41-44R
Plantinga, Alvin C. 1932- CANR-11
Earlier sketch in CA 21-24R
See also DLB 279
Plantinga, Leon B(rooks) 1935- 21-24R
Planz, Allen 1937- 53-56
See also CP 1, 2
Plaskovitis, Spyros 1917- .... EWL 3
Plaskow, Judith (Ellen) 1947- CANR-53
Brief entry 108
Earlier sketch in CA 126
See also FW
Plass, Adrian 222
Plastaras, James C(onstantine) 1931- 21-24R
Plate, Andrea 1952- 130
Plate, Andrea Darvi
See Plate, Andrea
Plate, Robert 1918-2005 .... 17-20R
Obituary 239
Plate, Thomas 1944- CANR-46
Earlier sketches in CA 69-72, CANR-23
Platen, August von 1796-1835 .... DLB 90
Plater, Alan (Frederick) 1935- 85-88
See also CBD
See also CD 5, 6
Plater, William M(armaduke) 1945- 85-88
Plath, David W(illiam) 1930- CANR-3
Earlier sketch in CA 9-12R
Plath, Sylvia 1932-1963 .... CANR-101
Earlier sketches in CAP-2, CA 19-20, CANR-34
See also AAYA 13
See also AMWR 2
See also AMWS 1
See also BPFB 3
See also CDALB 1941-1968
See also CLC 1, 2, 3, 5, 9, 11, 14, 17, 50, 51, 62, 111
See also DA
See also DA3
See also DAB
See also DAC
See also DAM MST, POET
See also DLB 5, 6, 152
See also EWL 3
See also EXPN
See also EXPP
See also FL 1:6
See also FW
See also LAIT 4
See also MAL 5
See also MAWW
See also MTCW 1, 2
See also MTFW 2005
See also NFS 1
See also PAB
See also PC 1, 37
See also PFS 1, 15
See also RGAL 4
See also SATA 96
See also TUS
See also WLC
See also WP
See also YAW
Platig, E(mil) Raymond 1924- 37-40R
Plato c. 428B.C.-347B.C. .... AW 1
See also CDWLB 1
See also DA
See also DA3
See also DAB
See also DAC
See also DAM MST
See also DLB 176
See also LAIT 1
See also LATS 1:1
See also RGWL 2, 3
See also WLCS
Plato, Ann 1824(?)-(?) .... DLB 239
Platon 1737-1812 .... DLB 150
Platonov, Andrei
See Klimentov, Andrei Platonovich
Platonov, Andrei Platonovich
See Klimentov, Andrei Platonovich
See also DLB 272
Platonov, Andrey Platonovich
See Klimentov, Andrei Platonovich
See also EWL 3
Platov, Mariquita (Villard) 1905-2000 .... 5-8R
Platt, Anthony M. 1942- 25-28R
Platt, Charles 1945- CANR-80
Earlier sketches in CA 21-24R, CANR-24
See also DLB 261
See also SFW 4
Platt, Christopher
See Platt, D(esmond) C(hristopher St.) M(artin)
Platt, Colin (Peter Sherard) 1934- 152
Platt, D(esmond) C(hristopher St.) M(artin) 1934-1989
Obituary 129
Brief entry 109
Platt, David 1903-1992 152
Platt, Eugene (Robert) 1939- CANR-104
Earlier sketches in CA 49-52, CANR-3
Platt, Frederick 1946- 61-64
Platt, Gerald M. 1933- CANR-17
Earlier sketch in CA 97-100
Platt, Harlan D. 1950- 123
Platt, Harrison Gray 1902-1992 .... 41-44R
Platt, James R. 1972- 232
Platt, Jennifer (Ann) 1937- 29-32R
Platt, John Rader 1918-1992 .... 17-20R
Obituary 138
Platt, Kin 1911- CANR-11
Earlier sketch in CA 17-20R
See also AAYA 11
See also CLC 26
See also JRDA
See also SAAS 17
See also SATA 21, 86
See also WYA
Platt, Lyman De 1943- 102
Platt, Michael 1942- 122
Platt, Peter G(odfrey) 1961- 170
Platt, Randall (Beth) 1948- 144
See also AAYA 44
See also SATA 95
Platt, Richard 1953- 191
See also SATA 120
Platt, Rutherford 1894-1975
Obituary 61-64
Platt, Rutherford H. 1940- 148
Platt, Washington 1890-1965 .... 1-4R
Obituary 120
Platten, David (P.) 219
Platten, Thomas George 1899- CAP-1
Earlier sketch in CA 11-12
Plattner, Andy 231
Platts, Beryl 1918- 61-64
Platzker, David 1965- 201
Plauger, P(hillip) J(ames) 1944- 57-60
Plaut, Allene Talmey 1903-1986
Obituary 118
Plaut, Eric A. 1927- 147
Plaut, Joshua Eli 1957- 157
Plaut, Thomas F(ranz) A(lfred) 1925-2004 .... 25-28R
Obituary 229
Plaut, W(olf) Gunther 1912- CANR-17
Earlier sketches in CA 5-8R, CANR-2
Plautus c. 254B.C.-c. 184B.C. .... AW 1
See also CDWLB 1
See also DC 6
See also DLB 211
See also RGWL 2, 3
Plawin, Paul 1938- 89-92
Player, Gary (Jim) 1935- CANR-108
Earlier sketch in CA 101
Player, Ian 1927- 49-52
Playfair, Giles 1910-1996 133
Playfair, Guy Lyon 1935- CANR-47
Earlier sketches in CA 106, CANR-23
Playfellow, Robin
See Ellis, Edward S(ylvester)
Playford, John fl. 1647-1684 .... DLB 170
Playsted, James
See Wood, James Playsted
Pleasant, Barbara 232
Pleasants, Henry, Jr. 1884-1963 .... 1-4R
Pleasants, Henry 1910-2000 107
Obituary 188
Pleasants, Samuel A(ugustus III) 1918- 77-80
Plecas, Jennifer 1966- .... SATA 84, 149
Pleck, Elizabeth
See Pleck, Elizabeth Hafkin
Pleck, Elizabeth H.
See Pleck, Elizabeth Hafkin
Pleck, Elizabeth Hafkin 1945- 129
Brief entry 115
Pleck, Joseph H(ealy) 1946- CANR-23
Earlier sketches in CA 57-60, CANR-7
Pleier, Der fl. c. 1250- .... DLB 138
Pleij, Herman 1943- 227
Pleijel, Agneta (Christina) 1940- CANR-117
Earlier sketch in CA 142
See also DLB 257
Plekker, Robert J(ohn) 1929- 69-72
Plemons, Marti 1949- 197
Plendello, Leo
See Saint, Andrew (John)
Plender, Richard O(wen) 1945- 101
Plenzdorf, Ulrich 1934- 186
See also DLB 75
Pleshakov, Constantine 1959- 209
Pleshcheev, Aleksei Nikolaevich 1825(?)-1893 .... DLB 277
Plesko, Les 1954- 147
Pless, Vera 1931- 161
Plessen, Elisabeth (Charlotte Marguerite) 1944- 185
See also DLB 75
Plesset, Isabel R(osahoff) 1912-1985 103
Plesur, Milton 1927-1987 .... CANR-24
Earlier sketch in CA 45-48
Pletcher, Barbara A. 1946- 123
Pletcher, David M(itchell) 1920- 1-4R
Pletcher, Eldon L(ee) 1922- 133
Pletnev, Petr Aleksandrovich 1792-1865 .... DLB 205
Pletsch, Carl (Erich) 1943- 137
Pleydell, Susan
See Senior, Isabel J(anet Couper Syme)
Pliatzky, Leo 1919-1999 218
Plick et Plock
See Simenon, Georges (Jacques Christian)
Plieksane, Elza Rozenberga
See Aspazija
Plieksans, Janis
See Rainis, Janis
Plievier, Theodor 1892-1955 185
See also DLB 69
Plimmer, Charlotte 1916- 104
Plimmer, Denis 1914-1981 104
Plimpton, George (Ames) 1927-2003 .... CANR-133
Obituary 224
Earlier sketches in CA 21-24R, CANR-32, 70, 103
See also AITN 1
See also CLC 36
See also DLB 185, 241
See also MTCW 1, 2
See also MTFW 2005
See also SATA 10
See also SATA-Obit 150
Plimpton, Ruth Talbot 1916- 13-16R
Pliny the Elder c. 23-79 .... DLB 211
Pliny the Younger c. 61-c. 112 .... AW 2
See also DLB 211
Plischke, Elmer 1914- CANR-40
Earlier sketches in CA 1-4R, CANR-2, 18
Plitt, Jane R. 1948- 232
Plochmann, George Kimball 1914- 5-8R
Ploeg, Johannes P(etrus) M(aria) van der
See van der Ploeg, Johannes P(etrus) M(aria)
Ploeger, Katherine (M.) 1955- 193
Plog, Fred (Thomas III) 1944- CANR-12
Earlier sketch in CA 25-28R
Plog, Stanley C. 1930- CANR-15
Earlier sketch in CA 41-44R
Ploghoft, Milton E(rnest) 1923- 104
Plomer, William Charles Franklin 1903-1973 .... CANR-34
Earlier sketches in CAP-2, CA 21-22
See also AFW
See also BRWS 11
See also CLC 4, 8
See also CN 1
See also CP 1, 2
See also DLB 20, 162, 191, 225
See also EWL 3
See also MTCW 1
See also RGEL 2
See also RGSF 2
See also SATA 24
Plomley, Roy 1914-1985
Obituary 116
Brief entry 107
Plommer, (William) Hugh (?)-1983
Obituary 109
Plopper, Julie Jynelle 1916- 69-72
Ploscowe, Morris 1904-1975 .... CANR-2
Obituary 61-64
Earlier sketch in CA 45-48
Ploss, Sidney I. 1932- 13-16R
Plossl, George W. 1918- 21-24R
Plotinus 204-270 .... CDWLB 1
See also DLB 176
Plotkin, Diane M. 1942- 169
Plotkin, Fred 1956(?)- 237
Plotnick, Alan R(alph) 1926- 17-20R
Plotnick, Charles K(eith) 1931- 114
Plotnicov, Leonard 1930- 21-24R
Plotnik, Arthur 1937- CANR-20
Earlier sketch in CA 69-72
Plotz, Helen Ratnoff 1913-2000 .... CANR-8
Obituary 189
Earlier sketch in CA 9-12R
See also SATA 38
Plourde, Lynn 1955- .... SATA 122
Plous, Scott 1959- 144
Plowden, Alison 1931- CANR-114
Earlier sketches in CA 33-36R, CANR-15
Plowden, David 1932- 33-36R
See also SATA 52
Plowden, G(eoffrey) F(rank) C(hichele) 1929- 116
Plowden, Gene 1906-1985 .... 21-24R
Obituary 117
Plowden, Martha Ward 1948- 166
See also BW 3
See also SATA 98
Plowhead, Ruth Gipson 1877-1967 .... SATA 43
Plowman, E(dward) Grosvenor 1899-1984 .... 13-16R
Plowman, Edward E(arl) 1931- 37-40R
Plowman, Piers
See Kavanagh, Patrick (Joseph)
Plowman, Stephanie 1922- CANR-5
Earlier sketch in CA 53-56
See also CWRI 5
See also SATA 6
Plowright, Teresa 1952- .... DLB 251
Pluckrose, Henry (Arthur) 1931- CANR-120
Earlier sketch in CA 33-36R
See also SATA 13, 141
Pluff, Barbara Littlefield 1926- 5-8R
Plum, J.
See Wodehouse, P(elham) G(renville)
Plum, Jennifer
See Kurland, Michael (Joseph)
Plum, Lester Virgil 1906-1972 .... 1-4R
Obituary 37-40R
Plum, Patrick
See McConville, Michael (Anthony)
Plumb, Barbara Louise Brown 1934- CANR-15
Earlier sketch in CA 89-92
Plumb, Beatrice
See Hunzicker, Beatrice Plumb
Plumb, Charles P. 1900(?)-1982
Obituary 105
See also SATA-Obit 29
Plumb, Charlie
See Plumb, Joseph Charles, Jr.
Plumb, J(ohn) H(arold) 1911-2001 ...... CANR-3
Obituary 202
Earlier sketch in CA 5-8R
Plumb, Joseph Charles, Jr. 1942- CANR-3
Earlier sketch in CA 49-52
Plume, Ilse .... SATA-Brief 43
Plume, Thomas 1630-1704 .... DLB 213
Plumly, Stanley (Ross) 1939- CANR-97
Brief entry 108
Earlier sketch in CA 110
Interview in CA-110
See also CLC 33
See also CP 7
See also DLB 5, 193
Plumme, Don E.
See Katz, Bobbi
Plummer, Alfred 1896-1978 .... 29-32R
Plummer, Ben
See Bingley, David Ernest
Plummer, Beverly J. 1918- 29-32R
Plummer, Brenda Gayle 1946- 202
Plummer, Catharine 1922- 21-24R
Plummer, Clare (Emsley) 1912-1980 .... CANR-87
Earlier sketch in CA 25-28R
Plummer, Kenneth 1946- 73-76
Plummer, L. Gordon 1904-1999 .... CAP-2
Earlier sketch in CA 33-36
Plummer, Margaret 1911- CAP-2
Earlier sketch in CA 25-28
See also SATA 2
Plummer, Mark A(llen) 1929- 37-40R
Plummer, William (Halsey Jr.) 1945- 102
Plummer, William J(oseph) 1927- 53-56
Plumpe, Friedrich Wilhelm 1888-1931
Brief entry 112
See also TCLC 53
Plumpp, Sterling D(ominic) 1940- CANR-24
Earlier sketch in CA 45-48
See also CAAS 21
See also BW 1
See also DLB 41
Plumptre, Arthur Fitzwalter Wynne 1907-1977 109
Obituary 106
Plumstead, A(rthur) William 1933- CANR-11
Earlier sketch in CA 25-28R
Plum-Ucci, Carol .... AAYA 60
See also BYA 16
Plunket, Robert 1945- 115
Plunkett, Charles Hare
See Benson, A(rthur) C(hristopher)
Plunkett, James
See Kelly, James Plunkett
See also CN 4, 5, 6, 7
See also DLB 14
Plunkett, Thomas J. 1921- 33-36R
Plunkett, Walter 1902-1982 .... IDFW 3, 4
Plutarch c. 46-c. 120 .... AW 2
See also CDWLB 1
See also DLB 176
See also RGWL 2, 3
See also TWA
Plutchik, Robert 1927- CANR-11
Earlier sketch in CA 21-24R
Pluto, Terry 1955- CANR-89
Earlier sketch in CA 107
Plutonius
See Mehta, Rustam Jehangir
Plutschow, Herbert Eugen 1939- CANR-18
Earlier sketch in CA 102
Plutzik, Roberta Ann 1948- 110
Plymell, Charles 1935- CANR-11
Earlier sketch in CA 21-24R
See also CAAS 11
See also CP 1
See also DLB 16
Plympton, Bill
See Plympton, William M.
Plympton, William M. 1946- CANR-107
Earlier sketch in CA 110

Poag, James F(itzgerald) 1934-
Brief entry ... 107
Poage, Godfrey Robert 1920-2001 ... 5-8R
Obituary ... 196
Poage, Scott T(abor) 1931- ... 53-56
Poague, Leland A(llen) 1948- ... CANR-6
Earlier sketch in CA 57-60
Pobo, Kenneth 1954- ... CANR-113
Earlier sketch in CA 104
Pochin, Edward (Eric) 1909-1990
Obituary ... 130
Pochljobkin, W. V.
See Pokhlebkin, William (Vassilievich)
Pochmann, Henry A(ugust) 1901-1973 ... 37-40R
Pochmann, Ruth Fouts 1903-1993 ... CAP-2
Earlier sketch in CA 25-28
Pochocki, Ethel (Frances) 1925- ... 143
See also SATA 76
Pocius, Gerald L(ewis) 1950- ... 137
Pocknell, Pauline ... 210
Pocock, Douglas C. D. 1935- ... 129
Pocock, H(ugh) R(aymond) S(pilsbury)
1904- ... 25-28R
Pocock, J(ohn) G(reville) A(gard) 1924- ... 198
Pocock, Nick 1934- ... 53-56
Pocock, Robert
See Pocock, (Henry) Roger (Ashwell)
Pocock, (Henry) Roger (Ashwell)
1865-1941 ... TCWW 1, 2
Pocock, Thomas Allcot Guy 1925- . CANR-103
Earlier sketches in CA 103, CANR-23, 49
Pocock, Tom
See Pocock, Thomas Allcot Guy
Podbielski, Gisele 1918- ... 53-56
Podell, Diane K(opperman) 1931- ... 149
Podell, Janet 1954- ... 124
Podendorf, Illa (E.) 1903(?)-1983 ... CANR-28
Obituary ... 110
Earlier sketch in CA 81-84
See also SATA 18
See also SATA-Obit 35
Podeschi, John B(attista) 1942- ... 110
Podesta, Jose J. 1858-1937 ... DLB 305
Podhajsky, Alois 1898-1973 ... 69-72
Podhoretz, John 1961- ... 239
Podhoretz, Norman 1930- ... CANR-135
Earlier sketches in CA 9-12R, CANR-7, 78
See also AMWS 8
See also CLC 189
Podhradsky, Gerhard 1929- ... 21-24R
Podlecki, Anthony J(oseph) 1936- ... CANR-3
Earlier sketch in CA 49-52
Podmarsh, Rollo
See Salter, Donald P. M.
Podoliak, Boris
See Kostiuk, Hryhory
Podro, Michael (Isaac) 1931- ... CANR-90
Earlier sketch in CA 132
Podrug, Junius 1947- ... 219
Podulka, Fran 1933- ... 49-52
Poduschka, Walter 1922- ... 107
Podwal, Mark 1945- ... CANR-98
Earlier sketch in CA 147
See also SATA 101, 160
Poe, Charlsie 1909- ... CAP-2
Earlier sketch in CA 23-24
Poe, Edgar Allan 1809-1849 ... AAYA 14
See also AMW
See also AMWC 1
See also AMWR 2
See also BPFB 3
See also BYA 5, 11
See also CDALB 1640-1865
See also CMW 4
See also DA
See also DA3
See also DAB
See also DAC
See also DAM MST, POET
See also DLB 3, 59, 73, 74, 248, 254
See also EXPP
See also EXPS
See also GL 3
See also HGG
See also LAIT 2
See also LATS 1:1
See also LMFS 1
See also MSW
See also PAB
See also PC 1, 54
See also PFS 1, 3, 9
See also RGAL 4
See also RGSF 2
See also SATA 23
See also SCFW 1, 2
See also SFW 4
See also SSC 1, 22, 34, 35, 54
See also SSFS 2, 4, 7, 8, 16
See also SUFW
See also TUS
See also WLC
See also WP
See also WYA
Poe, James 1921-1980 ... 113
Obituary ... 93-96
See also DLB 44
Poe, Ty (Christopher) 1975- ... SATA 94
Poen, Monte Mac 1930- ... 107
Poeppel, Ernst 1940- ... 158
Poern, Ingmar 1935- ... 33-36R
Poesch, Jessie (Jean) 1922- ... CANR-109
Earlier sketches in CA 128, CANR-62
Poethen, Johannes 1928-2001 ... 237
Poetker, Frances Jones 1912- ... 85-88
Poet of Titchfield Street, The
See Pound, Ezra (Weston Loomis)
Poetzl, Pamela Major
See Major-Poetzl, Pamela
Poewe, Karla 1941- ... 124
Poey, Delia ... 202
Poganski, Donald J(ohn) 1928- ... 25-28R
Pogany, Andras H(enrik) 1919- ... 21-24R
Pogany, Hortenzia Lers ... 21-24R
Pogany, William Andrew 1882-1955
See Pogany, Willy
See also SATA 44
Pogany, Willy
See Pogany, William Andrew
See also SATA-Brief 30
Poggi, Emil J. 1928- ... 29-32R
Poggi, Gianfranco 1934- ... 85-88
Poggi, Jack
See Poggi, Emil J.
Poggie, John J(oseph), Jr. 1937-
Brief entry ... 107
Poggioli, Renato 1907-1963 ... CANR-2
Earlier sketch in CA 1-4R
Pogodin, Mikhail Petrovich
1800-1875 ... DLB 198
Pogorel'sky, Antonii
See Perovsky, Aleksei Alekseevich
Pogrebin, Letty Cottin 1939- ... CANR-143
Earlier sketches in CA 29-32R, CANR-15, 33
Pogue, Bill
See Pogue, William R.
Pogue, Charles (Edward), Jr. 1950- ... 164
Pogue, Forrest Carlisle 1912-1996 ... CANR-3
Obituary ... 154
Earlier sketch in CA 5-8R
Pogue, William R. 1930- ... 137
Poh, Caroline (Anne) 1938- ... 61-64
Pohanka, Brian C. ... 165
Pohl, Frances K. 1952- ... 219
Pohl, Frederick Julius 1889-1991 ... CANR-27
Earlier sketches in CA 1-4R, CANR-5
Pohl, Frederik 1919- ... 188
Earlier sketches in CA 61-64, CANR-11, 37, 81, 140
Interview in ... CANR-11
Autobiographical Essay in ... 188
See also CAAS 1
See also AAYA 24
See also CLC 18
See also CN 1, 2, 3, 4, 5, 6
See also DLB 8
See also MTCW 1, 2
See also MTFW 2005
See also SATA 24
See also SCFW 1, 2
See also SFW 4
See also SSC 25
Pohl, Janice
See Davidson, MaryJanice
Pohle, Linda C(arol) 1947- ... 45-48
Pohle, Robert W(arren), Jr. 1949- ... 81-84
Pohlen, Jerome 1964(?)- ... 223
Pohlman, Edward 1933- ... 33-36R
Pohlmann, Lillian (Grenfell) 1902-1997 .. 9-12R
See also SATA 11
Pohl-Weary, Emily ... 225
Pohndorf, Richard Henry 1916-1977
Obituary ... 73-76
Pohrt, Tom 1953- ... SATA 67, 152
Poignant, Raymond 1917- ... 29-32R
Poinar, G. O., Jr.
See Poinar, George
Poinar, George 1936- ... 188
Poinar, Roberta ... 202
Poincare, (Jules) Henri 1854-1912 ... 170
Poincelot, Raymond P. 1944- ... 122
Poindexter, Clarence Albert 1902(?)-1984
Obituary ... 111
Poindexter, David 1929- ... 29-32R
Poindexter, Hally Beth Walker 1927-
Brief entry ... 110
Poindexter, Marian J(ean) 1929- ... 29-32R
Poinsett, Alex(ander) Ceasar 1926- ... 29-32R
Pointer, Larry 1940- ... 101
Pointer, Michael 1927- ... 57-60
Pointer, Richard W(ayne) 1955- ... 131
Pointon, Marcia R(achel) 1943- ... 33-36R
Pointon, Robert
See Rooke, Daphne (Marie)
Points, Larry (Gene) 1945- ... 202
See also SATA 133
Poirier, Frank E(ugene) 1940- ... CANR-3
Earlier sketch in CA 49-52
Poirier, Louis 1910- ... CANR-141
Brief entry ... 122
Earlier sketch in CA 126
See also Gracq, Julien
Poirier, Mark Jude ... 202
Poirier, Normand 1928(?)-1981
Obituary ... 102
Poirier, Philip P(atrick) 1920-1979 ... 133
Brief entry ... 113
Poirier, Richard 1925- ... CANR-89
Earlier sketches in CA 1-4R, CANR-3, 40
Poirier-Bures, Simone 1944- ... 153
Poirion, Daniel 1927-1996 ... 221
Pois, Joseph 1905-2001 ... CAP-1
Obituary ... 199
Earlier sketch in CA 13-16
Poitier, Sidney 1927- ... CANR-94
Earlier sketch in CA 117
See also AAYA 60
See also BW 1
See also CLC 26
Poitras, Geoffrey 1954- ... 221
Pojman, Louis P. 1935- ... 221
Pokagon, Simon 1830-1899 ... DAM MULT
See also NNAL
Pok Chong-Hui
See Park Chung Hee
Pokeberry, P. J.
See Mitchell, B(etty) J(o)
Pokhlebkin, V. V.
See Pokhlebkin, William (Vassilievich)
Pokhlebkin, William (Vassilievich) 1923- ... 197
Pokrant, Marvin A. 1943- ... 201
Pokrovsky, Boris Aleksandrovich 1912-
Brief entry ... 109
POLA
See Watson, Pauline
Polacco, Patricia Ann 1944- ... CANR-101
Earlier sketch in CA 185
See also CLR 40
See also CWRI 5
See also MAICYA 2
See also MAICYAS 1
See also SATA 74, 123
Polacek, Karel 1892-1945 ... CDWLB 4
See also DLB 215
Polach, Jaroslav G(eorge) 1914-1993 ... 9-12R
Polack, Albert Isaac 1892- ... CAP-1
Earlier sketch in CA 9-10
Polak, Ada Buch 1914- ... 195
Brief entry ... 111
Polak, Alfred
See Polgar, Alfred
Polak, Jacques Jacobus 1914- ... 104
Polakoff, Keith Ian 1941- ... 49-52
Polakoff, Murray Emanuel 1922- ... 186
Brief entry ... 114
Polakow, Valerie (Suransky) 1950- ... 111
Polan, Dana ... 212
Polanco, Vincente Geigel
See Geigel Polanco, Vicente
Poland, Dorothy (Elizabeth Hayward)
1937- ... CANR-20
Earlier sketch in CA 103
Poland, Larry 1939- ... 101
Poland, Marguerite 1950- ... CWRI 5
Polanski, Roman 1933- ... 77-80
See also CLC 16, 178
Polansky, Norman A. 1918-2002 ... 85-88
Polansky, Ronald M. 1948- ... 144
Polansky, Stephen 1949- ... 202
Polanyi, Michael 1891-1976 ... CANR-28
Obituary ... 65-68
Earlier sketch in CA 81-84
See also DLB 100
Polatnick, Florence T. 1923- ... 29-32R
See also SATA 5
Polcher, Egon
See Anschel, Eugene
Polder, Markus
See Kruss, James
Poldervaart, Arie 1909-1969 ... 1-4R
Obituary ... 103
Pole, J(ack) R(ichon) 1922- ... CANR-8
Earlier sketch in CA 17-20R
Pole, Reginald 1500-1558 ... DLB 132
Polebaum, Elliot E(dward) 1950- ... 107
Poleman, Thomas T(heobald) 1928- ... 13-16R
Polen, Nehemia 193(?)- ... 219
Polenberg, Richard 1937- ... 21-24R
Polese, Carolyn 1947- ... 127
See also SATA 58
Polese, James 1914- ... 152
See also SATA 87
Polese, Marcia Ann 1949- ... 65-68
Polese, Mario 1943- ... 218
Polette, Nancy (Jane) 1930- ... CANR-45
Earlier sketches in CA 57-60, CANR-6, 21
See also SATA 42
Polevoi, Boris
See Kampov, Boris Nikolayevich
Polevoi, Nikolai Alekseevich
1796-1846 ... DLB 198
Polezhaev, Aleksandr Ivanovich
1804-1838 ... DLB 205
Polgar, Alfred 1873-1955 ... EWL 3
Polglase, Van Nest 1898-1968 ... IDFW 3, 4
Polgornek
See Laine, Daniel
Polhamus, Jean Burt 1928- ... 103
See also SATA 21
Polhemus, Robert M(ackinlay) 1935- ... 130
Poli, Bernard 1929- ... 21-24R
Poliakoff, Michael B. 1953- ... 127
Poliakoff, Stephen 1952- ... CANR-116
Earlier sketch in CA 106
See also CBD
See also CD 5, 6
See also CLC 38
See also DLB 13
Poliakov, Leon 1910-1997 ... 104
Obituary ... 163
Police Captain Howard
See Senarens, Luis P(hilip)
Police, The
See Copeland, Stewart (Armstrong) and Sting and Summers, Andrew James
Policoff, Stephen Phillip 1948- ... 145
See also SATA 77
Polidori, John William 1795-1821 ... DLB 116
See also HGG
Polier, Justine Wise 1903-1987 ... 104
Obituary ... 123
Polikoff, Barbara G(arland) 1929- ... 145
See also SATA 77, 162
Polin, Raymond 1918- ... 37-40R
Poling, Daniel Alfred 1884-1968
Obituary ... 93-96
Poling, David 1928- ... CANR-116
Earlier sketch in CA 85-88
Poling(-Kempes), Lesley 1954- ... 136
Polinger, Elliot Hirsch 1898-1970
Obituary ... 104
Polis, A(lbert) Richard 1937- ... CANR-6
Earlier sketch in CA 57-60
Polisar, Barry Louis 1954- ... CANR-92
Earlier sketch in CA 145
See also SATA 77, 134
Polisensky, Josef V. 1915-
Brief entry ... 107
Polish, David 1910-1995 ... 13-16R
Obituary ... 148
Polishook, Irwin H. 1935- ... 21-24R
Polite, Carlene Hatcher 1932- ... CANR-25
Earlier sketch in CA 21-24R
See also BW 1
See also DLB 33
Polite, Frank (C.) 1936- ... CANR-92
Earlier sketch in CA 125
Politella, Dario 1921- ... 13-16R
Politella, Joseph 1910-1975 ... CAP-2
Earlier sketch in CA 21-22
Politi, Leo 1908-1996 ... CANR-47
Obituary ... 151
Earlier sketches in CA 17-20R, CANR-13
See also CLR 29
See also MAICYA 1, 2
See also MAICYAS 1
See also SATA 1, 47
See also SATA-Obit 88
Politicus
See Kulski, Wladyslaw W(szebor)
Politkovskaya, Anna 1958(?)- ... 214
Polito, Robert 1951- ... 152
Polito, Sol 1892-1960 ... IDFW 3, 4
Politzer, Heinrich 1910-1978 ... CANR-3
Obituary ... 81-84
Earlier sketch in CA 5-8R
Politzer, Heinz
See Politzer, Heinrich
Politzer, Robert L. 1921-1998 ... 5-8R
Polivka, Bolek
See Polivka, Boleslav
Polivka, Boleslav 1949- ... 216
Polivy, Janet 1951- ... 115
Poliziano, Angelo 1454-1494 ... WLIT 7
Polizzotti, Mark 1957- ... 152
Poljanski, Hristo Andonov
See Andonov-Poljanski, Hristo
Polk, Cara Saylor 1945- ... CANR-38
Earlier sketch in CA 116
Polk, Dora (Beale) 1923- ... 49-52
Polk, Edwin Weiss 1916- ... 37-40R
Polk, James 1939- ... CANR-23
Earlier sketch in CA 105
Polk, James R. 1937- ... 69-72
Polk, Judd (Knox) 1913(?)-1975
Obituary ... 57-60
Polk, Kenneth 1935- ... CANR-1
Earlier sketch in CA 1-4R
Polk, Mary (Tasker) 1898- ... CAP-1
Earlier sketch in CA 11-12
Polk, Noel E(arl) 1943- ... CANR-49
Earlier sketch in CA 123
Polk, Ralph Lane, Jr. 1940-1985
Obituary ... 118
Polk, Ralph Weiss 1890-1978 ... 37-40R
Obituary ... 77-80
Polk, Stella Gipson 1901-1998 ... CANR-16
Earlier sketch in CA 93-96
Polk, William R(oe) 1929- ... CANR-91
Earlier sketch in CA 25-28R
Polking, Kirk 1925- ... CANR-30
Earlier sketches in CA 29-32R, CANR-12
See also SATA 5
Polkingharn, Anne T(oogood) 1937- ... 109
Polkinghorne, John Charlton
1930- ... CANR-103
Earlier sketch in CA 170
Polkinhorn, Harry 1945- ... CANR-139
Earlier sketch in CA 159
See also CAAS 25
Poll, Richard Douglas 1918- ... 101
Pollack, Cecelia 1909- ... 29-32R
Pollack, Eileen 1956- ... CANR-95
Earlier sketch in CA 138
Pollack, Ervin H(arold) 1913-1972 ... CAP-1
Earlier sketch in CA 13-16
Pollack, (Wilburt) Erwin 1935- ... 49-52
Pollack, Harvey 1913-1981 ... 5-8R
Pollack, Herman 1907- ... 69-72
Pollack, Howard 1952- ... CANR-88
Earlier sketch in CA 145
Pollack, Jack H(arrison) 1915(?)-1984
Obituary ... 113
Pollack, Jill S. 1963- ... 152
See also SATA 88
Pollack, Kenneth M(ichael) 1966- ... 225
Pollack, Marcelo ... 228
Pollack, Merrill S. 1924-1988 ... 5-8R
Obituary ... 124
See also SATA-Obit 55
Pollack, Neal 1970- ... 205
Pollack, Norman 1933- ... 13-16R
Pollack, Peter 1911-1978 ... 81-84
Obituary ... 77-80
Pollack, Rachel 1933- ... 203
Pollack, Rachel (Grace) 1945- ... CANR-106
Earlier sketch in CA 157
See also FANT
See also SFW 4
Pollack, Reginald 1924-2001 ... 37-40R
Obituary ... 202
Pollack, Robert (Elliot) 1940- ... CANR-100
Earlier sketch in CA 159
Pollack, Robert H(arvey) 1927- ... 49-52
Pollack, Sandra (Barbara) 1937- ... CANR-43
Earlier sketch in CA 119

Cumulative Index 463 Pope

Pollack, Seymour V(ictor) 1933- 25-28R
Pollack, William S(helley) CANR-133
Earlier sketch in CA 177
Pollaczek-Geiringer, Hilda
See Geiringer, Hilda
Pollak, Felix 1909-1987 .... CANR-10
Earlier sketch in CA 25-28R
Pollak, Kurt 1919- 29-32R
Pollak, Louis Heilprin 1922- 17-20R
Pollak, Mark 1947- 169
Pollak, Martha D. 1941- 140
Pollak, Michael 1918- CANR-103
Earlier sketches in CA 122, CANR-48
Pollak, Richard 1934- 186
Brief entry 111
Pollak, Vivian R. 1938- 136
Pollan, Michael 206
Pollan, Stephen M(ichael) 1929- 177
Polland, Barbara K(ay) 1939- 73-76
See also SATA 44
Polland, Madeleine A(ngela Cahill)
1918- CANR-91
Earlier sketches in CA 5-8R, CANR-3, 37
See also CWRI 5
See also MAICYA 1, 2
See also RHW
See also SAAS 8
See also SATA 6, 68
Pollard, A(nthony) J(ames) 1941- 132
Pollard, Alfred W(illiam) 1859-1944 184
See also DLB 201
Pollard, Arthur 1922-2002 206
Pollard, David 1942- 123
Pollard, Edward A. 1832-1872 .... DLB 30
Pollard, (Henry) Graham 1903-1976 179
Obituary 69-72
See also DLB 201
Pollard, Helen Perlstein 1946- 146
Pollard, Irina 1939- 150
Pollard, Jack 1926- CANR-58
Earlier sketches in CA 29-32R, CANR-30
Pollard, James E(dward) 1894-1979 ...... CAP-1
Obituary 89-92
Earlier sketch in CA 13-16
Pollard, Jann Lawrence 1942- 210
Pollard, John (Richard Thornhill) 1914- 5-8R
Pollard, (Joseph) Percival 1869-1911 185
See also DLB 71
Pollard, Sidney 1925-1998 .... CANR-91
Obituary 172
Earlier sketches in CA 17-20R, CANR-13, 44
Pollard, T(homas) E(van) 1921- 29-32R
Pollard, William G(rosvenor)
1911-1989 .... CANR-6
Earlier sketch in CA 13-16R
Pollefeyt, Didier 1965- 228
Pollema-Cahill, Phyllis 1958- .... SATA 123
Pollen, Daniel A. 1935- 144
Polley, Judith (Anne) 1938- 129
Polley, Robert L. 1933- 17-20R
Pollin, Burton R(alph) 1916- CANR-113
Earlier sketches in CA 129, CANR-67
Pollinger, Kenneth Joseph 1933- 57-60
Pollini, Francis 1930- CANR-1
Earlier sketch in CA 1-4R
Pollio, Howard R. 1937- 37-40R
Pollitt, Jerome J(ordan) 1934- 21-24R
Pollitt, Katha 1949- CANR-108
Brief entry 120
Earlier sketches in CA 122, CANR-66
See also CLC 28, 122
See also MTCW 1, 2
See also MTFW 2005
Pollitt, Michael G(erald) 1967- CANR-129
Earlier sketch in CA 162
Pollitt, Ronald 1939- 122
Pollitz, Edward A(lan), Jr. 1937- 127
Pollitzer, William S. 1923- 196
Pollock, Bruce 1945- CANR-23
Earlier sketches in CA 57-60, CANR-7
See also SATA 46
Pollock, Dale 1950- CANR-86
Earlier sketch in CA 130
Pollock, David H(arold) 1922-2001 49-52
Obituary 204
Pollock, George 1938- 61-64
Pollock, Harry 1920- 89-92
Pollock, Jackson 1912-1956 .... AAYA 32
Pollock, James K(err) 1898-1968 .... CAP-2
Obituary 29-32R
Earlier sketch in CA 21-22
Pollock, Jerry J. 1941- 220
Pollock, John (Charles) 1923- CANR-40
Earlier sketches in CA 5-8R, CANR-2, 18
Pollock, John 1945- 191
Pollock, John L(eslie) 1940- 37-40R
Pollock, Lansing R. 1943- 162
Pollock, Leland W(ells) 1943- 162
Pollock, Linda A(nne) 1955- CANR-39
Earlier sketch in CA 116
Pollock, Mary
See Blyton, Enid (Mary)
Pollock, Nancy J. 1934- 139
Pollock, Norman H(all), Jr. 1909-1998 .. CAP-2
Earlier sketch in CA 33-36
Pollock, Penny 1935- CANR-116
Earlier sketch in CA 101
See also SATA 44, 137
See also SATA-Brief 42
Pollock, Robert 1930- 45-48
Pollock, Seton 1910- 5-8R
Pollock, (Mary) Sharon 1936- CANR-132
Earlier sketch in CA 141
See also CD 5
See also CLC 50
See also CWD
See also DAC
See also DAM DRAM, MST
See also DFS 3
See also DLB 60
See also FW
Pollock, Sharon 1936- .... CD 6
See also DC 20
Pollock, Ted 1929- 85-88
Pollock, Thomas Clark 1902-1988 .... CAP-2
Obituary 125
Earlier sketch in CA 21-22
Pollock, William 1899-1982
Obituary 110
Pollowitz, Melinda Kilborn 1944- CANR-13
Earlier sketch in CA 77-80
See also SATA 26
Polmar, Norman 1938- 49-52
Polnaszek, Frank P(aul) 1947- 107
Polnay, Peter de
See De Polnay, Peter
Polner, Murray 1928- CANR-49
Earlier sketches in CA 13-16R, CANR-5, 23
See also SATA 64
Polo, Marco 1254-1324 .... WLIT 7
Poloma, Margaret Mary 1943- CANR-58
Earlier sketches in CA 111, CANR-30
Polome, Edgar (Ghislain) C(harles)
1920- CANR-13
Earlier sketch in CA 29-32R
Polon, Linda Beth 1943- CANR-46
Earlier sketches in CA 103, CANR-20
Polonsky, Abraham (Lincoln) 1910-1999 104
Obituary 187
Interview in CA-104
See also CLC 92
See also DLB 26
Polonsky, Antony Barry 1940- 73-76
Polonsky, Arthur 1925- .... SATA 34
Polonsky, Iakov Petrovich 1819-1898 . DLB 277
Polonsky, Michael Jay 1959- CANR-112
Earlier sketch in CA 154
Polony, Raymond
See Machan, Tibor R(ichard)
Polos, Nicholas C(hristopher) 1917- 17-20R
Polotsky, Simeon 1629-1680 .... DLB 150
Polowetzky, Michael 175
Pols, Edward 1919- 9-12R
Polsby, Nelson W(oolf) 1934- CANR-23
Earlier sketches in CA 53-56, CANR-5
Polselli, Joseph 1950- 122
Polseno, Jo 81-84
See also SATA 17
Polsgrove, Carol 1945- 201
Polsky, Abe 1935- 109
Polsky, Andrew J. 1955- 139
Polsky, Howard W. 1928- 25-28R
Polsky, Ned 1928- 25-28R
Polson, John 1965- 215
Polson, Willow A. 222
Polster, James 1947- 152
Poltawska, Wanda (Wiktoria) 1921- 136
Poltoratzky, N(ikolai) P(etrovich) 1921- ... 73-76
Poltroon, Milford
See Bascom, David
Polukhina, Valentina 1936- 135
Polunin, Nicholas (Vladimir) 1909-1997 . 65-68
Polunin, Oleg 1914-1985 85-88
Obituary 117
Polya, George 1887-1985
Obituary 117
Polya, Gyorgy
See Polya, George
Polyanin, Andrey
See Parnok, Sophia (Yakovlevna)
See also GLL 1
Polybius c. 200B.C.-c. 118B.C. .... AW 1
See also DLB 176
See also RGWL 2, 3
Pomada, Elizabeth 1940- CANR-8
Earlier sketch in CA 61-64
Pomaska, Anna 1946- .... SATA 117
Pomerance, Bernard 1940- CANR-134
Earlier sketches in CA 101, CANR-49
See also CAD
See also CD 5, 6
See also CLC 13
See also DAM DRAM
See also DFS 9
See also LAIT 2
Pomerans, Arno
See Pomerans, Arnold J(ulius)
Pomerans, Arnold J(ulius) 1920-2005 129
Obituary 239
Pomerantz, Charlotte 1930- CANR-101
Earlier sketches in CA 85-88, CANR-16, 38
See also CWRI 5
See also MAICYA 2
See also SATA 20, 80
Pomerantz, Edward 1934- 65-68
Pomerantz, Joel 1930- 29-32R
Pomerantz, Sidney I(rving) 1909-1975
Obituary 61-64
Pomeranz, Virginia E. 1925(?)-1986 134
Obituary 120
Pomerleau, Cynthia S(todola) 1943- 73-76
Pomerleau, Ovide F(elix) 1940- CANR-13
Earlier sketch in CA 73-76
Pomeroy, Charles A. 1930- 25-28R
Pomeroy, Earl 1915- 17-20R
Pomeroy, Elizabeth W(right) 1938- ... CANR-32
Earlier sketch in CA 113
Pomeroy, Florence Mary
See Powley, Florence Mary Pomeroy
Pomeroy, Hub(bard)
See Claassen, Harold
Pomeroy, John H(oward) 1918-1985
Obituary 115
Pomeroy, Kenneth B(rownridge) 1907-1975
Obituary 61-64
Pomeroy, Pete
See Roth, Arthur J(oseph)
Pomeroy, Ralph 1926- .... CP 1
Pomeroy, Sarah B(erman) 1938- 65-68
Pomeroy, Wardell B(axter)
1913-2001 .... CANR-1
Obituary 200
Earlier sketch in CA 1-4R
Pomeroy, William J(oseph) 1916- 85-88
Pomfret, Baron
See Dame, Lawrence
Pomfret, John 1667-1702 .... RGEL 2
Pomfret, John Edwin 1898-1981 .... CANR-3
Obituary 105
Earlier sketch in CA 1-4R
Pomfret, Richard 1948- CANR-42
Earlier sketch in CA 112
Pomialovsky, Nikolai Gerasimovich
1835-1863 .... DLB 238
Pomilio, Mario 1921-1990 .... DLB 177
Pommer, Erich 1889-1966 .... IDFW 3, 4
Pommer, Henry F(rancis) 1918- CANR-20
Earlier sketch in CA 1-4R
Pommer, Richard 1930- 137
Pommery, Jean 1932- 101
Pomorska, Krystyna 1928-1986 .... CANR-31
Earlier sketch in CA 41-44R
Pompa, Leon 1933- CANR-7
Earlier sketch in CA 57-60
Pompeia, Raul (d'Avila) 1863-1895 .... DLB 307
Pomper, Gerald M(arvin) 1935- CANR-41
Earlier sketches in CA 9-12R, CANR-5, 19
Pomper, Philip 1936- 77-80
Pompian, Richard O(wen) 1935- CANR-11
Earlier sketch in CA 29-32R
Pompidou, Georges (Jean Raymond) 1911-1974
Obituary 49-52
Pomplun, Tom 238
Pomrenke, Norman E. 1930- 21-24R
Pomroy, Martha 1943- 101
Ponce, Juan Garcia
See Garcia Ponce, Juan
Ponce, Mary Helen 1938- 176
See also DLB 122
See also HW 2
Ponce de Leon, Jose Luis S. 1931- 49-52
Ponce-Montoya, Juanita 1949- 181
See also DLB 122
Pond, Alonzo W(illiam) 1894-1986 .... CANR-1
Earlier sketch in CA 1-4R
See also SATA 5
Pond, Elizabeth (Ann) 129
Pond, Grace (Isabelle) 1910- CANR-5
Earlier sketch in CA 13-16R
Pond, L. W.
See Chute, Robert M.
Ponder, Catherine 1927- CANR-17
Earlier sketches in CA 1-4R, CANR-1
Ponder, James A(lton) 1933- 69-72
Ponder, Patricia
See Maxwell, Patricia
Pondrom, Cyrena N(orman) 1938-
Brief entry 111
Poneman, Daniel 1956- 130
Ponet, John 1516(?)-1556 .... DLB 132
Pong, David (B. P. T.) 1939- 149
Ponge, Francis 1899-1988 .... CANR-86
Obituary 126
Earlier sketches in CA 85-88, CANR-40
See also CLC 6, 18
See also DAM POET
See also DLBY 2002
See also EWL 3
See also GFL 1789 to the Present
See also RGWL 2, 3
Poniatowska, Elena 1933- CANR-107
Earlier sketches in CA 101, CANR-32, 66
See also CDWLB 3
See also CLC 140
See also CWW 2
See also DAM MULT
See also DLB 113
See also EWL 3
See also HLC 2
See also HW 1, 2
See also LAWS 1
See also WLIT 1
Ponicsan, Darryl 1938- CANR-21
Earlier sketch in CA 29-32R
Ponnamperuma, Cyril A. 1923-1994 101
Pons, Josep Sebastia 1886-1962 212
Pons, Maurice 1927- CANR-5
Earlier sketch in CA 53-56
Ponsard, Francois 1814-1867 .... DLB 192
Ponsonby, D(oris) A(lmon)
1907-1993 .... CANR-59
Earlier sketches in CA 5-8R, CANR-2
See also RHW
Ponsonby, Frederick Edward Neuflize
1913-1993 .... 13-16R
Obituary 143
Ponsonby, Laura 1935- 140
Ponsonby, William fl. 1577(?)-1604 .... DLB 170
Ponsot, Marie Birmingham CANR-86
Earlier sketch in CA 9-12R
Pont, Clarice Holt 1907- 5-8R
Ponte, Antonio Jose 1964- 219
Ponte, Lowell (Alton) 1946- 57-60
Ponte, Pierre Viansson
See Viansson-Ponte, Pierre
Pontes, Paulo 1941(?)-1976
Obituary 69-72
Ponti, Carlo 1910- .... IDFW 3, 4
Pontiero, Giovanni 1932- CANR-45
Earlier sketch in CA 29-32R
Pontiflet, Ted 1932- 105
See also SATA 32
Pontiggia, Giuseppe 1934- 211
See also DLB 196
Ponting, Clive 1947(?)- 235
Ponting, Kenneth 1913-1983
Obituary 109
Pontney, Jack A(rthur) 1931- 21-24R
Pontoppidan, Henrik 1857-1943 170
See also DLB 300
See also TCLC 29
Ponty, Maurice Merleau
See Merleau-Ponty, Maurice
Pool, Daniel 182
Pool, David de Sola 1885-1970
Obituary 29-32R
Pool, Elizabeth 1914- 114
Pool, Eugene (Hillhouse) 1943- 85-88
Pool, Ithiel de Sola 1917-1984 .... CANR-14
Obituary 112
Earlier sketch in CA 17-20R
Pool, Phoebe Dorothy 1913-1971 .... 5-8R
Pool, Robert 1955- 196
Pool, Tamar de Sola 1891(?)-1981
Obituary 104
Poole, Elizabeth (Anne) 1969- 233
Poole, Ernest 1880-1950
Brief entry 109
See also DLB 9
Poole, Fiona Farrell
See Farrell, Fiona
Poole, Frederick King 1934- 25-28R
Poole, Gary Thomas 1931- 107
Poole, Gray Johnson 1906- CANR-6
Earlier sketch in CA 5-8R
See also SATA 1
Poole, Herbert (Leslie) 103
Poole, Herbert Edmund 1912-1984
Obituary 115
Poole, John 1786-1872 .... RGEL 2
Poole, (Jane Penelope) Josephine
See Helyar, Jane Penelope Josephine
Poole, Josephine
See Helyar, Jane Penelope Josephine
See also CLC 17
See also SAAS 2
See also SATA 5
Poole, Lynn 1910-1969 .... 5-8R
See also SATA 1
Poole, Peggy 1925- CANR-103
Earlier sketches in CA 107, CANR-24, 49
See also SATA 39
Poole, Peter A(ndrews) 113
Poole, Richard 1945- 135
Poole, Robert M. 1950(?)- 237
Poole, Robert W(illiam), Jr. 1944- 112
Poole, Roger 1939-2003 102
Obituary 221
Poole, Scott 1951- 147
Poole, Seth
See Riemer, George
Poole, Sophia 1804-1891 .... DLB 166
Poole, Stafford 236
Poole, Susan 1926- 114
Poole, Victoria (Simes) 1927- 102
Pooler, Victor H(erbert), Jr. 1924- 13-16R
Pooley, Beverley J(ohn) 1934- 45-48
Pooley, Robert C(ecil) 1898-1978 .... CANR-7
Earlier sketch in CA 5-8R
Pooley, Roger 1947- 115
Poolla, Tirupati Raju
See Raju, Poolla Tirupati
Poolman, Jeremy 205
Poolman, Kenneth 1924- 223
Poon (Andersen), Irene 1941- 219
Poor, Harold Lloyd 1935- 45-48
Poor, Henry Varnum 1888(?)-1970
Obituary 37-40R
Poore, Benjamin Perley 1820-1887 ...... DLB 23
Poore, Charles (Graydon) 1902-1971
Obituary 29-32R
Poorman, Paul Arthur 1930-1992 106
Obituary 136
Poortinga, Y(pe) H. 1939- 202
Poortvliet, Rien 1932- 136
See also SATA 65
See also SATA-Brief 37
Poos, L. R. 1954- 141
Poots-Booby, Edna
See Larsen, Carl
Poovey, W(illiam) A(rthur)
1913-1995 .... CANR-10
Earlier sketch in CA 21-24R
Popa, Stefan 1922-
See Doinas, Stefan Augustin
Popa, Vasko 1922-1991 148
Brief entry 112
See also CDWLB 4
See also CLC 19
See also DLB 181
See also EWL 3
See also RGWL 2, 3
See also TCLC 167
Popcorn, Faith (Beryl) 1947(?)- CANR-80
Earlier sketch in CA 145
See also CPW
Pope, Abbie Hanscom 1858-1894 ...... DLB 140

Pope, Alexander 1688-1744 .... BRW 3
See also BRWC 1
See also BRWR 1
See also CDBLB 1660-1789
See also DA
See also DA3
See also DAB
See also DAC
See also DAM MST, POET
See also DLB 95, 101, 213
See also EXPP
See also PAB
See also PC 26
See also PFS 12
See also RGEL 2
See also WLC
See also WLIT 3
See also WP
Pope, Arthur Upham 1881-1969
Obituary 25-28R
Pope, Carl 1945- 113
Pope, Clifford Hillhouse 1899-1974 .... 1-4R
Obituary 103
Pope, Daniel 1946- 111
Pope, Deborah 136
Pope, Dudley (Bernard Egerton)
1925-1997 .... CANR-59
Obituary 157
Earlier sketches in CA 5-8R, CANR-2
See also RHW
Pope, Edwin 1928- 73-76
Pope, Elizabeth Marie 1917- 49-52
See also SATA 38
See also SATA-Brief 36
Pope, Generoso Paul, Jr. 1927-1988
Obituary 126
Pope, Harrison (Graham), Jr. 1947- 41-44R
Pope, James S. Sr. 1900(?)-1985
Obituary 118
Pope, Jamie 1957- 172
Pope, John Alexander 1906-1982
Obituary 107
Pope, Joya 1943- 124
Pope, Katherine Victoria 1939- 111
Pope, Marcel Cornis
See Cornis-Pope, Marcel (H.)
Pope, Maurice (Wildon Montague)
1926- 69-72
Pope, Michael James 1940- 101
Pope, Paul 1972(?)- 202
Pope, Phyllis Ackerman 1894(?)-1977
Obituary 69-72
Pope, Ray 1924- 29-32R
Pope, Rebecca A. 1955- 167
Pope, Richard Martin 1916- 17-20R
Pope, Robert G(ardner) 1936- 29-32R
Pope, Robert H. 1925- 33-36R
Pope, Thomas Harrington 1913-1999 73-76
Pope, Whitney 1935- 69-72
Pope, Willard Bissell 1903-1988
Obituary 127
Pope Benedict XVI 1927- 234
Pope-Hennessy, James 1916-1974 97-100
Obituary 45-48
Pope-Hennessy, John W(yndham)
1913-1994 .... CANR-83
Obituary 147
Earlier sketches in CA 1-4R, CANR-1, 35
Popenoe, David 1932- CANR-109
Earlier sketches in CA 29-32R, CANR-12, 28, 54
Popenoe, Paul (Bowman)
1888-1979 .... CANR-27
Earlier sketch in CA 1-4R
Popescu, Christine 1930- CANR-80
Earlier sketches in CA 13-16R, CANR-7, 20
See also Pullein-Thompson, Christine
See also CWRI 5
See also SATA 82
Popescu, D. R.
See Popescu, Dumitru Radu
Popescu, Dumitru Radu 1935-
Brief entry 122
See also EWL 3
Popescu, Julian (John Hunter)
1928- CANR-20
Earlier sketches in CA 1-4R, CANR-1
Popescu, Petru (Demetru) 1851-1935 ...... HGG
Popescu-Gopo, Ion 1923-1990 .... IDFW 3, 4
Popham, Arthur Ewart 1889-1970
Obituary 111
Popham, Estelle I. 1906-1984 .... CANR-5
Earlier sketch in CA 1-4R
Popham, Hugh 1920-1996 .... CANR-6
Earlier sketch in CA 5-8R
Popham, Margaret Evelyn 1895(?)-1982
Obituary 106
Popham, Melinda 1944- 49-52
Popham, Peter (Nicholas Home) 1952- 121
Popiel, Elda S(taver) 1915- 57-60
Popkin, Debra 1944- 118
Popkin, Jeremy D(avid) 1948- CANR-137
Earlier sketch in CA 102
Popkin, John William 1909- CAP-1
Earlier sketch in CA 13-14
Popkin, Richard H(enry) 1923-2005 . CANR-91
Obituary 238
Earlier sketch in CA 77-80
Popkin, Roy 1921- 25-28R
Popkin, Samuel L(ewis) 1942- 163
Popkin, Zelda (F.) 1898-1983 .... CANR-90
Popkin, Zelda F. 1898-1983 .... 25-28R
Obituary 109
Poplavsky, Boris 1903-1935 .... DLB 317
Poplawski, Paul 1957- 190
Poploff, Michelle 1956- 135
See also SATA 67
Popov, Aleksandr Serafimovich
See Serafimovich, Aleksandr Serafimovich
Popov, Dusko 1912(?)-1981
Obituary 105
Popov, Evgenii Anatol'evich
See Popov, Yevgeny
See also DLB 285
Popov, Haralan (Ivanov) 1907-1988 ...... 21-24R
Obituary 127
Popov, Linda Kavelin 233
Popov, Mikhail Ivanovich 1742-c.
1790 .... DLB 150
Popov, Yevgeny
See Popov, Evgenii Anatol'evich
See also CLC 59
Popovic, Aleksandar 1929-1996 234
See also DLB 181
Popovic, Nenad D(ushan) 1909-1997 ... CAP-2
Earlier sketch in CA 29-32
Popovic, Tanya
See Popovic, Tatyana (Vladana)
Popovic, Tatyana (Vladana) 1928- 130
Popovsky, Mark 1922- CANR-41
Earlier sketches in CA 102, CANR-19
Popowski, Bert (John) 1904-1982 ..... CANR-17
Earlier sketch in CA 1-4R
Popp, K. Wendy .... SATA 91
Poppe, Fred C(hristoph) 1923- CANR-35
Earlier sketch in CA 114
Poppe, Nicholas N(icolaevich)
1897-1991 73-76
Poppel, Ernst
See Poeppel, Ernst
Poppel, Hans 1942- .... SATA 71
Poppema, Suzanne T. 1948- 154
Popper, Frank J. 1944- CANR-12
Earlier sketch in CA 29-32R
Popper, Karl R(aimund) 1902-1994 .. CANR-61
Obituary 146
Earlier sketches in CA 5-8R, CANR-3, 20
See also DLB 262
See also MTCW 1, 2
Popperwell, Ronald G(eorge) (?)-1983 153
Obituary 111
Poppino, Rollie E(dward) 1922- 13-16R
Popple, James 1927- 107
Poppleton, Marjorie 1895- CAP-1
Earlier sketch in CA 13-14
Popplewell, Jack 1911-1996 .... 9-12R
Obituary 154
Poppo, Francine
See Rich, Francine Poppo
Poquelin, Jean-Baptiste
See Môliere
Porada, Edith 1912-1994 103
Obituary 144
Porath, Jonathan David 1944- 118
Porcari, Constance Kwolek 1933- 33-36R
Porcel, Baltasar 1937- CANR-120
Earlier sketch in CA 154
See also HW 2
Porcellino, John 1968- 227
Porch, Douglas 1944- 107
Porche, Simone (Benda) 1877(?)-1985
Obituary 118
Porcher, Mary F. Wickham
See Bond, Mary Fanning Wickham
Porcino, Jane 1923- 116
Pore, Renate (Elfriede) 1943- 113
Porell, Bruce 1947- 102
Porete, Marguerite (?)-1310 .... DLB 208
Porges, Arthur 1915- .... SFW 4
Porges, Paul Peter 1927- 124
Poriss, Martin 1948- 81-84
Poritz, Lily
See Miller, Lily Poritz
Porkert, Manfred (Bruno) 1933- 131
Porlock, Martin
See MacDonald, Philip
Porosky, P. H. 45-48
Porqueras-Mayo, Alberto 1930- CANR-49
Earlier sketches in CA 45-48, CANR-24
Porsche, Ferdinand (Anton Ernst)
1909-1998 89-92
Obituary 165
Porsche, Ferry
See Porsche, Ferdinand (Anton Ernst)
Port, M(ichael) H. 1930- 69-72
Port, Wymar
See Judy, Will(iam Lewis)
Porta, Antonio 1935-1989
See Paolazzi, Leo
See also DLB 128
See also EWL 3
Portal, Colette 1936- 53-56
See also SATA 6
Portal, Ellis
See Powe, Bruce
Portal, Francis Spencer 1903-1984
Obituary 114
Portalatin, Aida Cartagena 1918- 182
Portale, Alfred 239
Portales, Marco 1948- 225
Porte, Barbara Ann 1943- CANR-124
Earlier sketch in CA 159
See also SATA 57, 93, 152
See also SATA-Brief 45
Porte, Joan 1955- 154
Porte, Joel (Miles) 1933- CANR-24
Earlier sketches in CA 17-20R, CANR-8
Porten, Bezalel 1931- CANR-11
Earlier sketch in CA 25-28R
Porteous, (Leslie) Crichton 1901- 5-8R
Porteous, J(ohn) Douglas 1943- 228
Porter, A(nthony) P(eyton) 1945- 136
See also SATA 68
Porter, Alan
See Clark, Ruth C(ampbell)
Porter, Alan L(eslie) 1945- 115
Porter, Albert Wright 1923- 107
Porter, Alvin
See Rowland, D(onald) S(ydney)
Porter, Andrew 1928- CANR-23
Earlier sketches in CA 53-56, CANR-5
Porter, Andrew P. 1946- 219
Porter, Anna CANR-71
Earlier sketch in CA 130
Porter, Anna Maria 1780-1832 ... DLB 116, 159
Porter, Arthur T(homas) 1924- 5-8R
Porter, Barbara Nevling 1946- CANR-113
Earlier sketch in CA 152
Porter, Bern(ard Harden) 1911- CANR-24
Earlier sketches in CA 21-24R, CANR-9
Porter, Bernard (John) 1941- CANR-49
Earlier sketches in CA 107, CANR-24
Porter, Brian (Ernest) 1928- 25-28R
Porter, Bruce 1938- 124
Porter, Burton F(rederick) 1936- 106
Porter, C(edric) L(ambert) 1905-2000 .... CAP-2
Earlier sketch in CA 23-24
Porter, Carolyn (Jane) 1946- 131
Porter, Charles A(llan) 1932- 21-24R
Porter, Cole 1891-1964
Obituary 93-96
See also DLB 265
See also IDFW 3, 4
Porter, Connie (Rose) 1959(?)- CANR-109
Earlier sketches in CA 142, CANR-90
See also AAYA 65
See also BW 2, 3
See also CLC 70
See also SATA 81, 129
Porter, Darwin (Fred) 1937- CANR-118
Earlier sketches in CA 69-72, CANR-13, 30, 56
Porter, David 1780-1843 .... DLB 183
Porter, David L(indsey) 1941- CANR-101
Earlier sketches in CA 107, CANR-24, 50
Porter, David T. 1928- 17-20R
Porter, Dean A(llen) 1939- 198
Porter, Donald 1939- CANR-19
Earlier sketch in CA 103
Porter, Donald Clayton
See Gerson, Noel Bertram
Porter, Dorothy 182
Porter, Dorothy (Featherstone) 1954- 182
Porter, Edgar A(dwell) 1949- 168
Porter, Edward A. 1936- 21-24R
Porter, Eleanor H(odgman) 1868-1920
Brief entry 108
See also BYA 3
See also DLB 9
See also RHW
Porter, Elias H(ull) 1914- 9-12R
Porter, Eliot (Furness) 1901-1990 ...... CANR-42
Obituary 132
Earlier sketch in CA 5-8R
Porter, Ernest Graham 1889- 1-4R
Porter, Ethel K. 1901- CAP-2
Earlier sketch in CA 21-22
Porter, Fairfield 1907-1975
Obituary 61-64
Porter, Frank W(illiam) III 1947- 97-100
Porter, Gareth 1942- 130
Porter, Gene L. 1935- 25-28R
Porter, Gene(va Grace) Stratton
Brief entry 112
See also Stratton-Porter, Gene(va Grace)
See also BPFB 3
See also CWRI 5
See also RHW
See also TCLC 21
Porter, George 1920-2002 107
Obituary 207
Porter, Glenn 1944- 73-76
Porter, H(arry) Boone 1923-1999 .... CANR-8
Obituary 181
Earlier sketch in CA 5-8R
Porter, H(arry) C(ulverwell) 1927- 33-36R
Porter, Hal 1911-1984 .... CANR-60
Obituary 114
Earlier sketches in CA 9-12R, CANR-3
See also CN 1, 2, 3
See also CP 1, 2
See also DLB 260
See also RGEL 2
See also RGSF 2
See also RHW
Porter, Henry .... DLB 62
Porter, J(ene) M(iles) 1937- CANR-21
Earlier sketch in CA 103
Porter, J(oshua) R(oy) 1921- CANR-88
Earlier sketches in CA 53-56, CANR-5
Porter, Jack Nusan 1944- CANR-44
Earlier sketches in CA 41-44R, CANR-20
Porter, James A(rmer), Jr. 1922- 121
Porter, James A(mos) 1905-1970 155
See also BW 3
Porter, Jane 1776-1850 .... DLB 116, 159
Porter, Janice Lee 1953- .... SATA 68, 108
Porter, Joe Ashby 1942- CANR-112
Earlier sketches in CA 73-76, CANR-12
Porter, John 1919- 21-24R
Porter, Jonathan 1938- 77-80
Porter, Joseph C(harles) 1946- 116
Porter, Joyce 1924-1990 .... CANR-60
Obituary 133
Earlier sketches in CA 17-20R, CANR-8
See also CMW 4
Porter, Judith D(eborah) R(evitch) 1940- .. 81-84
Porter, Katherine Anne 1890-1980 ... CANR-65
Obituary 101
Earlier sketches in CA 1-4R, CANR-1
See also AAYA 42
See also AITN 2
See also AMW
See also BPFB 3
See also CDALBS
See also CLC 1, 3, 7, 10, 13, 15, 27, 101
See also CN 1, 2
See also DA
See also DA3
See also DAB
See also DAC
See also DAM MST, NOV
See also DLB 4, 9, 102
See also DLBD 12
See also DLBY 1980
See also EWL 3
See also EXPS
See also LAIT 3
See also MAL 5
See also MAWW
See also MTCW 1, 2
See also MTFW 2005
See also NFS 14
See also RGAL 4
See also RGSF 2
See also SATA 39
See also SATA-Obit 23
See also SSC 4, 31, 43
See also SSFS 1, 8, 11, 16
See also TCWW 2
See also TUS
Porter, Kathryn
See Swinford, Betty (June Wells)
Porter, Kenneth Wiggins 1905-1981 ... CANR-2
Earlier sketch in CA 5-8R
Porter, Laurence M(inot) 1936- CANR-130
Earlier sketches in CA 107, CANR-23, 47
Porter, Lewis 174
Porter, Lyman W(illiam) 1930- 21-24R
Porter, M. Gilbert 1937- 129
Porter, Margaret Eudine 1905-1975 .... CANR-8
Earlier sketch in CA 57-60
Porter, Mark
See Cox, James Anthony and
Leckie, Robert (Hugh)
Porter, McKenzie 1911- 69-72
Porter, Melinda Camber 1953- 127
Porter, Michael E. 1947- CANR-104
Earlier sketches in CA 105, CANR-22, 47
Porter, Michael Leroy 1947- 118
Porter, Monica 1952- 107
Porter, Peter (Neville Frederick) 1929- 85-88
See also CLC 5, 13, 33
See also CP 1, 2, 3, 4, 5, 6, 7
See also DLB 40, 289
See also WWE 1
Porter, Philip W(iley) 1900-1985 69-72
Obituary 116
Porter, R(obert) Russell 1908-1986
Obituary 120
Porter, Raymond J(ames) 1935- 85-88
Porter, Richard C(orbin) 1931- 9-12R
Porter, Robert 1946- CANR-48
Earlier sketch in CA 122
Porter, Roger B. 1946- 131
Porter, Roger J. 1936- 238
Porter, Roy S. 1946-2002 175
Obituary 209
Porter, S. F.
See Porter, Sylvia (Field)
Porter, Sheena 1935- CANR-80
Earlier sketch in CA 81-84
See also CWRI 5
See also SAAS 10
See also SATA 24
Porter, Spence 1948- 227
Porter, Sue
See Limb, Sue
Porter, Sue 1951- 143
See also SATA 76
Porter, Susan L(oraine) 1941-1993 142
Porter, Sylvia (Field) 1913-1991 .... CANR-82
Obituary 134
Earlier sketch in CA 81-84
Porter, Sylvia F.
See Porter, Sylvia (Field)
Porter, Theodore M(ark) 1953- CANR-50
Earlier sketch in CA 123
Porter, Thomas E. 1928- 29-32R
Porter, W(alter) Thomas, Jr. 1934- 29-32R
Porter, Willard H(all) 1920- 57-60
Porter, William E. 1918- CANR-13
Earlier sketch in CA 69-72
Porter, William Sydney 1862-1910 131
Brief entry 104
See also Henry, O.
See also CDALB 1865-1917
See also DA
See also DA3
See also DAB
See also DAC
See also DAM MST
See also DLB 12, 78, 79
See also MAL 5
See also MTCW 1, 2
See also MTFW 2005
See also TUS
See also YABC 2
Porter, William Trotter 1809-1858 ... DLB 3, 43, 250
Porterfield, Amanda 1947- CANR-104
Earlier sketch in CA 138
Porterfield, Bruce 1925- 21-24R
Porterfield, Nolan 1936- 33-36R

Cumulative Index 465 **Povod**

Portes, Alejandro 1944- CANR-36
Earlier sketches in CA 93-96, CANR-16
Porteus, Stanley D(avid) 1883-1972 . CANR-17
Earlier sketch in CA 1-4R
Portillo (y Pacheco), Jose Lopez
See Lopez Portillo (y Pacheco), Jose
Portillo Trambley, Estela 1927-1998 . CANR-32
See also Trambley, Estela Portillo
See also DAM MULT
See also DLB 209
See also HLC 2
See also HW 1
Portis, Charles (McColl) 1933- CANR-64
Earlier sketches in CA 45-48, CANR-1
See also BPFB 3
See also DLB 6
See also TCWW 1, 2
Portisch, Hugo 1927- CANR-36
Earlier sketch in CA 21-24R
Portland, Charles 1952- 163
Portlock, Rob 1952- 128
Portman, David N(athan) 1937- 45-48
Portner, Hans O. 1955- 161
Portnoy, Howard N. 1946- 81-84
Porto, Tony 1960- .... SATA 153
Portoghesi, Paolo 1931- 108
Portteus, Eleanora Marie Manthei
(?)-1983 .... SATA-Obit 36
Portugal, Franklin H. 1940-
Brief entry 116
Portuges, Paul 1945- 77-80
Portway, Christopher (John) 1923- 57-60
Portz, John 1953- 196
Porush, David H(illel) 1952- CANR-17
Earlier sketch in CA 93-96
Porzecanski, Teresa 1945- .... EWL 3
Porzelt, Paul 1902-1984 108
Posell, Elsa Z(eigerman) -1995 .... CANR-20
Earlier sketches in CA 1-4R, CANR-4
See also SATA 3
Posen, Barry R. 1952- 137
Posener, Georges (Henri) 1906-1988
Obituary 125
Posey, Alexander (Lawrence)
1873-1908 .... CANR-80
Earlier sketch in CA 144
See also DAM MULT
See also DLB 175
See also NNAL
Posey, Carl A(lfred, Jr.) 1933- CANR-30
Earlier sketch in CA 111
Posey, Lee 235
Posey, Sam 1944- 93-96
Posey, Walter B(rownlow) 1900-1988 ... CAP-1
Earlier sketch in CA 13-16
Posin, Daniel Q. 1909-2003 .... CAP-1
Obituary 217
Earlier sketch in CA 13-14
Posin, Jack A. 1900-1995 .... 13-16R
Posnack, Emanuel R. 1897-1989
Obituary 128
Posner, Alice
See Fins, Alice
Posner, Barry Z(ane) 1949- CANR-54
Earlier sketch in CA 111
Posner, David Louis 1938-1985 106
Obituary 117
Posner, Donald 1931-2005 202
Brief entry 115
Posner, Ernst (Maximilian) 1892-1980 ... 41-44R
Obituary 97-100
Posner, Gerald L. 1954- CANR-141
Earlier sketch in CA 147
Posner, Mitchell Jay 1949- 110
Posner, Richard 1944- CANR-20
Earlier sketches in CA 53-56, CANR-5
Posner, Richard A. 1939- CANR-120
Earlier sketch in CA 135
Posner, Steve 1953- 127
Pospelov, Pyotr Nikolayevich 1898-1979
Obituary 85-88
Pospesel, Howard Andrew 1937- 73-76
Pospielovsky, Dimitry V. 1935- 29-32R
Pospisil, J(aroslav) Leopold 1923- 13-16R
Posse, Abel .... CLC 70
Possehl, Gregory L. 1941- 236
Possley, Maurice 1949- 205
Possony, Stefan T(homas) 1913-1995
Obituary 148
Brief entry 117
Post, Austin 1922- 85-88
Post, C(harles) Gordon 1903-1997 .... CAP-1
Earlier sketch in CA 11-12
Post, Elizabeth L(indley) 1920- 49-52
Post, Emily Price 1873-1960 103
Obituary 89-92
Post, Felix 1913-2001 .... 21-24R
Post, Gaines, Jr. 1937- CANR-12
Earlier sketch in CA 73-76
Post, Gaines 1902-1986 .... CAP-1
Earlier sketch in CA 13-14
Post, Henry 1948- 61-64
Post, Homer A(very) 1888-1983 .... CAP-2
Earlier sketch in CA 25-28
Post, J(eremiah) B(enjamin) 1937- 97-100
Post, Jeffrey E. 1954- 167
Post, John F(rederic) 1936- 127
Post, Jonathan F(rench) S(cott)
1947- CANR-37
Earlier sketch in CA 115
Post, Joyce A(rnold) 1939- CANR-8
Earlier sketch in CA 61-64
Post, Marie J. 1919- 111
Post, Melville Davisson 1869-1930 202
Brief entry 110
See also CMW 4
See also TCLC 39
Post, Peggy 1945- 214
Post, Robert C(harles) 1937- CANR-135
Earlier sketch in CA 148
Post, Rose Zimmerman 1926- 230
Post, Steve(n A.) 1944- 103
Postal, Bernard 1905-1981 .... CANR-2
Obituary 103
Earlier sketch in CA 5-8R
Postan, Michael Moissey 1899-1981
Obituary 105
Postans, Marianne c. 1810-1865 .... DLB 166
Posten, Margaret L(ois) 1915- 29-32R
See also SATA 10
Poster, Carol 1956- 118
Poster, Cyril D(ennis) 1924- CANR-7
Earlier sketch in CA 13-16R
Poster, John B. 1939- 29-32R
Poster, Mark 1941- 33-36R
Posteuca, Vasile 1912-1972
Obituary 37-40R
Postgate, John (Raymond) 1922- 148
Postgate, Raymond (William)
1896-1971 .... CANR-3
Obituary 89-92
Earlier sketch in CA 5-8R
See also DLB 276
Posthuma, Sieb 1960- .... SATA 150
Posthumus, Cyril 1918- 104
Postl, Carl
See Sealsfield, Charles
Postlethwait, S(amuel) N(oel) 1918- ... CANR-8
Earlier sketch in CA 17-20R
Postlethwaite, Norman 228
Postlewait, Heidi 235
Postma, Johannes Menne 1935- 135
Postma, Lidia 1952- 101
Postma, Magdalena Jacomina 1908- 65-68
Postma, Minnie
See Postma, Magdalena Jacomina
Postman, Andrew 1961- 147
Postman, Neil 1931(?)-2003 102
Obituary 221
Poston, Larry (A.) 1952- CANR-93
Earlier sketch in CA 138
Poston, Richard W(averly) 1914-2000 65-68
Poston, Ted
See Poston, Theodore Roosevelt Augustus Major
See also DLB 51
Poston, Theodore Roosevelt Augustus Major
1906-1974 125
Obituary 104
See also Poston, Ted
See also BW
Poston, Walker S. Carlos (II) 1961- 193
Posvar, Wesley W(entz) 1925-2001 .... 17-20R
Obituary 201
Posy, Arnold 1894-1986 .... 9-12R
Potash, Betty 1933- 122
Potash, P. Jeffrey 1953- 142
Potash, Robert A(aron) 1921- CANR-19
Earlier sketch in CA 102
Poteet, G(eorge) Howard 1935- CANR-53
Earlier sketches in CA 33-36R, CANR-13, 29
Potekhin, Aleksei Antipovich
1829-1908 .... DLB 238
Pothan, Kap 1929- 29-32R
Potholm, Christian Peter II 1940- 29-32R
Potichnyj, Peter J(oseph) 1930- 41-44R
Potiphar
See Hern, (George) Anthony
Potok, Andrew 1931- CANR-134
Earlier sketch in CA 139
Potok, Chaim 1929-2002 .... CANR-98
Obituary 208
Earlier sketches in CA 17-20R, CANR-19, 35, 64
Interview in CANR-19
See also AAYA 15, 50
See also AITN 1, 2
See also BPFB 3
See also BYA 1
See also CLC 2, 7, 14, 26, 112
See also CLR 92
See also CN 4, 5, 6
See also DA3
See also DAM NOV
See also DLB 28, 152
See also EXPN
See also LAIT 4
See also MTCW 1, 2
See also MTFW 2005
See also NFS 4
See also SATA 33, 106
See also SATA-Obit 134
See also TUS
See also YAW
Potok, Herbert Harold -2002
See Potok, Chaim
Potok, Herman Harold
See Potok, Chaim
Potoker, Edward M(artin) 1931- 33-36R
Potokinov, Bohdan J.
See Krasko, Ivan
Pottebaum, Gerald A. 1934- CANR-5
Earlier sketch in CA 9-12R
Potter, A(lfred) Neal 1915- 13-16R
Potter, (Helen) Beatrix 1866-1943 .. CANR-107
Brief entry 108
Earlier sketch in CA 137
See also BRWS 3
See also CLR 1, 19, 73
See also CWRI 5
See also DLB 141
See also MAICYA 1, 2
See also MTCW 2
See also MTFW 2005
See also SATA 100, 132
See also TEA
See also WCH
See also YABC 1
Potter, Beverly A(nn) 1944- CANR-43
Earlier sketch in CA 119
Potter, Carol 1950- 152
Potter, Carole A. 1940- 123
Potter, Charles E(dward) 1916-1979 61-64
Obituary 135
Potter, Clare J. 1946- 122
Potter, Dan (Scott) 1932- 33-36R
Potter, David 1915- 29-32R
Potter, David Morris 1910-1971 108
See also DLB 17
Potter, Dennis (Christopher George)
1935-1994 .... CANR-61
Obituary 145
Earlier sketches in CA 107, CANR-33
See also BRWS 10
See also CBD
See also CLC 58, 86, 123
See also DLB 233
See also MTCW 1
Potter, Douglas A. 1956- 141
Potter, E. B. 1908-1997 .... 37-40R
Potter, Ellen 1960- 224
Potter, Eloise Fretz 1931- CANR-21
Earlier sketch in CA 105
Potter, Faith
See Toperoff, Sam
Potter, Frank N(ewton) 1911- 130
Potter, G(eorge) W(illiam, Jr.) 1930- 1-4R
Potter, Gail M(ac Leod) 1914-1996 .... 25-28R
Potter, George Richard 1900-1981 .... 5-8R
Potter, Giselle .... SATA 150
Potter, Harry (D.) 1954- 143
Potter, J(im) 1922- 21-24R
Potter, Jack M(ichael) 1936- 41-44R
Potter, James Gerrard 1944- 97-100
Potter, James H(arry) 1912-1978
Obituary 77-80
Potter, James L(ane) 1922- 107
Potter, Jay Hill
See Hanson, Vic(tor) J(oseph)
Potter, Jennifer 1949- 156
Potter, (Ronald) Jeremy 1922-1997 ... CANR-58
Obituary 162
Earlier sketches in CA 53-56, CANR-30
Potter, John Mason 1907- CAP-1
Earlier sketch in CA 11-12
Potter, Joy Hambuechen 1935- 123
Potter, Karl Harrington 1927- 5-8R
Potter, Kathleen 1929(?)-1987
Obituary 122
Potter, Kathleen Jill 1932- 104
Potter, Lois 1941- CANR-138
Earlier sketches in CA 41-44R, CANR-15
Potter, Loren D(avid) 1918- 121
Potter, M(aurice) David 1900-1983 .... CAP-2
Earlier sketch in CA 23-24
Potter, Margaret (Newman)
1926-1998 .... CANR-44
Obituary 169
Earlier sketches in CA 13-16R, CANR-6, 21
See also Betteridge, Anne
See also RHW
See also SATA 21
See also SATA-Obit 104
Potter, Marian 1915- CANR-1
Earlier sketch in CA 49-52
See also SATA 9
Potter, Miriam Clark 1886-1965 .... 5-8R
See also SATA 3
Potter, Philip 1907-1988
Obituary 125
Potter, Robert Alonzo 1934- CANR-1
Earlier sketch in CA 45-48
Potter, Robert D(ucharme) 1905-1978
Obituary 77-80
Potter, Simeon 1898-1976 .... CANR-4
Earlier sketch in CA 5-8R
Potter, Stephen 1900-1969 101
Obituary 25-28R
See also MTCW 1
Potter, Sulamith Heins 1944- 81-84
Potter, Van Rensselaer 1911-2001 .... 37-40R
Potter, Vincent G. 1928- 25-28R
Potter, William Hotchkiss 1914-2001 .... 1-4R
Potterton, Gerald 1931- 49-52
Potterton, Homan 1946- CANR-25
Earlier sketch in CA 108
Pottinger, Stanley 1940- 201
Pottker, Janice (Marie) 1948- CANR-123
Earlier sketches in CA 118, CANR-42
Pottle, Frederick A(lbert) 1897-1987 ... CANR-3
Obituary 122
Earlier sketch in CA 5-8R
See also DLB 103
See also DLBY 1987
Potts, Albert M(intz) 1914-2001 116
Potts, Charles 1943- 105
Potts, E(li) Daniel 1930- 25-28R
Potts, Eve 1929- 103
Potts, George Chapman 1898-1983 ...... CAP-1
Earlier sketch in CA 11-12
Potts, Jean (C.) 1910-1999 .... CANR-63
Earlier sketches in CA 5-8R, CANR-2
See also CMW 4
Potts, Paul (Hugh Patrick Howard) 1911-1990
Obituary 132
See also CP 1
Potts, Ralph Bushnell 1901-1991 57-60
Potts, Richard 1938- 103
Potts, Stephen W(ayne) 1949- 149
Potts, Willard (Charles) 1929- 123
Potvin, Denis (Charles) 1953-
Brief entry 113
Potvin, Georges C. 1928- 45-48
Potvin, Liza 225
Potvin, Raymond H(erve) 1924- 21-24R
Pou, Genevieve Long 1919-
Brief entry 114
Poucher, William Arthur 1891-1988 ...... CAP-1
Earlier sketch in CA 11-12
Pough, Frederick Harvey 1906- 81-84
Pouillon, Fernand 1912-1986 .... 29-32R
Poulakidas, Andreas K. 1934- 45-48
Poulakos, Takis 1952- 170
Poulet, Georges 1902-1991 .... 13-16R
Poulin, A(lfred A.), Jr. 1938-1996 ..... CANR-32
Obituary 152
Earlier sketches in CA 21-24R, CANR-12
See also CP 7
Poulin, Jacques 1937- 165
See also DLB 60
Poulin, Stephane 1961- 165
See also CLR 28
See also MAICYA 2
See also SATA 98
Poullada, Leon B(aqueiro) 1913-1987
Obituary 123
Poulos, Constantine 1916(?)-1986
Obituary 119
Poulson, Christine 232
Poulter, S(cott) L(arry) 1943- 49-52
Poultney, David 1939- 141
Poulton, Edith Eleanor (Diana) Chloe
1903- 85-88
Poulton, Helen Jean 1920-1971 .... CAP-2
Earlier sketch in CA 33-36
Poulton, Kimberly 1957(?)- .... SATA 136
Poulton, Richard (Christopher) 1938- 107
Pound, Arthur 1884-1966
Obituary 89-92
Pound, Ezra (Weston Loomis)
1885-1972 .... CANR-40
Obituary 37-40R
Earlier sketch in CA 5-8R
See also AAYA 47
See also AMW
See also AMWR 1
See also CDALB 1917-1929
See also CLC 1, 2, 3, 4, 5, 7, 10, 13, 18, 34, 48, 50, 112
See also CP 1
See also DA
See also DA3
See also DAB
See also DAC
See also DAM MST, POET
See also DLB 4, 45, 63
See also DLBD 15
See also EFS 2
See also EWL 3
See also EXPP
See also LMFS 2
See also MAL 5
See also MTCW 1, 2
See also MTFW 2005
See also PAB
See also PC 4
See also PFS 2, 8, 16
See also RGAL 4
See also TUS
See also WLC
See also WP
Pound, Merritt B(loodworth)
1898-1970 .... CAP-2
Earlier sketch in CA 19-20
Pound, Omar S(hakespear) 1926- CANR-45
Earlier sketches in CA 49-52, CANR-1, 16
Pound, Roscoe 1870-1964
Obituary 111
Pounds, Norman John Greville
1912- CANR-102
Earlier sketches in CA 1-4R, CANR-4
Pounds, Ralph Linnaeus 1910-1992 .... 5-8R
Poundstone, William 1955- CANR-89
Earlier sketch in CA 151
Poupeye, Veerle (Henriette Gabriella Maria)
1958- 176
Pournelle, Jerry (Eugene) 1933- CANR-103
Earlier sketches in CA 77-80, CANR-30
See also SATA 26, 91, 161
See also SFW 4
Pourrat, Henri 1887-1959 229
Poussaint, Alvin F(rancis) 1934- 53-56
Povelite, Kay 1955- .... SATA 102
Povenmire, (Edward) King(sley)
1904-1993 61-64
Poverman, C(harles) E. 1944- 228
Brief entry 115
See also DLB 234
Povey, John F. 1929- 85-88
Povey, Meic 1950- .... DLB 310
Povich, Maury 1939- 138
Povich, Shirley 1905-1998 196
See also DLB 171
Povod, Reinaldo 1959-1994 .... CANR-83
Obituary 146
Earlier sketch in CA 136
See also CLC 44

Pow, Tom 1950- 134
See also SATA 163
Powdermaker, Hortense 1900-1970 ...... CAP-1
Obituary 29-32R
Earlier sketch in CA 13-14
Powe, B(ruce) W. 1955- 133
Powe, Bruce 1925- 53-56
Powe, L. A. Scot
See Powe, Lucas A., Jr.
Powe, Lucas A., Jr. 1943- CANR-98
Earlier sketch in CA 155
Powe-Allred, Alexandra
See Allred, Alexandra Powe
Powell, A. M.
See Morgan, Alfred P(owell)
Powell, Adam Clayton, Jr.
1908-1972 .... CANR-86
Obituary 33-36R
Earlier sketch in CA 102
See also BLC 3
See also BW 1, 3
See also CLC 89
See also DAM MULT
Powell, Alan 1936- 158
Powell, Ann 1951- .... SATA-Brief 51
Powell, Anthony (Dymoke)
1905-2000 .... CANR-107
Obituary 189
Earlier sketches in CA 1-4R, CANR-1, 32, 62
See also BRW 7
See also CDBLB 1945-1960
See also CLC 1, 3, 7, 9, 10, 31
See also CN 1, 2, 3, 4, 5, 6
See also DLB 15
See also EWL 3
See also MTCW 1, 2
See also MTFW 2005
See also RGEL 2
See also TEA
Powell, Anton 184
Powell, Ardal 1958- 142
Powell, Barbara 1929- 119
Powell, Barry B. 1942- 136
Powell, Brian S(harples) 1934- 25-28R
Powell, Cecil Frank 1903-1969 157
Obituary 113
Powell, Clarence Alva 1905-1986 .... CAP-1
Earlier sketch in CA 11-12
Powell, Clilan B. 1894-1977
Obituary 73-76
Powell, Colin L(uther) 1937- 158
Powell, (John) Craig 1940- 77-80
See also CP 1, 2
Powell, D. A. 1963- 168
Powell, Dannye Romine 1941- 147
Powell, David 1925- 142
Powell, David A. 1952- 146
Powell, Dawn 1896(?)-1965 .... CANR-121
Earlier sketch in CA 5-8R
See also CLC 66
See also DLBY 1997
Powell, Donald M. 1914-1987 .... 13-16R
Powell, Dorothy Baden
See Baden-Powell, Dorothy
Powell, Dorothy M. 1914- 106
Powell, (Drexel) Dwane (Jr.) 1944- 89-92
Powell, E. Sandy 1947- .... SATA 72
Powell, Elwin H(umphreys) 1925- 81-84
Powell, Eric 235
Powell, Eric F(rederick) W(illiam)
1899-1991 .... CANR-6
Earlier sketch in CA 5-8R
Powell, Evan Arnold 1937- CANR-21
Earlier sketch in CA 69-72
Powell, Fern 1942- 25-28R
Powell, G. Bingham, Jr. 1942- CANR-11
Earlier sketch in CA 29-32R
Powell, Geoffrey (Stewart) 1914-2005 61-64
Obituary 235
Powell, Gordon (George) 1911- 1-4R
Powell, Grosvenor (Edward) 1932- 129
Powell, Ivor 1910-1998 .... CANR-38
Earlier sketches in CA 1-4R, CANR-17
Powell, J(ohn) Enoch 1912-1998 97-100
Powell, James 1932- CANR-65
Earlier sketch in CA 107
See also CMW 4
Powell, James 1942- .... TCWW 1, 2
Powell, James Lawrence 1936- 212
Powell, James M(atthew) 1930- CANR-8
Earlier sketch in CA 5-8R
Powell, James V(irgil) 1938- 104
Powell, John Roland 1889- CAP-1
Earlier sketch in CA 13-14
Powell, John Wesley 1834-1902 202
See also ANW
See also DLB 186
Powell, Joseph 1952- 203
Powell, Kenneth 1947- 215
Powell, Kevin 1966- 170
Powell, Kevin 1966- 170
Powell, L(awrence) F(itzroy) 1881-1975
Obituary 57-60
Powell, Larson Merrill 1932- 103
Powell, Lawrence Clark 1906-2001 . CANR-25
Obituary 195
Earlier sketches in CA 21-24R, CANR-8
Powell, Lawrence N(elson) 1943- 104
Powell, Lily
See Froissard, Lily Powell
Powell, Marcia (Leonora) 108
Powell, Margaret 1907(?)-1984 .... CANR-15
Obituary 112
Earlier sketch in CA 29-32R
Powell, Mark Allan 1953- 219
Powell, Marvin 1924- CANR-8
Earlier sketch in CA 21-24R
Powell, Meredith (Ann) 1936- 37-40R
Powell, Michael (Latham) 1905-1990 150
Obituary 130
Powell, Milton Bryan 1934- 21-24R
Powell, Neil
See Innes, Brian
Powell, Neil 1948- CANR-93
Earlier sketches in CA 85-88, CANR-15, 34
See also CP 7
Powell, (Caryll) Nicolas (Peter)
1920- CANR-12
Earlier sketch in CA 61-64
Powell, Norman J(ohn) 1908-1974 .... CAP-2
Obituary 49-52
Earlier sketch in CA 21-22
Powell, Padgett 1952- CANR-101
Earlier sketches in CA 126, CANR-63
See also CLC 34
See also CSW
See also DLB 234
See also DLBY 01
Powell, Pamela 1960- 146
See also SATA 78
Powell, Patricia Hruby 1966- 194
See also SATA 136
Powell, Paul W. 1933- 116
Powell, Peter 1908-1985
Obituary 116
Powell, Peter John 1928- 33-36R
Powell, Philip Wayne 1913-1987 85-88
Powell, Ralph L. 1917-1975
Obituary 57-60
Powell, Randy 1956- 190
See also AAYA 35
See also SATA 118
See also YAW
Powell, Raymond P(ark) 1922-1980
Obituary 97-100
Powell, Reed M(adsen) 1921- 29-32R
Powell, Richard (Pitts) 1908-1999 ...... CANR-4
Earlier sketch in CA 1-4R
Powell, Richard Stillman
See Barbour, Ralph Henry
Powell, Robert 1942- 170
Powell, Robert (Stephenson Smyth) Baden
See Baden-Powell, Robert (Stephenson Smyth)
Powell, Robert Richard 1909-1998 .... 5-8R
Powell, Ronald R(owe) 1944- 114
Powell, Shirley 1931- 106
Powell, Sidney W. 5-8R
Powell, Simon G. 1960- 144
Powell, Sophie 1980- 222
Powell, Stephanie 1953- 158
See also SATA 93
Powell, Sumner Chilton 1924- 5-8R
Powell, (Oval) Talmage 1920-2000 .. CANR-80
Earlier sketches in CA 5-8R, CANR-2
See also Queen, Ellery
Powell, Terry 1949- 103
Powell, Theodore 1919- 1-4R
Powell, Thomas F. 1933- 25-28R
Powell, Victor M(organ) 1919- 45-48
Powell, Violet Georgiana 1912-2002 103
Obituary 204
Powell, William S(tevens) 1919- 69-72
Powell, Yolanda White 1961- 169
Powell-Smith, Vincent (Walter Francis)
1939- CANR-30
Earlier sketch in CA 25-28R
Powelson, John Palen 1920- CANR-41
Earlier sketches in CA 1-4R, CANR-4, 19
Power, Arthur
See Dudden, Arthur P(ower)
Power, Brian 1918- 139
Power, Catherine
See Du Breuil, (Elizabeth) L(or)inda
Power, Edward John 1921- CANR-2
Earlier sketch in CA 5-8R
Power, Eileen (Edna Le Poer) 1889-1940 154
See also FW
Power, Francis C. 1909(?)-1987
Obituary 124
Power, J. Tracy 1958- 191
Power, John 1927- 61-64
Power, Jonathan 1941- CANR-120
Earlier sketch in CA 107
Power, M(aurice) S(tephen) 1935- 130
Power, Margaret (M.) 1945- .... SATA 75, 125
Power, Margaret 1950- CANR-115
Earlier sketches in CA 127, CANR-54
Power, Michael 1933- CAP-1
Earlier sketch in CA 11-12
Power, Nancy Goslee 1942- 154
Power, Nani 219
Power, Norman S(andiford) 1916- CANR-10
Earlier sketch in CA 65-68
Power, Patrick C(arthage) 1928- 146
Power, Paul F(rederick) 1925- 41-44R
Power, Rhoda (Dolores le Poer)
1890-1957 .... CWRI 5
Power, Richard 1928-1970 .... CAP-1
Earlier sketch in CA 9-10
Power, Samantha 1970- 211
Power, Susan 1961- CANR-135
Earlier sketch in CA 160
See also BYA 14
See also CLC 91
See also NFS 11
Power, Tyrone
See Guthrie, (William) Tyrone
Power, (Patrick) Victor 1930- CANR-13
Earlier sketch in CA 77-80
Power-Ross, Robert W. 1922- 102
Powers, Alan 1955- CANR-123
Earlier sketch in CA 140
Powers, Albert Theodore 1953- 227
Powers, Andy 1896-1992 .... CANR-6
Earlier sketch in CA 57-60
Powers, Ann 1964- 198
Powers, Anne
See Schwartz, Anne Powers
Powers, Barbara Hudson
See Dudley, Barbara Hudson
Powers, Bill 1931- 77-80
See also SATA 52
See also SATA-Brief 31
Powers, Bob
See Powers, Robert L(eroy) and
Repp, William
Powers, Charles T. 1943(?)-1996 169
Powers, David Guy 1911-1967 .... CAP-2
Earlier sketch in CA 19-20
Powers, Doris Cooper 1918- 105
Powers, Edward A(lvin) 1941- 77-80
Powers, Edward Alton 1927- 53-56
Powers, Edward D(oyle) 1900-1982 45-48
Powers, Edwin 1896-1990 73-76
Powers, Francis Gary 1929-1977
Obituary 109
Powers, George
See Infield, Glenn (Berton)
Powers, Georgia (Montgomery) Davis
1923- CANR-87
Earlier sketch in CA 150
Powers, Helen 1925- 97-100
Powers, J(ames) F(arl) 1917-1999 ..... CANR-61
Obituary 181
Earlier sketches in CA 1-4R, CANR-2
See also CLC 1, 4, 8, 57
See also CN 1, 2, 3, 4, 5, 6
See also DLB 130
See also MTCW 1
See also RGAL 4
See also RGSF 2
See also SSC 4
Powers, James Joseph Aloysius 1903-1995 . 205
See also Powers, Jimmy
Powers, Jeffrey W(ells) 1950- 61-64
Powers, Jimmy 1903-1995
See Powers, James Joseph Aloysius
See also DLB 241
Powers, J.L.
See Glasby, John S.
Powers, John 1948- 182
Powers, John 1951- 236
Powers, John J(ames) 1945- 69-72
See also Powers, John R.
Powers, John R.
See Powers, John J(ames)
See also CLC 66
Powers, Joseph M(ichael) 1926- 85-88
Powers, L. C.
See Tubb, E(dwin) C(harles)
Powers, Lyall H(arris) 1924- 145
Brief entry 115
Powers, M. L.
See Tubb, E(dwin) C(harles)
Powers, Mala 1931- 129
Powers, Margaret
See Heal, Edith
Powers, Mark James 1940- 110
Powers, Martha (Jean) 198
Powers, Meredith A(nn) 1949- 140
Powers, Nora
See Pykare, Nina
Powers, Patrick W(illiam) 1924- 13-16R
Powers, Richard (S.) 1957- CANR-80
Earlier sketch in CA 148
See also AMWS 9
See also BPFB 3
See also CLC 93
See also CN 6, 7
See also MTFW 2005
See also TCLE 1:2
Powers, Richard M(ichael) Gorman
1921-1996 .... 21-24R
Obituary 182
Powers, Robert L(eroy) 1924- 93-96
Powers, Robert M(aynard) 1942- CANR-14
Earlier sketch in CA 77-80
Powers, Ron(ald Dean) 1941- CANR-92
Earlier sketches in CA 97-100, CANR-56
Powers, Steve 1934- 145
Powers, Thomas (Moore) 1940- CANR-77
Earlier sketches in CA 37-40R, CANR-17
Interview in CANR-17
Powers, Tim(othy Thomas) 1952- ... CANR-118
Earlier sketches in CA 134, CANR-80
See also AAYA 49
See also FANT
See also MTFW 2005
See also SATA 107
See also SFW 4
Powers, Treval C(lifford) 1900- 158
Powers, William 1930- 45-48
Powers, William Edwards 1902-1993 .... CAP-2
Earlier sketch in CA 19-20
Powers, William K(eegan) 1934- 25-28R
Powers, William T(reval) 1926- 111
Powers, Willow Roberts 1943- 127
Powers-Beck, Jeffrey P(aul) 1964- 196
Powerscourt, Sheila
See Wingfield, Sheila (Claude)
Power-Waters, Alma Shelley
1896-1983 .... CANR-18
Earlier sketch in CA 1-4R
Power-Waters, Brian 1922- CANR-18
Earlier sketch in CA 93-96
Powicke, Michael Rhys 1920- CANR-8
Earlier sketch in CA 5-8R
Powledge, Fred 1935- CANR-58
Earlier sketches in CA 21-24R, CANR-9, 27
See also SATA 37
Powles, William E(arnest) 1919- 144
Powley, Edward Barzillai 1887-1968 ..... CAP-1
Earlier sketch in CA 13-14
Powley, Florence Mary Pomeroy 1892- . CAP-1
Earlier sketch in CA 13-16
Powling, Chris 1943- CANR-80
Earlier sketches in CA 121, CANR-49
See also CWRI 5
Pownall, David 1938- CANR-101
Earlier sketches in CA 89-92, 180, CANR-49
See also CAAS 18
See also CBD
See also CD 5, 6
See also CLC 10
See also CN 4, 5, 6, 7
See also DLB 14
Powrie, Peter James 1927- 21-24R
Powrie, Phil(ip Peter) 1951- CANR-143
Earlier sketch in CA 172
Powter, Susan 1957- 169
Powys, John Cowper 1872-1963 .... CANR-106
Earlier sketch in CA 85-88
See also CLC 7, 9, 15, 46, 125
See also DLB 15, 255
See also EWL 3
See also FANT
See also MTCW 1, 2
See also MTFW 2005
See also RGEL 2
See also SUFW
Powys, Llewelyn 1884-1939 204
See also DLB 98
Powys, T(heodore) F(rancis) 1875-1953 189
Brief entry 106
See also BRWS 8
See also DLB 36, 162
See also EWL 3
See also FANT
See also RGEL 2
See also SUFW
See also TCLC 9
Poyer, David 1949- CANR-135
Earlier sketches in CA 111, CANR-30, 73
Poyer, Joe
See Poyer, Joseph John (Jr.)
Poyer, Joseph John (Jr.) 1939- CANR-40
Earlier sketches in CA 49-52, CANR-1, 17
Poynor, Robin 1942- 150
Poynter, Dan(iel Frank) 1938- CANR-101
Earlier sketches in CA 89-92, CANR-24, 49
Poynter, Margaret 1927- CANR-36
Earlier sketches in CA 93-96, CANR-16
See also SATA 27
Poynter, Nelson 1903-1978 183
Obituary 77-80
See also DLB 127
Pozner, Vladimir 1934- 136
See also BEST 90:3
Pozzessere, Heather Graham CANR-80
Earlier sketch in CA 141
See also Graham, Heather
Pozzetta, George Enrico 1942- CANR-29
Earlier sketch in CA 111
Pozzo, Modesta
See Fonte, Moderata
Prabhavananda, Swami 1893-1976 .... CANR-8
Obituary 65-68
Earlier sketch in CA 17-20R
Prabhu, Pandharinath H(ari) 1911- CANR-7
Earlier sketch in CA 13-16R
Prabhupada, A. C. Bhaktivedanta
1896-1977 .... CANR-14
Earlier sketch in CA 73-76
Prabhupada, A. C. Bhaktivedanta Swami
See Prabhupada, A. C. Bhaktivedanta
Prachaticka, Marketa
See Kolibalova, Marketa
Prachatika, Marketa
See Kolibalova, Marketa
Prada, Juan Manuel de 1970- .... DLB 322
Prada, Manuel Gonzalez
See Gonzalez Prada, Manuel
Prada Oropeza, Renato 1937- CANR-32
Earlier sketch in CA 41-44R
See also HW 1
Prado, Adelia 1935- .... DLB 307
Prado, C(arlos) G(onzalez) 1937- CANR-52
Earlier sketches in CA 110, CANR-27
Prado, Holly 1938- CANR-137
Earlier sketch in CA 171
Prado (Calvo), Pedro 1886-1952 131
See also DLB 283
See also HW 1
See also LAW
See also TCLC 75
Pradon, Jacques 1644-1698 . GFL Beginnings to 1789
Prados, Emilio 1899-1962 .... DLB 134
Prados, John 1951- 106
Praed, Mrs. Campbell
See Praed, Rosa
See also HGG
Praed, Rosa 1851-1935
See Praed, Mrs. Campbell
See also DLB 230
Praed, Winthrop Mackworth
1802-1839 .... DLB 96
See also RGEL 2
Praetorius, Johannes 1630-1680 .... DLB 168
Prag, (Andrew) John (Nicholas Warburg)
1941- CANR-141
Earlier sketch in CA 173
Prager, Arthur CANR-12
Earlier sketch in CA 29-32R
See also SATA 44
Prager, Ellen J. 1962- 205
See also SATA 136

Cumulative Index 467 **Preziosi**

Prager, Emily 1952- 204
See also CLC 56
Prager, Jeffrey 1948- 184
Prager, Jonas 1938- 105
Prager, Karsten 1936-1998 73-76
Obituary 166
Prago, Albert 1911-1993 .... 29-32R
Prain, Ronald (Lindsay) 1907-1991 109
Prall, Stuart E(dward) 1929- CANR-94
Earlier sketch in CA 21-24R
Pramoedya, Ananta Toer 1925- 134
See also EWL 3
Pramoj, M(on) R(ajawong) Kukrit
1911-1995 206
See also Kukrit Pramoj
Prance, Claude A(nnett) 1906- CANR-43
Earlier sketches in CA 89-92, CANR-20
Prance, Ghillean Tolmie 1937- CANR-93
Earlier sketch in CA 145
Prance, June E(lizebeth) 1929- 69-72
Prandy, K(enneth) 1938- CANR-45
Earlier sketch in CA 117
Prange, Erwin (Edward) 1917- 113
Prange, Gordon W(illiam) 1910-1980 158
Obituary 97-100
Pranger, Robert J(ohn) 1931- CANR-10
Earlier sketch in CA 25-28R
Prantera, Amanda 1942- 130
Brief entry 126
Prasad, S(rinivas) Benjamin 1929- CANR-5
Earlier sketch in CA 53-56
Prassel, Frank Richard 1937- CANR-1
Earlier sketch in CA 49-52
Pratchett, Terry 1948- CANR-126
Earlier sketches in CA 143, CANR-87
See also AAYA 19, 54
See also BPFB 3
See also CLC 197
See also CLR 64
See also CN 6, 7
See also CPW
See also CWRI 5
See also FANT
See also MTFW 2005
See also SATA 82, 139
See also SFW 4
See also SUFW 2
Prater, Donald A(rthur) 1918-2001 ... CANR-60
Obituary 201
Earlier sketch in CA 128
Prater, John 1947- .... SATA 72, 103, 149
Prathap, G(angan) 1951- 148
Prather, Hugh 1938- CANR-2
Earlier sketch in CA 45-48
Prather, Richard S(cott) 1921- CANR-58
Earlier sketches in CA 1-4R, CANR-5
See also CMW 4
Pratley, Gerald 1923- 112
Pratney, William Alfred 1944- 124
Pratney, Winkie
See Pratney, William Alfred
Pratolini, Vasco 1913-1991 211
See also DLB 177
See also EWL 3
See also RGWL 2, 3
See also TCLC 124
Pratson, Frederick John 1935- 101
Pratt, Alexandra (J.) 1974- 223
Pratt, Allan D(aniel) 1933- 112
Pratt, Charles 1926-1976 .... CANR-21
Obituary 65-68
Earlier sketch in CA 69-72
Pratt, Chris (James) 1950- 118
Pratt, (Mildred) Claire 1921- 103
Pratt, Dallas 1914-1994 106
Obituary 145
Pratt, Denis
See Crisp, Quentin
Pratt, E(dwin) J(ohn) 1883(?)-1964 .... CANR-77
Obituary 93-96
Earlier sketch in CA 141
See also CLC 19
See also DAC
See also DAM POET
See also DLB 92
See also EWL 3
See also RGEL 2
See also TWA
Pratt, (Murray) Fletcher 1897-1956 161
Brief entry 113
See also FANT
See also SATA 102
See also SFW 4
Pratt, Fletcher 1897-1956 .... SUFW
Pratt, J(oseph) Gaither 1910-1979 ...... CANR-6
Obituary 89-92
Earlier sketch in CA 9-12R
Pratt, James Michael 193
Pratt, James Norwood 1942- 112
Pratt, Jane 1963(?)- CANR-77
Earlier sketch in CA 138
See also AAYA 9, 61
Pratt, John 1931-2001 .... CANR-1
Obituary 194
Earlier sketch in CA 1-4R
Pratt, John Clark 1932- CANR-104
Earlier sketches in CA 13-16R, CANR-17, 40
Pratt, John Lowell 1906-1968 .... CANR-3
Earlier sketch in CA 1-4R
Pratt, Julius W(illiam) 1888-1983 .... CAP-1
Earlier sketch in CA 11-12
Pratt, Keith L(eslie) 1938- 29-32R
Pratt, Kristin Joy 1976- .... SATA 87
Pratt, Mary 1935- 199
Pratt, Minnie Bruce 221
See also CSW
See also CWP
Pratt, Norman T(wombly), Jr. 1911-1999 118
Pratt, Pierre 1962- 160
See also SATA 95
Pratt, Robert Cranford 1926- 101
Pratt, Samuel Jackson 1749-1814 .... DLB 39
Pratt, T(erry) K(enneth) 1943- 177
Pratt, Theodore 1901-1969 .... CANR-4
Earlier sketch in CA 1-4R
Pratt, William C(rouch, Jr.) 1927- ... CANR-136
Earlier sketches in CA 13-16R, CANR-6
Pratt, William K. 1937- 215
Pratt, Willis Winslow 1908-
Brief entry 105
Pratt-Butler, Grace Kipp 1916- 103
Pratte, Richard (Norman) 1929- 93-96
Prattis, Percival L. 1895-1980
Obituary 97-100
Prawer, Joshua 1917- 41-44R
Prawer, S(iegbert) S(alomon) 1925- .. CANR-109
Earlier sketches in CA 103, CANR-29, 54
Pray, Lawrence M. 1947- 113
Praz, Mario 1896-1982 .... CANR-79
Obituary 106
Earlier sketch in CA 101
Prazniak, Roxann 199
Prchal, Mildred 1895-1983
Obituary 109
Prebble, John Edward Curtis
1915-2001 .... CANR-64
Obituary 192
Earlier sketches in CA 5-8R, CANR-3
See also TCWW 1, 2
Prebble, Marjorie Mary Curtis
1912- CANR-15
Earlier sketch in CA 17-20R
Prebish, Charles S(tuart) 1944- 57-60
Preble, Duane 1936- 61-64
Preble, Robert Curtis 1897-1983
Obituary 111
Prechtel, Martin 220
Prechter, Robert R(ougelot), Jr. 1949- 227
Preciado Martin, Patricia
See Martin, Patricia Preciado
See also DLB 209
Preda, Marin 1922-1980 .... EWL 3
Predmore, Michael P. 1938- CANR-86
Earlier sketches in CA 45-48, CANR-34
Predmore, Richard Lionel 1911-1987 .... 17-20R
Preece, Harold 1906-1992 .... 5-8R
Obituary 198
Preece, Rod(ney John) 1939- 113
Preedy, George
See Campbell, (Gabrielle) Margaret (Vere)
Preeg, Ernest H. 1934- 33-36R
Prefontaine, Yves 1937- 184
See also DLB 53
Pregel, Boris 1893-1976
Obituary 106
Preger, Paul D(aniel), Jr. 1926- 49-52
Preheim, Marion Keeney 1934- 25-28R
Preil, Gabriel (Joshua) 1911-1993 .... CANR-1
Obituary 141
Earlier sketch in CA 49-52
Preiser, Wolfgang F(riedrich) E(rnst)
1941- CANR-7
Earlier sketch in CA 57-60
Preisner, Zbigniew 1955- .... IDFW 4
Preiss, Byron (Cary) CANR-14
Earlier sketch in CA 69-72
See also SATA 47
See also SATA-Brief 42
Preiss, David (Lee) 1935- 69-72
Prejean, Helen 1939(?)- 147
Prelinger, Ernst 1926- 9-12R
Preller, James 1961- 152
See also SATA 88
Prelutsky, Jack 1940- CANR-118
Earlier sketches in CA 93-96, CANR-38
See also CLR 13
See also CWRI 5
See also DLB 61
See also MAICYA 1, 2
See also SATA 22, 66, 118
Prem, Dhani 1904(?)-1979
Obituary 93-96
Prem, Hanns J(uergen) 1941- CANR-116
Earlier sketch in CA 153
Premacanda
See Srivastava, Dhanpat Rai
Premack, Ann J(ames) 1929- 57-60
Premack, David 1925- 126
Premchand
See Srivastava, Dhanpat Rai
See also EWL 3
See also TCLC 21
Premchand, Munshi
See Srivastava, Dhanpat Rai
Prem Chand, Munshi
See Srivastava, Dhanpat Rai
Preminger, Alex 1915- 13-16R
Preminger, Erik Lee 1944- 132
Preminger, Marion Mill 1913-1972
Obituary 33-36R
Preminger, Otto (Ludwig) 1906(?)-1986 134
Obituary 119
Brief entry 110
Premont, Brother Jeremy
See Willett, Brother Franciscus
Prender, Bart
See King, Albert
Prendergast, Alan 1956- 124
Prendergast, Curtis 1915- 154
Prendergast, John 1958- 150
Prendergast, Karen A(nn) 1951- 117
Prendergast, Mark J(oseph Anthony) 1959- . 233
Prentice, Amy
See Kaler, James Otis
Prentice, Ann E(thelynd) 1933- CANR-6
Earlier sketch in CA 57-60
Prentice, Charlotte
See Platt, Charles
Prentice, George D. 1802-1870 .... DLB 43
Prentice, P(ierrepont) I(sham) 1899-1989
Obituary 127
Prenting, Theodore O(tto) 1933- 57-60
Prentis, Steve (?)-1987
Obituary 122
Prentiss, Augustin M. 1890-1977
Obituary 69-72
Preradovic, Paula von 1887-1951 .... EWL 3
Presberg, Miriam Goldstein
1919-1978 .... CANR-3
Earlier sketch in CA 1-4R
See also SATA-Brief 38
Prescott, Allen 1904(?)-1978
Obituary 73-76
Prescott, Caleb
See Bingley, David Ernest
Prescott, Casey
See Morris, Chris(topher Crosby)
Prescott, David M(arshall) 1926- 127
Brief entry 113
Prescott, H(ilda) F(rances) Margaret
1896-1972 .... CN 1
See also RHW
Prescott, J(ohn) R(obert) V(ictor)
1931- CANR-23
Earlier sketch in CA 107
Prescott, Jack
See Preston, John
See also GLL 1
Prescott, John Brewster 1919- CANR-64
Earlier sketch in CA 5-8R
See also TCWW 1, 2
Prescott, Kenneth W(ade) 1920- CANR-8
Earlier sketch in CA 57-60
Prescott, Michael 1960- 222
Prescott, Orville 1906-1996 .... 41-44R
Obituary 152
See also DLBY 1996
Prescott, Peter S(herwin)
1935-2004 .... CANR-14
Obituary 226
Earlier sketch in CA 37-40R
Interview in CANR-14
Prescott, William Hickling 1796-1859 ... DLB 1, 30, 59, 235
Preseren, France 1800-1849 .... CDWLB 4
See also DLB 147
Preshing, W(illiam) A(nthony) 1929- 85-88
Preslan, Kristina 1945- 106
Presland, John
See Bendit, Gladys Williams
Presley, Delma E(ugene) 1939- CANR-31
Earlier sketch in CA 112
Presley, James (Wright) 1930- CANR-10
Earlier sketch in CA 21-24R
Presley, Priscilla (Ann Beaulieu)
1945- CANR-106
Earlier sketch in CA 166
Presnall, Judith (Ann) Janda 1943- .. CANR-135
Earlier sketch in CA 161
See also SATA 96
Presnell, Barbara 1954- 202
Presnell, Robert (Jr.) 1915(?)-1986
Obituary 119
Presner, Lewis A. 1945- 142
Press, (Otto) Charles 1922- CANR-6
Earlier sketch in CA 13-16R
Press, Frank 1924- 130
Press, John (Bryant) 1920- CANR-3
Earlier sketch in CA 9-12R
See also CP 1
Press, Simone Juda 1943- 111
Press, Toni 1949- 108
Pressau, Jack Renard 1933- 77-80
Pressburger, Emeric 1902-1988 104
Obituary 124
Pressburger, Giorgio 1937- 228
Presseisen, Ernst L(eopold) 1928- 13-16R
Presser, (Gerrit) Jacob 1899-1970 .... CAP-2
Earlier sketch in CA 25-28
See also Presser, (Gerrit) Jacques
Presser, (Gerrit) Jacques
See Presser, (Gerrit) Jacob
Presser, Janice 1946- CANR-24
Earlier sketch in CA 107
Presser, Stephen B. 1946- 139
Pressfield, Steven 184
Pressler, Mirjam 1940- 234
See also SATA 155
Pressly, Thomas J(ames) 1919- 17-20R
Pressly, William Laurens 1944- 196
Pressman, David 1937- 89-92
Pressman, Jeffrey L(eonard) 1943- CANR-3
Earlier sketch in CA 45-48
Prest, Alan Richmond 1919-1985 93-96
Obituary 115
Prest, Thomas Peckett 1810-1859 .... HGG
Prest, Wilfred 1907-1985 111
Obituary 117
Prest, Wilfrid R(obertson) 1940- 112
Prestbo, John A(ndrew) 1941- CANR-2
Earlier sketch in CA 49-52
Prestera, Hector A(nthony) 1932- 65-68
Presthus, Robert 1917- CANR-20
Earlier sketches in CA 1-4R, CANR-5
Prestidge, Pauline 1922- 103
Preston, Ben
See Sanna, Ellyn
Preston, Caroline 170
Preston, Diana 1952- 203
Preston, Dickson J(oseph) 1914-1985 . CANR-8
Obituary 114
Earlier sketch in CA 61-64
Preston, Douglas 1956- CANR-100
Earlier sketch in CA 141
See also AAYA 32
See also SATA 113
Preston, Edna Mitchell 111
See also SATA 40
Preston, Edward
See Guess, Edward Preston
Preston, Fayrene .... RHW
Preston, Florence (Margaret) 1905- 103
Preston, Frances I(sabella) 1898- 61-64
Preston, Harry 1923- CANR-48
Earlier sketches in CA 57-60, CANR-23
Preston, Ivan L. 1931- 57-60
Preston, Ivy (Alice) Kinross 1914- CANR-58
Earlier sketches in CAP-1, CA 9-10, CANR-12, 30
See also RHW
Preston, James
See Unett, John
Preston, James 1913- CAP-1
Earlier sketch in CA 9-10
Preston, James J(ohn) 1941- CANR-27
Earlier sketch in CA 109
Preston, John 1945-1994 .... CANR-83
Obituary 145
Earlier sketch in CA 130
See also Hild, Jack and
MacAdam, Preston and McCray, Mike and
Prescott, Jack
See also GLL 1
Preston, John Hyde 1906-1980
Obituary 102
Preston, Julia 1955(?)- 230
Preston, Lee E. 1930- CANR-11
Earlier sketch in CA 21-24R
Preston, Lillian Elvira 1918- 108
See also SATA 47
Preston, Margaret Junkin 1820-1897 . DLB 239, 248
Preston, May Wilson 1873-1949 .... DLB 188
Preston, Michael B. 1933- 126
Preston, Nathaniel Stone 1928- 29-32R
Preston, Paul 1946- 224
Preston, Peter 1944- 192
Preston, Ralph C(lausius) 1908- CANR-6
Earlier sketch in CA 13-16R
Preston, Richard
See Lindsay, Jack
Preston, Richard (McCann) 1954- .. CANR-143
Earlier sketches in CA 128, CANR-66
See also AAYA 60
Preston, Richard Arthur 1910- CANR-18
Earlier sketches in CA 5-8R, CANR-3
Preston, Thomas 1537-1598 .... DLB 62
Preston, Thomas A(rthur) 1933- 112
Preston, Thomas R(onald) 1936- 186
Brief entry 109
Preston, William L(ee) 1949- 105
Preston-Mafham, Rod(ney Arthur)
1942- CANR-93
Earlier sketch in CA 146
Prestwich, Menna 1917- 21-24R
Prestwich, Michael (Charles) 1943- 134
Preti, Luigi 1914- 154
Pretorius, Hertha
See Kouts, Hertha Pretorius
Preto-Rodas, Richard (Anthony) 1936- 49-52
Prettyman, E(lijah) Barrett, Jr. 1925- 9-12R
Preus, Anthony 1936- 49-52
Preus, Herman Amberg 1896-1995 85-88
Obituary 198
Preus, Jacob A(ll) O(ttesen)
1920-1994 .... 33-36R
Preus, Johan Carl Keyser 1881-1983
Obituary 111
Preus, Robert 1924-1995 .... 33-36R
Preuss, Paul 1942- CANR-81
Earlier sketch in CA 130
See also SFW 4
Preussler, Otfried 1923- 77-80
See also CLC 17
See also SATA 24
Prevelakis, Pandelis 1909-1986
Obituary 118
See also EWL 3
Prevert, Jacques (Henri Marie)
1900-1977 .... CANR-61
Obituary 69-72
Earlier sketches in CA 77-80, CANR-29
See also CLC 15
See also DLB 258
See also EWL 3
See also GFL 1789 to the Present
See also IDFW 3, 4
See also MTCW 1
See also RGWL 2, 3
See also SATA-Obit 30
Previn, Andre (George) 1929- 115
See also IDFW 3, 4
Previn, Dor(oth)y (Langan) 1929(?)- 111
Prevost, (Antoine Francois)
1697-1763 .... DLB 314
See also EW 4
See also GFL Beginnings to 1789
See also RGWL 2, 3
Prevost, Alain 1930(?)-1971
Obituary 33-36R
Prevost, Marcel 1862-1941 187
Brief entry 116
Prevots, Naima 1935- 135
Prewitt, Kenneth 1936- CANR-12
Earlier sketch in CA 29-32R
Preziosi, Donald 1941- 93-96

Prezzolini, Giuseppi 1882-1982
Obituary 107
Pribam, Karl 1878(?)-1973
Obituary 41-44R
Pribbenow, Merle L. 1945- 232
Pribichevich, Stoyan 1905(?)-1976
Obituary 65-68
Price, Alan 1943- 149
Price, Alfred 1936- CANR-24
Earlier sketches in CA 21-24R, CANR-9
Price, Alice Lindsay 1927- CANR-121
Earlier sketch in CA 152
Price, Anthony 1928- CANR-61
Earlier sketches in CA 77-80, CANR-15, 33
See also CMW 4
See also DLB 276
Price, Archibald Grenfell 1892-1977 ...... 9-12R
Obituary 125
Price, Arnold H(ereward) 1912- 45-48
Price, Barbara Anne Ellvinger 1946(?)-1987
Obituary 122
Price, Barbara Pradal 103
Price, Beverley Joan 1931- CANR-104
Earlier sketches in CA 106, CANR-24, 49
See also SATA 98
Price, Bruce D(eitrick) 1941- 25-28R
Price, Byron 1891-1981
Obituary 104
Price, Cecil (John Layton) 1915-1991 ... 21-24R
Price, Charles 1925- 9-12R
Price, Charles C(oale) 1913-2001 107
Price, Charles F(red) 1938- 196
Price, Charles P(hilip) 1920-1999 115
Obituary 187
Price, Christine (Hilda) 1928-1980 ..... CANR-4
Obituary 93-96
Earlier sketch in CA 5-8R
See also SATA 3
See also SATA-Obit 23
Price, Daniel O('Haver) 1918- 21-24R
Price, (Paul) David 1940- CANR-89
Earlier sketch in CA 130
Price, David Deakins 1902-1983
Obituary 110
Price, Deb 1958- CANR-116
Earlier sketch in CA 152
See also GLL 2
Price, Derek (John) de Solla
1922-1983 .... CANR-3
Obituary 110
Earlier sketch in CA 1-4R
Price, Don C(ravens) 1937- 81-84
Price, Don K(rasher, Jr.) 1910-1995 73-76
Obituary 149
Price, E(dgar) Hoffmann (Trooper)
1898-1988 .... CANR-79
Obituary 125
Earlier sketches in CA 61-64, CANR-10
See also FANT
Price, Emerson 1902(?)-1977
Obituary 104
Price, Eugenia 1916-1996 .... CANR-18
Obituary 152
Earlier sketches in CA 5-8R, CANR-2
See also BEST 89:4
See also CPW
See also CSW
See also DAM POP
Price, Evadne 1896-1985
Obituary 116
See also CWRI 5
See also RHW
Price, Frances Brown 1895-1981 49-52
Price, Francis Wilson 1895-1974 .... CAP-1
Earlier sketch in CA 13-14
Price, Frank James 1917- 104
Price, Frank W.
See Price, Francis Wilson
Price, Garrett 1896-1979
Obituary 85-88
See also SATA-Obit 22
Price, George 1901-1995 103
Obituary 147
Price, George (Henry) 1910-(?) CAP-1
Earlier sketch in CA 13-14
Price, George R(ennie) 1909-1985 ..... CANR-4
Earlier sketch in CA 1-4R
Price, Glanville 1928- CANR-86
Earlier sketch in CA 132
Price, Glenn W(arren) 1918- 21-24R
Price, Harry 1881-1948
Brief entry 119
Price, Henry Habberley 1899-1984
Obituary 114
Price, Hugh B(ernard) 1941- 225
Price, J(oseph) H(enry) 1924- 25-28R
Price, Jacob M(yron) 1925- CANR-1
Earlier sketch in CA 45-48
Price, James Ligon, Jr. 1915- 1-4R
Price, Jennifer
See Hoover, Helen (Drusilla Blackburn)
Price, Jimmie
See White, John I(rwin)
Price, Joan 1931- CANR-54
Earlier sketch in CA 111
See also SATA 124
Price, John (T.) 1966- 232
Price, John A(ndrew) 1933- CANR-7
Earlier sketch in CA 57-60
Price, John Valdimir 1937- 17-20R
Price, Jonathan (Reeve) 1941- CANR-19
Earlier sketches in CA 45-48, CANR-3
See also SATA 46
Price, Karen 1957- 196
See also SATA 125
Price, Kenneth M(arsden) 1954- CANR-38
Earlier sketch in CA 115
Price, Kingsley Blake 1917- 21-24R
Price, Larkin B(url) 1927- 185
Brief entry 112
Price, Leo 1941- 77-80
Price, Lucie Locke
See Locke, Lucie
Price, Margaret (Evans) 1888-1973
Obituary 109
See also SATA-Brief 28
Price, Marion E(lizabeth) 1947- 111
Price, Marjorie 1929- 53-56
Price, Martin 1920- CANR-13
Earlier sketch in CA 17-20R
Price, Matthew A(rlen) 1960- 204
Price, Miles O(scar) 1890-1968 .... CAP-1
Earlier sketch in CA 13-16
Price, Molly 1903(?)-1984
Obituary 114
Price, Morgan Philips 1885-1973 .... CAP-1
Earlier sketch in CA 13-14
Price, (Lilian) Nancy (Bache) 1880-1970
Obituary 111
Price, Nancy 1925- CANR-137
Earlier sketch in CA 171
Price, Nelson Lynn 1931- CANR-24
Earlier sketches in CA 61-64, CANR-8
Price, Olive 1903-1991 .... 41-44R
See also SATA 8
Price, Paul 1912(?)-1985
Obituary 116
Price, R(onald) F(rancis) 1926- CANR-26
Earlier sketch in CA 29-32R
Price, R(ichard) G(eoffrey) G(eorge)
1910- CAP-1
Earlier sketch in CA 13-14
Price, Ray(mond John) 1931- 25-28R
Price, Ray Glenn 1903- CANR-2
Earlier sketch in CA 5-8R
Price, Raymond (Kissam, Jr.) 1930- 105
Price, (Edward) Reynolds 1933- CANR-128
Earlier sketches in CA 1-4R, CANR-1, 37, 57, 87
Interview in CANR-37
See also AMWS 6
See also CLC 3, 6, 13, 43, 50, 63, 212
See also CN 1, 2, 3, 4, 5, 6, 7
See also CSW
See also DAM NOV
See also DLB 2, 218, 278
See also EWL 3
See also MAL 5
See also MTFW 2005
See also NFS 18
See also SSC 22
Price, Rhys
See Price, George (Henry)
Price, Richard 1723-1791 .... DLB 158
Price, Richard 1941- CANR-27
Earlier sketch in CA 105
Price, Richard 1949- CANR-3
Earlier sketch in CA 49-52
See also CLC 6, 12
See also CN 7
See also DLBY 1981
Price, Robert 1900-1989 .... 33-36R
Price, Robert M. 1941- 139
Price, Robert W. 1925(?)-1979
Obituary 89-92
Price, Roger 1921-1990 .... 9-12R
Price, Roger (David) 1944- CANR-35
Earlier sketch in CA 107
Price, S(eymour) Stephen 1919- 25-28R
Price, Sally 1943- CANR-92
Earlier sketches in CA 106, CANR-27
Price, Stanley 1931- 13-16R
Price, Steven D(avid) 1940- CANR-37
Earlier sketches in CA 49-52, CANR-1, 16
Price, Susan 1955- CANR-108
Earlier sketches in CA 105, CANR-81
See also AAYA 42
See also CWRI 5
See also MAICYA 2
See also SATA 25, 85, 128
Price, V(incent) B(arrett) 1940- 69-72
Price, Victor 1930- 9-12R
Price, (Mary) Victoria 1962- 222
Price, Vincent (Leonard) 1911-1993 . CANR-83
Obituary 143
Earlier sketch in CA 89-92
Price, Walter K(leber) 1924- CANR-7
Earlier sketch in CA 17-20R
Price, Willadene Anton 1914- 5-8R
Price, Willard 1887-1983 .... CANR-82
Earlier sketches in CA 1-4R, CANR-1
See also CWRI 5
See also SATA 48
See also SATA-Brief 38
Price, William 1938- 37-40R
Price, Wilson T(itus) 1931- 37-40R
Price-Groff, Claire 197
See also SATA 127
Priceman, Marjorie .... SATA 81, 120
Price-Mars, Jean 1875-1969 .... CANR-87
Obituary 112
Earlier sketch in CA 153
See also BW 2
Price-Thompson, Tracy 1963- 202
Prichard, Caradog 1904-1980 .... CANR-81
Obituary 97-100
Earlier sketch in CA 103
Prichard, Doris (Smith) 1947- 116
Prichard, Hesketh 1876-1922 .... HGG
Prichard, James W(illiam) 1925- 13-16R
Prichard, K(atherine O'Brien) 1851-1935 . HGG
Prichard, Katharine Susannah
1883-1969 .... CANR-33
Earlier sketches in CAP-1, CA 11-12
See also CLC 46
See also DLB 260
See also MTCW 1
See also RGEL 2
See also RGSF 2
See also SATA 66
Prichard, Nancy S(awyer) 1924- 29-32R
Prichard, Peter S. 1944- 139
Prichard, Robert Williams 1923- 89-92
Prichard, Susan Perez 1953- 108
Prickett, (Alexander Thomas) Stephen
1939- CANR-29
Earlier sketch in CA 29-32R
Prida, Dolores 1943- .... LLW
Priddy, Fran(ces Rosaleen) 1931- CANR-17
Earlier sketch in CA 1-4R
Priddy, Laurance L. 1941- CANR-123
Earlier sketch in CA 144
Pride, Cletis 1925- 41-44R
Pride, J(ohn) B(ernard) 1929- 186
Brief entry 110
Prideaux, James 1935- 138
Prideaux, John 1578-1650 .... DLB 236
Prideaux, Tom 1908-1993 108
Obituary 141
See also SATA 37
See also SATA-Obit 76
Pridgen, Allen 1943- 215
Pridham, Geoffrey 1942- CANR-38
Earlier sketches in CA 97-100, CANR-17
Pridham, Radost 1922- 21-24R
Prieboy, Andy 236
Pries, Nancy R(uth) 1944- 118
Priesand, Sally J(ane) 1946- 65-68
Priest, Alice L. 1931- 102
Priest, Christopher 1943- 33-36R
See also DLB 14, 207, 261
See also SCFW 2
See also SFW 4
Priest, Dana 224
Priest, Harold Martin 1902-1982 73-76
Priest, John Michael 1949- CANR-92
Earlier sketch in CA 150
Priest, Lisa 1964- 140
Priest, Robert 1951- 118
Priest, Stephen 1954- 140
Priest, Susanna Hornig 223
Priestley, Alice 1962- .... SATA 95
Priestley, Barbara 1937- 33-36R
Priestley, Brian 1946- 129
Priestley, F(rancis) E(thelbert) L(ouis)
1905-1988 .... 21-24R
Priestley, Harold E(dford) 1901- 73-76
Priestley, J(ohn) B(oynton)
1894-1984 .... CANR-33
Obituary 113
Earlier sketch in CA 9-12R
See also BRW 7
See also CDBLB 1914-1945
See also CLC 2, 5, 9, 34
See also CN 1, 2, 3
See also DA3
See also DAM DRAM, NOV
See also DLB 10, 34, 77, 100, 139
See also DLBY 1984
See also EWL 3
See also MTCW 1, 2
See also MTFW 2005
See also RGEL 2
See also SFW 4
Priestley, Joseph 1733-1804 .... DLB 252
Priestley, Lee (Shore) 1904-1999 .... CANR-2
Earlier sketch in CA 5-8R
See also SATA 27
Priestley, Mary 1925- 61-64
Priestley, Philip 1939- 123
Priestly, Doug(las Michael) 1954- 195
See also SATA 122
Priestly, Mark
See Albert, Harold A.
Priestman, Martin 1949- 135
Prieto, Mariana Beeching 1912-1999 . CANR-5
Earlier sketch in CA 5-8R
See also SATA 8
Prigmore, Charles S(amuel) 1919- CANR-25
Earlier sketch in CA 45-48
Prigogine, Ilya 1917-2003 .... CANR-82
Obituary 216
Earlier sketch in CA 131
Prigov, Dmitrii Aleksandrovich 1940- . DLB 285
Prikkebeen
See Greshoff, Jan
Priley, Margaret (Ann) Hubbard
1909-1992 .... 1-4R
Obituary 199
See also SATA-Obit 130
Prill, Felician 1904- 103
Primack, Alice Lefler 1939- 143
Primack, Joel (Robert) 1945- 61-64
Primack, Richard B. 1950- 153
Primavera, Elise 1954- 180
See also SATA 58, 109
See also SATA-Brief 48
Primavesi, Oliver 1961- 228
Prime, Benjamin Young 1733-1791 ...... DLB 31
Prime, C(ecil) T(homas) 1909-1979 .... CANR-3
Earlier sketch in CA 49-52
Prime, Derek (James) 1931- CANR-50
Earlier sketches in CA 108, CANR-25
See also SATA 34
Prime, Jim H. 1948- 193
Primeau, Ronald 1946- 108
Primeaux, Walter J(oseph) Jr. 1928- 41-44R
Primm, Brother Orrin
See Willett, Brother Franciscus
Primm, James Neal 1918- 45-48
Primmer, Phyllis (Cora Griesbach) 1926- .. 5-8R
Primo, Albert T. 1935- 73-76
Primrose, Diana fl. 1630- .... DLB 126
Primrose, William 1904-1982 116
Obituary 106
Prince 1958- 213
See also CLC 35
Prince, Alison (Mary) 1931- CANR-52
Earlier sketches in CA 29-32R, CANR-26
See also CWRI 5
See also SATA 28, 86
Prince, Carl E. 1934- CANR-14
Earlier sketch in CA 21-24R
Prince, (Peter) Derek 1915-2003 ...... CANR-34
Obituary 221
Earlier sketch in CA 113
Prince, Don 1905(?)-1983
Obituary 110
Prince, F(rank) T(empleton)
1912-2003 .... CANR-79
Obituary 219
Earlier sketches in CA 101, CANR-43
See also CLC 22
See also CP 1, 2, 3, 4, 5, 6, 7
See also DLB 20
Prince, Gary Michael 1948- 89-92
Prince, Gerald (Joseph) 1942- 57-60
Prince, Hal
See Prince, Harold
Prince, Harold 1928- .... AAYA 58
Prince, Hugh C. 1927- CANR-123
Earlier sketch in CA 170
Prince, J(ack) H(arvey) 1908- 81-84
See also SATA 17
Prince, Maggie 169
See also SATA 102
Prince, Melvin 1932- 116
Prince, Morton 1854-1929
Brief entry 121
Prince, Nancy Gardner 1799-(?) .... DLB 239
Prince, Peter (Alan) 1942- CANR-98
Earlier sketch in CA 139
Prince, Stephen 1955- 193
Prince, Suzan D(enise) 1957- 111
Prince, Thomas 1687-1758 .... DLB 24, 140
Prince, Thomas Richard 1934- 13-16R
Prince Charming
See Thomas, Rosanne Daryl
Prince-Hughes, Dawn 1964- 231
Prince Ibis
See Randi, James
Prince Kropotkin
See Kropotkin, Peter (Aleksieevich)
Princess Anne
See Anne (Elizabeth Alice Louise Windsor), Princess
Princess Grace
See Kelly, Grace (Patricia)
Princess Soraya
See Bakhtiari, Soraya Esfandiari
Princeton, Michael
See Spencer, David
Principal, Victoria 1945- 207
Principale, Concettina
See Principal, Victoria
Prindl, A(ndreas) R(obert) 1939- 69-72
Prindle, David F. 1948- 147
Pring, Julian Talbot 1913-2001 .... 5-8R
Pring, Martin J(ohn) 1943- 111
Pringle, David (William) 1950- 134
Pringle, Denys 184
Pringle, Eric 209
See also SATA 138
Pringle, Henry F(owles) 1897-1958 227
Pringle, J(ohn) M(artin) Douglas
1912-1999 .... 13-16R
Pringle, Laurence P(atrick) 1935- ... CANR-139
Earlier sketches in CA 29-32R, CANR-14, 60
See also CLR 4, 57
See also CWRI 5
See also MAICYA 1, 2
See also SAAS 6
See also SATA 4, 68, 104, 154
Pringle, Mary Beth 1943- 177
Pringle, Mia (Lilly) Kellmer
1920(?)-1983 65-68
Obituary 109
Pringle, Peter 1940- CANR-102
Earlier sketches in CA 69-72, CANR-27
Pringle, Terrence Michael 1947- 136
Pringle, Terry
See Pringle, Terrence Michael
Pringle, Thomas 1789-1834 .... DLB 225
Pring-Mill, Robert D(uguid) F(orrest)
1924- 9-12R
Prins, Harald E. L. 1951- 164
Printz, Peggy 1945- 73-76
Printz, Wolfgang Caspar 1641-1717 ... DLB 168
Prinz, Joachim 1902-1988 .... CAP-1
Obituary 182
Earlier sketch in CA 11-12
Priolo, Pauline Pizzo 1907- 1-4R
Prior, A(rthur) N(orman) 1914-1969 ... CANR-3
Earlier sketch in CA 1-4R
Prior, Allan 1922- CANR-79
Earlier sketches in CA 65-68, CANR-10
Prior, Andrew 1940- 112
Prior, Ann 1949- 25-28R
Prior, Kenneth Francis William 1926- ... 17-20R
Prior, Lily 1966- 238
Prior, Matthew 1664-1721 .... DLB 95
See also RGEL 2
Prior, Natalie Jane 1963- 168
See also SATA 106

Prisco, Michele 1920- CANR-98
Earlier sketch in CA 53-56
See also CWW 2
See also DLB 177
See also EWL 3
Prisco, Salvatore III 1943- CANR-12
Earlier sketch in CA 61-64
Prishvin, Mikhail 1873-1954
See Prishvin, Mikhail Mikhailovich
See also TCLC 75
Prishvin, Mikhail Mikhailovich
See Prishvin, Mikhail
See also DLB 272
See also EWL 3
Prising, Robin 1933- 57-60
Pritam, Amrita 1919- .... CWW 2
Pritchard, Allan (Duncan) 1928- 157
Pritchard, Arnold 1949- 97-100
Pritchard, J(ohn) Harris 1923- 21-24R
Pritchard, Jack 1899-1992 177
Pritchard, James Bennett 1909-1997 .... 5-8R
Obituary 156
Pritchard, John 1964- .... HGG
Pritchard, John Paul 1902-1976 .... 9-12R
Obituary 126
Pritchard, John Wallace 1912-1998 81-84
Obituary 176
See also SFW 4
Pritchard, Leland J(ames) 1908-1991 ..... CAP-1
Earlier sketch in CA 11-12
Pritchard, Melissa 1948- CANR-122
Earlier sketches in CA 128, CANR-64
Pritchard, Norman Henry II 1939- 77-80
Pritchard, Paul Liam 1967- 187
Pritchard, R(onald) E(dward) 1936- 37-40R
Pritchard, R(obert) John 1945- 116
Pritchard, Ray 1952- 162
Pritchard, Sheila (Edwards) 1909- CAP-1
Earlier sketch in CA 13-16
Pritchard, William H(arrison) 1932- . CANR-95
Earlier sketches in CA 65-68, CANR-23
See also CLC 34
See also DLB 111
Pritchett, C(harles) Herman 1907- CANR-18
Earlier sketches in CA 1-4R, CANR-3
Pritchett, Elaine H(illyer) 1920- 108
See also SATA 36
Pritchett, John Perry 1902-1981 .... 1-4R
Pritchett, Kay 1946- 135
Pritchett, Price 1941- 123
Pritchett, Ron 1929- .... TCWW 2
Pritchett, V(ictor) S(awdon)
1900-1997 .... CANR-63
Obituary 157
Earlier sketches in CA 61-64, CANR-31
See also BPFB 3
See also BRWS 3
See also CLC 5, 13, 15, 41
See also CN 1, 2, 3, 4, 5, 6
See also DA3
See also DAM NOV
See also DLB 15, 139
See also EWL 3
See also MTCW 1, 2
See also MTFW 2005
See also RGEL 2
See also RGSF 2
See also SSC 14
See also TEA
Pritchett, W(illiam) Kendrick 1909- 97-100
Pritchrad, Jack 1899-1992 177
Pritikin, Nathan 1915-1985 .... CANR-27
Obituary 114
Earlier sketch in CA 89-92
Pritikin, Robert C(harles) 1929- 104
Prittie, Terence Cornelius Farmer
1913-1985 .... CANR-4
Obituary 116
Earlier sketch in CA 1-4R
Pritts, Kim Derek 1953- 150
See also SATA 83
Private 19022
See Manning, Frederic
Privateer, Paul Michael 1946- 135
Priyamvada, Usha
See Nilsson, Usha Saksena
Prizzia, Ross 1942- 119
Probert, Lowri
See Jones, R(obert) M(aynard)
Probert, Richard Ezra 195
Probert, Walter 1925- 77-80
Probst, Leonard 1921-1982 65-68
Obituary 106
Probst, Mark 1925- 130
See also CLC 59
Probyn, Clive T. 1944- CANR-93
Earlier sketch in CA 145
Probyn, Juliana Mary Louisa 1856(?)-1909 . 185
See also Probyn, May
Probyn, May (?)-
See Probyn, Juliana Mary Louisa
See also DLB 199
Procaccino, Michael
See Cristofer, Michael
Prochazkova, Iva 1953- 135
See also SATA 68
Prochnau, William W. 1937- CANR-55
Earlier sketch in CA 33-36R
Prochnow, Herbert V(ictor), Jr. 1931- 110
Prochnow, Herbert V. 1897-1998 .... CANR-4
Earlier sketch in CA 1-4R
Procktor, Richard (Edward Christopher)
1933- 53-56
Procopio, Mariellen
See Grutz, Mariellen Procopio
Procter, Adelaide Anne 1825-1864 ...... DLB 32, 199
Procter, Ben H. 1927- CANR-9
Earlier sketch in CA 5-8R
Procter, Bryan Waller 1787-1874 . DLB 96, 144
Procter, Maurice 1906-1973 .... CANR-62
Obituary 122
Earlier sketch in CA 5-8R
See also CMW 4
See also MSW
Proctor, Charles S(heridan) 1925- 29-32R
Proctor, (Philip) Dennis 1905-1983
Obituary 110
Proctor, Dorothea Hardy 1910- 61-64
Proctor, E(velyn) E(mma) S(tefanos)
1897-1980 103
Obituary 97-100
Proctor, Elsie 1902- 29-32R
Proctor, Everitt
See Montgomery, Rutherford George
Proctor, Geo(rge W.) 181
See also SFW 4
Proctor, Lillian Cummins 1900-1978 ..... CAP-2
Earlier sketch in CA 23-24
Proctor, Michael 237
Proctor, Mike
See Proctor, Michael
Proctor, Priscilla 1945- 65-68
Proctor, Raymond L(ambert) 1920- 45-48
Proctor, Robert 1868-1903 .... DLB 184
Proctor, Robert N. 1954- CANR-88
Earlier sketch in CA 138
Proctor, Samuel 1919- CANR-3
Earlier sketch in CA 9-12R
Proctor, Samuel D(eWitt) 1921-1997 133
Obituary 158
Brief entry 118
Proctor, Thelwall (True) 1912-1988 .... 29-32R
Obituary 174
Proctor, William (Gilbert, Jr.) 1941- .. CANR-99
Earlier sketches in CA 37-40R, CANR-16
Prodan, Mario 1911- 9-12R
Proeysen, Alf 1914-1970 136
See also Proysen, Alf
See also CLR 24
Proface, Dom
See Sheehy, Maurice S(tephen)
Professor Scribbler
See Hollingsworth, Mary
Proffer, Carl R(ay) 1938-1984 .... 41-44R
Obituary 113
Proffer, Ellendea 1944- CANR-1
Earlier sketch in CA 45-48
Proffitt, Charles G. 1896-1982
Obituary 108
Proffitt, Nicholas (Charles) 1943- 139
Brief entry 131
Interview in CA-139
Profumo, David 1955- CANR-79
Earlier sketch in CA 137
See also CN 6, 7
Proger, Samuel (Herschel) 1906-
Brief entry 106
Progoff, Ira 1921-1997 133
Obituary 163
Prohias, Antonio 1921-1998 104
Obituary 165
Projansky, Sarah 212
Prokasy, William F(rederick) 1930- 49-52
Prokes, Mary T(imothy) 1931- 163
Prokhorov, Aleksandr Mikhailovich
1916-2002 157
Obituary 203
Prokhorov, Vadim 219
Prokhovnik, Simon Jacques 1920- 107
Prokofiev, Aleksandr Andreyevich 1900-1971
Obituary 33-36R
Prokofiev, Camilla Gray 1938(?)-1971
Obituary 33-36R
Prokofiev, Sergei (Sergeevich) 1891-1953 166
Brief entry 112
See also IDFW 3, 4
Prokop, Phyllis Stillwell 1922- CANR-9
Earlier sketch in CA 21-24R
Prokopczyk, Czeslaw 1935- 108
Prokopovich, Feofan 1681(?)-1736 ..... DLB 150
Prokosch, Frederic 1908-1989 .... CANR-82
Obituary 128
Earlier sketch in CA 73-76
See also CLC 4, 48
See also CN 1, 2, 3, 4
See also CP 1, 2
See also DLB 48
See also MTCW 2
Prole, Lozania
See Bloom, Ursula (Harvey)
Promey, Sally M. 1953- 213
Promis, Jose 1940- 143
Pronin, Alexander 1927- 49-52
Pronko, Leonard Cabell 1927- CANR-1
Earlier sketch in CA 1-4R
Pronko, N(icholas) Henry 1908-1998 ..... 9-12R
Pronzini, Bill 1943- CANR-89
Earlier sketches in CA 49-52, CANR-1, 14, 32, 59
See also CMW 4
See also DLB 226
See also TCWW 2
Proosdij, Cornelis Van
See Van Proosdy, Cornelis
Propertius, Sextus c. 50B.C.-c. 16B.C. ..... AW 2
See also CDWLB 1
See also DLB 211
See also RGWL 2, 3
Propes, Stephen Charles 1942- CANR-1
Earlier sketch in CA 49-52
Propes, Steve
See Propes, Stephen Charles
Prophet, The
See Dreiser, Theodore (Herman Albert)
Propp, Karen 1957- 183
Propper, Dan 1937- 104
See also DLB 16
Prosch, Harry 1917- 13-16R
Prose, Francine 1947- CANR-132
Brief entry 109
Earlier sketches in CA 112, CANR-46, 95
See also CLC 45
See also DLB 234
See also MTFW 2005
See also SATA 101, 149
Prosek, James 1975- 166
Proske, Beatrice (Irene) Gilman 1899- ... CAP-1
Earlier sketch in CA 9-10
Proskouriakoff, Tatiana (Avenivovna) 1909-1985
Obituary 117
Prosper, John (joint pseudonym)
See Farrar, John C(hipman)
Prosper, Lincoln
See Cannon, Helen
Prosser, Eleanor 1922- 1-4R
Prosser, H(arold) L(ee) 1944- CANR-103
Earlier sketches in CA 77-80, CANR-15, 33, 57
Prosser, Lee
See Prosser, H(arold) L(ee)
Prosser, Michael H. 1936- CANR-17
Earlier sketch in CA 25-28R
Prostano, Emanuel Theodore, Jr. 1931- . 29-32R
Prostano, Joyce S. 126
Prosterman, Roy L. 1935- 57-60
Protagoras c. 490B.C.-420B.C. .... DLB 176
Protess, David L. 1946- 184
Prothero, R(alph) Mansell 1924- 41-44R
Prothero, Stephen (Richard) 1960- . CANR-130
Earlier sketch in CA 162
Prothro, Edwin Terry 1919- 53-56
Prothro, James W(arren) 1922- CANR-8
Earlier sketch in CA 5-8R
Protopapas, George 1917- 57-60
Prou, Suzanne (Marcelle Henriette)
1920- CANR-20
Earlier sketch in CA 33-36R
Proud, Robert 1728-1813 .... DLB 30
Proudfoot, J(ohn) J(ames) 1918- 21-24R
Proudfoot, Lindsay 1950- 153
Proudhon
See Cunha, Euclides (Rodrigues Pimenta) da
Proujan, Carl 1929- 81-84
Proulx, Annie
See Proulx, E(dna) Annie
Proulx, Danny 1947- 197
Proulx, E(dna) Annie 1935- CANR-110
Earlier sketches in CA 145, CANR-65
See also AMWS 7
See also BPFB 3
See also CLC 81, 158
See also CN 6, 7
See also CPW 1
See also DA3
See also DAM POP
See also MAL 5
See also MTCW 2
See also MTFW 2005
See also SSFS 18
Proulx, Monique 1952- CANR-129
Earlier sketch in CA 169
Proulx, Suzanne 217
Proussis, Costas M.
See Proussis, Kostas M(ichael)
Proussis, Kostas M(ichael)
1911-1993 .... CANR-15
Earlier sketch in CA 41-44R
Proust, (Valentin-Louis-George-Eugene) Marcel
1871-1922 .... CANR-110
Brief entry 104
Earlier sketch in CA 120
See also AAYA 58
See also BPFB 3
See also DA
See also DA3
See also DAB
See also DAC
See also DAM MST, NOV
See also DLB 65
See also EW 8
See also EWL 3
See also GFL 1789 to the Present
See also MTCW 1, 2
See also MTFW 2005
See also RGWL 2, 3
See also SSC 75
See also TCLC 7, 13, 33
See also TWA
See also WLC
Prout, W(illiam) Leslie 1922- 9-12R
Prouty, L. Fletcher 1917- 45-48
Prouty, Morton D(ennison), Jr.
1918- CANR-28
Earlier sketch in CA 1-4R
Prouty, Olive Higgins 1882(?)-1974 .... 9-12R
Obituary 49-52
Prouvost, Jean 1885-1978
Obituary 89-92
Provan, Jill E(llen) 1948- 117
Provence, Marcel
See Jouhandeau, Marcel Henri
Provence, Sally
See Provence, Sally A(nn)
Provence, Sally A(nn) 1916- 128
Provensen, Alice 1918- CANR-128
Earlier sketches in CA 53-56, CANR-5, 44
See also CLR 11
See also MAICYA 1, 2
See also SATA 9, 70, 147
Provensen, Martin (Elias)
1916-1987 .... CANR-44
Obituary 122
Earlier sketches in CA 53-56, CANR-5
See also CLR 11
See also MAICYA 1, 2
See also SATA 9, 70
See also SATA-Obit 51
Provenzo, Eugene (F., Jr.) 1949- CANR-121
Earlier sketch in CA 135
See also SATA 78, 142
Provine, Robert R(aymond) 1943- 204
Provist, d'Alain 1906-1989
See Diop, Birago (Ismael)
Provo, Frank 1913(?)-1975
Obituary 61-64
Provoost, Anne 1964- 238
Provost, Gail Levine 1944- 127
See also SATA 65
Provost, Gary (Richard) 1944-1995 133
See also SATA 66
Provus, Malcolm M. 1928- 184
Brief entry 108
Prowe, Diethelm (Manfred-Hartmut)
1941- 57-60
Prowell, Sandra West 162
Prowler, Don(ald) 1950- 121
Prowler, Harley
See Masters, Edgar Lee
Prown, Jonathan 167
Prown, Jules David 1930- 29-32R
Prowse, Brad A. 1935- 171
Proxmire, William 1915- CANR-31
Earlier sketch in CA 29-32R
Proysen, Alf
See Proeysen, Alf
See also SATA 67
Prozan, Charlotte (Krause) 1936- 167
Prpic, George J(ure) 1920- CANR-38
Earlier sketches in CA 25-28R, CANR-17
Prucha, Francis Paul 1921- CANR-38
Earlier sketches in CA 5-8R, CANR-2, 17
Prudden, Bonnie 1914- CANR-14
Earlier sketch in CA 77-80
Prude, Agnes George de Mille
1905-1993 .... CANR-79
Obituary 142
Earlier sketches in CA 65-68, CANR-30
Pruden, (James) Wesley, Jr. 1935- 17-20R
Prudentius, Aurelius Clemens 348-c.
405 .... EW 1
See also RGWL 2, 3
Prud'homme, Alex 233
Prudhomme, Rene Francois Armand
1839-1907 170
Prudhomme, Sully
See Prudhomme, Rene Francois Armand
Prue, Sally 238
Prueitt, Melvin L(ewis) 1932- 118
Pruessen, Ronald W. 1944- 158
Pruett, Candace (J.) 1968- 233
See also SATA 157
Pruett, John H(aywood) 1947- 102
Pruett, Kyle D(ean) 1943- 131
Pruett, Lynn 1960- 227
Prufer, Kevin 1969- 187
Prugh, Jeff(ery Douglas) 1939- 41-44R
Pruitt, David (Burton) 1948- 181
Pruitt, Evelyn L(ord) 1918-2000 .... 5-8R
Obituary 188
Pruitt, Ida 1888-1985 155
Obituary 116
Pruitt, Virginia (D.) 1943- 191
Pruitt, William O(badiah), Jr. 1922- 21-24R
Pruner, Leonora 1931- 114
Prunty, Jacinta 185
Prunty, Merle C(harles) 1917-1983 .... 37-40R
Obituary 109
Prunty, Morag 1964- 219
Prunty, (Eugene) Wyatt 1947- CANR-99
Earlier sketch in CA 110
See also CSW
See also DLB 282
Prus, Boleslaw 1845-1912 .... RGWL 2, 3
See also TCLC 48
Prusek, Jaroslav 1906-1980 129
Brief entry 117
Prusina, Katica 1935- 69-72
Pruter, Hugo R.
See Pruter, Karl
Pruter, Karl 1920- 211
Pruter, Robert 1944- 137
Pruthi, Surinder P(aul) S(ingh) 1934- 61-64
Prutkov, Koz'ma Petrovich
1803-1863 .... DLB 277
Pruyser, Paul W(illem) 1916- CANR-9
Earlier sketch in CA 21-24R
Prybyla, Jan S(tanislaw) 1927- 21-24R
Pryce, Malcolm 205
Pryce, Roy 1928- 29-32R
Pryce-Jones, David 1936- CANR-71
Earlier sketches in CA 13-16R, CANR-14, 45
Pryde, Philip Rust 1938- 61-64
Pryer, Pauline
See Roby, Mary Linn
Prymak, Thomas M. 1948- 167
Prynne, J(eremy) H(alward) 1936- CANR-79
Earlier sketches in CA 97-100, CANR-39
See also CP 1, 2, 3, 4, 5, 6, 7
See also DLB 40
Pryor, Adel
See Wasserfall, Adel
Pryor, Bonnie H. 1942- CANR-86
Earlier sketch in CA 130
See also SATA 69

Pryor, Boori (Monty) 1950- 184
See also MAICYA 2
See also SATA 112
Pryor, Frederic L(eRoy) 1933- CANR-2
Earlier sketch in CA 5-8R
Pryor, Helen Brenton 1897-1972 .... CAP-2
Earlier sketch in CA 33-36
See also SATA 4
Pryor, Josh 223
Pryor, Karen 1932- CANR-123
Earlier sketch in CA 119
Pryor, Larry
See Pryor, Lawrence A(lldercice)
Pryor, Lawrence A(lldercice) 1938- 85-88
Pryor, Michael 1957- 228
See also SATA 153
Pryor, Richard (Franklin Lenox Thomas)
1940- 152
Brief entry 122
See also CLC 26
Pryor, Vanessa
See Yarbro, Chelsea Quinn
Prys-Jones, Arthur Glyn 1888-1987 104
See also CP 1, 2
Przybos, Julian 1901-1970 .... EWL 3
Przybyszewska, Stanislawa 1901-1935
Przybyszewski, Stanislaw 1868-1927 160
See also DLB 66
See also EWL 3
See also TCLC 36
Psaila, Carmelo 1871-1961 .... EWL 3
Psathas, George 1929- 21-24R
Pseudo-Dionysius the Areopagite .... DLB 115
Ptacek, Kathryn (Anne) 1952- .... HGG
See also SUFW 2
Pteleon
See Grieve, C(hristopher) M(urray)
See also DAM POET
Ptushko, Alexander 1900- .... IDFW 3, 4
Pubantz, Jerry 1947- 188
Puccetti, Roland (Peter) 1924-1995 93-96
Obituary 171
Pucci, Albert John 1920- .... SATA 44
Pucci, Joseph M. 1957- 177
Pucci, Pietro 1927- CANR-93
Earlier sketch in CA 146
Pucciani, Oreste F(rancesco)
1916-1999 .... 21-24R
Puche, Jose Luis Castillo
See Castillo Puche, Jose Luis
Puchner, Martin 1969- 229
Puck, Wolfgang 1949- 124
Puck, Y. U.
See Andre, (Kenneth) Michael
Puckett, Lute
See Masters, Edgar Lee
Puckett, Robert Hugh 1935- 41-44R
Puckett, (William) Ronald 1936- 33-36R
Puckett, Ruby Parker 1932- 57-60
Puckey, Walter (Charles) 1899-1983 ..... CAP-2
Obituary 111
Earlier sketch in CA 29-32
Pudaite, Rochunga 1927- 120
Puddepha, Derek (Noel) 1930- 61-64
Pudney, John (Sleigh) 1909-1977 ..... CANR-81
Obituary 77-80
Earlier sketches in CA 9-12R, CANR-5
See also CN 1, 2
See also CP 1, 2
See also SATA 24
Pudovkin, V(sevolod) I(llarionovich)
1893-1953 181
Brief entry 112
Pue, W(illiam) Wesley (Thomas) 1954- 223
Puechner, Ray 1936-1987 .... 25-28R
Pueckler-Muskau, Hermann von
1785-1871 .... DLB 133
Puertolas (Villanueva), Soledad 1947- 172
See also DLB 322
Puette, William J(oseph) 1946- 77-80
Pufendorf, Samuel von 1632-1694 ..... DLB 168
Puffer, K(enneth) Hart 1910-1982 .... 5-8R
Pugh, Anthony (Roy) 1931- 53-56
Pugh, Charles 1948- 81-84
Pugh, Deborah 182
Pugh, Dianne G. 167
Pugh, Edwin William 1874-1930 .... DLB 135
Pugh, Ellen (Tiffany) 1920- 49-52
See also SATA 7
Pugh, Geoff(rey) 1953- 215
Pugh, Griffith T(hompson) 1908- 5-8R
Pugh, J(ohn) W(ilbur) 1912- 21-24R
Pugh, John Charles 1919- 110
Pugh, L(eslie) P(enrhys) 1895-1983
Obituary 110
Pugh, Ralph B(ernard) 1910-1982 .... CANR-28
Obituary 108
Earlier sketch in CA 25-28R
Pugh, Rod(erick) W(ellington) 1919- 45-48
Pugh, Samuel F(ranklin) 1904- CAP-1
Earlier sketch in CA 13-14
Pugh, Sheenagh 1950- CANR-82
Earlier sketch in CA 154
See also CP 7
See also CWP
Pugh, (Virginia) Wynette 1942-1998
Obituary 165
Brief entry 111
Pugin, A. Welby 1812-1852 .... DLB 55
Pugliese, Anthony J(ulian) 1912-1985
Obituary 117
Pugliese, Stanislao G. 1965- 196
Pugsley, Alex 154
Pugsley, Clement H. 1908- CAP-1
Earlier sketch in CA 13-14
Pugsley, John A. 1934- CANR-19
Earlier sketch in CA 103
Puharich, Henry (Andrija) Karl 1918- 85-88
Puhvel, Jaan 1932- CANR-31
Earlier sketch in CA 29-32R
Puig, Manuel 1932-1990 .... CANR-63
Earlier sketches in CA 45-48, CANR-2, 32
See also BPFB 3
See also CDWLB 3
See also CLC 3, 5, 10, 28, 65, 133
See also DA3
See also DAM MULT
See also DLB 113
See also DNFS 1
See also EWL 3
See also GLL 1
See also HLC 2
See also HW 1, 2
See also LAW
See also MTCW 1, 2
See also MTFW 2005
See also RGWL 2, 3
See also TWA
See also WLIT 1
Puiggros, Adriana (Victoria) 1941- 193
Puisieux, Madeleine d'Arsant de
1720-1798 .... DLB 314
Pulaski, Mary Ann Spencer
1916-1992 .... CANR-10
Obituary 137
Earlier sketch in CA 25-28R
Pulay, George 1923-1981 45-48
Obituary 135
Puleo, Nicole
See Miller, Nicole Puleo
Pulgar, Fernando del
See Pulgar, Hernando del
Pulgar, Hernando del c. 1436-c.
1492 .... DLB 286
Pulgram, Ernst 1915- 49-52
Puligandla, Ramakrishna 1930- CANR-7
Earlier sketch in CA 61-64
Pulis, Clifford A(lton) 1916- 116
Pulitzer, Joseph, Jr. 1885-1955 201
See also DLB 29
Pulitzer, Joseph 1847-1911
Brief entry 114
See also DLB 23
See also TCLC 76
Pulitzer, Roxanne 1951- CANR-60
Earlier sketch in CA 128
Pulkingham, Betty Carr 1928- CANR-51
Earlier sketches in CA 61-64, CANR-8, 26
Pulkingham, W(illiam) Graham 1926- 53-56
Pullapilly, Cyriac K(alapura) 1932- 61-64
Pullar, Philippa 1935-1997
Obituary 161
Brief entry 116
Pullein-Thompson, Christine
See Popescu, Christine
See also SATA 3
Pullein-Thompson, Denis
See Cannan, Denis
Pullein-Thompson, Diana
See Farr, Diana (Pullein-Thompson)
See also SATA 3
Pullein-Thompson, Joanna Maxwell
1898-1961 .... CANR-87
Earlier sketch in CA 106
See also Cannan, Joanna
See also CWRI 5
Pullein-Thompson, Josephine (Mary
Wedderburn) CANR-82
Earlier sketches in CA 5-8R, CANR-7, 20, 43
See also CWRI 5
See also SATA 3, 82
Pullen, John James 1913-2003 .... 17-20R
Obituary 215
Puller, Lewis B(urwell), Jr.
1945(?)-1994 .... CANR-83
Obituary 145
Earlier sketch in CA 142
Pulliam, Eugene C(ollins) 1889-1975
Obituary 89-92
See also AITN 2
See also DLB 127
Pulliam, H(oward) Ronald 1945- 114
Pulliam, Myrta 1947- 97-100
Pullias, Earl V(ivon) 1907-1994 .... CAP-1
Earlier sketch in CA 11-12
Pulling, Albert Van Siclen 1891-1980 53-56
Obituary 135
Pulling, Christopher Robert Druce
1893- CAP-1
Earlier sketch in CA 13-14
Pulling, Pierre
See Pulling, Albert Van Siclen
Pullman, Philip (Nicholas) 1946- ... CANR-134
Earlier sketches in CA 127, CANR-50, 77, 105
See also AAYA 15, 41
See also BYA 8, 13
See also CLR 20, 62, 84
See also JRDA
See also MAICYA 1, 2
See also MAICYAS 1
See also MTFW 2005
See also SAAS 17
See also SATA 65, 103, 150
See also SUFW 2
See also WYAS 1
See also YAW
Pullum, Geoffrey K(eith) 1945- CANR-136
Earlier sketch in CA 138
Pulman, Jack 1928(?)-1979
Obituary 85-88
Pulman, Michael Barraclough 1933- 33-36R
Pulos, William L(eroy) 1920- 45-48
Pulsford, Petronella 1946- 133
Pulsipher, Gerreld L(ewis) 1939- 101
Pultz, John Francisco 1952- 234
Pulver, Harry, Jr. 1960- .... SATA 129
Pulver, Mary Monica
See Kuhfeld, Mary Pulver
Pulver, Robin 1945- CANR-111
Earlier sketch in CA 143
See also SATA 76, 133
Pulzer, Peter George Julius 1929- 13-16R
Pumphrey, H(enry) George 1912- 13-16R
Pumroy, Donald K(eith) 1925- 49-52
Punch, Maurice 1941- 65-68
Pundeff, Marin 1921- 9-12R
Pundt, Helen Marie 1903(?)-1995 .... 5-8R
Obituary 149
Punekar, Shankar Mokashi
See Mokashi-Punekar, Shankar
Puner, Helen W(alker) 1915-1989 ...... CANR-2
Obituary 129
Earlier sketch in CA 5-8R
See also SATA 37
See also SATA-Obit 63
Puner, Morton 1921- 73-76
Punnett, R(obert) M(alcolm) 1936- 25-28R
Punshon, E(rnest) R(obertson)
1872-1956 .... CMW 4
Punter, John (V.) 219
Pupin, Michael (Idvorsky) 1858-1935 219
Purcal, John T(homas) 1931- 33-36R
Purcell, Anne G. 1932- 139
Purcell, Arthur Henry 1944- 102
Purcell, Ben(jamin H.) 1928- 139
Purcell, Deirdre 1945- .... DLB 267
Purcell, Donald 1916- 122
Purcell, Gillis Philip 1904-1987
Obituary 124
Purcell, H(ugh) D(ominic) 1932- CANR-17
Earlier sketch in CA 25-28R
Purcell, Katherine 196
Purcell, Leah 1970- 199
Purcell, Mary 1906-1991 .... CANR-2
Earlier sketch in CA 5-8R
Purcell, Roy E(verett) 1936- CANR-6
Earlier sketch in CA 57-60
Purcell, Sally 1944-1998 49-52
See also CP 2
Purcell, Susan Kaufman 1942- 186
Brief entry 114
Purcell, Theodore V(incent) 1911-1984 . 41-44R
Obituary 112
Purcell, Victor 1896-1965 .... 5-8R
Purchas, Samuel 1577(?)-1626 .... DLB 151
Purdom, Charles B(enjamin)
1883-1965 .... CAP-1
Earlier sketch in CA 9-10
Purdom, P(aul) Walton 1917- 57-60
Purdom, Thomas E(dward) 1936- CANR-82
Earlier sketch in CA 13-16R
See also SFW 4
Purdom, Tom
See Purdom, Thomas E(dward)
Purdon, Eric (Sinclaire) 1913-1989 93-96
Obituary 130
Purdue, A(rthur) W(illiam) 1941- 124
Purdue, Bill
See Purdue, A(rthur) W(illiam)
Purdum, Herbert .... TCWW 1, 2
Purdy, A(lfred) W(ellington)
1918-2000 .... CANR-66
Obituary 189
Earlier sketches in CA 81-84, CANR-42
See also CAAS 17
See also CLC 3, 6, 14, 50
See also CP 1, 2, 3, 4, 5, 6, 7
See also DAC
See also DAM MST, POET
See also DLB 88
See also PFS 5
See also RGEL 2
Purdy, Alexander 1890-1976
Obituary 65-68
Purdy, Anne S. 1902(?)-1987
Obituary 122
Purdy, (Charles) Anthony 1932- 17-20R
Purdy, Captain Jim
See Gillelan, G(eorge) Howard
Purdy, Carol 1943- CANR-98
Earlier sketch in CA 136
See also SATA 66, 120
Purdy, Dwight H(illiard) 1941- 131
Purdy, James (Amos) 1923- CANR-132
Earlier sketches in CA 33-36R, CANR-19, 51
Interview in CANR-19
See also CAAS 1
See also AMWS 7
See also CLC 2, 4, 10, 28, 52
See also CN 1, 2, 3, 4, 5, 6, 7
See also DLB 2, 218
See also EWL 3
See also MAL 5
See also MTCW 1
See also RGAL 4
Purdy, Jeannine M. 1959- 170
Purdy, Jedediah S. 1974- 200
Purdy, John David 1946- 122
Purdy, Ken W(illiam) 1913-1972 155
Obituary 37-40R
See also DLB 137
Purdy, Laura M. 1946- 137
Purdy, Richard Little 1904-1990
Obituary 132
Purdy, Susan G(old) 1939- CANR-101
Earlier sketches in CA 13-16R, CANR-10
See also SATA 8
Purdy, Theodore Martindale 1903-1979
Obituary 89-92
Pure, Simon
See Swinnerton, Frank Arthur
Puri, Shamlal 1951- 130
Purkey, Roy (Delbert) 1905-1981 .... CAP-2
Earlier sketch in CA 23-24
Purkey, William Watson 1929- 29-32R
Purkis, John 1933- 97-100
Purkiser, W(estlake) T(aylor)
1910-1992 .... CAP-1
Earlier sketch in CA 13-16
Purkiss, Diane 1961- 208
Purl, Sandy M. 1953- 122
Purmell, Ann 1953- .... SATA 147
Purnell, Idella 1901-1982 61-64
Obituary 182
See also SATA 120
Purpel, David E(dward) 1932- 49-52
Purpura, Lia 1964- 161
Purrington, Robert Daniel 1936- CANR-48
Earlier sketch in CA 122
Purscell, Phyllis 1934- 25-28R
See also SATA 7
Pursell, Carroll W(irth), Jr. 1932- 77-80
Purser, John Whitley 1942- 103
Purser, Philip John 1925- CANR-76
Earlier sketches in CA 104, CANR-21, 44
Purtill, Richard L. 1931- CANR-29
Earlier sketch in CA 37-40R
See also SATA 53
Purton, Rowland W(illiam Crisby)
1925- CANR-4
Earlier sketch in CA 53-56
Purves, Alan C(arroll) 1931- CANR-9
Earlier sketch in CA 21-24R
Purves, Libby 1950- CANR-86
Earlier sketch in CA 130
Purvis, Charles C. 1902(?)-1985
Obituary 115
Puryear, Alvin N(elson) 1937-
Brief entry 115
Puryear, Edgar F., Jr. 1930- 115
Pusey, Edward Bouverie 1800-1882 ..... DLB 55
Pusey, Merlo John 1902-1985 .... 9-12R
Obituary 117
Pusey, Nathan Marsh 1907-2001 109
Obituary 203
Pushkarev, Boris S. 1929- CANR-6
Earlier sketch in CA 5-8R
Pushkarev, Sergei Germanovich
1888-1984 .... CANR-6
Earlier sketch in CA 5-8R
Pushkareva, N(atalia) L(vovna) 192
Pushker, Gloria (Teles) 1927- 142
See also SATA 75, 162
Pushkin, Aleksandr Sergeevich
See Pushkin, Alexander (Sergeyevich)
See also DLB 205
Pushkin, Alexander (Sergeyevich) 1799-1837
See Pushkin, Aleksandr Sergeevich
See also DA
See also DA3
See also DAB
See also DAC
See also DAM DRAM, MST, POET
See also EW 5
See also EXPS
See also PC 10
See also RGSF 2
See also RGWL 2, 3
See also SATA 61
See also SSC 27, 55
See also SSFS 9
See also TWA
See also WLC
Pushkin, Dave
See Pushkin, David B.
Pushkin, David B. 1963- 215
Pushkin, Vasilii L'vovich 1766-1830 ... DLB 205
Pustay, John S(tephen) 1931- 17-20R
Pustz, Matthew 1968- 214
P'u Sung-ling 1640-1715 .... SSC 31
Putcamp, Luise jr. 1924- 29-32R
Puthoff, Harold E(dward) 1936- 191
Brief entry 113
Putinas
See Mykolaitis-Putinas, Vincas
Putnam, Alice 1916- CANR-96
Earlier sketches in CA 112, CANR-45
See also SATA 61
Putnam, Arnold Oscar 1922- 9-12R
Putnam, Arthur Lee
See Alger, Horatio, Jr.
Putnam, Carleton 1901-1998 65-68
Obituary 167
Putnam, Constance E(lizabeth) 1943- 140
Putnam, Donald F(ulton) 1903-1977 ..... CAP-2
Earlier sketch in CA 29-32
Putnam, Douglas T. 1953- 239
Putnam, George Palmer 1814-1872 ...... DLB 3,
79, 250, 254
Putnam, George Palmer 1887-1950
Brief entry 109
Putnam, Hilary 1926- CANR-141
Earlier sketch in CA 61-64
See also DLB 279
Putnam, J. Wesley
See Drago, Harry Sinclair
Putnam, Jackson K(eith) 1929- 29-32R
Putnam, John
See Beckwith, Burnham Putnam
Putnam, John Fay 1924(?)-1982
Obituary 106
Putnam, Michael Courtney Jenkins
1933- CANR-142
Earlier sketch in CA 105
Putnam, Peter B(rock) 1920-1998 85-88
Obituary 171
See also SATA 30
See also SATA-Obit 106

Cumulative Index 471 Quigley

Putnam, Robert D(avid) 1941- CANR-95
Earlier sketches in CA 65-68, CANR-10
Putnam, Robert E. 1933- CANR-41
Earlier sketches in CA 53-56, CANR-5, 19
Putnam, Roy Clayton 1928- 69-72
Putnam, Samuel Whitehall 1892-1950
Brief entry 107
See also DLB 4
Putnam, William L(owell) 1924- 148
Putney, Clifford 1963- 202
Putney, Gail J.
See Fullerton, Gail Jackson
Putney, Martha S. 1916- 143
Putney, Mary Jo CANR-98
Earlier sketch in CA 164
Putra, Kerala
See Panikkar, K(avalam) Madhava
Putt, Robert C. 1938- 120
Putt, S(amuel) Gorley 1913-1995 .... CANR-6
Earlier sketch in CA 5-8R
Puttenham, George 1529(?)-1590 .... DLB 281
Putter, Ad 1967- 149
Putter, Irving 1917- 65-68
Putter, Polly
See Adomeit, Ruth E(lizabeth)
Putterman, Louis (G.) 1952- CANR-98
Earlier sketch in CA 147
Putterman, Ron 1946- 108
Puttfarken, Thomas 1943- CANR-138
Earlier sketch in CA 122
Puttnam, David T(erence) 1941- 224
See also IDFW 3, 4
Putz, Louis J. 1909-1998 .... CAP-1
Obituary 181
Earlier sketch in CA 13-14
Putzar, Edward (David) 1930- 41-44R
Putzel, Max 1910- 9-12R
Putzel, Michael 1942- 73-76
Puxley, Ray 1948- 142
Puxon, Grattan 1939- 81-84
Puzo, Mario 1920-1999 .... CANR-131
Obituary 185
Earlier sketches in CA 65-68, CANR-4, 42, 65, 99
See also BPFB 3
See also CLC 1, 2, 6, 36, 107
See also CN 1, 2, 3, 4, 5, 6
See also CPW
See also DA3
See also DAM NOV, POP
See also DLB 6
See also MTCW 1, 2
See also MTFW 2005
See also NFS 16
See also RGAL 4
Pybrum, Steven 1951- 164
Pybus, Cassandra 170
Pybus, Rodney 1938- 107
See also CP 7
Pye, (John) David 1932- 25-28R
Pye, Jack
See Morton, James (Severs)
Pye, Lloyd (Anthony, Jr.) 1946- 77-80
Pye, Lucian W(ilmot) 1921- 21-24R
Pye, Michael (Kenneth) 1946- CANR-88
Earlier sketch in CA 149
Pye, Norman 1913- 109
Pye, Virginia (Frances Kennedy)
1901-1994 .... CWRI 5
Pyenson, Lewis (Robert) 1947- CANR-96
Earlier sketch in CA 146
Pye-Smith, Charlie 1951- 176
Pygge, Edward
See Barnes, Julian (Patrick)
Pyk, Ann Phillips 1937- 77-80
Pykare, Nina 1932- CANR-60
Earlier sketch in CA 130
See also RHW
Pykare, Nina Coombs
See Pykare, Nina
Pyke, David (Alan) 1921-2001 138
Obituary 194
Pyke, Helen Godfrey 1941- 29-32R
Pyke, Magnus 1908-1992 .... CANR-6
Earlier sketch in CA 13-16R
Pyle, A(lbert) M(offett) 1945- 123
Pyle, Ernest Taylor 1900-1945 160
Brief entry 115
See also Pyle, Ernie
Pyle, Ernie
See Pyle, Ernest Taylor
See also DLB 29
See also MTCW 2
See also TCLC 75
Pyle, (William) Fitzroy 1907- CAP-2
Earlier sketch in CA 29-32
Pyle, Gerald F. 1937- 148
Pyle, Hilary 1936- 77-80
Pyle, Howard 1853-1911 137
Brief entry 109
See also AAYA 57
See also BYA 2, 4
See also CLR 22
See also DLB 42, 188
See also DLBD 13
See also LAIT 1
See also MAICYA 1, 2
See also SATA 16, 100
See also TCLC 81
See also WCH
See also YAW
Pyle, Katharine 1863-1938 .... SATA 66
Pyle, Robert Michael 1947- CANR-89
Earlier sketch in CA 142
See also ANW
See also DLB 275
Pyles, Aitken
See McDavid, Raven I(oor), Jr.
Pyles, Thomas 1905-1980 .... 13-16R
Obituary 133
Pylyshyn, Zenon W(alter) 1937- 29-32R
Pym, Barbara (Mary Crampton)
1913-1980 .... CANR-34
Obituary 97-100
Earlier sketches in CAP-1, CA 13-14, CANR-13
See also BPFB 3
See also BRWS 2
See also CLC 13, 19, 37, 111
See also DLB 14, 207
See also DLBY 1987
See also EWL 3
See also MTCW 1, 2
See also MTFW 2005
See also RGEL 2
See also TEA
Pym, Christopher 1929-2001 .... 13-16R
Obituary 201
Pym, Denis 1936- 25-28R
Pym, Dora Olive (Ivens) 1890- CAP-1
Earlier sketch in CA 13-14
Pym, Michael 1890(?)-1983
Obituary 109
Pym, Peter and
Delores
See Sandlin, Tim
Pynchon, Thomas (Ruggles, Jr.)
1937- CANR-142
Earlier sketches in CA 17-20R, CANR-22, 46, 73
See also AMWS 2
See also BEST 90:2
See also BPFB 3
See also CLC 2, 3, 6, 9, 11, 18, 33, 62, 72, 123, 192, 213
See also CN 1, 2, 3, 4, 5, 6, 7
See also CPW 1
See also DA
See also DA3
See also DAB
See also DAC
See also DAM MST, NOV, POP
See also DLB 2, 173
See also EWL 3
See also MAL 5
See also MTCW 1, 2
See also MTFW 2005
See also RGAL 4
See also SFW 4
See also SSC 14, 84
See also TCLE 1:2
See also TUS
See also WLC
Pyne, Mable Mandeville 1903-1969 .... 1-4R
Obituary 103
See also SATA 9
Pyne, Stephen J(oseph) 1949- CANR-115
Earlier sketches in CA 106, CANR-54
Pynn, Ronald 1942- 85-88
Pyper, Andrew 1968- 191
Pyrnelle, Louise-Clarke 1850-1907 179
See also DLB 42
See also SATA 114
Pyros, John 1931- 77-80
Pytchely, R. F. St. B.
See Cowie, Donald
Pythagoras c. 582B.C.-c. 507B.C. .... DLB 176

Q

Q
See Quiller-Couch, Sir Arthur (Thomas)
Qabbani, Nizar 1923-1998 .... CWW 2
See also EWL 3
Qadar, Basheer
See Alexander, (Charles) K(halil)
Qaddafi, Muammar M(uhammad) al-
1942- 189
Qadiriy, Abdullah 1894-1940 .... EWL 3
Qanoat, Mu'min 1923- .... EWL 3
Qashu, Sayed
See Kashua, Sayed
Qays, Imru al-
See al-Qays, Imru
Qays ibn al-Mulawwah c. 680-710 .... DLB 311
Qazzaz, Ayad (Sayyid Ali) Al
See Al-Qazzaz, Ayad (Sayyid Ali)
Qi, Shouhua 1957- 219
Qian, Chongzhu
See Ch'ien, Chung-shu
Qian, Xiao 1910-1999 183
Qian Hao 1925- 111
Qian Zhongshu
See Ch'ien, Chung-shu
See also CWW 2
Qoboza, Percy 1938-1988
Obituary 124
Qoyawayma, Polingaysi 1892(?)-1990 212
Qroll
See Dagerman, Stig (Halvard)
Quackenbush, Margery (Carlson) 1943- 73-76
Quackenbush, Robert M(ead)
1929- CANR-112
Earlier sketches in CA 45-48, CANR-2, 17, 38, 78
See also MAICYA 1, 2
See also SAAS 7
See also SATA 7, 70, 133
See also SATA-Essay 133
Quad, M.
See Lewis, Charles Bertrand
Quade, E(dward) S(chaumberg) 1908-1988
Obituary 125
Quade, Quentin L(on) 1933-1999 .... CANR-107
Brief entry 106
Quaghebeur, Marc 1947- 194
Quaife, Darlene Barry 1948- 137
Quaife, Milo M(ilton) 1880-1959 189
Brief entry 114
Quain, Edwin A. 1906(?)-1975
Obituary 61-64
Quale, G(ladys) Robina 1931- 21-24R
Qualey, Carlton C(hester) 1904-1988 77-80
Qualey, Marsha 1953- 148
See also AAYA 39
See also SATA 79, 124
See also YAW
Qualles, Paris 182
Qualter, Terence H(all) 1925- 37-40R
Quammen, David 1948- CANR-79
Earlier sketches in CA 29-32R, CANR-28
See also ANW
See also SATA 7
Quanbeck, Philip A. 1927- 25-28R
Quandt, B. Jean 1932- 33-36R
Quandt, Richard E(meric) 1930- CANR-29
Earlier sketch in CA 45-48
Quandt, William B. 1941- CANR-35
Earlier sketch in CA 29-32R
Quantic, Diane Dufva 1941- CANR-109
Earlier sketch in CA 152
Quantrill, Malcolm 1931- CANR-35
Earlier sketch in CA 13-16R
Quaritch, Bernard 1819-1899 .... DLB 184
Quark, Jason
See Eldin, Peter
Quarles, Benjamin (Arthur)
1904-1996 .... CANR-16
Obituary 154
Earlier sketches in CA 1-4R, CANR-1
See also BW 1
See also SATA 12
Quarles, Francis 1592-1644 .... DLB 126
See also RGEL 2
Quarles, John R(hodes), Jr. 1935- CANR-15
Earlier sketch in CA 65-68
Quarm, Daisy 1948- 122
Quarmby, Arthur 1934- 45-48
Quarrie, Bruce (Roy Bryant) 1947- 103
Quarrington, Paul (Lewis) 1953- CANR-95
Earlier sketches in CA 129, CANR-62
See also CLC 65
Quarry, Nick
See Albert, Marvin H(ubert)
Quartermain, James
See Lynne, James Broom
Quartermain, Peter (Allan) 1934- CANR-40
Earlier sketch in CA 117
Quartz, Steven R. 227
Quasimodo, Salvatore 1901-1968 .... CAP-1
Obituary 25-28R
Earlier sketch in CA 13-16
See also CLC 10
See also DLB 114
See also EW 12
See also EWL 3
See also MTCW 1
See also PC 47
See also RGWL 2, 3
Quastel, J. H.
See Quastel, Juda Hirsch
Quastel, Juda Hirsch 1899-1987
Obituary 123
Quasten, Johannes 1900-1987 .... 9-12R
Quatermass, Martin
See Carpenter, John (Howard)
Quattlebaum, Mary 1958- CANR-114
Earlier sketch in CA 152
See also SATA 88, 134
Quay, Emma .... SATA 119
Quay, Herbert C. 1927- CANR-33
Earlier sketch in CA 13-16R
Quay, Stephen 1947- 189
See also CLC 95
Quay, Timothy 1947- 189
See also CLC 95
Quaye, Cofie 1947(?)- 143
See also BW 2
Quaye, Kofi
See Quaye, Cofie
Quayle, (John) Anthony 1913-1989
Obituary 130
Quayle, (James) Dan(forth) 1947- 148
Quayle, Eric 1921- CANR-36
Earlier sketch in CA 21-24R
Qubain, Fahim I(ssa) 1924- 1-4R
Quebedeaux, Richard (Anthony)
1944- CANR-30
Earlier sketches in CA 73-76, CANR-12
Queen, Ellery
See Dannay, Frederic and
Davidson, Avram (James) and
Deming, Richard and
Fairman, Paul W. and
Flora, Fletcher and
Hoch, Edward D(entinger) and
Kane, Henry and
Lee, Manfred B(ennington) and
Marlowe, Stephen and Powell, (Oval) Talmage and
Sheldon, Walter J(ames) and
Sturgeon, Theodore (Hamilton) and
Tracy, Don(ald Fiske) and
Vance, John Holbrook
See also BPFB 3
See also CLC 3, 11
See also CMW 4
See also MSW
See also RGAL 4
Queen, Ellery, Jr.
See Dannay, Frederic and
Holding, James (Clark Carlisle, Jr.) and
Lee, Manfred B(ennington)
Queen, Frank 1822-1882 .... DLB 241
Queen, Stuart Alfred 1890-1987 .... 21-24R
Queenan, Joe 1950- CANR-91
Earlier sketch in CA 140
Queen Noor
See Al Hussein, Noor
Queen Wilhelmina
See Nassau, Wilhelmina Helena Pauline Maria
Queiros, Eca de 1845-1900 .... DLB 287
Queiroz, Rachel de
See de Queiroz, Rachel
See also CWW 2
See also DLB 307
See also EWL 3
See also LAW
See also RGWL 2, 3
Quelch, John A(nthony) 1951- CANR-53
Earlier sketches in CA 112, CANR-29
Queller, Donald E(dward)
1925-1995 .... CANR-4
Earlier sketch in CA 53-56
Queneau, Raymond 1903-1976 .... CANR-32
Obituary 69-72
Earlier sketch in CA 77-80
See also CLC 2, 5, 10, 42
See also DLB 72, 258
See also EW 12
See also EWL 3
See also GFL 1789 to the Present
See also MTCW 1, 2
See also RGWL 2, 3
Quenelle, Gilbert 1914- 25-28R
Quennell, Marjorie Courtney
1884-1972 73-76
See also SATA 29
Quennell, Peter (Courtney)
1905-1993 .... CANR-69
Obituary 143
Brief entry 113
Earlier sketch in CA 115
See also CP 1
See also DLB 155, 195
Quental, Antero de 1842-1891 .... DLB 287
Quentin, Brad
See Bisson, Terry (Ballantine)
Quentin, Patrick
See Wheeler, Hugh (Callingham)
Querry, Ronald B(urns) 1943- 117
Query, William T(heodore), Jr. 1929- 41-44R
Quesada, Jose Luis 1948- .... DLB 290
Quesada, Roberto 1962- 226
Quesnel, Joseph 1746-1809 .... DLB 99
Quesnell, John G(eorge) 1936- CANR-1
Earlier sketch in CA 45-48
Quesnell, Quentin 1927- 120
Quest, Linda (Gerber) 1935- 77-80
Quest, (Edna) Olga W(ilbourne) Hall
See Hall-Quest, (Edna) Olga W(ilbourne)
Quest, Rodney CAP-2
Earlier sketch in CA 29-32
Quester, George H(erman) 1936- CANR-93
Earlier sketches in CA 25-28R, CANR-10, 34
Quest-Ritson, Charles 220
Quetchenbach, Bernard W. 1955- 232
Quezada, Abel 1920(?)-1991 .... 5-8R
Obituary 133
Quezada, J. Gilberto 1946- 187
Quiatt, Duane 1929- 149
Quichot, Dona
See Tomkiewicz, Mina
Quick, Amanda
See Krentz, Jayne Ann
Quick, Annabelle 1922-1986 .... 21-24R
See also SATA 2
Quick, Armand James 1894-1978
Obituary 73-76
Quick, Barbara 1954- 133
Quick, John 171
Quick, Philip
See Strage, Mark
Quick, Richard (John Worth) 1944- 127
Quick, Thomas L(ee) 1929-1992 .... CANR-34
Earlier sketch in CA 41-44R
Quick, W(illiam) T(homas) 172
Quick, William K(ellon) 1933- 137
Quickel, Stephen (Woodside) 1936- 73-76
Quie, Gretchen 1927- 117
Quiery, William H. 1926- 21-24R
Quigg, Jane (Hulda) (?)-1986
Obituary 120
See also SATA-Obit 49
Quigg, Philip W. 1920- CANR-35
Earlier sketch in CA 9-12R
Quigless, Helen Gordon 1944-
Brief entry 105
Quigley, Aileen 1930- 124
Brief entry 104
Quigley, Austin E(dmund) 1942- 101
Quigley, Carroll 1910-1977 .... CANR-27
Obituary 69-72
Earlier sketch in CA 37-40R
Quigley, Declan 1956- 146

Quigley, Eileen Elliott
See Vivers, Eileen Elliott
Quigley, Ellen 1955- ... 111
Quigley, Harold Scott 1889-1968 ... 1-4R
Obituary ... 103
Quigley, Joan 1927- ... CANR-43
Earlier sketch in CA 29-32R
See also BEST 90:3
Quigley, John 1927- ... 17-20R
Quigley, John M(ichael) 1942- ... 110
Brief entry ... 107
Quigley, Kevin F. F. 1952- ... 166
Quigley, Martin (Schofield), Jr.
1917- ... CANR-38
Earlier sketches in CA 1-4R, CANR-17
Quigley, Martin (Peter) 1913-2000 ... CANR-18
Obituary ... 188
Earlier sketch in CA 17-20R
Quilici, Folco 1930- ... 105
Quill
See Grange, Cyril
Quill, Barnaby
See Brandner, Gary (Phil)
Quill, Monica
See McInerny, Ralph (Matthew)
Quillen, Rita Sims 1954- ... 188
Quiller, Andrew
See Bulmer, (Henry) Kenneth and James, Laurence
Quiller-Couch, Sir Arthur (Thomas)
1863-1944 ... 166
Brief entry ... 118
See also DLB 135, 153, 190
See also HGG
See also RGEL 2
See also SUFW 1
See also TCLC 53
Quilligan, Maureen 1944- ... CANR-16
Earlier sketch in CA 89-92
Quilter, Deborah 1950- ... CANR-98
Earlier sketch in CA 147
Quilty, Rafe
See Witcombe, R(ick) T(rader)
Quimber, Mario
See Alexander, (Charles) K(halil)
Quimby, George Irving 1913-2003 .. CANR-34
Earlier sketch in CA 57-60
Quimby, Myron J. ... 25-28R
Quimby, Myrtle 1891-1980 ... CAP-2
Obituary ... 171
Earlier sketch in CA 25-28
Quin, Ann (Marie) 1936-1973 ... 9-12R
Obituary ... 45-48
See also CLC 6
See also CN 1
See also DLB 14, 231
Quin, Mike
See Ryan, Paul William
Quinan, Jack
See Quinan, John F.
Quinan, John F. 1939- ... 125
Quinault, Philippe c. 1635-1688 ... DLB 268
Quince, Peter
See Day, George Harold
Quince, Peter Lum
See Ritchie, (Harry) Ward
Quincey, Thomas de
See De Quincey, Thomas
Quincunx, Ramona J.
See Borgmann, Dmitri A(lfred)
Quincy, Samuel fl. 18th cent. - ... DLB 31
Quincy, Samuel 1734-1789 ... DLB 31
Quindlen, Anna 1953- ... CANR-126
Earlier sketches in CA 138, CANR-73
See also AAYA 35
See also CLC 191
See also DA3
See also DLB 292
See also MTCW 2
See also MTFW 2005
Quine, Judith Balaban 1932- ... 140
Quine, W. V.
See Quine, Willard Van Orman
See also DLB 279
Quine, Willard V.
See Quine, Willard Van Orman
Quine, Willard Van Orman
1908-2000 ... CANR-37
Obituary ... 191
Earlier sketches in CA 1-4R, CANR-1, 16
See also Quine, W. V.
Quin-Harkin, Janet 1941- ... CANR-104
Earlier sketches in CA 81-84, CANR-15, 33, 59
See also Bowen, Rhys
See also AAYA 6, 48
See also SATA 18, 90, 119
Quinion, Michael (Brian) 1942- ... 238
Quinlan, David 1942- ... 147
Quinlan, Red
See Quinlan, Sterling C(arroll)
Quinlan, Sterling C(arroll) 1916- ... CANR-8
Earlier sketch in CA 5-8R
Quinlan, Susan E(lizabeth) 1954- ... 152
See also SATA 88
Quinley, Harold E(arl) 1942- ... 61-64
Quinn, A(lexander) James 1932- ... 29-32R
Quinn, Anthony (Rudolph Oaxaca)
1915-2001 ... 155
Obituary ... 196
Brief entry ... 111
See also DLB 122
See also HW 1, 2
Quinn, Arthur 1942- ... 110
Quinn, (Mary) Bernetta 1915- ... 105
Quinn, C(osmas) Edward 1926-1989
Obituary ... 129
Quinn, Charles (Nicholas) 1930- ... 123
Brief entry ... 110
Interview in ... CA-123
Quinn, D. Michael 1944- ... CANR-117
Earlier sketch in CA 155
Quinn, Daniel 1935- ... CANR-89
Earlier sketch in CA 137
Quinn, David B(eers) 1909-2002 ... CANR-15
Obituary ... 203
Earlier sketch in CA 77-80
Quinn, Edward 1932- ... 77-80
Quinn, Elisabeth 1881-1962 ... SATA 22
Quinn, Esther Casier 1922- ... CANR-35
Earlier sketch in CA 5-8R
Quinn, Francis X. 1932- ... CANR-4
Earlier sketch in CA 9-12R
Quinn, Herbert F(urlong) 1910- ... CAP-1
Earlier sketch in CA 19-20
Quinn, James 1919- ... 13-16R
Quinn, James Brian 1928- ... CANR-35
Earlier sketch in CA 13-16R
Quinn, Jane Bryant 1939- ... 93-96
Quinn, John
See Wood, Edward D(avis), Jr.
Quinn, John ... CWRI 5
Quinn, John 1870-1924 ... DLB 187
Quinn, John F(rancis) 1925- ... 203
Quinn, John Francis 1925-
Brief entry ... 115
Quinn, John M(ichael) 1922- ... 45-48
Quinn, John Paul 1943- ... 33-36R
Quinn, John R. 1938- ... 97-100
Quinn, Julia 1970- ... 229
Quinn, Kenneth (Fleming) 1920- ... CANR-94
Earlier sketches in CA 25-28R, CANR-17
Quinn, Martin
See Smith, Martin Cruz
Quinn, Michael A(lan) 1945- ... CANR-25
Earlier sketch in CA 45-48
Quinn, Niall 1943- ... CANR-37
Earlier sketch in CA 108
Quinn, Pat 1947- ... 199
See also SATA 130
Quinn, Patrick 1950- ... SATA 73
Quinn, Peter 1947- ... 197
See also CLC 91
Quinn, R(obert) M(acLean) 1920- ... 21-24R
Quinn, Rob 1972- ... 208
See also SATA 138
Quinn, Sally 1941- ... CANR-27
Earlier sketch in CA 65-68
Interview in ... CANR-27
See also AITN 2
Quinn, Seabury (Grandin)
1889-1969 ... CANR-75
Obituary ... 104
Earlier sketch in CA 108
See also HGG
Quinn, Simon
See Smith, Martin Cruz
Quinn, Sister Bernetta
See Quinn, (Mary) Bernetta
Quinn, Sunny 1949- ... 165
Quinn, Susan 1940- ... CANR-113
Earlier sketch in CA 103
See also Jacobs, Susan
Quinn, Tara Taylor (a pseudonym) ... 225
Quinn, Terry 1945- ... CANR-18
Earlier sketch in CA 101
Quinn, Theodora K.
See Kroeber, Theodora (Kracaw)
Quinn, Vernon
See Quinn, Elisabeth
Quinn, Vincent 1926- ... 21-24R
Quinn, William Arthur 1920- ... 5-8R
Quinn, Zdenka (Hodbodova) 1942- ... 33-36R
Quinnell, A. J. 1939- ... 144
Quinnett, Paul G(uthrie) 1939- ... CANR-96
Earlier sketch in CA 114
Quinney, Richard 1934- ... CANR-126
Earlier sketches in CA 57-60, CANR-9
Quinones, Ricardo J(oseph) 1935- ... 153
Brief entry ... 112
Quinonez, Ernesto 1966(?)- ... 193
Quinonez, Naomi 1951- ... DLB 209
Quinsey, Mary Beth 1948- ... 132
Quint, Barbara Gilder 1928- ... 103
Quint, Bert 1930- ... 69-72
Quint, David 1950- ... 195
Quint, Howard H. 1917-1981 ... 97-100
Quint, Jeanne
See Benoliel, Jeanne Quint
Quint, Michel 1949- ... 230
Quintal, Claire 1930- ... 13-16R
Quintana, Anton 1937- ... 198
Quintana, Bertha B(eatrice) 1924-
Brief entry ... 113
Quintana, Frances
See Swadesh, Frances Leon
Quintana, Leroy V. 1944- ... CANR-139
Earlier sketches in CA 131, CANR-65
See also DAM MULT
See also DLB 82
See also HLC 2
See also HW 1, 2
See also PC 36
Quintana, Ricardo (Beckwith)
1898-1987 ... 25-28R
Quintana Ranck, Katherine 1942- ... 181
See also DLB 122
Quintanilla, (Maria) Aline (Griffith y Dexter)
1921- ... CANR-50
Earlier sketch in CA 9-12R
Quintero, Jose (Benjamin) 1924-1999 ... 153
Obituary ... 177
See also HW 1
Quintero, Ruben 1949- ... 143
Quintilian c. 40-c. 100 ... AW 2
See also DLB 211
See also RGWL 2, 3
Quinto, Leon 1926- ... 37-40R
Quinton, Ann 1934- ... 226
Quinton, Anthony Meredith 1925- ... CANR-10
Earlier sketch in CA 21-24R
Quirarte, Jacinto 1931- ... CANR-141
Earlier sketches in CA 45-48, CANR-32
See also HW 1
Quirin, G(eorge) David 1931- ... CANR-9
Earlier sketch in CA 21-24R
Quirin, William L(ouis) 1942- ... 93-96
Quirk, Anne (E.) 1956- ... 167
See also SATA 99
Quirk, James P(atrick) 1926- ... CANR-90
Earlier sketches in CA 57-60, CANR-7
Quirk, Joe 1966- ... 169
Quirk, John E(dward) 1920-1969 ... 5-8R
Quirk, Lawrence J. 1923- ... CANR-143
Earlier sketches in CA 25-28R, CANR-12, 27, 52
Quirk, Paul J. 1949- ... 108
Quirk, Randolph 1920- ... CANR-2
Earlier sketch in CA 5-8R
Quirk, Robert E. 1918- ... 1-4R
Quirk, Thomas Vaughan 1946- ... CANR-99
Earlier sketches in CA 122, CANR-48
Quirk, Tom
See Quirk, Thomas Vaughan
Quirk, William J. 1933- ... 154
Quiroga, Elena 1921-1995 ... CWW 2
Quiroga, Horacio (Sylvestre) 1878-1937 ... 131
Brief entry ... 117
See also DAM MULT
See also EWL 3
See also HLC 2
See also HW 1
See also LAW
See also MTCW 1
See also RGSF 2
See also TCLC 20
See also WLIT 1
Quiroga, Jose A. 1959- ... 197
Quiros, Armando 1925- ... 206
Quispel, Gilles 1916- ... 89-92
Quist, John W. 1960- ... 187
Quist, Susan 1944- ... 57-60
Quitslund, Sonya A(ntoinette) 1935- .. CANR-1
Earlier sketch in CA 49-52
Quittner, Joshua ... 182
Quixley, Jim 1931- ... SATA 56
Quoirez, Francoise 1935-2004 ... CANR-73
Obituary ... 231
Earlier sketches in CA 49-52, CANR-6, 39
See also Sagan, Francoise
See also CLC 9
See also MTCW 1, 2
See also MTFW 2005
See also TWA
Quoist, Michel 1921- ... 65-68
Quong, Rose Lanu 1879(?)-1972
Obituary ... 37-40R
Qureshi, Hazel 1949- ... 138
Qureshi, Ishtiaq Husain 1903-1980 ... CAP-1
Earlier sketch in CA 11-12
Quyth, Gabriel
See Jennings, Gary (Gayne)
Qvortrup, Mads 1967- ... 239

R

R., Ji
See Renaud, Jacques
Ra, Carol F. 1939- ... 143
See also SATA 76
Ra, Jong Oh 1945- ... 85-88
Raab, Evelyn 1951- ... 198
See also SATA 129
Raab, Lawrence E(dward) 1946- ... CANR-102
Earlier sketch in CA 65-68
Raab, Menachem 1923- ... 114
Raab, Robert Allen 1924- ... 29-32R
Raab, Selwyn 1934- ... 73-76
Raabe, Wilhelm (Karl) 1831-1910 ... 167
See also DLB 129
See also TCLC 45
Raack, R(ichard) C(harles) 1928- ... 41-44R
Raad, Virginia 1925- ... 154
Raadschelders, Jos C. N. 1955- ... 170
Ra'Anan, Gavriel D. 1954(?)-1983
Obituary ... 110
Ra'Anan, H. F. Frischwasser
See Ra'Anan, Uri
Ra'Anan, Uri 1926- ... CANR-25
Earlier sketch in CA 108
Raat, W(illiam) Dirk 1939- ... CANR-48
Earlier sketches in CA 106, CANR-23
Rabalais, J. Wayne 1944- ... 235
Rabalais, Maria 1921- ... 61-64
Raban, Jonathan 1942- ... CANR-65
Earlier sketches in CA 61-64, CANR-17
See also BRWS 11
See also DLB 204
Rabasa, George 1941- ... 169
Rabassa, Gregory 1922- ... 223
Earlier sketches in CA 45-48, CANR-2, 26, 51, 78
Autobiographical Essay in ... 223
See also CAAS 9
See also HW 1, 2
Rabasseire, Henri
See Pachter, Henry M(aximillian)
Rabate, Jean-Michel 1949- ... 139
Rabb, Jane M. 1938- ... 152
Rabb, Jonathan 1964- ... 169
Rabb, Theodore K. 1937- ... CANR-90
Earlier sketches in CA 21-24R, CANR-10
Rabbie
See Towers, Maxwell
Rabbitt, Thomas 1943- ... 57-60
Rabdau, Marianne
See Bakker-Rabdau, Marianne K(atherine)
Rabe, Berniece (Louise) 1928- ... CANR-1
Earlier sketch in CA 49-52
See also SAAS 10
See also SATA 7, 77, 148
See also SATA-Essay 148
Rabe, David (William) 1940- ... CANR-129
Earlier sketches in CA 85-88, CANR-59
See also CABS 3
See also CAD
See also CD 5, 6
See also CLC 4, 8, 33, 200
See also DAM DRAM
See also DC 16
See also DFS 3, 8, 13
See also DLB 7, 228
See also EWL 3
See also MAL 5
Rabe, John 1882-1949 ... 184
Rabe, Olive H(anson) (?)-1968 ... CAP-2
Earlier sketch in CA 19-20
See also SATA 13
Rabe, Stephen G(eorge) 1948- ... 108
Rabearivelo, Jean-Joseph 1901-1937 ... EWL 3
Rabelais, Francois 1494-1553 ... DA
See also DAB
See also DAC
See also DAM MST
See also EW 2
See also GFL Beginnings to 1789
See also LMFS 1
See also RGWL 2, 3
See also TWA
See also WLC
Rabemababjara, Jacques 1913- ... EWL 3
Raben, Joseph 1924- ... CANR-12
Earlier sketch in CA 69-72
Raber, David ... 203
Rabi, I(sidor) I(saac) 1898-1988
Obituary ... 125
Rabi'ah al-'Adawiyyah c. 720-801 ... DLB 311
Rabie, Jan 1920- ... 29-32R
Rabie, Mohamed 1940- ... CANR-109
Earlier sketch in CA 151
Rabier, Jean 1927- ... IDFW 3, 4
Rabikovitz, Dahlia ... CWW 2
Rabikovitz, Dalia 1936- ... 195
Brief entry ... 108
See also Ravikovitch, Dahlia and Ravikovitch, Dalia
Rabikowitz, Dalyah
See Rabikovitz, Dalia
Rabil, Albert, Jr. 1934- ... CANR-10
Earlier sketch in CA 25-28R
Rabin, A(lbert) I(srael) 1912- ... CANR-41
Earlier sketches in CA 53-56, CANR-4, 19
Rabin, Chaim 1915-1996 ... 105
Rabin, Edward H(arold) 1937- ... 49-52
Rabin, Leah 1928-2000 ... 160
Obituary ... 192
Rabin, Robert L. 1939- ... 148
Rabin, Staton 1958- ... 238
See also SATA 84, 162
Rabin, Yitzhak 1922-1995 ... 149
Brief entry ... 111
Rabinbach, Anson (Gilbert) 1945- ... 142
Rabiner, Susan 1948- ... 212
Rabinovich, Abraham 1933- ... 61-64
Rabinovich, Dalia ... 185
Rabinovich, Isaiah 1904-1972 ... CAP-2
Earlier sketch in CA 25-28
Rabinovich, Itamar 1942- ... 177
Rabinovitch, Sholem 1859-1916
Brief entry ... 104
See also Aleichem, Sholom
Rabinovitz, Rubin 1938- ... 21-24R
Rabinow, Paul 1944- ... CANR-93
Earlier sketches in CA 61-64, CANR-13
Rabinowich, Ellen 1946- ... 106
See also SATA 29
Rabinowicz, Mordka Harry 1919-2002 ... 5-8R
Obituary ... 203
Rabinowicz, Tzvi
See Rabinowicz, Mordka Harry
Rabinowitch, Alexander 1934- ... 21-24R
Rabinowitch, Eugene 1901-1973 ... 77-80
Obituary ... 41-44R
Rabinowitz, Alan 1927- ... CANR-127
Earlier sketches in CA 29-32R, CANR-27
Rabinowitz, Dorothy ... 232
Rabinowitz, Ezekiel 1892-1982 ... 25-28R
Rabinowitz, Howard Neil 1942-1998 ... 105
Rabinowitz, Ilana ... 238
Rabinowitz, Isaac 1909-1988
Obituary ... 126
Rabinowitz, Louis Isaac 1906-1984
Obituary ... 113
Rabinowitz, Paula 1951- ... CANR-55
Earlier sketch in CA 127
Rabinowitz, Peter MacGarr 1956- ... 104
Rabinowitz, Sandy 1954- ... 103
See also SATA 52
See also SATA-Brief 39
Rabinowitz, Solomon
See Rabinovitch, Sholem
Rabins, Peter V(incent) 1947- ... 109
Rabinyan, Dorit 1972- ... 170
See also CLC 119
Rabkin, Brenda 1945- ... 101

Cumulative Index 473 Rai

Rabkin, Eric S. 1946- CANR-4
Earlier sketch in CA 49-52
Rabkin, Gerald Edward 1930-
Brief entry 105
Rabkin, Norman C. 1930- CANR-73
Earlier sketches in CA 1-4R, CANR-4
Rabkin, Richard 1932- 33-36R
Rable, George C(alvin) 1950- 116
Raboff, Ernest Lloyd .... SATA-Brief 37
Rabon, Israel 1900-1941 .... EWL 3
Raboni, Giovanni 1932-2004 .... DLB 128
Raborg, Frederick A(shton), Jr.
1934- CANR-20
Earlier sketch in CA 103
Raboteau, Albert J(ordy) 1943- CANR-108
Earlier sketch in CA 151
Rabow, Gerald 1928- 25-28R
Raboy, Marc 1948- 135
Rabushka, Alvin 1940- 186
Brief entry 116
Rabuzzi, Kathryn Allen 1938- 113
Raby, Derek Graham 1927- 103
Raby, William L(ouis) 1927- CANR-23
Earlier sketches in CA 17-20R, CANR-8
Racan, Honorat de Bueil
1589-1670 .... GFL Beginnings to 1789
Race, Jeffrey 1943- 37-40R
Race, Robert Russell 1907-1984
Obituary 113
Racevskis, Karlis 1939- 117
Racheter, Donald P. 1947- 188
Rachilde
See Vallette, Marguerite Eymery and
Vallette, Marguerite Eymery
See also EWL 3
Rachins, Alan 1947- 172
Rachleff, Owen S(pencer) 1934- CANR-40
Earlier sketches in CA 21-24R, CANR-14
Rachleff, Peter (J.) 1951- 141
Rachlin, Carol K(ing) 1919- 57-60
See also SATA 64
Rachlin, Harvey (Brant) 1951- CANR-93
Earlier sketches in CA 107, CANR-26
See also SATA 47
Rachlin, Nahid CANR-120
Earlier sketches in CA 81-84, CANR-14
See also CAAS 17
See also SATA 64
Rachlis, Eugene (Jacob) 1920-1986 .... 5-8R
Obituary 121
See also SATA-Obit 50
Rachman, David Jay 1928- 57-60
Rachman, Stanley Jack 1934- 89-92
Rachow, Louis A(ugust) 1927- 57-60
Racin, Koco 1908-1943 .... DLB 147
Racina, Thom
See Raucina, Thomas Frank
Racine, Jean 1639-1699 .... DA3
See also DAB
See also DAM MST
See also DLB 268
See also EW 3
See also GFL Beginnings to 1789
See also LMFS 1
See also RGWL 2, 3
See also TWA
Racine, Michel 1942- 136
Racine, Philip N. 1941- CANR-101
Earlier sketch in CA 148
Rack, Henry D(enman) 1931- 13-16R
Racker, Efraim 1913-1991 89-92
Rackham, Arthur 1867-1939 179
See also AAYA 31
See also CLR 57
See also DLB 141
See also MAICYA 1, 2
See also SATA 15, 100
Rackham, John
See Phillifent, John Thomas
Rackham, Thomas W(illiam) 1919- 25-28R
Rackin, Phyllis 1933- 85-88
Rackman, Emanuel 1910- 29-32R
Rackowe, Alec 1897-1991 .... 25-28R
Obituary 171
Raczka, Bob 1963- 239
See also SATA 163
Raczymow, Henri 1948- .... DLB 299
Rad, Gerhard von
See von Rad, Gerhard
Radakovich, Anka 1957- 152
Radan, G. T.
See Radan, George T(ivadar)
Radan, George T(ivadar) 1923- CANR-39
Earlier sketch in CA 116
Radano, Ronald M. 1956- 149
Radauskas, Henrikas 1910-1970 ...... CDWLB 4
See also DLB 220
See also EWL 3
Radavich, David (Allen) 1949- 207
Radbill, Samuel X. 1901-1987 49-52
Obituary 174
Radcliff, Alan L(awrence) 1920- 49-52
Radcliff, Peter (Edward, Jr.) 1932- 21-24R
Radcliffe, Ann (Ward) 1764-1823 . DLB 39, 178
See also GL 3
See also HGG
See also LMFS 1
See also RGEL 2
See also SUFW
See also WLIT 3
Radcliffe, Donnie
See Radcliffe, Redonia
Radcliffe, George L. 1878(?)-1974
Obituary 53-56
Radcliffe, Janette
See Roberts, Janet Louise
Radcliffe, Lynn J(ames) 1896-1980 .... 1-4R
Obituary 176
Radcliffe, Philip (Fitzhugh) 1905-1986
Obituary 120
Radcliffe, Redonia CANR-98
Earlier sketch in CA 132
Radcliffe, Virginia
See Hurst, Virginia Radcliffe
Radcliffe-Brown, A(lfred) R(eginald)
1881-1955 212
Brief entry 114
Radcliff-Umstead, Douglas
1944-1992 .... CANR-13
Earlier sketch in CA 33-36R
Radclyffe-Hall, Marguerite
See Hall, (Marguerite) Radclyffe
Raddall, Thomas Head 1903-1994 ... CANR-77
Earlier sketches in CA 1-4R, CANR-28
See also CN 1, 2, 3, 4, 5
See also DLB 68
See also RHW
Radden, Jennifer H. 1943- CANR-121
Earlier sketch in CA 168
Raddysh, Garry
See Radison, Garry
Radel, John J(oseph) 1934- 29-32R
Radelet, Louis A(ugust) 1917-1991 89-92
Radelet, Michael L. 1950- 140
Radencich, Marguerite C. 1952-1998 148
See also SATA 79
Rader, Benjamin G(ene) 1935- 21-24R
Rader, Dotson 1942- CANR-11
Earlier sketch in CA 61-64
Rader, Melvin (Miller) 1903-1981 .... CANR-73
Earlier sketches in CA 13-16R, CANR-5
Rader, Ralph Wilson 1930- 13-16R
Rader, Randall R(ay) 1949- 121
Rader, Rosemary 1931- 112
Rader, (John) Trout (III) 1938- 37-40R
Radest, Howard B(ernard) 1928- 41-44R
Radford, Caroline Maitland 1858-1920 205
See also Radford, Dollie
Radford, Dollie 1858-1920
See Radford, Caroline Maitland
See also DLB 240
Radford, Edwin Isaac 1891-1973 ..... CANR-82
Earlier sketch in CA 104
Radford, Irene 1950- 152
Radford, John 1901-1967 .... CAP-2
Earlier sketch in CA 21-22
Radford, Richard F(rancis), Jr. 1939- . CANR-20
Earlier sketch in CA 104
Radford, Ruby L(orraine) 1891-1971 .. CANR-4
Earlier sketch in CA 1-4R
See also SATA 6
Radha, Sivananda 1911-1995 .... CANR-36
Earlier sketch in CA 114
Radha, Swami Sivananda
See Radha, Sivananda
Radhakrishnan, C(hakkorayil) 1939- 57-60
Radhakrishnan, Sarvepalli
1888-1975 .... CANR-73
Obituary 57-60
Earlier sketches in CAP-1, CA 13-16
Radi, Nuha 1941-2004 236
Radice, Barbara CANR-82
Earlier sketch in CA 133
Radice, Betty 1912-1985 .... CANR-12
Obituary 115
Earlier sketch in CA 25-28R
Radice, Giles 1936- CANR-142
Earlier sketches in CA 25-28R, CANR-17
Radichkov, Yordan 1929- .... DLB 181
Radichkov, Yordan Dimitrov 1929-2004 208
Obituary 222
Radiguet, Raymond 1903-1923 162
See also DLB 65
See also EWL 3
See also GFL 1789 to the Present
See also RGWL 2, 3
See also TCLC 29
Radimsky, Ladislaw 1898-1970
Obituary 29-32R
Radin, Beryl A(viva) 1936- 218
Radin, Edward D(avid) 1909-1966
Obituary 114
Radin, George 1896-1981
Obituary 102
Radin, Paul 1883-1959
Brief entry 120
Radin, Ruth Yaffe 1938- 124
See also SATA 56, 107
See also SATA-Brief 52
Radish, Kris 1953- 207
Radishchev, Aleksandr Nikolaevich
1749-1802 .... DLB 150
Radison, Garry 1949- 117
Radji, Parviz C(amran) 1936- 131
Radke, August C. 1922-2000 220
Radke, Don 1940- 57-60
Radl, Shirley L(ouise) 1935- CANR-12
Earlier sketch in CA 69-72
Radlauer, David 1952- 106
See also SATA 28
Radlauer, Edward 1921- CANR-30
Earlier sketches in CA 69-72, CANR-13
See also SATA 15
Radlauer, Ruth Shaw 1926- CANR-30
Earlier sketches in CA 81-84, CANR-13
See also SATA 15, 98
Radler, D(on) H. 1926- 13-16R
Radley, Eric John 1917- 109
Radley, Gail 1951- CANR-16
Earlier sketch in CA 89-92
See also SATA 25, 112
Radley, Paul John 1962- 121
Radley, Sheila
See Robinson, Sheila Mary
Radley, Virginia L. 1927-1998 .... 25-28R
Obituary 172
Radner, Gilda 1946-1989 129
Obituary 128
See also BEST 89:4
Radner, Joan Newlon 167
Radner, Roy 1927- 49-52
Radnoti, Miklos 1909-1944 212
Brief entry 118
See also CDWLB 4
See also DLB 215
See also EWL 3
See also RGWL 2, 3
See also TCLC 16
Rado, Alexander
See Rado, Sandor
Rado, James 1939- 105
See also CLC 17
Rado, Sandor 1900-1981 109
Obituary 105
Radoff, Morris L(eon) 1905-1978 85-88
Obituary 81-84
Radojcic-Kane, Natasha 1966- 220
Radom, Matthew 1905- 57-60
Radosh, Ronald 1937- CANR-57
Earlier sketch in CA 101
Radovanovic, Ivan 1961- 225
Radrigan, Juan 1937- .... DLB 305
Radstrom, Niklas 1953- 194
Radtke, Guenter 1920- 110
Radtke, Gunter
See Radtke, Guenter
Radvanyi, Janos 1922- 41-44R
Radvanyi, Netty 1900-1983 .... CANR-82
Obituary 110
Earlier sketch in CA 85-88
See also Seghers, Anna
Radwanski, Pierre A(rthur) 1903- CAP-2
Earlier sketch in CA 23-24
Radwanski-Szinagel, Dr. Pierre A.
See Radwanski, Pierre A(rthur)
Radway, Ann
See Geis, Richard E(rwin)
Radway, Janice A(nne) 1949- CANR-81
Earlier sketch in CA 121
Radyr, Tomos
See Stevenson, James Patrick (Haldane)
Radzienda, Tom 170
Radzinowicz, Leon 1906-1999 .... CANR-26
Obituary 188
Earlier sketch in CA 106
Radzinskii, Edvard (Stanislavovich)
See Radzinsky, Edvard (Stanislavovich)
See also CWW 2
Radzinsky, Edvard (Stanislavovich)
1936- CANR-72
Earlier sketch in CA 142
See also Radzinskii, Edvard (Stanislavovich)
See also EWL 3
Radzinsky, Edward
See Radzinsky, Edvard (Stanislavovich)
Rae, Ben
See Griffiths, Trevor
Rae, Daphne 1933- 109
Rae, (Margaret) Doris 1907- CANR-15
Earlier sketches in CAP-1, CA 11-12
Rae, Douglas W(hiting) 1939- 77-80
Rae, Evonne 1928-1974
Obituary 104
Rae, Gwynedd 1892-1977 .... CANR-76
Earlier sketch in CA 65-68
See also CWRI 5
See also SATA 37
Rae, Hugh C(rauford) 1935- CANR-55
Earlier sketches in CA 17-20R, CANR-8, 29
See also Crawford, Robert and
Stirling, Jessica
See also RHW
Rae, John B(ell) 1911-1988 .... CANR-73
Earlier sketch in CA 13-16R
Rae, John Malcolm 1931- CANR-4
Earlier sketch in CA 1-4R
Rae, Milford Andersen 1946- CANR-8
Earlier sketch in CA 61-64
Rae, Nicol C(ursiter) 1960- CANR-86
Earlier sketch in CA 131
Rae, Rusty
See Rae, Milford Andersen
Rae, Simon 1952- 185
Rae, Walter 1916- 57-60
Rae, Wesley D(ennis) 1932- 21-24R
Raebeck, Lois 1921- 13-16R
See also SATA 5
Raeburn, Antonia 1934- 101
Raeburn, John (Hay) 1941- 57-60
See also CLC 34
Raeburn, Michael 1940- 107
Raeburn, Michael 1943- 103
Raeburn, Paul 198
Raeder, Linda C. 1951- 231
Raef, Laura (Gladys) C(auble) -1995 . CANR-11
Earlier sketch in CA 29-32R
Raeff, Anne 1959- 223
Raeff, Marc 1923- CANR-73
Earlier sketch in CA 61-64
Rael, Elsa Okon 1927- .... CLR 84
Rael, Leyla 1948- 106
Raelin, Joseph A(lan) 1948- CANR-125
Earlier sketch in CA 125
Raeper, William 1959-1992 131
Raeschild, Sheila 1936- CANR-22
Earlier sketch in CA 105
Raetsch, Christian 1957- 144
Rafael, Gideon 1913-1999 129
Obituary 179
Brief entry 106
Rafat, Taufiq 1927- .... CP 1
RAF Casualty
See Gleave, T(homas) P(ercy)
Rafe, Stephen C. 1937- 132
Rafelson, Bob 128
Brief entry 112
Raffa, Frederick Anthony 1944- 53-56
Raffaele, Joseph A(ntonio) 1916- CANR-8
Earlier sketch in CA 5-8R
Raffel, Burton 1928- CANR-94
Earlier sketches in CA 9-12R, CANR-7, 30
See also CAAS 9
Raffel, Dawn 1957- 218
Raffelock, David 1897-1988 .... CAP-2
Obituary 182
Earlier sketch in CA 25-28
See also AITN 1
Raffer, Kunibert 1951- 222
Rafferty, Kathleen Kelly 1915-1981
Obituary 103
Rafferty, Max L. 1917-1982 .... CANR-1
Obituary 107
Earlier sketch in CA 1-4R
Rafferty, Milton 1932- 101
Rafferty, S. S.
See Hurley, John J(erome)
Raffi
See Cavoukian, Raffi
Raffin, Deborah 1953- 230
Raffini, James O. 1941- CANR-40
Earlier sketch in CA 117
Rafroidi, Patrick (Pierre) 1930-1989 132
Raftery, B(arry Joseph) 1944- 149
Raftery, Gerald (Bransfield)
1905-1986 .... CANR-73
Earlier sketches in CAP-1, CA 13-14
See also SATA 11
Ragan, David 1925- 65-68
Ragan, Sam(uel Talmadge) 1915-1996 .. 13-16R
Obituary 152
Ragan, William Burk 1896-1973 .... CANR-2
Earlier sketch in CA 1-4R
Ragan-Reid, Gale 1956- 155
See also SATA 90
Ragaway, Martin A(rnold)
1928(?)-1989 .... CANR-12
Obituary 128
Earlier sketch in CA 61-64
Ragen, Joseph E(dward) 1897-1971 .... CAP-2
Obituary 33-36R
Earlier sketch in CA 21-22
Ragen, Naomi 1949- CANR-129
Earlier sketches in CA 130, CANR-81
Raghavan, Manayath D. 1892- CAP-2
Earlier sketch in CA 19-20
Ragins, Sanford 117
Raglan, FitzRoy (Richard Somerset)
1885-1964 .... CANR-73
Earlier sketch in CA 5-8R
Ragni, Gerome 1942-1991 105
Obituary 134
See also CLC 17
Rago, Henry Anthony 1915-1969 .... CAP-2
Earlier sketch in CA 25-28
Rago, Louis J(oseph von) 1924-1973 .... 9-12R
Ragone, Helena 1955- 150
Ragosta, Millie J(ane) 1931- CANR-12
Earlier sketch in CA 73-76
Ragsdale, Ray W(aldo) 1909-1983 45-48
Ragsdale, W(arner) B(ernice) 1898-1986 . 73-76
Obituary 121
Raguin, Yves (Emile) 1912-1998 81-84
Ragusa, Olga (M.) 1922- 122
Raham, (R.) Gary 1946- 136
Rahaman, Vashanti 1953- 166
See also SATA 98
Rahe, Paul A. 1948- CANR-92
Earlier sketch in CA 145
Raheem 1929- .... CD 5
Rahill, Peter J(ames) 1910-1975 .... 5-8R
Rahim, Enayetur 1938- 107
Rahimi, Atiq 1962- 226
Rahl, James A(ndrew) 1917-1994 77-80
Rahm, David A. 1931-1976 57-60
Rahman, Abdul
See Wayman, Tony Russell
Rahman, F.
See Rahman, Fazlur
Rahman, Fazlur 1919-1988
Obituary 126
Rahman, Matiur 1940- 141
Rahn, Joan Elma 1929- CANR-13
Earlier sketch in CA 37-40R
See also SATA 27
Rahnema, Ali 1952- 192
Rahner, Karl 1904-1984 .... CANR-82
Obituary 112
Earlier sketch in CA 109
Rahner, Raymond M. 1919-2004 101
Obituary 223
Rahsepar
See Yar-Shater, Ehsan O(llah)
Rahtjen, Bruce D(onald) 1933- 21-24R
Rahtz, Philip (Arthur) 1921- 149
Rahv, Betty T(homas) 1931- 105
Rahv, Philip
See Greenberg, Ivan
See also CLC 24
See also DLB 137
See also MAL 5
Rai, Bali 1971- 227
See also SATA 152
Rai, Kul B(husan) 1937- 105

Rai, Navab
See Srivastava, Dhanpat Rai
Raia, Anthony P(aul) 1928- ... 61-64
Raible, Alton (Robert) 1918- ... SATA 35
Raich, Semen Egorovich 1792-1855 ... DLB 205
Raichlen, Steven 1953- ... 176
Raickovic, Stevan 1928- ... DLB 181
Raiff, Stan 1930- ... 61-64
See also SATA 11
Railton, Esther P(auline) 1929- ... 101
Raimi, Sam(uel M.) 1959- ... CANR-55
Earlier sketch in CA 123
See also AAYA 67
Raimond, C. E.
See Robins, Elizabeth
Raimund, Ferdinand Jakob 1790-1836 . DLB 90
Raimy, Eric 1942- ... 93-96
Raimy, Victor 1913-1987 ... 81-84
Rain, Mary Summer 1945- ... 196
Rain, Patricia 1943- ... 235
Rainbird, George (Meadus) 1905-1986 ... 133
Obituary ... 120
Rainbolt, William 1946- ... 152
Rainbow-Wind, Shandor
See Weiss, (Paul) Shandor
Raine, Craig (Anthony) 1944- ... CANR-103
Earlier sketches in CA 108, CANR-29, 51
See also CLC 32, 103
See also CP 7
See also DLB 40
See also PFS 7
Raine, Jerry 1955- ... CANR-127
Earlier sketch in CA 161
Raine, Kathleen (Jessie)
1908-2003 ... CANR-109
Obituary ... 218
Earlier sketches in CA 85-88, CANR-46
See also CLC 7, 45
See also CP 1, 2, 3, 4, 5, 6, 7
See also DLB 20
See also EWL 3
See also MTCW 1
See also RGEL 2
Raine, Nancy Venable 1946- ... 202
Raine, Norman Reilly 1895-1971
Obituary ... 33-36R
Raine, Richard
See Sawkins, Raymond H(arold)
Raine, William MacLeod
1871-1954 ... TCWW 1, 2
Rainer, Dachine 1921- ... CP 1
Rainer, George
See Greenburger, Ingrid Elisabeth
Rainer, Julia
See Goode, Ruth
Rainer, Yvonne 1934- ... 133
Raines, Howell (Hiram) 1943- ... 73-76
Raines, Jeff 1958- ... 127
Raines, John C. 1933- ... 73-76
Raines, Robert A(rnold) 1926- ... CANR-7
Earlier sketch in CA 13-16R
Raines, Shirley C(arol) 1945- ... CANR-108
Earlier sketch in CA 113
See also SATA 128
Raines, Theron 1925- ... CANR-135
Earlier sketch in CA 127
Rainey, Bill G. 1926- ... 89-92
Rainey, Buck
See Rainey, Bill G.
Rainey, Gene E(dward) 1934- ... 25-28R
Rainey, Homer Price 1896-1985
Obituary ... 118
Rainey, Lawrence S. ... 173
Rainey, Patricia Ann 1937- ... 49-52
Rainey, W. B.
See Blassingame, Wyatt Rainey
Rainham, Thomas
See Barren, Charles (MacKinnon)
Rainis, Janis 1865-1929 ... 170
See also CDWLB 4
See also DLB 220
See also EWL 3
See also TCLC 29
Rainolde, Richard 1530(?)-1606 . DLB 136, 236
Rainolds, John 1549-1607 ... DLB 281
Rains, Rob 1956- ... 138
Rainsberger, Todd J(effrey) 1951- ... 106
Rainsford, George Nichols 1928-1993 49-52
Raintree, Lee
See Sellers, Con(nie Leslie, Jr.)
Rainwater, (Mary) Catherine 1953- ... CANR-99
Earlier sketch in CA 119
Rainwater, Dorothy T(hornton) 1918- . CANR-1
Earlier sketch in CA 45-48
Rainwater, Lee 1928- ... CANR-74
Earlier sketch in CA 53-56
Raistrick, Arthur 1896-1991 ... CANR-3
Earlier sketch in CA 9-12R
Raisz, Erwin J(osephus) 1893-1968 ... 1-4R
Obituary ... 103
Raitt, A(lan) W(illiam) 1930- ... 29-32R
Raizen, Senta A. 1924- ... 148
Raizis, M(arios) Byron 1931- ... 41-44R
Raizner, Bernard I. 1945- ... 127
Rajan, Balachandra 1920- ... CANR-139
Earlier sketches in CA 69-72, CANR-73
Rajan, M(annarswamighala) S(reeranga)
1920- ... CANR-13
Earlier sketch in CA 13-16R
Rajan, Tilottama 1951- ... 107
See also CP 1
Rajanen, Aini ... 109
Rajaram
See Iyengar, K(odaganallur) R(amaswami) Srinivasa
Rajasekharaiah, T(umkur) R(udraradhya)
1926- ... 33-36R
Rajec, Elizabeth M(olnar) 1931- ... 109
Rajic, Negovan 1923- ... CANR-82
Earlier sketch in CA 130
Rajiva, Stanley Frederick 1932- ... CP 1
Rajneesh, Acharya 1931-1990 ... 93-96
Obituary ... 130
Rajneesh, Bhagwan Shree
See Rajneesh, Acharya
Rajski, Raymond B. 1917-1996 ... 21-24R
Rajtar, Steve 1951- ... CANR-121
Earlier sketch in CA 160
Raju, Poolla Tirupati 1904-1992 ... 33-36R
Obituary ... 196
Rake, Alan 1933- ... 142
Rake, Jody 1961- ... 233
See also SATA 157
Rakel, Robert E(dwin) 1932- ... CANR-54
Earlier sketches in CA 107, CANR-26
Rakesh, Mohan 1925-1972 ... EWL 3
Rakic, Milan 1876-1938 ... CDWLB 4
See also DLB 147
Raknes, Ola 1887-1975 ... CAP-2
Earlier sketch in CA 29-32
Rako, Susan (Mandell) 1939- ... CANR-137
Earlier sketch in CA 117
Rakoff, Alvin 1927- ... 102
Rakoff, David 1966(?)- ... 214
Rakosi, Carl
Obituary ... 228
See also Rawley, Callman
See also CAAS 5
See also CLC 47
See also CP 1, 2, 3, 4, 5, 6, 7
See also DLB 193
Rakosi, Matyas 1892-1971
Obituary ... 29-32R
Rakotoson, Michele 1948- ... EWL 3
Rakove, Jack N(orman) 1947- ... CANR-112
Earlier sketch in CA 93-96
Rakove, Milton L(eon) 1918-1983 .... CANR-15
Obituary ... 111
Earlier sketch in CA 65-68
Rakow, Mary ... 212
Rakowski, James Peter 1945- ... 105
Rakowski, John 1922- ... 106
Raksin, David 1912-2004 ... IDFW 3, 4
Rakstis, Ted J(ay) 1932- ... 101
Ralbovsky, Martin P(aul) 1942- ... CANR-111
Earlier sketch in CA 49-52
Rale, Nero
See Burgess, Michael (Roy)
Ralegh, Sir Walter
See Raleigh, Sir Walter
See also BRW 1
See also RGEL 2
See also WP
Raleigh, Debbie 1961- ... 211
Raleigh, Donald J(oseph) 1949- ... CANR-111
Earlier sketches in CA 125, CANR-51
Raleigh, John Henry 1920- ... CANR-3
Earlier sketch in CA 1-4R
Raleigh, Michael 1947- ... CANR-70
Earlier sketch in CA 141
Raleigh, Richard
See Lovecraft, H(oward) P(hillips)
Raleigh, Walter (Alexander) 1861-1922 ... 190
Raleigh, Sir Walter 1554(?)-1618
See Ralegh, Sir Walter
See also CDBLB Before 1660
See also DLB 172
See also EXPP
See also PC 31
See also PFS 14
See also TEA
Raley, Harold (Cecil) 1934- ... 41-44R
Raley, Patricia E(ward) 1940- ... 73-76
Raley, Rowena
See McCulley, Johnston
Ralin, Radoy 1923- ... DLB 181
Rall, Ted 1963- ... 185
Rallentando, H. P.
See Sayers, Dorothy L(eigh)
Ralph, David Clinton 1922- ... CANR-2
Earlier sketch in CA 5-8R
Ralph, Edmond
See Michaelis, Karin
Ralph, Elizabeth K(ennedy) 1921-1993 . 33-36R
Ralph, James R., Jr. 1960- ... 145
Ralph, Julian 1853-1903 ... 204
See also DLB 23
Ralph, Margaret Nutting 1941- ... CANR-98
Earlier sketches in CA 121, CANR-47
Ralphs, Sheila 1923- ... 106
Ralston, Alma (Smith Payne) ... CANR-11
Earlier sketch in CA 17-20R
Ralston, Anthony 1930- ... 144
Ralston, Gilbert A(lexander)
1912-1999 ... CANR-2
Earlier sketch in CA 45-48
Ralston, James Kenneth 1896-1987 ... 49-52
Ralston, Jan
See Dunlop, Agnes M. R.
Ralston, Ken 1955- ... IDFW 3, 4
Ralston, Leonard F. 1925- ... 45-48
Ralston, Melvin B. 1937- ... 49-52
Ram, Immanuel
See Velikovsky, Immanuel
Rama
See Gupta, Ram Chandra
Rama
See Lenz, Frederick (P.), (Jr.)
Rama, Swami
See Swami Rama
Ramachandran, V(ilayanur) S(ubramanian)
1951- ... 184
Ramacharaka, Yogi
See Atkinson, William Walker
Ramage, Edwin S(tephen) 1929- ... 65-68
Ramage, James A(lfred) 1940- ... CANR-91
Earlier sketch in CA 61-64
Ramal, Walter
See de la Mare, Walter (John)
Ramamurty, K(otamraju) Bhaskara 1924- . 53-56
Raman, Chandrasekhara Venkata 1888-1970
Obituary ... 113
Ramana Maharshi 1879-1950 ... TCLC 84
Ramanujan, A(ttipat) K(rishnaswami)
1929-1993 ... CANR-24
Obituary ... 141
Earlier sketches in CA 17-20R, CANR-8
See also CP 1, 2
See also SATA 86
See also WWE 1
Ramanujan, Molly 1932- ... CANR-24
Earlier sketch in CA 29-32R
Ramanujan, Shouri
See Ramanujan, Molly
Ramapryia
See Gaulden, Albert Clayton
Rama Rao, K. V. S. 1967- ... 218
Rama Rau, Dhanvanthi (Handoo)
1893-1987 ... 183
Obituary ... 123
Brief entry ... 106
Rama Rau, Santha
See Wattles, Santha Rama Rau
Ramaswamy, Mysore 1902- ... CAP-1
Earlier sketch in CA 13-14
Ramat, Silvio 1939- ... DLB 128
Ramati, Alexander D. 1921- ... CANR-44
Earlier sketches in CA 13-16R, CANR-7
Ramati, Yohanan (Joseph) 1921- ... 111
Ramazani, Jahan 1960- ... CANR-108
Earlier sketch in CA 150
Ramazani, Nesta 1932- ... 223
Ramazani, Rouhollah K(aregar)
1928- ... CANR-26
Earlier sketches in CA 13-16R, CANR-10
Rambach, Peggy 1960(?)- ... 201
Rambam, Cyvia
See Rambert, Marie
Rambam, Myriam
See Rambert, Marie
Rambaud, Patrick 1946- ... 192
Rambeau, James (Morris) 1938- ... 117
Ramberg, Bennett 1946- ... 111
Rambert, Marie 1888-1982 ... 103
Obituary ... 107
Rambler
See Harrison, Susan Frances (Riley)
Rambo, Lewis Ray 1943- ... 109
Rambuss, Richard ... 145
Ramdin, Ron(ald Andrew) 1942- ... CANR-82
Earlier sketch in CA 131
Rame, David
See Divine, Arthur Durham
Rameh, Clea 1927- ... 53-56
Ramenofsky, Ann F. 1942- ... 125
Ramet, Carlos 1955- ... 192
Ramet, Sabrina Petra 1949- ... 190
Ramey, James W(alter) 1928-1995 ... 112
Ramey, Mary Ann 1947- ... 125
Ramge, Sebastian Victor 1930- ... 9-12R
Ramien, Th.
See Hirschfeld, Magnus
Ramirez (Rodriguez), Armando
See Ramirez (Rodriguez), Armando
Ramirez, Carolyn H(olmes) 1933- ... CANR-2
Earlier sketch in CA 5-8R
Ramirez, Juan 1949- ... 213
Ramirez, Juan Antonio 1948- ... 224
Ramirez, Sergio (Mercado) 1942- ... 184
See also CWW 2
See also DLB 145
See also EWL 3
See also HW 2
Ramirez, Susan E(lizabeth) 1946- ... CANR-82
Earlier sketch in CA 130
See also HW 1
Ramirez de Arellano, Diana (T. Clotilde)
1919-1997 ... CANR-94
Earlier sketches in CA 45-48, CANR-32
See also HW 1
Ramirez de Arellano, Rafael W(illiam)
1884- ... HW 1
Ramis, Harold (Allen) 1944- ... 128
Brief entry ... 124
See also AAYA 14
Ramis, Magali Garcia 1946- ... 194
Ramke, Bin 1947- ... CANR-31
Earlier sketches in CA 81-84, CANR-14
See also DLB 120
Ramler, Karl Wilhelm 1725-1798 ... DLB 97
Ramm, Bernard L(awrence) 1916-1992
Brief entry ... 112
Rammelkamp, Julian S(turtevant)
1917-1994 ... 17-20R
Obituary ... 196
Rammohan, V. Gowri 1951- ... 235
Ramo, Simon 1913- ... 191
Brief entry ... 111
Ramoacn y Cajal, Santiago
1852-1934 ... TCLC 93
Ramon, Juan
See Jimenez (Mantecon), Juan Ramon
Ramond, Charles K(night) 1930- ... 101
Ramon Ribeyro, Julio ... 181
See also Ribeyro, Julio Ramon
See also DLB 145
Ramon y Cajal, Santiago 1852-1934 ... 213
Ramos, Graciliano 1892-1953 ... 167
See also DLB 307
See also EWL 3
See also HW 2
See also LAW
See also TCLC 32
See also WLIT 1
Ramos, Henry A. J. 1959- ... 201
Ramos, Joseph R(afael) 1938- ... 139
Ramos, Luis Arturo 1947- ... 169
See also HW 2
Ramos, Manuel 1948- ... 239
See also DLB 209
Ramos, Suzanne 1942- ... 101
Ramos-Oliveira, Antonio 1907-1973
Obituary ... 104
Ramos Sucre, Jose Antonio
1890-1930 ... DLB 290
Ramous, Mario 1924-1999 ... DLB 128
Ramp, Eugene A(ugust) 1942- ... 49-52
Rampa, Tuesday Lobsang
See Hoskin, Cyril Henry
Rampersad, Arnold 1941- ... CANR-81
Brief entry ... 127
Earlier sketch in CA 133
Interview in ... CA-133
See also BW 2, 3
See also CLC 44
See also DLB 111
Ramphal, Shridath (Surendranath) 1928- 141
Rampling, Anne
See Rice, Anne
See also GLL 2
Rampton, Sheldon 1957- ... 170
Ramquist, Grace (Bess) Chapman
1907- ... CANR-3
Earlier sketch in CA 9-12R
Ramras-Rauch, Gila 1933-2005 ... 147
Obituary ... 236
Ramrus, Al 1930- ... 105
Rams, Edwin M(arion) 1922-1980 ... 17-20R
Ramsaur, Ernest Edmondson, Jr.
1915-1985 ... 41-44R
Ramsay, Allan 1686(?)-1758 ... DLB 95
See also RGEL 2
Ramsay, David 1749-1815 ... DLB 30
Ramsay, J(ames) A(rthur) 1909-1988
Obituary ... 124
Ramsay, Jay
See Campbell, (John) Ramsey
Ramsay, Jay 1958- ... 135
Ramsay, Martha Laurens 1759-1811 ... DLB 200
Ramsay, Raylene L(ammas) 1945- CANR-94
Earlier sketch in CA 145
Ramsay, Raymond (Henry) 1927- ... 77-80
Ramsay, William M(cDowell) 1922- . CANR-12
Earlier sketch in CA 13-16R
Ramsbottom, John 1885-1974
Obituary ... 53-56
Ramsdell, Kristin (Romeis) 1940- ... 125
Ramsden, E. H. ... 102
Ramsden, Herbert 1927- ... CANR-25
Earlier sketch in CA 108
Ramsden, John (Andrew) 1947- ... CANR-138
Earlier sketch in CA 108
Ramsell, Donald 1926(?)-1983
Obituary ... 110
Ramsett, David E. 1942- ... 29-32R
Ramsey, Charles E(ugene) 1923- ... 13-16R
Ramsey, Dan(ny Clarence) 1945- ... 101
Ramsey, Doug(las A.) 1934- ... CANR-93
Earlier sketch in CA 132
Ramsey, Eric
See Hagberg, David J(ames)
Ramsey, Frank Plumpton 1903-1930 ... 158
See also DLB 262
Ramsey, (Charles) Frederic, Jr. 1915-1995 . 5-8R
Ramsey, G(ordon) C(lark) 1941- ... CANR-9
Earlier sketch in CA 21-24R
Ramsey, George Wilson 1937- ... 113
Ramsey, Ian T(homas) 1915-1972 ... CANR-4
Earlier sketch in CA 5-8R
Ramsey, Jackson E. 1938- ... 122
Ramsey, Jarold 1937- ... 33-36R
Ramsey, John F(raser) 1907-1983 ... 49-52
Ramsey, Lee C(arter) 1935- ... 120
Ramsey, (Arthur) Michael
1904-1988 ... CANR-83
Obituary ... 125
Earlier sketches in CA 77-80, CANR-14
Ramsey, (Robert) Paul 1913-1988 ... CANR-1
Obituary ... 124
Earlier sketch in CA 1-4R
Ramsey, Paul 1924-1994 ... 41-44R
See also CP 1, 2
Ramsey, Paul W. 1905-1976
Obituary ... 69-72
Ramsey, Robert D. 1934- ... CANR-100
Earlier sketch in CA 25-28R
Ramsey, Roy S. 1920(?)-1976
Obituary ... 65-68
Ramsey, Russell W. 1935- ... 124
Ramseyer, John A(lvin) 1908-1968 ... CANR-4
Earlier sketch in CA 5-8R
Ramseyer, Lloyd L(ouis) 1899-1977 ... CAP-2
Earlier sketch in CA 19-20
Ramskill, Valerie Patricia Roskams ... CAP-1
Earlier sketch in CA 9-10
Ramsland, Katherine 1953- ... CANR-99
Earlier sketch in CA 136
Ramson, W(illiam) S(tanley) 1933- ... 45-48
Ramstad, Ralph L. 1919- ... SATA 115
Ramundo, Bernard A. 1925- ... 21-24R
Ramuz, Charles-Ferdinand 1878-1947 ... 165
See also EWL 3
See also TCLC 33

Rana, Indi
See Rana, Indira Higham
Rana, Indira Higham 1944- 149
See also SATA 82
Rana, J.
See Bhatia, Jamunadevi
Ranadive, Gail 1944- 53-56
See also SATA 10
Rance, Joseph
See Hoyle, Trevor
Rance, Patrick (Lowry Cole Holwell)
1918-1999 138
Obituary 183
Ranch, Hieronimus Justesen
1539-1607 .... DLB 300
Rancour-Laferriere, Daniel 138
Rand, Ann (Binkley) 106
See also MAL 5
See also SATA 30
Rand, Austin Loomer 1905-1982 ...... CANR-73
Earlier sketch in CA 89-92
Rand, Ayn 1905-1982 .... CANR-73
Obituary 105
Earlier sketches in CA 13-16R, CANR-27
See also AAYA 10
See also AMWS 4
See also BPFB 3
See also BYA 12
See also CDALBS
See also CLC 3, 30, 44, 79
See also CN 1, 2, 3
See also CPW
See also DA
See also DA3
See also DAC
See also DAM MST, NOV, POP
See also DLB 227, 279
See also MTCW 1, 2
See also MTFW 2005
See also NFS 10, 16
See also RGAL 4
See also SFW 4
See also TUS
See also WLC
See also YAW
Rand, Brett
See Norwood, Victor G(eorge) C(harles)
Rand, Christopher 1912-1968 .... CANR-73
Earlier sketch in CA 77-80
Rand, Clayton (Thomas) 1891-1971 .... 5-8R
Obituary 29-32R
Rand, Earl (James) 1933- 21-24R
Rand, Frank Prentice 1889-1971 .... CAP-1
Earlier sketch in CA 11-12
Rand, Glenn (Martin) 1944- 220
Rand, Gloria 1925- CANR-123
Earlier sketch in CA 168
See also SATA 101, 156
Rand, Harry 1947- 137
Rand, J. H.
See Holland, James R.
Rand, James S.
See Attenborough, Bernard George
Rand, Mat
See Heckelmann, Charles N(ewman)
Rand, Nicholas T(homas) 1953- 190
Rand, Paul 1914-1996 .... CANR-61
Obituary 154
Earlier sketch in CA 21-24R
See also SATA 6
Rand, Peter 1942- CANR-62
Earlier sketch in CA 77-80
Rand, Robert E.
See Meares, Leonard Frank
Rand, Willard J., Jr. 1913-1990 .... 9-12R
Randa, Laura E.
See Randa King, Laura
Randa King, Laura 1965- 173
Randal, Beatrice (a pseudonym) 1916- 61-64
Randal, Jonathan C. 1933- 239
Randal, Vera 1922- 9-12R
Randall, Alice
See Ewing, Alice Randall
Randall, Belle 1940- 118
Randall, Bob 1937-1995 106
Obituary 148
Randall, Carrie
See Ransom, Candice F.
Randall, Charles Edgar 1897-1986 .... 41-44R
Randall, Charles H(enry) 1920- 133
Randall, Charlotte 219
Randall, Clarence Belden 1891-1967 .... CAP-1
Earlier sketch in CA 13-14
Randall, Clay
See Adams, Clifton
Randall, Dale B(ertrand) J(onas)
1929- CANR-2
Earlier sketch in CA 5-8R
Randall, David 1972- 238
Randall, David A(nton) 1905-1975 193
Obituary 57-60
See also DLB 140
Randall, Deborah 1957- 131
Randall, Diane
See Ross, W(illiam) E(dward) D(aniel)
Randall, Donald A. 1933- 61-64
Randall, Dudley (Felker)
1914-2000 .... CANR-82
Obituary 189
Earlier sketches in CA 25-28R, CANR-23
See also BLC 3
See also BW 1, 3
See also CLC 1, 135
See also CP 1, 2
See also DAM MULT
See also DLB 41
See also PFS 5
Randall, Florence Engel 1917-1997 . CANR-77
Earlier sketch in CA 41-44R
See also SATA 5
Randall, Francis Ballard 1931- 9-12R
Randall, Henry S. 1811-1876 .... DLB 30
Randall, J. G.
See Randall, James Garfield
Randall, James G.
See Randall, James Garfield
See also DLB 17
Randall, James Garfield 1881-1953
Brief entry 118
See also Randall, James G.
Randall, Janet
See Young, Janet Randall and
Young, Robert W(illiam)
Randall, Jo Anne Yarus 1942- 118
Randall, John E(rnest, Jr.) 1924- 65-68
Randall, John Herman, Jr. 1899-1980 . CANR-1
Obituary 102
Earlier sketch in CA 1-4R
See also DLB 279
Randall, John L(eslie) 1933- 107
Randall, Joseph Hungerford 1897-1975 .... 1-4R
Randall, Joshua
See Randisi, Robert J(oseph)
Randall, Julia (Sawyer) 1923- 33-36R
See also CP 1, 2, 3, 4, 5, 6, 7
See also TCLE 1:2
Randall, Laura 1935- 37-40R
Randall, Lilian M(aria) C(harlotte)
1931- CANR-89
Earlier sketch in CA 21-24R
Randall, Margaret 1936- 41-44R
See also CP 1, 2, 3, 4, 5, 6, 7
Randall, Marta 1948- CANR-80
Earlier sketch in CA 107
Randall, Mary
See Colver, Alice Mary (Ross)
Randall, Mercedes M. 1895-1977 .... 13-16R
Obituary 69-72
Randall, Monica 1944- CANR-134
Earlier sketch in CA 97-100
Randall, Randolph C. 1900-1992 .... 17-20R
Randall, Richard H(arding), Jr. 1926-1997 .. 148
Obituary 159
Randall, Robert
See Garrett, (Gordon) Randall (Phillip) and
Silverberg, Robert
Randall, Rona .... RHW
Randall, Ruth (Elaine) Painter 1892-1971 . 1-4R
Obituary 103
See also SATA 3
Randall, Steven
See Andrews, Clarence A(delbert)
Randall, Tony 1920-2004 156
Obituary 228
Randall, Vernellia 1948- .... SFW 4
Randall, Willard Sterne 1942- 196
Earlier sketches in CA 69-72, CANR-95
Autobiographical Essay in 196
Randall, William Lowell 1950- CANR-117
Earlier sketch in CA 158
Randall-Mills, Elizabeth West
1906-1983 .... 13-16R
Randazzo, Mary Callahan 1950- 127
Randazzo, Renee
See Randazzo, Mary Callahan
Randel, William (Peirce) 1909-1996 ..... 13-16R
Randell, Beverley
See Price, Beverley Joan
Randell, John Bulmer 1918-1982 109
Obituary 106
Randell, Nigel 233
Randers-Pehrson, Justine Davis 1910-2004 . 111
Obituary 231
Randhawa, M(ohinder) S(ingh)
1909-1986 .... CANR-28
Earlier sketch in CA 29-32R
Randi, James 1928- 117
Randisi, Robert J(oseph) 1951- CANR-97
Earlier sketches in CA 116, CANR-60
See also TCWW 2
Randle, Kevin D. 1949- 226
Randle, Kristen (Downey) 1952- 156
See also AAYA 34
See also SAAS 24
See also SATA 92
See also SATA-Essay 119
Randles, Anthony V(ictor), Jr. 1942- 65-68
Randles, Jennifer Christine 1951- 142
Randles, Jenny
See Randles, Jennifer Christine
Randles, Slim
See Randles, Anthony V(ictor), Jr.
Randoll, Anthony
See Blacking, John (Anthony Randoll)
Randolph, A(sa) Philip 1889-1979 125
Obituary 85-88
See also BW 2
See also DLB 91
Randolph, Arthur C.
See Greene, Alvin Carl
Randolph, Boynton M.D.
See Ellis, Edward S(ylvester)
Randolph, David James 1934- CANR-3
Earlier sketch in CA 49-52
Randolph, (Mary) Elizabeth 1930- .. CANR-119
Earlier sketch in CA 135
Randolph, Ellen
See Ross, W(illiam) E(dward) D(aniel)
Randolph, Geoffrey
See Ellis, Edward S(ylvester)
Randolph, Georgiana Ann 1908-1957 219
Brief entry 116
Randolph, Gordon
See von Block, Bela W(illiam) and
von Block, Sylvia
Randolph, J. H.
See Ellis, Edward S(ylvester)
Randolph, John 1915-2004 45-48
Obituary 223
Randolph, Lieutenant J. H.
See Ellis, Edward S(ylvester)
Randolph, Marion
See Rodell, Marie F(reid)
Randolph, Melanie
See Ragosta, Millie J(ane)
Randolph, Nancy
See Robb, Inez (Callaway)
Randolph, Ruth Elizabeth 1964- 162
Randolph, Thomas 1605-1635 ..... DLB 58, 126
See also RGEL 2
Randolph, Vance 1892-1980 105
Random, Alan
See Kay, Ernest
Random, Alex
See Rowland, D(onald) S(ydney)
Rands, William Brighty 1823-1882 ..... SATA 17
Randsborg, Klavs 1944- 142
Ranelagh, John (O'Beirne) 1947- 128
Raney, Deborah 1955- 223
Raney, Ken 1953- .... SATA 74
Ranga (Nayakulu), N(idubrolu) G(ogineni)
1900-1995 .... 29-32R
Obituary 148
Ranganathan, S(hiyali) R(amamrita)
1892-1972 .... CANR-5
Earlier sketch in CA 5-8R
Range, Willard Edgar Allen 1910-1993 ..... 1-4R
Rangel, Carlos 1929-1988 104
Obituary 124
Rangell, Leo 1913- 105
Rangel-Ribeiro, Victor 1925- 192
Ranger, Ken
See Creasey, John
Ranger, Paul 1933- 37-40R
Ranger, T(erence) O(sborn) 1929- CANR-96
Earlier sketches in CA 25-28R, CANR-19
Rangoussis, Steven 1973- 172
Ranis, Gustav 1929- CANR-3
Earlier sketch in CA 9-12R
Ranis, Peter 1935- 41-44R
Ranjee
See Shahani, Ranjee
Rank, Benjamin (Keith) 1911-2002 109
Rank, Hugh (Duke) 1932- CANR-12
Earlier sketch in CA 73-76
Rank, J. Arthur 1888-1972 .... IDFW 3, 4
Rank, Mark Robert 1955- 237
Rank, Maureen Joy 1947- 117
Rank, Otto 1884-1939 .... TCLC 115
Ranke-Heinemann, Uta (Johanna Ingrid)
1927- 137
Ranki, Gyoergy 1930-1988
Obituary 124
Rankin, Daniel S(tanislaus) 1895-1972 .. CAP-1
Earlier sketch in CA 13-16
Rankin, David J. 1945- 108
Rankin, Herbert David 1931- 103
Rankin, Hugh F(ranklin) 1913-1989 . CANR-77
Earlier sketches in CA 1-4R, CANR-1, 74
Rankin, Ian (James) 1960- CANR-137
Earlier sketches in CA 148, CANR-81
See also BRWS 10
See also DLB 267
See also MTFW 2005
Rankin, Jeannette 1880-1973
Obituary 41-44R
Rankin, Joan 1940- .... SATA 88, 148
Rankin, Judith Torluemke 1945- 193
Brief entry 107
Rankin, Judy
See Rankin, Judith Torluemke
Rankin, Karl Lott 1898-1991 .... CAP-1
Earlier sketch in CA 13-16
Rankin, Paula C(lark) 1945- CANR-21
Earlier sketch in CA 104
Rankin, Robert 1915- 126
Brief entry 108
Rankin, Robert 1949- 216
Rankin, Robert Harry 1909-1990
Obituary 131
Rankin, Robert P(arks) 1912- 77-80
Rankin, Ruth (DeLone) I(rvine) 1924- 61-64
Rankin, Tom 1957- 196
Rankine, John
See Mason, Douglas R(ankine)
Rankine, Paul Scott 1909(?)-1983
Obituary 109
Ranly, Ernest W. 1930- 37-40R
Rann, Sheila 1952- 152
Rann, Shelly
See Rann, Sheila
Ranney, Agnes V. 1916-1985 .... 5-8R
See also SATA 6
Ranney, (Joseph) Austin 1920- 77-80
Rannit, Aleksis 1914-1985 184
Obituary 114
Brief entry 109
See also EWL 3
Ranous, Charles A. 1912-1998 .... 13-16R
Ransby, Barbara 1957- 224
Ransel, David L(orimer) 1939- 73-76
Ransford, Oliver (Neil) 1914-1993 ... CANR-83
Obituary 142
Earlier sketches in CA 21-24R, CANR-10
Ransford, Tessa 1938- 205
Ransley, Peter 1931- CANR-81
Earlier sketches in CA 69-72, CANR-21
See also CBD
Ransmayr, Christoph 1954- 180
Ransohoff, Paul M(artin) 1948- 103
Ransom, Bill 1945- CANR-116
Earlier sketches in CA 101, CANR-19, 44
Ransom, Candice F. 1952- CANR-113
Earlier sketches in CA 121, CANR-47
See also SATA 52, 89, 135
See also SATA-Brief 49
Ransom, Daniel
See Gorman, Edward
Ransom, Harry Howe 1922- 9-12R
Ransom, Harry Hunt 1908-1976 195
See also DLB 187
Ransom, Jane (Reavill) 1958- 158
Ransom, Jay Ellis 1914- CANR-44
Earlier sketches in CA 9-12R, CANR-3, 20
Ransom, John Crowe 1888-1974 ..... CANR-34
Obituary 49-52
Earlier sketches in CA 5-8R, CANR-6
See also AMW
See also CDALBS
See also CLC 2, 4, 5, 11, 24
See also CP 1, 2
See also DA3
See also DAM POET
See also DLB 45, 63
See also EWL 3
See also EXPP
See also MAL 5
See also MTCW 1, 2
See also MTFW 2005
See also PC 61
See also RGAL 4
See also TUS
Ransom, Ray A. 1957- 219
Ransom, William Michael 1945-
Brief entry 108
Ransom, William R. 1876-1973
Obituary 37-40R
Ransome, Arthur (Michell)
1884-1967 .... CANR-81
Earlier sketch in CA 73-76
See also CLR 8
See also CWRI 5
See also DLB 160
See also MAICYA 1, 2
See also SATA 22
See also TEA
See also WCH
Ransome, Eleanor 1915- 93-96
Ransome, James E. 1961- .... CLR 86
See also SATA 76, 123
Ransome, Stephen
See Davis, Frederick C(lyde)
Ransome-Davies, Basil
See Colley, Iain
Ransone, Coleman B(ernard), Jr.
1920-1986 45-48
Ranstorp, Magnus 172
Rant, Tol E.
See Longyear, Barry B(rookes)
Ranum, Orest Allen 1933- CANR-8
Earlier sketch in CA 9-12R
Ranum, Patricia M(cGroder) 1932- 45-48
Ranz, James 1921- 9-12R
Ranz, Jim
See Ranz, James
Ranzini, Addis Durning 1909-1983
Obituary 110
Rao, Aruna P. 1955- 141
Rao, B. Shiva 1900(?)-1975
Obituary 61-64
Rao, C. H. Hanumantha 1929- CANR-7
Earlier sketch in CA 17-20R
Rao, K(oneru) Ramakrishna 1932- 130
Rao, R(anganatha) P(admanabha)
1924- 13-16R
Rao, Raja 1909- CANR-51
Earlier sketch in CA 73-76
See also CLC 25, 56
See also CN 1, 2, 3, 4, 5, 6
See also DAM NOV
See also EWL 3
See also MTCW 1, 2
See also MTFW 2005
See also RGEL 2
See also RGSF 2
Raoul, Anthony
See Wilmot, Anthony
Rapaport, Herman 1947- CANR-35
Earlier sketch in CA 114
Rapaport, Ionel F. 1909(?)-1972
Obituary 37-40R
Rapaport, Stella F(read) CANR-75
Earlier sketch in CA 1-4R
Raper, Arthur F(ranklin) 1899-1979 .. CANR-12
Obituary 89-92
Earlier sketch in CA 61-64
Raper, J(ulius) R(owan) 1938- 33-36R
Raper, Jack
See Raper, J(ulius) R(owan)
Rapf, Joanna E. 1941- 175
Raphael 1483-1520 .... AAYA 65
Raphael, Bertram 1936- 97-100
Raphael, Beverley 1934- 117
Raphael, Chaim 1908-1994 .... CANR-73
Obituary 146
Earlier sketches in CA 85-88, CANR-16
See also CMW 4
Raphael, Dan (Ambrose) 1952- CANR-130
Earlier sketch in CA 104
Raphael, Dana 61-64
Raphael, David D(aiches) 1916- CANR-20
Earlier sketches in CA 5-8R, CANR-2
Raphael, Elaine
See Bolognese, Elaine (Raphael Chionchio)
See also SATA 23

Raphael, Frederic (Michael) 1931- ... CANR-86
Earlier sketches in CA 1-4R, CANR-1
See also CLC 2, 14
See also CN 1, 2, 3, 4, 5, 6, 7
See also DLB 14, 319
See also TCLE 1:2
Raphael, Jody ... 230
Raphael, Lev 1954- ... CANR-72
Earlier sketch in CA 134
See also GLL 1
Raphael, Marc Lee 1942(?)- ... 195
Brief entry ... 113
Raphael, Maryanne 1938- ... 175
Raphael, Phyllis 1940- ... CANR-111
Earlier sketch in CA 45-48
Raphael, Ray ... 224
Raphael, Rick 1919-1994 ... CANR-10
Obituary ... 198
Earlier sketch in CA 21-24R
Raphael, Robert 1927- ... 45-48
Raphael, Sandra (Joan) 1939- ... 104
Raphaelson, Elliot 1937- ... 124
Raphaelson, Samson 1896-1983 ... 65-68
Obituary ... 110
See also DLB 44
See also IDFW 3, 4
Rapkin, Chester 1918-2001 ... 17-20R
Obituary ... 193
Rapley, Robert 1926- ... 218
Rapoport, Alan M. 1942- ... 134
Rapoport, Amos 1929- ... 65-68
Rapoport, Anatol 1911- ... 41-44R
Rapoport, Janis 1946- ... CANR-40
Earlier sketches in CA 101, CANR-18
Rapoport, Judith L. ... BEST 89:3
Rapoport, Louis (Harvey) 1942-1991 ... 117
Rapoport, Nessa ... 231
Rapoport, Rhona (Ross) 1927- ... CANR-8
Earlier sketch in CA 61-64
Rapoport, Robert Norman
1924-1996 ... CANR-39
Obituary ... 154
Earlier sketches in CA 5-8R, CANR-2, 17
Rapoport, Roger 1946- ... 33-36R
Rapoport, Ron 1940- ... 89-92
Raposa, Michael L. ... 192
Raposo, Joseph Guilherme 1938-1989
Obituary ... 127
See also SATA-Obit 61
Rapp, Adam 1968(?)- ... CANR-130
Earlier sketch in CA 194
See also AAYA 41
See also SATA 148
Rapp, Doris Jean 1929- ... CANR-21
Earlier sketch in CA 37-40R
Rapp, George (Robert), Jr. 1930- ... 130
Rapp, Joel ... AITN 1
Rapp, Lynn ... AITN 1
Rapp, Rayna 1946(?)- ... 235
Rapp, Steven A. 1964- ... 217
Rappaport, Alfred 1932-
Brief entry ... 110
Rappaport, Armin H. 1916-1983
Brief entry ... 111
Rappaport, David 1907-2000 ... CAP-2
Obituary ... 192
Earlier sketch in CA 19-20
Rappaport, Doreen ... 226
See also SATA 151
Rappaport, Eva 1924- ... 29-32R
See also SATA 6
Rappaport, Julian 1942-
Brief entry ... 112
Rappaport, Roy A(braham) 1926-1997 .. 41-44R
Obituary ... 161
Rappaport, Sheldon R(aphael) 1926- ... 29-32R
Rappaport, Steve 1948- ... 134
Rappeneau, Jean-Paul 1932- ... IDFW 3, 4
Rappole, John H(ilton) 1946- ... 123
Rappoport, David Steven 1957- ... 133
Rappoport, Ken 1935- ... CANR-42
Earlier sketches in CA 53-56, CANR-4, 20
See also SATA 89
Rappoport, Leon 1932- ... 41-44R
Rappoport, Shloyme Zanul 1863-1920 ... 144
Rapson, Richard L(awrence) 1937- ... CANR-97
Earlier sketches in CA 21-24R, CANR-10
Rarick, Carrie 1911-2002 ... 115
See also SATA 41
Rasanayagam, Angelo ... 235
Rasberry, Robert W. 1945- ... 110
Rasberry, Salli 1940- ... CANR-46
Earlier sketches in CA 107, CANR-23
Rasch, Sunna Cooper 1925- ... 105
Raschka, Chris
See Raschka, Christopher
Raschka, Christopher 1959- ... 190
See also SATA 80, 117
Raschke, Carl A(llan) 1944- ... 104
Rascoe, Jesse Ed
See Bartholomew, Ed(ward Ellsworth)
Rascoe, Judith 1941(?)- ... 107
Rascol, Sabina I. ... SATA 159
Rascon Banda, Victor Hugo 1948- ... DLB 305
Rascovich, Mark 1918(?)-1976
Obituary ... 69-72
Rasey, Ruth M.
See Simpson, Ruth Mary Rasey
Rash, Andy ... SATA 162
Rash, Dora Eileen Agnew (Wallace)
1897-1989 ... CANR-2
Earlier sketch in CA 5-8R
Rash, J(esse) Keogh 1906-1981 ... 93-96
Rash, Nancy 1940- ... CANR-37
Rash, Ron 1953- ... 204
Rashad, Johari M(ahasin) 1951- ... 138
See also BW 2
Rashi c. 1040-1105 ... DLB 208
Rashid, Ahmed 1948- ... 198
Rashidof, Sharif Rashidovich
See Rashidov, Sharaf Rashidovich
Rashidov, Sharaf Rashidovich 1917(?)-1983
Obituary ... 111
Rashke, Richard L. 1936- ... CANR-24
Earlier sketch in CA 107
Rashkin, Elissa J(oy) 1968- ... 214
Raskin, A(braham) H(enry)
1911-1993 ... CANR-75
Obituary ... 143
Earlier sketch in CA 104
Raskin, Barbara 1935-1999 ... 129
Obituary ... 185
Brief entry ... 126
Raskin, Edith Lefkowitz 1908-1987 ... CANR-3
Earlier sketch in CA 9-12R
See also SATA 9
Raskin, Ellen 1928-1984 ... CANR-37
Obituary ... 113
Earlier sketch in CA 21-24R
See also BYA 4
See also CLR 1, 12
See also DLB 52
See also MAICYA 1, 2
See also SATA 2, 38, 139
See also YAW
Raskin, Eugene 1909-2004 ... 33-36R
Obituary ... 228
Raskin, Herbert A(lfred) 1919-1979 .. CANR-76
Obituary ... 122
Earlier sketch in CA 29-32R
Raskin, Jonah (Seth) 1942- ... CANR-64
Earlier sketch in CA 81-84
Raskin, Joseph 1897-1982 ... CANR-13
Obituary ... 105
Earlier sketch in CA 33-36R
See also SATA 12
See also SATA-Obit 29
Raskin, Marcus G. 1934- ... 37-40R
Rasky, Frank (John) 1923- ... 184
Brief entry ... 107
Rasky, Harry 1928- ... CANR-97
Earlier sketches in CA 105, CANR-31
Rasmusen, Henry N(eil) 1909-1970 ... 5-8R
Obituary ... 200
Rasmussen, Alis A. 1958- ... CANR-81
Earlier sketch in CA 148
See also FANT
Rasmussen, David (William) 1942- ... 53-56
Rasmussen, Douglas B(ruce) 1948- ... 119
Rasmussen, Greg 1964- ... 192
Rasmussen, Halfdan 1915- ... 196
Rasmussen, John Peter 1933-
Brief entry ... 110
Rasmussen, Knud Johan Victor 1879-1933 . 173
Brief entry ... 113
See also SATA-Brief 34
Rasmussen, Larry L. 1939- ... 118
Rasmussen, Louis J(ames, Jr.) 1921-1997 . 73-76
Rasmussen, R. Kent 1943- ... 93-96
Rasmussen, Steen Eiler 1898-1990
Obituary ... 132
Rasmussen, Wayne D(avid) 1915-2004 . 33-36R
Obituary ... 227
Rasmussen, William M. S. ... 197
Raso, Jack 1954- ... 148
Rasof, Henry 1946- ... 113
Rasor, Eugene L(atimer) 1936- ... 89-92
Raspberry, William J(ames) 1935- ... 122
Brief entry ... 110
Interview in ... CA-122
See also BW 2
Rasponi, Lanfranco 1914-1983 ... 17-20R
Obituary ... 109
Rasputin, Maria
See Bern, Maria Rasputin Soloviev
Rasputin, Valentin (Grigorevich)
1937- ... CANR-88
Brief entry ... 108
Earlier sketch in CA 127
See also CWW 2
See also DLB 302
See also EWL 3
Rass, Rebecca 1936- ... 105
Rast, Walter E(mil) 1930- ... 73-76
Rastell, John fl. 1509(?)-1536(?) .. DLB 136, 170
See also RGEL 2
Ratch, Jerry 1944- ... 118
Ratcliff, Carter 1941- ... CANR-114
Earlier sketches in CA 61-64, CANR-13, 64
Ratcliff, Donald 1951- ... 189
Ratcliff, John Drury 1903-1973 ... 108
Obituary ... 106
Ratcliff, Ruth 1905-1989 ... 121
Ratcliffe, Barrie M(ichael) 1940- ... 114
Ratcliffe, Donald J(ohn) 1942- ... 179
Ratcliffe, F(rederick) W(illiam)
1927- ... CANR-52
Earlier sketch in CA 125
Ratcliffe, James M(axwell) 1925- ... 21-24R
Ratcliffe, James P.
See Mencken, H(enry) L(ouis)
Ratcliffe, Sam DeShong 1952- ... 186
Ratcliffe, T(om) A(rundel) 1910- ... CAP-2
Earlier sketch in CA 25-28
Ratermanis, J(anis) B(ernhards)
1904-1995 ... 9-12R
Ratey, John J(oseph) 1948- ... CANR-142
Earlier sketches in CA 146, CANR-111
Rath, Frederick L(ouis), Jr. 1913-2001 ... 41-44R
Obituary ... 202
Rath, Patricia M(ink) ... 17-20R
Rath, R. John 1910- ... 37-40R
Rath, Sara 1941- ... 108
Rathbone, Belinda 1950- ... 151
Rathbone, Cristina ... 231
Rathbone, Julian 1935- ... CANR-73
Earlier sketches in CA 101, CANR-34
See also CLC 41
Rathbone, Lucy 1896-1990 ... 5-8R
Obituary ... 198
Rathbone, Ouida Bergere 1886(?)-1974
Obituary ... 53-56
Rathbone, Richard 1942- ... CANR-105
Earlier sketch in CA 144
Rathbone, Robert Reynolds 1916- ... 21-24R
Rathborne, St. George (Henry) 1854-1938
See Adams, Harrison
See also TCWW 1, 2
Rathe, Alex W(erner) 1912-1997 ... 17-20R
Rathe, Gustave 1921- ... 138
Rathenau, Walther 1867-1922 ... 237
Brief entry ... 121
Rather, Dan (Irvin) 1931- ... CANR-107
Earlier sketches in CA 53-56, CANR-9
Interview in ... CANR-9
See also AITN 1
Rather, L(elland) J(oseph) 1913-1989 ... 77-80
Rathje, William (Laurens) 1945- ... 143
Rathjen, Carl Henry 1909-1984 ... CANR-2
Obituary ... 196
Earlier sketch in CA 5-8R
See also SATA 11
Rathjen, Frederick W(illiam) 1929- ... 41-44R
Rathlesberger, James (H.) 1948-
Brief entry ... 114
Rathmann, Peggy 1953- ... CANR-142
Earlier sketch in CA 159
See also Crosby, Margaret
See also CWRI 5
See also MAICYA 2
See also MAICYAS 1
See also SATA 94, 157
Rathmell, George W(esley) 1931- ... CANR-140
Earlier sketch in CA 173
Rathmell, J(ohn) C. A. 1935- ... 9-12R
Rathmell, Neil 1947- ... 104
Ratigan, Eleanor Eldridge 1916-1981 ... 5-8R
Ratigan, William 1910-1984 ... 29-32R
Ratiu, Ion 1917-2000 ... 5-8R
Obituary ... 188
Ratliff, Charles Edward, Jr. 1926- ... CANR-1
Earlier sketch in CA 1-4R
Ratliff, Gerald Lee 1944- ... 107
Ratliff, Richard C(harles) 1922- ... 65-68
Ratliff, Thomas M. 1948- ... 190
See also SATA 118
Ratliff, William 1937- ... 144
Ratliffe, Sharon A(nn) 1939- ... 61-64
Ratner, Joseph 1901(?)-1979
Obituary ... 85-88
Ratner, Leonard G(ilbert) 1916- ... 21-24R
Ratner, Lorman 1932- ... CANR-143
Earlier sketches in CA 25-28R, CANR-10
Ratner, Marc L. 1926- ... 45-48
Ratner, Rochelle 1948- ... CANR-93
Earlier sketches in CA 33-36R, CANR-12
Ratner, Sidney 1908-1996 ... 21-24R
Obituary ... 151
Ratner, Stanley C(harles) 1925-1975 ... 13-16R
Ratosh, Yonatan. 1909-1981 ... 212
Ratsch, Christian
See Raetsch, Christian
Rattenbury, Arnold (Foster) 1921- ... 29-32R
Rattenbury, Ken(neth Miller) 1920- ... 134
Ratti, John 1933- ... 73-76
Ratti, Oscar ... CANR-112
Earlier sketch in CA 41-44R
Rattigan, Jama Kim 1951- ... 167
See also SATA 99
Rattigan, Terence (Mervyn) 1911-1977 ... 85-88
Obituary ... 73-76
See also BRWS 7
See also CBD
See also CDBLB 1945-1960
See also CLC 7
See also DAM DRAM
See also DC 18
See also DFS 8
See also DLB 13
See also IDFW 3, 4
See also MTCW 1, 2
See also MTFW 2005
See also RGEL 2
Rattner, David S(amuel) 1916-1997 ... 69-72
Ratto, Linda Lee 1952- ... 148
See also SATA 79
Rattray, Everett T(ennant) 1932-1980 ... 89-92
Obituary ... 97-100
Rattray, Simon
See Trevor, Elleston
Ratushinskaya, Irina 1954- ... CANR-68
Earlier sketch in CA 129
See also CLC 54
See also CWW 2
Ratzan, Scott C. 1962- ... 124
Ratz de Tagyos, Paul 1958- ... 143
See also SATA 76
Ratzinger, Joseph
See Pope Benedict XVI
Ratzinger, Joseph Cardinal
See Pope Benedict XVI
Rau, Dana Meachen 1971- ... 159
See also SATA 94
Rau, Dhanvanthi (Handoo) Rama
See Rama Rau, Dhanvanthi (Handoo)
*Rau, Margaret 1913- ... CANR-8
Earlier sketch in CA 61-64
See also CLR 8
See also SATA 9
Rau, Rama
See Rama Rau, Dhanvanthi (Handoo)
Rauber, Paul ... 237
Rauch, Basil 1908-1986 ... CAP-2
Obituary ... 119
Earlier sketch in CA 19-20
Rauch, Constance 1937- ... 57-60
Rauch, Earl Mac 1950(?)-
Brief entry ... 118
Rauch, Georg Von
See Von Rauch, Georg
Rauch, Gila Ramras
See Ramras-Rauch, Gila
Rauch, Irmengard 1933- ... CANR-11
Earlier sketch in CA 21-24R
Rauch, Jonathan (Charles) 1960- ... 144
Rauch, Joseph B(rian) 1965- ... 131
Rauch, Leo 1927-1997 ... 110
Rauch, Mabel Thompson 1888-1972 ... 5-8R
Obituary ... 103
See also SATA-Obit 26
Rauch, Rufus William, Jr. 1929-1977
Obituary ... 113
Rauch, William 1950- ... 144
Raucher, Alan R(ichard) 1939- ... 118
Raucher, Herman 1928- ... CANR-81
Earlier sketches in CA 29-32R, CANR-29
See also HGG
See also SATA 8
Raucina, Thomas Frank 1946- ... CANR-115
Earlier sketches in CA 73-76, CANR-12, 29
Raudive, Konstantin 1909-1974 ... 29-32R
Obituary ... 126
Rauf, Abdur 1924- ... CANR-42
Earlier sketches in CA 73-76, CANR-13
Rauf, Muhammad Abdul
See Abdul-Rauf, Muhammad
Raulston, J(ames) Leonard 1905-1987 ... 89-92
Rault, Walter
See Gorham, Maurice Anthony Coneys
Raum, Elizabeth 1949- ... 230
See also SATA 155
Rauner, Robert M(cKenzie) 1925- ... CANR-1
Earlier sketch in CA 1-4R
Raunikar, Robert 1931- ... 124
Raup, H(allock) F(loyd) 1901-1985 ... 37-40R
Obituary ... 196
Raup, Robert 1888(?)-1976
Obituary ... 65-68
Rausch, Edward N. 1919-1995 ... CANR-7
Earlier sketch in CA 13-16R
Rausch, Jane M(eyer) 1940- ... 119
Rauschenberg, Roy A(nthony) 1929- ... 45-48
Rauscher, Donald J. 1921-1997 ... 9-12R
Rauschning, Hermann 1887-1982
Obituary ... 109
Rause, Vince ... 200
Raush, Harold L(ester) 1921-
Brief entry ... 110
Raushenbush, Esther (Mohr)
1898-1980 ... CAP-1
Obituary ... 171
Earlier sketch in CA 13-16
Rauta, Arvi
See Jarnefelt, Arvid
Ravage, Barbara ... 232
Ravel, Aviva 1928- ... CANR-45
Earlier sketch in CA 119
Ravel, Edeet 1955- ... 227
Raven, Daniel
See Lazuta, Gene
Raven, Frithjof Andersen 1907-1966 ... CAP-1
Earlier sketch in CA 13-16
Raven, J(ohn) E(arle) 1914-1980 ... 103
Obituary ... 97-100
Raven, Ninette Helene Jeanty 1903-1990
Obituary ... 132
Raven, Ronald William 1904-1991 .. CANR-23
Obituary ... 136
Earlier sketch in CA 107
Raven, Simon (Arthur Noel)
1927-2001 ... CANR-86
Obituary ... 197
Earlier sketch in CA 81-84
See also CLC 14
See also CN 1, 2, 3, 4, 5, 6
See also DLB 271
Ravenal, Earl C(edric) 1931- ... 33-36R
Ravenel, Shannon 1938- ... CANR-95
Earlier sketches in CA 108, CANR-27
Ravenhill, Mark 1966- ... CD 5, 6
See also DLB 310
Ravenna, Michael
See Welty, Eudora (Alice)
Ravenna, Roger
See Horbach, Michael
Ravenscroft, Arthur 1924- ... CANR-29
Earlier sketch in CA 110
Ravenscroft, Edward c. 1643- ... IDTP
See also RGEL 2
Ravenswood, John
See Slauerhoff, Jan Jacob
RavenWolf, Silver 1956- ... 224
See also SATA 155
Ravetch, Irving 1920- ... 227
Brief entry ... 110
See also IDFW 3
Ravetz, Alison 1930- ... 116
Ravetz, Jerome R(aymond) 1929- ... 97-100
Ravetz, Jerry
See Ravetz, Jerome R(aymond)
Ravi, Bison
See Vian, Boris
Ravich, Robert A(lan) 1920-1992 ... 184
Brief entry ... 113

Ravielli, Anthony 1916-1997 ... CANR-11
Obituary ... 156
Earlier sketch in CA 29-32R
See also SATA 3
See also SATA-Obit 95
Ravikovitch, Dahlia
See Rabikovitz, Dalia
See also CWW 2
Ravikovitch, Dalia
See Rabikovitz, Dalia
See also WLIT 6
Ravikovitz, Dalia
See Rabikovitz, Dalia
Ravilious, Robin 1944- ... 145
See also SATA 77
Ravin, Neil 1947- ... 105
Ravindra, Ravi 1939- ... CANR-82
Earlier sketches in CA 114, CANR-35
Ravitch, Diane 1938- ... CANR-97
Earlier sketches in CA 53-56, CANR-4, 31, 65
See also MTCW 1
Ravitch, Mark M(itchell) 1910-1989
Obituary ... 128
Ravitch, Norman 1936- ... 37-40R
Ravitz, Abe Carl 1927- ... 9-12R
Ravitz, Shlomo 1885-1980
Obituary ... 103
Raviv, Dan 1954- ... CANR-121
Earlier sketch in CA 140
Ravnkilde, Adda 1862-1883 ... DLB 300
Ravven, Heidi M(iriam Morrison) 1952- ... 225
Ravvin, Norman 1963- ... CANR-138
Earlier sketch in CA 138
Raw, Isaias 1927- ... 57-60
Rawcliffe, (John) Michael 1934- ... 115
Rawding, F(rederick) W(illiam) 1930- .. SATA 55
Rawet, Samuel 1929-1985 ... 219
Rawford, W. C.
See Crawford, William (Elbert)
Rawick, George P(hilip) 1929- ... 61-64
Rawicz, Piotr 1919-1982 ... DLB 299
Rawitch, Robert Joe 1945- ... 133
Rawlence, Christopher 1945- ... 136
Rawles, Beverly A(rcher) 1930- ... 107
Rawles, Nancy 1958- ... 197
Rawley, Callman 1903-2004 ... CANR-91
Obituary ... 228
Earlier sketches in CA 21-24R, CANR-12, 32
See also Rakosi, Carl
Rawley, Donald 1957-1998 ... 171
Rawley, James A. 1916- ... 21-24R
Rawling, Thomas Jackson 1916- ... 114
Rawling, Tom
See Rawling, Thomas Jackson
Rawlings, Hunter Ripley III 1944- ... 103
Rawlings, Jane ... 223
Rawlings, John 1930(?)-1981(?)
Obituary ... 102
Rawlings, Louisa
See Baumgarten, Sylvia
Rawlings, Marjorie Kinnan
1896-1953 ... CANR-74
Brief entry ... 104
Earlier sketch in CA 137
See also AAYA 20
See also AMWS 10
See also ANW
See also BPFB 3
See also BYA 3
See also CLR 63
See also DLB 9, 22, 102
See also DLBD 17
See also JRDA
See also MAICYA 1, 2
See also MAL 5
See also MTCW 2
See also MTFW 2005
See also RGAL 4
See also SATA 100
See also TCLC 4
See also WCH
See also YABC 1
See also YAW
Rawlings, Maurice S(kaggs) 1922- ... 108
Rawlins, Clive Leonard 1940- ... CANR-22
Earlier sketch in CA 105
Rawlins, Dennis 1937- ... 45-48
Rawlins, Eustace Robert
See Barton, Eustace Robert
Rawlins, Jack P. 1946- ... 57-60
Rawlins, Jennie Brown 1910- ... CAP-2
Earlier sketch in CA 23-24
Rawlins, Winifred 1907-1997 ... 9-12R
Rawlinson, A(rthur) R(ichard) 1894-1984
Obituary ... 113
Rawlinson, Dick
See Rawlinson, A(rthur) R(ichard)
Rawlinson, Gloria 1918- ... CP 1
Rawlinson, Jane 1947- ... 138
Rawlinson, Peter (Anthony) 1919- ... 180
Rawlinson, Richard 1690-1755 ... DLB 213
Rawlinson, Thomas 1681-1725 ... DLB 213
Rawls, Eugene S. 1927-1966 ... 9-12R
Rawls, James J(abus) 1945- ... 112
Rawls, John (Bordley) 1921-2002 ... CANR-106
Obituary ... 213
Brief entry ... 114
Earlier sketches in CA 147, CANR-86
See also DLB 279
See also NCFS 3
Rawls, Philip
See Levinson, Leonard
Rawls, Walter Cecil, Jr. 1928- ... 111
Rawls, Walton (Hendry) 1933- ... CANR-103
Earlier sketches in CA 121, CANR-48
Rawls, Wendell L(ee), Jr. 1941- ... CANR-22
Earlier sketch in CA 73-76
Rawls, (Woodrow) Wilson
1913-1984 ... CANR-131
Earlier sketches in CA 1-4R, CANR-5
See also AAYA 21
See also AITN 1
See also BYA 12
See also CLR 81
See also JRDA
See also MAICYA 2
See also SATA 22
Rawlyk, George Alexander 1935- ... CANR-51
Earlier sketches in CA 109, CANR-26
See also SATA 64
Rawn, Melanie (Robin) 1954- ... 157
See also FANT
See also SATA 98
Raworth, Thomas Moore 1938- ... CANR-46
Earlier sketch in CA 29-32R
See also Raworth, Tom
See also CP 1
Raworth, Tom
See Raworth, Thomas Moore
See also CAAS 11
See also CP 2, 3, 4, 5, 6, 7
See also DLB 40
Rawski, Conrad H(enry) 1914- ... 73-76
Rawski, Evelyn S(akakida) 1939- ... 89-92
Rawson, Beryl 1933- ... 121
Rawson, C(laude) J(ulien) 1935- ... CANR-119
Earlier sketch in CA 25-28R
Rawson, Clayton 1906-1971 ... CANR-73
Obituary ... 29-32R
Earlier sketches in CA 5-8R, CANR-4
Rawson, Elizabeth (Donata) 1934-1988
Brief entry ... 115
Rawson, Margaret B(yrd) 1899-2001 ... 25-28R
Obituary ... 200
Rawson, Philip Stanley 1924-1995 ... CANR-21
Obituary ... 150
Earlier sketches in CA 5-8R, CANR-6
Rawson, Wyatt Trevelyan Rawson
1894-1980 ... 5-8R
Obituary ... 103
Ray, Ann 1937- ... 114
Ray, Arthur J. 1941- ... 127
Ray, Carl 1943-1978 ... 229
See also SATA 63
Ray, Clyde H. 1938- ... 157
Ray, Cyril 1908-1991 ... CANR-21
Obituary ... 135
Earlier sketches in CA 5-8R, CANR-5
Ray, D(avid) Michael 1935- ... CANR-9
Earlier sketch in CA 17-20R
Ray, Daryll E. 1943- ... 149
Ray, David (E.) 1932- ... 194
Earlier sketches in CA 9-12R, CANR-5, 47
Autobiographical Essay in ... 194
See also CAAS 7
See also CP 1, 2, 3, 4, 5, 6, 7
See also DLB 5
See also MAL 5
Ray, Deborah
See Kogan Ray, Deborah
See also SATA 8
Ray, Delia 1963- ... 138
See also SATA 70
Ray, Dixy Lee 1914-1994 ... CANR-75
Obituary ... 143
Earlier sketch in CA 134
Ray, Dorothy Jean 1919- ... CANR-12
Earlier sketch in CA 25-28R
Ray, Francis ... 180
Ray, George McNeill 1910-1972 ... 1-4R
Ray, Gordon N(orton) 1915-1986 ... CANR-75
Obituary ... 121
Earlier sketch in CA 57-60
See also DLB 103, 140
Ray, H(enrietta) Cordelia 1849(?)-1916 ... 124
Brief entry ... 122
See also BW 1
See also DLB 50
Ray, Irene
See Sutton, Margaret Beebe
Ray, Jane 1960- ... SATA 72, 152
Ray, Janisse 1962- ... 191
Ray, Jean
See Kremer, Raymond Jean Marie de
Ray, JoAnne 1935- ... 61-64
See also SATA 9
Ray, John (Philip) 1929- ... CANR-141
Earlier sketches in CA 25-28R, CANR-11
Ray, John B(ernard) 1930- ... 61-64
Ray, John R(obert) 1921- ... 37-40R
Ray, Joseph M(alchus) 1907- ... 41-44R
Ray, (Suzanne) Judy 1939- ... 111
Ray, Karen 1956- ... 108
Ray, Kenneth Clark 1901-1981 ... CAP-2
Earlier sketch in CA 19-20
Ray, Man 1890-1976 ... CANR-29
Obituary ... 69-72
Earlier sketch in CA 77-80
See also AAYA 35
Ray, Marcella Ridlen 1941- ... 228
Ray, Martin S(cott) 1955- ... 176
Ray, Mary (Eva Pedder) 1932- ... CANR-94
Earlier sketches in CA 29-32R, CANR-12
See also CWRI 5
See also SATA 2, 127
Ray, Mary Lyn 1946- ... CANR-59
See also SATA 90, 154
Ray, Michele S. 1938- ... 25-28R
Ray, N(ancy) L(ouise) 1918- ... CANR-51
Earlier sketches in CA 109, CANR-26
Ray, Oakley S(tern) 1931- ... 45-48
Ray, Paul C(harles) 1926- ... 104
Ray, Philip A(lexander) 1911-1970 ... CAP-2
Earlier sketch in CA 23-24
Ray, Rebbecca 1980(?)- ... 198
Ray, Robert H. 1940- ... 135
Ray, Robert J. 1935- ... 126
Ray, Russell
See Strait, Raymond
Ray, Ruth E. 1954- ... 199
Ray, Satyajit 1921-1992 ... 114
Obituary ... 137
See also CLC 16, 76
See also DAM MULT
Ray, Sibnarayan 1921- ... CANR-15
Earlier sketch in CA 21-24R
Ray, Talton F. 1939- ... 29-32R
Ray, Trevor 1934- ... 107
Ray, Wesley
See Gaulden, Ray
Ray, Wilbert S(cott) 1901-1977 ... CAP-2
Earlier sketch in CA 25-28
Rayaprol, Marthandam Srinivas 1925- ... CP 1
Rayback, Joseph G(eorge) 1914- ... CANR-74
Earlier sketch in CA 5-8R
Rayburn, James Chalmers III 1945- ... 121
Rayburn, Jim III
See Rayburn, James Chalmers III
Rayburn, Robert G(ibson) 1915- ... 25-28R
Raycraft, Donald R(obert) 1942- ... 41-44R
Raycraft, Stan
See Shaver, Richard S(harpe)
Rayevsky, Robert 1955- ... SATA 81
Rayfiel, David 1923- ... 139
Rayfiel, Thomas 1958- ... 198
Rayfield, David 1940- ... 45-48
Rayfield, (Patrick) Donald 1942- ... 103
Rayfield, Stanley C. 1901(?)-1983(?)
Obituary ... 108
Raygor, Alton Lamon 1922- ... 49-52
Raymaker, John 1936- ... 229
Rayman, Paula Marian 1947- ... 107
Raymer, Edward C. ... 173
Raymo, Chet 1936- ... 230
See also ANW
Raymond, Agnes G. 1916- ... 25-28R
Raymond, Alex(ander Gillespie)
1909-1956 ... 169
Brief entry ... 112
See also AAYA 67
Raymond, C. Elizabeth 1953- ... 139
Raymond, Charles
See Koch, Charlotte (Moskowitz) and Koch, Raymond
Raymond, Diana (Joan) 1916- ... 89-92
Raymond, E. V.
See Gallun, Raymond Z(inke)
Raymond, Ellsworth (Lester)
1912-1996 ... 37-40R
Obituary ... 153
Raymond, Ernest 1888-1974 ... 185
Obituary ... 89-92
See also CN 1
See also DLB 191
Raymond, Father M.
See Flanagan, Joseph David Stanislaus
Raymond, G. Alison
See Lanier, Alison Raymond
Raymond, Harold 1887-1975
Obituary ... 104
Raymond, Henry J. 1820-1869 ... DLB 43, 79
Raymond, James (Charles) 1940- ... 119
Raymond, James Crossley 1917-1981
Obituary ... 105
See also SATA-Obit 29
Raymond, Janice G. 1943- ... 89-92
Raymond, John
See Brosnan, John
Raymond, Jonathan ... 233
Raymond, Joseph H.
See Le Fontaine, Joseph (Raymond)
Raymond, Laurie W(atson) 1951- ... 166
Raymond, Lee
See Hill, Mary Raymond
Raymond, Margaret E(lmendorf) 1912- ... 104
Raymond, Mary
See Keegan, Mary Heathcott
Raymond, P. L.
See Gibson, Walter B(rown)
Raymond, Patrick (Ernest) 1924- ... 102
Raymond, Rene (Brabazon)
1906-1985 ... CANR-61
Obituary ... 115
Earlier sketch in CA 126
See also Chase, James Hadley
See also CMW 4
Raymond, Robert
See Alter, Robert Edmond
Raymond, Steve 1940- ... 49-52
Raymond, Walter J(ohn) 1930- ... 53-56
Raymond, William O. 1880-1970 ... CAP-2
Earlier sketch in CA 19-20
Raymond de Jesus, Mother
See Dion, Sister Anita
Raynal, Paul 1885(?)-1971
Obituary ... 33-36R
Rayne, Alan
See Tobin, James Edward
Rayner, Claire (Berenice) 1931- ... CANR-70
Earlier sketches in CA 21-24R, CANR-13
See also RHW
Rayner, E(dgar) G(eoffrey) 1927- ... CANR-10
Earlier sketch in CA 21-24R
Rayner, Hugh ... 226
See also SATA 151
Rayner, Jay 1966- ... 223
Rayner, John Desmond 1924- ... 103
Rayner, Mary 1933- ... CANR-80
Earlier sketches in CA 69-72, CANR-12, 29, 52
See also CLR 41
See also CWRI 5
See also MAICYA 2
See also MAICYAS 1
See also SATA 22, 87
Rayner, Moira ... 221
Rayner, Ray
See Rahner, Raymond M.
Rayner, Richard
See McIlwain, David
Rayner, Richard 1955- ... 209
Rayner, Shoo
See Rayner, Hugh
Rayner, William 1929- ... CANR-64
Earlier sketch in CA 77-80
See also SATA 55
See also SATA-Brief 36
See also TCWW 2
Raynolds, John F(iske III) 1929- ... 181
Raynor, David R(alph) 1948- ... 111
Raynor, Dorka ... 106
See also SATA 28
Raynor, Henry (Broughton) 1917- ... 85-88
Rayside, Betty 1931- ... 57-60
Rayside, David 1947- ... 171
Rayson, Hannie 1957- ... CD 5, 6
See also CWD
Rayson, Paul
See Jennings, Leslie Nelson
Rayson, Steven 1932- ... 106
See also SATA 30
Rayward, W(arden) Boyd 1939- ... 102
Raywid, Mary Anne ... 5-8R
Raz, Aviad E. ... 232
Raz, Hilda 1938- ... 172
Raz, Joseph 1939- ... CANR-144
Earlier sketch in CA 125
Raz, Simcha 1931- ... CANR-118
Earlier sketch in CA 157
Razaf, Andy 1895-1973
Obituary ... 41-44R
See also DLB 265
Razgon, Lev (Emmanuelivich) 1908-1999 .. 189
Razi, al- 865(?)-c. 925 ... DLB 311
Razik, Taher A. 1924- ... CANR-19
Earlier sketch in CA 25-28R
Razin, Assaf 1941- ... 136
Razon, Felix
See San Juan, Epifanio, Jr.
Razor Saltboy
See Louis, Ray Baldwin
Razran, Gregory 1901-1973 ... 41-44R
Obituary ... 45-48
Razzell, Arthur (George) 1925- ... 85-88
See also SATA 11
Razzell, Mary (Catherine) 1930- ... CANR-124
Earlier sketch in CA 160
See also SATA 102
Razzi, James 1931- ... CANR-5
Earlier sketch in CA 53-56
See also SATA 10
Re, Edward D(omenic) 1920- ... CANR-12
Earlier sketch in CA 21-24R
Rea, Domenico 1921-1994 ... EWL 3
Rea, Frederick B(eatty) 1908-1984 ... 9-12R
Rea, Gardner 1892-1966
Obituary ... 93-96
Rea, K(enneth) J(ohn) 1932- ... 184
Brief entry ... 107
Rea, Kenneth Wesley 1944- ... 107
Rea, Michael M. 1927-1996 ... DLBY 1997
Rea, Robert R(ight) 1922- ... CANR-28
Earlier sketch in CA 1-4R
Reach, Angus 1821-1856 ... DLB 70
Reach, James 1910(?)-1970
Obituary ... 29-32R
Read, Al 1919-1987
Obituary ... 123
Read, Anthony 1935- ... 107
Read, Bill 1917- ... 13-16R
Read, Brian (Ahier) 1927- ... 108
Read, Cecil B(yron) 1901-1972 ... CAP-1
Earlier sketch in CA 13-16
Read, David Haxton Carswell
1910-2001 ... CANR-3
Obituary ... 193
Earlier sketch in CA 1-4R
Read, Donald 1930- ... CANR-75
Earlier sketches in CA 1-4R, CANR-1
Read, Elfreida 1920- ... CANR-25
Earlier sketches in CA 21-24R, CANR-9
See also SATA 2
Read, Forrest 1926-1980
Obituary ... 112
Read, Gardner 1913- ... CANR-6
Earlier sketch in CA 13-16R
Read, Hadley 1918- ... 81-84
Read, Helen Appleton 1887(?)-1974
Obituary ... 53-56
Read, Herbert Edward 1893-1968 ... 85-88
Obituary ... 25-28R
See also BRW 6
See also CLC 4
See also DLB 20, 149
See also EWL 3
See also PAB
See also RGEL 2
Read, Jan
See Read, John Hinton
Read, John Hinton 1917- ... CANR-22
Earlier sketches in CA 77-80, CANR-15
Read, Kenneth E(yre) 1917- ... 101

Read, Leonard Edward 1898-1983 ... CANR-11
Obituary ... 109
Earlier sketch in CA 17-20R
Read, Martha Meredith ... DLB 200
Read, Maureen Hay 1937- ... 113
Read, Nicholas 1956- ... 220
See also SATA 146
Read, Opie (Percival) 1852-1939 ... 183
See also DLB 23
Read, Peter 1945- ... 202
Read, Peter G. 1927- ... 141
Read, Piers Paul 1941- ... CANR-86
Earlier sketches in CA 21-24R, CANR-38
See also CLC 4, 10, 25
See also CN 2, 3, 4, 5, 6, 7
See also DLB 14
See also SATA 21
Read, R. B. 1916-1982 ... CANR-13
Earlier sketch in CA 61-64
Read, Ritchard 1914- ... 57-60
Read, Sylvia Joan ... 103
Read, William M(erritt) 1901-1984 ... 33-36R
Reade, B(rian) Edmund 1913-1989 ... 21-24R
Reade, Charles 1814-1884 ... DLB 21
See also RGEL 2
Reade, Deborah 1949- ... SATA 69
Reade, Hamish
See Gray, Simon (James Holliday)
Reade, Lang
See Carter, David C(harles)
Reader, Dennis 1929- ... SATA 71
Reader, Dennis Joel 1939- ... 106
Reader, Desmond H. 1920- ... 21-24R
Reader, John 1937- ... CANR-123
Earlier sketch in CA 171
Reader, W(illiam) J(oseph)
1920-1990 ... CANR-39
Obituary ... 132
Earlier sketches in CA 37-40R, CANR-16
Reading, Peter 1946- ... CANR-96
Earlier sketches in CA 103, CANR-46
See also BRWS 8
See also CLC 47
See also CP 7
See also DLB 40
Reading, Richard P(atrick) 1962- ... 237
See also SATA 161
Readings, Bill 1960-1994 ... 139
Readman, Jo 1958- ... 155
See also SATA 89
Ready, Kirk L(ewis) 1943- ... 114
See also SATA 39
Ready, William B(ernard)
1914-1981 ... CANR-22
Earlier sketch in CA 25-28R
Reagan, Charles E(llis) 1942- ... 53-56
Reagan, Michael D(aniel) 1927- ... CANR-93
Earlier sketch in CA 49-52
Reagan, Nancy (Davis) 1923- ... CANR-103
Earlier sketches in CA 110, CANR-33
See also BEST 90:1
Reagan, Patricia Ann
See Davis, Patti
Reagan, Ronald (Wilson)
1911-2004 ... CANR-47
Obituary ... 228
Earlier sketch in CA 85-88
See also BEST 90:1
Reagan, Sydney C(handler) 1916- ... 41-44R
Reagan, Thomas (James) B(utler) 1916- . 37-40R
Reage, Pauline
See Aury, Dominique
Reagen, Edward P(aul) 1924- ... 49-52
Reagen, Michael V. 1942- ... 81-84
Reagin, Ewell Kerr 1900-1985 ... 41-44R
Reagon, Bernice Johnson 1942- ... CANR-116
Earlier sketch in CA 147
Real, Terrence 1950(?)- ... CANR-117
Earlier sketch in CA 167
Reaman, George Elmore 1889-1969 ... CAP-1
Earlier sketch in CA 11-12
Reamer, Judy 1940- ... 125
Reams, Bernard D(insmore), Jr.
1943- ... CANR-16
Earlier sketch in CA 93-96
Reamy, Tom 1935-1977 ... CANR-79
Earlier sketch in CA 81-84
See also SFW 4
Reaney, James 1926- ... CANR-42
Earlier sketch in CA 41-44R
See also CAAS 15
See also CD 5, 6
See also CLC 13
See also CP 1, 2, 3, 4, 5, 6, 7
See also DAC
See also DAM MST
See also DLB 68
See also RGEL 2
See also SATA 43
Rearden, Jim 1925- ... CANR-40
Earlier sketch in CA 65-68
Reardon, B(ernard) M(orris) G(arvin)
1914- ... CANR-2
Earlier sketch in CA 5-8R
Reardon, Dennis J(oseph) 1944- ... 113
Brief entry ... 110
Interview in ... CA-113
See also CAD
See also CD 5, 6
Reardon, Joan 1930-1988 ... 116
Reardon, John J(oseph) 1926- ... 61-64
Reardon, William R. 1920- ... CANR-2
Earlier sketch in CA 1-4R
Rearick, Charles Walter 1942- ... 102
Reaske, Christopher R(ussell) 1941- ... 21-24R
Reason, James T(ootle) 1938- ... 104
Reasoner, Harry 1923-1991 ... CANR-75
Obituary ... 135
Earlier sketch in CA 111
See also AITN 1
Reasoner, James M(orris) 1953- ... TCWW 2
Reat, N(oble) Ross 1951- ... 139
Reaven, Gerald M. ... 231
Reaver, Chap 1935-1993 ... CANR-79
Obituary ... 142
Earlier sketch in CA 137
See also AAYA 31
See also SATA 69
See also SATA-Obit 77
See also YAW
Reaver, Herbert R.
See Reaver, Chap
Reaver, J(oseph) Russell 1915- ... 33-36R
Reaves, J. Michael
See Reaves, (James) Michael
Reaves, (James) Michael 1950- ... 158
See also FANT
See also SATA 99
See also SFW 4
Reaves, Philip
See Kiester, Edwin, Jr.
Reaves, Sam 1954- ... 215
Reaves, Wendy Wick 1950- ... 114
Reavey, George 1907-1976
Obituary ... 69-72
Reavey, Jean (Bullowa) 1917(?)-1987
Obituary ... 123
Reavis, Dick J. 1945- ... 133
Reay, Barry 1950- ... CANR-121
Earlier sketch in CA 144
Reb, Paul 1924- ... 49-52
Rebatet, Lucien 1903-1972
Obituary ... 37-40R
Rebay, Luciano 1928- ... 45-48
Rebbot, Olivier 1951(?)-1981
Obituary ... 103
Rebeck, Theresa ... DFS 11
Rebel, Adam
See Roan, Tom
Rebellato, Dan ... 183
Rebelo, Marques 1907-1973 ... 178
Rebelsky, Freda Gould 1931- ... 41-44R
Rebert, M. Charles 1920- ... 53-56
Rebeta-Burditt, Joyce ... 81-84
Rebholz, Ronald A(lexander) 1932- ... 111
Rebhorn, Wayne A. 1943- ... 189
Rebhun, Joseph 1921- ... 203
Rebhun, Paul c. 1500-1546 ... DLB 179
Rebischung, James A. 1928- ... 53-56
Rebolledo, Tey Diana 1937- ... 179
Rebora, Clemente 1885-1957 ... 184
See also DLB 114
See also EWL 3
Rebreanu, Liviu 1885-1944 ... 165
See also DLB 220
See also EWL 3
See also TCLC 28
Rebuffat, Gaston (Louis Simon)
1921-1985 ... CANR-75
Obituary ... 116
Earlier sketch in CA 21-24R
Receveur, Betty Layman 1930-2003 ... 130
Obituary ... 222
Rechcigl, Miloslav, Jr. 1930- ... CANR-12
Earlier sketch in CA 17-20R
Rechy, John (Francisco) 1934- ... 195
Earlier sketches in CA 5-8R, CANR-6, 32, 64
Interview in ... CANR-6
Autobiographical Essay in ... 195
See also CAAS 4
See also CLC 1, 7, 14, 18, 107
See also CN 1, 2, 3, 4, 5, 6, 7
See also DAM MULT
See also DLB 122, 278
See also DLBY 1982
See also HLC 2
See also HW 1, 2
See also LLW
See also MAL 5
See also RGAL 4
Reck, Alma Kehoe 1901-1981 ... 1-4R
Reck, Andrew J(oseph) 1927- ... CANR-6
Earlier sketch in CA 13-16R
Reck, David 1935- ... 73-76
Reck, Franklin Mering 1896-1965
Obituary ... 109
See also SATA-Brief 30
Reck, Rima Drell 1933- ... 21-24R
Reck, W(aldo) Emerson 1903-1995 ... 61-64
Recker, Colane 1940- ... 113
Reckless, Walter Cade 1899-1988 ... 37-40R
Reck-Malleczewen, Friedrich Percyval
1884-1945 ... 198
Reck-Malleczewen, Fritz Percy
See Reck-Malleczewen, Friedrich Percyval
Recknagel, Marsha (Lee) ... 205
Reckord, Barry 1926- ... 77-80
See also CD 6
Record, Cy Wilson 1916- ... 9-12R
Record, Jane Cassels 1915-1981 ... CANR-5
Earlier sketch in CA 13-16R
Record, Jeffrey 1943- ... 180
Rector, Frank ... 106
Red, Tulsa
See Fulson, Lowell
Reday, Ladislaw 1913-1987 ... 112
Red Bird
See Bonnin, Gertrude
Red Butterfly
See Lauritsen, John (Phillip)
Redcam, Tom 1870-1933 ... TCLC 25
Redcliffe-Maud, John
See Redcliffe-Maud, John Primatt
Redcliffe-Maud, John Primatt 1906-1982 ... 129
Obituary ... 108
Redcliffe-Maud, Lord
See Redcliffe-Maud, John Primatt
Redd, (Newton) Lawrence 1941- ... 57-60
Redd, Louise 1967- ... 153
Reddan, Harold J. 1926- ... 13-16R
Reddaway, (Arthur Frederick) John 1916-1990
Obituary ... 132
Reddaway, Peter (Brian) 1939- ... CANR-10
Earlier sketch in CA 21-24R
Reddaway, W(illiam) Brian 1913-2002 . 17-20R
Obituary ... 206
Redden, James Erskine 1928- ... 41-44R
Redder, George
See Drummond, Jack
Reddick, DeWitt Carter 1904-1980 ... 5-8R
Obituary ... 182
Reddick, L(awrence) D(unbar)
1910-1995 ... 61-64
Obituary ... 149
Reddin, Keith 1956- ... CAD
See also CD 6
See also CLC 67
Reddin, Paul L. ... 198
Reddin, W(illiam) J(ames) 1930- ... 29-32R
Redding, Bud
See Redding, Edward C.
Redding, David A. 1923- ... CANR-3
Earlier sketch in CA 1-4R
Redding, Edward C. 1917-1984
Obituary ... 113
Redding, J(ay) Saunders 1906-1988 .. CANR-87
Obituary ... 124
Earlier sketches in CA 1-4R, CANR-5, 26
See also Redding, Saunders
See also BW 1
See also DLB 63, 76
Redding, Robert Hull 1919- ... CANR-28
Earlier sketches in CA 21-24R, CANR-11
See also SATA 2
Redding, Saunders
See Redding, J(ay) Saunders
See also RGAL 4
Redditt, Paul L. 1942- ... 192
Reddy, John F. X. 1912(?)-1975
Obituary ... 53-56
Reddy, Maureen T. 1955- ... CANR-87
Earlier sketch in CA 130
Reddy, Michael 1933- ... 61-64
Reddy, T. J. 1945- ... 45-48
Reddy, T(hammaiahgari) Ramakrishna
1937- ... 45-48
Redekop, Calvin Wall 1925- ... CANR-51
Earlier sketches in CA 25-28R, CANR-10, 26
Redekop, John Harold 1932- ... 21-24R
Redekopp, Elsa ... 127
See also SATA 61
Redel, Victoria 1959- ... 174
Reder, Philip 1924-1983
Obituary ... 110
Redfern, Elizabeth 1950- ... 234
Redfern, George B. 1910-1996 ... 9-12R
Redfern, W(alter) D(avid) 1936- ... CANR-75
Earlier sketch in CA 21-24R
Redfield, Alden 1941- ... 77-80
Redfield, Alfred Clarence 1890-1983
Obituary ... 109
Redfield, Clark
See McMorrow, Fred
Redfield, Dana 1944- ... 187
Redfield, James 1950- ... CANR-111
Earlier sketches in CA 158, CANR-91
Redfield, James M. 1935- ... 155
Redfield, Jennifer
See Hoskins, Robert (Phillip)
Redfield, Malissa
See Elliott, Malissa Childs
Redfield, Margaret Park 1899(?)-1977
Obituary ... 69-72
Redfield, Robert 1897-1958 ... 182
Brief entry ... 121
Redfield, William 1927-1976
Obituary ... 69-72
Redford, Donald B(ruce) 1934- ... 149
Redford, Emmette Shelburn 1904-1998 ... 112
Redford, Kent H(ubbard) 1955- ... 141
Redford, Polly 1925-1972 ... CANR-74
Earlier sketches in CAP-2, CA 33-36
Redford, (Charles) Robert, (Jr.) 1937- ... 107
See also AAYA 15
Red Fox, William 1871(?)-1976
Obituary ... 65-68
Redgate, John
See Kennedy, Adam
Redgrave, Corin 1939- ... 154
Redgrave, Deirdre 1939-1997 ... 157
Obituary ... 161
Redgrave, Lady
See Kempson, Rachel
Redgrave, Lynn (Rachel) 1943- ... 157
Redgrave, Michael (Scudamore)
1908-1985 ... 143
Obituary ... 115
Redgrave, Paul 1920- ... 5-8R
Redgrave, Vanessa 1937- ... 148
Redgrove, Peter (William)
1932-2003 ... CANR-77
Obituary ... 217
Earlier sketches in CA 1-4R, CANR-3, 39
See also BRWS 6
See also CLC 6, 41
See also CP 1, 2, 3, 4, 5, 6, 7
See also DLB 40
See also TCLE 1:2
Redhead, Brian 1929-1994 ... 128
Obituary ... 143
Redhill, Michael H. 1966- ... CANR-121
Earlier sketch in CA 200
Red Hog
See Martin, Dannie M.
Rediker, Marcus 1951- ... 229
Redinger, Ruby V(irginia) 1915-1981 ... 65-68
Obituary ... 120
Redish, Bessie Braid 1905-1974 ... CAP-2
Earlier sketch in CA 25-28
Redkey, Edwin S(torer) 1931- ... 29-32R
Redlich, Frederick C(arl) 1910-2004
Obituary ... 222
Brief entry ... 106
See also Redlich, Fritz (C.)
Redlich, Fritz (C.) ... 180
See also Redlich, Frederick C(arl)
Redman, Ben Ray 1896-1961
Obituary ... 93-96
Redman, Deborah A. 1957- ... 177
Redman, Eric 1948- ... 49-52
Redman, L(ister) A(ppleton) 1933- ... 108
Redmayne, John
See Wood, Herbert Fairlie
Redmayne, Paul (Brewis) 1900- ... 5-8R
Redmon, Anne
See Nightingale, Anne Redmon
See also CLC 22
See also DLBY 1986
Redmond, Eugene B. 1937- ... CANR-25
Earlier sketches in CA 25-28R, CANR-12
See also BW 2
See also DLB 41
Redmond, Gerald 1934- ... 37-40R
Redmond, Howard A(lexander) 1925- ... 13-16R
Redmond, Ian (Michael) 1954- ... 147
Redmond, Juanita
See Hipps, Juanita Redmond
Redmond, Layne ... 165
Redmont, Bernard Sidney 1918- ... 73-76
Redmont, Dennis Foster 1942- ... 77-80
Redner, Harry 1937- ... 110
Redol, Alves 1911-1969 ... DLB 287
Redol, Antonio Alves 1911-1969 ... EWL 3
Redon, Joel 1961- ... 131
Redonnet, Marie 1948- ... 154
Redpath, Alan (Ogle) 1907-1989
Obituary ... 128
Redpath, (Robert) Theodore (Holmes)
1913-1997 ... 104
Redpath, William 1893(?)-1985
Obituary ... 116
Red Rabbit
See Drew, Horace R. III
Redshaw, Peggy A(nn) 1948- ... CANR-122
Earlier sketch in CA 168
Redstone, Louis G(ordon) 1903- ... CANR-2
Earlier sketch in CA 49-52
Redway, Ralph
See Hamilton, Charles (Harold St. John)
Redway, Ridley
See Hamilton, Charles (Harold St. John)
Redwood, Alec
See Milkomane, George Alexis Milkomanovich
Redwood, John (Alan) 1951- ... CANR-41
Earlier sketches in CA 102, CANR-19
Ree, Jonathan 1948- ... 57-60
Reebs, Stephen G. ... 214
Reece, Benny R(amon) 1930- ... 41-44R
Reece, Colleen L. 1935- ... 188
See also SATA 116
Reece, Gabrielle 1970- ... 161
See also SATA 108
Reece, Jack Eugene 1941- ... 101
Reece, L. a.
See Griffiths, Rhys Adrian
Reece, Robert D(enton) 1939- ... 128
Reeck, Darrell (Lauren) 1939- ... 104
Reed, A(lfred) H(amish) 1875-1975 ... CANR-4
Obituary ... 57-60
Earlier sketch in CA 9-12R
Reed, A(lexander) W(yclif)
1908-1979 ... CANR-4
Earlier sketch in CA 9-12R
Reed, Adolph L., Jr. ... 196
Reed, Alison Touster 1952- ... 105
Reed, Barry
See Reed, Barry C(lement)
Reed, Barry C(lement) 1927-2002 ... CANR-23
Obituary ... 211
Earlier sketch in CA 29-32R
Reed, Betty Jane 1921- ... 29-32R
See also SATA 4
Reed, Bobbie (Butler) 1944- ... 77-80
Reed, Carroll E(dward) 1914- ... 103
Reed, Christopher (G.) 1961- ... CANR-123
Earlier sketch in CA 163
Reed, Daniel 1892(?)-1978
Obituary ... 77-80
Reed, David 1946- ... CANR-136
Earlier sketch in CA 167
Reed, Don C(harles) 1945- ... 106
Reed, Donald A(nthony) 1935-2001 ... 103
Obituary ... 194
Reed, Douglas 1895-1976 ... 103
Obituary ... 89-92
Reed, E.
See Evans, Mari
Reed, Edward W(ilson) 1913-1997 ... 29-32R
Reed, Eliot
See Ambler, Eric
Reed, Elizabeth Liggett 1895-1978 ... 77-80
Obituary ... 133
Reed, Elizabeth Stewart 1914- ... 1-4R
Reed, Emmett X.
See King, Florence
Reed, Evelyn 1905-1979 ... 102

Cumulative Index 479 Reger

Reed, Graham 1923- ... CANR-24
Earlier sketch in CA 45-48
Reed, Gwendolyn E(lizabeth) 1932- ... 25-28R
See also SATA 21
Reed, H(erbert) Owen 1910- ... CANR-42
Earlier sketches in CA 53-56, CANR-4, 19
Reed, Harold W(illiam) 1909-1992 ... 118
Reed, Harrison Merrick, Jr. 1898-1970(?) .. 1-4R
Obituary ... 134
Reed, Henry 1808-1854 ... DLB 59
Reed, Henry 1914-1986 ... CANR-78
Obituary ... 121
Earlier sketch in CA 104
See also CP 1, 2
See also DLB 27
Reed, Henry Clay 1899-1972
Obituary ... 111
Reed, Howard Alexander 1920- ... 13-16R
Reed, Ishmael (Scott) 1938- ... CANR-128
Earlier sketches in CA 21-24R, CANR-25, 48, 74
See also AFAW 1, 2
See also AMWS 10
See also BLC 3
See also BPFB 3
See also BW 2, 3
See also CLC 2, 3, 5, 6, 13, 32, 60, 174
See also CN 1, 2, 3, 4, 5, 6, 7
See also CP 1, 2, 3, 4, 5, 6, 7
See also CSW
See also DA3
See also DAM MULT
See also DLB 2, 5, 33, 169, 227
See also DLBD 8
See also EWL 3
See also LMFS 2
See also MAL 5
See also MSW
See also MTCW 1, 2
See also MTFW 2005
See also PC 68
See also PFS 6
See also RGAL 4
See also TCWW 2
Reed, J(ames) D(onald) 1940- ... 33-36R
Reed, James 1922- ... 102
Reed, James F(red) 1909-1993 ... CAP-1
Earlier sketch in CA 11-12
Reed, James Wesley 1944- ... CANR-140
Earlier sketch in CA 112
Reed, Jeremy 1951- ... 154
See also CP 7
Reed, John (Silas) 1887-1920 ... 195
Brief entry ... 106
See also MAL 5
See also TCLC 9
See also TUS
Reed, John 1909-1999 ... 125
Obituary ... 188
Reed, John F(ord) 1911-1989 ... 13-16R
Reed, John L(incoln) 1938- ... 57-60
Reed, John P(lume) 1921- ... 65-68
Reed, John Q(uincy) 1918-1978 ... CANR-78
Obituary ... 103
Earlier sketch in CA 45-48
Reed, John R(obert) 1938- ... CANR-143
Earlier sketches in CA 17-20R, CANR-8
Reed, John Shelton, (Jr.) 1942- ... CANR-5
Earlier sketch in CA 53-56
See also CSW
Reed, Joseph Verner 1902-1973
Obituary ... 45-48
Reed, Joseph W(ayne), Jr. 1932- ... 37-40R
Reed, Joy 1962- ... 221
Reed, Kenneth 1944- ... 57-60
Reed, Kenneth T(errence) 1937- ... 73-76
Reed, Kit 1932- ... CANR-80
Earlier sketches in CA 1-4R, CANR-1, 16, 36
See also SATA 34, 116
See also SFW 4
Reed, Lawrence
See Reday, Ladislaw
Reed, Linda 1955- ... 137
Reed, Lou
See Firbank, Louis
See also CLC 21
Reed, Louis S(chultz) 1902-1975
Obituary ... 61-64
Reed, Luther D(otterer) 1873-1972 ... 5-8R
Reed, M(athilda) N(ewman) 1905-1971(?) ... CANR-78
Obituary ... 134
Earlier sketch in CA 1-4R
Reed, Macon, Jr. 1911(?)-1986
Obituary ... 121
Reed, Marcia 1929- ... 120
Reed, Mark D(ouglas) Morrison
See Morrison-Reed, Mark D(ouglas)
Reed, Mark L(afayette) III 1935- ... 93-96
Reed, Mary Jane (Pobst) 1920- ... 25-28R
Reed, Michael 1930- ... CANR-50
Earlier sketch in CA 123
Reed, (Fred) Mort(on) 1912-1988 ... 61-64
Reed, Neil 1961- ... SATA 99
Reed, Nelson A. 1926- ... 9-12R
Reed, Paul 1956- ... CANR-109
Earlier sketch in CA 113
Reed, Peter J. 1935- ... 53-56
Reed, Philip (Chandler) 1952- ... 159
Reed, Philip G. 1908- ... SATA-Brief 29
Reed, Rex (Taylor) 1938- ... CANR-68
Earlier sketches in CA 53-56, CANR-9, 27
See also AITN 1
See also DLB 185
Reed, Robert 1956- ... 127
See also SFW 4
Reed, Robert C(arroll) 1937- ... CANR-10
Earlier sketch in CA 65-68
Reed, Robert Rentoul, Jr. 1911-1995 ... 33-36R
Reed, Ronald F. 1945- ... CANR-91
Earlier sketch in CA 116
Reed, S(amuel) Kyle 1922- ... 41-44R
Reed, Sampson 1800-1880 ... DLB 1, 235
Reed, Talbot Baines 1852-1893 ... CLR 76
See also DLB 141
Reed, Thomas (James) 1947- ... 103
See also SATA 34
Reed, Thomas C. 1934- ... 230
Reed, Thomas Harrison 1881-1971
Obituary ... 110
Reed, Thomas Thornton 1902- ... 107
Reed, Victor (Brenner) 1926- ... 33-36R
Reed, Walter Logan 1943- ... 102
Reed, William Maxwell 1871-1962 ... SATA 15
Reed, Willis 1942- ... 104
Reeder, Carolyn 1937- ... 135
See also AAYA 32
See also CLR 69
See also MAICYA 2
See also MAICYAS 1
See also SATA 66, 97
Reeder, Colin (Dawson) 1938- ... 141
See also SATA 74
Reeder, Colonel Red
See Reeder, Russell P(otter), Jr.
Reeder, John P., Jr. 1937- ... 101
Reeder, Ray 1931- ... 158
Reeder, Russell P(otter), Jr. 1902-1998 ... CANR-5
Obituary ... 165
Earlier sketch in CA 1-4R
See also SATA 4
See also SATA-Obit 101
Reeder, Stephanie Owen 1951- ... 169
See also SATA 102
Reed-Jones, Carol 1955- ... 184
See also SATA 112
Reedstrom, Ernest Lisle 1928- ... 89-92
Reedy, George E(dward) 1917-1999 ... 29-32R
Obituary ... 179
Reedy, Jerry Edward 1936- ... 119
Reedy, John Louis 1925-1983
Obituary ... 111
Reedy, Pat
See Reedy, Patricia M.
Reedy, Patricia M. 1940- ... 181
Reedy, William A. 1916(?)-1975
Obituary ... 61-64
Reedy, William James 1921- ... 13-16R
Reedy, William Marion 1862-1920 ... 204
See also DLB 91
Reef, Catherine 1951- ... 198
See also SATA 73, 128
Reefe, Thomas Q(uentin) 1943- ... 123
Brief entry ... 116
Reekie, Jocelyn (Margaret) 1947- ... 218
See also SATA 145
Reel, A(dolph) Frank 1907-2000 ... 93-96
Obituary ... 189
Reeman, Douglas Edward 1924- ... CANR-59
Earlier sketches in CA 1-4R, CANR-3
See also RHW
See also SATA 63
See also SATA-Brief 28
Reems, Harry 1947- ... 61-64
Reens, Mary
See Singleton, Betty
Reep, Edward 1918- ... 33-36R
Rees, Alan M(axwell) 1929- ... 106
Rees, Albert (Everett) 1921-1992 ... CANR-78
Obituary ... 139
Earlier sketches in CA 29-32R, CANR-12
Rees, Alun William 1937- ... CP 1
Rees, Barbara (Elizabeth) 1934- ... CANR-9
Earlier sketch in CA 53-56
Rees, Brian 1929- ... CANR-86
Earlier sketch in CA 133
Rees, C. Roger 1946- ... 146
Rees, Celia 1949- ... AAYA 51
See also BYA 15
See also SATA 124
Rees, Clair (Francis) 1938- ... 117
Rees, David (Edward Bernard) 1928-2004 ... CANR-74
Obituary ... 228
Earlier sketches in CA 9-12R, CANR-11
Rees, David (Bartlett) 1936-1993 ... CANR-80
Obituary ... 141
Earlier sketches in CA 105, CANR-47
See also CWRI 5
See also MAICYA 1, 2
See also MAICYAS 1
See also SAAS 5
See also SATA 36, 69
See also SATA-Obit 76
Rees, David Morgan 1904-1980 ... 104
Rees, Dilwyn
See Daniel, Glyn (Edmund)
Rees, Elizabeth 1947- ... 190
Rees, Ennis (Samuel, Jr.) 1925- ... CANR-2
Earlier sketch in CA 1-4R
See also SATA 3
Rees, Frank D. 1950- ... 226
Rees, (Morgan) Goronwy 1909-1979 ... CANR-74
Earlier sketches in CA 45-48, CANR-3
Rees, Helen Christina Easson (Evans) 1903-1970 ... CANR-76
Obituary ... 89-92
Earlier sketch in CA 5-8R
Rees, Henry 1916- ... 107
Rees, Ioan Bowen 1929-1999 ... 29-32R
Rees, Jean A(nglin) 1912- ... CANR-1
Earlier sketch in CA 1-4R
Rees, Joan 1927- ... CANR-29
Earlier sketches in CA 25-28R, CANR-12
Rees, Joan Alice Gladys
See Rees, Joan
Rees, (George) Leslie (Clarence) 1905-2000 ... CANR-80
Earlier sketches in CA 104, CANR-26
See also CWRI 5
See also SATA 105
See also SATA-Obit 135
Rees, Lucy 1943- ... 107
Rees, Margaret A(nn) 1933- ... CANR-39
Earlier sketches in CA 101, CANR-18
Rees, Meriel
See Lambot, Isobel
Rees, Nigel (Thomas) 1944- ... CANR-86
Earlier sketch in CA 132
Rees, Paul Stromberg 1900-1991 ... 5-8R
Rees, Richard (Lodowick Edward Montagu) 1900-1970 ... CANR-4
Obituary ... 89-92
Earlier sketch in CA 5-8R
Rees, Richard-Lewis 1950- ... 142
Rees, Robert A(lvin) 1935- ... 81-84
Rees, Roberta ... 166
Rees, Roger 1944- ... 197
Rees, (Margaret) Una 1920- ... 124
Rees, William 1887-1978(?) ... CANR-76
Obituary ... 104
Earlier sketch in CA 5-8R
Reesby, Ralph (Harold) 1911-1999 ... 154
Reese, Alexander 1881-1969 ... 97-100
Reese, Algernon B(everly) 1896-1981
Obituary ... 105
Reese, Bob
See Reese, Robert A.
Reese, Carolyn Johnson 1938- ... 112
See also Reese, Lyn
Reese, Curtis W(illiford) 1887-1961
Obituary ... 110
Reese, Della 1931(?)- ... 180
See also SATA 114
Reese, Edward, Jr. 1928- ... 113
Reese, Francesca Gardner 1940- ... 65-68
Reese, Gustave 1899-1977
Obituary ... 73-76
Reese, Heloise (Bowles) 1919-1977 ... 9-12R
Obituary ... 73-76
Reese, Jim E(anes) 1912-1976 ... 13-16R
Obituary ... 134
Reese, John (Henry) 1910-1981 ... CANR-66
Earlier sketch in CA 102
See also TCWW 1, 2
Reese, Laura 1950- ... CANR-101
Earlier sketch in CA 156
Reese, Lizette Woodworth 1856-1935 ... 180
See also DLB 54
See also PC 29
Reese, Lyn
See Reese, Carolyn Johnson
See also SATA 64
Reese, M(ax) M(eredith) 1910-1987 . CANR-74
Obituary ... 123
Earlier sketches in CA 9-12R, CANR-3
Reese, Mason 1966- ... 97-100
Reese, Peter 1932- ... 221
Reese, Robert A. 1938- ... 114
See also SATA 60
See also SATA-Brief 53
Reese, Roger R(oi) 1959- ... 159
Reese, Sammy
See Reese, Samuel Pharr
Reese, Samuel Pharr 1930-1985 ... CANR-78
Obituary ... 117
Earlier sketch in CA 49-52
Reese, (John) Terence 1913-1996 ... 109
Obituary ... 151
See also SATA 59
Reese, Thomas 1742-1796 ... DLB 37
Reese, Thomas J(oseph) 1945- ... 106
Reese, Thomas R. 1890(?)-1974
Obituary ... 53-56
Reese, Trevor Richard 1929- ... 9-12R
Reese, William Lewis 1921- ... CANR-103
Earlier sketches in CA 17-20R, CANR-8
Reese, William S(herman) 1955- ... 111
Reese, Willis L(ivingston) M(esier) 1913-1990 ... 57-60
Reesink, Maryke 1919- ... CANR-45
Earlier sketch in CA 25-28R
Rees-Jones, Deryn ... 185
Rees-Mogg, William 1928- ... 142
Reeve, Agnesa B. 1927- ... 138
Reeve, Arthur B(enjamin) 1880-1936 ... 212
Reeve, Christopher 1952-2004 ... CANR-125
Obituary ... 232
Earlier sketch in CA 173
Reeve, Clara 1729-1807 ... DLB 39
See also RGEL 2
Reeve, F(ranklin) D(olier) 1928- ... 180
Earlier sketches in CA 77-80, CANR-125
Autobiographical Essay in ... 180
See also CP 1, 2
Reeve, Frank D(river) 1899-1967 ... CAP-1
Earlier sketch in CA 11-12
Reeve, G. Joan (Price) 1901-1983 ... 13-16R
Reeve, Joel
See Cox, William R(obert)
Reeve, Kirk 1934- ... 189
See also SATA 117
Reeve, Philip ... 230
Reeve, Richard M(ark) 1935- ... 37-40R
Reeve, Simon 1972- ... 191
Reeve, W(ilfred) D(ouglas) 1895- ... CAP-1
Earlier sketch in CA 13-14
Reeve, William Charles 1943- ... 93-96
Reeves, Alexander Stuart Frere
See Frere-Reeves, Alexander Stuart
Reeves, Amber
See Blanco White, Amber
Reeves, (Richard) Ambrose 1899-1980
Obituary ... 105
Reeves, Bruce Douglas 1940- ... CANR-11
Earlier sketch in CA 21-24R
Reeves, Charles Everand 1889-1975 ... 5-8R
Reeves, Diane Lindsey 1959- ... 145
Reeves, Donald 1952- ... 37-40R
Reeves, Dorothea D(resser) 1901-2000 . CAP-1
Earlier sketch in CA 11-12
Reeves, Earl J(ames, Jr.) 1933- ... 61-64
Reeves, Elton T(raver) 1912-1985 ... 29-32R
Reeves, Faye Couch 1953- ... 143
See also SATA 76
Reeves, Fionnuala 1943- ... 112
Reeves, Floyd (Wesley) 1890-1979
Obituary ... 89-92
Reeves, Gareth 1947- ... 119
Reeves, Gene (Arthur) 1933- ... 61-64
Reeves, Gregory Shaw 1950- ... 77-80
Reeves, Hubert 1932- ... 132
Reeves, James
See Reeves, John Morris
See also CP 1, 2
See also DLB 161
See also SATA 15
Reeves, Jeni 1947- ... SATA 111
Reeves, Joan Wynn 1910-1972 ... CAP-2
Earlier sketch in CA 21-22
Reeves, John 1926- ... 113
See also DLB 88
Reeves, John K(night) 1907- ... CAP-2
Earlier sketch in CA 25-28
Reeves, John Morris 1909-1978 ... CANR-91
Earlier sketch in CANR-44
See also Reeves, James
See also CWRI 5
See also SATA 87
Reeves, Joyce 1911- ... CANR-80
Earlier sketches in CA 73-76, CANR-12
See also CWRI 5
See also SATA 17
Reeves, Lawrence F. 1926- ... 105
See also SATA 29
Reeves, Marjorie E(thel) 1905-2003 . CANR-42
Obituary ... 221
Earlier sketches in CA 13-16R, CANR-5, 20
Reeves, Martha (Rose) 1941- ... 147
Reeves, Martha Emilie 1941- ... 65-68
Reeves, Mavis Mann 1921- ... CANR-25
Earlier sketch in CA 45-48
Reeves, Nancy 1913- ... 33-36R
Reeves, Paschal 1917-1976 ... 81-84
Reeves, Patricia Houts 1947- ... 126
Reeves, Richard 1936- ... CANR-110
Earlier sketches in CA 69-72, CANR-28
Reeves, Rosser 1910-1984 ... CANR-76
Obituary ... 111
Earlier sketch in CA 89-92
Reeves, Ruth Ellen
See Ranney, Agnes V.
Reeves, Thomas C(harles) 1936- ... CANR-9
Earlier sketch in CA 57-60
Reeves, Thomas Carl 1939- ... 33-36R
Reeves, Trish
See Reeves, Patricia Houts
Reeves, William Pember 1857-1932 ... RGEL 2
Reeves-Stevens, (Francis) Garfield 1953- ... DLB 251
See also HGG
Reff, Theodore Franklin 1930- ... 89-92
Refregier, Anton 1905-1979 ... 5-8R
Regalado, Nancy Freeman 1935- ... 17-20R
Regalbuto, Robert J. 1949- ... 175
Regalia, Nanzi
See Collins, Nancy A(verill)
Regan, Brad
See Norwood, Victor G(eorge) C(harles)
Regan, Cronan 1925- ... 45-48
Regan, Dian Curtis 1950- ... CANR-112
Earlier sketch in CA 142
See also SATA 75, 133, 149
See also SATA-Essay 149
Regan, Donald T(homas) 1918-2003 ... 127
Obituary ... 217
Brief entry ... 106
Regan, Geoffrey 1946- ... 129
Regan, John J. 1929-1995 ... 131
Obituary ... 149
Regan, Larry
See Strong, Charles S(tanley)
Regan, Milton C., Jr. 1952- ... CANR-100
Earlier sketch in CA 145
Regan, Pamela C. 1966- ... 232
Regan, Richard Joseph 1930- ... 5-8R
Regan, Robert (Charles) 1930- ... 17-20R
Regan, Stephen 1957- ... 142
Regan, Thomas Howard 1938- ... CANR-110
Earlier sketch in CA 104
Regan, Tom
See Regan, Thomas Howard
Regardie, (Francis) Israel 1907-1985 ... 85-88
Regehr, Lydia 1903-1991 ... 45-48
See also SATA 37
Regehr, T. D. 1937- ... 168
Regelski, Thomas A(dam) 1941- ... 57-60
Regenstein, Lewis 1943- ... 57-60
Regensteiner, Else (Friedsam) 1906-2003
Obituary ... 214
Brief entry ... 111
Reger, Gary 1954- ... 150
Reger, James P. 1952- ... 176
See also SATA 106

Reger, Roger 1933- 21-24R
Regester, Charlene B. 1956- 229
Reggiani, Renee 1925- CANR-36
Earlier sketch in CA 85-88
See also SATA 18
Reghaby, Heydar 1932- 29-32R
Regin, Deric (Wagenvort) 37-40R
Reginald
See Burgess, Michael (Roy)
Reginald, R.
See Burgess, Michael (Roy)
Reginald, Robert
See Burgess, Michael (Roy)
Reginald, Robert
See Burgess, Michael (Roy)
Regio, Jose
See Pereira, Jose Maria dos Reis
See also DLB 287
See also EWL 3
Region, Oscar
See Trimpey, John P.
Regis, Ed
See Regis, Edward, Jr.
Regis, Edward, Jr. 1944- CANR-138
Earlier sketches in CA 132, CANR-91
See also MTFW 2005
Regis, Sister Mary 1908- CAP-1
Earlier sketch in CA 13-14
Register, Cheri
See Register, Cheryl Lynn
Register, Cheryl Lynn 1945- 126
Register, William Wood 1958- 207
Register, Willie Raymond 1937- 45-48
Register, Woody
See Register, William Wood
Regler, Gustav 1898-1963 .... EWL 3
Regnard, Jean-Francois
1655-1709 .... GFL Beginnings to 1789
Regnery, Henry 1912-1996 .... CANR-88
Earlier sketch in CA 101
Interview in CA-101
Regnier, Mathurin 1573-1613 .. GFL Beginnings to 1789
Rego, Jose Lins do
See do Rego, Jose Lins
See also DLB 307
See also EWL 3
Regoli, Robert M. 1950- 116
Regosin, Richard L(loyd) 1937-
Brief entry 109
Regueiro, Helen 1943- 104
Regulus, Evelyn Judy
See Buehler, Evelyn Judy
Rehak, Peter (Stephen) 1936- 77-80
Rehbein, Edna Aguirre 1955- 145
Rehberg, Hans 1901-1963 .... DLB 124
Rehder, Ben 225
Rehder, Helmut 1905-1977 .... CANR-4
Earlier sketch in CA 5-8R
Rehder, Jessie Clifford 1908-1967 .... CAP-1
Earlier sketch in CA 9-10
Rehder, William J. 1947(?)- 227
Rehfeld, Barry J. 1946- 132
Rehfisch, Hans Jose 1891-1960 .... DLB 124
Rehfuss, John Alfred 1934- 85-88
Rehg, William (Richard) 1952- 149
Rehm, Diane 1936- 198
Rehm, John B. 1930- 224
Rehm, Karl M. 1935- .... SATA 72
Rehnquist, William H(ubbs)
1924-2005 .... CANR-106
Earlier sketch in CA 140
Rehrauer, George 1923- 53-56
Reibel, Paula
See Schwartz, Paula
Reibetanz, John 1944- 201
Reibstein, Janet 1946- 214
Reich, Ali
See Katz, Bobbi
Reich, Athena 1976- 229
Reich, Bernard 1941- CANR-32
Earlier sketches in CA 81-84, CANR-14
Reich, Cary 1950(?)-1998 229
Reich, Charles Alan 1928- CANR-64
Earlier sketch in CA 108
Interview in CA-108
Reich, Christopher 1961- 170
Reich, Deborah 1960- 130
Reich, Ebbe Klovedal 1940- .... DLB 214
See also EWL 3
Reich, Edward 1903(?)-1983
Obituary 109
Reich, Howard 1954- CANR-135
Earlier sketch in CA 143
Reich, Ilse Ollendorff 1909- 49-52
Reich, John Theodore 1906-1988
Obituary 124
Reich, Kenneth 1938- 69-72
Reich, Lee 1947- 142
Reich, Nancy B(assen) CANR-55
Earlier sketch in CA 126
Reich, Peter M(aria) 1929- 85-88
Reich, Robert B(ernard) 1946- CANR-104
Earlier sketches in CA 141, CANR-86
Reich, Sheldon 1931- 112
Reich, Simon (F.) 1959- 162
Reich, Steve 1936- CANR-122
Earlier sketches in CA 61-64, CANR-8
Reich, Susanna 1954- 185
See also SATA 113
Reich, Tova Rachel 1942- CANR-66
Earlier sketch in CA 103
Reich, Walter 1943- CANR-65
Earlier sketch in CA 129
Reich, Wilhelm 1897-1957 199
See also TCLC 57
Reichard, Gary Warren 1943- CANR-26
Earlier sketches in CA 61-64, CANR-10
Reichard, Robert S. 1923- 21-24R
Reichard, William 1963- 189
Reichardt, Jasia 1933- CANR-2
Earlier sketch in CA 5-8R
Reichardt, Mary R. 1956- CANR-126
Earlier sketch in CA 167
Reichart, Elisabeth 1953- CANR-106
Earlier sketch in CA 132
Reichart, Walter A(lbert) 1903-1999 .... 5-8R
Reiche, Dietlof 1941- 235
See also SATA 159
Reiche, Reimut 1941- 41-44R
Reichek, Morton A(rthur) 1924- 85-88
Reichel, Aaron I(srael) 1950- 130
Reichel, Mary 1946- 125
Reichel, O. Asher 1921- 45-48
Reichel, Sabine 1946- 132
Reichenbach, Bruce R. 1943- 33-36R
Reichenberger, Arnold G(ottfried)
1903-1977 .... 17-20R
Reichert, Edwin C(lark) 1909-1988
Obituary 126
See also SATA-Obit 57
Reichert, Herbert W(illiam)
1917-1978 .... CANR-24
Earlier sketch in CA 45-48
Reichert, Mickey Zucker
See Reichert, Miriam Zucker
Reichert, Miriam Zucker 1962- CANR-101
Earlier sketches in CA 128, CANR-87
See also FANT
See also SATA 85
Reichert, Tom 225
Reichert, Victor Emanuel 1897-1990 .... 13-16R
Obituary 200
Reichertz, Ronald R. 1933- 173
Reichhold, Jane(t E.) 1937- 221
See also SATA 147
Reichl, Ernst 1900-1980
Obituary 102
Reichl, Ruth (Molly) 1948- CANR-107
Earlier sketch in CA 61-64
Reichler, Joseph Lawrence
1915-1988 .... CANR-76
Obituary 127
Earlier sketch in CA 103
Reichley, (Anthony) James 1929- CANR-144
Earlier sketch in CA 1-4R
Reichmann, Felix 1899- 104
Reich-Ranicki, Marcel 1920- 206
Reichs, Kathleen J. 174
Reichs, Kathy
See Reichs, Kathleen J.
Reicke, Bo I(var) 1914- 13-16R
Reid, Aaron C. 1976- 178
Reid, Alan 1915(?)-1987
Obituary 123
Reid, Alastair 1926- CANR-3
Earlier sketch in CA 5-8R
See also BRWS 7
See also CP 1, 2, 3, 4, 5, 6, 7
See also DLB 27
See also SATA 46
Reid, Albert Clayton 1894-1988 53-56
Reid, Alfred S(andlin) 1924-1976 .... CANR-2
Earlier sketch in CA 45-48
Reid, Amelia 1942- .... CD 5
Reid, Anna 223
Reid, Anthony 1916- 29-32R
Reid, B(enjamin) L(awrence)
1918-1990 .... CANR-76
Obituary 133
Earlier sketch in CA 17-20R
See also DLB 111
Reid, Barbara 1922- CANR-12
Earlier sketch in CA 25-28R
See also SATA 21
Reid, Barbara (Jane) 1957- .... CLR 64
See also MAICYA 2
See also MAICYAS 1
See also SATA 93
Reid, Brian (Thomas) Holden 1952- 186
Reid, Charles (Stuart) 1900-1987 .... CANR-76
Obituary 121
Earlier sketch in CA 101
Reid, Charles K(er) II 1912-1969(?) CAP-1
Earlier sketch in CA 19-20
Reid, Charles L(loyd) 1927- 37-40R
Reid, Charles R(obert) 1926- 114
Reid, Christina 1942- 230
See also CBD
See also CD 6
See also CWD
Reid, Christopher (John) 1949- CANR-89
Earlier sketch in CA 140
See also CLC 33
See also CP 7
See also DLB 40
See also EWL 3
Reid, Cindy 1964(?)- 226
Reid, Clyde H. 1928- CANR-12
Earlier sketch in CA 25-28R
Reid, Constance (Bowman) 1918- CANR-80
Earlier sketch in CA 148
Reid, Daniel P. (Jr.) 1948- 125
Reid, David 1940- CANR-103
Earlier sketch in CA 147
Reid, Desmond
See McNeilly, Wilfred (Glassford) and Moorcock, Michael (John)
Reid, Donald (Matthew) 1952- 124
Reid, Dorothy M(arion) (?)-1974
Obituary 109
See also SATA-Brief 29
Reid, E. Emmet 1872-1973
Obituary 45-48
Reid, Ela 1907-1982
Obituary 107
Reid, Elwood 226
Reid, Escott (Meredith) 1905-1999 .... CANR-20
Earlier sketch in CA 101
Reid, Esmond 1945- 123
Reid, Eugenie Chazal 1924- 13-16R
See also SATA 12
Reid, Forrest 1875-1947 .... DLB 153
See also RGEL 2
Reid, Frances (Marion) P(ugh) 1910- .. CANR-2
Earlier sketch in CA 5-8R
Reid, Gavin 1950- 181
Reid, H. 1925- 17-20R
Reid, Helen Rogers 1882-1970 182
Obituary 115
See also DLB 29
Reid, Hilda (Stewart) 1898-1982
Obituary 106
Reid, Ian 1915-1984
Obituary 113
Reid, Inez Smith 49-52
Reid, J(ohn) C(owie) 1916-1972 .... CANR-76
Obituary 103
Earlier sketch in CA 9-12R
Reid, Jack 1925- 236
Reid, James .... DLB 31
Reid, James Macarthur 1900-1970 .... CAP-1
Earlier sketch in CA 9-10
Reid, James Malcolm 1902-1982 .... CANR-74
Obituary 107
Earlier sketch in CA 5-8R
Reid, James W. 1912-1970(?) CAP-2
Earlier sketch in CA 25-28
Reid, Jan 1945- CANR-135
Earlier sketch in CA 61-64
Reid, Jim 1929- 61-64
Reid, John
See Tobias, Andrew (Previn)
Reid, John Calvin CANR-11
Earlier sketch in CA 25-28R
See also SATA 21
Reid, John Kelman Sutherland 1910- . CANR-3
Earlier sketch in CA 1-4R
Reid, John Phillip 1930- CANR-41
Earlier sketches in CA 25-28R, CANR-19
Reid, John T(urner) 1908-1978 81-84
Reid, Leslie Hartley 1895- CAP-1
Earlier sketch in CA 13-14
Reid, Loren (Dudley) 1905- CANR-1
Earlier sketch in CA 1-4R
Reid, Louis Arnaud 1895-1986 .... CAP-1
Earlier sketch in CA 13-14
Reid, Malcolm 1941- 53-56
Reid, Margaret (Isabel) 1925-1992 ... CANR-75
Obituary 139
Earlier sketch in CA 130
Reid, (Thomas) Mayne 1818-1883 .... DLB 21, 163
See also SATA 24
Reid, Meta Mayne 1905-1991 .... CANR-87
Earlier sketch in CA 13-16R
See also SATA 58
See also SATA-Brief 36
Reid, Michaela (Ann) 1933- 128
Reid, Mildred I. 1908-1994 .... 21-24R
Reid, P(atrick) R(obert) 1910-1990
Obituary 131
Reid, Panthea 1940- CANR-103
Earlier sketches in CA 57-60, CANR-7
Reid, Pat
See Reid, P(atrick) R(obert)
Reid, Philip
See Ingrams, Richard (Reid) and Osmond, Andrew
Reid, R(obert) W(illiam)
1933-1990(?) CANR-75
Obituary 132
Earlier sketch in CA 29-32R
Reid, Randall 1931- 25-28R
Reid, Robert G(eorge) B(urnside) 1939- 119
Reid, Robin (Nicole) 1969- 218
See also SATA 145
Reid, Seerley 1909(?)-1972
Obituary 37-40R
Reid, Sue Titus 1939- CANR-58
Earlier sketches in CA 37-40R, CANR-14, 31
Reid, Suzanne Elizabeth 1944- 220
Reid, T. R. 202
Reid, Thomas 1710-1796 .... DLB 31, 252
Reid, Tim
See Reid, Timothy E. H.
Reid, Timothy E. H. 1936- 17-20R
Reid, Van 172
Reid, Vic(tor Stafford) 1913-1987 .... CANR-81
Earlier sketches in CA 65-68, CANR-16
See also BW 1
See also CN 1, 2, 3, 4, 5, 6
See also DLB 125
See also RGEL 2
Reid, W(illiam) Stanford 1913-1996 . CANR-18
Earlier sketches in CA 49-52, CANR-1
Reid, Whitelaw 1837-1912 184
See also DLB 23
Reid, William (Ronald) 1920-1998 212
Reid, William 1926- 85-88
Reid, William H(oward) 1945- CANR-37
Earlier sketches in CA 93-96, CANR-16
Reid, William J(ames) 1928-2003 .... CANR-39
Obituary 221
Earlier sketches in CA 77-80, CANR-17
Reida, Bernice 1915- 93-96
Reid Banks, Lynne 1929- CANR-87
Earlier sketches in CA 1-4R, CANR-6, 22, 38
See also Banks, Lynne Reid
See also AAYA 49
See also CLR 24
See also CN 1, 2, 3, 7
See also JRDA
See also MAICYA 1, 2
See also SATA 22, 75, 111
See also YAW
Reidel, Carl Hubert 1937- 107
Reidel, James 226
Reidel-Geubtner, Virginia 1921- 116
Reidenbaugh, Lowell (Henry) 1919- . CANR-48
Earlier sketch in CA 121
Reider, Katja 1960- .... SATA 126
Reidinger, Paul 1959- 201
Reid Jenkins, Debra 1955- .... SATA 87
Reidy, John Patrick 1930- 17-20R
Reidy, Joseph 1920- 53-56
Reidy, Sue 183
Reierson, Gary B(ruce) 1948- CANR-36
Earlier sketch in CA 114
Reif, Rita 1929- 41-44R
Reif, Stefan C. 1944- 195
Reife, Abraham 1931- 163
Reifen, David 1911- 93-96
Reiff, Henry 1899-1983
Obituary 110
Reiff, Robert (Frank) 1918-1982 .... CANR-75
Obituary 135
Earlier sketch in CA 17-20R
Reiff, Stephanie Ann 1948- 93-96
See also SATA 47
See also SATA-Brief 28
Reiffel, Leonard 1927- 101
Reifler, Samuel 1939- 93-96
Reifsnyder, William E(dward) 1924- 65-68
Reig, June 1933- 105
See also SATA 30
Reigelman, Milton Monroe 1942- 65-68
Reiger, George (Wesley) 1939- CANR-18
Earlier sketch in CA 101
Reiger, John F(ranklin) 1943- 57-60
Reiger, Kurt (Edward) 1956- 116
Reigot, Betty Polisar 1924- 111
See also SATA 55
See also SATA-Brief 41
Reigstad, Paul (Matthew) 1921- 81-84
Reik, Theodor 1888-1969 .... CANR-5
Obituary 25-28R
Earlier sketch in CA 5-8R
Reiken, Frederick 1966- 172
Reile, Louis 1925- 29-32R
Reill, Peter Hanns 1938- 101
Reilly, Bernard F. 1925- CANR-89
Earlier sketch in CA 142
Reilly, Catherine W(inifred) 1925- 118
Reilly, Christopher T(homas) 1924- 101
Reilly, D(avid) Robin 1928- CANR-8
Earlier sketch in CA 5-8R
Reilly, Edward R(andolph) 1929- 93-96
Reilly, Edwin David, Jr. 1932- 111
Reilly, Esther H(untington) 1917- 33-36R
Reilly, Francis E(agan) 1922- 29-32R
Reilly, Harold J. 1895(?)-1987
Obituary 123
Reilly, Helen 1891-1962 203
Reilly, James A. 1954- 235
Reilly, John H(urford) 1934- 77-80
Reilly, John M(arsden) 1933-2004 .... CANR-94
Obituary 223
Earlier sketches in CA 104, CANR-48
Reilly, Judith G(ladding) 1935- 61-64
Reilly, Mary 1920- 128
Brief entry 114
Reilly, Mary Lonan 1926- 33-36R
Reilly, Matthew 1974- 197
Reilly, Michael (Francis) 1910(?)-1973
Obituary 41-44R
Reilly, Patrick 1932- CANR-37
Earlier sketch in CA 115
Reilly, Patrick D.
See Rogers, Peter D(amien)
Reilly, Paul 1912-1990 .... CANR-75
Obituary 132
Earlier sketch in CA 125
Reilly, Richard Paul 1958- 186
See also AAYA 40
Reilly, Rick
See Reilly, Richard Paul
Reilly, Robert Thomas 1922-2004 .... CANR-2
Earlier sketch in CA 5-8R
Reilly, Robin 1928- CANR-5
Earlier sketch in CA 53-56
Reilly, Thomas 238
Reilly, William J(ohn) 1899-1970 .... CAP-2
Earlier sketch in CA 19-20
Reilly, William K.
See Creasey, John
Reim, Melanie (K.) 1956- .... SATA 104
Reiman, Donald H(enry) 1934- CANR-119
Earlier sketches in CA 33-36R, CANR-14, 31
Reiman, Jeffrey H. 1942- 93-96
Reimann, Brigitte 1933-1973 .... DLB 75
Reimann, Guenter (Hans)
1904-2005 .... CANR-74
Obituary 236
Earlier sketch in CA 25-28R
Reimann, Katya 1965- CANR-144
Earlier sketch in CA 168
Reimann, Lewis C. 1890-1961
Obituary 113
Reimann, Viktor 1915- 69-72
Reimer, Bennett 1932- CANR-3
Earlier sketch in CA 45-48
Reimers, David 1931- 115

Cumulative Index 481 Renken

Rein, Irving J. 1937- CANR-28
Earlier sketch in CA 25-28R
Rein, Martin 1928- 93-96
Rein, Mercedes 131
See also HW 1
Rein, Raanan 1960- CANR-96
Earlier sketch in CA 146
Rein, Richard
See Smith, Richard Rein
Reina, Ruben E. 1924- 49-52
Reinach, Jacquelyn (Krasne)
1930-2000 .... CANR-22
Obituary 189
Earlier sketch in CA 105
See also SATA 28
Reincheld, Bill 1946- 57-60
Reindorp, George E(dmund)
1911-1990 .... CANR-5
Earlier sketch in CA 5-8R
Reindorp, Reginald C(arl) 1907- 25-28R
Reinecke, Ian 1945- 117
Reinemer, Vic 1923- 21-24R
Reiner, Carl 1922- CANR-89
Brief entry 112
Earlier sketch in CA 138
See also SATA 151
Reiner, Joseph H. 1912(?)-1983
Obituary 111
Reiner, Laurence E(rwin) 102
Reiner, Max
See Caldwell, (Janet Miriam) Taylor (Holland)
Reiner, Rob(ert) 1945- 138
See also AAYA 13
Reiner, Thomas 1959- 226
Reiner, William B(uck) 1910-1976 ..... CANR-3
Obituary 61-64
Earlier sketch in CA 45-48
See also SATA 46
See also SATA-Obit 30
Reinerman, Alan J(erome) 1935- 114
Reinert, Paul C(lare) 1910-2001 85-88
Obituary 201
Reines, Alvin J. 1926-2004 53-56
Obituary 233
Reinfeld, Fred 1910-1964 .... CAP-1
Earlier sketch in CA 9-10
See also SATA 3
Reinfeld, Linda M. 1940- 141
Reingold, Nathan 1927-2004 140
Obituary 232
Reinhard, David W(illiam) 1952- 118
Reinhard, Ernst
See Frank, Rudolf
Reinhardt, Ad(olph Frederick) 1913-1967
Obituary 111
Reinhardt, Gottfried 1913-1994 .... CANR-76
Obituary 146
Earlier sketch in CA 93-96
Reinhardt, James Melvin 1894-1974 .. CANR-4
Obituary 49-52
Earlier sketch in CA 1-4R
Reinhardt, Jon M(c Ewen) 1936- 41-44R
Reinhardt, Kurt F(rank) 1896-1983 ..... CANR-1
Earlier sketch in CA 1-4R
Reinhardt, Richard W. 1927- CANR-31
Earlier sketches in CA 25-28R, CANR-13
Reinhart, Bruce Aaron 1926- 5-8R
Reinhart, Charles (Franklin) 1946- 104
Reinhart, Matthew .... SATA 161
Reinhart, Peter 1950- 136
Reinhart, Theodore R(ussell) 1938- 125
Reinhartz, Dennis 1944- 123
Reinharz, Jehuda 1944- CANR-49
Earlier sketches in CA 65-68, CANR-9, 24
Reinharz, Shulamit 1946- 138
Reinhold, Meyer 1909-2002 .... CANR-51
Obituary 211
Earlier sketches in CA 5-8R, CANR-5, 26
Reinhold, Robert 1941-1996 133
Obituary 153
Reinicke, Wolfgang H. 1955- 154
Reinig, Christa 1926- .... GLL 2
Reiniger, Lotte 1899-1981
Obituary 108
See also IDFW 3, 4
See also SATA 40
See also SATA-Obit 33
Reining, Conrad C(opeland)
1918-1984 .... CANR-76
Obituary 114
Earlier sketch in CA 21-24R
Reinisch, June M(achover) 1943- 138
Reinitz, Richard (Martin) 1934- 89-92
Reinke, William A(ndrew) 1928- CANR-49
Earlier sketches in CA 45-48, CANR-24
Reinmar der Alte c. 1165-c. 1205 .... DLB 138
Reinmar von Zweter c. 1200-c. 1250 . DLB 138
Reinmuth, Oscar William 1900-1984 ... 37-40R
Reinsma, Carol 1949- 155
See also SATA 91
Reinsma, Tjit 1945- 239
Reinsmith, Richard
See Smith, Richard Rein
Reinstedt, Randall A. 1935- 168
See also SATA 101
Reinstedt, Randy
See Reinstedt, Randall A.
Reis, Claire Raphael 1889-1978
Obituary 77-80
Reis, Ricardo
See Pessoa, Fernando (Antonio Nogueira)
Reis, Richard H(erbert) 1930- 41-44R
Reisberg, Mira 1955- .... SATA 82
Reisberg, Veg
See Reisberg, Mira
Reisch, Walter 1903-1983 185
Obituary 109
See also DLB 44
See also IDFW 3, 4
Reischauer, August Karl 1879-1971 .... CAP-2
Earlier sketch in CA 19-20
Reischauer, Edwin O(ldfather)
1910-1990 .... CANR-75
Obituary 132
Earlier sketch in CA 17-20R
Reischauer, Haru Matsukata 1915-1998 145
Obituary 172
Reiser, Lynn (Whisnant) 1944- 209
See also SATA 81, 138
Reiser, Martin 1927- 53-56
Reiser, Morton F(rancis) 1919- 124
Reiser, Oliver Leslie 1895-1974 .... CANR-4
Obituary 49-52
Earlier sketch in CA 1-4R
Reiser, Paul 1957- 153
Reiser, William (Edward) 1943- 114
Reisfeld, Bert 1906-1991 112
Reisgies, Teresa (Maria) 1966- .... SATA 74
Reising, Robert W(illiam) 1933- 89-92
Reisinger, William M. 1957- 138
Reisman, Arnold 1934- CANR-12
Earlier sketch in CA 33-36R
Reisman, George Gerald 1937- 104
Reisman, John M(ark) 1930- CANR-8
Earlier sketch in CA 21-24R
Reisman, Nancy 188
Reisner, George
See Ben-Ephraim, Gavriel
Reisner, Marc P. 1948-2000 144
Obituary 189
See also NCFS 2
Reisner, Robert George 1921-1974 .. CANR-74
Obituary 135
Earlier sketch in CA 9-12R
Reisner, Thomas Andrew 1935- 113
Reiss, Albert J(ohn), Jr. 1922- CANR-49
Earlier sketches in CA 21-24R, CANR-9, 24
Reiss, Alvin 1932- 61-64
Reiss, Alvin H(erbert) 1930- 81-84
Reiss, Barbara Eve 1941- CANR-15
Earlier sketch in CA 41-44R
Reiss, Benjamin 1964- 229
Reiss, Bob 209
Reiss, David S. 1953- 108
Reiss, Edmund (Allan) 1934- CANR-10
Earlier sketch in CA 21-24R
Reiss, Edward 1964- 146
Reiss, Ira L(eonard) 1925- 13-16R
Reiss, James 1941- CANR-97
Earlier sketch in CA 33-36R
Reiss, Johanna (de Leeuw) 1929(?)- 85-88
See also CLR 19
See also JRDA
See also SATA 18
See also YAW
Reiss, John J. 106
See also SATA 23
Reiss, Julie H. 1962- 206
Reiss, Kathryn 1957- CANR-127
Earlier sketch in CA 143
See also SATA 76, 144
Reiss, Mitchell 1957- 152
Reiss, Oscar 1925- CANR-122
Earlier sketch in CA 167
Reiss, Stephen (Charles) 1918-1999 57-60
Obituary 187
Reiss, Timothy James 1942- 107
Reiss, Tom 1963(?)- 239
Reissig, Herman F. 1899(?)-1985
Obituary 116
Reissig, Julio Herrera y
See Herrera y Reissig, Julio
Reissman, Leonard 1921-1975 .... CANR-4
Obituary 53-56
Earlier sketch in CA 5-8R
Reister, Floyd Nester 1919- 69-72
Reit, Seymour Victory 1918-2001 .... CANR-16
Obituary 204
Earlier sketch in CA 93-96
See also SATA 21
See also SATA-Obit 133
Reit, Sy
See Reit, Seymour Victory
Reitan, E(arl) A(aron) 1925- 17-20R
Reitci, John G(eorge) 1922-1983
Obituary 109
Reitci, Rita Krohne 1930- 5-8R
Reitemeyer, John Reinhart 1898-1979
Obituary 85-88
Reiter, Charles Jules 1928- 25-28R
Reiter, Robert E. 1932- 25-28R
Reiter, Seymour 1921- 101
Reiter, Victoria (Kelrich) 139
Reiterman, Carl 1921- 49-52
Reiterman, Tim 1947- 109
Reith, Charles C. 1953- 122
Reith, J. C. W.
See Reith, John Charles Walsham
Reith, John Charles Walsham 1889-1971
Obituary 113
Reither, Joseph 1903-1992 109
Reitlinger, Gerald R. 1900(?)-1978
Obituary 104
Reitman, Judith 1951- 142
Reitmeister, Louis Aaron 1903-1975 49-52
Obituary 61-64
Reitsch, Hanna 1912(?)-1979
Obituary 89-92
Reitz, Donald J(oseph) 1932- 25-28R
Reitz, Miriam 1935- 143
Reitze, Arnold W(infred), Jr. 1938- 49-52
Reizbaum, Marilyn 203
Reizei Mochikazu
See Reizei Mochitame
Reizenstein, Elmer Leopold
See Rice, Elmer (Leopold)
See also EWL 3
Rejai, Mostafa 1931- CANR-13
Earlier sketch in CA 37-40R
Rejali, Darius M. 1959- CANR-117
Earlier sketch in CA 153
Rejaunier, Jeanne 1934- 29-32R
Rekai, Kati 1921- 105
Rekdal, Paisley 1970- 204
Rekers, George A(lan) 1948- 119
Relesh, A.
See Sheller, Aleksandr Konstantinovich
Relf, Patricia 1954- 203
See also SATA 71, 134
Relgis, Eugene 1895- 81-84
Relis, Harry
See Endore, (Samuel) Guy
Rella, Ettore 1907(?)-1988
Obituary 126
Relyea, Harold C. 1944- 175
Relyea, Suzanne 1945- 77-80
Remak, Henry H. H. 1916- 17-20R
Remak, Joachim 1920- CANR-3
Earlier sketch in CA 1-4R
Remarque, Erich Maria 1898-1970 77-80
Obituary 29-32R
See also AAYA 27
See also BPFB 3
See also CDWLB 2
See also CLC 21
See also DA
See also DA3
See also DAB
See also DAC
See also DAM MST, NOV
See also DLB 56
See also EWL 3
See also EXPN
See also LAIT 3
See also MTCW 1, 2
See also MTFW 2005
See also NFS 4
See also RGWL 2, 3
Rembar, Charles (Isaiah) 1915-2000 ...... 25-28R
Obituary 192
Rembrandt 1606-1669 .... AAYA 50
Remen, (Rachelle) Naomi 1938- 122
Brief entry 118
Remenih, Maurine 1916(?)-1985
Obituary 118
Remer, Gary 1957- 157
Remer, Theodore G. 1899-1989 .... CAP-1
Earlier sketch in CA 13-16
Remi, Georges 1907-1983 .... CANR-31
Obituary 109
Earlier sketch in CA 69-72
See also Herge
See also SATA 13
See also SATA-Obit 32
Remington, Ella-Carrie 1914- 69-72
Remington, Frederic S(ackrider)
1861-1909 169
Brief entry 108
See also DLB 12, 186, 188
See also SATA 41
See also TCLC 89
See also TCWW 2
Remington, Mark
See Bingley, David Ernest
Remington, Robin Alison 1938- CANR-12
Earlier sketch in CA 33-36R
Remini, Robert V(incent) 1921- CANR-93
Earlier sketches in CA 9-12R, CANR-3, 20, 44
Remizov, A.
See Remizov, Aleksei (Mikhailovich)
Remizov, A. M.
See Remizov, Aleksei (Mikhailovich)
Remizov, Aleksei (Mikhailovich)
1877-1957 133
Brief entry 125
See also Remizov, Alexey Mikhaylovich
See also DLB 295
See also TCLC 27
Remizov, Alexey Mikhaylovich
See Remizov, Aleksei (Mikhailovich)
See also EWL 3
Remkiewicz, Frank 1939- 145
See also SATA 77, 152
Remley, David A. 1931- 45-48
Remley, Mary L(ouise) 1930- 102
Remmers, H(ermann) H(enry)
1892-1969 .... CANR-75
Obituary 103
Earlier sketch in CA 1-4R
Remmling, Gunter W(erner) 1929- 41-44R
Remnick, David J. 1958- CANR-92
Earlier sketch in CA 154
Remoff, Heather T(rexler) 1938- 117
Remonda-Ruibal, Jorge Silvestre 1928- 108
Rempel, William C. 1947- 141
Remsberg, Bonnie K(ohn) 1937- 69-72
Remsberg, Charles A(ndruss) 1936- CANR-7
Earlier sketch in CA 57-60
Remsberg, Rich 1965- 197
Remson, Irwin 1923- 53-56
Remy
See Renault, Gilbert (Leon Etienne Theodore)
Remy, Georges
See Remi, Georges
Remy, Pierre-Jean
See Angremy, Jean-Pierre
Remy, Richard C. 1942- CANR-29
Earlier sketch in CA 111
Rena, Sally
See Rena, Sarah Mary
Rena, Sarah Mary 1941- 103
Renan, Joseph Ernest 1823-1892 .. GFL 1789 to the Present
Renan, Sheldon (Jackson) 1941- CANR-14
Earlier sketch in CA 21-24R
Renard, Alexandre Charles 1906-1983
Obituary 111
Renard, Jules(-Pierre) 1864-1910 202
Brief entry 117
See also GFL 1789 to the Present
See also TCLC 17
Renard, Maurice 1875-1939 162
See also SFW 4
Renaud, Bernadette 1945- 134
See also SATA 66
Renaud, Jacques 1943- 204
See also DLB 60
Renauer, Albin (J.) 1959- 133
Renault, Gilbert (Leon Etienne Theodore)
1904-1984
Obituary 113
Renault, Mary
See Challans, Mary
See also BPFB 3
See also BYA 2
See also CLC 3, 11, 17
See also CN 1, 2, 3
See also DLBY 1983
See also EWL 3
See also GLL 1
See also LAIT 1
See also RGEL 2
See also RHW
Renault, Rick
See Wallmann, Jeffrey M(iner)
Renaut, Alain 1948- 156
Renaux, Sigrid 1938- 148
Renay, Liz 1926- 33-36R
Rencher, Alvin C. 1934- 216
Rendall, Justine 1954(?)-2004 155
Rendall, Steven 1939- 139
Rendall, Ted S. 101
Rendel, George William 1889-1979 . CANR-76
Obituary 103
Earlier sketch in CA 5-8R
Rendel, John 1906(?)-1978
Obituary 104
Rendell, Joan CANR-23
Earlier sketches in CA 61-64, CANR-7
See also SATA 28
Rendell, Ruth (Barbara) 1930- CANR-127
Earlier sketches in CA 109, CANR-32, 52, 74
Interview in CANR-32
See also Vine, Barbara
See also BPFB 3
See also BRWS 9
See also CLC 28, 48
See also CN 5, 6, 7
See also CPW
See also DAM POP
See also DLB 87, 276
See also MSW
See also MTCW 1, 2
See also MTFW 2005
Render, Sylvia Lyons 1913-1986 ...... CANR-15
Earlier sketch in CA 41-44R
Rendina, Laura (Jones) Cooper
1902- CANR-74
Earlier sketch in CA 9-12R
See also SATA 10
Rendleman, Danny L(ee) 1945- CANR-88
Earlier sketch in CA 65-68
Rendon, Armando B. 1939- 37-40R
Rendon, Marcie R. 1952- 164
See also SATA 97
Rendon, Maria 1965- .... SATA 116
Rendra 1935- .... RGWL 3
Rene, Leon (T.) 1902-1982
Obituary 107
Rene, Natalia 1908(?)-1977
Obituary 69-72
Renee
See Jones, Renee Gertrude
See also CD 6
Renee, Janina 1956- 211
See also SATA 140
Renehan, Edward J(ohn), Jr. 1956- .. CANR-121
Earlier sketch in CA 140
Renehan, Robert (Francis Xavier) 1935- 191
Brief entry 108
Renetzky, Alvin 1940- 101
Renfield, Richard L. 1932- 29-32R
Renfrew, (Andrew) Colin 1937- CANR-88
Earlier sketch in CA 158
Renfrew, Jane Margaret 1942- 49-52
Renfro, Ed 1924- .... SATA 79
Renfroe, Martha Kay 1938- CANR-101
Earlier sketches in CA 65-68, CANR-9
Rengert, George F. 1940- CANR-118
Earlier sketch in CA 158
Rengertsz, Jan
See Elburg, Joannes Gommert
Renich, Fred C. 1916-1979 115
Renich, Jill 1916- 25-28R
Renich-Meyers, Jill
See Renich, Jill
Renick, Marion (Lewis) 1905-1983 .... CANR-1
Earlier sketch in CA 1-4R
See also SATA 1
Renier, Elizabeth
See Baker, Betty D(oreen Flook)
Renk, Kathleen J. 1952- 190
Renken, Aleda 1907- CANR-12
Earlier sketch in CA 21-24R
See also SATA 27

Renker, Elizabeth 1961- ... 158
Renkiewicz, Frank 1935- ... CANR-26
Earlier sketch in CA 45-48
Renlie, Frank H. 1936- ... SATA 11
Renn, Casey
See Crim, Keith R(enn)
Renn, Ludwig
See Vieth von Golssenau, Arnold Friedrich
Renn, Thomas E(dward) 1939- ... 29-32R
Rennahan, Ray 1896-1980 ... IDFW 3, 4
Renne, Roland Roger 1905-1989 ... 1-4R
Rennell, Tony ... 226
Renner, Al G. 1912-1994 ... 89-92
Renner, Beverly Hollett 1929- ... 85-88
Renner, Bruce 1944- ... 33-36R
Renner, Gerald A(nthony) 1932- ... 230
Renner, John Wilson 1924- ... 41-44R
Renner, K(enneth) Edward 1936- ... 101
Renner, Thomas C(hoate)
1928-1990 ... CANR-75
Obituary ... 130
Earlier sketch in CA 73-76
Renner, Tom
See Renner, Thomas C(hoate)
Rennert, Maggie 1922- ... CANR-13
Earlier sketch in CA 61-64
Rennert, Richard Scott 1956- ... 135
See also SATA 67
Rennick, Robert M(orris) 1932- ... CANR-119
Earlier sketches in CA 122, CANR-48
Rennie, Bradford James 1960- ... 232
Rennie, Bryan S. 1954- ... 193
Rennie, Christopher
See Ambrose, Eric (Samuel)
Rennie, Eric 1947- ... 45-48
Rennie, James Alan 1899-1969 ... CAP-1
Earlier sketch in CA 11-12
Rennie, Ysabel Fisk 1918- ... CANR-2
Earlier sketch in CA 5-8R
Rennison, Louise 1951- ... 217
See also AAYA 52
See also BYA 15
See also SATA 149
Reno, Clint
See Ballard, (Willis) Todhunter
Reno, Dawn E(laine) 1953- ... CANR-97
Earlier sketch in CA 125
See also SATA 130
Reno, Marie R(oth) ... CANR-10
Earlier sketch in CA 65-68
Reno, Mark
See Keevill, Henry J(ohn)
Reno, Ottie W(ayne) 1929- ... 41-44R
Reno, Philip 1913-1981
Obituary ... 111
Renoir, Alain 1921- ... 77-80
Renoir, Claude 1914-1993 ... IDFW 3, 4
Renoir, Jean 1894-1979 ... 129
Obituary ... 85-88
See also CLC 20
Renoir, Pierre-Auguste 1841-1919 ... AAYA 60
Renouf, Alan 1919- ... 108
Rensberger, Boyce 1942- ... CANR-66
Earlier sketch in CA 81-84
Rensch, Bernhard (Carl Emmanuel)
1900-1990 ... 102
Renshaw, Corinne 1929- ... CANR-112
Earlier sketch in CA 156
Renshaw, Domeena C(ynthia) 1929- ... 89-92
Renshaw, Patrick (Richard George)
1936- ... 21-24R
Renshaw, Samuel 1892-1981 ... CANR-75
Obituary ... 133
Earlier sketch in CA 77-80
Renshon, Stanley Allen 1943-
Brief entry ... 109
Rensie, Willis
See Eisner, Will(iam Erwin)
Renstrom, Peter G. 1943- ... 223
Renta, Francoise de Langiade de la
See de la Renta, Francoise de Langiade
Renton, Cam
See Armstrong, Richard
Renton, Julia
See Cole, Margaret Alice
Renton, N(ick) E. 1931- ... 217
Rentschler, Eric 1949- ... CANR-42
Earlier sketch in CA 118
Renvoize, Jean ... CANR-74
Earlier sketch in CA 41-44R
See also SATA 5
Renwick, Ethel Hulbert 1910-1999 ... 5-8R
Renwick, Fred B(lackwell) 1930- ... 33-36R
Renzi, Thomas C. 1948- ... 143
Renzulli, L(ibero) Marx, Jr. 1934-
Brief entry ... 108
Repcheck, Jack 1957(?)- ... 223
Repetto, Robert C. ... 129
Replansky, Naomi 1918- ... CANR-124
Earlier sketches in CA 33-36R, CANR-68
See also CP 1
See also CWP
Repp, Arthur C(hristian) 1906-1994 ... CAP-1
Earlier sketch in CA 13-16
Repp, Ed(ward) Earl 1900(?)-1979
Obituary ... 85-88
See also TCWW 1, 2
Repp, William 1936- ... 110
Reppetto, Thomas A. 1932(?)- ... 232
Repplier, Agnes 1858-1950 ... DLB 221
Reps, John W(illiam) 1921- ... CANR-39
Earlier sketches in CA 45-48, CANR-1, 18
Reps, (Saladin) Paul 1895-1990 ... CANR-75
Obituary ... 132
Earlier sketches in CA 5-8R, CANR-6
ReQua, Eloise Gallup 1902-1989 ... CAP-1
Earlier sketch in CA 13-16
Resch, John Phillips 1940- ... 184
Brief entry ... 108
Rescher, Nicholas 1928- ... CANR-111
Earlier sketches in CA 21-24R, CANR-12, 55
Reschly, Steven D. 1953- ... 220
Resciniti, Angelo G. 1952- ... SATA 75
Rescoe, A(ntoine) Stan(ley) 1910- ... 5-8R
Reshetar, John S(tephen) Jr. 1924- ... CANR-75
Earlier sketch in CA 5-8R
Reshetnikov, Fedor Mikhailovich
1841-1871 ... DLB 238
Reshevsky, Samuel Herman 1911-1992 ... 65-68
Resick, Matthew C(larence) 1916- ... 57-60
Resis, Albert 1921- ... 145
Reske, Hermann (W.) 1911-1989 ... 45-48
Reskind, John
See Wallmann, Jeffrey M(iner)
Resnais, Alain 1922- ... CLC 16
Resnick, H(arvey) L(ewis) P(aul) 1930- .. 21-24R
Resnick, Marvin D. 1933- ... 21-24R
Resnick, Michael D(iamond) 1942- .. CANR-90
Earlier sketches in CA 107, CANR-24
See also AAYA 38
See also SATA 38, 106, 159
See also SFW 4
Resnick, Mike
See Resnick, Michael D(iamond)
Resnick, Nathan 1910-1977 ... CAP-2
Obituary ... 73-76
Earlier sketch in CA 19-20
Resnick, Patricia 1953- ... 135
Resnick, Rose ... 61-64
Resnick, Seymour 1920- ... 73-76
See also SATA 23
Resnick, Sylvia (Safran) 1927- ... CANR-30
Earlier sketch in CA 93-96
Resnicow, Herbert 1921-1997 ... 237
Resnik, H(arvey) L(ewis) P(aul)
1930- ... CANR-10
Earlier sketch in CA 21-24R
Resnik, Hank
See Resnik, Henry S.
Resnik, Henry S. 1940- ... CANR-29
Earlier sketch in CA 29-32R
Resnik, Michael D(avid) 1938- ... 116
Resposo, Epifania R. Castro 1922-1974
Obituary ... 113
Ressler, Alice 1918- ... 53-56
Ressner, Phil(ip) 1922- ... 13-16R
Rest, Friedrich Otto 1913-1997 ... CANR-38
Earlier sketches in CA 5-8R, CANR-2, 17
Rest, Karl H(einrich) A(lbert) 1908-1994 ... 5-8R
Restak, Richard M(artin) 1942- ... CANR-90
Earlier sketches in CA 61-64, CANR-8, 24
Restall, Matthew 1964- ... 171
Restall Orr, Emma 1965- ... 199
Restany, Pierre 1930-2003 ... 130
Obituary ... 216
Restivo, Sal 1940- ... 112
Restivo, Valerie
See Alia, Valerie
Restle, Frank (Joseph) 1927-1982(?) .. CANR-75
Obituary ... 133
Earlier sketch in CA 41-44R
Reston, James (Barrett) 1909-1995 ... CANR-58
Obituary ... 150
Earlier sketches in CA 65-68, CANR-31
See also AITN 1, 2
Reston, James B(arrett), Jr. 1941- ... CANR-109
Earlier sketches in CA 37-40R, CANR-31, 60
Reston, Jody ... AITN 2
Reston, Richard ... AITN 2
Reston, Scotty
See Reston, James (Barrett)
Restrepo, Laura ... 185
Retallack, Joan ... CWP
Retamar, Roberto Fernandez
See Fernandez Retamar, Roberto
Retif de la Bretonne, Nicolas-Anne-Edme
1734-1806 ... DLB 314
See also GFL Beginnings to 1789
Retla, Robert
See Alter, Robert Edmond
Retner, Beth A.
See Brown, Beth
Rettenbacher, Simon 1634-1706 ... DLB 168
Rettie, Dwight F. 1930- ... 153
Rettig, Edward B(ertram) 1940- ... 57-60
Rettig, Jack L(ouis) 1925- ... 57-60
Retz, Jean-Francois-Paul de Gondi
1613-1679 ... DLB 268
See also GFL Beginnings to 1789
Reuben, Bryan G. 1934- ... CANR-118
Earlier sketch in CA 160
Reuben, David 1933- ... 41-44R
See also AITN 1
Reuben, Shelly 1945- ... 127
Reubens, Paul 1952- ... 165
Reuber, Grant L(ouis) 1927- ... CANR-3
Earlier sketch in CA 49-52
Reuchlin, Johannes 1455-1522 ... DLB 179
Reul, R(ose) Myrtle 1919- ... 21-24R
Reuland, Rob 1963- ... 202
Reuman, Robert E(verett) 1923- ... 37-40R
Reumann, John (Henry Paul) 1927- ... CANR-5
Earlier sketch in CA 1-4R
Reuss, Carl F(rederick) 1915- ... 41-44R
Reuss, Frederick 1960- ... 233
Reuss, Frederick G(ustav) 1904-1985 ... CAP-1
Earlier sketch in CA 11-12
Reuss, Henry S(choellkopf)
1912-2002 ... CANR-6
Obituary ... 200
Earlier sketch in CA 9-12R
Reuss-Ianni, Elizabeth 1946- ... 130
Reuter, Bjarne (B.) 1950- ... CANR-121
Earlier sketch in CA 137
See also SATA 68, 142
Reuter, Carol (Joan) 1931- ... 21-24R
See also SATA 2
Reuter, Christian 1665-1712(?) ... DLB 168
Reuter, Frank T. 1926- ... 21-24R
Reuter, Fritz 1810-1874 ... DLB 129
Reuter, Gabriele 1859-1941 ... 204
See also DLB 66
Reuther, David L(ouis) 1946- ... CANR-57
Earlier sketches in CA 112, CANR-31
Reuther, Ruth E. 1917- ... CANR-12
Earlier sketch in CA 33-36R
Reuther, Victor G(eorge) 1912-2004 ... 77-80
Obituary ... 228
Reutter, Mark 1950- ... 129
Rev, B.
See Eisner, Betty Grover
Reval, Jacques
See Laver, James
Revankar, Ratna G. 1937- ... 33-36R
Revard, Carter (Curtis) 1931- ... CANR-81
Earlier sketch in CA 144
See also NNAL
See also PFS 5
Revard, Stella Purce 1933- ... 97-100
Reve, Gerard (Kornelis van het) 1923- ... 192
See also CWW 2
Reve, Karel van het
See van het Reve, Karel
Reve, Simon van het
See Reve, Gerard (Kornelis van het)
Revel, Jean-Francois 1924- ... CANR-93
Brief entry ... 109
Earlier sketches in CA 127, CANR-55
Reveley, Edith 1930- ... 123
Reveley, W(alter) Taylor III 1943- ... 126
Revell, Donald 1954- ... CANR-39
Earlier sketch in CA 116
Revell, J(ohn) R(obert) S(tephen)
1920-2004 ... CANR-51
Obituary ... 233
Earlier sketches in CA 25-28R, CANR-11, 26
Revell, Jack
See Revell, J(ohn) R(obert) S(tephen)
Revell, Peter 1929-1983 ... CANR-13
Earlier sketch in CA 29-32R
ReVelle, Charles S. 1938- ... 45-48
Revelle, Jack B. 1935- ... 216
ReVelle, Penelope 1941- ... 49-52
Revena
See Wright, Betty Ren
Reventlow, Franziska Grafin zu
1871-1918 ... DLB 66
Reverdy, Pierre 1889-1960 ... 97-100
Obituary ... 89-92
See also CLC 53
See also DLB 258
See also EWL 3
See also GFL 1789 to the Present
Revere, Michael Rigsby 1951- ... 163
Reverend Mandju
See Su, Chien
Reves, Emery 1904-1981
Obituary ... 105
Reville, Alma 1899-1982 ... IDFW 3, 4
Revoyr, Nina 1969- ... 224
Revsbech, Vicki
See Liestman, Vicki
Revueltas, Jose
See Revueltas, Jose (Sanchez)
See also EWL 3
Revueltas, Jose (Sanchez) 1914-1976 ... 191
See also Revueltas, Jose
See also LAWS 1
Rewald, John 1912-1994 ... CANR-44
Obituary ... 144
Earlier sketches in CA 9-12R, CANR-5
Rewoldt, Stewart H(enry) 1922- ... 37-40R
Rex, Barbara (Clayton) 1904- ... 77-80
Rex, John A(rderne) 1925- ... CANR-24
Earlier sketches in CA 5-8R, CANR-6
Rex, Walter E(dwin) 1927- ... 45-48
Rexine, John E(fstratios) 1929-1993 .. CANR-46
Obituary ... 146
Earlier sketches in CA 37-40R, CANR-15
Rex-Johnson, Braiden 1956- ... 139
Rexrode-Johnston, F.
See Johnston, Francine R.
Rexroth, Kenneth 1905-1982 ... CANR-63
Obituary ... 107
Earlier sketches in CA 5-8R, CANR-14, 34
Interview in ... CANR-14
See also BG 1:3
See also CDALB 1941-1968
See also CLC 1, 2, 6, 11, 22, 49, 112
See also CP 1, 2
See also DAM POET
See also DLB 16, 48, 165, 212
See also DLBY 1982
See also EWL 3
See also MAL 5
See also MTCW 1, 2
See also MTFW 2005
See also PC 20
See also RGAL 4
Rey, Bret ... TCWW 2
Rey, Faustina ... GLL 2
Rey, H(ans) A(ugusto) 1898-1977 ... CANR-90
Obituary ... 73-76
Earlier sketches in CA 5-8R, CANR-6
See also CLR 5, 93
See also CWRI 5
See also DLB 22
See also MAICYA 1, 2
See also SATA 1, 26, 69, 100
Rey, Margret (Elisabeth) 1906-1996 .. CANR-38
Obituary ... 155
Earlier sketch in CA 105
See also CLR 5, 93
See also CWRI 5
See also MAICYA 1, 2
See also MAICYAS 1
See also SATA 26, 86
See also SATA-Obit 93
Rey, Michael Stephan 1946- ... 113
Rey, Stephane
See Burtot, Gerald
Reyam
See Mayer, Charles Leopold
Reybold, Malcolm 1911(?)-1988
Obituary ... 124
Reyburn, Wallace (Macdonald)
1913-2001 ... CANR-1
Earlier sketch in CA 49-52
Reyes, Adelaida 1930- ... 191
Reyes, Alfonso 1889-1959 ... 131
See also EWL 3
See also HLCS 2
See also HW 1
See also LAW
See also TCLC 33
Reyes, Carlos 1935- ... CANR-3
Earlier sketch in CA 49-52
Reyes, Carlos Jose 1941- ... CANR-87
See also DLB 305
See also HW 1
Reyes, Gabriel de los
See de los Reyes, Gabriel
Reyes Schramm, Adelaida
See Reyes, Adelaida
Reyes y Basoalto, Ricardo Eliecer Neftali
See Neruda, Pablo
Reyher, Becky
See Reyher, Rebecca Hourwich
Reyher, Rebecca Hourwich 1897-1987
Obituary ... 121
See also SATA 18
See also SATA-Obit 50
Reyhner, Jon (Allan) 1944- ... 139
Reyles, Carlos 1868-1938 ... 153
See also EWL 3
See also HW 1
Reymont, Wladyslaw (Stanislaw) 1868(?)-1925
Brief entry ... 104
See also EWL 3
See also TCLC 5
Reyna, Rudy de
See de Reyna, Rudy
Reynolds, Alan 1942- ... 61-64
Reynolds, Alastair 1966- ... 236
Reynolds, Ann
See Bly, Carol(yn)
Reynolds, Anne
See Steinke, Ann E(lizabeth)
Reynolds, Arlene 1947- ... 148
Reynolds, Barbara 1914- ... CANR-109
Earlier sketches in CA 9-12R, CANR-29, 54
Reynolds, Barbara (Ann) 1942- ... 73-76
Reynolds, Barrie (Gordon Robert)
1932- ... CANR-75
Earlier sketch in CA 13-16R
Reynolds, Bart
See Emblen, D(onald) L(ewis)
Reynolds, Bede 1893(?)-1989
Obituary ... 130
Reynolds, Bertha Capen 1885-1978 ... CAP-2
Earlier sketch in CA 19-20
Reynolds, Bessie
See Aitken, Rosemary
Reynolds, Bill 1945- ... 166
Reynolds, C. Buck 1957- ... SATA 107
Reynolds, Charles O. 1921- ... 9-12R
Reynolds, (Alfred) Christopher 1911- ... 104
Reynolds, Clark G(ilbert) 1939- ... CANR-56
Earlier sketches in CA 25-28R, CANR-12, 27
Reynolds, Clark Winton 1934- ... CANR-8
Earlier sketch in CA 21-24R
Reynolds, Clay 1949- ... TCWW 2
Reynolds, (Richard) Clay 1949- ... CANR-90
Earlier sketch in CA 139
Reynolds, Dallas McCord
1917-1983 ... CANR-86
Earlier sketches in CA 5-8R, CANR-9
See also Reynolds, Mack
See also SFW 4
Reynolds, David (J.) 1952- ... CANR-96
Earlier sketch in CA 148
Reynolds, David K(ent) 1940- ... CANR-25
Earlier sketches in CA 65-68, CANR-9
Reynolds, David S(pencer) 1948- ... 124
Reynolds, Dickson
See Reynolds, Helen Mary Greenwood Campbell
Reynolds, Donald E. 1931- ... 33-36R
Reynolds, Elaine A. 1957- ... 192
Reynolds, Elizabeth
See Steinke, Ann E(lizabeth)
Reynolds, Ernest (Randolph) 1910- ... CANR-6
Earlier sketch in CA 13-16R
Reynolds, Frank 1923-1983 ... 114
Obituary ... 109
Reynolds, G. Scott 1925- ... 29-32R
Reynolds, G. W. M. 1814-1879 ... DLB 21
See also HGG
See also SUFW
Reynolds, (Arthur) Graham 1914- ... CANR-17
Earlier sketch in CA 13-16R
Reynolds, Graham 1944- ... 138
Reynolds, Harry W., Jr. 1924- ... 13-16R

Cumulative Index 483 Rice

Reynolds, Helen Mary Greenwood Campbell
1884-1969 .... CANR-75
Obituary 103
Earlier sketch in CA 5-8R
See also SATA-Obit 26
Reynolds, Henry 1938- 198
Reynolds, Jack
See Jones, Jack
Reynolds, Jan 1925- 145
Reynolds, Joe
See Steward, Samuel M(orris)
See also GLL 1
Reynolds, John
See Whitlock, Ralph
Reynolds, John 1901- 9-12R
Reynolds, John Hamilton 1794-1852 ... DLB 96
Reynolds, John J(oseph) 1924- 37-40R
Reynolds, John Lawrence 1939- 179
Reynolds, Jonathan 1942- CANR-28
Earlier sketch in CA 65-68
See also CLC 6, 38
Reynolds, Joshua 1723-1792 .... DLB 104
Reynolds, Julia Louise 1883(?)-1980
Obituary 102
Reynolds, Kenyon L.
See Reynolds, Bede
Reynolds, Kevin 1952- 160
Reynolds, Kimberley (Griffith) 1955- 135
Reynolds, Larry T(homas) 1938- 134
Brief entry 107
Reynolds, Lloyd (George)
1910-2005 .... CANR-15
Obituary 238
Earlier sketch in CA 21-24R
Reynolds, Louis B. 1917- 41-44R
Reynolds, Mack
See Reynolds, Dallas McCord
See also DLB 8
Reynolds, Madge
See Whitlock, Ralph
Reynolds, Malvina 1900-1978 114
Obituary 105
See also SATA 44
See also SATA-Obit 24
Reynolds, Margaret 1957- 230
Reynolds, Marie E. 1912-2000 .... 17-20R
Reynolds, Marilyn (M.) 1935- 192
See also BYA 14
See also SAAS 23
See also SATA 121
Reynolds, Marilynn 1940- 212
See also SATA 80, 141
Reynolds, Marjorie 1944- 169
Reynolds, Marjorie Harris 1903-1989 .... 5-8R
Reynolds, Mary T(rackett) 1914-2000 109
Obituary 189
Reynolds, Michael S(hane)
1937-2000 .... CANR-97
Obituary 189
Earlier sketches in CA 65-68, CANR-9, 89
See also CLC 44
Reynolds, (Marjorie) Moira Davison
1915- CANR-45
Earlier sketches in CA 105, CANR-21
Reynolds, Morgan O(wen) 1942- 117
Reynolds, Oliver 1957- 195
Reynolds, Pamela 1923- 103
See also SATA 34
Reynolds, Paul Davidson 1938- CANR-12
Earlier sketch in CA 33-36R
Reynolds, Paul R(evere) 1904-1988 . CANR-76
Obituary 125
Earlier sketch in CA 102
Reynolds, Peter C(arlton) 1943- 105
Reynolds, Peter H. 1961- .... SATA 128
Reynolds, Philip Alan 1920- CANR-3
Earlier sketch in CA 5-8R
Reynolds, Quentin (James) 1902-1965 73-76
Reynolds, Robert Leonard
1902-1966 .... CANR-76
Obituary 103
Earlier sketch in CA 1-4R
Reynolds, Roger 1934- 53-56
Reynolds, Ruth Sutton 1890(?)-1977
Obituary 69-72
Reynolds, Sheri 1967- 147
See also CSW
Reynolds, Susan (Mary Grace) 1929- 117
Reynolds, Terry S(cott) 1946- CANR-43
Earlier sketch in CA 117
Reynolds, Theodore (Andrus) 1938- 158
Reynolds, Timothy (Robin) 1936- CANR-8
Earlier sketch in CA 9-12R
See also CP 1
Reynolds, Valrae 1944- 93-96
Reynolds, Vernon 1935- CANR-86
Earlier sketch in CA 132
Reynolds, William H. 1910-1997 .... IDFW 3, 4
Reynolds, William Howard 1922-1972
Obituary 107
Reynolds, William J. 1956- CANR-62
Earlier sketch in CA 123
Reynolds, William Jensen 1920- CANR-7
Earlier sketch in CA 5-8R
Rey-Rosa, Rodrigo 1958- 131
Reys, Otto P.
See Greshoff, Jan
Reza, Yasmina 1959- 171
See also DFS 19
See also DLB 321
Rezits, Joseph 1925- 107
Rezler, Julius Stephen 1911-2001 .... 25-28R
Rezmerski, John Calvin 1942- CANR-27
Earlier sketch in CA 29-32R
Rezneck, Samuel 1897-1983 .... CANR-24
Obituary 110
Earlier sketch in CA 45-48
Reznek, Lawrie 183
Reznikoff, Charles 1894-1976 .... CAP-2
Obituary 61-64
Earlier sketch in CA 33-36
See also AMWS 14
See also CLC 9
See also CP 1, 2
See also DLB 28, 45
See also WP
Reznikov, Hanon 1950- .... CD 5, 6
Rezny, Arthur A(dolph) 1910- CAP-2
Earlier sketch in CA 19-20
Rezzori (d'Arezzo), Gregor von
1914-1998 136
Obituary 167
Brief entry 122
See also CLC 25
Rhea, Claude H(iram), Jr. 1927- 103
Rhea, Gordon Campbell 1945- CANR-93
Earlier sketch in CA 146
Rhea, Joseph Tilden 1967- 173
Rhea, Nicholas
See Walker, Peter N.
Rhees, Rush 1905(?)-1989(?)
Obituary 129
Rheims, Christine
See Orban, Christine
Rheims, Maurice 1910-2003 153
Obituary 215
Rhein, Francis Bayard 1915- 17-20R
Rhein, Phillip H(enry) 1923- 81-84
Rheingold, Howard (E.) 1947- CANR-135
Earlier sketch in CA 147
Rheinstein, Max 1899-1977
Obituary 73-76
Rhenisch, Harold (Arthur) 1958- 113
Rhett, Robert Barnwell 1800-1876 .... DLB 43
Rhie, Marylin M. 191
Rhie, Schi-Zhin 1936- 77-80
Rhine, Charles D. 1938- 175
Rhine, J(oseph) B(anks) 1895-1980 ..... CANR-4
Obituary 93-96
Earlier sketch in CA 5-8R
Rhine, Louisa (Weckesser) E.
1891-1983 .... CANR-4
Earlier sketch in CA 1-4R
Rhine, Richard
See Silverstein, Alvin and
Silverstein, Virginia B(arbara Opshelor)
Rhinehart, Luke
See Cockcroft, George Powers
Rhinehart, Marilyn D. 1948- 139
Rhinehart, Susan Oneacre 1938- 1-4R
Rhoades, Diane 1952- 155
See also SATA 90
Rhoades, Jonathan
See Olsen, John Edward
Rhoades, Judith G(rubman) 1935- 97-100
Rhoads, Dorothy M(ary) 1895-1986 ...... CAP-2
Earlier sketch in CA 19-20
Rhoads, Edward J(ohn) M(ichael)
1938- 33-36R
Rhoads, Jonathan E(vans) 1907-2002 104
Obituary 204
Rhode, Arvid
See Brekke, Paal (Emanuel)
Rhode, Austen
See Francis, Basil (Hoskins)
Rhode, Deborah L. 1952- 236
Rhode, Eric 1934- 21-24R
Rhode, Irma 1900-1982
Obituary 106
Rhode, John
See Street, Cecil J(ohn) C(harles)
See also DLB 77
Rhode, Robert B(artlett) 1916- 17-20R
Rhode, Robert D(avid) 1911- 93-96
Rhode, William 1972- 223
Rhode, Winslow
See Roe, F(rederic) Gordon
Rhodehamel, Josephine DeWitt
1901-2000 61-64
Rhodes, Albert 1916-1977 .... CANR-14
Earlier sketch in CA 21-24R
Rhodes, Anthony (Richard Ewart)
1916-2004 .... CANR-75
Obituary 230
Earlier sketch in CA 9-12R
Rhodes, Arnold Black 1913-2002 .... 13-16R
Rhodes, Bennie (Loran) 1927- 108
See also SATA 35
Rhodes, Carolyn Hodgson 1925- 122
Rhodes, Chip
See Rhodes, Winthrop G.
Rhodes, Clifford Oswald 1911-1985 65-68
Obituary 118
Rhodes, Colin 1963- CANR-103
Earlier sketch in CA 153
Rhodes, Daniel .... HGG
Rhodes, David 1946- 57-60
Rhodes, Dennis Everard 1923- 13-16R
Rhodes, Donna McKee 1962- 152
See also SATA 87
Rhodes, Elvi 1930- .... RHW
Rhodes, Ernest Lloyd 1915- 119
Rhodes, Eugene Manlove 1869-1934 198
See also DLB 256
See also TCLC 53
See also TCWW 1, 2
Rhodes, Evan H. 1929- CANR-10
Earlier sketch in CA 57-60
Rhodes, Frank Harold Trevor 1926- 107
See also SATA 37
Rhodes, Ginger 1955- 160
Rhodes, Hari 1932-1992 .... 17-20R
Rhodes, Irwin Seymour 1901-1985 73-76
Rhodes, James A(llen) 1909-2001
Obituary 195
Brief entry 105
Rhodes, James Ford 1848-1927 204
See also DLB 47
Rhodes, James M. 1940- 89-92
Rhodes, Jewell Parker 179
Rhodes, John J(acob II) 1916-2003 103
Obituary 219
Rhodes, Laura
See Robinson, Lisa
Rhodes, Leland
See Paine, Lauran (Bosworth)
Rhodes, Margaret 1915- 45-48
Rhodes, Martha 199
Rhodes, Norman (L.) 1942- 152
Rhodes, Olin E(ugene), Jr. 1960- 158
Rhodes, Philip 1922- 107
Rhodes, R. A. W. 1944- 139
Rhodes, Richard (Lee) 1937- CANR-111
Earlier sketches in CA 45-48, CANR-1, 20, 58
See also BEST 90:1
See also DLB 185
See also NCFS 1
Rhodes, Robert E(dward) 1927- 122
Rhodes, Robert Hunt 1937- 136
Rhodes, Robert I. 1942- 69-72
Rhodes, William C(onley) 1918- 81-84
Rhodes, Winthrop G. 1965- 189
Rhodes, Zandra (Lindsey) 1940- 153
Rhodes James, Robert (Vidal)
1933-1999 .... CANR-14
Obituary 179
Earlier sketch in CA 101
Rhodin, Eric Nolan 1916- CANR-3
Earlier sketch in CA 1-4R
Rhoidis, E.
See Bierbaum, Otto Julius
Rhone, Trevor (Dave) 1940- CANR-80
Earlier sketch in CA 127
See also BW 1
See also CD 5, 6
See also EWL 3
R'hoone, Lord
See Balzac, Honore de
Rhue, Morton
See Strasser, Todd
Rhydderch, Ieuan
See Jones, Evan David
Rhymer, Joseph 1927- CANR-9
Earlier sketch in CA 21-24R
Rhyne, Nancy 1926- 133
See also SATA 66
Rhynes, Martha E. 1939- 212
See also SATA 141
Rhys, Frank
See Rees, Clair (Francis)
Rhys, Ioan
See Rees, Ioan Bowen
Rhys, J(ohn) Howard W(inslow) 1917- .. 17-20R
Rhys, Jean 1890-1979 .... CANR-62
Obituary 85-88
Earlier sketches in CA 25-28R, CANR-35
See also BRWS 2
See also CDBLB 1945-1960
See also CDWLB 3
See also CLC 2, 4, 6, 14, 19, 51, 124
See also CN 1, 2
See also DA3
See also DAM NOV
See also DLB 36, 117, 162
See also DNFS 2
See also EWL 3
See also LATS 1:1
See also MTCW 1, 2
See also MTFW 2005
See also NFS 19
See also RGEL 2
See also RGSF 2
See also RHW
See also SSC 21, 76
See also TEA
See also WWE 1
Rhys, Kate
See Donald, Anabel
Rhys, Keidrych 1915-1987
Obituary 122
See also CP 1
Rhys Jones, Griff(ith)
See Jones, Griff(ith) Rhys
Riach, Alan 1957- CANR-80
Earlier sketch in CA 141
See also CP 7
Riad, Mahmoud 1917-1992 .... CANR-76
Obituary 136
Earlier sketch in CA 131
Riahi-Belkaoui, Ahmed 1943- 140
Riasanovsky, Nicholas V(alentine)
1923- CANR-3
Earlier sketch in CA 5-8R
Riba, Carles 1893-1959 208
See also EWL 3
Ribal, Joseph E(dward) 1931- 61-64
Ribalow, Harold U(riel) 1919-1982 .... CANR-2
Obituary 108
Earlier sketch in CA 5-8R
Ribalow, Meir Z(vi) 1948- 144
Ribar, Joe 1943- 77-80
Ribbons, Ian 1924- 108
See also SAAS 3
See also SATA 37
See also SATA-Brief 30
Ribeiro, Aileen 1944- CANR-138
Earlier sketch in CA 124
Ribeiro, Aquilino 1885-1963 .... EWL 3
Ribeiro, Bernardim fl. 1475-1526 .... DLB 287
Ribeiro, Darcy 1922-1997 .... 33-36R
Obituary 156
See also CLC 34
See also EWL 3
Ribeiro, Joao Ubaldo (Osorio Pimentel)
1941- 81-84
See also CLC 10, 67
See also CWW 2
See also EWL 3
Ribera Chevremont, Evaristo 1896-1976 . HW 1
Ribeyro, Julio Ramon 1929-1994 180
See also DLB 145
See also EWL 3
Ribicoff, Abraham (Alexander) 1910-1998 . 108
Obituary 167
Ribman, Ronald (Burt) 1932- CANR-80
Earlier sketches in CA 21-24R, CANR-46
See also CAD
See also CD 5, 6
See also CLC 7
Ribner, Irving 1921-1972 .... CANR-3
Obituary 37-40R
Earlier sketch in CA 1-4R
Ribon, Pamela 1975- 223
Riboud, Barbara (Dewayne Tosi) Chase
See Chase-Riboud, Barbara (Dewayne Tosi)
Ribowsky, Mark 1951- 146
Ribuffo, Leo P(aul) 1945- 118
Ricapito, Joseph V. 1933- 158
Ricardo, Cassiano 1895-1974 .... EWL 3
Ricardo, David 1772-1823 .... DLB 107, 158
Ricardo, Harry R(alph) 1885-1974
Obituary 114
Ricardo, Jack 1940- 140
Ricardo-Campbell, Rita CANR-26
Earlier sketches in CA 57-60, CANR-8
Ricardou, Jean 1932- .... DLB 83
See also EWL 3
Ricart, Josep Gudiol i
See Gudiol i Ricart, Josep
Riccards, Michael P(atrick) 1944- 61-64
Ricchiuti, Paul B(urton) 1925- 107
Ricci, David M. 1940- 143
Ricci, Franco 1953- 220
Ricci, Larry J. 1948- 109
Ricci, Nino (Pio) 1959- CANR-130
Earlier sketch in CA 137
See also CCA 1
See also CLC 70
Ricciardi, Lorenzo 1930- 109
Ricciotti, Hope 1963- 239
Ricciuti, Edward R(aphael) 1938- 41-44R
See also SATA 10
Riccoboni, Marie-Jeanne 1713-1792 .. DLB 314
Rice, A(lbert) Kenneth 1908- 5-8R
Rice, Albert
See Leventhal, Albert Rice
Rice, Albert R(ichard) 1951- 142
Rice, Alice (Caldwell) Hegan
1870-1942 .... CWRI 5
See also SATA 63
Rice, Allan Lake 1905-1984 .... CANR-27
Earlier sketch in CA 37-40R
Rice, Anne 1941- CANR-133
Earlier sketches in CA 65-68, CANR-12, 36, 53, 74, 100
See also Rampling, Anne
See also AAYA 9, 53
See also AMWS 7
See also BEST 89:2
See also BPFB 3
See also CLC 41, 128
See also CN 6, 7
See also CPW
See also CSW
See also DA3
See also DAM POP
See also DLB 292
See also GL 3
See also GLL 2
See also HGG
See also MTCW 2
See also MTFW 2005
See also SUFW 2
See also YAW
Rice, Arnold Sanford 1928- 113
Rice, Bebe Faas 1932- 155
See also SATA 89
Rice, Berkeley 1937- 21-24R
Rice, C(harles) David 1941- CANR-41
Earlier sketch in CA 118
Rice, C(harles) Duncan 1942- CANR-10
Earlier sketch in CA 57-60
Rice, Charles D(uane) 1910-1971
Obituary 104
See also SATA-Obit 27
Rice, Charles E. 1931- CANR-1
Earlier sketch in CA 1-4R
Rice, Charles L(ynvel) 1936- 65-68
Rice, Christopher 1978- 198
See also AAYA 61
Rice, Condoleezza 1954- 154
Rice, Craig
See Randolph, Georgiana Ann
Rice, Cy 1905-1971 .... CAP-1
Obituary 33-36R
Earlier sketch in CA 11-12
Rice, Dale R(ichard) 1948- 116
See also SATA 42
Rice, David G(ordon) 1938- 101
Rice, David Talbot 1903-1972 .... CANR-5
Earlier sketch in CA 9-12R
Rice, Desmond Charles 1924- CANR-21
Earlier sketches in CA 9-12R, CANR-5
Rice, Dick
See Rice, R. Hugh

Rice, Donald L. 1938- CANR-14
Earlier sketch in CA 37-40R
Rice, Dorothy Mary 1913- 9-12R
Rice, Earle (Wilmont), Jr. 1928- CANR-109
Earlier sketch in CA 156
See also SATA 92, 151
Rice, Edmund C. 1910(?)-1982
Obituary 106
Rice, Edward 1918-2001 CANR-47
Obituary 201
Earlier sketches in CA 49-52, CANR-1
See also BEST 90:4
See also SATA 47
See also SATA-Brief 42
Rice, Edward E(arl) 1909- 41-44R
Rice, Elinor
See Hays, Elinor Rice
Rice, Elizabeth 1913-1976 21-24R
See also SATA 2
Rice, Elmer (Leopold) 1892-1967 CAP-2
Obituary 25-28R
Earlier sketch in CA 21-22
See also Reizenstein, Elmer Leopold
See also CLC 7, 49
See also DAM DRAM
See also DFS 12
See also DLB 4, 7
See also IDTP
See also MAL 5
See also MTCW 1, 2
See also RGAL 4
Rice, Eugene F(ranklin), Jr. 1924- 29-32R
Rice, Eve (Hart) 1951- CANR-4
Earlier sketch in CA 53-56
See also SATA 34, 91
Rice, Frank M(artin) 1908-1983 45-48
Rice, George H(all), Jr. 1923- 53-56
Rice, Graham 1950- 203
Rice, Grantland 1880-1954
Brief entry 114
See also DLB 29, 171
Rice, Helen Steiner 1900(?)-1981 133
Rice, Homer C(ranston) 1927- 73-76
Rice, Inez 1907- 29-32R
See also SATA 13
Rice, James 1934- CANR-65
Earlier sketches in CA 61-64, CANR-8
See also SATA 22, 93
Rice, John F. 1958- SATA 82
Rice, John R(ichard) 1895-1980 CANR-5
Earlier sketch in CA 5-8R
Rice, Joseph Peter 1930- 29-32R
Rice, Julius 1923- 41-44R
Rice, Keith A(lan) 1954- 109
Rice, Lawrence D. 1929- 33-36R
Rice, Linda Lightsey 1950- 166
Rice, Louise 191
Rice, Luanne 1955- CANR-93
Earlier sketch in CA 139
Rice, Martin P(aul) 1938- 57-60
Rice, Max M(cGee) 1928- 93-96
Rice, Michael 1928- 137
Rice, Mitchell F. 1948- 138
See also BW 2
Rice, Otis K(ermit) 1919- CANR-27
Earlier sketch in CA 29-32R
Rice, Patricia 1949- 206
Rice, Patty 218
Rice, R. B.
See Chapman, Frank M(onroe)
Rice, R. Hugh 1929- 187
See also SATA 115
Rice, Richard H.
See Rice, R. Hugh
Rice, Ross R(ichard) 1922- 45-48
Rice, Stan 1942-2002 CANR-128
Obituary 214
Earlier sketches in CA 77-80, CANR-36, 127
Rice, Tamara (Abelson) Talbot 1904-
Brief entry 111
Rice, Thomas Jackson 1945- CANR-18
Earlier sketch in CA 101
Rice, Tim(othy Miles Bindon) 1944- CANR-46
Earlier sketch in CA 103
See also CLC 21
See also DFS 7
Rice, Virginia Hill 197
Rice, Wayne 1945- 89-92
Rice, William (Edward) 1938- 118
Rice, William C(arroll) 1911- 9-12R
Rich, Adrienne (Cecile) 1929- CANR-128
Earlier sketches in CA 9-12R, CANR-20, 53, 74
See also AMWR 2
See also AMWS 1
See also CDALBS
See also CLC 3, 6, 7, 11, 18, 36, 73, 76, 125
See also CP 1, 2, 3, 4, 5, 6, 7
See also CSW
See also CWP
See also DA3
See also DAM POET
See also DLB 5, 67
See also EWL 3
See also EXPP
See also FL 1:6
See also FW
See also MAL 5
See also MAWW
See also MTCW 1, 2
See also MTFW 2005
See also PAB
See also PC 5
See also PFS 15
See also RGAL 4
See also WP
Rich, Alan 1924- 9-12R
Rich, B. Ruby 183
Rich, Barbara
See Graves, Robert (von Ranke)
Rich, Barnaby 1542-1617 RGEL 2
Rich, Bennett M(ilton) 1909-1984 134
Rich, Daniel Catton 1904-1976 73-76
Obituary 69-72
Rich, Doris L. 1920- 138
Rich, Edwin Ernest 1904-1979
Obituary 89-92
Rich, Elaine Sommers 1926- CANR-103
Earlier sketches in CA 17-20R, CANR-9, 24, 49
See also SATA 6
Rich, Elizabeth 1935- 29-32R
Rich, (Ora) Everett 1900-1985 CAP-1
Earlier sketch in CA 11-12
Rich, Francine Poppo 1967- 193
Rich, Frank (Hart) 1949- CANR-99
Earlier sketch in CA 73-76
Rich, Gerry
See Brandon, Johnny
Rich, (David) Gibson 1936- 57-60
Rich, Harvey L. 1944- 218
Rich, Joe 1935- 57-60
Rich, John H., Jr. 1917- 81-84
Rich, John Martin 1931- 21-24R
Rich, Josephine Bouchard 1912- 5-8R
See also SATA 10
Rich, Katherine Russell 1955- 193
Rich, Louise Dickinson 1903-1991 73-76
Obituary 134
See also SATA 54
See also SATA-Obit 67
Rich, Mark J. 1948- SATA-Brief 53
Rich, Matty 1971- 140
See also BW 2
Rich, Michael B(enjamin) 1935- 29-32R
Rich, Norman 1921- 45-48
Rich, Paul B(enjamin) 1950- 124
Rich, Rhonda 212
Rich, Robert
See Trumbo, Dalton
Rich, Russell R(ogers) 1912-1988 101
Rich, Thomas H(ewitt) 1941- 204
Richard, Adrienne 1921- 29-32R
See also SAAS 9
See also SATA 5
Richard, Arthur Windsor
See Windsor-Richards, Arthur (Bedlington)
Richard, Betty Byrd 1922- 106
Richard, Carl J(ohn) 1962- 150
Richard, George
See Stubbs, Harry C(lement)
Richard, James Robert
See Bowen, Robert Sydney
Richard, John 1954- 106
Richard, Keith
See Richards, Keith
See also CLC 17
Richard, Lee
See Le Pelley, Guernsey
Richard, Lionel (Camille Paul) 1938- 93-96
Richard, Lucien J(oseph) 1931- 105
Richard, Mark 1955- CANR-88
Earlier sketch in CA 145
See also CSW
See also DLB 234
Richard, Marthe 1889-1962
Obituary 110
Richard, Michel Paul 1933- 45-48
Richard, Olga 1914- 103
Richard, Oscar G. Iii 1921- 202
Richard, Susan
See Ellis, Julie
Richard, Thelma (J.) Shinn 1942- 176
Richard-Allerdyce, Diane 1958- 170
Richard-Amato, Patricia (Abbott) 1940- 126
Richard de Fournival 1201-c. 1259 DLB 208
Richards, Alayna
See Posner, Richard
Richards, Alfred (Luther) 1939- 45-48
Richards, Allen
See Rosenthal, Richard A.
Richards, Alun (Morgan)
1929-2004 CANR-17
Obituary 228
Earlier sketch in CA 65-68
Richards, Amelia M. 1970- 225
Richards, Amy
See Richards, Amelia M.
Richards, Arlene Kramer 1935- CANR-11
Earlier sketch in CA 65-68
Richards, Audrey I(sabel)
1899-1984 CANR-27
Obituary 113
Earlier sketch in CA 21-24R
Richards, Beah 1920-2000 153
Obituary 189
See also BW 2
Richards, Ben 1964- 186
Richards, Blair P(atton) 1940- 69-72
Richards, Cara E(lizabeth) 1927- CANR-1
Earlier sketch in CA 49-52
Richards, Carl Edward, Jr. 1933- CANR-24
Earlier sketch in CA 45-48
Richards, Caroline 1939- 77-80
Richards, Charles
See Marvin, John T.
Richards, Clare
See Titchener, Louise
Richards, Clay
See Crossen, Kendell Foster
Richards, David
See Bickers, Richard (Leslie) Townshend
Richards, David 1940- 166
Richards, David A. J. 1944- 167
Richards, David Adams 1950- CANR-110
Earlier sketches in CA 93-96, CANR-60
See also CLC 59
See also CN 7
See also DAC
See also DLB 53
See also TCLE 1:2
Richards, David P. 1950- 166
Richards, Denis (George) 1910-2004 9-12R
Obituary 233
Richards, Dennis L(ee) 1938- 102
Richards, Dorothy B(urney) 1894-1985 85-88
Richards, Duane
See Hurley, Vic
Richards, Dusty 1937- 232
Richards, E. B.
See Bayley, Edwin (Richard)
Richards, Edward
See Tubb, E(dwin) C(harles)
Richards, Emilie 1948- 203
See also RHW
Richards, Eric 1940- CANR-99
Earlier sketch in CA 148
Richards, Eugene 1944- CANR-137
Earlier sketch in CA 154
Richards, Francis
See Lockridge, Frances Louise and Lockridge, Richard
Richards, Frank
See Hamilton, Charles (Harold St. John)
Richards, Fred
See Richards, Alfred (Luther)
Richards, George 1760(?)-1814 DLB 37
Richards, Guy 1905-1979 CANR-11
Obituary 81-84
Earlier sketch in CA 61-64
Richards, H(arold) M(arshall) S(ylvester)
1894-1985 CAP-2
Obituary 116
Earlier sketch in CA 23-24
Richards, Hilda
See Hamilton, Charles (Harold St. John)
Richards, Horace G(ardiner) 1906-1984 5-8R
Richards, Hubert J. 1921- CANR-125
Earlier sketches in CA 128, CANR-67
Richards, I(vor) A(rmstrong)
1893-1979 CANR-74
Obituary 89-92
Earlier sketches in CA 41-44R, CANR-34
See also BRWS 2
See also CLC 14, 24
See also CP 1, 2
See also DLB 27
See also EWL 3
See also MTCW 2
See also RGEL 2
Richards, J(ohn) Howard 1916- CANR-18
Earlier sketches in CA 45-48, CANR-2
Richards, J(ames) M(aude)
1907-1992 CANR-25
Earlier sketches in CA 5-8R, CANR-5
Richards, Jack W(esley) 1933- 33-36R
Richards, Jackie 1925- 169
See also SATA 102
Richards, James O(lin) 1936- 37-40R
Richards, Jane 1934- 33-36R
Richards, Janet Radcliffe 1944- 133
Richards, Jean 1940- 204
See also SATA 135
Richards, Jeffrey (Michael) 1945- CANR-13
Earlier sketch in CA 73-76
Richards, Jock 1918- 107
Richards, Joe 1909-1992 CAP-1
Obituary 136
Earlier sketch in CA 9-10
Richards, John 1939- 57-60
Richards, John F(olsom) 1938- 115
Richards, John Marvin 1929- 13-16R
Richards, Kathleen
See Dale, Kathleen
Richards, Kay
See Baker, Susan (Catherine)
Richards, Keith 1943- CANR-77
Earlier sketch in CA 107
See also Richard, Keith
Richards, Kenny
See Broderick, Richard L(awrence)
Richards, Kent David 1938- 104
Richards, Larry
See Richards, Lawrence O.
Richards, Laura E(lizabeth Howe)
1850-1943 137
Brief entry 120
See also CLR 54
See also CWRI 5
See also DLB 42
See also MAICYA 1, 2
See also WCH
See also YABC 1
Richards, Lawrence O. 1931- CANR-42
Earlier sketches in CA 29-32R, CANR-20
Richards, Lewis A(lva) 1925- 45-48
Richards, M(ary) C(aroline) 1916-1999 108
Obituary 185
Richards, Mark
See Ra'Anan, Uri
Richards, Martin P(aul) M(eredith)
1940- CANR-49
Earlier sketches in CA 61-64, CANR-8, 23
Richards, Matt 1968- 162
Richards, Max D(eVoe) 1923- CANR-16
Earlier sketch in CA 21-24R
Richards, Nat
See Richardson, James Nathaniel
Richards, Norman 1932- CANR-31
Earlier sketch in CA 112
See also SATA 48
Richards, Owain Westmacott 1901-1984
Obituary 114
Richards, Pamela Spence 1941- 111
Richards, Peter
See Monger, (Ifor) David
Richards, Peter Godfrey 1923-1987 108
Obituary 123
Richards, Phyllis
See Auty, Phyllis
Richards, R(onald) C(harles) W(illiam)
1923- CANR-26
Earlier sketches in CA 21-24R, CANR-10
See also SATA 59
See also SATA-Brief 43
Richards, Robert J. 144
Richards, Stanley 1918-1980 25-28R
Obituary 101
Richards, Susan 1948- 135
Richards, Tim 1960- 180
Richards, Todd
See Sutphen, Richard Charles
Richards, Vernon 1915-2001 206
Richards, Victor 1918- 57-60
Richards, Walter Alden (Jr.) 1907-1988
Obituary 125
See also SATA-Obit 56
Richards, William Carey 1818-1892 DLB 73
Richardson, Alan 1923- 29-32R
Richardson, Andrew (William)
1986- SATA 120
Richardson, Ann 1942- CANR-45
Earlier sketch in CA 119
Richardson, Anne
See Roiphe, Anne (Richardson)
Richardson, Arleta 1923- CANR-36
Earlier sketches in CA 93-96, CANR-16
Richardson, Beth
See Gutcheon, Beth R(ichardson)
Richardson, Betty 1935- 53-56
Richardson, Beulah
See Richards, Beah
Richardson, Bill 1955- 229
Richardson, Bonham C. 1939- 135
Richardson, Bradley M. 1928- 49-52
Richardson, C.
See Munsey, Cecil (Richard, Jr.)
Richardson, Carl 1950- 143
Richardson, Carol 1932- SATA 58
Richardson, Cecil Antonio 1928-1991 121
Obituary 136
Brief entry 115
Interview in CA-121
Richardson, Charles E(verett) 1928- 57-60
Richardson, Charles F(rancis) 1851-1913 231
See also DLB 71
Richardson, Charles R(ay) 1935- 219
Richardson, Cyril Charles 1909-1976 37-40R
Obituary 69-72
Richardson, Don(ald MacNaughton)
1935- CANR-9
Earlier sketch in CA 65-68
Richardson, Donald P(orter) 1932- CANR-44
Earlier sketch in CA 119
Richardson, Dorothy Lee 1900-1986 106
Obituary 121
Richardson, Dorothy Miller 1873-1957 192
Brief entry 104
See also DLB 36
See also EWL 3
See also FW
See also RGEL 2
See also TCLC 3
Richardson, Dorsey 1896-1981
Obituary 105
Richardson, (Robert) Douglas 1893-1989
Obituary 128
Richardson, Edgar Preston 1902-1985 110
Obituary 115
Richardson, Elliot L(ee) 1920-1999
Obituary 188
Brief entry 111
Richardson, Elmo (R.) 1930- CANR-11
Earlier sketch in CA 13-16R
Richardson (Robertson), Ethel Florence Lindesay
1870-1946 190
Brief entry 105
See also Richardson, Henry Handel
See also DLB 230
See also RHW
Richardson, Evelyn M(ay Fox)
1902-1976 CAP-1
Earlier sketch in CA 13-14
Richardson, Frank Howard 1882-1970
Obituary 104
See also SATA-Obit 27
Richardson, Frank McLean
1904-1996 CANR-20
Earlier sketch in CA 103
Richardson, Gayle E(lwin) 1911-1998 9-12R
Richardson, George Barclay 1924- 1-4R
Richardson, Gladwell 1903-1980 CANR-90
Earlier sketch in CA 123
See also TCWW 2
Richardson, Grace Lee
See Dickson, Naida
Richardson, H(arold) Edward 1929- CANR-15
Earlier sketch in CA 29-32R
Richardson, Harry V(an Buren)
1901-1990 69-72
Richardson, Harry W(ard) 1938- CANR-27
Earlier sketch in CA 29-32R
Richardson, Henrietta
See Richardson (Robertson), Ethel Florence Lindesay

Richardson, Henry Handel
See Richardson (Robertson), Ethel Florence Lindesay
See also DLB 197
See also EWL 3
See also RGEL 2
See also RGSF 2
See also TCLC 4
Richardson, Henry V(okes) M(ackey) 1923- 25-28R
Richardson, Howard (Dixon) 1917-1984 .... 41-44R
Obituary 114
Richardson, Isla Paschal 1886-1971 ...... CAP-1
Earlier sketch in CA 9-10
Richardson, Ivan L(eRoy) 1920- 101
Richardson, Ivor Lloyd Morgan 1930- 9-12R
Richardson, J. G.
See Richardson, Jacques (Gabriel)
Richardson, Jack (Carter) 1935- 5-8R
See also CAD
See also DLB 7
Richardson, Jacques (Gabriel) 1924- 125
Richardson, James 1950- CANR-81
Earlier sketch in CA 77-80
Richardson, James F(rancis) 1931- 29-32R
Richardson, James L(ongden) 1933- 21-24R
Richardson, James Nathaniel 1942- 53-56
Richardson, James R(ussell) 1908-1982 ..... 1-4R
Richardson, James T. 1941- 139
Richardson, Jean (Mary) 127
See also SATA 59
Richardson, Jeremy John 1942- CANR-27
Earlier sketch in CA 29-32R
Richardson, Joanna CANR-51
Earlier sketches in CA 13-16R, CANR-10, 26
Richardson, Joe M(artin) 1934- CANR-26
Earlier sketch in CA 45-48
Richardson, John 1796-1852 .... CCA 1
See also DAC
See also DLB 99
Richardson, John 1924- CANR-91
Earlier sketch in CA 140
Richardson, John Adkins 1929- 57-60
Richardson, John Martin, Jr. 1938- ... CANR-12
Earlier sketch in CA 33-36R
Richardson, Judith Benet 1941- .... SATA 77
Richardson, Justin 1900(?)-1975
Obituary 61-64
Richardson, Kenneth Ridley 1934- 29-32R
Richardson, Laurel 1938- 111
Richardson, Laurence E(aton) 1893-1985 .... CAP-1
Earlier sketch in CA 11-12
Richardson, (Stewart) Lee (Jr.) 1940- ... CANR-9
Earlier sketch in CA 21-24R
Richardson, Leopold John Dixon 1893-1979(?)
Obituary 104
Richardson, Malcolm 1947- 120
Richardson, Mark 1963- 173
Richardson, Midge Turk 1930- 33-36R
Richardson, Miles (Edward) 1932- 33-36R
Richardson, Mozelle Groner 1914- 33-36R
Richardson, Neil R(yan) 1944- 103
Richardson, Nola 1936- 57-60
See also BW 1
Richardson, Paul 1963- 226
Richardson, (George) Peter 1935- CANR-43
Earlier sketch in CA 114
Richardson, R. C. 1944- CANR-137
Earlier sketch in CA 162
Richardson, R(alph) Daniel 1931- 109
Richardson, Richard C(olby), Jr. 1933- CANR-13
Earlier sketch in CA 77-80
Richardson, Richard Judson 1935- 29-32R
Richardson, Robert 1940- 149
Richardson, Robert D(ale), Jr. 1934- . CANR-29
Earlier sketches in CA 29-32R, CANR-12
Richardson, Robert Galloway 1926- .. CANR-7
Earlier sketch in CA 13-16R
Richardson, Robert S(hirley) 1902-1981 .... CANR-87
Earlier sketch in CA 49-52
See also SATA 8
See also SFW 4
Richardson, Rupert Norval 1891-1988 .. 17-20R
Richardson, Ruth 1951- 136
Richardson, S(tanley) D(ennis) 1925- CANR-28
Earlier sketches in CA 21-24R, CANR-10
Richardson, Samuel 1689-1761 .... BRW 3
See also CDBLB 1660-1789
See also DA
See also DAB
See also DAC
See also DAM MST, NOV
See also DLB 39
See also RGEL 2
See also TEA
See also WLC
See also WLIT 3
Richardson, Sandy 1949- 188
See also SATA 116
Richardson, Stephen A. 1920- CANR-94
Earlier sketch in CA 61-64
Richardson, Thomas Dow 1887- 5-8R
Richardson, Tony
See Richardson, Cecil Antonio
Richardson, Vicky 1968- 213
Richardson, Vokes
See Richardson, Henry V(okes) M(ackey)
Richardson, W(alter) C(ecil) 1902-1983 .... CANR-1
Earlier sketch in CA 1-4R
Richardson, William John 1920- 21-24R
Richardson, Willis 1889-1977 124
See also BW 1
See also DLB 51
See also HR 1:3
See also SATA 60
Richason, Benjamin F(ranklin, Jr.) 1922- 41-44R
Richberg, Donald R(andall) 1881-1960
Obituary 113
Richburg, Keith B(ernard) 1958- 171
Riche, Barnabe 1542-1617 .... DLB 136
Riche, Pierre 1921- 123
Riche, Robert 1925- 108
Riche, William Harding le
See le Riche, William Harding
Richelieu, Peter
See Robinson, P. W.
Richelson, Geraldine 1922- 106
See also SATA 29
Richelson, Jeffrey T(albot) 1949- CANR-110
Earlier sketches in CA 119, CANR-43
Richemont, Enid 1940- 149
See also SATA 82
Richens, Richard Hook 1919-1984
Obituary 114
Richepin, Jean 1849-1926 184
See also DLB 192
Riches, David 1947- 128
Riches, John (Kenneth) 1939- CANR-94
Earlier sketch in CA 117
Riches, Pierre 1927- CANR-44
Earlier sketch in CA 118
Richette, Lisa Aversa 1928- 25-28R
Richetti, John J(oseph) 1938- 110
Richey, David 1939- CANR-10
Earlier sketch in CA 57-60
Richey, Dorothy Hilliard CANR-6
Earlier sketch in CA 9-12R
Richey, Elinor 1920- 45-48
Richey, Margaret Fitzgerald 1883(?)-1974
Obituary 53-56
Richey, Robert W(illiam) 1912-1978 .... CANR-17
Obituary 116
Earlier sketch in CA 25-28R
Richey, Russell E(arle) 1941- CANR-91
Earlier sketch in CA 69-72
Richie, Alexandra 183
Richie, Donald 1924- CANR-106
Earlier sketches in CA 17-20R, CANR-8, 24, 49
See also CAAS 20
Richland, W(ilfred) Bernard 1909-2003 102
Obituary 219
Richler, Daniel 1956- 137
Richler, Emma 207
Richler, Mordecai 1931-2001 .... CANR-111
Obituary 201
Earlier sketches in CA 65-68, CANR-31, 62
See also AITN 1
See also CCA 1
See also CLC 3, 5, 9, 13, 18, 46, 70, 185
See also CLR 17
See also CN 1, 2, 3, 4, 5, 7
See also CWRI 5
See also DAC
See also DAM MST, NOV
See also DLB 53
See also EWL 3
See also MAICYA 1, 2
See also MTCW 1, 2
See also MTFW 2005
See also RGEL 2
See also SATA 44, 98
See also SATA-Brief 27
See also TWA
Richler, Nancy 1957- 225
Richman, Barry M(artin) 1936-1978 . CANR-17
Earlier sketch in CA 21-24R
Richman, Irwin 1937- 165
Richman, Linda 1942- 203
Richman, Milton (Saul) 1922-1986 69-72
Obituary 119
Richman, Phyllis C(hasanow) 1939- . CANR-66
Earlier sketch in CA 89-92
Richman, Robert (Maxwell) 1914-1987
Obituary 124
Richman, Saul 1917(?)-1979
Obituary 85-88
Richman, Sophia 1941- 213
See also SATA 142
Rich-McCoy, Lois
See McCoy, Lois (Rich)
Richmond, Al 1913-1987 .... 41-44R
Obituary 124
Richmond, Anthony H(enry) 1925- 21-24R
Richmond, Cindy Packard 1948- 112
Richmond, Claire
See Titchener, Louise
Richmond, Cynthia 1956- 201
Richmond, Dick 1933- 61-64
Richmond, Douglas W(ertz) 1946- 111
Richmond, Grace
See Marsh, John
Richmond, H(ugh) M(acrae) 1932- CANR-3
Earlier sketch in CA 9-12R
Richmond, Hugh
See Young, Gordon
Richmond, Ian Archibald 1902-1965
Obituary 111
Richmond, John C(hristopher) B(lake) 1909-
Brief entry 106
Richmond, Julius B(enjamin) 1916- 29-32R
Richmond, Lee 1943- 49-52
Richmond, Lee J(oyce) 1934- 113
Richmond, Leigh (Tucker) 1911-1995 .... CANR-87
Obituary 199
Earlier sketch in CA 21-24R
See also SFW 4
Richmond, Peter 1953- 147
Richmond, Roaldus Fredrick 1910-1986(?) CANR-64
Earlier sketch in CA 114
See also Richmond, Roe
Richmond, Robert P. 1914- 21-24R
Richmond, Robert W(illiam) 1927- 53-56
Richmond, Robin 1951- 142
See also SATA 75
Richmond, Rod
See Glut, Donald F(rank)
Richmond, Roe
See Richmond, Roaldus Fredrick
See also TCWW 1, 2
Richmond, Samuel B(ernard) 1919- 41-44R
Richmond, Sandra 1948- 117
Richmond, (John) Stanley 1906- 45-48
Richmond, Velma E. B(ourgeois) 1931- ... 61-64
Richmond, W(illiam) Kenneth 1910- CANR-10
Earlier sketch in CA 25-28R
Richmond, Walt(er F.) 1922-1977 .. CANR-108
Obituary 117
Earlier sketch in CA 21-24R
See also SFW 4
Richoux, Pat(ricia) 1927- 25-28R
See also SATA 7
Richstatter, Thomas 1939- 112
Richter, Alice 1941- 105
See also SATA 30
Richter, C(harles) F(rancis) 1900-1985
Obituary 117
Richter, Conrad (Michael) 1890-1968 .... CANR-23
Obituary 25-28R
Earlier sketch in CA 5-8R
See also AAYA 21
See also BYA 2
See also CLC 30
See also DLB 9, 212
See also LAIT 1
See also MAL 5
See also MTCW 1, 2
See also MTFW 2005
See also RGAL 4
See also SATA 3
See also TCWW 1, 2
See also TUS
See also YAW
Richter, Daniel K(arl) 1954- CANR-123
Earlier sketch in CA 143
Richter, David H. 1945- CANR-92
Earlier sketch in CA 101
Richter, Derek 1907- 101
Richter, Dorothy 1906-1993 .... 29-32R
Richter, Gerard R(ichard) 1905-1995 .... 5-8R
Richter, Gerhard 1967- 191
Richter, Gisela M(arie) A(ugusta) 1882-1972 .... CANR-4
Earlier sketch in CA 5-8R
Richter, Gregory C. 1955- 146
Richter, Hans 1888-1976 .... CANR-30
Obituary 65-68
Earlier sketch in CA 73-76
Richter, Hans Peter 1925-1993 .... CANR-2
Earlier sketch in CA 45-48
See also BYA 1
See also CLR 21
See also MAICYA 1, 2
See also SAAS 11
See also SATA 6
See also YAW
Richter, Hans Werner 1908-1993 97-100
See also DLB 69
Richter, Harvena 1919- CANR-3
Earlier sketch in CA 5-8R
Richter, Horst-Eberhard 1923- CANR-20
Earlier sketches in CA 53-56, CANR-5
Richter, Irving 1911-1989 57-60
Richter, J. H(ans) 1901-1976 .... CAP-1
Earlier sketch in CA 13-16
Richter, Jean Paul
See Richter, Johann Paul Friedrich
See also EW 5
Richter, Joan 1930- 101
Richter, Johann Paul Friedrich 1763-1825
See Richter, Jean Paul
See also CDWLB 2
See also DLB 94
Richter, Lin 1936- 73-76
Richter, Linda K. 1942- 117
Richter, Maurice N(athaniel), Jr. 1930- 49-52
Richter, Melvin 1921- 201
Brief entry 110
Richter, Roland Suso 1961- 208
Richter, Stacey 1965- 195
Richter, Valentin
See Pick, Robert
Richter, Vernon
See Hutchcroft, Vera
Richter, W(alter) D(uch) 1945- 156
Richter, William L. 1942- CANR-52
Earlier sketch in CA 126
Rickard, Bob
See Rickard, Robert J(ohn) M(oberley)
Rickard, Cole
See Barrett, Geoffrey John
Rickard, Graham 1949- .... SATA 71
Rickard, John S. 238
Rickard, Robert J(ohn) M(oberley) 1945- 106
Rickards, Colin (William) 1937- 25-28R
Rickards, John 1977- 231
Rickards, Maurice 1919- 103
Rickel, Annette U. 1941- 123
Rickels, Karl 1924- CANR-1
Earlier sketch in CA 45-48
Rickels, Laurence A. 1954- 200
Rickels, Milton H. 1920- 5-8R
Rickenbacker, Eddie
See Rickenbacker, Edward Vernon
Rickenbacker, Edward Vernon 1890-1973 .. 101
Obituary 41-44R
Ricker, George Marvin 1922- CANR-20
Earlier sketch in CA 89-92
Rickert, Corinne Holt
See Sawyer, Corinne Holt
Rickert, John E(arl) 1923- CANR-24
Earlier sketch in CA 45-48
Rickett, Frances 1921- 107
Rickett, Harold William 1896-1989 ...... 17-20R
Ricketts, C(arl) E(verett) 1906- 57-60
Ricketts, Mac Linscott 1930- 130
Ricketts, Maurice L. 1922- 212
Ricketts, Norma B(aldwin) 1921- 126
Ricketts, Ralph Robert 1902-1998 116
Obituary 169
Ricketts, Viva Leone (Harris) 1900-1993 .... CAP-1
Earlier sketch in CA 11-12
Rickey, Don, Jr. 1925- CANR-9
Earlier sketch in CA 5-8R
Rickey, George Warren 1907-2002 65-68
Obituary 206
Rickey, Mary Ellen 1929- 21-24R
Rickford, John R(ussell) 1949- 126
Ricklefs, Roger 1940- 127
Rickman, Geoffrey (Edwin) 1932- 29-32R
Rickman, H(ans) P(eter) 1918- CANR-68
Earlier sketches in CA 17-20R, CANR-14, 32
Rickman, Phil
See Rickman, Philip
Rickman, Philip 239
See also HGG
Rickman, Thomas 165
Rickover, H. G.
See Rickover, Hyman G(eorge)
Rickover, Hyman G(eorge) 1900-1986 156
Obituary 119
Ricks, Chip
See Ricks, Nadine
Ricks, Christopher (Bruce) 1933- CANR-90
Earlier sketches in CA 9-12R, CANR-7, 23, 47
Ricks, David F(rank) 1927- CANR-10
Earlier sketch in CA 21-24R
Ricks, David Trulock 1936- 25-28R
Ricks, Don(ald) M(ax) 1936- 25-28R
Ricks, James 1975- 168
Ricks, Nadine 1925- CANR-53
Earlier sketches in CA 77-80, CANR-13, 29
Ricks, Patricia W. B. 1950- 228
Ricks, Thomas E. 1955(?)- 183
Rickstad, Eric 198
Rickword, (John) Edgell 1898-1982 .. CANR-36
Obituary 106
Earlier sketch in CA 101
See also CP 1, 2
See also DLB 20
See also RGEL 2
Rico, Don(ato) 1917-1985 .... CANR-28
Obituary 115
Earlier sketch in CA 81-84
See also SATA-Obit 43
Rico, Gabriele Lusser 1937- 110
Ricoeur, (Jean) Paul (Gustave)
See Ricoeur, Paul
Ricoeur, Paul 1913-2005 .... CANR-10
Earlier sketch in CA 61-64
Ricostranza, Tom
See Ellis, Trey
Ricou, Laurence (Rodger) 1944- CANR-108
Earlier sketches in CA 61-64, CANR-8, 25, 50
Riday, George E(mil) 1912- 13-16R
Ridd, Stephen (John) 1948- 149
Riddel, Frank S(tephen) 1940- 85-88
Riddel, Joseph N(eill) 1931-1991 .... CANR-5
Earlier sketch in CA 9-12R
Riddell, Alan 1927-1977 104
See also CP 1, 2
Riddell, Charlotte 1832-1906 165
See also Riddell, Mrs. J. H.
See also DLB 156
See also TCLC 40
Riddell, Chris(topher Barry) 1962- .. CANR-135
Earlier sketch in CA 186
See also SATA 114
Riddell, Edwina 1955- .... SATA 82
Riddell, Elizabeth (Richmond) 1907- CANR-80
Earlier sketch in CA 154
See also CP 1
See also CWP
Riddell, Mrs. J. H.
See Riddell, Charlotte
See also HGG
See also SUFW
Riddell, John 1942- 142
Riddell, Peter G. 1951- 239
Ridden, Brian (John) 1934- 194
See also SATA 123
Ridder, Bernard J. 1913-1983
Obituary 110
Ridder, Joseph B(ernard) 1920-1989
Obituary 127
Ridder, Marie 1925- 73-76
Ridderbos, Herman N(icolaas) 1909- 57-60
Riddle, Donald H(usted) 1921-1999 ...... 9-12R
Obituary 187
Riddle, Jean
See Weihs, Jean

Riddle, John M(arion) 1937- ... 45-48
Riddle, Kenneth Wilkinson 1920- ... 1-4R
Riddle, Maxwell 1907- ... CANR-3
Earlier sketch in CA 5-8R
Riddle, Paxton 1949- ... 217
Riddle, Thomas Wilkinson 1886-1983
Obituary ... 110
Riddle, Tohby 1965- ... SATA 74, 151
Riddleberger, Patrick Williams 1915- ... 21-24R
Riddles, Libby 1956- ... 211
See also SATA 140
Riddy, Felicity (Jacqueline) 1940- ... 128
Ride, Sally (Kristen) 1951- ... 158
Rideau, Wilbert 1942- ... 144
Ridenhour, Carlton 1960- ... 178
See also BW 3
Ridenour, Fritz 1932- ... CANR-50
Earlier sketches in CA 108, CANR-25
Ridenour, George M(eyer) 1928- ... 93-96
Ridenour, Ron 1939- ... 69-72
Rider, Alice Damon 1895-1984 ... 69-72
Rider, Brett
See Gooden, Arthur Henry
Rider, (Arthur) Fremont 1885-1962
Obituary ... 89-92
Rider, J. W.
See Stevens, Shane
Rider, John R. 1923- ... 25-28R
Ridge, Antonia (Florence) (?)-1981 ... CANR-80
Obituary ... 104
Earlier sketch in CA 9-12R
See also SATA 7
See also SATA-Obit 27
Ridge, George Ross 1931- ... 1-4R
Ridge, John Rollin 1827-1867 ... 144
See also DAM MULT
See also DLB 175
See also NNAL
Ridge, Julie 1956- ... 120
Ridge, Lola (Rose Emily) 1873-1941 ... 180
See also DLB 54
Ridge, Martin 1923-2003 ... CANR-98
Obituary ... 220
Earlier sketches in CA 121, CANR-47
See also SATA 43
Ridge, William Pett c. 1859-1930 ... 185
See also DLB 135
Ridgely, Beverly S(ellman) 1920- ... CANR-17
Earlier sketch in CA 25-28R
Ridgely, Joseph Vincent 1921- ... 5-8R
Ridgeway, James Fowler 1936- ... 106
Ridgeway, Jason
See Marlowe, Stephen
Ridgeway, Marian E(lizabeth)
1913-1982 ... 33-36R
Ridgeway, Rick 1949- ... CANR-88
Earlier sketch in CA 93-96
Ridgway, Brunilde Sismondo 1929- ... CANR-1
Earlier sketch in CA 45-48
Ridgway, John M. 1938- ... 25-28R
Ridgway, Judith 1939- ... CANR-26
Earlier sketch in CA 109
Ridgway, Judy
See Ridgway, Judith
Ridgway, Keith 1965- ... CANR-144
Earlier sketch in CA 172
See also CLC 119
Ridgway, Ronald S(idney) 1923- ... 45-48
Ridgway, Whitman H(awley) 1941- ... 101
Riding, Alan 1943- ... 122
Riding, Laura
See Jackson, Laura (Riding)
See also CLC 3, 7
See also CP 1, 2
See also RGAL 4
Ridington, Robin 1939- ... 139
Ridle, Julia Brown 1923- ... 1-4R
Ridler, Anne Barbara 1912-2001 ... CANR-80
Obituary ... 202
Earlier sketches in CA 5-8R, CANR-3
See also CBD
See also CD 5, 6
See also CP 1, 2, 3, 4, 5, 6, 7
See also CWD
See also DLB 27
Ridley, Anthony 1933- ... 107
Ridley, Arnold 1896-1984
Obituary ... 112
Ridley, B(rian) K(idd) 1931- ... 104
Ridley, Charles P(rice) 1933- ... 73-76
Ridley, Elizabeth J(ayne) 1966- ... 142
Ridley, Jane 1953- ... CANR-135
Earlier sketch in CA 149
Ridley, Jasper (Godwin)
1920-2004 ... CANR-118
Obituary ... 230
Earlier sketches in CA 13-16R, CANR-6, 22, 45
Ridley, John 1965- ... 182
Ridley, Mark (K.) 1956- ... CANR-109
Earlier sketch in CA 133
Ridley, Matt(hew White) 1958- ... CANR-107
Earlier sketch in CA 149
Ridley, Nat, Jr. ... CANR-26
Earlier sketches in CAP-2, CA 19-20
Ridley, Nicholas 1929-1993 ... 141
Ridley, Philip ... 140
See also SATA 88
Ridley, Ronald T(homas) 1940- ... 143
Ridlington, Sandy 1944- ... 162
Ridlon, Marci
See Balterman, Marcia Ridlon
See also SATA 22
Ridout, Albert K(ilburn) 1905-1998 ... CAP-2
Earlier sketch in CA 19-20
Ridout, James W. IV 1962- ... 188
Ridout, Ronald 1916-1994 ... CANR-20
Obituary ... 147
Earlier sketch in CA 103
Ridpath, Ian (William) 1947- ... 77-80
Ridpath, M(ichael) G(errans) 1926- ... 139
Ridpath, Michael 1961- ... CANR-99
Earlier sketch in CA 151
Ridruejo (Jimenez), Dionisio 1913(?)-1975 ... 176
Obituary ... 57-60
See also DLB 108
See also HW 2
Rieber, Alfred J(oseph) 1931- ... 9-12R
Rieber, R(obert) W(olff) 1932- ... CANR-3
Earlier sketch in CA 45-48
Riede, David G(eorge) 1951- ... 131
Riedel, Eunice 1931(?)-1986
Obituary ... 120
Riedel, Richard Langham 1908-1988 ... CAP-2
Obituary ... 127
Earlier sketch in CA 29-32
Riedel, Walter E(rwin) 1936- ... CANR-24
Earlier sketch in CA 45-48
Rieder, Marge ... 143
Riedesel, C(lark) Alan 1930- ... 25-28R
Riedl, John O(rth) 1905-1992 ... CAP-2
Earlier sketch in CA 21-22
Riedling, Ann Marlow 1952- ... 193
Riedman, Sarah R(egal) 1902-1995 ... CANR-37
Earlier sketches in CA 1-4R, CANR-1
See also SATA 1
Riefe, Alan 1925- ... CANR-9
Earlier sketch in CA 61-64
See also RHW
Riefe, Barbara
See Riefe, Alan
Riefenstahl, Berta Helene Amalia
1902-2003 ... 108
Obituary ... 220
See also Riefenstahl, Leni
Riefenstahl, Leni
See Riefenstahl, Berta Helene Amalia
See also CLC 16, 190
Rieff, David Sontag 1952- ... 202
Rieff, Philip 1922- ... 49-52
Riegel, Robert Edgar 1897-1983 ... 5-8R
Rieger, James H(enry) 1936- ... 93-96
Rieger, Shay 1929- ... 29-32R
Riegert, Eduard Richard 1932- ... 69-72
Riegert, Ray 1947- ... 105
Riegle, Donald W(ayne), Jr. 1938- ... CANR-43
Earlier sketch in CA 61-64
Riel, Louis 1844-1885 ... DLB 99
Rielage, Dale C. 1970- ... 235
Rielly, Edward J(ames) 1943- ... 194
Riely, John (Cabell) 1945- ... CANR-32
Earlier sketch in CA 113
Riemer, Andrew P. 1936- ... 192
Riemer, George 1920-1973 ... CAP-2
Obituary ... 41-44R
Earlier sketch in CA 25-28
Riemer, Johannes 1648-1714 ... DLB 168
Riemer, Neal 1922- ... 21-24R
Rienits, Rex 1909-1971 ... CAP-1
Obituary ... 29-32R
Earlier sketch in CA 13-14
Rienow, Leona Train 1903(?)-1983 ... 111
Rienow, Robert 1909-1989 ... CANR-36
Earlier sketch in CA 21-24R
Rienstra, Debra 1965- ... 212
Rienstra, Ellen Walker 1940- ... CANR-49
Earlier sketch in CA 123
Riepe, Dale (Maurice) 1918- ... 37-40R
Riera, Carme 1948- ... DLB 322
See also EWL 3
Ries, Al 1926- ... CANR-45
Earlier sketch in CA 120
Ries, Estelle H. 1896-1981 ... 25-28R
Ries, John C(harles) 1930- ... 13-16R
Ries, Laura ... 234
Ries, Lawrence R(obert) 1940- ... 65-68
Riese, Walther 1890-1976 ... 49-52
Rieseberg, Harry E(arl) 1892-1970 ... 5-8R
Rieselbach, Leroy N(ewman) 1934- ... CANR-24
Earlier sketches in CA 21-24R, CANR-9
Riesenberg, Felix, Jr. 1913-1962 ... 101
See also SATA 23
Riesenberg, Peter 1925- ... 145
Riesenberg, Saul H(erbert) 1911-1994 ... 49-52
Rieser, Dolf 1898-1983
Obituary ... 109
Riesman, David, Jr. 1909-2002 ... CANR-34
Obituary ... 208
Earlier sketch in CA 5-8R
Riesman, Evelyn Thompson
1912-1998 ... 21-24R
Riesner, Rainer 1950- ... 148
Riess, Claudia 1937- ... 110
Riess, Jana ... 231
Riess, Oswald George Lorenz 1896-1987 ... 5-8R
Riess, Steven A(llan) 1947- ... 112
Riess, Walter 1925- ... 17-20R
Riessen, Martin Clare 1941- ... 41-44R
Riessman, Frank 1924-2004 ... CANR-6
Obituary ... 225
Earlier sketch in CA 1-4R
Riesterer, Berthold P(hillip) 1935- ... 41-44R
Rieth, Marian
See Amft, M(arian) J(anet)
Rietz, Sandra A. 1943- ... 123
Rieu, E(mile) V(ictor) 1887-1972 ... CANR-80
Obituary ... 103
Earlier sketches in CA 1-4R, CANR-15
See also CWRI 5
See also SATA 46
See also SATA-Obit 26
Riewald, J(acobus) G(erhardus)
1910- ... CANR-44
Earlier sketches in CA 57-60, CANR-6, 21
Rifaat, Alifa
See Rifaat, Fatma Abdalla
Rifaat, Fatma Abdalla 1930- ... CANR-50
Earlier sketch in CA 123
Rifbjerg, Klaus (Thorvald) 1931- ... CANR-99
Brief entry ... 124
Earlier sketch in CA 137
See also CWW 2
See also DLB 214
See also EWL 3
Rife, J(ohn) Merle 1895-1990 ... 61-64
Rife, Joanne 1932- ... 110
Rife, Rosemary
See Nusbaum, Rosemary
Riffaterre, Michael 1924- ... 183
See also DLB 67
Riffe, Ernest
See Bergman, (Ernst) Ingmar
Riffel, Herman H(arold) 1916- ... 112
Rifkin, Adam 1972(?)- ... 157
Rifkin, Glenn H(oward) 1953- ... 229
Rifkin, Jeremy 1945- ... CANR-89
Brief entry ... 121
Earlier sketches in CA 129, CANR-50
Interview in ... CA-129
Rifkin, Libbie 1969- ... 196
Rifkin, Paul 1942- ... 127
Rifkin, Shepard 1918- ... CANR-64
Earlier sketches in CA 1-4R, CANR-1
See also TCWW 2
Rifkind, Carole 1935- ... 85-88
Rifkind, Simon H(irsch) 1901-1995 ... 109
Obituary ... 150
Rift, Valerie
See Bartlett, Marie (Swan)
Riga, Frank P(eter) 1936- ... 89-92
Riga, Peter J(ohn) 1933- ... CANR-37
Earlier sketch in CA 5-8R
Rigault, Andre 1922- ... 45-48
Rigbey, Liz 1960(?)- ... 156
Rigby, Andrew 1944- ... 61-64
Rigby, Ida Katherine 1944- ... CANR-10
Earlier sketch in CA 65-68
Rigby, Paul H(erbert) 1924- ... 17-20R
Rigby, T(homas) H(enry Richard)
1925- ... CANR-36
Earlier sketches in CA 17-20R, CANR-10
Rigden, John S. 1934- ... CANR-130
Earlier sketch in CA 127
Rigdon, Raymond M. 1919- ... 29-32R
Rigdon, Walter 1930- ... 13-16R
Rigelhof, T(errance) F(rederick) 1944- ... 112
Rigg, A(rthur) G(eorge) 1937- ... 37-40R
Rigg, H(enry Hemmingway) K(ilburn)
1911-1980 ... 29-32R
Obituary ... 93-96
Rigg, John Linton 1894- ... 5-8R
Rigg, Patricia Diane 1951- ... 206
Rigg, Robinson P(eter) 1918- ... 33-36R
Rigg, Sharon
See Creech, Sharon
Riggan, (John) Rob(inson) 1943- ... 115
Riggan, William (Edward, Jr.) 1946- ... 103
See also DLBY 2002
Riggio, Anita 1952- ... SATA 73, 148
Riggio, Thomas P(asquale) 1943- ... 109
Riggs, Cynthia 1931- ... 201
Riggs, David (Ramsey) 1941- ... 133
Riggs, Dionis Coffin 1898-1997 ... CAP-2
Earlier sketch in CA 29-32
Riggs, Fred(erick) W(arren) 1917- ... CANR-16
Earlier sketch in CA 25-28R
Riggs, James (Lear) 1929- ... 33-36R
Riggs, John R(aymond) 1945- ... CANR-73
Earlier sketches in CA 115, CANR-37
Riggs, (Rolla) Lynn 1899-1954 ... 144
See also DAM MULT
See also DLB 175
See also NNAL
See also TCLC 56
Riggs, Paula Detmer 1944- ... 162
Riggs, Robert E. 1927- ... CANR-8
Earlier sketch in CA 13-16R
Riggs, Sidney Noyes 1892-1975 ... 1-4R
Obituary ... 103
See also SATA-Obit 28
Riggs, Stephanie 1964- ... 208
See also SATA 138
Riggs, Webster, Jr. 1934- ... 168
Riggs, William (George) 1938- ... 61-64
Righter, Anne
See Barton, Anne
Righter, Carroll (Burch) 1900-1988 ... 93-96
Obituary ... 125
Righter, James H(aslam) 1916-1984
Obituary ... 113
Righter, Robert Willms 1933- ... 108
Righter, Walter C(ameron) 1923- ... 172
Right Honourable Lord Denning
See Denning, Alfred Thompson
Rightmire, G. Philip 1942- ... 135
Rigney, James Oliver, Jr. 1948- ... CANR-111
Earlier sketches in CA 140, CANR-62
See also Jordan, Robert
See also SATA 95
Rigoni, Orlando (Joseph)
1897-1987 ... CANR-11
Earlier sketch in CA 13-16R
Rigoulot, Pierre 1944- ... 207
Rigsby, Howard 1909-1975 ... CANR-70
Earlier sketch in CA 9-12R
See also TCWW 1, 2
Rigutti, Mario 1926- ... 131
Riha, Thomas 1929- ... 9-12R
Riis, Jacob A(ugust) 1849-1914 ... 168
Brief entry ... 113
See also DLB 23
See also TCLC 80
Riis, Sharon 1947- ... 136
Rijkens, Rein 1913- ... 143
Riker, H. Jay
See Keith, William H(enry), Jr., Jr.
Riker, John H. 1943- ... 111
Riker, Leigh 1941- ... CANR-129
Earlier sketches in CA 119, CANR-45
Riker, Tom L. 1936- ... 104
Riker, William H(arrison)
1920-1993 ... CANR-24
Obituary ... 141
Earlier sketch in CA 1-4R
Rikhoff, James C. 1931- ... 13-16R
Rikhoff, Jean 1928- ... 61-64
See also SATA 9
Rikhye, Indar Jit 1920- ... CANR-17
Earlier sketch in CA 93-96
Rikki
See Ducornet, Erica
Rikon, Irving 1931- ... 29-32R
Riley, Barry 1942- ... 136
Riley, Carroll L(averne) 1923- ... CANR-70
Earlier sketches in CA 25-28R, CANR-10
Riley, Charles A. II 1958- ... 150
Riley, Clara (Mae Deatherage) 1931- ... 25-28R
Riley, Dan 1946- ... 135
Riley, Dawn 1964- ... 150
Riley, Denise Kathleen 1947- ... CWP
Riley, Dick 1946-
See Riley, Richard Anthony
Riley, E(dward) C(alverley) 1923-2001 ... 9-12R
Riley, G. Micheal 1934- ... 45-48
Riley, Georgia
See Cooper, Carolyn (Joy)
Riley, Glenda 1938- ... CANR-88
Earlier sketches in CA 106, CANR-23, 46
Riley, Gregory J. 1947- ... 207
Riley, Helene M. 1939- ... 225
Riley, Helene M. Kastinger
See Riley, Helene M.
Riley, James 1777-1840 ... DLB 183
Riley, James A. 1939- ... CANR-108
Earlier sketch in CA 149
See also SATA 97
Riley, James C. 1943- ... 133
Riley, James F(rederic) 1912-1985 ... 29-32R
Obituary ... 134
Riley, James Whitcomb 1849-1916 ... 137
Brief entry ... 118
See also DAM POET
See also MAICYA 1, 2
See also PC 48
See also RGAL 4
See also SATA 17
See also TCLC 51
Riley, Jeannie C(arolyn Stephenson) 1945- ... 129
Riley, Joan 1958- ... 143
Riley, Jocelyn (Carol) 1949- ... CANR-39
Earlier sketch in CA 115
See also SATA 60
See also SATA-Brief 50
Riley, John 1937-1978 ... 184
See also DLB 40
Riley, Judith (Astria) Merkle 1942- ... CANR-90
Earlier sketches in CA 105, CANR-35
See also Merkle, Judith A.
Riley, Lawrence 1897(?)-1975
Obituary ... 61-64
Riley, Lee
See Vare, Ethlie Ann
Riley, Linda Capus 1950- ... SATA 85
Riley, Madeleine 1933- ... 25-28R
Riley, Martin 1948- ... 149
See also SATA 81
Riley, Matilda White 1911- ... 132
Brief entry ... 114
Riley, Miles O'Brien 1937- ... CANR-21
Earlier sketch in CA 104
Riley, (Thomas) Nord 1914-2001 ... 13-16R
Obituary ... 202
Riley, Pat(rick James) 1945- ... 147
Riley, R. David 1944(?)-1983
Obituary ... 111
Riley, Richard Anthony 1946- ... CANR-120
Earlier sketch in CA 101
Riley, (Hugh) Ridge(ly, Jr.) 1907-1976 ... 101
Riley, Roy, Jr. 1943(?)-1977
Obituary ... 73-76
Riley, Sam G. 1939- ... 136
Riley, Sandra 1938- ... 104
Riley, Tex
See Creasey, John
Riley, Thomas J. 1901(?)-1977
Obituary ... 73-76
Riley, Tim 1960- ... 129
Riley-Smith, Jonathan (Simon Christopher)
1938- ... 21-24R
Riling, Raymond L. J. 1896(?)-1974
Obituary ... 53-56

Cumulative Index 487 Ritsos

Rilke, Rainer Maria 1875-1926 ... CANR-99
Brief entry ... 104
Earlier sketches in CA 132, CANR-62
See also CDWLB 2
See also DA3
See also DAM POET
See also DLB 81
See also EW 9
See also EWL 3
See also MTCW 1, 2
See also MTFW 2005
See also PC 2
See also PFS 19
See also RGWL 2, 3
See also TCLC 1, 6, 19
See also TWA
See also WP
Rilla, Wolf 1925- ... 49-52
Rils
See Bohr, R(ussell) L(eRoi)
Rima
See Amir, Javed
Rima, I(ngrid) H(ahne) 1925- ... 21-24R
Rimanelli, Giose 1925- ... 184
See also DLB 177
Rimanoczy, Richard Stanton 1902-1991 . 73-76
Rimbaud, (Jean Nicolas) Arthur 1854-1891 . DA
See also DA3
See also DAB
See also DAC
See also DAM MST, POET
See also DLB 217
See also EW 7
See also GFL 1789 to the Present
See also LMFS 2
See also PC 3, 57
See also RGWL 2, 3
See also TWA
See also WLC
See also WP
Rimberg, John 1929- ... 57-60
Rimel, Duane (Weldon) 1915-1996 ... 29-32R
Obituary ... 203
Rimer, Barbara K. 1949- ... 136
Rimer, J. Thomas ... 130
Rimes, (Margaret) LeAnn 1982- ... 229
See also SATA 154
Rimington, Critchell 1907-1976
Obituary ... 61-64
Rimington, Dame Stella 1935- ... 214
Rimland, Bernard 1928- ... CANR-6
Earlier sketch in CA 13-16R
Rimland, Ingrid 1936- ... CANR-91
Earlier sketch in CA 61-64
Rimler, Walter 1946- ... 139
Rimlinger, Gaston V. 1926- ... 37-40R
Rimmer, C(harles) Brandon 1918- ... CANR-12
Earlier sketch in CA 61-64
Rimmer, Douglas 1927- ... 111
Rimmer, Robert H(enry) 1917-2001 . CANR-20
Obituary ... 201
Earlier sketches in CA 9-12R, CANR-4
See also CAAS 10
Rimmer, Steve
See Rimmer, Steven William
Rimmer, Steven William ... 183
Rimmer, W. J.
See Rowland, D(onald) S(ydney)
Rimmington, Gerald T(horneycroft)
1930- ... 17-20R
Rimpoche, (Nawang) Gelek 1939- ... 203
Rimstead, Roxanne L. 1953- ... 226
Rinaldi, Ann 1934- ... CANR-95
Earlier sketch in CA 111
See also AAYA 15
See also BYA 6, 7, 8
See also CLR 46
See also JRDA
See also MAICYA 2
See also MAICYAS 1
See also SATA 51, 78, 117, 161
See also SATA-Brief 50
See also WYA
See also YAW
Rinaldi, Nicholas Michael 1934- ... CANR-108
Earlier sketches in CA 104, CANR-22
Rinaldini, Angiolo
See Battisti, Eugenio
Rinard, Judith E(llen) 1947- ... CANR-119
Earlier sketch in CA 97-100
See also SATA 44, 140
Rinchen, Byambyn 1905(?)-1977
Obituary ... 69-72
Rinder, Lenore 1949- ... 156
See also SATA 92
Rinder, Walter (Murray) 1934- ... CANR-11
Earlier sketch in CA 69-72
Rinderle, Walter 1940- ... 140
Rindfleisch, Norval (William) 1930- ... 65-68
Rindo, Ron(ald J.) 1959- ... 155
Rinehart, Frederick Roberts 1903(?)-1981
Obituary ... 104
Rinehart, Mary Roberts 1876-1958 ... 166
Brief entry ... 108
See also BPFB 3
See also RGAL 4
See also RHW
See also TCLC 52
Rinehart, Stanley Marshall, Jr. 1897-1969
Obituary ... 29-32R
Rinehart, Steven ... 208
Riney-Kehrberg, Pamela 1963- ... 190
Ring, Alfred A. 1905- ... 29-32R
Ring, Daniel F(rank) 1945- ... 113
Ring, Douglas
See Prather, Richard S(cott)
Ring, Elizabeth 1912- ... 103
Ring, Elizabeth 1920- ... SATA 79
Ring, Jennifer 1948- ... 140
Ring, Kenneth 1935- ... 180
Ring, Malvin E. 1919- ... 120
Ring, Nancy G. 1956- ... 157
Ring, Raymond H. 1949- ... 128
Ringdal, Nils Johan 1952- ... 228
Ringdalh, Mark
See Longyear, Barry B(rookes)
Ringe, Donald A(rthur) 1923- ... 1-4R
Ringelblum, Emmanuel 1900-1944
Ringenbach, Paul T(homas) 1936- ... CANR-25
Earlier sketch in CA 45-48
Ringenberg, William C(arey) 1939- ... 191
Ringer, Alexander L(othar)
1921-2002 ... CANR-49
Obituary ... 209
Earlier sketches in CA 45-48, CANR-24
Ringer, Barbara Alice 1925- ... 9-12R
Ringer, Fritz (Franz) K(laus) 1934- ... 73-76
Ringer, R. Jeffrey 1957- ... 147
Ringer, Robert J. ... CANR-100
Earlier sketch in CA 81-84
Ringgold, Faith 1930- ... CANR-88
Earlier sketch in CA 154
See also AAYA 19
See also CLR 30
See also CWRI 5
See also MAICYA 2
See also MAICYAS 1
See also SATA 71, 114
Ringgold, Gene 1918- ... 25-28R
Ringgren, (Karl Vilhelm) Helmer
1917- ... CANR-3
Earlier sketch in CA 5-8R
Ringi, Kjell (Arne Soerensen) 1939- ... CANR-1
Earlier sketch in CA 45-48
See also SATA 12
Ringkamp, Jonathan 1929-1986 ... 153
Obituary ... 120
Ringler, Dick
See Ringler, Richard Newman
Ringler, Richard Newman 1934- ... 233
Ringler, William A(ndrew), Jr.
1912-1987(?) ... 5-8R
Obituary ... 121
Ringmaster, The
See Mencken, H(enry) L(ouis)
Ringo, John 1963- ... 199
Ringo, Johnny
See Keevill, Henry J(ohn)
Ringold, Clay
See Hogan, (Robert) Ray
Ringold, May Spencer 1914- ... 21-24R
Ringquist, Evan J. 1962- ... 146
Ringrose, David R. 1938- ... 53-56
Ringuet
See Panneton, Philippe
See also DLB 68
See also EWL 3
Ringwald, Donald C(harles)
1917-1987 ... CANR-36
Obituary ... 122
Earlier sketch in CA 21-24R
Ringwood, Gwen(dolyn Margaret) Pharis
1910-1984 ... 148
Obituary ... 112
See also CLC 48
See also DLB 88
Rinhart, Floyd (Lincoln) 1915-1996 .. CANR-96
Earlier sketches in CA 25-28R, CANR-10
Rinhart, Marion (Hutchinson)
1916- ... CANR-100
Earlier sketches in CA 25-28R, CANR-10
Rink, Oliver A(lbert) 1947- ... 125
Rinker, Rosalind Beatrice 1906-2002 . CANR-5
Earlier sketch in CA 5-8R
Rinkoff, Barbara Jean (Rich)
1923-1975 ... CAP-2
Obituary ... 57-60
Earlier sketch in CA 19-20
See also SATA 4
See also SATA-Obit 27
Rinn, Miriam 1946- ... 197
See also SATA 127
Rinpoche
See Chogyam Trungpa
Rinser, Luise 1911-2002 ... 188
Obituary ... 205
See also DLB 69
See also EWL 3
Rintels, David 1939- ... 73-76
Rinvolucri, Mario (Francesco Giuseppe)
1940- ... CANR-53
Earlier sketches in CA 21-24R, CANR-10, 26
Rinvolucri, Mina Josephine Moore
See Moore-Rinvolucri, Mina Josephine
Rinzema, Jakob 1931- ... 102
Rinzler, Alan 1938- ... CANR-12
Earlier sketch in CA 21-24R
Rinzler, Carol Ann 1937- ... 135
Rinzler, Carol Eisen (Gene) 1941-1990 ... 49-52
Obituary ... 133
Rio, Michel 1945(?)- ... 201
See also CLC 43
Riols, Noreen 1926- ... 124
Riopelle, Arthur J. 1920- ... 37-40R
Riordan, Dan
See Cook, Will(iam Everett)
Riordan, J. W.
See Feist, Gene
Riordan, James 1936- ... CANR-122
Earlier sketches in CA 69-72, CANR-11, 69
See also SATA 95
Riordan, James 1949- ... CANR-130
Earlier sketch in CA 111
Riordan, Mary Marguerite 1931- ... 106
Riordan, Michael 1946- ... CANR-37
Earlier sketch in CA 106
Riordan, Rick ... 201
Riordon, Michael 1944- ... 133
Rios, Alberto (Alvaro) 1952- ... CANR-137
Earlier sketches in CA 113, CANR-34, 79
See also AAYA 66
See also AMWS 4
See also CP 7
See also DLB 122
See also HW 2
See also MTFW 2005
See also PC 57
See also PFS 11
Rios, Francisco Giner de los
See Giner de los Rios, Francisco
Rios, Isabella
See Lopez, Diana
See also DLB 82
Rios, Julian 1941- ... 180
Earlier sketch in CA 154
Rios, Marlene Dobkin De
See Dobkin De Rios, Marlene
Rios, Tere
See Versace, Marie Teresa Rios
Riot, Pat
See Stroffolino, Chris
Riotta, Gianni 1954- ... 237
Riotte, Louise 1909-1998 ... 57-60
Riotto, Guy Michael 1943- ... 73-76
Riou, Roger 1909- ... 61-64
Ripa, Karol 1895-1983
Obituary ... 109
Ripken, Cal(vin Edward), Jr. 1960- ... 160
See also SATA 114
Ripley, Alexandra (Braid)
1934-2004 ... CANR-58
Obituary ... 224
Earlier sketches in CA 119, CANR-38
See also DA3
See also DAM POP
See also RHW
Ripley, Alvin
See King, Albert
Ripley, Ann ... 180
Ripley, Arthur 1895-1961 ... DLB 44
Ripley, C. Peter 1941- ... 218
Ripley, Catherine 1957- ... 149
See also SATA 82
Ripley, Elizabeth Blake 1906-1969 ... CANR-3
Earlier sketch in CA 1-4R
See also BYA 2
See also SATA 5
Ripley, Francis Joseph 1912- ... CANR-39
Earlier sketches in CA 1-4R, CANR-3, 18
Ripley, George 1802-1880 . DLB 1, 64, 73, 235
Ripley, Jack
See Wainwright, John
Ripley, Michael David 1952- ... CANR-70
Earlier sketch in CA 130
Ripley, Mike
See Ripley, Michael David
Ripley, Randall B(utler) 1938- ... CANR-41
Earlier sketches in CA 53-56, CANR-5, 19
Ripley, S(idney) Dillon II 1913-2001 ... 57-60
Obituary ... 194
Ripley, Sheldon N(ichols) 1925- ... 5-8R
Ripley, Stephens 1901(?)-1984
Obituary ... 111
Ripley, Theresa M(argaret) 1944- ... 85-88
Ripley, (William Young) Warren
1921- ... CANR-33
Earlier sketches in CA 33-36R, CANR-15
Rippa, S(ol) Alexander 1925- ... 53-56
Ripper, Charles L(ewis) 1929- ... CANR-1
Earlier sketch in CA 1-4R
See also SATA 3
Ripper, Chuck
See Ripper, Charles L(ewis)
Ripperger, Helmut Lothar 1897-1974
Obituary ... 53-56
Ripperger, Henrietta
See Hawley, Henrietta Ripperger
Rippey, Mari 1939- ... 112
Rippey, Robert (Max) 1926- ... 45-48
Ripple, Paula ... 112
Ripple, Richard E. 1931- ... CANR-22
Earlier sketch in CA 33-36R
Ripple Comin, Paula
See Ripple, Paula
Rippley, La Vern J. 1935- ... 33-36R
Rippon, Angela 1944- ... 126
Rippon, Marion E(dith) 1921- ... CANR-1
Earlier sketch in CA 49-52
Ripps, Susan
See Shapiro, Susan Ripps
Rippy, Frances (Marguerite) Mayhew
1929-2003 ... 89-92
Obituary ... 223
Rips, Ervine M(ilton) 1921- ... 101
Rips, Geoffrey 1950- ... 108
Rips, Rae Elizabeth 1914-1970
Obituary ... 104
Riq
See Atwater, Richard (Tupper)
Riquelme, John Paul 1946- ... 119
Risatti, Howard A(nthony) 1943- ... 49-52
Rischin, Moses 1925- ... CANR-3
Earlier sketch in CA 9-12R
Rise, Eric W. 1963- ... 151
Risebero, Bill 1938- ... 130
Riseley, Jerry B(urr, Jr.) 1920- ... CANR-13
Earlier sketch in CA 21-24R
Riseling, John J. W. 1888(?)-1977
Obituary ... 73-76
Risenhoover, Morris 1940- ... 65-68
Riser, Wayne H. 1909- ... CAP-1
Earlier sketch in CA 13-14
Rish, David 1955- ... 180
See also SATA 110
Rishell, Lyle 1927- ... 144
Risjord, Norman K(urt) 1931- ... CANR-47
Earlier sketches in CA 17-20R, CANR-7, 22
Riskin, Mary (Winifred) Walters 1949- ... 163
Riskin, Robert 1897-1955 ... 194
See also DLB 26
See also IDFW 3, 4
Riskind, Mary 1944- ... CANR-26
Earlier sketch in CA 108
See also SATA 60
Risley, Albert G. 1915- ... 168
Riss, Richard 1952- ... 81-84
Risse, Heinz 1898-1989 ... DLB 69
Rissi, Mathias 1920- ... 45-48
Rissinger, Matt 1956- ... 159
See also SATA 93
Rissman, Art
See Sussman, Susan
Rissman, Susan
See Sussman, Susan
Risso, Eduardo 1959- ... 238
Rissover, Fredric 1940- ... 33-36R
Rist, Johann 1607-1667 ... DLB 164
Rist, John M(ichael) 1936- ... CANR-18
Earlier sketch in CA 101
Rist, Ray C(harles) 1944- ... CANR-3
Earlier sketch in CA 49-52
Ristaino, Marcia R.
See Ristaino, Marcia Reynders
Ristaino, Marcia Reynders 1939- ... CANR-135
Earlier sketch in CA 127
Rist Arnold, Elisabeth 1950- ... 65-68
Riste, Olav 1933- ... CANR-12
Earlier sketch in CA 29-32R
Ristic, Dragisha N. 1909- ... CAP-2
Earlier sketch in CA 21-22
Ristikivi, Karl 1912-1977 ... DLB 220
See also EWL 3
Ristow, Walter W(illiam) 1908- ... 17-20R
Rit, Jean Qui
See Arkell, David
Ritcheson, Charles R(ay) 1925-
Brief entry ... 112
Ritchey, John A(rthur) 1919- ... 21-24R
Ritchie, (John) Andrew 1943- ... 85-88
Ritchie, Andrew Carnduff 1907-1978
Obituary ... 81-84
Ritchie, Anna Cora (Ogden) Mowatt
1819-1870 ... DLB 3, 250
Ritchie, Anne Thackeray 1837-1919 ... 180
See also DLB 18
Ritchie, Barbara Gibbons ... 73-76
See also SATA 14
Ritchie, Bill
See Edgar, Frank Terrell Rhoades
Ritchie, C(icero) T(heodore) 1914- ... 9-12R
Ritchie, Claire -1979 ... RHW
Ritchie, Daniel E. 1955- ... 162
Ritchie, Dennis (MacAlistair) 1941- ... 158
Ritchie, Donald A(rthur) 1945- ... CANR-98
Brief entry ... 106
Earlier sketches in CA 122, CANR-48
Ritchie, Donald D(irk) 1914- ... 112
Ritchie, Edwin 1921- ... CANR-35
Earlier sketch in CA 29-32R
Ritchie, Elisavietta (Yurievna
Artamonoff) ... CANR-2
Earlier sketch in CA 49-52
Ritchie, G(eorge) Stephen 1914- ... 13-16R
Ritchie, Guy 1968- ... 201
Ritchie, Harry 1958- ... 143
Ritchie, Jack
See Reitci, John G(eorge)
Ritchie, James A. 1953- ... 151
Ritchie, James McPherson 1927- ... 25-28R
Ritchie, James T. R. 1908-1998 ... CAP-2
Earlier sketch in CA 19-20
Ritchie, John C(ollins) 1927- ... 49-52
Ritchie, M(iller) A(lfred) F(ranklin)
1909-2000 ... CAP-2
Earlier sketch in CA 29-32
Ritchie, Paul 1923- ... 21-24R
Ritchie, Rebecca (T.) 1949- ... 223
Ritchie, Rita
See Reitci, Rita Krohne
Ritchie, Ruth 1900-1997 ... CANR-2
Earlier sketch in CA 1-4R
Ritchie, Simon
See Fodden, Simon R.
Ritchie, Thomas 1778-1854 ... DLB 43
Ritchie, (Harry) Ward 1905-1996 ... CANR-46
Obituary ... 151
Earlier sketches in CA 57-60, CANR-7, 22
Ritchie, William A(ugustus)
1903-1995 ... CANR-24
Earlier sketch in CA 45-48
Ritchie-Calder, Peter Ritchie
1906-1982 ... CANR-72
Obituary ... 105
Earlier sketches in CA 1-4R, CANR-4
Ritner, Peter Vaughn 1927(?)-1976 ... 77-80
Obituary ... 69-72
Ritschl, Dietrich 1929- ... CANR-24
Earlier sketches in CA 21-24R, CANR-9
Ritsos, Giannes
See Ritsos, Yannis

Ritsos, Yannis 1909-1990 ... CANR-61
Obituary ... 133
Earlier sketches in CA 77-80, CANR-39
See also CLC 6, 13, 31
See also EW 12
See also EWL 3
See also MTCW 1
See also RGWL 2, 3
Rittenhouse, Mignon 1904-1988 ... 41-44R
Ritter, Alan 1937- ... 117
Brief entry ... 113
Ritter, Ed 1917- ... 17-20R
Ritter, Erika 1948(?)- ... CD 5, 6
See also CLC 52
See also CWD
Ritter, Felix
See Kruss, James
Ritter, Gerhard 1888-1967
Obituary ... 111
Ritter, Henry, Jr. 1920- ... 93-96
Ritter, Jess(e P., Jr.) 1930- ... 37-40R
Ritter, John H. 1951- ... 195
See also AAYA 43
See also MAICYA 2
See also SATA 129, 137
Ritter, Lawrence S(tanley)
1922-2004 ... CANR-22
Obituary ... 225
Earlier sketch in CA 21-24R
See also SATA 58
See also SATA-Obit 152
Ritter, Naomi 1937- ... 138
Ritter, (William) Scott, Jr. 1960- ... 218
Ritterbush, Philip C. 1936- ... CANR-6
Earlier sketch in CA 9-12R
Ritthaler, Shelly 1955- ... 155
See also SATA 91
Ritts, Paul 1920(?)-1980
Obituary ... 102
See also SATA-Obit 25
Ritvala, M.
See Waltari, Mika (Toimi)
Ritvo, Harriet 1946- ... CANR-81
Earlier sketch in CA 124
Ritz, Charles 1891-1976
Obituary ... 65-68
Ritz, David 1943- ... CANR-123
Earlier sketches in CA 85-88, CANR-40
Ritz, Jean-Georges 1906- ... 5-8R
Ritz, Joseph P. 1929- ... 21-24R
Ritz, Karen 1957- ... SATA 80
Ritzenthaler, Pat 1914- ... 25-28R
Ritzer, George 1940- ... CANR-20
Earlier sketches in CA 53-56, CANR-5
Riva, Maria 1925(?)- ... 144
Rivard, Adjutor 1868-1945 ... 209
See also DLB 92
Rivard, David 1953- ... CANR-94
Earlier sketch in CA 159
Rivarol, Antoine Rivaroli
1753-1801 ... GFL Beginnings to 1789
Rivas, Gilberto Lopez y
See Lopez Y Rivas, Gilberto
Rivas, Manuel 1957- ... 204
Rive, Richard (Moore) 1931-1989 ... CANR-80
Obituary ... 128
Earlier sketches in CA 13-16R, CANR-27
See also BW 2, 3
See also DLB 125, 225
See also EWL 3
See also RGSF 2
Rivel, Isade
See Cuevas, Clara
Rivele, Stephen J. 1949- ... 142
Rivenburgh, Viola K(leinke) 1897-1990 . 17-20R
Rivera, Beatriz 1957- ... 195
See also SSFS 15
Rivera, (Jose) Diego 1886-1957 ... AAYA 38
Rivera, Edward 1939(?)-2001 ... 206
Rivera, Elena ... 201
Rivera, Feliciano (Moreno) 1932- ... CANR-24
Earlier sketch in CA 45-48
Rivera, Geraldo (Miguel) 1943- ... CANR-32
Earlier sketch in CA 108
See also HW 1
See also SATA 54
See also SATA-Brief 28
Rivera, Jose 1955- ... 200
See also DLB 249
Rivera, Jose Eustasio 1889-1928 ... 162
See also EWL 3
See also HW 1, 2
See also LAW
See also TCLC 35
Rivera, Marina 1942- ... 181
See also DLB 122
Rivera, Nemesio R. Canales y
See Canales, Nemesio R.
Rivera, Oswald 1944- ... 186
Rivera, Tomas 1935-1984 ... CANR-32
Earlier sketch in CA 49-52
See also DLB 82
See also HLCS 2
See also HW 1
See also LLW
See also RGAL 4
See also SSFS 15
See also TCWW 2
See also WLIT 1
Rivera-Valdes, Sonia ... 198
Rivere, Alec
See Nuetzel, Charles (Alexander)
Rivero, Eliana Suarez 1942- ... 41-44R
Rivers, Anthony 1944-1999 ... 183
Rivers, Caryl 1937- ... CANR-22
Earlier sketches in CA 49-52, CANR-4
Rivers, Clarence Joseph 1931- ... 77-80
Rivers, Conrad Kent 1933-1968 ... 85-88
See also BW 1
See also CLC 1
See also DLB 41
Rivers, Elfrida
See Bradley, Marion Zimmer
See also GLL 1
Rivers, Elias L(ynch) 1924- ... 17-20R
Rivers, Francine (Sandra) 1947- ... CANR-58
Earlier sketch in CA 130
See also RHW
Rivers, Joan
See Molinsky, Joan Sandra
Rivers, Julian Alfred Pitt
See Pitt-Rivers, Julian Alfred
Rivers, Karen 1970- ... 200
See also SATA 131
Rivers, Larry
Obituary ... 214
See also Grossberg, Yitzroch Loiza
Rivers, Patrick 1920- ... 131
Rivers, Reggie 1968- ... 239
Rivers, William L. 1925- ... CANR-7
Earlier sketch in CA 17-20R
Rivers-Coffey, Rachel 1943- ... 73-76
Riverside, John
See Heinlein, Robert A(nson)
Rives, Leigh
See Seward, William W(ard), Jr.
Rives, Stanley G(ene) 1930- ... CANR-11
Earlier sketch in CA 21-24R
Rives, William T. 1911(?)-1983
Obituary ... 111
Rivet, A(lbert) L(ionel) F(rederick)
1915-1993 ... CANR-24
Obituary ... 142
Earlier sketches in CA 21-24R, CANR-9
Rivett, Carol
See Rivett, Edith Caroline
Rivett, Edith Caroline 1894-1958
Brief entry ... 110
See also CMW 4
Rivett, Rohan (Deakin) 1917-1977 ... 25-28R
Obituary ... 135
Rivett-Carnac, Charles Edward
1901-1980 ... CAP-2
Earlier sketch in CA 19-20
Rivette, Marc 1916- ... 5-8R
Riviere, Bill
See Riviere, William Alexander
Riviere, Claude 1932- ... 102
Riviere, Jim (E.) 1953- ... 235
Riviere, Peter Gerard 1934- ... 103
Riviere, William 1954- ... 173
Riviere, William Alexander 1916- ... CANR-8
Earlier sketch in CA 5-8R
Rivington, James 1724(?)-1802 ... DLB 43
Rivkin, Allen (Erwin) 1903-1990 ... CANR-28
Obituary ... 130
Earlier sketches in CA 65-68, CANR-11
See also DLB 26
Rivkin, Ann 1920- ... 112
See also SATA 41
Rivkin, Arnold 1919-1968 ... CANR-3
Earlier sketch in CA 1-4R
Rivkin, Ellis 1918- ... 33-36R
Rivlin, Alice M(itchell) 1931- ... 33-36R
Rivlin, Gary 1958- ... CANR-118
Earlier sketch in CA 139
Rivlin, Harry N. 1904-1991 ... 17-20R
Rivlin, Paul Anthony 1952- ... 144
Rivoire, Jean 1929- ... CANR-21
Earlier sketches in CA 9-12R, CANR-5
Rivoli, Mario 1943- ... SATA 10
Rix, Donna
See Rowland, D(onald) S(ydney)
Rix, (Edward) Martyn 1943- ... 224
Rizkalla, John 1935- ... 129
Rizzo, Betty 1926- ... 111
Rizzo, Margaret ... 203
Rizzo, Mario 1948- ... 124
Rizzoli, Andrea 1914-1983
Obituary ... 109
Rizzoli, Angelo 1889-1970
Obituary ... 104
Rizzolo, S(uzanne) K(aye) 1962- ... 209
Rizzuto, Anthony 1937- ... 106
Rizzuto, James J(oseph) 1939- ... 107
Rizzuto, Jim
See Rizzuto, James J(oseph)
Rizzuto, Rahna Reiko ... 238
Ro, Ronin ... 238
Roa (y Garcia), Raul 1908-1982
Obituary ... 107
Roa Bastos, Augusto (Jose Antonio)
1917-2005 ... 131
Obituary ... 238
See also CLC 45
See also CWW 2
See also DAM MULT
See also DLB 113
See also EWL 3
See also HLC 2
See also HW 1
See also LAW
See also RGSF 2
See also WLIT 1
Roach, Archie 1955- ... 171
Roach, Catherine M. ... 226
Roach, E(ric) M. 1904- ... CP 1
Roach, Hal 1892-1992 ... IDFW 3, 4
Roach, Helen P(auline) 1903-1997 ... CAP-1
Earlier sketch in CA 11-12
Roach, Hildred 1937- ... 57-60
Roach, Jack L(eslie) 1925- ... 184
Brief entry ... 109
Roach, James P. 1907-1978
Obituary ... 77-80
Roach, Jay 1956- ... AAYA 42
Roach, Joyce Gibson 1935- ... CANR-40
Earlier sketches in CA 101, CANR-18
Roach, Marilynne K(athleen) 1946- .. CANR-12
Earlier sketch in CA 57-60
See also SATA 9
Roach, Marion 1956- ... 120
Roach, Mary C. 1959- ... 219
Roach, Mary Ellen 1921- ... 17-20R
Roach, Portia
See Takakjian, Portia
Roadarmel, Gordon 1932-1972
Obituary ... 104
Roadarmel, Paul 1942- ... 93-96
Roaden, Arliss L. 1930- ... 37-40R
Roads, Michael J. 1937- ... 208
Roadstrum, William H(enry) 1915- ... 25-28R
Roalfe, William R(obert) 1896-1979 ... 93-96
Roam, Pearl (Sovern) 1920- ... 1-4R
Roan, Tom -1958 ... TCWW 1, 2
Roark, Albert E(dward) 1933- ... 85-88
Roark, Dallas M(organ) 1931- ... 37-40R
Roark, Garland 1904-1985 ... CANR-63
Obituary ... 115
Earlier sketches in CA 1-4R, CANR-1
See also Garland, George
Roark, James L. 1941- ... CANR-19
Earlier sketch in CA 85-88
Roarke, Mike
See Kosser, Mike
Roazen, Paul 1936- ... CANR-81
Earlier sketch in CA 25-28R
Roback, A(braham) A(aron) 1890-1965 ... 5-8R
Robacker, Earl Francis 1904-1985 ... CANR-37
Earlier sketch in CA 53-56
Robakidse, Grigol 1884-1962 ... EWL 3
Robana, Abderrahman 1938- ... 65-68
Robard, Jackson
See Wallmann, Jeffrey M(iner)
Robards, Karen 1954- ... CANR-101
Earlier sketches in CA 122, CANR-42
Robards, Sherman M(arshall) 1939- .. CANR-37
Earlier sketch in CA 61-64
Robards, Terry
See Robards, Sherman M(arshall)
Robathan, Dorothy M(ae) 1898-1991 ... 41-44R
Robb, Brian 1913-1979 ... 113
Robb, Candace 1950- ... 203
Robb, David L. ... 232
Robb, David M(etheny) 1903-1990
Obituary ... 131
Brief entry ... 113
See also AITN 1
Robb, (George) Douglas 1899-1974
Obituary ... 114
Robb, Frank Thomson 1908- ... 57-60
Robb, Graham (MacDonald) 1958- .. CANR-90
Earlier sketch in CA 136
Robb, Inez (Callaway) 1901(?)-1979 ... 97-100
Obituary ... 85-88
Robb, J. D.
See Roberts, Nora
Robb, J(ohn) Wesley 1919- ... 5-8R
Robb, James H(arding) 1920- ... 9-12R
Robb, James Willis 1918- ... 41-44R
Robb, Kenneth
See Phipps, Joe (Kenneth)
Robb, Laura 1937- ... 160
See also SATA 95
Robb, Mary K(unkle) 1908-1993 ... CAP-2
Earlier sketch in CA 19-20
Robb, Nesca A(deline) 1905-1976 ... 9-12R
Robb, Peter ... 173
Robb, Peter (G.) 1945- ... CANR-142
Earlier sketch in CA 171
Robbe-Grillet, Alain 1922- ... CANR-115
Earlier sketches in CA 9-12R, CANR-33, 65
See also BPFB 3
See also CLC 1, 2, 4, 6, 8, 10, 14, 43, 128
See also CWW 2
See also DLB 83
See also EW 13
See also EWL 3
See also GFL 1789 to the Present
See also IDFW 3, 4
See also MTCW 1, 2
See also MTFW 2005
See also RGWL 2, 3
See also SSFS 15
Robben, John 1930- ... 93-96
Robbers, James E. 1934- ... 202
Robbert, Louise Buenger 1925- ... 41-44R
Robbin, (Jodi) Luna 1936- ... 103
Robbin, Tony 1943- ... 142
Robbins, Alexandra 1976- ... 214
Robbins, Anthony J. 1960- ... 126
Robbins, Brother Gerald 1940- ... 13-16R
Robbins, Bruce 1949- ... 200
Robbins, Caroline 1903-1999 ... 107
Robbins, Ceila Dame 1943- ... 118
Robbins, Daniel 1933-1995 ... CANR-3
Obituary ... 147
Earlier sketch in CA 45-48
Robbins, David L. 1954- ... 189
Robbins, Frank 1917-1994(?) ... 109
See also SATA 42
See also SATA-Brief 32
Robbins, Glaydon Donaldson 1908-1985 . 5-8R
Robbins, Harold 1916-1997 ... CANR-112
Obituary ... 162
Earlier sketches in CA 73-76, CANR-26, 54
See also BPFB 3
See also CLC 5
See also DA3
See also DAM NOV
See also MTCW 1, 2
Robbins, Henry 1928(?)-1979
Obituary ... 89-92
Robbins, Horace 1909-1982
Obituary ... 107
Robbins, Ira A(braham) 1954- ... 123
Robbins, J(ohn) Albert 1914- ... 17-20R
Robbins, Jane (Borsch) 1939- ... CANR-38
Robbins, Jane Marla 1943- ... CANR-138
Earlier sketch in CA 134
Robbins, June ... 61-64
Robbins, Kay
See Hooper, Kay
Robbins, Keith (Gilbert) 1940- ... CANR-28
Earlier sketches in CA 25-28R, CANR-11
Robbins, Ken 1945- ... SATA 94, 147
See also SATA-Brief 53
Robbins, Kenneth 1944- ... 128
Robbins, Lawrence H. 1938- ... 140
Robbins, Lionel (Charles) 1898-1984
Obituary ... 112
Robbins, Martin 1931- ... CANR-12
Earlier sketch in CA 29-32R
Robbins, Marty
See Robinson, Martin David
Robbins, Matthew ... 129
Brief entry ... 110
Robbins, Mildred Brown ... CAP-2
Earlier sketch in CA 33-36
Robbins, Millie
See Robbins, Mildred Brown
Robbins, Paul R(ichard) 1930- ... CANR-86
Earlier sketches in CA 114, CANR-35
Robbins, Raleigh
See Hamilton, Charles (Harold St. John)
Robbins, Richard (H.) 1922- ... 163
Robbins, Richard 1953- ... 200
Robbins, Richard G., Jr. 1939- ... 53-56
Robbins, Rossell Hope 1912-1990 ... CANR-2
Obituary ... 131
Earlier sketch in CA 45-48
Robbins, Roy M(arvin) 1904-1981 ... CANR-36
Earlier sketch in CA 65-68
Robbins, Ruth 1917(?)- ... 73-76
See also SATA 14
Robbins, S(allie) A(nn) 1940- ... 21-24R
Robbins, Sam
See Potter, Carole A.
Robbins, Thomas Eugene 1936- ... CANR-139
Earlier sketches in CA 81-84, CANR-29, 59, 95
See also Robbins, Tom
See also CN 7
See also CPW
See also CSW
See also DA3
See also DAM NOV, POP
See also MTCW 1, 2
See also MTFW 2005
Robbins, Tod 1888-1949 ... HGG
Robbins, Tom
See Robbins, Thomas Eugene
See also AAYA 32
See also AMWS 10
See also BEST 90:3
See also BPFB 3
See also CLC 9, 32, 64
See also CN 3, 4, 5, 6, 7
See also DLBY 1980
Robbins, Tony
See Pashko, Stanley
Robbins, Trina 1938- ... 128
See also AAYA 61
See also CLC 21
Robbins, Vesta O(rdelia) 1891-1985 ... 53-56
Robbins, Wayne
See Cox, William R(obert)
Robbins-Carter, Jane
See Robbins, Jane (Borsch)
Robe, Stanley L(inn) 1915- ... CANR-6
Earlier sketch in CA 5-8R
Robeck, Mildred C(oen) 1915- ... 57-60
Robel, S. L.
See Fraustino, Lisa Rowe
Roberge, Earl 1918- ... 85-88
Roberson, (Charles) Ed(win) 1939- ... 77-80
Roberson, Gloria Grant 1945- ... 238
Roberson, Jennifer 1953- ... CANR-91
Earlier sketches in CA 117, CANR-41
See also FANT
See also SATA 72
Roberson, John R(oyster) 1930- ... 129
See also SATA 53
Roberson, Marie
See Hamm, Marie Roberson
Roberson, Ricky James 1956- ... 101
Roberson, William H(oward) 1952- ... 110
Robert, Adrian
See St. John, Nicole
Robert, Dana L. 1956- ... CANR-127
Earlier sketch in CA 168
Robert, Marc 1927- ... 114
Robert, Marika Barna ... 9-12R
Robert, Paul 1911(?)-1980
Obituary ... 101
Robert, Paul A.
See Roubiczek, Paul (Anton)
Robert, Shaaban 1909-1962 ... EWL 3
Robertiello, Richard C. 1923- ... CANR-3
Earlier sketch in CA 9-12R

Cumulative Index 489 Robertson

Roberto, Brother
See Mueller, Gerald F(rancis)
Roberts, (Edward) Adam 1940- CANR-123
Earlier sketches in CA 21-24R, CANR-9
Roberts, Allen 1914- 29-32R
Roberts, Alvin 1930- 172
Roberts, Andrew 1963- CANR-120
Earlier sketch in CA 135
Roberts, Anthony
See Watney, John B(asil)
Roberts, Archibald Edward 1915- CANR-6
Earlier sketch in CA 57-60
Roberts, Arthur O. 1923- 25-28R
Roberts, Arthur Sydney 1905(?)-1978 85-88
Obituary 81-84
Roberts, Barney 1920- 202
Roberts, Barrie 1939- 151
Roberts, Ben
See Eisenberg, Benjamin
Roberts, Benjamin Charles 1917- 102
Roberts, Bethany .... SATA 133
Roberts, Bill
See Roberts, J. A. G.
Roberts, Bill 1914(?)-1978
Obituary 81-84
Roberts, Bleddyn J(ones) 1906-1977 ..... CAP-1
Earlier sketch in CA 13-14
Roberts, Brian 1930- CANR-12
Earlier sketch in CA 29-32R
Roberts, Bruce (Stuart) 1930- CANR-6
Earlier sketch in CA 9-12R
See also SATA 47
See also SATA-Brief 39
Roberts, Brynley F(rancis) 1931- 214
Roberts, C(atherine) 1917- 21-24R
Roberts, Carey 1935- 106
Roberts, Carlos A.
See Avila, Charles
Roberts, Carol A. 1933- 37-40R
Roberts, Cecil (Edric Mornington)
1892-1976 .... CAP-2
Obituary 69-72
Earlier sketch in CA 29-32
Roberts, Chalmers M(cGeagh)
1910-2005 .... 41-44R
Obituary 238
Roberts, Charles G(eorge) D(ouglas)
1860-1943 188
Brief entry 105
See also CLR 33
See also CWRI 5
See also DLB 92
See also RGEL 2
See also RGSF 2
See also SATA 88
See also SATA-Brief 29
See also TCLC 8
Roberts, Charles Wesley 1916-1992 ..... 17-20R
Obituary 136
Roberts, (Ray) Clayton, (Jr.) 1923- 159
Roberts, Clete 1910(?)-1984
Obituary 113
Roberts, Cokie 1943- CANR-100
Earlier sketch in CA 167
Roberts, Colette Jacqueline 1910-1971
Obituary 115
Roberts, Colin H(enderson) 1909-1990 132
Roberts, Dan
See Ross, W(illiam) E(dward) D(aniel)
Roberts, Daniel (Frank) 1922- CANR-6
Earlier sketch in CA 9-12R
Roberts, David
See Cox, John Roberts
Roberts, David Arthur 1924-1987 134
Obituary 122
Roberts, David D(ion) 1943- 101
Roberts, David S(tuart) 1943- CANR-98
Earlier sketch in CA 33-36R
Roberts, Dell
See Fendell, Bob
Roberts, Dennis W(ayne) 1947- 109
Roberts, Denys (Tudor Emil) 1923- CAP-1
Earlier sketch in CA 9-10
Roberts, Denys Kilham 1904(?)-1976
Obituary 65-68
Roberts, Derrell C(layton) 1927- 29-32R
Roberts, Donald Alfred 1897-1978
Obituary 77-80
Roberts, Donald Frank, Jr. 1939- 107
Roberts, Doreen 1922- 145
Earlier sketch in CA 108
Roberts, Dorothy (Gostwick) 1906- 183
See also CP 1
See also DLB 88
Roberts, Dorothy James 1903-1990 .... CAP-1
Obituary 131
Earlier sketch in CA 13-14
Roberts, Edgar V. 1928- 21-24R
Roberts, Edward B(aer) 1935- CANR-9
Earlier sketch in CA 21-24R
Roberts, Edward Barry 1900-1972 .... CAP-2
Earlier sketch in CA 19-20
Roberts, Edward Dryhurst 1904-1989
Obituary 129
Roberts, Edwin A(lbert), Jr. 1932- 21-24R
Roberts, Elfed Vaughan 1946- 143
Roberts, Elizabeth 1944- CANR-108
Earlier sketch in CA 148
See also SATA 80
Roberts, Elizabeth H. 1913-1998 61-64
Roberts, Elizabeth Madox 1886-1941 166
Brief entry 111
See also CLR 100
See also CWRI 5
See also DLB 9, 54, 102
See also RGAL 4
See also RHW
See also SATA 33
See also SATA-Brief 27
See also TCLC 68
See also TCWW 2
See also WCH
Roberts, Elizabeth (Allan) Mauchline 1936-
Brief entry 114
Roberts, Ellen Elizabeth Mayhew
1946- CANR-26
Earlier sketch in CA 108
Roberts, Elliott B. 1899-1988 .... 1-4R
Obituary 126
Roberts, Eric 1914- 5-8R
Roberts, Estelle (Wills) 1889-1970
Obituary 112
Roberts, Eugene (Leslie, Jr.) 1932- 97-100
Interview in CA-97-100
Roberts, Evelyn Lutman 1917-2005 65-68
Obituary 239
Roberts, F(rederick) David 1923- 5-8R
Roberts, F(rancis) X. 1932- 175
Roberts, Florence Bright 1941- 65-68
Roberts, Frances C(abaniss) 1916- 9-12R
Roberts, Francis Warren 1916- 13-16R
Roberts, Geoffrey R(ansford) 1924- 101
Roberts, Gillian
See Greber, Judith
Roberts, Gostwick
See Roberts, Gostwick
Roberts, Grant
See Wallmann, Jeffrey M(iner)
Roberts, Harold 1896(?)-1982
Obituary 108
Roberts, Harold S(elig) 1911-1970 .... CAP-2
Earlier sketch in CA 23-24
Roberts, Henry L(ithgow) 1916-1972
Obituary 37-40R
Roberts, Hortense Roberta 89-92
Roberts, Howard R(adclyffe) 1906-1982 109
Roberts, I.
See Roberts, Irene
Roberts, I(olo) F(rancis) 1925- 29-32R
Roberts, I. M.
See Roberts, Irene
Roberts, Irene 1925- CANR-88
Earlier sketches in CA 13-16R, CANR-6, 21
See also RHW
Roberts, Ivor
See Roberts, Irene
Roberts, J(ohn) A(lexander) Fraser 1899-1987
Obituary 121
Roberts, J. A. G. 1935- 192
Roberts, J(ohn) Kimberley 1935- 117
Roberts, J. R.
See Randisi, Robert J(oseph)
Roberts, James Deotis 1927- CANR-15
Earlier sketch in CA 33-36R
Roberts, James Hall
See Duncan, Robert L(ipscomb)
Roberts, Jane
See Butts, Jane Roberts
Roberts, Janet Louise 1925-1982 ...... CANR-88
Earlier sketches in CA 61-64, CANR-13
Roberts, Jason
See Bock, Fred
Roberts, Jeanne Addison 89-92
Roberts, Jim
See Bates, Barbara S(nedeker)
Roberts, Joan Ila 1935- 29-32R
Roberts, Joe
See Saltzman, Joseph
Roberts, John
See Bingley, David Ernest
Roberts, John
See Swynnerton, Thomas
Roberts, John G(aither) 1913-1993 49-52
See also SATA 27
Roberts, John M(ilton) 1916- 37-40R
Roberts, John M(orris) 1928-2003 .. CANR-141
Obituary 216
Earlier sketches in CA 85-88, CANR-16, 75
Roberts, John Maddox 1947- 183
See also FANT
Roberts, John R. 1934- CANR-12
Earlier sketch in CA 33-36R
Roberts, John Storm 1936- CANR-93
Earlier sketches in CA 25-28R, CANR-12
Roberts, John Stuart 1939(?)- 237
Roberts, Jon H. 1947- 208
Roberts, Joseph B(oxley), Jr. 1918- 41-44R
Roberts, Judy I. 1957- .... SATA 93
Roberts, Julian
See Bardens, Dennis (Conrad)
Roberts, K.
See Lake, Kenneth R(obert)
Roberts, K(enneth) B(ryson) 1923- 139
Roberts, Kate 1891-1985 107
Obituary 116
See also CLC 15
See also DLB 319
Roberts, Katherine 1962- 227
See also SATA 152
Roberts, Keith (John Kingston)
1935-2000 .... CANR-46
Earlier sketch in CA 25-28R
See also BRWS 10
See also CLC 14
See also DLB 261
See also SFW 4
Roberts, Keith 1937(?)-1979
Obituary 85-88
Roberts, Ken
See Lake, Kenneth R(obert)
Roberts, Kenneth (Lewis) 1885-1957 199
Brief entry 109
See also DLB 9
See also MAL 5
See also RGAL 4
See also RHW
See also TCLC 23
Roberts, Kenneth B. 1940- 207
Roberts, Kenneth H(arris) 1930- 33-36R
Roberts, Kevin E(rnest) A(lbert) 1940- 113
Roberts, Lawrence
See Fish, Robert L(loyd)
Roberts, Lee
See Martin, Robert (Lee)
Roberts, Leigh
See Smith, Lora R(oberts)
Roberts, Len
See Roberts, Leonard
See also CAAS 27
Roberts, Leonard 1947- CANR-119
Earlier sketches in CA 113, CANR-32
See also Roberts, Len
Roberts, Leonard W(ard)
1912-1983 .... CANR-28
Earlier sketch in CA 33-36R
Roberts, Les 1937- CANR-98
Earlier sketches in CA 128, CANR-62
Roberts, Leslie 1896-1980 103
Roberts, Lionel
See Fanthorpe, R(obert) Lionel
Roberts, Lisa
See Turner, Robert (Harry)
Roberts, Lois J. 1920- 199
Roberts, Lora
See Smith, Lora R(oberts)
Roberts, M. L.
See Mattern, Joanne
Roberts, MacLennan
See Terrall, Robert
Roberts, Madge Thornall 1929- 152
Roberts, Marguerite 1905(?)-1989
Obituary 128
Roberts, Mary D(uffy) 1925- 1-4R
Roberts, Mervin F(rancis) 1922- CANR-24
Earlier sketches in CA 65-68, CANR-9
Roberts, Michael 1945- 69-72
Roberts, Michael Symmons 1963- 238
Roberts, Michele (Brigitte) 1949- CANR-120
Earlier sketches in CA 115, CANR-58
See also CLC 48, 178
See also CN 6, 7
See also DLB 231
See also FW
Roberts, Monty 1935- CANR-119
Earlier sketch in CA 164
Roberts, Myron 1923-1992 .... CANR-31
Obituary 139
Earlier sketch in CA 29-32R
Roberts, Nancy Correll 1924- CANR-6
Earlier sketch in CA 9-12R
See also SATA 52
See also SATA-Brief 28
Roberts, Nancy N(orma) 1957- CANR-113
Earlier sketch in CA 150
Roberts, Neil 1953- 198
Roberts, Noel Keith 1929- 192
Roberts, Nora 1950- CANR-129
Earlier sketches in CA 123, CANR-45, 80
See also AAYA 35
See also BYA 14
See also MTFW 2005
See also RHW
Roberts, Oral 1918- 41-44R
Roberts, Patricia L(ee) 1936- 209
Roberts, (Thomas) Patrick 1920- 61-64
Roberts, Paul Craig 1939- CANR-22
Earlier sketch in CA 33-36R
Roberts, Paul McHenry 1917-1967 .... 1-4R
Obituary 103
Roberts, Paul William 1950- 141
Roberts, Percival R(udolph) III 1935- 41-44R
Roberts, Phil
See Roberts, Philip J.
Roberts, Philip Davies 1938- CANR-26
Earlier sketch in CA 109
Roberts, Philip J. 1948- 232
Roberts, Phyllis Barzillay 1932- 41-44R
Roberts, Rachel 1927-1980
Obituary 115
Roberts, Rand
See Parham, Robert Randall
Roberts, Randy (W.) 1951- CANR-106
Earlier sketch in CA 134
Roberts, Richard J(erome) 1928- 5-8R
Roberts, Richard W. 1935-1978
Obituary 73-76
Roberts, Rinalda
See Cudlipp, Edythe
Roberts, Robert B. 1911-1986 117
Roberts, Robert C(ampbell) 1942- CANR-31
Earlier sketches in CA 69-72, CANR-14
Roberts, Ron E. 1939- 33-36R
Roberts, Roy Allison 1887-1967
Obituary 89-92
Roberts, Rufus Putnam 1926- 1-4R
Roberts, Russell D. 1954- 200
Roberts, Sally
See Jones, Sally Roberts
See also CP 1
Roberts, Sam 210
Roberts, Sheila 1942- CANR-123
Earlier sketch in CA 102
Roberts, Spencer Eugene 1920- 89-92
Roberts, Steven V(ictor) 1943- 61-64
Roberts, Susan F. 1919- 104
Roberts, Suzanne 1931- 106
Roberts, Sydney (Castle) 1887-1966 ...... CAP-1
Earlier sketch in CA 13-16
Roberts, Tansy Rayner 1978- 201
Roberts, Terence
See Sanderson, Ivan T(erence)
Roberts, Theodore Goodridge 1877-1953 .. 212
See also DLB 92
Roberts, Thom(as Sacra) 1940- CANR-15
Earlier sketch in CA 81-84
Roberts, Thomas J(ohn) 1925- 41-44R
Roberts, Tom
See Thomas, R(obert) Murray
Roberts, Trev
See Trevathan, Robert E(ugene)
Roberts, Ursula (Wyllie) 1888-1975 201
See also Miles, Susan
Roberts, Vera Mowry 1918- 17-20R
Roberts, Virginia
See Dean, Nell Marr
Roberts, Walter Orr 1915- 131
Roberts, Walter R(onald) 1916- CANR-1
Earlier sketch in CA 49-52
Roberts, Warren (Errol) 1933- 73-76
Roberts, Warren Aldrich 1901-1990 ...... CAP-1
Earlier sketch in CA 11-12
Roberts, Wayne
See Overholser, Wayne D.
Roberts, Wesley K. 1946- CANR-120
Earlier sketch in CA 147
Roberts, Wess
See Roberts, Wesley K.
Roberts, William 1767-1849 .... DLB 142
Roberts, William 1868-1959
Brief entry 122
Roberts, William H(oward) 1950- 187
Roberts, William P(utnam) 1931- CANR-66
Earlier sketches in CA 113, CANR-32
Roberts, Willo Davis 1928-2004 .... CANR-112
Obituary 235
Earlier sketches in CA 49-52, CANR-3, 19, 47
See also AAYA 13
See also CLR 95
See also JRDA
See also MAICYA 1, 2
See also MAICYAS 1
See also RHW
See also SAAS 8
See also SATA 21, 70, 133, 150
See also SATA-Essay 150
See also SATA-Obit 160
See also YAW
Roberts, Willow
See Powers, Willow Roberts
Roberts, Yvonne 1949- 173
Robertshaw, (James) Denis 1911- 65-68
Roberts-Jones, Philippe 1924- 207
Robertson, Alec
See Robertson, Alexander Thomas Parke Anthony Cecil
Robertson, Alexander Thomas Parke Anthony
Cecil 1892-1982 104
Obituary 105
Robertson, Andrew (Beaumont)
1921-1986 134
Obituary 120
Robertson, Arthur Henry 1913-1984 .... 9-12R
Obituary 113
Robertson, Barbara (Anne) 1931- 25-28R
See also SATA 12
Robertson, Brian 1951- 101
Robertson, C(harles) K(evin) 1964- 233
Robertson, Carol P. 1934- 123
Robertson, Charles L(angner) 1927- 21-24R
Robertson, Cliff(ord Parker III) 1925- 208
Robertson, Colin 1906- 9-12R
Robertson, Constance (Pierrepont Noyes)
1896(?)-1985 .... 29-32R
Obituary 116
Robertson, Cordelia Biddle 1898(?)-1984
Obituary 114
Robertson, D(onald) J(ames)
1926-1970 .... CANR-10
Earlier sketch in CA 5-8R
Robertson, D(urant) W(aite), Jr.
1914-1992 .... CANR-9
Obituary 139
Earlier sketch in CA 61-64
Robertson, Dale 1923-
Brief entry 107
Robertson, David (Allan, Jr.) 1915- 81-84
Robertson, David 1947- 183
Robertson, Dede 1927- 114
Robertson, Denise 1933- 196
Robertson, Don 1929-1999 .... CANR-23
Obituary 179
Earlier sketches in CA 9-12R, CANR-7
See also SATA 8
See also SATA-Obit 113
Robertson, Donald S. 1918- 123
Robertson, Dorothy Lewis 1912- 25-28R
See also SATA 12
Robertson, Dougal 1924-1991 61-64
Obituary 135
Robertson, E(smonde) M(anning)
1923-1987 .... 29-32R
Obituary 121
Robertson, Edith Anne (Stewart)
1883-1973(?) CAP-1
Earlier sketch in CA 11-12
See also CP 1
Robertson, Edwin (Hanton) 1912- 130
Robertson, Elizabeth Chant 1899-1982 ... 49-52

Robertson, Ellis
See Ellison, Harlan (Jay) and Silverberg, Robert
Robertson, Eric Desmond 1914-1987
Obituary ... 122
Robertson, Frank C(hester)
1890-1969 ... CANR-64
Earlier sketches in CA 1-4R, CANR-4
See also TCWW 1, 2
Robertson, Geoffrey R. 1946- ... CANR-101
Earlier sketch in CA 147
Robertson, H(ector) M(enteith) 1905-1984
Obituary ... 113
Robertson, Heather Margaret 1942- . CANR-37
Earlier sketches in CA 93-96, CANR-17
Robertson, Howard Stephen 1931- ... 41-44R
Robertson, Ian (Campbell) 1928- ... CANR-90
Earlier sketch in CA 132
Robertson, James (Irvin), Jr. 1930- ... CANR-6
Earlier sketch in CA 9-12R
Robertson, James 1911-1988 ... 5-8R
Robertson, James Douglas 1904-1984 ... 5-8R
Robertson, James Louis 1907-1994 ... CAP-2
Obituary ... 144
Earlier sketch in CA 29-32
Robertson, James Oliver 1932- ... 111
Brief entry ... 106
Robertson, James Wilson 1899-1983 ... 109
Obituary ... 110
Robertson, Janet (E.) 1935- ... 137
See also SATA 68
Robertson, Jean (K.) 1913-1990
Obituary ... 132
Robertson, Jennifer Sinclair
1942-1998 ... CANR-5
Earlier sketch in CA 53-56
See also SATA 12
Robertson, Jenny
See Robertson, Jennifer Sinclair
Robertson, Joel C. 1952- ... 154
Robertson, John (Charles) 1951- ... 124
Robertson, Keith (Carlton)
1914-1991 ... CANR-87
Obituary ... 135
Earlier sketches in CA 9-12R, CANR-37
See also BYA 2
See also CWRI 5
See also MAICYA 1, 2
See also SAAS 15
See also SATA 1, 85
See also SATA-Obit 69
See also YAW
Robertson, Leon S(purgeon) 1936- ... 41-44R
Robertson, Lisa 1961- ... 229
Robertson, Lynn C. 1946- ... 169
Robertson, M(arion) G(ordon)
1930- ... CANR-58
Earlier sketch in CA 111
Robertson, Marian 1921- ... 111
Robertson, Martin
See Robertson, (Charles) Martin
Robertson, (Charles) Martin 1911-2004 ... 104
Obituary ... 234
Robertson, Mary D(emmond) 1927- ... 102
Robertson, Mary Elsie 1937- ... CANR-33
Earlier sketches in CA 81-84, CANR-15
Robertson, Nan 1926- ... 121
Robertson, Olive Hope 1909- ... CP 1
Robertson, Olivia (Melian) 1917- ... 9-12R
Robertson, Pat
See Robertson, M(arion) G(ordon)
Robertson, Patrick 1940- ... 61-64
Robertson, Priscilla (Smith) 1910-1989 . CAP-2
Obituary ... 130
Earlier sketch in CA 23-24
Robertson, Ray 1966- ... 214
Robertson, Robin (G.) 1953- ... 174
Robertson, Robin 1955- ... CANR-141
Earlier sketch in CA 172
Robertson, Roland 1938- ... 29-32R
Robertson, Roland Edward 1912- ... CP 1, 2
Robertson, Stephen
See Walker, Robert W(ayne)
Robertson, Thomas Anthony 1897- ... CAP-1
Earlier sketch in CA 13-16
Robertson, Thomas William 1829-1871
See Robertson, Tom
See also DAM DRAM
Robertson, Tom
See Robertson, Thomas William
See also RGEL 2
Robertson, Wally
See Robertson, Walter
Robertson, Walter 1892-1983
Obituary ... 109
Robertson, Wilfrid 1892- ... 5-8R
Robertson, William 1721-1793 ... DLB 104
Roberts-Wray, Kenneth (Owen)
1899-1983 ... CAP-2
Earlier sketch in CA 25-28
Robertus, Polly M. 1948- ... SATA 73
Robeson, Eslanda Cardoza Goode
1896-1965 ... 141
Robeson, Gerald B(yron) 1938- ... 65-68
Robeson, Kenneth
See Dent, Lester and Goulart, Ron(ald Joseph)
Robeson, Kenneth
See Johnson, (Walter) Ryerson
Robeson, Paul, Jr. 1927- ... CANR-108
Earlier sketch in CA 143
Robeson, Paul (Leroy Bustill) 1898-1976 ... 124
Obituary ... 109
See also AAYA 63
See also BW 1
Robey, Daniel 1944- ... 111
Robey, David ... 226
Robey, Edward George (Haydon) 1900-1983
Obituary ... 109
Robey, Harriet 1900- ... 107
Robey, Ralph W(est) 1899-1972
Obituary ... 37-40R
Robhs, Dwight
See Monaco, Richard
Robichaud, Gerald A(laric) 1912-1979
Obituary ... 85-88
Robichaud, Gerard 1908- ... CAP-2
Earlier sketch in CA 17-18
Robichon, Jacques 1920- ... 101
Robie, Bill
See Robie, William A., Jr.
Robie, Edward H(odges) 1886-1984 ... CAP-2
Earlier sketch in CA 19-20
Robie, William A., Jr. 1947- ... 146
Robilliard, Eileen Dorothy 1921- ... 21-24R
Robilliard, St. John Anthony 1953- ... 124
Robin
See Roberts, Eric
Robin, Arthur de Quetteville 1929-1990 ... 104
Robin, Harry 1915- ... 147
Robin, Leo 1900(?)-1984
Obituary ... 114
See also DLB 265
Robin, Ralph 1914- ... 65-68
Robin, Richard S(hale) 1926- ... 21-24R
Robinet, Harriette Gillem 1931- ... CANR-42
Earlier sketch in CA 69-72
See also AAYA 50
See also BW 2
See also BYA 13, 14, 15
See also CLR 64
See also MAICYA 2
See also SATA 27, 104
Robinett, Betty Wallace 1919- ... 41-44R
Robinett, Stephen (Allen) 1941- ... 101
Robinette, Joseph A. 1939- ... 131
Robinowitz, Carolyn B. 1938- ... 136
Robins, Corinne 1934- ... 118
Robins, Denise (Naomi)
1897(?)-1985 ... CANR-70
Obituary ... 116
Earlier sketches in CA 65-68, CANR-10, 19
See also RHW
Robins, Deri 1958- ... SATA 117
Robins, Dorothy B.
See Robins-Mowry, Dorothy B(ernice)
Robins, Eli 1921-1994 ... 109
Obituary ... 147
Robins, Elizabeth 1862(?)-1952 ... 195
Brief entry ... 116
See also DLB 197
Robins, Gina
See Feddersen, Connie
Robins, Harry Franklin 1915- ... 5-8R
Robins, Lee N(elken) 1922- ... CANR-14
Earlier sketch in CA 21-24R
Robins, Madeleine E. 1953- ... 234
Robins, Michael H(arvey) 1941- ... 133
Robins, Natalie S. 1938- ... 17-20R
Robins, Patricia
See Clark, Patricia Denise
Robins, Robert Henry 1921-2000 ... 5-8R
Obituary ... 189
Robins, Robert S. 1938- ... 144
Robins, Rollo, Jr.
See Ellis, Edward S(ylvester)
Robins, Seelin
See Ellis, Edward S(ylvester)
Robins-Mowry, Dorothy B(ernice)
1921- ... 25-28R
Robinson, A(ntony) M(eredith) Lewin
1916- ... CANR-9
Earlier sketch in CA 21-24R
Robinson, A(gnes) Mary F(rances)
1857-1944 ... 205
See also DLB 240
Robinson, A(rthur) N(apoleon) R(aymond)
1926- ... 33-36R
Robinson, Abby 1947- ... 117
Robinson, Adjai 1932- ... 45-48
See also SATA 8
Robinson, Alan R(onald) 1920- ... CAP-1
Earlier sketch in CA 11-12
Robinson, Albert J(ohn) 1926- ... 53-56
Robinson, Alex
See Robinson, Wayne Alexander
Robinson, Alice Gram 1896(?)-1984
Obituary ... 111
Robinson, Alice M(erritt) 1920-1983 ... 108
Obituary ... 109
Robinson, Aminah Brenda Lynn
1940- ... SATA 77, 159
Robinson, Andrew 1957- ... CANR-93
Earlier sketch in CA 146
Robinson, Anthony (Christopher)
1931- ... CANR-1
Earlier sketch in CA 1-4R
Robinson, Archie W. 1906(?)-1987
Obituary ... 123
Robinson, B(asil) W(illiam) 1912- ... CANR-3
Earlier sketch in CA 5-8R
Robinson, Barbara (Webb) 1927- ... 1-4R
See also MAICYA 2
See also SATA 8, 84
Robinson, Barry (James) 1938- ... 25-28R
Robinson, Betsy Julia 1951- ... 109
Robinson, Bill
See Robinson, William Wheeler
Robinson, Blackwell P(ierce) 1916- .. CANR-24
Earlier sketch in CA 45-48
Robinson, Blake 1932- ... 143
Robinson, Brooks (Calbert, Jr.) 1937- ... 116
Robinson, Bruce 1946- ... CANR-90
Earlier sketch in CA 131
Robinson, Budd
See Robinson, David
Robinson, C(harles) A(lexander), Jr.
1900-1965 ... CANR-4
Earlier sketch in CA 1-4R
See also SATA 36
Robinson, C(hester) Kelly 1970- ... 205
Robinson, (Kenneth) Casey 1903-1979 ... 189
See also DLB 44
See also IDFW 3
Robinson, Cecil 1921- ... 13-16R
Robinson, Cervin 1928- ... 61-64
Robinson, Chaille Howard (Payne) ... 13-16R
Robinson, Charles 1870-1937 ... SATA 17
Robinson, Charles 1922- ... 194
Robinson, Charles 1931- ... CANR-2
Earlier sketch in CA 49-52
See also SATA 6
Robinson, Charles E(dward) 1941- ... CANR-13
Earlier sketch in CA 77-80
Robinson, Charles Knox (Jr.) 1909-1980 ... 103
Obituary ... 97-100
Robinson, Charles M. III 1949- ... CANR-92
Earlier sketches in CA 120, CANR-46
Robinson, Charles P. III 1950- ... 156
Robinson, Chuck
See Robinson, Charles P. III
Robinson, Corinne H(ogden) 1909- ... 93-96
Robinson, Daniel N. 1937- ... 33-36R
Robinson, Daniel Sommer 1888-1977 .. 29-32R
Obituary ... 125
Robinson, David 1915- ... 81-84
Robinson, David A. 1925- ... 17-20R
Robinson, David L. 1942- ... 177
Robinson, Dean (Stewart) 1946- ... CANR-82
Earlier sketches in CA 114, CANR-36
Robinson, Debbie
See Robinson, Deborah A.
Robinson, Deborah A. 1958- ... 156
Robinson, Derek 1932- ... CANR-143
Earlier sketch in CA 77-80
See also DLBY 2002
Robinson, Donald 1913-1991 ... 25-28R
Obituary ... 135
Robinson, Donald H(oy) 1910- ... CAP-2
Earlier sketch in CA 33-36
Robinson, Donald L(eonard) 1936- ... 41-44R
Robinson, Donald W(ittmer)
1911-1980 ... CANR-12
Earlier sketch in CA 21-24R
Robinson, Dorothy W. 1929- ... SATA 54
Robinson, Douglas Hill 1918- ... CANR-8
Earlier sketch in CA 5-8R
Robinson, Earl (Hawley) 1910-1991 . CANR-43
Obituary ... 135
Earlier sketches in CA 45-48, CANR-2
Robinson, Eden 1968- ... 171
Robinson, Edgar Eugene 1887-1977
Obituary ... 73-76
Robinson, Edward G. 1893-1973
Obituary ... 45-48
Robinson, Edward L(ouis) 1921- ... 41-44R
Robinson, Edwin Arlington 1869-1935 ... 133
Brief entry ... 104
See also AMW
See also CDALB 1865-1917
See also DA
See also DAC
See also DAM MST, POET
See also DLB 54
See also EWL 3
See also EXPP
See also MAL 5
See also MTCW 1, 2
See also MTFW 2005
See also PAB
See also PC 1, 35
See also PFS 4
See also RGAL 4
See also TCLC 5, 101
See also WP
Robinson, Elwyn B(urns) 1905-1985 ... CAP-2
Earlier sketch in CA 19-20
Robinson, Eric 1924- ... 49-52
Robinson, Eugene (Harold) 1954- ... 193
Robinson, Eve
See Tanselle, Eve
Robinson, Forrest G(len) 1940- ... 41-44R
Robinson, Francis (Arthur) 1910-1980
Obituary ... 97-100
Robinson, Francis (Christopher Rowland)
1944- ... 112
Robinson, Frank M(elvin), Jr. 1928- ... 57-60
Robinson, Frank M(alcolm) 1926- ... CANR-80
Earlier sketches in CA 49-52, CANR-3, 19
See also SFW 4
Robinson, Frank S(teven) 1947- ... 97-100
Robinson, Fred Colson 1930- ... 37-40R
Robinson, Fred Miller 1942- ... 107
Robinson, Glen(dal P.) 1953- ... 156
See also SATA 92
Robinson, Godfrey Clive 1913- ... 13-16R
Robinson, Greg 1966- ... 228
Robinson, Gustavus H. 1881-1972
Obituary ... 37-40R
Robinson, H(enry) Basil 1919- ... CANR-82
Earlier sketch in CA 131
Robinson, Haddon W. 1931- ... 73-76
Robinson, Halbert B(enefiel)
1925-1981 ... CANR-9
Earlier sketch in CA 17-20R
Robinson, Harlow (Loomis) 1950- ... 128
Robinson, Helen Caister
1899-1986 ... CANR-16
Earlier sketch in CA 93-96
Robinson, Helen Mansfield 1906-1988 . 13-16R
Robinson, Helene M. ... 13-16R
Robinson, Henry Crabb 1775-1867 ... DLB 107
Robinson, Henry Morton 1898-1961
Obituary ... 116
Robinson, Herbert Spencer ... 93-96
Robinson, Horace W(illiam) 1909- ... 93-96
Robinson, Howard 1885-1977 ... CAP-1
Earlier sketch in CA 13-14
Robinson, Hubbell 1905-1974
Obituary ... 53-56
Robinson, Ira E(dwin) 1927- ... 81-84
Robinson, J(ohn) Lewis 1918- ... 107
Robinson, J(ohn) W(illiam) 1934- ... 17-20R
Robinson, James A(rthur) 1932- ... 17-20R
Robinson, James Harvey 1863-1936 ... 184
See also DLB 47
Robinson, James K(eith) 1916- ... 17-20R
Robinson, James L. 1945- ... 149
Robinson, James M(cConkey) 1924- ... 13-16R
Robinson, Jan M. 1933- ... 61-64
See also SATA 6
Robinson, Jancis (Mary) 1950- ... CANR-118
Earlier sketches in CA 128, CANR-60
Robinson, Jane 1959- ... 224
Robinson, Janet O(live) 1939- ... 33-36R
Robinson, Janice S(tevenson) 1941- ... 111
Robinson, Jay (Luke) 1932- ... 41-44R
Robinson, Jean O. 1934- ... 29-32R
See also SATA 7
Robinson, Jeffrey 1945- ... CANR-98
Earlier sketches in CA 121, CANR-37
Robinson, Jerry 1922-
Brief entry ... 112
See also SATA-Brief 34
Robinson, Jill 1936- ... CANR-120
Earlier sketch in CA 102
Interview in ... CA-102
See also CLC 10
Robinson, Jo Ann Ooiman 1942- ... 111
Robinson, Joan (Violet) 1903-1983 ... CANR-6
Obituary ... 110
Earlier sketch in CA 9-12R
See also MTCW 1
Robinson, Joan (Mary) G(ale Thomas)
1910-1988 ... CANR-80
Earlier sketches in CA 5-8R, CANR-5
See also CWRI 5
See also SATA 7
Robinson, John A(rthur) T(homas)
1919-1983 ... CANR-6
Obituary ... 111
Earlier sketch in CA 5-8R
Robinson, John W(esley) 1929- ... CANR-2
Earlier sketch in CA 49-52
Robinson, Joseph 1927-1999 ... 45-48
Obituary ... 181
Robinson, Joseph Frederick 1912-1982 . 13-16R
Robinson, Joseph William 1908- ... CAP-2
Earlier sketch in CA 25-28
Robinson, Julian 1931- ... 172
Robinson, Karl Frederic 1904-1967 ... CANR-5
Earlier sketch in CA 5-8R
Robinson, Kathleen
See Robinson, Chaille Howard (Payne)
Robinson, Kenneth (Ernest) 1914-2005 ... 5-8R
Obituary ... 235
Robinson, Kevin 1951- ... 145
Robinson, Kim Stanley 1952- ... CANR-139
Earlier sketches in CA 126, CANR-113
See also AAYA 26
See also CLC 34
See also CN 6, 7
See also MTFW 2005
See also SATA 109
See also SCFW 2
See also SFW 4
Robinson, L(eonard) W(allace)
1912-1999 ... 69-72
Robinson, Laura (Jane) 1958- ... 177
Robinson, Leah Ruth ... 176
Robinson, Lee 1948- ... 172
See also SATA 110
Robinson, (Esme Stuart) Lennox 1886-1958
Brief entry ... 120
See also DLB 10
See also RGEL 2
Robinson, Leonard A. 1904(?)-1980 ... 97-100
Robinson, Lewis 1971- ... 223
Robinson, Lillian S. 1941- ... 172
Robinson, Linda 1960- ... 143
Robinson, Lisa 1936- ... 93-96
Robinson, Lloyd
See Silverberg, Robert
Robinson, Logan Gilmore 1949- ... 108
Robinson, Louie, Jr. 1926- ... 107
Robinson, Lynda S(uzanne) 1951- ... CANR-71
Earlier sketch in CA 145
See also SATA 107
Robinson, Lytle W(ebb) 1913-1997 ... 61-64
Robinson, Mabel Louise 1874-1962 ... 191
Obituary ... 113
See also DLB 22
Robinson, Mairi 1945- ... 123
Robinson, Margaret A(twood) 1937- ... 107
Robinson, Marguerite S. 1935- ... 49-52
Robinson, Marileta 1942- ... 101
See also SATA 32
Robinson, Marilynne 1944- ... CANR-140
Earlier sketches in CA 116, CANR-80
See also CLC 25, 180
See also CN 4, 5, 6, 7
See also DLB 206
See also MTFW 2005
Robinson, Martin David 1925-1982
Obituary ... 108
Robinson, Mary 1758-1800 ... DLB 158
See also FW

Cumulative Index 491 Rodden

Robinson, Matt(hew Thomas, Jr.)
1937-2002 45-48
Obituary 209
Robinson, Maudie Millian Oller
1914- CANR-8
Earlier sketch in CA 61-64
See also SATA 11
Robinson, Maurice R(ichard) 1895-1982
Obituary 106
See also SATA-Obit 29
Robinson, Max (C.) 1939-1988 124
Obituary 127
Brief entry 110
Interview in CA-124
See also BW 1
Robinson, Michael J(ay) 1945- 113
Robinson, Nancy K(onheim)
1942-1994 .... CANR-24
Obituary 144
Earlier sketch in CA 106
See also SATA 32, 91
See also SATA-Brief 31
See also SATA-Obit 79
Robinson, Nancy (Lou) M(ayer) 1930- 61-64
Robinson, Norman H(amilton) G(alloway)
1912- 13-16R
Robinson, O(liver) Preston 1903-1990 .. 13-16R
Robinson, (Frances) Olvis 1923- 53-56
Robinson, P. W. 1893- 103
Robinson, Patricia
See Goedicke, Patricia (McKenna)
Robinson, Patricia Colbert 1923- 77-80
Robinson, Patrick 1940- CANR-95
Earlier sketch in CA 154
Robinson, Paul 1940- 81-84
Robinson, Paul H. 1948- 171
Robinson, Peter 1950- CANR-110
Earlier sketches in CA 147, CANR-67
See also CN 6, 7
Robinson, Peter (Mark) 1957- CANR-99
Earlier sketch in CA 149
Robinson, Phil Alden 1950- 139
Robinson, Philip (Bedford) 1926- CANR-16
Earlier sketch in CA 21-24R
Robinson, Philip (Samuel) 1946- 129
Robinson, Phyllis C(umins) 1924- 148
Robinson, Randall 1941- 191
Robinson, Ras 1935- 105
Robinson, Ray(mond Kenneth)
1920- CANR-98
Earlier sketch in CA 77-80
See also SATA 23
Robinson, Ray Charles 1932(?)-2004
Obituary 228
Brief entry 115
Robinson, Raymond Henry 1927- 41-44R
Robinson, Richard c. 1545-1607 .... DLB 167
Robinson, Richard 1924- 175
Robinson, Richard 1945- CANR-13
Earlier sketch in CA 57-60
Robinson, Richard Dunlop 1921- 5-8R
Robinson, Robert 1886-1975
Obituary 113
Robinson, Robert (Reginald) 1922- ... CANR-14
Earlier sketch in CA 41-44R
Robinson, Robert 1927- 9-12R
Robinson, Robert H(ouston) 1936- CANR-6
Earlier sketch in CA 5-8R
Robinson, Roland Inwood 1907- CANR-1
Earlier sketch in CA 1-4R
Robinson, Rollo S(mith) 1915- 41-44R
Robinson, Rose 77-80
Robinson, Roxana (Barry) CANR-58
Earlier sketch in CA 128
Robinson, Sally 1933- 145
Robinson, Selma 1899(?)-1977
Obituary 73-76
Robinson, Shari
See McGuire, Leslie (Sarah)
Robinson, Sharon 1950- CANR-87
Earlier sketch in CA 154
See also SATA 162
Robinson, Sheila Mary 1928- CANR-62
Brief entry 126
Earlier sketch in CA 131
Interview in CA-131
Robinson, Sidney K. 1943- CANR-33
Earlier sketch in CA 113
Robinson, Sister Marian Dolores 1916- ... 9-12R
Robinson, Smokey
See Robinson, William, Jr.
See also CLC 21
Robinson, Sondra Till 1931- CANR-7
Earlier sketch in CA 53-56
Robinson, Spider 1948- CANR-87
Earlier sketches in CA 65-68, CANR-11
See also AAYA 35
See also SATA 118
See also SFW 4
See also YAW
Robinson, Sue
See Robinson, Susan Maria
Robinson, Susan Maria 1955- 173
See also SATA 105
Robinson, Suzanne
See Robinson, Lynda S(uzanne)
Robinson, T(homas) H(eath)
1869-1950 .... SATA 17
Robinson, T(homas) M(ore) 1936- 29-32R
Robinson, Terry 1916- 108
Robinson, Therese 1797-1870
See Talvj
See also DLB 59
Robinson, Thomas W. 1935- 33-36R
Robinson, Trevor 1929- 53-56
Robinson, Vaughan 1957- CANR-93
Earlier sketch in CA 132
Robinson, (Wanda) Veronica 1926- 105
See also SATA 30
Robinson, Vince
See Newton, Michael
Robinson, Virgil E. 1908-1985 .... 21-24R
Robinson, W(illiam) Gordon
1903-1977 .... CANR-5
Earlier sketch in CA 5-8R
Robinson, W(illiam) Heath
1872-1944 .... SATA 17
Robinson, W(illiam) R(onald) 1927- 21-24R
Robinson, W. Stitt
See Robinson, W(alter) Stitt, Jr.
Robinson, W(alter) Stitt, Jr. 1917- CANR-53
Brief entry 105
Earlier sketch in CA 126
Robinson, Wayne 1916- 1-4R
Robinson, Wayne A(ustin) 1937- 73-76
Robinson, Wayne Alexander 1969- 226
Robinson, Wayne C. 1955- 156
Robinson, Wilhelmena S(impson)
1912- 25-28R
Robinson, Willard B(ethurem) 1935- 57-60
Robinson, William, Jr. 1940-
Brief entry 116
See also Robinson, Smokey
Robinson, William Childs 1897-1982 .... 1-4R
Obituary 116
Robinson, William F(rank) 1946- 118
Robinson, William H. 1912-1984
Obituary 111
Robinson, William H(enry) 1922- CANR-25
Earlier sketch in CA 37-40R
See also BW 1
Robinson, William I. 1959- 127
Robinson, William P(owell) 1910-1984 .... 5-8R
Robinson, William Wheeler 1918- ... CANR-18
Earlier sketches in CA 5-8R, CANR-3
Robison, Bonnie 1924- 57-60
See also SATA 12
Robison, David V. 1911(?)-1978 93-96
Obituary 81-84
Robison, Mabel Otis 1891-1978 .... CAP-1
Earlier sketch in CA 11-12
Robison, Mary 1949- CANR-87
Brief entry 113
Earlier sketch in CA 116
Interview in CA-116
See also CLC 42, 98
See also CN 4, 5, 6, 7
See also DLB 130
See also RGSF 2
Robison, Nancy L(ouise) 1934- 93-96
See also SATA 32
Robison, Sophia Moses 1888-1969 .... 5-8R
Obituary 103
Robitscher, Jonas B(ondi, Jr.)
1920-1981 .... CANR-19
Obituary 103
Earlier sketch in CA 21-24R
Robles, Emmanuel 1914-1995 81-84
Obituary 148
See also DLB 83
See also EWL 3
Robles, Harold E. 1948- 151
See also SATA 87
Robles, Mireya 1934- 81-84
See also HW 1
Robley, Grace 1918- 61-64
Robley, Rob
See Robley, Wendell
Robley, Wendell 1916- 61-64
Robo, Etienne 1879- CAP-1
Earlier sketch in CA 11-12
Robock, Stefan H. 1915- 17-20R
Robotham, Rosemarie 1957- 181
Robottom, John 1934- CANR-38
Earlier sketches in CA 29-32R, CANR-16
See also SATA 7
Robsjohn-Gibbings, Terence Harold 1905-1976
Obituary 69-72
Robson, B(rian) T(urnbull) 1939- 29-32R
Robson, D(erek) I(an) 1935- 25-28R
Robson, Dirk
See Robinson, Derek
Robson, E(manuel) W(alter) 1897- 65-68
Robson, Elizabeth 1942- 101
Robson, Eric 1939- .... SATA 82
Robson, Ernest (Mack)
1902-1988(?) CANR-24
Earlier sketch in CA 45-48
Robson, James 1890-1981 .... 5-8R
Robson, Jeremy 1939- CANR-4
Earlier sketch in.CA 5-8R
See also CP 1, 2
Robson, John M(ercel) 1927- CANR-28
Earlier sketch in CA 29-32R
Robson, Justina 1968- 195
Robson, L(eslie) L(loyd) 1931-1990 132
Robson, Lucia St. Clair 1942- CANR-51
Earlier sketches in CA 108, CANR-27
See also TCWW 2
Robson, Marion M. 1908- 89-92
Robson, Roy R(aymond) 1963- CANR-137
Earlier sketch in CA 162
Robson, Ruthann 1956- 139
See also GLL 2
Robson, W(illiam) W(allace) 1923-1993 158
Robson, William Alexander 1895-1980 103
Obituary 97-100
Robson, William N. .... AITN 1
Roby, Kimberla Lawson 1965- 187
Roby, Kinley E. 1929- 77-80
Roby, Mary Linn CANR-103
Earlier sketches in CA 13-16R, CANR-7
Roby, Pamela A. 1942- 29-32R
Roby, Robert C(urtis) 1922- 5-8R
Robyns, Gwen 1917- 93-96
Roca-Pons, Josep 1914- 49-52
Roccapriore, Marie 1933- 115
Roccatagliata Ceccardi, Ceccardo
1871-1919 .... DLB 114
Roch, John H(enry) 1916- 102
Rocha, Adolfo 1907-1995 141
Obituary 147
See also Torga, Miguel
Rocha, Adolfo Correia da
See Rocha, Adolfo
Rocha, Guy Louis 1951- 128
Rocha, Rina Garcia
See Garcia Rocha, Rina
Rochard, Henri
See Charlier, Roger H(enri)
Rochat, Philippe 1950- 212
Rochberg-Halton, Eugene 1950- 111
Roche, A. K.
See Abisch, Roslyn Kroop and
Kaplan, Boche
Roche, Alex F. 1921- 144
Roche, Alphonse Victor 1895-1991 104
Roche, Billy
See Roche, William (Michael)
See also CD 6
Roche, Daniel(-Robert) 1935- CANR-95
Earlier sketch in CA 128
Roche, Denis (Mary) 1967- 167
See also SATA 99
Roche, Douglas J. 1929- 101
Roche, George Charles III 1935- 29-32R
Roche, J. Jeffrey 1916(?)-1975
Obituary 61-64
Roche, John
See Le Roi, David (de Roche)
Roche, John P(earson) 1923-1994 69-72
Roche, Judith 210
Roche, Kennedy Francis 1911- 61-64
Roche, Orion 1948- 61-64
Roche, Owen I. A. 1911(?)-1973
Obituary 41-44R
Roche, P(atricia) K. 1935- 158
Brief entry 112
See also SATA 57
See also SATA-Brief 34
Roche, Paul 1928- CANR-4
Earlier sketch in CA 5-8R
See also CP 1, 2, 3, 4, 5, 6, 7
Roche, T(homas) W(illiam) E(dgar)
1919-1970(?) CAP-2
Earlier sketch in CA 21-22
Roche, Terry
See Poole, Peggy
Roche, Thomas P(atrick), Jr. 1931- 106
Roche, William (Michael) 1949- 205
See also Roche, Billy
See also CBD
See also CD 5
See also DLB 233
Rochefort, Christiane 1917- .... CWW 2
See also GLL 2
Rochelle, Jay C. 1938- 53-56
Rochelle, Mercedes 1955- 140
Rochemont, Louis de
See de Rochemont, Louis
Rocher, Guy 1924- CANR-108
Earlier sketches in CA 45-48, CANR-24, 49
Rocher, Ludo 1926- 185
Brief entry 106
Rochester
See Wilmot, John
See also RGEL 2
Rochester, Devereaux 1917- 105
Rochester, Harry A(rthur) 1897(?)-1983
Obituary 109
Rochester, J. Martin 1945- CANR-144
Earlier sketch in CA 37-40R
Rochester, Jack B. 1944- 122
Rochlin, Doris 1932- CANR-67
Earlier sketch in CA 128
Rochlin, Gregory 1912-2000 49-52
Rochlin, Harriet 1924- 117
Rochlitz, Rainer 1946- 162
Rochman, Hazel 1938- 144
See also SATA 105
Rochmis, Lyda N(onne) 1912- 29-32R
Rochon, Esther 1948- .... DLB 251
Rock, Andrea 229
Rock, Chris 1966- 222
Rock, David (Peter) 1945- CANR-19
Earlier sketch in CA 101
Rock, Gail 201
Brief entry 111
See also SATA-Brief 32
Rock, Howard 1911-1976 .... DLB 127
Rock, Howard B. 1944- CANR-120
Earlier sketch in CA 139
Rock, Irvin 1922- CANR-10
Earlier sketch in CA 21-24R
Rock, James M(artin) 1935- 102
Rock, Joanne T. 221
Rock, John 1890-1984 156
Obituary 114
Rock, Maxine 1940- 113
See also SATA 108
Rock, Milton L(ee) 1921- 49-52
Rock, Peter 1967- 206
Rock, Phillip 1927-2004 101
Obituary 227
Rock, Richard
See Mainprize, Don
Rock, Stanley A(rthur) 1937- 101
Rock, William R(ay) 1930- 41-44R
Rockar, Lee 1928- CANR-92
Earlier sketch in CA 13-16R
Rockcastle, Verne N(orton) 1920- 73-76
Rocke, Russell 1945- 33-36R
Rockefeller, David 1915- 214
Rockefeller, John D(avison Sr.) 1839-1937 . 169
Brief entry 116
Rockefeller, John Davison III 1906-1978 . 81-84
Obituary 77-80
Rockefeller, John William, Jr. 1899(?)-1987
Obituary 122
Rocker, Fermin 1907- .... SATA 40
Rockfern, Danielle
See Nolan, Frederick William
Rockingham, Montague
See Nye, Nelson C(oral)
Rockland, Mae Shafter 1937- 65-68
Rockland, Michael Aaron 1935- CANR-64
Earlier sketches in CA 37-40R, CANR-32
Rockley, L(awrence) E(dwin)
1916-1995 .... CANR-27
Earlier sketch in CA 29-32R
Rocklin, Joanne 1946- CANR-110
Earlier sketch in CA 151
See also SATA 86, 134
Rocklin, Ross Louis 1913-1988 .... CANR-80
Obituary 182
Earlier sketch in CA 61-64
See also SFW 4
Rocklynne, Ross
See Rocklin, Ross Louis
Rockman, Alexis 1962- 173
Rockmore, Tom 1942- 127
Rockne, Dick 1939- 61-64
Rockowitz, Murray 1920- 25-28R
Rocks, Burton 227
Rocks, Lawrence 1933- 85-88
Rockwell, Anne F(oote) 1934- CANR-87
Earlier sketches in CA 21-24R, CANR-22, 45
See also CWRI 5
See also MAICYA 1, 2
See also SAAS 19
See also SATA 33, 71, 114, 162
Rockwell, Bart
See Pellowski, Michael (Joseph)
Rockwell, F(rederick) F(rye) 1884-1976 ... 49-52
Obituary 103
Rockwell, Gail .... SATA-Brief 36
Rockwell, Harlow 1910-1988 .... CANR-45
Obituary 125
Earlier sketches in CA 109, CANR-22
See also SATA 33
See also SATA-Obit 56
Rockwell, Jane 1929- 65-68
Rockwell, John (Sargent) 1940- 126
Brief entry 114
Interview in CA-126
Rockwell, Kiffin Ayres 1917- 37-40R
Rockwell, Matt
See Rowland, D(onald) S(ydney)
Rockwell, Norman (Percevel)
1894-1978 89-92
Obituary 81-84
See also AAYA 54
See also DLB 188
See also SATA 23
Rockwell, Theodore (III) 1922- 140
Rockwell, Thomas 1933- CANR-44
Earlier sketch in CA 29-32R
See also CLR 6
See also MAICYA 1, 2
See also SATA 7, 70
Rockwell, Wilson (Miller) 1909- CAP-2
Earlier sketch in CA 19-20
Rockwood, Joyce 1947- CANR-6
Earlier sketch in CA 57-60
See also SATA 39
Rockwood, Louis G. 1925- 45-48
Rockwood, Roy CANR-27
Earlier sketches in CAP-2, CA 19-20
See also McFarlane, Leslie (Charles) and
Stratemeyer, Edward L.
See also CCA 1
See also SATA 1, 67
Rod, Edouard 1857-1910 .... TCLC 52
Rodahl, Kaare 1917- 9-12R
Rodale, J(erome) I(rving) 1898-1971
Obituary 29-32R
Rodale, Robert (David) 1930-1990 53-56
Obituary 132
Rodan, Paul N. Rosenstein
See Rosenstein-Rodan, Paul N.
Rodanas, Kristina 1952- .... SATA 155
Rodari, Gianni 1920-1980 219
See also CLR 24
Rodarmor, William 1942- 140
Rodaway, Angela 1918- 120
Rodberg, Leonard S(idney) 1932- CANR-24
Earlier sketch in CA 45-48
Rodberg, Lillian 1936- 29-32R
Rodburg, Maxine 185
Rodd, Kathleen Tennant
See Rodd, Kylie Tennant
See also SATA 57
See also SATA-Obit 55
Rodd, Kylie Tennant 1912-1988 .... CANR-26
Obituary 124
Earlier sketches in CA 5-8R, CANR-5
See also Rodd, Kathleen Tennant and
Tennant, Kylie
See also MTCW 1
Rodda, Charles 1891-1976 .... 5-8R
Rodda, Emily 1948- CANR-127
Earlier sketch in CA 164
See also CLR 32
See also SATA 97, 146
Rodda, Peter (Gordon) 1937-2003 81-84
Obituary 216
Roddam, Franc(is George) 1946- 208
Rodden, John (Gallagher) 1956- 131

Roddenberry, Eugene Wesley
1921-1991 .... CANR-37
Obituary 135
Earlier sketch in CA 110
See also Roddenberry, Gene
See also SATA 45
See also SATA-Obit 69
Roddenberry, Gene
See Roddenberry, Eugene Wesley
See also AAYA 5
See also CLC 17
See also SATA-Obit 69
Roddick, Alan (Melven) 1937- CANR-15
Earlier sketch in CA 77-80
See also CP 2
Roddick, Anita (Lucia) 1942- CANR-104
Earlier sketch in CA 140
Roddick, Ellen 1936- 41-44R
See also Meade, Ellen
Roddie, Shen .... SATA 153
Roddis, Louis Harry 1887-1969 .... 5-8R
Roddis, Roland J. 1908- 5-8R
Rodd-Marling, Yvonne 1912-1982
Obituary 107
Roddy, Lee 1921- 123
See also SATA 57
Rodefer, Stephen 1940- CANR-23
Earlier sketch in CA 107
Rodell, Fred 1907-1980
Obituary 97-100
Rodell, Marie F(reid) 1912-1975
Obituary 61-64
Roden, Claudia CANR-143
Earlier sketch in CA 159
Roden, Michael 1962- 156
Rodenas, Paula .... SATA 73
Rodenberg, Julius 1884-1970
Obituary 104
Rodenburg, Patsy 1953- 223
Roder, Wolf 1932- 17-20R
Roderus, Frank 1942- CANR-87
Earlier sketches in CA 89-92, CANR-17, 38
See also TCWW 1, 2
Rodes, John E(dward) 1923-2000 .... 13-16R
Obituary 192
Rodes, Robert Emmet, Jr. 1927- 112
Rodewyk, Adolf 1894- 65-68
Rodge, Mary King 1914- 187
Rodger, Alec
See Rodger, Thomas Alexander
Rodger, Anne 1910-1983
Obituary 111
Rodger, Ian (Graham) 1926- CANR-4
Earlier sketch in CA 5-8R
Rodger, N(icholas) A(ndrew) M(artin)
1949- 172
Rodger, Richard 1947- 143
Rodger, Thomas Alexander 1907-1982
Obituary 106
Rodgers, Alan (Paul) 1959- 168
See also HGG
Rodgers, Audrey T(ropauer) 1923- 148
Rodgers, Betsy (Aikin-Sneath) 1907- CAP-1
Earlier sketch in CA 13-14
Rodgers, Betty June (Flint) 1921- 9-12R
Rodgers, Brian 1910-1987 .... 29-32R
Rodgers, Buck
See Rodgers, Francis G.
Rodgers, Carolyn M(arie) 1945- CANR-70
Earlier sketches in CA 45-48, CANR-2, 27
See also CAAS 13
See also BW 2, 3
See also CP 2, 3, 4, 5, 6, 7
See also CWP
See also DLB 41
Rodgers, Daniel T(racy) 1942- 124
Rodgers, Dorothy F(einer) 1909-1992 89-92
Obituary 139
Rodgers, Eamonn 1941- 202
Rodgers, Eugene 1939- 132
Rodgers, Francis G. 1926- 123
Rodgers, Frank
See Infield, Glenn (Berton)
Rodgers, Frank 1944- 137
See also SATA 69
Rodgers, Frank P(eter) 1924- 9-12R
Rodgers, Franklin C. 1931- 133
Rodgers, Gordon 1952- 218
Rodgers, Harrell R(oss), Jr. 1939- CANR-50
Earlier sketches in CA 53-56, CANR-7, 25
Rodgers, Joann Ellison 1941- 77-80
Rodgers, John (Charles) 1906-1993 .... CAP-1
Earlier sketch in CA 11-12
Rodgers, Joni 1962- 197
Rodgers, Marie (E.) 1943- 177
Rodgers, Mary 1931- CANR-90
Earlier sketches in CA 49-52, CANR-8, 55
Interview in CANR-8
See also BYA 5
See also CLC 12
See also CLR 20
See also CWRI 5
See also JRDA
See also MAICYA 1, 2
See also SATA 8, 130
Rodgers, Pepper
See Rodricks, Daniel J.
Rodgers, Raboo 1945- 119
Rodgers, Richard (Charles) 1902-1979 89-92
See also AAYA 52
See also DFS 1
Rodgers, Rick 1953- 177
Rodgers, Shirlaw Johnston .... TCWW 2
Rodgers, Stanley 1928-1977
Obituary 106
Rodgers, W(illiam) R(obert) 1909-1969 85-88
See also CLC 7
See also DLB 20
See also RGEL 2
Rodgers, William H. 1918- 17-20R
Rodgers, William Henry 1947- 101
Rodham Clinton, Hillary
See Clinton, Hillary Rodham
Rodi, Robert 1956- 228
See also GLL 2
Rodick, Burleigh Cushing 1889-1983 .... 5-8R
Rodimer, Eva 1895-1982 .... CAP-2
Earlier sketch in CA 21-22
Rodimstev, Aleksandr 1905(?)-1977
Obituary 69-72
Rodin, Alvin E(li) 1926-1999 .... CANR-44
Earlier sketch in CA 119
Rodin, Arnold W. 1917- 89-92
Rodin, Auguste 1840-1917 .... AAYA 48
Rodin, Robert L. 172
Rodini, Robert J(oseph) 1936- 29-32R
Rodinson, Maxime 1915- CANR-4
Earlier sketch in CA 53-56
Roditi, Edouard Herbert 1910-1992 .... CANR-50
Obituary 137
Earlier sketch in CA 101
See also CAAS 14
See also CP 1, 2
Rodli, Agnes Sylvia 1921- 9-12R
Rodman, Bella (Kashin) 1903-1983 .... CAP-2
Earlier sketch in CA 19-20
Rodman, Dennis (Keith) 1961- 155
Rodman, Emerson
See Ellis, Edward S(ylvester)
Rodman, Eric
See Silverberg, Robert
Rodman, F(rancis) Robert 1934- 122
Brief entry 117
Rodman, Howard 1920(?)-1985
Obituary 118
See also CLC 65
Rodman, Hyman 1931- CANR-25
Earlier sketches in CA 17-20R, CANR-8
Rodman, Maia
See Wojciechowska, Maia (Teresa)
Rodman, (Cary) Selden 1909-2002 .... CANR-51
Obituary 214
Earlier sketches in CA 5-8R, CANR-5, 25
See also SATA 9
Rodney, Bob
See Rodrigo, Robert
Rodney, Howard
See Koch, Howard
Rodney, Lester 1911- 208
See also DLB 241
Rodney, Robert M(orris) 1911-2001 77-80
Rodney, Walter 1942-1980 125
Rodney, William 1923- 25-28R
Rodnick, David 1908-1980 .... 33-36R
Rodnitzky, Jerome L(eon) 1936- 212
Rodnitzky, Jerry L.
See Rodnitzky, Jerome L(eon)
Rodo, Jose Enrique 1871(?)-1917 178
See also EWL 3
See also HLCS 2
See also HW 2
See also LAW
Rodolph, Utto
See Ouologuem, Yambo
Rodoreda, Merce (i Gurgui)
1909-1983 .... DLB 322
See also EWL 3
See also RGSF 2
Rodowick, D(avid) N(orman) 1952- 183
Rodowsky, Colby F. 1932- CANR-98
Earlier sketches in CA 69-72, CANR-23
Interview in CANR-23
See also AAYA 23
See also SAAS 22
See also SATA 21, 77, 120
See also WYA
Rodricks, Daniel J. 1954- 133
Rodrigo, Robert 1928- 13-16R
Rodrigues, Jose Honorio
1913-1987 .... CANR-13
Earlier sketch in CA 29-32R
Rodrigues, Nelson 1912-1980 .... DLB 307
See also EWL 3
See also IDTP
See also LAWS 1
See also RGWL 2, 3
Rodriguez, Abraham, Jr. 1961- 180
See also LLW
Rodriguez, Aleida 1953- 195
Rodriguez, Alejo 1941- 150
See also SATA 83
Rodriguez, Alfred 1932- 145
Rodriguez, Ana 1938- 150
Rodriguez, Andres 1955- 151
Rodriguez, Clara E. 1944- CANR-126
Earlier sketch in CA 170
Rodriguez, Claudio 1934-1999 188
See also CLC 10
See also DLB 134
Rodriguez, Joe D. 1943- .... DLB 209
Rodriguez, Judith Green 1936- CANR-80
Earlier sketches in CA 107, CANR-23
See also CP 7
See also CWP
See also FW
Rodriguez, Junius P. 1957- CANR-125
Earlier sketch in CA 170
Rodriguez, Luis J. 1954- CANR-116
Earlier sketches in CA 142, CANR-103
See also CAAS 29
See also AAYA 40
See also DLB 209
See also LLW
See also MTFW 2005
See also SATA 125
Rodriguez, Manuel 1940- 227
Rodriguez, Mario 1922- 17-20R
Rodriguez, Richard 1944- CANR-116
Earlier sketches in CA 110, CANR-66
See also AMWS 14
See also CLC 155
See also DAM MULT
See also DLB 82, 256
See also HLC 2
See also HW 1, 2
See also LAIT 5
See also LLW
See also MTFW 2005
See also NCFS 3
See also WLIT 1
Rodriguez, Robert 1968- 182
Rodriguez, Spain
See Rodriguez, Manuel
Rodriguez, Walter 1948- 142
Rodriguez-Alcala, Hugo (Rosendo)
1917- CANR-14
Earlier sketch in CA 21-24R
See also HW 1
Rodriguez-Alcala, Sally 1938- 21-24R
Rodriguez Cepeda, Enrique 1939- 45-48
Rodriguez Delgado, Jose M(anuel)
See Delgado, Jose Manuel R(odriguez)
Rodriguez Julia, Edgardo
See Rodriguez Julia, Edgardo
Rodriguez Julia, Edgardo 1946- 195
See also DLB 145
Rodriguez Monegal, Emir 1921-1985 131
Obituary 117
Brief entry 115
See also HW 1
Rodriguez O(rdonez), Jaime E(dmundo)
1940- 110
See also HW 1
Rodway, Allan 1919- 13-16R
Rodwin, Lloyd 1919-1999 .... CANR-42
Obituary 188
Earlier sketches in CA 5-8R, CANR-4, 19
Rodwin, Victor G(eorge) 1950- 120
Rodzinski, Halina 1904-1993 69-72
Obituary 141
Roe, Anne 1904-1991 .... 17-20R
Roe, Barbara L(ouise) 1947- 141
Roe, Caroline 165
Roe, Daphne A(nderson) 1923-1993 93-96
Obituary 142
Roe, Derek A(rthur) 1937- CANR-23
Earlier sketch in CA 107
Roe, Dorothy
See Lewis, Dorothy Roe
Roe, E. P. 1838-1888 .... DLB 202
Roe, F(rederic) Gordon 1894-1985 .... 9-12R
Obituary 115
Roe, Gerald 1940- 117
Roe, Harry Mason CANR-26
Earlier sketches in CAP-2, CA 19-20
Roe, JoAnn 143
Roe, Kathleen Robson 1910- 93-96
Roe, Keith E. 1937- 127
Roe, Richard L(ionel) 1936- CANR-100
Earlier sketches in CA 65-68, CANR-15
Roe, Sue (Lynn) 1953- 227
Roe, W(illiam) G(ordon) 1932- 21-24R
Obituary 185
Roe, William Henry 1918- 5-8R
Roeber, Edward C(harles) 1913-1969 .... CANR-5
Earlier sketch in CA 5-8R
Roebuck, Carl Angus 1914-
Brief entry 105
Roebuck, Deborah Britt 1952- 196
Roebuck, Derek 1935- CANR-54
Earlier sketches in CA 111, CANR-29
Roebuck, Janet 1943- 49-52
Roebuck, Julian B(aker) 1920- 101
Roebuck, Peter (Michael) 1956- 119
Roeburt, John 1909(?)-1972
Obituary 33-36R
Roecker, W(illiam) A. 1942- 61-64
Roeder, Bill 1922-1982
Obituary 107
Roeder, George H., Jr. 1944-2004 147
Obituary 231
Roeder, Ralph Leclerq 1890-1969
Obituary 104
Roeder, Virginia Marsh 1926- .... SATA 98
Roederer, Scott (L.) 213
Roediger, David R(andall) 1952- CANR-122
Earlier sketch in CA 142
Roehr, George L. 1931(?)-1983
Obituary 110
Roehrig, Catharine H. 1949- 134
See also SATA 67
Roehrs, Walter R(obert) 1901-1996 103
Roeiker, Nancy Lyman 1915- 9-12R
Roelants, Maurice 1895-1966 192
See also EWL 3
Roelofs, H. Mark 1923- 111
Roelvaag, O(le) E(dvart) 1876-1931 171
Brief entry 117
See also Rolvaag, O(le) E(dvart) and
Rolvaag, O(le) E(dvart)
Roemer, Astrid H. 1947- .... EWL 3
Roemer, Joan (Phylis Akre) 1933- 132
Roemer, Kenneth Morrison 1945- CANR-106
Earlier sketches in CA 112, CANR-32
Roemer, Lawrence John 1916(?)-1989
Obituary 129
Roemer, Michael 1937-1996 111
Roemer, Milton I(rwin) 1916-2001 .... CANR-47
Obituary 192
Earlier sketches in CA 57-60, CANR-6, 21
Roemer, Norma H. 1905-1973 .... CAP-2
Earlier sketch in CA 19-20
Roemer, William F., Jr. 1926-1996 132
Roeming, Robert Frederick 1911- 29-32R
Roennfeldt, Robert 1953- .... SATA 78
Roepke, Wilhelm (Theodor)
1899-1966 .... CAP-1
Earlier sketch in CA 9-10
Roer, Berniece Marie 9-12R
Roer Neal, Berniece
See Roer, Berniece Marie
Roes, Nicholas 1926- 29-32R
Roes, Nicholas A. 1952- 124
Roesch, Roberta F(leming) 1919- CANR-2
Earlier sketch in CA 5-8R
Roesch, Ronald 1947- 106
Roeseler, Robert O(swald) 1882-1971 .... CAP-2
Earlier sketch in CA 17-18
Roeseler, W(olfgang) G(uenter) 1925- 111
Roeske, Paulette 1945- CANR-134
Earlier sketch in CA 153
Roesler, Robert Harry 1927- 120
Roessel, Monty 196
Roessel-Waugh, C. C.
See Waugh, Carol-Lynn Rossel and
Waugh, Charles G(ordon)
Roessler, Carl (Fred) 1933- 117
Roessner, Michaela(-Marie) 1950- CANR-90
Earlier sketch in CA 155
See also FANT
See also SFW 4
Roethenmund, Robert 1956- 103
Roethke, Theodore (Huebner)
1908-1963 81-84
See also CABS 2
See also AMW
See also CDALB 1941-1968
See also CLC 1, 3, 8, 11, 19, 46, 101
See also DA3
See also DAM POET
See also DLB 5, 206
See also EWL 3
See also EXPP
See also MAL 5
See also MTCW 1, 2
See also PAB
See also PC 15
See also PFS 3
See also RGAL 4
See also WP
Roets, Lois F. 1937- .... SATA 91
Roett, Riordan Joseph Allenby III 1938- 57-60
Roetter, Charles Frederick 1919- 61-64
Roetzel, Calvin J. 1931- 112
Roever, J(oan) M(arilyn) 1935- 105
See also SATA 26
Rofe, (Fevzi) Husein 1922- CAP-1
Earlier sketch in CA 9-10
Rofes, Eric Edward 1954- 106
See also SATA 52
Roff, William R(obert) 1929- 57-60
Roffey, Maureen 1936- 108
See also SATA 33
Roffman, Howard 1953- 61-64
Roffman, Roger A. 1942- 110
Roffman, Sara
See Hershman, Morris
Rofheart, Martha 1925- 149
Rogak, Lisa Angowski 1962- 148
See also SATA 80
Rogal, Samuel J. 1934- CANR-39
Earlier sketches in CA 25-28R, CANR-17
Rogaly, (Henry) Joseph 1935- 104
Rogan, Barbara 1951- CANR-88
Earlier sketch in CA 124
Rogan, Donald L(ynn) 1930- 29-32R
Rogan, Johnny 1953- CANR-86
Earlier sketch in CA 130
Rogan, Josh
See Mathison, Melissa
Rogasky, Barbara 1933- CANR-127
Earlier sketches in CA 130, CANR-51, 79
See also SATA 86, 144
See also YAW
Roger
See Sanchez Flores, Daniel
Roger, Jacques 1920-1990 171
Roger, Mae Durham 57-60
Rogers, A(mos) Robert 1927- CANR-8
Earlier sketch in CA 61-64
Rogers, Agnes
See Allen, Agnes Rogers
Rogers, Alan 1933- CANR-28
Earlier sketches in CA 21-24R, CANR-11
Rogers, (Thomas) Alan (Stinchcombe)
1937- CANR-18
Earlier sketch in CA 25-28R
See also SATA 2, 81
Rogers, Annie G. 156
Rogers, Augustus James III 1929- 33-36R
Rogers, Barbara 1945- CANR-17
Earlier sketch in CA 65-68
Rogers, Ben F. 1935- 185
Rogers, Berto 1903-1974 .... CAP-2
Earlier sketch in CA 29-32
Rogers, Bettye 1858-1919 170
See also SATA 103
Rogers, Bruce 1870-1957
Brief entry 123

Cumulative Index 493 **Rollins**

Rogers, Carl R(ansom) 1902-1987 .... CANR-18
Obituary 121
Earlier sketches in CA 1-4R, CANR-1
See also MTCW 1
See also TCLC 125
Rogers, (Grenville) Cedric (Harry) 1915- CANR-1
Earlier sketch in CA 1-4R
Rogers, Charles B. 1911-1987 89-92
Rogers, Chris 1944- 218
Rogers, Cindy 1950- 155
See also SATA 89
Rogers, Clara Coltman
See Vyvyan, C(lara) C(oltman Rogers)
Rogers, Colin D(arlington) 1936- 155
Rogers, Cyril A(lfred) 1923-1993 .... 5-8R
Obituary 141
Rogers, Cyril H(arold) 1907- CANR-20
Earlier sketches in CA 9-12R, CANR-5
Rogers, Dale Evans 1912-2001 103
Obituary 193
Interview in CA-103
Rogers, David 1930- 29-32R
Rogers, David C(harles) D(rummond) 1931- CANR-5
Earlier sketch in CA 9-12R
Rogers, Deborah D(ee) 1953- 175
Rogers, Donald I(rwin) 1918-1980 57-60
Obituary 102
Rogers, Dorothy 1914-1986 .... CANR-1
Obituary 118
Earlier sketch in CA 1-4R
Rogers, Douglass Marcel 1925- 127
Rogers, Edith R(andam) 1924- 117
Rogers, Elizabeth F(rances) 1892-1974 .... 5-8R
Obituary 53-56
Rogers, Elyse M(acFadyen) 1932- 102
Rogers, Emma 1951- .... SATA 74
Rogers, Evelyn 1935- CANR-123
Earlier sketch in CA 165
Rogers, Florence K(atherine) 1936- 101
Rogers, Floyd
See Spence, William John Duncan
Rogers, Frances 1888-1974 .... 5-8R
See also SATA 10
Rogers, Francis M(illet) 1914- CANR-1
Earlier sketch in CA 1-4R
Rogers, Franklin R(obert) 1921- 1-4R
Rogers, Fred B(aker) 1926- 109
Rogers, Fred McFeely 1928-2003 107
Obituary 208
See also SATA 33
See also SATA-Obit 138
Rogers, Garet -1996 .... 1-4R
Rogers, Gayle 1923- 69-72
Rogers, George Calvin, Jr. 1922- CANR-1
Earlier sketch in CA 1-4R
Rogers, George W(illiam) 1917- CANR-1
Earlier sketch in CA 1-4R
Rogers, H(ugh) C(uthbert) Basset 1905- CANR-14
Earlier sketch in CA 73-76
Rogers, Hal
See Sirimarco, Elizabeth
Rogers, Helen Spelman 1913(?)-1990
Obituary 132
Rogers, Henry C. 1914-1995 102
Obituary 148
Rogers, Ingrid 1951- 116
Rogers, Jack 1934- 93-96
Rogers, James Allen 1929- 13-16R
Rogers, James T(racy) 1921- 45-48
Rogers, Jane 1952- CANR-99
Earlier sketch in CA 113
See also DLB 194
Rogers, Jean 1919- 115
See also SATA 55
See also SATA-Brief 47
Rogers, Jeanne F. 1926(?)-1984
Obituary 113
Rogers, JoAnn V. 1940- 89-92
Rogers, Joel (Edward) 1952- 207
Rogers, Joel Augustus 1880(?)-1966 153
See also BW 2
Rogers, Joel Townsley 1896-1984
Obituary 114
Rogers, John 1906-1985 .... 5-8R
Rogers, Josephine 1925- 61-64
Rogers, Kate Ellen 1920- 13-16R
Rogers, Katharine M(unzer) 1932- .. CANR-139
Earlier sketches in CA 21-24R, CANR-8
Rogers, Kenneth Paul 1940- 53-56
Rogers, Kenneth Ray 85-88
Rogers, Kenny
See Rogers, Kenneth Ray
Rogers, Lesley J. 1943- 192
Rogers, Linda (Hall) 1944- 77-80
Rogers, Marian H. 1932- 140
Rogers, Matilda 1894-1976 .... CAP-2
Earlier sketch in CA 29-32
See also SATA 5
See also SATA-Obit 34
Rogers, Max Gray 1932- 53-56
Rogers, Michael 234
Rogers, Michael (A.) 1950- CANR-28
Earlier sketches in CA 49-52, CANR-1
Rogers, Mick
See Glut, Donald F(rank)
Rogers, Millard F(oster), Jr. 1932- 101
Rogers, Neville William 1908-1985 108
Rogers, P. P.
See Rogers, Paul (Patrick)
Rogers, Pamela 1927- CANR-4
Earlier sketch in CA 49-52
See also SATA 9
Rogers, Pat 1938- 85-88
Rogers, Pattiann (Tall) 1940- CANR-109
Earlier sketches in CA 109, CANR-26
See also DLB 105
See also PFS 18
Rogers, Paul (Patrick) 1900-1989 .... 41-44R
Rogers, Paul 1950- 123
See also SATA 54, 98
Rogers, Paul P.
See Rogers, Paul (Patrick)
Rogers, Paul T(aylor) 1936-1984 119
Obituary 113
Rogers, Peter 1934- 101
Rogers, Peter D(amien) 1942- CANR-38
Earlier sketch in CA 116
Rogers, Raymond A(rthur) 1911- 21-24R
Rogers, Richard 172
Rogers, Richard 183
Rogers, Richard 1933- 172
Rogers, Robert
See Hamilton, Charles (Harold St. John)
Rogers, Robert F. 1930- 150
Rogers, Rolf E(rnst) 1931- 57-60
Rogers, Rosemary 1932- CANR-113
Earlier sketches in CA 49-52, CANR-3, 23
Interview in CANR-23
See also AITN 1
See also CPW
See also DA3
See also DAM POP
See also MTCW 1
See also RHW
Rogers, Roy 1911-1998 112
Obituary 169
Rogers, Rutherford D(avid) 1915-
Brief entry 109
Rogers, Samuel 1763-1855 .... DLB 93
See also RGEL 2
Rogers, Sarah F. 1923(?)-1976
Obituary 69-72
Rogers, Thomas Hunton 1927- 89-92
Interview in CA-89-92
See also CLC 57
Rogers, Timothy (John Godfrey) 1927- CANR-1
Earlier sketch in CA 45-48
Rogers, (George) Truett 1931- 69-72
Rogers, Tyler Stewart 1895-1967 .... 5-8R
Obituary 134
Rogers, Vincent R(obert) 1926-
Brief entry 115
Rogers, W(illiam) G(arland) 1896-1978 .. 9-12R
Obituary 77-80
See also SATA 23
Rogers, Wade
See Madlee, Dorothy (Haynes)
Rogers, Warren
See Brucker, Roger W(arren)
Rogers, Warren (Joseph, Jr.) 1922-2003 .... CANR-13
Obituary 219
Earlier sketch in CA 77-80
Rogers, Will(iam Penn Adair) 1879-1935 ... 144
Brief entry 105
See also DA3
See also DAM MULT
See also DLB 11
See also MTCW 2
See also NNAL
See also TCLC 8, 71
Rogers, William C(ecil) 1919- 17-20R
Rogers, William D(ill) 1927- 41-44R
Rogers, William Elford 1944- 113
Rogers, William R(aymond) 1932- 104
Rogers, William Warren 1929- 127
Brief entry 112
Rogerson, J(ohn) W(illiam) 1935- CANR-38
Earlier sketch in CA 115
Rogerson, John
See Rogerson, J(ohn) W(illiam)
Rogg, Eleanor H(ertha) Meyer 1942- 57-60
Rogg, Sanford G. 1917-1976 .... 17-20R
Obituary 134
Rogge, Oetje John 1903-1981 .... 1-4R
Obituary 103
Rogin, Gilbert 1929- CANR-15
Earlier sketch in CA 65-68
See also CLC 18
Rogin, Michael Paul 1937-2001 .... CANR-43
Earlier sketch in CA 101
Roginski, J(ames) W. 1945- 119
Roginski, Jim
See Roginski, J(ames) W.
Rogler, Lloyd H(enry) 1930- 17-20R
Roglieri, John Louis 1939- 105
Rogness, Alvin N. 1906-1992 .... CANR-8
Earlier sketch in CA 21-24R
Rogness, Michael 1935- 101
Rogo, D. Scott 1950-1990 .... CANR-28
Earlier sketches in CA 33-36R, CANR-13
Rogoff, Barbara 1950- CANR-42
Earlier sketch in CA 118
Rogoff, Harry 1882-1971
Obituary 33-36R
Rogosin, (William) Donn 1947- 123
Rogovin, Anne 1918-2003 97-100
Obituary 218
Rogovin, Sheila Anne 1931- 195
Rogow, Arnold Austin 1924- CANR-1
Earlier sketch in CA 1-4R
Rogow, Roberta 1942- 140
Rogow, Zack 1952- 177
Earlier sketch in CA 146
Autobiographical Essay in 177
See also CAAS 28
Rogowski, Ronald (Lynn) 1944- CANR-58
Earlier sketch in CA 125
Roh, Jae Min 1927- 117
Rohan, Koda
See Koda Shigeyuki
Rohan, M. S.
See Rohan, Michael Scott
Rohan, Maurice Desmond
See Harrison, Michael
Rohan, Michael Scott 1951- CANR-121
Earlier sketch in CA 157
See also FANT
See also SATA 98
Rohan, Mike Scott
See Rohan, Michael Scott
Rohan, Zina 1946- 137
Rohatgi, Pauline 183
Rohatyn, Dennis 1949- 69-72
Rohatyn, Felix G(eorge) 1928- 118
Rohde, David S. 1967- 167
Rohen, Edward 1931- CANR-4
Earlier sketch in CA 53-56
See also Connors, Bruton
Rohlen, Tom 1940- 85-88
Rohlfs, Anna Katharine Green
See Green, Anna Katharine
Rohmann, Eric 1957- .... CLR 100
Rohmer, Eric
See Scherer, Jean-Marie Maurice
See also CLC 16
Rohmer, Harriet 1938- .... SATA 56
Rohmer, Richard 1924- CANR-19
Earlier sketch in CA 103
Rohmer, Sax
See Ward, Arthur Henry Sarsfield
See also DLB 70
See also MSW
See also SUFW
See also TCLC 28
Rohn, Arthur H(enry, Jr.) 1929- CANR-25
Earlier sketch in CA 45-48
Rohner, Ronald P(reston) 1935- CANR-32
Earlier sketch in CA 37-40R
Rohr, John A. 1934- 33-36R
Rohrbach, Peter Thomas 1926- CANR-1
Earlier sketch in CA 1-4R
Rohrbaugh, Joanna Bunker 1943- 101
Rohrberger, Mary 1929- CANR-1
Earlier sketch in CA 45-48
Rohrbough, Malcolm J(ustin) 1932- 29-32R
Rohrer, Alyce Stevens 1922- 123
Rohrer, Daniel M(organ) 1941- 33-36R
Rohrer, Doug 1962- 155
See also SATA 89
Rohrer, Matthew 172
Rohrer, Norman B(echtel) 1929- CANR-16
Earlier sketch in CA 93-96
Rohrer, Wayne C(urry) 1920- 21-24R
Rohrig, Walter 1897-1945 .... IDFW 3, 4
Rohrl, Vivian J. (Lober) 110
Rohrlich, Chester 1900(?)-1974
Obituary 53-56
Rohrlich, George F(riedrich) 1914- ... CANR-14
Earlier sketch in CA 37-40R
Rohrlich, Ruby CANR-5
Earlier sketch in CA 53-56
Rohrlich-Leavitt, Ruby
See Rohrlich, Ruby
Rohrlick, Paula 1955- 111
Rohrman, Nicholas L(eroy) 1937- 29-32R
Rohwer, Jim 1949-2001 202
Rohwer, Juergen 1924- 65-68
Rohwer, Jurgen
See Rohwer, Juergen
Roider, Karl A(ndrew), Jr. 1943- 111
Roig, Montserrat 1946-1991 .... DLB 322
Roiphe, Anne (Richardson) 1935- ... CANR-138
Earlier sketches in CA 89-92, CANR-45, 73
Interview in CA-89-92
See also CLC 3, 9
See also DLBY 1980
Roiphe, Katie 1968(?)- CANR-110
Earlier sketches in CA 145, CANR-73
Roisman, Hanna 198
Roizen, Michael F. 1946- 212
Roizman, Owen 1936- .... IDFW 3
Rojan
See Rojankovsky, Feodor (Stepanovich)
Rojankovsky, Feodor (Stepanovich) 1891-1970 77-80
See also MAICYA 2
See also MAICYAS 1
See also SATA 21
Rojany, Lisa 159
See also SATA 94
Rojas, A. R.
See Rojas, Arnold R.
Rojas, Arnold R. 1896(?)-1988 153
See also DLB 82
See also HW 1
Rojas, Carlos 1928- CANR-49
Earlier sketches in CA 17-20R, CANR-7, 22
Rojas, Fernando de 1475-1541 .... DLB 286
See also HLCS 1, 2
See also RGWL 2, 3
Rojas, Gonzalo 1917- 178
See also HLCS 2
See also HW 2
See also LAWS 1
Rojas, Guillermo 1938- 153
See also HW 1
Rojas (Sepulveda), Manuel 1896-1973 153
See also DNFS 1
See also EWL 3
See also HW 1
See also LAW
Rojas, Ricardo 1882-1957 207
See also LAW
Rojko, Anthony J. 1918(?)-1978
Obituary 77-80
Rojo, Antonio Benitez
See Benitez-Rojo, Antonio
See also EWL 3
Rojo, Ricardo 1923- 25-28R
Rokeach, Milton 1918-1988 .... CANR-5
Obituary 127
Earlier sketch in CA 1-4R
Rokeby-Thomas, Anna E(lma) 1911- 77-80
See also SATA 15
Roker, Al(bert Lincoln) 1954- 223
Rokes, Willis Park 1926- 25-28R
Rokkan, Elizabeth 1925- 140
Roland, Albert 1925-2002 61-64
Obituary 203
See also SATA 11
Roland, Betty 1903-1996 103
Roland, Charles G. 1933- CANR-94
Earlier sketch in CA 146
Roland, Charles P(ierce) 1918- 41-44R
Roland, Gerard 1954- 212
Roland (de la Platiere), Marie-Jeanne 1754-1793 .... DLB 314
Roland, Mary
See Lewis, Mary (Christianna)
Roland, Nicholas
See Walmsley, Arnold Robert
Roland Holst, Adriaan 1888-1976 .... EWL 3
Roland Holst(-Van Der Schalk), Henriette (Goverdine Anna) 1869-1952 193
See also EWL 3
Roland Smith, Gordon 1931- 102
Rolant, Rene
See Fanthorpe, R(obert) Lionel
Rolde, Neil 1931- CANR-119
Earlier sketch in CA 148
Roldos Aguilera, Jaime 1940-1981
Obituary 108
Roleder, George 1928- CANR-21
Earlier sketch in CA 105
Roleff, Tamara L. 1959- 215
See also SATA 143
Rolens, Sharon 1932- 197
Rolerson, Darrell A(llen) 1946- 49-52
See also SATA 8
Roley, Brian Ascalon 1966- 199
Rolf, David 1938- 130
Rolfe, Bari 1916-2002 .... CANR-32
Obituary 214
Earlier sketch in CA 113
Rolfe, Edwin 1909-1954 .... DLB 303
Rolfe, Eugene (Edward Musgrave) 1914- 13-16R
Rolfe, Franklin P(rescott) 1902-1985
Obituary 117
Rolfe, Frederick (William Serafino Austin Lewis Mary) 1860-1913 210
Brief entry 107
See also Al Siddik
See also DLB 34, 156
See also RGEL 2
See also TCLC 12
Rolfe, Lionel (Menuhin) 1942- CANR-28
Earlier sketch in CA 110
Rolfe, Sheila Constance 1935- 102
Rolfe, Sidney 1921-1976 69-72
Obituary 65-68
Rolfsrud, Erling Nicolai 1912-1994 65-68
Rolin, Dominique 1913- 196
Roll, Charles W(eissert), Jr. 1928-2002 .... CANR-1
Obituary 208
Earlier sketch in CA 45-48
Roll, Eric 1907-2005 102
Obituary 237
Roll, Richard J(effrey) 1952- 124
Roll, Samuel 1942- 124
Roll, William George, Jr. 1926- 81-84
Roll, Winifred 1909-1998 49-52
See also SATA 6
Rolland, Barbara J(une) 1929- 77-80
Rolland, Romain 1866-1944 197
Brief entry 118
See also DLB 65, 284
See also EWL 3
See also GFL 1789 to the Present
See also RGWL 2, 3
See also TCLC 23
Rolle, Andrew Frank 1922- CANR-3
Earlier sketch in CA 1-4R
Rolle, Richard c. 1300-c. 1349 .... DLB 146
See also LMFS 1
See also RGEL 2
Roller, David C(harles) 1937- 107
Roller, Duane H(enry) D(uBose) 1920- 61-64
Rolleston, James Lancelot 1939- 85-88
Rollin, Bernard Elliot 1943- 108
Rollin, Betty 1936- CANR-22
Earlier sketches in CA 13-16R, CANR-7
Interview in CANR-22
Rollin, Lucy 198
Rollin, Roger Best 1930- CANR-8
Earlier sketch in CA 17-20R
Rollini, Arthur 1912-1993 127
Rollins, Alden M(ilton) 1946- 139
Rollins, Alfred Brooks, Jr. 1921- 5-8R
Rollins, Bryant 1937- 49-52
Rollins, C(alvin) D(wight) 1918- 41-44R
Rollins, Charlemae Hill 1897-1979 .... 9-12R
Obituary 104
See also BW 1
See also SATA 3
See also SATA-Obit 26
Rollins, Ed(ward J.) 1943(?)- 156
Rollins, Henry 1961- CANR-129
Earlier sketch in CA 154
Rollins, Judith CANR-76
Earlier sketch in CA 122

Rollins, Kelly (a pseudonym) 1924- ... 106
Rollins, Peter C(ushing) 1942- ... CANR-26
Earlier sketch in CA 108
Rollins, Richard M(eryl) 1945- ... 121
Rollins, Royce
See Pepper, Choral
Rollins, Steed 1916-1985
Obituary ... 118
Rollins, Wayne G(ilbert) 1929- ... CANR-3
Earlier sketch in CA 9-12R
Rollison, William D(ewey) 1897-1971 .. CAP-2
Earlier sketch in CA 19-20
Rollo, Vera Foster 1924- ... 81-84
Rollock, Barbara T(herese) 1924- ... SATA 64
Rolls, Anthony
See Vulliamy, Colwyn Edward
Rolls, Charles J(ubilee) 1887- ... 107
Rolls, Eric C(harles) 1923- ... CANR-13
Earlier sketch in CA 33-36R
See also CP 1
Rollyson, Carl
See Rollyson, Carl E(dmund), Jr.
Rollyson, Carl E(dmund), Jr. 1948- . CANR-133
Earlier sketches in CA 129, CANR-65
See also DLBY 1997
Rollyson, Carl Sokolnicki
See Rollyson, Carl E(dmund), Jr.
Rolo, Charles J(acques) 1916-1982 ... 101
Obituary ... 108
Rolo, Paul Jacques Victor 1917- ... 21-24R
Roloff, Leland Harold 1927- ... 49-52
Roloff, Michael 1937- ... 130
Rolph, C. H.
See Hewitt, Cecil Rolph
Rolph, Earl R(obert) 1910-1988 ... CAP-2
Earlier sketch in CA 23-24
Rolston, Holmes III 1932- ... CANR-101
Earlier sketches in CA 113, CANR-32
Rolston, Holmes 1900-1977 ... CANR-3
Earlier sketch in CA 1-4R
Rolt, Francis 1955- ... 127
Rolt, L(ionel) T(homas) C(aswall)
1910-1974 ... CANR-81
Earlier sketches in CA 1-4R, CANR-1
See also HGG
Rolt-Wheeler, Francis William 1876-1960
Obituary ... 89-92
Rolvaag, O(le) E(dvart)
See Roelvaag, O(le) E(dvart)
See also DLB 9, 212
See also MAL 5
See also NFS 5
See also RGAL 4
See also TCLC 17
Rolvaag, O(le) E(dvart)
See Roelvaag, O(le) E(dvart)
See also TCWW 1, 2
Rolvaag, O. E.
See Roelvaag, O(le) E(dvart)
Rom, M. Martin 1946- ... 81-84
Romack, Janice Reed
See LeNoir, Janice
Romagnoli, G(ian) Franco 1926- ... CANR-123
Earlier sketch in CA 73-76
Romagnoli, Margaret O'Neill 1922- ... 73-76
Romain, Trevor ... 203
See also SATA 134
Romain Arnaud, Saint
See Aragon, Louis
Romaine, Lawrence B. 1900-1967 ... CAP-1
Earlier sketch in CA 13-14
Romaine, Paul
See Bleamer, Burton
Romaine, Suzanne 1951- ... 206
Romaine-Davis, Ada 1929- ... 142
Romains, Jules 1885-1972 ... CANR-34
Earlier sketch in CA 85-88
See also CLC 7
See also DLB 65, 321
See also EWL 3
See also GFL 1789 to the Present
See also MTCW 1
Roman, Daniel (David) 1921- ... 41-44R
Roman, Eric 1926- ... CANR-1
Earlier sketch in CA 1-4R
Roman, Howard (Edgar) 1916(?)-1988
Obituary ... 127
Roman, Lawrence 1921- ... 237
Roman, Murray 1920-1984
Obituary ... 112
Roman, Nancy Grace 1925- ... 161
Roman, Peter 1941- ... 199
Roman, Stephen B(oleslav) 1921- ... 189
Brief entry ... 112
Romanell, Patrick 1912-2002 ... 21-24R
Romanelli, Charles S. 1930- ... 13-16R
Romanelli, Giandomenico 1945- ... 168
Romanenko, Vitaliy 1962- ... SATA 101
Romano, Clare 1922- ... CANR-24
Earlier sketch in CA 41-44R
See also Ross, Clare
Romano, Deane Louis 1927- ... 25-28R
Romano, Don
See Turner, Robert (Harry)
Romano, Enotrio
See Carducci, Giosue (Alessandro Giuseppe)
Romano, John 1948- ... 133
Romano, Lalla 1906- ... DLB 177
Romano, Louis G. 1921- ... CANR-8
Earlier sketch in CA 17-20R
See also SATA 35
Romano, Melora A. 1966- ... SATA 118
Romano, Octavio I. 1932- ... 153
See also DLB 122
See also HW 1
Romanoff, Alexis Lawrence
1892-1980 ... CANR-5
Earlier sketch in CA 9-12R
Romanoff, Harry 1892(?)-1970
Obituary ... 104
Romanow, Roy (John) 1939- ... 132
Romanowski, Nick 1954- ... 212
Romanowski, Patricia
See Bashe, Patricia Ann Romanowski
Romans, J(ohn) Thomas 1933- ... 13-16R
Romanszkan, Gregor de
See de Romaszkan, Gregor
Romanucci-Ross, Lola 1928- ... CANR-18
Earlier sketch in CA 101
Romanus, Charles Franklin 1915-1983 . 21-24R
Obituary ... 111
Romanyshyn, Robert Donald 1942- ... 108
Romasco, Albert U(go) 1930- ... 110
Romberger, Judy 1940- ... 106
Rome, Anthony
See Albert, Marvin H(ubert)
Rome, Beatrice K(aufman) 1913-2000 .. 13-16R
Rome, David 1910-1996 ... 142
Rome, Elaine
See Barbieri, Elaine
Rome, Florence 1910-1997 ... 33-36R
Rome, Harold 1908-1993 ... DLB 265
Romein, J. M.
See Romein, Jan (Marius)
Romein, Jan (Marius) 1893-1962
Obituary ... 111
Romer, Alfred 1906-1998 ... 37-40R
Romer, (Louis) John 1941- ... 110
Romer, Stephen 1957- ... CANR-89
Earlier sketch in CA 125
Romeril, John (Henry) 1945- ... 229
See also CD 5, 6
Romero, George A(ndrew) 1940- ... CANR-104
Brief entry ... 116
Earlier sketch in CA 147
Romero, Gerry
See Neyland, James (Elwyn)
Romero, Jose Ruben 1890-1952 ... 131
Brief entry ... 114
See also EWL 3
See also HW 1
See also LAW
See also TCLC 14
Romero, Leo 1950- ... 181
See also DLB 122
Romero, Lin 1947- ... 184
See also DLB 122
Romero, Luis 1916- ... 184
Brief entry ... 111
Romero, Orlando 1945- ... CANR-80
Earlier sketch in CA 69-72
See also DLB 82
See also HW 1, 2
Romero, Patricia W. 1935- ... CANR-31
Romerstein, Herbert 1931- ... 9-12R
Romey, Bill
See Romey, William D(owden)
Romey, William D(owden) 1930- ... 57-60
Romig, Edna Davis 1889-1978 ... 45-48
Obituary ... 103
Romig, Walter 1903-1977
Obituary ... 110
Romijn, Johanna Maria Kooyker
See Kooyker-Romijn, Johanna Maria
Romilly, Jacqueline (Davis) de
See de Romilly, Jacqueline (David)
Romine, Gregory S. 1949- ... 197
Romm, Ethel Grodzins 1925- ... 33-36R
Romm, Joseph J. ... 236
Romm, Sharon 1942- ... 118
Rommel, (Mimi) Dayton ... 5-8R
Rommetveit, Ragnar 1924- ... 57-60
Romney, George W(ilcken) 1907-1995
Obituary ... 149
Brief entry ... 106
Romney, Rodney Ross 1931- ... 102
Romney, Ronna 1943- ... 116
Romney, Steve
See Bingley, David Ernest
Romo, Ricardo 1943- ... 111
Romo-Carmona, Mariana 1952- ... 174
See also HW 2
Romoser, George K(enneth) 1929- ... 41-44R
Rompkey, Ronald (George) 1943- ... CANR-37
Earlier sketch in CA 118
Romtvedt, David 1950- ... 125
Romulo, Carlos P(ena)
1899(?)-1985 ... CANR-10
Obituary ... 118
Earlier sketch in CA 13-16R
Romyn, Johanna Maria Kooyker
See Kooyker-Romijn, Johanna Maria
Rona, Peter A(rnold) 1934- ... 108
Ronald, Ann 1939- ... 124
Ronald, David William 1937- ... 65-68
Ronald, Hugh 1912(?)-1983
Obituary ... 109
Ronalds, Mary Teresa 1946- ... 25-28R
Ronaldson, Agnes S. 1916- ... 17-20R
Ronan, Charles E. 1914-2004 ... 224
Obituary ... 226
Ronan, Colin A(listair) 1920-1995 ... CANR-6
Obituary ... 148
Earlier sketch in CA 5-8R
Ronan, Frank 1963- ... 138
Ronan, Georgia
See Crampton, Georgia Ronan
Ronan, Margaret 1918- ... 102
Ronan, Thomas Matthew 1907-1976 ... CAP-1
Earlier sketch in CA 9-10
Ronan, Tom
See Ronan, Thomas Matthew
Ronan, William W. 1917- ... 33-36R
Ronay, Gabriel Ernest 1930- ... 85-88
Roncalli, Angelo Giuseppe
See John XXIII, Pope
Ronck, Ronn 1946- ... 121
Ronda, James P(aul) 1943- ... 134
Brief entry ... 113
Rondell, Florence 1907- ... 57-60
Ronder, Paul 1940(?)-1977
Obituary ... 73-76
Rondinelli, Dennis A(ugust) 1943- ... 111
Rondinone, P. J.
See Rondinone, Peter J.
Rondinone, Peter J. 1954- ... 171
Rondthaler, Edward 1905- ... 13-16R
Ronell, Avital 1956- ... CANR-122
Earlier sketch in CA 133
Ronen, Dov 1933- ... CANR-28
Earlier sketches in CA 57-60, CANR-10
Roney, Ruth Anne
See McMullin, Ruth R(oney)
Rong, Zhong
See Liu, Shaozhong
Rongen, Bjoern 1906- ... CAP-2
Earlier sketch in CA 29-32
See also SATA 10
Rongen, Bjorn
See Rongen, Bjoern
Rongione, Louis Anthony 1912-1980 ... 57-60
Ronk, Martha C(lare) 1940- ... 152
Ronken, Harriet
See Lynton, Harriet Ronken
Ronne, Finn 1899-1980 ... CANR-1
Obituary ... 97-100
Earlier sketch in CA 1-4R
Ronnie, Art(hur William) 1931- ... 41-44R
Ronning, C. Neale 1927- ... 5-8R
Ronning, Chester A. 1894-1984
Obituary ... 114
Ronns, Edward
See Aarons, Edward S(idney)
Ronsard, Pierre de 1524-1585 ... EW 2
See also GFL Beginnings to 1789
See also PC 11
See also RGWL 2, 3
See also TWA
Ronsheim, Sally B(ober) 1917(?)-1990 ... 57-60
Obituary ... 133
Ronsin, Jean
See Rodinson, Maxime
Ronsley, Joseph 1931- ... CANR-10
Earlier sketch in CA 25-28R
Ronsman, M. M.
See Nowak, Mariette
Ronson, Jon ... 206
Ronson, Mark
See Alexander, Marc
Rood, Allan 1894-1971 ... CAP-1
Earlier sketch in CA 13-14
Rood, John (Hiram) 1902-1974 ... 5-8R
Obituary ... 120
Rood, Karen Lane 1946- ... 102
Rood, Robert Thomas 1942- ... 107
Rood, Ronald (N.) 1920- ... CANR-50
Earlier sketches in CA 21-24R, CANR-9, 24
See also SATA 12
Roodenburg, Nancy McKee 1909-1972
Obituary ... 104
Roof, Wade Clark 1939- ... CANR-118
Earlier sketch in CA 114
Rook, (William) Alan 1909- ... 97-100
See also CP 1, 2
Rook, Clarence 1863-1915 ... DLB 135
Rook, Earnest Robert 1917- ... 104
Rook, Tony 1932- ... 69-72
Rooke, Constance 1942- ... 126
Rooke, Daphne (Marie) 1914- ... 53-56
See also CN 1, 2, 3, 4, 5, 6, 7
See also SATA 12
Rooke, Leon 1934- ... CANR-53
Earlier sketches in CA 25-28R, CANR-23
See also CCA 1
See also CLC 25, 34
See also CPW
See also DAM POP
Rooke, P(atricia) T. 1938- ... 127
Rookmaaker, Hendrik Roelof
1922-1977 ... CANR-26
Earlier sketch in CA 57-60
Rooks, Conrad 1934- ... 183
Rooks, George (M.) 1951- ... CANR-22
Earlier sketch in CA 105
Rooks, Judith P. 1941- ... 168
Rooksby, Rikky 1958- ... 144
Room, Adrian 1933- ... CANR-102
Earlier sketches in CA 97-100, CANR-16
Roome, Katherine Ann Davis 1952- ... 85-88
Rooney, Andrew A(itken) 1919- ... CANR-125
Earlier sketches in CA 5-8R, CANR-9, 45, 65
Interview in ... CANR-9
See also Rooney, Andy
See also MTCW 1
Rooney, Andy ... CANR-9
See also Rooney, Andrew A(itken)
Rooney, David Douglas 1924- ... CANR-11
Earlier sketch in CA 21-24R
Rooney, Elmo
See Perry, Charles
Rooney, James 1938- ... 101
Rooney, James R(owell) 1927- ... 61-64
Rooney, Jim
See Rooney, James
Rooney, John F(rancis), Jr. 1939- ... 101
Rooney, Lucy 1926- ... 135
Rooney, Miriam Theresa ... 81-84
Rooney, Patrick C. 1937- ... 29-32R
Rooney, William Richard 1938- ... 102
Roop, Connie
See Roop, Constance (Betzer)
Roop, Constance (Betzer) 1951- ... CANR-94
Earlier sketches in CA 122, CANR-49
See also SATA 54, 116
See also SATA-Brief 49
Roop, Peter (G.) 1951- ... CANR-101
Earlier sketches in CA 122, CANR-48
See also SATA 54, 116
See also SATA-Brief 49
Roorbach, Bill 1953- ... CANR-98
Earlier sketch in CA 137
Roos, Audrey (Kelley) 1912-1982 ... CANR-91
Obituary ... 108
Earlier sketch in CA 128
Roos, Charles A. 1914(?)-1974
Obituary ... 53-56
Roos, Hans
See Meissner, Hans-Otto
Roos, Hans Dietrich 1919- ... 17-20R
Roos, Johan 1961- ... 145
Roos, Kelley
See Roos, Audrey (Kelley)
Roos, Leslie L(eon), Jr. 1940- ... 33-36R
Roos, Murphre (joint pseudonym)
See Mele, Jim
Roos, Noralou P(reston) 1942- ... 33-36R
Roos, Stephen 1945- ... CANR-108
Earlier sketches in CA 112, CANR-31
See also JRDA
See also SATA 47, 77, 128
See also SATA-Brief 41
Roosa, Robert V(incent) 1918-1993 ... 25-28R
Obituary ... 143
Roose, Ronald 1945- ... 81-84
Roose-Evans, James 1927- ... CANR-91
Earlier sketches in CA 29-32R, CANR-35
See also SATA 65
Roosen, William (James) 1940- ... 117
Roosenburg, Henriette 1920-1972
Obituary ... 37-40R
Roosevelt, Archibald Bulloch, Jr.
1918-1990 ... 127
Obituary ... 131
Roosevelt, Archie
See Roosevelt, Archibald Bulloch, Jr.
Roosevelt, Edith Kermit 1926- ... 69-72
Roosevelt, (Anna) Eleanor 1884-1962
Obituary ... 89-92
See also SATA 50
Roosevelt, Elliott 1910-1990 ... CANR-90
Obituary ... 132
Earlier sketch in CA 105
See also AITN 1
Roosevelt, Felicia Warburg 1927- ... 57-60
Roosevelt, Franklin Delano 1882-1945 ... 173
Brief entry ... 116
See also LAIT 3
See also TCLC 93
Roosevelt, James 1907-1991 ... CANR-12
Obituary ... 135
Earlier sketch in CA 69-72
Roosevelt, Nicholas 1893-1982
Obituary ... 106
Roosevelt, Selwa 1929- ... 134
Roosevelt, Theodore 1858-1919 ... 170
Brief entry ... 115
See also DLB 47, 186, 275
See also TCLC 69
Root, Betty ... SATA 84
Root, Deane L(eslie) 1947- ... CANR-47
Earlier sketches in CA 107, CANR-23
Root, Deborah 1953- ... 164
Root, E(dward) Merrill 1895-1973 ... CAP-1
Earlier sketch in CA 13-16
Root, Franklin Russell 1923- ... 5-8R
Root, Judith C(arol) ... 65-68
Root, Lin (Segal) ... 69-72
Root, Oren 1911-1995 ... 85-88
Root, Phyllis 1949- ... CANR-125
Earlier sketches in CA 123, CANR-50
See also SATA 55, 94, 145
See also SATA-Brief 48
Root, Robert L., Jr. ... 188
Root, Shelton L., Jr. 1923-1986 ... SATA-Obit 51
Root, Waverley (Lewis) 1903-1982 .. CANR-29
Obituary ... 108
Earlier sketch in CA 25-28R
See also DLB 4
Root, William Pitt 1941- ... CANR-12
Earlier sketch in CA 25-28R
See also CAAS 11
See also CP 1, 2, 3, 4, 5, 6, 7
See also DLB 120
Root-Bernstein, Michele 1953- ... 167
Root-Bernstein, Robert Scott 1953- .. CANR-82
Earlier sketch in CA 132
Rooth, Gerhard Theodore 1898(?)-1983
Obituary ... 110
Rootham, Jasper (St. John)
1910-1990 ... CANR-41
Earlier sketches in CA 5-8R, CANR-4, 19
Roots, Clive (George) 1935-
Brief entry ... 111
Roots, Ivan Alan 1921- ... 9-12R
Roots, John McCook 1904(?)-1988
Obituary ... 126
Rooze, Gene E(dward) 1934- ... 120
Rope, Henry Edward George 1880-1978 .. 5-8R
Obituary ... 103
Roper, Gayle G(ordinier) 1940- ... 97-100
Roper, H(ugh) R(edwald) Trevor
See Trevor-Roper, H(ugh) R(edwald)
Roper, John Herbert 1948- ... 128
Roper, John Stephen 1924(?)-1980
Obituary ... 102

Cumulative Index 495 Rosenberg

Roper, Lanning 1912-1983
Obituary ... 109
Roper, Laura (Newbold) Wood
1911-2003 ... 57-60
Obituary ... 224
See also SATA 34
See also SATA-Obit 150
Roper, Mark 1951- ... 188
Roper, Robert 1946- ... CANR-121
Earlier sketches in CA 73-76, CANR-111
See also SATA 78, 142
Roper, Ronnalie J. 1936- ... 41-44R
Roper, Steve 1941- ... 103
Roper, Susan Bonthron 1948- ... 81-84
Roper, William L(eon) 1897-1990 ... 33-36R
Obituary ... 130
Ropes, Linda Brubaker 1942- ... 140
Ropke, Wilhelm (Theodor)
See Roepke, Wilhelm (Theodor)
Ropp, Theodore 1911-2000 ... 5-8R
Roppolo, Joseph Patrick 1913- ... 13-16R
Rops, Daniel
See Petiot, Henri Jules Charles
Roquebrune, Robert (Laroque) de
1889-1978 ... 148
See also DLB 68
Roquelaure, A. N.
See Rice, Anne
Roquemore, Kathleen (Ann) 1941- ... 61-64
Roraback, Robin (Ellan) 1964- ... SATA 111
Rorabaugh, William Joseph 1945- ... CANR-94
Earlier sketch in CA 101
Rorby, Ginny 1944- ... 159
See also SATA 94
Rorem, Ned 1923- ... CANR-109
Earlier sketches in CA 17-20R, CANR-32
See also GLL 1
Rorer, Abigail 1949- ... SATA 85
Roripaugh, Robert A(lan) 1930- ... CANR-64
Earlier sketch in CA 13-16R
See also TCWW 2
Rorke, Margaret (Curry) 1915- ... 110
Rorty, Amelie Oksenberg 1932- ... 107
Rorty, James 1891(?)-1973
Obituary ... 41-44R
Rorty, Richard M(cKay) 1931- ... CANR-135
Earlier sketches in CA 21-24R, CANR-9
See also DLB 246, 279
Rorty, Winifred Raushenbush 1894(?)-1979
Obituary ... 93-96
Rorvik, David M(ichael) 1946- ... CANR-38
Earlier sketch in CA 85-88
See also CP 7
Rosa, Alexis Gomez
See Gomez Rosa, Alexis
See also HW 1
Rosa, Alfred F(elix) 1942- ... 41-44R
Rosa, Joao Guimaraes 1908-1967
Obituary ... 89-92
See also Guimaraes Rosa, Joao
See also CLC 23
See also DLB 113, 307
See also EWL 3
See also HLCS 1
See also WLIT 1
Rosa, Joseph G. 1932- ... 13-16R
Rosa, Nicholas 1926- ... 110
Rosage, David E. 1913- ... CANR-21
Earlier sketches in CA 13-16R, CANR-6
Rosaldo, Michelle Z(imbalist) 1944-1981 ... 101
Obituary ... 108
Rosaldo, Renato I(gnacio), Jr. 1941- ... 89-92
Rosaler, Robert C. 1920- ... 155
Rosales, Francisco A(rturo) 1942- ... 131
See also HW 1
Rosales, Luis 1910-1992 ... DLB 134
Rosamel, Godeleine de 1968- ... SATA 151
Rosa Mendes, Pedro 1968- ... 235
Rosand, David 1938- ... 111
Rosa-Nieves, Cesareo 1901-1974 ... 57-60
See also HW 1
Rosanoff, Nancy 1949- ... 212
Rosario, Nelly 1972- ... 214
Rosario Green (de Heller), Maria del
1941- ... CANR-87
Earlier sketch in CA 130
See also HW 1
Rosato, Dominick V. 1921-2004 ... 166
Rosberg, Carl G(ustaf) 1923-1996 ... 239
Rosbottom, Ronald C(arlisle) 1942- ... 61-64
Rosbrow-Reich, Susan 1946- ... 212
Rosca, Ninotchka ... 127
Roschelle, Anne R. ... 231
Rosco, Jerry 1953- ... 225
Roscoe, A(drian) A(lan) 1939- ... 49-52
Roscoe, Charles
See Rowland, D(onald) S(ydney)
Roscoe, D(onald) T(homas) 1934- ... 113
See also SATA 42
Roscoe, Edwin Scott 1896-1978 ... 5-8R
Obituary ... 103
Roscoe, George B(oggs) 1907-1996 ... 65-68
Obituary ... 152
Roscoe, Patrick 1962- ... 151
Roscoe, Will 1955- ... CANR-88
Earlier sketch in CA 148
See also GLL 2
Roscoe, William 1753-1831 ... DLB 163
Rosdail, Jesse Hart 1914(?)-1977
Obituary ... 73-76
Rose, A(rthur) James 1927- ... 17-20R
Rose, Ada Campbell 1902(?)-1976
Obituary ... 65-68
Rose, Al 1916- ... 97-100
Rose, Alan Henry 1938- ... 93-96
Rose, Albert H(enry) 1903-1996 ... 41-44R
Rose, Alison (C.) ... 233
Rose, Alvin E(manuel) 1903-1983
Obituary ... 109
Rose, Andrew (Wyness) 1944- ... 136
Rose, Angelica 1960- ... 217
Rose, Anna Perrott
See Wright, Anna (Maria Louisa Perrott) Rose
Rose, Anne ... CANR-2
Earlier sketch in CA 49-52
See also SATA 8
Rose, Anthony Lewis 1939- ... 101
Rose, Arnold 1916-1983
Obituary ... 109
Rose, Arnold M(arshall) 1918-1968 ... 5-8R
Rose, Barbara E. 1937-
Brief entry ... 111
Rose, Betsy
See Rose, Elizabeth
Rose, Billy 1899-1966
Obituary ... 116
Rose, Brian Waldron 1915- ... 97-100
Rose, Camille Davied 1893-1988 ... CAP-2
Earlier sketch in CA 21-22
Rose, Carl 1903-1971
Obituary ... 29-32R
See also SATA-Brief 31
Rose, Clarkson 1890-1968 ... 5-8R
Rose, Clive (Martin) 1921- ... 121
Rose, Constance Hubbard 1934- ... CANR-16
Earlier sketch in CA 29-32R
Rose, Daniel M. 1940- ... 33-36R
Rose, David 1959- ... 225
Rose, David S. 1947- ... 121
Rose, Deborah Lee 1955- ... SATA 71, 124
Rose, Dilys 1954- ... 174
See also DLB 319
Rose, Don 1955- ... SFW 4
Rose, Elinor K(iess) 1920- ... 29-32R
Rose, Elizabeth 1915- ... 73-76
Rose, Elizabeth (Jane Pretty) 1933- ... CANR-9
Earlier sketch in CA 5-8R
See also SATA 68
See also SATA-Brief 28
Rose, (Edward) Elliot 1928- ... 65-68
Rose, Ernst A(ndreas) G(ottlieb)
1899-1990 ... CANR-4
Earlier sketch in CA 5-8R
Rose, Florella
See Carlson, Vada F.
Rose, Frank 1949- ... 103
Rose, Gerald (Hembdon Seymour)
1935- ... CANR-42
Earlier sketches in CA 65-68, CANR-9
See also SATA 68
See also SATA-Brief 30
Rose, Gilbert J(acob) 1923- ... 103
Rose, (Arthur) Gordon 1920-1975 ... CANR-4
Earlier sketch in CA 1-4R
Rose, Grace B(erne) 1914- ... 108
Rose, H(orace) E(dgar) 1913-1999 ... 206
Rose, Hannah T. 1909(?)-1976
Obituary ... 69-72
Rose, Harold 1921-1967 ... 5-8R
Obituary ... 103
Rose, Harold Wickliffe 1896-1970 ... CAP-1
Earlier sketch in CA 9-10
Rose, Helen 1904(?)-1985
Obituary ... 117
See also IDFW 3, 4
Rose, Hilary
See Mackinnon, Charles Roy
Rose, Homer C. 1909-1967 ... CAP-1
Earlier sketch in CA 13-16
Rose, Jacqueline (S.) 1949- ... 224
Rose, James M. 1941- ... 102
Rose, Jeanne 1940- ... CANR-16
Earlier sketch in CA 93-96
Rose, Jennifer
See Weber, Nancy
Rose, Jerome G. 1926- ... CANR-8
Earlier sketch in CA 13-16R
Rose, Jerry D. 1933- ... 33-36R
Rose, Joel 1948- ... CANR-120
Earlier sketches in CA 129, CANR-66
Rose, Jonathan 1952- ... 191
Rose, June 1926- ... 172
Rose, Kenneth (Vivian) 1924- ... 128
Brief entry ... 123
Rose, Kenneth D(avid) 1946- ... 205
Rose, Kenneth Jon 1954- ... CANR-38
Earlier sketch in CA 115
Rose, Laurel L. 1952- ... 144
Rose, Lawrence F.
See Fearn, John Russell
Rose, Leo E. 1926- ... 85-88
Rose, Lisle A(bbott) 1936- ... CANR-10
Earlier sketch in CA 65-68
Rose, Lynn Edmondson 1934-
Brief entry ... 105
Rose, Malcolm 1953- ... 213
See also SATA 107
Rose, Marcia
See Kamien, Marcia and
Novak, Rose
Rose, Margaret A. 1947- ... 138
Rose, Marilyn Gaddis 1930- ... 33-36R
Rose, Mark 1939- ... CANR-10
Earlier sketch in CA 25-28R
Rose, Michael (Simon) 1937- ... 133
Rose, Mike ... 232
Rose, Nancy (Ann) 1934- ... 37-40R
Rose, Nancy A.
See Sweetland, Nancy A(nn)
Rose, Norman Anthony 1934- ... CANR-103
Earlier sketch in CA 104
Rose, Paul (Bernard) 1935- ... 103
Rose, Pete(r Edward) 1942- ... 183
Brief entry ... 113
Rose, Peter I(saac) 1933- ... CANR-5
Earlier sketch in CA 13-16R
Rose, Phyllis
See Thompson, Phyllis Hoge
Rose, Phyllis 1942- ... CANR-45
Earlier sketch in CA 135
Rose, R(obert) B(arrie) 1929- ... 61-64
Rose, Ralph 1911(?)-1984
Obituary ... 112
Rose, Reginald 1920-2002 ... CANR-42
Obituary ... 209
Earlier sketch in CA 73-76
See also DLB 26
See also LAIT 4
Rose, Rex 1962- ... 223
Rose, Richard 1933- ... CANR-120
Earlier sketches in CA 21-24R, CANR-10, 27
Rose, Rose K. 1927- ... 176
Rose, Seraphim 1934-1982 ... 182
Rose, Stephen C. 1936- ... 129
Rose, Steven 1938- ... 168
Rose, Stuart 1899(?)-1975
Obituary ... 61-64
Rose, Susan (Phyllida) 1938- ... 111
Rose, Ted 1940- ... SATA 93
Rose, Thomas 1938- ... 33-36R
Rose, Tricia ... 227
Rose, Wendy 1948- ... CANR-51
Earlier sketches in CA 53-56, CANR-5
See also CLC 85
See also CWP
See also DAM MULT
See also DLB 175
See also NNAL
See also PC 13
See also PFS 13
See also RGAL 4
See also SATA 12
Rose, Will(iam Palen) 1889-1977 ... 57-60
Obituary ... 134
Rose, William 1920(?)-1987
Obituary ... 121
Rose, Willie Lee (Nichols) 1927- ... 13-16R
Rose-Ackerman, Susan 1942- ... 111
Roseberry, Cecil R. 1902-1990 ... 21-24R
Roseboom, Eugene Holloway 1892-1984 . 5-8R
Roseboro, John, Jr. 1933-2002 ... 102
Obituary ... 207
Rosebrock, Ellen Fletcher 1947- ... CANR-10
Earlier sketch in CA 57-60
Rosebury, Theodor 1904-1976 ... CAP-2
Obituary ... 69-72
Earlier sketch in CA 25-28
Rosecrance, Francis Chase 1897-1979 ... 5-8R
Rosecrance, Richard (Newton)
1930- ... CANR-91
Brief entry ... 111
Rosedale, Valerie
See Harron, Don(ald)
Rosefielde, Steven 1942- ... CANR-25
Earlier sketch in CA 45-48
Rosegger, Peter 1843-1918 ... DLB 129
Rosegrant, Susan 1954- ... 144
Rosei, Peter 1946- ... 183
See also DLB 85
See also EWL 3
Roseliep, Raymond 1917- ... CANR-6
Earlier sketch in CA 9-12R
See also CP 1, 2
Rosell, Steven A. ... 201
Roselle, Daniel 1920- ... 13-16R
Roseller, David
See Timms, E(dward) V(ivian)
Roseman, Ellen Barbara 1947- ... 124
Roseman, Janet Lynn 1954- ... 205
Roseman, Kenneth David 1939- ... 110
See also SATA-Brief 52
Roseman, Mark 1958- ... 210
Rosemeyer, Nita (Mary) 1907- ... 119
Rosemond, John K(irk) 1947- ... 110
Rosemont, Henry, Jr. 1934- ... 41-44R
Rosemont, Penelope 1942- ... 194
Rosen, Barbara 1929- ... 37-40R
Rosen, Barry 1944- ... 136
Rosen, Benson 1942- ... 120
Rosen, Bernard Carl 1922- ... 181
Rosen, Billi 1942- ... BYA 13
Rosen, Carol (Cynthia) 1950- ... 119
Rosen, Charles ... 201
Rosen, Charles (Welles) 1927- ... CANR-88
Earlier sketches in CA 126, CANR-50
Rosen, Charley
See Rosen, Charles
Rosen, Corey 1948- ... 138
Rosen, Dorothy 1916- ... CANR-100
Earlier sketches in CA 119, CANR-43
Rosen, Edward 1906-1985 ... 21-24R
Obituary ... 115
Rosen, Elliot A(lfred) 1928- ... 93-96
Rosen, Frederick 1938- ... CANR-93
Earlier sketches in CA 120, CANR-45
Rosen, George 1910-1977 ... CANR-31
Obituary ... 73-76
Earlier sketch in CA 81-84
Rosen, George 1920- ... 57-60
Rosen, Gerald 1938- ... 177
Earlier sketch in CA 33-36R
Autobiographical Essay in ... 177
See also CAAS 29
Rosen, Haiim B(aruch)
See Rosen, Haiim B(aruch)
Rosen, Haiim B(aruch) 1922- ... CANR-49
Earlier sketches in CA 1-4R, CANR-20
Rosen, Hjalmar 1922- ... 17-20R
Rosen, Ira 1954- ... 114
Rosen, James Alan 1908(?)-1972
Obituary ... 37-40R
Rosen, Jay 1956- ... 195
Rosen, Jeffrey 1964- ... 203
Rosen, Joe
See Rosen, Joseph
Rosen, Jonathan ... 183
Rosen, Joseph 1937- ... CANR-9
Earlier sketch in CA 65-68
Rosen, Laura 1948- ... 116
Rosen, Lawrence R(onald) 1938- ... 57-60
Rosen, Leonard 1954- ... 125
Rosen, Leora N(adine) 1950- ... 159
Rosen, Lillian (Diamond) 1928- ... 108
See also SATA 63
Rosen, Martin Meyer
See Rosen, Moishe (Martin)
Rosen, Marvin 1933- ... 237
See also SATA 161
Rosen, Marvin J(erold) 1929- ... 69-72
Rosen, Michael (Wayne) 1946- ... CANR-92
Earlier sketches in CA 25-28R, CANR-15, 32, 52
See also CLR 45
See also CWRI 5
See also MAICYA 2
See also SATA 48, 84, 137
See also SATA-Brief 40
Rosen, Michael J(oel) 1954- ... CANR-136
Earlier sketches in CA 132, CANR-49
See also CWRI 5
See also SATA 86
Rosen, Milt ... 231
Rosen, Moishe (Martin) 1932- ... CANR-4
Earlier sketch in CA 49-52
Rosen, Mortimer (Gilbert) 1931- ... 101
Rosen, Norma (Gangel) 1925- ... 33-36R
See also DLB 28
Rosen, Paul L(yon) 1939- ... 61-64
Rosen, Philip 1928- ... 177
Rosen, R. D.
See Rosen, Richard (Dean)
Rosen, Richard (Dean) 1949- ... CANR-120
Earlier sketches in CA 77-80, CANR-62
Interview in ... CANR-30
See also CLC 39
See also CMW 4
Rosen, Robert C(harles) 1947- ... 106
Rosen, Robert H. 1955- ... 139
Rosen, Ruth (E.) 1945- ... CANR-95
Earlier sketch in CA 125
Rosen, S. McKee 1902(?)-1978
Obituary ... 77-80
Rosen, Sam 1920- ... 5-8R
Rosen, Samuel 1897-1981
Obituary ... 108
Rosen, Seymour Michael 1924- ... 33-36R
Rosen, Sheldon 1943- ... 109
Rosen, Shirley 1933- ... 105
Rosen, Sidney 1916- ... CANR-101
Earlier sketch in CA 9-12R
See also SATA 1
Rosen, Stanley H. 1929- ... 25-28R
Rosen, Stephen 1934- ... 65-68
Rosen, Sybil Fran 1950- ... 205
Rosen, Trix 1947- ... 116
Rosen, Winifred 1943- ... CANR-32
Earlier sketch in CA 29-32R
See also SATA 8
Rosenak, Charles B. 1927- ... 134
Rosenak, Chuck
See Rosenak, Charles B.
Rosenak, Jan(ice M.) 1930- ... 134
Rosenast, Eleanor S(trauss) 1929- ... 97-100
Rosenau, Helen ... 101
Rosenau, James N(athan) 1924- ... CANR-18
Earlier sketches in CA 1-4R, CANR-2
Rosenau, Pauline Vaillancourt 1943- ... 144
Rosenauer, Johnnie L(ee) 1951- ... 110
Rosenbach, A. S. W. 1876-1952 ... DLB 140
Rosenbach, A(braham) S(imon) W(olf)
1876-1952 ... 199
Rosenbaum, Alan S(helby) 1941- ... 124
Brief entry ... 106
Rosenbaum, Alvin 1945- ... 113
Rosenbaum, Bernard L. 1937- ... 107
Rosenbaum, Edward E. 1915- ... 139
Rosenbaum, Eileen 1936- ... 21-24R
Rosenbaum, Ernest H. 1929- ... 97-100
Rosenbaum, H. Jon 1941- ... 41-44R
Rosenbaum, Jean 1927- ... 17-20R
Rosenbaum, Jonathan 1943- ... CANR-104
Earlier sketch in CA 130
Rosenbaum, Kurt 1926- ... 13-16R
Rosenbaum, Maurice 1907- ... 17-20R
See also SATA 6
Rosenbaum, Max 1923- ... 41-44R
Rosenbaum, Nathan 1897-1984 ... CAP-2
Earlier sketch in CA 23-24
Rosenbaum, Patricia L(eib) 1932- ... 105
Rosenbaum, Peter S. 1940- ... CANR-14
Earlier sketch in CA 21-24R
Rosenbaum, Ron 1946- ... 172
See also DLB 185
Rosenbaum, S(tanford) P(atrick) 1929- .. 13-16R
Rosenbaum, Samuel R(awlins) 1888-1972
Obituary ... 37-40R
Rosenbaum, Thane 1960- ... 214
See also DLB 299
Rosenbaum, Veryl 1936- ... CANR-1
Earlier sketch in CA 49-52
Rosenbaum, Walter A(nthony) 1937- ... 21-24R
Rosenberg, Alexander 1946- ... 132
Rosenberg, Amye 1950- ... SATA 74
Rosenberg, Arthur D(onald) 1939- ... 61-64
Rosenberg, Betty 1916- ... 113
Rosenberg, Blanca 1913-1998 ... 142
Obituary ... 172
Rosenberg, Bruce A(lan) 1934- ... 29-32R

Rosenberg, Charles E(rnest) 1936- 97-100
Rosenberg, Claude N(ewman), Jr.
1928- CANR-5
Earlier sketch in CA 1-4R
Rosenberg, David 1943- 147
Rosenberg, David A(aron) 1940- 93-96
Rosenberg, Debra Gilbert 223
Rosenberg, Dorothy 1906- CANR-18
Earlier sketches in CA 45-48, CANR-2
See also SATA 40
Rosenberg, Edgar 1925- 13-16R
Rosenberg, Emily S(chlaht) 1944- 108
Rosenberg, Eth(el) Clifford
1915-1953 .... CANR-57
Earlier sketches in CA 29-32R, CANR-16
See also Clifford, Eth
See also MAICYA 2
See also SATA 3
Rosenberg, George S(tanley) 1930- 29-32R
Rosenberg, Harold 1906-1978 .... CANR-39
Obituary 77-80
Earlier sketch in CA 21-24R
Rosenberg, Harry E. 1932- 57-60
Rosenberg, Isaac 1890-1918 188
Brief entry 107
See also BRW 6
See also DLB 20, 216
See also EWL 3
See also PAB
See also RGEL 2
See also TCLC 12
Rosenberg, Israel 1909-1978 49-52
Rosenberg, J(ehiol) Mitchell
1906-2000 .... 37-40R
Rosenberg, Jakob 1893-1980
Obituary 97-100
Rosenberg, James L. 1921- 13-16R
Rosenberg, Jane 1949- CANR-106
Earlier sketches in CA 121, CANR-47
See also SATA 58
Rosenberg, Janet 1930- 117
Rosenberg, Jerome Roy 1926- 104
Rosenberg, Jerry M. 1935- CANR-24
Earlier sketches in CA 21-24R, CANR-9
Rosenberg, Jessie 1941- 21-24R
Rosenberg, Joel 1954- CANR-137
Earlier sketch in CA 115
Rosenberg, John D(avid) 1929- CANR-5
Earlier sketch in CA 1-4R
Rosenberg, John J.
See Ramati, Yohanan (Joseph)
Rosenberg, Joseph
See Ramati, Yohanan (Joseph)
Rosenberg, Judith K(aren) 1945- 57-60
Rosenberg, Kenyon Charles 1933- 57-60
Rosenberg, Liz 1958- CANR-109
Earlier sketches in CA 142, CANR-89
See also SATA 75, 129
Rosenberg, Marvin 1912-2003 .... 1-4R
Obituary 214
Rosenberg, Maurice 1919- 81-84
Rosenberg, Maxine B(erta) 1939- CANR-65
Earlier sketches in CA 117, CANR-41
See also SATA 55, 93
See also SATA-Brief 47
Rosenberg, Morris 1922- CANR-2
Earlier sketch in CA 5-8R
Rosenberg, Nancy (Sherman) 1931- . CANR-22
Earlier sketches in CA 1-4R, CANR-5
See also SATA 4
Rosenberg, Nancy Taylor 1946- CANR-101
Earlier sketches in CA 140, CANR-62
See also CMW 4
Rosenberg, Nathan 1927- CANR-98
Brief entry 113
Earlier sketch in CA 147
Rosenberg, Neil V. 1939- 122
Rosenberg, Norman J(ack) 1930- 57-60
Rosenberg, Norman L(ewis) 1942- ... CANR-48
Earlier sketch in CA 122
Rosenberg, Otto 1927-2001 208
Rosenberg, Philip 1942- CANR-129
Earlier sketch in CA 103
Interview in CA-103
Rosenberg, Robert 1951- CANR-105
Earlier sketch in CA 160
Rosenberg, Ron 172
Rosenberg, Rosalind 1946- 108
Rosenberg, Samuel 1912-1996 53-56
Obituary 151
Rosenberg, Sharon 1942- CANR-10
Earlier sketch in CA 57-60
See also SATA 8
Rosenberg, Shirley Sirota 1925- CANR-12
Earlier sketch in CA 21-24R
Rosenberg, Stephen N(icholas) 1941- 111
Rosenberg, Stuart E. 1922-1990 .... CANR-9
Obituary 131
Earlier sketch in CA 5-8R
Rosenberg, Tina 1960- CANR-53
Earlier sketch in CA 136
Rosenberg, William Gordon 1938- 61-64
Rosenberg, Wolfgang 1915- CANR-9
Earlier sketch in CA 65-68
Rosenberger, Francis Coleman
1915- CANR-15
Earlier sketch in CA 41-44R
Rosenberger, Harleigh M. 1913- 21-24R
Rosenberger, Homer Tope
1908-1982 .... CANR-8
Earlier sketch in CA 17-20R
Rosenberry, Vera 1948- .... SATA 83, 144
Rosenblatt, Arthur
See Rosenblatt, Arthur S.
Rosenblatt, Arthur S. 1938- 134
See also SATA 68
See also SATA-Brief 45
Rosenblatt, Bernard A(braham)
1886-1970 .... CAP-1
Earlier sketch in CA 13-14
Rosenblatt, Fred 1914- 41-44R
Rosenblatt, Gary 1947- 77-80
Rosenblatt, Jason P. 1941- 137
Rosenblatt, Joe
See Rosenblatt, Joseph
See also CLC 15
See also CP 7
Rosenblatt, Jon M(ichael) 1947- 89-92
Rosenblatt, Joseph 1933- 89-92
Interview in CA-89-92
See also Rosenblatt, Joe
See also CP 1, 2, 3, 4, 5, 6
Rosenblatt, Kathleen Ferrick 1947- 218
Rosenblatt, Lily 1956- .... SATA 90
Rosenblatt, Louise M(ichelle)
1904-2005 49-52
Obituary 236
Rosenblatt, Milton B. 1908(?)-1975
Obituary 53-56
Rosenblatt, Roger 1940- CANR-136
Earlier sketches in CA 85-88, CANR-34
Rosenblatt, Samuel 1902-1983 53-56
Rosenblatt, Stanley M. 1936- 29-32R
Rosenblatt, Suzanne Maris 1937- 69-72
Rosenblith, Judy F(rancis) 1921- 25-28R
Rosenbloom, Bert 1944- 109
Rosenbloom, David H(arry) 1943- 73-76
Rosenbloom, David L. 1944- 45-48
Rosenbloom, Jerry S(amuel) 1939- 129
Brief entry 110
Rosenbloom, Joseph 1928- CANR-21
Earlier sketches in CA 57-60, CANR-6
See also SATA 21
Rosenbloom, Joseph R. 1928- 29-32R
Rosenbloom, Noah H. 1915- CANR-14
Earlier sketch in CA 37-40R
Rosenblum, Art 1927- 57-60
Rosenblum, Davida 1927- 93-96
Rosenblum, Gershen 1924- 41-44R
Rosenblum, Helen Faye 1941- 121
Rosenblum, Joseph 1947- 111
Rosenblum, Leonard A. 1936- CANR-11
Earlier sketch in CA 57-60
Rosenblum, Marc J. 1936- 29-32R
Rosenblum, Martin J(ack) 1946- CANR-40
Earlier sketches in CA 45-48, CANR-2, 18
See also CAAS 11
Rosenblum, Mary 1952- 183
Rosenblum, Mort 1943- CANR-103
Earlier sketch in CA 73-76
Rosenblum, Nancy L. 1947- CANR-137
Earlier sketch in CA 133
Rosenblum, Ralph 1925-1995 .... IDFW 3, 4
Rosenblum, Richard 1928- CANR-9
Earlier sketch in CA 65-68
See also SATA 11
Rosenblum, Robert H. 1927- CANR-91
Earlier sketches in CA 1-4R, CANR-5
Rosenbluth, Gideon 1921- 61-64
Rosenburg, Ellis Howard 1936(?)-1986
Obituary 121
Rosenburg, John M. 1918- 21-24R
See also SATA 6
Rosenburg, Robert K(emper) 1920- CANR-4
Earlier sketch in CA 5-8R
Rosendall, Betty 1916- 49-52
Rosendorfer, Herbert 1934- 189
Rosenfarb, Chawa 1923- 53-56
Rosenfeld, Albert (Hyman) 1920- CANR-11
Earlier sketch in CA 65-68
Rosenfeld, Alvin (Z.) 1919-1992 73-76
Obituary 139
Rosenfeld, Alvin H(irsch) 1938- CANR-24
Earlier sketches in CA 49-52, CANR-4
Rosenfeld, Arnold (Solomon) 1933- 65-68
Rosenfeld, Arthur 232
Rosenfeld, Dina 1962- CANR-125
Earlier sketch in CA 167
See also SATA 99
Rosenfeld, Edward J(ulius) 1943- 41-44R
Rosenfeld, Harry M(orris) 1929- 69-72
Rosenfeld, Harvey 1939- 110
Rosenfeld, Isaac 1918-1956 200
See also DLB 28
Rosenfeld, Isadore 1926- CANR-111
Earlier sketches in CA 81-84, CANR-40
Rosenfeld, Jeffrey P(hilip) 1946- 115
Rosenfeld, Louis 1925- 189
Rosenfeld, Lucinda 1969(?)- 228
Rosenfeld, Lulla 1914- 85-88
Rosenfeld, Marthe 1928- 45-48
Rosenfeld, Nancy (G.) 1941- 148
Rosenfeld, Oskar 1884-1944 224
Rosenfeld, Richard N. 176
Rosenfeld, Sam 1920- 9-12R
Rosenfeld, Samuel
See Tzara, Tristan
Rosenfeld, Stephanie 1968- 225
Rosenfeld, Sybil (Marion) 1903-1996 119
Obituary 154
Rosenfelt, David 224
Rosenfield, Isadore 1893-1980
Obituary 97-100
Rosenfield, Israel 1939- 128
Rosenfield, James A(lexander) 1943- 49-52
Rosenfield, John M(ax) 1924- CANR-14
Earlier sketch in CA 21-24R
Rosenfield, Leonora Cohen 1909-1982 . 41-44R
Obituary 105
Rosenfield, Paul 1948-1993 139
Rosengart, Oliver A. 1941- 49-52
Rosengarten, David 1950- 193
Rosengarten, Frank 1927- 73-76
Rosengarten, Frederic (Jr.) 1916- 118
Rosengarten, Herbert (J.) 1940- 138
Rosengarten, Lucille 1936- 212
Rosengarten, Theodore 1944- 103
Rosengren, William R(udolph) 1929-
Brief entry 114
Rosenhaupt, Hans 1911-1985
Obituary 116
Rosenheim, Andrew 1955- 139
Rosenheim, Edward W(eil), Jr. 1918- 25-28R
Rosenheim, Lucile G. 1902-1990
Obituary 132
Rosenhouse, Archie 1878-1972 .... CAP-2
Earlier sketch in CA 21-22
Rosenkrantz, Linda 1934- CANR-11
Earlier sketch in CA 25-28R
Rosenkranz, E. Joshua 1961- 159
Rosenkranz, Richard S. 1942- 37-40R
Rosenman, John B(rown) 1941- 106
Rosenman, Leonard 1924- .... IDFW 3, 4
Rosenman, Ray H(arold) 1920- 97-100
Rosenman, Samuel I(rving) 1896-1973
Obituary 41-44R
Rosenmeyer, Patricia A. 1958- 142
Rosenmeyer, Thomas Gustav 1920- 111
Rosenn, Keith S(amuel) 1938- 111
Rosenof, Theodore 1943- CANR-10
Earlier sketch in CA 65-68
Rosenow, John E(dward) 1949- 97-100
Rosenquist, Carl M(artin) 1895-1973 ..... CAP-2
Earlier sketch in CA 29-32
Rosenrauch, Heinz Erich
See Rosen, Haiim B(aruch)
Rosensaft, Menachem Z. 1948- 21-24R
Rosenstein-Rodan, Paul N. 1902-1985 107
Obituary 116
Rosenstiel, Annette 1911- 115
Rosenstiel, Leonie 1947- 85-88
Rosenstiel, Tom 1956- 142
Rosenstock, (Patricia) Janet (Stearns)
1933- 108
Rosenstock, Sami
See Tzara, Tristan
Rosenstock, Samuel
See Tzara, Tristan
Rosenstock-Huessy, Eugen 1888-1973 .. CAP-1
Obituary 41-44R
Earlier sketch in CA 13-16
Rosenstone, Robert A(llan) 1936- CANR-52
Earlier sketches in CA 29-32R, CANR-28
Rosenstone, Steven J(ay) 1952- 104
Rosenthal, A(braham) M(ichael)
1922- CANR-27
Earlier sketch in CA 21-24R
Rosenthal, Alan 1936- CANR-92
Earlier sketch in CA 105
Rosenthal, Albert H(arold) 1914- 21-24R
Rosenthal, Andrew 1918(?)-1979
Obituary 89-92
Rosenthal, Bernard G(ordon)
1922-1993 .... CANR-11
Obituary 141
Earlier sketch in CA 29-32R
Rosenthal, Bernice (Glatzer) 1938- 121
Rosenthal, David 1916- 41-44R
Rosenthal, Debra J. 1964- CANR-123
Earlier sketch in CA 169
Rosenthal, Donald B. 1937- CANR-14
Earlier sketch in CA 37-40R
Rosenthal, Douglas E(urico) 1940- 57-60
Rosenthal, Earl E(dgar) 1921- 41-44R
Rosenthal, Edwin Stanley 1914- 77-80
Rosenthal, Eric 1905-1983 .... CANR-6
Earlier sketch in CA 9-12R
Rosenthal, Erwin Isak Jacob 1904-1991 102
Rosenthal, F(rank) F(ranz) 1911(?)-1979
Obituary 89-92
Rosenthal, Harold 1914-1999 .... CANR-135
Earlier sketch in CA 111
See also DLB 241
See also SATA 35
Rosenthal, Harold (David) 1917-1987 ...... 5-8R
Obituary 122
Rosenthal, Harry F(rederick) 1927- 65-68
Rosenthal, Harry Kenneth 1941- 57-60
Rosenthal, Henry Moses 1906-1977
Obituary 73-76
Rosenthal, Jack
See Rosenthal, Jacob
Rosenthal, Jack (Morris) 1931-2004 140
Obituary 229
Rosenthal, Jacob 1935- 161
Rosenthal, Jean 1912-1969 213
Rosenthal, Joe
See Rosenthal, Joseph J.
Rosenthal, Joel T(homas) 1934- 57-60
Rosenthal, Joseph J. 1911- 69-72
Rosenthal, Judy 234
Rosenthal, Jules M. 1924- 17-20R
Rosenthal, Ken S. 1951- CANR-126
Earlier sketch in CA 169
Rosenthal, Lucy (Gabrielle) 1933- 144
Rosenthal, M(acha) L(ouis)
1917-1996 .... CANR-51
Obituary 152
Earlier sketches in CA 1-4R, CANR-4
See also CAAS 6
See also CLC 28
See also CP 1, 2
See also DLB 5
See also SATA 59
Rosenthal, Mark 1945- 130
Rosenthal, Mark A(lan) 1946- .... SATA 64
Rosenthal, Michael 223
Rosenthal, Mitchell S(tephen) 1935- 104
Rosenthal, Nan 1937- 193
Rosenthal, Naomi B(raun) 1940- 204
Rosenthal, Norman (Leon) 1944- 209
Rosenthal, Odeda 1934- 161
Rosenthal, Pam (Ritterman) 1945- 229
Rosenthal, Peggy 1944- 121
Rosenthal, Renee (?)-1975
Obituary 57-60
Rosenthal, Richard A. 1925- 1-4R
Rosenthal, Ricky 1930(?)-1984
Obituary 114
Rosenthal, Robert 1933- CANR-42
Earlier sketches in CA 41-44R, CANR-16
Rosenthal, Shirley Lord 1934- CANR-57
Earlier sketches in CA 65-68, CANR-11, 27
Rosenthal, Steven T. 220
Rosenthal, Stuart 1934- 117
Rosenthal, Sylvia Dworsky
1911-1994 .... CANR-27
Earlier sketch in CA 109
Rosenthal, T(homas) G(abriel) 1935- 227
Rosenus, Alan (Harvey) 1940- 73-76
Rosenwald, Henry M(artin) 1905-1978 . 33-36R
Rosenwald, Lessing J. 1891-1979 .... DLB 187
Rosenwald, Lessing J(ulius) 1891-1979 199
Rosenwasser, Dorothy Eckmann 1917- 1-4R
Rosenzweig, Michael L(eo) 1941- 101
Rosenzweig, Norman 1924- CANR-6
Earlier sketch in CA 57-60
Rosenzweig, Peter M. 1949- 139
Rosenzweig, Robert Myron 1931- 113
Rosenzweig, Roy 1950- CANR-86
Earlier sketches in CA 113, CANR-35
Rosenzweig, Saul 1907- 141
Roses, Lorraine Elena 1943- 166
Rosett, Arthur (Irwin) 1934- 69-72
Rosette, Bennetta Jules
See Jules-Rosette, Bennetta (Washington)
Rosetti, Minerva
See Rowland, D(onald) S(ydney)
Roseveare, Helen Margaret 1925- 73-76
Rosewell, Paul Truman 1926- 17-20R
Roseyear, John 1936- 21-24R
Roshco, Bernard 1929- 5-8R
Rosher, Charles 1885-1974 .... IDFW 3, 4
Rosher, Grace (?)-1980
Obituary 111
Roshwalb, Irving 1924- 45-48
Roshwald, Aviel 1962- 145
Roshwald, Miriam Mindla 1925-1998 188
Roshwald, Mordecai Marceli
1921- CANR-107
Earlier sketch in CA 1-4R
Rosi, Eugene J(oseph) 1931- 61-64
Rosichan, Richard H(arry) 1941- 45-48
Rosie, George 1941- 120
Rosier, Bernard 1931- CANR-12
Earlier sketch in CA 29-32R
Rosier, James L(ouis) 1932-1992 .... CANR-22
Obituary 145
Earlier sketch in CA 1-4R
Rosillo-Calle, Francisco 1945- 121
Rosis, Brendan
See Tilly, Chris
Rositzke, Harry A(ugust) 1911-2002 . CANR-29
Obituary 212
Earlier sketch in CA 45-48
Roskamp, Karl Wilhelm 1923- 13-16R
Roske, Ralph Joseph 1921- 122
Roskies, David G(regory) 1948- CANR-88
Earlier sketch in CA 120
Roskies, Ethel 1933- CANR-25
Earlier sketch in CA 45-48
Roskill, Mark W(entworth) 1933- CANR-6
Earlier sketch in CA 5-8R
Roskill, Stephen W(entworth)
1903-1982 .... CANR-6
Obituary 108
Earlier sketch in CA 13-16R
Rosko, Milt 1930- 41-44R
Roskolenko, Harry 1907-1980 .... CANR-17
Obituary 101
Earlier sketch in CA 13-16R
Roslavleva, Natalia
See Rene, Natalia
Rosman, Abraham 1930- 89-92
Rosman, Steven M(ichael) 1956- 149
See also SATA 81
Rosmond, Babette 1921-1997 .... CANR-6
Earlier sketch in CA 5-8R
Rosner, Bob 1956- 166
Rosner, David K(arl) 1947- 112
Rosner, Elizabeth J. 1959- 204
Rosner, Fred 1935- CANR-32
Earlier sketch in CA 113
Rosner, Joseph 1914- 57-60
Rosner, Lisa 1958- 140
Rosner, Lynn 1944- 61-64
Rosner, Martin C. 1932- 212
Rosner, Stanley 1928- 41-44R
Rosnow, Ralph L(eon) 1936- CANR-28
Earlier sketches in CA 21-24R, CANR-10
Rosochacki, Daniel 1942- 45-48
Rosoff, Meg 1956- 236
See also SATA 160
Rosoff, Sidney D. 1924- 1-4R
Rosovsky, Henry 1927- 184
Brief entry 105
Rosow, Irving 1921- 85-88
Rosow, Jerome M(orris) 1919-2002 81-84
Obituary 211
Rosowski, Susan J(ean) 1942-2004 ... CANR-95
Obituary 233
Earlier sketches in CA 111, CANR-29, 54
Ross, Adrian 1859-1933 .... HGG
Ross, Alan
See Warwick, Alan R(oss)
Ross, Alan 1922-2001 .... CANR-44
Earlier sketches in CA 9-12R, CANR-6, 21
See also CP 1, 2, 3, 4, 5, 6, 7

Cumulative Index 497 Rosskam

Ross, Alan M. 1951- 212
Ross, Alan O(tto) 1921-1993 .... 41-44R
Obituary 143
Ross, Alan Strode Campbell 1907-1980 .. 9-12R
Obituary 102
Ross, Albert
See Jarrett, Philip (Martin)
Ross, Alec 1926- 29-32R
Ross, Alex(ander) 1909- .... SATA-Brief 29
Ross, Alex 1970- .... AAYA 53
Ross, Alexander 1591-1654 .... DLB 151
Ross, Alf (Niels Christian Hansen)
1899-1979 53-56
Ross, Andrew 1956- CANR-130
Earlier sketch in CA 172
Ross, Angus
See Giggal, Kenneth
Ross, Angus 1911-2000 .... 21-24R
Ross, Barnaby
See Dannay, Frederic
Ross, Becki L. 1959- 153
Ross, Bernard H(arvey) 1934- 102
Ross, Bernard L.
See Follett, Ken(neth Martin)
Ross, Bette M. 1932- 106
Ross, Betty 69-72
Ross, Bill D. 1921-1994 123
Obituary 146
Ross, Billy I(rvan) 1925- 57-60
Ross, Brian (Elliot) 1948- 126
Brief entry 119
Interview in CA-126
Ross, Caroline
See Nicolson, Catherine
Ross, Catherine
See Beaty, Betty
Ross, Charles (Derek) 1924(?)-1986
Obituary 118
Ross, Charles D. 1958- 206
Ross, Charles L(ouis) 1945- 176
Ross, Charlotte (Brand) 1921- 117
Ross, Christine 1950- .... SATA 83
Ross, Clare
See Romano, Clare
See also SATA 48, 111
Ross, Clarissa
See Ross, W(illiam) E(dward) D(aniel)
Ross, Colin
See Roskolenko, Harry
Ross, Corinne Madden 1931- 106
Ross, Dallas
See Reynolds, Dallas McCord
Ross, Dan
See Ross, W(illiam) E(dward) D(aniel)
Ross, Dana
See Ross, W(illiam) E(dward) D(aniel)
Ross, Dana Fuller
See Cockrell, Amanda and
Gerson, Noel Bertram
Ross, Daniel W(illiam) 1952- 189
Ross, Dave
See Ross, David
See also SATA 32
Ross, David 1896-1975 65-68
Obituary 61-64
See also SATA 49
See also SATA-Obit 20
Ross, David 1949- CANR-112
Earlier sketch in CA 111
See also Ross, Dave
See also SATA 133
Ross, David O(liver), Jr. 1936-
Brief entry 117
Ross, David P(reston), Jr. 1908-1984
Obituary 112
Ross, David William 1922- 181
Ross, Davis R. B. 1934- 33-36R
Ross, Diana
See Denney, Diana
Ross, Diana 1944- 146
Ross, Donald H. 1928- 159
Ross, Donald K. 1943- 49-52
Ross, Dorothy 1936- 137
Ross, Edward S(hearman) 1915- .... SATA 85
Ross, Eileen 1950- 187
See also SATA 115
Ross, Elizabeth Irvin 1942- 121
Ross, Ellen 1942- 147
Ross, Emory 1887-1973
Obituary 41-44R
Ross, Eric (De Witt) 1929- 29-32R
Ross, Erin
See Tallman, Shirley
Ross, Eulalie Steinmetz 1910-1975 .... 17-20R
Obituary 134
Ross, Eva J(eany) 1903-1969 .... CAP-2
Earlier sketch in CA 23-24
Ross, Floyd H(iatt) 1910-1998 73-76
Ross, Frances Aileen 1909- CAP-1
Earlier sketch in CA 9-10
Ross, Frank (Xavier), Jr. 1914- CANR-16
Earlier sketch in CA 93-96
See also SATA 28
Ross, Frank E. 1925- 17-20R
Ross, Gary 1948- CANR-38
Earlier sketch in CA 115
Ross, George
See Morgan-Grenville, Gerard (Wyndham)
Ross, H(ugh) Laurence 1934- CANR-13
Earlier sketch in CA 77-80
Ross, Hal 1941- 65-68
Ross, Harold Raymond 1904-1980 .... CAP-2
Earlier sketch in CA 19-20
Ross, Harold W(allace) 1892-1951
Brief entry 119
See also DLB 137
Ross, Helaine
See Daniels, Dorothy
Ross, Helen 1890(?)-1978 85-88
Obituary 81-84
Ross, Hugh (Norman) 1945- 181
Ross, Ian
See Rossmann, John F(rancis)
Ross, Ian Campbell 1950- 216
Ross, Ian Simpson 1930- CANR-3
Earlier sketch in CA 45-48
Ross, Irwin 1919- 97-100
Ross, Ishbel 1897-1975 93-96
Obituary 61-64
Ross, Ivan T.
See Rossner, Robert
Ross, J. H.
See Lawrence, T(homas) E(dward)
Ross, James Davidson 1924- 49-52
Ross, James F(rancis) 1931- CANR-11
Earlier sketch in CA 21-24R
Ross, James Frederick Stanley 1886- 9-12R
Ross, James McLaren
See MacLaren-Ross, Julian
Ross, James R(odman) 1950- CANR-94
Earlier sketch in CA 145
Ross, James S(tiven) 1892-1975
Obituary 57-60
Ross, Jane 1961- .... SATA 79
Ross, Janet 1914- 37-40R
Ross, Janice L(ynn) 1950- 195
Ross, Jerry 1926-1955 .... DLB 265
Ross, Joel E(lmore, Jr.) 1922- 29-32R
Ross, John 1921- 108
See also SATA 45
Ross, John A(ddison) 1919- 17-20R
Ross, John Hume
See Lawrence, T(homas) E(dward)
Ross, John Munder 1945- 127
Ross, John O'C(onnell) 1916- 25-28R
Ross, Jonathan
See Rossiter, John
Ross, Joseph
See Wrzos, Joseph Henry
Ross, Judith Wilson 1937- 114
Ross, Judy 1942- .... SATA 54
Ross, K. G. M. (?)-1985
Obituary 116
Ross, Kate -1998 238
See also CMW 4
Ross, Katharine (Reynolds) 1948- .... SATA 89
Ross, Katherine
See Walter, Dorothy Blake
Ross, Kenneth (Michael Andrew) 1941- 107
Ross, Kenneth Lynn 1940- 125
Ross, Kenneth N(eedham)
1908-1970 .... CANR-5
Earlier sketch in CA 5-8R
Ross, Kent 1956- 155
See also SATA 91
Ross, Lanson Clifford, Jr. 1936- 120
Ross, Laura
See Mincieli, Rose Laura
Ross, Leah
See Webb, Mary H(aydn)
Ross, Leonard
See Rosten, Leo C(alvin)
Ross, Leonard M(ichael) 1945-1985 . CANR-29
Obituary 116
Earlier sketch in CA 29-32R
Ross, Leonard Q.
See Rosten, Leo C(alvin)
Ross, Lillian 1927- CANR-68
Earlier sketches in CA 9-12R, CANR-46
See also DLB 185
Ross, Lillian Hammer 1925- 140
See also SATA 72
Ross, Lola Romanucci
See Romanucci-Ross, Lola
Ross, Lynne Nannen
See Ross-Robertson, Lynne Nannen
Ross, Mabel (Irene) H(ughes) 1909- 81-84
Ross, Malcolm
See Ross-Macdonald, Malcolm J(ohn)
Ross, Marc H(ansen) 1928- 114
Ross, Marilyn
See Ross, W(illiam) E(dward) D(aniel)
Ross, Marilyn (Ann) Heimberg
1939- CANR-57
Earlier sketches in CA 81-84, CANR-14, 31
Ross, Marjorie Drake Rhoades
1901-1997 .... 1-4R
Ross, Mark C. 208
Ross, Martha 1951- 103
Ross, Martin 1862-1915
See Martin, Violet Florence
See also DLB 135
See also GLL 2
See also RGEL 2
See also RGSF 2
Ross, Martin J. 1912- 53-56
Ross, Marvin C(hauncey) 1904-1977 .... CAP-2
Obituary 69-72
Earlier sketch in CA 19-20
Ross, Mary Adelaide Eden
See Phillpotts, (Mary) Adelaide Eden
Ross, Michael 1905- 85-88
Ross, Michael Elsohn 1952- CANR-107
Earlier sketch in CA 148
See also SATA 80, 127
Ross, Michael W(allis) 1952- 118
Ross, Mitchell S(cott) 1953- 81-84
Ross, Murray George 1912-2000 .... 17-20R
Ross, Nancy
See DeRoin, Nancy
Ross, Nancy Wilson 1910-1986 97-100
Obituary 118
Ross, Nathaniel 1904-1986 .... 21-24R
Ross, Oakland 1952- 169
Ross, Pat(ricia Kienzle) 1943- 128
See also SATA 53
See also SATA-Brief 48
Ross, Patricia
See Baxter, Patricia E. W.
Ross, Paul
See Crawford, William (Elbert)
Ross, Philip 1939- 69-72
Ross, Phyllis (Freedman) 1926-1970 ..... CAP-2
Earlier sketch in CA 17-18
Ross, Prudence Leith
See Leith-Ross, Prudence
Ross, Ralph Gilbert 1911-2000 .... 13-16R
Ross, Ramon R(oyal) 1930- .... SATA 62
Ross, Raymond S(amuel) 1925- CANR-27
Earlier sketches in CA 21-24R, CANR-8
Ross, Richard 1944- 163
Ross, Robert 1949- 195
Ross, Robert H(enry), Jr. 1916- 13-16R
Ross, Robert Horace 106
Ross, Robert S(amuel) 1940- 57-60
Ross, Robert W.
See Power-Ross, Robert W.
Ross, Ronald 1857-1932 157
Ross, Rosetta E. 235
Ross, Russell M. 1921- 21-24R
Ross, Ruth 1930(?)-1986
Obituary 119
Ross, Sam 1912-1998 .... 13-16R
Obituary 166
Ross, Sheila Muriel 1925- 106
Ross, (James) Sinclair 1908-1996 ..... CANR-81
Earlier sketch in CA 73-76
See also CLC 13
See also CN 1, 2, 3, 4, 5, 6
See also DAC
See also DAM MST
See also DLB 88
See also RGEL 2
See also RGSF 2
See also SSC 24
See also TCWW 1, 2
Ross, Stanley R(obert) 1921- CANR-7
Earlier sketch in CA 17-20R
Ross, Stanley Ralph 1940-2000 .... CANR-20
Obituary 189
Earlier sketch in CA 97-100
Ross, Stephen David 1935- CANR-97
Earlier sketches in CA 41-44R, CANR-17, 39
Ross, Stephen M. 1943- 171
Ross, Steven Thomas 1937- 41-44R
Ross, Stewart 1947- CANR-127
Earlier sketch in CA 156
See also SAAS 23
See also SATA 92, 134
Ross, Stewart Halsey 1928- 162
Ross, Stuart 1950- 155
Ross, Sutherland
See Callard, Thomas Henry
Ross, T(heodore) J(ohn) 1924- 57-60
Ross, Terrence 1947- 103
Ross, Thomas B(ernard) 1929-2002 ...... 29-32R
Obituary 212
Ross, Thomas W(ynne) 1923- CANR-107
Earlier sketch in CA 41-44R
Ross, Timothy A(rrowsmith) 1936- 57-60
Ross, Tom 1958- .... SATA 84
Ross, Tony 1938- CANR-90
Earlier sketches in CA 77-80, CANR-35
See also CWRI 5
See also MAICYA 1, 2
See also SATA 17, 65, 130
Ross, Veronica 1946- CANR-73
Earlier sketch in CA 113
Ross, W(illiam) E(dward) D(aniel)
1912-1995 .... CANR-32
Earlier sketches in CA 81-84, CANR-14
See also HGG
See also TCWW 2
Ross, W(illiam) Gordon 1900-1990 45-48
Ross, W. W. E(ustace) 1894-1966 202
See also DLB 88
Ross, Wilda 1915- 85-88
See also SATA 51
See also SATA-Brief 39
Ross, William
See Dewart, Leslie
Ross, William B. 1915-2003 .... 25-28R
Obituary 219
Ross, Z. H.
See Ross, Zola Helen
Ross, Zola Helen 1912-1989 .... CANR-64
Obituary 130
Earlier sketch in CA 53-56
See also TCWW 1, 2
Rossabi, Morris 1941- 102
Rossant, Colette 1932- 199
Rossant, Murray J(oseph) 1923-1988
Obituary 125
Rossbach, Richard M. 1915(?)-1987
Obituary 123
Rossbacher, Lisa A(nn) 1952- 117
Rossberg, Robert H. 1926- 45-48
Rosse, Ian
See Straker, J(ohn) F(oster)
Rosse, Susanna
See Connolly, Vivian
Rossel, Seymour 1945- CANR-21
Earlier sketches in CA 53-56, CANR-5
See also SATA 28
Rossel, Sven H(akon) 1943- CANR-22
Earlier sketch in CA 105
Rosselli, Amelia 1930- .... CWP
See also DLB 128
Rossellini, Isabella 1952- 162
Rossellini, Roberto 1906-1977
Obituary 69-72
Rossel-Waugh, C. C.
See Waugh, Carol-Lynn Rossel
Rossen, Robert 1908-1966 185
Obituary 113
See also DLB 26
Rosser, Neill A(lbert) 1916-1973 .... CAP-1
Earlier sketch in CA 13-16
Rosser, Sue V(ilhauer) 1947- 156
Rosset, B(enjamin) C(harles) 1910-1974 .. 9-12R
Obituary 103
Rosset, Barnet Lee, Jr. 1922- 97-100
Interview in CA-97-100
See also Rosset, Barney
Rosset, Barney
See Rosset, Barnet Lee, Jr.
See also DLBY 2002
Rossetti, Christina (Georgina)
1830-1894 .... AAYA 51
See also BRW 5
See also BYA 4
See also DA
See also DA3
See also DAB
See also DAC
See also DAM MST, POET
See also DLB 35, 163, 240
See also EXPP
See also FL 1:3
See also LATS 1:1
See also MAICYA 1, 2
See also PC 7
See also PFS 10, 14
See also RGEL 2
See also SATA 20
See also TEA
See also WCH
See also WLC
Rossetti, Dante Gabriel 1828-1882 ..... AAYA 51
See also BRW 5
See also CDBLB 1832-1890
See also DA
See also DAB
See also DAC
See also DAM MST, POET
See also DLB 35
See also EXPP
See also PC 44
See also RGEL 2
See also TEA
See also WLC
Rossi, Aga
See Agarossi, Elena
Rossi, Agnes 1959- 195
Rossi, Alfred 1935- 29-32R
Rossi, Alice S(chaerr) 1922- CANR-17
Earlier sketches in CA 45-48, CANR-1
Rossi, Bruno
See Levinson, Leonard and
McCurtin, Peter
Rossi, Cristina Peri
See Peri Rossi, Cristina
Rossi, Ernest Lawrence 1933- CANR-14
Earlier sketch in CA 37-40R
Rossi, Hozy (Joe) 1965- 208
Rossi, Ino 89-92
Rossi, Jean-Baptiste 1931-2003 201
Obituary 215
See also Japrisot, Sebastien
Rossi, John P. 1936- 194
Rossi, John V. 1955- 152
Rossi, Joyce 1943- 188
See also SATA 116
Rossi, Lino 1923- 104
Rossi, Mario 1916- CANR-8
Earlier sketch in CA 5-8R
Rossi, Nicholas Louis, Jr. 1924- CANR-6
Earlier sketch in CA 13-16R
Rossi, Nick
See Rossi, Nicholas Louis, Jr.
Rossi, Paul A. 1929- 198
Brief entry 110
Rossi, Peter Henry 1921- CANR-41
Earlier sketches in CA 1-4R, CANR-4, 19
Rossi, Philip Joseph 1943- 115
Rossi, Roxanne 1962- 152
Rossi, Sanna Morrison Barlow 1917- 93-96
Rossi, William A(nthony) 1916- 65-68
Rossie, Jonathan Gregory 1935-
Brief entry 106
Rossi-Landi, Ferruccio 1921- 114
Rossing, Barbara 234
Rossini, Frederick A(nthony) 1939- ... CANR-12
Earlier sketch in CA 73-76
Rossit, Edward A. 1921- 17-20R
Rossiter, Charles 1942- 212
Rossiter, Charlie
See Rossiter, Charles
Rossiter, Clare
See Dawson, Janis
Rossiter, Clinton (Lawrence) 1917-1970
Obituary 25-28R
Rossiter, Frank R(aymond) 1937- 61-64
Rossiter, Ian
See Ross Williamson, Hugh
Rossiter, Jane
See Ross, W(illiam) E(dward) D(aniel)
Rossiter, John 1916- CANR-59
Earlier sketch in CA 33-36R
See also CMW 4
Rossiter, Margaret W(alsh) 1944- CANR-13
Earlier sketch in CA 77-80
Rossiter, Sarah 1942- 136
Rossiter, (Percival) Stuart (Bryce) 1923- ... 85-88
Rosskam, Edwin 1903(?)-1985
Obituary 115

Rosskopf 498 CONTEMPORARY AUTHORS

Rosskopf, Myron Frederick
1907-1973 ... CANR-5
Obituary ... 41-44R
Earlier sketch in CA 5-8R
Ross-Macdonald, Malcolm J(ohn)
1932- ... CANR-48
Earlier sketches in CA 65-68, CANR-13
Rossman, Charles Raymond 1938- ... CANR-90
Earlier sketches in CA 113, CANR-34
Rossman, Evelyn
See Rothchild, Sylvia
Rossman, Jack E(ugene) 1936- ... 49-52
Rossman, Marlene L. 1948- ... CANR-91
Earlier sketch in CA 124
Rossman, Martin L. 1945- ... 214
Rossman, Michael Dale 1939- ... 101
Rossman, (George) Parker 1919- ... 69-72
Rossman, Vadim 1964- ... 234
Rossmann, John F(rancis) 1942- ... 101
Rossner, Judith (Perelman) 1935- ... CANR-73
Earlier sketches in CA 17-20R, CANR-18, 51
Interview in ... CANR-18
See also AITN 2
See also BEST 90:3
See also BPFB 3
See also CLC 6, 9, 29
See also CN 4, 5, 6, 7
See also DLB 6
See also MAL 5
See also MTCW 1, 2
See also MTFW 2005
Rossner, Robert 1932- ... CANR-1
Earlier sketch in CA 1-4R
Rosso, Julee 1944- ... 139
Rossoff, Martin 1910- ... 9-12R
Rossol, Monona 1936- ... CANR-121
Earlier sketch in CA 140
Rossomando, Frederic William 1924- ... 49-52
Rosson, Hal 1895-1988 ... IDFW 3, 4
Rossotti, Hazel Swaine 1930- ... 142
See also SATA 95
Ross-Robertson, Lynne Nannen
1936- ... CANR-25
Earlier sketch in CA 107
Ross Williamson, Hugh 1901-1978 ... CANR-8
Earlier sketch in CA 17-20R
Rostand, Edmond (Eugene Alexis)
1868-1918 ... 126
Brief entry ... 104
See also DA
See also DA3
See also DAB
See also DAC
See also DAM DRAM, MST
See also DC 10
See also DFS 1
See also DLB 192
See also LAIT 1
See also MTCW 1
See also RGWL 2, 3
See also TCLC 6, 37
See also TWA
Rostand, J.
See Rostand, Jean
Rostand, Jean 1894-1977 ... 126
Brief entry ... 124
Rostand, Robert
See Hopkins, Robert S(ydney)
Rosten, Leo C(alvin) 1908-1997 ... CANR-6
Obituary ... 156
Earlier sketch in CA 5-8R
Interview in ... CANR-6
See also CN 1, 2, 3, 4, 5, 6
See also DLB 11
Rosten, Norman 1914-1995 ... CANR-21
Obituary ... 147
Earlier sketch in CA 77-80
Rostenberg, Leona 1908-2005 ... CANR-109
Obituary ... 237
Earlier sketches in CA 5-8R, CANR-5
See also DLB 140
Rostkowski, Margaret I. 1945- ... CANR-87
Earlier sketches in CA 127, CANR-54
See also AAYA 22
See also SATA 59
See also YAW
Rostler, Bill
See Rotsler, (Charles) William
Roston, Murray 1928- ... CANR-5
Earlier sketch in CA 53-56
Rostopchina, Evdokiia Petrovna
1811-1858 ... DLB 205
Rostov, Stefan
See Hutson, Shaun
Rostovsky, Dimitrii 1651-1709 ... DLB 150
Rostow, Eugene Victor 1913-2002 ... 5-8R
Obituary ... 212
Rostow, Walt W(hitman) 1916-2003 ... CANR-8
Obituary ... 214
Earlier sketch in CA 13-16R
Interview in ... CANR-8
Rostvold, Gerhard N(orman) 1919- ... CANR-10
Earlier sketch in CA 21-24R
Rostworowski, Karol Hubert
1877-1938 ... EWL 3
Roszak, Betty 1933- ... 29-32R
Roszak, Theodore 1933- ... CANR-81
Earlier sketches in CA 77-80, CANR-45
See also HGG
Rota, (Cyril) Bertram 1903-1966 ... 185
See also DLB 201
Rota, Gian-Carlo 1932-1999 ... 126
Obituary ... 178
Rota, Nino 1911-1979 ... IDFW 3, 4
Rotarius
See Kerekes, Tibor
Rotberg, Robert I. 1935- ... CANR-107
Earlier sketches in CA 13-16R, CANR-6, 21
Rotblat, Joseph 1908-2005 ... CANR-26
Earlier sketch in CA 109
Rotchstein, Janice 1944- ... CANR-25
Earlier sketch in CA 106
Rote, Kyle 1928-2002 ... 21-24R
Obituary ... 211
Rotella, Carlo 1964- ... 194
Rotella, Guy Louis 1947- ... 115
Rotella, Mark 1967- ... 224
Rotelle, John E. 1939- ... 158
Rotello, Gabriel 1953- ... 171
Rotenberg, David ... 209
Rotenberg, Marc 1960- ... 169
Rotenberg, Yehoshu'a
See Rothenberg, Joshua
Rotenstreich, Nathan 1914- ... CANR-23
Earlier sketches in CA 61-64, CANR-8
Roth, Alexander
See Dunner, Joseph
Roth, Andrew 1919- ... 53-56
Roth, Ann 1950- ... 229
Roth, Arlen 1952- ... 103
Roth, Arnold 1929- ... 21-24R
See also SATA 21
Roth, Arthur 1920- ... 1-4R
Roth, Arthur J(oseph) 1925-1993 ... CANR-7
Obituary ... 140
Earlier sketch in CA 53-56
See also SAAS 11
See also SATA 43
See also SATA-Brief 28
See also SATA-Obit 75
Roth, Audrey J. 1927- ... 21-24R
Roth, Cecil 1899-1970 ... CANR-13
Obituary ... 25-28R
Earlier sketch in CA 9-12R
Roth, Charles E(dmund) 1934- ... 111
Roth, Claire Jarett 1923- ... 5-8R
Roth, Darlene R(ebecca) 1941- ... 149
Roth, David 1940- ... 106
See also SATA 36
Roth, David F(rancisco) 1939- ... 41-44R
Roth, David Lee 1954- ... 166
Roth, David M. 1874(?)-1971
Obituary ... 104
Roth, David M(orris) 1935- ... 57-60
Roth, Don A. 1927- ... 25-28R
Roth, Eric (R.) ... 231
Roth, Ernst 1896-1971 ... CAP-2
Earlier sketch in CA 25-28
Roth, Eugen 1895-1976
Obituary ... 65-68
Roth, Friederike 1948- ... 197
Roth, Geneen 1951- ... CANR-42
Earlier sketch in CA 111
Roth, Gerhard (Jurgen) 1942- ... 159
See also DLB 85, 124
Roth, Hal 1927- ... 37-40R
Roth, Harold ... SATA-Brief 49
Roth, Harold L(eo) 1919-1982
Obituary ... 108
Roth, Harry 1903(?)-1976
Obituary ... 65-68
Roth, Henry 1906-1995 ... CANR-63
Obituary ... 149
Earlier sketches in CAP-1, CA 11-12, CANR-38
See also AMWS 9
See also CLC 2, 6, 11, 104
See also CN 1, 2, 3, 4, 5, 6
See also DA3
See also DLB 28
See also EWL 3
See also MAL 5
See also MTCW 1, 2
See also MTFW 2005
See also RGAL 4
Roth, Herbert (Otto) 1917- ... 61-64
Roth, Herrick S. 1916- ... 77-80
Roth, Holly 1916-1964 ... CANR-61
Earlier sketches in CA 1-4R, CANR-6
See also CMW 4
Roth, Jack J(oseph) 1920- ... 21-24R
Roth, John D. 1960- ... 237
Roth, John K(ing) 1940- ... CANR-123
Earlier sketches in CA 25-28R, CANR-10, 26, 51
Roth, Jonathan P. 1955- ... 198
Roth, (Moses) Joseph 1894-1939 ... 160
See also DLB 85
See also EWL 3
See also RGWL 2, 3
See also TCLC 33
Roth, Julius A(lfred) 1924- ... 21-24R
Roth, June (Doris Spiewak)
1926-1990 ... CANR-19
Obituary ... 132
Earlier sketches in CA 9-12R, CANR-5
Roth, Klaus 1939- ... CANR-106
Earlier sketch in CA 150
Roth, Leland M(artin) 1943- ... CANR-16
Earlier sketch in CA 93-96
Roth, (Hyam) Leon 1896-1963
Obituary ... 106
Roth, Lillian 1910-1980
Obituary ... 97-100
Roth, Mark J(oseph) 1941- ... 77-80
Roth (Vanceburg), Martha 1938- ... 137
Roth, Martin 1924- ... 134
Roth, Marty
See Roth, Martin
Roth, Mary Jane ... 21-24R
Roth, Michael S. 1957- ... 127
Roth, Moira 1933- ... 121
Roth, Norman 1938- ... 150
Roth, Peggy (Meehan) (?)-1973
Obituary ... 104
Roth, Philip (Milton) 1933- ... CANR-132
Earlier sketches in CA 1-4R, CANR-1, 22, 36, 55, 89
See also AAYA 67
See also AMWR 2
See also AMWS 3
See also BEST 90:3
See also BPFB 3
See also CDALB 1968-1988
See also CLC 1, 2, 3, 4, 6, 9, 15, 22, 31, 47, 66, 86, 119, 201
See also CN 3, 4, 5, 6, 7
See also CPW 1
See also DA
See also DA3
See also DAB
See also DAC
See also DAM MST, NOV, POP
See also DLB 2, 28, 173
See also DLBY 1982
See also EWL 3
See also MAL 5
See also MTCW 1, 2
See also MTFW 2005
See also RGAL 4
See also RGSF 2
See also SSC 26
See also SSFS 12, 18
See also TUS
See also WLC
Roth, Richard H(enry) 1949- ... 77-80
Roth, Robert Howard 1933- ... CANR-14
Earlier sketch in CA 41-44R
Roth, Robert J. 1920- ... 17-20R
Roth, Robert N(elson) 1928- ... 212
Roth, Robert Paul 1919- ... 61-64
Roth, Samuel 1894-1974
Obituary ... 49-52
Roth, Sister Mary Augustine 1926- ... CANR-3
Earlier sketch in CA 9-12R
Roth, Sol 1927- ... 65-68
Roth, Susan L. ... 196
See also SATA 134
Roth, Theodore W(illiam) 1916- ... 57-60
Roth, William 1942- ... 101
Roth, Wolfgang M(ax) W(ilhelm)
1930- ... 41-44R
Rotha, Paul 1907-1984 ... 9-12R
Obituary ... 112
Rothafel, Roxy
See Rothafel, Samuel L(ionel)
Rothafel, Samuel L(ionel) 1881(?)-1936(?) ... 181
Brief entry ... 123
Rothbard, Murray N(ewton)
1926-1995 ... CANR-22
Obituary ... 148
Earlier sketches in CA 5-8R, CANR-6
Rothbart, Harold A(rthur) 1917- ... 111
Rothbaum, Melvin 1926- ... 5-8R
Rothberg, Abraham 1922- ... 33-36R
See also SATA 59
Rothblatt, Ben 1924- ... 25-28R
Rothblatt, Donald N(oah) 1935- ... CANR-23
Earlier sketches in CA 61-64, CANR-8
Rothblatt, Henry B(arnett)
1916-1985 ... CANR-19
Obituary ... 117
Earlier sketch in CA 25-28R
Rothchild, Donald (Sylvester) 1928- ... CANR-14
Earlier sketches in CA 41-44R, CANR-31
Rothchild, Sylvia 1923- ... 77-80
Rothe, Dietmar (E.) 1934- ... 219
Rothel, David 1936- ... CANR-10
Earlier sketch in CA 65-68
Rothenberg, Alan B(aer) 1907-1977
Obituary ... 73-76
Rothenberg, Albert 1930- ... CANR-51
Earlier sketches in CA 57-60, CANR-8, 25
Rothenberg, B(arbara) Annye 1940- ... 107
Rothenberg, Diane Brodatz 1932- ... 115
Rothenberg, Gunther Eric 1923- ... CANR-8
Earlier sketch in CA 21-24R
Rothenberg, Jerome 1924- ... 29-32R
Rothenberg, Jerome 1931- ... CANR-106
Earlier sketches in CA 45-48, CANR-1
See also CLC 6, 57
See also CP 1, 2, 3, 4, 5, 6, 7
See also DLB 5, 193
Rothenberg, Joshua 1911-1990 ... 37-40R
Rothenberg, Laura 1981-2003 ... 226
Rothenberg, Lillian 1922- ... 9-12R
Rothenberg, Marc 1949- ... 115
Rothenberg, Michael ... 198
Rothenberg, Paula S. 1943- ... 200
Rothenberg, Polly 1916- ... 85-88
Rothenberg, Randall 1956- ... 118
Rothenberg, Rebecca 1948-1998 ... 230
Rothenberg, Robert E(dward)
1908-2002 ... 37-40R
Obituary ... 207
Rothenstein, John K(newstub) M(aurice)
1901-1992 ... CANR-1
Earlier sketch in CA 1-4R
Rothermere, Viscount
See Harmsworth, Esmond Cecil
Rothery, Brian 1934- ... CANR-1
Earlier sketch in CA 49-52
Rothfork, John 1946- ... 110
Roth-Hano, Renee 1931- ... CANR-110
Earlier sketch in CA 151
See also SATA 85
Rothkopf, Carol Z. 1929- ... 25-28R
See also SATA 4
Rothman, Barbara Katz 1948- ... CANR-29
Earlier sketch in CA 111
Rothman, Charles Warren 1952- ... 120
Rothman, Chuck
See Rothman, Charles Warren
Rothman, David B. 1956- ... 111
Rothman, David J. 1937- ... CANR-57
Earlier sketch in CA 33-36R
Rothman, Esther P. 1919- ... 37-40R
Rothman, Hal (K.) 1958- ... CANR-141
Earlier sketch in CA 130
Rothman, Joel 1938- ... 37-40R
See also SATA 7
Rothman, Judith
See Peters, Maureen
Rothman, Milton A. 1919- ... 41-44R
Rothman, Sheila M(iller) ... 230
Rothman, Stanley 1927- ... 93-96
Rothman, Theodore 1907- ... CAP-2
Earlier sketch in CA 29-32
Rothman, Tony 1953- ... CANR-33
Earlier sketches in CA 85-88, CANR-15
Rothman, William 1944- ... 232
Rothmiller, Mike 1950- ... 143
Rothmuller, Aron Marko 1908- ... 73-76
Rotholz, James M. 1951- ... 237
Rothrock, George A(bel) 1932- ... 61-64
Rothschild, Alfred 1894(?)-1972 ... 37-40R
Rothschild, Alfred Charles de
1842-1918 ... DLB 184
Rothschild, Anthony Nathan de
1810-1876 ... DLB 184
Rothschild, Dick
See Rothschild, Richard D.
Rothschild, Emma (Georgina) 1948- ... 207
Rothschild, Ferdinand James Anselm de
1839-1898 ... DLB 184
Rothschild, Fritz A(lexander) 1919-
Brief entry ... 106
Rothschild, Guy de
See de Rothschild, Guy (Edouard Alphonse Paul)
Rothschild, J(acquard) H(irshorn)
1907- ... CAP-2
Earlier sketch in CA 17-18
Rothschild, James Armand Edmond de
1878-1957 ... DLB 184
Rothschild, Joseph A. 1931-2000 ... CANR-3
Obituary ... 188
Earlier sketch in CA 9-12R
Rothschild, Kurt Wilhelm 1914- ... CANR-47
Earlier sketches in CA 102, CANR-23
Rothschild, Lincoln 1902-1983 ... CANR-12
Obituary ... 109
Earlier sketch in CA 45-48
Rothschild, Lionel Nathan de
1882-1942 ... DLB 184
Rothschild, Lionel Walter 1868-1937 ... DLB 184
Rothschild, Mayer Amschel
1743-1812 ... DLB 184
Rothschild, Mayer Amschel de
1818-1874 ... DLB 184
Rothschild, Miriam (Louisa)
1908-2005 ... CANR-92
Obituary ... 235
Earlier sketch in CA 145
Rothschild, Nathaniel Mayer Victor 1910-1990
Obituary ... 131
Rothschild, Norman 1913- ... 103
Rothschild, Richard Charles 1895-1986
Obituary ... 118
Rothschild, Richard D. 1923- ... 184
Rothstein, Arthur 1915-1985 ... CANR-6
Obituary ... 117
Earlier sketch in CA 57-60
Rothstein, Bo (A. M.) 1945- ... 183
Rothstein, Edward 1952- ... CANR-142
Earlier sketch in CA 136
Rothstein, Eric 1936- ... 73-76
Rothstein, Marian ... 197
Rothstein, Robert L. 1936- ... 199
Rothstein, Samuel 1902(?)-1978
Obituary ... 77-80
Rothstein, Samuel 1921- ... 61-64
Rothstein, Stanley William 1929- ... 120
Rothstein, William G(ene) 1937- ... 73-76
Rothweiler, Paul Roger 1931- ... CANR-10
Earlier sketch in CA 65-68
Rothwell, Bruce 1923(?)-1984
Obituary ... 114
Rothwell, Kenneth J(ames) 1925- ... CANR-14
Earlier sketch in CA 21-24R
Rothwell, Kenneth S(prague) 1921- ... CANR-95
Earlier sketch in CA 33-36R
Rothwell, Talbot (Nelson Conn) 1916-1981
Obituary ... 103
Rothwell, V(ictor) H(oward) 1945- ... 37-40R
Rothwell, William J. 1951- ... 158
Rotimi, E. G. O.
See Rotimi, (Emmanuel Gladstone) Ola(wale)
Rotimi, (Emmanuel Gladstone) Ola(wale)
1938- ... 124
See also AFW
See also BW 2
See also CD 5, 6
See also DLB 125
See also EWL 3
Rotimi, Olawale
See Rotimi, (Emmanuel Gladstone) Ola(wale)
Rotkin, Charles E. 1916- ... 5-8R
Rotmans, Elmer A. 1896-1964 ... 5-8R
Rotner, Shelley 1951- ... 143
See also SATA 76
Rotondi, Cesar 1926- ... 97-100
Rotrou, Jean 1609-1650 ... DLB 268
See also GFL Beginnings to 1789
Rotsler, William 1926- ... CANR-4
Earlier sketch in CA 53-56
See also SFW 4

Cumulative Index 499 Roy

Rotsler, (Charles) William 1926-1997
Obituary ... 176
See also Appleton, Victor
Rotstein, Abraham 1929- ... 104
Rotten, Johnny
See Lydon, John (Joseph)
Rottenberg, Dan(iel) 1942- ... CANR-120
Earlier sketches in CA 102, CANR-19, 40
Rottenberg, Isaac C. 1925- ... 13-16R
Rottensteiner, Franz 1942- ... CANR-33
Earlier sketches in CA 81-84, CANR-15
Rotter, Julian B(ernard) 1916- ... 33-36R
Rotter, Marion 1940(?)-1973
Obituary ... 104
Rotter, Pat ed. ... CLC 65
Rottman, S(usan) L(ynn) 1970- ... CANR-142
Earlier sketch in CA 176
See also AAYA 55
See also SATA 106, 157
Rotundo, Louis C. 1949- ... 146
Rotunno, Giuseppe 1923- ... IDFW 3, 4
Rouaud, Jean 1952- ... 228
Roubickova, Eva Mandlova 1921-
Roubiczek, Paul (Anton) 1898-1972
Obituary ... 115
Roubinek, Darrell L(eRoy) 1935- ... 57-60
Roucek, Joseph S(labey) 1902-1984 . CANR-32
Earlier sketch in CA 9-12R
Roud, Richard 1929-1989
Obituary ... 127
Roudaut, Jean ... 178
Roudiez, Leon S(amuel) 1917-2004 ... 37-40R
Obituary ... 228
Roudinesco, Elisabeth 1944- ... CANR-120
Earlier sketch in CA 142
Roudybush, Alexandra (Brown) 1911- ... 65-68
Roueche, Berton 1911-1994 ... CANR-48
Obituary ... 145
Earlier sketches in CA 1-4R, CANR-1
See also SATA 28
Roueche, John E(dward) 1938- ... 49-52
Rougeau, Remy 1948- ... 199
Rougemont, Denis de
See de Rougemont, Denis (Louis)
Rouget, Marie-Melanie
See Noel, Marie
Roughan, Howard ... 237
Roughsey, Dick 1921(?)-1985 ... CANR-80
Earlier sketch in CA 109
See also CLR 41
See also CWRI 5
See also SATA 35
Roughsey, Goobalathaldin
See Roughsey, Dick
Rougier, Louis (Auguste Paul)
1889-1982 ... CANR-13
Earlier sketch in CA 29-32R
Rougier, Nicole 1929- ... 29-32R
Rouhani, Fuad 1907-2004 ... 37-40R
Obituary ... 223
Roukes, Nicholas 1925- ... 25-28R
Roulac, Stephen E. 1945- ... 104
Rouleau, Raymond (Edgard Marie) 1904-1981
Obituary ... 108
Roulston, Marjorie Hillis 1890-1971
Obituary ... 104
Roumain, Jacques (Jean Baptiste)
1907-1944 ... 125
Brief entry ... 117
See also BLC 3
See also BW 1
See also DAM MULT
See also EWL 3
See also TCLC 19
Rounding, Virginia 1956- ... 224
Rounds, David 1930-1983
Obituary ... 111
Rounds, David 1942- ... 143
Rounds, Glen (Harold) 1906-2002 . CANR-114
Obituary ... 212
Earlier sketches in CA 53-56, CANR-7, 22, 44
See also CWRI 5
See also MAICYA 1, 2
See also SATA 8, 70, 112
See also SATA-Obit 141
Rouner, Arthur A(cy), Jr. 1929- ... CANR-5
Earlier sketch in CA 9-12R
Rouner, Leroy S(tephens) 1930- ... 73-76
Rountree, Owen
See Kittredge, William and
Krauzer, Steven M(ark)
Rountree, Thomas J. 1927- ... 25-28R
Rourke, Constance Mayfield 1885-1941 ... 200
Brief entry ... 107
See also MAL 5
See also TCLC 12
See also YABC 1
Rourke, Francis E(dward) 1922- ... CANR-6
Earlier sketch in CA 1-4R
Rourke, James
See Heckelmann, Charles N(ewman)
Rous, Stanley (Ford) 1895-1986 ... 108
Rous, Stephen N. 1931- ... 141
Rousculp, Charles G(ene) 1923- ... 29-32R
Rouse, Anne (Barrett) 1954- ... CANR-107
Earlier sketch in CA 149
Rouse, (Hubert) Blair 1912-1981 ... 1-4R
Rouse, (Benjamin) Irving, (Jr.) 1913- ... 9-12R
Rouse, John E(dward), Jr. 1942- ... 89-92
Rouse, John E(vans) 1892-1990 ... 73-76
Rouse, Mary A(mes) 1934- ... CANR-140
Earlier sketch in CA 141
Rouse, Parke (Shepherd), Jr. 1915- ... 17-20R
Rouse, Richard H(unter) 1933- ... CANR-140
Earlier sketch in CA 29-32R
Rouse, Russell 1913(?)-1987
Obituary ... 123
Rouse Jones, Lewis 1907- ... CAP-1
Earlier sketch in CA 13-14
Roush, Barbara 1940- ... 109
Roush, John H., Jr. 1923- ... 37-40R
Rousmaniere, John 1944- ... CANR-121
Earlier sketches in CA 93-96, CANR-17, 38
Rousmaniere, Leah Robinson
See Robinson, Leah Ruth
Roussan, Jacques de
See de Roussan, Jacques
Rousseau, George Sebastian 1941- ... CANR-11
Earlier sketch in CA 29-32R
Rousseau, Jean-Jacques 1712-1778 ... DA
See also DA3
See also DAB
See also DAC
See also DAM MST
See also DLB 314
See also EW 4
See also GFL Beginnings to 1789
See also LMFS 1
See also RGWL 2, 3
See also TWA
See also WLC
Rousseau, Richard W(ilfred) 1924- ... 110
Rousseau, Victor 1879-1960 ... 165
See also HGG
See also SFW 4
Roussel, Raymond 1877-1933 ... 201
Brief entry ... 117
See also EWL 3
See also GFL 1789 to the Present
See also TCLC 20
Rousselle, Aline 1939- ... 130
Rousselot, Philippe 1945- ... IDFW 4
Rousset, (Elisee) David 1912-1997 ... 144
Obituary ... 163
Roussin, Andre (Jean Paul Marie) 1911-1987
Obituary ... 124
Rout, Leslie B(rennan), Jr. 1936-1987 ... 57-60
Obituary ... 122
Routh, C(harles) R(ichard) N(airne)
1896- ... CAP-1
Earlier sketch in CA 13-14
Routh, Donald K(ent) 1937- ... 57-60
Routh, Francis John 1927- ... 13-16R
Routh, Jonathan ... 110
Routh, Porter W(roe) 1911-1987 ... 77-80
Routhier, Adolphe Basil 1839-1920 ... 213
Routhier, Adolphe-Basile 1839-1920 ... DLB 99
Routier, Simone 1901-1987 ... 153
See also CCA 1
See also DLB 88
Routledge, Paul 1943- ... 191
Routley, Erik (Reginald) 1917-1982 ... CANR-5
Obituary ... 108
Earlier sketch in CA 1-4R
Routley, (Bernarra) Jane 1962- ... 158
Routsong, Alma 1924- ... 49-52
See also Miller, Isabel
See also GLL 1
Routt, Mary Patterson 1890(?)-1986
Obituary ... 119
Routtenberg, Max Jonah 1909-1987 ... 77-80
Rouverol, Jean
See Butler, Jean Rouverol
Roux, Edward R(udolph) 1903-1966 ... 13-16R
Roux, Georges 1914- ... 17-20R
Roux, Willan Charles 1902-1978 ... CAP-2
Earlier sketch in CA 17-18
Rover, Constance (Mary) 1910- ... 21-24R
Rovere, Richard H(alworth)
1915-1979 ... CANR-3
Obituary ... 89-92
Earlier sketch in CA 49-52
Roversi, Roberto 1923- ... 182
See also DLB 128
Rovin, Ben
See Clevenger, Ernest Allen, Jr.
Rovin, Jeff 1951- ... 77-80
Rovinski, Samuel 1932- ... EWL 3
Rovit, Earl (Herbert) 1927- ... CANR-12
Earlier sketch in CA 5-8R
See also CLC 7
Row, Jess 1974- ... 238
Rowan, Andrew N(icholas) 1946- ... 124
Rowan, Carl T(homas) 1925-2000 ... CANR-46
Obituary ... 189
Earlier sketch in CA 89-92
See also BW 2
Rowan, Dan (Hale) 1922-1987
Obituary ... 125
Rowan, Deirdre
See Williams, Jeanne
Rowan, Ford 1943- ... CANR-29
Earlier sketch in CA 69-72
Rowan, Helen 1927(?)-1972
Obituary ... 37-40R
Rowan, Hester
See Robinson, Sheila Mary
Rowan, M. M.
See Rowan, Marie
See also TCWW 2
Rowan, Marie 1943-
See Rowan, M. M.
Rowan, Richard Lamar 1931- ... 9-12R
Rowan, Roy 1920- ... 156
Rowan, Stephen A(nthony) 1928- ... 45-48
Rowan, Steven William 1943- ... 116
Rowan-Robinson, Michael (Geoffrey)
1942- ... 191
Rowans, Virgina
See Tanner, Edward Everett III
Rowat, Donald C(ameron) 1921- ... CANR-42
Earlier sketches in CA 9-12R, CANR-5, 20
Rowatt, G(eorge) Wade, Jr. 1943- ... 126
Rowbotham, David (Harold) 1924- .. CANR-90
Brief entry ... 112
Earlier sketch in CA 149
See also CP 1, 2, 3, 4, 5, 6, 7
Rowbotham, Sheila 1943- ... CANR-116
Earlier sketches in CA 101, CANR-59
See also FW
Rowdon, Maurice 1922- ... 185
Brief entry ... 110
Rowe, A(lbert) W(ard) 1915- ... CANR-14
Earlier sketch in CA 21-24R
Rowe, C(hristopher) J(ames) 1944- ... 132
Rowe, Clarence J(ohn), Jr. 1916- ... 104
Rowe, David C. 1949-2003 ... 147
Rowe, David Knox 1924(?)-1989 ... 77-80
Obituary ... 129
Rowe, David Nelson 1905-1985 ... CANR-2
Earlier sketch in CA 5-8R
Rowe, Elizabeth Singer 1674-1737 ... DLB 39, 95
Rowe, Erna (Dirks) 1926- ... 93-96
Rowe, Frank (A.) 1921-1985 ... 130
Obituary ... 115
Rowe, Frederick William 1912- ... 101
Rowe, G(ail) S(tuart) 1936- ... 112
Rowe, George E(rnest), Jr. 1947- ... 93-96
Rowe, H. Edward 1927- ... 69-72
Rowe, James L(ester), Jr. 1948- ... 69-72
Rowe, James N(icholas) 1938-1989 ... 37-40R
Obituary ... 128
Rowe, Jeanne A. 1938- ... 29-32R
Rowe, Jeannette Louise 1947- ... 178
Rowe, Jennifer
See Rodda, Emily
Rowe, John (Seymour) 1936- ... CANR-28
Earlier sketch in CA 109
Rowe, John A. 1949- ... SATA 146
Rowe, John Carlos 1945- ... CANR-82
Earlier sketches in CA 114, CANR-36
Rowe, John L(eroy) 1914-1975(?) ... 17-20R
Obituary ... 135
Rowe, John W(allis) 1944- ... 178
Rowe, Margaret (Kevin) 1920- ... 13-16R
Rowe, Mary Budd 1925- ... 113
Rowe, Nicholas 1674-1718 ... DLB 84
See also RGEL 2
Rowe, Robert 1920- ... 17-20R
Rowe, Rosemary
See Aitken, Rosemary
Rowe, Terry ... AITN 2
Rowe, Timothy 1953- ... 187
Rowe, Viola Carson 1903-1969 ... 1-4R
Obituary ... 103
See also SATA-Obit 26
Rowe, Vivian C(laud) 1902-1978 ... CANR-2
Earlier sketch in CA 1-4R
Rowe, William (Neil) 1942- ... 131
Rowe, William D(avid) 1930- ... 114
Rowe, William L. 1931-
Brief entry ... 108
Rowell, Galen 1940-2002 ... CANR-113
Obituary ... 207
Earlier sketches in CA 65-68, CANR-18, 55
Rowell, (Douglas) Geoffrey 1943- ... CANR-142
Earlier sketch in CA 129
Rowell, George (Rignall) 1923- ... CANR-39
Earlier sketches in CA 5-8R, CANR-2, 18
Rowell, Henry T(hompson) 1904-1974 . CAP-1
Earlier sketch in CA 13-14
Rowell, John W(illiam) 1914- ... 33-36R
Rowell, Patricia Frances 1937- ... 222
Rowell, Patti
See Rowell, Patricia Frances
Rowell, Steve A. 1954- ... 228
Rowen, Betty (Jane Rose) 1920- ... 127
Brief entry ... 109
Rowen, Henry S(tanislaus) 1925- ... 123
Brief entry ... 118
Rowen, Herbert H(arvey) 1916- ... CANR-3
Earlier sketch in CA 9-12R
Rowen, Hobart 1918-1995 ... 9-12R
Obituary ... 148
Rowen, Lilian 1925- ... 108
Rowen, Ruth Halle 1918- ... 33-36R
Rower, Ann 1938- ... 211
Rowes, Barbara Gail ... 101
Rowett, Colin 1952- ... 128
Rowh, Mark 1952- ... 155
See also SATA 90
Rowland, Arthur R(ay) 1930- ... CANR-21
Earlier sketches in CA 13-16R, CANR-6
Rowland, Benjamin, Jr. 1904-1972
Obituary ... 37-40R
Rowland, Beryl ... 89-92
Rowland, Christopher (Charles) 1947- ... 116
Rowland, Claude K. 1943- ... 112
Rowland, D(onald) S(ydney) 1928- .. CANR-65
Earlier sketch in CA 21-24R
See also TCWW 1, 2
Rowland, David ... 192
Rowland, Diana 1950- ... 122
Rowland, Edna 1922- ... 139
Rowland, Florence Wightman
1900-1997 ... CANR-5
Obituary ... 174
Earlier sketch in CA 5-8R
See also SATA 8
See also SATA-Obit 108
Rowland, Ingrid D(rake) 1953- ... 197
Rowland, Iris
See Roberts, Irene
Rowland, J(ohn) R(ussell) 1925- ... 101
See also CP 1, 2
Rowland, Jon Thomas 1956- ... 177
Rowland, Judith 1944- ... 124
Rowland, Laura Joh 1954(?)- ... CANR-120
Earlier sketches in CA 156, CANR-73
Rowland, Lawrence S. 1942- ... 166
Rowland, Peter (Kenneth) 1938- ... 25-28R
Rowland, Robin F. 1950- ... 136
Rowland, Stanley J., Jr. 1928- ... 13-16R
Rowland, Virgil K(enneth) 1909-1974 ... 5-8R
Rowland, Wade 1944- ... 182
Rowland-Entwistle, (Arthur) Theodore (Henry)
1925- ... CANR-49
Earlier sketches in CA 107, CANR-24
See also SATA 31, 94
Rowlands, Ian 1964- ... DLB 310
Rowlands, John (Kendall) 1931- ... 219
Rowlands, John 1938- ... 221
Rowlands, John Robert 1947- ... 109
Rowlands, Peter
See Lovell, Mark
Rowlands, Samuel 1570(?)-1630 ... DLB 121
Rowlandson, Mary 1637(?)-1678 .. DLB 24, 200
See also RGAL 4
Rowlatt, Mary 1908- ... 5-8R
Rowley, Ames Dorrance
See Lovecraft, H(oward) P(hillips)
Rowley, Anthony 1939- ... 61-64
Rowley, Brian A(lan) 1923- ... 5-8R
Rowley, Charles (Dunford) 1906-1985 ... 103
Obituary ... 117
Rowley, Charles K(ershaw) 1939- ... 143
Rowley, Hazel 1951- ... CANR-113
Earlier sketch in CA 149
Rowley, Peter 1934- ... 65-68
Rowley, Peter T(empleton) 1929-
Brief entry ... 112
Rowley, (Richard) Trevor 1942- ... 131
Rowley, William 1585(?)-1626 ... DFS 22
See also DLB 58
See also RGEL 2
Rowley, William Dean 1939- ... 112
Rowling, J.K. 1966- ... CANR-128
Earlier sketch in CA 173
See also AAYA 34
See also BYA 11, 13, 14
See also CLC 137
See also CLR 66, 80
See also MAICYA 2
See also MTFW 2005
See also SATA 109
See also SUFW 2
Rowling, Joanne Kathleen
See Rowling, J.K.
Rowling, Marjorie A(lice Thexton) 1900- .. 5-8R
Rowlingson, Donald T(aggart) 1907- .. CANR-6
Earlier sketch in CA 1-4R
Rowlinson, Matthew 1956- ... 150
Rowney, Don Karl 1936- ... 108
Rowny, Edward L. 1917- ... 145
Rowse, A(lfred) L(eslie) 1903-1997 ... CANR-45
Obituary ... 161
Earlier sketches in CA 1-4R, CANR-1
See also CAAS 8
See also CP 1, 2
See also DLB 155
Rowsome, Frank (Howard), Jr. 1914-1983 .. 112
See also SATA 36
Rowson, Susanna Haswell
1762(?)-1824 ... AMWS 15
See also DLB 37, 200
See also RGAL 4
Rowthorn, Anne W(heeler) 1939- ... 113
Roxas, Savina A. ... 37-40R
Roxborough, Henry Hall 1891- ... 5-8R
Roxon, Lillian 1933(?)-1973
Obituary ... 111
Roy, Archibald Edmiston 1924- ... 102
Roy, Archie E.
See Roy, Archibald Edmiston
Roy, Arundhati 1960(?)- ... CANR-126
Earlier sketches in CA 163, CANR-90
See also CLC 109, 210
See also CN 7
See also DLBY 1997
See also EWL 3
See also LATS 1:2
See also MTFW 2005
See also NFS 22
See also WWE 1
Roy, Camille 1870-1943 ... DLB 92
Roy, Claude
See Orland, Claude
See also EWL 3
See also RGWL 3
Roy, David Tod 1933- ... 41-44R
Roy, Donald H. 1944- ... CANR-125
Earlier sketch in CA 163
Roy, Emil L. 1933- ... 25-28R
Roy, Ewell Paul 1929- ... 9-12R
Roy, F. Hampton 1937- ... 144
Roy, G(eorge) Ross 1924- ... 77-80
Roy, Gabrielle 1909-1983 ... CANR-61
Obituary ... 110
Earlier sketches in CA 53-56, CANR-5
See also CCA 1
See also CLC 10, 14
See also DAB
See also DAC
See also DAM MST
See also DLB 68
See also EWL 3
See also MTCW 1
See also RGWL 2, 3
See also SATA 104
See also TCLE 1:2
Roy, Gregor 1929- ... 21-24R
Roy, Jack
See Dangerfield, Rodney
Roy, Jacqueline 1954- ... 153
See also BW 2
See also SATA 74

Roy 500 CONTEMPORARY AUTHORS

Roy, James A(lexander) 1884-1973 .... CAP-1
Earlier sketch in CA 11-12
Roy, James Charles 1945- 204
Roy, Jessie Hailstalk 1895-1986
Obituary 121
See also SATA-Obit 51
Roy, Joaquin 1943- 77-80
Roy, John (Flint) 1913- 93-96
Roy, Jules 1907-2000 181
Obituary 188
See also DLB 83
Roy, Katherine (Morris) 1906- 1-4R
Roy, Liam
See Scarry, Patricia (Murphy)
Roy, Louis 1942- 229
Roy, Lucinda (H.) 168
Roy, Michael 1913-1976 .... CANR-10
Obituary 65-68
Earlier sketch in CA 61-64
Roy, Mike
See Roy, Michael
Roy, Patricia E. 137
Roy, Reginald H(erbert) 1922- 49-52
Roy, Robert L(ouis) 1947- 106
Roy, Robin 1946- CANR-36
Earlier sketch in CA 114
Roy, Ron(ald) 1940- 114
See also SATA 40, 110
See also SATA-Brief 35
Roy, Rustum 1924- 113
Roy, William G. 1946- 190
Royal, Claudia Smith 1904-1980 .... 5-8R
Royal, D.
See Du Breuil, (Elizabeth) L(or)inda
Royal, Dan
See Barrett, Geoffrey John
Royal, Denise 1935- 25-28R
Royal, Lauren 221
Royal, Priscilla 1944(?)- 239
Royal, Rosamond
See Hines, Jeanne
Royal, William Robert 1905-1997 101
Royale, A.
See Gibson, Arthur
Royall, Anne 1769-1854 .... DLB 43, 248
Royall, Vanessa
See Hinkemeyer, Michael T(homas)
Royalton-Kisch, Martin (Bruce)
1952- CANR-60
Earlier sketch in CA 128
Roybal, Laura (Husby) 1956- 152
See also SATA 85
Royce, Anya Peterson 1940- 101
Royce, James E(mmet) 1914-1996 .... CANR-34
Obituary 151
Earlier sketch in CA 1-4R
Royce, Josiah 1855-1916 .... DLB 270
Royce, Kenneth
See Gandley, Kenneth Royce
Royce, Patrick M(ilan) 1922- 13-16R
Royce, R(ussell) Joseph 1921- CANR-9
Earlier sketch in CA 21-24R
Roy Choudhury, Malay 1939- 215
Autobiographical Essay in 215
See also CAAS 14
Royde-Smith, Naomi 1875-1964 .... DLB 191
Royds, Caroline 1953- 123
See also SATA 55
Royer, Fanchon 1902- 5-8R
Royko, Mike 1932-1997 .... CANR-111
Obituary 157
Earlier sketches in CA 89-92, CANR-26
See also CLC 109
See also CPW
Roylance, William H(erbert) 1927- 61-64
Royle, Edward 1944- 61-64
Royle, Nicholas (John) 1957- CANR-81
Earlier sketch in CA 151
See also HGG
Royle, Selena 1904-1983
Obituary 109
Royle, Trevor 1945- CANR-116
Earlier sketches in CA 112, CANR-31
Royster, Charles 1944- 101
Royster, Philip M. 1943- CANR-13
Earlier sketch in CA 65-68
Royster, Salibelle 1895-1975 .... CAP-2
Earlier sketch in CA 25-28
Royster, Vermont (Connecticut)
1914-1996 .... 21-24R
Obituary 152
See also DLB 127
Royston, Angela 1945- CANR-136
Earlier sketches in CA 128, CANR-67
See also SATA 120
Royston, Olive 1904- 102
Royston, Richard fl. 1628-1686 .... DLB 170
Royte, Elizabeth 204
Rozakis, Gregory 1943(?)-1989
Obituary 129
Rozakis, Laurie E. 1952- CANR-94
Earlier sketch in CA 150
See also SATA 84
Rozan, S(hira) J. CANR-104
Earlier sketch in CA 165
See also AAYA 66
Rozanov, Vasilii Vasil'evich
See Rozanov, Vassili
See also DLB 295
Rozanov, Vasily Vasilyevich
See Rozanov, Vassili
See also EWL 3
Rozanov, Vassili 1856-1919
See Rozanov, Vasilii Vasil'evich and
Rozanov, Vasily Vasilyevich
See also TCLC 104
Rozbicki, Michael J. 1946- 170
Rozeboom, William W(arren) 1928- 17-20R
Rozek, Evalyn Robillard 1941- 61-64
Rozell, Mark J. 1959- 154
Rozemond, Marleen 184
Rozenberg, Joshua 1950- 235
Rozensztroch, Daniel 1944- 128
Rozental, Alek A(ron) 1920- 33-36R
Rozewicz, Tadeusz 1921- CANR-66
Earlier sketches in CA 108, CANR-36
See also CLC 9, 23, 139
See also CWW 2
See also DA3
See also DAM POET
See also DLB 232
See also EWL 3
See also MTCW 1, 2
See also MTFW 2005
See also RGWL 3
Rozhdestvensky, Vsevolod A. 1895(?)-1977
Obituary 73-76
Rozier, John W(iley) 1918- 107
Rozik, Eli 1932- 232
Rozin, Skip 1941- 89-92
Roziner, Felix (Yakovlevich) 1936- 142
Rozman, Deborah 1949- 115
Rozman, Gilbert Friedell 1943- CANR-51
Earlier sketches in CA 109, CANR-26
Rozovsky, Lorne Elkin 1942- CANR-24
Earlier sketch in CA 108
Rozovsky, Mark (Grigorievich) 1937- 181
Rozsa, Miklos 1907-1995 .... IDFW 3, 4
Rozwenc, Edwin C(harles) 1915-1974 .. CAP-1
Earlier sketch in CA 13-14
Ruan, Fang-fu 1937- 156
Ruane, Gerald P(atrick) 1934- 69-72
Ruano, Argimiro 1924- 33-36R
Ruano, Nazario
See Ruano, Argimiro
Ruark, Gibbons 1941- CANR-57
Earlier sketches in CA 33-36R, CANR-14, 31
See also CAAS 23
See also CLC 3
See also DLB 120
Ruark, Robert (Chester) 1915-1965 .... CAP-2
Obituary 25-28R
Earlier sketch in CA 19-20
See also BPFB 3
Ruas, Charles (Edward) 1938- 124
Rubadeau, Duane O. 1927- 29-32R
Rubadiri, David 1930- .... CP 1
Ruban, Vasilii Grigor'evich
1742-1795 .... DLB 150
Rubashov, Schneor Zalman
See Shazar, (Schneor) Zalman
Rubashov, Zalman
See Shazar, (Schneor) Zalman
Rubbra, Edmund 1901-1986
Obituary 119
Rubel, Arthur J. 1924- CANR-15
Earlier sketch in CA 41-44R
Rubel, James Lyon 1894-(?)
See Macrae, Mason
Rubel, Marc (Reid) 1949- CANR-54
Earlier sketch in CA 123
Rubel, Maximilien 1905-1996 .... CAP-1
Earlier sketch in CA 11-12
Rubel, Nicole 1953- CANR-69
Earlier sketch in CA 125
See also SATA 18, 95, 135
Rubel, Paula G(licksman) 1933- 89-92
Ruben, Brent David 1944- 41-44R
Ruben, Harvey L. 1941- 119
Rubens, Bernice (Ruth) 1923-2004 . CANR-128
Obituary 232
Earlier sketches in CA 25-28R, CANR-33, 65
See also CLC 19, 31
See also CN 1, 2, 3, 4, 5, 6, 7
See also DLB 14, 207
See also MTCW 1
Rubens, Jeff(rey Peter) 1941- CANR-39
Earlier sketches in CA 25-28R, CANR-17
Rubenson, Sven (Abel) 1921- 115
Rubenstein, Boris B. 1907(?)-1974
Obituary 53-56
Rubenstein, Harry R. 1951- 177
Rubenstein, Joshua 1949- 103
Rubenstein, Richard E(dward)
1938- CANR-127
Earlier sketches in CA 29-32R, CANR-32
Rubenstein, Richard L(owell) 1924- . CANR-17
Earlier sketch in CA 21-24R
Interview in CANR-17
Rubenstein, (Clarence) Robert 1926- 21-24R
Rubenstein, Roberta 1944- 89-92
Rubenstein, William B(ruce) 1960- 147
Rubenstone, Jessie 1912-2000 69-72
Rubia Barcia, Jose 1914-1997 .... CANR-41
Obituary 157
Earlier sketches in CA 103, CANR-19
Rubiao, Murilo 1916-1991 .... DLB 307
Rubicam, Harry Cogswell, Jr.
1902-1982 .... CAP-2
Earlier sketch in CA 17-18
Rubicon
See Lunn, Arnold
Rubies, Joan-Pau 213
Rubin, Alan (Michael) 1936- 113
Rubin, Amy Kateman 1945- 106
Rubin, Arnold P(erry) 1946- 69-72
Rubin, Barnett R(ichard) 1950- 154
Rubin, Barry (M.) 1950- CANR-32
Earlier sketch in CA 108
Rubin, Benny 1899-1986
Obituary 119
Rubin, Bruce Joel 1943(?)- 140
Rubin, Charles 1953- 168
Rubin, Charles J. 1950- 101
Rubin, Cynthia Elyce 1944- 97-100
Rubin, David Lee 1939- CANR-33
Earlier sketches in CA 41-44R, CANR-15
Rubin, David M. 1945- 77-80
Rubin, Dorothy 1932- CANR-41
Earlier sketches in CA 101, CANR-19
Rubin, Duane R(oger) 1931- 57-60
Rubin, Eli Z(under) 1922- 17-20R
Rubin, Ernest 1915-1978
Obituary 81-84
Rubin, Eva Johanna 1925- .... SATA 38
Rubin, Eva R(edfield) 1926- 113
Rubin, Frederick 1926- 33-36R
Rubin, Gayle .... FW
Rubin, Gretchen (Craft) 1966(?)- 226
Rubin, Hank 1916- CANR-124
Earlier sketch in CA 165
Rubin, Harold
See Robbins, Harold
Rubin, Harriet 1952- 228
Rubin, Ida Ely 1923- 107
Rubin, Isadore 1912-1970 .... CAP-1
Obituary 29-32R
Earlier sketch in CA 13-16
Rubin, Israel 1923- 37-40R
Rubin, Jacob A. 1910-1972 .... CAP-1
Obituary 37-40R
Earlier sketch in CA 11-12
Rubin, James Henry 1944- 106
Rubin, Jason 1970(?)- .... AAYA 55
Rubin, Jerry (C.) 1938-1994 69-72
Obituary 147
Rubin, Joan 1932- 102
Rubin, Joan Shelley 1947- 139
Rubin, Julia Danielle 1944- 113
Rubin, Larry (Jerome) 1930- CANR-98
Earlier sketches in CA 5-8R, CANR-47
See also CP 1
Rubin, Leona G(reenstone) 1920- 49-52
Rubin, Lillian B(reslow) 1924- CANR-143
Earlier sketches in CA 65-68, CANR-37
Rubin, Louis D(ecimus), Jr. 1923- CANR-97
Earlier sketches in CA 1-4R, CANR-6, 21, 47
See also CSW
Rubin, Mann 1927- 119
Rubin, Mark 1946- CANR-9
Earlier sketch in CA 53-56
Rubin, Michael 1935-1972 .... CANR-1
Earlier sketch in CA 1-4R
Rubin, Miri 1956- 236
Rubin, Morris H(arold) 1911-1980
Obituary 101
Rubin, Morton 1923- 41-44R
Rubin, Nancy 1944- 129
Rubin, Patricia Lee 1951- 152
Rubin, Rachel 1964- 192
Rubin, Rhea Joyce 1950- 195
Rubin, Rose M. 176
Rubin, Stanley 1928- 107
Rubin, Steven Jay 1951- 110
Rubin, Steven Joel 1943- 107
Rubin, Susan Goldman 1939- 150
See also SATA 84, 132
Rubin, Theodore Isaac 1923- 110
Brief entry 108
Interview in CA-110
See also AITN 1
Rubin, Vera (Dourmashkin) 1911-1985
Obituary 115
Rubin, Vitalii 1923-1981 69-72
Obituary 105
Rubin, William 1927- 77-80
Rubin, Zick 1944- CANR-1
Earlier sketch in CA 49-52
Rubina, Dina Il'inichna 1953- .... DLB 285
Rubin-Dorsky, Jeffrey 1947- 158
Rubinetti, Donald 1947- 156
See also SATA 92
Rubinfeld, William A. 1914(?)-1984
Obituary 113
Rubington, Earl 1923- 73-76
Rubini, Sergio 1959- 216
Rubino, Jane 166
Rubinoff, (M.) Lionel 1930- 25-28R
Rubinow, Sol (Isaac) 1923-1981
Obituary 103
Rubins, Harriett 1942- 120
Rubins, Jack L(awrence) 1916-1982 85-88
Obituary 107
Rubinshtein, Lev Semenovich 1947- .. DLB 285
Rubinsky, Holley 169
Rubinstein, Alvin Zachary 1927- CANR-39
Earlier sketches in CA 9-12R, CANR-3, 18
Rubinstein, Amnon 1931- CANR-99
Earlier sketches in CA 13-16R, CANR-7
Rubinstein, Arthur 1887(?)-1982 113
Obituary 108
Rubinstein, Daryl Reich 1938(?)-1981
Obituary 102
Rubinstein, David H(ugh) 1915- 109
Rubinstein, David M(ichael) 1942- 93-96
Rubinstein, E(lliott) 1936- 41-44R
Rubinstein, Edwin S. 1946- 166
Rubinstein, Erna F(erber) 1922- 120
Rubinstein, Gillian (Margaret)
1942- CANR-143
Earlier sketches in CA 136, CANR-86
See also AAYA 22
See also CLR 35
See also SAAS 25
See also SATA 68, 105, 158
See also SATA-Essay 116
See also YAW
Rubinstein, H(arold) F(rederick) 1891-1975
Obituary 115
Rubinstein, Helena 1871(?)-1965
Obituary 113
Rubinstein, Helge 1929- 134
Rubinstein, Hilary 1926- CANR-90
Earlier sketch in CA 57-60
Rubinstein, Isaak 1949- 150
Rubinstein, Lev (I.) 1914- 149
Rubinstein, Moshe F(ajwel) 1930- 57-60
Rubinstein, Patricia (Giulia Caulfield Kate)
-2003
Obituary 224
See also Forest, Antonia
See also SATA 29
See also SATA-Obit 149
Rubinstein, Paul (Arthur) CANR-7
Earlier sketch in CA 61-64
Rubinstein, Robert E(dward) 1943- 106
See also SATA 49
Rubinstein, Ruth P. 149
Rubinstein, S(amuel) Leonard 1922- 45-48
Rubinstein, Stanley (Jack) 1890-1975 .... CAP-2
Earlier sketch in CA 29-32
Rubinstein, W(illiam) D(avid) 1946- . CANR-81
Earlier sketch in CA 114
Rubio, Gwyn Hyman 204
Rublowsky, John M(artin) 1928- 17-20R
See also SATA 62
Rubsamen, Walter Howard 1911-1973 . 13-16R
Rubulis, Aleksis 1922- 37-40R
Ruby, Jay 1935- 136
Ruby, Kathryn 1947- 65-68
Ruby, Laura 230
See also SATA 155
Ruby, Lois (F.) 1942- 183
Earlier sketches in CA 97-100, CANR-18, 39,
69
Autobiographical Essay in 183
See also SATA 35, 95
See also SATA-Brief 34
See also SATA-Essay 105
See also YAW
Ruby, Robert Holmes 1921- CANR-7
Earlier sketch in CA 17-20R
Ruchames, Louis 1917-1976 .... CANR-2
Obituary 65-68
Earlier sketch in CA 1-4R
Ruchelman, Leonard I. 1933- CANR-28
Earlier sketch in CA 29-32R
Ruchlis, Hy(man) 1913-1992 .... CANR-47
Earlier sketches in CA 1-4R, 139, CANR-2
See also SATA 3
See also SATA-Obit 72
Ruchwarger, Gary 1949- 128
Ruck, Amy Roberta 1878-1978 .... CANR-69
Earlier sketches in CA 5-8R, CANR-5
See also RHW
Ruck, Berta
See Ruck, Amy Roberta
Ruck, Carl A(nton) P(aul) 1935- 25-28R
Ruck, Peter F(rederick) Carter
See Carter-Ruck, Peter F(rederick)
Rucka, Greg 209
Rucker, Brian R. 1961- 219
Rucker, Bryce W(ilson) 1921- 9-12R
Rucker, (Egbert) Darnell 1921- 41-44R
Rucker, Frank Warren 1886-1975 .... 1-4R
Obituary 103
Rucker, Helen (Bornstein) 1-4R
Rucker, Mike 1940- 155
See also SATA 91
Rucker, Patrick Michael 1974- 226
Rucker, Rudolf v(on) B(itter) 1946- 228
Brief entry 119
Earlier sketches in CA 124, CANR-77
Interview in CA-124
Autobiographical Essay in 228
See also SFW 4
Rucker, Rudy
See Rucker, Rudolf v(on) B(itter)
Rucker, W(infred) Ray 1920- 13-16R
Ruckman, Ivy 1931- CANR-61
Earlier sketch in CA 111
See also SATA 37, 93
Ruck-Pauquet, Gina 1931- 122
Brief entry 116
See also SATA 40
See also SATA-Brief 37
Rud, Nils Johan 1908-1993 239
Rudashevski, Yitskhok 1927-1943
Rudd, Anthony 1963- 146
Rudd, Enid 108
Rudd, Hughes (Day) 1921-1992 73-76
Obituary 139
Rudd, Margaret
See Newlin, Margaret Rudd
Rudd, Margaret T(homas) 1907-1999 .... 17-20R
Obituary 187
Rudd, Robert D(ean) 1924- 93-96
Rudd, Robert L. 1921- 117
Rudd, Steele
See Davis, Arthur Hoey
See also RGEL 2
Ruddell, Robert B(yron) 1937- 93-96
Rudder, Robert S(ween) 1937- CANR-119
Earlier sketches in CA 53-56, CANR-5
Rudder, Virginia L. 1941- 65-68
Ruddick, James 1923- 211
Ruddick, Nicholas 1952- 142
Ruddick, Sara 1935- 77-80
Ruddock, Ralph 1913-2002 53-56
Ruddock, Ted 1930- 139
Ruddy, Christopher 223
Ruddy, Frank C.
See Frank, Rudolf
Ruddy, T(homas) Michael 1946- 124
Rude, George F(rederick) E(lliot)
1910-1993 .... CANR-24
Obituary 140
Earlier sketches in CA 5-8R, CANR-5

Rudeen, Kenneth
  Brief entry ... 117
  See also SATA-Brief 36
Rudel, Hans-Ulrich 1916-1982
  Obituary ... 110
Rudelius, William 1931- ... CANR-29
  Earlier sketch in CA 45-48
Rudenko, Mykola 1920- ... EWL 3
Rudensky, Morris "Red"
  See Friedman, Max Motel
Rudenstine, Neil Leon 1935-
  Brief entry ... 105
Ruder, William 1921- ... 17-20R
Rudes, Blair Arnold 1951- ... 202
Rudgers, David F. 1941- ... 198
Rudgley, Richard 1961- ... 173
Rudhart, Alexander 1930- ... 61-64
Rudhyar, Dane 1895-1985 ... CANR-21
  Obituary ... 117
  Earlier sketch in CA 29-32R
Rudin, Jacob Philip 1902-1982
  Obituary ... 107
Rudin, Marcia Ruth 1940- ... 102
Rudinsky, Joseph F(rancis) 1891-1972 ... 5-8R
  Obituary ... 171
Rudis, Al 1943- ... 77-80
Rudisill, D(orus) P(aul) 1902-1978 ... 45-48
  Obituary ... 135
Rudkin, (James) David 1936- ... 89-92
  See also CBD
  See also CD 5, 6
  See also CLC 14
  See also DLB 13
Rudley, Stephen 1946- ... 106
  See also SATA 30
Rudloe, Jack 1943- ... 97-100
Rudman, Mark 1948- ... CANR-97
  Earlier sketches in CA 119, CANR-45
Rudman, Masha Kabakow 1933- ... CANR-27
  Earlier sketch in CA 110
Rudner, Barry Mathew 1954- ... 182
Rudner, Lawrence (Sheldon) 1947-1995 ... 204
Rudner, Rita 1955- ... 214
Rudnick, Hans H(einrich) 1935- ... 41-44R
Rudnick, Lois Palken 1944- ... 121
Rudnick, Milton Leroy 1927- ... CANR-3
  Earlier sketch in CA 1-4R
Rudnick, Paul 1957(?)- ... CANR-101
  Earlier sketch in CA 139
  See also DFS 22
  See also DLB 266
Rudnicki, Adolf 1909-1990 ... DLB 299
Rudnicki, Robert W. 1968- ... 190
Rudnik, Raphael 1933- ... 29-32R
  See also CLC 7
Rudofsky, Bernard 1905-1988 ... 17-20R
  Obituary ... 125
Rudolf, Anthony 1942- ... CANR-80
  Earlier sketches in CA 61-64, CANR-9, 24
  See also CP 7
Rudolf von Ems c. 1200-c. 1254 ... DLB 138
Rudolph, Alan 1943- ... 231
Rudolph, Albert
  See Frank, Rudolf
Rudolph, Donna Keyse 1934- ... 33-36R
Rudolph, Erwin Paul 1916- ... 33-36R
Rudolph, Frederick 1920- ... 9-12R
Rudolph, Kurt 1929- ... 158
Rudolph, L(avere) C(hristian) 1921- ... CANR-2
  Earlier sketch in CA 5-8R
Rudolph, Lee (Norman) 1948- ... CANR-7
  Earlier sketch in CA 57-60
Rudolph, Lloyd I(rving) 1927- ... 57-60
Rudolph, Marguerita 1908- ... CANR-13
  Earlier sketch in CA 33-36R
  See also SATA 21
Rudolph, Nancy 1923- ... 57-60
Rudolph, Paul (Marvin) 1918-1997 ... 185
Rudolph, Richard (H.) 1940- ... 128
Rudolph, Robert S. 1937- ... 41-44R
Rudolph, Susanne Hoeber 1930- ... 25-28R
Rudomin, Esther
  See Hautzig, Esther Rudomin
Rudrum, Alan (William) 1932- ... CANR-110
  Earlier sketches in CA 25-28R, CANR-36
Rudwick, Elliot M. 1927-1986(?) ... 104
  Obituary ... 118
Rudy, Ann 1927- ... 101
Rudy, Kathy 1956- ... 164
Rudy, Peter 1922- ... 53-56
Rudy, Willis 1920- ... 37-40R
Rue, John E. 1924- ... 21-24R
Rue, Leonard Lee III 1926- ... CANR-121
  Earlier sketches in CA 1-4R, CANR-1
  See also SATA 37, 142
Rue, Leslie W(aits) 1944- ... 110
Rue, Loyal D. 1944- ... 145
Rue, Nancy Naylor 1951- ... 122
Ruebsaat, Helmut J(ohannes) 1920- ... 61-64
Ruebsamen, Helga 1934- ... 197
Ruechelle, Randall C(ummings) 1920- ... 41-44R
Rueckert, William H(owe) 1926- ... 21-24R
Ruedi, Norma Paul
  See Ainsworth, Norma
Ruedy, John 1927- ... 145
Ruef, John S. 1927- ... 37-40R
Rueff, Jacques (Leon) 1896-1978 ... CANR-12
  Obituary ... 77-80
  Earlier sketch in CA 65-68
Ruefle, Mary 1952- ... 232
Ruege, Klaus 1934- ... CANR-11
  Earlier sketch in CA 65-68
Ruehle, Juergen 1924- ... 25-28R
Ruehlmann, William 1946- ... 105
Ruehmkorf, Peter
  See Ruhmkorf, Peter
Ruell, Patrick
  See Hill, Reginald (Charles)
Ruelle, Karen Gray 1957- ... SATA 84, 126
Ruel-Mezieres, Laurence 1957- ... 207
Ruemmler, John D(avid) 1948- ... 146
  See also SATA 78
Ruepp, Krista 1947- ... 216
  See also SATA 143
Ruesch, Hans 1913- ... 13-16R
Ruesch, Jurgen 1909-1995 ... 73-76
Rueschemeyer, Dietrich 1930- ... CANR-95
  Earlier sketch in CA 146
Rueschemeyer, Marilyn 1938- ... CANR-49
  Earlier sketch in CA 122
Rueschhoff, Phil H. 1924- ... 29-32R
Ruether, Rosemary Radford 1936- ... CANR-101
  Earlier sketches in CA 97-100, CANR-39
  See also FW
Rueveni, Uri 1933- ... 102
Ruf, Frederick J. 1950- ... 194
Ruff, Ann 1930-1993 ... 120
  Obituary ... 145
Ruff, Howard J. ... CANR-36
  Earlier sketch in CA 93-96
Ruff, Matt 1965(?)- ... 228
Ruffell, Ann 1941- ... CANR-23
  Earlier sketch in CA 107
  See also SATA 30
Ruffell, Thomas
  See Laslett, Peter
Ruffian, M.
  See Hasek, Jaroslav (Matej Frantisek)
Ruffin, C(aulbert) Bernard III 1947- ... CANR-27
  Earlier sketch in CA 109
Ruffin, Josephine St. Pierre 1842-1924 . DLB 79
Ruffin, Paul D. 1941- ... 207
Ruffini, (Jacopo) Remo 1942- ... 57-60
Ruffins, Reynold 1930- ... CANR-105
  Earlier sketches in CA 112, CANR-46
  See also MAICYA 1, 2
  See also SATA 41, 125
Ruffle, The
  See Tegner, Henry (Stuart)
Ruffner, Budge
  See Ruffner, Lester Ward
Ruffner, Kevin C(onley) 1960- ... 187
Ruffner, Lester Ward 1918- ... 89-92
Ruffo, Vinnie ... 25-28R
Rufin, Jean-Christophe 1952- ... 204
Rufo, Juan Gutierrez 1547(?)-1620(?) .. DLB 318
Rufus, Anneli S. 1959- ... 233
Ruganda, John 1941- ... 176
  See also BW 3
  See also CD 5, 6
  See also DLB 157
Rugel, Miriam 1911-1999 ... 101
Rugeley, Terry 1956- ... 233
Rugg, Dean S(prague) 1923- ... 41-44R
Rugg, Linda (Haverty) 1957- ... 170
Rugg, Paul ... 234
Ruggero, Ed(ward Joseph) ... 197
Ruggieri, Helen 1938- ... 207
Ruggiero, Guido 1944- ... 118
Ruggiers, Paul G(eorge) 1918- ... CANR-24
  Earlier sketch in CA 25-28R
Ruggles, Eleanor 1916- ... 5-8R
Ruggles, Henry Joseph 1813-1906 ... 213
  See also DLB 64
Ruggles, Joanne Beaule 1946- ... 73-76
Ruggles, Philip (Kent) 1944- ... 73-76
Rugh, Belle Dorman 1908- ... CAP-1
  Earlier sketch in CA 13-16
Rugh, Roberts 1903-1978 ... 93-96
  Obituary ... 81-84
Rugh, Susan Sessions ... 213
Rugman, Alan M. 1945- ... 221
Rugoff, Milton 1913- ... CANR-49
  Earlier sketch in CA 21-24R
  See also SATA 30
Ruhen, Olaf 1911-1989 ... CANR-20
  Earlier sketches in CA 1-4R, CANR-5
  See also SATA 17
Ruhlen, Merritt 1944- ... CANR-48
  Earlier sketch in CA 122
Ruhlman, Michael 1963- ... 224
Ruhmkorf, Peter 1929- ... 207
Ruibal, Jorge Silvestre Remonda
  See Remonda-Ruibal, Jorge Silvestre
Ruibal (Argibay), Jose 1925- ... CWW 2
Ruihley, Glenn Richard ... 107
Ruin, Hans 1961- ... 239
Ruitenbeek, Hendrik M(arinus)
  1928-1983 ... CANR-8
  Obituary ... 109
  Earlier sketch in CA 5-8R
Ruiz, Don Miguel
  See Ruiz, Miguel Angel
Ruiz, Jose Martinez
  See Martinez Ruiz, Jose
  See also CLC 11
Ruiz, K.
  See Lynn (Ruiz), Kathryn
Ruiz, Miguel Angel 1952- ... 195
Ruiz, Ramon Eduardo 1921- ... CANR-11
  Earlier sketch in CA 25-28R
  See also HW 1
Ruiz, Ricardo Navas
  See Navas-Ruiz, Ricardo
Ruiz, Roberto 1925- ... 41-44R
Ruiz, Vicki Lynn 1955- ... 127
Ruiz de Burton, Maria Amparo
  1832(?)-1895 ... DLB 209, 221
Ruiz-De-Conde, Justina (Malaxechevarria)
  1909- ... 73-76
Ruiz-Fornells, Enrique 1925- ... CANR-36
  Earlier sketch in CA 33-36R
Ruiz Zafon, Carlos 1964- ... 239
Ruja, Harry 1912-2002 ... 41-44R
Rukeyser, Louis 1933- ... CANR-88
  Earlier sketches in CA 65-68, CANR-36
Rukeyser, Merryle Stanley 1897-1988 ... CAP-2
  Obituary ... 127
  Earlier sketch in CA 23-24
Rukeyser, Muriel 1913-1980 ... CANR-60
  Obituary ... 93-96
  Earlier sketches in CA 5-8R, CANR-26
  See also AMWS 6
  See also CLC 6, 10, 15, 27
  See also CP 1, 2
  See also DA3
  See also DAM POET
  See also DLB 48
  See also EWL 3
  See also FW
  See also GLL 2
  See also MAL 5
  See also MTCW 1, 2
  See also PC 12
  See also PFS 10
  See also RGAL 4
  See also SATA-Obit 22
Rukeyser, William Simon 1939- ... CANR-37
  Earlier sketch in CA 69-72
Ruksenas, Algis 1942- ... 49-52
Ruland, Richard (Eugene) 1932- ... CANR-36
  Earlier sketch in CA 21-24R
Ruland, Vernon Joseph 1931- ... 17-20R
Rule, Ann 1935- ... CANR-140
  Earlier sketches in CA 145, CANR-65, 110
  See also BEST 90:2
  See also CPW
  See also DA3
  See also DAM POP
  See also MTCW 2
  See also MTFW 2005
Rule, Gordon Wade 1906-1982
  Obituary ... 107
Rule, James B(ernard) 1943- ... CANR-107
  Earlier sketches in CA 73-76, CANR-47
Rule, Jane (Vance) 1931- ... CANR-87
  Earlier sketches in CA 25-28R, CANR-12
  See also CAAS 18
  See also CLC 27
  See also CN 4, 5, 6, 7
  See also DLB 60
  See also FW
Rulfo, Juan 1918-1986 ... CANR-26
  Obituary ... 118
  Earlier sketch in CA 85-88
  See also CDWLB 3
  See also CLC 8, 80
  See also DAM MULT
  See also DLB 113
  See also EWL 3
  See also HLC 2
  See also HW 1, 2
  See also LAW
  See also MTCW 1, 2
  See also RGSF 2
  See also RGWL 2, 3
  See also SSC 25
  See also WLIT 1
Rulon, Philip Reed 1934- ... CANR-14
  Earlier sketch in CA 37-40R
Rumaker, Michael 1932- ... CANR-80
  Earlier sketches in CA 1-4R, CANR-2
  See also CN 2, 3, 4, 5, 6
  See also DLB 16
Rumanes, George N(icholas) 1925- ... 45-48
Rumbaugh, Duane M. 1929- ... 229
Rumbaut, Hendle 1949- ... 150
  See also SATA 84
Rumbelow, Donald 1940- ... 49-52
Rumberger, Russell W(illiam) 1949- . CANR-26
  Earlier sketch in CA 109
Rumble, Adrian 1945- ... 137
Rumble, Thomas C(lark) 1919- ... 13-16R
Rumble, Wilfrid E., Jr. 1931- ... 25-28R
Rumbold-Gibbs, Henry St. John Clair
  1913-1975 ... CANR-87
  Earlier sketches in CA 1-4R, CANR-3
Rumens, Carol(-Ann) 1944- ... CANR-90
  Earlier sketch in CA 131
  See also CP 7
  See also CWP
  See also DLB 40
Rumer, Boris ... 156
Rumer, Thomas Andrew 1942- ... 192
Rumford, James 1948- ... 188
  See also SATA 116
Rumi, Jalal al-Din 1207-1273 ... AAYA 64
  See also PC 45
  See also RGWL 2, 3
  See also WLIT 6
  See also WP
Rummel, Fran
  See Rummel, J(osiah) Francis
Rummel, J(osiah) Francis 1911- ... CANR-96
  Earlier sketches in CA 17-20R, CANR-45
Rummel, (Louis) Jack(son) 1950- ... 132
Rummel, R(udolph) J(oseph) 1932- ... 65-68
Rummo, Paul-Eerik 1942- ... DLB 232
Rumold, Rainer ... 180
Rumpleforeskin
  See Krassner, Paul
Rumscheidt, H(ans) Martin 1935- ... CANR-36
  Earlier sketch in CA 57-60
Rumsey, Marian (Barritt) 1928- ... 21-24R
  See also SATA 16
Rumstuckle, Cornelius
  See Brennan, J(ames) H(erbert)
Runcie, Robert (Alexander Kennedy)
  1921-2000 ... CANR-28
  Obituary ... 189
  Earlier sketch in CA 108
Runcie, Robert A. K.
  See Runcie, Robert (Alexander Kennedy)
Runciman, Lex 1951- ... 206
Runciman, (James Cochran) Steven(son)
  1903-2000 ... CANR-3
  Obituary ... 191
  Earlier sketch in CA 1-4R
Runco, Mark A. 1957- ... 202
Rundell, Walter, Jr. 1928- ... CANR-3
  Earlier sketch in CA 9-12R
Rundle, Anne -1989 ... CANR-88
  Earlier sketches in CA 57-60, CANR-12
Runes, Dagobert D(avid)
  1902-1982 ... CANR-26
  Obituary ... 108
  Earlier sketch in CA 25-28R
Runge, C(arlisle) Ford 1953- ... 122
Runge, William H(arry) 1927- ... 1-4R
Runia, Klaas 1926- ... CANR-45
  Earlier sketches in CA 5-8R, CANR-5, 20
Runkel, Philip J(ulian) 1917- ... CANR-11
  Earlier sketch in CA 29-32R
Runkel, Sylvan T(homas) 1906-1995 ... 225
Runkle, Gerald 1924- ... CANR-14
  Earlier sketch in CA 37-40R
Runnels, Curtis 1950- ... 126
Runnerstroem, Bengt Arne 1944- ... SATA 75
Running, Leona Glidden 1916- ... 89-92
Runte, Alfred 1947- ... CANR-41
  Earlier sketches in CA 102, CANR-19
Runyan, Harry (John) 1913-(?) ... CAP-2
  Earlier sketch in CA 23-24
Runyan, John
  See Palmer, Bernard (Alvin)
Runyan, Thora J. 1931- ... 69-72
Runyon, A(lfred) Milton 1905-1983
  Obituary ... 109
Runyon, Brent ... 236
Runyon, Catherine 1947- ... 61-64
  See also SATA 62
Runyon, Charles W. 1928-1987 ... 17-20R
Runyon, (Alfred) Damon 1884(?)-1946 ... 165
  Brief entry ... 107
  See also DLB 11, 86, 171
  See also MAL 5
  See also MTCW 2
  See also RGAL 4
  See also TCLC 10
Runyon, Daniel V. 1954- ... 120
Runyon, John H(arold) 1945- ... 33-36R
Runyon, Randolph Paul 1947- ... 148
Runyon, Richard P(orter) 1925- ... CANR-3
  Earlier sketch in CA 45-48
Ruoff, A. LaVonne Brown 1930- ... 143
  See also SATA 76
Ruoff, James E. 1925- ... 41-44R
Ruokanen, Miikka 1953- ... 146
Ruotolo, Andrew K(eogh) 1926(?)-1979 ... 103
  Obituary ... 89-92
Ruotolo, Lucio P(eter) 1927-2003 ... 41-44R
  Obituary ... 219
RuPaul
  See Charles, Rupaul Andre
RuPaul
  See Charles, Rupaul Andre
RuPaul 1960- ... 155
Rupert, Hoover 1917- ... CANR-3
  Earlier sketch in CA 1-4R
Rupert, James C(layton) II 1957- ... 136
Rupert, Raphael Rudolph 1910- ... CAP-2
  Earlier sketch in CA 19-20
Ruple, Wayne Douglas 1950- ... 53-56
Rupp, E. G.
  See Rupp, E(rnest) Gordon
Rupp, E(rnest) Gordon 1910-1986 ... 124
  Brief entry ... 113
Rupp, Gordon
  See Rupp, E(rnest) Gordon
Rupp, James M. 1952- ... 142
Rupp, Joyce 1943- ... 203
Rupp, Leila J(ane) 1950- ... 81-84
Rupp, Richard H(enry) 1934- ... CANR-107
  Earlier sketch in CA 29-32R
Ruppenthal, Karl M. 1917- ... 17-20R
Ruppersburg, Hugh Michael 1950- ... 124
Ruppli, Michel 1934- ... 101
Ruprecht, Mary M(argaret Wyant) 1934- ... 118
Ruric, Peter
  See Sims, George (Carrol)
Rus, Vladimir 1931- ... 17-20R
Rusalem, Herbert 1918- ... 41-44R
Rusan, Otilia Valeria
  See Blandiana, Ana
Rusbridger, Alan 1953- ... 125
Rusbridger, James 1928-1994 ... CANR-39
  Obituary ... 144
  Earlier sketch in CA 134
Rusch, Hermann G. 1907- ... 61-64
Rusch, John J(ay) 1942- ... 106
Rusch, Kris
  See Rusch, Kristine Kathryn
Rusch, Kristine Kathryn 1960- ... CANR-122
  Earlier sketch in CA 157
  See also AAYA 59
  See also FANT
  See also SATA 113
  See also SFW 4
Rusco, Elmer R(itter) 1928-2004 ... 65-68
  Obituary ... 230
Ruscoe, (Steuart) James (Bailey) 1947- ... 116
Ruse, Gary Alan 1946- ... CANR-12
  Earlier sketch in CA 61-64

Ruse 502 CONTEMPORARY AUTHORS

Ruse, Michael E. 1940- ... CANR-91
Earlier sketch in CA 107
Rush, Alison 1951- ... 115
See also SATA 41
Rush, Anne Kent 1945- ... CANR-8
Earlier sketch in CA 61-64
Rush, Benjamin 1746-1813 ... DLB 37
Rush, Christopher 1944- ... 122
Rush, Elizabeth 1918- ... 115
Rush, James J. 1929- ... 120
Rush, Joseph H(arold) 1911- ... 5-8R
Rush, Joshua
See Pearlstein, Howard J.
Rush, Michael (David) 1937- ... 61-64
Rush, Myron 1922- ... 45-48
Rush, N(ixon) Orwin 1907- ... CANR-25
Earlier sketch in CA 45-48
Rush, Norman 1933- ... CANR-130
Brief entry ... 121
Earlier sketch in CA 126
Interview in ... CA-126
See also CLC 44
Rush, Patricia 1948- ... 188
Rush, Peter 1937- ... 111
See also SATA 32
Rush, Philip
See Lardner, Ring(gold Wilmer), Jr.
Rush, Philip 1908-1996 ... CANR-80
Earlier sketch in CA 104
See also CWRI 5
Rush, Ralph E(ugene) 1903-1965 ... 5-8R
Rush, Rebecca 1779-(?) ... DLB 200
Rush, Richard Henry 1915- ... CANR-6
Earlier sketch in CA 5-8R
Rush, Robert
See Barber, D(ulan) F(riar Whilberton)
Rush, Sharon E(lizabeth) 1951- ... 198
Rush, Theressa Gunnels 1945- ... 104
Rushbrook Williams, L(aurence) F(rederic)
1890-1978 ... 97-100
Rushby, Kevin ... 196
Rushdie, (Ahmed) Salman 1947- ... CANR-133
Brief entry ... 108
Earlier sketches in CA 111, CANR-33, 56, 108
Interview in ... CA-111
See also AAYA 65
See also BEST 89:3
See also BPFB 3
See also BRWS 4
See also CLC 23, 31, 55, 100, 191
See also CN 4, 5, 6, 7
See also CPW 1
See also DA3
See also DAB
See also DAC
See also DAM MST, NOV, POP
See also DLB 194
See also EWL 3
See also FANT
See also LATS 1:2
See also LMFS 2
See also MTCW 1, 2
See also MTFW 2005
See also NFS 22
See also RGEL 2
See also RGSF 2
See also SSC 83
See also TEA
See also WLCS
See also WLIT 4
Rushdoony, Rousas J(ohn) 1916-2001 ... 93-96
Obituary ... 195
Rusher, William A(llen) 1923- ... CANR-28
Earlier sketch in CA 103
Rushfield, Richard ... 208
Rushford, Patricia H(elen) 1943- ... CANR-112
Earlier sketches in CA 115, CANR-37
See also SATA 134
Rushforth, Peter (Scott) 1945- ... 101
See also CLC 19
Rushin, Steve 1966- ... 172
Rushing, Francis W(illard) 1939- ... CANR-31
Earlier sketch in CA 112
Rushing, Jane Gilmore 1925-1997 ... CANR-64
Earlier sketch in CA 49-52
See also BYA 8
See also TCWW 1, 2
Rushing, William A. 1930- ... 81-84
Rushkoff, Douglas 1961- ... 164
Rushmer, Robert F(razer) 1914-2001 ... 134
Obituary ... 199
Brief entry ... 111
Rushmore, Helen 1898-1994 ... 25-28R
See also SATA 3
Rushmore, Robert (William)
1926-1986 ... 25-28R
Obituary ... 120
See also SATA 8
See also SATA-Obit 49
Rusholm, Peter
See Powell, Eric F(rederick) W(illiam)
Rushton, J(ohn) Philippe 1943- ... CANR-66
Earlier sketch in CA 111
Rushton, Julian (Gordon) 1941- ... CANR-90
Earlier sketch in CA 132
Rushton, William Faulkner 1947- ... CANR-22
Earlier sketch in CA 101
Rusi, Alpo M. 1949- ... 167
Rusinek, Alla 1949- ... 45-48
Rusinko, Susan 1922- ... 133
Rusinow, Dennison I. 1930- ... 85-88
Rusk, (David) Dean 1909-1994 ... 141
Obituary ... 147
Rusk, Howard A(rchibald) 1901-1989 ... 103
Obituary ... 130
Rusk, Ralph Leslie 1888-1962 ... 5-8R
See also DLB 103
Rusk, Richard (Geary) 1946- ... 138
Ruskan, John ... 231
Ruskay, Joseph A. 1910- ... CAP-2
Earlier sketch in CA 29-32
Ruskay, Sophie 1887-1980 ... 69-72
Obituary ... 97-100
Ruskin, Ariane
See Batterberry, Ariane Ruskin
Ruskin, John 1819-1900 ... 129
Brief entry ... 114
See also BRW 5
See also BYA 5
See also CDBLB 1832-1890
See also DLB 55, 163, 190
See also RGEL 2
See also SATA 24
See also TCLC 63
See also TEA
See also WCH
Ruskin, Ronald 1944- ... 115
Ruslanov, Sviatoslav
See Krasnov, Vladislav Georgievich
Russ, Joanna 1937- ... CANR-65
Earlier sketches in CA 25-28, CANR-11, 31
See also BPFB 3
See also CLC 15
See also CN 4, 5, 6, 7
See also DLB 8
See also FW
See also GLL 1
See also MTCW 1
See also SCFW 1, 2
See also SFW 4
Russ, Laurence 1943- ... 114
Russ, Lavinia (Faxon) 1904-1992 ... 25-28R
Obituary ... 137
See also SATA 74
Russ, Martin 1931- ... CANR-88
Earlier sketch in CA 106
Russ, Richard Patrick
See O'Brian, Patrick
Russ, William Adam, Jr. 1903-1981 ... 1-4R
Russak, Ben 1912-1988
Obituary ... 127
Russek, Henry I(rving) 1911-1990
Obituary ... 131
Russel, Myra T(eicher) 1920- ... CANR-93
Earlier sketch in CA 145
Russel, Robert R(oyal) 1890-1996 ... 13-16R
Russell, Alan 1956- ... 168
See also CMW 4
Russell, Alan K.
See Leventhal, Lionel
Russell, Albert
See Bixby, Jerome Lewis
Russell, Allan Melvin 1930- ... 122
Russell, Andrew (George Alexander)
1915- ... CANR-26
Earlier sketches in CA 21-24R, CANR-10
Russell, Annie V(est) 1880(?)-1974
Obituary ... 49-52
Russell, Arthur (Wolseley) 1908- ... CANR-16
Earlier sketches in CAP-1, CA 13-14
Russell, (Muriel) Audrey 1906(?)-1989(?)
Obituary ... 129
Russell, Benjamin 1761-1845 ... DLB 43
Russell, Bertrand (Arthur William)
1872-1970 ... CANR-44
Obituary ... 25-28R
Earlier sketches in CAP-1, CA 13-16
See also DLB 100, 262
See also MTCW 1, 2
See also TEA
Russell, Bill
See Russell, William Felton
Russell, C(harles) Allyn 1920- ... 65-68
Russell, Carroll Mason 1898(?)-1983
Obituary ... 111
Russell, Charles 1941(?)- ... 224
Russell, Charles 1944- ... 111
Russell, Charles Edward 1860-1941 ... 194
See also DLB 25
Russell, Charles M(arion) 1864(?)-1926 ... 204
See also DLB 188
See also TCWW 1, 2
Russell, Charlie
See Russell, Charles
Russell, Charlotte
See Rathjen, Carl Henry
Russell, Cheryl 1953- ... 150
Russell, Ching Yeung 1946- ... SATA 107
Russell, Claude Vivian 1919- ... 17-20R
Russell, Clifford S(pringer) 1938- ... CANR-12
Earlier sketch in CA 73-76
Russell, Colin Archibald 1928- ... 45-48
Russell, Conrad (Sebastian Robert)
1937-2004 ... 33-36R
Obituary ... 232
Russell, D(avid) S(yme) 1916- ... 13-16R
Russell, Daniel 1937- ... 41-44R
Russell, David L. 1946- ... 195
Russell, David O(wen) 1958- ... 201
Russell, Diana E(lizabeth) H(amilton)
1938- ... CANR-34
Earlier sketches in CA 61-64, CANR-8
Russell, Diarmuid 1902(?)-1973
Obituary ... 45-48
Russell, Dick
See Russell, Richard B.
Russell, Don(ald Bert) 1899-1986 ... CANR-1
Obituary ... 118
Earlier sketch in CA 1-4R
See also SATA-Obit 47
Russell, Donald Andrew (Frank Moore)
1920- ... 110
Russell, Dora (Winifred Black) 1894-1986 ... 125
Obituary ... 119
Russell, Douglas A(ndrew) 1927- ... CANR-16
Earlier sketch in CA 41-44R
Russell, E(nid) S(herry) 1924- ... 139
Russell, Earl
See Russell, Conrad (Sebastian Robert)
Russell, Edward (Frederick Langley)
1895-1981 ... 107
Obituary ... 103
Russell, Eric Frank 1905-1978 ... CANR-80
Obituary ... 102
Earlier sketch in CA 124
See also DLB 255
See also SCFW 1, 2
See also SFW 4
Russell, Foster Meharry 1907- ... 111
Russell, Francis 1910-1989 ... 25-28R
Obituary ... 128
Russell, Frank
See Fearn, John Russell
Russell, Frank D. 1923- ... 126
Russell, Franklin (Alexander) 1926- ... CANR-11
Earlier sketch in CA 17-20R
See also SATA 11
Russell, Fred(erick McFerrin) 1906-2003 ... 208
See also DLB 241
Russell, Fred 1906-2003
See Russell, Fred(erick McFerrin)
Russell, Frederick S(tratten) 1897-1984 ... 157
Obituary ... 113
Russell, George 1923- ... 166
Russell, George William 1867-1935 ... 153
Brief entry ... 104
See also A.E. and
Baker, Jean H.
See also BRWS 8
See also CDBLB 1890-1914
See also DAM POET
See also EWL 3
See also RGEL 2
Russell, Gertrude Barrer
See Barrer-Russell, Gertrude
Russell, (Sydney) Gordon 1892-1980 ... CAP-2
Earlier sketch in CA 29-32
Russell, Gordon 1930(?)-1981
Obituary ... 102
Russell, H(elen) Diane 1936-2004 ... 110
Obituary ... 225
Russell, Harold (John) 1914-2002 ... 129
Obituary ... 203
Russell, Helen Ross 1915- ... 33-36R
See also SATA 8
Russell, Herb
See Russell, Herbert K.
Russell, Herbert K. 1943- ... 177
Russell, Howard Lewis 1962- ... 136
Russell, Howard S(ymmes) 1887-1980 ... 105
Russell, I(saac) Willis 1903-1985 ... 118
Russell, Ina (Dillard III) 1936- ... 236
Russell, Ivy E(thel Southern) 1909- ... 5-8R
Russell, J.
See Bixby, Jerome Lewis
Russell, J(effrey) P(eter) 1954- ... 112
Russell, James
See Harknett, Terry (Williams)
Russell, James 1933- ... SATA 53
Russell, James E. 1916-1975
Obituary ... 57-60
Russell, Jan Jarboe 1951- ... 233
Russell, Jeffrey Burton 1934- ... CANR-52
Earlier sketches in CA 25-28R, CANR-11, 28
See also CLC 70
Russell, Jeremy Longmore 1935- ... 110
Russell, Jim
See Russell, James
Russell, Joan Mercedes 1921- ... 102
Russell, Joan Plummer 1930- ... 210
See also SATA 139
Russell, John
See Fearn, John Russell
Russell, John 1919- ... CANR-34
Earlier sketch in CA 13-16R
Russell, John David 1928- ... 9-12R
Russell, John L(owry), Jr. 1921- ... 9-12R
Russell, John L(eonard) 1906- ... 13-16R
Russell, John Malcolm 1953- ... 149
Russell, Josh ... 196
Russell, Josiah Cox 1900-1996 ... 41-44R
Russell, Katie
See Holmes, Katie
Russell, (Henry) Ken(neth Alfred) 1927- ... 105
See also CLC 16
Russell, Ken(neth Victor) 1929- ... CANR-11
Earlier sketch in CA 25-28R
Russell, Letty M(andeville) 1929- ... CANR-8
Earlier sketch in CA 57-60
Russell, Lois Ann 1931- ... 113
Russell, Lynne 1946- ... 223
Russell, Mariann Barbara 1935- ... 109
Russell, Mark 1932- ... 113
Brief entry ... 108
Interview in ... CA-113
Russell, Martin 1934- ... CANR-61
Earlier sketch in CA 73-76
See also CMW 4
Russell, Mary Annette Beauchamp
1866-1941 ... 167
See also von Arnim, Elizabeth
Russell, Mary Doria 1950- ... CANR-139
Earlier sketch in CA 162
See also MTFW 2005
Russell, Maud 1893(?)-1989
Obituary ... 130
Russell, Maurin
See Russell, Maurine (Fletcher)
Russell, Maurine (Fletcher) 1899- ... CAP-1
Earlier sketch in CA 9-10
Russell, Meg ... 224
Russell, Norma Hull Lewis 1902- ... 5-8R
Russell, Norman H(udson), Jr.
1921- ... CANR-45
Earlier sketch in CA 49-52
Russell, O(live) Ruth 1897-1979 ... 57-60
Obituary ... 133
Russell, P(hilip) Craig 1951- ... CANR-127
Earlier sketch in CA 148
See also AAYA 58
See also SATA 80, 162
Russell, P(eggy) J(ean) 1934- ... 97-100
Russell, Pamela Redford 1950- ... 81-84
Russell, Patrick
See Sammis, John
Russell, Paul (Gary) 1942- ... SATA 57
Russell, Paul 1956- ... CANR-118
Earlier sketch in CA 133
Russell, (Irwin) Peter 1921-2003 ... CANR-97
Obituary ... 212
Earlier sketches in CA 97-100, CANR-44
See also CP 2, 3, 4, 5, 6, 7
Russell, Ray 1924-1999 ... CANR-81
Obituary ... 179
Earlier sketches in CA 1-4R, CANR-6
See also HGG
Russell, Richard B. 1947- ... CANR-130
Earlier sketch in CA 152
Russell, Rinaldina 1934- ... 167
Russell, Robert W(allace) 1912-1992 ... 160
Russell, Robert W(illiam) 1924- ... CANR-34
Earlier sketch in CA 1-4R
Russell, Ronald (Stanley) 1904-1974 ... CAP-1
Earlier sketch in CA 11-12
Russell, Ronald 1924- ... 102
Russell, Rosalind 1908-1976 ... 116
Obituary ... 111
Russell, Ross 1909-2000 ... CANR-34
Obituary ... 189
Earlier sketch in CA 1-4R
Russell, Roy 1918- ... CANR-26
Earlier sketch in CA 107
Russell, Russell
See Meades, Jonathan (Turner)
Russell, Sarah
See Laski, Marghanita
Russell, Sean 1952- ... 213
Russell, Shane
See Norwood, Victor G(eorge) C(harles)
Russell, Sharman Apt 1954- ... CANR-92
Earlier sketch in CA 142
See also ANW
See also SATA 123
Russell, Sharon 1941- ... 175
Russell, Shirley 1935- ... IDFW 3
Russell, Solveig Paulson 1904-1985 ... CANR-5
Earlier sketch in CA 1-4R
See also SATA 3
Russell, Thaddeus ... 207
Russell, Thomas 1902(?)-1984
Obituary ... 114
Russell, Victor L. 1948- ... 192
Russell, William ... CMW 4
Russell, William F(rank) 1945- ... CANR-67
Earlier sketch in CA 126
Russell, William Felton 1934- ... 108
Russell, William H(enry) 1911-1991 ... 61-64
Russell, William Martin 1947- ... CANR-107
Earlier sketch in CA 164
See also Russell, Willy
Russell, Willy
See Russell, William Martin
See also CBD
See also CD 5, 6
See also CLC 60
See also DLB 233
Russell-Smith, Enid (Mary Russell) 1903-1989
Obituary ... 129
Russell Taylor, Elisabeth 1930- ... CANR-34
Earlier sketches in CA 81-84, CANR-15
Russell-Wood, A(nthony) J(ohn) R(ussell)
1939- ... CANR-7
Earlier sketch in CA 57-60
Russert, Tim 1950- ... 237
Russett, Bruce M(artin) 1935- ... CANR-2
Earlier sketch in CA 5-8R
Russett, Cynthia Eagle 1937- ... 21-24R
Russman, Thomas A. 1944- ... 128
Russo, Albert 1943- ... 227
Russo, Anthony 1933- ... 61-64
Russo, Ferdinando 1866-1927 ... 214
Russo, Giuseppe Luigi 1884-1971 ... CAP-1
Earlier sketch in CA 9-10
Russo, Gus ... 181
Russo, J. Edward ... 206
Russo, Jack
See Russo, John A.
Russo, John A. 1939- ... 239
See also HGG
Russo, John Paul 1944- ... 41-44R
Russo, Joseph Louis
See Russo, Giuseppe Luigi
Russo, Marisabina 1950- ... 176
See also SATA 106, 151
Russo, Monica J. 1950- ... SATA 83
Russo, Richard 1949- ... CANR-114
Brief entry ... 127
Earlier sketches in CA 133, CANR-87
See also AMWS 12
See also CLC 181
Rusoo, Richard Paul 1954- ... CANR-76
Earlier sketch in CA 129
Russo, Sarett Rude 1918(?)-1976
Obituary ... 65-68
Russo, Susan 1947- ... 106
See also SATA 30
Russo, Thomas A. 1932- ... 203

Cumulative Index 503 **Rylands**

Russo, Vito 1946-1990 107
See also GLL 1
Russon, Allien R. 1905-1986 105
Russon, Anne E(leanor) 1947- 191
Russon, L(eslie) J(ohn) 1907- 17-20R
Rust, Brian Arthur Lovell 1922- CANR-2
Earlier sketch in CA 45-48
Rust, Claude 1916- 109
Rust, Doris (Dibblin) 13-16R
Rust, Eric C(harles) 1910-1991 .... 13-16R
Rust, Graham (Redgrave) 1942- 171
Rust, Marina (Marshall) 1964- 141
Rust, Richard Dilworth 1937- 29-32R
Rusticus
See Martin, Brian P(hilip)
Rustin, Bayard 1910(?)-1987 .... CANR-25
Obituary 123
Earlier sketch in CA 53-56
See also BW 1
Rustmann, F(rederick). W. Jr 213
Rustomji, Nari Kaikhosru 1919- 101
Rustow, Dankwart A(lexander) 1924-1996 .... CANR-1
Obituary 153
Earlier sketch in CA 1-4R
Ruta, Suzanne 1940- 127
Rutan, Dick 1938- 149
Rutan, J. Scott 1940- 142
Rutan, Richard Glenn
See Rutan, Dick
Rutberg, Sidney 1924- 69-72
Rutebeuf fl. c. 1249-1277 .... DLB 208
Rutenber, Culbert G(erow) 1909- CAP-2
Earlier sketch in CA 17-18
Rutgers, Leonard Victor 1964- CANR-110
Earlier sketch in CA 152
Rutgers van der Loeff, An
See Rutgers van der Loeff-Basenau, An(na) Maria Margaretha
Rutgers van der Loeff-Basenau, An(na) Maria Margaretha 1910- CANR-7
Earlier sketch in CA 9-12R
See also SATA 22
Ruth, Babe
See Ruth, George Herman (Jr.)
Ruth, Claire (Merritt) 1900-1976
Obituary 69-72
Ruth, David
See Cannell, (Humberston) Skipwith, Jr.
Ruth, Elizabeth 1968- 206
Ruth, George Herman (Jr.) 1895-1948
Brief entry 116
Ruth, John L(andis) 1930- 73-76
Ruth, Kent Ringelman 1916- CANR-2
Earlier sketch in CA 5-8R
Ruth, Rod 1912-1987 .... SATA 9
Ruthchild, Rochelle Goldberg 1940- 152
Rutherford, Andrew 1929-1998 .... CANR-9
Obituary 165
Earlier sketch in CA 5-8R
Rutherford, Douglas
See McConnell, James Douglas Rutherford
Rutherford, Edward
See Wintle, Francis Edward
Rutherford, Ernest 1871-1937 156
Rutherford, Malcolm 1939-1999 119
Rutherford, Margaret 1882-1972
Obituary 33-36R
Rutherford, Mark
See White, William Hale
See also DLB 18
See also RGEL 2
See also TCLC 25
Rutherford, Meg 1932- 29-32R
See also SATA 34
Rutherford, Michael (Andrew) 1946- CANR-26
Earlier sketch in CA 45-48
Rutherford, Phillip Roland 1939- 37-40R
Rutherford, Ward 1927-1999 .... CANR-14
Earlier sketch in CA 77-80
Ruthin, Margaret
See Catherall, Arthur
See also SATA 4
Ruthstrom, Dorotha 1936- 107
Ruthven, Beverly (M.) 1953- 149
Ruthven, K(enneth) K(nowles) 1936- CANR-51
Earlier sketches in CA 25-28R, CANR-26
Rutkoff, Peter M. 1942- CANR-93
Earlier sketches in CA 116, CANR-39
Rutkowski, Edwin H(enry) 1923- 37-40R
Rutkowski, Thaddeus 1954- 184
Rutland, Dodge
See Singleton, Betty
Rutland, Elizabeth
See Fearn, John Russell
Rutland, Robert A(llen) 1922- CANR-2
Earlier sketch in CA 45-48
Rutland, Suzanne D. 1946- 233
Rutledge, Aaron L(eslie) 1919- 45-48
Rutledge, Albert J(ohn) 1934- 33-36R
Rutledge, Archibald (Hamilton) 1883-1973 .... CANR-5
Obituary 45-48
Earlier sketch in CA 5-8R
Rutledge, Brett
See Paul, Elliot (Harold)
Rutledge, Dom Denys
See Rutledge, Edward William
Rutledge, Edward William 1906- 5-8R
Rutledge, Harley Dean 1926- 107
Rutledge, Howard Elmer 1929(?)-1984
Obituary 113
Rutledge, Jill Zimmerman 1951- 230
See also SATA 155
Rutledge, Leigh W. 1957- 151
Rutman, Darrett B(ruce) 1929- CANR-6
Earlier sketch in CA 13-16R
Rutman, Gilbert L(ionel) 1935- 25-28R
Rutman, Leo 1935- CANR-121
Earlier sketch in CA 45-48
Rutsala, Vern 1934- CANR-80
Earlier sketches in CA 9-12R, CANR-6, 20, 43
See also CP 1, 2, 3, 4, 5, 6, 7
Rutstein, David D(avis) 1909-1986 .... 33-36R
Obituary 118
Rutstein, Harry Sidney 1929- 108
Rutstein, Nat(han) 1930- 53-56
Rutstrum, Calvin 1895-1982 .... CANR-1
Obituary 106
Earlier sketch in CA 1-4R
Rutt, M. E.
See Shah, Amina
Rutt, Richard 1925- CANR-6
Earlier sketch in CA 9-12R
Ruttan, Vernon W(esley) 1924- 41-44R
Ruttenberg, Joseph 1889-1983
Obituary 109
See also IDFW 3, 4
Ruttenberg, Stanley H(arvey) 1917-2001 .... 33-36R
Obituary 194
Rutter, Barbara A. 1943- 118
Rutter, Eileen Joyce 1945- CANR-80
Earlier sketches in CA 61-64, CANR-10
See also Chant, (Eileen) Joy
Rutter, Jeremy B. 1946- 163
Rutter, Michael (Llewellyn) 1933- CANR-53
Earlier sketches in CA 109, CANR-29
Rutter, Virginia Beane 176
Ruttkowski, Wolfgang Victor 1935- .. CANR-15
Earlier sketch in CA 41-44R
Ruttle, Lee 1909-1985 81-84
Rutz, Viola Larkin 1932- 21-24R
See also SATA 12
Rutzebeck, (Hans) Hjalmar 1889-1980 ... 9-12R
Ruud, Charles A(rthur) 1933- CANR-48
Earlier sketch in CA 121
Ruud, Josephine Bartow 1921- 73-76
Ruurs, Margriet 1952- CANR-134
Earlier sketch in CA 164
See also SATA 97, 147
Ruusbroec, John 1293-1381 .... LMFS 1
Ruusuvuori, Aarno (Emil) 1925-1992 231
Ruuth, Marianne 1937- CANR-21
Earlier sketches in CA 57-60, CANR-6
Rux, Carl Hancock 1970- 228
Ruxin, Robert H(arris) 1953- 110
Ruxton, George Frederick 1821-1848 . DLB 186
Ruyerson, James Paul
See Rothweiler, Paul Roger
Ruy-Sanchez, Alberto 1951- 207
Ruyslinck, Ward
See Belser, Reimond Karel Maria de
See also CLC 14
Ruz, Fidel Castro
See Castro (Ruz), Fidel
Ruzic, Neil P. 1930- CANR-39
Earlier sketches in CA 17-20R, CANR-8
Ruzicka, Rudolph 1883-1978
Obituary 81-84
See also SATA-Obit 24
Ruzzante c. 1495-1542 .... RGWL 2, 3
Ruzzier, Sergio 1966- .... SATA 159
R-va, Zeneida
See Gan, Elena Andreevna
Ryall, Edward W(illiam) 1902- 61-64
Ryall, George (Francis Trafford) 1887(?)-1979 103
Obituary 89-92
Ryalls, Alan 1919- 102
Ryals, Clyde de L(oache) 1928-1998 ..... 21-24R
Obituary 169
Ryan, Alan 1940- CANR-49
Earlier sketch in CA 29-32R
See also HGG
Ryan, Allan A(ndrew), Jr. 1945- 124
Ryan, Alvan Sherman 1912-1996 .... 17-20R
Ryan, Bernard, Jr. 1923- CANR-6
Earlier sketch in CA 5-8R
Ryan, Betsy
See Ryan, Elizabeth (Anne)
Ryan, Bob 1946- CANR-4
Earlier sketch in CA 49-52
Ryan, Bryce F(inley) 1911- 81-84
Ryan, Charles W(illiam) 1929- 57-60
Ryan, Charles W(illiam) 1932- 93-96
Ryan, Cheli Duran 102
See also SATA 20
Ryan, Chris 1945- 206
Ryan, Claude 1925-2004
Obituary 223
Brief entry 111
Ryan, Cornelius (John) 1920-1974 .... CANR-38
Obituary 53-56
Earlier sketch in CA 69-72
See also CLC 7
Ryan, Craig 1953- 153
Ryan, Desmond 1893-1964
Obituary 113
Ryan, Desmond 1943- 130
Ryan, Dorothy (Barger) 1942- CANR-13
Earlier sketch in CA 73-76
Ryan, Edwin 1916- 5-8R
Ryan, Elizabeth (Anne) 1943- CANR-7
Earlier sketch in CA 61-64
See also SATA 30
Ryan, Frank 1944- 145
Ryan, Gig (Elizabeth) 1956- CANR-80
Earlier sketch in CA 154
See also CP 7
See also CWP
Ryan, Gordon W. 1943- 236
Ryan, Halford (Ross) 1943- 175
Ryan, Henry Butterfield 1931- 187
Ryan, Herbert J(oseph) 1931- 41-44R
Ryan, James 1952- .... DLB 267
Ryan, James G(ilbert) 1947- CANR-93
Earlier sketch in CA 165
Ryan, James H(erbert) 1928- 53-56
Ryan, Jeanette Mines
See Mines, Jeanette (Marie)
Ryan, Jessica Cadwalader 1915(?)-1972
Obituary 33-36R
Ryan, Joan 1960(?)- 158
Ryan, John (Gerald Christopher) 1921- CANR-16
Earlier sketches in CA 49-52, CANR-1
See also SATA 22
Ryan, John Barry 1933- CANR-7
Earlier sketch in CA 57-60
Ryan, John Fergus 1931- 73-76
Ryan, John J. 1922(?)-1977
Obituary 69-72
Ryan, John Julian 1898-1983 73-76
Ryan, John K(enneth) 1897-1981 ...... CANR-16
Earlier sketch in CA 13-16R
Ryan, Joseph A. 1920- 138
Ryan, Joseph J. 1910(?)-1976
Obituary 69-72
Ryan, Juanita 1949- 120
Ryan, Kathryn Morgan 1925-1993 102
Obituary 140
Interview in CA-102
Ryan, Kay 1945- 208
Ryan, Kay 1945- .... DLB 282
Ryan, Kevin 1932- CANR-139
Earlier sketches in CA 29-32R, CANR-12
Ryan, Lawrence Vincent 1923- 5-8R
Ryan, Leonard Eames 1930- 9-12R
Ryan, Marah Ellis 1866(?)-1934
Brief entry 122
See also TCWW 1, 2
Ryan, Margaret 1950- CANR-106
Earlier sketch in CA 146
See also SATA 78
Ryan, Marleigh Grayer 1930- 17-20R
Ryan, Mary E(lizabeth) 1953- .... SATA 61
Ryan, Mary P(atricia) 1945- 134
Brief entry 113
Ryan, Maureen Jones
See Jones-Ryan, Maureen
Ryan, Michael 1946- CANR-109
Earlier sketch in CA 49-52
See also CLC 65
See also DLBY 1982
Ryan, Milo 1907- 5-8R
Ryan, Neil Joseph 1930- 13-16R
Ryan, Oscar 1904- 181
See also DLB 68
Ryan, Pam(ela) Munoz 201
See also AAYA 47
See also BYA 15
See also SATA 134
Ryan, Pat M(artin) 1928- CANR-13
Earlier sketch in CA 33-36R
Ryan, Patrick 1957- 209
See also SATA 138
Ryan, Patrick J. 1902-1978 .... CAP-1
Earlier sketch in CA 11-12
Ryan, Paul B(rennan) 1913-1987 ...... CANR-15
Earlier sketch in CA 81-84
Ryan, Paul William 1906-1947
Brief entry 114
Ryan, Peter (Charles) 1939- 61-64
See also SATA 15
Ryan, Peter Allen 1923- 109
Ryan, R(achel) R. .... HGG
Ryan, Rachel
See Brown, Sandra
Ryan, Regina (Claire) 1938- 118
Ryan, Regina S(ara) 1945- 119
Ryan, Richard 1946- .... CP 1
Ryan, Robert Michael 1934- 29-32R
Ryan, Sister Joseph Eleanor 61-64
Ryan, Susan Elizabeth 1948- 190
Ryan, T. Antoinette 1924- 41-44R
Ryan, Terry 1947(?)- 202
Ryan, Tex
See Fearn, John Russell
Ryan, Thomas Arthur 1911- 41-44R
Ryan, Thomas Richard 1897-1981 .... 29-32R
Obituary 122
Ryan, Tim
See Dent, Lester
Ryan, Tom 1938- CANR-10
Earlier sketch in CA 57-60
Ryan, Tracy 1964- 196
Ryan, William (Howard) 1914- 104
Ryan, William (Michael) 1948- 122
Ryan, William H. 1928(?)-1986
Obituary 121
Ryan, William M(artin) 1918- 33-36R
Ryang, Sonia 1960- 165
Ryan-Lush, Geraldine 1949- .... SATA 89
Ryans, David Garriott 1909-1986 .... 5-8R
Ryans, John K(elley), Jr. 1932- 61-64
Ryavec, Karl W(illiam) 1936- 137
Ryback, Eric 1952- 37-40R
Ryback, Tim
See Ryback, Timothy W.
Ryback, Timothy W. 236
Rybak, Nathan 1913-1978(?)
Obituary 81-84
Rybakov, Anatoli (Naumovich) 1911-1998 . 135
Obituary 172
Brief entry 126
See also Rybakov, Anatolii (Naumovich)
See also CLC 23, 53
See also SATA 79
See also SATA-Obit 108
Rybakov, Anatolii (Naumovich)
See Rybakov, Anatoli (Naumovich)
See also DLB 302
Rybalka, Michel 1933- 41-44R
Rybczynski, Witold (Marian) 1943- CANR-138
Earlier sketches in CA 110, CANR-29, 96
See also MTFW 2005
Rybka, Edward F(rank) 1928- 33-36R
Rybolt, Thomas R(oy) 1954- .... SATA 62
Rybot, Doris
See Ponsonby, D(oris) A(lmon)
Rychlak, Joseph F(rank) 1928- CANR-14
Earlier sketch in CA 37-40R
Rychlak, Ronald (J.) 1957- 193
Ryckmans, Pierre 1935- CANR-16
Earlier sketch in CA 85-88
Rycroft, Charles (Frederick) 1914-1998 .... CANR-11
Obituary 169
Earlier sketch in CA 21-24R
Ryczek, William J. 1953- 143
Rydberg, Ernest E(mil) 1901-1993 .... 13-16R
See also SATA 21
Rydberg, Lou(isa Hampton) 1908- 69-72
See also SATA 27
Rydel, Christine A(nn) 1944- 118
Rydell, Forbes
See Forbes, DeLoris (Florine) Stanton
Rydell, Katy 1942- 155
See also SATA 91
Rydell, Robert W(illiam) 1952- CANR-52
Earlier sketch in CA 126
Rydell, Wendell
See Rydell, Wendy
Rydell, Wendy 33-36R
See also SATA 4
Ryden, Ernest Edwin 1886-1981
Obituary 102
Ryden, Hope CANR-59
Earlier sketches in CA 33-36R, CANR-14
See also ANW
See also SATA 8, 91
Rydenfelt, Sven 1911- 132
Ryder, A(rthur) J(ohn) 1913-1993 .... 21-24R
Ryder, Eileen 1908- 117
Ryder, Ellen 1913- 29-32R
Ryder, Frank G(lessner) 1916- 5-8R
Ryder, Frederick Bushnell 1871-1936 208
See also DLB 241
Ryder, Jack 1871-1936
See Ryder, Frederick Bushnell
Ryder, Joanne (Rose) 1946- CANR-90
Brief entry 112
Earlier sketch in CA 133
See also CLR 37
See also CWRI 5
See also MAICYA 1, 2
See also SATA 65, 122, 163
See also SATA-Brief 34
Ryder, John 1917- CANR-5
Earlier sketch in CA 5-8R
Ryder, Jonathan
See Ludlum, Robert
Ryder, M(ichael) L(awson) 1927- 102
Ryder, Meyer S. 1909-1986 .... 21-24R
Ryder, Norman B(urston) 1923- 37-40R
Ryder, Pamela
See Lamb, Nancy
Ryder, Richard D. 1940- 139
Ryder, Ron 1904-1994 61-64
Ryder, Rowland (Vint) 1914-1996 85-88
Ryder, T(homas) A(rthur) 1902- 5-8R
Ryder, Thom
See Harvey, John (Barton)
Rydill, Jessica 227
Ryding, Erik (S.) 1953- 215
Ryding, William W. 1924- 77-80
Rye, Anthony
See Youd, (Christopher) Samuel
Rye, Bjoern Robinson 1942- 61-64
Ryerson, Eric
See Coffey, Wayne
Ryerson, Margery (Austin) 1886-1989
Obituary 128
Ryerson, Martin 1907- CANR-8
Earlier sketch in CA 13-16R
Ryersson, Scot D. 1960- CANR-90
Earlier sketch in CA 174
Ryf, Robert S. 1918-1985 .... 17-20R
Obituary 117
Ryfa, Juras T. 1964- 187
Ryga, George 1932-1987 .... CANR-90
Obituary 124
Earlier sketches in CA 101, CANR-43
See also CCA 1
See also CLC 14
See also DAC
See also DAM MST
See also DLB 60
Ryken, Leland 1942- CANR-144
Earlier sketches in CA 29-32R, CANR-12, 28, 52
Rykwert, Joseph 1926- CANR-97
Earlier sketches in CA 69-72, CANR-11
Ryland, Lee
See Arlandson, Leone
Rylands, Enriqueta Augustina Tennant 1843-1908 210
See also DLB 184

Rylands, John 1801-1888 ... DLB 184
Rylands, Philip 1950- ... 144
Rylant, Cynthia 1954- ... CANR-140
Earlier sketches in CA 136, CANR-79
See also AAYA 10, 45
See also BYA 6, 7
See also CLR 15, 86
See also CWRI 5
See also JRDA
See also MAICYA 1, 2
See also MAICYAS 1
See also SAAS 13
See also SATA 50, 76, 112, 160
See also SATA-Brief 44
See also WYAS 1
See also YAW
Ryle, Anthony 1927- ... 107
Ryle, Gilbert 1900-1976 ... 73-76
Obituary ... 69-72
See also DLB 262
Ryle, Martin (H.) 1918-1984 ... 133
Ryle, Michael 1927- ... 133
Ryleev, Kondratii Fedorovich
1795-1826 ... DLB 205
Rylski, Aleksander Scibor
See Scibor-Rylski, Aleksander
Rylsky, Maxym 1895-1964 ... EWL 3
Ryman, Geoff(rey Charles) 1951- ... CANR-90
Earlier sketch in CA 134
See also FANT
See also SFW 4
Ryman, Rebecca
Brief entry ... 184
Rymer, Alta May 1925- ... CANR-1
Earlier sketch in CA 49-52
See also SATA 34
Rymer, James Malcolm 1804-1884 ... HGG
Rymer, Russ 1952- ... 186
Rymer, Thomas 1643(?)-1713 ... DLB 101
Rymes, Thomas Kenneth 1932- ... 37-40R
Rymkiewicz, Jaroslaw (Marek) 1935-
Ryn, Claes G. 1943- ... 129
Rynearson, Edward H(arper) 1901-1987
Obituary ... 121
Rynew, Arden N. 1943- ... 37-40R
Rynne, Xavier
See Murphy, Francis Xavier
Ryrie, Charles C(aldwell) 1925- ... CANR-39
Earlier sketches in CA 9-12R, CANR-3, 18
Ryskamp, Charles (Andrew) 1928- ... 104
Ryskamp, John Henry 1954- ... 179
Ryskind, Morrie 1895-1985 ... 198
Obituary ... 117
Brief entry ... 109
See also DLB 26
See also IDFW 3
Rystrom, Kenneth 1932- ... 110
Ryufu, Zenshin
See Whalen, Philip (Glenn)
Ryuhoku 1837-1884 ... MJW
Rywell, Martin 1905-1971 ... CAP-2
Earlier sketch in CA 19-20
Rywkin, Michael 1925- ... 13-16R
Ryzl, Milan 1928- ... 29-32R
Rzepka, Charles J(ulian) 1949- ... 127
Rzhevsky, Aleksai Andreevich
1737-1804 ... DLB 150
Rzhevsky, Leonid 1905-1986 ... CANR-14
Earlier sketch in CA 41-44R
Rzhevsky, Nicholas 1943- ... 115

S

S. H.
See Hartmann, Sadakichi
S. L. C.
See Clemens, Samuel Langhorne
S. S.
See Sassoon, Siegfried (Lorraine)
S. S. E.
See Sperry, (Sally) Baxter
S., Svend Otto
See Soerensen, Svend Otto
S., Tayeb
See Djaout, Tahar
Saab, E(velyn) Ann Pottinger 1934- ... 107
Saab, Edouard 1929-1976
Obituary ... 65-68
Saabye Christensen, Lars 1953- ... 216
See also DLB 297
Sa'adawi, al- Nawal
See El Saadawi, Nawal
See also AFW
See also EWL 3
Saadawi, Nawal El
See El Saadawi, Nawal
See also WLIT 2
Saaf, Donald W(illiam) 1961- ... SATA 124
Saal, Jocelyn
See Sachs, Judith
Saalman, Howard 1928- ... CANR-74
Earlier sketches in CA 1-4R, CANR-1
Saar, James 1949- ... 131
Saari, Carolyn 1939- ... 140
Saarikoski, Pentti (Ilmari) 1937-1983 ... 162
See also EWL 3
Saarinen, Aline B(ernstein Louchheim)
1914-1972
Obituary ... 37-40R
Saarinen, Eero 1910-1961 ... 184
Obituary ... 113
See also AAYA 65
Saatkamp, Herman J(oseph), Jr.
1942- ... CANR-53
Earlier sketch in CA 126
Saaty, Thomas L(orie) 1926- ... CANR-8
Earlier sketch in CA 57-60
Saavedra, Luis Spota
See Spota (Saavedra), Luis
Saba, Umberto 1883-1957 ... CANR-79
Earlier sketch in CA 144
See also DLB 114
See also EWL 3
See also RGWL 2, 3
See also TCLC 33
Sabais, Heinz Winfried 1922-1981
Obituary ... 114
Sabaliunas, Leonas 1934- ... 61-64
Saban, Cheryl (Lynn) 1951- ... 144
Sabar, Yona 1939- ... CANR-30
Earlier sketch in CA 112
Sabaroff, Rose Epstein 1918- ... 85-88
Sabatier, Paul 1854-1941 ... 156
Sabatier, Robert 1923- ... CANR-39
Earlier sketches in CA 102, CANR-18
Sabatine, Jean A. 1941- ... 158
Sabatini, Rafael 1875-1950 ... 162
See also BPFB 3
See also RHW
See also TCLC 47
Sabatini, Sandra 1959- ... 203
Sabato, Ernesto (R.) 1911- ... CANR-65
Earlier sketches in CA 97-100, CANR-32
See also CDWLB 3
See also CLC 10, 23
See also CWW 2
See also DAM MULT
See also DLB 145
See also EWL 3
See also HLC 2
See also HW 1, 2
See also LAW
See also MTCW 1, 2
See also MTFW 2005
Sabato, Haim ... 225
Sabato, Larry (J.) 1952- ... CANR-103
Earlier sketches in CA 108, CANR-27
Sabbag, Robert 1946- ... CANR-115
Earlier sketch in CA 101
Sabbagh, Karl ... 198
Sabbah, Hassan i
See Butler, William Huxford
Sabbeth, Carol (Landstrom) 1957- ... 196
See also SATA 125
Sabe, Quien
See Bates, Harry
Sabel, Charles F(rederick) 1947- ... CANR-110
Earlier sketch in CA 129
Saberhagen, Fred(erick Thomas)
1930- ... CANR-104
Earlier sketches in CA 57-60, CANR-7, 27, 33, 64
See also DLB 8
See also FANT
See also HGG
See also MTCW 1
See also SATA 37, 89
Saberhagen, Joan 1943- ... 219
Sabiad
See White, Stanhope
Sabin, Albert B(ruce) 1906-1993 ... 156
Sabin, Arthur J. 1930- ... 144
Sabin, E(lenora) Rose ... 220
Sabin, Edwin L(egrand) 1870-1952 ... YABC 2
Sabin, Florence Rena 1871-1953 ... 156
Sabin, Francene ... CANR-11
Earlier sketch in CA 69-72
See also SATA 27
Sabin, Joseph 1821-1881 ... DLB 187
Sabin, Katharine Cover 1910- ... 57-60
Sabin, Lou
See Sabin, Louis
Sabin, Louis 1930- ... CANR-11
Earlier sketch in CA 69-72
See also SATA 27
Sabin, Mark
See Fox, Norman A(rnold)
Sabin, Roger (John) 1961- ... 202
Sabin, Thomas D. 1936- ... 147
Sabina, Maria ... WP
Sabine, B(asil) E. V. 1914- ... CANR-28
Earlier sketch in CA 97-100
Sabine, Ellen S. (Borcherding)
1908-1986 ... CANR-74
Earlier sketches in CAP-1, CA 17-18
Sabine, Gordon Arthur 1917- ... CANR-41
Earlier sketch in CA 117
Sabine, Waldo
See Sabine, William H(enry) W(aldo)
Sabine, William H(enry) W(aldo)
1903-1994 ... CANR-4
Earlier sketch in CA 53-56
Sabines, Jaime 1925(?)-1999 ... 153
Obituary ... 179
See also EWL 3
See also HW 1
See also LAWS 1
Sabini, John Anthony 1921- ... 9-12R
Sabino, Fernando (Tavares)
1923-2004 ... DLB 307
Sabino, Osvaldo R(uben) 1950- ... 192
Sabisch, Christian 1955- ... 129
Sabki, Hisham M. 1934- ... 193
Brief entry ... 106
Sable, Martin Howard 1924- ... CANR-29
Earlier sketches in CA 33-36R, CANR-12
Sableman, Mark (Stephen) 1951- ... 163
Sabloff, Jeremy A(rac) 1944- ... CANR-8
Earlier sketch in CA 61-64
Sablosky, Irving L. 1924- ... 124
Sabom, Michael Bruce 1944- ... 109
Sabourin, Anne Winifred 1910- ... 101
Sabourin, Justine
See Sabourin, Anne Winifred
Sabourin, Leopold 1919- ... CANR-11
Earlier sketch in CA 65-68
Sabre, Dirk
See Laffin, John (Alfred Charles)
Sabri-Tabrizi, Gholam-Reza 1934- ... 61-64
Sabuda, Robert (James) 1965- ... CANR-106
Earlier sketch in CA 149
See also SATA 81, 120
Sa-Carneiro, Mario de 1890-1916 ... DLB 287
See also EWL 3
See also TCLC 83
Sacastru, Martin
See Bioy Casares, Adolfo
See also CWW 2
Saccio, Peter (Churchill) 1941- ... 61-64
Sacco, Joe 1960- ... CANR-139
Earlier sketch in CA 199
See also AAYA 57
See also MTFW 2005
Sacer, Gottfried Wilhelm 1635-1699 ... DLB 168
Sach, Nathan
See Zach, Nathan
Sachar, Abram Leon 1899-1993 ... CANR-74
Obituary ... 142
Earlier sketch in CA 97-100
Sachar, Emily 1958- ... 135
Sachar, Howard Morley 1928- ... CANR-120
Earlier sketches in CA 5-8R, CANR-6
Sachar, Louis 1954- ... CANR-131
Earlier sketches in CA 81-84, CANR-15, 33
See also AAYA 35
See also CLR 28, 79
See also CWRI 5
See also JRDA
See also MAICYA 2
See also MAICYAS 1
See also SATA 63, 104, 154
See also SATA-Brief 50
See also WYAS 1
Sacharoff, Shanta Nimbark 1945- ... 61-64
Sachdev, Paul ... 115
Sachem, E. B.
See Creel, Stephen Melville
Sacher, Jack, Jr. 1931- ... 57-60
Sacher-Masoch, Alexander 1902(?)-1972
Obituary ... 37-40R
Sachs, Albert Louis 1935- ... CANR-14
Earlier sketch in CA 21-24R
Sachs, Albie
See Sachs, Albert Louis
Sachs, Alexander 1893-1973
Obituary ... 41-44R
Sachs, Elizabeth-Ann 1946- ... 111
See also SATA 48
Sachs, Georgia
See Adams, Georgia Sachs
Sachs, Hans 1494-1576 ... CDWLB 2
See also DLB 179
See also RGWL 2, 3
Sachs, Harley L. 1931- ... 206
Sachs, (Stewart) Harvey 1946- ... 85-88
Sachs, Herbert L. 1929- ... 25-28R
Sachs, Judith 1947- ... CANR-103
Earlier sketches in CA 122, CANR-48
See also SATA 52
See also SATA-Brief 51
Sachs, Lewis Benjamen 1938- ... 61-64
Sachs, Margaret 1948- ... 206
Brief entry ... 115
Sachs, Marianne 1945- ... 114
Sachs, Marilyn (Stickle) 1927- ... CANR-47
Earlier sketches in CA 17-20R, CANR-13
See also AAYA 2
See also BYA 6
See also CLC 35
See also CLR 2
See also JRDA
See also MAICYA 1, 2
See also SAAS 2
See also SATA 3, 68
See also SATA-Essay 110
See also WYA
See also YAW
Sachs, Mary P(armly) K(oues) 1882(?)-1973
Obituary ... 45-48
Sachs, Mendel 1927- ... CANR-12
Earlier sketch in CA 29-32R
Sachs, Michael L(eo) 1951- ... CANR-37
Earlier sketch in CA 115
Sachs, Murray 1924- ... CANR-14
Earlier sketch in CA 37-40R
Sachs, Nelly 1891-1970 ... CANR-87
Obituary ... 25-28R
Earlier sketches in CAP-2, CA 17-18
See also CLC 14, 98
See also EWL 3
See also MTCW 2
See also MTFW 2005
See also PFS 20
See also RGWL 2, 3
Sachs, Robert 1952- ... 231
Sachs, Wolfgang 1946- ... 143
Sachse, William L(ewis) 1912- ... 25-28R
Sack, Allen L. 1945- ... 175
Sack, Daniel (Edward) 1962- ... 220
Sack, James J(ohn) 1944- ... 101
Sack, John 1930-2004 ... CANR-68
Obituary ... 225
Earlier sketches in CA 21-24R, CANR-14, 50
See also DLB 185
Sack, Kevin 1959- ... 228
Sack, Saul 1912- ... 53-56
Sackerman, Henry
See Kahm, H(arold) S.
Sackett, Jeffrey 1949- ... HGG
Sackett, L(eyland) H(ugh) 1928- ... 119
Sackett, S(amuel) J(ohn) 1928- ... CANR-6
Earlier sketch in CA 1-4R
See also SATA 12
Sackett, Susan 1943- ... CANR-22
Earlier sketch in CA 106
Sackett, Theodore Alan 1940- ... 89-92
Sackett, Walter W(allace), Jr. 1905-1985 ... 5-8R
Obituary ... 117
Sackheim, Maxwell 1890-1982
Obituary ... 108
Sackler, Howard (Oliver)
1929-1982 ... CANR-30
Obituary ... 108
Earlier sketch in CA 61-64
See also CAD
See also CLC 14
See also DFS 15
See also DLB 7
Sackman, Harold 1927- ... CANR-12
Earlier sketch in CA 21-24R
Sackrey, Charles 1936- ... 77-80
Sacks, Benjamin 1903- ... CAP-2
Earlier sketch in CA 23-24
Sacks, Claire
See Sprague, Claire S(acks)
Sacks, David Harris 1942- ... 139
Sacks, Howard L. 1949- ... 147
Sacks, Judith Rose 1952- ... 152
Sacks, Karen 1941- ... CANR-26
Earlier sketch in CA 109
Sacks, Norman P(aul) 1914- ... 45-48
Sacks, Oliver (Wolf) 1933- ... CANR-76
Earlier sketches in CA 53-56, CANR-28, 50
Interview in ... CANR-28
See also CLC 67, 202
See also CPW
See also DA3
See also MTCW 1, 2
See also MTFW 2005
Sacks, Peter
See Sacks, Peter M.
Sacks, Peter M. 1950- ... CANR-127
Earlier sketch in CA 124
Sacks, Sheldon 1930-1979 ... 17-20R
Obituary ... 122
Sacks, Steven 1968- ... 225
Sackson, Sid 1920- ... CANR-12
Earlier sketch in CA 69-72
See also SATA 16
Sackton, Alexander H(art) 1911-1992 ... 37-40R
Sackville, Charles 1638-1706
See Dorset
See also BRW 2
See also DLB 131
See also PAB
Sackville, Lady Margaret
See Sackville, Margaret
See also DLB 240
Sackville, Margaret 1881-1963 ... 205
See also Sackville, Lady Margaret
Sackville, Thomas 1536-1608 ... DAM DRAM
See also DLB 62, 132
See also RGEL 2
Sackville-West, Edward (Charles)
1901-1965 ... 206
See also DLB 191
Sackville-West, V(ictoria Mary)
1892-1962 ... CANR-60
Obituary ... 93-96
Earlier sketches in CA 104, CANR-40
See also DLB 34, 195
See also MTCW 1, 2
See also MTFW 2005
Sacre, Antonio 1968- ... 227
See also SATA 152
Sadakichi
See Hartmann, Sadakichi
(el-)Sadat, Anwar 1918-1981 ... CANR-77
Obituary ... 104
Earlier sketch in CA 101
Sa'dawi, Nawal al-
See El Saadawi, Nawal
See also CWW 2
Sadd, Susan 1951- ... 103
Saddhatissa, Hammalawa 1914- ... CANR-17
Earlier sketch in CA 97-100
Saddlemyer, (Eleanor) Ann 1932- ... CANR-134
Earlier sketch in CA 17-20R
Saddler, Allen
See Richards, R(onald) C(harles) W(illiam)
Saddler, K. Allen
See Richards, R(onald) C(harles) W(illiam)
Sade, Donatien Alphonse Francois
1740-1814 ... DLB 314
See also EW 4
See also GFL Beginnings to 1789
See also RGWL 2, 3
Sade, Marquis de
See Sade, Donatien Alphonse Francois
Sadecky, Petr Milos 1943- ... 41-44R
Sadeh, Pinhas 1929-1994 ... CANR-34
Obituary ... 143
Earlier sketches in CA 25-28R, CANR-13
Sa de Miranda, Francisco de
1481-1558(?) ... DLB 287
Sader, Emir 1943- ... 142
Sa'di, Muslih-al-Din 1209-1292 ... RGWL 2, 3
Sadick, Neil (S.) 1951- ... 138
Sadie, Stanley (John) 1930-2005 ... CANR-115
Obituary ... 237
Earlier sketches in CA 17-20R, CANR-9
See also SATA 14
Sadiq, Muhammad 1898-1984 ... CANR-18
Earlier sketch in CA 17-20R
Sadiq, Nazneen 1944- ... 160
See also SATA 101

Cumulative Index 505 St. John

Sadker, Myra Pollack 1943-1995 ...... CANR-46
Obituary 148
Earlier sketches in CA 53-56, CANR-5, 22
Sadler, Amy 1924- .... TCWW 2
Sadler, Arthur Lindsay 1882-1970 .... 5-8R
Sadler, Barry 1940-1989 129
Sadler, Catherine Edwards 1952- 154
See also SATA 60
See also SATA-Brief 45
Sadler, Christine 1908-1983 .... CAP-1
Obituary 110
Earlier sketch in CA 11-12
Sadler, Ella Jo 1942- 57-60
Sadler, Geoff
See Sadler, Jeff
Sadler, Geoffrey
See Sadler, Jeff
Sadler, Glenn Edward 1935- 97-100
Sadler, Jeff 1943- .... TCWW 2
Sadler, Julius Trousdale, Jr. 1923- 65-68
Sadler, Marilyn (June) 1950- .... MAICYA 2
See also SATA 79
Sadler, Mark
See Lynds, Dennis
Sadler, William A(lan), Jr. 1931- CANR-92
Earlier sketch in CA 25-28R
Sadlier, Darlene J(oy) 1950- CANR-127
Earlier sketch in CA 139
Sadlier, Mary Anne 1820-1903 181
See also DLB 99
Sadock, Benjamin James 1933- 185
Brief entry 105
Sadoff, Ira 1945- CANR-109
Earlier sketches in CA 53-56, CANR-5, 21
See also CLC 9
See also DLB 120
Sadoveanu, Mihail 1880-1961 .... DLB 220
See also EWL 3
Sadowsky, Jonathan Hal 201
Sadri, Ahmad 1953- 145
Sadrin, Anny 1935- 150
Sadun, Elvio H. 1918(?)-1974
Obituary 49-52
Sadur, Nina Nikolaevna 1950- .... DLB 285
Sa'edi, Gholam-Hossein 1935-1985 .... EWL 3
Saenz, Andres 1927-
See Saenz, Andres
Saenz, Andres 1927- 220
Saenz, Benjamin Alire 1954- CANR-121
Earlier sketch in CA 159
See also DLB 209
Saenz, Dalmiro
See Saenz, Dalmiro A.
Saenz, Dalmiro A. 1926- .... HW 1
Saenz, Jaime 1921-1986 176
See also DLB 145, 283
See also HW 2
Saer, Juan Jose 1937- 219
See also CWW 2
See also LAWS 1
See also RGWL 3
Saerchinger, Cesar 1889-1971
Obituary 33-36R
Saetone
See Camus, Albert
Safa, Helen M. Icken 1930- CANR-57
Earlier sketches in CA 45-48, CANR-1, 30
Safarian, Albert Edward 1924- 105
Safarik, Allan 1948- 114
Safdie, Moshe 1938- CANR-116
Earlier sketches in CA 69-72, CANR-73
Safer, Daniel J. 1934- CANR-11
Earlier sketch in CA 69-72
Safer, Elaine Berkman 1937- 41-44R
Safer, Morley 1931- 93-96
See also AITN 2
See also CCA 1
Saferstein, Dan 231
Saffell, David C(lyde) 1941- CANR-11
Earlier sketch in CA 61-64
Saffer, Barbara 217
See also SATA 144
Saffin, John 1626(?)-1710 .... DLB 24
Saffle, Michael 1946- 139
Saffron 1942- .... CD 5
Saffron, Morris Harold 1905-1993 45-48
Saffron, Robert 1918(?)-1985
Obituary 114
Safi, Omid 219
Safian, Jill
See Bharti, Ma Satya
Safilios-Rothschild, Constantina
1936- CANR-31
Earlier sketch in CA 45-48
Safina, Carl 1955- CANR-121
Earlier sketch in CA 173
Safir, Howard 1942- 227
Safir, Leonard 1921-1992 109
Obituary 140
Safire, William 1929- CANR-91
Earlier sketches in CA 17-20R, CANR-31, 54
See also CLC 10
Safran, Claire 1930- 101
Safran, Nadav 1925-2003 .... 5-8R
Obituary 218
Safran, William 1930- CANR-64
Earlier sketches in CA 113, CANR-32
Safranski, Rudiger 180
Safransky, Sy 1945- 145
Sagall, Elliot L. 1918- 29-32R
Sagalyn, Lynne B. 1947- CANR-137
Earlier sketch in CA 134
Sagan, Carl (Edward) 1934-1996 ...... CANR-74
Obituary 155
Earlier sketches in CA 25-28R, CANR-11, 36
See also AAYA 2, 62
See also CLC 30, 112
See also CPW
See also DA3
See also MTCW 1, 2
See also MTFW 2005
See also SATA 58
See also SATA-Obit 94
Sagan, Dorion 1959- CANR-138
Earlier sketch in CA 131
Sagan, Eli 1927- CANR-116
Earlier sketch in CA 124
Sagan, Francoise
See Quoirez, Francoise
See also CLC 3, 6, 9, 17, 36
See also CWW 2
See also DLB 83
See also EWL 3
See also GFL 1789 to the Present
See also MTCW 2
Sagan, Leonard A. 1928-1997 49-52
Sagan, Miriam (Anna) 1954- CANR-123
Earlier sketch in CA 77-80
Sagar, Keith (Milsom) 1934- CANR-119
Earlier sketches in CA 21-24R, CANR-14, 45
Sagara, Michelle 1963- 180
See also West, Michelle Sagara
Sagarin, Edward 1913-1986 .... CANR-4
Earlier sketch in CA 5-8R
See also GLL 1
Sagarin, Mary 1903-1990 81-84
Sagarra, Eda 1933- CANR-11
Earlier sketch in CA 65-68
Sagastizabal, Patricia 1953- 208
Sage, Angie 239
Sage, George Harvey 1929- 61-64
Sage, Joe
See Sage, Joseph
Sage, Jonathan 1953- 129
Sage, Joseph 1921-1987
Obituary 122
Sage, Juniper
See Brown, Margaret Wise and
Hurd, Edith Thacher
Sage, Leland L(ivingston) 1899-1989 61-64
Sage, Lorna 1943-2001 216
Sage, (Frank) Norman 1910- 150
Sage, Robert 1899-1962 106
See also DLB 4
Sagel, Jim 1947-1998 131
Obituary 166
See also DLB 82
See also HW 1
Sagendorf, Bud
See Sagendorf, Forrest C(owles)
Sagendorf, Forrest C(owles) 1915-1994
Brief entry 112
Sagendorph, Robb Hansell
1900-1970 .... CANR-7
Obituary 29-32R
Earlier sketch in CA 5-8R
See also DLB 137
Sager, Carole Bayer 1947- 146
Sager, Clifford J. 1916- CANR-12
Earlier sketch in CA 29-32R
Sager, Ruth 1918-1997 158
Sager, Samuel 1923- 123
Sageser, A(delbert) Bower 1902-1990 ... 29-32R
Saget, Bob 1956- 173
Saggs, Henry W(illiam) F(rederick) 1920- .. 5-8R
Saghir, Marcel T(awfic) 1937- 49-52
Sagnier, Thierry (Bright) 1946- 53-56
Sagola, Mario J.
See Kane, Henry
Sagsoorian, Paul 1923- .... SATA 12
Sagstetter, Karen 1941- 105
Saha, P(rosanta) K(umar) 1932- .... CP 1
Sahagun, Carlos 1938- 180
See also DLB 108
Sahakian, Lucille 1894-1982 53-56
Sahakian, Mabel Lewis 1921-1982 .... 21-24R
Sahakian, William S(ahak)
1921-1986 .... CANR-8
Earlier sketch in CA 17-20R
Sahgal, Nayantara (Pandit) 1927- CANR-88
Earlier sketches in CA 9-12R, CANR-11
See also CLC 41
See also CN 1, 2, 3, 4, 5, 6, 7
Sahihi, Ashkan 1963- 141
Sahl, Hans 1902-1993 144
See also DLB 69
Sahl, Mort(on Lyon) 1927- 148
Brief entry 113
Sahlins, Marshall
See Sahlins, Marshall D(avid)
Sahlins, Marshall D(avid) 1930- CANR-117
Brief entry 114
Earlier sketch in CA 133
Sahn, Seung 1927- 113
Sahni, Balbir S. 1934- CANR-3
Earlier sketch in CA 45-48
Sahni, Chaman L. 1933- 128
Sahota, Gian Singh 1924- 142
Said, Abdul Aziz 1930- 81-84
Sa'id, Ali Ahmad 1930-
See Adonis and
Adunis
Said, Edward W. 1935-2003 .... CANR-131
Obituary 220
Earlier sketches in CA 21-24R, CANR-45, 74, 107
See also CLC 123
See also DLB 67
See also MTCW 2
See also MTFW 2005
Said, Laila
See Abou-Saif, Laila
Saida
See LeMair, H(enriette) Willebeek
Saidel, Rochelle G. 1942- 121
Saidenberg, Jocelyn 1963- 224
Sa'Idi, Ghulam Husayn 1936-1985
Obituary 119
Saidman, Anne 1952- 142
See also SATA 75
Saidy, Anthony Fred 1937- 89-92
Saidy, Fareed Milhem 1907-1982
Obituary 106
Saidy, Fred M.
See Saidy, Fareed Milhem
Saigyo 1118-1190 .... DLB 203
See also RGWL 3
Saijo, Albert 1926- .... DLB 312
Saiki, Jessica K(awasuna) 1928- 138
Saiko, George (Emmanuel) 1892-1962 182
See also DLB 85
Sail, Lawrence (Richard) 1942- CANR-80
Earlier sketch in CA 132
See also CP 7
Saille, Davydd ap
See Seals, David
Sailor, Charles 1947- 97-100
Sailor, Merlin F(orrest) 1906-1965 .... CAP-1
Earlier sketch in CA 13-16
Saine, Thomas P(rice) 1941- 41-44R
Sainer, Arthur 1924- CANR-3
Earlier sketch in CA 49-52
See also CAD
See also CD 5, 6
Saini, B(alwant) S(ingh) 1930- 107
Sainsbury, Eric (Edward) 1925- CANR-13
Earlier sketch in CA 33-36R
Sainsbury, John A. 1946- 127
Sainsbury, Maurice Joseph 1927- 108
Saint, Andrew (John) 1946- 65-68
Saint, Assotto 1957-1994 .... GLL 2
Ste. Croix, G(eoffrey) E(rnest) M(aurice) de
See de Ste. Croix, G(eoffrey) E(rnest) M(aurice)
Saint, Dora Jessie 1913- CANR-46
Earlier sketches in CA 13-16R, CANR-7, 22
See also SATA 10
Saint, H(arry) F. 1941- 127
See also CLC 50
Saint, Phil(ip) 1912- 61-64
St. Andre, Lucien
See Mott, Vincent Valmon
St. Andrews, B(onnie). A. 1950- 215
St. Angelo, Douglas 1931- 45-48
St. Antoine, Sara L. 1966- 150
See also SATA 84
St. Antoine, Theodore J(oseph) 1929- 41-44R
St. Aubin de Teran, Lisa 1953- 126
Brief entry 118
Interview in CA-126
See also Teran, Lisa St. Aubin de
See also CN 6, 7
St. Aubyn, F(rederic) C(hase) 1921- 25-28R
St. Aubyn, Fiona 1952- CANR-23
Earlier sketch in CA 106
St. Aubyn, Giles 1925- CANR-19
Earlier sketches in CA 5-8R, CANR-4
St. Bruno, Albert Francis 1909- CAP-1
Earlier sketch in CA 9-10
St. Clair, (Howard) Barry 1945- CANR-46
Earlier sketch in CA 120
St. Clair, Byrd Hooper 1905-1976 .... CANR-85
Obituary 103
Earlier sketch in CA 1-4R
See also SATA-Obit 28
St. Clair, Clovis
See Skarda, Patricia Lyn
St. Clair, David 1932- CANR-81
Earlier sketch in CA 33-36R
See also HGG
St. Clair, Elizabeth
See Cohen, Susan (Lois)
St. Clair, Katherine
See Huff, T(om) E.
St. Clair, Leonard 1916-1986 101
Obituary 118
St. Clair, Margaret 1911-1995 49-52
See also CAAS 8
See also SCFW 1, 2
See also SFW 4
St. Clair, Philip
See Howard, Munroe
St. Clair, Robert James 1925- 9-12R
St. Clair, William CANR-74
Earlier sketch in CA 77-80
St. Claire, Erin
See Brown, Sandra
St. Cyr, Cyprian
See Berne, Eric (Lennard)
St. Cyr, Margaret 1920- 29-32R
Saint-Cyran, Jean Duvergier de Hauranne
1581-1643 .... GFL Beginnings to 1789
Saint-Denis, Michel Jacques
1897-1971 .... CAP-2
Obituary 33-36R
Earlier sketch in CA 19-20
St. Denis, Ruth 1879-1968 213
St. Denny, Douglas 180
Saint Dorliae
See Dorliae, Peter Gondro
St. E. A. of M. and
S
S
See Crowley, Edward Alexander
Sainte-Beuve, Charles Augustin
1804-1869 .... DLB 217
See also EW 6
See also GFL 1789 to the Present
Saint-Eden, Dennis
See Foster, Don(ald)
Sainte-Marie, Beverly 1941- 107
Sainte-Marie, Buffy
See Sainte-Marie, Beverly
Saint-Evremond, Charles de Marquetel de
Saint-Denis 1614-1703 ..... GFL Beginnings to 1789
Saint-Exupery, Antoine (Jean Baptiste Marie
Roger) de 1900-1944 132
Brief entry 108
See also AAYA 63
See also BPFB 3
See also BYA 3
See also CLR 10
See also DA3
See also DAM NOV
See also DLB 72
See also EW 12
See also EWL 3
See also GFL 1789 to the Present
See also LAIT 3
See also MAICYA 1, 2
See also MTCW 1, 2
See also MTFW 2005
See also RGWL 2, 3
See also SATA 20
See also TCLC 2, 56, 169
See also TWA
See also WLC
Saint-Gall, Auguste Amedee de
See Strich, Christian
St. George, Andrew 1962- 146
St. George, Arthur
See Paine, Lauran (Bosworth)
St. George, David
See Markov, Georgi
St. George, Edith
See Delatush, Edith G.
St. George, George 1904-1977 .... CANR-74
Earlier sketch in CA 25-28R
St. George, Harry
See Rathborne, St. George (Henry)
St. George, Judith 1931- CANR-14
Earlier sketch in CA 69-72
See also AAYA 7
See also CLR 57
See also JRDA
See also SAAS 12
See also SATA 13, 99, 161
St. George, LaVerne 1954- 223
St. George, Margaret
See Osborne, Margaret Ellen
St. George, Noel
See Green, Jonathon
St. Germain, Gregory
See Wallmann, Jeffrey M(iner)
St. Germain, Sheryl 1954- 189
St. Hereticus
See Brown, Robert McAfee
Saint-Jacques, Bernard 1928- CANR-37
Earlier sketches in CA 41-44R, CANR-16
St. James, Bernard
See Treister, Bernard W(illiam)
St. James, Blakely
See Gottfried, Theodore Mark and
Platt, Charles
St. James, Lyn 1947- 216
Saint James, Synthia 1949- .... SATA 84, 152
St. Jean, Yanick 166
St. John, Beth
See John, Elizabeth Beaman
St. John, Bob J. 1937- 146
Brief entry 122
St. John, Bruce (Carlisle) 1923- 107
See also CP 7
St. John, David
See Hunt, E(verette) Howard, (Jr.)
St. John, David 1949- CANR-108
Earlier sketch in CA 148
See also CP 7
St. John, Elizabeth
See John, Elizabeth Beaman
St. John, Henry 1678-1751 .... DLB 101
St. John, J. Allen 1872-1957 .... DLB 188
St. John, J(ames) Allen 1872-1957 199
St. John, J. Hector
See Crevecoeur, Michel Guillaume Jean de
St. John, John 1917-1988 .... CANR-5
Obituary 127
Earlier sketch in CA 5-8R
St. John, Lauren 1966- 224
St. John, Leonie
See Bayer, William and
Jenkins, Nancy (Harmon)
St. John, Lisa
See Sanford, Annette
St. John, Mabel .... RHW
St. John, Madeleine 1942- .... DLB 267
St. John, Nicole CANR-32
See also Johnston, Norma
See also AAYA 57
See also CLR 46
See also SAAS 7
See also SATA 89, 143
See also SATA-Essay 143

St. John, Patricia Mary 1919-1993 ... CANR-86
Obituary ... 142
Earlier sketches in CA 5-8R, CANR-3
See also SATA-Obit 79
St. John, Philip
See del Rey, Lester
St. John, Primus 1939- ... 113
See also BW 1
St. John, Robert 1902-2003 ... CANR-5
Obituary ... 213
Earlier sketch in CA 1-4R
St. John, Ronald Bruce 1943- ... 141
St. John, Tina 1966- ... 230
St. John, Wylly Folk 1908-1985 ... 21-24R
Obituary ... 117
See also SATA 10
See also SATA-Obit 45
Saint-John Perse
See Leger, (Marie-Rene Auguste) Alexis Saint-Leger
See also EW 10
See also EWL 3
See also GFL 1789 to the Present
See also RGWL 2
St. Johns, Adela Rogers 1894-1988 ... 108
Obituary ... 126
Interview in ... CA-108
See also AITN 1
See also DLB 29
St. John-Stevas, Norman Anthony Francis 1929- ... CANR-4
Earlier sketch in CA 49-52
St. John Thomas, David
See Thomas, David St. John
St. Martin, Hardie 1924- ... 153
St. Max, E. S.
See Ellis, Edward S(ylvester)
St. Meyer, Ned
See Stratemeyer, Edward L.
St. Mox, E. A.
See Ellis, Edward S(ylvester)
St. Myer, Ned
See Stratemeyer, Edward L.
St. Omer, Garth ... 73-76
See also BW 2
See also CN 1, 2, 3, 4, 5, 6, 7
See also DLB 117
St. Onge, Keith R. 1920- ... 139
Saint Phalle, Thibaut de
See de Saint Phalle, Thibaut
St. Pierre, Dorothy
See Nyren, Dorothy Elizabeth
Saint Pierre, Michel de 1916-1987 ... 217
See also DLB 83
St. Pierre, Paul 1923- ... 113
Saint-Pol-Roux
See Roux, Paul
Saintsbury, George (Edward Bateman) 1845-1933 ... 160
See also DLB 57, 149
See also TCLC 31
Saint-Simon, Louis de Rouvroy 1675-1755 ... DLB 314
See also GFL Beginnings to 1789
St. Tamara
See Kolba, St. Tamara
St. Vincent, Paul
See Markham, E(dward) A(rchibald)
St. Vivant, M.
See Bixby, Jerome Lewis
Sainty, John Christopher 1934- ... 93-96
Sainz, Gustavo 1940- ... CANR-80
Earlier sketch in CA 131
See also EWL 3
See also HW 1
Sainz de la Maza, Regino 1896-1981
Obituary ... 108
Saiokuken Socho 1448(?)-1532 ... DLB 203
Saipradit, Kulap 1905-1974
See Siburapha
Saisselin, Remy G(ilbert) 1925- ... 9-12R
Sait Faik
See Abasiyanik, Sait Faik
See also TCLC 23
Saito, Fred
See Saito, Hiroyuki
Saito, Hiroyuki 1917- ... 61-64
Saito, Michiko
See Fujiwara, Michiko
Saix, Tyler De
See Stacpoole, H(enry) de Vere
Sajdak, Bruce T. 1945- ... 142
Saje, Natasha ... PFS 23
Sajna, Mike 1950-2000 ... CANR-116
Earlier sketch in CA 141
Sakai, Kazuo 1952- ... 174
Sakai, Stan 1953- ... AAYA 64
Sakamaki, Shunzo 1906-1973 ... 1-4R
Obituary ... 103
Sakamoto, Kerri 1959- ... 171
Sakamoto, Yoshikazu 1927- ... 133
Sakell, Achilles Nicholas 1906-1987 ... 1-4R
Obituary ... 123
Sakers, Don 1958- ... 127
See also SATA 72
Sakers, George 1950- ... 108
Sakharnov, S.
See Sakharnov, Svyatoslav (Vladimirovich)
Sakharnov, Svyatoslav (Vladimirovich) 1923- ... CANR-82
Earlier sketch in CA 133
See also SATA 65
Sakharov, Andrei D(mitrievich) 1921-1989 . 157
Obituary ... 130
Brief entry ... 105
Saki
See Munro, H(ector) H(ugh)
See also BRWS 6
See also BYA 11
See also LAIT 2
See also RGEL 2
See also SSC 12
See also SSFS 1
See also SUFW
See also TCLC 3
Saklatvala, Beram 1911-1976 ... 89-92
Sakoian, Frances 1912-1989 ... 65-68
Sakol, Jeannie 1928- ... CANR-11
Earlier sketch in CA 5-8R
Sakran, Frank Charles 1895(?)-1983
Obituary ... 111
Saks, Elmer Eliot
See Fawcett, F(rank) Dubrez
Saks, Elyn R. 1955- ... 230
Saks, Katia 1939- ... 29-32R
Saks, Mike 1952- ... 140
Saksena, Kate ... 222
See also SATA 148
Sakurai, Gail 1952- ... CANR-137
Earlier sketch in CA 152
See also SATA 87, 153
Sakwa, Richard 1953- ... 236
Sala, Charles 1924- ... 116
Sala, Richard 1956- ... 235
Salaam, Kalamu ya 1947- ... 126
See also CAAS 21
See also BW 2
See also DLB 38
Salacrou, Armand 1899-1989 ... DLB 321
See also EWL 3
See also GFL 1789 to the Present
See also IDTP
Saladino, Salvatore 1922- ... 33-36R
Salaff, Janet W. 1940- ... 112
Salam, Abdus 1926-1996 ... 157
Salama, Hannu 1936- ... CLC 18
See also EWL 3
Salaman, Esther 1900-1995 ... 61-64
Salaman, Nicholas 1936- ... CANR-107
Brief entry ... 116
Earlier sketch in CA 146
Salamanca, J(ack) R(ichard) 1922- ... 193
Earlier sketch in CA 25-28R
Autobiographical Essay in ... 193
See also CLC 4, 15
Salamanca, Lucy
See del Barco, Lucy Salamanca
Salamatullah
See Ullah, Salamat
Salamon, Julie 1953- ... CANR-144
Earlier sketch in CA 136
Salamon, Lester M(ilton) 1943- ... 89-92
Salamon, Sonya 1939- ... 146
Salamun, Tomaz 1941- ... CANR-99
Earlier sketch in CA 169
See also CDWLB 4
See also CWW 2
See also DLB 181
See also EWL 3
Salant, Nathan N(athaniel) 1955- ... 106
Salant, Walter S. 1911-1999 ... CANR-2
Obituary ... 179
Earlier sketch in CA 5-8R
Salarrue
See Salazar Arrue, Salvador
See also EWL 3
Salas, Floyd Francis 1931- ... CANR-93
Earlier sketches in CA 119, CANR-44, 75
See also CAAS 27
See also DAM MULT
See also DLB 82
See also HLC 2
See also HW 1, 2
See also MTCW 2
See also MTFW 2005
Salas, Rafael M(ontinola) 1928-1987 ... 129
Obituary ... 121
Salassi, Otto R(ussell) 1939-1993 ... 106
Obituary ... 142
See also SATA 38
See also SATA-Obit 77
Salat, Cristina ... CANR-108
Earlier sketch in CA 149
See also SATA 82
Salazar, Antonio de Oliveira 1889-1970
Obituary ... 113
Salazar, Carles 1961- ... 162
Salazar, Dixie 1947- ... 149
Salazar, Fred A. 1942- ... 21-24R
Salazar, Michael (Brien) 1941- ... 194
Salazar, Rachel 1954- ... 123
Salazar, Ruben 1928-1970
Obituary ... 115
Salazar Arrue, Salvador 1899-1975
See Salarrue
See also LAW
Salazar Bondy, Sebastian 1924-1965 ... EWL 3
See also HW 1
Salaz-Marquez, Ruben (Dario) 1935- ... 182
See also DLB 122
Salber, Eva J. 1916-1990 ... 125
Salcedo, Hugo 1964- ... DLB 305
Salda, Frantisek Xaver 1867-1937 ... EWL 3
Saldana, Theresa 1955- ... 158
Saldutti, Denise 1953- ... SATA 39
Sale, Cornelius Calvin, Jr.
See Byrd, Robert C(arlyle)
Sale, J. Kirkpatrick
See Sale, Kirkpatrick
Sale, Kirkpatrick 1937- ... CANR-10
Earlier sketch in CA 13-16R
See also CLC 68
Sale, Larry L(owell) 1939- ... 194
Brief entry ... 113
Sale, Richard (Bernard) 1911-1993 ... CANR-61
Obituary ... 140
Earlier sketch in CA 9-12R
See also CMW 4
Sale, Roger 1932- ... CANR-93
Earlier sketches in CA 21-24R, CANR-33
Sale, Tim 1956- ... SATA 153
Sale, William (Merritt III) 1929- ... 45-48
Saleh, Dennis 1942- ... CANR-13
Earlier sketch in CA 33-36R
Salem, Elie Adib 1930- ... 49-52
Salem, James M. 1937- ... CANR-99
Earlier sketch in CA 21-24R
Salem, Kay 1952- ... SATA 92
Salem, Sema'an I. 1927- ... 142
Salemme, Lucia (Autorino) 1919- ... 89-92
Salemson, Harold J(ason) 1910-1988 ... 110
Obituary ... 126
Brief entry ... 108
Interview in ... CA-110
See also DLB 4
Saler, Benson 1930- ... CANR-138
Earlier sketch in CA 173
Salerno, Lynn M(cCormick) 1926- ... 119
Sales, Francois de 1567-1622 .. GFL Beginnings to 1789
Sales, Grover 1919-2004 ... 65-68
Obituary ... 223
Sales, Jane M(agorian) 1931-1974 ... 49-52
Sales, M(ary) E(ileen) 1936- ... 29-32R
Sales, M(illard) Vance 1929- ... 53-56
Salesbury, William 1520(?)-1584(?) ... DLB 281
Saleth, Rathinasamy Maria 1955- ... 221
Saletore, Bhasker Anand 1900- ... 5-8R
Salgado, Gamini 1929- ... 102
Salgado, Maria Antonia 1933- ... 41-44R
Salgado, Sebastiao 1944- ... AAYA 49
Saliba, George 1939- ... 149
Saliba, John A. 1937- ... CANR-35
Earlier sketch in CA 114
Saliers, Don E(arl) 1937- ... 119
Salih, al-Tayyib 1929-
See Salih, Tayeb
See also AFW
See also CWW 2
Salih, H(alil) Ibrahim 1939- ... 93-96
Salih, Tayeb
See Salih, al-Tayyib
See also WLIT 2
Salin, Mary Wolff
See Wolff-Salin, Mary
Salinas, Luis Omar 1937- ... CANR-81
Earlier sketch in CA 131
See also AMWS 13
See also CLC 90
See also DAM MULT
See also DLB 82
See also HLC 2
See also HW 1, 2
Salinas (y Serrano), Pedro 1891(?)-1951
Brief entry ... 117
See also DLB 134
See also EWL 3
See also TCLC 17
Saline, Carol 1939- ... 128
Salinger, Herman 1905-1983 ... CAP-1
Earlier sketch in CA 13-14
Salinger, J(erome) D(avid) 1919- ... CANR-129
Earlier sketches in CA 5-8R, CANR-39
See also AAYA 2, 36
See also AMW
See also AMWC 1
See also BPFB 3
See also CDALB 1941-1968
See also CLC 1, 3, 8, 12, 55, 56, 138
See also CLR 18
See also CN 1, 2, 3, 4, 5, 6, 7
See also CPW 1
See also DA
See also DA3
See also DAB
See also DAC
See also DAM MST, NOV, POP
See also DLB 2, 102, 173
See also EWL 3
See also EXPN
See also LAIT 4
See also MAICYA 1, 2
See also MAL 5
See also MTCW 1, 2
See also MTFW 2005
See also NFS 1
See also RGAL 4
See also RGSF 2
See also SATA 67
See also SSC 2, 28, 65
See also SSFS 17
See also TUS
See also WLC
See also WYA
See also YAW
Salinger, Margaretta 1908(?)-1985
Obituary ... 115
Salinger, Pierre (Emil George) 1925-2004 ... CANR-14
Obituary ... 232
Earlier sketch in CA 17-20R
Salis, Jean-Rodolphe de
See Von Salis, Jean-R.
Salisachs, Mercedes (Rovilralta) 1916- ... 211
Salisbury, Carola
See Butterworth, Michael
Salisbury, Carola (Isobel Julien) 1943- ... 89-92
Salisbury, Charlotte Y. 1914- ... CANR-75
Earlier sketch in CA 129
Salisbury, Dorothy (Kendall Cleveland) 1891(?)-1976
Obituary ... 69-72
Salisbury, Edward J(ames) 1886-1978 ... CAP-1
Earlier sketch in CA 13-14
Salisbury, Frank 1930- ... 108
Salisbury, Frank B(oyer) 1926- ... CANR-8
Earlier sketch in CA 17-20R
Salisbury, Gay ... 223
Salisbury, Graham 1944- ... CANR-123
Earlier sketch in CA 143
See also AAYA 26
See also MAICYA 2
See also MAICYAS 1
See also SATA 76, 108, 161
See also WYA
See also YAW
Salisbury, Harrison E(vans) 1908-1993 ... CANR-30
Obituary ... 141
Earlier sketches in CA 1-4R, CANR-3
Interview in ... CANR-30
See also CAAS 15
See also MTCW 1
Salisbury, John
See Caute, (John) David
Salisbury, Joyce E(llen) 1944- ... CANR-111
Earlier sketch in CA 135
See also SATA 138
Salisbury, Mike 1942- ... 136
Salisbury, Ralph 1926- ... CANR-15
Earlier sketch in CA 41-44R
Salisbury, Ray(mond Eric) 1942- ... CANR-31
Earlier sketch in CA 110
Salisbury, Richard Frank 1926- ... CANR-9
Earlier sketch in CA 5-8R
Salisbury, Robert H(olt) 1930- ... 9-12R
Salisbury, Ruth 1921- ... 73-76
Salisbury-Jones, Guy 1896-1985
Obituary ... 115
Salitan, Laurie P. ... 146
Salivarova, Zdena
See Skvorecka, Zdena Salivarova
Salk, Erwin Arthur 1918-2000 ... 81-84
Obituary ... 189
Salk, Jonas Edward 1915-1995 ... 49-52
Salk, Lee 1926-1992 ... 104
Obituary ... 137
See also AITN 1
Salkeld, Audrey 1936(?)- ... 220
Salkeld, Robert J(ohn) 1932- ... CANR-31
Earlier sketch in CA 29-32R
Salkever, Louis R(omov) 1914-1995 ... 17-20R
Salkey, (Felix) Andrew (Alexander) 1928-1995 ... CANR-80
Obituary ... 148
Earlier sketches in CA 5-8R, CANR-13, 27
See also BW 1, 3
See also CN 1, 2, 3, 4, 5, 6
See also DLB 125
See also EWL 3
See also SATA 35, 118
Salkin, Jeffrey (K.) 1954- ... 194
Sallada, Logan Henry 1942-1987
Obituary ... 123
Sallah, Tijan M. 1958- ... EWL 3
Sallaska, Georgia 1933- ... 25-28R
Sallaway, George H(enry) 1930- ... 21-24R
Sallee, Wayne Allen 1959- ... 213
Salles Gomes, Paulo Emilio
See Gomes, Paulo Emilio Salles
Sallis, James 1944- ... CANR-101
Earlier sketches in CA 33-36R, CANR-58
See also CMW 4
See also CN 7
See also CSW
See also SFW 4
Sallis, John C(leveland) 1938- ... 41-44R
Sallis, Susan (Diana) 1929- ... RHW
See also SATA 55
Sallnow, Michael (Julian) 1949-1990
Obituary ... 131
Salls, Betty Ruth 1926- ... 49-52
Sallust c. 86B.C.-35B.C. ... AW 2
See also CDWLB 1
See also DLB 211
See also RGWL 2, 3
Salm, Peter 1919-1990 ... CANR-74
Obituary ... 132
Earlier sketch in CA 41-44R
Salma, Abu
See Karmi, Abdul Karim
Salmansohn, Karen 1960- ... 148
Salmen, Walter (Heinrich) 1926- ... CANR-86
Earlier sketch in CA 132
Salmon, Andre 1881-1969 ... 208
See also GFL 1789 to the Present
Salmon, Annie Elizabeth 1899- ... CANR-12
Earlier sketch in CA 69-72
See also SATA 13
Salmon, Charles Gerald 1930- ... 49-52
Salmon, Edward T(ogo) 1905-1988 ... CANR-2
Earlier sketch in CA 5-8R
Salmon, H. Morrey 1892(?)-1985
Obituary ... 116
Salmon, J(ohn) B(rynmor) 1942- ... 118
Salmon, J(ohn) H(earsey) M(cMillan) 1925-2005 ... 25-28R
Obituary ... 236
Salmon, Jacqueline L. 1957- ... CANR-119
Earlier sketch in CA 156
Salmon, James F(rancis) 1925- ... 111
Salmon, John Tenison 1910-1999 ... 13-16R
Salmon, Margaret Belais 1921- ... CANR-8
Earlier sketch in CA 17-20R
Salmon, Nathan (Ucuzoglu) 1951- . CANR-119
Earlier sketches in CA 109, CANR-27

Cumulative Index 507 Sanchez

Salmon, Tim(othy) 1942- ... 128
Salmon, Wesley C(harles) 1925-2001 ... CANR-23
Obituary ... 195
Earlier sketches in CA 17-20R, CANR-8
Salmond, John A(lexander) 1937- ... CANR-112
Earlier sketches in CA 114, CANR-53
Salmond, Mary Anne 1945- ... 142
Salmonson, Jessica Amanda 1950- ... CANR-58
Earlier sketches in CA 114, CANR-36
See also FANT
See also SFW 4
Salmonson, R(oland) F(rank) 1922-1997 ... CANR-17
Earlier sketch in CA 25-28R
Salom, Philip 1950- ... 154
See also CP 7
Saloma, John S. III 1935(?)-1983
Obituary ... 110
Salomon, Albert 1891-1966 ... 5-8R
Salomon, Herman Prins 1930- ... 41-44R
Salomon, I(sidore) L(awrence) 1899-1985 ... 73-76
Obituary ... 116
See also CP 1
Salomon, Irving 1897-1979
Obituary ... 85-88
Salomon, Janet Lynn (Nowicki) 1953- ... 61-64
Salomon, Julian Harris 1896-1987
Obituary ... 123
Salomon, Richard Geoffrey 1948- ... 198
Salomon, Roger Blaine 1928- ... 1-4R
Salomon, Sir Walter
See Salomon, Walter (Hans)
Salomon, Walter (Hans) 1906-1987
Obituary ... 123
Salomone, A(rcangelo) William 1915-1989 ... 13-16R
Obituary ... 127
Salop, Lynne
See Hawes, Lynne Gusikoff Salop
Salot, Lorraine 1914- ... 17-20R
Saloutos, Theodore 1910-1980 ... 9-12R
Salper, Roberta Linda 1940- ... 105
Salpeter, Eliahu (Arnost) 1927- ... 93-96
Salpukas, Agis 1939-2000 ... 128
Obituary ... 188
Salsbury, Barbara G(race) 1937- ... 121
Brief entry ... 118
Salsbury, Edith Colgate 1907-1971 ... CAP-2
Earlier sketch in CA 17-18
Salsbury, Kathryn H(errick) 1924- ... 107
Salsbury, Stephen 1931-1998 ... CANR-11
Earlier sketch in CA 21-24R
Salsi, Lynn 1947- ... 199
See also SATA 130
Salsini, Paul E(dward) 1935- ... 77-80
Salsitz, Norman 1920- ... 219
Salsitz, R. A. V.
See Salsitz, Rhondi Vilott
See also AAYA 67
Salsitz, Rhondi Vilott ... 180
See also Salsitz, R. A. V.
See also SATA 115
Salt, Beryl (Winifred) 1931- ... 110
Salt, Waldo 1914-1987 ... CANR-77
Obituary ... 121
Earlier sketch in CA 111
Interview in ... CA-111
See also DLB 44
Salten, Felix
See Salzmann, Siegmund
See also WCH
Salter, Anna C. ... 180
Salter, Cedric
See Knight, Francis Edgar
Salter, Charles A. 1947- ... 127
Salter, David F. 1961- ... 175
Salter, Donald P. M. 1942- ... 93-96
Salter, Elizabeth 1918-1981 ... CANR-9
Obituary ... 103
Earlier sketch in CA 53-56
Salter, Elizabeth 1925-1980 ... 105
Obituary ... 97-100
Salter, James 1925- ... CANR-107
Earlier sketch in CA 73-76
See also AMWS 9
See also CLC 7, 52, 59
See also DLB 130
See also SSC 58
Salter, Lionel (Paul) 1914-2000 ... CANR-3
Earlier sketch in CA 5-8R
Salter, Margaret Lennox
See Donaldson, Margaret
Salter, Mary D.
See Ainsworth, Mary D(insmore) Salter
Salter, Mary Jo 1954- ... CANR-144
Earlier sketches in CA 119, CANR-45
See also CP 7
See also CWP
See also DLB 120, 282
See also EWL 3
See also PFS 22
See also TCLE 1:2
Salter, Paul Sanford 1926- ... 61-64
Salter, Robbie
See Salter, Robina
Salter, Robina ... 123
Salter, Stefan 1908(?)-1985
Obituary ... 115
Salter, W(illiam) H(enry) 1880-1970
Obituary ... 112
Salter-Mathieson, Nigel Cedric Stephen 1937- ... 1-4R
Salthe, Stanley N(orman) 1930- ... 53-56
Saltman, Jack 1936- ... 129
Saltman, Judith 1947- ... CANR-53
Earlier sketch in CA 126
See also SATA 64
Saltman, Juliet 1923- ... 101
Saltonstall, Richard, Jr. 1937-1981 ... 33-36R
Obituary ... 103
Saltonstall, William G(urdon) 1905(?)-1989
Obituary ... 130
Saltus, Edgar (Everton) 1855-1921
Brief entry ... 105
See also DLB 202
See also RGAL 4
See also TCLC 8
Saltus, Edgar 1855-1921 ... 210
Saltykov, Mikhail Evgrafovich 1826-1889 ... DLB 238:
Saltykov-Shchedrin, N.
See Saltykov, Mikhail Evgrafovich
Saltz, Donald 1933- ... 102
Saltz, Eli 1926- ... 184
Brief entry ... 108
Saltzberg, Barney 1955- ... SATA 135
Saltzgaber, Jan M. 1933- ... 115
Saltzman, Arthur M(ichael) 1953- ... CANR-118
Earlier sketch in CA 136
Saltzman, Cynthia ... 174
Saltzman, David (Charles Laertes) 1967-1990 ... SATA 86
Saltzman, Joe
See Saltzman, Joseph
Saltzman, Joseph 1939- ... 81-84
Saltzman, Lisa R. ... 185
Saltzman, Marvin L(ouis) 1922- ... 85-88
Salu, Mary 1919- ... 93-96
Salupo, Victor Thomas 1929- ... 175
Salusinszky, Imre 1955- ... 126
Salutin, Rick 1942- ... 131
Salvadori, Joyce
See Lussu, Joyce (Salvadori)
Salvadori, Mario (George) 1907-1997 ... 178
Obituary ... 159
Earlier sketch in CA 108
Autobiographical Essay in ... 178
See also CAAS 25
See also SATA 40, 97
Salvadori, Massimo
See Salvadori-Paleotti, Massimo
Salvadori, Max (William)
See Salvadori-Paleotti, Massimo
Salvadori-Paleotti, Massimo 1908-1992 ... CANR-7
Obituary ... 138
Earlier sketch in CA 9-12R
Salvaggio, John 1933- ... 144
Salvan, Jacques-Leon 1898- ... 1-4R
Salvato, Larry 1948- ... 118
Salvato, Sharon 1938- ... CANR-15
Earlier sketch in CA 65-68
Salvatore, Diane 1960- ... 139
Salvatore, Nicholas 1943- ... CANR-65
Earlier sketches in CA 109, CANR-32
Salvatore, Nick
See Salvatore, Nicholas
Salvatore, Paul A. 1959- ... YAW
Salvatore, R(obert) A(nthony) 1959- ... CANR-102
Earlier sketch in CA 166
See also AAYA 31
See also FANT
Salvatore, Ricardo D(onato) 1954- ... 229
Salvatores, Gabriele 1950- ... 208
Salvendy, Gavriel 1938- ... 49-52
Salverson, Laura Goodman 1890-1970 ... CANR-78
Earlier sketch in CA 153
See also DLB 92
See also RHW
Salviris, Jacob
See Sime, Jessie Georgina
Salwak, Dale (Francis) 1947- ... 137
Salway, Peter 1932- ... 148
Salwen, Michael B(rian) 1954- ... 142
Salwolke, Scott 1964- ... 146
Salwood, F. K.
See Kilworth, Garry (D.)
Salyer, Lucy E. 1956- ... 159
Salzano, F(rancisco) M(auro) 1928- ... CANR-45
Earlier sketches in CA 29-32R, CANR-12
Salzberg, Allen 1953- ... 137
Salzberg, Sharon ... 217
Salzer, Felix 1904-1986 ... 109
Obituary ... 120
Salzer, L. E.
See Wilson, Lionel
Salzer, Linda P(arsons) 1951- ... 122
Salzinger, Kurt 1929- ... 134
Brief entry ... 107
Salzman, Eric 1933- ... CANR-13
Earlier sketch in CA 25-28R
Salzman, Eva (Frances) 1960- ... 139
Salzman, Jack 1937- ... CANR-11
Earlier sketch in CA 25-28R
Salzman, Marian 1959- ... 146
See also SATA 77
Salzman, Mark (Joseph) 1959- ... CANR-137
Earlier sketches in CA 136, CANR-101
See also MTFW 2005
Salzman, Neil 1940- ... 139
Salzman, Paul 1953- ... CANR-118
Earlier sketches in CA 125, CANR-58
Salzman, Yuri ... SATA-Brief 42
Salzmann, Siegmund 1869-1945 ... 137
Brief entry ... 108
See also Salten, Felix
See also MAICYA 1, 2
See also SATA 25
Salzmann, Zdenek 1925- ... CANR-82
Earlier sketches in CA 97-100, CANR-16, 36
Samachson, Dorothy (Mirkin) 1914-1997 ... 9-12R
See also SATA 3
Samachson, Joseph 1906-1980 ... 17-20R
Obituary ... 122
See also SATA 3
See also SATA-Obit 52
Samain, Albert 1858-1900 ... DLB 217
Samar, Vincent J(oseph) 1953- ... 170
Samarakis, Andonis
See Samarakis, Antonis
See also EWL 3
Samarakis, Antonis 1919-2003 ... CANR-36
Obituary ... 224
Earlier sketch in CA 25-28R
See also Samarakis, Andonis
See also CAAS 16
See also CLC 5
Samaras, Anastasia P. ... 220
Samarin, William J. 1926- ... 93-96
Samartha, S(tanley) J(edidiah) 1920- ... CAP-1
Earlier sketch in CA 11-12
Samay, Sebastian 1926- ... 37-40R
Sambrook, Arthur James 1931- ... CANR-40
Earlier sketch in CA 13-16R
Sambrot, William 1920- ... 25-28R
Samek, Hana 1953- ... 126
Samelson, William 1928- ... CANR-37
Earlier sketches in CA 25-28R, CANR-17
Samenow, Stanton E(than) 1941- ... 129
Sametz, Arnold W(illiam) 1919- ... CANR-1
Earlier sketch in CA 1-4R
Samford, Clarence D(ouglas) 1905-1991 ... CAP-2
Earlier sketch in CA 19-20
Samford, Doris E. 1923- ... 21-24R
Samhaber, Ernst Marzell 1901-1974 ... 9-12R
Obituary ... 122
Samigli, E.
See Schmitz, Aron Hector
Samkange, S. J. T.
See Samkange, Stanlake (John Thompson)
Samkange, Stanlake (John Thompson) 1922-1988 ... CANR-28
Obituary ... 125
Earlier sketch in CA 29-32R
See also BW 2
Samli, A. Coskun 1931- ... CANR-22
Earlier sketch in CA 105
Samman, Ghada
See al-Samman, Ghadah
Sammartino, Peter 1904-1992 ... CANR-7
Obituary ... 137
Earlier sketch in CA 57-60
Sammis, John 1942- ... 29-32R
See also SATA 4
Sammon, Paul M. 1949- ... 171
Sammons, David 1938- ... 73-76
Sammons, Jeffrey L(eonard) 1936- ... CANR-19
Earlier sketch in CA 21-24R
Samoiloff, Louise Cripps
See Cripps, L(ouise) L(ilian)
Samolin, William 1911-1992 ... 61-64
Samora, Julian 1920-1996 ... 37-40R
Obituary ... 151
See also HW 1
Samore, Theodore 1924-1992
Brief entry ... 108
Sampedro, Jose Luis 1917- ... CANR-11
Earlier sketch in CA 21-24R
Sampford, Michael 1924(?)-1983
Obituary ... 109
Sampley, Arthur M(cCullough) 1903-1975 ... 41-44R
Sampley, J(ohn) Paul 1935- ... 105
Sampson, A(ylwin) A(rthur) 1926- ... 117
Sampson, Anthony (Terrell Seward) 1926-2004 ... CANR-123
Obituary ... 234
Earlier sketches in CA 1-4R, CANR-3, 63
Sampson, Curt 1952- ... CANR-123
Earlier sketch in CA 139
Sampson, Edward C(oolidge) 1920- ... 57-60
Sampson, Edward E. 1934- ... CANR-14
Earlier sketch in CA 37-40R
Sampson, Emma (Keats) Speed 1868-1947 . 135
See also SATA 68
Sampson, Fay (Elizabeth) 1935- ... CANR-90
Earlier sketches in CA 101, CANR-18, 40
See also FANT
See also SATA 42, 151
See also SATA-Brief 40
Sampson, Geoffrey 1944- ... 97-100
Sampson, H(erbert) Grant 1932- ... 45-48
Sampson, Henry T(homas) 1934- ... 117
See also BW 2
Sampson, Michael 1952- ... CANR-122
Earlier sketch in CA 160
See also SATA 95, 143
Sampson, R(obert) Neil 1938- ... CANR-58
Earlier sketches in CA 106, CANR-31
Sampson, R(onald) V(ictor) 1918-1999 ... CANR-5
Earlier sketch in CA 9-12R
Sampson, Richard Henry ... 186
See also Hull, Richard
Sampson, Robert C. 1909-1995 ... 21-24R
Sampson, Roy J(ohnson) 1919- ... CANR-1
Earlier sketch in CA 1-4R
Sampson, Wallace 1930- ... 199
Samra, Cal 1931- ... 37-40R
Samraj, Adi Da
See Jones, Franklin Albert
Samreto, Regina 1930-
See Ezera, Regina
Sams, Candace 1956- ... 223
Sams, David R. 1958- ... 138
Sams, Eric 1926-2004 ... CANR-49
Obituary ... 231
Earlier sketch in CA 123
Sams, Ferrol, (Jr.) 1922- ... 146
See also CN 7
See also CSW
Sams, Jonathan Carter 1942- ... 194
Brief entry ... 110
Samsell, R(ay) L(ane) 1925-1993 ... 69-72
Samson, Anne S(tringer) 1933- ... 25-28R
See also SATA 2
Samson, Gloria Garrett 1934- ... 177
Samson, Jack
See Samson, John G(adsden)
Samson, Jane (Dianne) 1962- ... 180
Samson, (Thomas) Jim 1946- ... 129
Samson, Joan 1937-1976 ... 73-76
See also SATA 13
Samson, John G(adsden) 1922- ... 134
Brief entry ... 109
Samson, Lisa 1964- ... 189
Samson, Naomi 1933- ... 190
Samson, Suzanne M. 1959- ... 155
See also SATA 91
Samsonov, Leon
See Maximov, Vladimir (Yemelyanovich)
Samstag, Nicholas 1903-1968 ... 5-8R
Obituary ... 25-28R
Samter, Linda Bantel
See Bantel, Linda
Samtur, Susan J(oy) 1944- ... 97-100
Samuel, Alan E(douard) 1932- ... CANR-37
Earlier sketches in CA 73-76, CANR-17
Samuel, Athanasius Y.
See Samuel, Yeshue
Samuel, Barbara 1959- ... 205
Samuel, Dorothy T(ucker) 1918- ... 45-48
Samuel, Edwin Herbert 1898-1978 ... CANR-2
Earlier sketch in CA 1-4R
Samuel, Irene 1915-1991 ... 17-20R
Obituary ... 134
Samuel, Lorenzo
See Wiley, Lawrence Samuel
Samuel, Maurice 1895-1972 ... 102
Obituary ... 33-36R
Samuel, Sealhenry Olumide
See Seal
Samuel, Vivette 1919- ... 211
Samuel, Yeshue 1907-1995 ... CAP-2
Obituary ... 148
Earlier sketch in CA 21-22
Samuels, Charles 1902-1982 ... CANR-5
Obituary ... 106
Earlier sketch in CA 1-4R
See also SATA 12
Samuels, Charles Thomas 1936-1974 ... 41-44R
Obituary ... 49-52
Samuels, Cynthia K(alish) 1946- ... 135
See also SATA 79
Samuels, E. A.
See Tiffany, E. A.
Samuels, Ernest 1903-1996 ... CANR-43
Obituary ... 151
Earlier sketches in CAP-1, CA 11-12
See also DLB 111
Samuels, Gayle Brandow ... 220
Samuels, Gertrude 1910(?)-2003 ... CANR-6
Obituary ... 218
Earlier sketch in CA 9-12R
See also SATA 17
See also SATA-Obit 147
Samuels, Harold 1917-2002 ... 93-96
Obituary ... 207
Samuels, Harry 1893- ... 13-16R
Samuels, Jayne Newcomer 1914- ... 150
Samuels, Lesser 1894(?)-1980
Obituary ... 102
Samuels, M(ichael) L(ouis) 1920- ... 41-44R
Samuels, Peggy 1922- ... 97-100
Samuels, Shirley 1957- ... 144
Samuels, Warren J. 1933- ... CANR-14
Earlier sketch in CA 21-24R
Samuelson, Arnold 1912(?)-1981
Obituary ... 116
Samuelson, Hyman 1919- ... 154
Samuelson, Paul A(nthony) 1915- ... CANR-40
Earlier sketch in CA 5-8R
Samuelson, Robert J(acob) 1945- ... 155
Samuelsson, Bengt Ingemar 1934- ... 168
Samura, Hiroaki 1970- ... 228
Samway, Patrick H(enry) 1939- ... CANR-71
Earlier sketches in CA 105, CANR-21
Samyn, Mary Ann 1970- ... 191
Sanborn, B. X.
See Ballinger, William Sanborn
Sanborn, Duane 1914-1996 ... CANR-1
Earlier sketch in CA 1-4R
See also SATA 38
Sanborn, Franklin Benjamin 1831-1917 ... 201
See also DLB 1, 223
Sanborn, Margaret 1915- ... CANR-4
Earlier sketch in CA 53-56
Sanborn, Patricia F. 1937- ... 25-28R
Sanborn, Ruth Cummings 1917- ... 29-32R
Sancha, Sheila 1924- ... CANR-11
Earlier sketch in CA 69-72
See also SATA 38
Sanchez, Alberto Ruy
See Ruy-Sanchez, Alberto
Sanchez, Alex 1957- ... 226
See also AAYA 51
See also SATA 151
Sanchez, David A(lan) 1933- ... CANR-87
Earlier sketch in CA 157

Sanchez, Federico
See Semprun, Jorge
Sanchez, Florencio 1875-1910 ... 153
See also DLB 305
See also EWL 3
See also HW 1
See also LAW
See also TCLC 37
Sanchez (y Sanchez), George I(sidore) 1906-1972 ... 153
See also HW 1
Sanchez, Jose M(ariano) 1932- ... CANR-118
Earlier sketch in CA 9-12R
Sanchez, Jose M(ariano) 1932-
See Sanchez, Jose M(ariano)
Sanchez, Luis Rafael 1936- ... 128
See also CLC 23
See also DLB 305
See also EWL 3
See also HW 1
See also WLIT 1
Sanchez, Maria Bruscino 1964- ... CANR-135
Earlier sketch in CA 174
Sanchez, Oscar Arias
See Arias Sanchez, Oscar
Sanchez, Patrick 1970- ... 211
Sanchez, Phil
See Sanchez, Philomeno
Sanchez, Philomeno
See Sanchez, Philomeno
See also DLB 122
Sanchez, Philomeno 1917- ... 181
See also Sanchez, Philomeno
Sanchez, Ramiro Guerra y
See Guerra y Sanchez, Ramiro
Sanchez, Ray 1964- ... 220
Sanchez, Ricardo 1941-1995 ... CANR-32
Obituary ... 149
Earlier sketch in CA 73-76
See also DAM MULT
See also DLB 82
See also HW 1
See also RGAL 4
Sanchez, Saul 1943- ... DLB 209
Sanchez, Sonia 1934- ... CANR-115
Earlier sketches in CA 33-36R, CANR-24, 49, 74
See also BLC 3
See also BW 2, 3
See also CLC 5, 116
See also CLR 18
See also CP 2, 3, 4, 5, 6, 7
See also CSW
See also CWP
See also DA3
See also DAM MULT
See also DLB 41
See also DLBD 8
See also EWL 3
See also MAICYA 1, 2
See also MAL 5
See also MTCW 1, 2
See also MTFW 2005
See also PC 9
See also SATA 22, 136
See also WP
Sanchez, Thomas 1944- ... CANR-87
Earlier sketches in CA 45-48, CANR-2, 32
See also BEST 90:1
See also HW 1
Sanchez, Trinidad, Jr. ... 167
See also HW 2
Sanchez Albornoz (y Mediuna), Claudio 1893-1984 ... 127
Obituary ... 113
Sanchez-Boudy, Jose 1927- ... 178
See also HW 2
Sanchez de Arevalo, Rodrigo 1404-1470 ... DLB 286
Sanchez de Badajoz, Diego (?)-1552(?) ... DLB 318
Sanchez Ferlosio, Rafael 1927- ... EWL 3
Sanchez Flores, Daniel 1960(?)-1990
Obituary ... 132
Sanchez-Hidalgo, Efrain Sigisfredo 1918-1974 ... 57-60
Sanchez-Korrol, Virginia (E.) 1936- ... CANR-87
Earlier sketch in CA 131
See also HW 1
Sanchez-Scott, Milcha 1953(?)- ... CANR-79
Earlier sketch in CA 131
See also CAD
See also CD 5, 6
See also CWD
See also HW 1, 2
Sanchez-Silva, Jose Maria 1911- ... 73-76
See also CLR 12
See also MAICYA 1, 2
See also SATA 16, 132
Sanctuary, Gerald 1930- ... CANR-12
Earlier sketch in CA 29-32R
Sand, Arne 1927-1963 ... 238
Sand, Dave
See Newton, D(wight) B(ennett)
Sand, George 1804-1876 ... DA
See also DA3
See also DAB
See also DAC
See also DAM MST, NOV
See also DLB 119, 192
See also EW 6
See also FL 1:3
See also FW
See also GFL 1789 to the Present
See also RGWL 2, 3
See also TWA
See also WLC
Sand, George X. ... 13-16R
See also SATA 45
Sand, Margaret 1932- ... 85-88
Sand, Richard E(ugene) 1924- ... 33-36R
Sandage, Allan R(ex) 1926- ... 167
Sandak, Cass R(obert) 1950-2001 ... 108
See also SATA 51
See also SATA-Brief 37
Sandall, Roger 1933- ... 207
Sandars, N(ancy) K(atharine) 1914- ... 61-64
Sanday, Peggy Reeves 1937- ... CANR-144
Earlier sketch in CA 157
Sandbach, Francis Henry 1903-1991 ... 93-96
Obituary ... 135
Sandbach, Mary (Warburton) 1901- ... 25-28R
Sandberg, (Karin) Inger 1930- ... CANR-52
Earlier sketches in CA 65-68, CANR-11, 26
See also SATA 15
Sandberg, John H(ilmer) 1930- ... 49-52
Sandberg, Karl C. 1931- ... 49-52
See also SATA 35
Sandberg, Larry
See Sandberg, Lawrence H.
Sandberg, Lars G(unnarsson) 1939- ... 53-56
Sandberg, Lasse (E. M.) 1924- ... SATA 15
Sandberg, Lawrence H. 1944- ... CANR-136
Earlier sketch in CA 77-80
Sandberg, Margaret M(ay) 1919- ... 61-64
Sandberg, Peter Lars 1934- ... CANR-24
Earlier sketches in CA 61-64, CANR-9
Sandberg, R. N. 1948- ... 187
Sandbrook, Dominic ... 228
Sandbrook, K(eith) Richard J(ames) 1943- ... CANR-82
Earlier sketches in CA 97-100, CANR-16, 36
Sandburg, Carl (August) 1878-1967 ... CANR-35
Obituary ... 25-28R
Earlier sketch in CA 5-8R
See also AAYA 24
See also AMW
See also BYA 1, 3
See also CDALB 1865-1917
See also CLC 1, 4, 10, 15, 35
See also CLR 67
See also DA
See also DA3
See also DAB
See also DAC
See also DAM MST, POET
See also DLB 17, 54, 284
See also EWL 3
See also EXPP
See also LAIT 2
See also MAICYA 1, 2
See also MAL 5
See also MTCW 1, 2
See also MTFW 2005
See also PAB
See also PC 2, 41
See also PFS 3, 6, 12
See also RGAL 4
See also SATA 8
See also TUS
See also WCH
See also WLC
See also WP
See also WYA
Sandburg, Charles
See Sandburg, Carl (August)
Sandburg, Charles A.
See Sandburg, Carl (August)
Sandburg, Helga 1918- ... CANR-5
Earlier sketch in CA 1-4R
See also CP 1
See also SAAS 10
See also SATA 3
Sande, Theodore Anton 1933- ... CANR-12
Earlier sketch in CA 65-68
Sandeen, Ernest (Emanuel) 1908-1997 ... 13-16R
Obituary ... 159
Sandeen, Ernest Robert 1931- ... CANR-1
Earlier sketch in CA 45-48
Sandel, Cora
See Fabricius, Sara (Cecilie Margarete Gjorwell)
See also DLB 297
Sandelowski, Margarete J. 1946- ... 116
Sandemose, Aksel 1899-1965 ... 202
See also DLB 297
See also EWL 3
Sander, August 1876-1964 ... 197
Sander, (Jane) Ellen 1944- ... 41-44R
Sander, Heather L. 1947- ... 233
See also SATA 157
Sander, Joseph Lincoln 1926-
Brief entry ... 108
Sander, Volkmar 1929- ... 113
Sanderlin, David 1943- ... 123
Sanderlin, George 1915- ... CANR-74
Earlier sketch in CA 13-16R
See also SATA 4
Sanderlin, Owenita (Harrah) 1916- ... CANR-7
Earlier sketch in CA 17-20R
See also SATA 11
Sanders, Albert
See Davidson, David
Sanders, Andrew 1946- ... 145
Sanders, Ann(a Pearl Goodman) 1935- ... 5-8R
Sanders, Arthur 1955- ... 143
Sanders, Bill 1951- ... 137
Sanders, Brett
See Barrett, Geoffrey John
Sanders, Buck
See Frentzen, Jeffrey
Sanders, Byrne Hope
See Sperry, Byrne Hope
Sanders, Charles (Wesley) ... TCWW 2
Sanders, Charles 1935- ... 25-28R
Sanders, Charles L. 1932(?)-1990
Obituary ... 132
Sanders, Clinton R. 1944- ... 139
Sanders, Coyne Steven 1956- ... 142
Sanders, D(onald) G(len) 1899-1990 ... 85-88
Sanders, David (Scott, Jr.) 1926- ... 25-28R
Sanders, (Franklin) David 1934- ... 41-44R
Sanders, Deion (Luwynn) 1967- ... 191
Sanders, Dennis 1949- ... 108
Sanders, Donald 1915(?)-1979
Obituary ... 89-92
Sanders, Donald H. 1932- ... CANR-10
Earlier sketch in CA 25-28R
Sanders, Dori(nda) 1935(?)- ... 206
See also CSW
Sanders, Dorothy Lucie 1917-1987 ... 33-36R
See also Walker, Lucy
Sanders, (James) Ed(ward) 1939- ... CANR-78
Earlier sketches in CA 13-16R, CANR-13, 44
See also Sanders, Edward
See also CAAS 21
See also BG 1:3
See also CLC 53
See also CP 1, 2, 3, 4, 5, 6, 7
See also DAM POET
See also DLB 16, 244
Sanders, Ed Parish 1937- ... 105
Sanders, Edward
See Sanders, (James) Ed(ward)
See also DLB 244
Sanders, Eve Rachele ... 232
Sanders, Frederick K(irkland) 1936- ... 65-68
Sanders, Gerald D(eWitt) 1895-1983 ... CAP-1
Earlier sketch in CA 13-14
Sanders, Gladys (Shultz) 1919(?)-1988
Obituary ... 125
Sanders, Harland 1890-1980 ... 114
Obituary ... 102
Sanders, Herbert H(arvey) 1909-1988 ... 13-16R
Sanders, Ivan 1944- ... CANR-44
Earlier sketch in CA 119
Sanders, J(ohn) Oswald 1902-1992 ... CANR-21
Earlier sketches in CA 13-16R, CANR-6
Sanders, Jack T(homas) 1935- ... 37-40R
Sanders, Jacquin 1922- ... CANR-74
Earlier sketch in CA 1-4R
Sanders, James ... 204
Sanders, James A(lvin) 1927- ... CANR-14
Earlier sketch in CA 21-24R
Sanders, James Bernard 1924- ... 41-44R
Sanders, James Edward 1911-1998 ... 103
Sanders, Jeanne
See Rundle, Anne
Sanders, Jennings B(ryan) 1901-1990 ... CAP-2
Earlier sketch in CA 25-28
Sanders, Joan Allred 1924- ... 9-12R
Sanders, John H. 1941- ... 162
Sanders, Joseph Lee 1940- ... 105
Sanders, Kent
See Wilkes-Hunter, R(ichard)
Sanders, Lawrence 1920-1998 ... CANR-62
Obituary ... 165
Earlier sketches in CA 81-84, CANR-33
See also BEST 89:4
See also BPFB 3
See also CLC 41
See also CMW 4
See also CPW
See also DA3
See also DAM POP
See also MTCW 1
Sanders, Leonard 1929- ... CANR-3
Earlier sketch in CA 9-12R
Sanders, Leslie Catherine 1944- ... 129
Sanders, Margaret ... 5-8R
Sanders, Marion K. 1905-1977 ... 33-36R
Obituary ... 73-76
Sanders, Mark A. 1963- ... 218
Sanders, Marlene 1931- ... 65-68
Sanders, Michael S. 1961- ... 223
Sanders, Nancy I. 1960- ... CANR-112
Earlier sketch in CA 155
See also SATA 90, 141
Sanders, Noah
See Blount, Roy (Alton), Jr.
Sanders, Norman (Joseph) 1929- ... 9-12R
Sanders, Peter B(asil) 1938- ... 105
Sanders, Pieter 1912- ... CANR-12
Earlier sketch in CA 29-32R
Sanders, (Charles) Richard 1904-1998 ... 53-56
Sanders, Richard (Kinard) 1940- ... CANR-129
Earlier sketch in CA 171
Sanders, Ronald 1932-1991 ... CANR-20
Obituary ... 133
Earlier sketch in CA 21-24R
Sanders, Scott Russell 1945- ... CANR-130
Earlier sketches in CA 85-88, CANR-15, 35, 86
See also ANW
See also SATA 56, 109
Sanders, Sol (Witner) 1926- ... CANR-2
Earlier sketch in CA 49-52
Sanders, Stephen (Jesse, Jr.) 1919- ... 29-32R
Sanders, Thomas E. 1926- ... 21-24R
Sanders, Thomas Griffin 1932- ... 9-12R
Sanders, Tobi Gillian
See Hammes, Tobi Gillian Sanders
Sanders, Tony 1957- ... 203
Sanders, William B(rauns) 1944- ... CANR-10
Earlier sketch in CA 65-68
Sanders, William T(imothy) 1926- ... CANR-3
Earlier sketch in CA 45-48
Sanders, Winston P.
See Anderson, Poul (William)
Sanderson, Irma 1912- ... 135
See also SATA 66
Sanderson, Isabel S(aunders) 1913-1987
Obituary ... 123
Sanderson, Ivan T(erence) 1911-1973 ... 37-40R
Obituary ... 41-44R
See also SATA 6
Sanderson, James L(ee) 1926-
Brief entry ... 111
Sanderson, Jayne 1943- ... 21-24R
Sanderson, Jim 1953- ... 184
Sanderson, Lennox, Jr.
See Slide, Anthony (Clifford)
Sanderson, Margaret Love
See Keats, Emma and Sampson, Emma (Keats) Speed
Sanderson, (John) Michael 1939- ... 127
Sanderson, Milton W(illiam) 1910- ... CANR-9
Earlier sketch in CA 9-12R
Sanderson, Peter (Crawshaw) 1929- ... 33-36R
Sanderson, Robert 1587-1663 ... DLB 281
Sanderson, Ruth (L.) 1951- ... 180
See also SATA 41, 109
Sanderson, Sabina W(arren) 1931- ... CANR-3
Earlier sketch in CA 9-12R
Sanderson, Stewart (Forson) 1924- ... 108
Sanderson, Warren 1931- ... 105
Sandford, Cedric Thomas 1924-2004 ... CANR-68
Obituary ... 226
Earlier sketches in CA 113, CANR-32
Sandford, Christopher 1902-1983
Obituary ... 109
Sandford, Christopher 1956- ... 186
Sandford, John
See Camp, John (Roswell)
Sandford, John Loren 1929- ... CANR-86
Earlier sketches in CA 101, CANR-36
Sandford, Nell Mary 1936- ... 81-84
See also Dunn, Nell (Mary)
See also CD 5
See also CN 7
Sandford, Paula 1931- ... CANR-36
Earlier sketch in CA 101
Sandford, William P(hillips) 1896-1975 ... CAP-2
Earlier sketch in CA 17-18
Sandhaus, Paul 1923- ... 25-28R
Sandhu, Daya S(ingh) 1943- ... 196
Sandifer, Durward Valdamir 1900-1981
Obituary ... 108
Sandifer, Linda P(rophet) 1951- ... 120
Sandiford, Keith A(rlington) P(atrick) 1936- ... 195
Sandin, Joan 1942- ... CANR-137
Earlier sketch in CA 159
See also SATA 12, 94, 153
Sandin, Robert T(heodore) 1927- ... 111
Sandison, Alan 1932- ... 21-24R
Sandison, Janet
See Cameron, Elizabeth Jane
Sandle, Floyd Leslie 1913-2002 ... 185
Brief entry ... 106
Sandler, Adam (Richard) 1966- ... 176
Sandler, Benjamin P. 1902(?)-1979
Obituary ... 85-88
Sandler, Irving (Harry) 1925- ... CANR-31
Earlier sketch in CA 29-32R
Sandler, Kevin S. 1969- ... 168
Sandler, Lucy Freeman 1930- ... CANR-31
Brief entry ... 113
Sandler, Martin W. ... 236
See also SATA 160
Sandler, Stanley Lawrence 1937- ... CANR-56
Earlier sketch in CA 113
Sandlin, Joann S(chepers) De Lora 1935- ... CANR-4
Earlier sketch in CA 53-56
Sandlin, John L(ewis) 1908-1993 ... CANR-4
Earlier sketch in CA 1-4R
Sandlin, Tim 1950- ... CANR-75
Earlier sketch in CA 126
Sandman, Peter M(ark) 1945- ... 25-28R
Sandmel, Samuel 1911-1979 ... CANR-2
Earlier sketch in CA 1-4R
Sando, Joe S. 1923- ... 123
Sandom, J. Gregory 1956- ... 137
Sandon, Henry 1928- ... 81-84
Sandon, J. D.
See Harvey, John (Barton) and Wells, Angus
Sandor, Bela I(mre) 1935- ... 102
Sandor, Gyorgy ... 108
Sandor, Marjorie ... 208
Sandoval, Lynda 1965(?)- ... 237
Sandoz, (George) Ellis, (Jr.) 1931- ... CANR-122
Earlier sketches in CA 37-40R, CANR-14
Sandoz, Mari(e Susette) 1900-1966 ... CANR-64
Obituary ... 25-28R
Earlier sketches in CA 1-4R, CANR-17
See also CLC 28
See also DLB 9, 212
See also LAIT 2
See also MTCW 1, 2
See also SATA 5
See also TCWW 1, 2
Sandrof, Ivan 1912(?)-1979 ... 93-96
Obituary ... 85-88
Sandroff, Ronni 1943- ... 102
Sandrow, Edward T. 1906-1975
Obituary ... 61-64
Sands, Dave
See Powell, (Oval) Talmage
Sands, Donald B. 1920- ... 13-16R
Sands, Dorothy 1893-1980
Obituary ... 102
Sands, Edith Sylvia (Abeloff) 1912- ... 21-24R
Sands, John Edward 1930- ... 13-16R
Sands, Kathleen M.
See Sands, Kathleen Mullen

Cumulative Index 509 Sargent

Sands, Kathleen Mullen CANR-41
Earlier sketch in CA 118
Sands, Leo G(eorge) 1912-1984 .... CANR-29
Obituary 114
Earlier sketch in CA 17-20R
See also Craig, Lee A(llen)
Sands, Lynsay 239
Sands, Marella 183
Sands, Martin
See Burke, John (Frederick)
Sands, Melissa 1949- 109
Sandstorm, R. O. C.
See Campbell, Bruce
Sandstroem, Yvonne L. 1933- 140
Sandstrom, Alan R(ussell) 1945- 139
Sandstrom, Eve K. 1936- 141
Sandstrom, Pamela Effrein 1954- 139
Sandu, Gabriel 1954- 141
Sandusky, Annie Lee 1900(?)-1976
Obituary 69-72
Sandved, Arthur O. 1931- 33-36R
Sandweiss, Martha A(nn) 1954- CANR-142
Earlier sketch in CA 136
Sandwell, B(ernard) K(eble) 1876-1954 184
See also DLB 92
Sandy, Max
See Saunders, Carl Maxon
Sandy, Stephen 1934- 177
Earlier sketches in CA 49-52, CANR-5, 22, 101
Autobiographical Essay in 177
See also CAAS 29
See also CP 1, 2, 3, 4, 5, 6, 7
See also DLB 165
Sandys, Celia 1943- CANR-101
Earlier sketch in CA 152
Sandys, Elspeth (Somerville) 1940- ... CANR-26
Earlier sketch in CA 108
Sandys, George 1578-1644 .... DLB 24, 121
Saner, Reg(inald Anthony) 1931- 65-68
See also CLC 9
See also CP 7
Sanfield, Steve 1937- 124
Sanfilip, Thomas 1952- 57-60
Sanford, Abigail
See Foster, Jeannette Howard
See also GLL 1
Sanford, Agnes (White) 1897-1976 .... 17-20R
See also SATA 61
Sanford, Annette 1929- CANR-141
Earlier sketch in CA 130
Sanford, Charles B(elding) 1920- 113
Sanford, Charles Le Roy 1920- 5-8R
Sanford, David (Boyer) 1943-
Brief entry 114
Sanford, Doris 1937- 138
See also SATA 69
Sanford, Fillmore H(argrave) 1914-1967 ... 1-4R
Obituary 103
Sanford, George 1943- 118
Sanford, Harry Allen 1929- 1-4R
Sanford, Jack D(onald) 1925- 5-8R
Sanford, John 1904-2003 .... CANR-106
Obituary 215
Brief entry 117
Earlier sketches in CA 123, CANR-50
Interview in CA-123
Sanford, John A. 1929- CANR-50
Earlier sketches in CA 25-28R, CANR-10
Sanford, John B.
See Sanford, John
Sanford, Kate
See Sanford, Kathleen (D.)
Sanford, Kathleen (D.) 1952- 163
Sanford, Kathy
See Sanford, Kathleen (D.)
Sanford, Leda 1933- CANR-12
Earlier sketch in CA 65-68
Sanford, Richard 1950- 152
Sanford, Terry 1917-1998 .... 17-20R
Obituary 167
Sanford, Thomas K(yle), Jr. 1921-1977 73-76
Sanger, Andrew 1948- 123
Sanger, Clyde 1928- CANR-82
Earlier sketches in CA 114, CANR-36
Sanger, David E. 1960- 136
Sanger, Elliott M(axwell) 1897-1989
Obituary 129
Sanger, Margaret (Higgins) 1879-1966
Obituary 89-92
See also FW
Sanger, Marjory Bartlett 1920- 37-40R
See also SATA 8
Sanger, Richard H. 1905(?)-1979
Obituary 85-88
Sangiuliano, Iris (Agatha) 1923- 184
Brief entry 114
Sangrey, Dawn 1942- CANR-15
Earlier sketch in CA 85-88
Sangster, Charles 1822-1893 .... DLB 99
Sangster, Ian 1934- 61-64
Sangster, Jimmy 1927- CANR-14
Earlier sketch in CA 21-24R
Sangster, Margaret E(lizabeth) 1894-1981
Obituary 105
Sanguineti, Edoardo 1930- .... DLB 128
Sanguinetti, Elise Ayers 1926- CANR-1
Earlier sketch in CA 1-4R
Sang Ye
See Shen, Dajun
Saniel, Josefa M. 1925- 13-16R
Sanin Cano, Baldomero 1861-1957 178
See also HW 2
Sanjek, David 1952- 163
Sanjian, Avedis K(rikor) 1921-1995 .... 33-36R
Obituary 149
Sanjonishi Sanetaka 1455-1537 .... DLB 203
San Juan, Epifanio, Jr. 1938- CANR-130
Earlier sketches in CA 25-28R, CANR-10, 44
See also CP 1
Sankar, Andrea (Patrice) 1948- 139
Sankar, D(evarakonda) V(enkata) Siva
1927- 53-56
Sankey, Alice (Ann-Susan) 1910- 61-64
See also SATA 27
Sankey, Jay 1963- 206
Sankhala, Kailash S. 1925- 101
Sankichi, Toge 1917-1953 .... MJW
San Martin, Marta 1942- 102
Sann, Paul 1914-1986 .... CANR-5
Obituary 120
Earlier sketch in CA 13-16R
Sanna, Ellyn 1957- 171
Sannazaro, Jacopo 1456(?)-1530 ..... RGWL 2, 3
See also WLIT 7
Sannebeck, Norvelle (Harrison)
1909-1995 97-100
Obituary 171
Sanneh, Lamin CANR-92
Earlier sketch in CA 172
Sano, Furumi
See Mallett, Daryl F(urumi)
Sanoff, Alvin P. 1941- 136
San Pedro, Diego de fl. 1492- .... DLB 286
Sansay, Leonora (?)-1823(?) .... DLB 200
Sansom, Arthur B(aldwin) II 1920-1991 112
Obituary 134
Sansom, C. J. 226
Sansom, Clive 1910-1981 104
Sansom, Ian 236
Sansom, Peter 1958- 133
Sansom, William 1912-1976 .... CANR-42
Obituary 65-68
Earlier sketch in CA 5-8R
See also CLC 2, 6
See also CN 1, 2
See also DAM NOV
See also DLB 139
See also EWL 3
See also MTCW 1
See also RGEL 2
See also RGSF 2
See also SSC 21
Sanson, Jerry Purvis 1952- 188
Sansone, Sam J(ohn) 1915- 115
San Souci, Daniel 161
See also SATA 96
San Souci, Robert D. 1946- CANR-143
Earlier sketches in CA 108, CANR-46, 79
See also CLR 43
See also MAICYA 2
See also MAICYAS 1
See also SATA 40, 81, 117, 158
Sansweet, Stephen Jay 1945- 61-64
Sant, Thomas 1948- 136
Santa Ana, Julio de
See de Santa Ana, Julio
Santa Cruz (Gamarra), Nicomedes
1925- .... HW 1
Santa Maria
See Powell-Smith, Vincent (Walter Francis)
Santana, Dharmi 1914-2002 .... CANR-20
Obituary 208
Earlier sketch in CA 101
Santangelo, Elena 194
Sant'Anna, Affonso Romano de
1937- .... DLB 307
Santareno, Bernardo 1920-1980
Santas, Joan Foster 1930- 17-20R
Santayana, George 1863-1952 194
Brief entry 115
See also AMW
See also DLB 54, 71, 246, 270
See also DLBD 13
See also EWL 3
See also MAL 5
See also RGAL 4
See also TCLC 40
See also TUS
Sant Cassia, Paul 1954- 143
Sante, Luc 1954- CANR-98
Earlier sketch in CA 147
Santee, Ross 1889(?)-1965 .... CANR-64
Earlier sketch in CA 108
See also TCWW 1, 2
Santee, Walt
See King, Albert
Santesson, Hans Stefan 1914(?)-1975 93-96
Obituary 57-60
See also SATA-Obit 30
Santhi, S. 1934- .... CP 1
Santi, Enrico Mario 1950- 116
Santiago, Danny
See James, Daniel (Lewis)
See also CLC 33
See also DLB 122
Santiago, Esmeralda 1948- CANR-130
Earlier sketch in CA 179
See also AAYA 43
See also BYA 12
See also LLW
See also SATA 129
Santiago, Silviano 1936- 219
Santiago, Soledad 179
Santillana, Giorgio Diaz de
See de Santillana, Giorgio Diaz
Santillana, Inigo Lopez de Mendoza, Marques
de 1398-1458 .... DLB 286
Santini, Rosemarie 81-84
Santlofer, Jonathan 1946- 217
Santmire, H(arold) Paul 1935- 53-56
Santmyer, Helen Hooven
1895-1986 .... CANR-33
Obituary 118
Earlier sketches in CA 1-4R, CANR-15
See also CLC 33
See also DLBY 1984
See also MTCW 1
See also RHW
See also TCLC 133
Santoka, Taneda 1882-1940 .... TCLC 72
Santoli, Al 1949- 105
Santoni, Georges V. 1938- 103
Santoni, Ronald E(rnest) 1931- 5-8R
Santoro, Carlo Maria 1935- 143
Santoro, Gene 207
Santoro, Michael A(nthony) 1954- 203
Santos, Bienvenido N(uqui)
1911-1996 .... CANR-46
Obituary 151
Earlier sketches in CA 101, CANR-19
See also AAL
See also CLC 22
See also CP 1
See also DAM MULT
See also DLB 312
See also EWL
See also RGAL 4
See also SSFS 19
See also TCLC 156
Santos, Eduardo 1888-1974
Obituary 89-92
Santos, Helen
See Griffiths, Helen
Santos, Michael (Gerard) 1964- 236
Santos, Michael W(ayne) 1956- 231
Santos, Miguel
See Mihura, Miguel
Santos, Sherod (A.) 1948- 132
Santos-Febres, Mayra 1966- 198
Santos Silva, Loreina 1933- 189
Santostefano, Sebastiano 1929- 41-44R
Santosuosso, Antonio 1936- 208
Santrey, Louis
See Sabin, Louis
Santucci, Barbara 1948- .... SATA 130
Sanville, Jean 1918- 89-92
Sanvitale, Francesca 1928- 199
See also DLB 196
Sanwal, B(hairava) D(at) 1917- 17-20R
Saperstein, Alan 103
Saperstein, David 1937- 130
Saphier, Michael 1911-1987 .... 25-28R
Saphire, Saul 1896(?)-1974
Obituary 53-56
Sapia, Yvonne (V.) 1946- CANR-56
Earlier sketch in CA 126
Sapidus, Joannes 1490-1561 .... DLB 179
Sapiets, Janis 1921-1983(?)
Obituary 109
Sapieyevski, Anne Lindbergh 1940-1993 115
Obituary 143
Brief entry 113
See also Feydy, Anne Lindbergh and
Lindbergh, Anne
See also SATA 35, 78
Sapin, Jean 187
Sapinsley, Alvin 1921-2002 .... CANR-21
Obituary 207
Earlier sketch in CA 104
Sapinsley, Barbara 137
Sapir, Edward 1884-1939 211
See also DLB 92
See also TCLC 108
Sapir, Richard (Ben) 1936-1987 .... CANR-79
Obituary 121
Earlier sketches in CA 69-72, CANR-13
See also CMW 4
Sapiro, Virginia 1951- CANR-53
Earlier sketch in CA 126
Sapolsky, Robert M. 1957- 203
Sapori, Armando 1892-1975 .... 33-36R
Saport, Linda 1954- .... SATA 123
Saporta, Marc(el) 1923- 21-24R
Saporta, Sol 1925- 17-20R
Saposnik, Irving Seymour 1936- 97-100
Saposs, David Joseph 1886-1968 ..... CANR-75
Obituary 103
Earlier sketches in CA 1-4R, CANR-15
Sapp, Allen 1929- .... SATA 151
Sapp, Phyllis Woodruff 1908-2001 ..... CANR-1
Earlier sketch in CA 1-4R
Sappell, Joel 1953- 133
Sapper
See McNeile, Herman Cyril
See also TCLC 44
Sapper, Laurence Joseph 1922-1989
Obituary 129
Sapphire
See Sapphire, Brenda
Sapphire, Brenda 1950- .... CLC 99
Sappho fl. 6th cent. B.C.- .... CDWLB 1
See also DA3
See also DAM POET
See also DLB 176
See also FL 1:1
See also PC 5
See also PFS 20
See also RGWL 2, 3
See also WP
Sappington, Roger E(dwin) 1929- 13-16R
Sara
See Blake, Sally Mirliss
Sara, Dorothy 1897(?)-1976
Obituary 69-72
Sarac, Roger
See Caras, Roger A(ndrew)
Saracevic, Tefko 1930- 37-40R
Saracino, Mary 1954- 207
Sarah, Duchess of York
See Ferguson, Sarah (Margaret)
Sarah, Edith 1921- 149
Sarah, Robyn 1949- 237
Earlier sketches in CA 112, CANR-31
Autobiographical Essay in 237
Saramago, Jose 1922- CANR-96
Earlier sketch in CA 153
See also CLC 119
See also CWW 2
See also DLB 287
See also EWL 3
See also HLCS 1
See also LATS 1:2
Saran, Parmatma 1943- 129
Sarano, Jacques 1920- 29-32R
Sarant, P(eter) C. 1933(?)-1979
Obituary 89-92
Sarantakes, Nicholas Evan 1966- 192
Sarasin, Jennifer
See Sachs, Judith
Sarason, Seymour Bernard 1919- 120
Sarasy, Phyllis Powell 1930- 13-16R
Sarat, Austin Dean 1947- 106
Sarban
See Wall, John W.
See also DLB 255
See also HGG
See also SFW 4
See also SUFW
Sarde, Philippe 1945- .... IDFW 3, 4
SarDesai, D(amodar) R. 1931- CANR-11
Earlier sketch in CA 25-28R
Sardeson, Charles T. 1921- 5-8R
Sardi, Jan 1953- 164
Sardou, Victorien 1831-1908 185
See also DLB 192
See also GFL 1789 to the Present
Sarducci, Father Guido
See Novello, Don
Sarduy, Severo 1937-1993 .... CANR-81
Obituary 142
Earlier sketches in CA 89-92, CANR-58
See also CLC 6, 97
See also CWW 2
See also DLB 113
See also EWL 3
See also HLCS 2
See also HW 1, 2
See also LAW
See also TCLC 167
Sarett, Alma (Johnson) 1908-1982 .... CAP-2
Earlier sketch in CA 17-18
Sarett, Morton R(euben) 1916- 93-96
Sarewitz, Daniel 1955- 158
Sareyan, Alex 1913-2001 149
Sarf, Wayne M(ichael) 1957- 114
Sarfoh, Joseph A. 1936- 145
Sarg, Anthony Frederick
See Sarg, Tony
Sarg, Tony 1882-1942 .... YABC 1
Sargant, Norman 1909-1982
Obituary 107
Sargant, William (Walters) 1907- 65-68
Sargeant, Howland H(ill) 1911-1984
Obituary 112
Sargeant, Winthrop 1903-1986 .... CANR-75
Obituary 120
Earlier sketch in CA 29-32R
Sargent, Alice G(oldstein)
1939-1988 .... CANR-88
Obituary 125
Earlier sketch in CA 110
Sargent, Alvin 1927- CANR-48
Brief entry 111
Earlier sketch in CA 121
See also IDFW 3, 4
Sargent, Ben 1948- 118
Brief entry 113
Interview in CA-118
Sargent, Brian (Lawrence) 1927- 97-100
Sargent, Daniel 1890-1987
Obituary 121
Sargent, David R(utledge) 1920- 93-96
Sargent, Frederic O(berlin) 1919- 41-44R
Sargent, Inge 1932- 147
Sargent, Jean Vieth 1918- 106
Sargent, John Richard 1925- 13-16R
Sargent, Judy Tam 1968- 196
Sargent, Lyman Tower 1940- CANR-15
Earlier sketch in CA 29-32R
Sargent, Pamela 1948- 200
Earlier sketches in CA 61-64, CANR-8, 41, 78
Autobiographical Essay in 200
See also CAAS 18
See also AAYA 18
See also DLB 8
See also SATA 29, 78
See also SFW 4
See also YAW
Sargent, Ralph M(illard) 1904-1985 ...... 37-40R
Obituary 116
Sargent, Robert 1933- 21-24R
See also SATA 2
Sargent, Ruth (Sexton) 1920- 112
Sargent, Sarah 1937- 106
See also SATA 44
See also SATA-Brief 41
Sargent, Shirley 1927-2004 .... CANR-2
Obituary 234
Earlier sketch in CA 1-4R
See also SATA 11
Sargent, (Francis) William, (Jr.)
1946- CANR-143
Earlier sketch in CA 106
Sargent, Wyn 49-52

Sargeson, Frank 1903-1982 .... CANR-79
Obituary 106
Earlier sketches in CA 25-28R, CANR-38
See also CLC 31
See also CN 1, 2, 3
See also EWL 3
See also GLL 2
See also RGEL 2
See also RGSF 2
See also SSFS 20
Sarhan, Samir 1941- 103
Sari
See Fleur, Anne
Saricks, Ambrose 1915- 17-20R
Sariego, Patricia Treece
See Treece, Patricia
Sarif, Shamim 1971(?)- 203
Sariola, Sakari 1919- 41-44R
Sarjeant, William A(ntony) S(within)
1935-2002 105
See also FANT
Sarkar, Asoke 1911(?)-1983
Obituary 109
Sarkar, (Anvil) Kumar 1912-1997 .... 37-40R
Sarkar, Prabhat Ranjan
See Anandamurti, Shrii Shrii
Sarkesian, Sam C(harles) 1927- 57-60
Sarkodie-Mensah, Kwasi 1955- 225
Sarlos, Robert Karoly 1931- 109
Sarma, G. V. L. N. 1925- 17-20R
Sarmiento, Domingo Faustino
1811-1888 .... HLCS 2
See also LAW
See also WLIT 1
Sarmiento, Felix Ruben Garcia
See Dario, Ruben
Sarna, Igal 1952- 217
Sarna, Jonathan D(aniel) 1955- CANR-59
Earlier sketches in CA 109, CANR-27
Sarna, Nahum M(attathias) 1923- 17-20R
Sarnat, Marshall 1929- CANR-26
Earlier sketches in CA 21-24R, CANR-10
Sarndal, Carl Erik 1937- 105
Sarner, Harvey 1934- 17-20R
Sarno, Arthur D. 1921(?)-1982
Obituary 106
Sarno, Ronald A(nthony) 1941- CANR-27
Earlier sketches in CA 29-32R, CANR-12
Sarnoff, David 1891-1971
Obituary 113
Sarnoff, Dorothy 1917- 33-36R
Sarnoff, Irving 1922- CANR-8
Earlier sketch in CA 17-20R
Sarnoff, Jane 1937- CANR-9
Earlier sketch in CA 53-56
See also SATA 10
Sarnoff, Paul 1918- CANR-40
Earlier sketches in CA 5-8R, CANR-2, 18
Sarnoff, Stanley Jay 1917-1990
Obituary 131
Sarnoff, Suzanne 1928- 97-100
Saro-Wiwa, Ken(ule Beeson)
1941-1995 .... CANR-60
Obituary 150
Earlier sketch in CA 142
See also BW 2
See also CLC 114
See also DLB 157
Saroyan, Aram 1943- CANR-114
Earlier sketches in CA 21-24R, CANR-30
See also CAAS 5
See also CP 1, 2
Saroyan, Arshalyus 1923-1974
Obituary 53-56
Saroyan, William 1908-1981 .... CANR-30
Obituary 103
Earlier sketch in CA 5-8R
See also AAYA 66
See also CAD
See also CDALBS
See also CLC 1, 8, 10, 29, 34, 56
See also CN 1, 2
See also DA
See also DA3
See also DAB
See also DAC
See also DAM DRAM, MST, NOV
See also DFS 17
See also DLB 7, 9, 86
See also DLBY 1981
See also EWL 3
See also LAIT 4
See also MAL 5
See also MTCW 1, 2
See also MTFW 2005
See also RGAL 4
See also RGSF 2
See also SATA 23
See also SATA-Obit 24
See also SSC 21
See also SSFS 14
See also TCLC 137
See also TUS
See also WLC
Sarpi, Emilio
See Ca'Zorci, Giacomo
Sarrantonio, Al 1952- CANR-140
Earlier sketches in CA 120, CANR-70
See also HGG
Sarratt, Reed 1918(?)-1986
Obituary 118
Sarraute, Nathalie 1900-1999 .... CANR-134
Obituary 187
Earlier sketches in CA 9-12R, CANR-23, 66
See also BPFB 3
See also CLC 1, 2, 4, 8, 10, 31, 80
See also CWW 2
See also DLB 83, 321
See also EW 12
See also EWL 3
See also GFL 1789 to the Present
See also MTCW 1, 2
See also MTFW 2005
See also RGWL 2, 3
See also TCLC 145
Sarrazin, Albertine (Damien) 1937-1967 184
See also DLB 83
Sarre, Winifred Turner 1931- 29-32R
Sarri, Rosemary C(onzemius) 1926- 111
Sarrinikolaou, George 1970- 238
Sarris, Andrew 1928- 21-24R
Sarris, Greg(ory M.) 1952- CANR-90
Earlier sketch in CA 172
See also DLB 175
See also LATS 1:2
Sarsfield, C. P.
See Marshner, Connaught Coyne
Sartain, Aaron Quinn 1905-1998 .... 1-4R
Sarti, Roland 1937- 37-40R
Sarti, Ron 1947- 154
Sarto, Ben
See Fawcett, F(rank) Dubrez
Sarton, (Eleanor) May 1912-1995 ... CANR-116
Obituary 149
Earlier sketches in CA 1-4R, CANR-1, 34, 55
Interview in CANR-34
See also AMWS 8
See also CLC 4, 14, 49, 91
See also CN 1, 2, 3, 4, 5, 6
See also CP 1, 2
See also DAM POET
See also DLB 48
See also DLBY 1981
See also EWL 3
See also FW
See also MAL 5
See also MTCW 1, 2
See also MTFW 2005
See also PC 39
See also RGAL 4
See also SATA 36
See also SATA-Obit 86
See also TCLC 120
See also TUS
Sartor, Margaret 1959- CANR-117
Earlier sketches in CA 125, CANR-51
Sartori, Giovanni 1924- CANR-38
Earlier sketches in CA 5-8R, CANR-2, 17
Sartre, Jean-Paul 1905-1980 .... CANR-21
Obituary 97-100
Earlier sketch in CA 9-12R
See also AAYA 62
See also CLC 1, 4, 7, 9, 13, 18, 24, 44, 50, 52
See also DA
See also DA3
See also DAB
See also DAC
See also DAM DRAM, MST, NOV
See also DC 3
See also DFS 5
See also DLB 72, 296, 321
See also EW 12
See also EWL 3
See also GFL 1789 to the Present
See also LMFS 2
See also MTCW 1, 2
See also MTFW 2005
See also NFS 21
See also RGSF 2
See also RGWL 2, 3
See also SSC 32
See also SSFS 9
See also TWA
See also WLC
Sartwell, Crispin 1958- 168
Sarvepalli, Gopal 1923- 81-84
Sarver, Hannah
See Nielsen, Jean Sarver
Sarvig, Ole 1921-1981 192
See also EWL 3
Sasaki, R. A. 1952- 136
Sasaki, Tazu 1932- CANR-10
Earlier sketch in CA 25-28R
Saseen, Sharon (Dillon) 1949- .... SATA 59
Sasek, Lawrence A(nton) 1923- CANR-1
Earlier sketch in CA 1-4R
Sasek, Miroslav 1916-1980 73-76
Obituary 101
See also CLR 4
See also SATA 16
See also SATA-Obit 23
Saskin, E.
See Steiner, Evgeny
Saslow, Helen 1926- 105
Saslow, James M(axwell) 1947- 199
Sasnett, Martena T(enney) 1908- 53-56
Saso, Michael R. 1930- 112
Sass, Lorna Janet 1945- CANR-112
Earlier sketch in CA 102
Sass, Stephen L. 1940- 167
Sass, Steven A(rthur) 1949- 116
Sassen, Saskia 1949- 154
Sasser, Charles W(ayne) 1942- CANR-100
Earlier sketches in CA 122, CANR-48
Sasso, Sandy Eisenberg 1947- CANR-117
Earlier sketch in CA 151
See also SATA 86, 116, 162
Sasson, Jean P. 1947- CANR-110
Earlier sketch in CA 144
Sasson, Sarah Diane Hyde 1946- 125
Sassoon, Beverly Adams 65-68
Sassoon, Rosemary 1931- CANR-99
Earlier sketches in CA 118, CANR-48
Sassoon, Siegfried (Lorraine)
1886-1967 .... CANR-36
Obituary 25-28R
Earlier sketch in CA 104
See also BRW 6
See also CLC 36, 130
See also DAB
See also DAM MST, NOV, POET
See also DLB 20, 191
See also DLBD 18
See also EWL 3
See also MTCW 1, 2
See also MTFW 2005
See also PAB
See also PC 12
See also RGEL 2
See also TEA
Sassoon, Vidal 1928- CANR-15
Earlier sketch in CA 65-68
Sassower, Raphael 1955- 190
Sastre (Salvador), Alfonso 1926- .... CWW 2
Sasuly, Richard 1913- 109
Sata Ineko 1904- .... DLB 180
Satchidananda, Sri Swami
See Santana, Dharmi
Satchidananda, Swami 1914-2002
See Santana, Dharmi
Satchwell, John .... SATA-Brief 49
Satel, Sally L. 197
Sater, William F(rederick) 1937- 118
Sateren, Leland B. 1913- 141
Sather, Julia Coley Duncan 1940- 103
Sathre, Vivian 1952- 202
See also SATA 79, 133
Satiafa
See Gordon, Vivian V(erdell)
Satin, Joseph 1922- 9-12R
Satin, Mark 1946- 41-44R
Satir, Virginia (Mildred) 1916-1988
Obituary 126
Satiricus
See Roetter, Charles Frederick
Satler, Gail R. 1951- 191
Sato, Esther Masako Tateishi 1915- 108
Sato, Hiro
See Sato, Hiroaki
Sato, Hiroaki 1942- CANR-93
Earlier sketch in CA 145
Satprem 1923- CANR-35
Earlier sketches in CA 85-88, CANR-15
Satran, Pamela Redmond 1953- 110
Satrapi, Marjane 1969- .... AAYA 55
Sattelmeyer, Robert 1946- 125
Satter, Beryl E. 1959- 206
Satter, Ellyn 1942- 145
Satter, Robert 1919- 139
Satterfield, Archie 1933- CANR-14
Earlier sketch in CA 57-60
Satterfield, Charles
See del Rey, Lester and
Pohl, Frederik
Satterlund, Donald R(obert) 1928- 53-56
Satterly, Weston
See Sunners, William
Satterthwait, Walter 1946- CANR-62
Earlier sketch in CA 127
See also CMW 4
Sattgast, L. J.
See Sattgast, Linda J.
Sattgast, Linda J. 1953- 155
See also SATA 91
Sattin, Anthony (Neil) 1956- CANR-96
Earlier sketch in CA 126
Sattler, Helen Roney 1921-1992 .... CANR-31
Earlier sketches in CA 33-36R, CANR-14
See also CLR 24
See also SATA 4, 74
Sattler, Henry V(ernon) 1917- CANR-7
Earlier sketch in CA 5-8R
Sattler, Jerome M(urray) 1931- 49-52
Sattler, Warren 1934- 65-68
Sattley, Helen R(owland) -1999 .... 1-4R
Satyamurti, Carole 1939- CANR-106
Earlier sketches in CA 127, CANR-55
See also CP 7
See also CWP
Satyremont
See Peret, Benjamin
Satz, Paul 1932- 61-64
Satz, Ronald Norman 1944- CANR-8
Earlier sketch in CA 61-64
Saucy, Robert L(loyd) 1930- 123
Brief entry 118
Saudek, Jan 1935- 205
Sauder, Robert A(lden) 1943- 148
Sauer, Carl Ortwin 1889-1975 .... CANR-9
Earlier sketch in CA 61-64
Sauer, Elizabeth M. 1964- CANR-129
Earlier sketch in CA 164
Sauer, Julia Lina 1891-1983 .... CANR-83
Earlier sketch in CA 81-84
See also CWRI 5
See also SATA 32
See also SATA-Obit 36
Sauer, Muriel Stafford -1994 .... 13-16R
Sauer, Peter 1937- 139
Sauer, Val John, Jr. 1938- 107
Sauerhaft, Stan 1926- 85-88
Sauerlaender, Willibald
See Sauerlander, Willibald
Sauerlander, Willibald
See Sauerlander, Willibald
Sauerlander, Willibald 1924- CANR-127
Earlier sketch in CA 118
Sauers, Michael P(atrick) 1970- 227
Sauers, Richard A(llen) 1954- 164
Sauers, Richard James 1930- 53-56
Sauers, Wendy 1958- 116
Sauerwein, Leigh 1944- 230
See also SATA 155
Saul, Carol P. 1947- 182
See also SATA 78, 117
Saul, George Brandon 1901-1986 ...... CANR-6
Obituary 120
Earlier sketch in CA 13-16R
Saul, John (W. III) 1942- CANR-81
Earlier sketches in CA 81-84, CANR-16, 40
See also AAYA 10, 62
See also BEST 90:4
See also CLC 46
See also CPW
See also DAM NOV, POP
See also HGG
See also SATA 98
Saul, John Ralston 1947- CANR-82
Earlier sketch in CA 133
Saul, Leon J(oseph) 1901-1983 .... CANR-10
Earlier sketch in CA 21-24R
Saul, Mary 105
Saul, Nigel Edward 1952- 117
Saul, Norman E(ugene) 1932- CANR-116
Earlier sketch in CA 53-56
Saul, Oscar
See Halpern, Oscar Saul
Saul, (Ellen) Wendy 1946- CANR-81
Earlier sketch in CA 114
See also SATA 42
Saulnier, Beth 1969- 226
Saulnier, Christine Flynn 1950- 197
Saulnier, Jacques 1928- .... IDFW 3, 4
Saulnier, Karen Luczak 1940- 148
See also SATA 80
Saulnier, Raymond Joseph
1908-1996 .... CANR-65
Earlier sketch in CA 5-8R
Sauls, Roger 1944- 33-36R
Saum, Karen 1935- 137
Saumarez Smith, Charles Robert 1954- 144
Saunders, Allen 1899-1986 69-72
Obituary 118
Saunders, Ann Loreille 1930- 103
Saunders, Aretas (Andrews) 1884-1970 . CAP-1
Earlier sketch in CA 11-12
Saunders, B(ernard) C(harles) 1903-1983
Obituary 115
Saunders, Beatrice 49-52
Saunders, Blanche 1906- CAP-1
Earlier sketch in CA 13-14
Saunders, Caleb
See Heinlein, Robert A(nson)
Saunders, Carl Maxon 1890-1974
Obituary 89-92
Saunders, Charles B(askerville), Jr. 1928- . 61-64
Saunders, Charles R(obert) 1946- 172
See also FANT
Saunders, Christopher T(homas)
1907-2000 119
Saunders, Dave 1939- .... SATA 85
Saunders, David
See Sontup, Dan(iel)
Saunders, Doris E(vans) 1921- 77-80
Saunders, E. Dale 1919- 5-8R
Saunders, Ernest 1901(?)-1983
Obituary 109
Saunders, Francis J. 1927- 131
Saunders, Frank
See Saunders, Francis J.
Saunders, Gail 1944- 145
Saunders, George (W.) 1958- CANR-98
Earlier sketch in CA 164
Saunders, Helen E(lizabeth) 1912- 25-28R
Saunders, Hilary Aidan St. George 1898-1951
Brief entry 121
Saunders, Ione
See Cole, Margaret Alice
Saunders, J(ohn) W(hiteside) 1920- .. CANR-39
Earlier sketch in CA 116
Saunders, James (Arthur)
1925-2004 .... CANR-83
Obituary 222
Brief entry 124
Earlier sketch in CA 139
See also CBD
See also CD 5, 6
See also DLB 13
Saunders, James Robert 1953- CANR-87
Earlier sketch in CA 153
Saunders, Jason Lewis 1922-
Brief entry 106
Saunders, Jean 1932- CANR-83
Earlier sketches in CA 102, CANR-19
See also RHW
Saunders, Jeanne
See Rundle, Anne
Saunders, John
See Nickson, Arthur
Saunders, John Monk 1897-1940 185
See also DLB 26
See also IDFW 3, 4
Saunders, John Turk 1929-1974 .... CAP-2
Earlier sketch in CA 21-22
Saunders, Julie 1939- .... SATA 85
Saunders, (William) Keith 1910-1994 57-60
See also SATA 12
Saunders, Mack
See Ketchum, Philip (L.)

Cumulative Index 511 Sayers

Saunders, Madelyn
See Day, Dianne
Saunders, Margaret Marshall 1861-1947 195
See also DLB 92
Saunders, Max 1957- CANR-130
Earlier sketch in CA 164
Saunders, Peter 1950- CANR-36
Earlier sketch in CA 114
Saunders, Richard 1947- CANR-21
Earlier sketch in CA 105
Saunders, Robert 1914- .... CP 1
Saunders, Roy 1911- CAP-1
Earlier sketch in CA 11-12
Saunders, Rubie (Agnes) 1929- 49-52
See also SATA 21
Saunders, Sally Love 1940- 125
Saunders, Susan 1945- CANR-68
Earlier sketch in CA 106
See also SATA 46, 96
See also SATA-Brief 41
Saunders, Thomas 1909- CANR-12
Earlier sketch in CA 73-76
See also CP 1
Saunders, Trevor J(ohn) 1934-1999 206
Saura (Atares), Carlos 1932-1998 ..... CANR-79
Brief entry 114
Earlier sketch in CA 131
See also CLC 20
See also HW 1
Sauret, Martine 218
Sauro, Regina Calderone 1924- 9-12R
Sause, George G(abriel) 1919-1996 ...... 41-44R
Sauser, Frederic Louis
See Sauser-Hall, Frederic
Sauser-Hall, Frederic 1887-1961 ...... CANR-62
Obituary 93-96
Earlier sketches in CA 102, CANR-36
See also Cendrars, Blaise
See also CLC 18
See also MTCW 1
Saussure, Eric de
See de Saussure, Eric
Saussure, Ferdinand de
See de Saussure, Ferdinand
Saussure, Ferdinand de 1857-1913 .... DLB 242
See also TCLC 49
Sautel, Maureen Ann 1951- 61-64
Sauter, Doris Elaine 231
Sauter, Edwin Charles Scott, Jr. 1930- ... 13-16R
Sauter, Eric 1948- CANR-62
Earlier sketch in CA 117
See also CMW 4
Sauter, Van Gordon 1935- 73-76
Sautet, Claude 1924-2000 143
Obituary 189
Sautter, Hermann 1938- 230
Sautter, Udo 1934- 144
Sauvage, Franck
See Horn, Maurice
Sauvage, Leo 1913(?)-1988
Obituary 127
Sauvage, Roger 1917-1977
Obituary 73-76
Sauvage, Tristan
See Schwarz, Arturo (Umberto Samuele)
Sauvageau, Juan 1917- CANR-11
Earlier sketch in CA 65-68
Sauvain, Philip Arthur 1933- CANR-103
Earlier sketches in CA 104, CANR-21, 49
See also SATA 111
Sauvant, Karl P(eter) 1944- 77-80
Sauvy, Jean (Maurice Paul) 1916- 65-68
Sauvy, Simonne 1922- 65-68
Sava, George
See Milkomane, George Alexis Milkomanov-
ich
Savacool, John K(enneth) 1917-1998 45-48
Savadier, Elivia 1950- .... SATA 79
Savage, Alan
See Nicole, Christopher (Robin)
Savage, (Maria) Ania 1941- 202
Savage, Augusta 1892(?)-1962 .... AAYA 45
Savage, Blake
See Goodwin, Harold L(eland)
Savage, Brian 1933- 41-44R
Savage, Candace (M.) 1949- CANR-121
Earlier sketch in CA 123
See also AAYA 60
See also SATA 142
Savage, Carlton Raymond 1897-1990
Obituary 131
Savage, Catharine
See Brosman, Catharine Savage
Savage, Charles 1918- 53-56
Savage, Christina
See Newcomb, Kerry and
Schaefer, Frank
Savage, Christopher I(vor)
1924-1969 .... CANR-6
Earlier sketch in CA 5-8R
Savage, D(ouglas) J(oseph) 1950- 118
Savage, D(erek) S(tanley) 1917- 104
Savage, Dan 183
Savage, Daniel M. 1956- 220
Savage, Deborah 1955- 143
See also BYA 8
See also SATA 76
Savage, Elizabeth Fitzgerald
1918-1989 .... CANR-69
Earlier sketches in CA 1-4R, CANR-1
See also RHW
Savage, Ernest 1918- CANR-83
Earlier sketch in CA 112
Savage, Felicity 1975- 169
Savage, Frances Higginson (Fuller)
1898-1984 .... CAP-1
Earlier sketch in CA 19-20
Savage, (Leonard) George (Gimson)
1909- CANR-75
Earlier sketches in CA 9-12R, CANR-5
Savage, Georgia 138
Savage, Helen 1915- 97-100
Savage, Henry, Jr. 1903-1990 .... CAP-2
Earlier sketch in CA 25-28
Savage, Herbert
See Picot, Derek
Savage, James 1784-1873 .... DLB 30
Savage, James F(rancis) 1939- 73-76
Savage, Jeff 1961- 164
See also SATA 97
Savage, Jon
See Sage, Jonathan
Savage, Joseph P. 1895(?)-1977
Obituary 69-72
Savage, Katharine James 1905-1989 ..... 13-16R
Obituary 128
See also SATA-Obit 61
Savage, Kirk 1958- 173
Savage, Lee 1928- 101
Savage, Leonard J(immie) 1917-1971 .... CAP-2
Obituary 33-36R
Earlier sketch in CA 17-18
Savage, Les, Jr. 1922-1958 .... TCWW 2
Savage, Marc 1945- 65-68
Savage, Marmion 1803(?)-1872 .... DLB 21
Savage, Michael D(onald) 1946- 101
Savage, Mildred (Spitz) 1919- 9-12R
Savage, Minot Judson 1841-1918
Brief entry 115
Savage, Naomi 1927- 204
Savage, Richard 1697(?)-1743 .... DLB 95
See also RGEL 2
Savage, Robert L(ynn) 1939- CANR-46
Earlier sketch in CA 109
Savage, Roth
See Kehrer, Daniel M(ark)
Savage, Sean J. 1964- 161
Savage, Teresa 1950- 113
Savage, Terry 196
Savage, Thomas 1915-2003 132
Obituary 218
Brief entry 126
Interview in CA-132
See also CAAS 15
See also CLC 40
See also CN 6, 7
See also SATA-Obit 147
See also TCWW 2
Savage, Thomas Gerard 1926- 49-52
Savage, Tom 1948- 171
Savage, W(illiam) Sherman 1890-1980 ... 69-72
Savage, William W(oodrow), Jr. 1943- 57-60
Savage, William W(oodrow) 1914- 37-40R
Savageau, Cheryl 1950- 152
See also SATA 96
Savain, Petion (?)-1973
Obituary 41-44R
Savan, Bruce (Sheldon) 1927-1987 .... 5-8R
Obituary 122
Savan, Glenn 1953-2003 225
See also CLC 50
Savard, Felix-Antoine 1896-1982 148
See also DLB 68
Savard, Jeannine 1950- 216
Savarese, Julia 37-40R
Savarin
See Courtine, Robert
Savary, Louis M(ichael) 1936- CANR-49
Earlier sketches in CA 21-24R, CANR-9, 24
Savas, E(manuel) S(tephen) 1931- 17-20R
Savas, Jason F. 1954- 182
Saveland, Robert N(elson) 1921- 41-44R
Savelev, Boris 1947- 212
Savell, Don P(atrick) 1939- 119
Savelle, Max(well H.) 1896-1979 .... 21-24R
Obituary 174
Savery, Constance (Winifred)
1897-1999 .... CANR-7
Earlier sketch in CA 9-12R
See also SATA 1
Savery, Henry 1791-1842 .... DLB 230
See also RGEL 2
Savery, Ranald 1903(?)-1974
Obituary 104
Saveson, John E(dward) 1923- 41-44R
Saveth, Edward N(orman) 1915- 21-24R
Savigneau, Josyane 228
Saville, Diana 1943- 160
Saville, Eugenia (Curtis) 1913- 41-44R
Saville, Lloyd (Blackstone) 1913-1988 .. 21-24R
Saville, (Leonard) Malcolm
1901-1982 .... CANR-83
Obituary 107
Earlier sketch in CA 101
See also DLB 160
See also SATA 23
See also SATA-Obit 31
Savin, Marc 1948- 106
Savini, Tom 1946- .... IDFW 3, 4
Savinio, Alberto 1891-1952 .... DLB 264
Saviotti, Paolo
See Saviotti, Pier Paolo
Saviotti, Pier Paolo 1944- 198
Saviozzi, Adriana
See Mazza, Adriana
Savir, Uri 170
Savitch, Jessica 1948-1983 108
Obituary 110
Savitt, Ronald 1939- 33-36R
Savitt, Sam 1917(?)-2000 .... CANR-17
Obituary 191
Earlier sketches in CA 1-4R, CANR-1
See also SATA 8
See also SATA-Obit 126
Savitt, Todd Lee 1943- 102
Savitz, Harriet May 1933- CANR-64
Earlier sketches in CA 41-44R, CANR-14, 32
See also AAYA 57
See also MAICYA 1, 2
See also SAAS 9, 26
See also SATA 5, 72
See also YAW
Savitz, Leonard D. 1926- CANR-8
Earlier sketch in CA 21-24R
Savoca, Nancy 1959- 219
Savoie, Donald J(oseph) 1947- 112
Savoie, Paul 1946- 113
Savonarola, Girolamo 1452-1498 .... LMFS 1
Savory, Alan Forsyth 1905- 9-12R
Savory, Hubert Newman
1911-2001 .... CANR-26
Obituary 193
Earlier sketches in CA 25-28R, CANR-10
Savory, Jerold 1933- CANR-10
Earlier sketch in CA 25-28R
Savory, Teo 1907-1989 .... CANR-31
Earlier sketch in CA 29-32R
See also CP 1, 2
Savory, Theodore Horace 1896-1980 . CANR-6
Earlier sketch in CA 5-8R
Savours, Ann (Margaret) 1927- CANR-90
Earlier sketch in CA 57-60
Savoy, Lauret E. 139
Savoy, Mark
See Turner, Robert (Harry)
Sawai, Gloria Ostrem CANR-127
Earlier sketch in CA 113
Saward, Dudley 1913-1994 147
Saward, Michael 1932- 97-100
Sawatsky, Harry Leonard 1931- 89-92
Sawatsky, John 1948- 144
Sawer, Geoffrey 1910- 17-20R
Sawey, Orlan (Lester) 1920- CANR-12
Earlier sketch in CA 29-32R
Sawhill, Isabel V(an Devanter) 1937- 130
Sawicki, Marianne 1950- CANR-36
Earlier sketch in CA 114
Sawicki, Mary 1950- .... SATA 90
Sawin, Martica 1927- 124
Sawin, Philip 1933- 137
Sawkins, Raymond H(arold) 1923- 103
See also Forbes, Colin
Sawley, Petra
See Marsh, John
Sawrey, Robert D. 1948- 144
Sawyer, Albert E(rnest) 1898-1972 .... 5-8R
Sawyer, Charles 1887-1979 .... CAP-2
Obituary 85-88
Earlier sketch in CA 25-28
Sawyer, Christopher
See Sawyer-Laucanno, Christopher
Sawyer, Clyde Lynwood, Jr. 1951- 219
Sawyer, Corinne Holt CANR-73
Earlier sketch in CA 17-20R
Sawyer, Diane K. 1945(?)- 115
Brief entry 109
Interview in CA-115
Sawyer, (Frederick) Don(ald) 1947- .. CANR-86
Earlier sketch in CA 133
See also SATA 72
Sawyer, Jack 1931- 61-64
Sawyer, Jesse O. 1918- 17-20R
Sawyer, John
See Foley, (Cedric) John
Sawyer, Joy 1960- 194
Sawyer, Kem Knapp 1953- 150
See also SATA 84
Sawyer, Mark
See Greenhood, (Clarence) David
Sawyer, Mary R. 1944- 148
Sawyer, P(eter) H(ayes) 1928- CANR-6
Earlier sketch in CA 9-12R
Sawyer, R(obert) McLaran 1929- 45-48
Sawyer, Ralph Alanson 1895-1978
Obituary 81-84
Sawyer, Robert J(ames) 1960- 212
Earlier sketches in CA 149, CANR-83, 132
Autobiographical Essay in 212
See also DLB 251
See also SATA 81, 149
See also SFW 4
Sawyer, Roger 1931- 123
Sawyer, Ruth 1880-1970 .... CANR-83
Earlier sketches in CA 73-76, CANR-37
See also BYA 3
See also CLR 36
See also CWRI 5
See also DLB 22
See also MAICYA 1, 2
See also SATA 17
See also WCH
Sawyer, Shiva
See Sawyer, Clyde Lynwood, Jr.
Sawyer, W(alter) W(arwick) 1911- 53-56
Sawyer-Laucanno, Christopher
1951- CANR-82
Earlier sketches in CA 114, CANR-36
Sawyerr, Harry (Alphonso Ebun)
1909-1986 .... 37-40R
Obituary 120
Sax, Boria 1946- 216
Sax, Gilbert 1930- 21-24R
Sax, Joseph L. 1936- 33-36R
Sax, Karl 1892-1973
Obituary 45-48
Sax, Richard 1949-1995 125
Obituary 149
Sax, Robert
See Johnson, Robert
Sax, Saville 1924- 97-100
Saxberg, Borje O(svald) 1928- 41-44R
Saxby, H. M.
See Saxby, (Henry) Maurice
Saxby, (Henry) Maurice 1924- .... SATA 71
Saxe, Isobel
See Rayner, Claire (Berenice)
Saxe, Richard W(arren) 1923- 49-52
Saxe, Thomas E., Jr. 1903-1975
Obituary 61-64
Saxon, A(rthur) H(artley) 1935- CANR-37
Earlier sketches in CA 25-28R, CANR-16
Saxon, Alex
See Pronzini, Bill and
Quennell, Peter (Courtney)
Saxon, Andrew
See Arthur, Robert, (Jr.)
Saxon, Antonia
See Sachs, Judith
Saxon, Bill
See Wallmann, Jeffrey M(iner)
Saxon, Charles D(avid) 1920-1988
Obituary 127
Brief entry 118
Saxon, Gladys Relyea 5-8R
Saxon, Grant Tracy
See Raucina, Thomas Frank
Saxon, John
See Rumbold-Gibbs, Henry St. John Clair
Saxon, Lyle 1891-1946 202
Brief entry 119
Saxon, Peter
See McNeilly, Wilfred (Glassford)
Saxon, Van
See Henderson, M(arilyn) R(uth)
Saxon, William
See Mayleas, William
Saxton, Alexander P(laisted) 1919- ... CANR-73
Earlier sketch in CA 105
Saxton, Josephine (Mary) 1935- CANR-56
Earlier sketch in CA 29-32R
See also SFW 4
Saxton, Judith 1936- CANR-101
Earlier sketch in CA 105
See also RHW
Saxton, Lloyd 1919- 29-32R
Saxton, Mark 1914-1988 .... CANR-75
Obituary 124
Earlier sketch in CA 93-96
Saxton, Martha 1945- 81-84
Saxton, Robert
See Johnson, Robert
Saxton, Ruth O. 1941- 150
Say, Allen 1937- CANR-30
Earlier sketch in CA 29-32R
See also CLR 22
See also CWRI 5
See also JRDA
See also MAICYA 1, 2
See also MAICYAS 1
See also SATA 28, 69, 110, 161
Saya, Peter
See Peterson, Robert E(ugene)
Sayce, Richard Anthony 1917- 61-64
Saydah, J. Roger 1939-1976 .... CANR-88
Obituary 120
Earlier sketch in CA 25-28R
Saye, Albert B(erry) 1912-1989 .... CANR-5
Earlier sketch in CA 5-8R
Sayeed, Khalid B. 1926- 25-28R
Sayegh, Fayez A(bdullah)
1922-1980 .... CANR-86
Obituary 102
Earlier sketch in CA 9-12R
Sayer, Angela 1935- 89-92
Sayer, Derek 184
Sayer, Ian (Keith Terence) 1945- 139
Sayer, Karen (Anne) 1967- CANR-117
Earlier sketch in CA 153
Sayer, Mandy 1963- 171
Sayer, Paul 1955- 132
Sayers, Dorothy L(eigh) 1893-1957 .. CANR-60
Brief entry 104
Earlier sketch in CA 119
See also BPFB 3
See also BRWS 3
See also CDBLB 1914-1945
See also CMW 4
See also DAM POP
See also DLB 10, 36, 77, 100
See also MSW
See also MTCW 1, 2
See also MTFW 2005
See also RGEL 2
See also SSC 71
See also SSFS 12
See also TCLC 2, 15
See also TEA
Sayers, Frances Clarke 1897-1989 .... CANR-77
Obituary 129
Earlier sketches in CA 17-20R, CANR-74
See also SATA 3
See also SATA-Obit 62
Sayers, Gale 1943- 73-76
Sayers, James Denson
See Bardwell, Denver
Sayers, Janet 1945- 134
Sayers, Kari 1941- 204
Sayers, Peig 1873-1958
Brief entry 113
Sayers, Raymond S. 1912-1994 .... CANR-10
Earlier sketch in CA 25-28R
Sayers, Richard Sidney 1908-1989
Obituary 128
Sayers, Sean (Philip) 1942- 224
Sayers, Valerie 1952- CANR-61
Earlier sketch in CA 134
See also CLC 50, 122
See also CSW

Sayigh, Tawfiq 1923-1971 ... EWL 2
Sayle, Alexei (David) 1952- ... 197
Sayle, Charles Edward 1864-1924 ... DLB 184
Sayles, E(dwin) B(ooth) 1892-1977 ... CANR-74
Earlier sketches in CAP-2, CA 25-28
Sayles, Elizabeth 1956- ... SATA 108, 163
Sayles, George O(sborne)
1901-1994 ... CANR-74
Obituary ... 144
Earlier sketches in CA 53-56, CANR-4
Sayles, John (Thomas) 1950- ... CANR-84
Earlier sketches in CA 57-60, CANR-41
See also CLC 7, 10, 14, 198
See also DLB 44
Sayles, Leonard Robert 1926- ... CANR-1
Earlier sketch in CA 1-4R
Sayles, Nettie Leitch Major 1903(?)-1984
Obituary ... 113
Sayles, Ted
See Sayles, E(dwin) B(ooth)
Saylor, David J(onathan) 1945- ... 89-92
Saylor, Irene 1932- ... 33-36R
Saylor, J(ohn) Galen 1902-1998 ... CANR-9
Earlier sketch in CA 17-20R
Saylor, Neville 1922- ... 61-64
Saylor, Steven 1956- ... CANR-99
Earlier sketches in CA 142, CANR-67
See also CMW 4
Saylor-Marchant, Linda 1963- ... 149
See also SATA 82
Sayre, Anne 1923-1998 ... 61-64
Obituary ... 167
Sayre, April Pulley 1966- ... 152
See also SATA 88, 131
Sayre, Eleanor Axson 1916-2001 ... 25-28R
Obituary ... 197
Sayre, Gordon M. 1964- ... 168
Sayre, Henry M(arshall) 1948- ... 119
Sayre, J(ohn) Woodrow 1913- ... CANR-5
Earlier sketch in CA 9-12R
Sayre, Joel 1900-1979
Obituary ... 89-92
Sayre, John L(eslie) 1924- ... 53-56
Sayre, Kenneth Malcolm 1928- ... CANR-3
Earlier sketch in CA 9-12R
Sayre, Leslie C. 1907- ... CAP-1
Earlier sketch in CA 11-12
Sayre, Nora (Clemens) 1932-2001 ... CANR-55
Obituary ... 201
Earlier sketch in CA 118
Sayre, Robert F(reeman) 1933- ... CANR-104
Earlier sketch in CA 9-12R
Sayre, Shay 1942- ... 227
Sayre, Wallace S. 1905-1972
Obituary ... 33-36R
Sayres, Alfred Nevin 1893-1972(?) ... CAP-1
Earlier sketch in CA 17-18
Sayres, William C(ortlandt) 1927-1993 . 17-20R
Obituary ... 140
Sayrs, Henry John 1904-1995 ... 5-8R
Saywell, John T(upper) 1929- ... 13-16R
Sayyab, al- Badr Shakir 1926-1964 ... EWL 3
Sazer, Nina 1949- ... 69-72
See also SATA 13
Sbarbaro, Camillo 1888-1967 ... 213
See also DLB 114
See also EWL 3
Scabrini, Janet 1953- ... SATA 13
Scacco, Anthony M., Jr. 1939- ... 109
Scaduto, Anthony ... 104
Scaduto, Tony
See Scaduto, Anthony
Scaer, David P(aul) 1936- ... CANR-12
Earlier sketch in CA 33-36R
Scagell, Robin 1946- ... SATA 107
Scaglione, Aldo D(omenico) 1925- ... CANR-21
Earlier sketches in CA 13-16R, CANR-6
Scaglione, Cecil F(rank) 1934- ... 81-84
Scagnetti, Jack 1924- ... CANR-4
Earlier sketch in CA 49-52
See also SATA 7
Scala, James 1934- ... 124
Scalapino, Leslie 1947- ... CANR-103
Earlier sketches in CA 123, CANR-67
See also CP 7
See also CWP
See also DLB 193
Scalapino, Robert A(nthony) 1919- ... CANR-40
Earlier sketches in CA 1-4R, CANR-2, 18
Scales, Barbara 1926- ... 140
Scales, James Ralph 1919- ... 120
Scales, Junius Irving 1920-2002 ... 126
Obituary ... 206
Scales, Pat(sy) R. 1944- ... 122
Scales-Trent, Judy 1940- ... 158
Scali, John (Alfred) 1918-1995 ... 65-68
Scalia, Antonin 1936- ... 168
Scalia, Laura J. 1959- ... 237
Scalia, Toni 1939- ... 133
Scally, M. A.
See Scally, Sister (Mary) Anthony
Scally, Robert James 1937- ... 61-64
Scally, Sister (Mary) Anthony 1905-1992 ... 110
Scally, Sister Mary Anthony
See Scally, Sister (Mary) Anthony
Scalzo, Joe 1941- ... 49-52
Scambray, Kenneth 1945- ... 190
Scamehorn, H(oward) Lee 1926- ... 69-72
Scamell, Ragnhild 1940- ... 145
See also SATA 77
Scammell, Michael 1935- ... 156
See also CLC 34
Scammell, William 1939-2000 ... CP 7
Scammell, William McConnell
1920- ... CANR-6
Earlier sketch in CA 5-8R
Scammon, John H(umphrey) 1905-1994 . 53-56
Scammon, Richard M(ontgomery)
1915-2001 ... 61-64
Obituary ... 194
Scandura, Joseph M(ichael) 1931- ... CANR-5
Earlier sketch in CA 53-56
Scanlan, James P(atrick) 1927- ... 9-12R
Scanlan, Lawrence ... 191
Scanlan, Michael 1931- ... CANR-23
Earlier sketches in CA 57-60, CANR-7
Scanlan, Patricia 1956- ... 218
Scanlan, Patrick F. 1895(?)-1983
Obituary ... 109
Scanlan, Thomas J. 1934- ... 114
Scanlon, Bill ... 239
Scanlon, David G. 1921-1990 ... 13-16R
Obituary ... 132
Scanlon, James Edward 1940- ... 125
Scanlon, Kathryn I(da) 1909-1998 ... CAP-1
Earlier sketch in CA 11-12
Scanlon, Marion Stephany ... 5-8R
See also SATA 11
Scanlon, T(homas) M(ichael, Jr.) 1940- ... 187
Scannell, Donal ... 185
Scannell, Francis P. 1915-1988
Obituary ... 125
Scannell, Frank
See Scannell, Francis P.
Scannell, Vernon 1922- ... CANR-143
Earlier sketches in CA 5-8R, CANR-8, 24, 57
See also CLC 49
See also CN 1, 2
See also CP 1, 2, 3, 4, 5, 6, 7
See also CWRI 5
See also DLB 27
See also SATA 59
Scanzoni, John H. 1935- ... CANR-24
Earlier sketches in CA 21-24R, CANR-9
Scanzoni, Letha Dawson 1935- ... CANR-14
Earlier sketch in CA 57-60
Scaperlanda, Maria (de Lourdes) Ruiz
1960- ... 207
Scaperlanda, Michael A(nthony) 1960- ... 238
Scarberry, Alma Sioux 1899-1990
Obituary ... 131
Scarborough, Alma May C. 1913- ... 5-8R
Scarborough, Dorothy 1877-1935 . TCWW 1, 2
Scarborough, Elizabeth (Ann) 1947- . CANR-58
Earlier sketch in CA 120
See also AAYA 28
See also FANT
See also SATA 98
See also SFW 4
Scarborough, John 1940- ... CANR-15
Earlier sketch in CA 41-44R
Scarborough, Ruth 1904-1990 ... 115
Scarborough, Vernon L(ee) 1950- ... 139
Scarborough, William Kauffman 1933- . 17-20R
Scarbrough, George (Addison)
1915- ... CANR-38
Earlier sketches in CA 77-80, CANR-16
Scarbrough, Jan 1950- ... 229
Scardino, Albert (James) 1948- ... 129
Brief entry ... 119
Scaretti, Marjorie (?)-1982
Obituary ... 107
Scarf, Maggi
See Scarf, Maggie
Scarf, Maggie 1932- ... CANR-53
Earlier sketches in CA 29-32R, CANR-22
See also SATA 5
Scarfe, Allan (John) 1931- ... CANR-13
Earlier sketch in CA 25-28R
Scarfe, Francis Harold 1911-1986
Obituary ... 118
See also CP 1
Scarfe, Wendy (Elizabeth) 1933- ... CANR-13
Earlier sketch in CA 25-28R
Scargall, Jeanne Anna 1928- ... 93-96
Scargill, (David) Ian 1935- ... CANR-12
Earlier sketch in CA 61-64
Scariano, Margaret M. 1924- ... 151
See also SATA 86
Scarisbrick, J(ohn) J(oseph) 1928- ... CANR-18
Earlier sketch in CA 25-28R
Scarlett, Elizabeth 1961- ... 150
Scarlett, Roger
See Page, Evelyn
Scarlett, Susan
See Streatfeild, (Mary) Noel
Scarne, John 1903-1985 ... 159
Obituary ... 116
Scarpelli, Furio 1919-
See Age and
Scarpelli
Scarpetta, Frank
See McCurtin, Peter
Scarpitti, Frank R(oland) 1936- ... CANR-14
Earlier sketch in CA 41-44R
Scarr, Dee 1948- ... 122
Scarr, Deryck (Antony) 1939- ... CANR-94
Earlier sketch in CA 132
Scarr(-Salapatek), Sandra (Wood) 1936- ... 126
Scarron 1847-1910
See Mikszath, Kalman
Scarron, Paul 1610-1660 ... GFL Beginnings to 1789
See also RGWL 2, 3
Scarrott, Michael
See Fisher, A(rthur) Stanley T(heodore)
Scarrow, Howard A(lbert) 1928- ... 110
Scarrow, Simon 1962- ... 224
Scarry, Elaine (Margaret) 1946- ... CANR-90
Earlier sketch in CA 137
Scarry, Huck
See Scarry, Richard McClure, Jr.
Scarry, Patricia (Murphy) 1924- ... 17-20R
See also SATA 2
Scarry, Patsy
See Scarry, Patricia (Murphy)
Scarry, Richard (McClure)
1919-1994 ... CANR-83
Obituary ... 145
Earlier sketches in CA 17-20R, CANR-18, 39
See also CLR 3, 41
See also CWRI 5
See also DLB 61
See also MAICYA 1, 2
See also MAICYAS 1
See also SATA 2, 35, 75
See also SATA-Obit 90
Scarry, Richard McClure, Jr. 1953- ... 130
See also SATA 35
Scarth, Alwyn ... 225
Scates, Shelby 1931- ... 169
Scavullo, Francesco 1921-2004 ... CANR-43
Obituary ... 222
Earlier sketch in CA 102
Sceve, Maurice 1501(?)-1564 ... GFL Beginnings to 1789
Schaaf, C(arl) Hart 1912-1995 ... 5-8R
Schaaf, Martha Eckert 1911- ... CANR-1
Earlier sketch in CA 1-4R
Schaaf, Peter 1942- ... 106
Schaafsma, David 1953- ... 149
Schaafsma, Polly 1935- ... 57-60
Schaal, John H. 1908- ... 73-76
Schaap, Dick
See Schaap, Richard J(ay)
Schaap, James C(alvin) 1948- ... CANR-41
Earlier sketch in CA 118
Schaap, Richard J(ay) 1934-2001 ... CANR-5
Obituary ... 204
Earlier sketch in CA 9-12R
Schaar, John H(omer) 1928- ... CANR-31
Earlier sketch in CA 1-4R
Schaarwachter, Jurgen
See Schaarwaechter, Juergen
Schaarwaechter, Georg 1929- ... 25-28R
Schaarwaechter, Juergen 1967- ... 180
Schabert, Kyrill S. 1909(?)-1983
Obituary ... 109
Schach, Paul 1915- ... 142
Schachner, Judith Byron 1951- ... SATA 88
Schachner, Nathan(iel) 1895-1955 ... 156
Brief entry ... 120
See also SFW 4
Schacht, Al(exander) 1894(?)-1984
Obituary ... 113
Schacht, Hjalmar (Horace Greeley) 1877-1970
Obituary ... 113
Schacht, Richard (Lawrence) 1941- ... CANR-31
Earlier sketch in CA 29-32R
Schachtel, Ernest G(eorge) 1903-1975 .. 37-40R
Schachtel, Hyman Judah 1907- ... 49-52
Schachtel, Roger (Bernard) 1949- ... 106
See also SATA 38
Schachter, Gustav 1926- ... 17-20R
Schachter, Michael 1941- ... 102
Schachter, Oscar 1915-2003 ... 65-68
Obituary ... 222
Schachter, Stanley 1922-1997 ... 37-40R
Obituary ... 159
Schachterle, Nancy (Lange) 1925- ... 101
Schachtman, Max 1903-1972
Obituary ... 37-40R
Schack, Hans Egede 1820-1859 ... DLB 300
Schack, William 1898-1988
Obituary ... 128
Schackne, Stewart 1905-1975
Obituary ... 61-64
Schacter, Daniel L. 1952- ... 202
Schad, Christian 1894-1982 ... 204
Schad, Jasper G(ripper) 1932- ... 110
Schad, Wilhelm
See Reichert, Herbert W(illiam)
Schade, Jens August 1903-1978 ... EWL 3
Schadeberg, Jurgen 1931- ... 213
Schaechter, Elio
See Schaechter, Moselio
Schaechter, Mordkhe 1927- ... 41-44R
Schaechter, Moselio 1928- ... 164
Schaedel, Richard P. 1920- ... 45-48
Schaedler, Sally ... SATA 116
Schaef, Anne Wilson 1934- ... 118
Schaefer, Charles E. 1933- ... 37-40R
Schaefer, Claude 1913- ... 33-36R
Schaefer, Claudia 1949- ... 162
Schaefer, Eric P. 1959- ... 231
Schaefer, Frank 1936- ... CANR-10
Earlier sketch in CA 65-68
Schaefer, George (Louis) 1920-1997 ... 170
Schaefer, Jack (Warner) 1907-1991 .. CANR-64
Obituary ... 133
Earlier sketches in CAP-1, CA 17-20R, CANR-15
See also BPFB 3
See also BYA 3, 4
See also CWRI 5
See also DLB 212
See also LAIT 2
See also SATA 3, 66
See also SATA-Obit 65
See also TCWW 1, 2
Schaefer, John 1958- ... 126
Schaefer, John H(arrison) 1937- ... 57-60
Schaefer, Josephine O'Brien 1929- ... 37-40R
Schaefer, Leah Cahan 1920- ... 49-52
Schaefer, Lola M. 1950- ... CANR-126
Earlier sketch in CA 155
See also SATA 91, 144
Schaefer, Nicola Caroline 1939- ... 104
Schaefer, Peter 1943- ... 180
Schaefer, Ted 1939- ... 77-80
Schaefer, Vincent J(oseph)
1906-1993 ... CANR-46
Obituary ... 142
Earlier sketch in CA 120
Schaefer, Walter Erich 1901-1982(?)
Obituary ... 106
Schaefer, William D. 1928- ... 134
Schaeffer, Albrecht 1885-1950 ... 216
See also DLB 66
Schaeffer, Claude Frederic Armand 1898-1982
Obituary ... 108
Schaeffer, Edith (Seville) 1914- ... 77-80
Schaeffer, Elizabeth 1939- ... 45-48
Schaeffer, Francis A(ugust) 1912-1984 ... 77-80
Obituary ... 112
Schaeffer, Frank 1952- ... 140
Schaeffer, K(laus) H(eymann) 1921- ... 61-64
Schaeffer, Mark 1956- ... 140
Schaeffer, Mead 1898- ... SATA 21
Schaeffer, Neil 1940- ... CANR-91
Earlier sketch in CA 107
Schaeffer, Norma 1924-1985 ... 119
Schaeffer, Susan Fromberg 1941- ... CANR-65
Earlier sketches in CA 49-52, CANR-18
See also CLC 6, 11, 22
See also CN 4, 5, 6, 7
See also DLB 28, 299
See also MTCW 1, 2
See also MTFW 2005
See also SATA 22
Schaeffer-Forrer, Claude F. A.
See Schaeffer, Claude Frederic Armand
Schaeling, Marianne
See Amft, M(arian) J(anet)
Schaeper, Kathleen ... 235
Schaeper, Thomas J(erome) 1948- ... 109
Schaer, Brigitte 1958- ... 184
See also SATA 112
Schaeren, Beatrix 1941- ... 29-32R
Schaerf, Carlo 1935- ... 133
Schaetzel, J(oseph) Robert 1917-2003 ... 65-68
Obituary ... 221
Schaetzel, Wendy 1950- ... 136
Schafer, Charles (Louis) 1916- ... 61-64
Schafer, Edward Hetzel 1913-1991 .. CANR-77
Earlier sketches in CA 1-4R, CANR-1, 74
Schafer, Elisabeth 1945- ... 166
Schafer, Grant C. 1926- ... 21-24R
Schafer, R(aymond) Murray 1933- ... 77-80
Schafer, Robert 1942- ... 108
Schafer, Stephen 1911-1976 ... 37-40R
Schafer, Violet (Christine) 1910-2001 ... 61-64
Schafer, William J. 1937- ... 49-52
Schaff, Adam 1913- ... CANR-12
Earlier sketch in CA 25-28R
Schaff, David 1943- ... 33-36R
Schaff, Philip 1819-1893 ... DLBD 13
Schaffer, (Benjamin) Bernard 1925-1984
Obituary ... 113
Schaffer, Daniel 1950- ... 114
Schaffer, Dylan 1964(?)- ... 238
Schaffer, Frank 1910- ... 103
Schaffer, Jeff(rey P.) 1943- ... CANR-22
Earlier sketch in CA 105
Schaffer, Kay 1945- ... 185
Schaffer, Lewis A(dam) 1934- ... 101
Schaffer, Marion 1931- ... 111
Schaffer, Talia C. 1968- ... 190
Schaffer, Ulrich 1942- ... CANR-31
Earlier sketch in CA 69-72
Schaffner, Bradley L(ewis) 1959- ... 152
Schaffner, Cynthia V. A. 1947- ... 121
Schaffner, Ingrid 1961(?)- ... 218
Schaffner, Kenneth 1939- ... 45-48
Schaffner, Nicholas 1953-1991 ... CANR-15
Obituary ... 135
Earlier sketch in CA 85-88
Schaffner, Val(entine) 1951- ... 107
Schaflander, Gerald M(aurice) 1920- ... 37-40R
Schagrin, Morton L(ouis) 1930- ... 25-28R
Schaie, K(laus) Warner 1928- ... CANR-86
Earlier sketches in CA 41-44R, CANR-15, 34
Schain, Richard J. 1930- ... 225
Schakne, Robert 1926-1989 ... 65-68
Obituary ... 129
Schakovskoy, Zinaida 1908-2001 ... CANR-74
Earlier sketches in CA 17-20R, CANR-8
Schaldenbrand, Mary 1922- ... 49-52
Schaleben, Arville Orman 1907- ... CANR-1
Earlier sketch in CA 1-4R
Schalit, Joel 1967- ... 214
Schalk, Adolph F(rancis) 1923- ... 33-36R
Schalk, David L(ouis) 1936- ... 89-92
Schall, James V(incent) 1928- ... CANR-116
Earlier sketches in CA 9-12R, CANR-6, 20, 42
Schall, Lucy 1946- ... 204
Schaller, George B(eals) 1933- ... CANR-9
Earlier sketch in CA 5-8R
See also SATA 30
Schaller, Lyle E(dwin) 1923- ... 131
Schaller, Michael 1947- ... 126
Brief entry ... 110
Schaller, Susan 1957(?)- ... 145
Schalluck, Paul 1922-1976 ... EWL 3
Schally, Andrew V(ictor) 1926- ... 156
Schalm, Bernard 1928-1974 ... 1-4R
Obituary ... 103
Scham, Alan (Myron) 1937- ... 29-32R
Schama, Simon (Michael) 1945- ... CANR-91
Earlier sketches in CA 105, CANR-39
See also BEST 89:4
See also CLC 150
Schami, Rafik 1946- ... 194
Schamus, James 1959- ... IDFW 4
Schanberg, Sydney H(illel) 1934- ... 69-72

Cumulative Index 513 **Schiller**

Schanche, Don(ald) A(rthur)
1926-1994 .... CANR-86
Obituary 147
Earlier sketches in CA 5-8R, CANR-6
Schandler, Herbert Y(ale) 1928- 69-72
Schang, Frederick C., (Jr.)
1893-1990 .... CANR-13
Obituary 182
Earlier sketch in CA 33-36R
Schank, Roger C(arl) 1946- CANR-96
Earlier sketch in CA 132
Schanke, Robert A(nders) 1940- 141
Schanker, D(avid) R. 200
Schanz, John P(hilip) 1924- 107
Schanzer, George O(swald) 1914- 41-44R
Schanzer, Ros
See Schanzer, Rosalyn (Good)
Schanzer, Rosalyn (Good) 1942- 209
See also SATA 77, 138
Schanzer, Roz
See Schanzer, Rosalyn (Good)
Schaper, Edzard (Hellmuth) 1908-1984 195
See also DLB 69
Schapiro, Amy 1970- 224
Schapiro, Barbara 1952- 145
Schapiro, J(acob) Salwyn 1879-1973 .. CANR-5
Obituary 45-48
Earlier sketch in CA 5-8R
Schapiro, Leonard (Bertram)
1908-1983 .... CANR-13
Obituary 111
Earlier sketch in CA 65-68
Schapiro, Meyer 1904-1996 .... CANR-104
Obituary 151
Earlier sketch in CA 97-100
Schappell, Elissa 218
Schapper, Beatrice Aronson 1906-1974 .. 9-12R
Obituary 45-48
Schappes, Morris U(rman) 1907-2004 49-52
Obituary 228
Schapsmeier, Edward L(ewis)
1927- CANR-101
Earlier sketch in CA 29-32R
Schapsmeier, Frederick H(erman)
1927- 29-32R
Schara, Ron 1942- 69-72
Scharbach, (John) Alexander 1909-1991 114
Scharbach, J. Alexander
See Scharbach, (John) Alexander
Scharf, Bertram 1931- 53-56
Scharf, J. Thomas 1843-1898 .... DLB 47
Scharf, Michael P(aul) 1963- 171
Scharfenberg, Doris 1925- 108
Scharff, Edward E. 1946- 123
Scharfstein, Ben-Ami 1919- CANR-79
Earlier sketch in CA 101
Scharfstein, Zevi 1884-1972
Obituary 37-40R
Scharine, Richard G. 1938- 123
Brief entry 118
Scharlatt, Hal 1936(?)-1974
Obituary 104
Scharlemann, Dorothy Hoyer 1912- 65-68
Scharlemann, Martin H(enry)
1910-1982 .... 13-16R
Scharlemann, Robert Paul 1929- 9-12R
Scharnhorst, Gary (Francis) 1950- .. CANR-109
Earlier sketch in CA 119
Scharper, (C.) Diane 1942- 191
Scharper, Phillip (Jenkins)
1919-1985 .... CANR-79
Obituary 116
Earlier sketch in CA 73-76
Scharrer, Berta (Vogel) 1906-1995 158
Schary, Dore 1905-1980 .... CANR-1
Obituary 101
Earlier sketch in CA 1-4R
See also DFS 17
See also IDFW 3, 4
Schary, Jill
See Robinson, Jill
Schatell, Brian 124
See also SATA 66
See also SATA-Brief 47
Schatkin, Margaret 1944- 118
Schatkin, Sidney B. 1903-1997 .... 25-28R
Schatt, Stanley 1943- CANR-26
Earlier sketch in CA 69-72
Schatten, Fritz (Max Robert) 1930- 13-16R
Schatten, Robert 1911-1977
Obituary 73-76
Schatz, Mark N(orton) 1929- 113
Schatz, Ronald W. 1949- 125
Schatz, Sayre P(erry) 1922- 41-44R
Schatzki, Walter 1899- .... SATA-Brief 31
Schatzkin, Paul 225
Schau, Michael 1945- 85-88
Schaub, Marilyn McNamara 1928- 17-20R
Schaub, Mary H(unter) 1943- 140
Schaub, Thomas Hill 1947- 105
Schauensee, Rodolphe Meyer de
See De Schauensee, Rodolphe Meyer
Schauer, Frederick Franklin 1946- CANR-42
Earlier sketch in CA 112
Schauf, George Edward 1925- 41-44R
Schaufele, William E., Jr. 1923- 111
Schawlow, Arthur L(eonard) 1921-1999 157
Obituary 179
Scheader, Catherine 1932- 85-88
Schealer, John M(ilton) 1920- CANR-74
Earlier sketch in CA 5-8R
Schechner, Richard 1934- CANR-17
Earlier sketches in CA 45-48, CANR-1
Schechter, A(bel) A(lan) 1907-1989
Obituary 128
Schechter, Alan H(enry) 1936- 9-12R
Schechter, Betty (Goodstein) 1921- .. CANR-74
Earlier sketch in CA 5-8R
See also SATA 5
Schechter, Bruce 206
Schechter, Harold 1948- CANR-101
Earlier sketch in CA 108
Schechter, Joel 1947- 222
Schechter, Ruth Lisa 1927-1989 .... CANR-49
Earlier sketch in CA 33-36R
Schechter, William 1934- 21-24R
Schechtman, Joseph B. 1891-1970 ..... CANR-3
Earlier sketch in CA 1-4R
Scheck, Barry C. 1949- 192
Schecter, Barnet 227
Schecter, Darrow 1961- 143
Schecter, Ellen 1944- .... SATA 85
Schecter, Jerrold L. 1932- CANR-49
Earlier sketch in CA 21-24R
Schede, Paul Melissus 1539-1602 ...... DLB 179
Scheeder, Louis 1946- 212
See also SATA 141
Scheel, J(oergen) D(itlev) 1918- 9-12R
Scheele, Adele M. 1938- CANR-18
Earlier sketch in CA 97-100
Scheele, Carl H(arry) 1928- 85-88
Scheer, George F(abian) 1917-1996 . CANR-74
Obituary 151
Earlier sketch in CA 13-16R
Scheer, Julian (Weisel) 1926-2001 49-52
Obituary 202
See also SATA 8
Scheer, Robert 1936- 106
Scheer, Wilbert E. 1909- CANR-17
Earlier sketch in CA 25-28R
Scheese, Don 1954- 225
Scheff, Thomas Joel 1929- 105
Scheffel, Joseph Viktor von
1826-1886 .... DLB 129
Scheffer, Kathy J(ean) 1955- 169
Scheffer, Nathalie P. 1890(?)-1981
Obituary 105
Scheffer, Victor B(lanchard) 1906- CANR-11
Earlier sketch in CA 29-32R
See also SATA 6
Scheffler, Harold W(alter) 1932- 17-20R
Scheffler, Israel 1923- CANR-1
Earlier sketch in CA 1-4R
Scheffler, Johann 1624-1677 .... DLB 164
Scheffler, Ursel 1938- 149
See also SATA 81
Scheffrin-Falk, Gladys 1928- .... SATA 76
Scheflen, Albert E. 1920-1980 .... CANR-3
Obituary 101
Earlier sketch in CA 45-48
Scheft, Bill 1957- 216
Schefter, Jim 1940- 89-92
Schehade, Georges 1905-1989 .... DLB 321
Scheibe, Karl E(dward) 1937- CANR-105
Earlier sketches in CA 29-32R, CANR-11
Scheiber, Bela 1949- 200
Scheiber, Harry N(oel) 1935- CANR-1
Earlier sketch in CA 1-4R
Scheiber, Jane L(ang) 1937- 93-96
Scheiberg, Susan L. 1962- 233
Scheibla, Shirley 1919-2000 .... 41-44R
Scheick, William J(oseph) 1941- CANR-97
Earlier sketches in CA 49-52, CANR-1, 17, 38
Scheid, Francis J(ames) 1920- 17-20R
Scheidl, Gerda Marie 1913- 152
See also SATA 85
Scheidler, Joseph M. 1927- 122
Scheier, Ivan Henry 1926- CANR-7
Earlier sketch in CA 5-8R
Scheier, Libby 1946- 136
Scheier, Michael 1943- CANR-36
Earlier sketch in CA 115
See also SATA 40
See also SATA-Brief 36
Scheimann, Eugene 1897-1993 .... 33-36R
Obituary 140
Schein, Clarence J(acob) 1918- 65-68
Schein, James Arns 1920(?)-1983
Obituary 110
Schein, Jerome D(aniel) 1923- 118
Schein, Lorraine 1953- 149
Schein, Muriel
See Dimen, Muriel
Scheindlin, Raymond P(aul) 1940- ... CANR-94
Earlier sketch in CA 146
Scheiner, Seth M(ordecai) 1933- 17-20R
Scheinfeld, Aaron 1899-1970 .... CAP-2
Earlier sketch in CA 29-32
Scheinfeld, Amram 1897-1979 .... 17-20R
Obituary 89-92
Scheingold, Stuart A(llen) 1931- 53-56
Scheleen, Joseph C(arl) 1904-1985
Obituary 116
Scheler, Max G. 1928- 206
Schell, Bunny
See Schell, Rolfe F(inch)
Schell, Edgar T(homas) 1931- 45-48
Schell, Herbert S(amuel)
1899-1994 .... CANR-21
Earlier sketch in CA 1-4R
Schell, Jim 1936- 142
Schell, Jonathan 1943- CANR-117
Earlier sketches in CA 73-76, CANR-12
See also CLC 35
Schell, Maximilian 1930- 172
Brief entry 116
Schell, Mildred 1922- 113
See also SATA 41
Schell, Orville (Hickok) 1940- CANR-95
Earlier sketch in CA 25-28R
See also SATA 10
Schell, Rolfe F(inch) 1916- CANR-7
Earlier sketch in CA 57-60
Schellenberg, Helene Chambers 13-16R
Schellenberg, James A. 1932- 37-40R
Schellenberg, Theodore R.
1903-1970(?) CAP-1
Earlier sketch in CA 17-18
Schelle-Noetzel, A. H.
See Bronnen, Arnolt
Scheller, Melanie 1953- .... SATA 77
Schellie, Don 1932- 101
See also SATA 29
Schelling, Andrew 1953- CANR-118
Earlier sketch in CA 158
Schelling, Friedrich Wilhelm Joseph von
1775-1854 .... DLB 90
Schelling, Thomas Crombie 1921- ... CANR-49
Earlier sketch in CA 1-4R
Schelly, William 1951- 114
Schembechler, Bo 1929- 139
Schembri, Jim 1962- .... SATA 124
Schemering, (Crien) Christopher 1956- 123
Schemm, Mildred Walker
1905-1998 .... CANR-1
Obituary 169
Earlier sketch in CA 1-4R
See also Walker, Mildred
See also SATA 21
See also SATA-Obit 103
Schemmer, Benjamin F(ranklin)
1932-2003 .... CANR-144
Obituary 221
Earlier sketch in CA 61-64
Schemmer, Kenneth E(dwin) 1936- 110
Schenck, Anita A(llen) 1909-1982 89-92
Schenck, Hilbert (van Nydeck) 1926- 166
See also SFW 4
Schenck, Janet Daniels 1883(?)-1976
Obituary 69-72
Schenck, Joseph 1878-1961 .... IDFW 3, 4
Schenck, Nicholas 1881-1969 .... IDFW 3, 4
Schendel, Dan 1934- 148
Schendler, Sylvan 1925- 25-28R
Schenk, George (Walden) 1929- 139
Schenk, H(ans) G(eorg) 1912- 21-24R
Schenkar, Joan 1946- CANR-82
Earlier sketch in CA 133
See also CAD
See also CD 5, 6
See also CWD
Schenken, Howard 1904(?)-1979 93-96
Obituary 85-88
Schenken, Suzanne O'Dea 1950- 199
Schenker, Alexander M(arian) 1924- 33-36R
Schenker, Dona 1947- CANR-112
Earlier sketch in CA 135
See also SATA 68, 133
Schenker, Eric 1931- 37-40R
Schenkkan, Robert (Frederic), (Jr.)
1953- CANR-124
Earlier sketch in CA 132
See also DFS 10
Scheper, Nancy
See Scheper-Hughes, Nancy
Scheper-Hughes, Nancy 1944- 89-92
Schepers, Maurice B. 1928- 13-16R
Scheponik, P(eter) C. 1952- 187
Scheps, Clarence 1915- 33-36R
Scher, Helene L(enz) 1935- 123
Brief entry 118
Scher, Les 1946- 101
Scher, Paula 1948- 115
See also SATA 47
Scher, Steven Paul 1936- CANR-3
Earlier sketch in CA 49-52
Schere, Monroe 1913-1996 85-88
Scherer, F(rederic) M(ichael) 1932- ... CANR-12
Earlier sketch in CA 29-32R
Scherer, Frances Schlosser 1912- 69-72
Scherer, Jack F(ranklin) 1939- 69-72
Scherer, Jacqueline Rita 1931- 53-56
Scherer, Jean-Marie Maurice 1920- 110
See also Rohmer, Eric
Scherer, Joanna Cohan 1942- 107
Scherer, Klaus R(ainer) 1943- 101
Scherer, Lester B(uryl) 1931- 132
Scherer, Migael 1947- 144
Scherer, Paul (Ehrman) 1892-1969 .... 5-8R
Obituary 134
Scherer, Priscilla 1948- 119
Scherer, Ray(mond Lewis) 1919-2000 104
Obituary 189
Scherer, Wilhelm 1841-1886 .... DLB 129
Scherer, William F(rederick) 1939- 41-44R
Scherf, Kathleen D. 1960- 142
Scherf, Margaret 1908-1979 .... CANR-62
Earlier sketches in CA 5-8R, CANR-6
See also CMW 4
See also SATA 10
Scherfig, Hans 1905-1979 .... DLB 214
Scherle, Victor 1935- 25-28R
Scherman, Bernadine Kielty 1890(?)-1973
Obituary 45-48
Scherman, David E(dward) 1916-1997 102
Obituary 158
Scherman, Katharine 1915- CANR-27
Earlier sketches in CA 5-8R, CANR-11
Scherman, Thomas K(ielty) 1917-1979
Obituary 106
Schermbrucker, Bill
See Schermbrucker, William (Gerald)
Schermbrucker, William (Gerald) 1938- 155
Schermer, Judith (Denise) 1941- 106
See also SATA 30
Schermerhorn, Richard A(lonzo)
1903-1991 .... 37-40R
Scherr, George Harry 1920- 114
Scherr, Max 1916(?)-1981
Obituary 105
Schertenleib, Charles 1905-1972
Obituary 37-40R
Schertle, Alice 1941- CANR-128
Earlier sketches in CA 107, CANR-23, 59
See also SATA 36, 90, 145
Scherzer, Carl John 1901-1966 .... 1-4R
Schetzen, Martin 1928- 236
Scheub, Harold 1931- 61-64
Scheuer, Joseph F(rancis) 1918-1975
Obituary 61-64
Scheuer, Philip K(atz) 1902-1985
Obituary 115
Scheuerle, William H(oward) 1930- 33-36R
Scheuerman, Richard D(ean) 1951- . CANR-27
Earlier sketch in CA 57-60
Scheuring, Lyn 1937- 73-76
Scheuring, Tom 1942- 73-76
Schevill, James (Erwin) 1920- 5-8R
See also CAAS 12
See also CAD
See also CD 5, 6
See also CLC 7
See also CP 1, 2
Schevill, Maqrgot Blum 1931- 150
Schevitz, Jeffrey M(orrie) 1941- 65-68
Scheyer, Ernst 1900-1985 .... 13-16R
Schiaparelli, Elsa 1890-1973
Obituary 113
Schiappa, Barbara D(ublin) 1943- 109
Schiappa, (Anthony) Edward (Jr.) 1954- 141
Schiavone, Giuseppe 1938- 146
Schiavone, James 1933- CANR-9
Earlier sketch in CA 5-8R
Schick, Alice 1946- CANR-15
Earlier sketch in CA 81-84
See also SATA 27
Schick, Eleanor 1942- CANR-125
Earlier sketches in CA 49-52, CANR-4, 19, 41
See also SATA 9, 82, 144
Schick, Frank L(eopold) 1918-1992 132
Schick, George B(aldwin Powell)
1903-1990 .... 41-44R
Schick, Joel 1945- 107
See also SATA 31
See also SATA-Brief 30
Schick, Lawrence 1955- 139
Schick, Renee 1919- 149
Schickel, Julia Whedon 1936- 49-52
Schickel, Richard (Warren) 1933- CANR-91
Earlier sketches in CA 1-4R, CANR-1, 34
See also AITN 1
Schickele, Peter 1935- 85-88
Schickele, Rene 1883-1940 217
See also DLB 66
Schickler, David 208
Schiddel, Edmund 1909-1982 .... CANR-86
Obituary 107
Earlier sketch in CA 5-8R
Schieber, Phyllis 1953- 180
Schiebinger, Londa (L.) 1952- 187
Schiefelbein, Michael E. 1958(?)- 224
Schiefelbusch, Richard L. 1918- CANR-11
Earlier sketch in CA 25-28R
Schieffer, Bob 1937- 69-72
Schields, Gretchen 1948- .... SATA 75
Schier, Donald (Stephen) 1914- 29-32R
Schier, Ernest L. 1918- 77-80
Schier, Flint 1954(?)-1988
Obituary 126
Schiff, Dorothy 1903-1989 121
Obituary 129
Brief entry 114
Interview in CA-121
See also DLB 127
Schiff, Harold (Irvin) 1923- 89-92
Schiff, Irwin A(llan) 1928- CANR-25
Earlier sketch in CA 65-68
Schiff, Isaac 1944- 153
Schiff, Jacqui Lee 1934- 37-40R
Schiff, James A(ndrew) 1958- CANR-93
Earlier sketch in CA 143
Schiff, Ken(neth Roy) 1942- 49-52
See also SATA 7
Schiff, Lewis J. 1969- 229
Schiff, Michael 1915- 13-16R
Schiff, Stacy 206
Schiff, Sydney (Alfred) 1868(?)-1944 203
See also Hudson, Stephen
Schiff, Ze'ev 1932- 144
Schiffer, Irvine 1917-
Brief entry 114
Schiffer, James (M.) 1948- 202
Schiffer, Michael 1948- 106
Schiffer, Michael B(rian) 1947- CANR-52
Earlier sketches in CA 110, CANR-27
Schifferes, Justus J(ulius) 1907-1997 ... CANR-5
Obituary 156
Earlier sketch in CA 5-8R
Schiffhorst, Gerald J. 1940- CANR-38
Earlier sketch in CA 17-20R
Schiffman, Jack 1921- 49-52
Schiffman, Joseph Harris 1914-1999 .... 17-20R
Schiffman, Stephan 218
Schiffrin, Andre 1935- 197
Schiffrin, Harold Z. 1922- 29-32R
Schifrin, Lalo 1932- .... IDFW 3, 4
Schildgen, Brenda Deen 1942- 209
Schiler, Marc (Eugene) 1951- 106
Schillaci, Anthony
See Schillaci, Peter Paul
Schillaci, Peter Paul 1929- 29-32R
Schillebeeckx, Edward (Cornelis Florentius
Alfons) 1914- 127
Brief entry 111
Schiller, A. Arthur 1902-1977 .... CANR-20
Obituary 73-76
Earlier sketch in CA 37-40R

Schiller, Andrew 1919- 41-44R
See also SATA 21
Schiller, Barbara (Heyman) 1928- 17-20R
See also SATA 21
Schiller, Bob
See Schiller, Robert Achille
Schiller, Bradley R(obert) 1943- 57-60
Schiller, Craig 1951- 81-84
Schiller, Dan(iel T.) 1951- 131
Schiller, Dorothea E. 1898(?)-1987
Obituary 123
Schiller, Friedrich von 1759-1805 .... CDWLB 2
See also DAM DRAM
See also DC 12
See also DLB 94
See also EW 5
See also RGWL 2, 3
See also TWA
Schiller, Greta 1954- CANR-118
Earlier sketch in CA 158
Schiller, Herbert I(rving) 1919-2000 ...... 29-32R
Obituary 188
Schiller, Jerome P(aul) 1934- 25-28R
Schiller, JoAnn 1949- 140
Schiller, Justin G. 1943-
Brief entry 110
See also SATA-Brief 31
Schiller, Lawrence (Julian) 1936- CANR-121
Earlier sketch in CA 163
Schiller, Lee Virginia Chambers
See Chambers-Schiller, Lee Virginia
Schiller, Mayer
See Schiller, Craig
Schiller, Pamela (Byrne) 197
See also SATA 127
Schiller, Robert Achille 1918- 123
Brief entry 118
Interview in CA-123
Schiller, Rose Leiman
See Goldemberg, Rose Leiman
Schilling, Betty 1925- 106
Schilling, Heinz 1942- 191
Schilling, Mark R. 1949- 176
Schilling, S. Paul 1904-1994 .... CANR-16
Earlier sketches in CA 1-4R, CANR-1
Schilling, Warner R(oller) 1925-
Brief entry 112
Schilpp, Madelon Golden 117
Schilpp, Paul A(rthur) 1897-1993 ..... CANR-88
Obituary 142
Earlier sketches in CA 1-4R, CANR-4, 19
Schilz, Thomas F. 1950- 125
Schimel, John L(ouis) 1916- 25-28R
Schimel, Lawrence 1971- 180
Schimmel, Annemarie (Brigitte)
1922-2003 132
Obituary 212
Brief entry 120
Schimmel, Betty 1929(?)- 209
Schimmel, Herbert D(avid) 1927- 117
Schimmel, Solomon 1941- CANR-135
Earlier sketch in CA 139
Schimmels, Cliff 1937- 115
Schimpf, Ann L.
See Linnea, Ann
Schimpff, Jill Wagner 1945- 135
Schinagl, Mary S(onora) 1914- 17-20R
Schindel, John 1955- 187
See also SATA 77, 115
Schindel, Robert 1944-
Schindeler, Fred(erick) Fernand 1934- ... 41-44R
Schindelman, Joseph 1923- .... SATA 67
See also SATA-Brief 32
Schindler, Emilie 1907-2001 206
Schindler, Marvin Samuel 1932-
Brief entry 106
Schindler, S(teven) D. 1952- .... SATA 75, 118
See also SATA-Brief 50
Schine, Cathleen 1953- 149
Schinhan, Jan Philip 1887-1975 .... CAP-2
Obituary 61-64
Earlier sketch in CA 23-24
Schinto, Jeanne 1951- CANR-69
Earlier sketch in CA 133
See also SATA 93
Schioetz, Aksel 1906-1975
Obituary 111
Schiotz, Aksel
See Schioetz, Aksel
Schipf, Robert G(eorge) 1923- 61-64
Schipper, Mineke
See Schipper, W(ilhelmina) J(anneke) J(osepha)
Schipper, W(ilhelmina) J(anneke) J(osepha)
1938- CANR-143
Earlier sketch in CA 156
Schippers, K.
See Stigter, Gerard
Schirmer, Daniel B(oone) 1915- 41-44R
Schirmer, David 1623-1687 .... DLB 164
Schirmer, Gregory A(lan) 1944- 117
Schirmer, Henry W. 1922- 107
Schirmer, Jennifer G(ay) 1947- 113
Schirmerhorn, Clint
See Riemer, George
Schirokauer, Conrad M(ax) 1929- 107
Schisgal, Murray (Joseph) 1926- CANR-86
Earlier sketches in CA 21-24R, CANR-48
See also CAD
See also CD 5, 6
See also CLC 6
See also MAL 5
Schisgall, Oscar 1901-1984 .... CANR-88
Obituary 112
Earlier sketches in CA 53-56, CANR-9
See also SATA 12
See also SATA-Obit 38
Schissler, Hanna 1946- 209
Schivelbusch, Wolfgang 1941- CANR-101
Earlier sketches in CA 105, CANR-45
Schjeldahl, Peter 1942-
Brief entry 113
See also CP 1
Schkade, Lawrence L. 1930- CANR-7
Earlier sketch in CA 17-20R
Schlabach, Theron F(rederick) 1933- 25-28R
Schlabrendorff, Fabian von
See von Schlabrendorff, Fabian
Schlachter, Gail Ann 1943- CANR-60
Earlier sketches in CA 77-80, CANR-14, 31
Schlachter, Susan
See Thaler, Susan
Schlaepfer, Gloria G. 1931- 229
See also SATA 154
Schlaf, Johannes 1862-1941 .... DLB 118
Schlafly, Phyllis 1924- CANR-52
Earlier sketches in CA 25-28R, CANR-26
See also AITN 1
See also MTCW 1
Schlain, Bert H(oward) 1898-1986 .... 17-20R
Schlamm, William S(iegmund)
1904-1978 93-96
Obituary 81-84
Schlanger, Henry 1918(?)-1984
Obituary 113
Schlant, Ernestine 1935- 81-84
Schlapbach-Oberhansli, Trudi 1944- 21-24R
Schlatter, Richard 1912-1987 .... 21-24R
Obituary 123
Schlauch, Margaret 1898-1986 .... CAP-1
Obituary 119
Earlier sketch in CA 13-14
Schlayer, Mary Elizabeth 1915-1987 129
Schlebecker, John T(homas) 1923- 9-12R
Schleck, Charles A. 1925- CANR-6
Earlier sketch in CA 5-8R
Schlee, Ann 1934- CANR-88
Earlier sketches in CA 101, CANR-29
See also CLC 35
See also SATA 44
See also SATA-Brief 36
Schlee, Guenther 1951- 135
Schlee, Gunther
See Schlee, Guenther
Schlee, Susan 93-96
See also Baur, Susan (Whiting)
Schleef, Einar 1944-2001 206
Schlegel, August Wilhelm von
1767-1845 .... DLB 94
See also RGWL 2, 3
Schlegel, Dorothea 1763-1839 .... DLB 90
Schlegel, Dorothy (Mildred) B(adders)
1910-1998 .... 37-40R
Schlegel, Friedrich 1772-1829 .... DLB 90
See also EW 5
See also RGWL 2, 3
See also TWA
Schlegel, John Henry 1942- 154
Schlegel, Richard 1913-1982 65-68
Schlegel, Stuart A(llen) 1932- 61-64
Schlegelmann, V. E.
See Hartz, Fred R.
Schleh, Eugene 1939- 137
Schleicher, Charles P. 1907- 9-12R
Schleichert, Elizabeth 1945- 145
See also SATA 77
Schleier, Curt 1944- 89-92
Schleier, Gertrude 1933- 1-4R
Schleiermacher, Friedrich 1768-1834 ... DLB 90
Schleifer, James T(homas) 1942- 97-100
Schleifer, Ronald 1948- CANR-43
Earlier sketch in CA 118
Schlein, Miriam 1926-2004 .... CANR-87
Obituary 233
Earlier sketches in CA 1-4R, CANR-2, 52
See also CLR 41
See also CWRI 5
See also MAICYA 2
See also SATA 2, 87, 130
See also SATA-Obit 159
Schleiner, Winfried 1938- 29-32R
Schlem
See Prevost, Marcel
Schlender, William E(lmer) 1920- CANR-14
Earlier sketch in CA 17-20R
Schlenker, Elizabeth D. (Wallace)
1912- 17-20R
Schlenther, Boyd (Stanley) 1936- 41-44R
Schlepp, Wayne Allen 1931- 29-32R
Schlereth, Howard (Hewitt) 1936- 57-60
Schlereth, Thomas J(ohn) 1941- 97-100
Schlesier, Karl H. 234
Schlesinger, Alfred Cary 1900-1993 ...... CAP-1
Earlier sketch in CA 13-14
Schlesinger, Allen B(rian) 1924- 149
Schlesinger, Arthur M(eier), Jr.
1917- CANR-105
Earlier sketches in CA 1-4R, CANR-1, 28, 58
Interview in CANR-28
See also AITN 1
See also CLC 84
See also DLB 17
See also MTCW 1, 2
See also SATA 61
Schlesinger, Arthur Meier 1888-1965 . CANR-5
Obituary 25-28R
Earlier sketch in CA 5-8R
Schlesinger, Benjamin 1928- CANR-46
Earlier sketches in CA 17-20R, CANR-7, 22
Schlesinger, Bruno Walter 1876-1962 116
Obituary 111
Schlesinger, Elizabeth Bancroft 1886-1977
Obituary 69-72
Schlesinger, Hilde S(tephanie) CANR-6
Earlier sketch in CA 53-56
Schlesinger, Joseph A(braham) 1922- 61-64
Schlesinger, Lawrence E(rwin) 1921- 41-44R
Schlesinger, Leon 1884-1949 .... IDFW 3, 4
Schlesinger, Leonard A. 1952- 126
Schlesinger, Marian Cannon 1912- 89-92
Schlesinger, Roger 1943- 126
Schlesinger, Stephen C(annon)
1942- CANR-28
Earlier sketch in CA 57-60
Schlesinger, Thomas O(tto) 1925- 41-44R
Schlessinger, Laura (Catherine)
1947- CANR-112
Earlier sketch in CA 152
See also SATA 110, 160
Schlessinger, Philip J. 1914- 5-8R
Schleunes, Karl A(lbert) 1937- 29-32R
Schley, Jim 1956- 118
Schlichting, Harold E(ugene, Jr.) 1926- 112
Schlicke, Priscilla 1945- 146
Schlimbach, Alice (Paula) 1898-1992 ... CAP-1
Earlier sketch in CA 13-16
Schlink, Basilea
See Schlink, Klara
Schlink, Bernhard 1944- CANR-116
Earlier sketch in CA 163
See also CLC 174
Schlink, Frederick John 1891-1995 65-68
Obituary 147
Schlink, Klara 1904-2001 .... CANR-49
Earlier sketch in CA 101
Schlink, M. Basilea
See Schlink, Klara
Schlink, Mother Basilea
See Schlink, Klara
Schlissel, Lillian 1930- CANR-53
Earlier sketches in CA 25-28R, CANR-13, 29
Schlitzer, Albert Lawrence 1902-1985 ...... 1-4R
Schloat, G. Warren, Jr. 1914-2000 .... 21-24R
Obituary 189
See also SATA 4
Schlobin, Roger Clark 1944- CANR-18
Earlier sketch in CA 102
Schlosberg, H. J.
See May, H(enry) J(ohn)
Schlosberg, Suzanne 1971(?)- 232
Schloss, Arthur David
See Waley, Arthur (David)
Schlossberg, Dan 1948- CANR-19
Earlier sketch in CA 101
Schlossberg, Edwin (Arthur) 1945-
Brief entry 112
Schlossberg, Herbert 1935- 111
Schlosser, Eric 1960(?)- 229
See also AAYA 60
Schlossman, Beryl 1955- 124
Schlossman, Steven L(awrence)
1947- CANR-16
Earlier sketch in CA 81-84
Schlossstein, Steven 1941- 122
Schlueter, June 1942- CANR-32
Earlier sketch in CA 101
Schlueter, Paul (George) 1933- CANR-32
Earlier sketches in CA 13-16R, CANR-11
Schlumberger, Daniel 1904-1972
Obituary 37-40R
Schlumberger, Jean 1877-1968 155
Obituary 116
See also DLB 65
Schmacher, Evelyn A(nn) 1919- 130
Schmalenbach, Werner 1920- CANR-53
Earlier sketches in CA 73-76, CANR-13, 29
Schmalz, Rosemary 1940- 148
Schmandt, Henry J. 1918- CANR-9
Earlier sketch in CA 5-8R
Schmandt, Jurgen 1929- 144
Schmandt, Raymond H(enry, Jr.)
1925-2005 .... 9-12R
Obituary 236
Schmandt-Besserat, Denise 1933- CANR-42
Earlier sketches in CA 69-72, CANR-20
Schmeck, Harold M(arshall), Jr. 1923- ... 17-20R
Schmeidler, Gertrude Raffel 1912- 37-40R
Schmeiser, Douglas Albert 1934- CANR-3
Earlier sketch in CA 9-12R
Schmeling, Gareth L(on) 1940- 73-76
Schmeling, Marianne 1930- 101
Schmeltz, Susan Alton 111
Schmeltz, Susan M.
See Schmeltz, Susan Alton
Schmeltz, William Frederick 1924- 41-44R
Schmemann, Alexander 1921-1983 117
Obituary 111
Schmemann, Serge 1945- 136
Schmertz, Herb(ert) 1930- 120
Schmid, A. Allan 1935- 37-40R
Schmid, Carlo 1896-1979
Obituary 97-100
Schmid, Carol L(ouise) 1946- 105
Schmid, Claus-Peter 1942- 61-64
Schmid, Ed
See Schmid, Eduard
Schmid, Eduard 1890-1966
Obituary 113
See also Edschmid, Kasimir
Schmid, Eleonore 1939- CANR-106
Earlier sketches in CA 53-56, CANR-5, 21
See also SATA 12, 84, 126
Schmid, John 1926- 133
Schmid, Mark J(oseph) 1901-1971(?) CAP-1
Earlier sketch in CA 13-14
Schmid, W. George
See Schmid, Wolfram George
Schmid, Walter T(homas) 1946- 145
Schmid, Wolfram George 1930- CANR-127
Earlier sketch in CA 143
Schmiderer, Dorothy 1940- 85-88
See also SATA 19
Schmidgall, Gary 1945- 77-80
Schmidhauser, John R(ichard) 1922- ... CANR-1
Earlier sketch in CA 45-48
Schmidt, Albert J(ohn) 1925- 37-40R
Schmidt, Alice M(ahany) 1925- 65-68
Schmidt, Alvin J(ohn) 1932- CANR-1
Earlier sketch in CA 45-48
Schmidt, Annie M. G. 1911-1995 135
Obituary 152
See also CLR 22
See also SATA 67
See also SATA-Obit 91
Schmidt, Arno (Otto) 1914-1979 128
Obituary 109
See also CLC 56
See also DLB 69
See also EWL 3
Schmidt, Arthur 1943- 158
Schmidt, Charles T., Jr. 1934- 25-28R
Schmidt, Claire Harman 1957- 109
Schmidt, Dana Adams 1915- 9-12R
Schmidt, Diane 1953- .... SATA 70
Schmidt, Dolores Barracano 1931- 41-44R
Schmidt, Dorothea
See Wender, Dorothea
Schmidt, Elizabeth 1915- .... SATA 15
Schmidt, Emerson Peter 1899-1976
Obituary 111
Schmidt, Fred H(artz) 1918- 85-88
Schmidt, Frederick G. 1924- 49-52
Schmidt, Gary D. 1957- CANR-113
Earlier sketch in CA 158
See also SATA 93, 135
Schmidt, George P. 1894(?)-1989
Obituary 130
Schmidt, Hans 1938- 61-64
Schmidt, Helmut Dan 1915- 9-12R
Schmidt, Hubert (Glasgow) 1905-1980
Obituary 112
Schmidt, J(akob) E(dward) 1906-2000 ... 13-16R
Schmidt, James Norman 1912-1983 . CANR-88
Earlier sketches in CA 1-4R, CANR-1
See also SATA 21
Schmidt, James W. 1947- 121
Schmidt, Jerry A(rthur) 1945- CANR-28
Earlier sketch in CA 69-72
Schmidt, Joel (Paul Armand) 1937- 130
Schmidt, John 1905-1969 .... CAP-1
Earlier sketch in CA 19-20
Schmidt, Karen Lee 1953- .... SATA 94
Schmidt, Karl H. 1955- 168
Schmidt, Karl M. (Jr.) 1917- 13-16R
Schmidt, Laura M(arie) 1952- CANR-16
Earlier sketch in CA 65-68
Schmidt, Lawrence K(ennedy) 1949- 190
Schmidt, Leigh Eric 1961- CANR-96
Earlier sketch in CA 133
Schmidt, Lyle D(arrel) 1933- 61-64
Schmidt, Lynette 1952- .... SATA 76
Schmidt, Margaret Fox 1925-1979 65-68
Obituary 125
Schmidt, Mark Ray 1953- 197
Schmidt, Marlene 133
Schmidt, Michael 1945- 210
Schmidt, Michael (Norton) 1947- CANR-88
Earlier sketches in CA 49-52, CANR-2
See also CP 2, 3, 4, 5, 6, 7
See also DLB 40
Schmidt, Michael Jack 1949- 126
Schmidt, Mike
See Schmidt, Michael Jack
Schmidt, Nancy Jeanne 1936- CANR-7
Earlier sketch in CA 57-60
Schmidt, Paul Frederic 1925- CANR-89
Earlier sketches in CA 1-4R, CANR-1
Schmidt, Peggy Jeanne 1951- 109
Schmidt, Rick
See Schmidt, William R(ichard) III
Schmidt, Robert Milton 1930- 5-8R
Schmidt, Royal Jae (Jr.) 1915- 41-44R
Schmidt, Samuel 1950- 141
Schmidt, Sandra
See Oddo, Sandra (Schmidt)
Schmidt, Sarah 1934- 152
Schmidt, Stanley (Albert) 1944- CANR-84
Earlier sketches in CA 61-64, CANR-8, 24
See also SFW 4
Schmidt, Steven (Thomas) 1927- 33-36R
Schmidt, Warren H(arry) 1920- CANR-99
Earlier sketches in CA 45-48, CANR-1
Schmidt, Werner Felix 1923- 9-12R
Schmidt, Werner H. 1935- CANR-86
Earlier sketch in CA 131
Schmidt, William E. 1947- 73-76
Schmidt, William R(ichard) III 1949- 110
Schmidt, Wilson Emerson 1927- 103
Schmidt, Winsor C. Jr. 1949- 156
Schmidtbonn, Wilhelm August
1876-1952 .... DLB 118
Schmidt-Nielsen, Knut 1915- CANR-96
Earlier sketch in CA 106
Schmidt-Nowara, Christopher 1966- 238
Schmiechen, James A. 1940- 126
Schmiechen, Peter 1938- 159
Schmieding, Holger 1958- 144
Schmier, Louis Eugene 1940- 112
Schmit, Patricia Brady
See Brady, Patricia
Schmithals, Walter 1923- CANR-9
Earlier sketch in CA 65-68
Schmitt, Abraham 1927- CANR-17
Earlier sketch in CA 97-100
Schmitt, Albert R(ichard) 1929- 73-76
Schmitt, Bernadotte Everly 1886-1969 ...... 1-4R
Obituary 103
Schmitt, Charles 1934(?)-1986
Obituary 119

Cumulative Index 515 **Schonborg**

Schmitt, David (Edward) 1940- 53-56
Schmitt, Eric-Emmanuel 1960- 206
Schmitt, Gladys 1909-1972 .... CANR-2
Obituary 37-40R
Earlier sketch in CA 1-4R
Schmitt, Hans A. 1921- CANR-5
Earlier sketch in CA 1-4R
Schmitt, Heinrich 1894-1976
Obituary 115
Schmitt, Jean-Claude 214
Schmitt, Karl Michael 1922- 41-44R
Schmitt, Marshall L. 1919- 13-16R
Schmitt, Martin (Ferdinand)
1917-1978 .... CANR-9
Earlier sketch in CA 53-56
Schmitt, Peter 1958- 215
Schmitt, Raymond L(ouis) 1936- 93-96
Schmitt, Richard 1927- CANR-105
Earlier sketch in CA 118
Schmitter, Dean Morgan 1917- 41-44R
Schmitter, Phillipe Charles 1936- 115
Schmitthoff, Clive M(acmillan)
1903-1990 .... CANR-18
Obituary 132
Earlier sketches in CA 5-8R, CANR-3
Schmittroth, John (William), Jr.
1949- CANR-19
Earlier sketch in CA 97-100
Schmittroth, John 1924-1988 49-52
Obituary 125
Schmitz, Aron Hector 1861-1928 122
Brief entry 104
See also Svevo, Italo
See also MTCW 1
Schmitz, Carl August 1920-1966
Obituary 116
Schmitz, Cecilia M. 1960- 154
Schmitz, Charles Henry 1904-1995 .... 5-8R
Schmitz, David F. 1956- 132
Schmitz, Dennis 1937- CANR-84
Earlier sketch in CA 29-32R
See also CP 1, 2, 3, 4, 5, 6, 7
Schmitz, James H(enry) 1911-1981 .. CANR-58
Earlier sketch in CA 103
See also BPFB 3
See also DLB 8
See also SFW 4
Schmitz, Joseph William 1905-1966 .... 5-8R
Schmitz, Michael J. 1934- 21-24R
Schmitz, Neil 237
Schmitz, Robert L(enzen) 1914- 145
Schmitz, Virginia
See Pasley, Virginia Schmitz
Schmoeller, David (Lee) 1947- 144
Schmokel, Wolfe W(illiam) 1933- 9-12R
Schmoller, Hans 1916-1985
Obituary 117
Schmook, Kathy Grizzard 1947- 127
Schmookler, Andrew Bard 1946- 135
Schmuck, Richard A(llen) 1936- 13-16R
Schmucke, Anne
See Strich, Christian
Schmuhl, Robert (Philip) 1948- 135
Schmuller, Angelo Aaron 1910-1988 53-56
Schmurz, Adolph
See Vian, Boris
Schnabel, Billie H(agen) 1944(?)-1980
Obituary 101
Schnabel, Johann Gottfried 1692-c.
1760 .... DLB 168
Schnabel, Julian 1951- 156
Schnabel, Timothy B. 1963- 237
Schnabel, Truman Gross, Jr. 1919- 105
Schnacke, Dick
See Schnacke, Richard N(ye)
Schnacke, Richard N(ye) 1919- 61-64
Schnackenberg, Gjertrud (Cecelia)
1953- CANR-100
Brief entry 116
See also AMWS 15
See also CLC 40
See also CP 7
See also CWP
See also DLB 120, 282
See also PC 45
See also PFS 13
Schnackenburg, Rudolf 1914- CANR-45
Earlier sketches in CA 29-32R, CANR-12
Schnall, Maxine (Swarttz) 1934- 17-20R
Schnapper, Dominique 1934- 130
Schnarch, David M(orris) 1946- CANR-123
Earlier sketch in CA 160
Schnaubelt, Franz Joseph 1914-1994 65-68
Schneck, Jerome M. 1920- 17-20R
Schneck, Stephen 1933-1996 .... CANR-10
Obituary 155
Earlier sketch in CA 13-16R
Schnee, Charles 1916-1963 .... IDFW 3, 4
Schneebaum, Tobias 1921- CANR-98
Earlier sketches in CA 29-32R, CANR-15
Schneede, Uwe M(ax) 1939- 235
Brief entry 111
Schneemann, Carolee 1939- CANR-111
Earlier sketch in CA 155
Schneer, Jonathan 1948- 191
Schneewind, Elizabeth Hughes
1940- CANR-2
Earlier sketch in CA 45-48
Schneewind, J(erome) B(orges) 1930- 25-28R
Schneidau, Herbert N. 1935- 29-32R
Schneider, Abram Leopoldovich
See Schneider, Alan (Leo)
Schneider, Alan (Leo) 1917-1984 145
Schneider, Alfred R. 1926- 201
Schneider, Andrew (J.) 1942- 132
Brief entry 127
Interview in CA-132
Schneider, Anna
See Sequoia, Anna
Schneider, Antonie 1954- .... SATA 89
Schneider, Barbara 203
Schneider, Bart 1951- 180
Schneider, Ben Ross, Jr. 1920- 37-40R
Schneider, Benjamin 1938- 41-44R
Schneider, Bill
See Schneider, William
Schneider, Carl D(avid) 1942- 69-72
Schneider, Christine M. 1972(?)- 191
See also SATA 120
Schneider, Clement J(oseph)
1927-1972 .... 41-44R
Schneider, Daniel J(ohn) 1927- 61-64
Schneider, David 1918- 114
Schneider, David M(urray) 1918-
Brief entry 112
Schneider, Deborah Lucas 1943- 168
Schneider, Delwin Byron 1926- 37-40R
Schneider, Dick
See Schneider, Richard H(enry)
Schneider, Duane 1937- 103
Schneider, Elisa
See Kleven, Elisa
Schneider, Elisabeth Wintersteen
1897-1985 .... CAP-1
Earlier sketch in CA 11-12
Schneider, Elizabeth (Susan) 1943- ... CANR-82
Earlier sketches in CA 93-96, CANR-16, 36
Schneider, Fred B. 1953- 150
Schneider, Gertrude 1928- 175
Schneider, Hans J(uergen) 1935- 73-76
Schneider, Harold K(enneth) 1925- 33-36R
Schneider, Helga 1937- 239
Schneider, Helmuth 1946- 227
Schneider, Herbert Wallace
1892-1984 .... 13-16R
Obituary 114
Schneider, Herman 1905-2003 .... CANR-16
Obituary 218
Earlier sketch in CA 29-32R
See also SATA 7
See also SATA-Obit 148
Schneider, Howie .... AITN 2
Schneider, Isidor 1896-1977 .... CAP-1
Obituary 73-76
Earlier sketch in CA 13-14
Schneider, Jo Anne 1959- 149
Schneider, John C(harles) 1945- 102
Schneider, Joyce Anne 1942- 107
Schneider, Karen 1948- 168
Schneider, Kenneth Ray 1927- 49-52
Schneider, Lambert 1900-1970
Obituary 104
Schneider, Laurence Allen 1937- 81-84
Schneider, Laurie
See Adams, Laurie
Schneider, Leo 1916- 5-8R
Schneider, Leonard Alfred 1925-1966 89-92
See also Bruce, Lenny
Schneider, Louis 1915-1979 .... CANR-13
Earlier sketch in CA 57-60
Schneider, Martina
See Duettmann, Martina (Friederike)
Schneider, Myles J(ay) 1943- 116
Schneider, Myra 1936- CANR-24
Earlier sketch in CA 107
Schneider, Nicholas A. 1930- 25-28R
Schneider, Nina 1913- CANR-15
Earlier sketch in CA 29-32R
See also SATA 2
Schneider, Paul 1923- 201
Schneider, Paul 1962- 234
Schneider, Peter 1940- 223
Schneider, Rex 1937- 122
See also SATA 44
Schneider, Richard H(enry) 1922- 97-100
Schneider, Richard J. 1945- 216
Schneider, Robert G. 1930- 112
Schneider, Robert T(homas) 1925- 5-8R
Schneider, Robert W. 1933- 13-16R
Schneider, Rolf 1932- 130
Brief entry 112
Schneider, Ronald M(ilton) 1932- 53-56
Schneider, Sara K. 1962- 150
Schneider, Sherrie 1959- CANR-114
Earlier sketch in CA 161
Schneider, Stanley D(ale) 1921- 17-20R
Schneider, Stephen H(enry) 1945- CANR-66
Earlier sketches in CA 69-72, CANR-12
Schneider, Steven A. 1952- 120
Schneider, Susan Weidman 1944- 118
Schneider, Wayne (Joseph) 1950- 233
Schneider, William CANR-19
Earlier sketch in CA 29-32R
Schneiderman, Beth Kline 97-100
Schneiderman, David 1958- 175
Schneiderman, Harry 1885-1975
Obituary 61-64
Schneiderman, L(awrence) J(erome)
1932- CANR-143
Earlier sketch in CA 57-60
Schneiderman, Stuart (Alan) 1943- ... CANR-66
Earlier sketch in CA 114
Schneiders, Alexander A(loysius)
1909-1968 .... CAP-1
Earlier sketch in CA 17-18
Schneiders, Sandra M(arie) 1936- 191
Schneier, Edward V(incent), Jr. 1939- ... 29-32R
Schneier, Marc 1959- 198
Schneir, Miriam 1933- 77-80
Schnell, George A(dam) 1931- CANR-57
Earlier sketches in CA 29-32R, CANR-12, 27
Schnell, R(odolph) L(eslie) 1931- 113
Schnell, William J(acob) 5-8R
Schnelle, Kenneth E(dward) 1914- 21-24R
Schneller, Robert John, Jr. 1957- 196
Schnepper, Jeff A(lan) 1947- CANR-21
Earlier sketch in CA 85-88
Schneps, Maurice 1917- 1-4R
Schnessel, S. Michael 1947- CANR-14
Earlier sketch in CA 73-76
Schneyder, J. F.
See Taylor, (Frank Herbert) Griffin
Schniedewind, William M. 1962- 239
Schnirel, James R. 1931- 69-72
See also SATA 14
Schnitter, Jane T. 1958- 152
See also SATA 88
Schnitter, Nicholas J. 1927- 148
Schnitzer, Martin C(olby) 1925- 134
Brief entry 110
Schnitzlein, Danny .... SATA 134
Schnitzler, Arthur 1862-1931
Brief entry 104
See also CDWLB 2
See also DC 17
See also DLB 81, 118
See also EW 8
See also EWL 3
See also RGSF 2
See also RGWL 2, 3
See also SSC 15, 61
See also TCLC 4
Schnore, Leo F(rancis) 1927- 17-20R
Schnur, Steven 1952- CANR-124
Earlier sketches in CA 140, CANR-92
See also SATA 95, 144
Schnurnberger, Lynn (Edelman) 1950(?)- 239
Schnurre, Wolfdietrich 1920-1989
Obituary 129
See also DLB 69
See also SATA-Obit 63
Schob, David Eugene 1941- 61-64
Schoberle, Cecile 1949- .... SATA 80
Schochet, Gordon J(oel) 1937- 45-48
Schochet, J(acob) Immanuel 1935- CANR-1
Earlier sketch in CA 45-48
Schock, Pauline 1928- 111
See also SATA 45
Schocken, Theodore 1914-1975
Obituary 104
Schodek, Daniel L(ewis) 1941- 127
Schoder, Raymond V(ictor)
1916-1987 .... CANR-1
Obituary 122
Earlier sketch in CA 1-4R
Schodt, Frederick L(owell) 1950- 132
Schoeck, Richard J(oseph) 1920- CANR-5
Earlier sketch in CA 1-4R
Schoeffler, Oscar E(dmund) 1899-1979 ... 73-76
Obituary 85-88
Schoell, William 1951- 186
See also SATA 160
Schoemaker, Paul J. H. 1949- 218
Schoeman, Karel 1939- 101
Schoemperlen, Diane 1954- CANR-107
Earlier sketches in CA 133, CANR-60
Schoen, Barbara (Taylor) 1924-1993 ..... 21-24R
Obituary 142
See also SATA 13
Schoen, Elin 1945- 101
Schoen, Juliet P. 1923- 69-72
Schoen, Robert 1947(?)- 235
Schoenbach, Carrie 1928- 120
Schoenbaum, S(amuel) 1927-1996 ... CANR-28
Obituary 151
Earlier sketch in CA 107
Schoenbaum, Thomas John 1939- 104
Schoenberg, Arnold Franz Walter
1874-1951 188
Brief entry 109
See also TCLC 75
Schoenberg, B(ernhardt) Mark 1928- 97-100
Schoenberg, Bernard 1927-1979 .... CANR-2
Obituary 85-88
Earlier sketch in CA 45-48
Schoenberg, Robert J. 1933- 141
Schoenberg, Ronald 1942- 126
Schoenberg, Wilfred Paul 1915- 9-12R
Schoenberger, Guido L. 1891-1974
Obituary 53-56
Schoenberger, Karl 1954- 195
Schoenberger, Nancy 1950- CANR-110
Earlier sketch in CA 126
Schoenberger, Walter Smith 1920- 29-32R
Schoenberner, Franz 1892-1970
Obituary 104
Schoenbohm, Wilko B. 1913-1998 .... 17-20R
Schoenbrod, David 1942- 146
Schoenbrun, Amy
See Glazer, Ellen Sarasohn
Schoenbrun, David (Franz)
1915-1988 .... CANR-3
Obituary 125
Earlier sketch in CA 49-52
Schoendoerffer, Pierre 1928-
Brief entry 111
Schoener, Allon 1926- 144
Schoenewolf, Gerald 1941- 136
Schoenfeld, Bruce 235
Schoenfeld, Clarence Albert 1918- CANR-6
Earlier sketch in CA 1-4R
Schoenfeld, David 1923- CANR-12
Earlier sketch in CA 17-20R
Schoenfeld, Eugene 1935-
Brief entry 118
Schoenfeld, Hanns Martin W(alter)
1928- CANR-6
Earlier sketch in CA 57-60
Schoenfeld, Maxwell Philip 1936- 33-36R
Schoenfield, Allen 1896(?)-1979
Obituary 85-88
Schoenherr, John (Carl) 1935- 136
See also MAICYA 1, 2
See also SAAS 13
See also SATA 37, 66
Schoenherr, Karl 1867-1943
See Schonherr, Karl
See also DLB 118
Schoenherr, Richard Anthony
1935-1996 .... CANR-21
Obituary 151
Earlier sketch in CA 29-32R
Schoenholtz, Larry 1948- 57-60
Schoenl, William 1941- 192
Schoenman, Ralph 1935- 25-28R
Schoenstein, Paul 1902-1974
Obituary 89-92
Schoenstein, Ralph 1933- 13-16R
Schoenwald, Richard L. 1927- 17-20R
Schoep, Arthur Paul 1920- 53-56
Schoepfer, Virginia B. 1934- 33-36R
Schoepflin, George A. 1939- 29-32R
Schoeps, Hans-Joachim 1909-1980 230
Brief entry 106
Schoeps, Karl-Heinz 1935- CANR-50
Earlier sketches in CA 107, CANR-24
Schoer, Lowell A(ugust) 1931- 29-32R
Schoeser, Mary 1950- CANR-86
Earlier sketch in CA 133
Schoettle, Lynn 49-52
Schofer, Lawrence 1940- 77-80
Schoffman, Nachum 1930- 137
Schofield, B(rian) B(etham) 1895-1984 . 21-24R
Obituary 114
Schofield, Carey 1955- 130
Schofield, (Edward) Guy 1902-1990
Obituary 131
Schofield, J(ohn) N(oel) 1899-1986
Obituary 120
Schofield, Janet Ward 1946- 215
Schofield, Jonathan
See Streib, Dan(iel Thomas)
Schofield, Mary Anne 1948- 124
Schofield, Michael 1919- CANR-14
Earlier sketch in CA 41-44R
Schofield, Paul
See Tubb, E(dwin) C(harles)
Schofield, Robert E(dwin) 1923- 162
Schofield, Roger Snowden 1937- 181
Schofield, Sandy
See Rusch, Kristine Kathryn
Schofield, Sylvia Anne 1918- CANR-13
Earlier sketch in CA 73-76
Schofield, W(ilfred) B(orden) 1927- 134
Schofield, William 1921- 9-12R
Schofield, William G(reenough)
1909-1996 .... CANR-2
Earlier sketch in CA 5-8R
Schogt, Henry G(ilius) 1927- 154
Scholastica, Sister Mary
See Jenkins, Marie M(agdalen)
Scholberg, Henry 1921- 77-80
Scholder, Henry 1948- 229
Scholderer, (Julius) Victor 1880-1971 191
Obituary 104
See also DLB 201
Scholefield, A. T.
See Scholefield, Alan
Scholefield, Alan 1931- CANR-34
Earlier sketch in CA 97-100
See also SATA 66
Scholefield, Edmund O.
See Butterworth, W(illiam) E(dmund III)
Scholem, Gershom (Gerhard)
1897-1982 .... CANR-39
Obituary 106
Earlier sketch in CA 45-48
Scholer, David M(ilton) 1938- 101
Scholes, Katherine 1959- 123
Scholes, Marie V(ielmetti) 1916- 29-32R
Scholes, Robert (Edward) 1929- CANR-88
Earlier sketches in CA 9-12R, CANR-14, 46
Scholes, Walter V(inton) 1916-1975 ...... CAP-2
Earlier sketch in CA 29-32
Scholey, Arthur 1932- 93-96
See also SATA 28
Scholl, John 1922- 9-12R
Scholl, Lisette 1945- 89-92
Scholl, Sabine 1959- 194
Scholl, Sharon L. 1932- 41-44R
Scholl, William M(athias) 1882-1968
Obituary 113
Scholnick, Ellin Kofsky 1936- 170
Scholt, Grayce 1925- 104
Scholz, Albert A(ugust) 1899-1972(?) CAP-2
Earlier sketch in CA 29-32
Scholz, Carter 1953- CANR-114
Earlier sketch in CA 119
Scholz, Jackson Volney 1897-1986 .... 5-8R
Obituary 120
See also SATA-Obit 49
Scholz, William 1916- 5-8R
Schom, Alan (Morris) 1937- CANR-111
Earlier sketches in CA 128, CANR-52
Schomaker, Mary Zimmeth 1928- 108
Schomp, Gerald 1937- 29-32R
Schon, Donald A(lan) 1930- 17-20R
Schon, Isabel 1940- 110
See also HW 1
Schonberg, Arnold
See Schoenberg, Arnold Franz Walter
Schonberg, Harold C(harles) 1915-2003 112
Obituary 218
Schonberg, Leonard A. 1935- 164
Schonberg, Rosalyn Krokover 1913(?)-1973
Obituary 41-44R
Schonberger, Richard J. 1937- 110
Schonborg, Virginia 1913-1981 77-80

Schone, Mark 1960- 213
Schone, Virginia 97-100
See also SATA 22
Schonell, Fred(erick) Joyce
1900-1969 .... CANR-2
Earlier sketch in CA 1-4R
Schonfeld, William R(ost) 1942- CANR-17
Earlier sketch in CA 37-40R
Schonfield, Hugh J(oseph)
1901-1988 .... CANR-46
Obituary 124
Earlier sketch in CA 9-12R
Schongut, Emanuel 1936- .... SATA 52
See also SATA-Brief 36
Schonherr, Karl 1867-1943 197
See also Schoenherr, Karl
Schoolcraft, Jane Johnston
1800-1841 .... DLB 175
Schooler, Carmi 1933- 114
Schooler, (Seward) Dean, Jr. 1941- 73-76
Schooler, Lynn 216
Schoolfield, George C(larence) 1925- . CANR-6
Earlier sketch in CA 1-4R
Schoolland, Marian M(argaret)
1902-1984 .... CANR-2
Earlier sketch in CA 5-8R
Schoonhoven, Calvin R(obert) 1931- 21-24R
Schoonmaker, Alan N. 1936- 25-28R
Schoonmaker, Ann 1928- 73-76
Schoonmaker, Frank 1905-1976
Obituary 61-64
Schoonmaker, Thelma 1945- .... IDFW 3, 4
Schoonover, Frank (Earle) 1877-1972 106
See also SATA 24
Schoonover, Jason 1946- CANR-129
Earlier sketch in CA 129
Schoonover, Lawrence Lovell
1906-1980 .... CANR-4
Obituary 97-100
Earlier sketch in CA 1-4R
Schoonover, Melvin E(ugene) 1926-
Brief entry 114
Schoonover, Shirley 1936- 77-80
Schoonover, Thelma I(rene) 1907- 41-44R
Schoonover, Thomas D(avid) 1936- . CANR-96
Earlier sketches in CA 120, CANR-45
Schoor, Gene 1921- CANR-29
Earlier sketch in CA 29-32R
See also SATA 3
Schopenhauer, Arthur 1788-1860 .... DLB 90
See also EW 5
Schopenhauer, Johanna 1766-1838 ...... DLB 90
Schopf, J(ames) William 1941- CANR-90
Earlier sketch in CA 133
Schopflin, George A.
See Schoepflin, George A.
Schoppert, James 1947-1992 216
Schoppert, Jim
See Schoppert, James
Schor, Amy 1954- 105
Schor, Juliet B. 1955- CANR-102
Earlier sketch in CA 140
Schor, Lynda 1938- 73-76
Schor, Naomi 1943-2001 .... CANR-16
Obituary 203
Earlier sketch in CA 89-92
Schor, Sandra (M.) 1932(?)-1990
Obituary 132
See also CLC 65
Schorb, E(dwin) M(arsh) 1940- 61-64
Schorer, Mark 1908-1977 .... CANR-7
Obituary 73-76
Earlier sketch in CA 5-8R
See also CLC 9
See also CN 1, 2
See also DLB 103
Schories, Pat 1952- 188
See also SATA 116
Schorr, Alan Edward 1945- 85-88
Schorr, Alvin L. 1921- CANR-15
Earlier sketch in CA 29-32R
Schorr, Daniel (Louis) 1916- CANR-107
Earlier sketch in CA 65-68
See also AITN 2
Schorr, Jerry 1934- 29-32R
Schorr, Jonathan 215
Schorr, Lisbeth B. 1931- 136
Schorr, Mark 1953- CANR-62
Earlier sketch in CA 122
See also CMW 4
Schorsch, Ismar 1935-
Brief entry 115
Schorsch, Laurence 1960- 149
Schorske, Carl E(mil) 1915- CANR-90
Earlier sketch in CA 85-88
Schosberg, Paul A. 1938- 13-16R
Schossberger, Emily Maria 1905-1979
Obituary 104
Schott, Jeffrey J. 1949- 126
Schott, John R(obert) 1936- CANR-7
Earlier sketch in CA 57-60
Schott, Penelope Scambly 1942- 77-80
Schott, Richard Lockwood 1939- 117
Schott, Webster 1927- 49-52
Schottelius, Justus Georg 1612-1676 .. DLB 164
Schottenfeld, Barbara 134
Schotter, Roni CANR-137
Earlier sketch in CA 160
See also SATA 105, 149
Schottland, Charles Irwin 1906-1995 .... 13-16R
Obituary 149
Schouler, James 1839-1920 220
See also DLB 47
Schoultz, Solveig von 1907-1996 202
See also CWW 2
See also DLB 259
Schouvaloff, Alexander 1934- 143
Schow, David J. 1955- .... HGG
See also SUFW 2
Schowalter, John E(rwin) 1936- 109
Schoyer, B. Preston 1912(?)-1978
Obituary 77-80
Schrader, Constance 1933- CANR-18
Earlier sketch in CA 101
Schrader, George A(lfred), Jr. 1917- 21-24R
Schrader, Leonard 173
Schrader, Maria 1965- 201
Schrader, Paul (Joseph) 1946- CANR-41
Earlier sketch in CA 37-40R
See also CLC 26, 212[001b]'
See also DLB 44
Schrader, Richard James 1941- CANR-92
Earlier sketch in CA 85-88
Schrader, Robert F(ay) 1931- 119
Schraepler, Hans-Albrecht 1934- 157
Schraff, Anne E(laine) 1939- CANR-59
Earlier sketches in CA 49-52, CANR-1, 17, 39
See also SATA 27, 92
Schraff, Francis Nicholas 1937- 101
Schraffenberger, Nancy 1933- CANR-16
Earlier sketch in CA 93-96
Schrag, Adele Frisbie 1921- 105
Schrag, Calvin O. 1928- 203
Schrag, Calvin Orville 1928- CANR-1
Earlier sketch in CA 1-4R
Schrag, Myles 1969- 219
Schrag, Oswald O. 1916- 49-52
Schrag, Peter 1931- CANR-8
Earlier sketch in CA 13-16R
Schrag, Philip G(ordon) 1943- 102
Schrager, Jeanne Hart 1919- 127
Schrager, Sam(uel Alan) 202
Schram, Martin 1942- CANR-115
Earlier sketches in CA 69-72, CANR-13
Schram, Peninnah 1934- 190
See also SATA 119
Schram, Stuart R(eynolds) 1924- 97-100
Schramm, David N(orman) 1945-1997 135
Obituary 163
Schramm, Laurier L. 1954- CANR-93
Earlier sketch in CA 146
Schramm, Percy Ernst 1894-1970
Obituary 104
Schramm, Richard (Howard) 1934- 41-44R
Schramm, Sarah Slavin 1942- 93-96
Schramm, Wilbur (Lang)
1907-1987 .... CANR-88
Obituary 124
Earlier sketches in CA 105, CANR-22
Schrank, Ben 238
Schrank, Jeffrey 1944- 29-32R
Schrank, Joseph 1900-1984 .... CANR-20
Obituary 112
Earlier sketch in CA 5-8R
See also SATA-Obit 38
Schreber, Daniel 1842-1911 .... TCLC 123
Schrecengost, Maity
See Schrecengost, S. Maitland
Schrecengost, S. Maitland 1938- 190
See also SATA 118
Schreck, Alan (Edward) 1951- CANR-95
Earlier sketch in CA 124
Schreck, Everett M. 1897-1991 .... CAP-2
Earlier sketch in CA 33-36
Schreck, Harley Carl 1948 204
Schrecker, Ellen 1938- 184
Schrecker, John (Ernest) 1937-
Brief entry 112
Schrecker, Judie 1954- 155
See also SATA 90
Schreiber, Daniel 1909-1981 .... CAP-1
Obituary 103
Earlier sketch in CA 13-14
Schreiber, Elizabeth Anne (Ferguson)
1947- 69-72
See also SATA 13
Schreiber, Flora Rheta 1918-1988 .... CANR-87
Obituary 127
Earlier sketches in CA 53-56, CANR-11
Interview in CANR-11
See also AITN 1
Schreiber, Georges 1904-1977
Obituary 109
See also SATA-Brief 29
Schreiber, Hermann (Otto Ludwig)
1920- CANR-36
Earlier sketch in CA 25-28R
Schreiber, Jan 1941- 65-68
Schreiber, Jean-Jacques Servan
See Servan-Schreiber, Jean-Jacques
Schreiber, Joseph 1969- 147
Schreiber, Le Anne 1945- 140
See also BEST 90:2
Schreiber, Mark 1960- 116
Schreiber, Michael 1937- 116
Schreiber, Ralph W(alter) 1942- 69-72
See also SATA 13
Schreiber, Ron 1934-2004 .... 41-44R
Obituary 229
Schreiber, Roy E. 1941- 142
Schreiber, Ted
See Schreiber, V. Theodore
Schreiber, V. Theodore 1905-1986 124
Schreiber, Vernon R(oy) 1925- 61-64
Schreiber-Wicke, Edith 1943- 123
Schreider, Frank(lin David) 1924-1994 ...... 5-8R
Obituary 145
Schreiner, George F(rederic) 1949- 117
Schreiner, Lee
See Schreiner, George F(rederic)
Schreiner, Olive (Emilie Albertina)
1855-1920 154
Brief entry 105
See also AFW
See also BRWS 2
See also DLB 18, 156, 190, 225
See also EWL 3
See also FW
See also RGEL 2
See also TCLC 9
See also TWA
See also WLIT 2
See also WWE 1
Schreiner, Samuel A(gnew), Jr.
1921- CANR-52
Earlier sketches in CA 65-68, CANR-9, 26
See also SATA 70
Schreiner, Thomas R. 1954- 185
Schreiner-Mann, Joan 1939- 45-48
Schreiter, Rick 1936- 21-24R
Schreivogel, Paul A. 1930- 25-28R
Schrepfer, Susan R(ita) 1941- 117
Schreuder, D(eryck) M(arshall) 1942- 120
Schreyer, George M(aurice) 1913-1986 ..... 5-8R
Schriber, Mary Suzanne 1938- 126
Schrier, Arnold 1925- 49-52
Schrier, Nettie Vander
See Vander-Schrier, Nettie
Schrier, William 1900-1973 .... 41-44R
Schrift, Shirley 1922(?)- 113
Brief entry 110
Schriftgiesser, Karl (John) 1903-1988 ..... CAP-1
Obituary 126
Earlier sketch in CA 11-12
Schrijvers, Peter 1963- 175
Schrire, Theodore 1906- 21-24R
Schrock, Kathleen 1957- 201
Schrock, Simon 1938- 113
Schroder, Amund A. Schulze 1925- ... CANR-5
Earlier sketch in CA 13-16R
Schroder, John Henry Erle 1895-1980 ... CAP-1
Earlier sketch in CA 13-14
Schroder, Walter K. 1928- 149
Schrodinger, Erwin
See Schroedinger, Erwin
Schrodt, Philip A(ndrew) 1951- 111
Schroedel, Jean Reith 1951- CANR-97
Earlier sketch in CA 122
Schroeder, Alan 1961- CANR-100
Earlier sketch in CA 133
See also SATA 66, 98
Schroeder, Albert H(enry) 1914- CANR-14
Earlier sketch in CA 41-44R
Schroeder, Andreas (Peter) 1946- CANR-37
Earlier sketches in CA 93-96, CANR-16
See also CP 2
See also DLB 53
Schroeder, Barbet 1941- 143
Schroeder, Binette
See Nickl, Barbara (Elisabeth)
Schroeder, David 1924- 21-24R
Schroeder, David P. 1946- 192
Schroeder, Eric 1904-1971 .... CAP-1
Earlier sketch in CA 13-14
Schroeder, Fred E(rich) H(arald) 1932- .. 41-44R
Schroeder, Frederick W(illiam)
1896-1982 .... 1-4R
Schroeder, Gerald L. 202
Schroeder, Glenna R.
See Schroeder-Lein, Glenna R(uth)
Schroeder, Henry A(lfred) 1906-1975 .... CAP-2
Earlier sketch in CA 25-28
Schroeder, Joan V(annorsdall) 1951- 153
Schroeder, John H(erman) 1943- 49-52
Schroeder, Karl 1962- 215
Schroeder, Manfred (Robert) 1926- 138
Schroeder, Mary 1903- 73-76
Schroeder, Oliver Charles, Jr. 1916- . CANR-30
Earlier sketch in CA 110
Schroeder, Paul Walter 1927- 5-8R
Schroeder, Rudolf Alexander
See Schroder, Rudolf Alexander
Schroeder, Russell (K.) 1943- .... SATA 146
Schroeder, Ted 1931(?)-1973 .... SATA-Obit 20
Schroeder, W(illiam) Widick 1928-
Brief entry 111
Schroeder-Lein, Glenna R(uth) 1951- 147
Schroedinger, Erwin 1887-1961
Obituary 113
Schroeter, James 1927- 21-24R
Schroeter, Louis C(larence) 1929- 29-32R
Schroeter, Wolfgang G(unther)
See Schroter, Wolfgang G(unther)
Schroetter, Hilda Noel 1917- 29-32R
Schroll, Herman T(heodore III) 1946- ... 33-36R
Schroter, Wolfgang G(unther) 1928- 205
Schroth, Richard J. 218
Schruben, Francis W(illiam) 1918- 45-48
Schruth, Peter Elliott 1917-1979
Obituary 89-92
Schryer, Frans J(osef) 1946- 171
Schubart, Christian Friedrich Daniel
1739-1791 .... DLB 97
Schubart, Mark Allen 1918-2000 105
Obituary 188
Schubel, J(erry) R(obert) 1936- 126
Schubel, Vernon James 152
Schubert, Delwyn George 1919- 9-12R
Schubert, Dieter 1947- CANR-28
Earlier sketch in CA 111
See also SATA 62, 101
Schubert, Frank N. 1943- CANR-118
Earlier sketch in CA 154
Schubert, Glendon 1918- CANR-44
Earlier sketches in CA 5-8R, CANR-6, 21
Schubert, Gotthilf Heinrich
1780-1860 .... DLB 90
Schubert, Kurt 1923- 5-8R
Schubert-Gabrys, Ingrid 1953- CANR-28
Earlier sketch in CA 111
See also SATA 62, 101
Schuberth, Christopher J. 1933- CANR-18
Earlier sketch in CA 25-28R
Schuchman, Joan 1934- 101
Schuck, Peter H. 1940- 129
Schudson, Charles B(enjamin) 1950- 130
Schudson, Michael 1946- CANR-42
Earlier sketches in CA 101, CANR-19
Schuecking, Levin 1814-1883 .... DLB 133
Schueler, Donald G(ustave) 1929- 106
Schueler, G(eorge) F(rederick)
1944- CANR-115
Earlier sketch in CA 154
Schuerer, Ernst 1933- CANR-37
Earlier sketches in CA 45-48, CANR-1, 17
Schuerger, Michele R. 180
See also SATA 110
Schuessler, Hermann E. 1929(?)-1975
Obituary 61-64
Schuessler, Karl F(rederick) 1915- 105
Schuett, Stacey 1960- .... SATA 75
Schuettinger, Robert Lindsay 1936- 33-36R
Schuetz, David
See Schuetz, David
Schuetz, John Howard 1933- 97-100
Schuetz, Stefan
See Schutz, Stefan
Schuetze, Armin William 1917- 57-60
Schufftan, Eugen -1977 .... IDFW 3, 4
Schug, Willis E(rvin) 1924- 49-52
Schuh, Dwight R(aymond) 1945- 101
Schuh, G(eorge) Edward 1930- CANR-30
Earlier sketch in CA 29-32R
Schuker, Stephen Alan 1939- 69-72
Schul, Bill D(ean) 1928- CANR-8
Earlier sketch in CA 61-64
Schulberg, Budd (Wilson) 1914- CANR-87
Earlier sketches in CA 25-28R, CANR-19
See also BPFB 3
See also CLC 7, 48
See also CN 1, 2, 3, 4, 5, 6, 7
See also DLB 6, 26, 28
See also DLBY 1981, 2001
See also MAL 5
Schulberg, Herbert C(harles) 1934- CANR-8
Earlier sketch in CA 61-64
Schulberg, Stuart 1922-1979
Obituary 89-92
Schulder, Diane Blossom 1937- 37-40R
Schulenberg, David (Louis) 1955- .. CANR-103
Earlier sketch in CA 145
Schuler, Betty Jo 1934- 229
Schuler, Carol Ann 1946- 106
Schuler, Douglas 1954(?)- 176
Schuler, Edgar A(lbert) 1905-1999 .... CAP-2
Earlier sketch in CA 23-24
Schuler, Robert 1939- 194
Schuler, Stanley Carter 1915- CANR-5
Earlier sketch in CA 5-8R
Schulhofer, Stephen J(oseph) 1942- 185
Schulian, John 1945- 129
Schulke, Flip Phelps Graeme 1930- . CANR-22
Earlier sketch in CA 105
See also SATA 57
Schulkind, Eugene (Walter) 1923- 97-100
Schull, (John) Joseph 1916-1980 .... CANR-8
Earlier sketch in CA 53-56
Schuller, Gunther 1925- CANR-73
Earlier sketches in CA 69-72, CANR-28
Schuller, Robert (Harold) 1926- CANR-117
Earlier sketches in CA 9-12R, CANR-14, 46
Schullery, Paul (David) 1948- CANR-123
Earlier sketches in CA 111, CANR-30, 57
Schulman, Arlene 1961- CANR-143
Earlier sketch in CA 173
See also SATA 105
Schulman, Arnold
See Trumbo, Dalton
Schulman, Arnold 1925- 103
Schulman, Audrey 1963- CANR-93
Earlier sketch in CA 146
Schulman, Bob
See Schulman, Robert
Schulman, Bruce J. 1959- 222
Schulman, Grace 1935- CANR-103
Earlier sketch in CA 65-68
Schulman, Helen 1961- CANR-115
Earlier sketch in CA 128
Schulman, Ivan A(lbert) 1931- 131
Schulman, J(oseph) Neil 1953- 89-92
Schulman, Janet 1933- CANR-116
Earlier sketch in CA 101
See also SATA 22, 137
Schulman, L(ester) M(artin) 1934- CANR-12
Earlier sketch in CA 33-36R
See also SATA 13
Schulman, Michael D. 1948- 137
Schulman, Robert 1916- 77-80
Schulman, Rosalind 1914- 41-44R
Schulman, Sam 1924- 45-48
Schulman, Sarah 1958- CANR-72
Earlier sketch in CA 118
Schulman, Tom 1951(?)- 133
Schulmerich, Alma 1902(?)-1985
Obituary 115
Schulte, Elaine L(ouise) 1934- CANR-28
Earlier sketches in CA 73-76, CANR-12
See also SATA 36
Schulte, Henry F(rank) 1924-2004 .... 25-28R
Obituary 230
Schulte, Paul C(larence) 1890-1984
Obituary 112
Schulte, Rainer 1937- 21-24R
See also CP 1

Cumulative Index 517 Schwartz

Schulten, Susan 239
Schultes, Richard Evans 1915-2001 . CANR-50
Obituary 202
Earlier sketches in CA 108, CANR-25
Schultheis, Rob 1943- CANR-109
Earlier sketch in CLC 111
Schulthess, Emil 1913-1996 65-68
Schults, Raymond L. 1926- 105
Schultz, Alfred W. 1920- 162
Schultz, Barbara 1923- 21-24R
Schultz, Barbara A. 117
Schultz, (Reynolds) Bart(on) 1951- 142
Schultz, Betty K(epka) 1932- .... SATA 125
Schultz, David E. 1952- 180
Schultz, Dodi 1930- CANR-36
Earlier sketches in CA 45-48, CANR-1, 16
Schultz, Donald O. 1939- CANR-17
Earlier sketch in CA 25-28R
Schultz, Duane P(hilip) 1934- 29-32R
Schultz, Ed 1933- 45-48
Schultz, Edna Moore 1912- 13-16R
Schultz, Edward W(illiam) 1936- CANR-1
Earlier sketch in CA 45-48
Schultz, George F(ranklin) 1908-1992 ... CAP-2
Earlier sketch in CA 19-20
Schultz, George J(oseph) 1932-
Brief entry 109
Schultz, Gerard 1902-1974
Obituary 110
Schultz, Gladys Denny 1896(?)-1984
Obituary 113
Schultz, Gwendolyn 65-68
See also SATA 21
Schultz, Harold John 1923- 103
Schultz, Harry D. CANR-14
Earlier sketch in CA 21-24R
Schultz, James Willard 1859-1947
Brief entry 121
See also YABC 1
Schultz, John (Ludwig) 1932- CANR-15
Earlier sketch in CA 41-44R
Schultz, Joseph P(enn) 1928- 113
Schultz, Mark 1935- 116
Schultz, Mort(on) J(oel) 1930- CANR-28
Earlier sketches in CA 73-76, CANR-12
Schultz, Pearle Henriksen 1918- CANR-1
Earlier sketch in CA 49-52
See also SATA 21
Schultz, Philip 1945- CANR-125
Earlier sketch in CA 104
Schultz, Samuel J(acob) 1914- CANR-12
Earlier sketch in CA 25-28R
Schultz, Sigrid (Lillian) 1893-1980
Obituary 97-100
Schultz, Stanley K(enton) 1938-
Brief entry 116
Schultz, Susan M. 201
Schultz, Terri 1946- CANR-10
Earlier sketch in CA 65-68
Schultz, Theodore William 1902-1998 85-88
Obituary 165
Schultz, Vernon B(urdette) 1924- 9-12R
Schultz, Ward
See Schultz, (Reynolds) Bart(on)
Schultze, Charles L(ouis) 1924-
Brief entry 114
Schultze, Quentin J(ames) 1952- 217
Schultze, William Andrew 1937- 37-40R
Schulyer Van Rensselaer, Mrs.
See Van Rensselaer, Mariana Griswold
Schulz, Ann Tibbitts 1938- 116
Schulz, Anne Markham 1938- 121
Schulz, Bruno 1892-1942 .... CANR-86
Brief entry 115
Earlier sketch in CA 123
See also CDWLB 4
See also DLB 215
See also EWL 3
See also MTCW 2
See also MTFW 2005
See also RGSF 2
See also RGWL 2, 3
See also SSC 13
See also TCLC 5, 51
Schulz, Charles M(onroe)
1922-2000 .... CANR-132
Obituary 187
Earlier sketches in CA 9-12R, CANR-6
Interview in CANR-6
See also AAYA 39
See also CLC 12
See also MTFW 2005
See also SATA 10
See also SATA-Obit 118
Schulz, Clare Elmore 1924- 13-16R
Schulz, David A. 1933- CANR-30
Earlier sketch in CA 29-32R
Schulz, Dorothy Moses 1946- 199
Schulz, Ernst B(ernhard) 1896-1985 73-76
Schulz, Florence 1908-1994 .... CAP-2
Earlier sketch in CA 21-22
Schulz, James Henry 1936- 89-92
Schulz, John E. 1939- 29-32R
Schulz, Juergen 1927- 41-44R
Schulz, Max F(rederick) 1923- 5-8R
Schulz, Monte 194
Schulz, Phillip Stephen 1946- CANR-50
Earlier sketch in CA 123
Schulz, William F(rederick) 1949- 217
Schulz-Behrend, George 1913- 45-48
Schulze, Dallas 164
Schulze, Franz 1927- 125
Schulze, Gene 1912- 85-88
Schulze, Hertha 1935- 122
Schulze, Ingo 1962- CANR-111
Earlier sketch in CA 168
Schulzinger, Robert D(avid) 1945- 61-64
Schumacher, Alvin J. 1928- 13-16R
Schumacher, E(rnst) F(riedrich)
1911-1977 .... CANR-85
Obituary 73-76
Earlier sketches in CA 81-84, CANR-34
See also CLC 80
Schumacher, Evelyn A(nn) 1919- 130
Schumacher, Jim 1955- 234
Schumacher, Joel 1939- 213
Schumacher, John N(orbert, Jr.)
1927- CANR-90
Earlier sketch in CA 131
Schumacher, Julie (Alison) 1958- 239
Schumacher, Michael 234
Schumaker, Lyn(ette) 229
Schumaker, Paul 1946- 139
Schumaker, Ward 1943- 161
See also SATA 96
Schuman, Ben N. 1923- 17-20R
Schuman, David Feller 1942- CANR-17
Earlier sketch in CA 97-100
Schuman, Frederick Lewis 1904-1981 45-48
Obituary 135
Schuman, Howard 1928- 124
Schuman, Michael A. 1953- CANR-111
Earlier sketch in CA 152
See also SATA 85, 134
Schuman, Patricia Glass 1943- CANR-14
Earlier sketch in CA 33-36R
Schumann, Elizabeth Creighton 1907- .. CAP-1
Earlier sketch in CA 11-12
Schumann, Paul L. 1955- 112
Schumer, Fran 1953- 148
Schumm, Ruth Frances 1921-1988
Obituary 125
Schunk, Laurel 180
Schuon, Frithjof 1907-1998 .... CANR-108
Earlier sketches in CA 73-76, CANR-13
Schuon, Karl Albert 1913-1984 .... CANR-86
Obituary 114
Earlier sketch in CA 13-16R
Schupack, Deborah 234
Schupp, Johann Balthasar 1610-1661 . DLB 164
Schur, Edwin M(ichael) 1930- CANR-7
Earlier sketch in CA 13-16R
Schur, Maxine
See Schur, Maxine Rose
Schur, Maxine Rose 1948- CANR-82
Earlier sketch in CA 129
See also MAICYA 2
See also SATA 53, 98, 135
See also SATA-Brief 49
See also SATA-Essay 135
Schur, Norman W(arren) 1907- CANR-37
Earlier sketches in CA 41-44R, CANR-17
Schurer, Ernst
See Schuerer, Ernst
Schurer, Leopold (Sidney) Launitz, Jr.
See Launitz-Schurer, Leopold (Sidney), Jr.
Schurfranz, Vivian 1925- 61-64
See also SATA 13
Schurke, Paul 1955- 126
Schurmacher, Emile C. 1903(?)-1976
Obituary 69-72
Schurman, D(onald) M. 1924- 37-40R
Schurman, Nona 1909- 216
Schurr, Cathleen 9-12R
Schurz, Carl 1829-1906 209
See also DLB 23
Schuschnigg, Kurt von
See von Schuschnigg, Kurt
Schusky, Ernest L(ester) 1931- CANR-8
Earlier sketch in CA 17-20R
Schussler Fiorenza, Elisabeth 1858-1944 .... FW
Schuster, George 1873-1972
Obituary 37-40R
Schuster, George 1881-1982
Obituary 107
Schuster, Louis A. 1916- 13-16R
Schuster, Marilyn R. 1943- 148
Schuster, Max Lincoln 1897-1970
Obituary 29-32R
Schutte, Anne Jacobson 1940- CANR-114
Earlier sketch in CA 139
Schutte, William Metcalf 1919- 5-8R
Schutz, Alfred 1899-1959 215
Schutz, Anton Friedrich Joseph
1894-1977 81-84
Obituary 73-76
Schutz, Benjamin Merrill 1949- CANR-111
Earlier sketch in CA 107
Schutz, David 1941- .... EWL 3
Schutz, John Adolph 1919- 5-8R
Schutz, John Howard
See Schuetz, John Howard
Schutz, Susan Polis 1944- 105
Schutz, Wallace J. 1908-1996 135
Schutz, Wilhelm Wolfgang 1911- 25-28R
Schutz, William C(arl) 1925-2002 ..... CANR-10
Obituary 212
Earlier sketch in CA 25-28R
Schutze, Gertrude 1917- 17-20R
Schutze, Jim 1946- 123
Schutzer, A. I. 1922- 25-28R
See also SATA 13
Schutzer, Amy 1956- 198
Schutzman, Steven 1947- 114
Schuyler, David 1950- CANR-52
Earlier sketch in CA 126
Schuyler, George Samuel
1895-1977 .... CANR-42
Obituary 73-76
Earlier sketch in CA 81-84
See also BW 2
See also DLB 29, 51
See also HR 1:3
Schuyler, James Marcus 1923-1991 101
Obituary 134
Interview in CA-101
See also CLC 5, 23
See also CP 1, 2
See also DAM POET
See also DLB 5, 169
See also EWL 3
See also MAL 5
See also WP
Schuyler, Jane 1943- 65-68
Schuyler, Joseph B(ernard) 1921- 1-4R
Schuyler, Judy
See Eshbach, Lloyd Arthur
Schuyler, Keith C. 1919- CANR-12
Earlier sketch in CA 29-32R
Schuyler, Pamela R. 1948- 106
See also SATA 30
Schuyler, Philippa Duke 1934-1967 .... 5-8R
See also BW 1
Schuyler, Robert Livingston 1883-1966 . CAP-1
Earlier sketch in CA 11-12
Schvaneveldt, Jay D. 1937- 103
Schvey, Henry I(van) 1948- 133
Schwab, Arnold T. 1922- 9-12R
Schwab, George 1931- CANR-37
Earlier sketches in CA 45-48, CANR-1, 16
Schwab, James C. 1949- 128
Schwab, Jim
See Schwab, James C.
Schwab, John J. 1923- 85-88
Schwab, Joseph J(ackson) 1909-1988 . CANR-5
Earlier sketch in CA 5-8R
Schwab, Paul Josiah 1894-1966 .... 5-8R
Obituary 103
Schwab, Peter 1940- CANR-110
Earlier sketches in CA 41-44R, CANR-14
Schwabacher, Ethel K(remer) 1903-1984
Obituary 114
Schwabe, William
See Cassidy, William L(awrence Robert)
Schwaber, Paul 1936- 13-16R
Schwab Pomerantz, Carrie 1941(?)- 223
Schwadron, Abraham A(be) 1925-1987
Obituary 123
Schwager, Jack D. 1948- 197
Schwager, Raymund 1935-2004 165
Schwager, Tina 1964- 180
See also SATA 110
Schwalberg, Carol(yn Ernestine Stein)
1930- 69-72
Schwaller, John Frederick 1948- 126
Schwamm, Ellen 1934- 122
Schwandt, Stephen (William) 1947- 126
See also SATA 61
Schwantes, Carlos A(rnaldo) 1945- . CANR-142
Earlier sketch in CA 150
Schwarberg, Guenther 1926- 130
Schwarcz, Vera 1947- 152
Schwark, Mary Beth 1954- .... SATA 51
Schwartau, Winn 1952- 151
Schwartz, Al(bert) 1911(?)-1988
Obituary 125
Schwartz, Alfred 1922- 17-20R
Schwartz, Alvin 1927-1992 .... CANR-86
Obituary 137
Earlier sketches in CA 13-16R, CANR-7, 24, 49
See also CLR 3, 89
See also MAICYA 1, 2
See also SATA 4, 56
See also SATA-Obit 71
Schwartz, Amy 1954- CANR-130
Earlier sketches in CA 110, CANR-29, 57
Interview in CANR-29
See also CLR 25
See also MAICYA 2
See also MAICYAS 1
See also SAAS 18
See also SATA 47, 83, 131
See also SATA-Brief 41
Schwartz, Anna J(acobson) 1915- 125
Schwartz, Anne Powers 1913-1987 .... CANR-1
Earlier sketch in CA 1-4R
See also SATA 10
Schwartz, Arthur Nathaniel 1922- CANR-28
Earlier sketches in CA 61-64, CANR-8
Schwartz, Audrey James 1928- 89-92
Schwartz, Barry 1938- CANR-111
Earlier sketch in CA 77-80
Schwartz, Barry N. 1942- 33-36R
Schwartz, Benjamin I(sadore)
1916-1999 .... 13-16R
Obituary 186
Schwartz, Bernard 1923-1997
Obituary 163
Brief entry 117
Schwartz, Bernard (Sherman) 1945- 106
Schwartz, Bertie G. 1901(?)-1976
Obituary 69-72
Schwartz, Betty 1927- 93-96
Schwartz, Carol 1954- .... SATA 77
Schwartz, Charles 73-76
Schwartz, Charles W(alsh) 1914- 13-16R
See also SATA 8
Schwartz, Cheryl (A.) 1965- 154
Schwartz, Daniel (Bennet)
1929- .... SATA-Brief 29
Schwartz, David (E.) 1916-1989
Obituary 130
Schwartz, David B. 1948- 165
Schwartz, David C. 1939- 37-40R
Schwartz, David J(oseph), Jr. 1927- .. CANR-13
Earlier sketch in CA 17-20R
Schwartz, David M(artin) 1951- 118
See also SATA 59, 110
Schwartz, Delmore (David)
1913-1966 .... CANR-35
Obituary 25-28R
Earlier sketches in CAP-2, CA 17-18
See also AMWS 2
See also CLC 2, 4, 10, 45, 87
See also DLB 28, 48
See also EWL 3
See also MAL 5
See also MTCW 1, 2
See also MTFW 2005
See also PAB
See also PC 8
See also RGAL 4
See also TUS
Schwartz, Donald E(dward) 1930-1988
Obituary 127
Schwartz, Douglas W(right) 1929- ... CANR-17
Earlier sketch in CA 25-28R
Schwartz, E(arl) A(lbert) 169
Schwartz, Eleanor Brantley 1937- 57-60
Schwartz, Eli 1921- CANR-34
Earlier sketch in CA 1-4R
Schwartz, Elias 1923- 41-44R
Schwartz, Elizabeth Reeder 1912- 13-16R
See also SATA 8
Schwartz, Elkanah 1937- 21-24R
Schwartz, Ellen 1949- 189
See also SATA 117
Schwartz, Elliott S. 1936- 13-16R
Schwartz, Emanual K. 1912-1973 .... 37-40R
Obituary 41-44R
Schwartz, Ernst
See Ozu, Yasujiro
Schwartz, Eugene M. 1927-1995 .... 13-16R
Obituary 149
Schwartz, Evan I. 217
Schwartz, Gail Garfield 117
Schwartz, Gary (David) 1940- 145
Schwartz, Gary E. 1944- 211
Schwartz, George 1908-1974
Obituary 104
Schwartz, George Leopold 1891-1983
Obituary 109
Schwartz, George R. 1942- CANR-17
Earlier sketch in CA 97-100
Schwartz, Gerald 1932- 120
Schwartz, Gil (Stanley Bing) 170
Schwartz, Harry W. 1903(?)-1984
Obituary 114
Schwartz, Helen 1935- 111
Schwartz, Helene E(nid) 1941- 65-68
Schwartz, Herman 1931- 218
Schwartz, Hillel 1948- CANR-43
Earlier sketches in CA 102, CANR-20
Schwartz, Howard 1945- CANR-116
Earlier sketches in CA 49-52, CANR-5, 22
Schwartz, Israel J(acob) 1885-1971
Obituary 33-36R
Schwartz, Jason 1967- 188
Schwartz, Jeffrey H. 1948- 231
Schwartz, Jeffrey M. 1951- 224
Schwartz, Jerome L.
See Lawrence, Jerome
Schwartz, Joan 1938- 144
Schwartz, Joel 1942- 144
Schwartz, Joel L. 1940- 121
See also SATA 54
See also SATA-Brief 51
Schwartz, John Burnham 1965- CANR-116
Earlier sketch in CA 132
See also CLC 59
Schwartz, Jonathan 1938- 97-100
See also DLBY 1982
Schwartz, Joseph 1925- CANR-90
Earlier sketch in CA 33-36R
Schwartz, Joyce R. 1950- 159
See also SATA 93
Schwartz, Julius 1907-2004 109
See also SATA 45
Schwartz, K(arlene) V. 1936- 104
Schwartz, Kessel 1920- CANR-6
Earlier sketch in CA 1-4R
Schwartz, Larry 1922- 53-56
Schwartz, Laurens R. 1951- 127
Schwartz, Leon 1922- 113
Schwartz, Leslie (A.) 1962- 218
Schwartz, Lester J(erome) 1927-2000 113
Obituary 188
Schwartz, Lewis M(arvin) 1935- 45-48
Schwartz, Lita Linzer 1930- 29-32R
Schwartz, Lloyd 1941- CANR-101
Earlier sketch in CA 112
Schwartz, Lois C. 1935- 33-36R
Schwartz, Loretta 1943- 97-100
Schwartz, Louis B(rown) 1913-2003 ..... 21-24R
Obituary 214
Schwartz, Lynne Sharon 1939- CANR-89
Earlier sketches in CA 103, CANR-44
See also CLC 31
See also DLB 218
See also MTCW 2
See also MTFW 2005
Schwartz, Marie Jenkins 1946- 193
Schwartz, Martin D(avid) 1945- 118
Schwartz, Mel 1950- 173
Schwartz, Melvin 1932- 168
Schwartz, Michael 1942- 113
Schwartz, Mildred A(nne) 1932- CANR-9
Earlier sketch in CA 21-24R
Schwartz, Mimi 206
Schwartz, Morris S. 1916- 17-20R
Schwartz, Mortimer (Donald) 1922- 116
Schwartz, Muriel A.
See Eliot, T(homas) S(tearns)
Schwartz, Murray M. 1942- 116
Schwartz, Nancy Lynn 1952-1978 107

Schwartz, Norman B(oris) 1932- 111
Schwartz, Paula 1925-2003 .... CANR-41
Obituary 222
Earlier sketches in CA 85-88, CANR-18
Interview in CANR-18
Schwartz, Pedro 1935- CANR-24
Earlier sketch in CA 107
Schwartz, Pepper 1945- 33-36R
Schwartz, Perry 1942- 142
See also SATA 75
Schwartz, Richard Alan 1951- CANR-129
Earlier sketch in CA 165
Schwartz, Richard B. 1941- CANR-141
Earlier sketches in CA 85-88, CANR-15
Schwartz, Richard D(erecktor) 1925- .. CANR-6
Earlier sketch in CA 1-4R
Schwartz, Ronald 1937- 65-68
Schwartz, Ruth L. 1962- 218
Schwartz, S.
See Starr, S(tephen) Frederick
Schwartz, Samuel M. 1929- 144
Schwartz, Sanford 1946- 238
Schwartz, Selwyn S. 1907(?)-1988
Obituary 125
Schwartz, Sheila (Ruth) 1929- CANR-30
Earlier sketches in CA 25-28R, CANR-11
See also SATA 27
Schwartz, Shloime
See Schwartz, Selwyn S.
Schwartz, Stephan A(ndrew) 1942- 130
Schwartz, Stephen (Lawrence) 1948- 85-88
See also CAAS 26
See also SATA 19
Schwartz, Stephen 1948- .... IDFW 4
Schwartz, Stephen (Alfred) 1948- CANR-141
Earlier sketches in CA 144, CANR-68
Schwartz, Steven 1950- 118
Schwartz, Stuart B. 1940- 126
Brief entry 108
Schwartz, Virginia Frances 1950- 200
See also SATA 131
Schwartz, William 1916-1982
Obituary 107
Schwartzberg, Julie 1943- 29-32R
Schwartzman, Aaron 1900(?)-1981
Obituary 102
Schwartzman, David 1924- 41-44R
Schwartzman, Edward 1927- 73-76
Schwartzman, Simon 1939- 143
Schwartzman, Sylvan D(avid)
1913-1994 .... CANR-21
Earlier sketch in CA 41-44R
Schwartzmann, Mischa 1919- 29-32R
Schwartz-Nobel, Loretta 232
Schwarz, Adam 1961- 152
Schwarz, Adele Aron
See Greenspun, Adele Aron
Schwarz, Alfred 1925-
Brief entry 118
Schwarz, Arturo (Umberto Samuele)
1924- CANR-136
Earlier sketch in CA 166
Schwarz, Boris 1906-1983 .... CANR-29
Obituary 111
Earlier sketch in CA 37-40R
Schwarz, Christina 192
Schwarz, Daniel R(oger) 1941- CANR-98
Earlier sketch in CA 131
Schwarz, Egon 1922- 57-60
Schwarz, Fred(erick) Charles 1913- .. CANR-69
Earlier sketches in CA 1-4R, CANR-32
Schwarz, Hans 1939- CANR-144
Earlier sketch in CA 41-44R
Schwarz, Henry G(uenter) 1928- 37-40R
Schwarz, Jack
See Schwarz, Jacob
Schwarz, Jacob 1924- 103
Schwarz, John E. 1939- 171
Schwarz, Jordan A(braham) 1937- CANR-45
Earlier sketch in CA 105
Schwarz, Karen 1957- 138
Schwarz, Leo W(alder) 1906-1967 .... 5-8R
Schwarz, Liese O'Halloran 1963- 133
Schwarz, Philip J. 1940- 232
Schwarz, Richard W(illiam) 1925- CANR-12
Earlier sketch in CA 29-32R
Schwarz, Robert 1921- 77-80
Schwarz, Robin 233
Schwarz, Sibylle 1621-1638 .... DLB 164
Schwarz, Solomon M. 1882(?)-1973
Obituary 45-48
Schwarz, Ted
See Schwarz, Theodore R., Jr.
Schwarz, Theodore R., Jr. 1945- CANR-91
Earlier sketches in CA 65-68, CANR-10, 26
Schwarz, Vera 1947- 152
Schwarz, (Silvia Tessa) Viviane 1977- 212
See also SATA 141
Schwarz, Walter 1930- 13-16R
Schwarz, Wilhelm Johannes 1929- 65-68
Schwarz-Bart, Andre 1928- CANR-109
Earlier sketch in CA 89-92
See also CLC 2, 4
See also DLB 299
Schwarz-Bart, Simone 1938- CANR-117
Earlier sketch in CA 97-100
See also BLCS
See also BW 2
See also CLC 7
See also EWL 3
Schwarzenberger, Georg 1908-1991 ..... 13-16R
Schwarzenegger, Arnold 1947- CANR-143
Earlier sketches in CA 81-84, CANR-21
See also AAYA 19, 59
Schwarzkopf, H. Norman 1934- 145
Schwarzkopf, LeRoy C(arl) 1920- CANR-38
Earlier sketch in CA 115
Schwarzkopf-Legge, Elisabeth 1915- 109
Schwarzschild, Bettina 1925- 29-32R
Schwarzschild, Stuart 1918- 5-8R
Schwarzweller, Harry K(arl) 1929- 37-40R
Schwebel, Milton 1914- 17-20R
Schwebel, Stephen M(yron) 1929- 77-80
Schwebell, Gertrude C(lorius) 9-12R
Schwed, Peter 1911-2003 .... CANR-56
Obituary 218
Earlier sketches in CA 57-60, CANR-13, 31
Schweickart, Patrocinio P. 1942- 138
Schweid, Eliezer 1929- CANR-18
Earlier sketches in CA 45-48, CANR-1
Schweid, Richard M. 1946- CANR-111
Earlier sketch in CA 106
Schweik, Robert C(harles) 1927- CANR-57
Earlier sketches in CA 45-48, CANR-31
Schweikart, Larry (Earl) 1951- 134
Schweitzer, Albert 1875-1965
Obituary 93-96
See also DLB 284
Schweitzer, Arthur 1905- 9-12R
Schweitzer, Byrd Baylor
See Baylor, Byrd
Schweitzer, Christoph E(ugen) 1922-
Brief entry 107
Schweitzer, Darrell (Charles) 1952- .. CANR-85
Earlier sketches in CA 116, CANR-39
See also FANT
Schweitzer, George K(eene) 1924- 17-20R
Schweitzer, Gertrude 1909-1996 85-88
Schweitzer, Iris 156
Brief entry 117
See also SATA 59
See also SATA-Brief 36
Schweitzer, Jerome William
1908-1988 .... 41-44R
Schweitzer, John C. 1934- 17-20R
Schweizer(-Hanhart), Eduard 1913- .. CANR-20
Earlier sketches in CA 13-16R, CANR-5
Schweizer, Karl W. 1946- CANR-97
Earlier sketch in CA 136
Schweizer, Niklaus R. 1939- 206
Schweizer, Peter 1964- 214
Schwendeman, J(oseph) R(aymond)
1897-1984 81-84
Schweninger, Ann 1951- 107
See also SATA 29, 98
Schweninger, Loren (Lance) 1941- 101
Schwerin, Doris H(alpern) 1922- CANR-9
Earlier sketch in CA 65-68
See also SATA 64
Schwerin, Jules 1919- 144
Schwerin, Kurt 1902-1995 45-48
Schwerner, Armand 1927-1999 .... CANR-85
Obituary 179
Earlier sketches in CA 9-12R, CANR-50
See also CP 2
See also DLB 165
See also PC 42
Schwertfeger, Ruth 1941- 132
Schwichtenberg, Cathy 1953- 142
Schwiebert, Ernest G(eorge)
1895-2000 .... CAP-1
Earlier sketch in CA 13-16
Schwieder, Dorothy 1933- 89-92
Schwimmer, Walter 1903-1989
Obituary 129
Schwitters, Kurt (Hermann Edward Karl Julius)
1887-1948 158
See also TCLC 95
Schwitzgebel, Robert L. 1934- 41-44R
Schwob, Marcel (Mayer Andre)
1867-1905 168
Brief entry 117
See also DLB 123
See also GFL 1789 to the Present
See also TCLC 20
Schwoerer, Lois G(reen) 1927- CANR-15
Earlier sketch in CA 77-80
Schydlowsky, Daniel M(oses) 1940- . CANR-27
Earlier sketch in CA 45-48
Schyffert, Bea Uusma 239
Sciabarra, Chris Matthew 1960- 155
Scialiano, Robert (G.) 1925- 9-12R
Scianna, Ferdinando 1943- 211
Sciascia, Leonardo 1921-1989 .... CANR-35
Obituary 130
Earlier sketch in CA 85-88
See also CLC 8, 9, 41
See also DLB 177
See also EWL 3
See also MTCW 1
See also RGWL 2, 3
Scibetta, Barbara Smith 1949- 129
Scibor-Rylski, Aleksander 1927(?)-1983
Obituary 109
See also IDFW 3, 4
Scicluna, Hannibal Publius 1880-1981(?)
Obituary 106
Scieszka, Jon 1954- CANR-84
Earlier sketch in CA 135
See also AAYA 21
See also CLR 27
See also CWRI 5
See also MAICYA 2
See also MAICYAS 1
See also SATA 68, 105, 160
Scifres, Bill(y N.) 1925- 103
Scigaj, Leonard M. -2005 198
Obituary 238
Scillian, Devin .... SATA 128
Scimecca, Joseph A. 1940- 129
Sciolino, Elaine 237
Scioscia, Mary (Hershey) 1926- .... SATA 63
Scipes, Kim 1951- 162
Scipio
See Watson, (John Hugh) Adam
Scire
See Gardner, G(erald) B(rosseau)
Scism, Carol K. 1931- 41-44R
Scithers, George H(arry) 1929- 57-60
Scitovsky, Tibor 1910-2002 104
Obituary 206
Scivener, Michael (Henry) 1948- 130
Scliar, Moacyr 1937- 136
See also EWL 3
Scoales, William 1933- 33-36R
Scobbie, Irene 1930- 191
Scobel, Donald N. 1929- 122
Scobey, Joan 1927- CANR-46
Earlier sketches in CA 57-60, CANR-7
Scobey, Mary-Margaret 1915- CANR-1
Earlier sketch in CA 1-4R
Scobie, James R(alston) 1929-1981 .... CANR-6
Obituary 104
Earlier sketch in CA 9-12R
Scobie, Stephen 1943- 111
Scoby, Donald R(ay) 1931- 33-36R
Scoffham, E. R.
See Scoffham, Ernie
Scoffham, Ernie 1939- 188
Scofield, Gregory 1966- 169
Scofield, Jonathan
See Levinson, Leonard and
Rothweiler, Paul Roger and
Toombs, John
Scofield, Martin (Paul) 1945- 132
Scofield, Norma Margaret Cartwright
1924- 103
Scofield, Penrod 1933- .... SATA 62
See also SATA-Obit 78
Scofield, Sandra (Jean) 1943- CANR-84
Earlier sketch in CA 146
Scofield, William H. 1915- 17-20R
Scoggin, Margaret C(lara) 1905-1968 .. SATA 47
See also SATA-Brief 28
Scoggins, James (Lawrence) 1934- 21-24R
Scoles, Eugene F(rancis) 1921- CANR-15
Earlier sketch in CA 37-40R
Scollan, E. A.
See O'Grady, Anne
Scolnick, Sylvan 1930(?)-1976
Obituary 69-72
Scoltock, Jack 1942- 212
See also SATA 72, 141
Scopes, John T. 1900-1970
Obituary 29-32R
Scoppettone, Sandra 1936- CANR-73
Earlier sketches in CA 5-8R, CANR-41
See also Early, Jack
See also AAYA 11, 65
See also BYA 8
See also CLC 26
See also GLL 1
See also MAICYA 2
See also MAICYAS 1
See also SATA 9, 92
See also WYA
See also YAW
Scorer, Richard 1919- 77-80
Scorsese, Martin 1942- CANR-85
Brief entry 110
Earlier sketches in CA 114, CANR-46
See also AAYA 38
See also CLC 20, 89, 207
Scortia, Thomas N(icholas)
1926-1986 .... CANR-85
Obituary 119
Earlier sketches in CA 1-4R, CANR-6
See also SFW 4
Scorza, Manuel 1928-1983 131
Obituary 113
See also HW 1
Scorza, Thomas J. 1948- 132
Scot, Chesman
See Bulmer, (Henry) Kenneth
Scot, Michael
See Rohan, Michael Scott
Scot, Reginald 1538(?)-1599 .... DLB 136
Scotchie, Joseph 1956- 235
Scotellaro, Rocco 1923-1953 182
See also DLB 128
Scotford, John Ryland 1888-1976 .... 5-8R
Obituary 103
Scotland, Andrew 1905- 5-8R
Scotland, James 1917-1983 .... CANR-36
Obituary 110
Earlier sketch in CA 33-36R
Scotland, Jay
See Jakes, John (William)
Scotson, John L(loyd) 1928-1980 .... 21-24R
Obituary 134
Scotson, Linda 1945- 128
Scott
See Charlier, Roger H(enri)
Scott, A(dolphe) C(larence) 1909- CANR-2
Earlier sketch in CA 5-8R
Scott, Agnes Neill
See Muir, Willa
Scott, Alan (B.) 1957- 141
Scott, Alastair
See Allen, Kenneth S.
Scott, Alexander 1920- 105
See also CP 1, 2
Scott, Alicia Anne 1810-1900 207
See also DLB 240
Scott, Allan
See Shiach, Allan G.
Scott, Allan (James Julius) 1952- .... FANT
Scott, Allen John 1938- 97-100
Scott, Amanda 1944- 217
Scott, Amoret (Scudamore) 1930- CANR-10
Earlier sketch in CA 21-24R
Scott, Andrew (Paul) 1947- 215
Scott, Andrew M(acKay) 1922- 17-20R
Scott, Ann Herbert 1926- CANR-119
Earlier sketches in CA 21-24R, CANR-68
See also SATA 56, 94, 140
See also SATA-Brief 29
See also SATA-Essay 140
Scott, Anne Firor 1921- 33-36R
Scott, Anthony
See Dresser, Davis
Scott, Anthony Dalton 1923- CANR-29
Earlier sketches in CA 65-68, CANR-11
Scott, Arthur Finley 1907- CANR-41
Earlier sketches in CA 5-8R, CANR-2, 18
Scott, Arthur L(incoln) 1914- 21-24R
Scott, Austin (Wakeman) 1885(?)-1981
Obituary 103
Scott, Beth (Bailey) 1922-1994 .... CANR-137
Earlier sketch in CA 132
Scott, Bill
See Scott, William N(eville)
Scott, Bill 1920(?)-1985
Obituary 117
See also SATA-Obit 46
Scott, Bonnie Kime 1944- CANR-98
Earlier sketches in CA 119, CANR-43
Scott, C(ecil) Winfield 1905-1997 .... 5-8R
Scott, Cal
See Lazenby, Norman
Scott, Casey
See Kubis, Pat
Scott, Catharine Amy Dawson
See Dawson-Scott, C(atharine) A(my)
See also DLB 240
Scott, Cecil Alexander 1902(?)-1981
Obituary 104
Scott, Charles R(alph), Jr. 1914- CANR-16
Earlier sketch in CA 89-92
Scott, Charles T. 1932- 21-24R
Scott, Charles W(esley) 1932- 116
Scott, Charlotte Angas 1858-1931 169
Scott, Christopher 1930- 21-24R
Scott, Claudia 1948-1979
Obituary 114
Scott, Clinton Lee 1890-1985 .... CAP-2
Earlier sketch in CA 19-20
Scott, Cora Annett (Pipitone) 1931- 17-20R
See also SATA 11
Scott, Cynthia 229
Scott, Cyril (Meir) 1879-1970
Obituary 111
Scott, Dan
See Barker, S(quire) Omar
Scott, Dan CANR-27
Earlier sketches in CAP-2, CA 19-20
Scott, Dana
See Robertson, Constance (Pierrepont Noyes)
Scott, Daryl Michael 1958- 166
See also BW 3
Scott, David (Aubrey) 1919- 109
Scott, David 1944- 190
Scott, David (Henry Tudor) 1948- 127
Scott, David A. 1949- 168
Scott, David L. 1942- 167
Scott, David W(infield) 1916- 109
Scott, Denise 114
Scott, Dennis (Courtney) 1939-1991 143
See also BW 2
See also CP 1
See also DLB 125
See also EWL 3
Scott, Derek B. 1950- 137
Scott, Dixon 1881-1915 184
See also DLB 98
Scott, Donald F(letcher) 1930- 89-92
Scott, Dorothea Hayward 93-96
Scott, Duncan Campbell 1862-1947 153
Brief entry 104
See also DAC
See also DLB 92
See also RGEL 2
See also TCLC 6
Scott, Edward M. 1919- 33-36R
Scott, Elaine 1940- CANR-137
Earlier sketches in CA 105, CANR-21, 50
See also SATA 36, 90
Scott, Eleanor 1921- 61-64
Scott, Ellis L(averne) 1915- 49-52
Scott, Eve
See Rodgers, Joann Ellison
Scott, Evelyn 1893-1963 .... CANR-64
Obituary 112
Earlier sketch in CA 104
See also CLC 43
See also DLB 9, 48
See also RHW
Scott, F(rancis) R(eginald)
1899-1985 .... CANR-87
Obituary 114
Earlier sketch in CA 101
Interview in CA-101
See also CLC 22
See also CP 1, 2
See also DLB 88
See also RGEL 2
Scott, Frances V.
See Wing, Frances (Scott)
Scott, Frank
See Scott, F(rancis) R(eginald)
Scott, Frank 1949- 141
Scott, Franklin D(aniel) 1901-1994 .. CANR-85
Obituary 146
Earlier sketches in CA 5-8R, CANR-5
Scott, Frederick George 1861-1944 216
See also DLB 92

Cumulative Index **519** **Scumbag**

Scott, Gail 1945- 127
Scott, Gavin 1936- 77-80
Scott, Geoffrey 1884-1929 .... DLB 149
Scott, Geoffrey 1952- 106
Scott, George (Edwin) 1925-1988 ..... CANR-85
Obituary 127
Earlier sketch in CA 29-32R
Scott, George Walton 1921- 21-24R
Scott, Grant F. 1961- CANR-112
Earlier sketch in CA 151
Scott, Grover
See King, Albert
Scott, (Peter) Hardiman 1920-1999 144
Obituary 185
Scott, Harold George 1925- 61-64
Scott, Harold Richard 1887-1969 .... 5-8R
Scott, Harold W(illiam) 1906-1998 118
Scott, Harvey W(hitefield) 1838-1910 218
See also DLB 23
Scott, Helen G. 1915(?)-1987
Obituary 124
Scott, Herbert 1931- CANR-6
Earlier sketch in CA 53-56
Scott, Hilda 1915- 124
Scott, Holden
See Mezrich, Ben
Scott, Ira O(scar), Jr. 1918- 17-20R
Scott, J(ohn) D(ick) 1917-1980 77-80
Obituary 97-100
See also CN 1, 2
Scott, J. K(eith) L. 1966- 210
Scott, J(ames) M(aurice) 1906-1986 105
Obituary 118
Scott, Jack B(rown) 1928- 77-80
Scott, Jack Denton 1915-1995 .... CANR-86
Earlier sketches in CA 108, CANR-48
See also CLR 20
See also MAICYA 1, 2
See also MAICYAS 1
See also SAAS 14
See also SATA 31, 83
Scott, Jack S.
See Escott, Jonathan
Scott, James A. 1946- 123
Scott, James B(urton) 1926- 85-88
Scott, James C(ampbell) 1936- 29-32R
Scott, James F(razier) 1934- CANR-47
Earlier sketches in CA 77-80, CANR-22
Scott, Jane
See McElfresh, (Elizabeth) Adeline
Scott, Jane (Harrington) 1931- .... SATA 55
Scott, Jay 1949-1993 133
Obituary 142
Scott, Jean
See Muir, Marie
Scott, Jeffrey
See Usher, Shaun
Scott, Joan .... CLC 65
Scott, Joanna 1960- CANR-92
Earlier sketches in CA 126, CANR-53
See also CLC 50
Scott, Joanna C.
See Scott, Joanna Catherine
Scott, Joanna Catherine 1943- 228
Scott, Joanne 212
Scott, Jody 81-84
Scott, John 1912-1976 .... CANR-6
Obituary 69-72
Earlier sketch in CA 5-8R
See also RGEL 2
See also SATA 14
Scott, John (Peter) 1949- 126
Scott, John A. 1948- CANR-85
Earlier sketch in CA 135
See also CP 7
Scott, John Anthony 1916- CANR-23
Earlier sketches in CA 9-12R, CANR-6
See also SATA 23
Scott, John Irving E(lias) (?)-1981 73-76
Obituary 133
Scott, John M(artin) 1913- CANR-50
Earlier sketches in CA 65-68, CANR-10, 25
See also SATA 12
Scott, Johnie Harold 1946- CANR-14
Earlier sketch in CA 33-36R
See also CP 1
Scott, Jonathan 1958- CANR-96
Earlier sketch in CA 132
Scott, (Henry) Joseph 1917- 57-60
Scott, Joseph Reid 1926- 41-44R
Scott, Judith Unger 1916- 5-8R
Scott, Justin CANR-75
Earlier sketches in CA 104, CANR-26
Scott, Kathleen 1955- 224
Scott, Kay W. 169
Scott, Kenneth 1900-1993 .... CANR-26
Obituary 143
Earlier sketches in CA 69-72, CANR-11
Scott, Kenneth J. 1933(?)-1983
Obituary 111
Scott, Kim 1957- 217
Scott, Lady John
See Scott, Alicia Anne
Scott, Lalla (McIntosh) 1893-1981 .... CAP-2
Earlier sketch in CA 21-22
Scott, Latayne Colvett 1952- CANR-17
Earlier sketch in CA 97-100
Scott, Lauren
See Frentzen, Jeffrey
Scott, Laurence Prestwich 1909-1983
Obituary 110
Scott, Leonard B. III 1948- 143
Scott, Lloyd
See Turner, George E(ugene)
Scott, Lloyd F. 1926- 21-24R
Scott, Louise Binder 1910- CANR-4
Earlier sketch in CA 1-4R
Scott, Lucy 1928- 175
See also CWRI 5
See also YAW
Scott, Manda 225
Scott, Marcia (Adele Morse) 1943- 97-100
Scott, Margaret (Allan Bennett) 1928- 145
Scott, Margaret B(rodie) (?)-1976
Obituary 61-64
Scott, Martin
See Gehman, Richard (Boyd)
Scott, Marvin B(ailey) 1944-
Brief entry 118
Scott, Mary
See Mattern, Joanne
Scott, Mary Jane W(ittstock) 1949- 129
Scott, Mel(lier Goodin) 1906-1988 .... 29-32R
Scott, Melissa 1960- CANR-102
Earlier sketch in CA 161
See also AAYA 37
See also SATA 109
See also SFW 4
Scott, (Guthrie) Michael 1907-1983 130
Obituary 110
Scott, Michael 1924(?)-1989
Obituary 129
See also HGG
Scott, (Robert James) Munroe 1927- 130
Scott, Natalie Anderson 1906-1983 .... CAP-2
Earlier sketch in CA 23-24
Scott, Nathan A(lexander), Jr. 1925- . CANR-20
Earlier sketches in CA 9-12R, CANR-5
See also BW 2
Scott, Nerissa
See Ring, Elizabeth
Scott, Nina M. 1937- CANR-100
Earlier sketch in CA 146
Scott, Norford
See Rowland, D(onald) S(ydney)
Scott, Otto J. 1918- 85-88
Scott, Owen Le Grand 1898-1985
Obituary 117
Scott, P(aul) H(enderson) 1920- 142
Scott, P. T.
See Poage, Scott T(abor)
Scott, Patrick (Greig) 1945- 112
Scott, Paul (Mark) 1920-1978 .... CANR-33
Obituary 77-80
Earlier sketch in CA 81-84
See also BRWS 1
See also CLC 9, 60
See also CN 1, 2
See also DLB 14, 207
See also EWL 3
See also MTCW 1
See also RGEL 2
See also RHW
See also WWE 1
Scott, Peter (Markham) 1909-1989 101
Obituary 129
Scott, Peter Dale 1929- CANR-103
Earlier sketches in CA 21-24R, CANR-9
Scott, Peter Graham
See Graham Scott, Peter
Scott, R(obert) B(algarnie) Y(oung) 1899-1987
Obituary 124
Scott, Rachel (Ann) 1947- 103
Scott, Ralph S(amuel) 1927- 41-44R
Scott, Rebecca J(arvis) 1950- 128
Scott, Regina
See Lundgren, Regina (E.)
Scott, Richard
See Rennert, Richard Scott
Scott, Richard A(llen) 1931- 25-28R
Scott, Ridley 1937- .... AAYA 13, 43
See also CLC 183
Scott, Robert A. 1936- 89-92
Scott, Robert Adrian 1901(?)-1972
Obituary 37-40R
Scott, Robert E(dwin) 1923- CANR-1
Earlier sketch in CA 1-4R
Scott, Robert F(alcon) 1868-1912 184
Brief entry 115
Scott, Robert Garth 1957- 137
Scott, Robert Haney 1927- 17-20R
Scott, Robert Ian 1931- 106
Scott, Robert Lee, Jr. 1908- CAP-1
Earlier sketch in CA 11-12
Scott, Robert Lee 1928- CANR-3
Earlier sketch in CA 5-8R
Scott, Robin
See Wilson, Robin Scott
Scott, Roger (Dennis) 1939- 97-100
Scott, Ronald Bodley 1906-1982 109
Obituary 106
Scott, Ronald Guthrie McNair
See McNair Scott, Ronald (Guthrie)
Scott, Roney
See Gault, William Campbell
Scott, Rosie 1948- .... CN 7
Scott, Roy Vernon 1927- CANR-1
Earlier sketch in CA 1-4R
Scott, Sally 1909-1978 116
See also SATA 43
Scott, Sally (Elisabeth) 1948- 125
See also SATA 44
Scott, Sarah 1723-1795 .... DLB 39
Scott, Sheila
See MacIntyre, Sheila Scott
Scott, Sheila (Christine) 1927-1988 53-56
Obituary 126
Scott, Sophfronia 1966(?)- 235
Scott, Stanley
See Fagerstrom, Stan
Scott, Stephen E. 1948- CANR-43
Earlier sketch in CA 115
Scott, Steve
See Crawford, William (Elbert)
Scott, Stuart
See Aitken, W(illiam) R(ussell)
Scott, Tirsa Saavedra 1920- 13-16R
Scott, Tom 1918-1995 .... 9-12R
See also CP 1, 2
See also DLB 27
Scott, Trevor 216
Scott, Valerie
See Rowland, D(onald) S(ydney)
Scott, Virgil (Joseph) 1914- CANR-2
Earlier sketch in CA 5-8R
Scott, Virginia M(uhleman) 1945- CANR-92
Earlier sketch in CA 121
Scott, W(illiam) E(dgar), Jr. 1929- 49-52
Scott, W. N.
See Scott, William N(eville)
Scott, W(illiam) Richard 1932- 17-20R
Scott, Sir Walter 1771-1832 .... AAYA 22
See also BRW 4
See also BYA 2
See also CDBLB 1789-1832
See also DA
See also DAB
See also DAC
See also DAM MST, NOV, POET
See also DLB 93, 107, 116, 144, 159
See also GL 3
See also HGG
See also LAIT 1
See also PC 13
See also RGEL 2
See also RGSF 2
See also SSC 32
See also SSFS 10
See also SUFW 1
See also TEA
See also WLC
See also WLIT 3
See also YABC 2
Scott, Warwick
See Trevor, Elleston
Scott, Whitney 1945- CANR-93
Earlier sketch in CA 145
Scott, Willard H., Jr. 1934- CANR-140
Earlier sketch in CA 109
Scott, William Abbott 1926- CANR-9
Earlier sketch in CA 5-8R
Scott, William B(utler) 1945- 126
Scott, William Bell 1811-1890 .... DLB 32
See also RGEL 2
Scott, William C(lyde) 1937- 119
Scott, William G(eorge) 1926- CANR-11
Earlier sketch in CA 21-24R
Scott, William Henry 1921- 132
Scott, William L.
See Finley, Joseph E(dwin)
Scott, William N(eville) 1923- CANR-85
Earlier sketches in CA 132, CANR-52
See also CWRI 5
See also SATA 87
Scott, William R(eese) 1907- 77-80
Scott, William R(alph) 1918-1992 101
Obituary 136
Scott, Wilson L(udlow) 1909-1983 ... CANR-34
Obituary 111
Earlier sketch in CA 45-48
Scott, Winfield H(arker) 1932-1992 ...... 21-24R
Obituary 136
Scott, Winfield Townley 1910-1968 .... CANR-7
Obituary 25-28R
Earlier sketch in CA 5-8R
See also MAL 5
Scott-Clark, Cathy 1965- 216
Scott-Drennan, Lynne
See Scott, Amanda
Scott-Giles, C(harles) W(ilfred) 1893-1982(?)
Obituary 106
Scott-Heron, Gil 1949- CANR-90
Earlier sketches in CA 45-48, CANR-24
See also BW 1
See also DLB 41
Scotti, Anna
See Coates, Anna
Scotti, Anna
See Coates, Anna
Scotti, Paul C(arl) 1943- 118
Scotti, R. A. 1946- CANR-103
Earlier sketches in CA 122, CANR-48
Scott-James, Anne Eleanor 1913- 105
Scott-Moncrieff, David (William Hardy)
1907-1987
Obituary 123
Scott-Moncrieff, George (Irving)
1910-1999(?) CAP-1
Earlier sketch in CA 11-12
Scott Moncrieff, Martha Christian 1897- . 61-64
Scotto, Robert M(ichael) 1942- 57-60
Scottoline, Lisa 1956(?)- 186
See also AAYA 30
Scott-Stokes, Henry J. M. 128
Brief entry 117
Scott-Taggart, John 1897-1979
Obituary 104
Scott Thorn, Ronald
See Wilkinson, Ronald
Scouten, Arthur Hawley 1910-1995 . CANR-11
Obituary 148
Earlier sketches in CAP-1, CA 13-14
Scovel, Myra (Scott) 1905-1994 .... CANR-2
Earlier sketch in CA 5-8R
Scovell, Brian (Souter) 1935- CANR-86
Earlier sketch in CA 130
Scovell, E(dith) J(oy) 1907-1999 .... CANR-85
Obituary 187
Earlier sketch in CA 136
See also CP 1, 2
Scovell, Jane (Frances) 1934- CANR-90
Earlier sketch in CA 116
Scoville, Herbert, Jr. 1915-1985 .... CANR-43
Obituary 116
Earlier sketch in CA 29-32R
Scoville, James G(riffin) 1940- 29-32R
Scoville, Warren Candler 1913-1969 . CANR-2
Earlier sketch in CA 1-4R
Scowcroft, Richard P(ingree) 1916-2001 . 9-12R
Obituary 202
Scraton, Phil 1949- 128
Screech, M(ichael) A(ndrew) 1926- 140
Scriabine, Helene (A. Gorstrine)
1906-1996 .... CANR-45
Earlier sketches in CA 21-24R, CANR-14
Scribe, (Augustin) Eugene
1791-1861 .... DAM DRAM
See also DC 5
See also DLB 192
See also GFL 1789 to the Present
See also RGWL 2, 3
Scribner, Charles, Jr. 1921-1995 69-72
Obituary 150
See also DLBD 17
See also DLBY 1995
See also SATA 13
See also SATA-Obit 87
Scribner, Charles III 1951- 126
Scribner, Joanne L. 1949- .... SATA 33
Scribner, Keith 1962(?)- 209
Scribner, Kimball 1917- .... SATA 63
Scribner, Sylvia 1923-1991 133
Scrimgeour, Gary J(ames) 1934- 108
Scrimger, Richard 1957- 190
See also MAICYA 2
See also SATA 119
Scrimshaw, Nevin Stewart 1918- 89-92
Scrimsher, Lila Gravatt 1897-1974 .... 1-4R
Obituary 103
See also SATA-Obit 28
Scripps, E(dward) W(yllis) 1854-1926
Brief entry 118
See also DLB 25
Scripps, James G. 1911-1986
Obituary 121
Scriven, Michael (John) 1928- CANR-14
Earlier sketch in CA 21-24R
Scrivener, Michael (Henry) 1948- CANR-86
Earlier sketch in CA 130
Scriver, Bob
See Scriver, Robert MacFie
Scriver, Robert MacFie 1914-1999 115
Obituary 174
Scrivner, Wilma Possien 1915- 107
Scroder, Walter K. 1928- .... SATA 82
Scroggins, Daniel C(oy) 1937- 33-36R
Scroggins, Deborah 1961- 224
Scroggs, Robin (Jerome) 1930- 116
Scruggs, C(harles) Eugene 1937- 113
Scruggs, Sandy 1961- 155
See also SATA 89
Scrum, R.
See Crumb, R(obert)
Scruton, Roger 1944- CANR-105
Earlier sketches in CA 89-92, CANR-16, 39
Scudamore, Pauline 1936- 129
Scudder, Brooke 1959- .... SATA 154
Scudder, C(leo) W(ayne) 1915- CANR-3
Earlier sketch in CA 1-4R
Scudder, Horace E(lisha) 1838-1902
Brief entry 119
See also DLB 42, 71
Scudder, Kenyon J. 1890-1977
Obituary 73-76
Scudder, Mildred Lee 1908- CANR-85
Earlier sketch in CA 9-12R
See also Lee, Mildred
See also YAW
Scudder, Rogers V(aughn) 1912- 17-20R
Scudder, Thayer 1930- 126
Brief entry 106
Scudder, Townsend (III) 1900-1988
Obituary 126
Scudder, Vida Dutton 1861-1954 183
See also DLB 71
Scudery, Georges de
1601-1667 .... GFL Beginnings to 1789
Scudery, Madeleine de 1607-1701 ..... DLB 268
See also GFL Beginnings to 1789
Sculatti, (Eu)Gene 1947- 110
Scull, Andrew 1947- CANR-122
Earlier sketches in CA 81-84, CANR-15, 33
Scull, Florence Doughty 1905-1982 ...... CAP-1
Earlier sketch in CA 11-12
Scull, Marie-Louise 1943-1993 .... SATA 77
Scullard, Howard Hayes 1903-1983 .. CANR-3
Obituary 109
Earlier sketch in CA 9-12R
Sculle, Keith A. 1941- 232
Sculley, John 1939- 127
Scully, Frank 1892-1964 .... 5-8R
Scully, Gerald William 1941- 65-68
Scully, Helen 1977- 239
Scully, James 1937- 175
Earlier sketches in CA 25-28R, CANR-11
Autobiographical Essay in 175
See also CAAS 30
See also CP 1, 2, 3, 4, 5, 6, 7
Scully, Julia S(ilverman) 1929- 103
Scully, Pamela (Frederika) 1962- 170
Scully, Vincent (Joseph, Jr.) 1920- ... CANR-139
Brief entry 113
Earlier sketch in CA 147
Scum
See Crumb, R(obert)
Scumbag, Little Bobby
See Crumb, R(obert)

Scuorzo, Herbert E(rnest) 1928- 21-24R
Scupham, John Peter 1933- CANR-9
Earlier sketch in CA 65-68
See also CP 2, 3, 4, 5, 6, 7
See also DLB 40
Scuro, Vincent 1951- CANR-40
Earlier sketches in CA 53-56, CANR-5
See also SATA 21
Scutt, Ronald 1916- 97-100
Sczesnoczkawasm, Jun
See Smith, Warren Allen
Seaberg, Stanley 1929- 21-24R
Seaborg, Glenn T(heodore)
1912-1999 .... CANR-2
Obituary 179
Earlier sketch in CA 49-52
Seabough, Ed(ward Ellis) 1932- 29-32R
Seabright, John
See Tubb, E(dwin) C(harles)
Seabrook, David 239
Seabrook, Jeremy 1939- CANR-111
Earlier sketch in CA 108
See also CBD
See also CD 6
Seabrook, John
See Hubbard, L(afayette) Ron(ald)
Seabrook, John M., Jr. 1959- 227
Seabrook, Mike 1950- 147
Seabrook, William B(uehler) 1886-1945
Brief entry 107
See also DLB 4
Seabrooke, Brenda 1941- CANR-130
Earlier sketch in CA 107
See also SATA 30, 88, 148
Seabury, Paul 1923-1990
Obituary 132
Brief entry 115
Seabury, Samuel 1729-1796 .... DLB 31
Seacole, Mary Jane Grant 1805-1881 . DLB 166
Seaford, Richard 235
Seagal, Steve
See Seagal, Steven
Seagal, Steven 1952- 174
Seagears, Clayton B. 1902(?)-1983
Obituary 110
Seager, Allan 1906-1968 .... 5-8R
Obituary 25-28R
Seager, Ralph William 1911- CANR-6
Earlier sketch in CA 9-12R
Seager, Robert II 1924-2004 .... CANR-6
Obituary 230
Earlier sketch in CA 5-8R
Seager, Stephen B. 1950- 139
Seager, Walter H(arold) T(ennant) 1938- 120
Seagle, Janet 1924- 102
Seagle, William 1898-1977 .... 5-8R
Obituary 73-76
Seagoe, May V(iolet) 1906-1980 ...... CANR-10
Earlier sketch in CA 13-16R
Seagrave, Sterling 1937- CANR-91
Brief entry 125
Earlier sketch in CA 135
Interview in CA-135
Seagroatt, Margaret 1920- CANR-13
Earlier sketch in CA 73-76
Seagull, Louis Martin 1941- 112
Seal 1963- 156
Seal, Anil 1938- 25-28R
Seal, Basil
See Kavanagh, Dan(iel)
Seal, Jeremy 1962- 209
Seale, Alan 1955- 164
Seale, Bobby
See Seale, Robert George
Seale, Ervin 1910(?)-1990
Obituary 130
Seale, John 1943- .... IDFW 4
Seale, Patrick 1930- 97-100
Seale, Robert George 1936- 110
See also BW 1
Seale, William 1939- CANR-7
Earlier sketch in CA 17-20R
Sealey, Bruce
See Sealey, D(onald) Bruce
Sealey, D(onald) Bruce 1929- 121
Sealey, Danguole 1931- 33-36R
Sealey, Leonard (George William) 1923- 103
Sealey, (Bertram) Raphael (Izod) 1927- 65-68
Sea-Lion
See Bennett, Geoffrey (Martin)
Sealock, Richard Burl 1907- CAP-2
Earlier sketch in CA 23-24
Seals, David 1947- 145
Sealsfield, Charles 1793-1864 .... DLB 133, 186
Sealts, Merton M(iller), Jr. 1915- 13-16R
Sealy, I(rwin) Allan 1951- 136
See also CLC 55
See also CN 6, 7
Seaman, Ann Rowe 231
Seaman, Augusta Huiell 1879-1950
Brief entry 110
See also SATA 31
Seaman, Barbara 1935- CANR-142
Earlier sketch in CA 29-32R
Seaman, (A.) Barrett 1945- 73-76
Seaman, Don F(erris) 1935- 77-80
Seaman, Donald (Peter) 1922-1997 155
Obituary 161
Brief entry 114
Seaman, Elizabeth Cochrane 183
See also Cochrane, Elizabeth
Seaman, Gerald Roberts 1934- 25-28R
Seaman, John E(ugene) 1932- 89-92
Seaman, L(ewis) C(harles) B(ernard)
1911- 57-60
Seaman, P. David 1932- 143
Seaman, Sylvia S(ybil Bernstein)
1901(?)-1995 .... CAP-2
Obituary 147
Earlier sketch in CA 23-24
Seaman, William M(illard) 1907- 41-44R
Seamands, John Thompson 1916- 9-12R
Seamands, Ruth 1916- 45-48
See also SATA 9
Sear, Frank 1944- 121
Seara Vazquez, M(odesto) 1931- CANR-14
Earlier sketch in CA 17-20R
Search, Alexander
See Pessoa, Fernando (Antonio Nogueira)
Search-Light
See Frank, Waldo (David)
Searcy, David 1946- 203
Searcy, Margaret Zehmer 1926- 81-84
See also SATA 54
See also SATA-Brief 39
Seare, Nicholas
See Whitaker, Rod(ney)
Searight, Mary W(illiams) 1918- 29-32R
See also SATA 17
Searing, Donald D. 1942- 148
Searing, Helen E. 1933- 111
Searing, Susan Ellis 1950- 122
Searle, Elizabeth 1962- CANR-109
Earlier sketch in CA 164
Searle, G(eoffrey) R(ussell) 1940- 171
Searle, Humphrey 1915-1982 .... 9-12R
Obituary 106
Searle, John R(ogers) 1932- CANR-51
Earlier sketches in CA 25-28R, CANR-26
See also DLB 279
Searle, Kathryn Adrienne 1942- 29-32R
See also SATA 10
Searle, Leroy F(rank) 1942- 73-76
Searle, Mark 1941- 114
Searle, Ronald (William Fordham)
1920- CANR-87
Earlier sketches in CA 9-12R, CANR-25, 50
See also MAICYA 1, 2
See also SATA 42, 70
Searle, Verna (Ruth) 1919- 132
Searles, (William) Baird 1934-1993 123
Searles, Herbert L(eon) 1891-1980 45-48
Searles, John 1968(?)- 207
Searles, P. D(avid) 1933- 164
Searles, Richard B. 1936- 139
Searls, David 1947- 233
Searls, Doc
See Searls, David
Searls, Hank
See Searls, Henry Hunt, Jr.
Searls, Henry Hunt, Jr. 1922- CANR-85
Earlier sketches in CA 13-16R, CANR-28
See also SFW 4
Sears, Barry 1947- 154
Sears, David 1951- 184
Sears, David O'Keefe 1935- 29-32R
Sears, Deane
See Rywell, Martin
Sears, Donald A(lbert) 1923- CANR-6
Earlier sketch in CA 5-8R
Sears, Edward I. 1819(?)-1876 .... DLB 79
Sears, Francis W. 1898-1975
Obituary 61-64
Sears, Hal D(on) 1942- 122
Sears, James T(homas) 1951- CANR-113
Earlier sketch in CA 164
Sears, Joe 1949- 160
Sears, Martha 1945- 210
Sears, Paul Bigelow 1891-1990 .... 17-20R
Sears, Paul M(cCutcheon) 1920- 1-4R
Sears, Pauline Snedden 1908-1993 .... 29-32R
Sears, Peter 1937- 110
Sears, Richard 225
Sears, Robert R(ichardson) 1908-1989 .. 17-20R
Obituary 128
Sears, Sallie 1932- 41-44R
Sears, Stephen W. 1932- CANR-96
Earlier sketches in CA 33-36R, CANR-45
See also SATA 4
Sears, Val 1927- 73-76
Sears, William (P.) 1939- CANR-123
Earlier sketch in CA 160
Sears, William P(aul), Jr. 1902-1976
Obituary 61-64
Seary, E(dgar) R(onald) 1908-1984 .... 41-44R
Seashore, Stanley E. 1915- CANR-24
Earlier sketch in CA 33-36R
Seasoltz, R(obert) Kevin 1930- 9-12R
Seasongood, Murray 1878-1983
Obituary 109
Seat, William R(obert), Jr. 1920- 13-16R
Seaton, Beryl
See Platts, Beryl
Seaton, Don Cash(ius) 1902-1986 .... CAP-1
Earlier sketch in CA 9-10
Seaton, Douglas P(aul) 1947- 107
Seaton, Frederick Andrew 1909-1974
Obituary 89-92
Seaton, George 1911-1979 105
Obituary 89-92
Interview in CA-105
See also DLB 44
Seaton, J(erome) P. 1941- 166
Seaton, Mary Ethel (?)-1974
Obituary 53-56
Seaton, Matt 1965- 212
Seaton, William Winston 1785-1866 .... DLB 43
Seator, Lynette 214
Seaver, George (Fenn) 1890-1976 .... CAP-1
Earlier sketch in CA 13-14
Seaver, Kirsten A. 1934- 191
Seaver, Paul S(iddall) 1932- 29-32R
Seay, James 1939- 29-32R
See also CSW
Seay, Jody 227
Seay, Thomas A(ustin) 1942- 97-100
Sebag Montefiore, Simon
See Sebag-Montefiore, Simon
Sebag-Montefiore, Simon 1965- 136
Sebald, Hans 1929- 73-76
Sebald, W(infried) G(eorg)
1944-2001 .... CANR-98
Obituary 202
Earlier sketch in CA 159
See also BRWS 8
See also CLC 194
See also MTFW 2005
Sebald, William J(oseph) 1901-1980 ..... CAP-1
Obituary 101
Earlier sketch in CA 13-16
Sebastian, Jeanne
See Newsome, Arden J(eanne)
Sebastian, Lee
See Silverberg, Robert
Sebastian, Margaret
See Gladstone, Arthur M.
Sebastian, Mihail
See Hechter, Iosif
Sebastian, Richard
See Golder, Herbert (Alan)
Sebastian, Tim 1952- 139
Sebastian Owl
See Thompson, Hunter S(tockton)
Sebba, Anne (Marietta) 1951- CANR-94
Earlier sketches in CA 127, CANR-55
Sebbar, Leila 1941- 199
See also EWL 3
Sebenthall, R(oberta) E(lizabeth)
1917-1979 .... 33-36R
Sebeok, Thomas A(lbert)
1920-2001 .... CANR-96
Obituary 200
Earlier sketches in CA 9-12R, CANR-46
Seberg, Jean 1938-1979
Obituary 89-92
Sebes, Joseph (Schobert) 1915-1990
Obituary 131
Sebesta, Sam L(eaton) 1930- 85-88
Sebestyen, Gyorgy 1930- CANR-6
Earlier sketch in CA 9-12R
Sebestyen, Igen
See Sebestyen, Ouida
Sebestyen, Ouida 1924- CANR-114
Earlier sketches in CA 107, CANR-40
See also AAYA 8
See also BYA 7
See also CLC 30
See also CLR 17
See also JRDA
See also MAICYA 1, 2
See also SAAS 10
See also SATA 39, 140
See also WYA
See also YAW
Sebold, Alice 1963(?)- 203
See also AAYA 56
See also CLC 193
See also MTFW 2005
Seboldt, Roland H(enry) A(ugust) 1924- 5-8R
Sebree, Charles 1914-1985
Obituary 117
Sebrey, Mary Ann 1951- 116
See also SATA 62
Secchiaroli, Tazio 1925-1998 205
Secher, Bjorn 1929- 33-36R
Sechrest, Lee 1929- 17-20R
Sechrist, Elizabeth Hough 1903-1991 .... 5-8R
See also SATA 2
Seckel, Al 1958- CANR-144
Earlier sketch in CA 122
Seckler, David William 1935- 115
Secombe, Harry (Donald) 1921-2001 57-60
Obituary 194
Secondari, John Hermes 1919-1975 61-64
Obituary 57-60
Second Duke of Buckingham
See Villiers, George
Secor, Robert 1939- CANR-15
Earlier sketch in CA 89-92
Secrest, Meryle 1930- CANR-113
Earlier sketch in CANR-50
Secretan, Lance H. K. 1939- 130
Secrist, Margaret C(rystal) 1905- 111
Secrist Schmedes, Barbera 1952- 238
Secunda, Sholom 1894-1974
Obituary 49-52
Secunda, Victoria (H.) 1939- CANR-95
Earlier sketch in CA 141
Secundus, H. Scriblerus
See Fielding, Henry
Secundus, Petrus Lotichius
1528-1560 .... DLB 179
Sedaine, Michel-Jean
1719-1797 .... GFL Beginnings to 1789
Sedaitis, Judith B. 165
Sedaka, Neil 1939- 103
Sedaris, Amy 1961- 226
Sedaris, David 1957(?)- CANR-138
Earlier sketches in CA 147, CANR-68, 100
See also AAYA 47
See also MTFW 2005
Seddon, Andrew M. 1959- 155
Sederberg, Arelo Charles 1930- 37-40R
Sederberg, Peter C(arl) 1943- 65-68
Sedges, John
See Buck, Pearl S(ydenstricker)
Sedgewick, Ellery 1872-1960
Obituary 89-92
See also DLB 91
Sedgwick, Alexander 1930- 17-20R
Sedgwick, Arthur George 1844-1915 185
See also DLB 64
Sedgwick, Catharine Maria 1789-1867 . DLB 1,
74, 183, 239, 243, 254
See also FL 1:3
See also RGAL 4
Sedgwick, Eve Kosofsky 1950- CANR-90
Earlier sketch in CA 145
See also DLB 246
Sedgwick, Fred 1945- CANR-85
Earlier sketch in CA 154
See also CP 7
Sedgwick, Jeffrey Leigh 1951- 116
Sedgwick, John 1954- CANR-94
Earlier sketch in CA 145
Sedgwick, Marcus 1968- 238
See also SATA 160
Sedgwick, Michael Carl 1926-1983 89-92
Obituary 111
Sedgwick, Peter 1934-1983
Obituary 110
Sedgwick, Walter (Bradbary) 1885- CAP-1
Earlier sketch in CA 13-14
Sedlacek, William E(dward) 1939- 69-72
Sedlar, Jean W. 1935- 147
Sedler, Robert Allen 1935- 41-44R
Sedley, Sir Charles 1639-1701 .... BRW 2
See also DLB 131
See also RGEL 2
Sedley, David Neil 1947- 195
Sedley, Kate
See Clarke, Brenda (Margaret Lilian)
Sed-Rajna, Gabrielle 1927- CANR-123
Earlier sketches in CA 168, CANR-122
Seduro, Vladimir 1910-1995 .... 41-44R
Sedwick, B(enjamin) Frank 1924- 9-12R
Sedych, Andrei
See Zwibak, Jacques
See, Carolyn (Penelope) 1934- CANR-84
Earlier sketches in CA 29-32R, CANR-25, 50
Interview in CANR-25
See also CAAS 22
See also CN 6, 7
See, (Nadine) Ingram 1904-1997 112
See, Lisa
See Kendall, Lisa See
See, Ruth Douglas 1910- CANR-35
Earlier sketches in CA 1-4R, CANR-1
Seeber, Edward Derbyshire 1904-1983 . 13-16R
Seeber, Gerd Christian 1941- 113
Seeberg, Peter 1925-1999 .... DLB 214
See also EWL 3
Seebohm, Caroline 1940- CANR-114
Earlier sketch in CA 102
Seebord, G. R.
See Soderberg, Percy Measday
Seed, Cecile Eugenie 1930- CANR-83
Earlier sketches in CA 21-24R, CANR-26, 51
See also Seed, Jenny
See also CWRI 5
See also SATA 86
Seed, David 1946- CANR-93
Earlier sketch in CA 150
Seed, Jenny
See Seed, Cecile Eugenie
See also CLR 76
See also SATA 8
Seed, Sheila Turner 1937(?)-1979
Obituary 89-92
See also SATA-Obit 23
Seedman, Albert A. 1918-
Brief entry 112
Seefeldt, Carol 1935-2005 146
Obituary 235
Seeger, Alan 1888-1916 185
See also DLB 45
Seeger, Charles Louis 1886-1979 101
Obituary 85-88
Seeger, Elizabeth 1889-1973
Obituary 45-48
See also BYA 4
See also SATA-Obit 20
Seeger, Murray (Amsdell) 1929- 152
Seeger, Pete(r R.) 1919- CANR-118
Earlier sketches in CA 69-72, CANR-33
See also SATA 13, 139
Seegers, Kathleen Walker 1915- 21-24R
Seeley, Barbara J. 1964- 214
Seeley, John R(onald) 1913- 25-28R
Seeley, Laura L. 1958- .... SATA 71
Seelhammer, Ruth 1917- 41-44R
Seelig, Sharon Cadman 1941- 119
Seely, Gordon M. 1930- 37-40R
Seely, Norma 1942- 113
Seely, Rebecca Z(ahm) 1935- 104
Seelye, H(ugh) Ned 1934- 102
Seelye, John (Douglas) 1931- CANR-70
Earlier sketch in CA 97-100
Interview in CA-97-100
See also CLC 7
See also TCWW 1, 2
Seeman, Bernard 1911-1990 .... 21-24R
Seeman, Elizabeth (Brickel) 1904-1994 . CAP-1
Earlier sketch in CA 19-20
Seeman, Ernest Albright 1887-1979 85-88
Seers, Dudley 1920-1983 129
Obituary 109
Seers, Eugene 1865-1945 178
See also Dantin, Louis
Seese, Ethel Gray 1903-1998 89-92
Seese, June Akers 1935- 134
Seet, Leonard
See Sheet, Lenny
Seever, R.
See Reeves, Lawrence F.
Sefa Dei, George J. 1954- 198

Cumulative Index 521 **Sellers**

Seferiades, Giorgos Stylianou
1900-1971 .... CANR-36
Obituary 33-36R
Earlier sketches in CA 5-8R, CANR-5
See also Seferis, George
See also MTCW 1
Seferis, George
See Seferiades, Giorgos Stylianou
See also CLC 5, 11
See also EW 12
See also EWL 3
See also PC 66
See also RGWL 2, 3
Sefler, George Francis 1945- 81-84
Sefozo, Mary 1925- .... SATA 82
Sefton, Catherine
See Waddell, Martin
Sefton, James E(dward) 1939- 21-24R
Segal, Abraham 1911(?)-1977
Obituary 69-72
Segal, Alan F(ranklin) 1945- CANR-44
Earlier sketch in CA 119
Segal (Freilich), Ariel 1965- 229
Segal, Bernice G. 1929-1989
Obituary 128
Segal, Charles Paul 1936-2002 .... CANR-92
Obituary 204
Earlier sketches in CA 41-44R, CANR-16, 39
Segal, David I. 1928(?)-1970
Obituary 104
Segal, David R(obert) 1941- CANR-52
Earlier sketches in CA 111, CANR-28
Segal, Elliot A(lan) 1938- 93-96
Segal, Erich (Wolf) 1937- CANR-113
Earlier sketches in CA 25-28R, CANR-20, 36, 65
Interview in CANR-20
See also BEST 89:1
See also BPFB 3
See also CLC 3, 10
See also CPW
See also DAM POP
See also DLBY 1986
See also MTCW 1
Segal, Fred 1924(?)-1976 69-72
Obituary 65-68
Segal, Gerald 1953- 117
Segal, Geraldine R(osenbaum) 1908- 113
Segal, Hanna M(aria) 1918- 101
Segal, Harold S. 1903-1985 .... 29-32R
Segal, Harriet 1931- CANR-103
Earlier sketches in CA 123, CANR-50
Segal, Harvey H(irst) 1922-1994 ...... CANR-85
Obituary 144
Earlier sketch in CA 1-4R
Segal, Helen Gertrude 1929- .... CP 1
Segal, Henry 1901(?)-1985
Obituary 116
Segal, Howard P. 1948- 144
Segal, Jeanne (Sandra) 1939- 108
Segal, Joyce 1940- 101
See also SATA 35
Segal, Julia (Clare) 1950- 145
Segal, Julius 1924-1994 184
Brief entry 112
Segal, Lore (Groszmann) 1928- CANR-5
Earlier sketch in CA 13-16R
See also DLB 299
See also SAAS 11
See also SATA 4, 66, 163
Segal, Lynne 1943- 133
Segal, Marilyn 1927- CANR-23
Earlier sketches in CA 17-20R, CANR-8
Segal, Martin -1982 .... CANR-1
Earlier sketch in CA 1-4R
Segal, Melvin J(ames) 1910-1995 .... 37-40R
Segal, Mendel 1914- 49-52
Segal, Muriel 1913- 121
Segal, Nancy (L.) 1951- 190
Segal, Naomi (Dinah) 1949- 128
Segal, Robert M(ilton) 1925- CANR-32
Earlier sketch in CA 29-32R
Segal, Ronald (Michael) 1932- CANR-144
Earlier sketches in CA 21-24R, CANR-14
Segal, S(tanley) S. 1919-1994 .... 25-28R
Segal, Susan 1956- 204
Segalen, Martine 1940- 130
Segalman, Ralph 1916- 106
Segar, E(lzie) C(risler) 1894-1938 .... SATA 61
Segedin, Petar 1909- .... DLB 181
See also EWL 3
Segel, Harold B(ernard) 1930- CANR-127
Earlier sketch in CA 21-24R
Segel, Thomas D(onald) 1931- 93-96
Segell, Michael 1951- 186
Seger, Bob 1945- .... CLC 35
Seger, Maura 1951- .... RHW
Segerberg, Osborn, Jr. 1924- 115
Segev, Tom 1945- 207
Segger, Sydney Walter 1902-(?) CAP-1
Earlier sketch in CA 13-16
Seghers
See Radvanyi, Netty
Seghers, Anna
See Radvanyi, Netty
See also CDWLB 2
See also CLC 7
See also DLB 69
See also EWL 3
Seghers, Jan
See Altenburg, Matthias
Segler, Franklin Morgan 1907- 17-20R
Segovia, Andres 1893(?)-1987 147
Obituary 122
Brief entry 111
See also SATA-Obit 52
Segrave, Edmond 1904-1971
Obituary 29-32R
Segrave, Elisa 1949- 150
Segraves, Kelly L(ee) 1942- CANR-13
Earlier sketch in CA 61-64
Segre, Claudio Giuseppe 1937- 53-56
Segre, Dan V(ittorio) 1922- 104
Segre, Emilio (Gino) 1905-1989 .... CANR-13
Obituary 128
Earlier sketch in CA 33-36R
Segre, Roberto 1934- 172
Segrest, James 1961- 236
Segrest, Mab 1949- .... GLL 2
Segriff, Larry 1960- CANR-111
Earlier sketch in CA 153
Seguin, Marilyn W(eymouth)
1951- CANR-111
Earlier sketch in CA 155
See also SATA 91
Seguin-Fontes, Marthe 1924- 171
See also SATA 109
Segun, Mabel D(orothy Aig-Imoukhuede)
1930- .... CP 1
See also CWP
See also CWRI 5
Segundo, Bart
See Rowland, D(onald) S(ydney)
Segy, Ladislas 1904-1988 .... CANR-30
Earlier sketch in CA 45-48
Seib, Kenneth Allen 1938- 29-32R
Seib, Philip 1949- CANR-108
Earlier sketch in CA 129
Seibel, C(lifford) W(inslow) 1890-1984 . CAP-2
Earlier sketch in CA 25-28
Seibel, Hans Dieter 1941- CANR-29
Earlier sketches in CA 65-68, CANR-11
Seibold, J. Otto 1960- .... SAAS 22
See also SATA 83, 149
Seid, Ruth 1913-1995 .... 5-8R
Obituary 148
See also Sinclair, Jo
Seide, Diane 1930- CANR-31
Earlier sketches in CA 73-76, CANR-14
Seide, Michael 1911-2001 111
Seidel, Frederick (Lewis) 1936- CANR-99
Earlier sketches in CA 13-16R, CANR-8
See also CLC 18
See also CP 1, 2, 3, 4, 5, 6, 7
See also DLBY 1984
Seidel, George J(oseph) 1932- 13-16R
Seidel, Ina 1885-1974 180
Obituary 116
See also DLB 56
Seidel, Kathleen G(illes) 1951- CANR-83
Earlier sketch in CA 112
See also RHW
Seidel, Michael Alan 1943- 93-96
Seidel, Ross 160
See also SATA 95
Seidelman, James Edward 1926- 25-28R
See also SATA 6
Seiden, Art(hur) .... SATA 107
See also SATA-Brief 42
Seiden, Martin H. 1934- 13-16R
Seiden, Morton Irving 1921- 17-20R
Seidenbaum, Art(hur David)
1930-1990 .... 29-32R
Obituary 132
Seidenberg, Robert 1920- 25-28R
Seidenberg, Roderick 1890(?)-1973
Obituary 45-48
Seidensticker, Edward G. 1921- 89-92
Seidick, Kathryn A(melia) 1943- CANR-123
Earlier sketch in CA 108
Seidler, Ann (G.) 1925- 25-28R
See also SATA 131
Seidler, Grzegorz Leopold 1913- CANR-28
Earlier sketches in CA 29-32R, CANR-12
Seidler, Lee J. 1935- 73-76
Seidler, Murray Benjamin 1924- 5-8R
Seidler, Tor 1952- CANR-134
Earlier sketch in CA 123
See also MAICYA 2
See also SATA 52, 98, 149
See also SATA-Brief 46
Seidlin, Oskar 1911-1984 .... 41-44R
Seidman, Ann (Willcox) 1926- 81-84
Seidman, Harold 1911-2002 .... 29-32R
Obituary 208
Seidman, Hugh 1940- CANR-85
Earlier sketches in CA 29-32R, CANR-35
See also CP 7
Seidman, Jerome M(artin) 1911-1986 45-48
Seidman, Joel 1906-1977 .... CANR-9
Earlier sketch in CA 5-8R
Seidman, L. William 1921- 144
Seidman, Laurence Ivan 1925- 77-80
See also SATA 15
Seidman, Richard 218
Seidman, Robert J(erome) 1941- 73-76
Seidmann, Ginette
See Spanier, Ginette
Seidner, Diane
See Seide, Diane
Seife, Charles 193
Seiferheld, Alfredo M. 1950-1988
Obituary 125
Seiferle, Rebecca 1951- CANR-104
Earlier sketch in CA 150
Seifert, Anne 1943- 105
Seifert, Elizabeth
See Gasparotti, Elizabeth Seifert
Seifert, Harvey (J.D.) 1911-1998 .... CANR-3
Earlier sketch in CA 9-12R
Seifert, Jaroslav 1901-1986 127
See also CDWLB 4
See also CLC 34, 44, 93
See also DLB 215
See also EWL 3
See also MTCW 1, 2
See also PC 47
Seifert, Shirley L(ouise) 1888-1971 ..... CANR-2
Obituary 33-36R
Earlier sketch in CA 1-4R
Seiffert, Rachel 1971- 205
Seifman, Eli 1936- 37-40R
Seifrid, Thomas 1956- 139
Seifullina, Lidiia Nikolaevna
1889-1954 .... DLB 272
Seigel, Catharine F. 1933- 146
Seigel, Jerrold (Edward) 1936- 85-88
Seigel, Jules 1931- 93-96
Seigel, Kalman 1917-1998 .... 25-28R
Obituary 169
See also SATA 12
See also SATA-Obit 103
Seigenthaler, John (Lawrence) 1927-
Brief entry 113
See also DLB 127
Seignobosc, Francoise 1897-1961 73-76
See also SATA 21
Seignolle, Claude 1917- 21-24R
Seiho
See Sullivan, M(ichael) J(ustin)
Seiler, John A(ndrew) 1927- 21-24R
Seiler, Robert E. 1925- 17-20R
Seilhamer, Frank Henry 1933- 85-88
Seim, Richard K(nudt) 1928- 102
Seimer, Stanley J(ames) 1918- CANR-28
Earlier sketch in CA 1-4R
Seinfel, Ruth
See Goode, Ruth
Seinfeld, Jerry 1954- CANR-128
Earlier sketch in CA 140
See also AAYA 11
See also SATA 146
Seinfelt, Mark 236
Seip, Terry Lee 1944- 113
Seiter, Ellen 1957- 196
Seitlin, Charlotte 1907(?)-1979
Obituary 89-92
Seitz, Frederick 1911- 167
Seitz, Georg J(osef) 1920- 13-16R
Seitz, Jacqueline 1931- .... SATA 50
Seitz, John F. 1893-1979 .... IDFW 3, 4
Seitz, Nick 1939- 97-100
Seitz, Raymond (G. H.) 1940- 176
Seitz, William Chapin 1914-1974 ...... CANR-2
Obituary 53-56
Earlier sketch in CA 1-4R
Seixas, Judith S. 1922- 85-88
See also SATA 17
Sejima, Yoshimasa 1913- 33-36R
See also SATA 8
Sejnowski, Terrence J(oseph) 1947- 214
Sejour, Victor 1817-1874 .... DC 10
See also DLB 50
Sejour Marcou et Ferrand, Juan Victor
See Sejour, Victor
Sekaxsu, Petakwonexnajunkis 1950- 133
Sekers, Simone 1945- 119
Sekirin, Peter 1960- 180
Sekler, Eduard F(ranz) 1920- 69-72
Sekora, John 1939- 189
Brief entry 106
Sekowski, Jozef-Julian
See Senkovsky, Osip Ivanovich
Selavy, Rrose
See Duchamp, (Henri-Robert) Marcel
Selberg, Ingrid (Maria) 1950- 136
See also SATA 68
Selbourne, David 1937- CANR-38
Earlier sketches in CA 89-92, CANR-16
See also CBD
See also CD 5, 6
Selby, Bettina 1934- CANR-41
Earlier sketch in CA 117
See also DLB 204
Selby, Curt
See Piserchia, Doris (Elaine)
Selby, Donald Joseph 1915- CANR-24
Earlier sketch in CA 1-4R
Selby, Edward B(urford), Jr. 1938- 45-48
Selby, Elliot
See Nicholson, Hubert
Selby, Hazel Barrington 1889-1972 .... CAP-2
Earlier sketch in CA 17-18
Selby, Henry A. 1934- 37-40R
Selby, Hubert, Jr. 1928-2004 .... CANR-85
Obituary 226
Earlier sketches in CA 13-16R, CANR-33
See also CLC 1, 2, 4, 8
See also CN 1, 2, 3, 4, 5, 6, 7
See also DLB 2, 227
See also MAL 5
See also SSC 20
Selby, James Winford III 1947- 108
Selby, John (Allen) 1897-1980 .... CANR-86
Obituary 97-100
Earlier sketch in CA 1-4R
Selby, John M(illin) 1905- 25-28R
Selcamm, George
See Machlis, Joseph
Selcer, Richard F. 1950- 139
Selcher, Wayne A(lan) 1942- CANR-10
Earlier sketch in CA 65-68
Selden, George
See Thompson, George Selden
See also CLR 8
See also DLB 52
Selden, John 1584-1654 .... DLB 213
Selden, Mark 1938- 81-84
Selden, Neil R(oy) 1931- 106
See also SATA 61
Selden, Raman 1937-1991 127
Obituary 134
Selden, Samuel 1899-1979 .... CANR-3
Earlier sketch in CA 1-4R
Selden, William K(irkpatrick) 1911- 1-4R
Seldes, George (Henry) 1890-1995 .... CANR-2
Obituary 149
Earlier sketch in CA 5-8R
Seldes, Gilbert (Vivian) 1893-1970 .... 5-8R
Obituary 29-32R
Seldes, Marian (Hall) 1928- CANR-19
Earlier sketch in CA 85-88
Seldin, Maury 1931- CANR-34
Earlier sketches in CA 29-32R, CANR-15
Seldis, Henry 1925-1978
Obituary 77-80
Seldon, Anthony 1953- 136
Seldon, James R(alph) 1944- 112
Seldon, Mary Elisabeth 1921- 37-40R
Seldon, W(endell) Lynn, Jr. 1961- 167
Seldon-Truss, Leslie 1892-1990 .... 5-8R
Selegen, Galina V(assily) 1899-1981 ..... 41-44R
Selekman, Matthew D. 1957- 236
Selement, George Joseph 1946- 113
Selenic, Slobodan 1933-1995 193
See also DLB 181
Self, Carolyn Shealy 1931- CANR-16
Earlier sketch in CA 93-96
Self, Edwin F(orbes) 1920- 69-72
See also DLB 137
Self, Huber 1914- 73-76
Self, Jerry M(arvin) 1938- 61-64
Self, Margaret Cabell 1902-1996 .... CANR-3
Earlier sketch in CA 5-8R
See also SATA 24
Self, Peter J(ohn) O(tter) 1919-1999 . CANR-47
Earlier sketch in CA 120
Self, Will(iam) 1961- CANR-126
Earlier sketches in CA 143, CANR-83
See also BRWS 5
See also CN 6, 7
See also DLB 207
Self, William L(ee) 1932- 122
Selg, Herbert 1935- 69-72
Selig, Elaine Booth 1935- 104
Selig, Robert L. 1932- 152
Selig, Sylvie 1942- .... SATA 13
Selig, William N. 1864-1948 .... IDFW 3, 4
Seligman, Barnard 1923- 113
Seligman, Ben B(aruch) 1912-1970 .... CANR-2
Obituary 29-32R
Earlier sketch in CA 1-4R
Seligman, Craig 233
Seligman, Daniel 1924-
Brief entry 113
Seligman, Edwin R. A. 1861-1939 .... DLB 47
Seligman, Edwin Robert Anderson
1861-1939 185
Seligman, Eustace 1889(?)-1976
Obituary 69-72
Seligman, Germain 1893-1978
Obituary 77-80
Seligman, Lester George 1918- 13-16R
Seligman, Linda H(elen Goldberg) 1944- 114
Seligman, Martin E. P. 1942- CANR-144
Earlier sketch in CA 150
Seligman, Susan Meilach 1950 105
Seligmann, G(ustav) L(eonard) Jr. 1934- ... 45-48
Seligmann, Herbert J(acob) 1891-1984
Obituary 112
Seligmann, Nancy 1948- 57-60
Seligson, Mitchell A(llan) 1945- 119
Seligson, Tom 1946- 33-36R
Selimovic, Mehmed 1910-1982 184
Obituary 108
See also Selimovic, Mesa
Selimovic, Mesa -1982
See Selimovic, Mehmed
See also CDWLB 4
See also DLB 181
See also EWL 3
Seljouk, Mehdi Ali 1935- .... CP 1
Selke, William L(ee) 1947- 144
Selkirk, Jane
See Chapman, John Stanton Higham
Sell, Betty (Marie) H(aas) 1928- 102
Sell, Charles M(urray) 1933- 113
Sell, DeWitt E(llsworth) 1915- 1-4R
Sell, Francis Edmund 1902-1993 .... 5-8R
Sell, Henry Blackman 1889-1974
Obituary 89-92
Sell, Joseph
See Haley, William (John)
Sell, Kenneth D(aniel) 1928- 102
Sell, Louis (D.) 1947- 210
Sell, Roger D(avid) 1944- 116
Sell, Ted 1928-1989 69-72
Obituary 128
Sellars, Jane 1951- 149
Sellars, Wilfrid Stalker 1912-1989
Obituary 129
See also DLB 279
Sellen, Robert W(alker) 1930- 45-48
Seller, Maxine Schwartz 1935- 104
Sellerberg, Ann-Mari 1943- CANR-87
Earlier sketch in CA 154
Sellers, Alexandra 1865-1943 .... RHW
Sellers, Bettie M(ixon) 1926- 77-80
Sellers, Charles Coleman
1903-1980 .... CANR-11
Earlier sketch in CA 17-20R
Sellers, Christopher C. 1958- 166

Sellers, Con(nie Leslie, Jr.)
1922-1992 .... CANR-37
Obituary 136
Earlier sketch in CA 97-100
Sellers, Heather (Laurie) 1964- 199
Sellers, James Earl 1926- 113
Sellers, Naomi
See Flack, Naomi John White
Sellers, Robert Victor 1894-1973 .... CAP-1
Obituary 89-92
Earlier sketch in CA 13-14
Sellers, Ronnie 1948- 115
Sellery, C(larence) Morley 1894-1990 ... CAP-2
Obituary 199
Earlier sketch in CA 21-22
Sellew, Gladys 1887-1977 .... CAP-1
Earlier sketch in CA 11-12
Sellier, Andre 1920- 239
Sellin, Eric 1933- CANR-22
Earlier sketches in CA 17-20R, CANR-7
Sellin, Paul R(oland) 1930- 45-48
Sellings, Arthur
See Ley, Arthur Gordon
See also DLB 261
Sellman, Hunton Dade 1900-1992 .... 5-8R
Sellman, Roger R(aymond) 1915- CANR-1
Earlier sketch in CA 1-4R
Sellmann, James D. 1956- 222
Sells, Arthur Lytton 1895-1978 .... CANR-6
Earlier sketch in CA 5-8R
Sells, Iris (Esther) Lytton
See Lytton-Sells, Iris (Esther)
Sells, S(aul) B. 1913-1988 .... CANR-19
Earlier sketches in CA 1-4R, CANR-4
Selltiz, Claire (Alice) 1914- 5-8R
Selman, LaRue W. 1927- .... SATA 55
Selman, Robyn 1959- 152
Selmark, George
See Seldon-Truss, Leslie
Selness, Craig A(lan) 1955- 119
Selormey, Francis 1927- 21-24R
See also BW 1
Selous, Frederick Courteney
1851-1917 .... DLB 174
Selous, Trista 142
Selsam, Howard 1903-1970
Obituary 29-32R
Selsam, Millicent E(llis) 1912-1996 .. CANR-38
Obituary 154
Earlier sketches in CA 9-12R, CANR-5
See also CLR 1
See also MAICYA 1, 2
See also MAICYAS 1
See also SATA 1, 29
See also SATA-Obit 92
Seltzer, Alvin J(ay) 1939- 65-68
Seltzer, Charles Alden 1875-1942 . TCWW 1, 2
Seltzer, Chester E. 1915-1971 131
See also Muro, Amado (Jesus)
See also HW 1
Seltzer, Daniel 1933-1980 89-92
Obituary 97-100
Seltzer, David 1920(?)- 170
Brief entry 110
Seltzer, George 1924- 73-76
Seltzer, Leon E(ugene) 1918-1988 89-92
Obituary 124
Seltzer, Leon F(rancis) 1940- 33-36R
Seltzer, Louis B(enson) 1897-1980
Obituary 97-100
Seltzer, Marc 1940- .... HGG
Seltzer, Meyer 1932- .... SATA 17
Seltzer, Richard (Warren, Jr.) 1946- .. CANR-90
Earlier sketch in CA 105
See also SATA 41
Selvadurai, Shyam 1965(?)- CANR-88
Earlier sketch in CA 167
See also CN 7
Selver, (Percy) Paul 1888-1970 .... CAP-2
Earlier sketch in CA 29-32
Selvidge, Marla J(ean) 1948- 162
Selvin, David F(rank) 1913- 25-28R
Selvin, Hanan C(harles) 1921- 9-12R
Selvin, Joel 1950- 133
Selvon, Sam
See Selvon, Samuel (Dickson)
See also CDWLB 3
See also CN 5
See also DLB 125
Selvon, Samuel (Dickson) 1923-1994 128
Obituary 146
Brief entry 117
See also Selvon, Sam
See also BW 2
See also CN 1, 2, 3, 4
See also EWL 3
See also MTCW 1
See also RGEL 2
Selway, Martina 1940- .... SATA 74
Selwyn, David G. 1938- 188
Selwyn, Francis 1935- .... CMW 4
Selwyn-Clarke, Selwyn 1893-1976
Obituary 65-68
Selwyn-Lloyd, John S. B. 1904-1978
Obituary 110
Selye, Hans 1907-1982 .... CANR-85
Obituary 108
Earlier sketches in CA 5-8R, CANR-2
Selz, Peter (Howard) 1919- CANR-96
Earlier sketches in CA 1-4R, CANR-29, 53
Selzer, Jack
See Selzer, John L.
Selzer, Joae Graham 1926- 53-56
Selzer, John L. 176
Selzer, Michael (I.) 1940- CANR-9
Earlier sketch in CA 53-56
Selzer, Richard 1928- CANR-106
Earlier sketches in CA 65-68, CANR-14
See also CLC 74
Selznick, Brian 1966- .... SATA 79, 117
Selznick, David O(liver) 1902-1965
Obituary 110
See also IDFW 3, 4
Selznick, Irene Mayer 1907-1990
Obituary 132
Semaan, Khalil I. H. 1920- 37-40R
Sembene, Ousmane
See Ousmane, Sembene
See also AFW
See also EWL 3
See also WLIT 2
Semchyshyn, Stefan 1940- 134
Semeiks, Jonna Gormely 1944- 109
Semel, Nava 1954- .... DLB 299
See also SATA 107
Semenov, Julian
See Lyandres, Yulian Semenovich
Semenov, Julian Semenovich
See Lyandres, Yulian Semenovich
Semenov, Nikolai N(ikolaevich)
1896-1986 157
Semenov, Yulian
See Lyandres, Yulian Semenovich
Semkiw, Virlyana
See Bishop, Tania Kroitor
Semler, H. Eric 1965- 125
Semler, Ricardo 1959- 149
Semloh
See Holmes, Peggy
Semmel, Bernard 1928- 77-80
Semmelroth, Otto 1912-1979 .... CANR-10
Earlier sketch in CA 13-16R
Semmens, James P(ike) 1919- 61-64
Semmes, Clovis E. 1949- 176
Semmes, Raphael 1809-1877 .... DLB 189
Semmes, Stephen (William) 1962- 178
Semmler, Clement (William) 1914- ... CANR-45
Earlier sketches in CA 21-24R, CANR-14
Semonche, John E(rwin) 1933- CANR-30
Earlier sketch in CA 45-48
Sempa, Francis P. 1959- 237
Sempell, Charlotte 1909-1998 .... 41-44R
Semple, Gordon
See Neubauer, William Arthur
Semple, Lorenzo, Jr. 129
Brief entry 125
Semprun, Jorge 1923- CANR-87
Brief entry 111
Earlier sketch in CA 158
See also IDFW 4
Semrud-Clikeman, Margaret 1950- 232
Semyonov, Julian
See Lyandres, Yulian Semenovich
Semyonov, Moshe 1946- 139
Semyonov, Yulian
See Lyandres, Yulian Semenovich
Sen, Amartya K(umar) 1933- CANR-91
Earlier sketch in CA 147
Sen, Ela
See Reid, Ela
Sen, Pradip 1926- .... CP 1
Sen, Sudhir 1906-1989 .... 33-36R
Obituary 129
Sen, Zekai 1947- 153
Sena, John F(rancis) 1940- 110
Sena, Jorge de
See de Sena, Jorge
See also DLB 287
See also EWL 3
Senac, Jean 1926-1973(?) .... EWL 3
Senancour, Etienne Pivert de
1770-1846 .... DLB 119
See also GFL 1789 to the Present
Senarens, Luis P(hilip) 1865-1939 164
See also SCFW 1, 2
See also SFW 4
Senate, Melissa 204
Sencourt, Robert
See George, Robert Esmonde Gordon
Sencourt, Robert Esmonde
See George, Robert Esmonde Gordon
Sendak, Jack 1924(?)-1995 .... CANR-85
Obituary 147
Earlier sketch in CA 77-80
See also SATA 28
Sendak, Maurice (Bernard) 1928- ... CANR-112
Earlier sketches in CA 5-8R, CANR-11, 39
Interview in CANR-11
See also CLR 1, 17, 74
See also CWRI 5
See also DLB 61
See also MAICYA 1, 2
See also MTCW 1, 2
See also MTFW 2005
See also SATA 1, 27, 113
See also TUS
Sender, Ramon (Jose) 1902-1982 .... CANR-8
Obituary 105
Earlier sketch in CA 5-8R
See also CLC 8
See also DAM MULT
See also DLB 322
See also EWL 3
See also HLC 2
See also HW 1
See also MTCW 1
See also RGWL 2, 3
See also TCLC 136
Sender, Ruth M(insky) 1926- .... SATA 62
Sender Barayon, Ramon 1934- 130
See also HW 1
Sendler, David A. 1938- 65-68
Sendrey, A(ladar) Alfred 1884-1976 ...... 13-16R
Sendy, Jean 1910-1978 .... CANR-12
Earlier sketch in CA 53-56
Seneca, Lucius Annaeus c. 4B.C.-c. 65 ... AW 2
See also CDWLB 1
See also DAM DRAM
See also DC 5
See also DLB 211
See also RGWL 2, 3
See also TWA
Senecal, Eva 1905- 185
See also DLB 92
Seneca the Elder c. 54B.C.-c. 40 .... DLB 211
Sened, Yonat 1926- 210
Senelick, Laurence P(hilip) 1942- CANR-91
Earlier sketches in CA 106, CANR-22, 47
Senesh, Hannah 1921-1944 183
Brief entry 119
Senesi, Mauro 1931- 17-20R
Seng, Peter J. 1922- 17-20R
Senghor, Leopold Sedar
1906-2001 .... CANR-134
Obituary 203
Brief entry 116
Earlier sketches in CA 125, CANR-47, 74
See also AFW
See also BLC 3
See also BW 2
See also CLC 54, 130
See also CWW 2
See also DAM MULT, POET
See also DNFS 2
See also EWL 3
See also GFL 1789 to the Present
See also MTCW 1, 2
See also MTFW 2005
See also PC 25
See also TWA
Sengler, Johanna 1924- .... SATA 18
Sengstacke, John H(erman Henry)
1912-1997 101
Obituary 158
See also BW 1
See also DLB 127
Sen Gupta, Pranati 1938- 102
Sen Gupta, Rajeswar 1908- CAP-1
Earlier sketch in CA 9-10
Senick, Gerard J(oseph) 1953- 97-100
Senie, Harriet F. 1943- CANR-93
Earlier sketch in CA 146
Senior, Clarence (Ollson) 1903-1974 65-68
Obituary 53-56
Senior, Donald 1940- CANR-53
Earlier sketches in CA 77-80, CANR-13, 29
Senior, Isabel J(anet Couper Syme) CANR-9
Earlier sketch in CA 5-8R
Senior, Michael 1940- 103
Senior, Nancy 1941- 119
Senior, Olive (Marjorie) 1941- CANR-126
Earlier sketches in CA 154, CANR-86
See also BW 3
See also CN 6
See also CP 7
See also CWP
See also DLB 157
See also EWL 3
See also RGSF 2
See also SSC 78
Senior, W(illiam) A. 1953- 155
Senisi, Ellen B(abinec) 1951- 189
See also SATA 116
Senkevitch, Anatole, Jr. 1942- CANR-19
Earlier sketch in CA 101
Senkovsky, Osip Ivanovich
1800-1858 .... DLB 198
Senn, Alfred Erich 1932- 134
Brief entry 112
Senn, Bryan 1962- 145
Senn, Frank C(olvin) 1943- CANR-39
Earlier sketch in CA 115
Senn, Fritz 1928- 41-44R
Senn, J(oyce) A(nn) 1941- 187
See also SATA 115
Senn, Milton J(ohn) E(dward)
1902-1990 81-84
Senn, Peter R(ichard) 1923- 33-36R
Senn, Steve 1950- 105
See also SATA 60
See also SATA-Brief 48
Senna, Carl 1944- CANR-19
Earlier sketches in CA 49-52, CANR-4
Senna, Danzy 1970- CANR-130
Earlier sketch in CA 169
See also CLC 119
Sennett, Frank (Ronald, Jr.) 1968- 226
Sennett, Richard 1943- CANR-87
Earlier sketch in CA 73-76
Sennett, Ted 1928- CANR-38
Earlier sketch in CA 33-36R
Sennholz, Hans F. 1922- CANR-47
Brief entry 118
Earlier sketch in CA 120
Senning, Cindy Post 220
Senoa, August 1838-1881 .... CDWLB 4
See also DLB 147
Senoh, Kappa 1930- .... NCFS 5
Sensabaugh, George Frank 1906- CAP-1
Earlier sketch in CA 13-14
Senser, Robert A(nton) 1921- 5-8R
Sensibar, Judith L(evin) 1941- 144
Senter, Florence H.
See Ellis, Florence Hawley
Senter, Sylvia 1921- 113
Sentner, David P. 1898-1975
Obituary 57-60
Sentner, Mary Steele 1900(?)-1983
Obituary 110
Senungetuk, Joseph (Engasongwok) 1940- .. 212
Seo, Audrey Yoshiko 231
Seoane, Rhoda 1905-1991 .... CAP-2
Earlier sketch in CA 25-28
Sepamla, (Sydney) Sipho 1932- CANR-86
Earlier sketch in CA 154
See also BW 3
See also CP 7
See also DLB 157, 225
Sepetys, Jonas 1901-1988 57-60
Sepheriades, Georgios
See Seferiades, Giorgos Stylianou
Sepia
See Holmvik, Oyvind
September, Anna
See Manner, Eeva-Liisa
Sepulveda, Luis 1949- 205
Sequoia, Anna 109
Serafian, Michael
See Martin, Malachi
Serafimovich, Aleksandr Serafimovich
1863-1949 .... DLB 272
Serafini, Anthony Louis 1943- 112
Serafinowicz, Leszek 1899-1956
See Lechon, Jan
Serage, Nancy 1924- 65-68
See also SATA 10
Seraile, William 1941- 193
Serandrei, Mario 1907-1966 .... IDFW 3
Seranella, Barbara 217
Seranus
See Harrison, Susan Frances (Riley)
Serao, Matilde 1856-1927 .... DLB 264
Serb, Ann Toland 1937- 81-84
Serban, George 1926- 129
Serban, William M(ichael) 1949- 102
Serebriakoff, Victor 1912-2000 148
Obituary 190
Serebryakova, Galina Iosifovna 1905-1980
Obituary 102
Seredy, Kate 1899-1975 .... CANR-83
Obituary 57-60
Earlier sketch in CA 5-8R
See also BYA 1, 4
See also CLR 10
See also CWRI 5
See also DLB 22
See also MAICYA 1, 2
See also SATA 1
See also SATA-Obit 24
See also WCH
Serels, M. Mitchell 1948- 144
Sereni, Vittorio 1913-1983 184
Obituary 109
See also DLB 128
See also EWL 3
Sereny, Gitta
See Serenyi, Gitta
Serenyi, Gitta 1923- CANR-113
Earlier sketch in CA 119
See also Sereny, Gitta
Serenyi, Peter 1931- 61-64
Seres, William fl. 1546(?)-1579(?) .... DLB 170
Seret, Roberta 1945- 146
Serfaty, Simon 1940- CANR-26
Earlier sketches in CA 25-28R, CANR-10
Serfozo, Mary 1925- 149
Sergeant, Harriet 1954- 132
Sergeant, (Herbert) Howard
1914-1987 .... CANR-20
Obituary 121
Earlier sketches in CA 5-8R, CANR-5
See also CP 1, 2
Sergeev, Sergei Nikolaevich
See Sergeev-Tsensky, Sergei Nikolaevich
Sergeev-Tsensky, Sergei Nikolaevich
1875-1958 .... DLB 272
Sergel, Ruth
See Perry, Ruth (Fuller)
Sergent, Bernard 1946- CANR-82
Earlier sketch in CA 133
Sergievsky, Orest 1911-1984
Obituary 114
Sergio, Elisa 1905-1989 .... CANR-86
Obituary 129
Earlier sketch in CA 61-64
Sergio, Lisa
See Sergio, Elisa
Sergios, Paul A. 1961- 145
Seriel, Jerome
See Vallee, Jacques F.
Serif, Med 1924- 17-20R
Serig, Beverly J. 1934- 101
Serin, Judith Ann 1949- 209
Serious, Yahoo 1953- 208
Serjeant, Robert Bertram 1915-1993 139
Serle, (Alan) Geoffrey 1922-1998 .... 13-16R
Serling, Carol 1929- 140
Serling, Robert J(erome) 1918- CANR-1
Earlier sketch in CA 45-48
Serling, (Edward) Rod(man) 1924-1975 162
Obituary 57-60
See also AAYA 14
See also AITN 1
See also CLC 30
See also DLB 26
See also SFW 4
Serna, Ramon Gomez de la
See Gomez de la Serna, Ramon
Serna-Maytorena, Manuel Antonio
1932- CANR-3
Earlier sketch in CA 45-48
Sernett, Milton C(harles) 1942- 61-64
Sernine, Daniel 156
See also Lortie, Alain
See also DLB 251
See also SFW 4

Cumulative Index 523 **Seyton**

Seroff, Victor I(ilyitch) 1902-1979 ... 25-28R
Obituary ... 85-88
See also SATA 12
See also SATA-Obit 26
Seroka, James H. 1950- ... 124
Seroka, Jim
See Seroka, James H.
Serote, Mongane Wally 1944- ... CANR-81
Earlier sketch in CA 142
See also BW 2, 3
See also CP 7
See also DLB 125, 225
Seroussi, Karyn 1965- ... 209
Serpieres
See Guillevic, (Eugene)
Serra, Diana
See Cary, Peggy-Jean Montgomery
Serraillier, Ian (Lucien) 1912-1994 ... CANR-83
Obituary ... 147
Earlier sketches in CA 1-4R, CANR-1
See also BYA 3, 4
See also CLR 2
See also DLB 161
See also MAICYA 1, 2
See also MAICYAS 1
See also SAAS 3
See also SATA 1, 73
See also SATA-Obit 83
See also YAW
Serrano, Lucienne J. 1936- ... 131
Serrano, Miguel 1917- ... 132
Serrano, Napoleon Diestro Valeriano
See Valeriano, Napoleon D(iestro)
Serrano, Nina 1934- ... 182
See also DLB 122
Serrano, Richard A. 1953- ... 172
Serrano Plaja, Arturo 1909-1979 ... CANR-13
Earlier sketch in CA 29-32R
Serrifile, F. O. O.
See Holmes, William Kersley
Serron, Luis A(ugusto) 1930- ... 102
Serry, Victor
See Serebriakoff, Victor
Sert, Josep Lluis 1902-1983 ... 184
Obituary ... 109
Servadio, Gaia 1938- ... CANR-11
Earlier sketch in CA 25-28R
Servan-Schreiber, Jean-Jacques 1924- ... 102
Servello, Joe 1932- ... SATA 10
Serventy, Vincent (Noel) ... CANR-27
Earlier sketches in CA 65-68, CANR-10
Server, Lee ... CANR-107
Earlier sketch in CA 146
Service, Alastair (Stanley Douglas) 1933- ... 130
Service, Elman Rogers 1915- ... 112
Service, Grace 1879-1954 ... 142
Service, John S(tewart) 1909(?)-1999 ... 142
Obituary ... 179
Brief entry ... 113
Service, Pamela F. 1945- ... CANR-85
Earlier sketches in CA 120, CANR-47
See also AAYA 20
See also SATA 64
See also YAW
Service, Robert
See Service, Robert W(illiam)
See also BYA 4
See also DAB
See also DLB 92
Service, Robert (Edward) ... 189
Service, Robert W(illiam)
1874(?)-1958 ... CANR-84
Brief entry ... 115
Earlier sketch in CA 140
See also Service, Robert
See also DA
See also DAC
See also DAM MST, POET
See also PFS 10
See also RGEL 2
See also SATA 20
See also TCLC 15
See also WLC
Servid, Carolyn 1953- ... 201
Servieres, Jules
See Halevy, Ludovic
Servin, Manuel P(atrick) 1920- ... 37-40R
Serviss, Garrett P(utnam) 1851-1929 ... 160
Brief entry ... 119
See also SCFW 1, 2
See also SFW 4
Serwadda, W(illiam) Moses 1931- ... 107
See also SATA 27
Serwer-Bernstein, Blanche L(uria)
1910-1997 ... 65-68
See also SATA 10
Serwicher, Kurt 1912-1979
Obituary ... 89-92
Sescoe, Vincent E. 1938- ... 194
See also SATA 123
Seshadri, Vijay 1954- ... 156
Seskin, Eugene P(aul) 1948- ... 89-92
Sesonske, Alexander 1917- ... 13-16R
Sessa, Valerie I. 1964- ... 203
Sessions, Kyle Cutler 1934-
Brief entry ... 106
Sessions, Roger Huntington 1896-1985 ... 93-96
Obituary ... 115
Sessions, W. A.
See Sessions, William A(lfred)
Sessions, Will 1905-1998 ... 1-4R
Sessions, William A(lfred) 1938- ... 233
Sessler, Charles 1854-1935 ... DLB 187
Sessoms, H(anson) Douglas 1931- ... 41-44R
Sesti, Giuseppe Maria 1942- ... 137
Seth, Mary
See Lexau, Joan M.
Seth, Ronald (Sydney) 1911-1985 ... 106
Obituary ... 115
Seth, Vikram 1952- ... CANR-131
Brief entry ... 121
Earlier sketches in CA 127, CANR-50, 74
Interview in ... CA-127
See also BRWS 10
See also CLC 43, 90
See also CN 6, 7
See also CP 7
See also DA3
See also DAM MULT
See also DLB 120, 271, 282
See also EWL 3
See also MTCW 2
See also MTFW 2005
See also WWE 1
Sethi, Narendra Kumar 1935- ... CANR-14
Earlier sketch in CA 37-40R
Sethi, Robbie Clipper 1951- ... 193
Sethi, S. Prakash 1934- ... 41-44R
Sethi, Sunil 1954- ... 192
Sethna, Jehangir Minocher 1941- ... 37-40R
Sethna, Minocher Jehangirji 1911-1993 ... 9-12R
Seth-Smith, Elsie K.
See Murrell, Elsie Kathleen Seth-Smith
Seth-Smith, Leslie James 1923- ... 104
Seth-Smith, Michael 1928- ... CANR-16
Earlier sketch in CA 29-32R
Setien, Miguel Delibes
See Delibes Setien, Miguel
Seton, Anya 1904(?)-1990 ... CANR-69
Obituary ... 133
Earlier sketch in CA 17-20R
See also RHW
See also SATA 3
See also SATA-Obit 66
Seton, Cynthia Propper 1926-1982 ... CANR-7
Obituary ... 108
Earlier sketch in CA 5-8R
See also CLC 27
Seton, Elizabeth Ann 1774-1821 ... DLB 200
Seton, Ernest (Evan) Thompson
1860-1946 ... 204
Brief entry ... 109
See also ANW
See also BYA 3
See also CLR 59
See also DLB 92
See also DLBD 13
See also JRDA
See also SATA 18
See also TCLC 31
Seton, John c. 1509-1567 ... DLB 281
Seton, Marie 1910-1985 ... 105
Seton, Nora Janssen ... 194
Seton-Thompson, Ernest
See Seton, Ernest (Evan) Thompson
Seton-Watson, Christopher 1918- ... CANR-11
Earlier sketch in CA 21-24R
Seton-Watson, (George) Hugh (Nicholas)
1916-1984 ... 117
Obituary ... 114
Setouchi Harumi 1922- ... 184
See also DLB 182
Settanni, Harry 1945-1999 ... 146
Settel, Gertrude S. 1919- ... CANR-86
Earlier sketch in CA 17-20R
Settel, Irving 1916- ... 17-20R
Settel, Trudy S.
See Settel, Gertrude S.
Setterberg, Fred 1951- ... 144
Settle, Edith
See Andrews, (William) Linton
Settle, Elkanah 1648-1724 ... RGEL 2
Settle, Mary Lee 1918-2005 ... CANR-126
Earlier sketches in CA 89-92, CANR-44, 87
Interview in ... CA-89-92
See also CAAS 1
See also BPFB 3
See also CLC 19, 61
See also CN 6, 7
See also CSW
See also DLB 6
Setton, Kenneth M. 1914- ... CANR-39
Earlier sketches in CA 9-12R, CANR-3, 18
Setzekorn, William David 1935- ... 65-68
Setzer, (Cynthia) Lynn 1955- ... 167
Setzler, Frank M(aryl) 1902-1975
Obituary ... 57-60
Seufert, Karl Rolf 1923- ... CANR-28
Earlier sketch in CA 9-12R
Seuling, Barbara 1937- ... CANR-125
Earlier sketches in CA 61-64, CANR-8, 26, 52
See also SAAS 24
See also SATA 10, 98, 145
Seume, Johann Gottfried 1763-1810 ... DLB 94
Seung, Thomas Kaehao 1930- ... CANR-82
Earlier sketches in CA 108, CANR-36
Seuphor, Michel
See Arp, Jean
Seuren, Pieter A. M. 1934- ... 49-52
Seuse, Heinrich c. 1295-1366 ... DLB 179
See also LMFS 1
Seuss, Dr.
See Dr. Seuss and
Geisel, Theodor Seuss and
LeSieg, Theo. and
Stone, Rosetta
Sevag, Barouyr
See Ghazarian, Barouyr Raphael
See also EWL 3
Sevareid, (Arnold) Eric 1912-1992 ... 69-72
See also AITN 1
Sevela, Efraim 1928- ... CANR-30
Earlier sketch in CA 69-72
See also Sevela, Ephraim
Sevela, Ephraim
See Sevela, Efraim
See also BYA 8
Seventeenth Earl of Oxford
See de Vere, Edward
Severance, Carol (Ann Wilcox) 1944- ... 155
See also FANT
Severance, John B(ridwell) 1935- ... CANR-133
Earlier sketch in CA 164
Severianin, Igor'
See Lotarev, Igor' Vasil'evich
See also DLB 295
Severin, Dorothy Sherman 1942- ... 229
Severin, Mark (Fernand) 1906-1987 ... 107
Severin, (Giles) Timothy 1940- ... CANR-111
Earlier sketches in CA 21-24R, CANR-10
See also DLB 204
Severino, Alexandrino E(usebio) 1931- ... 41-44R
Severino, Carol (J.) 1949- ... 168
Severn, Bill
See Severn, William Irving
Severn, David
See Unwin, David S(torr)
Severn, Donald
See Nolan, Frederick William
Severn, Sue 1918- ... 5-8R
Severn, William Irving 1914- ... CANR-36
Earlier sketches in CA 1-4R, CANR-1, 16
See also SATA 1
Severo, Richard 1932- ... 73-76
Severs, Jerome
See Wooley, John (Steven)
Severs, Vesta-Nadine 1935- ... CANR-15
Earlier sketch in CA 89-92
Seversky, Alexander P(rocofieff) De
See De Seversky, Alexander P(rocofieff)
Severson, John H(ugh) 1933- ... 13-16R
Severson, Richard 1955- ... 175
Sevier, Richard P(utnam) 1931- ... 229
Sevigne, Marie (de Rabutin-Chantal) 1626-1696
See Sevigne, Marie de Rabutin Chantal
See also GFL Beginnings to 1789
See also TWA
Sevigne, Marie de Rabutin Chantal
See Sevigne, Marie (de Rabutin-Chantal)
See also DLB 268
Sewall, Gilbert T. ... CANR-144
Earlier sketch in CA 173
Sewall, Joseph 1688-1769 ... DLB 24
Sewall, Laura 1955- ... 198
Sewall, Marcia 1935- ... CANR-97
Earlier sketches in CA 45-48, CANR-1, 18
See also MAICYA 1, 2
See also SATA 37, 69, 119
Sewall, Mary Franklin 1884-1971(?) ... CAP-2
Earlier sketch in CA 21-22
Sewall, Richard B(enson) 1908-2003 ... 93-96
Obituary ... 216
Interview in ... CA-93-96
See also DLB 111
Sewall, Samuel 1652-1730 ... DLB 24
See also RGAL 4
Seward, Anna 1742-1809 ... RGEL 2
Seward, Desmond 1935- ... CANR-127
Brief entry ... 114
Earlier sketch in CA 158
Seward, Jack
See Seward, John Neil
Seward, James H(odson) 1928- ... 65-68
Seward, John Neil 1924- ... CANR-8
Earlier sketch in CA 21-24R
Seward, Prudence 1926- ... SATA 16
Seward, Robert (Allen) 1942- ... 208
Seward, William W(ard), Jr. 1913- ... 9-12R
Sewart, Alan 1928- ... CANR-25
Earlier sketch in CA 108
Sewel, John 1946- ... 103
Sewell, Anna 1820-1878 ... BYA 1
See also CLR 17
See also DLB 163
See also JRDA
See also MAICYA 1, 2
See also NFS 22
See also SATA 24, 100
See also WCH
Sewell, Brocard 1912-2000 ... 107
Obituary ... 189
Sewell, (Margaret) Elizabeth 1919-2001 ... 49-52
Obituary ... 192
Sewell, Helen (Moore) 1896-1957 ... CANR-85
Brief entry ... 123
Earlier sketch in CA 137
See also CWRI 5
See also MAICYA 1, 2
See also SATA 38
Sewell, J. Leslie 1923- ... 21-24R
Sewell, James Patrick 1930- ... 73-76
Sewell, Lisa 1960- ... 171
Sewell, Marilyn ... CANR-112
Earlier sketch in CA 166
Sewell, Michael (John) 1934- ... 171
Sewell, Richard H(erbert) 1931- ... 186
Brief entry ... 117
Sewell, Stephen 1953- ... CD 5, 6
Sewell, W. R. Derrick 1931- ... CANR-9
Earlier sketch in CA 21-24R
Sewell, William H(amilton) 1909-2001 ... 45-48
Obituary ... 199
Sewell, Winifred 1917-2002 ... 102
Obituary ... 210
Sewny, Kathryn Wiehe 1909-1983 ... CAP-1
Earlier sketch in CA 13-16
Sexton, Albert Charles 1912- ... 89-92
Sexton, A(da) Jeanette 1924- ... 65-68
Sexton, Adam 1962- ... 142
Sexton, Anne (Harvey) 1928-1974 ... CANR-36
Obituary ... 53-56
Earlier sketches in CA 1-4R, CANR-3
See also CABS 2
See also AMWS 2
See also CDALB 1941-1968
See also CLC 2, 4, 6, 8, 10, 15, 53, 123
See also CP 1, 2
See also DA
See also DA3
See also DAB
See also DAC
See also DAM MST, POET
See also DLB 5, 169
See also EWL 3
See also EXPP
See also FL 1:6
See also FW
See also MAL 5
See also MAWW
See also MTCW 1, 2
See also MTFW 2005
See also PAB
See also PC 2
See also PFS 4, 14
See also RGAL 4
See also SATA 10
See also TUS
See also WLC
Sexton, James D(ean) 1942- ... 113
Sexton, Linda Gray 1953- ... CANR-36
Earlier sketch in CA 101
Sexton, Michael J(oseph) 1939- ... 45-48
Sexton, Patricia Cayo 1924- ... 141
Sexton, Richard J(oseph) 1912-1997 ... 45-48
Sexton, Virgil Wesley 1918- ... 33-36R
Sexton, Virginia Staudt 1916- ... 29-32R
Sexton, William C(ottrell) 1928- ... 133
Seybold, Patricia B. ... 202
Seybolt, Peter J(ordan) 1934- ... CANR-86
Earlier sketches in CA 53-56, CANR-35
Seydel, Mildred Woolley 1890(?)-1988 ... 37-40R
Obituary ... 124
Seydell, Mildred
See Seydel, Mildred Woolley
Seydor, Paul 1947- ... 97-100
Seyer, Philip C. 1941- ... 119
Seyersted, Brita Lindberg
See Lindberg-Seyersted, Brita
Seyersted, Per 1921- ... CANR-15
Earlier sketch in CA 29-32R
Seyfert, Carl K(eenan) 1938- ... 57-60
Seyfettin, Omer 1884-1920 ... WLIT 6
Seyffert, Kenneth D. 1927- ... 215
Seyler, Dorothy U(pton) 1938- ... 109
Seymour, A(rthur) J(ames) 1914- ... CANR-29
Earlier sketch in CA 97-100
See also BW 2
See also CP 1, 2
Seymour, Alan
See Wright, S(ydney) Fowler
Seymour, Alan 1927- ... 53-56
Seymour, Alta Halverson ... CAP-1
Earlier sketch in CA 11-12
See also SATA 10
Seymour, Anne
See Morton, Phyllis Digby
Seymour, Charles, Jr. 1912-1977 ... 9-12R
Obituary ... 69-72
Seymour, Digby G. 1923- ... 17-20R
Seymour, Dorothy Jane Z(ander) 1928- ... 89-92
Seymour, Emery W. 1921- ... 13-16R
Seymour, Forrest W. 1905-1983
Obituary ... 111
Seymour, Gerald (William Herschel Kean)
See Seymour, (William Herschel Kean) Gerald
See also CMW 4
Seymour, (William Herschel Kean) Gerald
1941- ... CANR-115
Earlier sketches in CA 101, CANR-45, 68
See also Seymour, Gerald (William Herschel Kean)
Seymour, Harold 1910-1992 ... 138
Seymour, Henry
See Hartmann, Helmut Henry
Seymour, James D. 1935- ... 162
Seymour, Jane 1951- ... 210
See also SATA 139
Seymour, John 1914-2004 ... CANR-127
Obituary ... 231
Earlier sketches in CA 13-16R, CANR-9
Seymour, Miranda
See Sinclair, Miranda (Jane)
Seymour, Raymond B(enedict)
1912-1991 ... CANR-44
Earlier sketches in CA 73-76, CANR-13
Seymour, Rogers James 1942- ... 110
Seymour, Stephan A(ndrew) 1920- ... 21-24R
Seymour, Tres 1966- ... 149
See also SATA 82
Seymour, W(illiam) Douglas 1910- ... 49-52
Seymour, Whitney North, Jr. 1923- ... CANR-14
Earlier sketch in CA 81-84
Seymour, William Kean 1887-1975 ... 9-12R
Obituary ... 126
Seymour, William Napier 1914- ... 77-80
Seymour-Smith, Martin 1928-1998 ... CANR-54
Obituary ... 169
Earlier sketch in CA 5-8R
See also CP 1, 2
See also DLB 155
Seymour-Ure, Colin K. 1938- ... CANR-18
Earlier sketch in CA 25-28R
Seyppel, Joachim (Hans) 1919- ... 194
Seyton, Marion
See Saxon, Gladys Relyea

Seznec, Jean J. 1905-1983
Obituary ... 111
Sgard, Jean ... 223
Sgorlon, Carlo 1930- ... DLB 196
Sgroi, Peter Philip 1936- ... 57-60
Sgroi, Suzanne M(ary) 1943- ... 108
Shaaban, Bouthaina 1953- ... 137
Shaaber, M. A.
See Shaaber, Matthias A(dam)
Shaaber, Matthias A(dam) 1897-1979
Obituary ... 111
Shaara, Jeff 1952- ... CANR-109
Earlier sketch in CA 163
See also CLC 119
See also CN 7
See also MTFW 2005
Shaara, Michael (Joseph, Jr.)
1929-1988 ... CANR-85
Obituary ... 125
Earlier sketches in CA 102, CANR-52
See also AITN 1
See also BPFB 3
See also CLC 15
See also DAM POP
See also DLBY 1983
See also MTFW 2005
Shabad, Theodore 1922-1987 ... CANR-86
Obituary ... 122
Earlier sketches in CA 25-28R, CANR-10
Shabbi, Abu al-Qasim 1909-1934 ... AFW
See also EWL 3
Shabecoff, Philip 1934- ... 203
Shabel'skaia, Aleksandra Stanislavovna
1845-1921 ... DLB 238
Shaber, Sarah R. 1951- ... 209
Shabtai, Yaakov 1934-1981 ... EWL 3
Shacham, Mordechai 1942- ... 188
Shachtman, Tom 1942- ... CANR-91
Earlier sketch in CA 89-92
See also SATA 49
Shack, William A(lfred) 1923-2000 ... 113
Obituary ... 189
Shackelford, Jean A. 1946- ... CANR-43
Earlier sketch in CA 105
Shacket, Sheldon R(ubin) 1941- ... 102
Shackford, Martha Hale 1875-1963 ... 1-4R
Shackford, R(oland) H(erbert) 1908-1998 .. 1-4R
Obituary ... 165
Shackle, G(eorge) L(ennox) S(harman)
1903-1992 ... CANR-2
Obituary ... 137
Earlier sketch in CA 5-8R
Shackleford, Bernard L. 1889-1975 ... CAP-2
Earlier sketch in CA 29-32
Shackleford, Ruby P(aschall) 1913- ... 57-60
Shackleton, C. C.
See Aldiss, Brian W(ilson)
Shackleton, Doris (Cavell) 1918- ... 93-96
Shackleton, Edward Arthur Alexander
1911-1994 ... 13-16R
Shackleton, Ernest Henry 1874-1922 ... 219
Brief entry ... 118
Shackleton, Keith Hope 1923- ... 5-8R
Shackleton, Philip 1923- ... 101
Shackleton, Robert 1919-1986 ... CANR-86
Obituary ... 120
Earlier sketch in CA 1-4R
Shackleton Bailey, D(avid) R(oy)
1917- ... CANR-19
Earlier sketches in CA 5-8R, CANR-3
Shackley, Myra (Lesley) 1949- ... 115
Shackley, Theodore (George), Jr. 1927-2002
Obituary ... 210
Brief entry ... 117
Shacochis, Bob
See Shacochis, Robert G.
See also CLC 39
Shacochis, Robert G. 1951- ... CANR-100
Brief entry ... 119
Earlier sketch in CA 124
Interview in ... CA-124
See also Shacochis, Bob
Shadbolt, Doris 1918- ... 196
Shadbolt, Maurice (Francis Richard)
1932-2004 ... CANR-114
Obituary ... 232
Earlier sketches in CA 13-16R, CANR-5, 84
See also CAAS 3
See also CN 1, 2, 3, 4, 5, 6, 7
See also RGEL 2
See also RGSF 2
Shade, Eric 1970- ... 224
Shade, Rose (Marian) 1927- ... 57-60
Shade, William G(erald) 1939- ... 41-44R
Shade, William L(eonard) 1945-
Brief entry ... 113
Shadegg, Stephen C. 1909-1990 ... 13-16R
Obituary ... 131
Shader, Rachel
See Sofer, Barbara
Shadi, Dorothy Clotelle Clarke
1908-1992 ... 13-16R
Shadid, Anthony 1969(?)- ... 237
Shadily, Hassan 1920- ... 105
Shadlick, Harold (Ernest) 1902-1993 ... 41-44R
Shadoian, Jack 1940- ... 105
Shadowitz, Albert 1915- ... 69-72
Shadwell, Delvenia G. 1938- ... 192
Shadwell, Thomas
See Cover, Arthur Byron
Shadwell, Thomas 1641(?)-1692 ... DLB 80
See also IDTP
See also RGEL 2
Shadyac, Tom 1959- ... AAYA 36
Shadyland, Sal
See Cooper, Louise
Shaevitz, Marjorie Hansen 1943- ... CANR-91
Earlier sketch in CA 101
Shaevitz, Morton H(erbert) 1935- ... 102
Shafarevich, Igor Rostislavovich 1923- ... 105
Shafer, Boyd Carlisle 1907- ... 17-20R
Shafer, Byron E. 1947- ... CANR-131
Earlier sketch in CA 165
Shafer, D. Michael 1953- ... 134
Shafer, Glenn (Ray) 1946- ... CANR-136
Earlier sketch in CA 168
Shafer, Neil 1933- ... 33-36R
Shafer, Robert E(ugene) 1925- ... CANR-10
Earlier sketch in CA 57-60
See also SATA 9
Shafer, Robert Jones 1920- ... 37-40R
Shafer, Ronald G. 1939- ... CANR-10
Earlier sketch in CA 65-68
Shafer, Thomas 1910(?)-1986
Obituary ... 119
Shafer, Yvonne 1936- ... 175
Shaff, Albert L(averne) 1937- ... 29-32R
Shaffer, Anthony (Joshua) 1926-2001 ... 116
Obituary ... 200
Brief entry ... 110
See also CBD
See also CD 5, 6
See also CLC 19
See also DAM DRAM
See also DFS 13
See also DLB 13
Shaffer, Betty
See Shaffer, Elizabeth (Nickerson)
Shaffer, Brian W. 1960- ... 209
Shaffer, Dale Eugene 1929- ... 37-40R
Shaffer, David R. 1946- ... 218
Shaffer, Elizabeth (Nickerson) 1925- ... 113
Shaffer, Harry George 1919- ... CANR-6
Earlier sketch in CA 5-8R
Shaffer, Helen B. 1909(?)-1978 ... 85-88
Obituary ... 81-84
Shaffer, Jeffrey 1953- ... 151
Shaffer, Jerome A(rthur) 1929- ... 37-40R
Shaffer, K(atherine) Stevenson
1902-1990 ... CAP-2
Earlier sketch in CA 17-18
Shaffer, Karen A. 1947- ... CANR-57
Earlier sketch in CA 127
Shaffer, Kenneth R(aymond) 1914- ... 5-8R
Shaffer, Laurance Frederic 1903-1976
Obituary ... 65-68
Shaffer, Louise ... 152
Shaffer, Peter (Levin) 1926- ... CANR-118
Earlier sketches in CA 25-28R, CANR-25, 47, 74
See also BRWS 1
See also CBD
See also CD 5, 6
See also CDBLB 1960 to Present
See also CLC 5, 14, 18, 37, 60
See also DA3
See also DAB
See also DAM DRAM, MST
See also DC 7
See also DFS 5, 13
See also DLB 13, 233
See also EWL 3
See also MTCW 1, 2
See also MTFW 2005
See also RGEL 2
See also TEA
Shaffer, Rosalind Keating 1896-1990
Obituary ... 131
Shaffer, Samuel 1910-1995 ... 104
Shaffer, Terea 1968- ... SATA 79
Shaffer, Thomas Lindsay 1934- ... 37-40R
Shaffer, Wilma L. 1916- ... 17-20R
Shafferman, Barbara 1928- ... 178
Shafi'i, Muhammad ibn Idris al-
767-820 ... DLB 311
Shafik, Viola 1961- ... 209
Shafir, Michael 1944- ... 129
Shafquat, Sofia 1959- ... 141
Shafritz, Jay M(ichael) 1944- ... 117
Shaftel, Oscar 1912-2000 ... 57-60
Obituary ... 189
Shaftner, Dorothy 1918- ... 25-28R
Shagan, Steve 1927- ... CANR-6
Earlier sketch in CA 53-56
Shaginian, Marietta Sergeevna
See Shaginyan, Marietta (Sergeyevna)
See also DLB 272
Shaginyan, Marietta (Sergeyevna)
1888-1982 ... 129
Obituary ... 106
See also Shaginian, Marietta Sergeevna
Shah, A(ruind) M(anilal) 1931- ... 73-76
Shah, Amina 1918- ... 49-52
Shah, Diane K(iver) 1945- ... 73-76
Shah, (Sayed) Idries 1924-1996 ... CANR-47
Obituary ... 154
Earlier sketches in CA 17-20R, CANR-7, 22
Shah, Jami J. 1950- ... 159
Shah, Krishna B. 1933- ... 17-20R
Shah, Tahir 1966- ... 188
Shaha, Rishikesh 1925- ... CANR-47
Earlier sketch in CA 69-72
Shahan, Lynn 1941- ... 106
Shahan, Sherry 1949- ... 156
See also SATA 92, 134
Shahane, Vasant Anant 1923- ... CANR-12
Earlier sketch in CA 25-28R
Shahani, Ranjee 1904-1968 ... CANR-2
Earlier sketch in CA 1-4R
Shahar, David 1926- ... 65-68
Shaheen, Jack G(eorge) 1935- ... 124
Shaheen, Naseeb 1931- ... CANR-86
Earlier sketches in CA 65-68, CANR-34
Shahid, Irfan Arif 1926- ... 197
Shahn, Ben(jamin) 1898-1969 ... 121
Obituary ... 89-92
See also SATA-Obit 21
Shahn, Bernarda Bryson
See Bryson, Bernarda
Shahnon Ahmad 1933- ... EWL 3
Shah of Iran
See Pahlevi, Mohammed Riza
Shaik, Fatima ... 186
See also SATA 114
Shain, Henry 1941- ... 57-60
Shain, Merle 1935-1989 ... 61-64
See also AITN 1
Shain, Milton 1949- ... 149
Shain, Yossi 1956- ... CANR-112
Earlier sketches in CA 131, CANR-100
Shainberg, Lawrence 1936- ... 137
Brief entry ... 131
Interview in ... CA-137
Shainmark, Eliezer L. 1900-1976
Obituary ... 104
Shainmark, Lou
See Shainmark, Eliezer L.
Shairp, (Alexander) Mordaunt 1887-1939
Brief entry ... 110
See also DLB 10
Shakabpa, Tsepon W(angchuk) D(eden)
1907-1989 ... CAP-2
Obituary ... 128
Earlier sketch in CA 21-24R
Shakar, Alex 1968- ... 203
Sha'Ked, Ami 1945- ... 101
Shaked, Gershon 1929- ... CANR-95
Earlier sketch in CA 131
Shaked, Haim 1939- ... 130
Shakeri, Khosrow 1938- ... 154
Shakesby, Paul S(tewart) 1946- ... 57-60
Shakespeare, Geoffrey (Hithersay) 1893-1980
Obituary ... 105
Shakespeare, (William Richmond) Nicholas
1957- ... CANR-92
Earlier sketch in CA 145
See also DLB 231
Shakespeare, William 1564-1616 ... AAYA 35
See also BRW 1
See also CDBLB Before 1660
See also DA
See also DA3
See also DAB
See also DAC
See also DAM DRAM, MST, POET
See also DFS 20, 21
See also DLB 62, 172, 263
See also EXPP
See also LAIT 1
See also LATS 1:1
See also LMFS 1
See also PAB
See also PFS 1, 2, 3, 4, 5, 8, 9
See also RGEL 2
See also TEA
See also WLC
See also WLIT 3
See also WP
See also WS
See also WYA
Shakey, Bernard
See Young, Neil
Shakhova, Elisaveta Nikitichna
1822-1899 ... DLB 277
Shakhovskoi, Aleksandr Aleksandrovich
1777-1846 ... DLB 150
Shakoor, Jordana Y. 1956- ... 209
Shakoori, Ali 1962- ... 225
Shakow, David 1901-1981
Obituary ... 108
Shakur, Sanyika 1963- ... 148
Shakur, Tupac (Amaru) 1971-1996 ... 156
Shakya, Tsering 1959- ... 183
Shalamov, Varlam (Tikhonovich)
1907-1982 ... 129
Obituary ... 105
See also CLC 18
See also DLB 302
See also RGSF 2
Shalant, Phyllis 1949- ... 225
See also SATA 150
Shale, Richard 1947- ... 89-92
Shales, Thomas William 1948- ... CANR-139
Brief entry ... 110
Earlier sketch in CA 112
Interview in ... CA-112
Shales, Tom
See Shales, Thomas William
Shalett, Anita Effron 1917(?)-1984
Obituary ... 112
Shalev, Meir 1948- ... 210
Shalev, Zeruya 1959- ... 206
Shalhope, Robert E. 1941- ... 85-88
Shalit, Beatrice 1945- ... 142
Shalit, Wendy 1975- ... 189
Shallcrass, John James 1922- ... CANR-20
Earlier sketch in CA 103
Shallenberger, David 1950- ... 166
Shallit, Jeffrey (Outlaw) 1957- ... 164
Shallow, Robert
See Atkinson, Frank
Shaloff, Stanley 1939- ... CANR-43
Earlier sketch in CA 29-32R
Shalom, Stephen Rosskamm 1948- ... 112
Shalvey, Thomas (Joseph) 1937- ... 105
Shambaugh, David L. 1953- ... 142
Shambaugh, George E. 1963- ... 189
Shamblin, Gwen ... 192
Shamburger, (Alice) Page ... 9-12R
Shames, Germaine W. ... 217
Shames, Laurence 1951- ... CANR-73
Earlier sketch in CA 124
Shamir, Moshe 1921-2004 ... 210
Obituary ... 230
Shamir, Yitzhak 1915- ... 150
Shamloo, Ahmad
See Shamlu, Ahmad
Shamlou, Ahmad
See Shamlu, Ahmad
Shamlu, Ahmad 1925-2000 ... 216
See also CLC 10
See also CWW 2
Shammas, Anton 1951- ... 199
See also CLC 55
Shamon, Albert Joseph 1915- ... 13-16R
Shamroy, Leon 1901-1974 ... IDFW 3, 4
Shamsie, Kamila 1973- ... 208
Shan, Darren
See O'Shaughnessy, Darren
See also AAYA 48
Shan, Yeh
See Wang, C(hing) H(sien)
Shanahan, Daniel (A.) 1947- ... 139
Shanahan, Eileen 1924-2001 ... 102
Obituary ... 204
Shanahan, Michael Edward 1952- ... 225
Shanahan, Mike
See Shanahan, Michael Edward
Shanahan, William J. 1935- ... 29-32R
Shanberg, Karen
See Shragg, Karen (I.)
Shand, Rosa 1937- ... 206
Shandler, Sara ... 192
Shandling, Arline
See Berriault, Gina
Shandling, Garry 1949- ... 216
Shands, Harley Cecil 1916-1981 ... 109
Obituary ... 105
Shane, Alex M(ichael) 1933- ... 45-48
Shane, Bart
See Rowland, D(onald) S(ydney)
Shane, C(harles) Donald 1895-1983
Obituary ... 109
Shane, Don (Graves) 1933- ... 53-56
Shane, Harold Gray 1914-1993 ... CANR-21
Obituary ... 141
Earlier sketches in CA 9-12R, CANR-3
See also SATA 36
See also SATA-Obit 76
Shane, John
See Durst, Paul
Shane, Mark
See Norwood, Victor G(eorge) C(harles)
Shane, Maxwell 1905(?)-1983
Obituary ... 111
Shane, Rhondo
See Norwood, Victor G(eorge) C(harles)
Shane, Scott 1954- ... 146
Shane, Steve
See Gribble, Leonard (Reginald)
Shaner, Madeleine 1932- ... 73-76
Shanes, Eric 1944- ... 134
Shanet, Howard (Stephen) 1918- ... 130
Shanfara, al- fl. 6th cent. - ... DLB 311
Shange, Ntozake 1948- ... CANR-131
Earlier sketches in CA 85-88, CANR-27, 48, 74
See also CABS 3
See also AAYA 9, 66
See also AFAW 1, 2
See also BLC 3
See also BW 2
See also CAD
See also CD 5, 6
See also CLC 8, 25, 38, 74, 126
See also CP 7
See also CWD
See also CWP
See also DA3
See also DAM DRAM, MULT
See also DC 3
See also DFS 2, 11
See also DLB 38, 249
See also FW
See also LAIT 4, 5
See also MAL 5
See also MTCW 1, 2
See also MTFW 2005
See also NFS 11
See also RGAL 4
See also SATA 157
See also YAW
Shank, Alan 1936- ... 53-56
Shank, David Arthur 1924- ... 29-32R
Shank, Joseph E(lmer) 1892-1980 ... CAP-2
Earlier sketch in CA 25-28
Shank, Margarethe Erdahl 1910- ... CAP-2
Earlier sketch in CA 19-20
Shank, Theodore
See Shank, Theodore J(unior)
Shank, Theodore J(unior) 1929- ... CANR-135
Earlier sketches in CA 129, CANR-65
Shankar, Ravi 1920- ... IDFW 3, 4
Shankar, S(ubramanian) 1962- ... CANR-136
Earlier sketch in CA 171
Shankel, George Edgar 1894-1976 ... CAP-2
Earlier sketch in CA 23-24
Shankland, Peter Macfarlane
1901-1995 ... CANR-16
Earlier sketches in CAP-1, CA 11-12
Shankle, Ralph O(tis) 1933- ... 9-12R
Shanklin, William L(eslie) 1941- ... 120
Shankman, Arnold M(ichael) 1945- ... 129
Shankman, Florence V(ogel) 1912- ... 41-44R
Shankman, Paul (Andrew) 1943- ... 93-96
Shankman, Sarah ... 186

Cumulative Index 525 Sharrock

Shanks, Ann Zane (Kushner) 53-56
See also SATA 10
Shanks, Bob 1932- 101
Shanks, Bruce .... AITN 1
Shanks, Hershel 1930- CANR-79
Brief entry 106
Earlier sketches in CA 126, CANR-52
Shanks, Michael (James) 1927-1984 ... CANR-8
Obituary 111
Earlier sketch in CA 5-8R
Shanley, John Patrick 1950- CANR-83
Brief entry 128
Earlier sketch in CA 133
See also AMWS 14
See also CAD
See also CD 5, 6
See also CLC 75
Shanley, Mary Kay 1943- 158
Shanley, Mary L(yndon) 1944- CANR-135
Earlier sketch in CA 163
Shann, Renee 1907(?)-1979
Obituary 89-92
Shannon, Claude (Elwood) 1916-2001 162
Obituary 193
Shannon, David 1959- .... CLR 87
See also SATA 107, 152
Shannon, David Allen 1920- CANR-43
Earlier sketch in CA 1-4R
Shannon, Dell
See Linington, (Barbara) Elizabeth
Shannon, Doris 1924- CANR-62
Earlier sketches in CA 61-64, CANR-8, 23
See also CMW 4
Shannon, Edgar F(inley), Jr. 1918- 9-12R
Shannon, Elaine 1946- 212
Shannon, Elizabeth (McNelly) 1937- 147
Shannon, Ellen 1927- 77-80
Shannon, Foster (Houts) 1930- 106
Shannon, Fred Albert 1893-1963
Obituary 111
Shannon, George (William Bones)
1952- CANR-122
Earlier sketches in CA 106, CANR-23, 69
See also SATA 35, 94, 143
Shannon, Harry 1948- 232
Shannon, Jacqueline .... SATA 63
Shannon, Jade
See Tanner, Janet
Shannon, Jasper Berry 1903-1984 .... 1-4R
Obituary 114
Shannon, John 1943- CANR-108
Earlier sketch in CA 57-60
Shannon, Lyle William 1920- 61-64
Shannon, M.
See Geddie, John
Shannon, Margaret
See Silverwood, Margaret Shannon
Shannon, Mike 1951- 127
Shannon, Monica 1905(?)-1965
Obituary 109
See also BYA 1
See also CWRI 5
See also SATA 28
Shannon, Pat(ricia) 1933- 229
Shannon, Richard 1945- 73-76
Shannon, Robert
See Wieder, Robert S(hannon)
Shannon, Robert C. 1930- 13-16R
Shannon, Robert L(eroy) 1926- 93-96
Shannon, Steve
See Bouma, J(ohanas) L.
Shannon, Terry
See Mercer, Jessie
See also SATA 21
Shannon, Terry Miller 1951- 222
See also SATA 148
Shannon, Thomas A(nthony) 1940- .. CANR-42
Earlier sketches in CA 53-56, CANR-5, 20
Shannon, William H(enry) 1917- 45-48
Shannon, William V(incent)
1927-1988 .... CANR-86
Obituary 126
Earlier sketches in CA 9-12R, CANR-6
Shanor, Donald Read 1927- CANR-30
Earlier sketches in CA 61-64, CANR-12
Shanwa
See Haarer, Alec Ernest
Shao, Stephen P(inyee) 1924- CANR-11
Earlier sketch in CA 21-24R
Shapard, Robert (Perry) 1942- 126
Shapcott, Jo 1958- CANR-141
Earlier sketch in CA 135
See also CWP
Shapcott, Thomas W(illiam) 1935- . CANR-103
Earlier sketches in CA 69-72, CANR-49, 83
See also CLC 38
See also CP 1, 2, 3, 4, 5, 6, 7
See also DLB 289
Shapell, Nathan 1922- 49-52
Shapera, Robert J.
See Evans, Robert
Shapere, Dudley 1928- 17-20R
Shapin, Steven 1943- 164
Shapir, Ol'ga Andreevna 1850-1916 .. DLB 295
Shapiro, Alan 1952- CANR-99
Earlier sketch in CA 125
See also CAAS 23
Shapiro, Alan E(lihu) 1942- 128
Shapiro, Andrew L. 184
Shapiro, Ann R. 1937- 188
Shapiro, Barbara J(une) 1934- 130
Shapiro, Barry M. 1944- 146
Shapiro, Bonnie L. 150
Shapiro, Cecile 85-88
Shapiro, Charles K. 1926- 5-8R
Shapiro, Dan(iel) 1966- 234
Shapiro, Dani (J.) 167
Shapiro, David (Joel) 1947- CANR-83
Earlier sketches in CA 13-16R, CANR-45
See also CP 1, 2, 3, 4, 5, 6, 7
Shapiro, David A. 1957- 220
Shapiro, David S(idney) 1923-1983 . CANR-85
Obituary 109
Earlier sketches in CA 1-4R, CANR-1
Shapiro, Deborah 1923- 106
Shapiro, Dolph
See Sharp, Dolph
Shapiro, Edward 1920- 17-20R
Shapiro, Edward S. 1938- CANR-103
Earlier sketch in CA 148
Shapiro, Eileen C. CANR-101
Earlier sketch in CA 152
Shapiro, Elizabeth Klein
See Klein, Elizabeth
Shapiro, Fred(eric) C(harles)
1931-1993 .... 17-20R
Obituary 143
Shapiro, Fred R(ichard) 1954- 145
Shapiro, Gerald 1950- 183
Shapiro, Gilbert 1926- 207
Shapiro, Harold I(srael) 1931- 45-48
Shapiro, Harold T(afler) 1935- 132
Shapiro, Harry L(ionel) 1902-1990 49-52
Shapiro, Harvey 1924- CANR-83
Earlier sketches in CA 41-44R, CANR-15, 34
See also CP 1, 2, 3, 4, 5, 6, 7
Shapiro, Henry D(avid) 1937-2004 .... CANR-3
Obituary 225
Earlier sketch in CA 9-12R
Shapiro, Herbert 1929- 37-40R
Shapiro, Herman 1922- 13-16R
Shapiro, Howard I(ra) 1937- 73-76
Shapiro, Irving 1917- 29-32R
Shapiro, Irwin 1911-1981 .... CANR-45
Earlier sketch in CA 81-84
See also SATA 32
Shapiro, James E(arnest) 1946- 108
Shapiro, James S. 1955- 228
Shapiro, Jane 1942- 196
See also CLC 76
Shapiro, Jane P.
See Zacek, Jane Shapiro
Shapiro, Jerrold Lee 1943- 144
Shapiro, Jim
See Shapiro, James E(arnest)
Shapiro, Joan Hatch 1928- 33-36R
Shapiro, Judith 1953- 144
Shapiro, Julian L.
See Sanford, John
Shapiro, Karl (Jay) 1913-2000 .... CANR-66
Obituary 188
Earlier sketches in CA 1-4R, CANR-1, 36
See also CAAS 6
See also AMWS 2
See also CLC 4, 8, 15, 53
See also CP 1, 2, 3, 4, 5, 6
See also DLB 48
See also EWL 3
See also EXPP
See also MAL 5
See also MTCW 1, 2
See also MTFW 2005
See also PC 25
See also PFS 3
See also RGAL 4
Shapiro, Kenneth A(llan) 1942- 118
Shapiro, Laura 1946- 145
Shapiro, Laurie Gwen 1966- 174
Shapiro, Lillian L(adman) 1913- 102
Shapiro, Linda Gaye 1953- 65-68
Shapiro, Lisa 1962- 186
Shapiro, Lisa Wood 1961- 236
Shapiro, Marianne (Goldner) 1940- 123
Brief entry 118
Shapiro, Martin M(athew) 1933- 102
Shapiro, Max 1912(?)-1981
Obituary 105
Shapiro, Mel 1937- CANR-140
Earlier sketch in CA 101
Shapiro, Melisse 1953- 197
Shapiro, Michael 1952- 187
Shapiro, Milton J. 1926- 81-84
See also SATA 32
Shapiro, Nat(haniel M.) 1922-1983 .. CANR-15
Obituary 111
Earlier sketch in CA 29-32R
Shapiro, Norman R(ichard) 1930- .. CANR-108
Earlier sketch in CA 93-96
Shapiro, Paulett
See Tumay, Paulett
Shapiro, Robert 1935- 113
Shapiro, Robert L(eslie) 1942- CANR-110
Earlier sketch in CA 156
Shapiro, Robert Y. 1953- 142
Shapiro, Rochelle Jewel 1947(?)- 235
Shapiro, Samuel 1927- CANR-1
Earlier sketch in CA 1-4R
Shapiro, Sidney 1915- 136
Shapiro, Stanley 1925-1990
Obituary 132
Shapiro, Stewart (David) 1951- 171
Shapiro, Stuart C(harles) 1944- 127
Shapiro, Sue A. 1947- 109
Shapiro, Susan R.
See Shapiro, Susan Ripps
Shapiro, Susan Ripps 1954- 180
Shapiro, Tricia
See Andryszewski, Tricia
Shapiro, William E. 1934- CANR-20
Earlier sketch in CA 25-28R
Shapiro-Barash, Susan
See Shapiro, Susan Ripps
Shaplen, June Herman 1924(?)-1982
Obituary 108
Shaplen, Robert (Modell) 1917-1988 ...... 9-12R
Obituary 125
Shapley, Fern Rusk 1890-1984 .... 41-44R
Obituary 114
Shapley, Harlow 1885-1972
Obituary 37-40R
Shapley, John 1890(?)-1978
Obituary 81-84
Shapo, Marshall S(chambelan)
1936- CANR-15
Earlier sketch in CA 41-44R
Shapp, Charles M(orris) 1906-1989 57-60
Obituary 127
See also SATA-Obit 61
Shapp, Martha Glauber 1910- CANR-2
Earlier sketch in CA 1-4R
See also SATA 3
Shappiro, Herbert (Arthur)
1899(?)-1975 .... CANR-68
Obituary 57-60
Earlier sketches in CAP-2, CA 21-22
See also Arthur, Burt
Sharabi, H(isham) B(ashir)
1927-2005 .... CANR-2
Obituary 235
Earlier sketch in CA 5-8R
Sharaff, Irene 1910-1993 .... IDFW 3, 4
Sharansky, Anatoly
See Sharansky, Natan (Borisovich)
Sharansky, Natan (Borisovich) 1948- 236
Sharat Chandra, G(ubbi) S(hankara Chetty)
1938-2000 171
Earlier sketch in CA 53-56
Sharfman, Amalie 73-76
See also SATA 14
Sharif, M(ohammad) Nawaz 1942- .. CANR-36
Earlier sketch in CA 114
Sharif, Omar
See Chalhoub, Michael
Sharkansky, Ira 1938- 29-32R
Sharkawi, A(bdel)-R(ahman) 1920-1987
Obituary 125
Sharkey, Bernarda 1934- 33-36R
Sharkey, Jack
See Sharkey, John Michael
Sharkey, Joe 1946- 146
Sharkey, John Michael 1931-1992 .... CANR-83
Earlier sketches in CA 1-4R, CANR-3
See also SFW 4
Sharkey, Olive (Margaret Mary) 1954- 128
Sharkey, (Neil) Owen 1917- 61-64
Sharlet, Robert (Stewart) 1935- 37-40R
Sharlin, Harold I(ssadore) 1925- 9-12R
Sharma, Akhil 1972- 197
See also SSFS 21
Sharma, Arun K. 1950- 218
Sharma, Arvind 1940- CANR-103
Earlier sketch in CA 152
Sharma, Chandradhar 1920- 13-16R
Sharma, Govind Narain 1927- 45-48
Sharma, Haresh 1965(?)- 198
Sharma, Jagdish Prasad 1934- 81-84
Sharma, Partap 1939- CANR-14
Earlier sketch in CA 77-80
See also SATA 15
Sharma, Rashmi
See Singh, Rashmi Sharma
Sharma, Ravindra N(ath) 1944- 110
Sharma, Robin S(hilp) 1964- 220
Sharma, Shripad Rama 1879- CAP-2
Earlier sketch in CA 29-32
Sharma, Sohan L(al) 1927- 128
Sharman, Alison
See Leonard, Alison
Sharman, Gopal 1935- .... CP 1
Sharman, Maisie
See Bolton, Maisie Sharman
Sharman, Miriam
See Bolton, Maisie Sharman
Sharman, Nick 1952- .... HGG
Sharmat, Marjorie Weinman 1928- . CANR-112
Earlier sketches in CA 25-28R, CANR-12, 39, 84
See also CWRI 5
See also JRDA
See also MAICYA 1, 2
See also SATA 4, 33, 74, 133
Sharmat, Mitchell 1927- CANR-96
Earlier sketches in CA 104, CANR-46
See also SATA 33, 127
Sharon, Donna Haye
See Scharlemann, Dorothy Hoyer
Sharon, Rose
See Merril, Judith
Sharon, Sylvia
See Little, Paul H(ugo)
Sharot, Stephen 1943- 109
Sharouni, Yusuf
See Al Sharouni, Youssef
Sharov, Vladimir Aleksandrovich
1952- .... DLB 285
Sharp, Aaron John 1904-1997 .... 9-12R
Obituary 162
Sharp, Adrienne 210
Sharp, Alan 1934- 13-16R
Sharp, Andrew 1906-1974 .... CANR-3
Earlier sketch in CA 1-4R
Sharp, Ann Margaret 1942- 81-84
Sharp, Anne Wallace 1947- 217
See also SATA 144
Sharp, Ansel M(iree) 1924- 77-80
Sharp, Buchanan 1942- 105
Sharp, Clifford Henry 192?- 108
Sharp, Daniel A(sher) 1932- 49-52
Sharp, Dolph 1914- 29-32R
Sharp, Donald Bruce 1938- 29-32R
Sharp, Doreen Maud 1920- CANR-25
Earlier sketch in CA 108
Sharp, Dorothea Elizabeth 21-24R
Sharp, Edith Lambert 1917- 5-8R
Sharp, Ernest Jack
See Sharpsteen, Ernest Jack
Sharp, Francis Michael 1941- 106
Sharp, Hal
See Sharp, Harold W(ilson)
Sharp, Harold S(pencer) 1909-1990 ... CANR-3
Earlier sketch in CA 9-12R
Sharp, Harold W(ilson) 1914- 93-96
Sharp, Helen
See Paine, Lauran (Bosworth)
Sharp, James
See Kinghorn, A(lexander) M(anson)
Sharp, James Roger 1936- 29-32R
Sharp, John Kean 1892-1979
Obituary 93-96
Sharp, John R. 1921- 17-20R
Sharp, Laure M(etzger) 1921-2005 .... 29-32R
Obituary 236
Sharp, Luke
See Barr, Robert
Sharp, Luke
See Alkiviades, Alkis
Sharp, Margery 1905-1991 .... CANR-85
Obituary 134
Earlier sketches in CA 21-24R, CANR-18
See also CLR 27
See also CN 1, 2, 3, 4
See also CWRI 5
See also DLB 161
See also MAICYA 1, 2
See also SATA 1, 29
See also SATA-Obit 67
Sharp, Martin 1900(?)-1987
Obituary 124
Sharp, Maurice L. 1933- 145
Sharp, Paula 1957- CANR-97
Earlier sketch in CA 128
Sharp, Robert P(hillip) 1911-2004 168
Obituary 227
Sharp, Roger (William) 1935-1986 ... CANR-86
Obituary 119
Earlier sketch in CA 73-76
Sharp, Ronald A(lan) 1945- CANR-49
Earlier sketch in CA 123
Sharp, Saundra 1942- 45-48
See also BW 1
Sharp, Shirley I. 1934- 45-48
Sharp, Sister Mary Corona 1922- 13-16R
Sharp, William 1855-1905 160
See also Macleod, Fiona
See also DLB 156
See also RGEL 2
See also TCLC 39
Sharp, Zerna A. 1889-1981
Obituary 104
See also SATA-Obit 27
Sharpe, Genell J(ackson) Subak
See Subak-Sharpe, Genell J(ackson)
Sharpe, Grant W(illiam) 1925- 69-72
Sharpe, J(ames) A(nthony) 1946- 117
Sharpe, Jon
See Duncan, Alice and
Knott, William C(ecil, Jr.) and
Messman, Jon
See also TCWW 2
Sharpe, Kevin (M.) 1949- CANR-104
Earlier sketch in CA 136
Sharpe, Lawrence A(lbright) 1920- 49-52
Sharpe, Lucretia
See Burgess, Michael (Roy)
Sharpe, Matthew 1962- 179
Sharpe, Mitchell R(aymond) 1924- 29-32R
See also SATA 12
Sharpe, Myron E(manuel) 1928- 136
Sharpe, Roger Carter 1948- 93-96
Sharpe, Shane E.
See Meares, Leonard Frank
Sharpe, Susan 1946- .... SATA 71
Sharpe, Thomas Ridley 1928- CANR-85
Brief entry 114
Earlier sketch in CA 122
Interview in CA-122
See also Sharpe, Tom
Sharpe, Tom
See Sharpe, Thomas Ridley
See also CLC 36
See also CN 4, 5, 6, 7
See also DLB 14, 231
Sharpe, Tony 1952- 227
Sharpe, William Chapman 1951- 139
Sharpe, William D(onald) 1927- 17-20R
Sharpes, Donald K(enneth) 1934- CANR-1
Earlier sketch in CA 45-48
Sharples, Win(ston S.), Jr. 1932- 45-48
Sharpless, F(rancis) Parvin 1929- 25-28R
Sharpless, Rebecca 1958- 214
Sharpsteen, Ernest Jack 1880-1976
Obituary 110
Sharpton, Al(fred Charles, Jr.) 1954- 224
Sharpton, Alfred Charles, Jr.
See Sharpton, Al(fred Charles, Jr.)
Sharpton, Robert E(arl) 1936- 104
Sharratt, Mary 1964- 192
Sharratt, Nick 1962- CANR-137
Earlier sketch in CA 171
See also SATA 104, 153
Sharrock, David 183
Sharrock, Roger (Ian) 1919-1991(?) CANR-2
Obituary 133
Earlier sketch in CA 5-8R

Sharwood Smith, Bryan Evers
1899-1983 ... CANR-85
Obituary ... 111
Earlier sketches in CAP-2, CA 29-32
Shary, Timothy (Matthew) 1967- ... 221
Shasha, Dennis (E.) 1955- ... 143
Shasha, Mark 1961- ... SATA 80
Shatner, William 1931- ... CANR-85
Earlier sketch in CA 146
See also CCA 1
Shatrov, Mikhail ... CLC 59
Shatto, Gloria M. 1931-1999 ... 41-44R
Shattock, Ernest (Henry) 1904-1985 ... 102
Shattuc, Jane ... 238
Shattuck, Charles H(arlen)
1910-1992 ... CANR-47
Obituary ... 139
Earlier sketches in CA 5-8R, CANR-2
Shattuck, George C. 1927- ... 137
Shattuck, Jessica ... 230
Shattuck, Roger (Whitney) 1923- ... CANR-71
Earlier sketches in CA 5-8R, CANR-7, 47
See also SATA 64
Shattuck, Sim 1950- ... 220
Shatzkin, Leonard 1919- ... 109
Shatzky, Joel 1943- ... 175
Shaughnessy, Alfred (James) 1916- ... 134
Shaughnessy, Dan ... 236
Shaughnessy, Edward J(oseph, Jr.) 1934- ... 110
Shaughnessy, Edward L(awrence) 1932- ... 130
Shaughnessy, Mary Alice 1951- ... 141
Shaughnessy, Robert 1962- ... 189
Shaul, Frank
See Rowland, D(onald) S(ydney)
Shaull, (Millard) Richard 1919-2002 . CANR-11
Obituary ... 210
Earlier sketch in CA 21-24R
Shave, Gordon A(shton) 1922- ... 101
Shavelson, Lonny 1952- ... CANR-113
Earlier sketch in CA 147
Shavelson, Melville 1917- ... CANR-4
Earlier sketch in CA 53-56
Shaver, James P. 1933- ... CANR-7
Earlier sketch in CA 17-20R
Shaver, Phillip (Robert) 1944- ... 130
Shaver, Richard S(harpe) 1907-1975 ... 166
See also SFW 4
Shaver-Crandell, Anne (Elizabeth) 1941- ... 113
Shaver-Crandell, Annie
See Shaver-Crandell, Anne (Elizabeth)
Shavin, Norman 1926- ... 81-84
Shaw, Alan George Lewers 1916- ... CANR-9
Earlier sketch in CA 21-24R
Shaw, Albert 1857-1947 ... 185
See also DLB 91
Shaw, Alison 1957- ... 130
Shaw, Arnold 1909-1989 ... CANR-44
Obituary ... 129
Earlier sketches in CA 1-4R, CANR-1
See also SATA 4
See also SATA-Obit 63
Shaw, Artie 1910-2004 ... 144
Obituary ... 234
Shaw, B(iswanath) N. 1923- ... 37-40R
Shaw, Barton C(arr) 1947- ... 123
Shaw, Bernard
See Shaw, George Bernard
See also DLB 10, 57, 190
Shaw, Bernard 1940- ... 119
Brief entry ... 109
Interview in ... CA-119
See also BW 1
Shaw, Bob 1931-1996 ... CANR-85
Obituary ... 151
Earlier sketches in CA 49-52, CANR-1, 19, 41
See also SFW 4
Shaw, Brian
See Tubb, E(dwin) C(harles)
Shaw, Bruce 1941- ... 119
Shaw, Bruno 1905-1984
Obituary ... 114
Shaw, Bryan
See Fearn, John Russell
Shaw, Bud
See Shaw, Henry I(var), Jr.
Shaw, Bynum (Gillette) 1923- ... CANR-4
Earlier sketch in CA 1-4R
Shaw, Carleton Ford 1908-1992 ... CAP-1
Obituary ... 196
Earlier sketch in CA 13-16
Shaw, Carlos M. Fernandez
See Fernandez-Shaw, Carlos M(anuel)
Shaw, Carolyn Hagner 1903(?)-1977
Obituary ... 69-72
Shaw, Carolyn V. 1934- ... 155
See also SATA 91
Shaw, Charles (Green) 1892-1974 ... CAP-1
Earlier sketch in CA 17-18
See also SATA 13
Shaw, Charles R(aymond) 1921- ... CANR-14
Earlier sketch in CA 21-24R
Shaw, Chester Lee 1898(?)-1985
Obituary ... 118
Shaw, Christine 1952- ... CANR-93
Earlier sketch in CA 146
Shaw, Colin 1928- ... 212
Shaw, David 1943-2005 ... 49-52
Shaw, David W. 1961- ... CANR-103
Earlier sketch in CA 167
Shaw, Dawn
See Shaw, Thelma
Shaw, Donald Leslie 1930- ... 195
Shaw, Donald Lewis 1936- ... 61-64
Shaw, Earl Bennett 1889-1979 ... CAP-1
Earlier sketch in CA 17-18
Shaw, Edward P(ease) 1911-1986 ... CANR-85
Obituary ... 118
Earlier sketch in CA 21-24R
Shaw, Elizabeth
See Prance, June E(lizabeth)
Shaw, Ellen Torgerson
See Torgerson Shaw, Ellen
Shaw, Evelyn S. 1927- ... 104
See also SATA 28
Shaw, Felicity 1918-1989 ... CANR-61
Earlier sketch in CA 104
See also CMW 4
Shaw, Fiona ... 239
Shaw, Flora Louisa
See Lugard, Flora Louisa Shaw
Shaw, Fred (?)-1972
Obituary ... 104
Shaw, Frederick 1912-1991 ... CANR-1
Earlier sketch in CA 45-48
Shaw, Frederick W. 1916(?)-1983
Obituary ... 111
Shaw, G. Bernard
See Shaw, George Bernard
Shaw, Gaylord 1942- ... 81-84
Shaw, George
See Bickham, Jack M(iles)
Shaw, George Bernard 1856-1950 ... 128
Brief entry ... 104
See also Shaw, Bernard
See also AAYA 61
See also BRW 6
See also BRWC 1
See also BRWR 2
See also CDBLB 1914-1945
See also DA
See also DA3
See also DAB
See also DAC
See also DAM DRAM, MST
See also DC 23
See also DFS 1, 3, 6, 11, 19, 22
See also EWL 3
See also LAIT 3
See also LATS 1:1
See also MTCW 1, 2
See also MTFW 2005
See also RGEL 2
See also TCLC 3, 9, 21, 45
See also TEA
See also WLC
See also WLIT 4
Shaw, Graham 1944- ... 118
Shaw, Harold 1916(?)-1986
Obituary ... 118
Shaw, Harry (Lee, Jr.) 1905-1998 ... 81-84
Shaw, Harry Edmund 1946- ... 114
Shaw, Helen 1913-1985 ... CANR-20
Earlier sketch in CA 103
See also CP 1
Shaw, Henry I(var), Jr. 1926-2000 ... 33-36R
Obituary ... 188
Shaw, Henry Wheeler 1818-1885 ... DLB 11
See also RGAL 4
Shaw, Howard 1934- ... 106
Shaw, Irene
See Roberts, Irene
Shaw, Irwin 1913-1984 ... CANR-21
Obituary ... 112
Earlier sketch in CA 13-16R
See also AITN 1
See also BPFB 3
See also CDALB 1941-1968
See also CLC 7, 23, 34
See also CN 1, 2, 3
See also CPW
See also DAM DRAM, POP
See also DLB 6, 102
See also DLBY 1984
See also MAL 5
See also MTCW 1, 21
See also MTFW 2005
Shaw, J(oseph) Thomas 1919- ... 17-20R
Shaw, Janet 1937- ... CANR-127
Earlier sketch in CA 127
See also CLR 96
See also SATA 61, 146
Shaw, Janet Beeler
See Shaw, Janet
Shaw, John Bennett 1913-1994 ... 21-24R
Shaw, John Mackay 1897-1984 ... CANR-13
Earlier sketch in CA 29-32R
Shaw, Joseph M(inard) 1925- ... 140
Shaw, Joseph Thompson 1874-1952 ... 215
Shaw, Joseph Thompson 1874-1952 ... 215
See also DLB 137
Shaw, Lau
See Shu, Ch' ing-ch'un
Shaw, Lawrence H(ugh) 1940- ... 69-72
Shaw, Leroy R(obert) 1923- ... 13-16R
Shaw, Linda 1938- ... CANR-46
Earlier sketches in CA 106, CANR-23
Shaw, Lisa 1966- ... 227
Shaw, Luci N(orthcote) 1928- ... CANR-94
Earlier sketches in CA 101, CANR-17, 39
Shaw, Malcolm Edwin 1926- ... CANR-1
Earlier sketch in CA 1-4R
Shaw, Margret 1940- ... 136
See also SATA 68
Shaw, Marion ... 209
Shaw, Mark 1945- ... 147
Shaw, Martin 1947- ... 143
Shaw, Marvin E(vert) 1919- ... 21-24R
Shaw, Mary 1854-1929 ... DLB 228
Shaw, Maxine 1945- ... 57-60
Shaw, Murray 1908- ... 134
Shaw, Nancy 1946- ... 196
See also SATA 71, 162
Shaw, Nancy Stoller 1942- ... 57-60
Shaw, Patrick W. 1938- ... 143
Shaw, Peter 1936-1995 ... CANR-9
Obituary ... 149
Earlier sketch in CA 65-68
Shaw, Priscilla Washburn 1930- ... 13-16R
Shaw, Ralph R(obert) 1907-1972
Obituary ... 37-40R
Shaw, Randy 1956- ... 190
Shaw, Ray ... 33-36R
See also SATA 7
Shaw, Richard 1923- ... 37-40R
See also SATA 12
Shaw, Robert (H.) 1916- ... 167
Shaw, Robert (Archibald) 1927-1978 .. CANR-4
Obituary ... 81-84
Earlier sketch in CA 1-4R
See also AITN 1
See also CLC 5
See also CN 1, 2
See also DLB 13, 14
Shaw, Robert B. 1947- ... 137
See also DLB 120
Shaw, Robert Byers 1916- ... 37-40R
Shaw, Ron W. 1951- ... 145
Shaw, Ronald D(uncan) M(ackintosh)
1883- ... CAP-1
Earlier sketch in CA 13-14
Shaw, Ronald E. 1923- ... 17-20R
Shaw, Russell B(urnham) 1935- ... CANR-3
Earlier sketch in CA 1-4R
Shaw, Scott 1958- ... 170
Shaw, Simon ... 166
Shaw, Sophia 1969- ... 152
Shaw, Stanford Jay 1930- ... CANR-6
Earlier sketch in CA 5-8R
Shaw, Steven John 1918- ... 17-20R
Shaw, T. D. W.
See Shaw, Thelma
Shaw, T. E.
See Lawrence, T(homas) E(dward)
Shaw, Terrence 1934- ... 170
Shaw, Thelma ... 25-28R
Shaw, Thurstan 1914- ... 103
Shaw, Timothy Milton 1945- ... CANR-30
Earlier sketch in CA 112
Shaw, Vivian
See Seldes, Gilbert (Vivian)
Shaw, W. David 1937- ... 29-32R
Shaw, (Harold) Watkins 1911-1996 ... 1-4R
Shaw, Wayne E(ugene) 1932- ... 53-56
Shaw, William 1959- ... 143
Shaw, William Harlan 1922- ... CANR-15
Earlier sketch in CA 41-44R
Shawchuck, Norman 1935- ... 126
Shawcross, John T. 1924- ... 13-16R
Shawcross, William (Hartley Hume)
1946- ... CANR-97
Earlier sketch in CA 105
Shawhan, Ralph 1903(?)-1990
Obituary ... 130
Shawn, Allen 1948- ... 205
Shawn, Clyde B.
See Meares, Leonard Frank
Shawn, Edwin Meyers 1891-1972
Obituary ... 33-36R
Shawn, Frank S.
See Goulart, Ron(ald Joseph)
Shawn, Ted
See Shawn, Edwin Meyers
Shawn, Wallace 1943- ... 112
See also CAD
See also CD 5, 6
See also CLC 41
See also DLB 266
Shawn, William 1907-1992 ... CANR-86
Obituary ... 140
Earlier sketch in CA 108
See also DLB 137
Shawver, Lois 1939- ... 150
Shay, Art
See Shay, Arthur
Shay, Arthur 1922- ... CANR-100
Earlier sketches in CA 33-36R, CANR-46
See also SATA 4
Shay, Jonathan 1941- ... 225
Shay, Kathryn ... 226
Shay, Lacey
See Shebar, Sharon Sigmond
Shaykh, al- Hanan
See al-Shaykh, Hanan
See also CWW 2
See also EWL 3
Shayne, Gordon
See Winter, Bevis (Peter)
Shaynoux, Bucky
See Landau, Paul Stuart
Shayon, Robert Lewis ... 49-52
Shayon, Samuel 1904(?)-1984
Obituary ... 112
Shazar, Rachel
See Katznelson-Shazar, Rachel
Shazar, (Schneor) Zalman 1889-1974 ... 101
Obituary ... 53-56
Shcharansky, Anatoly
See Sharansky, Natan (Borisovich)
Shchedrin, N.
See Saltykov, Mikhail Evgrafovich
Shcherbakova, Galina Nikolaevna
1932- ... DLB 285
Shcherbina, Nikolai Fedorovich
1821-1869 ... DLB 277
Shea, Christina 1963- ... 195
Shea, Cornelius ... TCWW 1, 2
Shea, Donald F(rancis) 1925- ... 73-76
Shea, George 1940- ... CANR-49
Earlier sketch in CA 108
See also SATA 54
See also SATA-Brief 42
Shea, George E., Jr. 1902-1980
Obituary ... 97-100
Shea, James J. 1890(?)-1977
Obituary ... 69-72
Shea, John 1941- ... 73-76
Shea, John Gerald 1906-1980 ... 9-12R
Shea, John Gilmary 1824-1892 ... DLB 30
Shea, John S. 1933- ... 21-24R
Shea, Lisa 1953- ... 147
See also CLC 86
Shea, Mark P. 1958- ... 202
Shea, Michael (Sinclair MacAuslan) 1938- . 130
Shea, Michael 1946- ... CANR-85
Earlier sketch in CA 112
See also FANT
See also SUFW 2
Shea, Patrick 1908-1986 ... 130
Shea, Pegi Deitz 1960- ... CANR-116
Earlier sketch in CA 145
See also SATA 77, 137
Shea, Robert (Joseph) 1933-1994 ... 101
Obituary ... 144
Shea, Sandra ... 222
Shea, Shirley 1924- ... 121
Shea, Suzanne Strempek ... 211
Sheaffer, Louis 1912-1993 ... 192
Obituary ... 142
See also DLB 103
Sheaffer, Mike 1950- ... 170
Sheaffer, Robert M(errill) 1949- ... 106
Sheagren, Thomas G(eorge) 1949- ... 118
Sheahan, Henry Beston
See Beston, Henry
Sheahan, John (B.) 1923- ... CANR-91
Earlier sketch in CA 17-20R
Sheahan, Richard T(homas) 1942- ... CANR-15
Earlier sketch in CA 65-68
Shealy, C(lyde) Norman 1932- ... CANR-7
Earlier sketch in CA 57-60
Shean, Glenn (Daniel) 1939- ... 53-56
Shear, Jeff 1947- ... 147
Shear, Jonathan 1940- ... 198
Shear, Walter 1932- ... 232
Sheard, Kevin 1916- ... 41-44R
Sheard, Robert 1960- ... 229
Sheard, Sarah 1953- ... 141
Sheard, Virna 1865-1943 ... RHW
Shearer, Douglas 1899-1971 ... IDFW 3, 4
Shearer, Harry (Julius) 1943- ... 165
Shearer, Jill 1936- ... CD 5, 6
See also CWD
Shearer, John 1947- ... 125
See also CLR 34
See also SATA 43
See also SATA-Brief 27
Shearer, Ronald A(lexander) 1932- ... 77-80
Shearer, Ted 1919- ... SATA 43
Shearing, Joseph
See Campbell, (Gabrielle) Margaret (Vere)
See also DLB 70
Shearman, Hugh (Francis) 1915- ... 13-16R
Shearman, John (Kinder Gowran)
1931-2003 ... 13-16R
Obituary ... 219
Shears, Billie
See Watson, O(scar) Michael
Sheats, Mary Boney 1918- ... 13-16R
Sheats, Paul Douglas 1932- ... 101
Shebar, Sharon Sigmond 1945- ... CANR-41
Earlier sketches in CA 103, CANR-19
See also SATA 36
Shebbeare, John 1709-1788 ... DLB 39
Shebl, James M(ichael) 1942- ... CANR-23
Earlier sketches in CA 61-64, CANR-8
Shechner, Mark E. 1940- ... 124
Sheck, Laurie 1953- ... 213
Sheckley, Robert 1928- ... 223
Earlier sketches in CA 1-4R, CANR-2, 85
Autobiographical Essay in ... 223
See also DLB 8
See also SCFW 1, 2
See also SFW 4
Shecter, Ben 1935- ... 81-84
See also SATA 16
Shecter, Leonard 1926-1974
Obituary ... 45-48
Shedd, Charlie W. 1915- ... 17-20R
Shedd, Clarence Prouty 1887-1973
Obituary ... 45-48
Shedd, Margaret Cochran 1900-1986
Obituary ... 118
Shedd, Warner 1934- ... CANR-118
Earlier sketch in CA 151
See also SATA 87, 147
Shedd, William G. T. 1820-1894 ... DLB 64
Shedley, Ethan I.
See Beizer, Boris
Sheean, Diana 1915(?)-1987
Obituary ... 124
Sheean, (James) Vincent 1899-1975 ... 61-64
Sheed, F. J.
See Sheed, Francis Joseph
Sheed, Francis J.
See Sheed, Francis Joseph
Sheed, Francis Joseph 1897-1981 ... 129
Obituary ... 105
Sheed, Frank
See Sheed, Francis Joseph
Sheed, Frank J.
See Sheed, Francis Joseph

Cumulative Index 527 **Shepardson**

Sheed, Wilfrid (John Joseph) 1930- ... CANR-66
Earlier sketches in CA 65-68, CANR-30
See also CLC 2, 4, 10, 53
See also CN 1, 2, 3, 4, 5, 6, 7
See also DLB 6
See also MAL 5
See also MTCW 1, 2
See also MTFW 2005
Sheedy, Alexandra Elizabeth 1962- 85-88
See also SATA 19, 39
Sheedy, Ally 1962- 173
Sheehan, Arthur 1910(?)-1975
Obituary 61-64
Sheehan, Aurelie 1963- 147
Sheehan, Bernard W(illiam) 1934- 41-44R
Sheehan, Donald Henry 1917-1974 ... CANR-2
Earlier sketch in CA 1-4R
Sheehan, Ethna 1908-2000 61-64
See also SATA 9
Sheehan, George (Augustine)
1918-1993 .... CANR-13
Obituary 143
Earlier sketch in CA 73-76
Sheehan, Helen E(lizabeth) 1944- 146
Sheehan, James J(ohn) 1937- CANR-11
Earlier sketch in CA 17-20R
Sheehan, John F(rancis) X(avier) 1933- 122
Brief entry 118
Sheehan, Joseph Green 1918-1983
Obituary 111
Sheehan, Julie 1964- 239
Sheehan, Margaret A(nne) 1956- 111
Sheehan, Michael J. 1939- 203
Sheehan, Neil 1936- CANR-40
Earlier sketch in CA 29-32R
See also BEST 89:2
See also MTFW 2005
Sheehan, Patrick Augustine
See O Siochain, P(adraig) A(ugustine)
Sheehan, Patty 1945- 145
See also SATA 77
Sheehan, Paul V(incent) 1904-1978 ...... 33-36R
Sheehan, Sean 1951- CANR-135
Earlier sketch in CA 151
See also SATA 86, 154
Sheehan, Sister Helen 1904-1982 .... CAP-1
Earlier sketch in CA 17-18
Sheehan, Susan 1937- CANR-87
Earlier sketches in CA 21-24R, CANR-12, 40
Sheehan, Thomas 1941- 122
Sheehan, Valerie Harms
See Harms, Valerie
Sheehan, William 1954- 139
Sheehy, Eugene P(aul) 1922- 9-12R
Sheehy, Gail 1937- CANR-92
Earlier sketches in CA 49-52, CANR-1, 33, 55
See also CLC 171
See also CPW
See also MTCW 1
Sheehy, Helen 1948- CANR-86
Earlier sketch in CA 133
Sheehy, Jeanne 1939- 110
Sheehy, John F. 1925- 199
Sheehy, Maurice S(tephen) 1898-1972
Obituary 111
Sheekman, Arthur 1901-1978 81-84
Obituary 73-76
Sheen, Barbara 1949- 216
See also SATA 143
Sheen, Fulton J(ohn) 1895-1979 .... CANR-5
Obituary 89-92
Earlier sketch in CA 5-8R
See also MTCW 1
Sheeran, James Jennings 1932- 65-68
Sheerin, John Basil 1906-1992 .... CANR-4
Obituary 136
Earlier sketch in CA 1-4R
Sheerman, Barry 1940- 144
Sheers, Owen 1974- 230
Sheet, Lenny 1965- 185
Sheets, Bob
See Sheets, Robert C.
Sheets, Elva (Darah) 1898-1988 57-60
Obituary 196
Sheets, John R(ichard) 1922- 25-28R
Sheets, Kenneth Ray 1936- 136
Sheets, Millard (Owen) 1907-1989
Obituary 128
Sheets, Robert C. 1937- 212
Sheets, Robin Lauterbach 1943- 131
Sheets-Pyenson, Susan -1998 163
Sheetz, Ann Kindig 1934- 101
Shefelman, Janice Jordan 1930- CANR-96
Earlier sketches in CA 120, CANR-45
See also SATA 58, 129
Shefelman, Tom (Whitehead) 1927- .... SATA 58
Sheffer, H. R.
See Abels, Harriette S(heffer)
Sheffer, Isaiah 1935- 17-20R
Sheffield, Charles 1935-2002 .... CANR-103
Obituary 211
Earlier sketch in CA 162
See also AAYA 38
See also SATA 109
See also SFW 4
Sheffield, James Rockwell 1936-
Brief entry 106
Sheffield, Janet N. 1926- 65-68
See also SATA 26
Sheffield, Suzanne Le-May 1967- 228
Sheffy, Lester Fields 1887- CAP-1
Earlier sketch in CA 13-14
Sheftel, Victor O. 1936- 152
Sheftell, Fred D. 1941- 137
Shefter, Harry 1910- 9-12R
Shefter, Martin 1943- 136
Shefts, Joelle .... SATA-Brief 49
Shehadeh, Lamia Rustrum 1940- 227
Shehadeh, Raja 1951- CANR-120
Earlier sketch in CA 141
Shehadi, Fadlou 1926- 162
Shehan, Lawrence Joseph 1898-1984 117
Shehyn, Audrey E. 1967- 191
Sheikh, Nazneen
See Sadiq, Nazneen
Shein, Brian 1947- 110
Shein, Louis J(ulius) 1914- 25-28R
Sheinberg, Marcia 1943- 211
Sheindlin, Judith 1942(?)- 199
Sheiness, (Lee) Marsha 1940- CANR-15
Earlier sketch in CA 89-92
Sheinin, David (M. K.) 1960- 154
Sheinwold, Alfred 1912-1997 61-64
Obituary 157
Sheinwold, Patricia
See Fox-Sheinwold, Patricia
Shek, Ben-Zion 1927- 110
Shekerjian, Regina Tor .... SATA 16
Shelbourne, Cecily
See Goodwin, Suzanne
Shelby, Anne 1948- 151
See also SAAS 26
See also SATA 85
See also SATA-Essay 121
Shelby, Brit
See Grady, James (Thomas)
Shelby, Carroll Hall 1923- 17-20R
Shelby, Cole
See King, Albert
Shelby, Graham 1940- 102
Shelby, Philip 183
Shelby, Susan
See Kinnicutt, Susan Sibley
Shelden, Michael 1951- 141
Sheldon, Alan 1933- 114
Sheldon, Alice Hastings Bradley
1915(?)-1987 .... CANR-34
Obituary 122
Earlier sketch in CA 108
Interview in CA-108
See also Tiptree, James, Jr.
See also MTCW 1
Sheldon, Ann CANR-27
Earlier sketches in CAP-2, CA 19-20
See also SATA 1, 67
Sheldon, Ann
See Antle, Nancy
Sheldon, Aure 1917-1976 61-64
See also SATA 12
Sheldon, Charles Harvey 1929- 107
Sheldon, Charles S(tuart) II 1917-1981
Obituary 105
Sheldon, Deyan 53-56
Sheldon, Edward 1886-1946 .... DLB 7
See also RGAL 4
Sheldon, Edward Brewster 1886-1946 200
Sheldon, Eleanor Bernert 1920- 85-88
Sheldon, Esther K. 1906-1984 .... 37-40R
Sheldon, Garrett Ward 1954- 139
Sheldon, George E.
See Stahl, LeRoy
Sheldon, John
See Bloch, Robert (Albert)
Sheldon, Joseph K(enneth) 1943- 143
Sheldon, Lee
See Lee, Wayne C(yril)
Sheldon, Mary 1955- 239
Sheldon, Michael 1918- 17-20R
Sheldon, Muriel 1926- CANR-18
Earlier sketch in CA 101
See also SATA 45
See also SATA-Brief 39
Sheldon, Ned
See Sheldon, Edward Brewster
Sheldon, Peter 1922- 25-28R
Sheldon, Raccoona
See Sheldon, Alice Hastings Bradley
Sheldon, Richard (Robert) 1932- 33-36R
Sheldon, Roy .... AITN 1
Sheldon, Roy
See Tubb, E(dwin) C(harles)
Sheldon, Scott
See Wallmann, Jeffrey M(iner)
Sheldon, Sidney 1917- CANR-100
Earlier sketches in CA 29-32R, CANR-33
See also AAYA 65
See also AITN 1
See also BEST 89:1
See also BPFB 3
See also CPW
See also DA3
See also DAM NOV, POP
See also MTCW 1, 2
Sheldon, Suzanne Eaton 1928(?)-1985
Obituary 117
Sheldon, Walt
See Sheldon, Walter J(ames)
Sheldon, Walter J(ames) 1917-1996 . CANR-10
Earlier sketch in CA 25-28R
See also Queen, Ellery
See also AITN 1
Sheldon, William (Herbert) 1898-1977 . 25-28R
Obituary 116
Sheldon, William Denley 1915- 17-20R
Sheldrake, Rupert 1942- CANR-91
Earlier sketches in CA 127, CANR-55
Sheldrick, Daphne 1934- CANR-3
Earlier sketch in CA 49-52
Shelemay, Kay Kaufman 1948- 142
Sheler, Jeffery (L.) 1949(?)- 228
Shell, Ellen Ruppel 1952- CANR-142
Earlier sketch in CA 138
Shell, G. Richard 198
Shell, Ray 215
Shell, Robert C(arl)-H(einz) 1949- 152
Shell, Susan Meld 1948- 239
Shell, Virginia Law 1923- 21-24R
Shellabarger, Samuel 1888-1954 163
See also BPFB 3
See also RHW
Sheller, Aleksandr Konstantinovich
1838-1900 .... DLB 238
Shelley, Bruce L(eon) 1927- CANR-9
Earlier sketch in CA 21-24R
Shelley, Bryan Keith 1949- 212
Shelley, Dolores 1937- 122
Shelley, Florence D(ubroff) 1921- 65-68
Shelley, Frances
See Wees, Frances Shelley
Shelley, John L(ascola) 1907- .... TCWW 1, 2
Shelley, Lillian
See Koppel, Lillian and
Koppel, Shelley R(uth)
Shelley, Louise I(sabel) 1952- 108
Shelley, Mack Clayton II 1950- CANR-118
Earlier sketches in CA 126, CANR-56
Shelley, Mary Wollstonecraft (Godwin)
1797-1851 .... AAYA 20
See also BPFB 3
See also BRW 3
See also BRWC 2
See also BRWS 3
See also BYA 5
See also CDBLB 1789-1832
See also DA
See also DA3
See also DAB
See also DAC
See also DAM MST, NOV
See also DLB 110, 116, 159, 178
See also EXPN
See also FL 1:3
See also GL 3
See also HGG
See also LAIT 1
See also LMFS 1, 2
See also NFS 1
See also RGEL 2
See also SATA 29
See also SCFW 1, 2
See also SFW 4
See also TEA
See also WLC
See also WLIT 3
Shelley, Noreen 1920- 104
Shelley, Percy Bysshe 1792-1822 .... AAYA 61
See also BRW 4
See also BRWR 1
See also CDBLB 1789-1832
See also DA
See also DA3
See also DAB
See also DAC
See also DAM MST, POET
See also DLB 96, 110, 158
See also EXPP
See also LMFS 1
See also PAB
See also PC 14, 67
See also PFS 2
See also RGEL 2
See also TEA
See also WLC
See also WLIT 3
See also WP
Shelley, Rebecca 1887(?)-1984
Obituary 111
Shelly, Adrienne 1966- 207
Shelly, (Michael) Bruce 1929- 57-60
Shelly, Judith A(llen) 1944- CANR-38
Earlier sketch in CA 115
Shelly, Maynard W(olfe) 1928- CANR-7
Earlier sketch in CA 13-16R
Shelly, Peter
See Dresser, Davis
Shelmerdine, Cynthia Wright 1949- 117
Shelnutt, Eve (Brown) 1941- 132
See also CAAS 14
See also CSW
See also DLB 130
Shelp, Earl E(dward) 1947- 116
Shelton, Barrett C(linton) 1903(?)-1984
Obituary 112
Shelton, Beth Anne 1957- 143
Shelton, Hal T(erry) 1935- 150
Shelton, (Austin) Jess(e), Jr. 1926- CANR-25
Earlier sketch in CA 1-4R
Shelton, Kathleen J. 1946-1990
Obituary 131
Shelton, Lola
See Klaue, Lola Shelton
Shelton, Mark L(ogan) 1958- 135
Shelton, Napier 1931- 189
Shelton, Regina Maria 1927- 112
Shelton, Richard 1933- CANR-13
Earlier sketch in CA 33-36R
See also CP 2, 3, 4, 5, 6, 7
Shelton, Ron(ald W.) 1945- 166
Shelton, Suzanne
See Buckley, Suzanne Shelton
Shelton, William Roy 1919-1995 ..... CANR-11
Obituary 198
Earlier sketch in CA 5-8R
See also AITN 1
See also SATA 5
See also SATA-Obit 129
Shem, Samuel 1944- CANR-80
Earlier sketch in CA 144
Shemesh, Haim 1954- 142
Shemie, Bonnie (Jean Brenner)
1949- CANR-135
Earlier sketches in CA 133, CANR-70
See also SATA 96
Shemin, Margaretha (Hoeneveld)
1928- 13-16R
See also SATA 4
Shen, Congwen 1902-1988
Obituary 125
See also RGSF 2
Shen, Dajun 1955- 168
Shen, Fan (A.) 1955- 235
Shen, James C. H. 1909- 126
Shen, Peter 110
Shen, Tong 1968- 135
Shengold, Leonard 1925- CANR-88
Earlier sketch in CA 136
Shenk, David 1967(?)- CANR-114
Earlier sketch in CA 167
Shenk, David W(itmer) 1937- 106
Shenk, Lois (Landis) 1944- 114
Shenk, Marcia Ann 1953- 73-76
Shenk, Wilbert R. 1935- CANR-94
Earlier sketch in CA 21-24R
Shenkin, Elizabeth Shoemaker (?)-1975
Obituary 61-64
Shenkman, Richard (Bennett) 1954- 144
Shennan, Joseph Hugh 1933- 103
Shennan, Margaret 1933- 215
Shenon, Philip 1959- 136
Shenoy, B(ellikoth) R(aghunath)
1905-1978 77-80
Shen Rong 1935- .... CWW 2
Shenstone, Susan (Burgess) 1927- 212
Shenstone, William 1714-1763 .... DLB 95
See also RGEL 2
Shenton, Edward 1895-1977 .... SATA 45
Shenton, Edward H(eriot) 1932- CANR-17
Earlier sketch in CA 25-28R
Shenton, James P(atrick) 1925-2003 ... CANR-2
Obituary 218
Earlier sketch in CA 5-8R
Shepard, Aaron 1950- 142
See also SATA 75, 113
Shepard, Alan B., Jr. 1923-1998 158
Obituary 169
Shepard, Charles E. 1954- 145
Shepard, David W. 1922- 93-96
Shepard, Elaine (Elizabeth) 1923-1998 .. 21-24R
Shepard, Ernest Howard 1879-1976 . CANR-86
Obituary 65-68
Earlier sketches in CA 9-12R, CANR-23
See also CLR 27
See also DLB 160
See also MAICYA 1, 2
See also SATA 3, 33, 100
See also SATA-Obit 24
Shepard, Francis P(arker) 1897-1985 .... 13-16R
Obituary 169
Shepard, Gary 1939- 97-100
Shepard, Jean H(eck) 1930- 49-52
Shepard, Jim 1956- CANR-104
Earlier sketches in CA 137, CANR-59
See also CLC 36
See also SATA 90
Shepard, Jon M(ax) 1939- CANR-7
Earlier sketch in CA 57-60
Shepard, Leslie (Alan) 1917-2004 ...... CANR-8
Obituary 230
Earlier sketch in CA 17-20R
Shepard, Leslie Albert 1929- 29-32R
Shepard, Lucius 1947- CANR-124
Brief entry 128
Earlier sketches in CA 141, CANR-81
See also CLC 34
See also HGG
See also SCFW 2
See also SFW 4
See also SUFW 2
Shepard, Martin 1934- CANR-96
Earlier sketch in CA 33-36R
Shepard, Mary
See Knox, (Mary) Eleanor Jessie
Shepard, Neil 1951- CANR-102
Earlier sketch in CA 140
Shepard, Odell 1884-1967 .... CANR-3
Obituary 25-28R
Earlier sketch in CA 5-8R
Shepard, Paul (Howe) 1925-1996 .... CANR-10
Obituary 152
Earlier sketch in CA 21-24R
Shepard, Richard F. 1922-1998 115
Obituary 167
Shepard, Richmond 1929- 29-32R
Shepard, Sam 1943- CANR-140
Earlier sketches in CA 69-72, CANR-22, 120
See also CABS 3
See also AAYA 1, 58
See also AMWS 3
See also CAD
See also CD 5, 6
See also CLC 4, 6, 17, 34, 41, 44, 169
See also DA3
See also DAM DRAM
See also DC 5
See also DFS 3, 6, 7, 14
See also DLB 7, 212
See also EWL 3
See also IDFW 3, 4
See also MAL 5
See also MTCW 1, 2
See also MTFW 2005
See also RGAL 4
Shepard, Thomas I 1604(?)-1649 .... DLB 24
Shepard, Thomas II 1635-1677 .... DLB 24
Shepard, Thomas Rockwell, Jr. 1918- 105
Shepardson, Mary (Thygeson) 1906- 29-32R

Shephard, Esther 1891-1975 .... CAP-2
Obituary 57-60
Earlier sketch in CA 25-28
See also SATA 5
See also SATA-Obit 26
Shephard, John (Brownlow) 1900- CAP-1
Earlier sketch in CA 13-14
Shephard, Roy J(esse) 1929- CANR-11
Earlier sketch in CA 29-32R
Shepherd, Cybill (Lynne) 1950- 173
Shepherd, (Richard) David 1931- 65-68
Shepherd, David Gwynne 1924- 5-8R
Shepherd, Donald (Lee) 1932- CANR-86
Earlier sketch in CA 61-64
Shepherd, Donna Walsh
See Walsh Shepherd, Donna
Shepherd, Elizabeth 33-36R
See also SATA 4
Shepherd, Geoffrey (Seddon)
1898-1984 .... CANR-20
Earlier sketch in CA 1-4R
Shepherd, George W., Jr. 1926- CANR-6
Earlier sketch in CA 1-4R
Shepherd, Gordon
See Brook-Shepherd, (Frederick) Gordon
Shepherd, J(ohn) Barrie 1935- CANR-29
Earlier sketch in CA 111
Shepherd, Jack 1937- CANR-43
Earlier sketch in CA 57-60
Shepherd, James L(eftwich) III 1921- 21-24R
Shepherd, Jean (Parker) 1929(?)-1999 77-80
Obituary 187
See also AITN 2
Shepherd, Joan
See Buchanan, Betty (Joan)
Shepherd, John
See Ballard, (Willis) Todhunter
Shepherd, John Scott 1964- 239
Shepherd, L. P. 53-56
Shepherd, Leon H. 1957- 212
Shepherd, Loraine MacKenzie 1958- 230
Shepherd, Luke .... DLB 136
Shepherd, Massey H., Jr.
See Shepherd, Massey Hamilton, Jr.
Shepherd, Massey Hamilton
See Shepherd, Massey Hamilton, Jr.
Shepherd, Massey Hamilton, Jr.
1913-1990 122
Shepherd, Michael
See Ludlum, Robert
Shepherd, Nan 1893-1981 105
Shepherd, Naomi 210
Shepherd, Neal
See Morland, Nigel
Shepherd, Reginald 1963- 217
Shepherd, Robert 1949- 136
Shepherd, Robert Henry Wishart
1888-1971 .... CAP-1
Earlier sketch in CA 13-14
Shepherd, Simon 1951- 120
Shepherd, Thomas W. 1946- 212
Shepherd, Walter Bradley 1904- 105
Shepherd, William C(hauncey)
1942- CANR-18
Earlier sketch in CA 25-28R
Shepley, James R(obinson) 1917-1988
Obituary 127
Brief entry 112
Sheppard, Alice 1945- 152
Sheppard, Anne
See Sheppard, Anne D(eborah) R(aphael)
Sheppard, Anne D(eborah) R(aphael)
1951- 128
Sheppard, Barry 1937- 61-64
Sheppard, Cynthia A(nne) 1955- 108
Sheppard, David Stuart 1929-2005 103
Obituary 237
Sheppard, Don(ald D.) 1930- 138
Sheppard, Eugenia (Benbow)
1900(?)-1984 103
Obituary 114
Sheppard, Francis Henry Wollaston
1921- 21-24R
Sheppard, Harold L(loyd) 1922-1997 . CANR-1
Obituary 159
Earlier sketch in CA 45-48
Sheppard, Joseph 1930- CANR-23
Earlier sketches in CA 61-64, CANR-8
Sheppard, Lancelot C(apel) 1906- CANR-5
Earlier sketch in CA 5-8R
Sheppard, Lila (Brooks) 1906- CAP-1
Earlier sketch in CA 13-14
Sheppard, Mary 29-32R
Sheppard, Mary C. 217
Sheppard, Rob 235
Sheppard, Roger 1939- 77-80
Sheppard, Sally 1917- 69-72
Sheppard, Stephen 1945- 105
Sheppard, Thomas F(rederick) 1935- 73-76
Sheppard, Walter Lee, Jr. 1911-2000 69-72
Sheppard-Jones, Elisabeth 1920- 13-16R
Shepperson, Wilbur Stanley
1919-1991 .... CANR-6
Earlier sketch in CA 1-4R
Sheps, Cecil G(eorge) 1913-2004 .... 9-12R
Obituary 224
Sheps, Mindel (Cherniack) 1913-1973
Obituary 37-40R
Sher, Anthony 1951- 185
Sher, Barbara 1935- 132
Sher, Eva CAP-2
Earlier sketch in CA 23-24
Sher, Gerson S(amuel) 1947- 81-84
Sher, Gila 142
Sher, Ira G. 1970- 227
Sher, Jack 1913-1988
Obituary 126
Sher, Zelig 1888-1971
Obituary 104
Shera, Jesse Hauk 1903-1982 .... CANR-2
Obituary 106
Earlier sketch in CA 5-8R
Sherar, Mariam G(hose) 1924- 45-48
Sherashevski, Boris
See Brown, John J.
Sheraton, Mimi 1926- CANR-104
Earlier sketch in CA 126
Sheraton, Neil
See Smith, Norman Edward Mace
Sheratsky, Rodney E(arl) 1933- 25-28R
Sherbaniuk, Richard 234
Sherblom, Liz 1942- 154
Sherbo, Arthur 1918- 185
Brief entry 113
Sherburne, Donald W(ynne) 1929- 1-4R
Sherburne, Edward 1616-1702 .... DLB 131
Sherburne, James (Robert) 1925- 33-36R
Sherburne, Zoa (Lillian Morin)
1912-1995 .... CANR-37
Obituary 176
Earlier sketches in CA 1-4R, CANR-3
See also AAYA 13
See also CLC 30
See also MAICYA 1, 2
See also SAAS 18
See also SATA 3
See also YAW
Sherby, Linda B(arbara) 1946- 108
Shercliff, Jose 1902(?)-1985
Obituary 115
Sherdeman, Ted 1910(?)-1987
Obituary 123
Shere, Dennis 1940- 77-80
Sherek, Henry 1900-1967 .... CAP-1
Earlier sketch in CA 13-16
Sherer, Mary Louise 1901-1992 101
Sherer, Michael W. 1952- CANR-105
Earlier sketch in CA 127
Sherer, Robert G(lenn, Jr.) 1940- 69-72
Sheret, Rene (Dundee) 1933- 29-32R
Sherfey, Mary Jane 1933-1983
Obituary 109
Shergold, N(orman) D(avid) 1925- 25-28R
Sheridan, Adora
See Hong, Jane Fay and
Pavlik, Evelyn Marie
Sheridan, Alan 1934- 190
Sheridan, Anne-Marie 1948- 85-88
Sheridan, Chris 212
Sheridan, Dorothy Elizabeth 1948- 116
Sheridan, Eugene Robert 1945- CANR-23
Earlier sketch in CA 107
Sheridan, Frances 1724-1766 .... DLB 39, 84
Sheridan, James E(dward) 1922- 21-24R
Sheridan, James F(rancis), Jr. 1927- 29-32R
Sheridan, Jane
See Winslow, Pauline Glen
Sheridan, Jim 1949- 238
Sheridan, John V. 1915- CANR-3
Earlier sketch in CA 9-12R
Sheridan, L(ionel) A(stor) 1927- CANR-9
Earlier sketch in CA 21-24R
Sheridan, Lane
See Winslow, Pauline Glen
Sheridan, Lee
See Lee, Elsie
Sheridan, Marion Campbell 17-20R
Sheridan, Martin 1914-2003 104
Obituary 222
Sheridan, Naomi 236
Sheridan, Noel 1936- 220
Sheridan, Peter 1952- 187
Sheridan, Polly
See Oates, Jeannette
Sheridan, Richard B. 1918- 45-48
Sheridan, Richard Brinsley 1751-1816 .. BRW 3
See also CDBLB 1660-1789
See also DA
See also DAB
See also DAC
See also DAM DRAM, MST
See also DC 1
See also DFS 15
See also DLB 89
See also WLC
See also WLIT 3
Sheridan, Thomas 1938- 61-64
Sheridan, Thomas L. 1926- 37-40R
Sherif, Carolyn W(ood) 1922- 17-20R
Sherif, Muzafer 1906-1988 .... CAP-1
Obituary 126
Earlier sketch in CA 13-14
Sheriff, John K(eith) 1944- CANR-47
Earlier sketch in CA 120
Sherlock, John 1932- CANR-3
Earlier sketch in CA 9-12R
Sherlock, Patti .... SATA 71
Sherlock, Philip Manderson
1902-2000 .... CANR-6
Earlier sketch in CA 5-8R
See also CP 1
Sherlock, Richard 1947- 126
Sherlock, Dame Sheila (Patricia Violet)
1918-2001 206
Sherman, A(lan) Robert 1942- 57-60
Sherman, Allan 1924-1973 101
Obituary 45-48
Sherman, Arnold 1932- CANR-14
Earlier sketch in CA 33-36R
Sherman, Arthur W(esley), Jr. 1917- . CANR-21
Earlier sketch in CA 1-4R
Sherman, Barbara H(ayes) 1942- 25-28R
Sherman, Bernard 1929- 29-32R
Sherman, Cecil E(dwin) 1927- 127
Brief entry 110
Sherman, Charles Bezalel 1896-1971 .... 1-4R
Obituary 103
Sherman, Charlotte A.
See Sherman, Jory (Tecumseh)
Sherman, Charlotte Watson 1958- 143
See also BW 2
Sherman, Cindy 1954- .... AAYA 41
Sherman, Claire Richter 1930- CANR-143
Earlier sketch in CA 106
Sherman, Constance D(enise)
1909-1987 45-48
Sherman, D(enis) R(onald) 1934- CANR-8
Earlier sketch in CA 13-16R
See also SATA 48
See also SATA-Brief 29
Sherman, Dan(iel Michael) 1950- 77-80
Sherman, (Cor)delia (Caroline) 1951- 205
Sherman, Delia 1951- .... FANT
Sherman, Diane (Finn) 1928- CANR-5
Earlier sketch in CA 9-12R
See also SATA 12
Sherman, Edmund 1927- 139
Sherman, Eileen Bluestone 1951- CANR-45
Earlier sketch in CA 119
Sherman, Eleanor Rae 1929- 13-16R
Sherman, Elizabeth
See Friskey, Margaret (Richards)
Sherman, Eric 1947- 69-72
Sherman, Francis 1871-1926 .... DLB 92
Sherman, Francis (Joseph) 1871-1926 184
Sherman, Franklin (Eugene) 1928- 57-60
Sherman, G(eorge) W(itters) 1903-1988 117
Sherman, Harold (Morrow) 1898-1987 ... 77-80
See also SATA 37
See also SATA-Obit 137
Sherman, (Marcus) Harvey 1917-1985 .. 21-24R
Obituary 114
Sherman, Howard J. 1931- CANR-10
Earlier sketch in CA 13-16R
Sherman, Ingrid 1919- 103
Sherman, James E(dward) 1939- 25-28R
Sherman, Janann 1944- 190
Sherman, Jane 1908- CANR-12
Earlier sketch in CA 73-76
Sherman, Janette D. 1930- 203
Sherman, Jason 1962- CANR-143
Earlier sketch in CA 165
Sherman, Jerry 1924- 97-100
Sherman, Joan
See Dern, Erolie Pearl Gaddis
Sherman, Joe 1945- 137
Sherman, John W. 1960- 175
Sherman, Jonathan Marc 1968- 230
See also CLC 55
Sherman, Jory (Tecumseh) 1932- CANR-98
Earlier sketches in CA 69-72, CANR-11, 28, 53
See also Mitchum, Hank
Sherman, Josepha 127
See also SATA 75, 163
Sherman, Julia A(nn) 1934- 37-40R
Sherman, Kenneth 1950- CANR-40
Earlier sketch in CA 117
Sherman, L. L.
See Armentrout, Fred S(herman)
Sherman, Lawrence W(illiam) 1949- .. CANR-7
Earlier sketch in CA 57-60
Sherman, Lynn
See Obrecht, Jas
Sherman, Martin 1941(?)- CANR-86
Brief entry 116
Earlier sketch in CA 123
See also CAD
See also CD 5, 6
See also CLC 19
See also DFS 20
See also DLB 228
See also GLL 1
See also IDTP
Sherman, Michael
See Lowndes, Robert A(ugustine) W(ard)
Sherman, Michele 1945- CANR-36
Earlier sketch in CA 114
Sherman, Murray H(erbert) 1922- 17-20R
Sherman, Nancy
See Rosenberg, Nancy (Sherman)
Sherman, Patrick 1928- 103
Sherman, Peter Michael
See Lowndes, Robert A(ugustine) W(ard)
Sherman, Philip M(artin) 1930- 29-32R
Sherman, Ray W(esley) 1884-1971
Obituary 33-36R
Sherman, Richard B. 1929- 29-32R
Sherman, Richard M(orton) 1928-
Brief entry 107
Sherman, Robert 1928- 142
Sherman, Robert B(ernard) 1925-
Brief entry 108
Sherman, Roger 1930- 37-40R
Sherman, Spencer E. 1936- 112
Sherman, Steve (Barry) 1938- 37-40R
Sherman, Stuart 1955- .... CAD
See also CD 5, 6
Sherman, Susan Jean 1939- CANR-95
Earlier sketch in CA 1-4R
Sherman, T. P. 1917-1976 .... CAP-2
Earlier sketch in CA 29-32
Sherman, Theodore A(llison)
1901-1981 .... CANR-86
Obituary 134
Earlier sketch in CA 17-20R
Sherman, Vincent 1906- 159
Sherman, William David 1940- CANR-21
Earlier sketch in CA 105
Sherman, William H. 1966- CANR-107
Earlier sketch in CA 150
Sherman, William Lewis 1927- 105
Shermer, Michael 1954- 170
Shero, Fred (Alexander) 1925- 105
Sherover, Charles M. 25-28R
Sherr, Lynn B(eth) 1942- 165
Brief entry 109
Sherr, Paul C(linton) 1920- 77-80
Sherraden, Michael (Wayne) 1948- 137
Sherrard, Philip (Owen Arnould)
1922-1995 .... CANR-7
Obituary 148
Earlier sketch in CA 13-16R
Sherrard, Valerie (Anne) 1957- 212
See also SATA 141
Sherred, T(homas) L. 1915-1985 ...... CANR-86
Earlier sketch in CA 153
See also SFW 4
Sherrer, Quin(ton M.) 1933- CANR-118
Earlier sketch in CA 163
Sherriff, R(obert) C(edric) 1896-1975 85-88
Obituary 61-64
See also DLB 10, 191, 233
See also IDFW 3, 4
See also RGEL 2
Sherriffs, Ronald E(verett) 1934-
Brief entry 112
Sherrill, Dorothy 1901-1990 69-72
Sherrill, Elizabeth 1928- 110
Sherrill, Henry Knox 1890-1980
Obituary 97-100
Sherrill, John L. 1923- 110
Sherrill, Kenneth S. 1942- 145
Sherrill, Martha 229
Sherrill, Robert G(lenn) 1925- CANR-15
Earlier sketch in CA 21-24R
Sherrill, Suzanne
See Woods, Sherryl
Sherrin, Edward George 1931- CANR-15
Earlier sketch in CA 21-24R
Sherrin, Ned
See Sherrin, Edward George
Sherrington, Richard (Wallace) 1940-1977 . 108
Sherrod, Blackie 1919- 225
See also AITN 2
See also DLB 241
Sherrod, Drury 1943- 109
Sherrod, Jane
See Singer, Jane Sherrod
Sherrod, Robert (Lee) 1909-1994 77-80
Sherry, Clifford J. 1943- 150
See also SATA 84
Sherry, James (Terence) 1946- CANR-41
Earlier sketch in CA 112
Sherry, John (Olden) 1923- 119
Sherry, John E(rnest) H(orwath)
1932- CANR-37
Earlier sketches in CA 89-92, CANR-16
Sherry, Michael S(tephen) 1945- CANR-81
Earlier sketch in CA 73-76
Sherry, (Michael) Norman 1935- CANR-34
Earlier sketch in CA 49-52, 170
See also BEST 89:4
See also DLB 155
Sherry, Patrick 1938- 138
Sherry, Pearl Andelson 1899-1996 109
Sherry, Richard 1506-1551(?) .... DLB 236
Sherry, Suzanna 1954- CANR-141
Earlier sketch in CA 167
Sherry, (Dulcie) Sylvia 1932- CANR-85
Earlier sketches in CA 49-52, CANR-34
See also CWRI 5
See also SATA 8, 122
Sherry, Vincent B(ernard), Jr. 1948- .. CANR-39
Earlier sketch in CA 116
Shershow, Scott Cutler 1953- 123
Shertzer, Bruce E(ldon) 1928- CANR-3
Earlier sketch in CA 9-12R
Sherven, Judith 1943- 219
Sherwan, Earl 1917- 5-8R
See also SATA 3
Sherwin, Byron L(ee) 1946- CANR-49
Earlier sketch in CA 123
Sherwin, J. Stephen 1923- 199
Sherwin, Judith Johnson CANR-85
See also Johnson, Judith (Emlyn)
See also CP 2
See also CWP
Sherwin, Martin J(ay) 1937-
Brief entry 110
Sherwin, Oscar 1902-1976 .... 1-4R
Obituary 65-68
Sherwin, Richard E(lliott) 1933- 69-72
Sherwin, Richard K(enneth) 197
Sherwin, Sidney 1920- 65-68
Sherwin, Sterling
See Hagen, John Milton
Sherwin-White, A(drian) N(icholas)
1911-1993 119
Obituary 143
Sherwonit, Bill 1950- 237
Sherwood, Ben 1964- 200
Sherwood, Debbie
See Sherwood, Deborah
Sherwood, Deborah 25-28R
Sherwood, Dennis H. 1949- 236
Sherwood, Dolly 138
Sherwood, Frances 1940- 220
Earlier sketch in CA 146
Autobiographical Essay in 220
See also CLC 81
Sherwood, Frank Persons 1920- CANR-9
Earlier sketch in CA 5-8R
Sherwood, Hugh C. 1928- 29-32R

Cumulative Index 529 Shivpuri

Sherwood, John (Herman Mulso)
1913- CANR-61
Earlier sketches in CA 5-8R, CANR-6, 21
See also CMW 4
Sherwood, John C(ollingwood) 1918- ... 13-16R
Sherwood, John J(oseph) 1933- 29-32R
Sherwood, Jonathan
See London, Jonathan (Paul)
Sherwood, Lyn 1937- 212
Sherwood, Marika 1937- 219
Sherwood, Martin (Anthony) 1942- .. CANR-19
Earlier sketch in CA 102
Sherwood, Mary Martha 1775-1851 ... DLB 163
Sherwood, Michael 1938-1976 .... CAP-2
Earlier sketch in CA 29-32
Sherwood, Morgan B(ronson)
1929-(?) CANR-6
Earlier sketch in CA 13-16R
Sherwood, Nelson
See Bulmer, (Henry) Kenneth
Sherwood, Robert D(an) 1949- 118
Sherwood, Robert E(mmet)
1896-1955 .... CANR-86
Brief entry 104
Earlier sketch in CA 153
See also DAM DRAM
See also DFS 11, 15, 17
See also DLB 7, 26, 249
See also IDFW 3, 4
See also MAL 5
See also RGAL 4
See also TCLC 3
Sherwood, Shirley 1933- 230
Sherwood, Tom 1946- 147
Sherwood, Valerie
See Hines, Jeanne
Sherwood, William Robert 1929- 21-24R
Shesgreen, Sean N(icholas) 1939- 45-48
Shestack, Alan 1938- 33-36R
Shestack, Jerome J(oseph) 1925- 118
Shestack, Melvin (Bernard) 1931- 120
Shestov, Lev 1866-1938 .... TCLC 56
Sheth, Jagdish N(anchand) 1938- CANR-97
Earlier sketches in CA 61-64, CANR-11
Shetter, William Z(eiders, Jr.) 1927- 81-84
Shetterly, Will(iam Howard) 1955- ... CANR-85
Earlier sketch in CA 119
See also FANT
See also SATA 78
See also SATA-Essay 106
Shettles, Landrum B(rewer)
1909-2003 .... CANR-13
Obituary 214
Earlier sketch in CA 77-80
Shetty, C(handrashekar) M(ajur)
1927- CANR-10
Earlier sketch in CA 13-16R
Shetty, Manohar 1953- CANR-84
Earlier sketch in CA 154
See also CP 7
Shetty, Sharat 1940- 73-76
Shev, Edward E(lmer) 1919- 93-96
Shevchenko, A. N.
See Shevchenko, Arkady N(ikolaevich)
Shevchenko, Arkady N(ikolaevich)
1930-1998 129
Obituary 165
Shevchuk, Tetiana
See Bishop, Tania Kroitor
Shevchuk, Valery 1939- .... EWL 3
Shevelove, Burt 1915-1982
Obituary 106
Shevin, David (Avram) 1951- 77-80
Shevory, Thomas C. 1955- 212
Shevrin, Aliza 1931- 129
Shevtsova, Lilia (Fedorovna) 230
Shevyrev, Stepan Petrovich
1806-1864 .... DLB 205
Shew, E(dward) Spencer 1908-1977 ... CANR-3
Obituary 69-72
Earlier sketch in CA 1-4R
Shewbridge, Edythe A(nne) 1943- 41-44R
Shewell-Cooper, W(ilfred) E(dward)
1900-1982 .... CANR-7
Earlier sketch in CA 9-12R
Shewmaker, Kenneth E. 1936- 33-36R
Shewring, Walter Hayward (Francis)
1906(?)-1990
Obituary 132
Shi, David Emory 1951- CANR-28
Earlier sketch in CA 106
Shi, Yanfei 1963- 230
Shiach, Allan G. 1941- CANR-84
Earlier sketch in CA 136
Shiarella, Robert 1936- 57-60
Shibles, Warren 1933- CANR-12
Earlier sketch in CA 29-32R
Shiboleth, Myrna 1947- 217
Shibutani, Tamotsu 1920- 17-20R
Shideler, John C(lement) 1949- 118
Shideler, Mary McDermott 1917- 25-28R
Shidle, Norman G(lass) 1895-1978 .... 17-20R
Shiefman, Vicky 1942- 57-60
See also SATA 22
Shieh, Francis S(hih-hoa) 1926- 37-40R
Shiel, M(atthew) P(hipps) 1865-1947 160
Brief entry 106
See also Holmes, Gordon
See also DLB 153
See also HGG
See also MTCW 2
See also MTFW 2005
See also SCFW 1, 2
See also SFW 4
See also SUFW
See also TCLC 8
Shield, Benjamin 183
Shield, Renee Rose 1948- 115
Shields, Allan (Edwin) 1919- 65-68
Shields, Brenda Desmond (Armstrong)
1914- 5-8R
See also SATA 37
Shields, Carol (Ann) 1935-2003 ..... CANR-133
Obituary 218
Earlier sketches in CA 81-84, CANR-51, 74, 98
See also AMWS 7
See also CCA 1
See also CLC 91, 113, 193
See also CN 6, 7
See also CPW
See also DA3
See also DAC
See also MTCW 2
See also MTFW 2005
Shields, Charles 1944- .... SATA 10
Shields, Currin Vance 1918- 1-4R
Shields, David (Jonathan) 1956- CANR-112
Earlier sketches in CA 124, CANR-48, 99
See also CLC 97
Shields, Donald J(ames) 1937- 53-56
Shields, Gerald R. 1925- 110
Shields, Jody 1952- 203
Shields, John M(ackie) 1954- CANR-99
Earlier sketch in CA 147
Shields, Joyce Farley 1930-
Brief entry 109
Shields, Laurie 1922(?)-1989
Obituary 128
Shields, Nancy E. 1928- 146
Shiell, Timothy C. 1959- 183
Shiels, Barbara
See Adams, Barbara Johnston
Shiels, Frederick L(ambert) 1949- 118
Shiels, George 1886-1949
Brief entry 111
See also DLB 10
Shiels, W(illiam) Eugene 1897-1976 ..... CAP-1
Earlier sketch in CA 9-10
Shiers, George 1908-1983 73-76
Shiff, Nathan A. 1914- 25-28R
Shiff, Richard 225
Shiffert, Edith (Marcombe) 1916- CANR-6
Earlier sketch in CA 13-16R
Shifflett, Crandall A(vis) 1938- 135
Shiffman, Lena 1957- .... SATA 101
Shiffrin, Nancy 1944- 81-84
Shiflet, Kenneth E(lwood) 1918-1978 . CANR-2
Obituary 81-84
Earlier sketch in CA 1-4R
Shiflett, Lee
See Shiflett, Orvin Lee
Shiflett, Orvin Lee 1947- 115
Shiga, Naoya 1883-1971 101
Obituary 33-36R
See also Shiga Naoya
See also CLC 33
See also MJW
See also RGWL 3
See also SSC 23
Shiga Naoya
See Shiga, Naoya
See also DLB 180
See also EWL 3
See also RGWL 3
Shigekuni, Julie CANR-134
Earlier sketch in CA 171
Shigley, Forrest Dwight 1930- 1-4R
Shih, Chih-yu 1958- 143
Shih, Chung-wen 81-84
Shih, Vincent Y(u) C(hung) 1903-2000 ... 77-80
Shih Hsio-Yen 1933- 119
Shiina, Makoto 1944- 150
See also SATA 83
Shiina Rinzo 1911-1973 .... DLB 182
Shikes, Ralph E. 1912-1992 .... CANR-12
Obituary 137
Earlier sketch in CA 29-32R
Shikishi Naishinno 1153(?)-1201 .... DLB 203
Shillaber, Benjamin Penhallow
1814-1890 .... DLB 1, 11, 235
Shiller, Jack G(erald) 1928- 73-76
Shiller, Robert J. 1946- CANR-143
Earlier sketch in CA 136
Shilling, Arthur 1941-1986 215
Shilling, Dana 1953- CANR-29
Earlier sketch in CA 109
Shilling, N(ed) 1924- 29-32R
Shillinglaw, Gordon 1925- CANR-7
Earlier sketch in CA 17-20R
Shillingsburg, Miriam J.
See Shillingsburg, Miriam (Carolyn) Jones
Shillingsburg, Miriam (Carolyn) Jones
1943- 130
Shillingsburg, Peter L(eRoy) 1943- 139
Shillony, Ben-Ami 1937- 73-76
Shiloah, Amnon 1928- 158
Shiloh, Ailon 1924- 33-36R
Shiloh, Ilana 1949- 238
Shils, Edward B. 1915- CANR-6
Earlier sketch in CA 5-8R
Shilton, Lance(lot) R(upert) 1921- 5-8R
Shilts, Randy 1951-1994 .... CANR-45
Obituary 144
Brief entry 115
Earlier sketch in CA 127
Interview in CA-127
See also AAYA 19
See also CLC 85
See also DA3
See also GLL 1
See also MTCW 2
See also MTFW 2005
Shim, Jae K. 1943- 142
Shimada, Masahiko 1961- 143
Shimao, Toshio 1917-1986
See Shimao Toshio
Shimao Toshio
See Shimao, Toshio
See also DLB 182
Shimazaki, Haruki 1872-1943 .... CANR-84
Brief entry 105
Earlier sketch in CA 134
See also Shimazaki Toson and Toson
See also RGWL 3
Shimazaki Toson
See Shimazaki, Haruki
See also DLB 180
See also EWL 3
See also TCLC 5
Shimberg, Benjamin 1918-2003 45-48
Obituary 221
Shimberg, Elaine Fantle 1937- CANR-31
Earlier sketch in CA 112
Shimer, Dorothy Blair 1911-1990 45-48
Shimin, Symeon 1902-1984 81-84
See also MAICYA 1, 2
See also SATA 13
Shimkin, Michael B(oris) 1912-1989
Obituary 127
Shimko, Bonnie 1941- 217
Shi Mo
See Zhenkai, Zhao
Shimoda, Todd 1955- 213
Shimomura, Tsutomu 1965(?)- 155
Shimoni, Yaacov 1915- 141
Shimoniak, Wasyl 1923-
Brief entry 108
Shimose, Pedro 1940- .... DLB 283
Shimota, Helen
See Gross, Helen Shimota
Shimpock, Kathy E(lizabeth) 1952- 201
Shinagel, Michael 1934- 25-28R
Shindell, Sidney 1923- 13-16R
Shinder, Jason (Scott) 1955- CANR-106
Earlier sketch in CA 133
Shindler, Colin 1946- 227
Shine, Andrea 1955- .... SATA 104
Shine, Deborah 1932- CANR-44
Earlier sketch in CA 110
See also SATA 71
Shine, Frances L(ouise) 1927- 25-28R
Shine, Richard 1950- 139
Shine, Ted 1931- CANR-24
Earlier sketches in CA 77-80, CANR-13
See also BW 1
See also DLB 38
Shineberg, Dorothy (Lois) 1927- 210
Shiner, David 1951- 201
Shiner, Larry (Ernest) 1934- 21-24R
Shiner, Lewis 1950- 174
Autobiographical Essay in 174
See also CAAS 30
Shiner, Roger A(lfred) 1940-
Brief entry 109
Shingleton, John D. CANR-37
Earlier sketch in CA 115
Shingleton, Royce (Gordon Sr.)
1935- CANR-107
Earlier sketches in CA 29-32R, CANR-12
Shinichi, Kano
See Jackson, G. Mark
Shinkei 1406-1475 .... DLB 203
Shinkle, James D. 1897(?)-1973
Obituary 104
Shinkle, Tex
See Shinkle, James D.
Shinkman, Elizabeth Benn 1907-1999 185
Shinn, Everett 1876-1953 .... SATA 21
Shinn, Larry Dwight 1942- 107
Shinn, Roger L(incoln) 1917- CANR-40
Earlier sketches in CA 1-4R, CANR-18
Shinn, Sharon 1957- CANR-98
Earlier sketch in CA 155
See also SATA 110
Shinn, Thelma J.
See Richard, Thelma (J.) Shinn
Shinnie, Peter Lewis 1915- 103
Shinoda, Minoru 1915- 5-8R
Shinohara, Kazuo 1925- 206
Shinoyama, Kishin 1930- 205
Shinwell, Emanuel 1884-1986
Obituary 119
Ship, Reuben 1915-1975 148
See also Davis, Reuben
See also CCA 1
See also DLB 88
Shipler, David K(arr) 1942- CANR-111
Earlier sketches in CA 103, CANR-21
Shiplett, June Lund 1930- CANR-36
Earlier sketches in CA 81-84, CANR-16
Shipley, David
See Holden, David (Shipley)
Shipley, David O. 1925- 37-40R
Shipley, Joseph T(wadell) 1893-1988 . CANR-9
Obituary 125
Earlier sketch in CA 13-16R
Shipley, Nan (Sommerville) 9-12R
Shipley, Peter (Samuel) 1946- CANR-20
Earlier sketch in CA 103
Shipley, (Howard) Thorne 1927- 5-8R
Shipman, David 1932-1996 .... CANR-30
Obituary 152
Earlier sketches in CA 29-32R, CANR-12
Shipman, Harry L(ongfellow) 1948- . CANR-85
Earlier sketches in CA 65-68, CANR-10, 32
Shipman, Pat 1949- CANR-105
Earlier sketch in CA 141
Shipnuck, Alan 1973- 208
Shipp, Nelson (McLester) 1892-1979 57-60
Shipp, Steve 1937- 160
Shipp, Thomas J. 1918- 13-16R
Shippen, Katherine B(inney)
1892-1980 .... CANR-86
Obituary 93-96
Earlier sketch in CA 5-8R
See also CLR 36
See also SATA 1
See also SATA-Obit 23
Shipper, Frank M(artin) 1945- 119
Shippey, Frederick Alexander
1908-1994 .... CAP-1
Earlier sketch in CA 13-14
Shippey, (Henry) Lee 1884-1969
Obituary 89-92
Shippey, T(homas) A(lan) 1943- CANR-121
Earlier sketch in CA 108
See also SATA 143
Shipps, Jan (Barnett) 1929- 127
Shippy, Richard W. 1927- 81-84
Shipton, Clifford K(enyon) 1902-1973 ... CAP-2
Earlier sketch in CA 17-18
Shipton, Eric Earle 1907-1977 65-68
Obituary 69-72
See also SATA 10
Shipway, George 1908- 25-28R
Shirakawa, Yoshikazu 1935- CANR-14
Earlier sketch in CA 73-76
Shiras, Wilmar H(ouse) 1908-1990 160
See also SFW 4
Shiratori, Rei 1937- 133
Shirazi, Faegheh 1952- 212
Shire, Helena (Mary) Mennie
1912-1991 .... CANR-27
Obituary 136
Earlier sketch in CA 29-32R
Shirer, William L(awrence)
1904-1993 .... CANR-92
Obituary 143
Earlier sketches in CA 9-12R, CANR-7, 55
See also DLB 4
See also MTCW 1, 2
See also MTFW 2005
See also SATA 45
See also SATA-Obit 78
Shires, Henry M(illis) 1913-1980 .... 17-20R
Obituary 134
Shires, Linda M(arguerite) 1950- 118
Shirinian, Lorne 1945- 210
Shirinsky-Shikhmatov, Sergii Aleksandrovich
1783-1837 .... DLB 150
Shirk, Evelyn Urban 1918- 17-20R
Shirk, George H(enry) 1913-1977 .... 17-20R
Shirk, Martha 228
Shirk, Susan L(ee) 1945- 108
Shirkey, Albert P(atterson) 1904-1990 ... CAP-2
Obituary 133
Earlier sketch in CA 17-18
Shirley, Dennis 1955- 137
Shirley, Donna 1941- 199
Shirley, Edward 1949- 169
Shirley, Frances A(nn) 1931- CANR-2
Earlier sketch in CA 5-8R
Shirley, Gayle C(orbett) 1955- CANR-144
Earlier sketch in CA 161
See also SATA 96
Shirley, Glenn 1916- 89-92
Shirley, Hardy L(omax) 1900-1996 .... 37-40R
Shirley, James 1596-1666 .... DC 25
See also DLB 58
See also RGEL 2
Shirley, Jean 1919- 138
See also SATA 70
Shirley, John 1953- CANR-81
Earlier sketch in CA 126
See also HGG
See also SFW 4
See also SUFW 2
Shirley, John William 1908-1988 126
Brief entry 114
Shirley, Ralph 1865-1946
Brief entry 117
Shirley, Shirley 1934- 162
Shirley-Smith, Hubert 1901-1981
Obituary 113
Shirow, Masamune 1961- .... AAYA 61
Shirreffs, Gordon D(onald)
1914-1996 .... CANR-86
Earlier sketches in CA 13-16R, CANR-6, 21, 49
See also SATA 11
See also TCWW 2
Shirts, Morris A(lpine) 1922- 73-76
See also SATA 63
Shishkov, Aleksandr Semenovich
1753-1841 .... DLB 150
Shissler, Barbara Johnson
See Nosanow, Barbara Shissler
Shi Tuo 1910-1988 .... RGSF 2
Shiva, Vandana 1952- 215
Shivanandan, Mary 1932- CANR-12
Earlier sketch in CA 73-76
Shively, Donald H(oward) 1921-2005
Brief entry 115
Shively, George Jenks 1893(?)-1980
Obituary 97-100
Shivers, Alfred Samuel 1929- 41-44R
Shivers, Frank R(emer), Jr. 1924- CANR-93
Earlier sketch in CA 130
Shivers, Jay S(anford) 1930- CANR-52
Earlier sketches in CA 33-36R, CANR-12, 27
Shivers, Louise 1929- 136
Shivers, Samuel A.
See Shivers, Alfred Samuel
Shivpuri, Gopi Krishna 1903-1984 ... CANR-42
Obituary 113
Earlier sketch in CA 101

Shklovsky, Iosif Samuilovitch 1916-1985
Obituary ... 115
Shklovsky, Viktor Borisovich 1893-1984 ... 144
Obituary ... 114
Shlaim, Avi 1945- ... CANR-96
Earlier sketch in CA 136
Shlapentokh, Dmitry (V.) 1950- ... 195
Shlechter, Theodore M. 1952- ... 144
Shlemon, Barbara Leahy 1936- ... CANR-31
Earlier sketch in CA 112
Shlichta, Joe 1968- ... SATA 84
Shlonsky, Abraham 1898(?)-1973
Obituary ... 41-44R
Shloss, Carol (Loeb) ... 238
Shmanske, Stephen 1954- ... 139
Shmelev, I. S. 1873-1950 ... DLB 317
Shmeruk, Chone 1921-1997 ... 166
Shmueli, Adi 1941- ... CANR-1
Earlier sketch in CA 45-48
Shmurak, Carole B. 1944- ... 190
See also SATA 118
Shnayerson, Michael 1954- ... CANR-141
Earlier sketch in CA 132
Shneerson, Grigory Mikhailovich 1901-1982
Obituary ... 106
Shneiderman, Ben A. 1947- ... 115
Shneiderman, Samuel L(oeb) 1906- ... 97-100
Shneidman, Conalee Levine
See Levine-Shneidman, Conalee
Shneidman, Edwin S. 1918- ... CANR-82
Earlier sketches in CA 29-32R, CANR-36
Shneidman, J(erome) Lee 1929- ... 37-40R
Shneidman, N(oah) N(orman) 1924- ... 136
Shneour, Elie A(lexis) 1925- ... 37-40R
Shoaf, Diann Blakely 1957- ... 237
See also Blakely, Diann
Shoaf, Richard Allen 1948- ... CANR-96
Earlier sketches in CA 119, CANR-45
Shoales, Ian
See Kessler, Merle (Bruce)
Shoben, Edward Joseph, Jr. 1918- ... 21-24R
Shober, Joyce Lee 1932- ... 1-4R
Shoberg, Lore 1949- ... 33-36R
Shobin, David 1945- ... CANR-102
Earlier sketches in CA 104, CANR-20
Shoblad, Richard H(anson) 1937- ... 41-44R
Shock, Julian
See Williamson, Gerald Neal
Shock, Nathan W(etherill) 1906-1989 ... 5-8R
Obituary ... 130
Shockley, Ann Allen 1927- ... CANR-59
Earlier sketches in CA 49-52, CANR-1
See also BW 1
See also DLB 33
See also FW
Shockley, Donald G(rady) 1937- ... 103
Shockley, William (Bradford) 1910-1989 ... 215
Obituary ... 129
Brief entry ... 113
Shoe, Lucy T.
See Meritt, Lucy Shoe
Shoemaker, Bill
See Shoemaker, William Lee
Shoemaker, Don(ald) C(leavenger)
1912-1998 ... 97-100
Shoemaker, Donald J(ay) 1927- ... 37-40R
Shoemaker, Leonard Calvin 1881-1973 . CAP-1
Earlier sketch in CA 13-16
Shoemaker, Lloyd R. 1921- ... 133
Shoemaker, Lynn Henry 1939- ... CANR-9
Earlier sketch in CA 65-68
Shoemaker, Richard H(eston)
1907-1970 ... CAP-1
Earlier sketch in CA 11-12
Shoemaker, Robert B(rink) 1956- ... 142
Shoemaker, Robert G(ardner) 1941- ... 142
Shoemaker, Robert John 1919- ... 13-16R
Shoemaker, Robin 1949- ... 108
Shoemaker, Sarah
See Wolf, Sarah (Elizabeth)
Shoemaker, William H(utchinson)
1902-1989 ... 13-16R
Shoemaker, William Lee 1931-2003 ... 154
Obituary ... 221
Brief entry ... 115
Shoemaker, Willie
See Shoemaker, Willie and
Skocpol, Theda (Ruth)
Shoenight, Aloise 1914- ... 77-80
Shoesmith, Kathleen A(nne) 1938- ... CANR-86
Earlier sketches in CA 49-52, CANR-1, 17
See also RHW
Shofner, Jerrell H(arris) 1929- ... 57-60
Shofner, Robert D(ancey) 1933- ... 57-60
Shogan, Robert 1930- ... CANR-110
Earlier sketch in CA 153
Shokeid, Moshe 1936- ... CANR-16
Earlier sketch in CA 41-44R
Sholinsky, Jane 1943- ... 89-92
Sholokhov, Mikhail (Aleksandrovich)
1905-1984 ... 101
Obituary ... 112
See also CLC 7, 15
See also DLB 272
See also EWL 3
See also MTCW 1, 2
See also MTFW 2005
See also RGWL 2, 3
See also SATA-Obit 36
Shomaker, Dianna 1934- ... 109
Shomer, Enid ... CANR-111
Earlier sketch in CA 143
Shomon, Joseph James 1914- ... 73-76
Shomon, Mary J. 1961- ... 229
Shomroni, Reuven
See von Block, Bela W(illiam)
Shone, Anna
See Shone, Bridget Ann
Shone, Bridget Ann 1947- ... 150
Shone, Patric
See Hanley, James
Shone, Richard (N.) 1949- ... CANR-97
Earlier sketch in CA 141
Shone, Robert 1906-1992 ... 109
Shone, Ronald 1946- ... CANR-20
Earlier sketch in CA 103
Shonfield, Andrew (Akiba) 1917-1981 ... 105
Obituary ... 102
Shonk, Katherine ... 236
Shono, Junzo 1921- ... 184
See also Shono Junzo
Shono Junzo
See Shono, Junzo
See also DLB 182
Shontz, Franklin C(urtis) 1926- ... 17-20R
Shook, Karel 1920-1985
Obituary ... 117
Shook, Laurence K(ennedy) 1909-1993 ... 73-76
Shook, Robert L. 1938- ... CANR-46
Earlier sketches in CA 61-64, CANR-8, 23
Shookman, Ellis 1957- ... CANR-136
Earlier sketch in CA 166
Shoolbred, C(laude) F(rederick) 1901- ... CAP-2
Earlier sketch in CA 25-28
Shooter, James (Charles) 1951- ... 136
Shooter, Jim
See Shooter, James (Charles)
Shor, Elizabeth N(oble) 1930- ... 110
Shor, Franc(is Marion Luther) 1914-1974
Obituary ... 111
Shor, Ira 1945- ... CANR-55
Earlier sketch in CA 126
Shor, Joel 1919- ... 89-92
Shor, Pekay 1923- ... 45-48
Shor, Ronald (Edwin) 1930- ... 61-64
Shorb, Wil(bert Hanson, Jr.) 1938- ... 45-48
Shore, Anne
See Sanford, Annette
Shore, Arabella 1820(?)-1901 ... 195
See also DLB 199
Shore, Bernard (Alexander Royle) 1896-1985
Obituary ... 116
Shore, Jane 1947- ... CANR-66
Earlier sketch in CA 77-80
Shore, June Lewis ... 105
See also AITN 1
See also SATA 30
Shore, Louisa 1824-1895 ... DLB 199
Shore, Nancy 1960- ... SATA 124
Shore, Norman
See Smith, Norman Edward Mace
Shore, Paul J(ohn) 1956- ... 118
Shore, Philippa
See Holbeche, Philippa Jack
Shore, Robert 1924- ... SATA 39
Shore, Sidney 1921-1981
Obituary ... 103
Shore, Stephen (Eric) 1947- ... 205
Shore, William B(urton) 1925- ... 53-56
Shore, Wilma 1913- ... 13-16R
Shores, David L(ee) 1933- ... 123
Brief entry ... 118
Shores, Louis 1904-1981 ... CANR-8
Obituary ... 104
Earlier sketch in CA 13-16R
Shorris, Earl 1936- ... CANR-142
Earlier sketches in CA 65-68, CANR-10, 34
Shorrock, William I(rwin) 1941- ... 65-68
Shors, John 1969- ... 232
Short, Alan Lennox
See Lennox-Short, Alan
Short, Alison 1920- ... 61-64
Short, Bobby
See Short, Robert Waltrip
Short, Brian (Michael) 1944- ... 136
Short, Bryan C. ... 139
Short, (Charles) Christopher (Dudley)
(?)-1978 ... CANR-2
Earlier sketch in CA 1-4R
Short, Clarice 1910-1977 ... 45-48
Obituary ... 103
Short, Edmund C(oen) 1931- ... 25-28R
Short, Howard E(lmo) 1907- ... 61-64
Short, Jackson ... 53-56
Short, James F(ranklin, Jr.) 1924- ... CANR-25
Earlier sketches in CA 5-8R, CANR-8
Short, James R. 1922(?)-1980
Obituary ... 103
Short, K(enneth) R(ichard) M(acDonald)
1936- ... 131
Short, Kathy G(nagey) 1952- ... CANR-103
Earlier sketch in CA 150
Short, Luke
See Glidden, Frederick D(illey)
See also TCWW 1, 2
Short, Michael 1937- ... CANR-42
Earlier sketch in CA 117
See also SATA 65
Short, Peter fl. 1589-1603 ... DLB 170
Short, Philip 1945- ... CANR-91
Earlier sketch in CA 105
Short, Robert L(ester) 1932- ... 77-80
Short, Robert Stuart 1938- ... 29-32R
Short, Robert Waltrip 1924(?)-2005
Obituary ... 237
Brief entry ... 107
Short, Roger
See Arkin, Alan (Wolf)
Short, Roger, Jr.
See Eyen, Tom
Short, Roy Hunter 1902-1994 ... 120
Short, Ruth Gordon ... CANR-6
Earlier sketch in CA 1-4R
Short, Thayne R(edford) 1929- ... 108
Short, Wayne 1926- ... 9-12R
Shortall, Leonard W. ... 81-84
See also SATA 19
Shorter, Aylward 1932- ... 81-84
Shorter, Carl
See Schwalberg, Carol(yn Ernestine Stein)
Shorter, Dora Sigerson 1866-1918 ... 206
See also DLB 240
Shorter, Edward 1941- ... CANR-46
Earlier sketch in CA 73-76
Shorter, Frank C(harles) 1947- ... 132
Shorthouse, Joseph Henry 1834-1903 ... 164
Brief entry ... 121
See also DLB 18
See also RGEL 2
Shorto, Harry L(eonard) 1919- ... 5-8R
Shortridge, James R. 1944- ... 136
Shortsleeve, Kevin 1965- ... 183
Shortt, Terence Michael 1911-1986 ... 77-80
Shortt, Tim(othy Donald) 1961- ... 161
See also SATA 96
Shostak, Arthur B. 1937- ... 108
Shostak, Jerome 1913- ... CANR-7
Earlier sketch in CA 17-20R
Shostak, Stanley 1938- ... 117
Shostakovich, Dmitri (Dmitrievich)
1906-1975 ... CANR-117
Obituary ... 113
Earlier sketch in CA 148
See also IDFW 3, 4
Shosteck, Robert 1910-1979 ... CANR-11
Obituary ... 85-88
Earlier sketch in CA 61-64
Shotetsu 1381-1459 ... DLB 203
Shott, James R. 1925- ... 139
Shotwell, Louisa Rossiter
1902-1993 ... CANR-86
Earlier sketches in CA 1-4R, CANR-4
See also SATA 3
Shouksmith, George A. 1931- ... 49-52
Shoumatoff, Alex(ander) 1946- ... CANR-48
Earlier sketches in CA 53-56, CANR-9
Shoup, Barbara 1947- ... CANR-116
Earlier sketch in CA 151
See also SAAS 24
See also SATA 86, 156
See also YAW
Shoup, Carl S(umner) 1902-2000 ... 49-52
Obituary ... 189
Shoup, Laurence H(enry) 1943- ... CANR-43
Earlier sketch in CA 102
Shoup, Paul S(nedden) 1929- ... CANR-88
Earlier sketch in CA 106
Shover, John L. 1927- ... 21-24R
Showalter, Dennis 1942- ... 89-92
Showalter, Elaine 1941- ... CANR-106
Earlier sketches in CA 57-60, CANR-58
See also CLC 169
See also DLB 67
See also FW
See also GLL 2
Showalter, English, Jr. 1935- ... 53-56
Showalter, Jean B(reckinridge) ... 21-24R
See also SATA 12
Showalter, Ronda Kerr 1942- ... 37-40R
Showell, Ellen Harvey 1934- ... 85-88
See also SATA 33
Showers, Paul C. 1910-1999 ... CANR-59
Obituary ... 183
Earlier sketches in CA 1-4R, CANR-4, 38
See also CLR 6
See also MAICYA 1, 2
See also SAAS 7
See also SATA 21, 92
See also SATA-Obit 114
Showers, Renald E(dward) 1935- ... CANR-13
Earlier sketch in CA 77-80
Showers, Victor 1910- ... 53-56
Shoy, Lee Ang
See Sheridan, L(ionel) A(stor)
Shoyo, Tsubouchi
See Yuzo, Tsubouchi
Shpakow, Tanya 1959(?)- ... 159
See also SATA 94
Shpitalnik, Vladimir 1964- ... SATA 83
Shrader, Charles R. 1943- ... 153
Shrady, Maria 1924- ... 49-52
Shragg, Karen (I.) 1954- ... 213
See also SATA 142
Shragin, Boris 1926-1990 ... 102
Obituary ... 132
Shrake, Bud
See Shrake, Edwin
Shrake, Budd
See Shrake, Edwin
Shrake, Edwin 1931- ... CANR-86
Brief entry ... 116
Earlier sketch in CA 144
See also TCWW 1, 2
Shrayer, Maxim D. 1967- ... 191
Shreeve, Elizabeth 1956- ... SATA 156
Shreffler, Philip A. 1948- ... 138
Shrestha, Nanda R. 1949- ... 235
Shreve, Anita 1946- ... CANR-136
Earlier sketches in CA 139, CANR-80
See also CN 7
See also DLB 292
See also MTFW 2005
Shreve, Gene R. 1943- ... 191
Shreve, L(evin) G(ale) 1910-1998 ... 101
Shreve, Porter 1966- ... 236
Shreve, Susan
See Shreve, Susan Richards
Shreve, Susan Richards 1939- ... CANR-100
Earlier sketches in CA 49-52, CANR-5, 38, 69
See also CAAS 5
See also CLC 23
See also MAICYA 1, 2
See also SATA 46, 95, 152
See also SATA-Brief 41
Shriber, Ione Sandberg 1911-1987
Obituary ... 121
Shrimpton, Gordon Spencer 1941- ... 115
Shrimsley, Anthony 1934-1984
Obituary ... 114
Shrimsley, Bernard 1931- ... 103
Shrivastava, Paul 1951- ... 133
Shriver, Donald W(oods), Jr. 1927- ... CANR-1
Earlier sketch in CA 45-48
Shriver, George H(ite), Jr. 1931- ... CANR-94
Earlier sketch in CA 21-24R
Shriver, Harry C(lair) 1904-1986 ... CANR-10
Earlier sketch in CA 65-68
Shriver, Jean Adair 1932- ... 142
See also SATA 75
Shriver, Lionel 1957- ... CANR-140
Earlier sketches in CA 134, CANR-72
Shriver, Maria (Owings) 1955- ... 196
See also SATA 134
Shriver, Peggy (Ann) L(eu) 1931- ... 107
Shriver, Phillip Raymond 1922- ... 13-16R
Shriver, Rosalia (Oliver) 1927-1987 .. CANR-85
Obituary ... 135
Earlier sketch in CA 115
Shrode, Mary
See Hollingsworth, Mary
Shroder, Maurice Z(orensky) 1933- ... 1-4R
Shrodes, Caroline 1908-1991 ... CANR-4
Earlier sketch in CA 1-4R
Shropshire, Kenneth (L.) 1955- ... 160
Shropshire, W(alter), Jr. 1932- ... 118
Shrosbree, Colin (John) 1938- ... 130
Shrout, Richard Neil 1931- ... 144
Shrout, Thomas R(euben) 1919- ... 41-44R
Shroyer, Frederick B(enjamin)
1916-1983 ... CANR-13
Earlier sketch in CA 13-16R
Shryock, (Edwin) Harold 1906- ... CANR-8
Earlier sketch in CA 21-24R
Shryock, Richard Harrison 1893-1972 .. CAP-2
Obituary ... 33-36R
Earlier sketch in CA 17-18
Shtainmets, Leon ... 105
See also SATA 32
Shteiger, Anatolii 1907-1944 ... DLB 317
Shtemenko, Sergei Matveyevich
1907-1976 ... 103
Shternfeld, Ari A(bramovich) 1905-1980
Obituary ... 105
Shteynbarg, Eliezer 1880-1932 ... EWL 3
Shteyngart, Gary 1972- ... 217
Shtromas, Alexander 1931-1999 ... CANR-90
Earlier sketch in CA 132
Shu, Austin Chi-wei 1915- ... 29-32R
Shu, Ch' ing-ch'un 1899-1966
Obituary ... 109
See also Lao She
Shua, Ana Maria 1951- ... EWL 3
Shub, Beth
See Pessen, Beth
Shub, David 1887-1973
Obituary ... 41-44R
Shub, Elizabeth 1915(?)-2004 ... CANR-15
Obituary ... 228
Earlier sketch in CA 41-44R
See also SATA 5
Shubik, Martin 1926- ... CANR-2
Earlier sketch in CA 5-8R
Shubin, Seymour 1921- ... CANR-141
Earlier sketch in CA 1-4R
Shucard, Alan R(obert) 1935- ... CANR-51
Earlier sketches in CA 61-64, CANR-26
Shuchman, Abraham 1919-1978
Obituary ... 77-80
Shue, Larry 1946-1985 ... 145
Obituary ... 117
See also CLC 52
See also DAM DRAM
See also DFS 7
Shuffelton, Frank 1940- ... CANR-38
Earlier sketch in CA 115
Shuford, Cecil Eugene 1907- ... 13-16R
See also AITN 1
Shuford, Gene
See Shuford, Cecil Eugene
Shugart, Herman H(enry, Jr.) 1944- ... 145
Shughart, William F. (II) 1947- ... CANR-114
Earlier sketch in CA 154
Shugrue, Michael F(rancis) 1934- ... 21-24R
Shu-Jen, Chou 1881-1936
Brief entry ... 104
See also Lu Hsun
Shuken, Julia 1948- ... 150
See also SATA 84
Shukert, Elfrieda Berthiaume 1948- ... 129
Shukman, Harold 1931- ... CANR-127
Earlier sketches in CA 53-56, CANR-66
Shukman, Henry 1962- ... 236
Shukshin, V.
See Shukshin, Vasily (Makarovich)
Shukshin, V. M.
See Shukshin, Vasily (Makarovich)
Shukshin, Vasilii (Makarovich)
See Shukshin, Vasily (Makarovich)
See also DLB 302
Shukshin, Vasily (Makarovich)
1929-1974 ... CANR-87
Earlier sketch in CA 135
See also Shukshin, Vasilii (Makarovich)
See also EWL 3

Shula
See Reinharz, Shulamit
Shula, Don(ald Francis) 1930- 182
Brief entry 106
Shulberg, Alan
See Wilkes-Hunter, R(ichard)
Shuldinger, Herbert 1929- 130
Shuler, Linda Lay 128
Shulevitz, Uri 1935- CANR-3
Earlier sketch in CA 9-12R
See also CLR 5, 61
See also CWRI 5
See also DLB 61
See also MAICYA 1, 2
See also SATA 3, 50, 106
Shull, Fremont Adam, Jr. 1924- CANR-1
Earlier sketch in CA 1-4R
Shull, Margaret Anne Wyse 1940- 77-80
Shull, Michael Slade 1949- 212
Shull, Peg
See Shull, Margaret Anne Wyse
Shull, Steven A. 1943- CANR-93
Earlier sketch in CA 147
Shulman, Albert M(aimon) 1902-1997 49-52
Shulman, Alix Kates 1932- CANR-43
Earlier sketch in CA 29-32R
See also CLC 2, 10
See also FW
See also SATA 7
Shulman, Arnold 1914- 29-32R
Shulman, Bernard H. 1922- 108
Shulman, Charles E. 1904-1968 .... CAP-1
Earlier sketch in CA 13-14
Shulman, David Dean 1949- CANR-103
Earlier sketch in CA 102
Shulman, Dee 1957- .... SATA 146
Shulman, Fay Grissom Stanley 1925(?)-1990
Obituary 133
Shulman, Frank Joseph 1943- CANR-60
Earlier sketches in CA 29-32R, CANR-12, 30
Shulman, Harry 1903-1955
Brief entry 112
Shulman, Harry Manuel 1899-1984 .... 1-4R
Shulman, Irving 1913-1995 .... CANR-6
Obituary 148
Earlier sketch in CA 1-4R
See also SATA 13
Shulman, Lisa M. 220
Shulman, Mark R(ussell) 1963- 147
Shulman, Marshall Darrow 1916- 1-4R
Shulman, Max 1919-1988 89-92
Obituary 126
See also DLB 11
See also SATA-Obit 59
Shulman, Milton 1913-2004 .... CANR-89
Obituary 229
Earlier sketch in CA 103
See also SATA-Obit 154
Shulman, Morton 1925- CANR-14
Earlier sketch in CA 21-24R
See also AITN 1
See also CCA 1
Shulman, Neil B(arnett) 1945- CANR-53
Earlier sketches in CA 65-68, CANR-9, 26
See also SATA 89
Shulman, Neville 1945- 184
Shulman, Sandra (Dawn) 1944- CANR-9
Earlier sketch in CA 21-24R
Shulman, Seth 1960- 239
Shults, Sylvia 1968- 195
Shultz, George P(ratt) 1920- CANR-49
Earlier sketch in CA 104
Shultz, Gladys Denny 1895-1984 49-52
Shultz, Suzanne M. 1947- 144
Shultz, William J(ohn) 1902-1970 .... CANR-16
Obituary 103
Earlier sketch in CA 1-4R
Shulvass, Moses A. 1909-1988 .... 13-16R
Shumaker, Peggy 1952- CANR-86
Earlier sketch in CA 154
See also CP 7
Shumaker, Wayne 1910- 5-8R
Shuman, Bruce A(lan) 1941- 110
Shuman, James B(urrow) 1932- 61-64
Shuman, Nicholas R(oman) 1921- 109
Shuman, R(obert) Baird 1929- CANR-4
Earlier sketch in CA 1-4R
Shuman, Samuel I(rving) 1925- CANR-3
Earlier sketch in CA 9-12R
Shumsky, Zena
See Collier, Zena
Shumway, Floyd M(allory, Jr.)
1917-1997 .... CANR-29
Obituary 162
Earlier sketch in CA 29-32R
Shumway, George (Alfred, Jr.) 1928- 9-12R
Shumway, Mary L. 1926- CANR-7
Earlier sketch in CA 17-20R
Shupe, Anson 1948- CANR-67
Earlier sketch in CA 129
Shupp, Mike 1946- 121
Shura, Mary Francis
See Craig, Mary (Francis) Shura
Shurden, Walter B(yron) 1937- CANR-21
Earlier sketch in CA 69-72
Shurin, Aaron 1947- 192
Shurkin, Joel N. 1938- CANR-14
Earlier sketch in CA 69-72
Shurr, Emily Grey 1972- 147
Shurr, William H(oward) 1932- CANR-18
Earlier sketch in CA 41-44R
Shurter, Robert L(e Fevre) 1907-1974 . CANR-2
Earlier sketch in CA 1-4R
Shurtleff, Malcolm C., Jr. 1922- 5-8R
Shurtleff, Michael 1930- 41-44R
Shurtleff, William 1941- CANR-16
Earlier sketch in CA 93-96
Shusei, Tokuda
See Sueo, Tokuda
Shuseki, Hayashi
See Hubbell, Lindley Williams
Shu She-Yu 1899-1966 189
Shuster, Albert H., Jr. 1917- 17-20R
Shuster, Alvin 1930-
Brief entry 113
Shuster, Bud
See Shuster, E. G.
Shuster, E. G. 1932- 138
Shuster, George Nauman 1894-1977 77-80
Obituary 69-72
Shuster, Joe 1914-1992 .... AAYA 50
See also CLC 21
Shuster, Ronald L(owell) 1927- 45-48
Shusterman, David 1912- 25-28R
Shusterman, Neal 1962- CANR-99
Earlier sketch in CA 133
See also AAYA 21
See also MAICYA 2
See also MAICYAS 1
See also SATA 85, 121, 140
See also SATA-Essay 140
Shusterman, Richard (M.) 1949- 136
Shute, Alberta V(an Horn) 1906- CANR-7
Earlier sketch in CA 57-60
Shute, Gary Brana
See Brana-Shute, Gary
Shute, Henry A(ugustus) 1856-1943 184
See also DLB 9
Shute, Jenefer 1956- CANR-93
Earlier sketch in CA 138
Shute, Nerina 1908-2004 101
Obituary 232
Shute, Nevil
See Norway, Nevil Shute
See also BPFB 3
See also CLC 30
See also DLB 255
See also NFS 9
See also RHW
See also SFW 4
Shute, Plupy
See Shute, Henry A(ugustus)
Shute, R(eginald) Wayne 1933- 29-32R
Shute, Wallace B. 1911- 29-32R
Shute, Wilfred Eugene 1907- 105
Shuter, Jane (Margaret) 1955- CANR-135
Earlier sketch in CA 155
See also SATA 90, 151
Shuttle, Penelope (Diane) 1947- CANR-108
Earlier sketches in CA 93-96, CANR-39, 84, 92
See also CLC 7
See also CP 7
See also CWP
See also DLB 14, 40
Shuttlesworth, Dorothy Edwards CANR-4
Earlier sketch in CA 1-4R
See also SATA 3
Shuttleworth, John 1937- .... AITN 1
Shuval, Judith T(annenbaum) 1925- . CANR-25
Earlier sketch in CA 45-48
Shuy, Roger W(ellington) 1931- CANR-13
Earlier sketch in CA 61-64
Shvarts, Elena 1948- 147
See also PC 50
Shvarts, Evgenii L'vovich 1896-1958 .. DLB 272
Shvets, Yuri B. 1953- 147
Shvidkovsky, Dimitri 1959- 157
Shwadran, Benjamin 1907- CANR-20
Earlier sketches in CA 13-16R, CANR-5
Shwartz, Susan (Martha) 1949- CANR-118
Earlier sketches in CA 109, CANR-56
See also FANT
See also SATA 94
See also SFW 4
Shwayder, David S(amuel) 1926- 106
Shweder, Richard A. 224
Shy, John W(illard) 1931- CANR-3
Earlier sketch in CA 5-8R
Shyamalan, M. Night 1970- 195
See also AAYA 41
Shyer, Charles (Richard) 1941- 138
Shyer, Christopher 1961- 157
See also SATA 98
Shyer, Marlene Fanta CANR-11
Earlier sketch in CA 69-72
See also SATA 13
Shyne, Ann W(entworth) 1914- 115
Shynnagh, Frank
See Will, Frederic
Shyre, Paul 1929(?)-1989 103
Obituary 130
Siano, Mary M(artha) 1924- 77-80
Sibawayhi c. 750-c. 795 .... DLB 311
Sibbes, Richard 1577-1635 .... DLB 151
Siberell, Anne 104
See also SATA 29
Siberry, (Jane) Elizabeth 1957- 122
Sibiriak, D.
See Mamin, Dmitrii Narkisovich
Sibley, Agnes M(arie) 1914- 61-64
Sibley, Celestine 1917-1999 .... CANR-73
Obituary 183
Earlier sketch in CA 85-88
Sibley, David Allen 1962- 223
Sibley, Don 1922- .... SATA 12
Sibley, Elbridge 1903-1994 .... CAP-1
Earlier sketch in CA 13-14
Sibley, Katherine A. S. 1961- 156
Sibley, Marilyn McAdams 1923- 21-24R
Sibley, Mulford Quickert 1912-1989 .. CANR-6
Earlier sketch in CA 5-8R
Sibley, Patricia (Hayles) 1928- 97-100
Sibley, Susan
See Kinnicutt, Susan Sibley
Sibley, William Jack 1952- 207
Sibly, John 1920- 1-4R
Sibson, Caroline
See Dracup, Angela
Sibum, Norm 1947- 225
Siburapha
See Saipradit, Kulap
See also EWL 3
See also RGWL 3
Siburt, Ruth 1951- 192
See also SATA 121
Sices, David 1933- 25-28R
Sichel, Deborah (Anne) 195
Sichel, Kim Deborah 1955- 202
Sichel, Peter M(ax) F(erdinand) 1922- 65-68
Sichel, Pierre (Laugier) 1915- 1-4R
Sichel, Werner 1934- CANR-47
Earlier sketches in CA 21-24R, CANR-8, 23
Sicherman, Carol 1937- 135
Sichol, Marcia W. 1940- 135
Sichov, Vladimir 1945- 108
Sichrovsky, Peter 1947- 148
Sicignano, Robert 1946- 116
Siciliano, Enzo 1934- 147
Siciliano, Vincent Paul 1911-1989 .... CAP-2
Earlier sketch in CA 29-32
Sicinski, Andrzej 1924- CANR-40
Earlier sketch in CA 115
Sick, Gary G(ordon) 1935- 144
Sickels, Noelle 1945- 153
Sickels, Robert J(udd) 1931- 41-44R
Sicker, Martin 1931- 146
Sicker, Philip 1951- 103
Sickles, William Russell 1913- 57-60
Sickman, Laurence C(halfant) S(tevens)
1906-1988 .... CAP-1
Obituary 125
Earlier sketch in CA 11-12
Siculan, Daniel 1922- .... SATA 12
Sidahmed, Abdel Salam 1956- 159
Sidak, J. Gregory 1955- 148
Sidaoru'ang 1943- .... EWL 3
Siddal, Elizabeth Eleanor 1834-1862 .. DLB 199
Siddall, William R(ichard) 1928- 41-44R
Siddiqi, Akhtar Husain 1925- 61-64
Siddiqui, Ashraf (Hossain) 1927- CANR-2
Earlier sketch in CA 5-8R
Siddle, Sheila 1931- 238
Siddons, (Sybil) Anne Rivers 1936- . CANR-131
Earlier sketches in CA 101, CANR-33, 53, 81
See also BEST 89:2
See also CPW
See also CSW
See also DA3
See also DAM POP
See also HGG
See also MTCW 1, 2
See also MTFW 2005
Siddons, Robert 1952- 119
Sidel, John T. 1966- 237
Sidel, Victor W(illiam) 1931- CANR-9
Earlier sketch in CA 65-68
Sider, Don 1933- 77-80
Sider, Robert Dick 1932- CANR-16
Earlier sketch in CA 37-40R
Sider, Ronald J(ames) 1939- CANR-91
Earlier sketches in CA 93-96, CANR-17, 39
Siders, Ellis L(eroy) 1920- 17-20R
Sides, W(ade) Hampton 1962- 139
Sidetracked Home Executives
See Jones, Peggy and
Young, Pam
Sidey, Hugh (Swanson) 1927- 124
Brief entry 111
Sidgwick, Ethel 1877-1970 183
See also DLB 197
See also SATA 116
Sidgwick, Henry 1838-1900
Brief entry 120
See also DLB 262
Sidhwa, Bapsi
See Sidhwa, Bapsy (N.)
See also CN 6, 7
Sidhwa, Bapsy (N.) 1938- CANR-57
Earlier sketches in CA 108, CANR-25
See also Sidhwa, Bapsi
See also CLC 168
See also FW
Sidhwa, Keki R(attanshah) 1926- 69-72
Sidjakov, Nicolas 1924- .... SATA 18
Sidky, H. 1956- CANR-124
Earlier sketch in CA 171
Sidley, Nathan T(heodore) 1929- 113
Sidman, Joyce 1956- 218
See also SATA 145
Sidnell, Michael John 1935- 113
Sidney, Frank
See Warwick, Alan R(oss)
Sidney, Jonathan
See Cooper, Emmanuel
Sidney, Kathleen M(arion) 1944- 103
Sidney, Margaret
See Lothrop, Harriet Mulford Stone
Sidney, Mary 1561-1621
See Sidney Herbert, Mary
Sidney, Neilma
See Gantner, Neilma
Sidney, Sir Philip 1554-1586 .... BRW 1
See also BRWR 2
See also CDBLB Before 1660
See also DA
See also DA3
See also DAB
See also DAC
See also DAM MST, POET
See also DLB 167
See also EXPP
See also PAB
See also PC 32
See also RGEL 2
See also TEA
See also WP
Sidney-Fryer, Donald 1934- CANR-46
Earlier sketch in CA 45-48
Sidney Herbert, Mary
See Sidney, Mary
See also DLB 167
Sidowski, Joseph B(oleslaus) 1925- 21-24R
Sidran, Ben H. 1943- 102
Sidransky, Ruth 1929- 135
Sidwell, Keith 1948- 185
Sidwell, Mark (Edward) 1958- 185
Siebel, Fritz (Frederick) 1913- ..... SATA-Brief 44
Siebenheller, Norma 1937- 107
Siebenschuh, William R(obert) 1942- 89-92
Sieber, Joan E. 1937- CANR-35
Earlier sketch in CA 114
Sieber, Roy 1923- 102
Sieber, Sam Dixon 1931- 13-16R
Siebert, Charles 183
Siebert, Fred(rick) Seaton 1901-1982 .... 21-24R
Siebert, Muriel 1932(?)- 220
Siebold, Cathy 1951- 145
Siebold, Jan 1953- 175
Siebrasse, Glen 1934- .... CP 1, 2
Siedel, Frank 1914- 25-28R
Siedel, James M. 1937- 25-28R
Siedlecki, Janusz Nel 1916-2000
Sieff, Jeanloup 1933-2000 205
Siegal, Aranka 1930- 112
See also AAYA 5
See also SATA 88
See also SATA-Brief 37
Siegal, Diana Laskin 1931- 127
Siegal, Harvey A. 1945- 127
Siegal, Mordecai 1934- 102
Siegal, Sanford (Sherwin) 1928- 105
Siegan, Bernard H(erbert) 1924- CANR-45
Earlier sketch in CA 65-68
Siegbahn, Kai M. 1918- 161
Siegbahn, Karl M(anne) G(eorg)
1886-1978 161
Siegel, Adrienne 1936- CANR-12
Earlier sketch in CA 61-64
Siegel, Arthur (Sidney) 1913-1978 203
Siegel, Barry 196
Siegel, Beatrice CANR-40
Earlier sketches in CA 101, CANR-18
See also SATA 36
Siegel, Ben 1925- 77-80
Siegel, Benjamin 1914-1991 .... CANR-4
Obituary 135
Earlier sketch in CA 1-4R
Siegel, Bernard S.
See Siegel, Bernie S(hepard)
Siegel, Bernie S(hepard) 1932- CANR-49
Earlier sketch in CA 123
See also BEST 89:4
Siegel, Bertram M. 1936- 25-28R
Siegel, Daniel M. 1939- 144
Siegel, Dorothy (Schainman) 1932- 9-12R
Siegel, Eli 1902-1978 .... CANR-9
Obituary 81-84
Earlier sketch in CA 17-20R
See also CP 1, 2
Siegel, Ernest 1922- 73-76
Siegel, Esther 1949- 102
Siegel, Fred 1941- 167
Siegel, Frederick F(ein) 1945- 133
Siegel, Gonnie McClung 1928- 110
Siegel, Helen
See Siegl, Helen
Siegel, Irving H(erbert) 1914-1988 ... CANR-85
Obituary 125
Earlier sketches in CA 21-24R, CANR-9
Siegel, Jack
See Siegel, Jacob
Siegel, Jacob 1913- 17-20R
Siegel, James 217
Siegel, James T. 1937-
Brief entry 113
Siegel, Jan
See Askew, Amanda Jane
Siegel, Jerome 1914-1996 169
Obituary 151
Brief entry 116
See also Siegel, Jerry
See also CLC 21
Siegel, Jerry
See Siegel, Jerome
See also AAYA 50
Siegel, Joel 1943- 232
Siegel, June 1929- 77-80
Siegel, Katherine A. S.
See Sibley, Katherine A. S.
Siegel, Lee 1945- CANR-71
Earlier sketch in CA 126
Siegel, Marcia B. 1932- CANR-37
Earlier sketch in CA 69-72
Siegel, Mark Richard 1949-2003 ...... CANR-29
Earlier sketch in CA 110
Siegel, Martin 1933- 33-36R
Siegel, Mary-Ellen (Kulkin) 1932- CANR-40
Earlier sketch in CA 116

Siegel, Max 1904-1972
Obituary ... 104
Siegel, Maxwell E(dward) 1933- ... 101
Siegel, Paul N. 1916- ... 37-40R
Siegel, Rachel Josefowitz 1924- ... CANR-123
Earlier sketch in CA 163
Siegel, Richard L(ewis) 1940- ... 73-76
Siegel, Robert (Harold) 1939- ... CANR-110
Earlier sketches in CA 53-56, CANR-5, 21, 50
See also SATA 39
Siegel, Seymour 1927-1988
Obituary ... 124
Siegel, Sheldon ... 209
Siegel, Stanley E(lliott) 1928- ... 41-44R
Siegelbaum, Lewis H. 1949- ... CANR-102
Earlier sketch in CA 144
Siegel-Gorelick, Bryna 1954- ... 115
Siegelman, James Howard 1951- ... 81-84
Siegelman, Jim
See Siegelman, James Howard
Siegelson, Kim L. 1962- ... 234
See also SATA 114
Siegener, Ray(mond) 1931- ... 123
Brief entry ... 118
Siegfried, Tom 1950- ... 217
Sieghart, (Henry Laurence) Paul (Alexander) 1927-1988
Obituary ... 127
Siegl, Helen 1924- ... SATA 34
Siegle, Bernard A(ndrew) 1914- ... 89-92
Siegler, Frederick Adrian 1932- ... 49-52
Siegler, Ilene C. 1946- ... 114
Siegler, Naomi
See Savage, Naomi
Siegman, Gita 1939- ... CANR-31
Earlier sketch in CA 112
Siegmeister, Elie 1909-1991 ... CANR-46
Obituary ... 133
Earlier sketches in CA 1-4R, CANR-1
Siegner, C(larence) Vernon, Jr. 1920- ... 1-4R
Sieh, Kerry (Edward) 1950- ... 182
Sielaff, Theodore J. 1920- ... 13-16R
Sieller, William Vincent 1917- ... 29-32R
Siemanowski, Richard F. 1922(?)-1981
Obituary ... 104
Siemens, Alfred H. 1932- ... 139
Siemens, Reynold Gerrard 1932- ... 41-44R
Siemon, James Ralph 1948- ... 121
Siemon, Jeff 1950- ... 103
Siena, Catherine of 1347-1380 ... LMFS 1
Sienkiewicz, Henryk (Adam Alexander Pius) 1846-1916 ... CANR-84
Brief entry ... 104
Earlier sketch in CA 134
See also EWL 3
See also RGSF 2
See also RGWL 2, 3
See also TCLC 3
Sienkiewicz-Mercer, Ruth 1950- ... 136
Sienko, Michell J. 1923-1983
Obituary ... 111
Siepmann, Charles Arthur 1899-1985 ... CANR-85
Obituary ... 115
Earlier sketch in CA 1-4R
Siepmann, Mary Aline
See Wesley, Mary (Aline)
Sierakowiak, Dawid 1924-1943
Sierpinski, Waclaw 1882-1969 ... 161
Sierra, Gregorio Martinez
See Martinez Sierra, Gregorio
Sierra, Judy 1945- ... CANR-80
Earlier sketch in CA 128
See also SATA 104, 162
Sierra, Maria (de la O'LeJarraga) Martinez
See Martinez Sierra, Maria (de la O'LeJarraga)
Sierra, Patricia ... 166
Sierra, Ruben 1946-1998 ... 176
See also DLB 122
See also HW 2
Sies, Luther F(rank) 1927- ... CANR-144
Earlier sketch in CA 111
Sieswerda, Paul L. 1942- ... 221
See also SATA 147
Siev, Asher 1913- ... 57-60
Sievers, Allen M. 1918- ... 89-92
Sievers, Harry J(oseph) 1920-1977 ... 25-28R
Obituary ... 73-76
Sievers, W(ieder) David 1919-1966 ... 1-4R
Obituary ... 103
Sievert, Philipp 1970- ... 150
Sievert, Terri
See Dougherty, Terri (L.)
Siewert, Frances E. (Cornelius) 1881-1967 ... CAP-1
Earlier sketch in CA 11-12
Sifakis, G(regory) M(ichael) 1935- ... 25-28R
Siffert, Robert S(pencer) 1918- ... 109
Sifford, (Charles) Darrell 1931- ... CANR-15
Earlier sketch in CA 77-80
Sifry, Micah L. ... 210
Sifton, Claire 1897(?)-1980
Obituary ... 93-96
Sifton, Paul F. 1893(?)-1972
Obituary ... 33-36R
Sigal, Clancy 1926- ... CANR-85
Earlier sketch in CA 1-4R
See also CLC 7
See also CN 1, 2, 3, 4, 5, 6, 7
Sigal, Leon V(ictor) 1942- ... 186
Brief entry ... 114
Sigaloff, Jane 1973- ... 220
Sigaud, Dominique 1959- ... 185
Sigband, Norman Bruce 1920- ... CANR-17
Earlier sketches in CA 5-8R, CANR-2
Sigel, Efrem 1943- ... 121
Sigelschiffer, Saul 1902-1994 ... 81-84
Siger of Brabant 1240(?)-1284(?) ... DLB 115
Sigerson, Davitt ... 237
Siggins, Lorna 1958- ... 169
Siggins, Maggie 1942- ... 165
Sigler, Hollis 1948-2001 ... 195
Sigler, Jamie-Lynn
See DiScala, Jamie-Lynn
Sigler, Jay A(drian) 1933- ... 25-28R
Sigler, John W(illiam) 1946- ... 127
Sigler, William F. ... 128
Sigmund, Paul E(ugene) 1929- ... CANR-39
Earlier sketches in CA 5-8R, CANR-2, 18
Signoret, Simone 1921-1985 ... 135
Obituary ... 117
Sigogo, Ndabezinhle S. 1932- ... CP 1
Sigourney, Andre R. ... 132
Sigourney, Lydia H.
See Sigourney, Lydia Howard (Huntley)
See also DLB 73, 183
Sigourney, Lydia Howard (Huntley) 1791-1865
See Sigourney, Lydia H. and Sigourney, Lydia Huntley
See also DLB 1
Sigourney, Lydia Huntley
See Sigourney, Lydia Howard (Huntley)
See also DLB 42, 239, 243
Siguenza y Gongora, Carlos de 1645-1700 ... HLCS 2
See also LAW
Sigurbjarnardottir, Jakobina 1883-1977
See Johnson, Jakobina
Sigurdardottir, Frida A. 1940- ... DLB 293
Sigurdardottir, Steinunn 1950- ... DLB 293
Sigurdsson, Olafur Johann 1918-1988 ... DLB 293
See also EWL 3
Sigurdsson, Stefan 1887-1933
See Hvitadal, Stefan fra
Sigurjonsson, Johann
See Sigurjonsson, Johann
Sigurjonsson, Johann 1880-1919 ... 170
See also DLB 293
See also EWL 3
See also TCLC 27
Sigworth, Oliver F(rederic) 1921- ... 13-16R
Sihanouk, Norodom
See Norodom Sihanouk (Varman), Samdech Preah
Siirala, Aarne 1919-1991 ... 13-16R
Sijie, Dai 1954- ... 208
Sik, Endre 1891-1978
Obituary ... 77-80
Sikelianos, Angelos 1884-1951 ... EWL 3
See also PC 29
See also RGWL 2, 3
See also TCLC 39
Sikelianos, Eleni ... 217
Sikes, Gini 1957- ... 239
Sikes, Herschel Moreland 1928- ... 17-20R
Sikes, Melvin P. 1917- ... 146
Sikes, Walter W(allace) 1925- ... 57-60
Sikora, Frank J(oseph) 1936- ... CANR-40
Earlier sketch in CA 115
Sikora, Joseph (John) 1932-1967 ... CAP-2
Earlier sketch in CA 17-18
Sikora, Stefan
See Rey, Michael Stephan
Sikorski, Radek (Tomasz) 1963- ... 164
Sikorsky, Igor I(van) 1889-1972 ... 157
Obituary ... 113
Sikov, Ed ... CANR-122
Earlier sketch in CA 189
Siks, Geraldine Brain 1912- ... 25-28R
Sikula, Andrew F(rank) 1944- ... CANR-2
Earlier sketch in CA 49-52
Silangan, Manuel
See Yabes, Leopoldo Y(abes)
Silard, Bela (A.) 1900- ... 140
Silas
See McCay, (Zenas) Winsor
Silbajoris, Frank
See Silbajoris, Rimvydas
Silbajoris, Rimvydas 1926- ... 25-28R
Silber, Diana 1936- ... 134
Silber, Evelyn (Ann) 1949- ... 124
Silber, Irwin 1925- ... 9-12R
Silber, Joan 1945- ... CANR-97
Earlier sketches in CA 104, CANR-20
Silber, Kate 1902-1979 ... 77-80
Silber, Mark 1946- ... CANR-43
Earlier sketch in CA 45-48
Silber, Nina 1959- ... 140
Silber, Norman I. 1951- ... 114
Silber, William L. 1942- ... CANR-29
Earlier sketch in CA 29-32R
Silberberg, R(ein) 1932-2001 ... 149
Obituary ... 201
Silberg, Moshe 1900-1975
Obituary ... 61-64
Silberg, Richard 1942- ... 21-24R
Silberger, Julius 1929- ... CANR-21
Earlier sketch in CA 105
Silberkleit, Louis Horace 1905-1986
Obituary ... 118
Silberman, Arlene ... 133
Silberman, Charles E(liot) 1925- ... CANR-7
Earlier sketch in CA 9-12R
Silberman, James H(enry) 1927- ... 133
Silberman, Jerome
See Wilder, Gene
Silberman, Marc (D.) 1948- ... 162
Silberman, Neil Asher 1950- ... CANR-102
Earlier sketch in CA 108
Silberman, Robert (Bruce) 1950- ... 206
Silbermann, Eileen Z(ieget) 1925- ... 114
Silbersack, John (Walter) 1954- ... CANR-33
Earlier sketch in CA 107
Silberschlag, Eisig 1903-1988 ... CANR-17
Earlier sketches in CA 1-4R, CANR-1
Silberschmidt, Max 1899- ... 65-68
Silberstang, Edwin 1930- ... CANR-3
Earlier sketch in CA 49-52
Silberstein, Gerard Edward 1926- ... 37-40R
Silberstein, Howard E. 1907(?)-1984
Obituary ... 112
Silberstein, Warren P(aul) 1948- ... 110
Silberstein-Storfer, Muriel (Rosoff) ... 111
Silbey, Joel H. 1933- ... 21-24R
Silbiger, Alexander 1935- ... 136
Silcock, Sara Lesley 1947- ... SATA 12
Silcock, Thomas H(enry) 1910- ... 9-12R
Silcox, David Phillips 1937- ... 109
Silen, Juan Angel 1938- ... 33-36R
Siler, Jenny 1971- ... 217
Silesky, Barry 1949- ... CANR-112
Earlier sketch in CA 135
See also CAAS 29
Silet, Charles L(oring) P(rovine) 1942- ... CANR-108
Earlier sketches in CA 93-96, CANR-17
Silex, Edgar Gabriel 1958- ... 150
Silinsh, Edgar A. 1927- ... 152
Siliotti, Alberto 1950- ... 169
Silitch, Clarissa MacVeagh 1930- ... CANR-31
Earlier sketch in CA 112
Silje, Par
See Gyllensten, Lars (Johan Wictor)
Silk, Andrew 1953(?)-1981
Obituary ... 106
Silk, Dennis (Peter) 1928-1998 ... 161
See also CP 7
Silk, Gerald 1947- ... CANR-82
Earlier sketch in CA 133
Silk, Joseph (Ivor) 1942- ... 149
Silk, Leonard S(olomon) 1918-1995 ... CANR-46
Obituary ... 147
Earlier sketches in CA 1-4R, CANR-4
Silke, James R. ... FANT
Silkin, Jon 1930-1997 ... CANR-89
Earlier sketch in CA 5-8R
See also CAAS 5
See also CLC 2, 6, 43
See also CP 1, 2, 3, 4, 5, 6
See also DLB 27
Silko, Leslie (Marmon) 1948- ... CANR-118
Brief entry ... 115
Earlier sketches in CA 122, CANR-45, 65
See also AAYA 14
See also AMWS 4
See also ANW
See also BYA 12
See also CLC 23, 74, 114, 211
See also CN 4, 5, 6, 7
See also CP 7
See also CPW 1
See also CWP
See also DA
See also DA3
See also DAC
See also DAM MST, MULT, POP
See also DLB 143, 175, 256, 275
See also EWL 3
See also EXPP
See also EXPS
See also LAIT 4
See also MAL 5
See also MTCW 2
See also MTFW 2005
See also NFS 4
See also NNAL
See also PFS 9, 16
See also RGAL 4
See also RGSF 2
See also SSC 37, 66
See also SSFS 4, 8, 10, 11
See also TCWW 1, 2
See also WLCS
Sill, Cathryn 1953- ... 212
See also SATA 74, 141
Sill, Geoffrey M(ichael) 1944- ... 111
Sill, Gertrude Grace ... 69-72
Sill, John 1947- ... 211
See also SATA 74, 140
Sill, Sterling Welling 1903-1994 ... CANR-6
Earlier sketch in CA 57-60
Sillanpaa, Frans Eemil 1888-1964 ... 129
Obituary ... 93-96
See also CLC 19
See also EWL 3
See also MTCW 1
Sillars, Stuart 1951- ... 205
Sillem, Edward 1916-1964 ... 5-8R
Sillen, Samuel 1911(?)-1973
Obituary ... 41-44R
Sillery, Anthony 1903-1976 ... CANR-5
Obituary ... 65-68
Earlier sketch in CA 5-8R
Silliker, Bill, Jr. 1947- ... 181
Silliman, Benjamin 1779-1864 ... DLB 183
Silliman, Ron(ald Glenn) 1946- ... CANR-115
Earlier sketches in CA 45-48, CANR-46, 85
See also CAAS 29
See also CP 7
See also DLB 169
Silliphant, Stirling (Dale) 1918-1996 ... CANR-130
Obituary ... 152
Earlier sketches in CA 73-76, CANR-14, 42
See also DLB 26
Sillitoe, Alan 1928- ... 191
Earlier sketches in CA 9-12R, CANR-8, 26, 55, 139
Autobiographical Essay in ... 191
See also CAAS 2
See also AITN 1
See also BRWS 5
See also CDBLB 1960 to Present
See also CLC 1, 3, 6, 10, 19, 57, 148
See also CN 1, 2, 3, 4, 5, 6
See also CP 1, 2
See also DLB 14, 139
See also EWL 3
See also MTCW 1, 2
See also MTFW 2005
See also RGEL 2
See also RGSF 2
See also SATA 61
Sillitoe, Linda 1948- ... 152
Sillman, Leonard (Dexter) 1908-1982
Obituary ... 105
Sills, Beverly 1929- ... 89-92
Sills, David Lawrence 1920- ... 33-36R
Sills, Frank D(reyer) 1914- ... 1-4R
Sills, Jennifer
See Lewis, Stephen
Sills, Judith 1948(?)- ... 144
Sills, Leslie (Elka) 1948- ... CANR-109
Earlier sketch in CA 130
See also SATA 129
Sills, Ruth C(urtis) ... 29-32R
Sills, Vaughn 1946- ... 217
Silly, E. S.
See Kraus, (Herman) Robert
Silman, Roberta 1934- ... 101
See also DLB 28
Silone, Ignazio 1900-1978 ... CANR-34
Obituary ... 81-84
Earlier sketches in CAP-2, CA 25-28
See also CLC 4
See also DLB 264
See also EW 12
See also EWL 3
See also MTCW 1
See also RGSF 2
See also RGWL 2, 3
Silone, Ignazione
See Silone, Ignazio
Silsbe, Brenda 1953- ... SATA 73
Siltanen
See Aho, Juhani
Siluriensis, Leolinus
See Jones, Arthur Llewellyn
Silva, Beverly 1935- ... CANR-95
Earlier sketch in CA 131
See also DLB 122
See also HW 1
Silva, Clara 1905-1976 ... DLB 290
Silva, Daniel ... 173
Silva, David B. 1950- ... 202
See also HGG
Silva, Eduardo Neale
See Neale-Silva, Eduardo
Silva, Jose Asuncion 1865-1896 ... DLB 283
See also LAW
Silva, Joseph
See Goulart, Ron(ald Joseph)
Silva, Julian 1927- ... 115
Silva, Julio A(lberto) 1933- ... 17-20R
Silva, Ruth C(aridad) 1920-1995 ... 13-16R
Obituary ... 148
Silvanus
See Strasser, Bernard Paul
Silvaroli, Nicholas J. 1930- ... CANR-12
Earlier sketch in CA 29-32R
Silveira de Queiroz, Dinah 1911-1982 ... LAW
Silver, A(aron) David 1941- ... 124
Silver, A(aron) Henry 1891-1986
Obituary ... 121
Silver, Abba Hillel 1893-1963 ... 1-4R
Silver, Alain (Joel) 1947- ... CANR-10
Earlier sketch in CA 57-60
Silver, Alfred 1951- ... CANR-15
Earlier sketch in CA 85-88
Silver, Anna Krugovoy ... 227
Silver, Brenda R. 1942- ... 202
Silver, Carol ... GLL 1
Silver, Carole G(reta) 1937- ... 132
Silver, Daniel Jeremy 1928-1989 ... CANR-86
Obituary ... 130
Earlier sketches in CA 5-8R, CANR-3
Silver, Gary (Thomas) 1944- ... 89-92
Silver, Gerald A(lbert) 1932- ... CANR-58
Earlier sketches in CA 33-36R, CANR-13, 30
Silver, Harold 1928- ... CANR-10
Earlier sketch in CA 21-24R
Silver, Isidore 1934- ... 53-56
Silver, James W(esley) 1907-1988 ... 9-12R
Obituary ... 126
Silver, Joan Micklin 1935- ... 121
Brief entry ... 114
Interview in ... CA-121
See also CLC 20
Silver, Jody 1942- ... 109
Silver, Lee M(errill) 1952- ... CANR-124
Earlier sketch in CA 169
Silver, Marisa 1960- ... 203
Silver, Marjorie A. 1948- ... 93-96
Silver, Nathan 1936- ... CANR-11
Earlier sketch in CA 21-24R
Silver, Nicholas
See Faust, Frederick (Schiller)
Silver, Norman 1946- ... YAW
Silver, Pat
See Carleton, Barbara
Silver, Philip Warnock 1932- ... CANR-91
Earlier sketch in CA 106

Cumulative Index 533 Simon

Silver, Richard
  See Bulmer, (Henry) Kenneth
Silver, Rollo G(abriel) 1909-1989 .... CAP-1
  Earlier sketch in CA 19-20
Silver, Roy R. 1918-1979
  Obituary 89-92
Silver, Ruth
  See Chew, Ruth
Silver, Samuel 1915(?)-1976
  Obituary 69-72
Silver, Samuel M. 1912- CANR-11
  Earlier sketch in CA 21-24R
Silver, Warren A. 1914- 65-68
Silvera, Alain 1930- 21-24R
Silvera, Makeda 1955- 220
  See also GLL 2
Silverberg, Ira 1962- 139
Silverberg, Robert 1935- 186
  Earlier sketches in CA 1-4R, CANR-1, 20, 36, 85, 140
  Interview in CANR-20
  Autobiographical Essay in 186
  See also CAAS 3
  See also AAYA 24
  See also BPFB 3
  See also BYA 7, 9
  See also CLC 7, 140
  See also CLR 59
  See also CN 6, 7
  See also CPW
  See also DAM POP
  See also DLB 8
  See also MAICYA 1, 2
  See also MTCW 1, 2
  See also MTFW 2005
  See also SATA 13, 91
  See also SATA-Essay 104
  See also SCFW 1, 2
  See also SFW 4
  See also SUFW 2
Silverblatt, Art 1949- 175
Silverburg, Sanford R. 1940- 143
Silverglate, Harvey A. 1942- 210
Silverlock, Anne
  See Titchener, Louise
Silverman, Al 1926- 9-12R
Silverman, Alvin Michaels 1912-1999 .... 9-12R
  Obituary 174
Silverman, Burt(on Philip) 1928- 103
Silverman, Corinne 1930- 5-8R
Silverman, David 1907- CAP-2
  Earlier sketch in CA 21-22
Silverman, Erica 1955- 184
  See also SATA 78, 112
Silverman, Franklin H(arold) 1933- 195
Silverman, Gerry 1938- 133
Silverman, Harold M(artin) 1945- 112
Silverman, Hillel E. 1924- CANR-11
  Earlier sketch in CA 21-24R
Silverman, Hirsch Lazaar 1915- 45-48
Silverman, Hugh J(erald) 1945- 118
Silverman, Janis L. 1946- 197
  See also SATA 127
Silverman, Jason H(oward) 1952- ... CANR-107
  Earlier sketch in CA 110
Silverman, Jerry 1931- CANR-7
  Earlier sketch in CA 13-16R
Silverman, Jonathan 1955- 138
Silverman, Joseph H(erman) 1924- 170
Silverman, Judith 1933- 103
Silverman, Kaja 1947- CANR-123
  Earlier sketch in CA 132
  See also DLB 246
Silverman, Kenneth 1936- CANR-128
  Earlier sketches in CA 57-60, CANR-17, 71
  See also DLB 111
Silverman, Mark Philip 1945- CANR-119
  Earlier sketch in CA 147
Silverman, Mel(vin Frank) 1931-1966 .... 5-8R
  See also SATA 9
Silverman, Milton (M.) 1910-1997 152
Silverman, Milton J. 1944- 108
Silverman, Morris 1894-1972
  Obituary 33-36R
Silverman, Oscar Ansell 1903-1977
  Obituary 69-72
Silverman, Robert A(llan) 1943- 57-60
Silverman, Robert E(ugene) 1924- 41-44R
Silverman, Robert J(ay) 1940- 101
Silverman, Robin L(andew) 1954- 161
  See also SATA 96
Silverman, Rose
  See Millstein, Rose Silverman
Silverman, S(ol) Richard 1911-2000 107
Silverman, Samuel .... AITN 1
Silverman, Stephen M. 1951- 135
Silverman, Sue William 1946- 212
Silverman, Sydel 1933- 77-80
Silverman, Sylvia W. 1907-1992 139
Silverman, Willa Z. 1959- 155
Silverman, William B. 1913-2001 49-52
Silvern, Leonard C. 1919- CANR-7
  Earlier sketch in CA 17-20R
Silvers, Phil
  See Silversmith, Philip
Silvers, Robert B. 1929- CANR-116
  Earlier sketch in CA 165
Silvers, Vicki 1941- 93-96
Silversmith, Philip 1912-1985
  Obituary 117
  Brief entry 111
Silverstein, Alvin 1933- CANR-2
  Earlier sketch in CA 49-52
  See also CLC 17
  See also CLR 25
  See also JRDA
  See also MAICYA 1, 2
  See also SATA 8, 69, 124
Silverstein, Charles 1935- 73-76
Silverstein, Herma 1945- 176
  See also SATA 106
Silverstein, Josef 1922- CANR-58
  Earlier sketches in CA 37-40R, CANR-14, 31
Silverstein, Mel(vin Jerome) 1940- 101
Silverstein, Norman 1922-1974 .... 37-40R
  Obituary 49-52
Silverstein, Robert Alan 1959- ..... SATA 77, 124
Silverstein, Shel(don Allan)
  1932-1999 .... CANR-81
  Obituary 179
  Earlier sketches in CA 107, CANR-47, 74
  See also AAYA 40
  See also BW 3
  See also CLR 5, 96
  See also CWRI 5
  See also JRDA
  See also MAICYA 1, 2
  See also MTCW 2
  See also MTFW 2005
  See also PC 49
  See also SATA 33, 92
  See also SATA-Brief 27
  See also SATA-Obit 116
Silverstein, (Hyman) Theodore 1904-2001 . 106
  Obituary 202
Silverstein, Virginia B(arbara Opshelor)
  1937- CANR-2
  Earlier sketch in CA 49-52
  See also CLC 17
  See also CLR 25
  See also JRDA
  See also MAICYA 1, 2
  See also SATA 8, 69, 124
Silverstone, Lou 1928- 108
Silverstone, Paul H. 1931- 21-24R
Silvert, Kalman H(irsch) 1921-1976 ... CANR-6
  Obituary 65-68
  Earlier sketch in CA 13-16R
Silverthorn, J(ames) E(dwin) 1906- CAP-1
  Earlier sketch in CA 13-16
Silverthorne, Elizabeth 1930- 89-92
  See also SATA 35
Silverton, Michael 1935- 65-68
Silverton, Nancy 1954- 164
Silverwood, Jane
  See Titchener, Louise
Silverwood, Margaret Shannon
  1966- CANR-116
  Earlier sketch in CA 150
  See also SATA 83, 137
Silvester, Christopher (Paul Victor) 1959- 167
Silvester, Frank
  See Bingley, David Ernest
Silvester, P(eter) P. 1935-1996 135
Silvester, Peter (John) 1934- 133
Silvester, Victor CAP-1
  Earlier sketch in CA 13-14
Silvestri, Richard 1944- 81-84
Silvey, Anita 1947- 237
Silvey, Diane F. 1946- 204
  See also SATA 135
Silving, Helen 1906- 41-44R
Silvis, Randall 1950- CANR-107
  Earlier sketch in CA 136
Silvius, G(eorge) Harold 1908-1981 ... CANR-3
  Obituary 104
  Earlier sketch in CA 5-8R
Sim, David 1953- .... SATA 162
Sim, Dorrith M. 1931- 161
  See also SATA 96
Sim, Georges
  See Simenon, Georges (Jacques Christian)
Sim, John Cameron 1911-1990 .... 25-28R
  Obituary 132
Sim, Katharine (Thomasset) 1913- 13-16R
Sim, Myre 1915- 61-64
Sim, Yawsoon 1937- 108
Sima, Carol Ann 1956- 216
Simak, Clifford D(onald)
  1904-1988 .... CANR-35
  Obituary 125
  Earlier sketches in CA 1-4R, CANR-1
  See also CLC 1, 55
  See also DLB 8
  See also MTCW 1
  See also SATA-Obit 56
  See also SCFW 1, 2
  See also SFW 4
Simard, Real 1951- 129
Simbari, Nicola 1927- CANR-1
  Earlier sketch in CA 1-4R
Simbeck, Rob 1952- 236
Simckes, L(azarre) S(eymour) 1937- 9-12R
Simcoe, Elizabeth 1762-1850 .... DLB 99
Simcox, Carroll E(ugene) 1912- 132
Simcox, Edith Jemima 1844-1901 ...... DLB 190
Simcox, George Augustus 1841-1905 220
  See also DLB 35
Sime, Georgina
  See Sime, Jessie Georgina
Sime, Jessie Georgina 1868-1958 180
  See also DLB 92
Sime, Mary 1911- 53-56
Simecka, Martin M. 1957- 151
Simenon, Georges (Jacques Christian)
  1903-1989 .... CANR-35
  Obituary 129
  Earlier sketch in CA 85-88
  See also BPFB 3
  See also CLC 1, 2, 3, 8, 18, 47
  See also CMW 4
  See also DA3
  See also DAM POP
  See also DLB 72
  See also DLBY 1989
  See also EW 12
  See also EWL 3
  See also GFL 1789 to the Present
  See also MSW
  See also MTCW 1, 2
  See also MTFW 2005
  See also RGWL 2, 3
Simeon, Mother Mary 1888- CAP-1
  Earlier sketch in CA 13-14
Simeon, Richard 1943- CANR-9
  Earlier sketch in CA 61-64
Simeone, Diane A. 1953(?)-1983
  Obituary 109
Simes, Dimitri (Konstantin) 1947- 195
Simeti, Mary Taylor 1941- CANR-114
  Earlier sketch in CA 144
Simic, Andrei 1930- 93-96
Simic, Charles 1938- CANR-140
  Earlier sketches in CA 29-32R, CANR-12, 33, 52, 61, 96
  See also CAAS 4
  See also AMWS 8
  See also CLC 6, 9, 22, 49, 68, 130
  See also CP 2, 3, 4, 5, 6, 7
  See also DA3
  See also DAM POET
  See also DLB 105
  See also MAL 5
  See also MTCW 2
  See also MTFW 2005
  See also PFS 7
  See also RGAL 4
  See also WP
Simic, Goran 1952- 168
Simini, Joseph Peter 1921- CANR-8
  Earlier sketch in CA 17-20R
Simionescu, Mircea Horia 1928- .... DLB 232
Simirenko, Alex 1931- 13-16R
Simis, Konstantin 1919- 130
Simister, Florence Parker 1913-1981 .. CANR-2
  Earlier sketch in CA 5-8R
Simkin, C(olin) G(eorge) F(rederick)
  1915- 29-32R
Simkin, Penny 1938- 116
Simkin, Tom 1933- CANR-87
  Earlier sketch in CA 132
Simkin, William E(dward) 1907- 45-48
Simkins, Lawrence D(avid) 1933-1998 . 41-44R
Simley, Anne 1891-1992 .... 5-8R
Simmel, Edward C(lemens) 1932- CANR-31
  Earlier sketch in CA 45-48
Simmel, Georg 1858-1918 157
  See also DLB 296
  See also TCLC 64
Simmel, Johannes M(ario) 1924- 81-84
  See also DLB 69
Simmel, Marianne L(enore) 1923- 21-24R
Simmes, Valentine fl. 1589(?)-1623(?) . DLB 170
Simmie, James Martin 1941- CANR-38
  Earlier sketch in CA 115
Simmie, Lois (Ann) 1932- CANR-137
  Earlier sketch in CA 165
  See also SATA 106
Simmonds, A(ndrew) J(effrey) 1943- 81-84
Simmonds, George W. 1929- 21-24R
Simmonds, James D(udley) 1933- 104
Simmonds, John 1942- 135
Simmonds, Posy 1945- 199
  See also CLR 23
  See also SATA 130
Simmonds, Walter H(enry) C(live) 1917- 118
Simmons, A(lan) John 1950- 106
Simmons, Andra 1939- 212
  See also SATA 141
Simmons, Anthony 1922- 103
Simmons, Billy E. 1931- CANR-10
  Earlier sketch in CA 21-24R
Simmons, Blake
  See Wallmann, Jeffrey M(iner)
Simmons, Cal 1951(?)- 203
Simmons, Charles (Paul) 1924- 89-92
  Interview in CA-89-92
  See also CLC 57
Simmons, Charles A(lexander) 1933- 170
Simmons, Cynthia Francene 1949- 231
Simmons, D(avid) R(oy) 1930- CANR-118
  Earlier sketches in CA 110, CANR-28, 56
Simmons, Dan 1948- CANR-126
  Earlier sketches in CA 138, CANR-53, 81
  See also AAYA 16, 54
  See also CLC 44
  See also CPW
  See also DAM POP
  See also HGG
  See also SUFW 2
Simmons, David
  See Gold, Alan R(obert)
Simmons, Dawn Langley 1923(?)-2000 . 29-32R
  Obituary 189
Simmons, Diane E. 1948- 202
Simmons, Earl 1970- 235
Simmons, Edwin Howard 1921- 89-92
Simmons, Elly 1955- .... SATA 134
Simmons, Ernest J(oseph) 1903-1972 , CANR-3
  Earlier sketch in CA 1-4R
  See also DLB 103
Simmons, Geoffrey 1943- 104
Simmons, Gloria Mitchell 1932-1993 ... 37-40R
  Obituary 143
Simmons, Henry T. 1927(?)-1986
  Obituary 120
Simmons, Herbert A(lfred) 1930- 1-4R
  See also BW 1
  See also DLB 33
Simmons, Ian 1937- 106
Simmons, J(oseph) Edgar (Jr.)
  1921-1979 .... CANR-49
  Earlier sketch in CA 21-24R
Simmons, J(erry) L(aird) 1933- 29-32R
Simmons, Jack 1915-2000 .... CANR-38
  Obituary 189
  Earlier sketches in CA 5-8R, CANR-2
Simmons, James (Stewart Alexander)
  1933- 105
  See also CAAS 21
  See also CLC 43
  See also CP 1, 2, 3, 4, 5, 6, 7
  See also DLB 40
Simmons, James C(oleman) 1939- 144
Simmons, James E(dwin) 1923- 41-44R
Simmons, James W(illiam) 1936- CANR-12
  Earlier sketch in CA 17-20R
Simmons, Jane 231
Simmons, Jerold L. 1941- 129
Simmons, John Edwards 1918-1986
  Obituary 121
Simmons, Joseph Larry 1935- 65-68
Simmons, Judy Dothard 1944- 77-80
Simmons, Mabel Clark 1899-1988
  Obituary 124
Simmons, Marc 1937- CANR-51
  Earlier sketches in CA 25-28R, CANR-10, 26
Simmons, Mary Kay 1933- 81-84
Simmons, Matty 1926- 29-32R
Simmons, Merle Edwin 1918- CANR-2
  Earlier sketch in CA 5-8R
Simmons, Michael 1935- CANR-66
  Earlier sketch in CA 128
Simmons, Otis D(avis) 1928- 57-60
Simmons, Ozzie Gordon 1919-1988 ...... 9-12R
  Obituary 127
Simmons, Patricia A. 1930- 93-96
Simmons, Paul D(ewayne) 1936- CANR-58
  Earlier sketches in CA 45-48, CANR-31
Simmons, Richard 1948- 192
Simmons, Robert R. 1940- 97-100
Simmons, S. H.
  See Simmons, Sylvia
Simmons, Suzanne 1946- 200
Simmons, Sylvia 49-52
Simmons, Thomas 1956- 150
Simmons, Trana Mae 220
Simmons, William S(cranton) 1938- 121
Simms, Anastatia 1953- 170
Simms, Brendan 216
Simms, D(enton) Harper 1912-2001 ..... 29-32R
Simms, Eric Arthur 1921- 101
Simms, George (Otto) 1910-1991 ..... CANR-25
  Obituary 136
  Earlier sketch in CA 108
Simms, Laura 1947- 182
  See also SATA 117
Simms, Michael 1954- 208
Simms, Peter (F. J.) 1925- 21-24R
Simms, Ruth P. 1937- 17-20R
Simms, Suzanne
  See Simmons, Suzanne
Simms, Willard S. 1943- 29-32R
Simms, William Gilmore 1806-1870 ..... DLB 3, 30, 59, 73, 248, 254
  See also RGAL 4
Simner, Janni Lee 176
  See also SATA 113
Simon, Alfred (Edward) 1907-1991 .... 41-44R
  Obituary 134
Simon, Alvah 1950(?)- 234
Simon, Andre (Louis) 1877-1970
  Obituary 29-32R
Simon, Andrea 1945- 212
Simon, Anne Elizabeth 1956- 195
Simon, Anne W(ertheim) 1914-1996 105
  Obituary 152
Simon, Arthur 1930- 33-36R
Simon, Barney 1933- .... CD 5, 6
Simon, Bennett 1933- 101
Simon, Boris-Jean 1913(?)-1972
  Obituary 33-36R
Simon, Carl P(aul) 1945- 107
Simon, Carly 1945- 105
  See also CLC 26
Simon, Charlie May
  See Fletcher, Charlie May Hogue
Simon, Christopher Fitz
  See Fitz-Simon, Christopher
Simon, Claude (Eugene Henri)
  1913-2005 .... CANR-117
  Earlier sketches in CA 89-92, CANR-33
  See also CLC 4, 9, 15, 39
  See also CWW 2
  See also DAM NOV
  See also DLB 83
  See also EW 13
  See also EWL 3
  See also GFL 1789 to the Present
  See also MTCW 1
Simon, Clea 1961- 214
Simon, Daniel (Martin) 1957- 147
Simon, David 1960- CANR-139
  Earlier sketch in CA 136
  See also MTFW 2005
Simon, David R(eese) 1944- 223
Simon, Diane 227

Simon, Disney
See Simon, Sidney B.
Simon, Eckehard 1939- 61-64
Simon, Edith 1917- 13-16R
Simon, Francesca 1955- CANR-142
Earlier sketch in CA 172
See also SATA 111
Simon, Fritz B(ernhard) 1948- 156
Simon, Gabriel 1972- SATA 118
Simon, George T(homas)
1912-2001 CANR-17
Obituary 193
Earlier sketch in CA 25-28R
Simon, Harvey B(ruce) 1942- 217
Simon, Henry W(illiam) 1901-1970 CANR-4
Obituary 29-32R
Earlier sketch in CA 5-8R
Simon, Herbert 1898(?)-1974
Obituary 53-56
Simon, Herbert A(lexander)
1916-2001 CANR-85
Obituary 193
Earlier sketches in CA 13-16R, CANR-9, 49
Simon, Hilda Rita 1921- 77-80
See also CLR 39
See also SATA 28
Simon, Howard 1903-1979 33-36R
Obituary 89-92
See also SATA 32
See also SATA-Obit 21
Simon, Hubert K. 1917- 13-16R
Simon, James
See Elliott, Bill
Simon, James E(dward) 1954- CANR-44
Earlier sketch in CA 119
Simon, James F. 1939- CANR-111
Earlier sketch in CA 134
Simon, Jo Ann 1946- 106
Simon, Joan L. 1921- 13-16R
Simon, Joe
See Simon, Joseph H.
Simon, John (Ivan) 1925- 21-24R
Simon, John G. 1928- 37-40R
Simon, John Y. 1933- CANR-53
Earlier sketches in CA 25-28R, CANR-12, 29
Simon, Joseph H. 1913- 29-32R
See also SATA 7
Simon, Julian L(incoln) 1932-1998 CANR-45
Obituary 165
Earlier sketch in CA 33-36R
Simon, Kate (Grobsmith)
1912-1990 CANR-61
Obituary 130
Brief entry 115
Earlier sketch in CA 127
Interview in CA-127
See also MTCW 1
Simon, Leonard 1922- 9-12R
Simon, Linda 1946- CANR-13
Earlier sketch in CA 73-76
Simon, Lizzie 1975(?)- 235
Simon, Lorena Cotts 1897-1995 5-8R
Simon, Louis M(ortimer) 1906-1996 77-80
Obituary 154
Simon, Marcia L. 1939- 93-96
Simon, Martin P(aul William)
1903-1969 CAP-1
Earlier sketch in CA 11-12
See also SATA 12
Simon, Mary of the Angels 1897(?)-1985
Obituary 116
Simon, Matila 1908-1997 17-20R
Simon, Michael 1963- 236
Simon, Michael A(rthur) 1936- CANR-13
Earlier sketch in CA 33-36R
Simon, Mina Lewiton
See Lewiton, Mina
Simon, Morton J. 1913-1996 17-20R
Simon, Myles
See Follett, Ken(neth Martin)
Simon, (Marvin) Neil 1927- CANR-126
Earlier sketches in CA 21-24R, CANR-26, 54, 87
See also AAYA 32
See also AITN 1
See also AMWS 4
See also CAD
See also CD 5, 6
See also CLC 6, 11, 31, 39, 70
See also DA3
See also DAM DRAM
See also DC 14
See also DFS 2, 6, 12, 18
See also DLB 7, 266
See also LAIT 4
See also MAL 5
See also MTCW 1, 2
See also MTFW 2005
See also RGAL 4
See also TUS
Simon, Norma (Feldstein) 1927- CANR-109
Earlier sketches in CA 5-8R, CANR-6, 21, 44
See also MAICYA 1, 2
See also SATA 3, 68, 129
Simon, Paul (Martin) 1928-2003 CANR-43
Obituary 222
Earlier sketch in CA 81-84
Simon, Paul (Frederick) 1941(?)- 153
Brief entry 116
See also CLC 17
Simon, Pierre-Henri 1903-1972
Obituary 37-40R
Simon, Rachel 1959- 217
Simon, Rita James 1931- CANR-8
Earlier sketch in CA 21-24R
Simon, Robert
See Musto, Barry
Simon, Robert A. 1897(?)-1981
Obituary 103
Simon, Robin (John Hughes) 1947- 128
Simon, Roger 1948- 169
Simon, Roger David 1943- 109
Simon, Roger L(ichtenberg) 1943- CANR-136
Earlier sketches in CA 137, CANR-63
See also CMW 4
Simon, Samuel A(lan) 1945- 117
Simon, Scott 1952- 193
Simon, Seymour 1931- CANR-117
Earlier sketches in CA 25-28R, CANR-11, 29
See also CLR 9, 63
See also MAICYA 1, 2
See also SATA 4, 73, 138
Simon, Sheldon W(eiss) 1937- CANR-51
Earlier sketches in CA 25-28R, CANR-10, 26
Simon, Shirley (Schwartz) 1921- CANR-16
Earlier sketches in CA 1-4R, CANR-1
See also SATA 11
Simon, Sidney B(lair) 1927- 101
Simon, Sidney B. 1927- 21-24R
Simon, Solomon 1895-1970
Obituary 104
See also SATA 40
Simon, (Edward) Ted 1931- 105
Simon, Tony 1921- 5-8R
Simon, Ulrich E(rnst) 1913-1997 29-32R
Obituary 159
Simon, Uriel 1929- CANR-130
Earlier sketch in CA 168
Simon, Walter G(old) 1924- 17-20R
Simon, William 1927- 9-12R
Simon, William E(dward) 1927-2000 81-84
Obituary 188
Simon, William L(eonard) 1930- 210
Simonds, John Ormsbee 1913- 77-80
Simonds, Merilyn 1949- 193
Simonds, Roger (Tyrrell) 1929- 93-96
Simonds, Rollin Head 1910- 1-4R
Simonds, William Adams 1887-1963(?) CAP-1
Earlier sketch in CA 11-12
Simone
See Porche, Simone (Benda)
Simone, Albert Joseph 1935- 17-20R
Simone, Charles B(rian) 1949- 116
Simonelli, Frederick J. 189
Simonelli, Jeanne M(arie) 1947- 170
Simonelli, Maria Picchio 1921- 49-52
Simonet, Thomas Solon 1942- 116
Simonetta, Joseph R. 1943- 217
Simonetta, Linda 1948- 77-80
See also SATA 14
Simonetta, Sam 1936- 77-80
See also SATA 14
Simonhoff, Harry 1891-1966 5-8R
Simoni, John Peter 1911-
Brief entry 106
Simonin, Albert (Charles) 1905-1980
Obituary 104
Simonini, R(inaldo) C(harles), Jr.
1922-1967 CAP-1
Earlier sketch in CA 11-12
Simonon, Paul 1956(?)- CLC 30
Simonov, Konstantin (Kirill) Mikhailovich
1915-1979
Obituary 89-92
See also Simonov, Konstantin Mikhaylovich
See also DLB 302
Simonov, Konstantin Mikhaylovich
See Simonov, Konstantin (Kirill) Mikhailovich
See also EWL 3
Simons, Barbara B(rooks) 1934- 108
See also SATA 41
Simons, Beverley 1938- 104
See also CD 5, 6
See also CWD
Simons, David G(oodman) 1922- 17-20R
Simons, Donald L. 1945- 138
Simons, Elwyn LaVerne 1930- CANR-22
Earlier sketch in CA 105
Simons, Eric N(orman) 1896- 13-16R
Simons, Geoff(rey Leslie) 1939- 182
Simons, Hans 1893-1972
Obituary 33-36R
Simons, Harry 1912-1997 1-4R
Simons, Howard 1929-1989 65-68
Obituary 128
Simons, James Marcus 1939- 106
Simons, Jim
See Simons, James Marcus
Simons, John D(onald) 1935- 41-44R
Simons, Joseph 1933- 81-84
Simons, Katherine Drayton Mayrant
1892(?)-1969 9-12R
Obituary 112
See also DLBY 1983
Simons, Lewis M(artin) 1939- 128
Brief entry 123
Interview in CA-128
Simons, Margaret A. 1946- 157
Simons, Michelle Blake 195
Simons, Myron (Bud) 1920- 113
Simons, Paullina 1963- 204
Simons, Rae
See Sanna, Ellyn
Simons, Rita Dandridge
See Dandridge, Rita B(ernice)
Simons, Robin 1951- 65-68
Simons, Thomas G(erald) 1950- 111
Simons, Thomas W(inston), Jr. 1938- 134
Simons, William Edward 1927- 17-20R
Simonsen, Thordis 1944- 145
Simonson, Conrad 1931- 49-52
Simonson, Eric 1960- 214
Simonson, Harold P(eter) 1926- 33-36R
Simonson, Lee 1888-1967 9-12R
Simonson, Mary Jane
See Wheeler, Mary Jane
Simonson, Rick ed. CLC 70
Simonson, Solomon S. 1914- 21-24R
Simont, Marc 1915- CANR-106
Earlier sketches in CA 61-64, CANR-38, 86
See also MAICYA 1, 2
See also SATA 9, 73, 126
Simontacchi, Carol 1947- 165
Simonton, Dean Keith 1948- CANR-43
Earlier sketch in CA 119
Simonton, Stephanie
See Matthews-Simonton, Stephanie
Simoons, Frederick J. 1922- CANR-23
Earlier sketch in CA 1-4R
Simos, Miriam 1951- 104
See also FW
Simosko, Vladimir 1943- 200
Simper, Robert 1937- CANR-46
Earlier sketches in CA 61-64, CANR-8, 23
Simpich, Frederick, Jr. 1911-1975 61-64
Obituary 57-60
Simpkin, Richard E(velyn) 1921-1986 124
Simplex
See Kusenberg, Kurt
Simpson, A(lfred) W. Brian 1931- CANR-96
Earlier sketches in CA 5-8R, CANR-46
Simpson, Adrienne 1943- 235
Simpson, Alan 1912-1998 CANR-30
Obituary 169
Earlier sketch in CA 1-4R
Simpson, Allen 1934- 208
Simpson, Anne 1956- 227
Simpson, Brooks D. 208
Simpson, Cedric Keith 1907-1985 111
Obituary 117
Simpson, Claude M(itchell), Jr.
1910-1976 5-8R
Obituary 65-68
Simpson, Colin 1908-1983 CANR-5
Earlier sketch in CA 53-56
See also SATA 14
Simpson, Craig M(ichael) 1942- 119
Simpson, D(avid) P(enistan) 1917- 9-12R
Simpson, Dick 1940- CANR-30
Earlier sketches in CA 33-36R, CANR-13
Simpson, Doris 1913- CANR-68
Simpson, Dorothy 1933- CANR-95
Earlier sketches in CA 107, CANR-30, 62
Interview in CANR-30
See also CMW 4
See also MTCW 1
Simpson, E(rvin) P(eter) Y(oung)
1911-2000 17-20R
Simpson, Eileen (Patricia) B(erryman)
1918-2002 139
Obituary 214
Simpson, Elizabeth 1947- 163
Simpson, Elizabeth Alice Hilts 1921-1989
Obituary 130
Simpson, Elizabeth Leonie 33-36R
Simpson, Ethel 1937- 117
Simpson, (John) Evan 1940- 97-100
Simpson, George E(dward) 1944- 101
Simpson, George Eaton 1904-1998 77-80
Simpson, George Gaylord
1902-1984 CANR-61
Obituary 114
Earlier sketches in CAP-1, CA 19-20, CANR-16
See also MTCW 1
Simpson, Harold Brown 1917- CANR-4
Earlier sketch in CA 9-12R
Simpson, Harriette
See Arnow, Harriette (Louisa) Simpson
Simpson, Hassell A(lgernon) 1930- 41-44R
Simpson, Helen (De Guerry) 1897-1940
Brief entry 109
See also DLB 77
Simpson, Helen 1957- CANR-106
Earlier sketches in CA 134, CANR-56
Simpson, Hilary 1954- 131
Simpson, Howard Russell
1925-1999 CANR-1
Obituary 179
Earlier sketch in CA 1-4R
Simpson, Ian J(ames) 1895- CAP-1
Earlier sketch in CA 13-14
Simpson, Ida Harper 1928- 17-20R
Simpson, Jacqueline (Mary) 1930- CANR-103
Earlier sketches in CA 13-16R, CANR-5
Simpson, Jacynth Hope
See Hope Simpson, Jacynth
Simpson, James (Jay) B(easley)
1926-2002 CANR-9
Obituary 231
Earlier sketch in CA 5-8R
Simpson, Jean I(rwin) 1896-1982 5-8R
Simpson, Jeffrey (Carl) 1949- CANR-119
Earlier sketch in CA 153
Simpson, Jerry H(oward, Jr.) 1925- 138
Simpson, Joan Murray 1918-1977
Obituary 89-92
See also CP 1
Simpson, John (Cody Fidler) 1944- 140
Simpson, John (Andrew) 1953- CANR-48
Earlier sketch in CA 122
Simpson, John E(dwin) 1951- 140
Simpson, John Frederick Norman Hampson
See Hampson, John
Simpson, John L(iddle) 9-12R
Simpson, John Warfield 232
Simpson, Judith H(olroyd) 1941- 110
Simpson, Kemper 1893-1970 CAP-1
Earlier sketch in CA 11-12
Simpson, Kirke L(arue) 1882(?)-1972
Obituary 37-40R
Simpson, Leo 1934- 101
See also AITN 2
Simpson, Lesley 1963- SATA 150
Simpson, Lewis P(earson) 1916- CANR-8
Earlier sketch in CA 17-20R
Simpson, Louis (Aston Marantz)
1923- CANR-140
Earlier sketches in CA 1-4R, CANR-1, 61
See also CAAS 4
See also AMWS 9
See also CLC 4, 7, 9, 32, 149
See also CP 1, 2, 3, 4, 5, 6, 7
See also DAM POET
See also DLB 5
See also MAL 5
See also MTCW 1, 2
See also MTFW 2005
See also PFS 7, 11, 14
See also RGAL 4
Simpson, Marc 173
Simpson, Margaret 1943- 198
See also SATA 128
Simpson, Matt(hew William) 1936- CANR-90
Earlier sketch in CA 131
Simpson, Michael Andrew 1944- 89-92
Simpson, Mona (Elizabeth) 1957- CANR-103
Brief entry 122
Earlier sketches in CA 135, CANR-68
See also CLC 44, 146
See also CN 6, 7
See also EWL 3
Simpson, Myrtle L(illias) 1931- CANR-11
Earlier sketch in CA 21-24R
See also SATA 14
Simpson, N(orman) F(rederick) 1919- 13-16R
See also CBD
See also CLC 29
See also DLB 13
See also RGEL 2
Simpson, Norman T. 1919(?)-1988
Obituary 125
Simpson, O(renthal) J(ames) 1947- CANR-50
Earlier sketch in CA 103
Simpson, Peter L. Phillips 1951- 169
Simpson, Philip L. 1964- 238
Simpson, R(onald) A(lbert) 1929- CANR-14
Earlier sketch in CA 77-80
See also CP 1, 2, 3, 4, 5, 6, 7
Simpson, Ray H. 1907- 1-4R
Simpson, Richard L(ee) 1929- 9-12R
Simpson, Robert (Wilfred Levick) 1921- 103
Simpson, Robert 1924- 49-52
Simpson, Robert H. 1912- 108
Simpson, Ruth 1926- 73-76
Simpson, Ruth Mary Rasey 1902- CANR-1
Earlier sketch in CA 1-4R
Simpson, (Robert) Smith 1906- CAP-2
Earlier sketch in CA 21-22
Simpson, Stanhope Rowton 1903-1999 73-76
Simpson, Thomas W(illiam) 1957- 137
Simpson, W. W.
See Simpson, William Wynn
Simpson, (Bessie) Wallis Warfield (Spencer)
1896(?)-1986 211
Simpson, Warwick
See Ridge, William Pett
Simpson, William Hays 1903-1989 41-44R
Simpson, William Kelly 1928- 105
Simpson, William Wynn 1907-1987
Obituary 123
Sims, Anastatia 1953- 170
Sims, Bernard John 1915- 13-16R
Sims, Blanche (L.) SATA 75
Sims, Bobbi 1931- 117
Sims, Charles A(gustus) 1901-1983
Obituary 111
Sims, Edward H. 1923- CANR-6
Earlier sketch in CA 1-4R
Sims, Edward J(ames) 1927- 41-44R
Sims, Elizabeth 225
Sims, George (Carrol) 1902-1966 234
See also Cain, Paul
Sims, George (Frederick Robert)
1923-1999 CANR-58
Earlier sketches in CA 25-28R, CANR-12
See also CMW 4
See also DLB 87
Sims, George R(obert) 1847-1922 185
See also DLB 35, 70, 135
Sims, Harold D(ana) 1935- 41-44R
Sims, Henry P., Jr. 1939- CANR-116
Earlier sketch in CA 156
Sims, James H(ylbert) 1924- CANR-46
Earlier sketch in CA 1-4R
Sims, Janet L.
See Sims-Wood, Janet L(ouise)
Sims, John
See Hopson, William (L.)
Sims, Lois Dorothy Lang
See Lang-Sims, Lois Dorothy
Sims, Lt. A. K.
See Whitson, John H(arvey)
Sims, Mary Sophia Stephens 1886-1976
Obituary 65-68
Sims, Michael 1958- 227
Sims, Naomi (Ruth) 1949- CANR-26
Earlier sketch in CA 69-72
Sims, Norman (Howard) 1948- 132
Sims, Patsy 1938- 135
Brief entry 110
Sims, Patterson 1947- 124
Sims, Phillip L(eon) 1940- 105
Sims, William Sowden 1858-1936 220
Simson, Eve 1937- 73-76
Simsova, Sylva 1931- CANR-12
Earlier sketch in CA 29-32R
Sims-Wood, Janet L(ouise) 1945- 108

Cumulative Index 535 Sinyavsky

Simundsson, Elva 1950- .... SATA 63
Sinai, I(saac) Robert 1924- CANR-10
Earlier sketch in CA 21-24R
Sinan, Rogelio
See Alba, Bernardo Dominguez
See also DLB 145, 290
See also LAW
Sinclair, Andrew (Annandale) 1935- . CANR-91
Earlier sketches in CA 9-12R, CANR-14, 38
See also CAAS 5
See also CLC 2, 14
See also CN 1, 2, 3, 4, 5, 6, 7
See also DLB 14
See also FANT
See also MTCW 1
Sinclair, Bennie Lee 1939-2000 .... CANR-1
Earlier sketch in CA 49-52
Sinclair, Bertrand William 1881-1972 148
See also DLB 92
Sinclair, Brett J(ason) 1942- 141
Sinclair, Bruce A. 1929- 126
Brief entry 106
Sinclair, Carla 160
Sinclair, Catherine 1800-1864 .... DLB 163
Sinclair, Clive (John) 1948- CANR-56
Earlier sketch in CA 127
See also DLB 319
Sinclair, Clover
See Gater, Dilys
Sinclair, David 1945- 220
Sinclair, Donna 1943- CANR-46
Earlier sketches in CA 106, CANR-23
Sinclair, Elizabeth
See Smith, Marguerite
Sinclair, Emil
See Hesse, Hermann
Sinclair, (Allan) Gordon 1900-1984 102
Obituary 112
Interview in CA-102
See also AITN 1
Sinclair, Grace
See Wallmann, Jeffrey M(iner)
Sinclair, Grant
See Drago, Harry Sinclair
Sinclair, Harold (Augustus) 1907-1966 ...... 5-8R
Sinclair, Heather
See Johnston, William
Sinclair, Iain 1943- CANR-81
Earlier sketch in CA 132
See also CLC 76
See also CP 7
See also HGG
Sinclair, Iain MacGregor
See Sinclair, Iain
Sinclair, Ian
See Foley, (Cedric) John
Sinclair, Irene
See Griffith, D(avid Lewelyn) W(ark)
Sinclair, James
See Staples, Reginald Thomas
Sinclair, Jeff 1958- .... SATA 77
Sinclair, Jo
See Seid, Ruth
See also CN 1, 2, 3, 4
See also DLB 28
Sinclair, John L(eslie) 1902-1993 105
Obituary 143
Sinclair, Julian
See Sinclair, Mary Amelia St. Clair
Sinclair, Keith 1922-1993 .... 17-20R
Obituary 142
See also CP 1, 2
Sinclair, Lister (Shedden) 1921- 105
See also DLB 88
Sinclair, Marjorie (Jane) 1913- 132
Sinclair, Mary Amelia St. Clair 1865(?)-1946
Brief entry 104
See also Sinclair, May
See also HGG
See also RHW
Sinclair, Max 1945- 113
Sinclair, May 166
See also Sinclair, Mary Amelia St. Clair
See also DLB 36, 135
See also EWL 3
See also RGEL 2
See also SUFW
See also TCLC 3, 11
Sinclair, Michael
See Shea, Michael (Sinclair MacAuslan)
Sinclair, Miranda (Jane) 1948- CANR-110
Earlier sketch in CA 77-80
Sinclair, Murray 1950- 108
Sinclair, Olga 1923- CANR-85
Earlier sketches in CA 61-64, CANR-11, 26, 51
See also RHW
See also SATA 121
Sinclair, Rose
See Smith, Susan Vernon
Sinclair, Roy
See Griffith, D(avid Lewelyn) W(ark)
Sinclair, Sandra 1940- 120
Sinclair, Sonia 1928- 126
Sinclair, Stephen (Kennedy) 1956- .... CD 5, 6
Sinclair, Upton (Beall) 1878-1968 ...... CANR-7
Obituary 25-28R
Earlier sketch in CA 5-8R
Interview in CANR-7
See also AAYA 63
See also AMWS 5
See also BPFB 3
See also BYA 2
See also CDALB 1929-1941
See also CLC 1, 11, 15, 63
See also DA
See also DA3
See also DAB
See also DAC
See also DAM MST, NOV
See also DLB 9
See also EWL 3
See also LAIT 3
See also MAL 5
See also MTCW 1, 2
See also MTFW 2005
See also NFS 6
See also RGAL 4
See also SATA 9
See also TCLC 160
See also TUS
See also WLC
See also YAW
Sinclair-Stevenson, Christopher 1939- 102
Sincoff, Michael Z(olman) 1943- 85-88
Sinden, Donald (Alfred) 1923- 132
Sindermann, Carl J(ames) 138
Sindler, Allan Paul 1928- 97-100
Sinel, Allen 1936- 45-48
Siner, Howard W(alter) 1946- 117
Sinetar, Marsha 182
Sinfield, Alan 1941- CANR-68
Earlier sketches in CA 113, CANR-32
Sing, Lung
See Chan, Jackie
Singal, Daniel Joseph 1944- CANR-92
Earlier sketch in CA 129
Singe, (Edmund) J(ohn) M(illington)
1871-1909 .... WLC
Singer, A. L.
See Lerangis, Peter
Singer, Adam
See Karp, David
Singer, Alan 1948- 156
Singer, Amanda
See Brooks, Janice Young
Singer, Armand Edwards 1914- CANR-14
Earlier sketch in CA 41-44R
Singer, Arthur 1917-1990 .... SATA 64
Singer, Barry 1957- 144
Singer, Bayla 1940- 227
Singer, Benjamin D. 1931- 37-40R
Singer, Beth J(udith) 1927- 113
Singer, Bryan 1965- 197
See also AAYA 44
Singer, Burns
See Singer, James Hyman
Singer, C(harles) Gregg 1910-1999 ... CANR-12
Earlier sketch in CA 73-76
Singer, Daniel 1926- 188
Singer, David L(in) 1937- 73-76
Singer, Fred J. 1931- 21-24R
Singer, Irving 1925- CANR-100
Earlier sketch in CA 21-24R
Singer, Isaac
See Singer, Isaac Bashevis
Singer, Isaac Bashevis 1904-1991 ... CANR-106
Obituary 134
Earlier sketches in CA 1-4R, CANR-1, 39
See also AAYA 32
See also AITN 1, 2
See also AMW
See also AMWR 2
See also BPFB 3
See also BYA 1, 4
See also CDALB 1941-1968
See also CLC 1, 3, 6, 9, 11, 15, 23, 38, 69, 111
See also CLR 1
See also CN 1, 2, 3, 4
See also CWRI 5
See also DA
See also DA3
See also DAB
See also DAC
See also DAM MST, NOV
See also DLB 6, 28, 52, 278
See also DLBY 1991
See also EWL 3
See also EXPS
See also HGG
See also JRDA
See also LAIT 3
See also MAICYA 1, 2
See also MAL 5
See also MTCW 1, 2
See also MTFW 2005
See also RGAL 4
See also RGSF 2
See also SATA 3, 27
See also SATA-Obit 68
See also SSC 3, 53, 80
See also SSFS 2, 12, 16
See also TUS
See also TWA
See also WLC
Singer, Israel Joshua 1893-1944 169
See also EWL 3
See also TCLC 33
Singer, J(oel) David 1925- CANR-49
Earlier sketches in CA 1-4R, CANR-6
Singer, Jack W(olfe) 1942- 104
Singer, James Hyman 1928-1964 102
Obituary 89-92
Singer, Jane Sherrod 1917-1985 .... CANR-17
Obituary 115
Earlier sketch in CA 25-28R
See also SATA 4
See also SATA-Obit 42
Singer, Jerome L(eonard) 1924- 132
Singer, Joe
See Singer, Joseph
Singer, Jonathan 183
Singer, Joseph 1923-(?) CANR-2
Earlier sketch in CA 45-48
Singer, Joseph I.
See Singer, Joseph
Singer, Joy Daniels 1928- 29-32R
Singer, Judith 1926- 61-64
Singer, Julia 1917- 65-68
See also SATA 28
Singer, June (Kurlander) 1918-2004 .. CANR-10
Obituary 223
Earlier sketch in CA 41-44R
Interview in CANR-10
Singer, June Flaum 1933- 106
Singer, Katie 1960- 185
Singer, Kurt D(eutsch) 1911- CANR-2
Earlier sketch in CA 49-52
See also SATA 38
Singer, Marcus George 1926- CANR-3
Earlier sketch in CA 1-4R
Singer, Margaret
See Singer, Margaret Thaler
Singer, Margaret Thaler 1921-2003 237
Singer, Marilyn 1948- CANR-105
Earlier sketches in CA 65-68, CANR-9, 39, 85
See also CLR 48
See also JRDA
See also MAICYA 1, 2
See also SAAS 13
See also SATA 48, 80, 125, 158
See also SATA-Brief 38
See also SATA-Essay 158
See also YAW
Singer, Mark 1950- CANR-68
Earlier sketch in CA 138
See also DLB 185
Singer, Marshall R. 1932- 41-44R
Singer, Max 1931- 145
Singer, Maxine 1931- 160
Singer, Michael A(lan) 1947- 57-60
Singer, Milton Borah 1912-1994 ...... CANR-49
Obituary 147
Earlier sketches in CA 105, CANR-23
Singer, Muff 1942-2005 171
Obituary 235
See also SATA 104
See also SATA-Obit 160
Singer, Neil M(ichael) 1939- 93-96
Singer, Norman 1925- 41-44R
Singer, Peter (Albert David) 1946- .. CANR-102
Earlier sketches in CA 57-60, CANR-8, 51, 85
Singer, Phylis
See Morrison, Phylis
Singer, Ray (Eleazer) 1916-1992 105
Obituary 140
Singer, Richard G. 1943- 89-92
Singer, (Dennis) Robert 1931- 49-52
Singer, Robert N. CANR-50
Earlier sketches in CA 53-56, CANR-5, 25
Singer, Rochelle 1939- CANR-20
Earlier sketch in CA 104
Singer, S(iegfried) Fred 1924-
Brief entry 118
Singer, Samuel L(oewenberg) 1911- 65-68
Singer, Sarah 1915- 81-84
Singer, Shelley
See Singer, Rochelle
Singer, Sholom A. 1924-1987
Obituary 123
Singer, Susan (Mahler) 1941- 61-64
See also SATA 9
Singerman, Robert 1942- 110
Singh, Ajit 1940- 109
Singh, Amritjit 1945- 102
Singh, Arjan 1917- 49-52
Singh, Avtar 1929- 65-68
Singh, Baljit 1929-1980 .... CANR-49
Earlier sketch in CA 41-44R
Singh, Bawa Satinder 1932- 101
Singh, Chetan 1955- 138
Singh, D(asharath) 1937- 167
Singh, Darshan 1921-1989 133
Singh, Dayanita 1961- 205
Singh, G(han Shyam) 1929- CANR-43
Earlier sketches in CA 9-12R, CANR-5, 20
Singh, Harbans 1921- 17-20R
Singh, Karan 1931- 13-16R
Singh, Khushwant 1915- CANR-84
Earlier sketches in CA 9-12R, CANR-6
See also CAAS 9
See also CLC 11
See also CN 1, 2, 3, 4, 5, 6, 7
See also EWL 3
See also RGEL 2
Singh, Lalita Prasad 1936- 21-24R
Singh, Madanjeet 1924- 17-20R
Singh, Nagendra 1914- CANR-7
Earlier sketch in CA 17-20R
Singh, Patwant 1925- 150
Singh, R. K. Janmeja 1932- 37-40R
Singh, Raghubir 1942-1999 205
Singh, Rashmi Sharma 1952- .... SATA 90
Singh, Rina 1955- 180
Singh, St. Nihal 1884- 105
Singh, Simon 1964- CANR-130
Earlier sketches in CA 166, CANR-98
See also MTFW 2005
Singh, Surender 1932- 49-52
Singh, Surendra Nihal
See Nihal Singh, Surendra
Singh, Vijai Pratap 1939-
Brief entry 106
Singhal, D(amodar) P(rasad) 1925- 49-52
Singher, Martial (Jean-Paul) 1904-1990
Obituary 131
Singing Nun, The
See Deckers, Jeanine
Singletary, Otis Arnold, Jr. 1921-2003 45-48
Obituary 221
Singleton, Ann
See Benedict, Ruth (Fulton)
Singleton, Betty 1910- CAP-2
Earlier sketch in CA 25-28
Singleton, Charles S(outhward) 1909-1985 . 155
Obituary 117
Brief entry 113
Singleton, Elyse
See Singleton, Janet Elyse
Singleton, Frederick Bernard 1926- 89-92
Singleton, George 1958- 238
Singleton, Ira C(uster) 1920- 5-8R
Singleton, Jack 1911- 13-16R
Singleton, Janet Elyse 233
Singleton, John 1930- 21-24R
Singleton, John 1968(?)- CANR-82
Earlier sketches in CA 138, CANR-67
See also AAYA 50
See also BW 2, 3
See also CLC 156
See also DAM MULT
Singleton, Linda Joy 1957- .... SATA 88
Singleton, M(arvin) K(enneth) 1933- 1-4R
Singleton, Mary Ann 1934- 57-60
Singleton, Mary Montgomerie
See Currie, Mary Montgomerie Lamb Singleton
Singleton, Ralph Herbert 1900-1982 ..... 13-16R
Singleton, Rebecca (Jane) 1948- 121
Singleton, Rupert
See Pitt-Kethley, Fiona
Singleton, V(ernon) L(eRoy) 1923- 25-28R
Singley, Carol (J.) 1951- 189
Singmaster, Elsie 1879-1958
Brief entry 110
See also DLB 9
Sington, David 208
Sington, Philip 1962- 161
Singular, Stephen 1950- 139
Sinha, Indra 1950- 208
Sinha, Krishna N(andan) 1924- 13-16R
Sinha, Manisha 1962- 218
Sinha, Phulgenda 1924- 130
Sinha, Sasadhar 1901- 17-20R
Siniavskii, Andrei (Donatovich)
See Siniavsky, Andrei
See also CWW 2
Siniavskii, Andrei
See Sinyavsky, Andrei (Donatevich)
See also CWW 2
Siniavsky, Andrei 1925-1997
See Siniavskii, Andrei (Donatovich)
See also DLB 302
Sinibaldi, Fosco
See Kacew, Romain
Sinick, Daniel 1913-1984 .... CANR-45
Earlier sketch in CA 45-48
Sinicropi, Giovanni Andrea 1924- CANR-42
Earlier sketch in CA 45-48
Sinisalo, Johanna 1958- 239
Sinisgalli, Leonardo 1908-1981
Obituary 103
See also DLB 114
Sinjohn, John
See Galsworthy, John
Sinjun
See John, Elizabeth Beaman
Sinkankas, John 1915-2002 .... CANR-6
Obituary 208
Earlier sketch in CA 1-4R
Sinkler, George 1927- 85-88
Sinn, Hans-Werner 1948- 201
Sinnema, John R(alph) 1911-1999 .... 41-44R
Sinnen, Jeanne 1926-1976
Obituary 104
Sinnett, Mark C. 1963- 234
Sinnette, Elinor Des Verney 1925- 132
Sinnigen, William G. 1928- 13-16R
Sinning, Wayne E. 1931- 77-80
Sinofsky, Esther R. 1951- 126
Sinopoli, Carla M. 1956- 141
Sinopoli, Richard C. 1956-1997 138
Obituary 158
Sinor, Denis 1916- CANR-6
Earlier sketch in CA 1-4R, 183
Sinor, John 1930-1996 .... CANR-11
Obituary 153
Earlier sketch in CA 69-72
Sin Phe Mran
See Thein Pe Myint
Sinsabaugh, Art(hur Reeder) 1924-1983 205
Sinyavsky, Andrei (Donatevich)
1925-1997 85-88
Obituary 159
See also Siniavskii, Andrei and Sinyavsky, Andrey Donatovich and Tertz, Abram
See also CLC 8
Sinyavsky, Andrey Donatovich
See Sinyavsky, Andrei (Donatevich)
See also EWL 3

Sinykin, Sheri(l Terri) Cooper
1950- CANR-121
Earlier sketch in CA 202
See also SATA 72, 133, 142
See also SATA-Essay 142
Siodmak, Curt 1902-2000 .... CANR-81
Obituary 189
Brief entry 111
Earlier sketch in CA 113
See also DLB 44
See also HGG
See also IDFW 3, 4
See also SFW 4
Sion, Georges S. 1913-2001 198
Sion, Mari
See Jones, R(obert) M(aynard)
Sionil Jose, F(rancisco)
See Sionil Jose, F(rancisco)
Sionil Jose, F(rancisco) 1924- CANR-103
Earlier sketches in CA 21-24R, CANR-10, 60
See also CN 4, 5, 6, 7
See also RGSF 2
Sions, Harry 1906-1974
Obituary 104
Siotis, Jean 1931- 25-28R
Sipherd, Ray 1935- CANR-123
Earlier sketch in CA 144
Sipiera, Paul P., (Jr.) 1948- CANR-116
Earlier sketch in CA 155
See also SATA 89, 144
Siple, Molly 1942- CANR-114
Earlier sketch in CA 156
Siporin, Steve 1947- 139
Sippl, Charles J. 1924- CANR-18
Earlier sketch in CA 21-24R
Sipress, David 1947- CANR-101
Earlier sketch in CA 130
Siracusa, Catherine (Jane) 1947- 149
See also SATA 82
Siracusa, Joseph 1929- CANR-1
Earlier sketch in CA 45-48
Siracusa, Joseph M(arcus) 1944- CANR-12
Earlier sketch in CA 73-76
Sirageldin, Ismail A(bdel-Hamid)
1930- CANR-16
Earlier sketch in CA 29-32R
Siraisi, Nancy Gillian 1932- 182
Sirandrews, Mark
See Serandrei, Mario
Sirbu, Ion D. 1919-1989 .... DLB 232
Sirc, Ljubo 1920- 103
Sircar, Badal 1925- .... CWW 2
Sire, H. J. A. 1949- 146
Sire, James W(alter) 1933- CANR-52
Earlier sketches in CA 29-32R, CANR-11, 28
Sirera, Rodolf 1948- 238
Sirett, Dawn (Karen) 1966- .... SATA 88
Siri, Giuseppe 1906-1989
Obituary 128
Sirica, John J(oseph) 1905-1992 110
Sirimarco, Elizabeth 1966- 234
See also SATA 158
Sirin, V.
See Nabokov, Vladimir (Vladimirovich)
Siringo, Charles A(ngelo) 1855-1928 185
See also DLB 186
Siris, Peter 1944- 117
Sirius
See Beuve-Mery, Hubert
Sirius, R. U.
See Goffman, Ken
Sirjamaki, John 1911-1988 .... 13-16R
Sirkin, Gerald 1920- 25-28R
Sirkis, Nancy 1936- 102
Sirlin, Rhoda 1949- 225
Sirluck, Ernest 1918- 25-28R
Sirof, Harriet 1930- CANR-43
Earlier sketches in CA 104, CANR-20
See also SATA 37, 94
Sirois, Allen L. 1950- 143
See also SATA 76
Sirowitz, Hal 1949- 176
Sirr, Peter 1960- CANR-115
Earlier sketch in CA 172
Sirrom, Wes
See Weiss, Morris S(amuel)
Sirvaitis (Chernyaev), Karen (Ann) 1961- 148
See also SATA 79
Sis, Peter 1949- CANR-132
Earlier sketch in CANR-98
See also Sis, Peter
See also SATA 149
Sis, Peter 1949- 128
See also Sis, Peter
See also CLR 45
See also MAICYAS 1, 2
See also SATA 67, 106
Sisco, John I(sodore) 1931- 41-44R
Sisk, David W. 1963- 175
Sisk, Dorothy Poole 1897-1983
Obituary 111
Sisk, Frank A., Jr. 1915-1985
Obituary 115
Sisk, Henry L(ybran) 1914- 49-52
Sisk, John P(aul) 1914-1997 .... 29-32R
Siskel, Gene 1946-1999 113
Obituary 179
Brief entry 110
Siskind, Aaron 1903-1991 228
Sisler, Harry Hall 1917- 109
Sisler, Rebecca 1932- 104
Sisley, Emily L(ucretia) 1930-
Brief entry 113
Sisman, Adam 222
Sisman, Robyn 238
Sisoko, Fa-Digi .... WLIT 2
Sissle, Noble 1889-1975
Obituary 112
Sissman, L(ouis) E(dward)
1928-1976 .... CANR-13
Obituary 65-68
Earlier sketch in CA 21-24R
See also CLC 9, 18
See also CP 2
See also DLB 5
Sisson, A(lbert) F(ranklin) 1901-1984 .... 5-8R
Sisson, C(harles) H(ubert)
1914-2003 .... CANR-84
Obituary 220
Earlier sketches in CA 1-4R, CANR-3, 48
See also CAAS 3
See also BRWS 11
See also CLC 8
See also CP 1, 2, 3, 4, 5, 6, 7
See also DLB 27
Sisson, Rosemary Anne 1923- CANR-84
Earlier sketches in CA 13-16R, CANR-12, 29
See also RHW
See also SATA 11
Sister Agnes Martha
See Westwater, Agnes Martha
Sister Carol Anne O'Marie
See O'Marie, Carol Anne
Sister Luc-Gabrielle
See Deckers, Jeanine
Sister M. Victoria
See Maria Del Rey, Sister
Sister Magdeleine de Jesus
See Hutin, Magdeleine
Sister Mary Annette
See Buttimer, Anne
Sister Mary Jeremy
See Finnegan, Mary Jeremy
Sister Mary Terese
See Donze, Mary Terese
Sister Maura
See Eichner, Maura
Sister Smile
See Deckers, Jeanine
Sister Teresa Margaret
See Rowe, Margaret (Kevin)
Sister Wendy
See Beckett, Wendy
Sisyphus
See Barthelmes, (Albert) Wes(ley, Jr.)
Sita
See Tourgee, Albion W.
Sita, Lisa 1962- 151
See also SATA 87
Sitaram, K(ondavagil) S(urya) 1935- 69-72
Sitarz, Paula (Gaj) 1955- CANR-119
Earlier sketches in CA 122, CANR-48
Sitchin, Zecharia 1920- CANR-22
Earlier sketch in CA 69-72
Sites, James N(eil) 1924- 1-4R
Sites, Paul 1926- 53-56
Sithole, Ndabaningi 1920-2000
Obituary 191
Brief entry 110
Sitomer, Harry 1903-1985 101
See also SATA 31
Sitomer, Mindel 1903-1987 101
See also SATA 31
Sitter, John E(dward) 1944- CANR-87
Brief entry 114
Earlier sketch in CA 130
Sitterly, Charlotte Emma Moore
See Moore, Charlotte E(mma)
Sitting Bull 1831(?)-1890 .... DA3
See also DAM MULT
See also NNAL
Sittler, Joseph 1904-1987
Obituary 124
Sitton, Claude (Fox) 1925- 154
Brief entry 122
Sittser, Gerald L(awson) 1950- CANR-142
Earlier sketch in CA 166
Sittser, Jerry
See Sittser, Gerald L(awson)
Sitwell, Dame Edith 1887-1964 .... CANR-35
Earlier sketch in CA 9-12R
See also BRW 7
See also CDBLB 1945-1960
See also CLC 2, 9, 67
See also DAM POET
See also DLB 20
See also EWL 3
See also MTCW 1, 2
See also MTFW 2005
See also PC 3
See also RGEL 2
See also TEA
Sitwell, (Francis) Osbert (Sacheverell)
1892-1969 .... CAP-2
Obituary 25-28R
Earlier sketch in CA 21-22
See also DLB 100, 195
See also RGEL 2
See also TEA
Sitwell, Sacheverell 1897-1988 .... CANR-86
Obituary 126
Earlier sketch in CA 21-24R
See also CP 1, 2
See also RGEL 2
See also TEA
Sitzfleisch, Vladimir
See Spirer, Herbert F(rederick)
Siu, Helen 1950- 114
Siu, R(alph) G(un) H(oy) 1917-1998 . CANR-10
Obituary 172
Earlier sketch in CA 25-28R
Sive, Helen R(obinson) 1951- 107
See also SATA 30
Sive, Mary Robinson 1928- CANR-10
Earlier sketch in CA 65-68
Siverling, Mike 233
Siverson, Randolph M. 1940- 138
Siviero, Rodolpho 1912(?)-1983
Obituary 111
Sivulich, Sandra (Jeanne) Stroner 1941- .. 61-64
See also SATA 9
Sivulka, Juliann 1950- 207
Siwaarmill, H. P.
See Sharp, William
Siwek, Manuel 1908-1976
Obituary 65-68
Siwundhla, Alice Msumba 1928- 45-48
Sixel, Friedrich W. 1934- 226
Sixsmith, Eric Keir Gilborne
1904-1986 .... 33-36R
Obituary 118
Siy, Robert Y(oung), Jr. 1955- CANR-45
Earlier sketch in CA 119
Sizemore, Burlan A. 1933- 45-48
Sizemore, Chris(tine) Costner 1927- 81-84
Sizemore, Christine Wick 1945- 134
Sizemore, Deborah Lightfoot 1956- 138
Sizemore, Margaret D(avidson) CAP-2
Earlier sketch in CA 19-20
Sizer, John 1938- CANR-12
Earlier sketch in CA 29-32R
Sizer, Mona D.
See Sizer, Mona Young
Sizer, Mona Young 1934- CANR-94
Earlier sketch in CA 146
Sizer, Nancy F(aust) 1935- 45-48
Sizer, Theodore R(yland) 1932- CANR-13
Earlier sketch in CA 33-36R
Sjoberg, Leif 1925- 65-68
Sjoeberg, Birger 1885-1929
See Sjoberg, Birger
Sjoeberg, Leif
See Sjoberg, Leif
Sjoestrand, Sven-Erik 1945- 147
Sjoewall, Maj 1935- CANR-73
Earlier sketch in CA 65-68
See also Sjowall, Maj
See also CLC 7
Sjostedt, Ulf (Georg) 1935- 208
Sjostrand, Osten 1925- 197
Sjostrand, Sven-Erik
See Sjoestrand, Sven-Erik
Sjowall, Maj
See Sjoewall, Maj
See also BPFB 3
See also CMW 4
See also MSW
Skaar, Grace Brown 1903-1986 69-72
Skacel, Jan 1922-1989 .... DLB 232
Skaer, Peter M(acKall) 1953- 103
Skagen, Kiki
See Munshi, Kiki Skagen
Skagestad, Tormod 1920-1997 196
Skaggs, David Curtis (Jr.) 1937- CANR-107
Earlier sketch in CA 41-44R
Skaggs, (Barbara) Gayle 1952- 237
Skaggs, Jimmy M(arion) 1940- CANR-39
Earlier sketches in CA 45-48, CANR-1
Skaggs, Merrill Maguire 1937- CANR-96
Earlier sketches in CA 45-48, CANR-45
Skaine, Rosemarie 1936- 210
Skal, David J. 1952- 235
See also HGG
Skala, John J. 1923- 17-20R
Skalbe, Karlis 1879-1945 .... DLB 220
See also EWL 3
Skaldaspillir, Sigfridur
See Broxon, Mildred Downey
Skallerup, Harry R(obert) 1927- 73-76
Skard, Sigmund 1903- CANR-22
Earlier sketches in CA 17-20R, CANR-7
Skarda, Patricia Lyn 1946- 106
Skardal, Dorothy Burton 1922- 61-64
Skardon, Alvin W(ilson, Jr.) 1912- 53-56
Skaria, Ajay 204
Skarmeta, Antonio 1940- CANR-80
Earlier sketch in CA 131
See also CDWLB 3
See also CWW 2
See also DLB 145
See also EWL 3
See also HW 1, 2
See also LAWS 1
See also RGWL 3
See also SATA 57
Skarsaune, Oskar 1946- 136
Skarsten, Malvin O. 1892-1993 .... CAP-1
Earlier sketch in CA 13-16
Skartvedt, Dan (L.) 1945- 77-80
Skates, John R(ay) 1934- 97-100
Skau, Michael 1944- 210
Skavronsky, A.
See Danilevsky, Grigorii Petrovich
Skeaping, John Rattenbury 1901-1980 108
Obituary 97-100
Skeaping, Mary 1902-1984
Obituary 112
Skeat, Walter W(illiam) 1835-1912 193
See also DLB 184
Skeates, Robin 1965- 180
Skedgell, Marian Jay 1921- CANR-14
Earlier sketch in CA 17-20R
Skeel, Dorothy J(une) CANR-8
Earlier sketch in CA 61-64
Skeen, Carl Edward 1937- 113
Skeet, Ian 1928- 145
Skegg, P(eter) D(onald) G(raham) 1944- 127
Skehan, James W(illiam) 1923- 57-60
Skei, Allen B(ennet) 1935-1985 .... CANR-31
Earlier sketch in CA 108
Skei, Hans H. 1945- 223
Skellings, Edmund 1932- 77-80
Skelly, James R(ichard) 1927- 85-88
See also SATA 17
Skelly, Madge 1903-1993 .... 41-44R
Obituary 198
Skelton, Barbara 1918-1996 136
Obituary 151
Skelton, Eugene (Lamar) 1914- CANR-1
Earlier sketch in CA 45-48
Skelton, Geoffrey (David) 1916- CANR-40
Earlier sketches in CA 49-52, CANR-1, 18
Skelton, John 1460(?)-1529 .... BRW 1
See also DLB 136
See also PC 25
See also RGEL 2
Skelton, John E. 1934- 37-40R
Skelton, Peter 1928- 13-16R
Skelton, Red 1913-1997 104
Obituary 161
Skelton, Richard
See Skelton, Red
Skelton, Robin 1925-1997 .... CANR-89
Obituary 160
Earlier sketches in CA 5-8R, CANR-28
See also Zuk, Georges
See also CAAS 5
See also AITN 2
See also CCA 1
See also CLC 13
See also CP 1, 2
See also DLB 27, 53
Skelton, Roger
See Horn, Peter (Rudolf Gisela)
Skelton, William B(arott) 1939- 140
Skema, Antanas 1910-1961 .... DLB 220
Skemp, Joseph Bright 1910-1992 106
Obituary 140
Skemp, Richard R(owland) 1919- 107
Skempton, A(lec) W(estley) 1914-2001 206
Skendi, Stavro 1906- 25-28R
Skene-Melvin, Ann (Patricia) 1936- 108
Skene-Melvin, (Lewis) David (St. Columb)
1936- 108
Skerpan, Elizabeth (Penley) 1955- 142
Skeyne, Oliver
See Lardner, Ring(gold Wilmer), Jr.
Skibbe, Eugene M(oritz) 1930- 21-24R
Skibell, Joseph 180
Skibo, James M. 1960- 191
Skidelsky, Robert 1939- CANR-70
Earlier sketches in CA 25-28R, CANR-11
Skidmore, David (G. II) 1958- 161
Skidmore, Ian 1929- CANR-10
Earlier sketch in CA 61-64
Skidmore, Max J(oseph Sr.) 1933- CANR-12
Earlier sketch in CA 29-32R
Skidmore, Rex A(ustin) 1914-1998 .... 13-16R
Skidmore, Thomas E. 1932- 21-24R
Skiles, Jacqueline D(ean) 1937- 108
Skilken, Patricia S(tout) 1943- 119
Skilling, H(arold) Gordon 1912-2001 . CANR-7
Earlier sketch in CA 13-16R
Skillings, R(oger) D(eering) 1937- CANR-115
Earlier sketch in CA 61-64
Skilliter, S(usan) A. 1931(?)-1985
Obituary 117
Skillman, Don 1932- 169
Skilton, John H. 1906- 37-40R
Skimin, Robert (Elwayne) 1929- CANR-99
Earlier sketch in CA 108
Skinner, Ainslie
See Gosling, Paula
Skinner, Anthony David
See David, Anthony
Skinner, B(urrhus) F(rederic)
1904-1990 .... CANR-42
Obituary 132
Earlier sketches in CA 9-12R, CANR-18
See also MTCW 1, 2
Skinner, Charles Edward 1891-1983 .... CAP-1
Earlier sketch in CA 17-18
Skinner, Constance Lindsay 1877-1939 209
See also DLB 92
See also YABC 1
Skinner, Cornelia Otis 1901-1979 .... 17-20R
Obituary 89-92
See also SATA 2
Skinner, Elliott P(ercival) 1924- 13-16R
Skinner, G(eorge) William 1925- CANR-2
Earlier sketch in CA 49-52
Skinner, Gloria Dale 1951- 167
Skinner, Gordon S(weetland) 1924- 13-16R
Skinner, Jeffrey 1949- CANR-113
Earlier sketches in CA 126, CANR-52
Skinner, John 1945- 220
Skinner, John Emory 1925- 5-8R
Skinner, John Stuart 1788-1851 .... DLB 73
Skinner, June O'Grady 1922- CANR-85
Earlier sketch in CA 5-8R
Skinner, Knute (Rumsey) 1929- CANR-85
Earlier sketches in CA 17-20R, CANR-9, 24, 49
See also CP 1, 2, 3, 4, 5, 6, 7
Skinner, Margaret 1942- 147
See also CSW
Skinner, Michael 1953- 134
Skinner, Mike 1924- .... TCWW 2
Skinner, Robert (Earle) 1948- 190
Skinner, Rulon Dean 1931- 61-64
Skinner, Stephen 1948- 239
Skinner, Thomas Edward 1909-1991 109
Skinner, Tom 1942-1994 .... 25-28R
Obituary 145
Skinner-Linnenberg, Virginia (M.) 1951- 193
Skiold, Birgit (?)-1982
Obituary 107

Cumulative Index 537 Sljivic-Simsic

Skipp, John (Mason) 1957- 239
See also HGG
Skipp, Victor (Henry Thomas) 1925- 123
Brief entry 118
Skipper, Betty
See Barr, Betty
Skipper, G. C. 1939- CANR-14
Earlier sketch in CA 77-80
See also SATA 46
See also SATA-Brief 38
Skipper, James K(inley), Jr.
1934-1993 .... CANR-85
Obituary 140
Earlier sketches in CA 17-20R, CANR-12
Skipsey, Joseph 1832-1903 184
See also DLB 35
Skipwith, Sofka 1907-1994 .... 29-32R
Obituary 144
Skira, Albert 1904-1973
Obituary 104
Skirpa, Kazys 1895(?)-1979
Obituary 89-92
Skjei, Eric William 1947- 97-100
Sklansky, Amy E(dgar) 1971- 218
See also SATA 145
Sklansky, Morris Aaron 1919- 17-20R
Sklar, Dusty 1928- 65-68
Sklar, George 1908-1988 .... CANR-85
Obituary 125
Earlier sketch in CA 1-4R
Sklar, Kathryn Kish 1939- CANR-40
Earlier sketches in CA 45-48, CANR-3, 18
Sklar, Lawrence 1938- 105
Sklar, Michael Joel 1945(?)-1984
Obituary 112
Sklar, Morty 1935- CANR-13
Earlier sketch in CA 77-80
Sklar, Richard L(awrence) 1930- 9-12R
Sklar, Robert 1936- CANR-111
Earlier sketches in CA 21-24R, CANR-8
Sklar, Scott 1950- 131
Sklare, Arnold B(eryl) 1924- 17-20R
Sklare, Marshall 1921-1992 .... CANR-12
Obituary 137
Earlier sketch in CA 21-24R
Sklarew, Myra 1934- CANR-112
Earlier sketches in CA 109, CANR-30
Sklarewitz, Norman 1924- 69-72
Sklenicka, Carol 1948- 218
Skloot, Floyd 1947- CANR-137
Earlier sketch in CA 171
Skobtsova, Elizaveta Kuz'mina-Karavaeva
1891-1945
See Mat' Mariia
Skocpol, Theda (Ruth) 1947- CANR-93
Brief entry 105
Earlier sketch in CA 154
Skofield, James 156
See also SATA 95
See also SATA-Brief 44
Skoglund, Elizabeth 1937- CANR-34
Earlier sketches in CA 41-44R, CANR-15
Skoglund, Goesta 1904- 65-68
Skoglund, John Egnar 1912- 9-12R
Skold, Betty Westrom 1923- 112
See also SATA 41
Skolimowski, Jerzy 1938- 128
See also CLC 20
Skolnick, Jerome H(erbert) 1931-
Brief entry 114
Skolnik, Alfred 1920(?)-1977
Obituary 69-72
Skolnik, Peter L(aurence) 1944- 57-60
Skolnikoff, Eugene B. 1928- 21-24R
Skolsky, Sidney 1905-1983 .... CANR-85
Obituary 109
Earlier sketch in CA 103
Skom, Edith 184
Skoog, Folke Karl 1908-2001 162
Obituary 193
Skornia, Harry J(ay) 1910-1991 .... CAP-2
Earlier sketch in CA 17-18
Skorpen, Liesel Moak 1935- 25-28R
See also SATA 3
Skorpios, Antares
See Barlow, Jane
Skorupski, John 1946- CANR-93
Earlier sketch in CA 146
Skotheim, Robert Allen 1933- 21-24R
Skott, Maria
See Nikolajeva, Maria
Skouen, Arne 1913- 207
Skoug, Kenneth N., Jr. 1931- 176
Skou-Hansen, Tage 1925- CANR-6
Earlier sketch in CA 13-16R
See also DLB 214
Skousen, Mark 104
Skousen, W(illard) Cleon 1913- CANR-5
Earlier sketch in CA 5-8R
Skover, David M. 1951- CANR-118
Earlier sketch in CA 152
Skovron, Alex 1948- 220
Skowronek, Stephen 1951- CANR-93
Earlier sketch in CA 146
Skowronski, JoAnn 108
Skoyles, John 1949- CANR-116
Earlier sketch in CA 104
Skrade, Carl 1935- 65-68
Skram, Amalie (Bertha) 1847-1905 165
See also TCLC 25
Skramstad, Susan 1942- 139
Skrivanek, John M(arion) 1913- 49-52
Skrypuch, Marsha Forchuk 1954- 203
See also SATA 134
Skrzynecki, Peter 1945- 128
See also CP 7
See also DLB 289
Skulicz, Matthew V. 1944- 37-40R
Skulsky, Harold Lawrence 1935- 107
Skura, Meredith Anne 1944- 117
Skurdenis, Julliann V.
See Skurdenis-Smircich, Julliann V(eronica)
Skurdenis-Smircich, Julliann V(eronica)
1942- 77-80
Skurnik, W. A. E. 1926- 41-44R
Skurzynski, Gloria (Joan) 1930- CANR-100
Earlier sketches in CA 33-36R, CANR-13, 30, 58
See also AAYA 38
See also SAAS 9
See also SATA 8, 74, 122, 145
See also SATA-Essay 145
Skutch, Alexander F(rank)
1904-2004 .... CANR-104
Obituary 227
Earlier sketches in CA 33-36R, CANR-21, 49
Skutch, Ira 1921- 194
Skutch, Margaret F. 1932- 105
Skutch, Robert 1925- 155
See also SATA 89
Skutsch, Otto 1906- 126
Skvorecka, Zdena Salivarova 1933- 41-44R
Skvorecky, Josef (Vaclav) 1924- CANR-108
Earlier sketches in CA 61-64, CANR-10, 34, 63
See also CAAS 1
See also CDWLB 4
See also CLC 15, 39, 69, 152
See also CWW 2
See also DA3
See also DAC
See also DAM NOV
See also DLB 232
See also EWL 3
See also MTCW 1, 2
See also MTFW 2005
Sky, Kathleen
See Goldin, Kathleen Mckinney
Sky, Michael 1951- 144
Skye, Christina 204
Skye, Ione 1971- 172
Skye, Maggie
See Werner, Herma
Skyler, Heather 235
Skynner, (Augustus Charles) Robin
1922-2000 141
Obituary 189
Skyrms, Brian 1938- CANR-26
Earlier sketch in CA 108
Slaatte, Howard A(lexander) 1919- ... CANR-31
Earlier sketches in CA 41-44R, CANR-14
Slabbert, F(rederik) Van Zyl 1940- 133
Slaby, Andrew Edmund 1942- CANR-7
Earlier sketch in CA 57-60
Slack, Adrian (Charles) 104
Slack, Charles W(illiam) 1929- 61-64
Slack, Kenneth 1917-1987
Obituary 123
Slack, Paul Alexander 1943- 190
Slack, Robert C(harles) 1914-1998 81-84
Slack, Walter H. 1932- 21-24R
Slackjaw
See Knipfel, Jim
Slackman, Charles B. 1934- .... SATA 12
Slade, Afton J. 1919-1993 89-92
Obituary 140
Slade, Arthur G(regory) 1967- CANR-132
Earlier sketch in CA 176
See also MAICYA 2
See also SATA 106, 149
Slade, Bernard 1930-
See Newbound, Bernard Slade
See also CAAS 9
See also CCA 1
See also CD 6
See also CLC 11, 46
See also DLB 53
Slade, Caroline (Beach) 1886-1975
Obituary 61-64
Slade, Jack
See Ballard, (Willis) Todhunter and
Germano, Peter B. and
Haas, Ben(jamin) L(eopold)
Slade, Joseph W(arren) 1941- 89-92
Slade, Leonard A., Jr. 1942- 148
Slade, Madeleine 1892-1982
Obituary 115
Slade, Michael .... HGG
Slade, Peter 1912- 13-16R
Slade, Richard 1910-1971 .... CAP-2
Earlier sketch in CA 23-24
See also SATA 9
Slade, Tony 1936- 33-36R
Sladek, John 1937-2000 .... 25-28R
See also SFW 4
Sladen, Kathleen 1904- 69-72
Sladen, Norman St. Barbe (?)-1969 .... CAP-1
Earlier sketch in CA 13-14
Slader, John M. 1924- 154
Slaght, Lawrence T(ownsend)
1912-1983 73-76
Slakter, Malcolm J(ulian) 1929- 41-44R
Slamecka, Vladimir 1928- 5-8R
Slamnig, Ivan 1930- .... DLB 181
Slancekova, Bozena
See Timrava
Slane, Andrea 1964- 220
Slaney, George Wilson 1884-1978 .... CAP-1
Earlier sketch in CA 13-14
Slangerup, Erik Jon 1969- 199
See also SATA 130
Slapikoff, Saul A(braham) 1931- 141
Slappey, Sterling G(reene) 1917-2001 65-68
Obituary 200
Slatalla, Michelle 177
Slataper, Scipio 1888-1915 .... DLB 264
Slate, Caroline 1934- CANR-120
Earlier sketch in CA 142
Slate, John
See Fearn, John Russell
Slate, Joseph 1927- 45-48
Slate, Joseph (Frank) 1928- 110
See also SATA 38, 122
Slate, Sam J(ordan) 1909-1981 49-52
Slaten, Yeffe Kimball 1914(?)-1978
Obituary 77-80
Slater, Charlotte (Wolpers) 1944- 65-68
Slater, Dashka 1963- 188
Slater, Eliot (Trevor Oakeshott)
1904-1983 53-56
Slater, Harrison Gradwell 220
Slater, Ian 1941- CANR-34
Earlier sketch in CA 85-88
Slater, James (Derrick)
See Slater, Jim
Slater, Jerome N(orman) 1935- 17-20R
Slater, Jim 1929- 144
Brief entry 112
See also SATA-Brief 34
Slater, John Clarke 1900-1976 156
Slater, Judith 1951- 204
Slater, Lauren 1962(?)- 182
Slater, Layton Ernest Alfred 1916-1984
Obituary 114
Slater, Leonard 1920- 13-16R
Slater, Lydia (Elizabeth) Pasternak 1902-1989
Obituary 128
Slater, Mariam K(reiselman) 1922- 123
Brief entry 118
Slater, Mary Louise 1923- 29-32R
Slater, Maya 1941- 119
Slater, Miriam 1931- 120
Slater, Niall W. 1954- CANR-137
Earlier sketch in CA 126
Slater, Nigel 1944- CANR-18
Earlier sketch in CA 102
Slater, Patrick 1880-1951 .... DLB 68
Slater, Peter Gregg 1940- 81-84
Slater, Philip E(lliot) 1927- CANR-40
Earlier sketch in CA 21-24R
Slater, Ralph P(hipps) 1915- 21-24R
Slater, Ray
See Lansdale, Joe R(ichard)
Slater, Robert 1943- CANR-43
Earlier sketch in CA 119
Slater, Robert (Henry) Lawson
1896-1984 .... CAP-1
Earlier sketch in CA 13-14
Slater, Stuart 1934- .... CP 1
Slater, Thomas J. 1955- 140
Slater, Veronica
See Sullivan, Victoria
Slatin, John M. 1952- 126
Slatkin, Charles Eli 1907-1977
Obituary 73-76
Slatoff, Walter J(acob) 1922-1991 .... 9-12R
Obituary 133
Slaton, Mary Leta Dorothy
See Lamour, Dorothy
Slatta, Richard W(ayne) 1947- CANR-94
Earlier sketch in CA 133
Slattery, Dennis Patrick 1944- 233
Slattery, Marty 1938- 134
Slattery, Timothy Patrick 1911- 25-28R
Slattery, William J(ames) 1930- 101
Slatzer, Robert F(ranklin) 1927-2005
Obituary 238
Brief entry 113
Slauerhoff, Jan Jacob 1898-1936 .... EWL 3
Slaughter, Anne-Marie 239
Slaughter, Anson
See Athanas, (William) Verne
Slaughter, Carolyn 1946- CANR-85
Earlier sketch in CA 85-88
See also CLC 56
See also CN 5, 6, 7
Slaughter, Eugene Edward 1909-1995 ... 37-40R
Slaughter, Frank G(ill) 1908-2001 ..... CANR-85
Obituary 197
Earlier sketches in CA 5-8R, CANR-5
Interview in CANR-5
See also AITN 2
See also CLC 29
See also RHW
Slaughter, Guy 1919- 151
Slaughter, Hope 1940- .... SATA 84
Slaughter, Howard K(ey) 1927- 45-48
Slaughter, Jane M(undy) 1908-1990 73-76
Slaughter, Jean
See Doty, Jean Slaughter
Slaughter, Jim
See Paine, Lauran (Bosworth)
Slaughter, Karin 216
Slaughter, M(ary) M(artina) 1940- 131
Slaughter, Tom 1955- .... SATA 152
Slavens, Thomas P(aul) 1928- CANR-46
Earlier sketches in CA 104, CANR-22
Slavet, Joseph S. 1920- 61-64
Slaveykov, Pencho 1866-1912 .... DLB 147
See also EWL 3
Slavic, Rosalind Welcher
See Welcher, Rosalind
Slavicek, Louise Chipley 1956- 217
See also SATA 144
Slavicek, Milivoj 1929- 208
See also DLB 181
Slavick, William H(enry) 1927- 104
Slavin, Arthur Joseph 1933- CANR-3
Earlier sketch in CA 9-12R
Slavin, Bill 1959- .... SATA 76, 148
Slavin, Julia 236
Slavin, Morris 1913- CANR-41
Earlier sketch in CA 118
Slavin, Neal 1941- 208
Slavin, Robert E(dward) 1950- 146
Slavin, Stephen L(oren) 1939- 111
Slavitt, David R(ytman) 1935- CANR-83
Earlier sketches in CA 21-24R, CANR-41
See also CAAS 3
See also CLC 5, 14
See also CN 1, 2
See also CP 1, 2, 3, 4, 5, 6, 7
See also DLB 5, 6
Slavson, Samuel R(ichard) 1890-1981 ... 17-20R
Obituary 182
Slavutych, Yar 1918- CANR-38
Earlier sketches in CA 45-48, CANR-2, 17
Slawson, Ron(ald L.) 1932- 128
Slawson, William David 1931- 110
Slaymaker, Melissa Eskridge 1958- ..... SATA 158
Slaymaker, R(edsecker) Samuel II 1923- .. 65-68
Slayton, Donald K(ent) 1924-1993 159
Slayton, Mariette (Elizabeth) Paine
1908- 65-68
Slayton, Robert A(llen) 1951- 204
Sleator, William (Warner III) 1945- ... CANR-97
Earlier sketches in CA 29-32R, CANR-46, 83
See also AAYA 5, 39
See also BYA 4, 6, 7, 8, 9, 10, 11, 16
See also CLR 29
See also JRDA
See also LAIT 5
See also MAICYA 1, 2
See also SATA 3, 68, 118, 161
See also WYA
See also YAW
Sledd, James Hinton 1914- 17-20R
Sledge, Linda Ching 1944- 108
Sledge, Michael 1962- 151
Slee, Debora A. 1949- CANR-96
Earlier sketch in CA 146
Slee, Vergil N(elson) 1917- 146
Sleem, Patricia Anne 1948- 222
Sleem, Patty
See Sleem, Patricia Anne
Sleeper, James A. 1947- 133
See also Sleeper, Jim
Sleeper, Jim CANR-81
See also Sleeper, James A.
Slegers, Liesbet 1975- .... SATA 154
Slegman, Ann 1954- 202
Sleigh, Barbara 1906-1982 .... CANR-83
Obituary 106
Earlier sketches in CA 13-16R, CANR-6, 51
See also CWRI 5
See also SATA 3, 86
See also SATA-Obit 30
Sleigh, Burrows Willcocks Arthur
1821-1869 .... DLB 99
Sleigh, Dan(iel) 236
Sleigh, (Brocas) Linwood 1902- 5-8R
Sleigh, Robert Collins, Jr. 1932- 37-40R
Sleigh, Tom 1953- CANR-139
Earlier sketch in CA 171
Sleight, Robert B(enton) 1922- 41-44R
Slemrod, Joel (B.) 202
Slepian, Jan(ice B.) 1921- CANR-83
Earlier sketch in CA 136
See also AAYA 20
See also JRDA
See also MAICYA 1, 2
See also SAAS 8
See also SATA 51, 85
See also SATA-Brief 45
See also YAW
Sleptsov, Vasilii Alekseevich
1836-1878 .... DLB 277
Slesar, Henry 1927-2002 .... CANR-61
Obituary 205
Earlier sketches in CA 1-4R, CANR-1
See also CMW 4
Slesin, Suzanne 1944- 123
Slesinger, Doris P(eyser) 1927- 113
Slesinger, Reuben E. 1916- 5-8R
Slesinger, Tess 1905-1945 199
Brief entry 107
See also DLB 102
See also TCLC 10
Slesinger, Warren 1933- 33-36R
Slesser, Malcolm 1926- 17-20R
Slessor, Kenneth 1901-1971 102
Obituary 89-92
See also CLC 14
See also DLB 260
See also RGEL 2
Slethaug, Gordon E. 1940- 140
Sletholt, Erik 1919- 77-80
Slezak, Walter 1902-1983
Obituary 109
Slicer, Margaret O. 1920- 25-28R
See also SATA 4
Slick, Grace (Wing) 1939- CANR-106
Earlier sketch in CA 183
Slide, Anthony (Clifford) 1944- CANR-142
Earlier sketches in CA 33-36R, CANR-12, 29, 53
Slier, Debby
See Shine, Deborah
Slim, William Joseph 1891-1970
Obituary 107
Slimming, John 1927-1979 .... 25-28R
Obituary 89-92
Slinger, Joey 1943(?)- 164
Slitor, Richard Eaton 1911-1982 .... CANR-32
Earlier sketch in CA 45-48
Slive, Seymour 1920- 103
Sliwa, Curtis 1954- 111
Sljivic-Simsic, Biljana 1933- 41-44R

Sloan, Alfred P(ritchard), Jr. 1875-1966
Obituary 113
Sloan, Allan 1944- 118
Sloan, Anthony
See Feist, Gene
Sloan, Bill
See Sloan, William E. III
Sloan, Carolyn 1937- CANR-117
Earlier sketches in CA 127, CANR-55
See also SATA 58, 116
Sloan, Don 1928- 142
Sloan, Edward William III 1931- 37-40R
Sloan, Glenna (Davis) 1930- 191
See also SATA 120
Sloan, Harold Stephenson 1887-1988 ... CAP-1
Earlier sketch in CA 17-18
Sloan, Irving J. 1924- CANR-7
Earlier sketch in CA 17-20R
Sloan, James Park (Jr.) 1944- CANR-63
Earlier sketch in CA 29-32R
Sloan, Jane 1946- 145
Sloan, John 1871-1951 232
See also DLB 188
Sloan, John 1948- 153
Sloan, Kay 1951- CANR-99
Earlier sketch in CA 108
Sloan, Mark 218
Sloan, Michael 1946- 130
Sloan, Pat(rick Alan) 1908-1978 .... CANR-43
Earlier sketch in CA 65-68
Sloan, Phillip R(eid) 1938- 109
Sloan, Raymond Paton 1893-1983 .... CAP-1
Obituary 109
Earlier sketch in CA 19-20
Sloan, Ruth Catherine 1898(?)-1976
Obituary 65-68
Sloan, Stephen 1936- 33-36R
Sloan, Susan R. 211
Sloan, Thomas 1928- 93-96
Sloan, Tod (Stratton) 1952- 140
Sloan, William E. III 1935- 207
Sloan, William Wilson 1901-1991 .... 1-4R
Sloane, Arthur A(llan) 1931- 33-36R
Sloane, Eric 1910(?)-1985 108
Obituary 115
See also SATA 52
See also SATA-Obit 42
Sloane, Eugene A(nthony) 1926- 65-68
Sloane, Howard N(orman) 1932- 81-84
Sloane, Joseph C(urtis) 1909-1998 .... CAP-1
Earlier sketch in CA 11-12
Sloane, Leonard 1932- 21-24R
Sloane, Martin 1940- 132
Sloane, Peter J(ames) 1942- 108
Sloane, R(obert) Bruce 1923- 53-56
Sloane, Sara
See Bloom, Ursula (Harvey)
Sloane, Thomas O. 1929- 37-40R
Sloane, Todd 1955- .... SATA 88
Sloane, William M. 1906-1974
Obituary 53-56
See also DLB 284
See also HGG
See also SFW 4
Sloat, Teri 1948- 138
See also SATA 70, 106
Sloate, Daniel 1931- CANR-32
Earlier sketch in CA 113
Slobin, Dan Isaac 1939- CANR-11
Earlier sketch in CA 65-68
Slobin, Mark 1943- CANR-106
Earlier sketch in CA 93-96
Slobodin, Richard 1915- 102
Slobodkin, Florence Gersh 1905-1994 ...... 1-4R
Obituary 170
See also SATA 5
See also SATA-Obit 107
Slobodkin, Lawrence (B.) 1928- 137
Slobodkin, Louis 1903-1975 .... CANR-83
Obituary 57-60
Earlier sketch in CA 13-16R
See also CWRI 5
See also MAICYA 1, 2
See also SATA 1, 26
Slobodkina, Esphyr 1908-2002 .... CANR-84
Obituary 209
Earlier sketches in CA 1-4R, CANR-1
See also CWRI 5
See also SAAS 8
See also SATA 1
See also SATA-Obit 135
Slochower, Harry 1900-1991 .... CANR-2
Obituary 134
Earlier sketch in CA 49-52
Slocombe, Douglas 1913- .... IDFW 3, 4
Slocum, Bill
See Slocum, William J(oseph Michael), Jr.
Slocum, Donald Barclay 1911-1983
Obituary 110
Slocum, Frank 1925-1997 136
Obituary 158
Slocum, John W(esley), Jr. 1940- 112
Slocum, Joshua 1844-1910(?) 211
Slocum, Michael
See Slocum, William J(oseph Michael), Jr.
Slocum, Milton Jonathan
1905-1993 .... CANR-86
Obituary 140
Earlier sketch in CA 126
Slocum, Robert Bigney 1922- 9-12R
Slocum, Robert Boak 1952- 206
Slocum, Walter L(ucius) 1910-1975 ...... 21-24R
Slocum, William J(oseph Michael), Jr.
1912(?)-1974
Obituary 53-56
Sloggatt, Arthur H(astings) 1917(?)-1975
Obituary 61-64
Sloggett, Nellie 1851-1923 .... SATA 44
Sloma, Richard Stanley 1929- CANR-19
Earlier sketch in CA 103
Sloman, Albert Edward 1921- 5-8R
Sloman, Larry 1948- CANR-20
Earlier sketch in CA 81-84
Slomovitz, Philip 1896-1993 81-84
Obituary 201
Slomp, Hans 1945- 175
Slonczewski, Joan (Lyn) 1956- .... SFW 4
Slone, Dennis 1930-1982
Obituary 106
Slone, Verna Mae 1914- 89-92
Slonim, Marc 1894-1976
Obituary 65-68
Slonim, Morris J(ames) 1909-2004 .... 1-4R
Obituary 228
Slonim, Reuben 1914- 97-100
Slonim, Ruth 1918- 17-20R
Slonimski, Antoni 1895-1976
Obituary 65-68
See also EWL 3
Slonimsky, Mikhail Leonidovich
1897-1972 .... DLB 272
Slonimsky, Nicolas 1894-1995 .... CANR-97
Obituary 150
Earlier sketch in CA 17-20R
Slonimsky, Yuri 1902-1978
Obituary 77-80
Slosberg, Mike 1934- 69-72
Slosberg, Myron
See Slosberg, Mike
Sloss, Lesley Lord 1965- .... SATA 72
Slosser, Bob G(ene) 1929- CANR-10
Earlier sketch in CA 65-68
Slosson, Preston (William)
1892-1984 .... CANR-8
Earlier sketch in CA 61-64
Slote, Alfred 1926- 203
See also CLR 4
See also CWRI 5
See also JRDA
See also MAICYA 1, 2
See also SAAS 21
See also SATA 8, 72
Slote, Bernice D. 1915(?)-1983
Obituary 109
Slote, Elizabeth 1956- .... SATA 80
Slote, Michael A(nthony) 1941- 61-64
Slote, Stanley J(ames) 1917- 61-64
Slotkin, Richard S(idney) 1942- CANR-97
Earlier sketches in CA 102, CANR-41
Slotnick, Daniel L(eonid) 1931-1985
Obituary 117
Slotten, Ross A. 1954- 233
Slouka, Mark CANR-116
Earlier sketch in CA 156
Slovenko, Ralph 1926- 17-20R
Slovo, Gillian 1952- .... CMW 4
Slovo, Joe 1926-1995 161
Slowacki, Juliusz 1809-1849 .... RGWL 3
Slowikowski, M. Z. Rygor 1896-1989(?)
Obituary 129
Sloyan, Gerard Stephen 1919- CANR-40
Earlier sketches in CA 5-8R, CANR-2, 18
Sluchevsky, Konstantin Konstantinovich
1837-1904 .... DLB 277
Sluckin, W(ladyslaw) 1919-1985 .... 21-24R
Obituary 116
Slung, Louis Sheaffer
See Sheaffer, Louis
Slung, Michele (Beth) 1947- 102
Slusher, Howard S. 1937- 25-28R
Slusser, Dorothy M. 1922- 33-36R
Slusser, George Edgar 1939- CANR-13
Earlier sketch in CA 69-72
Slusser, Gerald H(erbert) 1920- 13-16R
Slusser, Robert M(elville) 1916- CANR-3
Earlier sketch in CA 1-4R
Slutsky, Boris (Abramovich) 1919-1986 193
Slye, Leonard Franklin
See Rogers, Roy
Smaerup Sorensen, Jens
See Sorensen, Jens Smaerup
Smaldone, William 1958- 185
Smale, Stephen 1930- 162
Small, Albion Woodbury 1854-1926 213
Small, Bertrice 1937- CANR-84
Earlier sketches in CA 77-80, CANR-13, 29, 53
See also RHW
Small, David 1937- CANR-39
Earlier sketch in CA 108
Small, David 1945- .... CLR 53
See also MAICYA 2
See also SATA 50, 95, 126
See also SATA-Brief 46
Small, Dwight Hervey 1919- CANR-8
Earlier sketch in CA 61-64
Small, Ernest
See Lent, Blair
Small, Gary W(illiam) 1951- CANR-122
Earlier sketch in CA 127
Small, George L(eroy) 1924- 85-88
Small, George Raphael 1918- 57-60
Small, Hugh 1943- 208
Small, Jocelyn Penny 1945- 186
Small, Kenneth A(lan) 1945- CANR-43
Earlier sketch in CA 112
Small, Melvin 1939- CANR-92
Earlier sketches in CA 29-32R, CANR-12, 30, 58
Small, Miriam Rossiter 1899-1985 .... 1-4R
Obituary 199
Small, Norman M. 1944- 41-44R
Small, Terry 1942- 142
See also SATA 75
Small, William
See Eversley, D(avid) E(dward) C(harles)
Smallcomb, Pam 1954- .... SATA 159
Smallenburg, Harry W. 1907- CAP-1
Earlier sketch in CA 13-14
Smalley, Barbara Martin 1926- 105
Smalley, Beryl 1905-1984 103
Obituary 112
Smalley, Donald (Arthur) 1907- 17-20R
Smalley, Gary 192
Smalley, Ruth E(lizabeth) 1903-1979 ..... CAP-2
Earlier sketch in CA 21-22
Smalley, Stephen Stewart 1931- 103
Smalley, Stuart
See Franken, Al
Smalley, William A. 1923-1997 .... CANR-1
Obituary 163
Earlier sketch in CA 45-48
Smallman, Basil 1921- CANR-103
Earlier sketch in CA 150
Smalls, Irene
See Smalls-Hector, Irene
Smalls-Hector, Irene 1950- 220
See also CLR 103
See also SATA 73, 146
Smallwood, Arwin D. 1965- 192
Smallwood, Carol 1939- CANR-138
Earlier sketches in CA 122, CANR-45, 90
Smallwood, Frank(lin) 1927- 123
Brief entry 118
Smallwood, James (Milton) 1944- 115
Smallwood, Joseph R(oberts)
1900-1991 .... CANR-43
Earlier sketch in CA 105
Smallwood, Norah (Evelyn) 1910(?)-1984
Obituary 114
See also SATA-Obit 41
Smarandache, Florentin 1954- 204
Smaridge, Norah (Antoinette)
1903-1994 .... 37-40R
See also SATA 6
Smart, (Peter) Alastair (Marshall)
1922-1992 .... CANR-96
Earlier sketch in CA 37-40R
Smart, Albert Davis 1931(?)-1989
Obituary 130
Smart, Barry 1946- 117
Smart, Carol 1948- CANR-37
Earlier sketches in CA 73-76, CANR-16
Smart, Carolyn (Alexandra) 1952- CANR-38
Earlier sketch in CA 116
Smart, Charles Allen 1904-1967 .... CAP-1
Earlier sketch in CA 11-12
Smart, Christopher 1722-1771 .... DAM POET
See also DLB 109
See also PC 13
See also RGEL 2
Smart, David A. 1892-1952 .... DLB 137
Smart, Elizabeth 1913-1986 81-84
Obituary 118
See also CLC 54
See also CN 4
See also DLB 88
Smart, Graydon F. 1906(?)-1984
Obituary 111
Smart, Harold R(obert) 1892-1979 .... CAP-1
Earlier sketch in CA 9-10
Smart, Ian Isidore 1944- 142
See also BW 2
Smart, J(ohn) J(amieson) C(arswell)
1920- CANR-82
Earlier sketches in CA 13-16R, CANR-7, 36
See also DLB 262
Smart, James D(ick) 1906-1982 .... CANR-8
Obituary 105
Earlier sketch in CA 57-60
Smart, Mary (Spencer Simpson) 1915- 159
Smart, Mollie S(tevens) 1916- 61-64
Smart, (Roderick) Ninian
1927-2001 .... CANR-56
Obituary 192
Earlier sketches in CA 29-32R, CANR-12, 30
Smart, S(tephen) Bruce, Jr. 1923- 142
Smart, William (Edward, Jr.) 1933- CANR-7
Earlier sketch in CA 13-16R
Smartt, J(oseph) 1931- 138
Smead, (Edwin) Howard 1953- 124
Smedes, Lewis B. 1921-2002 .... CANR-36
Obituary 211
Earlier sketches in CA 69-72, CANR-11
Smedley, Agnes 1892-1950 154
See also FW
See also TCWW 2
Smedley, Audrey 147
Smedley, Hester Marsden
See Marsden-Smedley, Hester
Smedley, Menella Bute 1820(?)-1877 . DLB 199
Smedley, Philip Marsden
See Marsden-Smedley, Philip
Smeds, Dave 1955- CANR-123
Earlier sketch in CA 118
Smee, John (Charles) Odling
See Odling-Smee, John (Charles)
Smee, Nicola 1948- .... SATA 76
Smeed, J. W. 1926- CANR-55
Earlier sketch in CA 127
Smeeton, Miles (Richard) 1906-1988 .... 13-16R
Obituary 126
Smeijers, Fred 1961- 189
Smelianskii, Anatolii M.
See Smeliansky, Anatoly
Smeliansky, Anatoly 208
Smellie, Jim 1955- 133
Smellie, K.
See Smellie, Kingsley Bryce (Speakman)
Smellie, K. B.
See Smellie, Kingsley Bryce (Speakman)
Smellie, Kingsley Bryce (Speakman)
1897-1987 .... 5-8R
Obituary 124
Smelser, Marshall 1912-1978 .... 17-20R
Obituary 135
Smelser, Neil J(oseph) 1930- CANR-8
Earlier sketch in CA 17-20R
Smelser, William T. 1924- 29-32R
Smeltzer, C(larence) H(arry)
1900-1970(?) CANR-15
Earlier sketch in CA 1-4R
Smelyakov, Yaroslav 1913(?)-1972
Obituary 37-40R
Smerk, George M(artin) 1933- 107
Smertenko, Johan J. 1897(?)-1983
Obituary 109
Smerud, Warren D(ouglas) 1928- 49-52
Smetana, Josette 1928- 93-96
Smethurst, Mae J. 1935- 133
Smethurst, Susan E. 1951- 187
Smethurst, William (Knowles) 1945- 117
Smidt, Kristian 1916- 17-20R
Smigel, Erwin O. 1917-1973 .... 41-44R
Obituary 45-48
Smigel, Robert 1960- 232
Smil, Vaclav 1943- CANR-105
Earlier sketches in CA 112, CANR-30
Smilansky, Moshe 1874-1953 213
Smiles, Sam 175
Smiles, Samuel 1812-1904 .... DLB 55
Smiley, Charles W(esley) 1940- 113
Smiley, David L(eslie) 1921- 5-8R
Smiley, Jane (Graves) 1949- CANR-96
Earlier sketches in CA 104, CANR-30, 50, 74
Interview in CANR-30
See also AAYA 66
See also AMWS 6
See also BPFB 3
See also CLC 53, 76, 144
See also CN 6, 7
See also CPW 1
See also DA3
See also DAM POP
See also DLB 227, 234
See also EWL 3
See also MAL 5
See also MTFW 2005
See also SSFS 19
Smiley, Sam Max 1931- 105
Smiley, Tavis 1964- 206
Smiley, Virginia Kester 1923- CANR-28
Earlier sketches in CA 29-32R, CANR-12
See also SATA 2
Smiraglia, Richard P(aul) 1952- CANR-134
Earlier sketch in CA 169
Smirnoff, Marc 1963(?)- 234
Smirnov, Sergei Sergeevich 1915-1976
Obituary 65-68
Smith, Liz 1923-
See Smith, Mary Elizabeth
Smith, A(nthony) C(harles) H(ockley)
1935- CANR-44
Brief entry 116
Earlier sketch in CA 119
Smith, A(lexander) G(raham) Cairns
See Cairns-Smith, A(lexander) G(raham)
Smith, A(lbert) H(ugh) 1903-1967 .... 5-8R
Smith, A(lbert) J(ames) 1924-1991 65-68
Obituary 136
Smith, A(rthur) J(ames) M(arshall)
1902-1980 .... CANR-4
Obituary 102
Earlier sketch in CA 1-4R
See also CLC 15
See also CP 1, 2
See also DAC
See also DLB 88
See also RGEL 2
Smith, A. Robert 1925- 73-76
Smith, A. Weston 1900(?)-1975
Obituary 57-60
Smith, Abbot E(merson) 1906-1983
Obituary 109
Smith, Ada Beatrice Queen Victoria Louisa Virginia 1894-1984
Obituary 111
Smith, Adam
See Goodman, George J(erome) W(aldo)
See also DLB 185
Smith, Adam 1723(?)-1790 .... DLB 104, 252
See also RGEL 2
Smith, Alan M(cKinley) 1937- 41-44R
Smith, Alexander 1829-1867 .... DLB 32, 55
Smith, Alexander McCall 1948- 215
Smith, Alfred Edward 1895-1969 .... CAP-1
Earlier sketch in CA 11-12
Smith, Alfred G(oud) 1921- CANR-4
Earlier sketch in CA 9-12R
Smith, Ali 1962- CANR-88
Earlier sketch in CA 150
Smith, Alice K(imball) 1907- 138
Smith, Alice Upham 1908-1998 45-48
Smith, Allen William 1938- 61-64
Smith, Alson Jesse 1908-1965 .... 1-4R
Obituary 103
Smith, Alton E. 1917- 17-20R
Smith, Amanda (Dale) 203
Smith, Amanda 1837-1915 .... DLB 221
Smith, Andrew F. 1946- 191
Smith, Angel
See Masterton, Graham
Smith, Anna Deavere 1950- CANR-103
Earlier sketch in CA 133
See also CD 5, 6
See also CLC 86
See also DFS 2, 22

Cumulative Index 539 Smith

Smith, Anna H(ester) 1912- CANR-6
Earlier sketch in CA 57-60
Smith, Anna Piszczan-Czaja 1920- 110
Smith, Anne Mollegen 1940- 81-84
Smith, Anne Warren 1938- 111
See also SATA 41
See also SATA-Brief 34
Smith, Annick 1936- CANR-95
Earlier sketch in CA 149
Smith, Anthony (John Francis)
1926- CANR-45
Earlier sketches in CA 9-12R, CANR-3
Smith, Anthony 1938- CANR-10
Earlier sketch in CA 53-56
Smith, Anthony D(avid) 1939- 101
Smith, Anthony Peter 1912-1980
Obituary 105
Smith, April 1949- CANR-99
Earlier sketch in CA 151
Smith, Arnold Cantwell 1915-1994 109
Smith, Arthur 1948- 120
Smith, Arthur C. 1916- 21-24R
Smith, Arthur L(ee)
See Asante, Molefi Kete
Smith, Arthur L(ee), Jr. 1927- 37-40R
Smith, Arthur M(umford) 1903-1968 ..... CAP-2
Earlier sketch in CA 17-18
Smith, Audrey D(owling) 1930- 119
Smith, Barbara 1929- 206
Smith, Barbara 1946- 142
See also BW 2
See also FW
See also GLL 1
Smith, Barbara 1949- 189
Smith, Barbara B(urnett) 183
Smith, Barbara Clark 1951- 124
Smith, Barbara Dawson 206
Smith, Barbara Herrnstein 1932- 13-16R
Smith, Bardwell L(eith) 1925- 41-44R
Smith, Barry (Edward Jervis) 1943- ...... SATA 75
Smith, Barry D(ecker) 1940- 29-32R
Smith, Beatrice S(chillinger) CANR-10
Earlier sketch in CA 57-60
See also SATA 12
Smith, Ben A(rwood) 1916- 1-4R
Smith, Benjamin Franklin 1902-1987 .... 41-44R
Smith, Bernard (William) 1916- CANR-17
Earlier sketches in CA 1-4R, CANR-1
Smith, Bert Kruger 1915- CANR-11
Earlier sketch in CA 13-16R
Smith, Betsy Covington 1937- 111
See also SATA 43, 55
Smith, Betty (Wehner) 1904-1972 .... 5-8R
Obituary 33-36R
See also BPFB 3
See also BYA 3
See also CLC 19
See also DLBY 1982
See also LAIT 3
See also RGAL 4
See also SATA 6
Smith, Beulah Fenderson 1915- 13-16R
Smith, Bob 1958- 183
Smith, Bobbi
See Walton, Bobbi Smith
Smith, Bonnie G(ene) 1940- CANR-50
Earlier sketches in CA 108, CANR-25
Smith, Boyd M. 1888(?)-1973
Obituary 41-44R
Smith, Bradford 1909-1964 .... CANR-16
Earlier sketch in CA 1-4R
See also SATA 5
Smith, Bradley 1910-1997 .... CANR-19
Obituary 160
Earlier sketches in CA 5-8R, CANR-2
Smith, Bradley A. 1958- 203
Smith, Bradley F. 1931- CANR-43
Earlier sketch in CA 108
Smith, Brenda 1946- 149
See also SATA 82
Smith, Brian 1949- 139
Smith, Brian C(live) 1938- CANR-30
Earlier sketch in CA 110
Smith, Brian R. 1939- CANR-70
Earlier sketch in CA 129
Smith, Bromley K(eables) 1911-1987
Obituary 121
Smith, Bruce 1949- 108
Smith, Bruce L. R. 1936- 141
Smith, Bruce R. 1946- CANR-88
Earlier sketch in CA 139
Smith, Bryan Evers Sharwood
See Sharwood Smith, Bryan Evers
Smith, C. Busby
See Smith, John (Charles)
Smith, C. Pritchard
See Hoyt, Edwin P(almer), Jr.
Smith, C. Ray 1929-1988 .... CANR-28
Obituary 126
Earlier sketch in CA 109
Smith, C(lifford) T(horpe) 1924- 21-24R
Smith, C(ora) U. 1901-1993 .... 41-44R
Smith, C(hristopher) U(pham) M(urray)
1930- 33-36R
Smith, C(harles) W(illiam) 1940- 61-64
See also TCWW 2
Smith, C. Willard 1899(?)-1979
Obituary 89-92
Smith, Caesar
See Trevor, Elleston
Smith, Cameron Mitchell 1935- 133
Smith, Carleton 1910-1984
Obituary 112
Smith, Carlton
See Rocklin, Ross Louis
Smith, Carmichael
See Linebarger, Paul M(yron) A(nthony)
Smith, Carol H(ertzig) 1929- 5-8R
Smith, Carol Sturm 1938- CANR-25
Earlier sketch in CA 25-28R
See also DLBY 1981
Smith, Carole 1935- 101
Smith, Carolyn J. 1946- 175
Smith, (Charles) Carter (Jr.) 1930- 107
Smith, Catherine C. 1929- 29-32R
Smith, Cecil (Howard III) 1917- 69-72
Smith, Celina Janson
See Janson-Smith, Celina
Smith, Chard Powers 1894-1977 .... 5-8R
Obituary 73-76
Smith, Charles
See Heckelmann, Charles N(ewman)
Smith, Charles E(dward) 1904-1970
Obituary 29-32R
Smith, Charles Harvard Gibbs
See Gibbs-Smith, Charles Harvard
Smith, Charles Henry 1826-1903
Brief entry 119
See also DLB 11
Smith, Charles Merrill (?)-1985
Obituary 115
Smith, Charles R., (Jr.) 1969- .... SATA 159
Smith, Charles W(illiam) (Frederick)
1905-1993 .... 13-16R
Obituary 142
Smith, Charlie 1947- CANR-97
Earlier sketch in CA 143
Smith, Charlotte (Turner) 1749-1806 ... DLB 39, 109
See also RGEL 2
See also TEA
Smith, Cherry 1931- 120
Smith, Chet 1899-1973 200
See also DLB 171
Smith, Christian 1960- 186
Smith, Christine 1945- 143
Smith, Clagett G. 1930- 37-40R
Smith, Clark Ashton 1893-1961 .... CANR-81
Earlier sketch in CA 143
See also CLC 43
See also FANT
See also HGG
See also MTCW 2
See also SCFW 1, 2
See also SFW 4
See also SUFW
Smith, Clifford Neal 1923- 41-44R
Smith, Clint E(rnest) 1930- 198
Smith, Clodus R(ay) 1928- CANR-8
Earlier sketch in CA 21-24R
Smith, (Christopher) Colin 1927- 102
Smith, Constance Babington
See Babington Smith, Constance
Smith, Cordelia (Meda) Titcomb
1902-1994 .... CAP-1
Obituary 198
Earlier sketch in CA 11-12
Smith, Cordwainer
See Linebarger, Paul M(yron) A(nthony)
See also DLB 8
See also SCFW 1, 2
Smith, Cornelius C(ole, Jr.) 1913- CANR-22
Earlier sketch in CA 21-24R
Smith, Courtland L(ester) 1939- 81-84
Smith, Craig 1955- .... SATA 81, 117
Smith, Craig R(alph) 1944- 81-84
Smith, Curt 1951- 81-84
Smith, Curtis C. 1939- 127
Smith, Cynthia Leitich 1967- 227
See also AAYA 51
See also SATA 152
Smith, Cynthia S. 1924- CANR-81
Earlier sketch in CA 106
Smith, Cyril 1928- 109
Smith, Cyril James 1909-1974
Obituary 53-56
Smith, D(avid) Howard 1900-1987 .... 25-28R
Obituary 123
Smith, D. MacLeod
See Smith, David MacLeod
Smith, D(wight) Moody, Jr. 1931- CANR-42
Earlier sketches in CA 41-44R, CANR-20
Smith, D(onald) V(incent) 1933-1978 ... 25-28R
Obituary 117
Smith, D(avid) W(arner) 1932- CANR-12
Earlier sketch in CA 17-20R
Smith, Dale L(ee) 1953- CANR-144
Earlier sketch in CA 146
Smith, Dale O(rville) 1911-1998 73-76
Smith, Dan Throop 1908-1982
Obituary 106
Smith, Dana Prom 1927- 49-52
Smith, Daniel M(alloy) 1922-1976 ..... CANR-8
Earlier sketch in CA 17-20R
Smith, Daniel S(omers) 1961- 147
Smith, Danyel 1965(?)- 219
Smith, Darren L. 1958- 124
Smith, Datus C(lifford), Jr.
1907-1999 .... CANR-11
Obituary 186
Earlier sketches in CAP-1, CA 11-12
See also SATA 13
See also SATA-Obit 116
Smith, Dave
See Smith, David (Jeddie)
See also CAAS 7
See also CLC 22, 42
See also DLB 5
Smith, David
See Allyn, David S(mith)
Smith, David 1906-1965
Obituary 113
Smith, David (Jeddie) 1942- CANR-120
Earlier sketches in CA 49-52, CANR-1, 59
See also Smith, Dave
See also CP 7
See also CSW
See also DAM POET
Smith, David (Anthony) 1943- 128
Smith, David 1970- 173
Smith, David A(lden) 1956- 162
Smith, David Alexander 1953- 143
Smith, David C(layton) 1929- 49-52
Smith, David C. 1931- 69-72
Smith, David C. 1952- 120
Smith, David Elvin 1939- 29-32R
Smith, David Fay 1939- 112
Smith, David G. 1948- 206
Smith, David H. 1939- 93-96
Smith, David Horton 1939- CANR-97
Earlier sketches in CA 57-60, CANR-7
Smith, David James 183
Smith, David L(awrence) 1963- 149
Smith, David M(arshall) 1936- CANR-12
Earlier sketch in CA 29-32R
Smith, David MacLeod 1920- CANR-5
Earlier sketch in CA 53-56
Smith, David Osmond
See Osmond-Smith, David
Smith, David Shiverick 1918- 108
Smith, David T. 1935- 53-56
Smith, David W. 1921-1981 110
Obituary 108
Smith, Dean (Edwards) 1931- 189
Smith, Dean E(llis) 1923- CANR-4
Earlier sketch in CA 9-12R
Smith, Deborah 1955- CANR-103
Earlier sketch in CA 143
Smith, Debra 1955- .... SATA 89
Smith, Delia 149
Smith, Delos Owen 1905-1973
Obituary 41-44R
Smith, Denis 1932- 175
Smith, Denison Langley 1924- 13-16R
Smith, Dennis 1940- CANR-90
Earlier sketches in CA 61-64, CANR-10
Smith, Derek 1943- 212
See also SATA 141
Smith, Desmond 1927- 103
Smith, Dian G. 1946- 120
Smith, Diana Kappel
See Kappel-Smith, Diana
Smith, Diane 217
Smith, Dick 1908-1974 .... CAP-1
Earlier sketch in CA 19-20
See also IDFW 3, 4
Smith, Dick King
See King-Smith, Dick
Smith, Dinitia 1945- CANR-82
Earlier sketch in CA 136
Smith, Dodie
See Smith, Dorothy Gladys
See also CBD
See also CWD
See also DLB 10
Smith, Don(ald Taylor) 1909- 49-52
Smith, Don Ian 1918- 45-48
Smith, Donal Ian Bryce 1934- 41-44R
Smith, Donald Eugene 1927- 9-12R
Smith, Donald G. 1927- 13-16R
Smith, Doris Buchanan 1934-2002 ... CANR-11
Obituary 211
Earlier sketch in CA 69-72
See also DLB 52
See also JRDA
See also MAICYA 1, 2
See also SAAS 10
See also SATA 28, 75
See also SATA-Obit 140
See also YAW
Smith, Doris E(dna Elliott)
1919-1994 .... CANR-18
Earlier sketch in CA 25-28R
See also RHW
Smith, Dorothea Fuller 1927- 196
Smith, Dorothy Gladys 1896-1990 ... CANR-37
Obituary 133
See also Smith, Dodie
See also MAICYA 1, 2
See also SATA 82
See also SATA-Obit 65
Smith, Dorothy Stafford 1905- 21-24R
See also SATA 6
Smith, Dorothy Valentine 1908- 29-32R
Smith, Douglas 1918- 73-76
Smith, Douglas 1949- 113
Smith, Douglas K. 1949- 160
Smith, Duane A(llan) 1937- CANR-47
Earlier sketches in CA 21-24R, CANR-8, 23
Smith, Dwight C(hichester), Jr. 1930- 77-80
Smith, Dwight L. 1918- CANR-103
Earlier sketches in CA 33-36R, CANR-24, 49
Smith, Dwight R. 1921- 106
Smith, E(lmer) Boyd 1860-1943 .... YABC 1
Smith, E(dric) Brooks 1917- 5-8R
See also SATA 40
Smith, E(ric) D(avid) 1923- CANR-41
Earlier sketch in CA 118
Smith, E. E.
See Smith, Edward Elmer
Smith, E. E. "Doc"
See Smith, Edward Elmer
Smith, Edgar H(erbert) 1934- 25-28R
Smith, Edna Hopkins 1932(?)-1979
Obituary 89-92
Smith, Edward Conrad 1891-1982 45-48
Smith, Edward E.
See Smith, Edward Elmer
Smith, Edward E. "Doc"
See Smith, Edward Elmer
Smith, Edward Ellis 1921- 25-28R
Smith, Edward Elmer 1890-1965 118
Obituary 102
See also DLB 8
See also SCFW 1, 2
See also SFW 4
Smith, Edward W(illiam) 1920-1975
Obituary 57-60
Smith, Edwin H. 1920- 13-16R
Smith, Elbert B(enjamin) 1920- 21-24R
Smith, Lady Eleanor (Furneaux)
1902-1945 .... HGG
See also RHW
Smith, Eleanor Touhey 1910- 25-28R
Smith, Elihu Hubbard 1771-1798 .... DLB 37
Smith, Elinor Goulding 1917- CANR-3
Earlier sketch in CA 1-4R
Smith, Eliot Fremont
See Fremont-Smith, Eliot
Smith, Elizabeth A(ngele) T(aft)
1958- CANR-86
Earlier sketch in CA 133
Smith, Elizabeth Oakes (Prince) 1806-1893
See Oakes Smith, Elizabeth
See also DLB 1
Smith, Elliott Dunlap 1890(?)-1976
Obituary 61-64
Smith, Elsdon C(oles) 1903-1996 .... CANR-6
Earlier sketch in CA 1-4R
Smith, Elske v(an)P(anhuys) 1929- 77-80
Smith, Elton E(dward) 1915- CANR-14
Earlier sketch in CA 13-16R
Smith, Elva Sophronia 1871-1965
Obituary 107
See also SATA-Brief 31
Smith, Elwyn Allen 1919- CANR-9
Earlier sketch in CA 5-8R
Smith, Emma 1923- 73-76
See also CN 1, 2, 3, 4, 5, 6, 7
See also SATA 52
See also SATA-Brief 36
Smith, Eric Ledell 1949- 144
Smith, Erin A(nn) 1970- 232
Smith, Ernest A(llyn) 1911-1977 .... 1-4R
Obituary 103
Smith, Ethel Morgan 1952- 198
Smith, Ethel Sabin 1887-1981 .... CAP-1
Earlier sketch in CA 13-16
Smith, Eugene L(ewis) 1912-1986 .... 21-24R
Obituary 118
Smith, Eugene Waldo 1905-1990 .... CAP-1
Earlier sketch in CA 9-10
Smith, Eunice 1757-1823 .... DLB 200
Smith, (Katherine) Eunice (Young)
1902-1993 .... CANR-2
Earlier sketch in CA 5-8R
See also SATA 5
Smith, Evans Lansing 1950- 187
Smith, Evelyn E. 1927-2000
Brief entry 113
See also SFW 4
Smith, F(rederick) G(eorge) Walton
1909-1989 .... CANR-44
Obituary 130
Earlier sketch in CA 45-48
Smith, F(rancis) Hopkinson 1838-1915 213
See also DLBD 13
Smith, F. Joseph 1925- CANR-2
Earlier sketch in CA 45-48
Smith, F. Todd 1957- 152
Smith, Fay Jackson 1912- 25-28R
Smith, Faye McDonald 1950- CANR-87
Earlier sketch in CA 157
Smith, Florence Margaret
1902-1971 .... CANR-35
Obituary 29-32R
Earlier sketches in CAP-2, CA 17-18
See also Smith, Stevie
See also DAM POET
See also MTCW 1, 2
See also TEA
Smith, Ford
See Friend, Oscar
See also TCWW 2
Smith, Frances C(hristine) 1904-1986 . CANR-1
Earlier sketch in CA 1-4R
See also SATA 3
Smith, Frances Scott Fitzgerald Lanahan
1921-1986
Obituary 119
Smith, Francis 1949- 195
Smith, Francis Hopkinson
See Smith, F(rancis) Hopkinson
Smith, Frank (Arthur) 1917- 69-72
Smith, Frank E(llis) 1918-1997 .... 17-20R
Obituary 160
Smith, Frank E. 1919-1984
Obituary 114
See also CMW 4
Smith, Frank Kingston 1919- CANR-18
Earlier sketch in CA 102
Smith, Frank O. M. (?)-1983
Obituary 109
Smith, Frank Seymour 1898-1972 .... CANR-86
Obituary 89-92
Earlier sketch in CA 9-12R
Smith, (David) Fred(erick) 1898(?)-1976
Obituary 69-72
Smith, Frederick E(screet) 1922- CANR-44
Earlier sketches in CA 5-8R, CANR-3, 19
Smith, Frederick W(illiam) 1920- 73-76
Smith, Frederick William Robin 1936-1985
Obituary 115

Smith, Frederick Winston Furneaux
1907-1975 65-68
Obituary 57-60
Smith, Fredrika Shumway 1877-1968
Obituary 109
See also SATA-Brief 30
Smith, G(eorge) E(verard) Kidder
1913-1997 .... 9-12R
Obituary 162
Smith, Gaddis 1932- 21-24R
Smith, Garry (Van Dorn) 1933- 5-8R
Smith, Gary (Milton) 1943- 97-100
Smith, Gary R. 1932- 69-72
See also SATA 14
Smith, Gary V(incent) 1943- 101
Smith, Gavin D. 1960- 144
Smith, (John) Geddeth, Jr. 1934- 175
Smith, Gene 1924- 77-80
Smith, Gene 1929- 81-84
Smith, Genevieve Love 1917- 21-24R
Smith, Geof 1969- 169
See also SATA 102
Smith, Geoffrey (John) 1943- 120
Smith, Geoffrey (Francis) Hattersley
See Hattersley-Smith, Geoffrey (Francis)
Smith, Geoffrey Sutton 1941- 49-52
Smith, George (Henry) 1922-1996 103
See also SFW 4
Smith, George D. 1870-1920 .... DLB 140
Smith, George E. 1938- 37-40R
Smith, George Harmon 1920- 49-52
See also SATA 5
Smith, George Ivan 1915-1995 121
Obituary 150
Smith, George O(liver) 1911-1981 ... CANR-28
Obituary 103
Earlier sketch in CA 97-100
See also DLB 8
See also SFW 4
Smith, George P(atrick) II 1939- CANR-96
Earlier sketch in CA 131
Smith, Gerald A(lfred) 1921- 37-40R
Smith, Gerald B. 1909- CAP-2
Earlier sketch in CA 25-28
Smith, Gerald L(yman) K(enneth) 1898-1976
Obituary 65-68
Smith, Gerald Stanton 1938- 123
Smith, Glenn C. 1924- 123
Smith, Glenn Robert 1952- 145
Smith, Godfrey 1926- 9-12R
Smith, Goldwin 1823-1910 .... DLB 99
Smith, Goldwin (Albert) 1912-1994 ...... 41-44R
Smith, Gordon Roland
See Roland Smith, Gordon
Smith, Gordon Ross 1917- 5-8R
Smith, Gordon T. 1953- 223
Smith, Grahame 1933- 25-28R
Smith, Greg Leitich 227
See also SATA 152
Smith, Gregory Blake 1951- 141
Smith, Gregory White 1951- CANR-118
Earlier sketch in CA 144
Smith, Gretchen L. (?)-1972
Obituary 104
Smith, Grover C(leveland) 1923- 33-36R
Smith, Gudmund J(ohn) W(ilhelm) 1920- ... 102
Smith, Guy N(ewman) 1939- .... HGG
Smith, Guy-Harold 1895-1976 .... CAP-2
Earlier sketch in CA 19-20
Smith, H(arry) Allen 1907-1976 .... CANR-5
Obituary 65-68
Earlier sketch in CA 5-8R
See also AITN 2
See also DLB 11, 29
See also SATA-Obit 20
Smith, H. Jeff 1957- 150
Smith, H(arold) Wendell 1923- 111
Smith, Hale G(illiam) 1918- 61-64
Smith, Hallett (Darius) 1907-1996 .... 21-24R
Obituary 153
Smith, Harmon L. 1930- 29-32R
Smith, Harold F. 1923- 195
Smith, Harold Ivan 1947- 121
Smith, Harold L(ester) 1942- 125
Smith, Harris (Gordon) 1921- 49-52
Smith, (Oliver) Harrison 1888-1971
Obituary 29-32R
Smith, Harry 1936- CANR-29
Earlier sketches in CA 77-80, CANR-13
Smith, Harry B. 1860-1936 .... DLB 187
Smith, Harry E(dmund) 1928-2002 .... 25-28R
Obituary 211
Smith, Harry W(illiam) 1937- 112
Smith, Harvey K(ennedy) 1904-1968 .... CAP-1
Earlier sketch in CA 13-14
Smith, Hazel Brannon 1914-1994 ...... DLB 127
Smith, Hedrick (Laurence) 1933- CANR-41
Earlier sketches in CA 65-68, CANR-11
Smith, Helen Zenna
See Price, Evadne
Smith, Helene 1937- 213
See also SATA 142
Smith, Helmut Walser 1962- 217
Smith, Henry
See Smith, Henry DeWitt II
Smith, Henry 1560-1591 .... DLB 136
Smith, Henry 1905-1988
Obituary 124
Smith, Henry B(ache) 1860-1936 184
Smith, Henry Clay 1913- 1-4R
Smith, Henry DeWitt II 1940- 119
Smith, Henry Holmes 1909-1986 209
Smith, Henry Lee, Jr. 1913-1972
Obituary 37-40R
Smith, Henry Nash 1906-1986 .... CANR-2
Obituary 119
Earlier sketch in CA 1-4R
Smith, Henry Peter 1910-1968 .... 1-4R
Obituary 103
Smith, Herbert F(rancis) 1922- CANR-58
Earlier sketches in CA 77-80, CANR-13, 30
Smith, Herbert F. A. 1915-1969 .... CAP-1
Earlier sketch in CA 13-16
Smith, Hermon Dunlap 1900-1983
Obituary 109
Smith, Hilda Worthington 1889(?)-1984
Obituary 112
Smith, Hobart M(uir) 1912- CANR-9
Earlier sketch in CA 65-68
Smith, Holly A. 1956- 224
Smith, Hope M(ayhew) 1916- 1-4R
Smith, Horatio (Horace) 1779-1849 .... DLB 96, 116
Smith, Howard E(verett), Jr. 1927- CANR-21
Earlier sketch in CA 25-28R
See also SATA 12
Smith, Howard K(ingsbury)
1914-2002 .... CANR-71
Obituary 205
Earlier sketches in CA 45-48, CANR-2
Smith, Howard R(oss) 1917- 1-4R
Smith, Howard Van 1910(?)-1986 .... 5-8R
Obituary 120
Smith, Hubert Shirley
See Shirley-Smith, Hubert
Smith, Hugh L(etcher) 1921-1968 .... CAP-2
Earlier sketch in CA 25-28
See also SATA 5
Smith, Huston (Cummings) 1919- .. CANR-106
Earlier sketch in CA 61-64
Smith, Hyrum W. 1943- 145
Smith, I(rving) Norman 1909-1989 107
Smith, Iain Crichton 1928-1998 .... 21-24R
Obituary 171
See also BRWS 9
See also CLC 64
See also CN 1, 2, 3, 4, 5, 6
See also CP 1, 2
See also DLB 40, 139, 319
See also RGSF 2
Smith, Imogene Henderson 1922- 5-8R
See also SATA 12
Smith, Irene 1903- 73-76
Smith, Irving H(arold) 1932- 49-52
Smith, Irwin 1892-1977 .... 5-8R
Obituary 73-76
Smith, Isadore Leighton Luce
1901-1985 .... CANR-85
Obituary 118
Earlier sketch in CA 101
Smith, J. Allen 1860-1924 185
See also DLB 47
Smith, J. C. S.
See Smith, Jane S.
Smith, J(ohn) Holland 1932- 17-20R
Smith, J(ames) L(eonard) B(rierley)
1897-1968 .... CAP-1
Earlier sketch in CA 13-14
Smith, J(ohn) Malcolm 1921- 49-52
Smith, J(oseph) Russell 1874-1966 .... CAP-1
Earlier sketch in CA 13-14
Smith, J(oe) W(illiam) Ashley 1914- 5-8R
Smith, Jack (Clifford) 1916-1996 ...... CANR-12
Obituary 151
Earlier sketch in CA 69-72
Smith, Jack (Prescott) 1945-2004 127
Obituary 227
Smith, Jack Martin .... IDFW 3, 4
Smith, Jackie M. 1930- 93-96
Smith, Jackson Algernon 1917-
Brief entry 105
Smith, Jacqueline B. 1937- .... SATA 39
Smith, Jada Pinkett 1971- 163
See also SATA 161
Smith, James 1775-1839 .... DLB 96
Smith, James 1904-1972 85-88
Smith, James A. 1914-1983(?) CANR-39
Earlier sketch in CA 21-24R
Smith, James D(ale) 1940- 121
Smith, James D. 1955- 171
Smith, James L(eslie Clarke) 1936- 25-28R
Smith, James Monroe 1975- 164
Smith, James Morton 1919- 103
Smith, James R. 1941- 101
Smith, James Roy 1920- 21-24R
Smith, James T(homas) 1939- 198
Smith, Jane F(rances) 1916- 123
Brief entry 117
Smith, Jane I(dleman) 1937- CANR-118
Earlier sketch in CA 107
Smith, Jane S. 1947- 118
Smith, Janet (Buchanan) Adam
See Adam Smith, Janet (Buchanan)
Smith, Janet L. 167
Smith, Janice Lee 1949- 230
See also SATA 54, 155
Smith, Janna M(alamud) 1952- 164
Smith, Jaune Quick-To-See 1940- 210
Smith, Jean
See Smith, Frances C(hristine)
Smith, Jean DeMouthe 1949- 65-68
Smith, Jean Edward 1932- CANR-107
Earlier sketch in CA 37-40R
Smith, Jean Pajot 1945- 53-56
See also SATA 10
Smith, Jeanne Rosier 1966- 231
Smith, Jeff(rey Alan) 1958- CANR-144
Earlier sketches in CA 132, CANR-66
See also AAYA 38
See also SATA 93, 161
Smith, Jeff Allen
See Smith, Jeff(rey Alan)
Smith, Jennifer 1949- 193
Smith, Jenny 1963- .... SATA 90
Smith, Jerome F(ranken) 1928- 107
Smith, Jessica 1895-1983 .... CANR-2
Earlier sketch in CA 49-52
Smith, Jessie
See Kunhardt, Edith
Smith, Jessie Carney 1930- CANR-39
Earlier sketches in CA 89-92, CANR-17
See also BW 2
Smith, Jessie Willcox 1863-1935 190
See also CLR 59
See also DLB 188
See also MAICYA 1, 2
See also SATA 21
Smith, Jim 1920-
Brief entry 115
See also SATA-Brief 36
Smith, Joan (Mary) 1933- .... SATA 54
See also SATA-Brief 46
Smith, Joan 1935-2004 61-64
Obituary 231
Smith, Joan Gerarda 1932- 145
See also RHW
Smith, Joan K(aren) 1939- 93-96
Smith, Joanmarie 1932- CANR-16
Earlier sketch in CA 85-88
Smith, Jody Brant 1943- 113
Smith, John
See Herrick, Marvin Theodore
Smith, John 1580(?)-1631 .... DLB 24, 30
See also TUS
Smith, John 1618-1652 .... DLB 252
Smith, John fl. 1656-1665 .... DLB 281
Smith, John (Charles) 1924- 103
See also CP 1, 2, 3, 4, 5, 6, 7
Smith, John Chabot 1915- 69-72
Smith, John Coventry 1903-1984 115
Smith, John David 1949- CANR-99
Earlier sketches in CA 111, CANR-30, 60
Smith, John Edwin 1921- 103
Smith, John F(erris) 1934- CANR-119
Earlier sketch in CA 81-84
Smith, John H(azel) 1928- 9-12R
Smith, John M. 1942- 139
Smith, John Norton
See Norton-Smith, John
Smith, Johnston
See Crane, Stephen (Townley)
Smith, Jon R(ichard) 1946- 77-80
Smith, Jonathan 1942- 144
Smith, Jonathan M(ark) 1957- CANR-125
Earlier sketch in CA 165
Smith, Jordan 1954- 110
Smith, Jos(eph) A. 1936- .... SATA 73, 120
Smith, Joseph B(urkholder) 1921- 65-68
Smith, Joseph Fielding 1876-1972
Obituary 37-40R
Smith, Joseph H(enry) 1913-1981
Obituary 105
Smith, Josiah 1704-1781 .... DLB 24
Smith, Judie R. 1936- 148
See also SATA 80
Smith, Julia Floyd 1914- 85-88
Smith, Julia Frances 1911-1989
Obituary 128
Smith, Julian 1937- 61-64
Smith, Julian C(leveland, Jr.) 1919- 144
Smith, Julian W. 1901-1975 .... 13-16R
Smith, Julie 1944- 230
Earlier sketches in CA 112, CANR-32, 63
Autobiographical Essay in 230
See also CMW 4
See also CSW
Smith, Julie Dean 1960- .... FANT
Smith, Justin Harvey 1857-1930 209
Smith, K(ermit) Wayne 1938- 29-32R
Smith, Karl U(lrich) 1907-1994 .... CANR-46
Earlier sketches in CA 61-64, CANR-9
Smith, Kate
See Smith, Kathryn Elizabeth
Smith, Kathleen J(oan) 1929- 103
Smith, Kathryn Elizabeth 1907(?)-1986
Obituary 119
Smith, Kay
See Smith, Catherine C.
Smith, Kay Nolte 1932-1993 .... CANR-66
Obituary 142
Earlier sketches in CA 101, CANR-18, 43
See also CMW 4
Smith, Keith V(an) 1937-1998 172
Smith, Ken(neth Danforth)
1902-1991 .... CANR-1
Earlier sketch in CA 45-48
Smith, Ken(neth John) 1938-2003 .... CANR-39
Obituary 217
Earlier sketch in CA 33-36R
See also CP 1, 2, 3, 4, 5, 6, 7
See also DLB 40
Smith, Kenneth Lee 1925- 77-80
Smith, Kenneth M(anley) 1892-1981
Obituary 108
Smith, Kerri S. 1960- 139
Smith, Kevin 1970- CANR-131
Earlier sketch in CA 166
See also AAYA 37
Smith, Kurtis 1958- 163
Smith, L(eonard) Glenn 1939- 93-96
Smith, L. J. 1964(?)- .... AAYA 53
Smith, L(ester) Neil 1946- 144
Smith, Lacey Baldwin 1922- CANR-6
Earlier sketch in CA 5-8R
Smith, Lafayette
See Higdon, Hal
Smith, Lane 1959- 143
See also AAYA 21
See also CLR 47
See also MAICYA 2
See also MAICYAS 1
See also SATA 76, 131
Smith, Larry 1940- 49-52
Smith, Larry (R.) 1943- 191
Smith, Laura I(vory) 1902- 17-20R
Smith, Laura J. 144
Smith, Lauren B. 1963- 202
Smith, Laurence D. 1950- 123
Smith, Lavon B(enson) 1921- 21-24R
Smith, Lawrence Berk 1939- CANR-13
Earlier sketch in CA 73-76
Smith, Lawrence R(ichard) 1945- 117
Smith, Lee
See Albion, Lee Smith
Smith, Lee 1937- 73-76
Smith, Lee 1944- CANR-118
Brief entry 114
Earlier sketches in CA 119, CANR-46
Interview in CA-119
See also CLC 25, 73
See also CN 7
See also CSW
See also DLB 143
See also DLBY 1983
See also EWL 3
See also RGAL 4
Smith, Lee L. 1930- 29-32R
Smith, Lena (Kennedy) 1914- 93-96
Smith, Lendon H(oward) 1921- 81-84
See also SATA 64
Smith, LeRoi Tex 1934- 29-32R
Smith, Leslie F(rancis) 1901-1999 .... CAP-1
Earlier sketch in CA 19-20
Smith, Leslie James Seth
See Seth-Smith, Leslie James
Smith, Leslie R(aymond) 1904-1986 .... 1-4R
Smith, Lew
See Floren, Lee
Smith, Lillian (Eugenia) 1897-1966 .. CANR-72
Obituary 25-28R
Earlier sketches in CAP-2, CA 17-18
See also FW
See also TCLE 1:2
Smith, Lillian H(elena) 1887-1983
Obituary 111
See also SATA-Obit 32
Smith, Linda Wasmer
See Andrews, Linda Wasmer
Smith, Linell Nash 1932- 5-8R
See also SATA 2
Smith, Logan Pearsall 1865-1946 184
See also AMWS 14
See also DLB 98
Smith, Lora R(oberts) 1949- CANR-121
Earlier sketch in CA 153
Smith, Lou 1918- 73-76
Smith, Louis
See Barzini, Luigi (Giorgio, Jr.)
Smith, Louis M(ilde) 1929- 17-20R
Smith, Lucia B. 1943- 108
See also SATA 30
Smith, Lynnette 1951- 116
Smith, M(ahlon) Brewster 1919- 61-64
Smith, M. Estellie 1935- CANR-8
Earlier sketch in CA 61-64
Smith, M. J. 1955- 175
Smith, M. Weston
See Weston-Smith, M.
Smith, Malcolm 1938- 97-100
Smith, Malcom N(orman) 1919(?)-1985
Obituary 116
Smith, Manuel (Juan) 1934- 105
Smith, Marcus J(oel) 1918- 73-76
Smith, Margaret (Middleton) 1931- 162
Smith, Margaret Bayard 1778-1844 .... DLB 248
Smith, Margaret (Madeline) Chase
1897-1995 73-76
Obituary 148
Smith, Margaret Emily Noel Nuttall
See Nuttall-Smith, Margaret Emily Noel
Smith, Margaret F(oltz) 1915- 102
Smith, Margaret Mary 1916- 108
Smith, Margaret Ruth 1902-1991 .... CAP-1
Earlier sketch in CA 19-20
Smith, Margarita G. 1923(?)-1983
Obituary 109
Smith, Marguerite 1940- 162
Smith, Marie D. 13-16R
Smith, Marilyn Cochran
See Cochran-Smith, Marilyn
Smith, Marion Hagens 1913- 17-20R
See also SATA 12
Smith, Marion Jaques 1899-1987 ..... CANR-11
Earlier sketch in CA 69-72
See also SATA 13
Smith, Marisa 1956- 147
Smith, Mark (Richard) 1935- CANR-44
Earlier sketches in CA 13-16R, CANR-10
See also DLBY 1982
Smith, Mark Eddy 1967- 220
Smith, Mark Haskell 227
Smith, Mark M. 1968- 169
Smith, Marny 1932- 108
Smith, Martha Nell 1953- 208
Smith, Martin
See Smith, Martin Cruz

Cumulative Index 541 Smith

Smith, Martin Cruz 1942- CANR-119
Earlier sketches in CA 85-88, CANR-6, 23, 43, 65
Interview in CANR-23
See also BEST 89:4
See also BPFB 3
See also CLC 25
See also CMW 4
See also CPW
See also DAM MULT, POP
See also HGG
See also MTCW 2
See also MTFW 2005
See also NNAL
See also RGAL 4
Smith, Martin J. 1956- 180
Smith, Martin R. 1934- 144
Smith, Mary Ann 1934- 126
Smith, Mary Benton 1903- CAP-2
Earlier sketch in CA 17-18
Smith, Mary Burnett 1931- 237
Smith, Mary C. 1936- 176
Smith, Mary Elizabeth 1923- CANR-104
Earlier sketch in CA 65-68
Smith, Mary Elizabeth 1932- 41-44R
Smith, Mary Ellen 69-72
See also SATA 10
Smith, Marya 1945- 146
See also SATA 78
Smith, Mason McCann 1952- 108
Smith, Maxwell A(ustin) 1894-1985 ...... 37-40R
Smith, (Albert) Merriman 1913-1970 .. CANR-2
Obituary 29-32R
Earlier sketch in CA 1-4R
Smith, Merritt Roe 1940- CANR-141
Earlier sketch in CA 77-80
Smith, Michael 1698-1771(?) .... DLB 31
Smith, Michael (Townsend) 1935- CANR-11
Earlier sketch in CA 21-24R
See also CAD
See also CD 5, 6
Smith, Michael 1942- .... CP 1, 2
Smith, Michael 1946- 132
Smith, Michael 1952- 234
Smith, Michael A(nthony) 1942- 102
Smith, Michael Marshall 1965- CANR-117
Earlier sketch in CA 162
See also HGG
Smith, Michael P(eter) 1942- 65-68
Smith, Michael R(obert) 1946- 144
Smith, Michael Ray 1955- 220
Smith, Michael Stephen 1944- 103
Smith, Michael W(hitaker) 1958- 166
Smith, Mike
See Smith, Mary Ellen
Smith, Mildred C(atharine) 1891-1973 101
Obituary 45-48
Smith, Mildred Nelson 1918- 69-72
Smith, Mitchell 1935- CANR-136
Earlier sketch in CA 136
Smith, Molly (Easo) 1958- 185
Smith, Morris 1928- 164
Smith, Mortimer B(rewster) 1906-1981 107
Obituary 104
Smith, Morton 1915-1991 .... CANR-85
Obituary 134
Earlier sketches in CA 5-8R, CANR-6
Smith, Morton Howison 1923- 45-48
Smith, Murphy D(e Witt) 1920- CANR-42
Earlier sketches in CA 37-40R, CANR-13
Smith, Murray G(ordon) 1952- 120
Smith, Myron J(ohn), Jr. 1944- CANR-96
Earlier sketches in CA 45-48, CANR-1, 16, 38
Smith, N(orman) J(ames) 1930- CANR-20
Earlier sketch in CA 103
Smith, N. V.
See Smith, Neil(son Voyne)
Smith, Nancy Covert 1935- CANR-10
Earlier sketch in CA 57-60
See also SATA 12
Smith, Nancy Taylor 57-60
Smith, Neil(son Voyne) 1939- 133
Smith, Neil Homer 1909(?)-1972
Obituary 37-40R
Smith, Nicholas D. 1949- 137
Smith, Nicola 1960- 237
Smith, Nigel J(ohn) H(arwood) 1949- 109
Smith, Nila Banton 1890-1976 .... CANR-85
Obituary 120
Earlier sketch in CA 21-24R
Smith, Nina Slingsby 1928- 119
Smith, Noel W. 1933- 144
Smith, Norman Edward Mace 1914- 103
Smith, Norman F. 1920- CANR-44
Earlier sketch in CA 29-32R
See also SATA 5, 70
Smith, Norman Lewis 1941- 77-80
Smith, Norris Kelly 1917- 21-24R
Smith, Norris Parker 1929- 171
Smith, Ophia D(elilah) Smith 1891-1994 .. 5-8R
Smith, Oswald J(effrey) 1889-1986
Obituary 119
Smith, (Charles) Page 1917-1995 .... CANR-2
Obituary 149
Earlier sketch in CA 1-4R
Smith, Pamela (A.) 1947- 175
Smith, Patricia Clark 1943- CANR-126
Earlier sketch in CA 161
See also SATA 96
Smith, Patricia Jean Adam
See Adam-Smith, Patricia Jean
Smith, Patricia Juliana 236
Smith, Patrick 1936- 77-80
Smith, Patrick D(avis) 1927- 77-80
Smith, Patrick J(ohn) 1932- 41-44R
Smith, Patrick Wykeham Montague
See Montague-Smith, Patrick Wykeham
Smith, Patti 1946- CANR-63
Earlier sketch in CA 93-96
See also CLC 12
Smith, Pattie Sherwood 1909(?)-1974
Obituary 53-56
Smith, Paul CANR-2
Earlier sketch in CA 1-4R, 144
Smith, Paul B(rainerd) 1921- CANR-28
Earlier sketches in CA 13-16R, CANR-10
Smith, Paul C. 1908-1976
Obituary 65-68
Smith, Paul F. 1919- 57-60
Smith, Paul H(ubert) 1931- 89-92
Smith, Paul Jordan
See Jordan-Smith, Paul
Smith, Paul Julian 1956- 138
Smith, Paula
See Allen, Paula Smith
Smith, Pauline (Urmson) 1882-1959 .. DLB 225
See also EWL 3
See also TCLC 25
Smith, Pauline (Janet) 1882-1959 .... RGSF 2
Smith, Pauline C.
See Arthur, Robert, (Jr.)
Smith, Pauline C(oggeshall)
1908-1994 .... 29-32R
See also SATA 27
Smith, Percival Gardner
See Gardner-Smith, Percival
Smith, Perry McCoy 1934- 29-32R
Smith, Peter 1897-1982
Obituary 107
Smith, Peter C(harles Horstead)
1940- CANR-118
Earlier sketches in CA 57-60, CANR-7, 30, 56
Smith, Peter H(opkinson) 1940- 41-44R
Smith, Peter J(ohn) 1931- 114
Smith, Philip Chadwick Foster 1939- 77-80
Smith, Philip E(dward II) 1943- 25-28R
Smith, Philip L. 1943- 108
Smith, Philip Warren 1936- .... SATA 46
Smith, R(ichard) A(lbert) N(ewton)
1908- 9-12R
Smith, R(eginald) C(harles) 1907- 65-68
Smith, R(eginald) D(onald) 1914-1985 117
Obituary 140
Smith, R(obert) Philip 1907- 81-84
Smith, R(ichard) Selby 1914- 108
Smith, Ralph (Bernard) 1939- 33-36R
Smith, Ralph Alexander 1929- 77-80
Smith, Ralph B. 1894(?)-1985
Obituary 115
Smith, Ralph Carlisle 1910-1989 124
Smith, Ralph Lee 1927- CANR-1
Earlier sketch in CA 1-4R
Smith, Ray 1915- CANR-11
Earlier sketch in CA 13-16R
Smith, Ray 1941- CANR-18
Earlier sketch in CA 101
See also CN 7
Smith, Ray Campbell 1916- CANR-134
Earlier sketch in CA 171
Smith, Ray Winfield 1897-1982
Obituary 110
Smith, Rebecca 1946- .... SATA 123
Smith, Red
See Smith, Walter W(ellesley)
See also DLB 29, 171
Smith, Rex Alan 1921- 61-64
Smith, Rhea Marsh 1907- CAP-1
Earlier sketch in CA 17-18
Smith, Richard 1941- 81-84
Smith, Richard A(ustin) 1911- 17-20R
Smith, Richard C(hristopher) 1948- 81-84
Smith, Richard Harris 1946- 41-44R
Smith, Richard Joseph 1944- CANR-42
Earlier sketches in CA 97-100, CANR-20
Smith, Richard K(ent) 1936- 41-44R
Smith, Richard L. 1950- 152
Smith, Richard M(ills) 1946- 73-76
Smith, Richard N. 1937- 21-24R
Smith, Richard P(aul) 1949- CANR-56
Earlier sketches in CA 111, CANR-30
Smith, Richard Rein 1930- 97-100
Smith, Robert A(rthur) 1944- 69-72
Smith, Robert Allan 1909-1980
Obituary 105
Smith, Robert C(hester) 1912-1975
Obituary 114
Smith, Robert C(harles) 1947- 111
Smith, Robert Charles 1938- 65-68
Smith, Robert D. 1937- 37-40R
Smith, Robert Dickie 1928- 9-12R
Smith, Robert Eliot 1899-1983 .... 37-40R
Smith, Robert Ellis 1940- CANR-16
Earlier sketch in CA 89-92
Smith, Robert Freeman 1930- CANR-1
Earlier sketch in CA 1-4R
Smith, Robert G(illen) 1913- CANR-42
Earlier sketch in CA 45-48
Smith, Robert G(ordon) 1947- 102
Smith, Robert Griffin, Jr. 1920- 41-44R
Smith, Robert Houston 1931- 105
Smith, Robert J(ohn) 1927- 53-56
Smith, Robert Kimmel 1930- CANR-42
Earlier sketches in CA 61-64, CANR-8
See also JRDA
See also MAICYA 2
See also MAICYAS 1
See also SATA 12, 77
Smith, Robert Lee 1928- 111
Smith, Robert Paul 1915-1977 73-76
Obituary 69-72
See also SATA 52
See also SATA-Obit 30
Smith, Robert S(idney) 1904-1969 .... CAP-1
Earlier sketch in CA 13-16
Smith, Robert W(ayne) 1926- 45-48
Smith, Robert W(illiam) 1926- CANR-109
Earlier sketch in CA 13-16R
Smith, Robin Baird
See Baird-Smith, Robin
Smith, Rockwell Carter 1908-1996 53-56
Smith, Rodney P(ennell), Jr. 1930- 29-32R
Smith, Roger 1953- CANR-140
Earlier sketch in CA 172
Smith, Roger H(askell) 1932-1980 69-72
Obituary 101
Smith, Roger Montgomery 1915(?)-1975
Obituary 57-60
Smith, Rogers M(ood) 1953- 120
Smith, Roland 1951- 179
See also SATA 115, 161
Smith, Roland B(eatcher) 1909- 1-4R
Smith, Rolando (R.) Hinojosa
See Hinojosa(-Smith), Rolando (R.)
Smith, Rollin 1942- 144
Smith, Ronald Gregor 1913-1968 .... CAP-1
Earlier sketch in CA 9-10
Smith, Ronald L(ande) 1952- CANR-36
Earlier sketch in CA 110
Smith, Rosamond
See Oates, Joyce Carol
Smith, Rosemary 1942- 150
Smith, Rosie 1954- 139
Smith, Roswell 1829-1892 .... DLB 79
Smith, Rowland (James) 1938- CANR-43
Earlier sketch in CA 45-48
Smith, Roy C(yrus) 1896-1989 124
Smith, Roy H(armon) III 1936- 25-28R
Smith, Roy H. 1945- 236
Smith, Russell E. 1932- 77-80
Smith, Russell F. W. 1915(?)-1975
Obituary 61-64
Smith, Ruth Leslie 1902- CAP-2
Earlier sketch in CA 29-32
See also SATA 2
Smith, Ruth Schluchter 1917- CANR-26
Earlier sketches in CA 69-72, CANR-11
Smith, S(idney) G(erald) Denis 1932- 103
Smith, Sally Bedell 1948- CANR-98
Earlier sketch in CA 140
Smith, Sally Liberman 1929- CANR-11
Earlier sketch in CA 21-24R
Smith, Sam(uel Frederic Houston) 1937- . 73-76
Smith, Sam 1948- 141
Smith, Samantha 1972-1985
Obituary 117
See also SATA-Obit 45
Smith, Samuel 1904-1994 .... CANR-11
Earlier sketch in CA 29-32R
Smith, Samuel Harrison 1772-1845 ...... DLB 43
Smith, Samuel Stanhope 1751-1819 ..... DLB 37
Smith, Sandra 1940- 122
Smith, Sandra Lee 1945- 142
See also SATA 75
Smith, Sarah 1832-1911
Brief entry 112
See also Stretton, Hesba
Smith, Sarah (Winthrop) 1947- CANR-98
Earlier sketch in CA 147
Smith, Sarah Pogson 1774-1870 .... DLB 200
Smith, Sarah Stafford
See Smith, Dorothy Stafford
Smith, Scott 1965(?)- 145
Smith, Scottie
See Smith, Frances Scott Fitzgerald Lanahan
Smith, Scottie Fitzgerald
See Smith, Frances Scott Fitzgerald Lanahan
Smith, Seba 1792-1868 .... DLB 1, 11, 243
Smith, Sharon 1947- 77-80
See also SATA 82
Smith, Sheila Kaye
See Kaye-Smith, Sheila
Smith, Shelley
See Bodington, Nancy H(ermione) and Shelley, Dolores and Smith, Sandra
Smith, Sherri L. 1971- 231
See also SATA 156
Smith, Sherry L. 1951- CANR-86
Earlier sketch in CA 133
Smith, Sherwin 1924(?)-1985
Obituary 116
Smith, Sherwood 1951- CANR-111
Earlier sketch in CA 149
See also SATA 82, 140
Smith, Shirley M(ae) 1923- CANR-42
Earlier sketches in CA 53-56, CANR-4
Smith, Shirley Raines
See Raines, Shirley C(arol)
Smith, Sid 1949- 197
Smith, Stan(ley William) 1943- 120
Smith, Stan(ley Roger) 1946- 85-88
Smith, Stanley H. 1920- 138
Smith, Stephen 1961- 239
Smith, Stephen Murray
See Murray-Smith, Stephen
Smith, Steve(n R.) 1947- 118
Smith, Steven A(lbert) 1939- 57-60
Smith, Steven D. 1952- 173
Smith, Steven G(arry) 1953- 139
Smith, Steven Phillip 1943- CANR-10
Earlier sketch in CA 57-60
Smith, Steven Trent 1947- 201
Smith, Stevie
See Smith, Florence Margaret
See also BRWS 2
See also CLC 3, 8, 25, 44
See also CP 1
See also DLB 20
See also EWL 3
See also PAB
See also PC 12
See also PFS 3
See also RGEL 2
Smith, Susan Carlton 1923- .... SATA 12
Smith, Susan M. 1942- 137
Smith, Susan Mathias 1950- 114
See also SATA 43
See also SATA-Brief 35
Smith, Susan Vernon 1950- CANR-19
Earlier sketch in CA 102
See also Mendonca, Susan
See also SATA 48
Smith, Susy 1911-2001 .... CANR-6
Earlier sketch in CA 5-8R
Smith, Suzanne E. 1964- 215
Smith, Sydney 1771-1845 .... BRWS 7
See also DLB 107
Smith, Sydney Bernard 1936- .... CP 1
Smith, Sydney Goodsir 1915-1975 101
Obituary 57-60
See also CP 1, 2
See also DLB 27
See also EWL 3
See also RGEL 2
Smith, T(ed) C. 1915- 49-52
Smith, T(homas) E(dward) 1916- 13-16R
Smith, T(homas) Lynn 1903-1976 ..... CANR-42
Earlier sketch in CA 5-8R
Smith, Talbot 1899-1978 .... CAP-1
Earlier sketch in CA 11-12
Smith, Taylor 1952- 195
Smith, Terence (Fitzgerald) 1938- 73-76
Smith, Terrence L(ore) 1942-1988
Obituary 127
Smith, Terri McFerrin 1954- 129
Smith, Sir Thomas 1513-1577 .... DLB 132
Smith, Thomas B(ell) 1923- 122
Smith, Thomas G. 1945- 123
Smith, Thomas Malcolm 1921-
Brief entry 106
Smith, Thomas R. 180
Smith, Thorne 1892-1934 162
See also BPFB 3
See also FANT
See also SFW 4
See also SUFW
Smith, Tilman R(ay) 1903-2000 113
Smith, Tim(othy R.) 1945- 226
See also SATA 151
Smith, Timothy Dudley
See Dudley-Smith, Timothy
Smith, Timothy L(awrence) 1924- 116
Smith, Timothy Wilson
See Wilson-Smith, Timothy
Smith, Toby 1946- CANR-43
Earlier sketch in CA 119
Smith, Tony 93-96
Smith, Tony
See Smith, Anthony Peter
Smith, Ursula 1934- .... SATA 54
Smith, V(incent) Kerry 1945- 111
Smith, Varrel Lavere 1925- 29-32R
Smith, Verla Lee 1927(?)-1982
Obituary 106
Smith, Vernon Lomax 1927- CANR-6
Earlier sketch in CA 1-4R
Smith, Vesta (Henderson) 1933- 5-8R
Smith, Vian (Crocker) 1920-1969 .... CANR-3
Earlier sketch in CA 1-4R
See also SATA 11
Smith, Victor C(lyde) 1902- 5-8R
Smith, Vincent E(dward) 1915-1972
Obituary 33-36R
Smith, Violet
See Gibson, Margaret Dunlop
Smith, Virginia Carlson 1944- 49-52
Smith, Virginia Masterman
See Masterman-Smith, Virginia
Smith, Virginia Whatley 1939- 228
Smith, Vivian (Brian) 1933- CANR-23
Earlier sketches in CA 61-64, CANR-8
See also CP 1, 2, 3, 4, 5, 6, 7
Smith, Vivian Bickford
See Bickford-Smith, Vivian
Smith, W(illiam) David 1928- 77-80
Smith, W(illiam) Eugene 1918-1978 142
Obituary 81-84
Smith, W. Gordon 1928-1996 .... DLB 310
Smith, Wade
See Snow, Charles H(orace)
Smith, Walter W(ellesley)
1905-1982 .... CANR-62
Obituary 105
Earlier sketches in CA 77-80, CANR-36
See also Smith, Red
Smith, Wanda VanHoy 1926- 133
See also SATA 65
Smith, Ward
See Goldsmith, Howard
Smith, Warren Allen 1921- 195
Smith, Warren L(ounsbury) 1914-1972 .. CAP-2
Earlier sketch in CA 21-22
Smith, Warren Sylvester 1912-1984 ...... 21-24R
Smith, Warren T(homas) 1923-1986 117
Obituary 119
Smith, Webster
See Coleman, Clayton W(ebster)

Smith 542 CONTEMPORARY AUTHORS

Smith, Wendell 1914-1972 ... 193
Obituary ... 104
See also DLB 171
Smith, Wendell I(rving) 1921- ... 13-16R
Smith, Wendy 1956- ... 138
Smith, Wesley D(ale) 1930-
Brief entry ... 111
Smith, Wesley E. 1938- ... 29-32R
Smith, Wesley J. 1949- ... CANR-118
Earlier sketch in CA 160
Smith, Whitney, Jr. 1940- ... 97-100
Smith, Wilbur (Addison) 1933- ... CANR-134
Earlier sketches in CA 13-16R, CANR-7, 46, 66
See also CLC 33
See also CPW
See also MTCW 1, 2
See also MTFW 2005
Smith, Wilbur M(oorehead) 1894-1976 . 17-20R
Smith, Wilda M(axine) 1924- ... 137
Smith, Wilford E(mery) 1916- ... 49-52
Smith, Wilfred Cantwell 1916-2000 ... CANR-7
Obituary ... 188
Earlier sketch in CA 13-16R
Smith, Wilfred R(obert) 1915- ... 13-16R
Smith, Will(ard) 1968- ... 166
Smith, Willard L(aurence) 1927- ... 5-8R
Smith, William 16th cent. - ... DLB 136
Smith, William 1727-1803 ... DLB 31
Smith, William 1728-1793 ... DLB 30
Smith, William A. 1918- ... SATA 10
Smith, William A. 1929- ... 45-48
Smith, William Allen 1904- ... 45-48
Smith, William C(harles) 1881-1972
Obituary ... 111
Smith, William Dale 1929- ... 49-52
Smith, William E(rnest) 1892-1969 ... 5-8R
Smith, William Frank 1925- ... 103
Smith, William Gardner 1926-1974 ... 65-68
Obituary ... 53-56
See also BW 1
See also DLB 76
Smith, William Henry 1808-1872 ... DLB 159
Smith, William I. 1932- ... 29-32R
Smith, William J. 1907(?)-1986
Obituary ... 118
Smith, William Jay 1918- ... CANR-106
Earlier sketches in CA 5-8R, CANR-44
See also AMWS 13
See also CLC 6
See also CP 1, 2, 3, 4, 5, 6, 7
See also CSW
See also CWRI 5
See also DLB 5
See also MAICYA 1, 2
See also SAAS 22
See also SATA 2, 68, 154
See also SATA-Essay 154
See also TCLE 1:2
Smith, William Martin 1911- ... 105
Smith, William S. 1917- ... 13-16R
Smith, William Scott 1926- ... 117
Smith, William Stevenson 1907-1969 ... CAP-2
Earlier sketch in CA 21-22
Smith, (Francis) Wilson 1922- ... 81-84
Smith, Winsome 1935- ... 115
See also SATA 45
Smith, Woodrow Wilson
See Kuttner, Henry
Smith, Woodruff D(onald) 1946- ... 85-88
Smith, Z. Z.
See Westheimer, David
Smith, Zadie 1976- ... 193
See also AAYA 50
See also CLC 158
See also MTFW 2005
Smith-Ankrom, M. E. 1942- ... 193
See also SATA 130
Smith-Ayala, Emilie 1964- ... 155
Smith Brindle, Reginald 1917- ... 89-92
See also Brindle, Reginald Smith
Smith-Brown, Fern 1939- ... 168
Smithdas, Robert Joseph 1925- ... 17-20R
Smithee, Alan
See Frankenheimer, John (Michael)
Smithells, Roger (William) 1905- ... CAP-1
Earlier sketch in CA 13-14
Smither, Elizabeth (Edwina) 1941- ... CANR-44
Earlier sketch in CA 107
See also CP 7
See also CWP
Smitherman, Geneva 1940- ... 130
Smitherman, P(hilip) H(enry) 1910- ... 21-24R
Smithers, Don LeRoy 1933- ... 45-48
Smithers, Peter Henry Berry Otway
1913- ... 29-32R
Smithgall, Elizabeth
See Watts, Elizabeth (Bailey) Smithgall
Smith-Griswold, Wendy 1955- ... SATA 88
Smithies, Arthur 1907-1981
Obituary ... 104
Smithies, Edward (Draper) 1941- ... 132
Smithies, Richard H(ugo) R(ipman)
1936- ... 21-24R
Smith-Rex, Susan J. 1950- ... 159
See also SATA 94
Smithsen, Richard
See Pellowski, Michael (Joseph)
Smithson, Alison (Margaret)
1928-1993 ... CANR-116
Earlier sketches in CA 25-28R, CANR-5
Smithson, Norman 1931- ... 33-36R
Smithson, Peter (Denham)
1923-2003 ... CANR-116
Obituary ... 215
Earlier sketches in CA 53-56, CANR-5
Smithson, Rulon N(ephi) 1927- ... 45-48
Smithyman, (William) Kendrick
1922-1995 ... 101
See also CP 1, 2
See also EWL 3
Smithyman, Mary Isobel 1919- ... CP 1
Smits, Teo
See Smits, Theodore R(ichard)
Smits, Theodore R(ichard) 1905-1996 ... 77-80
See also SATA 45
See also SATA-Brief 28
Smitten, Jeffrey Roger 1941- ... 105
Smitten, Richard 1940- ... 136
Smock, Audrey Chapman
See Chapman, Audrey R.
Smocovitis, Vassiliki Betty 1955- ... 186
Smoke, Jim ... 109
Smoke, Richard 1944- ... CANR-10
Earlier sketch in CA 65-68
Smolansky, Oles M. 1930- ... CANR-1
Earlier sketch in CA 45-48
Smolar, Boris (Ber) 1897-1986 ... 41-44R
Obituary ... 118
Smolens, John (Harrison), (Jr.)
1949- ... CANR-110
Earlier sketch in CA 151
Smoley, Richard 1956- ... 235
Smolich, Yurik K. 1899(?)-1976
Obituary ... 69-72
Smolin, C. Roger 1948- ... 110
Smolin, Lee 1955- ... 218
Smolinski, Dick 1932- ... SATA 86
Smoll, Frank L(ouis) 1941- ... 115
Smolla, Rod
See Smolla, Rodney A(lan)
Smolla, Rodney A(lan) 1953- ... CANR-105
Earlier sketch in CA 121
Smoller, Bruce M. 1944- ... 113
Smoller, Sanford J(erome) 1937- ... 57-60
Smollett, Tobias (George) 1721-1771 ... BRW 3
See also CDBLB 1660-1789
See also DLB 39, 104
See also RGEL 2
See also TEA
Smoluchowski, Louise 1922- ... 126
Smoodin, Roberta 1952- ... 147
Smooha, Sammy 1941- ... 101
Smoot, Dan 1913- ... CANR-1
Earlier sketch in CA 1-4R
Smothers, Ethel Footman 1944- ... CANR-133
Earlier sketch in CA 143
See also SATA 76, 149
Smothers, Frank A(lbert) 1901-1981
Obituary ... 104
Smout, T(homas) C(hristopher)
1933- ... CANR-118
Earlier sketches in CA 21-24R, CANR-9
Smucker, Barbara (Claassen) 1915- ... CANR-23
Earlier sketch in CA 106
See also CLR 10
See also CWRI 5
See also JRDA
See also MAICYA 1, 2
See also SAAS 11
See also SATA 29, 76, 130
Smucker, Donovan E(bersole) 1915- ... 149
Smucker, Leonard 1928- ... 21-24R
Smullyan, Arthur Francis 1912-1998 ... 1-4R
Smullyan, Raymond
See Smullyan, Raymond M(errill)
Smullyan, Raymond M(errill) 1919- ... 125
Brief entry ... 120
Interview in ... CA-125
Smurl, James F(redrick) 1934- ... 45-48
Smurr, John Welling 1922- ... 1-4R
Smurthwaite, Ronald 1918-1975 ... CAP-2
Earlier sketch in CA 21-22
Smyer, Richard 1935- ... 102
Smyers, Karen (A.) 1954- ... 185
Smykay, Edward W(alter) 1924- ... CANR-12
Earlier sketch in CA 17-20R
Smylie, James H(utchinson) 1925- ... CANR-14
Earlier sketch in CA 37-40R
Smylie, Mark A. 1954- ... 111
Smyllie, J. S.
See Smellie, Jim
Smyrl, Frank H(erbert) 1938- ... 113
Smyser, Adam A(lbert) 1920- ... 77-80
Smyser, H(amilton) M(artin) 1901-1980 . CAP-1
Earlier sketch in CA 13-16
Smyser, Jane Worthington 1914-1975 ... 65-68
Obituary ... 61-64
Smyth, Alice M.
See Hadfield, Alice M(ary)
Smyth, David 1929- ... CANR-12
Earlier sketch in CA 61-64
Smyth, Dame Ethel Mary 1858-1944 ... 232
See also FW
Smyth, Gerry 1961- ... 184
Smyth, H. D.
See Smyth, Henry DeWolf
Smyth, H(arriet) Rucker (Crowell) 1926- ... 1-4R
Smyth, Henry DeWolf 1898-1986
Obituary ... 120
Smyth, Howard McGaw 1901-1975
Obituary ... 61-64
Smyth, Iain 1959- ... CANR-139
Earlier sketch in CA 173
See also SATA 105
Smyth, Jacqui (Marie) 1960- ... 124
Smyth, John (George) 1893-1983 ... CANR-11
Obituary ... 109
Earlier sketch in CA 61-64
Smyth, Paul 1944- ... CANR-8
Earlier sketch in CA 61-64
Smyth, R(obert) L(eslie) 1922- ... CANR-10
Earlier sketch in CA 9-12R
Smyth, William J. 1949- ... 135
Smythe, Colin 1942- ... CANR-16
Earlier sketch in CA 97-100
Smythe, Daniel Webster 1908-1981 ... 13-16R
Smythe, David Mynders 1915- ... 1-4R
Smythe, Dion C. 1959- ... 197
Smythe, Donald 1927- ... 41-44R
Smythe, Francis S(ydney) 1900-1949 ... 202
Smythe, Francis Sydney 1900-1949 ... DLB 195
Smythe, Frank S.
See Smythe, Francis S(ydney)
Smythe, Hugh H(eyne) 1913-1977 ... 9-12R
Obituary ... 69-72
Smythe, Mabel M(urphy) 1918- ... 37-40R
Smythe, Reginald 1918(?)-1998 ... AITN 1
Smythe, Ted Curtis 1932- ... 101
Smythies, Bertram E(velyn) 1912-1999 ... 189
Smythies, J(ohn) R(aymond) 1922- ... 37-40R
Snadowsky, Alvin M. 1938- ... 61-64
Snailham, (George) Richard 1930- ... 37-40R
Snaith, Norman Henry 1898-1982
Obituary ... 106
Snaith, William Theodore 1908-1974 ... 110
Obituary ... 106
Snape, H(enry) Currie 1902- ... 9-12R
Snape, R(ichard) H(al) 1936- ... 29-32R
Snapes, Joan 1925- ... 107
Snavely, Adam A. 1930- ... 25-28R
Snavely, Ellen Bartow 1910-1990 ... CAP-2
Earlier sketch in CA 21-22
Snavely, Guy Everett 1881-1974 ... 5-8R
Obituary ... 49-52
Snavely, Tipton Ray 1890-1995 ... 17-20R
Snavely, William P(ennington) 1920- ... 17-20R
Snead, Rodman Eldredge 1931- ... 73-76
Snead, Sam(uel Jackson) 1912-2002
Obituary ... 209
Brief entry ... 114
Snedeker, Bonnie 1947- ... 119
Snedeker, Caroline Dale (Parke)
1871-1956 ... YABC 2
Snedeker, Michael ... 236
Sneden, Robert Knox 1832-1918 ... 220
Sneed, Joseph Donald 1938- ... 49-52
Sneed, Joseph Tyree 1920- ... 21-24R
Sneider, Vern(on) John 1916-1981 ... CANR-13
Obituary ... 103
Earlier sketch in CA 5-8R
Snell, Bruno (Karl Johannes Richard)
1896-1986 ... CAP-1
Earlier sketch in CA 13-16
Snell, Daniel C. 1947- ... 166
Snell, David 1936- ... 77-80
Snell, Foster Dee 1898-1980
Obituary ... 108
Snell, Frank 1920- ... 1-4R
Snell, George Davis 1903-1996 ... 106
Obituary ... 152
Snell, John Leslie, Jr. 1923-1972 ... CANR-3
Obituary ... 33-36R
Earlier sketch in CA 5-8R
Snell, John Nicholas Blashford
See Blashford-Snell, John (Nicholas)
Snell, (H.) Michael 1945- ... 216
Snell, Michael 1945- ... 140
Snell, Nigel (Edward Creagh) 1936- ... 111
See also SATA 57
See also SATA-Brief 40
Snell, Tee Loftin ... 105
See also Loftin, T(helma) L(ois)
Snell, William R(obert) 1930- ... 216
Sneller, Delwyn Lee 1945- ... 111
Snellgrove, David L(lewellyn) 1920- ... 147
Brief entry ... 115
Snellgrove, L(aurence) E(rnest)
1928- ... CANR-23
Earlier sketches in CA 9-12R, CANR-3
See also SATA 53
Snellgrove, Louis 1928- ... 45-48
Snelling, Dennis (Wayne) 1958- ... 150
See also SATA 84
Snelling, Lauraine ... 231
Snelling, Lois ... 5-8R
Snelling, O(swald) F(rederick) 1916- ... 17-20R
Snelling, W(illiam) Rodman 1931- ... 93-96
Snelling, William Joseph 1804-1848 ... DLB 202
Snellings, Rolland
See Toure, Askia Muhammad Abu Bakr el
Snepp, Frank (Warren III) 1943- ... CANR-88
Earlier sketch in CA 105
Interview in ... CA-105
Snetsinger, John (Goodall) 1941- ... 73-76
Snetsinger, Robert 1928- ... 107
Sneve, Virginia Driving Hawk
1933- ... CANR-68
Earlier sketches in CA 49-52, CANR-3
See also CLR 2
See also SATA 8, 95
Snicket, Lemony 1970- ... 195
See also Handler, Daniel
See also AAYA 46
See also BYA 15
See also MTFW 2005
See also SATA 126
Snider, Delbert A(rthur) 1914- ... 1-4R
Snider, Jim ... 141
Snider, Lewis W. ... 119
Sniderman, Florence (Lama) 1915- ... 33-36R
Sniechowski, James ... 218
Snipes, Wilson Currin 1924- ... 29-32R
Snively, Susan 1945- ... 117
Snively, W(illiam) D(aniel), Jr.
1911-1992 ... 29-32R
Snoddy, Theo 1922- ... 168
Snodgrass, A(nthony) M(cElrea)
1934- ... CANR-88
Earlier sketches in CA 21-24R, 185, CANR-10
Snodgrass, Ann 1958- ... 220
Snodgrass, Donald R(ay) 1935- ... 112
Snodgrass, Joan Gay 1934- ... 77-80
Snodgrass, Jon 1941- ... 113
Snodgrass, Mary Ellen 1944- ... 142
See also SATA 75
Snodgrass, Milton M(oore) 1931- ... 29-32R
Snodgrass, Quentin Curtius
See Clemens, Samuel Langhorne
Snodgrass, Thomas Jefferson
See Clemens, Samuel Langhorne
Snodgrass, W(illiam) D(e Witt)
1926- ... CANR-85
Earlier sketches in CA 1-4R, CANR-6, 36, 65
See also AMWS 6
See also CLC 2, 6, 10, 18, 68
See also CP 1, 2, 3, 4, 5, 6, 7
See also DAM POET
See also DLB 5
See also MAL 5
See also MTCW 1, 2
See also MTFW 2005
See also RGAL 4
See also TCLE 1:2
Snoek, J(aap) Diedrick 1931- ... 49-52
Snoke, Albert W(aldo) 1907- ... 125
Snook, Barbara (Lillian) 1913-1976 ... 109
See also SATA 34
Snook, I(van) A(ugustine) 1933- ... CANR-14
Earlier sketch in CA 77-80
Snook, Jean M(cGregor) 1952- ... CANR-105
Earlier sketch in CA 150
Snook, John B. 1927- ... 106
Snoop Doggy Dogg 1972- ... 207
Snorri Sturluson 1179-1241 ... RGWL 2, 3
Snortum, Niel K(lendenon) 1928- ... 21-24R
Snow, C(harles) P(ercy) 1905-1980 ... CANR-28
Obituary ... 101
Earlier sketch in CA 5-8R
See also BRW 7
See also CDBLB 1945-1960
See also CLC 1, 4, 6, 9, 13, 19
See also CN 1, 2
See also DAM NOV
See also DLB 15, 77
See also DLBD 17
See also EWL 3
See also MTCW 1, 2
See also MTFW 2005
See also RGEL 2
See also TEA
Snow, Charles Ernest 1910-1967
Obituary ... 116
Snow, Charles H(orace) 1877-1967 .. TCWW 1, 2
Snow, Chet B. 1945- ... 213
Snow, D(avid) W(illiam) 1924- ... 65-68
Snow, Davis W. 1913(?)-1975
Obituary ... 61-64
Snow, Donald 1951- ... 138
Snow, Donald Clifford 1917-1979 ... 85-88
See also SATA 16
Snow, Donald M(erritt) 1943- ... CANR-52
Earlier sketches in CA 106, CANR-27
Snow, Dorothea J(ohnston) 1909- ... CANR-27
Earlier sketches in CA 1-4R, CANR-3
See also SATA 9
Snow, Dorothy Mary Barter 1897- ... CAP-1
Earlier sketch in CA 13-14
Snow, Edgar Parks 1905-1972 ... CANR-38
Obituary ... 33-36R
Earlier sketch in CA 81-84
Snow, Edward Rowe 1902-1982 ... CANR-6
Obituary ... 106
Earlier sketch in CA 9-12R
Snow, Frances Compton
See Adams, Henry (Brooks)
Snow, George (D'Oyly) 1903-1977 ... 5-8R
Snow, Helen Foster 1907-1997 ... CANR-46
Obituary ... 156
Earlier sketch in CA 57-60
Snow, John Hall 1924- ... 37-40R
Snow, Karen (a pseudonym) 1923- ... 120
Snow, Kathleen 1944- ... 81-84
Snow, Keith Ronald 1943- ... 110
Snow, Lois Wheeler 1920- ... 57-60
Snow, Lucy
See Aubert, Rosemary
Snow, Michael (James Aleck) 1929- ... 209
Snow, Peter G(ordon) 1933- ... 21-24R
Snow, Philip (Albert) 1915- ... CANR-54
Earlier sketches in CA 9-12R, CANR-28
Snow, Philip 1952- ... 130
Snow, Richard F(olger) 1947- ... 106
See also SATA 52
See also SATA-Brief 37
Snow, Robert L. 1949- ... 193
Snow, Roslyn 1936- ... CANR-9
Earlier sketch in CA 21-24R
Snow, Russell E(lwin) 1938- ... 65-68
Snow, Sinclair 1909-1972 ... CAP-2
Earlier sketch in CA 25-28
Snow, Vernon F. 1924-1998 ... 37-40R
Obituary ... 181
Snow, (Charles) Wilbert 1884-1977 ... 9-12R
Obituary ... 73-76
Snow, William George Sinclair 1908- ... 5-8R
Snowden, Frank M(artin), Jr. 1911- ... 41-44R
Snowdon
See Armstrong-Jones, Antony (Charles Robert)
Snowdon, David A. 1952- ... 211
Snowman, Daniel 1938- ... CANR-110
Earlier sketches in CA 53-56, CANR-4, 33
Snukal, Robert (Martin) 1942- ... 45-48

Snyder, Anne 1922-2001 ... CANR-14
Obituary ... 193
Earlier sketch in CA 37-40R
See also SATA 4
See also SATA-Obit 125
Snyder, Bernadette McCarver 1930- . CANR-37
Earlier sketch in CA 115
See also SATA 97
Snyder, Brad M. 1972- ... 225
Snyder, Carl Dean 1921-
Brief entry ... 113
Snyder, Carol 1941- ... 85-88
See also SATA 35
Snyder, Cecil K., Jr. 1927- ... 29-32R
Snyder, Charles M. 1909-1996 ... 49-52
Snyder, Charles Royce 1924- ... 105
Snyder, Christopher A. 1966- ... 187
Snyder, Chuck 1933- ... 122
Snyder, Don J. 1950- ... CANR-124
Earlier sketch in CA 126
Snyder, E(ugene) V(incent) 1943- ... 41-44R
Snyder, Eldon E. 1930- ... 49-52
Snyder, Eloise C(olleen) 1928- ... 29-32R
Snyder, Francis Gregory 1942- ... CANR-22
Earlier sketches in CA 17-20R, CANR-7
Snyder, Fred A. 1931- ... 37-40R
Snyder, Gary (Sherman) 1930- ... CANR-125
Earlier sketches in CA 17-20R, CANR-30, 60
See also AMWS 8
See also ANW
See also BG 1:3
See also CLC 1, 2, 5, 9, 32, 120
See also CP 1, 2, 3, 4, 5, 6, 7
See also DA3
See also DAM POET
See also DLB 5, 16, 165, 212, 237, 275
See also EWL 3
See also MAL 5
See also MTCW 2
See also MTFW 2005
See also PC 21
See also PFS 9, 19
See also RGAL 4
See also WP
Snyder, George Sergeant 1952- ... 122
Snyder, Gerald S(eymour) 1933- ... CANR-12
Earlier sketch in CA 61-64
See also SATA 48
See also SATA-Brief 34
Snyder, Glenn Herald 1924- ... CANR-18
Earlier sketch in CA 1-4R
Snyder, Graydon F. 1930- ... 13-16R
Snyder, Guy (Eugene, Jr.) 1951- ... 57-60
Snyder, Henry Leonard 1929- ... 41-44R
Snyder, Howard A(lbert) 1940- ... CANR-82
Earlier sketches in CA 113, CANR-34
Snyder, Jack (Lewis) 1951- ... 189
Snyder, James E(dward) 1928-1990 ... 123
Obituary ... 132
Brief entry ... 117
Snyder, Jane McIntosh 1943- ... 130
Snyder, Jerome 1916-1976
Obituary ... 65-68
See also SATA-Obit 20
Snyder, Joan 1943- ... 41-44R
Snyder, John P(arr) 1926-1997 ... CANR-31
Obituary ... 157
Earlier sketch in CA 41-44R
Snyder, John William 1924- ... 1-4R
Snyder, Keith 1966- ... CANR-110
Earlier sketch in CA 164
Snyder, Laura (Lillie) 1940- ... 120
Snyder, Leslie 1945- ... 114
Snyder, Leslie Crocker 1942- ... 215
Snyder, Louis L(eo) 1907-1993 ... CANR-34
Obituary ... 143
Earlier sketches in CA 1-4R, CANR-2
Snyder, Marilyn 1936- ... 120
Snyder, Midori 1954- ... 167
See also FANT
See also SATA 106
Snyder, (Donald) Paul 1933- ... CANR-1
Earlier sketch in CA 45-48
Snyder, Paul A. 1946- ... 196
See also SATA 125
Snyder, Rachel 1924- ... 9-12R
Snyder, Richard C(arlton) 1916-1997 ... 61-64
Obituary ... 163
Snyder, Robert Edward 1943- ... CANR-46
Earlier sketch in CA 120
Snyder, Robert L. 1928- ... 25-28R
Snyder, Robert W. 1955- ... 195
Snyder, Solomon H(albert) 1938- ... CANR-14
Earlier sketch in CA 37-40R
Snyder, Susan (Brooke) 1934-2001 ... 93-96
Obituary ... 203
Snyder, Tom 1936- ... 121
Brief entry ... 109
Interview in ... CA-121
Snyder, William 1951- ... 104
Snyder, William M. 1956- ... 213
Snyder, William P(aul) 1928- ... 13-16R
Snyder, William S(tover) 1927- ... 123
Brief entry ... 118
Snyder, Zilpha Keatley 1927- ... CANR-38
Earlier sketch in CA 9-12R
See also AAYA 15
See also BYA 1
See also CLC 17
See also CLR 31
See also JRDA
See also MAICYA 1, 2
See also SAAS 2
See also SATA 1, 28, 75, 110, 163
See also SATA-Essay 112, 163
See also YAW
Snyderman, Reuven K. 1922- ... 29-32R
See also SATA 5
So, Meilo ... SATA 162
Soames, Jane
See Nickerson, Jane Soames (Bon)
Soames, Mary 1922- ... 111
Soard, Lori 1969- ... 229
Soares, Anthony T(homas) 1923- ... 45-48
Soares, Bernardo
See Pessoa, Fernando (Antonio Nogueira)
Soares-Prabhu, George M. 1929-1995 ... 228
Sobacos, Juan, Jr.
See Mallett, Daryl F(urumi)
Sobczak, A(ndrew) J(ames) 1962- ... 163
Sobel, B. Z. 1933- ... 77-80
Sobel, Bernard 1887-1964 ... 5-8R
Sobel, Brian M. 1954- ... 107
Sobel, Dava 1947- ... CANR-138
Earlier sketches in CA 154, CANR-91
See also MTFW 2005
Sobel, David T. 1949- ... 227
Sobel, Harold W(illiam) 1933- ... 61-64
Sobel, Ileene Smith 1953- ... 217
Sobel, Irwin Philip 1901-1991 ... 45-48
Obituary ... 134
Sobel, Jordan Howard 1929- ... 213
Sobel, June 1950- ... SATA 149
Sobel, Lester A(lbert) 1919- ... CANR-9
Earlier sketch in CA 21-24R
Sobel, Michael I. 1939- ... 128
Sobel, Robert 1931-1999 ... CANR-31
Obituary ... 181
Earlier sketches in CA 5-8R, CANR-8
Sobel, Russell S(teven) 1968- ... 175
Sobell, Morton 1917- ... 53-56
Sober, Elliott (Reuben) 1948- ... CANR-82
Earlier sketch in CA 132
Soberman, Richard M. 1937- ... CANR-10
Earlier sketch in CA 25-28R
Sobh, A.
See Shamlu, Ahmad
Sobh, Alef
See Shamlu, Ahmad
Sobieski, Carol (O'Brien) 1939-1990 ... 129
Obituary ... 132
Brief entry ... 124
Interview in ... CA-129
Sobieszek, Robert A(llan) 1943- ... 184
Sobiloff, Hy(man Jordan) 1912-1970 ... 226
Obituary ... 29-32R
See also CP 1
See also DLB 48
Sobin, A. G.
See Sobin, Anthony
Sobin, Anthony 1944- ... 116
Sobin, Gustaf 1935-2005 ... CANR-94
Earlier sketches in CA 115, CANR-38
Sobin, Julian M(elvin) 1920- ... 132
Sobir, Bozor 1938- ... EWL 3
Sobirov, Bozor
See Sobir, Bozor
Soble, Alan 1947- ... 122
Soble, Jennie
See Cavin, Ruth (Brodie)
Sobol, Donald J. 1924- ... CANR-38
Earlier sketches in CA 1-4R, CANR-1, 18
See also CLR 4
See also CWRI 5
See also JRDA
See also MAICYA 1, 2
See also SATA 1, 31, 73, 132
Sobol, Harriet Langsam 1936- ... CANR-8
Earlier sketch in CA 61-64
See also SATA 47
See also SATA-Brief 34
Sobol, Joseph Daniel ... 224
Sobol, Joshua 1939- ... 200
See also Sobol, Yehoshua
See also CLC 60
Sobol, Louis 1896-1986 ... CAP-2
Obituary ... 118
Earlier sketch in CA 29-32
Sobol, Rose 1931- ... 101
See also SATA 76
Sobol, Yehoshua 1939-
See Sobol, Joshua
See also CWW 2
Sobolev, Leonid (Sergeevich) 1898-1971
Obituary ... 29-32R
Sobosan, Jeffrey G. 1946- ... CANR-52
Earlier sketch in CA 126
Sobott-Mogwe, Gaele 1956- ... 152
See also SATA 97
Soboul, Albert Marius 1914-1982
Obituary ... 107
Sobre, Judith Berg 1941- ... 139
Sobrino, Josephine 1915- ... CANR-36
Earlier sketch in CA 45-48
Soby, James Thrall 1906-1979 ... 103
Socarides, Charles William 1922- ... 194
Brief entry ... 118
Sochen, June 1937- ... CANR-88
Earlier sketches in CA 41-44R, CANR-14, 43
So Chong-ju 1915- ... EWL 3
Sockman, Ralph W(ashington)
1889-1970 ... CANR-86
Obituary ... 89-92
Earlier sketch in CA 5-8R
Socolofsky, Homer E(dward) 1922- ... CANR-1
Earlier sketch in CA 1-4R
Socolow, Robert H(arry) 1937- ... 37-40R
Sodaro, Craig 1948- ... CANR-40
Earlier sketches in CA 101, CANR-18
Soddy, Frederick 1877-1956 ... 167
Soden, Dale E. 1951- ... 226
Soden, Garrett ... 226
Soderberg, Hjalmar 1869-1941 ... DLB 259
See also EWL 3
See also RGSF 2
See also TCLC 39
Soderberg, Paul Stephen 1949- ... CANR-19
Earlier sketch in CA 103
Soderberg, Percy Measday 1901-1969 .. CAP-1
Earlier sketch in CA 9-10
Soderbergh, Steven 1963- ... AAYA 43
See also CLC 154
Sodergran, Edith (Irene) 1892-1923 ... 202
See also Soedergran, Edith (Irene)
See also DLB 259
See also EW 11
See also EWL 3
See also RGWL 2, 3
Soderholm, Marjorie Elaine 1923- ... 13-16R
Soderlind, Arthur E(dwin) 1920- ... 69-72
See also SATA 14
Soderlund, Jean Ruth 1947- ... 127
Soderstrom, Edward Jonathan
1954- ... CANR-30
Earlier sketch in CA 111
Sodowsky, Roland (E.) 1938- ... 134
Soedergran, Edith (Irene) 1892-1923
See Sodergran, Edith (Irene)
See also TCLC 31
Soedjatmoko 1922-1989
Obituary ... 130
Soehnlein, Karl M. ... 203
Soekarno
See Sukarno, (Ahmed)
Soelle, Dorothee 1929-2003 ... CANR-11
Obituary ... 219
Earlier sketch in CA 69-72
Soentpiet, Chris 1970- ... MAICYA 2
Soentpiet, Chris K. 1970- ... SATA 97, 159
Soerensen, Georg
See Sorensen, Georg
Soerensen, Svend Otto 1916- ... 132
See also SATA 67
Soeur Sourire
See Deckers, Jeanine
Sofen, Edward 1919- ... 9-12R
Sofer, Barbara 1949- ... 163
See also SATA 109
Sofer, Cyril 1921- ... 5-8R
Sofer, Rachel
See Sofer, Barbara
Sofer, Rachel
See Sofer, Barbara
Soffer, Reba N(usbaum) 1934- ... 85-88
Soffici, Ardengo 1879-1964 ... DLB 114, 264
Sofola, 'Zulu 1938- ... 163
See also CD 5, 6
See also CWD
See also DLB 157
Softly, Barbara Frewin 1924- ... CANR-2
Earlier sketch in CA 5-8R
See also CWRI 5
See also SATA 12
Softly, Edgar
See Lovecraft, H(oward) P(hillips)
Softly, Edward
See Lovecraft, H(oward) P(hillips)
Soghomonian, Eghishe 1897-1937
See Charents, Eghishe
Soglow, Otto 1900-1975 ... 93-96
Obituary ... 57-60
See also SATA-Obit 30
Sogolow, Rosalie (K.) 1939- ... 153
Sohl, Frederic J(ohn) 1916- ... 21-24R
See also SATA 10
Sohl, Jerry 1913-2002 ... CANR-15
Obituary ... 211
Earlier sketch in CA 81-84
See also SFW 4
Sohl, Robert (Allen) 1941- ... 103
Sohn, Amy 1973- ... 208
Sohn, David A. 1929- ... CANR-6
Earlier sketch in CA 9-12R
Sohn, Louis B(runo) 1914- ... 101
Sojourner, Mary ... 218
Sokal, Alan D. 1955- ... 181
Sokel, Walter H(erbert) 1917- ... CANR-6
Earlier sketch in CA 5-8R
Sokhanskaia, Nadezhda Stepanovna
1823(?)-1884 ... DLB 277
Sokil, Ya.
See Sokolyszyn, Aleksander
Sok-Kyong, Kang 1951- ... 176
Sokol, Anthony E. 1897-1982 ... 37-40R
Sokol, Bill
See Sokol, William
Sokol, David M(artin) 1942- ... CANR-16
Earlier sketches in CA 49-52, CANR-1
Sokol, Stanley S. 1923- ... 213
Sokol, William 1923- ... SATA 37
Sokoloff, Alice Hunt 1912- ... 25-28R
Sokoloff, Boris Theodore 1889-1979 ... 89-92
Sokoloff, Kiril 1947- ... 108
Sokoloff, Naomi B. 1953- ... 144
Sokoloff, Natalie B.
See Scott, Natalie Anderson
Sokoloff, Natalie J(ean) 1944- ... CANR-44
Earlier sketch in CA 113
Sokolov, Alexander V(sevolodovich)
1943- ... 73-76
See also Sokolov, Sasha
Sokolov, Kirill 1930- ... SATA 34
Sokolov, Raymond 1941- ... 85-88
See also CLC 7
Sokolov, Sasha
See Sokolov, Alexander V(sevolodovich)
See also CLC 59
See also CWW 2
See also DLB 285
See also EWL 3
See also RGWL 2, 3
Sokolov, Valentin 1925(?)-1984
Obituary ... 114
Sokolow, Jayme Aaron 1946- ... 113
Sokolowski, Robert (Stanley)
1934- ... CANR-116
Earlier sketch in CA 89-92
Sokolski, Alan 1931- ... 13-16R
Sokolsky, George Ephraim 1893-1962
Obituary ... 89-92
Sokolyszyn, Aleksander 1914- ... 132
Solano, Solita 1888-1975 ... 117
Obituary ... 61-64
See also DLB 4
Solares, Ignacio 1945- ... 193
See also EWL 3
Solari, A. G.
See Rimanelli, Giose
Solaun, Mauricio 1935- ... 138
Brief entry ... 106
Solberg, Carl 1915- ... CANR-12
Earlier sketch in CA 73-76
Solberg, Carl Edward 1940- ... 61-64
Solberg, Gunard 1932- ... 29-32R
Solberg, Richard W. 1917- ... CANR-3
Earlier sketch in CA 9-12R
Solberg, S(ammy) E(dward) 1930- ... 21-24R
Solberg, Winton U(dell) 1922- ... 41-44R
Solbert, Romaine G. 1925- ... 29-32R
See also SATA 2
Solbert, Ronni
See Solbert, Romaine G.
Solbrig, Dorothy J. 1945- ... 146
Solbrig, Otto T(homas) 1930- ... CANR-9
Earlier sketch in CA 21-24R
Soldati, Mario 1906-1999 ... 108
Obituary ... 181
See also CWW 2
See also DLB 177
See also EWL 3
See also RGSF 2
Soldo, John J(oseph) 1945- ... CANR-14
Earlier sketch in CA 77-80
Soldofsky, Robert Melvin 1920- ... CANR-1
Earlier sketch in CA 1-4R
Sole, Carlos A(lberto) 1938- ... 53-56
Sole, Robert ... 238
Solecki, Ralph S(tefan) 1917-
Brief entry ... 109
Soledad
See Zalmudio, Adela
Solem, (George) Alan 1931- ... 57-60
Solensten, John M(artin) 1929- ... CANR-28
Earlier sketch in CA 110
Soleri, Paolo 1919- ... CANR-116
Earlier sketch in CA 106
Soley, Lawrence C(harles) 1949- ... 150
Solheim, Bruce O. 1958- ... 188
Solheim, James ... 202
See also SATA 133
Soliday, Gerald Lyman 1939- ... CANR-12
Earlier sketch in CA 61-64
Solinas, Franco 1927-1982 ... IDFW 3, 4
Solinger, Dorothy J(ane) 1945- ... CANR-66
Earlier sketches in CA 113, CANR-32
Solinger, Rickie 1947- ... 208
Solis, Octavio ... CD 5, 6
Soljan, Antun 1932-1993 ... 190
See also DLB 181
Solkin, David H. 1951- ... 213
Solkoff, Joel 1947- ... 133
Soll, Ivan 1938- ... CANR-108
Earlier sketch in CA 29-32R
Sollberger, Edmond (Albert) 1920-1989
Obituary ... 129
Solle, Dorothee
See Soelle, Dorothee
Sollers, Philippe 1936- ... 184
See also CWW 2
See also DLB 83
See also EWL 3
Solley, Charles Marion, Jr. 1925- ... 1-4R
Sollogub, Vladimir Aleksandrovich
1813-1882 ... DLB 198
Sollors, Werner 1943- ... CANR-106
Earlier sketches in CA 119, CANR-45, 96
See also DLB 246
Sollosy, Judith 1946- ... CANR-116
Earlier sketch in CA 149
Solman, Paul 1944- ... 148
Brief entry ... 119
Solmi, Sergio 1899-1981 ... DLB 114
Solmon, Lewis C(alvin) 1942- ... 41-44R
Solmsen, Friedrich (Rudolf Heinrich)
1904-1989 ... 53-56
Obituary ... 127
Solmssen, Arthur R(obert) G(eorge) 1928- .. 143
Solnick, Bruce B. 1933- ... 29-32R
Solnit, Albert J(ay) 1919-2002 ... 103
Obituary ... 207
Solnit, Rebecca 1961- ... 224
Solo, Jay
See Ellison, Harlan (Jay)
Solo, Robert A(lexander) 1916- ... CANR-37
Earlier sketches in CA 45-48, CANR-1, 17
Sologub, Fedor
See Teternikov, Fyodor Kuzmich
See also DLB 295

Sologub, Fyodor
See Teternikov, Fyodor Kuzmich
See also EWL 3
See also TCLC 9
Solomita, Stephen ... 233
Solomon, Andrew 1963- ... CANR-119
Earlier sketch in CA 140
Solomon, Barbara H. 1936- ... CANR-42
Earlier sketches in CA 73-76, CANR-13
Solomon, Barbara Probst 1928- ... 5-8R
Solomon, Barry D. 1955- ... 141
Solomon, Bernard S(imon) 1924- ... 61-64
Solomon, Brad 1945- ... 103
Earlier sketch in CA 101
Solomon, Carl 1928- ... 21-24R
See also DLB 16
Solomon, Charles J. 1906(?)-1975
Obituary ... 61-64
Solomon, Daniel 1933- ... 9-12R
Solomon, David J. 1925- ... 17-20R
Solomon, Deborah 1957- ... 127
Solomon, Dorothy Allred 1949- ... CANR-142
Earlier sketch in CA 119
Solomon, Edward ... 173
Solomon, Esther Riva 1921-1969 ... 5-8R
Obituary ... 135
Solomon, Evan ... 208
Solomon, Ezra 1920-2002 ... CANR-17
Obituary ... 211
Earlier sketch in CA 85-88
Solomon, Flora 1895(?)-1984
Obituary ... 114
Solomon, George 1940- ... 45-48
Solomon, Goody L(ove) ... 57-60
Solomon, Henry A. 1937- ... 123
Solomon, Irving I. 1922- ... CANR-16
Earlier sketch in CA 21-24R
Solomon, Janis Little 1938- ... CANR-15
Earlier sketch in CA 41-44R
Solomon, Jay 1960- ... 135
Solomon, Joan 1930- ... CANR-28
Earlier sketch in CA 109
See also SATA 51
See also SATA-Brief 40
Solomon, Kenneth Ira 1942- ... 49-52
Solomon, Leonard 1930- ... 45-48
Solomon, Margaret C(laire) 1918- ... 29-32R
Solomon, Marion F. 1935- ... 146
Solomon, Maynard (Elliott) 1930- ... 41-44R
Solomon, Michael M(aurice)
1909-1994 ... 97-100
Solomon, Miriam 1958- ... 238
Solomon, Morris J. 1919- ... 13-16R
Solomon, Neil 1932- ... CANR-27
Earlier sketch in CA 65-68
Solomon, Nina 1961- ... 226
Solomon, Norman 1951- ... CANR-9
Earlier sketch in CA 57-60
Solomon, Philip 1951- ... 205
Solomon, Richard H(arvey) 1937- ... 103
Solomon, Robert 1921- ... 108
Solomon, Robert C(harles) 1942- ... CANR-93
Earlier sketches in CA 41-44R, CANR-15, 32
Solomon, Ruth (Freeman) 1908-1996 ... 21-24R
Solomon, Samuel 1904-1988 ... 53-56
Obituary ... 126
Solomon, Shirl 1928- ... 93-96
Solomon, Stanley J. 1937- ... 41-44R
Solomon, Stephen D(avid) 1950- ... 69-72
Solomon, Steve 1942- ... 117
Solomon, Susan 1956- ... CANR-116
Earlier sketch in CA 158
Solomons, David 1912-1995 ... 13-16R
Obituary ... 148
Solomons, Ikey Esquir
See Thackeray, William Makepeace
Solomonson, Katherine M. ... 208
Solon, Gregory Kent 1923(?)-1985
Obituary ... 117
Solonevich, George 1915-2003 ... SATA 15
Solorzano, Carlos 1922- ... CANR-79
Earlier sketch in CA 153
See also CWW 2
See also DLB 305
See also EWL 3
See also HW 1, 2
Solot, Mary Lynn 1939- ... 49-52
See also SATA 12
Solotaroff, Ivan 1956- ... 204
Solotaroff, Robert David 1937- ... 57-60
Solotaroff, Ted
See Solotaroff, Theodore
See also CAAS 2
Solotaroff, Theodore 1928- ... CANR-8
Earlier sketch in CA 9-12R
Interview in ... CANR-8
See also Solotaroff, Ted
Soloukhin, Vladimir (Alekseevich) 1924-1997
Brief entry ... 111
See also CWW 2
See also DLB 302
See also EWL 3
Solov'ev, Sergei Mikhailovich
1885-1942 ... DLB 295
Solov'ev, Vladimir Sergeevich
See Solovyov, Vladimir Sergeyevich
See also DLB 295
Solovyov, Vladimir Sergeyevich
1853-1900 ... CANR-106
Earlier sketch in CA 183
See also Solov'ev, Vladimir Sergeevich
Solow, Martin 1920-1991 ... 81-84
Obituary ... 135
Solow, Robert Merton 1924- ... 187
Solow, Ruth
See Combs, Maxine
Soloway, Richard Allen 1934- ... 118
Solsona, S.
See Schwartz, Stephen (Alfred)
Solstad, Dag 1941- ... DLB 297
See also EWL 3
Solt, Mary Ellen (Bottom) 1920- ... 17-20R
See also CP 2
See also CWP
Soltau, T(heodore) Stanley 1890-1972 ... 5-8R
Solter, Aletha J(auch) 1945- ... 166
Soltis, Andrew (Eden, Jr.) 1947- ... CANR-4
Earlier sketch in CA 49-52
Soltis, Andy
See Soltis, Andrew (Eden, Jr.)
Soltis, Jonas F(rancis) 1931- ... CANR-31
Earlier sketches in CA 37-40R, CANR-14
Soltow, James H(arold) 1924- ... 109
Soltow, Lee 1923- ... 108
Soltow, Martha-Jane 1924- ... 110
Solum, John 1935- ... CANR-92
Earlier sketch in CA 145
Solway, David 1941- ... CANR-97
Earlier sketch in CA 112
See also DLB 53
Solway, Diane 1958- ... 147
Solwoska, Mara
See French, Marilyn
Solyn, Paul 1951- ... 77-80
Solzhenitsyn, Aleksandr I(sayevich)
1918- ... CANR-116
Earlier sketches in CA 69-72, CANR-40, 65
See also Solzhenitsyn, Aleksandr Isaevich
See also AAYA 49
See also AITN 1
See also BPFB 3
See also CLC 1, 2, 4, 7, 9, 10, 18, 26, 34, 78, 134
See also DA
See also DA3
See also DAB
See also DAC
See also DAM MST, NOV
See also DLB 302
See also EW 13
See also EXPS
See also LAIT 4
See also MTCW 1, 2
See also MTFW 2005
See also NFS 6
See also RGSF 2
See also RGWL 2, 3
See also SSC 32
See also SSFS 9
See also TWA
See also WLC
Solzhenitsyn, Aleksandr Isaevich
See Solzhenitsyn, Aleksandr I(sayevich)
See also CWW 2
See also EWL 3
Soma, Daniel
See Lange, Martin
Soman, Alfred 1934- ... CANR-36
Earlier sketch in CA 45-48
Soman, Jean Powers 1949- ... 122
Soman, Shirley Camper ... CANR-3
Earlier sketch in CA 9-12R
Some, Malidoma Patrice 1956- ... 145
Somekh, Emile 1915- ... 53-56
Somer, John (Laddie) 1936- ... CANR-94
Earlier sketch in CA 37-40R
Somerlott, Robert 1928-2001 ... 105
See also SATA 62
Somers, Albert B(ingham) 1939- ... 115
Somers, Bart
See Fox, G(ardner) F(rancis)
Somers, Gerald G(eorge) 1922-1977 ... CANR-5
Earlier sketch in CA 13-16R
Somers, Herman Miles 1911-1991 ... CANR-1
Obituary ... 134
Earlier sketch in CA 1-4R
Somers, Jane
See Lessing, Doris (May)
Somers, Jeff 1971- ... 203
Somers, Paul
See Winterton, Paul
Somers, Paul P(reston), Jr. 1942- ... 182
Somers, Robert H(ough) 1929- ... 45-48
Somers, Suzanne
See Daniels, Dorothy
Somers, Suzanne 1946- ... 139
Somerset, Anne 1955- ... 145
Somerset, FitzRoy Richard
See Raglan, FitzRoy (Richard Somerset)
Somerset, Henry Hugh Arthur FitzRoy
1900-1984
Obituary ... 112
Somerset Fry, (Peter George Robin) Plantagenet
1931- ... 104
Somerset-Ward, Richard 1942- ... 177
Somervill, Barbara A(nn) 1948- ... 211
See also SATA 140
Somerville, Edith Oenone 1858-1949 ... 196
See also DLB 135
See also RGEL 2
See also RGSF 2
See also SSC 56
See also TCLC 51
Somerville, (James) Hugh (Miller)
1922-1992 ... 9-12R
Obituary ... 137
Somerville, James 1947- ... 128
Somerville, John (P. M.) 1905-1994 ... CANR-29
Obituary ... 143
Earlier sketch in CA 45-48
Somerville, (Henry) Lee 1915- ... 69-72
Somerville, Mollie ... CANR-12
Earlier sketch in CA 29-32R
Somerville, Rose M(aurer) 1908- ... 45-48
Somerville, William 1675-1742 ... RGEL 2
Somerville & Ross
See Martin, Violet Florence and
Somerville, Edith Oenone
Somerville-Large, Peter 1928- ... CANR-20
Earlier sketch in CA 97-100
Somit, Albert 1919- ... 81-84
Somkin, Fred 1924- ... 25-28R
Somkin, Steven 1941- ... 149
Sommer, Angela
See Sommer-Bodenburg, Angela
Sommer, Carl 1930- ... 196
See also SATA 126
Sommer, Doris 1947- ... 187
Sommer, Elyse 1929- ... CANR-2
Earlier sketch in CA 49-52
See also SATA 7
Sommer, Frederick 1905-1999 ... 209
Sommer, Jason ... 208
Sommer, Joellen 1957- ... 45-48
Sommer, John 1941- ... 29-32R
Sommer, John D(aniel) 1929- ... 213
Sommer, Mark 1945- ... 140
Sommer, Piotr 1948- ... CWW 2
Sommer, Richard J(erome) 1934- ... CANR-1
Earlier sketch in CA 45-48
Sommer, Robert 1929- ... CANR-18
Earlier sketches in CA 9-12R, CANR-3
See also SATA 12
Sommer, Scott 1951- ... 106
See also CLC 25
Sommer-Bodenburg, Angela 1948- ... 132
See also SATA 63
Sommer-Bodenburg, Angela 1948- ... SATA 113
Sommerdorf, Norma (Jean) 1926- ... 200
See also SATA 131
Sommerfeld, Ray(nard) M(atthias)
1933- ... CANR-28
Earlier sketch in CA 105
Sommerfeld, Richard Edwin 1928- ... 13-16R
Sommerfeldt, John R(obert) 1933- ... CANR-3
Earlier sketch in CA 49-52
Sommerfelt, Aimee 1892-1975 ... 37-40R
See also BYA 3
See also SATA 5
Sommerfield, Sylvie 1931-1994 ... 236
See also RHW
Sommerness, Martin David 1954- ... 116
Sommers, Christina Hoff 1950- ... CANR-95
Earlier sketch in CA 153
See also CLC 197
Sommers, David
See Smith, Howard Van
Sommers, Fred(eric Tamler) 1923- ... 113
Sommers, Jay 1917(?)-1985
Obituary ... 117
Sommers, Joseph 1924-1979 ... CANR-29
Earlier sketch in CA 25-28R
Sommers, Lawrence M(elvin)
1919- ... CANR-116
Earlier sketches in CA 126, CANR-53
Sommers, Robert (Thomas) 1926- ... 151
Sommers, Tish 1914(?)-1985
Obituary ... 117
Sommerville, C(harles) John 1938- ... 137
Somorjai, Gabor Arpad 1935- ... 105
Somov, Orest Mikhailovich
1793-1833 ... DLB 198
Somtow, S. P.
See Sucharitkul, Somtow
See also SUFW 2
Son, John ... 236
See also SATA 160
Sondak, Norman E(dward) 1931- ... 112
Sonderby, Knud
See Sonderby, Knud
See also DLB 214
Sonderby, Knud 1909-1966 ... 192
See also Sonderby, Knud
Sondermann, Fred A. 1923- ... 49-52
Sonders, Scott (Alejandro) 1953- ... CANR-56
Earlier sketch in CA 132
Sondheim, Stephen (Joshua) 1930- ... CANR-125
Earlier sketches in CA 103, CANR-47, 67
See also AAYA 11, 66
See also CLC 30, 39, 147
See also DAM DRAM
See also DC 22
See also LAIT 4
Sondrup, Steven P(reece) 1944- ... 103
Sone, Monica 1919- ... AAL
See also DLB 312
Sonenberg, Maya 1960- ... 131
Sonenblick, Jerry 1931- ... 104
Sonenblum, Sidney 1924- ... 29-32R
Sonenscher, Michael 1947- ... 118
Sonero, Devi
See Pelton, Robert W(ayne)
Sones, Sonya ... 200
See also AAYA 51
See also MAICYA 2
See also SATA 131
Song, Ben (Chunho) 1937- ... 37-40R
Song, Cathy 1955- ... CANR-118
Earlier sketch in CA 154
See also AAL
See also CWP
See also DLB 169, 312
See also EXPP
See also FW
See also PC 21
See also PFS 5
Song, C(hoan-)S(eng) 1929- ... 115
Song, Miri ... 192
Songe, Alice Heloise 1914- ... 102
Songer, C. J. ... 237
Soni, P.R. 1953- ... 238
Soniat, Katherine (Thompson) 1942- ... 207
Sonkin, Robert 1911(?)-1980
Obituary ... 97-100
Sonn, Richard D. ... 144
Sonne, Jorgen 1925- ... 196
Sonne, Juergen
See Sonne, Jorgen
Sonneborn, Harry L(ee) 1919- ... 77-80
Sonneborn, Ruth (Cantor) 1899-1974 ... CAP-2
Obituary ... 49-52
Earlier sketch in CA 21-22
See also SATA 4
See also SATA-Obit 27
Sonneborn, Tracy Morton 1905-1981
Obituary ... 108
Sonneman, Eve 1950- ... 208
Sonnenberg, Ben 1936- ... 139
Sonnenfeld, Barry 1953- ... AAYA 26
Sonnenfeld, Marion (Wilma) 1928- ... 37-40R
Sonnenmark, Laura A. 1958- ... SATA 73
Sonnenschein, Allan 1941- ... 133
Sonneveld, A.
See Stolk, Anthonie
Sonnevi, Goeran
See Sonnevi, Goran
Sonnevi, Goran 1939- ... 193
See also DLB 257
Sonnichsen, C. L. 1901-1991 ... CANR-39
Earlier sketches in CA 1-4R, CANR-2, 17
Sonntag, Jacob 1905-1984
Obituary ... 113
Sono, Ayako
See Miura, Chizuko
See also DLB 182
Son of the Soil
See Fletcher, J(oseph) S(mith)
Sons, Raymond W(illiam) 1926- ... 136
Sonstegard, Manford Aldrich 1911- ... CANR-2
Earlier sketch in CA 49-52
Sonstroem, David 1936- ... 29-32R
Sontag, Alan 1946- ... 85-88
Sontag, Frederick (Earl) 1924- ... CANR-1
Earlier sketch in CA 1-4R
Sontag, Frederick H(erman) 1924- ... 81-84
Sontag, Raymond J(ames) 1897-1972
Obituary ... 37-40R
Sontag, Susan 1933-2004 ... CANR-97
Obituary ... 234
Earlier sketches in CA 17-20R, CANR-25, 51, 74
See also AMWS 3
See also CLC 1, 2, 10, 13, 31, 105, 195
See also CN 1, 2, 3, 4, 5, 6, 7
See also CPW
See also DA3
See also DAM POP
See also DLB 2, 67
See also EWL 3
See also MAL 5
See also MAWW
See also MTCW 1, 2
See also MTFW 2005
See also RGAL 4
See also RHW
See also SSFS 10
Sontheimer, Morton ... 101
Sontup, Dan(iel) 1922- ... 1-4R
Soong, Ching-ling 1890-1981
Obituary ... 108
Soos, Troy 1957- ... CANR-119
Earlier sketch in CA 164
Soper, Alexander Coburn 1904-1993 ... 105
Obituary ... 140
Soper, Donald Oliver 1903-1998 ... 109
Obituary ... 172
Soper, Eileen A(lice) 1905-1990(?) ... 9-12R
Obituary ... 131
Soper, Eileen Louise 1900- ... 103
Soper, Fred L. 1894(?)-1977
Obituary ... 69-72
Soper, Paul L(eon) 1906- ... 5-8R
Soper, Tony 1939- ... CANR-22
Earlier sketch in CA 105
Soper-Cook, JoAnne (M.) ... 218
Sopher, Sharon Isabel 1945- ... 101
Sophia -1844 ... FW
Sophocles 496(?)B.C.-406(?)B.C. ... AW 1
See also CDWLB 1
See also DA
See also DA3
See also DAB
See also DAC
See also DAM DRAM, MST
See also DC 1
See also DFS 1, 4, 8
See also DLB 176
See also LAIT 1
See also LATS 1:1
See also LMFS 1
See also RGWL 2, 3
See also TWA
See also WLCS
Sophron fl. 430B.C.- ... LMFS 1
Sopko, Eugen 1949- ... SATA 58
Sopov, Aco 1923-1982 ... DLB 181
Soras, George 1930-
Brief entry ... 184
Sorauf, Francis Joseph 1928- ... 9-12R
Sorauf, Frank J.
See Sorauf, Francis Joseph
Sorden, L(eland) G(eorge) 1898-1981 ... CANR-1
Earlier sketch in CA 1-4R
Sorel, Byron
See Yatron, Michael
Sorel, Charles 1599(?)-1674 ... DLB 268
See also GFL Beginnings to 1789

Cumulative Index 545 Spacks

Sorel, Edward 1929- CANR-106
Earlier sketches in CA 9-12R, CANR-33
See also SATA 65, 126
See also SATA-Brief 37
Sorel, Georges 1847-1922 188
Brief entry 118
See also TCLC 91
Sorel, Julia
See Drexler, Rosalyn
Sorel, Nancy Caldwell 1934- CANR-90
Earlier sketch in CA 37-40R
Sorel-Cameron, James (Robert) 1948- 136
Sorell, Walter 1905-1997 .... 21-24R
Obituary 156
Sorensen, Andrew Aaron 1938- 65-68
Sorensen, Chris 1942- 107
Sorensen, Georg 1948- CANR-93
Earlier sketch in CA 145
Sorensen, Henri 1950- 187
See also SATA 77, 115
Sorensen, Jacki 1942- 110
Sorensen, Robert C(haikin) 1923- 45-48
Sorensen, Roy A. 1957- 139
Sorensen, Svend Otto
See Soerensen, Svend Otto
Sorensen, Theodore C(haikin) 1928- .. CANR-2
Earlier sketch in CA 45-48
Sorensen, Thomas C. 1926- 21-24R
Sorensen, Villy 1929-2001 184
Obituary 203
See also CWW 2
See also DLB 214
See also EWL 3
Sorensen, Virginia 1912-1991 .... CANR-22
Earlier sketch in CA 13-16R, 139
See also BYA 2
See also CWRI 5
See also DLB 206
See also MAICYA 1, 2
See also SAAS 15
See also SATA 2
See also SATA-Obit 72
See also TCWW 1, 2
Sorensen, W. Conner 1942- 155
Sorenson, Georgia L(ynn Jones) 1947- 188
Sorenson, Herbert 1898-1995 .... 21-24R
Obituary 198
Sorenson, Jane 1926- .... SATA 63
Sorenson, John L. 1924- 169
Sorenson, Margo 1946- CANR-130
Earlier sketch in CA 161
See also SATA 96
Sorenson, Marian 1925-1968 .... CAP-1
Earlier sketch in CA 11-12
Sorescu, Marin 1936-1996 147
Obituary 155
See also CWW 2
See also EWL 3
Sorestad, Glen (Allan) 1937- CANR-57
Earlier sketches in CA 112, CANR-31
Sorge, Reinhard Johannes 1892-1916 . DLB 118
Sorgman, Mayo 1912- 13-16R
Soria, Regina 1911- CANR-55
Earlier sketch in CA 126
Soriano, Osvaldo 1943-1997 .... EWL 3
Sorin, Gerald 1940- CANR-57
Earlier sketches in CA 77-80, CANR-31
Sorine, Stephanie Riva 1954- 105
Sorkin, Aaron 1961- .... AAYA 55
Sorkin, Adam J. 1943- 143
Sorkin, Alan Lowell 1941- CANR-57
Earlier sketches in CA 41-44R, CANR-14, 31
Sorkin, David 1953- 192
Sorley, Charles Hamilton 1895-1915 .... RGEL 2
Sorley, Lewis 1934- 117
Sorley Walker, Kathrine CANR-6
Earlier sketch in CA 5-8R
See also SATA 41
Sorokin, Boris 1922- 116
Sorokin, Elena 1894(?)-1975
Obituary 61-64
Sorokin, Pitirim A(lexandrovitch)
1889-1968 .... CANR-5
Obituary 25-28R
Earlier sketch in CA 5-8R
Sorokin, Vladimir
See Sorokin, Vladimir Georgievich
See also CLC 59
Sorokin, Vladimir Georgievich
See Sorokin, Vladimir
See also DLB 285
Soromenho, Fernando Monteiro de Castro
1910-1968 .... EWL 3
Soros, George 1930- 184
Soros, Susan (Weber) 1955- 190
Soroush, Abdolkarim 1945- 225
Sorrell, Alan 1904-1974 93-96
Sorrell, J(ohn) E(dward) 1954- 137
Sorrells, Dorothy C. 9-12R
Sorrells, Helen 1908- 37-40R
Sorrells, Robert T. 1932- 127
Sorrells, Walter 196
Sorrentino, Gilbert 1929- CANR-115
Earlier sketches in CA 77-80, CANR-14, 33
Interview in CANR-14
See also CLC 3, 7, 14, 22, 40
See also CN 3, 4, 5, 6, 7
See also CP 1, 2, 3, 4, 5, 6, 7
See also DLB 5, 173
See also DLBY 1980
Sorrentino, Joseph N. 1937- CANR-3
Earlier sketch in CA 49-52
See also SATA 6
Sorrentino, Steven 1957- 238
Sorret, Ludovico
See Noonan, Tom
Sorrow, Barbara Head 1945- 147
Sorsby, Arnold 1900-1980 85-88
Sortor, June Elizabeth 1939- 61-64
See also SATA 12
Sortor, Toni
See Sortor, June Elizabeth
Sorum, Paul Clay 1943- 103
Sosa, Ernest 1940- 53-56
Sosa, Roberto 1930- CANR-87
Earlier sketch in CA 131
See also DLB 290
See also EWL 3
See also HW 1
Sosa de Quesada, Aristides V.
1908-2000 53-56
Soseki
See Natsume, Soseki
See also MJW
Sosin, Danielle 1959- 213
Soskice, Janet Martin 1951- 124
Soskin, V. H.
See Ellison, Virginia H(owell)
Sosna, Morton 1945- 102
Sosnick, Stephen H(oward) 1930- 45-48
Sosnow, Eric 1910-1987
Obituary 121
Sosnowski, David (J.) 1959- 159
Sossaman, Stephen 1944- 77-80
Soteriou, Alexandra 233
Soth, Lauren (Kephart) 1910-1998 .... CAP-1
Obituary 165
Earlier sketch in CA 17-18
Sotheby, James 1682-1742 .... DLB 213
Sotheby, John 1740-1807 .... DLB 213
Sotheby, Samuel 1771-1842 .... DLB 213
Sotheby, Samuel Leigh 1805-1861 ..... DLB 213
Sotheby, William 1757-1833 .... DLB 93, 213
Soto, Gary 1952- CANR-107
Brief entry 119
Earlier sketches in CA 125, CANR-50, 74
Interview in CA-125
See also AAYA 10, 37
See also BYA 11
See also CLC 32, 80
See also CLR 38
See also CP 7
See also DAM MULT
See also DLB 82
See also EWL 3
See also EXPP
See also HLC 2
See also HW 1, 2
See also JRDA
See also LLW
See also MAICYA 2
See also MAICYAS 1
See also MAL 5
See also MTCW 2
See also MTFW 2005
See also PC 28
See also PFS 7
See also RGAL 4
See also SATA 80, 120
See also WYA
See also YAW
Soto, Lourdes Diaz 211
Soto, Pedro Juan 1928- 131
Brief entry 114
See also EWL 3
See also HW 1
Soto, Shirlene A(nn) 1947- CANR-87
Earlier sketch in CA 131
See also HW 1
Sotomayor, Antonio 1902-1985 73-76
See also SATA 11
Sotomayor, Sally .... GLL 2
Sotter, Fred
See Lake, Kenneth R(obert)
Souci, Robert D. San
See San Souci, Robert D.
Soucie, Gary (Arnold) 1937- 127
Soucy, Robert J(oseph) 1933- CANR-30
Earlier sketch in CA 45-48
Souder, William 1949- 236
Soudley, Henry
See Wood, James Playsted
Soueif, Ahdaf 1950- CANR-98
Earlier sketch in CA 168
See also DLB 267
Souerwine, Andrew H(arry) 1924- CANR-19
Earlier sketch in CA 81-84
Souhami, Diana 1940- CANR-76
Earlier sketch in CA 130
Soukup, James R(udolph) 1928- 9-12R
Soukup, Martha (Clare) 1959- .... SFW 4
Soule, Gardner (Bosworth)
1913-2000 .... CANR-2
Earlier sketch in CA 5-8R
See also SATA 14
Soule, George (Henry, Jr.) 1887-1970 .... CAP-2
Obituary 29 32R
Earlier sketch in CA 21-22
Soule, George (Alan) 1930- 57-60
Soule, Isabel Walker 1898(?)-1972
Obituary 37-40R
Soule, Jean Conder 1919- 5-8R
See also SATA 10
Soule, Sandra W(olf) 1946- 137
Souljah, Sister 1964- CANR-87
Earlier sketch in CA 154
Sounes, Howard 1965- 182
Soupault, Philippe 1897-1990 147
Obituary 131
Brief entry 116
See also CLC 68
See also EWL 3
See also GFL 1789 to the Present
See also LMFS 2
Soupcoff, Murray 1943- 101
Souper, Patrick Charles 1928- 110
Sour, Robert B(andler) 1905-1985
Obituary 115
Sourian, Peter 1933- 1-4R
Souritz, Elizabeth 1923- 135
Sourkes, Theodore L(ionel) 1919- 17-20R
Sours, John Appling 1931-1983 .... CANR-9
Obituary 110
Earlier sketch in CA 21-24R
Sourvinou-Inwood, Christiane 1945- 143
Sousa, Geraldo (U. de) 1952- 189
Sousa, Marion 1941- 65-68
Soussloff, Catherine M. 1951- 165
Soustelle, Jacques (Emile) 1912-1990
Obituary 132
Souster, (Holmes) Raymond 1921- ... CANR-53
Earlier sketches in CA 13-16R, CANR-13, 29
See also CAAS 14
See also CLC 5, 14
See also CP 1, 2, 3, 4, 5, 6, 7
See also DA3
See also DAC
See also DAM POET
See also DLB 88
See also RGEL 2
See also SATA 63
Soutar, William 1898-1943 192
See also EWL 3
South, Clark
See Swain, Dwight V(reeland)
South, Cris 1950- 118
South, Grace
See Clark, Gail
South, Malcolm Hudson 1937- 107
South, Sheri Cobb 1959- 149
See also SATA 82
Southall, Aidan (William) 1920- 77-80
Southall, Ivan (Francis) 1921- CANR-47
Earlier sketches in CA 9-12R, CANR-7
See also AAYA 22
See also BYA 2
See also CLR 2
See also JRDA
See also MAICYA 1, 2
See also SAAS 3
See also SATA 3, 68, 134
See also SATA-Essay 134
See also YAW
Southam, B(rian) C(harles) 1931- CANR-26
Earlier sketches in CA 13-16R, CANR-10
Southard, Frank Allan, Jr. 1907- 107
Southard, Helen Fairbairn 1906- 5-8R
Southard, Samuel 1925- CANR-3
Earlier sketch in CA 1-4R
Southerington, F(rank) R(odney) 1938- 57-60
Southerland, Ellease 1943- 107
Interview in CA-107
See also BW 1
See also DLB 33
Southern, David W. 1938- 25-28R
Southern, Eileen (Jackson)
1920-2002 .... CANR-31
Obituary 211
Earlier sketches in CA 37-40R, CANR-14
Southern, Richard 1903-1989
Obituary 129
Southern, Richard William 1912-2001 .... 9-12R
Obituary 193
Southern, Terry 1924(?)-1995 .... CANR-107
Obituary 150
Earlier sketches in CA 1-4R, CANR-1, 55
See also AMWS 11
See also BPFB 3
See also CLC 7
See also CN 1, 2, 3, 4, 5, 6
See also DLB 2
See also IDFW 3, 4
Southerne, Thomas 1660-1746 .... DLB 80
See also RGEL 2
Southey, Caroline Anne Bowles
1786(?)-1854 .... DLB 116
Southey, Robert 1774-1843 .... BRW 4
See also DLB 93, 107, 142
See also RGEL 2
See also SATA 54
Southgate, Martha 205
See also AAYA 56
Southgate, Minoo S. CANR-90
Earlier sketch in CA 132
Southgate, Vera 109
See also SATA 54
Southgate, W(yndham) M(ason)
1910-1998 .... CAP-2
Earlier sketch in CA 23-24
Southouse-Cheney, Reginald
See Cheyney, (Reginald Evelyn) Peter (Southouse)
Southwell, Eugene A. 1928- 17-20R
Southwell, Robert 1561(?)-1595 .... DLB 167
See also RGEL 2
See also TEA
Southwell, Samuel B(eall) 1922- 17-20R
Southwick, Charles H(enry) 1928- 65-68
Southwick, Karen 1951-2004 235
Southwick, Leslie H. 1950- 172
Southworth, Emma Dorothy Eliza Nevitte
1819-1899 .... DLB 239
Southworth, Herbert Rutledge
1908-1999 85-88
Southworth, Horton C. 1926- 17-20R
Southworth, James G(ranville)
1896-1980 .... CAP-2
Earlier sketch in CA 33-36
Southworth, John Van Duyn
1904-1986 .... CANR-6
Obituary 118
Earlier sketch in CA 5-8R
Southworth, Louis
See Grealey, Thomas Louis
Southworth, Warren H(ilbourne)
1912-1999 .... 37-40R
Soutter, Fred
See Lake, Kenneth R(obert)
Souvarine, Boris
See Lifchitz, Boris
Souza, Ernest
See Scott, Evelyn
Souza, Marcio 1946- 145
See also DAM MULT
Souza, Raymond D(ale) 1936- CANR-104
Earlier sketches in CA 69-72, CANR-13, 30
See also HW 1
Souza, Steven M. 1953- 49-52
Souza Filho, Henrique de 1945(?)-1988
Obituary 124
Sova, Dawn B(everly) 1949- 195
Sovak, Jan 1953- 187
See also SATA 115
Sovik, E(dward) A(nders) 1918- 186
Brief entry 112
Sowande, Bode 1948- .... AFW
See also CD 5, 6
See also DLB 157
Sowards, J(esse) K(elley) 1924- 73-76
Sowards, Jack B. 183
Sowden, Celeste
See Walters, Celeste
Sowden, Lewis 1905-1974 .... CAP-1
Earlier sketch in CA 9-10
Sowell, David 1948- 228
Sowell, David (Lee) 1952- 139
Sowell, Mike 1948- 131
Sowell, Thomas 1930- CANR-98
Earlier sketches in CA 41-44R, CANR-26, 61
See also BW 2
Sowerby, A(rthur) L(indsay) M(cRae)
1899- CAP-1
Earlier sketch in CA 9-10
Sowerby, E(mily) Millicent 1883-1977 ... CAP-2
Obituary 73-76
Earlier sketch in CA 25-28
Sowers, Miriam R. 1922- 89-92
Sowers, Robert (Watson) 1923- 17-20R
Sowers, Sidney Gerald, Jr. 1935- 17-20R
Sow Fall, Aminata 1941-
See Fall, Aminata Sow
See also EWL 3
Sowle, Tace fl. 1691-1749 .... DLB 170
Sowls, Lyle K. 1916- 165
Sowter, Nita .... SATA 69
Sox, (Harold) David 1936- 124
Soyer, Raphael 1899-1987 81-84
Obituary 124
Soyfer, Jura 1912-1939 185
See also DLB 124
See also EWL 3
Soyinka, Wole 1934- CANR-136
Earlier sketches in CA 13-16R, CANR-27, 39, 82
See also AFW
See also BLC 3
See also BW 2, 3
See also CD 5, 6
See also CDWLB 3
See also CLC 3, 5, 14, 36, 44, 179
See also CN 6, 7
See also CP 1, 2, 3, 4, 5, 6 ,7
See also DA
See also DA3
See also DAB
See also DAC
See also DAM DRAM, MST, MULT
See also DC 2
See also DFS 10
See also DLB 125
See also EWL 3
See also MTCW 1, 2
See also MTFW 2005
See also RGEL 2
See also TWA
See also WLC
See also WLIT 2
See also WWE 1
Spaak, Charles 1903-1975 .... IDFW 3, 4
Spaak, Paul-Henri 1899-1972
Obituary 37-40R
Spaatz, Carl A(ndrew) 1891-1974
Obituary 49-52
Spach, John Thom 1928- 29-32R
Spache, Evelyn B(ispham) 1929- CANR-30
Earlier sketch in CA 29-32R
Spache, George D(aniel) 1909-1996 .. CANR-6
Earlier sketch in CA 5-8R
Spack, Ruth 1947- 239
Spackman, Doc
See Spackman, Robert R., Jr.
Spackman, Robert R., Jr. 1917-1984 . CANR-86
Obituary 111
Earlier sketch in CA 13-16R
Spackman, W(illiam) M(ode) 1905-1990 . 81-84
Obituary 132
See also CLC 46
Spacks, Barry (Bernard) 1931- CANR-109
Earlier sketches in CA 154, CANR 33
See also CLC 14
See also CP 7
See also DLB 105
Spacks, Patricia Meyer 1929- CANR-1
Earlier sketch in CA 1-4R

Spada 546 CONTEMPORARY AUTHORS

Spada, James 1950- CANR-137
Earlier sketches in CA 57-60, CANR-7, 28
Interview in CANR-28
Spade, Mark
See Balchin, Nigel (Marlin)
Spade, Rupert
See Pawley, Martin Edward
Spaemann, Robert 1927- 216
Spaeth, Anthony 1955- 133
Spaeth, David A(nthony) 1941- 119
Spaeth, Eloise O'Mara 1904-1998 104
Spaeth, Gerold 1939- CANR-24
Earlier sketches in CA 65-68, CANR-9
See also Spath, Gerold
See also DLB 75
Spaeth, Harold J(oseph) 1930- CANR-32
Earlier sketch in CA 45-48
Spaeth, Robert L(ouis) 1935- 119
Spaeth, Sigmund 1885-1965 .... 5-8R
Spafford, Suzy 1945- .... SATA 160
Spagnoli, Cathy 1950- 203
See also SATA 79, 134
Spahn, Mary Attea 1929- CANR-7
Earlier sketch in CA 57-60
Spain, Daphne 1949- CANR-103
Earlier sketch in CA 111
Spain, David H. 1939- 57-60
Spain, James W(illiam) 1926- 5-8R
Spain, John
See Adams, Cleve F(ranklin)
Spain, Nancy (Brooker) 1917-1964 ...... CMW 4
Spain, Nicholas
See Skinner, Mike
Spain, Rufus B(uin) 1923- 21-24R
Spain, Sahara Sunday 1991- 202
See also SATA 133
Spake, Amanda 1947- 77-80
Spalatin, Christopher 1909-1994 49-52
Obituary 169
Spalding, Andrea 1944- CANR-135
Earlier sketches in CA 160, CANR-108
See also SATA 101, 150
Spalding, David A(lan) E(dwin) 1937- 195
Spalding, Frances 1950- CANR-93
Earlier sketches in CA 104, CANR-26
See also DLB 155
Spalding, Graydon (Edward) 1911-1993 .. 89-92
Spalding, Henry D(aniel) 1915- CANR-11
Earlier sketch in CA 25-28R
Spalding, Jack 1913-2003 69-72
Spalding, Linda 1943- CANR-119
Earlier sketches in CA 128, CANR-62
Spalding, Lucile
See Spalding, Ruth
Spalding, P(hilip) A(nthony) 1911- 5-8R
Spalding, (Billups) Phinizy
1930-1994 .... CANR-85
Obituary 144
Earlier sketches in CA 41-44R, CANR-16, 39
Spalding, R. W.
See Spalding, Ronald W(olcott)
Spalding, Ronald W(olcott) 1904-1983 ... 81-84
Spalding, Ruth 104
Spalek, John M. 1928- 104
Spallone, Patricia 1951- 144
Spalter, Max 1929- 21-24R
Spanbauer, Tom CANR-115
Earlier sketch in CA 142
Spanfeller, James J(ohn) 1930-
See Spanfeller, Jim
See also MAICYA 1, 2
See also SATA 19
Spanfeller, Jim
See Spanfeller, James J(ohn)
See also SAAS 8
Spangenberg, Judith Dunn 1942- CANR-12
Earlier sketch in CA 29-32R
See also SATA 5
Spanger, Hans-Joachim 1953- 145
Spangler, Ann (Elizabeth) 1950- 205
Spangler, Catherine 233
Spangler, David 1945- 203
Spangler, Earl 1920- CANR-5
Earlier sketch in CA 5-8R
Spanidou, Irini 1946- 185
See also CLC 44
Spanier, David 1932-2000 .... CANR-39
Obituary 189
Earlier sketches in CA 101, CANR-18
Spanier, Ginette 1904-1987
Obituary 125
Spanier, John W(inston) 1930- CANR-2
Earlier sketch in CA 1-4R
Spanier, Sandra Whipple 1951- 141
Spann, Edward K(enneth) 1931- CANR-107
Earlier sketch in CA 45-48
Spann, Gloria Carter 1926-1990 ...... CANR-85
Obituary 131
Earlier sketch in CA 77-80
Spann, Meno H. 1903-1991 .... CANR-21
Obituary 136
Earlier sketch in CA 1-4R
Spann, Philip O. 1941- 128
Spann, Weldon O(ma) 1924- 17-20R
Spano, Charles 1948- 93-96
Spanos, William V(aios) 1925- CANR-11
Earlier sketch in CA 21-24R
Spanyol, Jessica 1965- .... SATA 137
Spar, Jerome 1918- 25-28R
See also SATA 10
Sparano, Vin(cent) T(homas) 1934- .. CANR-22
Earlier sketch in CA 45-48
Sparer, Joyce
See Adler, Joyce Sparer
Spargo, John 1876-1966
Obituary 89-92
Spark, Debra (Alison) 1962- CANR-110
Earlier sketches in CA 122, CANR-45
Spark, Muriel (Sarah) 1918- CANR-131
Earlier sketches in CA 5-8R, CANR-12, 36, 76, 89
Interview in CANR-12
See also BRWS 1
See also CDBLB 1945-1960
See also CLC 2, 3, 5, 8, 13, 18, 40, 94
See also CN 1, 2, 3, 4, 5, 6, 7
See also CP 1, 2, 3, 4, 5, 6, 7
See also DA3
See also DAB
See also DAC
See also DAM MST, NOV
See also DLB 15, 139
See also EWL 3
See also FW
See also LAIT 4
See also MTCW 1, 2
See also MTFW 2005
See also NFS 22
See also RGEL 2
See also SSC 10
See also TEA
See also WLIT 4
See also YAW
Spark, Richard F. 1937- 216
Sparke, (George) Archibald 1871-1970 . CAP-2
Earlier sketch in CA 21-22
Sparke, Michael fl. 1607-1653 .... DLB 170
Sparke, Penny 1948- CANR-93
Earlier sketch in CA 146
Sparkes, Boyden 1890-1954 214
Sparkes, Ivan G(eorge) 1930- CANR-38
Earlier sketch in CA 115
Sparkia, Roy (Bernard) 1924- 77-80
Sparkman, Brandon B(uster) 1929- ... CANR-13
Earlier sketch in CA 61-64
Sparkman, G(rady) Temp 1932- CANR-15
Earlier sketch in CA 89-92
Sparkman, William
See Roper, William L(eon)
Sparks, Allister (Haddon) 1933- 150
Sparks, Asa H(oward) 1937- CANR-19
Earlier sketch in CA 97-100
Sparks, Barbara 1942- .... SATA 78
Sparks, Beatrice (Mathews) 1918- ... CANR-143
Earlier sketch in CA 97-100
See also BYA 14
See also SATA 44
See also SATA-Brief 28
Sparks, Bertel M(ilas) 1918- 21-24R
Sparks, Donald B. 1931- 124
Sparks, Donald L. 1953- 143
Sparks, Edgar H(erndon) 1908-1996 ..... 13-16R
Sparks, Fred 1916(?)-1981
Obituary 103
Sparks, Jack Norman 1928- 102
Sparks, James Allen 1933- 109
Sparks, Jared 1789-1866 .... DLB 1, 30, 235
Sparks, John 1939- CANR-44
Earlier sketch in CA 103
Sparks, Mary W. 1920- .... SATA 15
Sparks, Merla Jean
See McCormick, Merla Jean
Sparks, Merrill 1922- 21-24R
Sparks, Micah 1964- 234
Sparks, Nicholas 1965- CANR-125
Earlier sketch in CA 192
Sparks, Paul 1955- 230
Sparks, Will (R.) 1924-1987 .... CANR-85
Obituary 124
Earlier sketch in CA 37-40R
Sparrow, Bartholomew H. 1959- 198
Sparrow, Elizabeth 1928- 237
Sparrow, (John Walter) Gerald 1903- 49-52
Sparrow, John (Hanbury Angus)
1906-1992 .... CANR-105
Earlier sketch in CA 103
Sparrow, Phil
See Steward, Samuel M(orris)
Sparrow, Philip
See Steward, Samuel M(orris)
See also GLL 1
Sparrowdancer, Mary 217
Sparse Grey Hackle
See Miller, Alfred W.
Sparshott, F. E.
See Sparshott, Francis (Edward)
Sparshott, Francis (Edward) 1926- CANR-51
Earlier sketches in CA 25-28R, CANR-10, 26
See also CAAS 15
See also CP 2, 3, 4, 5, 6, 7
See also DLB 60
Spartacus, Deutero
See Fanthorpe, R(obert) Lionel
Spartacus, Tertius
See Burgess, Michael (Roy)
Spash, Clive L(aurence) 1962- 153
Spate, O(skar) H(ermann) K(hristian)
1911-2000 .... CANR-29
Earlier sketches in CA 25-28R, CANR-10
Spater, George (Alexander) 1909-1984 145
Obituary 113
Spath, Gerold
See Spaeth, Gerold
See also DLB 75
Spatola, Adriano 1941-1988 .... DLB 128
Spatz, (Kenneth) Chris(topher, Jr.)
1940- 37-40R
Spatz, Jonas 1935- 29-32R
Spaugh, Jean Christopher 171
Spaulding, Dayton M(athewson) 1922- ... 61-64
Spaulding, Douglas
See Bradbury, Ray (Douglas)
Spaulding, Leonard
See Bradbury, Ray (Douglas)
Spaulding, Norma .... SATA 107
Spaulding, Robert K(ilburn) 1898-1992 ..... 5-8R
Spaulding, William E(llsworth) 1898-1979
Obituary 93-96
Spaull, Hebe (Fanny Lily) 1893- 9-12R
Spawforth, Antony (James Stuart) 1950- 189
Spaziani, Maria Luisa 1924- 210
See also DLB 128
Speaight, George Victor 1914- CANR-12
Earlier sketch in CA 29-32R
Speaight, Robert (William)
1904-1976 .... CANR-12
Earlier sketch in CA 13-16R
Speak, Dorothy 1950- 185
Speakes, Larry (Melvin) 1939- 137
Speakwell, Justus
See Humez, Nicholas (David)
Spear, Allan Henry 1937- 21-24R
Spear, Benjamin
See Henisch, Heinz K.
Spear, Charles 1910- .... CP 1, 2
Spear, George E(lliott) 1925- 102
Spear, Hilda D(oris) 1926- CANR-108
Earlier sketches in CA 107, CANR-23, 47
Spear, (Thomas George) Percival
1901-1982 106
Obituary 108
Spear, Peta 1959- 191
Spear, Richard E(dmund) 1940- 45-48
Spear, Roberta 1948- 113
Speare, Elizabeth George 1908-1994 .... 1-4R
Obituary 147
See also BYA 1, 3
See also CLR 8
See also JRDA
See also MAICYA 1, 2
See also MAICYAS 1
See also SATA 5, 62
See also SATA-Obit 83
See also YAW
Spearing, Judith (Mary Harlow)
1922- CANR-3
Earlier sketch in CA 49-52
See also SATA 9
Spearman, Arthur Dunning 1899- CAP-2
Earlier sketch in CA 21-22
Spearman, Frank H(amilton)
1859-1937 .... TCWW 1, 2
Spearman, Walter (Smith) 1908-1987 .... CAP-2
Earlier sketch in CA 29-32
Spears, Betty (Mary) 1918- CANR-6
Earlier sketch in CA 1-4R
Spears, Dorothea (Johnson) 1901- CAP-1
Earlier sketch in CA 13-14
Spears, Edward (Louis) 1886-1974 .... CAP-2
Obituary 45-48
Earlier sketch in CA 23-24
Spears, Heather 1934- .... CP 1
Spears, Jack 1919- 29-32R
Spears, Monroe K(irk) 1916-1998 .... CANR-2
Obituary 167
Earlier sketch in CA 5-8R
Spears, Richard A(lan) 1939- CANR-21
Earlier sketch in CA 104
Spears, Ross 1947- 122
Spears, Sally 1938- 171
Spears, Woodridge 1913-1989 .... 13-16R
Spears Jones, Patricia Kay 1951- 231
See also CSW
See also CWP
Spear-Swerling, Louise 1954- 158
Speart, Jessica 195
Specht, Ernst Konrad 1926- 29-32R
Specht, Harry 1929-1995 .... CANR-8
Obituary 148
Earlier sketch in CA 53-56
Specht, Robert 1928- 103
Specht, Walter F(rederick) 1912-1999 ... 97-100
Speck, Bruce W. 1948- 145
Speck, Gordon 1898-1986 .... CAP-2
Earlier sketch in CA 17-18
Speck, Nancy 1959- 171
See also SATA 104
Speck, Ross V(ictor) 1927- 125
Brief entry 107
Specking, Inez 1890-1960(?) 5-8R
See also SATA 11
Spectator
See Popovic, Nenad D(ushan)
Spector, Craig 1958- 206
See also HGG
Spector, Debra 1953- 109
Spector, Irwin 1916- 45-48
Spector, Ivar 1898-1989 .... 1-4R
Spector, Jack J. 1925- 29-32R
Spector, Leonard S. 1945- 122
Spector, Marshall 1936- 45-48
Spector, Robert Donald 1922- CANR-94
Earlier sketch in CA 13-16R
Spector, Ronald (Harvey) 1943- 57-60
Spector, Samuel I(ra) 1924- 77-80
Spector, Sheila A. 1946- 231
Spector, Sherman David 1927- CANR-22
Earlier sketch in CA 1-4R
Spector, Shmuel 1925(?)- 205
Spector, Shushannah 1903- 9-12R
Spector, Stanley 1924- 9-12R
Spector, Stephen 1946- 138
Spectorsky, A(uguste) C(omte)
1910-1972 .... CAP-2
Obituary 33-36R
Earlier sketch in CA 17-18
Spedding, (Alison Louise) 1962- 155
See also FANT
Spedding, C(olin) R(aymond) W(illiam)
1925- 53-56
Spedding, Frank Harold 1902-1984 162
Spedding, James 1808-1881 .... DLB 144
Speed, Eric CANR-27
Earlier sketches in CAP-2, CA 19-20
Speed, F(rederick) Maurice 1912(?)-1998 ... 107
Obituary 169
Speed, Frank Warren 104
Speed, (Herbert) Keith 1934- 115
Speed, Nell
See Keats, Emma and
Sampson, Emma (Keats) Speed
Speed, Nell (Ewing) 1878-1913 135
See also SATA 68
Speel, Erika 1932- 170
Speelman, Arlene 1916- 41-44R
Speer, Albert 1905-1981 .... CANR-40
Obituary 104
Earlier sketch in CA 65-68
Speer, Bonnie Stahlman 1929- 175
See also SATA 113
Speer, David G(ordon) 1913- 45-48
Speer, Laurel 1940- 132
Speer, Michael L. 1934- 93-96
Speer-Lyon, Tammie L. 1965- .... SATA 89
Speeth, Kathleen Riordan 1937- 89-92
Speght, Rachel 1597-c. 1630 .... DLB 126
Spehar, Betty M. 1924- 45-48
Spehr, Paul C(hristopher) 1931- 163
Speicher, Helen Ross S(mith) 1915- CANR-4
Earlier sketch in CA 5-8R
See also SATA 8
Speicher, John 1934(?)-1986
Obituary 119
Speidel, Hans 1897-1984 133
Obituary 114
Speidel, Michael P(aul) 1937- 108
Speier, Hans 1905-1990 .... CANR-9
Obituary 131
Earlier sketch in CA 21-24R
Speight, Harold 1916- 5-8R
Speight, Johnny 1921(?)-1998
Obituary 169
Brief entry 117
See also CBD
See also CD 5, 6
Speir, Nancy 1958- .... SATA 81
Speirs, John (Hastie) 1906- 61-64
Speirs, Logan 1938- 37-40R
Speirs, Russell 1901-1975 .... CANR-4
Obituary 61-64
Earlier sketch in CA 45-48
Speiser, Jean 69-72
Speiser, Stuart Marshall 1923-
Brief entry 106
Speitel, H. H.
See Speitel, Hans(-Henning)
Speitel, Hans(-Henning) 1937- 123
Speizman, Morris 1905- 77-80
Speke, John Hanning 1827-1864 .... DLB 166
Spekke, Arnolds 1887-1972
Obituary 37-40R
Spektor, Shemu'el
See Spector, Shmuel
Spelios, Thomas 1930- 25-28R
Spelling, Aaron 1923(?)- 184
Brief entry 184
Spellman, Alfred B. 1935- 97-100
See also BW 1
See also DLB 41
Spellman, Cathy Cash 1941- 121
See also RHW
Spellman, Francis (Joseph) 1889-1967
Obituary 113
Spellman, Francis Cardinal
See Spellman, Francis (Joseph)
Spellman, Frank R. 1944- 165
Spellman, John W(illard) 1934- 13-16R
See also SATA 14
Spellman, Paul N. 1948- 194
Spellman, Roger G.
See Cox, William R(obert)
Spellman, W. M. 1956- 141
Spelman, Cornelia Maude 1946- CANR-123
Earlier sketch in CA 161
See also SATA 96, 144
Spelman, Elizabeth V. 230
Spelman, Mary 1934- CANR-13
Earlier sketch in CA 77-80
See also SATA 28
Spelvin, George
See Phillips, David Atlee
Spemann, Hans 1869-1941 162
Spence, Alan 1947- 174
See also CN 5, 6, 7
Spence, Andrew 1947-2000 .... CN 7
Spence, Bill
See Spence, William John Duncan
Spence, Catherine Helen 1825-1910 .. DLB 230
See also FW
Spence, Clark C(hristian) 1923- CANR-6
Earlier sketch in CA 1-4R
Spence, Cynthia
See Eble, Diane
Spence, Donald P(ond) 1926- 154
Brief entry 109
Spence, Duncan
See Spence, William John Duncan
Spence, Eleanor (Rachel) 1928- CANR-3
Earlier sketch in CA 49-52
See also CLR 26
See also SATA 21
See also YAW
Spence, Gerald (Leonard) 1929- CANR-125
Earlier sketches in CA 118, CANR-71
Spence, Geraldine 1931- .... SATA 47

Cumulative Index 547 Spink

Spence, Gerry
See Spence, Gerald (Leonard)
Spence, Gordon William 1936- 25-28R
Spence, Hartzell 1908-2001 .... 5-8R
Obituary 200
Spence, J. A. D.
See Eliot, T(homas) S(tearns)
Spence, J(ohn) E(dward) 1931- 25-28R
Spence, James R(obert) 1927- 25-28R
Spence, Jo 1934-1992 209
Spence, Jonathan D(ermot) 1936- CANR-91
Earlier sketches in CA 21-24R, CANR-23, 54
See also BEST 90:4
Spence, June 180
Spence, (James) Lewis (Thomas Chalmers)
1874-1955 188
Brief entry 115
Spence, Mary Lee 1927- 45-48
Spence, Piers 1959- 149
Spence, Polly 1914-1998 222
Spence, Richard B. 1951- 223
Spence, Thomas 1750-1814 .... DLB 158
Spence, Vernon Gladden 1924- 37-40R
Spence, William John Duncan
1923- CANR-43
Earlier sketches in CA 103, CANR-20
See also Bowden, Jim
Spencer
See Herz, Jerome Spencer
Spencer, Aida Besancon 1947- 178
Spencer, Ann 1918- 29-32R
See also SATA 10
Spencer, Anne 1882-1975 161
See also BW 2
See also DLB 51, 54
See also HR 1:3
Spencer, Benjamin T(ownley) 1904-1996 ... 124
Spencer, (Charles) Bernard 1909-1963
Obituary 115
See also RGEL 2
Spencer, Bonnell 1909-1996 106
Spencer, Brent 1952- CANR-141
Earlier sketches in CA 149, CANR-111
Spencer, Catherine (Marie-Louise) 1960- 144
Spencer, Charles 1674-1722 .... DLB 213
Spencer, Charles 1920- 49-52
Spencer, Christopher 1930- 13-16R
Spencer, Colin 1933- CANR-132
Earlier sketches in CA 21-24R, CANR-12
See also CBD
See also CN 2, 3, 4, 5, 6, 7
Spencer, Cornelia
See Yaukey, Grace S(ydenstricker)
Spencer, Dale R(ay) 1925- 57-60
Spencer, David 1954- CANR-108
Earlier sketch in CA 149
Spencer, Donald D(ean) 1931- 108
See also SATA 41
Spencer, Dorothy 1909- .... IDFW 3, 4
Spencer, Duncan 1940- 144
Spencer, Edgar Winston 1931- 41-44R
Spencer, Elizabeth 1921- CANR-87
Earlier sketches in CA 13-16R, CANR-32, 65
See also CLC 22
See also CN 1, 2, 3, 4, 5, 6, 7
See also CSW
See also DLB 6, 218
See also EWL 3
See also MTCW 1
See also RGAL 4
See also SATA 14
See also SSC 57
Spencer, Frank 1941-1999 139
Obituary 179
Spencer, Frederick J(ohn) 1923- 228
Spencer, George John 1758-1834 .... DLB 184
Spencer, Hanna 1913- 216
Spencer, Harold (Edwin) 1920- CANR-23
Earlier sketch in CA 45-48
Spencer, Herbert 1820-1903 .... DLB 57, 262
Spencer, J(oseph) E(arle) 1907-1984 . CANR-22
Earlier sketch in CA 45-48
Spencer, James 1932- 109
Spencer, Jean E(lizabeth) 1933- 17-20R
Spencer, Jeffry Withers B(urress) 1927- ... 45-48
Spencer, John
See Vickers, Roy C.
Spencer, John (Walter) 1922- 9-12R
Spencer, John Hall 1928- 5-8R
Spencer, John Hathaway 1907- 112
Spencer, Jon Michael CANR-87
Earlier sketch in CA 159
Spencer, LaVyrle 1943- CANR-82
Earlier sketches in CA 102, CANR-34
See also BEST 89:3
See also CPW
See also DA3
See also DAM POP
See also RHW
Spencer, Leonard G.
See Garrett, (Gordon) Randall (Phillip) and Silverberg, Robert
Spencer, Lloyd Neville 1955- 121
Spencer, Margaret 1916- 21-24R
Spencer, Mark 1956- 154
Spencer, Metta Wells 1931- 69-72
Spencer, Michael (Clifford) 1936- 57-60
Spencer, Milton Harry 1926- CANR-6
Earlier sketch in CA 1-4R
Spencer, Paul 1932- 186
Spencer, Raine 132
Spencer, Robert Allan 1920- 5-8R
Spencer, Robert F(rancis) 1917-
Brief entry 108
Spencer, Robert H. 1950- 232
Spencer, Ross (Harrison) 1921-1998 101
Obituary 169
Spencer, Scott 1945- CANR-51
Earlier sketch in CA 113
See also CLC 30
See also DLBY 1986
Spencer, Sharon Dougherty 1933- CANR-13
Earlier sketch in CA 5-8R
Spencer, Sidney 5-8R
Spencer, Steven M. 1905-1985 .... CAP-1
Earlier sketch in CA 13-14
Spencer, Stewart 1949- 121
Spencer, Stuart S. 1957- 226
Spencer, Terence (John Bew) 1915-1978
Obituary 77-80
Spencer, Warren F(rank) 1923- 29-32R
Spencer, William 1922- CANR-23
Earlier sketches in CA 17-20R, CANR-8
See also SATA 9
Spencer, William Browning 1946- CANR-86
Earlier sketches in CA 133, CANR-60
See also HGG
Spencer, William David (III) 1947- 186
Spencer, Zane A(nn) 1935- 89-92
See also SATA 35
Spencer-Churchill, Laura 1915-1990
Obituary 131
Spencer-Fleming, Julia 218
Spender, Dale 1943- 125
Brief entry 120
Interview in CA-125
See also FW
Spender, (John) Humphrey 1910-2005 206
Obituary 237
Spender, J(ohn) A(lfred) 1862-1942 186
Spender, J. A. 1862-1942 .... DLB 98
Spender, Lynne 1946- 119
Spender, Matthew 1945- 193
Spender, Stephen (Harold)
1909-1995 .... CANR-54
Obituary 149
Earlier sketches in CA 9-12R, CANR-31
See also BRWS 2
See also CDBLB 1945-1960
See also CLC 1, 2, 5, 10, 41, 91
See also CP 1, 2
See also DA3
See also DAM POET
See also DLB 20
See also EWL 3
See also MTCW 1, 2
See also MTFW 2005
See also PAB
See also PFS 23
See also RGEL 2
See also TEA
Spener, Philipp Jakob 1635-1705 .... DLB 164
Spengemann, William Charles 1932- 102
Spengler, Edwin H(arold) 1906-1981
Obituary 104
Spengler, Oswald (Arnold Gottfried)
1880-1936 189
Brief entry 118
See also TCLC 25
Spenser, Daniela 1948- 197
Spenser, Edmund 1552(?)-1599 .... AAYA 60
See also BRW 1
See also CDBLB Before 1660
See also DA
See also DA3
See also DAB
See also DAC
See also DAM MST, POET
See also DLB 167
See also EFS 2
See also EXPP
See also PAB
See also PC 8, 42
See also RGEL 2
See also TEA
See also WLC
See also WLIT 3
See also WP
Sper, Emily 1957- 213
See also SATA 142
Sperber, A(nn) M. 1935-1994 .... CANR-79
Earlier sketch in CA 126
Sperber, Al E(lias) 1916- 65-68
Sperber, Manes 1905-1984 124
Obituary 112
See also EWL 3
Sperber, Murray A(rnold) 1940- 196
Earlier sketches in CA 61-64, CANR-12
Autobiographical Essay in 196
Sperber, Perry Arthur 1907- 37-40R
Sperber, Philip 1944- CANR-26
Earlier sketch in CA 109
Speregen, Devra Newberger 1964- 150
See also SATA 84
Sperelakis, Nicholas Sr. 1930- 162
Spergel, Irving A. 1924 .... CANR 11
Earlier sketch in CA 21-24R
Sperka, Joshua S. 1905-1982 49-52
Sperlich, Peter W. 1934- 37-40R
Sperling, Dan(iel Lee) 1949- 112
See also SATA 65
Sperling, John G(len) 1921- 49-52
Sperling, L(eslie) H. 1932- 170
Sperling, Milton M. 1912-1988
Obituary 126
Sperling, Vatsala 1960- 214
Spero, Sterling D. 1896-1976 65-68
Obituary 61-64
Speroni, Charles 1911-1984 93-96
Obituary 113
Sperr, Martin 1944- 196
See also DLB 124
Sperry, Armstrong W. 1897-1976 .... CAP-1
Obituary 107
Earlier sketch in CA 9-10
See also BYA 4
See also CWRI 5
See also MAICYA 1, 2
See also SATA 1
See also SATA-Obit 27
Sperry, (Sally) Baxter 1914- CANR-16
Earlier sketches in CA 49-52, CANR-1
Sperry, Byrne Hope 1902- 69-72
Sperry, J. E.
See Eisenstat, Jane Sperry
Sperry, Kip 1940- CANR-105
Earlier sketches in CA 101, CANR-19
Sperry, Len 1943- CANR-12
Earlier sketch in CA 61-64
Sperry, Margaret 1905-1986 .... 37-40R
Sperry, Ralph A(ddison) 1944- 106
Sperry, Raymond
See Garis, Howard R(oger)
Sperry, Raymond, Jr. CANR-26
Earlier sketches in CAP-2, CA 19-20
See also SATA 1
Sperry, Roger W(olcott) 1913-1994 157
Sperry, Stuart M(ajor) 1929- 49-52
Speshock, Phyllis (Nieboer) 1925- 17-20R
Spetter, Jung-Hee 1969- 196
See also SATA 134
Spewack, Bella 1899-1990
Obituary 131
See also Spewack, Bella Cohen
Spewack, Bella Cohen
See Spewack, Bella
See also DLB 266
Spewack, Samuel 1899-1971
Obituary 33-36R
See also DLB 266
Speyer, Leonora von Stosch 1872-1956 224
Spheeris, Penelope 1945- 213
See also AAYA 46
Spicci, Joan
See Saberhagen, Joan
Spice, Ginger
See Halliwell, Geraldine Estelle
Spice, Marjorie Davis 1924- 9-12R
Spicehandler, Daniel 1923- 1-4R
Spicehandler, Ezra 1921- 214
Spicer, Bart 1918- CANR-61
Earlier sketch in CA 103
See also CMW 4
Spicer, Chrystopher J. 1953- 213
Spicer, Dorothy Gladys -1975 .... CANR-4
Earlier sketch in CA 1-4R
See also SATA 32
Spicer, Jack 1925-1965 85-88
See also BG 1:3
See also CLC 8, 18, 72
See also DAM POET
See also DLB 5, 16, 193
See also GLL 1
See also WP
Spicer, James 1928(?)-1979
Obituary 85-88
Spicer, Michael 1943- 135
Spicer, Ron
See Kelly, Ronald
Spicher, Julia
See Kasdorf, Julia
Spicker, Stuart Francis 1937- CANR-30
Earlier sketch in CA 65-68
Spidle, Jake Wilton, Jr. 1941- 127
Spiegel, Allen D(avid) 1927- 139
Spiegel, David 1945- 204
Spiegel, Don(ald Elwin) 1926- 41-44R
Spiegel, Henry William 1911-1995 .... 1-4R
Spiegel, John P(aul) 1911-1991 103
Obituary 135
Spiegel, Joseph 1928- 9-12R
Spiegel, Richard Alan 1947- CANR-58
Earlier sketches in CA 104, CANR-30
Spiegel, Robert H. 1922- 81-84
Spiegel, Sam 1903-1985 .... IDFW 3, 4
Spiegel, Shalom 1899-1984
Obituary 112
Spiegel, Steven L(ee) 1941- 77-80
Spiegel, Ted 1934-
Brief entry 105
Spiegelberg, Herbert 1904-1990 .... 9-12R
Obituary 132
Spiegelman, Annie 225
Spiegelman, Art 1948- CANR-124
Earlier sketches in CA 125, CANR-41, 55, 74
See also AAYA 10, 46
See also CLC 76, 178
See also DLB 299
See also MTCW 2
See also MTFW 2005
See also SATA 109, 158
See also YAW
Spiegelman, Ian 1974- 227
Spiegelman, J(oseph) Mavvin 1926- 57-60
Spiegelman, Judith 1942- 101
Spiegelman, Judith M. 21-24R
See also SATA 5
Spiegelman, Katia 1959- 143
Spiegler, Charles G. 1911-1989 .... CANR-3
Earlier sketch in CA 9-12R
Spiegler, Michael D(avid) 1943- 61-64
Spiel, Hilde (Maria) 1911-1990 .... CANR-14
Obituary 133
Earlier sketches in CAP-1, CA 9-10
Spielberg, Peter 1929- CANR-48
Earlier sketches in CA 5-8R, CANR-4
See also CLC 6
See also DLBY 1981
Spielberg, Steven 1947- CANR-32
Earlier sketch in CA 77-80
See also AAYA 8, 24
See also CLC 20, 188
See also SATA 32
Spielberger, Charles D(onald) 1927- 102
Spielberger, Walter Jakob 1925- CANR-16
Earlier sketch in CA 21-24R
Spielhagen, Friedrich 1829-1911 .... DLB 129
Spielman, John P. 1930- 144
Spielman, Patrick E. 1936- CANR-22
Earlier sketches in CA 13-16R, CANR-7
Spielmann, Peter James 1952- 97-100
Spier, Peter (Edward) 1927- CANR-41
Earlier sketch in CA 5-8R
See also CLR 5
See also CWRI 5
See also DLB 61
See also MAICYA 1, 2
See also SATA 4, 54
Spier, Robert F(orest) G(ayton) 1922- 41-44R
Spier, William H. 1907(?)-1973
Obituary 41-44R
Spierenburg, Petrus Cornelis 1948- .. CANR-93
Earlier sketch in CA 132
Spierenburg, Pieter
See Spierenburg, Petrus Cornelis
Spiering, Frank 1938- CANR-10
Earlier sketch in CA 25-28R
Spiers, Edward M(ichael) 1947- CANR-43
Earlier sketch in CA 119
Spies, Werner 1937- CANR-123
Earlier sketch in CA 37-40R
Spigel, Irwin M(yron) 1926- 17-20R
Spigelgass, Leonard 1908-1985 103
Obituary 115
Spike, John T(homas) 1951- CANR-111
Earlier sketch in CA 140
Spike, Paul 1947- 120
Spikes, Brian S. J. 101
Spikes, Daniel 1953- 149
Spilhaus, Athelstan (Frederick)
1911-1998 .... CANR-31
Obituary 165
Earlier sketch in CA 17-20R
See also SATA 13
See also SATA-Obit 102
Spilka, Arnold 1917- 49-52
See also SATA 6
Spilka, Mark 1925- CANR-58
Earlier sketches in CA 81-84, CANR-31
Spilke, Francine S. 101
Spillane, Frank Morrison 1918- CANR-125
Earlier sketches in CA 25-28R, CANR-28, 63
See also Spillane, Mickey
See also DA3
See also MTCW 1, 2
See also MTFW 2005
See also SATA 66
Spillane, John D(avid) 1909(?)-1985
Obituary 117
Spillane, Mickey
See Spillane, Frank Morrison
See also BPFB 3
See also CLC 3, 13
See also CMW 4
See also DLB 226
See also MSW
Spillard, Anne 1932- 128
Spiller, Burton L(owell) 1886- 5-8R
Spiller, Earl A(lexander), Jr. 1934- 21-24R
Spiller, Gene A(lan) 1927- CANR-144
Earlier sketch in CA 133
Spiller, Robert E. 1896-1988 .... CANR-4
Earlier sketch in CA 5-8R
Spillman, Ken 1959- 190
Spillmann, Betty Evelyn 1920- 53-56
Spilman, Richard 1946- 132
Spilsbury, Richard J(oy) 1919-1984 104
Obituary 113
Spina, Tony 1914- 69-72
Spinage, Clive A(lfred) 1933- 13-16R
Spindler, Arthur 1918- 104
Spindler, Erica 1957- 219
Spindler, George Dearborn 1920- 21-24R
Spindler, Konrad 1939- 147
Spindler, Louise Schaubel 1917-1997 49-52
Spindler, Michael (James) 1948- 116
Spinella, Marcello 1970- 218
Spinelli, Altiero 1907-1986 .... CANR-16
Obituary 119
Earlier sketch in CA 21-24R
Spinelli, Eileen 1942- 107
See also SATA 38, 101, 150
Spinelli, Jerry 1941- CANR-119
Earlier sketches in CA 111, CANR-30, 45
See also AAYA 11, 41
See also BYA 7, 10
See also CLR 26, 82
See also JRDA
See also MAICYA 1, 2
See also SATA 39, 71, 110, 158
See also WYA
See also YAW
Spinelli, Marcos 1904-1970
Obituary 29-32R
Sping, Dan
See Spalding, Henry D(aniel)
Spingarn, Lawrence P(erreira) 1917- . CANR-46
Earlier sketches in CA 1-4R, CANR-6, 23
Spingarn, Natalie Davis 1922-2000 85-88
Obituary 188
Spinifex
See Martin, David
Spink, Alfred H(enry) 1854(?)-1928 219
Spink, Ian (Walter Alfred) 1932- 185
Brief entry 113

Spink, J. G. Taylor 1888-1962 ... DLB 241
Spink, J(ohn) G(eorge) Taylor 1888-1962 ... 208
Spink, John Stephenson 1909-1985
  Obituary ... 116
Spink, Reginald (William)
  1905-1994 ... CANR-41
  Earlier sketches in CA 53-56, CANR-4, 19
  See also SATA 11
Spink, Walter M. 1928- ... 61-64
Spinka, Matthew 1890-1972 ... CANR-2
  Obituary ... 37-40R
  Earlier sketch in CA 1-4R
Spinka, Penina Keen 1945- ... 218
  See also SATA 72
Spinks, G(eorge) Stephens 1903-1978 ... CAP-2
  Earlier sketch in CA 23-24
Spinks, John William Tranter 1908-1987 ... 109
Spinner, Stephanie 1943- ... CANR-59
  Earlier sketches in CA 45-48, CANR-32
  See also SATA 38, 91, 132
Spinner, Thomas J(ohn), Jr. 1929- ... 45-48
Spinner-Halev, Jeff 1964- ... 223
Spinney, David
  See Spinney, J(ohn) D(avid)
Spinney, J(ohn) D(avid) 1912-1988 ... 29-32R
Spinossimus
  See White, William, Jr.
Spinrad, Norman (Richard) 1940- ... 233
  Earlier sketches in CA 37-40R, CANR-20, 91
  Interview in ... CANR-20
  Autobiographical Essay in ... 233
  See also CAAS 19
  See also BPFB 3
  See also CLC 46
  See also DLB 8
  See also SFW 4
Spinrad, William 1917- ... 29-32R
Spira, Ruth Rodale 1928- ... 61-64
Spire, Andre 1868-1966 ... GFL 1789 to the Present
Spirer, Herbert F(rederick) 1925- ... CANR-16
  Earlier sketch in CA 93-96
Spires, Elizabeth 1952- ... CANR-88
  Earlier sketches in CA 106, CANR-28, 52
  See also CP 7
  See also CWP
  See also DLB 120
  See also PFS 21
  See also SATA 71, 111
  See also TCLE 1:2
Spires, Robert C(ecil) 1936- ... 125
Spirin, Gennadii
  See Spirin, Gennady
Spirin, Gennadij
  See Spirin, Gennady
Spirin, Gennady 1948- ... CLR 88
  See also CWRI 5
  See also MAICYA 2
  See also MAICYAS 1
  See also SATA 95, 134
Spiro, Edward 1908- ... 25-28R
Spiro, Herbert J(ohn) 1924- ... CANR-6
  Earlier sketch in CA 1-4R
Spiro, Herzl Robert 1935- ... 104
Spiro, Howard M(arget) 1924- ... CANR-58
  Earlier sketch in CA 125
Spiro, Jack D. 1933- ... CANR-6
  Earlier sketch in CA 9-12R
Spiro, Melford E(lliot) 1920- ... CANR-1
  Earlier sketch in CA 45-48
Spirt, Diana L(ouise) 1925- ... 17-20R
Spisak, James W(illiam) 1951- ... 117
Spit, Sam
  See Schneck, Stephen
Spittel, Richard Lionel 1881-1969 ... CAP-1
  Earlier sketch in CA 13-14
Spitteler, Carl (Friedrich Georg) 1845-1924
  Brief entry ... 109
  See also DLB 129
  See also EWL 3
  See also TCLC 12
Spitz, A. Edward 1923- ... 73-76
Spitz, Allan A(ugust) 1928- ... 13-16R
Spitz, David 1916-1979 ... 41-44R
  Obituary ... 85-88
Spitz, Ellen Handler 1939- ... CANR-129
  Earlier sketch in CA 147
Spitz, Lewis W(illiam) 1922-1999 ... CANR-64
  Earlier sketches in CA 1-4R, CANR-6, 32
Spitz, Mark (Andrew) 1950-
  Brief entry ... 115
Spitz, Reuben T. 1954- ... 165
Spitzer, Abe 1912(?)-1984
  Obituary ... 112
Spitzer, E(rwin) E(dwin) 1910-1996 ... CAP-2
  Earlier sketch in CA 21-22
Spitzer, Herbert Frederick 1906- ... CAP-1
  Earlier sketch in CA 13-14
Spitzer, John 1956- ... CANR-18
  Earlier sketch in CA 102
Spitzer, Leo 1939- ... 61-64
Spitzer, Lyman (Jr.) 1914-1997 ... 116
  Obituary ... 157
Spitzer, Morton Edward ... 41-44R
Spitzer, Nicholas R. 1950- ... 142
Spitzer, Robert J(ames) 1953- ... CANR-118
  Earlier sketches in CA 112, CANR-30, 56
Spitzer, Robert S(idney) 1926- ... 61-64
Spivack, Charlotte K(esler) 1926- ... 21-24R
Spivack, Ellen Sue 1937- ... 106
Spivack, George 1927-
  Brief entry ... 109
Spivack, Kathleen (Romola Drucker)
  1938- ... 49-52
  See also CLC 6
Spivack, Robert (Gerald) 1915-1970
  Obituary ... 104
Spivak, Dawnine ... 168
  See also SATA 101
Spivak, Gayatri Chakravorty 1942- ... CANR-91
  Brief entry ... 110
  Earlier sketch in CA 154
  See also FW
  See also LMFS 2
Spivak, John L(ouis) 1897-1981
  Obituary ... 105
Spivak, Lawrence E. 1900-1994 ... 216
  See also DLB 137
Spivak, Mel 1937- ... 57-60
Spivak, Talbot 1937- ... 77-80
Spivakovsky, Erika 1909-1998 ... 49-52
Spivey, Nigel
  See Spivey, Nigel (Jonathan)
Spivey, Nigel (Jonathan) 1958- ... CANR-111
  Earlier sketch in CA 139
Spivey, Richard L. 1937- ... CANR-130
  Earlier sketch in CA 115
Spivey, Robert Atwood 1931- ... 186
  Brief entry ... 106
Spivey, Ted R(ay) 1927- ... 105
Spizer, Joyce 1941- ... 221
Splane, Richard B. 1916- ... 17-20R
Splaver, Sarah ... 85-88
  See also SATA-Brief 28
Spletter, Mary 1946- ... 111
Splichal, Jan 1929- ... 209
Splichal, Joachim 1954- ... 153
Spock, Benjamin (McLane)
  1903-1998 ... CANR-65
  Obituary ... 166
  Earlier sketches in CA 21-24R, CANR-35
  Interview in ... CANR-35
  See also AITN 1
  See also MTCW 1, 2
Spodek, Bernard 1931- ... CANR-105
  Earlier sketches in CA 17-20R, CANR-7, 22, 49
Spoehr, Alexander 1913-1992 ... 109
  Obituary ... 139
Spoehr, John ... 189
Spoelstra, Nyle (Ray) 1939- ... 29-32R
Spoerri, Elka (Zagaroff) 1924-2002 ... 196
  Obituary ... 206
Spofford, Harriet (Elizabeth) Prescott
  1835-1921 ... 201
Spofford, Harriet Prescott 1835-1921 .. DLB 74, 221
Spofford, Walter O(smon), Jr. 1936- ... 107
Spohn, David 1948- ... SATA 72
Spohn, Kate 1962- ... SATA 87, 147
Spohn, William C. 1944- ... 202
Spollen, Christopher 1952- ... SATA 12
Spolsky, Bernard 1932- ... CANR-45
  Earlier sketches in CA 45-48, CANR-1
Spolsky, Ellen 1943- ... CANR-45
  Earlier sketch in CA 119
Spolter, Pari (Dokht) 1930- ... 163
Spong, John Shelby 1931- ... CANR-96
  Earlier sketch in CA 104
Spooner, David 1941- ... 230
Spooner, Frank (Clyffurde) 1924- ... 85-88
Spooner, Frederick Percy 1898- ... CAP-1
  Earlier sketch in CA 13-14
Spooner, Jane R(oss) 1922- ... 5-8R
Spooner, John D. 1937- ... 21-24R
Spooner, Mary Helen 1951- ... 150
Spooner, Michael (Tim) 1954- ... CANR-111
  Earlier sketch in CA 156
  See also SATA 92
Spooner, (Glenda) Victoria Maude (Graham)
  1897- ... CAP-1
  Earlier sketch in CA 9-10
Spores, Ronald 1931- ... 21-24R
Spot, Ryhen
  See Post, Henry
Spota, Luis
  See Spota (Saavedra), Luis
  See also EWL 3
Spota (Saavedra), Luis 1925-1985 ... 153
  Obituary ... 114
  See also Spota, Luis
  See also HW 1
Spotnitz, Hyman 1908- ... CANR-6
  Earlier sketch in CA 1-4R
Spoto, Donald 1941- ... CANR-93
  Earlier sketches in CA 65-68, CANR-11, 57
  See also CLC 39
Spotte, Stephen 1942- ... CANR-1
  Earlier sketch in CA 45-48
Spottiswood, Alicia Anne
  See Scott, Alicia Anne
Spottiswoode, Raymond J. 1913-1970
  Obituary ... 104
Spotts, Charles D(ewey) 1899-1974(?) ... CAP-2
  Earlier sketch in CA 19-20
Spotts, Frederic 1930- ... CANR-144
  Earlier sketch in CA 101
Spowart, Robin 1947- ... SATA 82
Sprackland, Jean 1962- ... 235
Spradley, James P(hillip) 1933-1982 . CANR-13
  Earlier sketch in CA 29-32R
Spradling, Mary Elizabeth Mace 1911- ... 104
Spragens, Thomas A(rthur), Jr. 1942- ... 85-88
Spragens, William C(lark) 1925- ... 41-44R
Spragg, Mark 1952- ... 191
Spraggett, Allen (Frederick) 1932- ... CANR-18
  Earlier sketch in CA 25-28R
Sprague, Arthur Colby 1895-1991 ... 89-92
Sprague, Carter
  See Merwin, (W.) Sam(uel Kimball), Jr.
Sprague, Charles Arthur 1887-1969
  Obituary ... 89-92
Sprague, Claire S(acks) 1926- ... 25-28R
Sprague, Gretchen (Burnham) 1926- ... 13-16R
  See also SATA 27
Sprague, Howard B(ennet) 1898-1988 .. 41-44R
Sprague, Irvine H(enry, Jr.)
  1921-2004 ... CANR-51
  Obituary ... 224
  Earlier sketch in CA 123
Sprague, Ken 1945- ... 108
Sprague, Marshall 1909-1994 ... CANR-1
  Obituary ... 146
  Earlier sketch in CA 1-4R
Sprague, Richard E. 1921- ... 29-32R
Sprague, Rosamond Kent 1922- ... CANR-2
  Earlier sketch in CA 5-8R
Sprague, Rosemary ... 17-20R
Sprague, Stuart Seely 1937- ... 161
Sprague, W. D.
  See von Block, Bela W(illiam) and von Block, Sylvia
Spraos, John 1926- ... 5-8R
Spratt, Hereward Philip 1902- ... 5-8R
Spray, Pauline 1920- ... CANR-10
  Earlier sketch in CA 25-28R
Spray, Sherrad L(ee) 1935- ... 104
Spreiregen, Paul D. 1931- ... 21-24R
Sprengel, Donald P(hilip) 1938- ... 53-56
Sprengnether, Madelon ... 180
Spretnak, Charlene 1946- ... 145
  See also FW
Spriegel, William R(obert) 1893-1972 ... 5-8R
Sprigel, Olivier
  See Avice, Claude (Pierre Marie)
Sprigg, C(hristopher) St. John 1907-1937
  Brief entry ... 120
  See also Caudwell, Christopher
Sprigg, June 1953- ... 65-68
Sprigge, Elizabeth (Miriam Squire)
  1900-1974 ... 13-16R
  See also RHW
  See also SATA 10
Sprigge, Timothy L(auro) S(quire) 1932- .. 57-60
  See also DLB 262
Sprinchorn, Evert Manfred 1923- ... 107
Spring, Bob
  See Spring, Robert W(alton)
Spring, David 1918- ... 81-84
Spring, Eileen 1923- ... 147
Spring, Gerald M(ax) 1897-1980 ... 61-64
Spring, (Robert) Howard 1889-1965 ... CAP-1
  Earlier sketch in CA 9-10
  See also DLB 191
  See also SATA 28
Spring, Ira L. 1918-2003 ... CANR-7
  Obituary ... 217
  Earlier sketch in CA 57-60
Spring, Joel Henry 1940- ... CANR-3
  Earlier sketch in CA 49-52
Spring, Justin D. 1962- ... 196
Spring, Matthew ... 206
Spring, Michelle
  See Stanworth, Michelle
Spring, Norma 1917- ... 61-64
Spring, Robert W(alton) 1918- ... CANR-7
  Earlier sketch in CA 57-60
Springborg, Robert 1944- ... 119
Springer, Axel 1912-1985
  Obituary ... 117
Springer, Bernhard J. 1907(?)-1970
  Obituary ... 29-32R
Springer, Brian
  See Dwight, Jeffry
Springer, Claudia 1956- ... 159
Springer, E(ustace) Laurence
  1903-1984 ... 21-24R
Springer, Haskell S(aul) 1939- ... CANR-29
  Earlier sketch in CA 111
Springer, John (Shipman) 1916-2001 ... 53-56
  Obituary ... 203
Springer, John L(awrence) 1915- ... CANR-25
  Earlier sketch in CA 1-4R
Springer, L(ois) Elsinore 1911-1992 ... 69-72
Springer, Margaret 1941- ... CANR-96
  Earlier sketch in CA 146
  See also SATA 78
Springer, Marilyn Harris 1931- ... CANR-9
  Earlier sketch in CA 21-24R
  See also NFS 14
  See also RHW
  See also SATA 47
Springer, Marlene Ann 1937- ... 107
Springer, Mary Doyle 1918- ... 116
Springer, Nancy 1948- ... CANR-106
  Earlier sketches in CA 101, CANR-18, 41
  See also AAYA 32
  See also BYA 15
  See also FANT
  See also SATA 65, 110
  See also SFW 4
Springer, Nelson P(aul) 1915- ... 115
Springer, Nesha Bass 1930-1990 ... CANR-86
  Obituary ... 132
  Earlier sketch in CA 81-84
Springer, Otto 1905-1991 ... CAP-1
  Earlier sketch in CA 13-14
Springer, Sally P(earl) 1947- ... 108
Springfield
  See Kelly, Maurice Anthony
Springfield, David
  See Lewis, (John) Roy(ston)
Springs, Elliott White 1896-1959 ... DLB 316
Springs, Nadia
  See Obrecht, Jas
Springsted, Eric Osmon 1951- ... 113
Springsteen, Bruce (F.) 1949- ... 111
  See also CLC 17
Springstubb, Tricia 1950- ... CANR-46
  Earlier sketches in CA 105, CANR-21
  See also SATA 46, 78
  See also SATA-Brief 40
Sprinkel, Beryl W(ayne) 1923- ... 9-12R
Sprinker, Michael 1950- ... 129
Sprinkle, Annie (M.) 1954- ... 234
Sprinkle, Joe M. 1953- ... 187
Sprinkle, Patricia Houck 1943- ... CANR-97
  Earlier sketch in CA 133
Sprinthall, Richard C(lark) 1930- ... 45-48
Sprinzak, Ehud (Zelig) 1940-2002 ... 139
  Obituary ... 214
Sproat, Iain (MacDonald) 1938- ... 152
Sproat, John G(erald) 1921- ... 25-28R
Sproat, Robert 1944- ... 144
Sproston, John
  See Scott, Peter Dale
Sprott, Duncan 1952- ... 158
Sprott, W(alter) John Herbert
  1897-1971 ... CANR-16
  Obituary ... 103
  Earlier sketch in CA 1-4R
Sproul, Barbara Chamberlain 1945- ... 105
Sproul, Dorothy Noyes
  See Noyes-Kane, Dorothy
Sproul, R(obert) C(harles) 1939- ... CANR-30
  Earlier sketch in CA 111
Sprouse, Mary L. 1948- ... 108
Sprout, Harold 1901-1980 ... CANR-6
  Obituary ... 102
  Earlier sketch in CA 1-4R
Spruch, Grace Marmor 1926- ... 57-60
Spruch, Larry 1923- ... 102
Sprug, Joseph W(illiam) 1922- ... 21-24R
Spruill, Charles R(ay) 1946- ... 117
Spruill, Steven G(regory) 1946- ... CANR-59
  Earlier sketch in CA 73-76
  See also SFW 4
Sprunger, Keith L(a Verne) 1935- ... CANR-119
  Earlier sketch in CA 41-44R
Sprunt, Alexander, Jr. 1898-1973
  Obituary ... 37-40R
Spry, Irene Mary 1907- ... 163
Spudvilas, Anne 1951- ... SATA 94
Spufford, Francis 1964- ... 171
Spuhler, J(ames) N(orman) 1917- ... CANR-3
  Earlier sketch in CA 1-4R
Spulber, Nicolas 1915- ... CANR-3
  Earlier sketch in CA 9-12R
Spuler, Bertold 1911- ... 81-84
Spungen, Deborah 1937- ... 119
Spungin, Charlotte I(sabelle) 1929- ... 158
Spuris, Egons 1931-1990 ... 209
Spurling, (Susan) Hilary 1940- ... CANR-94
  Earlier sketches in CA 104, CANR-25, 52
  See also CLC 34
Spurling, John 1936- ... CANR-50
  Earlier sketches in CA 45-48, CANR-1, 25
  See also CBD
  See also CD 5, 6
Spurll, Barbara 1952- ... SATA 78
Spurlock, Clark P.
  See Stuart, Colin
Spurlock, Jeanne (M.) 1921-1999 ... 202
Spurr, Clinton
  See Rowland, D(onald) S(ydney)
Spurr, David Anton 1949- ... 118
Spurr, Russell 1922- ... 144
Spurr, Stephen Hopkins 1918- ... 81-84
Spurr, William A(lfred) 1905-1975 ... 5-8R
Spurrier, William A(twell) 1916- ... 53-56
Spycket, Jerome 1928- ... 145
Spyers-Duran, Peter 1932- ... CANR-23
  Earlier sketches in CA 17-20R, CANR-8
Spyker, John Howland
  See Elman, Richard (Martin)
Spykman, E(lizabeth) C(hoate) 1896-1965 .. 101
  See also CLR 35
  See also CWRI 5
  See also SATA 10
Spyri, Johanna (Heusser) 1827-1901 ... 137
  See also BYA 2
  See also CLR 13
  See also MAICYA 1, 2
  See also SATA 19, 100
  See also WCH
Spyridakis, Stylianos 1937- ... 89-92
Squared, A.
  See Abbott, Edwin A.
Squibob
  See Derby, George Horatio
Squier, Charles L(a Barge) 1931- ... 17-20R
Squier, E(phraim) G(eorge)
  1821-1888 ... DLB 189
Squier, Susan Merrill 1950- ... 120
Squire, Elizabeth 1919- ... 13-16R
Squire, Elizabeth Daniels 1926-2001 ... 164
Squire, Jason E(dward) 1948- ... CANR-23
  Earlier sketch in CA 45-48
Squire, Norman 1907-1991 ... CANR-3
  Earlier sketch in CA 9-12R
Squire, Robin 1937- ... 105
Squire, Russel Nelson 1908-1997 ... 1-4R
Squire, Susan 1950- ... 112
Squires, Eric
  See Ball, Sylvia Patricia
Squires, James (David) 1943- ... 119
Squires, James Duane 1904-1981 ... 5-8R
Squires, Michael (George) 1941- ... CANR-137
  Earlier sketch in CA 61-64
Squires, Patricia
  See Ball, Sylvia Patricia
Squires, Phil
  See Barker, S(quire) Omar

Cumulative Index 549 **Standard**

Squires, (James) Radcliffe
1917-1993 ... CANR-21
Obituary ... 140
Earlier sketches in CA 1-4R, CANR-6
See also CLC 51
See also CP 1, 2
Squires, Richard D(onald) 1957- ... 150
Squires, Susan ... 213
Sraffa, Piero 1898-1983 ... CANR-27
Obituary ... 110
Earlier sketch in CA 45-48
Srba, Lynne ... SATA 98
Sreenivasan, Jyotsna 1964- ... 156
See also SATA 101
Srere, Benson M. 1928- ... 77-80
Srikanth, Rajini 1957- ... 197
Srinawk, Khamsing 1930-
See Lao Khamhom
S-Ringi, Kjell
See Ringi, Kjell (Arne Soerensen)
Srinivas, M(ysore) N(arasimhachar)
1916(?)-1999 ... 186
Srinivasan, T. N. 1933- ... 174
Srivastav, Dhanpat Ray
See Srivastava, Dhanpat Rai
Srivastav, Dheanpatrai
See Srivastava, Dhanpat Rai
Srivastava, C(handrika) P(rasad)
1920- ... CANR-118
Earlier sketch in CA 153
Srivastava, Dhanpat Rai 1880(?)-1936 ... 197
Brief entry ... 118
See also Premchand
Srivastava, Jane Jonas 1941- ... 119
See also SATA-Brief 37
Srivastava, Ramesh K(umar) 1940- ... CANR-55
Earlier sketch in CA 127
Srivastava, Satyendra 1935- ... CWW 2
Srivastava, Vinayak N. 1961- ... 217
Srodes, James 1940- ... 188
Srole, Leo 1908-1993 ... 125
Brief entry ... 107
Ssapir, Richard ... CMW 4
Staaf, Robert J(ames) 1939- ... 93-96
Staake, Bob 1957- ... 217
Staal, Cyril 1912-
Brief entry ... 113
Staal, J(ohan) F(rederik) 1930- ... 45-48
Staal, Julius D(irk) W(illem) 1917-1986
Obituary ... 120
Staal, Stephanie 1972- ... 198
Staal-Delaunay, Marguerite-Jeanne Cordier de
1684(?)-1750 ... DLB 314
Staar, Richard F(elix) 1923- ... CANR-38
Earlier sketches in CA 1-4R, CANR-1, 16
Staats, Arthur (Wilbur) 1924- ... 13-16R
Staats, Marilyn Dorn 1939- ... 139
Stabb, Martin S(anford) 1928- ... 21-24R
Stabenow, Dana 1952- ... CANR-98
Earlier sketch in CA 164
See also AAYA 31
See also CMW 4
Stabile, Donald R(obert) 1944- ... CANR-105
Earlier sketch in CA 149
Stabile, Toni ... 85-88
Stableford, Brian (Michael) 1948- ... CANR-90
Earlier sketches in CA 57-60, CANR-29, 55
See also DLB 261
See also HGG
See also SFW 4
See also SUFW 2
Stablein, Marilyn 1946- ... 120
Stabler, Arthur P(hillips) 1919- ... CANR-14
Earlier sketch in CA 41-44R
Stabley, Fred(erick) W(illiam) 1915- ... 112
Stace, Christopher 1942- ... 97-100
Stace, Walter Terence 1886-1967 ... CANR-2
Earlier sketch in CA 1-4R
Stacey, C(harles) P(erry) 1906- ... CANR-19
Earlier sketch in CA 101
Stacey, Cherylyn 1945- ... 161
See also SATA 96
Stacey, Frank Arthur 1923-1977 ... 57-60
Obituary ... 135
Stacey, Judith 1943- ... CANR-56
Earlier sketch in CA 125
Stacey, Kathryn
See Fenton, Kate
Stacey, Margaret 1922-2004 ... CANR-38
Obituary ... 223
Earlier sketches in CA 29-32R, CANR-17
Stacey, Michelle 1959- ... CANR-113
Earlier sketch in CA 150
Stacey, Nicholas Anthony Howard 1920- . 5-8R
Stacey, Roy 1919- ... 9-12R
Stacey, Susannah
See Staynes, Jill
Stacey, Thomas Charles Gerard
1930- ... CANR-47
Earlier sketches in CA 9-12R, CANR-21
See also Stacey, Tom
Stacey, Tom
See Stacey, Thomas Charles Gerard
See also CN 1, 2
Stach, Patricia Burgess
See Burgess, Patricia
Stachel, John (Jay) 1928- ... CANR-141
Earlier sketch in CA 172
Stachow, Hasso G(ert) 1924- ... 109
Stachys, Dimitris
See Constantelos, Demetrios J.
Stack, Andy
See Rule, Ann
Stack, Eddie 1955- ... 222
Stack, Edward M(acGregor) 1919- ... CANR-28
Earlier sketch in CA 1-4R
Stack, Frank H(untington) 1937- ... CANR-9
Earlier sketch in CA 61-64
Stack, George J. 1931- ... 37-40R
Stack, Herbert James 1893-1967 ... CANR-3
Earlier sketch in CA 1-4R
Stack, Nicolete Meredith 1896- ... 13-16R
Stack, Robert
See Stacy, R(obert) H(arold)
Stackelberg, Roderick 1935- ... 189
Stackhouse, John (G.), Jr. 1960- ... 189
Stackhouse, Max L. 1935- ... 21-24R
Stackhouse, Reginald 1925- ... 21-24R
Stackpole, Edouard Alexander
1903-1993 ... CANR-16
Obituary ... 142
Earlier sketches in CA 1-4R, CANR-1
Stackpole, Edward J(ames) 1894-1967 ... 1-4R
Obituary ... 103
Stackpole, Michael A(ustin) 1957- .. CANR-120
Earlier sketch in CA 153
Stacks, Don W. 1949- ... 227
Stacks, John F(ultz) 1942- ... 113
Stacpoole, H(enry) de Vere
1863-1951 ... DLB 153
Stacton, David (Derek) 1925-1968 ... CANR-6
Obituary ... 25-28R
Earlier sketch in CA 5-8R
Stacy, Bruce
See Elliott, Bruce (Walter Gardner Lively Stacy)
Stacy, Donald
See Pohl, Frederik
Stacy, Donald L. 1925- ... 29-32R
Stacy, Jan 1948(?)-1989
Obituary ... 129
Stacy, Judith Minthorn 1943- ... 189
Stacy, Judy
See Stacy, Judith Minthorn
Stacy, Pat(ricia A.) 1941- ... 118
Stacy, R(obert) H(arold) 1919- ... 73-76
Stacy, Walter
See Elliott, Bruce (Walter Gardner Lively Stacy)
Staddon, John (E. R.) 1937- ... 148
Stade, George 1933- ... CANR-46
Earlier sketch in CA 29-32R
Stadelman, S(ara) L(ee) 1917- ... 81-84
Stadler, Karl R(udolph) 1913-1987 ... 21-24R
Stadler, Matthew 1959- ... CANR-89
Earlier sketch in CA 140
Stadley, Pat (Anna May Gough) 1918-
Brief entry ... 114
Stadt, Ronald W(ilmer) 1935- ... CANR-16
Earlier sketch in CA 93-96
Stadter, Philip A(ustin) 1936- ... 104
Stadtfeld, Curtis K(arl) 1935- ... 49-52
Stadtler, Bea 1921- ... 65-68
See also SATA 17
Stadtman, Verne A. 1926- ... 29-32R
Staebler, Edna ... 101
Staebler, Neil 1905-2000 ... 77-80
Staebler, Warren 1912- ... 45-48
Staehle, Albert 1899-1974 ... AITN 1
Stael
See Stael-Holstein, Anne Louise Germaine Necker
See also EW 5
See also RGWL 2, 3
Stael, Germaine de
See Stael-Holstein, Anne Louise Germaine Necker
See also DLB 119, 192
See also FL 1:3
See also FW
See also GFL 1789 to the Present
See also TWA
Stael-Holstein, Anne Louise Germaine Necker
1766-1817
See Stael and
Stael, Germaine de
Staender, Gilbert F(rank) 1930- ... 104
Staender, Vivian 1923- ... 97-100
Staff, Adrienne 1947- ... 123
Staff, Frank 1908-1994 ... 25-28R
Staffel, Megan 1952- ... CANR-118
Earlier sketch in CA 128
Staffeldt 1769-1826 ... DLB 300
Stafford, Barbara Maria 1941- ... CANR-106
Earlier sketch in CA 149
Stafford, Caroline
See Watjen, Carolyn L. T.
Stafford, David (Alexander Tetlow)
1942- ... CANR-97
Earlier sketches in CA 104, CANR-21
Stafford, David (Christopher) 1943- ... 103
Stafford, Edward Peary 1918- ... 135
Stafford, Fiona (Jane) 1960- ... CANR-90
Earlier sketch in CA 131
Stafford, Gilbert Wayne 1938- ... CANR-118
Earlier sketches in CA 112, CANR-31, 56
Stafford, Irvin G. 1936- ... 114
Stafford, Jean 1915-1979 ... CANR-65
Obituary ... 85-88
Earlier sketches in CA 1-4R, CANR-3
See also CLC 4, 7, 19, 68
See also CN 1, 2
See also DLB 2, 173
See also MAL 5
See also MTCW 1, 2
See also MTFW 2005
See also RGAL 4
See also RGSF 2
See also SATA-Obit 22
See also SSC 26
See also SSFS 21
See also TCWW 1, 2
See also TUS
Stafford, Kenneth R(ay) 1922- ... 17-20R
Stafford, Kim R(obert) 1949- ... CANR-46
Earlier sketches in CA 69-72, CANR-22
Stafford, Liliana 1950- ... 212
See also SATA 141
Stafford, Linda (Crying Wind) 1943- ... 108
Stafford, Muriel
See Sauer, Muriel Stafford
Stafford, Paul 1966- ... 188
See also SATA 116
Stafford, Peter
See Tabori, Paul
Stafford, Robert A(ndrew) 1953- ... 133
Stafford, Tim ... 135
Stafford, William (Edgar)
1914-1993 ... CANR-22
Obituary ... 142
Earlier sketches in CA 5-8R, CANR-5
Interview in ... CANR-22
See also CAAS 3
See also AMWS 11
See also CLC 4, 7, 29
See also CP 1, 2
See also DAM POET
See also DLB 5, 206
See also EXPP
See also MAL 5
See also PFS 2, 8, 16
See also RGAL 4
See also WP
Stafford, William B(utler) 1931- ... 53-56
Stafford, William T(almadge) 1924- .. CANR-25
Earlier sketch in CA 1-4R
Stafford-Clark, David 1916-1999 ... 21-24R
Obituary ... 185
Stafford-Deitsch, Jeremy 1958- ... 141
Staffordshire Knot
See Wrottesley, A(rthur) J(ohn) F(rancis)
Stagaman, David 1935- ... 195
Stageberg, Norman C(lifford)
1905-1984 ... CAP-1
Earlier sketch in CA 11-12
Stage Door Jimmy
See Starr, James (A.)
Stagg, Albert 1903-1989 ... 85-88
Stagg, Evelyn 1914- ... 85-88
Stagg, Frank 1911-2001 ... CANR-18
Earlier sketches in CA 1-4R, CANR-1
Stagg, James Martin 1900-1975
Obituary ... 61-64
Stagg, Paul L. 1914- ... 21-24R
Stagge, Jonathan
See Wheeler, Hugh (Callingham)
Staggenborg, Suzanne 1955- ... 140
Staggs, Sam ... 221
Stagner, Lloyd Ernest 1923- ... 101
Stagner, Ross 1909-1997 ... CANR-5
Earlier sketch in CA 5-8R
Stahl, Ben(jamin) 1910-1987 ... 29-32R
Obituary ... 123
See also SATA 5
See also SATA-Obit 54
Stahl, Donald 1935- ... 25-28R
Stahl, Fred Alan 1944- ... 45-48
Stahl, Gustav Richard 1888(?)-1978
Obituary ... 81-84
Stahl, Hilda 1938-1993 ... CANR-40
Obituary ... 142
Earlier sketch in CA 116
See also SATA 48
See also SATA-Obit 77
Stahl, J(ohn) D(aniel) 1952- ... 149
Stahl, Jerry 1954- ... 220
Stahl, LeRoy 1908-1987 ... CAP-1
Earlier sketch in CA 11-12
Stahl, Lesley R(ene) 1941- ... 107
Interview in ... CA-107
See also AITN 2
Stahl, Nancy 1937- ... 104
Stahl, Naomi
See Mosiman, Billie Sue (Stahl)
Stahl, Norman 1931- ... 85-88
Stahl, O(scar) Glenn 1910-2002 ... CANR-14
Obituary ... 204
Earlier sketch in CA 41-44R
Stahl, Saul 1942- ... CANR-125
Earlier sketch in CA 165
Stahl, William Harris 1908-1969
Obituary ... 111
Stahlecker, Lotar V(ictor) 1915- ... 21-24R
Stahler, David, Jr. ... 238
See also SATA 162
Stahlman, James Geddes 1893-1976
Obituary ... 89-92
Stahnke, Arthur A(llan) 1935- ... 65-68
Stahnke, Astrida B. 1935- ... 123
Stahr, John W. 1904-1981
Obituary ... 104
Staib, Bjorn O. 1938- ... 17-20R
Staicar, Thomas Edward 1946- ... 108
Staicar, Tom
See Staicar, Thomas Edward
Staiger, Janet 1946- ... 123
Stainback, Berry 1935- ... 161
Stainback, Susan Bray 1947- ... CANR-31
Earlier sketches in CA 57-60, CANR-7, 14
Stainback, William (Clarence)
1943- ... CANR-31
Earlier sketches in CA 77-80, CANR-14
Staincliffe, Cath 1956- ... 207
Stainer, Pauline 1941- ... 154
See also CP 7
See also CWP
Staines, David 1946- ... CANR-109
Earlier sketches in CA 125, CANR-52
Staines, Trevor
See Brunner, John (Kilian Houston)
Stainsby, Charles 1925-1985
Obituary ... 118
Stainton, Leslie 1955- ... 193
Stainton, Robert J.(H.) 1964- ... 217
Stair, Gobin (John) 1912- ... SATA 35
Stairs, Denis (Winfield) 1939- ... 185
Brief entry ... 114
Stairs, Gordon
See Austin, Mary (Hunter)
Stalder, Valerie ... 41-44R
See also SATA 27
Staley, Allen (Percival Green) 1935- ... 146
Brief entry ... 115
Staley, Charles E(arl) 1927- ... 45-48
Staley, (Alvah) Eugene 1906- ... 77-80
Staley, Lynn 1947- ... 151
Staley, Thomas F(abian) 1935- ... CANR-60
Earlier sketches in CA 77-80, CANR-13, 30
Stalheim, O(le) H. V. 1917- ... 149
Stalin, Joseph 1879-1953 ... TCLC 92
Stalker, John 1939- ... 127
Stalker, Peter 1944- ... 213
Stall, Katharine 1950- ... 127
Stallabrass, Julian 1960- ... 224
Stallaerts, Robert 1947- ... 151
Stallard, John (Richard) 1935-1985 ... 49-52
Obituary ... 116
Stalley, Rodney E(dward) 1930- ... 116
Stalley, Roger 1945- ... 101
Stallibrass, (Helen) Alison 1916- ... 104
Stallich, Jan 1907-1973 ... IDFW 3, 4
Stalling, Carl ... IDFW 3, 4
Stallings, Constance L(ee) 1932- ... CANR-17
Earlier sketch in CA 97-100
Stallings, James O. 1938- ... CANR-19
Earlier sketch in CA 103
Stallings, Laurence 1894-1968 ... 182
Obituary ... 89-92
See also DLB 7, 44, 316
Stallman, Richard Matthew 1953- ... 226
Stallman, Robert 1930-1980 ... HGG
Stallman, Robert Wooster 1911-1982 . CANR-3
Earlier sketch in CA 1-4R
Stallone, Sylvester (Enzio) 1946- ... 77-80
Stallwood, Veronica ... 162
Stallworth, Anne Nall 1935- ... 85-88
Stallworthy, Jon (Howie) 1935- ... CANR-139
Earlier sketches in CA 9-12R, CANR-8
See also BRWS 10
See also CP 1, 2, 3, 4, 5, 6, 7
See also DLB 40
Stallybrass, Oliver (George Weatherhead)
1925-1978 ... CANR-24
Earlier sketch in CA 29-32R
Stalvey, Lois Mark 1925- ... CANR-14
Earlier sketch in CA 29-32R
Stam, James H(enry) 1937- ... 49-52
Stam, Robert 1941- ... 115
Stamaty, Mark Alan 1947- ... CANR-15
Earlier sketch in CA 61-64
See also SATA 12
Stambaugh, Joan 1932- ... 89-92
Stambaugh, Sara 1936- ... CANR-43
Earlier sketch in CA 119
Stamberg, Susan 1938- ... 103
Interview in ... CA-103
Stambler, Helen
See Latner, Helen (Stambler)
Stambler, Irwin 1924- ... CANR-2
Earlier sketch in CA 5-8R
See also SATA 5
Stambolian, George 1938-1991 ... CANR-72
Obituary ... 136
Earlier sketch in CA 41-44R
See also GLL 2
Stambuk, George 1927-2004 ... 5-8R
Obituary ... 234
Stames, Ward
See Steward, Samuel M(orris)
See also GLL 1
Stamey, Sara (Lucinda) 1953- ... CANR-127
Earlier sketch in CA 126
Stamford Krause, Shari 1961- ... 157
Stamm, Keith R(oman) 1941- ... 116
Stamm, Martin L. 1917- ... CANR-19
Earlier sketch in CA 37-40R
Stamm, Peter 1963- ... 231
Stammers, Neil 1950- ... 119
Stamp, L(aurence) Dudley 1898-1966 ... CAP-1
Earlier sketch in CA 13-14
Stamp, Robert M(iles) 1937- ... 126
Stampa, Aquiles
See Coma, Javier
Stampa, Gaspara c. 1524-1554 ... PC 43
See also RGWL 2, 3
See also WLIT 7
Stamper, Alexander
See Kent, Arthur William Charles
Stampfer, Judah (Leon) 1923-1996 ... 25-28R
Obituary ... 154
Stampfle, Felice 1912-2000 ... 105
Obituary ... 191
Stampflinger, K. A.
See Benjamin, Walter
Stampp, Kenneth M. 1912- ... 13-16R
See also DLB 17
Stanbury, David 1933- ... 104
Stanbury, Walter A. 1910-1976
Obituary ... 65-68
Stancliffe, Michael (Staffurth) 1916-1987 ... 124
Stancu, Zaharia 1902-1974 ... 97-100
Obituary ... 53-56
Stancykowna
See Szymborska, Wislawa
Standage, Tom 1969- ... 183
Standard, William L. 1900(?)-1978
Obituary ... 77-80

Stander, Siegfried 1935- CANR-19
Earlier sketches in CA 9-12R, CANR-4
Standifer, Leon(idas) C(almet, Jr.) 1925- 176
Standiford, Les(ter Alan) 1945- CANR-141
Earlier sketches in CA 77-80, CANR-73
Standiford, Natalie 1961- 149
See also SATA 81
Standing, Edwin (Mortimer) 1887- CAP-1
Earlier sketch in CA 9-10
Standing, Sue 1952- 119
Standing Bear, Luther 1868(?)-1939(?) 144
Brief entry 113
See also DAM MULT
See also NNAL
Standish, Buck
See Paine, Lauran (Bosworth)
Standish, Carole
See Koehler, Margaret (Hudson)
Standish, Robert 1898(?)-1981
Obituary 105
Standley, Fred L(loyd) 1932- 41-44R
Standon, Anna (Slater) 1929- 17-20R
Standring, Gillian 1935- 69-72
Stands In Timber, John 1884-1967 154
Stanek, Carolyn 1951- 107
Stanek, Lou Willett 1931- .... SATA 63
Stanek, Muriel (Novella) 1915-
Brief entry 112
See also SATA-Brief 34
Stanescu, Nichita 1933-1983 .... DLB 232
See also EWL 3
Stanev, Emiliyan
See Stanev, Nikola (Stoyanov)
See also DLB 181
Stanev, Nikola (Stoyanov) 1907-1979 108
See also Stanev, Emiliyan
Stanfield, Nancy Fisher Clay 1905- CAP-1
Earlier sketch in CA 9-10
Stanfield, Vernon Latrelle 1920- 97-100
Stanford, Alfred (Boller) 1900-1985 .... CAP-1
Obituary 115
Earlier sketch in CA 17-18
Stanford, Ann 1916-1987 .... CANR-32
Obituary 123
Earlier sketches in CA 9-12R, CANR-4
See also CP 1, 2
See also DLB 5
Stanford, Barbara Dodds 1943- 37-40R
Stanford, Craig (Britton) 1956- 208
Stanford, Derek 1918- CANR-45
Earlier sketch in CA 9-12R
See also CP 1
Stanford, Don
See Stanford, Donald E(lwin)
Stanford, Don(ald Kent) 1918- 53-56
Stanford, Donald E(lwin)
1913-1998 .... CANR-28
Earlier sketches in CA 13-16R, CANR-5
Stanford, Edward V(alentine) 1897-1966 ... 5-8R
Stanford, Gene 1944- 37-40R
Stanford, J(ohn) K(eith) 1892-1971 .... 5-8R
Obituary 199
Stanford, Melvin Joseph 1932- CANR-16
Earlier sketch in CA 89-92
Stanford, Miles J(oseph) 1914- 65-68
Stanford, Neal 1906(?)-1988
Obituary 127
Stanford, Peter 1961- 194
Stanford, Quentin Hunt 1935- 45-48
Stanford, Sally 1903-1982
Obituary 105
Stanford, Sondra .... RHW
Stanford, William Bedell 1910-1984 85-88
Obituary 115
Stanforth, Deirdre 1924- 102
Stang, Ivan 1949- 129
Stang, Judit 1921-1977 .... CANR-8
Earlier sketch in CA 5-8R
See also SATA 29
Stang, Judy
See Stang, Judit
Stang, Sondra J. 1928- CANR-90
Earlier sketch in CA 131
Stange, G(eorge) Robert 1919- 21-24R
Stanger, Frank Bateman 1914- 109
Stanger, Ila (Ann) 1940- 65-68
Stangerup, Helle 1939- 132
Stangerup, Henrik 1937-1998 147
Obituary 169
See also CWW 2
See also DLB 214
See also EWL 3
Stangl, (Mary) Jean 1928- 136
See also SATA 67
Stangos, Nicolas 1936-2004 146
Obituary 227
Stangos, Nikos
See Stangos, Nicolas
Stanhope, Eric
See Hamilton, Charles (Harold St. John)
Stanhope, Philip Dormer 1694-1773 .. DLB 104
Stanier, John (Wilfred) 1925- 169
Stanier, Maida Euphemia Kerr 1909- 101
Staniforth, (John Hamilton) Maxwell
1893- CAP-2
Earlier sketch in CA 25-28
Stanihurst, Richard 1547-1618 .... DLB 281
Stanish, Charles 1956- 233
Stanislavsky, Konstantin (Sergeivich)
1863(?)-1938
Brief entry 118
See also TCLC 167
Stanislawski, Dan 1903-1997 .... CANR-3
Earlier sketch in CA 5-8R
Stanislawski, Michael 1952- 119
Stanitsky, N.
See Panaeva, Avdot'ia Iakovlevna
Stanke, Alain 1934- 81-84
Stanke, Don E(dward) 1929- 61-64
Stankevich, Boris 1928- 21-24R
See also SATA 2
Stankevich, Nikolai Vladimirovich
1813-1840 .... DLB 198
Stankiewicz, Edward 1920- CANR-43
Earlier sketch in CA 45-48
Stankiewicz, Marketa Goetz
See Goetz-Stankiewicz, Marketa
Stankiewicz, W(ladyslaw) J(ozef)
1922- CANR-1
Earlier sketch in CA 45-48
Stanko, Elizabeth Anne 1950- CANR-38
Earlier sketch in CA 116
Stankovic, Bora
See Stankovic, Borisav
Stankovic, Borisav 1876-1927 .... CDWLB 4
See also DLB 147
Stankus, Tony 1951- 215
Stanley, Alexander O. 1910-1990 .... 5-8R
Stanley, Autumn 144
Stanley, Bennett
See Hough, S(tanley) B(ennett)
Stanley, C(laude) Maxwell 1904-1984 114
Stanley, Carol
See White, Carol
Stanley, Chuck
See Strong, Charles S(tanley)
Stanley, Dave
See Dachs, David
Stanley, David 1944- CANR-39
Earlier sketch in CA 115
Stanley, David T(aylor) 1916-
Brief entry 107
Stanley, Debby
See Stanley, Deborah B.
Stanley, Deborah B. 1950- 206
Stanley, Diana 1909- .... SATA-Brief 30
Stanley, Diane 1943- CANR-132
Earlier sketches in CA 112, CANR-32, 64
See also CLR 46
See also CWRI 5
See also MAICYA 2
See also MAICYAS 1
See also SAAS 15
See also SATA 37, 80, 115
See also SATA-Brief 32
Stanley, Fay Grissom
See Shulman, Fay Grissom Stanley
Stanley, George 1934-
Brief entry 114
See also CP 1, 2
Stanley, George Edward 1942- CANR-142
Earlier sketches in CA 97-100, CANR-17, 39
See also Dixon, Franklin W. and
Hope, Laura Lee and
Keene, Carolyn
See also SATA 53, 111, 157
Stanley, George F(rancis) G(ilman)
1907- CANR-15
Earlier sketch in CA 41-44R
Stanley, Henry M(orton) 1841-1904 191
See also DLB 189
See also DLBD 13
Stanley, Jerry 1941- CANR-99
Earlier sketch in CA 148
See also SATA 79, 127
Stanley, John 1940- 21-24R
Stanley, John L(angley) 1937-1998 45-48
Obituary 167
Stanley, Julian C(ecil), Jr. 1918- CANR-8
Earlier sketch in CA 21-24R
Stanley, Leo Leonidas 1886-1976 69-72
Stanley, Liz 1947- CANR-96
Earlier sketches in CA 119, CANR-45
Stanley, Marge
See Weinbaum, Stanley Grauman
Stanley, Maurice F. 1945- 220
Stanley, Nora Kathleen Begbie Strange
1885- CAP-1
Earlier sketch in CA 11-12
Stanley, Patricia H. 138
Stanley, Peter (Alan) 1956- 118
Stanley, Peter W(illiam) 1940- 143
Stanley, Phil
See Ind, Allison
Stanley, Richard L. Sr. 1928- 171
Stanley, Richard P. 1944- 161
Stanley, Robert
See Hamilton, Charles (Harold St. John)
Stanley, Robert Henry 1940- 101
Stanley, Roy M. II 1936- 114
Stanley, Sandra Kumamoto 1954- 186
Stanley, Sanna 1962- .... SATA 145
Stanley, Steven M(itchell) 1941- 109
Stanley, T(om) (D.) 1959- 198
Stanley, Thomas 1625-1678 .... DLB 131
See also RGEL 2
Stanley, Thomas J. 196
Stanley, Timothy Wadsworth 1927-1997 . 77-80
Obituary 161
Stanley, Warwick
See Hilton, John Buxton
Stanley, William O(liver), Jr.
1902-1992 .... CANR-1
Earlier sketch in CA 1-4R
Stanley-Brown, Katherine (Oliver) 1893(?)-1972
Obituary 33-36R
Stanley-Jones, D(ouglas) 1905- 9-12R
Stanley-Wrench, Margaret 1916- 9-12R
Stanli, Sue
See Meilach, Dona Z(weigoron)
Stanlis, Peter J(ames) 1919- 101
Stanmeyer, William A(nthony) 1934- 118
Stann, Francis E. 1912(?)-1987
Obituary 124
Stannard, David E(dward) 1941- 65-68
Stannard, Martin 1947- 142
See also CLC 44
See also DLB 155
Stannard, Neville (George) 1949- 118
Stannard, Richard M. 1925- 141
Stannard, Una 1927- 73-76
Stanner, W(illiam) E(dward) H(anley) 1905-1981
Obituary 108
Stannus, (James) Gordon (Dawson)
1902-1989 65-68
Obituary 129
Stanovich, Betty Jo 1954- 118
See also SATA-Brief 51
Stans, Maurice H(ubert) 1908-1998
Obituary 167
Brief entry 113
Stansberger, Richard 1950- CANR-18
Earlier sketch in CA 101
Stansberry, Domenic (Joseph) 1952- . CANR-99
Earlier sketch in CA 149
Stansbury, Donald L. 1929- 37-40R
Stansby, William fl. 1597-1636 .... DLB 170
Stansfield, Richard Habberton 1921- 107
Stansfield, William D. 1930- 215
Stansky, Peter (David Lyman) 1932- . CANR-12
Earlier sketch in CA 17-20R
Stanstead, John
See Groom, Arthur William
Stanton, Andrew 1966(?)- 239
Stanton, Arch
See Wynorski, Jim
Stanton, Bob
See Stanton, Robert J.
Stanton, Dorothy
See Lamour, Dorothy
Stanton, Doug 203
Stanton, Edward F. 1942- CANR-118
Earlier sketches in CA 89-92, CANR-42, 56
Stanton, Elizabeth Cady 1815-1902 171
See also DLB 79
See also FL 1:3
See also FW
See also TCLC 73
Stanton, Frank Lebby 1857-1927 214
See also DLB 25
Stanton, Gerald B(arry) 1918- 9-12R
Stanton, Graham N(orman) 1940- 61-64
Stanton, Jessie Earl 1887-1976
Obituary 65-68
Stanton, Marietta (P.) 1948- 134
Stanton, Mary 1947- CANR-106
Earlier sketch in CA 150
See also FANT
Stanton, Maura 1946- CANR-123
Earlier sketches in CA 89-92, CANR-15
See also CLC 9
See also DLB 120
Stanton, Paul
See Beaty, (Arthur) David
Stanton, Peggy Smeeton 1939- 61-64
Stanton, Phoebe B(aroody) 1914- 37-40R
Stanton, Robert J. 1942- 187
Stanton, Royal (Waltz) 1916- 37-40R
Stanton, Schuyler
See Baum, L(yman) Frank
Stanton, Shelby L(ee) 1948- 147
Stanton, Tom H. 1960- 224
Stanton, Vance
See Avallone, Michael (Angelo, Jr.)
Stanton, Will 1918- 85-88
Stanton, William 1925- 1-4R
Stanton, William J(ohn, Jr.) 1919-
Brief entry 115
Stanwell-Fletcher, Theodora Hope 1906- . ANW
Stanwood, Brooks
See Kaminsky, Susan Stanwood
Stanwood, Brooks
See Kaminsky, Howard
Stanwood, P(aul) G(rant) 1933- 49-52
Stanworth, Michelle 209
Stanyer, Jeffrey 1936- 61-64
Staph, C. C.
See Carroll, Bob
Stapledon, (William) Olaf 1886-1950 162
Brief entry 111
See also DLB 15, 255
See also SCFW 1, 2
See also SFW 4
See also TCLC 22
Stapler, Harry (Bascom) 1919- CANR-13
Earlier sketch in CA 61-64
Staples, Brent (A.) 1951- CANR-139
Earlier sketch in CA 153
Staples, Mary Jane
See Staples, Reginald Thomas
Staples, Reginald Thomas 1911- CANR-43
Earlier sketches in CA 69-72, CANR-14
See also RHW
Staples, Robert (Eugene) 1942- CANR-2
Earlier sketch in CA 49-52
Staples, Suzanne Fisher 1945- CANR-82
Earlier sketch in CA 132
See also AAYA 26
See also BYA 15
See also CLR 60
See also MAICYA 2
See also MAICYAS 1
See also SATA 70, 105, 151
See also WYAS 1
See also YAW
Stapleton, Amy 1959- 154
Stapleton, Constance 1930- 104
Stapleton, G(eorge) Brian 1922- 25-28R
Stapleton, Jean 1942- 69-72
Stapleton, Katherine
See Kane, Henry
Stapleton, Lara 1967- 174
Stapleton, (Katharine) Laurence
1911-1998 .... 17-20R
Stapleton, Margaret (Lucy) 1903-1984 57-60
Stapleton, Marjorie (Winifred) 1932- 106
See also SATA 28
Stapleton, Richard John 1940- 89-92
Stapleton, Richard M. 1942- 147
Stapleton, Ruth Carter 1929-1983 81-84
Obituary 110
Stapp, Arthur D(onald) 1906-1972 ..... CANR-2
Obituary 33-36R
Earlier sketch in CA 1-4R
See also SATA 4
Stapp, William B. 1929- CANR-48
Earlier sketches in CA 45-48, CANR-2, 22
Stappenbeck, Herb(ert) Louis (Jr.) 1935- .. 65-68
Star, Angel
See Quigley, Joan
Star, Cima 1939- 110
Star, Jack 1920- 73-76
Star, Max 1890(?)-1986
Obituary 121
Star, Nancy 238
Star, Shirley A(nn) 1918-1976 .... 41-44R
Obituary 65-68
Starbird, Kaye 1916- CANR-38
Earlier sketch in CA 17-20R
See also CLR 60
See also MAICYA 1, 2
See also SATA 6
Starbuck, George (Edwin)
1931-1996 .... CANR-23
Obituary 153
Earlier sketch in CA 21-24R
See also CLC 53
See also CP 1, 2
See also DAM POET
Starbuck, William H(aynes) 1934- CANR-7
Earlier sketch in CA 57-60
Starch, Daniel 1883-1979 .... CANR-85
Obituary 133
Earlier sketch in CA 37-40R
Starchild, Adam (Aristotle) 1946- 123
Starchuk, Orest 1915- 5-8R
Stardust, Alvin 1942- 123
Stare, Fredrick J(ohn) 1910-2002 132
Obituary 205
Starenko, Ronald C(harles) 1930- 93-96
Starer, Daniel 1954- 144
Starer, Robert 1924-2001 125
Obituary 195
Starewicz, Ladislaw 1882-1965 .... IDFW 3, 4
Stargell, Willie
See Stargell, Wilver Dornel
Stargell, Wilver Dornel 1940-2001 146
Obituary 194
Brief entry 118
Starhawk
See Simos, Miriam
Starita, Joe 1948- 150
Stark, Bradford 1948-1979 .... CANR-3
Earlier sketch in CA 49-52
Stark, Claude Alan 1935-1980 .... CANR-85
Obituary 134
Earlier sketch in CA 57-60
Stark, Cruce 1942- 137
Stark, Elizabeth 1970- 220
Stark, Evan 1942- CANR-101
Earlier sketch in CA 146
See also SATA 78
Stark, Freya (Madeline) 1893-1993 .. CANR-47
Obituary 141
Earlier sketches in CA 5-8R, CANR-5
See also DLB 195
Stark, Gary Duane 1948- CANR-21
Earlier sketch in CA 105
Stark, George Washington 1884-1966
Obituary 89-92
Stark, Harry (Newman) 1895-1980 .... 1-4R
Stark, Irwin 1912-1994 .... 9-12R
Obituary 145
Stark, Jack
See Stark, John H.
Stark, James
See Goldston, Robert (Conroy)
Stark, John
See Godwin, John
Stark, John H. 1914- 49-52
Stark, John Olsen 1939- CANR-5
Earlier sketch in CA 53-56
Stark, Joshua
See Olsen, T(heodore) V(ictor)
Stark, Lucien 1929- 156
Stark, Marisa Kantor 1973- 170
Stark, Michael
See Lariar, Lawrence
Stark, Paul C. 1891(?)-1974
Obituary 53-56
Stark, Peter 1954- 213
Stark, R. J.
See Kikel, Rudy (John)
Stark, Ray 1915-2004 .... IDFW 3, 4
Stark, Raymond 1919- 73-76
Stark, Richard
See Westlake, Donald E(dwin)
Stark, Rodney 231
Stark, Stephen (Edward) 1958- 140
Stark, Steven D. 1951- 163
Stark, Ulf 1944- .... SATA 124
Stark, Werner 1909-1985 .... CANR-10
Earlier sketch in CA 21-24R
Starke, Aubrey (Harrison) 1905(?)-1972
Obituary 37-40R
Starke, Catherine Juanita 1913- 37-40R
Starke, J(oseph) G(abriel) 1911- 115
Starke, Roland 53-56

Cumulative Index 551 Steele

Starke, Ruth (Elaine) 1946- 198
See also SATA 129
Starkey, David CANR-105
Earlier sketch in CA 164
Starkey, Lycurgus M(onroe), Jr. 1928- 5-8R
Starkey, Marion L(ena) 1901-1991 ..... CANR-1
Earlier sketch in CA 1-4R
See also SATA 13
Starkey, Richard 1940- 174
Starkey, Thomas c. 1499-1538 ..... DLB 132
Starkie, Enid 1903(?)-1970 ..... CANR-2
Obituary 29-32R
Earlier sketch in CA 1-4R
Starkie, Walter F(itzwilliam) 1894-1976 .. 77-80
Obituary 69-72
See also DLB 195
Starkins, Edward 1946- 120
Starkloff, Carl F. 1933- 53-56
Starkman, Miriam K(osh) 1916- 65-68
Starkman, Moshe 1906-1975
Obituary 57-60
Starks, Richard 1947- 113
Starkweather, David 1935- 97-100
See also CAD
See also CD 5, 6
See also DLB 7
Starling, Boris 238
Starling, Thomas
See Hayton, Richard Neil
Star-Man's Padre
See Patrick, Johnstone G(illespie)
Starn, Randolph 1939- CANR-67
Earlier sketches in CA 45-48, CANR-32
Starnes, Richard 1922-
Brief entry 114
Starobin, Joseph R(obert) 1913-1976 45-48
Obituary 69-72
Starobin, Rosalind Gould 1912(?)-1983
Obituary 111
Starobinski, Jean 1920- CANR-101
Earlier sketch in CA 131
Starowicz, Mark (M.) 1946- 224
Starr, Anne
See Sanford, Annette
Starr, Cecile 1921- 65-68
Starr, Chauncey 1912- 109
Starr, Chester G. 1914-1999 ..... CANR-36
Obituary 185
Earlier sketches in CA 1-4R, CANR-1, 16
Starr, Douglas 1950- 180
Starr, Edward Caryl 1911-1996 ..... 13-16R
Starr, Frank 1938- 69-72
Starr, Harvey 1946- CANR-143
Earlier sketch in CA 172
Starr, Henry
See Bingley, David Ernest
Starr, Herbert F(rederick) 1932- 116
Starr, Isidore 1911- CANR-7
Earlier sketch in CA 13-16R
Starr, James (A.) 1904(?)-1990
Obituary 132
Starr, Jason 1966- 171
Starr, Jerold M. 1941- 77-80
Starr, Jimmy
See Starr, James (A.)
Starr, John
See Counselman, Mary Elizabeth
Starr, John 1914(?)-1980
Obituary 101
Starr, John A.
See Gillese, John Patrick
Starr, John Bryan 1939- 77-80
Starr, Judy
See Gelfman, Judith S(chlein)
Starr, June (O.) 1934-2001 140
Starr, Kenneth W(inston) 1946- 215
Starr, Kevin 1940- CANR-72
Earlier sketch in CA 120
Starr, Larry 1946- 143
Starr, Louis M(orris) 1917-1980 ..... CANR-86
Obituary 97-100
Earlier sketch in CA 53-56
Starr, Mark 1894-1985
Obituary 116
See also AITN 1
Starr, Martin Kenneth 1927- CANR-8
Earlier sketch in CA 17-20R
Starr, Patricia 1943- 145
Starr, Patti
See Starr, Patricia
Starr, Paul (Elliot) 1949- 127
Brief entry 123
Starr, Penelope
See Gelles-Cole, Sandi
Starr, Raymond 1937- 65-68
Starr, Ringo
See Starkey, Richard
Starr, Roger (Samuel) 1918-2001 ..... CANR-11
Obituary 203
Earlier sketch in CA 21-24R
Starr, Roland
See Rowland, D(onald) S(ydney)
Starr, S(tephen) Frederick 1940- CANR-17
Earlier sketch in CA 85-88
Starr, Stephen Z. 1909-1985 ..... CANR-17
Earlier sketch in CA 37-40R
Starr, Ward
See Manes, Stephen
Starr, William Thomas 1910-1999 ..... 41-44R
Starr, Wilmarth Holt 1913-1999 ..... 17-20R
Starratt, Alfred B(yron) 1914- 17-20R
Starret, William
See McClintock, Marshall
Starrett, (Charles) Vincent (Emerson)
1886-1974 ..... CANR-62
Obituary 45-48
Earlier sketches in CA 73-76, CANR-31
See also CMW 4
See also DLB 187
Starrs, James E(dward) 1930- 118
Starrs, Roy Anthony 1946- 185
Starr Taylor, Bridget 1959- ..... SATA 99
Starry, Donn Albert 1925- 109
Start, Clarissa
See Lippert, Clarissa Start
Starzl, Thomas E(arl) 1926- 140
Stasch, Stanley F. 1931- 41-44R
Stasheff, Christopher 1944- CANR-97
Earlier sketches in CA 65-68, CANR-10, 26, 58
See also FANT
See also SFW 4
Stasheff, (Adolph) Edward 1909- 5-8R
Stashower, Daniel (Meyer) 1960- CANR-95
Earlier sketch in CA 131
Stasiak, Krystyna ..... SATA 49
Stasio, Marilyn L(ouise) 1940- 33-36R
Stassinopoulos, Arianna
See Huffington, Arianna Stassinopoulos
Stasz, Clarice CANR-112
Earlier sketches in CA 61-64, CANR-7
Staten, Patricia S. 1945- 53-56
Staten, Vince 1947- 225
Statera, Gianni 1943- CANR-8
Earlier sketch in CA 57-60
States, Bert O(len) 1929- 73-76
Statham, E. Robert, Jr. 1963- CANR-110
Earlier sketch in CA 152
Statham, Frances P(atton) 1931- 101
Statham, Jane 1917- 13-16R
Statius c. 45-c. 96 ..... AW 2
See also DLB 211
Statlander, Jane (B.) 1943- 234
Statler, Oliver Hadley 1915- 5-8R
Staton, Knofel L. 1934- CANR-35
Earlier sketch in CA 114
Staton, Thomas Felix 1917- 5-8R
Statten, Vargo
See Fearn, John Russell
Staub, August W(illiam) 1931- CANR-2
Earlier sketch in CA 45-48
Staub, Ervin 1938- CANR-109
Earlier sketch in CA 133
Staub, Frank (Jacob) 1949- 188
See also SATA 116
Staub, Wendy Corsi 1964- 176
See also SATA 114
Staubach, Charles N(eff) 1906- CANR-4
Earlier sketch in CA 5-8R
Staubach, Roger (Thomas) 1942- 104
Stauber, John (Clyde) 1953- 176
Staudacher, Joseph M. 1914- 25-28R
Staudacher, Rosemarian V(alentiner)
1918- 5-8R
Staudenraus, P(hilip) J(ohn) 1928-1971 ..... 1-4R
Obituary 103
Stauder, Jack 1939- 37-40R
Stauderman, Albert P(hilip) 1910- CANR-39
Earlier sketches in CA 77-80, CANR-18
Staudinger, Hermann 1881-1965 162
Obituary 113
Staudohar, Paul D. 1940- 184
Staudt, Kathleen 1946- 172
Staudt, Virginia
See Sexton, Virginia Staudt
Stauffacher, Sue 1961- 230
See also SATA 155
Stauffer, Don
See Berkebile, Fred D(onovan)
Stauffer, Donald Barlow 1930- 57-60
Stauffer, Helen Winter 1922- CANR-30
Earlier sketch in CA 109
Stauffer, John 205
Staum, Martin Sheldon 1943- 103
Staunton, Michael 1967- 220
Staunton, Schuyler
See Baum, L(yman) Frank
Staunton, Ted 1956- 163
See also SATA 112
Staupers, Mabel Keaton 1890-1989
Obituary 129
Staurowsky, Ellen J. 1955- 176
Stauter, (Justin) Jay 1907-1986
Obituary 118
Stavans, Ilan 1961- CANR-104
Earlier sketch in CA 151
Stave, Bruce M(artin) 1937- CANR-12
Earlier sketch in CA 29-32R
Stave, Holly
See Stave, Shirley A.
Stave, Shirley A. 1952- 175
Staveacre, Tony 1942- CANR-93
Earlier sketch in CA 130
Staveley, Gaylord L(ee) 1931- 37-40R
Stavenhagen, Lee 1933- 104
Stavenhagen, Rodolfo 1932- CANR-12
Earlier sketch in CA 29-32R
Stavins, Robert N. 196
Stavis, Barrie 1906- 49-52
See also CAD
See also CD 5, 6
Stavis, Ben(edict) 1941- 29-32R
Stavitsky, Gail 1954- 225
Stavrakis, Peter J(acob) 1955- 171
Stavrianos, Leften Stavros 1913-2004 . CANR-6
Obituary 226
Earlier sketch in CA 5-8R
Stavros, Niko
See King, Florence
Stavrou, Theofanis G(eorge) 1934- ... CANR-48
Earlier sketch in CA 45-48
Stawinski, Jerzy Stefan 1921- ..... IDFW 3, 4
Stayer, James M(entzer) 1935- CANR-26
Earlier sketch in CA 45-48
Staynes, Jill 133
Stead, C(hristian) K(arlson) 1932- ... CANR-102
Earlier sketches in CA 57-60, CANR-6, 44
See also CN 5, 6, 7
See also CP 1, 2, 3, 4, 5, 6, 7
See also RGEL 2
Stead, Christina (Ellen) 1902-1983 ... CANR-40
Obituary 109
Earlier sketches in CA 13-16R, CANR-33
See also BRWS 4
See also CLC 2, 5, 8, 32, 80
See also CN 1, 2, 3
See also DLB 260
See also EWL 3
See also FW
See also MTCW 1, 2
See also MTFW 2005
See also RGEL 2
See also RGSF 2
See also WWE 1
Stead, Philip John 1916- 108
Stead, Robert J(ames) C(ampbell)
1880-1959 186
See also DLB 92
See also TCWW 1, 2
Stead, Thistle Yolette 1902-1990 107
Stead, William Thomas 1849-1912 167
See also TCLC 48
Steadman, David (Wilton) 1936- 107
Steadman, John M(arcellus III) 1918- 25-28R
Steadman, Mark 1930- CANR-115
Earlier sketch in CA 37-40R
See also DLB 6
Steadman, Ralph (Idris) 1936- CANR-101
Earlier sketches in CA 107, CANR-29
See also AAYA 45
See also SATA 32, 123
Steahly, Vivian Eugenia Emrick 1915- 61-64
Steakley, John 1951- 120
Stealingworth, Slim
See Wesselmann, Tom
Steamer
See Nason, Leonard H(astings)
Steamer, Robert J(ulius) 1920- 41-44R
Steane, J(ohn) B(arry) 1928- CANR-88
Earlier sketch in CA 9-12R
Steans, Jill A. 1961- 167
Steanson, Karen E(lizabeth) 1942- 116
Stearman, Kaye 1951- 190
See also SATA 118
Stearn, Gerald E. 1934(?)-1982
Obituary 108
Stearn, Jess -2002 97-100
Obituary 209
Stearn, William T(homas) 1911-2001 158
Stearns, Harold Edmund 1891-1943
Brief entry 107
See also DLB 4
Stearns, Marshall Winslow 1908-1966
Obituary 110
Stearns, Martha Genung 1886-1972 ..... 9-12R
Obituary 170
Stearns, Monroe (Mather) 1913-1987 . CANR-2
Obituary 124
Earlier sketch in CA 5-8R
See also SATA 5
See also SATA-Obit 55
Stearns, Pamela Fujimoto 1935- 65-68
Stearns, Peter N. 1936- CANR-92
Earlier sketches in CA 21-24R, CANR-10, 28, 55
Stearns, Raymond Phineas 1904-1970 .. CAP-1
Earlier sketch in CA 11-12
Steavenson, Wendell 1970- 234
Stebbins, G(eorge) Ledyard 1906-2000 ... 45-48
Obituary 190
Stebbins, Richard P(oate) 1913- CANR-2
Earlier sketch in CA 5-8R
Stebbins, Robert A(lan) 1938- CANR-30
Earlier sketches in CA 29-32R, CANR-12
Stebbins, Robert C(yril) 1915- 49-52
Stebbins, Theodore E(llis), Jr. 1938- .. CANR-98
Earlier sketch in CA 89-92
Stebel, S(idney) L(eo) 1924- 29-32R
Stebenne, David 1960- 154
Steber, A. R.
See Palmer, Raymond A.
Steber, Rick 1946- 128
Stebnitsky, M.
See Leskov, Nikolai (Semyonovich)
Stecha, Pavel 1944- 209
Stecher, Miriam B(rodie) 1917- 106
Stechow, Wolfgang 1896-1974 ..... CANR-9
Obituary 53-56
Earlier sketch in CA 65-68
Steck, James S(perow) 1911-1997 ..... 41-44R
Steckel, William Reed 1915- 17-20R
Stecker, Ann Page 1942- 149
Steckler, Arthur 1921-1985 108
See also SATA 65
Steckler, Doug(las) 1948- 107
Steckler, Phyllis B. (Schwartzbard)
1933- 9-12R
Steding, Laurie 1953- 190
See also SATA 119
Stedman, Edmund Clarence 1833-1908 213
See also DLB 64
Stedman, James Murphy 1938- 77-80
Stedman, Jane W(inifred) 1920- 37-40R
Stedman, Murray S(alisbury), Jr. 1917- 17-20R
Stedman, R(aymond) William 1930- 29-32R
Stedman, Ray C. 1917- 104
Stedman Jones, Gareth 1942- CANR-31
Earlier sketch in CA 45-48
Stedmond, John Mitchell 1916- 103
Stedwell, Paki 1945- 103
Steed, Gitel P. 1914-1977 ..... 41-44R
Steed, Thomas Jefferson 1904-1983
Obituary 110
Steed, Tom
See Steed, Thomas Jefferson
Steedman, Carolyn (Kay) 1947- 152
Steedman, Marguerite Couturier
1908- CANR-1
Earlier sketch in CA 1-4R
Steefel, Lawrence D(inkelspiel Sr.)
1894-1976 ..... CAP-2
Obituary 169
Earlier sketch in CA 21-22
Steeger, Henry 1903-1990 ..... 41-44R
Obituary 133
Steeger, Henry 1929(?)-1978
Obituary 77-80
Steegmuller, Francis 1906-1994 ..... CANR-2
Earlier sketch in CA 49-52
See also CN 1, 2
See also DLB 111
Steel, Anthony Bedford 1900-1973 ..... 5-8R
Obituary 89-92
Steel, Byron
See Steegmuller, Francis
Steel, Danielle (Fernande) 1947- CANR-138
Earlier sketches in CA 81-84, CANR-19, 36, 65, 99
Interview in CANR-19
See also AAYA 23
See also BEST 89:1, 90:4
See also BPFB 3
See also CPW
See also DA3
See also DAM POP
See also MTCW 1, 2
See also MTFW 2005
See also RHW
See also SATA 66
Steel, David 1938- 145
Steel, Dawn 1946-1997 151
Obituary 163
Steel, Duncan (I.) 1955- 209
Steel, Edward M(arvin), Jr. 1918- 9-12R
Steel, Eric M. 1904-1980 89-92
Steel, Flora Annie (Webster) 1847-1929
Brief entry 116
See also DLB 153, 156
Steel, Gayla R(uth) 1933- 149
Steel, Joyce 1937- 164
Steel, Nigel 1962- 147
Steel, Ronald (Lewis) 1931- CANR-91
Earlier sketches in CA 9-12R, CANR-7
Steel, Tex
See Ross, W(illiam) E(dward) D(aniel)
Steele, A(rchibald) T(rojan) 1903-1992 .. CAP-2
Obituary 137
Earlier sketch in CA 19-20
Steele, Addison II
See Lupoff, Richard A(llen)
Steele, Alan 1905-1985
Obituary 115
Steele, Alexander 1958- 188
See also SATA 116
Steele, Allen 1958- CANR-81
Earlier sketch in CA 136
Steele, Arthur R(obert) 1916- 9-12R
Steele, Chester K. CANR-26
Earlier sketches in CAP-2, CA 19-20
Steele, Colin Robert 1944- 104
Steele, Curtis
See Davis, Frederick C(lyde)
Steele, Cynthia 1951- 156
Steele, Dale
See Glut, Donald F(rank)
Steele, Dirk
See Plawin, Paul
Steele, Elizabeth 1921- CANR-43
Earlier sketch in CA 45-48
Steele, Erskine
See Henderson, Archibald
Steele, Fletcher 1885-1971 ..... CAP-1
Earlier sketch in CA 13-14
Steele, Frank 1935- 37-40R
Steele, Fred I(rving) 1938- CANR-17
Earlier sketches in CA 45-48, CANR-2
Steele, Fritz
See Steele, Fred I(rving)
Steele, George P(eabody II) 1924- 1-4R
Steele, Gordon (Charles) 1892-1981 105
Obituary 102
Steele, Harwood E(lmes Robert)
1897-1978 ..... CANR-64
Earlier sketches in CAP-1, CA 13-16
See also TCWW 1, 2
Steele, Henry 1931- 41-44R
Steele, Howard
See Steele, Harwood E(lmes Robert)
Steele, I(an) K(enneth) 1937- 45-48
Steele, Jack 1914-1980 109
Obituary 102
Steele, James B(ruce, Jr.) 1943- CANR-98
Brief entry 110
Earlier sketch in CA 115
Interview in CA-115
Steele, Jessica
See Steele, Marcia (Glennys Howell)
See also RHW
Steele, Ken 1948-2000 201
Steele, Marcia (Glennys Howell) 1933- 239
See also Steele, Jessica
Steele, Mary 1930- 159
See also SATA 94

Steele, Mary Q(uintard Govan)
1922-1992 .... CANR-22
Obituary 139
Earlier sketches in CA 1-4R, CANR-6
See also CWRI 5
See also MAICYA 1, 2
See also MAICYAS 1
See also SATA 3, 51
See also SATA-Obit 72
Steele, (Henry) Max(well) 1922-2005 .... 25-28R
See also CSW
See also DLBY 1980
See also SATA 10
Steele, Michael R(hoads) 1945- CANR-143
Earlier sketch in CA 111
Steele, Peter (R.) 1935- 108
Steele, Philip 1948- CANR-106
Earlier sketch in CA 149
See also SATA 81, 140
Steele, Phillip W(ayne) 1934- 61-64
Steele, R. David 1931- 135
Steele, Richard 1672-1729 .... BRW 3
See also CDBLB 1660-1789
See also DLB 84, 101
See also RGEL 2
See also WLIT 3
Steele, Richard W(illiam) 1934- 134
Brief entry 107
Steele, Robert (Scott) 1917- 49-52
Steele, Shelby 1946- 155
Steele, Thomas J(oseph) 1933- 61-64
Steele, Timothy (Reid) 1948- CANR-92
Earlier sketches in CA 93-96, CANR-16, 50
See also CLC 45
See also CP 7
See also DLB 120, 282
Steele, Tommy
See Hicks, Thomas
Steele, Valerie (Fahnestock) 1955- .. CANR-106
Earlier sketch in CA 138
Steele, Wilbur Daniel 1886-1970 109
Obituary 29-32R
See also DLB 86
See also MAL 5
See also RGAL 4
Steele, William O(wen) 1917-1979 .. CANR-64
Earlier sketches in CA 1-4R, CANR-2
See also CWRI 5
See also MAICYA 1, 2
See also SATA 1, 51
See also SATA-Obit 27
See also TCWW 2
Steele-Perkins, Christopher Horace 1947- ... 211
Steelhammer, Ilona 1952- .... SATA 98
Steelman, Robert J(ames)
1914-1994 .... CANR-28
Earlier sketches in CA 69-72, CANR-11
See also TCWW 1, 2
Steelsmith, Shari 1962- .... SATA 72
Steely, John E(dward) 1922- 37-40R
Steen, Edwin B. 1901-1995 101
Steen, Frank
See Felstein, Ivor
Steen, John Warren, Jr. 1925- 13-16R
Steen, Malcolm Harold 1928-1983 .... 29-32R
Obituary 135
Steen, Marguerite 1894-1975 97-100
Obituary 61-64
See also RHW
Steen, Mike
See Steen, Malcolm Harold
Steen, Sara Jayne 1949- 106
Steenberg, Sven 1905- 37-40R
Steene, Birgitta 1928- 85-88
Steensma, Robert Charles 1930- 41-44R
Steenson, Gary P(aul) 1944- 107
Steer, Alfred G(ilbert), Jr. 1913- 45-48
Steer, Charlotte
See Hunter, Maud L(ily)
Steere, Daniel C(onrad) 1938- 93-96
Steere, Douglas V(an) 1901-1995 .... 13-16R
Obituary 147
Steere, Richard 1643(?)-1721 .... DLB 24
Steers, J(ames) A(lfred) 1899-1987 124
Steese, Edward 1902-1981
Obituary 105
Steese, Peter B(echler) 1933- 17-20R
Steeves, Frank Leslie 1921- 13-16R
Steeves, Harrison R(oss) 1881-1981
Obituary 104
Stefan, Jude 1930- 211
Stefan, Verena 1947- 154
See also FW
See also GLL 2
Stefanelli, Vladimir Clain
See Clain-Stefanelli, Vladimir
Stefaniak, Mary Helen 1951- 176
Stefanics, Charlotte L(ouise) 1927- 116
Stefanik, Alfred T. 1939- .... SATA 55
Stefanile, Felix 1920- CANR-1
Earlier sketch in CA 45-48
Stefanovski, Goran 1952- .... DLB 181
Stefansson, Evelyn
See Nef, Evelyn Stefansson
Stefansson, Thorsteinn 1912- CANR-29
Earlier sketch in CA 77-80
Stefansson fra Fagraskogi, David
1895-1964 .... DLB 293
Stefanyk, Vasyl 1871-1936 .... EWL 3
Steffan, Alice Kennedy 1907- 5-8R
Steffan, Jack
See Steffan, Alice Kennedy
Steffan, Siobhan R.
See Goulart, Frances Sheridan
Steffan, Truman Guy 1910-1996 .... 29-32R
Steffanson, Con
See Cassiday, Bruce (Bingham) and Goulart, Ron(ald Joseph)
Steffek, Edwin F(rancis) 1912-1985 89-92
Obituary 118
Steffen, Albert 1884-1963
Obituary 93-96
Steffen, Elizabeth Allen 194
Steffen, Jerome O(rville) 1942- 112
Steffen, Jonathan 1958- 135
Steffen, Lloyd H. 1951- 206
Steffens, Bradley 1955- 146
See also SATA 77
Steffens, (Joseph) Lincoln 1866-1936 198
Brief entry 117
See also DLB 303
See also MAL 5
See also TCLC 20
Steffensmeier, Darrell J. 1942- 123
Stefferud, Alfred (Daniel) 1903-1993 .... CAP-1
Earlier sketch in CA 13-16
Steffler, John (Earl) 1947- CANR-33
Earlier sketch in CA 110
See also CN 6, 7
Stefflre, Buford 1916- 5-8R
Steffy, J. Richard 1924- 151
Stegall, Carrie Coffey 1908-1985 .... CAP-2
Earlier sketch in CA 25-28
Stegeman, Janet Allais 1923- 128
See also Britton, Kate
See also SATA 53
See also SATA-Brief 49
Stegeman, John F(oster) 1918- 17-20R
Stegenga, James A. 1937- 25-28R
Steger, Shelby 1906- 49-52
Steglich, W(infred) G(eorge) 1921- ... CANR-30
Earlier sketch in CA 45-48
Stegman, Michael A(llen) 1940- 41-44R
Stegner, Lynn (Marie) 1957- 196
Stegner, Page 1937- CANR-10
Earlier sketch in CA 21-24R
Stegner, Wallace (Earle) 1909-1993 .. CANR-46
Obituary 141
Earlier sketches in CA 1-4R, CANR-1, 21
See also CAAS 9
See also AITN 1
See also AMWS 4
See also ANW
See also BEST 90:3
See also BPFB 3
See also CLC 9, 49, 81
See also CN 1, 2, 3, 4, 5
See also DAM NOV
See also DLB 9, 206, 275
See also DLBY 1993
See also EWL 3
See also MAL 5
See also MTCW 1, 2
See also MTFW 2005
See also RGAL 4
See also SSC 27
See also TCWW 1, 2
See also TUS
Stehling, Kurt R(ichard) 1919-1997 162
Obituary 157
Brief entry 110
Stehr, Hermann 1864-1940 209
See also DLB 66
Steible, Daniel J(oseph) 1912-1976 45-48
Obituary 103
Steichen, Edward 1879-1973
Obituary 41-44R
Steichen, Joanna T(aub) 1933- CANR-107
Earlier sketch in CA 132
Steichen, Paula 1943- 25-28R
Steig, Irwin 1901-1977
Obituary 73-76
Steig, William (H.) 1907-2003 .... CANR-119
Obituary 224
Earlier sketches in CA 77-80, CANR-21, 44
Interview in CANR-21
See also AITN 1
See also CLR 2, 15, 103
See also CWRI 5
See also DLB 61
See also MAICYA 1, 2
See also MTFW 2005
See also SATA 18, 70, 111
See also SATA-Obit 149
Steiger, Andrew Jacob 1900-1970 .... 5-8R
Steiger, Brad (E.) 1936- CANR-21
Earlier sketch in CA 33-36R
Steiger, Paul E(rnest) 1942- 77-80
Steigman, Benjamin 1889(?)-1974
Obituary 53-56
Steiman, Sidney 1922- 5-8R
Steimberg, Alicia 1933- 206
Steimle, Edmund A(ugustus) 1907- 121
Stein, Aaron Marc 1906-1985 .... CANR-63
Obituary 117
Earlier sketches in CA 9-12R, CANR-6
See also CMW 4
Stein, Arlene 1959- 197
Stein, Arnold (Sidney) 1915-2002
Obituary 214
Brief entry 114
Stein, Arthur (Benjamin) 1937- 29-32R
Stein, Ben
See Stein, Benjamin (Jeremy)
Stein, Benjamin (Jeremy) 1944- CANR-129
Earlier sketch in CA 106
Interview in CA-106
Stein, Bob 1920- 37-40R
Stein, Bruno 1930-1996 .... 37-40R
Obituary 151
Stein, Calvert 1903-1982 .... 29-32R
Obituary 125
Stein, Charles
See Schwalberg, Carol(yn Ernestine Stein)
Stein, Charles S. 1940- 21-24R
Stein, Charles W(arner) 1918- 116
Stein, Dan J(oseph) 1962- CANR-126
Earlier sketch in CA 166
Stein, Dona 77-80
Stein, Edith Sarah
See Sarah, Edith
Stein, Edward D. 1965- 162
Stein, Edward V(incent) 1920- 13-16R
Stein, Emanuel 1908-1985
Obituary 114
Stein, Eric 1913- 184
Stein, Eugene 1960- 149
Stein, George P(hilip) 1917- 65-68
Stein, Gertrude 1874-1946 .... CANR-108
Brief entry 104
Earlier sketch in CA 132
See also AAYA 64
See also AMW
See also AMWC 2
See also CDALB 1917-1929
See also DA
See also DA3
See also DAB
See also DAC
See also DAM MST, NOV, POET
See also DC 19
See also DLB 4, 54, 86, 228
See also DLBD 15
See also EWL 3
See also EXPS
See also FL 1:6
See also GLL 1
See also MAL 5
See also MAWW
See also MTCW 1, 2
See also MTFW 2005
See also NCFS 4
See also PC 18
See also RGAL 4
See also RGSF 2
See also SSC 42
See also SSFS 5
See also TCLC 1, 6, 28, 48
See also TUS
See also WLC
See also WP
Stein, Harry 1938- 61-64
Stein, Harry 1948- CANR-94
Brief entry 120
Earlier sketch in CA 128
Interview in CA-128
Stein, Harve 1904- .... SATA-Brief 30
Stein, Herb 1928- 65-68
Stein, Herbert 1916-1999 106
Obituary 185
Stein, Herman D(avid) 1917- CANR-30
Earlier sketch in CA 1-4R
Stein, Jack M(adison) 1914-1976 .... CANR-15
Obituary 103
Earlier sketch in CA 1-4R
Stein, Jan
See Hegeler, Sten
Stein, Jane Jacobson 1937- 97-100
Stein, Janice Gross 1943- CANR-55
Earlier sketch in CA 127
Stein, Jerome L(eon) 1928- 81-84
Stein, Jess 1914-1984
Obituary 113
Stein, Joseph 1912- CANR-125
Earlier sketches in CA 13-16R, CANR-31, 61
See also DFS 7
See also LAIT 3
Stein, Karen 1941- 190
Stein, Kevin 1954- CANR-102
Earlier sketch in CA 159
Stein, Leo Daniel 1872-1947 213
Brief entry 107
See also DLB 4
Stein, Leon 1910-2002 .... 17-20R
Obituary 206
Stein, Leon 1912-1990 .... CANR-7
Obituary 130
Earlier sketch in CA 17-20R
Stein, Leslie 1945- 202
Stein, Louis 1917- 138
Stein, M(eyer) L(ewis) 1920- CANR-13
Earlier sketch in CA 17-20R
See also SATA 6
Stein, Mark (Avrum) 1951- 118
Stein, Martha L(inda) 1942- 53-56
Stein, Mary Kay 1953- 193
Stein, Maurice Robert 1926- 49-52
Stein, Michael B. 1940- CANR-32
Earlier sketch in CA 45-48
Stein, Mini 29-32R
See also SATA 2
Stein, Morris I(saac) 1921- CANR-1
Earlier sketch in CA 1-4R
Stein, Murray 1943- 176
Stein, Peter (Gonville) 1926- 21-24R
Stein, Philip L(awrence) 1939- 61-64
Stein, R(ichard) Conrad 1937- CANR-138
Earlier sketches in CA 41-44R, CANR-22
See also SATA 31, 82, 154
Stein, Rita F. 1922-
Brief entry 106
Stein, Robert 1924- 49-52
Stein, Robert (A.) 1933- 182
Stein, Robert H(arry) 1935- 101
Stein, Roger B(reed) 1932- CANR-2
Earlier sketch in CA 45-48
Stein, Sandra Kovacs 1939- 106
Stein, Sara Bonnett .... SATA-Brief 34
Stein, Sherman K. 1926- CANR-141
Earlier sketch in CA 151
Stein, Sol 1926- CANR-2
Earlier sketch in CA 49-52
See also AITN 1
Stein, Stanley J. 1920-
Brief entry 108
Stein, Susan M. 1942- CANR-14
Earlier sketch in CA 37-40R
Stein, Thomas A. 1924- 45-48
Stein, Toby 1935- 5-8R
Stein, Walter 1924- 25-28R
Stein, Wendy 1951- 145
See also SATA 77
Stein, William B. 1915- 104
Stein, William W(arner) 1921- 1-4R
Steinarr, Steinn
See Kristmundsson, Aoalsteinn
See also DLB 293
See also EWL 3
Steinbach, Alexander Alan 1894-1978 85-88
Obituary 81-84
Steinbach, Meredith 1949- 107
Steinbeck, John (Ernst) 1902-1968 .... CANR-35
Obituary 25-28R
Earlier sketches in CA 1-4R, CANR-1
See also AAYA 12
See also AMW
See also BPFB 3
See also BYA 2, 3, 13
See also CDALB 1929-1941
See also CLC 1, 5, 9, 13, 21, 34, 45, 75, 124
See also DA
See also DA3
See also DAB
See also DAC
See also DAM DRAM, MST, NOV
See also DLB 7, 9, 212, 275, 309
See also DLBD 2
See also EWL 3
See also EXPS
See also LAIT 3
See also MAL 5
See also MTCW 1, 2
See also MTFW 2005
See also NFS 1, 5, 7, 17, 19
See also RGAL 4
See also RGSF 2
See also RHW
See also SATA 9
See also SSC 11, 37, 77
See also SSFS 3, 6
See also TCLC 135
See also TCWW 1, 2
See also TUS
See also WLC
See also WYA
See also YAW
Steinbeck, Nancy 1945- 202
Steinbeck, Thomas 215
Steinberg, Aaron Zacharovich 1891-1975
Obituary 61-64
Steinberg, Alfred 1917-1995 .... CANR-9
Obituary 147
Earlier sketch in CA 5-8R
See also SATA 9
Steinberg, Blema S. 1934- 163
Steinberg, Charles S(ide) 1913-1978 ... CANR-4
Earlier sketch in CA 49-52
Steinberg, Clarence B. 1929- 153
Steinberg, Danny D(avid Charles)
1931- CANR-14
Earlier sketch in CA 37-40R
Steinberg, David Joel 1937- 25-28R
Steinberg, Eleanor B(usick) 1936- 65-68
Steinberg, Erwin R(ay) 1920- CANR-142
Earlier sketches in CA 29-32R, CANR-12
Steinberg, Fannie 1899-1990 115
See also SATA 43
Steinberg, Fred J. 1933- 37-40R
See also SATA 4
Steinberg, Goodwin B. 1922- 232
Steinberg, Goody
See Stencel, Mark
Steinberg, Harriet 1954- 127
Steinberg, Israel 1903(?)-1983
Obituary 109
Steinberg, J(ay) Leonard 1930- 57-60
Steinberg, Jacob 1915- 141
Steinberg, Jacques 215
Steinberg, Jeffrey 1947(?)-1981
Obituary 104
Steinberg, Jonathan 1934- 21-24R
Steinberg, Joseph L(awrence) 1928- 25-28R
Steinberg, Judah 1861-1908
Brief entry 106
Steinberg, Laurence 1952- 146
Steinberg, Leigh (William) 1949- 182
Steinberg, Leo 1920- CANR-17
Earlier sketches in CA 45-48, CANR-1
Steinberg, M. W. 1918- 127
Steinberg, Mark D(avid) 1953- CANR-115
Earlier sketch in CA 153
Steinberg, Neil 1960- CANR-123
Earlier sketch in CA 139
Steinberg, Norman 1939- 159
Steinberg, Phillip Orso 1921- CANR-2
Earlier sketch in CA 5-8R
See also SATA 34
Steinberg, Rafael (Mark) 1927- CANR-9
Earlier sketch in CA 61-64
See also SATA 45
Steinberg, Rolf 1929- 132
Steinberg, S(igrid) H(enry) 1899-1969 ... CAP-1
Earlier sketch in CA 9-10

Steinberg, Saul 1914-1999 ... 89-92
  Obituary ... 179
  See also SATA 67
Steinberg, Ted
  See Steinberg, Theodore
Steinberg, Theodore 1961- ... 197
Steinberg, Warren 1944- ... 147
Steinberg, Wendy 1952- ... 146
Steinbergh, Judith W(olinsky) 1943- ... CANR-1
  Earlier sketch in CA 45-48
Steinbicker, Paul G(eorge) 1906- ... CAP-2
  Earlier sketch in CA 19-20
Steinbreder, Harry John, Jr. 1930-1985
  Obituary ... 117
Steinbreder, Sandy
  See Steinbreder, Harry John, Jr.
Steinbrook, Gordon L. 1942- ... 149
Steinbrueck, Victor 1911-1985 ... 13-16R
Steinbruner, John David 1941- ... 77-80
Steinbrunner, (Peter) Chris(tian)
  1933-1993 ... CANR-1
  Obituary ... 141
  Earlier sketch in CA 45-48
Steincrohn, Peter J(oseph) 1899-1986 ... 171
  Obituary ... 118
  Brief entry ... 112
Steinem, Gloria 1934- ... CANR-139
  Earlier sketches in CA 53-56, CANR-28, 51
  See also CLC 63
  See also DLB 246
  See also FW
  See also MTCW 1, 2
  See also MTFW 2005
Steiner, Barbara A(nnette) 1934- ... CANR-30
  Earlier sketches in CA 73-76, CANR-13
  See also SAAS 13
  See also SATA 13, 83
Steiner, Barry H(oward) 1942- ... 137
Steiner, Barry R(aymond) ... 115
Steiner, Charlotte 1900-1981 ... SATA 45
Steiner, Claude 1935- ... 97-100
Steiner, Evgeny 1955- ... 193
Steiner, Frederick 1949- ... CANR-39
  Earlier sketch in CA 116
Steiner, Gary A(lbert) 1931-1966 ... 9-12R
  Obituary ... 103
Steiner, George 1929- ... CANR-108
  Earlier sketches in CA 73-76, CANR-31, 67
  See also CLC 24
  See also DAM NOV
  See also DLB 67, 299
  See also EWL 3
  See also MTCW 1, 2
  See also MTFW 2005
  See also SATA 62
Steiner, George A(lbert) 1912- ... CANR-7
  Earlier sketch in CA 13-16R
Steiner, Gerolf 1908- ... 29-32R
Steiner, Gilbert Yale 1924- ... 160
  Brief entry ... 115
Steiner, H. Arthur 1905-1991 ... 5-8R
Steiner, Irene Hunter 1920- ... 97-100
Steiner, Jean-Francois 1938-
Steiner, Joan ... CANR-142
  Earlier sketch in CA 172
  See also SATA 110
Steiner, Jorg
  See Steiner, Jorg
Steiner, Jorg 1930- ... CANR-118
  Earlier sketches in CA 108, CANR-29, 56
  See also SATA 35
Steiner, K. Leslie
  See Delany, Samuel R(ay), Jr.
Steiner, Kurt 1912-2003 ... CANR-7
  Obituary ... 225
  Earlier sketch in CA 17-20R
Steiner, Lee R. 1901- ... CAP-1
  Earlier sketch in CA 13-14
Steiner, Max 1888-1971 ... IDFW 3, 4
Steiner, Michael C. 1947- ... 149
Steiner, Paul ... CANR-37
  Earlier sketches in CA 9-12R, CANR-4
Steiner, Peter O(tto) 1922- ... CANR-14
  Earlier sketch in CA 37-40R
Steiner, Ralph 1899-1986 ... 148
  Obituary ... 119
  Brief entry ... 113
Steiner, Roger J(acob) 1924- ... CANR-32
  Earlier sketch in CA 45-48
Steiner, Rudolf 1861-1925
  Brief entry ... 107
  See also TCLC 13
Steiner, Shari 1941- ... 73-76
Steiner, Stan(ley) 1925-1987 ... CANR-39
  Obituary ... 121
  Earlier sketches in CA 45-48, CANR-1, 16
  See also SATA 14
  See also SATA-Obit 50
Steiner, Susan Clemmer 1947- ... 115
Steiner, Thomas R(obert) 1934- ... 45-48
Steiner, Vera P(olgar) John
  See John-Steiner, Vera P(olgar)
Steiner, Wendy 1949- ... CANR-110
  Earlier sketches in CA 81-84, CANR-14, 61
Steiner, Zara S(hakow) 1928- ... 129
Steiner-Prag, Hugo 1880-1945 ... SATA-Brief 32
Steinert, Marlis G(ertrud) ... 81-84
Steinfels, Peter (Francis) 1941-
  Brief entry ... 116
Steingarten, Jeffrey ... 174
Steingold, Fred S(aul) 1936- ... 109
Steingraber, Sandra 1959- ... 172
Steinhardt, Anne Elizabeth 1941- ... 104
Steinhardt, Herschel S. 1910- ... CANR-40
  Earlier sketches in CAP-2, CA 23-24
Steinhardt, Milton 1909-1994 ... 77-80
Steinhardt, Nancy Shatzman 1954- ... 135
Steinhart, Carol E(lder) 1935- ... 57-60
Steinhart, Peter 1943- ... 148
Steinhauer, Harry 1905- ... CANR-1
  Earlier sketch in CA 1-4R
Steinhauer, Olen ... 237
Steinhaus, Arthur H. 1897-1970 ... CAP-1
  Earlier sketch in CA 19-20
Steinhaus, John Edward 1917- ... 127
Steinheimer, Richard (V.) 1929- ... CANR-50
  Earlier sketch in CA 123
Steinhoff, Dan 1911-1984 ... 77-80
Steinhoff, William (Richard) 1914- ... 85-88
Steinhowel, Heinrich c. 1411-1479 ... DLB 179
Steinitz, Kate T(rauman) 1889-1975 ... CAP-2
  Earlier sketch in CA 23-24
Steinitz, Paul 1909-1988 ... 104
Steinke, Ann E(lizabeth) 1946- ... CANR-32
  Earlier sketch in CA 113
Steinke, Peter L(ouis) 1938- ... 29-32R
Steinke, Rene 1964- ... 186
Steinkraus, Warren E(dward) 1922- ... 21-24R
Steinlauf, Michael C. 1947- ... 167
Steinle, John G(erard) 1916-1990 ... CANR-86
  Obituary ... 132
  Earlier sketch in CA 9-12R
Steinle, Paul (Michael) 1939- ... 77-80
Steinman, David 1958- ... 153
Steinman, Lisa Malinowski 1950- ... CANR-123
  Earlier sketch in CA 69-72
Steinman, Louise 1951- ... CANR-112
  Earlier sketch in CA 147
Steinman, Michael 1952- ... CANR-109
  Earlier sketch in CA 134
Steinman, Ron 1934- ... 199
Steinmann, Anne G. 1906(?)-1987
  Obituary ... 121
Steinmann, Martin, Jr. 1915- ... CANR-26
  Earlier sketch in CA 1-4R
Steinmetz, Eulalie
  See Ross, Eulalie Steinmetz
Steinmetz, Lawrence L(eo) 1938- ... CANR-11
  Earlier sketch in CA 21-24R
Steinmetz, Leon ... 136
Steinmetz, Paul B. 1928- ... 135
Steinmetz, Rollin C. 1912(?)-1986
  Obituary ... 121
Steinmetz, Urban G. 1920- ... CANR-10
  Earlier sketch in CA 25-28R
Steins, Richard 1942- ... 148
  See also SATA 79
Steinsaltz, Adin 1937- ... 189
Steinschreiber, Edith 1932-
  See Bruck, Edith
Steintrager, James A(lvin) 1936- ... 93-96
Steinwedel, Louis William 1943- ... 37-40R
Steirman, Hy 1921- ... 29-32R
Steiss, Alan Walter 1937- ... CANR-28
  Earlier sketches in CA 29-32R, CANR-12
Steitz, Edward S(tephen) 1920-1990 ... 69-72
  Obituary ... 131
Stekert, Ellen J(ane) 1935- ... 33-36R
Stekler, Herman O. 1932- ... 17-20R
Stell, Aaron 1911-1996 ... 57-60
Stell, Elizabeth P(arker) 1958- ... 166
Stell, Geoffrey (Percival) 1944- ... 124
Stella, Carmelo 1956- ... 219
Stella, Charlie
  See Stella, Carmelo
Stellingwerf, Steve(n Lee) 1962- ... 138
Stellman, Jeanne M(ager) 1947- ... 102
Stellman, Steven D(ale) 1945- ... 85-88
Steloff, Frances 1887-1989 ... DLB 187
Steltenkamp, Michael F(rancis) 1950- ... 112
Stelter, Gilbert Arthur 1933- ... CANR-15
  Earlier sketch in CA 41-44R
Steltzer, Ulli 1923- ... 104
Stelzer, Dick 1950- ... 107
Stelzig, Eugene Louis 1943- ... CANR-93
  Earlier sketch in CA 81-84
Stem, Jacqueline 1931- ... 180
  See also SATA 110
Stem, Thad(deus Garland), Jr.
  1916-1980 ... 97-100
  Obituary ... 101
Stember, Charles Herbert 1916-1982 ... 21-24R
  Obituary ... 135
Stemp, Isay 1922- ... 29-32R
Stemp, Robin (Jenniver Pamela) 1944- ... 107
Stempel, Guido H(ermann) III 1928- ... 77-80
Stempel, John Dallas 1938- ... 110
Stempel, Thomas Ritter 1941- ... CANR-141
  Earlier sketch in CA 110
Stempel, Tom
  See Stempel, Thomas Ritter
Sten, Christopher (W.) 1944- ... 137
Stenberger, Marten 1898-1973 ... CANR-5
  Earlier sketch in CA 5-8R
Stenbock, (Count) (Stanislaus) Eric
  1859-1895 ... HGG
Stencel, Mark ... 232
Stendahl, Krister 1921- ... CANR-12
  Earlier sketch in CA 17-20R
Stendhal 1783-1842 ... DA
  See also DA3
  See also DAB
  See also DAC
  See also DAM MST, NOV
  See also DLB 119
  See also EW 5
  See also GFL 1789 to the Present
  See also RGWL 2, 3
  See also SSC 27
  See also TWA
  See also WLC
Stendhal, Renate (Neumann) 1944- ... 148
Stene, Edwin O(tto) 1900-1992 ... CAP-2
  Earlier sketch in CA 21-22
Steneck, Nicholas H. 1940- ... 106
Steneman, Shep 1945- ... 107
  See also SATA 132
Stenerson, Douglas C. 1920- ... 37-40R
Stengel, Joyce A. 1938- ... 234
  See also SATA 158
Stengel, Richard 1955- ... CANR-100
  Earlier sketch in CA 136
Stenhouse, David 1932- ... 89-92
Stenius, George
  See Seaton, George
Stenross, Barbara 1946- ... 196
Stensboel, Ottar 1930- ... 69-72
Stenson, Frederick 1951- ... 113
Stenstreem, Ruth Marian
  See Babson, Marian
Stent, Gunther S(iegmund) 1924- ... 29-32R
Stentiford, Barry M. 1964- ... 232
Stenton, Doris Mary (Parsons) 1894-1971
  Obituary ... 104
Stenus
  See Huxley, Herbert H(enry)
Stenzel, Anne K(atherine) 1911- ... 57-60
Stenzel, George 1910- ... 45-48
Stepanchev, Stephen 1915- ... CANR-7
  Earlier sketch in CA 17-20R
  See also CP 1, 2, 3, 4, 5, 6, 7
Stepanek, Matthew J(oseph) T(haddeus)
  1990-2004 ... 219
  Obituary ... 228
Stepanek, Mattie J. T.
  See Stepanek, Matthew J(oseph) T(haddeus)
Stepanian, Michael 1939- ... 45-48
Stepaniants, Marietta 1935- ... 225
Stephan, Alexander 1946- ... 197
Stephan, John J(ason) 1941- ... CANR-96
  Earlier sketches in CA 41-44R, CANR-45
Stephan, Leslie (Bates) 1933- ... CANR-24
  Earlier sketches in CA 21-24R, CANR-9
Stephan, Ruth 1910-1974 ... 5-8R
  Obituary ... 145
Stephanie, Gordon
  See Gordon, Stephanie Jacob
Stephansson, Stephan G.
  See Gudmundsson, Stefan
  See also DLB 293
Stephen, Adeline Virginia
  See Woolf, (Adeline) Virginia
Stephen, Andrew ... 173
Stephen, David 1910-1989 ... 106
Stephen, Felix N. 1925- ... 153
  See also BW 2
Stephen, George 1926- ... 102
Stephen, Jaci ... 171
Stephen, Jan 1933- ... 1-4R
Stephen, Sir Leslie 1832-1904
  Brief entry ... 123
  See also BRW 5
  See also DLB 57, 144, 190
  See also TCLC 23
Stephen, Lily G(ebhardt) 1943- ... 215
Stephen, Martin 1949- ... 135
Stephen, Parel Lukose 1898- ... CAP-1
  Earlier sketch in CA 9-10
Stephen, R. J.
  See Barrett, Norman (S.)
Stephen, Sid 1942- ... 105
Stephen, Sir Leslie
  See Stephen, Sir Leslie
Stephen, Virginia
  See Woolf, (Adeline) Virginia
Stephens, A(lfred) G(eorge)
  1865-1933 ... DLB 230
Stephens, A. Ray 1932- ... CANR-13
  Earlier sketch in CA 77-80
Stephens, Alan 1925- ... 17-20R
  See also CP 1, 2, 3, 4, 5, 6, 7
Stephens, Alexander H. 1812-1883 ... DLB 47
Stephens, Alice Barber 1858-1932 ... 209
  See also DLB 188
  See also SATA 66
Stephens, Andy 1956- ... 146
Stephens, Ann Sophia (Winterbotham)
  1810-1886 ... DLB 3, 73, 250
Stephens, C(harles) Ralph 1943- ... CANR-48
  Earlier sketch in CA 122
Stephens, Casey
  See Wagner, Sharon B.
Stephens, Charles
  See Goldin, Stephen
Stephens, Charles Asbury 1844(?)-1931 ... 180
  See also DLB 42
Stephens, Donald G. 1931- ... 21-24R
Stephens, Edna Buell 1903-1989 ... CANR-14
  Earlier sketch in CA 37-40R
Stephens, Edward Carl 1924- ... 21-24R
Stephens, Eve
  See Ward-Thomas, Evelyn Bridget Patricia Stephens
Stephens, Evelyne Huber 1950- ... 145
Stephens, Frances
  See Bentley, Margaret
Stephens, Henrietta Henkle
  1909-1993 ... CANR-6
  Obituary ... 109
  Earlier sketch in CA 9-12R
  See also Buckmaster, Henrietta
Stephens, Ian Melville 1903-1984
  Obituary ... 112
Stephens, J(ohn) M(ortimer) 1901-2000 . 13-16R
Stephens, Jack Edward (Jr.) 1955- ... 133
Stephens, James 1882(?)-1950 ... 192
  Brief entry ... 104
  See also DLB 19, 153, 162
  See also EWL 3
  See also FANT
  See also RGEL 2
  See also SSC 50
  See also SUFW
  See also TCLC 4
Stephens, James Charles 1915-2000 ... CANR-3
  Obituary ... 189
  Earlier sketch in CA 5-8R
Stephens, Jeanne
  See Hager, Jean
Stephens, John D(avid) 1947- ... 145
Stephens, John Lloyd 1805-1852 ... DLB 183, 250
Stephens, Joyce 1941- ... 69-72
Stephens, Lester D(ow) 1933- ... CANR-32
  Earlier sketch in CA 45-48
Stephens, Martha (Thomas) 1937- .. CANR-119
  Earlier sketch in CA 77-80
Stephens, Mary Jo 1935- ... 37-40R
  See also SATA 8
Stephens, Meic 1938- ... 65-68
  See also CP 1, 2
Stephens, Michael (Gregory) 1946- .. CANR-43
  Earlier sketches in CA 49-52, CANR-3
  See also CN 6, 7
  See also DLB 234
Stephens, Michael D(awson) 1936- .. CANR-22
  Earlier sketches in CA 57-60, CANR-7
Stephens, Mitchell 1949- ... 136
Stephens, Otis H(ammond), Jr. 1936- ... 65-68
Stephens, Rebecca 1961- ... 212
  See also SATA 141
Stephens, Reed
  See Donaldson, Stephen R(eeder)
Stephens, Robert O(ren) 1928- ... 25-28R
Stephens, Rockwell R(ittenhouse)
  1900-1982 ... 53-56
  Obituary ... 170
Stephens, Rosemary 1924- ... 77-80
Stephens, Sharon
  See Camp, Candace (Pauline)
Stephens, Thomas M. 1931- ... 29-32R
Stephens, W(illiam) P(eter) 1934- ... CANR-52
  Earlier sketches in CA 29-32R, CANR-12, 28
Stephens, W(illiam) Richard 1932- ... 29-32R
Stephens, Wade C. 1932- ... 21-24R
Stephens, Walter 1949- ... 239
Stephens, Will Beth 1918- ... 37-40R
Stephens, William M(cLain) 1925- ... 57-60
  See also SATA 21
Stephens, William N(ewton) 1927- ... CANR-1
  Earlier sketch in CA 1-4R
Stephensen, A. M.
  See Manes, Stephen
Stephensen, P. R. 1901-1965 ... DLB 260
Stephenson, Alan M. G. (?)-1984
  Obituary ... 113
Stephenson, Andrew M(ichael) 1946- ... 124
  Brief entry ... 118
  See also SFW 4
Stephenson, Crocker 1956- ... 142
Stephenson, David 1947- ... 118
Stephenson, Donald Grier, Jr. 1942- ... 188
Stephenson, Fred, Jr. ... 210
Stephenson, Gilbert T(homas)
  1884-1972 ... CAP-1
  Obituary ... 37-40R
  Earlier sketch in CA 17-18
Stephenson, Howard 1893-1978 ... 37-40R
Stephenson, Hugh 1938- ... 219
Stephenson, Jean 1892-1979
  Obituary ... 85-88
Stephenson, John B(ell) 1937- ... 61-64
Stephenson, John Edward Drayton 1928-2001
  Obituary ... 197
  Brief entry ... 112
Stephenson, Matthew A(rnold) 1935- ... 45-48
Stephenson, Maureen 1927- ... CANR-38
  Earlier sketches in CA 85-88, CANR-16
Stephenson, Neal 1959- ... CANR-138
  Earlier sketches in CA 122, CANR-88
  See also AAYA 38
  See also CN 7
  See also MTFW 2005
  See also SFW 4
Stephenson, Pamela 1950- ... 211
Stephenson, (William) Ralph (Ewing)
  1910- ... 17-20R
Stephenson, Richard M(anning) 1918- ... 109
Stephenson, Wendell Holmes
  1899-1970 ... CANR-3
  Earlier sketch in CA 1-4R
Stepka, Milan
  See Benes, Jan
Stepp, Ann 1935- ... 106
  See also SATA 29
Stepp, Laura Sessions 1951- ... 202
Steppling, John 1951- ... CAD
  See also CD 5, 6
Stepto, Michele 1946- ... 128
  See also SATA 61
Stepto, Robert B(urns) 1945- ... 101
  See also BW 1
Steptoe, Andrew (R. A.) ... 162
Steptoe, Javaka 1971- ... MAICYA 2
  See also SATA 151

Steptoe, John (Lewis) 1950-1989 ...... CANR-81
Obituary 129
Earlier sketches in CA 49-52, CANR-3, 26
See also BW 1
See also CLR 2, 12
See also CWRI 5
See also MAICYA 1, 2
See also SATA 8, 63
Steptoe, Lydia
See Barnes, Djuna
See also GLL 1
Steptoe, Patrick Christopher 1913-1988 163
Obituary 125
Sterba, Gunther Hans Wenzel 1922- 5-8R
Sterba, James P. 1943- 228
Sterba, Jim
See Sterba, James P.
Sterba, Richard F(rancis) 1898- 124
Sterchi, Beat 1949- 203
See also CLC 65
Stercho, Peter George 1919- 49-52
Sterelny, Kim 1950- 210
Sterken, Christiaan (L.) 1946- 142
Sterland, E(rnest) G(eorge) 1919- 65-68
Sterling, Anna Kate
See Slide, Anthony (Clifford)
Sterling, Anthony
See Caesar, (Eu)Gene (Lee)
Sterling, Brett
See Bradbury, Ray (Douglas) and
Hamilton, Edmond and
Samachson, Joseph
Sterling, Bruce 1954- CANR-135
Earlier sketches in CA 119, CANR-44
See also CLC 72
See also CN 7
See also MTFW 2005
See also SCFW 2
See also SFW 4
Sterling, Bryan B. 1922- CANR-114
Earlier sketch in CA 164
Sterling, Chandler W(infield)
1911-1984 .... 21-24R
Sterling, Claire 1919-1995 123
Obituary 148
Sterling, David L. 1929- 139
Sterling, Donald J(ustus), Jr. 1927- 77-80
Sterling, Dorothy 1913- 201
Earlier sketches in CA 9-12R, CANR-5, 28
Autobiographical Essay in 201
See also CLR 1
See also JRDA
See also MAICYA 1, 2
See also SAAS 2
See also SATA 1, 83
See also SATA-Essay 127
Sterling, George 1869-1926 165
Brief entry 117
See also DLB 54
See also TCLC 20
Sterling, Helen
See Watts, Helen L. Hoke
Sterling, James 1701-1763 .... DLB 24
Sterling, John 1806-1844 .... DLB 116
Sterling, Keir B(rooks) 1934- 175
Sterling, Maria Sandra
See Floren, Lee
Sterling, Philip 1907-1989 49-52
Obituary 129
See also SATA 8
See also SATA-Obit 63
Sterling, Richard W(hitney) 1922- 45-48
Sterling, Robert
See Casil, Amy Sterling
Sterling, Robert R. 1931- CANR-28
Earlier sketch in CA 29-32R
Sterling, Sandra
See Floren, Lee
Sterling, Shirley (Anne) 1948- 160
See also SATA 101
Sterling, Susan Fisher 1955- 147
Sterling, Theodor D(avid) 1923- 25-28R
Sterling, Val
See Meares, Leonard Frank
Stermer, Bill 1947- 110
Stern, Alfred 1899-1980 53-56
Stern, Barbara L.
See Lang, Barbara
Stern, Bert 1929- 205
Stern, Bill 1907-1971
Obituary 89-92
Stern, Boris 1892-1984 .... CANR-85
Obituary 113
Earlier sketches in CAP-2, CA 17-18
Stern, Carl 1937- 97-100
Stern, Catherine B(rieger) 1894-1973
Obituary 37-40R
Stern, Clarence A. 1913-1991 .... 17-20R
Stern, Curt 1902-1981
Obituary 105
Stern, Daniel 1928- CANR-93
Earlier sketches in CA 5-8R, CANR-5
See also CN 2, 3, 6, 7
Stern, Daniel N. 1934- 136
Stern, David 1949- 138
Stern, Donald A. 1928(?)-1975
Obituary 57-60
Stern, E. Mark 1929- 37-40R
Stern, Edith Mendel 1901-1975
Obituary 57-60
Stern, Edward Severin 1924- 53-56
Stern, Eliahu 1948- 222
Stern, Elizabeth
See Uhr, Elizabeth
Stern, Ellen Norman 1927- CANR-14
Earlier sketch in CA 37-40R
See also SATA 26
Stern, Frances Meritt 1938- 112
Stern, Frederick Curtis 1929- 108
Stern, Frederick M. 1890(?)-1977
Obituary 69-72
Stern, Fritz (Richard) 1926- CANR-92
Earlier sketches in CA 1-4R, CANR-1
Stern, G(ladys) B(ertha) 1890-1973
Obituary 45-48
See also DLB 197
See also RHW
Stern, G(ladys) B(ronwyn) 1890-1973 204
Stern, George G(ordon) 1923-1974 .... CAP-2
Earlier sketch in CA 29-32
Stern, Gerald 1925- CANR-94
Earlier sketches in CA 81-84, CANR-28
See also AMWS 9
See also CLC 40, 100
See also CP 7
See also DLB 105
See also RGAL 4
Stern, Gerald M(ann) 1937- 69-72
Stern, Geraldine 1907- 101
Stern, Gerd Jacob 1928-
Brief entry 106
Stern, Guy 1922- CANR-99
Earlier sketch in CA 41-44R
Stern, Harold P. 1922-1977
Obituary 69-72
Stern, Harold S. 1923(?)-1976 153
Obituary 65-68
See also BW 2
Stern, Harry Joshua 1897-1985 69-72
Stern, Henry L. 1899-1990 97-100
Stern, Howard 1954- 146
Stern, Isaac 1920-2001 187
Obituary 203
Stern, J(ulius) David 1886-1971
Obituary 104
Stern, J(oseph) P(eter Maria)
1920-1991 .... CANR-10
Obituary 136
Earlier sketch in CA 21-24R
Stern, Jacqueline Lee
See Marten, Jacqueline (Lee)
Stern, James (Andrew) 1904-1993 .... CANR-85
Obituary 143
Earlier sketch in CA 21-24R
See also CN 1, 2, 3, 4
Stern, Jane 1946- CANR-141
Earlier sketches in CA 61-64, CANR-10
Stern, Jay B(enjamin) 1929- CANR-18
Earlier sketch in CA 25-28R
Stern, Jean Gordon 1904(?)-1985
Obituary 117
Stern, Jerome H(illel) 1938-1996 163
Stern, Judith M. 1951- 142
See also SATA 75
Stern, Karl 1906-1975 .... CANR-12
Obituary 61-64
Earlier sketch in CA 9-12R
Stern, Kathryn Glasgow 220
Stern, Kenneth S. 1953- 154
Stern, Laurence (Marcus) 1929-1979 85-88
Obituary 89-92
Stern, Lesley 210
Stern, Louis William 1935- CANR-18
Earlier sketch in CA 25-28R
Stern, Madeleine B(ettina) 1912- CANR-119
Earlier sketches in CA 17-20R, CANR-7, 22, 46
See also DLB 111, 140
See also SATA 14
Stern, Maggie 1953- .... SATA 156
Stern, Malcolm H(enry) 1915-1994 73-76
Obituary 143
Stern, Marie 1909- 45-48
Stern, Mario Rigoni 1921- 186
Stern, Martha Eccles Dodd 1908-1990
Obituary 132
Stern, Max
See Barrett, Geoffrey John
Stern, Michael 1910- CAP-2
Earlier sketch in CA 23-24
Stern, Michael 1946- 172
Stern, Milton R(alph) 1928- CANR-15
Earlier sketch in CA 41-44R
Stern, Nancy (B.) 1944- CANR-56
Earlier sketches in CA 110, CANR-28
Stern, Paul C(linton) 1944- 143
Stern, Paula 1945- 102
Stern, Philip M(aurice) 1926-1992 104
Obituary 137
Stern, Philip Van Doren 1900-1984 . CANR-86
Obituary 113
Earlier sketches in CA 5-8R, CANR-6
See also SATA 13
See also SATA-Obit 39
Stern, Richard (Gustave) 1928- CANR-120
Earlier sketches in CA 1-4R, CANR-1, 25, 52
Interview in CANR-25
See also CLC 4, 39
See also CN 1, 2, 3, 4, 5, 6, 7
See also DLB 218
See also DLBY 1987
Stern, Richard Martin 1915-2001 ..... CANR-70
Obituary 202
Earlier sketches in CA 1-4R, CANR-2, 18, 40
See also CMW 4
Stern, Robert 183
Earlier sketch in CA 168
Stern, Robert A. M. 1939- CANR-50
Earlier sketches in CA 29-32R, CANR-25
Stern, Robert M. 1927- CANR-10
Earlier sketch in CA 21-24R
Stern, Rudi 1936- 184
Brief entry 115
Stern, S. Alan 1957- 172
Stern, S. M.
See Stern, Samuel Miklos
Stern, Samuel Miklos 1920-1969
Obituary 111
Stern, Sheila (Frances) 1922- 136
Stern, Simon 1943- 89-92
See also SATA 15
Stern, Sol 1935- 227
Stern, Steve 1947- 132
Brief entry 126
Interview in CA-132
Stern, Stewart 1922-
Brief entry 113
See also DLB 26
Stern, Stuart
See Rae, Hugh C(rauford)
Stern, Susan (Tanenbaum) 1943-1976
Obituary 65-68
Stern, Sydney Ladensohn 1947- 134
Stern, Theresa
See Hell, Richard
Stern, Tracy 1953- 129
Stern, Vivien 239
Stern, William B(ernhard) 1910-1972 .... CAP-1
Earlier sketch in CA 13-16
Stern, Wilma 1940- 138
Stern, Zelda 1949- 116
Sternau, Cynthia 1956- 150
Sternberg, Cecilia 1908-1983 .... CANR-39
Obituary 111
Earlier sketch in CA 73-76
Sternberg, Jacques 1923-
Brief entry 111
Sternberg, Josef von 1894-1969 81-84
See also CLC 20
Sternberg, Martin L(eo) A(ltar) 1925- 107
Sternberg, Patricia 1930- 118
Sternberg, Robert J(effrey) 1949- CANR-127
Brief entry 119
Earlier sketch in CA 126
Interview in CA-126
Sternberg, Vernon (Arthur) 1915-1979
Obituary 104
Sternberg, William 173
Sternberger, Dolf 1907-1989 104
Sterne, Colin C(hase) 1921- 144
Sterne, Emma Gelders 1894- CANR-5
Earlier sketch in CA 5-8R
See also SATA 6
Sterne, Laurence 1713-1768 .... BRW 3
See also BRWC 1
See also CDBLB 1660-1789
See also DA
See also DAB
See also DAC
See also DAM MST, NOV
See also DLB 39
See also RGEL 2
See also TEA
See also WLC
Sterne, Richard Clark 1927- 150
Sterne, Richard S(tephen) 1921- 13-16R
Sterner, Jerry (Joseph) 1938-2001 161
Sterner, Lewis George 1894-1965 .... 5-8R
Sterner, R. Eugene 1912- CANR-3
Earlier sketch in CA 9-12R
Sternfeld, Robert 1917- 81-84
Sternfield, Allen 1930- 53-56
Sterngold, James (S.) 1954- 140
Sternheim, (William Adolf) Carl
1878-1942 193
Brief entry 105
See also DLB 56, 118
See also EWL 3
See also IDTP
See also RGWL 2, 3
See also TCLC 8
Sternhold, Thomas (?)-1549 .... DLB 132
Sternlicht, Sanford 1931- CANR-51
Earlier sketches in CA 25-28R, CANR-10, 26
Sternlieb, George 1928- CANR-25
Earlier sketches in CA 21-24R, CANR-8
Sterns, Kate 1961- 235
Sternsher, Bernard 1925- 9-12R
Sterrett, Cliff 1883-1964 155
Sterritt, David 1944- 186
Sterry, David Henry 1957- 218
Sterry, Rick 1938- 25-28R
Stertz, Bradley A. 1960- 199
Stertz, Eda 1921- 104
Stessin, Lawrence 1911- 9-12R
Stetler, Charles E(dward) 1927- 65-68
Stetler, Russell (Dearnley, Jr.) 1945- 41-44R
Stetson, Brad 1963- 175
Stetson, Charlotte Perkins
See Gilman, Charlotte (Anna) Perkins (Stetson)
Stetson, Damon 1915- 85-88
Stetson, Erlene 108
Stettler, Howard Frederic 1919- 5-8R
Stettner, Irving 1922- CANR-37
Earlier sketches in CA 77-80, CANR-16
Stettner, Louis 1922- 204
Steuart, David 1747-1824 .... DLB 213
Steuer, Faye B(rown) 1942- 229
Steuerle, C. Eugene 1946- 143
Steurt, Marjorie Rankin 1888-1978 .... 13-16R
See also SATA 10
Steven, Hugh 1931- CANR-14
Earlier sketch in CA 41-44R
Stevens, Ana Maria Diaz
See Diaz-Stevens, Ana Maria
Stevens, Andrew 1955- 175
Stevens, Anita 1911-
Brief entry 110
Stevens, Anthony (George) 1933- ... CANR-136
Earlier sketches in CA 110, CANR-71
Stevens, April 1963- 154
Stevens, Ardis 1921- 45-48
Stevens, Art 1935- 124
Stevens, (John) Austin 53-56
Stevens, Austin N(eil) 1930- 104
Stevens, Bernice A. 37-40R
Stevens, Blaine
See Whittington, Harry (Benjamin)
Stevens, Brooke 1957- 200
Stevens, Bryna 1924- 136
See also SATA 65
Stevens, Carl
See Obstfeld, Raymond
Stevens, Carla M(cBride) 1928- CANR-12
Earlier sketch in CA 69-72
See also SATA 13
Stevens, Cat
See Georgiou, Steven Demetre
Stevens, Chambers 1968- 198
See also SATA 128
Stevens, Charles W. 1955- 136
Stevens, Christopher
See Tabori, Paul
Stevens, Christopher 1948- 119
Stevens, Clifford 1926- CANR-6
Earlier sketch in CA 9-12R
Stevens, Clysle
See Wade, John Stevens
Stevens, Dan J.
See Overholser, Wayne D.
Stevens, David 232
Stevens, David Harrison 1884-1980 . CANR-85
Obituary 93-96
Earlier sketch in CA 77-80
Stevens, Denis William 1922-2004 .... CANR-3
Obituary 227
Earlier sketch in CA 9-12R
Stevens, Diane 1939- 159
See also SATA 94
Stevens, Diane 1944- 65-68
Stevens, Dick 1928- 143
Stevens, E. S.
See Drower, E(thel) S(tefana May)
Stevens, Edmund William 1910-1992 109
Obituary 137
Stevens, Edward 1928- CANR-11
Earlier sketch in CA 29-32R
Stevens, Edwin L(ockwood)
1913-1987 .... 21-24R
Obituary 122
Stevens, Eleanour V(irginia) 1926- 29-32R
Stevens, Elisabeth (Goss) 1929- 110
Stevens, Fae Hewston
See Stevens, Frances Isted
Stevens, Felton, Jr. 1970- 206
Stevens, Frances Isted 1907- CAP-1
Earlier sketch in CA 9-10
Stevens, Francis 1884-1939 .... FANT
See also SFW 4
Stevens, Franklin 1933- 29-32R
See also SATA 6
Stevens, Garry 239
Stevens, George (Cooper), Jr. 1932- 125
Brief entry 118
Interview in CA-125
Stevens, George 1904(?)-1985
Obituary 116
Stevens, George Putnam 1918- 45-48
Stevens, Georgiana G(erlinger) 1904- CAP-1
Earlier sketch in CA 17-18
Stevens, Gerald 1909-1981 .... 5-8R
Stevens, Glen
See Wlaschin, Ken
Stevens, Graeme R(oy) 1932- 118
Stevens, Greg
See Cook, Glen (Charles)
Stevens, Gwendolyn 1944- 104
See also SATA 33
Stevens, Halsey 1908-1989 .... 25-28R
Obituary 127
Stevens, Harold 1917- 89-92
Stevens, Harvey A(lonzo) 1913-1986 89-92
Stevens, Henry 1819-1886 .... DLB 140
Stevens, Holly 1924-1992 .... 25-28R
Obituary 137
Stevens, J. D.
See Rowland, D(onald) S(ydney)
Stevens, Jacqueline 1962- 197
Stevens, James (Richard) 1940- CANR-16
Earlier sketch in CA 93-96
Stevens, James F(loyd) 1892-1971
Obituary 33-36R
See also TCWW 1, 2
Stevens, Jan Romero 1953- 160
See also SATA 95
Stevens, Jane Greengold 1945- 108
Stevens, Janet 1953- .... SATA 90, 148
Stevens, Jay (Karl) 1950(?)- 166
Stevens, Joan 1908- CANR-2
Earlier sketch in CA 5-8R
Stevens, John
See Tubb, E(dwin) C(harles)
Stevens, John (Edgar) 1921-2002 221
Stevens, John Paul 1920- 176
Stevens, Joseph C(harles) 1929- 17-20R
Stevens, Joseph E. 1956- 128
Stevens, Joyce Ann 1948- 227
Stevens, Kathleen 1936- CANR-39
Earlier sketch in CA 116
See also SATA 49
Stevens, L(ewell) Robert 1932- 111
Stevens, Laird 1953- 128
Stevens, Lauren R(ogers) 1938- 5-8R
Stevens, Lawrence L.
See London, Lawrence Steven
Stevens, Lee
See Leigh, Stephen (W.)

Cumulative Index 555 **Stewart**

Stevens, Leonard A. 1920- CANR-12
Earlier sketch in CA 17-20R
See also SATA 67
Stevens, Leonie 1962- 167
Stevens, Lucile Vernon 1899-1994 61-64
See also SATA 59
Stevens, M. L. Tina (L.) 216
Stevens, Marcus 1959- 231
Stevens, Margaret Dean
See Aldrich, Bess Streeter
Stevens, Margaret M. 1920- 220
Stevens, Marjorie 1923- .... RHW
Stevens, Mark 1951- 122
See also CLC 34
Stevens, Martin 1927- 13-16R
Stevens, Michael 1919- 53-56
Stevens, Mitchell L. 1966- 215
Stevens, Norma Young 1927- 21-24R
Stevens, Pam
See Gilbert, George
Stevens, Patricia Bunning 1931- 53-56
See also SATA 27
Stevens, Paul 1946- 123
Stevens, Peter
See Geis, Darlene Stern
Stevens, Peter
See Geis, Darlene Stern
Stevens, Peter 1927- 93-96
See also CP 1, 2, 3, 4, 5, 6, 7
Stevens, Peter S(mith) 1936- 53-56
Stevens, R(obert) B(ocking) 1933- CANR-9
Earlier sketch in CA 21-24R
Stevens, R. L.
See Hoch, Edward D(entinger)
Stevens, Richard P. 1931- CANR-10
Earlier sketch in CA 21-24R
Stevens, Robert D(avid) 1921- 112
Stevens, Robert E(llis) 1942- 142
Stevens, Robert Tyler
See Staples, Reginald Thomas
Stevens, Robert Warren 1918-1987 .... CANR-1
Obituary 122
Earlier sketch in CA 45-48
Stevens, Roger (Bentham) 1906-1980
Obituary 105
Stevens, Rolland E(lwell) 1915- 81-84
Stevens, Rosemary (Anne) 1935- CANR-97
Earlier sketch in CA 85-88
Stevens, S. P.
See Palestrant, Simon S.
Stevens, S(tanley) S(mith) 1906-1973
Obituary 116
Stevens, Serita (Deborah) 1949- CANR-44
Earlier sketch in CA 119
See also SATA 70
Stevens, Shane 1941- CANR-43
Earlier sketch in CA 21-24R
Stevens, Sharon 1949- 77-80
Stevens, Shira
See Stevens, Serita (Deborah)
Stevens, Stuart CANR-116
Earlier sketch in CA 162
Stevens, Suzanne H. 1938- 136
Stevens, Sylvester K(irby) 1904-1974 ..... CAP-1
Obituary 45-48
Earlier sketch in CA 13-16
Stevens, Thomas Terry Hoar 1911-1990
Obituary 130
Stevens, Tricia
See Pearl, Jacques Bain
Stevens, Trisha
See Pearl, Jacques Bain
Stevens, Wallace 1879-1955 124
Brief entry 104
See also AMW
See also AMWR 1
See also CDALB 1929-1941
See also DA
See also DA3
See also DAB
See also DAC
See also DAM MST, POET
See also DLB 54
See also EWL 3
See also EXPP
See also MAL 5
See also MTCW 1, 2
See also PAB
See also PC 6
See also PFS 13, 16
See also RGAL 4
See also TCLC 3, 12, 45
See also TUS
See also WLC
See also WP
Stevens, William 1925- 21-24R
Stevens, William W(ilson) 1914- 37-40R
Stevens-Arroyo, Antonio M. 1941- 120
Stevenson, Adlai E(wing) 1900-1965 ..... CAP-1
Earlier sketch in CA 13-16
Stevenson, Andrew W. 1951- 222
Stevenson, Angus 229
Stevenson, Anna (M.) 1905- .... SATA 12
Stevenson, Anne (Katharine) 1933- . CANR-123
Earlier sketches in CA 17-20R, CANR-9, 33
See also CAAS 9
See also BRWS 6
See also CLC 7, 33
See also CP 7
See also CWP
See also DLB 40
See also MTCW 1
See also RHW
Stevenson, Augusta 1869(?)-1976 .... 1-4R
Obituary 85-88
See also SATA 2
See also SATA-Obit 26
Stevenson, (William) Bruce 1906- 49-52
Stevenson, Burton Egbert 1872-1962 102
Obituary 89-92
See also SATA 25
Stevenson, Carol Dornfeld 1931- 5-8R
Stevenson, Charles 1908(?)-1979
Obituary 85-88
Stevenson, Christopher Sinclair
See Sinclair-Stevenson, Christopher
Stevenson, David 1942- CANR-28
Earlier sketch in CA 109
Stevenson, David Lloyd 1910-1975 ...... CAP-2
Obituary 57-60
Earlier sketch in CA 23-24
Stevenson, Dorothy E(mily) 1892-1973 . CAP-1
Obituary 49-52
Earlier sketch in CA 13-16
See also DLB 191
See also RHW
Stevenson, Doug 1950- 232
Stevenson, Drew 1947- .... SATA 60
Stevenson, Dwight E(shelman) 1906- . CANR-1
Earlier sketch in CA 1-4R
Stevenson, Elizabeth 1919- CANR-26
Earlier sketch in CA 1-4R
Stevenson, Florence CANR-16
Earlier sketch in CA 97-100
Stevenson, Garth 1943- CANR-107
Earlier sketch in CA 148
Stevenson, George J(ames) 1924- 9-12R
Stevenson, Gloria 1945- 61-64
Stevenson, Grace Thomas 1900-1992 ... 37-40R
Stevenson, Harold W(illiam) 1921- 25-28R
Stevenson, Harvey 1960- .... SATA 80, 148
Stevenson, Henry M(iller) 1914- 77-80
Stevenson, Herbert Frederick 1906- ... CANR-2
Earlier sketch in CA 5-8R
Stevenson, Hugh A(lexander) 1935- 112
Stevenson, Ian (Pretyman) 1918- 158
Brief entry 115
Stevenson, Ian Ralph 1943- 102
Stevenson, J. P.
See Stevenson, James Patrick (Haldane)
Stevenson, James 1929- CANR-101
Earlier sketches in CA 115, CANR-47
See also CLR 17
See also CWRI 5
See also MAICYA 1, 2
See also SATA 42, 71, 113, 161
See also SATA-Brief 34
Stevenson, James Patrick
See Stevenson, James Patrick (Haldane)
Stevenson, James Patrick (Haldane)
1910- CANR-14
Earlier sketch in CA 45-48
Stevenson, Janet 1913- CANR-29
Earlier sketch in CA 13-16R
See also SATA 8
Stevenson, John (Edward) 1952- 160
Stevenson, John Albert 1890(?)-1979
Obituary 89-92
Stevenson, John P.
See Grierson, Edward
Stevenson, Jonathan 1956- CANR-117
Earlier sketch in CA 151
Stevenson, L(eland) W(ells) 1916- 107
Stevenson, Laura Caroline 1946- 120
Stevenson, Leslie (Forster) 1943- 65-68
Stevenson, (Arthur) Lionel 1902-1973 103
Obituary 45-48
See also DLB 155
Stevenson, Louise L. 1948- 143
Stevenson, Mary Lou K.
See Kohfeldt, Mary Lou (Stevenson)
Stevenson, Matthew 1954- 204
Stevenson, Michael Ian 1953- 103
Stevenson, Randall 1953- CANR-140
Earlier sketches in CA 128, CANR-74
Stevenson, Richard
See Lipez, Richard
Stevenson, Robert 1905-1986
Obituary 120
Stevenson, Robert (Murrell) 1916- CANR-1
Earlier sketch in CA 1-4R
Stevenson, Robert G. 1945- 148
Stevenson, Robert Louis III 1952- 174
Stevenson, Robert Louis (Balfour)
1850-1894 .... AAYA 24
See also BPFB 3
See also BRW 5
See also BRWC 1
See also BRWR 1
See also BYA 1, 2, 4, 13
See also CDBLB 1890-1914
See also CLR 10, 11
See also DA
See also DA3
See also DAB
See also DAC
See also DAM MST, NOV
See also DLB 18, 57, 141, 156, 174
See also DLBD 13
See also GL 3
See also HGG
See also JRDA
See also LAIT 1, 3
See also MAICYA 1, 2
See also NFS 11, 20
See also RGEL 2
See also RGSF 2
See also SATA 100
See also SSC 11, 51
See also SUFW
See also TEA
See also WCH
See also WLC
See also WLIT 4
See also WYA
See also YABC 2
See also YAW
Stevenson, Sucie 1956- 162
See also MAICYA 2
See also SATA 104
Stevenson, Suzanne Silvercruys 1898(?)-1973
Obituary 41-44R
Stevenson, T(homas) H(ulbert) 1919- 61-64
Stevenson, Terry 1953- 214
Stevenson, Tom 1899(?)-1982
Obituary 106
Stevenson, Vera Kemp 1920- 57-60
Stevenson, Victoria F. 1878(?)-1973
Obituary 41-44R
Stevenson, W(illiam) Taylor 1928- CANR-18
Earlier sketch in CA 25-28R
Stevenson, (Stanley) Warren 1933- 41-44R
Stevenson, William Henri 1924- CANR-41
Earlier sketch in CA 13-16R
Stevermer, C. J.
See Stevermer, Caroline
Stevermer, Caroline 1955- CANR-106
Earlier sketch in CA 136
See also FANT
Stevick, Philip T. 1930- 132
Steward, Dick 1942- 188
Steward, F(rederick) C(ampion)
1904-1993 .... 41-44R
Obituary 142
Steward, H. Leighton 1934- CANR-143
Earlier sketch in CA 173
Steward, Hal D(avid) 1922- 69-72
Steward, Helen 1965- 187
Steward, Julian H. 1902-1972
Obituary 33-36R
Steward, Samuel M(orris) 1909-1993 112
Obituary 143
See also Andros, Phil and
Bishop, Donald and
Cave, Thomas and
Kramer, Ted and
McAndrews, John and
Reynolds, Joe and
Sparrow, Philip and
Stames, Ward and
Young, Philip
Stewart, A(gnes) C(harlotte) 77-80
See also SATA 15
Stewart, A(nthony) T(erence) Q(uincey)
1929- CANR-110
Earlier sketch in CA 25-28R
Stewart, A(lfred) W(alter) 1880-1947 234
See also Connington, J. J.
Stewart, (John) Allan 1939- 1-4R
Stewart, Allegra 1899-1994 45-48
Stewart, Alva W. 1931- 197
Stewart, Angus (J. M.) 1936- 106
Stewart, Bertie Ann Gardner 1912-2000 ... 5-8R
Stewart, Bill 1942(?)-1979
Obituary 89-92
Stewart, Chantal 1945- .... SATA 121
Stewart, Charles
See Zurhorst, Charles (Stewart, Jr.)
Stewart, Charles J(oseph) 1936- 41-44R
Stewart, Charles T(odd), Jr. 1922- 101
Stewart, Chris 1951(?)- 196
Stewart, Christina Duff 1926- 65-68
Stewart, Cochrane
See Stewart, Kenneth
Stewart, D(avid) H(ugh) 1926- 21-24R
Stewart, Dan
See Linaker, Mike
Stewart, Daniel Blair 1951- 153
Stewart, Daniel K(enneth) 1925- 29-32R
Stewart, David
See Politella, Dario
Stewart, David W. 1929- 146
Stewart, Desmond (Stirling)
1924-1981 .... CANR-30
Obituary 104
Earlier sketch in CA 37-40R
Stewart, Devin J. 1962- 213
Stewart, Donald 1930-1999 188
Stewart, Donald Charles 1930-1992 ..... 37-40R
Stewart, Donald H(enderson) 1911- 29-32R
Stewart, Donald Ogden 1894-1980 . CANR-43
Obituary 101
Earlier sketch in CA 81-84
See also DLB 4, 11, 26
See also IDFW 3, 4
Stewart, Dorothy Mary 1917-1965
Obituary 104
See also RHW
Stewart, Douglas (Alexander)
1913-1985 81-84
See also CP 1, 2
See also DLB 260
See also RGEL 2
Stewart, Douglas Day 1940- 166
Stewart, Dugald 1753-1828 .... DLB 31
Stewart, Edgar I(rving) 1900-1971 .... 5-8R
Stewart, Edith Hamilton 1883-1968 ...... CAP-1
Earlier sketch in CA 11-12
Stewart, Elbert Wilton 1916- 37-40R
Stewart, Eleanor
See Porter, Eleanor H(odgman)
Stewart, Elinore Pruitt .... TCWW 2
Stewart, Elisabeth J(ane) 1927- 158
See also SATA 93
Stewart, Elizabeth Grey
See Reed, Elizabeth Stewart
Stewart, Elizabeth Laing 1907- 49-52
See also SATA 6
Stewart, Ella Winter 1898-1980
Obituary 101
Stewart, Eve
See Napier, Priscilla
Stewart, Frank 1946- CANR-42
Earlier sketches in CA 104, CANR-20
Stewart, Fred Mustard 1936- CANR-81
Earlier sketches in CA 37-40R, CANR-42
See also HGG
Stewart, Gail B. 1949- 202
See also SATA 141
Stewart, Garrett (Fitzgerald) 1945- 93-96
Stewart, Gary 1944- 145
Stewart, George, Jr. 1848-1906 179
See also DLB 99
Stewart, George 1892-1972
Obituary 33-36R
Stewart, George Rippey 1895-1980 .... CANR-3
Obituary 101
Earlier sketch in CA 1-4R
See also DLB 8
See also SATA 3
See also SATA-Obit 23
See also SFW 4
Stewart, Hal D(ouglas) 1899-1979 .... CAP-1
Earlier sketch in CA 13-16
Stewart, Harold C. 1891(?)-1976
Obituary 69-72
Stewart, Harold Frederick
1916-1995 .... CANR-48
Earlier sketch in CA 69-72
See also CP 1, 2
See also DLB 260
Stewart, Harris B(ates), Jr. 1922- CANR-35
Earlier sketch in CA 45-48
Stewart, Harry E. 1931- 150
Stewart, Hilary 1924- CANR-16
Earlier sketch in CA 93-96
Stewart, Horace Floyd, Jr. 1928- 49-52
Stewart, Ian (Nicholas) 1945- CANR-105
Earlier sketch in CA 139
Stewart, J(ohn) I(nnes) M(ackintosh)
1906-1994 .... CANR-47
Obituary 147
Earlier sketch in CA 85-88
See also Innes, Michael
See also CAAS 3
See also CLC 7, 14, 32
See also CMW 4
See also CN 1, 2, 3, 4, 5
See also MTCW 1, 2
Stewart, Jack (F.) 1935- 200
Stewart, James Alexander 1948- 113
Stewart, James B. 1957(?)- CANR-91
Earlier sketch in CA 146
Stewart, James Brewer 1940- CANR-86
Earlier sketches in CA 29-32R, CANR-32
Stewart, James S(tuart) 1896-1990 .... 9-12R
Obituary 132
Stewart, Jean
See Newman, Mona Alice Jean
Stewart, Jeffrey C. 1950- CANR-80
Earlier sketch in CA 152
See also BW 3
Stewart, Jennifer J(enkins) 1960- 198
See also SATA 128
Stewart, Jim
See Stewart, James Alexander
Stewart, Joel .... SATA 151
Stewart, John 1904(?)-1985
Obituary 116
Stewart, John (William) 1920- 33-36R
See also Cole, Jack
See also SATA 14
Stewart, John 1933- CANR-37
Earlier sketches in CA 97-100, CANR-16
Stewart, John 1941- 97-100
Stewart, John 1952- 142
Stewart, John B(enjamin) 1924- 9-12R
Stewart, John G(ilman) 1935-
Brief entry 112
Stewart, John L. 1925- 181
Stewart, Jon 1962- 209
See also AAYA 57
Stewart, Judith
See Polley, Judith (Anne)
Stewart, Judith Anne
See Maciel, Judi(th Anne)
Stewart, K(athleen) Alison Clarke
See Clarke-Stewart, K(athleen) Alison
Stewart, Katharine Jeanne (Dark) 1914- .. 9-12R
Stewart, Kathleen 1958- 232
Stewart, Kaye
See Howe, Doris Kathleen
Stewart, Kenneth 1918-1985
Obituary 118
Stewart, Kenneth L. 1949- CANR-98
Earlier sketch in CA 147
Stewart, Kenneth N. 1901-1978
Obituary 77-80
Stewart, Kerry
See Stewart, Linda
Stewart, Lawrence D(elbert) 1926- 89-92
Stewart, Lawrence H(oyle) 1922- 17-20R
Stewart, Leah 1973- 200
Stewart, Linda 101
Stewart, Logan
See Savage, Les, Jr.
Stewart, Lucretia 1952- 171
Stewart, Margaret 1912- CANR-18
Earlier sketch in CA 25-28R
Stewart, Maria W. 1803(?)-1879 .... DLB 239
Stewart, Marie M(cCaffery) 1899-1979 ..... 5-8R
Stewart, Mark Armstrong 1929- 89-92
Stewart, Mart A. 1947- 167
Stewart, Martha 1942(?)- 152
Stewart, Mary (Florence Elinor)
1916- CANR-130
Earlier sketches in CA 1-4R, CANR-1, 59

See also AAYA 29
See also BPFB 3
See also CLC 7, 35, 117
See also CMW 4
See also CPW
See also DAB
See also FANT
See also RHW
See also SATA 12
See also YAW
Stewart, Mary Anne 1831-1911 ... 225
See also Barker, Lady Mary Anne
Stewart, Mary Rainbow
See Stewart, Mary (Florence Elinor)
Stewart, Matthew 1963- ... 239
Stewart, Maxwell S(lutz) 1900-1990
Obituary ... 131
Stewart, Melissa 1968- ... 182
See also SATA 111
Stewart, Melville Y(orke) 1935- ... CANR-94
Earlier sketch in CA 146
Stewart, (Robert) Michael (Maitland) 1906-1990 ... CANR-22
Obituary ... 131
Earlier sketch in CA 106
Stewart, Michael 1924(?)-1987
Obituary ... 123
Stewart, Michael 1933- ... 116
Stewart, Michael 1945- ... 138
Stewart, Mike 1955- ... 220
Stewart, Natacha
See Ullman, Natacha
Stewart, Oliver 1895-1980 ... CANR-5
Earlier sketch in CA 5-8R
Stewart, Omer C(all) 1908-1991 ... 127
Stewart, Pat(ricia) 1944- ... 97-100
Stewart, Paul (James), (Jr.) 1929- ... 151
Stewart, Paul 1955- ... 186
See also SATA 114, 163
Stewart, Paul D(ekker) 1918- ... 1-4R
Stewart, Philip Robert 1940- ... 29-32R
Stewart, Phyllis Langton 1933- ... 194
Brief entry ... 106
Stewart, Ramona 1922- ... CANR-6
Earlier sketch in CA 1-4R
Stewart, Randall 1896-1964 ... CANR-1
Earlier sketch in CA 1-4R
See also DLB 103
Stewart, Rex William 1907-1967
Obituary ... 110
Stewart, Rhea Talley 1915- ... 41-44R
Stewart, Robert G(ordon) 1931- ... 65-68
Stewart, Robert Neil 1891-1972 ... 9-12R
See also SATA 7
Stewart, Robert T. 1920(?)-1977
Obituary ... 73-76
Stewart, Robert Wilson 1935- ... 49-52
Stewart, Ron(nie) 1956- ... 142
Stewart, Rosemary (Gordon) ... CANR-15
Earlier sketch in CA 37-40R
Stewart, Sally 1930- ... 221
Stewart, Sam
See Stewart, Linda
Stewart, Sarah ... 216
See also MAICYA 2
See also SATA 143
Stewart, Scott
See Zaffo, George J.
Stewart, (Michael) Sean 1965- ... CANR-94
Earlier sketch in CA 148
See also DLB 251
Stewart, Seumas 1919- ... 61-64
Stewart, Shelia 1928- ... 21-24R
Stewart, Shelley 1934- ... 214
Stewart, Stanley N(ordahl) 1931- ... 17-20R
Stewart, Susan 1952- ... 168
See also CWP
See also PFS 22
Stewart, Suzanne ... 61-64
Stewart, Thomas A(lan) 1948- ... 217
Stewart, Vincent (Astor, Jr.) 1939- ... 29-32R
Stewart, W(illiam) A(lexander) Campbell 1915- ... 13-16R
Stewart, W(alter) P. 1924- ... SATA 53
Stewart, Walter 1931- ... CANR-117
Earlier sketch in CA 129
Stewart, Walter Bingham 1913- ... CANR-16
Earlier sketch in CA 85-88
Stewart, Whitney 1959- ... CANR-89
Earlier sketch in CA 156
See also SATA 92
Stewart, Will
See Williamson, John Stewart
Stewart, William Stanley 1938- ... 89-92
Stewart, William T(homas) 1934- ... 127
Stewart, Wynn 1934-1985 ... 154
Obituary ... 116
Stewart, Zeph 1921- ... 41-44R
Stewig, John Warren 1937- ... CANR-69
Earlier sketches in CA 81-84, CANR-14, 32, 56
See also SATA 26, 110, 162
Steyaert, Thomas A(dolph) 1930- ... 37-40R
Steyer, James P(earson) ... 218
Steyer, Wesley W. 1923- ... 29-32R
Steyermark, Julian A(lfred) 1909-1988 ... CANR-17
Obituary ... 126
Earlier sketches in CAP-1, CA 13-14
Steyn, Mark ... 239
Sthen, Hans Christensen 1544-1610 ... DLB 300
Stibbe, Mark W. G. 1960- ... 143
Stibbs, Alan M(arshall) 1901- ... CANR-2
Earlier sketch in CA 1-4R
Stich, Rodney (Frank) 1923- ... 176
Stich, Stephen P(eter) 1943- ... 41-44R
Stick, David 1919- ... CANR-17
Earlier sketch in CA 97-100
Stickells, Austin T. 1914- ... 41-44R
Stickgold, Bob 1945- ... 104
Stickland, Caroline (Amanda) 1955- ... 127
Stickler, Soma Han 1942- ... SATA 128
Stickney, Benjamin D. 1940- ... 135
Stickney, (Joseph) Trumbull 1874-1904 ... 180
See also DLB 54
See also MAL 5
See also RGAL 4
Stidworthy, John 1943- ... SATA 63
Stieber, Jack 1919- ... CANR-6
Earlier sketch in CA 1-4R
Stiebing, William H(enry), Jr. 1940- ... 141
Stieglitz, Alfred 1864-1946 ... AAYA 59
Stiehm, Judith 1935- ... 61-64
Stieler, Caspar 1632-1707 ... DLB 164
Stierlin, Helm 1926- ... 29-32R
Stierwell, Jay
See Swicegood, Thomas L. P.
Stiff, Robert M(artin) 1931- ... 132
Stiffel, Frank 1916- ... 117
Stifle, June
See Campbell, Maria
Stifter, Adalbert 1805-1868 ... CDWLB 2
See also DLB 133
See also RGSF 2
See also RGWL 2, 3
See also SSC 28
Stigen, Terje 1922- ... 193
Stigger, Judith A. 1949- ... 111
Stigler, George J(oseph) 1911-1991 ... 41-44R
Obituary ... 136
Stigler, Stephen M(ack) 1941- ... 125
Stiglitz, Joseph E(ugene) 1943- ... 214
Stigter, Gerard 1936- ... 194
Stigum, Marcia (Lee) 1934- ... CANR-8
Earlier sketch in CA 61-64
Stigwood, Robert C. 1934- ... 102
Stiles, Ezra 1727-1795 ... DLB 31
Stiles, John R. 1916(?)-1976
Obituary ... 65-68
Stiles, Joseph 1903-2000 ... CAP-2
Earlier sketch in CA 17-18
Stiles, Lindley Joseph 1913- ... CANR-3
Earlier sketch in CA 5-8R
Stiles, Martha Bennett ... 37-40R
See also SATA 6, 108
Stiles, Merritt N. 1899-1975
Obituary ... 57-60
Stiles, Ned B(erry) 1932-2003 ... 17-20R
Obituary ... 214
Stiles, Norman B. 1942- ... 114
See also SATA-Brief 36
Stiles, T(imothy) J(udd) 1964- ... CANR-144
Earlier sketch in CA 152
Stilgoe, John R. ... 109
Still, C. Henry 1920- ... 9-12R
Still, Edgar
See Garber, Joseph R(ene)
Still, James 1906-2001 ... CANR-26
Obituary ... 195
Earlier sketches in CA 65-68, CANR-10
See also CAAS 17
See also CLC 49
See also CSW
See also DLB 9
See also DLBY 01
See also SATA 29
See also SATA-Obit 127
Still, Richard R(alph) 1921-1991 ... CANR-1
Earlier sketch in CA 1-4R
Still, William N(orwood), Jr. 1932- ... CANR-18
Earlier sketch in CA 25-28R
Stille, Alexander ... CANR-119
Earlier sketch in CA 159
Stille, Darlene R(uth) 1942- ... 196
See also SATA 126
Stiller, Ben 1965- ... 183
Stiller, Brian C(arl) 1942- ... CANR-41
Earlier sketch in CA 117
Stiller, Jerry 1927- ... 233
Stillerman, Marci ... 171
See also SATA 104
Stillerman, Robbie 1947- ... SATA 12
Stilley, Frank 1918- ... 61-64
See also SATA 29
Stillinger, Jack 1931- ... CANR-1
Earlier sketch in CA 1-4R
Stillman, Damie 1933- ... CANR-82
Earlier sketches in CA 45-48, CANR-36
Stillman, David A. ... 204
Stillman, Edmund O. 1924-1983
Obituary ... 111
Stillman, Frances (Jennings) 1910-1975 . CAP-1
Obituary ... 57-60
Earlier sketch in CA 13-16
Stillman, Irwin M(axwell) 1895-1975 ... 49-52
Obituary ... 61-64
Stillman, Myra Stephens 1915- ... CANR-6
Earlier sketch in CA 5-8R
Stillman, Nathan 1914- ... 5-8R
Stillman, Noam
See Stillman, Norman A(rthur)
Stillman, Norman A(rthur) 1945- ... 136
Stillman, Richard J. 1917- ... CANR-34
Earlier sketches in CA 37-40R, CANR-14
Stillman, (John) Whit(ney) 1952- ... CANR-99
Earlier sketch in CA 153
Stillson, Alan 1945- ... CANR-122
Earlier sketch in CA 171
Stillwaggon, Eileen 1949- ... CANR-144
Earlier sketch in CA 172
Stillwell, Margaret Bingham 1887-1984 ... 41-44R
Obituary ... 112
Stillwell, Norma Jamieson 1894-1978 ... CAP-1
Earlier sketch in CA 13-16
Stillwell, Paul (Lewis) 1944- ... CANR-140
Earlier sketch in CA 126
Stillwell, Richard 1899-1982
Obituary ... 111
Stilson, Max 1919- ... 9-12R
Stilton, Geronimo ... 234
See also SATA 158
Stilwell, Hart 1902- ... TCWW 1, 2
Stilwell, William E(arle) III 1936- ... 107
Stimmel, Barry 1939- ... CANR-11
Earlier sketch in CA 69-72
Stimpson, Catherine R(oslyn) 1936- ... 41-44R
Stimpson, Gerald
See Mitchell, Adrian
Stimson, Dorothy 1890-1988
Obituary ... 126
Stimson, Richard A(lden) 1923- ... 177
Stimson, Robbe Pierce 1948- ... 136
Stimson, William 1946- ... 122
Stinchcombe, Arthur L. 1933- ... CANR-23
Earlier sketches in CA 13-16R, CANR-8
Stinchcombe, William 1937- ... 105
Stinchecum, Amanda Mayer 1941- ... 139
Stine, G(eorge) Harry 1928-1997 ... CANR-30
Obituary ... 198
Earlier sketches in CA 65-68, CANR-9
See also SATA 10, 136
See also SFW 4
Stine, Hank
See Stine, Henry Eugene
Stine, Henry Eugene 1945- ... 133
Stine, Jovial Bob
See Stine, R(obert) L(awrence)
Stine, R(obert) L(awrence) 1943- ... CANR-109
Earlier sketches in CA 105, CANR-22, 53
See also AAYA 13
See also CLR 37
See also CPW
See also HGG
See also JRDA
See also MAICYA 2
See also MAICYAS 1
See also MTCW 2
See also MTFW 2005
See also SATA 31, 76, 129
See also WYAS 1
See also YAW
Stine, Scott A(aron) 1968- ... 226
Stine, Whitney Ward 1930- ... CANR-7
Earlier sketch in CA 57-60
See also AITN 1
Stineman, Esther F. 1947- ... CANR-17
Earlier sketch in CA 97-100
Stinetorf, Louise (Allender) 1900-1992 ... 9-12R
See also SATA 10
Sting 1951- ... 167
See also Sumner, Gordon Matthew
Stingel, Janine (Lianne) 1966- ... 232
Stinger, Charles L(ewis) 1944- ... 77-80
Stini, William A(rthur Anthony) 1930- ... 127
Brief entry ... 107
Stinnett, Caskie 1911-1998 ... 5-8R
Stinnett, Nick 1942- ... 110
Stinnett, Robert B. ... 233
Stinnett, Ronald F. 1929- ... 21-24R
Stinnett, Tim Moore 1901-1985 ... CANR-13
Obituary ... 115
Earlier sketch in CA 17-20R
Stinnette, Charles R(oy), Jr. 1914- ... 77-80
Stinson, James Emerson, Jr. 1937- ... CANR-45
Earlier sketch in CA 119
Stinson, Jim
See Stinson, James Emerson, Jr.
Stinson, Kathy 1952- ... 113
See also SATA 98
Stinson, Robert William 1941- ... 111
Stinton, T(homas) C(harles) W(arren) 1925-1985
Obituary ... 117
Stipe, (John) Michael 1960- ... 169
Stipe, Robert Edwin 1928- ... 49-52
Stirling, Alfred (Thorpe) 1902-1981 ... 110
Obituary ... 108
Stirling, Anna Maria Diana Wilhelmina (Pickering) 1865-1965 ... CAP-1
Earlier sketch in CA 9-10
Stirling, Arthur
See Sinclair, Upton (Beall)
Stirling, Betty Rutledge 1923- ... 9-12R
Stirling, (Thomas) Brents 1904-1995 ... CAP-2
Earlier sketch in CA 25-28
Stirling, Ian 1941- ... 145
See also SATA 77
Stirling, Jessica
See Coghlan, Margaret M. and Rae, Hugh C(rauford)
See also RHW
Stirling, Lilla (May Elderkin) 1902-1994 ... 107
Stirling, Matthew Williams 1896-1975
Obituary ... 53-56
Stirling, Monica 1916-1983 ... 81-84
Obituary ... 111
See also CN 1, 2, 3
Stirling, Nora B(romley) 1900-1997 ... CANR-3
Earlier sketch in CA 5-8R
See also SATA 3
Stirling, S(teve) M. 1953- ... 140
See also DLB 251
See also SFW 4
Stirner, Max 1806-1856 ... DLB 129
Stirnweis, Shannon 1931- ... SATA 10
Stirt, Joseph A. 1948- ... 140
Stitelman, Leonard (Arnold) 1932- ... 41-44R
Stites, Francis N(oel) 1938- ... 41-44R
Stites, Raymond S(omers) 1899-1974 ... 65-68
Obituary ... 53-56
Stith, John E(dward) 1947- ... CANR-40
Earlier sketch in CA 117
Stith, William 1707-1755 ... DLB 31
Stitskin, Leon D. 1910-1978 ... CANR-1
Earlier sketch in CA 1-4R
Stitt, Milan 1941- ... 69-72
See also CLC 29
Stitt, Peter 1940- ... CANR-52
Earlier sketch in CA 123
Stitz, Aline M. Stomfay
See Stomfay-Stitz, Aline M.
Stitzel, Thomas E(dward) 1936- ... 93-96
Stivale, Charles J. 1949- ... 175
Stiven, Tessa
See Ransford, Tessa
Stivender, Ed 1946- ... 141
Stivens, Dal(las George) 1911-1997 . CANR-14
Earlier sketch in CA 69-72
See also CN 1, 2, 3
See also DLB 260
Stiver, Mary Weeden 1909-1999 ... CAP-1
Earlier sketch in CA 13-14
Stivers, Robert L(loyd) 1940- ... 69-72
Stjernberg, Lloyd A(rmand) 1937- ... 25-28R
St-John Nevill, Barry
See Nevill, Barry St-John
Stoan, Stephen K(uzman) 1942- ... 111
Stob, Ralph 1894-1965 ... 1-4R
Obituary ... 103
Stobart, Thomas Ralph 1914- ... 13-16R
Stobaugh, Robert B. (Jr.) 1927- ... 101
Stobbs, John L(ouis) N(ewcombe) 1921- ... 13-16R
Stobbs, William 1914-2000 ... 81-84
Obituary ... 188
See also SATA 17
See also SATA-Obit 120
Stock, A(my) G(eraldine) 1902-1988
Obituary ... 126
Stock, Alfred 1876-1946 ... 158
Stock, Barbara R(uth) 1942- ... CANR-19
Earlier sketch in CA 112
Stock, Brian 1939- ... 41-44R
Stock, Carolmarie 1951- ... SATA 75
Stock, Catherine 1952- ... CANR-116
Earlier sketch in CA 119
See also SATA 65, 114, 158
Stock, Claudette 1934- ... 65-68
Stock, Ernest 1924- ... 21-24R
Stock, Francine 1958- ... 219
Stock, Gregory ... 227
Stock, Guy 1933- ... 124
Stock, Irvin 1920- ... 25-28R
Stock, Phyllis H(artman) 1930- ... 85-88
Stock, R(obert) D(ouglas) 1941- ... CANR-43
Earlier sketches in CA 41-44R, CANR-14
Stockanes, Anthony E(dward) 1935- ... 109
Stockard, James G. 1915(?)-2002 ... 220
Stockard, James Wright, Jr. 1935- ... 13-16R
Stockard, Jimmy
See Stockard, James Wright, Jr.
Stockbridge, Grant
See Page, Norvell W(ooten)
Stockdale, Eric 1929- ... 25-28R
Stockdale, James B(ond) 1923- ... 143
Stockdale, Jim
See Stockdale, James B(ond)
Stockdale, Susan 1954- ... 166
See also SATA 98
Stockel, H. Henrietta 1938- ... 139
Stockenberg, Antoinette 1943- ... CANR-112
Earlier sketch in CA 167
Stockenstroem, Wilma
See Stockenstrom, Wilma
Stockenstrom, Wilma 1933- ... 205
See also EWL 3
Stocker, Jeffrey D. 1958- ... 162
Stocker, Margarita 1955- ... 121
Stocker, Mark (Andrew) 1956- ... 131
Stockham, Peter (Alan) 1928- ... SATA 57
Stockhammer, Morris 1904-1972 ... 13-16R
Stocking, David M(ackenzie) 1919- ... 25-28R
Stocking, George W(ard), Jr. 1928- ... CANR-44
Earlier sketch in CA 73-76
Stocking, George Ward 1892-1975
Obituary ... 61-64
Stocking, Hobart E(bey) 1906- ... 101
Stocking, Kathleen 1945- ... 135
Stocking, Marion Kingston 1922- ... 25-28R
Stocking, S(usan) Holly 1945- ... 117
Stockler, Bruce 1960(?)- ... 226
Stockley, Grif 1944- ... CANR-70
Earlier sketch in CA 140
Stockman, David A(llen) 1946- ... 123
Stock-Morton, Phyllis N. 1930- ... 205
Stocks, Mary (Danvers Brinton) 1891-1975 ... CANR-85
Obituary ... 118
Earlier sketch in CA 13-16R
Stockton, Adrian James 1935-1981 .. CANR-85
Obituary ... 134
Earlier sketch in CA 29-32R
Stockton, Bayard 1930- ... 134
Stockton, Francis Richard 1834-1902 ... 137
Brief entry ... 108
See also Stockton, Frank R.
See also MAICYA 1, 2
See also SATA 44
See also SFW 4

Stockton, Frank R.
See Stockton, Francis Richard
See also BYA 4, 13
See also DLB 42, 74
See also DLBD 13
See also EXPS
See also SATA-Brief 32
See also SSFS 3
See also SUFW
See also TCLC 47
See also WCH
Stockton, J. Roy 1892(?)-1972
Obituary ... 37-40R
See also DLB 241
Stockton, Jim
See Stockton, Adrian James
Stockton, John R(obert) 1903-1994 ... 13-16R
Stockton, Ronald R. 1940- ... 118
Stockwell, Edward G(rant) 1933- ... 21-24R
Stockwell, Foster (Paul) 1929- ... 227
Stockwell, John R(obert) 1937- ... 104
Stockwell, Robert P(aul) 1925- ... 17-20R
Stockwin, (James) Arthur (Ainscow) 1935- .. 103
Stockwin, Julian 1944- ... 220
Stockwood, (Arthur) Mervyn 1913-1995 ... 183
Brief entry ... 117
Stoddard, Alexandra 1941- ... 183
Stoddard, Charles
See Kuttner, Henry and Strong, Charles S(tanley)
Stoddard, Charles Warren 1843-1909 ... 211
See also DLB 186
Stoddard, Edward G. 1923- ... 9-12R
See also SATA 10
Stoddard, Elizabeth Drew 1823-1902 ... 198
See also AMWS 15
See also DLB 202
Stoddard, Ellwyn R(eed) 1927- ... CANR-38
Earlier sketches in CA 45-48, CANR-1, 17
Stoddard, George Dinsmore 1897-1981
Obituary ... 106
Stoddard, Hope 1900-1987 ... 49-52
See also SATA 6
Stoddard, Richard 1942- ... 102
Stoddard, Richard Henry 1825-1903
Brief entry ... 114
See also DLB 3, 64, 250
See also DLBD 13
Stoddard, Robert H. 1928- ... CANR-82
Earlier sketch in CA 133
Stoddard, Roger E(liot) 1935- ... 220
Stoddard, Sandol 1927- ... CANR-8
Earlier sketch in CA 5-8R
See also Warburg, Sandol Stoddard
See also SATA 98
Stoddard, Solomon 1643-1729 ... DLB 24
Stoddard, Tom 1933- ... 37-40R
Stoddard, Whitney Snow 1913-2003 ... 109
Obituary ... 216
Stoddart, Brian 1946- ... 152
Stoddart, Jack Elliott 1916-1988
Obituary ... 124
Stodelle, Ernestine 1912- ... 117
Stoeckle, John D(uane) 1922- ... 128
Stoehr, C(arl) Eric 1945- ... 65-68
Stoehr, Shelley 1969- ... 168
See also AAYA 27
See also BYA 13
See also SATA 107
See also WYAS 1
Stoeke, Janet Morgan 1957- ... SATA 90, 136
Stoekl, Allan 1951- ... 144
Stoessinger, John G. 1927- ... CANR-9
Earlier sketch in CA 13-16R
Stoessl, Otto 1875-1936 ... EWL 3
Stoesz, David 1947- ... 206
Stoett, Peter J. 1963- ... 153
Stoetzer, O(tto) Carlos (Enrique) 1921- ... CANR-28
Earlier sketch in CA 109
Stoff, David M. ... 175
Stoff, Joshua 1958- ... 136
Stoff, Sheldon (Ptaschevitch) 1930- ... 21-24R
Stoffel, Albert Law 1909-2002 ... 65-68
Obituary ... 209
Stoffel, Betty W. 1922- ... 17-20R
Stoffel, Ernest Lee 1923- ... 114
Stoffel, Lester L(enneth, Jr.) 1920- ... 45-48
Stoffle, Carla J(oy) 1943- ... CANR-7
Earlier sketch in CA 61-64
Stofflet, Mary 1942- ... 127
Stogdill, Ralph M(elvin) 1904-1978 ... CANR-1
Earlier sketch in CA 1-4R
Stohl, Michael (Steven) 1947- ... CANR-25
Earlier sketch in CA 107
Stohlman, Martha Lou Lemmon 1913- ... 65-68
Stoianovich, Trajan 1921- ... 21-24R
Stoiber, Rudolph M(aria) 1925- ... 1-4R
Stoicheff, Peter 1956- ... 174
Stoiko, Michael 1919- ... 9-12R
See also SATA 14
Stoil, Michael Jon 1950- ... 53-56
Stojanovic, Svetozar 1931- ... 134
Brief entry ... 112
Stojic, Manya 1967- ... SATA 156
Stok, T.
See Stolk, Anthonie
Stokely, James R(orex), Jr. 1913-1977 ... 9-12R
Obituary ... 69-72
Stoker, Abraham 1847-1912 ... 150
Brief entry ... 105
See also Stoker, Bram
See also DA
See also DA3
See also DAC
See also DAM MST, NOV
See also HGG
See also MTFW 2005
See also SATA 29
Stoker, Alan 1930- ... CANR-24
Earlier sketches in CA 21-24R, CANR-9
Stoker, Bram
See Stoker, Abraham
See also AAYA 23
See also BPFB 3
See also BRWS 3
See also BYA 5
See also CDBLB 1890-1914
See also DAB
See also DLB 304
See also GL 3
See also LATS 1:1
See also NFS 18
See also RGEL 2
See also SSC 62
See also SUFW
See also TCLC 8, 144
See also TEA
See also WLC
See also WLIT 4
Stoker, H(oward) Stephen 1939- ... CANR-8
Earlier sketch in CA 61-64
Stoker, R. Bryan 1962- ... CANR-125
Earlier sketch in CA 170
Stoker, Richard 1938- ... CANR-123
Earlier sketch in CA 164
Stokes, Adrian Durham 1902-1972 ... CANR-5
Obituary ... 89-92
Earlier sketch in CA 13-16R
Stokes, Alec 1925- ... 144
Stokes, Bob
See Wilkening, Howard (Everett)
Stokes, Bruce 1948- ... 130
Stokes, Carl B(urton) 1927-1996 ... 69-72
Obituary ... 152
Stokes, Cedric
See Beardmore, George
Stokes, Charles (Herbert) 1932- ... 103
Stokes, Charles J(unius) 1922- ... CANR-10
Earlier sketch in CA 25-28R
Stokes, Daniel M. J. 1950- ... 57-60
Stokes, Donald (Hubert) 1913-1986
Obituary ... 119
Stokes, Donald Elkinton 1927-1997 ... CANR-1
Obituary ... 156
Earlier sketch in CA 1-4R
Stokes, Donald W. 1947- ... 132
Stokes, Doris 1919-1987
Obituary ... 122
Brief entry ... 115
Stokes, Edward 1922- ... 128
Stokes, Eric (Thomas) 1924-1981 ... 107
Obituary ... 103
Stokes, Gale 1933- ... 146
Stokes, Geoffrey 1940-1995 ... CANR-36
Obituary ... 149
Earlier sketch in CA 69-72
Stokes, Henry J. M. Scott
See Scott-Stokes, Henry J. M.
Stokes, Jack (Tilden) 1923- ... 29-32R
See also SATA 13
Stokes, James (D.) 1943- ... 169
Stokes, Lisa Odham 1953- ... 194
Stokes, Martin 1958- ... 127
Stokes, Olivia Pearl 1916- ... 37-40R
See also SATA 32
Stokes, Peg (Lee Ewing) ... 1-4R
Stokes, Penelope J. ... 238
Stokes, Robert
See Wilkening, Howard (Everett)
Stokes, Roy 1915- ... 17-20R
Stokes, Roy Eliot ... CANR-26
Earlier sketches in CAP-2, CA 19-20
Stokes, Simpson
See Fawcett, F(rank) Dubrez
Stokes, Thomas L(unsford, Jr.) 1898-1958 ... 179
See also DLB 29
Stokes, William Lee 1915- ... CANR-42
Earlier sketches in CA 41-44R, CANR-20
Stokesbury, James L(awton) 1934- ... CANR-38
Earlier sketches in CA 93-96, CANR-17
Stokesbury, Leon 1945- ... CANR-21
Earlier sketch in CA 69-72
See also CSW
See also DLB 120
Stokke, Baard Richard 1937- ... 25-28R
Stokoe, E(dward) G(eorge) 1919- ... TCWW 2
Stokoe, William C(larence), Jr. 1919-2000 ... 41-44R
Obituary ... 189
Stokstad, Marilyn 1929- ... CANR-15
Earlier sketch in CA 37-40R
Stolberg, Christian Graf zu 1748-1821 . DLB 94
Stolberg, Friedrich Leopold Graf zu 1750-1819 ... DLB 94
Stolberg, Mary M. 1956- ... CANR-144
Earlier sketch in CA 172
Stoler, Ann Laura 1949- ... 119
Stoler, Peter (Robert) 1935- ... CANR-44
Earlier sketch in CA 97-100
Stolk, Anthonie 1916- ... 131
Stoll, Clarice Stasz
See Stasz, Clarice
Stoll, Clifford 1950- ... CANR-88
Earlier sketch in CA 136
See also BEST 90:3
Stoll, Dennis G(ray) 1912-1987 ... 13-16R
Obituary ... 124
Stoll, Irma 1929- ... 135
Stoll, John E(dward) 1933- ... 49-52
Stoller, Debbie ... 239
Stoller, Robert J(esse) 1924-1991 ... 184
Obituary ... 135
Brief entry ... 117
Stollman, Aryeh Lev 1954- ... 173
Stollnitz, Fred 1939- ... 45-48
Stoloff, Carolyn 1927- ... CANR-9
Earlier sketch in CA 65-68
Stolorow, Robert D(avid) 1942- ... 102
Stolper, Wolfgang F(riedrich) 1912-2002 ... 21-24R
Obituary ... 209
Stolten, Jane (Henry) ... 97-100
Stoltenberg, Donald Hugo 1927- ... 89-92
Stoltenberg, John (Vincent) 1944- ... 146
Stoltzfus, Ben Franklin 1927- ... CANR-98
Earlier sketch in CA 103
Stoltzfus, (Mary) Louise 1952- ... 138
Stoltzfus, Nathan 1954- ... 194
Stolz, Lois (Hayden) Meek 1891-1984 .. CAP-2
Earlier sketch in CA 21-22
Stolz, Mary (Slattery) 1920- ... CANR-112
Earlier sketches in CA 5-8R, CANR-13, 41
See also AAYA 8
See also AITN 1
See also CLC 12
See also JRDA
See also MAICYA 1, 2
See also SAAS 3
See also SATA 10, 71, 133
See also YAW
Stolzenbach, Norma Frizzell 1904-1994 ... 41-44R
Stolzenberg, Mark 1950- ... 102
Stomfay-Stitz, Aline M. ... 147
Stommel, Henry Melson 1920-1992 ... 155
Stonberg, Selma F(ranks) ... 69-72
Stone, Alan
See Svenson, Andrew E(dward)
Stone, Alan A(braham) 1929- ... 17-20R
Stone, Albert E., Jr.
See Stone, Albert E(dward)
Stone, Albert E(dward) 1924- ... CANR-50
Earlier sketches in CA 17-20R, CANR-8
Stone, Alfred R. 1926- ... 17-20R
Stone, Alma 1908- ... 77-80
Stone, Babette Rosmond
See Rosmond, Babette
Stone, Barbara Haskins 1924(?)-1979
Obituary ... 89-92
Stone, Betty E. 1926- ... 9-12R
Stone, Bonnie (M.) Domrose 1941- .. CANR-82
Earlier sketch in CA 133
Stone, Brian 1919-1995 ... 13-16R
Stone, Charles Sumner, Jr. 1924- ... 77-80
See also BW 2
Stone, Christopher D(avid) 1937- ... 53-56
Stone, Chuck
See Stone, Charles Sumner, Jr.
Stone, Clarence N. 1935- ... CANR-30
Earlier sketch in CA 112
Stone, Cliffie 1917-1998 ... 200
Stone, Clifford A. 1951-1986
Obituary ... 118
Stone, David (Anthony) 1929- ... 5-8R
Stone, David K(arl) 1922- ... 85-88
See also SATA 9
Stone, David R. 1968- ... 216
Stone, David U. 1927- ... CANR-7
Earlier sketch in CA 17-20R
Stone, Deborah
See Navas, Deborah
Stone, Del, Jr. 1958(?)- ... 167
Stone, Donald (Adelbert), Jr. 1937- ... 29-32R
Stone, Donald D(avid) 1942- ... 81-84
Stone, Doris (Zemurray) 1909-1994 ... 105
Stone, Doris (Mary) 1918- ... 117
Stone, Edward 1913-1990 ... 37-40R
Stone, Edward Durell 1902-1978 ... 184
Stone, Elaine Murray 1922- ... CANR-38
Earlier sketches in CA 89-92, CANR-17
Stone, Elizabeth W(enger) 1918-2002 ... CANR-25
Obituary ... 205
Earlier sketch in CA 107
Stone, Ellery W(heeler) 1894-1981
Obituary ... 105
Stone, Elna ... CANR-5
Earlier sketch in CA 13-16R
Stone, Eugenia 1879-1971 ... 9-12R
See also SATA 7
Stone, Ferdinand Fairfax 1908-1989
Obituary ... 129
Stone, Frank A(ndrews) 1929- ... CANR-8
Earlier sketch in CA 61-64
Stone, G. H.
See Lynds, Gayle (Hallenbeck)
Stone, Gayle
See Lynds, Gayle (Hallenbeck)
Stone, Gene
See Stone, Eugenia
Stone, Geoffrey R(ichard) 1946- ... 236
Stone, George Winchester, Jr. 1907-2000 ... CANR-6
Obituary ... 188
Earlier sketch in CA 5-8R
Stone, Gerald (Charles) 1932- ... 104
Stone, Glenn D(avis) 1954- ... 164
Stone, Grace Zaring 1891-1991 ... CAP-2
Obituary ... 135
Earlier sketch in CA 25-28
Stone, Gregory P(rentice) 1921-1981 . CANR-1
Obituary ... 116
Earlier sketch in CA 49-52
Stone, Hal 1927- ... 228
Stone, Hampton
See Stein, Aaron Marc
Stone, Harris B. 1934- ... 57-60
Stone, Harry 1926- ... 130
Stone, Harry 1928- ... 13-16R
Stone, Helen V(irginia) ... 25-28R
See also SATA 6
Stone, Howard W. 1942- ... 124
Stone, Hoyt E(dward) 1935- ... 101
Stone, I(sidor) F(einstein) 1907-1989 ... CANR-40
Obituary ... 129
Earlier sketch in CA 61-64
Stone, Idella Purnell
See Purnell, Idella
Stone, Ikey
See Purnell, Idella
Stone, Irving 1903-1989 ... CANR-23
Obituary ... 129
Earlier sketches in CA 1-4R, CANR-1
Interview in ... CANR-23
See also CAAS 3
See also AITN 1
See also BPFB 3
See also CLC 7
See also CN 1, 2, 3, 4
See also CPW
See also DA3
See also DAM POP
See also MTCW 1, 2
See also MTFW 2005
See also RHW
See also SATA 3
See also SATA-Obit 64
Stone, James Champion 1916- ... 17-20R
Stone, James H(erbert) 1918- ... 41-44R
Stone, James S(tuart) 1919- ... 151
Stone, Jeanne C. Fawtier 1920- ... 144
Stone, Jennifer 1933- ... 174
Autobiographical Essay in ... 174
See also CAAS 30
Stone, Jerry 1942(?)-1987
Obituary ... 124
Stone, Joan Carol 1930- ... CANR-13
Earlier sketch in CA 77-80
Stone, Joel 1931- ... 138
Stone, John (Timothy, Jr.) 1933- ... 102
Stone, John H(enry) 1936- ... 89-92
Stone, Jon 1931-1997 ... 107
Obituary ... 157
See also SATA 39
See also SATA-Obit 95
Stone, Jonathan 1956- ... 223
Stone, Josephine Rector
See Dixon, Jeanne
Stone, Judith F. 1946- ... 162
Stone, Julius 1907-1985 ... CANR-5
Obituary ... 117
Earlier sketch in CA 53-56
Stone, Justin (Federman) 1916- ... 116
Stone, K. Franklin
See Stone, Kurt F(ranklin)
Stone, Katherine 1949- ... CANR-137
Earlier sketch in CA 171
Stone, Kurt F(ranklin) 1949- ... 196
Stone, L(awrence) Joseph 1912-1975
Obituary ... 61-64
Stone, Laurie 1946- ... 163
Stone, Lawrence 1919-1999 ... 13-16R
Obituary ... 181
Stone, Lesley
See Trevor, Elleston
Stone, Louis 1910(?)-1985
Obituary ... 115
Stone, Lucy 1818-1893 ... DLB 79, 239
Stone, Margaret N.
See Dresser, Norine
Stone, Martin
See Ryan, Oscar
Stone, Marvin Lawrence 1924-2000 ... 69-72
Obituary ... 188
Stone, Matt(hew) 1971- ... 168
See also AAYA 27
Stone, Melville E(lijah) 1848-1929 ... 179
See also DLB 25
Stone, Merlin 1931- ... CANR-39
Earlier sketches in CA 101, CANR-17
See also FW
Stone, Michael E(dward) 1938- ... CANR-82
Earlier sketch in CA 132
Stone, Mildred Fairbanks 1902- ... CAP-1
Earlier sketch in CA 11-12
Stone, Nancy (Young) 1925- ... 49-52
Stone, Natalie
See Goldenbaum, Sally and Staff, Adrienne
Stone, Oliver (William) 1946- ... CANR-125
Earlier sketches in CA 110, CANR-55
See also AAYA 15, 64
See also CLC 73
Stone, Patti 1926- ... 5-8R
Stone, Peter 1930-2003 ... CANR-128
Obituary ... 216
Earlier sketches in CA 9-12R, CANR-7
See also CD 5, 6
See also SATA 65
See also SATA-Obit 143
Stone, Peter B(ennet) 1933- ... 143
Stone, Phillip James III 1936- ... 21-24R
Stone, Phoebe ... SATA 134
Stone, Ralph A. 1934- ... 37-40R

Stone, Raymond CANR-26
Earlier sketches in CAP-2, CA 19-20
See also SATA 1
Stone, Reynolds 1909-1979
Obituary 89-92
Stone, Richard
See Delaney, Jack J(ames)
Stone, Richard 219
Stone, Richard H. CANR-26
Earlier sketches in CAP-2, CA 19-20
Stone, Robert (Anthony) 1937- CANR-95
Earlier sketches in CA 85-88, CANR-23, 66
Interview in CANR-23
See also AMWS 5
See also BPFB 3
See also CLC 5, 23, 42, 175
See also CN 4, 5, 6, 7
See also DLB 152
See also EWL 3
See also MAL 5
See also MTCW 1
See also MTFW 2005
Stone, Robert B. 1916- CANR-31
Earlier sketch in CA 29-32R
Stone, Rodney 1932- 140
Stone, Roger D. 1934- CANR-43
Earlier sketch in CA 119
Stone, Ronald H. 1939- CANR-40
Earlier sketches in CA 77-80, CANR-16
Stone, Rosetta
See Dr. Seuss and
Geisel, Theodor Seuss and
LeSieg, Theo. and
Seuss, Dr.
Stone, Rufus
See Cowie, Donald
Stone, Ruth 1915- CANR-91
Earlier sketches in CA 45-48, CANR-2
See also CP 7
See also CSW
See also DLB 105
See also PC 53
See also PFS 19
Stone, Samuel 1602-1663 .... DLB 24
Stone, Scott C(linton) S(tuart) 1932- . CANR-40
Earlier sketches in CA 25-28R, CANR-18
Stone, Shelley C(lyde, Jr.) 1928- 61-64
Stone, Shepard 1908-1990
Obituary 131
Stone, Sidra (L. Winkelman) 1937- 228
Stone, Susan Berch 1944- 61-64
Stone, Thomas H.
See Harknett, Terry (Williams)
Stone, Todd 1957- 140
Stone, Tom 219
Stone, Vernon A(lfred) 1929- 65-68
Stone, Walter 1955- 216
Stone, Wilfred (Healey) 1917- 21-24R
Stone, William F(rank) 1931- 41-44R
Stone, William Leete 1792-1844 .... DLB 202
Stone, William Sidney 1928-1995 .... 13-16R
Stone, Zachary
See Follett, Ken(neth Martin)
Stoneburner, (Charles Joseph) Tony
1926- 41-44R
Stonechild, A. Blair 180
Stoneham, A. M.
See Stoneham, (Arthur) Marshall
Stoneham, Gillian 1932- .... CP 1
Stoneham, (Arthur) Marshall 1940- 179
Stonehouse, Bernard 1926- CANR-119
Earlier sketches in CA 49-52, CANR-2, 19, 42
See also SATA 13, 80, 140
Stonehouse, John (Thomson) 1925- 112
Stonehouse, Merlin 1911-1987 .... 13-16R
Stoneman, Elvyn Arthur 1919-2002 ...... 17-20R
Obituary 209
Stoneman, Paul 1947- 115
Stoneman, Richard (John) 1951- 130
Stoneman, William H(arlan) 1904-1987
Obituary 122
Stonequist, Everett Verner 1901-1979
Obituary 85-88
Stoner, Carol Hupping 1949- 53-56
Stoner, K. Lynn 1946- 143
Stones, (Cyril) Anthony 1934- .... SATA 72
Stones, E(dgar) 1922- CANR-15
Earlier sketch in CA 37-40R
Stones, E(dward) L(ionel) G(regory) 1914-1987
Obituary 121
Stonesifer, Richard James 1922- 13-16R
Stong, Clair L. 1902(?)-1975
Obituary 61-64
Stong, Phil(ip Duffield) 1899-1957 ...... SATA 32
Stong, Red
See Stong, Clair L.
Stonich, Sarah 1958- 201
Stonier, Tom (Ted) 1927- 5-8R
Stonor, Oliver 1903- CAP-1
Earlier sketch in CA 13-16
Stonov (Vlodavsky), Dmitry 1898-1962 154
Stonov, Natasha 1932- 154
Stonum, Gary Lee 1947- 89-92
Stoodley, Bartlett Hicks 1907-1978 .... 1-4R
Obituary 103
Stookey, Richard 1938- 93-96
Stookey, Robert W(ilson) 1917- CANR-14
Earlier sketch in CA 81-84
Stoop, David 1937- 119
Stoop, Norma McLain 65-68
Stoops, Emery 1902- CANR-17
Earlier sketches in CA 1-4R, CANR-1
Stoops, Erik D(aniel) 1966- CANR-121
Earlier sketch in CA 146
See also SATA 78, 142
Stoops, John A(lbert) 1925- 29-32R
Stopelman, Francis
See Stoppelman, Frans
Stopes, M. C.
See Stopes, Marie (Charlotte) Carmichael
Stopes, Marie C.
See Stopes, Marie (Charlotte) Carmichael
Stopes, Marie (Charlotte) Carmichael
1880-1958 154
Brief entry 115
See also FW
Stopford, John M(orton) 1939- 140
Stopford, Robert Wright 1901-1976 ...... CAP-1
Earlier sketch in CA 13-14
Stopp, Elisabeth (Charlotte Vellar-Etscheit)
1911-1996 .... 5-8R
Stoppard, Miriam 1937- 120
Stoppard, Tom 1937- CANR-125
Earlier sketches in CA 81-84, CANR-39, 67
See also AAYA 63
See also BRWC 1
See also BRWR 2
See also BRWS 1
See also CBD
See also CD 5, 6
See also CDBLB 1960 to Present
See also CLC 1, 3, 4, 5, 8, 15, 29, 34, 63, 91
See also DA
See also DA3
See also DAB
See also DAC
See also DAM DRAM, MST
See also DC 6
See also DFS 2, 5, 8, 11, 13, 16
See also DLB 13, 233
See also DLBY 1985
See also EWL 3
See also LATS 1:2
See also MTCW 1, 2
See also MTFW 2005
See also RGEL 2
See also TEA
See also WLC
See also WLIT 4
Stoppelman, Francis
See Stoppelman, Frans
Stoppelman, Frans 1921- CAP-1
Earlier sketch in CA 9-10
Stoppelmoore, Cheryl Jean
See Ladd, Cheryl (Jean)
Stops, Sue 1936- 151
See also SATA 86
Storad, Conrad J. 1957- 190
See also SATA 119
Storaro, Vittorio 1940- .... IDFW 3, 4
Storch, Margaret 1941- 137
Storer, Doug(las) 1899-1985 57-60
Obituary 118
Storer, J(ames) D(onald) 1928- CANR-23
Earlier sketch in CA 107
Storer, Norman W(illiam) 1930- 41-44R
Storer, Tracy I(rwin) 1889-1973 .... 13-16R
Obituary 126
Stores, Teresa (T.) 1958- 154
Storey, Anthony 1928- CANR-2
Earlier sketch in CA 49-52
See also CN 2, 3
See also DLB 14
Storey, Arthur 1915- 45-48
Storey, David (Malcolm) 1933- CANR-36
Earlier sketch in CA 81-84
See also BRWS 1
See also CBD
See also CD 5, 6
See also CLC 2, 4, 5, 8
See also CN 1, 2, 3, 4, 5, 6
See also DAM DRAM
See also DLB 13, 14, 207, 245
See also EWL 3
See also MTCW 1
See also RGEL 2
Storey, Dee
See Storey, Denise Carol
Storey, Denise Carol 1950- 146
Storey, Edward 1930- 97-100
Storey, Edward J. 1901-1988 89-92
Storey, Gail Donohue 1947- 140
Storey, Graham 1920- 171
Storey, John W(oodrow) 1938- 121
Storey, Margaret 1926- CANR-1
Earlier sketch in CA 49-52
See also CWRI 5
See also SATA 9
Storey, Mark CANR-136
Earlier sketch in CA 167
Storey, P(eter) J. 1937- 238
Storey, R(obin) L(indsay) 1927- CANR-11
Earlier sketch in CA 21-24R
Storey, Richard
See Gold, H(orace) L(eonard)
Storey, Robert F(ranklin) 1945- 85-88
Storey, Victoria Carolyn 1945- 33-36R
See also SATA 16
Storey, W(illiam) George 1923- CANR-6
Earlier sketch in CA 5-8R
Storfer, Muriel (Rosoff) Silberstein
See Silberstein-Storfer, Muriel (Rosoff)
Storing, Herbert James 1928-1977
Obituary 73-76
Storke, Thomas More 1876-1971
Obituary 89-92
Storlie, Erik Fraser 1940- 168
Storm, Christopher
See Olsen, T(heodore) V(ictor)
Storm, Elizabeth
See Sandstrom, Eve K.
Storm, Eric
See Tubb, E(dwin) C(harles)
Storm, Hannah 1962- 214
Storm, Hester G(lory) 1903-1979 .... 9-12R
Storm, Hyemeyohsts 1935- CANR-45
Earlier sketch in CA 81-84
See also CLC 3
See also DAM MULT
See also NNAL
Storm, Lesley
See Clark, Mabel Margaret (Cowie)
Storm, Mallory
See Fairman, Paul W.
Storm, Marian 1892(?)-1975
Obituary 61-64
Storm, Russell
See Williams, Robert Moore
Storm, (Hans) Theodor (Woldsen)
1817-1888 .... CDWLB 2
See also DLB 129
See also EW
See also RGSF 2
See also RGWL 2, 3
See also SSC 27
Storm, Virginia
See Swatridge, Irene Maude (Mossop)
Stormcrow
See Talifero, Gerald
Storme, Peter
See Stern, Philip Van Doren
Storme, Sarah
See Baker, Sarah H.
Stormer, John A. 1928- 25-28R
Storni, Alfonsina 1892-1938 131
Brief entry 104
See also DAM MULT
See also DLB 283
See also HLC 2
See also HW 1
See also LAW
See also PC 33
See also TCLC 5
Storr, (Charles) Anthony 1920-2001 . CANR-41
Earlier sketches in CA 97-100, CANR-17
Storr, Catherine (Cole) 1913-2001 .... CANR-52
Obituary 192
Earlier sketches in CA 13-16R, CANR-23
See also CWRI 5
See also SATA 9, 87
See also SATA-Obit 122
Storrer, Carol Marchal 1949- 112
Storrer, William Allin 1936- 156
Storrow, H(ugh) A(lan) 1926- 21-24R
Storrow, James J., Jr. 1917-1984
Obituary 111
Storry, Richard 1914(?)-1982
Obituary 106
See also SFW 4
Storsve, LaVaughn (Ernestine Kipena)
1921- 1-4R
Story, Alice
See Shankman, Sarah
Story, E(ugenia) Macer
See Macer-Story, E(ugenia)
Story, Edward M. 1921-2001 .... 29-32R
Obituary 204
Story, G(eorge) M(orley) 1927- CANR-9
Earlier sketch in CA 21-24R
Story, Gertrude 1929- 129
Story, Jack Trevor 1917-1991 .... CANR-49
Obituary 136
Earlier sketch in CA 29-32R
Story, Jonathan 1940- 170
Story, Josephine
See Loring, Emilie (Baker)
Story, Ronald (D.) 1946- CANR-11
Earlier sketch in CA 65-68
Story, Thomas 1670(?)-1742 .... DLB 31
Story, William Wetmore 1819-1895 ...... DLB 1, 235
Stoskopf, Neal C. 1934- 148
Stossel, John 1947- 224
Stothart, Herbert 1885-1949 .... IDFW 3, 4
Stotko, Mary-Ann 1960- 229
See also SATA 154
Stotland, Ezra 1924-1993 .... 17-20R
Stott, D(enis) H(erbert) 1909-1988 ... CANR-85
Obituary 124
Earlier sketches in CA 13-16R, CANR-8
Stott, Dorothy (M.) 1958- 134
See also SATA 67, 99
Stott, Dot
See Stott, Dorothy (M.)
Stott, Douglas W(ayne) 1948- 109
Stott, Jane 1940- 85-88
Stott, John R. W. 1921- CANR-40
Earlier sketches in CA 5-8R, CANR-2, 18
Stott, Leland H(yrum) 1897-1981 .... 25-28R
Stott, (Charlotte) Mary 1907-2002 104
Obituary 209
Stott, Mike 1944- 104
See also CBD
See also CD 5, 6
Stott, Raymond Toole
See Toole Stott, Raymond
Stott, Rebecca (K.) 224
Stott, William (Merrell) 1940- 61-64
Stotter, Mike 1957- 178
See also SATA 108
See also TCWW 2
Stotts, Herbert Edward 1916- CANR-1
Earlier sketch in CA 1-4R
Stotts, Jack L. 1932- 49-52
Stotz, Charles Morse 1898-1985
Obituary 115
Stouck, David (Hamilton) 1940- 61-64
Stoudemire, Sterling A(ubrey)
1902-1992 .... CANR-86
Obituary 137
Earlier sketch in CA 37-40R
Stoudt, John Joseph 1911-1981 49-52
Stouffer, Allen P. 1937- 143
Stouffer, Samuel A(ndrew) 1900-1960 229
Stough, Furman C(harles) 1928-
Brief entry 107
Stoughton, Clarence Charles 1895-1975
Obituary 61-64
Stoughton, Gertrude K. 1901-1975 .... CAP-2
Earlier sketch in CA 25-28
Stoughton, William 1631-1701 .... DLB 24
Stout, Alan Ker 1900-1983
Obituary 110
Stout, Chris E. 1959- 154
Stout, David 1942- 136
Stout, Frances C.
See Suntree, Susan
Stout, Gardner Dominick 1903-1984
Obituary 111
Stout, George L(eslie) 1897-1978 81-84
Obituary 77-80
Stout, Glenn 1958- CANR-100
Earlier sketch in CA 138
Stout, Harry S. 1947- 201
Stout, Irving Wright 1903-1972 .... CANR-3
Earlier sketch in CA 1-4R
Stout, James (Harvey) 1954- 119
Stout, Janis P. 1939- CANR-101
Earlier sketch in CA 139
Stout, Jeffrey Lee 1950- 106
Stout, Joseph A(llen), Jr. 1939- CANR-2
Earlier sketch in CA 45-48
Stout, Maureen 233
Stout, Nancy 1942- 137
Stout, Neil Ralph 1932- 97-100
Stout, Rex (Todhunter) 1886-1975 .... CANR-71
Earlier sketch in CA 61-64
See also AITN 2
See also BPFB 3
See also CLC 3
See also CMW 4
See also CN 2
See also DLB 306
See also MSW
See also RGAL 4
Stout, Robert Joe 1936- 65-68
Stout, Russell, Jr. 1932- CANR-18
Earlier sketch in CA 101
Stout, Ruth 1884-1980 .... 33-36R
Obituary 120
Stout, Tim 1946- .... HGG
Stout, Wesley Winans 1889-1971
Obituary 89-92
Stout, William 1949- 126
See also SATA 132
Stoutamire, Albert 1921- 41-44R
Stoutenburg, Adrien (Pearl)
1916-1982 .... CANR-45
Obituary 176
Earlier sketch in CA 5-8R
See also CP 1, 2
See also SATA 3
Stoutland, Allison 1963- .... SATA 130
Stovall, Floyd 1896-1991 .... 9-12R
Obituary 171
Stovall, Tyler 1954- 163
Stove, D. C.
See Stove, David (Charles)
Stove, David (Charles) 1927-1994 136
Stover, Allan C(arl) 1938- CANR-12
Earlier sketch in CA 69-72
See also SATA 14
Stover, Bill
See Stover, W(illiam) H(arrison) M(owbray)
Stover, Deb 1957- 230
Stover, Jill (Griffin) 1958- .... SATA 82
Stover, Jo Ann 1931- 37-40R
Stover, John F(ord) 1912- CANR-1
Earlier sketch in CA 1-4R
Stover, Leon E(ugene) 1929- CANR-43
Earlier sketches in CA 49-52, CANR-2
Stover, Marjorie Filley 1914- CANR-31
Earlier sketch in CA 45-48
See also SATA 9
Stover, Matthew Woodring 1962- 200
Stover, W(illiam) H(arrison) M(owbray)
1898-1980 103
Obituary 97-100
Stover, Webster 1902-1984 53-56
Stow, John 1525-1605 .... DLB 132
See also RGEL 2
Stow, (Julian) Randolph 1935- CANR-33
Earlier sketch in CA 13-16R
See also CLC 23, 48
See also CN 1, 2, 3, 4, 5, 6, 7
See also CP 1, 2
See also DLB 260
See also MTCW 1
See also RGEL 2
Stowe, Charles E(dwin) Hambrick
See Hambrick-Stowe, Charles E(dwin)
Stowe, Cynthia (M.) 1944- CANR-93
Earlier sketch in CA 146
Stowe, David M. 1919- 9-12R

Cumulative Index 559 Street

Stowe, Harriet (Elizabeth) Beecher
1811-1896 ... AAYA 53
See also AMWS 1
See also CDALB 1865-1917
See also DA
See also DA3
See also DAB
See also DAC
See also DAM MST, NOV
See also DLB 1, 12, 42, 74, 189, 239, 243
See also EXPN
See also FL 1:3
See also JRDA
See also LAIT 2
See also MAICYA 1, 2
See also NFS 6
See also RGAL 4
See also TUS
See also WLC
See also YABC 1
Stowe, James L(ewis) 1950- ... 89-92
Stowe, Leland 1899-1994 ... CANR-53
Obituary ... 143
Earlier sketch in CA 77-80
See also DLB 29
See also SATA 60
See also SATA-Obit 78
Stowe, Noel James 1942- ... 106
Stowe, Richard S(cribner) 1925- ... 73-76
Stowe, Rosetta
See Ogan, George F. and
Ogan, Margaret E. (Nettles)
Stowe, William McFerrin 1913-1988 ... 5-8R
Stowe, William W. 1946- ... 145
Stowell, Joseph M(ishael) 1944- ... 119
Stowers, Carlton 1942- ... CANR-124
Earlier sketches in CA 81-84, CANR-31, 14
Stoy, R(ichard) H(ugh) 1910-1994 ... 57-60
Stoyanov, Dimitur Ivanov 1877-1949
See Elin Pelin
Strabo c. 64B.C.-c. 25 ... DLB 176
Strabolgi, Bartolomeo
See Tucci, Niccolo
Strachan, Hew (Francis Anthony)
1949- ... CANR-110
Earlier sketch in CA 61-64
Strachan, Ian 1938- ... 151
See also SATA 85
Strachan, J(ohn) George 1910-1996 ... 107
Strachan, Margaret Pitcairn 1908-1998 ... 5-8R
See also SATA 14
Strachan, T(ony) S(impson) 1920- ... 13-16R
Strachan, W. J.
See Strachan, Walter John
Strachan, Walter John 1903-1994 ... 120
Strachan, Winona Peacock 1918- ... 5-8R
Strachey, Alix 1892-1973 ... 133
Strachey, Barbara
See Halpern, Barbara Strachey
Strachey, Isobel 1907-1987
Obituary ... 122
Strachey, James 1888-1967 ... 128
Brief entry ... 124
Strachey, (Evelyn) John (St. Loe) 1901-1963
Obituary ... 93-96
Strachey, (Giles) Lytton 1880-1932 ... 178
Brief entry ... 110
See also BRWS 2
See also DLB 149
See also DLBD 10
See also EWL 3
See also MTCW 2
See also NCFS 4
See also TCLC 12
Strackbein, O(scar) R(obert)
1900-1993 ... 21-24R
Obituary ... 143
Straczynski, J(oseph) Michael 1954- . CANR-81
Earlier sketch in CA 109
See also AAYA 30
See also HGG
Strader, June (Sellers) 1925- ... 97-100
Stradley, Mark
See Smith, Richard Rein
Stradling, Harry 1901-1970 ... IDFW 3, 4
Stradling, Leslie Edward 1908-1998 ... 104
Obituary ... 165
Stradling, R. A. 1942- ... 144
Strafford, Mary
See Mayor, Flora MacDonald
Strage, Mark 1927- ... 81-84
Strahan, Randall (W.) 1954- ... 136
Strahinich, H. C.
See Strahinich, Helen C.
Strahinich, Helen C. 1949- ... CANR-94
Earlier sketch in CA 146
See also SATA 78
Strahl, Leonard E. 1926- ... 29-32R
Strahlem, Richard E(arl) 1909-1990 ... 37-40R
Strahler, Arthur N(ewell) 1918- ... 139
Straight, Michael (Whitney)
1916-2004 ... CANR-7
Obituary ... 222
Earlier sketch in CA 5-8R
See also CN 1, 2
See also TCWW 1, 2
Straight, Susan 1960- ... CANR-92
Earlier sketch in CA 145
See also CN 7
Strain, Dudley 1909-2000 ... CAP-1
Earlier sketch in CA 11-12
Strain, Frances Bruce (?)-1975 ... CAP-2
Earlier sketch in CA 29-32
Strain, Lucille Brewton ... 69-72
Strainchamps, Ethel (Reed) 1912-1991 ... 53-56
Strait, Raymond 1924- ... CANR-4
Earlier sketch in CA 53-56
Strait, Treva Adams 1909- ... 97-100
See also SATA 35
Straiton, E(dward) C(ornock) 1917- .. CANR-42
Earlier sketches in CA 45-48, CANR-3, 19
Straiton, Eddie
See Straiton, E(dward) C(ornock)
Straiton, John S(eal) 1922- ... 136
Straka, Andy 1958- ... 213
Straka, Gerald Milton 1931- ... CANR-2
Earlier sketch in CA 5-8R
Straker, J(ohn) F(oster) 1904-1987 ... CANR-11
Earlier sketch in CA 13-16R
Strakosch, Avery
See Denham, Avery Strakosch
Straley, John 1953- ... CANR-103
Earlier sketch in CA 166
Straley, John A(lonzo) 1894-1966 ... 1-4R
Obituary ... 103
Stramel, James S. 1960- ... 189
Stramm, August 1874-1915 ... 195
See also EWL 3
See also PC 50
Strand, Kenneth A(lbert) 1927- ... CANR-3
Earlier sketch in CA 9-12R
Strand, Mark 1934- ... CANR-100
Earlier sketches in CA 21-24R, CANR-40, 65
See also AMWS 4
See also CLC 6, 18, 41, 71
See also CP 1, 2, 3, 4, 5, 6, 7
See also DAM POET
See also DLB 5
See also EWL 3
See also MAL 5
See also PAB
See also PC 63
See also PFS 9, 18
See also RGAL 4
See also SATA 41
See also TCLE 1:2
Strand, Paul 1890-1976
Obituary ... 65-68
Strand, Paul E.
See Palestrant, Simon S.
Strand, Thomas 1944- ... 65-68
Strand, William K. 1931- ... 29-32R
Strandberg, Victor H(ugo) 1935- ... CANR-16
Earlier sketch in CA 89-92
Strane, Susan 1944- ... 136
Strang, Barbara M(ary) H(ope)
1925-1982 ... 37-40R
Obituary ... 106
Strang, Gerald 1908-1983 ... CAP-2
Earlier sketch in CA 25-28
Strang, Herbert 1867-1947 ... CWRI 5
Strang, Lennox ... GLL 1
Strang, Ruth May 1895-1971 ... CANR-2
Earlier sketch in CA 1-4R
Strang, Veronica 1957- ... 192
Strange, Dillon
See Norwood, Victor G(eorge) C(harles)
Strange, Jack Roy 1921- ... 17-20R
Strange, James F(rancis) 1938- ... CANR-42
Earlier sketch in CA 117
Strange, K(athleen) H(aidee) 1904- ... 113
Strange, Maureen 1948- ... 89-92
Strange, N. Blair
See Sargent, Brian (Lawrence)
Strange, Nora K.
See Stanley, Nora Kathleen Begbie Strange
Strange, (Thomas) Oliver 1871-1952 . TCWW 2
Strange, Philippa
See Coury, Louise Andree
Strange, Susan 1923-1998 ... 49-52
Obituary ... 171
Strangeland, Karin Michaelis
See Michaelis, Karin
Strangeland, Michaelis
See Michaelis, Karin
Stranger, Joyce
See Wilson, Joyce M(uriel Judson)
See also SAAS 24
Strangis, Joel 1948- ... SATA 124
Strankay, Sam J(ames) 1905-1983 ... 57-60
Strannigan, Shawn (Alyne) 1956- ... 158
See also SATA 93
Strasberg, Lee 1901-1982 ... CANR-29
Obituary ... 106
Earlier sketch in CA 13-16R
Strasberg, Susan (Elizabeth) 1938-1999
Obituary ... 174
Brief entry ... 120
Strasburger, Victor C. 1949- ... 112
Strassels, Paul N. ... 109
Strasser, Bernard Paul 1895-1981 ... CAP-1
Earlier sketch in CA 9-10
Strasser, Marland K(eith) 1915- ... CANR-6
Earlier sketch in CA 5-8R
Strasser, Otto (Johann Maximilian) 1897-1974
Obituary ... 53-56
Strasser, Stephan 1905-1991 ... 133
Strasser, Susan 1948- ... CANR-24
Earlier sketch in CA 107
Strasser, Todd 1950- ... CANR-130
Brief entry ... 117
Earlier sketches in CA 123, CANR-47
See also AAYA 2, 35
See also BYA 6, 8, 9, 12
See also CLR 11
See also JRDA
See also MAICYA 1, 2
See also SATA 41, 45, 71, 107, 153
See also WYA
See also YAW
Strassfeld, Michael J. 1950- ... CANR-139
Earlier sketch in CA 120
Strassfeld, Sharon M(arcia) 1950- ... 107
Strassmann, W(olfgang) Paul 1926- ... 41-44R
Strassova, Helena 1924- ... 49-52
Strate, Grant 1927- ... 210
Stratemeyer, Edward L. 1862-1930 ... CANR-27
Earlier sketches in CAP-2, CA 19-20
See also Adams, Harrison and
Appleton, Victor and
Dixon, Franklin W. and
Keene, Carolyn and
Rockwood, Roy and
Young, Clarence
See also DLB 42
See also MAICYA 1, 2
See also SATA 1, 67, 100
See also WYA
Stratford, H. Philip
See Bulmer, (Henry) Kenneth
Stratford, Michael
See Cassiday, Bruce (Bingham)
Stratford, Philip 1927- ... CANR-5
Earlier sketch in CA 9-12R
See also SATA 47
Strathern, Andrew (Jamieson) 1939- . CANR-19
Earlier sketches in CA 49-52, CANR-2
Strathern, Ann Marilyn 1941- ... CANR-3
Earlier sketch in CA 49-52
Strathern, Paul 1940- ... 199
Strati, Saverio 1924- ... CANR-48
Earlier sketches in CA 17-20R, CANR-7, 23
See also DLB 177
Stratman, Carl J(oseph) 1917-1972 ... CAP-2
Earlier sketch in CA 19-20
Straton, Hillyer H(awthorne)
1905-1969 ... CAP-1
Earlier sketch in CA 9-10
Stratton, Arthur M. 1910(?)-1975
Obituary ... 61-64
Stratton, George Malcolm 1865-1957
Brief entry ... 112
Stratton, Henry
See Nelson, Michael Harrington
Stratton, J. M.
See Whitlock, Ralph
Stratton, J(ohn) T(heodore) ... 61-64
Stratton, John R(ay) 1935- ... 45-48
Stratton, Jon 1950- ... 207
Stratton, Porter Andrew 1918- ... 37-40R
Stratton, Rebecca -1982
Brief entry ... 115
Stratton, Robert 1928- ... SFW 4
Stratton, Roy (Olin) ... CAP-2
Earlier sketch in CA 21-22
Stratton, Ted
See Stratton, J(ohn) T(heodore)
Stratton, Thomas
See Coulson, Robert S(tratton) and
DeWeese, Thomas Eugene
Stratton, William David 1896-1965 ... CAP-1
Earlier sketch in CA 9-10
Stratton-Porter, Gene(va Grace)
1863-1924 ... 137
See also Porter, Gene(va Grace) Stratton
See also ANW
See also CLR 87
See also DLB 221
See also DLBD 14
See also MAICYA 1, 2
See also SATA 15
Stratyner, Barbara Naomi Cohen
See Cohen-Stratyner, Barbara Naomi
Straub, Gerard Thomas 1947- ... CANR-129
Earlier sketch in CA 126
Straub, Peter (Francis) 1943- ... CANR-109
Earlier sketches in CA 85-88, CANR-28, 65
See also BEST 89:1
See also BPFB 3
See also CLC 28, 107
See also CPW
See also DAM POP
See also DLBY 1984
See also HGG
See also MTCW 1, 2
See also MTFW 2005
See also SUFW 2
Straubing, Harold (Elk) 1918- ... 126
Strauch, Carl F(erdinand) 1908-1989 ... 41-44R
Strauch, Judith V(ivian) 1942- ... 107
Strauch, Katina (Parthemos) 1946- ... 105
Straughan, Robert P(aul) L(ouis) 1924- ... 49-52
Straughn, Charles (Thomas II) 1933- ... 117
Straumann, Heinrich 1902-1991 ... 13-16R
Straus, Dennis ... CANR-23
Earlier sketch in CA 105
Straus, Dorothea 1916- ... CANR-72
Earlier sketch in CA 37-40R
Straus, Murray A(rnold) 1926- ... CANR-10
Earlier sketch in CA 21-24R
Straus, Nathan 1889-1961
Obituary ... 89-92
Straus, Richard 1925-1986 ... CANR-22
Earlier sketch in CA 1-4R
Straus, Robert 1923- ... CANR-6
Earlier sketch in CA 57-60
Straus, Roger A(ustin) 1948- ... 109
Strausbaugh, John ... 231
Strauss, Albrecht B(enno) 1921- ... 37-40R
Strauss, Anselm L(eonard) 1916-1996
Obituary ... 153
Brief entry ... 114
Strauss, Barry S. ... 238
Strauss, Bert(ram) Wiley 1901-1999 ... 13-16R
Strauss, Botho 1944- ... 157
See also CLC 22
See also CWW 2
See also DLB 124
Strauss, Darin ... 195
Strauss, David 1937- ... CANR-103
Earlier sketch in CA 89-92
Strauss, David Frederick 1808-1874 ... DLB 133
Strauss, David Levi ... 225
Strauss, Diane Wheeler 1943- ... 128
Strauss, Elaine Mandle 1916(?)-1982
Obituary ... 107
Strauss, Erich 1911-1981 ... 13-16R
Obituary ... 135
Strauss, Frances Goetzmann
1904-1991 ... CAP-2
Obituary ... 134
Earlier sketch in CA 29-32
Strauss, Gerald 1922- ... CANR-33
Earlier sketch in CA 9-12R
Strauss, Gwen 1963- ... 145
See also SATA 77
Strauss, Hans 1898(?)-1977
Obituary ... 69-72
Strauss, Harold 1907-1975
Obituary ... 104
Strauss, Helen M(arion) 1904(?)-1987
Obituary ... 122
Strauss, Herbert A(rthur) 1918- ... 133
Brief entry ... 121
Strauss, Jennifer 1933- ... 154
See also CP 7
See also CWP
Strauss, Joyce 1936- ... 93-96
See also SATA 53
Strauss, Leo 1899-1973 ... CANR-122
Obituary ... 45-48
Earlier sketch in CA 101
See also TCLC 141
Strauss, Lewis Lichtenstein 1896-1974
Obituary ... 45-48
Strauss, Linda Leopold 1942- ... 197
See also SATA 127
Strauss, (Mary) Lucille Jackson
1908-1994 ... CAP-1
Earlier sketch in CA 11-12
Strauss, Maurice B(enjamin)
1904-1974 ... CAP-2
Earlier sketch in CA 25-28
Strauss, Patricia (Frances O'Flynn) 1909-1987
Obituary ... 123
Strauss, Richard (Georg) 1864-1949
Brief entry ... 118
Strauss, Richard L(ehman) 1933- ... CANR-82
Earlier sketches in CA 49-52, CANR-1, 16, 36
Strauss, Susan (Elizabeth) 1954- ... 142
See also SATA 75
Strauss, Victor 1907(?)-1979
Obituary ... 89-92
Strauss, W(allace) Patrick 1923- ... 41-44R
Strauss, Walter A(dolf) 1923- ... 81-84
Strauss, Walter L(eopold)
1922-1988 ... CANR-28
Obituary ... 124
Earlier sketch in CA 81-84
Strauss, Werner 1930- ... 29-32R
Strauss, William 1947- ... CANR-101
Earlier sketch in CA 145
Strauss, William Louis 1914- ... 61-64
Strausz-Hupe, Robert 1903-2002 ... 9-12R
Obituary ... 209
Strausz-Hupe, Robert 1903-2002
See Strausz-Hupe, Robert
Stravinskas, Peter M. J. 1950- ... 216
Stravinski, Igor Fedorovich
See Stravinsky, Igor Fedorovich
Stravinsky, Igor Fedorovich
1882-1971 ... CANR-122
Obituary ... 29-32R
Earlier sketch in CA 107
Stravinsky, Vera 1888-1982 ... 106
Obituary ... 107
Stravitz, David 1940- ... 219
Straw, Deborah 1948- ... 216
Strawinsky, Igor Fedorovich
See Stravinsky, Igor Fedorovich
Strawn, Martha A. 1945- ... 176
Strawson, Galen 1952- ... 133
Strawson, John 1921- ... CANR-12
Earlier sketch in CA 29-32R
Strawson, P(eter) F(rederick) 1919- ... 25-28R
See also DLB 262
Strax, Philip 1909-1999 ... 61-64
Obituary ... 178
Stray, Christopher 1943- ... 142
Strayer, Barry L. 1932- ... 29-32R
Strayer, Brian E. 1950- ... 191
Strayer, E. Ward
See Stratemeyer, Edward L.
Strayer, Joseph Reese 1904-1987 ... 103
Obituary ... 123
Strayer, Sara Barker 1896(?)-1986
Obituary ... 118
Strean, Herbert S(amuel) 1931- ... CANR-19
Earlier sketch in CA 103
Streano, Vince(nt Catello) 1945- ... 53-56
See also SATA 20
Streatfeild, (Mary) Noel
1897(?)-1986 ... CANR-31
Obituary ... 120
Earlier sketch in CA 81-84
See also CLC 21
See also CLR 17, 83
See also CWRI 5
See also DLB 160
See also MAICYA 1, 2
See also SATA 20
See also SATA-Obit 48
Streb, Matthew J(ustin) 1974- ... 232
Streckert, Hal 1955- ... 175
Streebeck, Nancy 1934- ... 118
Street, Alicia (Kumpula) 1911- ... 5-8R
Street, Arthur George 1892-1966 ... CAP-1
Earlier sketch in CA 13-14

Street, Aurora
See Sova, Dawn B(everly)
Street, Brian Jeffrey 1955- ... 133
Street, Cecil J(ohn) C(harles) 1884-1964 ... 204
See also Rhode, John
Street, G(eorge) S(lythe) 1867-1936 ... DLB 135
Street, Harry 1919-1984
Obituary ... 112
Street, James H(arry) 1915-1988 ... CANR-4
Obituary ... 125
Earlier sketch in CA 53-56
Street, Janet Travell 1959- ... SATA 84
Street, Jay
See Slesar, Henry
Street, Julia Montgomery 1898-1993 .. CANR-2
Earlier sketch in CA 5-8R
See also SATA 11
Street, Lee
See Hampton, Kathleen
Street, Leslie
See Freemantle, Brian (Harry)
Street, Lucie ... 13-16R
Street, Margaret M(ary) 1907-1993 ... 65-68
Street, Mattie (Waters) 1896-1966 ... CAP-1
Earlier sketch in CA 13-16
Street, Pamela 1921- ... CANR-52
Earlier sketches in CA 45-48, CANR-27
Streeten, Paul Patrick 1917- ... CANR-53
Earlier sketches in CA 25-28R, CANR-11, 28
Streeter, Edward 1891-1976 ... CANR-2
Obituary ... 65-68
Earlier sketch in CA 1-4R
See also DLB 11
Streeter, Herbert Andrus 1918- ... 5-8R
Streeter, James (Jr.) ... 61-64
Streeter, Thomas Winthrop 1883-1965 ... 184
See also DLB 140
Strehlow, Theodor (George Heinrich) 1908-
Brief entry ... 106
Strehlow, Theodor George Henry
See Strehlow, Theodor (George Heinrich)
Streib, Dan(iel Thomas) 1928-1996 ... 106
Obituary ... 151
Streib, Gordon F(ranklin) 1918- ... 112
Streiker, Lowell D(ean) 1939- ... 49-52
Streisand, Barbra 1942- ... 144
Streissguth, Michael ... 238
Streissguth, Thomas 1958- ... 188
See also SATA 116
Streit, Clarence Kirshman 1896-1986 ... 1-4R
Obituary ... 119
Streit, Jindrich 1946- ... 209
Streithorst, Tom 1932(?)-1981
Obituary ... 103
Strelka, Joseph P(eter) 1927- ... CANR-51
Earlier sketches in CA 61-64, CANR-8, 26
Strelkoff, Tatiana 1957- ... CANR-113
Earlier sketch in CA 155
See also SATA 89
Strelow, Liselotte 1908-1981 ... 206
Strelsky, Katharine (Anderson) ... 108
Strempek, Carol Campbell ... 37-40R
Stren, Patti 1949- ... 124
Brief entry ... 117
See also CLR 5
See also SATA 88
See also SATA-Brief 41
Streng, Frederick J(ohn) 1933-1993 .. CANR-27
Obituary ... 141
Earlier sketch in CA 21-24R
Streng, William D(ietrich) 1909-1983 . CANR-1
Earlier sketch in CA 1-4R
Streng, William Paul 1937-
Brief entry ... 108
Streshinsky, Shirley G. 1934- ... CANR-94
Earlier sketches in CA 85-88, CANR-20, 45
Strete, Craig Kee 1950- ... CANR-69
Earlier sketch in CA 161
See also SATA 44, 96
See also SFW 4
Stretton, Barbara (Humphrey) 1936- . CANR-39
Earlier sketch in CA 116
See also SATA 43
See also SATA-Brief 35
Stretton, Charles
See Dyer, Charles (Raymond)
Stretton, Hesba
See Smith, Sarah
See also DLB 163, 190
Stretton, Hugh 1924- ... 104
Streuvels, Stijn 1871-1969 ... EWL 3
Stribling, T(homas) S(igismund)
1881-1965 ... 189
Obituary ... 107
See also CLC 23
See also CMW 4
See also DLB 9
See also RGAL 4
Stribrny, Zdenck 1922- ... 218
Strich, Christian 1930- ... 109
Strick, Ivy 1952- ... 85-88
Strick, Philip 1939-
Brief entry ... 109
Strick, Wesley 1954- ... 164
Stricker, George 1936- ... CANR-14
Earlier sketch in CA 37-40R
Stricker, Remy 1936- ... 220
Strickland, Arvarh E(unice) 1930- ... 21-24R
Strickland, (William) Brad(ley)
1947- ... CANR-122
Earlier sketch in CA 130
See also FANT
See also SATA 83, 137, 142
Strickland, Charles E(verett) 1930- ... 77-80
Strickland, Cowles 1903(?)-1971
Obituary ... 33-36R
Strickland, Craig (A.) 1956- ... 169
See also SATA 102
Strickland, D. A.
See Strickland, Donald A(llen)
Strickland, Donald A(llen) 1934-
Brief entry ... 109
Strickland, Dorothy S(alley) 1933- ... CANR-59
Earlier sketch in CA 108
See also SATA 89
Strickland, Glenn G. 1917- ... 97-100
Strickland, Joshua 1896- ... 81-84
Strickland, Margaret 1930- ... 116
Strickland, Margot 1927- ... CANR-10
Earlier sketch in CA 65-68
Strickland, Michael R. 1965- ... 217
See also SATA 83, 144
Strickland, Phil D. 1941- ... 29-32R
Strickland, Rennard (James) 1940- ... CANR-43
Earlier sketch in CA 21-24R
Strickland, Rex W(allace) 1897-1985 ... 45-48
Strickland, Ron(ald Gibson) 1943- ... 122
Strickland, Ruth Gertrude 1898-1987 . CANR-5
Earlier sketch in CA 5-8R
Strickland, Samuel 1804-1867 ... DLB 99
Strickland, Stephanie 1942- ... 188
Strickland, Stephen P(arks) 1933- ... CANR-3
Earlier sketch in CA 45-48
Strickler, Susan (Elizabeth) 1952- ... 124
Strickon, Arnold 1930- ... 127
Brief entry ... 108
Strieber, (Louis) Whitley 1945- ... CANR-81
Earlier sketches in CA 81-84, CANR-12, 43
Interview in ... CANR-12
See also HGG
Strieby, Irene Macy 1894-1987 ... CAP-1
Earlier sketch in CA 11-12
Strieder, Leon F. 1950- ... 227
Strieder, Peter (Adolf) 1913- ... CANR-73
Earlier sketch in CA 131
Striegel, Jana 1955- ... 211
See also SATA 140
Striegel-Wilson, Jana
See Striegel, Jana
Strier, Karen B. 1959- ... CANR-92
Earlier sketch in CA 145
Strietelmeier, John (Henry) 1920- ... 25-28R
Stright, Hayden Leroy 1898-1975 ... 37-40R
Strike, Jeremy
See Renn, Thomas E(dward)
Striker, Cecil Leopold 1932- ... 109
Striker, Lee
See Clark, Margaret (D.)
Striker, Susan 1942- ... SATA 63
Strimple, Earl O. 1938- ... 97-100
Strindberg, (Johan) August 1849-1912 ... 135
Brief entry ... 104
See also DA
See also DA3
See also DAB
See also DAC
See also DAM DRAM, MST
See also DC 18
See also DFS 4, 9
See also DLB 259
See also EW 7
See also EWL 3
See also IDTP
See also LMFS 2
See also MTCW 2
See also MTFW 2005
See also RGWL 2, 3
See also TCLC 1, 8, 21, 47
See also TWA
See also WLC
Stringer, Arthur 1874-1950 ... 161
See also DLB 92
See also TCLC 37
Stringer, Christopher 1947- ... 165
See also MTFW 2005
Stringer, David
See Roberts, Keith (John Kingston)
Stringer, Lauren 1957- ... SATA 129
Stringer, Lee 1952(?)- ... 195
Stringer, Lorene A(dair) 1908-1985 ... 37-40R
Stringer, Ruth M(arjorie) Pearson
1905-1987 ... 5-8R
Stringer, William Henry 1908-1976
Obituary ... 65-68
Stringfellow, (Frank) William
1928-1985 ... CANR-9
Obituary ... 115
Earlier sketch in CA 5-8R
Stringfield, Leonard H(arry) 1920-1994 ... 85-88
Stripp, Alan 1924- ... 144
Stritch, Elaine 1926(?)- ... 158
Strittmatter, Erwin 1912-1994 ... DLB 69
See also EWL 3
Stritzler-Levine, Nina 1959- ... 179
Strnisa, Gregor 1930-1987 ... DLB 181
Strobel, Frederick Richard 1937- ... 198
Strobel, Margaret 1946- ... 124
Strober, Gerald S. 1935- ... 85-88
Strober, Myra H. 1941- ... 196
Strobos, Robert Julius 1921- ... 102
Strobridge, Truman R(ussell) 1927- ... CANR-94
Earlier sketch in CA 41-44R
Strock, Carren (Elaine) 1944- ... 174
Strock, Herbert L. 1918- ... 223
Strock, Ian Randal 1966- ... 173
Strodach, George Kleppinger 1905-1971 .. 5-8R
Strode, Hudson 1892-1976 ... CANR-8
Obituary ... 69-72
Earlier sketch in CA 13-16R
Strode, William 1603-1645 ... DLB 126
See also RGEL 2
Strode, Woodrow Wilson Woolwine
1914-1994 ... 171
Strode, Woody
See Strode, Woodrow Wilson Woolwine
Strodtbeck, Fred L(ouis) 1919- ... 5-8R
Stroeyer, Poul 1923- ... CANR-14
Earlier sketch in CA 77-80
See also SATA 13
Stroffolino, Chris 1963- ... 187
Strogatz, Steven H(enry) ... 228
Stroh, Guy W(eston) 1931- ... 49-52
Stroh, Thomas F. 1924- ... CANR-11
Earlier sketch in CA 21-24R
Stroheim, Erich von 1885-1957 ... TCLC 71
Strohm, John
See Strohm, John L(ouis)
Strohm, John L(ouis) 1912-1987
Obituary ... 124
Strohm, Paul (Holzworth, Jr.) 1938- ... 187
Strohm, Reinhard 1942- ... 181
Strohmeyer, John 1924- ... 128
Brief entry ... 125
Interview in ... CA-128
Strohmeyer, Sarah ... 210
Strom, Dao 1973- ... 219
Strom, Deborah 1947- ... 123
Strom, Ingrid Mathilda 1912-1982 ... 13-16R
Strom, Leslie Winter
See Winter, Leslie
Strom, Robert D(uane) 1935- ... CANR-10
Earlier sketch in CA 25-28R
Strom, Yale 1957- ... 142
Stroman, Duane F(rederick) 1934- ... 104
Stroman, Susan 1954- ... AAYA 46
Stromberg, Gustaf (Benjamin) 1882-1962
Obituary ... 112
Stromberg, Hunt 1894-1968 ... IDFW 3, 4
Stromberg, Peter G. 1952- ... 145
Stromberg, Roland N(elson) 1916- ... CANR-46
Earlier sketches in CA 5-8R, CANR-6, 21
Strommen, Merton P. 1919- ... CANR-5
Earlier sketch in CA 9-12R
Stromoski, Rick 1958- ... 182
See also SATA 111
Stronach, Bruce 1950- ... 146
Strong, Albertine ... 170
Strong, Anna Louise 1885-1970
Obituary ... 29-32R
See also DLB 303
Strong, Carson 1946- ... 176
Strong, Charles
See Epstein, Beryl (M. Williams) and
Epstein, Samuel
Strong, Charles Olen 1925- ... 5-8R
Strong, Charles S(tanley) ... TCWW 2
Strong, Charles S(tanley) ... TCWW 2
Strong, David
See McGuire, Leslie (Sarah)
Strong, Donald Stuart 1912-1995 ... 41-44R
Strong, Douglas H(illman) 1935- ... 117
Brief entry ... 111
Strong, Douglas M. 1956- ... 167
Strong, Eithne 1923- ... 97-100
See also CP 1
Strong, Harrington
See McCulley, Johnston
Strong, J. J.
See Strong, Jeremy
Strong, Jeremy 1949- ... 108
See also SATA 36, 105
Strong, John S. 1956- ... 138
Strong, John W. 1930- ... 37-40R
Strong, John William 1935- ... 37-40R
Strong, Jonathan 1944- ... 37-40R
Strong, June 1928- ... 126
Strong, Kenneth William Dobson
1900-1982 ... 104
Obituary ... 105
Strong, L(eonard) A(lfred) G(eorge)
1896-1958 ... DLB 191
See also RGEL 2
Strong, Leah A(udrey) 1922- ... 21-24R
Strong, Lennox
See Grier, Barbara G(ene Damon)
See also GLL 1
Strong, Maggie
See Kotker, Zane
Strong, Pat
See Hough, Richard (Alexander)
Strong, Patience
See Cushing, Winifred
Strong, Philip Nigel Warrington
1899-1983 ... 109
Obituary ... 110
Strong, Roy (Colin) 1935- ... CANR-93
Earlier sketches in CA 49-52, CANR-1, 21
Strong, Rupert 1911-1984 ... 13-16R
Strong, Solange
See Hertz, Solange (Strong)
Strong, Stacie 1965- ... 141
See also SATA 74
Strong, Susan
See Rees, Joan
Strong, Terence 1946- ... 145
Strong, Tracy B(urr) 1943- ... 93-96
Strong, William S. 1951- ... 124
Strong, Zachary
See Mann, E(dward) B(everly)
Strongblood, Casper
See Webster, David Endicott
Stronge, James H. 1950- ... CANR-93
Earlier sketch in CA 146
Strongin, Lynn 1939- ... CANR-44
Earlier sketches in CA 49-52, CANR-1
Strongman, K(enneth) T(homas)
1940- ... CANR-10
Earlier sketch in CA 61-64
Strong Man of the Pen, The
See Olisah, Sunday Okenwa
Stroop, Helen E.
See Witty, Helen E. S(troop)
Stroot, Michel ... 173
Stross, Charles 1964- ... 232
Strossen, Nadine 1950- ... 171
Strother, David B(oyd) 1928- ... 25-28R
Strother, David Hunter 1816-1888 . DLB 3, 248
Strother, Elsie (Frances Warmoth Weitzel)
1912- ... CANR-28
Earlier sketches in CA 65-68, CANR-11
Strother, Horatio Theodore 1930- ... 5-8R
Strother, Pat Wallace 1929- ... CANR-29
Earlier sketches in CA 65-68, CANR-9
Strother, Patricia
See Strother, Pat Wallace
Strother, Raymond D. 1940- ... 228
Stroube, Hal 1921(?)-1983
Obituary ... 110
Stroud, Bettye 1939- ... 161
See also SATA 96
Stroud, Carsten 1946- ... 165
Stroud, Dorothy Nancy 1910-1997 ... 144
Stroud, Joe H(inton) 1936-2002 ... 103
Stroud, Jonathan 1970- ... CANR-144
Earlier sketch in CA 169
See also SATA 102, 159
Stroud, Kandy (Andrea) ... 108
Stroud, Patricia Tyson 1932- ... CANR-103
Earlier sketch in CA 138
Strouhal, Eugen 1931- ... 140
Stroup, Herbert H(ewitt) 1916- ... 13-16R
Stroup, Thomas B(radley) 1903-1992 ... 25-28R
Strouse, Jean 1945- ... CANR-93
Earlier sketch in CA 103
See also DLB 111
Strousse, Flora G. 1897(?)-1974
Obituary ... 49-52
Strout, (Sewall) Cushing (Jr.) 1923- ... 13-16R
Strout, Elizabeth 1956- ... 178
Strout, Richard L(ee) 1898-1990 ... CANR-86
Obituary ... 132
Earlier sketch in CA 69-72
Strover, Dorothea ... 9-12R
Strow, Mary R. 1946- ... 148
Stroyen, William Basil 1925- ... 25-28R
Stroyer, Poul
See Stroeyer, Poul
Stroynowski, Juliusz 1919- ... 132
Strozier, Charles B(urnett) 1944- ... CANR-103
Earlier sketches in CA 107, CANR-24, 50
Strozier, Robert M. 1934- ... 220
Strube, Cordelia 1960- ... 169
Struble, Mitch 1945- ... 93-96
Struble, Virginia
See Burlingame, Virginia (Struble)
Struever, Stuart McKee 1931- ... 104
Strug, Kerri 1977- ... 169
See also SATA 108
Strugatskii, Arkadii (Natanovich)
1925-1991 ... 106
Obituary ... 135
See also Strugatsky, Arkadii Natanovich
See also CLC 27
See also SFW 4
Strugatskii, Boris (Natanovich) 1933- ... 106
See also Strugatsky, Boris (Natanovich)
See also CLC 27
See also SFW 4
Strugatsky, Arkadii Natanovich
See Strugatskii, Arkadii (Natanovich)
See also DLB 302
Strugatsky, Boris (Natanovich)
See Strugatskii, Boris (Natanovich)
See also DLB 302
Struglia, Erasmus Joseph 1915- ... 13-16R
Struhl, Paula Rothenberg
See Rothenberg, Paula S.
Struik, Dirk Jan 1894-2000 ... CANR-6
Obituary ... 192
Earlier sketch in CA 5-8R
Struk, Danylo H(usar) 1940- ... CANR-55
Earlier sketch in CA 57-60
Strum, Philippa 1938- ... CANR-140
Earlier sketch in CA 61-64
Strummer, Joe 1952-2002 ... CLC 30
Strumpen-Darrie, Robert L. 1912-1994 . 13-16R
Strung, Norman 1941- ... CANR-14
Earlier sketch in CA 41-44R
Strunge, Michael 1958-1986 ... EWL 3
Strunk, (William) Oliver 1901-1980 ... 105
Obituary ... 97-100
Strunk, Orlo, Jr. 1925- ... CANR-1
Earlier sketch in CA 1-4R
Strunk, William, Jr. 1869-1946 ... 164
Brief entry ... 118
See also NCFS 5
See also TCLC 92
Strupp, Hans H(ermann) 1921- ... CANR-2
Earlier sketch in CA 1-4R
Struss, Karl 1886-1981 ... IDFW 3, 4
Struther, Jan 1901-1953 ... 227
Strutt, Malcolm 1936- ... 115
Strutton, William Harold 1918-2003 ... 77-80
Obituary ... 221
Strutz, Henry 1932- ... CANR-50
Earlier sketches in CA 5-8R, CANR-7, 24
Struve, Walter 1935- ... CANR-99
Earlier sketch in CA 49-52
Struyk, Raymond J(ay) 1944- ... 134
Brief entry ... 107
Strydom, (Barend) Piet(er) 1946- ... 207
Stryjkowski, Julian 1905-1996 ... CANR-30
Obituary ... 153
Earlier sketches in CA 49-52, CANR-3
Stryk, Dan 1951- ... 120

Cumulative Index 561 Suckling

Stryk, Lucien 1924- CANR-110
Earlier sketches in CA 13-16R, CANR-10, 28, 55
See also CP 1, 2, 3, 4, 5, 6, 7
See also PC 27
Stryker, Daniel
See Morris, Chris(topher Crosby) and Stump, Jane Barr
Stryker, (Philip) David 1916- 45-48
Stryker, Perrin 1908-1988 .... 5-8R
Stryker, Sheldon 1924- 9-12R
Stryker-Rodda, Harriet 1905-1996 81-84
Stryker-Rodda, Kenn 1903-1990 73-76
Obituary 132
Stuart, Aimee 1886(?)-1981
Obituary 103
Stuart, Alex
See Stuart, (Violet) Vivian (Finlay)
Stuart, Alice V(andockum) 1899- 13-16R
Stuart, Anthony
See Hale, Julian A(nthony) S(tuart)
Stuart, Charles
See Mackinnon, Charles Roy and Reid, Charles (Stuart)
Stuart, Clay
See Whittington, Harry (Benjamin)
Stuart, Colin 1910-1990 104
Stuart, Dabney 1937- CANR-68
Earlier sketches in CA 17-20R, CANR-8
See also CP 1, 2, 3, 4, 5, 6, 7
See also CSW
See also DLB 105
Stuart, David
See Hoyt, Edwin P(almer), Jr.
Stuart, Derek
See Foster, John L(ouis)
Stuart, Don A.
See Campbell, John W(ood, Jr.)
Stuart, Douglas (Keith) 1943- 115
Stuart, Forbes 1924- 69-72
See also SATA 13
Stuart, Francis 1902-2000 .... CANR-44
Obituary 188
Earlier sketch in CA 13-16R
See also CN 2, 3, 4, 5, 6
Stuart, Gloria 1910- 192
Stuart, Graham H(enry) 1887-1983 .... CAP-1
Earlier sketch in CA 13-14
Stuart, Ian
See MacLean, Alistair (Stuart)
Stuart, Ian 1927-1993 .... CANR-30
Earlier sketches in CA 73-76, CANR-13
Stuart, Irving R. 1916- CANR-14
Earlier sketch in CA 41-44R
Stuart, (Jessica) Jane 1942- CANR-31
Earlier sketch in CA 41-44R
Stuart, Jay Allison
See Tait, Dorothy
Stuart, Jesse (Hilton) 1906-1984 .... CANR-31
Obituary 112
Earlier sketch in CA 5-8R
See also CLC 1, 8, 11, 14, 34
See also CN 1, 2, 3
See also DLB 9, 48, 102
See also DLBY 1984
See also SATA 2
See also SATA-Obit 36
See also SSC 31
Stuart, Kenneth
See Cox, P(atrick) Brian
Stuart, Leslie
See Marlowe, Kenneth
Stuart, Logan .... TCWW 2
Stuart, Lyle 1922- 81-84
Stuart, Margaret
See Paine, Lauran (Bosworth)
Stuart, Mary 1926-2002 228
Stuart, Matt
See Holmes, L(lewellyn) P(erry)
Stuart, Monroe
See Shapiro, Max
Stuart, Reginald (Charles) 1943- CANR-38
Earlier sketch in CA 116
Stuart, Richard Bernard 1933- 41-44R
Stuart, Ruth McEnery 1849(?)-1917 182
See also DLB 202
See also SATA 116
Stuart, Sally E(lizabeth) 1940- 152
Stuart, Sarah Payne 1952- 136
Stuart, Sebastian 194
Stuart, Sheila
See Baker, Mary Gladys Steel
Stuart, Sidney
See Avallone, Michael (Angelo, Jr.)
Stuart, Simon (Walter Erskine)
1930-2002 .... 29-32R
Stuart, V. A.
See Stuart, (Violet) Vivian (Finlay)
Stuart, Virginia (Elaine) 1953- 128
Stuart, (Violet) Vivian (Finlay)
1914-1986 .... CANR-12
Earlier sketch in CA 13-16R
See also RHW
Stuart, W. J.
See MacDonald, Philip
Stuart, Warren
See MacDonald, Philip
Stuart-Clark, Christopher (Anthony)
1940- CANR-24
Earlier sketch in CA 107
See also SATA 32
Stuart-Jones, Edwyn Henry 1895-(?) CAP-1
Earlier sketch in CA 13-16
Stub, Ambrosius 1705-1758 .... DLB 300
Stub, Holger R(ichard) 1922- 41-44R
Stubbings, Hilda Uren
See U'Ren-Stubbings, Hilda
Stubblebine, Donald J(ames) 1925- 139
Stubblebine, James H(arvey)
1920-1987 97-100
Obituary 121
Stubblefield, Harold W. 1934- 17-20R
Stubblefield, Sally
See Trumbo, Dalton
Stubbs, Harry C(lement) 1922-2003 . CANR-26
Obituary 224
Earlier sketches in CA 13-16R, CANR-7
See also Clement, Hal
See also SFW 4
Stubbs, Jean 1926- CANR-43
Earlier sketch in CA 5-8R
See also CMW 4
See also RHW
Stubbs, Joanna 1940- .... SATA-Brief 53
Stubbs, John C(aldwell) 1936- 29-32R
Stubbs, P(eter) C(harles) 1937- 117
Stuber, Florian (Cy) 1947- CANR-24
Earlier sketch in CA 106
Stuber, Stanley I(rving) 1903-1985 .... CANR-85
Obituary 116
Earlier sketches in CAP-1, CA 13-14
Stubis, Talivaldis 1926- .... SATA 5
Stubley, Trevor (Hugh) 1932- .... SATA 22
Stuckenberg, Viggo 1863-1905 .... DLB 300
Stuckenschmidt, H(ans) H(einz)
1901-1988 .... CANR-85
Obituary 126
Earlier sketches in CA 25-28R, CANR-18
Stuckey, Elma 1907(?)-1988
Obituary 126
Stuckey, Gilbert B. 1912-1995 65-68
Stuckey, Peter J(ames) 1963- 171
Stuckey, Sterling 1932- 101
Stuckey, William Joseph 1923- 41-44R
Stuckey-French, Elizabeth 219
Stucki, Curtis W(illiam) 1928- 13-16R
Stucky, Naomi R. 1922- .... SATA 72
Stucky, Solomon 1923-1988 117
Obituary 140
Stucky, Steven 1949- 109
Stucley, Elizabeth
See Northmore, Elizabeth Florence
Studd, Stephen (Allen) 1946- CANR-91
Earlier sketch in CA 116
Studdert-Kennedy, (William) Gerald
1933- CANR-90
Earlier sketch in CA 131
Studebaker, J. W.
See Studebaker, John W(ard)
Studebaker, John W(ard) 1887-1989
Obituary 129
Studebaker, William V. 1947- .... DLB 256
Studer, Gerald C. 1927- 65-68
Studlar, Donley T(rent) 1947- 120
Studlar, Gaylyn 237
Studwell, William E. 1936- CANR-113
Earlier sketch in CA 152
Stueart, Robert D. 1935- 105
Stuebing, (Arthur) Douglas 1913-1995 .. 25-28R
Stueck, William Whitney, Jr. 1945- 105
Stuempke, Harald
See Steiner, Gerolf
Stuermann, Walter E(arl) 1919-1965 .... 5-8R
Stuermer, Nina Roberta 1933- 104
Stuerup, Georg Kristoffer 1905- 25-28R
Stuetzle, Walther 1941- 147
Stuever, Hank 1969(?)- 232
Stuewe, Paul 1943- 130
Stuhlmann, Gunther (Andrew)
1927- CANR-44
Earlier sketch in CA 25-28R
Stuhlmueller, Carroll 1923-1994 ...... CANR-24
Obituary 144
Earlier sketches in CA 13-16R, CANR-9
Stuhr(-Rommereim), Rebecca (Ann)
1958- CANR-125
Earlier sketch in CA 168
Stukas, David 239
Stulman, Julius 1906-1997 118
Stultifer, Morton
See Curtis, Richard (Alan)
Stultz, Newell M(aynard) 1933- 29-32R
Stump, Al(vin J.) 1916-1995 .... CANR-127
Earlier sketch in CA 149
See also DLB 241
Stump, Jane Barr 1936- 133
Stumpf, Bill
See Stumpf, William E.
Stumpf, Samuel Enoch 1918-1998 .... 41-44R
Stumpf, Stephen A(lan) 1949- CANR-34
Earlier sketch in CA 111
Stumpf, William E. 1936- 171
Stumpke, Harald
See Steiner, Gerolf
Stunkard, Albert J(ames) 1922- 117
Stunkel, Kenneth Reagan 1931- 127
Stuntz, Albert Edward 1902-1976
Obituary 65-68
Stuntz, Laurance F(itzhugh) 1908-1993 ... 61-64
Stupak, Ronald J(oseph) 1934- 29-32R
Stupples, Peter (Cecil) 1936- 133
Strucken, Frank 1929- 135
Sturdivant, Frederick D(avid) 1937- 41-44R
Sturdy, Carl
See Strong, Charles S(tanley)
Sture-Vasa, Mary
See Alsop, Mary O'Hara
Sturgeon, Foolbert
See Stack, Frank H(untington)
Sturgeon, Theodore (Hamilton)
1918-1985 .... CANR-103
Obituary 116
Earlier sketches in CA 81-84, CANR-32
See also Queen, Ellery
See also AAYA 51
See also BPFB 3
See also BYA 9, 10
See also CLC 22, 39
See also DLB 8
See also DLBY 1985
See also HGG
See also MTCW 1, 2
See also MTFW 2005
See also SCFW
See also SFW 4
See also SUFW
Sturgeon, Wina 85-88
Sturges, Patricia P(atterson) 1930- 69-72
Sturges, Preston 1898-1959 149
Brief entry 114
See also DLB 26
See also TCLC 48
Sturges, Robert S(tuart) 1953- CANR-97
Earlier sketch in CA 138
Sturgess, Philip J. M. 1946- 141
Sturgill, Claude C(arol) 1933- CANR-9
Earlier sketch in CA 13-16R
Sturgis, Ingrid 239
Sturgis, James L(averne) 1936- 37-40R
Sturm, Douglas E. 1929- CANR-93
Earlier sketch in CA 145
Sturm, Ernest 1932- 65-68
Sturm, James 1965- 214
Sturm, John E. 1927- 37-40R
Sturm, Rudolf 1912-2000
Brief entry 109
Sturm, Sara
See Sturm-Maddox, Sara Higgins
Sturmer, Michael 1938- CANR-125
Earlier sketch in CA 169
Sturmey, S(tanley) G(eorge) 1924- 9-12R
Sturm-Maddox, Sara Higgins 1938-
Brief entry 108
Sturmthal, Adolf F(ox) 1903-1986 .... CANR-86
Obituary 119
Earlier sketch in CA 9-12R
Sturrock, Jeremy
See Healey, Ben (James)
Sturrock, John 183
Sturrock, Peter A(ndrew) 1924- 189
Stursberg, Peter 1913- 101
Sturt, Mary 1896- CAP-2
Earlier sketch in CA 23-24
Sturtevant, A(lfred) H(enry) 1891-1970 158
Sturtevant, Catherine (?)-1970
Obituary 104
Sturtevant, David Reeves 1926- 104
Sturtevant, Katherine 1950- 199
See also SATA 130
Sturtevant, Peter M(ann), Jr. 1943- 69-72
Sturton, Hugh
See Johnston, H(ugh) A(nthony) S(tephen)
Sturtzel, Howard A(llison)
1894-1985 .... CANR-70
Earlier sketches in CA 1-4R, CANR-6
See also SATA 1
Sturtzel, Jane Levington 1903-1996 .... CANR-6
Earlier sketch in CA 1-4R
See also SATA 1
Sturup, Georg Kristoffer
See Stuerup, Georg Kristoffer
Stus, Vasyl 1938-1985 .... EWL 3
Stutler, Boyd B. 1889-1970 .... CAP-2
Earlier sketch in CA 23-24
Stutley, D(oris) J(ean) 1959- 213
See also SATA 142
Stutley, Margaret 1917- 228
Stutson, Caroline 1940- CANR-134
Earlier sketch in CA 171
See also SATA 104
Stutz, Bruce 1950- 139
Stutz, Robert Michael 1941-
Brief entry 110
Stutzle, Walther
See Stuetzle, Walther
Stutzman, Christian
See Mallett, Daryl F(urumi)
Stutzman, Linford L. 1950- 139
Stuve-Bodeen, Stephanie 1965- CANR-143
Earlier sketch in CA 179
See also SATA 114, 158
Stux, Erica 1929- 211
See also SATA 140
Styan, J(ohn) L(ouis) 1923-2002 .... CANR-6
Obituary 214
Earlier sketch in CA 5-8R
Stych, F(ranklin) S(amuel) 1916- 176
Stychin, Carl F. 1964- CANR-125
Earlier sketch in CA 162
Stycos, J(oseph) Mayone 1927- 13-16R
Style, Colin Thomas Elliot 1937- .... CP 1
Styles, Jimmie C(arter) 1931- 41-44R
Styles, (Frank) Showell 1908- CANR-60
Earlier sketches in CA 1-4R, CANR-6, 21
See also CMW 4
See also SATA 10
Stylla, Joanne
See Branden, Victoria (Fremlin)
Stynes, Barbara White 202
See also SATA 133
Styron, Alexandra 1966- 217
Styron, Rose (Burgunder) 1928- 17-20R
Styron, William 1925- CANR-126
Earlier sketches in CA 5-8R, CANR-6, 33, 74
Interview in CANR-6
See also AMW
See also AMWC 2
See also BEST 90:4
See also BPFB 3
See also CDALB 1968-1988
See also CLC 1, 3, 5, 11, 15, 60
See also CN 1, 2, 3, 4, 5, 6, 7
See also CPW
See also CSW
See also DA3
See also DAM NOV, POP
See also DLB 2, 143, 299
See also DLBY 1980
See also EWL 3
See also LAIT 2
See also MAL 5
See also MTCW 1, 2
See also MTFW 2005
See also NCFS 1
See also NFS 22
See also RGAL 4
See also RHW
See also SSC 25
See also TUS
Styx, Marguerite (Salzer) 1908(?)-1975
Obituary 53-56
Su, Chien 1884-1918
Brief entry 123
See also Su Man-shu
Su, Louis
See Kaufman, Lloyd
Suard, Jean-Baptiste-Antoine
1732-1817 .... DLB 314
Suares, Guy 1932- 103
Suarez, Clementina
See Suarez, Clementina
See also DLB 290
Suarez, Clementina 1902-1991
See Suarez, Clementina
See also EWL 3
Suarez, Ignacio Padilla
See Padilla, Ignacio
Suarez, Mario 1925- .... DLB 82
Suarez, Ray 1957- 193
Suarez, Virgil 1962- CANR-87
Earlier sketch in CA 131
See also Suarez, Virgilio
See also HW 1
Suarez, Virgilio
See Suarez, Virgil
See also LLW
Suarez Lynch, B.
See Bioy Casares, Adolfo and Borges, Jorge Luis
Suassuna, Ariano Vilar 1927- 178
See also DLB 307
See also HLCS 1
See also HW 2
See also LAW
Suba, Susanne 29-32R
See also SATA 4
Subak-Sharpe, Genell J(ackson)
1936- CANR-31
Earlier sketch in CA 112
Subbiah, B(ommireddi) V(enkata)
1917-1975 .... 41-44R
Subilia, Vittorio 1911-1988 .... CANR-4
Earlier sketch in CA 9-12R
Sublette, C(lifford) M(acClellan)
1887-1939 .... TCWW 1, 2
Sublette, Edith Blanche 1909- 17-20R
Sublette, Ned 1951- 238
Sublette, Walter (Edwards) 1940- ... CANR-107
Brief entry 117
Earlier sketch in CA 124
Subond, Valerie
See Grayland, Valerie (Merle Spanner)
Subotnik, Rena F. 1948- CANR-110
Earlier sketch in CA 153
Subrahmanyam, Sanjay 216
Such, David G. 1954- 154
Such, Peter 1939- 182
See also DLB 60
Sucharitkul, Somtow 1952- CANR-51
Earlier sketch in CA 118
See also Somtow, S. P.
See also HGG
See also SFW 4
Sucher, Dorothy 1933- 128
Sucher, Harry V(ictor) 1915- 89-92
Suchlicki, Jaime 1939- CANR-53
Earlier sketches in CA 29-32R, CANR-29
Suchman, Edward A(llen) 1915-1970(?) . CAP-1
Earlier sketch in CA 13-14
Suchocki, Marjorie Hewitt 1933- 109
Suchoff, Benjamin 1918- CANR-11
Earlier sketch in CA 69-72
Suchting, W. A. 1931- 142
Suckert, Kurt Erich
See Malaparte, Curzio
Suckiel, Ellen Kappy 1943- CANR-55
Earlier sketch in CA 127
Suckling, Sir John 1609-1642 .... BRW 2
See also DAM POET
See also DLB 58, 126
See also EXPP
See also FAB
See also PC 30
See also RGEL 2

Suckow, Ruth 1892-1960 193
Obituary 113
See also DLB 9, 102
See also RGAL 4
See also SSC 18
See also TCWW 2
Sucre, Guillermo 1933- .... HW 1
Suda, Issei 1940- 206
Suda, Zdenek (Ludvik) 1920- CANR-31
Earlier sketch in CA 29-32R
Sudbery, Rodie 1943- 104
See also CWRI 5
See also SATA 42
Sudek, Josef 1896-1976 205
Sudermann, Hermann 1857-1928 201
Brief entry 107
See also DLB 118
See also TCLC 15
Sudhalter, Richard M(errill) 1938- CANR-88
Earlier sketch in CA 101
Sudjic, Deyan 1952- 173
Sudman, Seymour 1928-2000 .... CANR-15
Obituary 188
Earlier sketch in CA 41-44R
Sue, Eugene 1804-1857 .... DLB 119
Sue, Judy
See Epstein, Judith Sue
Sue, Marie-Joseph 1804-1857 . GFL 1789 to the Present
Suedfeld, Peter 1935- 41-44R
Suelflow, August R(obert) 1922- 9-12R
Sueltz, Arthur Fay 1928- CANR-2
Earlier sketch in CA 49-52
Suen, Anastasia 1956(?)- 235
See also SATA 157
Suenens, Leon Joseph 1904-1996 61-64
Obituary 152
Sueskind, Patrick 1949-
See Suskind, Patrick
See also CLC 44, 182
Suetonius
See Morris, Roger
Suetonius c. 70-c. 130 .... AW 2
See also DLB 211
See also RGWL 2, 3
Sueyoshi, Akiko 1942- 132
Suffling, Mark
See Rowland, D(onald) S(ydney)
Sufrin, Mark 1925- 143
See also SATA 76
Sufrin, Sidney Charles 1910-1997 .... CANR-17
Obituary 159
Earlier sketches in CA 5-8R, CANR-2
Sugano, Takuo 1931- CANR-51
Earlier sketch in CA 123
Sugar, Bert Randolph 1937- CANR-9
Earlier sketch in CA 65-68
Sugarman, Daniel A(rthur) 1931- 21-24R
Sugarman, Joan G. 1917- .... SATA 64
Sugarman, Karlene A. 1969- 168
Sugarman, Tracy 1921- CANR-100
Earlier sketch in CA 21-24R
See also SATA 37
Sugden, John 1947- CANR-90
Earlier sketches in CA 120, CANR-51
Sugden, Mark 1902-1990 .... CAP-1
Obituary 130
Earlier sketch in CA 13-14
Sugerman, Danny 1954-2005 137
Obituary 235
Sugerman, Shirley 1919- 65-68
Sugg, Joyce (Marie) 1926- 131
Sugg, Redding S(tancill), Jr. 1922- CANR-2
Earlier sketch in CA 45-48
Sugg, Richard P(eter) 1941- CANR-93
Earlier sketch in CA 131
Suggs, George G(raham), Jr. 1929- . CANR-141
Earlier sketch in CA 41-44R
Suggs, M(arion) Jack 1924- CANR-3
Earlier sketch in CA 1-4R
Suggs, Robert Carl 1932- 9-12R
Suggs, Willie Kathryn 1950- 77-80
Sugihara, Seishiro 1941- 221
Sugimoto, Yoshio 1939- 130
Sugita, Yutaka 1930- 115
See also SATA 36
Sugiyama, Shinya 1949- CANR-90
Earlier sketch in CA 132
Sugnet, Charles (Joseph) 1944- 109
Sugrue, Thomas J(oseph) 1962- 188
Suh, Dae-Sook 1931- 21-24R
Suhl, Benjamin 49-52
Suhl, Yuri (Menachem) 1908-1986 ... CANR-38
Obituary 121
Earlier sketches in CA 45-48, CANR-2
See also CLR 2
See also MAICYA 1, 2
See also SAAS 1
See also SATA 8
See also SATA-Obit 50
Suhor, Charles 1935- CANR-142
Earlier sketches in CA 25-28R, CANR-10
Suhr, Elmer George 1902-1976 .... 9-12R
Obituary 65-68
Suhr, Joanne .... SATA 129
Su Hsuan-ying
See Su, Chien
Su Hsuean-ying
See Su, Chien
Suid, Lawrence Howard 1938- 101
Suid, Murray 1942- CANR-30
Earlier sketch in CA 97-100
See also SATA 27
Suinn, Richard M(ichael) 1933- 29-32R
Suits, Daniel B(urbidge) 1918- 29-32R
Suits, Gustav 1883-1956 .... CDWLB 4
See also DLB 220
Sujata, Anagarika 1948- 65-68
Suk, Julie CANR-38
Earlier sketch in CA 115
Sukarno, (Ahmed) 1901-1970
Obituary 113
Sukenick, Ronald 1932-2004 209
Obituary 229
Earlier sketches in CA 25-28R, CANR-32, 89
Autobiographical Essay in 209
See also CAAS 8
See also CLC 3, 4, 6, 48
See also CN 3, 4, 5, 6, 7
See also DLB 173
See also DLBY 1981
Sukhotin-Tolstoy, Tatyana
See Tolstoy, Tatyana (Sukhotin)
Sukhovo-Kobylin, Aleksandr Vasil'evich 1817-1903 .... DLB 277
Sukhwal, Bheru Lal 1929- 57-60
Sukiennik, Adelaide Weir 1938- 126
Suknaski, Andrew 1942- 101
See also CLC 19
See also CP 7
See also DLB 53
Sulayman, Muhammad ibn c. 1480-1556
See Fuzuli
Suleiman, Ezra N. 1941- 85-88
Suleiman, Michael W(adie) 1934- CANR-42
Earlier sketches in CA 21-24R, CANR-9
Suleiman, Susan Rubin CANR-28
Earlier sketch in CA 109
Suleri, Sara 1953- 136
Suleski, Ronald (Stanley) 1942- 220
Sulimirski, Tadeusz Joseph 1898-1983
Obituary 110
Sulitzer, Paul-Loup 1946- 126
Brief entry 122
Sulkin, Sidney 1918-1995 .... CANR-17
Obituary 149
Earlier sketches in CA 5-8R, CANR-2
Sullens, Idelle 1921-1997 .... 21-24R
Sullivan, A(loysius) M(ichael) 1896-1980 .... CAP-2
Obituary 97-100
Earlier sketch in CA 29-32
Sullivan, Alan 1868-1947 .... DLB 92
Sullivan, (Edward) Alan 1868-1947 .... CANR-103
Earlier sketch in CA 162
Sullivan, Alvin 1942-1991 .... 29-32R
Sullivan, Andrew 1963- 154
Sullivan, Anita T. 1942- 123
Sullivan, Barry
See Sullivan, Matthew Barry
Sullivan, Brad 1961- 199
Sullivan, Brian R. 1945- 141
Sullivan, C(harles) Gardner 1886(?)-1965 ... 196
Obituary 113
See also DLB 26
See also IDFW 3, 4
Sullivan, C(harles) W(illiam) III 1944- CANR-119
Earlier sketch in CA 139
Sullivan, Caroline 1958- 203
Sullivan, Chester L(amar) 1939- 53-56
Sullivan, Clara K(atherine) 1915- 21-24R
Sullivan, Claudia 1950- 193
Sullivan, Colleen (M.) 1950-1991 117
Obituary 133
Sullivan, D(ale) H(owill) 1936- 61-64
Sullivan, Dan(iel Joseph) 1935- 135
Sullivan, David 1942- 176
Sullivan, Dean A(lan) 1963- CANR-142
Earlier sketch in CA 156
Sullivan, Denis G(artland) 1929- 103
Sullivan, Dolores P. 1925- 148
Sullivan, Donald 1942(?)-1989
Obituary 130
Sullivan, Dulcie Turner 1895-1969 .... CAP-2
Earlier sketch in CA 25-28
Sullivan, Earl L. 1942- 124
Sullivan, Ed(ward Vincent) 1902(?)-1974
Obituary 89-92
Sullivan, Edmund V(incent) 1938- 61-64
Sullivan, Edward A(nthony) 1936- 115
Sullivan, Edward Daniel 1913-1995 .... 5-8R
Obituary 150
Sullivan, Eleanor (Regis) 1928-1991 139
Brief entry 112
Sullivan, Elizabeth L. 1904(?)-1985
Obituary 115
Sullivan, Evelin 1947- CANR-112
Earlier sketch in CA 142
Sullivan, Faith 1933- 134
Sullivan, Francis (Patrick) 1929- CANR-7
Earlier sketch in CA 57-60
Sullivan, Francis John 1892-1976 .... CAP-2
Obituary 65-68
Earlier sketch in CA 25-28
See also Sullivan, Frank
Sullivan, Frank
See Sullivan, Francis John
See also DLB 11
Sullivan, Frank 1912-1975 65-68
Obituary 61-64
Sullivan, Garrett A., Jr. 231
Sullivan, George (Edward) 1927- CANR-130
Earlier sketches in CA 13-16R, CANR-44
See also SATA 4, 89, 147
Sullivan, Henry W(ells) 1942- 149
Sullivan, J(ohn) P(atrick) 1930-1993 . CANR-26
Earlier sketches in CA 25-28R, CANR-10
Sullivan, Jack 1946- 119
Sullivan, James L(enox) 1910- 29-32R
Sullivan, Jerry (Martin) 1938-2000 115
Obituary 191
Sullivan, Jody
See Rake, Jody
Sullivan, John F. 1939- 222
Sullivan, John Jeremiah 1974- 235
Sullivan, John L. 1908- 21-24R
Sullivan, Judy 1936- 53-56
See also AITN 1
Sullivan, Kathryn A. 1954- 212
See also SATA 141
Sullivan, Kevin 228
Sullivan, Kevin 1918(?)-1987 .... CANR-34
Obituary 122
Earlier sketch in CA 1-4R
Sullivan, Larry E. 1944- 136
Sullivan, Louis (Henry) 1856-1924 184
Sullivan, Louis (Graydon) 1951- 134
Sullivan, M(ichael) J(ustin) 1940- 142
Sullivan, Marion F. 1899-1992 .... 37-40R
Sullivan, Mark J. III 228
Sullivan, Mark T. 1958- 198
Sullivan, Mark W(ilbur) 1927- 25-28R
Sullivan, Martin (Gloster) 1910-1980 107
Obituary 104
Sullivan, Martin (Richard Preece) 1934- 29-32R
Sullivan, Mary Ann 1954- 125
See also SATA 63
Sullivan, Mary B(arrett) 1918- 13-16R
Sullivan, Mary W(ilson) 1907- CANR-12
Earlier sketch in CA 73-76
See also SATA 13
Sullivan, Matthew Barry 1915-1997 132
Sullivan, Maurice William 1925- CANR-2
Earlier sketch in CA 5-8R
Sullivan, (Donovan) Michael 1916- CANR-3
Earlier sketch in CA 5-8R
Sullivan, Michael B. 1938-2000 77-80
Sullivan, Michael J(oseph III) 1941- 175
Sullivan, Nancy 1929- 17-20R
Sullivan, Navin 1929- 5-8R
Sullivan, Noelle 1965- 185
Sullivan, Otha Richard 1941- CANR-126
Earlier sketch in CA 170
See also BW 3
Sullivan, Pat
See Messmer, Otto
Sullivan, Paul 1939- 176
See also SATA 106
Sullivan, Paul (Robert) 1951- 133
Sullivan, Peggy (Anne) 1929- CANR-12
Earlier sketch in CA 29-32R
Sullivan, Prescott 1904(?)-1985
Obituary 116
Sullivan, Randall 1951- CANR-123
Earlier sketch in CA 154
Sullivan, Reese
See Lutz, Giles A(lfred)
Sullivan, Richard 1908-1981 77-80
Obituary 104
Sullivan, Richard E(ugene) 1921-
Brief entry 115
Sullivan, Robert E(rtel) 1947- 135
Sullivan, Roger J. 1928- CANR-90
Earlier sketch in CA 132
Sullivan, Rosemary 1947- CANR-114
Earlier sketches in CA 97-100, CANR-54
Sullivan, Ruth Christ 1924- 57-60
Sullivan, Sean Mei
See Sohl, Jerry
Sullivan, Sheila 1927- CANR-14
Earlier sketch in CA 77-80
Sullivan, Silky
See Makowski, Silvia Ann
Sullivan, Sister Bede 1915- 25-28R
Sullivan, Stanislaus 1930- 127
Sullivan, Steve (Joseph) 1954- 234
Sullivan, Sue
See Sullivan, Susan E.
Sullivan, Susan E. 1962- .... SATA 123
Sullivan, Thomas (William) 1940- 127
Sullivan, Thomas Joseph, Jr. 1947- 81-84
See also SATA 16
Sullivan, Tom
See Sullivan, Thomas Joseph, Jr.
Sullivan, Tony
See Sullivan, Stanislaus
Sullivan, Tricia 1968- 196
Sullivan, Vernon
See Vian, Boris
Sullivan, Victoria 1943- 65-68
Sullivan, Vincent F. 1899-1983 .... CAP-2
Earlier sketch in CA 29-32
Sullivan, Walter 1906- 13-16R
Sullivan, Walter (Laurence) 1924- .. CANR-106
Earlier sketch in CA 41-44R
Sullivan, Walter Seager 1918-1996 .... CANR-2
Obituary 151
Earlier sketch in CA 1-4R
Sullivan, William H(ealy) 1922- 133
Sullivan, William M. 1945- CANR-43
Earlier sketch in CA 109
Sullivan, Winona 1942- 141
Sullivan Harper, Akiba
See Sullivan Harper, Donna Akiba
Sullivan Harper, Donna Akiba 1954- CANR-87
Earlier sketch in CA 151
Sullivant, Robert S(cott) 1925- 1-4R
Sulloway, Alison G. 1917-
Brief entry 111
Sulloway, Frank J(ones) 1947- 124
Brief entry 118
Interview in CA-124
Sullum, Jacob (Z.) 1965- 239
Sully, (Lionel Henry) Francois 1927-1971 .... CAP-2
Obituary 29-32R
Earlier sketch in CA 25-28
Sully, Kathleen M. 1910- 13-16R
Sully, Nina (Rosemary) 1948- 110
Sully, Tom 1959- .... SATA 104
Sully Prudhomme, Rene-Francois-Armand 1839-1907 .... GFL 1789 to the Present
See also TCLC 31
Sulmasy, Daniel P. 1956- 170
Sulston, John (Edward) 1942- 227
Sultan, Alan 1948- 145
Sultan, Arne 1925-1986
Obituary 118
Sultan, Stanley 1928- CANR-93
Earlier sketches in CA 13-16R, CANR-10, 26
Sultana, Donald Edward 1924- 103
Sulte, Benjamin 1841-1923 179
See also DLB 99
Sulzberger, Arthur Hays 1891-1968
Obituary 89-92
See also DLB 127
Sulzberger, Arthur Ochs 1926- 182
See also DLB 127
Sulzberger, C(yrus) L(eo II) 1912-1993 .... CANR-23
Obituary 142
Earlier sketches in CA 53-56, CANR-7
Sulzberger, Iphigene (Bertha) Ochs 1892-1990
Obituary 131
Sulzberger, Marina Tatiana 1919(?)-1976
Obituary 111
Sum, Ngai-Ling 1952- 146
Su Man-shu
See Su, Chien
See also EWL 3
See also TCLC 24
Sumariwalla, Russy D(inshaw) 1934- 196
Sumarokov, Aleksandr Petrovich 1717-1777 .... DLB 150
Sumarsam 1944- 159
Sumichrast, Jozef 1948- .... SATA 29
Sumichrast, Michael M. 1921- CANR-21
Earlier sketch in CA 104
Sumida, Jon Tetsuro 1949- 124
Sumii, Sue 1902-1997 192
Sumiko
See Davies, Sumiko
Summer, Brian
See Du Breuil, (Elizabeth) L(or)inda
Summer, Charles Edgar 1923- 81-84
Summer, Jane 1954- 219
Summer, Lauralee 1976- 225
Summerfield, Harry L. 1940- 37-40R
Summerfield, Jack
See Summerfield, John D(udley)
Summerfield, Joanne 1940- 117
Summerfield, John D(udley) 1927- 21-24R
Summerfield, Lin(da Victoria) 1952- 132
Summerfield, Margie 1949- 89-92
Summerfield, Penny 1951- 119
Summerforest, Ivy B.
See Kirkup, James
Summerhawk, Barbara 1946- 203
Summerhayes, Victor Samuel 1897(?)-1974
Obituary 53-56
Summerhill, J. K.
See Schere, Monroe
Summerlin, Sam(uel A.) 1928- CANR-34
Earlier sketch in CA 45-48
Summerlin, Vernon CANR-124
Earlier sketch in CA 168
Summers, Andrew James 1942- .... CLC 26
Summers, Andy
See Summers, Andrew James
Summers, Anthony (Bruce) 1942- ... CANR-103
Earlier sketches in CA 69-72, CANR-23
Summers, Bre L. 1969- 190
Summers, Clyde Wilson 1918- 109
Summers, D. B.
See Barrett, Geoffrey John
Summers, Dennis
See Barrett, Geoffrey John
Summers, Essie
See Summers, Ethel Snelson
Summers, Ethel Snelson 1912-1998
Brief entry 116
See also RHW
Summers, Festus P(aul) 1895-1971 .... CAP-1
Earlier sketch in CA 11-12
Summers, Gene F(ranklin) 1936- CANR-12
Earlier sketch in CA 29-32R
Summers, Gordon
See Hornby, John (Wilkinson)
Summers, Hal
See Summers, Henry Forbes
See also CP 1
Summers, Harrison B(oyd) 1894-1980 .. 13-16R
Summers, Harry G(lenn), Jr. 1932-1999 123
Obituary 186
Summers, Henry Forbes 1911- 109
See also Summers, Hal
Summers, Hollis (Spurgeon, Jr.) 1916- CANR-3
Earlier sketch in CA 5-8R
See also CLC 10
See also CN 1, 2, 3
See also CP 1, 2
See also DLB 6
See also TCLE 1:2
Summers, Ian 1939- 105
Summers, James L(evingston) 1910-1973 .... 13-16R
See also SATA 57
See also SATA-Brief 28
Summers, JoAn 1943- 106

Cumulative Index 563 **Sutton**

Summers, John A.
See Lawson, H(orace) L(owe)
Summers, Joseph H(olmes) 1920-2003 . 41-44R
Obituary ... 214
Summers, Lionel M(organ) 1905-1975 45-48
Obituary ... 103
Summers, Marc ... 209
Summers, Merna 1933- ... 131
Summers, (Alphonsus Joseph-Mary Augustus) Montague 1880-1948 ... 163
Brief entry ... 118
See also TCLC 16
Summers, Ray 1910-1992 ... 13-16R
Summers, Robert 1922- ... 77-80
Summers, Robert E. 1918- ... 25-28R
Summers, Robert S(amuel) 1933- ... CANR-11
Earlier sketch in CA 69-72
Summers, Rowena
See Saunders, Jean
Summerscale, Kate 1965- ... 170
Summerscales, William 1921- ... 29-32R
Summersell, Charles Grayson 1908-1987 ... CANR-19
Earlier sketches in CA 1-4R, CANR-3
Summerskill, Edith 1901-1980
Obituary ... 93-96
Summerson, John (Newenham) 1904-1992
Brief entry ... 117
Summerson, Rachel (Elizabeth) 1944- ... 107
Summerton, Margaret ... RHW
Summertree, Katonah
See Windsor, Patricia
Summerville, James 1947- ... CANR-45
Earlier sketch in CA 119
Sumner, Charles 1811-1874 ... DLB 235
Sumner, Cid Ricketts 1890-1970 ... 5-8R
Obituary ... 29-32R
Sumner, Colin 1949- ... 111
Sumner, David (W. K.) 1937- ... 57-60
Sumner, David E. 1946- ... 163
Sumner, Eldon
See Bruno, James Edward
Sumner, Gordon Matthew
See Police, The and Sting
See also CLC 26
Sumner, Judith H. 1951- ... 213
Sumner, Lloyd Quinton 1943- ... 103
Sumner, Mark (C.) ... 235
Sumner, Melanie 1964(?)- ... 220
Sumner, Richard (William) 1949- ... 69-72
Sumner, William Graham 1840-1910 ... 216
See also DLB 270
Sumption, Jonathan (Philip Chadwick) 1948- ... CANR-100
Earlier sketch in CA 136
Sumrall, Amber Coverdale 1945- ... 147
Sumwalt, Martha Murray 1924- ... 69-72
Sun, Annalise
See Maxwell, Ann (Elizabeth)
Sun, Chyng Feng 1959- ... 155
See also SATA 90
Sun, Ruth Q(uinlan) 1907- ... 57-60
Sun, Yifeng
See Sun Yifeng
Sunagel, Lois A(nn) 1926- ... 93-96
Sund, Robert B(ruce) 1926- ... CANR-36
Earlier sketch in CA 29-32R
Sundahl, Daniel James 1947- ... 146
Sundarananda
See Nakashima, George Katsutoshi
Sundaresan, Indu ... 219
Sunday, Billy
See Sunday, William Ashley
Sunday, William Ashley 1862(?)-1935
Brief entry ... 120
Sundberg, Trudy James 1925- ... 17-20R
Sundbo, Jon 1945- ... 220
Sunde, Karen 1942- ... CANR-144
Earlier sketch in CA 172
See also CAD
See also CD 5, 6
See also CWD
Sundeen, Mark 1970- ... 227
Sundell, Roger H(enry) 1936- ... 21-24R
Sundelson, David 1946- ... 152
Sunder, Shyam 1944- ... 118
Sunderland, Eric 1930- ... CANR-21
Earlier sketch in CA 103
Sunderland, Glenn W. 1925- ... 25-28R
Sunderland, Lane V(on) 1945- ... 97-100
Sunderlin, Sylvia (S.) 1911-1997 ... 73-76
Obituary ... 162
See also SATA 28
See also SATA-Obit 99
Sunderman, James F. 1919- ... 17-20R
Sunderman, Lloyd Frederick 1905-1983
Obituary ... 109
Sundgaard, Arnold (Olaf) 1909- ... CANR-2
Earlier sketch in CA 45-48
Sundiata, Ibrahim K. 1944- ... CANR-87
Earlier sketch in CA 158
Sundman, Per Olof 1922-1992
Brief entry ... 111
See also DLB 257
See also EWL 3
Sundquist, Eric J. 1952- ... 129
Sundquist, James L(loyd) 1915- ... 29-32R
Sundquist, Ralph Roger, Jr. 1922-
Brief entry ... 106
Sung, Betty Lee ... CANR-10
Earlier sketch in CA 25-28R
See also SATA 26
Sung, P. M.
See Chun, Jinsie K(yung) S(hien)
Sungolowsky, Joseph 1931- ... CANR-97
Earlier sketch in CA 41-44R
Sunley, Margaret 1921-1990 ... 134
Sunners, William 1903-1988 ... CANR-85
Obituary ... 125
Earlier sketches in CAP-1, CA 9-10
Sunoo, Harold Hak-Won 1918- ... 41-44R
Sunseri, Alvin R(aymond) 1925- ... 93-96
Sunshine, John 1897(?)-1987
Obituary ... 123
Sunshine, Linda 1948- ... 154
Sunstein, Cass R. 1954- ... 172
Sunstein, Emily W(eisberg) 1924- ... 53-56
Suntree, Susan 1946- ... 213
Suny, Ronald Grigor 1940- ... CANR-55
Earlier sketches in CA 111, CANR-29
Sun Yat-sen, Madame
See Soong, Ching-ling
Sun Yefang 1908-1983
Obituary ... 109
Sun Yifeng ... 226
Suomi, Verner E(dward) 1915-1995 ... 161
Suonio, Aino
See Kallas, Aino (Julia Maria)
Supeene, Shelagh Lynne 1952- ... 228
See also SATA 153
Super, Donald E(dwin) 1910-1994 ... CANR-3
Earlier sketch in CA 1-4R
Super, R(obert) H(enry) 1914-1996 ... 13-16R
Super Santa
See Berman, Ed
Supervielle, Jules 1884-1960
Obituary ... 114
See also DLB 258
See also EWL 3
See also GFL 1789 to the Present
Suponev, Michael 1923- ... 65-68
Suppe, Frederick (Roy) 1940- ... 41-44R
Suppes, Patrick 1922- ... CANR-42
Earlier sketches in CA 1-4R, CANR-4, 20
Suppon, Charles 1949-1989
Obituary ... 128
Supraner, Robyn 1930- ... CANR-51
Earlier sketches in CA 69-72, CANR-26
See also SATA 20, 101
Supree, Burt(on) 1941-1992 ... 65-68
Obituary ... 137
See also SATA 73
Surace, Samuel J. 1919- ... 21-24R
Suran, Bernard G(regory) 1939- ... 81-84
Suran, Mark
See Serandrei, Mario
Suransky, Valerie Polakow
See Polakow, Valerie (Suransky)
Surdas 15th cent. - ... RGWL 2, 3
Suret-Canale, Jean 1921- ... CANR-1
Earlier sketch in CA 49-52
Surette, (Philip) Leon 1938- ... 110
Surface, Bill
See Surface, William E.
Surface, Mary Hall 1958- ... 197
See also SATA 126
Surface, William E. 1935-1980(?) ... CANR-13
Earlier sketch in CA 5-8R
Surge, Frank 1931- ... 69-72
See also SATA 13
Suri, Manil 1959- ... 190
Suria, Violeta Lopez
See Lopez Suria, Violeta
Surkin, Marvin 1938- ... 61-64
Surkov, Alexei Aleksandrovich 1899-1983
Obituary ... 110
Surles, Lynn 1917- ... 13-16R
Surman, Charles Edward 1901- ... 5-8R
Surmelian, Leon (Zaven) 1907- ... CAP-2
Earlier sketch in CA 25-28
Surowiecki, James (Michael) 1967- ... 227
Surplus, Robert W. 1923- ... 5-8R
Surrey, Henry Howard 1517-1574 ... BRW 1
See also PC 59
See also RGEL 2
Surrey, (Arthur) John 1933- ... 117
Surrey, Peter J. 1928- ... 106
Surrey, Richard
See Brooker, Bertram (Richard)
Surrey, Stanley Sterling 1910-1984
Obituary ... 113
Surtees, Robert L. 1906-1985 ... IDFW 3, 4
Surtees, Robert Smith 1805-1864 ... DLB 21
See also RGEL 2
Surtz, Edward 1910(?)-1973
Obituary ... 41-44R
Survant, Joe 1942- ... 191
Susac, Andrew 1929- ... 49-52
See also SATA 5
Susan
See Graham, (Maude Fitzgerald) Susan
Susanka, Sarah 1957- ... 196
Susann, Jacqueline 1921-1974 ... 65-68
Obituary ... 53-56
See also AITN 1
See also BPFB 3
See also CLC 3
See also MTCW 1, 2
Susanna (i Nadal), Alex 1957- ... 208
Su Shi
See Su Shih
See also RGWL 2, 3
Su Shih 1036-1101
See Su Shi
Susi, Geraldine Lee 1942- ... 165
See also SATA 98
Suskind, Patrick ... 145
See also Sueskind, Patrick
See also BPFB 3
See also CLC 182
See also CWW 2
Suskind, Richard 1925- ... CANR-9
Earlier sketch in CA 13-16R
Suskind, Ron(ald Steven) 1959- ... 171
Susko, Mario 1941- ... 181
Suslov, Alexander 1950- ... 105
Suslov, Mikhail Andreyevich 1902-1982
Obituary ... 105
Susman, Gerald I. 1941- ... 139
Susman, Warren (Irving) 1927-1985
Obituary ... 116
Suss, Elaine ... 102
Susser, Mervyn (Wilfred) 1921- ... CANR-1
Earlier sketch in CA 45-48
Susser, Samuel S. 1910-1994 ... 97-100
Sussex, Lucy (Jane) 1957- ... CANR-118
Earlier sketch in CA 159
See also SFW 4
Susskind, Charles 1921-2004 ... CANR-15
Obituary ... 228
Earlier sketch in CA 85-88
Sussman, Aaron 1903-
Brief entry ... 116
Sussman, Barry 1934- ... 53-56
Sussman, Cornelia Silver 1914-1999 ... CANR-13
Earlier sketch in CA 5-8R
See also SATA 59
Sussman, Gerald 1933(?)-1989
Obituary ... 130
Sussman, Henry 1947- ... CANR-43
Earlier sketch in CA 111
Sussman, Herbert L. 1937- ... 25-28R
Sussman, Irving 1908-1996 ... CANR-13
Earlier sketch in CA 77-80
See also SATA 59
Sussman, Leonard R(ichard) 1920- ... CANR-4
Earlier sketch in CA 53-56
Sussman, Marvin B(ernard) 1918- ... CANR-19
Earlier sketches in CA 9-12R, CANR-4
Sussman, Paul 1968(?)- ... 222
Sussman, Peter Y. 1941- ... 144
Sussman, Susan 1942- ... CANR-58
Earlier sketches in CA 111, CANR-30
See also SATA 48
Suster, Gerald 1951-2001 ... 238
See also HGG
Sutch, Richard C(harles) 1942- ... CANR-34
Earlier sketch in CA 107
Sutcliff, Rosemary 1920-1992 ... CANR-37
Obituary ... 139
Earlier sketch in CA 5-8R
See also AAYA 10
See also BYA 1, 4
See also CLC 26
See also CLR 1, 37
See also CPW
See also DAB
See also DAC
See also DAM MST, POP
See also JRDA
See also LATS 1:1
See also MAICYA 1, 2
See also MAICYAS 1
See also RHW
See also SATA 6, 44, 78
See also SATA-Obit 73
See also WYA
See also YAW
Sutcliffe, Anthony (Richard) 1942- ... CANR-94
Earlier sketches in CA 106, CANR-34
Sutcliffe, Jane 1957- ... 208
See also SATA 138
Sutcliffe, Katherine 1952- ... 208
Sutcliffe, Matthew 1550(?)-1629 ... DLB 281
Sutcliffe, William 1971- ... 202
See also DLB 271
Suter, Ronald 1930- ... 41-44R
Sutermeister, Robert Arnold 1913- ... 5-8R
Suther, Judith 1940- ... 181
Suther, Marshall E(dward), Jr. 1918- ... 1-4R
Sutherland, Allan T(homas) 1950- ... 132
Sutherland, Arthur Eugene, Jr. 1902-1973 ... CAP-1
Obituary ... 41-44R
Earlier sketch in CA 19-20
Sutherland, C(arol) Humphrey V(ivian) 1908- ... 13-16R
Sutherland, Colleen 1944- ... SATA 79
Sutherland, Daniel E(llyson) 1946- ... CANR-63
Earlier sketches in CA 109, CANR-26
Sutherland, Donald 1915- ... 37-40R
Sutherland, Donald W(ayne) 1931- ... 9-12R
Sutherland, Douglas 1919- ... 21-24R
Sutherland, Earl Wilbur 1915-1974 ... 163
Obituary ... 49-52
Sutherland, Efua (Theodora Morgue) 1924-1996 ... 105
See also AFW
See also BW 1
See also CWD
See also DLB 117
See also EWL 3
See also IDTP
See also SATA 25
Sutherland, Elizabeth
See Martinez, Elizabeth Sutherland
Sutherland, Elizabeth 1926- ... 85-88
Sutherland, Fraser 1946- ... 102
See also CP 7
Sutherland, Gordon (Brims Black McIvor) 1907-1980
Obituary ... 108
Sutherland, Grant ... 219
Sutherland, H(erbert) W(arren) 1917-1981 ... 13-16R
Obituary ... 134
Sutherland, Ivan (Edward) 1938- ... 181
Sutherland, J. A.
See Sutherland, John (A.)
Sutherland, James (Edward) 1948- ... CANR-2
Earlier sketch in CA 49-52
Sutherland, John (M. A.) 1919-1956 ... 179
See also DLB 68
Sutherland, John (Patrick) 1920-1988
Obituary ... 125
Sutherland, John (Anthony) 1933- ... CANR-16
Earlier sketch in CA 93-96
Sutherland, John (A.) 1938- ... 239
Sutherland, Jon Nicholas 1941-1977 ... CANR-32
Earlier sketch in CA 41-44R
Sutherland, Lucy Stuart 1903-1980 ... CAP-1
Obituary ... 105
Earlier sketch in CA 13-14
Sutherland, Luke 1971(?)- ... 233
Sutherland, Margaret 1941- ... CANR-14
Earlier sketch in CA 77-80
See also SATA 15
Sutherland, N(icola) M(ary) 1925- ... 49-52
Sutherland, R(ussell) Galbraith 1924- ... CAP-1
Earlier sketch in CA 9-10
Sutherland, Robert D(onald) 1937- ... 37-40R
Sutherland, Roger
See Hicks, Roger W(illiam)
Sutherland, Ronald 1933- ... 25-28R
Sutherland, (Norman) Stuart 1927-1998 .. 65-68
Obituary ... 172
Sutherland, (William) Temple (Gairdner) 1906- ... CAP-1
Earlier sketch in CA 9-10
Sutherland, Zena Bailey 1915-2002 ... 102
Obituary ... 209
See also SATA 37
See also SATA-Obit 137
Sutherland-Smith, James (Alfred) 1948- ... CP 7
Suthinee
See Ambhanwong, Suthilak
Suthren, Victor (James Henry) 1942- ... CANR-23
Earlier sketch in CA 107
Sutin, Lawrence 1951- ... 135
Sutnar, Ladislav 1897-1976
Obituary ... 104
Suto, Andras 1927- ... CWW 2
Su Tong
See Tong, Zhong Gui
See also RGWL 3
Sutphen, Dick
See Sutphen, Richard Charles
Sutphen, Joyce 1949- ... 195
Sutphen, Richard Charles 1937- ... CANR-53
Earlier sketches in CA 25-28R, CANR-11, 28
Sutphin, Winfield Blair 1919(?)-1990
Obituary ... 131
Sutphin, Wyn Blair
See Sutphin, Winfield Blair
Sutro, Alfred 1863-1933 ... 185
Brief entry ... 105
See also DLB 10
See also RGEL 2
See also TCLC 6
Sutro, John 1903(?)-1985
Obituary ... 117
Sutryn, Barbara M(ay) 1927- ... 120
Sutskever, Avrom 1913- ... EWL 3
Sutter, Barton 1949- ... 196
Sutter, Franz
See Strich, Christian
Sutter, Frederic Koehler 1938- ... 107
Sutter, Larabie
See Savage, Les, Jr.
Sutter, Paul S. ... 224
Sutter, Ruth E(laine) 1935- ... 45-48
Suttles, Gerald 1932- ... 85-88
Suttles, Shirley (Smith) 1922- ... 13-16R
See also SATA 21
Suttmeier, Richard Peter 1942- ... CANR-6
Earlier sketch in CA 57-60
Sutton, Allan 1952- ... 163
Sutton, Andrew
See Tubb, E(dwin) C(harles)
Sutton, Ann (Livesay) 1923- ... CANR-10
Earlier sketch in CA 5-8R
See also SATA 31
Sutton, Antony C. 1925- ... 97-100
Sutton, Barry 1919-1988
Obituary ... 125
Sutton, Carol 1933-1985
Obituary ... 115
Sutton, Caroline 1953- ... 106
Sutton, Christine 1950- ... 120
Sutton, Dana F. 1942- ... 145
Sutton, David (John) 1944- ... 116
Sutton, David 1947- ... 101
Sutton, Denys (Miller) 1917-1991 ... CANR-20
Obituary ... 133
Earlier sketches in CA 53-56, CANR-5
Sutton, Eve(lyn Mary) 1906-1992 ... CANR-10
Earlier sketch in CA 65-68
See also CWRI 5
See also SATA 26
Sutton, Felix 1910(?)-1973 ... 77-80
See also SATA 31
Sutton, George Miksch 1898-1982 ... CANR-86
Obituary ... 109
Earlier sketch in CA 107
Sutton, Gordon 1910-1998 ... 21-24R
Sutton, Henry
See Slavitt, David R(ytman)
Sutton, Horace (Ashley) 1919-1991 . CANR-10
Obituary ... 135
Earlier sketch in CA 13-16R
Sutton, Howard 1930- ... 65-68
Sutton, Ian 1929- ... 231
Sutton, James Winford 1916- ... 177

Sutton 564 CONTEMPORARY AUTHORS

Sutton, Jane 1950- ... 89-92
See also SATA 52
See also SATA-Brief 43
Sutton, Jeff
See Sutton, Jefferson (Howard)
Sutton, Jefferson (Howard)
1913-1979 ... CANR-10
Earlier sketch in CA 21-24R
Sutton, John G. 1949- ... 186
Sutton, John L(awrence) 1917- ... 105
Sutton, L(aurence) P(aul) Elwell
See Elwell-Sutton, L(aurence) P(aul)
Sutton, Larry M(atthew) 1931- ... CANR-14
Earlier sketch in CA 37-40R
See also SATA 29
Sutton, Margaret Beebe 1903-2001 ... 1-4R
Obituary ... 202
See also SATA 1
See also SATA-Obit 131
Sutton, Marilyn (Phyllis) 1944- ... 215
Sutton, Maurice Lewis 1927- ... CANR-64
Earlier sketch in CA 13-16R
See also Sutton, Stack
Sutton, Max Keith 1937- ... 93-96
Sutton, Myron Daniel 1925- ... 107
See also SATA 31
Sutton, Penny
See Wood, Christopher (Hovelle)
Sutton, Penny
See Cartwright, Justin
Sutton, Peter C. 1949- ... 132
Sutton, R. Anderson 1949- ... 142
Sutton, Remar 1941- ... 126
Sutton, Robert I. ... 204
Sutton, Robert M(ize) 1915- ... 77-80
Sutton, Robert P. 1940- ... 150
Sutton, Roberta Briggs 1899-1986 ... 5-8R
Sutton, Roger 1956- ... CANR-144
Earlier sketch in CA 159
See also SATA 93
Sutton, S(tephanne) B(arry) 1940- ... 29-32R
Sutton, Stack
See Sutton, Maurice Lewis
See also TCWW 2
Sutton, Tony C.
See Sutton, Antony C.
Sutton, Walter 1916- ... 85-88
Sutton, William A(lfred) 1915- ... 61-64
Sutton-Smith, Brian 1924- ... CANR-17
Earlier sketch in CA 29-32R
Sutton-Vane, Vane
See Vane, (Vane Hunt) Sutton
Sutton-Vane, Vane Hunt
See Vane, (Vane Hunt) Sutton
Suttor, T(imothy) L(achlan) 1926- ... 21-24R
Sutzkever, Abraham 1913- ... CWW 2
Suu Kyi, (Daw) Aung San 1945- ... 172
Suvin, Darko (Ronald) 1932- ... CANR-38
Earlier sketches in CA 89-92, CANR-16
Suvorov, Viktor (a pseudonym) ... 116
Su Xiaokang 1949- ... 200
Suyin, Han
See Han Suyin
Su Yuan-ying
See Su, Chien
Su Yuean-ying
See Su, Chien
Suzanne, Jamie
See Hawes, Louise and
Lantz, Francess L(in) and Singleton, Linda Joy and
Zach, Cheryl (Byrd)
Suzman, Helen 1917- ... 145
Suzuki, D. T.
See Suzuki, Daisetz Teitaro
Suzuki, Daisetz T.
See Suzuki, Daisetz Teitaro
Suzuki, Daisetz Teitaro 1870-1966 ... 121
Obituary ... 111
See also MTCW 1, 2
See also MTFW 2005
See also TCLC 109
Suzuki, David T(akayoshi) 1936- ... 209
See also SATA 138
Suzuki, Koji 1957- ... 226
Suzuki, Shunryu 1904-1971 ... 218
Suzuki, Teitaro
See Suzuki, Daisetz Teitaro
Suzuki, Tessa Morris
See Morris-Suzuki, Tessa
Suzuki, Yoshio 1931- ... 143
Svajian, Stephen G. 1906(?)-1977
Obituary ... 73-76
Svankmajer, Jan 1934- ... IDFW 3, 4
Svanstrom, Ragnar 1904(?)-1988
Obituary ... 127
Svareff, Count Vladimir
See Crowley, Edward Alexander
Svarlien, Oscar 1906- ... CAP-1
Earlier sketch in CA 13-16
Svartvik, Jan 1931- ... 21-24R
Svartvik, Jesper 1965- ... 211
Svatik, Donna 1976- ... 178
Svec, Carol ... 238
Svedberg, Theodor 1884-1971 ... 167
Sveinsson, Jon Stefan 1857-1944 ... DLB 293
Svejda, George J. 1927- ... 41-44R
Svenbro, Jesper 1944- ... PFS 23
Svendsen, Hanne Marie 1933- ... 134
See also DLB 214
Svendsen, Linda 1954- ... CANR-105
Earlier sketch in CA 139
Svendsen, Mark (Nestor) 1962- ... 191
See also SATA 120
Svenonius, Elaine 1933- ... 194
Svenson, Andrew E(dward)
1910-1975 ... CANR-27
Obituary ... 61-64
Earlier sketch in CA 5-8R
See also SATA 2
See also SATA-Obit 26
Svenson, Bo 1941- ... 216
Svenson, Peter 1944(?)- ... 239
Svensson, Arne 1929- ... 49-52
Svensson, Jon Stefan
See Sveinsson, Jon Stefan
Svenvold, Mark 1958- ... 225
Sverdlin, Hannah Grad 1911(?)-1989
Obituary ... 127
Svestka, Oldrich 1922-1983
Obituary ... 110
Svevo, Italo
See Schmitz, Aron Hector
See also DLB 264
See also EW 8
See also EWL 3
See also RGWL 2, 3
See also SSC 25
See also TCLC 2, 35
See also WLIT 7
Sviatopolk-Mirsky, Prince Dimitrii Petrovich
1890-1939
See Mirsky, Prince D. S.
Svich, Caridad 1963- ... 219
Svirsky, Grigori (Tsezarevich) 1921- .. CANR-42
Earlier sketch in CA 69-72
Svoboda, Frederic Joseph 1949- ... 116
Svoboda, Terese 1950- ... CANR-107
Earlier sketch in CA 147
Svoray, Yaron 1954(?)- ... 158
Swaan, Wim 1927-1995 ... CANR-18
Obituary ... 149
Earlier sketch in CA 25-28R
Swaanswijk, Lubertus Jacobus 1924-1994
See Lucebert
Swabey, Marie Collins 1890-1966 ... CANR-16
Earlier sketch in CA 1-4R
Swade, Doron 1946- ... 203
Swadesh, Frances Leon 1917- ... 120
Swadley, Elizabeth 1929- ... 21-24R
Swados, Elizabeth (A.) 1951- ... CANR-49
Earlier sketch in CA 97-100
Interview in ... CA-97-100
See also CLC 12
Swados, Harvey 1920-1972 ... CANR-6
Obituary ... 37-40R
Earlier sketch in CA 5-8R
See also CLC 5
See also CN 1
See also DLB 2
See also MAL 5
Swaffer, Hannen 1879-1962
Obituary ... 112
Swafford, Jan Johnson 1946- ... 167
Swaim, Alice Mackenzie 1911-1996 .. CANR-6
Earlier sketch in CA 9-12R
Swaim, Joan (Hewatt) 1934- ... 138
Swaim, Lawrence 1942- ... 69-72
Swain, Bruce M(cArthur) 1943- ... 101
Swain, Charles 1801-1874 ... DLB 32
Swain, Donald C(hristie) 1931- ... 29-32R
Swain, Dwight V(reeland)
1915-1992 ... CANR-37
Obituary ... 174
Earlier sketches in CA 17-20R, CANR-7
Swain, Frank G. 1893(?)-1975
Obituary ... 53-56
Swain, Gladys 1945-1995 ... 198
Swain, Gwenyth 1961- ... CANR-112
Earlier sketch in CA 150
See also SATA 84, 134
Swain, James E(dgar) 1897-1975 ... CAP-2
Earlier sketch in CA 25-28
Swain, Joseph P(eter) 1955- ... CANR-142
Earlier sketches in CA 136, CANR-73
Swain, Joseph Ward 1891-1971 ... CAP-2
Earlier sketch in CA 21-22
Swain, Margaret (Helen) 1909- ... 53-56
Swain, Mark
See Latimer, Dean
Swain, Marshall (William) 1940- ... 124
Brief entry ... 117
Swain, Martha H(elen) 1929- ... CANR-107
Earlier sketch in CA 85-88
Swain, Olive 1896-1985 ... 5-8R
Swain, Raymond Charles 1912-1982 ... 9-12R
Swain, Roger (Bartlett) 1949- ... CANR-41
Earlier sketch in CA 102
See also BYA 8
Swain, Ruth (Freeman) 1951- ... 190
See also SATA 119, 161
Swain, Su Zan (Noguchi) 1916- ... CANR-6
Earlier sketch in CA 5-8R
See also SATA 21
Swainson, Donald 1938- ... CANR-56
Earlier sketches in CA 109, CANR-30
Swainson, Eleanor Frances ... 111
Swale, Rose 1947-
Brief entry ... 116
Swale, Rosie
See Swale, Rose
Swales, Martin 1940- ... 81-84
Swallow, Alan 1915-1966 ... CANR-16
Obituary ... 25-28R
Earlier sketch in CA 1-4R
Swallow, Jean 1953-1995 ... 182
Swallow, Mark (Richard Crawley) 1963- ... 134
Swallow, Norman 1921- ... 21-24R
Swallow, Wendy 1954- ... 238
Swami Rama 1925-1996 ... 119
Swamp, Jake 1941- ... 165
See also SATA 98
Swamy, Subramanian 1939- ... 49-52
Swan, Annie S. -1943 ... RHW
Swan, Berta W(aterhouse) 1928- ... 29-32R
Swan, Bradford Fuller 1908(?)-1976
Obituary ... 65-68
Swan, Carroll J. 1914-1984
Obituary ... 112
Swan, Christopher C(ushing) 1946- ... 103
Swan, Gladys 1934- ... CANR-39
Earlier sketches in CA 101, CANR-17
See also CLC 69
See also TCLE 1:2
Swan, James H. 1946- ... 144
Swan, Jon 1929- ... 89-92
See also CP 1
Swan, Marie
See Bartlett, Marie (Swan)
Swan, Sharon ... 211
Swan, Susan 1944- ... SATA 22, 108
Swan, Susan 1945- ... CN 7
Swan, Thomas 1926- ... 162
Swanberg, W(illiam) A(ndrew)
1907-1992 ... CANR-8
Obituary ... 139
Earlier sketch in CA 5-8R
See also CAAS 13
See also DLB 103
Swander, Mary 1950- ... CANR-144
Earlier sketches in CA 122, CANR-48
Swanger, David 1940- ... CANR-113
Earlier sketch in CA 49-52
Swann, Brian (Stanley Frank)
1940- ... CANR-118
Earlier sketches in CA 37-40R, CANR-31, 56
See also SATA 116
Swann, Donald (Ibrahim)
1923-1994 ... CANR-41
Obituary ... 144
Earlier sketches in CA 21-24R, CANR-16
Swann, E. L.
See Lasky, Kathryn
Swann, Francis 1913-1983 ... CANR-4
Earlier sketch in CA 9-12R
Swann, Ingo 1933- ... 57-60
Swann, Lois 1944- ... CANR-12
Earlier sketch in CA 65-68
Swann, Peggy
See Geis, Richard E(rwin)
Swann, Peter C(harles) 1921- ... 5-8R
Swann, Ruth Rice 1920- ... SATA 84
Swann, S. Andrew
See Swiniarski, S(teven) A.
Swann, Thomas Burnett, Jr.
1928-1976 ... CANR-4
Earlier sketch in CA 5-8R
See also FANT
See also SUFW 1, 2
Swansea, Charleen 1932- ... CANR-16
Earlier sketch in CA 103
Swansen, Vern 1916- ... 49-52
Swanson, Arlene Collyer 1913-1981 ... 5-8R
Swanson, Austin D. 1930- ... 25-28R
Swanson, Bert E(lmer) 1924- ... 29-32R
Swanson, Carl P(ontius) 1911-1996 ... 45-48
Swanson, David 1935- ... 146
Swanson, Denise 1956- ... 215
Swanson, Don R(ichard) 1924- ... 13-16R
Swanson, Donald Roland 1927- ... 41-44R
Swanson, Doug J. 1953- ... CANR-99
Earlier sketch in CA 160
Swanson, Edward I. 1923- ... 29-32R
Swanson, Eric ... 231
Swanson, Gerald J. 1940- ... 147
Swanson, Gloria 1897(?)-1983 ... 142
Obituary ... 109
Swanson, Gloria Borseth 1927- ... 77-80
Swanson, Gustav A(dolph)
1910-1995 ... CANR-14
Earlier sketch in CA 77-80
Swanson, H(arold) N(orling) 1899-1991 ... 132
Swanson, Harold B(urdette) 1917- ... 37-40R
Swanson, Heather (Crichton) 1949- ... 135
Swanson, Helen M(cKendry) 1919- ... 159
See also SATA 94
Swanson, Jean 1943- ... 238
Swanson, Judith A(nn) 1957- ... 139
Swanson, June 1931- ... 143
See also SATA 76
Swanson, Logan
See Matheson, Richard (Burton)
Swanson, Mark
See Skinner, Mike
Swanson, Neil H(armon) 1896-1983
Obituary ... 109
See also RHW
Swanson, Roy Arthur 1925- ... CANR-93
Earlier sketch in CA 17-20R
Swanson, Susan Marie ... 174
Swanson, (Karl) Thor (Waldemar)
1922- ... CANR-22
Earlier sketch in CA 45-48
Swanson, Walter S. J. 1917- ... 29-32R
Swanson, Wayne 1951- ... 130
Swanton, Ernest William
1907-2000 ... CANR-18
Obituary ... 190
Earlier sketches in CA 5-8R, CANR-2
Swanton, Jim
See Swanton, Ernest William
Swanton, Molly (Butler) 1946(?)- ... 238
Swanwick, Michael 1950- ... CANR-119
Earlier sketches in CA 119, CANR-55
See also AAYA 60
See also SFW 4
Swarbrick, Andrew 1955- ... 120
Sward, Robert (Stuart) 1933- ... 206
Earlier sketches in CA 5-8R, CANR-5, 23
Autobiographical Essay in ... 206
See also CAAS 13
See also CP 1, 2, 3, 4, 5, 6, 7
Swardson, Harold Roland, Jr. 1925- ... 1-4R
Swarthout, Doris L(ouise) 1931- ... 77-80
Swarthout, Glendon (Fred)
1918-1992 ... CANR-47
Obituary ... 139
Earlier sketches in CA 1-4R, CANR-1
See also AAYA 55
See also CLC 35
See also CN 1, 2, 3, 4, 5
See also LAIT 5
See also SATA 26
See also TCWW 1, 2
See also YAW
Swarthout, Kathryn 1919- ... 41-44R
See also SATA 7
Swartley, David Warren 1950- ... 102
Swartley, Willard M(yers) 1936- ... CANR-41
Earlier sketch in CA 117
Swartwout, Susan 1950- ... 191
Swartz, Harry (Felix) 1911-1996 ... CANR-6
Earlier sketch in CA 57-60
Swartz, Jon D(avid) 1934- ... CANR-39
Earlier sketch in CA 69-72
Swartz, Marc J(erome) 1931- ... 21-24R
Swartz, Mark 1968- ... 232
Swartz, Marvin 1941- ... 101
Swartz, Mary I(sabelle) 1942- ... 97-100
Swartz, Melvin Jay 1930- ... 97-100
Swartz, Norman (Manuel) 1939- ... 127
Swartz, Paul 1927- ... 5-8R
Swartz, Robert D(avid) 1937- ... 41-44R
Swartz, Robert J(ason) 1936- ... 17-20R
Swartz, Susan F(rey) 1943- ... 174
Swartz, Willis George 1902-1965 ... 1-4R
Swartzlow, Ruby Johnson 1903-1981 ... CAP-1
Earlier sketch in CA 13-16
Swarzenski, Hanns (Peter Theophil) 1903-1985
Obituary ... 116
Swasy, Alecia 1963- ... 145
Swatridge, Charles (John) (?)-1964 ... CANR-34
Earlier sketches in CA 13-16R, CANR-7
Swatridge, Irene Maude (Mossop)
-1993 ... CANR-34
Earlier sketches in CA 29-32R, CANR-7
Swatuk, Larry A(nthony) 1957- ... 167
Sway, Marlene 1950- ... 129
Swaybill, Roger E(lliot) 1943-1991 ... 105
Obituary ... 133
Swayne, Geoffrey
See Campion, Sidney R(onald)
Swayne, Sam(uel F.) 1907- ... SATA 53
Swayne, Zoa (Lourana) 1905- ... SATA 53
Swayze, (Sarah) Beulah G(arland) 1907- ... 5-8R
Swayze, Carolyn (Norma) 1945- ... 127
Swayze, E(rnest) Harold 1930- ... 1-4R
Swayze, John Cameron 1906-1995 ... 102
Obituary ... 149
Swearengen, Thomas F. 1924- ... 17-20R
Swearer, Donald K(eeney) 1934- ... 37-40R
Swearingen, Arthur Rodger 1923- ... CANR-10
Earlier sketch in CA 5-8R
Sweat, Lynn 1934- ... SATA 57
Sweatman, Margaret (Lisa) 1953- ... 210
Sweazey, George E. 1905-1992 ... CANR-4
Earlier sketch in CA 1-4R
Swedberg, Richard 1948- ... 139
Swedburg, Wilma Adeline ... 5-8R
Swede, George 1940- ... CANR-64
Earlier sketches in CA 113, CANR-32
See also SATA 67
Sweeney, Amin 1938- ... 105
Sweeney, Barry
See Hand, G(eoffrey) J(oseph Philip Macaulay)
Sweeney, (Roderick) Charles (Hinton)
1922- ... CANR-16
Earlier sketch in CA 21-24R
Sweeney, Douglas (A.) ... 200
Sweeney, Eamonn 1968- ... 171
Sweeney, Earl M. 1937- ... 112
Sweeney, Emma ... 216
Sweeney, Francis 1916- ... 5-8R
Sweeney, Henry Whitcomb 1898-1967 . CAP-2
Earlier sketch in CA 17-18
Sweeney, James B(artholomew)
1910-1999 ... CANR-12
Earlier sketch in CA 29-32R
See also SATA 21
Sweeney, James Johnson 1900-1986 .. CANR-6
Obituary ... 119
Earlier sketch in CA 5-8R
Sweeney, John Thomas 1958- ... 209
Sweeney, Joyce (Kay) 1955- ... CANR-86
Earlier sketches in CA 116, CANR-35
See also AAYA 26
See also SATA 65, 68, 108
Sweeney, Julia 1960(?)- ... 160
Sweeney, Karen O'Connor
See O'Connor, Karen
Sweeney, (Charles) Leo 1918-2001 .. CANR-34
Obituary ... 203
Earlier sketches in CA 37-40R, CANR-15
Sweeney, Matthew (Gerard) 1952- ... 224
See also CP 7
See also CWRI 5
See also SATA 156
Sweeney, R. C. H.
See Sweeney, (Roderick) Charles (Hinton)
Sweeney, Robert Dale 1939- ... 45-48
Sweeney, Terrance (Allen) 1945- ... 142
Sweeney, Thomas J(ohn) 1936- ... 41-44R

Cumulative Index 565 Symons

Sweeney, William J(oseph) III 1922- . CANR-33
Obituary ... 161
Earlier sketch in CA 45-48
Sweeny, Mary K. 1923- ... 126
Sweet, Donald H(erbert) 1925- ... 112
Sweet, Franklyn Haley 1916- ... 9-12R
Sweet, Frederick A(rnold) 1903-1984 .... CAP-2
Earlier sketch in CA 17-18
Sweet, George Elliott 1904-1997 ... 45-48
Obituary ... 156
Sweet, J(ohn) P(hilip) M(cMurdo) 1927- ... 119
Sweet, James Stouder 1918- ... 41-44R
Sweet, Jeffrey 1950- ... CANR-130
Earlier sketches in CA 81-84, CANR-43
Sweet, Leonard Ira 1947- ... CANR-99
Earlier sketch in CA 97-100
Sweet, Muriel W. 1888-1977 ... 106
Sweet, O. Robin 1952- ... 139
Sweet, Paul R(obinson) 1907- ... 77-80
Sweet, Robert Burdette 1930- ... 85-88
Sweet, Sarah C.
See Jewett, (Theodora) Sarah Orne
Sweet, Waldo Earle 1912-1992 ... 1-4R
Sweet, William 1955- ... 217
Sweeting, George 1924- ... CANR-11
Earlier sketch in CA 65-68
Sweetkind, Morris 1898-1994 ... 13-16R
Sweetland, Nancy A(nn) 1934- ... SATA 48
Sweetland, Richard C. 1931- ... 119
Sweetman, David 1943-2002 ... CANR-97
Obituary ... 205
Earlier sketch in CA 141
Sweetman, Jack 1940- ... CANR-26
Earlier sketches in CA 25-28R, CANR-10
Sweetman, Rosita (Anne) 1948- ... 124
Brief entry ... 118
Sweets, John Frank 1945- ... 89-92
Sweetser, Mary (Chisholm) 1894-1978 .. 41-44R
Sweetser, Ted
See Sweetser, Mary (Chisholm)
Sweetser, Thomas P(atrick) 1939- ... 112
Sweetser, Wesley D(uaine) 1919- ... 37-40R
Sweezy, Alan Richardson 1907- ... 41-44R
Sweezy, Paul M(arlor) 1910-2004 ... CANR-5
Obituary ... 223
Earlier sketch in CA 1-4R
Sweigard, Lulu E. (?)-1974
Obituary ... 53-56
Swell, Lila ... 97-100
Sweney, Fredric 1912-1996 ... 1-4R
Swensen, Cole 1955- ... 215
Swenson, Allan A(rmstrong) 1933- ... 77-80
See also SATA 21
Swenson, Clifford H(enrik) Jr. 1926- ... 45-48
Swenson, Judy Harris 1947- ... 120
Swenson, Karen 1936- ... CANR-97
Earlier sketch in CA 53-56
See also CAAS 13
Swenson, Loyd S(ylvan), Jr. 1932- CANR-15
Earlier sketch in CA 41-44R
Swenson, May 1919-1989 ... CANR-131
Obituary ... 130
Earlier sketches in CA 5-8R, CANR-36, 61
See also AMWS 4
See also CLC 4, 14, 61, 106
See also CP 1, 2
See also DA
See also DAB
See also DAC
See also DAM MST, POET
See also DLB 5
See also EXPP
See also GLL 2
See also MAL 5
See also MTCW 1, 2
See also MTFW 2005
See also PC 14
See also PFS 16
See also SATA 15
See also WP
Swenson, Peggy
See Geis, Richard E(rwin)
Swenson, Peggye 1933- ... 73-76
Swensson, Paul S. 1907- ... 77-80
Swentzell, Rina 1939- ... SATA 79
Swerdlow, Amy (Miriam) G(alstuck) 1923- . 105
Swerling, Beverly 1949- ... 238
Swerling, Jo(seph) 1897-1964 ... 217
Swerling, Jo 1897-1964 ... DLB 44
See also IDFW 3, 4
Swerling, Jo, Jr. 1931- ... 173
Swetman, Glenn R(obert) 1936- ... CANR-4
Earlier sketch in CA 53-56
Swetnam, Evelyn (Frances) 1919- ... 93-96
Swetnam, Ford 1941- ... 215
Swetnam, Michael S. ... 210
Swets, John A(rthur) 1928- ... CANR-9
Earlier sketch in CA 21-24R
Swetz, Frank J. 1937- ... 135
Swezey, Kenneth M. 1905(?)-1972
Obituary ... 33-36R
Swicegood, Thomas L. P. 1930- ... 53-56
Swick, Clarence 1883(?)-1979
Obituary ... 89-92
Swick, Kevin J(ames) 1943- ... 111
Swick, Marly 1949- ... CANR-90
Earlier sketches in CA 135, CANR-60
Swick, Thomas 1952- ... 138
Swidler, Ann 1944- ... 132
Swidler, Arlene (Anderson) 1929- ... CANR-12
Earlier sketch in CA 61-64
Swidler, Leonard 1929- ... CANR-7
Earlier sketch in CA 17-20R
Swierenga, Robert P. 1935- ... 25-28R
Swift, Augustus
See Lovecraft, H(oward) P(hillips)
Swift, Benjamin
See McKimmey, James
Swift, Bryan
See Knott, William C(ecil, Jr.)
Swift, Carolyn Ruth 1928- ... 107
Swift, Clive 1936- ... 129
Swift, David
See Kaufmann, John
Swift, Donald C. 1937- ... 166
Swift, E(dward) M(cKelvy) 1951- ... 107
Swift, Earl 1958- ... 224
Swift, Edd
See Swift, Edward
Swift, Edward 1943- ... 37-40R
Swift, George B. 1902(?)-1983
Obituary ... 110
Swift, Graham (Colin) 1949- ... CANR-128
Brief entry ... 117
Earlier sketches in CA 122, CANR-46, 71
See also BRWC 2
See also BRWS 5
See also CLC 41, 88
See also CN 4, 5, 6, 7
See also DLB 194
See also MTCW 2
See also MTFW 2005
See also NFS 18
See also RGSF 2
Swift, Helen C(ecilia) 1920- ... 117
Swift, Helen Miller 1914- ... 1-4R
Swift, Hildegarde Hoyt 1890(?)-1977
Obituary ... 69-72
See also SATA-Obit 20
Swift, Howard W. 1908-1989 ... CAP-1
Earlier sketch in CA 9-10
Swift, Jamie 1951- ... 193
Swift, Joan 1926- ... 115
Swift, Jonathan 1667-1745 ... AAYA 41
See also BRW 3
See also BRWC 1
See also BRWR 1
See also BYA 5, 14
See also CDBLB 1660-1789
See also CLR 53
See also DA
See also DA3
See also DAB
See also DAC
See also DAM MST, NOV, POET
See also DLB 39, 95, 101
See also EXPN
See also LAIT 1
See also NFS 6
See also PC 9
See also RGEL 2
See also SATA 19
See also TEA
See also WCH
See also WLC
See also WLIT 3
Swift, Kate 1923- ... 69-72
Swift, Marshall S(tefan) 1936- ... 53-56
Swift, Mary Grace 1927- ... 29-32R
Swift, Merlin
See Leeming, Joseph
Swift, Patrick 1927-1983
Obituary ... 110
Swift, Richard N(ewton) 1924- ... CANR-34
Earlier sketch in CA 1-4R
Swift, Sally 1913- ... 172
Swift, Sue 1955- ... 226
Swift, W. Porter 1914- ... 29-32R
Swift, Will 1947- ... 239
Swigart, Rob 1941- ... CANR-28
Earlier sketches in CA 69-72, CANR-11
Swiger, Elinor Porter 1927- ... 37-40R
See also SATA 8
Swigg, Richard 1938- ... 103
Swihart, Altman K 1903-1979 ... 1-4R
Swihart, Thomas L(ee) 1929-1995 ... 107
Swinburne, Algernon Charles 1837-1909 ... 140
Brief entry ... 105
See also BRW 5
See also CDBLB 1832-1890
See also DA
See also DA3
See also DAB
See also DAC
See also DAM MST, POET
See also DLB 35, 57
See also PAB
See also PC 24
See also RGEL 2
See also TCLC 8, 36
See also TEA
See also WLC
Swinburne, Laurence (Joseph)
1924- ... CANR-15
Earlier sketch in CA 61-64
See also SATA 9
Swinburne, Richard 1934- ... CANR-52
Earlier sketches in CA 25-28R, CANR-10, 28
Swinburne, Stephen R. 1952- ... CANR-136
Earlier sketch in CA 177
See also SATA 150
Swinburne, Steve
See Swinburne, Stephen R.
Swindell, Larry (Nolan) 1929- ... 25-28R
Swindells, Madge ... 157
Swindells, Robert (Edward) 1939- .. CANR-135
Earlier sketches in CA 97-100, CANR-21
See also AAYA 20
See also JRDA
See also MAICYA 1, 2
See also MAICYAS 1
See also SAAS 14
See also SATA 50, 80, 150
See also SATA-Brief 34
See also YAW
Swinden, Patrick 1941- ... 49-52
Swindler, Daris R(ay) 1925- ... 178
Swindler, William F(inley) 1913-1984 ... 13-16R
Obituary ... 112
Swindoll, Charles R(ozell) 1934- ... 174
Swindoll, Chuck
See Swindoll, Charles R(ozell)
Swindoll, Luci 1932- ... 112
Swineford, Ada 1917- ... 61-64
Swineshead, Richard ... DLB 115
Swinfen, Ann ... 202
See also CLC 34
Swinfen, D(avid) B(erridge) 1936- ... 37-40R
Swinford, Betty (June Wells) 1927- ... CANR-7
Earlier sketch in CA 5-8R
See also SATA 58
Swinford, Bob
See Swinford, Betty (June Wells)
Swing, Raymond Gram 1887-1968
Obituary ... 89-92
Swing, Thomas Kaehao 1930- ... 9-12R
Swingle, Paul G(eorge) 1937- ... 41-44R
Swinglehurst, Edmund 1917- ... CANR-28
Earlier sketches in CA 57-60, CANR-8
Swiniarski, S(teven) A. ... 174
Swinnerton, A(rnold) R(eber) 1912- ... 106
Swinnerton, Frank (Arthur) 1884-1982 ... 202
Obituary ... 108
See also CLC 31
See also CN 1, 2, 3
See also DLB 34
Swinnerton, Frank Arthur 1884-1982
Obituary ... 108
See also CLC 31
See also DLB 34
Swinnerton, James Guilford 1875-1974
Obituary ... 93-96
Swinson, Arthur 1915-1970 ... CAP-2
Earlier sketch in CA 17-18
Swint, Henry L(ee) 1909-1987 ... 37-40R
Swinton, Elizabeth de Sabato 1937- ... 153
Swinton, George 1917- ... 85-88
Swinton, John 1939- ... 111
Swinton, Stanley M(itchell) 1919-1982
Obituary ... 107
Swinton, William E(lgin) 1900-1994 ... 13-16R
Obituary ... 145
Swinyard, Alfred W(ilbur) 1915- ... 9-12R
Swir, Anna ... PFS 21
Swire, Otta F(lora Macdonald Lois)
1898-1973 ... CAP-1
Earlier sketch in CA 13-14
Swisher, Carl Brent 1897-1968 ... CANR-16
Obituary ... 103
Earlier sketch in CA 1-4R
Swisher, (Frank) Earl 1902-1975 ... CAP-2
Earlier sketch in CA 29-32
Swisher, Robert K., Jr. 1947- ... 61-64
Swisher, Viola Hegyi 1904(?)-1990
Obituary ... 131
Swisshelm, Jane Grey 1815-1884 ... DLB 43
Swithen, John
See King, Stephen (Edwin)
Swithin, Antony
See Sarjeant, William A(ntony) S(within)
Switzer, Barry 1937- ... 143
Switzer, David Karl 1925- ... 57-60
Switzer, Ellen 1923- ... CANR-2
Earlier sketch in CA 45-48
See also SATA 48
Switzer, Jacqueline Vaughn
See Vaughn, Jacqueline
Switzer, Les 1935- ... CANR-119
Earlier sketch in CA 147
Switzer, (Perry) Richard 1925-1995 .. CANR-18
Obituary ... 161
Earlier sketch in CA 25-28R
Swivett, R. G. O.
See Trippett, Frank
Swomley, John M., Jr. 1915- ... 9-12R
Swonk, Diane (C.) 1962- ... 229
Swope, George S(teel) 1915- ... 29-32R
Swope, Herbert Bayard 1882-1958 ... 190
See also DLB 25
Swope, Sam(uel) ... 170
See also SATA 156
Swor, Chester E(ugene) 1907- ... 9-12R
Sword, Randall S(tanford) 1942- ... 114
Sword, Wiley 1937- ... 85-88
Swords, James (?)-1844 ... DLB 73
Swords, Thomas 1763-1843 ... DLB 73
Swortzell, Lowell (Stanley)
1930-2004 ... CANR-1
Obituary ... 229
Earlier sketch in CA 49-52
Swycaffer, Jefferson P(utnam) 1956- ... 119
Swyhart, Barbara Ann DeMartino 1942- . 61-64
Swynnerton, Thomas c. 1500-1554 .... DLB 281
Syal, Meera 1963(?)- ... CANR-96
Earlier sketch in CA 160
Syberberg, Hans-Juergen 1935- ... 93-96
Sybesma, Jetske
See Ironside, Jetske
Syburg, Jane 1927- ... 29-32R
Sydenham, Michael J(ohn) 1923- ... 17-20R
Sydney, Cynthia
See Tralins, S(andor) Robert
Sydney, Frank
See Warwick, Alan R(oss)
Sydnor, Charles W(right), Jr. 1943- ... 77-80
Sydnor, James Rawlings 1911- ... 5-8R
Sydnor, (Charles) William 1911-2000 ... 112
Obituary ... 188
Syed, Anwar H(ussain) 1926- ... 102
Syers, Ed
See Syers, William Edward
Syers, William Edward 1914- ... CANR-4
Earlier sketch in CA 1-4R
Sykes, (Richard) Adam 1940- ... 29-32R
Sykes, Alrene ... 77-80
Sykes, Bryan Clifford 1947- ... 236
Sykes, Charles J. ... 153
Sykes, Christopher (Hugh) 1907-1986 ... 29-32R
Obituary ... 121
Sykes, Ella C(onstance) 1869(?)-1939 . DLB 174
Sykes, Gerald 1903-1984 ... 134
Obituary ... 113
Sykes, Jay G(ilbert) 1922- ... 45-48
Sykes, John 1918- ... 17-20R
Sykes, Roosevelt 1906-1983
Obituary ... 110
Syktus, Jozef 1959- ... 155
Sylbert, Richard 1928- ... IDFW 3, 4
Sylva, Carmen
See Elisabeth (Ottilie Luise), Queen (Pauline)
Sylvander, Carolyn W(edin) 1939- ... 117
Sylvanus, Erwin 1917-1985
Sylvester, A(lbert) J(ames) 1889-1989 ... 101
Sylvester, Arline 1914- ... 65-68
Sylvester, Bob
See Sylvester, Robert (McPherson)
Sylvester, (Anthony) David (Bernard)
1924-2001 ... 168
Obituary ... 201
Sylvester, Dorothy 1906- ... 29-32R
Sylvester, Edward J(oseph) 1942- ... CANR-44
Earlier sketch in CA 118
Sylvester, Harold ... 215
Sylvester, Janet 1950- ... 162
Sylvester, Janet Hart 1917-1987
Obituary ... 123
Sylvester, Josuah 1562(?)-1618 ... DLB 121
See also RGEL 2
Sylvester, Judith L. 1952- ... 228
Sylvester, Kathryn F. 1901(?)-1983
Obituary ... 111
Sylvester, Natalie G(abry) 1922- ... 97-100
See also SATA 22
Sylvester, Richard Standish
1926-1978 ... CANR-2
Obituary ... 77-80
Earlier sketch in CA 1-4R
Sylvester, Robert (McPherson)
1907-1975 ... 61-64
Obituary ... 57-60
Sylvester, William (Arthur) 1918- ... CANR-34
Earlier sketch in CA 45-48
Sylvestre, (Joseph Jean) Guy 1918- ... 61-64
Sylvia
See Ashton-Warner, Sylvia (Constance)
Sylvin, Francis
See Seaman, Sylvia S(ybil Bernstein)
Symanski, Richard 1941- ... 111
Symcox, Geoffrey Walter 1938- ... 112
Syme, Ronald 1903-1989
Obituary ... 129
Syme, (Neville) Ronald 1913-1992 .... CANR-6
Earlier sketch in CA 9-12R
See also CWRI 5
See also SATA 2, 87
Symeonoglou, Sarantis 1937- ... 126
Symes, R. F. ... SATA 77
Symington, David 1904-1984 ... CAP-2
Obituary ... 113
Earlier sketch in CA 29-32
Symmes, Patrick 1964- ... 219
Symmes, Robert Edward
See Duncan, Robert (Edward)
Symmons, Sarah ... 239
Symmons-Symonolewicz, Konstantin
1909-1986 ... 37-40R
Symonds, Craig L. 1946- ... CANR-113
Earlier sketches in CA 126, CANR-52
Symonds, Deborah A(nn) 1951- ... 164
Symonds, Emily Morse
See Paston, George
Symonds, Helen Sanford 1899-1978 ... 5-8R
Symonds, John ... 105
Symonds, John Addington 1840-1893 . DLB 57, 144
Symonds, (John) Richard (Charters)
1918- ... 21-24R
Symons, A(lphonse) J(ames) A(lbert)
1900-1941 ... 213
Symons, A. J. A. 1900-1941 ... DLB 149
Symons, Allene 1944- ... 110
Symons, Arthur 1865-1945 ... 189
Brief entry ... 107
See also DLB 19, 57, 149
See also RGEL 2
See also TCLC 11
Symons, (Dorothy) Geraldine 1909- . CANR-75
Earlier sketch in CA 85-88
See also CWRI 5
See also SATA 33

Symons, Julian (Gustave)
1912-1994 ..... CANR-59
Obituary 147
Earlier sketches in CA 49-52, CANR-3, 33
See also CAAS 3
See also CLC 2, 14, 32
See also CMW 4
See also CN 1, 2, 3, 4, 5
See also CP 1
See also DLB 87, 155
See also DLBY 1992
See also MSW
See also MTCW 1
Symons, Leslie John 1926- CANR-26
Earlier sketch in CA 109
Symons, R(obert) D(avid) 1898-1973 ..... 41-44R
Symons, (Hugh Brennan) Scott
1933- CANR-70
Earlier sketch in CA 77-80
See also CN 1, 2, 3
See also DLB 53
Symons, Stuart
See Stanley, George Edward
Symynkywicz, Jeffrey B(ruce) 1954- 151
See also SATA 87
Synan, Edward A(loysius) 1918- 17-20R
Synan, (Harold) Vinson 1934- CANR-14
Earlier sketch in CA 37-40R
Synge, Allen 1930- 142
Synge, (Edmund) J(ohn) M(illington)
1871-1909 141
Brief entry 104
See also BRW 6
See also BRWR 1
See also CDBLB 1890-1914
See also DAM DRAM
See also DC 2
See also DFS 18
See also DLB 10, 19
See also EWL 3
See also RGEL 2
See also TCLC 6, 37
See also TEA
See also WLIT 4
Synge, (Phyllis) Ursula 1930- CANR-1
Earlier sketch in CA 49-52
See also BYA 4
See also SATA 9
Synnestvedt, Sig(fried T.) 1924-1977 ..... 37-40R
Syntax, John
See Dennett, Herbert Victor
Sypher, Francis Jacques, Jr. 1941- CANR-10
Earlier sketch in CA 57-60
Sypher, Lucy Johnston 1907- CANR-2
Earlier sketch in CA 45-48
See also SATA 7
Sypher, Wylie 1905-1987 ..... CANR-3
Earlier sketch in CA 1-4R
Syracuse, Marcella Pfeiffer 1930- 21-24R
Syrdal, Rolf A(rthur) 1902-1993 ..... 25-28R
Syred, Celia 1911- CANR-12
Earlier sketch in CA 29-32R
Syrett, David 1939-2004 190
Obituary 233
Brief entry 106
Syrett, Harold Coffin 1913-1984
Obituary 113
Syrett, Netta 1865-1943 ..... DLB 135, 197
Syrkin, Marie 1899-1989 ..... CANR-6
Obituary 127
Earlier sketch in CA 9-12R
Syrop, Konrad 1914-1998 ..... CANR-5
Earlier sketch in CA 9-12R
Syrotinski, Michael 1957- 190
Syruc, J.
See Milosz, Czeslaw
Sysyn, Frank E. 1946- 126
Syvertsen, Edythe 1921- 73-76
Syverud, Genevieve Wold 1914- 21-24R
Szabo, Denis 1929- CANR-43
Earlier sketches in CA 89-92, CANR-20
Szabo, Istvan 1938- 144
Szabo, Lorinc 1900-1957 ..... DLB 215
See also EWL 3
Szabo, Magda 1917- ..... DLB 215
Szabo, Sandor 1954- 153
Szabo, Stephen (Lee) 1940-2000 217
Szabolcsi, Bence 1899-1973
Obituary 116
Szajkowski, Zosa
See Frydman, Szajko
Szakolczai, A'rpa'd 1958- 147
Szalay, Miklos
See Szalay, Miklos
Szalay, Miklos 1940- CANR-136
Earlier sketch in CA 171
Szancer, Henryk (?)-1976
Obituary 61-64
Szaniawski, Jerzy 1886-1970
Obituary 29-32R
Szanto, George H(erbert) 1940- CANR-143
Earlier sketch in CA 41-44R
Szanton, Andrew (Emlew) 1963- 140
Szanton, Peter L(oeb) 1930- CANR-11
Earlier sketch in CA 69-72
Szasz, Ferenc Morton 1940- CANR-56
Earlier sketch in CA 125
Szasz, Kathleen 1912- 25-28R
Szasz, Margaret Connell 1935- 97-100
Szasz, Suzanne (Shorr) 1915-1997 ... CANR-18
Obituary 159
Earlier sketches in CA 5-8R, CANR-3
See also SATA 13
See also SATA-Obit 99
Szasz, Thomas (Stephen) 1920- CANR-9
Earlier sketch in CA 17-20R
Szathmary, Louis (Istvan) II 1919- 81-84
Szaz, Zoltan Michael 1930-2001 ..... CANR-3
Obituary 194
Earlier sketch in CA 1-4R
Szczesniak, Boleslaw (B.) 1908-1996 ..... 9-12R
Szczypiorski, Andrzej 1928- CANR-60
Earlier sketch in CA 133
Sze, Arthur C. 1950- CANR-93
Earlier sketch in CA 152
Szechter, Szymon 1920(?)-1983
Obituary 110
Szego, Gabor 1895-1985 170
Szekely, Endre 1922- 17-20R
Szekely, Istvan P(al) 1959- 151
Szekeres, Cyndy 1933- 137
See also CWRI 5
See also MAICYA 1, 2
See also SAAS 13
See also SATA 5, 60, 131, 157
See also SATA-Essay 157
Szekessy, Karin 1939- 216
Szekessy, Tanja 166
See also SATA 98
Szenberg, Michael 1934- 144
Szent-Gyoergyi, Albert (von Nagyrapolt)
1893-1986
Obituary 120
Brief entry 112
Szent-Gyorgyi, Albert (von Nagyrapolt)
See Szent-Gyoergyi, Albert (von Nagyrapolt)
Szep
See Szep, Paul (Michael)
Szep, Paul (Michael) 1941- CANR-111
Brief entry 110
Earlier sketch in CA 128
Interview in CA-128
Szeplaki, Joseph 1932- 73-76
Szerlip, Barbara 1949- CANR-3
Earlier sketch in CA 49-52
Szichman, Mario 1945- ..... EWL 3
Szigeti, Joseph 1892-1973 ..... CAP-1
Earlier sketch in CA 9-10
Szilard, Leo 1898-1964 158
Obituary 113
Szirtes, George 1948- CANR-117
Earlier sketches in CA 109, CANR-27, 61
See also CLC 46
See also CP 7
See also PC 51
Szittya, Ruth Outland 1910-1993 112
Szlengel, Wladyslaw -1943
Szoeverffy, Joseph 1920- CANR-40
Earlier sketches in CA 65-68, CANR-17
Szogyi, Alex 1929- CANR-35
Earlier sketch in CA 45-48
Szostak, Rick 1959- 139
Szpilman, Wladyslaw 1911-2000 186
Szporluk, Larissa 1967- 187
Szporluk, Roman 1933- CANR-1
Earlier sketch in CA 45-48
Szpur, Mary 1956- 128
Szpura, Beata 1961- ..... SATA 93
Sztompka, Piotr 1944- 141
Szudek, Agnes S(usan) P(hilomena) ..... SATA 57
See also SATA-Brief 49
Szulc, Tad 1926-2001 ..... CANR-96
Obituary 197
Earlier sketches in CA 9-12R, CANR-4, 23
Interview in CANR-23
See also SATA 26
Szumigalski, Anne 1922-1999 ..... CANR-82
Earlier sketches in CA 49-52, CANR-1, 16, 36
See also CP 7
See also CWP
Szumski, Bonnie 1958- 122
Szwajger, Adina Blady 1917-1993 140
Obituary 141
Szwarc, Josef 1947- 118
Szybist, Mary 1970- 239
Szydlow, Jarl
See Szydlowski, Mary Vigliante
Szydlowski, Mary Vigliante 1946- CANR-65
Earlier sketch in CA 104
See also SATA 94
Szydlowski, Roman 1918(?)-1983
Obituary 111
Szyliowicz, Joseph S. 1931- 41-44R
Szymanski, Albert (John) 1942(?)-1985
Obituary 115
Szymanski, Leszek 1933- 146
Szymanski, Lois 1957- 155
See also SATA 91
Szymanski, Richard
See Symanski, Richard
Szymborska, Wislawa 1923- CANR-133
Earlier sketches in CA 154, CANR-91
See also CDWLB 4
See also CLC 99, 190
See also CWP
See also CWW 2
See also DA3
See also DLB 232
See also DLBY 1996
See also EWL 3
See also MTCW 2
See also MTFW 2005
See also PC 44
See also PFS 15
See also RGWL 3
Szymczak, Leonard K. 1947- 159
Szyszkowitz, Gerald 1938- ..... EWL 3

T

T. B. D.
See James, William Milbourne
T. O., Nik
See Annensky, Innokenty (Fyodorovich)
Ta, Van Tai 1938- 133
Taaffe, Edward James 1921- 85-88
Taaffe, James G. 1932- 17-20R
Taaffe, Michael
See Maguire, R(obert) A(ugustine) J(oseph)
Taagepera, Rein 1933-1995 109
Tabachnik, Abraham B(er) 1902-1970
Obituary 29-32R
Taback, Simms 1932- 171
Brief entry 115
See also CLR 100
See also MAICYA 2
See also SATA 40, 104
See also SATA-Brief 36
Tabak, Israel 1904-1991
Obituary 171
Brief entry 105
Taban, Liyong
See Liyong, Taban lo
See also CP 7
Taban lo Liyong
See Liyong, Taban lo
See also CP 7
See also DLB 125
Tabard, Geoffrey
See McNelly, Willis E(verett)
Tabard, Peter
See Blake, L(eslie) J(ames)
Tabari, al- 839-923 ..... DLB 311
Tabb, Jay Yanai 1907-1976 ..... CAP-2
Earlier sketch in CA 29-32
Tabbi, Joseph 1960- 227
Taber, Anthony Scott 1944- 105
Taber, George M(cCaffrey) 1942- 65-68
Taber, Gladys (Bagg) 1899-1980 ..... CANR-4
Obituary 97-100
Earlier sketch in CA 5-8R
See also SATA-Obit 22
Taber, Julian Ingersoll 1929-
Brief entry 106
Taber, Robert 17-20R
Taber, Robert W(illiam) 1921- 73-76
Taber, Stephen Welton 1956- 200
Tabidze, Galaktion 1892-1959 ..... EWL 3
Tablada, Jose Juan 1871-1945 206
See also DLB 290
See also LAW
Tabler, Edward C. 1916-1977 ..... 5-8R
Tablet, Hilda
See Swann, Donald (Ibrahim)
Tabor, Nancy Maria Grande 1949- ..... SATA 89, 161
Tabor, Paul
See Tabori, Paul
Tabor, Stephen 1951- 127
Tabori, George 1914- CANR-69
Earlier sketches in CA 49-52, CANR-4
See also CBD
See also CD 5, 6
See also CLC 19
See also DLB 245
Tabori, Paul 1908-1974 ..... CANR-5
Obituary 53-56
Earlier sketch in CA 5-8R
Taborsky, Edward (Joseph)
1910-1996 ..... CANR-3
Earlier sketch in CA 1-4R
Tabouis, Genevieve 1892-1985
Obituary 117
Tabrah, Ruth Milander 1921- CANR-52
Earlier sketches in CA 13-16R, CANR-10, 28
See also SATA 14
Tabucchi, Antonio 1943- 205
See also CWW 2
See also DLB 196
See also EWL 3
Tacey, William S(anford) 1904-1986 ..... 37-40R
Obituary 174
Tachau, Frank 1929- CANR-55
Brief entry 111
Earlier sketch in CA 127
Tachau, Mary K(atherine) Bonsteel
1926-1990 85-88
Tache, Joseph-Charles 1820-1894 ..... DLB 99
Tacheron, Donald Glen 1928-1996 ..... 21-24R
Obituary 152
Tachihara Masaaki 1926-1980 ..... DLB 182
Tacitus c. 55-c. 117 ..... AW 2
See also CDWLB 1
See also DLB 211
See also RGWL 2, 3
Tack, Alfred 1906- 104
Tackach, James 1953- 194
See also SATA 123
Tackett, Timothy 1945- 223
Tademy, Lalita 206
Tadie, Jean-Yves 1936- 195
Tadijanovic, Dragutin 1905- ..... DLB 181
Tadjo, Veronique 1955- ..... EWL 3
Tadlock, Max R. 1919- 17-20R
Tadrack, Moss
See Caryl, Warren
Taegel, William S(tephens) 1940- 45-48
Taetzsch, Lyn 1941- CANR-8
Earlier sketch in CA 57-60
Taeuber, Alma Ficks 1933- 17-20R
Taeuber, Conrad F. 1906-1999 ..... CANR-28
Obituary 185
Earlier sketch in CA 45-48
Taeuber, Cynthia M. 1947- 161
Taeuber, Irene Barnes 1906-1974
Obituary 106
Taeuber, Karl E(rnst) 1936- CANR-28
Earlier sketch in CA 17-20R
Tae-yong, Ro
See Rutt, Richard
Tafdrup, Pia 1952- 189
See also CWP
See also CWW 2
See also DLB 214
See also EWL 3
Tafel, Edgar Allen 1912- 89-92
Taffy
See Llewellyn, D(avid) W(illiam) Alun
Tafolla, (Mary) Carmen 1951- 131
See also DLB 82
See also HW 1
Taft, Charles P(helps II) 1897-1983
Obituary 110
Brief entry 105
Taft, John (Thomas) 1950- 133
Taft, Pauline Dakin 1891-1981 ..... CAP-1
Obituary 176
Earlier sketch in CA 13-16
Taft, Philip 1902-1976
Obituary 69-72
Taft, Ronald 1920- 21-24R
Taft, William H(oward) 1915- 13-16R
Tafti, H. B. Dehqani
See Dehqani-Tafti, H. B.
Tafuri, Manfredo 1935- CANR-26
Earlier sketch in CA 69-72
Tafuri, Nancy (E.) 1946- CANR-44
Earlier sketch in CA 118
See also CLR 74
See also CWRI 5
See also MAICYA 1, 2
See also SAAS 14
See also SATA 39, 75, 130
Tagawa, Cary-Hiroyuki 1950- 215
Tager, Jack 1936-1987 ..... CANR-93
Earlier sketch in CA 118
Tager-Flusberg, Helen 1951- CANR-95
Earlier sketch in CA 145
Tageson, Carroll W(illiam) 1925- 53-56
Tagg, Christine Elizabeth 1962- 208
See also SATA 138
Taggard, Genevieve 1894-1948 166
See also DLB 45
Taggard, Mindy Nancarrow 1951- 143
Taggart, Dorothy T(rekell) 1917- 102
Taggart, (Paul) John 1942- CANR-1
Earlier sketch in CA 45-48
See also DLB 193
Taggart, John Scott
See Scott-Taggart, John
Taggart, Joseph Herman 1902-1984
Obituary 112
Taggart, Robert (III) 1945- 192
Brief entry 111
Tagger, Theodor 1891-1958
See Bruckner, Ferdinand
Tagiuri, Renato 1919- 77-80
Tagliabue, John 1923- 21-24R
See also CP 1, 2
Tagliaferri, Aldo 1931- 77-80
Tagliavia, Sheila 1936- 104
Tagliavini, Gabriela 1968- 202
Tagore, Amitendranath 1922- 61-64
Tagore, Rabindranath 1861-1941 120
Brief entry 104
See also DA3
See also DAM DRAM, POET
See also EWL 3
See also MTCW 1, 2
See also MTFW 2005
See also PC 8
See also PFS 18
See also RGEL 2
See also RGSF 2
See also RGWL 2, 3
See also SSC 48
See also TCLC 3, 53
See also TWA
Taguieff, Pierre-Andre 1946(?)- 231
Taha, Hamdy A(bdelaziz) 1937- 37-40R
Taha, Karen T(erry) 1942- 120
See also SATA 71, 156
Taha Husayn
See Hussein, Taha
See also AFW
Tahara, Mildred Machiko 1941- 104
Taher, Bahaa 1935- 219
Taheri, Amir 1942- 136
Tahir, Abe M(ahmoud), Jr. 1931- 69-72
Tahir, Kemal 1910(?)-1973
Obituary 45-48
Tahlaquah, David
See LeMond, Alan
Tahtinen, Dale R(udolph) 1945- 65-68
Tai, Hung-chao 1929- 73-76
Tai, Sharon O. 1963- 228
See also SATA 153
Taibbi, Matt 1970- 196
Taibo, Paco Ignacio II 1949- CANR-92
Earlier sketches in CA 131, CANR-58
See also HW 1
Taichert, Louise C(ecile) 1925- 89-92
Taikeff, Stanley 1940- 109
Taine, Hippolyte Adolphe 1828-1893 ..... EW 7
See also GFL 1789 to the Present
Taine, John
See Bell, Eric Temple
See also SCFW 1, 2
Taines, Beatrice (Green) 1923- CANR-14
Earlier sketch in CA 73-76
Tainter, Frank H(ugh) 1941- 159

Cumulative Index 567 **Tanner**

Taira, Koji 1926- 41-44R
Taishoff, Sol J(oseph) 1904-1982 ...... CANR-85
  Obituary 107
  Earlier sketch in CA 73-76
Tait, Alan A(nderson) 1934- CANR-10
  Earlier sketch in CA 21-24R
Tait, Arch 1943- 186
Tait, Dorothy 1902(?)-1972
  Obituary 33-36R
Tait, Douglas 1944- .... SATA 12
Tait, George E(dward) 1910-2000 .... 5-8R
Tait, Katharine 1923- 65-68
Tait, L(eslie) Gordon 1926- 45-48
Tait, Viola (Wilson) 1911-2002 230
Taitz, Emily 1937- 85-88
Tak, Sagetarius en Joost
  See Greshoff, Jan
Takabayashi, Mari 1960- 187
  See also SATA 115, 156
Takacs, Carol Addison 1926- 124
Takacs, Tibor 1954- 233
Takagi, Akimitsu 1920-1995 181
  Brief entry 108
Takagi, Dana Y. 1954- 141
Takahashi, Akira 1932- 29-32R
Takahashi, Mutsuo 1937- .... GLL 2
Takahashi, Rumiko 1957- 239
  See also AAYA 62
  See also SATA 163
Takahashi, Yasundo 1912-1996 .... CANR-14
  Obituary 182
  Earlier sketch in CA 41-44R
Takaki, Ronald T(oshiyuki) 1939- ... CANR-128
  Earlier sketches in CA 37-40R, CANR-75
Takakjian, Portia 1930- .... SATA 15
Takashima, Shizuye 1928- 45-48
  See also BYA 1
  See also CWRI 5
  See also SATA 13
Takayama, Akira 1932-1996 .... CANR-2
  Earlier sketch in CA 49-52
Takayama, Sandi 1962- 176
  See also SATA 106
Takdir Alisjahbana, Sutan 1908- .... EWL 3
Takeda, Pete(r M.) 1964- 222
  See also SATA 148
Takei, George (Hosato) 1937- 147
Takemae, Eiji 1930- 233
Takemitsu, Toru 1930- .... IDFW 3, 4
Takenaka, Heizo 1951- 142
Takeshita, Thomas Kohachiro 1891(?)-1973
  Obituary 45-48
Takeuchi, Naoko 1967- .... AAYA 53
Takeuchi, Yoshinori 1913- 132
Taki
  See Theodoracopulos, Taki
Taktsis, Costas 1927-1988 .... CANR-85
  Obituary 126
  Earlier sketch in CA 21-24R
  See also EWL 3
Talafous, Don (Francis) 1926- 113
Talalay, Kathryn M(arguerite) 1949- 154
Talamantes, Florence Williams 1931- . CANR-6
  Earlier sketch in CA 57-60
Talamini, John T(homas) 1940- 126
  Brief entry 113
Talarico, Ross 1945- 73-76
Talattof, Kamran 188
Talayesva, Don C. 1890-(?) .... NNAL
Talbert, Ansel Edward (McLaurine) 1912-1987
  Obituary 124
Talbert, Charles Gano 1912-1996 .... 5-8R
Talbert, Charles H(arold) 1934- CANR-99
  Earlier sketches in CA 41-44R, CANR-14, 31, 58
Talbert, Marc (Alan) 1953- CANR-130
  Earlier sketch in CA 136
  See also AAYA 25
  See also SATA 68, 99, 154
  See also SATA-Essay 154
  See also WYA
Talbot, Alice-Mary 1939- 112
Talbot, Allan R. 1934- CANR-10
  Earlier sketch in CA 21-24R
Talbot, Carol Terry 1913-2000 .... 13-16R
Talbot, Charlene Joy 1928- CANR-8
  Earlier sketch in CA 17-20R
  See also SATA 10
Talbot, Edward Hugh Frederick Chetwynd
  See Chetwynd-Talbot, Edward Hugh Frederick
Talbot, Emile J. 1941- 145
Talbot, Ethel 1888-1976 .... CWRI 5
Talbot, Godfrey (Walker) 1908-2000 107
  Obituary 189
Talbot, Gordon (Gray) 1928- CANR-14
  Earlier sketch in CA 69-72
Talbot, Hugh
  See Chetwynd-Talbot, Edward Hugh Frederick
Talbot, Kay
  See Rowland, D(onald) S(ydney)
Talbot, Lawrence
  See Bryant, Edward (Winslow, Jr.)
Talbot, Michael 1953-1992 .... CANR-81
  Obituary 137
  Earlier sketch in CA 119
  See also HGG
Talbot, Nathan B(ill) 1909-1994 104
  Obituary 196
Talbot, Norman (Clare) 1936- CANR-9
  Earlier sketch in CA 21-24R
  See also CP 1
Talbot, Ross B. 1919- 17-20R
Talbot, Toby 1928- CANR-29
  Earlier sketch in CA 21-24R
  See also SATA 14
Talbot Rice, David
  See Rice, David Talbot
Talbot Rice, Tamara (Abelson)
  See Rice, Tamara (Abelson) Talbot
Talbott, Basil 1899-1985
  Obituary 117
Talbott, Hudson 1949- CANR-137
  Earlier sketch in CA 128
  See also SATA 84, 131
Talbott, John E(dwin) 1940- 25-28R
Talbott, Lisa 219
Talbott, Robert D(ean) 1928- 57-60
Talbott, Strobe 1946- CANR-116
  Earlier sketches in CA 93-96, CANR-42
  See also AITN 1
Talcott, Dudley Vaill 1899-1986
  Obituary 119
Talens, Jenaro 1946- 212
Talent Family, The
  See Sedaris, David
Talese, Gay 1932- CANR-137
  Earlier sketches in CA 1-4R, CANR-9, 58
  Interview in CANR-9
  See also AITN 1
  See also CLC 37
  See also DLB 185
  See also MTCW 1, 2
  See also MTFW 2005
Talev, Dimiter 1898-1966 211
  See also DLB 181
  See also EWL 3
Talev, Dimitur
  See Talev, Dimiter
Taliaferro, H. E. 1811-1875 .... DLB 202
Taliaferro, John 1952- 191
Taliaferro, Tevi 1969- 229
Talifero, Gerald 1950- .... SATA 75
Talirunnilik, Joe 1899(?)-1976 214
Talker, T.
  See Rands, William Brighty
Talkin, Gil
  See Rosenthal, Alan
Talkington, Virginia Savage
  See McAlester, Virginia
Tall, Deborah 1951- CANR-114
  Earlier sketches in CA 105, CANR-22, 47
Tall, Stephen
  See Crook, Compton Newby
Talland, George A(lexander)
  1917-1968 .... CAP-2
  Earlier sketch in CA 25-28
Tallarico, Tony 1933- 188
  See also SATA 116
Tallcott, Emogene 29-32R
  See also SATA 10
Tallemant des Reaux, Gedeon
  1619-1692 .... GFL Beginnings to 1789
Tallent, Elizabeth (Ann) 1954- CANR-72
  Earlier sketch in CA 117
  See also CLC 45
  See also DLB 130
Tallent, Norman 1921-1994 .... 17-20R
Talleur, Richard W(iley) 1931- 97-100
Talley, Marcia 1943- 224
Talley-Morris, Neva B(ennett)
  1909-1996 57-60
Tallis, Frank 225
Tallis, (George) Michael 1931- 189
Tallis, Raymond 1946- 196
Tallis, Robyn
  See Coville, Bruce and
  Doyle, Debra and
  Macdonald, James D. and
  Smith, Sherwood and Zambreno, Mary Frances
Tallman, Albert 1902-1975 53-56
Tallman, Shirley 232
Tallmo, Karl-Erik 1953- 205
Tallmountain, Mary 1918-1997 146
  Obituary 161
  See also DLB 193
  See also NNAL
Tallon, Robert 1939- CANR-8
  Earlier sketch in CA 9-12R
  See also SATA 43
  See also SATA-Brief 28
Tally, Ted 1952- CANR-125
  Brief entry 120
  Earlier sketch in CA 124
  Interview in CA-124
  See also CAD
  See also CD 5, 6
  See also CLC 42
Talmadge, Herman Eugene 1913-2002 216
Talmadge, Marian .... SATA 14
Talmage, Anne
  See Powell, (Oval) Talmage
Talmage, Frank (Ephraim) 1938- 97-100
Talmey, Allene
  See Plaut, Allene Talmey
Talmon, Jacob L(aib) 1916-1980 ...... CANR-86
  Obituary 101
  Earlier sketch in CA 13-16R
Talmon, Shemaryahu 1920- CANR-112
  Earlier sketches in CA 29-32R, CANR-12, 28, 55
Talpalar, Morris 1900-1979 73-76
  Obituary 201
Talvi
  See Robinson, Therese
Talvik, Heiti 1904-1947 .... EWL 3
  See also TCLC 87
Talvio, Maila 1871-1951 .... EWL 3
Talvj
  See Robinson, Therese
  See also DLB 133
Talwar, Jennifer Parker 222
Tamaki, Norio 1940- CANR-85
  Earlier sketch in CA 128
Tamar, Erika 1934- CANR-122
  Earlier sketch in CA 168
  See also AAYA 30
  See also BYA 6
  See also SATA 62, 101, 150
Tamari, Meier 1927- 127
Tamarin, Alfred H. 1913-1980 .... CANR-4
  Obituary 102
  Earlier sketch in CA 29-32R
  See also SATA 13
Tamarkin, Jeff 226
Tamaro, Susanna 1958- CANR-129
  Earlier sketch in CA 172
Tamasi, Aron 1897-1966
  Obituary 114
  See also DLB 215
Tambasco, Anthony J(oseph) 1939- .. CANR-41
  Earlier sketch in CA 117
Tambi
  See Tambimuttu, Thurairajah
Tambiah, S. J.
  See Tambiah, Stanley Jeyaraja
Tambiah, Stanley J.
  See Tambiah, Stanley Jeyaraja
Tambiah, Stanley Jeyaraja 1929- CANR-125
  Earlier sketch in CA 123
Tambimuttu, Thurairajah 1915(?)-1983
  Obituary 110
Tambling, Jeremy (Charles Richard) 1948- .. 128
Tambs, Lewis Arthur 1927- CANR-4
  Earlier sketch in CA 53-56
Tamburine, Jean 1930- 9-12R
  See also SATA 12
Tamburri, Anthony Julian 1949- 138
Tambutti, Susana 1947- 211
Tamedly, Elisabeth L. 1931- 29-32R
Tames, Richard (Lawrence) 1946- 103
  See also SATA 67, 102
Tamir, Max Mordecai 1912- 29-32R
Tamir, Vicki 1924- 29-32R
Tamir, Zakariyya 1931- .... EWL 3
Tamm, Igor (Evgenievich) 1895-1971 162
Tamm, Igor Yevgenyevich
  See Tamm, Igor (Evgenievich)
Tammam, Abu c. 805-845 .... DLB 311
  See also WLIT 6
Tammaro, Thom(as Michael) 1951- 109
Tammeus, William David 1945- 136
Tamminga, Frederick W(illiam) 1934- 135
  See also SATA 66
Tammsaare, A(nton) H(ansen) 1878-1940 ... 164
  See also CDWLB 4
  See also DLB 220
  See also EWL 3
  See also TCLC 27
Tammuz, Benjamin 1919-1989 .... CANR-36
  Obituary 129
  Earlier sketch in CA 85-88
  See also EWL 3
  See also SATA-Obit 63
Tamny, Martin 1941- 37-40R
Tampion, John 1937- 73-76
Tam'si, Tchicaya U
  See Tchicaya, Gerald Felix
Tamsin
  See Summers, Ethel Snelson
Tamson, Janet
  See Smith, Pauline Janet (Urmson)
Tamulaitis, Vytas 1913-1982 .... 17-20R
Tamuno, Tekena N. 1932- 21-24R
Tamura, Linda 1949- 152
Tan, Amy (Ruth) 1952- CANR-132
  Earlier sketches in CA 136, CANR-54, 105
  See also AAL
  See also AAYA 9, 48
  See also AMWS 10
  See also BEST 89:3
  See also BPFB 3
  See also CDALBS
  See also CLC 59, 120, 151
  See also CN 6, 7
  See also CPW 1
  See also DA3
  See also DAM MULT, NOV, POP
  See also DLB 173, 312
  See also EXPN
  See also FL 1:6
  See also FW
  See also LAIT 3, 5
  See also MAL 5
  See also MTCW 2
  See also MTFW 2005
  See also NFS 1, 13, 16
  See also RGAL 4
  See also SATA 75
  See also SSFS 9
  See also YAW
Tan, Cecilia (Maureen) 1967- CANR-136
  Earlier sketch in CA 174
Tan, Fred 1955(?)-1990
  Obituary 131
Tan, Hwee-Hwee 1974- 191
Tan, Kok-Chor 1964- 233
Tana, Tomoe (Hayashima) 1913-1991 ... 21-24R
Tanahashi, Kazuaki 1933- 122
Tanaka, Beatrice 1932- 115
  See also SATA 76
Tanaka, Hideyuki 1940- 132
Tanaka, Shelley CANR-115
  Earlier sketch in CA 183
  See also MAICYA 2
  See also SATA 136
Tanaka, Yukiko 1940- 201
Tanaquil, Paul
  See Le Clercq, Jacques Georges Clemenceau
Tanay, Emanuel 1928- 93-96
Tanchuck, Nathaniel 1912-1978 .... 13-16R
Tancock, John (Leon) 1942- 105
Tancredi, Laurence R(ichard) 1940- .. CANR-39
  Earlier sketch in CA 116
Tandem, Felix
  See Spitteler, Carl (Friedrich Georg)
Tandon, Prakash 1911- 93-96
Tandori, Dezso 1938- .... DLB 232
Tandy, Clifford Ronald Vivien 1919(?)-1981
  Obituary 104
Taneda, Santoka 1882-1940 166
  See also Taneda Santoka
Taneda Santoka
  See Taneda, Santoka
  See also EWL 3
Taneda Shoichi
  See Taneda, Santoka
Tanenbaum, Jan Karl 1936- 61-64
Tanenbaum, Leora 1969- 185
Tanenbaum, Robert K. CANR-99
  Brief entry 116
  Earlier sketches in CA 128, CANR-60
Tanenhaus, Sam 163
Tang, Charles 1948- .... SATA 81
Tang, Peter Shen-Hao 1919- 1-4R
Tang, Victor 1942- 138
Tang, Xianzu 1550-1616 .... RGWL 3
Tang, You-Shan 1946- .... SATA 53
Tang, Yungmei 1940- 129
Tange, Kenzo 1913-2005 184
  Obituary 237
Tangerman, Elmer John 1907-1998 .. CANR-46
  Obituary 198
  Earlier sketches in CA 106, CANR-23
Tangherlini, Arne 1960-1999 189
Tangri, Shanti S. 1928- 25-28R
Tang Xianzu
  See Tang, Xianzu
Tangye, Nigel (Trevithick) 1909-1988 185
  Obituary 125
  Brief entry 117
Tanham, George K(ilpatrick)
  1922-2003 .... CANR-1
  Obituary 215
  Earlier sketch in CA 1-4R
Tania B.
  See Blixen, Karen (Christentze Dinesen)
Taniguchi, Kazuko 1946- 93-96
Taniguchi, Masaharu 1893-1985
  Obituary 116
Tanikawa, Shuntaro 1931- CANR-103
  Earlier sketches in CA 121, CANR-49
Tanis, James (Robert) 1928- 118
Tanis, Norman Earl 1929- 110
Tanizaki, Jun'ichiro 1886-1965 93-96
  Obituary 25-28R
  See also Tanizaki Jun'ichiro
  See also CLC 8, 14, 28
  See also MJW
  See also MTCW 2
  See also MTFW 2005
  See also RGSF 2
  See also RGWL 2
  See also SSC 21
Tanizaki Jun'ichiro
  See Tanizaki, Jun'ichiro
  See also DLB 180
  See also EWL 3
Tank, Herbert 1922(?)-1982
  Obituary 108
Tank, Ronald W(arren) 1929- 49-52
Tankard, Alice (Doumanian) 1926- 117
Tankard, James William, Jr. 1941- 73-76
Tanksley, Perry 1928- 37-40R
Tann, Jennifer 1939- 103
Tannahill, Reay 1929- CANR-59
  Earlier sketches in CA 49-52, CANR-2
  See also RHW
Tannehill, Robert C(ooper) 1934- CANR-51
  Earlier sketches in CA 45-48, CANR-26
Tannen, Deborah F(rances) 1945- CANR-95
  Earlier sketch in CA 118
  See also CLC 206
Tannen, Jack 1907-1991 .... CANR-87
  Obituary 136
  Earlier sketch in CA 114
Tannen, Mary 1943- CANR-51
  Earlier sketch in CA 105
  See also SATA 37
Tannenbaum, Arnold S(herwood)
  1925- 17-20R
Tannenbaum, Arthur C. 1941- 123
Tannenbaum, Beulah Goldstein
  1916- CANR-7
  Earlier sketch in CA 5-8R
  See also SATA 3
Tannenbaum, D(onald) Leb 1948- 115
  See also SATA 42
Tannenbaum, Edward R(obert) 1921- 17-20R
Tannenbaum, Frank 1893-1969 .... 9-12R
Tannenbaum, Harold E. 1914- 5-8R
Tannenbaum, Percy Hyman 1927-
  Brief entry 106
Tannenbaum, Robert 1915-2003 .... 21-24R
  Obituary 215
Tannenbaum, Stanley I. 1928-2001 144
  Obituary 197
Tanner, Adam 1964- 127
Tanner, C(harles) Kenneth 1938- 53-56
Tanner, Clara L(ee) 1905-1997 .... CANR-75
  Earlier sketch in CA 41-44R
Tanner, Daniel 1926- 17-20R
Tanner, Edward Everett III
  1921-1976 .... CANR-75
  Obituary 69-72
  Earlier sketch in CA 73-76
Tanner, Helen Hornbeck 1916- 61-64

Tanner, Henry 1918-1998 ... 73-76
Obituary ... 167
See also AAYA 49
Tanner, James M(ourilyan) 1920- ... CANR-5
Earlier sketch in CA 13-16R
Tanner, James T(homas) F(ontenot)
1937- ... 41-44R
Tanner, Jane 1946- ... SATA 74
Tanner, Janet 1941- ... 238
Tanner, Jo A. ... 145
Tanner, John
See Matcha, Jack
Tanner, John (Benedict Ian) 1927-2004 ... 103
Obituary ... 229
Tanner, John S. 1950- ... 138
Tanner, Karen Holliday (Olson)
1940- ... CANR-129
Earlier sketch in CA 168
Tanner, Louise S(tickney)
1922-2000 ... CANR-75
Obituary ... 188
Earlier sketch in CA 69-72
See also SATA 9
Tanner, Marcus ... CANR-111
Earlier sketch in CA 169
Tanner, Michael (K.) 1935- ... 168
Tanner, Nancy Makepeace 1933-1989
Obituary ... 129
Tanner, Norman P. 1943- ... 208
Tanner, Paul O(ra) W(arren) 1917- ... 61-64
Tanner, Roy L(ynn) 1947- ... 118
Tanner, Stephen L. 1938- ... 123
Tanner, Terence A(rthur) 1948-2003 ... 135
Obituary ... 222
Tanner, Thomas 1673(?)-1735 ... DLB 213
Tanner, Thomas 1936- ... 128
Tanner, Tony 1935-1998 ... 85-88
Obituary ... 172
Tanner, William
See Amis, Kingsley (William)
Tanner-Rutherford, C.
See Winchester, Clarence
Tanobe, Miyuki 1937- ... 69-72
See also SATA 23
Tanous, Peter (Joseph) 1938- ... CANR-7
Earlier sketch in CA 61-64
Tanselle, Eve 1933- ... SATA 125
Tanselle, G(eorge) Thomas 1934- ... CANR-52
Earlier sketches in CA 21-24R, CANR-11, 28
Tansi, Sony Labou
See Ntsoni, Marcel
See also EWL 3
Tansill, Charles Callan 1890-1964 ... 1-4R
Tanter, Raymond 1938- ... CANR-25
Earlier sketch in CA 45-48
Tantrist
See Cox, P(atrick) Brian
Tanyzer, Harold Joseph 1929- ... 9-12R
Tanzer, Lester 1929-2004 ... 17-20R
Obituary ... 234
Tanzer, Michael David 1935- ... 57-60
Tanzi, Rudolph E(mile) 1958- ... 203
Tanzi, Vito 1935- ... CANR-5
Earlier sketch in CA 53-56
Tao Lao
See Storni, Alfonsina
Tao Mulian
See Totten, George Oakley III
Tao Qian 365-427 ... RGWL 2, 3
Tapahonso, Luci 1953- ... CANR-127
Earlier sketches in CA 145, CANR-72
See also DLB 175
See also NNAL
See also PC 65
Tapert, Robert G. 1955(?)- ... 232
Tapia, Maria Del Carmen 1925- ... 190
Tapia, Ralph J(ohn) 1925-1989 ... 41-44R
Tapia, Richard A(lfred) 1939- ... 161
Tapio, Pat Decker
See Kines, Pat Decker
Tapley, Caroline 1934- ... 97-100
Taplin, Glen W(illiam) 1917-1993 ... 107
Taplin, Mark (Allard) 1957- ... 176
Taplin, Oliver 1943- ... CANR-117
Earlier sketch in CA 102
Taplin, Walter 1910-1986 ... CAP-1
Earlier sketch in CA 9-10
Taplinger, Cecily Lent 1943-1983
Obituary ... 110
Taplinger, Richard Jacques 1911-1973
Obituary ... 41-44R
Taplinger, Terry
See Taplinger, Cecily Lent
Tapon, Philippe ... 194
Tapp, Jack Thomas 1934- ... 49-52
Tapp, June Louin 1929- ... 41-44R
Tapp, Kathy Kennedy 1949- ... CANR-39
Earlier sketch in CA 116
See also SATA 88
See also SATA-Brief 50
Tapp, Robert B(erg) 1925- ... 41-44R
Tappan, Paul Wilbur 1911-1964 ... 5-8R
Tapper, Nancy
See Lindisfarne, Nancy
Tapper, Richard (Lionel) 1942- ... 238
Tappert, Theodore G(erhardt)
1904-1973 ... CANR-2
Earlier sketch in CA 1-4R
Tapply, H(orace) G(ardner) 1910- ... 13-16R
Tapply, William G(eorge) 1940- ... CANR-126
Earlier sketches in CA 118, CANR-41, 72
See also CMW 4
Tapscott, Stephen (J.) 1948- ... CANR-17
Earlier sketch in CA 89-92
Tapsell, R(obert) F(rederick) 1936- ... 21-24R
Taraborrelli, J. Randy 1956- ... CANR-111
Earlier sketch in CA 142
Taradash, Daniel (Irwin) 1913-2003 ... CANR-71
Obituary ... 214
Earlier sketch in CA 101
Interview in ... CA-101
See also DLB 44
See also IDFW 3, 4
Taragano, Martin 1959- ... 139
Taranovskii, Kirill Fyodorvich
See Taranovsky, Kiril (Fedorovich)
Taranovsky, Kiril (Fedorovich) 1911-1993 ... 114
Obituary ... 201
Taranow, Gerda ... 37-40R
Tarantino, Quentin (Jerome) 1963- ... CANR-125
Earlier sketch in CA 171
See also AAYA 58
See also CLC 125
Taras, Raymond (C.) 1946- ... 139
Tarascio, Vincent J(oseph) 1930- ... 45-48
Tarasov-Rodionov, Aleksandr Ignat'evich
1885-1938 ... DLB 272
Tarassoff, Lev
See Troyat, Henri
Tarassuk, Leonid (Ilyich) 1925-1990 ... 130
Obituary ... 132
Tarazaga, Santiago Genoves
See Genoves Tarazaga, Santiago
Tarbell, Ida M(inerva) 1857-1944 ... 181
Brief entry ... 122
See also DLB 47
See also TCLC 40
Tarbell, Roberta K. 1944- ... 139
Tarbert, Gary C(harles) 1937- ... 101
Tarbescu, Edith 1939- ... SATA 107
Tarbox, Katherine ... 194
Tarcher, Martin 1921- ... 17-20R
Tarcov, Nathan ... 171
Tardat, Claude 1949- ... 136
Tarde, Jean Gabriel 1843-1904 ... 214
Tardieu, Jean 1903-1995 ... 189
Brief entry ... 116
See also CWW 2
See also DLB 321
See also EWL 3
See also GFL 1789 to the Present
Tardieu d'Esclavelles, Louise-Florence-Petronille
See Epinay, Louise d'
Tardiff, Olive 1916- ... 73-76
Tardivel, J(ules)-P(aul) 1851-1905 ... 179
See also DLB 99
Tardos, Ann
See Tardos, Anne
Tardos, Anna
See Tardos, Anne
Tardos, Anne 1943- ... 190
Tardy, Gaye 1929(?)-1982
Obituary ... 108
Targ, Harry R. 1940- ... 118
Targ, Russell 1934- ... 104
Targ, William 1907-1999 ... 61-64
Obituary ... 185
Targan, Barry 1932- ... CANR-71
Earlier sketches in CA 73-76, CANR-17
See also DLB 130
Targ Brill, Marlene
See Brill, Marlene Targ
Target, G(eorge) W(illiam) 1924- ... CANR-7
Earlier sketch in CA 5-8R
Targetti, Ferdinando 1945- ... 146
Tarica, Ralph 1932- ... 113
Tarkenton, Fran(cis Asbury) 1940- ... 103
Tarkington, (Newton) Booth 1869-1946 ... 143
Brief entry ... 110
See also BPFB 3
See also BYA 3
See also CWRI 5
See also DLB 9, 102
See also MAL 5
See also MTCW 2
See also RGAL 4
See also SATA 17
See also TCLC 9
Tarkovskii, Andrei Arsen'evich
See Tarkovsky, Andrei (Arsenyevich)
Tarkovsky, Andrei (Arsenyevich)
1932-1986 ... 127
See also CLC 75
Tarling, (Peter) Nicholas 1931- ... 21-24R
Tarlock, A(nthony) Dan 1940- ... CANR-37
Earlier sketches in CA 97-100, CANR-16
Tarlov, I. M. 1905(?)-1977
Obituary ... 69-72
Tarlow, Nora
See Cohen, Nora
Tarlton, Gillian Leigh 1953- ... 119
Tarlton, John S. 1950- ... 233
Tarn, John Nelson 1934- ... 41-44R
Tarn, Nathaniel 1928- ... CANR-127
Earlier sketches in CA 9-12R, CANR-5, 30, 70
See also CAAS 16
See also CP 1, 2, 3, 4, 5, 6, 7
Tarnawski, Wit(old) 1894-1988
Obituary ... 126
Tarnawsky, Maxim 1955- ... 150
Tarnawsky, Ostap 1917- ... 73-76
Tarnman, Ian
See Fox, William L(yman)
Tarnopol, Lester 1913-1983 ... 77-80
Tarnopolsky, Yuri 1936- ... 153
Tarnower, Herman 1910-1980 ... CANR-87
Obituary ... 97-100
Earlier sketch in CA 89-92
Tarpey, Lawrence Xavier 1928-1987 ... 21-24R
Tarpley, Fred 1932- ... 41-44R
Tarpley, Natasha A(nastasia) 1971- ... CANR-128
Earlier sketch in CA 147
See also SATA 147
Tarpy, Roger M(aynard) 1941- ... 93-96
Tarr, Herbert 1929-1993 ... CANR-54
Obituary ... 143
Earlier sketch in CA 13-16R
Tarr, Joel A(rthur) 1934- ... CANR-38
Earlier sketches in CA 37-40R, CANR-14
Tarr, Judith 1955- ... CANR-112
Earlier sketches in CA 120, CANR-52
See also BPFB 3
See also FANT
See also SATA 64, 149
See also SFW 4
Tarr, Rodger L(eRoy) 1941- ... CANR-92
Earlier sketch in CA 110
Tarr, Yvonne Young 1929- ... CANR-8
Earlier sketch in CA 61-64
Tarrance, V(ernon) Lance, Jr. 1940- ... 37-40R
Tarrant, Desmond 1924- ... 21-24R
Tarrant, John
See Egleton, Clive (Frederick)
Tarrant, John J(oseph) 1924-1996 ... CANR-41
Earlier sketches in CA 53-56, CANR-4, 19
Tarrant, Wilma
See Sherman, Jory (Tecumseh)
Tarrok, Peer
See Zwerenz, Gerhard
Tarrow, Sidney G. 1938- ... CANR-138
Earlier sketch in CA 173
Tarry, Ellen 1906- ... CANR-69
Earlier sketch in CA 73-76
See also BW 1, 3
See also CLR 26
See also SAAS 16
See also SATA 16
Tarsaidze, Alexandre 1901-1978 ... 37-40R
Obituary ... 77-80
Tarshis, Jerome 1936- ... 61-64
See also SATA 9
Tarsis, Valery Yakovlevich 1906-1983
Obituary ... 109
Tarski, Alfred 1901(?)-1983 ... 157
Obituary ... 111
Tarsky, Sue 1946- ... CANR-31
Earlier sketch in CA 112
See also SATA 41
Tart, Charles T(heodore) 1937- ... 29-32R
Tarter, Donald E(dward) 1938- ... 112
Tartikoff, Brandon 1949-1997 ... 166
Tartre, Raymond S. 1901-1975 ... CAP-2
Earlier sketch in CA 21-22
Tartt, Donna 1964(?)- ... CANR-135
Earlier sketch in CA 142
See also AAYA 56
See also CLC 76
See also MTFW 2005
Tarver, Ben 1927- ... 113
Tarzan, Deloris Lehman
See Ament, Deloris Tarzan
Tas, Filip (Josef) 1918- ... 210
Tasca, Henry J. 1912-1979
Obituary ... 89-92
Tasca, Jules 1938- ... CANR-26
Earlier sketch in CA 109
See also AITN 1
Tasch, Peter A(nthony) 1933- ... 73-76
Taschdjian, Claire L(ouise) 1914-1998 ... 73-76
Obituary ... 199
Tashjian, Dickran (Levon) 1940- ... 61-64
Tashjian, Janet 1956- ... CANR-131
Earlier sketch in CA 169
See also MAICYA 2
See also SATA 102, 151
Tashjian, Virginia A. 1921- ... 29-32R
See also SATA 3
Tashlin, Frank 1913-1972 ... CANR-69
Obituary ... 110
Earlier sketch in CA 113
See also DLB 44
Tashmuhammad-oghli, Musa 1905-1968
See Aybek
Tasker, James 1908- ... 49-52
See also SATA 9
Tasker, Joe 1948-1982 ... 129
Obituary ... 108
Tasma
See Couvreur, Jessie
Tassin, Myron Jude 1933- ... 61-64
Tassin, Ray(mond Jean) 1926-1991 ... 53-56
Tasso, Torquato 1544-1595 ... EFS 2
See also EW 2
See also RGWL 2, 3
See also WLIT 7
Tata, Sam (Bejan) 1911- ... 216
Tatalovich, Raymond 1943- ... 152
Tatar, Maria M. 1945- ... 85-88
Tatarka, Dominik 1913-1989
Obituary ... 128
See also EWL 3
Tatarkiewicz, Wladyslaw 1886-1980 ... 103
Obituary ... 97-100
Tatchell, Peter 1952- ... CANR-52
Earlier sketch in CA 125
Tate, (John Orley) Allen
1899-1979 ... CANR-108
Obituary ... 85-88
Earlier sketches in CA 5-8R, CANR-32
See also AMW
See also CLC 2, 4, 6, 9, 11, 14, 24
See also CN 1, 2
See also CP 1, 2
See also DLB 4, 45, 63
See also DLBD 17
See also EWL 3
See also MAL 5
See also MTCW 1, 2
See also MTFW 2005
See also PC 50
See also RGAL 4
See also RHW
Tate, B. H.
See Boyer, Bruce Hatton
Tate, Carolyn E. 1952- ... 144
Tate, Claudia C. 1946-2002 ... 121
Obituary ... 211
Tate, Don(ald E.) ... SATA 159
Tate, Edward
See Dransfield, Michael (John Pender)
Tate, Eleanora E(laine) 1948- ... CANR-81
Earlier sketches in CA 105, CANR-25, 43
See also AAYA 25
See also BW 2, 3
See also CLR 37
See also CWRI 5
See also JRDA
See also MAICYA 2
See also MAICYAS 1
See also SATA 38, 94
Tate, Ellalice
See Hibbert, Eleanor Alice Burford
Tate, Gary 1930- ... 21-24R
Tate, George T(homas) 1931- ... 21-24R
Tate, Greg ... 226
Tate, Jackson R. 1899(?)-1978
Obituary ... 81-84
Tate, James (Vincent) 1943- ... CANR-114
Earlier sketches in CA 21-24R, CANR-29, 57
See also CLC 2, 6, 25
See also CP 1, 2, 3, 4, 5, 6, 7
See also DLB 5, 169
See also EWL 3
See also PFS 10, 15
See also RGAL 4
See also WP
Tate, Joan 1922- ... CANR-54
Earlier sketches in CA 49-52, CANR-1, 48
See also CWRI 5
See also SAAS 20
See also SATA 9, 86
Tate, Marilyn Freeman 1921- ... 13-16R
Tate, Mary Anne
See Hale, Arlene
Tate, Merle W(esley) 1903-1984 ... CAP-1
Earlier sketch in CA 17-18
Tate, Merze 1905-1996 ... 17-20R
Obituary ... 152
Tate, Nahum 1652(?)-1715 ... DLB 80
See also RGEL 2
Tate, Nikki ... 203
See also SATA 134
Tate, Peter 1940- ... 161
See also SFW 4
Tate, Richard
See Masters, Anthony (Richard)
Tate, Robin
See Fanthorpe, R(obert) Lionel
Tate, Suzanne 1930- ... SATA 91
Tate, Velma 1913-1997 ... 21-24R
Tatelbaum, Judith Ann 1938- ... 104
Tatelbaum, Judy
See Tatelbaum, Judith Ann
Tatem, Moira (Phillips) 1928- ... 133
Tatford, Brian F(rederick) B(arrington)
1927- ... CAP-1
Earlier sketch in CA 9-10
Tatford, Frederick Albert 1901- ... CANR-10
Earlier sketch in CA 13-16R
Tatgenhorst, John 1938- ... 65-68
Tatham, Andrew Francis 1949- ... 125
Tatham, Betty ... 213
See also SATA 142
Tatham, C. Ernest 1905-1997 ... CAP-1
Earlier sketch in CA 9-10
Tatham, Campbell
See Elting, Mary
Tatham, David 1932- ... 138
Tatham, John c. 1610- ... RGEL 2
Tatham, Julie
See Tatham, Julie Campbell
Tatham, Julie Campbell 1908-1999 ... 148
See also SATA 80
Tatham, Laura (Esther) 1919- ... 13-16R
Tati, Jacques
See Tatischeff, Jacques
Tatischeff, Jacques 1908-1982
Obituary ... 108
Tatlock, Ann 1959- ... 219
Tatlow, Antony 1935- ... CANR-48
Earlier sketch in CA 122
Taton, Rene 1915- ... 9-12R
Tatray, Istvan
See Rupert, Raphael Rudolph
Tattersall, Ian (Michael) 1945- ... CANR-130
Earlier sketch in CA 115
Tattersall, (Honor) Jill 1931- ... CANR-10
Earlier sketch in CA 25-28R
Tattersall, Lawrence H(olmes) 1933- ... 29-32R
Tattersall, M(uriel Joyce) 1931- ... CAP-1
Earlier sketch in CA 9-10
Tattlin, Isadora ... 216

Cumulative Index 569 Taylor

Tatu, Michel 1933- 25-28R
Tatum, Arlo 1923- 25-28R
Tatum, Billy Joe 1933- 61-64
Tatum, Charles M(ichael) 1943- CANR-29
Earlier sketch in CA 111
Tatum, Edward Lawrie 1909-1975
Obituary 113
Tatum, Jack
See Tatum, John David
Tatum, James (Harvey) 1942- 224
Tatum, John David 1948- 104
Taub, Harald (Jay) 1918- 110
Taube, Evert 1890-1976 212
Obituary 61-64
Taube, Lester S. 1920- 69-72
Taubenfeld, Howard J(ack) 1924- 13-16R
Tauber, Abraham 1915(?)-1977
Obituary 69-72
Tauber, Edward S(anford) 1908-1988
Obituary 124
Tauber, Gerald E(rich) 1922-1989 89-92
Tauber, Gilbert 1935- CANR-9
Earlier sketch in CA 21-24R
Tauber, Kurt P(hilip) 1922- 21-24R
Tauber, Maurice F(alcolm) 1908-1980 105
Obituary 102
Tauber, Peter 1947-2004 37-40R
Obituary 225
Taubert, Sigfred 1914- 120
Taubert, William H(owland) 1934- 103
Taubes, Frederic 1900-1981 CANR-9
Obituary 104
Earlier sketch in CA 17-20R
Taubes, Susan
See Feldmann, Susan Judith
Taubes, Timothy 1955- 148
Taubman, Bruce 1947- 141
Taubman, Jane A. 1942- 130
Taubman, Philip 1948- 225
Taubman, William 1941- CANR-130
Earlier sketch in CA 21-24R
Taubr, Paul Raymond 1937- 29-32R
Taucar, Christopher Edward 1968- 196
Taufer, Veno 1933- DLB 181
Taulbert, Clifton L(emoure) 1945- 143
See also BW 2
Tauler, Johannes c. 1300-1361 DLB 179
See also LMFS 1
Taunton, Eric
See Westcott-Jones, K(enneth)
Tauranac, John 1939- 124
Tausk, Petr 1927-1988 217
Taussig, Helen Brooke 1898-1986 163
Tavard, George H(enry) 1922- CANR-37
Earlier sketches in CA 1-4R, CANR-1, 16
Tavares, Matt SATA 159
Tavares, Salette 1922-1994 DLB 287
Tavcar, Ivan 1851-1923 DLB 147
Tave, Stuart M(alcolm) 1923- 104
Tavel, Ronald 1940- CANR-33
Earlier sketch in CA 21-24R
See also CAD
See also CD 5, 6
See also CLC 6
Taverne, Dick 1928- 85-88
Taverner, Richard 1505(?)-1575(?) DLB 236
Tavernier, Bertrand 1941- 123
Tavernor, Robert (William) 1954- CANR-135
Earlier sketch in CA 168
Taves, Ann 1952- 192
Taves, Ernest H(enry) 1916-2003 93-96
Obituary 221
Taves, Isabella 1915- CANR-8
Earlier sketch in CA 21-24R
See also SATA 27
Taviani, Paolo 1931- 153
See also CLC 70
Taviani, Vittorio 1929- 153
Taviss, Irene
See Thomson, Irene Taviss
Tavo, Gus
See Ivan, Martha Miller Pfaff
Tavor, Eve
See Bannet, Eve Tavor
Tavoularis, Dean 1932- IDFW 3, 4
Tavris, Carol (Anne) 1944- 143
Tavuchis, Nicholas 1934- 57-60
Tavy, Peter
See Hemery, Eric
Tawa, Nicholas E. 1923- CANR-135
Earlier sketch in CA 136
Tawfiq al-Hakim
See Hakim, Tawfiq al-
See also RGWL 2
Tawney, R(ichard) H(enry) 1880-1962
Obituary 93-96
Tax, Meredith (Jane) 1942- 144
Tax, Sol 1907-1995 5-8R
Taydo
See McDonald, Erwin L(awrence)
Tayler, Irene 136
Tayler, Jeffrey 1962(?)- 227
Taylor, A(lan) J(ohn) P(ercivale)
1906-1990 CANR-32
Obituary 132
Earlier sketch in CA 5-8R
See also MTCW 1, 2
See also MTFW 2005
Taylor, Alan 1955- 206
Taylor, Alan Carey 1905-1975
Obituary 114
Taylor, Alan R(os) 1926-1992 CANR-86
Obituary 139
Earlier sketch in CA 109
Taylor, Alastair 1959 SATA 130
Taylor, Alastair M(acDonald) 1915- 17-20R
Taylor, Albert E(dward) 1908- 89-92
Taylor, Alec Clifton
See Clifton-Taylor, Alec
Taylor, Alfred 1896-1973 105
Taylor, Alice J. 1909-1969 CAP-2
Earlier sketch in CA 25-28
Taylor, Alice L(ouise) 1911-1985 61-64
Obituary 116
Taylor, Alison 1927- 21-24R
Taylor, Alix 1921- 5-8R
Taylor, Allegra 1940- 136
Taylor, Andrew (McDonald) 1940- CANR-51
Earlier sketches in CA 69-72, CANR-11, 27
See also CP 1, 7
Taylor, Andrew 1944-1988 126
Taylor, Andrew (John Robert) 1951- CANR-97
Earlier sketches in CA 110, CANR-28, 52
See also CMW 4
See also SATA 70
Taylor, Anique 1946- 109
Taylor, Ann
See Smith, Richard Rein
Taylor, Ann 1782-1866 DLB 163
See also SATA 41
See also SATA-Brief 35
Taylor, Anna 1944- 25-28R
Taylor, Anne 1934- 140
See also HGG
Taylor, Anne (Gary) Pannell 1910-1984
Obituary 112
Taylor, Anne-Marie 1964- 225
Taylor, Apirana 1956- 128
Taylor, Archer 1890-1973
Obituary 107
Taylor, Arnold H. 1929- 33-36R
Taylor, Art(hur Stephen, Jr.) 1929-1995 122
Obituary 148
Taylor, Arthur Samuel 1894-1963 CANR-86
Obituary 103
Earlier sketch in CA 1-4R
Taylor, Audilee Boyd 1931- SATA 59
Taylor, Barbara G. 1942- 25-28R
Taylor, Barbara J. 1927- 53-56
See also SATA 10
Taylor, Bayard 1825-1878 DLB 3, 189, 250, 254
See also RGAL 4
Taylor, Ben
See Strachan, Ian
Taylor, Benjamin J. 1934- 21-24R
Taylor, Bernard (Irvin) 1934- CANR-81
Earlier sketches in CA 69-72, CANR-24
See also HGG
Taylor, Bert Leston 1866-1921
Brief entry 117
See also DLB 25
Taylor, Betty Jo 1933- 13-16R
Taylor, Beverly (White) 1947- 132
Taylor, Bob L(eslie) 1923- 33-36R
Taylor, Brad
See Smith, Richard Rein
Taylor, Bron Raymond 1955- 138
Taylor, Bruce 1947- 175
Taylor, Bruce E. 1947- 201
Taylor, C(ecil) P(hilip) 1929-1981 CANR-47
Obituary 105
Earlier sketch in CA 25-28R
See also CBD
See also CLC 27
Taylor, Carl 1937- 69-72
See also SATA 14
Taylor, Carl S. 1949- 146
Taylor, Carol MacKenzie 1957- 167
Taylor, Charlene M(ae) 1938- 33-36R
Taylor, Charles 1931- CANR-27
Earlier sketches in CA 13-16R, CANR-11
Taylor, Charles Alfred 1922-2002 109
Obituary 205
Taylor, Charles D(oonan) 1938- CANR-37
Earlier sketches in CA 101, CANR-17
Taylor, Charles Henry 1846-1921 166
See also DLB 25
Taylor, Charles Lewis 1935- CANR-13
Earlier sketch in CA 77-80
Taylor, Cheryl Munro 1957- SATA 96
Taylor, Clyde R(ussell) 1931- 45-48
Taylor, Clyde Willis 1904-1988
Obituary 125
Taylor, Constance Lindsay
1907-2000 CANR-75
Earlier sketch in CA 106
Taylor, Cora (Lorraine) 1936- CANR-125
Earlier sketch in CA 124
See also CLR 63
See also CWRI 5
See also SATA 64, 103
Taylor, Cora Sibal 1941(?)-1987
Obituary 123
Taylor, D. J. 1960- CANR-112
Earlier sketch in CA 122
Taylor, Dallas 1948- 157
Taylor, Dalmas A(rnold) 1933-1998 57-60
Obituary 164
Taylor, Daniel (William) 1948- 154
Taylor, Dave 1948- 146
See also SATA 78
Taylor, David
See Taylor, Dave
Taylor, David 1900-1965 1-4R
See also SATA 10
Taylor, David (Conrad) 1934- 105
Taylor, David Alan 1943- 108
Taylor, Dawson 1916- CANR-50
Earlier sketches in CA 13-16R, CANR-25
Taylor, Day
See Parkinson, Cornelia M. and Salvato, Sharon
Taylor, Dayna
See Parkinson, Cornelia M.
Taylor, (Joseph) Deems 1885-1966
Obituary 89-92
Taylor, Delores 138
Taylor, Demetria 1903-1977
Obituary 73-76
Taylor, (Edmund) Dennis 1940- CANR-43
Earlier sketch in CA 119
Taylor, Desmond 1930- CANR-45
Earlier sketch in CA 37-40R
Taylor, Diana 1950- 235
Taylor, Don(ald) 1910-1998 13-16R
Taylor, Don(ald) 1943-1999 219
Taylor, Don(ald D.) 1946- 192
Taylor, Donald L(avor) 1916- 17-20R
Taylor, Donald Stewart 1924- 190
Brief entry 106
Taylor, Donathan 1962- 193
Taylor, Donna June 1949- 37-40R
Taylor, Drew Hayden 1962- 208
Taylor, Duncan (Burnett) 1912- CANR-91
Earlier sketch in CA 25-28R
Taylor, Duncan Norton
See Norton-Taylor, Duncan
Taylor, Dwight 1902-1986(?)
Obituary 121
Taylor, Earl Aulick 1904-1965 CAP-1
Earlier sketch in CA 13-14
Taylor, Edith 1913- 45-48
Taylor, Edward 1642(?)-1729 AMW
See also DA
See also DAB
See also DAC
See also DAM MST, POET
See also DLB 24
See also EXPP
See also PC 63
See also RGAL 4
See also TUS
Taylor, Eleanor Ross 1920- CANR-70
Earlier sketch in CA 81-84
See also CLC 5
Taylor, Elisabeth (D.) 1931- 135
Taylor, Elisabeth Russell
See Russell Taylor, Elisabeth
Taylor, Elizabeth 1912-1975 CANR-70
Earlier sketches in CA 13-16R, CANR-9
See also CLC 2, 4, 29
See also CN 1, 2
See also DLB 139
See also MTCW 1
See also RGEL 2
See also SATA 13
Taylor, Elizabeth (Rosemond)
1932- CANR-144
Earlier sketch in CA 172
Taylor, Elizabeth Atwood 1936- 142
Taylor, Elizabeth Tebbetts 101
Taylor, Ethel Stoddard 1895(?)-1975
Obituary 57-60
Taylor, Eugene Jackson 1913-1978
Obituary 81-84
Taylor, Florance Walton 37-40R
See also SATA 9
Taylor, Florence M(arian Tompkins)
1892-1983 13-16R
See also SATA 9
Taylor, Frank
See Hutson, Shaun
Taylor, Frank J. 1894-1972 CAP-1
Obituary 37-40R
Earlier sketch in CA 13-14
Taylor, Fred James 1919- 107
Taylor, (George) Frederick 1928- 77-80
Taylor, Frederick Winslow 1856-1915 188
See also TCLC 76
Taylor, G(eorge) Jeffrey 1944- 116
Taylor, G(raham) P(eter) 1959(?)- 236
See also SATA 156
Taylor, Gage 1942-2000 SATA 87
Taylor, Gary 1953- 154
Taylor, George
See Parulski, George R(ichard), Jr.
Taylor, George A(lbert) 1942- 102
Taylor, George E(dward) 1905-2000 CANR-22
Obituary 189
Earlier sketch in CA 1-4R
Taylor, Gillian F. 1967- 218
Taylor, Gordon O(verton) 1938- 25-28R
Taylor, Gordon Rattray 1911-1981 85-88
Obituary 105
Taylor, Graham
See Taylor, G(raham) P(eter)
Taylor, Greg(ory Thomas) 1963- 200
Taylor, (Frank Herbert) Griffin 1917- 65-68
Taylor, H. Baldwin
See Waugh, Hillary Baldwin
Taylor, H. Kerr 1891(?)-1977
Obituary 73-76
Taylor, Harold 1914-1993 25-28R
Obituary 140
Taylor, Harold L(awrence) 1934- 110
Taylor, Harold McCarter 1907-1995 109
Obituary 150
Taylor, Harold S. 1901(?)-1985
Obituary 116
Taylor, Harry
See Granick, Harry
Taylor, Harry H. 1926- 57-60
Taylor, Helen 1947- CANR-86
Earlier sketch in CA 133
Taylor, Henry 1800-1886 CSW
See also DLB 32
Taylor, Henry (Splawn) 1942- CANR-31
Earlier sketch in CA 33-36R
See also CAAS 7
See also CLC 44
See also CP 7
See also DLB 5
See also PFS 10
Taylor, Henry J(unior) 1902-1984 CANR-86
Obituary 112
Earlier sketches in CAP-2, CA 23-24
Taylor, Herb(ert Norman, Jr.)
1942-1987 97-100
Obituary 123
See also SATA 22
See also SATA-Obit 54
Taylor, Howard F(rancis) 1939- 110
Taylor, Hugh 1917(?)-1987
Obituary 123
Taylor, Hugh A(lexander) 1920- 115
Taylor, Ian (R.) 1944- CANR-93
Earlier sketch in CA 77-80
Taylor, Ina (Margaret Kathleen) 1949- 119
Taylor, Irving A. 1925- 61-64
Taylor, J. David
See Taylor, Dave
Taylor, J. Thomas 1930- 107
See also Taylor, Tom
Taylor, Jack W(ilson) 1915- 9-12R
Taylor, James A(llan) 1925-2002 147
Obituary 207
Taylor, James B(entley) 1930- 37-40R
Taylor, James C(hapman) 1937- 77-80
Taylor, James R(owe) 1907- CAP-2
Earlier sketch in CA 17-18
Taylor, James R. 1928- 204
Taylor, James Spear 1897(?)-1979
Obituary 85-88
Taylor, James Stephen 1935- 121
Taylor, Jane 1783-1824 DLB 163
See also SATA 41
See also SATA-Brief 35
Taylor, Janelle (Diane Williams)
1944- CANR-112
Brief entry 118
Earlier sketches in CA 124, CANR-43, 67
Interview in CA-124
See also RHW
Taylor, (Samuel) Jared 1951- CANR-64
Earlier sketch in CA 122
Taylor, Jay
See Taylor, Joseph E. III
Taylor, Jay 1931- 199
Taylor, Jayne
See Krentz, Jayne Ann
Taylor, Jean 1947- 151
Taylor, Jed H(arbottle) 1902-1990 CAP-1
Earlier sketch in CA 13-16
Taylor, Jennifer (Evelyn) 1935- 128
Taylor, Jenny 1910- 105
Taylor, Jeremy c. 1613-1667 DLB 151
Taylor, Jeremy F. 1952- 137
Taylor, Jeremy James 1948- 128
Taylor, Jerome 1918- CANR-1
Earlier sketch in CA 1-4R
Taylor, Jerry D(uncan) 1938- 115
See also SATA 47
Taylor, Jesse
See Amidon, Bill (Vincent)
Taylor, Jim 239
Taylor, Jim 1937- 119
Taylor, Jim 1958- 214
Taylor, Joan du Plat (?)-1983
Obituary 109
Taylor, Joan E(lizabeth) 1958- CANR-130
Earlier sketch in CA 163
Taylor, Joe 1949- 159
Taylor, Joe Gray 1920- CANR-6
Earlier sketch in CA 57-60
Taylor, John 1577(?)-1653 DLB 121
Taylor, John 1916- 93-96
Taylor, John 1921-2003 CANR-16
Obituary 222
Earlier sketch in CA 21-24R
Taylor, John 1925- 81-84
Taylor, John (Alfred) 1931- 61-64
Taylor, John 1955- CANR-137
Earlier sketch in CA 124
Taylor, John F(rank) A(dams) 1915- 17-20R
Taylor, John G(erald) 1931- CANR-96
Earlier sketch in CA 29-32R
Taylor, John H(ilton) 1958- 138
Taylor, John Laverack 1937- CANR-1
Earlier sketch in CA 45-48
Taylor, John M(axwell) 1930- 25-28R
Taylor, John Randolph 1929-2002 1-4R
Obituary 203
Taylor, John Robert
See Taylor, Andrew (John Robert)
Taylor, John Russell 1935- CANR-91
Earlier sketches in CA 5-8R, CANR-37
Taylor, John Vernon 1914-2001 CANR-44
Obituary 192
Earlier sketches in CA 9-12R, CANR-5, 21
Taylor, John W(illiam) R(ansom)
1922-1999 49-52
Obituary 188
Taylor, Joseph E. III 1958- 191
Taylor, Joshua Charles 1917-1981 104
Taylor, Judith M. 1934- 195
Taylor, Judy
See Hough, Judy Taylor
Taylor, Kamala (Purnaiya) 1924-2004 77-80
Obituary 227
See also Markandaya, Kamala
See also MTFW 2005
See also NFS 13

Taylor 570 CONTEMPORARY AUTHORS

Taylor, Karen
See Malpede, Karen (Sophia)
Taylor, Karen E. 234
Taylor, Karl K. 1938- 41-44R
Taylor, Katharine Whiteside
1897-1989 .... CAP-2
Earlier sketch in CA 25-28
Taylor, Kathy 1950- CANR-110
Earlier sketch in CA 154
Taylor, Keith Weller 1946- 111
Taylor, Ken 1922- 108
Taylor, Kenneth N(athaniel)
1917-2005 .... CANR-8
Earlier sketch in CA 17-20R
See also AITN 2
See also SATA 26
Taylor, (Paul) Kent 1940- CANR-9
Earlier sketch in CA 17-20R
Taylor, L(aurie) A(ylma Sparer)
1939-1996 .... CANR-30
Obituary 200
Earlier sketch in CA 111
Taylor, L(ester) B(arbour), Jr. 1932- CANR-26
Earlier sketches in CA 57-60, CANR-11
See also SATA 27
Taylor, Larissa J(uliet) 1952- 138
Taylor, Lawrence 1942- 105
Taylor, (M.) Lee 1930- 41-44R
Taylor, Lester D(ean) 1938- 17-20R
Taylor, Lisa (Suter) 1933-1991 128
Obituary 134
Taylor, Liz McNeill
See Taylor, Elisabeth (D.)
Taylor, Liza Pennywitt 1955- 140
Taylor, Lloyd A(ndrew) 1921- 41-44R
Taylor, Lloyd C(hamberlain), Jr. 1923- 57-60
Taylor, Lois Dwight Cole
See Cole, Lois Dwight
Taylor, Lord
See Taylor, Stephen James Lake
Taylor, Louis 1900-1981 .... CANR-2
Earlier sketch in CA 5-8R
Taylor, Louise Todd 1939- 115
See also SATA 47
Taylor, Lucy (Campbell) 1950(?)- 174
Taylor, M(artin) J. 1952- 143
Taylor, Malcolm Gordon 1915- 109
Taylor, Margaret
See Burroughs, Margaret Taylor (Goss)
Taylor, Margaret
See Burroughs, Margaret Taylor (Goss)
Taylor, Margaret 1950- 176
See also SATA 106
Taylor, Margaret Stewart 89-92
Taylor, Marion Ansel 1904- 13-16R
Taylor, Mark 1927- 108
See also SATA 32
See also SATA-Brief 28
Taylor, Mark C. 1945- CANR-56
Earlier sketch in CA 125
Taylor, Mary Ann 1912-1984 97-100
Taylor, Mary F. 233
Taylor, Maureen 1956- 184
Taylor, Maxwell D(avenport) 1901-1987
Obituary 122
Brief entry 111
Taylor, Mel 1939- 194
Taylor, Michael J. 1924- CANR-7
Earlier sketch in CA 17-20R
Taylor, Michael J(ohn) H(addrick)
1949- CANR-93
Earlier sketches in CA 77-80, CANR-14, 34
Taylor, Michael M. 1944- 97-100
Taylor, Michael Ray 1959- 160
Taylor, Michelle 1968- 196
Taylor, Mildred D(elois) 1943- CANR-136
Earlier sketches in CA 85-88, CANR-25, 115
See also AAYA 10, 47
See also BW 1
See also BYA 3, 8
See also CLC 21
See also CLR 9, 59, 90
See also CSW
See also DLB 52
See also JRDA
See also LAIT 3
See also MAICYA 1, 2
See also MTFW 2005
See also SAAS 5
See also SATA 135
See also WYA
See also YAW
Taylor, Moddie Daniel 1912-1976 168
Taylor, Morris F. 1915- 37-40R
Taylor, Murry A. 1941- 191
Taylor, Nick 1945- CANR-95
Earlier sketch in CA 146
Taylor, Nina 1942- 197
Taylor, Norman 1883-1967 .... CAP-2
Earlier sketch in CA 23-24
Taylor, Owen Reece 1912(?)-1983
Obituary 111
Taylor, P(hilip) A. M. 1920- 136
Taylor, Pat Ellis 1941- 111
Taylor, Paul 1948- 121
Taylor, Paul B(eekman) 1930- CANR-87
Earlier sketch in CA 81-84
Taylor, Paul F. 1927- 146
Taylor, Paul S(chuster) 1895-1984 .... CANR-29
Obituary 112
Earlier sketch in CA 81-84
Taylor, Paul W(arren) 1923- CANR-21
Earlier sketch in CA 1-4R
Taylor, Paula (Wright) 1942- 122
Brief entry 111
See also SATA 48
See also SATA-Brief 33
Taylor, Peggy 1946- 120
Taylor, Peter (Hillsman) 1917-1994 .. CANR-50
Obituary 147
Earlier sketches in CA 13-16R, CANR-9
Interview in CANR-9
See also AMWS 5
See also BPFB 3
See also CLC 1, 4, 18, 37, 44, 50, 71
See also CN 1, 2, 3, 4, 5
See also CSW
See also DLB 218, 278
See also DLBY 1981, 1994
See also EWL 3
See also EXPS
See also MAL 5
See also MTCW 1, 2
See also MTFW 2005
See also RGSF 2
See also SSC 10, 84
See also SSFS 9
See also TUS
Taylor, Peter 1942- 221
Taylor, Philip Elbert 1908-1975
Obituary 61-64
Taylor, Phoebe Atwood 1909-1976
Obituary 61-64
See also CMW 4
Taylor, Phoebe Jean 1921(?)-1979
Obituary 89-92
Taylor, Quintard 1948- 168
Taylor, Ransom Theodore 1913-1992 45-48
Taylor, Ray J. 1918(?)-1977
Obituary 69-72
Taylor, Ray Ward 1908-1987 .... CAP-2
Earlier sketch in CA 19-20
Taylor, Rebe Prestwich 1911- 13-16R
Taylor, Regina (Annette) 1960(?)- 230
Taylor, Renee 1935- 178
Taylor, Rex 1921- 13-16R
Taylor, Richard 1919- 17-20R
Taylor, Richard K(night) 1933- CANR-39
Earlier sketches in CA 101, CANR-18
Taylor, Richard S(helley) 1912- CANR-38
Earlier sketch in CA 115
Taylor, Richard W(arren) 1924- CANR-19
Earlier sketches in CA 5-8R, CANR-3
Taylor, Robert, Jr. 1941- CANR-109
See also Taylor, Robert Love
Taylor, Robert 1925- 81-84
Taylor, Robert 1941- 217
Taylor, Robert 1943- 220
Taylor, Robert Allan 1958- 208
Taylor, Robert B(artley) 1926- 81-84
Taylor, Robert Brown 1936- CANR-12
Earlier sketch in CA 61-64
Taylor, Robert H(enry) 1943- 217
Taylor, Robert Lewis 1912-1998 .... CANR-64
Obituary 170
Earlier sketches in CA 1-4R, CANR-3
See also CLC 14
See also CN 1, 2
See also SATA 10
See also TCWW 1, 2
Taylor, Robert Love 1941- CANR-109
Earlier sketch in CA 118
See also Taylor, Robert, Jr.
Taylor, Robert Martin 1909-1978 .... CAP-2
Earlier sketch in CA 25-28
Taylor, Robert R(atcliffe) 1939- 53-56
Taylor, Rogan 1945- CANR-65
Earlier sketch in CA 152
Taylor, Roger CANR-110
Earlier sketch in CA 155
See also FANT
Taylor, Roland 1907- CAP-1
Earlier sketch in CA 13-14
Taylor, Ron(ald) W(illiam) 1922- CAP-1
Earlier sketch in CA 11-12
Taylor, Ronald (Jack) 1924- CANR-94
Earlier sketches in CA 93-96, CANR-26
Taylor, Ronald B. 1930- 142
Taylor, Ronald J. 1932-1998 143
Taylor, Ronald L(ee) 1938- 77-80
Taylor, Ross McLaury 1909(?)-1977
Obituary 69-72
Taylor, Rupert (Maurice) 1946- 45-48
Taylor, Ruth Mattson 1922- 101
Taylor, Samuel (Woolley)
1907-1997 .... CANR-28
Obituary 161
Earlier sketch in CA 73-76
Taylor, Samuel (Albert) 1912-2000 .... 25-28R
Obituary 188
Taylor, Sandra C. 1936- CANR-136
Earlier sketch in CA 123
Taylor, Sarah Stewart 1971- 227
Taylor, Sheila Ortiz 1939- 208
Taylor, Shelley Elizabeth 1946- 214
Taylor, Simona
See Carrington, Roslyn
Taylor, Stephen
See Taylor, Stephen James Lake
Taylor, Stephen 1948- CANR-82
Earlier sketch in CA 133
Taylor, Stephen James Lake 1910-1988
Obituary 124
Taylor, Sue 1949- 202
Taylor, Susie King 1848-1912 .... DLB 221
Taylor, Sybil (Renee) 1933- 122
Taylor, Sydney (Brenner)
1904(?)-1978 .... CANR-4
Obituary 77-80
Earlier sketch in CA 5-8R
See also CWRI 5
See also MAICYA 1, 2
See also SATA 1, 28
See also SATA-Obit 26
Taylor, T(homas) F(is) 1913- 136
Taylor, T. G.
See Taylor, T(homas) Geoffrey
Taylor, T(homas) Geoffrey 1918-1987
Obituary 123
Taylor, Telford 1908-1998 .... CANR-16
Obituary 181
Earlier sketch in CA 25-28R
Interview in CANR-16
See also MTCW 1
Taylor, Theodore 1921- CANR-108
Earlier sketches in CA 21-24R, CANR-9, 25, 38, 50
See also AAYA 2, 19
See also BYA 1
See also CLR 30
See also JRDA
See also MAICYA 1, 2
See also MAICYAS 1
See also SAAS 4
See also SATA 5, 54, 83, 128
See also WYA
See also YAW
Taylor, Theodore B(rewster) 1925-2004 102
Obituary 232
Taylor, Theodore W(alter) 1913-2005 119
Obituary 237
Taylor, Thomas 1934- 21-24R
Taylor, Thomas Lowe 1938- .... CAAS 26
Taylor, Tim 1920-1974 45-48
Obituary 53-56
Taylor, Timothy (F.) 1960- 237
Taylor, Timothy 1963(?)- 210
Taylor, Tom
See Taylor, J. Thomas
See also RGEL 2
Taylor, Valerie
See Tate, Velma
Taylor, Vernon L. 1922- 33-36R
Taylor, Verta 1948- 114
Taylor, W(illiam) H(odge) 1904-1984
Obituary 113
Taylor, Walter Fuller 1900-1966 .... 1-4R
Taylor, Walter Kingsley 1939- 227
Taylor, Walter W(illard) 1913-1997 61-64
Taylor, Warren 1903-1991 .... 21-24R
Taylor, Weldon J. 1908-2000 .... 1-4R
Taylor, Welford Dunaway 1938- 37-40R
Taylor, Wendell H(ertig) 1905-1985 102
Taylor, William 1930- CANR-15
Earlier sketch in CA 81-84
Taylor, William 1938- CANR-94
Earlier sketch in CA 146
See also CLR 63
See also CWRI 5
See also SATA 78, 113
Taylor, William C. 1959- 142
Taylor, William David, Jr. 1902-1975
Obituary 107
Taylor, William E(dwards) 1920- CANR-10
Earlier sketch in CA 25-28R
Taylor, William Ewart, Jr. 1927-1994 126
Obituary 152
Taylor, William Howland 1901-1966 208
See also DLB 241
Taylor, William L. 1937- 29-32R
Taylor, William N(athaniel), (Jr.) 1952- 153
Taylor, William R(obert) 1922- 138
Taylor, Yuval 1963- 209
Taylor, Zack 1927- 65-68
Taylor-Gooby, Peter 1947- CANR-41
Earlier sketch in CA 118
Taylor-Hall, Mary Ann 1937- CANR-89
Earlier sketch in CA 147
Taylor-Olson, Clara Mae 1899(?)-1988
Obituary 124
Taymor, Julie 1952- 222
See also AAYA 42
Taymur, Mahmud 1894-1973 .... EWL 3
See also WLIT 6
Taze, James E. 1938- 166
Tazewell, Charles 1900-1972
Obituary 37-40R
See also MAICYA 2
See also SATA 74
Tazieff, Haroun 1914-1998
Obituary 165
Brief entry 113
Tchaadaieff
See Sorokin, Pitirim A(lexandrovitch)
Tchana, Katrin Hyman 1963- .... SATA 125
Tchekhov, Anton
See Chekhov, Anton (Pavlovich)
Tchen, John Kuo Wei 1951- 190
Tchen, Richard 191
See also SATA 120
Tcherniak, Natasha
See Sarraute, Nathalie
Tchernichovsky, Saul (Gutmanovich)
1875-1943 212
Brief entry 116
See also Tchernichowsky, Saul
Tchernichowsky, Saul
See Tchernichovsky, Saul (Gutmanovich)
See also EWL 3
Tchicaya, Gerald Felix 1931-1988 .... CANR-81
Obituary 125
Earlier sketch in CA 129
See also Tchicaya U Tam'si
See also CLC 101
Tchicaya U Tam'si
See Tchicaya, Gerald Felix
See also EWL 3
Tchividjian, Gigi Graham 1945- 108
Tchobanoglous, George 1935- 102
Tchudi, Stephen N. 1942- CANR-22
Earlier sketch in CA 89-92
See also SATA 55
See also YAW
Tea, Michelle 1971(?)- 212
Teachout, Terry 1956- CANR-140
Earlier sketch in CA 133
Tead, Ordway 1891-1973
Obituary 45-48
Teaford, Jon C(hristian) 1946- CANR-94
Earlier sketches in CA 65-68, CANR-10
Teague, Bob
See Teague, Robert
Teague, Frances (N.) 1949- CANR-90
Earlier sketch in CA 139
Teague, Kathleen 1937- 97-100
Teague, Mark (Christopher) 1963- 136
See also SATA 68, 99
Teague, Michael (Noel) 1932-1999 109
Obituary 185
Teague, Robert 1929- 106
See also BW 2
See also SATA 32
See also SATA-Brief 31
Teahan, Sheila 1961- 153
Teal, G. Donn 1932- 33-36R
Teal, John J(erome), Jr. 1921-1982
Obituary 110
Teal, Val(entine M.) 1902-1997 61-64
Obituary 182
See also SATA 10
See also SATA-Obit 114
Teale, Edwin Way 1899-1980 .... CANR-2
Obituary 102
Earlier sketch in CA 1-4R
See also ANW
See also DLB 275
See also SATA 7
See also SATA-Obit 25
Teall, Edna (A.) West 1881-1968 201
Tearle, John L. 1917- 140
Teasdale, Sara 1884-1933 163
Brief entry 104
See also DLB 45
See also GLL 1
See also PC 31
See also PFS 14
See also RGAL 4
See also SATA 32
See also TCLC 4
See also TUS
Teasdale, Wayne (Robert) 1945- CANR-96
Earlier sketch in CA 158
Teasley, Lisa 1962- 239
Te Awekotuku, Ngahuia 154
Tebbel, John (William) 1912-2004 .... CANR-29
Obituary 232
Earlier sketch in CA 85-88
See also SATA 26
Tebbel, Robert E(verett) 1924- 5-8R
Tebbetts-Taylor, Elizabeth
See Taylor, Elizabeth Tebbetts
Tebbit, Norman 1931- 138
Tebeau, Charlton Watson 1904-2000 110
Tebelak, John-Michael 1949(?)-1985
Obituary 115
Tec, Leon 1919- 97-100
Tec, Nechama 1931- CANR-48
Earlier sketches in CA 9-12R, CANR-23
Techine, Andre 1943- 146
Teck, Alan 1934- 25-28R
TeCube, Leroy 1947- 187
Tecumseh 1768-1813 .... DAM MULT
See also NNAL
Tedder, Arthur William 1890-1967 .... CAP-2
Earlier sketch in CA 23-24
Tedder, Lord
See Tedder, Arthur William
Teddy, Paul
See Aldrich, Jonathan
Tedeschi, Giuliana (Brunelli) 1914-
Tedeschi, (Theodore) James, Jr. 1928- 41-44R
Tedeschi, Martha 1958- 187
Tedlock, E(rnest) W(arnock), Jr.
1910-1988 .... CAP-2
Earlier sketch in CA 17-18
Tedlow, Richard S. 1947(?)- 237
Tedone, David A. 1953- 132
Tedrow, John C. F. 1917- 142
Tedrow, R. L.
See Tedrow, Richard L(ove)
Tedrow, Richard L(ove) 1913(?)-1987
Obituary 121
Tee, John
See Meades, Jonathan (Turner)
Teece, David J(ohn) 1948- 138
Teed, Peter (Litterland) 1924- 143
Teegen, Otto John 1899-1983
Obituary 109
Teensma, Lynne Bertrand
See Bertrand, Lynne
Teer, Frank 1934- 53-56
Teeter, Don E(l) 1934- 73-76
Teeter, Karl V(an Duyn) 1929- 17-20R
Teeters, Negley K(ing) 1896-1971 .... CAP-2
Obituary 33-36R
Earlier sketch in CA 23-24
Teetor, Paul R(aymond) 1919- 113
Teets, Bruce E. 1914-1997 .... 37-40R
Teets, John Phillip 1948- 132
Tee-Van, Helen Damrosch 1893-1976 49-52
Obituary 65-68
See also SATA 10
See also SATA-Obit 27
Teevan, Richard C(ollier) 1919- CANR-4
Earlier sketch in CA 1-4R
Tefertiller, Casey (Orie) 1952- 165

Teffeteller, Gordon Lamar 1931- 115
Teffi, N. A. 1872-1952 .... DLB 317
Tefft, Bess H(agaman) 1915(?)-1977
Obituary 110
Tega, Vasile 1921- CANR-18
Earlier sketch in CA 102
Tegenfeldt, Herman G(ustaf) 1913-1981 .. 73-76
Tegerdine, Maria
See Morsy, Magali
Tegethoff, Wolf W. 1953- 144
Tegner, Bruce 1928- CANR-8
Earlier sketch in CA 61-64
See also SATA 62
Tegner, Henry (Stuart) 1901- CANR-12
Earlier sketch in CA 13-16R
Tehan, Arline Boucher 1930- 130
Tehranian, Majid 1937- 230
Teich, Albert H(arris) 1942- CANR-104
Earlier sketches in CA 45-48, CANR-25, 50
Teicher, Morton I(rving) 1920- CANR-11
Earlier sketch in CA 69-72
Teichgraeber, Richard F., III III
1950- CANR-56
Earlier sketch in CA 125
Teichman, Jenny 1930- CANR-141
Earlier sketches in CA 127, CANR-55
Teichman, Judith A. 1947- 163
Teichmann, Howard (Miles)
1916-1987 .... CANR-85
Obituary 123
Earlier sketches in CA 69-72, CANR-17
Teikmanis, Arthur L. 1914- 13-16R
Teil, Thierry
See Lhermitte, Thierry
Teilhard de Chardin, (Marie Joseph) Pierre
1881-1955 210
Brief entry 105
See also GFL 1789 to the Present
See also TCLC 9
Teilhet, Darwin L(eOra) 1904-1964 204
Teillier, Jorge 1935-1996 .... DLB 283
See also EWL 3
Teirlinck, Herman Louis-Cesar 1879-1967 . 191
See also EWL 3
Teiser, Ruth 1915-1994 109
Teish, Luisah 1948- 141
See also BW 2
Teissier du Cros, Janet 1906- CAP-2
Earlier sketch in CA 17-18
Teitelbaum, Harry 1930- 21-24R
Teitelbaum, Matthew 1956- 144
Teitelbaum, Michael 1953- 121
See also SATA 59, 116
Teitelbaum, Myron 1929- 13-16R
Teitelman, Robert 1954- 135
Teiwes, Helga 1930- 140
Teixeira, Bernardo 1926- 108
Teixeira, Ruy A. 196
Teixeira da Mota, Avelino (?)-1982
Obituary 106
Teixeira de Pascoaes
See Teixeira de Vasconcelos, Joaquim Pereira
See also EWL 3
Teixeira de Vasconcelos, Joaquim Pereira
1877-1952
See Teixeira de Pascoaes
Teja, Jesus F(rancisco) de la 1956- .. CANR-112
Earlier sketch in CA 154
See also HW 2
Tejima
See Tejima, Keizaburo
Tejima, Keizaburo 1931- .... CLR 20
See also SATA 139
Tekahionwake
See Johnson, E(mily) Pauline
Tekeyan, Charles 1927- 29-32R
Telander, Richard F(orster) 1948- 65-68
Telander, Todd (G.) 1967- .... SATA 88
Teleki, Geza 1943- CANR-19
Earlier sketches in CA 49-52, CANR-3
See also SATA 45
Telemaque, Eleanor Wong 1934- 104
See also SATA 43
Telemaque, Harold Mitton 1910- .... CP 1
Telescope, Tom
See Newbery, John
Telfair, Richard
See Jessup, Richard
Telfair, Richard .... TCWW 1
Telfer, Dariel (Doris) 1905-1987 .... CANR-86
Obituary 122
Earlier sketches in CAP-2, CA 25-28
Telfer, R(oss) 1937- 106
Telfer, W.
See Telfer, William
Telfer, William 1886-1968 .... CAP-1
Earlier sketch in CA 13-14
Telford, Charles W(itt) 1903-1992 65-68
Tell, Jack 1909(?)-1979
Obituary 89-92
Teller, Astro 1970- 169
Teller, Edward 1908-2003 .... CANR-114
Obituary 220
Earlier sketches in CAP-1, CA 13-14, CANR-33, 65
See also MTCW 1
Teller, James D(avid) 1906-1992 .... 41-44R
Teller, Judd L. 1912-1972
Obituary 33-36R
Teller, Neville 1931- CANR-49
Earlier sketches in CA 103, CANR-23
Teller, Walter (Magnus) 1910-1993 ... CANR-87
Obituary 140
Earlier sketches in CA 5-8R, CANR-2
Telles, Lygia Fagundes 1923(?)- 157
See also Fagundes Telles, Lygia
See also CWW 2
See also DLB 113, 307
See also EWL 3
See also HW 2
See also RGSF 2
Tellez, Gabriel
Tellis, Gerard J. 1950- 219
Tello, Carlos 1938- 112
Telmig, Akdov
See Wood, Edward D(avis), Jr.
Telnaes, Ann C. 1960- 231
Telser, Lester G(reenspan) 1931- 33-36R
Telushkin, Joseph 1948- 222
Tem, Melanie CANR-117
Earlier sketch in CA 165
Tem, Steve
See Tem, Steve Rasnic
Tem, Steve R.
See Tem, Steve Rasnic
Tem, Steve Rasnic 1950- CANR-117
Earlier sketch in CA 165
See also HGG
Temerson, Catherine 1944- 147
Temianka, Dan(iel) 1948- 152
Temianka, Henri 1906-1992 45-48
Obituary 196
Temin, Peter 1937- 13-16R
Temkin, Gabriel 1921- 173
Temkin, Pauline B. 1919- 25-28R
Temkin, Sara Anne Schlossberg
1913-1996 .... 1-4R
See also SATA 26
Temko, Allan 1924- 136
Temko, Florence CANR-37
Earlier sketches in CA 49-52, CANR-1, 17
See also SATA 13
Temmer, Mark J. 1922- 192
Brief entry 107
Temp, George (Edward) 1929- 45-48
Temperley, Howard 1932- 85-88
Temperley, Nicholas 1932- 107
Tempest, Jan
See Swatridge, Irene Maude (Mossop)
Tempest, Margaret Mary 1892-1982
Obituary 108
See also SATA-Obit 33
Tempest, Sarah
See Ponsonby, D(oris) A(lmon)
Tempest, Theresa
See Kent, Louise Andrews
Tempest, Victor
See Philipp, Elliot Elias
Templar, Maurice
See Groom, Arthur William
Temple, Ann
See Mortimer, Penelope (Ruth)
Temple, Arthur
See Northcott, (William) Cecil
Temple, Charles 1947- 148
See also SATA 79
Temple, Cliff 1947-1994 .... CANR-86
Obituary 143
Earlier sketch in CA 111
Temple, Dan
See Newton, D(wight) B(ennett)
Temple, Frances (Nolting) 1945-1995 151
See also AAYA 19
See also BYA 11
See also MAICYA 2
See also MAICYAS 1
See also SATA 85
See also YAW
Temple, Herbert 1919- .... SATA 45
Temple, Joe 1917-1990 97-100
Temple, Nigel (Hal Longdale)
1926-2003 .... 29-32R
Obituary 221
Temple, Norman J. 1947- CANR-104
Earlier sketch in CA 148
Temple, Paul
See McConnell, James Douglas Rutherford
Temple, Paul
See Durbridge, Francis (Henry)
Temple, Philip (Robert) 1939- CANR-22
Earlier sketch in CA 104
Temple, Robert (Kyle Grenville)
1945- CANR-40
Earlier sketches in CA 89-92, CANR-16
Temple, Robert M(ickler), Jr. 1935-
Brief entry 107
Temple, Ruth Z(abriskie) 1908-1999 61-64
Temple, Wayne C(alhoun) 1924- CANR-17
Earlier sketches in CA 1-4R, CANR-1
Temple, Willard H. 1912-1982 .... 1-4R
Temple, William 1881-1944 182
Brief entry 120
Temple, Sir William 1555(?)-1627 ...... DLB 281
Temple, Sir William 1628-1699 .... DLB 101
Temple, William F(rederick)
1914-1989 .... CANR-126
Earlier sketch in CA 166
See also DLB 255
See also SATA 107
See also SFW 4
Templeman, Eleanor Lee (Reading) 1906-1990
Obituary 131
Templer, Robert 1966- 190
Temple-Raston, Dina 1964- 219
Templeton, Charles B. 1915-2001 101
Templeton, Edith 1916- CANR-114
Earlier sketch in CA 53-56
Templeton, Fiona .... CWP
Templeton, Janet
See Hershman, Morris
Templeton, John J(oseph), Jr. 1928- 25-28R
Temrizov, A.
See Marchenko, Anastasiia Iakovlevna
Tenax
See Lean, Garth Dickinson
ten Berge, Hans Cornelis 1938-
See Berge, H(ans) C(ornelius) ten
Tenberken, Sabriye 1970- 234
ten Boom, Corrie 1892-1983 111
Obituary 109
Tenbrook, Gretchen W. 1972- 203
Tench, Watkin 1758-1833 .... DLB 230
Tencin, Alexandrine-Claude Guerin de
1682-1749 .... DLB 314
Tendriakov, Vladimir Fedorovich
See Tendryakov, Vladimir Fyodorovich
See also DLB 302
Tendryakov, Vladimir Fyodorovich
1923-1984(?) 104
Obituary 113
See also Tendriakov, Vladimir Fedorovich
See also EWL 3
Tenenbaum, Frances 1919- CANR-12
Earlier sketch in CA 73-76
Tenenbaum, Shea 1910-1989 .... CANR-1
Earlier sketch in CA 49-52
Tenenbaum, Shelly 1955- CANR-101
Earlier sketch in CA 146
Tener, Robert L(awrence) 1924- 110
Teng, S(su)-Y(u) 1906-1988 .... CANR-22
Obituary 145
Earlier sketch in CA 13-16R
Tengbom, Mildred 1921- CANR-39
Earlier sketches in CA 97-100, CANR-17
Tenggren, Gustaf 1896-1970 .... SATA 18
See also SATA-Obit 26
Ten Harmsel, Henrietta 1921- 106
Ten Hoor, Elvie (Marie Mortensen)
1900-1984 .... CANR-87
Obituary 112
Earlier sketch in CA 9-12R
TenHouten, Warren David 1939-
Brief entry 108
Tenhula, John 1951- 135
Tenison, Marika Hanbury
See Hanbury-Tenison, Marika
Tenison, Robin Hanbury
See Hanbury-Tenison, (Airling) Robin
Tenn, William 1919- .... DLB 8
See also SCFW 1, 2
See also SFW 4
Tennant, Alan 1943- 108
Tennant, Emma (Christina) 1937- CANR-88
Earlier sketches in CA 65-68, CANR-10, 38, 59
See also CAAS 9
See also BRWS 9
See also CLC 13, 52
See also CN 3, 4, 5, 6, 7
See also DLB 14
See also EWL 3
See also SFW 4
Tennant, Ivo (S.) 1955- 128
Tennant, Kylie
See Rodd, Kylie Tennant
See also CN 1, 2, 3, 4
See also RGEL 2
See also SATA 6
Tennant, Nora Jackson 1915- CANR-4
Earlier sketch in CA 9-12R
Tennant, (Charles) Roger 1919- 106
Tennant, Stephen (James Napier) 1906-1987
Obituary 122
Tennant, Veronica 1947- 103
See also SATA 36
Tennen, Howard 1948- 138
Tennenbaum, Silvia 1928- CANR-21
Earlier sketch in CA 77-80
Tenner, Edward 1944- CANR-138
Earlier sketch in CA 155
Tenneshaw, S. M.
See Beaumont, Charles and Garrett, (Gordon) Randall (Phillip) and Silverberg, Robert
Tenneson, Joyce 1945- 208
Tenness, George
See Delk, Robert Carlton
Tenney, H(orace) Kent 1892-1982
Obituary 107
Tenney, Merrill C(hapin) 1904-1985 . CANR-87
Obituary 115
Earlier sketches in CA 1-4R, CANR-4
Tenney, Tabitha Gilman 1762-1837 ..... DLB 37, 200
Tenniel, John 1820-1914
Brief entry 111
See also CLR 18
See also MAICYA 1, 2
See also SATA 74
See also SATA-Brief 27
Tennien, Mark A. 1900(?)-1983
Obituary 108
Tennies, Arthur C(ornelius) 1931- 53-56
Tennison, Patrick Joseph 1928- CANR-23
Earlier sketch in CA 106
Tennissen, Anthony C(ornelius) 1920-1982 . 114
Tennov, Dorothy 1928- 41-44R
Tennyson, Alfred 1809-1892 .... AAYA 50
See also BRW 4
See also CDBLB 1832-1890
See also DA
See also DA3
See also DAB
See also DAC
See also DAM MST, POET
See also DLB 32
See also EXPP
See also PAB
See also PC 6
See also PFS 1, 2, 4, 11, 15, 19
See also RGEL 2
See also TEA
See also WLC
See also WLIT 4
See also WP
Tennyson, Brian 1939- 193
Tennyson, Charles (Bruce Locker)
1879-1977 .... CANR-29
Obituary 73-76
Earlier sketch in CA 81-84
Tennyson, Frederick 1807-1898 .... DLB 32
Tennyson, G(eorg) B(ernhard) 1930- ... CANR-9
Earlier sketch in CA 21-24R
Tenorio, Arthur 1924- .... DLB 209
Tenpas, Kathryn Dunn 1963- 171
Tenpas, Margaret (Susan Lyon) 1923- 85-88
Tens, Isaac .... WP
Tensen, Ruth M(arjorie) 5-8R
Tent, Ned
See Dennett, Herbert Victor
Tenzin, Gyatso
See Gyatso, Tenzin
Tenzing, Tashi 1965- 214
TePaske, John J(ay) 1929- CANR-40
Earlier sketch in CA 117
Tepliakov, Viktor Grigor'evich
1804-1842 .... DLB 205
Teplitz, Paul V(ictor) 1940- 111
Tepper, Albert 1928- 25-28R
Tepper, Ellen Jean
See Glazer, Ellen Sarasohn
Tepper, Michael 1941- CANR-12
Earlier sketch in CA 73-76
Tepper, Sheri S. 1929- CANR-90
Earlier sketch in CA 137
See also AAYA 32
See also FANT
See also SATA 113
See also SCFW 2
See also SFW 4
Tepper, Terri P(atricia) 1942- 107
Terada, Alice M. 1928- 155
See also SATA 90
Teramis
See Christian, Deborah
Teran, Boston 235
Teran, Lisa St. Aubin de
See St. Aubin de Teran, Lisa
See also CLC 36
Terayama, Shuji 1935-1983
Obituary 109
ter Balkt, H(erman) H(endrik) 1938- 195
Terban, Marvin 1940- .... SATA 54
See also SATA-Brief 45
Terborgh, George (Willard) 1897-1989 .. CAP-2
Obituary 128
Earlier sketch in CA 23-24
Terborgh, John W. 1936- 199
Terbovich, John B. 1933-1969 .... CAP-2
Earlier sketch in CA 21-22
ter Braak, Menno 1902-1940 .... EWL 3
Terchek, Ronald John 1936- 49-52
Terdiman, Richard 1941- 73-76
Terence c. 184B.C.-c. 159B.C. .... AW 1
See also CDWLB 1
See also DC 7
See also DLB 211
See also RGWL 2, 3
See also TWA
Terenzio, Stephanie 1932- 118
Teresa of Avila, St.
See Teresa de Jesus, St.
Teresi, Judith M.
See Goldberger, Judith M.
Ter Haar, B. J. 1958- 144
ter Haar, Jaap 1922- 37-40R
See also Haar, Jaap ter
See also SATA 6
terHorst, J(erald) F(ranklin) 1922- 107
Interview in CA-107
See also AITN 1
ter Horst, Robert 1929- 116
Terhune, Albert Payson 1872-1942 136
Brief entry 111
See also CWRI 5
See also DLB 9
See also MAICYA 1, 2
See also SATA 15
Terhune, Mary Virginia 1830-1922 228
See also DLBD 13
Terhune, William B(arclay)
1893-1987 .... CANR-86
Obituary 122
Earlier sketch in CA 61-64
Terich, Thomas A. 1943- 125
Terkel, Louis 1912- CANR-132
Earlier sketches in CA 57-60, CANR-18, 45, 67
See also Terkel, Studs
See also DA3
See also MTCW 1, 2
See also MTFW 2005

Terkel, Studs
See Terkel, Louis
See also AAYA 32
See also AITN 1
See also CLC 38
See also MTCW 2
See also TUS
Terkel, Susan N(eiburg) 1948- CANR-38
Earlier sketch in CA 115
See also SATA 59, 103
Terlecki, Tymon Tadeusz J(ulian)
1905-2000 132
Obituary 191
Terlouw, Jan (Cornelis) 1931- 108
See also SATA 30
Terman, Douglas 1933- 136
Brief entry 112
Terman, Sibyl 1902(?)-1975
Obituary 57-60
Terme, Hilary
See Hay, Jacob
Terner, Janet 1938- 102
Terni-Cialente, Fausta 1900-1994 .... CANR-5
Earlier sketch in CA 5-8R
Terpigorev, Sergei Nikolaevich
1841-1895 .... DLB 277
Terpstra, John 1953- 171
Terpstra, Vern 1927- CANR-11
Earlier sketch in CA 21-24R
Terr, Lenore (C.) 1936- 134
Terr, Leonard B(rian) 1946- 73-76
Terrace, Edward L. B. 1936(?)-1973
Obituary 45-48
Terrace, Herbert S(ydney) 1936- CANR-43
Earlier sketch in CA 102
Terrace, Vincent 1948- CANR-50
Earlier sketches in CA 65-68, CANR-9, 25
Terraine, John (Alfred) 1921-2003 .... CANR-13
Obituary 222
Earlier sketch in CA 5-8R
Terrall, Robert 1914- 102
See also Halliday, Brett
Terranova, Elaine 1939- CANR-74
Earlier sketch in CA 139
Terras, Victor 1921- 128
Brief entry 113
Terrell, Carroll F(ranklin)
1917-2003 .... CANR-20
Obituary 221
Earlier sketch in CA 102
Terrell, Donna McManus 1908-1986 57-60
Terrell, John Upton 1900-1988 .... 29-32R
Obituary 127
See also SATA-Obit 60
Terrell, Robert L(ouis) 1943- CANR-17
Earlier sketch in CA 41-44R
Terres, John K(enneth) 1905- CANR-5
Earlier sketch in CA 5-8R
Terrien, Samuel Lucien 1911-2002 81-84
Obituary 203
Terrill, Marshall 1963- CANR-101
Earlier sketch in CA 145
Terrill, Ross 1938- CANR-35
Earlier sketch in CA 25-28R
Interview in CANR-35
Terrill, Tom E(dward) 1935- 41-44R
Terrio, Susan J. 1950- 225
Terris, Susan 1937- CANR-12
Earlier sketch in CA 29-32R
See also JRDA
See also SATA 3, 77
Terris, Virginia R(inaldy) 1917- 65-68
Terry, Arthur (Hubert) 1927-2004 85-88
Obituary 223
Terry, Bill 1931- 118
Terry, C. V.
See Slaughter, Frank G(ill)
Terry, Carol
See Talbot, Carol Terry
Terry, Charles S. 1926(?)-1982
Obituary 107
Terry, Doug(las) 1950- 120
Terry, Edith (Buchanan) 1952- 120
Terry, Edward D(avis) 1927- 29-32R
Terry, Irwin J. 1960- 150
Terry, James L. 1949- 226
Terry, Jennifer 1958- 190
Terry, John V(erlin) 1920- 144
Terry, Luther L(eonidas) 1911-1985 .. CANR-86
Obituary 115
Earlier sketches in CAP-2, CA 33-36
See also SATA 11
See also SATA-Obit 42
Terry, Margaret
See Dunnahoo, Terry Janson
Terry, Mark 1947- 37-40R
Terry (Northway), Marshall, (Jr.) 1931- 1-4R
Terry, Megan 1932- CANR-43
Earlier sketch in CA 77-80
See also CABS 3
See also CAD
See also CD 5, 6
See also CLC 19
See also CWD
See also DC 13
See also DFS 18
See also DLB 7, 249
See also GLL 2
Terry, Michael 1899-1981 104
Terry, Paul 1887-1971 .... IDFW 3, 4
Terry, Robert H(arold) 1935- 29-32R
Terry, Robert Meredith 1939- 41-44R
Terry, Robert W(illiam) 1937- 37-40R
Terry, Sarah Meiklejohn 1937- 111
Terry, Saralee
See Kaye, Marvin (Nathan)
Terry, Walter 1913-1982 .... CANR-10
Obituary 107
Earlier sketch in CA 21-24R
See also SATA 14
Terry, William
See Harknett, Terry (Williams)
Terry-Thomas
See Stevens, Thomas Terry Hoar
Terson, Peter 1932- CANR-127
Earlier sketches in CA 104, CANR-70
See also CBD
See also CD 5, 6
See also DLB 13
Terstall, Eddy 1964- 207
Terstegge, Mabel Alice 1905-1997 93-96
Tertis, Lionel 1876-1975 93-96
Obituary 57-60
Terts, Abram .... CWW 2
Tertz, Abram
See Sinyavsky, Andrei (Donatevich)
See also RGSF 2
Tervalon, Jervey 1958- 157
See also BW 3
See also LAIT 5
Tervapaa, Juhani
See Wuolijoki, Hella
Terwilliger, Robert E(lwin)
1917-1991 .... CANR-86
Obituary 134
Earlier sketch in CA 65-68
Terzakis, Anghelos 1907-1979 .... EWL 3
Terzani, Tiziano 1938-2004 .... CANR-110
Obituary 229
Earlier sketches in CA 77-80, CANR-14
Terzian, James P. 1915- 13-16R
See also SATA 14
Terzian, Kathryn
See Cramer, Kathryn
Terzian, Pierre 1948- 136
Terzian, Yervant 1939- 125
Tesanovic, Jasmina 1954- 205
TeSelle, Eugene (Arthur, Jr.) 1931- 37-40R
TeSelle, Sallie McFague
See McFague, Sallie
Teshigawara, Saburo 1953- 228
Tesich, Steve 1943(?)-1996 105
Obituary 152
See also CAD
See also CLC 40, 69
See also DLBY 1983
Teske, Edmund (Rudolph) 1911-1996 209
Teske, Paul Eric 1958- 152
Tesla, Nikola 1856-1943 .... TCLC 88
Tesla, Nikola 1856-1943 157
Teslik, Kennan Lee 1952- 113
Tessa, Delio 1886-1939 .... DLB 114
Tessaro, Kathleen 1965- 226
Tessendorf, K(enneth) C(harles) 1925-2003 . 142
Obituary 214
See also SATA 75
See also SATA-Obit 142
Tessier, (Ernst) M(aurice) 1885-1973 . CANR-95
Earlier sketches in CA 5-8R, CANR-3
Tessier, Thomas (Edward) 1947- 196
See also HGG
Tessina, Tina B. 1944- 198
Tessler, Mark A(rnold) 1941- CANR-37
Earlier sketches in CA 45-48, CANR-1, 16
Tessler, Stephanie Gordon
See Gordon, Stephanie Jacob
Testa, Judith 1943- 170
Tester, S. J(im) 1924-1986 140
Tester, Sylvia Root 1939- CANR-8
Earlier sketch in CA 9-12R
See also SATA 64
See also SATA-Brief 37
Testori, Giovanni 1923-1993 .... DLB 128, 177
Teta, Jon (Anthony) 1933- 25-28R
Tetel, Julie 1950- CANR-42
Earlier sketch in CA 118
Tetel, Marcel 1932-2004 .... 21-24R
Obituary 228
Tetens, Tete Harens 1899(?)-1976
Obituary 65-68
Teternikov, Fyodor Kuzmich 1863-1927
Brief entry 104
See also Sologub, Fedor and
Sologub, Fyodor
Tether, (Cynthia) Graham 1950- CANR-6
Earlier sketch in CA 57-60
See also SATA 46
See also SATA-Brief 36
Tetlow, Edwin 1905-2000 .... 17-20R
Tetlow, L. D. .... TCWW 2
Tetreault, Wilfred F. 1927-1992 106
Teubal, Savina J. 1926- 132
Teune, Henry 1936- CANR-3
Earlier sketch in CA 49-52
Teunissen, John James 1933- 112
Teuscher, Robert H(erman) 1934- 77-80
Teveth, Shabtai (Amotz) 1925- CANR-115
Brief entry 117
Earlier sketch in CA 156
Tevis, Walter 1928-1984 113
See also CLC 42
See also SFW 4
Tewkesbury, Joan 1936- 101
Interview in CA-101
Texier, Catherine 229
Texon, Meyer 1909- 124
Tey, Josephine
See Mackintosh, Elizabeth
See also DLB 77
See also MSW
See also TCLC 14
Teyber, Edward C. 1950- 141
Teynac, Francoise (Dolores Dupuis) 123
Teyte, Maggie 1888-1976
Obituary 65-68
Tezla, Albert 1915- CANR-57
Earlier sketches in CA 37-40R, CANR-14, 31
Tezuka, Osamu 1928-1989 214
See also AAYA 56
See also MTFW 2005
Thacher, Alida McKay 1951- CANR-11
Earlier sketch in CA 69-72
Thacher, James 1754-1844 .... DLB 37
Thacher, John Boyd 1847-1909 214
See also DLB 187
Thacher, Mary McGrath 1933- .... SATA 9
Thacher, Russell 1919(?)-1990
Obituary 132
Thackara, James 1944- CANR-119
Earlier sketch in CA 129
Thacker, Eric (Lee) 1923-
Brief entry 107
Thacker, Ernest W(ichman) 1914-1981 . 13-16R
Thacker, Jonathan W(illiam) 1967- 143
Thacker, Shelly 1963- 220
Thacker, Thomas William 1911-1984
Obituary 113
Thackeray, Frank W. 1943- 146
Thackeray, Milton G. 1914-1996 .... 13-16R
Thackeray, William Makepeace
1811-1863 .... BRW 5
See also BRWC 2
See also CDBLB 1832-1890
See also DA
See also DA3
See also DAB
See also DAC
See also DAM MST, NOV
See also DLB 21, 55, 159, 163
See also NFS 13
See also RGEL 2
See also SATA 23
See also TEA
See also WLC
See also WLIT 3
Thackray, Arnold 1939- 49-52
Thackray, Derek V(incent) 1926- 103
Thackrey, Russell I. 1904-1990 .... 37-40R
Thackrey, Ted, Jr. 1918- 132
Thaddeus, Janice Farrar
1933-2001 .... CANR-101
Obituary 202
Earlier sketch in CA 13-16R
Thaden, Edward Carl 1922- 17-20R
Thagard, Paul 1950- 149
Thahkin Ko-daw Hmaing
See U Lun
See also EWL 3
Thain, Chris 1937- 127
Thain, Donald H(ammond) 1928- CANR-25
Earlier sketch in CA 1-4R
Thakur, Shivesh Chandra 1936- 29-32R
Thakura, Ravindranatha
See Tagore, Rabindranath
Thalacker, Donald W(illiam) 1939-1987 127
Brief entry 108
Thalberg, Irving (Grant, Jr.) 1930-1987 .. 41-44R
Obituary 123
Thalberg, Irving G. 1899-1936 .... IDFW 3, 4
Thale, Jerome 1927-1981 .... 13-16R
Thaler, Alwin 1891-1977 .... CAP-1
Earlier sketch in CA 11-12
Thaler, M. N.
See Kerner, Fred
Thaler, Michael C. 1936- CANR-61
Earlier sketch in CA 124
See also SATA 56, 93
See also SATA-Brief 47
Thaler, Mike
See Thaler, Michael C.
Thaler, Shmuel 1958- 196
See also SATA 72, 126
Thaler, Susan 1939- 21-24R
Thalheimer, Ross 1905-1977 .... 41-44R
Thalia
See Bokum, Fanny Butcher
Thalmann, Rita Renee Line 1926- CANR-19
Earlier sketches in CA 53-56, CANR-4
Thalmann, William G. 1947- 233
Thamer, Katie
See Treherne, Katie Thamer
Thamer, Katie 1955- .... SATA 42
Thames, C. H.
See Marlowe, Stephen
Thames, Jack
See Ryan, John Fergus
Thames, Susan 1947- 158
Thamm, Robert 1933- 89-92
Thampi, Parvathi (Menon) 1925- 5-8R
Thandeka 1946- 171
Thane, (Lillian) Adele 1904-1998 .... 25-28R
Thane, Elswyth 1900-1984(?) CANR-60
Obituary 202
Earlier sketch in CA 5-8R
See also RHW
See also SATA 32
Thanet, Neil
See Fanthorpe, R(obert) Lionel
Thanet, Octave
See French, Alice
Thant, U 1909-1974
Obituary 108
Thapar, Romesh 1922-1987 133
Thapar, Valmik 1952- 139
Tharaud, Lucien Rostaing, Jr. 1953- 69-72
Tharaud, Ross
See Tharaud, Lucien Rostaing, Jr.
Tharoor, Shashi 1956- CANR-91
Earlier sketch in CA 141
See also CLC 70
See also CN 6, 7
Tharp, Louise (Marshall) Hall
1898-1992 .... CANR-33
Obituary 198
Earlier sketch in CA 1-4R
See also SATA 3
See also SATA-Obit 129
Tharp, Tim 1957- 185
Tharp, Twyla 1941- 210
Tharpe, Jac Lyndon 1928-1985 .... CANR-85
Obituary 117
Earlier sketches in CA 57-60, CANR-7
Tharps, Lori L. 1972- 219
't Hart, Maarten 1944- CANR-102
See also Hart, Martin
t'Hart, Marjolein C. 1955- CANR-93
Earlier sketch in CA 146
Tharu, Susie Jacob 1943- 142
Thass-Thienemann, Theodore
1900-1985 .... 25-28R
Thatcher, David 1922- 77-80
Thatcher, Dora (Fickling) 1912-1986 ..... 13-16R
Thatcher, Dorothy Southwell 1903- CAP-1
Earlier sketch in CA 13-14
Thatcher, Floyd W(ilson) 1917- 102
Thatcher, Joan (Claire) 1934- 106
Thatcher, Julia
See Bensen, Donald R.
Thatcher, Margaret (Hilda) 1925- CANR-119
Earlier sketch in CA 147
Thaw-da Hswei
See U Kyin Hswei
See also EWL 3
Thaxter, Celia 1835-1894 .... ANW
See also DLB 239
Thaxton, John 1949- 127
Thaxton, Ralph 1944- 114
Thayer, Caroline Matilda Warren
1785-1844 .... DLB 200
Thayer, Charles Wheeler
1910-1969 .... CANR-26
Obituary 103
Earlier sketch in CA 1-4R
Thayer, Cynthia 237
Thayer, Douglas H. 1929- .... DLB 256
Thayer, Emma R(edington) Lee
1874-1973 .... CAP-1
Obituary 45-48
Earlier sketch in CA 9-10
Thayer, Ernest Lawrence 1863-1940 168
Brief entry 119
See also EXPP
See also PFS 5
See also SATA 60
Thayer, Frederick C(lifton), Jr. 1924- . CANR-12
Earlier sketch in CA 73-76
Thayer, George (Chapman, Jr.)
1933-1973 .... CAP-2
Obituary 45-48
Earlier sketch in CA 25-28
Thayer, Geraldine
See Daniels, Dorothy
Thayer, H(orace) S(tandish) 1923- CANR-27
Earlier sketch in CA 45-48
Thayer, James Stewart 1949- CANR-108
Earlier sketch in CA 73-76
Thayer, Jane
See Woolley, Catherine
Thayer, Lee
See Thayer, Emma R(edington) Lee
Thayer, Lee (Osborne) 1927- CANR-18
Earlier sketches in CA 49-52, CANR-3
Thayer, Marjorie 1908-1992
Brief entry 116
See also SATA 74
See also SATA-Brief 37
Thayer, Mary Van Rensselaer
1903(?)-1983 .... CANR-85
Obituary 111
Earlier sketch in CA 97-100
Thayer, Molly
See Thayer, Mary Van Rensselaer
Thayer, Nancy 1943- 198
Thayer, Nathaniel B(owman) 1929- 45-48
Thayer, Peter
See Wyler, Rose
Thayer, Theodore 1904-1981
Obituary 103
Thayer, V(ivian) T(row) 1886-1979 .... CAP-2
Obituary 89-92
Earlier sketch in CA 17-18
Thayer-Bacon, Barbara J(ean) 1953- 196
Thayler, Carl 1933- CANR-69
Earlier sketch in CA 37-40R
See also CAAS 11
Thayne, Emma Lou 1924- 65-68
Thayne, Miria Greenwood 1907-1997 .. 21-24R
Theakston, Kevin 1958- 127
Theall, Donald Francis 1928- 105
Thebaud, Jo 1914- 49-52
Theberge, James D.
See Theberge, James Daniel
Theberge, James Daniel 1930-1988 . CANR-87
Obituary 124
Earlier sketch in CA 25-28R
Thede, Marion Draughon 1903-1998 .... CAP-2
Earlier sketch in CA 25-28
Thee, Marek 1918- 101
Theen, Rolf H(einz) W(ilhelm) 1937- 41-44R
Thegan fl. c. 850- .... DLB 148
Theil, Henri 1924-2000 .... CANR-22
Earlier sketches in CA 17-20R, CANR-7
Theiler, Max 1899-1972 164

Theiner, George (Fredric)
1927-1988 .... CANR-27
Earlier sketch in CA 29-32R
Thein Hpei Myint
See Thein Pe Myint
See also EWL 3
Thein Pe Myint 1914-1978 239
See also Thein Hpei Myint
Theis, John William 1911-1994
Brief entry 109
Theis, Paul A(nthony) 1923-2004 .... 41-44R
Obituary 225
Theisen, Jerome Paul 1930- 113
Theismann, Joe 1949- 171
Theismann, Joseph Robert
See Theismann, Joe
Theissen, Gerd 1943- CANR-41
Earlier sketch in CA 117
Theisz, R. D. 1941- 150
Thekaekara, Matthew P(othen)
1914-1976 77-80
Obituary 69-72
Thelen, David P(aul) 1939- 134
Brief entry 110
Thelen, Gil 1938- 73-76
Thelen, Herbert Arnold 1913- 108
Thelin, John R(obert) 1947- CANR-11
Earlier sketch in CA 69-72
Thelle, Notto R(eidar) 1941- CANR-117
Earlier sketches in CA 125, CANR-51
Thelwall, John 1764-1834 .... DLB 93, 158
Thelwell, Michael Miles 1939- 101
See also BW 2
See also CLC 22
Thelwell, Norman 1923-2004 .... CANR-4
Obituary 224
Earlier sketch in CA 5-8R
See also SATA 14
Themerson, Stefan 1910-1988 .... CANR-86
Obituary 126
Earlier sketches in CA 65-68, CANR-9, 28
See also SATA 65
Theo, Ion
See Theodorescu, Ion N.
Theobald, Lewis, Jr.
See Lovecraft, H(oward) P(hillips)
Theobald, Robert 1929-1999 .... 37-40R
Obituary 186
Theobald, William F. 1934- 156
Theocharis, Reghinos D(emetrios)
1929- CANR-11
Earlier sketch in CA 13-16R
Theocritus c. 310B.C.- .... AW 1
See also DLB 176
See also RGWL 2, 3
Theodoracopulos, Taki 1937- 129
Theodorakis, Michalis 1925-
Brief entry 105
See also Theodorakis, Mikis
Theodorakis, Mikis
See Theodorakis, Michalis
See also IDFW 3, 4
Theodorakopoulos, Ioannis 1900-1981
Obituary 108
Theodoratus, Robert J(ames) 1928- 41-44R
Theodore, Athena 1919- 41-44R
Theodore, Chris A(thanasios) 1920- 13-16R
Theodore, Sister Mary 1907- 5-8R
Theodore, Wayne 1958- 225
Theodorescu, Ion N. 1880-1967
Obituary 116
See also Arghezi, Tudor
Theodorson, George A. 1924- 29-32R
Theodulf c. 760-c. 821 .... DLB 148
Theoharis, Athan G(eorge) 1936- CANR-119
Earlier sketches in CA 29-32R, CANR-12, 30, 56
Theophile de Viau
See Viau, Theophile de
Theophrastus c. 371B.C.-c. 287B.C. ... DLB 176
See also RGWL 2, 3
Theorell, (Per Gunnar) Toeres 1942- 139
Theorell, (Per Gunnar) Tores
See Theorell, (Per Gunnar) Toeres
Theotokas, Yorghos (George)
1905-1966 .... EWL 3
Theriault, Albert A(ugustine), Jr. 1928- 53-56
Theriault, Joseph-Adrien 1925- CANR-116
Earlier sketch in CA 160
See also DLB 53
Theriault, Joseph-Adrien 1925-
See Theriault, Joseph-Adrien
Theriault, Reg 1924- 224
Theriault, Yves 1915-1983 102
See also CCA 1
See also CLC 79
See also DAC
See also DAM MST
See also DLB 88
See also EWL 3
Therio, Adrien
See Theriault, Joseph-Adrien
Therion, Master
See Crowley, Edward Alexander
See also GLL 1
Thermes, Jennifer 1966- .... SATA 155
Thernstrom, Abigail M. 1936- CANR-73
Earlier sketch in CA 127
Thernstrom, Stephan (Albert) 1934- 13-16R
Theron, Johan 1924- 140
Theroux, Alexander (Louis) 1939- CANR-63
Earlier sketches in CA 85-88, CANR-20
See also CLC 2, 25
See also CN 4, 5, 6, 7
Theroux, Joseph (Peter) 1953- 133
Theroux, Marcel 1968- 190
Theroux, Paul (Edward) 1941- CANR-133
Earlier sketches in CA 33-36R, CANR-20, 45, 74
See also AAYA 28
See also AMWS 8
See also BEST 89:4
See also BPFB 3
See also CDALBS
See also CLC 5, 8, 11, 15, 28, 46
See also CN 1, 2, 3, 4, 5, 6, 7
See also CP 1
See also CPW 1
See also DA3
See also DAM POP
See also DLB 2, 218
See also EWL 3
See also HGG
See also MAL 5
See also MTCW 1, 2
See also MTFW 2005
See also RGAL 4
See also SATA 44, 109
See also TUS
Theroux, Peter (Christopher Sebastian)
1956- CANR-90
Earlier sketch in CA 132
Theroux, Phyllis 1939- CANR-129
Earlier sketch in CA 110
Thersites
See Bram, Christopher
Thesen, Hjalmar Peter 1925- 107
Thesen, Sharon 1946- CANR-125
Earlier sketch in CA 163
See also CLC 56
See also CP 7
See also CWP
Thesiger, Wilfred (Patrick) 1910-2003 ... CAP-2
Obituary 219
Earlier sketch in CA 17-18
See also DLB 204
Thesing, William B(arney) 1947- CANR-32
Earlier sketch in CA 113
Thesman, Jean .... AAYA 16
See also JRDA
See also MAICYA 2
See also MAICYAS 1
See also SATA 74, 124
Thespis fl. 6th cent. B.C.- .... LMFS 1
Theunissen, Michael 1932- 132
Thevenin, Denis
See Duhamel, Georges
Thevoz, Michel 1936- CANR-93
Earlier sketch in CA 132
Thewlis, P(eter) J(ohn) 1944- 127
Thibaudeau, Colleen 1925- 113
See also DLB 88
Thibaudeau, May Murphy 1908- 131
Thibault, Jacques Anatole Francois
1844-1924 127
Brief entry 106
See also France, Anatole
See also DA3
See also DAM NOV
See also MTCW 1, 2
See also TWA
Thibault, John C(rowell) 1922- 77-80
Thibodeau, David 1969(?)- 195
Thibodeau, Serge Patrice 1959- 176
Thibodeaux, Mark E. 1970- 219
Thiebaud, Wayne 1920- 45-48
Thiebaux, Marcelle 1931- 122
Brief entry 110
Thieda, Shirley Ann 1943- 69-72
See also SATA 13
Thiede, Carsten (Peter) 1952-2004 . CANR-107
Obituary 234
Earlier sketch in CA 156
Thiel, Diane 1967- 202
Thiele, Colin (Milton) 1920- CANR-105
Earlier sketches in CA 29-32R, CANR-12, 28, 53
See also CLC 17
See also CLR 27
See also CP 1, 2
See also DLB 289
See also MAICYA 1, 2
See also SAAS 2
See also SATA 14, 72, 125
See also YAW
Thiele, Edwin R(ichard) 1895-1986 .... CAP-1
Earlier sketch in CA 19-20
Thiele, Leslie Paul 1959- 166
Thiele, Margaret Rossiter 1901-2000 ..... 21-24R
Thielen, Benedict 1903-1965 208
See also DLB 102
Thielen, Thoraf Theodore 1921- 5-8R
Thielens, Wagner P., Jr. 1925- 1-4R
Thielicke, Helmut 1908-1986 .... CANR-87
Obituary 118
Earlier sketches in CA 69-72, CANR-11
Thielman, Jeff(rey D.) 1963- 139
Thiem, E(zra) George 1897-1987 134
Obituary 123
Thiem, George
See Thiem, E(zra) George
Thiemann, Ronald F. 1946- CANR-118
Earlier sketch in CA 159
Thien-An, Thich 1926- 57-60
Thier, Herbert D(avid) 1932- 29-32R
Thier, Marlene 239
Thierauf, Robert J(ames) 1933- CANR-12
Earlier sketch in CA 29-32R
Thiering, Barbara (Elizabeth) 1930- 140
Thiery, Herman 1912-1978
See Daisne, Johan
Thiesenhusen, William C. 1936- 21-24R
Thiesing, Lisa 1958- .... SATA 95, 159
Thiessen, Elmer John 1942- 231
Thiessen, Jack 1931- CANR-34
Earlier sketches in CA 41-44R, CANR-15
Thiessen, John
See Thiessen, Jack
Thiessen, John C(aldwell) 1890-1966 .... 5-8R
Thiher, Allen (Ottah) 1941- CANR-112
Earlier sketches in CA 41-44R, CANR-14, 31, 57
Thiman, Eric Harding 1900-1975 .... CAP-1
Earlier sketch in CA 13-14
Thimblethorpe, June Sylvia 1926-
Brief entry 117
See also RHW
Thimm, Alfred L. 1923- CANR-8
Earlier sketch in CA 61-64
Thimmesch, Nicholas Palen
1927-1985 .... CANR-28
Obituary 116
Earlier sketch in CA 13-16R
Thimmesch, Nick
See Thimmesch, Nicholas Palen
Thimmesh, Catherine 236
Thirgood, J(ack) V(incent) 1924- 127
Thirion, Andre 1907-2001 101
Thirkell, Angela (Margaret)
1890-1961 .... CANR-118
Obituary 93-96
Earlier sketch in CA 140
See also RGEL 2
Thirkell, John Henry 1913- CANR-10
Earlier sketch in CA 13-16R
Thirlwall, A(nthony) P. 1941- 230
Thirlwall, John C(onnop, Jr.) 1904-1971 .. 69-72
Thirlwell, Adam 1978- 225
Thiroux d'Arconville, Marie-Genevieve
1720-1805 .... DLB 314
Thirsk, (Irene) Joan 1922- CANR-94
Earlier sketch in CA 25-28R
Thiry, Joan (Marie) 1926- 121
See also SATA 45
Thisby
See Turner, Dona M.
Thiselton, Anthony C(harles) 1937- .. CANR-92
Earlier sketch in CA 145
Thistle, Mel(ville William) 1914- 53-56
Thistlethwaite, Bel
See Wetherald, Agnes Ethelwyn
Thistlethwaite, Miles 1945- .... SATA 12
Thistlethwaite, Susan (Brooks) 1948- 127
Thobaben, Robert G. 1924- 229
Thoby-Marcelin, (Emile) Philippe
1904-1975 125
Obituary 61-64
See also BW 1
See also EWL 3
Thody, Philip (Malcolm Waller)
1928-1999 .... CANR-90
Earlier sketches in CA 5-8R, CANR-9
Thoene, Alma E(vans) 1903-1991 49-52
Thoene, (William) Brock 1952- CANR-108
Earlier sketch in CA 167
Thoene, Peter
See Bihalji-Merin, Oto
Thoene, William Brock
See Thoene, (William) Brock
Thoger, Marie 1923- CANR-11
Earlier sketch in CA 25-28R
Tholfsen, Trygve R(ainone) 1924- 134
Brief entry 108
Thollander, Earl 1922- CANR-18
Earlier sketch in CA 101
See also SATA 22
Thom, Alexander 1894-1985 133
Thom, James Alexander 1933- CANR-130
Earlier sketches in CA 77-80, CANR-15, 64
See also TCWW 2
Thom, Mary 1944- 128
Thom, Paul 1941- 139
Thom, Rene (Frederic) 1923-2002 161
Obituary 212
Thom, Robert 1929-1979 .... 21-24R
Obituary 85-88
Thom, Robert Anderson 1915-1980 61-64
Thom, Valerie M(acLaren) 1929- 124
Thoma, Henry F. 1909(?)-1983
Obituary 110
Thoma, Ludwig 1867-1921 .... DLB 66
Thoma, Richard 1902-1974 167
See also DLB 4
Thomae, Betty Kennedy 1920- 61-64
Thoman, Richard S(amuel) 1919- 65-68
Thomaneck, J(uergen) K. A. 1941- CANR-90
Earlier sketch in CA 132
Thomas, A(rthur) J(oshua), Jr.
1918-1982 .... CANR-10
Earlier sketch in CA 5-8R
Thomas, A. M. 1960- 175
Thomas, A(ndrew) R(owland) B(enedick)
1904- 65-68
Thomas, Abigail 1941- 173
See also SATA 112
Thomas, Abraham V(azhayil) 1934- 61-64
Thomas, Alan (Cedric) 1933- 81-84
Thomas, Alan G. 1911-1992 .... 25-28R
Thomas, Alexander 1914-2003 103
Obituary 212
Thomas, Andrea
See Hill, Margaret (Ohler)
Thomas, Ann Van Wynen 1919- CANR-10
Earlier sketch in CA 5-8R
Thomas, Anna (Irena) 1948- CANR-24
Earlier sketch in CA 41-44R
Thomas, Annabel (Crawford) 1929- .. CANR-85
Earlier sketch in CA 106
Thomas, Arline 1913-1989 49-52
Obituary 128
Thomas, Armstrong 1909(?)-1975
Obituary 57-60
Thomas, Art(hur Lawrence) 1952- 105
See also SATA 48
See also SATA-Brief 38
Thomas, Audrey (Callahan) 1935- 237
Earlier sketches in CA 21-24R, CANR-36, 58
Autobiographical Essay in 237
See also CAAS 19
See also AITN 2
See also CLC 7, 13, 37, 107
See also CN 2, 3, 4, 5, 6, 7
See also DLB 60
See also MTCW 1
See also RGSF 2
See also SSC 20
Thomas, Augustus 1857-1934 .... MAL 5
See also TCLC 97
Thomas, Barbara L(ee) 1939- 145
Thomas, Ben Bowen 1899-1977
Obituary 108
Thomas, Bill 1934- CANR-8
Earlier sketch in CA 61-64
Thomas, Bob
See Thomas, Robert J(oseph)
Thomas, Brook 1947- 139
Thomas, Bruce
See Paine, Lauran (Bosworth)
Thomas, Bruce 134
Thomas, C(harles) T. 1947- 196
Thomas, Calvin 1956- 189
Thomas, Carl H.
See Doerffler, Alfred
Thomas, Carol G. 1938- 191
Thomas, Carroll
See Ratliff, Thomas M. and Shmurak, Carole B.
Thomas, Chantal 225
Thomas, (Antony) Charles 1928- 119
Thomas, Charles W. 1903-1973
Obituary 41-44R
Thomas, Charles W(ellington) 1943- 65-68
Thomas, Claire Sherman 1923- 108
Thomas, Clara (McCandless) 1919- 25-28R
Thomas, Clarence 1948- 166
See also BW 3
Thomas, Claudia E. 1956- 170
Thomas, Conrad Ward 1914-1994 .... 37-40R
Thomas, Cornell 1955- CANR-93
Earlier sketch in CA 145
Thomas, Craig (David) 1942- 112
Brief entry 108
Interview in CA-112
Thomas, Cullen
See Kimes, Beverly Rae
Thomas, D(onald) M(ichael) 1935- CANR-75
Earlier sketches in CA 61-64, CANR-17, 45
Interview in CANR-17
See also CAAS 11
See also BPFB 3
See also BRWS 4
See also CDBLB 1960 to Present
See also CLC 13, 22, 31, 132
See also CN 4, 5, 6, 7
See also CP 1, 2, 3, 4, 5, 6, 7
See also DA3
See also DLB 40, 207, 299
See also HGG
See also MTCW 1, 2
See also MTFW 2005
See also SFW 4
Thomas, D(avid) O(swald) 1924- CANR-41
Earlier sketch in CA 117
Thomas, Dan
See Sanders, Leonard
Thomas, Daniel B.
See Bluestein, Daniel Thomas
Thomas, Daniel H(arrison) 1904-1999 .. 13-16R
Thomas, Danny 1912(?)-1991 143
Thomas, Dante 1922- 53-56
Thomas, Dave 1949- 152
Brief entry 115
Thomas, David 1931- 103
Thomas, David 1959- 143
Thomas, David A(rthur) 1925- 13-16R
Thomas, David Hurst 1945- CANR-102
Earlier sketch in CA 108
Thomas, David St. John 1929- CANR-30
Earlier sketch in CA 112
Thomas, David Winton 1901-1970 .... CAP-1
Earlier sketch in CA 9-10
Thomas, Denis 1922-2003 .... CANR-34
Obituary 214
Earlier sketches in CA 77-80, CANR-15
Thomas, Dian 1945- CANR-10
Earlier sketch in CA 65-68
Thomas, Diane Renee 1946(?)-1985
Obituary 117
Thomas, Donald 1926- 49-52
Thomas, Donald F. 1913-1998 .... 29-32R
Thomas, Donald Roff 1924-1979
Obituary 111
Thomas, Dorothy Swaine 1899-1977 .... CAP-2
Obituary 69-72
Earlier sketch in CA 17-18
Thomas, Douglas 1966- 214
Thomas, Dwight (Rembert) 1944- 127

Thomas, Dylan (Marlais) 1914-1953 ... CANR-65
Brief entry ... 104
Earlier sketch in CA 120
See also AAYA 45
See also BRWS 1
See also CDBLB 1945-1960
See also DA
See also DA3
See also DAB
See also DAC
See also DAM DRAM, MST, POET
See also DLB 13, 20, 139
See also EWL 3
See also EXPP
See also LAIT 3
See also MTCW 1, 2
See also MTFW 2005
See also PAB
See also PC 2, 52
See also PFS 1, 3, 8
See also RGEL 2
See also RGSF 2
See also SATA 60
See also SSC 3, 44
See also TCLC 1, 8, 45, 105
See also TEA
See also WLC
See also WLIT 4
See also WP
Thomas, E(ric) H(ubert) Gwynne
See Gwynne-Thomas, E(ric) H(ubert)
Thomas, Earl W(esley) 1915- ... 53-56
Thomas, Ed 1961- ... DLB 310
Thomas, Edison H(ugh) 1912- ... 85-88
Thomas, (Philip) Edward 1878-1917 ... 153
Brief entry ... 106
See also BRW 6
See also BRWS 3
See also DAM POET
See also DLB 19, 98, 156, 216
See also EWL 3
See also PAB
See also PC 53
See also RGEL 2
See also TCLC 10
Thomas, Edward Llewellyn
See Llewellyn-Thomas, Edward
Thomas, Edwin J(ohn) 1927- ... 21-24R
Thomas, Egbert S.
See Ellis, Edward S(ylvester)
Thomas, Elizabeth Ann 1952- ... 85-88
Thomas, Elizabeth Marshall 1931- ... CANR-95
Earlier sketch in CA 17-20R
Thomas, Emory M. 1939- ... 97-100
Thomas, Ernest Lewys 1904-1983 ... CANR-1
Earlier sketch in CA 1-4R
Thomas, Estelle Webb 1899-1982 ... 21-24R
See also SATA 26
Thomas, Evan (III) 1951- ... CANR-99
Earlier sketch in CA 152
Thomas, Evangeline 1904- ... 117
Thomas, F(ranklin) Richard 1940- ... CANR-55
Earlier sketches in CA 77-80, CANR-13, 29
Thomas, Frances 1943- ... CANR-124
Earlier sketches in CA 130, CANR-59
See also SATA 92
Thomas, Frank P(atrick) 1916- ... 119
Thomas, Frederick William 1806-1866 ... DLB 202
Thomas, G. K.
See Davies, L(eslie) P(urnell)
Thomas, G(regory) Scott 1955- ... 151
Thomas, (Thomas) George 1909- ... 126
Thomas, George Finger 1899-1977
Obituary ... 73-76
Thomas, George I. 1915- ... 25-28R
Thomas, George Leicester, Jr. 1907-1977 ... CAP-1
Earlier sketch in CA 11-12
Thomas, Gerrard
See Kempinski, Tom
Thomas, Gilbert (Oliver) 1891-1978 ... 5-8R
Thomas, Gordon 1933- ... CANR-40
Earlier sketch in CA 9-12R
Thomas, Gordon L. 1914- ... 37-40R
Thomas, Graham Stuart 1909-2003 . CANR-41
Obituary ... 216
Earlier sketches in CA 9-12R, CANR-4, 19
Thomas, Gwyn 1913-1981 ... CANR-9
Obituary ... 103
Earlier sketch in CA 65-68
See also CN 2
See also DLB 15, 245
Thomas, H. C.
See Keating, Lawrence A.
Thomas, H(ubert) Nigel 1947- ... CANR-104
Earlier sketch in CA 148
Thomas, Harold Becken 1888-1971
Obituary ... 104
Thomas, Heather Smith 1944- ... CANR-6
Earlier sketch in CA 57-60
Thomas, Helen A. 1920- ... 101
Thomas, Helen Shirley 1931-1968 ... 5-8R
Obituary ... 103
Thomas, Henri (Joseph Marie) 1912-1993 ... CAP-1
Earlier sketch in CA 9-10
Thomas, Henry 1886-1970
Obituary ... 29-32R
Thomas, Hugh Swynnerton 1931- ... CANR-5
Earlier sketch in CA 9-12R
Thomas, I(saac) D(avid) E(llis) 1921- ... 65-68
Thomas, Ianthe 1951- ... CLR 8
See also SATA 139
See also SATA-Brief 42
Thomas, Isaiah 1750-1831 ... DLB 43, 73, 187
Thomas, Ivo Herbert Christopher 1912-1976 ... 5-8R
Thomas, J(eremy) A(mbler) 1947- ... 118
Thomas, J. C. ... 57-60
Thomas, J(ames) D(avid) 1910- ... CANR-57
Earlier sketches in CA 57-60, CANR-6, 31
Thomas, J. James 1933- ... 53-56
Thomas, J. W. 1917- ... 101
Thomas, Jack Ray 1931- ... 41-44R
Thomas, Jack W(illiam) 1930- ... CANR-16
Earlier sketches in CA 49-52, CANR-1
Thomas, James H(arold) 1943- ... 119
Thomas, Jane Resh 1936- ... CANR-59
Earlier sketches in CA 106, CANR-24
See also SATA 38, 90
Thomas, Jeannette Grise 1935- ... 101
Thomas, Jerry D. 1959- ... SATA 91
Thomas, Jim
See Reagan, Thomas (James) B(utler)
Thomas, Joan Gale
See Robinson, Joan (Mary) G(ale Thomas)
Thomas, Johann 1624-1679 ... DLB 168
Thomas, John 1890- ... 49-52
Thomas, John Allen Miner 1900-1932
Brief entry ... 107
See also DLB 4
Thomas, John Clayton 1944- ... 139
Thomas, John Hunter 1928- ... 57-60
Thomas, John Lawrence 1910-1991 . CANR-86
Obituary ... 134
Earlier sketch in CA 5-8R
Thomas, Joyce Carol 1938- ... CANR-135
Brief entry ... 113
Earlier sketches in CA 116, CANR-48, 114
Interview in ... CA-116
See also AAYA 12, 54
See also BW 2, 3
See also CLC 35
See also CLR 19
See also DLB 33
See also JRDA
See also MAICYA 1, 2
See also MTCW 1, 2
See also MTFW 2005
See also SAAS 7
See also SATA 40, 78, 123, 137
See also SATA-Essay 137
See also WYA
See also YAW
Thomas, Julian (Stewart) 1959- ... 143
Thomas, June Manning 1950- ... 166
See also BW 3
Thomas, K.
See Fearn, John Russell
Thomas, K. H.
See Kirk, T(homas) H(obson)
Thomas, Keith (Vivian) 1933- ... CANR-82
Earlier sketches in CA 37-40R, CANR-15, 34
Thomas, Kenneth Bryn (?)-1978
Obituary ... 81-84
Thomas, Kurt 1956- ... 154
Brief entry ... 114
Thomas, Latta R(oosevelt) 1927- ... 65-68
Thomas, Laurence (Mordekhai) 1949- ... 227
Thomas, Lawrence L(eslie) 1924- ... 45-48
Thomas, Lee
See Floren, Lee
Thomas, Lee 1918- ... CANR-1
Earlier sketch in CA 1-4R
Thomas, Leslie (John) 1931- ... CANR-22
Earlier sketch in CA 13-16R
Thomas, Lew(is) (Christopher) 1932- ... 206
Thomas, Lewis 1913-1993 ... CANR-60
Obituary ... 143
Earlier sketches in CA 85-88, CANR-38
See also ANW
See also CLC 35
See also DLB 275
See also MTCW 1, 2
Thomas, Lewis H(erbert) 1917-1983 ... CANR-13
Earlier sketch in CA 73-76
Thomas, Lionel H(ugh) C(hristopher) 1922(?)-1978
Obituary ... 104
Thomas, Liz
See Thomas, Elizabeth Ann
Thomas, Lorenzo 1944- ... CANR-114
Earlier sketches in CA 73-76, CANR-25
See also BW 1
See also DLB 41
Thomas, Lowell (Jackson) 1892-1981 . CANR-3
Obituary ... 104
Earlier sketch in CA 45-48
See also AITN 1, 2
Thomas, Lowell Jackson, Jr. 1923- ... 85-88
See also SATA 15
Thomas, Lyn 1953- ... 232
Thomas, M. Carey 1857-1935 ... FW
See also TCLC 89
Thomas, M(ilton) Halsey 1903-1977 ... 25-28R
Obituary ... 73-76
Thomas, Mack
See Womack, Thomas Hale
Thomas, Mack 1928- ... 9-12R
Thomas, Maria
See Worrick, Roberta
Thomas, Marlo 1938- ... CANR-124
Earlier sketch in CA 165
Thomas, Mary Martha Hosford 1927- ... 53-56
Thomas, Mason P(age), Jr. 1928- ... CANR-22
Earlier sketch in CA 25-28R
Thomas, Meredith 1963- ... 190
See also SATA 119
Thomas, Mervyn
See Curran, Mona (Elisa)
Thomas, Michael
See Wilks, Michael Thomas
Thomas, Michael A. 1946- ... 202
Thomas, Michael M(ackenzie) 1936- ... 139
Thomas, (William) Miles (Webster) 1897-1980
Obituary ... 105
Thomas, Nicholas (Jeremy) 1960- ... CANR-90
Earlier sketch in CA 135
Thomas, Norman (Mattoon) 1884-1968 ... 101
Obituary ... 25-28R
See also DLB 303
Thomas, Norman C(arl) 1932- ... 17-20R
Thomas, Norman L(ee) 1925- ... 41-44R
Thomas, Owen Clark 1922- ... 9-12R
Thomas, Patricia J. 1934- ... 37-40R
See also SATA 51
Thomas, Paul
See Mann, (Paul) Thomas
Thomas, Paul 1908- ... CANR-22
Earlier sketches in CAP-1, CA 9-10
Thomas, Paul L. 1961- ... 224
Thomas, Peter 1928- ... 37-40R
Thomas, Peter David Garner 1930- ... 180
Thomas, Peter Wynne
See Wynne-Thomas, Peter
Thomas, Phillip Drennon 1938- ... 124
Thomas, Phyllis 1935- ... 119
Thomas, Piri 1928- ... 73-76
See also CLC 17
See also HLCS 2
See also HW 1
See also LLW
Thomas, Quentin
See Quick, W(illiam) T(homas)
Thomas, R. George 1914-2001 ... CANR-93
Earlier sketch in CA 146
Thomas, R(ichard) Hinton 1912-1983 ... CANR-5
Obituary ... 110
Earlier sketch in CA 5-8R
Thomas, R(obert) Murray 1921- ... CANR-22
Earlier sketches in CA 17-20R, CANR-7
Thomas, R(onald) S(tuart) 1913-2000 ... CANR-30
Obituary ... 189
Earlier sketch in CA 89-92
See also CAAS 4
See also CDBLB 1960 to Present
See also CLC 6, 13, 48
See also CP 1, 2, 3, 4, 5, 6, 7
See also DAB
See also DAM POET
See also DLB 27
See also EWL 3
See also MTCW 1
See also RGEL 2
Thomas, Ralph 1949- ... 196
Thomas, Richard (Earl) 1951- ... 107
Thomas, Rob 1965- ... CANR-136
Earlier sketch in CA 164
See also AAYA 25
See also BYA 13, 15
See also SATA 97
See also WYAS 1
See also YAW
Thomas, Robert 1930- ... 25-28R
Thomas, Robert C(harles) 1925-1993 ... 101
Obituary ... 141
Thomas, Robert J(oseph) 1922- ... CANR-13
Earlier sketch in CA 77-80
Thomas, Robert L. 1928- ... 195
Thomas, Rollin G(eorge) 1896-1972(?) .. CAP-1
Earlier sketch in CA 13-16
Thomas, Rosalind 1959- ... CANR-112
Earlier sketch in CA 132
Thomas, Rosanne Daryl 1956- ... CANR-90
Earlier sketch in CA 143
Thomas, Rosie 1947- ... 133
Brief entry ... 126
Interview in ... CA-133
See also RHW
Thomas, Ross (Elmore) 1926-1995 ... CANR-63
Obituary ... 150
Earlier sketches in CA 33-36R, CANR-22
See also CLC 39
See also CMW 4
Thomas, Roy 1940- ... 223
Thomas, Ruth 1944- ... 200
Thomas, S(idney) Claudewell 1932- ... 17-20R
Thomas, Sara (Sally) 1911(?)-1982
Obituary ... 106
Thomas, Scarlett 1972- ... 224
Thomas, Scott 1959- ... SATA 147
Thomas, Sewell 1884-1970 ... CAP-1
Earlier sketch in CA 9-10
Thomas, Sheree R(enee) ... 217
Thomas, Sherilyn 1948- ... CANR-13
Earlier sketch in CA 73-76
Thomas, Sherry
See Thomas, Sherilyn
Thomas, Shirley ... 5-8R
Thomas, Stanley 1933- ... 21-24R
Thomas, Stephen N(aylor) 1942- ... 89-92
Thomas, Sue
See Thomas, Susan-Jane
Thomas, Susan-Jane 1951- ... 143
Thomas, T. M(athai) 1933- ... 53-56
Thomas, Ted
See Thomas, Theodore L.
See also SFW 4
Thomas, Theodore L. 1920- ... 29-32R
See also Thomas, Ted
Thomas, Thom 1940- ... 108
Thomas, Tony 1947- ... 61-64
Thomas, Trisha R. 1964- ... 219
Thomas, Vaughan 1934- ... 81-84
Thomas, Vernon (Arthur) 1934- ... SATA 56
Thomas, Victoria
See DeWeese, Thomas Eugene and Kugi, Constance Todd
Thomas, Virginia Castleton
See Castleton, Virginia
Thomas, W(illiam) A(rthur) 1937- ... 127
Thomas, W(alter) Ian 1914- ... 17-20R
Thomas, Will 1958- ... 233
Thomas, William 1906- ... 73-76
Thomas, William E(dward) 1942- ... 111
Thomas, William F. 1924- ... 69-72
Thomas, William G(ordan) 1931- ... 93-96
Thomas, William Isaac 1863-1947 ... 214
Thomas, William J. 1946- ... 226
Thomas, William L(eRoy, Jr.) 1920- ... 41-44R
Thomas-Anderson, Gloria
See Anderson, Gloria T.
Thomas-El, Salome 1964- ... 197
Thomas-Graham, Pamela (Borders) 1963(?)- ... 171
Thomasin von Zerclaere c. 1186-c. 1259 ... DLB 138
Thomasius, Christian 1655-1728 ... DLB 168
Thomasma, David Charles 1939- ... CANR-44
Earlier sketches in CA 104, CANR-21
Thomasma, Kenneth R. 1930- ... 155
See also SATA 90
Thomason, A(lan) Mims 1910-1985
Obituary ... 117
Thomason, Burke C(urtis) 1943- ... 113
Thomason, George 1602(?)-1666 ... DLB 213
Thomason, John W(illiam), Jr. 1893-1944 ... TCWW 1, 2
Thomason, Tommy 1949- ... 73-76
Thomassie, Tynia 1959- ... CANR-136
Earlier sketch in CA 156
See also SATA 92
Thometz, Carol Estes 1938- ... 9-12R
Thomey, Tedd 1920- ... CANR-2
Earlier sketch in CA 5-8R
Thomis, Malcolm I(an) 1936- ... 172
Brief entry ... 118
Thomis, Wayne 1907-1988
Obituary ... 126
Thomison, Dennis 1937- ... 53-56
Thomlinson, Ralph 1925- ... 41-44R
Thommen, George S. 1896-1990 ... CAP-1
Earlier sketch in CA 13-16
Thompson, A(lbert) Gray 1928- ... 41-44R
Thompson, A(rthur) L(eonard) B(ell) 1917-1975 ... CANR-5
Obituary ... 61-64
Earlier sketch in CA 53-56
See also Clifford, Francis
Thompson, Alan Eric 1924- ... 109
Thompson, Alice ... 229
Thompson, Anne Armstrong 1939- ... 85-88
Thompson, Anne Hall Whitt 1930-1996 ... 119
Obituary ... 155
Thompson, Arthur A., Jr. 1940- ... 85-88
Thompson, Arthur W(illiam) 1920-1966 ... 1-4R
Thompson, Bard 1925-1987 ... CANR-1
Obituary ... 123
Earlier sketch in CA 1-4R
Thompson, Betty A(nne) 1926- ... 111
Thompson, Blanche Jennings ... 5-8R
Thompson, Brenda 1935- ... 106
See also SATA 34
Thompson, Brian 1935- ... CANR-139
Earlier sketch in CA 109
Thompson, Buck
See Paine, Lauran (Bosworth)
Thompson, C. Bradley ... 194
Thompson, C(harles) Hall ... TCWW 2
Thompson, C(lara) Mildred 1881-1975
Obituary ... 57-60
Thompson, Carol 1951- ... SATA 85
Thompson, Caroline 1956- ... 110
Thompson, Charles Lowell 1937- ... CANR-3
Earlier sketch in CA 49-52
Thompson, Charles P. 1933- ... 147
Thompson, Charles Waters, Jr.
See Thompson, Toby
Thompson, China
See Lewis, Mary (Christianna)
Thompson, Claude Holmes 1908-1971 . CAP-1
Earlier sketch in CA 11-12
Thompson, Claudia G(reig) 1953- ... 142
Thompson, Colin (Edward) 1942- ... CANR-126
Earlier sketch in CA 160
See also SATA 95, 163
Thompson, Corrie 1887-1986 ... 61-64
Thompson, Craig 1907-1986
Obituary ... 121
Thompson, Craig 1975- ... 235
See also AAYA 55
Thompson, Daniel (Calbert) 1916- ... 13-16R
Thompson, Daniel P(ierce) 1795-1868 ... DLB 202
Thompson, Darcy Wentworth 1860-1948 .. 164
See also NCFS 4
Thompson, David 1770-1857 ... DLB 99
Thompson, David (Bradford) 1938- ... 57-60
Thompson, David 1953- ... 127
Thompson, David H(ugh) 1941- ... 81-84
See also SATA 17
Thompson, Dennis F(rank) 1940- ... 53-56
Thompson, Dennis L. 1935- ... 41-44R
Thompson, (Arthur) Denys (Halstead) 1907-1988 ... CANR-4
Obituary ... 124
Earlier sketch in CA 9-12R
Thompson, Don(ald Arthur) 1935-1994 .. 53-56
Obituary ... 198
Thompson, Donald 1928- ... 140
Thompson, Donald Eugene 1913-1992 ... 109
Thompson, Donald L(ambert) 1930- ... 49-52

Cumulative Index 575 Thomson

Thompson, Donald Neil 1939- 37-40R
Thompson, Donnis Stark 1928- 21-24R
Thompson, Dorothy 1894-1961 179
Obituary 89-92
See also DLB 29
See also FW
Thompson, Dorothy (Katherine) 1923- 142
Thompson, Duane G(len) 1933- 73-76
Thompson, E. P. 1924-1993 .... DLB 242
Thompson, E(rnest) V(ictor) 1931- .... RHW
Thompson, Earl 1931(?)-1978 85-88
Obituary 81-84
Thompson, Edgar T(ristram) 1900-1989 .... 17-20R
Thompson, Edward Thorwald 1928- CANR-21
Earlier sketch in CA 105
See also CMW 4
Thompson, Eileen
See Panowski, Eileen Thompson
Thompson, Elizabeth Allen 1914-1984 119
Thompson, Emily 1962- 223
Thompson, Emma 1959(?)- CANR-125
Earlier sketch in CA 154
Thompson, Era Bell 1905-1986 89-92
Obituary 121
See also BW 2
Thompson, Eric
See Thompson, J(ohn) Eric S(idney)
Thompson, (Richard) Ernest 1949- CANR-128
Brief entry 115
Earlier sketch in CA 123
Thompson, Ernest Trice 1894-1985 .. CANR-86
Obituary 115
Earlier sketch in CA 1-4R
Thompson, Eugene Allen 1924-2001 .... CANR-26
Obituary 195
Earlier sketch in CA 104
Thompson, Evelyn Wingo 1921- 21-24R
Thompson, Ewa M(ajewska) 1937- 49-52
Thompson, Flora (Jane Timms) 1876(?)-1947
Brief entry 123
See also DLB 240
Thompson, Frances C(lements) 1906- ... CAP-1
Earlier sketch in CA 9-10
Thompson, Francis (Joseph) 1859-1907 189
Brief entry 104
See also BRW 5
See also CDBLB 1890-1914
See also DLB 19
See also RGEL 2
See also TCLC 4
See also TEA
Thompson, Francis Clegg
See Mencken, H(enry) L(ouis)
Thompson, Francis George 1931- CANR-23
Earlier sketch in CA 106
Thompson, Frank H., Jr. 1926- 25-28R
Thompson, Fred 1900-1987
Obituary 121
Thompson, Fred Dalton 1942- 69-72
Thompson, Fred P(riestly), Jr. 1917- 89-92
Thompson, G(ary) R(ichard) 1937- CANR-2
Earlier sketch in CA 45-48
Thompson, Gene
See Thompson, Eugene Allen
Thompson, Gene
See Lutz, Giles A(lfred)
Thompson, George Clifford 1920- 104
Thompson, George G(reene) 1914- 21-24R
Thompson, George H(yman) 1923- 125
Brief entry 117
Thompson, George Selden 1929-1989 .... CANR-37
Obituary 130
Earlier sketches in CA 5-8R, CANR-21
Interview in CANR-21
See also Selden, George
See also CWRI 5
See also FANT
See also MAICYA 1, 2
See also SATA 4, 73
See also SATA-Obit 63
Thompson, Gerald E(verett) 1924- 53-56
Thompson, Gertrude Caton
See Caton-Thompson, Gertrude
Thompson, Glenda
See Goss, Glenda Dawn
Thompson, Grant P(helps) 1940- 111
Thompson, Gregory Lee 1946- 154
Thompson, Harlan (Howard) 1894-1987 .... CAP-1
Obituary 123
Earlier sketch in CA 9-10
See also Holt, Stephen
See also SATA 10
See also SATA-Obit 53
Thompson, Harry 1960- 164
Thompson, Harry C. 1921(?)-1980
Obituary 97-100
Thompson, (Harry) Harwood 1894- 65-68
Thompson, Helen M. (Smith) 1903-1990 .... CAP-1
Earlier sketch in CA 13-14
Thompson, Helen M. 1950- 199
Thompson, Henry O(rrin) 1931- CANR-25
Earlier sketch in CA 45-48
Thompson, Henry Yates 1838-1928 ... DLB 184
Thompson, Hilary 1943- 127
See also SATA 56
See also SATA-Brief 49
Thompson, Hildegard (Steerstedter) 1901-1983 .... 17-20R
Thompson, Hunter S(tockton) 1937(?)-2005 .... CANR-133
Obituary 236
Earlier sketches in CA 17-20R, CANR-23, 46, 74, 77, 111
See also AAYA 45
See also BEST 89:1
See also BPFB 3
See also CLC 9, 17, 40, 104
See also CPW
See also CSW
See also DA3
See also DAM POP
See also DLB 185
See also MTCW 1, 2
See also MTFW 2005
See also TUS
Thompson, Ian B(entley) 1936- 37-40R
Thompson, Irene 1919- 110
Thompson, Isabel
See Kelsay, Isabel Thompson
Thompson, J(ohn) Eric S(idney) 1898-1975 65-68
Obituary 61-64
Thompson, J(esse) J(ackson) 1919-1993 .... 5-8R
Obituary 227
Thompson, Jack Maynard 1924- 41-44R
Thompson, Jacqueline 1945- CANR-38
Earlier sketches in CA 97-100, CANR-17
Thompson, James 1902-1983
Obituary 109
Thompson, James 1932- 73-76
Thompson, James Clay 1943- 127
Thompson, James D(avid) 1920-1973 ... CAP-2
Earlier sketch in CA 21-22
Thompson, James H.
See Freeman, G(raydon) L(a Verne)
Thompson, James Myers
See Thompson, Jim (Myers)
Thompson, James W. 1935- 105
Thompson, Janet A(nn) 1944- 150
Thompson, Jean 1950- CANR-88
Earlier sketch in CA 136
Thompson, Jeanie 1952- 172
Autobiographical Essay in 172
See also CAAS 28
Thompson, Jennifer Trainer
See Trainer, Jennifer
Thompson, Jewel Taylor 1935- 148
Thompson, Jill 1966- .... AAYA 52
Thompson, Jim (Myers) 1906-1977(?) 140
See also BPFB 3
See also CLC 69
See also CMW 4
See also CPW
See also DLB 226
See also MSW
Thompson, Joan 1943- 97-100
Thompson, Joan Berengild 1915- 17-20R
Thompson, Joanna Maxwell Pullein
See Pullein-Thompson, Joanna Maxwell
Thompson, Joe Allen 1936- 37-40R
Thompson, Joel A. 1950- CANR-100
Earlier sketch in CA 146
Thompson, John (Anderson) 1918-2002 .... 5-8R
Obituary 207
Thompson, John 1938-1976 148
See also DLB 60
Thompson, John Leslie 1917- 5-8R
Thompson, John M(eans) 1926- 129
Thompson, John N. 1951- 154
Thompson, John Reuben 1823-1873 ..... DLB 3, 73, 248
Thompson, Josiah 1935- CANR-48
Earlier sketch in CA 41-44R
Thompson, Judith (Clare Francesca) 1954- . 143
See also CD 5, 6
See also CLC 39
See also CWD
See also DFS 22
Thompson, Julian F(rancis) 1927- ... CANR-102
Earlier sketches in CA 111, CANR-30, 56
See also AAYA 9
See also CLR 24
See also JRDA
See also MAICYA 1, 2
See also SAAS 13
See also SATA 55, 99, 155
See also SATA-Brief 40
See also WYA
Thompson, Julius Eric 1946- 49-52
Thompson, K(athryn Carolyn) Dyble 1952- .... SATA 82
Thompson, Karl F. 1917- 37-40R
Thompson, Kathleen 1918- CANR-144
Earlier sketch in CA 169
Thompson, Kay 1912(?)-1998 85-88
Obituary 169
See also CLR 22
See also MAICYA 1, 2
See also SATA 16
Thompson, Ken D(avid) 1926- 65-68
Thompson, Kenneth W(infred) 1921- CANR-118
Earlier sketches in CA 9-12R, CANR-5, 29, 54
Thompson, Kent 1936- 49-52
Thompson, Kristin 1950- CANR-25
Earlier sketch in CA 108
Thompson, Laura (Maud) 1905-2000 53-56
Thompson, Lauren (Stevens) 1962- .... SATA 132
Thompson, Laurence C(assius) 1926- . CANR-7
Earlier sketch in CA 5-8R
Thompson, Laurence G(raham) 1920-2005 .... 37-40R
Thompson, Lawrance (Roger) 1906-1973 .... CANR-10
Obituary 41-44R
Earlier sketch in CA 5-8R
See also DLB 103
Thompson, Lawrence Sidney 1916-1986 .... CANR-85
Obituary 121
Earlier sketches in CA 9-12R, CANR-5
Thompson, Leon (Whitey) 1923- 145
Thompson, Leonard Monteath 1916- CANR-16
Earlier sketches in CA 1-4R, CANR-1
Thompson, Lewis 1915(?)-1972
Obituary 37-40R
Thompson, Lloyd A(rthur) 1932-1997 137
Obituary 160
Thompson, Loring M(oore) 1918- 45-48
Thompson, Luther Joe 1918- 21-24R
Thompson, M(ichael) W(elman) 1928- CANR-124
Earlier sketches in CA 128, CANR-65
Thompson, Margot 1914-2003 132
Obituary 223
Thompson, Marian Spitzer 1899(?)-1983
Obituary 110
Thompson, Marilyn W. 1952- 227
Thompson, Mark 1952- CANR-141
Earlier sketch in CA 142
Thompson, Mark 1956- 219
Thompson, Mark L. 1945- 137
Thompson, Mary Wolfe 1886-1970 107
Thompson, Maurice 1844-1901 ..... DLB 71, 74
Thompson, Mel(vin R.) 1929- 73-76
Thompson, Morris Mordecai 1912- 109
Thompson, Neil 1929- 108
Thompson, Neville 1938- CANR-88
Earlier sketch in CA 37-40R, 185
Thompson, Noel W. 1951- 123
Thompson, Patrick H. 1933- 196
Thompson, Paul (Richard) 1935- CANR-38
Earlier sketches in CA 21-24R, CANR-16
Thompson, Paul 1943- CANR-32
Earlier sketches in CA 77-80, CANR-14
Thompson, Phyllis Hoge 1926- CANR-36
Earlier sketches in CA 29-32R, CANR-13
Thompson, Ralph 1904-1979
Obituary 89-92
Thompson, (William) Ralph 1910- 53-56
Thompson, Randall 1899-1984
Obituary 113
Thompson, Richard 1924- 9-12R
Thompson, Richard A(rlen) 1930- 61-64
Thompson, Richard L. 1947- 227
Thompson, Robert (Grainger Ker) 1916-1992 49-52
Thompson, Robert Elliott 1921-2003 77-80
Obituary 221
See also AITN 2
Thompson, Robert Farris 1932- 103
Thompson, Robert Norman 1914- 106
Thompson, Robert Sidney 1918- 111
Thompson, Roger Francis 1933- CANR-13
Earlier sketch in CA 73-76
Thompson, Roy Anton 1897-1985 .... CAP-2
Earlier sketch in CA 29-32
Thompson, Russ
See Paine, Lauran (Bosworth)
Thompson, Ruth Plumly 1891-1976 134
Obituary 113
See also DLB 22
See also SATA 66
Thompson, Samuel M(artin) 1902-1983
Obituary 110
Thompson, Sandra (Jean) 1943- 121
Thompson, Sharon (Elaine) 1952- 190
See also SATA 119
Thompson, Stanbury Dugard 1905- CAP-1
Earlier sketch in CA 11-12
Thompson, Steven L(ynn) 1948- 114
Thompson, Stith 1885-1976 .... CANR-5
Obituary 61-64
Earlier sketch in CA 5-8R
See also SATA 57
See also SATA-Obit 20
Thompson, Sue Ellen 1948- 207
Thompson, Susan (Ayers) 1946- 132
Thompson, Susan L. 1945- 114
Thompson, Susan O(tis) 1931- 85-88
Thompson, Sylvia
See Thompson, Sylvia (Vaughn Sheekman)
Thompson, Sylvia (Vaughn Sheekman) 1935- CANR-51
Earlier sketches in CA 5-8R, CANR-26
Thompson, Thomas 1913- .... TCWW 1, 2
Thompson, Thomas 1933-1982 .... CANR-14
Obituary 108
Earlier sketch in CA 65-68
Thompson, Thomas Kirkland 1914- 13-16R
Thompson, Thomas L. 1939- 146
Thompson, Thomas Phillips 1843-1933 179
See also DLB 99
Thompson, Toby 1944- 65-68
Thompson, Tracy 1955- 152
Thompson, Travis I. 1937- 37-40R
Thompson, Victor A(lexander) 1912-1996 .... 25-28R
Thompson, Victoria (E.) 232
Thompson, Virginia
See Adloff, Virginia Thompson
Thompson, Virginia 1937- 108
Thompson, Virginia McLean
See Adloff, Virginia Thompson
Thompson, Vivian L(aubach) 1911- CANR-1
Earlier sketch in CA 1-4R
See also SATA 3
Thompson, W. Grant 1935- 146
Thompson, W(illard) Scott 1942- CANR-12
Earlier sketch in CA 25-28R
Thompson, Wayne C(urtis) 1943- 109
Thompson, Wayne N. 1914- 21-24R
Thompson, Wilbur R(ichard) 1923- 13-16R
Thompson, Willa 1916- 9-12R
Thompson, Willard Mead 1913- 5-8R
Thompson, William 1775-1833 .... DLB 158
Thompson, William A(ncker) 1931- 77-80
Thompson, William Bernard 1914- CAP-1
Earlier sketch in CA 9-10
Thompson, William C. L.
See Edwards, William B(ennett)
Thompson, William D. 1929- 17-20R
Thompson, William E(llison), Jr. 1923- .. 13-16R
Thompson, William Fletcher, Jr. 1929- 1-4R
Thompson, William Irwin 1938- CANR-66
Earlier sketches in CA 21-24R, CANR-9
Thompson, William J. 1939- 146
Thompson, William N. 1940- 135
Thompson, William Tappan 1812-1882 .... DLB 3, 11, 248
Thompson, Wolfe
See Thompson, Mary Wolfe
Thompson-Frey, Nancy 1955- 127
Thompson-Peters, Flossie E. 178
Thoms, Herbert 1885-1972
Obituary 110
Thoms, Peter 1960- 181
Thomsen, Christian W(erner) 1940- 190
Thomsen, Grimur 1820-1896 .... DLB 293
Thomsen, Harry 1928- 5-8R
Thomsen, Moritz 1915- 29-32R
Thomsen, Robert 1915(?)-1983
Obituary 117
Thomsen, Russel J(ohn) 1941- 37-40R
Thomsett, Michael C. 1948- 119
Thomson, Alice 194
Thomson, Alistair 1960- 151
Thomson, Andrew 1963(?)- 234
Thomson, Arthur Alexander (Malcolm) 1894-1969 .... CAP-1
Earlier sketch in CA 11-12
Thomson, Ashley 1946- 238
Thomson, Basil (Home) 1861-1939
Brief entry 110
Thomson, Beatrix 1900-1986
Obituary 120
Thomson, Betty Flanders 1913- 9-12R
Thomson, C(harles) Leslie 1914- 9-12R
Thomson, Daisy H(icks) 1918- CANR-20
Earlier sketch in CA 103
Thomson, Dale C(airns) 1923- 25-28R
Thomson, David 1912-1970 .... CANR-2
Obituary 29-32R
Earlier sketch in CA 1-4R
Thomson, David (Robert Alexander) 1914-1988 .... CANR-24
Obituary 124
Earlier sketch in CA 107
See also SATA 40
See also SATA-Obit 55
Thomson, David 1941- 187
Thomson, Derick S(mith) 1921- CANR-12
Earlier sketch in CA 25-28R
See also CP 2
Thomson, Douglas Ferguson Scott 1919- 41-44R
Thomson, Edward
See Tubb, E(dwin) C(harles)
Thomson, Edward William 1849-1924 179
See also DLB 92
Thomson, Elizabeth
See Thomson, Elizabeth M.
Thomson, Elizabeth M. 1957- 127
Thomson, F(rancis) P(aul) 1914-1998 .... 21-24R
Thomson, Frank S(elee) 1881-1975 57-60
Thomson, Garry 1925- 109
Thomson, George Derwent 1903-1987
Obituary 121
Thomson, George H(enry) 1924- 21-24R
Thomson, George Malcolm 1899-1996 .. 9-12R
Obituary 152
Thomson, George Paget 1892-1975 ... CANR-4
Obituary 61-64
Earlier sketch in CA 5-8R
Thomson, Hugh 1960(?)- 227
Thomson, (George) Ian F(alconer) 1912-1987 .... CANR-87
Obituary 122
Earlier sketch in CA 9-12R
Thomson, Irene Taviss 1941- 29-32R
Thomson, James 1700-1748 .... BRWS 3
See also DAM POET
See also DLB 95
See also RGEL 2
Thomson, James 1834-1882 .... DAM POET
See also DLB 35
See also RGEL 2
Thomson, James C(laude), Jr. 1931-2002 .... CANR-32
Obituary 209
Earlier sketch in CA 29-32R
Thomson, James C(utting) 1909- 61-64
Thomson, James Miln 1921- 109
Thomson, Joan
See Charnock, Joan
Thomson, John (Edward Palmer) 1936- 109
Thomson, John A(idan) F(rancis) 1934-2004 .... CANR-86
Obituary 231
Earlier sketch in CA 132
Thomson, John W(illiam) 1940- 125
Thomson, Jonathan H.
See Thomson, Daisy H(icks)
Thomson, Joseph 1858-1895 .... DLB 174

Thomson 576 CONTEMPORARY AUTHORS

Thomson, June (Valerie) 1930- CANR-44
Earlier sketches in CA 81-84, CANR-21
Interview in CANR-21
See also CMW 4
Thomson, Katherine 1955- .... CD 5, 6
Thomson, Keith (Nicholas Home)
1912-2001 .... 29-32R
Obituary 199
Thomson, Liz
See Thomson, Elizabeth M.
Thomson, Mortimer 1831-1875 .... DLB 11
Thomson, Pat 1939- CANR-96
Earlier sketch in CA 146
See also SATA 77, 122
Thomson, Peggy 1922- 85-88
See also SATA 31
Thomson, Peter 1913-1969 .... 5-8R
Thomson, Peter (William) 1938- CANR-93
Earlier sketch in CA 108
Thomson, Randall J(oseph) 1946- 109
Thomson, Robert 1921- 25-28R
Thomson, Robert 1943- 122
Thomson, Robert (James) 1961- 127
Thomson, Robert W(illiam) 1934- CANR-21
Earlier sketch in CA 104
Thomson, Rodney M(alcolm) 1946- 227
Thomson, Ronald William 1908- 25-28R
Thomson, Roy Herbert 1894-1976
Obituary 69-72
Thomson, Rupert 1955- 171
See also DLB 267
Thomson, S(amuel) Harrison
1895-1975 .... 41-44R
Obituary 61-64
Thomson, Susan Ruth 1941- 228
Thomson, Virgil (Garnett) 1896-1989 .... 41-44R
Obituary 129
See also IDFW 3, 4
Thomson, William 1927- CANR-94
Earlier sketch in CA 141
Thomson, William A. 1879-1971
Obituary 33-36R
Thomson, William A(rchibald) R(obson)
1906-1983 .... CANR-86
Obituary 111
Earlier sketch in CA 103
Thomy, Al(fred Marshall) 69-72
Thon, Melanie Rae 1957- CANR-112
Earlier sketches in CA 134, CANR-72
See also DLB 244
See also SATA 132
Thondup, Tulku 1939- CANR-116
Earlier sketch in CA 159
Thone, Ruth Raymond 1931- 170
Thonssen, Lester 1904-1997 .... 5-8R
Thor, Brad 217
Thor, Johannes
See Goll, Yvan
Thor, Tristan
See Goll, Yvan
Thorat, Sudhakar S. 1935- CANR-29
Earlier sketch in CA 45-48
Thorburn, David 1940- CANR-7
Earlier sketch in CA 53-56
Thorburn, Doug S. 1953- 202
Thorburn, Hugh G(arnet) 1924- 13-16R
Thorburn, John
See Goldsmith, John Herman Thorburn
Thorburn, Thomas 1913- 200
Thordarson, Agnar 1917- .... CWW 2
Thordarson, Thorbergur 1888-1974 .... DLB 293
See also EWL 3
Thoreau, Henry David 1817-1862 ...... AAYA 42
See also AMW
See also ANW
See also BYA 3
See also CDALB 1640-1865
See also DA
See also DA3
See also DAB
See also DAC
See also DAM MST
See also DLB 1, 183, 223, 270, 298
See also LAIT 2
See also LMFS 1
See also NCFS 3
See also PC 30
See also RGAL 4
See also TUS
See also WLC
Thorelli, Hans B(irger) 1921- CANR-6
Earlier sketch in CA 13-16R
Thoren, Arne 1927-2003 69-72
Obituary 214
Thoresen, Carl E. 1933- 57-60
Thorez, Maurice 1900-1964
Obituary 113
Thorlby, Anthony K. 1928- 25-28R
Thormaehlen, Marianne
See Thormahlen, Marianne
Thormahlen, Marianne 1949- CANR-108
Earlier sketch in CA 143
Thorman, Donald J. 1924-1977 .... 17-20R
Obituary 73-76
Thorman, Richard 1924- 105
Thorn, Barbara
See Paine, Lauran (Bosworth)
Thorn, John 1947- CANR-17
Earlier sketch in CA 97-100
See also SATA 59
Thorn, Richard S(emour) 1929- 17-20R
Thorn, Ronald Scott
See Wilkinson, Ronald
Thorn, William E. 1923- 9-12R
Thornber, Jean H(ewitt) 1919- 61-64
Thornbrook, Bill
See Turnbaugh, William A(rthur)
Thornbrough, Emma Lou -1994 .... 25-28R
Thornburg, Hershel D(ean)
1936-1987 .... CANR-14
Obituary 121
Earlier sketch in CA 37-40R
Thornburg, Newton K(endall) 1930- . CANR-71
Earlier sketches in CA 21-24R, CANR-9
See also CMW 4
Thorndike, A.
See Thorndike, A(nthony) E(dward)
Thorndike, A(nthony) E(dward) 1941- 117
Thorndike, E. L.
See Thorndike, Edward L(ee)
Thorndike, Edward L(ee) 1874-1949
Brief entry 121
See also TCLC 107
Thorndike, John 1942- 153
Thorndike, Joseph J(acobs), Jr. 1913-
Brief entry 117
Thorndike, (Everett) Lynn 1882-1965
Obituary 111
Thorndike, Robert Ladd 1910-1990 . CANR-86
Obituary 132
Earlier sketches in CA 1-4R, CANR-1
Thorndike, (Arthur) Russell 1885-1972
Obituary 37-40R
Thorndike, Susan 1944- 41-44R
Thorndike, Tony
See Thorndike, A(nthony) E(dward)
Thorndyke, Helen Louise CANR-27
Earlier sketches in CAP-2, CA 19-20
See also Benson, Mildred (Augustine Wirt)
See also SATA 1, 67
Thorne, Alice Dunn 1910-1973
Obituary 45-48
Thorne, Barrie 1942- 143
Thorne, Bliss K(irby) 1916-1987 .... 17-20R
Thorne, Bradley D.
See Glut, Donald F(rank)
Thorne, Christopher 1934-1992 .... CANR-86
Obituary 137
Earlier sketches in CA 21-24R, CANR-11, 29
Thorne, Florence Calvert 1878(?)-1973
Obituary 41-44R
Thorne, Hart
See Carhart, Arthur Hawthorne
Thorne, Hooper
See Sage, (Frank) Norman
Thorne, Ian
See May, Julian
Thorne, Jean Wright
See May, Julian
Thorne, Jim 1922- CANR-1
Earlier sketch in CA 1-4R
Thorne, John (H.) 1943- 136
Thorne, Julia 1944- 223
Thorne, Kip S. 1940- 144
Thorne, Matt Lewis 195
Thorne, Nicola
See Ellerbeck, Rosemary (Anne L'Estrange)
Thorne, Ramsay
See Cameron, Lou
Thorne, Ron
See Thorne-Finch, Ron(ald Barry)
Thorne, Sabina 1927- 106
Thorne, Sterling
See Fuller, Dorothy Mason
Thorne, Victoria
See Heley, Veronica
Thorne, William 1568(?)-1630 .... DLB 281
Thorne, William James 1898- 5-8R
Thorne-Finch, Ron(ald Barry) 1958- 146
Thornes, John B. 232
Thornhill, Alan 1907(?)-1988
Obituary 127
Thornhill, Jan 1955- 223
See also SATA 77, 148
Thornhill, John 1929- 206
Thornhill, Randy 1944- 196
Thorning, Joseph F(rancis) 1896-1985 ... CAP-1
Obituary 115
Earlier sketch in CA 9-10
Thornley, Diann 1957- 164
Thornley, Richard 1950- 117
Thornley, Stew 1955- 139
Thornton, Big Mama
See Thornton, Willie Mae
Thornton, Billy Bob 1955- 168
Thornton, Bruce S. 1953- CANR-124
Earlier sketch in CA 165
Thornton, Elizabeth 173
Thornton, Emma Shore 1908- 114
Thornton, Francis John 1938- 85-88
Thornton, Gene 93-96
Thornton, Hall
See Silverberg, Robert
Thornton, Ian 1926- 154
Thornton, J(onathan) Mills III 1943- 77-80
Thornton, James W., Jr. 1908- CANR-1
Earlier sketch in CA 1-4R
Thornton, Jerry
See Thornton, Emma Shore
Thornton, John Leonard 1913- CANR-4
Earlier sketch in CA 9-12R
Thornton, John W(illiam), Jr. 1948- 106
Thornton, John W(illiam) 1922- 106
Thornton, Lawrence 1937- 132
See also CN 7
See also LAIT 5
Thornton, Lee 1944- 73-76
Thornton, Margaret 139
Thornton, Mark 1960- 141
Thornton, Martin (Stuart Farrin) 1915- 9-12R
Thornton, Michael 1941- 105
Thornton, Peter (Kai) 1925- CANR-43
Earlier sketches in CA 102, CANR-20
Thornton, R(obert) K(elsey) R(ought) 1938- . 119
Thornton, Ralph 1922(?)-1989
Obituary 129
Thornton, Richard C. 1936- 81-84
Thornton, Robert J(ames) 1949- 148
Thornton, Thomas Perry 1931- 9-12R
Thornton, W. B.
See Burgess, Thornton Waldo
Thornton, Weldon 1934- 25-28R
Thornton, Willie Mae 1926-1984
Obituary 113
Thornton, Willis 1900-1965 .... CAP-1
Earlier sketch in CA 13-16
Thornton, Yvonne S(hirley) 1947- 153
See also SATA 96
Thorold, Peter 1930- 188
Thorp, Duncan Roy 1914-1994 .... 13-16R
Thorp, Edward O. 1932- 21-24R
Thorp, John 1947- 133
Thorp, Lillian 1914- 195
Thorp, Margaret Farrand 1891-1970
Obituary 104
Thorp, Roderick Mayne, Jr.
1936-1999 .... CANR-46
Obituary 179
Earlier sketches in CA 1-4R, CANR-6
Thorp, Rosemary 1940- 214
Thorp, Willard 1899-1992 .... CANR-3
Obituary 130
Earlier sketch in CA 5-8R
Thorp, Willard Long 1899-1992 .... CANR-85
Obituary 137
Earlier sketches in CA 1-4R, CANR-28
Thorpe, Adam 1956- CANR-92
Earlier sketch in CA 129
See also CLC 176
See also DLB 231
Thorpe, D(avid) R(ichard) 1943- CANR-135
Earlier sketches in CA 129, CANR-68
Thorpe, Donald W(illiam) 1928- 29-32R
Thorpe, E(ustace) G(eorge) 1916- 9-12R
See also SATA 21
Thorpe, Earl(ie) E(ndris) 1924-1989 61-64
Thorpe, Elliott R(aymond) 1897-1989 65-68
Obituary 129
Thorpe, George P. 1913(?)-1983
Obituary 110
Thorpe, J. K.
See Nathanson, Laura Walther
Thorpe, James 1915- CANR-17
Earlier sketches in CA 5-8R, CANR-2
Thorpe, Judith M(osier) 1941- 196
Thorpe, Kay .... RHW
Thorpe, Lee
See Meares, Leonard Frank
Thorpe, Lewis (Guy Melville)
1913-1977 .... CANR-10
Earlier sketch in CA 9-12R
Thorpe, Louis P(eter) 1893-1970 ...... CANR-20
Earlier sketch in CA 1-4R
Thorpe, Michael 1932- CANR-55
Earlier sketches in CA 21-24R, CANR-8
Thorpe, Peter 1932- 57-60
Thorpe, Sylvia
See Thimblethorpe, June Sylvia
Thorpe, Thomas Bangs 1815-1878 .. DLB 3, 11, 248
See also RGAL 4
Thorpe, Trebor
See Fanthorpe, R(obert) Lionel
Thorpe, Trevor
See Fanthorpe, R(obert) Lionel
Thorpe, William Homan 1902-1986 .. CANR-2
Obituary 119
Earlier sketch in CA 5-8R
Thorsell, Richard Lawrence 1938- 89-92
Thorsley, Peter L(arsen), Jr. 1929- 5-8R
Thorson, John E. 1946- 150
Thorson, Robert M. 1951- 214
Thorson, Thomas Landon 1934- 17-20R
Thorsson, Ornolfur 1953- 231
Thorstad, David 1941- 57-60
Thorstein, Eric
See Merril, Judith
Thorup, Kirsten 1942- 127
Brief entry 125
See also CWW 2
See also DLB 214
Thorvall, Kerstin 1925- CANR-13
Earlier sketch in CA 17-20R
See also SATA 13
Thorvall-Falk, Kerstin
See Thorvall, Kerstin
Thorwald, Juergen 1916- CANR-21
Earlier sketches in CA 49-52, CANR-1
Thott, Birgitte 1610-1662 .... DLB 300
Thouless, Robert H(enry)
1894-1984 .... CANR-85
Obituary 114
Earlier sketch in CA 77-80
Thrapp, Dan Lincoln 1913-1994 .... CANR-4
Obituary 145
Earlier sketch in CA 9-12R
Thrasher, Crystal (Faye) 1921- CANR-8
Earlier sketch in CA 61-64
See also BYA 7, 8
See also SATA 27
Thrasher, Travis 1971- 219
Threadgall, Colin 1941- .... SATA 77
Three Little Pigs
See Lantz, Francess L(in)
Threlkeld, Richard (Davis) 1937- CANR-107
Earlier sketch in CA 65-68
Thresher, B(rainard) Alden 1896-1984
Obituary 111
Thribb, E. J.
See Fantoni, Barry (Ernest)
Thring, M(eredith) W(ooldridge)
1915- CANR-86
Earlier sketch in CA 130
Throckmorton, Burton Hamilton, Jr.
1921- CANR-94
Earlier sketch in CA 5-8R
Throckmorton, Peter 1928-1990 ...... CANR-86
Obituary 131
Earlier sketch in CA 17-20R
Throneberry, Jimmy B. 1933- 89-92
Throneburg, James 5-8R
Thrower, Norman J(oseph) W(illiam)
1919- 41-44R
Thrower, Percy John 1913-1988 .... CANR-86
Obituary 125
Earlier sketches in CA 9-12R, CANR-4
Thruelsen, Richard (Delmar) 1908-1989
Obituary 129
Thubron, Colin (Gerald Dryden)
1939- CANR-95
Earlier sketches in CA 25-28R, CANR-12, 29, 59
See also CLC 163
See also CN 5, 6, 7
See also DLB 204, 231
Thubten, Jigme Norbu 1922-
Brief entry 109
Thucydides c. 455B.C.-c. 395B.C. .... AW 1
See also DLB 176
See also RGWL 2, 3
Thuery, Jacques (H. A.) 1951- 143
Thuesen, Gerald J(organ) 1938- 37-40R
Thuillier, Jacques 1928- CANR-7
Earlier sketch in CA 9-12R
Thulstrup, Niels 1924- CANR-26
Earlier sketches in CA 21-24R, CANR-10
Thulstrup, Thure de 1848-1930 .... DLB 188
Thum, Gladys 1920- 41-44R
See also SATA 26
Thum, Marcella CANR-49
Earlier sketches in CA 9-12R, CANR-6, 21
See also RHW
See also SATA 3, 28
Thumann, Albert 1942- 139
Thumboo, Edwin Nadason 1933- 194
See also CP 1
See also PC 30
Thumm, Garold W(esley) 1915- 13-16R
Thummel, Moritz August von
1738-1817 .... DLB 97
Thuna, Lee
See Thuna, Leonora
Thuna, Leonora 1929- CANR-16
Earlier sketch in CA 21-24R
Thundercloud, Katherine
See Witt, Shirley Hill
Thunder-Traveling-Over-The-Mountains
See Chief Joseph
Thundy, Zacharias Pontian 1936- 102
Thundyil, Zacharias Pontian
See Thundy, Zacharias Pontian
Thurber, Helen (Wismer) 1902(?)-1986 152
Obituary 121
Thurber, James (Grover) 1894-1961 . CANR-39
Earlier sketches in CA 73-76, CANR-17
See also AAYA 56
See also AMWS 1
See also BPFB 3
See also BYA 5
See also CDALB 1929-1941
See also CLC 5, 11, 25, 125
See also CWRI 5
See also DA
See also DA3
See also DAB
See also DAC
See also DAM DRAM, MST, NOV
See also DLB 4, 11, 22, 102
See also EWL 3
See also EXPS
See also FANT
See also LAIT 3
See also MAICYA 1, 2
See also MAL 5
See also MTCW 1, 2
See also MTFW 2005
See also RGAL 4
See also RGSF 2
See also SATA 13
See also SSC 1, 47
See also SSFS 1, 10, 19
See also SUFW
See also TUS
Thurber, Walter A(rthur) 1908- CANR-12
Earlier sketch in CA 21-24R
Thurian, Max 1921- 129
Thurkettle, James 1929- 69-72
Thurley, Geoffrey John 1936- CANR-13
Earlier sketch in CA 61-64
Thurley, Jon (Mark) CANR-42
Earlier sketch in CA 118
Thurley, Simon 1962- CANR-100
Earlier sketch in CA 146
Thurlo, Aimee CANR-121
Earlier sketch in CA 169
See also HW 2
See also SATA 161
Thurlo, David 181
See also SATA 161
Thurlow, David (Michael) 1932- 134
Thurm, Marian 168
See also Axelrod, Marian Thurm
Thurman, Christa C(harlotte) Mayer
1934- CANR-2
Earlier sketch in CA 49-52

Thurman, Howard 1900-1981 .... CANR-25
Obituary 103
Earlier sketch in CA 97-100
See also BW 1
Thurman, Judith 1946- CANR-1
Earlier sketch in CA 49-52
See also SATA 33
Thurman, Kelly 1914-1999 57-60
Thurman, Mark (Gordon Ian) 1948- 131
See also SATA 63
Thurman, Robert
See Thurman, Robert A(lexander) F(arrar)
Thurman, Robert A. F.
See Thurman, Robert A(lexander) F(arrar)
Thurman, Robert A(lexander) F(arrar) 1941- CANR-139
Earlier sketch in CA 172
Thurman, Wallace (Henry) 1902-1934 .... CANR-81
Brief entry 104
Earlier sketch in CA 124
See also BLC 3
See also BW 1, 3
See also DAM MULT
See also DLB 51
See also HR 1:3
See also TCLC 6
Thurman, Wayne L(averne) 1923- 49-52
Thurmond, Nancy Moore 1946- 132
Brief entry 114
Thurmond, (James) Strom 1902-2003 89-92
Obituary 217
Thurow, Lester C(arl) 1938- CANR-89
Earlier sketches in CA 81-84, CANR-45
Thursby, Vincent Victor 1918- 41-44R
Thurstan, Violetta CAP-1
Earlier sketch in CA 13-16
Thurston, Carol (M.) 1938(?)-2001 . CANR-135
Earlier sketch in CA 126
Thurston, David B. 1918- CANR-6
Earlier sketch in CA 5-8R
Thurston, Elliott Ladd 1895-1975
Obituary 89-92
Thurston, H. D.
See Thurston, H. David
Thurston, H. David 1927- 143
Thurston, Harry 1950- CANR-32
Earlier sketch in CA 113
Thurston, Hazel (Patricia) 1906- 57-60
Thurston, Jarvis 1914- 13-16R
Thurston, Lorrin P. 1900(?)-1984
Obituary 114
Thurston, Robert (Donald) 1936- CANR-15
Earlier sketch in CA 85-88
See also SFW 4
Thurston, Robert W. 1949- 239
Thut, I(saac) N(oah) -1975 .... CAP-1
Earlier sketch in CA 13-16
Thwaite, Ann (Barbara Harrop) 1932- CANR-41
Earlier sketch in CA 5-8R
See also CWRI 5
See also SATA 14
Thwaite, Anthony (Simon) 1930- CANR-143
Earlier sketches in CA 5-8R, CANR-41
See also CP 1, 2, 3, 4, 5, 6, 7
See also DLB 40
Thwaite, M(ary) F. (Austin) 21-24R
Thwaites, Michael 1915- 77-80
See also CP 1
Thwaites, Reuben Gold 1853-1913 159
See also DLB 47
Thwing, Leroy (L.) 1879-1967 .... 5-8R
Thybony, Scott 1948- CANR-108
Earlier sketch in CA 146
Thygerson, Alton L(uie) 1940- CANR-39
Earlier sketches in CA 45-48, CANR-1, 18
Thynn, Alexander (George) 1932- 132
Thynne, Alexander
See Thynn, Alexander (George)
Thyret, Isolde R. 1955- 209
Tiant, Luis 1940- 73-76
(al-)Tibawi, A(bdul-)L(atif) 1910-1981 .... CANR-24
Obituary 105
Earlier sketch in CA 25-28R
Tibber, Robert
See Friedman, (Eve) Rosemary (Tibber)
Tibber, Rosemary
See Friedman, (Eve) Rosemary (Tibber)
Tibbets, Albert B. 1888-1971 .... 5-8R
Tibbetts, Arnold M(acLean) 1927-2000 .... CANR-16
Earlier sketch in CA 93-96
Tibbetts, Charlene 1921-1999 93-96
Tibbetts, John C(arter) 1946- CANR-125
Earlier sketch in CA 89-92
Tibbetts, John W(esley) 1928- 25-28R
Tibbetts, Norris L. 1892(?)-1983
Obituary 108
Tibbetts, Orlando L(ailer), Jr. 1919- ... CANR-11
Earlier sketch in CA 29-32R
Tibbetts, Peggy 197
See also SATA 127
Tibbetts, William
See Brannon, William T.
Tibble, Anne 1912-1980 .... CANR-10
Obituary 102
Earlier sketch in CA 9-12R
Tibbles, Jean-Paul 1958- .... SATA 115
Tibbs, Ben 1907-1988 61-64
Tibbs, Virginia M.
See Scott, Virginia M(uhleman)
Tiber, Elliot 1935- 129
Tibi, Bassam 1944- CANR-92
Earlier sketch in CA 130
Tibo, Gilles 1951- CANR-139
Earlier sketch in CA 136
See also SATA 67, 107
Tibon, Gutierre
See Tibon, Gutierre
Tibon, Gutierre 1905-1999 189
Tibullus c. 54B.C.-c. 18B.C. .... AW 2
See also DLB 211
See also RGWL 2, 3
Tiburzi, Bonnie 1948- 136
See also SATA 65
Tice, George A(ndrew) 1938- CANR-142
Earlier sketches in CA 61-64, CANR-12
Ticheburn, Cheviot
See Ainsworth, William Harrison
Tichenor, Tom 1923-1992 .... 29-32R
See also SATA 14
Tichi, Cecelia 1942- 104
Tichnor, Richard 1959- .... SATA 90
Tichy, H(enrietta) J. 1912-1994 .... 21-24R
Tichy, Susan (Elizabeth) 1952- 123
Tichy, William 1924- 107
See also SATA 31
Tickell, Renee Oriana Haynes
See Haynes, Renee (Oriana Tickell)
Tickell, Thomas 1686-1740 .... RGEL 2
Tickle, Jack
See Chapman, Jane
Tickle, P(hyllis) A(lexander) 1934- CANR-49
Earlier sketches in CA 65-68, CANR-9, 24
Tickner, Fred(erick James) 1902-1980 .... CAP-1
Earlier sketch in CA 9-10
Tickner, Lisa 1944- CANR-101
Earlier sketch in CA 128
Ticknor, George 1791-1871 .... DLB 1, 59, 140, 235
Tidball, Derek J(ohn) 1948- 120
Tidy, Michael 1943- 113
Tidyman, Ernest 1928-1984 .... CANR-29
Obituary 113
Earlier sketch in CA 73-76
Tieck, (Johann) Ludwig 1773-1853 ... CDWLB 2
See also DLB 90
See also EW 5
See also IDTP
See also RGSF 2
See also RGWL 2, 3
See also SSC 31
See also SUFW
Tiede, Tom (Robert) 1937- CANR-119
Earlier sketch in CA 25-28R
Tiedt, Iris M(cClellan) 1928- CANR-49
Earlier sketches in CA 13-16R, CANR-7, 24
Tiedt, Sidney W(illis) 1927- CANR-24
Earlier sketch in CA 13-16R
Tiegreen, Alan F. 1935- .... SATA 94
See also SATA-Brief 36
Tiempo, Edith (Lopez) 1919- 104
See also CP 1, 2
Tien, H. Yuan 1926- 49-52
Tien, Hung-Mao 1938- 73-76
Tiernan, Cate 1961- .... AAYA 49
Tiernan, Frances Fisher
See Reid, Christian
Tierney, Brian 1922- 103
Tierney, Frank M. 1930- .... SATA 54
Tierney, Gene 1920-1991
Brief entry 116
Tierney, Helen 1928- 142
Tierney, John Lawrence 1892-1972 .... CAP-2
Earlier sketch in CA 21-22
Tierney, Kevin (Hugh) 1942- CANR-26
Earlier sketch in CA 29-32R
Tierney, M. Leo 1932(?)-1986
Obituary 118
Tierney, Michael 1894-1975
Obituary 114
Tierney, Nathan (L.) 1953- 195
Tierney, Neil 1913-2001 145
Tierney, Paul Ambrose 1895(?)-1979
Obituary 85-88
Tierney, Richard L(ouis) 1936- 111
Tierney, Ronald 1944- 140
Tierney, Tom 1928- CANR-47
Earlier sketches in CA 57-60, CANR-8, 23
See also SATA 113
Tierno, Michael 226
Tierno, Philip M(ario), Jr. 1943- 208
Tiersky, Ronald (S.) 1944- CANR-100
Earlier sketch in CA 118
Tiersten, Lisa 1959- 220
Tietenberg, T(homas) H(arry) 1942- 143
Tietjen, Jeanie (M.) 229
Tietjens, Eunice Strong (Hammond) 1884-1944 193
See also DLB 54
Tietze, Andreas 1914- 49-52
Tietze, Christopher 1908-1984
Obituary 112
Tiffany, Donald Wayne 1930-
Brief entry 108
Tiffany, E. A. 1911-1984 103
Tiffany, Grace 1958- 227
Tiffany, Phyllis G. 1932- 37-40R
Tiffany, William R(obert) 1920-1994 .... 5-8R
Tiffault, Benette W. 1955- .... SATA 77
Tiffin, Joseph 1905-1989 .... 17-20R
Tifft, Ellen CANR-1
Earlier sketch in CA 49-52
Tifft, Susan E. 1951- 135
Tifton, Leo
See Page, Gerald W(ilburn)
Tigar, Michael E(dward) 1941- 77-80
Tigay, Alan M(errill) 1947- 124
Tiger, Derry
See Ellison, Harlan (Jay)
Tiger, Jack
See Puechner, Ray
Tiger, John
See Wager, Walter H(erman)
Tiger, Lionel 1937- CANR-14
Earlier sketch in CA 25-28R
Tiger, Madeline 1934- CANR-42
Tiger, Theobald
See Tucholsky, Kurt
Tiger, Virginia Marie 1940-
Brief entry 106
Tiger Lily
See Blake, Lillie Devereux
Tigerman, Stanley 1930- CANR-36
Earlier sketch in CA 114
Tiger of the Snows
See Norgay, Tenzing
Tighe, Donald J. 1928- 29-32R
Tighe, Thomas B. 1907(?)-1983
Obituary 109
Tignor, Robert L(ee) 1933- 134
Brief entry 109
Tigue, Ethel Erkkila 1918- 21-24R
Tihanyi, Eva 1956- 171
Tijerina, Andres 1944- 187
Tikhomirov, Vladimir I. 1959- 201
Tikhonov, Nikolai Semyonovich 1896-1979
Obituary 85-88
Tikhonov, Valentin
See Payne, (Pierre Stephen) Robert
Tikkanen, Henrik 1924-1984 192
Tikkanen, Marta 1935- 195
See also DLB 257
See also EWL 3
Tikku, Girdhari L(al) 1925-1996 45-48
Tiktin, Carl 1930- CANR-13
Earlier sketch in CA 73-76
Tilberis, Liz 1947-1999 171
Tilden, Freeman 1884(?)-1980 97-100
Tildon, J(ames) Tyson 1931- 159
Tiles, J. E. 1944- 128
Tilford, Earl H., Jr. 1945- 142
Tilghman, Benjamin R(oss) 1927- 134
Brief entry 107
Tilghman, Christopher 1946- CANR-135
Earlier sketch in CA 159
See also CLC 65
See also CSW
See also DLB 244
Till, Barry 1923- 49-52
Till, Geoffrey 1945- 132
Till, Nicholas 1955- 141
Tillard, Jean-M(arie) Roger 1927- CANR-28
Earlier sketch in CA 45-48
Tillema, Herbert K(endall) 1942- 45-48
Tilleman, William Arthur 1932- 53-56
Tiller, Carl W(illiam) 1915-1991 108
Tiller, Ruth L. 1949- 150
See also SATA 83
Tiller, Ted
See Tiller, Theodore II
Tiller, Terence (Rogers) 1916-1987 ... CANR-86
Obituary 124
Earlier sketch in CA 101
See also CP 1, 2
Tiller, Theodore II 1913(?)-1988
Obituary 126
Tilles, Solomon H. 1932- 192
Brief entry 108
Tillett, Bill G(lenn) 1942- 118
Tillett, Gregory J. 1950- CANR-88
Earlier sketch in CA 110
Tilley, Ethel 1894-1972 .... CAP-1
Earlier sketch in CA 9-10
Tilley, Patrick 1928- CANR-55
Earlier sketch in CA 106
See also SFW 4
Tilley, (William) Roger (Montgomerie) 1905-1971 .... CAP-2
Earlier sketch in CA 25-28
Tillich, Hannah 1896-1988 73-76
Obituary 127
Tillich, Paul (Johannes) 1886-1965 ... CANR-33
Obituary 25-28R
Earlier sketch in CA 5-8R
See also CLC 131
See also MTCW 1, 2
Tillinghast, B(urette) S(tinson), Jr. 1930- ... 65-68
Tillinghast, David 195
Tillinghast, Pardon E(lisha) 1920- 9-12R
Tillinghast, Richard (Williford) 1940- CANR-96
Earlier sketches in CA 29-32R, CANR-26, 51
See also CAAS 23
See also CLC 29
See also CP 2, 3, 4, 5, 6, 7
See also CSW
Tillion, Diana (Rutzebeck) 1928-
Brief entry 110
Tillion, Germaine Marie Rosine 1907- 104
Tillis, Steve 208
Tillman, Barrett 1948- 132
Tillman, Deborah Lindsay 1953- 235
Tillman, Lynne CANR-144
Earlier sketch in CA 173
Tillman, Rollie, Jr. 1933- 21-24R
Tillman, Seth Phillip 1930- 1-4R
Tillman, Stephen Frederick 1900(?)-1977
Obituary 69-72
Tillotson, G(iles) H(enry) R(upert) 1960- 126
Tillotson, Geoffrey 1905-1969 .... CAP-1
Earlier sketch in CA 13-14
Tillson, Albert H., Jr. 1948- 139
Tilly, Charles 1929- CANR-20
Earlier sketch in CA 103
Tilly, Chris 1955- CANR-109
Earlier sketch in CA 159
Tilly, Louise A(udino) 1930- CANR-47
Earlier sketch in CA 120
Tilly, Meg 1960- 149
Tilly, Nancy 1935- 120
See also SATA 62
Tilly, Richard H(ugh) 1932- 17-20R
Tillyard, E(ustace) M(andeville) W(etenhall) 1889-1962
Obituary 93-96
Tillyard, Stella 164
Tilman, Harold William 1898-1978 103
Tilman, Robert O(liver) 1929- CANR-1
Earlier sketch in CA 45-48
Tilney, Edmund 1536(?)-1610 .... DLB 136
Tilson, Everett 1923- 41-44R
Tiltman, Hessell 1897(?)-1976
Obituary 69-72
Tiltman, Ronald Frank 1901- CAP-1
Earlier sketch in CA 9-10
Tilton, Alice
See Taylor, Phoebe Atwood
Tilton, Eleanor M(arguerite) 1913-1994
Brief entry 110
Tilton, John W(ightman) 1928-1983 122
Brief entry 118
Tilton, Madonna Elaine 1929- CANR-36
Earlier sketch in CA 114
See also SATA 41
Tilton, Rafael
See Tilton, Madonna Elaine
Tilton, Timothy Alan 1942- 61-64
Timanus, Boyd R. 1948- 230
Timanus, Rod
See Timanus, Boyd R.
Timasheff, Nicholas S. 1886-1970 .... 1-4R
Obituary 29-32R
Timberg, Robert 195
Timberlake, Amy .... SATA 156
Timberlake, Carolyn
See Dresang, Eliza (Carolyn Timberlake)
Timberlake, Charles E(dward) 1935- 41-44R
Timberlake, Richard Henry, Jr. 1922- 21-24R
Timberman, David G. 1955- 139
Timbrell, Charles 1942- CANR-90
Earlier sketch in CA 143
Timerman, Jacobo 1923-1999 .... CANR-32
Obituary 186
Brief entry 109
Earlier sketch in CA 120
See also HW 1
Timko, Michael 1925- 17-20R
Timlett, Peter Valentine 1933-
Brief entry 111
See also FANT
Timm, Bruce 1961- .... AAYA 66
Timm, Uwe 1940- 130
Timmen, Fritz 1918- 53-56
Timmerman, Frederick W., Jr. 1942- 186
Timmerman, Joan 1938- 118
Timmerman, John H(ager) 1945- CANR-118
Earlier sketches in CA 111, CANR-29, 56
Timmerman, John Johnson 1908- 111
Timmerman, Kenneth R. 1953- 141
Timmermans, Claire 1938- 104
Timmermans, Felix 1886-1947 193
See also EWL 3
Timmermans, Stefan 1968- 210
Timmermans, Tricia 1946- 167
Timmers, J(an) Joseph M(arie) 1907- CAP-1
Earlier sketch in CA 13-14
Timmins, Lois Fahs 1914- CANR-27
Earlier sketch in CA 45-48
Timmins, William F(rederick) .... SATA 10
Timmis, John Henry III 1934- 104
Timmons, Bascom N(olly) 1890-1987 104
Obituary 122
Timmons, Bonnie 1951- 120
Timmons, Jeffry A. 1941- 108
Timms, Arthur W(arren) 1940- 120
Timms, David 1946- 109
Timms, E(dward) V(ivian) 1895-1960 183
Brief entry 112
Timms, Edward 1937- 143
Timms, Kathleen 1943- 122
Timms, Noel 1927- CANR-16
Earlier sketch in CA 13-16R
Timoney, Francis 1938- 61-64
Timoshenko, Stephen P. 1878-1972
Obituary 33-36R
Timothy, Bankole 1920(?)- .... BW 2
Timothy, Hamilton B(aird) 1913- 102
Timothy, Peter 1725(?)-1782 .... DLB 43
Timpanelli, Gioia 1936- 197
Timpe, Eugene Frank 1926- 77-80
Timperley, Rosemary Kenyon 1920-1988 .... CANR-76
Earlier sketches in CA 97-100, CANR-17
See also HGG
Timrava 1867-1951 .... DLB 215
See also EWL 3
Timrod, Henry 1828-1867 .... DLB 3, 248
See also RGAL 4
Tinbergen, Jan 1903-1994 .... CANR-2
Obituary 145
Earlier sketch in CA 5-8R
Tinbergen, Niko(laas) 1907-1988 108
Obituary 127
See also SATA-Obit 60
Tindal, Henrietta 1818(?)-1879 .... DLB 199
Tindal, Mardi 1952- 219
Tindall, George Brown 1921- 85-88
Tindall, Gillian (Elizabeth) 1938- CANR-107
Earlier sketches in CA 21-24R, CANR-11, 65
See also CLC 7
See also CN 1, 2, 3, 4, 5, 6, 7
Tindall, Kenneth (Thomas) 1937- CANR-42
Earlier sketch in CA 29-32R

Tindall, P(eggy) E(leanor) N(ancy)
1927- ... 29-32R
Tindall, William York 1903-1981 ... CANR-16
Obituary ... 104
Earlier sketch in CA 1-4R
Tindell, Charles 1940- ... 184
Tiner, John Hudson 1944- ... CANR-40
Earlier sketches in CA 101, CANR-18
See also SATA 32
Tiner, Ralph W., Jr. 1948- ... CANR-103
Earlier sketch in CA 124
Ting
See Tingley, Merle R(andolph)
Ting, Jan C(hing-an) 1948- ... 37-40R
Ting, Samuel C. C. 1936- ... 157
Ting, Walasse 1929- ... 21-24R
Tingay, Lance 1915-1990 ... CANR-86
Obituary ... 131
Earlier sketch in CA 101
Tingen, Paul ... 224
Tingle, Dolli (?)-
See Brackett, Dolli Tingle
Tingley, Donald F(red) 1922- ... CANR-10
Earlier sketch in CA 25-28R
Tingley, Elizabeth 1955- ... 114
Tingley, Merle R(andolph) 1921- ... 129
Ting Ling
See Chiang, Pin-chin
See also EWL 3
Tingsten, Herbert 1896-1973
Obituary ... 45-48
Tingum, Janice 1958- ... 155
See also SATA 91
Tinic, Seha M(ehmet) 1941- ... 37-40R
Tinkelman, Murray 1933- ... SATA 12
Tinker, Beamish
See Jesse, F(ryniwyd) Tennyson
Tinker, Ben (Hill) 1903-1988 ... 102
Tinker, Chauncey Brewster 1876-1963 ... 184
See also DLB 140
Tinker, Edward Larocque 1881-1968 ... CAP-1
Earlier sketch in CA 13-14
Tinker, Grant A(lmerin) 1926- ... 147
Tinker, Hugh (Russell) 1921-2000 ... CANR-3
Obituary ... 189
Earlier sketch in CA 5-8R
Tinker, Jack (Samuel) 1938-1996 ... 132
Obituary ... 154
Tinker, Kristin Nelson 1945- ... 171
Tinker, Miles Albert 1893-1977 ... CANR-4
Earlier sketch in CA 5-8R
Tinker, Spencer Wilkie 1909-1999 ... 41-44R
Tinkham, Ace
See Tinkham, Harley
Tinkham, Harley 1923-1990
Obituary ... 132
Tinkle, (Julien) Lon 1906-1980 ... 104
See also SATA 36
Tinkle, Theresa ... 173
Tinling, Marion (Rose) 1904- ... 211
See also SATA 140
Tinling, Ted 1910-1990
Obituary ... 131
Tinling, Teddy
See Tinling, Ted
Tinne, Dorothea
See Strover, Dorothea
Tinne, E. D.
See Strover, Dorothea
Tinnin, David B(ruce) 1930- ... 49-52
Tinniswood, Adrian ... 204
Tinniswood, Peter 1936-2003 ... CANR-43
Obituary ... 212
Earlier sketch in CA 25-28R
See also CN 2, 3, 4, 5, 6, 7
Tinsley, Ernest John 1919-1992 ... 5-8R
Tinsley, James Robert 1921-2004 ... 13-16R
Tinsley, Jim Bob
See Tinsley, James Robert
Tinsley, Kevin (M.) ... 225
Tinsley, (John) Russell 1932- ... 17-20R
Tinterow, Gary 1953- ... 109
Tinti, Hannah 1973(?)- ... 228
Tintner, Adeline R. 1912-2003 ... CANR-89
Earlier sketches in CA 123, CANR-50
Tio (y Nazario de Figueroa), Aurelio
1907-1992 ... HW 1
Tiomkin, Dimitri 1899-1979
Obituary ... 93-96
See also IDFW 3, 4
Tipene, Tim 1972- ... 212
See also SATA 141
Tipler, Frank J(ennings III) 1947- ... 157
Tippett, James S(terling) 1885-1958 ... 135
See also SATA 66
Tippett, Maria 1944- ... 188
Tippett, Michael (Kemp) 1905-1998 ... CANR-27
Obituary ... 164
Earlier sketch in CA 109
Tippette, Giles 1934- ... CANR-93
Earlier sketches in CA 65-68, CANR-17, 37
See also TCWW 1, 2
Tipping, Marjorie Jean 1917- ... 122
Tippit, Sammy 1947- ... 104
Tipple, A(llan) Graham 1949- ... 188
Tipple, John Ord 1916-1983 ... 9-12R
Tipton, Charles Leon 1932- ... 41-44R
Tipton, David 1934-
Brief entry ... 111
Tipton, James (Sherwood) 1942- ... CANR-125
Earlier sketches in CA 57-60, CANR-8, 50
Tiptree, James, Jr.
See Sheldon, Alice Hastings Bradley
See also CLC 48, 50
See also DLB 8
See also SCFW 1, 2
See also SFW 4
Tirbutt, Honoria ... CANR-22
Earlier sketch in CA 106
Tirion, Wil 1943- ... 143
Tirone Smith, Mary-Ann 1944- ... CANR-113
Brief entry ... 118
Earlier sketch in CA 136
See also CLC 39
See also SATA 143
Tirro, Frank (Pascale) 1935- ... 81-84
Tirso de Molina 1580(?)-1648 ... DC 13
See also HLCS 2
See also RGWL 2, 3
Tirtha, Sada Shiva ... 169
Tiryakian, Edward A(shod) 1929- ... CANR-19
Earlier sketches in CA 5-8R, CANR-2
Tischauser, Leslie V. 1942- ... 176
Tischler, Barbara L. 1949- ... 123
Tischler, Hans 1915- ... CANR-6
Earlier sketch in CA 1-4R
Tischler, Nancy Marie (Patterson)
1931- ... CANR-110
Earlier sketch in CA 5-8R
Tischner, Rudolf (E.) 1879-1961
Obituary ... 112
Tisdale, Celes 1941- ... 57-60
Tisdale, Sallie 1957- ... CANR-103
Earlier sketch in CA 142
Tisdell, Clement Allan 1939- ... CANR-15
Earlier sketch in CA 25-28R
Tise, Larry Edward 1942- ... 102
Tish-Tash
See Tashlin, Frank
Tisma, Aleksandar 1924-2003 ... 160
Obituary ... 214
See also CWW 2
See also DLB 181
Tismaneanu, Vladimir ... 171
Tisse, Edward 1897-1961 ... IDFW 3, 4
Tisserand, Jacques
See Barnes, Jim
Tisserand, Michael (Joseph) 1963- ... 192
Tisseyre, Michelle 1947- ... 237
Titamgim, R. Dirk
See Dietrich, Richard V(incent)
Titan, Earl
See Fearn, John Russell
Titche, Leon 1939- ... 196
Titchener, James Lampton 1922- ... 45-48
Titchener, Louise 1941- ... CANR-48
Earlier sketch in CA 122
Titcomb, Margaret 1891-1982 ... CANR-5
Earlier sketch in CA 5-8R
Title, Elise ... 217
Titler, Dale M(ilton) 1926- ... 81-84
See also SATA 35
See also SATA-Brief 28
Titley, David Paul 1929- ... 110
Titley, E. Brian 1945- ... 128
Titley, Norah M(ary) 1920- ... 118
Titmarsh, Michael Angelo
See Thackeray, William Makepeace
Titmuss, Christopher ... 196
Titmuss, Richard M(orris) 1907-1973 ... 109
Obituary ... 107
Tito, Josip Broz 1911-1980
Obituary ... 97-100
Tito, Marshal
See Tito, Josip Broz
Titon, Jeff Todd 1943- ... CANR-37
Earlier sketches in CA 89-92, CANR-16
Titra, Stephen Andrew 1945- ... 97-100
Titterton, Ernest William 1916- ... 109
Tittle, Charles R(ay) 1939- ... CANR-15
Earlier sketch in CA 41-44R
Tittler, Jonathan (Paul) 1945- ... CANR-43
Earlier sketch in CA 119
Tittler, Robert 1942- ... CANR-15
Earlier sketch in CA 81-84
Tittmann, George Fabian 1915-1978 ... 5-8R
Obituary ... 81-84
Titunik, Irwin R(obert) 1929-1998 ... 126
Titus, A(lice) Costandina 1950- ... 127
Titus, Barry J(oseph) 1938- ... 1-4R
Titus, Charles 1942- ... CANR-93
Earlier sketch in CA 45-48
Titus, David Anson 1934- ... 97-100
Titus, Edward William 1870-1952 ... DLB 4
See also DLBD 15
Titus, Eve 1922- ... CANR-30
Earlier sketch in CA 29-32R
See also CWRI 5
See also SATA 2
Titus, Harold H(opper) 1896-1984 ... 5-8R
Titus, Warren Irving 1921-1984 ... 17-20R
Tiusanen, Timo 1936-1985 ... 85-88
Obituary ... 117
Tiutchev, Fedor Ivanovich
1803-1873 ... DLB 205
Tizard, Henry Thomas 1885-1959 ... 161
Tjader, Marguerite 1901-1986 ... 17-20R
Tjardes, Tamara J. 1961- ... 226
Tjepkema, Sandra L(ynn) 1953- ... 114
Tjernagel, Neelak S(erawlook) 1906- ... 17-20R
Tjong Khing, The 1933- ... SATA 76
Tjosvold, Dean 1948- ... 142
Tkacik, Arnold J(ohn) 1919- ... 81-84
Tkacz, Catherine Brown ... 230
Tlali, Miriam 1933- ... 164
See also BW 3
See also CN 5, 6, 7
See also DLB 157, 225
See also EWL 3
Toan, Arthur B(enjamin), Jr. 1915- ... 25-28R
Tobach, Ethel 1921- ... 81-84
Toback, James 1944- ... 41-44R
Tobe, John Harold 1907-1979 ... CANR-1
Earlier sketch in CA 1-4R
Tobey, George B., Jr. 1917- ... 49-52
Tobey, Kathrene McLandress
1908-2000 ... CAP-2
Earlier sketch in CA 29-32
Tobey, Mark 1890-1976
Obituary ... 65-68
Tobey, Ronald C(harles) 1942- ... 73-76
Tobias, Andrew (Previn) 1947- ... CANR-136
Earlier sketches in CA 37-40R, CANR-14
Tobias, Henry J(ack) 1925- ... 41-44R
Tobias, J(ohn) J(acob) 1925- ... 53-56
Tobias, Katherine
See Gottfried, Theodore Mark
Tobias, Michael (Charles) 1951- ... 140
Tobias, Phillip V. 1925- ... CANR-15
Earlier sketch in CA 37-40R
Tobias, Richard C(lark) 1925- ... 29-32R
Tobias, Ronald B(enjamin) 1948- ... CANR-28
Earlier sketch in CA 111
Tobias, Sheila 1935- ... CANR-65
Earlier sketch in CA 93-96
Tobias, Tobi 1938- ... CANR-135
Earlier sketches in CA 29-32R, CANR-16
See also CLR 4
See also SATA 5, 82
Tobin, Brian 1954- ... 221
Tobin, Gary A. 1949- ... 179
Tobin, Greg ... 192
Tobin, James ... 180
Tobin, James 1918-2002 ... CANR-92
Obituary ... 208
Earlier sketches in CA 53-56, CANR-5
Interview in ... CANR-5
Tobin, James Edward 1905-1968 ... CAP-2
Earlier sketch in CA 23-24
Tobin, Jean Holloway 1917(?)-1989
Obituary ... 130
Tobin, Juanita Brown 1915- ... CANR-117
Earlier sketch in CA 156
Tobin, Kay 1930- ... 37-40R
Tobin, Richard J. 1946- ... 137
Tobin, Richard Lardner 1910-1995 ... CANR-1
Obituary ... 149
Earlier sketch in CA 1-4R
Tobin, Sheldon S(idney) 1931- ... 134
Brief entry ... 110
Tobin, Terence 1938- ... 53-56
Tobino, Mario 1910-1991 ... 204
See also EWL 3
Toby, Liz
See Minsky, Betty Jane (Toebe)
Toby, Mark 1913(?)-1972
Obituary ... 37-40R
Toby-Potter, Ellen
See Potter, Ellen
Toch, Hans (Herbert) 1930- ... CANR-49
Earlier sketches in CA 17-20R, CANR-7, 23
Toch, Henry 1923- ... CANR-21
Earlier sketches in CA 9-12R, CANR-6
Toch, Thomas 1954- ... 145
Tocher, Michelle 1956- ... 239
Tocher, Timothy ... 238
Tocqueville, Alexis (Charles Henri Maurice
Clerel Comte) de 1805-1859 ... EW 6
See also GFL 1789 to the Present
See also TWA
Toczek, Nick 1950- ... 106
Tod, Ian J. 1945- ... 103
Tod, Osma Gallinger 1898-1982(?) ... CANR-86
Obituary ... 108
Earlier sketches in CAP-1, CA 9-10
Toda, Jusho 1928-1987 ... IDFW 3, 4
Todd, Alden 1918- ... CANR-6
Earlier sketch in CA 1-4R
Todd, Alexander (Robertus) 1907-1997 ... 146
Obituary ... 156
Todd, Ann 1909-1993 ... 129
Todd, Anne Ophelia
See Dowden, Anne Ophelia
Todd, Barbara Euphan 1890-1976 ... 104
See also CWRI 5
See also DLB 160
Todd, Barbara K(eith) 1917- ... 61-64
See also SATA 10
Todd, Burbank L. ... CANR-26
Earlier sketches in CAP-2, CA 19-20
Todd, Clark 1945(?)-1983
Obituary ... 110
Todd, Edgeley W(oodman) 1914-
Brief entry ... 109
Todd, Edward N. 1931- ... 53-56
Todd, Frances 1910-1989 ... 13-16R
Todd, Frederick Porter 1903-1977
Obituary ... 73-76
Todd, Galbraith Hall 1914- ... 1-4R
Todd, H(erbert) E(atton) 1908-1988 ... CANR-53
Earlier sketches in CAP-1, CA 9-10, CANR-12, 30
See also SATA 11, 84
Todd, Hollis N(elson) 1914-1998 ... 57-60
Todd, Ian A(lexander) 1941- ... CANR-31
Earlier sketch in CA 112
Todd, Ian Menzies 1923- ... 69-72
Todd, Jack 1946- ... 203
Todd, Janet M(argaret) 1942- ... CANR-108
Earlier sketches in CA 49-52, CANR-1, 28, 53
Todd, Jerry
See Vermilye, Jerry
Todd, Jerry D(ale) 1941- ... 53-56
Todd, John M(urray) 1918-1993 ... CANR-47
Obituary ... 141
Earlier sketch in CA 9-12R
Todd, Karen (Iris) Rohne (Pritchett) 1936-
Brief entry ... 111
Todd, Leonard 1940- ... 65-68
Todd, Loreto 1942- ... 107
See also SATA 30
Todd, Louise
See Sandweiss, Martha A(nn)
Todd, Malcolm 1939- ... 101
Todd, Mary 1947- ... 191
Todd, Olivier 1929- ... 168
Todd, Pamela 1950- ... 225
See also SATA 124
Todd, Paul
See Posner, Richard
Todd, Peter
See Hamilton, Charles (Harold St. John)
Todd, R. Larry 1952- ... CANR-60
Earlier sketch in CA 128
Todd, Richard (Killingworth) 1949- ... 125
Todd, Ruth Van Dorn 1889(?)-1976
Obituary ... 65-68
Todd, Ruthven 1914-1978 ... 81-84
See also CP 1, 2
Todd, Trisha 1961- ... 183
Todd, Virgil H(olcomb) 1921- ... 185
Brief entry ... 106
Todd, Vivian Edmiston 1912-1982 ... 17-20R
Todd, William Burton 1919- ... 41-44R
Todd, William Mills III 1944- ... 65-68
Todes, Samuel (Judah) 1927-1994 ... 233
Todhunter, Andrew ... 196
Todman, Bill
See Todman, William S.
Todman, John B. 1938- ... 204
Todman, William S. 1916-1979
Obituary ... 89-92
Todorov, Nikolai (Todorov)
1921-2003 ... CANR-93
Obituary ... 219
Earlier sketch in CA 132
Todorov, Tzvetan 1939- ... CANR-116
Earlier sketches in CA 73-76, CANR-64
See also DLB 242
Todrank, Gustave H(erman) 1924- ... 41-44R
Todras, Ellen H. 1947- ... 187
Todrin, Boris 1915-1999 ... 61-64
Toekes, Rudolf L(eslie) 1935- ... 21-24R
Toepfer, Ray Grant 1923-1996 ... 21-24R
Toeplitz, Jerzy 1909-1995 ... 65-68
Obituary ... 149
Toer, Pramoedya Ananta 1925- ... 197
See also CLC 186
See also RGWL 3
Tofani, Loretta 1953- ... 116
Brief entry ... 113
Interview in ... CA-116
Tofel, Richard J. 1957- ... 211
See also SATA 140
Toffler, Alvin 1928- ... CANR-67
Earlier sketches in CA 13-16R, CANR-15, 46
See also CLC 168
See also CPW
See also DAM POP
See also MTCW 1, 2
Toffler, Heidi 1929- ... 146
Toft, (Eric) John 1933- ... 103
Tofte, Arthur 1902-1980 ... 73-76
Obituary ... 103
Tofte, Robert c. 1561-c. 1619 ... DLB 172
Tofts, Darren (John) 1960- ... 202
Togawa, Masako 1933- ... 235
See also CMW 4
Togliatti, Palmiro 1893(?)-1964 ... 133
Obituary ... 113
Tohata, Seiichi 1899-1983
Obituary ... 110
Toibin, Colm 1955- ... CANR-81
Earlier sketch in CA 142
See also CLC 162
See also CN 7
See also DLB 271
Toka, Salchak Kalbakkhoreviich 1901-1973
Obituary ... 41-44R
Tokarczyk, Michelle M. 1953- ... 144
Tokayer, Marvin 1936- ... 102
Toker, Franklin K(arl) B(enedict) S(erchuk)
1944- ... CANR-134
Earlier sketches in CA 81-84, CANR-15
Tokes, Rudolf L(eslie) 1935-
Brief entry ... 114
Toklas, Alice B(abette) 1877-1967 ... 81-84
Obituary ... 25-28R
See also DLB 4
Tokmakoff, George 1928-1997 ... 123
Tokuda Shusei 1872-1943 ... DLB 180
Tolan, Stephanie S. 1942- ... CANR-122
Earlier sketches in CA 77-80, CANR-15, 34
See also AAYA 45
See also JRDA
See also SATA 38, 78, 142
See also WYAS 1
Toland, Gregg 1904-1948 ... IDFW 3, 4
Toland, John 1670-1722 ... DLB 252
Toland, John (Willard) 1912-2004 ... CANR-89
Obituary ... 223
Earlier sketches in CA 1-4R, CANR-6, 23, 46
See also MTCW 1, 2
See also SATA 38
Tolbert, E(lias) L(ake) 1915- ... CANR-3
Earlier sketch in CA 1-4R
Tolbert, Francis X(avier) Sr.
1912-1984 ... CANR-71
Obituary ... 111
Earlier sketches in CA 1-4R, CANR-16
See also TCWW 1, 2
Tolbert, Malcolm O(liver) 1924- ... 65-68
Tolbert, Mary Ann 1947- ... 116
Tolbert, Steve 1944- ... 216
See also SATA 143
Tolby, Arthur
See Infield, Glenn (Berton)

Cumulative Index 579 Toomer

Tolchin, Martin 1928- CANR-142
Earlier sketches in CA 120, CANR-46
Tolchin, Susan J(ane) 1941- CANR-142
Earlier sketch in CA 141
Toldson, Ivory L. 1943- 114
Toledano, Ralph de 1916- CANR-31
Earlier sketch in CA 9-12R
See also AITN 1
Toledano, Roulhac (Bunkley) 1938- 101
Tolegian, Aram 1909-1988 .... CANR-6
Earlier sketch in CA 1-4R
Toler, Violet M. 1941- 239
Toles, Thomas G. 1951- 126
Toles, Tom
See Toles, Thomas G.
Tolf, Robert W(alter) 1929- 73-76
Tolins, Robert B. 1952- 202
Tolischus, Otto D(avid) 1890-1967
Obituary 93-96
Toliver, George
See Masselink, Ben
Toliver, Hal
See Toliver, Harold E(arl)
Toliver, Harold E(arl) 1932- CANR-82
Earlier sketches in CA 21-24R, CANR-34
Toliver, Raymond F. 1914- CANR-86
Earlier sketches in CA 17-20R, CANR-35
Tolkien, J(ohn) R(onald) R(euel)
1892-1973 .... CANR-134
Obituary 45-48
Earlier sketches in CAP-2, CA 17-18, CANR-36
See also AAYA 10
See also AITN 1
See also BPFB 3
See also BRWC 2
See also BRWS 2
See also CDBLB 1914-1945
See also CLC 1, 2, 3, 8, 12, 38
See also CLR 56
See also CN 1
See also CPW 1
See also CWRI 5
See also DA
See also DA3
See also DAB
See also DAC
See also DAM MST, NOV, POP
See also DLB 15, 160, 255
See also EFS 2
See also EWL 3
See also FANT
See also JRDA
See also LAIT 1
See also LATS 1:2
See also LMFS 2
See also MAICYA 1, 2
See also MTCW 1, 2
See also MTFW 2005
See also NFS 8
See also RGEL 2
See also SATA 2, 32, 100
See also SATA-Obit 24
See also SFW 4
See also SUFW
See also TCLC 137
See also TEA
See also WCH
See also WLC
See also WYA
See also YAW
Tolkien, Simon 1959- 221
Tolkin, Michael 1950- CANR-127
Earlier sketch in CA 137
Toll, Emily
See Cannon, Eileen E(mily)
Toll, John .... IDFW 4
Toll, Nelly S. 1935- 146
See also SATA 78
Toll, Robert C(harles) 1938- 53-56
Toll, Seymour I. 1925- 29-32R
Toll, William 1941- 114
Tolland, W. R.
See Heitzmann, William Ray
Tollefson, James W(illiam) 1950- 144
Toller, Ernst 1893-1939 186
Brief entry 107
See also DLB 124
See also EWL 3
See also RGWL 2, 3
See also TCLC 10
Toller, Kate Caffrey
See Caffrey, Kate
Tollers, Vincent L(ouis) 1939- 57-60
Tolles, Frederick B(arnes)
1915-1975 .... CANR-87
Obituary 103
Earlier sketch in CA 5-8R
Tolles, Martha 1921- 49-52
See also SATA 8, 76
Tollet, Elizabeth 1694-1754 .... DLB 95
Tolley, A(rnold) T(revor) 1927- CANR-104
Earlier sketches in CA 123, CANR-50
Tolley, Howard B(oyd), Jr. 1943- 53-56
Tolley, Kemp 1908-2000 45-48
Obituary 191
Tolley, William Pearson 1900-1996 93-96
Obituary 151
Tolliver, Ruby C(hangos) 1922- 111
See also SATA 55, 110
See also SATA-Brief 41
Tolman, Newton F. 1908-1986 .... CANR-86
Obituary 120
Earlier sketch in CA 1-4R
Tolmie, Kenneth Donald 1941- 69-72
See also SATA 15
Tolmie Prance, Ghillean
See Prance, Ghillean Tolmie
Tolnai, Karoly
See De Tolnay, Charles Erich
Tolnai, Vagujhelyi Karoly
See De Tolnay, Charles Erich
Tolson, Jay 1948- 141
Tolson, M. B.
See Tolson, Melvin B(eaunorus)
Tolson, Melvin B(eaunorus)
1898(?)-1966 .... CANR-80
Obituary 89-92
Earlier sketch in CA 124
See also AFAW 1, 2
See also BLC 3
See also BW 1, 3
See also CLC 36, 105
See also DAM MULT, POET
See also DLB 48, 76
See also MAL 5
See also RGAL 4
Tolstaia, Tatiana (Nikitinichna)
See Tolstaya, Tatyana
See also CWW 2
See also RGSF 2
Tolstaya, Tatyana 1951- 130
See also Tolstaia, Tatiana (Nikitinichna)
See also DLB 285
See also EWL 3
See also RGWL 3
See also SSFS 14
Tolstoi, Aleksei Nikolaevich
See Tolstoy, Alexey Nikolaevich
Tolstoi, Lev
See Tolstoy, Leo (Nikolaevich)
See also RGSF 2
See also RGWL 2, 3
Tolstoy, Akeksei Konstantinovich
1817-1875 .... DLB 238
Tolstoy, Aleksei Nikolaevich
See Tolstoy, Alexey Nikolaevich
See also DLB 272
Tolstoy, Alexandra L(vovna)
1884-1979 .... CANR-42
Obituary 89-92
Earlier sketch in CA 65-68
Tolstoy, Alexey Nikolaevich 1882-1945 158
Brief entry 107
See also Tolstoy, Aleksei Nikolaevich
See also EWL 3
See also SFW 4
See also TCLC 18
Tolstoy, Dimitry 1912-1997 .... 29-32R
Tolstoy, Leo (Nikolaevich) 1828-1910 123
Brief entry 104
See also Tolstoi, Lev
See also AAYA 56
See also DA
See also DA3
See also DAB
See also DAC
See also DAM MST, NOV
See also DLB 238
See also EFS 2
See also EW 7
See also EXPS
See also IDTP
See also LAIT 2
See also LATS 1:1
See also LMFS 1
See also NFS 10
See also SATA 26
See also SSC 9, 30, 45, 54
See also SSFS 5
See also TCLC 4, 11, 17, 28, 44, 79
See also TWA
See also WLC
Tolstoy, Count Leo
See Tolstoy, Leo (Nikolaevich)
Tolstoy, Mary Koutouzov 1884(?)-1976
Obituary 69-72
Tolstoy(-Miloslavsky), Nikolai (Dimitrievich)
1935- CANR-45
Earlier sketch in CA 81-84
See also FANT
Tolstoy, Tatyana (Sukhotin) 1864-1950
Brief entry 117
Tolzmann, Don Heinrich 1945- CANR-38
Earlier sketches in CA 49-52, CANR-2, 17
Tom, Georgia
See Dorsey, Thomas A(ndrew)
Toma, David 1933- CANR-42
Earlier sketch in CA 118
Tomajczyk, S. F. 1960- 157
Tomalin, Claire 1933- CANR-88
Earlier sketches in CA 89-92, CANR-52
See also CLC 166
See also DLB 155
Tomalin, Nicholas 1931-1973
Obituary 45-48
Tomalin, Ruth CANR-29
Earlier sketches in CA 13-16R, CANR-13
See also SATA 29
Tomalonis, Alexandra 223
Toman, Walter 1920-2003 .... 5-8R
Tomas, Andrew Paul 1906-2001 ...... CANR-88
Earlier sketch in CA 73-76
Tomasek, Robert D(ennis) 1928- 17-20R
Tomaselli, Sylvana 1957- 137
Tomasevic, Nebojsa 1929- 81-84
Tomashevich, George Vid 1927- 133
Tomasi, Silvano M(ario) 1940- 115
Tomasi, Thomas E(dward) 1955- 139
Tomasic, D(inko) A(nthony) 1902-1975 . CAP-1
Earlier sketch in CA 19-20
Tomasi di Lampedusa, Giuseppe 1896-1957
Brief entry 111
See also Lampedusa, Giuseppe (Tomasi) di
See also DLB 177
See also EWL 3
See also WLIT 7
Tomasson, Katherine 1895- CAP-1
Earlier sketch in CA 9-10
Tomasson, Richard F(inn) 1928- CANR-1
Earlier sketch in CA 45-48
Tomaszewski, Tomasz 1953- 210
Tomatsu, Shomei 1930- 216
Tomb, David A(lan) 1944- CANR-40
Earlier sketch in CA 117
Tomek, Ivan 1939- 120
Tomeo, Javier 1932(?)- 212
Tomes, Margot (Ladd) 1917-1991 .... MAICYA 1, 2
See also SATA 36, 70
See also SATA-Brief 27
See also SATA-Obit 69
Tomes, Nancy (Jane) 1952- 186
Tomeski, Edward Alexander
1930-1989 .... 37-40R
Tomey, Ingrid 1943- CANR-92
Earlier sketch in CA 145
See also SATA 77
Tomfool
See Farjeon, Eleanor
Tomikel, John 1928- CANR-4
Earlier sketch in CA 53-56
Tomin, Zdena 1941- 123
Tomkiewicz, Mina 1917-1975 .... CAP-2
Earlier sketch in CA 29-32
Tomkins, Adam 226
Tomkins, Calvin 1925- CANR-8
Earlier sketch in CA 13-16R
Interview in CANR-8
Tomkins, Jasper
See Batey, Tom
Tomkins, Mary E(ileen) 1914-1998 61-64
Tomkinson, Constance
See Weeks, Constance Tomkinson
Tomkinson, Michael 1940- CANR-22
Earlier sketch in CA 93-96
Tomlan, Michael A. 1947- 137
Tomlin, E(ric) W(alter) F(rederick)
1913-1988(?) CANR-85
Obituary 124
Earlier sketches in CA 5-8R, CANR-3
Tomlin, Lily
See Tomlin, Mary Jean
See also CLC 17
Tomlin, Mary Jean 1939(?)-
Brief entry 117
See also Tomlin, Lily
Tomline, F. Latour
See Gilbert, W(illiam) S(chwenck)
Tomlins, Jack E(dward) 1929- 25-28R
Tomlinson, (Alfred) Charles 1927- CANR-33
Earlier sketch in CA 5-8R
See also CLC 2, 4, 6, 13, 45
See also CP 1, 2, 3, 4, 5, 6, 7
See also DAM POET
See also DLB 40
See also PC 17
See also TCLE 1:2
Tomlinson, Edward 1891(?)-1973
Obituary 45-48
Tomlinson, Gary (Alfred) 1951- 206
Tomlinson, Gerald (Arthur) 1933- 85-88
Tomlinson, H(enry) M(ajor) 1873-1958 161
Brief entry 118
See also DLB 36, 100, 195
See also TCLC 71
Tomlinson, Harry 1943- 135
Tomlinson, Janis A. 214
Tomlinson, Jill 1931-1976 .... CAP-2
Earlier sketch in CA 29-32
See also SATA 3
See also SATA-Obit 24
Tomlinson, Kenneth Y(oung) 1944- 65-68
Tomlinson, Reginald R(obert) 1885-1979(?)
Obituary 104
See also SATA-Obit 27
Tomlinson, T(homas) B(rian) 1925- 9-12R
Tomlinson, Theresa 1946- CANR-133
Earlier sketch in CA 170
See also BYA 11
See also CLR 60
See also MAICYA 2
See also SATA 103
Tomlinson-Keasey, Carol 1942- 101
Tommasini, Anthony 166
Tommeraasen, Miles 1923-1994 ....21-24R
Tommy the Turk
See Goltz, Thomas (Caufield)
Tompert, Ann 1918- CANR-137
Earlier sketches in CA 69-72, CANR-11, 59
See also SATA 14, 89, 139
Tompkins, C(linton) David 1937- 41-44R
Tompkins, Dorothy (Campbell)
1908-1998 .... 17-20R
Tompkins, E(dwin) Berkeley 1935- 29-32R
Tompkins, Everett Thomas 1931- 107
Tompkins, J(oyce) M(arjorie) S(anxter)
1897-1986
Obituary 121
Tompkins, Jane P(arry) 1940- CANR-39
Earlier sketches in CA 29-32R, CANR-17
Tompkins, Jerry R(obert) 1931- 17-20R
Tompkins, Julia (Marguerite Hunter Manchee)
1909- 29-32R
Tompkins, Kathleen Burns 1934- 93-96
Tompkins, Peter 1919- CANR-12
Earlier sketch in CA 9-12R
Tompkins, Ptolemy (Christian) 1962(?)- 168
Tompkins, Richard A. 1896(?)-1977
Obituary 73-76
Tompkins, Stuart R(amsay) 1886-1977 .. 37-40R
Tompkins, Tom
See Tompkins, Everett Thomas
Tompkins, Walker A(llison)
1909-1990(?) CANR-66
Obituary 182
Earlier sketch in CA 5-8R
See also TCWW 1, 2
Tompson, Benjamin 1642-1714 .... DLB 24
Toms, Bernard 1931- 17-20R
Toms, Carl 1927-1999
Obituary 183
Tomson, Bernard 1909-1978
Obituary 77-80
Tomson, Graham R.
See Watson, Rosamund Marriott
Ton, Mary Ellen 1933- 112
Ton'a 1289-1372 .... DLB 203
Tonashi
See Harrington, Mark Raymond
Tondelli, Pier Vittorio 1955-1991 195
See also DLB 196
Tone, Andrea 1964- 205
Tone, John Lawrence 1959- 151
Tone, Teona 1944- 112
Toner, Raymond John 1908-1986 .... 5-8R
See also SATA 10
Toney, Albert (Livingston, Jr.) 1933- 120
Toney, Anthony 1913-2004 .... CANR-9
Obituary 231
Earlier sketch in CA 17-20R
Tong, Gary S. 1942- 135
See also SATA 66
Tong, Raymond 1922- CANR-2
Earlier sketch in CA 5-8R
Tong, Te-kong 1920- CANR-8
Earlier sketch in CA 9-12R
Tong, Zhong Gui 1963- 144
Tongkat Waran
See Usman Awang
Tongren, Sally S(tetson) 1926- 118
Tonkin, Elizabeth 1934- 140
Tonkin, Humphrey 1939- CANR-38
Earlier sketches in CA 41-44R, CANR-16
Tonkin, Peter (Francis) 1950- CANR-77
Earlier sketch in CA 101
See also HGG
Tonkinson, Carole 1964- 150
Tonkinson, Robert 1928- 77-80
Tonks, A. Ronald 1934- 125
Tonks, Rosemary (D. Boswell) 89-92
See also CN 1, 2
See also CP 1, 2
See also DLB 14, 207
Tonn, Martin H. 1921- 5-8R
Tonna, Charlotte Elizabeth
1790-1846 .... DLB 163
Tonnies, Ferdinand
See Tonnies, Ferdinand
Tonnies, Ferdinand 1855-1936 214
Tonquedec, Joseph de 1868-1962
Obituary 112
Tonson, Jacob fl. 1655(?)-1736 .... DLB 170
Tonsor, Stephen (John) 1923-
Brief entry 114
Too, Adrian
See Shimoda, Todd
Too, Yun Lee 1965- 149
Toobin, Jeffrey (Ross) 1960- 203
Toobin, Jerome 1920(?)-1984
Obituary 111
Toohey, Catherine 1949- 109
Toohey, Robert E(ugene) 1935- 89-92
Took, Belladonna
See Chapman, Vera (Ivy May)
Tooke, Adrianne 1946- 191
Tooke, Ann (Mary Margaret) Hales
See Hales-Tooke, Ann (Mary Margaret)
Tooke, Louise Mathews 1950- 105
See also SATA 38
Tooke, Thomas (Renshaw) 1947- 73-76
Tooker, Elisabeth (Jane) 1927- 49-52
Tooks, Lance 1962- 223
Toolan, David S. 1935- 202
Toolan, Michael 1953- 196
Toole, F. X.
See Boyd, Jerry
Toole, John Kennedy 1937-1969 104
See also BPFB 3
See also CLC 19, 64
See also DLBY 1981
See also MTCW 2
See also MTFW 2005
Toole, K(enneth) Ross 1920-1981
Brief entry 112
Toole, Rex
See Tralins, S(andor) Robert
Toole, William Bell III 1930- 21-24R
Toole Stott, Raymond 1910-1982
Obituary 105
Tooley, John 1924- 197
Tooley, M. J.
See Tooley, Michael J(ohn)
Tooley, Michael J(ohn) 1942- CANR-24
Earlier sketch in CA 106
Tooley, R(onald) Vere 1898-1986 ..... CANR-86
Obituary 120
Earlier sketch in CA 9-12R
Toomay, Patrick J(ay) 1948- 65-68
Toombs, John 1927-1994 106
Toombs, Lawrence Edmund 1919- CANR-8
Earlier sketch in CA 5-8R
Toomer, Derek 1946- 65-68
Toomer, Eugene
See Toomer, Jean

Toomer, Eugene Pinchback
See Toomer, Jean
Toomer, Jean 1894-1967 ... 85-88
See also AFAW 1, 2
See also AMWS 3, 9
See also BLC 3
See also BW 1
See also CDALB 1917-1929
See also CLC 1, 4, 13, 22
See also DA3
See also DAM MULT
See also DLB 45, 51
See also EWL 3
See also EXPP
See also EXPS
See also HR 1:3
See also LMFS 2
See also MAL 5
See also MTCW 1, 2
See also MTFW 2005
See also NFS 11
See also PC 7
See also RGAL 4
See also RGSF 2
See also SSC 1, 45
See also SSFS 5
See also WLCS
Toomer, Nathan Jean
See Toomer, Jean
Toomer, Nathan Pinchback
See Toomer, Jean
Toomey, David 1956- ... 182
Tooming, Peter 1939- ... 208
Toon, Peter 1939- ... CANR-30
Earlier sketch in CA 112
Toona, Elin(-Kai) 1937- ... CANR-15
Earlier sketch in CA 81-84
Toonder, Martin
See Groom, Arthur William
Toop, David 1949- ... 195
Toothaker, Roy Eugene 1928- ... 65-68
See also SATA 18
Tooze, Ruth (Anderson) 1892-1972 ... 5-8R
See also SATA 4
Topaz, Jacqueline
See Hyman, Jackie (Diamond)
Tope, Rebecca 1948- ... 227
Topek, Susan Remick 1955- ... 146
See also SATA 78
Topel, L(ouis) John 1934- ... 118
Toperoff, Sam 1933- ... CANR-30
Earlier sketch in CA 45-48
Topitsch, Ernst 1919- ... 136
Topkins, Katharine 1927- ... 49-52
Topkins, Richard 1925- ... 25-28R
Toplin, Robert Brent 1940- ... CANR-130
Earlier sketches in CA 77-80, CANR-15
Topol, Allan 1941- ... 93-96
Topol, Edward 1938- ... 139
Topol, Josef 1935-
Topolnicki, Denise M. ... 201
Topolski, Daniel 1945- ... CANR-28
Earlier sketch in CA 110
Topolski, Feliks 1907-1989
Brief entry ... 112
Topor, Tom 1938- ... 105
Topper, Suzanne 1939- ... 128
Toppin, Edgar A(llan) 1928-2004 ... 21-24R
Obituary ... 234
Topping, Anne Marie ... 25-28R
Topping, Audrey R(onning) 1928- ... 41-44R
See also SATA 14
Topping, C(oral) W(esley) 1889-1988 ... 41-44R
Topping, Donald M(edley) 1929- ... 53-56
Topping, Keith A. 1963- ... 232
Topping, Seymour 1921- ... CANR-91
Earlier sketch in CA 49-52
Topping, Wesley
See Topping, C(oral) W(esley)
Topsfield, L(eslie) T(homas)
1920-1981 ... CANR-9
Obituary ... 105
Earlier sketch in CA 61-64
Topsoe, Vilhelm 1840-1881 ... DLB 300
Tor, Regina
See Shekerjian, Regina Tor
Torack, Richard M(aurice) 1927- ... 106
Torberg, Friedrich
See Kantor-Berg, Friedrich
See also DLB 85
See also EWL 3
Torbert, Floyd James 1922- ... 105
See also SATA 22
Torbert, William Rockwell 1944- ... 41-44R
Torbet, Laura 1942- ... CANR-16
Earlier sketch in CA 69-72
Torbet, Robert G(eorge) 1912-1995 ... 9-12R
Torbett, Harvey Douglas Louis 1921- ... 9-12R
Torchiana, Donald T(hornhill)
1923-2001 ... 17-20R
Obituary ... 197
Torchio, Menico 1932- ... 61-64
Torday, Ursula 1888- ... CANR-58
Earlier sketches in CA 97-100, CANR-28
See also RHW
Tordoff, William 1925- ... 120
Torekull, Bertil 1931- ... 231
Toren, Heller ... 77-80
Torga, Miguel
See Rocha, Adolfo
See also CWW 2
See also DLB 287
See also EWL 3
See also RGSF 2
See also RGWL 2, 3
Torgersen, Don Arthur 1934- ... 111
See also SATA 55
See also SATA-Brief 41
Torgersen, Eric 1943- ... 37-40R
Torgersen, Paul Ernest 1931- ... 81-84
Torgerson, Dial 1928-1983 ... 53-56
Torgerson Shaw, Ellen 1929(?)-1983
Obituary ... 109
Torgoff, Martin 1952- ... 109
Torgov, Morley 1927- ... 162
Torgovnick, Marianna 1949- ... CANR-82
Earlier sketches in CA 115, CANR-44
Torgovnick, Marianna DeMarco
See Torgovnick, Marianna
Torgownik, William
See Targ, William
Torley, Luke
See Blish, James (Benjamin)
Torme, Mel(vin Howard) 1925-1999 ... 143
Obituary ... 181
Brief entry ... 118
Tormey, John Connolly 1942- ... 61-64
Tornabene, Lyn 1930- ... 69-72
Tornabene, Wanda ... 204
Tornatore, Giuseppe 1956- ... 143
Torney, Judith V.
See Torney-Purta, Judith V(ollmar)
Torney-Purta, Judith V(ollmar)
1937- ... CANR-10
Earlier sketch in CA 65-68
Tornimparte, Alessandra
See Ginzburg, Natalia
Tornqvist, Egil
See Tornqvist, (Per) Egil
Tornqvist, (Per) Egil 1932- ... CANR-111
Earlier sketch in CA 29-32R, 149
Torode, Sam 1976- ... 210
Torok, Lou 1927- ... CANR-100
Earlier sketch in CA 49-52
Torok, Maria 1926(?)-1998 ... 232
Torosian, Michael 1952- ... 216
Torr, Iain
See Mackinnon, Charles Roy
Torrance, E(llis) Paul 1915-2003 ... CANR-40
Obituary ... 218
Earlier sketches in CA 1-4R, CANR-3, 18
Torrance, Robert M(itchell) 1939- ... 191
Torrance, Thomas F(orsyth) 1913- ... CANR-113
Earlier sketches in CA 9-12R, CANR-5, 29, 55
Torre, Francisco de la ... DLB 318
Torre, Jose de la
See de la Torre, Jose
Torre, Raoul della
See Mencken, H(enry) L(ouis)
Torre-Bueno, Lillian de la
See McCue, Lillian Bueno
Torregian, Sotere 1941- ... CANR-3
Earlier sketch in CA 45-48
Torrence, Ridgely 1874-1950 ... DLB 54, 249
See also MAL 5
See also TCLC 97
Torrence, (Frederic) Ridgely 1874-1950 ... 179
Torrens, Duncan
See Ripley, Michael David
Torrens, Robert George (?)-1981
Obituary ... 105
Torrent, Ferran 1951- ... 208
Torrente Ballester, Gonzalo 1910- ... DLB 322
See also EWL 3
Torrents, Nissa 1937- ... 128
Torres, Andres Segovia
See Segovia, Andres
Torres, Daniel 1958- ... 169
See also HW 2
See also SATA 102
Torres, Daniel 1961- ... 210
Torres, Edwin ... 111
Torres, Emmanuel 1932- ... 97-100
See also CP 1, 2
Torres, Gerald 1952- ... 217
Torres, John A(lbert) 1965- ... 159
See also SATA 94, 163
Torres, Jose Acosta 1925- ... CANR-32
Earlier sketch in CA 57-60
See also DLB 209
See also HW 1
Torres, Laura 1967- ... CANR-129
Earlier sketch in CA 151
See also SATA 87, 146
Torres, Leyla 1960- ... SATA 155
Torres, Luis Llorens
See Llorens Torres, Luis
Torres, Sergio
See Torres Gonzalez, Sergio A(ntonio)
Torres, Steven 1969- ... 232
Torres, Tereska
See Torres-Levin, Tereska (Szwarc)
Torres Bodet, Jaime 1902-1974 ... CANR-32
Obituary ... 49-52
Earlier sketch in CA 101
See also HW 1
See also LAW
See also MTCW 1
Torres Gonzalez, Sergio A(ntonio) 1929- ... 117
Torres-Levin, Tereska (Szwarc) ... CANR-15
Earlier sketch in CA 5-8R
Torres-Metzgar, Joseph V. 1933- ... 183
See also DLB 122
Torres Naharro, Bartolome de
1485(?)-1523(?) ... DLB 318
Torres-Rioseco, Arturo 1897-1971 ... CAP-1
Earlier sketch in CA 9-10
Torrey, E(dwin) Fuller 1937- ... CANR-71
Earlier sketch in CA 119
See also CLC 34
Torrey, Gordon H(oward) 1919-1995 ... 9-12R
Torrey, Joanna ... 179
Torrey, Norman Lewis 1894-1980 ... 1-4R
Obituary ... 102
Torrey, Therese von Hohoff 1898(?)-1974
Obituary ... 45-48
Torrey, Volta (Wray) 1905-1992 ... 69-72
Torrie, James H(iram) 1908-1976 ... 73-76
Torrie, Malcolm
See Mitchell, Gladys (Maude Winifred)
Torrington, Jeff ... 144
Torro, Pel
See Fanthorpe, R(obert) Lionel
Tors, Ivan (Lawrence) 1916-1983 ... CANR-86
Obituary ... 110
Earlier sketch in CA 103
Torsi, Johannes
See Goll, Yvan
Torsi, Tristan
See Goll, Yvan
Torsney, Cheryl B. 1955- ... 135
Torsvan, Ben Traven
See Traven, B.
Torsvan, Benno Traven
See Traven, B.
Torsvan, Berick Traven
See Traven, B.
Torsvan, Berwick Traven
See Traven, B.
Torsvan, Bruno Traven
See Traven, B.
Torsvan, Traven
See Traven, B.
Tortella Casares, Gabriel 1936- ... 218
Tortolano, William 1930- ... 77-80
Tortora, Daniel F(rancis) 1947- ... CANR-13
Earlier sketch in CA 73-76
Torvalds, Linus 1969- ... 205
Tory, Avraham 1909-2002 ... 140
Obituary ... 204
Toscano, Peter Ralph 1920-1999 ... 45-48
Tosches, Nick 1949- ... CANR-97
Earlier sketches in CA 81-84, CANR-45
Tosi, Henry L(ouis), Jr. 1936- ... 125
Tosics, Ivan 1952- ... 138
Toson
See Shimazaki, Haruki
See also MJW
Tostado, El
See Madrigal, Alfonso Fernandez de
Tosti, Donald Thomas 1935- ... 49-52
Toten, Teresa 1955- ... CANR-124
Earlier sketch in CA 160
See also SATA 99
Toth, Arpad 1886-1928 ... EWL 3
Toth, Charles W(illiam) 1919- ... CANR-10
Earlier sketch in CA 65-68
Toth, Emily 1944- ... CANR-88
Earlier sketch in CA 101
Toth, Endre
See de Toth, Andre
Toth, Jennifer 1967- ... CANR-111
Earlier sketch in CA 152
Toth, Lazlo
See Novello, Don
Toth, Robert Charles 1928- ... 102
Toth, Stephen, Jr. 1950- ... 69-72
Toth, Susan Erickson Allen 1940- ... 105
See also DLBY 1986
Totham, Mary
See Breinburg, Petronella
Totman, Conrad 1934- ... CANR-38
Earlier sketches in CA 101, CANR-17
Tottell, Richard fl. 1550-1593 ... DLB 170
Totten, George Oakley III 1922- ... CANR-48
Earlier sketches in CA 9-12R, CANR-5, 21
Totten, Mark D. 1962- ... 226
Totten, Martha Wescoat 1957- ... 118
Totten, Sam(uel) 1949- ... 118
Totten, W. Fred 1905-1984 ... 37-40R
Tougas, Gerald 1933- ... 174
Tougas, Gerard ... 174
Tough, Allen (MacNeill) 1936- ... 108
Touliatos, John 1944- ... 93-96
Toulmin, Stephen Edelston 1922- ... CANR-117
Earlier sketches in CA 9-12R, CANR-5, 20
Toulouse-Lautrec, Henri (Marie Raymond de)
1864-1901 ... AAYA 53
Toulouse-Lautrec, Marie-Pierre (Mapie) de
1901-1972
Obituary ... 37-40R
Toulson, Shirley 1924- ... CANR-38
Earlier sketches in CA 101, CANR-17
See also CP 1, 2
Toupin, Paul 1918- ... 171
Touponce, William F. 1948- ... 179
See also SATA 114
Touraine, Alain 1925- ... 85-88
Toure, Askia Muhammad
See Toure, Askia Muhammad Abu Bakr el
See also DLB 41
Toure, Askia Muhammad Abu Bakr el
1938- ... 124
See also Toure, Askia Muhammad
See also BW 2
Tourevski, Mark 1952- ... 142
Tourgee, Albion W. 1838-1905 ... 180
See also DLB 79
See also RGAL 4
Tournemir, Elizaveta Sailhas de
See Tur, Evgeniia
Tourneur, Cyril 1575(?)-1626 ... BRW 2
See also DAM DRAM
See also DLB 58
See also RGEL 2
Tourneur, Dina-Kathelijn 1934- ... 108
Tourney, Garfield 1927-1999 ... 57-60
Tourney, Leonard (Don) 1942- ... 225
See also CMW 4
Tournier, Michel (Edouard) 1924- ... CANR-74
Earlier sketches in CA 49-52, CANR-3, 36
See also CLC 6, 23, 36, 95
See also CWW 2
See also DLB 83
See also EWL 3
See also GFL 1789 to the Present
See also MTCW 1, 2
See also SATA 23
Tournier, Paul 1898-1986 ... CANR-29
Obituary ... 120
Earlier sketch in CA 81-84
Tournimparte, Alessandra
See Ginzburg, Natalia
Tours, Hugh Berthold 1910- ... CAP-1
Earlier sketch in CA 9-10
Tourtellot, Arthur Bernon 1913-1977 ... CANR-4
Obituary ... 73-76
Earlier sketch in CA 5-8R
Tourtellot, Jonathan B. 1946- ... 111
Tourville, Elsie A(lma) 1926- ... 57-60
Tousley, Clare M. 1889(?)-1985
Obituary ... 114
Toussaint, Jean-Phillipe 1957- ... 196
Toussaint, Stanley D. 1928- ... 115
Toussaint-Samat, Maguelonne 1926- ... 156
Tousseul, Jean
See Degee, Olivier
Touster, Alison
See Reed, Alison Touster
Touval, Saadia E. 1932- ... CANR-35
Earlier sketch in CA 45-48
Touw, Kathleen 1949- ... 109
Tovar, Juan 1941- ... 224
Tovey, Donald Francis 1875-1940 ... 214
Tovey, Doreen Evelyn 1918- ... 104
Tovo, Jerome 1936- ... 45-48
Towber, Chaim 1902(?)-1972
Obituary ... 33-36R
Towell, Julie E. 1953- ... 122
Tower, Ann
See Straubing, Harold (Elk)
Tower, Diana
See Smith, Richard Rein
Tower, Don
See Bower, Donald E(dward)
Tower, John G(oodwin) 1925-1991 ... 201
Brief entry ... 106
Tower, Margene 1939- ... 37-40R
Towers, Ivar
See Kornbluth, C(yril) M.
Towers, Maxwell 1909- ... 57-60
Towers, Regina
See Pykare, Nina
Towers, (Augustus) Robert
1923-1995 ... CANR-51
Obituary ... 148
Earlier sketch in CA 132
Towery, Twyman L. 1941- ... 189
Towey, Cyprian 1912-2000 ... 21-24R
Towle, Joseph W(alter) 1909-1989 ... CAP-1
Earlier sketch in CA 13-14
Towle, Philip 1945- ... 117
Towle, Tony 1939- ... 37-40R
See also CP 1
Towle, Wendy 1963- ... SATA 79
Towler, Juby Earl 1913- ... 13-16R
Town, Glenn P(atrick) 1949- ... 118
Town, Harold (Barling) 1924- ... CANR-15
Earlier sketch in CA 41-44R
Towne, Anthony 1928-1980 ... 25-28R
Obituary ... 117
Towne, Benjamin 1740(?)-1793 ... DLB 43
Towne, Marian K(leinsasser) 1933- ... 154
Towne, Mary
See Spelman, Mary
Towne, Peter
See Nabokov, Peter (Francis)
Towne, Robert (Burton) 1936(?)- ... 108
See also CLC 87
See also DLB 44
See also IDFW 3, 4
Towne, Stuart
See Rawson, Clayton
Towner, Donald (Chisholm)
1903-1985 ... CANR-86
Obituary ... 117
Earlier sketches in CAP-1, CA 19-20
Towner, Jason
See Smith, Harold Ivan
Towner, W. Sibley
See Towner, Wayne Sibley
Towner, Wayne Sibley 1933- ... 185
Brief entry ... 118
Townes, Charles H(ard) 1915- ... CANR-91
Earlier sketch in CA 154
Townley, Ralph 1923- ... 21-24R
Townley, Rod
See Townley, Roderick
Townley, Roderick 1942- ... CANR-29
Earlier sketches in CA 57-60, CANR-12
Towns, Elmer L(eon) 1932- ... CANR-2
Earlier sketch in CA 45-48
Towns, James E(dward) 1942- ... CANR-23
Earlier sketches in CA 61-64, CANR-8, 21
Towns, Jim
See Towns, James E(dward)
Townsend, Ann 1962- ... 216
Townsend, Brad W. 1962- ... 155
See also SATA 91
Townsend, Charles Bud 1929- ... 53-56
Townsend, Charles E(dward) 1932- ... 41-44R
Townsend, Charles R(ay) 1929- ... 69-72
Townsend, Doris McFerran 1914- ... CANR-19
Earlier sketch in CA 103
Townsend, Elizabeth A. 1945- ... 173
Townsend, Elsie Doig 1908-1994 ... 29-32R

Townsend, Harry 1925- 25-28R
Townsend, Irving 1920- 101
Townsend, J(ames) Benjamin
1918-1993 21-24R
Obituary 143
Townsend, J(acob) David 1888-1981 5-8R
Townsend, James B(arclay) J(ermain)
1910-1988 49-52
Townsend, Janet (Elizabeth) 1925- 107
Townsend, John Rowe 1922- CANR-41
Earlier sketch in CA 37-40R
See also AAYA 11
See also BYA 1
See also CLR 2
See also JRDA
See also MAICYA 1, 2
See also SAAS 2
See also SATA 4, 68, 132
See also SATA-Essay 132
See also YAW
Townsend, Larry 1935- 136
Townsend, Lawrence G. 1951- 214
Townsend, Lindsay 1960- 154
Townsend, Mark
See Wallmann, Jeffrey M(iner)
Townsend, Peter (Wooldridge)
1914-1995 CANR-28
Earlier sketch in CA 29-32R
Townsend, Ralph M. 1901(?)-1976
Obituary 65-68
Townsend, Reginald T. 1890-1977
Obituary 73-76
Townsend, Richard (Fraser) 1938- 140
Townsend, Richard E. 1897(?)-1975
Obituary 61-64
Townsend, Robert 1920-1998 45-48
Obituary 164
Townsend, Robert 1957- 162
See also AAYA 24
Townsend, Sue CANR-107
Brief entry 119
Earlier sketches in CA 127, CANR-65
Interview in CA-127
See also Townsend, Susan Lilian
See also AAYA 28
See also CBD
See also CD 5, 6
See also CLC 61
See also CPW
See also CWD
See also DAB
See also DAC
See also DAM MST
See also DLB 271
See also SATA 55, 93
See also SATA-Brief 48
See also YAW
Townsend, Susan Lilian 1946-
See Townsend, Sue
Townsend, Susanne Grayson 1941- 236
Townsend, Thomas L. 1944- 127
See also SATA 59
Townsend, Tom
See Townsend, Thomas L.
Townsend, William Cameron 1896-1982
Obituary 106
Townsend, William H(enry) 1890-1964
Obituary 111
Townsend Hall, Brenda P. 208
Townshend, Aurelian 1583(?)-1651(?) . DLB 121
See also RGEL 2
Townshend, Charles 205
Townshend, Pete
See Townshend, Peter (Dennis Blandford)
Townshend, Peter (Dennis Blandford)
1945- 107
See also CLC 17, 42
Townshend, Richard
See Bickers, Richard (Leslie) Townshend
Townson, Hazel CANR-112
Earlier sketches in CA 97-100, CANR-18
See also SATA 134
Towry, Peter
See Piper, David (Towry)
Towse, Ruth 1943- CANR-106
Earlier sketch in CA 150
Toy, Barbara 1908- 202
See also DLB 204
Toy, Henry, Jr. 1915-1987 37-40R
Toy, Maggie 1964- CANR-129
Earlier sketch in CA 162
Toye, Clive 1933(?)- SATA-Brief 30
Toye, John Francis 1883-1964 CAP-1
Earlier sketch in CA 9-10
Toye, William Eldred 1926- CANR-4
Earlier sketch in CA 1-4R
See also SATA 8
Toynbee, Arnold J(oseph)
1889-1975 CANR-36
Obituary 61-64
Earlier sketch in CA 5-8R
See also AITN 2
See also NCFS 1
Toynbee, Jocelyn M(ary) C(atherine)
1897-1985 CANR-86
Obituary 118
Earlier sketch in CA 37-40R
Toynbee, (Theodore) Philip
1916-1981 CANR-85
Obituary 104
Earlier sketches in CA 1-4R, CANR-4
See also CN 1, 2
See also CP 1, 2
Toynbee, Polly (Mary Louisa) 1946- ... CANR-9
Earlier sketch in CA 21-24R
Tozer, Katharine 1907-1943 CWRI 5
Tozer, Mary (Christine) 1947- 101
Tozzi, Federigo 1883-1920 CANR-110
Earlier sketch in CA 160
See also DLB 264
See also EWL 3
See also TCLC 31
See also WLIT 7
Traba, Marta 1930-1983 154
See also FW
Trabasso, Tom 1935- CANR-11
Earlier sketch in CA 21-24R
Trace, Arther Storrey, Jr. 1922- CANR-20
Earlier sketch in CA 1-4R
Tracey, Hugh (Travers) 1903-1977 CAP-2
Obituary 77-80
Earlier sketch in CA 29-32
Tracey, Lindalee 1957- 145
Tracey, Michael 177
Tracey, Patricia Cleland 1932- 5-8R
Trachman, Muriel Karlin CANR-15
Earlier sketch in CA 85-88
Trachte, Don(ald) 1915- 89-92
Trachtenberg, Alan 1932- 157
Trachtenberg, Inge 1923- 77-80
Trachtenberg, Marvin (Lawrence)
1939- CANR-123
Earlier sketch in CA 65-68
Trachtenberg, Paul 1948- 112
Trachtenberg, Stanley 119
Traci, Philip (Joseph) 1934-1984 CANR-85
Obituary 133
Earlier sketch in CA 41-44R
Tracy, Aloise
See Shoenight, Aloise
Tracy, Ann B(laisdell) 1941- 107
Tracy, Brian 192
Tracy, Charles (William) 1938- 128
Tracy, Clarence 1908- 9-12R
Tracy, David W. 1939- 101
Tracy, Diane (A.) 1951- 222
Tracy, Don(ald Fiske) 1905-1970(?) CANR-2
Obituary 176
Earlier sketch in CA 1-4R
See also Queen, Ellery
Tracy, Doris 1925- 61-64
Tracy, Honor (Lilbush Wingfield)
1913-1989 CANR-85
Obituary 128
Earlier sketches in CA 61-64, CANR-8, 24
See also CN 1, 2, 3, 4
See also DLB 15
Tracy, Hugh
See Evans, (Edwin) Stuart (Gomer)
Tracy, Jack W. 1945- 105
Tracy, James 1961- 164
Tracy, James D. 1938- CANR-98
Earlier sketch in CA 102
Tracy, John A(lvin) 1934- 53-56
Tracy, L(ee) Jack 1926- 9-12R
Tracy, Leland
See Tralins, S(andor) Robert
Tracy, Lorna 1934- 132
Tracy, Louise Treadwell 1896-1983
Obituary 114
Tracy, Margaret
See Klavan, Andrew
Tracy, Michael 1932- 13-16R
Tracy, Neil 1905- CP 1
Tracy, (John) Nicholas 1944- 141
Tracy, P. J.
See Lambrecht, P(atricia) J. and Lambrecht, Traci
Tracy, Powers
See Ward, Don(ald G.)
Tracy, Robert E. 1928- 89-92
Tracy, Steven C. 190
Tracy, Susan
See Marino, Carolyn Fitch
Tracy, Theodore J(ames) 1916- 29-32R
Tracy, Thomas F. 1948- 156
Tracy, Thomas Henry 1900-1972 CAP-2
Earlier sketch in CA 17-18
Tracz, Richard Francis 1944- CANR-17
Earlier sketch in CA 29-32R
Trader Vic
See Bergeron, Victor (Jules, Jr.)
Traeder, Tamara 1960- 166
Traer, James Frederick 1938- 102
Trafford, F. G.
See Riddell, Charlotte
Trafzer, Clifford Earl 1949- CANR-26
Earlier sketch in CA 109
Trager, Frank N(ewton) 1905-1984 ... CANR-85
Obituary 113
Earlier sketches in CA 17-20R, CANR-9
Trager, George L(eonard) 1906-1992 ..... 41-44R
Trager, Helen G. 1910- 69-72
Trager, James 1925- CANR-99
Earlier sketches in CA 37-40R, CANR-15, 34
Trager, Philip 1935- 209
Tragle, Henry Irving 1914-1991 37-40R
Trahan, Ronald 1950- 106
Traherne, Michael
See Watkins-Pitchford, Denys James
Traherne, Thomas 1637(?)-1674 BRW 2
See also BRWS 11
See also DLB 131
See also PAB
See also RGEL 2
Trahey, Jane 1923-2000 CANR-17
Earlier sketch in CA 188
See also SATA 36
See also SATA-Obit 120
Traill, Catharine Parr 1802-1899 DLB 99
Train, Arthur (Cheney) 1875-1945 159
Brief entry 112
See also DLB 86
See also DLBD 16
Train, Arthur K(issam) 1902(?)-1981
Obituary 104
Train, John 1928- CANR-30
Earlier sketch in CA 106
Traina, Richard P(aul) 1937- 25-28R
Trainer, David 1947- CANR-20
Earlier sketch in CA 25-28R
Trainer, Jennifer 1956- 108
Trainer, Orvel 1925- 45-48
Trainor, Bernard E. 1928- 153
Trainor, Kevin 228
Trainor, Richard
See Tralins, S(andor) Robert
Traister, Aaron 1904(?)-1976
Obituary 65-68
Traister, Barbara Howard 1943- 206
Trakas, Pedro N(icholas) 1923-1996 104
Trakhman, Mikhail (Anatol'evich)
1918-1976 217
Trakl, Georg 1887-1914 165
Brief entry 104
See also EW 10
See also EWL 3
See also LMFS 2
See also MTCW 2
See also PC 20
See also RGWL 2, 3
See also TCLC 5
Tralbaut, Mark-Edo 1902-1976 CAP-2
Earlier sketch in CA 29-32
Tralins, Bob
See Tralins, S(andor) Robert
Tralins, Robert S.
See Tralins, S(andor) Robert
Tralins, S(andor) Robert 1926- CANR-40
Earlier sketches in CA 21-24R, CANR-14
See also Miles, Keith
Trambley, Estela Portillo 77-80
See also Portillo Trambley, Estela
See also RGAL 4
See also TCLC 163
Tranel, Virginia 225
Trani, Eugene P(aul) 1939- CANR-29
Earlier sketch in CA 25-28R
Tranquilli, Secondino
See Silone, Ignazio
Transtroemer, Tomas Gosta
See Transtromer, Tomas (Goesta)
Transtromer, Tomas (Gosta)
See Transtromer, Tomas (Goesta)
See also CWW 2
Transtromer, Tomas (Goesta) 1931- . CANR-115
Brief entry 117
Earlier sketch in CA 129
See also Transtromer, Tomas (Gosta)
See also CAAS 17
See also CLC 52, 65
See also DAM POET
See also DLB 257
See also EWL 3
See also PFS 21
Transtromer, Tomas Gosta
See Transtromer, Tomas (Goesta)
Transue, Emily R. 1971(?)- 235
Transue, Jacob
See Matheson, Joan (Transue)
Transue, Joan
See Matheson, Joan (Transue)
Tranter, John
See Tranter, John Ernest
See also DLB 289
Tranter, John Ernest 1943- CANR-122
Earlier sketches in CA 110, CANR-121
See also Tranter, John
See also CP 7
Tranter, Nigel (Godwin)
1909-2000 CANR-103
Obituary 190
Earlier sketches in CA 9-12R, CANR-5, 20, 59
See also RHW
Tran Thi Nga 1927- 148
Trantino, Tommy 1938- 65-68
Trapani, Iza 1954- 188
See also SATA 80, 116
Trapido, Barbara 1941- 123
See also CN 6, 7
Trapier, Elizabeth du Gue 1893(?)-1974
Obituary 53-56
Trapnell, Coles 1911(?)-1999 181
Trapp, E(dward) Philip 1923- 45-48
Trapp, Frank Anderson 1922- 57-60
Trapp, J. B. 1925- 206
Trapp, (Kerwin) Kenneth R(aymond Stephen)
1943- 145
Trapp, Maria Augusta von
See von Trapp, Maria Augusta
See also SATA 16
Trapp, Stefan (Alfred Josef) 1962- 152
Traschen, Isadore 1915-1993 25-28R
Trask, Betty 1895-1983 RHW
Trask, David F(rederic) 1929- CANR-17
Earlier sketches in CA 1-4R, CANR-1
Trask, Haunani-Kay 1949- 188
Trask, John Jacquelin 1904(?)-1977
Obituary 69-72
Trask, Jonathan
See Levinson, Leonard
Trask, Larry 1944-2004 207
Obituary 225
Trask, Margaret Pope 1907- 1-4R
Trask, R. L.
See Trask, Larry
Trask, Roger R(eed) 1930- 41-44R
Trask, Willard (Ropes) 1900(?)-1980
Obituary 101
Trasko, Mary 1959- 144
Trasler, Gordon (Blair) 1929- CANR-3
Earlier sketch in CA 1-4R
Trattner, Walter I(rwin) 1936- CANR-13
Earlier sketch in CA 37-40R
Traub, Charles (Henry) 1945- 211
Traube, Ruy
See Tralins, S(andor) Robert
Traube, Shepard 1907-1983
Obituary 111
Traubel, Horace
See Traubel, Horace L(ogo)
Traubel, Horace L(ogo) 1858-1919
Brief entry 123
Traudl
See Flaxman, Traudl
Trauger, Wilmer K(ohl) 1898-1991 CAP-1
Earlier sketch in CA 9-10
Traugott, Elizabeth Closs 1939- 41-44R
Trauner, Alexandre 1906-1993 IDFW 3, 4
Traupman, John C. 1923- 41-44R
Trausti, Jon
See Magnusson, Gudmundur
See also DLB 293
Traut, Dennis 1953- 111
Trautman, Donald T. 1924- 37-40R
Trautman, Ray 1907- 45-48
Trautman, Victoria B. 1959- 195
Trautmann, Frederic 1936- 132
Trautmann, Thomas R(oger) 1940- 131
Travell, Janet (Graeme) 1901-1997 CAP-2
Earlier sketch in CA 29-32
Traven, B. 1882(?)-1969 CAP-2
Obituary 25-28R
Earlier sketch in CA 19-20
See also CLC 8, 11
See also DLB 9, 56
See also EWL 3
See also MTCW 1
See also RGAL 4
Traven, Beatrice
See Goldemberg, Rose Leiman
Traver, Robert
See Voelker, John D(onaldson)
See also CN 1, 2
Travers, Ben 1886-1980 133
Obituary 102
See also CBD
See also DLB 10, 233
See also RGEL 2
Travers, Col. J. M.
See Rathborne, St. George (Henry)
Travers, Kenneth
See Hutchin, Kenneth Charles
Travers, Louise Allderdice 1891- CAP-1
Earlier sketch in CA 9-10
Travers, P(amela) L(yndon)
1899-1996 CANR-30
Obituary 152
Earlier sketch in CA 33-36R
See also CLR 2, 93
See also CWRI 5
See also DLB 160
See also MAICYA 1, 2
See also MAICYAS 1
See also SAAS 2
See also SATA 4, 54, 100
See also SATA-Obit 90
See also TEA
Travers, Paul J(oseph) 1951- 138
Travers, Phil 1972- 217
Travers, Robert J. 1911(?)-1974
Obituary 49-52
Travers, Robert M(orris) W(illiam)
1913- CANR-2
Earlier sketch in CA 5-8R
Travers, Scott A(ndrew) 1961- 125
Travers, Susan 1909- 203
Travers, Virginia
See Coigney, Virginia
Travers, Will
See Rowland, D(onald) S(ydney)
Traversi, Derek A(ntona) 1912- 77-80
Travis, Aaron
See Saylor, Steven
Travis, Anthony S(tewart) 1943- CANR-104
Earlier sketch in CA 147
Travis, Charles S. 1943- 37-40R
Travis, Dempsey J(erome) 1920- CANR-104
Earlier sketches in CA 85-88, CANR-15, 49
Travis, Elizabeth (Frances Chandler) 1920- . 134
Travis, Frederick F. 1942- 135
Travis, Gerry
See Trimble, Louis P(reston)
Travis, Gretchen A. 103
Travis, Jack 1952- 141
Travis, John T. 1935- 25-28R
Travis, Lucille CANR-111
Earlier sketch in CA 152
See also SATA 88, 133
Travis, Neal 1940(?)-2002 103
Obituary 211
Travis, Stephen H(enry) 1944- 106
Travis, Tony
See Travis, Anthony S(tewart)
Travis, Walter Earl 1926- 21-24R
Travis, Will
See Keevill, Henry J(ohn)
Travis, William 1924- 25-28R
Travisano, Thomas (J.) 1951- CANR-136
Earlier sketch in CA 164
Travlos, John 1908(?)-1985
Obituary 118
Travolta, John 1954- 169
Trawick, Buckner Beasley 1914- 5-8R
Trawick, Leonard M. 1933- 137
Traxler, Arthur E(dwin) 1900-1975 CAP-2
Earlier sketch in CA 21-22

Traxler, Patricia 1947- CANR-112
Earlier sketch in CA 147
Traylor, Ellen Gunderson 1946- 122
Traylor, W. L. 1929- 37-40R
Traynor, Alex
See Lagerwall, Edna
TRB
See Strout, Richard L(ee)
Treacy, William 1919- 61-64
Treadgold, Donald W(arren) 1922-1994 . 9-12R
Treadgold, Mary 1910- 13-16R
See also CWRI 5
See also SATA 49
Treadgold, Warren 1949- 187
Treadway, John D(avid) 1950- 128
Treadway, Terry
See Treadway, Theresa
Treadway, Theresa 1941- 107
Treadwell, Lawrence P., Jr. 1928- 213
Treadwell, Sandy 1946- 124
Treadwell, Sophie 1885-1970 .... DFS 22
Treadwell, Theodore R. 1916- 218
Treadwell, Victor 238
Treahearne, Elizabeth
See Maxwell, Patricia
Treanor, John Holland 1903(?)-1978
Obituary 77-80
Treanor, Oliver 1949- CANR-73
Earlier sketch in CA 128
Trease, (Robert) Geoffrey
1909-1998 .... CANR-38
Obituary 165
Earlier sketches in CA 5-8R, CANR-7, 22
See also CLR 42
See also MAICYA 1, 2
See also SAAS 6
See also SATA 2, 60
See also SATA-Obit 101
See also YAW
Treaster, Joseph B. 1941- 128
Treasure, G(eoffrey) R(ussell) R(ichards)
1929- 77-80
Treat, Ida
See Bergeret, Ida Treat
Treat, James 1962- 239
Treat, John Whittier 1953- 128
Treat, Lawrence 1903-1998 .... CANR-64
Obituary 164
Earlier sketch in CA 49-52
See also CMW 4
See also MSW
See also SATA 59
Treat, Payson J(ackson) 1879-1972
Obituary 37-40R
Trebach, Arnold S. 1928- CANR-12
Earlier sketch in CA 9-12R
Trebay, Guy 1952- 149
Trebing, Harry M(artin) 1926- CANR-31
Earlier sketch in CA 29-32R
Trecker, Harleigh B(radley)
1911-1986 .... CANR-5
Earlier sketch in CA 5-8R
Trecker, Janice Law 1941- CANR-98
Earlier sketches in CA 65-68, CANR-9
Tredell, Nicolas (Samuel) 1950- CANR-103
Earlier sketch in CA 149
Tredennick, (George) Hugh (Percival Phair)
1899-1981 109
Obituary 105
Tredez, Alain 1926- 85-88
See also SATA 17
Tredez, Denise 1930- CANR-8
Earlier sketch in CA 5-8R
See also SATA 50
Tredgold, Nye
See Tranter, Nigel (Godwin)
Tredgold, Roger F(rancis) 1911-1975 .. CANR-5
Earlier sketch in CA 5-8R
Trediakovsky, Vasilii Kirillovich
1703-1769 .... DLB 150
Tree, Christina 1944- CANR-12
Earlier sketch in CA 73-76
Tree, Cornelia
See Nichols, Nina (Marianna) da Vinci
Tree, Gregory
See Bardin, John Franklin
Tree, Michael (John) 1926- 9-12R
Tree, Ronald 1897-1976 69-72
Obituary 65-68
Treece, Henry 1912-1966 .... CANR-60
Obituary 25-28R
Earlier sketches in CA 1-4R, CANR-6
See also BYA 4
See also CLR 2
See also DLB 160
See also MAICYA 1, 2
See also RHW
See also SATA 2
Treece, Patricia 1938- 110
Trefethen, Florence 1921- 29-32R
Trefethen, James B(yron, Jr.)
1916-1976 .... CANR-11
Obituary 69-72
Earlier sketch in CA 21-24R
Treffert, Darold A(llen) 1933- 131
Trefflich, Henry (Herbert Frederick)
1908-1978 .... CAP-2
Obituary 77-80
Earlier sketch in CA 23-24
Trefftzs, Kenneth Lewis 1911-2001 .... 13-16R
Obituary 194
Trefil, James S. 1938- CANR-91
Earlier sketches in CA 101, CANR-27
Trefor, Eirlys
See Williams, Eirlys O(lwen)
Trefousse, Hans Louis 1921- CANR-143
Earlier sketches in CA 37-40R, CANR-14
Tregarthen, Enys
See Sloggett, Nellie
Tregaskis, Hugh 1905(?)-1983
Obituary 110
Tregaskis, Richard 1916-1973 .... CANR-2
Obituary 45-48
Earlier sketch in CA 1-4R
See also SATA 3
See also SATA-Obit 26
Tregear, Thomas R(efoy) 1897- 21-24R
Treger, Harvey 1924- 61-64
Treggiari, Susan (Mary) 1940- 61-64
Tregidgo, Philip Sillince 1926-1992 105
Treglown, Jeremy (Dickinson)
1946- CANR-103
Brief entry 111
Earlier sketch in CA 114
Interview in CA-114
Trego, Walter
See Smith, W(illiam) Eugene
Tregoe, Benjamin B., Jr. 1927- 125
Tregonning, Kennedy Gordon 1923- 9-12R
Treherne, Katie Thamer 1955- .... SATA 76
Trehey, Harold F. 1902(?)-1978
Obituary 77-80
Trehub, Arnold 1923- 140
Treichel, Hans-Ulrich 1952- 185
Treichler, Jessie C(ambron) 1906(?)-1972
Obituary 37-40R
Treister, Bernard W(illiam) 1932- 101
Treitel, G(uenter) H(einz) 1928- 139
Treitel, Jonathan 1959- 210
See also CLC 70
See also DLB 267
Trejo, Arnulfo D(uenes) 1922-2002 .. CANR-32
Obituary 212
Earlier sketch in CA 57-60
See also HW 1
Trejo, Ernesto 1950-1991 175
See also DLB 122
See also HW 2
Trejos, Carlota 1920- 49-52
Trekell, Harold E(verett) 1910-1998 49-52
Trela, D(ale) J(ohn) 1958- 152
Trelawny, Edward John 1792-1881 .... DLB 110, 116, 144
Trelease, Allen William 1928- 108
Trelease, James J(oseph) 1941- 112
Trelease, Jim
See Trelease, James J(oseph)
Trelford, Donald Gilchrist 1937- 111
Trell, Bluma L(ee) 1903-1997 77-80
Obituary 159
Trell, Max 1900-1996 .... 41-44R
Obituary 174
See also SATA 14
See also SATA-Obit 108
Treloar, Dorothy 1920(?)-1983
Obituary 111
Treloar, James A(rthur) 1933- 45-48
Trelos, Tony
See Crechales, Anthony George
Tremain, Rose 1943- CANR-95
Earlier sketches in CA 97-100, CANR-44
See also CLC 42
See also CN 4, 5, 6, 7
See also DLB 14, 271
See also RGSF 2
See also RHW
Tremain, Ruthven 1922- CANR-95
Earlier sketch in CA 85-88
See also SATA 17
Tremaine, Jennie
See Chesney, Marion
Tremaine, Katherine
See Tremaine, Kit
Tremaine, Kit 1907-1997 139
Obituary 156
Tremayne, Jonathan
See Forrest-Webb, Robert
Tremayne, Ken(neth Eugene, Jr.) 1933- .. 17-20R
Tremayne, Peter
See Ellis, Peter Berresford
Tremayne, Sydney (Durward) 1912- ... CANR-5
Earlier sketch in CA 5-8R
See also CP 1, 2
Trembath, Don 1963- CANR-129
Earlier sketch in CA 161
See also SATA 96
See also YAW
Trembath, Kern R(obert) 1951- 144
Tremblay, Bill
See Tremblay, William (Andrew)
Tremblay, Florent A(lexander Joseph)
1933- 208
Tremblay, Marc-Adelard 1922- 41-44R
Tremblay, Michel 1942- 128
Brief entry 116
See also CCA 1
See also CLC 29, 102
See also CWW 2
See also DAC
See also DAM MST
See also DLB 60
See also EWL 3
See also GLL 1
See also MTCW 1, 2
See also MTFW 2005
Tremblay, William (Andrew) 1940- . CANR-111
Earlier sketches in CA 89-92, CANR-59
Tremble, Freda B. 1894-1979 73-76
Tremens, Del
See MacDonald, Amy
Treml, Vladimir G(uy) 1929- 25-28R
Tremlett, George (William) 1939- 142
Tremmel, William Calloley 1918- 97-100
Trench, (William Francis) Brinsley Le Poer
See Le Poer Trench, (William Francis) Brinsley
Trench, Charles (Pocklington) Chenevix
1914- CANR-45
Trench, John (Chenevix) 1920- .... CMW 4
Trench, Richard 1949- 133
Trench, Sally 1949- 195
Trendall, Arthur Dale 1909-1995 ...... CANR-46
Obituary 150
Earlier sketches in CA 53-56, CANR-5, 22
Treneer, Anne 1891-1966 .... CAP-1
Earlier sketch in CA 9-10
Trenerry, Walter N. 1917- 135
Trengove, Alan Thomas 1929- 108
Trenhaile, John (Stevens) 1949- 110
See also CMW 4
Trenholm, Virginia Cole 1902-1994 ...... 13-16R
Trenin, Dmitri V. 1955- 174
Trenker, Alois Franz 1892-1990
Obituary 131
Trenker, Luis
See Trenker, Alois Franz
Trennert, Robert A., Jr. 1937- 57-60
Trensky, Paul I. 1929- 93-96
Trent, Carol
See Brenchley, Chaz
Trent, James W(illiam) 1933-2001 .... 21-24R
Trent, Jimmie Douglas 1933- 49-52
Trent, May Wong 1939- 57-60
Trent, Olaf
See Fanthorpe, R(obert) Lionel
Trent, Robbie 1894-1988 .... CAP-1
Earlier sketch in CA 9-10
See also SATA 26
Trent, Timothy
See Malmberg, Carl
Trent, William 1919- CANR-3
Earlier sketch in CA 1-4R
Trent, William P(eterfield) 1862-1939 193
Brief entry 122
See also DLB 47, 71
Trento, Joseph John 1947- CANR-88
Earlier sketch in CA 45-48
Trento, Salvatore Michael 1952- 101
Trepp, Leo 1913- CANR-40
Earlier sketches in CA 5-8R, CANR-2, 18
Trepper, Leopold Leib 1904-1982(?)
Obituary 105
Tresch, John William, Jr. 1937-
Brief entry 106
Trescot, William Henry 1822-1898 .... DLB 30
Trescott, Paul B(arton) 1925- CANR-2
Earlier sketch in CA 1-4R
Trese, Leo J(ohn) 1902-1970 .... 5-8R
Treseder, Terry Walton 1956- .... SATA 68
Tresemer, David 1948- 108
Treshow, Michael 1926- 57-60
Tresidder, Argus John 1907-2002 .... CANR-5
Obituary 203
Earlier sketch in CA 5-8R
Tresilian, Liz
See Green, Elisabeth Sara
Tresilian, (Cecil) Stuart 1891-(?) .... SATA 40
Tresillian, Richard .... RHW
Tress, Arthur 1940- 101
Tressall, Robert
See Tressell, Robert
Tressell, Robert 1870-1911 186
See also DLB 197
See also RGEL 2
Tresselt, Alvin 1916-2000 .... CANR-1
Obituary 189
Earlier sketch in CA 49-52
See also CLR 30
See also CWRI 5
See also MAICYA 1, 2
See also SATA 7
Tressidy, Jim
See Norwood, Victor G(eorge) C(harles)
Tressilian, Charles
See Atcheson, Richard
Tressler, Donald K(iteley) 1894-1981 .. CANR-4
Obituary 103
Earlier sketch in CA 45-48
Trethewey, Natasha 1966- 203
Trethewey, Rachel 1967- 226
Trethowan, K(enneth) Illtyd
1907-1993 .... CANR-3
Earlier sketch in CA 1-4R
Tretick, (Aaron) Stanley 1921-1999 103
Obituary 185
Trettel, (Mario) Efrem 1921- 69-72
Treuenfels, Peter 1926- 37-40R
Treuer, David 1970- CANR-89
Earlier sketch in CA 153
Treuer, Robert 1926- 69-72
Trevanian
See Whitaker, Rod(ney)
See also CLC 29
Trevaskis, G(erald) K(ennedy) N(icholas)
1915-1990
Obituary 131
Trevaskis, John 1911-1968 .... CAP-1
Earlier sketch in CA 9-10
Trevaskis, Sir Kennedy
See Trevaskis, G(erald) K(ennedy) N(icholas)
Trevathan, Robert E(ugene) 1925- CANR-64
Earlier sketches in CA 1-4R, CANR-6
See also TCWW 2
Trevelyan, George Macaulay 1876-1962 . 89-92
See also BRW 6
Trevelyan, George Otto 1838-1928 .... DLB 144
Trevelyan, Humphrey 1905-1985 .... 37-40R
Obituary 115
Trevelyan, Julian O(tto) 1910-1988 .. CANR-85
Obituary 126
Earlier sketch in CA 9-12R
Trevelyan, Katharine 1908- CAP-1
Earlier sketch in CA 11-12
Trevelyan, Mary Caroline
See Moorman, Mary C(aroline Trevelyan)
Trevelyan, (Walter) Raleigh 1923- .. CANR-127
Earlier sketches in CA 13-16R, CANR-6, 22, 47
Trevelyan, Robert
See Forrest-Webb, Robert
Trever, John C(ecil) 1915- 17-20R
Treverton, Gregory F(rye) 1947- 118
Treves, Ralph 1906-1991 .... 13-16R
Trevino, Elizabeth B(orton) de 1904- .. CANR-9
Earlier sketch in CA 17-20R
See also BYA 2
See also CWRI 5
See also MAICYA 1, 2
See also SAAS 5
See also SATA 1, 29
Trevino, Elizabeth B(orton) de
1904- .... MAICYA 2
Trevino, Jesus Salvador 1946- 212
Trevino, Lee (Buck) 1939- 113
Trevisa, John c. 1342-c. 1402 .... BRWS 9
See also DLB 146
Trevisan, Dalton 1925- .... DLB 307
Trevor, Elleston 1920-1995 .... CANR-59
Obituary 149
Earlier sketch in CA 5-8R
See also Hall, Adam
See also CMW 4
See also SATA 28
Trevor, Frances
See Teasdale, Sara
Trevor, Glen
See Hilton, James
Trevor, (Lucy) Meriol 1919-2000 ...... CANR-16
Obituary 190
Earlier sketches in CA 1-4R, CANR-1
See also CWRI 5
See also SATA 10, 113
See also SATA-Obit 122
Trevor, Penelope 173
Trevor, William
See Cox, William Trevor
See also BRWS 4
See also CBD
See also CD 5, 6
See also CLC 7, 9, 14, 25, 71, 116
See also CN 1, 2, 3, 4, 5, 6, 7
See also DLB 14, 139
See also EWL 3
See also LATS 1:2
See also RGEL 2
See also RGSF 2
See also SSC 21, 58
See also SSFS 10
See also TCLE 1:2
Trevor-Roper, H(ugh) R(edwald)
1914-2003 101
Obituary 212
Trew, Antony (Francis) 1906-1996 ...... CANR-2
Earlier sketch in CA 45-48
Treweek, David 1947- 189
Trewin, Ion (Courtenay Gill) 1943- 69-72
Trewin, J(ohn) C(ourtenay) 1908-1990
Obituary 131
Brief entry 112
Treyz, Russell 1940- 132
Trez, Alain
See Tredez, Alain
Trez, Denise
See Tredez, Denise
Trezise, Percy (James) 1923- 132
See also CLR 41
See also CWRI 5
Trezise, Philip Harold 1912-2001 109
Obituary 199
Trezza, Alphonse F(iore) 1920- CANR-42
Earlier sketch in CA 118
Triana, Gaby 1971- 238
Triana, Jose 1931(?)- 131
See also DLB 305
See also EWL 3
See also HW 1
See also LAW
Triandis, Harry C(haralambos) 1926- 41-44R
Tribbe, Frank C(alvert) 1914- 117
Tribble, Edwin 1907-1986 142
Obituary 119
Tribble, Harold Wayland 1899-1986
Obituary 121
Tribe, David (Harold) 1931- 25-28R
Tribe, Ivan M(athews) 1940- CANR-104
Earlier sketches in CA 122, CANR-48
Tribe, Laurence H(enry) 1941- 133
Tribich, Susan 1945(?)-1985
Obituary 115
Trible, Phyllis 1932- CANR-118
Earlier sketch in CA 154
See also FW
Tribune
See Armstrong, Douglas Albert
Trice, Borough
See Allen, A(rthur) B(ruce)
Trice, Dawn Turner CANR-100
Earlier sketch in CA 166
See also BW 3
Trice, Harrison M. 1920-1994 .... 21-24R
Tricker, B(rian) J(ohn) K(ingsbury)
1937- 25-28R
Trickett, Joyce 1915- CANR-34
Earlier sketch in CA 105
Trickett, Mabel Rachel 1923-1999 101
See also CN 1, 2, 3, 4, 5, 6
Triece, Mary E. 1967- 188
Triegel, Linda (Jeanette) 1942- 117

Cumulative Index 583 True

Triem, Eve 1902-1992 .... CANR-9
Earlier sketch in CA 17-20R
Triere, Lynette 1941- 108
Trier Morch, Dea
See Morch, Dea Trier
See also CWW 2
Trieschman, Albert E(well)
1931-1984 .... CANR-85
Obituary 113
Earlier sketch in CA 29-32R
Triffin, Robert 1911-1993 .... CANR-3
Obituary 140
Earlier sketch in CA 1-4R
Trifkovic, Serge 226
Trifkovic, Srdja
See Trifkovic, Serge
Trifonov, Gennady 1945- .... GLL 2
Trifonov, Iurii (Valentinovich)
See Trifonov, Yuri (Valentinovich)
See also DLB 302
See also RGWL 2, 3
Trifonov, Yuri (Valentinovich) 1925-1981 126
Obituary 103
See also Trifonov, Iurii (Valentinovich) and Trifonov, Yury Valentinovich
See also CLC 45
See also MTCW 1
Trifonov, Yury Valentinovich
See Trifonov, Yuri (Valentinovich)
See also EWL 3
Trigg, George L. 1925- 139
Trigg, Harry Davis 1927- 61-64
Trigg, Joseph Wilson 1949- 118
Trigg, Louisa Hagner 1923- 200
Trigg, Roger (Hugh) 1941- 49-52
Trigg, Yolanda Lillian 1926- 61-64
Trigger, Bruce G(raham) 1937- CANR-29
Earlier sketches in CA 21-24R, CANR-9
Trigger, David S. 1953- 147
Triggs, Tony D. 1946- 138
See also SATA 70
Trigoboff, Joseph 1947- CANR-136
Earlier sketch in CA 81-84
Trillin, Calvin (Marshall) 1935- CANR-135
Earlier sketches in CA 85-88, CANR-20, 46, 67, 113
See also AITN 1
See also DLB 185
See also MTCW 1, 2
See also MTFW 2005
Trilling, Diana (Rubin) 1905-1996 .... CANR-46
Obituary 154
Earlier sketches in CA 5-8R, CANR-10
Interview in CANR-10
See also CLC 129
See also MTCW 1, 2
Trilling, Lionel 1905-1975 .... CANR-105
Obituary 61-64
Earlier sketches in CA 9-12R, CANR-10
Interview in CANR-10
See also AMWS 3
See also CLC 9, 11, 24
See also CN 1, 2
See also DLB 28, 63
See also EWL 3
See also MAL 5
See also MTCW 1, 2
See also RGAL 4
See also SSC 75
See also TUS
Trilussa 1871-1950 .... DLB 114
Trimball, W. H.
See Mencken, H(enry) L(ouis)
Trimble, Barbara Margaret 1921- CANR-62
Earlier sketch in CA 132
See also CMW 4
Trimble, Jacquelyn W(hitney) 1927- 13-16R
Trimble, John F(elix) 1925-1993 97-100
Trimble, Louis P(reston) 1917-1988 .. CANR-64
Obituary 171
Earlier sketches in CA 13-16R, CANR-6
See also SFW 4
See also TCWW 1, 2
Trimble, Marshall I(ra) 1939- CANR-122
Earlier sketches in CA 77-80, CANR-61
See also SATA 93
Trimble, Martha Scott 1914- 29-32R
Trimble, Stephen 1950- 149
Trimble, Vance H(enry) 1913- 49-52
Trimble, William Raleigh 1913-2002 ...... 9-12R
Trimby, Elisa 1948- 122
See also SATA 47
See also SATA-Brief 40
Trimiew, Darryl M. 1952- 158
Trimingham, J(ohn) Spencer 1904- CANR-3
Earlier sketch in CA 1-4R
Trimmer, Ellen McKay 1915- 9-12R
Trimmer, Eric J. 1923-1998 .... 9-12R
Trimmer, Joseph F(rancis) 1941- CANR-42
Earlier sketches in CA 77-80, CANR-13
Trimmer, Sarah 1741-1810 .... DLB 158
Trimpey, Jack
See Trimpey, John P.
Trimpey, John P. 1941- 139
Tring, A. Stephen
See Meynell, Laurence Walter
Trinh, T. Min-Ha 1952- 154
See also FW
Trinidad, Corky
See Trinidad, Francisco D., Jr.
Trinidad, David 1953- 188
See also GLL 2
Trinidad, Francisco D., Jr. 1939- 69-72
Trinkaus, Charles (Edward) 1911-1999 .. 29-32R
Obituary 185
Trinkaus, Erik 1948- 140
Trinkle, Dennis A. 1968- 219
Trinklein, Frederick E(rnst) 1924- 41-44R
Trinkner, Charles L. 1920- 29-32R
Trinquier, Roger Paul 1908- CANR-5
Earlier sketch in CA 9-12R
Triola, Mario F(rank) 1944- 57-60
Triolet, Elsa 1896-1970
Obituary 25-28R
See also DLB 72
Triplehorn, Charles A(lbert) 1927- 130
Triplett, Kenneth E(arl) 1926- 57-60
Triplett, Pimone 180
Triplett, Raymond (Francis) 1921- 117
Tripodi, Thomas Charles 1932-1999 141
Obituary 183
Tripodi, Tom
See Tripodi, Thomas Charles
Tripodi, Tony 1932- CANR-12
Earlier sketch in CA 29-32R
Tripp, C(larence) A(rthur) 1919-2003 73-76
Obituary 216
Tripp, Charles R(ees) H(oward) 1952- 158
Tripp, Dawn Clifton 1968(?)- 227
Tripp, Eleanor B(aldwin) 1936- 29-32R
See also SATA 4
Tripp, Janet 1942- 178
See also SATA 108
Tripp, John
See Moore, John Travers
Tripp, John 1927- 97-100
See also CP 1, 2
See also DLB 40
Tripp, Karen 1923-1993 .... CANR-47
Obituary 141
Earlier sketch in CA 53-56
See also Gershon, Karen
Tripp, L(ouis) Reed 1913-1994 .... 5-8R
Tripp, Miles (Barton) 1923-2000 ... ... CANR-98
Earlier sketches in CA 13-16R, CANR-12, 28, 60
See also CMW 4
Tripp, Nathaniel 1944- 161
See also SATA 101
Tripp, Paul 1916-2002 .... 21-24R
Obituary 208
See also SATA 8
See also SATA-Obit 139
Tripp, Valerie 1951- CANR-130
Earlier sketch in CA 146
See also SATA 78
Tripp, Wallace (Whitney) 1940- CANR-23
Earlier sketch in CA 106
See also SATA 31
Tripp, Wendell, Jr. 1928- 114
Trippett, Frank 1926-1998 .... CANR-88
Obituary 181
Earlier sketch in CA 21-24R
Trisco, Robert Frederick 1929- 41-44R
Triska, Jan Francis 1922-2003 .... CANR-7
Obituary 214
Earlier sketch in CA 5-8R
Trisler, Hank 1937- 121
Tristan
See Gomez de la Serna, Ramon
Tristan, Flora 1803-1844 .... FW
Tristan L'Hermite
1601(?)-1655 .... GFL Beginnings to 1789
Tristram
See Housman, A(lfred) E(dward)
Tristram, Claire 1959(?)- 228
Tritel, Barbara
See Quick, Barbara
Trites, Roberta Seelinger 1962- CANR-136
Earlier sketch in CA 168
Triton, A. N.
See Barclay, Oliver R(ainsford)
Tritt, Robert E(arl) 1921- 21-24R
Trittschuh, Travis Edward 1920- 5-8R
Trivas, A(lexander) Victor 1894-1970 ..... CAP-1
Obituary 29-32R
Earlier sketch in CA 19-20
Trivelpiece, Laurel 1926- 123
See also SATA 56
See also SATA-Brief 46
Trivers, Howard 1909-1987 73-76
Obituary 122
Trivett, Daphne Harwood 1940- 97-100
See also SATA 22
Trivizas, Eugene 1946- 150
See also SATA 84
Trnka, Jiri 1912-1969
Obituary 111
See also IDFW 3, 4
See also MAICYA 1, 2
See also SATA 43
See also SATA-Brief 32
Trobaugh, Augusta 1939- 188
Trobian, Helen R(eed) 1918- 5-8R
Trobisch, Ingrid (Hult) 1926- CANR-28
Earlier sketch in CA 97-100
Trocchi, Alexander 1925-1984 .... CANR-72
Obituary 112
Earlier sketch in CA 9-12R
See also CN 1, 2, 3
See also DLB 15
Troche, Rose 1964(?)- 147
Trocheck, Kathy Hogan 1954- 184
Trocme, Etienne 1924- 49-52
Troeger, Thomas H(enry) 1945- CANR-94
Earlier sketches in CA 89-92, CANR-15, 34
Troell, Jan (Gustaf) 1931- 207
Troelstrup, Arch William 1901-1994 ..... 17-20R
Troen, Selwyn K. 1940- 104
Trofimenko, Henry (Alexandrovich) 1929- .. 188
Trofimenkoff, Susan Mann 1941- 73-76
Trogdon, William (Lewis) 1939- CANR-89
Brief entry 115
Earlier sketches in CA 119, CANR-47
Interview in CA-119
See also Heat-Moon, William Least and Least Heat-Moon, William
See also AAYA 66
See also CPW
Trohan, Walter (Joseph) 1903-2003 81-84
Obituary 221
Troiden, Richard (Russell) 1946- 89-92
Troise, Joe 1942- 103
Troisgros, Jean (Georges) 1926-1983
Obituary 110
Troisi, Dante 1920-1989 .... DLB 196
Troitsky, Artemy 1955- 136
Trojan, Judith 1947- 131
Trojanowicz, John M.
See Troyanovich, John M(ichael)
Trojanowicz, Robert C(hester)
1941-1994 .... CANR-86
Obituary 144
Earlier sketches in CA 45-48, CANR-31
Trojanski, John 1943- 45-48
Trolander, Judith Ann 1942- 61-64
Trollope, Anthony 1815-1882 .... BRW 5
See also CDBLB 1832-1890
See also DA
See also DA3
See also DAB
See also DAC
See also DAM MST, NOV
See also DLB 21, 57, 159
See also RGEL 2
See also RGSF 2
See also SATA 22
See also SSC 28
See also WLC
Trollope, Frances 1779-1863 .... DLB 21, 166
Trollope, Joanna 1943- CANR-95
Earlier sketches in CA 101, CANR-58
See also CLC 186
See also CN 7
See also CPW
See also DLB 207
See also RHW
Troman, Morley 1918- 13-16R
Tromanhauser, Edward (Downer)
1932- 41-44R
Trombley, Charles C(yprian) 1928- 65-68
Trombley, Stephen 1954- 129
Trombold, Charles D(ickson) 1942- 143
Tromly, Fred(eric B.) 185
Tromp, S. W.
See Tromp, Solco Walle
Tromp, Solco W.
See Tromp, Solco Walle
Tromp, Solco Walle 1909-1983
Obituary 116
Tronchin-James, (Robert) Nevil 1916- CAP-1
Earlier sketch in CA 9-10
Troncoso, Sergio 188
Trondheim, Lewis 1964- 234
Tronvoll, Kjetil 229
Trooboff, Peter D(ennis) 1942- 65-68
Troop, Elizabeth 1931- 164
Brief entry 116
See also DLB 14
Troop, Miriam 1917- 13-16R
Troost, J. Maarten 236
Tropman, John E. 1939- CANR-113
Earlier sketch in CA 154
Tropp, Martin 1945- 65-68
Tropper, Jonathan 1970- 196
Trost, Cathy 1951- CANR-143
Earlier sketch in CA 125
Trost, Lucille W(ood) 1938- CANR-9
Earlier sketch in CA 61-64
See also SATA 12, 149
Trotman, Jack H(arry) 129
Trotsky, Leon 1879-1940 167
Brief entry 118
See also TCLC 22
Trott, Betty 1933- 155
See also SATA 91
Trott, Susan 1937- 97-100
Trotta, John 1936- 45-48
Trotta, Liz 206
Trotta, Maurice S. 1907-1976
Obituary 111
Trotter (Cockburn), Catharine
1679-1749 .... DLB 84, 252
Trotter, Charlie 1959- 196
Trotter, Grace V(iolet) 1900-1991 .... CANR-1
Earlier sketch in CA 1-4R
See also SATA 10
Trotter, Jesse McLane (?)-1983
Obituary 110
Trotter, Michael H(amilton) 1936- 165
Trotter, Patrick C. 1935- 126
Trotter, Robert J(oseph) 1943- 120
Trotter, Sallie (W. B.) 1915- 29-32R
Trotter, Sharland 1943(?)-1997 237
Trotter, Wilfred 1872-1939 .... TCLC 97
Trotter, William R., (Jr.) 1943- CANR-136
Earlier sketch in CA 141
Trotti, John H. 1936- 118
Trotti, Lamar (Jefferson) 1900-1952 179
See also DLB 44
See also IDFW 3, 4
Trottier, Chris .... AAYA 63
Trottier, Maxine 1950- 200
See also SATA 131
Trottier, Pierre 1925- .... DLB 60
Trotzig, Birgitta 1929- 194
See also DLB 257
See also EWL 3
Troughton, Joanna (Margaret) 1947- . CANR-26
Earlier sketch in CA 109
See also SATA 37
Trouncer, Margaret (Lahey)
1903-1982 .... CANR-10
Obituary 108
Earlier sketch in CA 5-8R
Troup, Cornelius V. 1902-1977 .... CAP-1
Earlier sketch in CA 9-10
Troupe, Quincy (Thomas, Jr.)
1943- CANR-126
Brief entry 113
Earlier sketches in CA 124, CANR-43, 90
See also BW 2
See also DLB 41
Trout, Charles Hathaway 1935- 113
Trout, Kilgore
See Farmer, Philip Jose
Trout, Richard E. 194
See also SATA 123
Trout, Robert J(ay) 1947- 142
Trout, Steven 1963- 234
Troutman, Charles (Henry) 1914-1990 69-72
Trouve, Roger 1882(?)-1984
Obituary 112
Trow, George W. S. 1943- CANR-91
Earlier sketch in CA 126
See also CLC 52
Trow, M(eirion) J(ames) 1949- CANR-98
Earlier sketch in CA 120
Trow, Martin A. 1926- 112
Trow, W(illiam) Clark 1894-1982 .... CANR-6
Earlier sketch in CA 5-8R
Trowbridge, Clinton W(hiting)
1928- CANR-10
Earlier sketch in CA 65-68
Trowbridge, John Townsend 1827-1916 220
See also DLB 202
Trowbridge, Keith W(ayne) 1920- 108
Trowbridge, Leslie Walter 1920- CANR-13
Earlier sketch in CA 77-80
Trowell, Kathleen Margaret 1904-1984 ... 65-68
Troxel, Karen
See Borrelli, Karen (Troxel)
Troxell, Eugene A(nthony) 1937- 73-76
Troxell, Mary D(earborn) 1907- 37-40R
Troy, George F(rancis), Jr.
1909-1969 .... CANR-87
Obituary 103
Earlier sketch in CA 1-4R
Troy, Judy 1951- CANR-82
Earlier sketch in CA 143
Troy, Katherine
See Buxton, Anne (Arundel)
Troy, Lawrence M. 1928- 21-24R
Troy, Nancy J. 1952- CANR-138
Earlier sketches in CA 115, CANR-37
Troy, Robin 1974- 188
Troy, Tevi 1967- 226
Troy, Una 1913-1993 .... CANR-3
Earlier sketch in CA 1-4R
Troy, William 1903-1961
Obituary 89-92
Troyan, Sasha (N.) 1962- 230
Troyanovich, John M(ichael) 1936- .. CANR-57
Earlier sketches in CA 49-52, CANR-31
Troyat, Henri 1911- CANR-117
Earlier sketches in CA 45-48, CANR-2, 33, 67
See also CLC 23
See also GFL 1789 to the Present
See also MTCW 1
Troyer, Byron L(eRoy) 1909-1980 65-68
Troyer, Johannes 1902-1969 .... SATA-Brief 40
Troyer, Warner 1932- 101
Interview in CA-101
Troyka, Lynn Quitman 1938- 37-40R
Troyna, Barry 1951- CANR-40
Earlier sketch in CA 117
Truax, Carol 1900-1986 .... CANR-5
Earlier sketch in CA 5-8R
Truax, Charles B. 1933-1970(?) CANR-13
Earlier sketches in CAP-2, CA 21-22
Truax, R. Hawley 1889(?)-1978
Obituary 81-84
Trubitt, Allen R(oy) 1931- 77-80
Trubo, Richard 1946- CANR-120
Earlier sketches in CA 61-64, CANR-11
Trubowitz, Sidney 1926- 21-24R
Truby, J(ohn) David 1938- CANR-24
Earlier sketches in CA 53-56, CANR-4
Truch, Stephen 1947- 115
Trudeau, G(arretson) B(eekman)
1948- CANR-31
Earlier sketch in CA 81-84
See also Trudeau, Garry B.
See also AAYA 60
See also SATA 35
Trudeau, Garry B.
See Trudeau, G(arretson) B(eekman)
See also AAYA 10
See also AITN 2
See also CLC 12
Trudeau, Margaret (Joan) 1948- 93-96
Trudeau, Noah Andre 1949- CANR-141
Earlier sketch in CA 132
Trudeau, (Joseph Philippe) Pierre (Yves) Elliott
1919-2000 .... CANR-3
Obituary 190
Earlier sketch in CA 45-48
Trudel, Jean-Louis 1967- .... DLB 251
Trudel, Marcel 1917- 104
Trudix, Marty
See Truman, Ruth
True, (Phaedra) Alianor 1975- 207
True, Cynthia 1969- 238
True, Dan 1924- 117

True, Michael (D.) 1933- CANR-37
Earlier sketches in CA 41-44R, CANR-17
Trueblood, Alan Stubbs 1917- 103
Trueblood, D(avid) Elton 1900-1994 41-44R
Trueblood, Paul Graham 1905-1997 CANR-12
Earlier sketches in CAP-1, CA 17-18
Trueblood, Ted Whitaker 1913-1982
Obituary 111
Trueheart, Charles 1951- 45-48
Trueman, Terry 1947- 199
See also AAYA 46
See also BYA 15
See also SATA 132
Truemper, David G(eorge) 1939- 112
Truesdale, C(alvin) W(illiam) 1929- CANR-30
Earlier sketch in CA 29-32R
Truesdell, Judy
See Mecca, Judy Truesdell
Truesdell, Leon E. 1881(?)-1979
Obituary 85-88
Truesdell, Sue
See Truesdell, Susan G.
Truesdell, Susan G. SATA 108
See also SATA-Brief 45
Truett, Fred M(oore) 1899-1991 CAP-2
Earlier sketch in CA 21-22
Truett, Joe C(lyde) 1941- 118
Truffaut, Francois 1932-1984 CANR-34
Obituary 113
Earlier sketch in CA 81-84
See also CLC 20, 101
Truillier-Lacombe, Joseph-Patrice 1807-1863 DLB 99
Truitt, Anne (Dean) 1921-2004 142
Obituary 234
Truitt, Deborah H(unsberger) 1945- 45-48
Truitt, Evelyn Mack 1931- 57-60
Truitt, Gloria A(nn) 1939- CANR-56
Earlier sketches in CA 111, CANR-30
Truitt, John O(liver) 1934- 117
Truitt, Willis H(arrison) 1936- 57-60
Trujillo, Carla (Mari) 228
Truman, Harry S 1884-1972 106
Obituary 37-40R
Truman, Jill 1934- CANR-65
Earlier sketch in CA 128
Truman, (Mary) Margaret 1924- CANR-96
Earlier sketches in CA 105, CANR-29, 54
See also BEST 90:1
See also CPW
See also DAM POP
See also MTCW 1
Truman, Ruth 1931- 53-56
Trumbach, Randolph Earl 1944- CANR-141
Earlier sketch in CA 180
Trumbauer, Lisa (Trutkoff) 1963- 223
See also SATA 149
Trumbo, Dalton 1905-1976 CANR-10
Obituary 69-72
Earlier sketch in CA 21-24R
See also CLC 19
See also CN 1, 2
See also DLB 26
See also IDFW 3, 4
See also YAW
Trumbull, Benjamin 1735-1820 DLB 30
Trumbull, Douglas 1942- IDFW 3, 4
Trumbull, John 1750-1831 DLB 31
See also RGAL 4
Trumbull, John 1759-1843 DLB 183
Trumbull, Robert 1912-1992 CANR-86
Obituary 139
Earlier sketches in CA 9-12R, CANR-5
Trump, Donald J.
See Trump, Donald J(ohn)
See also BEST 89:1
Trump, Donald J(ohn) 1946- 130
See also Trump, Donald J.
Trump, Fred(erick Leonard) 1924- 13-16R
Trump, Ivana M. 1949- 140
Trump, Richard F. 1912- 126
Trumpener, Ulrich 1930- 25-28R
Trumper, Hubert Bagster 1902- CAP-1
Earlier sketch in CA 9-10
Trundle, Robert C(hristner), Jr. 1943- 202
Trundlett, Helen B.
See Eliot, T(homas) S(tearns)
Trungpa, Chogyam
See Chogyam Trungpa
Trunk, Isaiah Elezer 1905-1981 89-92
Obituary 108
Interview in CA-89-92
Truong, Monique (T. D.) 1968- 224
Truong, Thanh-Dam 1949- 136
Trupin, James E. 1940- 37-40R
Trupp, Beverly Ann 1937- 105
Trupp, Philip (Zber) 206
Truscott, Alan (Fraser) 1925- 25-28R
Truscott, Lucian K(ing) IV 1947- CANR-65
Earlier sketch in CA 89-92
Truscott, Peter 1959- 227
Truscott, Robert Blake 1944- 77-80
Truse, Kenneth (Philip) 1946- 105
Truss, Jan 1925- 102
See also SATA 35
Truss, Lynne 1955(?)- 236
Truss, Seldon
See Seldon-Truss, Leslie
Trussell, C(harles) P(rescott) 1892-1968
Obituary 89-92
Trussler, Simon 1942- CANR-28
Earlier sketches in CA 25-28R, CANR-12
Trustman, Alan Robert 1930-
Brief entry 111
Truth, Sojourner 1797(?)-1883 DLB 239
See also FW
See also LAIT 2
Truumaa, Aare 1926- 49-52
Truzzi, Marcello 1935-2003 41-44R
Obituary 214
Try-Davies, J.
See Hensley, Sophie Almon
Tryon, Darrell Trevor 1942- 111
Tryon, Georgiana Shick 1945- 116
Tryon, Leslie SATA 139
Tryon, Ruth Wilson 1892(?)-1987
Obituary 123
Tryon, Thomas 1926-1991 CANR-77
Obituary 135
Earlier sketches in CA 29-32R, CANR-32
See also AITN 1
See also BPFB 3
See also CLC 3, 11
See also CPW
See also DA3
See also DAM POP
See also HGG
See also MTCW 1
Tryon, Tom
See Tryon, Thomas
Tryon, W(arren) S(tenson) 1901-1989 CANR-86
Obituary 129
Earlier sketches in CAP-1, CA 11-12
Trypanis, C(onstantine) A(thanasius) 1909-1993 CANR-85
Obituary 140
Earlier sketches in CA 5-8R, CANR-7, 24
See also CP 1, 2
Tryphe
See Barney, Natalie (Clifford)
Trythall, Anthony John 1927- 77-80
Trythall, J(ohn) W(illiam) D(onald) 1944- 29-32R
Tryzna, Tomek 1948- 185
Trzebinski, Errol 1936- CANR-97
Earlier sketch in CA 143
Trzynadlowski, Andrzej M. 1941- 217
Tsadick, Marta Gabre
See Gabre-Tsadick, Marta
Tsagaris, Ellen M. 191
Tsai, Shih-shan Henry 1940- CANR-112
Earlier sketch in CA 125
Tsaloumas, Dimitris 1921- CANR-112
Earlier sketch in CA 154
See also CP 7
Tsambassis, Alexander N(icholas) 1919- 21-24R
Ts'ao Yu
See Wan Chia-pao
See also EWL 2
Tsatoke, Monroe 1904-1937 220
Tsatsos, Jeanne 1909- CANR-13
Earlier sketch in CA 29-32R
Tschacbasov, Nahum 1899-1984
Obituary 112
Tschebotarioff, Gregory P. 1899-1985 13-16R
Tscherning, Andreas 1611-1659 DLB 164
Tschichold, Jan 1902(?)-1974
Obituary 53-56
Tschudy, James Jay 1925- 13-16R
Tschumi, Raymond Robert 1924- CANR-3
Earlier sketch in CA 5-8R
Tse, K. K. 1948- 125
Tseelon, Efrat 179
Tsegaye, Gabre-Medhin (Kawessa)
See Gabre-Medhin, Tsegaye (Kawessa)
Tseng Wen-Shing 1935- CANR-123
Earlier sketches in CA 114, CANR-35
Tsering, Diki 1901-1981 220
Tsernianski, Milos
See Crnjanski, Milos
Tsetskhladze, Gocha R(evazi) 1963- 199
Tshiamala, Kabasele (?)-1983(?)
Obituary 109
Tsien, Tsuen-hsuin 1909- CANR-23
Earlier sketches in CA 17-20R, CANR-7
Tsinhnahjinnie, Hulleah 1954- 217
Tsiolkovsky, Konstantin Eduardovich 1857-1935 164
Brief entry 119
See also SFW 4
Tsipenyuk, Yuri 1938- 170
Tsipis, Kosta 1934- 110
Tsirkas, Stratis
See Hadjiandreas, Yannis
See also EWL 2
Tso, Yiu-kam 1918(?)-1983
Obituary 110
Tsomo, Karma Lekshe 1944- 150
Tsongas, Paul Efthemios 1941-1997 108
Obituary 156
Tsou, Tang 1918-1999 CANR-8
Obituary 183
Earlier sketch in CA 5-8R
Tsubouchi Shoyo 1859-1935 DLB 180
Tsuburaya, Eiji 1901-1970 IDFW 3, 4
Tsuchida, Hiromi 1939- 214
Tsui, Kitty 1952- GLL 2
Tsuji, Jiro 1927- 231
Tsuji, Kunio 1925- 154
Tsuji, Shinichi
See Oiwa, Keibo
Tsuka, Kohei (Bong Woon Kim) 1948- 195
Tsukahira, Toshio George 1915- 21-24R
Tsukinabe, Isao
See Vermeule, Cornelius Clarkson III
Tsukiyama, Gail 221
Tsukui, Nobuko 1938- 133
Tsuneishi, Warren M(ichio) 1921- 17-20R
Tsuru, Shigeto 1912- 218
Tsurumi, Shunsuke 1922- 138
Tsurutani, Taketsugu 1935- 104
Tsushima, Satoko 1947- 154
See also Tsushima Yuko
Tsushima, Shuji 1909-1948
Brief entry 107
See also Dazai Osamu
Tsushima, Yuko
See Tsushima, Satoko
Tsushima Yuko
See Tsushima, Satoko
See also CWW 2
See also EWL 3
See also FW
See also RGSF 2, 3
Tsutsui, Yoriko 1945- 132
Tsuzuki, Chushichi 1926- CANR-3
Earlier sketch in CA 1-4R
Tsvetaeva (Efron), Marina (Ivanovna) 1892-1941 CANR-73
Brief entry 104
Earlier sketch in CA 128
See also DLB 295
See also EW 11
See also MTCW 1, 2
See also PC 14
See also RGWL 2, 3
See also TCLC 7, 35
Tswett, Mikhail Semyonovich 1872-1919 162
Tsypkin, Leonid 1926-1982 218
Tu, Wei-ming 1940- 65-68
Tuan, Yi-Fu 1930- CANR-107
Earlier sketches in CA 93-96, CANR-16, 37
Tuann, Lucy H(siu-mei) C(hen) 1938- 85-88
See also Chen Ruoxi
Tubb, E(dwin) C(harles) 1919- CANR-21
Earlier sketch in CA 101
See also SFW 4
See also TCWW 2
Tubb, Ernest (Dale) 1914-1984
Obituary 114
Tubb, Jonathan N. 1951- 146
See also SATA 78
Tubbs, Stewart L(ee) 1943- CANR-6
Earlier sketch in CA 57-60
Tubby, I. M.
See Kraus, (Herman) Robert
Tucci, Giuseppe 1894-1984
Obituary 112
Tucci, Niccolo 1908-1999 81-84
Obituary 188
See also CN 1, 2, 3, 4, 5, 6
Tucci, Stanley 1960- CANR-125
Earlier sketch in CA 165
Tuccille, Jerome 1937- CANR-12
Earlier sketch in CA 29-32R
Tuchinsky, Joseph S. 1937- CANR-10
Earlier sketch in CA 25-28R
Tuchman, Barbara W(ertheim) 1912-1989 CANR-24
Obituary 127
Earlier sketches in CA 1-4R, CANR-3
See also BEST 89:1
See also CPW
See also DAM POP
See also MTCW 1, 2
See also RGAL 4
Tuchman, Gaye 1943- 85-88
Tuchman, Maurice 1936- CANR-27
Earlier sketches in CA 49-52, CANR-4
Tuchman, Phyllis 1947- 114
Tuchock, Wanda 1898(?)-1985
Obituary 115
Tucholsky, Kurt 1890-1935 189
See also DLB 56
See also EWL 3
Tuck, (John) Anthony 1940- 124
Tuck, Dorothy
See McFarland, Dorothy Tuck
Tuck, James A(lexander) 1940- 37-40R
Tuck, Lily 1938- CANR-90
Earlier sketch in CA 139
See also CLC 70
Tuck, Lon 1938(?)-1987 133
Obituary 122
Tuck, Susan H. 1947- 118
Tucker, Ann
See Giudici, Ann Couper
Tucker, Anne 1945- CANR-19
Earlier sketch in CA 102
Tucker, Anthony 1924-1998 104
Obituary 170
Tucker, Archibald Norman 1904(?)-1980
Obituary 101
Tucker, Audrie Manley
See Manley-Tucker, Audrie
Tucker, Bob
See Tucker, (Arthur) Wilson
Tucker, Carll 1951- 133
Tucker, Caroline
See Nolan, Jeannette Covert
Tucker, Charlotte Maria 1821-1893 DLB 163, 190
Tucker, Cynthia Grant 1941- 135
Tucker, David M(ilton) 1937- 101
Tucker, Edward L(lewellyn) 1921- 17-20R
Tucker, Ernest E(dward) 1916-1969 61-64
Tucker, Eva 1929- 17-20R
Tucker, Frank H(ammond) 1923- CANR-10
Earlier sketch in CA 25-28R
Tucker, Gabe
See Tucker, Gaylord B(ob)
Tucker, Gaylord B(ob) 1915- 110
Tucker, Gene M(ilton) 1935- CANR-15
Earlier sketch in CA 37-40R
Tucker, George 1775-1861 DLB 3, 30, 248
Tucker, Georgina P. 1911- 97-100
Tucker, Gina
See Tucker, Georgina P.
Tucker, Glenn (Irving) 1892-1976 5-8R
Obituary 69-72
Tucker, Graham Harold 1925- 113
Tucker, Harry, Jr. 1921- 41-44R
Tucker, Helen 1926- CANR-11
Earlier sketch in CA 29-32R
Tucker, Herbert F(rederick) 1949- 189
Tucker, Irwin St. John 1886-1982
Obituary 105
Tucker, James 1808-1866 DLB 230
Tucker, James 1929- CANR-9
Earlier sketch in CA 21-24R
See also CMW 4
Tucker, John C. 1934- 170
Tucker, Jonathan B(rin) 1954- CANR-118
Earlier sketch in CA 109
Tucker, Karen 143
Tucker, Lael
See Wertenbaker, Lael (Tucker)
Tucker, Link
See Bingley, David Ernest
Tucker, Lisa 226
Tucker, Marcia 1940- 65-68
Tucker, Mark (D.) 1954-2000 155
Obituary 191
Tucker, Martin 1928- 17-20R
Tucker, Maurice E. 1946- 220
Tucker, Melvin J(ay) 1931- 113
Tucker, Michael R(ay) 1941- CANR-12
Earlier sketch in CA 61-64
Tucker, Nathaniel Beverley 1784-1851 DLB 3, 248
Tucker, Nicholas 1936- CANR-11
Earlier sketch in CA 65-68
Tucker, Patricia 1912-1999 65-68
Tucker, Paul Hayes 1950- CANR-99
Earlier sketch in CA 110
Tucker, Robert C(harles) 1918- CANR-3
Earlier sketch in CA 1-4R
Tucker, Robert W(arren) 1924- 134
Tucker, Robin 1950- 53-56
Tucker, Ruth A(nne) 1945- CANR-143
Earlier sketches in CA 117, CANR-40
Tucker, St. George 1752-1827 DLB 37
Tucker, Spencer (C.) 1937- CANR-121
Earlier sketches in CA 146, CANR-120
Tucker, Susan (Norris) 1950- 130
Tucker, Terry Ward 174
Tucker, Toba Pato 1935- 195
Tucker, Wallace H. 1939- 121
Tucker, William 1942- 163
Tucker, William E(dward) 1932- CANR-3
Earlier sketch in CA 9-12R
Tucker, William R(ayburn) 1923- 61-64
Tucker, (Arthur) Wilson 1914- 17-20R
See also SFW 4
Tucker-Fettner, Ann
See Giudici, Ann Couper
Tuckerman, Frederick Goddard 1821-1873 DLB 243
See also RGAL 4
Tuckerman, Henry Theodore 1813-1871 DLB 64, 254
Tuckett, Christopher M(ark) 220
Tuckey, John S(utton) 1921-1987 CANR-7
Earlier sketch in CA 5-8R
Tuckman, Bruce W(ayne) 1938- CANR-11
Earlier sketch in CA 25-28R
Tuckman, Howard P(aul) 1941- CANR-10
Earlier sketch in CA 57-60
Tuckner, Howard 1932(?)-1980
Obituary 101
Tudge, Colin 1943- CANR-103
Earlier sketch in CA 154
Tudhope, Richard
See Rodda, Peter (Gordon)
Tudor, Andrew Frank 1942- 107
Tudor, Dean 1943- CANR-8
Earlier sketch in CA 61-64
Tudor, Henry 1937- 147
Tudor, Nancy (Patricia Rice)
Brief entry 109
See also Krygsman, Nancy (Patricia Rice)
Tudor, Stephen H. 1933-1994 217
Tudor, Tasha 1915- 81-84
See also CLR 13
See also MAICYA 1, 2
See also SATA 20, 69, 160
Tudor-Craig, Pamela 1928- 124
Tudyman, Al 1914- 21-24R
Tuell, Jack Marvin 1923- 29-32R
Tuell, Steven S(hawn) 1956- 234
Tueni, Nadia (Hamade) 1935-1983
Obituary 110
Tuerck, David G(eorge) 1941- CANR-14
Earlier sketch in CA 21-24R
Tuerk, Hanne 1951- CANR-45
Earlier sketch in CA 118
See also SATA 71
Tufail, Muhammad 1921(?)-1984
Obituary 113
Tuffs, J(ack) Elsden 1922- 5-8R
Tufte, Edward R(olf) 1942- CANR-81
Earlier sketches in CA 49-52, CANR-1
Tufte, Virginia J(ames) 1918- 125
Brief entry 106
Tufts, Eleanor (May) 1927-1991 CANR-86
Obituary 136
Earlier sketch in CA 77-80
Tufty, Barbara 1923- 37-40R
Tufty, Esther Van Wagoner 1896-1986
Obituary 119

Tu Fu 712-770
See Du Fu
See also DAM MULT
See also PC 9
See also TWA
See also WP
Tugay, Emine Foat
See Foat Tugay, Emine
Tugend, Harry 1898(?)-1989
Obituary ... 129
Tugendhat, Christopher Samuel 1937- ... 89-92
Tuggener, Jakob 1904-1988 ... 224
Tuggle, Ann Montgomery 1942- ... 125
Tuggle, Richard (Allan) 1948- ... 139
Tuggy, Joy Turner 1922- ... 21-24R
Tugwell, Franklin 1942- ... 57-60
Tugwell, Rexford Guy 1891-1979 ... 85-88
Obituary ... 89-92
Tulasiewicz, J(an) B(runo) 1913-1981 ... 41-44R
Tulchin, Joseph S(amuel) 1939- ... 37-40R
Tulchin, Lewis 1905-1971 ... CAP-1
Earlier sketch in CA 19-20
Tulchinsky, Karen X. ... CANR-140
Earlier sketch in CA 174
Tuleja, Tad
See Tuleja, Thaddeus F(rancis)
Tuleja, Thaddeus F(rancis) 1944- ... 108
Tuli, Felix
See Wuolijoki, Hella
Tulis, Jeffrey K. 1950- ... CANR-56
Earlier sketches in CA 111, CANR-30
Tull, Charles Joseph 1931- ... 17-20R
Tull, Delena 1950- ... 125
Tull, Donald S(tanley) 1924- ... 81-84
Tull, James E. 1913-1989 ... CANR-13
Earlier sketch in CA 77-80
Tuller, Lawrence W. 1933- ... 145
Tullett, James Stuart 1912-1992 ... 106
Tullis, F. LaMond 1935- ... 81-84
Tulloch, G(ertrude) Janet 1924-2000 ... 65-68
Obituary ... 189
Tulloch, Lee 1954(?)- ... 220
Tulloch, Richard (George) 1949- ... 143
See also SATA 76
Tullock, Gordon 1922- ... CANR-3
Earlier sketch in CA 1-4R
Tullos, Allen 1950- ... 132
Tully, Andrew (Frederick, Jr.)
1914-1993 ... CANR-86
Obituary ... 142
Earlier sketch in CA 17-20R
Tully, Gordon F(rederick) 1935- ... 106
Tully, Grace George 1900-1984
Obituary ... 113
Tully, James (Hamilton) 1946- ... 222
Tully, John (Kimberley) 1923- ... CANR-53
Earlier sketches in CA 69-72, CANR-12, 28
See also SATA 14
Tully, (William) Mark 1935- ... 136
Tully, Mary Jo 1937- ... CANR-22
Earlier sketch in CA 105
Tully, Paul
See Gardner, Jerome
Tulsidas, Gosvami 1532(?)-1623 ... RGWL 2, 3
Tuma, Elias H. 1928-
Brief entry ... 115
Tuman, Myron C(hester) 1946- ... 139
Tumanov, Vladimir A. 1961- ... 209
See also SATA 138
Tumanova, Alla 1931- ... 217
Tumas, Juozas
See Vaizgantas
Tumay, Paulett 1945- ... 128
Tumelty, James J. 1921(?)-1979(?)
Obituary ... 104
Tumin, Melvin M(arvin) 1919-1994 .. CANR-86
Obituary ... 144
Earlier sketch in CA 45-48
Tumpson, Helen ... AITN 1
Tunbjork, Lars 1956- ... 214
Tung, Angela 1972- ... 180
See also SATA 109
Tung, Ling
See Tung, William L(ing)
Tung, Shih-tsin (Shih-chin) 1900-1984 ... 5-8R
Tung, William L(ing) 1907- ... 85-88
Tunick, Irve 1912-1987
Obituary ... 123
Tunick, Stanley B(loch) 1900-1988 ... CAP-1
Earlier sketch in CA 17-18
Tunink, Wilfrid Bernard 1920- ... 5-8R
Tunis, Edwin (Burdett) 1897-1973 ... CANR-7
Obituary ... 45-48
Earlier sketch in CA 5-8R
See also CLR 2
See also MAICYA 1, 2
See also SATA 1, 28
See also SATA-Obit 24
Tunis, John R(oberts) 1889-1975 ... CANR-62
Earlier sketch in CA 61-64
See also BYA 1
See also CLC 12
See also DLB 22, 171
See also JRDA
See also MAICYA 1, 2
See also SATA 37
See also SATA-Brief 30
See also YAW
Tunley, Roul 1912- ... 13-16R
Tunnadine, Prudence 1928- ... 129
Tunnard, Christopher 1910-1979 ... CANR-6
Obituary ... 85-88
Earlier sketch in CA 5-8R
Tunnell, Doug(las Alan) 1949- ... 97-100
Tunnell, Michael
See Tunnell, Michael O('Grady)
Tunnell, Michael O('Grady) 1950- . CANR-137
Earlier sketch in CA 170
See also SATA 103, 157
Tunner, William H(enry) 1906-1983 . CANR-86
Obituary ... 109
Earlier sketches in CAP-1, CA 13-16
Tunney, Gene
See Tunney, James Joseph
Tunney, James Joseph 1898(?)-1978
Obituary ... 111
Tunney, John V(arick) 1934- ... 61-64
Tunney, Kieran 1922-1998 ... 117
Tunnicliffe, C(harles) F(rederick)
1901-1979 ... 104
See also SATA 62
Tunstall, C. Jeremy 1934- ... CANR-42
Earlier sketches in CA 5-8R, CANR-4, 20
Tunstall, Cuthbert 1474-1559 ... DLB 132
Tunstall, Shana Barrett
See Tunstall, Velma
Tunstall, Velma 1914-1980 ... 53-56
Tunstroem, Goeran
See Tunstrom, Goran
Tunstrom, Goran 1937-2000 ... 192
See also DLB 257
Tunyogi, Andrew C(sapo) 1907-1984 ... CAP-2
Earlier sketch in CA 29-32
Tuohy, Frank
See Tuohy, John Francis
See also CLC 37
See also CN 1, 2, 3, 4, 5, 6, 7
See also DLB 14, 139
Tuohy, John Francis 1925- ... CANR-47
Obituary ... 178
Earlier sketches in CA 5-8R, CANR-3
See also Tuohy, Frank
Tuohy, William 1941- ... 37-40R
Tuohy, William Klaus 1926- ... 104
Tuohy, William S. 1938- ... 41-44R
Tupitsyn, Margarita 1955- ... 157
Tuplin, W(illiam) A(lfred) 1902-1975
Obituary ... 111
Tupper, Margo (Browne) 1919-1995 ... 17-20R
Obituary ... 148
Tupper, Martin (Farquhar) 1810-1889 ... RGEL 2
Tupper, Martin F. 1810-1889 ... DLB 32
Tuqan, Fadwa 1917-2003 ... 231
Tur, Evgeniia 1815-1892 ... DLB 238
Turabian, Kate L(arimore) 1893-1987
Obituary ... 123
Turan, Kenneth 1946- ... CANR-121
Earlier sketch in CA 132
Turbayne, Colin Murray 1916- ... CANR-24
Earlier sketch in CA 1-4R
Turbervile, George c. 1543-c. 1597 ... RGEL 2
Turbet, Richard 1948- ... 141
Turbeville, Deborah 1937- ... 214
Turbyfill, Mark 1896-1990 ... 108
See also DLB 45
Turchin, Valentin F(yodorovich) 1931- ... 101
Turck, Mary C. 1950- ... 217
See also SATA 144
Turco, Lewis (Putnam) 1934- ... CANR-51
Earlier sketches in CA 13-16R, CANR-24
See also CAAS 22
See also CLC 11, 63
See also CP 1, 2, 3, 4, 5, 6, 7
See also DLBY 1984
See also TCLE 1:2
Turco, Mary ... 206
Turco, Richard (Peter) 1943- ... 135
Turcotte, Gerry 1960- ... 212
Ture, Kwame 1941-1998
See Carmichael, Stokely
Turell, Dan
See Turell, Dan
Turell, Dan 1946-1993 ... EWL 3
Turell, Saul J. 1921-1986
Obituary ... 120
Turetzky, Bertram Jay 1933- ... 57-60
Turgenev, Aleksandr Ivanovich
1784-1845 ... DLB 198
Turgenev, Ivan (Sergeevich)
1818-1883 ... AAYA 58
See also DA
See also DAB
See also DAC
See also DAM MST, NOV
See also DC 7
See also DFS 6
See also DLB 238, 284
See also EW 6
See also LATS 1:1
See also NFS 16
See also RGSF 2
See also RGWL 2, 3
See also SSC 7, 57
See also TWA
See also WLC
Turgeon, Charlotte Snyder 1912- ... CANR-3
Earlier sketch in CA 5-8R
Turgeon, Lynn 1920-1999 ... 5-8R
Obituary ... 179
Turgeon, Pierre 1947- ... 163
Turgot, Anne-Robert-Jacques
1727-1781 ... DLB 314
Turiel, Isaac 1941- ... 122
Turing, John (Ferrier) 1908- ... CAP-2
Earlier sketch in CA 25-28
Turing, Penelope (Anne Tryon)
1925- ... CANR-90
Earlier sketch in CA 132
Turk, Dennis C. 1946- ... 221
Turk, Eleanor L. 1935- ... 194
Turk, Frances (Mary) 1915- ... CAP-1
Earlier sketch in CA 9-10
Turk, Hanne
See Tuerk, Hanne
Turk, Herman 1929- ... 45-48
Turk, Laurel H(erbert) 1903-1999 ... 21-24R
Turk, Midge
See Richardson, Midge Turk
Turk, Rudy H(enry) 1927- ... 97-100
Turk, Ruth 1917- ... CANR-135
Earlier sketch in CA 149
See also SATA 82
Turkel, Christopher 1955(?)-1983
Obituary ... 110
Turkel, Pauline
See Kesselman-Turkel, Judi
Turkel, Robin R. 1929(?)-1984
Obituary ... 113
Turkevich, Ludmilla Buketoff 1909-1995 .. 5-8R
Obituary ... 148
Turki, Fawaz 1940- ... 41-44R
Turkle, Brinton 1915- ... 25-28R
See also CWRI 5
See also MAICYA 2
See also MAICYAS 1
See also SATA 2, 79
Turkle, Sherry 1948- ... 102
Turkus, Burton B. 1902-1982
Obituary ... 108
Turley, Gerald H. 1931- ... 136
Turley, William S(tephen) 1943- ... CANR-21
Earlier sketch in CA 105
Turlington, Bayly 1919-1977 ... CANR-86
Obituary ... 122
Earlier sketch in CA 29-32R
See also SATA 5
See also SATA-Obit 52
Turlington, Catherine (Isabel) Hackett
1900(?)-1978
Obituary ... 77-80
Turlington, Henry E. 1918- ... 21-24R
Turnage, Anne Shaw 1927- ... 77-80
Turnage, Mac(lyn) N(eil) 1927- ... 77-80
Turnbaugh, William A(rthur) 1948- ... CANR-58
Earlier sketches in CA 112, CANR-31
Turnbull, Agnes Sligh 1888-1982 ... CANR-86
Obituary ... 105
Earlier sketches in CA 1-4R, CANR-2
See also SATA 14
Turnbull, Alexander H. 1868-1918 ... DLB 184
Turnbull, Andrew Winchester
1921-1970 ... CANR-3
Obituary ... 25-28R
Earlier sketch in CA 1-4R
See also DLB 103
Turnbull, Ann (Christine) 1943- ... 65-68
See also SATA 18, 160
Turnbull, Bob 1936- ... CANR-14
Earlier sketch in CA 37-40R
Turnbull, Colin M(acmillan)
1924-1994 ... CANR-3
Obituary ... 146
Earlier sketch in CA 1-4R
See also AITN 1
Turnbull, Gael Lundin 1928-2004 ... CANR-10
Obituary ... 230
Earlier sketch in CA 65-68
See also CAAS 14
See also CP 1, 2, 3, 4, 5, 6, 7
See also DLB 40
Turnbull, John G. 1913-1994 ... 1-4R
Turnbull, Malcolm John 1952- ... 197
Turnbull, Patrick Edward Xenophon
1908-1986 ... CANR-6
Earlier sketch in CA 5-8R
Turnbull, Peter (John) 1950- ... CANR-126
Earlier sketches in CA 130, CANR-74
See also CMW 4
Turnbull, Stephen (Richard) 1948- ... CANR-20
Earlier sketch in CA 104
Turnell, (George) Martin 1908-1979 . CANR-86
Obituary ... 103
Earlier sketch in CA 45-48
Turner, A(lmon) Richard 1932- ... 17-20R
Turner, Alberta Tucker 1919- ... CANR-17
Earlier sketches in CA 49-52, CANR-1
Turner, Alice K. 1940- ... 53-56
See also SATA 10
Turner, Amedee E. 1929- ... 9-12R
Turner, Ann W(arren) 1945- ... CANR-58
Earlier sketches in CA 69-72, CANR-14, 31
See also BYA 8
See also CWRI 5
See also SATA 14, 77, 113
Turner, (Henry) Arlin 1909-1980 ... CANR-6
Obituary ... 97-100
Earlier sketch in CA 5-8R
See also DLB 103
Turner, Arnella K. 1917- ... 138
Turner, Arthur C(ampbell) 1918- ... 17-20R
Turner, B. L. II 1945- ... 142
Turner, Barbara ... 171
Turner, Bessye Tobias 1917- ... 53-56
Turner, Bill
See Turner, W(illiam) Price
Turner, Bonnie 1932- ... 142
See also SATA 75
Turner, Brian (Lindsay) 1944- ... CANR-117
Earlier sketch in CA 154
See also CP 7
Turner, Bruce (Malcolm) 1922- ... 132
Turner, Bryan S(tanley) 1945- ... 115
Turner, Carole S(tevenson) 1949- ... 187
Turner, Charles (Tennyson) 1808-1879 .. DLB 32
Turner, Charles L. 1948- ... 167
Turner, Charles W(ilson) 1916- ... CANR-30
Earlier sketches in CA 37-40R, CANR-13
Turner, Clair (Elsmere) 1890-1974 ... CAP-1
Earlier sketch in CA 9-10
Turner, Clay
See Ballard, (Willis) Todhunter
Turner, D(avid) Harold 1912- ... 117
Turner, Daniel F(rank) 1947- ... 97-100
Turner, Darwin T(heodore Troy)
1931-1991 ... CANR-85
Obituary ... 133
Earlier sketches in CA 21-24R, CANR-11
See also BW 1
Turner, David 1927-1990 ... CBD
Turner, David R(euben) 1915- ... 57-60
Turner, Dean (Edson) 1927- ... 29-32R
Turner, Dennis C(lair) 1948- ... 61-64
Turner, Dona M. 1951- ... 103
Turner, E(rnest) S(ackville) 1909- ... 113
Turner, Edward R(euben) A(rthur) 1924- .. 81-84
Turner, Elizabeth 1774-1846 ... YABC 2
Turner, Eloise Fain 1906-1991 ... 5-8R
Turner, Eric Gardner 1911-1983
Obituary ... 109
Turner, Ethel (Sybil) 1872-1958 ... 202
Brief entry ... 111
See also DLB 230
Turner, Florence (Hayes) 1919- ... 128
Turner, Francis Joseph (Michael)
1929- ... CANR-22
Earlier sketch in CA 69-72
Turner, Frank M(iller) 1944- ... 220
Turner, Frederick (William III) 1937- . CANR-34
Earlier sketches in CA 37-40R, CANR-15
Turner, Frederick 1943- ... 227
Earlier sketches in CA 73-76, CANR-12, 30, 56
Autobiographical Essay in ... 227
See also CAAS 10
See also CLC 48
See also DLB 40, 282
Turner, Frederick C(lair) 1938- ... CANR-28
Earlier sketch in CA 25-28R
Turner, Frederick Jackson 1861-1932
Brief entry ... 113
See also DLB 17, 186
Turner, Georg
See Rehfisch, Hans Jose
Turner, George (Reginald)
1916-1997 ... CANR-21
Earlier sketch in CA 103
See also CN 1, 2, 3, 4, 5, 6
See also SFW 4
Turner, George Allen 1908-1998 ... CANR-10
Earlier sketch in CA 13-16R
Turner, George E(ugene) 1925-1999 ... CANR-5
Obituary ... 181
Earlier sketch in CA 53-56
Turner, George W(illiam)
1921-2003 ... CANR-49
Obituary ... 222
Earlier sketches in CA 104, CANR-24
Turner, Gladys T(ressia) 1935- ... CANR-13
Earlier sketch in CA 77-80
Turner, Glennette Tilley 1933- ... 133
See also SATA 71
Turner, Graham 1932- ... CANR-14
Earlier sketch in CA 21-24R
Turner, Guinevere 1968(?)- ... 147
Turner, Gwenda 1947-2001 ... CANR-42
Earlier sketch in CA 118
Turner, H(arold) W(alter) 1911- ... CANR-10
Earlier sketch in CA 21-24R
Turner, Henry Andrew, Jr. 1919-1998 ... 9-12R
Turner, Henry Ashby, Jr. 1932- ... CANR-106
Earlier sketches in CA 49-52, CANR-94
Turner, Henry Dicken 1919- ... 61-64
Turner, Henry Ernest William
1907-1995 ... CAP-1
Obituary ... 150
Earlier sketch in CA 9-10
Turner, Herbert Snipes 1891-1976 ... 41-44R
Turner, Howard M(oore), Jr. 1918- ... 13-16R
Turner, Hy B(enjamin) 1917- ... 187
Turner, J. M. W. 1775-1851 ... AAYA 57
Turner, J. Scott 1951- ... 196
Turner, James (Ernest) 1909-1975 ... HGG
Turner, Jamie Langston 1949- ... 212
Turner, John Elliot 1917- ... CANR-3
Earlier sketch in CA 5-8R
Turner, John F(reeland) 1942- ... 97-100
Turner, John Frayn 1923- ... CANR-3
Earlier sketch in CA 9-12R
Turner, John H(enry) 1938- ... 77-80
Turner, Jonathan H. 1942- ... CANR-14
Earlier sketches in CA 37-40R, CANR-32
Turner, Joseph Addison 1826-1868 ... DLB 79
Turner, Josie
See Crawford, Phyllis
Turner, Judy
See Saxton, Judith
Turner, Justin G(eorge) 1898-1976 ... CANR-32
Earlier sketch in CA 41-44R
Turner, Katharine Charlotte 1910-2001 .. CAP-2
Earlier sketch in CA 23-24
Turner, Kathleen J. 1952- ... 138
Turner, Kay 1932- ... 69-72
Turner, Kermit 1936- ... 104
Turner, L(eonard) C(harles) F(rederick)
1914- ... 29-32R
Turner, Len
See Floren, Lee
Turner, Lloyd 1924-1992 ... 103
Interview in ... CA-103
Turner, Louis (Mark) 1942- ... CANR-34
Earlier sketches in CA 37-40R, CANR-15
Turner, Lowell 1947- ... 138
Turner, Lynn Warren 1906-1982 ... 5-8R
Turner, Marjorie S. 1921- ... 145
Turner, Mark ... 216

Turner, Martha Anne (Bonner) 1904-1985 .. 134
Obituary 117
Turner, Martin 1948- 142
Turner, Mary
See Lambot, Isobel
Turner, Mason 1914- 123
Turner, Megan Whalen 1965- 156
See also AAYA 31
See also BYA 9, 14
See also SATA 94
Turner, Merfyn (Lloyd) 1915-1991 104
Obituary 135
Turner, Morrie
See Turner, Morris
Turner, Morris 1923- CANR-15
Earlier sketch in CA 29-32R
Turner, Mrs. G. D.
See Wilson, Margaret (Wilhelmina)
Turner, Myron 1935- 112
Turner, Nancy E(laine) 1953- 212
Turner, Nancy J. 1947- 142
Turner, Paul Digby Lowry 1917- 105
Turner, Paul R(aymond) 1929- 45-48
Turner, Paul V(enable) 236
Turner, Peter Paul
See Jeffery, Grant
Turner, Philip (William) 1925- CANR-27
Earlier sketches in CA 25-28R, CANR-11
See also CLR 89
See also CWRI 5
See also SAAS 6
See also SATA 11, 83
Turner, Ralph 1936-
Brief entry 107
Turner, Ralph H(erbert) 1919- 37-40R
Turner, Ralph Lilley 1888-1983 .... 5-8R
Obituary 109
Turner, Ralph V(ernon) 1939- 77-80
Turner, Richard Brent 1951- 165
Turner, Richard E(ugene) 1920- 29-32R
Turner, Robert (Harry) 1915-1980 .... CANR-1
Earlier sketch in CA 45-48
Turner, Robert C(lemens) 1908-1978 77-80
Turner, Robert Edward III 1938(?)- 120
Turner, Robert F(oster) 1944- CANR-30
Earlier sketches in CA 77-80, CANR-13
Turner, Robert Kean, Jr. 1926- 17-20R
Turner, Robert Y(ongue) 1927-
Brief entry 110
Turner, Robyn 1947- 145
See also SATA 77
Turner, Roger (Humphrey George) 1943- 123
Turner, Roland 1943- 106
Turner, Ronald Cordell 1939- 41-44R
Turner, Sheila
See Rowbotham, Sheila
Turner, Sheila 1906- CAP-1
Earlier sketch in CA 13-14
Turner, Sheila R.
See Seed, Sheila Turner
Turner, Silvie 1946- 117
Turner, Stansfield 1923- CANR-95
Brief entry 118
Earlier sketch in CA 124
Interview in CA-124
Turner, Stephen P(ark) 1951- CANR-86
Earlier sketches in CA 122, CANR-48
Turner, Steve
See Turner, Stephen P(ark)
Turner, (Clarence) Steven 1923- 29-32R
Turner, Susan 1952- 106
Turner, T. H. D. 1946- 122
Turner, Ted
See Turner, Robert Edward III
Turner, Thomas B(ourne) 1902-2002 ..... 41-44R
Obituary 209
Turner, Thomas Coleman 1927- 5-8R
Turner, Thomas N(oel) 1940- 113
Turner, Tina 1939- 147
Turner, Tom
See Turner, T. H. D.
Turner, Tom 1942- 136
Turner, Victor Witter 1920-1983 .... CANR-3
Obituary 111
Earlier sketch in CA 5-8R
Turner, Violet Bender 1902(?)-1990
Obituary 130
Turner, W(illiam) Price 1927- CANR-16
Earlier sketch in CA 21-24R
See also CP 1, 2
Turner, Wallace 1921- 17-20R
Turner, Wesley B. 1933- 230
Turner, William F. 1936(?)-1989
Obituary 130
Turner, William O(liver) 1914-1980 . CANR-64
Earlier sketches in CA 1-4R, CANR-3
See also AITN 1
See also TCWW 2
Turner, William W. 1927- CANR-12
Earlier sketch in CA 25-28R
Turney, Alfred (Walter) 1916- 73-76
Turney, Catherine 1906-1998 101
Obituary 172
Turney, Denise
See Campbell, Rhonda
Turney, Jon 176
Turngren, Annette 1902(?)-1980 .... 9-12R
Obituary 101
See also SATA-Obit 23
Turngren, Ellen (?)-1964 .... 5-8R
See also SATA 3
Turnill, Reginald 1915- CANR-15
Earlier sketch in CA 37-40R
Turnipseed, Erica Simone 1971- 226
Turnipseed, Joel 1968- 229
Turnock, David 1938- 109
Turnstile, Magnus
See Baistow, (Enoch) Thomas
Turock, Betty J(ane) CANR-30
Earlier sketch in CA 110
Turow, Joseph G(regory) 1950- CANR-57
Earlier sketches in CA 111, CANR-30
Turow, Rita P(astron) 1919- 101
Turow, Scott 1949- CANR-137
Earlier sketches in CA 73-76, CANR-40, 65, 111
See also AAYA 53
See also BEST 90:3
See also BPFB 3
See also CMW 4
See also CPW
See also DA3
See also DAM POP
See also MSW
See also MTCW 2
See also MTFW 2005
Turpin, James W(esley) 1927- 21-24R
Turpin, Jennifer 1961- 148
Turpin, Lorna 1950- 107
Turpin, Waters Edward 1910-1968 125
See also BW 1
See also DLB 51
Turrill, David A. 239
Turrini, Peter 1944- 209
See also DLB 124
Turska, Krystyna (Zofia) 1933- 106
See also SATA 31
See also SATA-Brief 27
Tursten, Helene 1954- 224
Tursun-Zade, Mirzo 1911-1977
Obituary 104
See also Tursunzoda, Mirzo
Tursunzoda, Mirzo
See Tursun-Zade, Mirzo
See also EWL 3
Turteltaub, H. N.
See Turtledove, Harry (Norman)
Turtledove, Harry (Norman) 1949- ... CANR-93
Earlier sketch in CA 153
See also AAYA 33
See also FANT
See also SATA 116
See also SFW 4
Turton, Godfrey (Edmund) 1901- 21-24R
Turton, James
See Crace, Jim
Turton-Jones, Edith Constance (Bradshaw) 1904-1968 .... CAP-1
Earlier sketch in CA 9-10
Turville-Petre, Edward Oswald Gabriel 1908-1978 .... 9-12R
Obituary 77-80
Turyn, Alexander 1900-1981
Obituary 104
Tusa, Ann 160
Tusa, Bobs M. 230
Tusa, John, (Jr.) 1936- CANR-88
Earlier sketch in CA 127
Tusa, Michael C(harles) 1953- 142
Tusa, Tricia 1960- 182
See also SATA 72, 111
Tusan, Stan 1936- 105
Tushingham, A(rlotte) Douglas 1914-2002 .... 41-44R
Obituary 205
Tushnet, Leonard 1908-1973 .... CAP-1
Obituary 45-48
Earlier sketch in CA 13-16
Tushnet, Mark V(ictor) 1945- CANR-112
Earlier sketch in CA 126
Tusiani, Joseph 1924- CANR-43
Earlier sketches in CA 9-12R, CANR-5, 20
See also SATA 45
Tuska, Jon 1942- CANR-13
Earlier sketch in CA 73-76
Tusquets (Guillen), Esther 1936- .... CWW 2
See also DLB 322
Tusser, Thomas c. 1524-1580 .... RGEL 2
Tussing, A(ubrey) Dale 1935- 17-20R
Tutaev, David 1916- 21-24R
Tute, Warren (Stanley) 1914- CANR-1
Earlier sketch in CA 1-4R
Tuten, Frederic 1936- CANR-120
Earlier sketch in CA 37-40R
Tuthill, John Wills 1910-1996 108
Obituary 153
Tutin, Thomas Gaskell 1908-1987
Obituary 123
Tutko, Thomas A(rthur) 1931- 69-72
Tutorow, Norman E. 1934- CANR-29
Earlier sketch in CA 25-28R
Tuttle, Alva M(aurice) 1900-1980 .... 5-8R
Tuttle, Day
See Tuttle, (Frank) Day, Jr.
Tuttle, (Frank) Day, Jr. 1902-1989 116
Tuttle, Frank W(aldo) 1896-1983 61-64
Tuttle, Howard Nelson 1935- 41-44R
Tuttle, Lisa 1952- 126
See also HGG
See also SFW 4
See also SUFW 2
Tuttle, Russell (Howard) 1939- 77-80
Tuttle, W(ilbur) C(oleman) 1883-1969(?) CANR-64
Earlier sketches in CAP-2, CA 21-22
See also TCWW 1, 2
Tuttle, William M., Jr. 1937- CANR-107
Earlier sketches in CA 29-32R, CANR-11
Tuttleton, James Welsey 1934-1998 ...... 41-44R
Tutu, Desmond M(pilo) 1931- CANR-81
Earlier sketches in CA 125, CANR-67
See also BLC 3
See also BW 1, 3
See also CLC 80
See also DAM MULT
Tutuola, Amos 1920-1997 .... CANR-66
Obituary 159
Earlier sketches in CA 9-12R, CANR-27
See also AFW
See also BLC 3
See also BW 2, 3
See also CDWLB 3
See also CLC 5, 14, 29
See also CN 1, 2, 3, 4, 5, 6
See also DA3
See also DAM MULT
See also DLB 125
See also DNFS 2
See also EWL 3
See also MTCW 1, 2
See also MTFW 2005
See also RGEL 2
See also WLIT 2
Tuuri, Anti 1944- 194
See also Tuuri, Antti
Tuuri, Antti
See Tuuri, Anti
See also EWL 3
Tuve, Merle Antony 1901-1982
Obituary 106
Tuve, Rosemond 1903-1964 .... CAP-1
Earlier sketch in CA 9-10
Tuveson, Ernest (Lee) 1915-1996 .... 17-20R
Tuwhare, Hone 1922- 103
See also CP 1, 2, 3, 4, 5, 6, 7
See also EWL 3
Tuwim, Julian 1894-1953 .... EWL 3
Tuzin, Donald F(rancis) 1945- 106
Tvardovsky, Alexandr Trifonovich 1910-1971 102
Obituary 33-36R
See also EWL 3
Twaddell, Kristie
See Miller, Kristie
Twaddell, W(illiam) F(reeman) 1906-1982 .... CANR-32
Earlier sketch in CA 81-84
Twaddle, Andrew C. 1938- 120
Twain, Mark
See Clemens, Samuel Langhorne
See also AAYA 20
See also AMW
See also AMWC 1
See also BPFB 3
See also BYA 2, 3, 11, 14
See also CLR 58, 60, 66
See also DLB 11
See also EXPN
See also EXPS
See also FANT
See also LAIT 2
See also MAL 5
See also NCFS 4
See also NFS 1, 6
See also RGAL 4
See also RGSF 2
See also SFW 4
See also SSC 6, 26, 34
See also SSFS 1, 7, 16, 21
See also SUFW
See also TCLC 6, 12, 19, 36, 48, 59, 161
See also TUS
See also WCH
See also WLC
See also WYA
See also YAW
Twark, Allan J(oseph) 1931- 49-52
Twedt, Dik Warren 1920-1985 .... CANR-14
Obituary 115
Earlier sketch in CA 37-40R
Tweed, Stephen C. 1949- 133
Tweed, Thomas A. 1954- 137
Tweedale, Douglas 1958(?)-1990
Obituary 132
Tweedale, J.
See Bickle, Judith Brundrett
Tweedale, Violet (Chambers) 1862-1936
Brief entry 116
Tweedie, Donald F(erguson), Jr. 1926- .. 13-16R
Tweedie, Ethel Brilliana c. 1860-1940 .... DLB 174
Tweeten, Luther 1931- 89-92
Tweit, Susan J(oan) 1956- 151
See also SATA 94
Twelveponies, Mary
See Cleveland, Mary
Twemlow, Stuart W(est) 1941- 128
Twersky, Isadore 1930-1997 120
Obituary 162
Twersky, Jacob 1920- 49-52
Tweton, D. Jerome 1933- .... SATA 48
Twichell, Chase 1950- CANR-56
Earlier sketch in CA 127
See also CP 7
See also CWP
Twigg, Alan (Robert) 1952- 125
Twigger, Robert 1964- 236
Twiggy
See Hornby, Leslie
Twin, Stephanie L. 1948- 101
Twinam, Ann 1946- 187
Twiname, Eric 1942(?)-1980
Obituary 102
Twine, France Winddance 175
Twine, Francine Winddance
See Twine, France Winddance
Twinem, Neecy 1958- .... SATA 92
Twining, Nathan F(arragut) 1897-1982
Obituary 106
Twining, William (Lawrence) 1934- CANR-115
Earlier sketches in CA 123, CANR-51
Twisleton-Wykeham-Fiennes, Richard Nathaniel 1909-1988 .... CANR-11
Earlier sketch in CA 21-24R
Twiss, Sumner B(arnes), Jr. 1944- 184
Brief entry 114
Twist, Ananias
See Nunn, William Curtis
Twiston Davies, David 1945- 199
Twitchell, James B(uell) 1943- CANR-90
Earlier sketches in CA 118, CANR-43
Twitchell, Paul 1908(?)-1971 132
Obituary 111
Twitchett, Carol Cosgrove 1943- CANR-26
Earlier sketch in CA 29-32R
Twitchett, Denis Crispin 1925-
Brief entry 106
Twohig, Elizabeth Shee 1946- 132
Twohill, Maggie
See Gaberman, Judie Angell
Twohy, David 167
Two Ladies of England
See Moore, Doris Langley
Twombly, Robert C(harles) 1940- ... CANR-127
Earlier sketch in CA 85-88
Twombly, Wells A. 1935-1977 .... CANR-137
Obituary 69-72
Earlier sketch in CA 41-44R
See also DLB 241
Two-Rivers, E(dmund) Donald 1945- 202
Tworkov, Jack 1900-1982
Obituary 107
See also SATA 47
See also SATA-Obit 31
Twyman, Gib
See Twyman, Gilbert Oscar III
Twyman, Gilbert Oscar III 1943- 109
Twysden, Sir Roger 1597-1672 .... DLB 213
Ty, Eleanor 1958- 188
Tyard, Pontus de 1522-1605 .... GFL Beginnings to 1789
Ty-Casper, Linda 1931- CANR-105
Earlier sketches in CA 107, CANR-24, 50
See also DLB 312
See also EWL 3
See also RGSF 2
Tychyna, Pavlo Hryhorovych 1891-1967 .... EW 10
Tyde, Eddie
See Meades, Jonathan (Turner)
Tydeman, William (Marcus) 1935- ... CANR-90
Earlier sketches in CA 119, CANR-43
Tydings, Joseph D(avies) 1928- 29-32R
Tye, Larry 192
Tye, Michael 1950- 158
Tyer, Shirley
See Coscarelli, Kate
Tyerman, Christopher 1953- 208
Tyerman, Hugo 1880-1977
Obituary 77-80
Tyers, Jenny 1969- .... SATA 89
Tyers, Kathy 1952- 149
See also SATA 82
See also SFW 4
Tygiel, Jules 1949- CANR-98
Earlier sketch in CA 132
Tyl, Noel 1936- 93-96
Tylden-Wright, David 1923- 25-28R
Tyldesley, Joyce (Ann) 1960- CANR-107
Earlier sketch in CA 155
Tylecote, Mabel (Phythian) 1896-1987 .. CAP-1
Obituary 121
Earlier sketch in CA 13-14
Tylecote, R(onald) F(rank) 1916-1990
Obituary 132
Tyler, A. E.
See Armstrong, (Annette) Elizabeth
Tyler, Alison
See Title, Elise
Tyler, Anne 1941- CANR-132
Earlier sketches in CA 9-12R, CANR-11, 33, 53, 109
See also AAYA 18, 60
See also AMWS 4
See also BEST 89:1
See also BPFB 3
See also BYA 12
See also CDALBS
See also CLC 7, 11, 18, 28, 44, 59, 103, 205
See also CN 1, 2, 3, 4, 5, 6, 7
See also CPW
See also CSW
See also DAM NOV, POP
See also DLB 6, 143
See also DLBY 1982
See also EWL 3
See also EXPN
See also LATS 1:2
See also MAL 5
See also MAWW
See also MTCW 1, 2
See also MTFW 2005
See also NFS 2, 7, 10
See also RGAL 4
See also SATA 7, 90
See also SSFS 17
See also TCLE 1:2
See also TUS
See also YAW
Tyler, Converse 1903(?)-1978
Obituary 81-84

Tyler, David B(udlong) 1899-1993 77-80
Obituary 140
Tyler, Elias S. 1904(?)-1977
Obituary 73-76
Tyler, Ellis
See King, Albert and Tyler, Ellis
Tyler, Gus 1911- 130
Tyler, Hamilton A(lden) 1917- CANR-5
Earlier sketch in CA 9-12R
Tyler, J. Allen 1924- 101
Tyler, James (Henry) 1940- 227
Tyler, John Ecclesfield (?)-1966 .... CAP-1
Earlier sketch in CA 9-10
Tyler, Kelsey
See Kingsbury, Karen
Tyler, Leona E(lizabeth) 1906-1993 .... 17-20R
Tyler, Linda
See Tyler, Linda W(agner)
Tyler, Linda W(agner) 1952- 136
See also SATA 65
Tyler, Mary Palmer 1775-1866 .... DLB 200
Tyler, Moses Coit 1835-1900 224
See also DLB 47, 64
Tyler, Parker 1907-1974 .... CANR-5
Obituary 49-52
Earlier sketch in CA 5-8R
See also GLL 1
Tyler, Patrick (Edward) 1951- 125
Tyler, (John) Poyntz 1907-1971 .... 1-4R
Obituary 103
Tyler, Ralph Winfred 1902-1994 109
Obituary 144
Tyler, Richard W(illis) 1917- CANR-24
Earlier sketch in CA 41-44R
Tyler, Robert L(awrence) 1922- 13-16R
Tyler, Rodney 1943- 127
Tyler, Ron(nie) C(urtis) 1941- CANR-53
Earlier sketches in CA 29-32R, CANR-12, 28
Tyler, Royall 1757-1826 .... DLB 37
See also RGAL 4
Tyler, S(amuel) Lyman 1920- 77-80
Tyler, Sandra 1963- 154
Tyler, Stephen A(lbert) 1932- 29-32R
Tyler, Steven 1948- 231
Tyler, Tom R(ichard) 1950- 135
Tyler, Varro Eugene 1926-2001 110
Obituary 201
Tyler, Vicki 1952- 121
See also SATA 64
Tyler, W. T.
See Hamrick, Samuel J., Jr.
Tyler, William R(oyall) 1910-2003 .... 37-40R
Obituary 221
Tyler, Zeke
See Marshall, Mel(vin D.)
Tyler-Whittle, Michael Sidney 1927-1994 .... CANR-4
Earlier sketch in CA 5-8R
Tylor, Edward Burnett 1832-1917 221
Brief entry 123
See also DLB 57
Tymchuk, Alexander J(ames) 1942- 57-60
Tymeson, Mildred McClary
See Petrie, Mildred McClary
Tymieniecka, Anna-Teresa CANR-9
Earlier sketch in CA 61-64
Tymms, Ralph Vincent 1913-1987
Obituary 123
Tymn, Marshall (Benton) 1937- 107
Tymon, Dorothy 85-88
Tynan, Katharine 1861-1931 167
Brief entry 104
See also DLB 153, 240
See also FW
See also TCLC 3
Tynan, Kathleen 1937(?)-1995 97-100
Obituary 147
Tynan, Kenneth (Peacock) 1927-1980 .... CANR-63
Obituary 101
Earlier sketches in CA 13-16R, CANR-22
See also MTCW 1, 2
See also MTFW 2005
Tynan, Ronan 1960- 226
Tyndale, William c. 1484-1536 .... DLB 132
Tyne, Joel
See Schembri, Jim
Tyre, Nedra 104
Tyre, Peg 1960- 146
Tyree, Omar (Rashad) 1969- CANR-136
Earlier sketch in CA 181
See also DLB 292
See also MTFW 2005
Tyrell, Donald J(ohn) 1929-
Brief entry 110
Tyrmand, Leopold 1920-1985 .... CANR-5
Obituary 115
Earlier sketch in CA 49-52
Tyrone, Paul
See Norwood, Victor G(eorge) C(harles)
Tyrrell, Bernard (James) 1933- 57-60
Tyrrell, Frances 1959- .... SATA 107
Tyrrell, Francis M(artin) 1916-
Brief entry 107
Tyrrell, Ian R(obert) 1947- 142
Tyrrell, Joseph M(orten) 1927- 41-44R
Tyrrell, R(obert) Emmett, Jr. 1943- CANR-25
Earlier sketch in CA 85-88
Interview in CANR-25
Tyrrell, Robert 1929- 41-44R
Tyrrell, William Blake 1940- 125
Tyrwhitt, (Mary) Jacqueline 1905-1983(?)
Obituary 109
Tyrwhitt, Janice 1928- 97-100
Tysdahl, B(joern) J(ohan) 1933- 25-28R
Tysliava, Valerie 1914(?)-1984
Obituary 112
Tyson, Alan (Walker) 1926-2000 128
Obituary 192
Tyson, Ann 1959- 171
Tyson, James (Levering, Jr.) 151
Tyson, Joseph B(lake) 1928- CANR-38
Earlier sketches in CA 37-40R, CANR-14
Tyson, Lois (M.) 150
Tyson, Nancy Jane 1949- 117
Tyson, Remer (Hoyt) 1934- 131
Tyson, Richard 1944- 69-72
Tyson, Salinda 1952- 162
Tyson, Timothy B. 1959- 192
Tysse, Agnes N. 1904-1997 101
Tytell, John 1939- CANR-127
Earlier sketch in CA 29-32R
Tytler, Graeme (Douglas Colville) 1934- 117
Tzannes, Nicolaos S(tamatios) 1937- 57-60
Tzara, Tristan 1896-1963 153
Obituary 89-92
See also CLC 47
See also DAM POET
See also EWL 3
See also MTCW 2
See also PC 27
See also TCLC 168
Tzeng, Rueyling 1959- 212
Tzitsikas, Helene 1926- 45-48
Tzonis, Alexander 1937- 101

U

Ubbelohde, Carl (William, Jr.) 1924- CANR-6
Earlier sketch in CA 1-4R
Ubelaker, Douglas H. 1946- 146
Ubell, Earl 1926- 37-40R
See also SATA 4
Ucelay, Margarita 1916- 21-24R
Uchida, Tadao 1939- 65-68
Uchida, Yoshiko 1921-1992 .... CANR-61
Obituary 139
Earlier sketches in CA 13-16R, CANR-6, 22, 47
See also AAL
See also AAYA 16
See also BYA 2, 3
See also CDALBS
See also CLR 6, 56
See also CWRI 5
See also DLB 312
See also JRDA
See also MAICYA 1, 2
See also MTCW 1, 2
See also MTFW 2005
See also SAAS 1
See also SATA 1, 53
See also SATA-Obit 72
Ucko, Barbara 1945- 136
Udall, Brady 1957(?)- CANR-121
Earlier sketch in CA 163
Udall, Jan Beaney 1938- CANR-35
Earlier sketch in CA 65-68
See also SATA 10
Udall, Morris K(ing) 1922-1998 .... CANR-1
Obituary 172
Earlier sketch in CA 45-48
Udall, Nicholas 1504-1556 .... DLB 62
See also RGEL 2
Udall, Stewart L(ee) 1920- CANR-93
Earlier sketch in CA 69-72
Ude, Wayne (Richard) 1946- CANR-64
Earlier sketches in CA 77-80, CANR-13
See also TCWW 1, 2
Udell, Jon G(erald) 1935- CANR-37
Earlier sketches in CA 45-48, CANR-1, 16
Udelson, Joseph H. 1943- 125
Uden, (Bernard Gilbert) Grant 1910- 102
See also SATA 26
Uderzo, Albert 1927- 230
See also CLR 37
Udo, Reuben Kenrick 1935- CANR-82
Earlier sketches in CA 77-80, CANR-35
Udoff, Yale M(aurice) 1935- CANR-12
Earlier sketch in CA 57-60
Udolf, Roy 1926- CANR-4
Earlier sketch in CA 53-56
Udovicki, Jasminka 171
Udovitch, Abraham Labe 1933-
Brief entry 105
Udry, J(oe) Richard 1928- 33-36R
Udry, Janice May 1928- CANR-6
Earlier sketch in CA 5-8R
See also SATA 4, 152
Udy, Stanley Hart, Jr. 1928-
Brief entry 106
Ueda, Makoto 1931- CANR-77
Earlier sketches in CA 21-24R, CANR-34, 74
Ueda, Shoji 1913-2000 213
Uegaki, Chieri 1969- .... SATA 153
Uehling, Carl Theodore 1927- 29-32R
Uehling, Theodore Edward, Jr. 1935- CANR-20
Earlier sketch in CA 104
Uekert, Brenda K. 1963- 175
Ueland, Leif 214
Uelsmann, Jerry N(orman) 1934- 210
Ueno, Noriko
See Nakae, Noriko
Uffelman, F. C.
See Gehman, Richard (Boyd)
Uffenbeck, Lorin A(rthur) 1924- 61-64
Ugama, LeRoi
See Smith, LeRoi Tex
Ugarte, Francisco 1910-1969 .... CAP-1
Earlier sketch in CA 9-10
Ugarte, Michael 1949- 114
Ugboajah, Frank
See Ugboajah, (Francis) Okwu
Ugboajah, (Francis) Okwu 1945- 93-96
Ugent, Donald 1933- 141
Uglow, Jennifer 180
Uglow, Jenny
See Uglow, Jennifer
Uglow, Loyd M. 1952- 220
Ugolini, Lydia 1916- 180
Ugresic, Dubravka 1949- CANR-90
Earlier sketch in CA 136
See also CWW 2
See also DLB 181
Uhalley, Stephen, Jr. 1930-
Brief entry 106
Uher, Lorna
See Crozier, Lorna
Uhl, Alexander H. 1899(?)-1976
Obituary 69-72
Uhl, Melvin John 1915- CANR-34
Earlier sketch in CA 5-8R
Uhlan, Edward 1912-1988
Obituary 127
Uhland, Ludwig 1787-1862 .... DLB 90
Uhlenbeck, Karen (Keskulla) 1942- 160
Uhlfelder, Myra L. 1923- 194
Brief entry 109
Uhlig, Susan 1955- 198
See also SATA 129
Uhlin, Donald M(acbeth) 1930-1981 49-52
Uhlinger, Susan J. 1942-1980 .... CANR-34
Obituary 120
Earlier sketch in CA 57-60
Uhlman, Fred 1901-1985(?) CANR-34
Obituary 116
Earlier sketch in CA 105
Uhnak, Dorothy 1933- CANR-63
Earlier sketches in CA 81-84, CANR-29
See also AITN 1
See also CMW 4
Uhr, Carl George 1911-1999 81-84
Uhr, Elizabeth 1929- 25-28R
Uhr, Leonard (Merrick) 1927- CANR-7
Earlier sketch in CA 5-8R
Uhry, Alfred 1936- CANR-112
Brief entry 127
Earlier sketch in CA 133
Interview in CA-133
See also CAD
See also CD 5, 6
See also CLC 55
See also CSW
See also DA3
See also DAM DRAM, POP
See also DFS 11, 15
See also MTFW 2005
Uitti, Karl David 1933-2003 .... CANR-10
Obituary 227
Earlier sketch in CA 17-20R
Ujayli, al- 'Abd al-Salam 1918(?)- .... EWL 3
Ujevic, Augustin 1891-1955
See Ujevic, Tin
See also DLB 147
Ujevic, Tin
See Ujevic, Augustin
See also EWL 3
Ujfalussy, Jozsef 1920-
Brief entry 114
Ujse, Bodo 1904-1963 .... DLB 69
Ukrayinka, Lesya
See Kvitka, Laryssa Kosach
See also EWL 3
U Kyin Hswei 1919-
See Thaw-da Hswei
Ulack, Richard 1942- 140
Ulam, Adam B(runo) 1922-2000 .... CANR-51
Obituary 189
Earlier sketches in CA 13-16R, CANR-7, 26
Ulam, S(tanislaw) M(arcin) 1909-1984 .... CANR-34
Obituary 112
Earlier sketch in CA 61-64
See also SATA 51
Ulanoff, Stanley M(elvin) 1922- CANR-23
Earlier sketches in CA 17-20R, CANR-7
Ulanov, Ann Belford 1938- CANR-38
Earlier sketches in CA 49-52, CANR-16
Ulanov, Barry 1918-2000 .... CANR-38
Obituary 189
Earlier sketches in CA 1-4R, CANR-16
Ulasi, Adaora Lily 1932- 167
See also BW 3
Ulbricht, Walter 1893-1973
Obituary 113
Ulc, Otto 1930- CANR-13
Earlier sketch in CA 77-80
Uldrich, Jack 1964- 235
Ulen, Eisa Nefertari 1968- 188
Ulene, Art(hur Lawrence) 1936- CANR-30
Earlier sketch in CA 103
Ulenhart, Niclas fl. 1600- .... DLB 164
Ulett, George A(ndrew) 1918- 21-24R
Ulevich, Neal Hirsch 1946- 108
Ulf, Haerved
See Strindberg, (Johan) August
Ulf, Harved
See Strindberg, (Johan) August
Ulfeldt, Leonora Christina 1621-1698 .... DLB 300
Ulibarri, Sabine R(eyes) 1919-2003 .... CANR-81
Obituary 214
Earlier sketch in CA 131
See also CLC 83
See also DAM MULT
See also DLB 82
See also HLCS 2
See also HW 1, 2
See also RGSF 2
Ulica, Jorge 1870-1926 .... DLB 82
Ulich, Robert 1890(?)-1977
Obituary 69-72
Ulitskaya, Ludmila 1943- 226
See also Ulitskaya, Lyudmila
Ulitskaya, Lyudmila 1943-
See Ulitskaya, Ludmila
See also DLB 285
Ulivi, Ferruccio 1912- 207
See also DLB 196
Ulizio, B. George 1889-1969 184
See also DLB 140
Ullah, Najib 1914-1965 .... 13-16R
Ullah, Salamat 1913-2002 .... 13-16R
Ulle, Robert F. 1948- 117
Ullendorff, Edward 1920- CANR-40
Earlier sketches in CA 1-4R, CANR-2, 18
Ullian, Joseph S(ilbert) 1930- 41-44R
Ullman, Allan 1909(?)-1982
Obituary 106
Ullman, Barbara
See Schwalberg, Carol(yn Ernestine Stein)
Ullman, Edward L(ouis) 1912-1976 45-48
Obituary 125
Ullman, Ellen 1950(?)- 226
Ullman, Elwood 1903(?)-1985
Obituary 117
Ullman, James Ramsey 1907-1971 .... CANR-3
Obituary 29-32R
Earlier sketch in CA 1-4R
See also SATA 7
Ullman, Leslie 1947- 104
Ullman, Michael (Alan) 1945- 103
Ullman, Montague 1916- CANR-28
Earlier sketch in CA 41-44R
Ullman, Natacha 1929(?)-1986
Obituary 119
Ullman, Pierre L(ioni) 1929- 33-36R
Ullman, Richard Henry 1933- CANR-3
Earlier sketch in CA 1-4R
Ullman, Sharon R. 1955- 186
Ullmann, Christian 1942- 165
Ullmann, John E(manuel) 1923- CANR-34
Earlier sketch in CA 17-20R
Ullmann, Leonard P(aul) 1930- 17-20R
Ullmann, Linn 1966- 198
Ullmann, Liv 1939- CANR-110
Earlier sketch in CA 102
Ullmann, Owen 1947- 144
Ullmann, Stephen 1914-1976 .... CANR-4
Obituary 65-68
Earlier sketch in CA 5-8R
Ullmann, Walter 1910-1983 .... CANR-10
Obituary 108
Earlier sketch in CA 21-24R
Ullrich, Helen D(enning) 1922- CANR-28
Earlier sketch in CA 109
Ullstein, Hermann 1875(?)-1943
Brief entry 116
Ullyot, Joan 1940- 73-76
Ulm, Robert 1934-1977 .... SATA 17
Ulman, William A. 1908(?)-1979 103
Obituary 89-92
Ulmer, (Roland) Curtis 1923- 103
Ulmer, Diane K. 1943- 122
Ulmer, Gregory L(eland) 1944- 136
Ulmer, Louise 1943- 113
See also SATA 53
Ulmer, Mari 189
Ulmer, Melville J(ack) 1911-2001 .... 21-24R
Obituary 193
Ulmer, S(hirley) Sidney 1923- 41-44R
Ulph, Owen 1914- 133
Ulrich, Anton 1633-1714 .... DLB 168
Ulrich, Betty Garton 1919- 29-32R
Ulrich, Carolyn F. 1881(?)-1970
Obituary 104
Ulrich, David O. 1953- 192
Ulrich, Heinz 1927(?)-1980
Obituary 97-100
Ulrich, (John) Homer 1906-1987 .... CANR-36
Obituary 124
Earlier sketches in CA 5-8R, CANR-2
Ulrich, Larry 171
Ulrich, Laurel Thatcher 1938- CANR-114
Earlier sketch in CA 142
Ulrich, Louis E., Jr. 1918- 13-16R
Ulrich, Roberta 1928- 221
Ulrich, Roger E(lwood) 1931- 41-44R
Ulrich von Liechtenstein c. 1200-c. 1275 .... DLB 138
Ulrich von Zatzikhoven c. 1194-c. 1214 .... DLB 138
Ultan, Lloyd 1929-1998 117
Ultee, (J.) Maarten 1949- CANR-37
Earlier sketch in CA 109
Ulughzoda, Sotim 1911-1997 .... EWL 3
U Lun 1876-1964
See Thahkin Ko-daw Hmaing
Ulyanov, V. I.
See Lenin
Ulyanov, Vladimir Ilyich
See Lenin
Ulyanov-Lenin
See Lenin
Ulyatt, Kenneth 1920- CANR-8
Earlier sketch in CA 61-64
See also SATA 14

Uman, Myron F. 1939- 149
Umansky, Kaye 1946- .... SATA 158
Umansky, Lauri 180
'Umar ibn Abi Rabi'ah 644-712(?) ...... DLB 311
Umen, Samuel 1917(?)-1990
Obituary 132
Umezawa, Rui 1959- 228
Umland, Craig (Owen) 1947- 61-64
Umland, Rebecca A. 1954- 177
Umland, Samuel J(oseph) 1954- 175
Umphlett, Wiley Lee 1931- CANR-73
Earlier sketches in CA 49-52, CANR-1, 34
Umpierre (Herrera), Luz Maria 1947- 153
See also HW 1, 2
Umrigar, Thrity 1961- 207
Umstatter, Jack 1950- CANR-118
Earlier sketch in CA 158
Umstead, William Lee 1921-1995 81-84
Unada
See Gliewe, Unada (Grace)
Unaipon, David 1872-1967 .... DLB 230
Unamuno (y Jugo), Miguel de
1864-1936 .... CANR-81
Brief entry 104
Earlier sketch in CA 131
See also DAM MULT, NOV
See also DLB 108, 322
See also EW 8
See also EWL 3
See also HLC 2
See also HW 1, 2
See also MTCW 1, 2
See also MTFW 2005
See also RGSF 2
See also RGWL 2, 3
See also SSC 11, 69
See also SSFS 20
See also TCLC 2, 9, 148
See also TWA
Unbegaun, Boris Ottokar 1898-1973
Obituary 41-44R
Uncle Carter
See Boucher, (Clarence) Carter
Uncle Gordon
See Roe, F(rederic) Gordon
Uncle Gus
See Rey, H(ans) A(ugusto)
Uncle Gus, Hans Augusto .... CWRI 5
Uncle Mac
See McCulloch, Derek (Ivor Breashur)
Uncle Ray
See Coffman, Ramon Peyton
Uncle Shelby
See Silverstein, Shel(don Allan)
Under, Marie 1883-1980 .... CDWLB 4
See also DLB 220
See also EWL 3
Undercliffe, Errol
See Campbell, (John) Ramsey
Underdown, David (Edward) 1925- .. CANR-98
Earlier sketches in CA 5-8R, CANR-11, 26, 51
Underhill, Alice Mertie (Waterman)
1900-1971 .... 1-4R
Obituary 103
See also SATA 10
Underhill, Charles
See Hill, Reginald (Charles)
Underhill, Evelyn 1875-1941 206
See also DLB 240
Underhill, Frank Hawkins 1889-1971 163
Underhill, Hal
See Underhill, Harold
Underhill, Harold 1926-1972 .... CAP-2
Earlier sketch in CA 25-28
Underhill, Hugh 1937- 145
Underhill, Liz 1948- 121
See also SATA 53
See also SATA-Brief 49
Underhill, Lois Beachy 151
Underhill, Miriam E. 1898(?)-1976
Obituary 61-64
Underhill, Paco 206
Underhill, Peter
See Soderberg, Percy Measday
Underhill, Ruth Murray 1884-1984 .. CANR-39
Obituary 114
Earlier sketches in CA 1-4R, CANR-3
Underwood, Aggie
See Underwood, Agness May Wilson
Underwood, Agness May Wilson 1902-1984
Obituary 113
Underwood, Barbara 1952- 101
Underwood, Benton J. 1915- CANR-34
Earlier sketch in CA 101
Underwood, (Mary) Betty 1921- 37-40R
Underwood, Gary Neal 1940-
Brief entry 113
Underwood, Helen 1914- 139
Underwood, Jane H(ammons) 1931- 61-64
Underwood, Jeffery S(cott) 1954- 137
Underwood, John Weeden 1932- CANR-35
Earlier sketch in CA 17-20R
Underwood, Lewis Graham
See Wagner, C(harles) Peter
Underwood, Mavis Eileen 1916-
Brief entry 108
Underwood, Michael
See Evelyn, (John) Michael
Underwood, Miles
See Glassco, John
Underwood, Norman 1878(?)-1974
Obituary 53-56
Underwood, Paul S(taats) 1915-1985 77-80
Obituary 118
Underwood, Peter 1923- CANR-44
Earlier sketches in CA 104, CANR-21
Underwood, Sam J(esse) 1922- CANR-2
Earlier sketch in CA 45-48
Underwood, Ted Leroy 1935- 115
Underwood, Tim (Edward) 1948- CANR-24
Earlier sketch in CA 105
Undine, P. F.
See Paine, Lauran (Bosworth)
Undset, Sigrid 1882-1949 129
Brief entry 104
See also DA
See also DA3
See also DAB
See also DAC
See also DAM MST, NOV
See also DLB 293
See also EW 9
See also EWL 3
See also FW
See also MTCW 1, 2
See also MTFW 2005
See also RGWL 2, 3
See also TCLC 3
See also WLC
Undy, R(oger) 1938- 115
Unett, John 13-16R
Ung, Loung 1970- 201
Ungar, Frederick 1898-1988
Obituary 127
Ungar, Sanford J. 1945- CANR-71
Earlier sketches in CA 37-40R, CANR-13, 29
Ungar, Sheldon (B.) 1948- 144
Ungar, Steven (Ronald) 1945- 126
Ungaretti, Giuseppe 1888-1970 .... CAP-2
Obituary 25-28R
Earlier sketch in CA 19-20
See also CLC 7, 11, 15
See also DLB 114
See also EW 10
See also EWL 3
See also PC 57
See also PFS 20
See also RGWL 2, 3
See also WLIT 7
Ungaro, Harold R(aymond) Mancusi, Jr.
See Mancusi-Ungaro, Harold R(aymond), Jr.
Ungaro, Susan Kelliher 1953- 103
Unger, Arthur 1924- 1-4R
Unger, Barbara 1932- CANR-40
Earlier sketches in CA 77-80, CANR-13
Unger, Craig 1949- 128
Unger, David 1950- CANR-87
Earlier sketch in CA 153
See also HW 1
Unger, Douglas 1952- CANR-94
Earlier sketch in CA 130
See also CLC 34
Unger, Friederike Helene 1741-1813 ... DLB 94
Unger, Hans 1915- 17-20R
Unger, Harlow G. 1931- 142
See also SATA 75
Unger, Henry F. 1912-1994 .... 13-16R
Unger, Irwin 1927- CANR-7
Earlier sketch in CA 9-12R
Unger, J(ames) Marshall 1947- 126
Unger, Jim 1937- CANR-13
Earlier sketch in CA 61-64
See also SATA 67
Unger, Len
See Unger, Leonard
Unger, Leonard 1916- CANR-34
Earlier sketch in CA 5-8R
Unger, Leonard 1934- 69-72
Unger, Marion
See Thede, Marion Draughon
Unger, Marvin H. 1936- 29-32R
Unger, Maurice Albert 1917-1996 ...... CANR-3
Earlier sketch in CA 9-12R
Unger, Merrill F. 1909-1980 .... CANR-6
Earlier sketch in CA 1-4R
Unger, Nancy C. 1956- 187
Unger, Peter K(enneth) 1942- 136
Brief entry 109
Unger, Richard (Lawrence) 1939- CANR-15
Earlier sketch in CA 65-68
Unger, Richard W. 1942- 121
Unger, Walter P(eter) 1939-
Brief entry 115
Unger, Zac 1974(?)- 228
Ungerer, Miriam 1929- 117
Ungerer, (Jean) Thomas 1931- 41-44R
See also Ungerer, Tomi
See also CWRI 5
See also MAICYA 1, 2
See also SATA 5, 33, 106
Ungerer, Tomi 1931-
See Ungerer, (Jean) Thomas
See also CLR 3, 77
Unger-Hamilton, Clive (Wolfgang)
1942- CANR-42
Earlier sketches in CA 101, CANR-19
Ungermann, Kenneth Armistead 1916- ... 9-12R
Ungs, Thomas D(ale) 1928- 81-84
Unkelbach, Kurt 1913-1992 .... CANR-8
Earlier sketch in CA 21-24R
See also SATA 4
Unklesbay, A. G. 1914- 143
Unkovic, Charles M. 1922-1995 45-48
Unnerstad, Edith (Totterman)
1900-1982 .... CANR-72
Earlier sketches in CA 5-8R, CANR-6
See also CLR 36
See also SATA 3
Uno, Chiyo 1897-1996 .... CANR-70
Earlier sketch in CA 154
See also Uno Chiyo
Uno, Kathleen S. 1951- 196
Uno, Koji 1891-1961 202
Unobagha, Uzo .... SATA 139
Uno Chiyo
See Uno, Chiyo
See also DLB 180
Unrau, Ruth 1922- 61-64
See also SATA 9
Unrau, William E. 1929- 37-40R
Unrue, Darlene Harbour 1938- 139
Unruh, Fritz von -1970
See Von Unruh, Fritz
See also DLB 56
Unruh, Glenys Grace (Green) 1910- 29-32R
Unruh, James A(rlen) 1941- 156
Unruh, John D., Jr. 1938(?)-1976
Obituary 105
Unser, Bobby
See Unser, Robert William
Unser, Robert William 1934- 97-100
Unstead, R(obert) J(ohn) 1915-1988 . CANR-94
Obituary 125
Earlier sketches in CA 9-12R, CANR-7, 23
See also SATA 12
See also SATA-Obit 56
Unsworth, Barry (Forster) 1930- CANR-125
Earlier sketches in CA 25-28R, CANR-30, 54
See also BRWS 7
See also CLC 76, 127
See also CN 6, 7
See also DLB 194
Unsworth, Geoffrey 1914-1978 .... IDFW 3, 4
Unsworth, Mair 1909- CANR-10
Earlier sketch in CA 25-28R
Unsworth, Walt(er) 1928- CANR-38
Earlier sketches in CA 29-32R, CANR-17
See also SATA 4
Unt, Mati 1944- .... DLB 232
Unterberger, Betty Miller 1923- 25-28R
Unterbrink, Mary 1937- 113
Unterecker, John (Eugene)
1922-1989 .... CANR-34
Obituary 127
Earlier sketch in CA 17-20R
Untereiner, Raymond Edward 1898-1983
Obituary 110
Unterman, Alan 1942- 97-100
Unterman, Issar Y(ehuda) 1886-1976
Obituary 61-64
Untermeyer, Bryna Ivens
1909-1985 .... CANR-31
Earlier sketches in CA 5-8R, CANR-3
See also SATA 61
Untermeyer, Jean Starr 1886-1970
Obituary 29-32R
Untermeyer, Louis 1885-1977 .... CANR-31
Obituary 73-76
Earlier sketch in CA 5-8R
See also AMWS 15
See also CP 1, 2
See also DLB 303
See also SATA 2, 37
See also SATA-Obit 26
Unthank, Luisa-Teresa 33-36R
Unthank, Tessa Brown
See Unthank, Luisa-Teresa
Unwalla, Darab B. 1928- 25-28R
Unwin, David S(torr) 1918- CANR-6
Earlier sketch in CA 9-12R
See also CWRI 5
See also SATA 14
Unwin, Derick (James) 1931- 21-24R
Unwin, Nora S(picer) 1907-1982 .... 21-24R
Obituary 120
See also SATA 3
See also SATA-Obit 49
Unwin, Peter 1956- 204
Unwin, Rayner S(tephens) 1925-2000 .... 1-4R
Obituary 191
Unwin, Simon 1952- 206
Unwin, Stanley 1884-1968 .... CANR-91
Earlier sketch in CA 5-8R
Unzner, Christa 1958- .... SATA 80, 141
Unzner-Fischer, Christa
See Unzner, Christa
Upadhyay, Samrat 207
Upcher, Caroline 1946- 229
Upchurch, Boyd (Bradfield) 1919- CANR-27
Earlier sketch in CA 25-28R
See also Boyd, John
See also SFW 4
Upchurch, Michael 1954- 155
Updike, David (H.) 1957- 128
Updike, John (Hoyer) 1932- CANR-133
Earlier sketches in CA 1-4R, CANR-4, 33, 51, 94
See also CABS 1
See also AAYA 36
See also AMW
See also AMWC 1
See also AMWR 1
See also BPFB 3
See also BYA 12
See also CDALB 1968-1988
See also CLC 1, 2, 3, 5, 7, 9, 13, 15, 23, 34, 43, 70, 139
See also CN 1, 2, 3, 4, 5, 6, 7
See also CP 1, 2, 3, 4, 5, 6, 7
See also CPW 1
See also DA
See also DA3
See also DAB
See also DAC
See also DAM MST, NOV, POET, POP
See also DLB 2, 5, 143, 218, 227
See also DLBD 3
See also DLBY 1980, 1982, 1997
See also EWL 3
See also EXPP
See also HGG
See also MAL 5
See also MTCW 1, 2
See also MTFW 2005
See also NFS 12
See also RGAL 4
See also RGSF 2
See also SSC 13, 27
See also SSFS 3, 19
See also TUS
See also WLC
Updike, L(eRoy) Wayne 1916- 49-52
Updyke, James
See Burnett, W(illiam) R(iley)
Updyke, Rosemary K. 1924- 170
See also SATA 103
Upfield, Arthur W(illiam) 1888-1964
Obituary 114
See also CMW 4
See also MSW
Upgren, Arthur P. 1897-1986
Obituary 120
Uphaus, Robert W(alter) 1942- 57-60
Uphaus, Willard Edwin 1890-1983 .... CAP-1
Obituary 111
Earlier sketch in CA 19-20
Uphoff, Norman T(homas) 1940- CANR-11
Earlier sketch in CA 29-32R
Uphoff, Walter H. 1913-1998 .... CANR-14
Earlier sketch in CA 25-28R
Upitis, Alvis .... SATA 109
Upits, Andrejs 1877-1970
Obituary 104
See also DLB 220
Upjohn, Everard M(iller) 1903-1978 ..... CAP-1
Obituary 81-84
Earlier sketch in CA 13-14
Uppal, Jogindar S. 1927- CANR-1
Earlier sketch in CA 45-48
Uppal, Priscila 1974- 220
Uppdal, Kristofer 1878-1961 190
See also EWL 3
Uppman, Jean Seward 1922- 136
Upright, Diane W(arner) 1947- 120
Upshaw, Margaret Mitchell
See Mitchell, Margaret (Munnerlyn)
Upson, Norma 1919- CANR-8
Earlier sketch in CA 61-64
Upson, William Hazlett 1891-1975 .... 5-8R
Obituary 57-60
Upton, Albert 1897-1986 .... CAP-2
Earlier sketch in CA 23-24
Upton, Anthony F. 1929- 17-20R
Upton, Arvin 1914-1990 81-84
Upton, Bertha (Hudson) 1849-1912
Brief entry 121
See also DLB 141
Upton, Charles 1948-
Brief entry 116
See also DLB 16
Upton, Dell 1949- CANR-50
Earlier sketch in CA 123
Upton, Florence K. 1873-1922 .... DLB 141
Upton, Joseph C(heshire) N(ash) 1946- ... 81-84
Upton, L(eslie) F(rancis) S(tokes)
1931-1980 61-64
Obituary 125
Upton, Lee 1953- CANR-94
Earlier sketch in CA 123
Upton, Mark
See Sanders, Lawrence
Upton, Monroe 1898-1990 .... CAP-2
Obituary 171
Earlier sketch in CA 17-18
Upton, Robert CANR-55
Earlier sketches in CA 73-76, CANR-13, 29
Upward, Allen 1863-1926 187
Brief entry 117
See also DLB 36
See also TCLC 85
Upward, Edward (Falaise) 1903- 77-80
See also CN 1, 2, 3, 4, 5, 6, 7
See also RGEL 2
Urakami, Hiroko 1937- 140
Urbach, Reinhard 1939-
Brief entry 113
Urban, Helle (Denise) 1957- .... SATA 149
Urban, Joao Aristeu 1943- 210
Urban, Mark 173
Urban, Michael E(dward) 1947- CANR-29
Earlier sketch in CA 111
Urban, Milo 1904-1982 .... DLB 215
Urban, Wilbur Marshall 1873-1952 183
Brief entry 119
Urban, William L(awrence) 1939- .. CANR-106
Earlier sketches in CA 45-48, CANR-2, 18
Urbanek, Mae (Bobb) 1903-1995 77-80
Obituary 171
Urbanek, Zdenek 1917- 140
Urban Griot
See Tyree, Omar (Rashad)
Urbano, Victoria (Eugenia) 1926- CANR-2
Earlier sketch in CA 45-48
Urbanska, Wanda (Marie) 1956- 124
Urbanski, Edmund Stefan
See Urbanski, Edmund Stephen
Urbanski, Edmund Stephen
1909-1996 .... CANR-23
Earlier sketch in CA 45-48
Urbanski, Marie M. Olesen 1922- 102
Urbina, Nicasio 1958- 219
Urch, Elizabeth 1921- 103
Urda, Nicholas 1922-1986 .... 21-24R
Urdang, Constance (Henriette)
1922-1996 .... CANR-24
Earlier sketches in CA 21-24R, CANR-9
See also CLC 47

Cumulative Index 589 Valdes-Rodriguez

See also CP 1, 2
See also CWP
Urdang, Laurence 1927- CANR-40
Earlier sketches in CA 89-92, CANR-17
Ure, Jean 1943- CANR-109
Earlier sketches in CA 125, CANR-48, 92
See also AAYA 33
See also BYA 6
See also CLR 34
See also JRDA
See also MAICYA 1, 2
See also SAAS 14
See also SATA 48, 78, 129
See also YAW
Ure, John (Burns) 1931- CANR-94
Earlier sketch in CA 144
Ure, Peter 1919-1969 .... CAP-1
Earlier sketch in CA 11-12
Ure, Susan 238
U'Ren, Andrea 1968- 217
See also SATA 142
Uren, Hilda
See U'Ren-Stubbings, Hilda
U'Ren, Hilda
See U'Ren-Stubbings, Hilda
Urena de Henriquez, Salome
1850-1897 .... DLB 283
U'Ren-Stubbings, Hilda 1914- CANR-49
Earlier sketch in CA 29-32R
Uretsky, Myron 1940- 53-56
Urey, Harold (Clayton) 1893-1981 157
Obituary 102
Urfe, Honore d' 1567(?)-1625 .... DLB 268
See also GFL Beginnings to 1789
See also RGWL 2, 3
Uri, Pierre (Emmanuel) 1911-1992 ... CANR-47
Obituary 138
Earlier sketch in CA 97-100
Uriel, Henry
See Faust, Frederick (Schiller)
Uris, Auren 1913-1999 .... CANR-22
Earlier sketch in CA 17-20R
Uris, Dorothy CANR-9
Earlier sketch in CA 61-64
Uris, Leon (Marcus) 1924-2003 ...... CANR-123
Obituary 217
Earlier sketches in CA 1-4R, CANR-1, 40, 65
See also AITN 1, 2
See also BEST 89:2
See also BPFB 3
See also CLC 7, 32
See also CN 1, 2, 3, 4, 5, 6
See also CPW 1
See also DA3
See also DAM NOV, POP
See also MTCW 1, 2
See also MTFW 2005
See also SATA 49
See also SATA-Obit 146
Urista (Heredia), Alberto (Baltazar)
1947- CANR-32
Earlier sketches in CA 182, CANR-2
See also Alurista
See also HLCS 1
See also HW 1
ur Kotlum, Johannes
See Johannes Ur Kotlum
Urkowitz, Steven 1941- 111
Urmson, J(ames) O(pie) 1915- 25-28R
Urmuz
See Codrescu, Andrei
Urmuz
See Demetrescu-Buzau, Demetru Dem.
See also EWL 3
Urness, Carol 1936-
Brief entry 111
Uroff, Margaret Dickie 1935- 93-96
Urofsky, Melvin I. 1939- CANR-31
Earlier sketches in CA 37-40R, CANR-14
Urquhart, Alvin W. 1931- 13-16R
Urquhart, Brian (Edward) 1919- CANR-51
Earlier sketches in CA 105, CANR-26
Urquhart, Caroline 1940- 118
Urquhart, Colin 1940- CANR-37
Earlier sketch in CA 115
Urquhart, Fred(erick Burrows)
1912-1995 .... CANR-72
Obituary 150
Earlier sketches in CA 9-12R, CANR-6, 21
See also CN 1, 2, 3, 4, 5, 6
See also DLB 139
See also RGSF 2
Urquhart, Guy
See McAlmon, Robert (Menzies)
Urquhart, Jane 1949- CANR-116
Earlier sketches in CA 113, CANR-32, 68
See also CCA 1
See also CLC 90
See also DAC
Urquhart, Judy 1942- 123
Urrea, Luis Alberto 1955- 181
See also DLB 209
Urrutia Lleo, Manuel 1901-1981
Obituary 104
Urry, David (Laurence) 1931- 85-88
Urry, John 1946- CANR-98
Earlier sketches in CA 122, CANR-48
Urry, W(illiam) G(eorge) 1913-1981
Obituary 103
Ursano, Robert J. 1947- CANR-103
Earlier sketch in CA 148
Ursell, Geoffrey 1943- 158
Ursini, James 1947- CANR-68
Earlier sketch in CA 61-64
Ursu, Anne 206
Urusevsky, Sergei 1908-1974 .... IDFW 4
Urvater, Michele 1946- 102
ur Vor, Jon
See Jonsson, Jon
See also DLB 293
Urwick, Lyndall Fownes 1891-1983 ...... CAP-1
Obituary 111
Earlier sketch in CA 13-14
Urwin, Derek W(illiam) 1939- 149
Urwin, Gregory J(ohn) W(illiam)
1955- CANR-36
Earlier sketch in CA 114
Ury, Allen B. 1954- 166
See also SATA 98
Ury, William L(anger) 1953- CANR-27
Earlier sketch in CA 109
Ury, Zalman F. 1924- CANR-17
Earlier sketch in CA 65-68
Urzidil, Johannes 1896-1970
Obituary 29-32R
See also DLB 85
Us
See Deal, Borden
Usabiaga (Ibanez), Carlos 1965- 204
Usatine, Richard P. 220
Usborne, Cornelie 1942- CANR-95
Earlier sketch in CA 145
Usborne, Richard Alexander 1910- 104
Uschan, Michael V. 1948- 198
See also SATA 129
Usco
See Stern, Gerd Jacob
Usdin, Gene (Leonard) 1922- 37-40R
Useem, Michael 1942- CANR-117
Earlier sketch in CA 61-64
Usene, Serge
See Seers, Eugene
Useni
See Perkins, (Useni) Eugene
Usher, Dan 1934- CANR-12
Earlier sketch in CA 29-32R
Usher, Frank (Hugh) 1909-1976 .... CANR-5
Earlier sketch in CA 5-8R
Usher, George 1930- 109
Usher, Margo Scegge
See McHargue, Georgess
Usher, Shaun 1937- 77-80
Usher, Stephen 1931- 29-32R
Usher-Wilson, Rodney N. 1908(?)-1983
Obituary 109
Usherwood, Elizabeth (Ada) 1923- ... CANR-51
Earlier sketch in CA 123
Usherwood, Stephen Dean
1907-2001 .... CANR-41
Obituary 196
Earlier sketches in CA 5-8R, CANR-3, 19
Usigli, Rodolfo 1905-1979 131
See also DLB 305
See also EWL 3
See also HLCS 1
See also HW 1
See also LAW
Usikota
See Brinitzer, Carl
Usk, Thomas (?)-1388 .... DLB 146
Uslaner, Eric M(ichael) 1947- 111
Uslar Pietri, Arturo 1906-2001 150
Obituary 193
See also DAM MULT
See also DLB 113
See also EWL 3
See also HW 1
See also LAW
Usman Awang 1929-2001 .... EWL 3
Usmiani, Renate 1931- 113
Uspensky, Gleb Ivanovich
1843-1902 .... DLB 277
Usry, Becky (S.) 1949- 152
Usry, Milton F. 1931- 17-20R
Ussher, (Percival) Arland
1899-1980 .... CANR-91
Obituary 102
Earlier sketches in CAP-1, CA 13-14, CANR-10
Ussher, James 1581-1656 .... DLB 213
Ussher, Jane M. 1961- 139
Ussher, Percy Arland
See Ussher, (Percival) Arland
Ustinov, D(mitri) F(edorovich) 1908-1984 .. 133
Obituary 114
Ustinov, Peter (Alexander)
1921-2004 .... CANR-51
Obituary 225
Earlier sketches in CA 13-16R, CANR-25
See also AITN 1
See also CBD
See also CD 5, 6
See also CLC 1
See also DLB 13
See also MTCW 2
Uston, Ken(neth Senzo) 1935-1987 108
Obituary 123
See also SATA 65
U Tam'si, Gerald Felix Tchicaya
See Tchicaya, Gerald Felix
U Tam'si, Tchicaya
See Tchicaya, Gerald Felix
Utechin, S(ergei) V(asilievich) 1921- 9-12R
Utgard, Russell O(liver) 1933- 49-52
Utgoff, Victor A. 237
Utke, Allen R(ay) 1936- 81-84
Utley, Francis Lee 1907-1974 .... CANR-2
Obituary 49-52
Earlier sketch in CA 1-4R
Utley, Freda 1898-1978 81-84
Obituary 77-80
Utley, (Clifton) Garrick 1939- CANR-102
Earlier sketch in CA 69-72
Utley, Jonathan G. 1942- 129
Utley, Ralph
See Cairns, Huntington
Utley, Robert M(arshall) 1929- CANR-94
Earlier sketches in CA 5-8R, CANR-2
Utley, Steven 1948- .... SFW 4
Utley, T(homas) E(dwin) 1921-1988
Obituary 125
Utt, Richard H. 1923- CANR-7
Earlier sketch in CA 9-12R
Utt, Walter C(harles) 1921-1985 .... 21-24R
Uttley, Alice Jane (Taylor)
1884-1976 .... CANR-52
Obituary 65-68
Earlier sketches in CA 53-56, CANR-7
See also Uttley, Alison
See also CWRI 5
See also SATA 3, 88
See also SATA-Obit 26
Uttley, Alison
See Uttley, Alice Jane (Taylor)
See also DLB 160
Uttley, John 1914- 21-24R
Utton, Albert Edgar 1931- CANR-1
Earlier sketch in CA 45-48
Utz, Lois (Marie) 1932-1986 .... 25-28R
Obituary 121
See also SATA 5
See also SATA-Obit 50
Utz, Robert T(homas) 1934- 53-56
Utzon, Joern
See Utzon, Jorn
Utzon, Jorn 1918- .... AAYA 55
Uu, David
See Harris, David W.
Uvalic, Milica 1952- 167
Uveges, Joseph A(ndrew), Jr. 1938- 41-44R
Uvezian, Sonia CANR-9
Earlier sketch in CA 57-60
Uviller, H(erman) Richard
1929-2005 .... CANR-65
Obituary 238
Earlier sketch in CA 129
Uyematsu, Amy 191
Uyl, Douglas J(ohn) Den
See Den Uyl, Douglas J(ohn)
Uys, Errol Lincoln 1943- 136
Uz, Johann Peter 1720-1796 .... DLB 97
Uzgiris, Ina Cepenas 1937-1998 184
Brief entry 108
Uzodinma, E(dmund) C(hukuemeka) C(hieke)
1936- 153
See also BW 2
Uzzell, J(ohn) Douglas 1937- 93-96
Uzzi, Brian 1960- 203
Uzzle, Burk 1938- 213

V

V. D. S.
See Scudder, Vida Dutton
V., Nina
See Vickers, Antoinette L.
Vac, Bertrand 1914- .... DLB 88
Vacca, Roberto 1927- CANR-1
Earlier sketch in CA 49-52
Vaccaro, Ernest B. 1905(?)-1979
Obituary 89-92
Vaccaro, Joseph P(ascal) 1935- 104
Vaccaro, Louis C(harles) 1930- CANR-1
Earlier sketch in CA 45-48
Vaccaro, Tony
See Vaccaro, Ernest B.
Vache, Warren W(ebster) 1914-2005 202
Obituary 236
Vachek, Josef 1909-1996 132
Vachell, Horace Annesley 1861-1955
Brief entry 120
Vachon, Brian 1941- 41-44R
Vachon, Christine 1962- .... IDFW 4
Vachon, John 1914-1975 213
Vachon, Mary L. S. 1945- 127
Vachss, Andrew (Henry) 1942- 214
Earlier sketches in CA 118, CANR-44, 95
Autobiographical Essay in 214
See also CLC 106
See also CMW 4
Vachss, Andrew H.
See Vachss, Andrew (Henry)
Vacietis, Ojars 1933-1983 .... DLB 232
See also EWL 3
Vaculik, Ludvik 1926- CANR-72
Earlier sketch in CA 53-56
See also CLC 7
See also CWW 2
See also DLB 232
See also EWL 3
Vaczek, Louis 1913-1983 .... CANR-21
Obituary 111
Earlier sketch in CA 9-12R
Vad, Poul 1927- 142
Vadakin, James C(harles) 1924-1981 ..... 29-32R
Obituary 134
Vadianus, Joachim 1484-1551 .... DLB 179
Vadim, Roger 1928-2000 143
Obituary 188
Vadney, Thomas E(ugene) 1939- 45-48
Vaeth, J(oseph) Gordon 1921- 5-8R
See also SATA 17
Vaggi, Gianni 1947- 127
Vagin, Vladimir (Vasilevich) 1937- .... SATA 142
Vago, Bela Adalbert 1922- 93-96
Vagts, Alfred (Hermann Friedrich)
1892-1986 .... 5-8R
Obituary 171
Vagts, Detlev F(rederick) 1929- 25-28R
Vagts, Miriam Beard 1901-1983
Obituary 110
Vahanian, Gabriel (Antoine) 1927- ... CANR-45
Earlier sketches in CA 1-4R, CANR-6, 22
Vaiciulaitis, Antanas 1906-1992 .... DLB 220
See also EWL 3
Vaiciunaite, Judita 1937- .... DLB 232
Vaid, Krishna Baldev 1927- CANR-8
Earlier sketch in CA 61-64
Vaid, Urvashi 1958- CANR-100
Earlier sketch in CA 156
See also GLL 2
Vaidhyanathan, Siva 1966- 232
Vaidon, Lawdom
See Woolman, David S.
Vaihinger, Hans 1852-1933 166
Brief entry 116
See also TCLC 71
Vail, (Marilyn) Elaine 1948- 109
Vail, Laurence 1891-1968 190
Obituary 112
See also DLB 4
Vail', Petr L'vovich 1949- .... DLB 285
Vail, Priscilla L. 1931- 101
Vail, Rachel 1966- 159
See also AAYA 33
See also SATA 94, 163
Vail, Robert William 1921-1988 .... CANR-12
Earlier sketch in CA 17-20R
Vaill, Amanda CANR-103
Earlier sketch in CA 170
Vaill, George D. 1911(?)-1986
Obituary 119
Vaillancourt, Jean-Guy 1937- CANR-21
Earlier sketch in CA 105
Vaillancourt, Pauline M(ariette) 104
Vaillancourt, Pauline Marie
See Rosenau, Pauline Vaillancourt
Vaillancourt, Renee J.
See McGrath, Renee J. Vaillancourt
Vailland, Roger (Francois)
1907-1965 .... CANR-70
Obituary 89-92
Earlier sketch in CA 103
See also DLB 83
See also EWL 3
Vaillant, George E. 1934- CANR-13
Earlier sketch in CA 77-80
Vaillant, Janet G. 1937- 136
Vainio, Pirkko 1957- .... SATA 76, 123
Vairo, Philip Dominic 1933- 102
Vaisse, Maurice 1942- 187
Vaitheeswaran, Vijay V. 1969- 236
Vaizey, Edward 1968- 215
Vaizey, Mrs. George de Horne 1857- ...... RHW
Vaizey, John 1929-1984 .... CANR-4
Obituary 113
Earlier sketch in CA 5-8R
Vaizey, Marina 1938- 116
Vaizgantas 1869-1933 .... DLB 220
Vajda, Edward (J.) 1958- 219
Vajda, Ernest 1887-1954
Brief entry 122
See also DLB 44
See also IDFW 3, 4
Vajda, Stephan 1926-1987 .... CANR-27
Earlier sketch in CA 29-32R
Vajk, J(oseph) Peter 1942- 117
Vakar, N(icholas) P(latonovich)
1897-1970 .... CANR-20
Obituary 103
Earlier sketch in CA 1-4R
Vala, Katri
See Heikel, Karin Alice
Valaoritis, Nanos 1921- 186
Autobiographical Essay in 186
See also CAAS 26
Valaskakis, Kimon Plato 1941- 89-92
Valberg, J. J. 1936- 144
Valbonne, Jean
See Leprohon, Pierre
Valbuena-Briones, Angel (Julian)
1928- CANR-3
Earlier sketch in CA 45-48
Valcarcel, Emilio Diaz
See Diaz Valcarcel, Emilio
Valcoe, H. Felix
See Swartz, Harry (Felix)
Valdata, Patricia 1952- 218
Valdemi, Maria I. 1947- 114
Valder, Peter 1928- CANR-90
Earlier sketch in CA 153
Valdes, Alfonso de 1490(?)-1532 .... DLB 318
Valdes, Donald M(anuel) 1922- 21-24R
Valdes, Gina 1943- 181
See also DLB 122
Valdes, Ivy 1921- 105
Valdes, Joan 1931- 49-52
Valdes, Jorge 1956- 194
Valdes, Juan de 1508-1541 .... DLB 318
Valdes, Mario J. 1934- CANR-44
Earlier sketches in CA 13-16R, CANR-6, 21
Valdes, Nelson P. 1945- CANR-38
Earlier sketch in CA 33-36R
Valdes, Zoe
See Valdes, Zoe
Valdes, Zoe 1959- 191
Valdes-Rodriguez, Alisa 1969- 224

Valdez, Luis (Miguel) 1940- ... CANR-81
Earlier sketches in CA 101, CANR-32
See also CAD
See also CD 5, 6
See also CLC 84
See also DAM MULT
See also DC 10
See also DFS 5
See also DLB 122
See also EWL 3
See also HLC 2
See also HW 1
See also LAIT 4
See also LLW
Valdez, Paul
See Yates, A(lan) G(eoffrey)
Valdman, Albert 1931- ... 103
Valdombre
See Grignon, Claude-Henri
Valduga, Patrizia 1953- ... 210
See also DLB 128
Vale, C(orwyn) P(hilip) 1921- ... 49-52
Vale, (Henry) Edmund (Theodoric) 1888-1969 ... CAP-1
Earlier sketch in CA 9-10
Vale, Eugene 1916-1997 ... CANR-12
Obituary ... 158
Earlier sketch in CA 57-60
Vale, Juliet (Elizabeth) 1952- ... 132
Vale, Lewis
See Oglesby, Joseph
Vale, Malcolm Graham Allan 1942- ... 191
Brief entry ... 109
Valen, Nanine 1950- ... 65-68
See also SATA 21
Valencak, Hannelore
See Mayer, Hannelore Valencak
See also SATA 42
Valencia, Guillermo 1873-1943 ... 206
See also LAW
Valency, Maurice 1903-1996 ... CANR-26
Obituary ... 153
Earlier sketches in CA 25-28R, CANR-10
Valens, Amy 1946- ... 138
See also SATA 70
Valens, E(vans) G(ladstone), Jr. 1920-1992 ... CANR-14
Earlier sketches in CA 5-8R, 81-84, CANR-3
See also SATA 1
Valenstein, Elliot S(piro) 1923- ... CANR-86
Earlier sketch in CA 132
Valenstein, Suzanne G(ebhart) 1928- ... 77-80
Valente, Jose Angel 1929-2000 ... 176
Obituary ... 189
See also DLB 108
See also HW 2
Valente, Justino
See Eidem, Odd
Valente, Michael F(eeney) ... 57-60
Valenti, Jack 1921- ... 73-76
Valentin, Thomas 1922-1981
Obituary ... 103
Valentine, Alan (Chester) 1901-1980 .. CANR-2
Obituary ... 101
Earlier sketch in CA 5-8R
Valentine, Charles A. 1929-1990 ... 25-28R
Valentine, Charles Wilfrid 1879-1964
Obituary ... 107
Valentine, D(onald) G(raham) 1929- ... 5-8R
Valentine, David
See Ludovici, Anthony M(ario)
Valentine, Douglas ... 139
Valentine, Douglas
See Williams, (George) Valentine
Valentine, Fawn 1949- ... 201
Valentine, Foy (Dan) 1923- ... CANR-10
Earlier sketch in CA 17-20R
Valentine, Helen
See Valentine, Sister Mary Hester
Valentine, Helen (Lachman) 1893-1986
Obituary ... 121
Valentine, James W(illiam) 1926- ... 126
Valentine, Jean 1934- ... CANR-98
Earlier sketches in CA 65-68, CANR-34
See also CP 2, 3, 4, 5, 6, 7
See also CWP
Valentine, Jo
See Armstrong, Charlotte
Valentine, Johnny ... SATA 72
Valentine, Lloyd Magnus 1922-
Brief entry ... 110
Valentine, Mark 1959- ... 155
Valentine, Roger
See Duke, Donald Norman
Valentine, Ruth 1945- ... 196
Valentine, Sister Mary Hester 1909-2000 ... CAP-2
Earlier sketch in CA 23-24
Valentine, Steven Richards 1956- ... 113
Valentine, Tom 1935- ... CANR-22
Earlier sketch in CA 45-48
Valentine, William Alexander 1905-1988 ... 57-60
Valentis, Mary 1945- ... 148
Valenzuela, Arturo A. 1944- ... 101
Valenzuela, Luisa 1938- ... CANR-123
Earlier sketches in CA 101, CANR-32, 65
See also CDWLB 3
See also CLC 31, 104
See also CWW 2
See also DAM MULT
See also DLB 113
See also EWL 3
See also FW
See also HLCS 2
See also HW 1, 2
See also LAW
See also RGSF 2
See also RGWL 3
See also SSC 14, 82
Valeo, Francis Ralph 1916-
Brief entry ... 108
Valera, Diego de 1412-1488 ... DLB 286
Valeran, A. B.
See Starr, S(tephen) Frederick
Valera y Alcala-Galiano, Juan 1824-1905
Brief entry ... 106
See also TCLC 10
Valeri, Diego 1887-1976 ... DLB 128
Valeri, Laura ... 232
Valeriani, Richard (Gerard) 1932- ... CANR-12
Earlier sketch in CA 65-68
Valeriano, Napoleon D(iestro) 1917(?)-1975
Obituary ... 53-56
Valerio, Anthony 1940- ... 165
Valerius Flaccus fl. 92- ... DLB 211
Valerius Maximus fl. 20- ... DLB 211
Valery, Bernard 1913(?)-1984
Obituary ... 113
Valery, (Ambroise) Paul (Toussaint Jules) 1871-1945 ... 122
Brief entry ... 104
See also DA3
See also DAM POET
See also DLB 258
See also EW 8
See also EWL 3
See also GFL 1789 to the Present
See also MTCW 1, 2
See also MTFW 2005
See also PC 9
See also RGWL 2, 3
See also TCLC 4, 15
See also TWA
Vales, Robert L(ee) 1933- ... 53-56
Valesio, Paolo 1939- ... 201
See also DLB 196
Valett, Robert E. 1927- ... CANR-22
Earlier sketches in CA 17-20R, CANR-7
Valette, Rebecca M(arianne Loose) 1938- ... CANR-8
Earlier sketch in CA 21-24R
Valgardson, W(illiam) D(empsey) 1939- ... CANR-135
Earlier sketches in CA 41-44R, CANR-38, 60
See also DAC
See also DAM MST
See also DLB 60
See also MAICYA 2
See also SATA 101, 151
Valgeirsdottir, Sigrieur 1919- ... 219
Valgemae, Mardi 1935- ... 41-44R
Vali, Ferenc Albert 1905-1984 ... CANR-37
Obituary ... 114
Earlier sketches in CA 1-4R, CANR-3
Valiani, Leo 1909-1999 ... CANR-18
Obituary ... 185
Earlier sketch in CA 101
Valiente, Doreen 1922-1999 ... 189
Valin, Jonathan Louis 1948- ... CANR-62
Earlier sketches in CA 101, CANR-38
See also CMW 4
Valin, Martial (Henry) 1898-1980
Obituary ... 105
Valis, Noel M(aureen Ritter) 1945- ... 110
Valkenier, Elizabeth Kridl 1926- ... 119
Valkepaa, Nils Aslak 1943- ... CWW 2
Valko, Peter 1950- ... 159
Vall, Seymour 1925(?)-1987
Obituary ... 124
Valla, Lorenzo 1405-1457 ... LMFS 1
Vallance, Elizabeth (Mary) 1945- ... CANR-40
Earlier sketch in CA 102
Vallbona, Rima-Gretel Rothe 1931- ... 146
Valle, Luz 1899-1971 ... DLB 290
Valle, Rafael Heliodoro 1891-1959 ... 207
See also LAW
Valle, Victor Manuel 1950- ... CANR-134
Earlier sketch in CA 176
See also DLB 122
See also HW 2
Valleau, Emily 1925- ... SATA 51
Valledor, Edgardo
See Goldenthal, Edgar J.
Vallee, Hubert P(rior) 1901-1986 ... CANR-2
Obituary ... 119
Earlier sketch in CA 1-4R
Vallee, Jacques F. 1939- ... CANR-10
Earlier sketch in CA 17-20R
Vallee, Lillian (Bozenna) 1949- ... 135
Vallee, Rudy
See Vallee, Hubert P(rior)
Vallee-Poussin, Charles Jean Gustave Nicolas de la 1866-1962 ... 170
Valle-Inclan, Ramon (Maria) del 1866-1936 ... CANR-80
Brief entry ... 106
Earlier sketch in CA 153
See also del Valle-Inclan, Ramon (Maria)
See also DAM MULT
See also DLB 134
See also EW 8
See also EWL 3
See also HLC 2
See also HW 2
See also RGSF 2
See also RGWL 2, 3
See also TCLC 5
Vallejo, Antonio Buero
See Buero Vallejo, Antonio
Vallejo, Armando 1949- ... 176
See also DLB 122
See also HW 2
Vallejo, Boris 1941- ... 167
See also AAYA 13
See also HW 2
Vallejo, Cesar (Abraham) 1892-1938 ... 153
Brief entry ... 105
See also DAM MULT
See also DLB 290
See also EWL 3
See also HLC 2
See also HW 1
See also LAW
See also RGWL 2, 3
See also TCLC 3, 56
Vallen, Jerome J(ay) 1928- ... 93-96
Vallentine, John F(ranklin) 1931- ... CANR-41
Earlier sketches in CA 53-56, CANR-4, 19
Vallerand, April Hazard 1957- ... 168
Valles, Jules 1832-1885 ... DLB 123
See also GFL 1789 to the Present
Vallette, Marguerite Eymery 1860-1953 ... 182
See also Rachilde
See also DLB 123, 192
See also TCLC 67
Valle Y Pena, Ramon del
See Valle-Inclan, Ramon (Maria) del
Vallhonrat, Javier 1953- ... 214
Vallieres, Pierre 1938-1998 ... 194
Vallinder, Torbjorn 1925- ... 155
Vallis, Val(entine Thomas) 1916- ... CP 1
Vallois
See Bove, Emmanuel
Vallone, Lynne 1962- ... CANR-115
Earlier sketch in CA 150
Vallone, Ralph, Jr. 1947- ... 147
Valmaggia, Juan S. 1895-1980
Obituary ... 97-100
Valsan, E. H. 1933- ... 29-32R
Valtz, Robert C. K. 1936- ... 13-16R
Value, Barbara Ann 1932-1986
Obituary ... 120
Valverde, Jose Maria 1926-1996 ... 176
See also DLB 108
See also HW 2
Vambe, Lawrence (Chinyani) 1917- ... 110
Vamos, Mara (Miriam) 1927-1997
Brief entry ... 114
Vampilov, Aleksandr Valentinovich 1937-1972
See Vampilov, Alexander
See also DLB 302
Vampilov, Alexander
See Vampilov, Aleksandr Valentinovich
Vamplew, Wray 1943- ... CANR-20
Earlier sketch in CA 103
Van Abbe, Derek Maurice 1916- ... 57-60
Van Abbe, Salaman 1883-1955 ... SATA 18
Van Allen, James (Alfred) 1914- ... 162
Van Allsburg, Chris 1949- ... CANR-120
Brief entry ... 113
Earlier sketches in CA 117, CANR-38
See also CLR 5, 13
See also CWRI 5
See also DLB 61
See also MAICYA 1, 2
See also SATA 37, 53, 105, 156
van Alphen, Ernst 1958- ... 143
Van Alstyne, Richard W(arner) 1900-1983 ... CANR-39
Earlier sketch in CA 9-12R
Van Alstyne, William W. 1934- ... 145
Van Anda, Carr 1864-1945 ... DLB 25
Van Andel, Jay 1924-2004 ... 181
Obituary ... 234
Van Anrooy, Francine 1924- ... 21-24R
See also SATA 2
Van Anrooy, Frans
See Van Anrooy, Francine
van Appledorn, Mary Jeanne 1927- .. CANR-51
Earlier sketches in CA 25-28R, CANR-10, 26
Vanardy, Varick
See Dey, Frederic (Merrill) Van Rensselaer
Van Arsdel, Rosemary T(horstenson) 1926- ... CANR-43
Earlier sketch in CA 108
Van Ash, Cay 1918-1994 ... 220
See also CLC 34
Van Atta, Winfred 1910-1990 ... CANR-1
Earlier sketch in CA 1-4R
Vanauken, Sheldon 1914-1996 ... CANR-94
Earlier sketches in CA 85-88, CANR-15, 35
Van Ausdale, Debra 1954- ... 232
Vanbalen, A.
See Stolk, Anthonie
van Beeck, Frans Jozef 1930- ... 115
van Belkom, Edo 1962- ... 182
van Belle, Gerald ... 146
Vanberg, Bent J(arl) 1915-1989 ... 118
van Bergeijk, Peter A(drianus) G(errit) 1959- ... CANR-108
Earlier sketch in CA 152
van Beusekom, Janneke 1956- ... 167
VanBibber, Max A(rnold) 1913(?)-1981
Obituary ... 103
van Brabant, Jozef M(artin) 1942- ... 141
Van Briggle, Margaret F(rances) Jessup 1917- ... 9-12R
Van Brocklin, Norm(an Mack) 1926-1983
Obituary ... 109
Vanbrugh, Sir John 1664-1726 ... BRW 2
See also DAM DRAM
See also DLB 80
See also IDTP
See also RGEL 2
Van Brunt, H. L.
See Van Brunt, (Howell) Lloyd
Van Brunt, (Howell) Lloyd 1936- ... CANR-35
Earlier sketch in CA 49-52
See also CAAS 15
Van Buitenen, J(ohannes) A(drian) B(ernard) 1928(?)-1979 ... 103
Obituary ... 89-92
Van Buren, Abigail
See Phillips, Pauline (Esther Friedman)
Van Buren, James G(eil) 1914- ... 57-60
van Buren, Paul (Matthews) 1924-1998 ... CANR-11
Obituary ... 169
Earlier sketch in CA 61-64
Van Buren, Raeburn 1891-1987 ... CANR-39
Earlier sketch in CA 103
VanBurkleo, Sandra F. ... 237
Van Caenegem, R(aoul) C(harles) 1927- ... CANR-23
Earlier sketch in CA 45-48
Van Campen, Karl
See Campbell, John W(ood, Jr.)
Van Caspel, Venita 1922- ... 104
van Cauwelaert, Didier
See Cauwelaert, Didier van
Vance, A. D.
See Vane-Wright, R(ichard) I(rwin)
Vance, Adrian 1936- ... 77-80
Vance, Barbara Jane 1934- ... 57-60
Vance, Bruce 1931- ... 33-36R
Vance, Cyrus R(oberts) 1917-2002 ... 121
Obituary ... 200
Vance, Edgar
See Ambrose, Eric (Samuel)
Vance, Eleanor Graham 1908-1985 ... 9-12R
See also SATA 11
Vance, Ethel
See Stone, Grace Zaring
Vance, Eugene 1934- ... 126
Vance, Gerald
See Garrett, (Gordon) Randall (Phillip) and Silverberg, Robert
Vance, Jack
See Vance, John Holbrook
See also CLC 35
See also DLB 8
See also FANT
See also SCFW 1, 2
See also SFW 4
See also SUFW 1, 2
Vance, Joel M. 1934- ... 238
Vance, John Holbrook 1916- ... CANR-65
Earlier sketches in CA 29-32R, CANR-17
See also Queen, Ellery and Vance, Jack
See also CMW 4
See also MTCW 1
Vance, Jonathan F(ranklin) 1963- ... 221
Vance, Lawrence L(ee) 1911-1978 ... CANR-39
Earlier sketch in CA 49-52
Vance, Louis Joseph 1879-1933
Brief entry ... 112
See also CMW 4
Vance, Marguerite 1889-1965
Obituary ... 109
See also SATA 29
Vance, (Robert) Norman (Colbert) 1950- ... CANR-48
Earlier sketch in CA 122
Vance, Rupert B(ayless) 1899-1975
Obituary ... 61-64
Vance, Samuel 1939- ... 29-32R
Vance, Sandra S. 1946- ... 147
Vance, Stanley 1915- ... CANR-3
Earlier sketch in CA 1-4R
Vance, Steve 1952- ... HGG
Vance, William E. 1911-1986 ... CANR-64
Obituary ... 119
Earlier sketch in CA 105
See also TCWW 1, 2
Vance, William L(ynn) 1934- ... CANR-93
Earlier sketch in CA 132
Vanceburg, Martha
See Roth (Vanceburg), Martha
Vance-Watkins, Lequita 1936- ... 151
Vancil, Richard F(ranklin) 1931-1996 ... CANR-40
Obituary ... 151
Earlier sketches in CA 5-8R, CANR-8
Van Cise, Jerrold G(ordon) 1910-1996 ... 114
Obituary ... 153
VanCleave, Janice 1942- ... CANR-95
Earlier sketch in CA 142
See also SATA 75, 116
See also SATA-Essay 123
Van Cleef, Eugene 1887-1973
Obituary ... 107
Van Cleve, John Walter 1950- ... CANR-48
Earlier sketch in CA 122

Cumulative Index 591 Van Hise

Van Cleve, Thomas Curtis 1888-1976 ... 41-44R
Obituary ... 65-68
Van Coevering, Jack
See Van Coevering, Jan Adrian
Van Coevering, Jan Adrian 1900-1978 .. CAP-1
Earlier sketch in CA 9-10
van Corstanje, Auspicius
See van Corstanje, Charles
van Corstanje, Charles 1913-1993 ... 107
Van Creveld, Martin L. 1946- ... 214
Van Cromphout, Gustaaf ... 206
van Croonenburg, Engelbert J(ohannes)
1909- ... 37-40R
Vancura, Vladislav 1891-1942 ... CDWLB 4
See also DLB 215
See also EWL 3
Van Dahm, Thomas E(dward) 1924- ... 65-68
Van Dalen, Deobold B(ertrude)
1911-1995 ... CANR-20
Earlier sketch in CA 1-4R
Van Dam, Ine 1947- ... 109
van Dam, J.
See Presser, (Gerrit) Jacob
Van Damme, Jean-Claude 1960- ... 214
Van Deburg, William L. 1948- ... 139
See also BW 2
Vande Kieft, Ruth Marguerite 1925- ... 17-20R
Van D'Elden, Karl H. 1923- ... 45-48
Van Delden, Maarten 1958- ... 169
Vandeman, George E(dward) 1916-2000
Obituary ... 191
Brief entry ... 114
Van De Mieroop, Marc 1956- ... 139
Vandenberg, Arthur Hendrick 1884-1951
Brief entry ... 120
Vandenberg, Donald 1931- ... 29-32R
Vandenberg, Philipp 1941- ... CANR-47
Earlier sketches in CA 61-64, CANR-8, 23
Vandenberg, T. F. 1941- ... 25-28R
Van Den Bergh, Nan 1947- ... 140
van den Berghe, Pierre L. 1933- ... CANR-5
Earlier sketch in CA 9-12R
Van Den Bogarde, Derek Jules Gaspard Ulric
Niven 1921-1999 ... 77-80
Obituary ... 179
See also Bogarde, Dirk
See also CLC 14
Vandenbosch, Amry 1894-1990 ... 61-64
Vandenbosch, Robert 1922-1978
Obituary ... 107
Vanden Bossche, Chris R. 1950- ... 141
van den Brink, Gijsbert 1963- ... 215
van den Brink, H(ans) M(aarten) 1956- ... 199
VandenBroeck, Andre 1923- ... 128
Vandenbroucke, Lucien S. 1951- ... 148
Vandenburg, Mary Lou 1943- ... 73-76
See also SATA 17
Vandenburgh, Jane ... 168
See also CLC 59
Vandenburgh, Mildred 1898-1984 ... 97-100
Vandenbusche, Duane (Lee) 1937- ... CANR-49
Earlier sketches in CA 45-48, CANR-24
van den Bussche, Henri O(mer) A(ntoine)
See Bussche, Henri O(mer) A(ntoine) Van den
van den Haag, Ernest 1914-2002 ... CANR-26
Obituary ... 203
Earlier sketches in CA 5-8R, CANR-6
van den Heuvel, Albert H(endrik)
1932- ... 17-20R
van den Heuvel, Cornelisz A. 1931- ... 13-16R
Vanden Heuvel, Jon 1963- ... 215
vanden Heuvel, Katrina 1959- ... CANR-135
Earlier sketch in CA 133
van den Hoven, Adrian T. 1939- ... 141
Van De Pitte, Frederick P. 1932- ... 45-48
Vander, Harry J(oseph) III 1913-1969(?) . CAP-2
Earlier sketch in CA 25-28
VanDerBeets, Richard 1932- ... CANR-35
Earlier sketch in CA 29-32R
van der Bent, Ans J(oachim) 1924-1995 ... 131
Vanderbes, Jennifer (Chase) 1974- ... 226
Vanderbilt, Amy 1908-1974 ... CANR-3
Obituary ... 53-56
Earlier sketch in CA 1-4R
Vanderbilt, Arthur T. II 1950- ... 122
Vanderbilt, Cornelius, Jr. 1898-1974 ... CAP-1
Obituary ... 49-52
Earlier sketch in CA 9-10
See also AITN 1
Vanderbilt, Gloria (Laura Morgan)
1924- ... CANR-60
Earlier sketches in CA 89-92, CANR-22
Interview in ... CANR-22
Vander Boom, Mae M. ... SATA 14
Vanderborg, Susan 1967- ... 220
Vanderburgh, R(osamond) M(oate) 1926- ... 105
Vander-Els, Betty 1936- ... SATA 63
van der Elsken, Ed(uard) 1925-1990 ... 224
Vander Goot, Mary 1947- ... 112
Vandergriff, (Lola) Aola 1920-1989 .. CANR-18
Obituary ... 128
Earlier sketch in CA 89-92
Interview in ... CANR-18
Vanderhaar, Gerard A(nthony) 1931- ... 125
Vanderhaeghe, Guy 1951- ... CANR-72
Earlier sketch in CA 113
See also BPFB 3
See also CLC 41
See also CN 7
Vanderham, Paul 1959(?)- ... 193
van der Heyden, A(ntonius) A(lphonsus) M(aria)
1922- ... CANR-7
Earlier sketch in CA 57-60
Vander Hill, C(harles) Warren 1937- ... 33-36R
VanDerhoof, Jack W(arner) 1921- ... 53-56
Van der Horst, Brian 1944- ... 41-44R
VanderKam, James C(laire) 1946- ... CANR-104
Earlier sketch in CA 148
Van der Kiste, John (Patrick Guy)
1954- ... CANR-106
Earlier sketch in CA 147
Vander Kooi, Ronald C(harles) ... CANR-2
Earlier sketch in CA 45-48
van der Kroef, Justus M(aria) 1925- .. CANR-14
Earlier sketch in CA 41-44R
van der Lemme, Arie
See van Hensbergen, Gijs
van der Linde, Laurel 1952- ... 146
See also SATA 78
Vanderlip, D(odava) George 1926- ... CANR-15
Earlier sketch in CA 77-80
Vander Lugt, Herbert 1920- ... CANR-18
Earlier sketch in CA 101
van der Marck, Jan 1929- ... 119
VanderMeer, Jeff 1968- ... 224
See also HGG
See also SUFW 2
van der Meer, Ron 1945- ... 152
See also SATA 98
van der Merwe, Nikolaas J(ohannes)
1940- ... CANR-82
Earlier sketches in CA 41-44R, CANR-35
Vandermerwe, Sandra ... 231
van der Meulen, Daniel 1894-1989 ... 117
VanderMolen, Robert 1947- ... CANR-36
Earlier sketch in CA 57-60
van der Plas, Rob(ert) 1938- ... 138
van der Ploeg, Johannes P(etrus) M(aria)
1909- ... CANR-42
Earlier sketches in CAP-1, CA 9-10, CANR-15
van der Poel, Cornelius J(ohannes)
1921- ... CANR-4
Earlier sketch in CA 53-56
Vanderpool, Harold Y(oung) 1936- ... 53-56
Vanderpool, James A(lbert) 1916-1983
Obituary ... 109
van der Poorten, Alf(red J.) 1942- ... 163
van der Post, Laurens (Jan)
1906-1996 ... CANR-35
Obituary ... 155
Earlier sketch in CA 5-8R
See also AFW
See also CLC 5
See also CN 1, 2, 3, 4, 5, 6
See also DLB 204
See also RGEL 2
Van Dersal, William R(ichard)
1907-1990 ... 77-80
Obituary ... 131
Vander-Schrier, Nettie 1922- ... 114
Vandersee, Charles (Andrew) 1938- . CANR-29
Earlier sketch in CA 41-44R
Van Der Slik, Jack R(onald) 1936- ... CANR-65
Earlier sketches in CA 29-32R, CANR-30
van der Smissen, Betty
See van der Smissen, Margaret Elisabeth
van der Smissen, Margaret Elisabeth
1927- ... CANR-9
Earlier sketch in CA 17-20R
van der Steen, Mensje Francine
See van Keulen, Mensje
van der Straaten, Jan 1935- ... CANR-139
Earlier sketch in CA 171
van der Vat, Dan(iel Francis Jeroen)
1939- ... CANR-55
Earlier sketches in CA 109, CANR-28
Vanderveen, Bareld Harmannus 1932- ... 103
Vanderveen, Bart H.
See Vanderveen, Bareld Harmannus
Van der Veer, Judy 1912-1982 ... 33-36R
Obituary ... 108
See also SATA 4
See also SATA-Obit 33
van der Veer, Peter 1953- ... 221
Van Derveer, Tara 1954- ... 169
Vandervelde, Marjorie (Mills) 1908- . CANR-10
Earlier sketch in CA 21-24R
Van der Veldt, James 1893(?)-1977
Obituary ... 73-76
van der Ven, Johannes A. 1940- ... 171
Van der Veur, Paul W. 1921- ... 21-24R
Van Der Voort, Richard Lee 1936- ... 37-40R
van der Vyfer, Thuys
See de Vries, Abraham H.
Vanderwall, Francis W(illiam)
1946- ... CANR-26
Earlier sketch in CA 108
Van der Wee, Herman (Frans Anna) 1928- . 133
Vanderwerff, Corrine 1939- ... 189
See also SATA 117
Vanderwerken, David L(eon) 1945- ... 119
Vanderwerth, W(illiam) C(onnor)
1904-1987 ... 73-76
Vanderwood, Paul J(oseph) 1929- ... CANR-28
Earlier sketch in CA 29-32R
Vander Zanden, James Wilfrid
1930- ... CANR-19
Earlier sketches in CA 13-16R, CANR-5
van der Zee, Barbara (Blanche) 1932- ... 146
van der Zee, Henri A(nthony) 1934- ... 185
Brief entry ... 114
Van Der Zee, James (Augustus Joseph)
1886-1983 ... 104
Obituary ... 109
van der Zee, John 1936- ... CANR-32
Earlier sketches in CA 21-24R, CANR-15
van der Zee, Karen 1874-1957 ... RHW
Vander Zee, Ruth ... SATA 159
Vanderzell, John H. 1924- ... 45-48
VanderZwaag, Harold J. 1929- ... CANR-23
Earlier sketch in CA 45-48
van Deurs, George 1901-1984 ... 25-28R
van Deursen, A. Th. 1931- ... 138
Van Deusen, Dayton G(roff) 1914-1991 .. 9-12R
Van Deusen, Glyndon Garlock
1897-1987 ... CANR-1
Earlier sketch in CA 1-4R
Van Deusen, L. Marshall 1922- ... 61-64
Van Deusen, Ruth B(rown) 1907- ... 5-8R
Van De Vall, Mark 1923-1993 ... CANR-30
Earlier sketches in CA 29-32R, CANR-12
Van Devander, Charles W(ood) 1902-1986
Obituary ... 121
Van Devanter, Lynda (Margaret)
1947-2002 ... 117
Obituary ... 210
Van de Vate, Dwight, Jr. 1928- ... 61-64
Vande Velde, Vivian 1951- ... CANR-120
Earlier sketch in CA 160
See also AAYA 32
See also BYA 6
See also MAICYA 2
See also SATA 62, 95, 141
VanDevelder, Paul 1951(?)- ... 232
Van Deventer, David E(arl) 1937-
Brief entry ... 115
Van Deventer, Fred 1903-1971 ... CAP-1
Earlier sketch in CA 13-16
VanDeventer, Robert ... 105
van de Waarsenburg, Hans 1943- ... 210
Van de Water, Frederic F(ranklyn) 1890-1968
Obituary ... 110
van de Wetering, Janwillem 1931- ... CANR-90
Earlier sketches in CA 49-52, CANR-4, 62
See also CLC 47
See also CMW 4
Van Dine, S. S.
See Wright, Willard Huntington
See also DLB 306
See also MSW
See also TCLC 23
Vandiver, Edward P(inckney), Jr.
1902-1993 ... CAP-1
Earlier sketch in CA 13-14
Vandiver, Frank E(verson)
1925-2005 ... CANR-124
Obituary ... 235
Earlier sketches in CA 5-8R, CANR-7
Vandivert, Rita (Andre) 1905-1986 ... CANR-6
Earlier sketch in CA 5-8R
See also SATA 21
Vando, Gloria 1936- ... 210
Van Domelen, John E(mory) 1935- ... 130
Van Dommelen, David B. 1929- ... CANR-93
Earlier sketches in CA 5-8R, CANR-35
Van Dongen, Helen 1909- ... IDFW 3, 4
van Dooren, Ingrid 1949- ... 114
van Dooren, L(eonard) A(lfred) T(heophile)
1912- ... CANR-19
Earlier sketches in CA 5-8R, CANR-3
Van Doren, Carl (Clinton) 1885-1950 ... 168
Brief entry ... 111
See also TCLC 18
Van Doren, Charles L. 1926- ... CANR-4
Earlier sketch in CA 5-8R
Van Doren, Dorothy Graffe 1896-1993 ... 1-4R
Obituary ... 141
Van Doren, Irita 1891-1966
Obituary ... 89-92
Van Doren, Mark 1894-1972 ... CANR-3
Obituary ... 37-40R
Earlier sketch in CA 1-4R
See also CLC 6, 10
See also CN 1
See also CP 1
See also DLB 45, 284
See also MAL 5
See also MTCW 1, 2
See also RGAL 4
Van Dorne, R.
See Wallmann, Jeffrey M(iner)
Vandour, Cyril
See Surmelian, Leon (Zaven)
Van Dover, J(ames) K(enneth) 1950- ... 139
Van Draanen, Wendelin ... 195
See also AAYA 36
See also MAICYA 2
See also SATA 122
Van Druten, John (William) 1901-1957 ... 161
Brief entry ... 104
See also DLB 10
See also MAL 5
See also RGAL 4
See also TCLC 2
Van Dusen, Albert E(dward)
1916-1999 ... CANR-3
Earlier sketch in CA 5-8R
Van Dusen, Clarence Raymond 1907- ... 5-8R
Van Dusen, Henry P(itney)
1897-1975 ... CANR-3
Obituary ... 57-60
Earlier sketch in CA 1-4R
Van Dusen, Robert LaBranche 1929- ... 41-44R
Van Duyn, Janet 1910- ... 69-72
See also SATA 18
Van Duyn, Mona (Jane)
1921-2004 ... CANR-116
Obituary ... 234
Earlier sketches in CA 9-12R, CANR-7, 38, 60
See also CLC 3, 7, 63, 116
See also CP 1, 2, 3, 4, 5, 6, 7
See also CWP
See also DAM POET
See also DLB 5
See also MAL 5
See also MTFW 2005
See also PFS 20
Van Duzee, Mabel 1895-1967 ... 5-8R
Van Duzer, Chet A. 1966- ... 153
Van Dyck, Karen (Rhoads) 1961- ... 181
Van Dyk, Jere
See Van Dyk, Wilmer Jerald
Van Dyk, Wilmer Jerald 1945- ... 131
Van Dyke, Annette 1943- ... 194
Van Dyke, Carolynn 1947- ... 116
Van Dyke, Dick 1925- ... 166
Brief entry ... 112
Van Dyke, Henry 1852-1933 ... DLB 71
See also DLBD 13
Van Dyke, Henry 1928- ... CANR-88
Earlier sketches in CA 49-52, CANR-25
See also BW 1
See also DLB 33
Van Dyke, John C. 1856-1932 ... ANW
See also DLB 186
Van Dyke, John Charles 1856-1932 ... 197
Van Dyke, Jon M. 1943- ... 29-32R
Van Dyke, Lauren A. 1906-1995 ... 29-32R
Van Dyke, Vernon Brumbaugh
1912-1998 ... CANR-46
Earlier sketches in CA 1-4R, CANR-23
Van Dyke, Willard (Ames) 1906-1986 ... 235
Van Dyne, Edith
See Baum, L(yman) Frank and
Sampson, Emma (Keats) Speed and
van Zantwijk, Rudolf (Alexander Marinus)
Vane, Brett
See Kent, Arthur William Charles
Vane, Howard (R.) 1951- ... 189
Vane, John R(obert) 1927-2004 ... 160
Obituary ... 233
Vane, Michael
See Humphries, Sydney Vernon
Vane, Roland
See McKeag, Ernest L(ionel)
Vane, (Vane Hunt) Sutton 1888-1963
Obituary ... 113
See also DLB 10
van Eeden, Frederik Willem
See Eeden, Frederik Willem van
Van Eenwyk, John R. 1946- ... 164
Van Eerde, Katherine S(ommerlatte)
1920- ... 61-64
Van Egmond, Peter (George) 1937- ... 61-64
Vanek, Jaroslav 1930- ... 103
Van Engen, John H. 1947- ... 117
Van Ermengem, Frederic 1881-1972
Obituary ... 33-36R
Van Erven, Eugene 1955- ... 138
Vanesch, Jean (Louis) 1950- ... 210
Van Ess, Dorothy 1885(?)-1975
Obituary ... 61-64
Van Ettinger, Jan 1902- ... CANR-21
Earlier sketch in CA 1-4R
Van Every, Dale 1896-1976 ... CANR-3
Earlier sketch in CA 1-4R
Van Ewijk, Casper 1953- ... 140
Vane-Wright, R(ichard) I(rwin) 1942- ... 121
Van Fossen, Richard W(aight) 1927- .. CANR-6
Earlier sketch in CA 5-8R
van Fraassen, Bastiaan Cornelis ... CANR-14
Earlier sketch in CA 37-40R
van Frankenhuyzen, Gijsbert 1951- ... SATA 132
van Geert, Paul 1950- ... 132
Van Geil, Mercury E. C. L.
See McGilvery, Laurence
van Gelder, Dora 1904-
Brief entry ... 116
Van Gelder, Gordon (Mark) 1966- ... 190
Van Gelder, Lindsy 1944- ... 97-100
Van Gelder, Richard George 1928- ... 73-76
Vangelisti, Paul 1945- ... CANR-111
Earlier sketches in CA 77-80, CANR-14, 31
Vangen, Roland Dean 1935- ... 105
Vanger, Milton Isadore 1925- ... CANR-34
Earlier sketch in CA 13-16R
Van Gieson, Judith 1941- ... 198
See also CMW 4
See also DLB 306
Van Ginneken, Jaap 1943- ... 142
Van Goethem, Larry 1934- ... 101
van Gogh, Vincent 1853-1890 ... AAYA 29
Van Greenaway, Peter 1929-1988 ... CMW 4
van Gulik, Robert Hans 1910-1967 . CANR-62
Obituary ... 25-28R
Earlier sketches in CA 1-4R, CANR-3
See also CMW 4
See also DLBD 17
See also MSW
VanGundy, Arthur B(oice), Jr. 1946- . CANR-29
Earlier sketch in CA 110
Van Haaften, Julia 1946- ... 109
van Hasselt, G.
See Claes, Ernest
Van Hassen, Amy
See Wiles, Domini
Van Hattum, Rolland J(ames)
1924-1987 ... CANR-21
Earlier sketch in CA 105
Van Hecke, B(resee) C(oleman)
1926-1990 ... 29-32R
Van Heerden, Ernst 1916-1997 ... 213
van Heerden, Etienne 1954- ... 143
Van Heijenoort, Jean 1912-1986 ... 161
Obituary ... 120
Van Helden, Albert 1940- ... 125
van Hensbergen, Gijs 1958- ... 227
Van Herik, Judith 1947- ... 108
van Herk, Aritha 1954- ... CANR-94
Earlier sketch in CA 101
van het Reve, Karel 1921- ... 49-52
Van Heusen, James 1913-1990 ... IDFW 3, 4
van Heyningen, Christina 1900- ... 17-20R
van Heyningen, William Edward
1911-1989 ... 112
Van Hise, Della 1955- ... 121

van Hoddis, Jakob
See Davidsohn, Hans
Van Hoesen, Walter H. 1898(?)-1977
Obituary ... 69-72
Van Hook, Beverly H. 1941- ... 167
See also SATA 99
Van Hook, Roger Eugene 1943- ... 29-32R
Van Hoose, William H. 1927- ... 89-92
Van Horn, Ray, Jr. 1970- ... 217
Van Horn, Richard L. 1932- ... 53-56
Van Horn, William 1939- ... 115
See also SATA 43
Van Horne, Harriet 1920-1998
Obituary ... 164
Brief entry ... 113
Van Houten, Lois 1918- ... CANR-34
Earlier sketch in CA 77-80
Van Huss, Wayne D(aniel) 1917- ... 61-64
Van Hyning, Thomas E. 1954- ... 154
Vanier, Jean 1928- ... 225
van Inwagen, Peter (Jan) 1942- ... CANR-39
Earlier sketch in CA 116
van Itallie, Jean-Claude 1936- ... CANR-48
Earlier sketches in CA 45-48, CANR-1
See also CAAS 2
See also CAD
See also CD 5, 6
See also CLC 3
See also DLB 7
Van Itallie, Philip H. 1899-1986 ... CAP-1
Earlier sketch in CA 9-10
Van Iterson, S(iny) R(ose) ... 102
See also SATA 26
van Jaarsveld, Floris Albertus 1922- ... CANR-7
Earlier sketch in CA 5-8R
van Kaam, Adrian (L.) 1920- ... CANR-52
Earlier sketches in CA 17-20R, CANR-10, 26
Van Kampen, Vlasta 1943- ... SATA 54, 163
van Kessel, Ineke 1948- ... 199
van Keulen, Mensje 1946- ... 195
Van Kleek, Peter Eric 1929- ... CANR-35
Earlier sketch in CA 53-56
Van Krevelen, Alice 1914- ... 45-48
Van Laan, Nancy 1939- ... CANR-126
Earlier sketch in CA 173
See also SATA 105
van Lawick, Hugo 1937- ... 85-88
van Lawick-Goodall, Jane
See Goodall, Jane
Vanleer, Jay
See Williams, June Vanleer
Van Leeuwen, Jean 1937- ... CANR-121
Earlier sketches in CA 25-28R, CANR-11, 28, 52
See also SAAS 8
See also SATA 6, 82, 132, 141
See also SATA-Essay 141
van Lemmen, Hans 1946- ... 144
Van Lente, Charles R(obert) 1941- ... 65-68
van Lhin, Erik
See del Rey, Lester
Van Lierde, John 1907- ... CAP-1
Earlier sketch in CA 9-10
Van Lierde, Peter Canisius
See Van Lierde, John
van Lint, June 1928- ... 65-68
Van Loan, Charles E(mmett) 1876-1919 ... 186
See also DLB 171
van Loon, Gerard Willem 1911-1980 ... 45-48
Van Loon, Hendrik Willem 1882-1944 ... 201
Brief entry ... 117
See also SATA 18
See also WCH
Van Loon, Karel Glastra 1962- ... 225
Van Loot, Cornelius Obenchain
See Roberts, Kenneth (Lewis)
Van Meerhaeghe, M(arcel) A(lfons) G(ilbert) 1921- ... CANR-13
Earlier sketch in CA 77-80
Van Melsen, Andreas G(erardus) M(aria) 1912- ... CANR-82
Earlier sketches in CA 1-4R, CANR-4, 34
Van Meter, Jonathan W. 1963- ... 226
VanMeter, Vandelia 1934- ... 142
Van Munching, Philip ... 180
Vann, J(erry) Don 1938- ... 29-32R
Vann, James Allen 1939- ... 110
Vann, Richard T(ilman) 1931- ... 21-24R
Vann, Robert L. 1887-1940 ... DLB 29
Vannatta, Dennis 1946- ... 138
Van Natta, Don, Jr. 1964- ... 225
Vanneman, Reeve 1945- ... 127
Van Ness, Peter 1933- ... 29-32R
van Niekerk, Marlene 1954- ... 229
Van Niel, Cornelius B(ernardus) 1897-1985
Obituary ... 115
Vannier, Maryhelen 1915- ... CANR-22
Earlier sketches in CA 1-4R, CANR-6
van Nieuwenhuijze, C(hristoffel) A(nthonie) O(livier) 1920- ... 25-28R
Van Nimmen, (Carol) Jane 1937- ... 125
Van Nooten, Barend A(drian) 1932- ... 45-48
Van Noppen, Ina (Faye) W(oestemeyer) 1906-1980 ... 5-8R
Obituary ... 103
Vannorsdall, John Warren 1924- ... 113
Van Nostrand, A(lbert) D(ouglass) 1922- ... CANR-16
Earlier sketch in CA 41-44R
Vannoy, Russell (Columbus) 1933- ... 119
Vano, Gerard S. 1943- ... 112
Vanocur, Edith C. 1924(?)-1975
Obituary ... 57-60
Vanocur, Sander 1928- ... 120
Brief entry ... 109
Interview in ... CA-120
van Onselen, Charles 1944- ... 154
van Oort, Jan 1921- ... CANR-31
Earlier sketch in CA 29-32R
Van Oosterzee, Penny 1955- ... 191
Van Orden, M(erton) D(ick) 1921- ... 37-40R
See also SATA 4
Van Orman, Bonny 1939(?)-1987
Obituary ... 122
Van Orman, Richard A(lbert) 1936- ... CANR-34
Earlier sketch in CA 21-24R
Van Osdol, William R(ay) 1927- ... 53-56
van Ostaijen, Paul
See Ostaijen, Paul van
van Ostaijen, Paul 1896-1928 ... 163
See also TCLC 33
Van Over, Raymond 1934- ... 184
Brief entry ... 112
van Overbeek, Johannes 1908-1988 ... CAP-1
Earlier sketch in CA 13-14
Van Parijs, Philippe 1951- ... CANR-118
Earlier sketch in CA 152
Van Patten, Dick 1928- ... 170
Van Peebles, Melvin 1932- ... CANR-82
Earlier sketches in CA 85-88, CANR-27, 67
See also BW 2, 3
See also CLC 2, 20
See also DAM MULT
Van Pelt, James ... 238
van Pelt, Robert-Jan 1955- ... 139
van Peursen, Cornelius Anthonie 1920-1996 ... 53-56
Van Praagh, David 1931- ... CANR-135
Earlier sketch in CA 165
Van Praagh, Margaret 1910-1990 ... CAP-2
Obituary ... 130
Earlier sketch in CA 17-18
Van Praagh, Peggy
See Van Praagh, Margaret
Van Proosdy, Cornelis 1919- ... CANR-5
Earlier sketch in CA 9-12R
Van Proyen, Mark 1954- ... CAAS 25
Van Raden, Kristine 1953- ... 165
van Ravenswaay, Charles 1911-1990 ... 119
Van Rensselaer, Alexander (Taylor Mason) 1892-1962 ... 73-76
See also SATA 14
van Rensselaer, Maria van Cortlandt 1645-1689 ... DLB 200
Van Rensselaer, Mariana Griswold 1851-1934 ... 179
See also DLB 47
Van Rheenen, Gailyn 1946- ... 69-72
Van Rij, Jan 1928- ... 200
van Rijn, Ignatius
See Ingram, Forrest L(eo)
Van Riper, Francis A(lbert) 1946- ... CANR-11
Earlier sketch in CA 69-72
Van Riper, Frank
See Van Riper, Francis A(lbert)
Van Riper, Guernsey, Jr. 1909-1995 ... CANR-6
Earlier sketch in CA 5-8R
See also SATA 3
Van Riper, Paul P(ritchard) 1916- ... CANR-31
Earlier sketch in CA 1-4R
Van Riper, Robert 1921- ... 37-40R
van Rjndt, Philippe 1950- ... CANR-14
Earlier sketch in CA 65-68
van Rooy, C(harles) A(ugust) 1923- ... 17-20R
van Ruler, Han
See van Ruler, J. A.
van Ruler, J. A. 1963- ... 152
Van Runkle, Theodora 1940- ... IDFW 3, 4
Van Rynbach, Iris 1952- ... 169
See also SATA 102
Van Saher, Lilla 1912-1968 ... CAP-1
Earlier sketch in CA 11-12
Vansant, Carl 1938- ... 37-40R
Van Sant, Gus 1952- ... 152
See also AAYA 17
Vansant, Rhonda Joy Edwards 1950- ... SATA 92
Van Schaick, Frances L. 1912(?)-1979
Obituary ... 89-92
van Schendel, Arthur(-Francois-Emile) 1874-1946 ... EWL 3
See also TCLC 56
Van Scyoc, Sydney J(oyce) 1939- ... CANR-33
Earlier sketches in CA 89-92, CANR-15
See also SFW 4
Van See, John
See Vance, John Holbrook
Van Sertima, Ivan Gladstone 1935- ... CANR-42
Earlier sketch in CA 104
See also BW 2
See also CP 1
Van Seters, John 1935- ... CANR-38
Earlier sketch in CA 115
Van Sickle, Emily 1910-2005 ... 140
Obituary ... 237
Van Sickle, John V(alentine) 1892-1975 ... CANR-35
Earlier sketch in CA 5-8R
Van Sickle, Neil D(avid) 1915- ... 41-44R
VanSickle, V. A.
See Carhart, Arthur Hawthorne
Vansina, Jan 1929- ... CANR-10
Earlier sketch in CA 65-68
Vansittart, Jane
See Moorhouse, Hilda Vansittart
Vansittart, Peter 1920- ... CANR-90
Earlier sketches in CA 1-4R, CANR-3, 49
See also CLC 42
See also CN 4, 5, 6, 7
See also RHW
Van Slingerland, Peter 1929- ... 21-24R
Van Slooten, Henry 1916- ... 1-4R
Van Slyck, Abigail A(yres) 1959- ... 161
Van Slyck, Philip 1920- ... 13-16R
Van Slyke, Donald Dexter 1883-1971
Obituary ... 104
Van Slyke, Helen (Lenore) 1919-1979 ... CANR-28
Obituary ... 89-92
Earlier sketch in CA 37-40R
See also RHW
Van Slyke, Lyman P(age) 1929- ... 21-24R
Van Smith, Howard
See Smith, Howard Van
van Someren, Liesje
See Lichtenberg, Elisabeth Jacoba
Van Staaveren, Jacob 1917- ... 153
Van Steenberghen, Fernand (Emmanuel) 1904-1993 ... 130
Van Steenhouse, Andrea 1943- ... 170
Van Steenwyk, Elizabeth (Ann) 1928- ... CANR-127
Earlier sketches in CA 101, CANR-18, 40
See also SATA 34, 89
Van Stockum, Hilda 1908- ... CANR-5
Earlier sketch in CA 9-12R
See also CWRI 5
See also SATA 5
Vanstone, W(illiam) H(ubert) 1923-1999 ... 183
van Straten, Florence W(ilhelmina) 1913-1992 ... 17-20R
Obituary ... 137
Vanstrum, Glenn S. ... 219
Van Sweden, James 1935- ... 223
Van Tassel, Alfred J. 1910-1993 ... 41-44R
Van Tassel, David Dirck 1928-2000 ... CANR-35
Earlier sketch in CA 103
Van Tassel, Dennie L(ee) 1939- ... CANR-35
Earlier sketches in CA 57-60, CANR-8
Van Tassel, George W. 1910-1978
Obituary ... 112
Van Tassel, Roger (Carleton) 1924- ... 45-48
van Thal, Herbert (Maurice) 1904-1983 ... CANR-30
Obituary ... 111
Earlier sketch in CA 65-68
Van Tighem, Patricia 1959(?)- ... 207
Van Til, Cornelius 1895-1987 ... CANR-3
Earlier sketch in CA 1-4R
Van Til, William 1911- ... CANR-10
Earlier sketch in CA 25-28R
Van Tilburg, Hans (Konrad) 1961- ... 170
Van Tilburg, Jo Anne 1942- ... CANR-93
Earlier sketch in CA 151
Van Tine, Warren R(ussell) 1942- ... 53-56
Van Trump, James D(enholm) 1908-1995 ... 41-44R
Van Tuyl, Barbara 1940- ... 53-56
See also SATA 11
van Tuyll, Hubert P. 1957- ... 203
Van Valkenburg, Samuel 1891-1976 ... 5-8R
Obituary ... 103
Van Valkenburgh, Paul 1941- ... 89-92
Van Vechten, Benjamin D(avenport) 1935- . 110
Van Vechten, Carl 1880-1964 ... 183
Obituary ... 89-92
See also AMWS 2
See also CLC 33
See also DLB 4, 9, 51
See also HR 1:3
See also RGAL 4
Van Vleck, David B. 1929- ... 101
Van Vleck, John Hasbrouck 1899-1980
Obituary ... 102
Van Vleck, L(loyd) Dale 1933- ... 53-56
Van Vleck, Sarita 1933- ... 13-16R
Van Vlissingen, Arthur 1894-1986
Obituary ... 120
van Vogt, A(lfred) E(lton) 1912-2000 ... CANR-28
Obituary ... 190
Earlier sketch in CA 21-24R
See also BPFB 3
See also BYA 13, 14
See also CLC 1
See also DLB 8, 251
See also SATA 14
See also SATA-Obit 124
See also SCFW 1, 2
See also SFW 4
Van Vooren, Monique 1933- ... 107
Van Voorhis, Linda Lyon 1902-1989
Obituary ... 129
Van Voorst, Robert (E.) 1952- ... 190
Van Voris, Jacqueline 1922- ... 57-60
Van Vugt, William E. 1957- ... 193
van Vuuren, Nancy 1938- ... CANR-35
Earlier sketch in CA 49-52
Van Wagenen, Gertrude 1893-1978
Obituary ... 77-80
van Wageningen, J.
See Presser, (Gerrit) Jacob
Van Wagner, Judy
See Collischan, Judy
Van Wagner, Judy Collischan
See Collischan, Judy
Van Wart, Alice 1948- ... 137
Van Waters, Miriam 1887-1974
Obituary ... 45-48
Van Weddingen, Marthe 1924- ... CANR-14
Earlier sketch in CA 81-84
Van Wert, William F(rancis) 1945- ... 105
Van Wie, Pat
See Lewin, Patricia
Van Winckel, Nance 1951- ... CANR-99
Earlier sketch in CA 131
See also CP 7
van Witsen, Leo 1912- ... 106
Van Woeart, Alpheus
See Halloway, Vance
Van Woerkom, Dorothy (O'Brien) 1924-1996 ... CANR-26
Earlier sketches in CA 57-60, CANR-11
See also SATA 21
Van Wormer, Joe
See Van Wormer, Joseph Edward
Van Wormer, Joseph Edward 1913-1998 ... CANR-5
Earlier sketch in CA 9-12R
See also SATA 35
Van Wormer, Laura (Eleanor) 1955- ... CANR-102
Earlier sketch in CA 127
van Wyk, Gary N(eville) 1960- ... 179
Van Young, Eric (Julian) 1946- ... 122
Van Zandt, E. F.
See Cudlipp, Edythe
Van Zandt, Roland 1918-1991 ... 17-20R
Obituary ... 134
Vanzant, Iyanla (Rhonda) 1952- ... CANR-106
Earlier sketch in CA 142
See also BW 2
Van Zante, Helen Johnson 1906-1990 .. 13-16R
Van Zanten, John W(illiam) 1913-1994 ... 101
van Zantwijk, Rudolf (Alexander Marinus) 1931- ... 133
van Zeller, Claud 1905-1984 ... CANR-6
Obituary ... 113
Earlier sketch in CA 1-4R
van Zeller, Hubert
See van Zeller, Claud
Vanzi, Max (Bruno) 1934- ... 123
Van Zwienen, Ilse Charlotte Koehn 1929-1991 ... CANR-35
Earlier sketch in CA 85-88
See also SATA 34
See also SATA-Brief 28
See also SATA-Obit 67
van Zwoll, James A. 1909-1987 ... CAP-1
Earlier sketch in CA 13-14
Van Zyle, Jon 1942- ... SATA 84
Van Zyl Slabbert, F.
See Slabbert, F(rederik) Van Zyl
Vapnyar, Lara 1971- ... 239
Vaqar, Nasrollah 1920- ... 41-44R
Vara, Albert C. 1931- ... CANR-35
Earlier sketch in CA 33-36R
Vara, Madeleine
See Jackson, Laura (Riding)
Varah, Chad 1911- ... 57-60
Varandyan, Emmanuel P(aul) 1904- ... 65-68
Varas, Florencia
See Olea, Maria Florencia Varas
Varda, Agnes 1928- ... 122
Brief entry ... 116
See also CLC 16
Vardaman, E. Jerry 1927- ... 17-20R
Vardaman, George T(ruett) 1920- ... CANR-4
Earlier sketch in CA 1-4R
Vardaman, James M(oney) 1921- ... 104
Vardaman, Patricia B(lack) 1931- ... 37-40R
Vardamis, Alex A. 1934- ... 77-80
Vardamis, Frances (Diem) 1935- ... 149
Vardeman, Robert E(dward) 1947- ... 158
See also Appleton, Victor
See also FANT
Varderi, Alejandro 1960- ... 178
See also HW 1, 2
Vardey, Lucinda 1949- ... 128
Vardre, Leslie
See Davies, L(eslie) P(urnell)
Vardy, Steven Bela 1936- ... CANR-93
Earlier sketches in CA 53-56, CANR-4, 19, 41
Vardys, V(ytautas) Stanley 1924-1993 ... CANR-5
Earlier sketch in CA 13-16R
Vare, Daniele 1880-1956 ... 185
Brief entry ... 119
Vare, Ethlie Ann 1953- ... CANR-104
Earlier sketches in CA 127, CANR-49
Vare, Robert 1945- ... 103
Varela, Blanca 1926- ... CWW 2
See also DLB 290
Varela, Francisco J. 1946- ... 220
Vareldzis, Georgia M. 1933- ... 149
Varenhorst, Barbara B(raden) 1928- ... 116
Varese, Louise 1890-1989 ... 41-44R
Obituary ... 129
Varesi, Anthony G. 1972- ... 217
Varey, Simon 1951- ... 135
Varg, Paul A(lbert) 1912-1994 ... 118
Obituary ... 144
Brief entry ... 113
Varga, Andrew Charles 1917-1994 ... 113
Varga, Balint Andras 1941- ... CANR-86
Earlier sketch in CA 132
Varga, Judy
See Stang, Judit
Varga, Susan 1943- ... 189
Vargas, Julie S. 1938- ... CANR-34
Earlier sketch in CA 57-60
Vargas, Margarita 1956- ... 149

Cumulative Index 593 **Venables**

Vargas Llosa, (Jorge) Mario (Pedro)
1936- CANR-140
Earlier sketches in CA 73-76, CANR-18, 32, 42, 67, 116
See also Llosa, (Jorge) Mario (Pedro) Vargas
See also BPFB 3
See also CDWLB 3
See also CLC 3, 6, 9, 10, 15, 31, 42, 85, 181
See also CWW 2
See also DA
See also DA3
See also DAB
See also DAC
See also DAM MST, MULT, NOV
See also DLB 145
See also DNFS 2
See also EWL 3
See also HLC 2
See also HW 1, 2
See also LAIT 5
See also LATS 1:2
See also LAW
See also LAWS 1
See also MTCW 1, 2
See also MTFW 2005
See also RGWL 2
See also SSFS 14
See also TWA
See also WLIT 1
Vargish, Thomas 1939- CANR-14
Earlier sketch in CA 37-40R
Varia, Radu 1940- 128
Varlay, Rene G. 1927-1994 .... 1-4R
Varley, Dimitry V. 1906-1984 .... CAP-1
Earlier sketch in CA 17-18
See also SATA 10
Varley, Gloria 1932- 101
Varley, H(erbert) Paul 1931- 77-80
Varley, John (Herbert) 1947- CANR-138
Earlier sketches in CA 69-72, CANR-25
See also BPFB 3
See also BYA 8
See also DLBY 1981
See also SFW 4
Varley, John Philip
See Mitchell, Langdon (Elwyn)
Varley, Susan 1961- .... SATA 63, 134
Varma, Baidya Nath 1921- 41-44R
Varma, Devendra P. 1923-1994 144
Obituary 147
Brief entry 113
Varma, Monika 1916- 77-80
See also CP 1, 2
Varma, Nirmal
See Verma, Nirmal
See also CWW 2
Varmus, Harold E(liot) 1939- 162
Varnac, d'Hugues
See Prevost, Alain
Varnado, Coravar
See Snoop Doggy Dogg
Varnado, Jewel Goodgame 1915- 9-12R
Varnalis, Costas 1884-1974
Obituary 53-56
See also Varnalis, Kostas
Varnalis, Kostas
See Varnalis, Costas
See also EWL 3
Varnedoe, (John) Kirk (Train) 1946-2003 187
Obituary 219
Varner, Jeannette J.
See Varner, Jeannette Johnson
Varner, Jeannette Johnson 1909-1992 132
Varner, John Grier 1905-1978 .... 25-28R
Obituary 120
Varner, Velma V. 1916-1972
Obituary 37-40R
Varney, Carleton B(ates) 1937- CANR-16
Earlier sketch in CA 89-92
Varney, Philip (Allen) 1943- CANR-114
Earlier sketch in CA 125
Varnhagen von Ense, Karl August
1785-1858 .... DLB 90
Varnhagen von Ense, Rahel
1771-1833 .... DLB 90
Varnum, Keith (A.) 1948- CANR-123
Earlier sketch in CA 164
Varoujan, Daniel
See Cheboukiarian, Daniel
See also EWL 3
Varro 116B.C.-27B.C. .... DLB 211
Vars, Gordon F(orrest) 1923- 21-24R
Varshavsky, Ilya 1909-1973 167
See also SFW 4
Vartan, Vartanig G(arabed) 1923-1988 61-64
Obituary 125
Vartanian, Aram 1922-1997 .... CANR-3
Earlier sketch in CA 1-4R
Varzi, Achille C. 1958- 149
Vasalis, M.
See Fortuyn-Leenmans, Margaretha Droogleever
Vasarely, Victor 1908-1997 .... AAYA 62
Vasconcelos (Calderon), Jose 1882-1959 191
Brief entry 118
See also LAW
Vas Dias, Robert (Leonard Michael)
1931- CANR-7
Earlier sketch in CA 17-20R
See also CP 1, 2, 3, 4, 5, 6, 7
Vasek, Vladimir 1867-1958
See Bezruc, Petr
Vasey, Lloyd Roland 113
Vash, Carolyn L(ee) 1934- CANR-46
Brief entry 116
Earlier sketch in CA 121
Vasil, R(aj) K(umar) 1931- CANR-14
Earlier sketch in CA 37-40R
Vasilenko, Svetlana Vladimirovna
1956- .... DLB 285
Vasileva, Tatiana
See Wassiljewa, Tatjana
Vasiliev, Valery 1949- .... SATA 80
Vasilieva, Tatiana
See Wassiljewa, Tatjana
Vasiliu, George
See Bacovia, George
Vasiliu, Gheorghe 189
Brief entry 123
See also Bacovia, George
Vasiliu, Mircea 1920- 21-24R
See also SATA 2
Vaske, Martin O. 1915- CANR-2
Earlier sketch in CA 5-8R
Vasoli, Robert H. 1925- 170
Vasquez, John A(nthony) 1945- 108
Vasquez, Richard 1928-1990 131
See also DLB 209
See also HW 1
Vasquez, Robert J. 1931- 180
Vass, George 1927- 37-40R
See also SATA 57
See also SATA-Brief 31
Vass, Winifred Kellersberger 1917- 57-60
Vassa, Gustavus
See Equiano, Olaudah
Vassalli, Sebastiano 1941- 191
See also DLB 128, 196
Vassanji, M(oyez) G. 1950- 136
See also CN 6, 7
See also EWL 3
Vassberg, David E(rland) 1936- CANR-73
Earlier sketch in CA 131
Vassi, Marco 1937- CANR-13
Earlier sketch in CA 61-64
Vassilikos, Vassilis 1933- CANR-75
Earlier sketch in CA 81-84
See also CLC 4, 8
See also EWL 3
Vassiliou, Yannis 1949- 117
Vasta, Edward 1928- 17-20R
Vasu, Nirmala-Kumara
See Bose, N(irmal) K(umar)
Vasvary, Edmund 1888-1977
Obituary 73-76
Vatikiotis, Michael R. J. 1957- 144
Vatikiotis, P(anayiotis) J(erasimos)
1928-1997 .... CANR-28
Earlier sketches in CA 13-16R, CANR-6
Vatsyayan, Sachchidanand Hiranand
1911-1987 158
Vatter, Harold Goodhue 1910-2000 .... 5-8R
Vattimo, Gianni 1936- 188
Vaucher, Andrea R. 1949- 142
Vauclair, Jacques 1947- 166
Vaudrin, Bill
See Vaudrin, William
Vaudrin, William 1943-1976 .... CAP-2
Earlier sketch in CA 29-32
Vaugelas, Claude Favre de
1585-1650 .... DLB 268
Vaughan, Adrian 1941- 120
Vaughan, Agnes Carr 1887-1974 .... CAP-1
Earlier sketch in CA 9-10
Vaughan, Alan 1936-2001 81-84
Obituary 194
Vaughan, Alden T. 1929- CANR-7
Earlier sketch in CA 17-20R
Vaughan, Beatrice 1909(?)-1972
Obituary 37-40R
Vaughan, Bill
See Vaughan, William E(dward)
Vaughan, Brian K. 1976(?)- 226
Vaughan, Carter A.
See Gerson, Noel Bertram
Vaughan, Clark (Alvord) 1924-1995 108
Vaughan, David 1924- 77-80
Vaughan, Denis 1920- 61-64
Vaughan, Donald S(hores) 1921- CANR-10
Earlier sketch in CA 17-20R
Vaughan, Frances E. 1935- CANR-51
Brief entry 107
Earlier sketch in CA 125
Vaughan, Frederick 1935- 120
Vaughan, Harold Cecil 1923- 29-32R
See also SATA 14
Vaughan, Henry 1621-1695 .... BRW 2
See also DLB 131
See also PAB
See also RGEL 2
Vaughan, Hilda
See Morgan, Hilda Campbell
Vaughan, J(ohn) G(riffith) 1926-2005 168
Obituary 239
Vaughan, James A(gnew) 1936- 49-52
Vaughan, John Edmund 1935- 61-64
Vaughan, Leo
See Lendon, Kenneth Harry
Vaughan, Marcia (K.) 1951- CANR-144
Earlier sketch in CA 160
See also SATA 60, 95, 159
Vaughan, Paul 1925- 29-32R
Vaughan, Richard
See Thomas, Ernest Lewys
Vaughan, Richard 1947- .... SATA 87
Vaughan, Richard Patrick 1919- 13-16R
Vaughan, Robert 1592(?)-1667 .... DLB 213
Vaughan, Robert (Richard) 1937- 103
Vaughan, Roger 1937- 85-88
Vaughan, Ronald G(eorge) 1952- 143
Vaughan, Sam(uel) 1928- 13-16R
See also DLBY 1997
See also SATA 14
Vaughan, Sheila Marie 1930- 21-24R
Vaughan, Susan C. 1941- CANR-143
Earlier sketch in CA 167
Vaughan, Thomas 1621-1666 .... DLB 131
Vaughan, Virginia M(ason) 1947- 110
Vaughan, William E(dward) 1915-1977 .... 5-8R
Obituary 69-72
Vaughan-Thomas, (Lewis John) Wynford
1908-1987 130
Vaughan-Whitehead, Daniel 1963- 177
Vaughan Williams, Ralph 1872-1958
Brief entry 115
Vaughan Williams, Ursula Wood
1911- CANR-24
Earlier sketches in CA 9-12R, CANR-6
Vaughn, Charles L(e Claire) 1911-1994 . 41-44R
Vaughn, Donald E(arl) 1932- 21-24R
Vaughn, Elizabeth Dewberry
See Dewberry, Elizabeth
Vaughn, Ellen Santilli 168
Vaughn, Eloise 200
Vaughn, Jack A(lfred) 1935- 85-88
Vaughn, Jacqueline 1950- 234
Vaughn, Jesse Wendell 1903-1968 .... 1-4R
Obituary 103
Vaughn, Lewis 1950- CANR-41
Earlier sketch in CA 111
Vaughn, Michael J(effery) 1943- 37-40R
Vaughn, Patrika 1933- CANR-101
Earlier sketch in CA 157
Vaughn, Richard C(lements) 1925- CANR-9
Earlier sketch in CA 21-24R
Vaughn, Robert (Francis) 1932- 61-64
Vaughn, Ruth 1935- CANR-15
Earlier sketch in CA 41-44R
See also SATA 14
Vaughn, Sally N(orthrop) 1939- 126
Vaughn, Sister Ann Carol 1922- 9-12R
Vaughn, Stephanie .... CLC 62
Vaughn, Stephen L. 1947- 101
Vaughn, Toni
See Du Breuil, (Elizabeth) L(or)inda
Vaughn, William Preston 1933- 73-76
Vaught, Jacque
See Brogan, Jacqueline Vaught
Vaupel, James W(alton) 1945- 111
Vaurie, Charles 1906-1975 .... CANR-4
Earlier sketch in CA 5-8R
Vause, L(aurence) Mikel 1952- 140
Vaussard, Maurice (Rene Jean Arthur Andre)
1888-1978 .... 9-12R
Vautier, Ghislaine 1932- 112
See also SATA 53
Vauvenargues, Luc de Clapiers
1715-1747 .... GFL Beginnings to 1789
Vaux, Lord Thomas 1509-1556 .... DLB 132
See also RGEL 2
Vavra, Robert James 1935- CANR-25
Earlier sketch in CA 25-28R
See also SATA 8
Vavra, Terry G. 1941- 143
Vawter, F(rancis) Bruce 1921-1986 ..... CANR-4
Earlier sketch in CA 1-4R
Vayda, Andrew P. 1931- 17-20R
Vayhinger, John Monroe 1916- 73-76
Vayle, Valerie
See Brooks, Janice Young
Vaz, Edmund (Winston) 1924- 108
Vaz, Mark Cotta 1954- 220
Vazakas, Byron 1905-1987 .... CAP-2
Earlier sketch in CA 25-28
Vazirani, Reetika 1962-2003 170
Obituary 218
Vazov, Ivan (Minchov) 1850-1921 167
Brief entry 121
See also CDWLB 4
See also DLB 147
See also TCLC 25
Vazquez, Carmen Inoa 1942- CANR-87
Earlier sketch in CA 154
Vazquez Amaral, Jose 1913-1987 153
See also HW 1
Vazquez-Gomez, Juana 1940- 175
Vazquez Montalban, Manuel
See Vazquez Montalban, Manuel
See also DLB 322
Vazquez Montalban, Manuel 1939-2003
See Vazquez Montalban, Manuel
See also DLB 134
Vazsonyi, Balint 1936- 187
Vazsonyi, Nicholas 1963- CANR-124
Earlier sketch in CA 168
Vea, Alfredo, Jr. 1950- 224
See also DLB 209
See also LLW
Veach, William B(rier) Templeton
1896- CAP-1
Earlier sketch in CA 9-10
Veaner, Allen B(arnet) 1929- 41-44R
Veatch, Henry Babcock 1911-1999 .... CANR-6
Earlier sketch in CA 5-8R
Veatch, Robert M(arlin) 1939- CANR-11
Earlier sketch in CA 69-72
Veber, Francis 1937- 135
Veblen, Thorstein B(unde) 1857-1929 165
Brief entry 115
See also AMWS 1
See also DLB 246
See also MAL 5
See also TCLC 31
Vecoli, Rudolph J(ohn) 1927- CANR-51
Earlier sketches in CA 17-20R, CANR-10, 26
Vecsey, George S. 1909(?)-1984
Obituary 114
Vecsey, George Spencer 1939- CANR-10
Earlier sketch in CA 61-64
See also SATA 9
Vedder, Amy (Louise) 1951- 222
Vedder, James S(herman) 1912-1995 117
Vedder, John K.
See Gruber, Frank
Vedder, Richard K(ent) 1940- 115
Vedel, Anders Sorensen 1542-1616 .... DLB 300
Vedeler, Harold C. 1903- 122
Veder, Bob 1940- 104
Vedral, Joyce L(auretta) 1943- CANR-127
Earlier sketches in CA 117, CANR-41
See also SATA 65
Veeck, Bill
See Veeck, William Louis, Jr.
Veeck, William Louis, Jr. 1914-1986
Obituary 118
Veedam, Voldemar 1912-1983
Obituary 109
Veenendaal, Cornelia 1924- 117
Vega, Ana Lydia 1946- 193
See also CWW 2
See also EWL 3
Vega (Yunque), Ed(gardo) 1936- 178
See also HW 2
See also LLW
Vega, Janine Pommy 1942- CANR-81
Earlier sketches in CA 49-52, CANR-2
See also DLB 16
Vega, Jose Luis 1948- 178
See also HW 2
Vega, L(uis) Eduardo 1939- 188
Vega, Lope de 1562-1635 .... EW 2
See also HLCS 2
See also RGWL 2, 3
Vega, Suzanne 1959- 183
Vegh, Claudine 1934- 142
Veglahn, Nancy (Crary) 1937- CANR-7
Earlier sketch in CA 17-20R
See also SATA 5
Vehr, Bill 1940(?)-1988
Obituary 126
Veidlinger, Jeffrey 1971- 197
Veiga, Jose J(acinto da) 1915-1999 ... CANR-33
Earlier sketches in CA 37-40R, CANR-15
Veiller, Anthony 1903-1965 179
See also DLB 44
See also IDFW 3, 4
Veiller, Major Tony
See Veiller, Anthony
Veillon, Lee 1942- 49-52
Veit, Fritz 1907-1998 111
Veit, Lawrence A. 1938- 184
Brief entry 115
Veit, Stan(ley Stanford) 1929- 110
Vekemans, Roger 1921- 37-40R
Velarde, Giles 1935- 233
Velarde, Pablita 1918- 211
Velasquez(-Trevino), Gloria (Louise)
1949- CANR-139
Earlier sketch in CA 174
See also Velasquez, Gloria (Louise)
See also DLB 122
Velasquez, Gloria (Louise) 1949-
See Velasquez(-Trevino), Gloria (Louise)
See also HW 2
See also SATA 113
Velasquez, Manuel G(onzales) 1942- 113
Velasquez, Mary Marden 1954- 207
Velazquez, Deigo 1599-1660 .... AAYA 65
Veler, Richard P(aul) 1936- 49-52
Veley, Margaret 1843-1887 .... DLB 199
Velez-Ibanez, Carlos G(uillermo) 1936- 118
See also HW 1
Velie, Alan R. 1937- CANR-99
Earlier sketches in CA 45-48, CANR-1
Velie, Lester 1908- CAP-2
Earlier sketch in CA 17-18
Velikovsky, Immanuel 1895-1979 .... CANR-15
Obituary 89-92
Earlier sketch in CA 69-72
Veliz, Claudio 1930- 25-28R
Veljanovski, (G.) Cento 1953- 128
Velkley, Richard L. 1949- 148
Vella, Walter F(rancis) 1924-1980 .... CANR-24
Earlier sketch in CA 45-48
Vellacott, Jo 1922- CANR-56
Earlier sketch in CA 126
Velleius Paterculus c. 20B.C.-c. 30 ..... DLB 211
Vellela, Tony 1945- 65-68
Velleman, Daniel J. 1954- 150
Velleman, Ruth A(nn) 1921- 110
Velmans, Edith 1925- 220
Veloso, Caetano 1942- 219
Veloz Maggiolo, Marcio E. 1936- .... DLB 145
See also EWL 3
See also HW 1
Velthuijs, Max 1923-2005 89-92
Obituary 235
See also SATA 53, 110
See also SATA-Obit 160
Vel'tman, Aleksandr Fomich
1800-1870 .... DLB 198
Veltman, Vera
See Panova, Vera (Fedorovna)
Veltri, George (M.) 1949- 150
Velvel, Lawrence R. 1939- 29-32R
Ven, Ton
See Bordewijk, Ferdinand
Venable, Alan (Hudson) 1944- 45-48
See also SATA 8
Venable, Tom C(alvin) 1921- 29-32R
Venable, Vernon 1906-1996 .... CAP-2
Obituary 152
Earlier sketch in CA 21-22
Venables, Stephen 1954- CANR-144
Earlier sketch in CA 144
Venables, Terry 1943- 152

Venafro 594 CONTEMPORARY AUTHORS

Venafro, Mark
 See Pizzat, Frank J(oseph)
Venardos, Thomas J(oseph) 1945- ... CANR-110
 Earlier sketch in CA 151
Vencent, Gabrielle (a pseudonym) 126
Venclova, Tomas 1937- CANR-96
 Earlier sketch in CA 158
Vendler, Helen (Hennessy) 1933- ... CANR-136
 Earlier sketches in CA 41-44R, CANR-25, 72
 See also CLC 138
 See also MTCW 1, 2
 See also MTFW 2005
Vendler, Zeno 1921- 126
 Brief entry 105
Vendrovskii, David Efimovich 1879-1971
 Obituary 33-36R
Vendrovsky, David
 See Vendrovskii, David Efimovich
Venegas, Daniel .... DLB 82
Veness, Molly 1900(?)-1985
 Obituary 118
Veness, (Winifred) Thelma 1919-1971 .... 5-8R
 Obituary 122
Venevitinov, Dmitrii Vladimirovich
 1805-1827 .... DLB 205
Venezia, Mike 1945- .... SATA 150
Venezis, Elias
 See Mellos, Elias
 See also EWL 3
Venezky, Richard L(awrence) 1938-2004 ... 199
Vengroff, Richard 1945- CANR-10
 Earlier sketch in CA 65-68
Venison, Alfred
 See Pound, Ezra (Weston Loomis)
Veniste, Richard Ben
 See Ben-Veniste, Richard
Venn, George (Andrew) 1943- 231
Venn, Grant 1919-1979 .... 13-16R
 Obituary 122
Vennard, Edwin (Wilson) 1902-1997 .... CAP-2
 Obituary 174
 Earlier sketch in CA 25-28
Vennema, Alje 1932- 101
Venner, J. G.
 See Lewis, John (Noel Claude)
Vennewitz, Leila 148
Venning, Corey 1924-1996 49-52
Venning, Hugh
 See van Zeller, Claud
Venning, Michael
 See Randolph, Georgiana Ann
Venolia, Jan(et G.) 1928- CANR-111
 Earlier sketch in CA 151
Venter, Al(bertus) J(ohannes) 1938- 117
Venton, W. B. 1898-1976 .... CAP-2
 Earlier sketch in CA 25-28
Ventsel, Elena Sergeevna 1907-2002 154
 See also Grekova, I. and
 Grekova, Irina
Venttsel', Elena Sergeevna
 See Ventsel, Elena Sergeevna
Ventura, Anthony
 See Pellowski, Michael (Joseph)
Ventura, Jeffrey
 See Feinman, Jeffrey
Ventura, Jesse 1951- 183
Ventura, Michael 1945- 146
Ventura, Piero (Luigi) 1937- CANR-39
 Earlier sketch in CA 103
 See also CLR 16
 See also MAICYA 1, 2
 See also SATA 61
 See also SATA-Brief 43
Venturi, Denise Scott Brown
 See Brown, Denise Scott
Venturi, Franco 1914- 130
Venturi, Marcello 1925- CANR-42
 Earlier sketches in CA 29-32R, CANR-13
Venturi, Robert 1925- CANR-117
 Earlier sketch in CA 61-64
Venuti, Lawrence (Michael) 1953- .. CANR-104
 Earlier sketches in CA 120, CANR-48
Vequin, Capini
 See Quinn, Elisabeth
Vera, Yvonne 1964-2005 .... CANR-125
 Obituary 238
 Earlier sketch in CA 168
Verb, M. L.
 See Tammeus, William David
Verba, Joan Marie 1953- CANR-93
 Earlier sketch in CA 146
 See also SATA 78
Verba, Sidney 1932- CANR-3
 Earlier sketch in CA 1-4R
Verbeke, Gerard 1910-2001 131
Verbitskaia, Anastasiia Alekseevna
 1861-1928 .... DLB 295
Verbitsky, Bernardo 1907- .... HW 1
Verboven, Agnes 1951- 170
 See also SATA 103
Verbrugge, Verlyn D(avid) 1942- 220
Vercors
 See Bruller, Jean (Marcel)
 See also EWL 3
Vercors, J. Bruller
 See Bruller, Jean (Marcel)
Vercoutter, Jean 1911-2000 142
Verde, Cesario 1855-1886 .... DLB 287
Verdecchia, Guillermo (Luis) 1962- 161
Verdelle, A. J. 1960- CANR-87
 Earlier sketch in CA 152
Verdenius, W(illem) J(acob) 1913- 25-28R
Verdery, John D(uane) 1917-1986 .... 9-12R
Verdery, Katherine (Maureen) 1948- 188
Verdi, Marie de
 See Mencken, H(enry) L(ouis)
Verdi, Richard 1941- 128
Verdick, Mary (Peyton) 1923- CANR-4
 Earlier sketch in CA 1-4R
Verdon, Dorothy
 See Tralins, S(andor) Robert
verDorn, Bethea (Stewart) 1952- .... SATA 76
Verdu, Matilde
 See Cela, Camilo Jose
Verduin, John R(ichard), Jr. 1931- CANR-49
 Earlier sketches in CA 21-24R, CANR-9, 24
Verduin, Leonard 1897-1999 61-64
Verene, Donald Phillip 1937- CANR-142
 Earlier sketches in CA 41-44R, CANR-15, 45
Verey, David (Cecil Wynter)
 1913-1984 .... CANR-15
 Obituary 113
 Earlier sketch in CA 65-68
Verey, Rosemary 1918-2001 130
 Obituary 197
Verga, Giovanni (Carmelo)
 1840-1922 .... CANR-101
 Brief entry 104
 Earlier sketch in CA 123
 See also EW 7
 See also EWL 3
 See also RGSF 2
 See also RGWL 2, 3
 See also SSC 21
 See also TCLC 3
 See also WLIT 7
Vergani, Luisa 1931- 21-24R
Vergara, Jose Manuel 1929- 97-100
Vergara, Joseph R. 1915- 29-32R
Vergara, Lisa 1948- 120
Vergara, William C(harles) 1923-1994 .... 1-4R
Verger, Pierre 1902-1996 174
Verger, Pierre Fatumbi
 See Verger, Pierre
Verghese, Abraham 1955- 150
Verghese, T. Paul
 See Gregorios, Paulos Mar
Vergil 70B.C.-19B.C.
 See Virgil
 See also AW 2
 See also DA
 See also DA3
 See also DAB
 See also DAC
 See also DAM MST, POET
 See also EFS 1
 See also LMFS 1
 See also PC 12
 See also WLCS
Vergil, Polydore c. 1470-1555 .... DLB 132
Verhaeren, Emile (Adolphe Gustave) 1855-1916
 Brief entry 109
 See also EWL 3
 See also GFL 1789 to the Present
 See also TCLC 12
Verhalen, Philip A(ndrew) 1934- 69-72
Verhey, Allen D. 1945- 220
Verheyen, Dirk 1957- 139
Verhoeven, Cornelis 1928- CANR-46
 Earlier sketches in CA 61-64, CANR-8, 23
Verhoeven, Paul 1901-1975
 Obituary 115
Verhonick, Phillis J. 1922(?)-1977
 Obituary 73-76
Verhoogen, John 1912-1993 109
Verin, Velko
 See Inkiow, (Janakiev) Dimiter
Verissimo, Erico (Lopes) 1905-1975 174
 Obituary 115
 See also DLB 145, 307
 See also EWL 3
 See also HW 2
 See also LAW
 See also SATA 113
Verlaine, Paul (Marie) 1844-1896 .. DAM POET
 See also DLB 217
 See also EW 7
 See also GFL 1789 to the Present
 See also LMFS 2
 See also PC 2, 32
 See also RGWL 2, 3
 See also TWA
Verluise, Pierre 1961- 154
Verma, Nirmal 1929- 225
 See also Varma, Nirmal
Verme, Louis J. 1924- 212
Vermeer, Jan 1632-1675 .... AAYA 46
Vermes, Geza 1924- CANR-108
 Earlier sketch in CA 57-60
Vermes, Jean C(ampbell Pattison)
 1907-1985 106
 Obituary 176
Vermes, Pamela 1918- 118
Vermeule, Cornelius Clarkson III 1925- . 41-44R
Vermeule, Emily D(ickinson) T(ownsend)
 1928-2001 .... 17-20R
 Obituary 193
Vermeylen, August 1872-1945 .... EWL 3
Vermillion, Robert 1915(?)-1987
 Obituary 122
Vermilye, Jerry 1931- 239
Vernadsky, George 1887-1973
 Obituary 41-44R
Vernam, Glenn R. 1896-1980 .... CANR-10
 Earlier sketch in CA 17-20R
Vernant, Jean-Pierre 1914- CANR-109
 Earlier sketches in CA 109, CANR-29, 54
Vernazza, Marcelle Wynn 1909- CANR-10
 Earlier sketch in CA 17-20R
Verne, Jules (Gabriel) 1828-1905 131
 Brief entry 110
 See also AAYA 16
 See also BYA 4
 See also CLR 88
 See also DA3
 See also DLB 123
 See also GFL 1789 to the Present
 See also JRDA
 See also LAIT 2
 See also LMFS 2
 See also MAICYA 1, 2
 See also MTFW 2005
 See also RGWL 2, 3
 See also SATA 21
 See also SCFW 1, 2
 See also SFW 4
 See also TCLC 6, 52
 See also TWA
 See also WCH
Vernelle, Marjorie 1948- 222
Verner, Coolie 1917-1979 .... CANR-7
 Earlier sketch in CA 53-56
Verner, Gerald 1897(?)-1980
 Obituary 102
 See also SATA-Obit 25
Vernerey, Denise 1947- 146
Verney, Douglas Vernon 1924- 13-16R
Verney, John 1913-1993 65-68
 Obituary 140
 See also CWRI 5
 See also SATA 14
 See also SATA-Obit 75
Verney, Michael P(almer) 1923- CANR-6
 Earlier sketch in CA 13-16R
Verney, Peter (Vivian Lloyd) 1930- ... CANR-19
 Earlier sketch in CA 81-84
Verney, Sarah
 See Holloway, Brenda W(ilmar)
Verney, Stephen Edmund 1919- 104
Vernick, Audrey
 See Shehyn, Audrey E.
Vernon, Amelia Wallace 1926- 149
Vernon, Betty D(esiree) 1917- 146
Vernon, Eddie
 See Stone, Hoyt E(dward)
Vernon, Edward
 See Coleman, Vernon
Vernon, (Georgina) Frances 1963-1991 110
 Obituary 135
Vernon, Glenn M(orley) 1920- 49-52
Vernon, James 1965- 146
Vernon, John (Edward) 1943- CANR-127
 Earlier sketch in CA 41-44R
Vernon, Judy 1945- 119
Vernon, Lee M.
 See von Block, Bela W(illiam)
Vernon, Lorraine 1921- 113
Vernon, (Elda) Louise A(nderson) 1914- .. 53-56
 See also SATA 14
Vernon, McCay 1928- 41-44R
Vernon, Olympia 1973- 229
Vernon, Philip Ewart 1905-1987 .... CANR-12
 Obituary 133
 Earlier sketch in CA 5-8R
Vernon, Raymond 1913-1999 .... CANR-40
 Obituary 183
 Earlier sketches in CA 5-8R, CANR-2, 18
Vernon, Roland 1961- 220
Vernon, Rosemary
 See Smith, Susan Vernon
Vernon, Thomas Bowater 1939- 118
Vernon, Thomas S. 1914- 25-28R
Vernon, Tom
 See Vernon, Thomas Bowater
Vernon, Walter N(ewton), Jr. 1907- .. CANR-12
 Earlier sketch in CA 17-20R
Vernon-Jackson, Hugh (Owen Hardinge)
 1925- 21-24R
Vernor, D.
 See Casewit, Curtis W(erner)
Verny, Tom 1936- 73-76
Verona, Stephen (Frederic) 1940- 154
Veronesi, Luigi (Mario) 1908-1998 234
Veronica, Sister Mary 1924-1977 .... 17-20R
 Obituary 134
Verplanck, Gulian C. 1786-1870 .... DLB 59
Verr, Harry Coe
 See Kunhardt, Edith
Verral, Charles Spain 1904-1990 .... CANR-37
 Obituary 131
 Earlier sketches in CAP-1, CA 9-10, CANR-16
 See also SATA 11
 See also SATA-Obit 65
Verreault, Sabine
 See Vonarburg, Elisabeth
Verrette, Joyce 1939- 129
Verrier, Suzanne 1942- 153
Verrier, Suzy
 See Verrier, Suzanne
Verrill, A(lpheus) Hyatt 1871-1954
 Brief entry 111
 See also SFW 4
Verrone, Robert J. 1935(?)-1984
 Obituary 113
 See also SATA-Obit 39
Versace, Marie Teresa Rios 1917- 17-20R
 See also SATA 2
Verschuur, Gerrit L(aurens) 1937- 142
Versenyi, Adam 1957- 149
Verstandig, Mark 1912- 172
Ver Steeg, Clarence L(ester) 1922- 13-16R
Versteeg, Robert John 1930- 1-4R
Vertinsky, Aleksandr 1889-1957 .... DLB 317
Vertreace, Martha M(odena) 1945- ... CANR-87
 Earlier sketch in CA 143
 See also BW 2
 See also SATA 78
Verus, Marcus Annius
 See Aurelius, Marcus
Verval, Alain
 See Lande, Lawrence (Montague)
Verweerd, Joke 1954- 205
Verwey, Albert 1865-1937 .... EWL 3
Verwilghen, A(lbert-) Felix 1916- 25-28R
Verwoerdt, Adriaan 1927- 17-20R
Very, Alice (N.) 1894-1977 .... 21-24R
 Obituary 120
Very, Jones 1813-1880 .... DLB 1, 243
 See also RGAL 4
Very, Rev. C.
 See Crowley, Edward Alexander
Veryan, Patricia
 See Bannister, Patricia Valeria
Vesaas, Halldis Moren 1907-1995 .... CWW 2
 See also DLB 297
Vesaas, Tarjei 1897-1970 190
 Obituary 29-32R
 See also CLC 48
 See also DLB 297
 See also EW 11
 See also EWL 3
 See also RGWL 3
Vesely, Erik 1905(?)-1970
 Obituary 57-60
Vesenyi, Paul E. 1911-1998 53-56
Veseth, Michael 1949- 135
Vesey, A(manda) 1939- 127
 See also SATA 62
Vesey, Godfrey (Norman Agmondisham)
 1923- 89-92
Vesey, Mark (David) 1958- .... SATA 123
Vesey, Paul
 See Allen, Samuel W(ashington)
Vesey-FitzGerald, Brian Seymour
 1900-1981 104
 Obituary 105
Vesper, Karl H(ampton) 1932- 115
Vess, David M(arshall) 1925- 89-92
Vessel, Matthew F. 1912-
 Brief entry 108
Vesselo, I(saac) Reginald 1903- CAP-2
 Earlier sketch in CA 17-18
Vest, Herb D. 1944- 145
Vest, Hilda 1933- 148
Vestal, David 1924- 89-92
Vestal, Edith Ballard 1884-1970 .... CAP-2
 Earlier sketch in CA 25-28
Vestdijk, Simon 1898-1971
 Obituary 89-92
 See also EWL 3
 See also RGWL 2, 3
Vester, Frederic 1925- 120
Vester, Horatio 1906-1985 .... CAP-1
 Obituary 117
 Earlier sketch in CA 13-14
Vesterman, William 1942- 89-92
Vestly, Anne-Cath(arina) 1920- CANR-41
 Earlier sketches in CA 85-88, CANR-18
 See also CLR 99
 See also SATA 14
Vet, T. V.
 See Straiton, E(dward) C(ornock)
Vetch, John (Hamilton) 1911-1997 150
Vetchinsky, Alex -1980 .... IDFW 3, 4
Vetere, Richard 1952- 104
Vetoe, Miklos 1936- 49-52
Vetter, Carole 1939- 25-28R
Vetter, Harold J. 1926- 29-32R
Vetterling-Braggin, Mary (Katherine) 1947- . 124
Veverka, Frank B. 1923(?)-1985
 Obituary 117
Vevers, (Henry) Gwynne 1916-1988 113
 Obituary 126
 See also SATA 45
 See also SATA-Obit 57
Vexillum
 See Banner, Hubert Stewart
Veysey, Arthur (Ernest) 1914-1997 133
 Obituary 160
Veysey, Laurence R(uss) 1932- 21-24R
Vezhinov, Pavel
 See Gougov, Nikola Delchev
Vial, Fernand (Louis) 1905-1985 .... CANR-21
 Obituary 182
 Earlier sketch in CA 1-4R
Vialis, Gaston
 See Simenon, Georges (Jacques Christian)
Viallaneix, Paul 1925- 181
Vian, Boris 1920-1959(?) CANR-111
 Brief entry 106
 Earlier sketch in CA 164
 See also DLB 72, 321
 See also EWL 3
 See also GFL 1789 to the Present
 See also MTCW 2
 See also RGWL 2, 3
 See also TCLC 9
Viana, Javier de 1868-1926 .... HW 1
Vianna, Hermano 1960- 184
Viano, Emilio C. 1942- 107
Viansson-Ponte, Pierre 1920-1979 101
 Obituary 85-88
Viator, Vacuus
 See Hughes, Thomas
Viau, Theophile de
 1590-1626 .... GFL Beginnings to 1789
Viaud, (Louis Marie) Julien 1850-1923
 Brief entry 107
 See also Loti, Pierre

Cumulative Index 595 Vincent

Viazemsky, Petr Andreevich
1792-1878 .... DLB 205
Vibert, Elizabeth 1962- 206
Vicar, Henry
See Felsen, Henry Gregor
Vicars, Thomas 1591-1638 .... DLB 236
Vicary, Dorothy
See Rice, Dorothy Mary
Vicchio, Stephen (John) 1950- 138
Vice, Lisa 1951- 156
Vicente, Gil 1465-c. 1536 .... DLB 318
See also IDTP
See also RGWL 2, 3
Vicente, Rafael Sebastian Guillen
See Marcos, Subcomandante Insurgente
Vichas, Robert P. 1933- CANR-14
Earlier sketch in CA 29-32R
Vick, Helen Hughes 1950- 152
See also SATA 88
Vicker, Angus
See Felsen, Henry Gregor
Vicker, Ray 1917-2000 61-64
Obituary 189
Vickers
See Kaufman, Wallace
Vickers, Antoinette L. 1942- 103
Vickers, Douglas 1924- CANR-11
Earlier sketch in CA 13-16R
Vickers, (Charles) Geoffrey 1894-1982 .. 41-44R
Obituary 106
Vickers, Hugo (Ralph) 1951- CANR-111
Brief entry 124
Earlier sketch in CA 128
Vickers, Jeanne 180
Vickers, Joanne F. 1941- 145
Vickers, John 1916-1976 .... 9-12R
Obituary 134
Vickers, Roy C. 1888(?)-1965 186
See also CMW 4
See also DLB 77
Vickers, Sheena 1960- .... SATA 94
Vickery, Amanda Jane 1962- 174
Vickery, Brian C(ampbell) 1918- 212
Vickery, Donald M(ichael) 1944- 101
Vickery, Florence E. 1906- 37-40R
Vickery, John B. 1925- 57-60
Vickery, Kate
See Kennedy, T(eresa) A.
Vickery, Margaret Birney 1963- 237
Vickery, Olga W(estland) 1925-1970 .. CANR-3
Earlier sketch in CA 1-4R
Vickery, Robert L. (Jr.) 1932- 49-52
Vickery, Sukey 1779-1821 .... DLB 200
Vickery, Tom Rusk 1935- 53-56
Vickrey, William (Spencer) 1914-1996 .. 41-44R
Obituary 154
Vico, Giambattista
See Vico, Giovanni Battista
See also WLIT 7
Vico, Giovanni Battista 1668-1744
See Vico, Giambattista
See also EW 3
Victor, Barbara 1946- CANR-118
Earlier sketch in CA 141
Victor, Charles B.
See Puechner, Ray
Victor, Daniel D(avid) 1944- 140
Victor, David 1910(?)-1989
Obituary 130
Victor, Ed(ward) 1939- 215
Victor, Edward 1914- CANR-3
Earlier sketch in CA 1-4R
See also SATA 3
Victor, George 168
Victor, Joan Berg 1942- 105
See also SATA 30
Victor, Mark 224
Victor, Sam
See Hershman, Morris
Victoria, Queen 1819-1901 188
See also DLB 55
Victoroff, Jeffrey Ivan 215
Vicuna, Cecilia 1948- 157
Vida, Nina 1933- CANR-121
Earlier sketches in CA 117, CANR-60
Vidal, (Eugene Luther) Gore 1925- . CANR-132
Earlier sketches in CA 5-8R, CANR-13, 45, 65, 100
Interview in CANR-13
See also Box, Edgar
See also AAYA 64
See also AITN 1
See also AMWS 4
See also BEST 90:2
See also BPFB 3
See also CAD
See also CD 5, 6
See also CDALBS
See also CLC 2, 4, 6, 8, 10, 22, 33, 72, 142
See also CN 1, 2, 3, 4, 5, 6, 7
See also CPW
See also DA3
See also DAM NOV, POP
See also DFS 2
See also DLB 6, 152
See also EWL 3
See also MAL 5
See also MTCW 1, 2
See also MTFW 2005
See also RGAL 4
See also RHW
See also TUS
Vidal, Mary Theresa 1814-1873 .... DLB 230
Vidal, Nicole 1928- 25-28R
Vidaver, Doris 108
Vidger, Leonard P(erry) 1920-2003 ...... CANR-5
Earlier sketch in CA 9-12R
Vidich, Arthur J. 1922- 115
Vidler, Alec R.
See Vidler, Alexander Roper
Vidler, Alexander Roper 1899-1991 ... CANR-5
Obituary 135
Earlier sketch in CA 5-8R
Vidler, Virginia (Ellen) 1928-1986 69-72
Obituary 121
Vidmer, Richards 1898-1978 206
See also DLB 241
Vidor, King (Wallis) 1894(?)-1982
Obituary 108
Vidrine, Beverly Barras 1938- 170
See also SATA 103
Viebig, Clara 1860-1952 .... DLB 66
Vieg, John A.
See Vieg, John Albert
Vieg, John Albert 1904-1988 .... 1-4R
Obituary 124
Vieira, Antonio S.J. 1608-1697 .... DLB 307
Vieira, Jose Luandino 1935- .... AFW
See also EWL 3
Vieira, Mark A. 1950- 223
Vieira, Sergio 1941- 146
Vier, Gene 1926- 105
Viereck, Ellen K. 1928- 53-56
See also SATA 14
Viereck, George S(ylvester) 1884-1962 182
Obituary 116
See also DLB 54
See also FANT
Viereck, Peter (Robert Edwin) 1916- . CANR-47
Earlier sketches in CA 1-4R, CANR-1
See also CLC 4
See also CP 1, 2, 3, 4, 5, 6, 7
See also DLB 5
See also MAL 5
See also PC 27
See also PFS 9, 14
Viereck, Phillip 1925- CANR-8
Earlier sketch in CA 5-8R
See also SATA 3
Vierny, Sacha 1919- .... IDFW 3, 4
Viertel, Janet 1915- 53-56
See also SATA 10
Viertel, Joseph 1915- 13-16R
Viertel, Peter 1920- CANR-52
Earlier sketch in CA 13-16R
Viessman, Warren, Jr. 1930- 53-56
Vieth, David M(uench) 1925- 5-8R
Vieth von Golssenau, Arnold Friedrich
1889-1979 89-92
Vietor, John A(dolf) 1914-1982
Obituary 108
Viets, Elaine 1950- 191
Viets, Roger 1738-1811 .... DLB 99
Viets, Wallace T(rowbridge) 1919- 17-20R
Vieyra, Antonio
See Vieira, Antonio S.J.
Vig, Norman Joseph 1939- 25-28R
Vigano, Renata 1900-1976 221
Vigee, Claude (Andre Strauss)
See Vigee, Claude (Andre Strauss)
Vigee, Claude (Andre Strauss)
1921- CANR-126
Earlier sketch in CA 157
Vigeland, Carl A. 1947- CANR-111
Earlier sketch in CA 122
Vigeveno, H(enk) S. 1925- 108
Vigfusson, Robin 1949- 106
Viggiani
See Viggiani, Guy
Viggiani, Guy 1932- 123
Vighi, Marco 1945- 154
Vigil, Angel 1947- 178
See also HW 2
Vigil, Diego
See Vigil, James Diego
Vigil, James Diego 1938- 130
Vigil, Lawrence
See Finnin, (Olive) Mary
Vigil-Pinon, Evangelina 1949- 181
See also DLB 122
See also HW 2
Vigliante, Mary
See Szydlowski, Mary Vigliante
Viglini, Janelle (Therese) 1933- 57-60
Vigna, Judith 1936- CANR-56
Earlier sketches in CA 77-80, CANR-13, 29
See also SATA 15, 102
Vigneault, Gilles 1928- 160
See also DLB 60
Vigneras, Louis-Andre 1903-1979 65-68
Vigness, David M(artell) 1922- 13-16R
Vigness, Paul G(erhardt) 1894-1990 ...... 41-44R
Obituary 196
Vignoles, R. H.
See Ford, Boris
Vignone, Joseph A. 1939- 37-40R
Vigny, Alfred (Victor) de
1797-1863 .... DAM POET
See also DLB 119, 192, 217
See also EW 5
See also GFL 1789 to the Present
See also PC 26
See also RGWL 2, 3
Vigoda, David 1946- 219
Vigolo, Giorgio 1894-1983 .... DLB 114
Viguers, Ruth Hill 1903-1971 .... CAP-1
Obituary 29-32R
Earlier sketch in CA 13-16
See also SATA 6
Viita, Lauri (Arvi) 1916-1965
See Vriesland, Victor Emanuel van
See also EWL 3
Vik, Bjorg
See Vik, Bjorg
Vik, Bjorg 1935- 192
See also CWW 2
See also DLB 297
See also RGSF 2
Vikis-Freibergs, Vaira 1937- 53-56
Viksnins, George J(uris) 1937- 105
Viktoria, Luise 1892-1980
Obituary 102
Vila, Bob
See Vila, Robert
Vila, Robert 1946- 106
Vilakazi, Benedict Wallet 1906-1947 168
See also TCLC 37
Vilalta, Maruxa 1932- 197
Vila-Matas, Enrique 1948- .... DLB 322
Vilanch, Bruce 1947- 167
Vilander, Barbara 1958- 199
Vilar, Esther 1935- CANR-8
Earlier sketch in CA 49-52
Vilar, Irene
See Mendes, Irene Vilar
Vilarino, Idea 1920- 153
See also HW 1
Vilde, Eduard 1865-1933 .... DLB 220
Vildrac, Charles
See Messager, Charles
Vile, Curt
See Moore, Alan
Vile, John R. 1951- 206
Vileisis, Ann 1967- 211
Vilhjalmsdottir, Linda 1958- .... DLB 293
Vilhjalmsson, Thor 1925- .... CWW 2
See also DLB 293
See also EWL 3
Vilinskaia, Mariia Aleksandrovna
See Markovich, Mariia Aleksandrovna
Viljoen, Helen Gill 1899-1974 45-48
Obituary 103
Vilkitis, James R(ichard) 1941- 61-64
Villa, Dana R. 215
Villa, Jose Garcia
See Villa, Jose Garcia
See also CP 1, 2
See also DLB 312
Villa, Jose Garcia 1914-1997 .... CANR-118
Earlier sketches in CA 25-28R, CANR-12
See also Villa, Jose Garcia
See also AAL
See also EWL 3
See also EXPP
See also PC 22
Villa, Susie Hoogasian
See Hoogasian-Villa, Susie
Villada, Gene Harold Bell
See Bell-Villada, Gene Harold
Villafane, Eldin 1940- 146
Villaggio, Paolo 1932- 215
Villa-Gilbert, Mariana 1937- 29-32R
Villalon, Leonardo A. 1957- 182
Villamil, Victoria Etnier 1940- 149
Villanueva, Alma Luz 1944- CANR-81
Earlier sketch in CA 131
See also CAAS 24
See also DLB 122
See also HW 1
See also RGAL 4
Villanueva, Tino 1941- CANR-109
Earlier sketches in CA 45-48, CANR-1
See also DLB 82
See also HW 1
See also LLW
Villard, Henry 1835-1900 .... DLB 23
Villard, Henry Hilgard 1911-1983
Obituary 111
Villard, Henry S(errano) 1900-1996 ...... 17-20R
Obituary 151
Villard, Oswald Garrison 1872-1949 162
Brief entry 113
See also DLB 25, 91
See also TCLC 160
Villarejo, Mary (Holan) 1915- 9-12R
Villarejo, Oscar M(ilton) 1909-1995 ...... 17-20R
Villari, Rosario 1925- CANR-98
Earlier sketch in CA 147
Villarreal, Edit 1944- .... DLB 209
Villarreal, Jose Antonio 1924- CANR-93
Earlier sketch in CA 133
See also DAM MULT
See also DLB 82
See also HLC 2
See also HW 1
See also LAIT 4
See also RGAL 4
Villars, Elizabeth
See Feldman, Ellen (Bette)
Villas, James 1938- 181
Villas, Martha Pearl 238
Villas Boas, Claudio 1916-1998
Obituary 166
Brief entry 117
Villas Boas, Orlando 1914-2002
Obituary 210
Brief entry 117
Villasenor, David V. 1913-1987 .... 13-16R
Villasenor, Edmund
See Villasenor, Victor E(dmundo)
Villasenor, Victor E(dmundo)
1940- CANR-118
Earlier sketches in CA 45-48, CANR-32, 67
See also DAM MULT
See also DLB 209
See also HW 1, 2
See also LLW
Villasmil, Omar (Santiago) 1942- 217
Villatoro, Marcos McPeek 199
Villaurrutia, Xavier 1903-1950 192
See also EWL 3
See also HW 1
See also LAW
See also TCLC 80
Villaverde, Cirilo 1812-1894 .... LAW
Villedieu, Madame de 1640(?)-1683 ... DLB 268
Villegas, Antonio de fl. 1560- .... DLB 318
Villegas, Daniel Cosio
See Cosio Villegas, Daniel
Villegas, Jose Luis 1960- 187
Villegas de Magnon, Leonor 1876-1955 178
See also DLB 122
See also HW 2
Villehardouin, Geoffroi de c. 1150-c.
1215 .... DLB 208
Villella, Edward 1936- 140
Villemaire, Yolande 1949- .... DLB 60
Villena, Enrique de c. 1382-1434 .... DLB 286
Villena, Luis Antonio de 1951- .... DLB 134
Villeneuve, Jocelyne 1941- 132
Villere, Sidney Louis 1900-1982 69-72
Obituary 196
Villers, Raymond 1911- CAP-2
Earlier sketch in CA 25-28
Villers, Robert 1921-1980
Obituary 93-96
Villet, Barbara 1931- 85-88
Villiard, Paul 1910-1974 .... CANR-10
Obituary 53-56
Earlier sketches in CAP-2, CA 25-28
See also SATA 51
See also SATA-Obit 20
Villiers, Alan (John) 1903-1982 .... CANR-1
Earlier sketch in CA 1-4R
See also SATA 10
Villiers, George 1628-1687 .... DLB 80
See also RGEL 2
Villiers, Guy
See Goulding, Peter Geoffrey
Villiers, Marie de
See Routier, Simone
Villiers, Marjorie 1903-1982
Obituary 107
Villiers de l'Isle Adam, Jean Marie Mathias Philippe Auguste 1838-1889 ... DLB 123, 192
See also GFL 1789 to the Present
See also RGSF 2
See also SSC 14
Villoldo, Alberto Pedro 1949- 108
Villon, Francois 1431-1463(?) .... DLB 208
See also EW 2
See also PC 13
See also RGWL 2, 3
See also TWA
Villum, Kjartan
See Flogstad, Kjartan
Vilmorin, Louise Leveque de 1902-1969
Obituary 104
Vilnay, Zev 1900-1988
Obituary 124
Vilott, Rhondi
See Salsitz, Rhondi Vilott
Vinacke, W(illiam) Edgar 1917-1991 .... 5-8R
Vinal, Harold 1891-1965
Obituary 89-92
Vinas, D.
See Vinas, David
Vinas, David 1929(?)- .... EWL 3
See also HW 1
Vinaver, Eugene 1899-1979 .... 13-16R
Vinaver, Michel 1927- .... CWW 2
See also DLB 321
See also IDTP
Vincent, Adrian 1917- 1-4R
Vincent, Andrew 1951- 141
Vincent, Charles 1945- 65-68
Vincent, Claire
See Allen, Charlotte Vale
Vincent, Clark E(dward) 1923- CANR-2
Earlier sketch in CA 1-4R
Vincent, David 1949- 187
Vincent, E. Lee
See Vincent, Elizabeth Lee
Vincent, Edgar 227
Vincent, Elizabeth Lee 1897-1974 .... CAP-2
Earlier sketch in CA 19-20
Vincent, Eric Douglas 1953- .... SATA 40
Vincent, Fay
See Vincent, Francis Thomas, Jr.
Vincent, Felix 1946- 118
See also SATA 41
Vincent, Francis Thomas, Jr. 1938- 222
Vincent, Gabrielle 1928-2000 .... CANR-99
Earlier sketch in CA 126
See also CLR 13
See also MAICYA 1, 2
See also SATA 61, 121
Vincent, Howard Paton 1904-1985 65-68
Vincent, Jack 1904-1999 .... 29-32R
Vincent, Jack E(rnest) 1932- CANR-19
Earlier sketch in CA 102
Vincent, Joan 1920- 21-24R
Vincent, John Carter 1900-1972
Obituary 37-40R
Vincent, John J(ames) 1929- CANR-51
Earlier sketches in CA 57-60, CANR-10, 26
Vincent, John R(ussell) 1937- 120
Vincent, K(enneth) Steven 1947- CANR-68
Earlier sketch in CA 128
Vincent, Leona
See Vincent, Elizabeth Lee
Vincent, Mary Keith
See St. John, Wylly Folk
Vincent, Peter 1944- 37-40R
Vincent, R(aymond) J(ohn) 1943-1990 77-80
Obituary 133

Vincent, Theodore G. 1936- ... CANR-13
Earlier sketch in CA 77-80
Vincent, William R.
See Heitzmann, William Ray
Vincent, William S(hafer) 1907- ... 41-44R
Vincenzi, Penny 1939- ... 239
Vince-Prue, Daphne 1926- ... 229
Vinciguerra, Mario 1887-1973
Obituary ... 104
Vincitorio, Gaetano L(eonard) 1921- ... 89-92
Vine, Barbara
See Rendell, Ruth (Barbara)
See also BEST 90:4
See also CLC 50
Vine, Louis L(loyd) 1922- ... CANR-3
Earlier sketch in CA 1-4R
Vine, Paul Ashley Laurence 1927- ... 21-24R
Vine, Phyllis 1945- ... 130
Vine, Sarah
See Rowland, D(onald) S(ydney)
Vineberg, Arthur (Martin) 1903-1988 ... 104
Obituary ... 125
Vineberg, Ethel (Shane) 1902-1998(?) ... 85-88
Vinegar, Tom
See Gregg, Andrew K.
Viner, George 1913(?)-1983
Obituary ... 109
Viner, Jacob 1892-1970
Obituary ... 104
Vines, Alice Gilmore 1923- ... 81-84
Vines, (Henry) Ellsworth (Jr.) 1911-1994
Obituary ... 144
Brief entry ... 109
Vines, Lois Davis 1939- ... 144
Vinest, Shaw
See Longyear, Barry B(rookes)
Viney, Donald Wayne 1953- ... 231
Viney, Ethna ... 166
Viney, Wayne 1932- ... 103
Vineyard, Edwin Earle 1926- ... 5-8R
Vineyard, Jerry D. 1935- ... 143
Vinge, Joan (Carol) D(ennison)
1948- ... CANR-72
Earlier sketch in CA 93-96
See also AAYA 32
See also BPFB 3
See also CLC 30
See also SATA 36, 113
See also SFW 4
See also SSC 24
See also YAW
Vinge, Vernor (Steffen) 1944- ... CANR-96
Earlier sketch in CA 101
See also AAYA 49
See also SFW 4
Vinikas, Vincent 1951- ... 161
Vining, Donald 1917- ... GLL 2
Vining, Elizabeth Gray 1902-1999 ... CANR-7
Obituary ... 186
Earlier sketch in CA 5-8R
See also Gray, Elizabeth Janet
See also MAICYA 1, 2
See also SATA 6
See also SATA-Obit 117
See also YAW
Vinograd, Julia 1943- ... CAAS 26
Vinogradov, Ivan M(atveyevich) 1891-1983
Obituary ... 109
Vinokur, Grigory
See Weinrauch, Herschel
Vinokurov, Yevgeny Mikhailovich 1925-
Brief entry ... 116
Vinovskis, Maris A. ... 238
Vinson, Elaine
See Rowland, D(onald) S(ydney)
Vinson, J(ohn) Chal(mers) 1919- ... 9-12R
Vinson, J(ohn) William 1916-1979
Obituary ... 89-92
Vinson, James (Albert) 1933- ... 120
Brief entry ... 118
Vinson, Jane 1927- ... 77-80
Vinson, Kathryn 1911-1995 ... 5-8R
See also SATA 21
Vinson, Rex Thomas 1935-2000 ... 101
See also SFW 4
Vinton, Bobby
See Vinton, Stanley Robert, Jr.
Vinton, Eleanor W(inthrop) 1899-1977 ... 61-64
Obituary ... 73-76
Vinton, Iris 1906(?)-1988 ... 77-80
Obituary ... 124
See also SATA 24
See also SATA-Obit 55
Vinton, John 1937- ... 73-76
Vinton, Stanley Robert, Jr. 1935(?)-
Brief entry ... 120
Vinton, Will 1947(?)- ... IDFW 3, 4
Vinyard, C. Dale 1932- ... 25-28R
Vinz, Mark 1942- ... 93-96
Viola, Herman J(oseph) 1938- ... CANR-91
Earlier sketches in CA 61-64, CANR-8, 23, 48
See also CLC 70
See also SATA 126
Viola, Lynne 1955- ... 135
Viola, Tom ... 180
Violet
See Blake, Lillie Devereux
Violet, Ultra
See Dufresne, Isabelle
Violett, Ellen 1925- ... 73-76
Violi, Paul 1944- ... CANR-88
Earlier sketches in CA 45-48, CANR-24, 49
Violis, G.
See Simenon, Georges (Jacques Christian)
Viorst, Judith 1931- ... CANR-101
Earlier sketches in CA 49-52, CANR-2, 26, 59
Interview in ... CANR-26
See also BEST 90:1
See also CLR 3, 90
See also CPW
See also CWRI 5
See also DAM POP
See also DLB 52
See also MAICYA 1, 2
See also SATA 7, 70, 123
Viorst, Milton 1930- ... CANR-116
Earlier sketches in CA 9-12R, CANR-26, 55
Vip
See Partch, Virgil Franklin II
Vipond, Don (Harry) 1932- ... 65-68
Vipond, Mary ... 152
Vipont, Charles
See Foulds, Elfrida Vipont
Vipont, Elfrida
See Foulds, Elfrida Vipont
See also DLB 160
Vira, Soma 1932- ... 174
Virahsawmy, Dev 1942- ... RGWL 3
Viramontes, Helena Maria 1954- ... 159
See also DLB 122
See also HLCS 2
See also HW 2
See also LLW
Viray, Manuel 1917- ... CP 1
Virden, Jenel 1954- ... 156
Virga, Vincent (Philip) 1942- ... CANR-93
Earlier sketch in CA 107
Virgil
See Vergil
See also CDWLB 1
See also DLB 211
See also LAIT 1
See also RGWL 2, 3
See also WP
Virgilio, Nicholas A(nthony) 1928-1989
Obituary ... 127
Virgines, George E. 1920- ... CANR-28
Earlier sketches in CA 25-28R, CANR-12
Virginius
See Connett, Eugene Virginius III
Virgo, Sean 1940- ... 161
Viroli, Maurizio ... 224
Virtanen, A(rtturi) I(lmari) 1895-1973 ... 168
Virtanen, Reino 1910-1987 ... CANR-4
Earlier sketch in CA 1-4R
Virtue, Doreen (L.) 1958- ... 187
Virtue, Noel 1947- ... 130
See also CN 5, 6, 7
Virtue, Vivian Lancaster 1911- ... CP 1
Virza, Edvarts
See Lieknis, Edvarts
See also EWL 3
Vis, William Ryerson 1886-1969
Obituary ... 110
Viscardi, Henry, Jr. 1912-2004 ... CANR-5
Obituary ... 226
Earlier sketch in CA 5-8R
Vischer, Friedrich Theodor
1807-1887 ... DLB 133
Vischer, Helen (Cassin Lombard) Carusi
1905(?)-1986
Obituary ... 119
Vischer, Lukas 1926- ... 131
Visconti, Luchino 1906-1976 ... CANR-39
Obituary ... 65-68
Earlier sketch in CA 81-84
See also CLC 16
Viscott, David S(teven) 1938-1996 ... CANR-26
Earlier sketch in CA 29-32R
See also AITN 1
See also SATA 65
Viscount Eccles
See Eccles, David (McAdam)
Viscusi, Robert 1941- ... 226
Viscusi, W. Kip 1949- ... CANR-123
Earlier sketch in CA 138
Vise, David A(llan) 1960- ... 203
Vise, Jean Donneau de
See Donneau de Vise, Jean
Visher, Emily B(rowning) 1918-2001 ... 109
Obituary ... 202
Visher, Halene Hatcher 1909- ... 45-48
Visher, John Sargent 1921- ... 109
Vishniac, Roman 1897-1990 ... 224
Vishniak, Mark 1883-1976
Obituary ... 69-72
Vishny, Michele 1932- ... 69-72
Visi, Baron
See Vian, Boris
Visiak, E(dward) H(arold) 1878-1972 ... HGG
Visocchi, Mark 1938- ... CANR-16
Earlier sketch in CA 93-96
Visotzky, Burton L. 1951- ... 138
Visram, Rozina 1939- ... 133
Visscher, Maurice B(olks) 1901-1983 ... 77-80
Obituary ... 182
Visser, Margaret 1940- ... CANR-72
Earlier sketch in CA 123
Visser, W(illem) F(rederik) H(endrik)
1900-1968 ... CAP-2
Earlier sketch in CA 25-28
See also SATA 10
Visser 't Hooft, Willem Adolf
1900-1985 ... 9-12R
Obituary ... 116
Visson, Lynn 1945- ... 134
Visson, Vladimir 1905(?)-1976
Obituary ... 69-72
Viswanathan, Gauri ... 190
Viswanathan, S(ubrahmanyam)
1933- ... CANR-82
Earlier sketch in CA 132
Visweswaran, Kamala 1962- ... 152
Vita-Finzi, Claudio 1936- ... 89-92
Vita-Finzi, Penelope (Jean) 1939- ... 133
Vital, David 1927- ... CANR-89
Earlier sketches in CA 29-32R, CANR-12, 44
Vitale, Ida 1923- ... LAWS 1
Vitale, Joseph T(homas) 1951- ... 107
Vitale, Philip H. 1913-1977 ... 17-20R
Vitale, Stefano 1958- ... 186
See also SATA 114
Vitali, Julius 1952- ... 153
Vitaliev, Vitali 1954- ... 219
Vitek, Donna
See Vitek, Donna Kimel
Vitek, Donna Kimel 1947- ... 131
See also RHW
Vitek, John D(ennis) 1942- ... 124
Vitelli, James R(obert) 1920- ... 29-32R
Viteritti, Joseph P. 1946- ... 210
Vitezovic, Tomislav
See Kuehnelt-Leddihn, Erik (Maria) Ritter von
Vitiello, Justin 1941- ... 139
Vitier, Cintio
See Vitier (y Bolanos), Cynthio
See also DLB 283
Vitier (y Bolanos), Cynthio 1921-
See Vitier, Cintio
See also HW 1
Vitola, Denise 1957- ... 159
Vitrac, Roger 1899-1952 ... DLB 321
Vitruvius c. 70B.C.-c. 16B.C. ... DLB 211
Vitry, Jacques de
See Jacques de Vitry
Vitry, Philippe de 1291-1361 ... DLB 208
Vittengl, Morgan John 1928- ... 5-8R
Vittitow, Mary L(ou) 1937- ... 139
Vittorini, Elio 1908-1966 ... 133
Obituary ... 25-28R
See also CLC 6, 9, 14
See also DLB 264
See also EW 12
See also EWL 3
See also RGWL 2, 3
Vitz, Robert C. 1938- ... 136
Vitzthum, Hilda 1902-1993 ... 143
Vitzthum, Richard Carleton 1936- ... 103
Vivanco, Luis Felipe 1907-1975 ... 176
See also DLB 108
See also HW 2
Vivante, Arturo 1923- ... CANR-72
Earlier sketches in CA 17-20R, CANR-10
See also CAAS 12
Vivante, Paolo 1921- ... 29-32R
Vivas, Eliseo 1901-1993 ... CANR-5
Obituary ... 176
Earlier sketch in CA 5-8R
Vivas, Julie 1947- ... 163
See also MAICYA 2
See also MAICYAS 1
See also SATA 96
Viveash, Cherry Jacqueline Lee 1929- ... CAP-1
Earlier sketch in CA 9-10
Vivekananda, Swami 1863-1902 ... TCLC 88
Vivelo, Jacqueline J. 1943- ... SATA 63
Vivers, Eileen Elliott 1905-1988 ... 41-44R
Obituary ... 174
Vives, Juan Luis 1493-1540 ... DLB 318
Vivian, Cordy Tindell 1924- ... 49-52
Vivian, E. Charles
See Cannell, Charles (Henry)
See also DLB 255
Vivian, Evelyn C. H.
See Cannell, Charles (Henry)
Vivian, Francis
See Ashley, (Arthur) Ernest
Vivian, Robert 1967- ... 209
Viviani, Cesare 1947- ... 210
See also DLB 128
Viviano, Benedict T(homas) 1940- ... CANR-10
Earlier sketch in CA 21-24R
Viviano, Frank 1947- ... 203
Vivien, Renee 1877-1909 ... 212
See also DLB 217
See also GLL 1
Vivien, Renee 1877-1909
See Vivien, Renee
Vivienne
See Entwistle, Florence Vivienne
Viviers, Jacobus Cornelius 1938-1999 ... 181
Vivion, Michael J. 1944- ... 140
Vizard, Stephen
See James, (David) Burnett (Stephen)
Vizedom, Monika B(asch) 1929- ... 69-72
Vizenor, Gerald Robert 1934- ... 205
Earlier sketches in CA 13-16R, CANR-5, 21, 44, 67
Autobiographical Essay in ... 205
See also CAAS 22
See also CLC 103
See also DAM MULT
See also DLB 175, 227
See also MTCW 2
See also MTFW 2005
See also NNAL
See also TCWW 2
Vizinczey, Stephen 1933- ... 128
Interview in ... CA-128
See also CCA 1
See also CLC 40
Vizzard, Jack
See Vizzard, John Anthony
Vizzard, John Anthony 1914- ... 29-32R
Vizzard, William J. 1944- ... 174
Vizzini, Ned 1981- ... 196
See also SATA 125
Vizzini, Salvatore 1926- ... 103
Vlach, John Michael 1948- ... 123
Vladeck, Bruce C. 1949- ... 101
Vladimirov, Leonid
See Finkelstein, Leonid Vladimirovitch
Vladimov, G.
See Vladimov, Georgii (Nikolaevich)
Vladimov, Georgii (Nikolaevich)
1931-2003 ... 123
Obituary ... 221
See also DLB 302
Vlahos, Olivia 1924- ... 21-24R
See also SATA 31
Vlasic, Bill 1954- ... 197
Vlasic, Bob
See Hirsch, Phil
Vlasic, Ivan Albert 1926- ... 9-12R
Vlasich, James A(nthony) 1944- ... 137
Vlastos, Gregory 1907-1991 ... 130
Obituary ... 135
Vlieghe, Hans ... 236
Vliet, R(ussell) G(ordon) 1929-1984 ... CANR-18
Obituary ... 112
Earlier sketch in CA 37-40R
See also CLC 22
See also CP 2
Vlock, Deborah (Michele) 1963- ... 230
Vlock, Laurel F(ox) 1926-2000 ... 37-40R
Obituary ... 189
Vloyantes, John P. 1918-1991 ... 61-64
Voaden, Herman Arthur 1903-1991 ... CANR-81
Earlier sketch in CA 103
See also DLB 88
Voake, Charlotte ... 180
See also MAICYA 2
See also SATA 114
Vo-Dinh, Mai 1933- ... CANR-53
Earlier sketches in CA 77-80, CANR-13, 29
See also SATA 16
Vodola, Thomas M(ichael)
1925-1993 ... CANR-19
Earlier sketches in CA 49-52, CANR-3
Voegeli, V(ictor) Jacque 1934- ... 21-24R
Voegelin, Eric (Herman Wilhelm)
1901-1985 ... CANR-122
Obituary ... 114
Earlier sketch in CA 132
Voehringer, Erich F(rederick)
1905-1973 ... CANR-2
Obituary ... 41-44R
Earlier sketch in CA 1-4R
Voeks, Robert A(llen) 1950- ... 171
Voeks, Virginia (Wilna) 1921- ... 13-16R
Voelcker, Hunce 1940- ... 77-80
Voelkel, Robert T(ownsend) 1933- ... 25-28R
Voelker, John D(onaldson)
1903-1991 ... CANR-42
Obituary ... 134
Earlier sketch in CA 1-4R
See also Traver, Robert
See also DAM POP
Voellner, Louada McCaughen 1888(?)-1986
Obituary ... 119
Voermans, Paul 1960- ... 168
Voet, H. L.
See Greshoff, Jan
Voeten, Teun 1961- ... 219
Vogan, Sara 1947-1991 ... 134
Vogau, Boris Andreevich
See Vogau, Boris Andreyevich
Vogau, Boris Andreyevich 1894-1938 ... 218
Brief entry ... 123
See also Pil'niak, Boris and
Pil'niak, Boris Andreevich and
Pilnyak, Boris
Vogel, Alfred T(ennyson) 1906-1992 ... 104
Vogel, Arthur A(nton) 1924- ... CANR-10
Earlier sketch in CA 25-28R
Vogel, Carole Garbuny 1951- ... 138
See also SATA 70, 105
Vogel, Dan 1927- ... 120
Vogel, David 1947- ... CANR-11
Earlier sketch in CA 65-68
Vogel, Donald Stanley 1917- ... 141
Vogel, Ezra F. 1930- ... CANR-30
Earlier sketch in CA 13-16R
Vogel, Frederick G. 1934- ... 153
Vogel, Helen Wolff 1918- ... 17-20R
Vogel, Hunter Bertram August 1903-1990
Obituary ... 131
Vogel, Ilse-Margret 1918- ... CANR-7
Earlier sketch in CA 13-16R
See also SATA 14
Vogel, Irving L. 1918- ... 122
Vogel, Jerry 1896(?)-1980
Obituary ... 101
Vogel, John H., Jr. 1950- ... 77-80
See also SATA 18
Vogel, Linda Jane 1940- ... 61-64
Vogel, Lise ... 217
Vogel, Lucy E(laine) ... 49-52
Vogel, Morris J. 1945- ... 128
Vogel, Paula A(nne) 1951- ... CANR-140
Earlier sketches in CA 108, CANR-119
See also CAD
See also CD 5, 6
See also CLC 76
See also CWD
See also DC 19
See also DFS 14
See also MTFW 2005
See also RGAL 4
Vogel, Shawna 1964- ... 149
Vogel, Speed
See Vogel, Irving L.

Cumulative Index 597 Vonnegut

Vogel, Stanley M(orton) 1921- 77-80
Vogel, Steve 1946- 132
Vogel, Steven 1940- 53-56
Vogel, Victor H(ugh) 1905-1978 .... CANR-3
Earlier sketch in CA 1-4R
Vogel, Virgil (Howard) J(oseph)
1918-1994 .... CANR-10
Obituary 143
Earlier sketch in CA 25-28R
Vogeler, Ingolf 1944- 107
Vogelgesang, Sandra Louise 1942- 57-60
Vogelgesang, Sandy
See Vogelgesang, Sandra Louise
Vogelman, Joyce 1936- 106
Vogelsang, Arthur 1942- 49-52
Vogelsinger, Hubert 1938- 25-28R
Vogelweide, Walther von der
See Walther von der Vogelweide
Vogenitz, David George 1930- 41-44R
Voget, Fred W. 1913-1997 61-64
Vogler, Roger E. 1938- 126
Voglino, Barbara 1940- 194
Vogt, Adolf Max 1920- 184
Vogt, Anton 1914- .... CP 1
Vogt, Bill
See Vogt, William McKinley
Vogt, Christian 1946- 216
Vogt, Esther Loewen 1915-1999 .... CANR-7
Earlier sketch in CA 17-20R
See also SATA 14
Vogt, Evon Zartman, Jr. 1918-2004 .. CANR-27
Obituary 228
Earlier sketch in CA 69-72
Vogt, Gregory .... SATA-Brief 45
Vogt, Gregory L. 153
See also SATA 94
Vogt, Gregory Max 1949- 137
Vogt, Joseph 1895-
Brief entry 112
Vogt, Marie Bollinger 1921- 57-60
See also SATA 45
Vogt, Walter 1927-1988 191
Vogt, William McKinley 1935- 89-92
Voiculescu, Vasile 1884-1963 .... EWL 3
Voien, Steven 1954- 166
Voight, Jon 1938- 179
Voight, Virginia Frances 1909-1989 . CANR-18
Earlier sketches in CA 5-8R, CANR-2
See also SATA 8
Voigt, Cynthia 1942- CANR-94
Earlier sketches in CA 106, CANR-18, 37, 40
Interview in CANR-18
See also AAYA 3, 30
See also BYA 1, 3, 6, 7, 8
See also CLC 30
See also CLR 13, 48
See also JRDA
See also LAIT 5
See also MAICYA 1, 2
See also MAICYAS 1
See also MTFW 2005
See also SATA 48, 79, 116, 160
See also SATA-Brief 33
See also WYA
See also YAW
Voigt, David Quentin 1926- CANR-32
Earlier sketches in CA 41-44R, CANR-14
Voigt, Ellen Bryant 1943- CANR-115
Earlier sketches in CA 69-72, CANR-11, 29, 55
See also CLC 54
See also CP 7
See also CSW
See also CWP
See also DLB 120
See also PFS 23
Voigt, Erna 1925- .... SATA 35
Voigt, Karsten D. 1941- 113
Voigt, Lieselotte E. Kurth
See Kurth-Voigt, Lieselotte E.
Voigt, Melvin J(ohn) 1911-2000 .... CANR-5
Earlier sketch in CA 13-16R
Voigt, Milton 1924- 9-12R
Voigt, Robert J(oseph) 1916-1994 93-96
Voigt, Stefan 1962- 225
Voigt, William, Jr. 1902-1991 73-76
Voigt-Rother, Erna
See Voigt, Erna
Voils, Jessie Wiley CAP-2
Earlier sketch in CA 29-32
Voinovich, Vladimir (Nikolaevich)
1932- CANR-67
Earlier sketches in CA 81-84, CANR-33
See also CAAS 12
See also CLC 10, 49, 147
See also CWW 2
See also DLB 302
See also MTCW 1
Voitle, Robert (Brown, Jr.) 1919-1994 .... 1-4R
Voiture, Vincent 1597-1648 . GFL Beginnings to 1789
Vojnovic, Ivo
See Vojnovik, Ivo
Vojnovik, Ivo 1857-1929 219
See also CDWLB 4
See also DLB 147
See also EWL 3
Vojtech, Anna 1946- .... SATA 42, 108
Volanski, John J. 1956- 218
Volbach, Walther R(ichard) 1897-1996 . 29-32R
Obituary 153
Volcker, Paul A(dolph) 1927- 129
Brief entry 114
Vold, Jan Erik 1939- 194
See also DLB 297
Vole, Zenobia N.
See Douglas, Lauren Wright
Volente, Deo
See DeVincentes-Hayes, Nan
Volgyes, Ivan 1936- CANR-20
Earlier sketch in CA 104
Volin, Michael 1911-1997 101
Volk, Hannah Marie
See Wormington, Hannah Marie
Volk, Patricia (Gay) 1943- CANR-111
Earlier sketch in CA 140
Volk, Toni 1944- 155
Volkan, Vamik D(jemal) 1932- CANR-19
Earlier sketch in CA 102
Volkart, Edmund H(owell) 1919-1992 ... 21-24R
Volkening, Henry T. 1902-1972
Obituary 37-40R
Volker, Roger 1934- 53-56
Volker, Roy 1924- 57-60
Volkman, Ernest 1940- 132
Volkman, Karen 1967- 206
Volkmar, Hans
See Holz, Arno
Volkoff, Vladimir 1932-2005 73-76
See also DLB 83
Volkogonov, Dmitri (A.) 1928-1995 157
Volkov, Leon 1920(?)-1974
Obituary 45-48
Volkov, Solomon (Moiseevich) 1944- 168
Volkova, Bronislava 1946- 195
Voll, John O(bert) 1936- CANR-67
Earlier sketch in CA 129
Vollbehr, Otto H. F. 1872(?)-1945(?) 189
See also DLB 187
Vollenweider, Richard 1922- 160
Vollers, Maryanne 1955- CANR-107
Earlier sketch in CA 150
Vollert, Cyril (Oscar) 1901-1980 61-64
Vollmann, William T. 1959- CANR-116
Earlier sketches in CA 134, CANR-67
See also CLC 89
See also CN 7
See also CPW
See also DA3
See also DAM NOV, POP
See also MTCW 2
See also MTFW 2005
Vollmer, Howard M. 1928- CANR-13
Earlier sketch in CA 17-20R
Vollstadt, Elizabeth Weiss 1942- 192
See also SATA 121
Vollstedt, Maryana 1925- 149
Volodin, Alexander 1919-
Vologdin
See Zasodimsky, Pavel Vladimirovich
Voloshin, Maksimilian Aleksandrovich
1877-1932 .... DLB 295
Voloshinov, V. N.
See Bakhtin, Mikhail Mikhailovich
Volpe, E(rminio) Peter 1927- CANR-15
Earlier sketch in CA 37-40R
Volpe, Edmond L(oris) 1922- CANR-1
Earlier sketch in CA 1-4R
Volpe, Vernon L(ewis) 1955- 135
Volponi, Paolo 1924-1994 199
See also CWW 2
See also DLB 177
See also EWL 3
Volsky, Paula CANR-137
Earlier sketch in CA 171
Volta, Ornella 1927- 158
Voltaire 1694-1778 .... BYA 13
See also DA
See also DA3
See also DAB
See also DAC
See also DAM DRAM, MST
See also DLB 314
See also EW 4
See also GFL Beginnings to 1789
See also LATS 1:1
See also LMFS 1
See also NFS 7
See also RGWL 2, 3
See also SSC 12
See also TWA
See also WLC
Voltz, Jeanne Appleton 1920-2002 ... CANR-21
Obituary 200
Earlier sketch in CA 104
Volz, Carl (Andrew) 1933-1998 .... 29-32R
Volz, Marlin M(ilton) 1917- 37-40R
von Abele, Rudolph (Radama) 1922-1989 .. 104
Obituary 127
Von Ahnen, Katherine 1922- 159
See also SATA 93
von Albertini, Rudolf 1923- 131
von Albrecht, Michael 1933- 188
Vonarburg, Elisabeth 1947- 208
Earlier sketches in CA 149, CANR-129
Autobiographical Essay in 208
See also DLB 251
See also SFW 4
von Arnim, Elizabeth
See Russell, Mary Annette Beauchamp
See also DLB 197
See also RHW
von Aschendrof, Baron Ignatz
See Ford, Ford Madox
von Baeyer, Hans Christian 1938- CANR-41
Earlier sketch in CA 117
von Balthasar, Hans U.
See von Balthasar, Hans Urs
von Balthasar, Hans Urs 1905-1988 130
Obituary 125
Brief entry 106
Von Bencke, Matthew Justin 1972- 164
von Berg, J(ohan) F(riedrich) (?)-1983(?)
Obituary 108
von Bertalanffy, Ludwig 1901-1972 .... CAP-2
Earlier sketch in CA 25-28
von Birken, Sigmund 1626-1681 .... DLB 164
von Block, Bela W(illiam) 1922-1991 104
von Block, Sylvia 1931- CANR-7
Earlier sketch in CA 53-56
von Bothmer, Dietrich Felix 1918- 106
von Brand, Theodor C. 1900(?)-1978
Obituary 81-84
Von Brandenstein, Patrizia .... IDFW 3, 4
von Braun, Wernher 1912-1977 .... CANR-9
Obituary 69-72
Earlier sketch in CA 5-8R
Von Canon, Claudia .... BYA 7
von Castlehun, Friedl
See Marion, Frieda
von Chamisso, Adelbert
See Chamisso, Adelbert von
von Cube, Irmgard 1900(?)-1977
Obituary 73-76
von Daeniken, Erich 1935- CANR-44
Earlier sketches in CA 37-40R, CANR-17
See also AITN 1
See also CLC 30
von Daniken, Erich
See von Daeniken, Erich
von Dassanowsky, Elfi 1924- .... IDFW 4
Von Dassanowsky, Robert
See Dassanowsky, Robert von
Vondel, Joost van den 1587-1679 ... RGWL 2, 3
von dem Werder, Diederich
1584-1657 .... DLB 164
von der Gruen, Max 1926-
See von der Grun, Max
See also DLB 75
von der Mehden, Fred R. 1927- 9-12R
Vonderplanitz, Aajonus 1947- 156
von der Vogelweide, Walther
See Walther von der Vogelweide
von Doderer, Heimito 1896-1966 183
Obituary 25-28R
See also Doderer, Heimito von
See also DLB 85
Vondra, J. Gert
See Vondra, Josef (Gert)
Vondra, Josef (Gert) 1941- CANR-99
Earlier sketch in CA 104
See also SATA 121
von Dreele, W(illiam) H(enry) 1924- 93-96
von Drehle, David 1961- CANR-127
Earlier sketch in CA 169
Vondung, Klaus 1941- 217
von Eckardt, Ursula M(aria) 1925- 13-16R
Von Eckardt, Wolf 1918-1995 .... 5-8R
Obituary 149
von Elbe, Joachim 1902-2000 132
Von Elsner, Don Byron 1909-1997 .... 1-4R
von Ende, Richard Chaffey 1907-1990 103
Von Erffa, Helmut (Hartmann) 1900-1979 .. 133
von Euler, Ulf (Svante) 1905-1983 158
Obituary 109
von Eyb, Albrecht 1420-1475 .... DLB 179
Von Falkenstein, Waldeen 1913-1993 233
von Finckenstein, Maria 1942- 193
von Frank, Albert J(ames) 1945- CANR-45
Earlier sketch in CA 120
von Franz, Marie-Louise
1915-1998 .... CANR-65
Obituary 165
Earlier sketch in CA 85-88
von Frisch, Karl (Ritter)
See Frisch, Karl (Ritter) von
von Frisch, Otto 1929- 101
von Fuerer-Haimendorf, Christoph
1909-1995 131
von Furstenberg, Egon (Edvard)
1946-2004 102
Obituary 228
von Furstenberg, George Michael
1941- CANR-10
Earlier sketch in CA 65-68
von Glahn, Gerhard E(rnst) 1911-1997 . 13-16R
von Graffenried, Michael 1957- 198
von Gronicka, Andre 1912-1999 .... 25-28R
von Grumbach, Argula 1492-1563(?) . DLB 179
von Grunebaum, G(ustave) E(dmund)
1909-1972 .... CANR-3
Earlier sketch in CA 1-4R
Von Gunden, Heidi Cecilia 1940- 125
Von Gunden, Kenneth 1946- 175
See also SATA 113
Vo Nguyen, Giap 1912(?)-
Brief entry 115
von Habsburg(-Lothringen), Geza Louis
Eusebius Gebhard Ralphael Albert Maria
1940- 161
von Hagen, Mark (L.) 168
Von Hagen, Victor Wolfgang 1908-1985 105
See also SATA 29
von Handel-Mazzetti, Enrica 1871-1955 177
Von Harbou, Thea 1888-1954 .... IDFW 3, 4
von Hartmann, Eduard 1842-1906 ..... TCLC 96
von Hassell, Fey 1918- 134
von Hayek, Friedrich August
See Hayek, F(riedrich) A(ugust von)
von Heidenstam, (Carl Gustaf) Verner
See Heidenstam, (Carl Gustaf) Verner von
von Heller, Marcus
See Zachary, Hugh
von Hertzen, Heikki 1913-2000(?) 37-40R
von Heyse, Paul (Johann Ludwig)
See Heyse, Paul (Johann Ludwig von)
von Hildebrand, Alice 1923- 21-24R
von Hildebrand, Dietrich
1889-1977 .... CANR-10
Obituary 69-72
Earlier sketch in CA 17-20R
Von Hilsheimer, George E(dwin III)
1934- 29-32R
von Hippel, Frank 1937- 93-96
von Hirsch, Andrew 1934- CANR-14
Earlier sketch in CA 81-84
von Hofe, Harold 1912- CANR-4
Earlier sketch in CA 1-4R
von Hoffman, Nicholas 1929- CANR-34
Earlier sketch in CA 81-84
von Hofmannsthal, Hugo
See Hofmannsthal, Hugo von
von Horn, Carl 1903- CAP-2
Earlier sketch in CA 21-22
von Horvath, Odon
See von Horvath, Odon
von Horvath, Odon
See von Horvath, Odon
von Horvath, Odon 1901-1938 194
Brief entry 118
See also von Horvath, Oedoen
See also DLB 85, 124
See also RGWL 2, 3
See also TCLC 45
von Horvath, Oedoen 184
See also von Horvath, Odon
von Kalnein, Wend 1914- 153
von Kaschnitz-Weinberg, Marie Luise
1901-1974 127
Obituary 93-96
See also Kaschnitz, Marie Luise
von Kellenbach, Katharina 1960- ... CANR-110
Earlier sketch in CA 151
von Kleist, Heinrich
See Kleist, Heinrich von
Von Klemperer, Klemens 1916- 21-24R
von Klopp, Vahrah
See Malvern, Gladys
von Koenigswald, (Gustav Heinrich) Ralph
1902-1982
Obituary 110
von Koerber, Hans Nordewin
1886-1979 .... 41-44R
von Kuffstein, Hans Ludwig
1582-1656 .... DLB 164
von Lang, Jochen
See von Lang-Piechocki, Joachim
von Langenfeld, Friedrich Spee
1591-1635 .... DLB 164
von Lang-Piechocki, Joachim 1925- 101
von Laue, Max Theodor Felix
See Laue, Max Theodor Felix von
Von Laue, Theodore Herman
1916-2000 .... 9-12R
von le Fort, Gertrud (Petrea)
See le Fort, Gertrud (Petrea) von
Von Leyden, Wolfgang Marius
1911-2004 .... CANR-3
Earlier sketch in CA 5-8R
von Liliencron, (Friedrich Adolf Axel) Detlev
See Liliencron, (Friedrich Adolf Axel) Detlev von
von Logau, Friedrich 1605-1655 .... DLB 164
von Maltitz, Horst 1905-1986 77-80
Von Manstein, Erich 1887-1973
Obituary 45-48
von Meck, Galina 1891-1985
Obituary 116
von Mehren, Arthur T(aylor) 1922- 17-20R
von Mendelssohn, Felix 1918- 13-16R
Von Mering, Otto Oswald, Jr. 1922- 1-4R
von Miklos, Josephine Bogdan 1900-1972
Obituary 37-40R
von Mises, Ludwig (Edler)
See Mises, Ludwig (Edler) von
von Mises, Margit
See Mises, Margit von
Von Mises, Richard (Martin Edler)
1883-1953 162
Von Mohrenschildt, Dimitri Sergius 1902-
Brief entry 106
Von Molnar, Geza (Walter Elemer)
1932-2001 .... 29-32R
Obituary 197
von Moltke, Helmuth James 1907-1945 140
von Moltke, Konrad 1941- CANR-19
Earlier sketch in CA 101
Von Moschzisker, Michael 1918- 37-40R
Vonnegut, Kurt, Jr. 1922- CANR-92
Earlier sketches in CA 1-4R, CANR-1, 25, 49, 75
See also AAYA 6, 44
See also AITN 1
See also AMWS 2
See also BEST 90:4
See also BPFB 3
See also BYA 3, 14
See also CDALB 1968-1988
See also CLC 1, 2, 3, 4, 5, 8, 12, 22, 40, 60, 111, 212
See also CN 1, 2, 3, 4, 5, 6, 7
See also CPW 1
See also DA
See also DA3
See also DAB
See also DAC
See also DAM MST, NOV, POP
See also DLB 2, 8, 152
See also DLBD 3
See also DLBY 1980
See also EWL 3
See also EXPN
See also EXPS
See also LAIT 4
See also LMFS 2
See also MAL 5
See also MTCW 1, 2
See also MTFW 2005

See also NFS 3
See also RGAL 4
See also SCFW
See also SFW 4
See also SSC 8
See also SSFS 5
See also TUS
See also WLC
See also YAW
Vonnegut, Mark 1947- 65-68
See also AITN 2
von Neumann, John 1903-1957
Brief entry 117
von Ost, Henry Lerner 1915-1994 101
Obituary 145
Von Rachen, Kurt
See Hubbard, L(afayette) Ron(ald)
von Rad, Gerhard 1901-1971
Obituary 104
von Rago, Louis J(oseph)
See Rago, Louis J(oseph von)
Von Rauch, Georg 1904-1991 73-76
von Reden, Sitta 232
von Rezzori (d'Arezzo), Gregor
See Rezzori (d'Arezzo), Gregor von
von Rhein, John (Richard) 1945- 120
von Riekhoff, Harald 1937- 89-92
von Rosenstiel, Helene 1944- 105
Von Salis, Jean-R. 1901-1971 .... 21-24R
von Salomon, Ernst 1902-1972
Obituary 37-40R
von Schilcher, Florian 1944- 118
von Schlabrendorff, Fabian 1907-1980
Obituary 105
von Schmidt, Eric 1931- CANR-13
Earlier sketch in CA 17-20R
See also SATA 50
See also SATA-Brief 36
Von Schmidt, Harold 1896(?)-1982
Obituary 107
von Schoenhoff, Ulrike
See Frank, Rudolf
von Schoultz, Solveig
See Schoultz, Solveig von
von Schuschnigg, Kurt 1897-1977 103
von Schwarzenfeld, Gertrude
See Cochrane de Alencar, Gertrude E. L.
von Staden, Heinrich 1939- 37-40R
von Staden, Wendelgard 1925- 110
von Stark, G.
See le Fort, Gertrud (Petrea) von
von Sternberg, Josef
See Sternberg, Josef von
von Storch, Anne B. 1910- CAP-2
Earlier sketch in CA 29-32
See also SATA 1
von Stroheim, Erich 1885-1957 190
Von Struensee, Vanessa M. G. 1958- 187
von Stubenberg, Johann Wilhelm
1619-1663 .... DLB 164
von Tepl, Johannes c. 1350-c. 1414 ... DLB 179
von Teuffel, Mrs.
See Howard, Blanche Willis
von Trapp, Maria Augusta 1905-1987 81-84
Obituary 122
See also Trapp, Maria Augusta von
von Trier, Lars 1956- 167
von Trotta, Margarethe 1942- 126
von Tunzelmann, G(eorge) N(icholas)
1943- 156
Von Unruh, Fritz 1885-1970
Obituary 29-32R
See also Unruh, Fritz von
See also DLB 118
von Wangenheim, Chris 1942-1981
Obituary 103
Von Ward, Paul 1939- 217
von Weizsaecker, Carl Friedrich 1912- 105
von Wiegand, Charmion 1898(?)-1983
Obituary 110
von Wiesenberger, Arthur 1953- 169
Von Wiren-Garczynski, Vera 1931- 41-44R
von Wodtke, Charlotte Buel Johnson
1918-1982 112
See also Johnson, Charlotte Buel
von Wohl-Musciny, Ludwig
See de Wohl, Louis
von Wuthenau, Alexander 1900- 65-68
von Wyle, Niklas c. 1415-1479 .... DLB 179
Von Zelewsky, Alexander 1936- 159
von Zesen, Philipp 1619-1689 .... DLB 164
von Ziegesar, Cecily 1970- .... AAYA 56
See also SATA 161
von Zuehlsdorff, Volkmar J(ohannes)
1912- CANR-20
Earlier sketch in CA 5-8R
Vooren, Monique Van
See Van Vooren, Monique
Voorhees, Richard J(oseph) 1916-1997 ..... 5-8R
Voorhies, Barbara 1939- 104
Voorhis, Horace Jeremiah
1901-1984 .... CANR-6
Obituary 113
Earlier sketch in CA 1-4R
Voorhis, Jerry
See Voorhis, Horace Jeremiah
Voorne, J. J. van
See Greshoff, Jan
Voos, Henry 1928-1987 .... 25-28R
Voos, Paula B. 1949- 150
Voranc, Prezihov 1893-1950 .... DLB 147
Vorhees, Melvin B. 1904(?)-1977
Obituary 69-72
Vorkapich, Slavko 1895-1976 .... IDFW 3, 4
Vorobeva, Maria 1892-1984
Obituary 113
Voronova, Lidiia Alekseevna 1875-1937
See Charskaia, Lidiia
Voronsky, Aleksandr Konstantinovich
1884-1937 .... DLB 272
Vorosmarty, Mihaly 1800-1855 .... RGWL 2, 3
Vorpahl, Ben Merchant 1937- 41-44R
Vorse, Mary Heaton 1874-1966 .... DLB 303
Vorspan, Albert 1924- CANR-13
Earlier sketch in CA 21-24R
Vorster, Gordon 1924- 133
See also CLC 34
Vorzimmer, Peter J. 1937- 93-96
Vos, Clarence J(ohn) 1920- 45-48
Vos, Ida 1931- CANR-99
Earlier sketch in CA 137
See also CLR 85
See also SATA 69, 121
See also YAW
Vos, Nelvin (LeRoy) 1932- 17-20R
Vosburgh, Leonard (W.) 1912- .... SATA 15
Vosce, Trudie
See Ozick, Cynthia
Vose, Clement E(llery) 1923-1985 .... 41-44R
Obituary 115
Vose, Ruth Hurst 1944- CANR-26
Earlier sketch in CA 109
Vosko, Leah F. 237
Voskovec, George 1905-1981
Obituary 104
See also Voskovec, Jiri (George)
Voskovec, Jiri (George)
See Voskovec, George
See also EWL 2
Voskuil, Dennis N(eal) 1944- 112
Voslensky, M(ichael) S(ergeevich) 1920- 128
Voss, Carl Hermann 1910-1995 .... CANR-10
Earlier sketch in CA 21-24R
Voss, E(rnst) Theodore 1928- 37-40R
Voss, Earl H. 1922- 9-12R
Voss, Frederick S. 1943- 172
Voss, George L. 1922- 57-60
Voss, James F(rederick) 1930- 41-44R
Voss, Johann Heinrich 1751-1826 .... DLB 90
Voss, Ralph F. 1943- 137
Voss, Sarah (Lou) 1945- 167
Voss, Thomas M(ichael) 1945- 105
vos Savant, Marilyn 1946- CANR-97
Earlier sketch in CA 154
Vosteen, Thomas R(aymond) 1944- 152
Vosti, Stephen A. 1955- 170
Votaw, Dow 1920- 17-20R
Voureka, Amalia
See Fleming, Amalia
Vournakis, John N(icholas) 1939- 57-60
Voute, J. Peter 1906-1996 125
Vovchok, Marko
See Markovich, Mariia Aleksandrovna
See also DLB 238
Vowell, Sarah 1969- 201
Vowles, Richard B(eckman) 1917- 25-28R
Voyageur
See Allen, Cecil J(ohn)
Voyant, Claire
See Ackerman, Forrest J(ames)
Voyce, Arthur 1889-1977 .... CAP-1
Earlier sketch in CA 13-14
Voyle, Mary
See Manning, Rosemary (Joy)
See also GLL 2
Voynich, E(thel) L(illian Boule) 1864-1960 . 179
Obituary 104
See also DLB 197
Voynovich, Vladimir Nikolaevich
1932- .... EWL 3
Voysey, Margaret 1945- 108
Voysey, Michael 1920-1987
Obituary 123
Vozenilek, Helen S. 1958- 140
Voznesensky, Andrei (Andreievich)
1933- CANR-37
Earlier sketch in CA 89-92
See also Voznesensky, Andrey
See also CLC 1, 15, 57
See also CWW 2
See also DAM POET
See also MTCW 1
Voznesensky, Andrey
See Voznesensky, Andrei (Andreievich)
See also EWL 3
Vranich, Joseph 1945- 138
Vrato, Elizabeth 1965- 224
Vrba, Rudolf 1924- 21-24R
Vrbovska, Anca 1905-1989 81-84
Vredenburg, Harvey L. 1921- 25-28R
Vreeland, Diana (Dalziel) 1903(?)-1989 111
Obituary 129
Vreeland, Jane D. 1915- 21-24R
Vreeland, Susan (Joyce) 1946- 204
Earlier sketch in CA 192
Autobiographical Essay in 204
Vrettos, Theodore 1919- CANR-118
Earlier sketches in CA 13-16R, CANR-27
Vreuls, Diane 57-60
Vriens, Jacques 1946- 226
See also SATA 151
Vries, Anne de
See de Vries, Anne
Vries, Leonard de 1919- 113
Vrkljan, Irena 1930- 233
Vroman, Leo 1915- 49-52
Vroman, Mary Elizabeth (Gibson)
1923-1967 125
Obituary 109
See also BW 1
See also DLB 33
Vroom, Victor H(arold) 1932- 9-12R
Vrooman, Jack Rochford 1929- 45-48
Vrugt, Johanna Petronella 1905-1960 191
See also Blaman, Anna
Vryonis, Speros (P.), Jr. 1928- 85-88
Vu, Tran Tri 206
Vucinich, Alexander S. 1914- 156
Brief entry 109
Vucinich, Wayne S. 1913-2005 .... 13-16R
Obituary 238
Vugteveen, Verna Aardema
See Aardema, Verna
See also CLR 17
See also MAICYA 1, 2
See also SAAS 8
See also SATA 4, 68, 107
See also SATA-Obit 119
Vu Hoang Chuong 1916-1976 .... EWL 3
Vuilleumier, Marion 1918- 81-84
Vujica, Stanko M(irko) 1909-1976 .... 41-44R
Vukcevich, Ray 203
Vukotic, Dusan 1927- .... IDFW 3, 4
Vuletic, Zivko
See Rajic, Negovan
Vulliamy, Colwyn Edward 1886-1971
Obituary 89-92
Vulture, Elizabeth T.
See Gilbert, Suzie
Vuong, Lynette Dyer 1938- CANR-46
Earlier sketch in CA 117
See also SATA 60, 110
Vuong g(ia) Thuy 1938- 69-72
Vurgun, Samed 1906-1956 .... EWL 3
Vyn, Kathleen 1949- 89-92
Vyner, Harriet 223
Vynnychenko, Volodymyr 1880-1951 .... EWL 3
Vysotsky, Vladimir 1938-1980 .... EWL 3
Vyverberg, Henry (Sabin) 1921- 109
Vyvyan, C(lara) C(oltman Rogers)
1885-1976 .... CAP-1
Earlier sketch in CA 9-10
Vyvyan, Nigel
See Nevill, Barry St-John

W

Waage, Frederick 1943- 104
Waagenaar, Sam 1908-1997 57-60
Waarsenburg, Hans van de
See van de Waarsenburg, Hans
Waas, Uli
See Waas-Pommer, Ulrike
Waas-Pommer, Ulrike 1949- .... SATA 85
Waber, Bernard 1924- CANR-140
Earlier sketches in CA 1-4R, CANR-2, 38, 68
See also CLR 55
See also CWRI 5
See also MAICYA 1, 2
See also SATA 47, 95, 155
See also SATA-Brief 40
Wabun
See James, Marlise Ann
Wace, Robert c. 1100-c. 1175 .... DLB 146
Wach, Kenneth 1944- 163
Wacher, J(ohn) S(tewart) 1927- 125
Brief entry 105
Wachhorst, Wyn 1938- CANR-114
Earlier sketch in CA 106
Wachowski, Andy 1967- .... AAYA 58
Wachowski, Larry 1965- .... AAYA 58
Wachs, Mark Marshall 1933- 25-28R
Wachs, Saul P(hilip) 1931- CANR-56
Earlier sketches in CA 112, CANR-30
Wachsberger, Ken(neth) 1949- 138
Wachsmann, Klaus Philipp 1907-1984
Brief entry 106
Wachsmann, Shelley 1950- 150
Wachtel, Albert 1939- CANR-50
Earlier sketch in CA 123
Wachtel, Eleanor 1947- 134
Wachtel, Howard M(artin) 1938- 49-52
Wachtel, Isidore H. 1909(?)-1979
Obituary 89-92
Wachtel, Michael 1960- 188
Wachtel, Paul L(awrence) 1940- 115
Wachtel, Paul Spencer 1947- 133
Wachtel, Shirley Russak 1951- 152
See also SATA 88
Wachter, Kenneth W. 1947- 139
Wachter, Oralee (Roberts) 1935- 122
See also SATA 61
See also SATA-Brief 51
Wachter, Susan M. 1943- 120
Wachtler, Sol 1930- 163
Wachtman, John B. 1928- 145
Waciuma, Wanjohi 1938- 77-80
Wackenroder, Wilhelm Heinrich
1773-1798 .... DLB 90
Wacker, Charles H(enry), Jr. 1925- 73-76
Wacker, Grant 1945- 207
Wackerbarth, Marjorie CAP-1
Earlier sketch in CA 13-14
Wackernagel, Wilhelm 1806-1869 ..... DLB 133
Wadbrook, William P. 1933- 45-48
Waddams, Herbert Montague 1911-1972
Obituary 107
Waddell, D(avid) A(lan) G(ilmour)
1927- CANR-23
Earlier sketch in CA 1-4R
Waddell, Eric (Wilson) 1939- 45-48
Waddell, Evelyn Margaret 1918- 53-56
See also SATA 10
Waddell, Helen (Jane) 1889-1965 102
See also DLB 240
See also RHW
Waddell, Jack O('Brien) 1933- 33-36R
Waddell, Martin 1941- CANR-107
Earlier sketches in CA 113, CANR-34, 56
See also AAYA 23
See also CLR 31
See also CWRI 5
See also MAICYA 2
See also MAICYAS 1
See also SAAS 15
See also SATA 43, 81, 127, 129
See also SATA-Essay 129
Waddell, Steve R(obert) 1961- 177
Waddell, Thomas F. 1937-1987 154
Wadden, Marie 1955- 139
Waddington, C(onrad) H(al)
1905-1975 .... CANR-6
Obituary 61-64
Earlier sketch in CA 13-16R
Waddington, Miriam 1917-2004 ...... CANR-30
Obituary 225
Earlier sketches in CA 21-24R, CANR-12
See also CCA 1
See also CLC 28
See also CP 1, 2, 3, 4, 5, 6, 7
See also DLB 68
Waddington, Patrick (Haynes)
1934- CANR-106
Earlier sketch in CA 149
Waddington, Raymond B(ruce) 1935- 53-56
Waddy, Charis 1909-2004 69-72
Obituary 229
Waddy, Lawrence (Heber) 1914- CANR-59
Earlier sketches in CA 13-16R, CANR-7
See also SATA 91
Wade, Alan
See Vance, John Holbrook
Wade, Bill
See Barrett, Geoffrey John
Wade, Bob
See Wade, Robert (Allison)
Wade, Brent James 1959- 179
Wade, Carlson 1928- 29-32R
Wade, David 1929- 103
Wade, Donald W(illiam) 1904-1988
Obituary 128
Wade, E(ileen) K(irkpatrick) 1892(?)-1985
Obituary 117
Wade, Edwin L. 1940- 126
Wade, Francis C(larence) 1907- CAP-1
Earlier sketch in CA 13-14
Wade, Graham 1940- CANR-25
Earlier sketch in CA 107
Wade, Harry Vincent 1894-1973
Obituary 89-92
Wade, Henry
See Aubrey-Fletcher, Henry Lancelot
See also DLB 77
Wade, Herbert
See Wales, Hugh Gregory
Wade, Hugh Mason 1913-1986
Obituary 118
Wade, Ira Owen 1896-1983 73-76
Obituary 109
Wade, Jack Warren, Jr. 1948- 131
Wade, Jennifer
See Wehen, Joy DeWeese
Wade, Jerry L(ee) 1941- 53-56
Wade, Jewel Millsap 1937-
Brief entry 107
Wade, Joanna
See Berckman, Evelyn Domenica
Wade, John Stevens 1927- CANR-6
Earlier sketch in CA 13-16R
Wade, Kit
See Carson, Xanthus
Wade, L(arry) L(ee) 1935- 33-36R
Wade, Lawrence 1949(?)-1990
Obituary 131
Wade, Mary Dodson 1930- 226
See also SATA 79, 151
Wade, Mason 1913-1986 .... 9-12R
Wade, Michael G. 1946- 198
Wade, Nicholas (Michael Landon)
1942- CANR-114
Earlier sketches in CA 77-80, CANR-16
Wade, Rex A(rvin) 1936- 61-64
Wade, Richard Clement 1922- 17-20R
Wade, Robert
See McIlwain, David
Wade, Robert (Allison) 1921-1981 ... CANR-62
Earlier sketch in CA 108
See also Miller, Wade
Wade, Roger
See Lankford, Terrill Lee
Wade, Rosalind Herschel
1909-1989(?) CAP-1
Obituary 127
Earlier sketch in CA 9-10
Wade, Sidney 1951- CANR-100
Earlier sketch in CA 136
Wade, Susan 1955- 171
Wade, Terence (L. B.) 1930- 141
Wade, Theodore E., Jr. 1936- .... SATA 37
Wade, (Sarah) Virginia 1945- 132
Wade, (Henry) William (Rawson)
1918-2004 .... CANR-4
Obituary 226
Earlier sketch in CA 1-4R
Wade, Wyn Craig 1944- 103
Wade-Gayles, Gloria Jean 142
See also BW 2
Wadekin, Karl-Eugen
See Waedekin, Karl-Eugen
Wadell, Paul J(oseph) 1951- 145
Wademan, Peter John 1946- .... SATA 122
Wademan, Spike
See Wademan, Peter John
Wadepuhl, Walter 1895-1989 61-64

Cumulative Index 599 **Walcott**

Wadham, Tim(othy Rex) 1962- ... 196
Wadia, Maneck S(orabji) 1931- ... CANR-13
Earlier sketch in CA 17-20R
Wadinasi, Sedeka
See Nall, Hiram Abiff
Wadley, Susan S(now) 1943- ... 77-80
Wadlington, Walter 1931- ... 33-36R
Wadlington, Warwick 1938- ... 73-76
Wadman, Anne Sijbe 1919- ... 210
Wadsworth, Barry James 1935- ... 37-40R
Wadsworth, Frank W(hittemore) 1919- ... 9-12R
Wadsworth, Ginger 1945- ... CANR-142
Earlier sketch in CA 134
See also SATA 103, 157
Wadsworth, Harrison (M.), Jr. 1924- ... 176
Wadsworth, James J(eremiah)
1905-1984 ... CAP-2
Obituary ... 112
Earlier sketch in CA 19-20
Wadsworth, Jerry
See Wadsworth, James J(eremiah)
Wadsworth, M(arshall) D. 1936- ... 45-48
Wadsworth, Michael E(dwin) J(ohn)
1942- ... 93-96
Wadsworth, Nelson B(ingham) 1930- ... 65-68
Waedekin, Karl-Eugen 1921- ... 73-76
Waegner, Elin
See Wagner, Elin (Mathilda Elisabeth)
Waehler, Charles A. 1956- ... 175
Waehrer, Helen (Youngelson) 1938- ... 53-56
Waelder, Robert 1900-1967 ... CAP-1
Earlier sketch in CA 13-14
Waelti-Walters, Jennifer (Rose)
1942- ... CANR-120
Earlier sketch in CA 136
Waengler, Hans-Heinrich B. 1921- ... CANR-20
Earlier sketch in CA 41-44R
Waerneryd, Karl-Erik
See Warneryd, Karl-Erik
Waffle, Harvey W(illiam) 1904-1988 ... 5-8R
Wagamese, Richard 1955- ... CANR-137
Earlier sketch in CA 163
Wagar, W(alter) Warren 1932-2004 ... CANR-3
Obituary ... 233
Earlier sketch in CA 5-8R
Wagatsuma, Hiroshi 1927- ... 21-24R
Wagemaker, Herbert, Jr. 1929- ... 93-96
Wagenaar, Theodore C(larence) 1948- ... 111
Wagener, Hans 1940- ... CANR-1
Earlier sketch in CA 45-48
Wagenheim, Kal 1935- ... CANR-26
Earlier sketch in CA 29-32R
See also SATA 21
Wagenheim, Olga
See Jiminez Wagenheim, Olga
Wagenknecht, Edward (Charles)
1900-2004 ... CANR-46
Obituary ... 229
Earlier sketches in CA 1-4R, CANR-6, 22
See also DLB 103
Wagenvoord, James 1937- ... 41-44R
Wager, Walter H(erman)
1924-2004 ... CANR-120
Obituary ... 230
Earlier sketches in CA 5-8R, CANR-8, 33
Wager, Willis Joseph 1911-1991 ... 37-40R
Waggaman, William Henry 1884(?)-1978
Obituary ... 77-80
Waggner, George 1894-1984
Obituary ... 114
Waggoner, Glen 1940- ... CANR-46
Earlier sketch in CA 121
Waggoner, Hyatt H(owe) 1913-1988 ... CANR-9
Obituary ... 126
Earlier sketch in CA 21-24R
Waggoner, Lawrence W. 1937- ... 128
Wagley, Charles (Walter)
1913-1991 ... CANR-10
Obituary ... 136
Earlier sketch in CA 13-16R
Waglow, Irving Frederick 1915-1998 ... 1-4R
Wagman, Fredrica 1937- ... 97-100
Interview in ... CA-97-100
See also CLC 7
Wagman, Morton 1925- ... 141
Wagman, Naomi 1937- ... 57-60
Wagman, Robert John 1942- ... 93-96
Wagner, Anthony Richard
1908-1995 ... CANR-42
Earlier sketches in CA 1-4R, CANR-5, 20
Wagner, Bruce 1954- ... CANR-118
Earlier sketch in CA 140
Wagner, C(harles) Peter 1930- ... CANR-49
Earlier sketches in CA 21-24R, CANR-9, 24
Wagner, Charles Abraham 1901-1986 ... 5-8R
Wagner, Daniel 1974- ... 235
Wagner, David 1950- ... CANR-119
Earlier sketch in CA 148
Wagner, David G(eorge) 1949- ... 114
Wagner, Denson
See Iannelli, Richard
Wagner, Doc
See Wagner, Edward J. Sr.
Wagner, Edward J. Sr. 1908(?)-1986
Obituary ... 118
Wagner, Edwin E(ric) 1930- ... 45-48
Wagner, Elaine 1939- ... 45-48
Wagner, Elin (Mathilda Elisabeth)
1882-1949 ... DLB 259
Wagner, Eliot 1917- ... 105
Wagner, Erica 1967- ... 166
Wagner, Francis S(tephen)
1911-1999 ... CANR-8
Earlier sketch in CA 61-64
Wagner, Frederick (Reese, Jr.) 1928- ... 5-8R
Wagner, Fritz Arno 1891-1958 ... IDFW 3, 4
Wagner, Geoffrey (Atheling) 1927- ... CANR-2
Earlier sketch in CA 1-4R
Wagner, Gillian (Mary Millicent) 1927- ... 141
Wagner, Gordon Parsons 1915-1987
Obituary ... 124
Wagner, Harvey M. 1931- ... CANR-6
Earlier sketch in CA 13-16R
Wagner, Heinrich Leopold 1747-1779 . DLB 94
Wagner, Helmut R(udolf)
1904-1989 ... CANR-19
Earlier sketches in CA 53-56, CANR-4
Wagner, Henry R(aup) 1862-1957 ... 184
See also DLB 140
Wagner, Jack Russell 1916- ... 49-52
Wagner, Jane ... CANR-42
Earlier sketch in CA 109
Wagner, Jean Pierre 1919- ... 21-24R
Wagner, Jenny 1939- ... CWRI 5
Wagner, Jon G(regory) 1944- ... 109
Wagner, Joseph Frederick 1900(?)-1974
Obituary ... 53-56
Wagner, Karl Edward 1945-1994 ... CANR-51
Earlier sketches in CA 49-52, CANR-3
See also FANT
Wagner, Ken(neth) 1911-1990 ... 37-40R
Wagner, Kenneth A. 1919- ... 53-56
Wagner, Lilya 1940- ... 112
Wagner, Linda W.
See Wagner-Martin, Linda (C.)
Wagner, Linda Welshimer
See Wagner-Martin, Linda (C.)
Wagner, Margaret D. 1949- ... 5-8R
Wagner, (Griegg) Marsden 1930- ... 69-72
Wagner, Michael G. 1951- ... 133
Wagner, Michele R. 1975- ... 233
See also SATA 157
Wagner, Nathaniel N(ed) 1930- ... 57-60
Wagner, Nike 1945- ... 208
Wagner, Peggy
See Wagner, Margaret D.
Wagner, Philip L(aurence) 1921- ... 41-44R
Wagner, Philip Marshall 1904-1996 ... 102
Obituary ... 155
Wagner, Ray(mond) David 1924- ... CANR-41
Earlier sketches in CA 5-8R, CANR-3, 19
Wagner, Ray Jay 1931- ... 77-80
Wagner, Richard 1813-1883 ... DLB 129
See also EW 6
Wagner, Richard Vansant 1935-
Brief entry ... 105
Wagner, Robert W(alter) 1918- ... 203
Wagner, Roy 1938- ... 41-44R
Wagner, Rudolph F(red) 1921- ... 37-40R
Wagner, Ruth H(ortense) 1909-1974 ... 29-32R
Wagner, Sharon B. 1936- ... CANR-10
Earlier sketch in CA 25-28R
See also SATA 4
Wagner, Stanley P(aul) 1923- ... 29-32R
Wagner, Tony ... 206
Wagner, Walter 1927(?)-1983(?)
Obituary ... 109
Wagner, Walter F(rederick), Jr.
1926-1985 ... CANR-26
Obituary ... 116
Earlier sketch in CA 69-72
Wagner, Wenceslas Joseph 1917- ... 37-40R
Wagner-Martin, Linda (C.) 1936- ... CANR-135
Earlier sketch in CA 159
See also CLC 50
Wagoner, David (Russell) 1926- ... CANR-71
Earlier sketches in CA 1-4R, CANR-2
See also CAAS 3
See also AMWS 9
See also CLC 3, 5, 15
See also CN 1, 2, 3, 4, 5, 6, 7
See also CP 1, 2, 3, 4, 5, 6, 7
See also DLB 5, 256
See also PC 33
See also SATA 14
See also TCWW 1, 2
Wagoner, Harless D. 1918-1973 ... 29-32R
Obituary ... 134
Wagoner, Jay J. 1923- ... 25-28R
Wagoner, John L(eonard) 1927-1984 ... 69-72
Obituary ... 112
Wagoner, Walter D. 1918-1998 ... 21-24R
Obituary ... 169
Wagonseller, Bill R(oss) 1933- ... 107
Wagschal, Harry 1939- ... 108
Wagschal, Peter H(enry) 1944- ... CANR-19
Earlier sketch in CA 102
Wagstaff, (John) Malcolm 1940- ... CANR-28
Earlier sketch in CA 109
Wah, Fred(erick James) 1939- ... 141
Brief entry ... 107
See also CLC 44
See also CP 1, 7
See also DLB 60
Waheenee
See Buffalo Bird Woman
Wahking, Harold L(eroy) 1931- ... 29-32R
Wahl, Jan (Boyer) 1933- ... CANR-38
Earlier sketches in CA 25-28R, CANR-12
See also CWRI 5
See also MAICYA 1, 2
See also SAAS 3
See also SATA 2, 34, 73, 132
Wahl, Jean 1888-1974
Obituary ... 49-52
Wahl, Paul 1922-1993 ... 9-12R
Wahl, Robert (Charles) 1948- ... CANR-1
Earlier sketch in CA 49-52
Wahl, Thomas (Peter) 1931- ... 9-12R
Wahlbeck, osten 1965- ... 209
Wahlberg, Rachel Conrad 1922- ... 93-96
Wahler, Robert G(ordon) 1936-
Brief entry ... 109
Wahlke, John C(harles) 1917- ... CANR-11
Earlier sketch in CA 21-24R
Wahloo, Per 1926-1975 ... CANR-73
Earlier sketch in CA 61-64
See also BPFB 3
See also CLC 7
See also CMW 4
See also MSW
Wahloo, Peter
See Wahloo, Per
Wahlroos, Sven 1931- ... 57-60
Wahrman, Miryam Z. 1956- ... 221
Wahtera, John (Edward) 1929-1985 ... 61-64
Obituary ... 117
Waiblinger, Wilhelm 1804-1830 ... DLB 90
Waid, Mark 1962- ... 220
Waide, Jan 1952- ... 105
See also SATA 29
Waidson, H(erbert) Morgan 1916- ... 5-8R
Waife, Marie
See Waife-Goldberg, Marie
Waife-Goldberg, Marie 1892-1985 ... CAP-2
Obituary ... 118
Earlier sketch in CA 25-28
Wailey, Anthony Paul 1947- ... 126
Wailey, Tony
See Wailey, Anthony Paul
Wain, Barry 1944- ... 122
Wain, John (Barrington) 1925-1994 .. CANR-54
Obituary ... 145
Earlier sketches in CA 5-8R, CANR-23
See also CAAS 4
See also CDBLB 1960 to Present
See also CLC 2, 11, 15, 46
See also CN 1, 2, 3, 4, 5
See also CP 1, 2
See also DLB 15, 27, 139, 155
See also EWL 3
See also MTCW 1, 2
See also MTFW 2005
Waine, Anthony 1946- ... 113
Wainer, Cord
See Dewey, Thomas B(lanchard)
Wainhouse, Austryn ... 228
Wainhouse, David Walter 1900-1976 ... 17-20R
Obituary ... 65-68
Wainscott, John Milton 1910-1981 ... SATA 53
Wainscott, Ronald H(arold) 1948- ... 131
Wainwright, A(lfred) 1907-1991 ... 140
Wainwright, Arthur William 1925- ... 114
Wainwright, Charles Anthony 1933- ... 37-40R
Wainwright, Clive 1942-1999 ... 188
Wainwright, David
See Stansfield, Richard Habberton
Wainwright, Geoffrey 1939- ... CANR-93
Earlier sketches in CA 37-40R, CANR-15, 34
Wainwright, Gordon Ray 1937- ... 113
Wainwright, Hilary 1949- ... 131
Wainwright, J(ohn) A(ndrew) 1946- ... 210
Wainwright, J(oseph) Allan 1921- ... 13-16R
Wainwright, Jeffrey 1944- ... CANR-107
Brief entry ... 122
Earlier sketch in CA 142
See also CP 7
See also DLB 40
Wainwright, John 1921- ... CANR-64
Brief entry ... 108
Earlier sketch in CA 110
Interview in ... CA-110
See also CMW 4
Wainwright, Ken
See Tubb, E(dwin) C(harles)
Wainwright, Loudon (Snowden) 1925(?)-1988
Obituary ... 127
Wainwright, Nicholas Biddle
1914-1986 ... 65-68
Wainwright, Richard M. 1935- ... SATA 91
Wainwright, William J(udson) 1935- ... 120
Waisanen, F(rederick) B(rynolf) 1923- ... 45-48
Waiser, Bill
See Waiser, William Andrew
Waiser, William Andrew 1953- ... CANR-131
Earlier sketch in CA 171
Waisman, Sergio Gabriel 1967- ... 152
Wait, Eugene M(eredith) 1936- ... 173
Wait, Lea 1946- ... 207
See also SATA 137
Waite, A(shley) D. 1930- ... 235
Waite, A. E.
See Waite, Arthur Edward
Waite, Arthur Edward 1857-1942
Brief entry ... 121
Waite, Helen Elmira 1903-1967 ... 1-4R
Waite, Judy ... 238
Waite, Michael P(hillip) 1960- ... 168
See also SATA 101
Waite, P(eter) B(usby) 1922- ... 9-12R
See also SATA 64
Waite, Robert G(eorge) L(eeson)
1919-1999 ... 9-12R
Obituary ... 187
Waite, William W(iley) 1903-1991 ... CAP-1
Earlier sketch in CA 13-16
Waith, Eugene M(ersereau) 1912- ... CANR-5
Earlier sketch in CA 5-8R
Waitley, Douglas 1927- ... CANR-94
Earlier sketches in CA 21-24R, CANR-9
See also SATA 30
Waitman, Katharine Lura 1956- ... 168
Waitman, Katie
See Waitman, Katharine Lura
Waitzkin, Fred ... 207
Waitzkin, Howard 1945- ... 141
Waitzmann, Dorothea 1915- ... 13-16R
Waiwaiole, Lono ... 237
Wajcman, Judy 1950- ... 140
Wajda, Andrzej 1926- ... 102
See also CLC 16
Wakefield, Celia 1910- ... 164
Wakefield, Connie LaVon 1948- ... 65-68
Wakefield, Dan 1932- ... 211
Earlier sketch in CA 21-24R
Autobiographical Essay in ... 211
See also CAAS 7
See also CLC 7
See also CN 4, 5, 6, 7
Wakefield, David 1950- ... 145
Wakefield, Donam Hahn 1927- ... 37-40R
Wakefield, Herbert Russell
1888-1965 ... CANR-77
Earlier sketch in CA 5-8R
See also HGG
See also SUFW
See also TCLC 120
Wakefield, Hubert George 1915-1984
Obituary ... 112
Wakefield, Hugh
See Wakefield, Hubert George
Wakefield, Jean L.
See Laird, Jean E(louise)
Wakefield, Norm(an) 1934- ... 195
Wakefield, R. I.
See White, Gertrude M(ason)
Wakefield, Robert A. 1916- ... 13-16R
Wakefield, Sherman Day 1894-1971
Obituary ... 29-32R
Wakefield, Tom 1935-1996 ... 101
Obituary ... 152
Wakefield, Walter Leggett 1911- ... 81-84
Wakefield Master 15th cent. - ... RGEL 2
Wakeford, John 1936-
Brief entry ... 112
Wakeham, Irene 1912- ... 29-32R
Wakeley, John H(albert) 1932- ... 41-44R
Wakelin, Martyn Francis 1935- ... 65-68
Wakelyn, Jon L(ouis) 1938- ... CANR-107
Earlier sketches in CA 45-48, CANR-1
Wakeman, Carolyn 1943- ... 126
Wakeman, Frederic (Evans), Jr. 1937- . CANR-1
Earlier sketch in CA 49-52
Wakeman, Geoffrey 1926- ... CANR-15
Earlier sketch in CA 37-40R
Wakeman, John 1928- ... 124
Wakeman, Robert Parker 1914(?)-1981
Obituary ... 104
Wakeman, Stephen H. 1859-1924 ... DLB 187
Wakerman, Elyce 1947- ... 128
Wakhevitch, Georges 1907-1984 ... IDFW 3, 4
Wakil, S(heikh) P(arvez) 1935- ... 85-88
Wakin, Daniel (Joseph) 1961- ... SATA 84
Wakin, Edward 1927- ... CANR-17
Earlier sketches in CA 5-8R, CANR-2
See also SATA 37
wa Kinyatti, Maina 1944- ... CANR-90
Earlier sketch in CA 132
Wakling, Christopher 1970- ... 233
Wako, Mdogo
See Nazareth, Peter
Wakoski, Diane 1937- ... 216
Earlier sketches in CA 13-16R, CANR-9, 60, 106
Interview in ... CANR-9
Autobiographical Essay in ... 216
See also CAAS 1
See also CLC 2, 4, 7, 9, 11, 40
See also CP 1, 2, 3, 4, 5, 6, 7
See also CWP
See also DAM POET
See also DLB 5
See also MAL 5
See also MTCW 2
See also MTFW 2005
See also PC 15
Wakoski-Sherbell, Diane
See Wakoski, Diane
Waksman, Selman A(braham)
1888-1973 ... CAP-1
Obituary ... 45-48
Earlier sketch in CA 13-16
Wakstein, Allen M. 1931- ... 29-32R
Walahfrid Strabo c. 808-849 ... DLB 148
Walas, Chris ... IDFW 3, 4
Walbank, F(rank) W(illiam) 1909- ... 142
Brief entry ... 111
Walberg, Herbert J(ohn) 1937- ... 61-64
Walbert, Kate 1961- ... 172
Walbridge, John 1950- ... 206
Walbridge, Linda S. 1946- ... 227
Walch, Timothy (George) 1947- ... CANR-21
Earlier sketch in CA 105
Walchars, John 1912-1992 ... 81-84
Walck, Henry Z. 1908(?)-1984
Obituary ... 114
See also SATA-Obit 40
Walcott, Charles E(liot) 1943- ... 152

Walcott, Derek (Alton) 1930- ... CANR-130
Earlier sketches in CA 89-92, CANR-26, 47, 75, 80
See also BLC 3
See also BW 2
See also CBD
See also CD 5, 6
See also CDWLB 3
See also CLC 2, 4, 9, 14, 25, 42, 67, 76, 160
See also CP 1, 2, 3, 4, 5, 6, 7
See also DA3
See also DAB
See also DAC
See also DAM MST, MULT, POET
See also DC 7
See also DLB 117
See also DLBY 1981
See also DNFS 1
See also EFS 1
See also EWL 3
See also LMFS 2
See also MTCW 1, 2
See also MTFW 2005
See also PC 46
See also PFS 6
See also RGEL 2
See also TWA
See also WWE 1
Walcott, Fred G. 1894-1984 ... 37-40R
Walcott, John 1949- ... 126
Walcott, Robert 1910-1988 ... CAP-1
Earlier sketch in CA 13-14
Walcutt, Charles Child 1908-1989 ... CANR-3
Obituary ... 128
Earlier sketch in CA 1-4R
Wald, Alan M(aynard) 1946- ... CANR-93
Earlier sketch in CA 129
Wald, Carol 1935- ... 65-68
Wald, Elijah 1959- ... 207
Wald, George 1906-1997 ... 159
Wald, Jerry 1911-1962 ... IDFW 3, 4
Wald, Kenneth D. 1949- ... 129
Wald, Malvin (Daniel) 1917- ... CANR-1
Earlier sketch in CA 45-48
Wald, Richard C(harles) ... 108
Waldbauer, Gilbert (P.) 1928- ... CANR-95
Earlier sketch in CA 157
Walde, Ralph E(ldon) 1943- ... 53-56
Waldeck, Peter Bruce 1940- ... 41-44R
Waldeen
See Von Falkenstein, Waldeen
Waldegrave, Robert fl. 1578-1603 ... DLB 170
Walden, Amelia Elizabeth ... CANR-2
Earlier sketch in CA 1-4R
See also SATA 3
Walden, Becky
See Usry, Becky (S.)
Walden, Daniel 1922- ... 25-28R
Walden, George (Gordon Harvey) 1939- ... 186
Walden, Herwarth
See Lewin, Georg
Walden, Howard T(albot) II 1897-1981 .. 45-48
Obituary ... 103
Walden, John C(layton) 1928- ... 53-56
Waldenfels, Hans 1931- ... CANR-82
Earlier sketch in CA 131
Walder, (Alan) David 1928-1978 ... CANR-17
Obituary ... 81-84
Earlier sketch in CA 65-68
Walder, Dennis 1943- ... 117
Walders, Joe 1948- ... 85-88
Waldheim, Kurt 1918- ... 89-92
Waldherr, Kris 1963- ... SATA 76
Waldhorn, Arthur 1918- ... CANR-3
Earlier sketch in CA 1-4R
Waldinger, Ernst 1896-1970
Obituary ... 104
See also EWL 3
Waldinger, Roger (David) 1953- ... 165
Waldis, Burkhard c. 1490-1556(?) ... DLB 179
Waldman, Anne (Lesley) 1945- ... CANR-116
Earlier sketches in CA 37-40R, CANR-34, 69
See also CAAS 17
See also BG 1:3
See also CLC 7
See also CP 1, 2, 3, 4, 5, 6, 7
See also CWP
See also DLB 16
Waldman, Ayelet 1964- ... 225
Waldman, Bruce 1949- ... SATA 15
Waldman, Diane 1936- ... CANR-135
Earlier sketches in CA 33-36R, CANR-26
Waldman, Eric 1914- ... 17-20R
Waldman, Harry 1945- ... 148
Waldman, Mark Robert ... 233
Waldman, Max 1919-1981 ... 105
Obituary ... 103
Waldman, Milton 1895-1976 ... 69-72
Obituary ... 65-68
Waldman, Neil 1947- ... CANR-122
Earlier sketches in CA 128, CANR-67
See also SATA 51, 94, 142
Waldmeir, Joseph John 1923- ... 9-12R
Waldner, Liz ... 207
Waldo, Anna Lee 1925- ... CANR-109
Earlier sketches in CA 85-88, CANR-64
See also TCWW 2
Waldo, Dale
See Clarke, D(avid) Waldo
See also TCWW 2
Waldo, Dave
See Clarke, D(avid) Waldo
See also TCWW 1
Waldo, E. Hunter
See Sturgeon, Theodore (Hamilton)
Waldo, Edward Hamilton
See Sturgeon, Theodore (Hamilton)
Waldo, Kay Cronkite 1938- ... 107
Waldo, Myra 1916(?)-2004 ... 93-96
Obituary ... 230
Waldo, Ralph Emerson III 1944- ... 102
Waldo, Terry
See Waldo, Ralph Emerson III
Waldo, Willis H. 1920- ... 13-16R
Waldock, (Claud) Humphrey (Meredith) 1904-1981
Obituary ... 108
Waldoff, Leon 1935- ... 227
Waldorf, Paul D(ouglass) 1908-1980 ... CAP-1
Earlier sketch in CA 13-16
Waldrep, Christopher (Reef) 1951- ... CANR-94
Earlier sketch in CA 146
Waldrep, (Alvis) Kent (II) 1954- ... 150
Waldrip, Louise B. 1912- ... 37-40R
Waldron, Ann Wood 1924- ... CANR-45
Earlier sketches in CA 13-16R, CANR-7
See also SATA 16
Waldron, Arthur (Nelson) 1948- ... 135
Waldron, D'Lynn
See Waldron-Shah, Diane Lynn
Waldron, Eli 1916(?)-1980
Obituary ... 101
Waldron, Ingrid 1939- ... 53-56
Waldron, Jeremy 1953- ... 194
Waldron, Martin O. 1925-1981
Obituary ... 103
Waldron, Peter 1956- ... 182
Waldron-Shah, Diane Lynn 1936- ... 9-12R
Waldrop, Howard 1946- ... CANR-126
Earlier sketches in CA 118, CANR-41
See also CSW
See also SCFW 2
See also SFW 4
See also SUFW 2
Waldrop, Keith 1932- ... CANR-113
Earlier sketch in CA 117
See also CAAS 30
Waldrop, M(orris) Mitchell 1947- ... CANR-112
Earlier sketch in CA 143
Waldrop, Rosmarie 1935- ... CANR-67
Earlier sketches in CA 101, CANR-18, 39
See also CAAS 30
See also CP 7
See also CWP
See also DLB 169
Waldrop, W. Earl 1910- ... 5-8R
Wale, Michael ... 81-84
Walen, Harry L(eonard) 1915- ... 41-44R
Wales, Hugh Gregory 1910-1995 ... CANR-2
Earlier sketch in CA 5-8R
Wales, Nym
See Snow, Helen Foster
Wales, Robert 1923-1994 ... 93-96
Wales, William
See Ambrose, David (Edwin)
Walesa, Lech 1943- ... 128
Waley, Arthur (David) 1889-1966 ... 85-88
Obituary ... 25-28R
Waley-Cohen, Joanna ... 236
Walford, Christian
See Dilcock, Noreen
Walford, Lionel Albert 1905-1979
Obituary ... 85-88
Walford, Roy L(ee, Jr.) 1924-2004 ... 111
Obituary ... 226
Walgenbach, Paul H(enry) 1923- ... 53-56
Walgren, Judy 1963- ... 190
See also SATA 118
Walhout, Donald 1927- ... CANR-2
Earlier sketch in CA 5-8R
Walicki, Andrzej 1930- ... 101
Walinsky, Louis J(oseph) 1908- ... CAP-2
Earlier sketch in CA 17-18
Walinsky, Ossip J. 1887(?)-1973
Obituary ... 41-44R
Waliullah, Syed 1922-1971 ... 21-24R
Obituary ... 134
Walkden, (George) Brian 1923- ... CANR-10
Earlier sketch in CA 13-16R
Walkenstein, Eileen 1923- ... CANR-14
Earlier sketch in CA 69-72
Walker, Addison
See Walker, (Addison) Mort
Walker, Alan (Edgar) 1911-2003 ... CANR-26
Obituary ... 212
Earlier sketches in CA 13-16R, CANR-7
Walker, Alan 1949- ... 129
Walker, Albert L(yell) 1907-1980 ... 41-44R
Walker, Alexander 1930-2003 ... 142
Obituary ... 218
Brief entry ... 116
Walker, Alice 1900-1982 ... 181
See also DLB 201
Walker, Alice (Malsenior) 1944- ... CANR-131
Earlier sketches in CA 37-40R, CANR-9, 27, 49, 66, 82
Interview in ... CANR-27
See also AAYA 3, 33
See also AFAW 1, 2
See also AMWS 3
See also BEST 89:4
See also BLC 3
See also BPFB 3
See also BW 2, 3
See also CDALB 1968-1988
See also CLC 5, 6, 9, 19, 27, 46, 58, 103, 167
See also CN 4, 5, 6, 7
See also CPW
See also CSW
See also DA
See also DA3
See also DAB
See also DAC
See also DAM MST, MULT, NOV, POET, POP
See also DLB 6, 33, 143
See also EWL 3
See also EXPN
See also EXPS
See also FL 1:6
See also FW
See also LAIT 3
See also MAL 5
See also MAWW
See also MTCW 1, 2
See also MTFW 2005
See also NFS 5
See also PC 30
See also RGAL 4
See also RGSF 2
See also SATA 31
See also SSC 5
See also SSFS 2, 11
See also TUS
See also WLCS
See also YAW
Walker, Anna Louisa 1836(?)-1907 ... DLB 240
Walker, Anne Collins 1939- ... 141
Walker, Ardis Manly 1901-1991 ... CANR-22
Earlier sketch in CA 37-40R
Walker, Augusta 1914-2000 ... 21-24R
Walker, Barbara G(oodwin) 1930- ... 73-76
Walker, Barbara (Jeanne) K(erlin) 1921- ... CANR-38
Earlier sketches in CA 33-36R, CANR-16
See also SATA 4, 80
Walker, Barbara M(uhs) 1928- ... SATA 57
Walker, Benjamin 1923- ... CANR-10
Earlier sketch in CA 25-28R
Walker, Bessie
See Henry, Bessie Walker
Walker, Betty A. ... 140
Walker, (James) Braz(elton) 1934-1983 ... 69-72
See also SATA 45
Walker, Brenda 1957- ... 194
Walker, Brian ... 238
Walker, Brooks R. 1935- ... 9-12R
Walker, Bruce (James) 1944- ... 85-88
Walker, Bryce S(tewart) 1934- ... 117
Walker, C(larence) Eugene 1939- ... CANR-52
Earlier sketches in CA 61-64, CANR-10, 28
Walker, Charles
See Gettings, Fred
Walker, Charles 1911- ... 17-20R
Walker, Charles R(umford) 1893-1974 .. CAP-2
Obituary ... 53-56
Earlier sketch in CA 17-18
Walker, Charlotte Zoe
See Mendez, Charlotte (Walker)
Walker, Cheryl 1947- ... 111
Walker, Claxton 1924- ... 101
Walker, Clive (Phillip) 1954- ... 124
Walker, D(aniel) P(ickering) 1914-1985 ... 85-88
Obituary ... 116
Walker, Dale L(ee) 1935- ... CANR-109
Earlier sketches in CA 57-60, CANR-8, 24, 49
Walker, Daniel Downing 1915- ... CANR-2
Earlier sketch in CA 1-4R
Walker, Danton (MacIntyre) 1899-1960
Obituary ... 93-96
Walker, David 1950- ... CANR-28
Earlier sketch in CA 104
Walker, David Clifton 1942- ... CANR-112
Earlier sketch in CA 69-72
Walker, David G(ordon) 1926- ... 110
See also SATA 60
Walker, David Harry 1911-1992 ... CANR-1
Obituary ... 137
Earlier sketch in CA 1-4R
See also CLC 14
See also CN 1, 2
See also CWRI 5
See also SATA 8
See also SATA-Obit 71
Walker, David J. ... 206
Walker, David M(axwell) 1920- ... CANR-46
Earlier sketches in CA 9-12R, CANR-5, 22
Walker, Deward E(dgar), Jr. 1935- ... CANR-43
Earlier sketches in CA 25-28R, CANR-19
Walker, Diana 1925- ... CANR-4
Earlier sketch in CA 49-52
See also SATA 9
Walker, Dianne Marie Catherine 1950-
See Walker, Kate
See also SATA 82
Walker, Dick
See Pellowski, Michael (Joseph)
Walker, Donald E(dwin) 1941- ... 152
Walker, Donald Smith 1918- ... 9-12R
Walker, Doreen 1920- ... 135
Walker, Earl Thomas 1891-1987 ... 105
Walker, Edward Joseph 1934-2004 ... CANR-53
Obituary ... 226
Earlier sketches in CA 21-24R, CANR-12, 28
See also Walker, Ted
Walker, Edward L(ewis) 1914-1997 .. CANR-11
Earlier sketch in CA 25-28R
Walker, Elinor 1911-1997 ... 13-16R
Walker, Eric Anderson 1886-1976 ... CAP-2
Obituary ... 65-68
Earlier sketch in CA 13-14
Walker, Ethel Valerie 1944- ... 53-56
Walker, Evan 1933(?)-1982
Obituary ... 107
Walker, Everett 1906-1983
Obituary ... 109
Walker, Frank 1931-2000 ... 69-72
See also SATA 36
Walker, Frank B. 1916(?)-1985
Obituary ... 117
Walker, Franklin (Dickerson) 1900-1979 ... 21-24R
Obituary ... 85-88
Walker, Geoffrey de Q(uincey) 1940- ... 131
Walker, Geoffrey James 1936- ... 93-96
Walker, George A. 1960- ... 191
Walker, George F(rederick) 1947- ... CANR-59
Earlier sketches in CA 103, CANR-21, 43
See also CD 5, 6
See also CLC 44, 61
See also DAB
See also DAC
See also DAM MST
See also DLB 60
Walker, Gerald 1928-2004 ... 9-12R
Obituary ... 223
Walker, Gilbert James 1907-1982
Obituary ... 107
Walker, Glen 1937- ... 108
Walker, Graham S. 1956- ... 122
Walker, Gregory P(iers) M(ountford) 1942- ... 73-76
Walker, Greta 1927- ... 77-80
Walker, Harold Blake 1904- ... 17-20R
Walker, Harry
See Waugh, Hillary Baldwin
Walker, Helen M(ary) 1891-1983
Obituary ... 109
Walker, Henry M(acKay) 1947- ... 151
Walker, Hill M(ontague) 1939- ... 93-96
Walker, Holly Beth
See Bond, Gladys Baker
Walker, Ira
See Walker, Irma Ruth (Roden)
Walker, Irma Ruth (Roden) 1921- ... CANR-46
Earlier sketches in CA 5-8R, CANR-6, 21
Walker, J.
See Crawford, John Richard
Walker, J(ohn) Ingram 1944- ... 112
Walker, Jack
See Thayer, Frederick C(lifton), Jr.
Walker, James Lynwood 1940- ... 37-40R
Walker, James R(obert) 1950- ... 164
Walker, Janet A(nderson) 1942- ... 119
Walker, Jeanne 1924- ... 61-64
Walker, Jeanne Murray 1944- ... 111
Walker, Jeremy D(esmond) B(romhead) 1936- ... 21-24R
Walker, Joan ... 5-8R
Walker, John 1906-1995 ... CANR-6
Earlier sketch in CA 5-8R
Walker, John 1933- ... 113
Walker, John (Bruce) 1938- ... 120
Walker, John 1947- ... 127
Walker, John A(lbert) 1938- ... 187
Walker, John Brisben 1847-1931 ... 179
See also DLB 79
Walker, Joseph 1892-1985
Obituary ... 117
See also IDFW 3, 4
Walker, Joseph A. 1935-2003 ... CANR-143
Earlier sketches in CA 89-92, CANR-26
See also BW 1, 3
See also CAD
See also CD 5, 6
See also CLC 19
See also DAM DRAM, MST
See also DFS 12
See also DLB 38
Walker, Joseph E(rdman) 1911-1987 ... 37-40R
Walker, Kara 1969- ... 224
Walker, Kate ... 149
See also Walker, Dianne Marie Catherine
Walker, Kath 1920-1992
See Noonuccal, Oodgeroo and Oodgeroo
Walker, Kathrine Sorley
See Sorley Walker, Kathrine
Walker, Keith 1934- ... 121
Walker, Kenneth Francis 1924- ... 33-36R
Walker, Kenneth Macfarlane 1882-1966 ... 5-8R
Walker, Kenneth R(oland) 1928- ... 37-40R
Walker, Kenneth Richard 1931-1989 ... 17-20R
Obituary ... 129
Walker, Kent 1962- ... 203
Walker, Laurence C(olton) 1924- ... 53-56
Walker, Lawrence David 1931- ... 53-56
Walker, Lenore E(lizabeth) 1942- ... 97-100
Walker, Leo ... 13-16R
Walker, Leslie 1953- ... 139
Walker, Lewis 1936- ... 222
Walker, Lou Ann 1952- ... CANR-53
Earlier sketch in CA 126
See also SATA 66
See also SATA-Brief 53

Cumulative Index 601 Wallach

Walker, Louise Jean 1891-1976
Obituary ... 110
See also SATA-Obit 35
Walker, Lucy
See Sanders, Dorothy Lucie
See also RHW
Walker, Mack 1929- ... 9-12R
Walker, Margaret (Abigail)
1915-1998 ... CANR-136
Obituary ... 172
Earlier sketches in CA 73-76, CANR-26, 54, 76
See also AFAW 1, 2
See also BLC
See also BW 2, 3
See also CLC 1, 6
See also CN 1, 2, 3, 4, 5, 6
See also CP 1, 2
See also CSW
See also DAM MULT
See also DLB 76, 152
See also EXPP
See also FW
See also MAL 5
See also MTCW 1, 2
See also MTFW 2005
See also PC 20
See also RGAL 4
See also RHW
See also TCLC 129
Walker, Margaret Pope 1901(?)-1980
Obituary ... 101
Walker, Margie 1952- ... 179
Walker, Marianne (Cascio) 1933- ... CANR-119
Earlier sketch in CA 144
Walker, Mark 1953- ... 117
Walker, Marshall (John) 1912-1989 ... 17-20R
Walker, Martin (Alan) 1947- ... CANR-98
Earlier sketch in CA 101
Walker, Mary Alexander 1927- ... 104
See also SATA 61
Walker, Mary Willis 1942- ... 161
See also CMW 4
Walker, Matthew
See Mewhinney, Bruce
Walker, Michael John 1932-1989(?)
Obituary ... 129
Walker, Mickey 1901-1981
Obituary ... 108
Walker, Mike ... 230
Walker, Mildred
See Schemm, Mildred Walker
See also CN 6
Walker, (Addison) Mort 1923- ... CANR-25
Earlier sketches in CA 49-52, CANR-3
See also SATA 8
Walker, Morton 1929- ... CANR-22
Earlier sketch in CA 85-88
Walker, Nancy A. 1942- ... 136
Walker, Nicolette (Daisy) Milnes 1943- . 41-44R
Walker, Nigel (David) 1917- ... 61-64
Walker, Obadiah 1616-1699 ... DLB 281
Walker, Pamela 1948- ... CANR-122
Earlier sketch in CA 69-72
See also SATA 24, 142
Walker, Paul E(rnest) 1941- ... CANR-98
Earlier sketch in CA 147
Walker, Paul Robert 1953- ... 222
See also SATA 154
Walker, Persia 1957- ... 220
Walker, Peter F(ranklin) 1931- ... 13-16R
Walker, Peter N. 1936- ... CANR-14
Earlier sketch in CA 77-80
Walker, Philip (Doolittle) 1924- ... 133
Walker, Philip Mitchell 1943- ... 29-32R
Walker, R. B. J. 1947- ... 145
Walker, Raymond Myerscough
See Myerscough-Walker, Raymond
Walker, Rebecca 1969- ... CANR-106
Earlier sketches in CA 154, CANR-87
See also FW
Walker, Reeve
See Heckelmann, Charles N(ewman)
Walker, Richard (John) 1952- ... 132
Walker, Richard L(ouis) 1922-2003 ... CANR-7
Obituary ... 218
Earlier sketch in CA 9-12R
Walker, Robert 1945- ... 211
Walker, Robert H(arris) 1924- ... CANR-48
Earlier sketches in CA 13-16R, CANR-7, 23
Walker, Robert Newton 1911-2002 ... 53-56
Walker, Robert W(ayne) 1948- ... CANR-77
Earlier sketches in CA 93-96, CANR-23, 48
See also HGG
See also SATA 66
Walker, Roger (Michael) 1938-1999 ... 181
Walker, Roger W(illiams) 1931- ... 45-48
Walker, Ronald G(ary) 1945- ... CANR-39
Earlier sketches in CA 93-96, CANR-16
Walker, Ruth
See Walker, Irma Ruth (Roden)
Walker, Sally M(acArt) 1954- ... 204
Walker, Sally M(acart) 1954- ... SATA 135
Walker, Samuel 1942- ... 85-88
Walker, Scott 1950- ... 120
Walker, Sheila S(uzanne) 1944- ... 127
Walker, Shel
See Sheldon, Walter J(ames)
Walker, Stanley 1898-1962
Obituary ... 93-96
Walker, Stella Archer 1907-2000 ... 61-64
Obituary ... 188
Walker, Stephen (Francis) 1941- ... 131
Walker, Stephen J. 1951- ... SATA 12
Walker, Stuart (Armstrong) 1880(?)-1941
Brief entry ... 120
Walker, Stuart H(odge) 1923- ... CANR-24
Earlier sketch in CA 45-48
Walker, Sydney III 1931- ... 21-24R
Walker, T. Michael 1937- ... 77-80
Walker, Ted
See Walker, Edward Joseph
See also CLC 13
See also CP 1, 2, 3, 4, 5, 6, 7
See also DLB 40
Walker, Theodore J. 1915-2003 ... 102
Obituary ... 215
Walker, Thomas W(illiam) 1940- ... 142
Walker, (Harold) Todd 1917-1998 ... 209
Walker, Walter (Colyear) 1912-2001 ... 117
Obituary ... 198
Walker, Walter (Herbert III) 1949- ... CANR-42
Earlier sketch in CA 117
Walker, Warren S(tanley) 1921- ... CANR-38
Earlier sketches in CA 9-12R, CANR-3, 16
Walker, Wendy (Alison) 1951- ... 131
Walker, Willard (Brewer) 1926- ... CANR-23
Earlier sketch in CA 45-48
Walker, William Edward 1925- ... 9-12R
Walker, William G(eorge) 1928-1995 ... 77-80
Walker, William H. 1913-1983 ... 17-20R
Walker, William Otis 1896-1981
Obituary ... 105
Walker, Wyatt Tee 1929- ... 127
Walker-Blondell, Becky 1951- ... 155
See also SATA 89
Walkerdine, Valerie 1947- ... 164
Walkerley, Rodney Lewis (de Burgh)
1905-1999 ... CAP-1
Earlier sketch in CA 9-10
Walker-Wright, A(nnie) D(oris)
1920-2002 ... 230
Walker-Wright, Dolly
See Walker-Wright, A(nnie) D(oris)
Walkinshaw, Colin
See Reid, James Macarthur
Walkinshaw, Lawrence H(arvey)
1904-1993 ... 45-48
Walkland, S(tuart) A(lan) 1925(?)-1989
Obituary ... 128
Walkowicz, Chris 1943- ... 135
Walkowitz, Daniel J(ay) 1942- ... 81-84
Wall, A(rthur) E(dward) P(atrick) 1925- ... 119
Wall, Alan ... 192
Wall, Barbara 1911- ... 97-100
Wall, Bennett H(arrison) 1914- ... 77-80
Wall, C. Edward 1942- ... 37-40R
Wall, Dorothy 1894-1942 ... CWRI 5
Wall, Elizabeth S(pooner) 1924- ... 93-96
Wall, Geoffrey
See Chadwick, Geoffrey
Wall, James M(cKendree) 1928- ... 134
Brief entry ... 113
Wall, James T. 1933- ... 202
Wall, John Nelson, Jr. 1945- ... 114
Wall, John W. 1910-1989 ... 166
See also Sarban
Wall, Joseph Barrye 1899(?)-1985
Obituary ... 117
Wall, Joseph Frazier 1920-1995 ... CANR-13
Obituary ... 149
Earlier sketch in CA 29-32R
Wall, Kathryn R. 1945- ... 226
Wall, Maggie 1937- ... 65-68
Wall, Margaret
See Wall, Maggie
Wall, Martha 1910-2000 ... CAP-2
Earlier sketch in CA 25-28
Wall, Mervyn (Eugene Welply) 1908-1997 . 129
Obituary ... 171
See also FANT
See also SUFW
Wall, Michael Morris 1942- ... 53-56
Wall, Mike
See Wall, Michael Morris
Wall, Patrick (Henry Bligh) 1916-1998 ... 104
Obituary ... 169
Wall, Patrick D(avid) 1925-2001 ... 17-20R
Obituary ... 202
Wall, Richard 1944- ... 41-44R
Wall, Robert Emmet, Jr. 1937- ... CANR-23
Earlier sketch in CA 45-48
Wall, Stephen D. 1948- ... 140
Wall, Steve 1946- ... 180
Wall, T. D.
See Wall, Toby (Douglas)
Wall, Toby (Douglas) 1946- ... 119
Wall, Toby D.
See Wall, Toby (Douglas)
Wall, Wendy Somerville 1942- ... 49-52
Wall, William 1955- ... 218
Wallace, Alexander Fielding
1918-1991 ... 33-36R
Obituary ... 135
Wallace, Alexander Ross 1891-1982
Obituary ... 107
Wallace, Alfred Russel 1823-1913
Brief entry ... 123
See also DLB 190
Wallace, Amy 1955- ... CANR-27
Earlier sketch in CA 81-84
Wallace, Andrew 1930- ... 37-40R
Wallace, Anthony F(rancis) C(larke)
1923- ... CANR-13
Earlier sketch in CA 61-64
Wallace, B. Alan 1950- ... CANR-107
Earlier sketch in CA 158
Wallace, Barbara Brooks 1922- ... CANR-115
Earlier sketches in CA 29-32R, CANR-11, 28
See also MAICYA 2
See also SAAS 17
See also SATA 4, 78, 136
Wallace, Ben J. 1937- ... 45-48
Wallace, Beverly Dobrin 1921- ... 101
See also SATA 19
Wallace, Bill
See Wallace, William Keith
See also SATA 101
See also SATA-Brief 47
Wallace, Bill
See Wallace, William N.
Wallace, Bronwen 1945- ... 112
Wallace, Bruce 1920- ... CANR-15
Earlier sketch in CA 85-88
Wallace, Catherine M(iles) 1950- ... 169
Wallace, Christine 1960- ... 195
Wallace, Claire 1956- ... 138
Wallace, Daisy
See Cuyler, Margery S(tuyvesant)
Wallace, Daniel 1959- ... 223
Wallace, David Foster 1962- ... CANR-133
Earlier sketches in CA 132, CANR-59
See also AAYA 50
See also AMWS 10
See also CLC 50, 114
See also CN 7
See also DA3
See also MTCW 2
See also MTFW 2005
See also SSC 68
Wallace, David H(arold) 1926- ... 25-28R
Wallace, David J. 1954- ... 124
Wallace, David Rains 1945- ... CANR-90
Earlier sketches in CA 81-84, CANR-31, 14
See also ANW
Wallace, Deborah 1945- ... 138
Wallace, (William Roy) DeWitt
1889-1981 ... 182
Obituary ... 103
See also DLB 137
Wallace, Dexter
See Masters, Edgar Lee
Wallace, Diana 1964- ... 211
Wallace, Doreen
See Rash, Dora Eileen Agnew (Wallace)
Wallace, Earl W. 1942- ... 164
Wallace, Ed(ward Tatum) 1906-1976
Obituary ... 69-72
Wallace, (Richard Horatio) Edgar
1875-1932 ... 218
Brief entry ... 115
See also CMW 4
See also DLB 70
See also MSW
See also RGEL 2
See also TCLC 57
Wallace, Edward C. 1946- ... 143
Wallace, Ernest 1906-1985 ... CANR-25
Earlier sketch in CA 13-16R
Wallace, F(loyd) L. ... SFW 4
Wallace, Francis 1894(?)-1977
Obituary ... 73-76
Wallace, G(erald) L. 1938- ... 97-100
Wallace, George C(orley) 1919-1998 ... 150
Obituary ... 170
Brief entry ... 114
Wallace, Helen Kingsbury 1897-1986 ... CAP-2
Earlier sketch in CA 25-28
Wallace, Helen M(argaret) 1913- ... CANR-12
Earlier sketch in CA 61-64
Wallace, Henry A(gard) 1888-1965 ... 105
Obituary ... 89-92
Wallace, Ian
See Pritchard, John Wallace
Wallace, Ian 1950- ... CANR-120
Earlier sketches in CA 107, CANR-25, 38, 50
See also CLR 37
See also CWRI 5
See also MAICYA 1, 2
See also SATA 53, 56, 141
Wallace, Irving 1916-1990 ... CANR-27
Obituary ... 132
Earlier sketches in CA 1-4R, CANR-1
Interview in ... CANR-27
See also CAAS 1
See also AITN 1
See also BPFB 3
See also CLC 7, 13
See also CPW
See also DAM NOV, POP
See also MTCW 1, 2
Wallace, James
See Barrett, Geoffrey John
Wallace, James 1947- ... 138
Wallace, James D. 1937- ... 162
Wallace, James Donald 1937- ... 108
Wallace, Jerry
See Vermilye, Jerry
Wallace, Joanne (M.) 1938- ... 117
Wallace, John 1966- ... 173
See also SATA 105, 155
Wallace, John A(dam) 1915-2004 ... 5-8R
Obituary ... 228
See also SATA 3
See also SATA-Obit 155
Wallace, John Malcolm 1928- ... 25-28R
Wallace, K(ay) K. 1949- ... 111
Wallace, Karen 1951- ... CANR-118
Earlier sketch in CA 150
See also SATA 83, 139
Wallace, Karl R(ichards) 1906-1973 ... 101
Wallace, Lew(is) 1827(?)-1905 ... 176
Brief entry ... 120
See also DLB 202
See also RGAL 4
Wallace, Lewis Grant 1910- ... CAP-2
Earlier sketch in CA 23-24
Wallace, Lila Bell Acheson 1889-1984
Obituary ... 112
Brief entry ... 105
See also DLB 137
Wallace, Lillian Parker 1890-1971 ... 1-4R
Obituary ... 103
Wallace, Luther T(ompkins) 1928- ... 13-16R
Wallace, Marc J., Jr. 1944- ... 114
Wallace, Marilyn (Weiss) 1941- ... 179
See also CMW 4
Wallace, Marjorie ... 101
Wallace, Mark I. 1956- ... 231
Wallace, Meredith 1965- ... 239
Wallace, Michael David 1943- ... 77-80
Wallace, Michele Faith 1952- ... CANR-58
Earlier sketch in CA 108
See also FW
Wallace, Mike 1918- ... CANR-108
Earlier sketch in CA 65-68
Wallace, Myron Leon
See Wallace, Mike
Wallace, Nancy Elizabeth 1948- ... SATA 141
Wallace, Naomi (French) 1960- ... 163
See also CD 5, 6
See also DLB 249
See also RGAL 4
Wallace, Nigel
See Hamilton, Charles (Harold St. John)
Wallace, Pamela 1949- ... 105
Wallace, Pat
See Strother, Pat Wallace
Wallace, Patricia M. ... 206
Wallace, Paul 1931- ... 61-64
Wallace, Paul A(nthony) W(ilson)
1891-1967 ... CAP-1
Earlier sketch in CA 13-16
Wallace, Paula S. ... 228
See also SATA 153
Wallace, Philip (Adrian) Hope
See Hope-Wallace, Philip (Adrian)
Wallace, Phyllis Ann 1920-1993 ... 105
Wallace, Rich 1957- ... CANR-143
Earlier sketch in CA 189
See also AAYA 34
See also SATA 117, 158
See also YAW
Wallace, Richard
See Ind, Allison
Wallace, Robert 1932-1999 ... CANR-10
Earlier sketch in CA 13-16R
See also SATA 47
See also SATA-Brief 37
Wallace, Robert Ash 1921- ... 1-4R
Wallace, Robert Kimball 1944- ... 69-72
Wallace, Robert M. 1947- ... 141
Wallace, Robin 1955- ... 128
Wallace, Roger
See Charlier, Roger H(enri)
Wallace, Ronald (William) 1945- ... CANR-109
Earlier sketches in CA 57-60, CANR-6, 20, 42
Wallace, Ronald S(tewart) 1911- ... CANR-5
Earlier sketch in CA 9-12R
Wallace, Ruby Ann 1923(?)- ... CANR-92
Earlier sketches in CA 112, CANR-26
See also Dee, Ruby
See also BW 1
Wallace, Samuel E(ugene) 1935- ... 41-44R
Wallace, Sarah Leslie 1914- ... 9-12R
Wallace, Sister M. Jean
See Paxton, Mary Jean Wallace
Wallace, Sylvia ... CANR-27
Earlier sketch in CA 73-76
Wallace, Tom 1874-1961
Obituary ... 93-96
Wallace, Vesna A. 1952- ... 158
Wallace, Walter L. 1927- ... 81-84
Wallace, Willard M(osher) 1911-2000 ... 13-16R
Wallace, William A(ugustine) 1918- ... 41-44R
Wallace, William A(lan) 1935- ... 49-52
Wallace, William Keith 1947- ... 124
See also Wallace, Bill
See also SATA 53
Wallace, William N. 1924- ... 13-16R
Wallace, William Stewart 1884-1970
Obituary ... 116
Wallace-Brodeur, Ruth 1941- ... 107
See also SATA 51, 88
See also SATA-Brief 41
Wallace-Clarke, George 1916- ... 117
Wallace-Crabbe, Chris(topher Keith)
1934- ... CANR-14
Earlier sketch in CA 77-80
See also BRWS 8
See also CP 1, 2, 3, 4, 5, 6, 7
See also DLB 289
Wallace-Hadrill, Andrew (Frederic)
1951- ... CANR-40
Earlier sketch in CA 117
Wallace-Hadrill, D(avid) S(utherland)
1920- ... 29-32R
Wallace-Hadrill, John Michael
1916-1985 ... 5-8R
Obituary ... 118
Wallach, Alan 1942- ... 147
Wallach, Erica Glaser 1922-1993 ... 21-24R
Obituary ... 143
Wallach, Ira 1913-1995 ... 9-12R
Obituary ... 150
Wallach, Janet 1942- ... CANR-143
Earlier sketches in CA 106, CANR-38
Wallach, Jeff 1960- ... 216
Wallach, John P(aul) 1943-2002 ... 139
Obituary ... 206
Wallach, Mark I(rwin) 1949- ... 69-72
Wallach, Michael A(rthur) 1933- ... CANR-51
Earlier sketches in CA 13-16R, CANR-11, 26

Wallach, Paul I. 1927- ... CANR-8
Earlier sketch in CA 17-20R
Wallach, Robert Charles 1935- ... 107
Wallach, Sidney 1905-1979 ... 103
Obituary ... 89-92
Wallach, Yona 1944-1985 ... 213
Wallance, Gregory Joseph 1948- ... 109
Wallant, Edward Lewis 1926-1962 ... CANR-22
Earlier sketch in CA 1-4R
See also CLC 5, 10
See also DLB 2, 28, 143, 299
See also EWL 3
See also MAL 5
See also MTCW 1, 2
See also RGAL 4
Wallas, Graham 1858-1932 ... TCLC 91
Wallechinsky, David 1948- ... CANR-55
Earlier sketches in CA 61-64, CANR-27
Wallek, Lee
See Johnson, Curt(is Lee)
Wallen, Carl J(oseph) 1931- ... 93-96
Wallenstein, Barry J(ay) 1940- ... CANR-11
Earlier sketch in CA 45-48
Wallenstein, Meir 1903- ... CAP-1
Earlier sketch in CA 13-16
Wallenstein, Peter 1944- ... 218
Wallenta, Adam 1974- ... SATA 123
Waller, Altina L(aura) 1940- ... 112
Waller, Brown
See Fraser, W(aller) B(rown)
Waller, Charles T(homas) 1934- ... 61-64
Waller, Douglas C. 1949- ... CANR-108
Earlier sketch in CA 146
Waller, Edmund 1606-1687 ... BRW 2
See also DAM POET
See also DLB 126
See also PAB
See also RGEL 2
Waller, G(ary) F(redric) 1944- ... CANR-31
Earlier sketch in CA 112
Waller, Gary
See Waller, G(ary) F(redric)
Waller, George Macgregor 1919- ... 9-12R
Waller, Gregory A(lbert) 1950- ... 127
Waller, Irene Ellen 1928- ... 109
Waller, J(ames) Irvin 1944- ... CANR-14
Earlier sketch in CA 61-64
See also CPW
Waller, Jane (Ashton) 1944- ... 132
Waller, John Stanier 1917-1995 ... 45-48
Obituary ... 147
Waller, Leslie 1923- ... CANR-2
Earlier sketch in CA 1-4R
See also SATA 20
Waller, Maureen ... 218
Waller, P(hilip) J(ohn) 1946- ... 143
Waller, Peter Louis 1935- ... 106
Waller, Robert J(ames) 1955- ... 117
Waller, Robert James 1939- ... CANR-65
Earlier sketch in CA 147
See also BPFB 3
See also CPW
See also DA3
See also DAM POP
Waller, Signe (Barbara Burke) 1938- ... 217
Waller, Susan (Stewart) 1948- ... 139
Wallerstein, Immanuel 1930- ... CANR-107
Earlier sketches in CA 21-24R, CANR-9, 24, 49
Wallerstein, Judith (Hannah) S(aretsky) 1921- ... CANR-99
Brief entry ... 105
Earlier sketch in CA 124
See also BEST 89:3
Wallerstein, Mitchel B(ruce) 1949- ... 105
Wallerstein, Robert S(olomon) 1921- ... CANR-12
Earlier sketch in CA 33-36R
Walley, Byron
See Card, Orson Scott
Walley, David G. 1945- ... CANR-37
Earlier sketch in CA 41-44R
Walley, Gay 1951- ... 187
Wallhauser, Henry T. 1930- ... 29-32R
Wallich, Henry C(hristopher) 1914-1988 ... CANR-6
Obituary ... 126
Earlier sketch in CA 1-4R
Wallich-Clifford, Anton 1923- ... 61-64
Wallig, Gaird (Elizabeth) 1942- ... 106
Wallin, Luke 1943- ... 130
Wallin, Pamela 1943- ... 226
Walling, William (Herbert) 1926- ... 103
Wallingford, Lee 1947- ... 142
Wallis, Charles L(angworthy) ... CANR-8
Earlier sketch in CA 5-8R
Wallis, Diz 1949- ... 145
See also SATA 77
Wallis, G. McDonald
See Campbell, Hope
Wallis, George A. 1892-1981 ... 17-20R
Wallis, Hal B. -1986
See Wallis, Harold Brent
See also IDFW 3, 4
Wallis, Harold Brent 1898(?)-1986 ... 153
Obituary ... 120
See also Wallis, Hal B.
Wallis, Jim 1948- ... CANR-97
Earlier sketches in CA 102, CANR-50
Wallis, Keith 1930- ... 25-28R
Wallis, Kenneth F(rank) 1938- ... CANR-24
Earlier sketch in CA 45-48
Wallis, Michael 1945- ... CANR-89
Earlier sketch in CA 139
Wallis, R(ichard) T(yrrell) 1941- ... 45-48
Wallis, Redmond Frankton 1933- ... 5-8R
Wallis, Robert 1900- ... CAP-2
Earlier sketch in CA 29-32
Wallis, Roy 1945- ... CANR-17
Earlier sketch in CA 97-100
Wallis, Ruth O(tis) S(awtell) 1895-1978
Obituary ... 73-76
Wallis, Velma 1960- ... 167
Wallis, W(ilson) Allen 1912-1998 ... 41-44R
Obituary ... 171
Wallison, Peter J. 1941- ... 224
Wallmann, Jeffrey M(iner) 1941- ... CANR-104
Earlier sketches in CA 77-80, CANR-14, 35
Wallmann, Margarethe 1904(?)-1992 ... 232
Wallmann, Margarita
See Wallmann, Margarethe
Wallmeyer, Dick
See Wallmeyer, Richard
Wallmeyer, Richard 1931- ... 133
Wallner, Alexandra 1946- ... CANR-13
Earlier sketch in CA 73-76
See also SATA 51, 98, 156
See also SATA-Brief 41
Wallner, John C. 1945- ... MAICYA 1, 2
See also SATA 10, 51, 133
Wallop, (John) Douglass III 1920-1985 ... CANR-13
Obituary ... 115
Earlier sketch in CA 73-76
Wallop, Lucille Fletcher 1912-2000 ... CANR-62
Obituary ... 189
Earlier sketch in CA 13-16R
See also CMW 4
Wallower, Lucille ... CANR-9
Earlier sketch in CA 21-24R
See also SATA 11
Wallraff, Barbara 1953- ... 197
Wallraff, Charles Fredric 1909-1991 ... 1-4R
Wallraff, Hans Gunter 1942- ... 195
Walls, David Stuart 1941- ... CANR-14
Earlier sketch in CA 37-40R
Walls, Dwayne E(stes) 1932- ... CANR-14
Earlier sketch in CA 41-44R
Walls, H(enry) J(ames) 1907-1988 ... 9-12R
Obituary ... 126
Walls, Ian G(ascoigne) 1922- ... 104
Walls, Ronald 1920- ... 103
Walls, William J(acob) 1885-1975 ... 81-84
Wallsten, Robert 1912- ... 101
Wallwork, Ernest (Edward) 1937- ... 41-44R
Walman, Jerome 1937- ... 125
Walmsley, Arnold Robert 1912-2000 ... 41-44R
Walmsley, Buck
See Walmsley, Haines
Walmsley, (Ronald) Charles 1910-1983
Obituary ... 110
Walmsley, Haines 1930(?)-1983
Obituary ... 111
Walmsley, Jane ... 128
Walmsley, Leo 1892-1966 ... CAP-1
Earlier sketch in CA 11-12
Walmsley, Lewis C(alvin) 1897-1968 ... 61-64
Walmsley, Robert 1905-1976 ... CAP-2
Earlier sketch in CA 29-32
Walmsley, Tom 1948- ... 126
Waln, Nora 1895-1964
Obituary ... 89-92
Walpole, Horace 1717-1797 ... BRW 3
See also DLB 39, 104, 213
See also GL 3
See also HGG
See also LMFS 1
See also RGEL 2
See also SUFW 1
See also TEA
Walpole, Hugh (Seymour) 1884-1941 ... 165
Brief entry ... 104
See also DLB 34
See also HGG
See also MTCW 2
See also RGEL 2
See also RHW
See also TCLC 5
Walpole, Ronald Noel 1903-1986 ... 106
Walpow, Nathan 1948- ... 198
Walrath, Douglas Alan 1933- ... 120
Walrath, Jane Dwyer 1939- ... 97-100
Walrond, Eric (Derwent) 1898-1966 ... 125
See also BW 1
See also DLB 51
See also HR 1:3
Walsch, Neale Donald ... 180
Walschap, Gerard 1898-1989 ... 103
See also EWL 3
Walsdorf, John J(oseph) 1941- ... 115
Walser, Martin 1927- ... CANR-46
Earlier sketches in CA 57-60, CANR-8
See also CLC 27, 183
See also CWW 2
See also DLB 75, 124
See also EWL 3
Walser, Richard (Gaither) 1908-1988 ... CANR-2
Earlier sketch in CA 5-8R
Walser, Robert 1878-1956 ... CANR-100
Brief entry ... 118
Earlier sketch in CA 165
See also DLB 66
See also EWL 3
See also SSC 20
See also TCLC 18
Walsh, Ann 1942- ... SATA 62
Walsh, Annmarie Hauck 1938- ... 25-28R
Walsh, Bren(dan) 1921- ... 121
Walsh, Chad 1914-1991 ... CANR-6
Obituary ... 133
Earlier sketch in CA 1-4R
See also CP 1, 2
Walsh, Clune J(oseph), Jr. 1928- ... 114
Walsh, Des 1954- ... 116
Walsh, Donald Devenish 1903-1980 ... CANR-3
Obituary ... 97-100
Earlier sketch in CA 49-52
Walsh, Edward J(oseph) 1937- ... 37-40R
Walsh, Edward N. 1925- ... 144
Walsh, Edward Warren 1930(?)-1986
Obituary ... 118
Walsh, Elizabeth M(iller) 1937- ... 120
Walsh, Ellen Stoll 1942- ... CANR-130
Earlier sketch in CA 104
See also SATA 49, 99, 147
Walsh, Ernest 1895-1926 ... 165
Brief entry ... 109
See also DLB 4, 45
Walsh, Frances ... 177
Walsh, George (Vincent) 1923- ... 109
Walsh, George (William) 1931- ... 118
Brief entry ... 114
Walsh, George B. 1947(?)-1989
Obituary ... 127
Walsh, George Johnston 1889-1981 ... SATA 53
Walsh, Gillian Paton
See Paton Walsh, Gillian
Walsh, Jack 1919(?)-1984
Obituary ... 114
Walsh, James
See Robinson, Frank M(alcolm)
Walsh, James 1920-1986(?)
Obituary ... 119
Walsh, James Edward 1891-1981
Obituary ... 104
Walsh, James J(erome) 1924- ... 9-12R
Walsh, James P(atrick) 1937- ... 111
Walsh, Jill Paton
See Paton Walsh, Gillian
See also CLC 35
See also CLR 2, 65
See also WYA
Walsh, John (Dixon) 1927- ... 17-20R
Walsh, John Evangelist 1927- ... CANR-97
Earlier sketches in CA 85-88, CANR-44
See also BYA 13
Walsh, Justin E(arl) 1933- ... CANR-10
Earlier sketch in CA 25-28R
Walsh, Kenneth T(homas) 1947- ... 227
Walsh, Lawrence Edward 1912- ... 167
Walsh, Lorena S. 1944- ... 194
Walsh, M. M. B. ... 101
Walsh, Marcus 1947- ... CANR-41
Earlier sketch in CA 118
Walsh, Marnie
See Walsh, M. M. B.
Walsh, Mary Caswell 1949- ... 190
See also SATA 118
Walsh, Mary Williams 1955- ... 136
Walsh, Maurice 1879-1964 ... 133
Brief entry ... 124
Walsh, Michael J. 1937- ... 106
Walsh, Myles E(ugene) 1937- ... 109
Walsh, P(atrick) G(erard) 1923- ... CANR-52
Earlier sketches in CA 25-28R, CANR-28
Walsh, Patricia L(ouise) 1942- ... 109
Walsh, Raoul 1887-1980
Obituary ... 102
Walsh, (Walter) Richard 1923- ... 25-28R
Walsh, Richard 1941- ... CANR-46
Earlier sketch in CA 120
Walsh, Robb 1952- ... CANR-138
Earlier sketch in CA 167
Walsh, Robert 1784-1859 ... DLB 59
Walsh, Robert L. 1933- ... 210
Walsh, Ronald A. 1934- ... 149
Walsh, Sheila 1928- ... 115
See also RHW
Walsh, (Michael) Stephen 1942- ... 37-40R
Walsh, (Richard) Taylor 1947- ... 73-76
Walsh, Thomas (Francis Morgan) 1908-1984
Obituary ... 114
See also CMW 4
Walsh, Timothy J(ames) 1927- ... 41-44R
Walsh, V. L.
See Walsh, Vivian
Walsh, Vivian 1960- ... SATA 120
Walsh, W(alter) Bruce 1936- ... 93-96
Walsh, Warren Bartlett 1909-1979 ... CAP-2
Earlier sketch in CA 13-14
Walsh, Wendy L(ee) ... 230
Walsh, William 1916-1996 ... CANR-11
Obituary ... 152
Earlier sketch in CA 65-68
See also RGEL 2
Walsh, William B(ertalan) 1920-1996 ... CANR-4
Obituary ... 155
Earlier sketch in CA 49-52
Walsh, William Henry 1913-1986
Obituary ... 119
Walsham, Alexandra 1966- ... 197
Walshe, M(aurice) O'C(onnell) 1911-1998 ... 5-8R
Walshe, Peter (Aubrey) 1934- ... CANR-86
Earlier sketch in CA 130
Walshe, R(obert) D(aniel) 1923- ... CANR-21
Earlier sketch in CA 104
Walsh Shepherd, Donna 1948- ... 146
See also SATA 78
Walster, Elaine Hatfield
See Hatfield, Elaine (Catherine)
Walster, G. William 1941- ... 85-88
Walston, Joseph
See Walston, Marie
Walston, Marie 1925- ... 41-44R
Walt, Lewis W(illiam) 1913-1989 ... 33-36R
Obituary ... 128
Waltari, Mika (Toimi) 1908-1979 ... 9-12R
Obituary ... 89-92
Waltch, Lilla M. 1932- ... 128
Walter, Bruno
See Schlesinger, Bruno Walter
Walter, Claire 1943- ... 81-84
Walter, Dorothy Blake 1908-1999 ... CAP-1
Earlier sketch in CA 11-12
Walter, Elizabeth ... CANR-77
Earlier sketches in CA 97-100, CANR-17, 38
See also HGG
Walter, Eugene (Ferdinand) 1921(?)-1998 ... CANR-119
Obituary ... 166
Earlier sketch in CA 9-12R
Walter, Eugene Victor 1925- ... 25-28R
Walter, Frances V. 1923- ... SATA 71
Walter, Gladys Mae 1901-1973 ... 41-44R
Walter, Hartmut 1940- ... 89-92
Walter, Ingo 1940- ... CANR-22
Earlier sketches in CA 17-20R, CANR-7
Walter, J(ulian) A(nthony) 1948- ... CANR-46
Earlier sketch in CA 120
Walter, Jess ... 217
Walter, John 1948- ... CANR-93
Earlier sketch in CA 134
Walter, Malcolm (Ross) 1944- ... 194
Walter, Mildred Pitts 1922- ... 138
See also BW 2
See also CLR 15, 61
See also CWRI 5
See also JRDA
See also MAICYA 1, 2
See also MAICYAS 1
See also SAAS 12
See also SATA 69, 133
See also SATA-Brief 45
See also YAW
Walter, Nancy
See Holmgren, Norah
Walter, Nina Willis 1900-1977 ... 5-8R
Walter, Otis M. 1921- ... 5-8R
Walter, Otto F. 1928- ... EWL 3
Walter, Richard 1944- ... CANR-87
Earlier sketch in CA 128
Walter, Robert H(enry) K(eamer, Jr.) 1922- ... 5-8R
Walter, Samuel 1916- ... 5-8R
Walter, Tony
See Walter, J(ulian) A(nthony)
Walter, Villiam Christian
See Andersen, Hans Christian
Walter, Virginia
See Walter, Virginia A.
See also SATA 134
Walter, Virginia A. ... CANR-112
Earlier sketch in CA 203
See also Walter, Virginia
Walter, William Grey 1910-1977 ... 103
Walters, A(lan) A(rthur) 1926- ... CANR-26
Earlier sketch in CA 29-32R
Walters, Anna L(ee) 1946- ... 73-76
See also NNAL
Walters, Audrey 1929- ... SATA 18
Walters, Barbara 1931- ... 65-68
See also AITN 2
Walters, Basil L(eon) 1896-1975
Obituary ... 89-92
Walters, C(harles) Glenn 1929- ... 81-84
Walters, Celeste 1938- ... 196
See also SATA 126
Walters, Chad
See Smith, Richard Rein
Walters, D(avid) Gareth 1948- ... 128
Walters, Derek 1936- ... 128
Walters, Dorothy (J.) 1928- ... CANR-121
Earlier sketch in CA 65-68
Walters, Dorothy Mae Wells 1924- ... CANR-2
Earlier sketch in CA 5-8R
Walters, Dottie
See Walters, Dorothy Mae Wells
Walters, Eleanor 1955- ... 108
Walters, Eric (Robert) 1957- ... CANR-140
Earlier sketch in CA 160
See also SATA 99, 155
Walters, Helen B. (?)-1987 ... 133
Obituary ... 121
See also SATA-Obit 50
Walters, Henry 1848-1931 ... 184
See also DLB 140
Walters, Hugh
See Hughes, Walter (Llewellyn)
Walters, J. Donald 1926- ... CANR-141
Earlier sketch in CA 132
Walters, Jack Edward 1896-1967 ... 5-8R
Obituary ... 134
Walters, James E. 1922- ... 144
Walters, James W. 1945- ... 144
Walters, Janet Lane 1936- ... 49-52
Walters, Jennifer Waelti
See Waelti-Walters, Jennifer (Rose)
Walters, John
See Lassally, Walter
Walters, John Beauchamp 1906- ... CANR-6
Earlier sketch in CA 5-8R
Walters, John Bennett, Jr. 1912-1979 ... 105
Walters, Kenneth D. 1941- ... 132
Walters, LeRoy (B., Jr.) 1940- ... 108
Walters, Mary
See Riskin, Mary (Winifred) Walters
Walters, Minette 1949- ... 160
See also CMW 4
Walters, Nell
See Muse, Patricia (Alice)
Walters, Richard P(aul) 1935- ... 107
Walters, Rick
See Rowland, D(onald) S(ydney)
Walters, Robert Mark 1938- ... 69-72
Walters, Robert S(tephen) 1941- ... 29-32R

Cumulative Index 603 Ward

Walters, Ronald 139
See also BW 2
Walters, Ronald G(ordon) 1942- 85-88
Walters, Roy W(ashington) 1918- 93-96
Walters, Shelly
See Sheldon, Walter J(ames)
Walters, Simon 213
Walters, Sister Annette 1910-1978 .... 37-40R
Walters, Stanley D(avid) 1931- 53-56
Walters, Thomas N(oble) 1935- 65-68
Walters, Vernon A(nthony) 1917-2002 122
Obituary 204
Walthall, Anne 182
Waltham, Antony Clive 1942- CANR-51
Earlier sketches in CA 65-68, CANR-10, 26
Walther, Eric H(arry) 1960- 140
Walther, Fritz R(udolf) 1921- CANR-90
Earlier sketch in CA 132
Walther, R(ichard) E(rnest) 1921- 41-44R
Walther, Regis (Hills) 1917-1983 .... CANR-8
Obituary 111
Earlier sketch in CA 17-20R
Walther, Thomas A. 1950- 107
See also SATA 31
Walther, Tom
See Walther, Thomas A.
Walther von der Vogelweide c. 1170-c. 1230 .... DLB 138
See also EW 1
See also RGWL 2, 3
Waltman, Jerold (Lloyd) 1945- CANR-112
Earlier sketch in CA 117
Waltman, John L. 1946- 120
Waltner, Elma 1912-1987 .... 17-20R
See also SATA 40
Waltner, Willard H. 1909- .... SATA 40
Walton, Alfred Grant 1887-1970 .... CAP-1
Earlier sketch in CA 13-14
Walton, Bobbi Smith 1949- 137
Walton, Bryce 1918-1988 .... 21-24R
Obituary 182
Walton, Chelle Koster 1954- 167
Walton, Clarence C. 1915- CANR-3
Earlier sketch in CA 1-4R
Walton, Clyde C(ameron) 1925- 29-32R
Walton, Craig 1934- 41-44R
Walton, Darwin McBeth 1926- 190
See also SATA 119
Walton, Donald William 1917- 112
Walton, Douglas N(eil) 1942- CANR-40
Earlier sketch in CA 117
Walton, Ed(ward Hazen) 1931- CANR-45
Earlier sketches in CA 105, CANR-22
Walton, Elizabeth Cheatham 5-8R
Walton, Evangeline
See Ensley, Evangeline
Walton, Fiona L. M. 1959- .... SATA 89
Walton, George (H.) 1904-1976 .... 17-20R
Walton, Hanes, Jr. 1942- 41-44R
Walton, Henry J(ohn) 1924- CANR-35
Earlier sketch in CA 53-56
Walton, Izaak 1593-1683 .... BRW 2
See also CDBLB Before 1660
See also DLB 151, 213
See also RGEL 2
Walton, J(ohn) Michael 1939- CANR-94
Earlier sketch in CA 117
Walton, Jo 213
Walton, John 1910-1991 .... CANR-5
Earlier sketch in CA 1-4R
Walton, John (Nicholas) 1922- CANR-55
Earlier sketch in CA 127
Walton, John 1937- 89-92
Walton, John K(immons) 1948- 124
Walton, Kendall L(ewis) 1939- 136
Walton, Luke
See Henderson, William Charles
Walton, Mary 1941- 166
Walton, Ortiz Montaigne 1933- CANR-26
Earlier sketch in CA 45-48
Walton, Priscilla L. 1957- CANR-107
Earlier sketch in CA 150
Walton, Richard Eugene 1931- 81-84
Walton, Richard J. 1928- 25-28R
See also SATA 4
Walton, Rick 1957- CANR-134
Earlier sketch in CA 168
See also SATA 101, 151
Walton, Robert Cutler 1932- 73-76
Walton, Ronald (Gordon) 1936- 65-68
Walton, Sam (Moore) 1918(?)-1992 144
Walton, Su 1944- 25-28R
Walton, Vicki (Elizabeth) 1949- 65-68
Walton, W. Robert 1902-1986 69-72
Walton, William 1909-1983 125
See also IDFW 3, 4
Waltrip, Lela (Kingston) 1904-1995 .... 5-8R
See also SATA 9
Waltrip, Mildred 1911- .... SATA 37
Waltrip, Robert
See Short, Robert Waltrip
Waltrip, Rufus (Charles) 1898-1988 .... 5-8R
See also SATA 9
Waltz, Jon R(ichard) 1929-2004 .... 17-20R
Obituary 222
Waltz, Kenneth N(eal) 1924- 37-40R
Waltz, Mitzi 1962- 230
Waltzer, Herbert 1930- 41-44R
Walvin, James 1942- CANR-37
Earlier sketches in CA 49-52, CANR-1, 17
Walvoord, John F(lipse) 1910-2002 ..... CANR-6
Obituary 210
Earlier sketch in CA 9-12R
Walwicz, Ania 1951- .... CWP
Walwik, Theodore J. 1937- 25-28R
Walworth, Alice
See Graham, Alice Walworth
Walworth, Arthur (Clarence) 1903-2005 .... 21-24R
Obituary 235
Walworth, Nancy Zinsser 1917- CANR-3
Earlier sketch in CA 5-8R
See also SATA 14
Walz, Audrey Boyers 1907(?)-1983
Obituary 109
Walz, Edgar 1914- 29-32R
Walz, Jay (Franklin) 1907-1991 49-52
Obituary 135
Walz, Marjorie A. 1939- 153
Walzer, Michael (Laban) 1935- CANR-127
Earlier sketches in CA 37-40R, CANR-15, 48
Walzer, Norman 1943- CANR-53
Earlier sketches in CA 111, CANR-29
Wamba, Philippe 1971-2002 192
Obituary 209
Wambaugh, Joseph (Aloysius), Jr. 1937- CANR-115
Earlier sketches in CA 33-36R, CANR-42, 65
See also AITN 1
See also BEST 89:3
See also BPFB 3
See also CLC 3, 18
See also CMW 4
See also CPW 1
See also DA3
See also DAM NOV, POP
See also DLB 6
See also DLBY 1983
See also MSW
See also MTCW 1, 2
Wamble, Gaston Hugh 1923- 5-8R
Wamble, Thelma 1916- 185
Brief entry 106
Wamsley, Gary L(ee) 1935- CANR-3
Earlier sketch in CA 49-52
Wamwere, Koigi wa 1949- 214
Wanamaker, A(llison) Temple 1918- 17-20R
Wan Chia-pao 1910-
See Cao Yu
Wand, (John) William (Charles) 1885-1977(?) 103
Wandel, Joseph 1918- 93-96
Wanderer, Zev W(illiam) 1932- 105
Wandesforde-Smith, Geoffrey Albert 1943- 29-32R
Wandor, Michelene (Dinah) 1940- 142
See also CBD
See also CD 5, 6
See also CWD
See also DLB 310
Wandrei, Donald 1908-1987 .... HGG
Wandro, Mark 1948- 106
Wandycz, Piotr Stefan 1923- CANR-2
Earlier sketch in CA 1-4R
Wang, An 1920-1990 132
Wang, Annie 1972- 218
Wang, Anyi 1954- 211
Wang, C(hing) H(sien) 1940- CANR-8
Earlier sketch in CA 61-64
Wang, (Fred) Fang Yu 1913-1997 .... 37-40R
Obituary 162
Wang, Hao 1921- 65-68
Wang, Hui-Ming 1922- 33-36R
Wang, J(en) Y(u) 1918- CANR-25
Earlier sketch in CA 45-48
Wang, Jing 1950- 175
Wang, John Ching-yu 1934- 41-44R
Wang, Julie C(aroline) 1947- 114
Wang, Leonard J(udah) 1926- 33-36R
Wang, Lucy 228
Wang, Meng 1934- 169
See also Wang Meng
Wang, Qun 1956- 191
Wang, Sabine E(isenberg) 1925- 37-40R
Wang, Sen 1959- 217
Wang, Shuo 1958- 171
Wang, Wallace E. 1961- 225
Wang, (John) Wayne 1949- 226
Wang, Xiufang 1956- 238
Wang, Yi Chu 1916- 61-64
Wang, Yun 1964- 227
Wang, Zhongshu 1925- CANR-41
Earlier sketch in CA 117
Wang Anyi 1954- .... EWL 3
Wangenheim, Chris von
See von Wangenheim, Chris
Wangensteen, Owen Harding 1898-1981 .. 103
Wangensteen, Sarah (Anne) D(avidson) 1908-1994 120
Wanger, Walter 1894-1968 .... IDFW 3, 4
Wangerin, Theodora Scharffenberg 1888-1978 .... 5-8R
Wangerin, Walter, Jr. 1944- CANR-100
Earlier sketches in CA 108, CANR-34
Interview in CA-108
See also FANT
See also SATA 45, 98
See also SATA-Brief 37
See also YAW
Wangermann, Ernst 1925- 103
Wang Gungwu 1930- CANR-10
Earlier sketch in CA 65-68
Wangh, Stephen 1943- 191
Wang Meng
See Wang, Meng
See also EWL 3
Wangmo, Isering 1967- 193
Wang Wei 699(?)-761(?) .... PC 18
See also TWA
Wangyal, Geshe 1901(?)-1983
Obituary 108
Waniek, Marilyn Nelson 1946- CANR-15
Earlier sketch in CA 89-92
See also Nelson, Marilyn
See also DLB 120
See also SATA 60
Wanissi, Zuhur 1936- .... EWL 3
Wan Jiabao
See Wan Chia-pao
Wankowicz, Melchior 1891-1974
Obituary 53-56
Wanlass, Stanley G(len) 1941- 61-64
Wanley, Humfrey 1672-1726 .... DLB 213
Wann, Kenneth D(ouglass) 1915-1974 ...... 5-8R
Wann, Marilyn 1966- 182
Wannamaker, Bruce
See Moncure, Jane Belk
Wannan, Bill
See Wannan, William Fielding
Wannan, William Fielding 1915- CANR-10
Earlier sketch in CA 21-24R
Wanniski, Jude 1936- 133
Wannus, Sa'dallah 1941- .... EWL 3
See also WLIT 6
Wanrooy, Willem F(rederik) 1925-1997 118
Wansell, (Stephen) Geoffrey 1945- 143
Wanshel, Jeff(rey Mark) 1947- CANR-13
Earlier sketch in CA 57-60
Wantland, William C(harles) 1934- 111
Wantling, William 1933-1974 105
Obituary 89-92
See also CP 1, 2
Waples, Douglas 1893-1978
Obituary 77-80
Waplington, Nick 1965- 213
Wapshott, Nicholas (Henry) 1952- 135
Warbler, J. M.
See Cocagnac, Augustin Maurice(-Jean)
Warbridge, C. W.
See Woods, Clee
Warburg, Fredric (John) 1898-1981 105
Warburg, James Paul 1896-1969 .... CAP-2
Obituary 25-28R
Earlier sketch in CA 21-22
Warburg, Otto (Heinrich) 1883-1970 158
Warburg, Sandol Stoddard
See Stoddard, Sandol
See also SATA 14
Warburton, Amber Arthun 1898(?)-1976
Obituary 61-64
Warburton, Clark (Abram) 1896-1979 73-76
Obituary 89-92
Warburton, Eileen 229
Warburton, Minnie 1949- 101
Warburton, Nigel 1962- 225
Warburton, William 1698-1779 .... DLB 104
Warch, Richard 1939- 105
Warcollier, Rene 1881-1962
Obituary 112
Ward, Aileen 1919- 5-8R
See also DLB 111
Ward, Alan Joseph 1936- 73-76
Ward, Allen M(ason) 1942- 89-92
Ward, Amanda Eyre 1972- 226
Ward, Andrew (Spencer) 1946- CANR-99
Earlier sketch in CA 81-84
Ward, Anne G. 1932- 77-80
Ward, Artemus
See Browne, Charles Farrar
See also RGAL 4
Ward, Arthur Henry Sarsfield 1883-1959 ... 173
Brief entry 108
See also Rohmer, Sax
See also CMW 4
See also HGG
Ward, Barbara
See Jackson, Barbara (Ward)
Ward, Benedicta 1933- CANR-118
Earlier sketches in CA 65-68, CANR-12, 28, 56
Ward, Brad
See Peeples, Samuel Anthony
Ward, Brendan Noel 1947- 129
Ward, Brian 1961- 202
Ward, Burt 1945- 167
Ward, Charles D(uane) 1935- 33-36R
Ward, Charles Dexter
See Taylor, John (Alfred)
Ward, Charlotte
See Chesney, Marion
Ward, Chester 1907-1977
Obituary 69-72
Ward, Chrissie 1949- 235
Ward, Colin 1924- 57-60
Ward, Craig 1892-1979
Obituary 85-88
Ward, David 1938- 29-32R
Ward, Dennis 1924- 13-16R
Ward, Diane (Lee) 1956- 154
See also CP 7
Ward, Don(ald G.) 1911-1984 .... 17-20R
Ward, Donald 1909- 109
Ward, Donald 1930- 37-40R
Ward, Douglas Turner 1930- CANR-27
Earlier sketch in CA 81-84
See also BW 1
See also CAD
See also CD 5, 6
See also CLC 19
See also DLB 7, 38
Ward, E. D.
See Gorey, Edward (St. John) and Lucas, E(dward) V(errall)
Ward, Ed
See Stratemeyer, Edward L.
Ward, Ed(mund O.) 1948- 114
Ward, Elizabeth 1952- 110
Ward, Elizabeth Campbell 1936- 45-48
Ward, Elizabeth Honor (Shedden) 1926- . 9-12R
Ward, Eric
See Ebon, Martin
Ward, Evelyn
See Everett-Green, Evelyn
Ward, Frank A. 1948- 203
Ward, Fred 1935- 85-88
Ward, Geoffrey C(hampion) 1940- . CANR-104
Earlier sketch in CA 141
Ward, Gregory 1951(?)- 171
Ward, Harry Merrill 1929- CANR-93
Earlier sketches in CA 1-4R, CANR-2
Ward, Helen 1962- .... SATA 72, 144
Ward, Herman Matthew 1914- CANR-39
Earlier sketches in CA 5-8R, CANR-2, 18
Ward, Hiley Henry 1929- CANR-2
Earlier sketch in CA 1-4R
Ward, Mrs. Humphry 1851-1920
See Ward, Mary Augusta
See also RGEL 2
Ward, J. Alan 1937- 114
Ward, J(oseph) Neville 1915- 77-80
Ward, J(ohn) P(owell) 1937- CANR-27
Earlier sketch in CA 109
Ward, James 1843-1925 .... DLB 262
Ward, James A(rthur) 1941- 49-52
Ward, James Myron 1919-1984
Obituary 112
Ward, Jane (A.) 1960(?)- 201
Ward, Jay 1920-1989 .... SATA-Obit 63
Ward, Jennifer 1963- .... SATA 146
Ward, John (Stanton) 1917- .... SATA 42
Ward, John M(anning) 1919- 21-24R
Ward, John Owen 1919- 13-16R
Ward, John Towers 1930-1987 .... CANR-7
Obituary 122
Earlier sketch in CA 109
Ward, John William 1922-1985 .... 5-8R
Obituary 116
Ward, Jonas
See Ard, William (Thomas) and Cox, William R(obert) and Garfield, Brian (Francis Wynne)
See also TCWW 1, 2
Ward, Jonathon
See Stine, Whitney Ward
Ward, Joseph A(nthony, Jr.) 1931- 1-4R
Ward, Jule DeJager 1942- 195
Ward, Justine Bayard Cutting 1879-1975
Obituary 61-64
Ward, (John Stephen) Keith 1938- CANR-37
Earlier sketches in CA 29-32R, CANR-16
Ward, Ken 1949- CANR-144
Earlier sketch in CA 136
Ward, Lester Frank 1841-1913 215
Ward, Lynd (Kendall) 1905-1985 .... 17-20R
Obituary 116
See also DLB 22
See also MAICYA 1, 2
See also SATA 2, 36
See also SATA-Obit 42
Ward, Maisie 1889-1975 69-72
Obituary 53-56
Ward, Margaret 1950- CANR-124
Earlier sketch in CA 168
Ward, Martha (Eads) 17-20R
See also SATA 5
Ward, Martha C(oonfield) 238
Ward, Mary Augusta 1851-1920
See Ward, Mrs. Humphry
See also DLB 18
See also TCLC 55
Ward, Mary Josephine
See Ward, Maisie
Ward, Matthew 1951(?)-1990
Obituary 132
Ward, Maurine Carr 1939- 157
Ward, Melanie
See Curtis, Richard (Alan) and Lynch, Marilyn
Ward, Michael 1939- 37-40R
Ward, Nathaniel 1578(?)-1652 .... DLB 24
Ward, Ned 1667-1731 .... RGEL 2
Ward, Norman 1918-1990 .... 41-44R
Ward, Olivia Tucker 1927- 57-60
Ward, Patricia A(nn) 1940- CANR-104
Earlier sketch in CA 57-60
Ward, Patricia Sarrafian 1969- 224
Ward, Paul W. 1905-1976
Obituary 69-72
Ward, Pearl L(ewis) 1920- 107
Ward, Peter
See Faust, Frederick (Schiller)
Ward, (William) Peter 1943- 134
Ward, Peter D(ouglas) 1949- 218
Ward, Philip 1938- CANR-56
Earlier sketches in CA 25-28R, CANR-12, 30
Ward, Philip C. 1932- 21-24R
Ward, R(ichard) H(eron) 1910-1969 ...... CAP-1
Earlier sketch in CA 11-12
Ward, R. Patrick
See Holzapfel, Rudolf Patrick
Ward, Ralph Gerard 1933- 107
Ward, Ralph T(homas) 1927- 49-52
Ward, Richard J(oseph) 1921- 41-44R
Ward, Ritchie R(unyan) 1906-1982 .... 29-32R
Ward, Robert 1943- CANR-44
Earlier sketch in CA 104
Ward, Robert E(rnest) 1927- 49-52
Ward, Robert Elmer 1937- 49-52
Ward, Ronald A(rthur) 1908- 53-56
Ward, Russel (Braddock) 1914-1995 .... CANR-22
Earlier sketch in CA 103
Ward, Russell A(very) 1947- 110
Ward, Stephen R(alph) 1938- 65-68
Ward, Stuart 215

Ward, Ted (Warren) 1930- ... CANR-16
Earlier sketch in CA 97-100
Ward, Terence 1953(?)- ... 218
Ward, Theodora 1890-1974 ... CAP-2
Obituary ... 53-56
Earlier sketch in CA 33-36
Ward, Theodore (James) 1902-1983 ... 125
Obituary ... 109
See also BW
See also DLB 76
Ward, Tom
See Stratemeyer, Edward L.
Ward, Virgil S(cott) 1916- ... 1-4R
Ward, W. R. 1925- ... CANR-94
Earlier sketch in CA 146
Ward, Waylon O. 1942- ... 114
Ward, Willa
See Ward-Royster, Willa
Ward, William Alan Heaton
See Heaton-Ward, William Alan
Ward, William Arthur 1921- ... 29-32R
Ward, William B(ethea) 1912-1996 ... 5-8R
Ward, William Ernest Frank
1900-1994 ... CANR-19
Earlier sketches in CA 9-12R, CANR-4
Ward, William G. 1929- ... 21-24R
Ward, William R(eed) 1918- ... 61-64
Ward, Winfred O('Neil) 1933- ... 106
Warddel, Nora Helen
See Heron-Allen, Edward
Warde, Alan 1949- ... CANR-67
Earlier sketches in CA 112, CANR-31
Warde, William F.
See Novack, George (Edward)
Wardell, Dean
See Prince, J(ack) H(arvey)
Wardell, Phyl(lis Robinson) 1909-1994 . CAP-1
Earlier sketch in CA 11-12
See also CWRI 5
Wardell, Steven (William) 1971- ... 148
Warden, G(erard) B(ryce) 1939- ... 29-32R
Warden, John 1936- ... 41-44R
Warden, Lewis (Christopher)
1913-1989 ... 13-16R
Warden, Rob(ert) 1940- ... CANR-97
Earlier sketch in CA 142
Wardhaugh, Ronald 1932- ... 37-40R
Wardlaw, Lee 1955- ... CANR-91
Earlier sketch in CA 148
See also SATA 79, 115
Wardle, Dan
See Snow, Charles H(orace)
Wardle, David 1930- ... 69-72
Wardle, (John) Irving 1929- ... 77-80
Wardle, Jane
See Hueffer, Oliver Madox
Wardle, Lynn D(ennis) 1947- ... 109
Wardle, Ralph Martin 1909-1988 ... CANR-5
Earlier sketch in CA 1-4R
See also DLB 103
Wardman, Alan (Edgar) 1926-1986 ... 77-80
Obituary ... 120
Wardman, Gordon 1948- ... 136
Ward-Perkins, John Bryan 1912-1981 ... 93-96
Obituary ... 108
Wardroper, John (Edmund) 1923- ... 29-32R
Wardropper, Bruce W(ear) 1919- ... 13-16R
Wardropper, Ian (Bruce) 1951- ... 137
Ward-Royster, Willa 1922- ... 162
Ward-Thomas, Evelyn Bridget Patricia Stephens
1928- ... CANR-58
Earlier sketches in CA 9-12R, CANR-5, 26
See also CMW 4
See also RHW
Wardwell, Allen 1935-1999 ... 151
Obituary ... 179
Ware, Caroline F. 1899-1990
Obituary ... 131
Ware, Cheryl 1963- ... 158
See also SATA 101
Ware, Chris 1967- ... CANR-119
Earlier sketch in CA 175
See also AAYA 47
See also MTFW 2005
See also SATA 140
Ware, Ciji 1942- ... 103
Ware, Clyde 1932- ... 33-36R
Ware, Emma 1896(?)-1975
Obituary ... 57-60
Ware, George W(hitaker) 1902-1984 ... 13-16R
Ware, Gilbert 1933- ... 65-68
Ware, Henry, Jr. 1794-1843 ... DLB 235
Ware, Jane (O.) 1936- ... CANR-86
Earlier sketch in CA 133
Ware, Jean (Jones) 1914- ... CAP-1
Earlier sketch in CA 11-12
Ware, Jim (Clark) 1953- ... 215
Ware, John
See Mabley, Edward (Howe)
Ware, Kallistos (Timothy Richard)
1934- ... CANR-24
Earlier sketches in CA 9-12R, CANR-7
Ware, Leon (Vernon) 1909-1976 ... CANR-2
Earlier sketch in CA 1-4R
See also SATA 4
Ware, Leonard 1900(?)-1976
Obituary ... 69-72
Ware, Monica
See Marsh, John
Ware, Runa Erwin ... CAP-2
Earlier sketch in CA 29-32
Ware, Sandra J. 1972- ... 235
Ware, Susan 1950- ... 171
Ware, Timothy
See Ware, Kallistos (Timothy Richard)
Ware, W. Porter 1904-1990 ... 105
Ware, Wallace
See Karp, David
Ware, William 1797-1852 ... DLB 1, 235
Wareham, John 1940- ... CANR-141
Earlier sketch in CA 101
Warenski, Marilyn L(iston) 1931- ... 117
Warfel, Harry R(edcay) 1899-1971 ... CAP-1
Earlier sketch in CA 13-14
Warfield, Catherine Ann 1816-1877 ... DLB 248
Warfield, (A.) Gallatin 1946- ... 140
Warfield, Gerald (Alexander) 1940- ... 117
Warford, Jeremy J(ames) 1938- ... 37-40R
Warga, Wayne 1937-1994 ... 152
Wargin, Kathy-jo 1965- ... 218
See also SATA 145
Wargo, Dan M. 1920- ... 21-24R
Wargon, Sylvia T(ruster) 1924- ... 221
Warhaft, Sidney 1921- ... 61-64
Warhol, Andy 1928(?)-1987 ... CANR-34
Obituary ... 121
Earlier sketch in CA 89-92
See also AAYA 12
See also BEST 89:4
See also CLC 20
Warhol, Robyn R. 1955- ... 135
Waring, Anna Letitia 1823-1910 ... 206
See also DLB 240
Waring, Belle 1951- ... 171
Waring, Brett
See Meares, Leonard Frank
Wark, David M(ayer) 1934- ... 33-36R
Wark, Ian W(illiam) 1899-1985 ... CAP-2
Earlier sketch in CA 29-32
Wark, McKenzie 1961- ... 196
Wark, Robert R(odger) 1924- ... CANR-8
Earlier sketch in CA 61-64
Wark, Wesley K. 1952- ... CANR-50
Earlier sketch in CA 123
Warkentin, Germaine (Therese) 1933- ... 109
Warkentin, John 1928- ... 9-12R
Warland, John
See Buchanan-Brown, John
Warlick, Ashley 1972- ... 154
Warlick, M(arjorie) E(lizabeth) ... 220
Warlimont, Walter 1894- ... CAP-1
Earlier sketch in CA 13-16
Warlum, Michael Frank 1940- ... 37-40R
Warm, Hermann 1889-1976 ... IDFW 3, 4
Warman, (William) Eric 1904- ... CAP-1
Earlier sketch in CA 13-14
Warman, Henry J(ohn) 1907-1982 ... 41-44R
Obituary ... 133
Warmbrand, Max 1896(?)-1976
Obituary ... 65-68
Warmbrunn, Werner 1920- ... 21-24R
Warmington, Brian Herbert 1924- ... 65-68
Warmington, E(ric) H(erbert) 1898-1987 ... 124
Warmington, William Allan 1922- ... 5-8R
Warmke, Roman F. 1929-1985 ... CANR-9
Earlier sketch in CA 17-20R
Warmond, Ellen
See Ypeyen, Pieternella Cornelia van
Warmuth, Donna Akers 1966- ... 231
Warnath, Charles F. 1925- ... 37-40R
Warne, Clinton L. 1921- ... 13-16R
Warne, Colston Estey 1900-1987
Obituary ... 122
Warne, Randi R(uth) 1952- ... 152
Warne, William E(lmo) 1905-1996 ... 41-44R
Obituary ... 151
Warneke, Sara ... CANR-106
Earlier sketch in CA 167
Warner, Alan 1912- ... 104
Warner, Alan 1964- ... 223
Warner, Alice Sizer 1929- ... 169
Warner, Anne (Richmond) 1869-1913 ... 185
See also DLB 202
Warner, B. F.
See Bowers, Warner Fremont
Warner, Bob
See Warner, Robert
Warner, Brian 1969(?)- ... 181
Warner, Charles Dudley 1829-1900 ... 182
See also DLB 64
See also RGAL 4
Warner, Daniel 1946- ... 141
Warner, Daniel S(umner)
1906-1983 ... CANR-16
Earlier sketch in CA 1-4R
Warner, Deborah Jean 1941- ... 108
Warner, Denis Ashton 1917- ... CANR-3
Earlier sketch in CA 5-8R
Warner, Edythe Records 1916-1980 ... 5-8R
Obituary ... 134
Warner, Elizabeth (Ann) 1940- ... 225
Warner, Emily S(mith) 1902(?)-1980
Obituary ... 97-100
Warner, Esther S.
See Dendel, Esther (Sietmann Warner)
Warner, Francis (Robert le Plastrier)
1937- ... CANR-11
Earlier sketch in CA 53-56
See also CLC 14
See also CP 1, 2
Warner, Frank
See Richardson, Gladwell
Warner, Frank A. ... CANR-26
Earlier sketches in CAP-2, CA 19-20
See also SATA 1, 67
Warner, Gary 1936- ... 21-24R
Warner, (George) Geoffrey John 1923- ... 1-4R
Warner, Gertrude Chandler
1890-1979 ... CANR-3
Earlier sketch in CA 1-4R
See also MAICYA 2
See also SATA 9
See also SATA-Obit 73
Warner, Glen 1947- ... CANR-46
Earlier sketch in CA 121
Warner, H(oyt) Landon 1911-1989 ... 13-16R
Warner, Harry, Jr. 1922- ... 29-32R
Warner, J(ohn) F. 1929- ... 142
See also SATA 75
Warner, Jack 1892-1978
Obituary ... 108
Warner, Jack L(eonard) 1892-1978
Obituary ... 108
See also IDFW 3, 4
Warner, James A(loysius) 1918- ... CANR-24
Earlier sketch in CA 45-48
Warner, Janine C. 1967- ... 232
Warner, Jessica ... 215
Warner, John Harley 1953- ... 127
Warner, Judith 1965- ... 142
Warner, Ken(neth Wilson, Jr.) 1928- . CANR-10
Earlier sketch in CA 65-68
Warner, Kenneth (Lewis) 1915- ... CAP-1
Earlier sketch in CA 9-10
Warner, Langdon 1881-1955
Brief entry ... 112
Warner, Lucien (Hynes) 1900-1963
Obituary ... 112
Warner, Lucille Schulberg ... CANR-11
Earlier sketch in CA 69-72
See also SATA 30
Warner, Malcolm 1953- ... 167
Warner, Malcolm-Jamal 1970- ... 229
Warner, Margaret
See Humphreys, Margaret
Warner, Marina 1946- ... CANR-118
Earlier sketches in CA 65-68, CANR-21, 55
See also CLC 59
See also CN 5, 6, 7
See also DLB 194
See also MTFW 2005
Warner, Martin 1940- ... 137
Warner, Matt
See Fichter, George S.
Warner, Michael 1958- ... 196
Warner, Oliver (Martin Wilson)
1903-1976 ... CANR-3
Obituary ... 69-72
Earlier sketch in CA 1-4R
See also SATA 29
Warner, Penny 1947- ... 165
Warner, Philip (Arthur William)
1914-2000 ... CANR-40
Obituary ... 190
Earlier sketches in CA 101, CANR-18
Warner, Rex (Ernest) 1905-1986 ... 89-92
Obituary ... 119
See also CLC 45
See also CN 1, 2, 3, 4
See also CP 1, 2
See also DLB 15
See also RGEL 2
See also RHW
Warner, Richard 1943- ... 120
Warner, Robert 1905-1992 ... 53-56
Warner, Robert M(ark) 1927- ... CANR-7
Earlier sketch in CA 9-12R
Warner, Sally 1946- ... 200
See also SATA 131
Warner, Sam Bass, Jr. 1928- ... CANR-39
Earlier sketches in CA 5-8R, CANR-2, 17
Warner, Seth 1927- ... 53-56
Warner, Sharon Oard 1952- ... CANR-99
Earlier sketch in CA 138
Warner, Sunny (B.) 1931- ... 178
See also SATA 108
Warner, Susan (Bogert) 1819-1885 .. DLB 3, 42, 239, 250, 254
Warner, Sylvia (Constance) Ashton
See Ashton-Warner, Sylvia (Constance)
Warner, Sylvia Townsend
1893-1978 ... CANR-104
Obituary ... 77-80
Earlier sketches in CA 61-64, CANR-16, 60
See also BRWS 7
See also CLC 7, 19
See also CN 1, 2
See also DLB 34, 139
See also EWL 3
See also FANT
See also FW
See also MTCW 1, 2
See also RGEL 2
See also RGSF 2
See also RHW
See also SSC 23
See also TCLC 131
Warner, Val 1946- ... CANR-23
Earlier sketch in CA 49-52
Warner, Virginia
See Brodine, Virginia Warner
Warner, W(illiam) Lloyd 1898-1970 ... CANR-2
Obituary ... 29-32R
Earlier sketch in CA 1-4R
Warner, Wayne E(arl) 1933- ... CANR-3
Earlier sketch in CA 49-52
Warner, William 1558-1609 ... DLB 172
See also RGEL 2
Warner, William W(hitesides) 1920- ... 134
Brief entry ... 114
Warner-Crozetti, R(uth G.) 1913- ... 101
Warneryd, Karl-Erik 1927- ... 189
Warnes, Tim(othy) 1971- ... 188
See also SATA 116
Warnick, Barbara 1946- ... 120
Warnick, Elsa 1942- ... 185
See also SATA 113
Warnke, Georgia 1951- ... 189
Warnock, G(eoffrey) J(ames)
1923-1995 ... 21-24R
Obituary ... 150
Warnock, (Helen) Mary (Wilson)
1924- ... CANR-89
Earlier sketches in CA 5-8R, CANR-8
Warr, Bertram 1917-1943 ... DLB 88
Warr, Peter B(ryan) 1937- ... 25-28R
Warrack, Graeme Matthew 1913-1985
Obituary ... 115
Warrack, John (Hamilton) 1928- ... CANR-139
Earlier sketches in CA 13-16R, CANR-5
Warraq, Ibn ... 210
Warre, Michael 1922-1987
Obituary ... 121
Warren, Andrea 1946- ... CANR-134
Earlier sketch in CA 165
See also SATA 98
Warren, Andrew
See Tute, Warren (Stanley)
Warren, Austin 1899-1986 ... 17-20R
Obituary ... 120
Warren, Betsy
See Warren, Elizabeth Avery
Warren, Bill 1943- ... 118
Warren, Billy
See Warren, William Stephen
Warren, Cathy 1951- ... 159
See also SATA 62
See also SATA-Brief 46
Warren, Charles 1868-1954 ... 219
Warren, Charles 1948- ... 147
Warren, Charles Marquis 1913(?)-1990
Obituary ... 132
See also TCWW 1, 2
Warren, Clay 1946- ... 219
Warren, Dave
See Wiersbe, Warren W(endell)
Warren, David 1943- ... 77-80
Warren, Dianne 1950- ... 227
Warren, Donald Irwin 1935-1997 ... CANR-1
Obituary ... 158
Earlier sketch in CA 45-48
Warren, Donald R. 1933- ... 111
Warren, Doug(las) 1935-2002 ... CANR-34
Obituary ... 210
Earlier sketch in CA 61-64
Warren, E(ugene) H(oward), Jr. 1943- ... 111
Warren, Earl 1891-1974 ... 123
Obituary ... 49-52
Warren, Elizabeth
See Supraner, Robyn
Warren, Elizabeth Avery 1916- ... CANR-8
Earlier sketch in CA 5-8R
See also SATA 46
See also SATA-Brief 38
Warren, (Francis) Eugene 1941- ... CANR-109
See also Doty, Gene Warren
Warren, Frank A. III 1933-
Brief entry ... 115
Warren, Gordon Harris 1944- ... 114
Warren, Harold Ostrander, Jr. 1910-1985
Obituary ... 116
Warren, Harris G(aylord) 1906-1988 .. CANR-5
Earlier sketch in CA 1-4R
Warren, Harry
See Guaragna, Salvatore
Warren, Jackie M. 1953- ... 204
See also SATA 135
Warren, James E(dward), Jr.
1908-1997 ... CANR-24
Earlier sketch in CA 21-24R
Warren, James Francis 1942- ... CANR-96
Earlier sketch in CA 146
Warren, James Hugo, Jr. 1928(?)-1983
Obituary ... 110
Warren, James Vaughn 1915-1990
Obituary ... 130
Warren, Jefferson T(rowbridge)
1912-1993 ... 41-44R
Warren, (William) John 1937- ... 138
Warren, John Byrne Leicester
See De Tabley, Lord
Warren, Joshua P(aul) 1976- ... SATA 107
Warren, Joyce W(illiams) 1935- ... 77-80
See also SATA 18
Warren, Karen J. 1947- ... 168
Warren, Kay B(arbara) 1947- ... 206
Warren, Kenneth 1931- ... 109
Warren, Kenneth W. 1957- ... 147
Warren, Lansing 1894-1987
Obituary ... 124
Warren, Lella 1899-1982 ... 199
Obituary ... 113
See also DLBY 1983
Warren, Leonard 1924- ... 180
Warren, Louis Austin 1885-1983 ... CANR-21
Obituary ... 110
Earlier sketch in CA 5-8R
Warren, Louise 1909(?)-1981
Obituary ... 104
Warren, Lucian (Crissey) 1913-1988 ... 101
Obituary ... 126
Warren, Mary Bondurant 1930- ... CANR-52
Earlier sketches in CA 73-76, CANR-12, 27
Warren, Mary Douglas
See Greig, Maysie
Warren, Mary Phraner 1929- ... CANR-5
Earlier sketch in CA 53-56
See also SATA 10
Warren, Matthew Madison 1907-1986
Obituary ... 119
Warren, Mercy Otis 1728-1814 ... DLB 31, 200
See also RGAL 4
See also TUS
Warren, Michael 1935- ... 112
Warren, Michael 1946- ... 174

Cumulative Index 605 Waterston

Warren, Mike
See Warren, Michael
Warren, Nagueyalti 1947- 190
Warren, Neil Clark 1934- 220
Warren, Patricia Nell 1936- CANR-89
Earlier sketches in CA 45-48, CANR-1
See also Kilina, Patricia
Warren, Peter Whitson 1941- CANR-5
Earlier sketch in CA 53-56
Warren, Richard (Andrew) 1961- 146
Warren, Richard M. 1925- 112
Warren, Rick 1954- 224
Warren, Robert Penn 1905-1989 ...... CANR-47
Obituary 129
Earlier sketches in CA 13-16R, CANR-10
Interview in CANR-10
See also AITN 1
See also AMW
See also AMWC 2
See also BPFB 3
See also BYA 1
See also CDALB 1968-1988
See also CLC 1, 4, 6, 8, 10, 13, 18, 39, 53, 59
See also CN 1, 2, 3, 4
See also CP 1, 2
See also DA
See also DA3
See also DAB
See also DAC
See also DAM MST, NOV, POET
See also DLB 2, 48, 152, 320
See also DLBY 1980, 1989
See also EWL 3
See also MAL 5
See also MTCW 1, 2
See also MTFW 2005
See also NFS 13
See also PC 37
See also RGAL 4
See also RGSF 2
See also RHW
See also SATA 46
See also SATA-Obit 63
See also SSC 4, 58
See also SSFS 8
See also TUS
See also WLC
Warren, Roland L(eslie) 1915- CANR-51
Earlier sketches in CA 57-60, CANR-10, 26
Warren, Rosanna 1953- 145
See also CP 7
See also PFS 13, 23
Warren, Samuel 1807-1877 .... DLB 190
Warren, Sandra K. 1944- 138
Warren, Scott S. 1957- 215
See also SATA 79
Warren, Sidney 1916- 25-28R
Warren, Thomas (Bratton) 1920- 103
Warren, Thomas L(eo) 1937- 111
Warren, Vernon
See Chapman, G(eorge) W(arren) Vernon
Warren, Victoria 1971- 202
Warren, Virginia Burgess 1913- 13-16R
Warren, W(ilfred) Lewis 1929-1994 . CANR-21
Earlier sketch in CA 1-4R
Warren, W(illiam) Preston 1901-1988 ... 37-40R
Warren, William Stephen 1882-1968 .... CAP-2
Earlier sketch in CA 21-22
See also SATA 9
Warrender, James Howard 1922-1985
Obituary 116
Warrick, Patricia Scott 1925- CANR-25
Earlier sketches in CA 61-64, CANR-8
See also SATA 35
Warrigal, Jack
See Furphy, Joseph
Warriner, Charles K(ing) 1920- 41-44R
Warriner, John 1907(?)-1987
Obituary 123
See also SATA-Obit 53
Warrington, Freda 1956- .... FANT
Warrner, Thomas W(endell) 1955- 118
Warry, J(ohn) G(ibson) 1916- 5-8R
Warsaw, Irene CAP-1
Earlier sketch in CA 13-16
Warsh
See Warshaw, Jerry
Warsh, David (Lewis) 1944- 118
Warsh, Lewis 1944- CANR-24
Earlier sketches in CA 61-64, CANR-9
See also CP 1, 2, 3, 4, 5, 6, 7
Warshaw, Jerry 1929- CANR-14
Earlier sketch in CA 37-40R
See also SATA 30
Warshaw, Leon J(oseph) 1917-2001 107
Obituary 192
Warshaw, Mary 1931- .... SATA 89
Warshawski, Morrie 207
Warshofsky, Fred 1931- CANR-94
Earlier sketches in CA 9-12R, CANR-45
See also SATA 24
Warshofsky, Isaac
See Singer, Isaac Bashevis
Wartels, Nat(han) 1902-1990
Obituary 130
Wartenberg, Thomas E. 1949- 195
Warth, Robert D(ouglas) 1921- 9-12R
Wartofsky, Marx W(illiam) 1928-1997 .. 41-44R
Obituary 157
Wartofsky, (William) Victor 1931- 29-32R
Warton, Joseph 1722-1800 .... DLB 104, 109
See also RGEL 2
Warton, Thomas 1728-1790 .... DAM POET
See also DLB 104, 109
See also RGEL 2
Wartski, Maureen (Ann Crane) 1940- 89-92
See also BYA 6, 7
See also SATA 50
See also SATA-Brief 37
See also YAW
Waruk, Kona
See Harris, (Theodore) Wilson
Warung, Price
See Astley, William
See also DLB 230
See also RGEL 2
See also TCLC 45
Warwick, Alan R(oss) 1900-1973 112
See also SATA 42
Warwick, Christopher 1949- 110
Warwick, Dennis 1930- 73-76
Warwick, Dolores
See Frese, Dolores Warwick
Warwick, Donald P(hillip) 1934- 118
Warwick, Granville
See Griffith, D(avid Lewelyn) W(ark)
Warwick, Jack 1930- 29-32R
Warwick, James 1894(?)-1983
Obituary 110
Warwick, Jarvis
See Garner, Hugh
See also CCA 1
Warwick, Ray 1911(?)-1983
Obituary 109
Warwick, Roger 1912-1991 109
Obituary 135
Warzeski, Walter C. 1929- 37-40R
Wasby, Stephen L(ewis) 1937- 139
Wa-Sha-Quon-Asin
See Belaney, Archibald Stansfeld
Wa-sha-quon-asin
See Belaney, Archibald Stansfeld
Washburn, (Henry) Bradford (Jr.)
1910- CANR-3
Earlier sketch in CA 49-52
See also SATA 38
Washburn, Charles 1890(?)-1972
Obituary 104
Washburn, Dorothy K(oster) 1945- ... CANR-24
Earlier sketch in CA 106
Washburn, Jan(ice) 1926- 93-96
See also SATA 63
Washburn, L(ivia) J(ane) 1957- .... TCWW 2
Washburn, Mark 1948- 77-80
Washburn, O(swell) A(aron) 1914-1993 .. 57-60
Washburn, Patrick S(cott) 1941- 145
Washburn, Sherwood L(arned) 1911-2000
Obituary 189
Brief entry 105
Washburn, Stan 1943- CANR-95
Earlier sketch in CA 146
Washburn, Wilcomb Edward
1925-1997 .... 41-44R
Obituary 156
Washburne, Carleton W(olsey)
1889-1968 .... CAP-1
Earlier sketch in CA 13-16
Washburne, Carolyn Kott 1944- 151
See also SATA 86
Washburne, Heluiz Chandler
1892-1970 .... CAP-1
Obituary 104
Earlier sketch in CA 11-12
See also SATA 10
See also SATA-Obit 26
Washington, Alex
See Harris, Mark
Washington, Booker T(aliaferro)
1856-1915 125
Brief entry 114
See also BLC 3
See also BW 1
See also DA3
See also DAM MULT
See also LAIT 2
See also RGAL 4
See also SATA 28
See also TCLC 10
Washington, Chester Lloyd 1902-1983
Obituary 110
Washington, Donna L. 1967- 166
See also SATA 98, 159
Washington, Ellis 1961- 228
Washington, George 1732-1799 .... DLB 31
Washington, Gladys J(oseph) 1931- 29-32R
Washington, Harold R(obert) 1935- 112
Washington, Ida Harrison 1924- CANR-35
Earlier sketch in CA 107
Washington, James Melvin 1948-1997 149
Obituary 158
Washington, Johnny 1946- 229
Washington, Joseph R(eed), Jr. 1930- 9-12R
Washington, (Catherine) Marguerite Beauchamp
1892-1972 .... CAP-1
Earlier sketch in CA 9-10
Washington, Mary Helen 1941- CANR-51
Earlier sketches in CA 65-68, CANR-26
See also BW 2, 3
Washington, Ned 1901-1976 .... DLB 265
Washington, Pat Beauchamp
See Washington, (Catherine) Marguerite Beauchamp
Washington, Warren M(orton) 1936- 168
Washton, Nathan S(eymour) 1916- 53-56
Wasiolek, Edward 1924- CANR-6
Earlier sketch in CA 1-4R
Waskin, Yvonne 1923- 21-24R
Waskow, Arthur I(rwin) 1933- CANR-103
Earlier sketches in CA 5-8R, CANR-4
Wasley, Robert S(echrist) 1918-1994 ..... 17-20R
Wasmuth, William J. 1925- CANR-24
Earlier sketch in CA 45-48
Wason, Betty
See Wason, Elizabeth
Wason, Elizabeth 1912- CANR-2
Earlier sketch in CA 1-4R
Wason, P(eter) C(athcart) 1924-2003 45-48
Obituary 216
Wasow, Mona 1933- 110
Wasowski, Sally
See Wasowski, Sara Ann
Wasowski, Sara Ann 1946- 223
Wass, Sir Douglas (William Gretton)
1923- 138
Wassenaar, Ella
See Wassenaar, Ella
Wassenbergh, Henri Abraham 1924- 21-24R
Wasser, Henry H. 1919- CANR-8
Earlier sketch in CA 21-24R
Wasserfall, Adel 1918- CANR-6
Earlier sketch in CA 1-4R
Wasserman, Aaron O(sias) 1927- 53-56
Wasserman, Burton 1929- 53-56
Wasserman, Dale 1917- 49-52
Wasserman, Earl R(eeves) 1913-1973 .... CAP-2
Earlier sketch in CA 17-18
Wasserman, Gary 1944- 69-72
Wasserman, Harriet 167
Wasserman, Harvey 1945- CANR-27
Earlier sketch in CA 45-48
Wasserman, Jack 1921- 61-64
Wasserman, Jerry 231
Wasserman, John L. 1938- 77-80
Wasserman, Lew 1913-2002 .... IDFW 3, 4
Wasserman, Mark 1946- CANR-118
Earlier sketches in CA 125, CANR-56
Wasserman, Max Judd 1895-1977 ..... CANR-4
Earlier sketch in CA 5-8R
Wasserman, Paul 1924- CANR-25
Earlier sketches in CA 1-4R, CANR-1
Wasserman, Pauline 1943- CANR-24
Earlier sketch in CA 110
Wasserman, Selma (Ginsberg) 1929- 5-8R
Wasserman, Sheldon 1940-1992 ...... CANR-24
Obituary 137
Earlier sketches in CA 65-68, CANR-9
Wassermann, (Karl) Jakob 1873-1934 163
Brief entry 104
See also DLB 66
See also EWL 3
See also TCLC 6
Wasserstein, Abraham 1921-1995 109
Wasserstein, Bernard (Mano Julius)
1948- CANR-90
Earlier sketch in CA 143
Wasserstein, Bruce 1947- 37-40R
Wasserstein, Susan 1952- 107
Wasserstein, Wendy 1950- CANR-128
Brief entry 121
Earlier sketches in CA 129, CANR-53, 75
Interview in CA-129
See also CABS 3
See also AMWS 15
See also CAD
See also CD 5, 6
See also CLC 32, 59, 90, 183
See also CWD
See also DA3
See also DAM DRAM
See also DC 4
See also DFS 5, 17
See also DLB 228
See also EWL 3
See also FW
See also MAL 5
See also MTCW 2
See also MTFW 2005
See also SATA 94
Wasserstrom, Richard Alan 1936- CANR-6
Earlier sketch in CA 1-4R
Wasserstrom, (Jacob) William
1922-1985 .... 9-12R
Obituary 115
Wassersug, Joseph D. 1912- 17-20R
Wassil, Aly 1930- 17-20R
Wassil-Grimm, Claudette 1948(?)- 237
Wassiljewa, Tatjana 1928- 176
See also SATA 106
Wassmer, Arthur C(harles) 1947- 103
Wassmo, Herbjorg 1942- 164
See also DLB 297
Wassner, Selig O. 1923- 25-28R
Wasson, Ben 1899(?)-1982
Obituary 114
Wasson, Chester R(eynolds)
1906-1987 .... CANR-10
Earlier sketch in CA 13-16R
Wasson, David Atwood 1823-1887 .... DLB 1, 223
Wasson, Donald 1914(?)-1976
Obituary 69-72
Wasson, John M. 1928- 45-48
Wasson, R(obert) Gordon 1898-1986 153
Brief entry 116
Wastberg, Per 1933- 193
See also CWW 2
See also EWL 3
Wasti, Syed R(azi) 1929- CANR-7
Earlier sketch in CA 13-16R
Waswo, Richard 1939- 53-56
Watada, Terry 1951- 164
Watanabe, Hitoshi 1919- 73-76
Watanabe, Ruth T(aiko) 1916- 37-40R
Watanabe, Shigeo 1928- CANR-45
Earlier sketch in CA 112
See also CLR 8
See also MAICYA 1, 2
See also SATA 39, 131
See also SATA-Brief 32
Watanabe, Yoshio 1907- 216
Watanna, Onoto
See Eaton, (Lillie) Winnifred
Waten, Judah
See Waten, Judah Leon
See also CN 1, 2, 3
See also DLB 289
Waten, Judah Leon 1911-1985 101
Water, Silas
See Loomis, Noel M(iller)
Waterfield, Gordon 1903-1987 61-64
Obituary 124
Waterfield, Robin (Everard) 1914-2002 ... 49-52
Obituary 201
Waterford, Van
See Wanrooy, Willem F(rederik)
Waterhouse, Carole A. 1957- 231
Waterhouse, Charles 1924- 29-32R
Waterhouse, Ellis K(irkham) 1905-1985 .. 65-68
Obituary 117
Waterhouse, Jane 1950(?)- .... BYA 12
Waterhouse, Keith (Spencer)
1929- CANR-109
Earlier sketches in CA 5-8R, CANR-38, 67
See also CBD
See also CD 6
See also CLC 47
See also CN 1, 2, 3, 4, 5, 6, 7
See also DLB 13, 15
See also MTCW 1, 2
See also MTFW 2005
Waterhouse, Larry G(ene) 1944- 37-40R
Waterhouse, Roger 1940- 129
Waterlow, Charlotte 1915- 25-28R
Waterman, Andrew (John) 1940- CANR-57
Earlier sketches in CA 109, CANR-31
See also CP 7
See also DLB 40
Waterman, Arthur E. 1926- 17-20R
Waterman, Bic
See Joseph, Stephen M.
Waterman, Cary (Martha) 1942- 103
Waterman, Charles F(rederick) 1913- 49-52
Waterman, Guy 1932-2000 97-100
Obituary 188
Waterman, John Thomas 1918- CANR-8
Earlier sketch in CA 5-8R
Waterman, Jonathan 1956- CANR-108
Earlier sketch in CA 151
Waterman, Laura 1939- 97-100
Waterman, Leroy 1875-1972 .... CAP-1
Obituary 33-36R
Earlier sketch in CA 19-20
Waterman, Margaret 1909-2001 .... 37-40R
Waterman, Richard Alan 1914-1971
Obituary 111
Waterman, Richard W. 1952- 192
Watermeier, Daniel J(ude) 1940- 73-76
Water Rat
See Jones, Stephen (Phillip)
Waters, Barbara 235
Waters, Bob 1921(?)-1987
Obituary 122
Waters, Brian Power
See Power-Waters, Brian
Waters, Catherine C.
See Cash, Catherine
Waters, Chocolate 1949- 77-80
Waters, Chris
See Waters, Harold A(rthur)
Waters, D(avid) W(atkin) 1911- 25-28R
Waters, Enoch P. 1910(?)-1987 134
Obituary 122
Waters, Ethel 1896-1977 81-84
Obituary 73-76
Waters, Frank (Joseph) 1902-1995 .. CANR-121
Obituary 149
Earlier sketches in CA 5-8R, CANR-3, 18, 63
See also CAAS 13
See also CLC 88
See also DLB 212
See also DLBY 1986
See also RGAL 4
See also TCWW 1, 2
Waters, Harold A(rthur) 1926- 53-56
Waters, James E. 1922-2002
Obituary 208
Waters, James E. 1922-2002
Obituary 208
Waters, John 1946- 130
Brief entry 126
Interview in CA-130
See also AAYA 16
Waters, John F(rederick) 1930- CANR-46
Earlier sketches in CA 37-40R, CANR-23
See also SATA 4
Waters, K(enneth) H(ugh) 1912- 120
Waters, Marianne
See Waters, Chocolate
Waters, Mary C. .... CLC 70
Waters, Mary Yukari 1965- 234
Waters, Mary-Alice 1942- CANR-9
Earlier sketch in CA 61-64
Waters, Michael 1949- CANR-142
Earlier sketches in CA 65-68, CANR-10, 27, 56
See also CP 7
See also DLB 120
Waters, Roger 1944- .... CLC 35
Waters, Sarah 1966- 206
Waters, Thomas F(rank) 1926- 81-84
Waters, Tony 1958- 142
See also SATA 75
Waters, William R(oland) 1920- 49-52
Waterston, Albert 1907-2001 .... CAP-1
Obituary 202
Earlier sketch in CA 13-14

Waterston, Alisse 1951- ... 146
Waterston, Barbara Johns 1940- ... 25-28R
Waterston, (Margaret) Elizabeth (Hillman) 1922- ... 69-72
Waterton, Betty (Marie) 1923- ... CANR-56
Earlier sketches in CA 111, CANR-28
See also SATA 37, 99
See also SATA-Brief 34
Watford, Christopher M. 1978- ... 226
Wathen, Richard B. 1917- ... 37-40R
Wathern, Peter 1947- ... 105
Watjen, Carolyn L. T. ... 85-88
Watkin, David 1925- ... IDFW 3, 4
Watkin, David (John) 1941- ... CANR-51
Earlier sketches in CA 29-32R, CANR-26
Watkin, Edward Ingram 1888-1981
Obituary ... 103
Watkin, Lawrence Edward 1901-1981 ... 81-84
Watkins, A(rthur) M(artin) 1924- ... CANR-7
Earlier sketch in CA 9-12R
Watkins, Alan (Rhun) 1933- ... 104
Watkins, Arthur Rich 1916- ... 41-44R
Watkins, Arthur Thomas Levi 1907-1965 .. 5-8R
Watkins, Arthur V(ivian) 1886-1973
Obituary ... 111
Watkins, Dawn L. ... SATA 126
Watkins, Dawn L. ... 196
Watkins, Elizabeth Siegel ... 187
Watkins, Evan Paul 1946- ... 104
Watkins, Floyd C. 1920-2000 ... CANR-18
Earlier sketches in CA 1-4R, CANR-2
Watkins, Frances Ellen
See Harper, Frances Ellen Watkins
Watkins, Gerrold
See Malzberg, Barry N(athaniel)
Watkins, Glenn (Elson) 1927-
Brief entry ... 117
Watkins, Gloria Jean 1952(?)- ... CANR-126
Earlier sketches in CA 143, CANR-87
See also BW 2
See also CLC 94
See also DLB 246
See also MTCW 2
See also MTFW 2005
See also SATA 115
Watkins, Gordon R(onald) 1930- ... 37-40R
Watkins, Grace F. 1927- ... 21-24R
Watkins, Graham 1944- ... 150
Watkins, Gwen(doline Mary) 1923- ... 116
Watkins, J(ohn) W(illiam) N(evill) 1924-1999 ... 21-24R
Obituary ... 185
Watkins, Jane 1929- ... 77-80
Watkins, Joan C.
See Casale, Joan T(herese)
Watkins, John C(umming), Jr. 1935- ... 113
Watkins, John G(oodrich) 1913- ... CANR-38
Earlier sketches in CA 1-4R, CANR-1, 17
Watkins, Keith 1931- ... 106
Watkins, Lois 1930- ... SATA 88
Watkins, Mark Hanna 1903-1976
Obituary ... 65-68
Watkins, Mary M. 1950- ... CANR-44
Earlier sketches in CA 104, CANR-20
Watkins, Mel 1940- ... CANR-117
Earlier sketch in CA 89-92
Watkins, Nicholas 1946- ... 148
Watkins, Paul 1964- ... CANR-98
Earlier sketches in CA 132, CANR-62
See also CLC 55
Watkins, Peter 1934- ... 109
See also SATA 66
Watkins, Ralph J(ames) 1896-1984 ... 45-48
Obituary ... 113
Watkins, (Arthur) Ronald (Dare) 1904-2001 ... 53-56
Obituary ... 193
Watkins, Ronald J(oseph) 1945- ... 133
Watkins, Stephen Hulme 1954- ... 165
Watkins, Steve
See Watkins, Stephen Hulme
Watkins, Steve 1954- ... 174
Watkins, T(homas) H(enry) 1936-2000 ... CANR-97
Earlier sketches in CA 37-40R, CANR-14, 31, 57
Watkins, Tobias 1780-1855 ... DLB 73
Watkins, Vernon Phillips 1906-1967 ... CAP-1
Obituary ... 25-28R
Earlier sketch in CA 9-10
See also CLC 43
See also DLB 20
See also EWL 3
See also RGEL 2
Watkins, William John 1942- ... CANR-58
Earlier sketches in CA 41-44R, CANR-56
See also SFW 4
Watkins, Yoko Kawashima 1933- ... 158
See also BYA 14
See also LAIT 4
See also SATA 93
Watkinson, John 1950- ... 143
Watkinson, Sandra
See Haarsager, Sandra (L.)
Watkinson, Valerie
See Elliston, Valerie Mae (Watkinson)
Watkins-Pitchford, Denys James 1905-1990 ... CANR-38
Obituary ... 132
Earlier sketches in CA 9-12R, CANR-4
See also CWRI 5
See also SAAS 4
See also SATA 6, 87
See also SATA-Obit 66
Watkyn, Arthur
See Watkins, Arthur Thomas Levi
Watland, Charles D(unton) 1913-1972 .. CAP-2
Earlier sketch in CA 25-28
Watling, James 1933- ... SATA 67, 117
Watlington, Patricia (Sue) 1933- ... 37-40R
Watmough, David 1926- ... CANR-33
Earlier sketches in CA 85-88, CANR-15
See also CN 3, 4, 5, 6, 7
See also DLB 53
Watney, John B(asil) 1915-1995 ... CANR-5
Obituary ... 148
Earlier sketch in CA 9-12R
Watney, Sanders (?)-1983
Obituary ... 109
Watney, Simon 1949- ... GLL 2
Watrous, James Scales 1908-1999 ... 141
Watrous, Livingston Vance 1943- ... 165
Watrous, Richard H. 1952- ... 189
Watson, (John Hugh) Adam 1914- ... CANR-17
Earlier sketch in CA 25-28R
Watson, Alan
See Watson, William Alexander Jardine
Watson, Alan D(ouglas) 1942- ... CANR-6
Earlier sketch in CA 57-60
Watson, Aldren A(uld) 1917- ... CANR-39
Earlier sketches in CA 81-84, CANR-4
See also SATA 42
See also SATA-Brief 36
Watson, Amy Zakrzewski 1965- ... 143
See also SATA 76
Watson, Andrew Samuel 1920- ... 45-48
Watson, Anthony I. 1926-1990
Obituary ... 132
Watson, B. S.
See Teitelbaum, Michael
Watson, Barbara Bellow ... 77-80
Watson, Ben 1956- ... CANR-94
Earlier sketch in CA 146
Watson, Benjamin A. 1961- ... 173
Watson, Bernard B(ennett) 1911-1977
Obituary ... 69-72
Watson, Billy 1938- ... 77-80
Watson, Brad ... 215
See also CSW
Watson, Burton (DeWitt) 1925- ... CANR-18
Earlier sketches in CA 5-8R, CANR-3
Watson, Carol 1949- ... 146
See also SATA 78
Watson, Charles N(elles, Jr.) 1939- ... 113
Watson, Charles S(t. Denis), Jr. 1934- ... 61-64
Watson, Clarissa ... 69-72
Watson, Clyde 1947- ... CANR-39
Earlier sketches in CA 49-52, CANR-4
See also CLR 3
See also MAICYA 1, 2
See also SATA 5, 68
Watson, Colin 1920-1983 ... CANR-60
Obituary ... 108
Earlier sketches in CA 1-4R, CANR-2
See also CMW 4
See also DLB 276
Watson, Cynthia 1957- ... 137
Watson, David 1934- ... CANR-49
Earlier sketches in CA 45-48, CANR-24
Watson, David Christopher Knight 1934(?)-1984
Obituary ... 112
Watson, David Robin 1935- ... 109
Watson, Derek 1948- ... 129
Watson, Donald 1946- ... 170
Watson, Donald Stevenson 1909-1983 . CAP-1
Earlier sketch in CA 13-14
Watson, E(lliot) L(ovegood) Grant 1885-1970 ... CAP-1
Earlier sketch in CA 11-12
Watson, Elaine 1921- ... 115
Watson, Ellen Dore 1950- ... 172
Watson, Ernest W(illiam) 1884-1969 ... 5-8R
Obituary ... 134
Watson, Eunice L. 1932- ... 65-68
Watson, F. J. B.
See Watson, Francis John Bagott
Watson, Fiona J. ... 228
Watson, Fletcher Guard (Jr.) 1912-1997 ... 5-8R
Obituary ... 158
Watson, Francis (Leslie) 1907-1988
Obituary ... 127
Watson, Francis John Bagott 1907-1992
Brief entry ... 116
Watson, Francis M(arion) 1921- ... 105
Watson, Frank
See Ames, Francis H.
Watson, Gayle Hudgens
See Hudgens, A(lice) Gayle
Watson, George (Grimes) 1927- ... CANR-42
Earlier sketches in CA 13-16R, CANR-5, 20
Watson, George (Henry) 1936- ... 77-80
Watson, Goodwin 1899(?)-1976
Obituary ... 69-72
Watson, Graham (Angus) 1913-2002 ... 104
Obituary ... 210
Watson, Harold M. 1924- ... 37-40R
Watson, Harry Legare 1949- ... 111
Watson, Helen Orr 1892-1978 ... 5-8R
Obituary ... 77-80
See also SATA-Obit 24
Watson, (George) Hugh (Nicholas) Seton
See Seton-Watson, (George) Hugh (Nicholas)
Watson, Ian 1943- ... CANR-119
Earlier sketches in CA 61-64, CANR-24, 54
See also AAYA 56
See also DLB 261
See also HGG
See also SCFW 2
See also SFW 4
Watson, Irving S.
See Mencken, H(enry) L(ouis)
Watson, J(ohn) R(ichard) 1934- ... CANR-144
Earlier sketches in CA 97-100, CANR-18, 39
Watson, J(ohn) Steven 1916- ... 5-8R
Watson, J(ames) Wreford 1915-1990 ... CANR-19
Obituary ... 132
Earlier sketch in CA 25-28R
See also Wreford, James
Watson, Jack Brierley 1927- ... 104
Watson, James 1936- ... CANR-4
Earlier sketch in CA 53-56
See also CWRI 5
See also SATA 10, 106
Watson, James B(ennett) 1918- ... 41-44R
Watson, James D(ewey) 1928- ... CANR-139
Earlier sketches in CA 25-28R, CANR-46, 116
See also MTFW 2005
See also NCFS 2
Watson, James Gray 1939- ... 29-32R
Watson, Jane Werner 1915- ... CANR-8
Earlier sketch in CA 5-8R
See also SATA 3, 54
Watson, Janet Lynch
See Lynch-Watson, Janet
Watson, Jean 1933- ... 211
Watson, Jean 1936- ... CANR-41
Earlier sketches in CA 89-92, CANR-16
Watson, John 1850-1907 ... CWRI 5
See also DLB 156
Watson, John A(rthur) F(ergus) 1903-1978 ... 65-68
Watson, John H.
See Farmer, Philip Jose
Watson, Julia 1943-1991 ... CANR-15
Earlier sketch in CA 41-44R
See also RHW
Watson, Ken 1925(?)-1984
Obituary ... 114
Watson, Larry 1947- ... CANR-103
Earlier sketch in CA 160
See also MTFW 2005
Watson, Leland Hale 1926-1989
Obituary ... 130
Watson, Lyall 1939- ... CANR-120
Earlier sketches in CA 57-60, CANR-8, 24, 62
Watson, Margaret Goodrich 1913-1979 ... 13-16R
Watson, Mark Skinner 1887-1966
Obituary ... 89-92
Watson, Mary 1953- ... SATA 117
Watson, Mary Ann 1944- ... 144
Watson, Mary Gordon
See Gordon-Watson, Mary
Watson, Michael (C.) 1958- ... 161
Watson, N. Cameron 1955- ... SATA 81
Watson, Nan Marriott
See Marriott-Watson, Nan
Watson, Nancy Dingman ... CANR-4
Earlier sketch in CA 49-52
See also SATA 32
Watson, O(scar) Michael 1936- ... 33-36R
Watson, Patricia Seets 1930-1997 ... 121
Watson, Patrick 1929- ... 97-100
Watson, Patty Jo (Andersen) 1932- ... CANR-13
Earlier sketch in CA 77-80
Watson, Pauline 1925- ... CANR-29
Earlier sketches in CA 69-72, CANR-11
See also SATA 14
Watson, Peter Frank Patrick 1943- . CANR-109
Earlier sketch in CA 147
Watson, Peter L(eslie) 1944- ... 53-56
Watson, Philip S(aville) 1909- ... 104
Watson, R(ichard) L(yness) 1945- ... 188
Watson, Richard A(bernethy) 1923- .. CANR-25
Earlier sketch in CA 45-48
Watson, Richard A(llan) 1931- ... CANR-93
Earlier sketch in CA 77-80
Watson, Richard F.
See Silverberg, Robert
Watson, Richard Jesse 1951- ... SATA 62
Watson, Richard L(yness), Jr. 1914-2000 ... 17-20R
Obituary ... 190
Watson, Robert (Winthrop) 1925- ... CANR-4
Earlier sketch in CA 1-4R
See also CP 1, 2, 3, 4, 5, 6, 7
Watson, Robert I(rving) 1909-1980
Obituary ... 111
Watson, Robert N(athaniel) 1953- ... 118
Watson, Roderick (Bruce) 1943- ... 102
See also CP 2
Watson, Rosamund Marriott 1860-1911 ... 207
See also DLB 240
Watson, Russell 1939- ... 77-80
Watson, Sally (Lou) 1924- ... CANR-3
Earlier sketch in CA 5-8R
See also SATA 3
See also YAW
Watson, Sara Ruth 1907-1995 ... 37-40R
Watson, Sheila 1909-1998 ... 155
See also AITN 2
See also CCA 1
See also DAC
See also DLB 60
Watson, Sophia 1962- ... 158
Watson, Stephen 1954- ... 211
Watson, Sterling ... 225
Watson, Steven 1947- ... 135
Watson, Thomas 1545(?)-1592 ... DLB 132
See also RGEL 2
Watson, Thomas J(ohn), Jr. 1914-1993 ... 138
Obituary ... 143
See also BEST 90:4
Watson, Thomas J(oel) 1948- ... 109
Watson, Tom, Jr. 1918- ... 21-24R
Watson, Wendy (McLeod) 1942- ... CANR-122
Earlier sketches in CA 49-52, CANR-4, 39
See also MAICYA 1, 2
See also SATA 5, 74, 142
Watson, Wilfred 1911-1998 ... 164
See also CP 1, 2
See also DLB 60
Watson, Will
See Floren, Lee
Watson, William 1858-1935 ... RGEL 2
Watson, William 1917- ... 9-12R
Watson, William Alexander Jardine 1933- ... CANR-12
Earlier sketch in CA 13-16R
Watson Taylor, Elizabeth 1915- ... SATA 41
Watson-Watt, Robert A(lexander) 1892-1973 ... CAP-1
Obituary ... 45-48
Earlier sketch in CA 13-14
Watstein, Esther 1928- ... 57-60
Watt, Alan 1901- ... 197
Watt, Alan 1965- ... 201
Watt, Ben 1962- ... 202
Watt, (John) David (Henry) 1932-1987 ... 133
Obituary ... 122
Watt, David Harrington 1957- ... 141
Watt, Donald 1938- ... 41-44R
Watt, Donald Beates 1893-1977
Obituary ... 73-76
Watt, Donald Cameron
See Cameron Watt, Donald
Watt, Donley 1940- ... CANR-88
Earlier sketch in CA 154
Watt, Douglas (Benjamin) 1914- ... 69-72
Watt, Frank Hedden 1889-1981
Obituary ... 105
Watt, Frederick B. 1901- ... 129
Watt, George Steven Harvie
See Harvie-Watt, George Steven
Watt, (Raymond Egerton) Harry 1906-1987
Obituary ... 122
Watt, Ian (Pierre) 1917-1999 ... CANR-106
Earlier sketch in CA 13-16R
Watt, James G(aius) 1938- ... 144
Watt, John Robertson 1934- ... 37-40R
Watt, Kelly 1958- ... 204
Watt, Kenneth E(dmund) F(erguson) 1929- ... 61-64
Watt, Melanie 1975- ... SATA 136
Watt, Richard M(artin) 1930- ... 5-8R
Watt, Ruth M. 1919- ... CANR-10
Earlier sketch in CA 57-60
Watt, Thomas 1935- ... 37-40R
See also SATA 4
Watt, W(illiam) Montgomery 1909- .. CANR-44
Earlier sketches in CA 1-4R, CANR-6, 21
Wattar, Al-Tahir 1936- ... EWL 3
Wattel, Harold Louis 1921- ... 126
Watten, Barrett 1948- ... DLB 193
Wattenbarger, James L(orenzo) 1922- ... 106
Wattenberg, Ben J. 1933- ... CANR-33
Earlier sketch in CA 57-60
Wattenberg, Martin P(aul) 1956- ... CANR-144
Earlier sketch in CA 142
Wattenberg, Miriam 1924-
See Berg, Mary
Wattenberg, William W(olff) 1911-1993 ... 21-24R
Wattenmaker, Richard J. 1941- ... 104
Watter, Lola Sheila 1925- ... CP 1
Watters, Barbara H(unt) 1907-1984 ... CANR-3
Obituary ... 111
Earlier sketch in CA 5-8R
Watters, Eugene Rutherford 1919- ... CP 1
Watters, (Walter) Pat(terson) 1927- ... CANR-8
Earlier sketch in CA 21-24R
Watters, R(eginald) E(yre) 1912-1979 ... 25-28R
Watterson, Bill 1958- ... CANR-141
Earlier sketch in CA 134
See also AAYA 9, 63
See also SATA 66
Watterson, Henry 1840-1921 ... 182
See also DLB 25
Watterson, Joseph 1900-1972 ... CAP-2
Obituary ... 33-36R
Earlier sketch in CA 25-28
Watt-Evans, Lawrence 1954- ... CANR-99
Earlier sketches in CA 102, CANR-32, 73
See also Evans, Lawrence Watt
See also SATA 121
Wattie, Margaret
See 'Espinasse, Margaret
Wattles, Santha Rama Rau 1923- ... CANR-1
Earlier sketch in CA 1-4R
Watts, A. J.
See Watts, Anthony J(ohn)
Watts, Al(bert) L. 1934- ... 85-88
Watts, Alan (Wilson) 1915-1973 ... CANR-32
Obituary ... 45-48
Earlier sketch in CA 41-44R
See also DLB 16
Watts, Alan (James) 1925- ... 108
Watts, Ann Chalmers 1938- ... 53-56
Watts, Anthony J(ohn) 1942- ... CANR-11
Earlier sketch in CA 25-28R
Watts, (Anna) Bernadette 1942- ... CANR-31
Earlier sketch in CA 29-32R
See also SATA 4, 103
Watts, Charles Edwin 1929- ... CANR-2
Earlier sketch in CA 5-8R
Watts, David 1935- ... 53-56
Watts, Duncan J. 1971- ... 223
Watts, Elizabeth (Bailey) Smithgall 1941- ... CANR-12
Earlier sketch in CA 73-76
Watts, Emily Stipes 1936- ... 81-84
Watts, Ephraim
See Horne, Richard Henry Hengist

Cumulative Index 607 Webb

Watts, Franklin (Mowry) 1904-1978 ... CANR-9
Obituary ... 89-92
Earlier sketches in CAP-2, CA 25-28
See also SATA 46
See also SATA-Obit 21
Watts, George W(illiam) 1952- ... 139
Watts, Harold H(olliday) 1906-1996 ... CAP-2
Earlier sketch in CA 13-14
Watts, Harriet M(ayor) 1933- ... 45-48
Watts, Helen L. Hoke 1903-1990 ... CANR-43
Obituary ... 131
See also Hoke, Helen
Watts, Irene N(aemi) 1931- ... SATA 56, 111
Watts, Isaac 1674-1748 ... DLB 95
See also RGEL 2
See also SATA 52
Watts, J(ulius) C(aesar), Jr. 1957- ... 224
Watts, J(ames) Wash(ington) 1896-1970(?) ... CANR-20
Earlier sketch in CA 1-4R
Watts, James K(ennedy) M(offitt) 1955- ... SATA 59
Watts, Jerry Gafio 1953- ... 206
Watts, John (Francis) 1926- ... CANR-21
Earlier sketch in CA 25-28R
Watts, John D. W. 1921- ... 21-24R
Watts, Julia 1969- ... 170
See also SATA 103
Watts, Leander 1956- ... 220
See also SATA 146
Watts, Lew 1922- ... 41-44R
Watts, Mabel Pizzey 1906-1994 ... CANR-3
Earlier sketch in CA 1-4R
See also SATA 11
Watts, May Theilgaard 1893-1975 ... 41-44R
Watts, Meredith W(ayne, Jr.) 1941- .. CANR-24
Earlier sketch in CA 45-48
Watts, Michael J(ohn) 1951- ... CANR-101
Earlier sketches in CA 122, CANR-48
Watts, Nigel 1957-1999 ... CANR-87
Earlier sketch in CA 130
See also SATA 121
Watts, Peter 1958- ... 238
Watts, Peter Christopher 1919-1983 . CANR-12
Earlier sketch in CA 69-72
See also Chisholm, Matt
Watts, Reginald John 1931- ... CANR-30
Earlier sketch in CA 29-32R
Watts, Richard (Jr.) 1898-1981
Obituary ... 102
Watts, Ronald L(ampman) 1929- ... 21-24R
Watts, Sarah Miles 1934- ... 65-68
Watts, Sheldon 1934- ... 176
Watts, Stephen 1910- ... 5-8R
Watts, Thomas D(ale) 1941- ... CANR-41
Earlier sketch in CA 117
Watts, Timothy 1957- ... 141
Watts, William 1930- ... CANR-1
Earlier sketch in CA 45-48
Watzlawick, Paul 1921- ... CANR-4
Earlier sketch in CA 9-12R
Waud, Alfred Rudolph 1828-1891 ... DLB 188
Waud, Elizabeth
See Tattersall, M(uriel Joyce)
Waugh, Albert E(dmund) 1902-1985 ... 37-40R
Obituary ... 115
Waugh, Alec
See Waugh, Alexander Raban
See also BRWS 6
See also CN 2, 3
Waugh, Alexander Raban 1898-1981 ... CANR-22
Obituary ... 104
Earlier sketch in CA 17-20R
See also Waugh, Alec
See also DLB 191
Waugh, Auberon (Alexander) 1939-2001 ... CANR-92
Obituary ... 192
Earlier sketches in CA 45-48, CANR-6, 22
See also CLC 7
See also CN 1, 2, 3
See also DLB 14, 194
Waugh, C. C. Roessel
See Waugh, Carol-Lynn Rossel and Waugh, Charles G(ordon)
Waugh, Carol-Lynn Rossel 1947- ... CANR-44
Earlier sketch in CA 107
See also SATA 41
Waugh, Charles
See Waugh, Charles G(ordon)
Waugh, Charles G(ordon) 1943- ... 123
Brief entry ... 118
Interview in ... CA-123
Waugh, Coulton 1896(?)-1973
Obituary ... 41-44R
Waugh, Dorothy -1996 ... CANR-1
Earlier sketch in CA 1-4R
See also SATA 11
Waugh, Evelyn (Arthur St. John) 1903-1966 ... CANR-22
Obituary ... 25-28R
Earlier sketch in CA 85-88
See also BPFB 3
See also BRW 7
See also CDBLB 1914-1945
See also CLC 1, 3, 8, 13, 19, 27, 44, 107
See also DA
See also DA3
See also DAB
See also DAC
See also DAM MST, NOV, POP
See also DLB 15, 162, 195
See also EWL 3
See also MTCW 1, 2
See also MTFW 2005
See also NFS 13, 17
See also RGEL 2
See also RGSF 2
See also SSC 41
See also TEA
See also WLC
See also WLIT 4
Waugh, Harriet 1944- ... CANR-22
Earlier sketch in CA 85-88
See also CLC 6
Waugh, Harry 1904- ... 21-24R
Waugh, Hillary Baldwin 1920- ... CANR-2
Earlier sketch in CA 1-4R
See also CMW 4
See also MSW
Waugh, John C(linton) 1929- ... CANR-142
Earlier sketch in CA 150
Waugh, Linda R(uth) 1942- ... CANR-16
Earlier sketch in CA 89-92
Waugh, Louisa 1970(?)- ... 227
Waugh, Nancy Collier 1930- ... 45-48
Waugh, Sylvia 1935- ... CWRI 5
Waugh, Teresa (Lorraine) 1940- ... 158
Waugh, Virginia
See Sorensen, Virginia
Waugh, William L., Jr. 1948- ... 192
Waughburton, Richard
See Sykes, Christopher (Hugh)
Wauthier, Claude Rene 1923- ... 73-76
Wautischer, Helmut 1954- ... 207
Wauzzinski, Robert A. 1950- ... 143
Wavell, Stewart Brooke 1921- ... 13-16R
Wax, Emmanuel 1911-1983
Obituary ... 109
Wax, Jimmy
See Wax, Emmanuel
Wax, Judith 1932(?)-1979 ... 101
Obituary ... 85-88
Wax, Murray L(ionel) 1922- ... 37-40R
Wax, Rosalie (Amelia) H. 1911-1998 ... 45-48
Wax, Sheldon 1928(?)-1979
Obituary ... 85-88
Wax, Wendy A. 1963- ... 220
See also SATA 73, 163
Wax, William Edward 1956- ... 133
Waxberg, Joseph David 1922- ... 108
Waxman, Chaim I(saac) 1941- ... CANR-19
Earlier sketch in CA 103
Waxman, Franz 1906-1967 ... IDFW 3, 4
Waxman, Ruth B(ilgray) 1916-1996 ... 93-96
Obituary ... 154
Waxman, Wayne 1956- ... 150
Way, Irene 1924- ... 93-96
Way, Margaret ... 162
Way, Peter (Howard) 1936- ... 163
Brief entry ... 115
Way, Robert E(dward) 1912- ... 57-60
Way, Walter L. 1931- ... 57-60
Way, Wayne
See Humphries, Adelaide M.
Wayans, Damon 1960- ... 229
Wayans, Keenen Ivory 1958- ... CANR-82
Earlier sketch in CA 140
See also AAYA 11, 66
See also BW 2
See also DAM MULT, POP
Wayans, Shawn 1971- ... 171
Wayburn, Peggy 1921-2002 ... CANR-24
Obituary ... 205
Earlier sketch in CA 45-48
Waycott, Edon 1943- ... 149
Waylan, Mildred
See Harrell, (Mildred) Irene B(urk)
Wayland, April Halprin 1954- ... CANR-122
Earlier sketch in CA 146
See also SAAS 26
See also SATA 78, 143
Wayland, Patrick
See O'Connor, Richard
Waymack, W(illiam) W(esley) 1888-1960
Obituary ... 93-96
Wayman, Alex 1921- ... 104
Wayman, Dorothy G. 1893-1975 ... 65-68
Obituary ... 61-64
Wayman, Norbury Lansing 1912-1990 . 41-44R
Wayman, Thomas Ethan 1945- ... 101
See also Wayman, Tom
Wayman, Tom
See Wayman, Thomas Ethan
See also CP 7
See also DLB 53
Wayman, Tony Russell 1929- ... 25-28R
Wayne, Alice
See Ressler, Alice
Wayne, Anderson
See Dresser, Davis
Wayne, David
See Balsiger, David (Wayne)
Wayne, Donald
See Dodd, Wayne (Donald)
Wayne, Doreen ... 29-32R
Wayne, Frances
See Wedge, Florence
Wayne, Jane Ellen 1936- ... CANR-144
Earlier sketches in CA 49-52, CANR-4, 20, 42
Wayne, (Anne) Jenifer 1917-1982 ... 105
Obituary ... 108
See also CWRI 5
See also SATA 32
Wayne, Jerry 1919- ... 29-32R
Wayne, John 1907-1979 ... 85-88
Wayne, Joseph
See Overholser, Wayne D.
Wayne, Joseph
See Patten, Lewis B(yford)
Wayne, Kyra Petrovskaya 1918- ... CANR-4
Earlier sketch in CA 1-4R
See also SATA 8
Wayne, Mary Collier 1913- ... 57-60
Wayne, Michael 1947- ... CANR-108
Earlier sketch in CA 112
Wayne, Philip
See Powell, Philip Wayne
Wayne, Richard
See Decker, Duane
Wayne, Stephen J(ay) 1939- ... CANR-44
Earlier sketches in CA 53-56, CANR-5, 20
Wayne, Valerie 1945- ... 137
Wayner, Peter 1964- ... 211
Wayre, Philip 1921- ... 89-92
Ways, C. R.
See Blount, Roy (Alton), Jr.
Ways, Max 1905-1985
Obituary ... 116
Wayshak, Deborah Noyes 1965- ... SATA 145
Waystaff, Simon
See Swift, Jonathan
Wazyk, Adam 1905-1982
Obituary ... 114
See also EWL 3
Wead, R(oy) Douglas 1946- ... CANR-20
Earlier sketch in CA 69-72
Weaks, Mary Louise 1961- ... 136
Weal, Michele 1936- ... 61-64
Weale, Anne ... 237
See also RHW
Weales, Gerald (Clifford) 1925- ... CANR-3
Earlier sketch in CA 5-8R
See also SATA 11
Wear, Ted Graham
See Wear, Theodore G(raham)
Wear, Theodore G(raham) 1902-1974 ... CAP-1
Earlier sketch in CA 9-10
Weare, Ralston B.
See La Barre, Weston
Weare, Walter B(urdette) 1938- ... 73-76
Wearin, Otha D(onner) 1903-1990 ... CANR-5
Obituary ... 131
Earlier sketch in CA 13-16R
Wearing, J. P. ... CANR-41
Earlier sketches in CA 102, CANR-19
Wearne, Alan (Richard) 1948- ... 126
See also CP 7
Weart, Edith L. 1898(?)-1977
Obituary ... 69-72
Weart, Spencer R(ichard) 1942- ... CANR-53
Earlier sketches in CA 25-28R, CANR-29
Weary, Ogdred
See Gorey, Edward (St. John)
Weatherall, Norman Leigh 1902- ... CAP-1
Earlier sketch in CA 11-12
Weatherby, Harold L(erow), Jr. 1934- ... 45-48
Weatherby, W(illiam) J(ohn) 1930(?)-1992 ... CANR-47
Obituary ... 139
Earlier sketches in CA 17-20R, CANR-12
Weathercock, The
See Romaine, Lawrence B.
Weatherfield, Molly
See Rosenthal, Pam (Ritterman)
Weatherford, Carole Boston 1956- ... 208
See also SATA 138
Weatherford, Doris 1943- ... 187
Weatherford, J. McIver
See Weatherford, Jack McIver
Weatherford, Jack
See Weatherford, Jack McIver
Weatherford, Jack McIver 1946- ... CANR-56
Earlier sketches in CA 111, CANR-30
Weatherford, Richard M(orris) 1939- ... 53-56
Weatherford, Willis Duke, Jr. 1916-1996 .. 5-8R
Weatherhead, A(ndrew) Kingsley 1923- ... CANR-3
Earlier sketch in CA 5-8R
Weatherhead, Leslie D(ixon) 1893-1976 ... CANR-4
Obituary ... 61-64
Earlier sketch in CA 5-8R
Weatherly, Edward H(owell) 1905-1984 ... 5-8R
Weatherly, (John) Max 1921- ... 13-16R
Weatherly, Myra (S.) 1926- ... 199
See also SATA 130
Weatherly, Owen M. 1915-1994 ... 5-8R
Weatherly, Tom 1942- ... CANR-25
Earlier sketch in CA 45-48
See also BW 1
See also DLB 41
Weathers, Wesley Wayne 1942- ... 111
Weathers, Winston 1926- ... CANR-8
Earlier sketch in CA 21-24R
Weatherwax, Rudd (B.) 1908(?)-1985
Obituary ... 115
Weatherwise, Abe
See Sagendorph, Robb Hansell
Weaver, Anthony Frederick 1913-1991 . 13-16R
Weaver, Bertrand 1908-1973 ... CAP-1
Obituary ... 45-48
Earlier sketch in CA 13-16
Weaver, C(lare) P(arsons) 1939- ... 184
Weaver, Carl H(arold) 1910-1994 ... 73-76
Weaver, Charley
See Arquette, Cliff(ord)
Weaver, Courtney 1965- ... 206
Weaver, David H(ugh) 1946- ... 111
Weaver, Denis 1906-1984
Obituary ... 114
Weaver, Earl S(idney) 1930- ... 116
Weaver, Earle
See Willets, Walter E.
Weaver, Frank Parks 1904-1983 ... 104
Weaver, Frederick S(tirton) 1939- ... 156
Weaver, Gordon (Allison) 1937- ... CANR-26
Earlier sketches in CA 25-28R, CANR-10
See also DLB 130
See also TCLE 1:2
Weaver, Harriett E. 1908-1993 ... CANR-20
Earlier sketches in CA 5-8R, CANR-5
See also SATA 65
Weaver, Helen 1931- ... 228
Weaver, Herbert 1905-1985 ... 61-64
Weaver, Horace R. 1915- ... 13-16R
Weaver, James H. 1933- ... 17-20R
Weaver, Jerry L(ee) 1939- ... 69-72
Weaver, John D(owning) 1912-2002 .. CANR-4
Obituary ... 211
Earlier sketch in CA 9-12R
Weaver, John L. 1949- ... 112
See also SATA 42
Weaver, Katherine Grey Dunlap 1910- . 37-40R
Weaver, Kitty
See Weaver, Katherine Grey Dunlap
Weaver, Leon Hiram 1913-1991 ... 5-8R
Weaver, Mateman
See Greene, Alvin Carl
Weaver, Michael D. 1961-1998 ... 126
Obituary ... 196
Weaver, Michael S. 1951- ... 149
Weaver, Pat
See Weaver, Sylvester L(aflin), Jr.
Weaver, Paul H. 1942- ... 174
Weaver, Peter 1925- ... CANR-15
Earlier sketch in CA 85-88
Weaver, Peter Malcolm 1927- ... 13-16R
Weaver, R(obert) Kent 1953- ... 138
Weaver, Richard 1910-1963 ... 206
Weaver, Richard L. II 1941- ... CANR-46
Earlier sketches in CA 106, CANR-23
Weaver, Robert 1921- ... 192
See also DLB 88
Weaver, Robert C(lifton) 1907-1997 ... 9-12R
Obituary ... 159
Weaver, Robyn
See Conley-Weaver, Robyn
Weaver, Robyn M.
See Conley-Weaver, Robyn
Weaver, Sylvester L(aflin), Jr. 1908-2002 ... 146
Obituary ... 208
Weaver, Thomas 1929- ... CANR-13
Earlier sketch in CA 61-64
Weaver, Walter P. 1934- ... 187
Weaver, Ward
See Mason, F(rancis) van Wyck
Weaver, Warren, Jr. 1923-1997 ... 41-44R
Obituary ... 156
Weaver, Warren 1894-1978 ... 89-92
Obituary ... 81-84
Weaver, Will(iam Weller) 1950- ... 143
See also AAYA 30
See also BYA 12
See also SATA 88, 109, 161
See also WYAS 1
See also YAW
Weaver, William 1923- ... 116
Brief entry ... 112
Interview in ... CA-116
Weaver, William Woys 1947- ... CANR-110
Earlier sketches in CA 123, CANR-51
Weaver-Gelzer, Charlotte 1950- ... 148
See also SATA 79
Weaver-Zercher, David L. 1960- ... 228
Webb, Alex 1952- ... CANR-125
Earlier sketch in CA 161
Webb, Aliske 1955(?)- ... 190
Webb, Anthony
See Wilson, N(orman) Scarlyn
Webb, Barbara (Helen) 1929- ... 103
Webb, (Stephen) Barry 1947- ... 135
Webb, Beatrice (Martha Potter) 1858-1943 ... 162
Brief entry ... 117
See also DLB 190
See also FW
See also TCLC 22
Webb, Bernice Larson ... CANR-15
Earlier sketch in CA 37-40R
Webb, Betty 1942- ... 204
Webb, Bob
See Forrest-Webb, Robert
Webb, C(harles) R(ichard), Jr. 1919- ... 5-8R
Webb, Charles (Richard) 1939- ... CANR-114
Earlier sketch in CA 25-28R
See also CLC 7
Webb, Christopher
See Wibberley, Leonard (Patrick O'Connor)
Webb, Clifford (Cyril) 1895-1972 ... 105
Webb, Eugene 1938- ... 29-32R
Webb, Forrest
See Forrest-Webb, Robert
Webb, Francis Charles 1925-1973 ... 101
See also CP 1, 2
See also DLB 260
See also RGEL 2

Webb 608 CONTEMPORARY AUTHORS

Webb, Frank J. ... DLB 50
Webb, Gary 1955-2004 ... 184
Obituary ... 234
Webb, George Ernest 1952- ... 113
Webb, Harri 1920-1994 ... 104
See also CP 1, 2
Webb, Harry 1887-1984
Obituary ... 113
Webb, Henry J(ameson) 1915- ... 17-20R
Webb, Herschel (F.) 1924-1983 ... 5-8R
Obituary ... 109
Webb, Holmes 1904-1997 ... CAP-2
Earlier sketch in CA 25-28
Webb, Igor 1941- ... 109
Webb, Jack 1916- ... 172
Webb, Jack (Randolph) 1920-1982 ... 174
Obituary ... 108
Brief entry ... 106
See also CMW 4
Webb, Jacqueline
See Pearce, Margaret
Webb, Jacquelyn
See Pearce, Margaret and
Pearce, Margaret
Webb, James (C. N.) 1946-1980 ... 103
Webb, James H(enry), Jr. 1946- ... 81-84
See also CLC 22
Webb, James Watson 1802-1884 ... DLB 43
Webb, Jane Carter ... 228
Webb, Janeen (S.) ... 200
Webb, Jean Francis (III) 1910-1991
Obituary ... 198
Webb, Jean Francis (III) 1910-1991 .. CANR-21
Obituary ... 198
Earlier sketches in CA 5-8R, CANR-6
See also SATA 35
Webb, Jon (Edgar) 1905(?)-1971
Obituary ... 104
Webb, Karl (Eugene) 1938- ... 105
Webb, Kaye 1914- ... SATA 60
Webb, Kempton E. 1931- ... 13-16R
Webb, Kenneth B(eals) 1902-1984 ... 97-100
Webb, Lance 1909-1995 ... CANR-10
Earlier sketch in CA 13-16R
Webb, Lionel
See Hershman, Morris
Webb, Lois Sinaiko 1922- ... 149
See also SATA 82
Webb, Lucas
See Burgess, Michael (Roy)
Webb, Margot 1934- ... 134
See also SATA 67
Webb, Margot S. 1914- ... 77-80
Webb, Martha G.
See Wingate, (Martha) Anne (Guice)
Webb, (Gladys) Mary 1881-1927 ... RGEL 2
Webb, Mary Gladys (Meredith)
1881-1927 ... 182
Obituary ... 123
See also DLB 34
See also FW
See also TCLC 24
Webb, Mary H(aydn) 1938- ... CANR-28
Earlier sketch in CA 61-64
Webb, Melody Rae 1946- ... 126
Webb, Mena 1915- ... 127
Webb, Michael (Dennis Puzey)
1937- ... CANR-118
Earlier sketch in CA 124
Webb, Michael (Jack) 1953- ... 137
Webb, Michael Gordon 1940- ... 109
Webb, Mrs. Sidney
See Webb, Beatrice (Martha Potter)
Webb, Muriel S(chlosberg)
1913-1977 ... CANR-36
Obituary ... 134
Earlier sketch in CA 17-20R
Webb, Nancy (Bukeley) 1915- ... CANR-21
Earlier sketch in CA 1-4R
Webb, Nancy Boyd 1932- ... 207
Webb, Neil
See Rowland, D(onald) S(ydney)
Webb, Pauline M(ary) 1927- ... CANR-49
Earlier sketches in CA 61-64, CANR-8, 24
Webb, Peggy (Elaine Hussey) 1942- ... 123
Webb, Peter B(randram) 1941- ... CANR-24
Earlier sketch in CA 106
Webb, Phyllis 1927- ... CANR-23
Earlier sketch in CA 104
See also CCA 1
See also CLC 18
See also CP 1, 2, 3, 4, 5, 6, 7
See also CWP
See also DLB 53
Webb, R(obert) K(iefer) 1922- ... 25-28R
Webb, Richard 1915-1993 ... CANR-47
Obituary ... 141
Earlier sketch in CA 37-40R
Webb, Robert 1947- ... 118
Webb, Robert Forrest-
See Forrest-Webb, Robert
Webb, Rodman B. 1941- ... CANR-28
Earlier sketch in CA 110
Webb, Ross A(llan) 1923-2003 ... 37-40R
Obituary ... 224
Webb, Rozana 1908-1990 ... 29-32R
Webb, Ruth Enid Borlase Morris 1926- ... 9-12R
Webb, Samuel C(lement) 1934- ... 69-72
Webb, Sharon 1936- ... CANR-32
Earlier sketch in CA 113
See also SATA 41
See also SFW 4
Webb, Sidney (James) 1859-1947 ... 163
Brief entry ... 117
See also DLB 190
See also TCLC 22
Webb, Sophie 1958- ... SATA 135
Webb, Spider
See Gohman, Fred Joseph
Webb, Stephen S(aunders) 1937- ... CANR-70
Earlier sketch in CA 104
Webb, T(erry) D(ouglas) 1949- ... 193
Webb, Todd 1905-2000 ... 211
Webb, Veronica 1965- ... 169
Webb, Victoria
See Baker, Will(iam Edwin)
Webb, Walter Prescott 1888-1963 ... 186
Obituary ... 113
See also DLB 17
Webb, Willard 1903-1978
Obituary ... 77-80
Webb, William (Griffin) 1919- ... 25-28R
Webb, Wilse B(ernard) 1920- ... CANR-3
Earlier sketch in CA 1-4R
Webbe, Gale D(udley) 1909-2000 ... 5-8R
Webbe, Gerald 1929-1999 ... 186
Webbe, William (?)-1591 ... DLB 132
Webber, Andrew Lloyd
See Lloyd Webber, Andrew
See also CLC 21
See also DFS 7
Webber, Bert
See Webber, Ebbert T(rue)
Webber, Charles Wilkins
1819-1856(?) ... DLB 202
Webber, Collin ... FANT
Webber, Ebbert T(rue) 1921- ... CANR-39
Earlier sketches in CA 45-48, CANR-2, 17
Webber, George J(ulius) 1899-1982(?)
Obituary ... 108
Webber, Gordon 1912-1986 ... 89-92
Obituary ... 120
Webber, Irma E(leanor Schmidt)
1904-1995 ... 69-72
See also SATA 14
Webber, Joan Malory 1930-1978 ... CANR-7
Earlier sketch in CA 5-8R
Webber, Robert (Eugene) 1933- ... CANR-97
Earlier sketches in CA 89-92, CANR-16, 37
Webber, (Edwin) Ronald 1915- ... CANR-4
Earlier sketch in CA 53-56
Webber, Ross A. 1934- ... 29-32R
Webber, Sabra J. 1945- ... 141
Webber, Thomas L(ane) 1947- ... 85-88
Weber, Alfons 1921- ... 29-32R
See also SATA 8
Weber, Andreas H. G. 1951- ... 185
Weber, Andy
See Weber, Andreas H. G.
Weber, Brom 1917-1998 ... 13-16R
Weber, Bruce 1942- ... CANR-98
Earlier sketches in CA 97-100, CANR-21, 49
See also SATA 73, 120
Weber, Burton Jasper 1934- ... 103
Weber, C(larence) A(dam)
1903-1998 ... CANR-37
Earlier sketches in CA 37-40R, CANR-13
Weber, Carl J(efferson) 1894-1966 ... CANR-3
Earlier sketch in CA 5-8R
Weber, David 1952- ... 199
See also AAYA 52
Weber, David J. 1940- ... CANR-14
Earlier sketch in CA 37-40R
Weber, David R(yder) 1943- ... 89-92
Weber, Debora 1955- ... SATA 58
Weber, Doron 1955- ... 138
Weber, Eric 1942- ... CANR-15
Earlier sketch in CA 101
Interview in ... CANR-15
Weber, Eugen 1925- ... CANR-2
Earlier sketch in CA 5-8R
Weber, Eugene (Mathew)
1939-1986 ... CANR-88
Earlier sketch in CA 41-44R
Weber, Francis J. 1933- ... CANR-69
Earlier sketches in CA 9-12R, CANR-4
Weber, Frank George 1932- ... 45-48
Weber, Gerard Peter 1918- ... 9-12R
Weber, Hans H. 1935- ... 61-64
Weber, Hans-Ruedi 1923- ... CANR-2
Earlier sketch in CA 5-8R
Weber, J(ohn) Sherwood 1918-1978 ... 37-40R
Obituary ... 77-80
Weber, James A(mbrose) 1932- ... 102
Weber, Janice ... CANR-100
Earlier sketches in CA 121, CANR-46
Weber, Jean-Paul 1917- ... 45-48
Weber, Jerome C(harles) 1938- ... 73-76
Weber, Jill 1950- ... SATA 127
Weber, Joe 1945- ... CANR-121
Earlier sketch in CA 141
Weber, Judith E(ichler) 1938- ... SATA 64
Weber, Katharine 1955- ... CANR-127
Earlier sketch in CA 157
Weber, Ken(neth J.) 1940- ... CANR-59
Earlier sketches in CA 116, CANR-39
See also SATA 90
Weber, Lenora Mattingly 1895-1971 ... CAP-1
Obituary ... 29-32R
Earlier sketch in CA 19-20
See also CLC 12
See also SATA 2
See also SATA-Obit 26
Weber, Marc 1950- ... CANR-1
Earlier sketch in CA 49-52
Weber, Maria 1951- ... 220
Weber, Max 1864-1920 ... 189
Brief entry ... 109
See also DLB 296
See also TCLC 69
Weber, Michael 1945- ... 151
See also SATA 87
Weber, Michael P. ... 127
Weber, Nan 1954- ... 195
Weber, Nancy 1942- ... CANR-108
Earlier sketch in CA 101
Weber, Nathan 1942- ... 111
Weber, Nicholas F(ox) 1947- ... CANR-116
Earlier sketch in CA 120
Weber, Paul J. 1937- ... 137
Weber, R. David 1941- ... 127
Weber, Ralph Edward 1926- ... CANR-2
Earlier sketch in CA 5-8R
Weber, Richard 1932- ... CP 1, 2
Weber, Robert J(ohn) 1936- ... CANR-99
Earlier sketch in CA 139
Weber, Robert L(emmerman) 1913-1997 . 53-56
Weber, Ronald 1934- ... CANR-118
Earlier sketches in CA 115, CANR-43
Weber, Rubin
See Rubinstein, S(amuel) Leonard
Weber, Sandra 1961- ... 234
See also SATA 158
Weber, Sarah Appleton
See Appleton, Sarah
Weber, Simon 1910(?)-1987
Obituary ... 124
Weber, Thomas 1950- ... CANR-118
Earlier sketch in CA 159
Weber, William 1950- ... 226
Weber, William A(lfred) 1918- ... 77-80
Weber, William J(ohn) 1927- ... CANR-25
Earlier sketch in CA 69-72
See also SATA 14
Weber, Wolfgang 1902-1985 ... 216
Weberman, Ben(jamin) 1923- ... 77-80
Webling, Lucy 1877-1952 ... 207
See also DLB 240
Webling, Peggy 1871-1949 ... DLB 240
Webster, Alice Jane Chandler 1876-1916
Brief entry ... 116
See also CWRI 5
See also RHW
See also SATA 17
Webster, Anthony 1923(?)-1987
Obituary ... 123
Webster, Augusta 1837-1894 ... DLB 35, 240
Webster, Brenda 1936- ... 172
Earlier sketches in CA 53-56, CANR-121
Autobiographical Essay in ... 172
See also CAAS 30
Webster, C(onstance) Muriel 1906- ... 49-52
Webster, Catherine 1946- ... 176
Webster, Charles 1936- ... 229
Webster, Cyril Charles 1909- ... CAP-2
Earlier sketch in CA 25-28
Webster, David 1930- ... 29-32R
See also SATA 11
Webster, David Endicott 1929- ... 25-28R
Webster, Donald 1926- ... 118
Webster, Donald Blake, Jr. 1933- ... 37-40R
Webster, Douglas 1920-1986 ... 13-16R
Obituary ... 118
Webster, Edna Robb 1896-1981 ... 69-72
Webster, Elizabeth 1918- ... CANR-40
Earlier sketch in CA 117
Webster, (Stanley) Eric 1919-1971 ... CAP-1
Earlier sketch in CA 17-18
Webster, Ernest 1923- ... 132
Webster, Frank V. ... CANR-27
Earlier sketches in CAP-2, CA 19-20
See also SATA 1, 67
Webster, Frederick E., Jr. 1937- ... CANR-14
Earlier sketch in CA 37-40R
Webster, Gary
See Garrison, Webb B(lack)
Webster, Graham 1915-2001 ... 49-52
Obituary ... 197
Webster, Grant T. 1933- ... 104
Webster, Harvey (Curtis) 1906-1988 ... 41-44R
Webster, J(ames) Carson 1905-1989 ... 45-48
Webster, James 1925-1981 ... CANR-29
Obituary ... 104
Earlier sketch in CA 73-76
See also SATA 17
See also SATA-Obit 27
Webster, James G. 1951- ... 171
Webster, Jan 1924- ... CANR-14
Earlier sketch in CA 77-80
Webster, Jason 1970- ... 226
Webster, Jean
See Webster, Alice Jane Chandler
Webster, John 1580(?)-1634(?) ... BRW 2
See also CDBLB Before 1660
See also DA
See also DAB
See also DAC
See also DAM DRAM, MST
See also DC 2
See also DFS 17, 19
See also DLB 58
See also IDTP
See also RGEL 2
See also WLC
See also WLIT 3
Webster, John 1925- ... 152
Webster, Josh (Lew) 1949- ... 113
Webster, Margaret 1905-1972
Obituary ... 37-40R
Webster, Noah
See Knox, William
Webster, Noah 1758-1843 .. DLB 1, 37, 42, 43, 73, 243
Webster, Norman William 1920- ... 104
Webster, Paul 1916- ... 41-44R
Webster, Paul Francis 1907-1984
Obituary ... 112
See also DLB 265
Webster, Randolph Wyatt 1900-1995 ... CAP-1
Earlier sketch in CA 19-20
Webster, Richard 1946- ... 198
Webster, Richard A. 1928- ... 21-24R
Webster, Sally 1938- ... 140
Webster, Staten Wentford 1928-1987 ... 21-24R
Webster, T. B. L.
See Webster, Thomas Bertram Lonsdale
Webster, Thomas Bertram Lonsdale
1905-1974 ... 105
Obituary ... 107
Webster, Tony
See Webster, Anthony
Wechman, Robert Joseph 1939- ... CANR-49
Earlier sketches in CA 45-48, CANR-24
Wechsberg, Joseph 1907-1983 ... CANR-34
Obituary ... 109
Earlier sketch in CA 105
Wechsler, David 1896-1981
Obituary ... 103
Wechsler, Harold S(tuart) 1946- ... 110
Wechsler, Henry 1932- ... CANR-7
Earlier sketch in CA 17-20R
Wechsler, Herbert 1909-2000 ... CANR-24
Obituary ... 189
Earlier sketch in CA 1-4R
Wechsler, Herman J. 1904-1976 ... 65-68
Obituary ... 61-64
See also SATA-Obit 20
Wechsler, James A(rthur) 1915-1983 ... 101
Obituary ... 110
Wechsler, Judith Glatzer 1940- ... CANR-42
Earlier sketches in CA 57-60, CANR-8
Wechsler, Louis K. 1905-1996 ... 65-68
Wechsler, Robert 1954- ... 187
Wechter, Nell (Carolyn) Wise
1913-1989 ... 57-60
Obituary ... 196
See also SATA 60, 127
Weck, Thomas L. 1942- ... 128
See also SATA 62
Wecker, David 1950- ... 148
Weckesser, Elden C(hristian) 1910- ... 139
Weckherlin, Georg Rodolf
1584-1653 ... DLB 164
Weckmann, Luis 1923- ... 143
Weckstein, Richard (Selig) 1924- ... 49-52
Wedberg, Anders 1913-1978
Obituary ... 77-80
Wedd, Kate
See Gregory, Philippa
Wedda, John A. 1911- ... 17-20R
Wedde, Ian 1946- ... 104
See also CN 5, 6
See also CP 2, 3, 4, 5, 6, 7
See also EWL 3
Wedderburn, Dorothy (Enid Cole) 1925- ... 185
Brief entry ... 113
Wedderburn, K(enneth) W(illiam) 1927- . 77-80
Wedding, Dan 1949- ... 93-96
Wedding, Donald Keith 1934- ... 41-44R
Weddington, Sarah (Ragle) 1945- ... 156
Weddle, David 1956- ... 231
Weddle, Ethel Harshbarger
1897-1996 ... CANR-4
Earlier sketch in CA 9-12R
See also SATA 11
Weddle, Ferris 1922-1985 ... 17-20R
Weddle, Robert S(amuel) 1921- ... 9-12R
Wedeck, Harry E(zekiel) 1894-1996 ... CANR-4
Obituary ... 152
Earlier sketch in CA 1-4R
Wedeen, Richard Peter 1934- ... 146
Wedeen, Shirley Ullman 1926-1992 ... 17-20R
Obituary ... 137
Wedekind, (Benjamin) Frank(lin)
1864-1918 ... CANR-122
Brief entry ... 104
Earlier sketches in CA 153, CANR-121
See also CDWLB 2
See also DAM DRAM
See also DLB 118
See also EW 8
See also EWL 3
See also LMFS 2
See also RGWL 2, 3
See also TCLC 7
Wedel, Alfred R(aphael) 1934- ... 117
Wedel, Alton F. ... 21-24R
Wedel, Cynthia Clark 1908-1986
Obituary ... 120
Wedel, Janine (R.) 1957- ... 132
Wedel, Leonard E. 1909- ... 21-24R
Wedel, Theodore Otto 1892-1970 ... CANR-4
Earlier sketch in CA 5-8R
Wedel, Waldo R(udolph) 1908-1996 ... 126
Brief entry ... 105
Wedell, Eberhard (Arthur Otto) George
1927- ... 104
Wedemeyer, Albert C(oady) 1897-1989
Obituary ... 130
Wedemeyer, Maria von 1924(?)-1977 ... 148
Wedge, Bryant (Miner) 1921-1987 ... CANR-10
Earlier sketch in CA 13-16R
Wedge, Florence 1919- ... 5-8R
Wedgwood, C(icely) V(eronica)
1910-1997 ... CANR-67
Obituary ... 157
Earlier sketches in CA 105, CANR-21
See also MTCW 1
Wedgwood, Pamela
See Tudor-Craig, Pamela
Wedlock, Eldon D(yment), Jr. 1942- ... 128
Weed, Florence C(ollins) 1897(?)-1983
Obituary ... 109
Weed, Joseph J(ohn) 1901-1978 ... 25-28R
Weeden, Robert B(arton) 1933- ... 85-88
Weedon, Chris 1952- ... 121
Weegee 1899-1968 ... 145

Weekes, Mark Kinkead
See Kinkead-Weekes, Mark
Weekes, Richard V. 1924-1999 .... 13-16R
Weekley, Carolyn 230
Weekley, Ian George 1933- 113
Weekly, William G(eorge) 1890(?)-1983
Obituary 111
Weeks, Albert L. 1923- 13-16R
Weeks, Brigitte 1943- 132
Weeks, Christopher 1930- 21-24R
Weeks, Constance Tomkinson 1915- 17-20R
Weeks, David (Joseph) 1944- 156
Weeks, (Norman) Donald
1921-2003 .... CANR-25
Obituary 223
Earlier sketch in CA 45-48
Weeks, Edward (Augustus)
1898-1989 .... CANR-36
Obituary 128
Earlier sketch in CA 85-88
See also DLB 137
Weeks, Edward J(oseph) 1902- CAP-1
Earlier sketch in CA 13-14
Weeks, Francis W(illiam) 1916-
Brief entry 111
Weeks, Grace E(zell) 1923- 49-52
Weeks, H(erbert) Ashley 1903-1992 45-48
Weeks, James Powell 1950- 226
Weeks, Jeffrey 1945- 108
See also GLL 1
Weeks, Jim
See Weeks, James Powell
Weeks, John (Stafford) 1928- 77-80
Weeks, John F. 1941- 141
Weeks, Kent M(cCuskey) 1937- 184
Brief entry 112
Weeks, Kent R. 181
Weeks, Lewis G(eorge) 1893-1977
Obituary 69-72
Weeks, Philip 1949- CANR-104
Earlier sketch in CA 110
Weeks, Robert Lewis 1924- 13-16R
Weeks, Robert P(ercy) 1915- 13-16R
Weeks, Sarah 234
See also SATA 158
Weeks, Sheldon G. 1931- CANR-30
Earlier sketches in CA 21-24R, CANR-13
Weeks, Stephen B. 1865-1918 200
See also DLB 187
Weeks, Thelma E(vans) 1921- 57-60
Weeks, Willet 1917- 203
Weems, Carrie Mae 1953- 206
Weems, David B(urnola) 1922- 148
See also SATA 80
Weems, J. Eddie, Jr.
See Weems, John Edward
Weems, John Edward 1924- CANR-19
Earlier sketches in CA 1-4R, CANR-4
Weems, Mason Locke 1759-1825 . DLB 30, 37, 42
Weenolsen, Hebe -1999 .... CANR-60
Earlier sketches in CA 111, CANR-34
Weenolsen, Patricia 1930- 157
Weer, William
See Kaufman, I(sadore)
Weerth, Georg 1822-1856 .... DLB 129
Weertman, Julia 1926- 160
Weerts, Richard Kenneth 1928- 49-52
Wees, Frances Shelley 1902-1982 .... CANR-3
Earlier sketch in CA 5-8R
See also SATA 58
Wees, W(ilfred) R(usk) 1899- 61-64
Weesner, Theodore 1935- CANR-89
Earlier sketch in CA 105
Weevers, Peter 1944- .... SATA 59
Wegela, Karen Kissel 1945- 168
Wegelin, Christof 1911- 45-48
Wegen, Ron(ald) .... SATA-Brief 44
Wegen, Ronald 1946-1985 154
See also SATA 99
Wegener, Alfred 1880-1930 161
Weglyn, Michi(ko Nishiura) 1926-1999 .. 85-88
Obituary 178
Wegman, William (George) 1943- .. CANR-113
Earlier sketches in CA 148, CANR-95
See also AAYA 15
See also SATA 78, 129, 135
Wegmann, Peter 1957- 146
Wegner, Fritz 1924- .... SATA 20
Wegner, Robert E. 1929- 17-20R
Wehen, Joy DeWeese CANR-3
Earlier sketch in CA 5-8R
Wehlitz, (Annie) Lou(ise) Rogers
1906-1998 .... 5-8R
Wehmeyer, Lillian (Mabel) Biermann
1933- CANR-8
Earlier sketch in CA 61-64
Wehr, Demaris .... CLC 65
Wehr, Wesley 1929- 196
Wehringer, Cameron K(ingsley)
1924-1997 .... 25-28R
Wehrle, Edmund S(heridan) 1930- 65-68
Wehrli, Eugene S(tanley) 1923- 45-48
Wehrwein, Austin C(arl) 1916- 77-80
Wei, Yung 1937- 49-52
Weibezahl, Robert 238
Weichel, Kim 1951- 107
Weida, Bill
See Weida, William J.
Weida, William J. 1942- 135
Weideger, Paula 1939- CANR-138
Earlier sketch in CA 65-68
Weideman, Ryan 1941- 137
Weidenbaum, Murray L(ew) 1927- ... CANR-14
Earlier sketch in CA 37-40R
Weidenfeld, (Arthur) George 1919- 153
Weidenfeld, Sheila Rabb 1943- 89-92
Weidenreich, Franz 1873-1948 164
Weider, Ben 1923- 108
Weidhorn, Manfred 1931- 53-56
See also SATA 60
Weidlein, Edward R(ay) 1887-1983
Obituary 110
Weidman, Jerome 1913-1998 .... CANR-1
Obituary 171
Earlier sketch in CA 1-4R
See also AITN 2
See also CAD
See also CD 1, 2, 3, 4, 5
See also CLC 7
See also DLB 28
Weidman, John 1946- 109
Weidman, Judith L(ynne) 1941- CANR-25
Earlier sketch in CA 107
Weidner, Edward William 1921- 13-16R
Weidt, Maryann N. 1944- 151
See also SATA 85
Weiers, Ronald M. 1941- CANR-19
Earlier sketch in CA 25-28R
Weigand, George R(obert) J(oseph)
1917- 13-16R
Weigand, Hermann J(ohn) 1892-1985 ... CAP-1
Obituary 117
Earlier sketch in CA 13-14
Weigel, George 1951- CANR-92
Earlier sketch in CA 125
Weigel, Gustave 1906-1964
Obituary 107
Weigel, John A(rthur) 1912-1998 57-60
Weiger, John George 1933- CANR-20
Earlier sketch in CA 104
Weigert, Andrew J(oseph) 1934- 109
Weigert, Edith 1894-1982 .... CAP-2
Earlier sketch in CA 29-32
Weigert, Hans Werner 1902(?)-1983
Obituary 111
Weight, Frank
See Tubb, E(dwin) C(harles)
Weightman, Gavin 1945- CANR-144
Earlier sketch in CA 120
Weightman, J(ohn) G(eorge)
1915-2004 .... CANR-5
Obituary 230
Earlier sketch in CA 9-12R
Weigl, Bruce 1949- CANR-97
Earlier sketches in CA 110, CANR-30
See also CP 7
See also DLB 120
See also TCLE 1:2
Weigle, Luther Allan 1880-1976 77-80
Obituary 69-72
Weigle, Marta 1944- CANR-26
Earlier sketches in CA 69-72, CANR-11
Weigle, Scott 1964- 177
Weigley, Russell F(rank) 1930-2004 . CANR-95
Obituary 225
Earlier sketches in CA 5-8R, CANR-2, 19
Weihofen, Henry 1904-1993 .... 37-40R
Weihs, Erika 1917- 93-96
See also SATA 15, 107
Weihs, Jean 1930- 153
Weihs, Jean Riddle
See Weihs, Jean
Wei Jingsheng 1951(?)- 162
Weik, Mary Hays 1898(?)-1979 .... 21-24R
Obituary 93-96
See also SATA 3
See also SATA-Obit 23
Weil, Andre 1906-1998 161
Obituary 169
Weil, Andrew (Thomas) 1942- CANR-95
Earlier sketches in CA 73-76, CANR-20, 43
Weil, Ann Yezner 1908-1969 .... 5-8R
Obituary 103
See also SATA 9
Weil, Dorothy 1929- CANR-118
Earlier sketch in CA 93-96
Weil, Gordon L(ee) 1937- CANR-12
Earlier sketch in CA 73-76
Weil, Herbert S., Jr. 1933- 21-24R
Weil, Irwin 1928- 21-24R
Weil, James L(ehman) 1929- CANR-36
Earlier sketches in CA 93-96, CANR-16
Weil, Jerry 1928- 1-4R
Weil, Jiri 1900-1959 141
See also DLB 299
Weil, Joseph 1875-1976
Obituary 65-68
Weil, Lisl 1910- CANR-2
Earlier sketch in CA 49-52
See also SATA 7
Weil, Mildred 45-48
Weil, Robert 1955- 125
Weil, Roman L(ee) 1940- CANR-44
Earlier sketches in CA 37-40R, CANR-14
Weil, Samuel
See Kaufman, Lloyd
Weil, Samuel L.
See Kaufman, Lloyd
Weil, Simone (Adolphine) 1909-1943 159
Brief entry 117
See also EW 12
See also EWL 3
See also FW
See also GFL 1789 to the Present
See also MTCW 2
See also TCLC 23
Weil, Ulric Henry 113
Weiland, Matt 176
Weilbacher, William Manning 1928- 108
Weiler, Joseph H. H. 183
Weilerstein, Sadie Rose 1894-1993 .... 5-8R
Obituary 141
See also SATA 3
See also SATA-Obit 75
Weill, Gus 1933- CANR-7
Earlier sketch in CA 53-56
Weill, Kurt (Julian) 1900-1950 183
Weiman, Eiveen 1925- 108
Weimann, Gabriel 1950- CANR-104
Earlier sketch in CA 149
Weimann, Jeanne Madeline 1943- 108
Weimar, Karl S(iegfried) 1916-1982 .... 5-8R
Weimer, Arthur M(artin) 1909-1987 .... 1-4R
Obituary 122
Weimer, Ferne 1950- 137
Weimer, Joan 1936- 144
Weimer, Maryellen 1947- 135
Wein, Elizabeth E(ve) 1964- CANR-135
Earlier sketch in CA 149
See also SATA 82, 151
Wein, George 1925- 228
Wein, Jacqueline 1938- 93-96
Weinbaum, Batya 1952- 223
Weinbaum, Marvin G. 1935- 150
Weinbaum, Raquel
See Vinas, David
Weinbaum, Stanley Grauman
1902(?)-1935 168
Brief entry 110
See also DLB 8
See also SCFW 1, 2
See also SFW 4
Weinberg, Arthur 1915-1989 .... CANR-15
Obituary 127
Earlier sketch in CA 25-28R
Weinberg, Bernard 1909-1973
Obituary 106
Weinberg, Bill 1962- 192
Weinberg, Daniel H. 1949- 120
Weinberg, Daniela 1936- 104
Weinberg, David Henry 1945- 89-92
Weinberg, Edgar 1917-1985
Obituary 117
Weinberg, Florence Byham
See Weinberg, Florence M(ay)
Weinberg, Florence M(ay) 1933- CANR-136
Earlier sketch in CA 37-40R
Weinberg, Gerald M(arvin) 1933- CANR-18
Earlier sketch in CA 89-92
Weinberg, Gerhard L(udwig) 1928- CANR-3
Earlier sketch in CA 9-12R
Weinberg, H. Barbara 134
Weinberg, Helen A(rnstein) 1927- 73-76
Weinberg, Herman G(ershon)
1908-1983 .... CANR-29
Obituary 111
Earlier sketch in CA 45-48
Weinberg, Ian 1938-1969 .... CAP-2
Earlier sketch in CA 21-22
Weinberg, Janet Hopson
See Hopson, Janet L(ouise)
Weinberg, Julius 1922- 37-40R
Weinberg, Julius R(udolph) 1908-1971 .. CAP-1
Earlier sketch in CA 17-18
Weinberg, Kenneth G. 1920- 41-44R
Weinberg, Kerry 29-32R
Weinberg, Kurt 1912-1996 .... 41-44R
Weinberg, Larry
See Weinberg, Lawrence (E.)
Weinberg, Lawrence (E.) .... SATA 92
See also SATA-Brief 48
Weinberg, Lila (Shaffer) 25-28R
Weinberg, Louise 169
Weinberg, Martin S(tephen) 1939- CANR-15
Earlier sketch in CA 41-44R
Weinberg, Meyer 1920-2002 .... CANR-4
Obituary 204
Earlier sketch in CA 1-4R
Weinberg, Nathan Gerald 1945- 104
Weinberg, Robert Charles 1901-1974
Obituary 45-48
Weinberg, Robert E(dward) 1946- .. CANR-123
Earlier sketches in CA 97-100, CANR-77
See also HGG
Weinberg, Samantha 1966- 197
Weinberg, Samuel Kirson 1912-2001 . CANR-1
Obituary 193
Earlier sketch in CA 1-4R
Weinberg, Sanford Bruce 1950- 109
Weinberg, Steve 1948- 142
Weinberg, Steven 1933- CANR-112
Earlier sketches in CA 53-56, CANR-5, 36
Weinberg, Thomas S(tephen) 1943- 151
Weinberg, Werner 1915-1997 .... CANR-16
Earlier sketch in CA 41-44R
Weinberger, Betty Kiralfy 1932- 65-68
Weinberger, Caspar W(illard)
1917- CANR-116
Earlier sketch in CA 133
Weinberger, David 1950- 191
Weinberger, Eliot 1949- CANR-105
Earlier sketches in CA 117, CANR-40
Weinberger, Everett 1964- 148
Weinberger, Leon J. 1926- 77-80
Weinberger, Marvin I(rvin) 1954- 113
Weinberger, Miro (Leonard) 1970- 135
Weinberger, Paul E. 1931-1983(?) 29-32R
Obituary 134
Weinberger, Tanya 1939- .... SATA 84
Weinbrot, Howard D. 1936-
Brief entry 107
Weiner, Andrew 1949- CANR-144
Earlier sketch in CA 161
See also DLB 251
See also SFW 4
Weiner, Andrew D(avid) 1943- 206
Brief entry 111
Weiner, Annette B. 1933-1997 93-96
Obituary 163
Weiner, Bernard 1935- 57-60
Weiner, Bernard 1940- .... CAAS 29
Weiner, Charles 1931- 134
Brief entry 109
Weiner, Dora B(ierer) 1924- 25-28R
Weiner, Edith M. 1948- 127
Weiner, Edmund (Simon Christopher)
1950- 139
Weiner, Egon 1906-1987 97-100
Obituary 123
Weiner, Elliot 1943- 122
Weiner, Florence 1931- 25-28R
Weiner, Hannah .... CP 1
Weiner, Henri
See Longstreet, Stephen
Weiner, Herbert 5-8R
Weiner, Howard L. 1944- CANR-55
Earlier sketch in CA 127
Weiner, Hyman J(oseph) 1926-1980 49-52
Weiner, Irving B(ernard) 1933- CANR-27
Earlier sketch in CA 29-32R
Weiner, J(oseph) S(idney) 1915-1982 114
Weiner, Jonathan (David) 1953- CANR-92
Earlier sketch in CA 123
Weiner, Kay Bain 1932- 136
Weiner, Leonard 1927- 21-24R
Weiner, Linda 1943- 114
Weiner, Marc A. 1955- 146
Weiner, Marcella Bakur 1925-
Brief entry 105
Weiner, Mark S(tuart) 235
Weiner, Myron 1931-1999 .... CANR-4
Obituary 181
Earlier sketch in CA 1-4R
Weiner, Neal (Orlove) 1942- 118
Weiner, Neil S(herman) 1936- 119
Weiner, Richard 1927- 89-92
Weiner, Sandra 1922- 49-52
See also SATA 14
Weiner, Shelley 1949- 139
Weiner, Skip
See Weiner, Stewart
Weiner, Stephen 1955- CANR-112
Earlier sketch in CA 155
Weiner, Steven
See Weiner, Stephen
Weiner, Stewart 1945- CANR-16
Earlier sketch in CA 89-92
Weiner, Susan 1946- 145
Weiner, Tim 1956- 135
Weiner, William J(errold) 1945- 204
Weiner-Davis, Michele 1952- 149
Weinerman, Lisa 1967- 149
Weinfield, Henry 1949- 37-40R
Weingand, Darlene E. 1937- 115
Weingarden, Lauren S. 1948- 128
Weingart, L(aurence) O. 1931- 17-20R
Weingarten, Henry 57-60
Weingarten, Roger 1945- CANR-10
Earlier sketch in CA 61-64
Weingarten, Violet (Brown)
1915-1976 .... CANR-7
Obituary 65-68
Earlier sketch in CA 9-12R
See also SATA 3
See also SATA-Obit 27
Weingartner, Charles 1922- 49-52
See also SATA 5
Weingartner, Herbert J. 1935- 148
Weingartner, James J(oseph) 1940- 93-96
Weingartner, Rudolph H(erbert) 1927- .. 13-16R
Weingast, David E(lliott) 1912- 5-8R
Weingrod, Herschel 1947- 234
Weinhaus, Carol L. 1947- 137
Weinhouse, Beth (R) 1957- CANR-68
Earlier sketch in CA 128
Weinig, Jean Maria 1920- CANR-12
Earlier sketch in CA 29-32R
Weinig, Sister Mary Anthony
See Weinig, Jean Maria
Weininger, Benjamin Isaac 1905-1988
Obituary 126
Weininger, Otto 1880-1903 .... TCLC 84
Weininger, Richard 1887(?)-1979
Obituary 89-92
Weinkauf, Mary S(tanley) 1938- 150
Weinland, James D(avid) 1894-1987 57-60
Weinman, Benzion 1897-1987
Obituary 121
Weinman, Irving 1937- 122
Weinman, Lynda (Susan) 1955(?)- 172
Weinman, Paul 1940- CANR-29
Earlier sketches in CA 77-80, CANR-13
Weinrauch, Herschel 1905-1983 .... CAP-1
Earlier sketch in CA 13-16
Weinreb, Lloyd L(obell) 1936- 69-72
Weinreich, Beatrice Silverman 1928- 129
Weinrich, A(nna) K(atharina) H(ildegard)
1933- CANR-37
Earlier sketches in CA 37-40R, CANR-16
Weinroth, Michelle 1959- 158
Weinryb, Bernard D(ov) 1905-1982 . CANR-25
Earlier sketch in CA 45-48
Weinstein, Allen 1937- CANR-135
Earlier sketches in CA 41-44R, CANR-26
Weinstein, Arnold 1927- 9-12R
See also CAD
See also CD 5, 6
Weinstein, Bernard L(ee) 1942- 111
Weinstein, Bob 1941- 120
Weinstein, Brian 1937- 21-24R
Weinstein, Cindy 1960- 149
Weinstein, Donald 1926- 13-16R
Weinstein, Fred 1931- 65-68
Weinstein, Gerald 1930- 25-28R

Weinstein, Grace W(ohlner) CANR-51
Earlier sketches in CA 61-64, CANR-10, 26
Weinstein, Howard 1954- CANR-23
Earlier sketch in CA 107
Weinstein, Jacob Joseph 1902-1974 110
Obituary 108
Weinstein, James 1926- CANR-127
Earlier sketch in CA 21-24R
Weinstein, Leo 1921-
Brief entry 110
Weinstein, Mark A. 1937- 25-28R
Weinstein, Marlene 1946- 45-48
Weinstein, Martin E. 1934- 85-88
Weinstein, Michael 1898- CAP-1
Earlier sketch in CA 13-14
Weinstein, Michael A(lan) 1942- CANR-65
Earlier sketch in CA 129
Weinstein, Nathan
See West, Nathanael
Weinstein, Nathan von Wallenstein
See West, Nathanael
Weinstein, Nina 1951- .... SATA 73
Weinstein, Norman Charles 1948- ... CANR-31
Earlier sketch in CA 37-40R
Weinstein, Philip M. 1940- 165
Weinstein, Robert A. 1914- 29-32R
Weinstein, Sol 1928- 13-16R
Weinstein, Warren 1941- 93-96
Weinstock, Herbert 1905-1971 .... CANR-2
Obituary 33-36R
Earlier sketch in CA 1-4R
Weinstock, John M(artin) 1936- 81-84
Weinstock, M(oshe) D(avid) 1922- 131
Weinstock, Nicholas 202
Weinstone, William W. 1898(?)-1985
Obituary 117
Weinswig, Melvin H. 1935- 185
Brief entry 107
Weintal, Edward 1901-1973
Obituary 41-44R
Weintraub, David 1949- 167
Weintraub, Dov 1926-1985 .... CANR-36
Earlier sketch in CA 109
Weintraub, Karl Joachim 1924-2004 ..... 25-28R
Obituary 225
Weintraub, Linda 1942- 135
Weintraub, Robert E. 1925-1983
Obituary 110
Weintraub, Rodelle (Selma) 1933- 97-100
Weintraub, Sidney 1914-1983 .... CANR-6
Obituary 110
Earlier sketch in CA 1-4R
Weintraub, Sidney 1922- CANR-26
Earlier sketch in CA 108
Weintraub, Stanley 1929- CANR-22
Earlier sketches in CA 1-4R, CANR-2
See also CAAS 20
See also DLB 111
Weintraub, Wiktor 1908-1988 .... CANR-3
Obituary 126
Earlier sketch in CA 5-8R
Weintraub, William 1926- CANR-130
Earlier sketch in CA 1-4R
Weinwurm, George F(elix) 1935- 33-36R
Weinzweig, Helen 1915- 106
Weir, Alice M.
See McLaughlin, Emma Maude
Weir, Alison 200
Weir, Ben(jamin M.) 1923- 144
Weir, Bob 1947- 143
See also SATA 76
Weir, Carol S. 1924- 125
Weir, Charlene 1937- CANR-112
Earlier sketch in CA 153
Weir, David (A.) 1947- 147
Weir, Diana (R.) Loiewski 1958- 182
See also SATA 111
Weir, Gary E. 1951(?)- 145
Weir, J(ohn) E(dward) 1935- 118
See also CP 1
Weir, Joan S(herman) 1928- CANR-58
Earlier sketches in CA 112, CANR-31
See also SATA 99
Weir, John
See Cross, Colin (John)
Weir, Judith 1954- 190
Weir, LaVada CANR-9
Earlier sketch in CA 21-24R
See also SATA 2
Weir, Molly 1920-2004 .... CANR-12
Obituary 233
Earlier sketch in CA 29-32R
Weir, Nancie MacCullough 1933- 65-68
Weir, Peter (Lindsay) 1944- 123
Brief entry 113
See also CLC 20
Weir, Robert E. 1952- 207
Weir, Robert M(cColloch) 1933- 93-96
Weir, Rosemary (Green) 1905-1994 . CANR-10
Earlier sketch in CA 13-16R
See also CWRI 5
See also SATA 21
Weir, Theresa 1954- 231
Weir, Thomas R(obert) 1912- 41-44R
Weir, Walter 1909-1996 .... 5-8R
Weir, Wendy 1949- 143
See also SATA 76
Weirich, Paul 1946- 192
Weis, Elisabeth 1944- 112
Weis, Jack 1932- 105
Weis, Lois 1948- 172
Weis, Margaret (Edith) 1948- CANR-94
Earlier sketches in CA 111, CANR-34, 59
See also AAYA 33
See also FANT
See also SATA 38, 92
See also YAW
Weis, Norman D(wight) 1923- 61-64
Weis, Rene (Jean Alphonse) 1953- 127
Weisberg, Barry 33-36R
Weisberg, Gabriel P(aul) 1942- CANR-87
Earlier sketch in CA 73-76
Weisberg, Harold 1913-2002 .... 41-44R
Obituary 207
Weisberg, Herbert F. 1941- 151
Weisberg, Joseph 215
Weisberg, Joseph Gotland 1911-1984
Obituary 112
Weisberg, Joseph S(impson) 1937- 107
Weisberg, Richard H(arvey) 1944- 128
Weisberger, Bernard A(llen) 1922- .. CANR-116
Earlier sketches in CA 5-8R, CANR-7
See also SATA 21
Weisberger, Eleanor (Burt) 1920- 97-100
Weisberger, Lauren 1977- 211
Weisbord, Albert 1900(?)-1977
Obituary 69-72
Weisbord, Marvin R(oss) 1931- CANR-9
Earlier sketch in CA 65-68
Weisbord, Robert G. 1933-
Brief entry 109
Weisbord, Vera Buch 1895-1987 73-76
Obituary 123
Weisbrod, Burton Allen 1931- CANR-21
Earlier sketches in CA 45-48, CANR-1
Weisbrot, Robert (S.) 1951- CANR-112
Earlier sketch in CA 131
Weisbuch, Robert 1946- 104
Weisburd, Martin Harold 1940(?)-1978
Obituary 77-80
Weise, Christian 1642-1708 .... DLB 168
Weise, R. Eric 1933- 41-44R
Weisenborn, Guenther 1902-1969
Obituary 114
See also Weisenborn, Gunther
See also DLB 69, 124
Weisenborn, Gunther
See Weisenborn, Guenther
See also DLB 69, 124
Weisenburger, Francis Phelps
1900-1980 .... CAP-1
Earlier sketch in CA 17-18
Weisenburger, Steven 196
Wei-Sender, Katherine 1930- 197
Weisenfeld, Murray 1923-1996 104
Weiser, David K. 1944- 127
Weiser, Eric 1907- 17-20R
Weiser, Marjorie P(hillis) K(atz) 1934- 103
See also SATA 33
Weisgal, Meyer W(olf) 1894-1977
Obituary 89-92
Weisgall, Deborah 194
Weisgall, Jonathan M. 1949- 154
Weisgard, Leonard (Joseph) 1916-2000 ... 9-12R
Obituary 190
See also MAICYA 1, 2
See also SAAS 19
See also SATA 2, 30, 85
See also SATA-Obit 122
Weisgerber, Charles A(ugust)
1912-1977 .... 41-44R
Weisgerber, Jean 1924- 65-68
Weisgerber, Robert A(rthur) 1929- 49-52
Weisheipl, James A(thanasius)
1923- CANR-15
Earlier sketch in CA 41-44R
Weisheit, Eldon 1933- CANR-14
Earlier sketch in CA 29-32R
Weisinger, Mort(imer) 1915-1978 ... CANR-144
Earlier sketch in CA 9-12R
Weiskopf, Bob
See Weiskopf, Robert J.
Weiskopf, Robert J. 1914-2001 123
Obituary 193
Brief entry 118
Interview in CA-123
Weisman, Alan H. 1947- 127
Weisman, Avery Danto 1913- 156
Weisman, Brent Richards 1952- 142
Weisman, Herman M. 1916- 9-12R
Weisman, John 1942- CANR-99
Earlier sketches in CA 45-48, 145, CANR-1, 40
Weisman, Larry 201
Weisman, Leslie Kanes 1945- 170
Weisman, Marilee 1939- 65-68
Weisman, Mary-Lou 1937- CANR-142
Earlier sketch in CA 109
Weismann, Donald L(eroy) 1914- 33-36R
Weismiller, Edward Ronald 1915- CANR-1
Earlier sketch in CA 1-4R
Weiss, Abraham 1895-1971
Obituary 104
Weiss, Adelle 1920- 81-84
See also SATA 18
Weiss, Allen 1918- 109
Weiss, Andrea 1956- 154
Weiss, Ann E(dwards) 1943- CANR-28
Earlier sketches in CA 45-48, CANR-1, 11
See also MAICYA 1, 2
See also SAAS 13
See also SATA 30, 69
Weiss, Arthur 1912-1980 .... 25-28R
Weiss, Bennet A., Jr. 1926(?)-1983
Obituary 109
Weiss, Beno 1933- 123
Weiss, Bernard J(acob) 1936- 109
Weiss, Brian L(eslie) 1944- 165
Weiss, Dale Eugene 1947- 114
Weiss, Daniel Evan 1953- CANR-99
Earlier sketch in CA 147
Weiss, David
See Halivni, David Weiss
Weiss, David 1909-2002 .... CANR-12
Obituary 211
Earlier sketch in CA 13-16R
Weiss, David W(alter) 1927- 185
Weiss, Edna
See Barth, Edna
Weiss, Edna Smith 1916- 5-8R
Weiss, Elizabeth S(chwartz) 1944- CANR-11
Earlier sketch in CA 61-64
Weiss, Ellen 1953- 113
See also SATA 44
Weiss, Ernst 1882-1940 .... DLB 81
See also EWL 3
Weiss, Francis Joseph 1899(?)-1975
Obituary 53-56
Weiss, G(ustav) A(dolf) M(ichael)
1922- 41-44R
Weiss, Gaea (Laughingbird) 1941- 119
Weiss, Gary (R.) 228
Weiss, Harry B(ischoff) 1883-1972 45-48
Weiss, Harvey 1922- CANR-38
Earlier sketches in CA 5-8R, CANR-6
See also CLR 4
See also MAICYA 1, 2
See also SAAS 19
See also SATA 1, 27, 76
Weiss, Herbert F. 1930- 21-24R
Weiss, Irving J. 1921- CANR-10
Earlier sketch in CA 17-20R
Weiss, Jaqueline Shachter 1926- CANR-130
Earlier sketch in CA 119
See also SATA 65
Weiss, Jeffrey S. 1958- 187
Weiss, Jess E(dward) 1926- CANR-38
Earlier sketch in CA 49-52
Weiss, Joan Talmage 1928- CANR-2
Earlier sketch in CA 5-8R
Weiss, John 1818-1879 .... DLB 1, 243
Weiss, John 1927- CANR-66
Earlier sketch in CA 17-20R
Weiss, Jonathan A(rthur) 1939- 93-96
Weiss, Julian 206
Weiss, Julian M. 1952-2001 206
Weiss, Kenneth M(onrad) 1941- 101
Weiss, Leatie 1928- 65-68
See also SATA-Brief 50
Weiss, Leonard W(inchell) 1925- CANR-6
Earlier sketch in CA 5-8R
Weiss, Lillian (?)-1972
Obituary 104
Weiss, Linda 1958- 189
Weiss, Louise 1893-1983
Obituary 109
Weiss, M(orton) Jerome 1926- CANR-9
Earlier sketch in CA 17-20R
Weiss, M. Jerry
See Weiss, M(orton) Jerome
Weiss, Malcolm E. 1928- CANR-11
Earlier sketch in CA 25-28R
See also SATA 3
Weiss, Margaret R. 1923(?)-1992 57-60
Obituary 137
Weiss, Melford Stephen 1937- 53-56
Weiss, Michael
See Weiss, Mike
Weiss, Michael J. 1952- 192
Weiss, Mike 1942- 141
Weiss, Miriam
See Schlein, Miriam
Weiss, Miriam (Strauss) 1905-1989 .... CAP-2
Earlier sketch in CA 29-32
Weiss, Mitch 1951- .... SATA 123
Weiss, Morris S(amuel) 1915- 89-92
Weiss, Nancy J(oan) 1944- CANR-13
Earlier sketch in CA 77-80
Weiss, Nicki 1954- CANR-129
Earlier sketches in CA 108, CANR-26
See also SATA 33, 86
Weiss, Paul
See Weiss, Paul A(lfred)
Weiss, Paul 1901-2002 .... CANR-3
Obituary 209
Earlier sketch in CA 5-8R
See also CAAS 12
See also DLB 279
Weiss, Paul A(lfred) 1898-1989
Obituary 129
Weiss, Peg 1933(?)-1996 125
Obituary 152
Weiss, Peter (Ulrich) 1916-1982 .... CANR-3
Obituary 106
Earlier sketch in CA 45-48
See also CLC 3, 15, 51
See also DAM DRAM
See also DFS 3
See also DLB 69, 124
See also EWL 3
See also RGWL 2, 3
See also TCLC 152
Weiss, Philip 1956(?)- 236
Weiss, Raymond L. 1930- 142
Weiss, Renee Karol 1923- 41-44R
See also SATA 5
Weiss, Robert M. 1929- 37-40R
Weiss, Robert S(tuart) 1925- 25-28R
Weiss, Roger W(illiam) 1930- 45-48
weiss, ruth 1928- 122
See also CAAS 24
Weiss, Samuel A(bba) 1922- 41-44R
Weiss, Sanford 1927- 25-28R
Weiss, (Paul) Shandor 1954- 120
Weiss, Tamara 239
Weiss, Theodore (Russell) 1916-2003 189
Obituary 216
Earlier sketches in CA 9-12R, CANR-46, 94
Autobiographical Essay in 189
See also CAAS 2
See also CLC 3, 8, 14
See also CP 1, 2, 3, 4, 5, 6, 7
See also DLB 5
See also TCLE 1:2
Weiss, Thomas Fischer 1934- 162
Weiss, Thomas G. 1946- CANR-99
Earlier sketch in CA 142
Weiss, Thomas J(oseph) 1942- 105
Weiss, Timothy F. 1949- 146
Weiss, Vikki 1969- 192
Weiss, Winfried (Ferdinand) 1937-1991 117
Obituary 140
Weissberg, Michael P. 1942- 126
Weissberger, L. Arnold 1907-1981
Obituary 103
Weissbort, Daniel 1935- CANR-2
Earlier sketch in CA 45-48
See also CP 2, 3, 4, 5, 6, 7
Weissbourd, Bernice (Targ) 1923- ... CANR-113
Earlier sketch in CA 153
Weissbourd, Richard 167
Weisse, Allen B(arry) 1929- 224
Weiße, Christian Felix 1726-1804 .... DLB 97
Weissenborn, Hellmuth 1898-1982
Obituary 107
See also SATA-Obit 31
Weisser, Henry 1935- 196
Weisser, Michael R. 1944- 143
Weisskopf, Kurt 1907- 25-28R
Weisskopf, Thomas E. 1940- CANR-87
Earlier sketch in CA 130
Weisskopf, Victor Frederick 1908-2002 107
Obituary 205
Weisskopf, Walter A(lbert) 1904-1991 ... 37-40R
Weissler, (Lenore E.) Chava 1947- 187
Weissman, Benjamin M(urry)
1917-1987 73-76
Weissman, Dick
See Weissman, Richard
Weissman, Jack 1921- 13-16R
Weissman, Karen 225
Weissman, Myrna M. 194
Weissman, Paul 1932- 45-48
Weissman, Philip 1911(?)-1972
Obituary 33-36R
Weissman, Richard 1935- 81-84
Weissman, Rozanne 1942- 101
Weissman, Stephen R(ichard) 1941- . CANR-11
Earlier sketch in CA 57-60
Weissman, Steve
See Weissman, Stephen R(ichard)
Weissmann, Ann B. 1934- 139
Weissmann, Gerald 1930- CANR-120
Earlier sketches in CA 126, CANR-52
Weissmuller, Johnny
See Weissmuller, Peter John
Weissmuller, Peter John 1904-1984
Obituary 111
Weisstein, Ulrich W(erner) 1925- 21-24R
Weisstub, D(avid) N(orman) 1944- ... CANR-44
Earlier sketch in CA 29-32R
Weist, Dwight 1910-1991 132
Weith, Warren 1926-1991 114
Weithorn, Stanley S(tephen) 1924- 13-16R
Weitling, Wilhelm 1808-1871 .... DLB 129
Weitz, Chris 1970- 230
Weitz, Henry 1911- 41-44R
Weitz, John 1923-2002 .... 29-32R
Obituary 211
Weitz, Mark A. 1957- 206
Weitz, Martin Mishli 1909-1992 ...... CANR-13
Earlier sketches in CAP-2, CA 17-18
Weitz, Morris 1916-1981 .... CANR-7
Obituary 102
Earlier sketch in CA 5-8R
Weitz, Paul 1966- 230
Weitz, Raanan 1913-1998 .... CANR-1
Earlier sketch in CA 45-48
Weitzel, Edwin A(nthony) 1905-1988
Obituary 127
Weitzel, Eugene Joseph 1927- 5-8R
Weitzel, Tony
See Weitzel, Edwin A(nthony)
Weitzel, William (Frederick) 1936- 143
Weitzenhoffer, Andre M(uller) 1921- 5-8R
Weitzman, Alan 1933- 29-32R
Weitzman, Arthur J(oshua) 1933- 53-56
Weitzman, David L. 1936- 195
See also SATA 122
Weitzman, Elliot D. 1929-1983
Obituary 110
Weitzman, Jacqueline Preiss 1964- 187
Weitzman, Martin L(awrence) 1942- 117
Weitzmann, Kurt 1904-1993 .... CANR-35
Obituary 141
Earlier sketch in CA 41-44R
Weixlmann, Joe
See Weixlmann, Joseph Norman
Weixlmann, Joseph Norman 1946- 109
Weizenbaum, Joseph 1923-
Brief entry 113
Weizman, Ezer 1924-2005 111
Obituary 238
Weizman, Savine Gross 1929- 131
Weizmann, Daniel 1967- 223
Weizsaecker, Carl Friedrich von
See von Weizsaecker, Carl Friedrich
Wekesser, Carol A. 1963- 143
See also SATA 76
Welber, Robert 104
See also SATA 26

Cumulative Index 611 **Wells**

Welbourn, F(rederick) B(urkewood) 1912- 21-24R
Welburn, Ron(ald Garfield) 1944- CANR-17
Earlier sketches in CA 45-48, CANR-1
See also BW 1
Welch, Amanda (Jane) 1945- .... SATA 75
Welch, Ann Courtenay (Edmonds) 1917-2002 .... CANR-18
Obituary 211
Earlier sketches in CA 9-12R, CANR-3
Welch, Bob
See Welch, Robert Lynn
Welch, Bob 1954- 236
Welch, Charles Scott
See Smith, LeRoi Tex
Welch, Claude E(merson), Jr. 1939- .. CANR-32
Earlier sketches in CA 41-44R, CANR-14
Welch, Cliff(ord Andrew) 236
Welch, Cyril 1939- 118
Welch, D. Don, (Jr.) 148
Welch, D'Alte Aldridge 1907-1970
Obituary 104
See also SATA-Obit 27
Welch, David 1950- 130
Welch, (Maurice) Denton 1915-1948 148
Brief entry 121
See also BRWS 8, 9
See also RGEL 2
See also TCLC 22
Welch, Don(ovan LeRoy) 1932- CANR-43
Earlier sketches in CA 104, CANR-20
Welch, Finis R. 1938- 118
Welch, George Patrick 1901-1976 .... CAP-1
Obituary 65-68
Earlier sketch in CA 13-14
Welch, Gita (Bernardo) Honwana 1948- 138
Welch, Herbert 1862-1969 .... CAP-1
Earlier sketch in CA 13-16
Welch, Holmes (Hinkley) 1921-1981 .... 21-24R
Welch, J(oseph) Edmund 1922- 57-60
Welch, James (Phillip) 1940-2003 .. CANR-107
Obituary 219
Earlier sketches in CA 85-88, CANR-42, 66
See also CLC 6, 14, 52
See also CN 5, 6, 7
See also CP 2, 3, 4, 5, 6, 7
See also CPW
See also DAM MULT, POP
See also DLB 175, 256
See also LATS 1:1
See also NNAL
See also PC 62
See also RGAL 4
See also TCWW 1, 2
Welch, Jean-Louise
See Kempton, Jean Welch
Welch, Jerome A. 1933- 65-68
Welch, Julie 228
Welch, June Rayfield 1927-1998 .... 41-44R
Welch, Kathleen E(thel) 1951- 136
Welch, Kathryn E. 1956- CANR-106
Earlier sketch in CA 184
Welch, Kenneth Frederick 1917- 105
Welch, Lew(is Barrett, Jr.) 1926-1971(?) 153
Obituary 113
See also BG 1:3
See also CP 1
See also DLB 16
Welch, Liliane 1937- CANR-27
Earlier sketch in CA 110
Welch, Martha McKeen 1914-
Brief entry 114
See also SATA-Brief 45
Welch, Martha Mckeen 1914- 206
Welch, Mary Ross 1918- 53-56
Welch, Mary-Scott (Stewart) 1919-1995 104
Obituary 149
Welch, Matthew 1958- 215
Welch, Michael Dylan 1962- 212
Welch, Michael Irene 1940- 97-100
Welch, Patrick
See Welch, George Patrick
Welch, Pauline
See Bodenham, Hilda Morris
Welch, Richard Edwin, Jr. 1924- 85-88
Welch, Robert 1947- CANR-117
Earlier sketch in CA 159
Welch, Robert H(enry) W(inborne), Jr. 1899-1985
Obituary 114
Welch, Robert Lynn 1956- 112
Welch, Ronald
See Felton, Ronald Oliver
Welch, Rowland
See Davies, L(eslie) P(urnell)
Welch, Sheila Kelly 1945- 199
See also SATA 130
Welch, Stuart Cary 1928- 103
Welch, Timothy L. 1935- 85-88
Welch, William 1918-1981(?) 154
Welch, William A. 1915(?)-1976
Obituary 65-68
Welch, Willy 1952- 159
See also SATA 93
Welcher, Jeanne K. 1922-
Brief entry 116
Welcher, Rosalind 1922- CANR-25
Earlier sketch in CA 45-48
Welchman, Gordon 1906(?)-1985
Obituary 117
Welch-Tyson, Delorys 235
Welcome, John
See Brennan, John N(eedham) H(uggard)
Weld, Angelina (Emily) Grimke
See Grimke, Angelina (Emily) Weld
See also FW
Weld, John 1905-2003 147
Obituary 218
Weld, Philip S(altonstall Sr.) 1914-1984
Obituary 114
Weld, William F(loyd) 1945- 186
Welding, Patsy Ruth 1924- 61-64
Weldon, Fay 1931- CANR-137
Earlier sketches in CA 21-24R, CANR-16, 46, 63, 97
Interview in CANR-16
See also BRWS 4
See also CDBLB 1960 to Present
See also CLC 6, 9, 11, 19, 36, 59, 122
See also CN 3, 4, 5, 6, 7
See also CPW
See also DAM POP
See also DLB 14, 194, 319
See also EWL 3
See also FW
See also HGG
See also MTCW 1, 2
See also MTFW 2005
See also RGEL 2
See also RGSF 2
Weldon, John 1890(?)-1963
Obituary 115
See also MacNamara, Brinsley
Weldon, John F(rederick Stover) 1948- 113
Weldon, Lynn Leroy 1930- 97-100
Weldon, Michael J(ames) 1952- 117
Weldon, Michele 1958- 187
Weldon, Rex
See Rimel, Duane (Weldon)
Weldon, (Nathaniel) Warren, (Jr.) 1919- 29-32R
Weldt-Basson, Helene Carol 1958- 145
Welfare, Humphrey 1950- 124
Welfare, Simon 1946- 133
Welfle, Richard A. 1901- CAP-1
Earlier sketch in CA 13-14
Welfling, Weldon 1912-1978
Obituary 111
Welford, A(lan) T(raviss) 1914- CANR-5
Earlier sketch in CA 13-16R
Welford, Sue 1942- 142
See also SATA 75
Welish, Marjorie 1944- 169
Welk, Lawrence 1903-1992 134
Brief entry 105
Welke, Elton 1941- 65-68
Welker, David 1917-1985 57-60
Welker, Robert Henry 1917-1991 89-92
Welker, Robert L(ouis) 1924- 9-12R
Welkowitz, Joan 1929- 53-56
Well, Alan Stewart
See Sewart, Alan
Welland, Colin
See Williams, Colin
Welland, Dennis (Sydney Reginald) 1919- CANR-2
Earlier sketch in CA 5-8R
Wellard, James (Howard) 1909-1987 . CANR-3
Obituary 122
Earlier sketch in CA 5-8R
Wellborn, Charles 1923- 29-32R
Wellborn, Fred W(ilmot) 1894-1982 .... 9-12R
Wellborn, Grace Pleasant 1906-1971(?) CAP-2
Earlier sketch in CA 17-18
Wellek, Rene 1903-1995 .... CANR-8
Obituary 150
Earlier sketch in CA 5-8R
Interview in CANR-8
See also CAAS 7
See also CLC 28
See also DLB 63
See also EWL 3
Wellen, Edward (Paul) 1919- CANR-108
Earlier sketch in CA 85-88
Weller, Allen Stuart 1907-1997 .... CANR-24
Earlier sketch in CA 1-4R
Weller, Anthony 1957- 234
Weller, Charles 1911-1997 .... 21-24R
Weller, George (Anthony) 1907-2002 65-68
Obituary 219
See also SATA 31
See also SATA-Obit 140
Weller, Jac 1913-1994 200
Weller, Mark 1962- 178
Weller, Michael 1942- 85-88
See also CAD
See also CD 5, 6
See also CLC 10, 53
Weller, Paul 1958- .... CLC 26
Weller, Robert P(aul) 1953- CANR-109
Earlier sketch in CA 118
Weller, Sam 1967- 236
Weller, Sheila 1945- 77-80
Weller, Vann K. 166
Weller, Worth H. 1946- 186
Wellershoff, Dieter 1925- CANR-37
Earlier sketches in CA 89-92, CANR-16
See also CLC 46
Welles, Benjamin 1916-2002 215
Welles, Elizabeth
See Roby, Mary Linn
Welles, Margery Miller 1923-1985
Obituary 115
Welles, (George) Orson 1915-1985 93-96
Obituary 117
See also AAYA 40
See also CLC 20, 80
Welles, Samuel Gardner 1913(?)-1981
Obituary 105
Welles, Winifred 1893-1939
Brief entry 112
See also SATA-Brief 27
Wellesbourne, Peter
See Williams, P(eter) F(airney)
Wellesley, Gerald 1885-1972
Obituary 104
Wellesley, Kenneth 1911-1995 106
Wellesz, Egon Joseph 1885-1974
Obituary 53-56
Wellford, Harrison 1940-
Brief entry 111
Wellford, Lin(da) 1951- 165
Wellham, John W(alter) G(eorge) 1919- 150
Welling, Kathryn M. 1952- 127
Welling, Peter J. 1947- .... SATA 135
Welling, William 1924- 81-84
Wellington, C(harles) Burleigh 1920- 1-4R
Wellington, Harry H(illel) 1926- 25-28R
Wellington, Jean Willett 1922- 1-4R
Wellington, John H. 1892-1981 .... CAP-2
Earlier sketch in CA 25-28
Wellington, Kate
See Schulze, Hertha
Wellington, Monica 1957- CANR-142
Earlier sketch in CA 136
See also SATA 67, 99, 157
Wellington, R(ichard) A(nthony) 1919- 61-64
Wellington, Sheila W(acks) 1932- 200
Wellisch, Hans H(anan) 1920-2004 102
Obituary 225
Wellisz, Leopold T. 1882-1972
Obituary 37-40R
Wellman, Alice 1900-1984 89-92
See also SATA 51
See also SATA-Brief 36
Wellman, Carl (Pierce) 1926- 37-40R
Wellman, Frederick L(ovejoy) 1897-1994 77-80
Wellman, Henry Q. 1945- 37-40R
Wellman, John McDowell 1945- 166
See also Wellman, Mac
See also CD 5
Wellman, Mac
See Wellman, John McDowell and Wellman, John McDowell
See also CAD
See also CD 6
See also CLC 65
See also RGAL 4
Wellman, Manly Wade 1903-1986 .. CANR-44
Obituary 118
Earlier sketches in CA 1-4R, CANR-6, 16
See also CLC 49
See also FANT
See also SATA 6
See also SATA-Obit 47
See also SFW 4
See also SUFW
Wellman, Paul I(selin) 1898-1966 .... CANR-64
Obituary 25-28R
Earlier sketches in CA 1-4R, CANR-16
See also SATA 3
See also TCWW 1, 2
Wellman, Sam(uel) 1939- 195
See also SATA 122
Wellman, William A(ugustus) 1896-1975
Obituary 61-64
Wellner, Alison S(tein) 1974- 163
Wellock, Thomas Raymond 1959- 196
Wells, Allen 1951- CANR-56
Earlier sketch in CA 125
Wells, Angus 1943- 167
See also FANT
See also TCWW 2
Wells, Anna Mary 1906- CANR-2
Earlier sketch in CA 5-8R
Wells, Arvin Robert 1927- 1-4R
Wells, Bella Fromm 1901(?)-1972
Obituary 104
Wells, C(olin) M(ichael) 1933- 41-44R
Wells, Carolyn 1869(?)-1942 185
Brief entry 113
See also CMW 4
See also DLB 11
See also TCLC 35
Wells, Catherine 1952- 164
Wells, Charles Jeremiah 1800-1879 ..... DLB 32
Wells, Daniel A. 1943- 177
Wells, David F. 229
Wells, Dee (Alberta) 1925-2003 85-88
Obituary 217
See also AITN 1
Wells, (William) Dicky 1910-1985 61-64
Wells, Donald A(rthur) 1917- 21-24R
Wells, Edward
See Wellsted, W. Raife
Wells, Ellen B(aker) 1934- 103
Wells, Evelyn 53-56
Wells, Gabriel 1862-1946 184
See also DLB 140
Wells, Gail (Elizabeth) 1952- 180
Wells, George A(lbert) 1926- CANR-32
Earlier sketches in CA 81-84, CANR-15
Wells, George Philip 1901-1985
Obituary 117
Wells, H(erbert) G(eorge) 1866-1946 121
Brief entry 110
See also AAYA 18
See also BPFB 3
See also BRW 6
See also CDBLB 1914-1945
See also CLR 64
See also DA
See also DA3
See also DAB
See also DAC
See also DAM MST, NOV
See also DLB 34, 70, 156, 178
See also EWL 3
See also EXPS
See also HGG
See also LAIT 3
See also LMFS 2
See also MTCW 1, 2
See also MTFW 2005
See also NFS 17, 20
See also RGEL 2
See also RGSF 2
See also SATA 20
See also SCFW 1, 2
See also SFW 4
See also SSC 6, 70
See also SSFS 3
See also SUFW
See also TCLC 6, 12, 19, 133
See also TEA
See also WCH
See also WLC
See also WLIT 4
See also YAW
Wells, Harold P(hilmore) 1925- CANR-10
Earlier sketch in CA 65-68
Wells, Harry Kohlsaat 1911-1976 .... 5-8R
Obituary 65-68
Wells, Helen
See Campbell, Hope
Wells, Helen 1910-1986 .... CANR-37
Earlier sketch in CA 29-32R
See also MAICYA 1, 2
See also SATA 2, 49
Wells, Helena 1758(?)-1824 .... DLB 200
Wells, Henry W(illis) 1895-1978 ...... CANR-28
Obituary 77-80
Earlier sketch in CA 81-84
Wells, Hondo
See Whittington, Harry (Benjamin)
Wells, J. Wellington
See de Camp, L(yon) Sprague
Wells, James B(uchanan) 1909-1996 45-48
Wells, James M. 1917- 17-20R
Wells, Jane 1961- 155
Wells, Jerome C(ovell) 1936- 41-44R
Wells, Jessica
See Buckland, Raymond
Wells, Joel F(reeman) 1930-2001 ..... CANR-23
Obituary 195
Earlier sketch in CA 13-16R
Wells, John Campbell 1936-1998 104
Obituary 164
Wells, John Jay
See Coulson, Juanita (Ruth)
Wells, John Warren 1938- CANR-4
Earlier sketch in CA 49-52
Wells, June
See Swinford, Betty (June Wells)
Wells, Ken 1948- 216
Wells, Kenneth McNeill 1905-1988 ...... CAP-1
Earlier sketch in CA 13-14
Wells, Lawrence 1941- 120
Wells, Leon W. 1925- 17-20R
Wells, Linton 1893-1976 97-100
Obituary 61-64
Wells, Lisa
See Raucina, Thomas Frank
Wells, Louis T(ruitt), Jr. 1937- 65-68
Wells, M. Gawain 1942- 101
Wells, Marian (Louise Bradfield) 1931- 113
Wells, Martha 1964- CANR-98
Earlier sketch in CA 142
See also FANT
Wells, Martin John 1928- 189
Wells, Mary Ann 1944- 155
Wells, Merle William 1918- CANR-37
Earlier sketches in CA 85-88, CANR-16
Wells, Miranda
See Winik, Marion (Lisa)
Wells, Nigel 1944- 118
Wells, Patricia 1946- CANR-115
Earlier sketch in CA 132
Wells, Peter D. 1936- 25-28R
Wells, Peter S. 217
Wells, Rebecca 1952- CANR-131
Earlier sketch in CA 172
See also DLB 292
Wells, Robert
See Welsch, Roger L(ee)
Wells, (Frank Charles) Robert 1929- 97-100
Wells, Robert 1947- 155
See also CP 7
See also DLB 40
Wells, Robert Vale 1943- CANR-12
Earlier sketch in CA 73-76
Wells, Robert W(ayne) 1918-1995 ..... CANR-2
Earlier sketch in CA 49-52
Wells, Roger 1947- 150
Wells, Ronald Vale 1913- CANR-14
Earlier sketch in CA 37-40R

Wells 612 CONTEMPORARY AUTHORS

Wells, Rosemary 1943- CANR-120
Earlier sketches in CA 85-88, CANR-48
See also AAYA 13
See also BYA 7, 8
See also CLC 12
See also CLR 16, 69
See also CWRI 5
See also MAICYA 1, 2
See also SAAS 1
See also SATA 18, 69, 114, 156
See also YAW
Wells, Samuel F(ogle, Jr.) 1935- 104
Wells, Samuel J(ames III) 1936- 123
Wells, Simon 1961- 225
Wells, Stanley W(illiam) 1930- CANR-112
Earlier sketches in CA 21-24R, CANR-10, 29
Wells, Susan (Mary) 1951- 146
See also SATA 78
Wells, Theodora (Westmont) 1926- 134
Brief entry 113
Wells, Tim 1954- 129
Wells, Tobias
See Forbes, DeLoris (Florine) Stanton
Wells, Tom H. 1917- 21-24R
Wells, Walter 1937- 25-28R
Wells, William D(eWitt) 1926- CANR-13
Earlier sketch in CA 61-64
Wells, William Thomas 1908-1990(?)
Obituary 130
Wells-Barnett, Ida B(ell) 1862-1931 182
See also DLB 23, 221
See also TCLC 125
Wellsted, W. Raife 1929- 125
Wellstone, Paul (David)
1944-2002 .... CANR-111
Obituary 212
Earlier sketch in CA 107
Wellwarth, George E(manuel) 1932- .. CANR-3
Earlier sketch in CA 9-12R
Welmers, William Evert 1916-1988 104
Welpott, Jack (Warren) 1923- 210
Wels, Alena 1938(?)-1985
Obituary 115
Wels, Byron G(erald) 1924-1993 .... CANR-8
Earlier sketch in CA 61-64
See also SATA 9
Wels, Susan 176
Welsbacher, Anne 1955- 155
See also SATA 89
Welsby, Paul A(ntony) 1920-2002 129
Obituary 209
Welsch, Erwin Kurt 1935- 17-20R
Welsch, Glenn Albert 1915- CANR-10
Earlier sketch in CA 13-16R
Welsch, Roger L(ee) 1936- CANR-9
Earlier sketch in CA 21-24R, 149
See also SATA 82
Welsh, Alexander 1933- CANR-127
Earlier sketches in CA 5-8R, CANR-6
Welsh, Andrew 1937- 110
Welsh, Anne 1922- 101
See also CP 1, 2
Welsh, David
See Hills, C(harles) A(lbert) R(eis)
Welsh, David J(ohn) 1920- 17-20R
Welsh, Frank (Reeson) 1931- CANR-140
Earlier sketch in CA 135
Welsh, George Schlager 1918- 17-20R
Welsh, Irvine 1958- 173
See also CLC 144
See also CN 7
See also DLB 271
Welsh, Jack (D.) 1928- 189
Welsh, James M(ichael)
1938-2003 .... CANR-105
Earlier sketches in CA 53-56, CANR-4, 20
Welsh, John R(ushing) 1916-1974 .... 37-40R
Welsh, Ken 1941- CANR-13
Earlier sketch in CA 77-80
Welsh, Louise 224
Welsh, Marion E. 1910-1996 118
Welsh, Mary
See Hemingway, Mary Welsh
Welsh, Mary Flynn 1910(?)-1984
Obituary 112
See also SATA-Obit 38
Welsh, Paul 1911- 104
Welsh, Peter C(orbett) 1926- 25-28R
Welsh, Stanley L. 1928- 103
Welsh, Susan
See Collins, Margaret (Brandon James)
Welsh, William A(llen) 1940- CANR-25
Earlier sketch in CA 45-48
Welsing, Frances Cress 1935- 142
See also BW 2
Welsman, Ernest 1912- 5-8R
Welsome, Eileen 1951- 198
Welt, Elly 127
Welt, Louis G(ordon) 1913-1974
Obituary 45-48
Welter, Erich 1900-1982
Obituary 107
Welter, Paul (R.) 1928- 121
Welter, Rush (Eastman) 1923-2001 ..... CANR-2
Earlier sketch in CA 5-8R
Weltge, Ralph (William) 1930- 21-24R
Weltge, Sigrid W(ortmann) 1935- ... CANR-106
Earlier sketch in CA 145
Weltge-Wortmann, Sigrid
See Weltge, Sigrid W(ortmann)
Welthy, Soni Halstead 1933- 13-16R
Weltman, Sharon Aronofsky 1957- 185
Weltmann, Lutz 1901- CAP-1
Earlier sketch in CA 11-12
Weltner, Linda R(iverly) 1938- 105
See also SATA 38
Weltner, Peter (Nissen) 1942- CANR-118
Earlier sketch in CA 160
Welton, Jude 1955- CANR-122
Earlier sketch in CA 148
See also SATA 79, 143
Weltsch, Robert 1891-1982
Obituary 108
Welty, Eudora (Alice) 1909-2001 .... CANR-128
Obituary 199
Earlier sketches in CA 9-12R, CANR-32, 65
See also CABS 1
See also AAYA 48
See also AMW
See also AMWR 1
See also BPFB 3
See also CDALB 1941-1968
See also CLC 1, 2, 5, 14, 22, 33, 105
See also CN 1, 2, 3, 4, 5, 6, 7
See also CSW
See also DA
See also DA3
See also DAB
See also DAC
See also DAM MST, NOV
See also DLB 2, 102, 143
See also DLBD 12
See also DLBY 1987, 2001
See also EWL 3
See also EXPS
See also HGG
See also LAIT 3
See also MAL 5
See also MAWW
See also MTCW 1, 2
See also MTFW 2005
See also NFS 13, 15
See also RGAL 4
See also RGSF 2
See also RHW
See also SSC 1, 27, 51
See also SSFS 2, 10
See also TUS
See also WLC
Welty, Joel Carl 1901-1986 .... CANR-2
Earlier sketch in CA 5-8R
Welty, S. F.
See Welty, Susan F.
Welty, Susan F. 1905- CAP-2
Earlier sketch in CA 17-18
See also SATA 9
Welwood, John 1943- CANR-46
Earlier sketch in CA 120
Welzenbach, Lanora F.
See Miller, Lanora
Welzenbach, Michael 1953(?)-2001 206
Wemple, Suzanne Fonay 1927- 106
Wen, Chihua 1958- 147
Wenar, Charles 1922- 93-96
Wende, Philip 1939- 29-32R
Wendel, Francois Jean 1905-(?) CAP-1
Earlier sketch in CA 13-14
Wendel, Natalja Rose 1900-1996 61-64
Wendel, Thomas H(arold) 1924- 53-56
Wendel, Tim 1956- 105
Wendelin, Rudolph 1910-2000 .... SATA 23
Wendell, Barrett 1855-1921 182
See also DLB 71
Wender, Dorothea 1934- CANR-24
Earlier sketch in CA 45-48
Wender, Paul H. 1934- CANR-51
Earlier sketches in CA 109, CANR-26
Wenderoth, Joe 1966- CANR-135
Earlier sketch in CA 150
Wenders, Wim 1945- 93-96
Wendland, Michael F(letcher) 1946- .. CANR-9
Earlier sketch in CA 65-68
Wendland, Mike
See Wendland, Michael F(letcher)
Wendling, Ronald C(harles) 1939- 152
Wendorf, Patricia 1928- 113
Wendorf, Richard (Harold) 1948- CANR-36
Earlier sketch in CA 114
Wendover, Robert W(arren) 1955- 145
Wendroff, Zalman
See Vendrovskii, David Efimovich
Wendrowsky, Zalman
See Vendrovskii, David Efimovich
Wendt, Albert 1939- 57-60
See also CN 3, 4, 5, 6, 7
See also CP 7
See also EWL 3
See also RGSF 2
Wendt, Gerald L(ouis) 1891-1973
Obituary 45-48
Wendt, Ingrid 1944- 117
Wendt, Jo Ann 1935- 109
Wendt, Lloyd 1908- CANR-25
Earlier sketch in CA 102
Wendt, Viola (Sophia) 1907-1986 104
Wendzel, Robert L. 1938- 112
Weng, Byron S. J. 1934- CANR-16
Earlier sketch in CA 41-44R
Weng, Hsing Ching
See Weng, Wan-go
Weng, Wan-go 1918- 97-100
Wengenroth, Edith Flack Ackley 1887-1970
Obituary 104
Wengenroth, Stow 1906-1978
Obituary 104
Wenger, Etienne 1952- 211
Wenger, (Anna) Grace 1919- 13-16R
Wenger, J(ohn) C(hristian)
1910-1995 .... CANR-21
Earlier sketches in CA 1-4R, CANR-6
Wengerd, Loren L. 1975- 227
Wengert, Norman Irving 1916- 85-88
Wengert, Timothy J. 1950- 172
Wengrov, Charles 1925- CANR-7
Earlier sketch in CA 5-8R
Wenham, David 1945- 152
Wenham, John W(illiam) 1913- 57-60
Wenhe, Mary B. 1910- 65-68
Wen I-to 1899-1946 .... EWL 3
See also TCLC 28
Wenk, Edward, Jr. 1920- 53-56
Wenkam, Robert 1920- CANR-4
Earlier sketch in CA 53-56
Wenkart, Heni
See Wenkart, Henny
Wenkart, Henny 1928- 9-12R
Wennblom, Ralph D. 1922(?)-1986
Obituary 121
Wenner, Jann S(imon) 1946- CA-101
Interview in 101
Wenner, Kate 1947- CANR-101
Earlier sketch in CA 77-80
Wenner, Lettie McSpadden 1937- 65-68
Wenner, Manfred W. 1936- 29-32R
Wenner, Sim 1922- 1-4R
Wennerstrom, Mary H(annah) 1939- 134
Brief entry 110
Wensing, Michael G. 1950- 118
Wensinger, Arthur S(tevens) 1926- CANR-33
Earlier sketches in CA 37-40R, CANR-15
Wentink, Andrew Mark 1948- 105
Wentworth, Barbara
See Pitcher, Gladys
Wentworth, Elise H(ughes) 1931- 77-80
Wentworth, Harold 1904-1973 .... CAP-1
Earlier sketch in CA 13-14
Wentworth, Michael J(ustin) 1938- 118
Wentworth, Patricia 1878-1961
See Elles, Dora Amy
See also CMW 4
Wentworth, Robert
See Hamilton, Edmond
Wentworth, Sally
See Hornsblow, Doreen
See also RHW
Wentworth, William Charles
1790-1872 .... DLB 230
Wentz, Frederick K(uhlman) 1921- 9-12R
Wentz, Walter B. 1929- CANR-10
Earlier sketch in CA 25-28R
Wenzel, Jean-Paul 1947- .... DLB 321
Wenzel, Siegfried 1928- 21-24R
Weores, Sandor 1913-1989
Obituary 127
See also EWL 3
See also RGWL 2, 3
Wepman, Dennis 1933- CANR-46
Earlier sketch in CA 120
Wepman, Joseph M. 1907-1982 45-48
Weppner, Robert S. 1936- 121
Werbach, Adam 1973- 170
Werber, Bernard 1961- 173
Werblow, Dorothy N. 1908-1972
Obituary 37-40R
Werckmeister, O(tto) K(arl) 1934- 140
Were, Gideon S(aulo) 1934- CANR-11
Earlier sketch in CA 65-68
Werenskiold, Marit 1942- CANR-87
Earlier sketch in CA 130
Werewere Liking 1950- .... EWL 3
Werfel, Franz (Viktor) 1890-1945 161
Brief entry 104
See also DLB 81, 124
See also EWL 3
See also RGWL 2, 3
See also TCLC 8
Werich, Jan 1905(?)-1980
Obituary 102
See also EWL 3
Werkema, Mark A. 1965- 209
Werking, Richard Hume 1943- 186
Brief entry 113
Werkley, Caroline E(lsea) 29-32R
Werkman, Sidney L(ee) 1927- 49-52
Werkmeister, Lucyle (Thomas)
1908-1999 .... 5-8R
Werkmeister, W(illiam) H(enry)
1901-1993 .... 21-24R
Werlich, David P(atrick) 1941- 81-84
Werlich, Robert (O'Donnell) 1924-1994 . 9-12R
Obituary 145
Werlin, Herbert Holland 1932- 61-64
Werlin, Nancy 1961- CANR-97
Earlier sketch in CA 151
See also AAYA 35
See also MAICYA 2
See also SATA 87, 119, 161
Werlock, Abby Holmes P(otter) 1942- 137
Werman, Golda 1930- 158
Werman, Robert 1929- 139
Wermiel, Sara E. 1950- 212
Wermuth, Paul C(harles Joseph) 1925- .. 13-16R
Wernberry, John
See Hensley, Sophie Almon
Wernblad, Annette 1958- 144
Werne, Benjamin 1904-1978
Obituary 77-80
Wernecke, Herbert Henry 1895-1975 .... 5-8R
Werner, Alfred 1911-1979
Obituary 89-92
Werner, D. Michael 1950- 120
Werner, Elsa Jane
See Watson, Jane Werner
Werner, Emmy Elizabeth 1929- CANR-144
Earlier sketch in CA 57-60
Werner, Eric 1901-1988 .... 13-16R
Obituary 126
Werner, Flora
See Gonzalez (Mandri), Flora
Werner, Hans 1946- 131
Werner, Hazen G. 1895-1988 .... 17-20R
Werner, Herma 1926- CANR-94
Earlier sketches in CA 85-88, CANR-15, 34
See also SATA 47
See also SATA-Brief 41
Werner, Jane
See Watson, Jane Werner
Werner, Jayne S(usan) 1944- 112
Werner, John R(oland) 1930- 41-44R
Werner, K.
See Casewit, Curtis W(erner)
Werner, Karl Ferdinand 1924- 131
Werner, M(orris) R(obert) 1897-1981 107
Obituary 104
Werner, Marta L. 1964- 235
Werner, Peter Howard 1944- CANR-4
Earlier sketch in CA 53-56
Werner, Victor (Emile) 1894-1980 .... 29-32R
Obituary 93-96
Werner, Vivian 1921- 105
Werner, Zacharias 1768-1823 .... DLB 94
Wernette, J(ohn) Philip 1903-1988 .... 5-8R
Wernheim, John
See Fearn, John Russell
Wernher der Gartenaere fl.
1265-1280 .... DLB 138
Wernick, Andrew (Lee) 1945- 142
Wernick, Robert 1918- 97-100
Wernick, Saul 1921-1982 81-84
Werning, Waldo J. 1921- CANR-10
Earlier sketch in CA 13-16R
Wernstedt, Frederick L(age) 1921- 21-24R
Werr, Donald F. 1920- 21-24R
Werry, Richard R. 1916-1987 .... 9-12R
Wersba, Barbara 1932- 182
Earlier sketches in CA 29-32R, CANR-16, 38
Autobiographical Essay in 182
See also AAYA 2, 30
See also BYA 6, 12, 13
See also CLC 30
See also CLR 3, 78
See also DLB 52
See also JRDA
See also MAICYA 1, 2
See also SAAS 2
See also SATA 1, 58
See also SATA-Essay 103
See also WYA
See also YAW
Wershoven, Carol Jean 1947- 112
Werstein, Irving 1914(?)-1971 73-76
Obituary 29-32R
See also SATA 14
Wert, Jeffry D. 206
Wert, Lynette L(emon) 1938- 106
Wertenbaker, Lael (Tucker)
1909-1997 .... CANR-18
Obituary 157
Earlier sketches in CA 5-8R, CANR-3
Wertenbaker, Thomas Jefferson
1879-1966 .... 5-8R
Wertenbaker, (Lael Louisiana) Timberlake
1951- CANR-139
Earlier sketch in CA 165
See also CBD
See also CD 6
See also CWD
Wertenbaker, William 1938- 97-100
Werth, Alexander 1901-1969 .... CAP-1
Obituary 25-28R
Earlier sketch in CA 13-16
Werth, Barry 1952- CANR-118
Earlier sketch in CA 173
Werth, Kurt 1896-1983 81-84
See also SATA 20
Wertham, Fredric 1895-1981 .... 5-8R
Obituary 105
Wertheim, Arthur Frank 1935- 97-100
Wertheim, Bill 1944- 37-40R
Wertheim, Stanley 1930- 41-44R
Wertheimer, Barbara M(ayer)
1926(?)-1983 129
Obituary 110
Wertheimer, Jack 1948- 144
Wertheimer, Leonard 1914- 116
Wertheimer, Linda (Cozby) 1943- 193
Brief entry 123
Wertheimer, Marilyn L(ou) 1928- 102
Wertheimer, Max 1880-1943
Brief entry 123
Wertheimer, Michael (Matthew)
1927- CANR-2
Earlier sketch in CA 1-4R
Wertheimer, Richard F(rederick) II
1943- 29-32R
Wertheimer, Roger 1942- 37-40R
Werther, William B(lanchfield), Jr.
1947- CANR-123
Earlier sketches in CA 105, CANR-21
Werthman, Michael S(cott) 1939- 89-92
Wertime, Richard (Allen) 1942- 203
Wertime, Theodore A(llen) 1919-1982 109
Obituary 106
Wertmueller, Lina 1928- CANR-78
Earlier sketches in CA 97-100, CANR-39
See also CLC 16
Werts, Margaret F(erguson) 1915-2003 102
Obituary 220
Wertsman, Vladimir (F.) 1929- CANR-94
Earlier sketches in CA 61-64, CANR-8, 20, 31, 50
Wertz, Richard W(ayne) 1933- 45-48
Wertz, S. K.
See Wertz, Spencer K.
Wertz, Spencer K. 1941- 125
Wesander, Bioern Kenneth
See Cox, P(atrick) Brian

Cumulative Index 613 Westlake

Wesberry, James Pickett 1906-1992 85-88
Weschcke, Carl L(ouis) 1930- 61-64
Wesche, L(ilburn) E(dgar) 1929- 93-96
Wesche, Percival A. 1912- 49-52
Weschler, Lawrence 1952- CANR-69
  Earlier sketch in CA 135
Weschler, Louis F(redrick) 1933- 41-44R
Wescott, Glenway 1901-1987 .... CANR-70
  Obituary 121
  Earlier sketches in CA 13-16R, CANR-23
  See also CLC 13
  See also CN 1, 2, 3, 4
  See also DLB 4, 9, 102
  See also MAL 5
  See also RGAL 4
  See also SSC 35
Wescott, Roger W. 1925- 25-28R
Wesencraft, Charles Frederick 1928- 61-64
Wesker, Arnold 1932- CANR-33
  Earlier sketches in CA 1-4R, CANR-1
  See also CAAS 7
  See also CBD
  See also CD 5, 6
  See also CDBLB 1960 to Present
  See also CLC 3, 5, 42
  See also DAB
  See also DAM DRAM
  See also DLB 13, 310, 319
  See also EWL 3
  See also MTCW 1
  See also RGEL 2
  See also TEA
Weslager, C(linton) A(lfred)
  1909-1994 .... CANR-24
  Obituary 146
  Earlier sketches in CA 21-24R, CANR-9
Wesley, Alison
  See Barnes, Michael
Wesley, Charles 1707-1788 .... DLB 95
  See also RGEL 2
Wesley, Charles H(arris) 1891-1987 101
  Obituary 123
Wesley, Doris A. 1952- 196
Wesley, Elizabeth
  See McElfresh, (Elizabeth) Adeline
Wesley, George R(andolph) 1931- 41-44R
Wesley, James
  See Rigoni, Orlando (Joseph)
Wesley, John 1703-1791 .... DLB 104
Wesley, Mary (Aline) 1912-2002 ...... CANR-66
  Obituary 211
  Earlier sketch in CA 49-52
  See also CN 5, 6, 7
  See also DLB 231
  See also MTCW 1
  See also RHW
  See also SATA 66
Wesley, Patricia Jabbeh 167
  See also BW 3
Wesley, Richard (Errol) 1945- CANR-27
  Earlier sketch in CA 57-60
  See also BW 1
  See also CAD
  See also CD 5, 6
  See also CLC 7
  See also DLB 38
Wesley, Valerie Wilson 1947- CANR-137
  Earlier sketch in CA 167
  See also BW 3
  See also SATA 106
Wesling, Donald 1939- 101
Wesner, Maralene 1935- 112
Wesner, Miles 1933- 112
Wess, Jane A. 1953- 150
Wess, Martin 1906(?)-1975
  Obituary 104
Wessel, Andrew E(rnest) 1925- 73-76
Wessel, Carl John 1911-1984
  Obituary 113
Wessel, Helen (Strain) 1924- CANR-11
  Earlier sketch in CA 13-16R
Wessel, Johan Herman 1742-1785 ..... DLB 300
Wessel, John 1952- 174
Wessel, Milton R(alph) 1923-1991 89-92
Wessel, Robert H. 1921- 1-4R
Wesselman, Hank (Henry Barnard) 1941- .. 153
Wesselmann, Debbie Lee 1959- 173
Wesselmann, Tom 1931-2004 108
  Obituary 234
Wessels, William L. 1889-1977 .... 5-8R
Wesser, Robert F. 1933- 21-24R
Wessler, Ruth Ann 1938- 29-32R
Wessman, Alden E(benhart) 1930- 21-24R
Wesson, Joan
  See Pittock, Joan (Hornby)
Wesson, Marianne 1948- 174
Wesson, Robert G(ale) 1920-1991 ... CANR-18
  Obituary 134
  Earlier sketches in CA 9-12R, CANR-3
West, Allan M(orrell) 1910- 109
West, Andrew
  See Arthur, Robert, (Jr.)
West, Anna 1938- 106
  See also SATA 40
West, Anthony (Panther) 1914-1987 . CANR-19
  Obituary 124
  Earlier sketches in CA 45-48, CANR-3
  See also CLC 50
  See also CN 1, 2, 3, 4
  See also DLB 15
West, Anthony C(athcart Muir)
  1910-1988 .... CANR-31
  Earlier sketch in CA 69-72
  See also CN 1, 2, 3, 4, 5, 6, 7
West, Barbara
  See Price, Olive
West, Betty 1921- CANR-7
  Earlier sketch in CA 5-8R
  See also SATA 11
West, Beverly Henderson 1939- 119
West, Bill
  See West, William G.
West, Bing
  See West, Francis J., Jr.
West, Bonnie 1946- 114
West, Bruce 1951- .... SATA 63
West, C. P.
  See Wodehouse, P(elham) G(renville)
West, Carroll Van 1955- 190
West, Charles Converse 1921- 81-84
West, Cheryl L. 1957- .... DLB 266
West, Colin 1951- 136
West, Cornel (Ronald) 1953- CANR-91
  Earlier sketch in CA 144
  See also BLCS
  See also CLC 134
  See also DLB 246
West, D(onald) J(ames) 1924- CANR-42
  Earlier sketches in CA 13-16R, CANR-5, 20
West, Darrell M. 1954- CANR-109
  Earlier sketch in CA 145
West, David (Alexander) 1926- 21-24R
West, Delno C(loyde), Jr. 1936- 57-60
  See also CLC 70
West, Dick Sheppard 1920-1989
  Obituary 130
West, Don 1928- 57-60
West, Dorothy
  See Benson, Mildred (Augustine Wirt)
West, Dorothy 1907-1998 143
  Obituary 169
  See also BW 2
  See also DLB 76
  See also HR 1:3
  See also TCLC 108
West, Douglas
  See Tubb, E(dwin) C(harles)
West, E(dwin) G(eorge) 1922- CANR-29
  Earlier sketch in CA 25-28R
West, Earle H(uddleston) 1925- 53-56
West, Edward 1949- 239
West, Edward Nason 1909-1990 .... CAP-2
  Earlier sketch in CA 19-20
West, Edwin
  See Westlake, Donald E(dwin)
West, Edwin G.
  See West, E(dwin) G(eorge)
West, Elizabeth
  See Wilson, Margaret (Wilhelmina)
West, Elliot 1924- CANR-85
  Earlier sketch in CA 17-20R
West, Elmer D(alton) 1907-1991 .... CAP-1
  Obituary 135
  Earlier sketch in CA 13-14
West, Emily Govan 1919- 109
  See also SATA 38
West, Emmy
  See West, Emily Govan
West, Eugenia Lovett 85-88
West, Ewan (D.) 1960- 142
West, Francis (James) 1927- CANR-3
  Earlier sketch in CA 5-8R
West, Francis Horner 1909-1999 118
West, Francis J., Jr. 1940- 227
West, Frank H.
  See West, Francis Horner
West, Fred 1918- 5-8R
West, G(eorge) Allen, Jr. 1915- 17-20R
West, George Algernon 1893-1980
  Obituary 97-100
West, Gertrude 110
West, Gordon 1896-1969 .... CAP-1
  Earlier sketch in CA 13-14
West, Henry Woolliscroft 1925- 41-44R
West, Herbert B(uell) 1916- 53-56
West, Herbert Faulkner 1898-1974 .... CAP-2
  Obituary 53-56
  Earlier sketch in CA 19-20
West, J. B.
  See West, J. Bernard
West, J. Bernard 1913(?)-1983 120
  Obituary 110
West, James
  See Withers, Carl A.
West, James King 1930- 45-48
West, James L(emuel) W(ills III)
  1946- CANR-86
  Earlier sketch in CA 131
West, James W. 1914(?)- 162
West, (Mary) Jane 1939(?)-1981
  Obituary 104
West, Jerry
  See Svenson, Andrew E(dward)
West, (Mary) Jessamyn 1902-1984 ... CANR-27
  Obituary 112
  Earlier sketch in CA 9-12R
  See also CLC 7, 17
  See also CN 1, 2, 3
  See also DLB 6
  See also DLBY 1984
  See also MTCW 1, 2
  See also RGAL 4
  See also RHW
  See also SATA-Obit 37
  See also TCWW 2
  See also TUS
  See also YAW
West, John
  See Arthur, Robert, (Jr.)
West, John Anthony 1932- 81-84
West, John Foster 1910- 13-16R
West, John Frederick 1929- 103
West, John G(ilbert) 1941- 142
West, Joyce (Tarlton) -1985 106
West, Kingsley .... TCWW 1, 2
West, Kirkpatrick
  See Harris, (Frank) Brayton
West, Leonard J(ordan) 1921- 41-44R
West, Lindsay
  See Weber, Nancy
West, M(artin) L(itchfield) 1937- CANR-104
  Earlier sketch in CA 147
West, Mae 1893-1980 89-92
  Obituary 102
  See also DLB 44
West, Marion B(ond) 1936- 101
West, Mark
  See Runyon, Charles W.
West, Mark I. 1955- 187
West, Michael Lee 1953- 236
  See also CSW
  See also DLB 292
West, Michelle
  See Sagara, Michelle
West, Michelle Sagara
  See Sagara, Michelle
  See also DLB 251
West, Morris L(anglo) 1916-1999 ..... CANR-64
  Obituary 187
  Earlier sketches in CA 5-8R, CANR-24, 49
  See also BPFB 3
  See also CLC 6, 33
  See also CN 1, 2, 3, 4, 5, 6
  See also CPW
  See also DLB 289
  See also MTCW 1, 2
  See also MTFW 2005
West, Muriel (Leitzell) 1903-1970(?) CAP-1
  Earlier sketch in CA 13-16
West, Naida 219
West, Nancy Richard
  See Westphal, Wilma Ross
West, Nathanael 1903-1940 125
  Brief entry 104
  See also AMW
  See also AMWR 2
  See also BPFB 3
  See also CDALB 1929-1941
  See also DA3
  See also DLB 4, 9, 28
  See also EWL 3
  See also MAL 5
  See also MTCW 1, 2
  See also MTFW 2005
  See also NFS 16
  See also RGAL 4
  See also SSC 16
  See also TCLC 1, 14, 44
  See also TUS
West, Owen
  See Koontz, Dean R(ay)
West, Pat
  See Strother, Pat Wallace
West, Paul 1930- CANR-136
  Earlier sketches in CA 13-16R, CANR-22, 53, 76, 89
  Interview in CANR-22
  See also CAAS 7
  See also CLC 7, 14, 96
  See also CN 1, 2, 3, 4, 5, 6, 7
  See also DLB 14
  See also MTCW 2
  See also MTFW 2005
West, Ray B(enedict), Jr. 1908-1990 ... CANR-3
  Earlier sketch in CA 1-4R
West, Rebecca 1892-1983 .... CANR-19
  Obituary 109
  Earlier sketch in CA 5-8R
  See also BPFB 3
  See also BRWS 3
  See also CLC 7, 9, 31, 50
  See also CN 1, 2, 3
  See also DLB 36
  See also DLBY 1983
  See also EWL 3
  See also FW
  See also MTCW 1, 2
  See also MTFW 2005
  See also NCFS 4
  See also RGEL 2
  See also TEA
West, Richard 1941- .... DLB 185
West, Richard S(edgewick), Jr.
  1902-1968 .... CAP-1
  Earlier sketch in CA 13-16
West, Richard Samuel 1955- 130
West, Robert C(raig) 1947- 89-92
West, Robert Frederick 1916- 5-8R
West, Robert H(unter) 1907-1988 .... 37-40R
West, Thomas R(eed) 1936- 124
  Brief entry 118
West, Token
  See Humphries, Adelaide M.
West, Tom 1895-1980(?) .... TCWW 1, 2
West, Trudy
  See West, Gertrude
West, Uta 1928- 85-88
West, V(ictoria Mary) Sackville
  See Sackville-West, V(ictoria Mary)
West, Walter
  See Soyfer, Jura
West, Ward
  See Borland, Harold Glen
West, William G. 1930- CANR-14
  Earlier sketch in CA 37-40R
Westall, Robert (Atkinson)
  1929-1993 .... CANR-68
  Obituary 141
  Earlier sketches in CA 69-72, CANR-18
  See also AAYA 12
  See also BYA 2, 6, 7, 8, 9, 15
  See also CLC 17
  See also CLR 13
  See also FANT
  See also JRDA
  See also MAICYA 1, 2
  See also MAICYAS 1
  See also SAAS 2
  See also SATA 23, 69
  See also SATA-Obit 75
  See also WYA
  See also YAW
Westaway, Jane 1948- 192
  See also SATA 121
Westberg, Granger E(llsworth)
  1913-1999 .... CANR-6
  Earlier sketch in CA 1-4R
Westbie, Constance 1910-1991 85-88
Westbrook, Adele CANR-112
  Earlier sketch in CA 41-44R
Westbrook, Max (Roger) 1927- 37-40R
Westbrook, Perry D(ickie)
  1916-1998 .... CANR-21
  Earlier sketches in CA 1-4R, CANR-6
Westbrook, Peter (J.) 1952- 164
Westbrook, Robert 1945- CANR-123
  Earlier sketch in CA 25-28R
Westbrook, Wayne W(illiam) 1939- 97-100
Westburg, Barry (Richard) 1938- 171
Westbury, Ian Douglas 1939-
  Brief entry 106
Westby, David L. 1929- 45-48
Westby-Gibson, Dorothy Pauline
  1920- 17-20R
Westcott, Cynthia 1898-1983 .... 5-8R
  Obituary 109
Westcott, Edward Noyes 1846-1898 .. DLB 202
Westcott, Jan Vlachos 1912- CANR-2
  Earlier sketch in CA 1-4R
  See also RHW
Westcott, Kathleen
  See Abrahamsen, Christine Elizabeth
Westcott, Nadine Bernard 1949- .... SATA 130
Westcott, Rich 209
Westcott, W(illiam) F(ranklin) 1949- 113
Westcott, Wayne L. 1949- CANR-122
  Earlier sketch in CA 171
Westcott-Jones, K(enneth) 1921- CANR-4
  Earlier sketch in CA 53-56
Westebbe, Richard (Manning) 1925- 45-48
Westell, Anthony 1926- 101
Westerberg, Christine 1950- 61-64
  See also SATA 29
Westerduin, Anne 1945- 173
  See also SATA 105
Westerfeld, Scott 218
  See also SATA 161
Westergaard, John (Harald) 1927- CANR-43
  Earlier sketches in CA 69-72, CANR-11
Westerhoff, John H(enry) III 1933- CANR-17
  Earlier sketches in CA 45-48, CANR-1
Westerink, Leendert Gerrit 1913-1990 93-96
Westerman, Percy F(rancis) 1876-1959
  Brief entry 110
  See also CWRI 5
Westermann, Claus 1909-2000 .... CANR-15
  Earlier sketch in CA 81-84
Westermann, Kurt-Michael 1951- 195
Westermarck, Edward 1862-1939 .... TCLC 87
Westermeier, Clifford P(eter) 1910-1986 .. 45-48
Westermeyer, Joseph John 1937- 109
Western, J(ohn) R(andle) 1928-1971 ...... CAP-2
  Earlier sketch in CA 21-22
Western, John (Charles) 1947- 105
Western, Mark
  See Crisp, Anthony Thomas
Western Spy, The
  See Dillon, John M(yles)
Westervelt, Saundra D(avis) 1968- 204
Westervelt, Virginia Veeder 1914- CANR-10
  Earlier sketch in CA 61-64
  See also SATA 10
Westfall, David 1927- 117
Westfall, Don C. 1928-1973 .... CAP-2
  Earlier sketch in CA 17-18
Westfall, Ralph (Libby) 1917- 5-8R
Westfall, Richard S(amuel) 1924-1996 .. 21-24R
  Obituary 153
Westfeldt, Lulie 1896- CAP-1
  Earlier sketch in CA 13-14
Westfried, Alex Huxley 1919- 231
Westheimer, David 1917- CANR-2
  Earlier sketch in CA 1-4R
  See also SATA 14
Westheimer, Ruth K(arola) 1928- 228
Westhues, Kenneth 1944- CANR-11
  Earlier sketch in CA 25-28R
Westin, Alan F(urman) 1929- CANR-10
  Earlier sketch in CA 13-16R
Westin, Av(ram) 1929- 77-80
Westin, Jeane Eddy 1931- 85-88
Westin, Richard A(xel) 1945- CANR-37
  Earlier sketch in CA 115
Westing, Arthur H(erbert) 1928- CANR-38
  Earlier sketches in CA 41-44R, CANR-17
Westing, John Howard 1911-2001 .... 9-12R
Westlake, Aubrey Thomas 1893-1985
  Obituary 119

Westlake 614 CONTEMPORARY AUTHORS

Westlake, Donald E(dwin) 1933- CANR-137
Earlier sketches in CA 17-20R, CANR-16, 44, 65, 94
Interview in CANR-16
See also CAAS 13
See also BPFB 3
See also CLC 7, 33
See also CMW 4
See also CPW
See also DAM POP
See also MSW
See also MTCW 2
See also MTFW 2005
Westlake, Helen Gum 1927- 41-44R
Westlake, Michael 1942- 127
Westland, Lynn
See Joscelyn, Archie L(ynn)
Westley, Bruce H(utchinson) 1915-1990 .... CANR-2
Earlier sketch in CA 1-4R
Westley, Dick
See Westley, Richard John
Westley, Richard John 1928- 112
Westley, William A. 1920- 37-40R
Westling, Louise (Hutchings) 1942- .. CANR-82
Earlier sketch in CA 133
Westlund, Joseph 1936- 118
Westmacott, Mary
See Christie, Agatha (Mary Clarissa)
Westmacott, Richard 1941- 141
Westman, Barbara 105
See also SATA 70
Westman, Daniel P. 1956- 139
Westman, Jack C(onrad) 1927- 93-96
Westman, Paul (Wendell) 1956- 106
See also SATA 39
Westman, Wesley C(harles) 1936- 29-32R
Westmeier, Karl-Wilhelm 1939- CANR-113
Earlier sketch in CA 151
Westminster, Aynn
See Mundis, Hester
Westmore, Ann 1953- 109
Westmore, Frank 1923(?)-1985
Obituary 116
Westmoreland, Reg(inald Conway) 1926- 29-32R
Westmoreland, Timothy A. 1966- 218
Westmoreland, William C(hilds) 1914-2005 101
See also SATA 63
Westoff, Charles Francis 1927- 81-84
Westoff, Leslie Aldridge 1928- 77-80
Weston, Alan J(ay) 1940- 73-76
Weston, Allen
See Hogarth, Grace (Weston Allen) and Norton, Andre
Weston, Allen 1912- .... FANT
See also SFW 4
Weston, Ann
See Pitcher, Gladys
Weston, Arthur
See Webling, Peggy
Weston, Brett (Theodore) 1911-1993 217
Weston, Burns H. 1933- 29-32R
Weston, Carol 1956- 198
See also SATA 135
Weston, Carolyn 1921- 107
Weston, Christine (Goutiere) 1904-1989
Obituary 128
Weston, Cole
See Randisi, Robert J(oseph)
Weston, Cole 1919- 214
Weston, Corinne Comstock 1919- CANR-21
Earlier sketch in CA 1-4R
Weston, Elizabeth Jane c. 1582-1612 . DLB 172
Weston, Glen E(arl) 1922- 49-52
Weston, Helen Gray
See Daniels, Dorothy
Weston, J(ohn) Fred(erick) 1916- CANR-1
Earlier sketch in CA 1-4R
Weston, John
See Davies, John Evan Weston
Weston, John (Harrison) 1932- 17-20R
See also SATA 21
Weston, Joseph H(arry) 1911(?)-1983
Obituary 111
Weston, Kath(leen M.) 1958- 183
Weston, Martha 1947- CANR-136
Earlier sketch in CA 129
See also SATA 53, 119
Weston, Michael 1931- 154
Weston, Paul B(rendan) 1910- 13-16R
Weston, Rubin Francis 1921- 104
Weston, Susan B(rown) 1943- 81-84
Weston-Smith, M. 1956- 93-96
Westphal, Arnold Carl 1897- .... SATA 57
Westphal, Barbara Osborne 1907-2000 .... CAP-1
Earlier sketch in CA 11-12
Westphal, Clarence 1904- CAP-2
Earlier sketch in CA 17-18
Westphal, Siegfried 1902-1982
Obituary 107
Westphal, Wilma Ross 1907-1987 .... 21-24R
Westphall, Victor 1913- 119
Westrum, Dexter 1944- 139
Westrum, Ron 1945- 194
Westrup, Hugh 169
See also SATA 102
Westrup, J(ack) A(llan) 1904-1975
Obituary 115
Westsmith, Kim 1945- 57-60
Westwater, Agnes Martha 1929- CANR-136
Earlier sketch in CA 21-24R
Westwater, Martha
See Westwater, Agnes Martha
Westwood, Gordon
See Schofield, Michael
Westwood, Gwen 1915- CANR-19
Earlier sketch in CA 25-28R
Westwood, J(ohn) N(orton) 1931- CANR-20
Earlier sketches in CA 13-16R, CANR-5
Westwood, Jennifer 1940- CANR-29
Earlier sketches in CA 65-68, CANR-9
See also SATA 10
Westwood, Perry
See Holmes, L(lewellyn) P(erry)
Westwood, Richard E. 1921- 137
Wetcheek, J. L.
See Feuchtwanger, Lion
Wetenhall, John 1957- 136
Wetering, Janwillem van de
See van de Wetering, Janwillem
Wetherald, Agnes Ethelwyn 1857-1940 202
See also DLB 99
See also TCLC 81
Wetherbee, Winthrop (III) 1938- CANR-28
Earlier sketches in CA 73-76, CANR-12
Wetherby, Terry (Lynne) 1943- 102
Wetherell, Donald G. 1949- 220
Wetherell, Elizabeth
See Warner, Susan (Bogert)
Wetherell, W(alter) D(avid) 1948- CANR-88
Earlier sketch in CA 138
See also DLB 234
Wetherell-Pepper, Joan Alexander 1920- . 9-12R
Wetherill, Peter Michael 1932- CANR-12
Earlier sketch in CA 61-64
Wethey, Harold E(dwin) 1902-1984 ... CANR-2
Obituary 113
Earlier sketch in CA 1-4R
Wetmore, Alexander 1886-1978 85-88
Obituary 81-84
Wetmore, Kevin J., (Jr.) 1969- 231
Wetmore, Ruth Y. 1934- 57-60
Wetmore, Thomas Hall 1915- 25-28R
Wetmore, William T. 1930- 9-12R
Wettenhall, Roger (Llewellyn) 1931- CANR-51
Earlier sketches in CA 109, CANR-26
Wetter, Gustav A(ndreas) 1911- 9-12R
Wetterhahn, Ralph (Francis) 1942- 207
Wettig, Gerhard 1934- 143
Wettlaufer, George 1935- 57-60
Wettlaufer, Nancy 1939- 57-60
Wettstein, Howard K(enneth) 1943- 105
Wettstein, Robert M. 1950- 170
Wetzel, Dan 197(?)- 221
Wetzel, David 218
Wetzel, (Earl) Donald 1921- 25-28R
Wetzel, Elizabeth 1930- 114
Wetzel, Friedrich Gottlob 1779-1819 ... DLB 90
Wetzel, James (Richard) 1959- 139
Wetzel, Lewis
See King, Albert
See also TCWW 2
Wetzel, Marlene Reed 1937- .... SSFS 17
Wetzel, Richard D(ean) 1935- 85-88
Weverka, Robert 1926- CANR-2
Earlier sketch in CA 49-52
Wevers, Richard Franklin 1933-
Brief entry 106
Wevill, David 1937- 13-16R
See also CP 1, 2, 3, 4, 5, 6, 7
Wexelblatt, Robert 226
Wexler, Alan 1947- 146
Wexler, Alice (Ruth) 1942- 144
Wexler, Haskell 1926- .... IDFW 3, 4
Wexler, Jean Stewart 1921- 65-68
Wexler, Jerome (LeRoy) 1923- 73-76
See also SATA 14
Wexler, Jerry 1917- 142
Wexler, Joyce Piell 1947- 97-100
Wexler, Laura E. 1971- 223
Wexler, Merin 227
Wexler, Nancy (Sabin) 1945- 161
Wexler, Norman 1926-1999 154
Obituary 183
Brief entry 116
Wexler, Richard 1953- 135
Wexley, John 1907-1985
Obituary 115
Wexley, Kenneth N. 93-96
Weyand, Alexander Mathias 1892-1982 ... 5-8R
Weybright, Victor 1903-1978
Obituary 89-92
Weyermann, Debra 1954- 147
Weygant, Noemi CANR-2
Earlier sketch in CA 45-48
Weyl, (Claus Hugo) Hermann 1885-1955 .. 157
Weyl, Joachim 1915-1977
Obituary 73-76
Weyl, Nathaniel 1910-2005 .... CANR-5
Obituary 238
Earlier sketch in CA 9-12R
Weyl, Woldemar A. 1901(?)-1975
Obituary 61-64
Weyland, Jack 1940- CANR-105
Earlier sketch in CA 149
See also SATA 81
Weyler, Rex 1947- 110
Weyman, Stanley J(ohn) 1855-1928 184
See also DLB 141, 156
See also RHW
Weyn, Suzanne 1955- 168
See also SATA 63, 101
Weyr, Garret
See Freymann-Weyr, (Rhoda) Garret (Michaela)
Weyr, Thomas 1927- 142
Weyrauch, Walter O(tto) 1919- CANR-10
Earlier sketch in CA 13-16R
Weyrich, Paul M(ichael) 1942- 118
Wezel, Johann Karl 1747-1819 .... DLB 94
Wezeman, Frederick Hartog 1915-1981 .... CANR-6
Obituary 106
Earlier sketch in CA 9-12R
Wezyk, Joanna 1966- .... SATA 82
Whale, James 1889-1957 .... TCLC 63
Whale, John (Hilary) 1931- 101
Whalen, Barbara G. 1928- 120
Whalen, Charles William, Jr. 1920- 105
Whalen, Edward L. 1936- 139
Whalen, George J. 1939- CANR-16
Earlier sketch in CA 89-92
Whalen, Philip (Glenn) 1923-2002 .. CANR-39
Obituary 209
Earlier sketches in CA 9-12R, CANR-5
See also BG 1:3
See also CLC 6, 29
See also CP 1, 2, 3, 4, 5, 6, 7
See also DLB 16
See also WP
Whalen, Richard J(ames) 1935- CANR-32
Earlier sketch in CA 13-16R
Whalen, Terry (Anthony) 1944- 127
Whalen, William Joseph 1926- CANR-4
Earlier sketch in CA 1-4R
Whaley, Barton Stewart 1928- 41-44R
Whaley, Donald L. 1934- 33-36R
Whaley, Joyce Irene 1923- .... SATA 61
Whaley, Russell Francis 1934- 57-60
Whalin, W. Terry 1953- .... SATA 93
Whalin, W. Terry 1953- 158
See also SATA 93
Whaling, Frank 1934- CANR-67
Earlier sketches in CA 113, CANR-32
Whalley, Dorothy 1911- CAP-1
Earlier sketch in CA 9-10
Whalley, George 1915-1983 101
See also DLB 88
Whalley, Janet 1945- 117
Whalley, Joyce Irene 103
Whalley, Peter 1946- .... CMW 4
Whalon, Marion K(elley) 1913- 119
Wharf, Michael
See Weller, George (Anthony)
Wharmby, Margot CANR-49
Earlier sketches in CA 17-20R, CANR-8, 24
See also SATA 63
Wharton, Annabel (Jane) CANR-50
Earlier sketch in CA 123
Wharton, Anthony
See McAllister, Alister
Wharton, Anthony P.
See McAllister, Alister
Wharton, Clifton R(eginald), Jr. 1926- ... 41-44R
Wharton, David B(ailey) 1914- 73-76
Wharton, Edith (Newbold Jones) 1862-1937 132
Brief entry 104
See also AAYA 25
See also AMW
See also AMWC 2
See also AMWR 1
See also BPFB 3
See also CDALB 1865-1917
See also DA
See also DA3
See also DAB
See also DAC
See also DAM MST, NOV
See also DLB 4, 9, 12, 78, 189
See also DLBD 13
See also EWL 3
See also EXPS
See also FL 1:6
See also GL 3
See also HGG
See also LAIT 2, 3
See also LATS 1:1
See also MAL 5
See also MAWW
See also MTCW 1, 2
See also MTFW 2005
See also NFS 5, 11, 15, 20
See also RGAL 4
See also RGSF 2
See also RHW
See also SSC 6, 84
See also SSFS 6, 7
See also SUFW
See also TCLC 3, 9, 27, 53, 129, 149
See also TUS
See also WLC
Wharton, Elizabeth Austin 1920-1985
Obituary 116
Wharton, Gary C(harles) 1940- 45-48
Wharton, George Frederick III 1952- 109
Wharton, James
See Mencken, H(enry) L(ouis)
Wharton, Joanna
See Hamel Peifer, Kathleen
Wharton, John Franklin 1894-1977 81-84
Obituary 73-76
Wharton, William (a pseudonym) 1925- . 93-96
Interview in CA-93-96
See also CLC 18, 37
See also CN 4, 5, 6, 7
See also DLBY 1980
Whateley, Leslie Violet Lucy Evelyn Mary 1899-1987
Obituary 123
Whately, Mary Louisa 1824-1889 .... DLB 166
Whately, Richard 1787-1863 .... DLB 190
Whatmore, Leonard Elliott 1912-1982 .. 13-16R
Whatmore, Richard 210
Whatmough, Joshua 1897-1964 .... 5-8R
Whealey, Robert 1930- 127
Wheat, Carolyn 1946- CANR-135
Earlier sketch in CA 152
See also CMW 4
Wheat, Cathleen Hayhurst 1904-1991 .. CAP-1
Earlier sketch in CA 17-18
Wheat, (Marcus) Ed(ward, Jr.) 1926- . CANR-42
Earlier sketch in CA 118
Wheat, Gilbert Collins, Jr. 1927- 1-4R
Wheat, Joe Ben 1916-1997 .... 41-44R
Obituary 159
Wheat, Leonard F. 1931- 29-32R
Wheat, Patte 1935- CANR-19
Earlier sketch in CA 101
Wheatcroft, Andrew (Jonathan Maclean) 1944- 110
Wheatcroft, Geoffrey 1945- 124
Wheatcroft, John 1925- CANR-14
Earlier sketch in CA 37-40R
Wheatcroft, Stephen F(rederick) 1921- 5-8R
Wheatley, Arabelle 1921- .... SATA 16
Wheatley, David 1970- 176
Earlier sketch in CA 174
Wheatley, Dennis (Yeats) 1897-1977 .... CANR-72
Obituary 73-76
Earlier sketches in CA 5-8R, CANR-9
See also CMW 4
See also DLB 77, 255
See also HGG
See also MTCW 1
See also SUFW
Wheatley, Jon 1931- 29-32R
Wheatley, Nadia 1949- 221
See also CWRI 5
See also SATA 147
Wheatley, Paul 1921-1999 200
Wheatley (Peters), Phillis 1753(?)-1784 .... AFAW 1, 2
See also BLC 3
See also CDALB 1640-1865
See also DA
See also DA3
See also DAC
See also DAM MST, MULT, POET
See also DLB 31, 50
See also EXPP
See also FL 1:1
See also PC 3
See also PFS 13
See also RGAL 4
See also WLC
Wheatley, Richard C(harles) 1904- CAP-1
Earlier sketch in CA 11-12
Wheatley, Ronald 1923(?)-1985
Obituary 115
Wheatley, Vera (Semple) CAP-1
Earlier sketch in CA 13-16
Wheat-Lieber, Patte
See Wheat, Patte
Wheaton, Anne (Williams) 1892-1977
Obituary 69-72
Wheaton, Barbara Ketcham 1931- 146
Wheaton, Bruce R. 1944- CANR-22
Earlier sketch in CA 104
Wheaton, Philip D(amon) 1916- 104
Wheaton, William L. C. 1913-1978 ... CANR-3
Earlier sketch in CA 1-4R
Whedbee, J. William 1938-2004 185
Obituary 224
Whedon, Joss 1964- 238
See also AAYA 50
Whedon, Julia
See Schickel, Julia Whedon
Whedon, Margaret B(runssen) 1926- 105
Whedon, Peggy
See Whedon, Margaret B(runssen)
Wheeler, Allen 1903-1984
Obituary 111
Wheeler, Anna Doyle 1785-1848(?) ... DLB 158
Wheeler, Bayard O. 1905- 41-44R
Wheeler, Bonnie G(rant) 1943- 109
Wheeler, Burton K(endall) 1882-1975
Obituary 53-56
Wheeler, Charles (Thomas) 1892-1974 . CAP-2
Obituary 53-56
Earlier sketch in CA 29-32
Wheeler, Charles Stearns 1816-1843 ..... DLB 1, 223
Wheeler, Cindy 1955- CANR-57
Earlier sketches in CA 110, CANR-31
See also SATA 49
See also SATA-Brief 40
Wheeler, David L. 1934- 37-40R
Wheeler, David Raymond 1942- 73-76
Wheeler, Deborah (Jean Ross) 1947- 150
See also SATA 83
Wheeler, Douglas L. 1937- CANR-99
Earlier sketch in CA 29-32R
Wheeler, Elizabeth A. 1959- 231
Wheeler, (Charles) Gidley 1938- CANR-24
Earlier sketch in CA 107
Wheeler, (John) Harvey 1918-2004 .. CANR-17
Obituary 231
Earlier sketches in CA 45-48, CANR-1
Wheeler, Helen Rippier CANR-14
Earlier sketches in CA 17-20R, CANR-31
Wheeler, Hugh (Callingham) 1912-1987 .... CANR-59
Obituary 123
Earlier sketch in CA 89-92
Interview in CA-89-92
See also CMW 4
See also DFS 19
Wheeler, J(oseph) Clyde 1910-1998 .... 1-4R
Wheeler, Janet D. CANR-26
Earlier sketches in CAP-2, CA 19-20
See also SATA 1

Cumulative Index 615 **White**

Wheeler, Jesse H(arrison), Jr. 1918- ... 45-48
Wheeler, Jill C. 1964- ... CANR-113
Earlier sketch in CA 151
See also SATA 86, 136
Wheeler, Jody 1952- ... SATA 84, 148
Wheeler, Joe L. 1936- ... 220
Wheeler, John Archibald 1911- ... 160
Wheeler, Kate 1955- ... CANR-94
Earlier sketch in CA 155
Wheeler, Keith 1911- ... CANR-7
Earlier sketch in CA 5-8R
Wheeler, Lesley 1967- ... 232
Wheeler, Leslie A. 1945- ... CANR-11
Earlier sketch in CA 65-68
Wheeler, Lisa 1963- ... SATA 162
Wheeler, Lora Jeanne 1923- ... 33-36R
Wheeler, Lyle 1905-1990 ... IDFW 3, 4
Wheeler, Margaret 1916- ... CAP-2
Earlier sketch in CA 25-28
Wheeler, Mary Jane ... 29-32R
Wheeler, Michael 1943- ... CANR-9
Earlier sketch in CA 65-68
Wheeler, Molly 1920- ... 29-32R
Wheeler, Monroe 1900-1988 ... 214
Obituary ... 126
See also DLB 4
Wheeler, (Robert Eric) Mortimer
1890-1976 ... CANR-32
Obituary ... 65-68
Earlier sketch in CA 77-80
Wheeler, Opal 1898- ... SATA 23
Wheeler, Paul 1934- ... 25-28R
Wheeler, Penny Estes 1943- ... 33-36R
Wheeler, Raymond Milner 1919-1982
Obituary ... 106
Wheeler, Richard 1922- ... CANR-50
Earlier sketches in CA 17-20R, CANR-8, 25
Wheeler, Richard Paul 1943- ... 108
Wheeler, Richard S(eabrook) 1928- ... 45-48
Wheeler, Richard S(haw) 1935- ... 215
See also TCWW 2
Wheeler, Robert C(ordell) 1913-1986 ... 61-64
Wheeler, Ron 1954- ... 136
Wheeler, Ruth Carr 1899-1996 ... 5-8R
Wheeler, Sara 1961- ... CANR-120
Earlier sketch in CA 169
Wheeler, Sessions S(amuel)
1911-1998 ... CANR-25
Earlier sketch in CA 17-20R
Wheeler, Shannon L. 1966- ... 226
Wheeler, Susan 1955- ... 171
Wheeler, Thomas ... 234
Wheeler, Thomas C. 1927- ... 104
Wheeler, Thomas H(utchin) 1947- ... CANR-40
Earlier sketch in CA 93-96
Wheeler, Tom
See Wheeler, Thomas H(utchin)
Wheeler, Tony 1946- ... 196
Wheeler, W(illiam) Lawrence 1925- ... 13-16R
Wheeler-Bennett, John 1902-1975 ... 65-68
Obituary ... 61-64
Wheelis, Allen B. 1915- ... CANR-91
Earlier sketch in CA 17-20R
Wheelock, Arthur Kingsland, Jr. 1943- ... 107
Wheelock, (Kinch) Carter 1924- ... 61-64
Wheelock, David C. 1960- ... 143
Wheelock, Frederic M(elvin)
1902-1987 ... 97-100
Obituary ... 124
Wheelock, John Hall 1886-1978 ... CANR-14
Obituary ... 77-80
Earlier sketch in CA 13-16R
See also CLC 14
See also CP 1, 2
See also DLB 45
See also MAL 5
Wheelock, Martha E. 1941- ... 25-28R
Wheelwright, Edward Lawrence
1921- ... CANR-50
Earlier sketches in CA 103, CANR-21
Wheelwright, John 1592(?)-1679 ... DLB 24
See also RGAL 4
Wheelwright, John (Brooks) 1897-1940 ... 182
See also DLB 45
See also MAL 5
Wheelwright, Julie (Diana) 1960- ... 130
Wheelwright, Philip (Ellis) 1901-1970 ... CAP-2
Earlier sketch in CA 23-24
Wheelwright, Richard 1936- ... 33-36R
Wheelwright, Steven C. 1943- ... 119
Wheen, Francis 1957- ... 194
Whelan, Elizabeth M(urphy) 1943- .. CANR-24
Earlier sketches in CA 57-60, CANR-8
See also SATA 14
Whelan, G(eraldine) V(alerie) 1952- ... 160
See also YAW
Whelan, Gloria (Ann) 1923- ... CANR-108
Earlier sketch in CA 101
See also AAYA 42
See also BYA 15
See also CLR 90
See also MAICYA 2
See also SATA 85, 128
Whelan, James Robert 1933- ... 102
Whelan, Joseph P(aul) 1932- ... 41-44R
Whelan, Michael 1950- ... AAYA 28
Whelan, Peter 1931- ... CBD
See also CD 5, 6
Whelan, Richard 1946- ... 144
Whelan, Tensie 1960- ... 141
Wheldon, David 1950- ... 146
Wheldon, Huw (Pyrs) 1916-1986 ... 107
Obituary ... 118
Whelehan, Imelda 1960- ... 153
Whelpton, (George) Eric 1894-1981 ... CANR-5
Obituary ... 103
Earlier sketch in CA 9-12R
Whelpton, Pascal K(idder)
1893-1964 ... CANR-16
Earlier sketch in CA 1-4R
Whelton, Clark 1937- ... 69-72
Whenham, (Ernest) John 1946- ... 127
Wherrett, Peter 1936- ... 190
Whetstone, Colonel Pete
See Noland, C. F. M.
Whetstone, George 1550-1587 ... DLB 136
See also RGEL 2
Whetten, Lawrence L. 1932- ... CANR-27
Earlier sketches in CA 61-64, CANR-11
Whetten, Nathan Laselle 1900-1984 ... 1-4R
Whewell, William 1794-1866 ... DLB 262
Whichcote, Benjamin 1609(?)-1683 ... DLB 252
Whicher, John F. 1919-1972 ... 17-20R
Whicher, Stephen E(merson) 1915-1961 ... 179
See also DLB 111
Whicker, Alan (Donald) 1925- ... 130
Whidden, Mary Bess 1936- ... 126
Whiffen, Marcus 1916- ... CANR-12
Earlier sketch in CA 61-64
Whigham, Peter (George)
1925-1987 ... CANR-28
Obituary ... 123
Earlier sketch in CA 25-28R
See also CP 1, 2
Whigham, Thomas 1955- ... 175
Whim-Wham
See Curnow, (Thomas) Allen (Monro)
Whinnery, John R(oy) 1916- ... 162
Whinney, Margaret Dickens 1897-1975
Obituary ... 61-64
Whinnom, Keith 1927-1986
Obituary ... 118
Whipkey, Kenneth Lee 1932- ... CANR-4
Earlier sketch in CA 53-56
Whipple, A(ddison) B(eecher) C(olvin)
1918- ... 125
See also SATA 64
Whipple, Beverly 1941- ... CANR-56
Earlier sketches in CA 109, CANR-30
Whipple, Cal
See Whipple, A(ddison) B(eecher) C(olvin)
Whipple, Chandler (Henry) 1905-1977 . 25-28R
Whipple, Dorothy 1893-1966 ... CAP-1
Earlier sketch in CA 13-14
Whipple, Edwin Percy 1819-1886 ... DLB 1, 64
Whipple, Fred L(awrence) 1906-2004 ... CAP-1
Obituary ... 230
Earlier sketch in CA 11-12
Whipple, George 1927- ... 119
Whipple, George Hoyt 1878-1976 ... 158
Whipple, James B. 1913-1988 ... 29-32R
Whipple, Maurine 1910-1992 ... 5-8R
Whisenand, Paul M. 1935- ... CANR-22
Earlier sketch in CA 69-72
Whisenhunt, Donald W(ayne) 1938- .. CANR-9
Earlier sketch in CA 57-60
Whisler, John A(lbert) 1951- ... 109
Whisler, Thomas L(ee) 1920- ... 154
Brief entry ... 115
Whisman, Dale ... 239
Whisnant, Charleen
See Swansea, Charleen
Whisnant, David E(ugene) 1938- ... 41-44R
Whisnant, Luke 1957- ... 144
Whistler, Laurence 1912-2000 ... CANR-19
Earlier sketches in CA 9-12R, CANR-3
See also CP 1, 2
Whistler, Reginald John 1905-1944 ... SATA 30
Whistler, Rex
See Whistler, Reginald John
Whiston, Lionel (Abney) 1895-1994 ... 69-72
Whitacre, Donald (DuMont) 1920- ... 69-72
Whitaker, Alexander 1585-1617 ... DLB 24
Whitaker, Arthur Preston 1895-1979
Obituary ... 112
Whitaker, Ben(jamin Charles George)
1934- ... 53-56
Whitaker, C(leophaus) S(ylvester), Jr.
1935- ... CANR-28
Earlier sketch in CA 29-32R
Whitaker, Carl A(lanson) 1912-1995
Obituary ... 148
Brief entry ... 114
Whitaker, Daniel K. 1801-1881 ... DLB 73
Whitaker, David 1930-1980 ... 21-24R
Obituary ... 134
Whitaker, Dorothy Stock 1925- ... 13-16R
Whitaker, Frederic 1891-1980 ... CANR-4
Obituary ... 97-100
Earlier sketch in CA 5-8R
Whitaker, Gilbert R(iley), Jr. 1931- ... 9-12R
Whitaker, Haddon 1908(?)-1982
Obituary ... 105
Whitaker, James 1931- ... 154
Whitaker, James W. 1936- ... 102
Whitaker, John O(gden), Jr. 1935- ... 105
Whitaker, Katie 1967- ... 235
Whitaker, Leslie 1940- ... 220
Whitaker, Malachi Taylor 1895-1976
Obituary ... 104
Whitaker, Mary 1896(?)-1976
Obituary ... 65-68
Whitaker, Peter 1952- ... 124
Whitaker, Phil 1966- ... 232
Whitaker, Reg(inald) 1943- ... 192
Whitaker, Rick 1968- ... 195
Whitaker, Robert 1953(?)- ... 229
Whitaker, Rod(ney) 1925- ... CANR-45
Earlier sketch in CA 29-32R
See also CMW 4
Whitaker, Rogers E(rnest) M(alcolm) 1899-1981
Obituary ... 103
Whitaker, Shelagh (Dunwoody) 1930- ... 125
Whitaker, T(ommy) J(ames) 1949- ... 53-56
Whitaker, Thomas R(ussell) 1925- ... 25-28R
Whitaker, Urban George, Jr. 1924- ... 9-12R
Whitaker, W(illiam) Denis 1915-2001 ... 128
Obituary ... 197
Whitbeck, George W(alter) 1932-2004 ... 73-76
Obituary ... 231
Whitbourn, John 1958- ... CANR-140
Earlier sketch in CA 155
See also FANT
Whitbread, Jane
See Levin, Jane Whitbread
Whitbread, Leslie George 1917-1988 ... 37-40R
Whitbread, Thomas (Bacon) 1931- ... 13-16R
See also CP 1, 2
Whitburn, Joel (Carver) 1939- ... CANR-112
Earlier sketches in CA 33-36R, CANR-15, 32, 67
Whitby, Henry Augustus Morton
1898-1969 ... CAP-1
Earlier sketch in CA 11-12
Whitby, Sharon
See Peters, Maureen
Whitby, Thomas J. 1919- ... 126
Whitcher, Frances Miriam 1814-1852 . DLB 11, 202
Whitcher, Susan (Godsil) 1952- ... CANR-137
Earlier sketch in CA 161
See also SATA 96
Whitcomb, Christopher 1959- ... 203
Whitcomb, Edgar D(oud) 1918- ... 21-24R
Whitcomb, Hale C(hristy) 1907- ... CAP-2
Earlier sketch in CA 29-32
Whitcomb, Helen Hafemann ... CANR-6
Earlier sketch in CA 13-16R
Whitcomb, Ian 1941- ... CANR-8
Earlier sketch in CA 57-60
Whitcomb, John C(lement) 1924- ... CANR-4
Earlier sketch in CA 1-4R
Whitcomb, Jon 1906-1988 ... CAP-1
Obituary ... 125
Earlier sketch in CA 13-16
See also SATA 10
See also SATA-Obit 56
Whitcomb, Meg W. 1930- ... CANR-50
Earlier sketch in CA 123
Whitcomb, Noel 1918(?)-1993 ... 134
Obituary ... 141
Whitcomb, Philip W(right) 1891-1986 ... 73-76
White, A(drian) N(icholas) Sherwin
See Sherwin-White, A(drian) N(icholas)
White, Alan ... CANR-60
Earlier sketches in CA 45-48, CANR-3
See also Fraser, James
White, Alan R(ichard) 1922-1992 ... 25-28R
Obituary ... 137
White, Alex Sandri 1916(?)-1983(?)
Obituary ... 108
White, Alice Violet 1922- ... CANR-13
Earlier sketch in CA 61-64
White, Alicen ... 77-80
White, Allon (H.) 1951-1988 ... 128
White, Amber Blanco
See Blanco White, Amber
White, Andrea 1942- ... 144
White, Andrew 1579-1656 ... DLB 24
White, Andrew Dickson 1832-1918 ... 182
See also DLB 47
White, Anne Hitchcock 1902-1970
Obituary ... 108
See also SATA-Brief 33
White, Anne S(hanklin) ... 93-96
White, Anne Terry 1896-1980 ... 9-12R
Obituary ... 135
See also SATA 2
White, Anthony Gene 1946- ... CANR-12
Earlier sketch in CA 73-76
White, Antonia 1899-1980 ... 104
Obituary ... 97-100
See also CN 1, 2
White, Augustus A(aron III) 1936- ... 168
White, Babington
See Braddon, Mary Elizabeth
White, Bailey 1950- ... CANR-88
Earlier sketch in CA 141
See also CSW
White, Barbara A(nne) 1942- ... CANR-56
Earlier sketches in CA 109, CANR-29
White, Barbara Ehrlich 1936- ... 136
White, Barry (Eugene) 1944-2003 ... 187
White, Beatrice (Mary Irene) 1902-1986
Obituary ... 119
White, Benjamin V(room) 1908- ... 101
White, Benton R. 1949- ... 124
White, Bessie (Felstiner) 1892(?)-1986
Obituary ... 121
See also SATA-Obit 50
White, Betty 1917- ... 5-8R
White, Brian Terence 1927- ... 105
White, Burton L(eonard) 1929- ... CANR-4
Earlier sketch in CA 45-48
White, Caramine 1966- ... 227
White, Carl M(ilton) 1903-1983 ... 13-16R
Obituary ... 111
White, Carol 1946- ... 111
White, Carol Hellings 1939- ... 81-84
White, Carolinne 1955- ... 142
White, Carolyn 1948- ... 199
See also SATA 130
White, (Edwin) Chappell 1920- ... 25-28R
White, Claire Nicolas 1925- ... CANR-25
Earlier sketch in CA 108
White, Curtis 1951- ... CANR-119
Earlier sketches in CA 110, CANR-27
White, Cynthia L(eslie) 1940- ... 37-40R
White, Dale
See Place, Marian T(empleton)
White, Dan S(eligsberger) 1939- ... 97-100
White, Dana
See Larsen, Anita
White, David Gordon 1953- ... CANR-136
Earlier sketch in CA 165
White, David Manning 1917-1993 ... CANR-4
Obituary ... 143
Earlier sketch in CA 1-4R
White, David Omar 1927- ... 17-20R
White, Dori 1919- ... 37-40R
See also SATA 10
White, Dorothy Shipley ... CAP-1
Earlier sketch in CA 13-14
White, Douglas M(alcolm) 1909- ... CANR-4
Earlier sketch in CA 1-4R
White, E(lwyn) B(rooks) 1899-1985 .. CANR-37
Obituary ... 116
Earlier sketches in CA 13-16R, CANR-16
See also AAYA 62
See also AITN 2
See also AMWS 1
See also CDALBS
See also CLC 10, 34, 39
See also CLR 1, 21
See also CPW
See also DA3
See also DAM POP
See also DLB 11, 22
See also EWL 3
See also FANT
See also MAICYA 1, 2
See also MAL 5
See also MTCW 1, 2
See also MTFW 2005
See also NCFS 5
See also RGAL 4
See also SATA 2, 29, 100
See also SATA-Obit 44
See also TUS
White, Edgar (B.) 1947- ... CANR-27
Earlier sketch in CA 61-64
See also BW 1
See also CD 5
See also DLB 38
White, Edgar Nkosi 1947- ... CAD
See also CD 6
White, Edmund (Valentine III)
1940- ... CANR-133
Earlier sketches in CA 45-48, CANR-3, 19, 36, 62, 107
See also AAYA 7
See also CLC 27, 110
See also CN 5, 6, 7
See also DA3
See also DAM POP
See also DLB 227
See also MTCW 1, 2
See also MTFW 2005
White, Edward M. 1933- ... 37-40R
White, Elijah (Brockenborough III)
1938- ... 69-72
White, Eliza Orne 1856-1947 ... CWRI 5
See also YABC 2
White, Elizabeth H(erzog) 1901(?)-1972
Obituary ... 37-40R
White, Elizabeth Wade 1906-1994 ... 97-100
White, Ellen E(merson) ... YAW
White, Elliott 1936- ... CANR-55
Earlier sketch in CA 127
White, Elmer G. 1926-1979 ... 21-24R
Obituary ... 134
White, Emily 1966- ... 224
White, Emmons E(aton) 1891-1982 ... 73-76
Obituary ... 133
White, Erdmute Wenzel ... 185
White, Eric Walter 1905-1985 ... CAP-1
Obituary ... 117
Earlier sketch in CA 11-12
White, Ethel Lina 1887-1944 ... 167
Brief entry ... 108
See also DLB 77
White, Eugene E. 1919- ... 13-16R
White, Evelyn C. 1954- ... 164
White, F(rederick) Clifton 1918-1993 ... 113
Obituary ... 140
White, Florence M(eiman) 1910- ... 41-44R
See also SATA 14
White, Frank 1944- ... 126
White, Franklin ... 173
White, G(eorge) Edward 1941- ... CANR-94
Earlier sketches in CA 69-72, CANR-12, 62
White, Geoffrey M(iles) 1949- ... CANR-107
Earlier sketch in CA 143
White, George Abbott 1943- ... 143
White, Gerald Taylor 1913-1989 ... CANR-2
Earlier sketch in CA 5-8R
White, Gertrude M(ason) 1915- ... 81-84
White, Gilbert 1720-1793 ... BRWS 6
White, Gillian Mary 1936- ... 17-20R
White, Glenn M. 1918(?)-1978 ... 93-96
Obituary ... 81-84
White, Gordon Eliot 1933- ... 101
White, H. T.
See Engh, Rohn
White, Harrison C(olyar) 1930- ... 45-48
White, Harry
See Whittington, Harry (Benjamin)
White, Hayden V. 1928- ... CANR-135
Earlier sketch in CA 128
See also CLC 148
See also DLB 246
White, Helen Constance 1896-1967 ... 5-8R
White, Henry Kirke 1785-1806 ... DLB 96
White, Hilda Crystal 1917- ... 5-8R
White, Horace 1834-1916
Brief entry ... 119
See also DLB 23
White, Howard 1945- ... 164

White, Howard Ashley 1913-1991 .... 29-32R
Obituary 133
White, Howard B. 1912(?)-1974
Obituary 53-56
White, Hugh Clayton 1936- 45-48
White, Hugh Vernon 1889-1984 .... 5-8R
White, Irvin L(inwood) 1932- CANR-8
Earlier sketch in CA 57-60
White, Ivan 1929- .... CP 1, 2
White, J(ay) P. 1952- 220
White, Jack
See White, W(illiam) J(ohn)
White, Jack Joseph 1954- 149
White, Jack McBride
See White, Jack Joseph
White, James 1913-2003 109
Obituary 217
White, James 1928-1999 .... CANR-4
Earlier sketch in CA 53-56
See also DLB 261
See also SFW 4
White, James Boyd 1938- CANR-117
Earlier sketches in CA 111, CANR-30
White, James Dillon
See White, Stanley
White, James F(loyd) 1932- CANR-105
Earlier sketches in CA 107, CANR-24, 49
White, James L. (?)-1981
Obituary 115
White, James P(atrick) 1940- CANR-99
Earlier sketches in CA 69-72, CANR-11, 42
White, Jane
See Brady, Jane
White, Jane Neal 1918- 110
White, Jerry E(ugene) 1937- 129
White, Jerry S. 1946- 130
White, Joan 1909-1999
Obituary 181
White, John 1924- CANR-20
See also CAD
White, John Albert 1910-2001 .... CAP-2
Earlier sketch in CA 23-24
White, John Baker
See Baker White, John
White, John H(oxland), Jr. 1933- CANR-126
Earlier sketches in CA 25-28R, CANR-42
White, John H(enry) 1945- 124
Brief entry 117
White, John I(rwin) 57-60
White, John K(enneth) 1952- CANR-99
Earlier sketches in CA 116, CANR-39
White, John Sylvester 1919- .... CD 5, 6
White, John W. 1939- CANR-13
Earlier sketch in CA 37-40R
White, John Wesley 1928- CANR-31
Earlier sketch in CA 29-32R
White, Jon (Ewbank) Manchip 1924- 197
Earlier sketches in CA 13-16R, CANR-15, 32, 67
Autobiographical Essay in 197
See also CAAS 4
See also CMW 4
See also CN 1, 2, 3
See also CP 1
White, Jonathan
See Harvey, John (Barton)
White, Jonathan 1956- 146
White, Joseph B. 1958- 147
White, Joyce C(arol) 1952- 112
White, Jude Gilliam 1947- CANR-89
Earlier sketches in CA 106, CANR-23, 41
See also Deveraux, Jude
See also CPW
See also DAM POP
See also RHW
White, K(enneth) D(ouglas)
1908-1998 .... CANR-12
Earlier sketch in CA 69-72
White, K(enneth) Owen 1902-1985 .... CAP-2
Earlier sketch in CA 17-18
White, Karen 1964- 226
White, Karol Koenigsberg 1938- 5-8R
White, Katharine S(ergeant Angell)
1892-1977 216
Obituary 104
White, Kenneth 1936- 25-28R
See also CP 1, 2, 3, 4, 5, 6, 7
White, Kenneth Steele 1922- 93-96
White, Kevin 1959- 144
White, Laurence B(arton), Jr. 1935- CANR-24
Earlier sketches in CA 65-68, CANR-9
See also SATA 10
White, Lawrence 1942- 115
White, Lawrence H(enry) 1954- 118
White, Lawrence J. 1943- CANR-31
Earlier sketches in CA 37-40R, CANR-14
White, Lee A. 1886-1971
Obituary 115
White, Leslie A(lvin) 1900-1975 .... CANR-3
Obituary 57-60
Earlier sketch in CA 1-4R
White, Leslie Turner 1903-1967(?) CAP-1
Earlier sketch in CA 13-14
White, Lionel 1905-1985 .... CANR-58
Earlier sketch in CA 103
See also CMW 4
White, Lonnie J(oe) 1931- 13-16R
White, Lucia 123
White, Lynn (Townsend), Jr.
1907-1987 .... CANR-2
Obituary 122
Earlier sketch in CA 5-8R
White, M(ary) E(llen) 1938- 21-24R
White, Margaret B(lackburn) 1936- 115
White, Martin 1943- .... SATA 51
White, Mary Alice 1920- 9-12R
White, Mary Wheeling 1965- 167
White, Matthew (Hagy) 1956- 129
White, Maurine
See Miller (Riis), Maurine
White, Maury 1919-1999 77-80
White, Melvin R(obert) 1911- CANR-40
Earlier sketches in CA 21-24R, CANR-18
White, Merry (I.) 1941- 141
White, Michael C(harles) CANR-107
Earlier sketch in CA 167
White, Mimi 1953- 145
White, Minor (Martin) 1908-1976 .... CANR-10
Obituary 65-68
Earlier sketch in CA 17-20R
See also AAYA 60
White, Morton Gabriel 1917- CANR-82
Earlier sketches in CA 5-8R, CANR-7, 35
White, Nancy 1942- 196
See also SATA 126
White, Nancy Bean 1922- 13-16R
White, Ned 1946- 129
White, Nicholas P. 1942- 73-76
White, Norval (Crawford) 1926- 77-80
White, Orion F(orrest) 1938- 53-56
White, Osmar (Egmont Dorkin)
1909-1991 130
Brief entry 105
White, Owen R(oberts) 1945- 41-44R
White, Patricia (Ann) 1937- CANR-43
Earlier sketch in CA 117
White, Patrick (Victor Martindale)
1912-1990 .... CANR-43
Obituary 132
Earlier sketch in CA 81-84
See also BRWS 1
See also CLC 3, 4, 5, 7, 9, 18, 65, 69
See also CN 1, 2, 3, 4
See also DLB 260
See also EWL 3
See also MTCW 1
See also RGEL 2
See also RGSF 2
See also RHW
See also SSC 39
See also TWA
See also WWE 1
White, Patrick C. T. 1924- 85-88
White, Paul Dudley 1886-1973
Obituary 45-48
White, Paul Hamilton Hume
1910-1992 .... CANR-23
Earlier sketches in CA 5-8R, CANR-7
White, Paulette Childress 1948- 111
White, Percival 1887-1970 .... CANR-2
Earlier sketch in CA 1-4R
White, Peter (O. G.) 1932- 139
White, Philip L(loyd) 1923- 81-84
White, Phillip M. 1950- CANR-111
Earlier sketch in CA 152
White, Phyllis Dorothy James
1920- CANR-112
Earlier sketches in CA 21-24R, CANR-17, 43, 65
See also James, P. D.
See also CMW 4
See also CN 7
See also CPW
See also DA3
See also DAM POP
See also MTCW 1, 2
See also MTFW 2005
See also TEA
White, Poppy Cannon 1906(?)-1975 65-68
Obituary 57-60
White, R. S. 1948- 127
White, Ramy Allison CANR-26
Earlier sketches in CAP-2, CA 19-20
See also SATA 1, 67
White, Randall 1945- 121
White, Randy Wayne 1950- CANR-129
Earlier sketch in CA 161
White, Ray Lewis 1941- CANR-9
Earlier sketch in CA 21-24R
White, Reginald E(rnest) O(scar)
1914-2003 .... CANR-44
Earlier sketches in CA 5-8R, CANR-5, 21
White, Reginald James 1905-1971 108
Obituary 104
White, Rhea A(melia) 1931- 77-80
White, Richard 1931- 110
White, Richard 1947- 196
White, Richard Alan 1944- 97-100
White, Richard C(lark) 1926- 45-48
White, Richard Grant 1821-1885 .... DLB 64
White, Richard W(eddington), Jr. 1936- 142
White, Robb 1909-1990 .... CANR-1
Earlier sketch in CA 1-4R
See also AAYA 29
See also CLR 3
See also SAAS 1
See also SATA 1, 83
See also YAW
White, Robert B(enjamin), Jr. 1930-
Brief entry 118
White, Robert I. 1908-1990 .... 1-4R
White, Robert Lee 1928- 17-20R
White, Robert Mitchell II 1915- 73-76
White, Robert R(ankin) 1942- 123
White, (William) Robin(son) 1928- CANR-20
Earlier sketches in CA 9-12R, CANR-4
White, Ronald C(edric), Jr. 1939- 93-96
White, Ruth (C.) 1942- CANR-95
Earlier sketch in CA 111
See also AAYA 41
See also BYA 10
See also SATA 39, 117
White, Ruth M(argaret) 1914- 17-20R
White, Ruth Morris 1902(?)-1978
Obituary 81-84
White, Ryan 1972-1990 141
White, Sarah Harriman 1929- 9-12R
White, Shane 1957- 220
White, Sheldon H(arold) 1928-2005 105
Obituary 237
White, Stanhope 1913-1998(?) 21-24R
White, Stanley 1913-1978 .... CANR-6
Earlier sketch in CA 9-12R
White, Stephanie F(rances) T(hirkell)
1942- 17-20R
White, Stephen (Leonard) 1945- 134
White, Stephen 1951- 183
White, Stephen D(aniel) 1945- 93-96
White, Stephen E. 1947- 145
White, Stephen K. 1949- CANR-93
Earlier sketch in CA 146
White, Steve
See McGarvey, Robert
White, Steven F(orsythe) 1955- CANR-118
Earlier sketches in CA 112, CANR-30, 56
White, Stewart Edward 1873-1946 ... TCWW 1, 2
White, Susan J. 1949- 126
White, Suzanne 1938- 77-80
White, Sybille
See Pearson, Sybille
White, T(erence) H(anbury)
1906-1964 .... CANR-37
Earlier sketch in CA 73-76
See also AAYA 22
See also BPFB 3
See also BYA 4, 5
See also CLC 30
See also DLB 160
See also FANT
See also JRDA
See also LAIT 1
See also MAICYA 1, 2
See also RGEL 2
See also SATA 12
See also SUFW 1
See also YAW
White, Ted
See White, Theodore Edwin
White, Tekla N. 1934- 187
See also SATA 115
White, Terence de Vere 1912-1994 .... CANR-3
Obituary 145
Earlier sketch in CA 49-52
See also CLC 49
White, Teri 1946- CANR-66
Brief entry 127
Earlier sketch in CA 132
Interview in CA-132
See also CMW 4
White, Theo Ballou 1903-1978
Obituary 111
White, Theodore Edwin 1938- CANR-12
Earlier sketch in CA 21-24R
See also SFW 4
White, Theodore H(arold)
1915-1986 .... CANR-64
Obituary 118
Earlier sketches in CA 1-4R, CANR-3, 33
See also DLB 255
See also MTCW 1, 2
White, Thomas Justin, Jr. 1919-1987
Obituary 122
White, Tim D. 1950- 143
White, Timothy (Thomas Anthony)
1952-2002 .... SATA 60
White, Tom 1923- 223
White, Tom 1923- .... SATA 148
White, Vanna (Marie) 1957- 216
White, Vibert Leslie, Jr. 1958- 194
White, W. D. 1926- 37-40R
White, W(illiam) J(ohn) 1920-1980 .... 13-16R
Obituary 97-100
White, Walter
See White, Walter F(rancis)
White, Walter F(rancis) 1893-1955 124
Brief entry 115
See also BLC 3
See also BW 1
See also DAM MULT
See also DLB 51
See also HR 1:3
See also TCLC 15
White, William, Jr. 1934- CANR-31
Earlier sketches in CA 37-40R, CANR-14
See also SATA 16
White, William 1910-1995 .... CANR-29
Earlier sketch in CA 21-24R
White, William A(nthony) P(arker)
1911-1968 .... CANR-67
Obituary 25-28R
Earlier sketches in CAP-1, CA 11-12
See also Boucher, Anthony
See also SFW 4
White, William Allen 1868-1944
Brief entry 108
See also DLB 9, 25
White, William D. 1945- 146
White, William F(rancis) 1928- CANR-1
Earlier sketch in CA 45-48
White, William Hale 1831-1913 189
Brief entry 121
See also Rutherford, Mark
White, William J(oseph) 1926- 97-100
White, William L(indsay) 1900-1973 101
Obituary 41-44R
White, William L. 1937-1985
Obituary 114
White, William Luther 1931- 29-32R
White, William S(mith) 1907-1994 .... 5-8R
Obituary 145
White, Zita
See Denholm, Therese Mary Zita White
Whitebird, J(oanie) 1951- CANR-25
Earlier sketch in CA 69-72
White-Bowden, Susan 1939- 120
Whitechurch, Victor L(orenzo) 1868-1933 . 160
Brief entry 116
See also DLB 70
Whited, Charles 1929- 141
White Elk, Michael
See Walker, T. Michael
Whitefield, Ann
See Stone, Susan Berch
Whiteford, Andrew H(unter) 1913- ... CANR-51
Earlier sketches in CA 45-48, CANR-26
Whiteford, Merry 1959- 229
Whiteford, Wynne (Noel) 1915-2002 ..... SFW 4
Whitefriar
See Hiscock, Eric
Whitehall, Harold 1905-1986 .... CAP-2
Obituary 118
Earlier sketch in CA 21-22
Whitehead, Alfred North 1861-1947 165
Brief entry 117
See also DLB 100, 262
See also TCLC 97
Whitehead, Barbara (Maude) 1930- 97-100
Whitehead, Barbara Dafoe 1944- 164
Whitehead, Catherine Sarah 1960- 131
Whitehead, Colson 1970- 202
Whitehead, David 1958- .... TCWW 2
Whitehead, Don(ald) F. 1908-1981 .... 9-12R
Obituary 102
See also SATA 4
Whitehead, E(dward) A(nthony)
1933- CANR-118
Earlier sketches in CA 65-68, CANR-58
See also Whitehead, Ted
See also CBD
See also CD 5
See also CLC 5
See also DLB 310
Whitehead, (Walter) Edward 1908-1978 . 81-84
Obituary 77-80
Whitehead, Evelyn Annette Eaton 1938- ... 104
Whitehead, Frank S. 1916-1998 .... 37-40R
Whitehead, G(eorge) Kenneth
1913-2004 .... CANR-8
Obituary 228
Earlier sketch in CA 61-64
Whitehead, Henry S(t. Clair) 1882-1932 .. HGG
Whitehead, James (T.) 1936-2003 77-80
Obituary 219
See also CP 1, 2
See also DLBY 1981
Whitehead, James D(ouglas) 1939- 105
Whitehead, Janet
See Whitehead, David
Whitehead, John (Randolph) 1924- 120
Whitehead, John W(ayne) 1946- CANR-109
Earlier sketch in CA 117
Whitehead, Kate
See Whitehead, Catherine Sarah
Whitehead, Neil L(ancelot) 1956- .. CANR-138
Earlier sketch in CA 174
Whitehead, Paxton 1937- 208
Whitehead, Raymond Leslie 1933- 77-80
Whitehead, Robert J(ohn) 1928- CANR-13
Earlier sketch in CA 37-40R
Whitehead, Ted
See Whitehead, E(dward) A(nthony)
See also CD 6
Whitehead, William 1715-1785 ... DLB 84, 109
See also RGEL 2
Whitehead, William Grant 1943-1987
Obituary 124
Whitehill, Arthur M(urray, Jr.) 1919- . CANR-13
Earlier sketch in CA 77-80
Whitehill, Walter Muir 1905-1978 ..... CANR-6
Obituary 77-80
Earlier sketch in CA 13-16R
Whitehorn, Alan (James) 1946- 138
Whitehorn, Katharine
See Lyall, Katharine Elizabeth
Whitehouse, Arch
See Whitehouse, Arthur George Joseph
Whitehouse, Arthur George Joseph
1895-1979 .... CANR-4
Obituary 89-92
Earlier sketch in CA 5-8R
See also SATA 14
See also SATA-Obit 23
Whitehouse, David (Bryn) 1941- CANR-93
Earlier sketch in CA 131
Whitehouse, Elizabeth S(cott)
1893-1968 .... CAP-1
Earlier sketch in CA 13-14
See also SATA 35
Whitehouse, Franklin S., Jr. 1934-1985
Obituary 117
Whitehouse, J(ohn) C(olin) 1932- 187
Whitehouse, Jack E(dward) 1933- 111
Whitehouse, Jeanne 103
See also Peterson, Jeanne Whitehouse
See also SATA 29
Whitehouse, Roger 1939- 57-60
Whitehouse, Ruth D(elamain) 1942- 118
Whitehouse, W(alter) A(lexander)
1915-2003 .... CANR-3
Obituary 216
Earlier sketch in CA 1-4R
Whitelaw, Billie 1932- 208
Whitelaw, Nancy 1933- 143
See also SATA 76

Cumulative Index 617 **Wibbelsman**

Whitelaw, William Menzies 1890(?)-1974
Obituary 45-48
Whiteley, Denys Edward Hugh 1914-1987
Obituary 123
Whiteley, George 1909(?)-1990
Obituary 132
Whiteley, Opal Stanley 1897-1992 237
Whiteley, Peter 1928- 165
Whitelock, Dorothy 1901-1982 129
Obituary 107
Whiteman, (David) Bruce 1952- CANR-93
Earlier sketch in CA 132
Whiteman, Maxwell 1914-1995 .... CANR-10
Earlier sketch in CA 21-24R
Whiteman, Paul 1890(?)-1967
Obituary 113
Whiteman, Roberta J. Hill 1947- 146
See also NNAL
Whiteman, Robin 1944- CANR-136
Earlier sketch in CA 167
Whitemore, Hugh (John) 1936- CANR-77
Earlier sketch in CA 132
Interview in CA-132
See also CBD
See also CD 5, 6
See also CLC 37
White-Parks, Annette 1935- 156
Whitesel, Cheryl Aylward 238
See also SATA 162
Whitesell, (James) Edwin 1909-1998 .... 41-44R
Whitesell, Faris Daniel 1895-1984 .... 5-8R
Obituary 146
Whiteside, Kathleen 1945- 212
Whiteside, Lynn W. 1908-1983 .... 25-28R
Whiteside, Robert L(eo) 1907-1995 53-56
Whiteside, Thomas 1918(?)-1997 161
Brief entry 109
Whitesitt, Linda (Marie) 1951- 129
Whiteson, Leon 1930- CANR-69
Earlier sketches in CA 21-24R, CANR-16
Whiteway, Doug(las) Alfred 1951- 164
Whitfield, Eileen 1951- 206
Whitfield, George J(oshua) N(ewbold) 1909-2000 .... CAP-1
Obituary 192
Earlier sketch in CA 11-12
Whitfield, James Monroe 1822-1871 .... DLB 50
Whitfield, John Humphreys 1906-1995 .. 9-12R
Whitfield, Phil(ip John) 1944- 97-100
Whitfield, Raoul 1897(?)-1945
Brief entry 109
See also CMW 4
See also DLB 226
Whitfield, Sarah 1942- 141
Whitfield, Shelby 1935- 49-52
Whitfield, Stephen J(ack) 1942- CANR-91
Earlier sketch in CA 61-64
Whitford, Bessie 1885(?)-1977
Obituary 69-72
Whitford, Frank 1941- CANR-50
Earlier sketch in CA 97-100
Whitgift, John c. 1533-1604 .... DLB 132
Whitin, Thomson McLintock 1923- CANR-3
Earlier sketch in CA 1-4R
Whiting, Allen S(uess) 1926- 125
Brief entry 105
Whiting, Beatrice Blyth 1914-2003 .... 5-8R
Obituary 221
Whiting, Charles (Henry) 1926- CANR-142
Earlier sketch in CA 173
Whiting, Charles E. 1914(?)-1980
Obituary 97-100
Whiting, Frank M. 1907-1977 101
Whiting, John (Robert) 1917-1963 102
Obituary 89-92
See also CBD
See also DLB 13
See also RGEL 2
Whiting, Kenneth R. 1913-1993 .... CANR-5
Earlier sketch in CA 5-8R
Whiting, Nathan 1946- 41-44R
Whiting, Percy H(ollister) 1880-1967 .... CAP-1
Earlier sketch in CA 13-16
Whiting, Robert 1942- 102
Whiting, Robert L(ouis) 1918- 17-20R
Whiting, Samuel 1597-1679 .... DLB 24
Whiting, Steven Moore 1953- 184
Whiting, Thomas A. 1917- CANR-3
Earlier sketch in CA 1-4R
Whitinger, R. D.
See Place, Marian T(empleton)
Whitington, R(ichard) S. 1912-1984 77-80
Whitlam, (Edward) Gough 1916- CANR-139
Earlier sketch in CA 109
Whitley, David S(cott) 1953- 193
Whitley, George
See Chandler, A(rthur) Bertram
Whitley, M. Stanley 1948- 212
Whitley, Mary Ann
See Sebrey, Mary Ann
Whitley, Oliver R. 1918-1978 77-80
Whitley, Peggy 1938- 211
See also SATA 140
Whitlock, Albert 1915-1999 .... IDFW 3, 4
Whitlock, Baird W(oodruff) 1924- 112
Whitlock, Brand 1869-1934 162
Brief entry 110
See also DLB 12
Whitlock, Glenn E(verett) 1917- 21-24R
Whitlock, Luder (G.), Jr. 1940- 193
Whitlock, Pamela 1921(?)-1982
Obituary 107
See also CWRI 5
See also SATA-Obit 31
Whitlock, Quentin A(rthur) 1937- 109
Whitlock, Ralph 1914-1995 .... CANR-45
Obituary 150
Earlier sketches in CA 101, CANR-20
See also SATA 35
Whitlock, Virginia Bennett (?)-1972
Obituary 37-40R
Whitlow, Roger 1940- 41-44R
Whitman, Albery Allson 1851-1901 176
See also BW 3
See also DLB 50
Whitman, Alden 1913-1990 .... CANR-29
Obituary 132
Earlier sketch in CA 17-20R
See also DLBY 1991
Whitman, Alice
See Marker, Sherry
Whitman, (Evelyn) Ardis 1905(?)-1990 .... 9-12R
Obituary 131
Whitman, Bertha Yerex 1892-1984
Obituary 114
Whitman, Cedric H(ubbell) 1916-1979 .... CANR-27
Obituary 120
Earlier sketch in CA 17-20R
Whitman, David (deFreudiger) 1955- 113
Whitman, Edmund Spurr 1900-1987 .... 17-20R
Whitman, Howard 1915(?)-1975
Obituary 53-56
Whitman, John 1944- CANR-11
Earlier sketch in CA 61-64
Whitman, Marina von Neumann 1935- CANR-89
Earlier sketch in CA 17-20R
Whitman, Martin J. 1924- 104
Whitman, Nancy C(hong) 1932- 199
Whitman, Richard Ray 1949- 234
Whitman, Robert Freeman 1925- 81-84
Whitman, Ruth (Bashein) 1922- CANR-31
Earlier sketches in CA 21-24R, CANR-12
See also CP 1, 2
Whitman, Sarah Helen (Power) 1803-1878 .... DLB 1, 243
Whitman, Sylvia (Choate) 1961- CANR-110
Earlier sketch in CA 151
See also SATA 85, 135
Whitman, T(orrey) Stephen 1950- 164
Whitman, Virginia Bruner 1901-1987 .... CANR-4
Earlier sketch in CA 5-8R
Whitman, W(illiam) Tate 1909- CAP-1
Earlier sketch in CA 11-12
Whitman, Walt(er) 1819-1892 .... AAYA 42
See also AMW
See also AMWR 1
See also CDALB 1640-1865
See also DA
See also DA3
See also DAB
See also DAC
See also DAM MST, POET
See also DLB 3, 64, 224, 250
See also EXPP
See also LAIT 2
See also LMFS 1
See also PAB
See also PC 3
See also PFS 2, 3, 13, 22
See also RGAL 4
See also SATA 20
See also TUS
See also WLC
See also WP
See also WYAS 1
Whitman, Wanda (?)-1976
Obituary 65-68
Whitmarsh, Anne (Mary Gordon) 1933- 106
Whitmont, Edward C. 1912-1998 115
Obituary 172
Whitmore, Arvella 1922- 196
See also SATA 125
Whitmore, Charles (Stanleigh) 1949- 117
Whitmore, Cilla
See Gladstone, Arthur M.
Whitmore, Eugene (Milton) 1895-1983 .... 5-8R
Whitmore, George 1945-1989 .... CANR-30
Obituary 128
Earlier sketch in CA 102
Whitnah, Donald R(obert) 1925- 9-12R
Whitnah, Dorothy L. 1926- CANR-16
Earlier sketch in CA 93-96
Whitnell, Barbara
See Hutton, Ann
Whitney, Alec
See White, Alan
Whitney, Alex(andra) 1922- 53-56
See also SATA 14
Whitney, Byrl A(lbert) 1901- CAP-1
Earlier sketch in CA 13-14
Whitney, Catherine (A.) 1950- 189
Whitney, Charles Allen 1929- 81-84
Whitney, Cornelius Vanderbilt 1899-1992 85-88
Whitney, Craig Richard 1943- 131
Whitney, Dallas (Cole) 1952- 117
Whitney, David
See Malick, Terrence
Whitney, David C(harles) 1921- CANR-5
Earlier sketch in CA 9-12R
See also SATA 48
See also SATA-Brief 29
Whitney, Eleanor Noss 1938- CANR-6
Earlier sketch in CA 13-16R
Whitney, Elizabeth Dalton 1906-1996 .. 21-24R
Whitney, Geoffrey 1552(?)-1601 .... DLB 136
Whitney, George D(ana) 1918- 93-96
Whitney, Gertrude Vanderbilt 1877-1942 .... AAYA 57
Whitney, Grace Lee 1930- 177
Whitney, Hallam
See Whittington, Harry (Benjamin)
Whitney, Isabella .... DLB 136
Whitney, J(ohn) D(enison) 1940- CANR-93
Earlier sketches in CA 49-52, CANR-3
Whitney, J. L. H.
See Trimble, Jacquelyn W(hitney)
Whitney, John Hay 1904-1982
Obituary 106
See also DLB 127
Whitney, John Raymond 1920- 105
Whitney, Kim Ablon 238
See also SATA 162
Whitney, Leon F(radley) 1894-1973 .... CANR-5
Earlier sketch in CA 5-8R
Whitney, Malika Lee 1946- 133
Whitney, Marie Louise (Schroeder) Hosford 1925(?)-
Brief entry 113
Whitney, Marylou
See Whitney, Marie Louise (Schroeder) Hosford
Whitney, Peter Dwight 1915- 9-12R
Whitney, Phyllis A(yame) 1903- CANR-60
Earlier sketches in CA 1-4R, CANR-3, 25, 38
See also AAYA 36
See also AITN 2
See also BEST 90:3
See also CLC 42
See also CLR 59
See also CMW 4
See also CPW
See also DA3
See also DAM POP
See also JRDA
See also MAICYA 1, 2
See also MTCW 2
See also RHW
See also SATA 1, 30
See also YAW
Whitney, Polly (Louise) 1948- CANR-137
Earlier sketch in CA 152
Whitney, Robert Frost 1906(?)-1986
Obituary 119
Whitney, Ruth Reinke 1928-1999 133
Obituary 181
Whitney, Sharon 1937- .... SATA 63
Whitney, Steve(n) 1946- 81-84
Whitney, Thomas P(orter) 1917- 104
See also SATA 25
Whiton, James Nelson 1932- 13-16R
Whitridge, Arnold 1891-1989 .... 9-12R
Obituary 127
Whitrow, Gerald James 1912-2000 .... CANR-3
Obituary 188
Earlier sketch in CA 5-8R
Whitson
See Warren, Peter Whitson
Whitson, John H(arvey) 1854-1936 .. TCWW 1, 2
Whitson, Skip 1944- 118
Whitson, Stephanie Grace (Irvin) 1952- 217
Whitt, Anne Hall
See Thompson, Anne Hall Whitt
Whitt, Richard 1944- 81-84
Whittaker, C(harles) R(ichard) 1929- 131
Whittaker, Kathryn Putnam 1931- 13-16R
Whittaker, Mark 238
Whittaker, Otto (Jr.) 1916- 25-28R
Whittaker, Robert Harding 1920-1980 105
Whittall, Arnold (Morgan) 1935- 195
Whittemore, Charles P(ark) 1921- 9-12R
Whittemore, Don 69-72
Whittemore, L(ouis) H(enry) 1941- 45-48
Whittemore, Mildred 1946- 9-12R
Whittemore, (Edward) Reed, Jr. 1919- 219
Earlier sketches in CA 9-12R, CANR-4, 119
Autobiographical Essay in 219
See also CAAS 8
See also CLC 4
See also CP 1, 2, 3, 4, 5, 6, 7
See also DLB 5
See also MAL 5
Whittemore, Robert Clifton 1921- 9-12R
Whitten, Jamie L(loyd) 1910-1995 .... CAP-2
Earlier sketch in CA 23-24
Whitten, Leslie H(unter), Jr. 1928- CANR-53
Earlier sketches in CA 17-20R, CANR-29
See also HGG
Whitten, Mary Evelyn 1922- 17-20R
Whitten, Norman E(arl), Jr. 1937- 17-20R
Whittet, G(eorge) S(orley) 1918- 21-24R
Whittet, T. D.
See Whittet, Thomas Douglas
Whittet, Thomas Douglas 1915-1987
Obituary 122
Whittick, Arnold 1898-1986 .... CAP-1
Earlier sketch in CA 11-12
Whittier, John Greenleaf 1807-1892 ... AMWS 1
See also DLB 1, 243
See also RGAL 4
Whitting, Philip (David) 1903-1988 97-100
Whittingham, Harry E(dward), Jr. 1918- 5-8R
Whittingham, Jack 1910-1972
Obituary 37-40R
Whittingham, Richard 1939-2005 .... CANR-82
Obituary 236
Earlier sketches in CA 37-40R, CANR-36
Whittington, Brad 1956- 226
Whittington, Geoffrey 1938- CANR-42
Earlier sketches in CA 104, CANR-20
Whittington, H(orace) G(reeley) 1929- .. 21-24R
Whittington, Harry (Benjamin) 1915-1989 .... CANR-58
Earlier sketches in CA 21-24R, CANR-5
Interview in CANR-5
See also Carter, Ashley
See also CMW 4
See also RHW
See also TCWW 1, 2
Whittington, Keith E. 1968- 200
Whittington, Mary K(athrine) 1941- .... SATA 75
Whittington, Peter
See Mackay, James (Alexander)
Whittington-Egan, Richard 1924- CANR-42
Earlier sketches in CA 9-12R, CANR-5, 20
Whittle, Amberys R(ayvon) 1935- 45-48
Whittle, Frank 1907-1996 162
Whittle, Tyler
See Tyler-Whittle, Michael Sidney
Whittlebot, Hernia
See Coward, Noel (Peirce)
Whittlesey, E(unice) S. 1907- 93-96
Whittlesey, Susan 1938- 29-32R
Whitton, Charlotte (Elizabeth) 1896-1975
Obituary 89-92
Whitton, David 1947- 149
Whitton, John Boardman 1892-1977 .... CAP-2
Earlier sketch in CA 23-24
Whitton, Kenneth S(tuart) 1925- CANR-90
Earlier sketch in CA 131
Whittow, J. B.
See Whittow, John B(yron)
Whittow, John B(yron) 1929- CANR-46
Earlier sketch in CA 120
Whitty, Jeff 1971- 238
Whitty, Julia 1958(?)- 216
Whitworth, John 1945- CANR-93
Earlier sketch in CA 131
See also SATA 123
Whitworth, John McKelvie 1942- 77-80
Whitworth, Rex (Henry) 1916-2004 144
Obituary 229
Whitworth, William 1937- 37-40R
Whitzman, Carolyn 1963- 152
Whiz, Walter
See Johnson, Curt(is Lee)
Wholey, Dennis 1937- 127
Whone, Herbert 1925- CANR-49
Earlier sketches in CA 108, CANR-24
Whorton, James C(lifton) 1942- CANR-143
Earlier sketch in CA 77-80
Whorton, M. Donald 1946- CANR-43
Earlier sketch in CA 117
Whozis, S. F.
See Bates, Harry
Whritner, John Alden 1935- 45-48
Whyard, Florence 1917- 129
Whyatt, Frances
See Boyd, Shylah
Whybray, Roger Norman 1923-1998 89-92
Obituary 166
Whybrow, Ian .... SATA 132
Whybrow, Peter C(harles) 1939- 187
Whynott, Douglas (Vernon) 1950- 137
Whyte, Fredrica (Harriman) 1905-1984 .... CAP-1
Earlier sketch in CA 11-12
Whyte, Henry Malcolm 1920- CANR-3
Earlier sketch in CA 5-8R
Whyte, Iain Boyd 1947- 132
Whyte, Jack 1940- 200
See also Whyte, John D.
See also AAYA 45
Whyte, James Huntington 1909-1962 .... 5-8R
Whyte, John D. 1940- 129
Whyte, John D. 1940- 200
See also Whyte, Jack
Whyte, Lancelot Law 1896-1972 .... CAP-1
Earlier sketch in CA 13-16
Whyte, Lewis (Gilmour) 1906-1986
Obituary 121
Whyte, Mal(colm Kenneth, Jr.) 1933- 106
See also SATA 62
Whyte, Martin King 1942- 81-84
Whyte, Mary 1953- CANR-118
Earlier sketch in CA 159
See also SATA 94, 148
Whyte, (Harry Archibald) Maxwell 1908- 105
Whyte, Robert Orr 1903-
Brief entry 106
Whyte, Ron 1942(?)-1989 132
Obituary 129
See also SATA-Obit 63
Whyte, Sibly
See Stine, Henry Eugene
Whyte, William Foote 1914-2000 .... CANR-40
Obituary 189
Earlier sketches in CA 1-4R, CANR-3, 18
Whyte, William H(ollingsworth) 1917-1999 .... 9-12R
Obituary 174
Whytock, Cherry 238
Wiarda, Howard J(ohn) 1939- CANR-119
Earlier sketches in CA 53-56, CANR-4, 21
Wiat, Philippa
See Ferridge, Philippa
Wiater, Stanley 1953- CANR-106
Earlier sketch in CA 150
See also SATA 84
Wibbelsman, Charles J(oseph) 1945- 128
See also SATA 59

Wibberley, Leonard (Patrick O'Connor)
1915-1983 .... CANR-3
Obituary 111
Earlier sketch in CA 5-8R
See also Holton, Leonard
See also CLR 3
See also SATA 2, 45
See also SATA-Obit 36
Wiber, Melanie G(ay) 1954- 151
Wiberg, Harald (Albin) 1908- .... SATA 93
See also SATA-Brief 40
Wicclair, Mark R. 1944- 149
Wice, Aubrey (Agnew) 1913(?)-1985
Obituary 119
Wice, Paul B(ernard) 1942- CANR-109
Earlier sketch in CA 57-60
Wick, Carter
See Wilcox, Collin
Wick, John W(illiam) 1935- CANR-15
Earlier sketch in CA 41-44R
Wick, Steve 1951- 159
Wick, Stuart Mary
See Freeman, Kathleen
Wick, Walter 1953- CANR-130
Earlier sketch in CA 208
See also MAICYA 2
See also SATA 148
Wick, Wendy
See Reaves, Wendy Wick
Wicke, Charles R(obinson) 1928- 37-40R
Wicke, Edith Schreiber
See Schreiber-Wicke, Edith
Wickenden, Elizabeth 1909-2001 .... 1-4R
Wickenden, Leonard Daniel 1913(?)-1989
Obituary 130
Wickens, Delos D(onald) 1909-1988 .... CAP-1
Earlier sketch in CA 13-16
Wickens, Elaine .... SATA 86
Wickens, James F. 1933- 57-60
Wicker, Brian 1929- 17-20R
Wicker, Ireene 1905(?)-1987 69-72
Obituary 124
See also SATA-Obit 55
Wicker, Randolfe Hayden 1938- 45-48
Wicker, Thomas Grey 1926- CANR-141
Earlier sketches in CA 65-68, CANR-21, 46
See also Wicker, Tom
Wicker, Tom
See Wicker, Thomas Grey
See also CLC 7
Wickers, David 1944- 77-80
Wickersham, Edward Dean 1927-1966 ..... 5-8R
Wickersham, Joan Barrett 1957- 105
Wickert, Erwin 1915- CANR-94
Earlier sketch in CA 132
Wickert, Frederic R(obinson) 1912- 21-24R
Wickes, George 1923- 9-12R
Wickes, Kim 1947- 109
Wickett, Ann 1942- 122
Wickett, William Harold, Jr. 1919- 108
Wickey, Gould 1891-1976 .... 25-28R
Wickham, Anna 1883-1947 .... DLB 240
Wickham, Christopher J. 1950- 144
Wickham, David 1944- 141
Wickham, Dewayne 1946- 217
Wickham, Edward Ralph 1911-1994 .... 5-8R
Wickham, Glynne (William Gladstone)
1922-2004 .... CANR-7
Obituary 223
Earlier sketch in CA 5-8R
Wickham, Jean 1903- 69-72
Wickham, Mary Fanning
See Bond, Mary Fanning Wickham
Wickham, Thomas Frederick 1926- 13-16R
Wickham-Crowley, Timothy P. 1951- 155
Wickham-Jones, C. R.
See Wickham-Jones, Caroline R.
Wickham-Jones, Caroline R. 1955- 188
Wicklein, John (Frederick) 1924- 106
Wicklund, Robert A. 1941- 144
Wickram, Georg c. 1505-c. 1561 .... DLB 179
Wickramasinghe, Nalin Chandra 1939- .... CP 1
Wickremasinghe, Esmond 1920(?)-1985
Obituary 117
Wickremasinghe, S(ugiswara) A(beywardena)
1901-1981
Obituary 108
Wicks, Ben 1926- 73-76
Wicks, Harold Vernon, Jr. 1931- 102
Wicks, Harry
See Wicks, Harold Vernon, Jr.
Wicks, Jared 1929- CANR-21
Earlier sketch in CA 25-28R
Wicks, John H. 1936- 17-20R
Wicks, Robert J(ohn) 1946- 113
Wicks, Robert S(igfrid) 1954- 210
Wicks, Robert Stewart 1923- 17-20R
Wicks, Susan 1947- CANR-144
Earlier sketch in CA 173
See also CWP
Wickstrom, Lois 1948- 106
Wickwar, (William) Hardy 1903-1999 57-60
Wickwire, Franklin B(acon) 1931- 21-24R
Wickwire, Mary Botts 1935- 104
Wicomb, Zoe 1948- CANR-106
Earlier sketch in CA 127
See also DLB 225
Wictor, Jan
See Gyllensten, Lars (Johan Wictor)
Widdecombe, Ann (Noreen) 1947- 225
Widdemer, Mabel Cleland 1902-1964 ...... 5-8R
See also SATA 5
Widdemer, Margaret 1897(?)-1978 ..... CANR-4
Obituary 77-80
Earlier sketch in CA 5-8R
Widder, (John) Arthur, (Jr.) 1928- 5-8R
Widder, Milton 1907(?)-1985
Obituary 118
Widdicombe, Richard Toby 1955- .. CANR-107
Earlier sketch in CA 150
Widdifield, Stacie G(raham) 1953- 168
Widdows, P(aul) F. 1918- 143
Widell, Helene 1912- 37-40R
Wideman, John Edgar 1941- CANR-140
Earlier sketches in CA 85-88, CANR-14, 42, 67, 109
See also AFAW 1, 2
See also AMWS 10
See also BLC 3
See also BPFB 4
See also BW 2, 3
See also CLC 5, 34, 36, 67, 122
See also CN 4, 5, 6, 7
See also DAM MULT
See also DLB 33, 143
See also MAL 5
See also MTCW 2
See also MTFW 2005
See also RGAL 4
See also RGSF 2
See also SSC 62
See also SSFS 6, 12
See also TCLE 1:2
Widener, Alice 1905(?)-1985
Obituary 114
Widener, Don(ald) 1930-2003 .... 37-40R
Obituary 216
Widener, Harry Elkins 1885-1912 ...... DLB 140
Widener, Terry 1950- .... SATA 105
Widenor, William C(ramer) 1937- 102
Widerberg, Siv 1931- 53-56
See also SATA 10
Widgery, Alban G(regory) 1887-1968 .... 5-8R
Widgery, David 1947-1992 .... CANR-47
Obituary 139
Earlier sketch in CA 69-72
Widgery, Jan 1920- 17-20R
Widick, B. J. 1910- 9-12R
Widicus, Wilbur W(ilson), Jr. 1932- 53-56
Widmaier, Eric P(aul) 1957- CANR-144
Earlier sketch in CA 172
Widman, F. Lisle 1919(?)-1983
Obituary 111
Widmer, Eleanor (Rackow) 1925- 17-20R
Widmer, Emmy Louise 1925- 29-32R
Widmer, Kingsley 1925- CANR-3
Earlier sketch in CA 1-4R
Widmer, Kurt 1962- 196
Widmer, Urs 1938- 195
Widner, Jennifer A(nne) 1958- CANR-109
Earlier sketch in CA 144
Widutis, Florence 1912(?)-1989 128
Wiebe, Donald 1943- 188
Wiebe, Katie Funk 1924- 132
Wiebe, M(elvin) G(eorge) 1939- 114
Wiebe, Robert H(uddleston) 1930-2000 .... 5-8R
Obituary 191
Wiebe, Rudy (Henry) 1934- CANR-123
Earlier sketches in CA 37-40R, CANR-42, 67
See also CLC 6, 11, 14, 138
See also CN 1, 2, 3, 4, 5, 6, 7
See also DAC
See also DAM MST
See also DLB 60
See also RHW
See also SATA 156
Wiebenson, Dora (Louise) 1926- 37-40R
Wiecek, William Michael 1938- 37-40R
Wiechert, Ernst (Emil) 1887-1950 .... DLB 56
See also EWL 3
Wiechmann, Barbara .... DFS 21
Wieck, Carl F. 1937- 239
Wieck, Fred D(ernburg) 1910-1973
Obituary 104
Wieckert, Jeanne E. (Lentz) 1939- 89-92
Wiecking, Anna M. 1887-1973 .... CAP-1
Earlier sketch in CA 13-14
Wieczynski, Joseph L. 1934- 37-40R
Wied, Alexander 1943- 188
Wied, Gustav 1858-1914 .... DLB 300
Wied, Martina 1882-1957 .... DLB 85
Wiedemann, Barbara 1945- 175
Wiedemann, Thomas (Ernst Josef)
1950-2001 138
Obituary 198
Wieder, Laurance 1946- CANR-8
Earlier sketch in CA 57-60
Wieder, Marcia 1956- 182
Wieder, Robert S(hannon) 1944- 85-88
Wiederumb, Trotzhard
See Steiner, Gerolf
Wiedman, John Charles 1949- 170
Wiedner, Donald L(awrence) 1930- 13-16R
Wiefels, Paul 1954- 221
Wiegand, Charmion von
See von Wiegand, Charmion
Wiegand, G(uenther) Carl 1906- 21-24R
Wiegand, Wayne A. 1946- CANR-136
Earlier sketch in CA 164
Wiegand, William G(eorge) 1928- 9-12R
Wieghart, James G. 1933- 77-80
Wiegner, Kathleen K(napp) 1938- 93-96
Wiehe, Evelyn May Clowes 1872(?)-1942 .. 213
See also DLB 174
Wiehl, Andrew (M.) 1904-1981 89-92
Wieland, Christoph Martin 1733-1813 . DLB 97
See also EW 4
See also LMFS 1
See also RGWL 2, 3
Wieland, George F(red) 1936- 89-92
Wieland, Heinrich Otto 1877-1957 167
Wieland, Liza 1960- 139
Wieler, Diana (Jean) 1961- 163
See also AAYA 36
See also MAICYA 2
See also SATA 109
See also YAW
Wiells, Helen
See Cameron, (Barbara) Anne
Wieman, Harold F(rancis) 1917- 61-64
Wieman, Henry N(elson) 1884-1975 61-64
Obituary 57-60
Wiemer, Rudolf Otto 1905-1998 ...... CANR-53
Earlier sketches in CA 21-24R, CANR-9, 25
Wienandt, Elwyn A(rthur) 1917-1993 .... 41-44R
Wienbarg, Ludolf 1802-1872 .... DLB 133
Wiencek, Henry 220
Wiene, Robert 1881-1938 .... TCLC 56
Wiener, Alexander (Solomon) 1907-1976 ... 158
Wiener, Allen J. 1943- CANR-53
Earlier sketch in CA 125
Wiener, Antje 1960- 169
Wiener, Daniel N(orman) 1921-1999 .... 37-40R
Wiener, Harvey Shelby 1940- 102
Wiener, Joan
See Bordow, Joan (Wiener)
Wiener, Joel H. 1937- CANR-14
Earlier sketches in CA 37-40R, CANR-31
Wiener, Jon
See Wiener, Jonathan M.
Wiener, Jonathan B(aert) 1962- 158
Wiener, Jonathan M. 1944- 115
Wiener, Joshua M(ark) 1949- 133
Wiener, Leigh Auston 1929-1993 ..... CANR-47
Obituary 141
Earlier sketch in CA 108
Wiener, Lori 1956- .... SATA 84
Wiener, M. Jean 1896-1982
Obituary 107
Wiener, Martin J. 1941- 85-88
Wiener, Norbert 1894-1964 157
Obituary 107
Wiener, Philip P(aul) 1905-1992 .... CAP-1
Obituary 137
Earlier sketch in CA 9-10
Wiener, Sally Dixon 1926- 101
Wiener, Sam
See Dolgoff, Sam
Wiener, Solomon 1915- CANR-7
Earlier sketch in CA 17-20R
Wieners, John 1934- 13-16R
See also BG 1:3
See also CLC 7
See also CP 1, 2, 3, 4, 5, 6, 7
See also DLB 16
See also WP
Wieners, Walter W. 1948- 212
Wieniewska, Celina
See Janson-Smith, Celina
Wienpahl, Paul D(e Velin) 1916-1980 .... 9-12R
Wier, Allen 1946- CANR-110
Earlier sketch in CA 77-80
See also CN 7
Wier, Dara 1949- CANR-143
Earlier sketches in CA 77-80, CANR-27, 53
See also CP 7
Wier, Ester (Alberti) 1910-2000 .... 9-12R
See also CWRI 5
See also DLB 52
See also SATA 3
Wiersbe, Warren W(endell) 1929- CANR-46
Earlier sketches in CA 5-8R, CANR-7, 23
Wiersma, Stanley M(arvin) 1930- CANR-11
Earlier sketch in CA 29-32R
Wiersma, William, Jr. 1931- CANR-1
Earlier sketch in CA 45-48
Wierwille, Victor Paul 1916-1985 ...... CANR-2
Obituary 116
Earlier sketch in CA 5-8R
Wierzynski, Gregory H(ieronim) 1939- ... 73-76
Wierzynski, Kazimierz 1894-1969
Obituary 115
See also EWL 3
Wiese, Arthur E(dward) 1946- 73-76
Wiese, Kurt 1887-1974 .... CANR-77
Obituary 49-52
Earlier sketch in CA 9-12R
See also CLR 86
See also MAICYA 1, 2
See also SATA 3, 36
See also SATA-Obit 24
Wiesel, Elie(zer) 1928- CANR-125
Earlier sketches in CA 5-8R, CANR-8, 40, 65
Interview in CANR-8
See also CAAS 4
See also AAYA 7, 54
See also AITN 1
See also CDALBS
See also CLC 3, 5, 11, 37, 165
See also CWW 2
See also DA
See also DA3
See also DAB
See also DAC
See also DAM MST, NOV
See also DLB 83, 299
See also DLBY 1987
See also EWL 3
See also LAIT 4
See also MTCW 1, 2
See also MTFW 2005
See also NCFS 4
See also NFS 4
See also RGWL 3
See also SATA 56
See also WLCS
See also YAW
Wieseltier, Meir 1941- 213
Wiesen, Allen E. 1939- 29-32R
Wiesen, S. Jonathan 1968- 225
Wiesenfarth, Joseph (John) 1933- CANR-8
Earlier sketch in CA 5-8R
Wiesenfeld, Joe 1947- 131
Wiesenthal, Simon 1908- CANR-13
Earlier sketch in CA 21-24R
See also AAYA 36
Wiesner, David 1956- 209
See also CLR 43, 84
See also CWRI 5
See also MAICYA 2
See also MAICYAS 1
See also SATA 72, 117, 139
Wiesner, Jerome B(ert) 1915-1994 .... 13-16R
Obituary 147
Wiesner, K. S.
See Wiesner, Karen Sue
Wiesner, Karen
See Wiesner, Karen Sue
Wiesner, Karen S.
See Wiesner, Karen Sue
Wiesner, Karen Sue 1969- 233
Wiesner, Merry E. 1952- CANR-99
Earlier sketch in CA 148
Wiesner, Portia
See Takakjian, Portia
Wiesner, William 1899-1984 .... 41-44R
See also SATA 5
Wiesner-Hanks, Merry E.
See Wiesner, Merry E.
Wiest, Claire (Johnson) 1930- CANR-34
Earlier sketch in CA 113
Wiffen, Joan 1922(?)- 208
Wigal, Donald 1933- CANR-14
Earlier sketch in CA 81-84
Wigan, Anthony (?)-1983
Obituary 110
Wigan, Bernard (John) 1918- 13-16R
Wigan, Christopher
See Bingley, David Ernest
See also TCWW 1
Wigan, Tony
See Wigan, Anthony
Wigforss, Ernst 1882(?)-1977
Obituary 69-72
Wigg, George (Edward Cecil) 1900-1983
Obituary 115
Wiggers, Raymond 1952- 149
See also SATA 82
Wiggin, Eric E(llsworth) 1939- 152
See also SATA 88
Wiggin (Riggs), Kate Douglas (Smith)
1856-1923 160
Brief entry 111
See also BYA 3
See also CLR 52
See also CWRI 5
See also DLB 42
See also MAICYA 1, 2
See also WCH
See also YABC 1
Wiggin, Maurice (Samuel) 1912- CANR-5
Earlier sketch in CA 9-12R
Wiggin, Paul 1934- 25-28R
Wiggins, Arthur W. 1938- 53-56
Wiggins, Charles W(illiam) 1937- 41-44R
Wiggins, David 1933- CANR-127
Earlier sketch in CA 118
Wiggins, Jack G(illmore) 1926- 41-44R
Wiggins, James B(ryan) 1935- 37-40R
Wiggins, James Russell 1903-2000 ... CANR-86
Obituary 191
Earlier sketch in CA 133
See also AITN 2
Wiggins, James Wilhelm 1914- 17-20R
Wiggins, Jerry S. 1931- 163
Wiggins, Marianne 1947- CANR-139
Earlier sketches in CA 130, CANR-60
See also BEST 89:3
See also CLC 57
See also CN 7
Wiggins, Melanie 1934- 159
Wiggins, Robert A. 1921- 13-16R
Wiggins, Sam P. 1919- 21-24R
Wiggins, VeraLee (Chesnut) 1928-1995 155
See also SATA 89
Wigginton, Eliot 1942- 101
See also AITN 1
Wigglesworth, Michael 1631-1705 .... DLB 24
See also RGAL 4
Wigglesworth, Vincent B(rian) 1899-1994 .. 157
Wiggs, Susan 201
See also CLC 70
Wigham, Eric Leonard 1904-1990 109
Wight, Darlene Coward 1948- 220
Wight, Frederick S.
See Wight, Frederick Stallknecht (Van Buren)
Wight, Frederick Stallknecht (Van Buren)
1902-1986
Obituary 120
Wight, James Alfred 1916-1995 77-80
See also Herriot, James
See also SATA 55
See also SATA-Brief 44
Wight, (Robert James) Martin
1913-1972 .... CAP-2
Earlier sketch in CA 21-22
Wightman, Edith Mary 1939(?)-1983(?)
Obituary 111
Wightman, George Brian Hamilton 1933- .. 107
See also CP 1
Wighton, Charles Ernest 1913- 5-8R
Wighton, Rosemary Neville 1925- 9-12R
Wigman, Mary 1886-1973 214
Wigmore
See Fabricius, Johan (Johannes)
Wignall, Anne 1912-1982 97-100

Wignell, Edel 1936- 137
See also SATA 69
Wigner, Eugene Paul 1902-1995 .... CAP-2
Obituary 147
Earlier sketch in CA 25-28
Wigoder, Geoffrey Bernard 1922-1999 105
Obituary 179
Wihl, Gary 120
Wiig, Howard (Calvert) 1940- 61-64
Wijasuriya, D(onald) E(arlian) K(ingsley) 1934- 81-84
Wijnberg, Ellen 151
See also SATA 85
Wik, Reynold M. 1910- CANR-14
Earlier sketch in CA 81-84
Wikan, Unni 1944- 147
Wikander, Matthew H. 1950- CANR-97
Earlier sketch in CA 125
Wikberg, Ron 1943(?)-1994 144
Obituary 147
Wike, Edward L. 1922-1999 .... 37-40R
Wikkramasinha, Lakdasa (Nimalasiri) 1941- .... CP 1
Wikland, Ilon 1930-
Brief entry 111
See also SATA 93
See also SATA-Brief 32
Wikler, Madeline 1943- 186
Earlier sketch in CA 117
See also SATA 114
Wiklund, Patricia 199
Wikramanayake, Marina 1938- 45-48
Wiksell, Milton J. 1910-1995 .... 5-8R
Wiksell, Wesley 1906-1991 .... CAP-1
Earlier sketch in CA 17-18
Wiktorowicz, Quintan 1970- 225
Wilber, Charles G(rady) 1916-1998 .. CANR-21
Obituary 169
Earlier sketch in CA 41-44R
Wilber, Charles K. 1935- 134
Brief entry 113
Wilber, Cynthia J. 1951- 140
Wilber, Donald N(ewton) 1907-1997 . CANR-2
Earlier sketch in CA 5-8R
See also SATA 35
Wilber, Ken 1949- 184
Wilberforce, William 1759-1833 .... DLB 158
Wilbers, Stephen 1949- 106
Wilbert, Johannes 1927- 124
Brief entry 118
Wilbourn, Carole C(ecile) 1940- CANR-14
Earlier sketch in CA 81-84
Wilbrandt, Adolf von 1837-1911 .... DLB 129
Wilbur, C. Keith 1923- CANR-57
Earlier sketches in CA 25-28R, CANR-11, 28
See also SATA 27
Wilbur, C(larence) Martin 1908-1997 85-88
Obituary 159
Wilbur, Crane 1887(?)-1973
Obituary 45-48
Wilbur, Frances 1921- .... SATA 107
Wilbur, James B(enjamin) III 1924- ... CANR-41
Earlier sketches in CA 37-40R, CANR-14
Wilbur, Marguerite Knowlton (Eyer) 1889-1982 .... CAP-1
Earlier sketch in CA 11-12
Wilbur, Richard (Purdy) 1921- CANR-139
Earlier sketches in CA 1-4R, CANR-2, 29, 76, 93
Interview in CANR-29
See also CABS 2
See also AMWS 3
See also CDALBS
See also CLC 3, 6, 9, 14, 53, 110
See also CP 1, 2, 3, 4, 5, 6, 7
See also DA
See also DAB
See also DAC
See also DAM MST, POET
See also DLB 5, 169
See also EWL 3
See also EXPP
See also MAL 5
See also MTCW 1, 2
See also MTFW 2005
See also PAB
See also PC 51
See also PFS 11, 12, 16
See also RGAL 4
See also SATA 9, 108
See also WP
Wilbur, William H(ale) 1888-1979 .... CAP-1
Earlier sketch in CA 13-14
Wilburn, Jean Alexander 1915- 21-24R
Wilburn, Kathy 1948- .... SATA 68
Wilburn, Ralph G(lenn) 1909-1986 .... CAP-1
Earlier sketch in CA 17-18
Wilburn, Reudene E. 210
Wilby, Basil Leslie 1930- CANR-41
Earlier sketches in CA 103, CANR-19
Wilcher, Robert 1942- 121
Wilcken, Lois 1949- CANR-93
Earlier sketch in CA 145
Wilckens, Ulrich 1928-
Brief entry 114
Wilcock, Donald E. 1944- 151
Wilcock, John 1927- CANR-2
Earlier sketch in CA 1-4R
Wilcocks, Julie 1943- 110
Wilcox, Bob
See Wilcox, Robert K(alleen)
Wilcox, Charlotte 1948- .... SATA 72
Wilcox, Clair 1898-1970 .... CANR-4
Earlier sketch in CA 5-8R
Wilcox, (William) Clyde 1953- 154
Wilcox, Collin 1924-1996 .... CANR-59
Obituary 152
Earlier sketches in CA 21-24R, CANR-14, 31
See also CMW 4
Wilcox, Daniel 1941- 53-56
Wilcox, Dennis L. 1941- CANR-14
Earlier sketch in CA 37-40R
Wilcox, Desmond (John) 1931-2000 .... CANR-21
Obituary 190
Earlier sketch in CA 69-72
Wilcox, Donald J(ames) 1938-1991 109
Obituary 134
Wilcox, Earl J(unior) 1933- 111
Wilcox, Francis (Orlando) 1908-1985 ... 37-40R
Obituary 115
Wilcox, Fred A(llen) 1940- 129
Wilcox, Helen (Elizabeth) 1955- 136
Wilcox, Herbert 1891-1977 57-60
Obituary 118
See also IDFW 3, 4
Wilcox, Howard 1913(?)-1987
Obituary 122
Wilcox, James (P.) 1949- CANR-72
Brief entry 125
Earlier sketch in CA 129
Interview in CA-129
See also CSW
See also DLB 292
Wilcox, Jess
See Hershman, Morris
Wilcox, John T(homas) 1933- 45-48
Wilcox, Laird (M.) 1942- 140
Wilcox, Michael (Denys) 1943- 77-80
Wilcox, Patricia (Anne Florence) 1932-2002 201
Wilcox, Paul L(orentus) 1899-1977 69-72
Wilcox, R(uth) Turner 1888-1970 .... 5-8R
Obituary 29-32R
See also SATA 36
Wilcox, Richard L. 1918-1978
Obituary 77-80
Wilcox, Robert K(alleen) 1943- CANR-96
Earlier sketches in CA 77-80, CANR-24
Wilcox, Roger
See Collins, Paul
Wilcox, Roger P. 1916- 21-24R
Wilcox, Stephen F. 1951- CANR-138
Earlier sketch in CA 141
Wilcox, Tamara 1940- CANR-19
Earlier sketch in CA 97-100
Wilcox, Virginia Lee 1911-1999 .... 37-40R
Wilcox, Walter 1920-1983
Obituary 110
Wilcox, Wayne Ayres 1932-1974 .... CANR-4
Obituary 49-52
Earlier sketch in CA 5-8R
Wilcoxon, George Dent, Jr. 1913- 93-96
Wild, (Robert) David (Fergusson) 1910-1995 139
Obituary 150
Wild, Jocelyn 1941- 116
See also SATA 46
Wild, John D(aniel) 1902-1972
Obituary 37-40R
Wild, Margaret 1948- 215
See also SATA 151
Wild, Peter 1940- 37-40R
See also CLC 14
See also CP 1, 2, 3, 4, 5, 6, 7
See also DLB 5
Wild, Robert A(nthony) 1940- 111
Wild, Robin (Evans) 1936- 116
See also SATA 46
Wild, Robyn 1947- 189
See also SATA 117
Wild, Rolf H(einrich) 1927- 81-84
Wildavsky, Aaron (B.) 1930-1993 .... CANR-30
Obituary 142
Earlier sketches in CA 1-4R, CANR-2
Wilde, Alan 1929- CANR-31
Earlier sketch in CA 110
Wilde, D. Gunther
See Hurwood, Bernhardt J.
Wilde, Daniel U(nderwood) 1937- 57-60
Wilde, Jean T(oeplitz) 1898-1973
Obituary 45-48
Wilde, Jennifer
See Huff, T(om) E.
Wilde, Jocelyn
See Toombs, John
Wilde, Kathey
See King, Patricia
Wilde, Kelley (Cotter) 1947(?)- 168
Wilde, Lady Jane Francesca 1821-1896 .... DLB 199
Wilde, Larry 1928- CANR-51
Earlier sketches in CA 25-28R, CANR-10, 26, 40
Wilde, Lyn Webster 231
Wilde, Meta Carpenter (Doherty) 1907-1994 81-84
Obituary 147
Wilde, Oscar (Fingal O'Flahertie Wills) 1854(?)-1900 .... CANR-112
Brief entry 104
Earlier sketch in CA 119
See also AAYA 49
See also BRW 5
See also BRWC 1, 2
See also BRWR 2
See also BYA 15
See also CDBLB 1890-1914
See also DA
See also DA3
See also DAB
See also DAC
See also DAM DRAM, MST, NOV
See also DC 17
See also DFS 4, 8, 9, 21
See also DLB 10, 19, 34, 57, 141, 156, 190
See also EXPS
See also FANT
See also GL 3
See also LATS 1:1
See also NFS 20
See also RGEL 2
See also RGSF 2
See also SATA 24
See also SSC 11, 77
See also SSFS 7
See also SUFW
See also TCLC 1, 8, 23, 41
See also TEA
See also WCH
See also WLC
See also WLIT 4
Wilde, Richard Henry 1789-1847 .... DLB 3, 59
Wilde, W(illiam) H(enry) 1923- CANR-11
Earlier sketch in CA 69-72
Wildeblood, Peter 1923-1999 65-68
Obituary 186
Wildeman, Marlene 1948- 141
Wilden, Anthony 1935- CANR-28
Earlier sketch in CA 37-40R
Wildenberg, Thomas 196
Wildenhain, Marguerite 1896-1985 77-80
Wilder, Alec
See Wilder, Alexander Lafayette Chew
Wilder, Alexander Lafayette Chew 1907-1980 104
Obituary 102
Wilder, Amos Niven 1895-1993 .... CANR-47
Obituary 141
Earlier sketch in CA 81-84
Wilder, Billy
See Wilder, Samuel
See also AAYA 66
See also CLC 20
See also DLB 26
Wilder, Buck
See Smith, Tim(othy R.)
Wilder, Charlotte Elizabeth 1898(?)-1980
Obituary 97-100
Wilder, Cherry
See Grimm, Cherry Barbara
Wilder, Effie Leland 1909-2001 .... CANR-88
Earlier sketch in CA 149
Wilder, Gene 1935- 142
Wilder, John Bunyan 1914- 5-8R
Wilder, Joseph 1895-1976
Obituary 116
Wilder, Laura (Elizabeth) Ingalls 1867-1957 137
Brief entry 111
See also AAYA 26
See also BYA 2
See also CLR 2
See also CWRI 5
See also DA3
See also DLB 22, 256
See also JRDA
See also MAICYA 1, 2
See also MTCW 2
See also MTFW 2005
See also SATA 15, 29, 100
See also TCWW 2
See also TUS
See also WCH
See also WYA
Wilder, Robert (Ingersoll) 1901-1974 .... CAP-2
Obituary 53-56
Earlier sketch in CA 13-14
Wilder, Robert D. 1916- 41-44R
Wilder, Roy (E.), Jr. 1914- 121
Wilder, Samuel 1906-2002 89-92
Obituary 205
See also Wilder, Billy
Wilder, Stephen
See Marlowe, Stephen
Wilder, Thornton (Niven) 1897-1975 .... CANR-132
Obituary 61-64
Earlier sketches in CA 13-16R, CANR-40
See also AAYA 29
See also AITN 2
See also AMW
See also CAD
See also CDALBS
See also CLC 1, 5, 6, 10, 15, 35, 82
See also CN 1, 2
See also DA
See also DA3
See also DAB
See also DAC
See also DAM DRAM, MST, NOV
See also DC 1, 24
See also DFS 1, 4, 16
See also DLB 4, 7, 9, 228
See also DLBY 1997
See also EWL 3
See also LAIT 3
See also MAL 5
See also MTCW 1, 2
See also MTFW 2005
See also RGAL 4
See also RHW
See also WLC
See also WYAS 1
Wilders, John (Simpson) 1927- 21-24R
Wilder-Smith, A(rthur) E(rnest) 1915- CANR-27
Earlier sketches in CA 57-60, CANR-11
Wildes, Harry Emerson 1890-1982 57-60
Wildgans, Anton 1881-1942 .... DLB 118
Wild Horse Annie
See Johnston, Velma B.
Wilding, Ann
See Budd, Mavis
Wilding, Eric
See Tubb, E(dwin) C(harles)
Wilding, Michael 1942- CANR-106
Earlier sketches in CA 104, CANR-24, 49
See also CLC 73
See also CN 4, 5, 6, 7
See also RGSF 2
See also SSC 50
Wildman, Allan K. 1927-1996 105
Wildman, Eugene 1938- CANR-88
Earlier sketch in CA 25-28R
Wildman, John Hazard 1911-1992 .... 37-40R
Wildman, Louis Robert 1941- CANR-5
Earlier sketch in CA 13-16R
Wildman, Stephen 192
Wildman, Steven S. 1948- 139
Wildmon, Donald E(llis) 1938- CANR-13
Earlier sketch in CA 61-64
Wildrick, Stanley B. 1894-1984
Obituary 112
Wilds, Nancy Alexander 1926- 13-16R
Wildsmith, Alan 1937- 97-100
Wildsmith, Brian 1930- CANR-35
Earlier sketch in CA 85-88
See also CLR 2, 52
See also MAICYA 1, 2
See also SAAS 5
See also SATA 16, 69, 124
Wile, Mary Lee 1947- 151
Wilenski, Peter Stephen 1939- 109
Wilenski, R(eginald) H(oward) 1887-1975 61-64
Obituary 57-60
Wilensky, Harold L. 1923- CANR-34
Earlier sketches in CA 41-44R, CANR-15
Wilentz, Amy 1954- 200
Wilentz, Gay (Alden) 1950- CANR-114
Earlier sketch in CA 138
Wilentz, Joan Steen 1930- 25-28R
Wilentz, Ted
See Wilentz, Theodore
Wilentz, Theodore 1915-2001 .... 29-32R
Obituary 197
Wiles, David K(imball) 1942- CANR-7
Earlier sketch in CA 53-56
Wiles, Domini 1942- 102
Wiles, Gordon Pitts 1909-1999 108
Wiles, John 1924- 9-12R
Wiles, Kimball 1913-1969 .... CANR-4
Earlier sketch in CA 5-8R
Wiles, Maurice Frank 1923- 108
Wiles, Peter John de la Fosse 1919-1997 .. 5-8R
Obituary 159
Wiles, Roy McKeen 1903-1974(?) CAP-1
Earlier sketch in CA 19-20
Wiley, Bell
See Strauss, Frances Goetzmann
Wiley, Bell I(rvin) 1906-1980 .... CANR-4
Obituary 97-100
Earlier sketch in CA 5-8R
See also DLB 17
Wiley, David Sherman 1935- CANR-29
Earlier sketches in CA 61-64, CANR-12
Wiley, Farida A(nna) 1887(?)-1986
Obituary 121
Wiley, Jack 1936- CANR-8
Earlier sketch in CA 61-64
Wiley, James (Milton) 1920- 154
Wiley, Jay Wilson 1913- 5-8R
Wiley, John P., Jr. 1936-2004 89-92
Obituary 224
Wiley, Karla H(ummel) 1918- 61-64
Wiley, Lawrence Samuel 1937- 187
Wiley, Margaret L.
See Marshall, Margaret Wiley
Wiley, Paul L(uzon) 1914-1979 .... CANR-10
Earlier sketch in CA 5-8R
Wiley, Peter (Booth) 1942- 131

Wiley, Ralph 1952-2004 ... 136
Obituary ... 228
Wiley, Raymond A(loysius) 1923- ... 37-40R
Wiley, Richard 1944- ... CANR-71
Brief entry ... 121
Earlier sketch in CA 129
See also CLC 44
Wiley, Roland John ... 237
Wiley, Stan
See Hill, John S(tanley)
Wiley, Tom 1906-1977 ... 25-28R
Wiley, William Leon 1903-1993 ... 111
Wilf, Alexander 1905(?)-1981
Obituary ... 103
Wilford, Allen 1948- ... 128
Wilford, Hugh 1965- ... 151
Wilford, John Noble 1933- ... CANR-105
Earlier sketches in CA 29-32R, CANR-15, 44
Wilford, Walton T. 1937- ... 49-52
Wilgus, A(lva) Curtis 1897-1981 ... CANR-3
Earlier sketch in CA 5-8R
Wilgus, D(onald) K(night) 1918-1989 ... 37-40R
Obituary ... 130
Wilhelm II
See Hohenzollern, Friedrich Wilhelm (Victor Albert)
Wilhelm, Gale 1908-1991 ... GLL 2
Wilhelm, Hans 1945- ... CANR-113
Earlier sketches in CA 119, CANR-48
See also CLR 46
See also SAAS 21
See also SATA 58, 135
Wilhelm, Hellmut 1905-1990 ... 5-8R
Wilhelm, James Jerome 1932- ... CANR-32
Earlier sketch in CA 17-20R
Wilhelm, John R(emsen) 1916-1994 ... 5-8R
Obituary ... 145
Wilhelm, Kate
Interview in ... CANR-17
See also Wilhelm, Katie (Gertrude)
See also CAAS 5
See also AAYA 20
See also BYA 16
See also CLC 7
See also DLB 8
See also SCFW 2
Wilhelm, Kathryn Stephenson 1915- ... 13-16R
Wilhelm, Katie (Gertrude) 1928- ... CANR-94
Earlier sketches in CA 37-40R, CANR-17, 36, 60
See also Wilhelm, Kate
See also MTCW 1
See also SFW 4
Wilhelm, Paul A. 1916- ... 61-64
Wilhelm, Walt 1893-1981 ... 29-32R
Wilhelmina
See Cooper, Wilhelmina (Behmenburg)
Wilhelmsen, Frederick D(aniel) 1923-1996 ... CANR-3
Earlier sketch in CA 1-4R
Wilhoit, Francis M(arion) 1920- ... 126
Brief entry ... 109
Wilk, David 1951- ... CANR-4
Earlier sketch in CA 53-56
Wilk, Gerard H(ermann) 1902-1990 ... 69-72
Wilk, Max 1920- ... CANR-37
Earlier sketches in CA 1-4R, CANR-1, 16
Wilk, Richard R(alph) 1953- ... 120
Wilke, Ekkehard-Teja 1941- ... 65-68
Wilke, Harold H(enry) 1914-2003 ... 132
Obituary ... 214
Wilke, Ulfert (Stephan) 1907-1987 ... CAP-1
Earlier sketch in CA 13-16
Wilken, Robert L(ouis) 1936- ... CANR-142
Earlier sketches in CA 29-32R, CANR-16
Wilkening, Howard (Everett) 1909-1995 ... 89-92
Obituary ... 150
Wilkens, Emily 1917-2000 ... 103
Obituary ... 191
Wilkerson, Cynthia
See Levinson, Leonard
Wilkerson, David R(ay) 1931- ... 41-44R
Wilkerson, Hugh 1939- ... 104
Wilkerson, Loree A. R(andleman) 1923- ... 17-20R
Wilkerson, Rich(ard Preston) 1952- ... 123
Wilkes, Charles 1798-1877 ... DLB 183
Wilkes, Edward T. 1889-1983
Obituary ... 111
Wilkes, George 1817-1885 ... DLB 79
Wilkes, Glenn Newton 1928- ... CANR-17
Earlier sketch in CA 1-4R
Wilkes, Ian (Henry) 1932- ... 41-44R
Wilkes, John W(illiam) 1924- ... 25-28R
Wilkes, Maurice (Vincent) 1913- ... 158
Wilkes, Paul 1938- ... CANR-91
Earlier sketches in CA 81-84, CANR-15, 42
Wilkes, Peter 1937- ... 125
Wilkes, William Alfred 1910-1982 ... 45-48
Wilkes-Hunter, R(ichard) ... 13-16R
Wilkie, Angus 1958- ... 128
Wilkie, Brian 1929- ... 13-16R
Wilkie, Curtis 1941(?)- ... 172
Wilkie, James W. 1936- ... 21-24R
Wilkie, Jane 1917-1996 ... 102
Wilkie, Katharine E(lliott) 1904-1980 ... 21-24R
Obituary ... 125
See also SATA 31
Wilkie, Kenneth 1942- ... 85-88
Wilkie, Pamela 1935- ... 175
Wilkin, Eloise 1904-1987 ... 124
See also MAICYA 1, 2
See also SATA 49
See also SATA-Obit 54
Wilkins, Alfred T., Jr. 1949- ... 129
Wilkins, Arnold J(onathan) 1946- ... 157
Wilkins, Beatrice (Brunson) 1928-1999 ... 61-64
Wilkins, Burleigh Taylor 1932- ... 105
Wilkins, Damien (John) 1963- ... CN 7
Wilkins, Ernest J. 1918- ... 53-56
Wilkins, Frances 1923- ... 73-76
See also SATA 14
Wilkins, H. Ford 1901(?)-1983
Obituary ... 111
Wilkins, John 1614-1672 ... DLB 236
Wilkins, Kathleen Sonia 1941- ... 104
Wilkins, Kay S.
See Wilkins, Kathleen Sonia
Wilkins, Kim ... 221
See also SATA 147
Wilkins, Kirby L. 1936- ... 127
Wilkins, Leslie T. 1915- ... CANR-22
Earlier sketches in CA 17-20R, CANR-7
Wilkins, Marilyn (Ruth) 1926- ... 105
See also SATA 30
Wilkins, Marne
See Wilkins, Marilyn (Ruth)
Wilkins, Mary
See Freeman, Mary E(leanor) Wilkins
Wilkins, Mary Huiskamp 1926- ... CANR-118
Earlier sketches in CA 5-8R, CANR-2, 18
See also Calhoun, Mary
See also MAICYA 2
See also MAICYAS 1
See also SATA 84, 139
Wilkins, Mary Huiskamp Calhoun
See Wilkins, Mary Huiskamp
Wilkins, Mesannie 1891-1980 ... CAP-2
Earlier sketch in CA 25-28
Wilkins, Mira 1931- ... 156
Brief entry ... 112
Wilkins, Roger (Wood) 1932- ... CANR-120
Brief entry ... 109
Earlier sketch in CA 117
See also BW 1
Wilkins, Ronald J(ohn) 1916- ... CANR-16
Earlier sketch in CA 93-96
Wilkins, Roy 1901-1981 ... 104
See also BW 1
Wilkins, Sally (E.D.) ... 225
Wilkins, Skip
See Wilkins, Alfred T., Jr.
Wilkins, Thurman 1915-1997 ... 5-8R
Wilkins, (William) Vaughan 1890-1959 ... 165
See also FANT
Wilkins, William R(ichard) 1933- ... 61-64
Wilkinson, Alec 1952- ... CANR-117
Earlier sketches in CA 109, CANR-44
Wilkinson, Anne (Cochran Boyd) 1910-1961 ... 148
See also DLB 88
See also RGEL 2
Wilkinson, (Thomas) Barry 1923- ... SATA 50
See also SATA-Brief 32
Wilkinson, Bertie 1898-1981 ... 9-12R
Wilkinson, Beth 1925- ... 148
See also SATA 80
Wilkinson, Bonaro
See Overstreet, Bonaro (Wilkinson)
Wilkinson, Brenda 1946- ... CANR-51
Earlier sketches in CA 69-72, CANR-26
See also BW 2
See also CLR 20
See also JRDA
See also MAICYA 2
See also MAICYAS 1
See also SATA 14, 91
See also WYA
See also YAW
Wilkinson, Bruce H. 1947- ... 211
Wilkinson, Bud
See Wilkinson, Charles B(urnham)
Wilkinson, (John) Burke 1913-2000 ... CANR-49
Obituary ... 191
Earlier sketch in CA 9-12R
See also SATA 4
Wilkinson, C. E. 1948- ... 109
Wilkinson, Charles B(urnham) 1916-1994 ... 105
Obituary ... 144
Wilkinson, Charles F. 1941- ... 239
Wilkinson, Charlotte Jefferson ... 69-72
Wilkinson, Christopher 1941- ... CBD
See also CD 6
See also DLB 310
Wilkinson, Clyde Winfield 1910-1994 ... 1-4R
Wilkinson, David ... 93-96
Wilkinson, David Marion 1957- ... 226
Wilkinson, Doris Yvonne 1936- ... 29-32R
Wilkinson, Eliza Yonge 1757-1813(?) ... DLB 200
Wilkinson, Elizabeth C. 1926- ... 123
Wilkinson, Ernest Leroy 1899-1978 ... CANR-3
Earlier sketch in CA 49-52
Wilkinson, G(eoffrey) K(edington) 1907- ... 1-4R
Wilkinson, Iris Guiver 1906-1939
See Hyde, Robin
Wilkinson, J(oseph) F. 1925- ... 105
Wilkinson, James Hardy 1919-1986
Obituary ... 120
Wilkinson, James Harvie III 1944- ... 101
Wilkinson, John (Donald) 1929- ... CANR-42
Earlier sketch in CA 9-12R
Wilkinson, John Thomas 1893-1980 ... 107
Obituary ... 104
Wilkinson, L(ancelot) P(atrick) 1907-1985 ... CANR-20
Obituary ... 116
Earlier sketches in CA 5-8R, CANR-3
Wilkinson, Lorna Hilda Kathleen 1909- ... CAP-1
Earlier sketch in CA 13-14
Wilkinson, Louis (Umfreville) 1881-1966
Obituary ... 116
Wilkinson, Maxwell Penrose 1905(?)-1985
Obituary ... 116
Wilkinson, Norman Beaumont 1910-1983 ... 37-40R
Obituary ... 126
Wilkinson, Patrick
See Wilkinson, L(ancelot) P(atrick)
Wilkinson, Paul 1937- ... CANR-14
Earlier sketch in CA 77-80
Wilkinson, Richard Gerald 1943- ... 45-48
Wilkinson, Richard H(erbert) 1951- ... CANR-137
Earlier sketch in CA 144
Wilkinson, (William) Roderick 1917- ... 13-16R
Wilkinson, Ronald 1920-1996 ... 5-8R
Obituary ... 152
Wilkinson, Rosemary C(halloner) 1924- ... CANR-42
Earlier sketches in CA 49-52, CANR-1, 17
Wilkinson, Rupert Hugh 1936- ... 9-12R
Wilkinson, Sylvia 1940- ... CANR-47
Earlier sketch in CA 17-20R
See also AITN 1
See also CSW
See also DLBY 1986
See also SATA 56
See also SATA-Brief 39
Wilkinson, Wallace G. 1941- ... CD 5
Wilkinson, Walter 1888-1970
Obituary ... 104
Wilkinson, (Arthur) Warren, (Jr.) 1945- ... CANR-120
Earlier sketch in CA 132
Wilkinson, William Cleaver 1833-1920 ... 190
See also DLB 71
Wilkinson, Winifred
See Hausmann, Winifred
Wilkomirski, Binjamin 1939(?)- ... 167
Wilkon, Jozef 1930- ... 107
See also MAICYA 1, 2
See also SATA 31, 71, 133
Wilks, Brian 1933- ... 69-72
Wilks, Ed 1928(?)-1984
Obituary ... 114
Wilks, John 1922- ... 73-76
Wilks, Michael Thomas 1947- ... 110
See also SATA 44
Wilks, Mike
See Wilks, Michael Thomas
Wilks, Yorick 1939- ... 73-76
Will
See Lipkind, William
Will, Clifford M(artin) 1946- ... 136
Will, Frederic 1928- ... CANR-118
Earlier sketches in CA 49-52, CANR-1, 16
See also CP 1
Will, Frederick L(udwig) 1909-1998 ... 13-16R
Will, George F(rederick) 1941- ... CANR-121
Earlier sketches in CA 77-80, CANR-32, 67
See also BEST 90:3
See also CPW
See also MTCW 1
See also TUS
Will, Lawrence Elmer 1893-1977 ... CAP-2
Earlier sketch in CA 17-18
Will, Lester J. 1908(?)-1984
Obituary ... 111
Will, Robert E(rwin) 1928- ... 17-20R
Will, W(ilbur) Marvin 1937- ... 118
Willan, Anne 1938- ... CANR-137
Earlier sketches in CA 57-60, CANR-6
Willan, Thomas Stuart 1910-1994 ... 9-12R
Willans, Jean Stone 1924- ... CANR-57
Earlier sketch in CA 65-68
Willard, Barbara (Mary) 1909-1994 ... CANR-15
Obituary ... 144
Earlier sketch in CA 81-84
See also CLR 2
See also DLB 161
See also MAICYA 1, 2
See also MAICYAS 1
See also SAAS 5
See also SATA 17, 74
See also YAW
Willard, Beatrice E(lizabeth) 1925- ... 41-44R
Willard, Charles
See Armstrong, John Byron
Willard, Charlotte 1914-1977 ... 81-84
Obituary ... 73-76
Willard, Dallas (Albert) 1935- ... CANR-141
Earlier sketch in CA 116
Willard, Emma Hart 1787-1870 ... DLB 239
See also FW
Willard, Frances E. 1839-1898 ... DLB 221
Willard, Fred 1939- ... CANR-126
Earlier sketch in CA 172
Willard, Mildred Wilds 1911-1978 ... 21-24R
Obituary ... 135
See also SATA 14
Willard, Nancy 1936- ... CANR-107
Earlier sketches in CA 89-92, CANR-10, 39, 68
See also BYA 5
See also CLC 7, 37
See also CLR 5
See also CP 2
See also CWP
See also CWRI 5
See also DLB 5, 52
See also FANT
See also MAICYA 1, 2
See also MTCW 1
See also SATA 37, 71, 127
See also SATA-Brief 30
See also SUFW 2
See also TCLE 1:2
Willard, Pat ... 216
Willard, Portman
See Norwood, Victor G(eorge) C(harles)
Willard, Samuel 1640-1707 ... DLB 24
Willcock, M(alcolm) M(aurice) 1925- ... 65-68
Willcox, A(lexander) R(obert) 1911-1993 ... 118
Obituary ... 142
Willcox, Donald J. 1933- ... 49-52
Willcox, Isobel 1907-1996 ... 111
See also SATA 42
Willcox, Sheila 1936- ... 73-76
Willcox, William Bradford 1907-1985 ... CANR-3
Obituary ... 117
Earlier sketch in CA 5-8R
Wille, Janet Neipris 1936- ... CANR-55
Earlier sketches in CA 109, CANR-30
Wille, Lois 1931- ... 163
Willee, Albert William 1916-1982 ... 109
Willeford, Betsy Ann 1939- ... 132
Willeford, Charles (Ray III) 1919-1988 ... CANR-48
Obituary ... 125
Earlier sketches in CA 33-36R, CANR-15
See also DAM POP
See also DLB 226
Willeford, William 1929- ... 25-28R
Willem, John M. 1909-1979 ... CAP-1
Obituary ... 93-96
Earlier sketch in CA 17-18
Willemen, Paul 1944- ... 156
Willems, Emilio 1905-1997 ... 105
Willems, J. Rutherford 1944- ... CANR-23
Earlier sketch in CA 45-48
Willems, Mo ... SATA 154
Willems, Paul 1912- ... CWW 2
Willems, Paul 1936- ... 195
Willen, Diane 1943- ... 117
Willens, Doris 1924- ... 127
Willens, Harold 1914-2003 ... 132
Obituary ... 215
Willensky, Elliot 1933-1990 ... 29-32R
Obituary ... 131
Willenson, Kim Jeremy 1937- ... 103
Willenz, June A. 1924- ... 121
Willerding, Margaret F(rances) 1919- ... 57-60
Willes, Mary (Janette) 1927- ... 120
Willesee, Amy ... 238
Willets, F(rederick) W(illiam) 1930- ... 21-24R
Willets, Walter E. 1924-1992 ... 25-28R
Willett, Brother Franciscus 1922- ... 13-16R
Willett, Edward (C.) 1959- ... 187
See also SATA 115
Willett, Edward R(ice) 1923- ... CANR-21
Earlier sketches in CA 5-8R, CANR-2
Willett, Frank 1925- ... 25-28R
Willett, Jincy 1946- ... 127
Willett, John (William Mills) 1917-2002 ... CANR-4
Obituary ... 207
Earlier sketch in CA 9-12R
Willett, Marcia 1945- ... 214
Willett, Ralph 1935- ... 161
Willett, T(erence) C(harles) 1918- ... 37-40R
Willett, Thomas D(unaway) 1942- ... 108
Willetts, R(onald) F(rederick) 1915-1999 ... CANR-2
Obituary ... 179
Earlier sketch in CA 5-8R
Willey, Basil 1897-1978 ... 9-12R
Obituary ... 135
Willey, Darrell S. 1925- ... 41-44R
Willey, Elizabeth ... FANT
Willey, F. T.
See Willey, Frederick Thomas
Willey, Fred
See Willey, Frederick Thomas
Willey, Frederick Thomas 1910-1987
Obituary ... 124
Willey, Gordon R(andolph) 1913-2002 ... CANR-2
Obituary ... 206
Earlier sketch in CA 5-8R
Willey, John C(offin) 1914-1990
Obituary ... 131
Willey, Keith (Greville) 1930- ... CANR-9
Earlier sketch in CA 21-24R
Willey, Margaret 1950- ... CANR-51
Earlier sketches in CA 117, CANR-40
See also AAYA 27
See also SATA 86
See also YAW
Willey, Peter (Robert Everard) 1922- ... 13-16R
Willey, R(oy) DeVerl 1910-1970(?) ... CAP-2
Earlier sketch in CA 19-20
Willey, Richard J(ames) 1934- ... 41-44R
Willey, Robert
See Ley, Willy
Willgoose, Carl E(dward) 1916- ... CANR-6
Earlier sketch in CA 13-16R
Willhelm, Sidney M(clarty) 1934- ... 9-12R
Willhoite, Michael A. 1946- ... GLL 2
See also SATA 71
William II
See Hohenzollern, Friedrich Wilhelm (Victor Albert)
William, Kate
See Armstrong, Jennifer
William, Maurice 1882(?)-1973
Obituary ... 45-48
William of Auvergne 1190(?)-1249 ... DLB 115
William of Conches 1090(?)-1154(?) ... DLB 115
William of Sherwood 1200(?)-1266(?) ... DLB 115
Williams, Alan F. 1933- ... 49-52
Williams, Alan L(arson) 1947- ... 139
Williams, (Timothy) Alden 1932- ... 41-44R
Williams, Alice Cary 1892-1983 ... 65-68
Obituary ... 111
Williams, Alice Davis 1901-1998 ... 113
Williams, Amanda Kyle 1957- ... 138

Cumulative Index 621 Williams

Williams, Ann, Jr. 1951-1985
Obituary 117
Williams, (Elisabeth) Ann 1937- 154
Williams, Anne
See Steinke, Ann E(lizabeth)
Williams, Aston R. 1912- 21-24R
Williams, Aubrey L(ake) 1922-1996 ... CANR-6
Earlier sketch in CA 1-4R
Williams, Barbara 1925- CANR-17
Earlier sketches in CA 49-52, CANR-1
See also CLR 48
See also MAICYA 2
See also SAAS 16
See also SATA 11, 107
Williams, Barbara 1937- .... SATA 62
Williams, Barnaby -2001(?) 237
Williams, Barry 1932- 29-32R
Williams, Ben A(mes), Jr. 1915- 116
Williams, Ben Ames 1889-1953 183
See also DLB 102
See also TCLC 89
Williams, Benjamin Buford 1923- 113
Williams, Benjamin H(arrison)
1889-1974 .... CANR-29
Earlier sketch in CA 37-40R
Williams, Bernard (Arthur Owen)
1929-2003 .... CANR-141
Obituary 217
Brief entry 112
Earlier sketch in CA 130
Williams, Bert Nolan 1930- 103
Williams, Beryl
See Epstein, Beryl (M. Williams)
Williams, Bill
See Crawford, William (Elbert)
Williams, Brad 1918- CANR-1
Earlier sketch in CA 1-4R
Williams, Brian (Peter) 1943- .... SATA 54
Williams, Bronwyn
See Browning, Dixie (Burrus)
Williams, Brooke 193
Williams, Bruce R(odda) 1919- 13-16R
Williams, Burton John 1927- 41-44R
Williams, Byron (Leigh) 1934- 29-32R
Williams, C(hester) Arthur, Jr.
1924-1998 .... CANR-2
Earlier sketch in CA 1-4R
Williams, C(lifford) Glyn 1928- 29-32R
Williams, C(hristopher) J(ohn) F(ardo)
1930- 103
Williams, C(harles) K(enneth)
1936- CANR-106
Earlier sketches in CA 37-40R, CANR-57
See also CAAS 26
See also CLC 33, 56, 148
See also CP 1, 2, 3, 4, 5, 6, 7
See also DAM POET
See also DLB 5
See also MAL 5
Williams, Carl C(arnelius) 1903-1989 45-48
Williams, Carla 1965- 226
Williams, Carol Lynch 1959- 180
See also AAYA 39
See also SATA 110
See also WYAS 1
Williams, Carol M. 1917- 65-68
Williams, Carol T(raynor) 1935- 112
Williams, Catharine M(elissa)
1903-1993 .... 37-40R
Williams, Cecil B(rown) 1901-1966 ...... CAP-1
Earlier sketch in CA 11-12
Williams, Chancellor 1905(?)-1992 142
See also BW 2
See also DLB 76
Williams, Charles
See Collier, James Lincoln
Williams, Charles (Walter Stansby)
1886-1945 163
Brief entry 104
See also BRWS 9
See also DLB 100, 153, 255
See also FANT
See also RGEL 2
See also SUFW 1
See also TCLC 1, 11
Williams, Charles 1909-1975 .... CMW 4
Williams, Charles 1933- 150
Williams, Chester
See Schechter, William
Williams, Christian 1943- 130
Williams, Christopher D(avis) 1968- 212
Williams, Cicely 1907-1985 57-60
Obituary 117
Williams, Claerwen 1938- 102
Williams, Claudette .... RHW
Williams, Clayton (Wheat) 1895-1983 125
Williams, Clifford 1943- 191
Williams, Clyde C. 1881-1974 .... CAP-2
Earlier sketch in CA 23-24
See also SATA 8
See also SATA-Obit 27
Williams, Coe
See Harrison, C(hester) William
Williams, Colin 1934- 109
Interview in CA-109
Williams, Colin W(ilbur) 1921- CANR-19
Earlier sketch in CA 25-28R
Williams, Colleen Madonna Flood 1963- ... 231
See also SATA 156
Williams, Conrad 1969- 222
Williams, Craig A(rthur) 1965- 207
Williams, Cris
See De Cristoforo, R(omeo) J(ohn)
Williams, Cynthia G. 1958- .... SATA 123
Williams, Cyril Glyndwr
1921-2004 .... CANR-15
Obituary 230
Earlier sketch in CA 37-40R
Williams, D.
See Ronald, David William
Williams, (Walter) Dakin 1919-
Brief entry 116
Williams, Daniel Day 1910-1973 .... CANR-1
Obituary 45-48
Earlier sketch in CA 1-4R
Williams, Daniel H(arrison) 1955- 206
Williams, Darren 1967- 214
Williams, David (Frank) 1909-1983
Obituary 109
Williams, David 1926- CANR-48
Earlier sketch in CA 122
See also CMW 4
Williams, David (Eliot) 1939- 123
Williams, David 1939- 73-76
Williams, David 1945- 97-100
Williams, David A. 1922- 29-32R
Williams, David Glenwood 1918-1998 .... 5-8R
Obituary 172
Williams, David L. 1940- CANR-10
Earlier sketch in CA 25-28R
Williams, David Rhys 1890-1970 .... 5-8R
Williams, David Ricardo
1923-1999 .... CANR-51
Earlier sketches in CA 101, CANR-26
Williams, Denis (Joseph Ivan)
1923-1998 .... CANR-80
Earlier sketches in CA 93-96, CANR-17, 41
See also BW 2, 3
See also DLB 117
Williams, Dennis A. 1951- 230
Williams, Diane 1946- 172
Williams, Donna 1963- 143
Williams, Donna Reilly 1945- 150
See also SATA 83
Williams, Dorian 1914- CANR-3
Earlier sketch in CA 9-12R
Williams, Dorothy
See Williams, Marcia (Dorothy)
Williams, (Marcia) Dorothy
See Williams, Marcia (Dorothy)
See also SATA 71
Williams, Duncan 1927- 41-44R
Williams, Dwight 1966- 156
Williams, E(ric) C(yril) 1918- 97-100
Williams, E(rnest) N(eville) 1917- 9-12R
Williams, Edward Ainsworth 1907-1976
Obituary 65-68
Williams, Edward Bennett 1920-1988 .... 1-4R
Obituary 126
Williams, Edward Christopher 1871-1929 .. 228
Williams, Edward Francis 1903-1970
Obituary 29-32R
Williams, Edward G. 1929- 29-32R
Williams, Edward J(erome) 1935- CANR-10
Earlier sketch in CA 21-24R
Williams, Edward K. 1923-1966 .... CAP-1
Earlier sketch in CA 13-16
Williams, Edward V(inson) 1935- 121
Williams, Edwin B(ucher) 1891-1975 .... 5-8R
Obituary 57-60
Williams, Edwin E(veritt) 1913- 45-48
Williams, Edwina Dakin 1885(?)-1980
Obituary 97-100
Williams, Eirlys O(lwen) CAP-1
Earlier sketch in CA 9-10
Williams, Elizabeth
See Dohen, Dorothy M.
Williams, Ella Gwendolen Rees
See Rhys, Jean
Williams, (George) Emlyn
1905-1987 .... CANR-36
Obituary 123
Earlier sketch in CA 104
See also CLC 15
See also DAM DRAM
See also DLB 10, 77
See also IDTP
See also MTCW 1
Williams, Emmett 1925- CANR-91
Earlier sketches in CA 45-48, CANR-2
See also CP 2, 3, 4, 5, 6, 7
Williams, Eric (Eustace) 1911-1981 125
Obituary 103
See also BW 2
Williams, Eric (Ernest) 1911-1983 ..... CANR-28
Obituary 111
Earlier sketch in CA 9-12R
See also SATA 14
See also SATA-Obit 38
Williams, Ernest Wells 1896(?)-1980
Obituary 97-100
Williams, Estelle S. 1908-1999 123
Williams, Esther (Jane) 1923- 186
Williams, Ethel L. 37-40R
Williams, F(rederick) Winston 1935- 103
Williams, Ferelith Eccles
See Eccles Williams, Ferelith
See also SATA 22
Williams, Forman A. 1934- 145
Williams, Frances 1935- 25-28R
Williams, Frances B.
See Browin, Frances Williams
Williams, Frances Leigh 1909-1978 ...... 13-16R
Williams, Frances Marion 1919- 57-60
Williams, Francis 1903-1970
Obituary 104
Williams, Francis Stewart 1921-1974 .... 37-40R
Williams, Frank B(royles), Jr. 1913- 118
Williams, Frank J. 1940- 228
Williams, Frederick (Dowell) 1933- 136
Williams, Frederick D(eForrest) 1918- 65-68
Williams, G(erhard) Mennen 1911-1988
Obituary 124
Williams, G. Robert 1948- 108
Williams, Garth (Montgomery) 1912-1996 . 134
Obituary 152
See also CLR 57
See also DLB 22
See also MAICYA 1, 2
See also MAICYAS 1
See also SAAS 7
See also SATA 18, 66
See also SATA-Obit 90
Williams, Gary J(ay) 188
Williams, Geoffrey (John) 1943- 29-32R
Williams, Geoffrey J(ames) 1936- 118
Williams, George (Joseph) III 1949- 125
Williams, George (Guion) 1902-1999 ... 13-16R
Williams, George C(hristopher) 1926- 73-76
Williams, George Huntston 1914- CANR-16
Earlier sketches in CA 1-4R, CANR-1
Williams, George M(ason, Jr.) 1940- 61-64
Williams, George W(alton) 1922- 9-12R
Williams, George Washington
1849-1891 .... DLB 47
Williams, Geraint 1942- 124
Williams, Gertrude 1897-1983
Obituary 109
Williams, Gilbert M. 1917- 61-64
Williams, Glanmor 1920-2005 .... 5-8R
Obituary 236
Williams, Glanville Llewelyn 1911-1997 106
Obituary 157
Williams, Gluyas 1888-1982
Obituary 108
See also AITN 2
Williams, Glyn 1932- 229
Williams, Glyndwr
See Williams, Glyn
Williams, Gordon
See Venables, Terry
Williams, Gordon
See Williams, Gordon M(aclean)
Williams, Gordon Leslie 1933- 110
Williams, Gordon M(aclean) 1934(?)- 130
Brief entry 116
Williams, Greer 1909-1986 .... CANR-10
Earlier sketch in CA 13-16R
Williams, Greg(ory) Alan 167
See also BW 3
Williams, Gregory 1952- 109
Williams, Gregory Howard 1943- CANR-87
Earlier sketch in CA 155
Williams, Griffith Wynne 1897-1972 .... CAP-2
Earlier sketch in CA 25-28
Williams, Gurney III 1941- CANR-30
Earlier sketch in CA 69-72
Williams, Guy Neal 1953- 77-80
Williams, Guy R(ichard) 1920- CANR-31
Earlier sketch in CA 13-16R
See also SATA 11
Williams, (David) Gwyn 1904-1990 103
See also CP 1
Williams, Hank, Jr. 1949- 182
Brief entry 117
Williams, Hank 1923-1953
See Williams, Hiram King
See also TCLC 81
Williams, Harold (Claude Noel) 1914-1990
Obituary 131
Williams, Harold A(nthony) 1916- 37-40R
Williams, Harold R(oger) 1935- 53-56
Williams, Harold S(tannett)
1898-1987 .... CANR-20
Earlier sketches in CA 9-12R, CANR-5
Williams, Harold Workman
See Wilson, Halsey William
Williams, Hawley
See Heyliger, William
Williams, Hazel Pearson 1914- 57-60
Williams, Heathcote 1941- CANR-49
Earlier sketch in CA 21-24R
See also CBD
See also CD 5, 6
See also DLB 13
Williams, Heather C. 1947- 223
Williams, Helen 1948- 145
See also SATA 77
Williams, Helen Maria 1761-1827 ..... DLB 158
Williams, Henry
See Manville, W(illiam) H(enry)
Williams, Henry Lionel 1895-1974
Obituary 45-48
Williams, Herbert (Lloyd) 1932- CANR-12
Earlier sketch in CA 29-32R
See also CP 1, 2
Williams, Herbert Lee 1918- CANR-29
Earlier sketch in CA 1-4R
Williams, Hermann Warner, Jr.
1908-1974 .... 5-8R
Obituary 53-56
Williams, Hiram D. 1917- 13-16R
Williams, Hiram Hank
See Williams, Hank
Williams, Hiram King 188
See also Williams, Hank
Williams, Hosea L(orenzo) 1926-2000 49-52
Obituary 191
Williams, Howard L(loyd) 1950- CANR-41
Earlier sketch in CA 117
Williams, Howard Russell 1915- 13-16R
Williams, Hugh (Anthony Glanmor)
1904-1969 .... CAP-2
Earlier sketch in CA 25-28
Williams, Hugh Aldersey
See Aldersey-Williams, Hugh
Williams, Hugh Steadman 1935- CANR-86
Earlier sketch in CA 132
Williams, Hugo (Mordaunt) 1942- .. CANR-119
Earlier sketches in CA 17-20R, CANR-45
See also CLC 42
See also CP 1, 2, 3, 4, 5, 6, 7
See also DLB 40
Williams, Ioan Miles 1941- CANR-11
Earlier sketch in CA 25-28R
Williams, Ira E., Jr. 1926- 53-56
Williams, Irving G(regory) 1915- 41-44R
Williams, Isaac 1802-1865 .... DLB 32
Williams, J(ames) David Lewis
See Lewis-Williams, J(ames) David
Williams, J(ohn) E(llis) Caerwyn
1912-1999 194
Williams, J(ames) Earl 1922- 41-44R
Williams, J(ohn) H(argreaves) Harley 9-12R
Williams, J. R.
See Williams, Jeanne
Williams, J(ohn) Rodman 1918- 81-84
Williams, J. Walker
See Wodehouse, P(elham) G(renville)
Williams, J. X.
See Ludwig, Myles Eric and
Offutt, Andrew J(efferson V)
Williams, Jacqueline (Block) 1934- .. CANR-92
Earlier sketch in CA 145
Williams, James C. 1942- 200
Williams, James G. 1936- 165
Williams, Jay 1914-1978 .... CANR-39
Obituary 81-84
Earlier sketches in CA 1-4R, CANR-2
See also CLR 8
See also MAICYA 1, 2
See also SATA 3, 41
See also SATA-Obit 24
Williams, Jay G(omer) 1932- 41-44R
Williams, Jayson 1968- 196
Williams, Jeanne 1930- CANR-67
Earlier sketches in CA 25-28R, CANR-64
See also SATA 5
See also TCWW 1, 2
Williams, Jeannie 1942- 228
Williams, (Edward) Jeffery 1920- CANR-105
Earlier sketch in CA 132
Williams, Jeffrey J(ames) 1958- 194
Williams, Jenny 1939- 112
See also SATA 60
Williams, Jeremy (Napier) Howard
See Howard-Williams, Jeremy (Napier)
Williams, Jerome 1926-2002 .... CANR-1
Obituary 208
Earlier sketch in CA 49-52
Williams, Jesse Lynch 1871-1929 197
Williams, Joan 1928- CANR-91
Earlier sketches in CA 1-4R, CANR-48
See also CSW
See also DLB 6
Williams, Joe
See Williams, Joseph Peter
Williams, Joel
See Jennings, John (Edward, Jr.)
Williams, John (Herbert) 1908-1976 . CANR-10
Earlier sketch in CA 13-16R
Williams, John (Edward) 1922-1994 ... CANR-2
Obituary 144
Earlier sketch in CA 1-4R
See also CN 2, 3, 4, 5
See also DLB 6
See also TCLE 1:2
See also TCWW 1, 2
Williams, John (Towner) 1932- .... IDFW 2, 3, 4
Williams, John 1954- 129
Williams, John A(lfred) 1925- 195
Earlier sketches in CA 53-56, CANR-6, 26, 51, 118
Interview in CANR-6
Autobiographical Essay in 195
See also CAAS 3
See also AFAW 2
See also BLC 3
See also BW 2, 3
See also CLC 5, 13
See also CN 1, 2, 3, 4, 5, 6, 7
See also CSW
See also DAM MULT
See also DLB 2, 33
See also EWL 3
See also MAL 5
See also RGAL 4
See also SFW 4
Williams, John Alden 1928- CANR-111
Earlier sketches in CA 1-4R, CANR-2
Williams, John B. 1919- 93-96
Williams, John Burr 1900-1989
Obituary 129
Williams, John D(elane) 1938- 57-60
Williams, John Edwin 1928- 93-96
Williams, John G(ordon) 1906- CAP-2
Earlier sketch in CA 23-24
Williams, John G. 1915- 120
Williams, John Hartley 1942- CANR-73
Earlier sketch in CA 130
Williams, John Henry 1887-1980
Obituary 105
Williams, John Hoyt 1940- 128
Williams, John R(yan) 1919- 37-40R
Williams, John Stanley 1925- CAP-1
Earlier sketch in CA 9-10
Williams, John Stuart 1920- 65-68
See also CP 1, 2
Williams, Jon
See Williams, Walter Jon

Williams, Jonathan (Chamberlain)
1929- CANR-108
Earlier sketches in CA 9-12R, CANR-8
See also CAAS 12
See also CLC 13
See also CP 1, 2, 3, 4, 5, 6, 7
See also DLB 5
Williams, Joseph Peter 1889-1972 208
See also DLB 241
Williams, Joy 1944- CANR-97
Earlier sketches in CA 41-44R, CANR-22, 48
See also CLC 31
Williams, Joyce E(layne) 1937- 104
Williams, Juan 1954- CANR-136
Earlier sketches in CA 125, CANR-84
See also BW 2
See also MTFW 2005
Williams, Juanita da Lomba Jones
1925- 37-40R
Williams, June Vanleer 131
Williams, Justin Sr. 1906- 101
Williams, Karen Lynn 1952- 133
See also SATA 66, 99
Williams, Kate
See Flynn, Donald R(obert)
Williams, Kenneth 1926-1988
Obituary 125
Williams, Kim 1924(?)-1986
Obituary 120
Williams, Kimmika L(yvette Hawes) 1959- . 153
See also BW 2
Williams, Kit 1946(?)- 107
See also CLR 4
See also SATA 44
Williams, Kyffin 1918- CANR-93
Earlier sketch in CA 145
Williams, L(aurence) F(rederic) Rushbrook
See Rushbrook Williams, L(aurence) F(rederic)
Williams, L(eslie) Pearce 1927- 65-68
Williams, Lady
See Williams, Gertrude
Williams, Lawrence 1916(?)-1983
Obituary 108
Williams, Lawrence K(enneth) 1930- 29-32R
Williams, Lee E(rskine) II 1946- 41-44R
Williams, Len 1937- 227
Williams, Lena (Marguerite) 1950- 216
Williams, LeRoy T. 1944- 120
Williams, Leslie 1941- 107
See also SATA 42
Williams, Lillian Serece 1944- 200
Williams, Linda 1946- CANR-119
Earlier sketch in CA 110
Williams, Linda 1948- .... SATA 59
Williams, Liz 1965- 227
Williams, Liza 1928- 102
Williams, Lori Aurelia .... AAYA 52
Williams, Loring G. 1924-1974 .... CAP-2
Earlier sketch in CA 29-32
Williams, Louise Bonino 1904(?)-1984
Obituary 114
See also SATA-Obit 39
Williams, Lovett E(dward), Jr. 1935- 109
Williams, Lynn
See Hale, Arlene
Williams, M(artin) A(nthony) J(ames)
1941- 141
Williams, Marcia 1932- 123
Williams, Marcia (Dorothy) 1945- .. CANR-144
Earlier sketch in CA 164
See also Williams, (Marcia) Dorothy
See also SATA 97, 159
Williams, Margaret (Anne) 1902- 21-24R
Williams, Margaret (Vyner) 1914-1993 . 25-28R
Williams, Margery
See Bianco, Margery Williams
Williams, Marie S(heppard) 1931- 164
Williams, Mark
See Arthur, Robert, (Jr.)
Williams, Mark 1951- 138
Williams, Mark London 1959- 211
See also SATA 140
Williams, Martha E(thelyn) 1934- 125
Williams, Martin 1924-1992 49-52
Obituary 137
Williams, Mary Alice 1949- 185
Brief entry 123
Williams, Mary C(ameron) 1923- 57-60
Williams, Mary E. 1960- 204
Williams, Mary Elizabeth 1909-1976
Obituary 65-68
Williams, Mary McGee 1925- 25-28R
See also HGG
Williams, Mary Pat 1946- 112
Williams, Mason 1938- 25-28R
Williams, Maureen 1951- 85-88
See also SATA 12
Williams, Melvin D(onald) 1933- 73-76
Williams, Merryn 1944- CANR-15
Earlier sketch in CA 41-44R
Williams, Michael
See St. John, Wylly Folk
Williams, Michael 1935- CANR-82
Earlier sketch in CA 133
Williams, Michael (Leon) 1952- .... FANT
Williams, Miller 1930- 198
Earlier sketches in CA 13-16R, CANR-67, 118
Autobiographical Essay in 198
See also CAAS 20
See also CP 1, 2, 3, 4, 5, 6, 7
See also CSW
See also DLB 105
See also TCLE 1:2
Williams, Mona (Goodwyn) 1916- 81-84
Williams, Nancy M(argaret) 1929- 122
Williams, Ned 1909-1978 .... 13-16R
Williams, Neville (John) 1924-1977
Obituary 111
Williams, Niall 1958- CANR-89
Earlier sketch in CA 167
Williams, Nick (Van) B(oddie) (Sr.)
1906-1992 214
Williams, Nigel 1948- CANR-103
Earlier sketch in CA 147
See also CBD
See also CD 5, 6
See also DLB 231
Williams, Noel Trevor St. John 1918- 41-44R
Williams, Norman 1952- 118
See also CLC 39
Williams, Oliver F(ranklin) 1939- CANR-82
Earlier sketches in CA 114, CANR-35
Williams, Oliver P(erry) 1925- 37-40R
Williams, Ora (Ruby) 1926- 73-76
Williams, Oscar 1900-1964 .... CANR-6
Earlier sketch in CA 1-4R
Williams, Otis (C.) 1941- 130
Williams, P(eter) F(airney) 1931- 121
Williams, Patricia J(oyce) 1951- CANR-87
Earlier sketch in CA 154
See also FW
Williams, Patrick 1950- 129
Williams, Patrick J.
See Butterworth, W(illiam) E(dmund III)
Williams, Patti 1936- 73-76
Williams, Paul (Revere) 1894-1980
Obituary 93-96
Williams, Paul (Hamilton) 1940- 121
Williams, Paul (Steven) 1948- 81-84
Williams, Paul K. 1966- 233
Williams, Paul O(sborne) 1935- CANR-24
Earlier sketch in CA 106
See also SFW 4
Williams, Penelope 1943- 212
Williams, Penry (Herbert) 1925- 128
Williams, Pete
See Faulknor, Cliff(ord Vernon)
Williams, Peter 1937- 138
Williams, Peter W(illiam) 1944- CANR-112
Earlier sketches in CA 112, CANR-30
Williams, Philip F. (C.) 1956- 146
Williams, Philip Lee 1950- CANR-65
Earlier sketch in CA 129
Williams, Philip Maynard 1920-1984
Obituary 114
Williams, Philip Middleton 1952- 145
Williams, Philip W(alter) 1941- CANR-11
Earlier sketch in CA 69-72
Williams, Phyllis S(awyer) 1931- 65-68
Williams, Pieter Daniel de Wet 1929- ...... CP 1
Williams, R(obert) D(eryck)
1917-1986 .... CANR-45
Obituary 120
Earlier sketch in CA 103
Williams, R(obert) J(oseph) P(aton) 1926- ... 143
Williams, Ralph Mehlin 1911-1975 .... 5-8R
Williams, Ralph Vaughan
See Vaughan Williams, Ralph
Williams, Randall Herbert Monier
See Monier-Williams, Randall Herbert
Williams, Raymond (Henry)
1921-1988 .... CANR-44
Obituary 124
Earlier sketches in CA 21-24R, CANR-33
See also CN 1, 2, 3, 4
See also DLB 14, 231, 242
See also MTCW 1
See also RGEL 2
Williams, Raymond (Brady) 1935- 132
Williams, Rebecca (Yancy) 1899-1976
Obituary 65-68
Williams, Richard 1933- .... IDFW 3, 4
Williams, Richard Hays 1912-1988 .... CANR-2
Earlier sketch in CA 1-4R
Williams, Richard Lippincott 1910-1989 101
Williams, Robert C. 1938- CANR-14
Earlier sketch in CA 37-40R
Williams, Robert Coleman 1940- 21-24R
Williams, Robert G. 1948- 125
Williams, Robert Hugh 1907(?)-1983
Obituary 109
Williams, Robert L(ewis)
1903-1989 .... CANR-10
Earlier sketch in CA 13-16R
Williams, Robert Moore 1907-1977
Obituary 102
See also SFW 4
Williams, Robert P. 1906(?)-1977
Obituary 69-72
Williams, Robin M(urphy), Jr. 1914- 13-16R
Williams, Robyn 1944- CANR-123
Earlier sketch in CA 165
Williams, Roger 1603(?)-1683 .... DLB 24
Williams, Roger J(ohn) 1893-1988 ..... CANR-7
Obituary 124
Earlier sketch in CA 17-20R
Williams, Roger L(awrence) 1923-
Brief entry 112
Williams, Roger M(iller) 1934- 37-40R
Williams, Roger Neville 1943- 37-40R
Williams, Ronald Ralph 1906-1979 .... CANR-7
Earlier sketch in CA 13-16R
Williams, Rosalind
See Fergusson, Rosalind (Joyce)
Williams, Rosalind H. 1944- 109
Williams, Rose
See Ross, W(illiam) E(dward) D(aniel)
Williams, Rowan (Douglas) 1950- .. CANR-111
Earlier sketch in CA 128
Williams, Rowland 1817-1870 .... DLB 184
Williams, Russell J(ohn) 1944- 104
Williams, S. P.
See Hart, Virginia
Williams, Sam .... SATA 124
Williams, Samm-Art
See Williams, Samuel Arthur
See also DLB 38
Williams, Samuel Arthur 1946- 123
Brief entry 117
See also Williams, Samm-Art
See also BW 1
Williams, Selma R(uth) 1925- CANR-1
Earlier sketch in CA 49-52
See also SATA 14
Williams, Sherley Anne 1944-1999 .. CANR-82
Obituary 185
Earlier sketches in CA 73-76, CANR-25
Interview in CANR-25
See also AFAW 2
See also BLC 3
See also BW 2, 3
See also CLC 89
See also DAM MULT, POET
See also DLB 41
See also SATA 78
See also SATA-Obit 116
Williams, Sheron 1955- 145
See also SATA 77
Williams, Shirley
See Williams, Sherley Anne
Williams, Shirley (Vivien Teresa Brittain)
1930- 158
Williams, Simon 1943- 133
Williams, Slim
See Williams, Clyde C.
Williams, Sophy 1965- .... SATA 135
Williams, Stanley W. 1917- 17-20R
Williams, Stephen 1926-
Brief entry 114
Williams, Stirling B(acot), Jr. 1943- 29-32R
Williams, Strephon Kaplan 1934- CANR-20
Earlier sketch in CA 102
Williams, Susan 1960- 141
Williams, Suzanne (Bullock) 1953- ..... SATA 71
Williams, T(erence) C(harles) 1925- 29-32R
Williams, T(homas) David 1929- 123
Williams, T(homas) Harry
1909-1979 .... CANR-3
Earlier sketch in CA 1-4R
See also DLB 17
Williams, (Robert Paul) Tad 1957- CANR-88
Earlier sketch in CA 146
See also AAYA 31
See also FANT
See also YAW
Williams, Ted
See Williams, Theodore Samuel
Williams, Tennessee 1911-1983 ..... CANR-132
Obituary 108
Earlier sketches in CA 5-8R, CANR-31
See also CABS 3
See also AAYA 31
See also AITN 1, 2
See also AMW
See also AMWC 1
See also CAD
See also CDALB 1941-1968
See also CLC 1, 2, 5, 7, 8, 11, 15, 19, 30, 39, 45, 71, 111
See also CN 1, 2, 3
See also DA
See also DA3
See also DAB
See also DAC
See also DAM DRAM, MST
See also DC 4
See also DFS 17
See also DLB 7
See also DLBD 4
See also DLBY 1983
See also EWL 3
See also GLL 1
See also LAIT 4
See also LATS 1:2
See also MAL 5
See also MTCW 1, 2
See also MTFW 2005
See also RGAL 4
See also SSC 81
See also TUS
See also WLC
Williams, Terrie (Michelle) 1954- 227
Williams, Terry Tempest 1955- CANR-106
Earlier sketch in CA 153
See also ANW
See also DLB 206, 275
Williams, Theodore C(urtis) 1930- 69-72
Williams, Theodore Samuel 1918-2002 220
Williams, Theresa 1956- 216
Williams, Thomas (Alonzo)
1926-1990 .... CANR-2
Obituary 132
Earlier sketch in CA 1-4R
See also CLC 14
Williams, Thomas (Andrew) 1931- 49-52
Williams, Thomas Howard 1935- 13-16R
Williams, Tia 1975- 229
Williams, Tina
See Wiles, Domini
Williams, Tod (Culpan) 1968- 229
Williams, Tony 1946- CANR-105
Earlier sketch in CA 147
Williams, Trevor Illtyd 1921-1996 109
Obituary 154
Williams, Ursula Moray
See Moray Williams, Ursula
See also DLB 160
See also SATA 3
Williams, (George) Valentine 1883-1946
Brief entry 111
See also CMW 4
See also DLB 77
Williams, Vera B(aker) 1927- CANR-123
Earlier sketches in CA 123, CANR-38
See also CLR 9
See also CWRI 5
See also MAICYA 1, 2
See also MAICYAS 1
See also SATA 53, 102
See also SATA-Brief 33
Williams, Vergil L(ewis) 1935- CANR-9
Earlier sketch in CA 57-60
Williams, Vernon J(ohnson, Jr.)
1948- CANR-87
Earlier sketch in CA 159
Williams, Virginia (Parrott) 1940- 185
Williams, W. S. C. 1929- 139
Williams, Wallace Edward 1926-
Brief entry 105
Williams, Walter
See Williams, Walter E(dward)
Williams, Walter E(dward) 1936- CANR-87
Brief entry 123
Earlier sketch in CA 154
Williams, Walter G(eorge) 1903-1983 ... CAP-1
Earlier sketch in CA 13-16
Williams, Walter Jon 1953- CANR-141
Earlier sketch in CA 152
See also AAYA 48
See also CPW
See also DAM POP
See also SFW 4
Williams, Walter L(ee) 1948- 127
Williams, (Margaret) Wetherby CANR-3
Earlier sketch in CA 45-48
Williams, Willard F(orest) 1921- 13-16R
Williams, William Appleman
1921-1990 .... CANR-3
Obituary 131
Earlier sketch in CA 1-4R
See also DLB 17
Williams, William C.
See Williams, William Carlos
Williams, William Carlos
1883-1963 .... CANR-34
Earlier sketch in CA 89-92
See also AAYA 46
See also AMW
See also AMWR 1
See also CDALB 1917-1929
See also CLC 1, 2, 5, 9, 13, 22, 42, 67
See also DA
See also DA3
See also DAB
See also DAC
See also DAM MST, POET
See also DLB 4, 16, 54, 86
See also EWL 3
See also EXPP
See also MAL 5
See also MTCW 1, 2
See also MTFW 2005
See also NCFS 4
See also PAB
See also PC 7
See also PFS 1, 6, 11
See also RGAL 4
See also RGSF 2
See also SSC 31
See also TUS
See also WP
Williams, William David 1917- 5-8R
Williams, William H(enry) 1936- CANR-82
Earlier sketches in CA 69-72, CANR-36
Williams, William P(roctor) 1939- CANR-47
Earlier sketches in CA 45-48, CANR-23
Williams, Wirt (Alfred, Jr.) 1921-1986 ..... 9-12R
Obituary 119
See also CN 1, 2, 3, 4
See also DLB 6
Williams-Andriani, Renee 1963- .... SATA 98
Williams-Ellis, (Mary) Amabel (Nassau Strachey)
1894-1984 105
Obituary 114
See also SATA 29
See also SATA-Obit 41
Williams-Ellis, (Bertram) Clough
1883-1978 .... 13-16R
Obituary 200
Williams-Garcia, Rita 1957- CANR-87
Earlier sketch in CA 159
See also AAYA 22
See also CLR 36
See also SATA 98, 160
See also WYAS 1
Williamson, A(lice) M(uriel) .... RHW
Williamson, Alan (Bacher) 1944- 57-60
Williamson, Anthony George 1932- 101
Williamson, Audrey (May)
1913-1986(?) CANR-3
Obituary 118
Earlier sketch in CA 49-52
Williamson, Bruce 1893-1984
Obituary 111
Williamson, Bruce 1930- 101
Williamson, C(harles) N(orris) .... RHW
Williamson, Chester Carlton
1948- CANR-144
Earlier sketch in CA 156
See also HGG
See also SUFW 2
Williamson, Chet
See Williamson, Chester Carlton
Williamson, Chilton, Jr. 1947- 102
Williamson, Chilton 1916- 13-16R

Cumulative Index 623 Wilson

Williamson, Claude C(harles) H.
1891-(?) ... CAP-1
Earlier sketch in CA 17-18
Williamson, Craig (Burke) 1943- ... CANR-16
Earlier sketch in CA 29-32R
Williamson, David (Geoffrey) 1927-2003 ... 134
Obituary ... 216
Williamson, David (Keith) 1942- ... CANR-41
Earlier sketch in CA 103
See also CD 5, 6
See also CLC 56
See also DLB 289
Williamson, David L(ouis) 1937- ... 111
Williamson, Deni
See Williamson, Denise
Williamson, Denise 1954- ... 193
Williamson, Donald I. 1922- ... CANR-92
Earlier sketch in CA 145
Williamson, Doug 1944- ... 136
Williamson, Duncan 1928- ... 123
Williamson, Edward 1908-1984
Obituary ... 113
Williamson, Ellen Douglas
1905-1984 ... CANR-39
Obituary ... 114
Earlier sketch in CA 17-20R
See also Douglas, Ellen
Williamson, Eugene L. (Jr.) 1930- ... 9-12R
Williamson, Geoffrey 1897- ... 9-12R
Williamson, Gerald Neal 1932- ... CANR-77
Earlier sketches in CA 112, CANR-34
See also HGG
Williamson, Glen 1909- ... CANR-9
Earlier sketch in CA 57-60
Williamson, Greg 1964- ... 154
See also CSW
Williamson, Gwyneth 1965- ... SATA 109
Williamson, H(enry) D(arvall) 1907- ... 65-68
Williamson, Harold Francis 1901-1989 ... 5-8R
Williamson, Henry (William)
1895-1977 ... CANR-110
Obituary ... 73-76
Earlier sketches in CA 81-84, CANR-36
See also CN 1, 2
See also CWRI 5
See also DLB 191
See also MTCW 1
See also RGEL 2
See also SATA 37
See also SATA-Obit 30
Williamson, J. N.
See Williamson, Gerald Neal
Williamson, J. Peter 1929- ... CANR-6
Earlier sketch in CA 1-4R
Williamson, J(erry) W(ayne) 1944- ... 148
Williamson, Jack
See Williamson, John Stewart
See also CAAS 8
See also CLC 29
See also DLB 8
See also SCFW 1, 2
Williamson, Jeffrey G(ale) 1935- ... CANR-39
Earlier sketches in CA 85-88, CANR-18
Williamson, Joanne S(mall) 1926- ... 13-16R
See also SATA 3, 122
Williamson, Joel (Roudolph) 1929- ... 144
Williamson, John 1937- ... 149
Williamson, John (Gordon) 1949- ... 138
Williamson, John Butler 1943- ... 89-92
Williamson, John G(rant) 1933- ... 45-48
Williamson, John Stewart 1908- ... CANR-70
Earlier sketches in CA 17-20R, CANR-23
See also Williamson, Jack
See also SFW 4
Williamson, Joseph 1895-1988 ... CAP-1
Obituary ... 125
Earlier sketch in CA 11-12
Williamson, Juanita V. 1917- ... 37-40R
Williamson, Karina 1928- ... 127
Williamson, Kevin 1965- ... 201
See also AAYA 30
Williamson, Lamar, Jr. 1926- ... 89-92
Williamson, Margaret 1947- ... 153
Williamson, Marianne 1952- ... CANR-91
Earlier sketch in CA 141
Williamson, Marilyn L. 1927- ... 225
Williamson, Moncrieff 1915- ... 102
See also CP 1
Williamson, Norma (Goff) 1934- ... 65-68
Williamson, Oliver E(aton) 1932- ... 81-84
Williamson, Philip G. 1955- ... 157
See also FANT
Williamson, Porter B(eyers) 1916- ... CANR-28
Earlier sketch in CA 110
Williamson, Rene de Visme
1908-1998 ... CANR-13
Earlier sketches in CAP-1, CA 17-18
Williamson, Richard 1930- ... 37-40R
Williamson, Richard 1935- ... 109
Williamson, Robert C(lifford) 1916- ... 21-24R
Williamson, Robin (Martin Eyre) 1938- . 29-32R
Williamson, Robin (Duncan Harry) 1943- .. 102
Williamson, Stanford Winfield 1916- ... 5-8R
Williamson, Timothy 1955- ... 187
Williamson, Tony
See Williamson, Anthony George
Williamson, William Bedford 1918- ... CANR-6
Earlier sketch in CA 1-4R
Williamson, William Landram 1920- ... 9-12R
Willie, Charles V(ert) 1927- ... CANR-58
Earlier sketches in CA 41-44R, CANR-14, 31
Willie, Frederick
See Lovecraft, H(oward) P(hillips)
Williford, Carolyn S. 1953- ... 224
Williford, (G.) Craig 1953- ... 232
Williford, Lex 1954- ... 145
Willig, George 1949- ... 102
Willig, John M. 1913-1982
Obituary ... 107
Willig, Rosette F. 1950- ... 114
Willimon, William H(enry) 1946- ... CANR-118
Earlier sketches in CA 106, 151, CANR-56
Willing, Jules Z. 1914-1981 ... 108
Willing, Martha Kent 1920- ... 37-40R
Willingham, Bill 1956- ... 227
Willingham, Calder (Baynard, Jr.)
1922-1995 ... CANR-3
Obituary ... 147
Earlier sketch in CA 5-8R
See also CLC 5, 51
See also CN 1, 2, 3, 4, 5
See also CSW
See also DLB 2, 44
See also IDFW 3, 4
See also MTCW 1
Willingham, John J. 1935- ... 37-40R
Willingham, John R(obert) 1919- ... 17-20R
Willings, David 1932- ... 111
Williram of Ebersberg c. 1020-1085 ... DLB 148
Willis, (George) Anthony Armstrong
1897-1976 ... 69-72
Willis, Arthur J(ames) 1895-1983 ... CANR-5
Obituary ... 111
Earlier sketch in CA 5-8R
Willis, Barry 1952- ... 148
Willis, Charles
See Clarke, Arthur C(harles)
Willis, Cleve E(dward) 1942- ... 123
Brief entry ... 118
Willis, Clint 1957- ... 198
Willis, Connie 1945- ... 203
Earlier sketches in CA 114, CANR-35, 91
Autobiographical Essay in ... 203
See also AAYA 30
See also CLR 66
See also CN 6, 7
See also FANT
See also MAICYA 2
See also SATA 110
See also SCFW 2
See also SFW 4
Willis, Corinne Denneny ... 21-24R
Willis, Deborah 1948- ... 227
Willis, Donald C(halmers) 1947- ... CANR-15
Earlier sketch in CA 41-44R
Willis, Donald J. 1919- ... 127
Willis, E(dward) David 1932- ... 37-40R
Willis, Edgar E(rnest) 1913- ... 5-8R
Willis, Edward Henry 1918-1992 ... CANR-65
Obituary ... 140
Earlier sketches in CA 9-12R, CANR-7, 23
See also Willis, Ted
See also CMW 4
Willis, Ellen Jane 1941- ... 106
Willis, F(rank) Roy 1930- ... 13-16R
Willis, Gordon 1931- ... IDFW 3, 4
Willis, Irene 1929- ... CANR-10
Earlier sketch in CA 65-68
Willis, James 1928- ... 109
Willis, Jeanne (Mary) 1959- ... CANR-101
Earlier sketch in CA 128
See also SATA 61, 123
Willis, Jennifer Schwamm 1957- ... 196
Willis, Jerry W. 1943- ... 85-88
Willis, John c. 1572-1625 ... DLB 281
Willis, John A(lvin) 1916- ... 17-20R
Willis, John C. 1961- ... 196
Willis, John H(oward), Jr. 1929- ... 37-40R
Willis, John Ralph 1938- ... 121
Willis, Julia 1949- ... 204
Willis, Margaret 1899-1986 ... CANR-19
Earlier sketches in CA 5-8R, CANR-3
Willis, Mary Pleshette ... 195
Willis, Maud
See Lottman, Eileen
Willis, Meredith Sue 1946- ... CANR-119
Earlier sketches in CA 85-88, CANR-16
See also SATA 101
Willis, Nancy Carol 1952- ... SATA 93, 139
Willis, Nathaniel Parker 1806-1867 ... DLB 3, 59, 73, 74, 183, 250
See also DLBD 13
See also RGAL 4
Willis, Paul J. 1955- ... 176
See also SATA 113
Willis, Resa 1949- ... 138
Willis, Roy (Geoffrey) 1927- ... CANR-17
Earlier sketch in CA 77-80
Willis, Samuel
See Parker, Hershel
Willis, Sarah 1954(?)- ... 228
Willis, Sharon O(zell) 1938- ... 37-40R
Willis, Stanley E. II 1923- ... 21-24R
Willis, Ted
See Willis, Edward Henry
See also CBD
See also DLB 310
Willis, Val 1946- ... 130
Willis, Wayne 1942- ... 29-32R
Willison, George F(indlay) 1896-1972 .. CAP-1
Obituary ... 37-40R
Earlier sketch in CA 13-14
Willison, Marilyn Murray 1948- ... 105
Willke, John Charles 1925- ... CANR-24
Earlier sketches in CA 65-68, CANR-9
Willkens, William H(enry) R(obert)
1919- ... 21-24R
Willkomm, Ernst Adolf 1810-1886 ... DLB 133
Willmington, Harold L. 1932- ... 49-52
Willmott, H(edley) P(aul) 1945- ... CANR-109
Earlier sketch in CA 157
Willmott, Peter 1923-2000 ... 21-24R
Willmott, Phyllis ... CANR-40
Earlier sketch in CA 117
Willms, Russ ... SATA 95
Willner, Ann Ruth 1924- ... 21-24R
Willner, Dorothy 1927-1993 ... 53-56
Obituary ... 140
Willnow, Ronald D. 1933- ... 77-80
Willock, Colin 1919-2005 ... CANR-10
Obituary ... 238
Earlier sketch in CA 13-16R
Willock, Ruth ... 13-16R
Willocks, Tim 1958(?)- ... 156
Willoughby, Bob 1927- ... 216
Willoughby, Cass
See Olsen, T(heodore) V(ictor)
Willoughby, Charles Andrew 1892-1972
Obituary ... 104
Willoughby, David P(atrick)
1901-1983 ... 37-40R
Willoughby, Elaine Macmann 1926- ... 101
Willoughby, Glynn
See Allentuck, Andrew
Willoughby, Hugh
See Harvey, Nigel
Willoughby, Lee Davis
See Avallone, Michael (Angelo, Jr.) and Brandner, Gary (Phil) and DeAndrea, William L(ouis) and Deming, Richard and Laymon, Richard (Carl) and Streib, Dan(iel Thomas) and Toombs, John and Webb, Jean Francis (III)
Willoughby, William Reid 1910- ... 1-4R
Willrich, Mason 1933- ... 77-80
Willrich, Ted L. 1924-1986 ... 29-32R
Wills, A(lfred) J(ohn) 1927- ... 21-24R
Wills, Chester
See Snow, Charles H(orace)
Wills, Christopher 1938- ... 132
Wills, Clair ... 228
Wills, David Hilary 1904-1985
Obituary ... 117
Wills, Garry 1934- ... CANR-88
Earlier sketches in CA 1-4R, CANR-1
See also DLB 246
Wills, Geoffrey
See Staal, Cyril
Wills, Jean 1929- ... CANR-22
Earlier sketch in CA 105
Wills, John E(lliot), Jr. 1936- ... CANR-44
Earlier sketch in CA 45-48
Wills, Jonathan 1947- ... 69-72
Wills, Maurice Morning 1932-
Brief entry ... 105
Wills, Maury
See Wills, Maurice Morning
Wills, Millicent A(gatha) 1901(?)-1988
Obituary ... 125
Wills, Philip Aubrey 1907-1978 ... 81-84
Wills, Thomas
See Ard, William (Thomas)
Willson, A(mos) Leslie, Jr. 1923- ... CANR-44
Earlier sketch in CA 9-12R
Willson, Leslie
See Willson, A(mos) Leslie, Jr.
Willson, Mary F(rances) 1938- ... 129
Willson, Meredith 1902-1984 ... 49-52
Obituary ... 113
See also DLB 265
Willson, Robina Beckles
See Beckles Willson, Robina (Elizabeth)
See also SATA 27
Willstaetter, Richard (Martin) 1872-1942 ... 161
Willstatter, Richard
See Willstaetter, Richard (Martin)
Willum, K.
See Flogstad, Kjartan
Willumsen, Dorrit (Kirsten) 1940- ... 131
See also DLB 214
Willumson, Glenn G(ardner) 1949- .. CANR-93
Earlier sketch in CA 146
Willwerth, James 1943- ... 57-60
Willy
See Colette, (Sidonie-Gabrielle)
Willy, Colette
See Colette, (Sidonie-Gabrielle)
See also GLL 1
Willy, Margaret (Elizabeth) 1919- ... 9-12R
See also PC 1, 2
Wilma, Dana
See Faralla, Dana
Wilmer, Clive 1945- ... CANR-112
Brief entry ... 122
Earlier sketch in CA 130
See also CP 7
See also DLB 40
Wilmer, Dale
See Miller, (H.) Bill(y) and Wade, Robert (Allison)
Wilmer, Valerie (Sybil) 1941- ... 85-88
Wilmerding, John 1938- ... 111
Wilmeth, Don B(urton) 1939- ... CANR-41
Earlier sketches in CA 102, CANR-19
Wilmore, Gayraud S(tephen, Jr.) 1921- ... 134
Brief entry ... 114
Wilmore, Jack H(arrison) 1938- ... 129
Wilmore, Sylvia (Joan) Bruce 1914- ... 89-92
Wilmot, Anthony 1933- ... 77-80
Wilmot, Jeanne ... 171
Wilmot, John 1647-1680
See Rochester
See also BRW 2
See also DLB 131
See also PAB
See also PC 66
Wilmot, William (Wallace) 1943- ... CANR-7
Earlier sketch in CA 57-60
Wilms, Barbara 1941- ... 57-60
Wilmshurst, Rea 1941- ... 127
Wilmut, Roger (Francis) 1942- ... CANR-19
Earlier sketch in CA 102
Wilner, Eleanor (Rand) 1937- ... CANR-113
Earlier sketches in CA 93-96, CANR-16, 37
Wilner, Herbert 1925-1977 ... CANR-3
Earlier sketch in CA 45-48
Wiloch, Thomas 1953- ... 164
Wilroy, Mary Edith (Farr) 1910-1987
Obituary ... 122
Wilsford, David 1956- ... 140
Wilsher, Ann
See Henisch, Bridget Ann
Wilshire, Bruce W(ithington)
1932- ... CANR-123
Earlier sketch in CA 77-80
Wilson, A(lfred) Jeyaratnam 1928- ... CANR-12
Earlier sketch in CA 61-64
Wilson, A(ndrew) N(orman) 1950- ... 122
Brief entry ... 112
See also BRWS 6
See also CLC 33
See also CN 4, 5, 6, 7
See also DLB 14, 155, 194
See also MTCW 2
Wilson, Abraham 1899(?)-1983
Obituary ... 110
Wilson, Adrian 1923-1988 ... 132
Obituary ... 125
Wilson, Alexander 1766-1813 ... ANW
Wilson, Alison M. 1932- ... 120
Wilson, Alton H(orace) 1925- ... 61-64
Wilson, Andrew 1923- ... 29-32R
Wilson, Andrew 1967- ... 239
Wilson, Angus (Frank Johnstone)
1913-1991 ... CANR-21
Obituary ... 134
Earlier sketch in CA 5-8R
See also BRWS 1
See also CLC 2, 3, 5, 25, 34
See also CN 1, 2, 3, 4
See also DLB 15, 139, 155
See also EWL 3
See also MTCW 1, 2
See also MTFW 2005
See also RGEL 2
See also RGSF 2
See also SSC 21
Wilson, April ... SATA 80
Wilson, Arthur 1595-1652 ... DLB 58
Wilson, Arthur M(cCandless) 1902-1979 . 61-64
Obituary ... 89-92
Wilson, August 1945-2005 ... CANR-128
Brief entry ... 115
Earlier sketches in CA 122, CANR-42, 54, 76
See also AAYA 16
See also AFAW 2
See also AMWS 8
See also BLC 3
See also BW 2, 3
See also CAD
See also CD 5, 6
See also CLC 39, 50, 63, 118
See also DA
See also DA3
See also DAB
See also DAC
See also DAM DRAM, MST, MULT
See also DC 2
See also DFS 3, 7, 15, 17
See also DLB 228
See also EWL 3
See also LAIT 4
See also LATS 1:2
See also MAL 5
See also MTCW 1, 2
See also MTFW 2005
See also RGAL 4
See also WLCS
Wilson, Augusta Jane Evans 1835-1909 ... 190
See also Evans, Augusta J. and Evans, Augusta Jane
See also DLB 42
Wilson, Barbara
See Janifer, Laurence M(ark)
Wilson, Barbara (Ellen) 1950- ... 200
See also TCWW 2
Wilson, Barbara Eleanore 1951- ... CMW 4
See also FW
Wilson, Barbara Ker
See Ker Wilson, Barbara
Wilson, Barry K. 1948- ... 201
Wilson, Beth P(ierre) ... CANR-1
Earlier sketch in CA 49-52
See also SATA 8
Wilson, Betty 1923- ... 97-100
Wilson, Bob Chuck
See Wilson, Robert Charles
Wilson, Brian (Douglas) 1942- ... 183
Wilson, Brian 1942- ... CLC 12
Wilson, Bryan R(onald) 1926-2004 .. CANR-41
Obituary ... 232
Earlier sketches in CA 5-8R, CANR-3, 19
Wilson, Budge 1927- ... 121
See also Wilson, Marjorie
See also SATA 55
See also YAW
Wilson, Callie C(oe) 1917- ... 124
Wilson, Camilla Jeanne 1945- ... 61-64
Wilson, Cammy
See Wilson, Camilla Jeanne
Wilson, Cara 1944- ... 150
Wilson, Carey 1889-1962 ... IDFW 3
Wilson, Carletta 1951- ... 141
See also BW 2
See also SATA 81
Wilson, Carlos 1941- ... 61-64

Wilson, Carole
See Wallmann, Jeffrey M(iner)
Wilson, Carolyn 1938- ... 21-24R
Wilson, Carroll L(ouis) 1910-1983 ... 89-92
Obituary ... 109
Wilson, Carter 1941- ... CANR-107
Earlier sketch in CA 17-20R
See also SATA 6
Wilson, Catherine 1951- ... 132
Wilson, (Lindsay) Charles 1932- ... 65-68
Wilson, Charles (P.) 1939- ... 135
Wilson, Charles McMoran 1882-1977 .. CAP-2
Obituary ... 69-72
Earlier sketch in CA 21-22
Wilson, Charles Morrow 1905-1977 .. CANR-4
Earlier sketch in CA 5-8R
See also SATA 30
Wilson, Charles Reagan 1948- ... 105
See also CSW
Wilson, Chris(topher Paul) 1949- ... 125
Wilson, Christine
See Geach, Christine
Wilson, Christopher B. 1910(?)-1985
Obituary ... 117
See also SATA-Obit 46
Wilson, Chuck
See Wilson, James Charles
Wilson, Cintra ... 230
Wilson, Clifford (Allan) 1923- ... 93-96
Wilson, Clifton E. 1919- ... 21-24R
Wilson, Clyde N(orman, Jr.) 1941- ... CANR-40
Earlier sketch in CA 116
Wilson, Colin (Henry) 1931- ... CANR-77
Earlier sketches in CA 1-4R, CANR-1, 22, 33
See also CAAS 5
See also CLC 3, 14
See also CMW 4
See also CN 1, 2, 3, 4, 5, 6
See also DLB 14, 194
See also HGG
See also MTCW 1
See also SFW 4
Wilson, Craig R. 1947- ... 57-60
Wilson, Crane
See O'Brien, Cyril C(ornelius)
Wilson, Cynthia ... 145
Wilson, D. A.
See Wilson, Derek (Alan)
Wilson, D(udley) B(utler) 1923- ... 21-24R
Wilson, Dagmar 1916- ... SATA-Brief 31
Wilson, Dale 1894-1987 ... CAP-1
Obituary ... 121
Earlier sketch in CA 13-14
Wilson, Daniel J(oseph) 1949- ... 117
Wilson, Darryl B(abe) 1939- ... 155
See also SATA 90
Wilson, Dave
See Floren, Lee
Wilson, David
See MacArthur, D(avid) Wilson
Wilson, (Anthony) David 1927- ... CANR-43
Earlier sketch in CA 97-100
Wilson, David 1942- ... CANR-38
Earlier sketches in CA 93-96, CANR-16
Wilson, David Allen 1926- ... CANR-7
Earlier sketch in CA 5-8R
Wilson, David Henry 1937- ... CANR-32
Earlier sketch in CA 113
See also FANT
Wilson, David L(ee) 1943- ... 112
Wilson, David M(ackenzie) 1931- ... CANR-94
Earlier sketch in CA 146
Wilson, David Niall 1959(?)- ... 175
Wilson, David Scofield 1931- ... 106
Wilson, David Sloan 1949- ... 223
Wilson, Deirdre (Susan Moir) 1941- ... 97-100
Wilson, Derek (Alan) 1935- ... CANR-111
Brief entry ... 115
Earlier sketch in CA 123
Interview in ... CA-123
Wilson, Derek A.
See Wilson, Derek (Alan)
Wilson, Diane 1948- ... 213
Wilson, Dick
See Wilson, Richard Garratt
Wilson, Dirk
See Pohl, Frederik
Wilson, Don(ald) 1932- ... 81-84
Wilson, Don E. 1944- ... 198
Wilson, Don W(hitman) 1942- ... 61-64
Wilson, (Alan) Doric 1939- ... 129
See also Aldon, Howard
See also CD 5
Wilson, Doric 1939- ... CAD
See also CD 6
See also GLL 1
Wilson, Dorothy Clarke 1904- ... CANR-6
Earlier sketch in CA 1-4R
See also SATA 16
Wilson, Douglas L. 1935- ... 37-40R
Wilson, Duff 1954(?)- ... 203
Wilson, (Archibald) Duncan 1911-1983 ... 103
Wilson, E(dward) Raymond 1896-1987 ... 61-64
Obituary ... 122
Wilson, (Harvey) Earl 1907-1987 ... 69-72
Obituary ... 121
Wilson, Earl (Dean) 1939- ... 118
Wilson, Edmund 1895-1972 ... CANR-110
Obituary ... 37-40R
Earlier sketches in CA 1-4R, CANR-1, 46
See also AMW
See also CLC 1, 2, 3, 8, 24
See also CN 1
See also DLB 63
See also EWL 3
See also MAL 5
See also MTCW 1, 2
See also MTFW 2005
See also RGAL 4
See also TUS
Wilson, Edmund Beecher 1856-1939 ... 159
Wilson, Edward A(rthur) 1886-1970
Obituary ... 116
See also SATA 38
Wilson, Edward M(eryon) 1906-1977
Obituary ... 114
Wilson, Edward O(sborne, Jr.)
1929- ... CANR-94
Earlier sketches in CA 61-64, CANR-16, 58
See also CAAS 16
See also MTCW 1, 2
See also MTFW 2005
Wilson, Edward T(homas) 1941- ... 129
Wilson, Elena 1907(?)-1979
Obituary ... 89-92
Wilson, Elizabeth 1947- ... CANR-90
Earlier sketch in CA 149
Wilson, Elizabeth Z. 1951- ... 123
Wilson, Ellen (Janet Cameron) (?)-1976 ... 49-52
Obituary ... 103
See also BYA 1
See also SATA 9
See also SATA-Obit 26
Wilson, Emma ... 226
Wilson, Eric (P.) ... 235
Wilson, Eric (H.) 1940- ... CANR-20
Earlier sketch in CA 101
See also SATA 34
See also SATA-Brief 32
Wilson, Erica ... CANR-23
Earlier sketches in CA 53-56, CANR-7
See also SATA 51
Wilson, Erle (Alexander Mann) 1898- ... 5-8R
Wilson, Ernest Charles 1896-1982 ... 29-32R
Wilson, Ethel Davis (Bryant) 1888(?)-1980 . 102
See also CLC 13
See also CN 1, 2
See also DAC
See also DAM POET
See also DLB 68
See also MTCW 1
See also RGEL 2
Wilson, Eugene E. 1887(?)-1974
Obituary ... 49-52
Wilson, Eugene Smith 1905-1981
Obituary ... 103
Wilson, Eunice ... 178
Wilson, Eva 1925- ... 146
Wilson, Evan M(orris) 1910-1984 ... 129
Obituary ... 112
Wilson, Everett K(eith) 1913-1999 ... 93-96
Wilson, F(rank) P(ercy) 1889-1963 ... CANR-1
Earlier sketch in CA 1-4R
See also DLB 201
Wilson, F(rancis) Paul 1946- ... CANR-71
Earlier sketch in CA 138
See also HGG
See also SFW 4
See also SUFW 2
Wilson, Florence Roma Muir 1891-1930
See Wilson, Romer
Wilson, Forbes (Kingsbury) 1910-1990 ... 126
Brief entry ... 112
Wilson, Forrest 1918- ... CANR-7
Earlier sketch in CA 53-56
See also SATA 27
Wilson, Fran
See Wilson, Frances Engle
Wilson, Frances Engle 1922- ... CANR-86
Earlier sketch in CA 130
Wilson, Francesca Mary 1888-1981
Obituary ... 103
Wilson, Francis Graham 1901-1976
Obituary ... 65-68
Wilson, Frank (Avray) 1914- ... CAP-1
Earlier sketch in CA 11-12
Wilson, Frank J. 1887-1970 ... CAP-1
Earlier sketch in CA 13-16
Wilson, Frank L(eondus) 1941- ... 57-60
Wilson, Frank R. ... 173
Wilson, Fred 1937- ... 37-40R
Wilson, G(eorge) B(ulkeley) L(aird)
1908-1984 ... 111
Obituary ... 114
Wilson, Gahan 1930- ... CANR-84
Earlier sketches in CA 25-28R, CANR-19
See also AAYA 55
See also SATA 35
See also SATA-Brief 27
Wilson, Gar
See Hoskins, Robert (Phillip) and
Linaker, Mike
Wilson, Garff B(ell) 1909-1998 ... 45-48
Wilson, George C. 1927- ... 124
Wilson, George M(acklin) 1937- ... 25-28R
Wilson, George W(ilton) 1928- ... CANR-7
Earlier sketch in CA 17-20R
Wilson, Gina 1943- ... CANR-53
Earlier sketch in CA 106
See also CWRI 5
See also SATA 36, 85
See also SATA-Brief 34
Wilson, Glenn Daniel 1942- ... CANR-46
Earlier sketches in CA 104, CANR-21
Wilson, (Leslie) Granville 1912- ... CANR-11
Earlier sketch in CA 69-72
See also SATA 14
Wilson, Gregory
See DeLamotte, Roy Carroll
Wilson, Gretchen 1956- ... 165
Wilson, H. W.
See Wilson, Halsey William
Wilson, Halsey William 1868-1954
Brief entry ... 118
Wilson, (James) Harold 1916-1995 .. CANR-16
Obituary ... 148
Earlier sketch in CA 53-56
Wilson, Harold Stacy 1935- ... 41-44R
Wilson, Harriet
See Wilson, Harriet E. Adams
See also DLB 239
Wilson, Harriet E.
See Wilson, Harriet E. Adams
See also DLB 243
Wilson, Harriet E. Adams 1827(?)-1863(?)
See Wilson, Harriet and
Wilson, Harriet E.
See also BLC 3
See also DAM MULT
See also DLB 50
Wilson, Harriett (Charlotte) 1916- ... CANR-16
Earlier sketch in CA 1-4R
Wilson, Harris W(ard) 1919- ... 21-24R
Wilson, Harry Leon 1867-1939 ... 160
Brief entry ... 108
See also DLB 9
See also TCWW 1, 2
Wilson, Hazel (Hutchins) 1898-1992 . CANR-6
Obituary ... 139
Earlier sketch in CA 1-4R
See also SATA 3
See also SATA-Obit 73
Wilson, Helen Helga (Mayne) -1991 .. CANR-4
Earlier sketch in CA 9-12R
Wilson, Helen Van Pelt 1901- ... 105
Wilson, Howard Allan 1927-
Brief entry ... 106
Wilson, Howard Hazen 1908-1978
Obituary ... 77-80
Wilson, Hugh 1943- ... 184
Wilson, Hughie
See Wilson, Hugh
Wilson, Ian (William) 1941- ... CANR-136
Earlier sketch in CA 85-88
Wilson, Iris Higbie
See Engstrand, Iris (H.) Wilson
Wilson, Isaiah Herbert 1909-1990
Obituary ... 131
Wilson, Ivor (Arthur) 1924- ... CAP-1
Earlier sketch in CA 11-12
Wilson, J(anice) J. 1936- ... 97-100
Wilson, J(erry) M. 1964- ... 192
See also SATA 121
Wilson, J(ohn) Tuzo 1908-1993 ... CANR-47
Obituary ... 141
Earlier sketch in CA 45-48
Wilson, Jack 1937- ... 21-24R
Wilson, Jacqueline 1945- ... CANR-137
Earlier sketches in CA 45-48, CANR-1, 17, 38
See also CWRI 5
See also MAICYA 2
See also SATA 61, 102, 153
See also SATA-Brief 52
Wilson, Jacques M(arcel) P(atrick) 1920- . 49-52
Wilson, James 1949- ... 232
Wilson, James C(lyde) 1948- ... 111
Wilson, James Charles 1951- ... 200
Wilson, James Orville 1895-1986 ... CAP-1
Earlier sketch in CA 11-12
Wilson, James Q(uinn) 1931- ... CANR-112
Brief entry ... 116
Earlier sketches in CA 128, CANR-65
Wilson, James Robert 1917- ... 1-4R
Wilson, James Vernon 1881- ... CAP-1
Earlier sketch in CA 9-10
Wilson, Janet 1952- ... MAICYA 2
Wilson, Janice Meredith
See Karon, Jan
Wilson, Jaye 1938- ... 104
Wilson, Jean Moorcroft ... 181
Wilson, Jeanne (Patricia Pauline)
1920- ... CANR-12
Earlier sketch in CA 69-72
Wilson, Jerry V(ernon) 1928- ... CANR-7
Earlier sketch in CA 57-60
Wilson, Jim
See Wilson, James Vernon
Wilson, Joan Hoff 1937- ... 134
Brief entry ... 105
See also Hoff, Joan
Wilson, Joe
See Wilson, Joseph T(homas)
Wilson, John 1588-1667 ... DLB 24
Wilson, John 1626-c. 1695 ... RGEL 2
Wilson, John 1785-1854 ... DLB 110
Wilson, John 1922- ... SATA 22
Wilson, (Richard) John (McMoran) 1924- ... 117
Wilson, John A. 1900(?)-1976
Obituary ... 69-72
Wilson, John A(braham) R(oss)
1911-1997 ... 41-44R
Wilson, John Boyd 1928-2003 ... CANR-5
Obituary ... 221
Earlier sketch in CA 9-12R
Wilson, John (Anthony) Burgess
1917-1993 ... CANR-46
Obituary ... 143
Earlier sketches in CA 1-4R, CANR-2
See also Burgess, Anthony
See also DA3
See also DAC
See also DAM NOV
See also MTCW 1, 2
See also MTFW 2005
See also NFS 15
See also TEA
Wilson, John C.
See Morrow, Felix
Wilson, John Dover 1881-1969 ... 102
Obituary ... 93-96
See also DLB 201
Wilson, John F(rederick) 1933-
Brief entry ... 117
Wilson, John Foster 1919-1999 ... 109
Obituary ... 186
Wilson, John Harold 1900-1982
Obituary ... 107
Wilson, John M.
See Wilson, John Morgan
Wilson, John Morgan 1945- ... 171
Wilson, John Oliver 1938- ... 129
Wilson, John R. M. 1944- ... 69-72
Wilson, John Stuart Gladstone
1916-1996 ... CANR-11
Earlier sketch in CA 13-16R
Wilson, John T(odd) 1914-1990
Obituary ... 132
Wilson, Johnniece Marshall 1944- ... 142
See also SATA 75
Wilson, Jonathan 1950- ... CANR-139
Earlier sketch in CA 152
Wilson, Joseph (Charles) (IV) 1949- ... 234
Wilson, Joseph T(homas) 1936- ... 117
Wilson, Joyce M(uriel Judson) ... CANR-122
Earlier sketches in CA 17-20R, CANR-12, 51
See also Stranger, Joyce
See also CWRI 5
See also SATA 21, 84
Wilson, Julia 1927- ... 21-24R
Wilson, Jussem
See Wilson, Nelly
Wilson, Justin 1914-2001 ... 116
Wilson, Katharine M(argaret) 1895- ... 89-92
Wilson, Keith 1927- ... 199
Earlier sketches in CA 21-24R, CANR-9
Autobiographical Essay in ... 199
See also CAAS 5
See also CP 1, 2, 3, 4, 5, 6, 7
Wilson, Keith 1929- ... CANR-49
Earlier sketch in CA 121
Wilson, Ken 1943- ... 168
Wilson, Kenneth G(eorge) 1923-2003 ... 5-8R
Obituary ... 215
Wilson, Kenneth L. 1897(?)-1979
Obituary ... 85-88
Wilson, Kenneth L(ee) 1916- ... 29-32R
Wilson, L(eland) Craig 1925- ... 37-40R
Wilson, Lanford 1937- ... CANR-96
Earlier sketches in CA 17-20R, CANR-45
See also CABS 3
See also CAD
See also CD 5, 6
See also CLC 7, 14, 36, 197
See also DAM DRAM
See also DC 19
See also DFS 4, 9, 12, 16, 20
See also DLB 7
See also EWL 3
See also MAL 5
See also TUS
Wilson, Larman C. 1930- ... CANR-14
Earlier sketch in CA 37-40R
Wilson, Larry 1930- ... 208
Wilson, Leigh Allison 1957- ... 117
Wilson, Leonard G(ilchrist) 1928- ... CANR-7
Earlier sketch in CA 57-60
Wilson, Libby
See Wilson, Elizabeth Z.
Wilson, Linda Miller 1936- ... 188
See also SATA 116
Wilson, Lionel 1924-2003 ... 105
Obituary ... 217
See also SATA 33
See also SATA-Brief 31
See also SATA-Obit 144
Wilson, Logan 1907-1990 ... 45-48
Wilson, Lois (M.) 1927- ... 134
Wilson, Louis D(oull) 1917- ... 93-96
Wilson, Louis E. 1939- ... 143
Wilson, Louis Round 1876-1980
Obituary ... 93-96
Wilson, Lyle (Giles) 1955- ... 211
Wilson, M(orris) Emett 1894-1987 ... 5-8R
Wilson, Major L(oyce) 1926- ... 57-60
Wilson, Margaret (Wilhelmina) 1882-1973 . 183
Obituary ... 113
See also DLB 9
Wilson, Margaret Gibbons 1943- ... 101
Wilson, Margery
See Strayer, Sara Barker
Wilson, Margo 1942- ... CANR-96
Earlier sketches in CA 110, CANR-31
Wilson, Marie B(eatrice) 1922- ... 53-56
Wilson, Marjorie
See Wilson, Budge
See also SATA-Brief 51
Wilson, Mary
See Roby, Mary Linn
Wilson, Mary C(hristina) 1950- ... 128
Wilson, Mary Elizabeth 1931- ... RHW
Wilson, Maurice (Charles John) 1914- . SATA 46

Cumulative Index 625 Wing

Wilson, Melba (Jean) 1947- 164
Wilson, (Daphne) Merna 1930- 109
Wilson, Michael 1914-1978 85-88
Obituary 77-80
See also DLB 44
See also IDFW 3, 4
Wilson, Michiko N(iikuni) 1945- 190
Wilson, Miles (Scott, Jr.) 1943- 139
Wilson, Mitchell 1913-1973 .... CANR-3
Obituary 41-44R
Earlier sketch in CA 1-4R
See also CN 1
Wilson, Mona 1872-1954 .... DLB 149
Wilson, Monica Hunter 1908-1982 .... CANR-6
Obituary 108
Earlier sketch in CA 1-4R
Wilson, Myoung Chung 1943- 193
Wilson, N(igel) G(uy) 1935- 127
Wilson, N(orman) Scarlyn 1901- CANR-5
Earlier sketch in CA 5-8R
Wilson, Nancy Hope 1947- CANR-117
Earlier sketch in CA 149
See also SATA 81, 138
Wilson, Neil 1944- 133
Wilson, Neill C(ompton) 1889-1973 .... 5-8R
Wilson, Nelly 1930- 106
Wilson, Nick
See Ellis, Edward S(ylvester)
Wilson, Noel Avon 1914-1985 73-76
Wilson, Owen (Cunningham) 1968- 214
Wilson, Pat 1910-1994 .... CANR-12
Earlier sketch in CA 29-32R
Wilson, Patrick Seymour 1926- .... CP 1
Wilson, Paul C(arroll) 1944- 77-80
Wilson, Paul R(ichard) 1942-
Brief entry 109
Wilson, Penelope Coker
See Hall, Penelope C(oker)
Wilson, Peter (Cecil) 1913-1984
Obituary 113
Wilson, Peter N. 1928-2004 .... 25-28R
Obituary 223
Wilson, Philip K(evin) 1961- 191
Wilson, Phillip (John) 1922- 57-60
Wilson, Phoebe Rous 1924(?)-1980
Obituary 101
Wilson, Phyllis Starr 1928- 69-72
Wilson, R(oger) H(arris) L(ebus) 1920- .. 13-16R
Wilson, R. Michael 1944- 166
Wilson, Rachel
See Duncan, Alice
Wilson, Raymond 1925-1995 .... CANR-17
Obituary 148
Earlier sketch in CA 97-100
See also CP 1
Wilson, Richard 1920-1987 .... SFW 4
Wilson, Richard Garratt 1928- 106
Wilson, Richard Guy 1940- CANR-45
Earlier sketches in CA 93-96, CANR-21
Wilson, Richard Lawson 1905-1981
Obituary 102
Wilson, Richard Trevor 1938- 118
Wilson, Richard W(hittingham) 1933- 73-76
Wilson, Rob
See Gore, Patrick Wilson
Wilson, Robert 1543-1600 .... RGEL 2
Wilson, Robert (Edward) 1951- 124
Wilson, Robert Anton 1932- CANR-52
Earlier sketches in CA 65-68, CANR-18
See also SFW 4
Wilson, Robert C. 1951- 166
Wilson, Robert Charles 1953- CANR-100
Earlier sketch in CA 159
See also DLB 251
See also SFW 4
Wilson, Robert L. 1925-1991 .... CANR-9
Obituary 134
Earlier sketch in CA 57-60
Wilson, Robert M(ills) 1929- CANR-25
Earlier sketches in CA 21-24R, CANR-9
Wilson, Robert M. 1941- CANR-41
Earlier sketches in CA 49-52, CANR-2
See also CAD
See also CD 5, 6
See also CLC 7, 9
See also MTCW 1
Wilson, Robert McLachlan 1916- 109
Wilson, Robert McLiam 1964- 132
See also CLC 59
See also DLB 267
Wilson, Robert N(eal) 1924-2002 .... 17-20R
Wilson, Robert R(athbun) 1914-2000 162
Obituary 190
Wilson, Robert Renbert 1898-1975 .. CANR-23
Earlier sketch in CA 45-48
Wilson, Robert W. 1917- 145
Wilson, Robin Scott 1928- 101
Wilson, Robley (Conant), Jr. 1930- . CANR-110
Earlier sketches in CA 77-80, CANR-14
See also DLB 218
Wilson, Rodney N. Usher
See Usher-Wilson, Rodney N.
Wilson, Roger Burdett 1919- 45-48
Wilson, Romer 1891-1930
See Wilson, Florence Roma Muir
See also DLB 191
Wilson, Ron(ald William) 1941- 112
See also SATA 38
Wilson, Ronald E(merson) 1932- 105
Wilson, Rosalind Baker 1923-2000 .. CANR-90
Obituary 192
Earlier sketch in CA 132
Wilson, (Edward) Ross (Armitage) 1914- ... 5-8R
Wilson, Rudy 1950- 136
Wilson, Sam 1946- 152
Wilson, Samuel, Jr. 1911-1993 .... CANR-6
Earlier sketch in CA 53-56
Wilson, Sandra 1944- CANR-116
Earlier sketch in CA 102
Wilson, Sarah 1934- CANR-121
Earlier sketch in CA 127
See also SATA 50, 142
Wilson, (Bryan) Scott 1953- 220
Wilson, Sharon Rose 1941- 152
Wilson, Sloan 1920-2003 .... CANR-44
Obituary 216
Earlier sketches in CA 1-4R, CANR-1
See also CLC 32
See also CN 1, 2, 3, 4, 5, 6
Wilson, Snoo 1948- 69-72
See also CBD
See also CD 5, 6
See also CLC 33
Wilson, Steve 1943- 73-76
Wilson, Susan 1951- CANR-93
Earlier sketch in CA 156
Wilson, Theodore A(llen) 1940- 37-40R
Wilson, Thomas 1523(?)-1581 .... DLB 132, 236
Wilson, Thomas C(ave) 1907-1984
Obituary 112
Wilson, Thomas Williams, Jr.
1912-1997 .... CANR-3
Obituary 162
Earlier sketch in CA 5-8R
Wilson, Tom 1931- 106
See also SATA 33
See also SATA-Brief 30
Wilson, Trevor (Gordon) 1928- CANR-118
Earlier sketch in CA 156
Wilson, Viola
See Tait, Viola (Wilson)
Wilson, W(illiam) Harmon 1905-1985 .. 37-40R
Wilson, Walt(er N.) 1939- 69-72
See also SATA 14
Wilson, Wayne 1946- 136
Wilson, Wesley M. 1927- 9-12R
Wilson, Wilfrid George 1910- CAP-2
Earlier sketch in CA 21-22
Wilson, William A(lbert) 1933- 105
Wilson, William E(dward)
1906-1988 .... CANR-2
Obituary 125
Earlier sketch in CA 5-8R
Wilson, William H(enry) 1935- 13-16R
Wilson, William J. 1935- CANR-1
Earlier sketch in CA 45-48
Wilson, William P. 1922- 124
Wilson, William Ritchie 1911-1986 ...... 41-44R
Wilson, William S(mith) 1932- 81-84
See also CLC 49
Wilson, (Thomas) Woodrow 1856-1924 166
See also DLB 47
See also TCLC 79
Wilson, Z. Vance 1950- 120
Wilson and
Warnke eds.
Warnke .... CLC 65
Wilson-Kastner, Patricia 1944- 126
Wilson-Max, Ken 1965- .... SATA 93
Wilson-Smith, Timothy 1936- CANR-143
Earlier sketch in CA 141
Wilt, David (Edward) 1955- 137
Wilt, Fred(erick Loren) 1920-1994 ..... CANR-9
Earlier sketch in CA 57-60
Wilt, Judith 1941- CANR-12
Earlier sketch in CA 57-60
Wiltenburg, Robert 1947- 139
Wiltgen, Ralph M(ichael) 1921- CANR-11
Earlier sketch in CA 25-28R
Wilton, (James) Andrew (Rutley)
1942- CANR-123
Earlier sketch in CA 97-100
Wilton, Dianne 1944- 196
Wilton, Elizabeth 1937- CANR-28
Earlier sketch in CA 69-72
See also SATA 14
Wilton, Hal
See Pepper, Frank S.
Wilton-Ely, John 1937- 128
Wiltse, Charles M(aurice) 1907-1990 . CANR-3
Obituary 131
Earlier sketch in CA 1-4R
Wiltse, David 1940- CANR-22
Earlier sketch in CA 105
Wiltsee, Joseph L. 1920- 110
Wiltshire, Susan Ford 1941- 140
Wiltz, Chris(tine) 1948- CANR-87
Earlier sketches in CA 106, CANR-24
See also CSW
Wiltz, John Edward 1930- 9-12R
Wilwerding, Walter Joseph 1891-1966 .. CAP-1
Earlier sketch in CA 13-16
See also SATA 9
Wimberley, (Amos) Darryl 204
Wimmer, Dick 1936- CANR-123
Earlier sketch in CA 172
Wimmer, Larry T(urley) 1935- 101
Wimmer, Mike 1961- .... SATA 70
Wimpfeling, Jakob 1450-1528 .... DLB 179
Wimpfen, Sheldon P(hillip) 1913- 171
Wimsatt, Billy
See Wimsatt, William Upski
Wimsatt, James I(rving) 1927- CANR-13
Earlier sketch in CA 61-64
Wimsatt, W(illiam) K(urtz), Jr.
1907-1975 .... CANR-3
Obituary 61-64
Earlier sketch in CA 1-4R
See also DLB 63
Wimsatt, William Upski 1972- 207
Winans, A(llan) D(avis, Jr.) 1936- CANR-112
Earlier sketches in CA 57-60, CANR-12
See also CAAS 28
Winans, Christopher 1950- 133
Winans, Edgar Vincent 1930- 5-8R
Winant, Fran 1943- CANR-70
Earlier sketch in CA 53-56
See also GLL 2
Winawer, Bonnie P. (Josephs) 1938- 17-20R
Winawer, Sidney Jerome 1931- 172
Winborn, Marsha (Lynn) 1947- .... SATA 75
Wincelberg, Shimon 1924-2004 .... CANR-46
Obituary 231
Earlier sketch in CA 45-48
Winch, D(avid) M(onk) 1933- 45-48
Winch, Donald N. 1935- 123
Winch, John
See Campbell, (Gabrielle) Margaret (Vere)
Winch, John 1944- 189
See also SATA 117
Winch, Julie 1953- CANR-119
Earlier sketch in CA 159
Winch, Michael Bluett 1907- CAP-1
Earlier sketch in CA 11-12
Winch, Peter G(uy) 1926-1997 .... 29-32R
Obituary 157
Winch, Robert F(rancis) 1911-1977 .. CANR-24
Earlier sketch in CA 25-28R
Winch, Terence 1945- 93-96
Winchell, Carol Ann 1936- CANR-7
Earlier sketch in CA 61-64
Winchell, Constance M(abel)
1896-1983 .... CAP-1
Obituary 109
Earlier sketch in CA 9-10
Winchell, Donna Haisty 1952- 145
Winchell, Wallace 1914-1995 53-56
Winchell, Walter 1897-1972 101
Obituary 33-36R
See also DLB 29
Winchester, A(lbert) M(cCombs)
1908-1994 .... 41-44R
Winchester, Clarence 1895-1981
Obituary 104
Winchester, Jack
See Freemantle, Brian (Harry)
Winchester, James H(ugh) 1917-1985 ... 17-20R
Obituary 117
See also SATA 30
See also SATA-Obit 45
Winchester, Otis 1933- 21-24R
Winchester, Simon 1944- CANR-130
Earlier sketches in CA 107, CANR-90
See also AAYA 66
Winchester, Stanley
See Youd, (Christopher) Samuel
Winchilsea .... RGEL 2
Winchilsea, Anne (Kingsmill) Finch 1661-1720
See Finch, Anne
See also RGEL 2
Winckelmann, Johann Joachim
1717-1768 .... DLB 97
Winckler, Martin 1955- 208
Winckler, Paul 1630-1686 .... DLB 164
Winckler, Paul A(lbert) 1926- 102
Wind, Barry 1942- 140
Wind, Edgar 1900-1971
Obituary 104
Wind, Herbert Warren 1916-2005 ... CANR-62
Obituary 239
Earlier sketches in CA 1-4R, CANR-6
See also DLB 171
Wind, Ruth
See Samuel, Barbara
Wind, Yoram (Jerry) 1938- 208
Windal, Floyd W(esley) 1930- 9-12R
Windawi, Thura al- 1983(?)- 237
Windchy, Eugene G. 1930- 41-44R
Windeler, Robert 1944- 102
Winder, Alvin E. 1923- 93-96
Winder, George Herbert 1895- CAP-1
Earlier sketch in CA 11-12
Winder, Mavis Areta 1907-1987 .... 21-24R
Winder, R(ichard) Bayly 1920-1988 ...... 17-20R
Obituary 126
Winders, Gertrude Hecker -1987 .... CANR-6
Earlier sketch in CA 1-4R
See also SATA 3
Windet, John fl. 1554-1610 .... DLB 170
Windham, Basil
See Wodehouse, P(elham) G(renville)
Windham, Donald 1920- CANR-6
Earlier sketch in CA 1-4R
See also CN 1, 2, 3
See also DLB 6
Windham, Douglas M(acArthur)
1943- CANR-43
Earlier sketch in CA 29-32R
Windham, Joan 1904- 21-24R
Windham, Kathryn T(ucker) 1918- ... CANR-11
Earlier sketch in CA 69-72
See also SATA 14
Windle, Janice Woods CANR-116
Earlier sketch in CA 164
Windle, Jeanette (M.) 1960- 197
Windle, William Frederick 1898-1985 108
Obituary 115
Windley, Carol 1947- 159
Windley, Charles Ellis 1942- 65-68
Windling, Terri 1958- 163
See also AAYA 59
See also SATA 151
Windmiller, Marshall 1924- 21-24R
Windmuller, John P. 1923- CANR-10
Earlier sketch in CA 25-28R
Windolph, F(rancis) Lyman 1889-1978 . 41-44R
Windrich, Elaine 1921- 131
Windrow, Martin
See Windrow, Martin Clive
Windrow, Martin C.
See Windrow, Martin Clive
Windrow, Martin Clive 1944- 134
Brief entry 110
See also SATA 68
Windsor, Alan 1931- 127
Windsor, Allen
See Smith, Warren Allen
Windsor, Annie
See Shull, Margaret Anne Wyse
Windsor, Claire
See Hamerstrom, Frances
Windsor, Duane 1947- 111
Windsor, Duke of
See Edward VIII
Windsor, Gerard (Charles) 1944- 124
Windsor, Laura Lynn 1959- 223
Windsor, Linda 1950- 201
See also SATA 124
Windsor, Merrill C(ranston, Jr.) 1924-1990 . 113
Obituary 133
Windsor, Patricia 1938- CANR-42
Earlier sketches in CA 49-52, CANR-4, 19
See also AAYA 23
See also BYA 7
See also MAICYA 2
See also MAICYAS 1
See also SAAS 19
See also SATA 30, 78
See also YAW
Windsor, Philip 1935- CANR-8
Earlier sketch in CA 5-8R
Windsor, Rex
See Armstrong, Douglas Albert
Windsor, Rudolph R. 1935- 185
Brief entry 107
Windsor, (Bessie) Wallis Warfield (Spencer)
Simpson 1896-1986
Obituary 119
Windsor-Liscombe, Rhodri 1946- 129
Windsor-Richards, Arthur (Bedlington)
1904- CAP-1
Earlier sketch in CA 11-12
Windsor-Smith, Barry .... AAYA 58
Wine, Dick
See Posner, Richard
Wine, Sherwin T. 1928- 93-96
Wineapple, Brenda 1949- CANR-82
Earlier sketches in CA 133, CANR-69
Winearls, Jane 1908- 103
Winearls, Joan 1937- 139
Wineberg, Henry J. 1905(?)-1983
Obituary 109
Winebrenner, D(aniel) Kenneth
1908-1975 .... CAP-1
Earlier sketch in CA 9-10
Winebrenner, Hubert W., Jr. 1937- 127
Winebrenner, Hugh
See Winebrenner, Hubert W., Jr.
Winecoff, Charles 1960- 162
Winegardner, Mark 1961- CANR-68
Earlier sketch in CA 127
Winegarten, Renee 1922- CANR-137
Earlier sketch in CA 65-68
Winehouse, Irwin 1922- 9-12R
Winek, Charles L(eone) 1936- 65-68
Wineman-Marcus, Irene 1952- .... SATA 81
Winer, Andrew 1966- 217
Winer, Bart 1919(?)-1989
Obituary 127
Winer, Deborah Grace 1961- 136
Winer, Elihu 1914- 192
Brief entry 111
Winer, Richard 1929- CANR-12
Earlier sketch in CA 73-76
Winer, Yvonne 1934- .... SATA 120
Winerip, Michael 160
Wines, Roger (Andrew) 1933- 21-24R
Winetrout, Kenneth 1912-1998 .... 21-24R
Winfield, Arthur M.
See Stratemeyer, Edward L.
Winfield, Edna
See Stratemeyer, Edward L.
Winfield, Fairlee E(lizabeth) 1929- 118
Winfield, Gerald Freeman 1908-1984
Obituary 113
Winfield, Julia
See Armstrong, Jennifer
Winfield, Leigh
See Youngberg, Norma Ione (Rhoads)
Winford, Donald C. 1945- 137
Winfrey, Dorman H(ayward) 1924- 17-20R
Winfrey, John Crawford 1935- 57-60
Winfrey, Lee 1932-2003 69-72
Obituary 215
Winfrey, Oprah (Gail) 1954- 213
See also AAYA 32
Wing, Betsy 1936- 140
Wing, Cliff W(aldron), Jr. 1922- 49-52
Wing, Donald Goddard 1904-1972 181
Obituary 37-40R
See also DLB 187
Wing, Elizabeth Nelson
See Wing, Betsy
Wing, Frances (Scott) 1907-1995 .... CAP-1
Earlier sketch in CA 17-18
Wing, George Douglas 1921- 17-20R
Wing, Grace Barnett
See Slick, Grace (Wing)
Wing, J(ohn) K(enneth) 1923- CANR-54
Earlier sketches in CA 29-32R, CANR-28
Wing, Jennifer Patai 1942- 57-60
Wing, John M. 1844-1917 .... DLB 187
Wing, John M(ansir) 1844-1917 204
Wing, Natasha (Lazutin) 1960- 149
See also SATA 82
Wing, R. L.
See Aero, Rita

Wing, Willis Kingsley 1899-1985
Obituary ... 116
Wingate, (Martha) Anne (Guice) 1943- ... 116
Wingate, Gifford W(endel) 1925- ... 65-68
Wingate, Isabel B(arnum) 1901-1987 ... 21-24R
Obituary ... 122
Wingate, John (Allan) 1920- ... CANR-24
Earlier sketch in CA 77-80
Wingate, John Williams 1899-1990 ... 9-12R
Wingate, Lisa ... 224
Wingenbach, Charles E.
See Wingenbach, Gregory C(harles)
Wingenbach, Gregory C(harles) 1938- ... 13-16R
Winger, Fred E. 1912-2000 ... 13-16R
Winger, Howard W(oodrow)
1914-1995 ... CANR-7
Earlier sketch in CA 17-20R
Wingert, Paul S. 1900(?)-1974
Obituary ... 53-56
Wingerter, J. Richard 1942- ... 227
Wingfield, Paul 1961- ... 140
Wingfield, Sheila (Claude) 1906-1992 ... 130
Obituary ... 136
Brief entry ... 108
See also CP 1, 2
Wingfield Digby, George (Frederick)
1911-1989 ... CAP-1
Obituary ... 127
Earlier sketch in CA 11-12
Wingler, Hans M(aria) 1920- ... CANR-14
Earlier sketch in CA 29-32R
Wingo, E(lvis) Otha 1934- ... 37-40R
Wingo, Glenn Max 1913-2001 ... 5-8R
Wingo, T(ullius) Lowdon, Jr. 1923- ... 21-24R
Wingo, Walter (Scott) 1931- ... 81-84
Wingrave, Anthony
See Wright, S(ydney) Fowler
Wingren, Gustaf F(redrik) 1910-2000 ... 13-16R
Wingrove, David (John) 1954- ... 133
See also CLC 68
See also SFW 4
Wingrove, Elizabeth Rose 1960- ... 237
Wings, Mary 1949- ... CANR-70
Earlier sketch in CA 145
See also CMW 4
See also GLL 2
Winick, Bruce J. 1944- ... 147
Winick, Charles 1922- ... 134
Brief entry ... 109
Winick, Judd 1970- ... 195
See also AAYA 41
See also SATA 124
Winick, Myron 1929- ... 107
Winick, Steven 1944- ... 61-64
Winik, Jay 1957- ... 228
Winik, Marion (Lisa) 1958- ... 172
Winiki, Ephriam
See Fearn, John Russell
Wininger, Kathleen (J.) 1953- ... 202
Wink, Richard L(ee) 1930- ... 93-96
Wink, Walter Philip 1935- ... CANR-82
Earlier sketches in CA 37-40R, CANR-15, 36
Winkelman, Betty J. 1936- ... 196
Winkelman, Carol ... 238
Winkelman, Donald M. 1934- ... 41-44R
Winkelman, Sidra
See Stone, Sidra (L. Winkelman)
Winkelman, Stanley J. 1922-1999 ... 215
Winkle, Kenneth J. ... 228
Winkler, Allan M(ichael) 1945- ... CANR-97
Earlier sketch in CA 81-84
Winkler, Anthony C. 1942- ... 123
Winkler, Bee (Finkelberg) 1919- ... 13-16R
Winkler, David F. 1958- ... 196
Winkler, Erhard M(ario) 1921- ... 89-92
Winkler, Ernst
See Hill, Crag
Winkler, Franz E. 1907-1972 ... 5-8R
Winkler, Henry (Franklin) 1945- ... 236
Winkler, Henry R(alph) 1916- ... CANR-10
Earlier sketch in CA 17-20R
Winkler, Irwin 1931- ... IDFW 3, 4
Winkler, John J(oseph) 1943-1990
Obituary ... 131
Winkler, Paul 1898-1982
Obituary ... 107
Winkler, Win Ann 1935- ... 73-76
Winkless, Nels(on Brock) III 1934- ... 57-60
Winkley, David (Ross) 1941- ... 224
Winks, Donald 1928-1999 ... 25-28R
Winks, Robin William 1930-2003 ... CANR-30
Obituary ... 216
Earlier sketches in CA 5-8R, CANR-3
See also SATA 61
Winkworth, Stephen 1939- ... 127
Winn, Albert Curry 1921- ... 106
Winn, Alison
See Wharmby, Margot
Winn, Bob
See Seuling, Barbara
Winn, Charles S. 1932- ... CANR-23
Earlier sketch in CA 69-72
Winn, Chris 1952- ... 117
See also SATA 42
Winn, Ira Jay 1929- ... 57-60
Winn, James Anderson 1947- ... 120
Winn, Janet Bruce 1928- ... 105
See also SATA 43
Winn, Laura Rocke 1902- ... CAP-1
Earlier sketch in CA 13-14
Winn, Marie 1936(?)- ... CANR-127
Earlier sketch in CA 111
See also SATA 38
Winn, Ralph Bubrich 1895-1975 ... 5-8R
Winn, Rowland (Denys Guy) 1916-1984
Obituary ... 114
Winn, Wilkins B(owdre) 1928- ... 49-52
Winnard, Frank
See Tubb, E(dwin) C(harles)
Winnegrad, Mark Harris 1948- ... 77-80
Winnemucca, Sarah 1844-1891 ... DAM MULT
See also DLB 175
See also NNAL
See also RGAL 4
Winner, Anna K(ennedy) 1900-1982 ... 29-32R
Winner, Irene P(ortis) 1923- ... CANR-14
Earlier sketch in CA 41-44R
Winner, Lauren F. 1975(?)- ... 225
Winner, Michael Robert 1935- ... 137
Winner, Percy 1899-1974
Obituary ... 45-48
Winner, Thomas G(ustav)
1917-2004 ... CANR-15
Obituary ... 226
Earlier sketch in CA 37-40R
Winner, Viola Hopkins 1928- ... CANR-4
Earlier sketch in CA 53-56
Winnett, Fred Victor 1903-1989 ... 37-40R
Winnett, Thomas 1921- ... CANR-22
Earlier sketches in CA 61-64, CANR-7
Winnick, Karen B(eth) B(inkoff) 1946- ... 73-76
See also SATA 51
Winnick, R. H. 1947- ... 144
Winnicott, Donald (Woods)
1896-1971 ... CAP-1
Earlier sketch in CA 13-14
Winnifrith, Thomas John 1938- ... CANR-103
Earlier sketches in CA 108, CANR-25, 50
See also DLB 155
Winnikoff, Albert 1930- ... 29-32R
Winningham, Geoff(rey) (L.) 1943- ... 216
Winnington, Alan 1910(?)-1983
Obituary ... 111
Winnington-Ingram, R(eginald) P(epys)
1904-1993 ... 129
Obituary ... 140
Winock, Michel 1937- ... 171
Winograd, Terry (Allen) 1946- ... CANR-67
Earlier sketch in CA 128
Winogrand, Garry 1928-1984 ... 169
Winokur, Joan Gelman 1935- ... 41-44R
Winokur, Jon 1947- ... 132
Winokur, Stephen 1941- ... 89-92
Winold, Allen 1929- ... 17-20R
Winsberg, Morton D. 1930- ... 13-16R
Winsborough, Hal (Liman) H. 1932- ... 9-12R
Winsett, Marvin Davis 1902-1979 ... 1-4R
Winsey, Valentine Rossilli ... 145
Winship, Elizabeth 1921- ... 41-44R
Winship, Laurence Leathe 1890-1975
Obituary ... 104
Winslade, John (Maxwell) 1953- ... 203
Winslade, William J(oseph) 1941- ... 118
Winsloe, Christa 1888-1944 ... DLB 124
See also GLL 1
Winslow, Anna Green 1759-1780 ... DLB 200
Winslow, Barbara 1947- ... 155
See also SATA 91
Winslow, Dean Hendricks, Jr.
1934-1972 ... 37-40R
Obituary ... 41-44R
Winslow, Don 1953- ... 145
Winslow, Donald
See Zoll, Donald Atwell
Winslow, Gerald A. ... 109
Winslow, John Hathaway 1932- ... 37-40R
Winslow, Martha
See Rickett, Frances
Winslow, Ola Elizabeth
1885(?)-1977 ... CANR-3
Obituary ... 73-76
Earlier sketch in CA 1-4R
Winslow, Pauline Glen ... CANR-69
Earlier sketches in CA 101, CANR-18, 41
Winslow, Pete
See Winslow, Dean Hendricks, Jr.
Winslow, Richard E(lliott) III 1934- ... 129
Winslow, Robert W(allace) 1940-
Brief entry ... 108
Winslow, Ron(ald A.) 1949- ... 103
Winslow, Thyra Samter 1893-1961
Obituary ... 89-92
Winslowe, John
See Richardson, Gladwell
Winslowe, John R.
See Richardson, Gladwell
Winsor, Justin 1831-1897 ... DLB 47
Winsor, Kathleen 1919-2003 ... CANR-62
Obituary ... 216
Earlier sketch in CA 97-100
See also RHW
Winsor, Mary P(ickard) 1943- ... 69-72
Winsor, Phil 1938- ... 142
Winsor, Roy (William) 1912-1987 ... 65-68
Obituary ... 122
Winspear, Alban Dewes 1899-1973 ... 45-48
Winspear, Jacqueline 1955- ... 229
Winspear, Violet 1928-1989 ... CANR-64
Earlier sketch in CA 122
See also RHW
Winstan, Matt
See Nickson, Arthur
See also TCWW 1
Winstanley, Michael J. 1949- ... 129
Winstanley, (Jane) Rita 1955- ... 128
Winston, Alexander 1909-1998 ... CAP-2
Earlier sketch in CA 25-28
Winston, Carl H(arold) -1992 ... 1-4R
Winston, Clara 1921-1983 ... CANR-44
Obituary ... 113
Earlier sketch in CA 25-28R
See also SATA 54
See also SATA-Obit 39
Winston, Daoma 1922- ... CANR-61
Earlier sketches in CA 45-48, CANR-1
See also RHW
Winston, Douglas Garrett ... 41-44R
Winston, Eric V(on) A(rthur) 1942- ... 29-32R
Winston, Henry 1911-1986
Obituary ... 121
Winston, Kenneth I(rwin) 1940- ... CANR-48
Earlier sketch in CA 117
Winston, Krishna 1944- ... CANR-136
Earlier sketch in CA 104
Winston, Lolly 1962(?)- ... 239
Winston, Mark L. 1950- ... CANR-127
Earlier sketch in CA 141
Winston, Martin Bradley 1948- ... 118
Winston, Michael R(ussell) 1941- ... 113
Winston, Mike
See King, Florence
Winston, R(obert) A(lexander)
1907-1974 ... CAP-2
Obituary ... 49-52
Earlier sketch in CA 25-28
Winston, Richard 1917-1979 ... 25-28R
Obituary ... 93-96
See also SATA 54
Winston, Sarah 1912-1994 ... 29-32R
Winston, Stan 1946- ... AAYA 45
See also IDFW 3, 4
Winstone, H(arry) V(ictor) F(rederick)
1926- ... CANR-44
Earlier sketches in CA 104, CANR-21
Wint, Guy 1910-1969 ... CANR-3
Earlier sketch in CA 1-4R
Winter, Abigail
See Schere, Monroe
Winter, Alice 1919- ... 13-16R
Winter, Bevis (Peter) 1918- ... CANR-8
Earlier sketch in CA 5-8R
Winter, Caryl 1944- ... 117
Winter, Colin O'Brien 1928-1981
Obituary ... 105
Winter, David Brian 1929- ... CANR-20
Earlier sketch in CA 103
Winter, David G(arrett) 1939- ... 57-60
Winter, Denis 1940- ... 118
Winter, Douglas E. 1950- ... CANR-105
Earlier sketches in CA 118, CANR-45
Winter, Edward H(enry) 1923- ... 1-4R
Winter, Elmer L(ouis) 1912- ... 13-16R
Winter, Gibson 1916- ... 49-52
Winter, Ginny Linville 1925- ... CANR-1
Earlier sketch in CA 1-4R
Winter, Gordon 1912-1993 ... CANR-14
Obituary ... 141
Earlier sketch in CA 77-80
Winter, H. G. Winter
See Bates, Harry
Winter, Herbert R(einhold) 1928- ... 45-48
Winter, J(erry) Alan 1937- ... 41-44R
Winter, J. M. 1945- ... 73-76
Winter, Janet 1926- ... SATA 126
Winter, Jeanette 1939- ... SATA 151
Winter, John F. 1913- ... 104
Winter, Kari J. 1960- ... 137
Winter, Keith 1906-1983
Obituary ... 109
Winter, Klaus 1928- ... 29-32R
Winter, Leslie 1940- ... CANR-6
Earlier sketch in CA 1-4R
Winter, Michael Morgan 1930- ... CAP-1
Earlier sketch in CA 11-12
Winter, Milo (Kendall) 1888-1956 ... SATA 21
Winter, Nathan H. 1926- ... 21-24R
Winter, Paula Cecelia 1929- ... 107
See also SATA 48
Winter, R. R.
See Winterbotham, R(ussell) R(obert)
Winter, Ralph K(arl, Jr.) 1935- ... 122
Brief entry ... 118
Winter, Roger 1931- ... 37-40R
Winter, Ruth (Nancy G.) 1930- ... CANR-139
Earlier sketch in CA 37-40R
Winter, Thomas 1961- ... 227
Winter, William D(avid) 1927- ... 25-28R
Winter, William O(rville) 1918- ... 49-52
Winterbotham, F(rederick) W(illiam)
1897-1990 ... 57-60
Obituary ... 130
Winterbotham, R(ussell) R(obert)
1904-1971 ... 1-4R
Obituary ... 103
See also SATA 10
Winterbotham, Russ
See Winterbotham, R(ussell) R(obert)
Winterfeld, Henry 1901-1990 ... 77-80
See also SATA 55
Wintergreen, Jane
See Duncan, Sara Jeannette
Wintergreen, John P.
See Ryskind, Morrie
Wintergreen, Warren
See Adamson, Joseph III
Winterich, John 1891-1970
Obituary ... 29-32R
Winteringham, F. Peter W. 1918- ... 144
Winternitz, Emanuel 1898-1983 ... CANR-20
Obituary ... 110
Earlier sketch in CA 25-28R
Winterowd, W. Ross 1930- ... 17-20R
Winters, Angela ... 236
Winters, Anne 1939- ... 122
Winters, Bayla 1921- ... 21-24R
Winters, Bernice
See Winters, Bayla
Winters, Catherine (Mary) 1951- ... 118
Winters, Donald L(ee) 1935- ... 29-32R
Winters, Francis Xavier 1933- ... 61-64
Winters, J. C.
See Cross, Gilbert B.
Winters, Janet Lewis
See Lewis, Janet
See also CLC 41
See also DLBY 1987
Winters, John D(avid) 1917- ... 9-12R
Winters, Jon
See Cross, Gilbert B.
Winters, Jonathan (Harshman) (III) 1925- ... 214
Winters, Katherine 1936- ... CANR-122
Earlier sketch in CA 170
See also SATA 103, 153
Winters, Kay
See Winters, Katherine
Winters, Laurie G. 1958- ... 188
Winters, Logan
See Lederer, Paul Joseph
See also TCWW 2
Winters, Marian 1924-1978 ... 101
Obituary ... 81-84
Winters, Marjorie
See Henri, Florette
Winters, Mick
See Wooley, John (Steven)
Winters, Mike 1930- ... 119
Winters, Nina 1944- ... SATA 62
Winters, Paul A. 1965- ... 176
See also SATA 106
Winters, Rebecca
See Burton, Rebecca B(rown)
Winters, Rosemary
See Breckler, Rosemary
Winters, Shelley
See Schrift, Shirley
Winters, (Arthur) Yvor 1900-1968 ... CAP-1
Obituary ... 25-28R
Earlier sketch in CA 11-12
See also AMWS 2
See also CLC 4, 8, 32
See also DLB 48
See also EWL 3
See also MAL 5
See also MTCW 1
See also RGAL 4
Winterson, Jeanette 1959- ... CANR-116
Earlier sketches in CA 136, CANR-58
See also BRWS 4
See also CLC 64, 158
See also CN 5, 6, 7
See also CPW
See also DA3
See also DAM POP
See also DLB 207, 261
See also FANT
See also FW
See also GLL 1
See also MTCW 2
See also MTFW 2005
See also RHW
Winterton, Gayle
See Adams, William Taylor
Winterton, Paul 1908-2001 ... CANR-58
Obituary ... 192
Earlier sketches in CA 5-8R, CANR-6
See also Garve, Andrew
See also CMW 4
Winther, Barbara 1926- ... CANR-17
Earlier sketch in CA 97-100
Winther, Christian 1796-1876 ... DLB 300
Winther, Oscar Osburn 1903-1970 ... CANR-2
Earlier sketch in CA 1-4R
Winther, Sophus Keith 1893-1983 ... CANR-66
Earlier sketch in CA 5-8R
See also TCWW 1, 2
Winthrop, Elizabeth ... CANR-110
See also Mahony, Elizabeth Winthrop
See also CLR 89
See also MAICYA 2
See also MAICYAS 1
See also SATA 76
See also SATA-Essay 116
Winthrop, Henry 1910-1980 ... 73-76
Winthrop, John, Jr. 1606-1676 ... DLB 24
Winthrop, John 1588-1649 ... DLB 24, 30
Winthrop, Margaret Tyndal
1591(?)-1647 ... DLB 200
Winthrop, Theodore 1828-1861 ... DLB 202
Wintle, Anne ... 29-32R
Wintle, Francis Edward 1948- ... 139
Wintle, Justin (Beecham) 1949- ... CANR-13
Earlier sketch in CA 77-80
Wintner, Robert 1948- ... 190
Winton, Calhoun 1927- ... 9-12R
Winton, Chester Allen 1941- ... 89-92
Winton, Harold R. 1942- ... 194
Winton, Harry N(athaniel) M(cQuillian)
1907-1977(?) ... CANR-29
Earlier sketch in CA 41-44R
Winton, Ian (Kenneth) 1960- ... SATA 76
Winton, John
See Pratt, John
Winton, Kate Barber 1882(?)-1974
Obituary ... 53-56
Winton, Tim 1960- ... CANR-118
Earlier sketch in CA 152
See also AAYA 34
See also CN 6, 7
See also SATA 98
Wintour, Charles (Vere) 1917-1999 ... 201
Wintrobe, Maxwell M(yer) 1901-1986 ... 133
Obituary ... 121
Wintterle, John F(rancis) 1927- ... 29-32R
Wintz, Cary D. 1943- ... CANR-105
Earlier sketch in CA 137
Wintz, Jack 1936- ... 109
Winwar, Frances 1900-1985 ... 89-92

Cumulative Index 627 Woestemeyer

Winward, Stephen Frederick 1911- 9-12R
Winward, (Richard) Walter 1938- 105
Wippel, John Francis 1933- 114
Wippler, Migene Gonzalez
See Gonzalez-Wippler, Migene
Wirkus, Tom E(dward) 1933- 37-40R
Wirnt von Grafenberg
1170(?)-1235(?) .... DLB 138
Wirsing, Marie E(milia) 1931- 45-48
Wirt, Ann
See Benson, Mildred (Augustine Wirt)
Wirt, Frederick M(arshall) 1924- CANR-90
Earlier sketches in CA 112, CANR-31
Wirt, Mildred A.
See Benson, Mildred (Augustine Wirt)
Wirt, Sherwood Eliot 1911- CANR-33
Earlier sketches in CA 41-44R, CANR-15
Wirt, William 1772-1834 .... DLB 37
Wirt, Winola Wells 1905(?)-1986 93-96
Obituary 120
Wirtenberg, Patricia Z(arrella) 1932- 61-64
See also SATA 10
Wirth, Arthur G. 1919- CANR-10
Earlier sketch in CA 21-24R
Wirth, Beverly 1938- 118
See also SATA 63
Wirth, John D(avis) 1936-2002 .... CANR-51
Obituary 207
Earlier sketches in CA 29-32R, CANR-26
Wirth, Louis 1897-1952 210
See also TCLC 92
Wirth, Niklaus 1934- CANR-21
Earlier sketch in CA 105
Wirth, Thomas 1941- 117
Wirths, Claudine (Turner) G(ibson)
1926-2000 .... CANR-53
Obituary 188
Earlier sketch in CA 126
See also SATA 64, 104
Wirtz, (William) Willard 1912- 101
Wisberg, Aubrey 1909(?)-1990 97-100
Obituary 131
Wisberg, Marian Aline 1923- 109
Wisbeski, Dorothy (Gross) 1929- 9-12R
Wisbey, Herbert Andrew, Jr. 1919- 13-16R
Wischnitzer, Rachel 1885(?)-1989
Obituary 130
Wisdom, (Arthur) John (Terence Dibben)
1904-1993 .... 25-28R
Obituary 143
Wisdom, Kenny
See Grogan, Emmett
Wisdome, Thomas
See Dunbar, Charles Stuart
Wise, Arthur 1923- 9-12R
Wise, Charles C(onrad), Jr. 1913- CANR-9
Earlier sketch in CA 21-24R
Wise, Christopher 1961- 222
Wise, David 1930- CANR-96
Earlier sketches in CA 1-4R, CANR-2, 42
Wise, Elia 230
Wise, Ernie
See Wiseman, Ernest
Wise, Gene 1936- 93-96
Wise, Helen Dickerson 1928-
Brief entry 106
Wise, Herbert H(erschel) 1928- 108
Wise, James E., Jr. 1930- 198
Wise, James Waterman 1901-1983
Obituary 111
Wise, Jessie (Mae Tench) 1937- 224
Wise, Joe 1939- CANR-129
Earlier sketch in CA 163
Wise, John 1652-1725 .... DLB 24
Wise, John E(dward) 1905-1974 .... CAP-1
Obituary 49-52
Earlier sketch in CA 13-16
Wise, Kelly 1932- 216
Wise, Leonard 77-80
Wise, Michael Z. 1957- 208
Wise, Mike 1964- 239
Wise, Nancy B(aker) 1921- 147
Wise, Raymond L(eo) 1895-1986 .... 21-24R
Wise, Robert L. 1939- 203
Wise, S(ydney) F(rancis) 1924- CANR-16
Earlier sketch in CA 21-24R
Wise, Stephen S(amuel) 1874-1949
Brief entry 117
Wise, Steven M. 1952(?)- 222
Wise, Steven W. 1948- CANR-123
Earlier sketch in CA 163
Wise, Terence 1935- 89-92
Wise, Thomas James 1859-1937 .... DLB 184
Wise, Victoria (Jenanyan) 1944- 148
Wise, William 1923- CANR-135
Earlier sketches in CA 13-16R, CANR-6
See also SATA 4, 163
Wise, Winifred E. 25-28R
See also SATA 2
Wisely, Rae 1938- 106
Wiseman, Adele 1928-1992 77-80
See also CN 1, 2, 3, 4, 5
See also DLB 88
Wiseman, Ann (Sayre) 1926- CANR-9
Earlier sketch in CA 65-68
See also SATA 31
Wiseman, Anne Marie (Murray) 1932- 5-8R
Wiseman, B(ernard) 1922-1995 .... CANR-24
Earlier sketches in CA 5-8R, CANR-8
See also SATA 4
Wiseman, Carter (Sterling) 1945- 208
Wiseman, Christopher S(tephen)
1936- CANR-44
Earlier sketch in CA 113
See also CP 1
Wiseman, David 1916- CANR-30
Earlier sketch in CA 109
See also SATA 43
See also SATA-Brief 40
Wiseman, Donald John 1918- 89-92
Wiseman, Ernest 1925-1999 129
Obituary 179
Wiseman, Francis Jowett 1905- CAP-1
Earlier sketch in CA 13-14
Wiseman, Frederick 1930- 159
See also CLC 20
Wiseman, James R(ichard) 1934- CANR-1
Earlier sketch in CA 45-48
Wiseman, John A. 1945- 139
Wiseman, Richard 1966- 233
Wiseman, Robert F(rederick) 1935- 77-80
Wiseman, T(imothy) P(eter) 1940- CANR-90
Earlier sketches in CA 45-48, CANR-1, 18, 40
Wiseman, Thomas 1931- 25-28R
Wisensale, Steven K. 1945- 213
Wisenthal, J. L. 1940- 126
Wiser, William CANR-106
Earlier sketch in CA 37-40R
Wish, Harvey 1909-1968 .... CANR-3
Earlier sketch in CA 1-4R
Wishard, Armin 1941- 37-40R
Wishart, David J(ohn) 1946- 124
Brief entry 118
Wishart, E(rnest) E(dward) 1902-1987
Obituary 123
Wishart, Henry
See Shepherd, Robert Henry Wishart
Wishinsky, Frieda 1948- CANR-137
Earlier sketch in CA 138
See also SATA 70, 112
Wishnia, Kenneth J. A. 1960- 194
Wiskemann, Elizabeth (?)-1971
Obituary 111
Wisker, Gina 1951- CANR-93
Earlier sketch in CA 145
Wisler, G(ary) Clifton 1950- 129
See also SATA 58, 103
See also SATA-Brief 46
See also TCWW 2
Wisler, Gene C(harles) 1920- 9-12R
Wisloff, Carl Johan Fredrik 1908- CAP-1
Earlier sketch in CA 13-14
Wisman, Ken(neth) 1947- .... HGG
Wismer, Donald (Richard) 1946- CANR-28
Earlier sketch in CA 109
See also SATA 59
Wisner, Bill
See Wisner, William L.
Wisner, George 1812-1849 .... DLB 43
Wisner, William H(arold) 1956- 213
Wisner, William L. 1914(?)-1983 111
Obituary 110
See also SATA 42
Wisneski, Henry 1940- 57-60
Wisnewski, David 1953-2002
See Wisniewski, David
Wisniewski, David 1953-2002 160
Obituary 209
See also CLR 51
See also CWRI 5
See also MAICYA 2
See also MAICYAS 1
See also SATA 95
See also SATA-Obit 139
Wisse, Ruth R(oskies) 1936- CANR-96
Earlier sketch in CA 37-40R
Wissmann, Ruth Leslie CANR-2
Earlier sketch in CA 5-8R
Wister, John C(aspar) 1887-1982
Obituary 109
Wister, Owen 1860-1938 162
Brief entry 108
See also BPFB 3
See also DLB 9, 78, 186
See also RGAL 4
See also SATA 62
See also TCLC 21
See also TCWW 1, 2
Wister, Sarah 1761-1804 .... DLB 200
Wistrich, Robert S(olomon) 1945- .. CANR-123
Earlier sketch in CA 107
Wiswall, F(rank) L(awrence), Jr. 1939- ... 29-32R
Wiswell, Ella Lury 1909- 111
Wiswell, Thomas George 1910-1998 . CANR-2
Earlier sketch in CA 5-8R
Wiswell, Tom
See Wiswell, Thomas George
Witchel, Alex CANR-114
Earlier sketch in CA 159
Witchel, Dinah B(rown) 1936- 105
Witcombe, R(ick) T(rader) 1943- 132
Witcover, Jules (Joseph) 1927- CANR-89
Earlier sketches in CA 25-28R, CANR-48
Witcutt, William Purcell 1907- CAP-1
Earlier sketch in CA 11-12
Witemeyer, Hugh 1939- 25-28R
Witham, (Phillip) Ross 1917- 105
See also SATA 37
Witham, W(illiam) Tasker 1914- 13-16R
Witheford, Hubert 1921-2000 102
See also CP 1, 2, 3, 4, 5, 6, 7
Wither, George 1588-1667 .... DLB 121
See also RGEL 2
Witheridge, Elizabeth P(lumb)
1907-1995 97-100
Witherington, Ben III 1951- CANR-142
Earlier sketch in CA 168
Withers, Audrey
See Kennett, (Elizabeth) Audrey
Withers, Carl A. 1900-1970 .... CANR-30
Earlier sketch in CA 73-76
See also SATA 14
Withers, Charles W. J. 1954- 128
Withers, E. L.
See Potter, G(eorge) W(illiam, Jr.)
Withers, Josephine 1938- 101
Withers, Sara Cook 1924- 17-20R
Withers, William 1905-1987 .... 13-16R
Obituary 121
Witherspoon, Frances 1887(?)-1973
Obituary 45-48
Witherspoon, Irene Murray 1913- CANR-1
Earlier sketch in CA 1-4R
Witherspoon, John 1723-1794 .... DLB 31
Witherspoon, Mary Elizabeth 1919- 77-80
Witherspoon, Naomi Long
See Madgett, Naomi Long
Witherspoon, Thomas E. 1934- 81-84
Witherup, William 1935- CANR-109
Earlier sketch in CA 133
Withey, J(oseph) A(nthony) 1918- 25-28R
Withim, Gloria 1929- 112
Withington, William Adriance
1924- CANR-14
Earlier sketch in CA 41-44R
Withorn, Ann 1947- 125
Withrow, Dorothy E. 1910-2000 .... 21-24R
Withrow, Sarah 1966- .... SATA 124
Withrow, William Henry 1839-1908 183
See also DLB 99
Witkacy
See Witkiewicz, Stanislaw Ignacy
Witke, Roxane 1938- 69-72
Witker, Kristi 77-80
Witkiewicz, Stanislaw Ignacy 1885-1939 ... 162
Brief entry 105
See also CDWLB 4
See also DLB 215
See also EW 10
See also EWL 3
See also RGWL 2, 3
See also SFW 4
See also TCLC 8
Witkin, Erwin 1926-1994 .... 37-40R
Witkin, Herman A. 1916-1979 .... CANR-1
Earlier sketch in CA 1-4R
Witkin, Joel-Peter 1939- 209
Witkin, Lee D(aniel) 1935-1984
Obituary 114
Witkin-Lanoil, Georgia Hope 1943- 120
Witmer, Helen L(eland) 1898-1979 .... CAP-2
Obituary 89-92
Earlier sketch in CA 25-28
Witmer-Gow, Karen
See Kary, Elizabeth N.
Witoszek, Nina 229
Witt, Dick 1948- .... SATA 80
Witt, Doris 187
Witt, Harold (Vernon) 1923-1995 ..... CANR-39
Earlier sketches in CA 1-4R, CANR-1, 17
Witt, Howell Arthur John 1920-1998 109
Obituary 169
Witt, Hubert 1935- CANR-28
Earlier sketches in CA 65-68, CANR-12
Witt, James F. 1937- 89-92
Witt, John (Clermont) 1907-1982
Obituary 106
Witt, Martha 239
Witt, Reginald Eldred 1907-1980 .... 37-40R
Obituary 97-100
Witt, Ronald Gene 1932- 126
Witt, Shirley Hill 1934- CANR-5
Earlier sketch in CA 53-56
See also SATA 17
Wittanen, Etolin 1907- .... SATA 55
Wittcoff, Harold A. 1918- 160
Witte, Ann Dryden 1942- CANR-26
Earlier sketch in CA 107
Witte, Glenna Finley 1925- CANR-26
Earlier sketches in CA 13-16R, CANR-10
See also AITN 1
Witte, John 1948- 93-96
Wittebols, James H. 1955- 178
Wittels, Harriet Joan 1938- 107
See also SATA 31
Witten, Herbert F. 1920- 5-8R
Witten, Ian H(ugh) 1947- CANR-28
Earlier sketch in CA 111
Wittenberg, Judith Bryant 1938- 102
Wittenberg, Philip 1895-1987 .... CAP-2
Obituary 122
Earlier sketch in CA 23-24
Wittenberg, Rudolph M. 1906-1986 . CANR-22
Earlier sketch in CA 69-72
Wittenwiler, Heinrich c. 1387-c.
1414 .... DLB 179
Wittermans, Elizabeth (Pino) 17-20R
Witters, Weldon L. 1929- 93-96
Wittfogel, Karl A(ugust) 1896-1988
Obituary 125
Wittgenstein, Ludwig (Josef Johann)
1889-1951 164
Brief entry 113
See also DLB 262
See also MTCW 2
See also TCLC 59
Wittich, Claus 1932- 113
Wittich, Walter A(rno) 1910- 49-52
Wittig, Alice J(osephine) 1929- 101
Wittig, Monique 1935-2003 .... CANR-143
Obituary 212
Brief entry 116
Earlier sketch in CA 135
See also CLC 22
See also CWW 2
See also DLB 83
See also EWL 3
See also FW
See also GLL 1
Wittig, Susan
See Albert, Susan Wittig
Witting, Amy 1918- CANR-100
Earlier sketch in CA 140
Witting, Clifford 1907- 1-4R
Wittke, Carl (Frederick) 1892-1971
Obituary 29-32R
Wittkofski, Joseph Nicholas 1912-1976 .. 9-12R
Wittkower, Rudolf 1901-1971
Obituary 33-36R
Wittkowski, Wolfgang 1925- CANR-24
Earlier sketches in CA 61-64, CANR-8
Wittliff, William D. 1940- CANR-54
Earlier sketch in CA 123
Wittlin, Alma S(tephanie) -1991 45-48
Wittlin, Jozef 1896-1976 .... CANR-3
Obituary 65-68
Earlier sketch in CA 49-52
See also CLC 25
See also EWL 3
Wittlin, Thaddeus (Andrew)
1909-1998 .... CANR-2
Obituary 171
Earlier sketch in CA 45-48
Wittlinger, Ellen 1948- CANR-119
Earlier sketches in CA 150, CANR-100
See also AAYA 36
See also SATA 83, 122
See also SATA-Essay 128
Wittman, Sally (Anne Christensen) 1941- ... 107
See also SATA 30
Wittmer, Joe 1937- 45-48
Wittmer, Pierre (Jean) 1942- 139
Wittner, Lawrence S(tephen) 1941- .. CANR-33
Earlier sketch in CA 25-28R
Witton, Dorothy 73-76
Witton-Davies, Carl(yle) 1913-1993 .... 9-12R
Obituary 141
Wittreich, Joseph Anthony, Jr.
1939- CANR-134
Earlier sketches in CA 29-32R, CANR-12, 28
Wittrock, M(erlin) C(arl) 1931- CANR-2
Earlier sketch in CA 49-52
Wittwer, Sylvan Harold 1917- CANR-35
Earlier sketch in CA 114
Witty, Helen E. S(troop) 1921- 105
Witty, Paul 1898-1976 73-76
Obituary 65-68
See also SATA 50
See also SATA-Obit 30
Witty, Robert G(ee) 1906- CAP-2
Earlier sketch in CA 23-24
Witucke, Virginia 1937- 37-40R
Witwer, Andrew S. 1920(?)-1990
Obituary 132
Witze, Claude 1909(?)-1977
Obituary 73-76
Witzel, Michael Karl 1960- 154
Wiwa, Ken 1968- 216
Wixman, Ronald 1947- 122
Wixom, Hartt 1933- 120
Wixson, Douglas 1933- CANR-101
Earlier sketch in CA 147
Wizard, Mariann G(arner) 1946- 37-40R
Wlaschin, Ken 1934- 187
Wobbe, R(oland) A(rthur) 1938- 102
Woddis, Hillel Chayim Keith 1914-
Brief entry 114
Woddis, Jack
See Woddis, Hillel Chayim Keith
Wodehouse, Lawrence 1934- CANR-41
Earlier sketches in CA 53-56, CANR-4, 19
Wodehouse, P(elham) G(renville)
1881-1975 .... CANR-33
Obituary 57-60
Earlier sketches in CA 45-48, CANR-3
See also AAYA 65
See also AITN 2
See also BRWS 3
See also CDBLB 1914-1945
See also CLC 1, 2, 5, 10, 22
See also CN 1, 2
See also CPW 1
See also DA3
See also DAB
See also DAC
See also DAM NOV
See also DLB 34, 162
See also EWL 3
See also MTCW 1, 2
See also MTFW 2005
See also RGEL 2
See also RGSF 2
See also SATA 22
See also SSC 2
See also SSFS 10
See also TCLC 108
Woden, George
See Slaney, George Wilson
Wodge, Dreary
See Gorey, Edward (St. John)
Wodhams, (Herbert) Jack 1931- 115
Woebcke, Mary-Jane 1933- 25-28R
Woehr, Richard (Arthur) 1942- 57-60
Woehrlin, William F(rederick) 1928- 45-48
Woelfel, James W(arren) 1937- 41-44R
Woelfl, Paul A(loysius) 1913- 17-20R
Woelfle, Gretchen 1945- 218
See also SATA 145
Woerner, Karl Heinrich 1910-1969
Obituary 110
Woessner, Nina C. 1933- 29-32R
Woessner, Warren (Dexter) 1944- CANR-14
Earlier sketch in CA 37-40R
Woestemeyer, Ina Faye
See Van Noppen, Ina (Faye) W(oestemeyer)

Woestendiek 628 CONTEMPORARY AUTHORS

Woestendiek, (William) John (Jr.) 1953- 133
Brief entry 127
Interview in CA-133
Woestijne, Karel van de 1878-1929 ...... EWL 3
Woetzel, Robert K(urt) 1930-1991 ...... CANR-6
Obituary 135
Earlier sketch in CA 5-8R
Woffinden, Bob 1948- 135
Wofford, Azile (May) 1896-1977 ...... 5-8R
Wofford, Harris (Llewellyn) 1926- 129
Wofsey, Marvin M(ilton) 1913-1993 105
Wogaman, J(ohn) Philip 1932- CANR-62
Earlier sketches in CA 25-28R, CANR-20
Wogaman, Philip
See Wogaman, J(ohn) Philip
Wohl, Anthony S(tephen) 1937- 220
Wohl, Ellen E. 1962- 237
Wohl, Gerald 1934- 17-20R
Wohl, James P(aul) 1937- 77-80
Wohl, Paul 1901(?)-1985
Obituary 115
Wohl, Robert 1936- 104
Wohlberg, Meg 1905-1990
Obituary 133
See also SATA 41
See also SATA-Obit 66
Wohlfeld, Valerie (Robin) 1956- 155
Wohlforth, Charles P. 1963- 228
Wohlgelernter, Maurice 1921- CANR-6
Earlier sketch in CA 13-16R
Wohl-Musciny, Ludwig von
See de Wohl, Louis
Wohlmuth, Ed 1935- 124
Wohlrabe, Raymond A. 1900-1977 ...... CANR-3
Earlier sketch in CA 1-4R
See also SATA 4
Wohlstetter, Albert J(ames) 1913-1997 129
Obituary 156
Wohmann, Gabriele 1932- 191
See also CWW 2
See also DLB 75
See also EWL 3
Woirol, Gregory R. 1948- 144
Woititz, Janet G(eringer) 1938-1994 . CANR-19
Obituary 145
Earlier sketch in CA 101
Woito, Robert (Severin) 1937- 120
Woiwode, L.
See Woiwode, Larry (Alfred)
Woiwode, Larry (Alfred) 1941- CANR-94
Earlier sketches in CA 73-76, CANR-16
Interview in CANR-16
See also CLC 6, 10
See also CN 3, 4, 5, 6, 7
See also DLB 6
Wojahn, David (Charles) 1953- CANR-143
Earlier sketch in CA 136
Wojciechowska, Maia (Teresa) 1927-2002 . 183
Obituary 209
Earlier sketches in CA 9-12R, CANR-4, 41
Autobiographical Essay in 183
See also AAYA 8, 46
See also BYA 3
See also CLC 26
See also CLR 1
See also JRDA
See also MAICYA 1, 2
See also SAAS 1
See also SATA 1, 28, 83
See also SATA-Essay 104
See also SATA-Obit 134
See also YAW
Wojciechowski, Susan CANR-106
Earlier sketch in CA 146
See also SATA 78, 126
Wojdowski, Bogdan 1930-1994 209
Wojtasik, Ted 228
Wojtyla, Karol (Jozef)
See John Paul II, Pope
Wojtyla, Karol (Josef)
See John Paul II, Pope
Wokeck, Marianne S(ophia) 231
Wolberg, Arlene Robbins 1907-1989
Obituary 130
Wolberg, Lewis Robert 1905-1988 ... CANR-19
Obituary 124
Earlier sketches in CA 45-48, CANR-2
Wolcot, John 1738-1819
See Pindar, Peter
See also DLB 109
Wolcott, Harry F(letcher) 1929- 65-68
Wolcott, James 1952- 220
Wolcott, Leonard Thompson CANR-28
Earlier sketches in CA 13-16R, CANR-11
Wolcott, Patty 1929- 57-60
See also SATA 14
Wolcott, Roger 1679-1767 ...... DLB 24
Wold, Allen L. 1943- CANR-22
Earlier sketch in CA 105
See also SATA 64
Wold, Donald J. 1945- 233
Wold, Jo Anne 1938- 61-64
See also SATA 30
Wold, Ruth 1923- 37-40R
Woldendorp, R(ichard) 1927- CANR-12
Earlier sketch in CA 29-32R
Woldin, Beth Weiner 1955- 102
See also SATA 34
Woldin, (Edwin) Judd 1925- 141
Brief entry 122
Wolf, Adolf Hungry
See Hungry Wolf, Adolf
Wolf, Arnold Jacob 1924- 29-32R
Wolf, Arnold Veryl 1916-1975
Obituary 104
Wolf, Barbara Herrman 1932- 57-60
Wolf, Bernard 1930-
Brief entry 115
See also SATA 102
See also SATA-Brief 37
Wolf, Charlotte (Elizabeth) 1926- 29-32R
Wolf, Christa 1929- CANR-123
Earlier sketches in CA 85-88, CANR-45
See also CDWLB 2
See also CLC 14, 29, 58, 150
See also CWW 2
See also DLB 75
See also EWL 3
See also FW
See also MTCW 1
See also RGWL 2, 3
See also SSFS 14
Wolf, Daniel 1955- 136
Wolf, Deborah Goleman 1938- 97-100
Wolf, Dick
See Wolf, Richard A.
Wolf, Donald J(oseph) 1929- 13-16R
Wolf, Edwin II 1911-1991 ...... CANR-4
Obituary 133
Earlier sketch in CA 1-4R
Wolf, Eric R(obert) 1923-1999 ...... 17-20R
Obituary 179
Wolf, Erica (Van Varick) 1978- ...... SATA 156
Wolf, Frank 1940- 57-60
Wolf, Frank L(ouis) 1924- 57-60
Wolf, Fred Alan 1934- 115
Wolf, Frederick
See Dempewolff, Richard F(rederic)
Wolf, Friedrich 1888-1953 189
See also DLB 124
See also EWL 3
Wolf, Gary K. 1941- 160
See also SFW 4
Wolf, George 1890(?)-1980
Obituary 97-100
Wolf, George D(ugan) 1923- 29-32R
Wolf, Gita 1956- 168
See also SATA 101
Wolf, Harold A. 1923- 13-16R
Wolf, Harvey 1935- 57-60
Wolf, Hazel Catharine 1907- 5-8R
Wolf, Herbert C(hristian) 1923-1987 ...... 13-16R
Wolf, Jack C(lifford) 1922- 57-60
Wolf, Jacqueline 1928- 109
Wolf, Janet 1957- ...... SATA 78
Wolf, Joan 208
Wolf, John B(aptist) 1907-1996 ...... 9-12R
Wolf, Karl E(verett) 1921- 17-20R
Wolf, Kirsten 1959- 137
Wolf, Leonard 1923- CANR-3
Earlier sketch in CA 49-52
Wolf, Margery 1933- 138
Wolf, Marguerite Hurrey 1914- 53-56
Wolf, Mark J(oseph) P(eter) 1967- 223
Wolf, Markus 1923- 162
Wolf, Martin (Harry) 1946- 236
Wolf, Marvin J(ules) 1941- CANR-134
Earlier sketch in CA 117
Wolf, Michael D(avid) 1953- 121
Wolf, Michele 208
Wolf, Miriam Bredow 1895-1975 ...... CAP-1
Earlier sketch in CA 9-10
Wolf, Naomi 1962- CANR-110
Earlier sketch in CA 141
See also CLC 157
See also FW
See also MTFW 2005
Wolf, Peter (Michael) 1935- 53-56
Wolf, Ray 1948- 107
Wolf, Reinhart 1930- 216
Wolf, Reva June 1956- 172
Wolf, Richard A. 1946- 139
Wolf, Robert Charles 1955- 109
Wolf, S. K.
See Wolf, Sarah (Elizabeth)
Wolf, Sallie 1950- ...... SATA 80
Wolf, Sarah (Elizabeth) 1936- 132
Wolf, Stewart (George, Jr.) 1914- 143
Wolf, Thomas H(oward) 1916-1996 69-72
Obituary 152
Wolf, William 1952-1974 103
Wolf, William B. 1920- CANR-26
Earlier sketches in CA 17-20R, CANR-10
Wolf, William C(harles), Jr. 1933- 41-44R
Wolf, William J(ohn) 1918- CANR-29
Earlier sketch in CA 111
Wolfbein, Seymour L(ouis)
1915-2001 ...... CANR-6
Obituary 198
Earlier sketch in CA 13-16R
Wolfe, Alan 1942- CANR-108
Earlier sketch in CA 108
Wolfe, Alvin William 1928- CANR-28
Earlier sketch in CA 1-4R
Wolfe, Art 1952- CANR-117
Earlier sketch in CA 143
See also SATA 76
Wolfe, Barbara (Lea) 1943- CANR-127
Earlier sketch in CA 149
Wolfe, Bernard 1915-1985 ...... CANR-3
Obituary 117
Earlier sketch in CA 1-4R
See also CN 1, 2, 3
See also SFW 4
Wolfe, Bertram D(avid) 1896-1977 .. CANR-40
Obituary 69-72
Earlier sketch in CA 5-8R
Wolfe, Burton H. 1932- 25-28R
See also SATA 5
Wolfe, Charles Keith 1943- CANR-90
Earlier sketches in CA 77-80, CANR-15, 34
Wolfe, Christopher (F.) 1949- CANR-51
Earlier sketch in CA 123
Wolfe, Don Marion 1902-1976
Obituary 65-68
Wolfe, (George) Edgar 1906- CAP-2
Earlier sketch in CA 25-28
Wolfe, Elizabeth
See Lederer, Paul Joseph
Wolfe, Frances 238
Wolfe, Gary K(ent) 1946- 129
Wolfe, Gene (Rodman) 1931- CANR-60
Earlier sketches in CA 57-60, CANR-6, 32
See also CAAS 9
See also AAYA 35
See also CLC 25
See also CPW
See also DAM POP
See also DLB 8
See also FANT
See also MTCW 2
See also MTFW 2005
See also SATA 118
See also SCFW 2
See also SFW 4
See also SUFW 2
Wolfe, George C. 1954- 149
See also BLCS
See also CAD
See also CD 5, 6
See also CLC 49
Wolfe, George Willoughby (Hooper)
1894(?)-1983
Obituary 111
Wolfe, Gerard R(aymond) 1926- CANR-11
Earlier sketch in CA 69-72
Wolfe, Harry Deane 1901-1975 ...... 41-44R
Wolfe, Harvey 1938- 45-48
Wolfe, Henry C. 1898(?)-1976
Obituary 69-72
Wolfe, Herbert S(now) 1898-1991 ...... CAP-1
Earlier sketch in CA 13-16
Wolfe, J(ames) N(athan) 1927-1988
Obituary 124
Wolfe, James H(astings) 1934- 93-96
Wolfe, Jane 1957- 133
Wolfe, John fl. 1576-1600 ...... DLB 170
Wolfe, John N. 1910(?)-1974
Obituary 53-56
Wolfe, Josephine Brace 1917- 5-8R
Wolfe, Linda 1935- 138
Brief entry 129
See also BEST 90:1
Wolfe, Linnie Marsh 1881-1945 191
Wolfe, Louis 1905-1985 ...... CANR-3
Obituary 196
Earlier sketch in CA 5-8R
See also SATA 8
See also SATA-Obit 133
Wolfe, Margaret Ripley 1947- CANR-103
Earlier sketch in CA 128
Wolfe, Martin 1920- 37-40R
Wolfe, Michael
See Williams, Gilbert M.
Wolfe, Michael 1945- 123
Wolfe, Peter (Bernard) 1929-1986
Obituary 121
Wolfe, Peter 1933- CANR-107
Earlier sketches in CA 21-24R, CANR-8
Wolfe, Reyner (Reginald) fl.
1543-1573 ...... DLB 170
Wolfe, Richard J(ames) 1928- CANR-56
Earlier sketches in CA 110, CANR-30
Wolfe, Rinna (Evelyn) 1925- 105
See also SATA 38
Wolfe, Ron 1945- 109
Wolfe, Roy I. 1917- 13-16R
Wolfe, Sidney M(anuel) 1937- 127
Wolfe, Susan 1950- 198
Wolfe, Swain 183
Wolfe, Thomas (Clayton)
1900-1938 ...... CANR-102
Brief entry 104
Earlier sketch in CA 132
See also AMW
See also BPFB 3
See also CDALB 1929-1941
See also DA
See also DA3
See also DAB
See also DAC
See also DAM MST, NOV
See also DLB 9, 102, 229
See also DLBD 2, 16
See also DLBY 1985, 1997
See also EWL 3
See also MAL 5
See also MTCW 1, 2
See also NFS 18
See also RGAL 4
See also SSC 33
See also SSFS 18
See also TCLC 4, 13, 29, 61
See also TUS
See also WLC
Wolfe, Thomas Kennerly, Jr. 1931- . CANR-104
Earlier sketches in CA 13-16R, CANR-9, 33, 70
Interview in CANR-9
See also Wolfe, Tom
See also CLC 147
See also DA3
See also DAM POP
See also DLB 185
See also EWL 3
See also MTCW 1, 2
See also MTFW 2005
See also TUS
Wolfe, Thomas W. 1914- 93-96
Wolfe, Tom
See Wolfe, Thomas Kennerly, Jr.
See also AAYA 8, 67
See also AITN 2
See also AMWS 3
See also BEST 89:1
See also BPFB 3
See also CLC 1, 2, 9, 15, 35, 51
See also CN 5, 6, 7
See also CPW
See also CSW
See also DLB 152
See also LAIT 5
See also RGAL 4
Wolfe, (William) Willard 1936- 93-96
Wolfe, Winifred 1929-1981 ...... CANR-10
Obituary 105
Earlier sketch in CA 17-20R
Wolfenden, George
See Beardmore, George
Wolfenden, John Frederick 1906-1985 106
Obituary 114
Wolfenstein, E. Victor 1940- 21-24R
Wolfenstein, Martha 1911(?)-1976
Obituary 69-72
See also DLB 221
Wolfer, Dianne 1961- CANR-130
Earlier sketch in CA 171
See also SATA 104
See also SATA-Essay 117
Wolferman, Kristie C(arlson) 1948- 154
Wolfers, Michael 1938- 136
Wolfert, Helen 1904-1985 ...... CAP-2
Earlier sketch in CA 17-18
Wolfert, Paula 1938(?)- 192
Wolff, Alexander (Nikolaus) 1957- 214
See also SATA 63, 137
Wolff, Anthony 1938- 49-52
Wolff, (Jenifer) Ashley 1956- CANR-56
Earlier sketch in CA 118
See also SATA 50, 81, 155
Wolff, Charlotte 1904-1986 ...... CANR-15
Obituary 120
Earlier sketch in CA 37-40R
Wolff, Christoph Johannes 1940- 196
Wolff, Craig 235
Wolff, Craig Thomas
See Wolff, Craig
Wolff, Cynthia Griffin 1936- 49-52
Wolff, David
See Maddow, Ben
See also IDFW 3
Wolff, Diane 1945- 77-80
See also SATA 27
Wolff, Edward N(athan) 1946- CANR-93
Earlier sketch in CA 132
Wolff, Egon 1926- 153
See also DLB 305
See also EWL 3
See also HW 1
See also LAW
Wolff, Ernst 1910- 73-76
Wolff, Ferida 1946- ...... SATA 79
Wolff, Geoffrey (Ansell) 1937- CANR-78
Earlier sketches in CA 29-32R, CANR-29, 43
See also CLC 41
Wolff, Hans Walter 1911- 130
Wolff, Helen 1906-1994 117
Obituary 144
Brief entry 113
Interview in CA-117
See also DLBY 1994
Wolff, Isabel 228
Wolff, Janet 1943- CANR-136
Earlier sketch in CA 77-80
Wolff, Janet L(oeb) 1924- 5-8R
Wolff, John U(lrich) 1932- CANR-18
Earlier sketch in CA 102
Wolff, Jurgen M(ichael) 1948- 57-60
Wolff, Konrad (Martin) 1907-1989 ...... 37-40R
Obituary 130
Wolff, Kurt H(einrich) 1912- CANR-39
Earlier sketches in CA 49-52, CANR-1, 17
Wolff, Maritta M(artin) 1918-2002 ...... 17-20R
Obituary 209
Wolff, Mary Evaline 1887-1964
Obituary 116
Wolff, Michael 1930- CANR-19
Earlier sketch in CA 25-28R
Wolff, Miles 1945- CANR-14
Earlier sketch in CA 73-76
Wolff, Milton 1915- 146
Wolff, Richard D(avid) 1942- 73-76
Wolff, Robert Jay 1905-1977 ...... 25-28R
Obituary 73-76
See also SATA 10
Wolff, Robert Lee 1915-1980
Obituary 102
Wolff, Robert Paul 1933- 103
Wolff, Ruth 1909(?)-1972
Obituary 37-40R
Wolff, Ruth (Rehrer) 1932- CANR-129
Earlier sketch in CA 165
Wolff, Sally 1954- 166
Wolff, Sonia
See Levitin, Sonia (Wolff)
Wolff, Theodore F. 1926- 162

Cumulative Index 629 Wood

Wolff, Tobias (Jonathan Ansell)
1945- CANR-96
Brief entry 114
Earlier sketches in CA 117, CANR-54, 76
Interview in CA-117
See also CAAS 22
See also AAYA 16
See also AMWS 7
See also BEST 90:2
See also BYA 12
See also CLC 39, 64, 172
See also CN 5, 6, 7
See also CSW
See also DA3
See also DLB 130
See also EWL 3
See also MTCW 2
See also MTFW 2005
See also RGAL 4
See also RGSF 2
See also SSC 63
See also SSFS 4, 11
Wolff, Victoria 1910-1992 111
Wolff, Virginia Euwer 1937- CANR-111
Earlier sketch in CA 107
See also AAYA 26
See also CLR 62
See also MAICYA 2
See also MAICYAS 1
See also SATA 78, 137
See also WYA
See also YAW
Wolffe, B. P.
See Wolffe, Bertram (Percy)
Wolffe, Bertram (Percy) 1923(?)-1988
Obituary 124
Wolff-Salin, Mary 1932- 122
Wolfgang, Marvin E(ugene) 1924-1998 ..... 5-8R
Obituary 167
Wolfinger, Raymond E(dwin) 1931- 156
Brief entry 112
Wolfle, Dael (Lee) 1906-2002 49-52
Obituary 211
Wolfman, Augustus 1908(?)-1974
Obituary 53-56
Wolfman, Bernard 1924- 41-44R
Wolfman, Judy 1933- 208
See also SATA 138
Wolf-Phillips, Leslie 1929- 21-24R
Wolfram, Stephen 203
See also AAYA 51
Wolfram, Walter A. 1941- 29-32R
Wolfram von Eschenbach c. 1170-c. 1220
See Eschenbach, Wolfram von
See also CDWLB 2
See also DLB 138
See also EW 1
See also RGWL 2
Wolfskill, George 1921- CANR-1
Earlier sketch in CA 1-4R
Wolfson, Evelyn 1937- .... SATA 62
Wolfson, Harry Austryn 1887-1974 .... CAP-2
Obituary 53-56
Earlier sketch in CA 19-20
Wolfson, Max
See Rosenberg, Robert
Wolfson, Murray 1927- 17-20R
Wolfson, P(incus) J(acob) 1903-1979 .... 5-8R
Obituary 200
Wolfson, Penny 222
Wolfson, Randy M(eyers) 1952- 120
Wolfson, Richard 227
Wolfson, Robert J(oseph) 1925- 93-96
Wolfson, Susan 1947-2002 120
Obituary 203
Wolfson, Susan J. 1948- 211
Wolfson, Victor 1910-1990 .... 33-36R
Obituary 131
Wolfthal, Diane (Bette) 1949- CANR-101
Earlier sketch in CA 135
Wolgast, Elizabeth H(ankins) 1929- 113
Wolgensinger, Bernard 1935- 37-40R
Wolin, Richard 214
Wolin, Sheldon S. 1922- 215
Wolin, Steven J. 1940- 143
Wolin, Sybil 143
Wolins, Leroy 1927- 107
Woliston, Jack 1916(?)-1990
Obituary 131
Wolitzer, Hilma 1930- CANR-40
Earlier sketches in CA 65-68, CANR-18
Interview in CANR-18
See also CLC 17
See also SATA 31
See also YAW
Wolitzer, Meg 1959- CANR-18
Earlier sketch in CA 107
See also AAYA 6, 63
Wolk, Allan 1936- 77-80
Wolk, Lauren 1956- 209
Wolken, Jerome J(ay) 1917-1999 154
Obituary 179
Wolker, Jiri 1900-1924 .... DLB 215
See also EWL 3
Wolkers, Jan (Hendrik) 1925-
Brief entry 116
See also CWW 2
Wolkoff, Judie (Edwards) 159
Brief entry 115
See also BYA 12
See also SATA 93
See also SATA-Brief 37
Wolkstein, Diane 1942- CANR-117
Earlier sketches in CA 37-40R, CANR-14, 32
See also SATA 7, 82, 138
Woll, Peter 1933- 13-16R
Wollaston, Nicholas 1926- 25-28R
Wolle, Muriel (Vincent) Sibell
1898-1977 .... CAP-1
Obituary 182
Earlier sketch in CA 13-14
Wollen, Peter 1938- CANR-137
Earlier sketch in CA 172
Wollheim, Donald A(llen)
1914-1990 .... CANR-19
Obituary 135
Earlier sketches in CA 1-4R, CANR-1
See also BYA 4
See also SATA-Obit 69
See also SFW 4
Wollheim, Richard Arthur
1923-2003 .... CANR-98
Obituary 221
Earlier sketch in CA 101
Wollman, Nathaniel 1915-
Brief entry 106
Wollstonecraft, Mary 1759-1797 .... BRWS 3
See also CDBLB 1789-1832
See also DLB 39, 104, 158, 252
See also FL 1:1
See also FW
See also LAIT 1
See also RGEL 2
See also TEA
See also WLIT 3
Wolman, Abel 1892-1989 168
Wolman, Benjamin B. 1908-2000 .... CANR-11
Earlier sketch in CA 13-16R
Wolman, Harold L. 1942- 37-40R
Wolman, William 1927- 1-4R
Wolmar, Christian 214
Wolny, P.
See Janeczko, Paul B(ryan)
Wolny, P.
See Janeczko, Paul B(ryan)
Woloch, Cecilia G. 1956- 202
Woloch, Isser 1937- CANR-114
Earlier sketches in CA 29-32R, CANR-12
Woloszynowski, Julian 1898-1978
Obituary 85-88
Wolozin, Harold 1920- 37-40R
Wolpe, Berthold (Ludwig) 1905-1989
Obituary 129
Wolpe, David J. 1958- 140
Wolpe, Hilda Morley
See Morley (Wolpe), Hilda
Wolpe, Joseph 1915-1997 .... 17-20R
Obituary 163
Wolper, Carol 239
Wolper, David L(loyd) 1928- 224
Wolpert, Lewis 1929- 190
Wolpert, Stanley A(lbert) 1927- CANR-107
Earlier sketches in CA 21-24R, CANR-15
Wolrige Gordon, Anne 1936- 103
Wolsch, Robert Allen 1925- 57-60
Wolseley, Roland E. 1904-1998 .... CANR-39
Obituary 181
Earlier sketches in CA 1-4R, CANR-1, 17
Wolsk, David 1930- 21-24R
Wolstein, Benjamin 1922-1998 .... 9-12R
Wolter, Allan B(ernard) 1913- 106
Wolters, O(liver) W(illiam) 1915-2000 .. 21-24R
Obituary 191
Wolters, Raymond 1938- 29-32R
Wolters, Richard A. 1920-1993 .... CANR-18
Obituary 143
Earlier sketches in CA 5-8R, CANR-3
See also SATA 35
Wolterstorff, Nicholas (Paul) 1932- .. CANR-44
Earlier sketch in CA 69-72
Woltman, Frederick (Enos) 1905-1970
Obituary 89-92
Wolton, Thierry 1951- 166
Wolverton, Cheryl 1963- 201
Wolverton, Dave 1957- 166
See also AAYA 55
See also SFW 4
Wolverton, Robert E(arl) 1925- 37-40R
Wolverton, Terry 1954- CANR-70
Earlier sketch in CA 150
See also GLL 2
Wolz, Carl 1933(?)-2002 233
Wolz, Henry G(eorge) 1905- 106
Wolzien, Valerie 170
Womack, Brantly 1947- 114
Womack, Craig S. 1960- 230
Womack, David A(lfred) 1933- CANR-7
Earlier sketch in CA 53-56
Womack, Don (L.) 1922- 25-28R
Womack, Jack 1956- CANR-112
Earlier sketch in CA 141
See also SFW 4
Womack, John, Jr. 1937- 45-48
Womack, Kenneth 1966- 187
Womack, Peter 1952- CANR-60
Earlier sketch in CA 128
Womack, Steven (James) 1952- CANR-72
Earlier sketch in CA 133
Womack, Thomas Hale 1952- 133
Womble, Vernon G. 1942(?)-1979
Obituary 89-92
Womer, Frank B(urton) 1921- 45-48
Womersley, Peter (John Walter) 1941- 118
Won, Ko
See Ko, Won
Wonder, Alvin
See Lourie, Dick
Wonder, Stevie
See Morris, Steveland Judkins
See also CLC 12
Wonders, Anne
See Passel, Anne W(onders)
Wonders, William C(lare) 1924- 41-44R
Wondratschek, Wolf 1943- .... DLB 75
Wondriska, William 1931- CANR-4
Earlier sketch in CA 1-4R
See also SATA 6
Wong, Baoswan Dzung
See Dzung Wong, Baoswan
Wong, Bing W. 1922- 73-76
Wong, Eleanor 1962- .... CD 5, 6
Wong, Elizabeth 1958- .... DLB 266
Wong, George Bernard 1918- 192
Wong, J(ohn) Y(ue-Wo) 1946- 126
Wong, Jade Snow 1922- CANR-91
Earlier sketch in CA 109
See also CLC 17
See also SATA 112
Wong, Janet S. 1962- CANR-132
Earlier sketch in CA 166
See also CLR 94
See also SATA 98, 148
Wong, Lin Ken 1931- 13-16R
Wong, May 1944- 25-28R
See also CP 1, 2
Wong, Molly 1920- 93-96
Wong, Nellie 1934- .... DLB 312
Wong, Norman 1963- 168
See also GLL 2
Wong, Roderick 1932- 65-68
Wong, Shawn (Hsu) 1949- 162
See also DLB 312
Wong, Wai Ching Angela 224
Wong, Wucius 1936- 212
Wong Phui Nam 1935- .... CP 1, 2
Wonnacott, Paul 1933- 21-24R
Wonnacott, Ronald J(ohnston)
1930- CANR-14
Earlier sketch in CA 29-32R
Wonnacott, Thomas H(erbert)
1935- CANR-14
Earlier sketch in CA 45-48
Wonodi, Okogbule 1936- .... CP 1
Woo, John 1946- .... AAYA 35
Woo, Wing Thye 1954- 170
Wood, A(rthur) Skevington 1916- CANR-40
Earlier sketches in CA 9-12R, CANR-3, 18
Wood, Abigail
See Marks, Jane (A. Steinberg)
Wood, Addie Robinson
See Wiggin, Eric E(llsworth)
Wood, Allen Tate 1947- 97-100
Wood, Allen W(illiam) 1942- CANR-110
Earlier sketches in CA 29-32R, CANR-17, 37
Wood, Ann
See Douglas, Ann
Wood, Ann Douglas
See Douglas, Ann
Wood, Anne (Savage) 1937- .... SATA 64
Wood, Anthony a 1632-1695 .... DLB 213
Wood, Audrey CANR-118
Earlier sketch in CA 137
See also CLR 26
See also MAICYA 1, 2
See also SATA 50, 81, 139
See also SATA-Brief 44
Wood, Audrey 1905-1985 .... CANR-56
Obituary 118
Earlier sketch in CA 153
Wood, Barbara 1947- CANR-109
Earlier sketches in CA 85-88, CANR-15, 44
See also RHW
Wood, Bari 1936- CANR-50
Earlier sketches in CA 81-84, CANR-13
Interview in CANR-13
See also HGG
Wood, Barry 1940- CANR-36
Earlier sketch in CA 29-32R
Wood, Benjamin 1820-1900
Brief entry 120
See also DLB 23
Wood, Bridget 1947- CANR-144
Earlier sketch in CA 155
See also FANT
Wood, Bruce 1943- 57-60
Wood, Bryce 1909-1985(?) CANR-19
Earlier sketch in CA 1-4R
Wood, Catherine
See Etchison, Birdie L(ee)
Wood, Charles Gerald 1932- 106
See also CBD
See also CD 5, 6
See also DLB 13
Wood, Charles Monroe 1944- 125
Wood, Charles Osgood III 1933- CANR-141
Earlier sketch in CA 109
Interview in CA-109
Wood, Charles T(uttle) 1933- CANR-30
Earlier sketch in CA 17-20R
Wood, Chauncey 1935- 37-40R
Wood, Christopher (Hovelle) 1935- . CANR-43
Earlier sketch in CA 29-32R
Wood, Christopher 1941- CANR-36
Earlier sketch in CA 103
Wood, Clement Biddle 1925-1994 .... 21-24R
Obituary 147
Wood, Crystal 1955- 178
Wood, Curtis W(illiam), Jr. 1941- 167
Wood, David 1944- CANR-141
Earlier sketches in CA 97-100, CANR-52
See also CWRI 5
See also SATA 87
Wood, David (Bowne) 1945- 93-96
Wood, David G. 1919- 126
Wood, David M(ichael) 1934-
Brief entry 109
Wood, Dennis (Michael) 1947- 140
Wood, Derek Harold 1930- CANR-16
Earlier sketch in CA 93-96
Wood, Don 1945- 136
See also CLR 26
See also MAICYA 1, 2
See also SATA 50
See also SATA-Brief 44
Wood, Donald 1926- 45-48
Wood, Donna (Marie) 1949- CANR-41
Earlier sketches in CA 97-100, CANR-18
Wood, Dorothy Adkins 1912-1975 .... CANR-6
Earlier sketch in CA 13-16R
Wood, Douglas (Eric) 1951- CANR-116
Earlier sketch in CA 149
See also MAICYA 2
See also SATA 81, 132
Wood, E(dward) Rudolf 1907- CANR-3
Earlier sketch in CA 9-12R
Wood, E. Thomas 1963- 220
Wood, Ed
See Wood, Edward D(avis), Jr.
Wood, Edgar A(llardyce) 1907-1998 77-80
See also SATA 14
Wood, Edward D(avis), Jr. 1924-1978 174
Wood, Edward John 1931- CANR-68
Earlier sketch in CA 141
See also CMW 4
Wood, Elizabeth A(rmstrong) 1912- .. CANR-30
Earlier sketch in CA 25-28R
Wood, Ellen Price -2000 .... RGEL 2
Wood, Esther
See Brady, Esther Wood
Wood, Forrest G(len) 1931- 25-28R
Wood, Frances Elizabeth 107
See also SATA 34
Wood, Frances M. 1951- 164
See also SATA 97
Wood, Fred M. 1921- CANR-26
Earlier sketches in CA 13-16R, CANR-10
Wood, Frederic C(onger), Jr.
1932-1970 .... CAP-2
Earlier sketch in CA 25-28
Wood, Frederick Thomas 1905- CANR-5
Earlier sketch in CA 5-8R
Wood, G(eorge) R(obert) Harding
1878-1968 .... CAP-1
Earlier sketch in CA 9-10
Wood, Gaby 225
Wood, Gerald C. 1944- CANR-139
Earlier sketch in CA 173
Wood, Gordon R(eid) 1913-1993 77-80
Wood, Gordon S(tewart) 1933- 25-28R
Wood, Graham R. 1945- 238
Wood, Harley Weston 1911-1984 109
Wood, Harold A(rthur) 1921- 17-20R
Wood, (Elizabeth) Harriet Harvey
See Harvey Wood, (Elizabeth) Harriet
Wood, Mrs. Henry 1814-1887 .... CMW 4
See also DLB 18
See also SUFW
Wood, Herbert Fairlie 1914-1967 110
Obituary 108
Wood, Ian N(icholas) 1950- 145
Wood, (David) Ira 1950- 142
Wood, J(ohn) Howard 1901-1988
Obituary 127
Wood, James 1889(?)-1975
Obituary 57-60
Wood, James (Alexander Fraser)
1918-1984 .... CANR-16
Earlier sketches in CA 1-4R, CANR-1
Wood, James 1965- 235
Wood, James E(dward), Jr. 1922- CANR-110
Earlier sketches in CA 29-32R, CANR-12, 28
Wood, James L(eslie) 1941- CANR-8
Earlier sketch in CA 57-60
Wood, James Playsted 1905- CANR-3
Earlier sketch in CA 9-12R
See also BYA 2, 3
See also SATA 1
Wood, Jamie (Martinez) 1967- 210
Wood, Jane Roberts 1927- 200
Wood, Janet L(ouise) Sims
See Sims-Wood, Janet L(ouise)
Wood, Jenny 1955- .... SATA 88
Wood, Joan Wentworth
See Morgan, Joan
Wood, Joanna E. 1867-1927 210
See also DLB 92
Wood, John 1947- 136
Wood, John A(rmstead, Jr.) 1932- 125
Brief entry 108
Wood, John C(unningham) 1952- 133
Wood, John Norris 1930- .... SATA 85
Wood, John Thomas 1939- 77-80
Wood, Jonathan 1945- 128
Wood, Joyce 1928- 25-28R
Wood, June Rae 1946- 191
See also AAYA 39
See also CLR 82
See also SATA 79, 120
Wood, June S(mallwood) 1931- 61-64
Wood, Kenneth 1922- CANR-26
Earlier sketches in CA 69-72, CANR-11
Wood, Kerry
See Wood, Edgar A(llardyce)
Wood, Kieron 1949- 231
Wood, Kim Marie 203
See also SATA 134
Wood, Kirk
See Stahl, LeRoy
Wood, Lana 1946- 139
Wood, Larry
See Wood, Marylaird
Wood, Laura N.
See Roper, Laura (Newbold) Wood
Wood, Lee Blair 1893-1982
Obituary 106
Wood, Leland Foster 1885-1981 .... 1-4R

Wood 630 CONTEMPORARY AUTHORS

Wood, Leon J(ames) 1918-1976 .... CANR-26
Earlier sketch in CA 29-32R
Wood, Leonard C(lair) 1923- 37-40R
Wood, Leslie A(lfred) 1930- 29-32R
Wood, (James) Lew(is) 1928- 65-68
Wood, Linda C(arol) 1945- 110
See also SATA 59
Wood, Lorna 1913- 69-72
Wood, M. Sandra 1947- 192
Wood, Marcia (Mae) 1956- 148
See also SATA 80
Wood, Margaret (Lucy Elizabeth)
1910- CANR-42
Earlier sketch in CA 13-16R
Wood, Margaret 1950- 211
Wood, Margaret I(sabel) 1926- 97-100
Wood, Marion N(ewman) 1909- 61-64
Wood, Mary 1915-2002 .... 21-24R
Wood, Marylaird CANR-21
Earlier sketch in CA 81-84
Wood, Maurice Arthur Ponsonby 1916- 109
Wood, Michael 1936- CANR-105
Earlier sketches in CA 37-40R, CANR-53
Wood, Monica 1953- 141
Wood, N. Lee 167
Wood, Nancy 1936- CANR-9
Earlier sketch in CA 21-24R
See also SATA 6
Wood, Neal (Norman) 1922- 1-4R
Wood, Nuria
See Nobisso, Josephine
Wood, Owen 1929- .... SATA 64
Wood, Pat
See Baxter, Patricia E. W.
Wood, Paul W(inthrop)
1922-2003 .... CANR-143
Earlier sketch in CA 61-64
Wood, Peggy 1892-1978
Obituary 77-80
Wood, Peter 1930- 93-96
Wood, Peter (W.) 1953- 237
Wood, Peter Weston 1953- 125
Wood, Phyllis Anderson 1923- CANR-43
Earlier sketches in CA 37-40R, CANR-14
See also SATA 33
See also SATA-Brief 30
Wood, R(ichard) Coke 1905-1979 ...... CANR-7
Earlier sketch in CA 53-56
Wood, Ralph C. 1942- 145
Wood, Ramsay 1943- 103
Wood, Raymund F(rancis) 1911-1998 61-64
Wood, Richard 1949- 180
See also SATA 110
Wood, Robert C(oldwell)
1923-2005 .... CANR-43
Obituary 238
Earlier sketch in CA 1-4R
Wood, Robert Chapman 1949- 139
Wood, Robert L. 1925- 21-24R
Wood, Robert Paul 1931- CANR-136
Earlier sketches in CA 53-56, CANR-5
Wood, Robert S(tephen) 1938- CANR-7
Earlier sketch in CA 57-60
Wood, Robin
See Wood, Robert Paul
Wood, Ruth C. 37-40R
Wood, Ruzena (Alenka Valda) 1937- 135
Wood, Sally Sayward Barrell Keating
1759-1855 .... DLB 200
Wood, Sara
See Bowen-Judd, Sara (Hutton)
See also RHW
Wood, Serry
See Freeman, G(raydon) L(a Verne)
Wood, Stephanie 1954- 169
See also HW 2
Wood, Susan 1946- 108
Wood, Susan Macduff 1941- 132
Wood, Sydney (Herbert) 1935- CANR-60
Earlier sketches in CA 112, CANR-31
Wood, Ted
See Wood, Edward John
Wood, Thomas W(esley), Jr. 1920-1998 .. 81-84
Wood, Tim(othy William Russell)
1946- .... SATA 88
Wood, Ursula
See Vaughan Williams, Ursula Wood
Wood, W(illiam) J. 1917-1997 135
Wood, Wallace 1927-1981
Obituary 108
See also SATA-Obit 33
Wood, Walter Hunt Sr. 1916(?)-1987
Obituary 124
Wood, William .... DLB 24
Wood, William P(reston) 1951- CANR-42
Earlier sketch in CA 118
Woodall, Clive 1957(?)- 236
Woodall, Corbet 1929(?)-1982
Obituary 106
Woodall, Mary 1901-1988
Obituary 125
Woodall, Ronald 1935- 73-76
Woodard, Bronte 1941(?)-1980
Obituary 101
Woodard, Carol 1929- 73-76
See also SATA 14
Woodard, Christopher R(oy)
1913-2001 .... 13-16R
Obituary 203
Woodard, Colin 1968- 192
Woodard, Gloria (Jean) H(iner) 1937- 45-48
Woodard, Helena 1953- 185
Woodard, Komozi 1949- 194
Woodard, Michael D. 1946- 169
Woodberry, George Edward 1855-1930 165
See also DLB 71, 103
See also TCLC 73
Woodberry, Joan (Merle) 1921- CANR-6
Earlier sketch in CA 9-12R
Woodbridge, Benjamin 1622-1684 ...... DLB 24
Woodbridge, Frederick J. E.
1867-1940 .... DLB 270
Woodbridge, Hensley Charles 1923- .. CANR-3
Earlier sketch in CA 9-12R
Woodbridge, Kenneth 1910-1988 127
Woodbridge, Linda 1945- 118
Woodbridge, (Barbara) Patricia 1946- 210
Woodbridge, Sally
See Woodbridge, Sally B(yrne)
Woodbridge, Sally B(yrne) 1930- CANR-67
Earlier sketch in CA 129
Woodburn, Arthur 1890-1978
Obituary 108
Woodburn, John Henry 1914- CANR-4
Earlier sketch in CA 1-4R
See also SATA 11
Woodbury, David Oakes 1896-1981 ... SATA 62
Woodbury, Frank
See Chapman, Frank M(onroe)
Woodbury, Lael J(ay) 1927- 81-84
Woodbury, Marda 1925- CANR-87
Earlier sketches in CA 97-100, CANR-17
Woodbury, Mildred Fairchild 1894-1975
Obituary 57-60
Woodbury, Richard B(enjamin) 1917-
Brief entry 109
Woodcock, Bruce 1948- 119
Woodcock, George 1912-1995 .... CANR-1
Obituary 147
Earlier sketch in CA 1-4R
See also CAAS 6
See also CP 1, 2
See also DLB 88
Woodcott, Keith
See Brunner, John (Kilian Houston)
Woodcraft, Elizabeth 215
Wooden, John 1910- 201
Wooden, Kenneth 1935- 81-84
Wooden, Warren W(alter) 1941-1983 132
Wooden, Wayne S(tanley) 1943- 109
Woodfield, Ian 1951- 222
Woodfield, William Read 1928-2001 ...... 9-12R
Obituary 203
Woodford, Arthur M(acKinnon)
1940- CANR-7
Earlier sketch in CA 53-56
Woodford, Bruce P(owers) 1919- 57-60
Woodford, Frank B(ury) 1903-1967 .... CAP-1
Earlier sketch in CA 13-16
Woodford, Jack
See Woolfolk, Josiah Pitts
Woodford, Peggy 1937- 104
See also SATA 25
Woodford, Susan 1938- 128
Woodforde, John 1925- CANR-10
Earlier sketch in CA 25-28R
Woodgate, Mildred Violet 9-12R
Woodger, Elin 1954- 233
Woodham-Smith, Cecil (Blanche Fitzgerald)
1896-1977 77-80
Obituary 69-72
Woodhead, Leslie 1937- 128
Woodhead, Peter 1944- 124
Woodhouse, Barbara (Blackburn)
1910-1988 .... CANR-30
Obituary 126
Earlier sketches in CA 5-8R, CANR-13
See also SATA 63
Woodhouse, C(hristopher) M(ontague)
1917-2001 155
Obituary 194
Brief entry 108
Woodhouse, Charles Platten 1915- 105
Woodhouse, Edward J(ames) 1946- 117
Woodhouse, Emma
See Harrod-Eagles, Cynthia
Woodhouse, John (Robert) 1937- 174
Woodhouse, Martin (Charlton)
1932- CANR-16
Earlier sketch in CA 21-24R
Woodhouse, S. T. 1958- 233
Woodhouse, Sarah 160
Woodhull, Victoria Claflin 1838-1927 180
See also DLB 79
Woodhull, Winifred 1950- 146
Woodin, Ann Snow 1926- 13-16R
Woodin, Noel 1929- 1-4R
Wooding, Dan 1940- 102
Wooding, Sharon
See Wooding, Sharon L(ouise)
Wooding, Sharon L(ouise) 1943- 136
See also SATA 66
Woodiwiss, Kathleen E(rin) 1939- CANR-99
Earlier sketches in CA 89-92, CANR-23, 41, 76
Interview in CANR-23
See also BEST 90:1
See also DA3
See also DAM POP
See also MTCW 1, 2
See also MTFW 2005
See also RHW
Woodiwiss, Michael J. 1950- 223
Wood-Legh, Kathleen Louise 1901-1981
Obituary 105
Woodley, Winifred
See Hedden, Worth Tuttle
Woodman, Allen 1954- 143
See also SATA 76
Woodman, Anthony John 1945- CANR-23
Earlier sketches in CA 61-64, CANR-8
Woodman, Bill
See Woodman, William
Woodman, David C(harles) 1956- 141
Woodman, Harold D. 1928- CANR-9
Earlier sketch in CA 21-24R
Woodman, James Monroe 1931- 17-20R
Woodman, Jim
See Woodman, James Monroe
Woodman, John E. 1932(?)-1983
Obituary 109
Woodman, Loring 1942- 45-48
Woodman, Marion (Boa) 1928- CANR-103
Earlier sketch in CA 162
Woodman, Richard 1944- CANR-97
Earlier sketch in CA 132
See also RHW
Woodman, William 1936- 125
Woodmason, Charles 1720(?)-(?) .... DLB 31
Woodrell, Daniel 1953- CANR-85
Earlier sketches in CA 121, CANR-46
Woodress, James (Leslie, Jr.) 1916- CANR-3
Earlier sketch in CA 5-8R
See also DLB 111
Woodrew, Greta 1930- 106
Woodrich, Mary Neville 1915- 25-28R
See also SATA 2
Woodring, Carl (Ray) 1919- CANR-96
Earlier sketch in CA 5-8R
Woodring, Jim 1952- 226
Woodring, Paul (Dean) 1907-1994 .... 17-20R
Woodrock, R. A.
See Cowlishaw, Ranson
Woodroffe, John
See Woodroffe, John George
Woodroffe, John George 1865-1936
Brief entry 121
Woodroof, Horace M(alcolm)
1906-1975 .... CAP-2
Earlier sketch in CA 29-32
Woodruff, Archibald Mulford, Jr.
1912-1984 105
Obituary 113
Woodruff, Asahel D(avis) 1904-1994 .... 1-4R
Woodruff, Elvira 1951- 138
See also SATA 70, 106, 162
Woodruff, J(ohn) Douglas 1897-1978 107
Obituary 104
Woodruff, Joan Leslie 1953- CANR-137
Earlier sketch in CA 171
See also SATA 104
Woodruff, Judy (Carline) 1946- CANR-13
Earlier sketch in CA 73-76
Woodruff, Marian
See Goudge, Eileen
Woodruff, Marian
See Goudge, Eileen
Woodruff, Nancy 1963- 203
Woodruff, Noah 1977- .... SATA 86
Woodruff, Philip
See Mason, Philip
Woodruff, Robert W.
See Mencken, H(enry) L(ouis)
Woodruff, Sue (Carolyn) 1943- 117
Woodruff, William 1916- 101
Woodrum, Lon 1901-1995 104
Woods, B(obby) W(illiam) 1930- CANR-19
Earlier sketch in CA 25-28R
Woods, Brenda (A.) 239
Woods, Clee 1893-1990 108
Woods, Constance
See McComb, K(atherine Woods)
Woods, Donald 1933-2001 .... CANR-78
Obituary 199
Brief entry 114
Earlier sketch in CA 121
Interview in CA-121
Woods, Donald H. 1933- 25-28R
Woods, Earl 1932- 161
Woods, Elizabeth 1940- 101
Woods, Frederick 1932- CANR-7
Earlier sketch in CA 17-20R
Woods, George A(llan) 1926-1988 .... 29-32R
Obituary 126
See also SATA 30
See also SATA-Obit 57
Woods, Geraldine 1948- 97-100
See also SATA 56, 111
See also SATA-Brief 42
Woods, Gerard
See Bosch, Henry G(erard)
Woods, Gregory 1953- 129
Woods, Harold 1945- 97-100
See also SATA 56
See also SATA-Brief 42
Woods, Harriett 1927- 194
Woods, James M. 1952- 125
Woods, Jeannie Marlin 1947- CANR-93
Earlier sketch in CA 145
Woods, Joan (LeSueur) 1932- 9-12R
Woods, John 1926- CANR-23
Earlier sketch in CA 13-16R
See also CP 1, 2, 3, 4, 5, 6, 7
Woods, John (Hayden) 1937- CANR-11
Earlier sketch in CA 57-60
Woods, John A(ubin) 1927- 13-16R
Woods, John B(arrie) 1933-
Brief entry 107
Woods, John David 1939- 37-40R
Woods, John E(dmund) 1938- 104
Woods, Kenneth F. 1930- 13-16R
Woods, L. B. 1938- 112
Woods, L(awrence) Milton 1932- 127
Woods, Lawrence
See Lowndes, Robert A(ugustine) W(ard)
Woods, Lawrence T(imothy) 1960- .. CANR-99
Earlier sketch in CA 147
Woods, Margaret 1921- 21-24R
See also SATA 2
Woods, Margaret L(ouisa) 1855-1945 204
Woods, Margaret L. 1855-1945 .... DLB 240
Woods, Margaret S(taeger)
1911-1999 .... CANR-44
Earlier sketch in CA 81-84
Woods, Michael 1952- 137
Woods, Nat
See Stratemeyer, Edward L.
Woods, Oliver (Frederick John Bradley)
1911-1972
Obituary 114
Woods, P. F.
See Bayley, Barrington J(ohn)
Woods, Pamela 1938- CANR-138
Earlier sketch in CA 106
Woods, Paula L. 1953- CANR-96
Earlier sketch in CA 146
Woods, Ralph L(ouis) 1904-1989 .... CANR-2
Earlier sketch in CA 5-8R
Woods, Randall Bennett 1944-
Brief entry 106
Woods, Richard (John) 1941- CANR-4
Earlier sketch in CA 53-56
Woods, Richard G(lenn) 1933- 109
Woods, Samuel H(ubert), Jr. 1926- 25-28R
Woods, Sara
See Bowen-Judd, Sara (Hutton)
Woods, Shadrach 1923-1973
Obituary 45-48
Woods, Sharon 1949- 125
Woods, Sherryl 1944- CANR-121
Earlier sketches in CA 120, CANR-65
See also RHW
Woods, Shirley E(dwards), Jr. 1934- 119
Woods, Sister Frances Jerome
1913-1992 .... 21-24R
Woods, Stockton
See Forrest, Richard (Stockton)
Woods, Stuart 1938- CANR-134
Earlier sketches in CA 93-96, CANR-72
See also CPW
See also HGG
Woods, William 1916- CANR-43
Earlier sketch in CA 77-80
Woods, William Crawford 1944- 29-32R
Woodside, Alexander Barton 1938- .. CANR-51
Earlier sketch in CA 123
Woodson, Carter G(odwin) 1875-1950 141
See also BW 2
See also DLB 17
Woodson, Jack
See Woodson, John Waddie Jr.
Woodson, Jacqueline (Amanda)
1964- CANR-129
Earlier sketches in CA 159, CANR-87
See also AAYA 54
See also CLR 49
See also GLL 2
See also MAICYA 2
See also MAICYAS 1
See also MTFW 2005
See also SATA 94, 139
See also WYAS 1
See also YAW
Woodson, Jeff
See Oglesby, Joseph
Woodson, John Waddie Jr. 1913- .... SATA 10
Woodson, Leslie H(arold) 1929- 41-44R
Woodson, Meg
See Baker, Elsie
Woodson, Robert L. 1937- 127
Woodson, Thomas (Miller) 1931- 104
Woodson, Wesley E(dward) 1918- 37-40R
Woodstone, Arthur 69-72
Woodstra, Christopher 1969- 145
Woodtor, Dee
See Woodtor, Delores Parmer
Woodtor, Dee Parmer 1945(?)-2002
See Woodtor, Delores Parmer
Woodtor, Delores Parmer
1945-2002 .... CANR-87
Obituary 209
Earlier sketch in CA 158
See also SATA 93
Wood-Trost, Lucille
See Trost, Lucille W(ood)
Woodward, Bob
See Woodward, Robert Upshur
Woodward, C. Hendrika
See Woodward, Caroline (Hendrika)
Woodward, C(omer) Vann
1908-1999 .... CANR-95
Earlier sketches in CA 5-8R, CANR-2, 17, 44
See also CSW
See also DLB 17
Woodward, Carl Raymond 1890-1974 . 41-44R
Woodward, Caroline (Hendrika) 1952- 146
Woodward, (Landon) Cleveland
1900-1986 .... SATA 10
See also SATA-Obit 48
Woodward, Daniel Holt 1931- 37-40R
Woodward, David 1909-1986
Obituary 120
Woodward, David B(rainerd) 1918- 65-68
Woodward, David Reid 1939- CANR-85
Earlier sketch in CA 114
Woodward, Douglas P. 1954- 135
Woodward, E. L.
See Woodward, Ernest Llewellyn
Woodward, Ernest Llewellyn 1890-1971
Obituary 111
Woodward, G(eorge) W(illiam) O(tway)
1924- CANR-3
Earlier sketch in CA 5-8R
Woodward, Gerard (Vaughan) 1961- 236
Woodward, Grace Steele 1899-1987 .... CAP-1
Earlier sketch in CA 9-10
Woodward, Helen Beal 1914(?)-1982
Obituary 108

Woodward, Helen Rosen 1882-1969 .... 5-8R
Woodward, Herbert N(orton) 1911- 65-68
Woodward, Hildegard 1898-1977 .... 5-8R
Woodward, James B(rian) 1935- CANR-2
Earlier sketch in CA 49-52
Woodward, John (William) 1920- 21-24R
Woodward, John (O.) 1922(?)-1988
Obituary 125
Woodward, John 1945- 113
Woodward, John Forster
See Woodward, Sandy
Woodward, Kenneth L. 1935- 141
Woodward, Lilian
See Marsh, John
See also RHW
Woodward, Llewellyn
See Woodward, Ernest Llewellyn
Woodward, Margaret E. 1950- 150
Woodward, Ralph Lee, Jr. 1934- 21-24R
Woodward, Robert B(urns) 1917-1979 161
Woodward, Robert H(anson) 1925- 17-20R
Woodward, Robert Upshur 1943- .. CANR-107
Earlier sketches in CA 69-72, CANR-31, 67
See also MTCW 1
Woodward, Sandy 1932- 143
Woodward, Stanley (Wingate) 1890-1970 . 5-8R
See also DLB 171
Woodward, Thomas B. 1937- 114
Woodward, W. Mary 1921- 45-48
Woodwell, George M. 1928- 142
Woodwell, William H., Jr. 208
Woodworth, Constance 1911-1983
Obituary 109
Woodworth, David (Perrin) 1932- 37-40R
Woodworth, G(eorge) Wallace
1902-1969 .... CAP-1
Earlier sketch in CA 13-16
Woodworth, G(eorge) Walter
1903-1993 .... CAP-1
Earlier sketch in CA 19-20
Woodworth, Hugh (MacCallum) 1906-1978
Obituary 107
Woodworth, Samuel 1785-1842 .... DLB 250
Woodworth, Steven E(dward) 1961- . CANR-93
Earlier sketch in CA 135
Woodworth, Viki 1952- .... SATA 127
Woody, Elizabeth (Ann) 1959- CANR-126
Earlier sketch in CA 152
Woody, Regina Jones 1894-1983 .... CANR-3
Earlier sketch in CA 5-8R
See also SATA 3
Woody, Robert H(enley) 1936- 93-96
Woody, Russell O(wen), Jr. 1934- 17-20R
Woodyard, David O. 1932- 21-24R
Woodyard, George 1934- 81-84
Woog, Adam 1953- CANR-105
Earlier sketch in CA 150
See also SATA 84, 125
Woog, Dan 1953- CANR-118
Earlier sketch in CA 167
Woolard, Edgar 1899(?)-1978
Obituary 77-80
Wooldridge, Adrian 1959- 152
Wooldridge, Connie Nordhielm
1950- CANR-117
Earlier sketch in CA 156
See also SATA 92, 143
Wooldridge, Frosty 1947- 209
Wooldridge, Frosty 1947- .... SATA 140
Wooldridge, Rhoda 1906-1988 77-80
See also SATA 22
Wooldridge, William C(harles)
1943- CANR-25
Earlier sketch in CA 45-48
Wooler, Thomas 1785(?)-1853 .... DLB 158
Woolery, George W(illiam) 1931- CANR-49
Earlier sketch in CA 122
Woolever, Cynthia A. 1954- 220
Wooley, John (Steven) 1949- CANR-119
Earlier sketch in CA 109
Wooley, Marilyn J. 1951- 201
Wooley, Peter 1934- 209
Wooley, Susan Frelick 1945- 175
See also SATA 113
Woolf, Alan D(avid) 1950- 193
Woolf, Daniel J(ames) 1916- 5-8R
Woolf, Douglas 1922-1992 .... CANR-2
Earlier sketch in CA 1-4R
See also CN 1, 2, 3, 4, 5
See also DLB 244
See also TCWW 1
Woolf, Greg 234
Woolf, Harry 1923-2003 .... CANR-1
Obituary 212
Earlier sketch in CA 1-4R
Woolf, James Dudley 1914- 37-40R
Woolf, Leonard S(idney) 1880-1969 . CANR-39
Obituary 25-28R
Earlier sketch in CA 5-8R
See also DLB 100
See also DLBD 10
Woolf, Paula 1950- 171
See also SATA 104
Woolf, Robert G(ary) 1928- 73-76
Woolf, S. J.
See Woolf, Stuart J(oseph)
Woolf, Stuart J(oseph) 1936- 153
Brief entry 118
Woolf, (Adeline) Virginia
1882-1941 .... CANR-132
Brief entry 104
Earlier sketches in CA 130, CANR-64
See also AAYA 44
See also BPFB 3
See also BRW 7
See also BRWC 2
See also BRWR 1
See also CDBLB 1914-1945
See also DA
See also DA3
See also DAB
See also DAC
See also DAM MST, NOV
See also DLB 36, 100, 162
See also DLBD 10
See also EWL 3
See also EXPS
See also FL 1:6
See also FW
See also LAIT 3
See also LATS 1:1
See also LMFS 2
See also MTCW 1, 2
See also MTFW 2005
See also NCFS 2
See also NFS 8, 12
See also RGEL 2
See also RGSF 2
See also SSC 7, 79
See also SSFS 4, 12
See also TCLC 1, 5, 20, 43, 56, 101, 123, 128
See also TEA
See also WLC
See also WLIT 4
Woolfe, F. X.
See Engel, Howard
Woolfe, H(arold) Geoffrey 1902- CAP-1
Earlier sketch in CA 11-12
Woolfe, Jennifer A(nne) 1944- 144
Woolfe, Sue 1950- 165
Woolfenden, John R(ichards) 1904-1988 113
Woolfolk, Joanna Martine 1940- 110
Woolfolk, Josiah Pitts 1894-1971
Obituary 29-32R
Woolfolk, Robert L(ee IV) 1947- 185
Brief entry 112
Woolfolk, William 1917-2003 113
Obituary 218
See also AAYA 64
Woolfson, Jonathan 195
Woolgar, C. M. 174
Woolgar, (George) Jack 1894-1987 .... 17-20R
Woollam, William Gifford 1921- 9-12R
Woollcott, Alexander (Humphreys)
1887-1943 161
Brief entry 105
See also DLB 29
See also TCLC 5
Woollen, Geoff 1945- 142
Woolley, A(lban) E(dward, Jr.)
1926- CANR-14
Earlier sketch in CA 41-44R
Woolley, Benjamin 235
Woolley, Bryan 1937- .... TCWW 2
Woolley, (Lowell) Bryan 1937- CANR-79
Earlier sketches in CA 49-52, CANR-4
Woolley, Catherine 1904-2005 .... CANR-6
Earlier sketch in CA 1-4R
See also SATA 3
Woolley, Davis Collier 1908-1971
Obituary 116
Woolley, Geoffrey Harold 1892-1968 ... CAP-1
Earlier sketch in CA 11-12
Woolley, Herbert B(allantyne) 1917-1978
Obituary 81-84
Woolley, Lisa 1960- 208
Woolley, Paul 1948- 146
Woolley, Peter J. 1960- 226
Woolley, Richard van der Riet 1906-1986
Obituary 121
Woolley, Robert (C.) 1944- 152
Woolley, (Alfred) Russell 1899-1986 .... 5-8R
Woolls, (Esther) Blanche 1935- CANR-39
Earlier sketch in CA 126
Woolman, David S. 1916- 29-32R
Woolman, John 1720-1772 .... DLB 31
Woolman, Steven 1969-2004 ...... SATA 90, 163
Woolner, Frank 1916- 53-56
Woolner, Thomas 1825-1892 .... DLB 35
Woolrich, Cornell
See Hopley-Woolrich, Cornell George
See also CLC 77
See also MSW
Woolrych, Austin (Herbert)
1918-2004 .... CANR-42
Obituary 231
Earlier sketch in CA 1-4R
Woolsey, Arthur (Wallace) 1906- 45-48
Woolsey, Gamel 1895(?)-1968 172
Woolsey, Janette 1904-1989 .... CANR-2
Obituary 200
Earlier sketch in CA 1-4R
See also SATA 3
See also SATA-Obit 131
Woolsey, Sarah Chauncy 1835(?)-1905
Brief entry 115
See also DLB 42
Woolson, Constance Fenimore
1840-1894 .... DLB 12, 74, 189, 221
See also RGAL 4
Woolson, Roland S., Jr. 1930(?)-1977
Obituary 104
Woolston, Mary
See Hensley, Sophie Almon
Woolverton, John F(rederick) 1926- 158
Woon, Basil 1894(?)-1974
Obituary 49-52
Wooster, Claire 1942- 101
Wooster, Ralph A(ncil) 1928- CANR-2
Earlier sketch in CA 5-8R
Wooster, Robert 1956- 124
Wooten, James (Terrell) 1937- 185
Brief entry 112
Wooten, Jim
See Wooten, James (Terrell)
Wootson, Alice (G.) 1937- 208
Wootten, Morgan 1931- 101
Wootters, John (Henry, Jr.) 1928- CANR-43
Earlier sketch in CA 113
Wootton, Anthony 1935- 129
Wootton, Barbara (Frances Adam) 1897-1988
Obituary 126
Wootton, (Devere) Gareth 1937- 117
Wootton, (John) Graham (George)
1917- CANR-10
Earlier sketch in CA 5-8R
Wootton, Richard .... BYA 9
Worblefister, Petunia
See Gribbin, Lenore S.
Worboys, Anne(tte Isobel) Eyre CANR-60
Earlier sketches in CA 65-68, CANR-9
See also RHW
Worcester, Dean A(mory), Jr. 1918- 21-24R
Worcester, Donald E(mmet) 1915- CANR-19
Earlier sketches in CA 1-4R, CANR-4
See also SATA 18
Worcester, Gurdon Saltonstall
1897-1978 .... CAP-1
Obituary 202
Earlier sketch in CA 11-12
Worcester, Joseph Emerson 1784-1865 .. DLB 1, 235
Worcester, Kent 1959- 157
Worcester, Robert M(ilton) 1933- ... CANR-138
Earlier sketch in CA 134
Worchel, Stephen 1946- CANR-37
Earlier sketches in CA 89-92, CANR-16
Word, Reagan 1944- .... SATA 103
Worden, Alfred M(errill) 1932- 101
Worden, J. William 168
Worden, William L. 1910-1982 .... CAP-1
Earlier sketch in CA 13-16
Wordsworth, Christopher 1807-1885 . DLB 166
Wordsworth, Dorothy 1771-1855 .... DLB 107
Wordsworth, Elizabeth 1840-1932 186
See also DLB 98
Wordsworth, Jonathan 1932- CANR-143
Earlier sketches in CA 29-32R, CANR-20
Wordsworth, William 1770-1850 .... BRW 4
See also BRWC 1
See also CDBLB 1789-1832
See also DA
See also DA3
See also DAB
See also DAC
See also DAM MST, POET
See also DLB 93, 107
See also EXPP
See also LATS 1:1
See also LMFS 1
See also PAB
See also PC 4, 67
See also PFS 2
See also RGEL 2
See also TEA
See also WLC
See also WLIT 3
See also WP
Worell, Judith 1928- CANR-7
Earlier sketch in CA 57-60
Work, Alison R. 1956- 128
Work, Robert E. 1928(?)-1986
Obituary 121
Work, Virginia 1946- 113
See also SATA 57
See also SATA-Brief 45
Working, Russell (Craig) 1959- 124
Workman, Fanny Bullock 1859-1925 182
See also DLB 189
Workman, Samuel K(linger)
1907-1988 .... CAP-2
Earlier sketch in CA 23-24
Workman, William D(ouglas), Jr.
1914-1990 .... 5-8R
Works, John 1949- 123
Worland, Stephen T. 1923- 21-24R
Worley, Robert Cromwell 1929-
Brief entry 108
Worline, Bonnie Bess 1914- 69-72
See also SATA 14
Worlock, Derek John Harford 1920-1996 .. 103
Obituary 151
Worm, Piet 1909- 81-84
Wormald, Francis 1904(?)-1972
Obituary 104
Wormald, Jenny 1942- CANR-32
Earlier sketch in CA 112
Wormald, (Charles) Patrick
1947-2004 .... CANR-75
Obituary 231
Earlier sketch in CA 132
Worman, Charles G(ordon) 1933- 119
Worman, Eli
See Weil, Roman L(ee)
Wormell, Christopher 1955- ...... SATA 103, 154
Wormell, Deborah 1946-1979
Obituary 114
Wormell, Mary 1959- CANR-119
Earlier sketch in CA 148
See also SATA 96
Wormington, Hannah Marie
1914-1994 .... CANR-3
Obituary 145
Earlier sketch in CA 45-48
Wormley, Cinda
See Kornblum, Cinda
Wormley, Stanton Lawrence
1909-1993 .... CANR-12
Obituary 142
Earlier sketch in CA 73-76
Wormser, Baron Chesley 1948- 110
Wormser, Rene A(lbert) 1896-1981 .. CANR-11
Obituary 104
Earlier sketch in CA 13-16R
Wormser, Richard (Edward)
1908-1977 .... TCWW 1, 2
Wormser, Richard 1933- 176
See also AAYA 38
See also SAAS 26
See also SATA 106
See also SATA-Essay 118
Wormser, Sophie 1897-1979 65-68
Obituary 199
See also SATA 22
Worner, Karl Heinrich
See Woerner, Karl Heinrich
Woroniak, Alexander 1920- 41-44R
Woronoff, Jon 1938- CANR-29
Earlier sketches in CA 29-32R, CANR-11
Woronov, Mary (Peter) 1946- CANR-142
Earlier sketch in CA 149
Woronov, Naomi 1938- 132
Worrall, Ambrose A(lexander)
1899-1972 .... CAP-2
Earlier sketch in CA 29-32
Worrall, Olga (Nathalie Ripich)
1906-1985 .... 29-32R
Obituary 182
Worrall, Simon 237
Worrell, Albert C(adwallader)
1913-2000 .... 37-40R
Worrell, Eric 1924-1987
Obituary 123
Worrell, Rupert DeLisle 1945- 146
Worrick, Roberta 1941-1989
Obituary 129
Worsham, Lynn 1953- 170
Worsley, Dale 1948- 104
Worsley, F(rank) A(rthur) 1872-1943 219
Worsley, Gump
See Worsley, Lorne (John)
Worsley, Lorne (John) 1929-
Brief entry 111
Worster, Donald E(ugene) 1941- CANR-42
Earlier sketches in CA 57-60, CANR-12
Worsthorne, Peregrine 1923- 45-48
Worswick, Clark 1940- CANR-138
Earlier sketches in CA 104, CANR-43
Worswick, G(eorge) D(avid) N(orman)
1916- 142
Worth, C. Brooke 1908-1984 101
Worth, Dean S(toddard) 1927-
Brief entry 112
Worth, Douglas 1940- CANR-9
Earlier sketch in CA 65-68
Worth, Fred L. 1943- 97-100
Worth, Helen 1913-2002 .... 13-16R
Worth, Katharine (Joyce) 1922- 161
Worth, Katherine J.
See Worth, Katharine (Joyce)
Worth, Margaret
See Strickland, Margot
Worth, Nicholas
See Page, Walter Hines
Worth, Richard
See Wiggin, Eric E(llsworth)
Worth, Richard 156
Worth, Richard 1945- .... SATA 59
See also SATA-Brief 46
Worth, Sol 1922(?)-1977 81-84
Obituary 73-76
Worth, Valerie -1994
See Bahlke, Valerie Worth
See also CLR 21
See also MAICYA 1, 2
See also SATA 8, 70
Wortham, John David 1941- 37-40R
Worthen, Blaine Richard 1936- CANR-15
Earlier sketch in CA 85-88
Worthen, John 225
Worthington, Edgar Barton 1905- 109
Worthington, Janet Evans 1942- 115
Worthington, Marjorie (Muir)
1898(?)-1976 .... CANR-2
Obituary 65-68
Earlier sketch in CA 1-4R
Worthington, Phoebe 1910- .... SATA-Brief 52
Worthington, Robin (Ann) 1932- 114
Worthley, Jean Reese 1925- 77-80
Worthy, James C(arson) 1910-1998 117
Worthy, Morgan 1936- 65-68
Worthylake, Mary Moore 1904-1994 . CANR-4
Earlier sketch in CA 1-4R
Wortis, Avi 1937- CANR-120
Earlier sketches in CA 69-72, CANR-12, 42
See also Avi and
Wortis, Edward (Irving)
See also JRDA
See also MAICYA 1, 2
See also MAICYAS 1
See also SATA 14
See also YAW
Wortis, Edward (Irving)
See Wortis, Avi
See also SATA 156
Wortley, Ben Atkinson 1907-1989 57-60
Obituary 129

Wortman, Marlene Stein 1937- 112
Wortman, Max S(idones), Jr. 1932- ... CANR-16
Earlier sketch in CA 21-24R
Wortman, Richard 1938- CANR-9
Earlier sketch in CA 21-24R
Wortman, (Leo) Sterling 1923-1981
Obituary 108
Worton, Stanley N(elson) 1923- 57-60
Wortsman, Peter 1952- 137
Wos, Joanna H(elena) 1951- 199
Woshinsky, Oliver H(anson) 1939- ... CANR-55
Brief entry 109
Earlier sketch in CA 127
Wosk, Julie 214
Wosmek, Frances 1917- CANR-51
Earlier sketches in CA 29-32R, CANR-11, 26
See also SATA 29
Wotton, Sir Henry 1568-1639 .... DLB 121
See also RGEL 2
Woudenberg, Paul Richard 1927- 69-72
Woudhuysen, Jan Frank 1942- 107
Woudstra, Marten H. 1922-1991 ..... CANR-19
Earlier sketch in CA 25-28R
Wouil, George
See Slaney, George Wilson
Wouk, Herman 1915- CANR-67
Earlier sketches in CA 5-8R, CANR-6, 33
Interview in CANR-6
See also BPFB 2, 3
See also CDALBS
See also CLC 1, 9, 38
See also CN 1, 2, 3, 4, 5, 6
See also CPW
See also DA3
See also DAM NOV, POP
See also DLBY 1982
See also LAIT 4
See also MAL 5
See also MTCW 1, 2
See also MTFW 2005
See also NFS 7
See also TUS
Woutat, Donald 1944- 136
Wouters, Liliane 1930- 209
Woy, James Bayly 1927- 13-16R
Woychuk, Denis 1953- .... SATA 71
Woychuk, N(icholas) A(rthur) 1915- 13-16R
Woytinsky, Emma S(hadkhan)
1893-1969 .... CAP-1
Earlier sketch in CA 17-18
Wozencraft, Kim 1955(?)- 187
Woznicki, Andrew N(icholas)
1931- CANR-111
Earlier sketches in CA 45-48, CANR-24, 49
Wrage, Ernest J. 1911-1965 .... 1-4R
Wragg, David William 1946- CANR-4
Earlier sketch in CA 53-56
Wragg, E(dward) C(onrad) 1938- CANR-47
Earlier sketches in CA 57-60, CANR-8, 23
Wragg, Joanna DiCarlo 1941- 133
Wraight, A(aron) Joseph 1913-1979 ...... 21-24R
Wray, John 1971- 217
Wrede, Patricia C(ollins) 1953- CANR-129
Earlier sketch in CA 134
See also AAYA 8, 53
See also FANT
See also MAICYA 2
See also MAICYAS 1
See also SATA 67, 146
See also YAW
Wreden, Nick 224
Wreen, Michael 1950- 117
Wreford, James
See Watson, J(ames) Wreford
See also DLB 88
Wreggitt, Andrew 1955- 138
Wren, Chris (?)-1982
Obituary 108
Wren, Sir Christopher 1632-1723 .... DLB 213
Wren, Christopher S(ale) 1936- CANR-104
Earlier sketch in CA 21-24R
Wren, Daniel Alan 1932- 41-44R
Wren, Ellaruth
See Elkins, Ella Ruth
Wren, M. K.
See Renfroe, Martha Kay
Wren, Melvin C(larence) 1910-1984 ..... 37-40R
Wren, Percival Christopher 1885-1941
Brief entry 123
See also DLB 153
See also RHW
Wren, Robert Meriwether 1928- 106
Wren, Thomas Edward 1938- 77-80
Wren, Wilfrid John 1930- 109
Wrench, David F(razer) 1932- 41-44R
Wrench, (John) Evelyn (Leslie)
1882-1966 .... 5-8R
Wrench, Sara J. 1961- 163
Wrench, Sarah
See Wrench, Sara J.
Wrenn, John H(aughton) 1920- 1-4R
Wrenn, John Henry 1841-1911 184
See also DLB 140
Wrenn, Lynette Boney 1928- 158
Wrenn, Robert L. 1933- 29-32R
Wrenn, Tony P(entecost) 1938- 89-92
Wrenn, Winnie Holden 1886(?)-1979
Obituary 89-92
Wreszin, Michael 1926- CANR-110
Earlier sketch in CA 145
Wriggins, Sally Hovey 1922- 97-100
See also SATA 17
Wriggins, W(illiam) Howard 1918- 61-64
Wright, A(nthony) Colin 1938- 120
Wright, A. D. 1947- CANR-68
Earlier sketch in CA 129
Wright, A(mos) J(asper) 1952- 93-96
Wright, Alexandra 1979- 170
See also SATA 103
Wright, Alice E(dwards) 1905-1980 104
Wright, Alison 1961- 187
Wright, Alison Elizabeth 1945-2000 202
Wright, Andrew (Howell) 1923- 17-20R
Wright, Anna (Maria Louisa Perrott) Rose
1890-1968
Obituary 109
See also SATA-Brief 35
Wright, Archie Lee 1916-1998
See Moore, Archie Lee
Wright, Arthur Frederick 1913-1976 . CANR-33
Obituary 69-72
Earlier sketch in CA 77-80
Wright, Austin 1904-1979 61-64
Wright, Austin (McGiffert) 1922- CANR-52
Earlier sketches in CA 1-4R, CANR-4
Wright, Barbara 1951- 149
Wright, Barton A(llen) 1920- CANR-8
Earlier sketch in CA 61-64
Wright, Basil Charles 1907-1987 105
Obituary 123
Wright, Beatrice A(nn) 1917- CANR-12
Earlier sketch in CA 21-24R
Wright, Benjamin Fletcher 1900-1976 77-80
Obituary 69-72
Wright, Betty Ren 147
See also JRDA
See also MAICYA 2
See also MAICYAS 1
See also SATA 63, 109
See also SATA-Brief 48
Wright, Bil 222
Wright, Brooks 1922- 25-28R
Wright, Bruce S(tanley) 1912-1975 .... CAP-2
Earlier sketch in CA 19-20
Wright, Burton 1917- 81-84
Wright, C(arolyn) D. 1949- CANR-111
Earlier sketch in CA 142
See also CAAS 22
See also AMWS 15
See also CP 7
See also CSW
See also CWP
See also DLB 120
Wright, Carolyne L(ee) 1949- 111
Wright, (Julia) Celeste Turner
1906-1999 .... CAP-1
Earlier sketch in CA 9-10
See also CP 1
Wright, Charles (Penzel, Jr.) 1935- .. CANR-135
Earlier sketches in CA 29-32R, CANR-23, 36, 62, 88
See also CAAS 7
See also AMWS 5
See also CLC 6, 13, 28, 119, 146
See also CP 7
See also DLB 165
See also DLBY 1982
See also EWL 3
See also MTCW 1, 2
See also MTFW 2005
See also PFS 10
Wright, Charles Alan 1927-2000 ...... CANR-37
Obituary 189
Earlier sketches in CA 45-48, CANR-1, 16
Wright, Charles David 1932-1978 104
Wright, Charles H(oward) 1918-2002 61-64
Obituary 204
Wright, Charles R(obert) 1927- CANR-1
Earlier sketch in CA 45-48
Wright, Charles Stevenson 1932- CANR-26
Earlier sketch in CA 9-12R
See also BLC 3
See also BW 1
See also CLC 49
See also CN 1, 2, 3, 4, 5, 6, 7
See also DAM MULT, POET
See also DLB 33
Wright, Chauncey 1830-1875 .... DLB 270
Wright, Christopher 1926- 9-12R
Wright, Cliff 1963- 143
See also SATA 76
Wright, Clifford A. 1951- CANR-110
Earlier sketch in CA 149
Wright, Cobina 1921(?)-1970
Obituary 115
Wright, (Charles) Conrad 1917- 21-24R
Wright, Constance Choate 1897-1987 .. 13-16R
Obituary 121
Wright, Courtni
See Wright, Courtni C(rump)
Wright, Courtni C(rump) 1950- CANR-87
Earlier sketch in CA 150
See also SATA 84
Wright, Courtni Crump
See Wright, Courtni C(rump)
Wright, Cynthia Challed 1953- CANR-41
Earlier sketch in CA 77-80
Wright, D(avid) G(ordon) 1937- 65-68
Wright, D(onald) I(an) 1934- CANR-3
Earlier sketch in CA 49-52
Wright, (Idonea) Daphne 1951- CANR-114
Earlier sketch in CA 157
Wright, Dare 1914(?)-2001 93-96
Obituary 192
See also SATA 21
See also SATA-Obit 124
Wright, David (John Murray)
1920-1994 .... CANR-3
Obituary 146
Earlier sketch in CA 9-12R
See also CAAS 5
See also CP 1, 2
Wright, David K. 1943- 184
See also SATA 73, 112
Wright, David McCord 1909-1968 .... CAP-2
Earlier sketch in CA 17-18
Wright, Deil S(pencer) 1930- 13-16R
Wright, Denis (Arthur Hepworth)
1911-2005 81-84
Obituary 239
Wright, Derek 1947- 144
Wright, Don(ald Conway) 1934- CANR-20
Earlier sketch in CA 104
Wright, Donald R(ichard) 1944- CANR-118
Earlier sketch in CA 160
Wright, Dorothy 1910- 13-16R
Wright, Doug 224
Wright, Edward A(rlington) 1906- 29-32R
Wright, Elizabeth Atwell 1919-1976
Obituary 65-68
Wright, Enid Meadowcroft (LaMonte)
1898-1966 .... CAP-2
Earlier sketch in CA 17-18
See also SATA 3
Wright, Eric 1929- CANR-98
Brief entry 127
Earlier sketches in CA 132, CANR-63
Interview in CA-132
See also CMW 4
Wright, Esmond 1915-2003 .... CANR-44
Obituary 219
Earlier sketches in CA 1-4R, CANR-6
See also SATA 10
Wright, Evan 236
Wright, F(rank) J(oseph) 1905- 9-12R
Wright, Frances 1795-1852 .... DLB 73
Wright, Frances Fitzpatrick 1897-1982 .. CAP-1
Earlier sketch in CA 13-14
See also SATA 10
Wright, Frances J.
See Crothers, J(essie) Frances
Wright, Francesca
See Robins, Denise (Naomi)
Wright, Frank Cookman, Jr. 1904-1982
Obituary 107
Wright, Frank Gardner 1931- 136
Wright, Frank Lloyd 1867-1959 174
See also AAYA 33
See also TCLC 95
Wright, Franz 1953- CANR-107
Earlier sketch in CA 139
Wright, G(eorge) Ernest 1909-1974 .... CANR-2
Obituary 53-56
Earlier sketch in CA 1-4R
Wright, G(eorg) H(enrik) von
1916-2003 .... CANR-118
Obituary 217
Brief entry 112
Earlier sketch in CA 157
Wright, Gavin Peter 1943- CANR-15
Earlier sketch in CA 89-92
Wright, George B(urton) 1912-1976 ...... 21-24R
Wright, George Nelson 1921- CANR-1
Earlier sketch in CA 45-48
Wright, George T(haddeus, Jr.) 1925- 5-8R
Wright, Gordon 1912-2000 .... 9-12R
Wright, Grahame 1947-1977 103
Wright, H(arold) Bunker 1907-2000 .... 5-8R
Wright, H(ugh) Elliott 1937- CANR-14
Earlier sketch in CA 37-40R
Wright, H(arry) Norman 1937- CANR-32
Earlier sketches in CA 57-60, CANR-8
Wright, Harold Bell 1872-1944
Brief entry 110
See also BPFB 3
See also DLB 9
See also TCWW 2
Wright, Harrison M(orris) 1928- 41-44R
Wright, (Mary) Helen Greuter
1914-1997 .... 9-12R
Obituary 162
Wright, Helen L(ouise) 1932- 116
Wright, Helena (Rosa Lowenfeld) 1887-1982
Obituary 110
Wright, Herbert Curtis 1928- 105
Wright, Howard W(ilson) 1915-1992 . CANR-3
Obituary 136
Earlier sketch in CA 5-8R
Wright, Ione Stuessy 1905-1992 .... CAP-1
Earlier sketch in CA 13-14
Wright, Irene Aloha 1879-1972
Obituary 33-36R
Wright, J. B.
See Barkan, Joanne
Wright, J(ames) Leitch, Jr. 1929- 21-24R
Wright, J(oseph) Patrick (Jr.) 1941- 103
Wright, J(ohn) Robert 1936- CANR-118
Earlier sketch in CA 111
Wright, J(ohn) Stafford 1905- CANR-11
Earlier sketch in CA 57-60
Wright, Jack R.
See Harris, Mark
Wright, James (Arlington)
1927-1980 .... CANR-64
Obituary 97-100
Earlier sketches in CA 49-52, CANR-4, 34
See also AITN 2
See also AMWS 3
See also CDALBS
See also CLC 3, 5, 10, 28
See also CP 1, 2
See also DAM POET
See also DLB 5, 169
See also EWL 3
See also EXPP
See also MAL 5
See also MTCW 1, 2
See also MTFW 2005
See also PC 36
See also PFS 7, 8
See also RGAL 4
See also TUS
See also WP
Wright, James Bowers 1950- 127
Wright, James C(laud), Jr. 1922- 49-52
Wright, James D(avid) 1947- CANR-144
Earlier sketch in CA 156
Wright, Jay 1935- CANR-82
Earlier sketch in CA 73-76
See also AFAW 2
See also BW 2, 3
See also CP 7
See also DAM MULT
See also DLB 41
Wright, Jim
See Wright, James Bowers
Wright, Jim
See Wright, James C(laud), Jr.
Wright, Jim
See Wright, James D(avid)
Wright, John C. 1961- 214
Wright, John D(ean), Jr. 1920- 117
Wright, John Eugene, Jr. 1931- 112
Wright, John J(oseph) 1909-1979 .... CANR-2
Earlier sketch in CA 1-4R
Wright, John L. 1937- CANR-86
Earlier sketch in CA 131
Wright, John S(hup) 1910-1989 .... 37-40R
Wright, John S(herman) 1920- CANR-6
Earlier sketch in CA 5-8R
Wright, Judith (Arundell)
1915-2000 .... CANR-93
Obituary 188
Earlier sketches in CA 13-16R, CANR-31, 76
See also CLC 11, 53
See also CP 1, 2, 3, 4, 5, 6, 7
See also CWP
See also DLB 260
See also EWL 3
See also MTCW 1, 2
See also MTFW 2005
See also PC 14
See also PFS 8
See also RGEL 2
See also SATA 14
See also SATA-Obit 121
Wright, Julie 1972- 232
Wright, Katrina
See Gater, Dilys
Wright, Keith 1963- 136
Wright, Kenneth
See del Rey, Lester
Wright, Kit 1944- CANR-109
Earlier sketch in CA 151
See also CP 7
See also CWRI 5
See also SATA 87
Wright, L(afayette) Hart 1917-1983 .. CANR-32
Obituary 109
Earlier sketch in CA 41-44
Wright, L(aurali) R. 1939- 138
See also CLC 44
See also CMW 4
Wright, Larry 1940- 140
Brief entry 122
Wright, Lawrence 1906-1983 162
Wright, Lawrence 1947- CANR-100
Earlier sketch in CA 93-96
Wright, Leigh Richard 1925- 93-96
Wright, Leonard M(arshall), Jr.
1923-2001 .... CANR-13
Obituary 199
Earlier sketch in CA 61-64
Wright, Leslie B(ailey) 1959- 155
See also SATA 91
Wright, Linda Raney 1945- CANR-11
Earlier sketch in CA 69-72
Wright, Louis Booker 1899-1984 .... CANR-1
Obituary 112
Earlier sketch in CA 1-4R
See also DLB 17
Wright, M(aureen) R(osemary) 131
Wright, Marshall D. 1956- 212
Wright, Mary Clabaugh 1917-1970
Obituary 109
Wright, Mary Pamela Godwin 1917- CAP-1
Earlier sketch in CA 9-10
Wright, Michael J(ohn) 1944- 144
Wright, Michael R(obert) 1901-1976 ..... CAP-1
Earlier sketch in CA 13-16
Wright, Monte Duane 1930- 41-44R
Wright, Muriel H(azel) 1889-1975
Obituary 57-60
Wright, N. T(om) 1948- CANR-124
Earlier sketch in CA 162
Wright, Nancy Means CANR-96
Earlier sketch in CA 104
See also SATA 38
Wright, Nathalia 1913- 120

Cumulative Index 633 **Wylie**

Wright, Nathan, Jr. 1923-2005 .... 37-40R
Obituary 236
Wright, Nathaniel, Jr.
See Wright, Nathan, Jr.
Wright, Nicholas 1940- .... CBD
See also CD 5, 6
Wright, Norman Edgar 1927- 101
Wright, Olgivanna Lloyd 1900(?)-1985
Obituary 115
Wright, (Mary) Patricia 1932- CANR-51
Earlier sketches in CA 65-68, CANR-10, 26
Wright, Patrick 1951- 220
Wright, Paul 1965- 229
Wright, Peter (Maurice) 1916-1995 128
Obituary 148
Wright, Philip Arthur 1908- CAP-1
Earlier sketch in CA 11-12
Wright, (Philip) Quincy 1890-1970 .... CANR-5
Obituary 29-32R
Earlier sketch in CA 5-8R
Wright, R(obert) Glenn 1932- 111
Wright, R(obert) H(amilton) 1906- CANR-7
Earlier sketch in CA 17-20R
See also SATA 6
Wright, R(ichard) I(rwin) Vane
See Vane-Wright, R(ichard) I(rwin)
Wright, Rachel 203
See also SATA 134
Wright, Rayburn B. 1922-1990
Obituary 131
Wright, Rebecca 1942- 105
Wright, Richard (Nathaniel)
1908-1960 .... CANR-64
Earlier sketch in CA 108
See also AAYA 5, 42
See also AFAW 1, 2
See also AMW
See also BLC 3
See also BPFB 3
See also BW 1
See also BYA 2
See also CDALB 1929-1941
See also CLC 1, 3, 4, 9, 14, 21, 48, 74
See also DA
See also DA3
See also DAB
See also DAC
See also DAM MST, MULT, NOV
See also DLB 76, 102
See also DLBD 2
See also EWL 3
See also EXPN
See also LAIT 3, 4
See also MAL 5
See also MTCW 1, 2
See also MTFW 2005
See also NCFS 1
See also NFS 1, 7
See also RGAL 4
See also RGSF 2
See also SSC 2
See also SSFS 3, 9, 15, 20
See also TCLC 136
See also TUS
See also WLC
See also YAW
Wright, Richard A(lan) 1953- 156
Wright, Richard B(ruce) 1937- CANR-120
Earlier sketch in CA 85-88
See also CLC 6
See also DLB 53
Wright, Richard J. 1935- 89-92
Wright, Rick 1945- .... CLC 35
Wright, Robert (Alan) 1957- CANR-99
Earlier sketch in CA 129
Wright, Robert Lee 1920- CANR-13
Earlier sketch in CA 17-20R
Wright, Robert Roy 1917- 9-12R
Wright, Robin (B.) 1948- CANR-114
Brief entry 119
Earlier sketch in CA 131
Wright, Robin M. 1950- 237
Wright, Ronald 1948- CANR-113
Earlier sketch in CA 139
Interview in CA-139
Wright, Ronald (William Vernon) Selby
1908-1995 .... CANR-6
Earlier sketch in CA 1-4R
Wright, Rosalie Muller 1942- 77-80
Wright, Rosalind 1952- 61-64
Wright, Rosemary Muir 1943- 158
Wright, Rowland
See Wells, Carolyn
Wright, Russel 1904-1976
Obituary 69-72
Wright, Russel O(wen) 1936- 155
Wright, S(ydney) Fowler
1874-1965 .... CANR-134
Earlier sketch in CA 156
See also DLB 255
See also SCFW 1, 2
See also SFW 4
Wright, Sally S. 224
Wright, Sarah E(lizabeth) 1928- 37-40R
See also BW 2
See also DLB 33
Wright, Sewall 1889-1988
Obituary 125
Wright, Stephen 1922- CANR-1
Earlier sketch in CA 49-52
Wright, Stephen 1946- 237
See also CLC 33
Wright, Stephen Caldwell 1946- 142
See also BW 2
Wright, Susan Kimmel 1950- 151
See also SATA 97
Wright, Sylvia 1917-1981 .... 29-32R
Obituary 104
Wright, T(errance) M(ichael)
1947- CANR-139
Earlier sketches in CA 120, CANR-77
See also HGG
Wright, T(erence) R(oy) 1951- 125
Wright, Theodore P(aul), Jr. 1926- CANR-9
Earlier sketch in CA 13-16R
Wright, Theon 1904-
Brief entry 109
Wright, Thomas E. 1927- 175
Wright, Vinita Hampton 1958- 211
Wright, Walter Francis 1912-1990 .... 5-8R
Wright, Weaver
See Ackerman, Forrest J(ames)
Wright, Will .... AAYA 60
Wright, Willard Hull 1894-1982
Obituary 107
Wright, Willard Huntington 1888-1939 189
Brief entry 115
See also Van Dine, S. S.
See also CMW 4
See also DLBD 16
Wright, William 1829-1898 .... DLB 186
Wright, William 1930- CANR-23
Earlier sketches in CA 53-56, CANR-7
See also CLC 44
Wright, William C(ook) 1939- 41-44R
Wright, William E(dward) 1926- 21-24R
Wrightfrierson
See Wright-Frierson, Virginia (Marguerite)
Wright-Frierson, Virginia (Marguerite)
1949- 180
See also SATA 58, 110
Wrightsman, Lawrence S(amuel), Jr.
1931- CANR-11
Earlier sketch in CA 21-24R
Wrightson, (Alice) Patricia 1921- CANR-36
Earlier sketches in CA 45-48, CANR-3, 19
See also AAYA 5, 58
See also BYA 5, 6
See also CLR 4, 14
See also DLB 289
See also FANT
See also JRDA
See also MAICYA 1, 2
See also SAAS 4
See also SATA 8, 66, 112
See also YAW
Wrigley, Chris (John) 1947- 129
Wrigley, E(dward) A(nthony) 1931- 129
Wrigley, Elizabeth S(pringer)
1915-1997 .... 41-44R
Obituary 157
Wrigley, Robert 1951- 203
See also DLB 256
Wriston, Henry M(erritt) 1889-1978 ...... CAP-1
Obituary 77-80
Earlier sketch in CA 11-12
Wriston, Walter B(igelow) 1919-2005 154
Obituary 235
Wrobel, David M. 1964- 139
Wrobel, Ignaz
See Tucholsky, Kurt
Wrobel, Sylvia (Burroughs) 1941- 65-68
Wroble, Lisa A. 1963- 203
See also SATA 134
Wroblewski, Sergius C(harles) 1918- .. CANR-8
Earlier sketch in CA 5-8R
Wrone, David R(ogers) 1933- CANR-6
Earlier sketch in CA 57-60
Wrong, Dennis H(ume) 1923- 81-84
Wronker, Lili
See Wronker, Lili Cassel
Wronker, Lili Cassel 1924- .... SATA 10
Wronski, Stanley P(aul) 1919- 13-16R
Wronsky, Gail (F.) 1956- 202
Wroth, Lawrence C(ounselman)
1884-1970 181
Obituary 29-32R
See also DLB 187
Wroth, Lady Mary 1587-1653(?) .... DLB 121
See also PC 38
Wrottesley, A(rthur) J(ohn) F(rancis)
1908- 45-48
Wryde, Dogear
See Gorey, Edward (St. John)
Wrzos, Joseph Henry 1929- 49-52
Wu, C(hien-) F(u) Jeff 1949- 203
Wu, Chien-Shiung 1912(?)-1997 159
Wu, Chin-Tao 226
Wu, David Y(en) H(o) 1940- 140
Wu, Duncan 1961- CANR-108
Earlier sketch in CA 142
Wu, Edna
See Wu, Qingyun
Wu, Frank H. 1967- 192
Wu, Harry 1937- CANR-101
Earlier sketch in CA 145
Wu, Hsiu-Kwang 1935- 17-20R
Wu, John C(hing) H(siung) 1899-1986 104
Obituary 118
Wu, Joseph S. 1934- 97-100
Wu, K(uo) C(heng) 1903-1984 .... 1-4R
Obituary 113
Wu, Nelson I(kon) 1919- 9-12R
Wu, Norbert 1961- 168
See also SATA 101, 155
Wu, Qingyun 1950- 154
Wu, Silas H. L. 1929- 37-40R
Wu, William F(ranking) 1951- 109
Wu, Xiao-bang 1906-1995 214
Wu, Yenna 1957- CANR-125
Earlier sketch in CA 164
Wu, Yuan-li CANR-12
Earlier sketch in CA 17-20R
Wuamett, Victor 1941- 134
Wubbels, Lance 1952- 150
Wubben, Hubert H(ollensteiner) 1928- 102
Wubben, John 1938- 65-68
Wub-e-ke-niew 1928-1997 188
Wucherer, Ruth Marie 1948- CANR-8
Earlier sketch in CA 61-64
Wu Ching-hsiung
See Wu, John C(hing) H(siung)
Wucker, Michele 1969- 208
WuDunn, Sheryl 1959- CANR-93
Earlier sketch in CA 132
Wuellner, Flora Slosson 1928- 53-56
Wuerch, William L. 1952- 176
Wuerpel, Charles E(dward) 1906-1979 105
Obituary 176
Wuerthner, George 1952- CANR-138
Earlier sketch in CA 168
Wuerzbach, Natascha 1933- 154
Wu Hung 1945- 163
Wul, Stefan
See Pairault, Pierre
Wulf, Helen Harlan 1913-2001 53-56
Wulfekoetter, Gertrude 1895-1986 .... 1-4R
Wulff, Lee 1905-1991 61-64
Obituary 134
Wulff, Robert M. 1926- 49-52
Wulffson, Don (L.) 1943- CANR-140
Earlier sketches in CA 102, CANR-19, 42
See also SATA 32, 88, 155
Wulforst, Harry David 1923- 125
Wuliger, Betty 1921- 65-68
Wullschlaeger, Jackie
See Wullschlager, Jackie
Wullschlager, Jackie 1962- 201
Wullstein, L(eroy) H(ughes) 1931- 29-32R
Wulstan, David 1937- 127
Wunder, John Remley 1945- CANR-37
Earlier sketch in CA 107
Wunderli, Richard (M.) 1940- 140
Wunderli, Stephen 1958- .... SATA 79
Wunderlich, Mark 1968- 197
Wunderlich, Ray C., Jr. 1929- 37-40R
Wunderlich, Roger 1914- 144
Wundt, Wilhelm
See de Mille, Richard
Wundt, Wilhelm (Max) 1832-1920
Brief entry 121
Wunnakyawhtin U Ohn Ghine
See Maurice, David (John Kerr)
Wunsch, James S(tevenson) 1946- 136
Wunsch, Josephine (McLean) 1914- . CANR-34
Earlier sketches in CA 1-4R, CANR-15
See also SATA 64
Wuolijoki, Hella 1886-1954 194
Wuori, G. K. 234
Wuorinen, John H(enry) 1897-1969
Obituary 111
Wuorio, Eva-Lis 1918- CANR-40
Earlier sketch in CA 77-80
See also SATA 34
See also SATA-Brief 28
Wurdemann, Audrey
See Auslander, Audrey (May) Wurdemann
Wurdinger, Scott D. 1958- 212
Wurfel, Seymour W(alter) 1907-1992 73-76
Obituary 174
Wurlitzer, Rudolph 1938(?)- 85-88
See also CLC 2, 4, 15
See also CN 4, 5, 6, 7
See also DLB 173
Wurm, Franz (Herbert) 1926- 150
Wurman, Richard Saul 1935- 162
Wurmbrand, (Heinrich) Richard
1909-2001 .... CANR-27
Obituary 195
Earlier sketch in CA 61-64
Wurmser, David 208
Wurmser, Leon 1931- 106
Wurtele, Margaret 223
Wurtman, Judith J(oy) 1937- 113
Wurts, Janny 1953- CANR-111
Earlier sketch in CA 157
See also FANT
See also SATA 98
Wurtzel, Elizabeth (Lena)
See Wurtzel, Elizabeth (Leigh)
Wurtzel, Elizabeth (Leigh) 1967- CANR-109
Earlier sketch in CA 149
Wurzbach, Natascha
See Wuerzbach, Natascha
Wurzburger, Walter S(amuel)
1920-2002 .... CANR-114
Obituary 208
Earlier sketch in CA 151
Wuthnow, Robert (J.) 1946- CANR-96
Earlier sketches in CA 65-68, CANR-15
Wu Tien-wei 1922- 118
Wu Yinxian 1900- 234
Wyandotte, Steve
See Thomas, Stanley
Wyant, William K(eblinger) 1913-1995 108
Obituary 150
Wyatt, Arthur R(amer) 1927- 1-4R
Wyatt, B. D.
See Robinson, Spider
Wyatt, Clarence R. 1956- 142
Wyatt, David K(ent) 1937- 29-32R
Wyatt, David M. 1948- CANR-75
Earlier sketch in CA 132
Wyatt, Don J. 1953- CANR-136
Earlier sketch in CA 166
Wyatt, Dorothea E(dith) 1909- CAP-2
Earlier sketch in CA 23-24
Wyatt, James
See Robinson, Louie, Jr.
Wyatt, Jane
See Bradbury, Bianca (Ryley)
Wyatt, Joan 1934- 97-100
Wyatt, John 1925- CANR-94
Earlier sketches in CA 105, CANR-22, 45
Wyatt, Rachel 1929- 101
Wyatt, Richard Jed 1939-2002 115
Obituary 207
Wyatt, Robert John 1931- 73-76
Wyatt, Robert Lee III 1940- CANR-124
Earlier sketch in CA 163
Wyatt, Stanley P(orter, Jr.) 1921-1980 ...... 9-12R
Obituary 120
Wyatt, Stephen (John) 1948- CANR-34
Earlier sketches in CA 81-84, CANR-15
Wyatt, Sir Thomas c. 1503-1542 .... BRW 1
See also DLB 132
See also EXPP
See also PC 27
See also RGEL 2
See also TEA
Wyatt, Wesley Butler
See Torme, Mel(vin Howard)
Wyatt, (Alan) Will 1942- 101
Wyatt, William F., Jr. 1932- 37-40R
Wyatt, Wilson (Watkins) (Sr.) 1905-1996 153
Wyatt, Woodrow Lyle 1918-1997 .... CANR-40
Obituary 163
Earlier sketch in CA 103
Wyatt, Zach
See Proctor, Geo(rge W.)
Wyatt-Brown, Anne M(arbury) 1939- 139
Wyatt-Brown, Bertram 1932- CANR-21
Earlier sketch in CA 25-28R
Wycherley, R(ichard) E(rnest) 1909- 77-80
Wycherley, William 1640-1716 .... BRW 2
See also CDBLB 1660-1789
See also DAM DRAM
See also DLB 80
See also RGEL 2
Wyckoff, Charlotte Chandler
1893-1966 .... CAP-2
Earlier sketch in CA 17-18
Wyckoff, D(onald) Daryl 1936-1985 .. CANR-7
Obituary 114
Earlier sketch in CA 57-60
Wyckoff, Edith Hay 1916- 107
Wyckoff, James M. 1918- CANR-39
Earlier sketch in CA 17-20R
Wyckoff, (Gregory) Jerome 1911- 9-12R
Wyckoff, Peter (Gerritsen) 1914-1996 ... 41-44R
Wyckoff, Ralph W(alter) G(raystone)
1897-1994 73-76
Obituary 147
Wyckoff, Russell L. 1916(?)-1984
Obituary 112
Wyclif, John c. 1330-1384 .... DLB 146
Wycliffe, John
See Bedford-Jones, H(enry James O'Brien)
Wycoff, Mary Elizabeth Jordon 1932- ... 13-16R
Wyden, Peter H. 1923-1998 .... CANR-110
Obituary 181
Earlier sketch in CA 105
Wydra, Nancilee 191
Wyer, Robert S., (Jr.) 1935- CANR-112
Earlier sketch in CA 153
Wyeth, Andrew 1917- .... AAYA 35
Wyeth, Betsy James 1921- 89-92
See also SATA 41
Wyeth, N(ewell) C(onvers)
1882-1945 .... DLB 188
See also DLBD 16
See also MAICYA 1, 2
See also SATA 17
Wyeth, Paul James Logan 1920-1982
Obituary 107
Wyeth, Sharon Dennis 239
Wykes, Alan 1914-1993 .... CANR-47
Obituary 141
Earlier sketches in CA 1-4R, CANR-2
Wykes, David 1941- 196
Wykstra, Ronald A. 1935-
Brief entry 106
Wyld, Lionel D(arcy) 1925- CANR-4
Earlier sketch in CA 1-4R
Wylder, Delbert E(ugene) 1923- CANR-12
Earlier sketch in CA 29-32R
Wylder, Edith (Perry) 1925- 29-32R
Wylder, Robert C. 1921- 9-12R
Wyle, Dirk
See Haynes, Duncan H(arold)
Wyler, Richard
See Linaker, Mike
Wyler, Rose 1909-2000 93-96
Obituary 188
See also SATA 18
See also SATA-Obit 121
Wyler, William 1902-1981
Obituary 108
Wylie, Betty Jane CANR-21
Earlier sketch in CA 105
See also SATA 48
Wylie, C(larence) Ray(mond), Jr.
1911-1995 .... CANR-36
Earlier sketch in CA 45-48
Wylie, Craig 1908-1976
Obituary 69-72
Wylie, Diana 1948- 225
Wylie, Elinor (Morton Hoyt) 1885-1928 162
Brief entry 105
See also AMWS 1
See also DLB 9, 45
See also EXPP
See also MAL 5
See also PC 23
See also RGAL 4
See also TCLC 8

Wylie, Francis E(rnest) 1905- CANR-37
Earlier sketch in CA 73-76
Wylie, Jeff
See Wylie, Francis E(rnest)
Wylie, Joanne 1928- 118
Wylie, John Anthony Hamilton 1919-1987
Obituary 123
Wylie, Jonathan 1945- 120
See also FANT
Wylie, Laura
See Matthews, Patricia (Anne)
Wylie, Laurence William 1909-1995 .... 21-24R
Wylie, Laurie
See Matthews, Patricia (Anne)
Wylie, Max (Melville) 1904-1975 97-100
Obituary 61-64
Wylie, Philip (Gordon) 1902-1971 .... CAP-2
Obituary 33-36R
Earlier sketch in CA 21-22
See also CLC 43
See also CN 1
See also DLB 9
See also SFW 4
Wylie, Ruth C(arol) 1920- 89-92
Wylie, Turrell V(erl) 1927- 41-44R
Wylie, William P(ercy) 1898- 5-8R
Wyller, Arne A(ugust) 1927- 190
Wyllie, Eugene D(onald) 1929- 123
Brief entry 118
Wyllie, John (Vectis Carew) 1914- CANR-5
Earlier sketch in CA 9-12R
Wyllie, John Cook 1908-1968 184
See also DLB 140
Wyllie, Peter J(ohn) 1930- CANR-5
Earlier sketch in CA 53-56
Wyllie, Stephen .... SATA 86
Wyly, Rachel Lumpkin 1892-1977 .... CAP-2
Obituary 171
Earlier sketch in CA 25-28
Wyman, Andrea 142
See also SATA 75
Wyman, Bill 1936- CANR-110
Earlier sketch in CA 146
Wyman, Bruce C. 1947- 139
Wyman, Carolyn 1956- 150
See also SATA 83
Wyman, David S. 1929- CANR-142
Earlier sketch in CA 25-28R
Wyman, Donald 1903-1993 .... CANR-2
Earlier sketch in CA 5-8R
Wyman, Leland C(lifton) 1897-1988
Obituary 124
Wyman, Lillie Buffum Chace 1847-1929 ... 180
See also DLB 202
Wyman, Marc
See Howith, Harry
Wyman, Mark 1938- CANR-36
Earlier sketch in CA 101
Wyman, Mary Alice 1889(?)-1976
Obituary 61-64
Wyman, Max 1939- 140
Wyman, Oliver
See Holmes, Olive
Wyman, Walker D(e Marquis)
1907-1999 .... CANR-36
Earlier sketch in CA 17-20R
Wymark, Olwen Margaret 1932- 104
See also CAD
See also CD 5, 6
See also CWD
See also CWRI 5
See also DLB 233
Wymelenberg, Suzanne 1929- 140
Wymer, Norman (George) 1911- 104
See also SATA 25
Wymer, Thomas L(ee) 1938- 105
Wynand, Derk 1944- CANR-17
Earlier sketch in CA 77-80
Wynants, Miche 1934- .... SATA-Brief 31
Wynar, Bohdan S(tephen) 1926- CANR-66
Earlier sketches in CA 17-20R, CANR-10, 27
Wynar, Christine L(oraine) 1933- 73-76
Wynar, Lubomyr R(oman) 1932- CANR-64
Earlier sketches in CA 73-76, CANR-14, 31
Wynard, Talbot
See Hamilton, Charles (Harold St. John)
Wynd, Oswald Morris 1913-1998 .... CANR-39
Obituary 169
Earlier sketches in CA 1-4R, CANR-1
See also Black, Gavin
Wynder, Mavis Areta
See Winder, Mavis Areta
Wyndham, Esther
See Lutyens, Mary
Wyndham, Everard Humphrey 1888- CAP-1
Earlier sketch in CA 13-14
Wyndham, Francis (Guy Percy)
1924- CANR-78
Brief entry 126
Earlier sketch in CA 131
Interview in CA-131
Wyndham, Joan 1921- 144
Wyndham, John
See Harris, John (Wyndham Parkes Lucas) Beynon
See also CLC 19
See also DLB 255
See also SCFW 1, 2
Wyndham, Lee
See Hyndman, Jane Andrews Lee
Wyndham, Robert
See Hyndman, Robert Utley
Wynes, Charles E. 1929- 9-12R
Wyness, (James) Fenton 1903- CAP-1
Earlier sketch in CA 11-12
Wynette, Tammy
See Pugh, (Virginia) Wynette
Wyn Griffith, Llewelyn 1890- .... CP 1
Wynia, Gary W. 1942- 133
Wynkoop, Mildred Bangs
1905-1997 .... CANR-40
Earlier sketch in CA 57-60
Wynkoop, Sally 1944- 41-44R
Wynkoop, William M. 1916- 21-24R
Wynman, Margaret
See Dixon, Ella Hepworth
Wynn, Alfred
See Brewer, Fredric (Aldwyn)
Wynn, Allan 1920-1987
Obituary 123
Wynn, Charles M. 1939- 163
Wynn, D(ale) Richard 1918- CANR-43
Earlier sketches in CA 1-4R, CANR-4
Wynn, Daniel Webster 1919-1983 .... 25-28R
Obituary 133
Wynn, Dianna R. 1963- 191
Wynn, Graeme 1946- 127
Wynn, John Charles 1920- CANR-2
Earlier sketch in CA 1-4R
Wynn, (Francis Xavier Aloysius James Jeremiah) Keenan 1916-1986
Obituary 120
Wynn, Neil A(lan) 1947- 113
Wynn, Patricia
See Ricks, Patricia W. B.
Wynn, Tracey Keenan 1945- 144
Wynne, Brian
See Dean (McGaughy), Dudley and Garfield, Brian (Francis Wynne)
Wynne, Edward A. 1928- 130
Wynne, Frank
See Garfield, Brian (Francis Wynne)
Wynne, Greville (Maynard) 1919-1990
Obituary 131
Wynne, John (Stewart) 149
Wynne, Lewis Nicholas 1943- 128
Wynne, Marcus 203
Wynne, May
See Knowles, Mabel Winifred
Wynne, Nancy Blue 1931- 85-88
Wynne, Paul 1943(?)-1990
Obituary 132
Wynne, Ronald D(avid) 1934- CANR-42
Earlier sketch in CA 102
Wynne, Thorne D. 1908-1979 .... 5-8R
Wynne-Davies, Marion 1958- 133
Wynne-Jones, Tim(othy) 1948- CANR-39
Earlier sketch in CA 105
See also AAYA 31
See also CLR 21, 58
See also CWRI 5
See also MAICYA 2
See also MAICYAS 1
See also SATA 67, 96, 136
See also SATA-Essay 136
Wynne-Thomas, Peter 1934- 118
Wynne-Tyson, Esme 1898-1972 .... 21-24R
See also DLB 191
Wynne-Tyson, (Timothy) Jon (Lyden)
1924- 17-20R
Wynn-Jones, Michael 1941- CANR-14
Earlier sketch in CA 69-72
Wynorski, Jim 1950- 215
Wynot, Edward D(avis), Jr. 1943- 105
Wynter, Edward (John) 1914- 69-72
See also SATA 14
Wynter, Leon E. 1953- 214
Wynter, Sylvia 1928- 153
See also BW 2
Wynveen, Tim 1951- 172
Wynward, Robin (Norman) 1945- 175
Wynyard, Talbot
See Hamilton, Charles (Harold St. John)
Wyon, Olive 1890-(?) CAP-1
Earlier sketch in CA 11-12
Wyrick, V(ictor) Neil, Jr. 1928- 13-16R
Wyschogrod, Edith 1930-
Brief entry 111
Wyschogrod, Michael 1928- 89-92
Wyse, Lois (Helene) 1926- CANR-46
Earlier sketch in CA 108
See also BEST 89:3
Wyse, Marion 1952- 123
Wyse, Sharon 214
Wysor, Bettie 1928- CANR-13
Earlier sketch in CA 77-80
Wyspianski, Stanislaw (Mateusz Ignacy)
1869-1907 .... EWL 3
See also RGWL 2, 3
Wyss, Hilary E. 1965- 196
Wyss, Johann David Von 1743-1818 .... CLR 92
See also JRDA
See also MAICYA 1, 2
See also SATA 29
See also SATA-Brief 27
Wyss, Johann Rudolph 1782-1830 .... BYA 4
Wyss, Max Albert 1908-1977 106
Wyss, Thelma Hatch 1934- CANR-119
Earlier sketch in CA 29-32R
See also SATA 10, 140
Wyss, Wallace A(lfred) 1944- 124
Brief entry 107
Wyszynski, Stefan 1901-1981
Obituary 108
Wyvis, Ben
See Munro, (Macfarlane) Hugh
Wyzanski, Charles E(dward), Jr.
1906-1986 .... CAP-1
Obituary 120
Earlier sketch in CA 17-18

X

Xaveria, M. Barton
See Barton, M. Xaveria
Xaveria, Sister
See Barton, M. Xaveria
Xavier, Father
See Hurwood, Bernhardt J.
Xavier I
See Horne, Frank (Smith)
Xeno
See Lake, Kenneth R(obert)
Xenophon c. 430B.C.-c. 354B.C. .... AW 1
See also DLB 176
See also RGWL 2, 3
Xenopoulos, Ghrighorios 1867-1951 ..... EWL 3
Xiang, Lanxin 1956- 152
Xiao, Hong 1911-1942 .... RGWL 3
Xiao Hong
See Xiao, Hong
Ximenes, Ben Cuellar, Jr. 1911- 5-8R
Xingjian, Gao 1940- 193
See also Gao Xingjian
See also DFS 21
See also RGWL 3
Xinran 1958- 214
Xi Xi
See Zhang Yan
See also EWL 2
Xixx, Jezebel Q.
See Borgmann, Dmitri A(lfred)
Xu, Meihong 1963(?)- 195
Xuan, YongSheng 1952- .... SATA 116
See also SATA-Essay 119
Xue, Hue
See Xinran

Y

Y. Y.
See Lynd, Robert
Yaari, Ehud 1945- 37-40R
Yabes, Leopoldo Y(abes) 1912-2000 101
Yablokoff, Herman 1903-1981
Obituary 108
Yablonsky, Lewis 1924- 21-24R
Yablonsky, Linda 1948- 166
Yabsley, Suzanne 1949- 124
Yabuki, Susumu 1938- 152
Yaccarino, Dan CANR-120
Earlier sketch in CA 174
See also SATA 141
Yaccarino, Michael Orlando 1963- .. CANR-95
Earlier sketch in CA 174
Yacine, Kateb 1929-1989 .... 9-12R
See also Kateb Yacine
See also WLIT 2
Yacorzynski, George Kassimer
1907-1997 .... 1-4R
Obituary 171
Yacovone, Donald 1952- 198
Yacowar, Maurice 1942- CANR-127
Earlier sketches in CA 41-44R, CANR-43
Yadav, Rajendra 1929- .... CWW 2
Yadin, (Rav-Aloof) Yigael 1917-1984 .. CANR-6
Obituary 113
Earlier sketch in CA 9-12R
See also SATA 55
Yaeger, Bart
See Strung, Norman
Yaeger, Don 1962- CANR-103
Earlier sketch in CA 144
Yafa, Stephen H. 1941- 21-24R
Yaffe, Alan
See Yorinks, Arthur
Yaffe, Barbara 1953- 85-88
Yaffe, Gideon 1971- 238
Yaffe, James 1927- CANR-12
Earlier sketch in CA 5-8R
See also CN 1, 2, 3, 4, 5, 6, 7
Yaffe, Richard 1903-1986 69-72
Yager, Jan 1948- CANR-30
Yager, Rosemary 1909-1993 .... 1-4R
Yaggy, Duncan 1938- 116
Yaggy, Elinor 1907-1996 89-92
Obituary 174
Yagher, Kevin 1962- 216
See also SATA 143
Yagoda, Ben 1954- CANR-93
Earlier sketch in CA 145
Yaguchi, Yorifumi 1932- .... CP 1
Yahil, Leni 29-32R
Yahraes, Herbert (C., Jr.) 1905-1984 81-84
Obituary 176
Yahuda, Joseph 1900- CAP-1
Earlier sketch in CA 11-12
Yakamochi 718-785 .... PC 48
Yaker, Henri (Marc) 1922-
Brief entry 109
Yakhlif, Yahya 1944- 232
Yakobson, Helen B(ates) 1913-2002 ..... 17-20R
Obituary 215
Yakobson, Sergius O. 1901-1979
Obituary 89-92
Yakovenko, L.
See Kopelev, Lev (Zinovievich)
Yakovetic, (Joseph Sandy) 1952- .... SATA 59
Yakovetic, Joe
See Yakovetic, (Joseph Sandy)
Yakovlev, Alexander 1923- 145
Yakumo Koizumi
See Hearn, (Patricio) Lafcadio (Tessima Carlos)
Yalden, Derek William 1940- 69-72
Yale, Kathleen Betsko 1939- 158
Yale, Wesley W(oodworth) 1900- CAP-2
Earlier sketch in CA 29-32
Yale, William 1888(?)-1975
Obituary 57-60
Yalem, Ronald J(oseph) 1926- 17-20R
Yalman, Ahmet Emin 1888-1972
Obituary 37-40R
Yalom, Irvin D(avid) 1931- CANR-118
Earlier sketch in CA 140
See also BEST 90:1
Yalom, Marilyn K. 1932- CANR-106
Earlier sketches in CA 117, CANR-40
Yalow, Rosalyn Sussman 1921- 157
Yamada, Mitsuye (May) 1923- 77-80
See also PC 44
Yamada, Nanako 1939- 143
Yamaguchi, J(ohn) Tohr 1932- 17-20R
Yamaguchi, Marianne (Illenberger)
1936- 29-32R
See also SATA 7
Yamaguchi, Yoji 1963- 165
Yamaka, Sara 1978- 156
See also SATA 92
Yamamoto, Hisaye 1921- 214
See also AAL
See also DAM MULT
See also DLB 312
See also LAIT 4
See also SSC 34
See also SSFS 14
Yamamoto, J(erry) Isamu 1947- 77-80
Yamamoto, Kaoru 1932- CANR-12
Earlier sketch in CA 25-28R
Yamamoto, Michiko 1936- 132
Yamamoto, Traise 1961- 184
Yamanaka, Lois-Ann 1961- CANR-103
Earlier sketch in CA 161
See also AAYA 40
See also CN 7
See also DLB 312
Yamanouchi, Hisaaki 1934- 93-96
Yamasaki, Minoru 1912-1986 155
Obituary 118
Yamashita, Karen Tei 1951- CANR-129
Earlier sketch in CA 166
See also DLB 312
Yamauchi, Edwin M(asao) 1937- CANR-41
Earlier sketches in CA 45-48, CANR-3, 19
Yamauchi, Wakako 1924- 214
See also AAL
See also DLB 312
Yamba, C(hristian) Bawa 1944- 163
Yampolsky, Mariana 1925- 216
Yan, Chiou-Shuang Jou 1934-
Brief entry 105
Yan, Geling 181
Yan, Martin 1948- 216
Yan, Mo
See Moye, Guan
See also RGWL 3
Yanaga, Chitoshi 1903-1985 .... CAP-2
Obituary 182
Earlier sketch in CA 25-28
Yanagimura, Shimpu
See Verwilghen, A(lbert-) Felix
Yancey, Diane 1951- CANR-118
Earlier sketch in CA 149
See also SATA 81, 138
Yancey, Philip D(avid) 1949- CANR-98
Earlier sketches in CA 101, CANR-18, 40
Yancey, Wes
See Lazenby, Norman
Yancey, William L(ayton) 1938- 21-24R
Yancy, Robert J(ames) 1944- 57-60
Yandell, Keith E. 1938- 37-40R
Yanev, Peter (Ivanov) 1946- 77-80
Yaney, George L(evings) 1930- 104
Yaney, Joseph P(aul) 1939- CANR-9
Earlier sketch in CA 65-68
Yanez, Agustin 1904-1980 131
See also EWL 3
See also HW 1
See also LAW
Yanez, Jose Donoso
See Donoso (Yanez), Jose
Yanez Cossio, Alicia 1929- 203
Yang, Belle 1960- 149
Yang, C(hing) K(un) 1911-1999 .... 5-8R
Yang, Chen Ning 1922- 157
Yang, Cunzhong
See Ruan, Fang-fu
Yang, Dali L. 139
Yang, Jay 1941- .... SATA 12
Yang, Linda (Gureasko) 1937- 57-60
Yang, Mingyi 1943- .... SATA 72
Yang, Philip Q. 1955- 178
Yang, Richard F. S. 1918- CANR-10
Earlier sketch in CA 25-28R
Yang, Sung Chul 1939- 117
Yang Chengye
See Yang Mo
Yang Chiang
See Yang Chi-k'ang
See also EWL 3
Yang Chi-k'ang 1911-
See Yang Chiang
Yang-Jen
See Shu, Austin Chi-wei
Yang Jiang
See Yang Chi-k'ang
Yang Lian 1955- .... CWW 2
Yang Mo 1914- .... CWW 2
Yang Zhong Mei 1945- 132
Yanikian, Gourgen Migirdic 1895-1984
Obituary 112
Yaniv, Avner 1942- 126

Cumulative Index 635 **Yim**

Yankelovich, Daniel 1924- CANR-90
Earlier sketch in CA 105
Yanker, Gary 1947- 37-40R
Yankowitz, Susan 1941- CANR-39
Earlier sketches in CA 45-48, CANR-1, 17
See also CAD
See also CD 5, 6
See also CWD
Yannarella, Philip A(nthony) 1942- 73-76
Yannatos, James 1929- 102
Yannella, Donald 1934- CANR-96
Earlier sketches in CA 57-60, CANR-8, 25
Yanni, Carla 1965- 201
Yanoff, Morris 1907-1996 108
Obituary 196
Yanouzas, John N(icholas) 1928- 41-44R
Yanovsky, Basile S.
See Yanovsky, V(assily) S(emenovich)
Yanovsky, V(assily) S(emenovich)
1906-1989 97-100
Obituary 129
See also CLC 2, 18
Yanow, Scott 239
Yans-McLaughlin, Virginia 1943- 89-92
Yant, Martin 1949- 134
Yao, Esther Lee 1944- CANR-56
Earlier sketches in CA 111, CANR-29
Yap, Arthur 1945- 154
See also CP 7
Yap Chior Hiong, Arthur 1943- .... CP 1
Yarber, Robert Earl 1929- 49-52
Yarbo, Steve
See King, Albert
Yarborough, Betty Hathaway 1927- 45-48
Yarborough, Sharon C(lare) 1937- 231
Yarbro, C. Q.
See Yarbro, Chelsea Quinn
Yarbro, Chelsea Quinn 1942- CANR-103
Earlier sketches in CA 65-68, CANR-9, 25, 77
See also AAYA 40
See also BPFB 3
See also BYA 6, 7
See also HGG
See also SFW 4
See also SUFW 2
Yarbrough, Camille 1938- 125
Brief entry 105
See also BW 2
See also CLR 29
See also SATA 79
Yarbrough, Ira 1910(?)-1983
Obituary 110
See also SATA-Obit 35
Yarbrough, Stephen R. 1950- 138
Yarbrough, Steve 1956- 200
Yarbrough, Tinsley E(ugene) 1941 ... CANR-96
Earlier sketch in CA 109
Yarde, Jeanne Betty Frances 1925- ... CANR-47
Earlier sketches in CA 105, CANR-23
Yardley, Alice 1913-
Brief entry 106
Yardley, Cathy 220
Yardley, Darrell G. 1948- 183
Yardley, Herbert O(sborn) 1889-1958
Brief entry 121
Yardley, Jonathan 1939- 73-76
Yardley, Richard Q(uincy) 1903-1979
Obituary 89-92
Yared, Nazik Saba 1928- CANR-123
Earlier sketch in CA 168
Yaremko, Michael 1914-1970 .... CAP-2
Earlier sketch in CA 25-28
Yarmey, A(lexander) Daniel 1938- CANR-17
Earlier sketch in CA 101
Yarmolinsky, Adam 1922-2000 .... 37-40R
Obituary 190
Yarmolinsky, Avrahm (Abraham)
1890-1975 .... CANR-7
Obituary 61-64
Earlier sketch in CA 5-8R
Yarmon, Morton 1916- 9-12R
Yarn, David H(omer), Jr. 1920- 17-20R
Yarnall, Sophia
See Jacobs, Sophia Yarnall
Yarnell, Allen 1942- 101
Yarnold, Barbara M(aria) 1961- 175
Yaroshinskaya, Alla 1953- 153
Yaroslava
See Mills, Yaroslava Surmach
Yarrow, Arnold 1920- 106
Yarrow, Marian J(eanette Radke) 1918-
Brief entry 105
Yarrow, P(hilip) J(ohn) 1917- 13-16R
Yarry, Mark Robert 1940- 110
Yar-Shater, Ehsan O(llah) 1920- 37-40R
Yartz, Frank Joseph CANR-97
Earlier sketch in CA 65-68
Yarwood, Doreen 1918- CANR-18
Earlier sketch in CA 101
Yaseen, Leonard C(layton) 1912-1989
Obituary 129
Yashar, Deborah J. 1963- 237
Yashima, Taro
See Iwamatsu, Jun Atsushi
See also CLR 4
Yastrzemski, Carl (Michael, Jr.) 1939- 104
Yasuoka, Shotaro 1920- 184
See also Yasuoka Shotaro
Yasuoka Shotaro
See Yasuoka, Shotaro
See also CWW 2
See also DLB 182
Yates, A(lan) G(eoffrey) 1923-1985 ... CANR-60
Obituary 116
Earlier sketches in CA 1-4R, CANR-3
See also Brown, Carter
Yates, Alan
See Yates, A(lan) G(eoffrey)
Yates, Alayne 1929- 81-84
Yates, Alfred 1917- 21-24R
Yates, Aubrey J(ames) 1925- 9-12R
Yates, Brock W(endel) 1933- 9-12R
Yates, David O.
See Womack, David A(lfred)
Yates, Donald A(lfred) 1930- 41-44R
Yates, Dornford
See Mercer, Cecil William
See also DLB 77, 153
Yates, Elizabeth 1905-2001 .... CANR-21
Obituary 198
Earlier sketches in CA 1-4R, CANR-6
See also BYA 1
See also JRDA
See also MAICYA 1, 2
See also SAAS 6
See also SATA 4, 68
See also SATA-Obit 128
See also YAW
Yates, Frances A(melia) 1899-1981 .. CANR-30
Obituary 105
Earlier sketch in CA 57-60
Yates, Gerard Francis 1907-1979
Obituary 89-92
Yates, J. Michael 1938- 21-24R
See also CP 1, 2, 3, 4, 5, 6, 7
See also DLB 60
Yates, Janelle K(aye) 1957- 145
See also SATA 77
Yates, John 1939- .... SATA 74
Yates, Madeleine 1937- 109
Yates, Norris W(ilson) 1923- 9-12R
Yates, Paul 1954-
Brief entry 117
Yates, Peter Bertram 1909-1976
Obituary 65-68
Yates, Philip 1958- 223
See also SATA 92, 149
Yates, Raymond F(rancis) 1895-1966
Obituary 110
See also SATA 31
Yates, Richard 1926-1992 .... CANR-43
Obituary 139
Earlier sketches in CA 5-8R, CANR-10
Interview in CANR-10
See also AMWS 11
See also CLC 7, 8, 23
See also CN 1, 2, 3, 4, 5
See also DLB 2, 234
See also DLBY 1981, 1992
Yates, W(illiam) E(dgar) 1938- 49-52
Yatron, Michael 1921- 37-40R
Yatsko, Pamela 207
Yau, John 1950- CANR-89
Earlier sketch in CA 154
See also CP 7
See also DLB 234, 312
See also PC 61
Yau, Shing-Tung 1949- CANR-118
Earlier sketch in CA 158
Yauch, Wilbur Alden 1904-1982
Obituary 106
Yaukey, David (William) 1927- 61-64
Yaukey, Grace S(ydenstricker)
1899-1994 .... CANR-1
Obituary 145
Earlier sketch in CA 1-4R
See also SATA 5, 80
Yavetz, Zvi 1925- CANR-16
Earlier sketch in CA 29-32R
Yavitz, Boris 1923- 114
Yavno, Max 1911-1985 216
Yavorov, Peyo 1878-1914 .... DLB 147
See also EWL 3
Yaw, Yvonne 1936- 65-68
Yawetz, Zwy
See Yavetz, Zvi
Yazdanfar, Farzin 1953- CANR-125
Earlier sketch in CA 167
Yazijian, Harvey Z. 1948- 107
Yazz, Beatien 1928- 212
Ye, Ting-xing 1952- 176
See also SATA 106
Ye, Zhaoyan 1957- 220
Yeadon, David 1942- CANR-116
Earlier sketch in CA 104
Yeager, Allan Edward 1943- 101
Yeager, Chuck 1923- 154
Yeager, Jeana 1952- 158
Yeager, Leland B(ennett) 1924- CANR-111
Earlier sketch in CA 125
Yeager, Peter C(leary) 1949- CANR-88
Earlier sketch in CA 131
Yeager, Randolph O. 1912-1991 130
Yeager, Robert Cushing 1942- 102
Yeager, W(illard) Hayes 1897-1978 .... CAP-2
Earlier sketch in CA 19-20
Yeakley, Marjory Hall 1908- CANR-2
Earlier sketch in CA 1-4R
See also SATA 21
Yeargers, Edward C. 1938- 144
Yearley, Clifton K(rebs), Jr. 1925- 13-16R
Yearns, W(ilfred) Buck 1918- 134
Yearsley, Ann 1753-1806 .... DLB 109
Yearwood, Richard M(eek) 1934- 37-40R
Yeates, Mabel
See Pereira, Harold Bertram
Yeates, Marian 1945- 198
Yeates, Maurice 1938- CANR-14
Earlier sketch in CA 41-44R
Yeatman, Linda 1938- 117
See also SATA 42
Yeats, Robert S(heppard) 1931- 201
Yeats, W. B.
See Yeats, William Butler
Yeats, William Butler 1865-1939 ...... CANR-45
Brief entry 104
Earlier sketch in CA 127
See also AAYA 48
See also BRW 6
See also BRWR 1
See also CDBLB 1890-1914
See also DA
See also DA3
See also DAB
See also DAC
See also DAM DRAM, MST, POET
See also DLB 10, 19, 98, 156
See also EWL 3
See also EXPP
See also MTCW 1, 2
See also MTFW 2005
See also NCFS 3
See also PAB
See also PC 20, 51
See also PFS 1, 2, 5, 7, 13, 15
See also RGEL 2
See also TCLC 1, 11, 18, 31, 93, 116
See also TEA
See also WLC
See also WLIT 4
See also WP
Yeats-Brown, F(rancis Charles Claypon)
1886-1944
Brief entry 119
Yeazell, Ruth Bernard 1947- CANR-117
Earlier sketches in CA 102, CANR-28, 52
Yeck, John D(avid) 1912-1999 .... 13-16R
Yee, Albert H(oy) 1929- CANR-1
Earlier sketch in CA 49-52
Yee, Brenda Shannon .... SATA 133
Yee, Chiang
See Chiang Yee
Yee, Lisa 1959- 236
See also SATA 160
Yee, Min S. 1938- 101
Yee, Paul (R.) 1956- CANR-122
Earlier sketches in CA 135, CANR-81
See also AAYA 24
See also CLR 44
See also CWRI 5
See also JRDA
See also MAICYA 2
See also MAICYAS 1
See also SATA 67, 96, 143
Yee, Shirley J. 1959- 141
Yee, Wong Herbert 1953- 187
See also SATA 78, 115
Yefremov, Ivan (Antonovich) 1907-1972 156
See also SFW 4
Yeganeh, Mohammed 1923- 5-8R
Yegul, Fikret K. 1942- 146
Yeh, Chun-Chan 1914- 148
See also Ye Junjian
See also SATA 79
Yeh, George K(ung)-C(hao) 1904-1981
Obituary 108
Yeh, Michelle (Mi-Hsi) 1955- 207
Yeh, Wei-lien
See Yip, Wai-lim
Yehiya, Eliezer Don
See Don-Yehiya, Eliezer
Yehoshua, A(braham) B. 1936- CANR-90
Earlier sketches in CA 33-36R, CANR-43
See also CLC 13, 31
See also CWW 2
See also EWL 3
See also RGSF 2
See also RGWL 3
See also WLIT 6
Ye Junjian
See Yeh, Chun-Chan
See also CWW 2
Yeldham, Peter 1927- 190
Yelin, Louise 1945- 198
Yelin, Shulamis S. 121
Yellen, Jack 1892-1991 .... DLB 265
Yellen, Samuel 1906-1983 .... 1-4R
See also CN 1, 2
Yellen, Sherman 1932- 29-32R
Yellin, Carol Lynn (Gilmer) 1920-1999 . 17-20R
Yellin, David G(ilmer) 1916- 158
Brief entry 115
Yellin, Emily 234
Yellin, Jean Fagan 1930- 41-44R
Yellow Bird
See Ridge, John Rollin
Yellowitz, Irwin 1933- CANR-4
Earlier sketch in CA 45-48
Yellow Robe, William S., (Jr.) 1950- 148
Yelton, David K. 1960- 229
Yelton, Donald Charles 1915-1993 106
Yeltsin, Boris (Nikolayevich) 1931- . CANR-103
Earlier sketch in CA 140
Yelverton, Eric Esskildsen 1888-1964 .... CAP-1
Earlier sketch in CA 9-10
Yen, Ching-hwang 1937- 136
Yenawine, Philip 1942- 151
See also SATA 85
Yen-Ping, Shen 1896(?)-1981
Obituary 103
See also Dun, Mao and
Mao Tun
Yenser, Stephen 1941- CANR-36
Earlier sketch in CA 114
Yensid, Retlaw
See Disney, Walt(er Elias)
Yeo, Cedric Arnold 1905-1987 .... CAP-1
Obituary 102
Earlier sketch in CA 17-18
Yeo, Robert 1940- 205
Yeo, Wilma (Lethem) 1918-1994 .... 25-28R
Obituary 146
See also SATA 24, 81
Yeoman, John 1934- 106
See also CLR 46
See also SATA 28, 80
Yeomans, Patricia Henry 1917- 97-100
Yep, Laurence Michael 1948- CANR-92
Earlier sketches in CA 49-52, CANR-1, 46
See also AAYA 5, 31
See also BYA 7
See also CLC 35
See also CLR 3, 17, 54
See also DLB 52, 312
See also FANT
See also JRDA
See also MAICYA 1, 2
See also MAICYAS 1
See also SATA 7, 69, 123
See also WYA
See also YAW
Yepsen, Roger B(ennet), Jr. 1947- CANR-82
Earlier sketches in CA 114, CANR-35
See also SATA 59
Yerbury, Grace (Helen) D(avies)
1899-1988 .... 37-40R
Obituary 176
Yerby, Frank G(arvin) 1916-1991 ..... CANR-52
Obituary 136
Earlier sketches in CA 9-12R, CANR-16
Interview in CANR-16
See also BLC 3
See also BPFB 3
See also BW 1, 3
See also CLC 1, 7, 22
See also CN 1, 2, 3, 4, 5
See also DAM MULT
See also DLB 76
See also MTCW 1
See also RGAL 4
See also RHW
Yergin, Daniel H(oward) 1947- CANR-117
Earlier sketch in CA 103
Yerian, Cameron John 73-76
See also SATA 21
Yerian, Margaret A. 73-76
See also SATA 21
Yerkes, James (O.) 1933- 198
Yermakov, Nicholas 1951- CANR-103
Earlier sketch in CA 118
See also FANT
See also SFW 4
Yerofeev, Venedikt 1938-1990 .... EWL 3
Yerushalmi, Yosef Hayim 1932- 160
Brief entry 112
Yerxa, Donald A(llan) 1950- 139
Yerxa, Leo 1947- .... CWRI 5
Yesalis, Charles E(dward) 1946- 144
Yeselson, Abraham 1921-1978
Obituary 77-80
Yesenin, Sergei Alexandrovich
See Esenin, Sergei (Alexandrovich)
Yesenin, Sergey
See Esenin, Sergei (Alexandrovich)
See also EWL 3
Yeshayahu, Yisrael 1910-1979
Obituary 89-92
Yeshurun, Avot 1904-1992 132
Obituary 136
Yessian, Mark R(obert) 1942- CANR-10
Earlier sketch in CA 25-28R
Yetiv, Steve(n) A. 238
Yetman, Norman R(oger) 1938- 29-32R
Yetska
See Ironside, Jetske
Yette, Samuel F(rederick) 1929- 102
Yeung Yue-man 1938- 110
Yevtushenko, Yevgeny (Alexandrovich)
1933- CANR-54
Earlier sketches in CA 81-84, CANR-33
See also Evtushenko, Evgenii Aleksandrovich
See also CLC 1, 3, 13, 26, 51, 126
See also DAM POET
See also EWL 3
See also MTCW 1
See also PC 40
Yew, Chay 196
Yezierska, Anzia 1885(?)-1970 126
Obituary 89-92
See also CLC 46
See also DLB 28, 221
See also FW
See also MTCW 1
See also RGAL 4
See also SSFS 15
Yezzo, Dominick 1947- 53-56
Yglesias, Helen 1915- CANR-95
Earlier sketches in CA 37-40R, CANR-15, 65
Interview in CANR-15
See also CAAS 20
See also CLC 7, 22
See also CN 4, 5, 6, 7
See also MTCW 1
Yglesias, Jose 1919-1995 .... CANR-32
Obituary 150
Earlier sketch in CA 41-44R
See also CN 2, 3, 4, 5, 6
See also HW 1
Yglesias, Rafael 1954- 37-40R
Yiannopoulos, A(thanassios) N(ikolaos)
1928- CANR-27
Earlier sketch in CA 1-4R
Yick, Joseph K(ong) S(ang) 1953- CANR-116
Earlier sketch in CA 157
[illegible], Sharon A. 1960- 112
Yim, Kwan Ha 1929- 101

Yin, Robert K(uo-zuir) 1941- CANR-1
Earlier sketch in CA 49-52
Ying, Hong 1962- 185
Ying, Hu 1962- 208
Yinger, J(ohn) Milton 1916- 89-92
Yinon, Jehuda 1935- 150
Yip, Wai-lim 1937- 33-36R
Yiu, Angela 1962- 236
Yllo, Kersti 1953- CANR-44
Earlier sketch in CA 119
Ylvisaker, Paul 1921-1992 ..... CANR-16
Obituary 137
Earlier sketches in CA 1-4R, CANR-1
Yngve, Victor H(use) 1920- 57-60
Yntema, Theodore O(tte) 1900-1985
Obituary 117
Y.O.
See Russell, George William
Yoakum, Robert 1922- 77-80
Yochelson, Ellis L. 1928- 235
Yochelson, Samuel 1906(?)-1976
Obituary 69-72
Yochim, Louise Dunn 1909- 37-40R
Yockey, Hubert P(almer) 1916- 146
Yockey, Ross Paul 1943- 192
Yocom, Charles Frederick 1914- CANR-7
Earlier sketch in CA 17-20R
Yoda, Yoshikata 1909- ..... IDFW 3, 4
Yoder, Carolyn P(atricia) 1953- 223
See also SATA 149
Yoder, (Theodore) Dale 1901-1990 ..... CANR-2
Obituary 174
Earlier sketch in CA 1-4R
Yoder, Don 1921- 85-88
Yoder, Dorothy Meenen 1921- 163
See also SATA 96
Yoder, Dot
See Yoder, Dorothy Meenen
Yoder, Edwin M(ilton), Jr. 1934- 239
Yoder, Glee 1916- CANR-9
Earlier sketch in CA 21-24R
Yoder, J(ames) Willard 1902-1989 ..... 37-40R
Yoder, Janice D(ana) 1952- 114
Yoder, Jess 1922- 45-48
Yoder, John C. 1942- 145
Yoder, John H(oward) 1927-1997 ..... 13-16R
Obituary 163
Yoder, Marie Angeline 1914-1987 ..... 5-8R
Yoder, Norman M. 1915-1990 ..... 21-24R
Yoder, Paton 1912- 93-96
Yoder, Sanford Calvin 1879-1975 ..... CAP-1
Obituary 171
Earlier sketch in CA 13-16
Yoder, Walter D. 1933- ..... SATA 88
Yoerg, Sonja I. 1959- 203
Yoffe, Elkhonon (Hona) 1928- 126
Yoffie, David B. 1954- 189
Yoggy, Gary A. 1938- 152
Yogiji, Harbhajan Singh Khalsa
1929-2004 93-96
Obituary 232
Yogman, Michael W. 1947- 126
Yohe, W(illiam) Frederick 1943- 49-52
Yohn, David Waite 1933- 41-44R
Yohn, Rick 1937- CANR-8
Earlier sketch in CA 61-64
Yoingco, Angel Q. 1921- CANR-11
Earlier sketch in CA 25-28R
Yoken, Melvin B(arton) 1939- 65-68
Yokomitsu, Riichi 1898-1947 170
See also EWL 3
See also TCLC 47
Yokoyama, Toshio 1947- 136
Yola, Yerima
See Kirk-Greene, Anthony (Hamilton Millard)
Yolen, Jane (Hyatt) 1939- CANR-126
Earlier sketches in CA 13-16R, CANR-11, 29, 56, 91
Interview in CANR-29
See also AAYA 4, 22
See also BPFB 3
See also BYA 9, 10, 11, 14, 16
See also CLR 4, 44
See also CWRI 5
See also DLB 52
See also FANT
See also JRDA
See also MAICYA 1, 2
See also MTFW 2005
See also SAAS 1
See also SATA 4, 40, 75, 112, 158
See also SATA-Essay 111
See also SFW 4
See also SUFW 2
See also WYA
See also YAW
Yolen, Steven H. 1942- 73-76
Yolen, Will(iam Hyatt) 1908-1985 ..... CANR-29
Obituary 118
Earlier sketches in CA 5-8R, CANR-5
Yolton, John W(illiam) 1921- CANR-14
Earlier sketch in CA 37-40R
Yone, Edward Michael Law
See Law Yone, Edward Michael
Yonemura, Margaret V. S. 1928- 29-32R
Yonge, Charlotte (Mary) 1823-1901 163
Brief entry 109
See also DLB 18, 163
See also RGEL 2
See also SATA 17
See also TCLC 48
See also WCH
Yonge, (Charles) Maurice 1899-1986
Obituary 118
Yonker, Nicholas J(unior) 1927- 117
Yoo, Grace S.
See Yoo, Young H(yun)
Yoo, Young H(yun) 1927- 41-44R
Yoo, Yushin 1940- CANR-2
Earlier sketch in CA 45-48
Yook, Wan-soon 1933- 233
Yooll, Andrew M(ichael) Graham
See Graham-Yooll, Andrew M(ichael)
Yoors, Jan 1922(?)-1977 81-84
Obituary 73-76
Yorburg, Betty 1926- CANR-16
Earlier sketch in CA 29-32R
Yorck, Ruth (Landshoff) 1909-1966
Obituary 25-28R
Yordan, Philip 1913(?)-2003 129
Obituary 214
Brief entry 116
Yorick, A. P.
See Tindall, William York
Yorinks, Arthur 1953- CANR-125
Earlier sketches in CA 106, CANR-38
See also CLR 20
See also CWRI 5
See also MAICYA 1, 2
See also SATA 33, 49, 85, 144
York, Alison
See Nicole, Christopher (Robin)
York, Amanda
See Dial, Joan
York, Andrew
See Nicole, Christopher (Robin)
York, Carol Beach 1928- CANR-6
Earlier sketch in CA 1-4R
See also BYA 7
See also JRDA
See also SATA 6, 77
York, Elizabeth
See York, Margaret Elizabeth
York, Georgia
See Hoffman, Lee
York, Helen 1918- CANR-4
Earlier sketch in CA 53-56
York, Herbert (Frank) 1921- 29-32R
York, Jeremy
See Creasey, John
York, Lorraine (M.) 1958- CANR-130
Earlier sketches in CA 129, CANR-66
York, Margaret Elizabeth 1927- 103
York, Michael (Otto) 1939- 224
York, Neil Longley 1951- 207
York, Pauline
See Howl, Marcia (Yvonne Hurt)
York, Phyllis 1937- 132
York, R. A. 1941- 199
York, Rebecca
See Buckholtz, Eileen (Garber) and Glick, Ruth (Burtnick)
York, Reginald O(scar) 1942- 117
York, Robert
See Estridge, Robin
York, Sarah 207
York, Simon
See Heinlein, Robert A(nson)
York, Susannah 1941- 130
York, Thomas (Lee) 1940- 73-76
York, William 1950- 107
Yorke, Amanda 1954- 139
Yorke, Christy 1965- 190
Yorke, Henry Vincent 1905-1974 85-88
Obituary 49-52
See also Green, Henry
See also CLC 13
Yorke, Katherine
See Ellerbeck, Rosemary (Anne L'Estrange)
Yorke, Malcolm 1938- CANR-129
Earlier sketch in CA 131
Yorke, Margaret
See Larminie, Margaret Beda
Yorke, Ritchie 1944- 77-80
Yorke, Roger
See Bingley, David Ernest
Yorke, Susan 1915- CANR-1
Earlier sketch in CA 1-4R
Yorkist
See Morrah, Dermot (Michael Macgregor)
Yosano Akiko 1878-1942 161
See also EWL 3
See also PC 11
See also RGWL 3
See also TCLC 59
Yoseloff, Martin 1919-1997 45-48
Yoseloff, Thomas 1913- 77-80
Yoshida, (Katsumi) Jim 1921- 41-44R
Yoshida, Shigeru 1878-1967
Obituary 113
Yoshida, Toshi 1911- ..... SATA 77
Yoshimasu, Gozo 1939- 126
Yoshimoto, Banana
See Yoshimoto, Mahoko
See also AAYA 50
See also CLC 84
See also NFS 7
Yoshimoto, Mahoko 1964- CANR-98
Earlier sketch in CA 144
See also Yoshimoto, Banana
See also SSFS 16
Yoshimura, Akira 1927- CANR-97
Earlier sketch in CA 156
Yoshioka Minoru
See Yoshioka, Minoru
Yoshiyuki, Junnosuke 1923-1994 184
Yoskowitz, Irving
See Younger, Irving
Yost, Charles W(oodruff) 1907-1981 ..... CANR-3
Obituary 104
Earlier sketch in CA 9-12R
Yost, David S(cott) 1948- 223
Yost, Edna 1889-1971 ..... 1-4R
Obituary 103
See also SATA-Obit 26
Yost, Elwy McMurran 1925- 126
Yost, F(rank) Donald 1927- 29-32R
Yost, Graham 1959- 129
Yost, Nellie Snyder 1905-1992 ..... CANR-16
Earlier sketch in CA 29-32R
Yost, Stanley K. 1924- 9-12R
Youcha, Geraldine 1925- CANR-51
Earlier sketch in CA 93-96
Youd, C. S.
See Youd, (Christopher) Samuel
See also SAAS 6
Youd, (Christopher) Samuel 1922- CANR-114
Earlier sketches in CA 77-80, CANR-37
See also Christopher, John and Youd, C. S.
See also JRDA
See also MAICYA 1, 2
See also SATA 47, 135
See also SATA-Brief 30
Youdale, Peter J. 1928- 45-48
Youman, Roger J(acob) 1932- 65-68
Youmans, E(lmer) Grant 1907-1999 ..... CAP-2
Earlier sketch in CA 23-24
Youmans, Marlene 1953- 77-80
Youmans, Marly 203
Young, A. S. Doc
See Young, Andrew Spurgeon Nash
Young, A. S. "Doc" 1919-1996 ..... DLB 241
Young, Agatha
See Young, Agnes Brooks
Young, Agnes Brooks 1898-1974
Obituary 109
Young, Ahdele Carrine 1923- CANR-41
Earlier sketch in CA 107
Young, Al(bert James) 1939- CANR-109
Earlier sketches in CA 29-32R, CANR-26, 65
See also BLC 3
See also BW 2, 3
See also CLC 19
See also CN 2, 3, 4, 5, 6, 7
See also CP 1, 2, 3, 4, 5, 6, 7
See also DAM MULT
See also DLB 33
Young, Alan 1930- CANR-6
Earlier sketch in CA 57-60
Young, Alan R(oger) 1941- 89-92
Young, Alison 1922- CANR-29
Earlier sketch in CA 53-56
Young, Allan Edward 1939- 125
Young, Allen 1941- CANR-39
Earlier sketches in CA 101, CANR-18
Young, Andre Ramelle
See Dre, Dr.
Young, Andrea 1956- 192
Young, Andrew (John) 1885-1971 ..... CANR-29
Earlier sketches in CA 5-8R, CANR-7
See also CLC 5
See also CP 1
See also RGEL 2
Young, Andrew (J.) 1932- 160
Young, Andrew Spurgeon Nash
1919-1996 207
Young, Angela
See Yardley, Alice
Young, Anne P(atricia) 1921- 65-68
Young, Anne Steele 1923- 129
Young, Arthur 1741-1820 ..... DLB 158
Young, Arthur C(lements) 1923- 25-28R
Young, Arthur N(ichols) 1890-1984 ..... 9-12R
Obituary 113
Young, Axel
See McDowell, Michael (McEachern)
Young, Barbara 1952- 141
Young, Bernice Elizabeth 1931- 37-40R
Young, Bertram Alfred 1912-2001 105
Obituary 200
Young, Bette Roth 1937- 149
Young, Billie 1936- 53-56
Young, Bob
See Young, James Robert and Young, Robert W(illiam)
Young, Brittany
See Young, Sandra
Young, C. Dale 1969- 203
Young, Carol 1945- 169
See also SATA 102
Young, Carol Ann
See Young, Casey
Young, Carrie
See Young, Ahdele Carrine
Young, Carter Travis
See Charbonneau, Louis (Henry)
See also TCWW 1, 2
Young, Casey 1951- 231
Young, Catherine
See Olds, Helen Diehl
Young, Catherine Alicia 1963- 136
Young, Cathy
See Young, Catherine Alicia
Young, Charles M(atthew) 1951- 93-96
Young, Charles R(obert) 1927- 13-16R
Young, Chesley Virginia 1919- 33-36R
Young, Chic
See Young, Murat Bernard (Chic)
Young, Clarence CANR-27
Earlier sketches in CAP-2, CA 19-20
See also Stratemeyer, Edward L.
See also SATA 1, 67
Young, Coleman A(lexander) 1918-1997 156
Obituary 162
Young, Collier
See Bloch, Robert (Albert)
Young, Collier 1908(?)-1980
Obituary 103
Young, Dallas M. 1914-1990 ..... 17-20R
Young, Dan 1952- ..... SATA 126
Young, David C(harles) 1937- 41-44R
Young, David M. 1940- 207
Young, David P(ollock) 1936- CANR-115
Earlier sketches in CA 21-24R, CANR-9, 24, 50
See also CP 1, 2, 3, 4, 5, 6, 7
Young, David S(amuel D'arcy) 1946- 113
Young, Dean (Wayne) 1938- 130
Young, Dean 1955- 211
Young, Delbert Alton 1907-1975 105
Young, Dennis R(alph) 1943-
Brief entry 107
Young, Dianne 1959- 152
See also SATA 88
Young, Dick 1918(?)-1987 181
Obituary 123
See also DLB 171
Young, Donald (Richard) 1933- CANR-46
Earlier sketches in CA 13-16R, CANR-12
Young, Donald J. 1930- 208
Young, Donald Ramsey 1898-1977
Obituary 69-72
Young, Dorothea Bennett 1924- CANR-13
Earlier sketch in CA 13-16R
See also SATA 31
Young, Douglas (Cuthbert Colquhoun)
1913-1973 ..... CAP-1
Obituary 45-48
Earlier sketch in CA 17-18
See also CP 1, 2
Young, Earle B. 1929- 194
Young, Ed (Tse-chun) 1931- CANR-100
Brief entry 116
Earlier sketch in CA 130
See also CLR 27
See also CWRI 5
See also MAICYA 1, 2
See also MAICYAS 1
See also SATA 10, 74, 122
Young, Edgar Berryhill 1908- 104
Young, Edith 49-52
Young, Edward
See Reinfeld, Fred
Young, Edward 1683-1765 ..... DLB 95
See also RGEL 2
Young, Edward J(oseph) 1907-1968 ..... CAP-1
Earlier sketch in CA 11-12
Young, (Cecil) Edwyn 1913-1988
Obituary 124
Young, Elaine L.
See Schulte, Elaine L(ouise)
Young, Eleanor R. 1918- 37-40R
Young, Elisabeth Larsh 1910-1999 81-84
Young, Elizabeth CANR-106
Earlier sketch in CA 108
Young, Ellin Dodge 1932- 106
Young, Everett
See Cosby, Yvonne Shepard
Young, Ezra P(orter) 1902-1990 113
Young, Fay
See Young, Frank A.
Young, Francis A(lfred) 1907-1995 130
Young, Francis Brett 1884-1954 205
Brief entry 122
See also DLB 191
Young, Frank A. 1884-1957 207
See also DLB 241
Young, Frank Carl 1907-1989 ..... CAP-1
Earlier sketch in CA 13-14
Young, Frank Wilbur 1928-
Brief entry 108
Young, Fred(erick) L(ee) 1922- 25-28R
Young, Freddie 1902- ..... IDFW 3, 4
Young, G(eorge) M(alcolm) 1882-1959
Brief entry 120
Young, Gary 1951- CANR-112
Earlier sketches in CA 117, CANR-40
Young, Gavin (David) 1928-2001 143
Obituary 192
See also DLB 204
Young, George Berkeley 1913-1988
Obituary 124
Young, George F(rederick) W(illiam)
1937- 57-60
Young, George Kennedy 1911-1990
Obituary 131
Young, Glennys 1959- 163
Young, Gordon 1886-1948 ..... TCWW 1, 2
Young, Gregory G. 1929-
Brief entry 110
Young, Harold Chester 1932- 129
Brief entry 109
Young, Harold H(erbert) 1903-1994 ..... CAP-2
Earlier sketch in CA 19-20
Young, Howard Thomas 1926- 9-12R
Young, Hugo (John Smelter)
1938-2003 ..... CANR-89
Obituary 221
Earlier sketches in CA 25-28R, CANR-28
Young, I(sador) S. 1902-1992 102
Young, Ian (George) 1945- CANR-52
Earlier sketches in CA 29-32R, CANR-11, 27
See also CP 2
Young, Iris Marion 1949- 190
Young, J(ames) Harvey 1915- CANR-6
Earlier sketch in CA 1-4R
Young, J(ohn) Michael 1944- 143
Young, J(ack) P. 1929- 157
Young, J(ohn) Z(achary) 1907-1997 ..... CANR-19
Obituary 159
Earlier sketch in CA 101
Young, James
See Graham, Ian
Young, James
See Graham, Ian

Cumulative Index 637 **Zacharias**

Young, James Allan 1934- 116
Young, James D(ean) 1925-
Brief entry 111
Young, James Douglas 1921- 25-28R
Young, James E. 1951- 159
Young, James J(oseph) 1940- CANR-16
Earlier sketch in CA 93-96
Young, James O(wen) 1943- 49-52
Young, James Robert 1921- 93-96
Young, James V(an) 1936- 69-72
Young, Jan
See Young, Janet Randall
Young, Janet Randall 1919-1994 .... CANR-5
Earlier sketch in CA 5-8R
See also SATA 3
Young, Jeff C. 1948- 201
See also SATA 132
Young, Jessica (Hankinson) Brett
See Brett-Young, Jessica (Hankinson)
Young, Jim 1930- 109
Young, Jock 1942- 104
Young, John
See Macintosh, Brownie
Young, John 1920- CANR-1
Earlier sketch in CA 45-48
Young, John 1934- 134
Young, John K(arl) 1951- 135
Young, John Orr 1886-1976
Obituary 65-68
Young, John Parke 1895-1988 .... 5-8R
Young, John Sacret 1947- 144
Young, John V. 1909-1999 121
Young, John Wesley 1951- 138
Young, John Wray 1907-1988 45-48
Young, Jordan Marten 1920- 21-24R
Young, Josh(ua D.) 210
Young, Judy 1956- 230
See also SATA 155
Young, Judy (Elaine) Dockrey 1949- .... SATA 72
Young, K(enneth) C. 1941- 155
Young, Karen M. 1942- 138
Young, Karen Romano 1959- 188
See also SATA 116
Young, Ken 1956- 151
See also SATA 86
Young, Kenneth 1916-1985 .... CANR-3
Obituary 118
Earlier sketch in CA 9-12R
Young, Kenneth Ray 1939- 150
Young, Kenneth T(odd) 1916-1972
Obituary 37-40R
Young, Kevin 175
Young, Leontine R(uth) 1910-1988 .... CAP-1
Obituary 126
Earlier sketch in CA 11-12
Young, Lesley 1949- 110
Young, Lois Horton 1911-1981 .... 9-12R
See also SATA 26
Young, Louisa .... SATA 161
Young, Louise B. 1919- CANR-10
Earlier sketch in CA 25-28R
See also SATA 64
Young, Louise Merwin 1903-1992 .... CAP-1
Obituary 139
Earlier sketch in CA 11-12
Young, M(erwin) Crawford 1931- 13-16R
Young, Mahonri (Sharp) 1911-1996 81-84
Obituary 152
Young, Margaret B(uckner) 1922- 21-24R
See also SATA 2
Young, Margaret Labash 1926- 134
Brief entry 110
Young, Marguerite (Vivian) 1909-1995 .. CAP-1
Obituary 150
Earlier sketch in CA 13-16
See also CLC 82
See also CN 1, 2, 3, 4, 5, 6
Young, Marjorie W(illis) -1994 85-88
Young, Mark 1960- 139
Young, Martin 1947- 127
Young, Mary 1940- 155
See also SATA 89
Young, Mary Elizabeth 1929- 37-40R
Young, Mary Elizabeth Reardon 1901(?)-1981
Obituary 105
Young, Mary Lou Daves 1918-1991 126
Obituary 135
Young, Mary Taylor 1955- 187
Young, Michael (Dunlop) 1915-2002 101
Obituary 201
Young, Michael W. 1937- 110
Young, Miriam 1913-1974 .... 37-40R
Obituary 53-56
See also SATA 7
Young, Morris N(athan) 1909-2002 .... 33-36R
Obituary 215
Young, Murat Bernard (Chic) 1901-1973
Obituary 41-44R
Young, Nacella
See Tate, Velma
Young, Nancy Beck 1963- 229
Young, Neil 1945- 110
See also CCA 1
See also CLC 17
Young, Noel (B.) 1922-2002 57-60
Obituary 207
Young, Noela 1930- .... SATA 89
Young, Norman J(ames) 1930- 77-80
Young, Oran R(eed) 1941- 112
Brief entry 109
Young, Otis E., Jr. 1925- 53-56
Young, Pam 1943- 109
Young, (Rodney Lee) Patrick (Jr.) 1937- ... 69-72
See also SATA 22
Young, Patrick 1937- 170
Young, Paul Thomas 1892-1978 .... CANR-3
Earlier sketch in CA 1-4R
Young, Pauline Vislick 1896- 5-8R
Young, Percy M(arshall) 1912-2004 . CANR-31
Obituary 229
Earlier sketch in CA 13-16R
See also SATA 31
See also SATA-Obit 154
Young, Perry Deane 1941- 57-60
Young, Peter 1915- 180
Earlier sketch in CA 13-16R
Young, Peter Alan 1934- 107
Young, Philip
See Steward, Samuel M(orris)
See also GLL 1
Young, Philip 1918-1991 .... CANR-6
Obituary 135
Earlier sketch in CA 9-12R
Young, Philip H(oward) 1953- 233
Young, R(obert) V(aughan) 1947- CANR-117
Earlier sketch in CA 127
Young, Ralph Aubrey 1902(?)-1980
Obituary 97-100
Young, Richard Alan 1946- 184
See also SATA 72
Young, Richard E(merson) 1932- 29-32R
Young, Richard Knox 1913-1974 .... 13-16R
Young, Richard Phillip 1940- 29-32R
Young, Robert
See Payne, (Pierre Stephen) Robert
Young, Robert 1944- 123
Young, Robert A. 1950- 153
Young, Robert Doran 1928- CANR-17
Earlier sketch in CA 29-32R
Young, Robert F(ranklin) 1915-1986 166
See also SFW 4
Young, Robert J(ohn) 1942- 101
Young, Robert W(illiam) 1916-1969 ... CANR-5
Earlier sketch in CA 5-8R
See also SATA 3
Young, Robert W. 1959- 187
Young, Roger (E.) 1942- 202
Young, Rosamond M. 1912- CANR-118
Earlier sketch in CA 154
Young, Rose
See Harris, Marion Rose (Young)
Young, Ross B. 1955- .... SATA 150
Young, Rusty 236
Young, Ruth 1884-1983
Obituary 111
Young, Ruth 1946- 136
See also SATA 67
Young, Sandra 1952- 124
Young, Scott A(lexander) 1918- CANR-20
Earlier sketches in CA 9-12R, CANR-5
See also SATA 5
Young, Seymour Dilworth 1897-1981 ... CAP-2
Earlier sketch in CA 29-32
Young, Stanley (Preston) 1906-1975
Obituary 57-60
Young, Stark 1881-1963 .... CANR-60
Obituary 89-92
Earlier sketch in CA 105
See also DLB 9, 102
See also DLBD 16
See also MAL 5
See also RHW
Young, Stephen M(arvin) 1889(?)-1984
Obituary 114
Young, T(heron) Kue 1948- CANR-103
Earlier sketch in CA 149
Young, Terence 1953- 226
Young, Thomas
See Yoseloff, Thomas
Young, Thomas Daniel 1919-1997 ... CANR-14
Obituary 156
Earlier sketch in CA 37-40R
Young, Toby 1963- 224
Young, Vernon 1912-1986 45-48
Obituary 120
Young, Victor 1900-1956 .... IDFW 3, 4
Young, Virginia Brady 1921- 61-64
Young, Virginia G(arton) 1919-2005 ..... 13-16R
Obituary 237
Young, Vivien
See Gater, Dilys
Young, Waldemar 1880-1938 183
See also DLB 26
See also IDFW 3
Young, Warren C(ameron) 1913- 13-16R
Young, Warren R(ichard) 1926- 21-24R
Young, Wayland 1923- 13-16R
Young, Whitney M(oore), Jr.
1921-1971 .... CANR-25
Earlier sketches in CAP-1, CA 13-14
See also BW 1
Young, William 1918- 45-48
Young, William C(urtis) 1928- 45-48
Young, William H(enry) 1912- 21-24R
Young, William J. 1938- 109
Young, Wilson
See Tippette, Giles
Young Bear, Ray A. 1950- 146
See also CLC 94
See also DAM MULT
See also DLB 175
See also MAL 5
See also NNAL
Youngberg, Norma Ione (Rhoads)
1896-1984 .... 9-12R
Youngberg, Ruth Tanis 1915- 107
Youngblood, Denise J. 1952- 139
Youngblood, Ila Dell 1926- 125
Youngblood, Ronald F. 1931- CANR-54
Earlier sketches in CA 37-40R, CANR-14, 30
Youngblood, Shay 1959- 168
See also CSW
Young-Bruehl, Elisabeth 1946- CANR-88
Earlier sketch in CA 131
Youngdahl, Benjamin E(manuel)
1897-1970 .... CAP-2
Earlier sketch in CA 21-22
Youngdahl, Reuben K(enneth Nathaniel)
1911-1968 .... 5-8R
Obituary 103
Younge, Gary 1969- 208
Younge, Sheila 1945(?)-1977
Obituary 73-76
Young-Eisendrath, Polly 1947- 143
Younger, Barbara 1954- .... SATA 108
Younger, Edward Eugene 1909-1979
Obituary 89-92
Younger, Irving 1932-1988
Obituary 125
Younger, James 234
Younger, Paul 1935- 101
Younger, R(onald) M(ichel) 1917- CANR-10
Earlier sketch in CA 17-20R
Younger, Richard D(avis) 1921- 9-12R
Youngholm, Thomas 1949- 164
Younghusband, Eileen (Louise) 1902-1981
Obituary 108
Younghusband, Francis (Edward) 1863-1942
Brief entry 113
Young Man, Alfred 1948- 211
Youngman, Henny 1906(?)-1998 134
Brief entry 107
Young-Mason, Jeanine Young 1938- 174
Youngquist, Walter 1921- 61-64
Youngren, J(ohn) Alan 1937- 108
Youngs, Betty 1934-1985 117
See also SATA 53
See also SATA-Obit 42
Youngs, Betty F(errell) 1928- 33-36R
Youngs, Frederic A., Jr. 1936-
Brief entry 112
Youngs, J. William T., Jr. 1941- CANR-10
Earlier sketch in CA 65-68
Youngs, Robert W(ells) 1913-2001 .... 13-16R
Youngs, Tim 227
Younie, William John 1932- 21-24R
Younin, Wolf 1908(?)-1984
Obituary 112
Younker, Lucas 1942- 65-68
Younkin, Paula 1942- 145
See also SATA 77
Yount, John A(lonzo) 1935- CANR-47
Earlier sketches in CA 45-48, CANR-5
Yount, Lisa (Ann) 1944- .... SATA 124
Yount, Lisa (Ann) 1944- 141
See also SATA 74, 124
Yount, Steven 1948- 146
Yourcenar, Marguerite 1903-1987 .... CANR-93
Earlier sketches in CA 69-72, CANR-23, 60
See also BPFB 3
See also CLC 19, 38, 50, 87
See also DAM NOV
See also DLB 72
See also DLBY 1988
See also EW 12
See also EWL 3
See also GFL 1789 to the Present
See also GLL 1
See also MTCW 1, 2
See also MTFW 2005
See also RGWL 2, 3
Yourdon, Edward Nash 176
Yourdon, Jennifer 235
Youree, Gary 1931-1982 .... CANR-2
Earlier sketch in CA 49-52
Yousaf, Muhammad 1937- 141
Youssef, Edwar Kolta Faltas
See al-Kharrat, Edwar
Youst, Lionel 1934- CANR-134
Earlier sketch in CA 167
Yousuf, Ahmed
See Essop, Ahmed
Youtie, Herbert Chayyim 1904-1980
Obituary 97-100
Yovkov, Yordan 1880-1937 209
See also CDWLB 4
See also DLB 147
See also EWL 3
Yow, Valerie Raleigh 1934- 202
Yowa
See McMurray, Nancy A(rmistead)
Yoxall, Harry W(aldo) 1896-1984 .... 13-16R
Obituary 113
Yoxen, Edward (John) 1950- 123
Yperen, Pieternella Cornelia van 1930- 195
Ysrael, Elie-Pierre
See Renaud, Jacques
Yu, Anthony C. 1938- 158
Brief entry 110
Yu, Beongcheon 1925- 189
Brief entry 108
Yu, Charles
See Targ, William
Yu, David C. 1918- 37-40R
Yu, Elena S. H. 1947- 125
Brief entry 109
Yu, Frederick T. C. 1921- 9-12R
Yu, George T(zuchiao) 1931- 17-20R
Yu, Hua 1960- 228
Yu, Ning 1954- 192
Yu, Pauline (Ruth) 1949- 122
Brief entry 118
Yu, Sui
See Chou, Eric
Yu, Ying-shih 1930- CANR-43
Earlier sketch in CA 25-28R
Yu, Zhuoyun 1918- 132
Yuan, Lei Chen
See De Jaegher, Raymond-Joseph
Yuan, Lou
See Chan, Jackie
Yuan, T'ung-li 1895-1965 .... CAP-1
Earlier sketch in CA 9-10
Yucel, Can 1926-1999 186
Yu Dafu 1896-1945 .... RGSF 2
Yudell, Lynn D. 1943- 29-32R
Yudelman, David 1944- 140
Yudewitz, Hyman 1906-1994 93-96
Yuditskaya, Tatyana 1964- .... SATA 75
Yudkin, John 1910-1995 .... 13-16R
Yudkin, Leon Israel 1939- CANR-12
Earlier sketch in CA 29-32R
Yudkin, Michael D(avid) 1938- 29-32R
Yudkoff, Alvin 1923- 188
Yudof, Mark G(eorge) 1944- 109
Yue, Gang 1955- 198
Yu Guangzhong
See Yu Kwang-chung
Yu-ho, Tseng
See Ecke, Betty Tseng Yu-ho
Yuill, Nicola M. 1965- 140
Yuill, P. B.
See Williams, Gordon M(aclean)
Yuill, P. D.
See Venables, Terry
Yuill, Phyllis Jean (Marquart) 1941- 65-68
Yuill, William Edward 1921- CANR-2
Earlier sketch in CA 1-4R
Yukawa, Hideki 1907-1981 163
Obituary 108
Yuki
See Inoue, Yukitoshi
Yukio, Agi
See Nosaka Akiyuki
Yu Kwang-chung 1928- .... EWL 3
Yule, Andrew 1936- 129
Yuma, Dan
See Dunham, Robert
Yumoto, Kazumi 1959- 200
See also BYA 16
See also MAICYA 2
See also SATA 153
Yun, Mia 238
Yun, Tan
See Lin, Adet J(usu)
Yunck, John A(dam) III 1917-1987 .... 9-12R
Yungblut, John R(ichard) 1913-1995 ..... 41-44R
Obituary 149
Yung-De Prevaux, Aude 1943- 203
Yunkel, Ramar
See Martin (Montes), Jose L(uis)
Yunker, James A. 237
Yunus Emre c. 1240-c. 1320 .... WLIT 6
Yurchenco, Henrietta 1916- 37-40R
Yurick, Sol 1925- CANR-25
Earlier sketch in CA 13-16R
See also CLC 6
See also CN 1, 2, 3, 4, 5, 6, 7
See also MAL 5
Yurieff, Zoya I(osifovna) 1922-
Brief entry 109
Yurka, Blanche 1887-1974 .... 9-12R
Obituary 120
Yuryenen, Sergey 1948- 202
Yushkevich, Semen 1868(?)-1927 .... DLB 317
Yusko, A(aron) A(llen) 1935- 65-68
Yuzyk, Paul 1913-1986 .... CANR-18
Earlier sketch in CA 101
Yzermans, Vincent Arthur 1925-1995 ... 13-16R

Z

Z
See Malia, Martin (Edward)
Zabaneh, Natalia (Shefka) 1946- 105
Zabeeh, Farhana 1919- 41-44R
Zabel, Diane 1957- CANR-109
Earlier sketch in CA 151
Zabih, Sepehr 1925- CANR-9
Earlier sketch in CA 21-24R
Zabilka, Gladys M. 1917- 5-8R
Zable, Arnold 1947-
Zablocki, Benjamin 1941- 37-40R
Zablocki, Clement J(ohn) 1912-1983
Obituary 111
Zabolotsky, Nikolai Alekseevich
1903-1958 164
Brief entry 116
See also Zabolotsky, Nikolay Alekseevich
See also TCLC 52
Zabolotsky, Nikolay Alekseevich
See Zabolotsky, Nikolai Alekseevich
See also EWL 3
Zabor, Rafi 1946- 165
Zaborowska, Magdalena J. 1963- 150
Zabrana, Jan .... CWW 2
Zabriskie, George 1919(?)-1989
Obituary 128
Zabytko, Irene 1954- 189
Zaccaria, Jerry A. 1945- 164
Zacek, Jane Shapiro 1938- 109
Zacek, Joseph Frederick 1930- 37-40R
Zach, Cheryl (Byrd) 1947- CANR-129
Earlier sketches in CA 124, CANR-69
See also AAYA 21
See also SAAS 24
See also SATA 58, 98
See also SATA-Brief 51
Zach, Natan
See Zach, Nathan
Zach, Nathan 1930- 156
Brief entry 105
See also CWW 2
Zacharia, Friedrich Wilhelm
1726-1777 .... DLB 97
Zacharias, Gary L. 1946- .... SATA 153

Zacharias, Lawrence S. 1947- 188
Zacharias, Lee
See Zacharias, Lela Ann
Zacharias, Lela Ann 1944- CANR-27
Earlier sketch in CA 85-88
Zacharias, Ravi K. 1946- 200
Zacharis, John C. 1936- 73-76
Zacharius, Walter 1923- 236
Zachary, Elizabeth 1928- 109
Zachary, G. Pascal 176
Zachary, Hugh 1928- CANR-47
Earlier sketches in CA 21-24R, CANR-13
See also SFW 4
Zachary, Saul 1934- 129
Zacher, Christian Keeler 1941- 105
Zacher, Mark W. 1938- 85-88
Zacher, Robert Vincent 1917-1997 .... 1-4R
Zack, Arnold M(arshall) 1931- CANR-42
Earlier sketches in CA 9-12R, CANR-3, 19
Zack, Bill 1956- 141
Zack, Naomi 1944- CANR-98
Earlier sketch in CA 147
Zackheim, Michele 1941- 188
Zacks, Mitch(ell) 226
Zacks, Richard 1955- 221
Zacks, Shelemyahu 1932- 141
Zade, Mirzo Tursun
See Tursun-Zade, Mirzo
Zadeh, Lotfi Asker 1921- 163
Zadeh, Norman 1950- 61-64
Zadoorian, Michael 1957- 187
Zadravec, Katharine E. 1933(?)-1989
Obituary 128
Zaehner, Robert Charles 1913-1974
Obituary 109
Zaffo, George J. (?)-1984 .... SATA 42
Zaffuto, Anthony A(ngelo) 1926- 101
Zafon, Carlos Ruiz
See Ruiz Zafon, Carlos
Zafren, Herbert C(ecil) 1925- CANR-50
Earlier sketches in CA 45-48, CANR-25
Zafzaf, Mohammed 1945- .... EWL 3
Zagajewski, Adam 1945- 186
See also DLB 232
See also EWL 3
See also PC 27
Zagar, J. Janko 1921- 121
Zagarell, Sandra A(belson) 1943- 118
Zagat, Arthur Leo 1895(?)-1949 169
Brief entry 110
See also SFW 4
Zagona, Salvatore Vincent 1920-
Brief entry 108
Zagoren, Marc Alan 1940-1996 132
Zagoren, Ruby 1922-1974 .... CAP-1
Earlier sketch in CA 17-18
Zagoria, Donald S. 1928- CANR-16
Earlier sketch in CA 21-24R
Zagorin, Perez 1920- CANR-82
Earlier sketches in CA 53-56, CANR-36
Zagorski, Paul W. 1946- 144
Zagoskin, Mikhail Nikolaevich
1789-1852 .... DLB 198
Zagst, Michael (Sidney) 1950- 121
Zagwyn, Deborah Turney 1953- .. SATA 78, 138
Zaharias, Babe Didrikson
See Zaharias, Mildred Ella Didrikson
Zaharias, Mildred Ella Didrikson 1913(?)-1956
Brief entry 117
Zaharopoulos, George K. 1933- 41-44R
Zahava, Irene 1951- 57-60
Zaheer, Hasan 1930-1998 149
Zahl, Paul Arthur 1910-1985
Obituary 117
Zahl, Paul F(rancis) M(atthew) 1951- 189
Zahler, Helene S. 1911-1981
Obituary 104
Zahn, Curtis 1912-1990 .... CANR-5
Earlier sketch in CA 5-8R
Zahn, Frank 1936- 97-100
Zahn, Gordon C(harles) 1918- 9-12R
Zahn, Muriel 1894-1970 .... 5-8R
Obituary 171
Zahn, Timothy 1951- CANR-138
Earlier sketches in CA 123, CANR-59, 63, 117
See also AAYA 14, 56
See also BPFB 3
See also CPW
See also DAM POP
See also SATA 91, 156
See also SFW 4
Zahniser, Marvin R(alph) 1934- 21-24R
Zahorchak, Michael G(eorge) 1929- . CANR-15
Earlier sketch in CA 41-44R
Zahorski, Kenneth J. 1939- 123
Zaid, Barry 1938- .... SATA 51
Zaid, Gabriel 1934- 193
Zaidenberg, Arthur 1908(?)-1990 108
Obituary 131
See also SATA 34
See also SATA-Obit 66
Zaidi, S(yed) M(ohammad) Hafeez
1929- CANR-25
Earlier sketch in CA 45-48
Zaillian, Steven 1953- CANR-124
Earlier sketch in CA 152
Zain, C. C.
See Benjamine, Elbert
Zainu'ddin, Ailsa
See Zainu'ddin, Ailsa G(wennyth) Thomson
Zainu'ddin, Ailsa G(wennyth) Thomson
1927- CANR-12
Earlier sketch in CA 29-32R
Zaitsev, Boris 1881-1972 .... DLB 317
Zajc, Dane 1929- 186
See also DLB 181
Zajonc, Robert Boleslaw 1923-
Brief entry 106
Zak, William F. 1945- 161
Zakaria, Fareed 1964- 171
Zakaria, Haji Ahmad 1947- 138
Zakarian, John J. 1937- 132
Zakarian, Richard H(achadoor) 1925- ... 41-44R
Zakia, Richard D(onald) 1925- CANR-9
Earlier sketch in CA 65-68
Zaknic, Ivan 1938- 138
Zakon, Alan J. 1935- 17-20R
Zakrzewski, Sigmund F. 1919-2005 142
Obituary 237
Zakuta, Leo 1925- 17-20R
Zalamea, Luis 1921- 17-20R
Zalan, Magda 1936- 112
Zalben, Jane Breskin 1950- CANR-98
Earlier sketches in CA 49-52, CANR-4
See also CLR 84
See also SATA 7, 79, 120
See also YAW
Zald, Mayer N(athan) 1931- CANR-28
Earlier sketches in CA 17-20R, CANR-8
Zaldivar, Fulgencio Batista y
See Batista y Zaldivar, Fulgencio
Zaleski, Eugene 1918- 77-80
Zaleski, Philip 1948- 186
Zaleznik, Abraham 1924- CANR-37
Earlier sketch in CA 73-76
Zalis, Paul 1952- 138
Zalite, Mara 1952- .... DLB 232
Zalkind, Sheldon S(tanley) 1922- 65-68
Zall, Paul M. 1922- CANR-20
Earlier sketches in CA 1-4R, CANR-6
Zallen, Doris Teichler 1941- 162
Zaller, Angeliki Bita CANR-82
Earlier sketches in CA 77-80, CANR-13, 36
Zaller, Robert 1940- CANR-92
Earlier sketches in CA 77-80, CANR-13, 32, 64
Zallinger, Jean (Day) 1918- ... SATA 14, 80, 115
Zallinger, Peter Franz 1943- 108
See also SATA 49
Zalmudio, Adela 1854-1928 .... DLB 283
Zaloga, Steven J(oseph) 1952- 150
Zalon, Jean E(ugenia) 1919- 102
Zaltkovich, Charles T(heodore) 1917- 5-8R
Zaltman, Gerald 1938- CANR-7
Earlier sketch in CA 17-20R
Zalygin, Sergei -2000 .... CLC 59
Zalygin, Sergei (Pavlovich) 1913-2000 . CLC 59
See also DLB 302
Zalzanick, Sheldon 1928- 77-80
Zamble, Edward 1942-
Brief entry 108
Zambrano, Maria 1904-1991 .... EWL 3
Zambrano, Myrna M. 1958- 165
Zambreno, Mary Frances 1954- CANR-119
Earlier sketch in CA 142
See also SATA 75, 140
Zamek, Jeff 1946- 228
Zamiatin, Evgenii
See Zamyatin, Evgeny Ivanovich
See also RGSF 2
See also RGWL 2, 3
Zamiatin, Evgenii Ivanovich
See Zamyatin, Evgeny Ivanovich
See also DLB 272
Zamiatin, Yevgenii
See Zamyatin, Evgeny Ivanovich
Zamir, Israel 1929- 154
Zamonski, Stanley W. 1919- 9-12R
Zamora, Bernice (B. Ortiz) 1938- CANR-80
Earlier sketch in CA 151
See also CLC 89
See also DAM MULT
See also DLB 82
See also HLC 2
See also HW 1, 2
Zamora, Daisy 1950- 180
Zamora, Lois Parkinson 1944(?)- 239
Zamoyski, Adam (Stefan Jan Maria Sariusz)
1949- CANR-101
Earlier sketch in CA 103
Zamoyta, Vincent C. 1921- 21-24R
Zampa, Luigi 1905-1991 157
Zampaglione, Gerardo 1917- CANR-14
Earlier sketch in CA 77-80
Zamyatin, Evgeny Ivanovich 1884-1937 166
Brief entry 105
See also Zamiatin, Evgenii and
Zamiatin, Evgenii Ivanovich and
Zamyatin, Yevgeny Ivanovich
See also SFW 4
See also TCLC 8, 37
Zamyatin, Yevgeny Ivanovich
See Zamyatin, Evgeny Ivanovich
See also EW 10
See also EWL 3
Zancanella, Don 1954- 166
Zand, Dale Ezra 1926- 111
Zand, Herbert 1923-1970 181
See also DLB 85
Zand, Roxanne 1952- 138
Zander, Alvin Frederick 1913-1998 .. CANR-19
Earlier sketch in CA 1-4R
Zanderbergen, George
See May, Julian
Zaner, Richard M(orris) 1933- CANR-16
Earlier sketch in CA 29-32R
Zanetti, J(oaquin) Enrique 1885-1974
Obituary 45-48
Zanetti (Lecuona), Oscar 1946- 184
Zang, David W(illiam) 1950- 148
Zangeneh, Hamid 1945- 141
Zangger, Eberhard 1958- 138
Zangrando, Robert L. 1932- 25-28R
Zangwill, Israel 1864-1926 167
Brief entry 109
See also CMW 4
See also DLB 10, 135, 197
See also RGEL 2
See also SSC 44
See also TCLC 16
Zangwill, Oliver Louis 1913-1987 109
Zanichkowsky, Stephen 1952- 220
Zanjani, Sally Springmeyer 1937- CANR-93
Earlier sketch in CA 120
Zanker, Paul 1937- 194
Zants, Emily 1937- 37-40R
Zanuck, Darryl F(rancis) 1902-1979
Obituary 93-96
See also IDFW 3, 4
Zanuck, Richard D. 1934- .... IDFW 3, 4
Zanussi, Krzysztof 1939- 149
Zanzotto, Andrea 1921- 208
See also CWW 2
See also DLB 128
See also EWL 3
See also PC 65
Zapata, Luis 1951- 194
See also GLL 2
Zapata Olivella, Manuel 1920- 153
See also DLB 113
See also EWL 3
See also HW 1
Zapoev, Timur Iur'evich
See Kibirov, Timur Iur'evich
Zappa, Francis Vincent, Jr.
1940-1993 .... CANR-57
Obituary 143
Earlier sketch in CA 108
See also Zappa, Frank
Zappa, Frank
See Zappa, Francis Vincent, Jr.
See also CLC 17
Zappler, Lisbeth 1930- CANR-4
Earlier sketch in CA 49-52
See also SATA 10
Zappulla, Elio 1933- 180
Zar, Rose 1923- 117
Zara, Louis 1910-2001 .... CAP-2
Obituary 200
Earlier sketch in CA 13-14
Zaranka, William 1944- 171
Zarb, Janet M. 1941- 144
Zarchy, Harry 1912-1987 .... CANR-2
Earlier sketch in CA 1-4R
See also SATA 34
Zarcone, Vincent P(eter), Jr. 1937- 61-64
Zardoya, Concha
See Conzalez, Maria Concepcion Zardoya
See also EWL 3
Zarefsky, David (Harris) 1946-
Brief entry 109
Zaremba, Eve 1930- 133
Zaremba, Joseph 1923-
Brief entry 112
Zaretsky, Eli 1940- CANR-37
Earlier sketch in CA 85-88
Zarifopol-Johnston, Ilinca Marina 139
Zarin, Cynthia 1959- 178
See also SATA 108
Zaring, Jane (Thomas) 1936- 108
See also SATA 40
Zarins, Joyce Audy
See dos Santos, Joyce Audy
See also SATA 57
Zariski, Raphael 1925- 49-52
Zarnecki, George 1915- CANR-10
Earlier sketch in CA 57-60
Zarnecki, Jerzy
See Zarnecki, George
Zarnow, Teryl 1951- 135
Zarnowitz, Victor 1919- 21-24R
Zarnowski, Frank 1943- 216
Zarro, Richard A(llen) 1946- 33-36R
Zartman, I(ra) William 1932- CANR-5
Earlier sketch in CA 9-12R
Zarucchi, Jeanne Morgan 1955- 138
Zaslavskaya, T. I.
See Zaslavskaya, Tatyana (Ivanovna)
Zaslavskaya, Tatyana (Ivanovna) 1924- 138
Zaslavsky, Claudia 1917- CANR-1
Earlier sketch in CA 49-52
See also SATA 36
Zasloff, J. J.
See Zasloff, Joseph J(ermiah)
Zasloff, Joseph J(ermiah) 1925- 129
Brief entry 116
Zaslow, Morris 1918- CANR-24
Earlier sketch in CA 45-48
Zasodimsky, Pavel Vladimirovich
1843-1912 .... DLB 238
Zassenhaus, Hiltgunt 1916- 49-52
See also AITN 1
Zastrow, Charles (H.) 1942- CANR-71
Earlier sketch in CA 127
Zastrow, Erika
See Massey, Erika
Zatlin, Phyllis 1938- CANR-36
Earlier sketches in CA 41-44R, CANR-15
Zatlin-Boring, Phyllis
See Zatlin, Phyllis
Zatlin Boring, Phyllis
See Zatlin, Phyllis
Zatsiorsky, Vladimir M. 1932- CANR-111
Earlier sketch in CA 156
Zatuchni, Gerald I. 1935- 37-40R
Zaturenska, Marya 1902-1982 .... CANR-22
Obituary 105
Earlier sketch in CA 13-16R
See also CLC 6, 11
See also CP 1, 2
Zauberman, Alfred 1903-1984
Obituary 112
Zaugg, Sandra L. 1938- 190
See also SATA 118
Zaugg, Sandy
See Zaugg, Sandra L.
Zaunders, Bo 1939- 207
See also SATA 137
Zavala, Albert 1930- 184
Brief entry 117
Zavala, Iris M(ilagros) 1936- CANR-32
Earlier sketches in CA 45-48, CANR-1
See also HW 1
Zavarzadeh, Mas'ud 1938- 106
Zavatsky, Bill
See Zavatsky, William Alexander
Zavatsky, William Alexander 1943- CANR-1
Earlier sketch in CA 49-52
Zavattini, Cesare 1902-1989 130
See also IDFW 3, 4
Zavin, Benjamin B. 1920(?)-1981
Obituary 103
Zavin, Theodora 1922-2004 53-56
Obituary 228
Zavrian, Suzanne (Ostro) 1928- 113
Zawadsky, Patience 1927- CANR-49
Earlier sketches in CA 21-24R, CANR-9, 24
Zawadzki, Edward S. 1914-1967 .... CAP-2
Earlier sketch in CA 17-18
Zawadzki, Marek 1958- .... SATA 97
Zawodny, J(anusz) K(azimierz)
1921- CANR-11
Earlier sketch in CA 13-16R
Zax, Melvin 1928- CANR-36
Earlier sketch in CA 37-40R
Zayas-Bazan, Eduardo 1935- CANR-37
Earlier sketch in CA 53-56
Zayas y Sotomayor, Maria de 1590-c.
1661 .... RGSF 2
Zaytsev, Boris Konstantinovich
1881-1972 .... EWL 3
Zazove, Philip 1951- 149
Zbarsky, Ilya 1913- 187
Zdenek, Marilee 1934- 102
Zea, Leopoldo 1912- CANR-16
Earlier sketch in CA 29-32R
Zeami 1363-1443 .... DC 7
See also DLB 203
See also RGWL 2, 3
Zeavin, Edna A. 1930- 138
Zebel, Sydney H. 1914-1993 .... 1-4R
Zebot, Cyril A. 1914-1989
Obituary 128
Zebouni, Selma A(ssir) 1930- 17-20R
Zebra, A.
See Scoltock, Jack
Zebrowski, Ernest, Jr. 1944- 189
Zebrowski, George (T.) 1945- 198
Earlier sketches in CA 41-44R, CANR-30
Autobiographical Essay in 198
See also CAAS 19
See also DLB 8
See also SATA 67
See also SFW 4
Zebrowski, Mark 1944-1999 186
Zec, Philip 1910(?)-1983
Obituary 110
Zech, Paul 1881-1946 181
See also DLB 56
Zeck, Gerald Anthony 1939- 114
See also SATA 40
Zeck, Gerry
See Zeck, Gerald Anthony
Zeckendorf, William 1905-1976 73-76
Zeckhauser, Richard J(ay) 1940- CANR-56
Earlier sketch in CA 126
Zed, Dr.
See Penrose, Gordon
Zeddies, Ann Tonsor 236
Zeder, Suzan L. 1948- .... CD 5, 6
Zedler, Beatrice H(ope) 1916- CANR-36
Earlier sketch in CA 41-44R
Zedler, Empress Young 1908- 41-44R
Zedric, Lance Q. 1961- 153
Zee, A. 138
Zeeveld, W(illiam) Gordon 1902-1975 . 41-44R
Zeff, Eleanor E. 1948- 212
Zeff, Stephen A(ddam) 1933- CANR-19
Earlier sketches in CA 9-12R, CANR-3
Zeffirelli, Franco 1923- 203
Zegart, Amy B. 1967- 238
Zegart, Arthur 1917(?)-1989
Obituary 127
Zegart, Dan 1955- 190
Zegger, Robert Elie 1932- 41-44R
Zegura, Elizabeth Chesney 1949- 144
Zehme, Bill 1958- 191
Zehna, Peter W(illiam) 1925- CANR-1
Earlier sketch in CA 1-4R
Zehnle, Richard F(rederick) 1933- 29-32R
Zehnpfennig, Gladys (Sophia) Burandt
1910-1986 .... CANR-5
Obituary 174
Earlier sketch in CA 5-8R
Zehring, John William 1947- 117
Zei, Alki 1925- 77-80
See also BYA 13
See also CLR 6
See also SATA 24
Zeidenstein, Harvey 1932- 57-60
Zeidman, Irving 1908- CAP-2
Earlier sketch in CA 21-22
Zeidner, Lisa 1955- 179
Earlier sketch in CA 110
Autobiographical Essay in 179
See also CAAS 24
See also DLB 120

Cumulative Index

Zuercher, Erik Jan
See Zuercher, Erik-Jan
Zuercher, Erik-Jan 1953- 158
Zuesse, Evan M. 1940- 105
Zug, George R. 1938- 239
Zug, Margaret Philbrook 1945(?)-1976 69-72
Zugger, Christopher Lawrence 1954- 209
Zugsmith, Leane 1903-1969
Obituary 115
Zuidervaart, Lambert 1950- 141
Zuiker, Anthony .... AAYA 64
Zuk, Georges
See Skelton, Robin
See also CCA 1
Zukav, Gary 204
Zukerman, Eugenia 1944- 110
Zukin, Sharon 131
Zukofsky, Louis 1904-1978 .... CANR-39
Obituary 77-80
Earlier sketch in CA 9-12R
See also AMWS 3
See also CLC 1, 2, 4, 7, 11, 18
See also CP 1, 2
See also DAM POET
See also DLB 5, 165
See also EWL 3
See also MAL 5
See also MTCW 1
See also PC 11
See also RGAL 4
Zukor, Adolph 1873-1976 .... IDFW 3, 4
Zulaika, Joseba 1948- 137
Zulauf, Sander W(illiam) 1946- 101
Zulawski, Marek 1908-1985
Obituary 116
Zulli, Floyd (Jr.) 1922-1980 .... 37-40R
Obituary 108
Zumbo, Jim 1940- 109
Zumoff, Barnett 1926- 149
Zumwalt, Elmo Russell, Jr. 1920-2000 85-88
Obituary 190
Zumwalt, Elmo Russell III 1946(?)-1988
Obituary 126
Zumwalt, Eva 1936- CANR-9
Earlier sketch in CA 65-68
Zundel, Alan F. 1952- 216

Zundel, Veronica (Elsa) 1953- 120
Zunder, William (Limbery) 1938- 117
Zuniga, Jose M. 1969- 146
Zunkel, Charles Edward 1905-1992 57-60
Zunkel, Cleda 1903- 57-60
Zunser, Jesse 1898-1985
Obituary 118
Zunz, Olivier J. 1946- 110
Zupa, G. Anthony
See Zeck, Gerald Anthony
Zupan, Vitomil 1914-1987 .... DLB 181
Zupancic, Oton 1878-1949 185
See also CDWLB 4
See also DLB 147
See also EWL 3
Zupko, Ronald Edward 1938- CANR-13
Earlier sketch in CA 37-40R
Zupnick, I(rving) L(awrence) 1920- 45-48
Zuravleff, Mary Kay 1960(?)- 238
Zurbo, Matt(hew) 1967- 166
See also SATA 98
Zurcher, Arnold John 1903(?)-1974
Obituary 49-52
Zurcher, Bernard 1953- 229
Zurcher, Erik Jan
See Zuercher, Erik-Jan
Zurcher, Erik-Jan
See Zuercher, Erik-Jan
Zurcher, Louis A(nthony), Jr. 1936- ... CANR-15
Earlier sketch in CA 41-44R
Zurhorst, Charles (Stewart, Jr.)
1913-1989 .... CANR-1
Earlier sketch in CA 45-48
See also SATA 12
Zuriff, G(erald) E(ugene) 1943- 123
Zurita (Canessa), Raul 1951- CANR-87
Earlier sketch in CA 131
See also HW 1
Zurlo, Tony 1941- 218
See also SATA 145
zur Muehlen, Hermynia 1883-1951
See zur Muhlen, Hermynia
zur Muhlen, Hermynia .... DLB 56
Zurndorfer, Lotte 1929- .... CP 1, 2
Zuroff, Efraim 1948- CANR-103
Earlier sketch in CA 149

Zuromskis, Diane
See Stanley, Diane
Zuromskis, Diane Stanley
See Stanley, Diane
Zusak, Markus 1975- 223
See also SATA 149
Zusne, Leonard 1924- 81-84
Zuwaylif, Fadil H. 1932- CANR-25
Earlier sketch in CA 45-48
Zuwiyya, Jalal (Zakariya) 1932- 77-80
Zwaanstra, Henry 1936-
Brief entry 105
Zwahlen, Diana 1947- 152
See also SATA 88
Zwar, Desmond (Laurence) (Gaudin)
1931- 107
Zwartenstern, Hendrik 1913-1976 .... 5-8R
Obituary 103
Zwart, Piet 1885-1977 214
Zwart, Pieter (Hendrik) 1938- 53-56
Zweibel, Alan 1950- 187
Zweifel, Frances W. 1931- CANR-12
Earlier sketch in CA 73-76
See also SATA 14
Zweig, Arnold 1887-1968 189
Obituary 115
See also DLB 66
See also EWL 3
Zweig, David 1950- CANR-137
Earlier sketch in CA 140
Zweig, Ferdynand 1896-1988
Obituary 125
Zweig, Friderike Maria Burger Winternitz)
1882-1971
Obituary 114
Zweig, Paul 1935-1984 85-88
Obituary 113
See also CLC 34, 42
Zweig, Ronald W. 1949- 124
Zweig, Stefan 1881-1942 170
Brief entry 112
See also DLB 81, 118
See also EWL 3
See also TCLC 17
Zweigenthaft, Richard L. 1945- CANR-135
Earlier sketch in CA 169

Zwerdling, Alex 1932- 57-60
Zwerenz, Gerhard 1925- 33-36R
Zwerger, Lisbeth 1954- .... CLR 46
See also MAICYA 1, 2
See also SAAS 13
See also SATA 66, 130
Zwerling, L. Steven 1938- 61-64
Zwibak, Jacques 1902-1994 77-80
Obituary 143
Zwick, Peter Ronald 1942- 116
Zwicker, Steven N(athan) 1943- 188
Zwicky, (Julia) Fay 1933- 154
See also CP 7
See also CWP
Zwicky, Fritz 1898-1974
Obituary 49-52
Zwicky, Jan 1955- CP-7
Zwiebach, Burton 1933- 57-60
Zwillinger, Frank Gerhard 1909-1989 .... EWL 3
Zwinger, Ann (H.) 1925- CANR-30
Earlier sketches in CA 33-36R, CANR-13
See also ANW
See also DLB 275
See also SATA 46
Zwinger, Susan .... ANW
Zwingli, Huldrych 1484-1531 .... DLB 179
Zwirn, Jerrold 1943- 109
Zworykin, Vladimir Kosma 1889-1982 157
Obituary 107
Zygalski, Zdzislaw 1921- 145
Zyla, Wolodymyr T(aras) 1919- CANR-2
Earlier sketch in CA 45-48
Zylberberg, Michael 1907-1971 .... CAP-2
Earlier sketch in CA 29-32
Zylbercweig, Zalman 1894-1972
Obituary 37-40R
Zylicz, Tomasz 1951- 203
Zymet, Cathy After 1965- 192
See also SATA 121
Zyskind, Harold 1917-1990 57-60
Obituary 130
Zysman, John 1946- 149
Zytaruk, George John 1927- 110
Zytowski, Donald G(lenn) 1929- 29-32R